**Biographical Reference Works
Published by Marquis Who's Who**

Who's Who in the South and Southwest

Who's Who
in the South and Southwest ®

Including Alabama, Arkansas, the District of
Columbia, Florida, Georgia, Kentucky,
Louisiana, Mississippi, North Carolina,
Oklahoma, South Carolina, Tennessee, Texas,
Virginia, Puerto Rico and the Virgin Islands.

14th edition
1975-1976

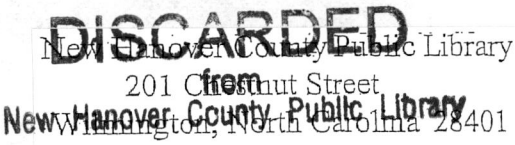
MARQUIS

Who's Who

Marquis Who's Who, Inc.
200 East Ohio Street
Chicago, Illinois 60611 U.S.A.

R
920
W

1975-76 ed.

Library of Congress Catalog Card Number 50-58231
ISBN 0-8379-0814-0

Distributed in the United Kingdom by
George Prior Associated Publishers
Rugby Chambers, 2 Rugby Street
London WC 1N 3 QU

Manufactured in the United States of America by
Kingsport Press, Inc., Kingsport, Tennessee 37662

Table of Contents

Preface

Table of Contents

During the past decade, the Southern and Southwestern areas of the United States have witnessed startling increases in population and in commercial and industrial activity. Population in these areas has grown significantly; numerous nationally recognized industrial corporations and financial institutions have expanded their operations in the South and Southwest. Today Atlanta, Miami, Houston, Dallas, Jacksonville, and Mobile are among the fastest growing business centers in the country. This progress could not have been accomplished without the work of educated, experienced, and responsible individuals who, on a daily basis, must concern themselves with the problems of a complex urban and suburban environment as well as with those problems that arise in their own professions. These individuals are of decided reference interest both locally and nationally. Thus, it is appropriate to record in the pages of this new edition of *Who's Who in the South and Southwest* the biographies of those men and women who have made outstanding contributions to their professional fields and to the communities in which they live.

This Fourteenth Edition of *Who's Who in the South and Southwest* represents the editors' attempts to recognize particular merit and to satisfy reference interest—to record the latest as well as the continuing accomplishments of individuals involved in all significant fields of endeavor.

Painstakingly reviewed, revised, and amended, the Fourteenth Edition provides up-to-the-minute coverage of a broad range of key individuals based on position or individual achievement. Our editors have made every effort to present a balanced image of achievement in the South and Southwest. To assure such balance in compilation of the volume, our list of essential names has been expanded. This list is made up of those men and women who are so eminent that their omission would fault the usefulness of the book. Should such individuals fail to furnish their own data, Marquis staff members compile the information through careful original research. Sketches compiled in this way are indicated by an asterisk. As in previous editions, however, nearly all biographees have furnished their own data and have checked pre-publication proofs of their sketches to make certain they are correct.

Marquis Who's Who editors exercise the utmost care in preparing each biographical sketch for publication. Occasionally, however, errors do occur, despite all precautions taken to minimize such occurrences. All users of this directory are requested to draw the attention of the publisher to any errors found, so that corrections can be made in a later edition.

The Fourteenth Edition contains approximately 18,500 names from the region embracing Alabama, Arkansas, the District of Columbia, Florida, Georgia, Kentucky, Louisiana, Mississippi, North Carolina, Oklahoma, South Carolina, Tennessee, Texas, Virginia, Puerto Rico, and the Virgin Islands. In addition, Mexico, because of its own importance and its contiguity to the southwestern United States, is also covered in this volume.

The persons sketched in this book include leading executives and officials in government, business, education, religion, the press, civic affairs, the arts, cultural affairs, law, and other fields. This edition also includes leading names in the managerial phase of professional and collegiate athletics, top figures in contemporary art and music and persons responsible for the latest developments in science.

Frequently, Marquis Who's Who editors are asked: "How do people get into a Who's Who volume?" Selection is based on the fundamental principle of reference value. Many individuals are eligible by virtue of positions achieved through election or appointment to office; others have distinguished themselves by outstanding achievement in their respective careers.

Biographees of *Who's Who in the South and Southwest* can be classified into two basic categories: (1) Persons who are of regional reference importance to colleagues, librarians, researchers, scholars, the press, historians, biographers, participants in business and civic affairs, and others with special or general inquiry needs; (2) Individuals of national reference interest who also are of such regional and local importance that their inclusion in the book is appropriate. In these names there is a minimum of duplication between this volume and *Who's Who in America*. In recognition of the complementary relationship between *Who's Who in America* and *Who's Who in the South and Southwest*, however, the Thirty-Eighth Edition of *Who's Who in America* includes for the first time, a listing of those individuals whose sketches appear in *Who's Who in the South and Southwest*. This list, which constitutes a special section of *Who's Who in America*, refers the book's users to the listee's biography in *Who's Who in the South and Southwest*.

The task of compiling this volume demands a keen knowledge not only of the South and Southwest, but of the entire continent. The people of a region, to be evaluated fairly, must be viewed objectively in a universal context. Marquis Who's Who is uniquely qualified to provide this combined knowledge, as publishers of *Who's Who in America* (thirty-eight editions since 1898); *Who Was Who in America* (a six-volume set of notables of America's past); *Who's Who in the World;* seven specialized biographical reference works of national or international scope; and four regional directories corresponding to the geographic regions of North America.

In the editorial evaluation that resulted in the ultimate selection of the names in this directory, an individual's desire to be listed was not sufficient reason for inclusion; rather it was the individual's demonstrated merit that determined inclusion. Similarly, wealth or social position was not a criterion; only occupational stature or achievement in some field affecting the development of the Southern and Southwestern regions of North America influenced selection. Indeed, many of the biographees are engaged in fields marked far more by service than by monetary reward. And, of course, this volume lists worthy individuals regardless of their race or ethnic origin.

Thus, on every level, this Fourteenth Edition of *Who's Who in the South and Southwest* carries on the tradition of excellence established years ago with the publication of the First Edition of *Who's Who in America*. The essence of that tradition is reflected in our unceasing effort to produce reference works that are responsive to the needs of their users throughout the world.

Standards of Admission

The foremost consideration in determining who will be admitted to the pages of *Who's Who in the South and Southwest* is the extent of an individual's reference interest. Such reference interest is judged on either of two factors: (1) The position of responsibility held, or (2) The level of significant achievement attained.

Admissions based on the factor of position include:

Members of the U.S. Congress.

Federal judges.

Governors of states covered by this volume.

Premiers of Canadian provinces covered by this volume.

State attorneys general.

Judges of state and territorial courts of highest appellate jurisdiction.

Mayors of major cities.

Heads of the major universities and colleges.

Officers on active duty beginning with the rank of major general in the Army, Air Force, and Marine Corps; and with rear admiral in the Navy.

Heads of leading philanthropic, educational, cultural, and scientific societies.

Selected members of the National Academy of Sciences, the National Academy of Design, the American Academy of Arts and Letters, and the National Institute of Arts and Letters.

Bishops and chief ecclesiastics of the principal religious denominations.

Principal officers of national and international businesses.

Others chosen because of incumbency, authorship, or membership.

Admission based on individual achievement, on the other hand, must be decided by a judicious process of evaluating qualitative factors. To be selected on this basis, a person must have accomplished some conspicuous achievement—something that distinguishes him from the vast majority of his contemporaries. He or she may scarcely be known in the local community, but may be widely recognized in some special field of endeavor. Such a person often is one whose work is better known than he is himself.

Key to Information in this Directory

① FULTON, Samuel Gardner, ② banker; **③** b. Roanoke, Va., May 9, 1923; **④** s. Oliver and Lorraine (Gardner) F.; **⑤** B.A., Furman U., 1944; **⑥** m. Rachel Harrison, Dec. 24, 1946; **⑦** children—Sallie Jo (Mrs. Garrett Potter), Walter James, Frances Ruth, Cecily Louise. **⑧** Teller, Union Nat. Bank, Decatur, Ga., 1947-50, trust officer, 1950-57, v.p. trusts, 1957-65, pres., 1965—, also dir. **⑨** Lectr. banking Decatur Jr. Coll., 1968—. **⑩** Chmn. Decatur United Fund, 1969; active Decatur chpt. A.R.C. **⑪** Mem. Decatur City Council, 1965-68. **⑫** Bd. dirs. Salvation Army Home. **⑬** Served with USNR, 1944-46; PTO. **⑭** Named Man of Year, Decatur Jaycees, 1969; decorated Bronze Star. **⑮** Mem. Am. Banker's Assn., A.I.M., Decatur Banker's League (pres. 1967-68), Phi Delta Theta. **⑯** Democrat. **⑰** Baptist. **⑱** Mason (Shriner). Clubs: **⑲** Decatur Country, Decatur Athletic. **⑳** Contbr. articles profl. jours. **㉑** Home: 28 Hidden Hollow Rd Decatur GA 30032. Office: **㉒** 350 Peachtree St Decatur GA 30034

Key

- ① Name
- ② Position
- ③ Vital statistics
- ④ Parents
- ⑤ Education
- ⑥ Marital status
- ⑦ Children
- ⑧ Career
- ⑨ Career related activities
- ⑩ Civic activities
- ⑪ Political activities
- ⑫ Non-professional directorships
- ⑬ Military record
- ⑭ Decorations and awards
- ⑮ Professional and other memberships
- ⑯ Political affiliation
- ⑰ Religion
- ⑱ Lodges
- ⑲ Clubs
- ⑳ Writings
- ㉑ Home address
- ㉒ Office address

The biographical listings in *Who's Who in the South and Southwest* are arranged in alphabetical order according to the first letter of the last name of the biographee. Each sketch is presented in a uniform order as in the sample sketch above. The many abbreviations used in the sketches are explained in the Table of Abbreviations.

Table of Abbreviations

The following abbreviations and symbols are frequently used in this Directory

* Following a sketch indicates that it was researched and written by the Marquis Who's Who editorial staff and has not been verified by the biographee.

A.A., Associate in Arts.
A.A.A., Agricultural Adjustment Administration; Anti-Aircraft Artillery.
A.A.A.S., American Association for the Advancement of Science.
AAC, Army Air Corps.
A. and M., Agricultural and Mechanical.
AAF, Army Air Force.
A.A.H.P.E.R., American Association for Health, Physical Education, and Recreation.
AB, Alberta.
A.B., Bachelor of Arts.
ABC, American Broadcasting Company.
A.,B.&C.R.R., Atlanta, Birmingham & Coast R.R.
AC, Air Corps.
acad., academy; academic.
A.C.L.R.R., Atlantic Coast Line R.R.
A.C.P., American College of Physicians.
A.C.S., American College of Surgeons.
a.d.c., aide-de-camp.
adj., adjutant; adjunct.
adm., admiral.
adminstr., administrator.
adminstrn., administration.
adminstrv., administrative.
adv., advocate; advisory.
advt., advertising.
A.E., Agricultural Engineer.
A.E. and P., Ambassador Extraordinary and Plenipotentiary.
AEC, Atomic Energy Commission.
AEF, American Expeditionary Forces.
aero., aeronautical, aeronautic.
AFB, Air Force Base.
A.F.D., Doctor of Fine Arts.
AFL (or A.F. of L), American Federation of Labor.
A.F.T.R.A., American Federation TV and Radio Artists.
agr., agriculture.
agrl., agricultural.
agt., agent.
agy., agency.
A.I.A., American Institute of Architects.
AID, Agency for International Development.
A.I.M., American Institute of Management.
AK, Alaska.
AL, Alabama.
Ala., Alabama.
A.L.A., American Library Association.
Alta., Alberta.
Am., American, America.
A.M., Master of Arts.
A.M.A., American Medical Association.
A.M.E., African Methodist Episcopal.
Am. Inst. E.E., American Institute of Electrical Engineers.
Am. Soc. C.E., American Society of Civil Engineers.
Am. Soc. M.E., American Society of Mechanical Engineers.
A.N.A., Associate National Academician.
anat., anatomical.
ann., annual.
ANTA, American National Theatre and Academy.
anthrop., anthropological.
A.P., Associated Press.
apptd., appointed.

apt., apartment.
AR, Arkansas.
A.R.C., American Red Cross.
archeol., archaeological.
archtl., architectural.
Ariz., Arizona.
Ark., Arkansas.
ArtsD., Doctor of Arts.
arty., artillery.
AS, Air Service.
A.S.C.A.P., American Society of Composers, Authors and Publishers.
ASF, Air Service Force.
assn., association.
asso., associate; associated.
asst., assistant.
astron., astronomical.
astrophys., astrophysical.
ATSC, Air Technical Service Command.
A., T. & S. F. Ry., Atchison, Topeka & Santa Fe Ry.
atty., attorney.
AUS, Army of the United States.
Aux., Auxiliary.
Av., Avenue.
AZ, Arizona.

b., born.
B., Bachelor.
B.A., Bachelor of Arts.
B.Agr., Bachelor of Agriculture.
Balt., Baltimore.
Bapt., Baptist.
B. Arch., Bachelor of Architecture.
B. & A. R.R., Boston & Albany R.R.
B.A.S., Bachelor of Agricultural Science.
B.B.A., Bachelor of Business Administration.
BBC, British Broadcasting Corp.
BC, British Columbia.
B.C., British Columbia.
B.C.E., Bachelor of Civil Engineering.
B.Chir., Bachelor of Surgery.
B.C.L., Bachelor of Civil Law.
B.C.S., Bachelor of Commercial Science.
bd., Board.
B.D., Bachelor of Divinity.
B.Di., Bachelor of Didactics.
B.E., Bachelor of Education.
B.E.E., Bachelor of Electrical Engineering.
BEF, British Expeditionary Force.
B.F.A., Bachelor of Fine Arts.
bibl., biblical.
bibliog., bibliographical.
biog., biographical.
biol., biological.
B.J., Bachelor of Journalism.
Bklyn., Brooklyn.
B.L., Bachelor of Letters.
bldg., building.
B.L.S., Bachelor of Library Science.
Blvd., Boulevard.
B. & M. R.R., Boston & Maine R.R.
Bn., Battalion.
B.O., Bachelor of Oratory.
B. & O. R.R., Baltimore & Ohio R.R.
bot., Botanical.
B.P., Bachelor of Painting.
B.P.E., Bachelor of Physical Education.
B.Pd., Bachelor of Pedagogy.
B.Py., Bachelor of Pedagogy.
br., branch.
B.R.E., Bachelor of Religious Education.
brig. gen., brigadier general.
Brit., British; Britannica.

Bro., Brother.
B.S., Bachelor of Science.
B.S.A., Bachelor of Agricultural Science.
B.S.D., Bachelor of Didactic Science.
B.S.T., Bachelor of Sacred Theology.
B.Th., Bachelor of Theology.
bull., bulletin.
bur., bureau.
bus., business.
B.W.I., British West Indies.

CA, California.
Cal., California.
C.Am., Central America.
CAA, Civil Aeronautics Adminstrn.
CAB, Civil Aeronautics Board.
CAC, Coast Artillery Corps.
Can., Canada.
capt., captain.
Cath., Catholic.
cav., cavalry.
CBI, China, Burma, India Theatre of Operations.
C.B. & Q. R. R., Chicago, Burlington & Quincy R.R. Co.
CBS, Columbia Broadcasting System.
CCC, Commodity Credit Corporation.
C.,C.,C. & St.L. Ry., Cleveland, Cincinnati, Chicago & St. Louis Ry.
C.E., Civil Engineer, Corps of Engineers.
CEF, Canadian Expeditionary Force.
C. & E.I. R.R., Chicago & Eastern Illinois R.R.
C.G.W. R.R., Chicago Great Western Ry.
ch., church.
Ch.D., Doctor of Chemistry.
chem., chemical.
Chem.E., Chemical Engineer.
Chgo., Chicago.
Chirurg., Chirurgical.
chmm., Chairman.
chpt., Chapter.
Cia. (Spanish), Company.
CIA, Central Intelligence Agency.
CIC, Counter Intelligence Corps.
C.,I. & L. Ry., Chicago, Indianapolis & Louisville Ry.
Cin., Cincinnati.
CIO, Congress of Industrial Organizations.
Cleve., Cleveland.
climatol., Climatological.
clin., clinical.
clk., clerk.
C.L.U., Chartered Life Underwriter.
C.M., Master in Surgery.
C.M., St.P. & P. R.R., Chicago, Milwaukee, St. Paul & Pacific R.R. Co.
C. & N.-W. Ry., Chicago & Northwestern Ry.
CO, Colorado.
Co., Company.
C. of C., Chamber of Commerce.
C.O.F., Catholic Order of Foresters.
C. of Ga. Ry., Central of Georgia Ry.
col., colonel.
coll., college.
Colo., Colorado.
com., committee.
comd., commanded.
comdg., commanding.
comdr., commander.
comdt., commandant.
commd., commissioned.
comml., commercial.
commn., commission.
commr., commissioner.
condr., conductor.

conf., conference.
Congl., Congregational; Congressional.
Conglist., Congregationalist.
Conn., Connecticut.
cons., consulting, consultant.
consol., consolidated.
constl., constitutional.
constn., constitution.
constrn., construction.
contbd., contributed.
contbg., contributing.
contbn., contribution.
contbr., contributor.
conv., convention.
coop. (or **co.op**), cooperative.
corp., corporation.
corr., correspondent; corresponding; correspondence.
C. & O. Ry., Chesapeake & Ohio Ry. Co.
C.P.A., Certified Public Accountant.
C.P.C.U., Chartered Property and Casualty Underwriter.
C.P.H., Certificate of Public Health.
cpl., corporal.
C.P. Ry., Canadian Pacific Ry. Co.
C.,R.I. & P. Ry., Chicago, Rock Island & Pacific Ry. Co.
C.R.R. of N.J., Central Railroad Co. of New Jersey.
C.S., Christian Science.
C.S.B., Bachelor of Christian Science.
C.S.D., Doctor of Christian Science.
C. & S. Ry. Co., Colorado & Southern Ry. Co.
C.,St.P.,M. & O. Ry., Chicago, St. Paul, Minneapolis & Omaha Ry. Co.
CT, Connecticut.
ct., court.
C.T., Candidate in Theology.
C.Vt. Ry., Central Vermont Ry.
C. & W.I. R.R., Chicago & Western Indiana R.R. Co.
CWS, Chemical Warfare Service.
cyclo., cyclopedia.
C.Z., Canal Zone.
CZ, Canal Zone.
d., daughter.
D., Doctor.
D.Agr., Doctor of Agriculture.
D.A.R., Daughters of the American Revolution.
dau., daughter.
D.A.V., Disabled American Veterans.
D.C., District of Columbia.
DC, District of Columbia.
D.C.L., Doctor of Civil Law.
D.C.S., Doctor of Commercial Science.
D.D., Doctor of Divinity.
D.D.S., Doctor of Dental Surgery.
DE, Delaware.
dec., deceased.
Def., Defense.
Del., Delaware.
del., delegate.
Dem., Democratic; Democrat.
D.Eng., Doctor of Engineering.
denom., denominational.
dep., deputy.
dept., department.
dermatol., dermatological.
desc., descendant.
devel., development.
D.F.C., Distinguished Flying Cross.
D.H.L., Doctor of Hebrew Literature.
D. & H. R.R., Delaware & Hudson R.R. Co.
dir., director.
disch., discharged.

dist., district.
distbg., distributing.
distbn., distribution.
distbr., distributor.
div., division; divinity; divorce proceedings.
D.Litt., Doctor of Literature.
D., L. & W. R.R., Delaware, Lackawanna & Western R.R. Co.
D.M.D., Doctor of Dental Medicine.
D.M.S., Doctor of Medical Science.
D.O., Doctor of Osteopathy.
DPA, Defense Production Administration.
D.P.H., Diploma in Public Health.
Dr., Doctor, Drive.
D.R., Daughters of the Revolution.
D.R.E., Doctor of Religious Education.
D. & R.G.W. R.R. Co., Denver & Rio Grande Western R.R. Co.
Dr.P.H., Doctor of Public Health, Doctor of Public Hygiene.
D.Sc., Doctor of Science.
D.S.C., Distinguished Service Cross.
D.S.M., Distinguished Service Medal.
D.S.T., Doctor of Sacred Theology.
D.T.M., Doctor of Tropical Medicine.
D.V.M., Doctor of Veterinary Medicine.
D.V.S., Doctor of Veterinary Surgery.

E., East.
E. and P., Extraordinary and Plenipotentiary.
ECA, Economic Cooperation Administration.
eccles., ecclesiastical.
ecol., ecological.
econ., economic.
ECOSOC, Economic and Social Council (of the UN).
ed., educated.
E.D., Doctor of Engineering.
Ed.B., Bachelor of Education.
Ed.D., Doctor of Education.
edit., edition.
Ed.M., Master of Education.
edn., education.
ednl., educational.
E.E., Electrical Engineer.
E.E. and M.P., Envoy Extraordinary and Minister Plenipotentiary.
Egyptol., Egyptological.
elec., electrical.
electrochem., electrochemical.
electrophys., electrophysical.
E. M., Engineer of Mines.
ency., encyclopaedia.
Eng., England.
engr., engineer.
engring., engineering.
entomol., entomological.
ethnol., ethnological.
ETO, European Theater of Operations.
Evang., Evangelical.
exam., examination; examining.
exec., executive.
exhbn., exhibition.
expdn., expedition.
expn., exposition.
expt., experiment.
exptl., experimental.

F.A., Field Artillery.
FAA, Federal Aviation Agency.
FAO, Food and Agriculture Organization (of the UN).
FBI, Federal Bureau of Investigation.

FCA, Farm Credit Administration.
FCC, Federal Communications Commission.
FCDA, Federal Civil Defense Administration.
FDA, Food and Drug Administration.
FDIA, Federal Deposit Insurance Administration.
F.E., Forest Engineer.
Fed., Federal.
Fedn., Federation.
Fgn., Foreign.
FHA, Federal Housing Administration.
FL, Florida.
Fla., Florida.
FOA, Foreign Operations Administration.
Found., Foundation.
frat., fraternity.
FSA, Federal Security Agency.
Ft., Fort.
FTC, Federal Trade Commission, Federal Tariff Commission.

G.-1 (or other number), Division of General Staff.
GA, Georgia.
Ga., Georgia.
gastroent., gastroenterological.
GATT, General Agreement on Tariffs and Trade.
G.,C. & S.F. Ry., Gulf, Colorado & Santa Fe Ry. Co.
G.D., Graduate in Divinity.
gen., general.
geneal., genealogical.
geod., geodetic.
geog., geographical; geographic.
geol., geological.
geophys., geophysical.
G.H.Q., General Headquarters.
G.,M. & N. R.R., Gulf, Mobile & Northern R.R. Co.
G.,M. & O. R.R., Gulf, Mobile & Ohio R.R. Co.
G.N. Ry., Great Northern Ry. Co.
gov., Governor.
govt., government.
govtl., governmental.
grad., graduated; graduate.
Gt., Great.
G.T. Ry., Grand Trunk Ry. System.
GU, Guam.
G.W. Ry. of Can., Great Western Ry. of Canada.
gynecol., genecological.

Hdqrs., Headquarters.
H.H.D., Doctor of Humanities.
HHFA, Housing and Home Finance Agency.
HI, Hawaii.
H.I., Hawaiian Islands.
H.M., Master of Humanics.
hist., Historical.
HOLC, Home Owners Loan Corporation.
homeo., homeopathic.
hon., honorary; honorable.
Ho. of Dels., House of Delegates.
Ho. of Reps., House of Representatives.
Hort., Horticultural.
hosp., hospital.
H.T., Territory of Hawaii.
Hwy., Highway.
hydrog., hydrographic.

IA, Iowa.
Ia., Iowa.
IAEA, International Atomic Energy Agency.
IBM, International Business Machines Corp.
ICA, International Cooperation Administration.
ICC, Interstate Commerce Commn.
I.C. R.R., Illinois Central R.R. System.
ID, Idaho.

Ida., Idaho.
I.E.E.E., Institute of Electrical and Electronics Engineers.
IFC, International Finance Corp.
I.G.N. R.R., International–Great Northern R.R.
IGY, International Geophysical Year.
IL, Illinois.
Ill., Illinois.
illus., illustrated.
ILO, International Labor Orgn.
IMF, International Monetary Fund.
IN, Indiana.
Inc., Incorporated.
Ind., Indiana.
ind., independent.
Indpls., Indianapolis.
indsl., industrial.
inf., infantry.
ins., insurance.
insp., inspector.
inst., institute.
instl., institutional.
instn., institution.
instr., instructor.
instrn., instruction.
internat., international.
intro., introduction.
I.R.E., Institute of Radio Engineers.

J.B., Jurum Baccalaureus.
J.C.B., Juris Canonici Bachelor.
J.C.L., Juris Canonici Lector.
J.D., Doctor of Jurisprudence.
j.g., junior grade.
jour., journal.
jr., junior.
J.S.D., Doctor of Juristic Science.
jud., Judicial.
J.U.D., Juris Utriusque Doctor: Doctor of Both (Canon and Civil) Laws.

Kan., Kansas.
K.C., Knight of Columbus.
K.P., Knight of Pythias.
K.C.S. Ry., Kansas City Southern Ry.
KS, Kansas.
K.T., Knight Templar.
KY, Kentucky.
Ky., Kentucky.

LA, Louisiana.
lab., laboratory.
lang., language.
laryngol., laryngological.
LB, Labrador.
lectr., lecturer.
L.H.D., Doctor of Humane Letters.
L.I., Long Island.
L.I. R.R., Long Island R.R. Co.
lit., literary; literature.
Litt.B., Bachelor of Letters.
Litt.D., Doctor of Letters.
LL.B., Bachelor of Laws.
LL.D., Doctor of Laws.
LL.M., Master of Laws.
L. & N. R.R., Louisville & Nashville R.R.
L.R.C.P., Licentiate Royal Coll. Physicians.
L.R.C.S., Licentiate Royal Coll. Surgeons.
L.S., Library Science.
lt., lieutenant.
Ltd., Limited.
Luth., Lutheran.
L.V. R.R., Lehigh Valley R.R. Co.

m., marriage ceremony.
M., Master.
MA, Massachusetts.
M.A., Master of Arts.
mag., magazine.
M.Agr., Master of Agriculture.
maj., major.
Man., Manitoba.
M.Arch., Master in Architecture.
Mass., Massachusetts.
math., mathematical, mathematics.
MB, Manitoba.
M.B., Bachelor of Medicine.
M.B.A., Master of Business Administration.
MBS, Mutual Broadcasting System.
M.C., Medical Corps.
M.C.S., Master of Commercial Science.
M.C.E., Master of Civil Engineering.
mcht., merchant.
M.C. R.R., Michigan Central R.R.
MD, Maryland.
Md., Maryland.
M.D., Doctor of Medicine.
M.Di., Master of Didactics.
M.Dip., Master in Diplomacy.
mdse., merchandise.
M.D.V., Doctor of Veterinary Medicine.
ME, Maine.
Me., Maine.
M.E., Mechanical Engineer.
mech., mechanical.
M.E. Ch., Methodist Episcopal Church.
M.Ed., Master of Education.
med., medical.
Med. O.R.C., Medical Officers' Reserve Corps.
Med. R.C., Medical Reserve Corps.
M.E.E., Master of Electrical Engineering.
mem., member.
Meml., Memorial.
merc., mercantile.
met., metropolitan.
metall., metallurgical.
Met.E., Metallurgical Engineer.
meteorol., meteorological.
Meth., Methodist.
metrol., metrological.
M.F., Master of Forestry.
M.F.A., Master of Fine Arts (carries title of Dr.).
mfg., manufacturing.
mfr., manufacturer.
mgmt., management.
mgr., manager.
M.H.A., Master of Hospital Administration.
MI, Michigan.
M.I., Military Intelligence.
Mich., Michigan.
micros., microscopical.
mil., military.
Milw., Milwaukee.
mineral., mineralogical.
Minn., Minnesota.
M.-K.-T. R.R., Missouri-Kansas-Texas R.R. Co.
M.L., Master of Laws.
M.L.D., Magister Legnum Diplomatic.
M.Litt., Master of Literature.
Minn., Minnesota.
Miss., Mississippi.
Mlle., Mademoiselle.
M.L.S., Master of Library Science.
Mme., Madame.
M.M.E., Master of Mechanical Engineering.
MN, Minnesota.
mng., managing.

MO, Missouri.
Mo., Missouri.
Moblzn., Mobilization.
Mont., Montana.
M.P., Member of Parliament.
M.Pd., Master of Pedagogy.
M.P.E., Master of Physical Education.
M.P.H., Master of Public Health.
M.P.L., Master of Patent Law.
Mpls., Minneapolis.
M.P. R.R., Missour Pacific R.R.
M.R.E., Master of Religious Education.
MS, Mississippi.
M.S., Master of Science.
M.Sc., Master of Science.
M.S.F., Master of Science of Forestry.
M.S.T., Master of Sacred Theology.
M. & St. L. R. R., Minneapolis & St. Louis R.R. Co.
M.,St.P. & S.S.M. Ry., Minneapolis, St. Paul & Sault Ste. Marie Ry.
M.S.W., Master of Social Work.
MT, Montana.
Mt., Mount.
MTO, Mediterranean Theater of Operations.
mus., museum; musical.
Mus.B., Bachelor of Music.
Mus.D., Doctor of Music.
Mus. M., Master of Music.
Mut., Mutual.
mycol., mycological.

N., North.
N.A., National Academician; National Army.
N.A.A.C.P., National Association for the Advancement of Colored People.
NACA, National Advisory Committee for Aeronautics.
N.A.D., National Academy of Design.
N.Am., North America.
N.A.M., National Association of Manufacturers.
NASA, National Aeronautics and Space Administration.
nat., national.
NATO, North Atlantic Treaty Organization.
NATOUSA, North African Theater of Operations, U.S. Army.
nav., navigation.
NB, New Brunswick.
N.B., New Brunswick.
NBC, National Broadcasting Company.
NC, North Carolina.
N.C., North Carolina.
N.,C. & St.L. Ry., Nashville, Chattanooga & St. Louis Ry.
ND, North Dakota.
N.D., North Dakota.
NDRC, National Defense Research Committee.
NE, Nebraska.
N.E., Northeast.
N.E.A., National Education Association.
Neb., Nebraska.
neurol., neurological.
Nev., Nevada.
New Eng., New England.
NF, Newfoundland.
Nfld., Newfoundland.
N.G., National Guard.
NH, New Hampshire.
N.H., New Hampshire.
NIH, National Institutes of Health.
NJ, New Jersey.
N.J., New Jersey.
NLRB, National Labor Relations Bd.
NM, New Mexico.

N.M., New Mexico.
No., Northern.
NPA, National Production Authority.
N.P. Ry., Northern Pacific Ry.
nr., near.
NRA, National Recovery Administrn.
NRC, National Research Council.
NS, Nova Scotia.
N.S., Nova Scotia.
NSC, National Security Council.
NSF, National Science Foundation.
NSRB, National Security Resources Board.
NT, Northwest Territories.
N.T., New Testament.
numis., numismatic.
NV, Nevada.
N.W., Northwest.
N. & W. Ry., Norfolk & Western Ry.
N.W.T., Northwest Territories.
NY, New York.
N.Y., New York.
N.Y.C., New York City.
N.Y.C. RR., New York Central R.R. Co.
N.Y.,C. & St.L. R.R., New York, Chicago & St. Louis R.R. Co.
N.Y.,N.H. & H. R.R., New York, New Haven & Hartford R.R. Co.
N.Y.,O. & W. Ry., New York, Ontario & Western Ry.

O., Ohio.
OAS, Organization of American States.
O.B., Bachelor of Oratory.
obs., observatory.
obstet., obstetrical.
OCDM, Office of Civil and Defense Mobilization.
ODM, Office of Defense Mobilization.
OECD, Organization European Cooperation and Development.
OEEC, Organization European Economic Co-operation.
ofcl., official.
OH, Ohio.
OK, Oklahoma.
Okla., Oklahoma.
ON, Ontario.
Ont., Ontario.
OPA, Office of Price Administration.
ophthal., ophthalmological.
OPM, Office of Production Management.
OPS, Office of Price Stabilization.
O.Q.M.G., Office of Quartermaster General.
OR, Oregon.
O.R.C., Officers' Reserve Corps.
orch., orchestra.
Ore., Oregon.
orgn., organization.
ornithol., ornithological.
O.S.L. R.R., Oregon Short Line R.R.
OSRD, Office of Scientific Research and Development.
OSS, Office of Strategic Services.
osteo., osteopathic.
O.T., Old Testament.
O.T.C., Officers Training Camp.
otol., Otological.
otolaryn., otolaryngological.
O.T.S., Officers Training School.

O.U.A.M., Order United American Mechanics.
OWI, Office of War Information.
O.-W. R.R. & N. Co., Oregon-Washington R.R. & Navigation Co.

PA, Pennsylvania.
Pa., Pennsylvania.
paleontol., paleontological.
Pa. R.R., Pennsylvania R.R.
path., pathological.
Pd.B., Bachelor of Pedagogy.
Pd.D., Doctor of Pedagogy.
Pd.M., Master of Pedagogy.
PE, Prince Edward Island.
P.E., Protestant Episcopal.
Pe.B., Bachelor of Pediatrics.
P.E.I., Prince Edward Island.
P.E.N., Poets, Playwrights, Editors, Essayists and Novelists (Internat. Assn.).
penol., penological.
pfc., private first class.
PHA, Public Housing Administration.
pharm., pharmaceutical.
Pharm.D., Doctor of Pharmacy.
Pharm.M., Master of Pharmacy.
Ph.B., Bachelor of Philosophy.
Ph.C., Pharmaceutical Chemist.
Ph.D., Doctor of Philosophy.
Ph.G., Graduate in Pharmacy.
Phila., Philadelphia.
philol., philological.
philos., philosophical.
photog., photographic.
phys., physical.
Phys. and Surg., Physicians and Surgeons (College at Columbia U.).
physiol., physiological.
P.I., Philippine Islands.
Pitts., Pittsburgh.
Pkwy., Parkway.
Pl., Place.
P. & L.E. R.R., Pittsburgh & Lake Erie R.R.
P.M. R.R., Pere Marquette R.R. Co.
P.O., Post Office.
polit., political.
poly., polytechnic; polytechnical.
pomol., pomological.
PQ, Quebec (province).
PR, Puerto Rico.
P.R., Puerto Rico.
prep., preparatory.
pres., president.
Presbyn., Presbyterian.
presdl., presidential.
prin., principal.
proc., proceedings.
prod., produced (play production).
prodn., production.
prof., professor.
profl., professional.
prog., progressive.
propr., proprietor.
pros. atty., prosecuting attorney.
pro tem, pro tempore (for the time being).
psychiat., psychiatric.
psychol., psychological.
P.T.A., Parent-Teacher Association.
PTO, Pacific Theater of Operations.
pub., public; publisher; publishing; published.
publ., publication.
pvt., private.
PWA, Public Works Administration.

q.m., quartermaster.
Q.M.C., Quartermaster Corps.
Q.M.O.R.C., Quartermaster Officers' Reserve Corps.
quar., quarterly.
Que., Quebec (province).

radiol., Radiological.
RAF, Royal Air Force.
R.C., Roman Catholic.
RCA, Radio Corporation of America.
RCAF, Royal Canadian Air Force.
Rd., Road.
R.D., Rural Delivery.
R.E., Reformed Episcopal.
rec., recording.
ref., reformed.
regt., regiment.
regtl., regimental.
rehab., rehabilitation.
Rep., Republican.
rep., representative.
Res., Reserve.
ret., retired.
rev., review, revised.
RFC, Reconstruction Finance Corp.
R.F.D., Rural Free Delivery.
rhinol., rhinological.
RI, Rhode Island.
R.I., Rhode Island.
R.N., Registered Nurse.
roentgenol., roentgenological.
R.O.S.C., Reserve Officers' Sanitary Corps.
R.O.T.C., Reserve Officers' Training Corps.
R.P., Reformed Presbyterian.
R.R., Railroad.
R.T.C., Reserve Training Corps.
Ry., Railway.

s., son.
S., South.
S.A., (Spanish) Sociedad Anonima: (French) societe Anonyme.
SAC, Strategic Air Command.
S.A.L. Ry., Seaboard Air Line Ry.
S.Am., South America.
san., sanitary.
S.A.R., Sons of the Am. Revolution.
Sask., Saskatchewan.
S.A.T.C., Student's Army Training Corps.
Sat. Eve. Post, Saturday Evening Post.
savs., savings.
S.B., Bachelor of Science.
SC, South Carolina.
S.C., South Carolina.
SCAP, Supreme Command Allies Pacific.
Sc.B., Bachelor of Science.
Sc.D., Doctor of Science.
S.C.D., Doctor of Commercial Science.
sch., school.
sci., science; scientific.
S.C.V., Sons of Confederate Veterans.
SD, South Dakota.
S.D., South Dakota.
S.E., Southeast.
SEATO, Southeast Asia Treaty Organization.
SEC, Securities and Exchange Commn.
sec., secretary.
sect., section.
seismol., seismological.
sem., seminary.
sgt., sergeant.
SHAEF, Supreme Headquarters, Allied Expeditionary Forces.
SHAPE, Supreme Headquarters Allied Powers in Europe.
S.I., Staten Island.
S.J., Society of Jesus (Jesuit).
SK, Saskatchewan.
S.J.D., Doctor Juristic Science.

S.M., Master of Science.
So., Southern.
soc., society.
sociol., sociological.
SOS, Service of Supply.
S.P. Co., Southern Pacific Co.
spl., special.
splty., specialty.
Sq., Square.
sr., senior.
S.R., Sons of the Revolution.
S.S., Steamship.
SSS, Selective Service System.
St., Saint; Street.
sta., station.
statis., statistical.
S.T.B., Bachelor of Sacred Theology.
Stblzn., Stabilization.
S.T.D., Doctor of Sacred Theology.
S.T.L., Licentiate in Sacred Theology; Lector of Sacred Theology.
St.L.-S.F. R.R., St. Louis-San Francisco Ry. Co.
supr., supervisor.
supt., superintendent.
surg., surgical.
S.W., Southwest.

T.A.P.P.I., Technical Association Pulp and Paper Industry.
Tb, Tuberculosis.
tchr., teacher.
tech., technical, technology.
technol., technological.
Tel. & Tel., Telephone and Telegraph.
temp., temporary.
Tenn., Tennessee.
Ter., Territory.
Tex., Texas.
T.H., Territory of Hawaii.
Th.D., Doctor of Theology.
Th.M., Master of Theology.
theol., theological.
TN, Tennessee.
tng., training.
topog., topographical.
T. & P. Ry., Texas & Pacific Ry. Co.
trans., transactions; transferred.
transl., transition.
transp., transportation.
treas., treasurer.

TV, Television.
TVA, Tennessee Valley Authority.
Twp., Township.
TX, Texas.
Ty., Territory.
typog., typographical.

U., University.
UAR, United Arab Republic.
U.A.W., International Union United Automobile, Aircraft, and Agricultural Implement Workers of American-AFL-CIO.
U.B., United Brethren in Christ.
U.D.C., United Daughters of the Confederacy.
U.K., United Kingdom.
UN, United Nations.
UNESCO, United Nations Educational, Scientific and Cultural Organization.
UNICEF, United Nations International Childrens Emergency Fund.
univ., university.
UNRRA, United Nations Relief and Rehabilitation Administration.
U.P., United Presbyterian.
U.P.I., United Press International.
U.P. R.R., Union Pacific R.R.
urol., urological.
U.S., United States.
U.S.A., United States of America.
USAAF, United States Army Air Force.
USAC, United States Air Corps.
USAF, United States Air Force.
USCG, United States Coast Guard.
USCGR, U.S. Coast Guard Reserve.
USES, United States Employment Service.
USIA, United States Information Agency.
USIS, United States Information Service.
USMC, United States Marine Corps.
USMCR, U.S. Marine Corps Reserve.
USMHS, United States Marine Hospital Service.
USN, United States Navy.
U.S.N.A., United States National Army.
U.S.N.G., United States National Guard.
USNR, United States Naval Reserve.
USNRF, United States Naval Reserve Force.
U.S.O., United Service Organizations.
USOM, United States Operations Mission.
USPHS, United States Public Health Service.
U.S.S., United States Ship.

USSR, Union of Soviet Socialist Republics.
U.S.V., United States Volunteers.
UT, Utah.

VA, Virginia.
Va., Virginia.
VA, Veterans Administration.
vet., Veteran; veterinary.
V.F.W., Veterans of Foreign Wars.
VI, Virgin Islands.
V.I., Virgin Islands.
vice pres., vice president.
vis., visiting.
vol., volunteer; volume.
v.p., vice president.
vs., versus.
VT, Vermont.
Vt., Vermont.

W., West.
WA, Washington.
WAC, Women's Army Corps.
Wash., Washington (state).
WAVES, Womens Reserve, U.S. Naval Reserve.
W.C.T.U., Women's Christian Temperance Union.
WHO, World Health Organization (of the UN).
WI, Wisconsin.
W.I., West Indies.
Wis., Wisconsin.
W. & L.E. Ry., Wheeling & Lake Erie Ry. Co.
WPA, Works Progress Administration.
WPB, War Production Board.
W.P.R.R. Co., Western Pacific R.R. Co.
WSB, Wage Stabilization Board.
WV, West Virginia.
W. Va., West Virginia.
WY, Wyoming.
Wyo., Wyoming.

YMCA, Young Men's Christian Assn.
YMHA, Young Men's Hebrew Assn.
YM and YWHA, Young Men's and Young Women's Hebrew Assn.
Y. & M.V. R.R., Yazoo & Mississippi Valley R.R.
YT, Yukon Territory.
Y.T., Yukon Territory.
YWCA, Young Women's Christian Assn.

zool., zoological.

Alphabetical Practices

Names are arranged alphabetically according to the surnames, and under identical surnames according to the first given name. If both surnames and first given names are identical, names are arranged alphabetically according to the second given name. Where full names are identical, they are arranged in order of age—those of the elder being put first.

Surnames beginning with De, Des, Du, etc., however capitalized or spaced, are recorded with the prefix preceding the surname and arranged alphabetically, under the letter D.

Surnames beginning with Mac are arranged alphabetically under M. This also holds for names beginning with Mc, that is, all names beginning Mc will be found in alphabetical order after those beginning Mac.

Surnames beginning with Saint or St. all appear after names that would begin Sains, and such surnames are arranged according to the second part of the name, e.g., St. Clair would come before Saint Dennis.

Surnames beginning with prefix Van are arranged alphabetically under letter V.

Surnames containing the prefix Von or von are usually arranged alphabetically under letter V; any exceptions are noted by cross reference (Von Kleinsmid, Rufus Bernhard; see Kleinsmid, Rufus Bernhard von).

Compound hyphenated surnames are arranged according to the first member of the compound.

Compound unhyphenated surnames common in Spanish are not rearranged but are treated as hyphenated names.

Since Chinese names have the family name first, they are so arranged, but without comma between family name and given name (as Lin Yutang).

Parentheses used in connection with a name indicate which part of the full name is usually deleted in common usage. Hence Abbott, W(illiam) Lewis indicates that the usual form of the given name is W. Lewis. In alphabetizing this type, the parentheses are not considered.

Who's Who in the South and Southwest

AARONSON, ALFRED ENOCH, real estate exec.; b. N.Y.C., Oct. 31, 1893; s. Lionel E. Z. and Cynthia Thelma (Robins) A.; student Columbia, 1911-12; m. Millicent Lubetkin, Oct. 5, 1915; children—Grace (Mrs. Judah Goldin), Alice (Mrs. Dov Zlotnick). Pres. Tuloma Oil Co., Tulsa, 1915-26; v.p. Leavell Coal Co., Tulsa, 1920-45; v.p. Commonwealth Co., Tulsa, 1925-35; pres. Court Arcade Bldg. Co., Tulsa, 1936—; dir. 4th Nat. Bank Tulsa. Chmn. Keep Gilcrease Mus. for Tulsa, 1954-55; chmn. Downtown Bus. Com., Tulsa Met. Area Bus. Com., 1959; chmn. Tulsa City and County Library Com., 1960-66; chmn. bldg. com. Tulsa Psychiat. Found., 1962; organizer Tulsa County Hist. Soc., 1962; mem. Tulsa Community Relations Com., 1962-66; mem. Okla. Human Rights Commn., 1963-66, hon. mem., 1967—; hon. mem. S.W. Center Human Relations, U. Okla., 1962; hon. mem. Urban League, 1963, Nat. Conf. Christians and Jews, 1964; pres. Tulsa Jewish Community Council, 1944, Gilcrease Inst. Am. History and Art, 1956-58. Recipient Distinguished Service award U. Okla., 1966, Sertoma award, 1969, Okla. Library Assn. award, 1966, awards City of Tulsa, 1967, 69; named Distinguished Hon. Alumnus, Langston U., 1966; Civitan Leadership award, Tulsa, 1973. Fellow U. Okla., 1970—. Mem. Tulsa Bldg. Owners and Mgrs. Assn. (past pres.). Mason (Shriner), Lion (hon.), Rotarian (hon.); mem. B'nai B'rith. Club: Summit (Tulsa). Home: 1782 E 30th St Tulsa OK 74114 Office: Court Arcade Bldg 6th and Boulder Av Tulsa OK 74103

ABBEY, JOE BEVERLY, lawyer; b. Dallas, Dec. 7, 1935; s. Ralph Jerome and Iva Ellan (Carter) A.; B.B.A., So. Meth. U., 1958, LL.B., 1960; m. Nancy Carolyn Cochran, Aug. 20, 1966; children—Christy Lee, Diana Beverly. Admitted to Tex. bar, 1960; practiced in Dallas, 1964—; mem. firm Haynes & Boone, 1968-71, partner, 1971—. Dir. Dallas Internat. Bank. Served to capt. USAF, 1960-63. Mem. Am., Fed., Tex., Dallas bar assns., Sigma Alpha Epsilon, Alpha Phi Omega, Phi Alpha Delta. Republican. Baptist. Home: 4341 Fairfax Dallas TX 75205 Office: 2900 LTV Tower Dallas TX 75201

ABBOTT, BENJAMIN EDWARD, JR., corp. exec.; b. Washington, Dec. 7, 1928; s. Benjamin Edward and Agnes (Campbell) A.; B. Indls. Engring., U. Fla., 1953; m. Ellianna Gray, May 22, 1955; children—Celeni, Dawn, Mark, Scott. Began career as industrial engineer with E. I. DuPont de Nemours & Company, Martinsville, Va., 1951, Allis Chalmers, Milw., 1953, Pensacola (Fla.) Naval Air Sta., 1955-61; mem. exec. staff Dr. Wernher von Braun, Marshall Space Flight Center, NASA, Huntsville, Ala., 1961-68; v.p., dir. Investors Corp. of Am., Birmingham, 1968—, Internat. Resorts, Inc., 1970—; dir. Pacific Am. Corp., San Francisco, Life Ins. Co. of Am., Birmingham, Ala. Served to lt. (j.g.) USNR, 1953-55. Registered profl. engr., Ala., Fla. Mem. Am. Inst. Indsl. Engrs. (sr.), Nat. Soc. Profl. Engrs., Ret. Officers Assn., Am. Inst. Aeros. and Astronautics, Pi Kappa Phi. Home: Route 2 Box 116-B Alpine AL 35014 Office: Investors Corp Am 1545 Montgomery Hwy Birmingham AL 35216

ABBOTT, CHARLES WARREN, lawyer; b. Miami, Fla., Jan 16, 1930; s. Voyle Eben and Katherine (Paschall) A.; B.S., U. Fla., 1951 LL.B., 1953; m. Betty Jo Eckholdt, Jan. 9, 1959; children—Brenda Jean, Katherine Louise, Abigail Jill. Admitted to Fla. bar, 1953; practiced in Orlando, Fla., 1955—; mem. firm Maguire, Voorhis and Wells, 1955—. Commr., Goldenrod-Dommerich Fire Control Dist., 1966—, chmn., 1972—. Dir. Orange County Assn. for Retarded Children, 1971—, Orange County Emergency Services Council, 1972—. Served with USAF, 1953-55. Mem. Am. Bar Assn., Fla. Bar, Fla. Def. Lawyers Assn., Alpha Tau Omega, Fla. Blue Key, Phi Delta Phi. Clubs: University (Orlando, Fla.); Sertoma (Winter Park, Fla.) Home: 515 Lightning Maitland FL 32751 Office: 135 Wall St Orlando FL 32802

ABBOTT, ROBERT FRANKLIN, psychologist, state ofcl.; b. Nashville, Oct. 19, 1927; s. Henry Preston and Nuffie Mae (Allen) A.; B.A., Cumberland U., 1951; M.A., George Peabody Coll., 1952; Ed.D., U. Tenn., 1963; m. Betty Blanche Sullivan, July 7, 1950; children—Robert Preston, Gerald Franklin. Tchr., prin. pub. schs. Maury County, Davidson County, Tenn., 1952-55; counselor, state supr. div. Vocational Rehab. Tenn., 1955-59; mem. faculty Middle Tenn. State U. 1959-67; prof., chmn. counselor edn. and psychology div. Ark. State U., Jonesboro, 1967-72; dir. regional integrated services Ark. Dept. Social and Rehabilitive Services, 1972—; pvt. practice counseling psychology. Sch. psychologist Tenn. Dept. Edn., 1965-67; lectr. grad. studies McGill U., 1966. Mem. Am., Ark. psychol. assns., Nat. Rehab. Assn. Home: 1107 Thrush Rd Jonesboro AR 72401

ABBOTT, THOMAS BENJAMIN, educator; b. Atlasburg, Pa., June 27; s. Thomas Rankin and Emma Elizabeth (Behling) A.; B.A., Muskingum Coll., 1943; M.A., Case Western Res. U., 1948; Ph.D., U. Fla., 1957; m. Lee Margaret Parsons, Dec. 29, 1945; children—John P., Amy P. Dir. speech therapy programs RoseMary Home for Crippled Children, Cleve., 1948-49; asst. prof. speech Minn. Stat. Coll. at St. Cloud, 1949-53; instr. U. Fla. at Gainesville, 1955-57; lectr. U. So. Cal., Los Angeles, 1957-58; prof. Baylor U., Waco, Tex., 1958-63; prof. speech U. Fla. at Gainesville, 1963—. Cons. Office Edn., 1966—; mem. adv. council Commr. Edn. Fla., 1969-72. Bd. dirs. Fla. Easter Seal Soc., 1966-73, pres., 1968-70. Served with AUS, 1943-45. Fellow Am. Speech and Hearing Assn.; mem. Fla. Speech and Hearing Assn. (pres. 1968-69), Speech Communication Assn., Nat. Council for Exceptional Children. Edit. cons. Jour. Speech and Hearing Disorders, 1966-69. Home: 1502 NW 31st St Gainesville FL 32605 Office: Dept Speech Univ Florida Gainesville FL 32611

ABDULRAHMAN, MUSTAFA SALIH, educator; b. Sulaimaniah, Iraq, June 15, 1930; s. Salih and Ammina Al-Haj (Mohammad) A.; came to U.S., 1956; B.S., Baghdad (Iraq) U., 1952; M.S., Rutgers U., 1958; Ph.D., Ia. State U., 1964. Chief engr. Baghdad U., 1964-65; asso. prof. civil engring. U. Miss., University, 1965—. Cons. engr., land developer, Oxford, Miss., 1968—. Named Outstanding Tchr., Sch. Engring., U. Miss., 1968. Mem. Am. Soc. C.E., Am. Soc. Engring. Edn., Am. Concrete Inst., Miss. Engring. Soc., Chi Epsilon. Home: 2204 Church St Oxford MS 38655 Office: PO Box 1251 University MS 38677

ABELS, LARRY JOSEPH, retail jewelry exec.; b. Ardmore, Okla., Feb. 11, 1939; s. Jerome Sylvin and Zipprea (Levine) A.; student U. Okla., 1957-59; m. Felice Seligson, Nov. 20, 1960; children—Jerome Todd, Lisa Gay, Mark Phillip. Partner, Jerome Abels Machine & Supply, Healdton, Okla., 1960-61; v.p. MACC Industries, Oklahoma City, 1961-62; salesman Peacock Jewelers, Oklahoma City, 1962, mgr., 1963, diamond sorter, grader Selco, Inc., Tulsa, 1964, diamond buyer, 1965, sec.-treas., 1966-67, v.p., 1968-69, exec. v.p., 1970—. Partner, Massie So. Hills Drug, Tulsa, 1973—. Mem. Air N.G., USAF, 1962-68. Mem. Okla. Retail Jewelers Assn. (v.p. 1973, dirs.), Sigma Alpha Mu. Democrat. Mason, Elk. Office: 4107 S Yale Av Tulsa OK 74135

ABELSON, LLOYD ARVID, govt. ofcl.; b. Butterfield, Minn., Feb. 20, 1922; s. Andrew and Amanda Elizabeth (Anderson) A.; B.S., Mankato State U., 1953; m. Mildred Jeanette Swenstad, Aug. 24, 1946; children—Diane, Alan, Julie, Mark, Gail, Scott. Tchr. history Pipestone (Minn.) Pub. Schs., 1953-58; historian, Pipestone, 1958-60; supervisory historian Nat. Park Service, Cumberland Gap Nat. Hist. Park, Middlesboro, Ky., 1960-68, supt. Andrew Johnson Nat. Historic Site, Greeneville, Tenn., 1968—; initiated planning and supervision Restoration of Hensley Settlement, 1963-68. Job Corps work coordinator, state liaison officer Tenn. Historic Landmarks; adviser Ky. Parks Commn., historic sites survey Bearea Coll., U. Louisville, Ky. Sch. for Blind. Co-chmn. Tri-State Civil War Centennial, 1962, Greeneville Art Guild hobby Fair, 1968—. Bd. dirs. Greene County Heritage Trust, Nolichuckey dist. C and A com. Boy Scouts Am. Served with USNR, 1943-46. Recipient Nat. Park Service Spl. Acts awards, 1959, 69; Spl. Services award Eastern Nat. Parks and Monument Assns., 1970; Boy Scouts Am. award for establishment 20 mile Mischa Mokwa Scout Trail, 1966. Mem. Am. Assn. for State and Local History, Greeneville Hist. Soc., V.F.W. Lutheran (deacon). Lion, Rotarian. Home: 121 Monument Av Greeneville TN 37743 Office: Depot St Greeneville TN 37743

ABERCROMBIE, RALPH MCCALL, JR., hosp. adminstr.; b. Charlotte, N.C., Sept. 26, 1928; s. Ralph McCall and Mamie (Schenck) A.; A.B., U. N.C., 1958; m. Elizabeth Joanne Hovis, Feb. 7, 1953; children—Ralph M. III, Jeffrey H., James M., Anne Elizabeth. Preceptorship hosp. adminstrn. Charlotte (N.C.) Meml. Hosp., 1958-60; asst. adminstr. Spartanburg (S.C.) Gen. Hosp., 1960-63; adminstr. Tuomey Hosp., Sumter, S.C., 1963—. Pres. Santee Wateree Health Adv. Council, 1971—. Bd. dirs. Carolinas Hosp. and Health Service, pres., 1973; bd. dirs. Carolinas Virginas Hosp. Conf., Blue Cross of S.C., Sumter, Santee Waterlee Mental Health Bd., Hosp. Edn. and Research Found. of S.C. Served with AUS, 1950-52. Mem. Am. Coll. Hosp. Adminstrs., S.C. Hosp. Assn. Assn. (pres. 1969-70), Alpha Phi Omega (state chmn. 1964-66). Methodist. Rotarian (pres. 1971-72). Club: Sunset Country (pres. 1974, dir. 1972-75). Home: 84 Nash St Sumter SC 29150 Office: 16-18 W Calhoun St Sumter SC 29150

ABERNETHY, BRUCE CATLIN, elec. engr.; b. Charlotte, N.C., June 6, 1936; s. Bruce B. and Opal Jean (Catlin) A.; B.S., Duke, 1961; postgrad. U.S. Naval Anti Submarine Sch., 1965, USAF Air Ground Operations Sch., 1966; m. Sharon Marie Cohen, June 6, 1971; children—Verna Clare, Bruce Gregory, Barry Todd, Brett Daniel. Digital design engr. Aircraft Armaments, Inc., Cockeysville, Md., 1961-62; sr. engr. NAA, Columbus, 1962-64; dir. data systems E Systems, Inc., Dallas, 1964—. Served with Signal Corps, AUS, 1954-57. Mem. I.E.E.E., Soc. for Information Display, N.Dallas Soccer Assn. (league pres. 1972, sch. coordinator 1973). Patentee sonic boom display. Home: 4805 Harvest Hill St Dallas TX 75234 Office: PO Box 6118 Dallas TX 75222

ABERNETHY, DONALD DOUGLAS, film co. exec.; b. Newton, N.C., Aug. 8, 1931; s. Ernest Glenn and Lottie Elizabeth (Shaw) A.; B.A., Lenoir Rhyne Coll., 1953; M.Ed., Appalachian State U., 1958, East Carolina U., 1962, Mich. State U., 1967, Duke, 1959; postgrad. U. Ga., 1968; m. Iris Buford Grigg, June 17, 1956; children—Douglas, Jeffrey, Jonathan, Beth, Robert. Tchr., prin. Catawba (N.C.) Elementary Sch., 1955-60; prin. Wallace-Rose Hill High Sch., Teachey, N.C., 1960-64, Hoke County High Sch., 1964-67; dir. student teaching Pembroke (N.C.) State U., 1967; supt. Hoke County Schs., Raeford, N.C., 1967-74; N.C. rep. Coronet Films, 1974—. Chmn. budget com. United Fund, 1968-71; chmn. Hoke County Bd. Health, 1971-73. Served with AUS, 1953-55. Mem. Horace Mann League, Am. Assn. Sch. Adminstrs., N.C. Assn. Edn. (pres. dist. supts. div. 1971-72), Grange. Democrat. Baptist. Kiwanian. Home: 603 N Fulton St Raeford NC 28376

ABERNETHY, ROBERT BRUCE, aircraft co. engr.; b. Albany, N.Y., July 12, 1930; s. Albert Clarence and Anne Frances (Conoby) A.; B.S. in Mech. Engring. (USN R.O.T.C. scholar), Rensselaer Poly. Inst., 1952, M.Sc. in Indsl. Mgmt., 1958; Ph.D. (Fulbright scholar), U. London, 1965; m. Eugenia M. Calvo, July 1954 (dec. 1971); children—Lynn M., James R.; m. 2d, Sally Kay Couzier, May 5, 1972; stepchildren—John S. Sabah, Nancy L. Sabah. With Pratt and Whitney Aircraft Co., West Palm Beach, Fla., 1955—, sr. project engr., dir. reliability, 1963—. Adj. prof. London Royal Coll. Sci., 1964-65, U. Fla., 1966-67, Fla. Atlantic U., 1968-69. Served to lt. USNR, 1948-55. Fellow Royal Statis. Soc.; mem. Am. Statis Soc. (pres. Fla. chpt. 1968-69), Tau Beta Pi, Pi Tau Sigma, Theta Chi. Patentee bleed bypass jet engine. Home: 536 Oyster Rd North Palm Beach FL 33408

ABERNETHY, WILBUR MURRAH, dentist; b. Troy, Miss., June 28, 1910; s. Bobby Luster and Nelle Olive (Dunlap) A.; student Chickasaw Coll., Pontotoc, Miss., 1929; B.A., U. Miss., 1933, postgrad., 1958; D.D.S., U. Tenn., 1942; m. Jamie C. Hickman, July 24, 1941; children—Sylvia Nelle (Mrs. William Byron Harvey), Wilbur Murrah II. Individual practice dentistry, Pontotoc, summer 1942, Oxford, Miss., 1946—. Served to maj. AUS, 1942-46. Mem. Lafayette County Alumni Assn. U. Miss. (past pres.), Oxford Jr. C. of C., Pierre Fauchard Acad., Miss. Dental Soc., N.E. Miss. Dental Soc., Am. Dental Assn., Psi Omega, Pi Kappa Alpha. Baptist. Rotarian. Home: 1949 Douglass Dr Oxford MS 38655 Office: 419 S Lamar St Oxford MS 38655

ABIDIN, RICHARD ROBERT, JR., psychologist, educator; b. N.Y.C., Sept. 5, 1938; s. Richard S. and Anna (Gennaro) A.; B.A., Rutgers U., 1960, M.Ed., 1962, Ed.D., 1964; m. Mary Louise Caiaccio, May 30, 1958; children—Richard Robert, Lynn, Michael, Joseph. Clin. sychologist USAF Wilford Hall Hosp., San Antonio, 1964-67; asst. prof. U. Va., Charlottesville, 1967—; child-clin. psychologist Bexar County Guidance Center, San Antonio, 1965-67; cons. Va. Dept. Edn., 1967-69, U.S. Office Edn., 1969—. Mem. Charlottesville-Albemarle Mental Health Bd., 1969-70; mem. Va. State Bd. Psychology, 1972—. Bd. dirs. Oakland Farm Sch. Served to capt. USAF, 1964-67. Diplomate Am. Bd. Psychologists. Mem. Am., Va. psychol. assns., Internat. Soc. Study Symbols (treas., dir.), Beta Theta Pi, Phi Delta Kappa, Kappa Delta Pi. Home: 2915 Idlewood Dr Charlottesville VA 22901

ABLON, ARNOLD NORMAN, accountant; b. Ft. Worth, July 12, 1921; s. Esir R. and Hazel (Dreeben) A.; B.S., La. State U., 1941; M.B.A., Northwestern, 1942; m. Carol Sarbin, July 25, 1962; children—Jan Ellen, Elizabeth Jane, William Neal, Robert Jack. Lectr. accounting So. Methodist U., 1946-47; auditor Levine's Dept. Stores, 1947-49; accountant Peat, Marwick, Mitchell & Co., 1946-47; sr. partner Arnold N. Ablon and Co., C.P.A.'s, Dallas, 1949—; partner Troth & Ablon, investments; dir. Mangum Mfg. Co., Troth Enterprises, Inc., 1st Continental Enterprises, Inc., Wolf Textile Co. Served as capt. F.A., AUS, World War II. Mem. Am. Inst. C.P.A.'s, Tex. Soc. C.P.A.'s, Nat. Assn. Accountants. Mason (Shriner). Clubs: Variety International, Dallas Athletic, Columbian, City, Engineers, Lancers. Home: 6929 Prestonshire Lane Dallas TX 75225 Office: Republic Nat Bank Bldg Dallas TX 75201

ABLON, BENJAMIN MANUEL, accountant; b. Dallas, Feb. 12, 1929; s. Esir R. and Hazel (Dreeben) A.; B.B.A., So. Meth. U., 1948; M.B.A., Northwestern, 1949; LL.B., Harvard, 1956; m. Renee Angrist, Jan. 6, 1962 (div. Oct. 1969); 1 son, Edward Lawrence. Admitted to Tex. bar, 1956, D.C. bar, 1957; with tax rulings div. IRS, Washington, 1956-60; asso. law firm, N.Y.C., 1960-62; accountant, tax mgr. Price Waterhouse & Co., N.Y.C., 1963-68; accountant, partner Arnold N. Ablon & Co., C.P.A.'s, Dallas, 1968—. Served to lt. USAF, 1951-53. Mem. Am. Inst. C.P.A.'s, Tex. Soc. C.P.A.'s, State Bar Tex., Am. Assn. Attys.-C.P.A.'s, Dallas Estate Planning Council, Beta Gamma Sigma. Contbr. articles to profl. jours. Home: 5916 Birchbrook St Dallas TX 75206 Office: Republic National Bank Bldg Dallas TX 75201

ABNEY, JAMES MARION, JR., dentist; b. Macon, Ga., Oct. 14, 1939; s. James Marion and Mae (Lockeby) A.; A.B., Emory U., 1961, D.D.S., 1966; m. Sandra Stewman, June 22, 1963; children—Marian Lynn, Mary Kate. Individual practice dentistry, Smyrna, Ga., 1968—; asso. prof. Emory U. Sch. Dentistry, 1968-70; asst. chief dental service Cobb Gen. Hosp., 1971—, cons. gen. dentistry cleft palate team. Mem. Cobb County C. of C., Am., Ga. dental assns., Northwestern Dist., Cobb County dental socs., Atlanta Gnathological Soc., Psi Omega, Sigma Alpha Epsilon. Republican. Mem. Ch. of God. Club: Chattahoochee Plantation (Marietta, Ga.). Home: 333 Hunters Ridge Marietta GA 30060 Office: 2131 Old Concord Rd Smyrna GA 30080

ABRAHAM, CLAUDE KURT, educator; b. Lorsch, Germany, Dec. 13, 1931; s. Siegmund and Johanna (Wachenheimer) A.; brought to U.S., 1946, naturalized, 1952; A.B., U. Cin., 1953, M.A., 1956; Ph.D., Ind. U., 1959; m. Marcia Edythe Phillips, June 3, 1956; children—Susan, Stephen, Catherine, Linda. Instr. French, U. Ill., 1959-62, asst. prof., 1962-64; asso. prof. French, U. Fla., Gainesville, 1964-70, prof., 1970—, asst. dean grad. sch., 1972—. Served with AUS, 1953-55. Nat. Endowment for the Humanities grantee, 1969; recipient award South-Atlantic Modern Language Assn., 1970. Mem. Modern Lang. Assn. (bibliography com. 1960-66, chmn. French 3, 1974), Midwest Modern Lang. Assn. (chmn. French I, 1964), South-Atlantic Modern Lang. Assn. (chmn. French I, 1969), Am. Assn. Tchrs. French (chpt. pres. 1971-73), Am. Council Teaching Fgn. Langs. (adv. assembly 1968-69), Conf. on 17th Century French Lit. (exec. council 1972). Author: Gaston d'Orleans et sa cour, 1963, rev. 1964; The Strangers, 1966, Enfin Malherbe, 1971, Corneille, 1972. Contbr. articles to profl. pubs. Home: 1820 N W 46th St Gainesville FL 32601

ABRAM, HARRY SHORE, psychiatrist; b. Roanoke, Va., Mar. 25, 1931; s. Edgar Nathan and Anna (Shore) A.; B.S., Northwestern U., 1952; M.D., U. Va., 1956; m. Mary Lou Combs, June 18, 1956; children—Rebecca, Harry, Sarah, Adam, Jessica. Intern, U. Va., Charlottesville, 1956-57, resident 1957-59, instr. psychiatry U. Va. Sch. Medicine, 1961-64, asst. prof., 1964-67, asso. prof., 1967-70, co-dir. Hosp. Renal Dialysis Unit, 1965-70, program dir. undergrad. tng. in psychiatry, 1965-70; research fellow Harvard Med Sch., Cambridge, Mass., 1959-61; practice medicine specializing in psychiatry, 1961—; prof. psychiatry Vanderbilt U. Sch. Med., Nashville, 1970—, mem. staff U. Med. Center. Recipient Career Tchr. award, Nat. Inst. Mental Health, 1961-63. Mem. Nashville Acad. Medicine, Am., Tenn. med. assns., Am. Psychiat. Assn., Am. Psychoanalytic Assn., Sigma Xi. Contbr. articles to profl. jours. Home: 2516 Fairfax Ave Nashville TN 37212

ABRAMS, MAYNARD ALVIN, lawyer; b. Chgo., Nov. 15, 1916; s. Isidor John and Pauline (Feldman) A.; student U. Fla., 1934-36; J.D., U. Miami, 1950; m. Gertrude Mendelson, Apr. 11, 1945; children—Michael Lee, Susan (Mrs. Kenneth Heyder), Jeffrey Alan. Owner, prin. Hollywood Airpark (Fla.), 1946-52; admitted to Fla. bar, 1950; since practiced in Hollywood; partner firm Abrams, Anton, Robbins, Resnick and Schneider. Chmn. bd. 1st Nat. Bank Hollywood, 1st Nat. Bank Hallandale (Fla.), 2d Nat. Bank West Hollywood, 1st Nat. Bank Miramar, Fla. Bankshares, Inc. dir. Lawyers' Title Services, Fort Lauderdale, Fla., 1967-69. Pres. Broward County League Municipalities, 1959-60; founder Hollywood-San Salvador Sister City Program, 1962. Commr. City Hollywood, 1959-66, mayor, 1966-69. Mem. exec. bd. So. Fla. council Boy Scouts Am., 1968—. Served with AAC, 1943-45. Named Hon. Seminole Chief, 1969; recipient Citizen Year award Hollywood, 1963; Eleanor Roosevelt Israel Humanitarian award, 1964. Mem. S. Broward (past bd. dirs.), Broward County bar assns., Fla. Bar, Am. Legion, Tau Epsilon Phi. Democrat. Elk. Club: Civitan (Hollywood). Home: 1231 Adams St Hollywood FL 33020 Office: PO Box 650 1720 Harrison St Hollywood FL 33022

ABRAMSON, DAVID CHARLES, physician; b. Phila., Mar. 30, 1938; s. George and Frances (Weiner) A.; B.S., Muhlenbern Coll., 1960; postgrad. Temple U., 1961-62; M.D. magna cum laude, Georgetown U., 1966; m. Kathryn Haddad, 1961 (div. Nov. 1972); children—Maia Sharon, Gabrielle, Benjamin. Intern Georgetown U. Hosp., Washington, 1966-67, resident, 1967-69; practice medicine, specializing in pediatric neonatology, Washington, 1970—; dir.

nurseries Georgetown U. Hosp., 1970—; mem. staff Columbia Hosp. for Women, Arlington County Hosp., Fairfax County Hosp.; asst. prof. dept. pediatrics Med. Center, Georgetown U., 1970—. Physician, Head Start Program, Washington, 1966-67; mem. Drug Abuse Panel, Washington Pub. Schs., 1969-70, Washington Free Clinic, 1969; mem. ad hoc com. neonatal cardiac care Met. Washington Regional Med. Program, 1970. NIH research grantee, 1969-71. Diplomate Am. Bd. Pediatrics. Mem. Am. Heart Assn., Soc. Obstetrical Anesthesia and Perinatology (chmn. neonatology com. 1971), N.Y. Acad. Scis., Am. Acad. Pediatrics (co-chmn. com. fetus and newborn Washington chpt.), Alpha Omega Alpha, Sigma Chi. Home: 2910 Garfield St NW Washington DC 20008 Office: 3800 Reservoir Rd NW Washington DC 20007

ABRAMSON, HYMAN NORMAN, research instn. adminstr.; b. San Antonio, Mar. 4, 1926; s. Nathan and Pearl (Westerman) A.; B.S., Stanford, 1950, M.S., 1951; Ph.D. (Southwestern Fund fellow), U. Tex., 1956; m. Idelle Rebecca Ringel, Apr. 20, 1947; children—Phillip David, Mark Donald. Project engr. Chance Vought Aircraft Co., Dallas, 1952; asso. prof. aero. engring. Tex. A. and M. U., College Station, 1952-56; tech. v.p. Southwest Research Inst., San Antonio, 1956—. Served with USNR, 1943-45. Registered profl. engr., Tex. Fellow Am. Soc. M.E., Am. Inst. Aeros. and Astronautics, A.A.A.S.; mem. Soc. Naval Architects and Marine Engrs. Author: Dynamics of Airplanes, 1958. Editor: Applied Mechanics Surveys, 1966. Contbr. articles on aero. engring. to profl. publs. Home: 1511 Spanish Oaks Dr San Antonio TX 78213

ABRAMSON, SAMUEL RALPH, physician; b. Lafayette, La., Mar. 12, 1917; s. Nathan and Ula (Coronna) A.; B.S., U. Southwestern La., 1937; M.D., Tulane U., 1939; m. Gwen Daly, Oct. 19, 1953; children—Ralph Keith, Robert Coronna, Suzanne Denise. Intern Touro Infirmary, New Orleans, 1939, resident in surgery, 1940-41; gen. practice medicine, Marksville, La., 1946—. Vice pres. Union Bank, Marksville, 1968—. Mem. Avoyelles Parish Sch. Bd., 1960-66, pres., 1960-62. Chmn. State Central Com. Am. party of La., 1969—; coordinator Wallace campaign for Pres., La., 1968. Served with M.C., AUS, 1941-46; MTO. Diplomate Am. Bd. Family Practice. Mem. A.M.A., Am. Assn. Physicians and Surgeons, Am. Physicians Guild, La. Physicians Guild, Am. Assn. Ry. Surgeons, So. Med. Assn., La., Avoyelles Parish med. socs., La. Acad. Gen. Practice, John Birch Soc. (chpt. leader). Home: 608 S Washington Marksville LA 71351 Office: 423 N Washington Marksville LA 71351

ABREGO, GILBERT FREDERICK, JR., accountant; b. Mission, Tex., Jan. 5, 1934; s. Gilbert Frederick and Geraldine (Meister) A.; B.S. in Indsl. Engring. and Indsl. Mgmt., U. Ark., 1956; m. Mary Ann Walker, June 15, 1956; children—Frederick Douglas, Anne Meister. Jr. accountant Douglas Walker & Co., Fort Smith, Ark., 1959-64, jr. partner, 1964-65, gen. partner, 1965—. Finance officer Fort Smith Civil Air Patrol, 1965—; treas., dir. Fort Smith Art Center, 1967; mem. Western Ark. Estate Planning Council, 1967—; coach Ch. League Baseball, 1967; mem. finance com. Mt. Magazine council Girl Scouts U.S.A., 1967-68. Served to capt. USAFR, 1956-59. C.P.A., Ark. Mem. Am. Inst. C.P.A.'s (financial mgmt. and controls com. 1968-69, tech. studies com. 1970), Ark. Soc. C.P.A.'s (dir. 1969-71, pres. western Ark. chpt. 1967-68, chmn. speakers bur. 1971-72), C.P.A. Assos. (practice mgmt. com. 1968-69, exec. com. 1973-74), Nat. Assn. Accountants (treas., dir. 1966-67), Air Force Assn., So. States Conf. C.P.A.'s (chmn. publicity and promotion com. 1972), Fort Smith C. of C. (vice chmn. aviation com. 1966-67), Sigma Nu. Lutheran (mem. new sch. constrn. com. 1969—). Clubs: Town of Fort Smith, Hardscrabble Country (Fort Smith). Home: 4325 S P St Fort Smith AR 72901 Office: Mchts Bank Bldg Fort Smith AR 72901

ABSHER, LEE ALTON, physician; b. Sugar Grove, Tenn., Jan. 26, 1905; s. Lytle Asberry and Ella Harriet (Perdue) A.; B.S., U. Tenn., 1927, M.D., 1928; m. Della Lucille Cathey, Mar. 25, 1931 (dec. Jan. 1952). Extern Shelby County Hosp., Memphis, 1926-28; intern Knoxville (Tenn.) Gen. Hosp., 1928-29; surg. preceptor, Newport News, Va., 1929-30; practice medicine and surgery, Portland, Tenn., 1931-38; practice medicine and surgery, Midland, Tex., 1938-42, also part owner Western Clinic Hosp.; practice medicine and surgery, Knoxville, 1946—; mem. staff Ft. Sanders Presbyn. Hosp., Knoxville, St. Mary's Meml. Hosp., Knoxville, East Tenn. Bapt. Hosp., Knoxville, U. Tenn. Meml. Hosp., Knoxville. Served from capt. to maj., M.C. AUS, World War II; ETO. Fellow Am. Acad. Family Physicians (charter); mem. A.M.A., So., Tenn. med. assns., Knoxville Acad. Medicine, Tenn. Soc. S.O.R., Scabbard and Blade, Sigma Nu, Alpha Kappa Kappa. Democrat. Baptist. Mason. Clubs: University Tennessee President's (founding mem.), Cherokee Country (Knoxville). Editor: Some Early Settlers of Upper Sumner County, Tennessee, 1966. Office: 3501 Broadway NE Knoxville TN 37917 Home: 2408 N Park Blvd Knoxville TN 37917

ACERS, ADNELL OWEN, JR., state ofcl.; b. Oklahoma City, Nov. 24, 1927; s. Adnell Owen and Audria (French) A.; B.Mus., Oklahoma City U., 1949; M.Mus.Ed., U. Okla., 1955, postgrad., 1957-62; postgrad. Okla. State U., 1960; m. Mary Louise Freeman, May 28, 1954; children—Kent Owen, Tamara Lynn, James Kevin. Tchr. music Taft Jr. High Sch., Oklahoma City, 1952-56; guidance counselor Marshall High Sch., Oklahoma City, 1956-59; asst. prin. Classen High Sch., Oklahoma City, 1959-62; mgr. information systems design Okla. State Dept. Edn., Oklahoma City, 1972—. Cons. ednl. data processing, 1962-72. Served with AUS, 1950-52. Decorated Bronze Star. Mem. Assn. Ednl. Data Systems, Okla. Edn. Assn., Phi Mu Alpha. Republican. Methodist. Home: 4018 NW 59th St Oklahoma City OK 73112 Office: State Dept Edn State Capitol Oklahoma City OK 73105

ACHEE, ROLAND JOSEPH, lawyer; b. New Orleans, Dec. 12, 1922; s. Benjamin Elphege and Marie J. (Cazenave) A.; B.A., Centenary Coll., 1944; LL.B., La. State U., 1949; m. Jean W. Lant, Feb. 19, 1955; 1 dau., Marie Alaine. Admitted to La. bar, 1949; practiced in Shreveport, 1949—; partner Ferris & Achee, attys., 1952-72, Nelson & Achee, Ltd., 1974—. Chmn. Draft Bd., Shreveport, 1964-67, vice chmn., 1967-70, sec., 1972—. Served to lt. (j.g.) USNR, 1944-46. Mem. Am., La., Shreveport (exec. com. 1964-65) bar assns., La. State Law Inst. (jr. hon.), Centenary Coll. Alumni Assn. (dir. 1969—), 40 and 8, Am. Legion (post comdr. 1961-62), Order of Coif, Omicron Delta Kappa. Elk (Shreveport exalted ruler 1958-59, trustee 1959-69). Editor-in-chief La. Law Review, 1948. Home: 182 Bruce Av Shreveport LA 71101 Office: Henry C Beck Bldg Shreveport LA 71101

ACHORN, FRANK PERRON, chem. engr.; b. Biloxi, Miss., Mar. 23, 1923; s. Glenwood Bryant and Leona (Weatherbee) A.; B.S. in Chem. Engring., U. Louisville, 1947; m. Jane Showalter, Sept. 29, 1945; children—Frank Perron, Judith (Mrs. P. Linden Reeder), Ted. Chem. engr. TVA, Muscle Shoals, Ala., 1947-57, head process and product improvement sect., 1959—; asst. plant mgr. Coastal Chem. Corp., Pascagoula, Miss., 1957-59. Dir. Fertilizer Industry Round Table; internat. fertilizer cons., Brazil, Afghanistan, Japan, Philippines, Sweden, Spain. Adviser Local Naval Res. Unit, Fertilizer Inst., Nat. Fertilizer Solutions Assn. Served to comdr. USNR. Mem. Am. Chem. Soc., Nat. Fertilizer Solutions Assn. (hon.). Presbyn. Lion. Author: (with Thomas Cox) Fertilizer Technology and Use, 1970. Contbr. articles to profl. jours. Patentee in field. Home: 2315 Sherrod Av Florence AL 35630 Office: F237 NFDC TVA Muscle Shoals AL 35660

ACKEL, FRED JOHN, dentist; b. Gloversville, N.Y., Mar. 28, 1927; s. Fred and Anna Azar (Ackel) A.; student Clarkson Coll. Tech., 1944-45, U.S. Merchant Marine Acad., 1945-46; B.S., Hartwick Coll., 1950; D.D.S., Georgetown U., 1954; m. Mildred Krause, July 15, 1950 (div. Oct. 1969); children—Debra Ann, Gary Fredric, Kimberly Jean. Individual practice dentistry, Ft. Lauderdale, Fla., 1957—. Mem. Fla. State Bd. Health, 1967-68; mem. Fla. State Racing Commn., 1968-71. Pres. Broward County Young Republicans, 1961-63; chmn. Young Ams. for Freedom, 1962-65; del. Rep. Nat. Conv., 1964; chmn. Citizens for Goldwater-Miller, Nat. Draft Goldwater Com., Broward County, 1964; chmn. Rep. Citizens Com., Broward County, 1965-71. Trustee Coral Oaks Med. Dental Bldg. Enterprises. Served from 1st lt. to capt. USAF, 1954-56. Fellow Acad. Gen. Dentistry; mem. Am. Dental Assn. (chmn. dels. ann. meeting 1969), Pierre Fauchard Acad., Navy League, Broward County Dental Soc. (pres. 1965-66), Fla. Dental Assn. (trustee 1972—). Roman Catholic. K.C. Club: Coral Ridge Country (Ft. Lauderdale). Editor Broward County Dental Review, 1968—, Atlantic Coast Dental Explorer, 1973—. Home: 4821 NE 26th Av Fort Lauderdale FL 33308 Office: 2655 E Oakland Park Blvd Fort Lauderdale FL 33306

ACKER, ARTHUR MALCOLM, glass co. marketing exec.; b. Boston, May 11, 1930; s. Robert Henry and Irene Agnes (Reed) A.; B.A., Northeastern U., Boston, 1955; m. Barbara Arabelle Rundlett, Dec. 19, 1953; 1 son, John Arthur. Estimator PPG Industries, Boston, 1951-52, contract salesman, 1953-54, contract mgr., 1955-56; dist. mgr. ASG Industries, Kingsport, Tenn., 1956-61, regional mgr., 1962-68, gen. sales mgr., 1968-70, v.p. sales, 1970-71, v.p. sales and marketing, 1971—. Dir. United Fund, Kingsport, Tenn., 1972-74; bd. govs. U. Tenn. Exec. Devel. Program, Knoxville, 1973. Served with USAF, 1948-49, 1950-51. Recipient Distinguished Salesman award Sales Exec. Club Pitts., 1958. Republican. Presbyn. Elk, Moose. Home: 3217 Parkcliffe Dr Kingsport TN 37664 Office: 1500 Lincoln St Kingsport TN 37662

ACKER, JOSEPH EDINGTON, JR., physician; b. Knoxville, Tenn., Oct. 19, 1918; s. Joseph Edwan and Kate Loubelle (Edington) A.; B.S., U. Tenn., 1941, M.D., 1941; m. Elizabeth Chase Gutch, Nov. 14, 1942; children—Joseph Edington III, Judith Ann (Mrs. Don Mitchell), Julia Chase (Mrs. Gordon Van Mol), John Howard, Janet Sue. Intern Kansas City Gen. Hosp., 1941-42; resident Cleve. City Hosp., 1946-48; pvt. practice internal medicine, Knoxville, 1948-55, cardiology, Knoxville, 1955—; mem. Knoxville Cardiovascular Group, 1962—; mem. staff U. Tenn. Meml. Hosp., St. Mary's Meml. Hosp., East Tenn. Bapt. Hosp., Ft. Sanders Presbyn. Hosp.; asso. prof. clin. medicine Meml. Research Center and Hosp. U. Tenn., 1957—, chief cardiac work evaluation clinic, 1956-72; chief cardiac work evaluation clinic Knoxville Gen. Hosp., 1948-56. Served to lt. comdr. USNR, 1942-46. Diplomate Am. Bd. Internal Medicine. Fellow A.C.P., Council Clin. Cardiology Am. Heart Assn., Am. Coll. Cardiology; mem. East Tenn. Heart Assn. (pres. 1956), Tenn. Heart Assn. (pres. 1961-63). Author: (with Erb and Mann) Physicians Handbook for Evaluation of Cardiovascular and Physical Fitness, 1970. Home: Weisgarber Rd Knoxville TN 37919 Office: 1928 Alcoa Hwy Knoxville TN 37920

ACKER, WARREN HARLAN, petroleum co. exec.; b. Junction City, Kan., Mar. 21, 1919; s. Samuel and Anna (Joltz) A.; B.S. in Chem. Engring., Kan. State Coll., 1942; m. Jacqueline Ann Folck, May 17, 1942; children—Mark E., Michael W. With Phillips Petroleum Co., Borger, Tex., 1946—, supt. mfg. Philback plant, 1964-65, mgr. plant, 1965-72, mgr. butadiene plant, 1972—. Bd. dirs. A.R.C. Hutchinson County, Tri-City United Fund, Borger. Served to lt. USNR, 1943-45. Mem. C. of C. (pres.), West Tex. C. of C. (dir.). Methodist (past pres. bd. stewards). Patentee in field. Home: 305 Riney Dr Phillips TX 79071 Office: Box 1526 Borger TX 79007

ACKERMAN, RICHARD HENRY, bishop; b. Pitts., Aug. 30, 1903; s. John and Josephine (Richard) A.; B.A., Duquesne U., 1923, Litt. D., 1961; student St. Mary's Seminary, Norwalk, Conn., U. Fribourg, Switzerland, U. Mich.; LL.D., Niagara U., 1953. Ordained priest Roman Cath. Ch., 1926; prof. philosophy, 1930-35, prin. high sch., 1935-40; nat. dir. Pontifical Assn. of Holy Childhood, internat. papal mission-aid soc. for benefit underprivileged children, 1940-56, pres. bd. dirs., v.p. superior council, Paris, France; consecrated titular bishop of Lares, auxiliary bishop of San Diego, 1956; vicar gen. Diocese of San Diego; bishop Covington, Ky., 1960—. Decorated Pro Ecclesiae et Pontifice, 1947. K.C. (4 deg.). Clubs: New York Athletic; Pittsburgh Athletic. Editor: The Paraclete, 1928-30; Annals of Holy Childhood, 1940-56. Address: 1140 Madison Av Covington KY 41011

ACKERS, GARY ROBERT, broadcasting co. exec.; b. Abilene, Tex., Jan. 21, 1941; s. Dale and Johnnie Robert (Weatherby) A.; B.F.A., Tex. Christian U., 1963; m. Virginia Ann Chase, May 23, 1970; 1 son, Brandon Dale. Salesman, gen. sales mgr. KRIO Radio, McAllen, Tex., 1964-69; v.p., sec., gen. sales mgr. KHEY, Inc., El Paso, Tex., 1969—; v.p., sec. KRMD, Inc., Shreveport, La.; v.p. Radio Abilene, Inc. KRBC. Co-chmn. Heart Fund, 1967; dist. comml. chmn. United FUnd, 1967-69; mem. spl. gifts com. Cancer Radiation Treatment Fund, 1972; mem. big gifts div. Pub. TV Fund drive, 1972. Served with USAF, 1963-64. Mem. Nat., Tex. assns. broadcasters, Kappa Sigma. Methodist. Home: 409 Indian Bluff St El Paso TX 79912 Office: 2419 N Piedras St El Paso TX 79930

ACOSTA, WILLIAM CAPERS, clergyman; b. Lexington, Ky., Aug. 18, 1912; s. William Wingate and Margaret Buchanan (Foster) A.; B.S., U. Ky., 1936; certificate theology Bexley Hall, Kenyon Coll., 1940, B.D., 1966, M.Div., 1973; postgrad. U. of South, 1949, 50, 51, 66; m. Virginia Sigrid Baker, June 28, 1941; children—Virginia Johanne (Mrs. Richard Edmund Smith), William Capers II. Ordained to ministry Episcopal Ch. as deacon, 1940, priest, 1940; missionary in charge, rector St. Mary's and Grace South Ch., Cleve., 1938-41; rector Christ Ch., Hudson, 1941-43; asst. rector St. Andrew's Ch., Louisville, 1944-46, Incarnation Ch., Dallas, 1946-49; rector St. John's Ch., Corsicana, Tex., 1949-50, Messiah Ch., Gonzales, Tex., also St. James Ch., Hallettsville, Tex., 1950-52, Annunciation Ch., New Orleans, 1952-65, Episcopal Ch. of Nativity, Dothan, Ala., 1965—. Dep. to provincial synod of Ky., 1944, 45, La., 1956, 63; chmn. youth and coll. work Ky. Dept. Christian Edn., 1944-46, Coll. Preachers, 1945, 48; co-chmn. dept. promotion Dallas, 1948-50; pres. Corsicana Ministerial Alliance, 1950; mem. bd. Camp Capers, W. Tex., 1950; pres. Ministerial Union, New Orleans, 1954; sec. bd. Gaudet Home, New Orleans, 1955-57; sec. Christian social relations dept. Diocese of La., 1955, chmn. dept. pub. relations, 1956-60; Episcopal chmn. Billy Graham Crusade, New Orleans, mem. La. Diocesan Council, 1956-62; chmn. La. Dept. Stewardship, 1961-62; sec. New Orleans Clericus, 1964-65; dean Dothan Convocation, Diocese of Ala., 1967; mem. com. charter and canons Diocese Central Gulf Coast, 1973—, host rector 2d ann. conv., 1973. Mem. adv. bd. Salvation Army, 1966—. Mem. Dothan Ministerial Union (sec.-treas. 1966-67). Home: 1811 Northside Dr Dothan AL 36301 Office: 205 S Denton St Dothan AL 36301

ACREE, WILLIAM BYRNES, physician; b. Memphis, Dec. 8, 1919; s. George T. and Helen Hunt (Byrnes) A.; M.D., U. Tenn., 1942; m. Eva Kersenia McClintock, Dec. 20, 1942; children—William B., George Michael. Intern, Knoxville (Tenn.) Gen. Hosp., 1943; individual practice medicine, Ridgely, Tenn., 1946—. Pres. West Tenn. Heart Assn., 1966-67. Alderman City of Ridgely, 1961-71, vice mayor, 1966-71; magistrate Lake County, Tenn., 1966-71. Served to capt., M.C. AUS, 1942-46. Named Man of Year Ridgely, 1969. Fellow am. Acad. Family Physicians (charter); mem. A.M.A., Am. Assn. Family Practice, N.Y. Acad. Scis., Tenn. Med. Assn., N.W. Tenn. Acad. Medicine (pres. 1965—), Royal Soc. Health. Mason, Rotarian (pres. 1956). Home: Hwy 78 Ridgely TN 38080 Office: 115 S Main Ridgely TN 38080

ACUFF, CLAUDE ROGER, JR., packaging co. exec.; b. Middlesboro, Ky., May 14, 1938; s. Claude Roger and Gladys Mildred (Ashton) A.; B.S., Middle Tenn. State U., 1960; m. Patricia Anne Rose, Feb. 5, 1965; children—Tracy Lynn, Kimberly Donnita. Asst. plant mgr. Rock City Packaging, Inc., Lebanon, Tenn., 1964-65, sales rep., 1966-67; sales mgr. Southeastern Box Corp., Gallatin, Tenn., 1968-69, gen. mgr., pres., 1969—; dir. Rock City Packaging, Inc. Served with AUS, 1960-63. Republican. Methodist. Moose. Home: Route 5 Lebanon TN 37087 Office: Hartsville Pike Gallatin TN 37066

ACUFF, FREDERICK GENE, educator; b. Stinesville, Ind., Sept. 13, 1931; s. George and Beryl (Canada) A.; B.A., Manhattan Christian Coll., 1957; M.S., Kan. State U., 1959, Ph.D., U. Mo., 1967; m. Phyllis Jo Surface, June 3, 1962; children—Jo Shelley (Mrs. Thomas Friedemann), Rod Worth Smith, Gene Taylor. Teaching asst., research asso. Kan. State U., 1958-60; instr. sociology U. Mo., 1959-60: asst. prof. sociology Phillips U., 1960-62; asst. prof. sociology Okla. State U., Stillwater, 1962-67, asso. prof., 1968-69, prof., 1969—, acting chmn. dept. sociology, 1967-68, chmn., 1968—. Faculty Midwest Council Social Research In Aging. Served with AUS, 1952-54. NSF fellow, 1966-67. Mem. Am. Sociol. Assn., Mid-West, S.W. sociol. socs. Mem. Disciples of Christ Ch. (lay minister). Author: (with Donald E. Allen and Lloyd Taylor) From Man to Society, 1973. Contbr. articles to profl. jours. Home: Route 1 Stillwater OK 74074

ACUFF, JOHN EDGAR, lawyer; b. Chattanooga, July 20, 1940; s. White Hollis and Estelle (Johnson) A.; B.A., David Lipscomb Coll., 1962; J.D., Vanderbilt U., 1969; m. Carolyn Elizabeth Howell, Sept. 6, 1963; children—John Edgar, William Ira Howell, Karl David. Admitted to Tenn. bar, 1969; asso. Cable, McDaniel, Bowie & Bond, Balt., 1969; law clk. to chief judge, U.S. Ct. Appeals for 6th Circuit, Nashville, 1969-70; asso. Crawford & Barnes, Cookeville, Tenn., 1970; partner Crawford, Barnes & Acuff, Cookeville, 1971—. Cons., lectr. to Tenn. Tech. program for low income families in Upper Cumberland region, 1971—. Pres., Law Students for Nixon, Nashville, 1968. Bd. dirs. Koinonia. Served with USNR, 1962-66. Mem. Am., Tenn., Putnam County (sec., treas. 1971) bar assns., Tenn. Trial Lawyers Assn. Home: Crossroads Farm Route 8 Box 309 A Sparta TN 38583 Office: Box 828 Cookeville TN 38501

ADAIR, ROBERT HOWARD, aero. engr.; b. New Orleans, Aug. 4, 1931; s. Howard Leon and Thelma Estelle (Hewett) A.; B.S. in Aero. Engring., U. Ala., 1958; postgrad. U. Fla., 1972; m. Rachael Dana Boone, Oct. 4, 1958; children—Robert Howard, Jr., David Lee. Aerospace engr. Brookley AFB, Ala., 1958-64, supervisory aerospace engr., 1964-65; research engr. Boeing Co., Huntsville, Ala., 1965-67; gen. engr. Elgin AFB, Fla., 1967—. Chmn. bldg. com. Boy Scouts Am., Shalimar, Fla., 1972-74, mem. adult adv. council, 1972-74. Served with USAF, 1951-55. Recipient Sustained Superior Performance award Elgin AFB, Fla., 1972-73. Registered profl. engr., Ala. Mem. Pi Kappa Alpha. Baptist. Home: 13 Maple Av Shalimar FL 32579 Office: Prodn Engring Branch Elgin AFB FL 32542

ADAIR, (WILLIAM) RALPH, cafeteria chain exec.; b. Temple, Okla., Apr. 19, 1908; s. James Williams and Margaret (Verhines) A.; student Southwestern Coll. Okla., 1925-28, Okla. U., 1931; m. Velma Elizabeth Pulley, May 4, 1933; children—James William, Gerald Paul, Reba Jane. Sales mgr. New State Ice Co., Oklahoma City, 1929-37; owner, gen. mgr. Eastside Ice Co., Oklahoma City, 1938-60, Bethany Ice Co., Oklahoma City, 1938-60; owner Ralph's Supermarket, Oklahoma City, 1948-58; pres., prin. owner Wyatt Airpark, Inc., Oklahoma City. Mem. Oklahoma County Bd. Commrs., 1953-73, chmn., 1973—. Contbr. articles, polit. cartoons to newspapers. Home: 117 Lake Aluma St Oklahoma City OK 73121 Office: 320 Robert S Kerr St Oklahoma City OK 73102

ADAMCIK, JOE ALFRED, educator; b. Taylor, Tex., June 28, 1930; s. Joseph John and Pearle Mae (Offield) A.; B.S., U. Tex., 1951, M.A., 1954; Ph.D., U. Ill., 1958. Asst. prof. Tex. Tech U., Lubbock, 1957-61, asso. prof., 1961—. Served from ensign to lt. (j.g.) USNR, 1951-53. Mem. Am. Chem. Soc. (chmn. com. on constn. and bylaws), Chem. Soc. (London), Am. Geophys. Union, A.A.A.S., Sigma Xi, Phi Kappa Phi (mem. editorial adv. bd. 1972—). Contbr. articles to profl. jours. Home: 5223 42d St Lubbock TX 79414

ADAMS, ADDISON (ADDIE) FRANK, land title abstracter; b. Abbott, Texas, Jan. 3, 1904; s. John Blair and Addie Frances (Forrest) A.; student Baylor U., Waco, Tex., 1922-24; grad. Sch. Social Sci., Civic Fedn., Dallas, 1937; m. Iva Dell Miller, Oct. 14, 1928 (div. 1930); 1 son John Blair; m. 2d Beulah Grace Jenkins, Dec. 26, 1938; children—Forrest Jenkins, Alice Ann. Resident mgr. R. C. Winters and Co., C.P.A.'s, McCamey, Tex., 1926-30; asso. F. A. Hornbeck, gen. land agt. Kansas City, Mexico and Orient R.R., 1926-30; pub. accountant, 1930-36; investigator Tex. Old Age Assistance Commn., 1936-40; sec.-mgr. Bastrop County Abstract Co., Bastrop, Tex., 1940-59, pres., 1960—. Mem. Am., Tex. land title assns., Am. Assn. Petroleum Landmen, Tex. Geneal. Soc. Baptist. Address: 1707 Pecan St Bastron TX 78602

ADAMS, ALFRED BERNARD, JR., chem. engr.; b. Asbury Park, N.J., Oct. 15, 1920; s. Alfred Bishop and Julia Ruth (Wiseman) A.; B.S., Ga. Inst. Tech., 1943; postgrad. Wayne U., 1946-47; m. Claudia Neff, Dec. 28, 1942; children—Alfred B. III, Tamara (Mrs. Carl Edward Dohn, Jr.), Carla (Mrs. William H. York, Jr.). Sr. project engr. Pennwalt Corp., Wyandotte, Mich., 1946-50; sales mgr. Goslin-Birmingham Mfg. Co. (Ala.), 1950-61; field chem. engr. Eimco Corp., Birmingham, 1961-62; prin. engr. Thiokol Chem. Co., Brunswick, Ga., 1962-64; sr. staff air pollution engr. Rust Engring. Co., Birmingham, 1964—. Tchr. air pollution course Auburn U. Extension Sch.; guest lectr. tech. soc. meetings. Mem. Pub. and Environmental Health Adv. Com. for 5 counties in Ala., 1973—. Served with AUS, World War II; ETO. Decorated Purple Heart. Registered profl. engr., Ala., Fla., Mich. Mem. T.A.P.P.I., Air Pollution Control Assn. (past chmn. So. sect.). Home: 1827 Mara Dr Birmingham AL 35215 Office: Rust Engring Co PO Box 101 Birmingham AL 35201

ADAMS, A(LFRED) HUGH, coll. pres.; b. Punta Gorda, Fla., Mar. 8, 1928; s. Alfred and Irene (Gatewood) A.; B.S., Fla. State U., 1950, M.S., 1956, Ed.D., 1962; m. Joyce Morgan, Nov. 11, 1954; children—Joy, Al, Paul. Asst. dir. housing, instr. edn. Fla. State U., 1958-62, asst. dean men, asst. prof. edn., 1962-64; supt. pub. instrn.

Charlotte County, Fla., 1965-68; vice chmn., coordinator Gov.'s Commn. for Quality Edn., 1968-70; pres. Broward Community Coll., Ft. Lauderdale, Fla., 1968—. Founding pres. Educators Investment Corp. Fla., 1966; mem. Fla. Gov.'s Adv. Com. Edn., 1966-70; mem. regional council Southeastern Edn. Corp., 1966-69; trustee South Fla. Edn. Center, Inc., Pub. Service TV. Del. U.S. Dept. State Nat. Fgn. Policy Conf. for Edn. Leaders, 1968; mem. Fla. State Tchr. Edn. Adv. Council, Profl. Practices Commn.; mem. Fla. Inter-agy. Law Enforcement Planning Council. Pres., United Way, vice chmn., 1971; bd. dirs. Broward chpt. A.R.C. Served to comdr. USNR, 1945-73. Decorated Knight Internat. Constantinian Order. Mem. N.E.A., Am. Assn. Sch. Adminstrs., Fla. Assn. Colls. and Univs. (pres.), Fla. Edn. Council (ethics com.), Fla. Assn. Deans and Counselors, Greater Ft. Lauderdale C. of C. (dir.), Omicron Delta Kappa. Kiwanian. Club: Metropolitan Dinner (dir.) (Ft. Lauderdale). Home: 105 N Victoria Park Fort Lauderdale FL 33301

ADAMS, BEULAH GRACE JENKINS (MRS. ADDISON FRANK ADAMS), abstract co. exec.; b. Bastrop, Tex., Nov. 29, 1909; d. Hartford and Beulah Alice (Hemphill) Jenkins; B.A., Baylor U., 1930; postgrad. U. Tex., 1933, 39, U. Colo., 1934; m. Addison Frank Adams, Dec. 26, 1938; children—Forrest Jenkins, Alice Ann (Mrs. Charles Woodrow Miller). Tchr., Bastrop (Tex.) Pub. Schs., 1930-41; v.p., mgr. Bastrop County Abstract Co., Inc., Tex., 1942—. Mem. Am. Assn. U. Women, Tex. State Geneal. Soc., Am., Tex. land title assns., Am. Assn. Petroleum Landmen, Delta Kappa Gamma. Baptist. Home: 1707 Pecan St Bastrop TX 78602 Office: 901 Main St PO Box 550 Bastrop TX 78602

ADAMS, CLIFFORD LOWELL, univ. adminstr.; b. nr. Vincennes, Ind., Jan. 28, 1915; s. George Washington and Estalla Mae (Baldwin) A.; B.S. in Physics, Ind. State U., 1940; M.S. in physics, U. Mo. at Rolla, 1950; postgrad. U. Md., 1951-53; m. Lillian Opal Ratliff, Dec. 24, 1943; children—Terry (Mrs. Walter Sparrow), Gerri Lea. Instr., Morehead (Ky.) State Coll., 1942-44; tchr. Kentland (Ind.) High Sch., 1944-46; asst. prof. Tri-State Coll., Angola, Ind., 1946-48; instr. U. Mo. at Rolla, 1948-50; asso. prof. Union U., Jackson, Tenn., 1950-51; asst. prof. U.S. Naval Acad., Annapolis, Md., 1951-55, asso. prof., 1955-56; asso. prof. N.E. La. State Coll., Monroe, 1956-58; chmn. dept. physics Old Dominion U., Norfolk, Va., 1958-68, research adminstr., 1966—, dir. research found., 1966—. Cons. USPHS Hosp., Norfolk, 1970-72; dir. Model Neighborhood Devel. Corp., Norfolk, 1972—. Founder, Norfolk Fedn. Civic Leagues, 1959-61; mem. Norfolk City Planning Commn., 1962-66; mem. Norfolk Area Med. Center Adv. Com., 1963—;pres. Norfolk chpt. Am. Field Service, 1963-65; mem. Norfolk Fine Arts Com., 1968-72; active Boy Scouts Am., 1966-68. AEC grantee, 1961; NSF grantee, 1962, 64. Mem. A.A.A.S., Am. Phys. Soc., Am. Assn. Physics Tchrs. (pres. Va. area 1966-69), Norfolk C. of C., Sigma Xi, Phi Kappa Phi. Democrat. Presbyn. Club: Norfolk Yacht and Country. Author: Research-Energy Levels in Potassium Chloride, 1950; Laboratory Manual for General Physics, 1956; General Physics Laboratory Manual, 1959. Home: 1325 Monterey Av Norfolk VA 23508

ADAMS, CRAWFORD WILLIAM, cardiologist; b. Springfield, Mass., Sept. 15, 1915; s. E. Crawford and Doris (Roane) A.; B.S., U. Mass., 1938; M.D., Boston U., 1942; m. Barbara Ann Simpkins, Nov. 27, 1943; children—Jeffrey Paul, Patricia Ann, Cynthia Louise (Mrs. Thomas T. Sumerville), Stephen Roane, Barbara Jean (Mrs. Lee G. Langston), Crawford William, Doris Elizabeth, Diane Elaine, Nancy Marie, John Thomas, Joan Theresa, Anne Melissa. Intern Boston City Hosp., 1942-43, resident, 1942-43, 46-47; practice medicine specializing in cardiology, Nashville, 1945—; mem. staff St. Thomas Hosp., Vanderbilt U., Bapt., Nashville Met., Nashville Meml. hosps. Asso. clin. prof. medicine Vanderbilt U. Med. Sch., Nashville, 1966—, Meharry Med. Sch., Nashville, 1950—. Chmn. Brentwood Acad. Fund Drive, 1971-72; pres. Middle Tenn. council Boy Scouts Am., 1967-69, bd. dirs., 1963-74; mem. at large Nat. council, 1965-74. Bd. dirs. Jr. Achievement, 1968-69. Served to maj. USAAF, 1943-46. Recipient Beaver award Boy Scouts Am., 1963, Eagle Scout Recognition dinner, 1972; named hon. citizen Tenn., 1967. Fellow Am. Coll. Chest Physicians (exec. council 1966—), Am. Coll. Angiology, Am. Coll. Cardiology (bd. govs. 1973-76), Internat. Cardiovascular Soc., Am. Geriatrics Soc.,Sci. Council and Internat. Coll. Angiology, Council on Clin. Cardiology Am. Heart Assn., A.C.P., Royal Soc. Health Gt. Britian; mem. Tenn. (dir. 1967—), Middle Tenn. (dir. 1959—, chmn. bd. dirs. 1968-69) heart assns., Nashville Acad. Medicine and Davidson County Med. Soc. (chmn. program com. 1964-65), Nashville Soc. Internal Medicine (chmn. program com. 1962-64), Upper Cumberland Med. Soc. (pres. 1963-64), Clin. Cardiac Research Found. (chmn. bd. dirs. 1968—), A.M.A. (chmn. sect. chest diseases 1966-67), Nashville Cardiovascular Soc. (pres. 1974-75). Author: Clinical Electrocardiography, 1964. Asso. editor Diseases of the Chest, 1965-67, sr. editor, 1967-72; edit. cons. Am. Jour. Cardiology, 1968—. Home: 963 Overton Lea Rd Nashville TN 37203 Office: 402 21st and Hayes Med Bldg Nashville TN 37203

ADAMS, DAVID HOLMES, lawyer, constrn. co. exec.; b. Paintsville, Ky., Oct. 6, 1948; s. Stuart Holmes and Geneva L. (Honeycutt) A.; B.S., Pikeville Coll., 1970; J.D., U. Louisville, 1972. Vice pres. Adams Constrn. Corp., Pikeville, Ky., 1970—; admitted to Ky. bar, 1972; asso. Hinton, Hall & Todd, 1972—; v.p. Adams Corps., WLSI Radio Sta. Mem. Phi Delta Tau, Delta Theta Phi. Home: 100 N Mayo Trail Pikeville KY 41501 Office: Box 2008 Pikeville KY 41501

ADAMS, DONALD PAUL, banker; b. Chauvin, La., Mar. 31, 1939; s. Clarence J. and Thelma (Pellegrin) A.; grad. Dale Carnegie Course, 1958; grad. Sch. of Banking of South, La. State U., 1972; m. Loretta Roberts, Dec. 28, 1957; children—Bryan, Debra, Lisa, Keith. Bookkeeper Terrebonne & Trust Co., Houma, La., 1957, teller, 1958, exchange window teller, 1959, note teller, 1960, asst. br. mgr., 1961, br. mgr., 1962, asst. cashier, 1963-68, asst. v.p., 1968-69, sr. v.p., br. bank adminstr., 1971—; owner Goodwill Advt. Co., 1965—, Bankers Advt. Service, 1967—, House of Gifts, 1968—, Income Protection Plan, 1967—, Adams Pub. House, 1969— (all Chauvin, La.); v.p. Adams & Lecompte Inc., Chauvin, 1966—, Co-chmn. Terrebonne Parish March of Dimes, 1968—; dir. Terrebonne Parish Recreation Dist. 7, 1966—. Mem. Advt. Specialty Inst., Houma-Terrebonne C. of C. Roman Catholic (chmn. finance com.). K.C. (4 deg.). Home: Star Route Box 690 A Chauvin LA 70344 Office: PO Box 173 Chauvin LA 70344

ADAMS, EDWARD QUINCY, broadcasting co. exec.; b. Chgo., Oct. 3, 1926; s. Edward Richmond and Frances Ruth (Cummings) A.; B.S., Northwestern U., 1950; m. Nancy Lane Thomas, Jan. 10, 1959; children—Marion Frances, Abigail Quincy. Salesman TV Advt. Reps., 1959-65; gen. sales mgr. sta. KDKA-TV, Pitts., 1965-68; v.p., gen. mgr. sta. WCIX-TV Coral TV Corp., Miami, Fla., 1968—. Served with USNR, 1944-46, 50-52. Home: 12855 Old Cutler Rd Miami FL 33156 Office: 1111 Brickell Av Miami FL 33131

ADAMS, ERNEST CORTLAND, cons. engr.; b. Dieterich, Ill., May 31, 1913; s. Ernest and Ollie (Higgins) A.; B.S., U. Ill., 1937; M.S., Harvard, 1947; student U.S. Army War Coll., 1957-58; m. Dorothy Sims, Feb. 12, 1965; children—James E., Richard B., Daniel E., Stephen C. Commd. 2d lt. C.E., U.S. Army, 1937, advanced through grades to col., 1952; exec. officer amphibious brigade, World War II, regimental comdr. Korean War, dep. engr. Hdqrs. 2d Army, dist. engr., Kansas City, Mo., chief of constrn. div. Dept. Army, chief logistics officer, Alaskan Command; ret., 1964; cons. engr. Frank G. Bryant & Assos., Austin, Tex., 1964—, exec. v.p., dir., 1965—. Decorated Legion of Merit with 2 oak leaf clusters, Bronze Star medal; Croix de Guerre (France). Registered profl. engr., Tex., D.C. Mem. Am. Soc. C.E., Nat. Soc. Profl. Engrs., Soc. Am. Mil. Engrs., Sigma Xi, Tau Beta Pi, Phi Kappa Phi. Patentee in field. Home: 305 Briarwood Trail Austin TX 78746 Office: 1107 W Gibson St Austin TX 78704

ADAMS, EZRA JOHN, educator; b. Darnell, La., Aug. 30, 1923; s. John Washington and Corinne (Hargrove) A.; B.A. in Journalism, N.E. La. State Coll., 1956; M.A., La. State U., 1964; m. Catherine Geraldine Ward, Nov. 2, 1956; children—(adopted) Janet Hawsey, Gayla Dawn. Reporter, state editor Morning World, Monroe, La., 1954-56; pub. relations dir. Parish Recreation and Parks Commn., Baton Rouge, 1956-57; salesman, newsman radio sta, WJBO, Baton Rouge, 1957-58; reporter Morning Adv., Baton Rouge, 1958; mng. editor Rural La., Assn. La. Elec. Coops., Opelousas, 1959-63; pub. information rep. La. Dept. Agr., Baton Rouge, 1963-64; dir. publs. Southeastern La. Coll., Hammond, 1964-66, asst. prof. journalism, 1964-66; pub. relations rep. Internat. Paper Co., Bastrop, La., 1966-68; student Am. history doctoral program Northwestern State U. La., Natchitoches, 1968-69, asso. prof. journalism, 1969—. Served with USAAF, 1942-46, USAF, 1951-53. Mem. Assn. Edn. in Journalism (charter mem. newspaper div.), Sigma Delta Chi, Tau Kappa Epsilon. Democrat. Baptist. Lion, Mason.

ADAMS, FRANCIS BOWEN, JR., physician; b. Florence, S.C., Oct. 2, 1925; s. Francis Bowen and Norma (Gignilliat) A.; student Clemson Coll., 1942-43; M.D., Emory U., 1948; m. Gloria Cox Poitevint, Oct. 2, 1948; children—Norma (Mrs. A. L. King, Sr.), Frank Bowen III. Intern, Pledmont Hosp., 1948-49; gen. practice medicine, Kingsport, Tenn., 1950-52, Seneca, S.C., 1954—; mem. staff Meml. Clinic, Seneca; chief medicine Oconee Meml. Hosp., 1945-48, chief obstetrics, 1970-72, chief staff, 1973-74. Chmn. Oconee County chpt. A.R.C., 1955-56, Am. Heart Assn., 1970-72. Served with M.C., USNR, 1949-50, 52-54. Diplomate Am. Bd. Family Practice. Fellow Am. Acad. Family Practice; mem. A.M.A., So. Med. Assn., Oconee County Med. Soc. (pres. 1957-58). Presbyn. Home: 401 S Pine Circle Seneca SC 29678 Office: PO Box 1174 Seneca SC 29678

ADAMS, FRANK JACKSON, JR., judge; b. Cornelia, Ga., July 15, 1916; s. Frank Jackson and Julia (Littlefield) A.; student Piedmont Coll.; LL.B., Atlanta Law Sch., 1940; m. Joye Hipps, Apr. 4, 1941; 1 son, Steven Charles. Admitted to Ga. bar, 1940; law practice, Clarkesville and Cornelia, Ga., 1945—; judge State Ct. of Habersham County, 1947—. Mem. Govs. Commn. on Jud. Selection, 1972—, Commn. on State Compensation, 1971—. Served with USAAF, 1942-45. Decorated D.F.C., Air medal with three clusters. Mem. C. of C. (past pres.), Am. Legion (past comdr.), Am., Ga. (gov. 1961—, exec. com. 1963-64, 67—, pres. 1973-74) bar assns., Jud. Council Ga., Am. Judicature Soc. Baptist. Kiwanian (past pres.). Address: Cornelia GA 30531

ADAMS, FREDERICK DAVID, civil engr.; b. Jalapa, Mexico, Mar. 1, 1918; s. Frederick and Natalia (Rodriguez) A.; brought to U.S., 1927, naturalized, 1957; student St. Mary's U., 1935-37; B.S. in C.E., Tex. A. & M. U., 1940; Civil Engr., Nat. U. Mexico, 1941; m. Mary Frances Martinez, Oct. 12, 1940; children—Frederick, Diane (Mrs. Robert Newton Neddo), Elizabeth (Mrs. Howard Baugh), David. Chief engr. Chalmers & Borton, Hutchinson, Kan., 1952-58; pvt. cons. B. M. Heede, Inc., Rye, N.Y., 1959-60, Door-Oliver Engring., Bartow, Fla., 1960-61; chief engr. Bunge Corp., N.Y.C., 1962-67; prin. F. Adams & Assos., Memphis, 1967—. Sec. Prairie Players, Hutchinson, 1956. Mem. Am. Soc. C.E., Aircraft Owners and Pilots Assn. Roman Catholic. Club: Falcon Aero (Manila, Philippines). Home: Gilarmi Apt Hotel Makati Rizal D708 Philippines Office: 2074 Elvis Presley Blvd Memphis TN 38106

ADAMS, GEORGE COTTON SMITH, educator; b. N.Y.C., June 1, 1911; s. Edward Leverett and Amanda (Smith) A.; student U. S.C., 1929-30, Middlebury Coll. (Ecole Francaise), summer 1935; A.B., U. N.C., 1933, A.M., 1934, Ph. D., 1950; certificate La Sorbonne, Paris, 1951; m. Adaline Holaday, Aug. 31, 1940 children—Charles Edward, George Holaday. Tchr. French, English, Dunbarton, S.C., 1935; service fellowship dept. romance langs. U. N.C., 1936-38, instr. French, 1938-39; instr. Spanish, English Tusculum Coll., 1939-40; asst. prof. romance langs. W. Ga. Coll., 1940-50, prof., head dept., 1950-52; asso. prof. Wofford Coll., 1952-56, prof. romance langs., 1957—, chmn. dept. fgn. langs., 1960—; prof. Spanish, U. Ariz., summer 1962. Recipient Cristobal Colon award Sigma Delta Pi, 1967, Don Quijote award, 1972. Mem. Modern Lang. Assn., Am. Assn. Tchrs. French (pres. Ga. chpt. 1950-51, pres. S.C. chpt. 1964-66), South Atlantic Modern Lang. Assn. (chmn. folklore sect. 1952, 56, 59, mem. exec. com. 1968-71), Southeastern Folklore Soc. (past pres.), Linguistic Soc. Am., Am. Assn. Tchrs. Spanish and Portuguese (past pres. S.C. chpt., state coordinator, Cervantes award 1970), Am. Assn. U. Profs., Phi Beta Kappa. Episcopalian (vestryman). Clubs: Sunrise Civitan (editor Civitan Notes 1965-72, pres. 1967-68) (Spartanburg, S.C.); University (N.Y.). Home: 100 Swansea Rd PO Box 3161 Spartanburg SC 29302

ADAMS, HAMPTON COLLIER, contractor; b. Lexington, Ky., Jan. 21, 1904; s. James J. and Maggie (Roberts) A.; B.S. in Mech. Engring., U. Ky., 1926; m. Emily Catherine Carey, June 27, 1928; children—Catherine Carey (Mrs. Courtney Ford Ellis), Hampton Collier. Staff Lexington (Ky.) Herald, 1920-27; employed in constrn. industry, 1927—; self employed H.C. Adams, Contractor, 1939-53; partner Carey Constrn. Co., Lexington, Ky., 1953—, H.C. Adams, Lexington, 1953—; pres. Carey-Adams, Inc., Lexington, from 1963, now chmn. bd. Pres. U. Ky. Sr. Assos., 1965. Recipient Achievement award, Boy Scouts, 1959, U. Ky. Achievement award, 1970. Fellow U. Ky., 1970. Mem. Am. Road Builders Assn. (div. dir.), Ky. Assn. Hwy Contractors (pres. 1950), Ky. Plantmix Asphalt Industry (pres. 1958), Ky. C. of C., Lambda Chi Alpha, Omicron Delta Kappa (hon.). Episcopalian (sr. warden 1969—). Clubs: Lexington (pres. 1954), Idle Hour, Lexington Optimist (pres. 1956), South Lexington Optimist (hon. life) Home; Versailles Rd Route 8 Lexington KY 40504 Office: 2216 Young Dr Lexington KY 40505

ADAMS, HARRY WESLEY, civil engr.; b. Muncie, Ind., July 10, 1908; s. Curtis Elva and Anna Josepha (Madden) A.; student U. Tenn. Jr. Coll., 1926-27, U. Chgo., 1927-29, U. Cin., 1938-42; m. Sarah Elizabeth Irwin, Nov. 24, 1934; children—Judith (Mrs. Albert L. Goldsmith, Jr.) and Janet (Mrs. Gilbert Resnik) (twins). With U.S. Army C.E., Louisville, 1930-37, Ohio River Div., Cin., Columbus, O., 1937-46, spl. engring. div. Panama Canal, Diablo Heights, Canal Zone, 1946-48, with Engring. Div., Civil Works, Office of Chief of Engrs., Washington, 1948-54, asst. chief, planning div., 1954-59, asst. exec. dir. U.S. Study Commn., S.E. River Basins, Atlanta, 1959-62; cons. on nat. and fgn. water resources devel. to various pvt. and pub. engring. agys., cons. cos., 1963—. Mem. engring. adv. com. Lake-Sumter Community Coll., Leesburg, Fla., 1970—. Registered profl. engr., Ohio, Va., Fla. Fellow Am. Soc. C.E.; mem. Am. Geophys. Union (life), Internat. Commn. on Irrigation and Drainage, Nat. Soc. Profl. Engrs., Fla. Engring. Soc. (sr. mem.), Alpha Tau Omega. Contbr. articles to profl. lit. Address: 1522 Park Dr Leesburg FL 32748

ADAMS, HAZEL GREENLEE REDFEARN (MRS. PAYTON F. ADAMS II), educator; b. Monroe, N.C., Nov. 12, 1905; d. Ephraim Eugene and Rebecca (Laney) Redfearn; student Radford Coll., 1924; A.B., U. Ky., 1940, M.A., 1953; postgrad. U. Neb., 1955; m. Payton F. Adams II, July 11, 1928; children—Payton F. III, Juliette Greenlee (Mrs. J. B. Hawk). Elementary tchr. Larchmont Sch., Norfolk, Va., 1924-28, Winchester (Ky.) City Schs., 1943-53; supr. Clark County (Ky.) Schs., 1953-61; supr. student tchrs. Ky. Wesleyan Coll., 1945-48; instr. Wesleyan Coll., Macon, Ga., 1960; named asst. prof. edn. Dakota Wesleyan U., Mitchell, S.D., 1961, asso. prof. edn. and psychology, 1961-70; asso. prof. early childhood edn. Pfeiffer Coll., Misenheimer, N.C., 1970—, adviser Student Edn. Assn., 1972-73. Chmn., Clark County Community Council, 1950-52, Clark County Recreation Bd., 1955-60; supr. Teen-Town, Winchester, 1954-60. Recipient Honor award State of Ky., 1960. Mem. Am. Assn. U. Women, Am. Assn. U. Profs., N.E.A., S.D. Edn. Assn., D.A.R., Assn. Supervision Curriculum Devel., Assn. for Childhood Edn., Mitchell Bus. and Profl. Women, Albemarle Bus. and Profl. Women (pres. 1972-73), Phi Kappa Phi (pres. 1964-66), Delta Kappa Gamma (pres. 1964-66), Pi Gamma Mu. Methodist. Mem. Order Eastern Star. Author: The Inimitable Educator: Robert E. Lee. Home: 136 College St Winchester KY 40391 Office: Pfeiffer Coll Misenheimer NC 28109

ADAMS, HELLEN ANNE HUTCHINSON, educator; b. Hamilton, Miss., Aug. 25, 1935; d. James Perry and Lois (Wright) Hutchinson; student Miss. State U., 1953-54; B.S., Miss. State Coll. Women, 1956; M.Ed., Duke, 1957; Ed.D., U. Miss., 1966; postgrad. U. Ga., 1966-67; m. Charles Floyd Adams, June 27, 1959; (div. 1970); son, Charles Floyd. Elementary tchr., Atlanta, 1957-59, Tampa, 1959-60, Hattiesburg, Miss., 1960-61, Oxford, Miss., 1961-64; dir. elementary edn., Columbus, Ga., 1965-67; dir. edn. LeFlore County Sch. Dist., Greenwood, Miss., 1967-69; asst. prof. edn., asso. dir. staff tng. of exemplary early edn. centers U. Tex., Austin, 1969-71; prof. edn. Duke U., Durham, N.C., 1971—. Mem. faculty U. Miss., 1964, U. Ga., 1966; mem. nat. adv. bd. J. B. Lippincott Co., 1966—; reading cons., Ga., Miss., Ala., La.; dir. Diagnostic and Remedial Reading Center, Columbus, 1967—, Duke U. Reading Clinic, 1971—. Named Outstanding Young Woman of Am., Miss. State Coll. Women, 1967, one of Outstanding Personalities of the South, 1966. Mem. Assn. Coll. Profs. Reading (pres. 1973—), Internat. Platform Assn., Phi Delta Epsilon, Alpha Delta Kappa, Pi Gamma Mu, Chi Omega. Author: The Reading Clinic, 1971; The Random House Reading Program, 1969; Threshold Learning Abilities for Children With Handicaps, 1972; Sounds for Me, 1971; The Clock Struck One, 1973; also scripts for The Look at you series of films. Contbr. articles to profl. jours. Home: 2727 Spencer St Durham NC 27705

ADAMS, HENRY BETHUNE, psychologist; b. Charlotte, N.C., Aug. 26, 1925; s. Hal Bethune and Mabel (Cooper) A.; A.B., U. N.C., 1949; M.A., Duke, 1953; Ph.D., Purdue U., 1956. Trainee VA Hosp., Marion, Ind., 1954-55, VA Regional Office, Indpls., 1955-56; instr. med. psychology U. Neb. Coll. Medicine, Omaha, 1956-59; psychologist Neb. Psychiat. Inst., 1956-59; research psychologist VA Hosp., Richmond, Va., 1959-63; psychologist Nat. Tng. Sch., Washington, 1963-64; chief psychol. services Fed. Reformatory, Alderson, W.Va., 1964-67; clin. asso. dept. psychology W.Va. U., Morgantown, 1965-67; supervisory psychologist Area C Community Health Center, 1967-72, coordinator psychol. services, 1972—. Served with AUS, 1943-46. Fellow Internat. Council Psychologists; mem. Am., D.C. (treas. 1970-73), Richmond (past pres.) psychol. assns. Contbr. articles to profl. jours. Home: 3001 Branch Av SE Washington DC 20031 Office: 1905 E St SE Washington DC 20001

ADAMS, HUGH LYNN, mech. engr.; b. Memphis, Dec. 16, 1926; s. William Watson and Ivah Edith (Wroten) A.; grad. Cleve. Engring. Inst., 1950; postgrad. U. Tenn., 1962; m. Ann Robertis Eatmon, June 27, 1954; children—Hugh Lynn, Robert Wroten. Project engr. Delta Products Co., Wilson, Ark., 1950-54; chief engr. Crompton-Osceola Co., Inc., Osceola, Ark., 1954—. Served with AUS, 1944-46; ETO. Registered profl. engr., Ark. Mem. Am. Soc. M.E., Nat., Ark. (pres. 1973-74) socs. profl. engrs. Baptist. Mason. Home: PO Box 13 Bassett AR 72313 Office: PO Drawer 309 Osceola AR 72370

ADAMS, JAMES IRWIN, r.r. exec.; b. Ackerman, Miss., Apr. 1, 1926; s. Irwin Asa and Josie (Morehead) A.; B.S., U. Tenn., 1948; m. Barbara Joyce Sullivan, Dec. 20, 1946; children—James R., David A., Elizabeth A., Robert A. Supr., Pa. R.R., Phila., Chgo., Johnstown and Harrisburg, Pa., Harrington, Del., Williamsport, Pa., Pitts., 1949-63; gen. supt. communications and signals L. & N. R.R., Louisville, 1963-69, chief engr., 1969-73, asst. v.p. engring., 1973—. Scoutmaster, mem. council Boy Scouts Am. Served with USAAF, 1944-45. Named Ky. col. Registered profl. engr., Pa., Ky. Mem. I.E.E.E., Am. Assn. Railroads, Am. Ry. Engring. Assn., Eta Kappa Nu, Kappa Alpha. Republican. Baptist. Club: L & N Golf (dir.). Home: 5416 Old Heady Rd Jeffersontown KY 40299 Office: 908 W Broadway Louisville KY 40201

ADAMS, JAMES LLEWELLYN, lawyer; b. Atlanta, Aug. 19, 1937; s. Oscar Llewellyn and Katherine (Crawford) A.; B.A., Emory U., 1959, LL.B., 1962-3m. Marilynn Elizabeth Pulliam, Aug. 22, 1959; children—Lisa Louise, James Benjamin, Dennis Paul. Admitted to Ga. bar, 1961; practiced in Atlanta, 1961-71; asso. Arnall, Golden & Gregory, Atlanta, 1962-67, partner, 1967-71; pres. AMI Realty & Mortgage Investors & Advisors, Inc., Shreveport, La., 1971—, also dir. gen. counsel; dir.; gen. counsel AMI, Inc.; dir., chmn. exec. com. Bossier Bank and Trust Co. Bd. dirs. Ga. Conservancy, 1968-71. Mem. Ga. Bar Assn., Atlanta Lawyers Club, Atlanta Jr. C. of C., Ga. Sportsmen's Fedn. (pres. 1966-68, exec. sec.-treas. 1968-70), Alpha Tau Omega, Phi Delta Phi. Clubs: Cherokee Appaloosa, Kadodacho Appaloosa; Atlanta Retriever. Home: 480 Railsback Rd Shreveport LA 71106 Office: 6001 Financial Plaza Shreveport LA 71130

ADAMS, JAMES WAYNE, JR., dentist; b. South Boston, Va., Dec. 26, 1934; d. James Wayne and Dorothy (Evans) A.; B.S., Coll. William and Mary, 1957; D.D.S., Med. Coll. Va., 1968; m. Janet Lee Lloyd, June 27, 1959; children—Anne Livingston, James Wayne III. Comml. mgr. Chesapeake & Potomac Telephone Co., Balt., 1957-62; salesman Shaw Real Estate Co., Alexandria, Va., 1962-64; pvt. practice dentistry, South Boston, Va., 1968—. Mem. South Boston (Va.) City Sch. Bd., 1970-72. Mem. Am., Va. State dental assns., Acad. Gen. Dentistry, Southeastern Analgesia Soc., Va. Assns. Professions, Piedmont Dental Soc., Delta Sigma Delta, Alpha Sigma Chi. Presbyn. (deacon 1972). Clubs: Sertoma (v.p. 1969-70, 73-74 dir. 1970-72) (South Boston, Va.); Halifax Country (dir. 1970-73). Office: Profl Bldg South Boston VA 24592

ADAMS, JESSE EARL, physician, surgeon; b. Lexington, Ky., Dec. 5, 1925; s. Jesse E. and Esther Francis (Nicholson) A.; B.S., U. Ky., 1945; M.D., Harvard, 1948; m. Hattie Boeswetter, Feb. 21, 1959; 1 son, Jesse Earl III. Rotating intern Harper Hosp., Detroit, 1948-49; intern in surgery Vanderbilt Hosp., 1949-50, resident, 53-55; resident

Med. Coll. Va. Hosp., 1950-51, U. Va. Hosp., 1955-56; vis. surgeon Rigshospitolet, Copenhagen, Denmark, 1956; asst. prof. surgery Vanderbilt U. Sch. Medicine, Nashville, 1956-60, dir. S.R. Light Lab. for Surg. Research, 1958-60; mem. Assn. Thoracic and Cardiovascular Surgery, Chattanooga, 1961—. Past pres. bd. dirs., mem. exec. com. Chattanooga Area Heart Assn.; chmn. Chattanooga-Hamilton County Air Pollution Control Bd. Served with USAF, 1951-52. Diplomate Am. Bd. Surgery, Am. Bd. Thoracic Surgery. Fellow A.C.S.; mem. Am. (past rep. councilor), So. thoracic socs., Am. Coll. Chest Physicians, A.M.A., Tenn. Med. Assn., Am. Assn. Thoracic Surgery, Southeastern Surg. Congress, Soc. Thoracic Surgeons, Tenn thoracic Soc. (past pres., mem. exec. com.), Tenn. Tb and Respiratory Disease Assn. (mem. exec. com.), Tenn. Heart Assn. (pres., dir., past chmn. program com.). Contbr. articles on cardiac, thoracic and vascular surgery to med. jours. Home: 224 N Crest Rd Chattanooga TN 37404 Office: 1000 E 3d St Chattanooga TN 37403

ADAMS, JEWEL HAMILTON, realtor; b. Bryant, Ark., May 15, 1924; d. Andrew Wilson and Bessie Jane (Hughes) Hamilton; student realty U. So. Ala., 1971; m. Shelley Bain Adams, June 1, 1941; children—Sherley Lewis II, Andrew W. Hamilton, Carol Lynn. Editor soc. newspapers Morehouse Enterprise, Bastrop, La., 1950-52; salesman mut. funds Investors Diversified Services, Mobile, Ala., 1958; sales exec. real estate Robert Bros., Inc., Mobile, 1960-72; v.p. Adams Real Estate, Inc., Mobile, 1972—. Residential chmn. A.R.C., 1949-50, Cancer Soc., 1951-52; mem. Mobile Beautification Bd. Mem. Ala. Assn. Realtors (dir.), Mobile County Bd. Realtors (bd. dirs., 1969-70), Million Dollar Sales Club, Nat. Assn. Real Estate Bds. (women's council), Nat. Inst. Real Estate Brokers. Republican. Methodist. Clubs: Skyline Country. Home: 3808 N Llewelyn Dr Mobile AL 36608 Office: Box 8524 Mobile AL 36608

ADAMS, JOHN CECIL, JR., civil engr.; b. N.Y.C., Apr. 5, 1924; s. John Cecil and Henriette Morrell (Umland) A.; B.S., Mass. Inst. Tech., 1948; m. Audrey Hale Tompkins, Feb. 2, 1946; children—Sandra Hale, Johnsie Morrell (Mrs. Jay MacDougall). With New Rochelle Water Co. (N.Y.), 1941, Metcalf & Eddy, cons. engrs., Boston, 1947; with Coffin & Richardson, Inc., cons. engrs., Boston, 1948—, chief engr., 1956-57, v.p., chief engr., 1958-62, pres., 1962—; partner Coffin & Richardson Assos., Boston, 1965—; pres. Coffin & Richardson Service Co., Inc., Sarasota, Fla., 1967—. Mem. evening faculty Mass. Inst. Tech., 1953-58. Registered profl. engr., 23 states and D.C. Mem. Am. Inst. Cons. Engrs., Am. Water Works Assn., Am. Soc. Appraisers, Am. Soc. Testing Materials, Boston Soc. C.E., Me. Water Utilities Assn., Mass. Water Works Assn., Nat., Mass. socs. profl. engrs., Nat. Water Co. Conf., New Eng. Water Works Assn. Clubs: Corinthian Yacht, Tedesco Country (Marblehead, Mass.). Home: 722 Spanish Dr S Sarasota FL 33577 Office: 141 Milk St Boston MA 02109

ADAMS, K.S., JR., bus. exec.; b. Bartlesville, Okla., 1923; ed. U. Kan., 1943. Chmn., pres. Ada Resources, Inc., Houston, Bud Adams Enterprises, Inc., Adams Petroleum Center, Inc., Bud Adams Ranches, Houston Oilers Profl. Football Team, Inc., River Garden Farms, S.W. Lincoln-Mercury, Inc., S.W. Motor Leasing; adv. dir. First City Nat. Bank of Houston, Am. Bank & Trust Co., Houston. Address: 6910 Fannin St Houston TX 77001

ADAMS, LOUIS WILLIAM, clergyman; b. Fort Worth, Dec. 29, 1929; s. James Oran and Marguerite Elizabeth (Horony) A.; B.A., Tex. Christian U., 1954, Th.M., 1973; B.D., Austin Presbyn. Theol. Sem., 1966, postgrad., 1967-68; m. Dolores Ann Reid, July 19, 1967; 1 dau., Wendy Kaye. Commd. 2d lt. USAF, 1954, advanced through grades to capt., 1960; ret., 1963; ordained to ministry Presbyn. Ch., 1966; asso. exec. sec. Presbyn. Synod Tex., chaplain Ramsey unit Tex. Dept. Corrections, Rosharon, Tex., 1966-73; dir. N.E. Pastoral Care and Counseling Center, Fort Worth, 1973—. Cons., Bishop's Com. on Rehab. and Parole, Episcopal Diocese Dallas. Chaplain, Civil Air Patrol, 1973-74. Bd. dirs. Tex. Corrections Assn., Assn. Specialized Ministries Presbyn. Ch. in U.S. Mem. Am. Protestant Correctional Chaplains Assn. (regional v.p. 1969-72), Internat. Transactional Analysis Assn., Assn. for Clin. Pastoral Edn., Presbyn. Assn. Diversified Ministries (v.p.), Nat. Council on Crime and Deliquency. Home: 2913 Carson St Fort Worth TX 76117

ADAMS, MYRON JOHN, physician; b. Athol, Mass., Oct. 23, 1905; s. John Myron and Grace Mabel (Terry) A.; A.B., Harvard, 1928; M.D., Yale, 1932; m. Lillias Wood Duncan, June 8, 1935; 1 son, Myron John. Intern, resident N.Y. Hosp.-Cornell Med. Center, N.Y.C., 1932-35; practice medicine, specializing in pediatrics, Kingsport, Tenn., 1936—; sr. partner Childrens Clinic, Kingsport; chmn. pediatric dept., past pres. Holston Valley Hosp.; med. dir. Tenn.-Va. Cerebro-palsy Center. Mem. exec. com. Community Chest, 1950-56; chmn. S. Central region Yale Med. Sch. Alumni Fund, 1955-70. Served to capt. M.C., AUS, 1943-46. Fellow Am. Acad. Pediatrics; mem. A.M.A., Am. Coll. Allergists, Tenn., Kingsport pediatric socs. Episcopalian. Clubs: Harvard Varsity, Ridgefields Country. Home: 1500 Fairidge Dr Kingsport TN 37664 Office: 1200 Wilcox Dr Kingsport TN 37660

ADAMS, NON QUINCY, banker; b. Mobile, Ala., June 1, 1925; s. Samuel Boyd and Dora (Williams) A.; B.S., U. Ala., 1949, LL.B., 1950; m. Eran Izard Jobe, Nov. 26, 1952; children—Laura A., Samuel Russell. Admitted to Ala. bar, 1950; practice law, Mobile, 1950-51; trust officer 1st Nat. Bank Mobile, 1951-55, asst. v.p., trust officer, 1955-62, v.p., trust officer, 1962-69, sr. v.p., 1969-72, exec. v.p., 1972—. Chmn., Allied Arts Drive, 1969; pres. Mobile chpt. A.R.C., 1969-71; co-chmn. indsl. div. United Fund, 1971—. Bd. dirs., sec. Gordon Smith Center, 1969—; bd. dirs. Community Chest Mobile. Served to lt. (j.g.), USNR, 1943-46. Hon. fellow Mobile Coll. Mem. Ala. Bankers Assn. (pres. trust div.), C. of C. (chmn. legislative com.). Kiwanian. Clubs: Mobile Country (pres. 1967), Athelstan Bienville (Mobile); Lakewood Golf (Point Clear, Ala.). Office: PO Drawer 1467 Mobile AL 36601 Home: 58 Clarise Circle Mobile AL 36608

ADAMS, PERRY RONALD, coll. pres.; b. Parkersburg, W.Va., Sept. 16, 1921; s. Russell Douglas and Beulah Grace (Cunningham) A.; A.B., U. Ky., 1943, M.A., 1948; Ed.D. (Kellogg fellow), U. Fla., 1965; m. Ann Mallory Gillespie, Dec. 25, 1943; children—Suzanne (Mrs. Frank Markwell), Sally (Mrs. Robert Barrios). Instr., U. Ky., 1948-53; dir. music U. Fla., 1953-63; dean instrn. Polk Jr. Coll., Winter Haven, Fla., 1965-69; provost No. Va. Community Coll., Annandale, 1969-70; pres. Paul D. Camp Community Coll., Franklin, Va., 1970—. Adjudicator various high sch. music contests, 1953—; mem. finance adv. com. Va. Council Higher Edn., 1970—; mem. adv. council of pres. Va. Community Coll. System; dir. United Va. Bank Va. Trustee, Southampton Hosp. Served with USNR, 1942-47; MTO, ETO, PTO. Mem. Am. Assn. Jr. Colls., So. Assn. Colls. and Schs. (accreditation com.), Phi Mu Alpha (nat. councilman), Ruritan Club (dir.), Phi Delta Kappa, Kappa Delta Pi. Baptist (bd. deacons). Rotarian. Home: 117 Beechwood Dr Franklin VA 23851 Office: PO Box 611 Franklin VA 23851

ADAMS, RICHARD LEON, bank exec.; b. Scottsbluff, Neb., July 19, 1921; s. Clyde Charles and Elizabeth (Sullivan) A.; student Okla. A. and M. Coll., 1940; diploma La. State U. Sch. Banking, 1963; m. Mildred Catherine Moody, Oct. 29, 1945; children—Janine Elaine, Richard Leon, Nancy Sue (Mrs. Dennis Yawn), Charles C., Donna Jo. Clk. Scottsbluff Nat. Bank, 1937-41, teller, loan clk., 1945-47; with First Nat. Bank in Palm Beach (Fla.), 1947—, auditor, 1947-51, asst. cashier, 1953-57, asst. v.p., 1957-61, v.p., 1961-68, exec. v.p., 1968—; pres., vice chmn. bd. Palm Beach Mall Bank, West Palm Beach, Fla., 1970—. Vice pres. Palm Beach County Heart Assn., 1971-72; adv. bd. Salvation Army, 1970—; bd. dirs. Palm Beach County Comprehensive Community Mental Health Center, Palm Beach Symphonette; bd. dirs. Fla. Bankers Assn. Ednl. Found., chmn., 1971-72. Served to maj. USAAF, 1941-46, USAF, 1951-53. Decorated D.F.C., Air Medal with cluster. Mem. Am. (exec. com. real estate and housing), Fla. (chmn. credit div. 1972-73) bankers assns., Soc. Real Estate Appraisers, Palm Beach Sales and Marketing Assn., Palm Beach Islanders (treas., bd. dirs.), Air Force Assn., Navy League. Palm Beach (dir.), West Palm Beach (dir.) chambers commerce, Quiet Birdmen, Flying Alligators. Methodist (mem. ch. bd., trustee 1960—). Kiwanian (dir.). Club: Sailfish (bd. govs. 1970—). Home: 4401 North Terrace West Palm Beach FL 33407 Office: 255 S County Rd Palm Beach FL 33480

ADAMS, ROBERT LEROY, TV sta. ofcl.; b. Lakeview, Mich., Mar. 13, 1937; s. Clyde Leroy and Ruth Mary (Mills) A.; B.A. (Regents Alumni scholar, Robert L. Drake All Around scholar, Robert L. Drake Athletic scholar), U. Mich., 1960; m. Judith C. Walkington, Nov. 30, 1957; children—Jeffry R., Mark D., Cynthia L., Robert D. News reporter Sta. WPAG, Ann Arbor, Mich., 1958-60; stage mgr. WRC-TV, NBC, Washington, 1960-62, producer, dir., 1962-67, prodn. mgr., 1967-72, mgr. programs, 1972—. Broadcast cons. Balt. Conf., United Meth. Ch., 1971—. Pres., Mill Creek Towne P.T.A., 1972; active Mill Creek Towne Civic Assn., Mill Creek Towne Recreation Assn. Recipient Emmy award for producing and directing children's programming, 1965. Mem. Nat. Assn. Television Program Execs., Nat. Acad. Television Arts and Scis. (1st v.p., gov. Washington chpt.), U. Mich. Alumni Assn., Gaithersburg Sports Assn. Methodist. Home: 7509 Park Mill Ct Rockville MD 20855 Office: 4001 Nebraska Av NW Washington DC 20016

ADAMS, SAMUEL KEITH, educator; b. Salisbury, Md., Mar. 1, 1938; s. Samuel Cleveland and Belle Jackson (Schoble) A.; grad. Germantown Acad., 1956; B. Mgmt. Engring., Rensselaer Poly. Inst., 1960; M.S.E., Ariz. State U., 1962, Ph.D. (Research Found. fellow 1962-63), 1966; m. Eileen Peggy Telinde, Aug. 27, 1966; children—Douglas Scott, Carey Margaret. Adminstrv. asst. Citizens Utilities Co., Stamford, Conn., 1960; research asst. Ariz. State U., Tempe, 1960-62, research fellow, 1962-63; human factors engr. Aberdeen Proving Ground, Aberdeen, Md., 1962; mem. faculty Okla. State U., Stillwater, 1965—, asso. prof. indsl. engring. and mgmt., 1970—. Spl. staff asst. Western Electric Co., Oklahoma City, also Kansas City, Mo., 1966, indsl. engr., 1968; research engr. Eastman Kodak Co., Rochester, N.Y., 1970; cons. indsl. safety and health Employers Ins. of Wausau, Milw., 1973. Recipient NSF grant, 1966-67, NASA Summer Faculty fellowship Langley Research Center, Hampton, Va., 1972. Registered profl. engr., Okla. Mem. Am. Inst. Indsl. Engrs., Human Factors Soc., Am. Soc. Engring. Edn., Sigma Xi. Mem. Ch. of Christ. Mem. editorial staff Jour. Indsl. Engring., AIIE Transactions, 1967—. Contbr. articles to various publs. Home: 831 W Knapp Av Stillwater OK 74074 Office: Okla State U Stillwater OK 74074

ADAMS, TOM, lt. gov. Florida; b. Jacksonville, Fla., Mar. 11, 1917; s. Thomas Burton and Carolyn (Hamilton) A.; grad. The Hill Sch., Pottstown, Pa., 1936; A.B., U. Mich., 1940; student U. Fla. Law Sch., 1948; H.D. Space Edn., Fla. Inst. Tech.; H.H.D., Trinity Coll.; m. Frances Brewer, Sept. 8, 1973; children by previous marriage—Carolyn (Mrs. James A. DeHaven, Jr.), Augusta (Mrs. T. Buckingham Bird), Frances. Real estate, property mgmt. H. P. Holmes, Inc. Detroit, 1940-42; plant supt. Foremost Dairies, Jacksonville and Daytona Beach, Fla., 1942-44; owner, operator dairy farm, Orange Park, 1944-48; timber dealer, property mgmt. Orange Park Properties (Fla.), 1948-61; farmer, Fla., 1942-61; mem. Fla. Senate, 29th Dist., 1956-60, chmn. com. reorgn. Fla. Dept. Agr.; sec. state Florida, 1961-70, lt. gov., 1970—. Pres. Leon County United Fund, 1964; state campaign chmn. Fla. Mental Health Assn., 1964. Decorated Order of San Carlos (Colombia); named most outstanding freshman senator 1957 Session, Fla. Legislature, also recipient agrl. award 1957 Session; named most valuable mem. legislature 1959 Session, named most effective state adminstr. 1961, 63, 65. Mem. U.S. Commn. Southeast River Basins (mem. resources adv. bd.), Nat. Rivers and Harbors Congress (dir.), Nat. Waterways Conf. (chmn. 1964-65, pres. 1965-67), Miss. Valley Assn. (pres. 1968, dir.), Fla. Colombia Alliance (founder 1963), Fla. State U. Gold Key Soc., Newcomen Soc., U. Fla. Alumni Assn., Blue Key, Phi Delta Theta, Alpha Kappa Psi. Baptist. Moose (state pres. 1966-67), Rotarian. Home: Gadsden County FL Office: State Capitol Tallahassee FL 32304

ADAMS, WARREN ERNEST, supt. schs.; b. Danville, Ark., Dec. 3, 1933; s. Orville Cletus and Mildred Ernestine (Waid) A.; B.A., Coll. Ozarks, 1958; M.Edn., Northeastern State Coll. at Tahlequah, Okla., 1965; certificate adminstrn. Okla. State U., Stillwater, 1970; D.Ed., Walden U., 1971; m. Doris Anita Reed, Apr. 9, 1954; children—Warren Lynn, Loren Keith, Eric Brian, Alicia Renee. Tchr. pub. schs., Livermore, Cal., 1958-62; tchr., prin. Delaware County Pub. Schs., Jay, Okla., 1962-68; supt. schs. Glencoe, Okla., 1968-70, Waurika, Okla., 1970—. Bd. dirs. United Fund, 1973, Jefferson County Bd. Health, 1971-73. Mem. Okla. Edn. Assn., Okla. Addn. Sch. Adminstrn., Am. Assn. Sch. Adminstrs. Methodist. Mason (32 deg.), Lion. Club: Waurika Country (dir. 1971-73). Home: 521 E Florida St Waurika OK 73573 Office: 600 E Florida St Waurika OK 73573

ADAMS, WILLIAM CARROLL, educator; b. Star City, Ark., July 15, 1930; s. Allie L. and Ila (Miles) A.; B.A. in Econs., State Coll. Ark., 1951; M.A., U. Ark., 1953, Ph.D. (Gen. Elec. fellow), 1963. With Graybar Elec. Co., St. Louis, 1953-54; instr. U. Ark., 1957-60; faculty E. Tex. State U., Commerce, 1960—, prof. bus. adminstrn., 1965—. Pub. utility cons. Bd. dirs. Commerce Pub. Library, Carmichael Found., Conway Ark. Served with AUS, 1954-57. Bus. Exchange fellow, 1964; Ill. Bell fellow, 1966. Mem. Am., So., Western econ. assns., Beta Gamma Sigma. Author: The Inflationary Erosion of Capital—A Case Study, 1964; A Checklist for Acquisitions, 1964. Home: Box 3064 ET Station Commerce TX 75428

ADAMS, WILLIAM GORDON, chem. co. exec.; b. Gadsden, Ala., May 5, 1934; s. Forrest B. and Mary Sue (Wadsworth) A.; student King Coll., 1952-53; B.S. in Indsl. Engring., U. Ala., 1958; postgrad. U. Tenn., 1959-68; m. Marian Gainey, Aug. 25, 1963; children—Lauren Brooke and Leigh Elizabeth (twins), Andrea Karen. Indsl. engr. Tenn. Eastman Co., Kingsport, Tenn., 1958-67, dir. wage and salary adminstrn. and indsl. engring., 1968-73, asst. supt. plastics div., 1973—. Registered profl. engr., Tenn. Mem. Am. Inst. Indsl. Engrs. (sr.), Tau Beta Pi, Alpha Pi Mu. Presbyn. (elder 1967—). Moose. Club: Civitan (Kingsport). Office: PO Box 511 Kingsport TN 37662

ADAMS, WILLIAM YEWDALE, educator; b. Los Angeles, Aug. 6, 1927; s. William F. and Lucy M. (Wilcox) A.; A.B., U. Cal. at Berkeley, 1948; Ph.D., U. Ariz., 1958; m. Nettie Alice Kesseler, June 7, 1955; children—Ernest W., Edward K. Dir., Glen Canyon archeol. salvage project Mus. No. Ariz., Flagstaff, 1957-59; dir. Sudan Antiquities Service archeol. salvage program, liaison officer UNESCO, 1959-66; prof. anthropology U. Ky. at Lexington, 1966—; vis. lectr. Archeol. Inst. Am., 1968-72. Served with USNR, 1945-46. Fellow A.A.A.S., Am. Anthrop. Assn., Soc. for Applied Anthropology. Author: Shonto: A Study of the Role of the Trader in a Modern Navaho Community, 1963. Home: 957 Wolf Run Rd Lexington KY 40504

ADAMSON, DOUGLAS VAN FLEET, computer co. exec.; b. Houston, Sept. 26, 1930; s. Arthur Douglas and Nora Maud (Harriman) A.; B.B.A., Tex. A. and M. U., 1952; M.S., So. Meth. U., 1962; m. Martha Lynn Kelfer, May 27, 1966; children—Douglas, Elaine, Mary, Marshall. Jr. salesman IBM, 1954-56, sr. salesman, 1957-63; trust officer Rep. Nat. Bank, 1964-65; sales mgr. Mgmt. Assistance Inc. Equipment Corp., 1966-67, gen. br. mgr., 1967-68; exec. v.p. Data Automation Services, 1969-70; v.p. marketing Gen. Computer Systems, Dallas, 1971-72; dir. bus. and product planning Harris Communications Systems, Inc., 1972—. Served from 2d lt. to 1st lt. USAF, 1952-54. Mem. Data Processing Mgmt. Assn. Episcopalian. Clubs: Corinthian Sailing, Martha Turner Reilly Dads (pres. 1963) (Dallas). Home: Route 1 Argyle TX 76226 Office: Harris Communications Systems Inc 13617 Neutron Dr Dallas TX 75234

ADANALIAN, ALICE ARAXIE, research scientist; b. Turkey; d. Garabed and Vartouhie (Manisalian) Adanalian; came to U.S., 1920, naturalized, 1927; student U. Pa., 1926-28; B.A., Northwestern U., 1930; M.A., Columbia, 1935; post-grad. Johns Hopkins, 1954, 57. Exec. sec. Bus. and Profl. Women's Program YWCA, Yonkers, N.Y., 1930-37; dir. Cleve. Guidance Service, 1937-39; exec. sec. group work-recreation employment-guidance div. Welfare Council N.Y., 1939-44; welfare specialist Middle East mission UNRRA, Egypt, Italy, 1944-45; chief liaison officer UN mission, Austria, 1946-47; head leaders and specialist div. Inst. Internat. Edn., 1948-51; Africa-Middle East specialist U.S. Govt., Washington, 1951-67; dep. chief Middle East Africa br. Center Research of Social Systems, Am. U., Washington, 1967-69; cons. Am. Inst. for Research, 1969—. Sec. exec. com. Community Chest, Yonkers, 1936-37; mem. program planning bd. Nat. Youth Adminstrn., Yonkers, 1936-37; sec. fair Employment Practice Com. N.Y., 1943-44. Bd. missions Meth. Ch., 1960-68. Mem. Nat. Vocational Guidance Assn. (chmn. internat. relations com. 1949-51), Am. Personnel and Guidance Assn., Africa Studies Assn., Johns Hopkins Alumni Assn., Columbia Tchrs. Coll. Alumni Assn., Am. Polit. and Social Sci. Assn., Nat. Capital Area Councilors Assn. (dir.), Acad. Am. Polit. and Social Scis. Contbr. articles to profl. jours. Home: 4600 Connecticut Av NW Washington DC 20008 Office: Kenwood MD 04102

ADDEN, ROBERT SPENCER, educator; b. Orangeburg, S.C., Jan. 1, 1923; s. John Augustus and Mary Elizabeth (Heggie) A.; B.S., The Citadel, 1947; M.B.A., U. Pa., 1948; Ph.D., U. N.C., 1960; m. Sue Sligh, Dec. 27, 1953; children—Carolyn, Robert Spencer, Virginia. Mem. faculty dept. bus. adminstrn. The Citadel, Charleston, S.C., 1947—, prof., 1962—, head dept., 1962—. Lectr. Sch. for Bank Adminstrn., 1970—. Bd. advisers Salvation Army, Charleston. Served with AUS, 1943-46. Decorated Bronze Star, Purple Heart. Mem. So. Econ. Assn., Am. Accounting Assn. Rotarian. Home and Office: The Citadel Charleston SC 29409 The Citadel Charleston SC 29409

ADDISCOTT, DEREK HERBERT, publisher; b. Plymouth, Eng., Apr. 14, 1910; s. Herbert C. and Claire (Roberts) A.; student Oundle Coll., Eng., 1924-28, Stevens Inst. Tech. 1928-29; m. Katharine W. Bray, Nov. 23, 1944; children—Gayle K., Lynn C. Office mgr. Hamilton Watch Co., Lancaster, Pa., 1939-41; mgr. orgn. planning and procedures div. RCA, Camden, N.J., 1941-50; mgr. indsl. engring. PanAm. Airways, Cape Kennedy, Fla., 1954-58, mgr. data processing, 1958-67; pub. Eau Gallie, Fla., 1967—. Councilman, Town of Palm Shores, Fla., 1960-61, vice mayor, 1961-63, mayor, 1963—. Mem. Planning Zoning Commn., Palm Shores, Brevard County Civilian-Mil. Relations Council. Mem. Am. Mgmt. Assn., Nat. Office Mgmt. Assn., Moonwalk Commemorative Assn. (pres. 1972), Sigma Nu. Democrat. Episcopalian. Home: Box 76 Route 1 Palm Shores FL 32935 Office: PO Box 399 Eau Gallie FL 32935

ADDISON, STAYTON DOUGLAS, hotel exec.; b. Toledo, May 13, 1935; s. John Nelson and Florence Mae (Smith) A.; B.A., Mich. State U., 1959; m. Joan Ellen Kohrman, Sept. 4, 1959; children—Stayton Douglas, Rodger Alan. Dir. of food Sheraton Hawaii Corp., Honolulu, 1960-63; resident mgr. Bismarck Hotel, Chgo., 1963-65; mgr. Hospitality Motor Inns, Columbus, O., 1965-69; v.p. Gardens Services, Inc., Pine Mountain, Ga., 1969—. Served with AUS, 1954-56. Mem. Am., Ga. (pres. 1973) hotel and motel assns., Hotel Sales Mgrs. Assn., Ga. C. of C. Home: PO Box 512 Pine Mountain GA 31822 Office: Callaway Gardens Pine Mountain GA 31822

ADDISON, WILLIAM PIERCE, physician; b. Ida, La., Apr. 6, 1909; s. William Pierce and Susan (Antony) A.; B.A., La. Coll., 1927; M.D., Tulane U., 1931; student Mass. Inst. Tech., summer 1953, U. Chgo., 1961-62; m. Edelweiss Buswell, June 6, 1938; 1 dau., Mary Elise (Mrs. J. G. Dupree). Intern, Tri-State Hosp., Shreveport, La., 1931-32; practice medicine, Shreveport, La., 1932-51; resident Langley Porter Psychiat. Inst. 1955-57; dir. Lake County Mental Health Clinic, Painesville, O., 1957; asst. supt. State Hosp., Columbus, O., 1957-60; asst. commr. Ohio Div. Mental Hygiene, Columbus, 1960-64; dir. Baton Rouge Regional Mental Health Center, 1964-66; commr. Mental Health State of La., Baton Rouge, 1966—; clin. prof. psychiatry Tulane U., 1964—, La. State U., 1971—; staff psychiatrist La. State U. Student Mental Health, 1965—. Served from lt. to lt. col. USAAF, 1942-46. Diplomate Am. Bd. Psychiatry and Neurology. Mem. Am., La. psychiat. assns., A.M.A., La. Med. Soc., Pi Kappa Phi, Phi Chi. Democrat. Home: 3719 Jolly Dr Baton Rouge LA 70808 Office: 655 N 5th St Baton Rouge LA 70804

ADEM, JULIAN, research meteorologist; b. Tuxpan, Veracruz, Mexico, Jan. 8, 1924; s. Jorge and Almas (Chahin) A.; Civil Engr., Nat. U. Mexico, 1948; Ph.D., Brown U., 1953; postgrad. in Meteorology, Internat. Meteorol. Inst., Stockholm, Sweden, 1955-56; m. Martha Diaz de Leon, Sept. 8, 1958; children—Julian, Alejandro. Research asst. U. Mexico, Mexico City, 1948-50, prof., 1954, 57-65, 71—; research asst. Brown U., Providence, 1952-53; research asso. Internat. Meteorol. Inst., Stockholm, 1955-56; asst. dir. Inst. Geophysics, Mexico City, Mexico, 1957-59, dir., 1959-62, 71—. Vis. prof. U. Hamburg (Germany) 1961-62; research meteorologist Nat. Weather Service, Washington, 1965-71. Mem. Am. Geophys. Union, Am. Meteorol. Soc., Union Geofisica Mexicana (pres. 1960—), Sociedad Mexicana de Fisica, Sociedad Matematica Mexicana, Academia de la Investigacion Cientifica, N.Y. Acad. Scis, Geofisica Internacional (dir. jour. 1960—). Contbr. articles to profl. jours. Home: 14 Privada de la Cerrada del Oliva Mexico City 20 DF Mexico Office: Torre de Ciencias Tercer Piso Giudad Universitaria Mexico City 20 DF Mexico

ADEN, GREGORY ALLEN (MIKE), bus. broker; b. Del Norte, Colo., Mar. 11, 1942; s. Carl William and Bobbie Irene (Allen) A.; B.A., U. Colo., 1964, M.A. (Ford Found. scholar), 1965; m. Sarah Elizabeth Jennings, Aug. 10, 1963; children—John Randall and Jarrod Dean (twins), Joy Tara. Bus. tng. course trainee computer div. Gen. Electric Co., Phoenix, 1965-66; asso. cons. mgmt. services Touche Ross & Co., Houston, 1969-72; owner, broker Del Lingco Corp., Houston, 1972—; instr. accounting and econs. Cameron State Coll., Lawton, Okla. Served to 1st lt. AUS, 1966-69. Decorated Army Commendation medal. Mem. Planning Execs. Inst. (v.p. membership), Houston Chpt. C.P.A.'s (chmn. Speakers Bur.), Lambda Chi Alpha. Presbyn. Club: Magic Circle Exchange. Home: 10047 Haddington St Houston TX 77055 Office: 5433 Westheimer Rd Houston TX 77027

ADEN, ROBERT CLARK, educator; b. Paris, Tenn., Jan. 13, 1927; s. Robert Franklin and Esther (Clark) A.; B.A., U. N.M., 1947; M.A., Murray State U., 1953; Ph.D., George Peabody Coll. for Tchrs., 1955; m. Martha Elizabeth Irby, Apr. 4, 1958; children—Robert Paul, Martha Lucille. Vis. prof. Bemidji (Minn.) State Coll., summer 1955; head dept. edn. and psychology Bethel Coll., McKenzie, Tenn., 1955-60; asst. prof. edn. N. Tex. State U., Denton, 1960-63, asso. prof., 1963-67; prof. edn. Middle Tenn. State U., Murfreesboro, 1967—, dean of the graduate school, 1968—. Cons. Cal. Test Bur., 1961—, Tex. Small Schs. Assn., 1960-67; asso. dir. N. Tex. area Met. Center Supplementary Ednl. Services, 1966-67. Served with AUS, 1950-52. Mem. N.E.A., Nat. Soc. Study Edn., Tenn. Edn. Assn., Phi Delta Kappa, Pi Gamma Mu, Phi Kappa Phi, Kappa Delta Pi. Author: Teacher Training in Guatemala, 1955; (with Crosthwait) Adolescent Psychology Achievement Test, 1963; Status of the Social Studies in Texas Secondary Schools in 1964-65, 1966. Contbr. articles to profl. jours. Home: 419 Minerva Dr Murfreesboro TN 37130

ADERHOLT, HARRY CHANEY, physician; b. Birmingham, Ala., Jan. 22, 1938; s. William Lewis and Lempi (Pernu) A.; B.S., U. Ala., 1960; M.D., U. Ala., 1964; m. Sandra Joy Doyle, Sept. 8, 1958; children—Mark C., Ashley Ayn. Intern Brooke Gen. Hosp., San Antonio, 1964; resident radiology U. Ala., 1968-71; practice medicine specializing in radiology, Winfield, Ala., Guin, Ala., Hamilton, Ala., Haleyville, Ala.; mem. staffs Rankin Fite Meml. Hosp., Winfield, Burdick West Meml. Hosp., Haleyville. Served with AUS, 1964-68. Mem. Phi Beta Kappa, Sigma Phi Epsilon, Phi Eta Sigma. Baptist. Home: 3341 Stone Ridge Lane Birmingham AL 35243 Office: 1529 N 25th St Birmingham AL 35233

ADKINS, CEPHAS JOE, JR., psychologist, educator; b. Gainesville, Fla., Apr. 18, 1925; s. Cephas Joe and Eloise (Cox) A.; B.A., U. Fla., 1946, M.A., 1947; Ph.D., Ohio State U., 1957. Asst. prof. psychology Bridgewater (Va.) Coll., 1948-51; asso. prof. psychology Carson-Newman Coll., Jefferson City, Tenn., 1954-57; asso. prof. psychology High Point (N.C.) Coll., 1957-61; asso. prof. psychology Old Dominion U., Norfolk, Va., 1961-66, prof., 1966—. Organist High Point Friends, 1960-61, Second Presbyn. Ch., Norfolk, 1968—. Fellow A.A.A.S.; mem. Am. Psychol. Assn., Am. Assn. U. Profs., So. Soc. for Philosophy and Psychology, Va. Acad. Sci., Psi Chi, Theta Chi. Presbyn. Home: 7832 Sea Wolf Dr Norfolk VA 23518

ADKINS, GEORGE BOZEMAN, JR., technical adviser; b. Ft. Worth, July 30, 1921; s. George Bozeman and Ethel (Hough) A.; B.S., U. Mo., 1950, M.A., ; m. Edith G. Mercer, Aug. 16, 1958; 1 dau., Virginia Ann. Chief statistician Gen. Motors Corp., Kansas City, Kan., 1951-53, Dept. Air Force, Kansas City, Mo., 1952-54, Dept. Def., 1953-56 chief math. statistics br. AEC, Washington, 1956-60; chief operation and intelligence br. Strategy and Tactics Analysis Group, Dept. Army, 1960-62; charge operations research group FAA, Washington, 1962-66; tech. adviser Def. Communication Agy., 1966—. Served with USN, 1940-46. Recipient Outstanding award Navy Dept., 1955, Superior Performance award, 1955. Mem. A.A.A.S., Inst. Math. Statistics. Author: (with others) The Management of Nuclear Materials, 1960; Operational Evaluation of Flight Inspections of Instrument Landing Systems, 1968. Research in electronics, ship propulsion, nuclear materials mgmt. Home: 4801 Kenmore Av Alexandria VA 22304 Office: Pentagon Washington DC 20301

ADKINS, JOHN MCLEAN, chem. co. engr.; b. Wheeling, W. Va., June 7, 1910; s. John McLean and Stella Agnes (Baltz) A.; B.S. in Engring., W. Va. U., 1934; m. Thelma R. Adkins, Dec. 21, 1934; children—Valdan C., Richard C. Chief draftsman, also civil engr., Am. Cyanamid Co., Bridgeville, Pa., 1946-53, project engr., New Orleans, 1953—. Mem. Collier Township Sch. Bd., 1950-53; radio officer New Orleans Civil Def., 1960-70. Served to lt. col., Signal Corps, AUS, 1942-46. Registered profl. engr., La. Mem. I.E.E.E. (chmn. chpt. 1960-61), M.T.A. Radio Club, Jefferson Radio Club, Pi Kappa Phi. Home: 611 Mayflower Dr Metairie LA 70001 Office: PO Box 10008 New Orleans LA 70121

ADKINS, RICHARD EUGENE, petroleum co. exec.; b. Bakersfield, Cal., Feb. 4, 1922; s. Walter Edwin and Addie (Woodward) A.; A.A., Bakersfield Coll., 1941; B.S., U. So. Cal., 1948; m. Mimi Thornton, Feb. 15, 1946 (dec. Dec. 1967); children—Corey (Mrs. Chester Robinson), Anthony, Scott, Lorraine; m. 2d, Jo Ann Yeager, Apr. 3, 1969. With Petrolane, Inc., Atlanta, 1951—, v.p., 1967—. Served with USAAF, 1942-45. Decorated D.F.C. Mem. Wash., Mont., Ga. Liquid Petroleum gas assns., Atlanta C. of C. Rotarian, Lion. Home: 2826 Evans Dale Circle Atlanta GA 30340 Office: 2965 Flowers Rd S 109 Atlanta GA 30341

ADKISSON, DAVID FLINTOFF, coll. pres.; b. Ashland City, Tenn,. Aug. 21, 1912; s. Samuel Henry and Ruth (Flintoff) A.; B.S., Middle Tenn. State Coll., 1935; M.A., George Peabody Coll., 1946; Ed.D., U. Tenn., 1960 ; m. Odessa Duncan, Feb. 2, 1940; 1 dau., Barbara Ann. Tchr. pub. schs., Cheatham County, Tenn., 1935-42, prin., South Fulton, Tenn., 1942-44, Bristol, Tenn., 1946-50; supt. schs., Watertown, Tenn., 1944-46, Bristol, Tenn., 1956-67; regional supr. Tenn. Dept. Edn., 1950-53; county dir. instrn. Knox County, Tenn., 1953-55; instr. U. Tenn., 1955-56; pres. Cleveland (Tenn.) State Community Coll., 1967—. Mem. Nat. (life), Tenn. (life) congresses parents and tchrs., Nat., Tenn. edn. assns., Phi. Kappa Phi, Phi Delta Kappa. Methodist. Mason, Rotarian. Home: 1211 Greenwood Trail Cleveland TN 37311

ADKISSON, GEORGE BILLY JOE, sales exec.; b. Rushville, Ill., June 29, 1918; s. Aaron Arthur and Clara A. (Ritchey) A.; student pub. schs.; m. Ruth E. Whitefield, Sept. 19, 1942; 1 dau., Karen Nannette (Mrs. Clude S. Bloomfield). Space salesman, classified mgr. Macomb (Ill.) Daily Jour., 1936-41; sales mgr. radio sta. KBUR, Burlington, Ia., 1941-47; gen. mgr. radio sta. KOKX and KOKX-FM, Keokuk, Ia., 1947-51; sales and pub. relations radio sta. KSTP, Mpls., 1951-53; asst. sales mgr. Midwest div. Peters, Griffin, Woodward, Inc., Chgo., 1953-63; sales, adminstrv. and personnel cons., Chgo., 1963-67; sales and radio sta. relations H-R Reps., Inc., Chgo., 1967-69; gen. sales mgr. radio sta. KFRE and KFRE-FM, Fresno, Cal., 1969-71; gen. sales mgr. radio sta. KGNC and KGNC-FM, Amarillo, Tex., 1970—. Served with USNR, 1944-45. Mem. Am. Legion, Nat. Rifle Assn., Internat. Platform Assn. Mem. Christian Ch. Mason (33 deg., Shriner). Home: 4207 Tulia Dr Amarillo TX 79109

ADKISSON, PERRY LEE, educator; b. Hickman, Ark., Mar. 11, 1929; s. Robert Louis and Imogene (Perry) A.; B.S., U. Ark., 1950, M.S., 1954; Ph.D. in Entomology, Kan. State U., 1956; m. Frances Rozelle, Dec. 29, 1956; 1 dau., Jean Amanda. Asst. prof. U. Mo., 1956-58; asso. prof. Tex. A. and M. U. at College Station, 1958-63, prof. entomology, 1963—, head dept., 1967—. Cons. Internat. AEC, Vienna, Austria, 1969, Hazardous Materials Adv. Com. and Office Water Programs Environmental Protection Agy., 1971-72; chmn. sci. adv. panel to Gov. Tex. on Agrl. Chems., 1970-72; chmn. Tex. Pesticide Adv. Com., 1971—; mem. panel experts on integrated pest control UN/FAO, Rome, Italy, 1971—; mem. Structural Pest Control Bd. Tex., 1971—; So. Agrl. Expt. Sta. Dirs. rep. to So. Regional Pest Mgmt. Working Group; mem. study group problems pest mgmt. environmental scis. bd. Nat. Acad. Sci.-Nat. Acad. Engring., 1972—; mem. com. pest mgmt. strategies NRC, 1973—; cons. OECD, Paris, France, 1973. Served with M.C., AUS, 1951-53. USPHS spl. post-doctoral fellow Harvard, 1963-64. Fellow A.A.A.S.; mem. Entomol. Soc. Am. (mem. governing bd. 1971-73, Bussart Meml. award 1967, pres. 1974), Kan. Entomol. Soc., Am. Inst. Biol. Scis., Internat. Orgn. Biol. Control (ad hoc com. integrated pest mgmt. 1973—), Sigma Xi. Contbr. numerous articles profl. jours. Mem. editorial com. Ann. Rev. Entomology, 1973—. Research in insect photoperidism, integrated control of cotton insects. Home: 305 W Brookside St Bryan TX 77801

ADLER, DAVID, broadcasting exec.; b. Louisville, May 28, 1945; s. Paul and Edna Lillian (Brazin) Sonnheim; student U. Louisville, 1963-65, Ray Shelton Radio Sch., summer 1966. Announcer radio sta. WCND, Shelbyville, Ky., 1966-67; program dir. radio sta. WSTM-FM, Louisville, 1967—. Mem. B'nai B'rith (pres. Bluegrass lodge). Composer: Spring, Measured Moments, Theme from Nowhere, My Heart Wanders in Ecstasy. Home: 1967 Goldsmith Lane Apt F 17 Louisville KY 40218

ADLER, LAWRENCE, educator; b. N.Y.C., June 6, 1923; s. Bertram and Serena (Katz) A.; A.B., N.Y.U., 1946; B.S., Columbia, 1949; M.S., U. Utah, 1953; Ph.D., U. Ill., 1964; m. Joan M. Anderson June 29, 1957; children—Charles, Lauri Jo, Albert. Jr. engr. N.Am. Aviation Co. Los Angeles, 1951; asst. civil engr. City Los Angeles, 1952-55; asst. prof. mining engring. U. Mo., Rolla, 1955-56, Lehigh U., Bethlehem, Pa., 1956-58, Mich. Technol. U., Houghton, 1958-61; asso. prof. mining engring. Va. Poly. Inst. and State U., Blacksburg, 1963-69, prof., 1969—, pres. engring. faculty orgn., 1971-72; cons. Rand Corp., Calumet & Hecla Co., Freeport Mining Co., Nat. Gypsum Co., U.S. Gypsum Co. Served with USAAF, 1943-45. Decorated Air medal, Purple Heart with one oak leaf cluster. Registered profl. engr., Va. Mem. Am. Soc. C.E., Am. Inst. Mining, Metall. and Petroleum Engrs., Sigma Xi. Mem. Disciples of Christ Ch. (deacon). Author: Ground Control; Excavation and Materials Handling. Contbr. articles to profl. jours. Coordinating editor, contbr. Mining Engring. Handbook. Patentee field roof support device. Home: 600 Preston Av Blacksburg VA 24060

ADLER, ROBERT, photog. co. exec.; b. N.Y.C., Dec. 25, 1906; s. Hyman and Freida (Byers) A.; student Ohio State U., 1925-27; m. Rosa Schuman, Aug. 5, 1933; 1 son, Michael Frederic. With advt., editorial depts. Cleve. Plain Dealer, 1927-32; advt. mgr. Lorain (O.) Times Herald, 1933-34; pub. Lorain Shopper, 1935-37; pub. Springfield (O.) Shopper, 1935-41; pub. Springfield Tabloid Times, Springfield Jour., 1939; owner Robert Adler Advt. Agy., Springfield, 1941-45; pres. Click Camera Shops, Inc., Springfield, 1945-63, Rapid Photo, Inc., Springfield, 1953-62, A & H Realty Co., Springfield; pres. Tru-Foto, Inc., Springfield 1953-64, now chmn. bd.; chmn. bd. Foto-Color Co., Dayton, O., 1960—, Rapid Mail Co., Dayton, Kisco Photo Co., Columbus, O., Photo Enterprises, Indpls., Progressive Industries Corp., Dayton. Mem. 4th Study Mission to Israel, 1957, Springfield Commn. Downtown Improvement Com., 1962. Pres. Retail Mchts. Council Springfield, United Jewish Appeal, Bonds for Israel; bd. dirs. Springfield Devel. Council, Boy Scouts Am., Jr. Achievement. Chmn. bd. So. Ohio Coll., Cin. Mem. Springfield (dir.), Woodlands Ft. Lauderdale chambers commerce. Jewish religion (v.p. dir. temple). Mason, Rotarian: mem. B'nai B'rith. Club: Meadowbrook Country (Dayton). Author, producer, photographer (films), Hong Kong Clicking, 1960, Israel, 1961. Home: 5719 Coco Palm Dr Ft Lauderdale FL 33313 Office: 2030 Kuntz Rd Dayton OH 45404

AFFLECK, BERT, educator; b. Childress, Tex., Apr. 22, 1934; s. Bert and Reba Marie (Wilson) A.; B.A., McMurry Coll., 1955; B.D., Perkins Sch. Theology, 1958; Ph.D. (Grad. fellow 1958-59), Drew U., 1968; m. Patsy Green, Dec. 27, 1955; children—Ellen Marie, Scott. Ordained to ministry Methodist Ch., 1956; asst. minister St. Mark's Meth. Ch., Midland, Tex., 1955-57, First Meth. Ch., Big Spring, Tex., 1957; minister Andover (N.J.) Meth. Ch., 1959-61; minister, asst. prof. religion McMurry Coll., Abilene, Tex., 1961-64, minister, asso. prof. religion, 1968-73, minister, prof. religion and philosophy, 1973—; minister United Meth. Ch., Pond Eddy, N.Y., 1964-68. Vol. co-pastor St. James United Meth. Ch., 1968-69; cons. multi-media team teaching in religion, 1968—; mem. bd. ministry N.W. Tex. conf. United Meth. Ch., 1968—, chmn. sem. com. bd. ministry, 1972—, chmn. ministerial recruitment, 1969—, chmn. mission work area Abilene dist., 1973, 74; dean Indian Meth. Pastor's Sch., Okla., 1974—; adj. prof. Perkins Sch. Theology, summers 1972, 73, winter 1974; leader missions tour, Mexico, 1973, study tour, Eng., 1972. Recipient Selecman Greek award Perkins Sch. Theology, 1958. Jesse Jones Edn. grantee, 1964-65, 65-66. Mem. Soc. Ch. History, Am. Acad. Religion, Am. Soc. Missiology (charter), Am. Assn. U. and Coll. Chaplains, West Tex.-N.M. Philos. Soc., Fellowship Christian Athletes, Alpha Chi. Democrat. Methodist. Co-author: Exploring Religious Meaning, 1974. Home: 1601 Sayles Blvd Abilene TX 79605

AFFLERBACH, RAYMOND ERNEST, leather goods mfg. co. exec.; b. Yoakum, Tex., June 1, 1921; s. Walter O. and Hildagarde (Raymond) A.; student St. Edwards U., 1937-38; m. Audrey C. Dvorak, June 6, 1942; children—Kathleen (Mrs. Roger M. Kirby), Michael Raymond, Jeanne (Mrs. Dan Barry), Walter Francis. Insp. Aircraft Supplies, Kelly AFB, San Antonio, 1942-46; payroll mgr. Tex Tan, Yoakum, Tex., 1946-50; accounting supr. IBM, Yoakum, Tex., 1950-59; credit and customer service mgr. Tex Tan Welhausen Co. div. Tandy Corp., Yoakum, Tex., 1959—, dir., 1962—. Home: PO Box 701 Yoakum TX 77995 Office: PO Box 431 Yoakum TX 77995

AFFRONTI, JOSEPH ANTHONY, paint co. exec.; b. Chgo., Feb. 26, 1932; s. Charles Vincent and Rose (Pantano) A.; B.A., Ia. Wesleyan Coll., 1955; M.B.A., U. Chgo., 1960; m. Nondace Vonee Anderson, Aug. 2, 1952; children—Teresa Lynn, Joseph Anthony. Mail order re-buyer Spiegels, Inc., Chgo., 1955-56; mail order buyer Co-op Electric Supply Co., Chgo., 1956-61; discount store buyer Aldens-Shoppers World, Inc., Chgo., 1961-64; with Mary Carter Industries, Tampa, Fla., 1964—, vice pres. sales, 1969-72, pres., 1972—. Dir. Trade World Commn., 1973. Com. of 100, 1972—. Served with AUS, 1952-54. Mem. Am. Marketing Assn. (pres. W. Coast chpt. 1969-70). Clubs: Temple Terrace Golf and Country. Home: 922 River Hills Dr Temple Terrace FL 33617 Office: PO Box 23387 Tampa FL 33622

AFFRONTI, LEWIS FRANCIS, educator, microbiologist; b. Rochester, N.Y., Aug. 12, 1928; s. John and Mary (Least) A.; B.A., U. Buffalo, 1950, M.A., 1951; Ph.D., Duke, 1958; m. Aileen Ledford, June 2, 1956; children—John, Lewis, Mary Louise, Eileen. Research asso. Buffalo VA Hosp., 1951-52, Roswell Meml. Cancer Inst., 1954; research asso. in Tb Henry Phipps Inst. U. Pa., 1957-58; commd. officer USPHS, 1958-62; asst. prof. George Washington U. Sch. Medicine, Washington, 1962-65, asso. prof., 1965-72, prof. microbiology, 1972—, chmn. dept. microbiology, 1973—. Cons. AVCO Research Corp., VA Hosp., Martinsburg, W.Va., VA Hosp. Center, Wilmington, Del. U.S. rep. WHO Conf. on Skin Test Antigens and Vaccines, Geneva, 1966. Mem. med. adv. bd. VA, Wilmington, Del. Served with USAF, 1952-54. NIH Spl. fellow, 1969; Nat. Tb fellow for Internat. Conf. on Tb, Moscow, 1971, Tokyo, 1973. Recipient WHO Exchange Research Workers award, 1970. Mem. Am. Soc. Microbiology, Am. Assn. for Immunologists, Reticuloendothelial Soc., Am. Thoracic Soc., Assembly on Microbiologists and Immunologists (sec. 1971-72), Wash. Acad. Sci. K.C. Club: Toastmasters Internat. (Atlanta). Home: 5003 Woodland Way Annandale VA 22003 Office: Dept Microbiology George Washington U Med Center 2300 Eye St Washington DC 20037

AGAMEMNON, GEORGE JOSEPH, transp. co. exec.; b. N.Y.C., Dec. 20, 1916; s. Emmanuel G. and Margaret (Rein) A.; student N.Y.U., 1944, Alexander Hamilton Inst., 1948, U.N.C., 1954, LaSalle Extension U., 1962, U. Mich., 1967; m. Helen A. Preston, Oct. 10, 1942 children—G. Richard, John Paul. Rate clk. Horton Motor Lines, N.Y.C., 1939-41 (merged with Asso. Transport, Inc. 1941), sales asst., 1943-44, asst. to v.p., 1946-59; asst. mgr. trucking Burlington Industries Inc. (N.C.), 1959-62, mgr., 1962—, v.p. trucking and warehousing, 1968—. Lectr. in field. Vice pres. Am. Cancer Soc., Alamance County, N.C., 1969-70, pres., 1973-74; chmn. campaign United Fund, Alamance County, 1967-68; mem. Alamance County Civil Def. Commn., 1969-72, chmn., 1973-74. Mem. Am. Trucking Assn. (indsl. relations com. 1964—), Am. Mgmt. Assn. (planning council 1968—), Pvt. Carrier Conf. (dir.), Burlington-Alamance County C. of C. (chmn. transp. com. 1972, employee relations com. 1973), N.C. Motor Carriers Assn. (dir. 1973-74), Va. Hwy. Users Assn., Burlington Traffic Club, Internat. Platform Assn., Central Motor Freight Assn. Roman Catholic. (chmn. adv. bd. 1969-71, chmn. finance com. 1971-72). Elk, K.C. (4 deg.). Home: Rt 7 Box 114 Collingwood Dr Burlington NC 27215 Office: Tucker St Extension PO Box 691 Burlington NC 27215

AGEE, HERNDON ROYCE, entomologist; b. Cottonburg, Ky., Dec. 21, 1933; s. Burdett and Marie (Long) A.; B.S., Berea Coll., 1958; student Eastern Ky. U., 1957; M.S., U. Minn., 1960; Ph.D., Tufts U., 1968; m. Juanita Hensley, Apr. 17, 1953; children—Herndon Douglas, Lois Annette. Research entomologist Dept. Agr., Florence, S.C., 1960-73, insect sensory physiologist, Gainesville, Fla., 1973—. Com. chmn. Troop 409 Boy Scouts Am., 1966—. Served with AUS, 1954. Mem. Entomol. Soc. Am., Fla. Entomol. Soc. Club: Toastmasters Internat. (dist. sec. 1971-72). Home: 401 NW 91st St Gainesville FL 32601 Office: 1700 SW 23d Dr PO Box 14565 Gainesville FL 32601

AGINS, BARNETT ROBERT, mathematician; b. N.Y.C., May 19, 1922; s. Isidore Robert and Rhea Kathryn (Orkow) A.; B.E.E., N.Y. U., 1952, M.E.E., 1956; M.Sc., Stanford, 1961; m. Esther Klein, Mar. 26, 1945; children—Ira, Harriet. Served with USAAF, 1942-45; engring. insp. U.S. Army, 1946-50; commd. 2d lt. USAF, 1944, advanced through grades to lt. col., 1966; project engr. Wright-Patterson AFB, 1956-59; chief applied math. div. Air Force Office Sci. Research, 1961-67; ret., 1967; asst. to dir. Courant Inst. Math. Scis., N.Y. U., 1967-69; program dir. applied math. and statistics NSF, Washington, 1969—. Professorial lectr. Am. U., 1962-72. Decorated Air Force Commendation medal with 2 oak leaf clusters. Mem. I.E.E.E., Soc. Indsl. and Applied Math. Asso. editor: Jour. of Optimization Theory and Applications, 1967—. Office: NSF Washington DC 20550

AGLIO, THOMAS JOSEPH, social agy. exec.; b. Boston, Nov. 22, 1931; s. Joseph Michael and Mary (Rossetti) A.; B.S., Boston Coll., 1953, M.S.W., 1955; m. Margaret Mary Cronin, Sept. 17, 1955; children—Susan M., Teresa E., Mariana, Stephen J., Elizabeth J. Philip G., Kathleen M. Caseworker, acting dir. social service Albany (N.Y.) Med. Center, 1955-58; supr. social service St. Vincent Hosp., Worcester, Mass., 1958-61; adminstr. Camp St. John for Cuban Refugees, Jacksonville, Fla., 1962; dir. Catholic Social Services, Inc., Orlando, Fla., 1962, asso. diocesan dir., 1968—; adminstr. Maris Stella Villa Maternity Home, Winter Park, Fla., 1964-69. Instr. Albany Med. Coll., Union U., Albany, N.Y., 1957-58; lectr. Russell Sage Sch. Nursing, Albany, N.Y., 1956-58; cons. Catholic Charities Diocese, Worcester, Mass., 1961. Mem. Acad. Certified Social Workers, Nat. Assn. Social Workers, Fla. Community Services Assn., Fla. Health and Welfare Council, Am. Pub. Health Assn., Profl. Community Service League, Nat. Conf. Catholic Charities. Home: 367 Fitzhugh Rd Winter Park FL 32789 Office: 550 N Bumby Av Orlando FL 32803

AGNELLO, SAMUEL ANTHONY, audiovisual media exec.; b. Jamestown, N.Y., Mar. 25, 1917; s. Guiseppi and Maria (LoPresti) A.; A.B., Duke, 1939; m. Myra Lois Crumpacker, Jan. 27, 1940; 1 dau., Maria LoPresti. Research asst. dept. anatomy Duke, 1941-55, adminstrv. asst., 1955-59, project dir. med. television, 1959-64, coordinator med. television Duke Med. Center, Durham, N.C., 1964-66, dir. div. audiovisual edn., 1966—. Pres., N. State Signal Co., Inc. Mem. Health Scis. Communications Assn. (sec.), Biol. Photog. Assn., Nat. Assn. Ednl. Broadcasters, Assn. Med. Illustrators, Internat. Soc. for Edn. in Health Scis. Editor: Health Sciences TV Bull., 1964-71; asso. editor Visual Medicine, 1965-68. Contbr. articles to profl. jours. Home: 1208 Woodburn Rd Durham NC 27705 Office: Box 3163 Duke U Med Center Durham NC 27710

AGNEW, DONALD BURNS, govt. ofcl.; b. Ogden, Ill., Aug. 10, 1922; s. Theodore Lee and Agnes (Faris) A.; B.S. (Sears Roebuck scholar 1938-1940), U. Ill., 1941; postgrad. Am. U., 1955, U. Md., 1957-65; m. Virginia L. Penn, Feb. 14, 1946 (div. June 1966); children—Donald Burns Lee, Melissa Louise; m. 2d, Joan Lee Parker, June 28, 1969; 1 dau., Leslye Ann. Began career as research asst. econ. entomology Ill. Natural History Survey, Urbana, 1940-41; economist Bur. Land Mgmt., U.S. Interior Dept., Cheyenne, Wyo., also Washington, 1946-48, with U.S. Dept. Agr., 1948—, economist Agrl. Marketing Service, also Prodn. and Marketing Adminstrn., 1948-62, economist Econ. Research Service, Washington, 1962—; dir. Spl. Econ. Surveys, Washington, 1954-58; econ. cons. U.S. AID Mission in Panama, 1972; cons. on food irradiation studies to AEC and food industry; lectr. various univs., dairy and livestock industry meetings; instr. econs. U. Md., 1969-73. Served with inf. AUS, 1941-46; PTO. Recipient citation for meritorious research U.S. Dept. Agr., 1952, 72, 73; commendation Nat. Commn. Food Marketing, 1966. Mem. A.A.A.S., Am. Agrl. Econ. Assn., Northeastern Agrl. Econ. Council, Am. Marketing Assn., Western Farm Econs. Assn., Anteaters Assn., Internat. Assn. Agrl. Economists, Orgn. Profl. Employees Dept. Agr., Alpha Zeta. Contbr. to Readings in Agricultural Marketing, 1954; also articles to profl. jours. Complier: Readings in Linear Programming: Applications to Agricultural Problems, 1956. Home: 6108 Rivanna Dr

Springfield VA 22150 Office: South Agriculture bldg 14th and C Sts SW Washington DC 20250 also 500 C St SW Washington DC

AGNEW, JEANNE LECAINE (MRS. THEODORE AGNEW, JR.), educator; b. Port Arthur, Ont., Can., May 3, 1917; d. Hubert Clarence and Susie Elma (Smith) LeCaine; B.A., Queen's U., Kingston, Ont., 1937, M.A. (Marty Meml. fellow), 1938; Ph.D., Radcliffe Coll., 1941; m. Theodore L. Agnew, Jr., Dec. 25, 1942; children—Theodore Agnew III, Susan Elizabeth (Mrs. Edward L. Dollmeyer), Hugh LeCaine, Peter Wallace, Marion Jeanne. Traveling fellow Canadian Fedn. U. Women, 1939; instr. Smith Coll., 1941-42; jr. research physicist NRC Can., 1942-46; asst. prof. math. Okla. State U., Stillwater, 1956-62, asso. prof., 1962-69, prof., 1969—. Vis. asso. prof. Ga. State Coll., 1966-67. Named Outstanding Tchr., Okla. State U. Alumni Assn., Blue Key, 1964. Mem. Math. Assn. Am., Am. Math. Soc., Phi Beta Kappa, Sigma Xi, Pi Mu Epsilon. Methodist. Author: Explorations in Number Theory, 1972. Contbr. articles to profl. jours. Home: 1216 N Lincoln St Stillwater OK 74074

AGNEW, SAMUEL CALVIN, automotive parts co. exec.; b. Jackson, Miss., Feb. 23, 1903; s. Sam C. and Katherine May (Pridgen) A.; student pub. schs.; m. Edith Velma Short, Apr. 11, 1929. Auto mechanic, 1920-25; parts salesman Robinson Bros., Jackson, 1925-28; salesman Ryan Supply, Jackson, 1928-32, gen. mgr., 1935-54, v.p., 1954-60; founder, pres. Automotive Warehouse Co., Jackson, 1960—. Bd. dirs. So. Automotive Show, 1970-72. Mem. Miss. Automotive Wholesalers Assn. (pres. 1967). Mason (Shriner), Lion. Club: Patio (Jackson). Home: 1512 Rosewell Dr Jackson MS 39211 Office: 701 E Silas Brown St Jackson MS 39207

AGNEW, THEODORE LEE, JR., historian; b. Ogden, ILL., Dec. 21, 1916; s. Theodore Lee and Agnes (Faris) A; B.A., U. Ill., 1937, M.A., 1938; A.M., Harvard U., 1939, Ph.D., 1954; M. Jeanne Starrett LeCaine, Dec. 25, 1942; children—Theodore (dec.), Theodore Lee III, Susan Elizabeth (Mrs. Edward L. Dollmeyer), Hugh LeCaine, Peter Wallace, Marion Jeanne. Grad. research asst. U. Ill., 1938; asst. prof. history Okla. State U., 1947-54, asso. prof., 1954-60, prof., 1960—; vis. prof. history Emory U., 1964, 1966-67. Served with USNR, 1942-46. Mem. Am. Hist. Assn., Orgn. Am. Historians, So. Hist. Assn., Western History Assn., Am. Soc. Ch. History, Ill., Okla. hist. socs., Am. Assn. U. Profs. (mem. council 1960-63), Am. Studies Assn., Phi Beta Kappa, Phi Kappa Phi, Phi Alpha Theta, Alpha Kappa Lambda, Omicron Delta Kappa. Democrat. Methodist. Home: 1216 N Lincoln St Stillwater OK 74074

AGUAYO, JORGE, librarian; b. Havana, Cuba, Dec. 4, 1903; D.C.L., U. Havana, 1925; studies in librarianship (Rockefeller fellow) Columbia, 1941. Asst. dir. gen. library U. Havana, 1937-59, dir. gen. library, 1959-60, prof. cataloging and classification, 1950-60; head br. librarian Columbus Meml. Library, Washington, 1962-69, chief librarian, 1969-73. Mem. A.L.A. Contbr. articles to profl. jours. Address: 2800 Quebec St NW Washington DC 20008

AGUILA, DANIEL DUMUK, broadcasting exec.; b. Manila, Philippines, Sept. 24, 1928; s. Doroteo A. and Donata B. (Dumuk) A.; B.F.A., U. Philippines, 1952; grad. student mass communications, ednl. TV, Syracuse (N.Y.) U.; m. Norma Alampay, Sept. 24, 1960; children—Normalinda, Dina Belle, Daniel Bliss. Came to U.S., 1967. Co. artist Philippines Am. Life Ins. Co., Manila, 1952-56; tech. expert mass communication Philippine Rural Reconstn. Movement, Manila, 1960-62; art dir., v.p. Asian newsweekly Examiner, Philippines, 1965-67; art cons. The Upper Room, Nashville, 1967-68; art dir. Robert G. Fields Advt., Nashville, 1967-72, channel 8, WDCN-TV, Nashville, 1972—, Philippine Times, Chgo.; lectr. mass. communications U. Philippines, 1963-64; free-lance writer, 1956—. Vice pres. Art Assn. Philippines, 1965-67; Philippines dir. Nat. Press Club Philippines, 1965-66; pres. Soc. Philippine Illustrators and Cartoonists, 1965-66; mem. Citizens Council for Mass Media, Manila, 1963-67. Pub. relations dir. Friends of Marcos, presdl. campaign, 1965. Recipient awards in art, journalism and broadcasting. Roman Roces art scholar, 1948-49; Harold Stassen grantee, 1956-58. Mem. Art Dirs. Club Nashville. Methodist (adminstrv. bd. 1973—). Editor: The First Couple of the Philippines, 1965. Home: 3906 Wallace Lane Nashville TN 37215 Office: PO Box 12555 Nashville TN 37212

AGUILAR, RODOLFO J., architect, engr.; b. San Jose, Costa Rica, Sept. 28, 1936; s. Hector Jesus and Nora Noemi (Espinosa) A.; student U. Santo Domingo, Dominican Republic, 1953-55; B.S. in Archtl. Engring., La. State U., 1958, M.S. in Civil Engring. (Latin-Am. fellow), 1960, B.Arch., 1961; postgrad. Ill. Inst. Tech., summer 1962; Ph.D. in Civil Engring. (Ford Found. fellow), N.C. State U., 1964; m. Nellyn Mariana Carias, Oct. 5, 1956; children—Rodolfo J., Ricardo A., Roberto J., Nora N. Came to U.S., 1955, naturalized, 1966. Architect, engr. Bodman, Murrell and Smith, Baton Rouge, La., summer 1959; architect, structural engr. J. Wesley Leake and Assos., Baton Rouge, 1959-62; cons. engr. Kahn & Furbush, Raleigh, N.C., summer 1964, Alfred G. Rayner, Baton Rouge, 1964; v.p. Systems Analysis and Design Optimization, Inc., Baton Rouge, 1966-70; pres. Corporate Devel. Group, Inc., Baton Rouge. Structural examiner La. Bd. Archtl. Examiners, 1965-66. Recipient Halliburton award for Excellence in Teaching Halliburton Co. and La. State U., 1967. NSF grantee, 1962, 65, 66; Ford Found. fellow, grantee, 1962-64. Mem. Am. Soc. C.E., A.I.A., Am. Soc. Engring. Edn., Operations Research Soc. Am., La. Engring. Soc. (certificate of Merit, 1958), Sigma Xi, Tau Beta Pi, Phi Kappa Phi, Chi Epsilon. Author: Systems Analysis and Design in Engineering, Architecture, Construction and Planning. Contbr. articles to tech. jours. Home: 4866 Whitehaven Baton Rouge LA 70808 Office: 5551 Corporate Blvd Suite 3 J Baton Rouge LA 70808

AGUIRRE, ARTURO REYMUNDO, lawyer; b. El Paso, Tex., Sept. 7, 1928; s. Lorenzo Delgado and Anita Angela (Gonzalez) A.; B.A., Tex. Western Coll., 1952; m. Estela Escalante, Oct. 21, 1950; children—Leonor, Arturo, David, Robert, Steven, Lawrence. Admitted to Tex. bar, 1956; U.S. Supreme Ct. bar; practiced in El Paso, 1956—. Mem. State Bar Com. on Services to Poor, 1972—; chmn. Com. on Mexican-Am. Affairs, 1973. Chmn. legal div. Fund for Excellence U. Tex., El Paso. Served with USNR, 1945-46, AUS, 1952-53. Mem. El Paso County Bar Assn. (dir.), Am. Arbitration Assn. (nat. panel). Democrat. Roman Catholic. Elk. Home: 6111 Tejas Dr El Paso TX 79905 Office: 806 SW Center El Paso TX 79901

AHEARN, MICHAEL JOHN, biologist; b. Jacksonville, Tex., June 22, 1936; s. John Tom and Reba (Raye) A.; B.A., U. Tex., 1958, M.A., 1961, Ph.D., 1965; m. Joyce Donaho Ramey, June 6, 1964. Teaching asst. U. Tex., Austin, 1961-63, lectr., 1963-65; asst. biologist M.D. Anderson Hosp. and Tumor Inst., Houston, 1965—; faculty asso. U. Tex. Grad. Sch. Biomed. Scis., Houston, 1972—. Mem. Am. Soc. Cell Biology, N.Y. Acad. Sci., Tex. Soc. Electron Microscopy, Electron Microscope Soc. Am., Sigma Xi. Home: 2236 S Piney Point Rd Houston TX 77042 Office: MD Anderson Hosp Houston TX 77025

AHERN, HUGH STEPHEN, editor; b. Edwards, Miss., July 22, 1894; s. James and Hannah (Lynch) A.; student Georgetown U., 1934-35; m. Lillian Mae Peaster, May 27, 1917. Reporter, editor sports Jackson (Miss.) Daily News, 1920-25; corr. AP, Tallahassee, 1925-30; regional information rep., depts. Labor and Commerce, Birmingham, Ala., 1940-45, Atlanta, 1946-62; dir. field office Commerce Dept., Atlanta, 1963-64; research editor So. Advt.-Markets, Atlanta, also research specialist Am. Bldg. Supplies and Sports Merchandiser, Atlanta, 1965—. Recipient Meritorious Service award Dept. Commerce, 1959. Mem. Am. Marketing Assn. (pres., 1955-56), Atlanta Assn. Fed. Execs. (pres., 1957). Home: 2254 Virginia Pl NE Atlanta GA 30305

AHLGREN, FRANK RICHARD, editor; b. Superior, Wis., June 25, 1903; s. Oscar John and Beatrice Marie (Gibson-Taylor) A.; student Superior (Wis.) State Tchrs. Coll., 1922-25, Memphis U. Law Sch., 1926-28; D.C.L., Southwestern Coll.; m. Elizabeth Alley, Feb. 25, 1932; children—Frank Richard, Gibson-Taylor, Calvin Lane. Reporter Superior Eve. Telegram, 1923-24, Duluth (Minn.) Herald, 1924-25, Milw. Jour., 1925-26, Memphis Eve. Appeal, 1926-33, Tex. Newspaper Pubs. Assn., Houston, 1934-36, Cleve. Press, 1936-37; editor Memphis Comml. Appeal, 1937-69. Trustee U. Tenn.; bd. dirs. Meth. Hosp., Memphis Pub. Library, Memphis-Ark. Bridge Commn. Mem. Sigma Delta Chi, Kappa Tau Alpha. Episcopalian. Mason, Rotarian. Clubs: Tennessee, Memphis Country, Hunt and Polo (Memphis). Home: 2714 Lombardy Memphis TN 38111 Office: Box 3120 100 N Main St Memphis TN 38101

AHLGREN, JAMES DAVID, electronics exec.; b. Washington, Feb. 17, 1934; s. Charles David and Dorothy Elizabeth (Webb) A.; B.S., Mass. Inst. Tech., 1955; postgrad. George Washington U., 1956-57, U. Cal. at Los Angeles, 1961, Georgetown U., 1972-73, Am. U., 1973; m. Barbara Jean Donelko, Sept. 7, 1957; children—Gillian W., Nils W. Chief engr. McIntosh Electronics Co., Binghamton, N.Y., 1954-56; with Reed Research Co., Washington, 1956-58; asst. dir. research and devel. Page Communications Engrs., Washington, 1958-63; v.p., pres., dir. Telcom, Inc., McLean, Va., 1963—. Mem. electronics adv. bd. No. Va. Community Coll. Mem. I.E.E.E. (chmn. geophysics electronics group Washington 1970-71), Am. Meteorol. Soc., Am. Geophys. Union, Am. Assn. Med. Instrumentation, Washington Philos. Soc. Republican. Lutheran. Home: 6800 Hampshire Rd McLean VA 22101 Office: 8027 Leesburg Pike McLean VA 22101

AHMANN, DONALD HENRY, mfg. co. exec.; b. Struble, Ia., Jan. 9, 1920; s. Henry F. and Philomena (Wictor) A.; student Trinity Coll., 1937-39; B.S. in Chemistry, Ia. State U., Ames, 1941, Ph.D., 1948; m. H. Anne Harvey, Sept. 24, 1945; children—Richard S., Carol (Mrs. Thomas P. Beresford), Rebecca (Mrs. Patrick Mahoney), Sarah, Kathryn, Elizabeth. Jr. chemist AEC Ames Lab. Ia. State U., Ames, 1942-48; research asso. Knolls Atomic Power Lab., Gen. Electric Co., Schenectady, 1948-50, mgr. phys. chemistry, 1950-55, mgr. chemistry and chem. engring., 1955-57, mgr. chemistry and chem. engring. Vallecitos Atomic Lab., Pleasanton, Cal., 1957-67, mgr. chemistry and metallurgy Vallecitos Atomic Lab., Pleasanton, 1967, mgr. materials sci. and tech. Nuclear Systems Programs, Cin., 1967-69, mgr. engring. Neutron Devices Dept., St. Petersburg, Fla., 1969—. Mem. Am. Chem. Soc., Am. Soc. for Metals, Am. Nuclear Soc., Am. Vacuum Soc., Phi Kappa Phi, Phi Lambda Upsilon. Home: 660 Bluff View Dr Belleair Bluffs FL 33540 Office: PO Box 11508 St Petersburg FL 33733

AHRABI, ROBERT, petroleum co. exec.; b. Tabriz, Iran, Aug. 23, 1933; s. Abolhasan and Mobara Ahrabi; came to U.S., 1955, naturalized, 1965; student Queens Coll., N.Y.C., 1955, Norfolk Jr. Coll., 1955-56, U. Houston, 1956-57; B.S., U. Southwestern La., Lafayette, 1959, M.S., 1961; postgrad. seminars Baton Rouge Vocational Tech. Sch., 1969, Teche Area Vocational Tech. Sch., Abbeville, La., 1971; m. Lou Ella Boutin, Feb. 20, 1961; children—Mitra, Ronald, Brenda, Ryan. Draftsman, engring. asst. Sunray Midcontinent Oil Co., Lafayette, 1959-61; engr. Central Excavation Co., Lafayette, 1961-62; v.p. Oil Center Research, Inc., Lafayette, 1962—. Registered profl. engr., La. Mem. Am. Inst. Mining, Metall. and Petroleum Engrs., Am. Petroleum Inst. (Teche chpt.), Nat. Assn. Corrosion Engrs., Soc. Petroleum Engrs. (judge Gulf Coast Region Student Paper Contest 1973), Internat. Relations Assn. Acadiana. Patentee in field. Home: 208 Birch Dr Lafayette LA 70501 Office: 320 Heymann Blvd Lafayette LA 70501

AIKEN, BEDFORD ELIAS (DICK), JR., advt. agy. exec.; b. Rocky Mount, N.C., July 30, 1916; s. Bedford Elias and Anna (Simmons) A.; student, Rollins Conservatory of Music (Winter Park, Fla.), 1947; m. Anne Shepherd Wright, July 2, 1939; children—Dian Shepherd (Mrs. Paul Leslie Martz), Bedford Elias III, Anne Wright (Mrs. Charles Denver Hayes, Jr.), John Charles, David Sutherland, Margaret Ava, Dick Seaborn, Michael Hamilton, Timothy Clay, Mary Simmons. Wholesale produce broker, Winston Salem, N.C. and Sanford, Fla., 1932-47; profl. singer (tenor), 1947-52; comml. mgr. WTRR Radio, Sanford, Fla., 1950-52; owner, operator Aiken Advt. Agy., Sanford, Fla., 1952—; spl. promotion adviser Sanford Herald, 1961-65. Winner, all-Florida Talent Contest, 1947, Arthur Godfrey Talent Scout Show, 1947. Mason (Shriner). Home: 444 Elliott Av Sanford FL 32771 Office: 208 S Sanford Av Sanford FL 32771

AILES, STEPHEN, lawyer; b. Romney, W.Va., Mar. 25, 1912; s. Eugene Elliot and Sallie (Cornwell) A.; grad. Episcopal High Sch., Alexandria, Va., 1929; A.B., Princeton, 1933; LL.B., W.Va. U., 1936; m. Helen Wales, June 24, 1939; children—Hester A. Nettles, Stephen Cornwell, Walter Brady, Richard Arvine. Admitted to W.Va. bar, 1936, D.C. bar, 1946; asst. prof. law W.Va. U., 1937-40; practice in Martinsburg, W.Va., 1936-37, 40-42; mem. legal staff OPA, 1942-46, asst. gen. counsel, 1945-46; counsel U.S. Econ. Mission to Greece, 1947; practice in Washington, 1946-61, 65-70; partner Steptoe & Johnson, 1948-61, 65-70; under sec. Army, 1961-64, sec. Army, 1964-65. Pres. Assn. Am. Railroads, 1971—. Mem. Bar Assn. D.C., Am., Fed. bar assns. Clubs: Chevy Chase (Md.); Burning Tree (Bethesda, Md.); Metropolitan (Washington). Home: 4521 Wetherill Rd Westmoreland Hills Washington DC 20016

AILOR, WILLIAM HENRY, JR., metallurgist; b. Knoxville, Tenn., July 15, 1917; s. William Henry and Eda Mae (Hacker) A.; B.S. cum laude, U. Tampa, 1939; B. Chem. Engring., N.C. State U., 1948; m. Clara Louise Horne, May 1, 1942; children—William H., James Richard, David Callahan. Research chemist A.C.L. R.R., Jacksonville, Fla., 1948-53; spl. lectr., research engr. N.C. State U., Raleigh, 1953-54; research engr. Reynolds Metals Co., Richmond, Va., 1954—. Adj. prof. math. Va. Commonwealth U., Richmond, 1959—. Pres. Westwood Civic Assn., 1966—. Bd. dirs. Richmond council Boy Scouts Am. Served with USNR, 1942-46, 52-53. Recipient Silver Beaver award Boy Scouts Am. Fellow Am. Soc. for Testing and Materials (award of merit 1970); mem. Nat. Assn. Corrosion Engrs., U.S. Naval Inst. Democrat. Methodist. Mason. Editor: Metal Corrosion in the Atmosphere, 1966; Handbook on Corrosion Testing and Evaluation, 1971. Home: 6009 S Crestwood Av Richmond VA 23226 Office: Metallurgical Research Div Reynolds Metals Co Richmond VA 23218

AINSLIE, RICHARD CLAYTON, architect; b. Monroe, Mich., July 27, 1936; s. John Clayton and Dorothy Mae (Brown) A.; B.Arch., U. Mich., 1961; postgrad. U. Houston, 1966-67; m. Marjorie Jean West, Nov. 1959; children—Richard D., Deborah D., David K. Project leader Rex W. Allen, Architects, San Francisco, 1962-64; planner Wurster, Bernardi, Emmons-Architects, San Francisco, 1964-65; owner Ainslie & Assos., Houston, 1966—. Club: Lakewood Yacht (Houston). Home: 2100 Tanglewilde Houston TX 77042 Office: 4507 Mt Vernon Houston TX 77006

AINSWORTH, MAX MCCABE, finance co. exec.; b. Bay Springs, Miss., July 13, 1921; s. Jessie Valerie and Nancy (Robbins) A.; student Miss. Coll., 1938-40; B.A., Tulane U., 1950, LL.B., 1950; m. Myrtle Louise Chatham, June 16, 1946; children—John Max, Robert Chatham. Admitted to La. bar, 1950; asso. firm Deutsch, Kerrigan & Stiles, New Orleans, 1950-51; with Indsl. Finance and Thrift Corp., New Orleans, 1951—, chief exec. officer, 1960—, pres., 1970—, also chmn. bd.; dir. First Pennsylvania Financial Services, Inc., Phila. Bd. dirs. Met. Crime Commn., Internat. House, both New Orleans; trustee So. Baptist Hosp., La. Coll. Served with USNR, 1942-46. Mem. New Orleans C. of C. (past dir.), New Orleans, La., Am. bar assns., Phi Alpha Delta. Baptist. Club: New Orleans Country. Home: 5558 Jacquelyn Ct New Orleans LA 70124 Office: 546 Carondelet St New Orleans LA 70130

AJELLO, LIBERO, med. mycologist; b. N.Y.C., Jan. 19, 1916; s. Joseph and Aurelia (Surdi) A.; A.B., Columbia, 1939, M.A., 1940, Ph.D., 1948; m. Gloria Claire Louise Wolff, Dec. 19, 1942; 1 son, Marc. Dir. mycology div. Center for Disease Control USPHS U.S. Dept. Health, Edn. and Welfare, Atlanta, 1947—. WHO expert adv. panel on parasitic diseases, 1959—. Pres. Italian Cultural Soc., Atlanta, 1968-69. Recipient Kimble Methodology Research award, 1972. Mem. A.A.A.S., Am. Soc. Microbiology, Mycol. Soc. Am., Internat. Soc. Human and Animal Mycology (pres. 1971—). Editor: Coccidioidomycosis, 1967; (with Chick and Furcolow) Histoplasmosis, 1971. Home: 2190 Spring Creek Rd Decatur GA 30033 Office: 1600 Clifton Rd Atlanta GA 30333

AKAMATSU, YASUYUKI, pathologist, educator; b. Hyokogen, Japan, Apr. 18, 1928; s. Suteji and Shieko (Momose) A.; M.D., Nara Med. Coll., 1950; Ph.D., Osaka (Japan) U. Med. Sch., 1957; m. Noriko Maki, May 1, 1960; children—Yuki, Maho, Takosi. Came to U.S., 1968. Intern, Nissei Hosp., Osaka, 1950-51; resident in pathology Osaka U. Med. Sch., 1951-55, instr., 1957; pathologist Atomic Bomb Casualty Commn., Hiroshima, Japan, 1955-57; jr. research pathologist U. Cal. at Los Angeles, 1960; asst. prof. pathology Osaka U. Inst. for Cancer Research, 1961-68; asst. prof. pathology, Med. Coll. Ga., Augusta, 1968—; attending physician VA Hosp., Augusta, Ga., 1972—. Fellow, Rockefeller Found., 1958, Am. Cancer Soc., 1959. Fellow Am. Soc. Clin. Pathologists; mem. Am. Assn. Cancer Research, Am. Assn. Pathologists and Bacteriologists, Internat. Acad. Pathologists, A.M.A., A.A.A.S., Ga., Pan Am. med assns., N.Y. Acad. Sci., Japanese Soc. Pathologists. Home: 535 Martin Lane Augusta GA 30904

AKERMAN, JOSEPH LAX, physician; b. Savannah, Ga., June 24, 1921; s. Walter E. and Marian (Lax) A.; student Vanderbilt U., 1940-42; M.D., Tulane U. Sch. Medicine, 1951; m. Orfa Mae Palko, Jan. 2, 1950; children—Joseph Lax, Marian Beth, Amos Tappan, John Michaels, Mary Louise. Intern USPHS, Galveston, Tex., 1951-52; resident USPHS Hosp., Memphis, 1952, med. staff, 1952; individual practice medicine, Apopka, Fla., 1953—; physician Plymouth Citrus Products Coop. plant, 1958—, Plymouth Citrus Growers Assn. (Fla.), 1958—, Gen. Electric Lamp Plant, Plymouth, 1969—; cons. physician for numerous owners in foliage plant industry. Pres. Central Fla. council Boy Scouts Am., 1968, 69, 70, council commr., 1966, 67, 71-73, mem. nat. council, 1965—, program chmn. Area VI, 1972-74; mem. nat. council Cub Scout Com., 1968—. Served with AUS, 1943-46, USAF, 1946-51; ATO, ETO. Recipient Silver Beaver award Fla. council Boy Scouts Am., Vigil Honor, Order of Arrow, 1968, named Man of Yr. Orange County YMCA, 1969, 1 of Top 10 Citizens Apopka, 1968, 69, 70. Mem. Kappa Alpha. Presbyn. (ruling elder). Club: Apopka Sertoma (charter pres.; chmn. bd. 1969-70, 70-71; named Distinguished Club pres., gov. Heart of Fla. dist. 1973-74). Home: 220 N Washington St Apopka FL 32703 Office: 125 S Park PO Box 1107 Apopka FL 32703

AKERS, THOMAS JEFFERSON, JR., petroleum co. exec.; b. Wenatchee, Wash., Oct. 30, 1930; s. Thomas Jefferson and Mary Aldyth (Owen) A.; B.S. in Organic Chemistry, Ore. State Coll., 1952, M.S. in Biochemistry (AEC fellow), 1954; m. Rosemary Ester Poole, June 11, 1954; children—Alice Ann, Patricia Ellen, Thomas Jay. Chemist, Wood River (Ill.) Research Lab., Shell Oil Co., 1954-66, sr. engr. product application dept., Chgo., 1966-70, sr. engr. MTM research and devel., 1970-72, sr. engr. indsl. sales dept. tech. services, Houston, 1972—. Mem. Soc. Automotive Engrs., Am. Soc. for Testing Materials. Patentee in field. Home: 6415 Bayonne St Spring TX 77373 Office: 2 Shell Plaza Houston TX 77002

AKIN, FRANCIS JAMES, architect; b. Beaumont, Tex., July 18, 1935; s. Hardy D. and Lillian Naida (Alexander) A.; B.Arch., Tex. A. and M. U., 1958; m. 2d, Elizabeth Ann Deskin, June 20, 1970; children by previous marriage—Kelly Ann, James Hardy. With Neuhaus Assos.; with Ford & Heesch; pvt. practice architecture, Houston, 1970—. Sec. Cosmopolitan Internat., Houston, 1972-73. Served to capt. AUS, 1958-65. Mem. Constrn. Specifications Inst. Mem. Christian Ch. (mem. ofcl. bd. 1972-74, deacon 1972-74). Home: 7405 S Gessner St Houston TX 77036 Office: 6440 Hillcroft 206 Houston TX 77036

AKIN, HENRY DAVID, JR., lawyer; b. Amarillo, Tex., Apr. 30, 1927; s. Henry D. and Catherine (Clark) A.; B.A., U. Tex., 1946, LL.B., 1950; m. Mary Ella Jones, Sept. 2, 1949; children—Catherine Anita, Henry David, John Stewart, Matthew Clark, Mary Haydon, Admitted to Tex. bar, 1950; practice law firm Leachman, Matthews, Gardere, Akin & Porter, 1950-53; partner Williams & Akin, 1953-57, Akin, Viai, Hamilton, Koch & Tubb, (all Dallas), 1957-72; dir. Capital S.W. Corp., Dallas, 1962-65, 1st Bank & Trust, Richardson, Tex., 1964—, Richardson Savs. & Loan Assn., 1957—, Federated Financial Corp., (both Dallas), 1961—, Vice pres. bd. Richardson Ind. Sch. Dist., 1958-64; active Baylor U. Hosp. Dr., 1967—, Meth. Hosp., Dallas, 1967—, Goals for Dallas Dr., 1968—, Dallas United Fund, 1968—; bd. dirs. YMCA, Richardson, 1965-71, Campfire Girls, Dallas, 1966-71. Judge, Richardson, 1956-57. Served with USNR, 1944-46. Named Outstanding Young Lawyer Dallas Jr. Bar Assn., 1967. Mem. Dallas (dir. 1958-59, 68-69, 2d v.p. 1967), Richardson (dir. 1956), Am. bar assns., Southwestern Legal Found., Tex. Bar Found. Methodist (chmn. bd.). Clubs: Northwood (Dallas), Dallas Gun. Home: 7249 Elmridge Dr Dallas TX 75240 Office: Suite 170 One Metro Sq Dallas TX 75234

AKIN, J. REGINALD, elec. machinery mfg. co. exec.; b. Carrollton, Ga., Aug. 29, 1936; s. T. Roy and Virginia (Tant) A.; student Atlanta Sch. Electronics, 1954-55; m. Betty Jean Allen, June 18, 1955; children—Deborah Lynne, Donna Leigh. Dealer rep. Economy Auto Stores Inc., Atlanta, 1954-60; territory mgr. Westinghouse Appliance Sales Co., Macon, Ga., 1960-62, 65-66; pres. Elec. Appliance, Inc., Atlanta, 1962-65; mgr. So. div. Kelvinator, Inc., Atlanta, 1966-69; v.p., mgr. appliance div. Carolina Sales Corp., Greenville, N.C., 1969—. Pres. Akin Appliance, Inc., Macon, Ga., 1962-65; v.p. Kelvinator Distr. Honor Council, 1973, pres., 1974. Republican. Mem. Christian Ch. (deacon, bd. dirs.). Mason (32 deg., Shriner).

Club: Greenville Golf and Country. Home: 201 W Martinsborough Rd Greenville NC 27834 Office: PO Box 1927 Greenville NC 27834

AKIN, TED MARTIN, judge; b. Pasadena, Cal., Jan. 5, 1932; s. Ted and Lillian (Jones) A.; B.A., So. Meth. U., 1952, J.D., 1955; m. Gloria Lille Dahl, Dec. 17, 1954; children—Laurel Sheffield, George Leighton, Adrienne Lillian, Ashley Griffin. Admitted to Tex. bar, 1955, U.S. Supreme Ct. bar, 1963; with firm Bradford & Pritchard, 1957-59, Edwards, Fortson, Sowell & Akin, 1959-61, Cervin, Stanford & Akin, 1961-63, Akin, Steinberg & Stanford, 1969-71, Akin, Stanford & Gilliland, 1971-72 (all Dallas); judge County Ct. at Law Dallas, 1963-69, 95th Dist. Ct., Dallas, 1972—. Founder, chmn. bd. Liberty Nat. Bank, Dallas, 1964-69. Served to 1st lt. USAF, 1955-57. Recipient certificate of Appreciation, Circle Ten council Boy Scouts Am., 1965. Mem. Tex., Dallas bar assns., Am. Judicature Soc., Sigma Alpha Epsilon (pres. 1971-72). Home: 5323 N Dentwood Dr Dallas TX 75220 Office: Dallas County Courthouse Dallas TX 75202

ALARIO, ROBERT JOSEPH, off-shore marine contracting co. exec.; b. Golden Meadow, La., June 3, 1938; s. Juan Victor and Victoria (Rebstock) A.; B.A. (Univ. scholar), U. Southwestern La., 1959; student Law Sch., La. State U., 1959-61; M.S. in Fgn. Service, Georgetown U., 1963; postgrad. in bus. Tulane U., 1968; m. Joan Carole Whitman, Jan. 21, 1961; children—Mitzi Louise, Robert Christopher. Clk., asso. dir. publs. Com. on Un-American Activities, U.S. Ho. of Reps., Washington, 1962-63; with Texaco Inc., various internat. locations, 1963-68, asst. to mgr., Port-au-Prince, Haiti, 1964-66, acting mgr., Conakry, Guinea, 1963-64; asst. to pres. Nolty J. Theriot, Inc., New Orleans, 1968-70, v.p., sec., 1970—, also dir.; pres., chmn. bd. Offshore Tugs Inc., New Orleans, 1971—; dir. Internat. Hotel Corp., New Orleans; pres. Internat. Imports Inc., New Orleans, 1972—. Mem. subcom. on manning, licensing and stability Nat. Offshore Operations Adv. Panel, 1969—; tech. adviser La. Adv. Commn. Coastal and Marine Resources, 1972—. Bd. dirs., vice chmn. Indsl. Found. South; bd. dirs. Council for Devel. French in La.; pres., chmn. bd. dirs. Offshore Marine Service Assn. Edn. Fund, 1971—. K.C. fellow, 1962; Ill. Central R.R. fellow, 1956. Mem. Offshore Marine Service Assn. (chmn. 1970—), Nat. Ocean Industries Assn. (mem. industry and govt. liaison com. 1973, mem. congl. action com. 1973), Pi Sigma Alpha, Kappa Sigma. K.C., Toastmaster. Clubs: Colonial Gulf and Country (Metairie, La.); Mystic Krewe of Louisianians (Washington). Office: 706 Odeco Bldg 1600 Canal St New Orleans LA 70112 Home: 16 Colonial Lane Harahan LA 70123

ALATIS, JAMES EFSTATHIOS, univ. dean; b. Weirton, W.Va., July 13, 1926; s. Efstathios and Vasiliki (Galanoudis) A.; B.A., W.Va. U., 1948; M.A., Ohio State U., 1953, Ph.D., 1966; m. Penelope Mastorides, Dec. 30, 1951; children—William, Stephen, Anthony. Fulbright lectr. English, U. Athens, 1955-57; English testing and teaching specialist Dept. State, 1959-61; specialist for lang. research U.S. Office Edn., 1961-65, chief lang. sect., 1965-66; asso. dean Sch. Langs. and Linguistics, Georgetown U., Washington, 1966-73, dean, 1973—; exec. sec. Tchrs. of English to Speakers of Other Langs., 1966—; prin. investigator team to evaluate English as second lang. programs Navajo Area Schs., Bur. Indian Affairs, 1969-70. Mem. adv. council ERIC Clearinghouse on Linguistics, 1966-71; bd. dirs. CONPASS, 1966-70. Served with USNR, 1944-46. Recipient Mary Glide Goethe prize Am. Name Soc., 1954. Am. Council Learned Socs. study grantee in linguistics U. Mich., 1954. Fellow A.A.A.S.; mem. Am. Council on Teaching Fgn. Langs. (adv. assembly), Linguistic Soc. Am. (del. 1966-69), Nat. Council Tchrs. English, Modern Lang. Assn. Am., Nat. Assn. Fgn. Student Affairs (dir. 1965-66), Fedn. Internationale des Professeurs de Langues Vivantes (exec. com.), Phi Beta Kappa. Editor: Studies in Honor of Albert H. Marckwardt, 1972. Contbr. articles to profl. jours. Home: 5108 Sutton Pl Alexandria VA 22304 Office: Sch Langs and Linguistics Georgetown U Washington DC 20007

ALBERT, CARL BERT, congressman; b. McAlester, Okla., May 10, 1908; s. Ernest Homer and Leona Ann (Scott) A.; A.B., U. Okla., 1931; B.A. (Rhodes scholar), Oxford U., Eng., 1933, B.C.L., 1934; m. Mary Harmon, Aug 20, 1942; children—Mary Frances, David. Admitted to Okla. bar, legal clk. FHA, 1934-37; atty., accountant Sayre Oil Co., Oklahoma City, 1937-38; legal dept. Ohio Oil Co., Marshall, Ill., Findlay, O., 1939-40; gen. practice law, Oklahoma City, 1938, Mattoon, Ill., 1938-39, McAlester, Okla., 1946-47; mem. 80th to 93d congresses from 3d Okla. Dist., majority leader. Served from pvt. to lt. col. U.S. Army, 1941-46. Decorated Bronze Star. medal. Democrat. Methodist. Home: 827 E Osage McAlester OK 74501 Address: Capitol Bldg Washington DC 20515

ALBERT, IRENE HOLT, ret. journalist, author; b. Moline, Ill., Jan. 4, 1910; d. George Edmund and Jean (Cox) Holt; student pvt. tutors and Internat. Sch. of Tangier, Morocco, schs. in N.Y. and Ill.; student Sorbonne U., 1927-30; m. John Jacob Albert III, June 10, 1939; 1 son, John J. IV (dec.). Staff writer Moline (Ill.) Dispatch, 1925-26, fgn. corr., 1927-30; accredited corr. U.S. Senate Press Gallery, 1926-27; contbr. to Paris edits. N.Y. Herald Tribune, Paris Times, 1927-30; contbr. book reviews Washington Post, 1937-39, short stories and poetry to nat. publs., 1940—; stringer for Time, Inc., 1957-58; spl. news reporter, art writer and columnist, feature writer Clearwater (Fla.) Sun, 1955-74; pub. relations Fla. Gulf Coast Art Center, 1958-68; pub. relations counselor Jr. Ballet Guild Found. Fla., 1964-70. Recipient first prize McCall's Home of Tomorrow, 1945; 2d pl. pub. short story Nat. League Am. Pen Women, 1962; 2d place interview Fla. Women's Press Club, 1959; spl. award Fla. State Poetry Contest, 1961; Press award Cuban Resistance, 1963; award in features, A.P. (Fla.), 1964; award for interviews, Fla. Women's Press Club, 1964; biennial awards lyrics Nat. League Am. Pen Women, 1965; Hadassah award for contbn. to journalism, 1966; Merit award Am. Heart Assn.; Grand prize poetry Americana Folk Festival, 1970; poetry prize Fla. competition, 1971, others. Mem. Nat. Soc. Arts and Letters, Nat. League Am. Pen-women (pres. Clearwater br. 1958-60). Nat. League Women Voters, Fla. Gulf Coast Art Center, St. Petersburg Mus. Fine Arts, Womens Aux. A.I.A., Women in Communications. Club: Washington Press. Home: 1321 Murray Av Clearwater FL 33515 Office: 1321 Murray Av Clearwater FL 33515

ALBERT, WILLIAM CHARLES, social worker, educator; b. Great Falls, Mont., June 17, 1941; s. William Merrill and Eva Rose (Cooper) A.; B.A. in Edn., Eastern Wash. State Coll., 1963; M.S.W., U. Wash., 1966; postgrad. U. So. Cal., 1971-73; m. Bertha May Wurl, June 9, 1963; children—Jon, Lisa. Social work supr., also social service tng. specialist Wash. State Dept. Pub. Assistance, Spokane, 1966-68, Wash. State Dept. Instns., Medical Lake, 1968-69; asst. prof. Eastern Wash. State Coll., Cheney, 1969-71; asst. prof. social work Va. Commonwealth U., Richmond, 1973—. Cons., Spokane Family Counseling Services, 1967-68; counselor Home of the Good Shepherd, Spokane, 1967-71. Mem. Va. Council Social Welfare. Bd. dirs. Wash. Assn. Social Welfare. 1968-69, Wash. Assn. Retarded Children, Spokane chpt., 1968-71. Mem. Nat. Assn. Social Workers (sec.-treas. Wash. council 1970-71, pres. Spokane chpt. 1970-71), Gerontology Soc., Alpha Kappa Delta, Pi Gamma Mu. Home 2715 Scarsborough Dr Richmond VA 23235

ALBERTS, HAROLD, lawyer; b. San Antonio, Apr 3, 1920; s. Bernard H. and Rose (Cassel) A.; LL.B., U. Tex., 1942; m. Rose M. Gaskin, Mar. 25, 1945; children—Linda Rae, Barry Lawrence. Tchr., U. Tex., 1942; admitted to Tex. bar, 1943; gen. practice law, Corpus Christi, Tex., 1946—. Pres., Jewish Welfare Fund Corpus Christi, 1948; charter vice chmn. of the Southwest Regional Anti-Defamation League, 1953, chmn., 1969-72; also chmn. Brotherhood Week, 1957; chmn Nueces County chpt. A.R.C., 1959-61; mem. campaign exec. com., chmn. meetings United Community Services, 1961; vice chmn. Coastal Bend Council on Alcoholism; v.p. Combined Jewish Appeal, 1972-73; v.p. Little Theatre Corpus Christi, 1964—. Chmn. Corpus Christi Nat. Conf. Christians and Jews, 1967-69; bd. dirs. Tex. State Assn. for Mental Health. Served to lt. USNR, 1942-46. Mem. Am., Tex., Nueces County bar assns. Mason, Kiwanian (pres. 1962); mem. B'nai B'rith (pres. 1955, past v.p. Tex.). Home: 618 Dolphin Pl Corpus Christi TX 78411 Office: Wilson Tower Corpus Christi TX 78401

ALBERTSON, HAROLD D., elec. engr., educator; b. Parsons, Kan., Dec. 28, 1931; s. George Dewey and Mamie Irene (Harrell) A.; B.S. in Math. and Elec. Engring., U. Houston, 1953; M.S. in Elec. Engring., So. Methodist U., 1960; Ph.D. (Tex. Instruments fellow), U. Tex., 1968; m. Margaret Elna Bodden, Aug. 8, 1953; 1 dau., Anne. Systems engr. Chance Vought Aircraft, Dallas, 1953-58; design engr. Tex. Instruments, Inc., Dallas, 1958-61, program mgr., 1961-65, mem. tech. staff, 1968-73; instr. physics Eastfield Coll., Dallas, 1972-73; instr. electro-mech. and fluid power tech., Richland Coll., Dallas, 1973—. Mem. steering com. Southwest Simulation Council, 1971-72. Mem. I.E.E.E. (chmn. Dallas chpt. 1971-72), Sigma Xi, Tau Beta Pi. Home: 7660 Chalkstone St Dallas TX 75240 Office: 12800 Abrams Rd Dallas TX 75231

ALBERTSON, JOHN NEWMAN, JR., mil. officer; b. New Haven, Jan. 18, 1933; s. John Newman and Catherine Marie (Davis) A.; B.A., U. Conn., 1954; M.S., Hahnemann Med. Coll., 1964; diploma U.S. Army Command and Gen. Staff Coll., 1968; m. Mary Anne Healey, Jan. 29, 1955; children—Laura Lee, Kurt David, Paul Douglas, Eric James, Nina Marie, Derek John, Luke Thomas. Commd. 2d. lt. U.S. Army, 1954, advanced through grades to col., 1974; asst. chief Dept. Immunology and Serology, U.S. Army Med. Lab., Landstuhl, Germany, 1954-59; chief clin. pathology and bacteriologist, Valley Forge Gen. Hosp., Phoenixville, Pa., 1959-62; research asso. Hahnemann Med. Coll., Phila., 1962-64; chief bacteriology and virology divs. First U.S. Army Med. Lab., Ft. George G. Meade, Md., 1964-67; chief med. and biol. scis. br. Office Chief Research and Devel., Hdqrs., Dept. Army, Washington, 1968-70, exec. officer, research directorate, 1970-71; comdg. officer 9th Med. Lab., Saigon, Vietnam, 1971-72; exec. officer Walter Reed Army Inst. of Research, Washington, 1972—. Decorated Legion of Merit, Meritorious Service medal, U.S. Army Commendation medal; Civic Action award (Republic of Vietnam). Diplomate Am. Bd. Microbiology. Fellow A.A.A.S.; mem. Am. Acad. Microbiology, Am. Soc. Microbiology (mil. chmn. 1960, 69), Sigma Xi. Mason (32 deg.). Contbr. articles to various publs. Home: 5226 Ferndale St Springfield VA 22151 Office: Walter Reed Army Inst Research Washington DC 20012

ALBRIGHT, BOYCE SINGLETON, supt. schs.; b. Haleyville Ala., Apr. 27, 1924; s. Virgie Hugh and Tiney (Posey) A.; student U. Ala., 1943; B.A., Howard Coll., 1948; M.A., George Peabody Coll., 1952. Head coordinator Vets. Tng. Program, Haleyville, 1948-61; tchr. Haleyville Schs., 1952-61, supt. schs., 1971—; coordinator trade and indsl. edn. Haleyville High Sch., 1960-61; supt. schs. Winston County (Ala.), 1961-71; state chmn. Profl. Relations and Tchr. Welfare Com. Mem. Ala. Com. for Better Schs., 1961—. Trustee N.W. Ala. State Jr. Coll. Served with AUS, World War II. Mem. Ala. Edn. Assn. (mem. state legislative com.; dist. pres. elect, state chmn. joint com.), Ala. Assn. Sch. Adminstrs. (state exec. com.), N.E. A., Distributive Edn. Clubs Am. (hon. life), Ala. Congress Parents and Tchrs. (hon. life), Internat. Platform Assn., Am. Legion, V.F.W., C. of C., Kappa Phi Kappa. Alpha Phi Omega, Omicron Delta Kappa, Pi Kappa Alpha. Mason., Lion (pres., dep. dist. gov., zone chmn.). Home: PO Box 149 Haleyville AL 35565 Office: 1800 E 20th St Haleyville AL 35565

ALBRIGHT, JERE BAXTER, SR., lawyer; b. Humboldt, Tenn., Feb. 18, 1933; s. Charles Wesley and Mettie Gladys (White) A.; B.B.A., Memphis State U., 1958; J.D., U. Tenn., 1961; m. Marian Knowles, Aug. 24, 1958; children—Lucinda Gaye, Jere Baxter, Jr., Marian. Admitted to Tenn. bar, 1961; pvt. practice law, Humboldt, Tenn., 1962-63, 1966—; asst. U.S. atty., Memphis, 1964-66. Del. Tenn. Bar Ho. of Dels., 1973—. Served with AUS, 1954-56. Mem. Humboldt C. of C. (bd. dirs. 1967-72; pres. 1971), Am., Tenn., Gibson County bar assns., Sigma Alpha Epsilon, Phi Delta Phi. Rotarian (bd. dirs. 1968-73; pres. 1972-73). Home: 2235 Lalatta Lane Humboldt TN 38343 Office: Mcht State Bank Bldg Humboldt TN 38343

ALBRIGHT, SPENCER DELANCEY, JR., educator; b. Nashville; s. Spencer Delancey and Sarah Anne (Lang) A.; B.A., U. Ark., 1922; A.M., U. Chgo., 1932; Ph. D., U. Tex., 1940; m. Margaret McCain Hyatt, July 23, 1929; children—Spencer Delancey III, Sarah Katherine (Mrs. William Karl Sipfle). Tchr. high sch., Earle, 1922-23, Fayetteville, Stuttgart, 1925-30 (all Ark.); faculty Crane Coll., Chgo., 1930-32, George Williams Coll., 1933-34, Central YMCA Coll., Chgo., 1934-35, U. Ark., 1935-37, U. Tex., Austin, 1937-39, Tex. Technol. Coll., 1939-40, Reed Coll., Portland, Ore., 1940-42, U. Wash., Seattle, 1942-43, U. Wis., summer 1946; prof. polit. sci. U. Richmond (Va.), 1946—, chmn. dept. history and polit. sci., 1967—; tchr. summer sessions U. S.D., 1947-49, Emory U., 1950, 52, 57, 61, 64. Served with U.S. Army, 1918; to capt. USAF, 1943-46. Mem. Am., So. polit. sci. assns., Am. Acad. Polit. and Social Sci., Va. Social Sci. Assn., Am. Soc. Pub. Administrn., N.E.A., Scabbard and Blade, Pi Sigma Alpha, Omicron Delta Kapa, Kappa Delta Pi, Pi Delta Epsilon, Phi Alpha Theta, Tau Kappa Alpha. Democrat. Baptist. Author: The American Ballot, 1942. Contbr. articles to profl. publs. Home: 6611 Three Chopt Rd Richmond VA 23226

ALBRIGHT, W(ILLIAM) DOUGLAS, lawyer; b. West Lafayette, Ind., Jan. 19, 1939; s. William Purvis and Dorothy (Wilbanks) A.; A.B., Duke, 1961; LL.B., Am. U., 1964; m. Mary Egerton,Apr. 1, 1961; children—Jon Douglas, David Erik, Robert Stuart, Lawrence Ethan. Admitted to N.C. bar, 1964; pvt. practice law, Greensboro, N.C., 1964-66; asst. solicitor Guilford County Superior Ct., Greensboro, 1966-68; chief dist. prosecutor 18th Jud. Dist., Greensboro, N.C., 1968-69, dist. atty., 1971—; dist. solicitor 12th Solicitorial Dist., 1969-71. Mem. N.C., Greensboro bar assns., N.C. State Bar, Optimist Internat., N.C. Jud. Council, N.C. Dist. Attys. Assn. (pres.), Phi Beta Kappa. Home: Red Forest Ct Greensboro NC 27410 Office: Guilford County Courthouse Greensboro NC 27408

ALBRITTON, WILLIAM HAROLD, III, lawyer; b. Andalusia, Ala., Dec. 19, 1936; s. Robert Bynum and Carrie (Veal) A.; diploma Marion Inst. (Ala.), 1955; A.B., U. Ala., 1959, LL.B., 1960; m. Jane Rollins Howard, June 2, 1958; children—William Harold IV, Benjamin Howard, Thomas Bynum. Admitted to Ala. bar, 1960, since practice law firm Albrittons & Rankin, Andalusia, 1962—, asso., 1962-66, partner, 1966—. Dir. TV Cable Co., Andalusia. Chmn. Andalusia Bd. Zoning Adjustment, 1963-64. Mem. Ala. Republican Exec. Com., 1967—; mem. Covington County Rep. Exec. Com., 1967—, chmn., 1970—. Bd. dirs. Covington County chpt. Ala. Soc. Crippled Children and Adults, 1970—. Served to capt. AUS, 1960-62. Mem. Am., Ala. (mem. exec. council young lawyers 1965-70), Covington County (pres. 1973) bar assns., Andalusia C. of C. (pres. 1967-68), Nat. Assn. R.R. Trial Counsel, Am. Judicature Soc., Ala. Def. Lawyers Assn. (dir. 1970-72, v.p. 1972-73), L.Q.C. Lamar Soc. (dir. Ala. chpt. 1972—), U. Ala. Farrah Law Soc., Phi Beta Kappa, Phi Delta Phi, Omicron Delta Kappa, Alpha Tau Omega. Presbyn. (elder). Rotarian. Home: 730 Albritton Rd Andalusia AL 36420 Office: 109 Opp Av Andalusia AL 36420

ALBURY, CHARLES BAUGHMAN, pub., editor, writer; b. Millersburg, O., Aug. 17, 1925; s. Charles R. and Ruth (Baughman) A.; B.A., Bowling Green State U., 1950; m. Maxine Marie Finley, June 11, 1955; children—Janice Michelle, Suzanne Marie, Cherie Babette, Charles Lloyd. Asst. sports editor Mansfield (O.) News-Jour., 1950-55; feature writer, photographer Lakeland (Fla.) Ledger, 1955; Clearwater bur. chief St. Petersburg (Fla.) Times, 1956-60, Enterprise writer, 1960—; editor, pub. Sr. Golfer mag., 1964—, also pres. Sr. Golf Publs. Co., 1964—; contbr. to Golf Digest, Book of Golf, Golf World; pub. Am. Srs. Golf Assn. yearbook, Fla. Profl. Golfers Assn. Sect. Annual. Served as sgt., AUS, 1943-45. Mem. Golf Writers Assn. Am., Softball Writers and Broadcasters Assn., YMCA, Clearwater C. of C., Clearwater Advt. Club. Republican. Methodist. Home: 1716 Verde Dr Clearwater FL 33515 Office: 311 S Osceola Av Clearwater FL 33516

ALCIATORE, JULES C(ESAR), educator; b. New Orleans, Nov. 18, 1901; s. Jules L. and Marie Althea (Roy) A.; A.B., Tulane U., 1922; A.M., U. of Ill., 1929; Ph.D., Univ. Chicago, 1938; m. Miss Audrey S. Bond, June 11, 1929; 1 son, Jules L. Asst. in French, U. of Ill., 1927-29; instr. French, Northwestern, 1929-31, 1934-35; instr. Romance lang., Catholic U. of Am., 1938-41; asso. prof. French, U. of Ga. 1947-49, prof., 1959-64, Alumni Found. prof., 1957, emeritus, 1964; vis. lectr. U. Chgo., summer 1948, vis. asso. prof., summer 1950. Served at lt. (s.g.), USNR, 1943-46. Recipient Carnegie grant-in-aid. 1951; M. G. Michael award, 1953. Mem. Modern Lang. Assn. (chmn. French VI 1958), S. Atlantic Modern Lang. Assn. (v.p. 1960), Am. Assn. Tchrs. of French, Societe d'Histoire Litteraire de la France, Assn. des Amis de Stendhal, Am. Assn. Teachers Italian, Am. Assn. U. Profs., Sigma Phi Epsilon, Phi Kappa Phi, Pi Delta Phi. Author: Abstract of dissertation; Stendhal et Helvetius; Les Sources de la philosophie de Stendhal (Geneve Librairie Droz, 1952); Stendhal et Maine de Biran (Geneve Librarie Droz, 1954). Home: 118 Mulberry Dr Metairie LA 70005

ALCORN, ROY ANVIL, ednl. adminstr.; b. Williamsville, Mo., Dec. 3, 1925; s. Scott and Delia Ann (Boxx) A.; B.S. in Edn., Southeast Mo. State Coll., 1955; M.A., George Peabody Coll. for Tchrs., 1958, Ed.D. in Edn., 1963; m. Virgie Lois Carter, Oct. 23, 1953; children—Martha Lynn, Daniel Sheridan, Joseph Dean, Elizabeth Ann, Walter Lee. Tchr. Mo. pub. schs., 1946-51; congl. aide to Mo. congressman, 1953-56; prin., high sch. Waynesville, Mo., 1956-58; supt. of schs., Eminence, Mo., 1958-61; asst. supt. schs., Wilmington, Del., 1963-65; supt. schs., Chesterfield County, Va., 1965-69, Roanoke City, 1969-72; chmn. edn. dept. George Peabody Coll. Tchrs., Nashville, 1972-73. Mem. exec. bd. Central Va. Ednl. TV, 1965-69. Trustee, Madison Coll., Harrisonburg, Va., 1972-73. Served with AUS, 1944-46, USAF, 1950-52. Recipient Freedom's Found. award, 1969. Mem. Am. Assn. Sch. Adminstrs., Va. Edn. Assn., N.E.A., Phi Delta Kappa, Kappa Delta Pi. Rotarian. Died Apr. 10, 1973. Home: 6067 Smith Springs Rd Antioch TN 37013

ALDAY, GONZALO, computer systems engr.; b. Habana, Cuba, Feb. 27, 1941; s. Gerardo Eloy and Hilda Caridad (Urioste) A.; came to U.S., 1960, naturalized, 1966; B.S. in Elec. Engring., U. Fla., 1964, M.S. in Engring., 1966; m. Marta R. Perdomo, Nov. 23, 1963; children—Marta Elena, Gonzalo Luis, Juan Antonio, Carolina Maria. Systems engr. data processing div. IBM Corp., Jacksonville, Fla., 1966—, adv. systems engr., 1971—. Instr., Lake City (Fla.) Community Coll., 1971. Active Boys Club of Gainesville. Mem. I.E.E.E., Phi Kappa Phi. Club: Big Five (Miami, Fla.). Home: 903 NW 36th Terrace Gainesville FL 32601 Office: 1403 NW 13th St Gainesville FL 32601

ALDERDICE, NOMER WOODROW, ret. retail trade exec.; b. nr. Mayfield, Ky., Feb. 23, 1913; s. Calvin Arnie and Bertha Alma (Foy) A.; student Murray State Tchrs. Coll., 1930-31, 32-33; m. Grace W. Boulton, Aug. 15, 1936; children—Jimmy, Donna (Mrs. Scott Lingo). Tchr. Graves County (Ky.) Sch. System, 1931-32, 34-37; prodn. worker B.F. Goodrich Co., Akron, O., 1933-34; mgr. Western Auto Store, Mayfield, 1937-38, 45-49, mgr. Marion, Ky., 1938-42, owner, mgr., 1949-73; prodn. supr. Nat. Fireworks 20MM Plant, Viola, 1942-45; dir. Peoples Bank, Marion. Mayor, City of Marion, 1956-58. Democrat. Mem. Ch. of Christ (tchr., treas. 1949—). Rotarian (pres. 1956-57). Home: 515 W Gum St Marion KY 42064

ALDERDICE, ROBERT JAMES, architect; b. Pitts., Jan. 29, 1929; s. William Patterson and Hilda (Karlen) A.; B.Arch., Carnegie Inst. Tech. (now Carnegie-Mellon U.), 1952; m. Jane M. Hanley, Jan. 23, 1957. With Tasso Katselas, Architect, Pitts., 1953-54, Rene D. Ramirez, A.I.A., Santurce, P.R., 1955-57, Schmidt & McDade, Architects, Santurce, 1957-58; architect Robert J. Alderdice, A.I.A. & Assos., Santurce, San Juan, P.R., 1958—. Served with USAF, 1946-49. Mem. A.I.A. (chpt. sec. 1966), Ingenieros y Agrimensores, Colegio de Arquitectos, Nat. Council Archtl. Registration Bds. Republican. Club: San Juan Exchange (Condado, Santurce, P.R.). Archtl. works includes El Conquistador Hotel, Gen. Foods, Inc., San Juan Star newspaper plant. Office: 1351 Ashford Av Condado San Juan PR 00907

ALDERMAN, LOUIS CLEVELAND, JR., coll. pres.; b. Douglas, Ga., Aug. 12, 1924; s. Louis Cleveland and Minnis Amelia (Wooten) A.; A.A., S.Ga. Coll., 1942; A.B., Emory U., 1946; M.S., U. Ga., 1949; postgrad. Columbia, summers 1951-54; Ed.D. (Ford Found. fellow), Auburn U., 1959; m. Anne Augusta Whipple, Dec. 31, 1952; children—Amelia Anne, Louis Cleveland III, Fielding Dillard, Jonathan Augustus. USPHS grad. research asst. U. Ga., 1948-49, instr. biology, Rome Center, 1949-50, dir., asst. prof. biology, Savannah Center, 1950-51, Rome Center, 1951-56, Columbus Center, 1956-59; dir. U. Ky., Henderson Coll., 1959-64; pres. Middle Ga. Coll., Cochran, 1964—. Mem. adv. bd. Union Fed. Savs. & Loan Assn.; mem. adv. council U. System of Ga. Bd. dirs. Bleckley County Hosp. Authority, Bleckley Recreation Assn., Cochran Community House. Served to sgt. AUS, 1942-46; PTO. Recipient Good Citizenship award Civitan Club, 1955, Club Service award Rotary Internat., 1968-69, Community Leaders of Am. award, 1969-70. Mem. Assn. Higher Edn., Ga. Hist. Soc., S.A.R., Order Ky. Cols., N.E.A., Ga. Assn. Colls., Ga. Assn. Educators, Ga. Assn. Jr. Colls. (exec. com. 1967-70, pres. 1968-69), Phi Delta Kappa, Phi Theta Kappa, Sigma Nu. Democrat. Baptist (chmn. bd. deacons). Rotarian (bd. dirs. 1965-69, pres. 1967-68), Barons, Descendants Knight of the Garter. Clubs: Uchee Trail Country, Magna Charta. Author: Focus on Change, 1964; Fifty Years as Middle Georgia College, 1967. Contbr. articles profl. jours. Home: Old Chester Rd Cochran GA 31014

ALDERSON, VETTRA GLENN, lawyer; b.Oxford, Miss., Oct. 10, 1940; s. Vettra Curtis and Louise (Mathis) A.; B.P.A., U. Miss., 1963, J.D., 1966; m. Jackie Lovell, Aug. 11, 1961; children—Vettra Glenn, Laura Lovell. Admitted to Miss. bar, 1966; pvt. practice law, Oxford, 1966—, also pros. atty. Lafayette County, City of Oxford, 1968—. Pres. Lafayette County Heart Assn., 1967-68. Mem. Lafayette County (pres.), Miss. Jr. (dir.), Am., Miss., 5th Circuit bar assns., Oxford C. of C. (dir.), Kappa Sigma, Phi Alpha Delta. Baptist. Mason. Home: 314 Garner Oxford MS 38655 Office: 1120 1/2 Van Buren Av Oxford MS 38655

ALDRIDGE, RICHARD CAMPBELL, JR., nurseryman; b. Center Point, Tex., Mar. 9, 1925; s. Richard Campbell (Sr.) and Tweena (Lange) A.; grad. high sch.; m. Meredith Emily Bailey, May 7, 1941; children—Donald Wayne, Mark Vinton, Connie Lynn (Mrs. Gerald Brannan), Gwenda (Mrs. Greg Neel), David Richard. With Aldridge Nursery, Inc., Von Omy, Tex., 1940—, gen. mgr., 1960—. Bd. trustees S.W. Ind. Sch. Dist., 1957, v.p., 1960-62, pres., 1963—. Mem. exec. com. Bexar County Fedn. Sch. Bds., 1970-73, Bexar County Mental Health and Mental Retardation Assn., 1971-73. Served with USCG, 1943-46; PTO. Mem. Am. (lt. gov. 1973), Tex. (regional dir. 1973) assns. nurserymen, Youth for Christ Assn. Democrat. Baptist. Address: Route 1 Von Ormy TX 78073

ALEPA, (FRANCIS) PAUL, physician; b. Bronx, N.Y., Dec. 29, 1932; s. Frank P. and Carmelina (Maiuzzo) A.; B.S., Lebanon Valley Coll., Anniville, Pa., 1954; M.D., Georgetown U., 1958. Intern, Cin. Gen. Hosp., 1958-59; resident D.C. Gen Hosp., Washington, 1959-60, resident internal medicine VA Hosp., Washington, 1960-62 postdoctoral fellow Nat. Inst. Arthritis Metabolic Diseases, NIH, Bethesda, Md., 1962-64, sr. investigator, acting asst. chief arthritis br., 1964-65; med. attendant VA Hosp., Washington, 1962—, chief rheumatology service, 1972—; asst. prof. medicine Georgetown U., 1965-71, asso. prof., 1971—, dir. div. rheumatic diseases, 1970—. Diplomate Am. Bd. Internal Medicine. Mem. D.C. Rheumatism Soc. (pres. 1971-72), Am. Rheumatism Assn. Home: 7211 Barnett Rd Bethesda MD 20034 Office: Georgetown U Hosp Washington DC 20007

ALESSANDRO, VICTOR NICHOLAS, symphony condr.; b. Waco, Tex., Nov. 27, 1915; s. Victor and Josephine (Kemendo) A.; Mus. B., U. Rochester, 1937, Mus.D. (hon.), 1948; L.H.D., So. Meth. U., 1956; student Mozarteum Acad., Salzburg, Austria, 1937, Santa Cecilia Acad., Rome, Italy, 1938; m. Ruth Drisko, May 1, 1955; children—Victor Tabbut, Ruth Ann. Musical dir. Oklahoma City Symphony, 1938-51, San Antonio Symphony Orch. and San Antonio Grand Opera Festival, 1951—; European conducting debut with Oslo Philharmonic, 1968. Trustee U. Rochester. Decorated cavalier Order Star of Solidarity (Italy); recipient Alice M. Ditson award Columbia, 1956; citation for outstanding service to Am. music Nat. Music Council, 1964. Mem. Internat. Alliance Theatrical and Stage Employees (hon.), Am. Fedn. Musicians (hon.), Phi Mu Alpha (hon.). Club: Torch (San Antonio). Home: 711 Garraty Rd San Antonio TX 78209 Office: Symphony Soc of San Antonio 600 Hemisfair Plaza Way San Antonio TX 78209

ALEXANDER, A. E., gas co. exec.; b. Kirksville, Mo., Apr. 23, 1913; s. George A. and Ettie (Hammond) A.; student Drake U., 1931-36; LL.B., So. Meth. U., 1937; m. Charlotte Agnus, Sept. 3, 1937;children—Jane, Nancy Ruth. Various positions The Cal. Co., New Orleans, 1937-50; v.p. Hibernia Nat. Bank, New Orleans, 1950-64; vice chmn. bd. La. Delta Offshore, New Orleans, 1964-65; pres. Crestwave Offshore Services, Inc., New Orleans, 1966-73, also pres. Crestwave Internat., Inc., Crestwave Overseas, Ltd.; spl. project rep. Tex. Gas Corp., 1973—; dir. Tex. Gas Transmission Corp.; trustee Grandison Land Co. Bd. mem. Tb Assn. Greater New Orleans, 1951—, pres., 1968-69. Mem. New Orleans C. of C. (com. chmn. 1962-64). Methodist (bd. mem. 1963-66, 67-70). Mason (Jester). Clubs: New Orleans Country (bd. mem. 1959-67); Houston; Plimsoll (New Orleans). Home: 25 Versailles Blvd New Orleans LA 70125 Office: PO Drawer J 500 Vets Memorial Blvd Metairie LA 70005

ALEXANDER, DOROTHY MOSES, ballet dancer, choreographer; b. Atlanta, Apr. 22, 1904; d. Frank Hamilton and Cora Mina (Thibadeau) Moses; A.B., Oglethorp U., 1930; postgrad. U. Ga., Sadlers Wells Ballet Sch., Eng., others U.S.; m. Marion Davis Alexander, June 1926 (dec.). Concert dancer in early 20's and 30's; founder Atlanta Ballet Co., 1929, now cons.; founder Atlanta Sch. Ballet, 1922, now cons.; spearheaded Regional Ballet Movement in Am., 1956; introduced, supervised phys. fitness through dance program Atlanta Pub. Schs.; choreographer numerous ballets, 1929-69. Mem. dance com. Atlanta Arts Council, 1970; Pres., v.p. nat. bd. dirs. Regional Ballet; trustee Atlanta Arts Alliance. Recipient Nat. Dance Mag. award, 1960; named Atlanta's Woman of Year in Arts, 1947. Mem. Assn. Am. Dance Cos. (Nat. Distinguished Service award 1971), Atlanta Symphony Womens Assn., High Mus. Art, Phi Sigma Alpha. Episcopalian. Contbr. articles profl. jours. Home: 9 Ansley Dr Atlanta GA 30309 Office: 3215 Cains Hill Pl NW Atlanta GA 30305

ALEXANDER, EVA ETHEL GALLMAN, bus. exec.; b. Spartanburg, S.C., Feb. 23, 1898; d. Joe and Etta Emily (Lancaster) Gallman; m. George F. Alexander, Apr. 24, 1923 (div. June 1930); children—Frank Harold, Wilbur Gallman, Mary Fay (Mrs. Jay Bodenheimer). With accounting dept. City of High Point, N.C., 1930-35; sec. bookkeeper Rhodes Press, 1935-56; owner, operator Arts by Alexander, High Point, 1956—; pres., treas. Alexander Press, Inc., High Point, 1960—. Chmn., High Point Crippled Children and Adults Soc., 1959; hon. mem. Boy's Home of Lake Waccamaw, N.C., 1963; treas. High Point Fine Arts Guild, 1969-70. Mem. Democratic Com., 1964. Recipient Medallion award for oil Guildford County Fine Arts Exhbn., 1956; silver cup for oil Sears Traveling Exhibit, 1964; 1st prize in High Point Fine Art Juried Show, 1967; Beautification award High Point Garden Council. Mem. Am., N.C. iris socs., Carolina Club Printing House Craftsmen, Printing Industry High Point (sec.-treas. 1958—), High Point C. of C. (civic com. 1964-68), Nat. Home Fashions League. Baptist. Club: Pilot (pres. High Point 1962, chmn. extension com. 1964-66, dist. extension chmn. 1965-66, internat. extension com. mem. 1966-68, chmn. safety com.). Home: 708 Willoubar Terrace High Point NC 27262 Office: 701 Greensboro Rd High Point NC 27260

ALEXANDER, FRED J., coll. adminstr.; b. Childress, Tex., May 14, 1935; s. E. C. and Tillie (Branum) A.; B.S., Abilene Christian Coll., 1958, M.Ed., 1959; postgrad. U. Mich., 1962-63; m. Claudette Harris, May 31, 1957; children—Joe Frederick, Beverly Ellen, Denise Kay. Instr. Moran (Tex.) High Sch., 1956-58, Baird (Tex.) High Sch., 1958-59; instr. Mich. Christian Jr. Coll., Rochester, 1959-64, registrar, dir. admissions, 1964-68; dir. jr. coll. relations Harding Coll., Searcy, Ark., 1968-69, dir. admissions, 1969—. Served with USNR, 1953-60. Mem. Am., Mich., Ark. assns. collegiate registrars and admissions officers. Home: 15 Indian Trail Searcy AR 72143

ALEXANDER, JAMES ATWELL, poultryman; b. Stony Point, N.C. July 23 1911; s. J. Will and Mary Emma (Alexander) A.; A.B. Davidson Coll., 1929, M.A., 1931; student Colo. Sch. Mines, 1930, postgrad. U. N.C., 1932-34 ; m. Anna Pauline Hill, Dec. 23, 1938; children—Mary Anna, Eva Pauline. Seismologist Shell Oil Co., Houston, 1937-40; owner, mgr. Alexander Poultry Farm, Stony Point, 1940— bd. of dirs. Alexander County Water Corp. Chmn. Alexander County Poultry Council, 1953-55, Catawaba Soil Conservation Dist. Conservation Dist. Suprs., 1949-51; mem. adv. com. poultry test, 1958—; mem. gen. bd. Northwestern Bank, 1971—. Mem. Bd. Commrs., Alexander County, 1950-54, Welfare Bd., 1952-54, Alexander County Planning Bd., 1969—; mem. N.C. State Bd. Agr., 1955—; mem. Gov's. Adv. Com. Nuclear Energy, N.C., 1957—; mem. N.C. Gov.'s Council on Occupational Health, N.C. Gov.'s Council on Rehabilitation; chmn. N.C. Gov.'s Adv. Com. Agr., 1965—; mem. exec. com. Gov's Council for Econ. Devel. Mem. Fair Commn., Dixie Classic Fair, Winston-Salem, N.C. Bd. dirs. Alexander County Hosp.; exec. com. N.C. Agricultural Found., 1965—, v.p., 1967; adv. com. Sch. Agr. N.C. State U. Named Man of the year by Grange of Alexander County, N.C., 1957, BY Alexander County C. of C., 1967; N.C. Outstanding Farm Manager, 1965, N.C. County Agrl. Agts. award, 1971. Mem. N.C. Acad. Science, N.W. N.C. Devel. Assn. (pres., chmn agrl. div. award 1969), C. of C. (dir.), N.C. Egg Marketing Assn. (pres. 1961-62), N.C. Poultry Council (pres. 1963), N.C. Vocational Agrl. Tchrs. Assn. (hon.), N.C. Agribusiness Council (exec. com.), Sigma Xi, Gamma Sigma Epsilon, Gamma Sigma Delta, Sigma Gamma Epsilon. Democrat. Lion (charter mem., zone chmn.). Home: Stony Point NC 28678

ALEXANDER, JAMES RICHARD, lawyer; b. Cleveland Heights, O., Nov. 2, 1923; s. Harry Morton and Helen (Sharpe) A.; B.B.A., So. Methodist U., 1943; postgrad. Northwestern U. Law Sch., 1943-44; J.D., U. Tex., 1946. Admitted to Tex. bar, 1946; Supreme Ct. of U.S.; partner Goldberg, Alexander & Sullivan and predecessor firms, Dallas, 1948—. Dir., gen. counsel Drawing Bd., Inc., Glenn Petroleum Corp. Mem. Dallas Council on World Affairs, Am. Jewish Com., Am. Jewish Hist. Soc., Nat. Conf. Christians and Jews, Am. Civil Liberties Union. Mem. Am., Tex., Dallas bar assns., Dallas C. of C., Tau Epsilon Rho, Sigma Alpha Mu (nat. sec. 1964-65). Democrat. Jewish religion. Mason (32 deg., Shriner); mem. B'nai B'rith. Club: Columbian Country. Home: 2812 Binkley St Dallas TX 75205 Office: Fidelity Union Life Bldg Dallas TX 75201

ALEXANDER, LARRY JOE, gas compression mfg. co. exec.; b. Harrison, Ark., Dec. 2, 1936; s. Dewey Franklin and Viola Anita (Curtis) A.; B.A., Benjamin Franklin U., 1965; m. Sandra Sue Groblebe, July 28, 1961; children—David Franklin, Dawn Michele, James Matthew. Asst. treas. United Planning Orgn., Washington, 1966-67; analyst N.Am. Rockwell, Tulsa, 1968-69; with Knight Industries, Inc., Broken Arrow, Okla., 1970—, v.p., 1971—; v.p., dir. Gas Compressor Services, Inc., Tulsa, 1971—, Knight Canadian, Ltd., Calgary, Alta., 1972—, Knight Compression Services, Inc., Tulsa, 1972—. Served with USNR, 1955-59. Home: 524 W Ithica St Broken Arrow OK 74012 Office: Box 348 Broken Arrow OK 74012

ALEXANDER, LOUIS, writer, educator; b. N.Y.C., Mar. 15, 1917; s. Louis I. and Gertrude (Seydel) A.; B.S. in Marketing, U. Newark, 1941; M. Letters in Journalism, U. Houston, 1961 m. Paulette Marlowe, Dec. 23, 1948 (div. Dec. 20, 1968); children—Kathryn, Marjory Lynn. Reporter, county editor Houston Chronicle, 1947-57; free-lance writer for mags. and newspapers, 1957—; instr. journalism U. Houston, 1954-69, asst. prof. journalism, 1969—. Corr., Wall Street Jour., 1959—, Nat. Observer, 1961—, Nat. Pub. Radio, 1972—. Mem. Bellaire Parks and Recreation Commn., 1957-60, vice chmn., 1960. Served with USAAF, 1942-45; to capt. USAF, 1951-52; lt. col. Res. Decorated D.F.C., Air medal with three oak leaf clusters. Mem. Aviation/Space Writers Assn. (gen. chmn. nat. conv. 1958), Assn. Petroleum Writers, Assn. Edn. in Journalism, Nat. Conf. Editorial Writers. Club: Press (Houston). Contbr. to Historic Decade, 1960. Home: 704 Mulberry Lane Bellaire TX 77401 Office: Communications Dept U Houston TX 77004

ALEXANDER, MARY LOUISE, educator; b. Ennis, Tex., Jan. 15, 1926; d. Emmett F. and Florence (Hill) Alexander; B.A., U. Tex., 1947, M.A., 1949, Ph.D., 1951. Instr., research asst. Genetics Found., U. Tex., Austin, 1944-51, postdoctoral research fellow, 1952-55, research scientist Genetics Found., 1962-68; postdoctoral fellow biology div. AEC, Oak Ridge, 1951-52; research asso. U. Tex.-M.D. Anderson Hosp. and Tumor Inst., Houston, 1956-58, asst. biologist, 1959-62; asso. prof. biology S.W. Tex. State U., San Marcos, 1967-69, prof., 1969—. Research cons. Brookhaven Nat. Lab., Upton, N.Y., 1955; research participant Oak Ridge Inst. Nuclear Studies, Tenn., 1951—. Nat. Cancer Inst. fellow Inst. Animal Genetics, Edinburgh, Scotland, 1960-61. Mem. Genetics Soc. Am., Radiation Research Soc., Am. Soc. Human Genetics, Sigma Xi, Gamma Phi Beta, Phi Sigma, Alpha Epsilon Delta. Home: Hunter's Glen Route 2 Box 119 San Marcos TX 78666

ALEXANDER, PAULINE HILL (MRS. JAMES ATWELL ALEXANDER), educator, clubwoman; b. Stony Point, N.C., Apr. 7, 1916; d. James Lolo and Eva (Shuford) Hill; student Mitchell Coll., 1932-34, Lenoir Rhyne Coll., 1935-36, Western Carolina Tchrs. Coll., 1937, U. Houston, 1939; m. James Atwell Alexander, Dec. 23, 1938; children—Mary Anna, Eva Pauline. Tchr. Central High Sch., Statesville, N.C., 1934-45, dramatics coach, 1939-41. Leader Stony Point Council Girl Scouts U.S., 1951-60; adult leader 4-H Clubs, Alexander County, N.C., 1958-61; 4-H Club sponsor, 1967—; area chmn. Mitchell Coll. Endowment, 1956; choir dir. Elk Shoals A.R. Presbyn. Ch., 1958-64. Recipient oratorical and essay awards Am. Legion, 1931, W.C.T.U., 1933; named Woman of the Year, Alexander County, 1959. Mem. D.A.R. (dir., chpt. conservation chmn. chpt. regent 1965, local nat. def. chmn. 1967—), Mitchell Coll. Alumni Assn. (pres. 1963-64), Colonial Daus. 17th Century. Democrat. Presbyn. (home mission sec. Women of Ch.) Club: Stony Point Woman's (pres. 1953-54). Home: Stony Point NC 28678

ALEXANDER, RALPH LAWRENCE, lawyer; b. Edinburg, Tex., Sept. 9, 1928; s. Robert Lawrence and Patye (Thornton) A.; B.A., U. Tex., 1950, J.D., 1953; m. Lu Ann Allen, Mar. 22, 1958; children—Sharon Ann, Ralph Lawrence, Cynthia Lu. Admitted to Tex. bar, 1953, since practiced in Edinburg; partner firm Kelley, Looney, Alexander & Hiester, 1963—. Vice pres., dir. Atlantic Oil Corp., Edinburg, 1963-70, Stag Sales Co., Inc., Edinburg, 1964—. Sec., Greater Edinburg Council, 1972-73. Mem. Edinburg Capital Improvement Bd. and Model Cities Planning Council, 1970—; chmn. Edinburg Econ. Devel. Bd., 1969—; mem. Hidalgo County Democratic Exec. Com., 1968—. Bd. regents Pan Am. Coll., 1965-70; bd. dirs., v.p. Edinburg Indsl. Found., pres., 1969-73; bd. dirs. Tip O' Tex. Girl Scout Council, 1970-71; bd. dirs., pres. Community Coordinated Child Care, Inc., 1972—. Recipient Community Leader of Am. award, 1969; Small Bus. Adminstrn. Pub. Service award, 1962. Served with AUS, 1946-49, 50-51. Mem. Hidalgo County Bar Assn. (past dir.), State Bar Tex., Edinburg C. of C. (pres. 1968-69), Am. Legion (past comdr.), Phi Delta Phi. Democrat. Baptist. Lion (pres. Edinburg 1959, zone chmn. 1960, dep. dist. gov. 1970). Club: Racket. Home: 1415 S 16th St Edinburg TX 78539 Office: 316 S Closner St Edinburg TX 78539

ALEXANDER, ROBERT LAFONSO, JR., mfg. co. exec.; b. Shenandoah, Va., Sept. 14, 1918; s. Robert LaFonso and Elsie Rose (Hawse) A.; grad. high sch.; m. Gale Bowens, May 14, 1938; children—Joan (Mrs. John A. Ward), Michael. With Briggs Filtration Co., Bethesda, Md., 1939-47; owner Alexander's Machine Shop, New Market, Va., 1948-52; works mgr. East Coast Aeronautics, Pelham Manor, N.Y., 1953-55; shop supt. West Engring. Co., Richmond, Va., 1956-62; with Precision Machine Co., Inc., Richmond, 1955—, pres., 1964—. Mem. Indsl. Mgmt. Club Richmond. Mason (Shriner), Rotarian (pres. 1948). Club: Richmond Country. Home: 1002 Westham Pkwy Richmond VA 23229 Office: 2915 W Leigh St Richmond VA 23230

ALEXANDER, WILLIAM MORTIMER, educator; b. Jacksonville, Fla., Dec. 5, 1928; s. Leon Wilson and Ruth Louise (Chesebrough) A.; A.B., Davidson Coll., 1950; B.D., Louisville Presbyn. Sem., 1953; S.T.M., Harvard, 1957; Ph.D., Princeton Theol. Sem., 1961; m. Katherine Alice Fryer, June 5, 1953; children—John Edward, Susan Dorman, David Leon. Asst. prof. St Andrews Coll., Laurinburg, N.C., 1961-63, asso. prof., 1963-67, prof. religion and philosophy, 1967—. Served with AUS, 1953-56. Research grantee Am. Council Learned Socs., 1966. Piedmont U. Center, 1969-71. Mem. Am. Philos. Assn., Am. Acad. Religion, Am. Assn. U. Profs., Soc. for Philosophy and Pub. Affairs. Presbyn. Author: Johann Georg Hamann: Philosophy and Faith, 1966. Home: Shepherd Av Laurinburg NC 28352

ALEXANDER, WILLIAM VOLLIE, JR., congressman; b. Memphis, Jan. 16, 1934; s. William V. and Spencer (Buck) A.; student U. Ark., 1951-53; B.A., Southwestern, Memphis, 1957; LL.B Vanderbilt U., 1960; m. Marjorie Gwendolyn Haven, Feb. 5, 1957; one dau., Alyse Haven. Admitted to Tenn. bar, 1960, Ark. bar, 1963; law clk. to chief judge U.S. Dist. Ct., Memphis, 1960-61; asso. Montedonico, Bonne, Gilliland, Heiskell & Loch, Memphis, 1961-63; partner Swift & Alexander, Osceola, Ark., 1963-69; former dir. Osceola Riverport Authority; former commr., Arkansas Waterways Commn. Mem. 91st-93d Congresses, 1st dist. Ark., asst. Democratic whip. Former bd. dirs. Osceola YMCA; East Ark. council Boy Scouts Am.; bd. dirs. Mississippi County YMCA. Southwestern at Memphis. Mem. Am. Acad. Polit. and Social Sci., Nat. Assn. Underwater Driving Instrs., Kappa Sigma, Phi Delta Phi. Episcopalian. Mason. Clubs: Rotary (pres., dir.). Office: Cannon House Office Bldg Washington DC 20515

ALEXEFF, IGOR, educator; b. Pitts., Jan. 5, 1931; s. Alexander and Tamara (Tchirkow) A.; B.A., Harvard, 1952; M.S., U. Wis., 1955, Ph.D., 1959; m. Anne I. Fabina, Feb. 4, 1954; children—Alexander, Helen. Research engr. Westinghouse Corp., Pitts., 1952-53; NSF postdoctoral fellow U. Zurich, Switzerland, 1959-60; group leader controlled thermonuclear fusion Oak Ridge Nat. Lab., 1960-71; prof. elec. engring. U. Tenn., 1971—. Vis. prof. Inst. Plasma Physics, Nagoya, Japan, 1973. Fellow Am. Phys. Soc.; mem. I.E.E.E. Contbr. articles to profl. jours. Home: 2790 Turnpike Oak Ridge TN 37830 Office: Ferris Hall U Tenn Knoxville TN 37916

ALFORD, FLORENCE MARSHALL, educator; b. Bowling Green, Ky., June 29, 1920; d. William Henry and Mabel Clair (Williams) Marshall; B.A., George Peabody Coll. for Tchrs., 1946; M.A., Western Ky. U., 1967; m. Earl Foster Alford, June 3, 1947. Tchr. pub. schs. Butler County, Morgantown, Ky., 1941-42, Hardin County, Elizabethtown, Ky., 1942-45, high sch. Clarksville, Tenn., 1946-47, pub. schs. Bowling Green, Ky., 1948—. Violinist, Nashville Symphony Orch., 1945-46. Chmn. Jr. Red Cross, Bowling Green, 1947-49; mem. Bowling Green-Warren County Tb Assn., 1947—, pres., 1957-59, 63-65. Mem. Bowling Green, Ky. edn. assns., N.E.A., Assn. Childhood Edn. Internat. (pres. 1969-71), Am. Assn. U. Women (treas. 1956-58), Alpha Delta Kappa (pres. 1966-68). Baptist. Home: 2837 Nashville Rd Bowling Green KY 42101 Office: Durbin Dr Bowling Green KY 42101

ALFORD, MARION ELMER, supt. schs.; b. Perry, Fla., Dec. 29, 1919; s. William D. and Jessie (McHargue) A.; B.S., Middle Tenn. State Coll., 1941; M.A., George Peabody Coll., 1947; Ed.D., U. Va., 1958; m. Eva Davis, Sept. 18, 1944; 1 son, William Andrew. Tchr. pub. schs., Taylor County, Fla., 1941-42; master tchr., Portsmouth, Va., 1946-47; prin. elementary sch., Hickory, Va., 1947-48; prin. demonstration sch. Ala. State Coll. for Women, 1948-49; prin. high sch., Great Bridge, Va., 1949-51; dir. instrn. Norfolk County Sch. Bd., Va., 1951-56, asst. supt. schs., 1957-60; prof. George Peabody Coll., Nashville, 1960-61, asso. dir. div. surveys and field services, 1961-62, ednl. adminstrn. cons. field services and survey team; pres. Frederick Coll., Portsmouth, Va., 1962-65; supt. Portsmouth Pub. Schs., 1965—. Mem. bd. edn. Commn. Higher Edn., Va. Conf. Meth. Chs., 1964—. Trustee Ferrum Jr. Coll., 1968-72; trustee Tidewater Community Coll., 1968-72, chmn., 1967-69. Served ensign to lt. USNR, 1942-45; now lt. comdr. Res. Mem. Va. Edn. Assn., Nat. Sch. Pub. Relations Assn., Am. Assn. Sch. Administrs. (participant internat. field study mission to USSR 1968), Portsmouth C. of C. (trustee 1965—), Assn. Supervision and Curriculum Devel., Phi Delta Kappa, Kappa Delta Pi. Methodist (bd. stewards chs. 1949—). Rotarian (pres. Portsmouth club 1968). Contbr. articles to profl. jours. Home: 37 Early Dr Portsmouth VA 23701 Office: Board Edn Portsmouth VA 23705

ALFORD, SAMUEL JACKSON, JR., physician; b. Orlando Fla., June 10, 1923; s. Samuel Jackson and Ada Lee (Jacobs) A.; student So. Jr. Coll., Collegedale, Tenn., 1942-43, Washington Missionary Coll., 1943-44; M.D., Med.-Coll. of Med. Evangelists, 1949; m. Margie LaVerne Morgan, June 19, 1945 (div. Aug. 1971); children—Michael Lee, Stephen Douglas, Joni Gail. Intern St. Luke's Hosp., Jacksonville, Fla., 1948-49, resident, 1949-50; practice medicine, specializing in obstetrics, also family practice, Jacksonville, Fla., 1953—; mem. staff St. Luke's Hosp., Jacksonville, 1953—, chmn. emergency room dept., 1960—, pres. staff, 1965-66, chmn. dept. family practice, 1971—. Pilot, group flight surgeon Civil Air Patrol, Jacksonville, 1953-72. Served to capt. M.C., USAF, 1951-53. Mem. Fla. Acad. Gen. Practice (bd. dirs. 1966-72, editor jour. 1966—). Club: Jacksonville Police Pistol (pres. 1955-71). Home: 33 W Ashly St Jacksonville FL 32211 Office: 33 W Ashley St Jacksonville FL 32202

ALFRIEND, SUE LANDON, banker, advt. exec.; b. North Wilkesboro, N.C.; d. Henry Clayton and Sue (Ennis) Landon; student Salem Coll., 1944-46; A.B., Randolph-Macon Woman's Coll., 1948; M.S., U. N.C., 1951; postgrad. Northwestern U., 1962; m. Richard Jeffrey Alfriend III, Jan. 12, 1952 (div. July 1958); 1 dau., Sue Landon. Tchr., Norfolk (Va.) City Schs., 1953-55; tchr. elementary sch. Princess Anne County (Va.), 1955-56; advt. mgr. Northwestern Bank, North Wilkesboro, N.C., 1958-61, asst. treas., 1961-62, asst. v.p. in charge advt. dept., 1962-69, v.p., 1969-73, v.p. in charge marketing div., 1973—. Chmn. publicity Wilkes United Fund, 1962-63, mem. publicity com., 1965. Bd. dirs. Tarheel Triad council Girl Scouts, U.S.A. Mem. Bank Marketing Assn., N.C. Bankers Assn., Wilkes C. of C. (chmn. mchts. div.), Delta Delta Delta. Presbyn. Home: 611 8th St North Wilkesboro NC 28659 Office: 924 B St North Wilkesboro NC 28659

ALISAGO, ANDRES SUMAYO, JR., physician; b. Nabua, Cam Sur, Philippines, Sept. 19, 1934; s. Andres Lirio and Martiniana (Sumayo) A.; B.S. in Zoology, U. Philippines, 1956; M.D., U. of East, Philippines, 1961; m. Hilda Navera, Apr. 24, 1965; children—James Andrew, Josephine, Andrew David. Came to U.S., 1963. Pvt. practice medicine, Philippines, 1961-63; rotating intern St. Vincent Hosp.,

Toledo, 1963-64; resident surgery Lakewood Hosp., 1964-66; resident anesthesiology Vanderbilt U. Hosp., Nashville, 1968-70; practice medicine, specializing in anesthesiology, Chattanooga, 1970—; clin. chief anesthesiology Baroness Erlanger Hosp., T.C. Thompson Children's Hosp. Diplomate Am. Bd. Anesthesiology. Fellow Am. Coll. Anesthesiologists, Am. Coll. Chest Physicians. Home: 1900 Skyline Dr Chattanooga TN 37421 Office: 241 Wiehl St Chattanooga TN 37403

ALISON, JAMES CONRAD, city ofcl.; b. Dyersburg, Tenn., Sept. 7, 1922; s James Dailey Jr. and Gladys Beatrix (Sudbury) A.; student Fla. Mil. Inst., Haines City, 1937, Gordon Mil. Coll., Barnesville, Ga., 1938-40, Officer Tng. Sch. USMC, Quantico, Va., 1945, Naval Law Sch., Port Hueneme, Cal., 1946, Staff and Command Sch., 1959; 1 son, Conrad Daley. Enlisted U.S. Marine Corps, 1940, Commd. 2d lt. U.S. Marine Corps, 1945, advanced through grades to lt. col.; various assignments including comdg. officer automotive maintenance, Tientsin, China, 1947-48, comdg. officer tng. center, Memphis, 1962-66, ret., 1966; dir. maintenance, head municipal maintenance dept. City of St. Petersburg, Fla., 1966—. Recipient Nat. award Am. Cities Mag. for leadership in field of automotive and equipment maintenance, 1968. Mason. Home: 2200 Bayou Grande Blvd St Petersburg FL 33703 Office: Municipal Maintenance Dept 619 19th St N St Petersburg FL 33713

ALLAN, JERRY DUANE, film and record co. exec.; b. N.Y.C., Apr. 2, 1924; s. Max Charles and Esther (Fingold) Schwartz; student Roosevelt U., 1946-48; B.Speech, Columbia Coll., Chgo., 1951; m. Pauline Brown, June 22, 1968. Announcer, master of ceremonies, also actor radio, TV, films, Chgo. area, 1948-52; field press rep. Ind. and Ky. terr. Metro-Goldwyn-Mayer, Indpls., 1954-55; promotion agt. Audio Fidelity Record Co., also Metro-Goldwyn-Mayer Records, Chgo., 1955-59; mng. dir. Variety Publicity Assos., Masque Artist Mgmt., J.A. Music Pub., also The Big Four, Indpls., 1959—; pres. Allan Records, Ludlow, Ky., also mng. dir. Organizer Shows for vets. and handicapped children's hosps., schs., orgns., cerebral palsy telethons, 1948—. Active A.R.C. Served with AUS, 1943-46; ETO. Mem. World War II Vets. of Ludlow, Hon. Order Ky. Cols., Bromley Swim Club Bear Boosters. Rotarian. Clubs: Variety, Antelope, Advertising. Address: PO Box 202 Ludlow KY 41016

ALLAN, ROGER DEMUTH, profl. assn. exec.; b. Waterloo, Ia., Oct. 12, 1933; s. Stuart Eugene and Clara (Demuth) A.; B.A., U. Notre Dame, 1957; m. Catherine Justine Baumann, Oct. 29, 1960; children—Theresa Joan, Susan Marie. Journalist, Covington (Va.) Virginian, 1957-59; with Homestead Hotel, Hot Springs, Va., 1959-61, Nat. Assn. Real Estate Bd., Washington, 1961-63, Asso. Gen. Contractors, 1963-66, C. of C. of U.S., 1966-67; account exec., pub. relations Ketchum McLeod & Grove, Pitts., 1967-68; dir. pub. relations Electronic Industries Assn., Washington, 1968-73; dir. hwy. div. Asso. Gen. Contractors, Washington, 1973—. Active United Givers Fund, Washington, 1971-72. Served with AUS, 1956. mem. Pub. Relations Soc. Am. (chmn. chpt. publicity com. 1971—, editor chpt. newsletter com. 1972-74, dir. 1973-74). Democrat. Roman Catholic. Club: Nat. Press (profl. relations com. 1971-72) (Washington). Home: 1903 Windmill Lane Alexandria VA 22307 Office: 1957 E St NW Washington DC 20006

ALLAN, WALTER EVERETT, ednl. adminstr.; b. Providence, Mar. 14, 1919; s. Everett William and Annabel Lane (Hall) A.; B.S. in Mech. Engring., Tufts U., 1940; M.Ed., U. Fla., 1972; m. Daphne Patience Pierce, June 2, 1951; children—Elizabeth Jean, Patience Alison, Susan Piper. Trainee to tool control engr. Waterbury Mfg. div. Chase Brass and Copper Co., Waterbury, Conn., 1940-44; tool engr. to works mgr. Fabricated Metal Goods div. Anaconda Co., Waterbury, 1946-66; pres. Woodbury Corp., 1968—; dir. Indium Corp. Am., Utica, N.Y., 1964-66. Instr. Lake Sumter Community Coll., Leesburg, Fla., 1968-69, dir. continuing edn., 1970—; vis. lectr. U. Conn., 1947-48, 51; chmn. dept. engring. Tech. Central Fla. Community Coll., 1969-70. Mem. bldg. com. Waterbury Hosp.; bd. dirs. Melon Patch Players, Inc., Leesburg, Fla. Served with C.E., AUS, 1944-46. Registered profl. engr., Fla., Conn. Mem. Am. Soc. M.E. (chmn. state gen. com. 1949-50), Am. Soc. Tool Engrs., Fla. Assn. Community Colls., Delta Upsilon (Tufts chpt.). Mason (life), Rotarian. Club: University (pres. Waterbury 1948-49). Home: Lake Shore Dr PO Box 398 Howey-in-The-Hills FL 32737 Office: Lake Sumter Community Coll Leesburg FL 32748

ALLBAUGH, LELAND GIRARD, econ. cons.; b. Leon, Ia., Oct. 6, 1896; s. William Alvin and Laura (Gammon) A.; B.S., Ia. State U., 1919, M.S., 1928; Ph.D., Harvard, 1951; m. Cora Emelia Oleson, Dec. 24, 1919; children—Robert Dean, James William. Asst. farm mgmt. demonstrator Ia. State U., 1918-19, asst. prof. agrl. econs., 1922-30, asso. prof., 1931-41; farmer, Humboldt County, Ia., 1920; county agt., Carroll County, Ia., 1921; chief farm plan and loan sect. FSA, Washington, 1941-42; asso. dir. Agrl. Extension Service, Ames, Ia., 1942-43; chief agrl. supplies Fgn. Econ. Adminstrn., Washington, 1944; dir. agrl. subcommn. Allied Control Commn., Rome, Italy, 1944-45; chief test-demonstration br. TVA, Knoxville, Tenn., 1946-47, dir. div. agrl. relations, 1952-61; econ. cons. UN Spl. Fund, Afghanistan, in 1963, FAO, Taiwan and Egypt, Korea, Ethiopia, 1964, Korea, Rome, Sudan, 1965, Tanzania, 1966, UNDP, Sudan, 1966, UNDP, Sudan, Iraq, West Irian, Indonesia, and Geneva, 1967; assistant dir. social scis. Rockefeller Found., N.Y.C., 1948-50; agrl. economist Inst. InterAm. Affairs, Washington, Asuncion, Paraguay, Port-au-Prince, Haiti, 1951-52. Lectr. agrl. econs. So. Ill. U., 1962. Served with U.S. Army, 1918. Recipient Medal of Freedom, U.S. Army, 1945; Distinguished Achievement citation Ia. State U. Alumni Assn., 1969. Mem. Am. Farm Econ. Assn., Internat. Assn. Agrl. Economists; Am. Forestry Assn., Am. Soc. Agronomy, Phi Kappa Phi, Gamma Sigma Delta, Lambda Chi Alpha. Methodist. Mason. Club: Torch (Knoxville). Author: Crete, 1953; also numerous articles in profl. jours. Address: 6830 Sheffield Dr Knoxville TN 37919

ALLDERDICE, THOMAS GILMORE, mech. engr.; b. Hagerstown, Md., Aug. 13, 1916; s. Fitzhugh Berry and Lillian Fletcher (Martin) A.; student St. Petersburg Jr. Coll., 1934-35; B.C.E., U. Fla., 1948; m. Ada Frances Runyon, Mar. 11, 1950; 1 dau., Mary Frances. With Russell & Axon, cons. engrs., Daytona Beach, Fla., 1948-49; with Reynolds, Smith & Hills, architects, engrs. and planners, Jacksonville, Fla., 1949—, now prin. design engr. Served with AUS, 1935-41, 42-46. Decorated Purple Heart, Combat Infantryman's Badge. Registered profl. engr., Fla. Mem. Nat. Soc. Profl. Engrs., Am. Soc. M.E., Fla. Engring. Soc., Tau Beta Pi, Sigma Tau. Presbyn. Patentee water system freeze protection valve. Home: 12816 Aladdin Rd Jacksonville FL 32223 Office: PO Box 4850 Jacksonville FL 32201

ALLEGER, DANIEL E(UGENE), ret. agrl. economist; b. East Stroudsburg, Pa., Oct. 18, 1903; s. Frank H. and Lena (Ruff) A.; B.S. in Agrl. Econs., Pa. State Coll., 1926, M.S. in Rural Sociology, 1943; m. Carolyn Breckenridge, May 6, 1933; 1 dau., Martha Alice. Agrl. prodn. and research United Fruit Co. in Honduras and Guatemala, 1926-31; agt. Met. Life Ins. Co., 1931-41; product supr. shells Bethlehem Steel Co., 1942-45; asso. agrl. economist Fla. Agrl. Expt. Sta., U. Fla., 1945-73, asso. prof. emeritus, 1973—. Cons. agrl. econs. to Govt. of Costa Rica, 1956; chief of party U. Fla. Mission to Costa Rica, 1960. Mem. Rural Sociol. Soc., Internat. Assn. Agrl. Economists, So. Agrl. Econs. Assn., Omicron Delta Epsilon, Gamma Sigma Delta. Editor: Fertile Lands of Friendship, 1963; Social Change and Aging in the Twentieth Century, 1964; Adventures on the Mosquito Shore (by Samuel Bard 1855), 1965. Compiler: The Genesis of the Allegers, 1970. Home: 1710 SW 49th Pl Gainesville FL 32608

ALLEN, ALBERT BINKLEY, beverage mfg. co. exec.; b. Nashville, Aug. 3, 1911; s. John Otis and Lucy (Mayberry) A.; B.S. in Chem. Engring., Auburn U., 1932, M.S., 1933; m. Sarah Griffin, Sept. 5, 1939; children—Albert Griffin, Margaret Allen (Mrs. L.M. Hanawald). With Coca-Cola Co. and subsidiaries, various locations, 1945—, head product research and devel., Atlanta, 1961-65, head quality standards dept., 1966—. Served to col. USAAF, 1941-45; PTO. Fellow Am. Inst. Chemists (chmn. Piedmont chpt. 1962-63); mem. Am. Chem. Soc. Home: 1159 Harrogate Lane NE Atlanta GA 30328 Office: PO Drawer 1734 Atlanta GA 30301

ALLEN, BENJAMIN HARRISON, state ofcl.; b. Goldsboro, N.C., Apr. 7, 1931; s. Benjamin Harrison and Nancy (Jones) A.; A.B. magna cum laude, Wofford Coll., 1956; M.A., Peabody Coll., 1957, Ph.D., 1962; m. Martha L. Payne, Aug. 10, 1952; children—Martha Jean and Mary Joan (twins), John Charles. Psychologist, City Schs., Nashville, 1959-61; cons. mental health Dept. Pub. Health, Wilmington, N.C., 1961-63; asso. prof. psychology East Carolina Coll., 1963-65; asst. prof. spl. edn. Fla. State U., 1965-68, U. Ga., 1968-69; dir. Div. Mental Retardation, Ala. Dept. Mental Health, Montgomery, 1969-70; program cons. Fla. Div. Retardation, 1970; dir. programs and services Sunland Tng. Center, Fort Meyers, Fla., 1971—. Evaluator div. Mental Retardation, Social Rehab. Services, Washington, 1965-68. Served with USN, 1949-53. Mem. Am. Psychol. Assn., Am. Assn. Mental Deficiency, Phi Beta Kappa. Home: 4028 Manning Av Fort Myers FL 33902 Office: Sunland Tng Center Fort Myers FL 33901

ALLEN, CARTER RANDOLPH, lawyer; b. Elkins, W.Va., Aug. 28, 1921; s. James Edward and Susan Hackney (Garrott) A.; A.B., Marshall U., 1943; LL.B., Washington and Lee U., 1948; m. Helen Porter Coley, Feb. 25, 1945; children—Charlotte (Mrs. Ronald W. Mason), Elizabeth Carter, Mary Dudley, Catherine Garrott. Admitted to Va. bar, 1948; since practiced in Waynesboro; commonwealth's atty., City of Waynesboro, 1955-70, County of Augusta, 1959-60; city atty. City of Waynesboro, 1950-54, 60—. Dir. First Fed. Savs. & Loan Assn., First & Mchts. Nat. Bank, Builders Center, Inc. Pres., Community Chest, 1952-53, YMCA, 1949-56. Bd. dirs. Waynesboro Community Hosp. Served with USNR, 1942-46. Mem. C. of C. (pres. 1954-55). Presbyn. (elder 1961—). Lion. Home: 601 Cherry Ave Waynesboro VA 22980 Office: PO Box 219 Waynesboro VA 22980

ALLEN, CHARLES GUY, physician; b. Denison, Tex., Aug. 9, 1923; s. Charlie Guy and Minnie Pearl (Church) A.; B.A., Union Coll., Lincoln, Neb., 1944; M.D., Loma Linda U., 1948; m. Cordelia Williamson, Sept. 30, 1945; children—Larry Guy, Jackie Charles. Intern, Loma Linda Sanitarium and Hosp., 1947-48, resident obstetrics and gynecology, 1948-50; gen. practice medicine, Strong, Ark., 1950-51, Itasca, Tex., 1953—, also owner clinic. City health officer, Itasca, 1967—. Served with AUS, 1951-53. Mem. Com. of 100 Southwestern Union Coll., Keene, Tex. 7th Day Adventist (elder). Club: 500 (Itasca). Home and office: Box 147 Itasca TX 76055

ALLEN, CLARENCE BOYCE, civic leader; b. Latta, S.C., Mar. 17, 1899; s. William Benjamin and Theodossi (Cox) A.; B.A., Furman U., 1921; postgrad. Yale, 1925-27; J.D., U. S.C., 1932, M.A., 1938; m. Eupha Lee McComas, Nov. 11, 1936; 1 dau., Martha Lee (Mrs. James Andrew Elkins, Jr.). Admitted to S.C. bar, 1932; mem. firm Dargan & Paulling, Darlington, S.C., 1933-34; farmer nr. Latta, 1935-71; tchr. pub. schs., Georgetown County, S.C., 1947-53, Lee County, S.C., 1953-56, Dillon County, S.C., 1956-71. Mem. Pee Dee Regional Devel. and Planning Council Task Force, 1972—; vice chmn. Dillon County Hist. Preservation Commn., 1972—. Chmn. bd. trustees Dillon County Library, 1973—. Mem. Dillon County Hist. Soc. (pres. 1971-72), Phi Beta Kappa. Baptist (deacon 1938). Mason, Lion. Club: Civitan. Author: Edwin Arlington Robinson: A Critical Analysis of His Poetic Contributions, 1938; English for Everyday Use, 1967; History of Dalcho Lodge, 1970; History of Catfish Creek Baptist Church, 1971; History of Antioch Baptist Church, 1973; William Benjamin and Theodosia Allen Family, 1973. Address: 311 Richardson St Latta SC 29565

ALLEN, CLIFTON JUDSON, clergyman, editor; b. Latta, S.C., Nov. 7, 1901; s. William Benjamin and Theodosia (Cox) A.; B.A., Furman U., 1923, D.D., 1960; Th.M., So. Baptist Theol. Sem., 1928, Ph.D., 1932; m. Hattie Bell McCracken, Aug. 22, 1930; children—Judson Boyce, Rosalind (Mrs. John C. Barker), Robert Moore. Prin., Minturn (S.C.) High Sch., 1923-25; tutor Greek N.T., So. Bapt. Theol. Sem., 1928-31; ordained to ministry So. Bapt. Ch., 1926; pastor in McHenry, Ky., 1926-29, Utica, Ky., 1929-32, Fairmont, N.C., 1932-36, Statesville, N.C., 1936-37; asso. editorial sec. Sunday sch. bd. So. Bapt. Conv., 1937-44, editorial sec., 1945-68; rec. sec. So. Bapt. Conv., 1966—. Sec. commn. Christian teaching and tng. Bapt. World Alliance, 1957-65, chmn., 1965-70; mem. exec. com. Bapt. Conv. N.C., 1935-37; mem. internat. Sunday sch. lesson com. div. Christian edn. Nat. Council Chs., 1942-68, chmn., 1960-67, mem. div. assembly. div., 1957-63; radio broadcaster, 1945-72. Recipient E.Y. Mullins Denominational Service award So. Baptist Theol. Sem., 1970. Democrat. Rotarian. Quarternion. Author: The Gospel According to Paul, 1956; Points for Emphasis (ann.), 1953-74; Affirmation of Our Faith, 1972; also curricular materials. Chmn. editorial com. Ency. of Southern Baptists, 1958; gen. editor Broadman Bible Commentary, 12 vols., 1969-72. Home: 1019 Kearns Av Winston-Salem NC 27106

ALLEN, DON LEE, coll. adminstr.; b. Burlington, N.C., Mar. 13, 1934; s. William Arthur and Gena (Davis) A.; student Elon Coll., 1952-55; D.D.S., U. N.C., 1959; M.S. in Periodontics, U. Mich., 1964; m. M. Winifred Rouse, Aug. 2, 1958; children—Don Lee, Michael Denmark, Susan Winifred. Faculty, U. N.C. Sch. Dentistry, Chapel Hill, 1959-70, asso. prof., 1965-70, prof., 1969-70; prof., asso. dean U. Fla. Coll. Dentistry, Gainesville, 1970—, interim dean, 1973—. Cons. USPHS, Council Dental Edn., VA Hosp., Gainesville. Mem. Orange County (N.C.) Cancer Soc., 1966-68, Y-Indian Guides, Chapel Hill, 1968-70, Gainesville, 1973—. Recipient teaching award U. N.C. Class of 1966. Fellow Am. Coll. Dentists; mem. Am. Acad. Periodontology, Am. Dental Assn., Am. Assn. Dental Schs., Internat. Assn. Dental Research, A.A.A.S., Omicron Kappa Upsilon. Presbyn. (elder). Author: (with G. Hunter, W. McFall) Periodontics for the Dental Hygienist, 1968. Home: 3611 SW 63d Lane Gainesville FL 32601

ALLEN, DONALD COLE, mfg. exec.; b. Dallas, Sept. 9, 1922; s. Raymond Daniel and Anne Elizabeth (Cole) A.; student Murray State Tchrs. Coll., 1943, U. Ga., 1945, So. Meth. U., 1948; J.D., LaSalle U., 1968; A.B., B.L.S., Syracuse U., 1972; m. Mary Jane Dunn, July 11, 1942; children—Dianne (Mrs. Charles Taylor Ashworth), Cynthia (Mrs. Phil Messer). Sales rep. Rice Stix Co., St. Louis. 1950-55; terr. mgr. Ely & Walker Co., Memphis, 1955-62, regional sales mgr., 1962-65, 1st v.p., gen. sales mgr., 1965-69, pres., 1969—. Asso. mem. Field Sales Mgmt. Inst., Syracuse U., 1962-63; research asso. So. Meth. U., 1950-65. Served with USNR, 1942-45. Mem. Sales Exec. Club, Sales and Marketing Execs. Internat. Methodist. Contbr. articles in field to profl. jours. Home: 3641 Woodglade Cove Memphis TN 38116 Office: 823 E Holmes Rd Memphis TN 38116

ALLEN, EDWARD PATRICK, educator, scientist; b. Dallas, Sept. 20, 1943; s. Jack Christopher and Dorothy (Holloway) A.; student So. Meth. U., 1961-65; D.D.S., Baylor U., 1969, Ph.D. (NIH fellow 1969-72), 1972; m. Joe Karen Callaway, Mar. 5, 1965; children—Karen Elizabeth, Edward Patrick, Everett Hunter. Research asso. endrocinrology Baylor U. Med. Center, Dallas, 1966-69; v.p. Specialized Biomed. Testing, Inc., Dallas, 1972-72; asst. prof. dept. periodontics Med. Coll. Va., Richmond, 1972—. Mem. Park Cities Com. for Water Fluoridation, 1971-72. Recipient Joe H. Smith award S.W. Soc. Periodontists, 1969. Mem. Am. Acad. Periodontology, Am., Tex. dental assns., Dallas County Dental Soc., Internat. Assn. Dental Research, Sigma Xi. Methodist. Contbr. articles to profl. lit. Home: 1506 Park Av Richmond VA 23220

ALLEN, EMORY RAWORTH, educator; b. Augusta, Ga., Jan. 21, 1935; s. Ernest Mason and Virginia (Williamson) A.; B.S. in Biol. Scis., U. Md., 1959; postgrad. Brown U., 1959; Ph.D. in Anatomy, U. Pa., 1964; m. Rae Heine, Dec. 19, 1957; children—Ronald Joseph, Dennis Raymond, Raworth Douglas, Robert Francis. Asst. instr. dept. anatomy U. Pa., Phila., 1964-65; instr. U. Pitts., 1965-66, asst. prof., 1966-71; asso. prof. dept. anatomy Med. Center, La. State U., New Orleans, 1971—. Mem. Fountain Estates Homeowners' Assn., 1971—. Served with USNR, 1954-56. USPHS predoctoral fellow, 1960-64, postdoctoral fellow, 1964-65; Muscular Dystrophy Assn. grantee, 1968-72. Mem. Internat. Acad. Pathology (lectr. 1970), Sigma Xi. Episcopalian. Contbr. profl. jours. Home: 126 DeWald Lane Slidell LA 70458 Office: 1100 Florida Av New Orleans LA 70119

ALLEN, ENSIL ROSS, reptile inst. exec.; b. Pitts., Jan. 2, 1908; s. Charles Leslie and Florence May (Martin) A.; student Stetson U., 1928; m. Jeanette Frances Perritt, Feb. 24, 1961; children—Kenneth Martin, Craig Lawrence, Sidney Janes. Founder, dir. Ross Allen's Reptile Inst., Silver Springs, Fla., 1929—; owner Indian Prairie Farm, 1970—. Mem. Fla. Commn. on Indian Affairs, 1969-71. Recipient Conservation award Fla. Dept. Agr., 1965; certificate of merit Fla. Bd. Conservation, 1965; Fla. Govs.'s Conservation award, 1970; award for contbn. to Fla. exhibit World's Fair, 1964; Silver Beaver award Boy Scouts Am., 1963, Distinguished Eagle Scout award, 1972; awards Tex. Med. Assn., Pa. Athletic Club. Mem. Internat. Crocodilian Soc. (founder, pres.), Nat. Audubon Soc. (pres. Ft. King chpt. 1968-70), Phila. Zool. Soc. (life). Contbr. numerous publs. in field to profl. jours. Discoverer several reptile species. Address: PO Box 217 Silver Springs FL 32688

ALLEN, FRANK SUTTON, physician; b. Talladega, Ala., Mar. 20, 1921; s. Arthur Hawkins and Julia Caskey (Sutton) A.; student Memphis State U., 1938-41; M.D., U. Tenn., 1944; m. Catherine Birna Stevens, Dec. 24, 1944; children—Anita Fran, Patricia Kay, Frank Sutton, James Edward, Michael Darryl. Intern, Baptist Meml. Hosp., Memphis, 1945; resident St. Joseph Hosp., Memphis, 1948-51, W. Tenn. Chest Hosp., 1951-52; practice medicine, specializing in surgery, Memphis, 1952—; chief of surgery Memphis St. Joseph Hosp. Served with AUS, 1941-44, 45-48. Fellow A.C.S.; mem. Memphis, Shelby County med. socs., Memphis Surg. Soc., Southeastern Surg. Congress, Phi Rho Sigma. Baptist (deacon 1948—). Home: 1002 Fair Meadow St Memphis TN 38117 Office: 1450 Poplar St Memphis TN 38104

ALLEN, GEORGE, football coach; b. Detroit, Apr. 29, 1922; s. Earl R. and Loretta (Hannigan) A.; B.A., M.A., U. Mich.; postgrad. U. So. Cal.; m. Etty L. Lumbroso, May 26, 1951; children—George, Gregory, Gerald, Jennifer. Formerly football coach Morningside Coll., Sioux City, Ia., Whittier (Cal.) Coll.; defensive coach Chgo. Bears, 1958-65; head coach Los Angeles Rams, 1966-70; head coach, gen. mgr., v.p. Washington Redskins, 1970—. Served with USNR, 1943-46. Author books. Office: Washington Redskins Box 17247-Dulles Washington DC 20041

ALLEN, GEORGE IRVING, electronic engr.; b. Bridgeport, Conn., Sept. 7, 1940; s. G.I. and Estelle Wilma (Lencewicz) A.; B.E.E., Miss. State U., 1965; m. Norma Sue Arthur, Apr. 14, 1965; children—Daye, Bethanie. Electronic engr. U.S. Navy Mine Def. Lab., Panama City, Fla., 1965-69, U.S. Naval Ship Research and Devel. Lab., Panama City, 1969-72, Naval Coastal Systems Lab., Panama City, 1972—. Electronics instr. Gulf Coast Jr. Coll., 1966-69, Tom Haney Vocational Sch., 1966-69. Mem. I.E.E.E. (chmn. local chpt. program com. 1972-73), Alpha Psi Omega (chpt. pres. 1964-65). Baptist (tchr. Sunday sch. 1972-73). Home: 2604 Dade Av Panama City FL 32401 Office: West Hwy 98 Panama City FL 32401

ALLEN, HERBERT, steel works exec.; b. Ratcliff, Tex., May 2, 1907; s. Jasper and Leona (Matthews) A.; B.S. in Mech. Engring., Rice Inst., 1929; m. Helen Daniels, Aug. 28, 1937; children—David Daniels, Anne (Mrs. Jonathan Taft Symonds), Michael Herbert. Engaged in miscellaneous research, 1929-31; chief engr. Abercrombie Pump Co., Houston, 1931-35; chief engr. Cameron Iron Works, Inc., 1935-41, v.p. engring. and mfg., 1942-50, v.p., gen. mgr., 1950-66, pres., 1966-73, chmn. bd., 1973—, also dir.; dir. Tenneco Inc., Tex. Commerce Bank. Bd. dirs. Tex. Tech. U., 1963-69, Houston Symphony Soc., 1971—; trustee St. Stephen's Episcopal Sch., 1967-70, S.W. Research Inst., 1956-64; trustee, chmn. bd. William Marsh Rice U. Named Engr. of Year, San Jacinto chpt. Tex. Soc. Profl. Engrs. Registered profl. engr., Tex. Fellow Am. Soc. M.E. (hon. mem.); mem. C. of C. (bd. dirs. 1952-54, 62, v.p. 1954-55), Am. Inst. Mining, Metall. and Petroleum Engrs., Am. Petroleum Inst., Philos. Soc. Tex., Newcomen Soc. N. Am., Tex. Soc. Profl. Engrs., Houston Engring. and Sci. Soc., Houston Philos. Soc., Tau Beta Pi, Episcopalian. Clubs: Ramada, River Oaks Country, Petroleum, Houston, Bayou. Patentee in field. Home: 3262 Huntingdon Pl Houston TX 77019 Office: PO Box 1212 Katy and Silber Rds Houston TX 77001

ALLEN, JAMES BROWNING, U.S. senator; b. Gadsden, Ala., Dec. 28, 1912; s. George C. and Mary Ethel (Browning) A.; student U. Ala., 1928-31, U. Ala. Law Sch., 1932-33; m. Marjorie Jo Stephens, Mar. 16, 1940 (dec. Jan. 1956); children—James Browning, Mary Rebecca, Debbie; m. 2d, Maryon Pittman Mullins, Aug. 7, 1964; stepchildren—J. Sanford Mullins III, John Pittman Mullins, Maryon Foster Allen. Admitted to Ala. bar, 1935, since practiced in Gadsden; mem. Ala. Legislature from Etowah County, 1939-43, mem. Ala. Senate, 1947-51; lt. gov. Ala., 1951-55, 63-67; U.S. senator from Ala., 1968—. Del. Democratic Nat. Conv., 1952. Served to lt. (j.g.) USNR, 1943-46. Home: 1321 Bellevue Dr Gadsden AL 35901 also 7405 Hallcrest Dr McLean VA 22101 Office: 6205 New Senate Office Bldg Washington DC 20510

ALLEN, JAMES DILLINO III, electronics engr.; b. Coshocton, O., Dec. 7, 1939; s. James Dillino and Beulah Mae (Simmons) A.; student Baldwin Wallace Coll., 1957-58; B.E.E., Ohio State U., 1962; M.S. in Elec. Engring., Va. Poly. Inst., 1966; postgrad. Mass., Inst. Tech., 1970-71, Northwestern U., 1967-68; m. Edna Marie McCall, Apr. 24,

1965; children—Shanua Kae, James Bryan, Ann Marie. Product design engr. Gen. Electric Co., Salem, Va., 1962-65; research engr. North Am. Aviation, Downey, Cal., 1965; mem. tech. staff Sci. Data Systems, El Segundo, Cal., 1966-67, Honeywell, Inc., St. Petersburg, Fla., 1967—. Registered profl. engr. NSF fellow, 1965. Mem. I.E.E.E. Club: Optimist. Contbr. articles on electronics to profl. jours. Home: 1873 Princeton Dr Clearwater FL 33515 Office: Honeywell Inc 13350 U S Hwy 19 N St Petersburg FL 33733

ALLEN, JAMES SCRIBNER, assn. exec.; b. Proctor, Vt., Oct. 6, 1919; s. Sinclair Tousey and Katharine (Scribner) A.; B.S., Norwich U., 1943; postgrad. N.Y. Law Sch., 1953, Alexander Hamilton, 1954; m. Virginia James Claudon, Mar. 5, 1947; children—Pamela Beckwith, Jeffrey James. Design engr. Gen. Electric Co., Pittsfield, Mass., 1946-49, product application engr., N.Y.C., 1949-52, Gen. Electric Internat., 1952-56; econ. devel. cons. Ebasco Internat., 1956-59; mgr. Edison Electric. Inst., Washington, 1959-71, coordinator indsl. relations, 1973—; mgr. Electric Energy Assn., Washington, 1971-73. Treas., Community Westmoreland Citizens Assn., 1968-70. Served with Signal Corps, AUS, 1943-47; PTO. Mem. Washington Soc. Assn. Execs., Producers Council (past pres.), Am. Marketing Assn. (dir. 1963-65), I.E.E.E., Soc. Am. Mil Engrs. Clubs: Washington Coal (pres. 1969), University (Washington); Chevy Chase. Home: 5208 Portsmouth Rd Washington DC 20016 Office: 1140 Connecticut Av Washington DC 20036

ALLEN, J(ESSE) DANIEL, printing sales exec.; b. Louisville, Aug. 6, 1921 Thomas Conway and Bettie (Kincheloe) A.; student pub schs.; m. Ester McKinney, Sept. 17, 1948; 1 dau., Dana Dee. With Courier-Jour. Lithographing Co., Louisville, 1939-72, asst. v.p., 1962-63, v.p. sales, 1963-72, also dir.; v.p. dir. Courier-Jour. Job Printing Co., Louisville, 1965-72, Ins. Field Co., Louisville, 1965-72; past pres., dir. Courier-Jour. Lithographing Co. of Ga., Inc., Atlanta; sales devel. Ky. Lithographing Co., Louisville, 1973—; dir. Clothiers, Ltd., Inc. Pres., bd. dirs. River City Endeavor, 1973—, Toonerville Enterprises, Inc., 1973—. Served with USMCR, 1942-46, 1951-52. Mem. Printing Salesmens Club Atlanta (past pres.), Lithograph Mfrs. Assn. (past pres.), Bank Stationers Assn. (past pres.). Methodist. Clubs: Louisville Boat, Jefferson (Louisville). Home: 515 Blankenbaker Lane Louisville KY 40207 Office: 600 E Main St Louisville KY 40202

ALLEN, JOHN ALEXANDER, educator; b. Chevy Chase, Md., Apr. 25, 1922; s. Emanuel Alexander and Ann (Allen) Goldenweiser; B.A., Swarthmore Coll., 1943; B.A., Oxford U., 1948, M.A., 1952; Ph.D., U. N.C., 1954; m. Josephine Haynes, June 2, 1951; children—Margaret Haynes, Elizabeth Alexander. Instr. English, U. Rochester, 1952-55; asst. prof. English, Hollins Coll., Va., 1955-60, asso. prof., 1960-67, prof., 1967—, chmn. dept. English, 1967-70. Served to lt. (j.g.) USNR, 1943-46. Mem. Modern Lang. Assn. Am., Renaissance Soc. Am. Author: The Lean Divider, 1968; Hero's Way: Contemporary Poems, 1971. Address: Hollins Coll Hollins College VA 24020

ALLEN, JOHN CHILES, architect; b. Grapeland, Tex., Oct. 24, 1913; s. John Andrew and Mary Kathryn (Chiles) A.; student Tex. A. and M. Coll., 1932-35; B.S. in Archtl. Engring., Tex. U., 1950; m. Elizabeth Iona Johnson, Mar. 17, 1939; 1 son, Robert Lewis. Asso. architect Haynes and Strange, Architects, Lubbock, Tex., 1941-42, Giesecke, Kuehne and Brooks, architects, Austin, Tex., 1942-45, John Linn Scott and Assos., Austin, 1947-53; prin. John Chiles Allen, architect, Austin, 1953—. Served to lt. C.E., AUS, 1945-46. Mem. A.I.A., Tex. Soc. Architects, Nat. Soc. Profl. Engrs., Constrn. Specifications Inst. (pres. Austin chpt.). Rotarian. Prin. works include Groveton Community Hosp., 1969; Hearne Housing Devel., 1972; North Runnels Hosp., 1973. Home: 901 W 30th St Austin TX 78705 Office: 2914 Pearl St Austin TX 78705

ALLEN, JOHN ELDRIDGE, hist. researcher; b. Morehead City, N.C., Sept. 11, 1911; s. Arthur Vincent and Annie (Willis) A.; B.B.A., U. Miami (Fla.), 1934; M.A., George Washington U., 1937; postgrad. Am. U., 1937; m. Mary Josephine Edwards, June 11, 1949, 1 son, Mark Edwards. Information aid NRA, Washington, 1935; tech. aid Dept. Treasury, 1935-39; records asst. Dept. Agr., 1940-41; social research supr. Works Progress Adminstrn. Fed. Works Agy., 1941-42; analyst Depts. Army and Defense, 1948-57; asst. exec. dir. Lincoln Sesquicentennial Commn., Nat. Archives, 1958-59; research, writer Abraham Lincoln Sesquicentennial Tributes, 1959-61; instr. social sciences U. Miami, 1961-62, housing asst. Dept. Residence Halls, 1963-73; research and writing, 1962—. Vice chmn. joint birthday celebration honoring George Washington, 1952, also program dir. pub. celebration honoring Thomas Jefferson, Washington, 1952; chmn. 150th birthday anniversary program Lincoln Mus., Washington, 1959; speaker program honoring U.S. Grant, Washington, 1959; mem. div. historic sites and bldgs. Nat. Capital Sesquicentennial Commn., Washington, 1950. Served from ensign to lt. comdr., USNR, 1942-46. Recipient Lincoln medallion Lincoln Sesquicentennial Commn., 1960; Service plaque Hialeah Boy Scouts Am. Cub Pack, 1961; Service plaque Beta Sigma Rho Fraternity, 1962. Mem. Columbia Hist. Soc. (past v.p.), Lincoln Group D.C. (past pres., charter), S.A.R. (past pres. D.C., Presidential Insignia medal 1957, service certificate 1968; nat. trustee 1953-54), Am. Econ. Assn., U.S. Capitol Hist. Soc. (founding mem.), George Washington Law Assn., Renaissance Soc. Am. (founding mem.), U. Miami Gen. Alumni Assn. (bd. dirs., 1961-64, chmn. Spring reunion 1962; chmn. devel. council 1962-63), U. Miami Alumni Fund Century Club (charter). Democrat. Methodist. Club: University (sec. 50th Anniversary Celebration com. 1954) (Washington). Editor and indexer: Allen Personal Papers and Journals, 1973—. Home: 7339 SW 82nd St South Miami FL 33143

ALLEN, JOSEPH PERCIVAL, astronaut; b. Crawfordsville, Ind., June 27, 1937; s. Joseph P. and Harriet (Taylor) A.; B.A., DePauw U., 1959; student Christian Albrechts U., Kiel, Germany, 1959-60; M.S., Yale, 1961, Ph.D., 1965; m. Bonnie Jo Darling, July 9, 1961. Guest research asso. Brookhaven Nat. Lab., 1962-65; staff physicist Nuclear Structure Lab., Yale, 1965; research asso. U. Wash., 1966; scientist-astronaut NASA-Manned Spacecraft Center, Houston, 1967—. Rector scholar, 1955-59; Fulbright scholar, 1959-60. Mem. Am. Phys. Soc., Am. Astronautical Soc., N.Y. Acad. Scis., Am. Astron. Soc., A.A.A.S., Phi Beta Kappa, Sigma Xi, Beta Theta Pi, Phi Eta Sigma. Author articles in field.Home: 1410 Antigua Lane Nassau Bay TX 77058 Office: NASA Manned Spacecraft Center CB Houston TX 77058

ALLEN, L. SCOTT, clergyman. Ordained to ministry Methodist Ch., now bishop, Knoxville, Tenn. Address: 502 Gay St SW Suite 314 Knoxville IN 37902

ALLEN, LAURENCE EDMUND (LARRY), war corr.; b. Mt. Savage, Md., Oct. 19, 1908; s. Laurence Bernard and Mary Caroline (Crowe) A.; student schools of several states; grad. high sch.; m. Helen Fazakerley Quisenberry. Reporter Balt. News, 1926, later on Washington Herald and Huntington (W.Va.) Evening Herald; reporter, telegraph editor Charleston (W.Va.) Daily Mail, 1927-33; with Asso. Press, 1933-60, as reporter and state editor Charleston bur., 1933-35 reporter Washington bur., 1935-37, fgn. cables desk, N.Y.C., 1937-38, European war corr., 1938-44, corr. Poland, 1945, 47, 49, chief Moscow bur., 1949, in Tel Aviv, 1950, war corr., S.E. Asia, Singapore, 1951, French Union and Vietminh Indochina, 1951-55, Malaya, Thailand, Burma, 1956, Caribbean area, 1957-61; organized Am. Press Service specializing Latin Am., 1960—. Recipient Bronze Star for defending freedom press as prisoner of war, 1945; Croix de Guerre Fr. High Command, Indo China, frontline reporting, Nov. 1952. Received first award Nat. Headliners Club, 1941, for best news-reporting in covering Brit. Fleet operations; awarded Pulitzer prize for reporting on internat. affairs, May 5, 1942; decorated Order of British Empire by King George VI, 1947. Republican. Contbr. many short stories to various publs., 1925-33. Home: Rio Amazonas 78 Mexico City 5 Mexico

ALLEN, MACK KENT, banker; b. Columbus, Tex., Sept. 9, 1924; s. Dee Hansworth and Anna (Hemans) A.; B.S., Tex. A. and M. U., 1950; m. Lillian Rodgers, Aug. 18, 1946; children—David Kent, Tricia Lynn, Nancy Kathryn. Tchr. agr. Vets. Vocational Tex. Edn. System, 1950-55; salesman Met. Life Ins. Co., Houston, 1955-61, cons., 1958-62; appraiser and loan officer Colo. County Fed. Savs. and Loan, Columbus, Tex., 1962-67; cashier Katy Nat. Bank (Tex.), 1967-69, v.p., 1969-71; dir. North Shore Bank of Houston, 1968-70. Tchr., Savs. and Loan Inst., 1962-63. Cons. soil conservation Boy Scouts of Am., 1953-64; adviser, coordinator Jr. Achievement, Katy, 1967-69; chmn. Colorado County (Tex.) chpt. Red Cross, 1962-67; Bd. dirs., trustee Houston Harris County United Fund; bd. dirs. Houston Harris County Red Cross 1968-71. Served with USNR, 1943-46, PTO. Methodist (trustee 1963-67). Mason, Rotarian (pres. 1971—), Lion (pres. Columbus 1966-67). Home: 809 Aster St Katy TX 77450 Office: 5622 3rd St Katy TX 77450

ALLEN, MARSHALL EDMUNDE, ednl. TV exec.; b. Chgo., Sept. 20, 1937; s. Marshall C. and Mildred (Zabel) A.; B.A., Miami U., Oxford, O., 1959, M.A., 1961; m. Joyce Sylvia Huff, Nov. 28, 1959; children—Terri Sue, David Marshall. Stage mgr. sta. WLWI-TV, Indpls., 1959-60; asst. dir. univ. broadcasting services So. Ill. U., 1961-67; asso. prof. journalism and broadcasting, head ednl. TV services Okla. State U., 1967—; cons. Okla. Ednl. TV Authority, 1968—, Okla. Consortium on Research Devel., 1969, Langston U., 1970, Higher Edn. Alumni Council Okla., 1972, Bacone Coll., 1973. Mem. Nat. Assn. Ednl. Broadcasters, Town and Gown Community Theater. Home: 2702 Fox Ledge Dr Stillwater OK 74074 Office: 307 Communications Bldg Stillwater OK 74074

ALLEN, MARYON PITTMAN (MRS. JAMES BROWNING ALLEN), columnist; b. Meridian, Miss., Nov. 30, 1925; d. John D. and Tellie (Chism) Pittman; student U. Ala., 1944-47; m. Joshua Sanford Mullins, Jr., Oct. 17, 1946 (div. Jan. 1959); children—Joshua Sanford, III, John Pittman, Maryon Foster; m. 2d, James Browning Allen (U.S. Senator from Ala.), Aug. 7, 1964; 1 stepson, James Browning Allen. Office mgr. Dr. Alston Callahan, Birmingham, Ala., 1959-60; bus. mgr. psychiat. clinic U. Ala. Med. Center, Birmingham, 1960-61; agt. Protective Life Ins. Co., Birmingham, 1961-62; women's editor Sun Newspapers, Birmingham, 1962-64; staff writer, columnist The Birmingham News, 1964—; v.p. Emerald Valley Corp., partner J. D. Pittman Partnership Co., Birmingham. Mem.-at-large Ala. Hist. Commn. Democratic presdl. elector Dem. primary, 1968. Bd. dirs. Children's Fresh Air Farm, Birmingham, Mamie Fogarty com. Birmingham Festival of Arts. Recipient 1st place award Ala. Press Assn. 1962, 63; also various awards in typography, fashion writing, food pages. Mem. Birmingham Com. 100 for Women, Ala. Writers Conclave, Ala. Hist. Commn. (mem.-at-large), Nat. League Am. Pen Women, Arlington Hist. Assn., Antiquarian Soc. Gadsen, Gadsen Art Assn., Capitol Hist. Soc., Nat. Trust Historic Preservation. Presbyn. Clubs: 1925 F Street, Mountain Laurel Garden. Home: 7405 Hallcrest Dr Mclean VA 22101 also 1321 Bellevue Dr Gadsden AL 35901

ALLEN, MATTHEW CARTWRIGHT, JR., cotton compressing co. exec.; b. Dallas, Dec. 3, 1934; s. Matthew Cartwright and Flossie Cleona (Davis) A.; B.S., West Tex. State U., 1958; m. Teddie Jean Trulove, May 30, 1959; children—Sandra Kay, Sue Lynn. With Memphis Compress Co. (Tex.), 1959—, crew pusher, 1959-60, supt., 1961-65, v.p. and gen. mgr., 1966—; dir. First Nat. Bank. Mem. Memphis Vol. Fire Dept., 1967—, chmn. Girl Scout Fund drive, 1970. Mem. Memphis Sch. Bd., 1971—. Bd. dirs. Hall County Indsl. Found, treas., 1968—. Recipient Community Service award radio sta. KCTX, 1970. Mem. Southwestern Cotton Compress and Warehouse Assn. (dir. 1961-71, pres. 1970-71), Nat. Cotton Council (del. 1968-70), C. of C. (dir. 1966-68, 70—). Mem. Ch. of Christ (deacon 1964—). Lion (dir. 1965-67). Home: 910 North 18th St Memphis TX 79245 Office: 820 Lucille St Memphis TX 79245

ALLEN, MILLER SHANNON, JR., pathologist, educator; b. White Gate, Va., Sept. 23, 1922; s. Miller Shannon and Ethel Catherine (Bird) A.; B.A., U. Va., 1943, M.S., 1951; M.D., U. Va., 1945; m. Anita Alice Pugh, Jan. 8, 1952; children—Mary Scott, Miller Shannon, Nancy Leigh, Catherine Bird. Intern Presbyn. Hosp., N.Y.C., 1945-46; resident surgery U. Va. Hosp., Charlottesville, 1948-51; practice medicine specializing in surgery, Kingsport, Tenn., 1952-57; mem. staffs Halston Valley Community Hosp.; mem. faculty U. Va. Sch. Medicine, Charlottesville, 1957—, prof., 1968—. Served to capt. M.C., AUS, 1946-48. Diplomate Am. Bd. Surgery, Am. Bd. Pathology. Mem. Raven Soc., Alpha Omega Alpha. Club: Farmington Country (Charlottesville). Contbr. articles to profl. jours. Home: 1607 St Anne's Rd Charlottesville VA 22901

ALLEN, NELL RUTH, speech pathologist, audiologist; b. Winnfield, La.; d. Columbus Willma and Caroline (Long) Allen; B.A., Northwestern State Coll., 1950; M.Ed., Wayne U., 1957; postgrad. N.Y. U. at Buffalo, summer 1951, Tulane U., 1957, La State U. Med. Sch., 1963-66, 66. Dept. head, speech therapist La. Spastic Sch., Alexandria, 1950-51, Detroit Cerebral Palsy Center, 1951-54, N.E. Cerebral Palsy Sch., Monroe, La., 1954-55, Rapides Parish Rehab. Center, Alexandria, 1955-57; dept head., dir. speech and hearing clinic. Crippled Children's Hosp., New Orleans, 1959—; spl. lectr. speech La. State U., 1963; instr. speech pathology and audiology Tulane U., 1966—; supr. speech therapy majors St. Mary's Dominican Coll., New Orleans, Northwestern State Coll., Natchitoches, La., Tulane U., 1960—; lectr. civic orgns. Recipient scholarship United Cerebral Palsy Assn. La., 1954, scholarship Office Vocational Rehab., 1957; awarded clin. competence in speech pathology, audiology Am. Speech and Hearing Assn., 1965, 67. Mem. Am., La. (past pres.) speech and hearing assns., Internat. Platform Assn. Research pertaining to hearing acuity of muscular dystrophic individuals. Home: 6755 River Rd New Orleans LA 70123 Office: 200 Henry Clay Av New Orleans LA 70118

ALLEN, OLLIE JAMES, supt. schs.; b. nr. Clayhole, Ky., Oct. 20, 1911; s. Ethan and Elizabeth (Combs) A.; B.S., Murray (Ky.) State U., 1941, M.A., 1958; m. Ruth Wallis, Feb. 11, 1940; children—Maura (Mrs. John A. Armes), J. Phillip, Jeanne A. (Mrs Darry A. Lieb). Tchr. pub. schs., Breathitt County, Ky., 1932-39, Trigg County, Ky., 1940, Ohio County, Ky., 1957; tchrs., coach, Ballard County, Ky., 1941-44; prin. Cunningham (Ky.) High Sch., 1944-57; prin., coach Fordsville (Ky.) High Sch., 1957-58; supt. schs. Breckinridge County Sch., Hardinsburg, 1958—. Bd. dirs. North Central Found., J. Town Vocational Area Sch. Mason, Rotarian, Lion. Address: Hardinsburg KY 40143

ALLEN, PHILLIP ELWOOD, lawyer; b. Joplin, Mo., Jan. 18, 1931; s. Elwood A. and Opal (Calhoun) A.; B.S., U. Ark., 1959, J.D., 1962; m. Lorraine V. Miller, July 12, 1952; children—Linda Denise, Karen Diane, Bradley Phillip. Admitted to Ark. bar, 1962, Ky. bar, 1971; asso. Rose, Meek, partner firm Allen, Dahlen & Young, Little Rock, Ark., 1968-71; pvt. practice law, Louisville, 1971—. Served with AUS, 1949-52, 52-57. Mem. Am., Ark., Ky bar assns., Tau Kappa Alpha, Beta Gamma Sigma Omicron Delta Kappa, Phi Eta Sigma, Delta Theta Phi. Home: 4720 Fox Den Ct Louisville KY 40222 Office: 400 Sherburn Lane Louisville Ky 40207

ALLEN, RICHARD SWEETNAM, educator; b. Pekin, Ill., Nov. 9, 1896; s. William Henry and Margaret Anne (Olt) A.; student U. Chgo., 1917-18, 26-27, 36-37; B.S., U. Rochester, 1922, M.S., 1925; m. Leone M.S. McLoughlin, Aug. 23, 1924; 1 son, William Henry II. Research asso. U. Rochester, 1922-23, asst., 1923-25; physiol. chemist Wilson Research Lab., Chgo., 1923; phys. chemist Western Elec. Co., Chgo., 1924; instr. Coll. Medicine, U. Tenn., 1925-26; asst. prof. anatomy and physiology U. Ky., Lexington, 1927-29, asso. prof., 1929-36, prof., 1936-67, head dept., 1931-67, prof. physiology Med. Sch., 1960-67, prof. emeritus, 1967—, faculty asst. to dean Coll. Arts and Scis., 1966-67. Served with U.S. Army, 1918-19. Mem. Assn. Am. Med. Colls., A.A.A.S., Am. Genetic Soc., Nat. Geog. Soc., Am. Legion (chmn. jr. athletic coms. local and state 1941-49), U. Ky. Research Club (sec. 1931-36), Sigma Xi, Alpha Epsilon Delta. Democrat. Contbr. articles to profl. jours. Home: 1836 McDonald Rd Lexington KY 40503

ALLEN, ROBERT ARTHUR, lawyer; b. Decatur, Ill., May 16, 1940; s. Glen F. and Catherine B. (Heer) A.; B.A. in Econs., U. Tex., 1966; LL.B., Baylor U., 1968; m. Cherryl Elaine Cuda, Aug. 24, 1972; children—Christopher Shane, Audrey Kay, Clifford Lewis, Brandon Trent. Admitted to Tex. bar, 1968; mem. firm Wiley & Plumb, San Antonio, 1968-70, Wiley, Plumb & Plunkett, San Antonio, 1970-71; mem. firm, sec. Wiley, Plunkett, Gibson & Allen, 1971—. Chmn., Concerned Young Lawyers Com., 1971. Recipient James P. Alexander award Baylor Sch. Law, 1968. Mem. Am., Tex., San Antonio, Tex. State Jr. bar assns., Tex. Assn. Def. Counsel, Delta Theta Phi. Home: 8710 Datapoint San Antonio TX 78228 Office: 1222 N Main Av San Antonio TX 78212

ALLEN, ROBERT DEE, lawyer; b. Tulsa, Oct. 13, 1928; s. Harve and Olive Jean (Brown) A.; B.A., U. Okla., 1951, LL.B., 1955, J.D., 1970; m. Mary Latimer Conner, May 18, 1957; children—Scott, Randy, Blake. Admitted to Okla. bar, 1955; asso. Abernathy & Abernathy, Shawnee, Okla., 1955; law clk. for Hon. A. P. Murrah, judge 10th U.S. Ct. Appeals, Denver, 1956, Hon. Ross Rizley, judge Western Dist. Okla., 1956-57; asst. ins. commr., counsel Okla. Ins. Dept., 1957-63; partner firm DeBois, Allen & Batchelor, Oklahoma City, 1963-65, DeBois & Allen, 1965-66; counsel Am. Tel. & Tel., Washington, 1966-67, gen. atty. Southwestern Bell Telephone Co., Okla., 1967—. Exec. com. local council Boy Scouts Am.; mem. Gov.'s Ad Valorem Tax Structure and Sch. Finance Commn., 1972. Bd. dirs. Oklahoma County Legal Aid Soc., 1973—. Served to sgt. AUS, 1946-48; maj. Res. Mem. Am. Judicature Soc., Am., Fed., Okla., Oklahoma County bar assns., Order of Coif, Phi Delta Phi, Sigma Phi Epsilon (dir.). Presbyn. Home: 3021 Robin Ridge Rd Oklahoma City OK 73120 Office: 707 N Robinson Oklahoma City OK 73102

ALLEN, ROBERT ERWIN, physiologist; b. Lufkin, Tex., Oct. 9, 1941; s. John Franklin and Bonnie Mae (Smith) A.; B.A., Stephen F. Austin State Coll., 1963; Ph.D., Vanderbilt Med. Sch., 1969; m. Roma Leah Trobaugh, Oct. 18, 1970; 1 dau., Jennifer Kay. With NASA Marshall Space Flight Center, Huntsville, Ala., 1969—, chief biometrics, 1972—. Home: 1221 Briar Hollow Trail Huntsville AL 35802 Office: Marshall Space Flight Center NASA Huntsville AL 35812

ALLEN, ROBERT G., physician; b. Memphis, June 14, 1928; student Southwestern at Memphis, Johns Hopkins, 1945-47; M.D., U. Tenn., 1950. Intern John Gaston Hosp., Memphis, 1951-52, now mem. staff; resident Boston Children's Hosp., 1952-53, sr. resident, 1956-57, chief resident, 1957-58; resident Kennedy Vets. Hosp., 1953-54; dir. cardiovascular surgery Le Bonheur Children's Hosp., Memphis, 1959—, chief surgery, 1964-68; mem. active staff W.F. Bowld Hosp.; mem. courtesy staff Bapt. Meml. Hosp., Meth. Hosp., St. Joseph Hosp. Served with USNR, 1954-56. Diplomate Am. Bd. Surgery. Mem. A.C.S., Am. Acad. Pediatrics, Am. Coll. Cardiology, A.M.A., Am. Pediatric Surg. Assn. (charter), Lilliputian Surg. Soc. (founder), Bowers Surg. Soc. (founder), Memphis, Shelby County med. socs., Memphis Thoracic Soc., Tenn., Memphis pediatric socs., Southeastern Surg. Congress, So. Soc. for Pediatric Research, Memphis Surg. Soc., Jour. Rev. Club, Memphis Staff and Serpent Jour. Club (pres. 1963), Alpha Omega Alpha. Contbr. articles to profl. jours. Address: 4111 Gwynne Rd Memphis TN 38117

ALLEN, ROBERT LEWIS, physician; b. Spartanburg, S.C., Feb. 13, 1930; s. Dudley Allen and Edna (Moore) A.; B.S. magna cum laude, Wofford Coll., 1951; M.D., Tulane U., 1955; m. Sterling Peebles, May 31, 1955; children—Elizabeth, Catherine, Deborah. Intern, Meyer Meml. Hosp., Buffalo, 1955-56; resident Kennedy Vets. Hosp., Memphis, 1956-59; pvt. practice internal medicine, Cleveland, Tenn., 1961—; dir. nuclear medicine Bradley Meml. Hosp., Cleveland Bd. dirs. YMCA. Mem. Cleveland City Planning Commn., 1966—. Served to capt. AUS, 1959-61. Diplomate Am. Bd. Internal Medicine. Mem. A.M.A., Am. Heart Assn., Soc. Nuclear Medicine, Bradley County Med. Soc. (pres. 1968), Phi Beta Kappa, Nu Sigma Nu. Home: 3545 Edgewood Circle Cleveland TN 37311 Office: 755 Broad St Cleveland TN 37311

ALLEN, ROBERT WATSON, transport co. exec.; b. Cambridge, Mass., Jan. 25, 1929; s. Ralph Watson and Dorothy Caroline (Dansie) A.; A.B. cum laude, Bowdoin Coll., 1950; M.B.A., Harvard, 1952; m. Ann Everette Stevens, May 17, 1958; children—Dansie Lee, Scott Thornton, Andrew Stevens. With W.R. Grace & Co., 1954—, Dewey & Almy Chem. Div., Cambridge, Mass., Chgo., Montreal and Toronto, 1954-62, Cryovac Div., 1962-71, treas., 1969-71, gen. mgr. Grace Distbn. Services, 1972—; dir. Rocky Mount Cord Co. Pres. Charles Lea Center, 1974—; treas. Council for Spartanburg Country, 1967—. Served with Finance Corp. AUS, 1952-54. Mem. Beta Theta Pi. Episcopalian. Home: 1090 Partridge Rd Spartanburg SC 29302 Office: PO Box 308 Duncan SC 29334

ALLEN, ROBERT WILSON, lawyer, educator; b. Los Angeles, Sept. 13, 1919; s. Albert V. and Myrtle Isabel (Hogg) A.; A.B., U. Cal. at Los Angeles, 1942; M.A., So. Meth. U., 1947; Dr. de L'Univ. de Paris, 1952; LL.B., John Marshall U., 1961, J.D., 1962. Instr. fgn. langs. Oxford Coll., Emory U., 1953-57, chrmn. div., 1957-67; admitted to Ga. bar, 1963; gen. practice Oxford, Ga., 1963—. Justice 1525th Dist. Ga. Militia, Newton County, 1965—. Served with AUS, 1942-46. Mem. Am. Trial Lawyers Assn., Ga. State Bar, Covington Bar, Nat., Ga. edn. assns., Alliance Francaise, Atlanta Symphony Guild, Pi Delta Phi, Alpha Mu Gamma, Lambda Phi Alpha. Democrat. Methodist. Mason. Contbr. articles to profl. jours. Home:

309 W Stone St Oxford GA 30267 Office: Starr Bldg Covington GA 30209

ALLEN, ROGER WILLIAMS, coll. dean; b. Birmingham, Ala., Mar. 29, 1897; s. Charles Morehead and Nannie Arabella (Thomson) A.; B.S., Auburn U., 1918, M.S., 1919; A.M., U. Mich., 1921; Ph.D., Columbia, 1927; m. Margaret Ann Chruch, Nov. 22, 1927; children—Patsy Jane, Roger W. Chemist, D. C. Pickard, cons. chemists, summer 1917, with E. I. du Pont de Nemours & Co., Washburn, Wis., summer 1918; with U.S. Chem. Warfare Service, Cleve., 1918; chemist Ala. State Chem. Lab., Auburn, 1919, U.S. Dept. Entomology, summer 1921; prof. chemistry Howard Coll., Birmingham, Ala., 1921-22, 1923-26; chemist Inecto, Inc., and Marinello Co., N.Y.C., 1926-28; prof. chemistry Auburn (Ala.) U., 1928-41, dean sch. sci. and lit., 1941-67, dean emeritus, 1967—. Dir. Auburn Community Chest Drive, 1940. Mem. Ala. Acad. Sci., Ala. Ednl. Assn., Sigma Xi, Phi Kappa Phi. Phi Lambda Upsilon, Omicron Delta Kappa, Delta Sigma Pi, Alpha Epsilon Delta, Pi Kappa Alpha, Phi Eta Sigma. Author: Fundamentals of Chemistry, 1930. Home: 572 Wright's Mill Rd Auburn AL 36830

ALLEN, ROLAND HAROLD, asst. atty. gen. Tex.; b. Waco, Tex., Apr. 16, 1921; s. Albert Sidney and Ida (Neel) A.; J.D., Baylor University, Waco, Tex., 1951; m. Elnora Lee Daniel, July 18, 1953; children—Donna Carol, James Edwin, William Harold. Admitted to Tex. bar, 1951; law clk., liaison with mil. and vets. reps. Office U.S. Congressman, Washington, 1951-52; asso. firm Eugene E. Piper, Borger, Tex., 1953; partner Gassaway & Allen and predecessor firms, Borger, 1954-68; asst. atty. gen. of Tex., Austin, 1969—. Engaged in oil gas bus., Borger, 1955—, real estate investments, 1958—; sec., dir. Indsl. Dynamics, Inc., Borger, 1961-69; atty. Panhandle Bank & Trust Co., Borger, 1954-68, 1st Savs. & Loan Assn., Borger, 1955-68. Dist. chmn. Nat. Fedn. Ind. Bus., 1963-68; mem. Tax Equalization Bd., Borger, 1965-67, chmn., 1967. Precinct chmn. Democratic party, 1960-62. Bd. dirs. Hutchinson County Child Welfare, 1967-69; trustee land trust, Amarillo, Tex., 1965-69; trustee, sec. N.W. Tex. Masonic Home and Sch. Ednl. Found. 1963—. Served with USMC, 1942-46; PTO. Decorated Purple Heart. Mem. Am., Borger (pres. 1957), Travis County bar assns., State Bar Tex., Am. Judicature Soc., Am. Legion, Delta Theta Phi. Baptist. Mason (Shriner, 32 deg.). Clubs: Exchange (pres. 1957), Country (Borger, Tex.). Home: 2903 Clarice Ct Austin TX 78731 Office: Supreme Ct Bldg Austin TX 78711

ALLEN, SIDNEY MITCHELL GREMILLION (MRS. JOHN HORTON ALLEN), civic worker; b. Alexandria, La., Nov. 8, 1921; d. Forrest and Neta Belle (Mitchell) Gremillion; B.A. Northwestern State Coll., Natchitoches, La., 1942; M.Ed., La. State U., 1951; m. John Horton Allen, July 14, 1943; children—John Horton, Lisa Jane. Elementary tchr. Caddo Parish Schs., La., 1942-44, 46-47; supervising tchr., instr. edn. Southeastern La. Coll., Hammond, 1947-51; summer workshop cons. La. State U., 1950-51, supervising tchr. Coll. Area Joint Schs., State Coll., Pa., 1951-52; prin. supervising tchr. Primary Sch., 1952-53; cons., supervising tchr. Pa. State U., 1952, 53, in service tchr. tng. cons., 1952, 53; elementary tchr. Hattiesburg (Miss.) Pub. Schs., 1954, 57-60. Vol. tchr. art appreciation Hattiesburg, (Miss.) Pub. Schs., 1964-69. Vice pres., bd. dirs. Shreveport Art Guild; bd. dirs. Shreveport Symphony Guild, Shreveport Civic Opera Assn., Northwest La. Heart Assn., YWCA, Caddo chpt. A.R.C. Mem. Am. Assn. U. Women (past br. pres.), Nat. Assn. Jr. Auxilaries (chpt. pres.), Hattiesburg. Panhellenic Assn., Alpha Sigma Alpha, Phi Alpha Theta, Kappa Delta Pi, Phi Kappa Phi, Delta Kappa Gamma, Alpha Sigma Alpha (nat. alumnae dir.). Home: 254 Rutherford Shreveport LA 71104

ALLEN, THOMAS HUNTER, health service physiologist; b. Davenport, Ia., Sept. 24, 1914; s. Victor V. and Norma C. (Haller) A.; B.A., U. Ia., 1936, Ph.D., 1941; m. Helen Herndon Moore, Dec. 28, 1940; children—Beverley (Mrs. Richard Wilschke), Rebecca (Mrs. Duane Brannon), Thomas M. (dec.). Instr. physiology Columbia, 1946-47, asst. prof., 1947-51, asso. prof., 1951-56; chief physiologist U.S. Army Med. Research and Nutrition Lab., Denver, 1956-61; chief physiologist U.S. Air Force Sch. Aerospace Medicine, San Antonio, 1961-70; sci. adviser Sch. Aerospace Medicine, Brooks AFB, Tex., 1970—. Served to 1st lt. USAAC, 1942-46. Mem. Am. Physiol. Soc., Aerospace Med. Assn. (pres. aerospace physiology sect. 1969-70), Am. Inst. Nutrition, Am. Soc. Clin. Nutrition, Soc. Exptl. Biology and Medicine. Contbr. articles to profl. jours. Home: 633 Balfour St San Antonio TX 78239 Office: Brooks Air Force Base TX 78235

ALLEN, WENDALL EARL, univ. dean; b. Elizabethtown, Ky., Nov. 16, 1936; s. Van Earl and Rudell (Brawner) A.; B.A., Vanderbilt U., 1958, M.A., 1961; Ph.D., U. Ky., 1968; m. Wende Joyce Winters, Nov. 7, 1966; 1 son, Stephen Van. Instr. biology U. Ala., Montevallo, 1961-63; research asso. U. Ky., Lexington, 1965-67; asst. prof. biology E. Carolina U., Greenville, N.C., 1967—, asst. dean, 1970—. Mem. Am. Soc. Microbiology, A.A.A.S., Assn. S.E. Biologists. Contbr. articles to sci. jours. Home: Azalea Gardens Greenville NC 27834

ALLEN, WILLIAM HUBERT, govt. ofcl.; b. Yakima, Wash., Oct. 9, 1916; s. Hubert Douglas and Claire (Burris) A.; student U. Portland, 1935-37; B.A. in Math., U. Tex., 1951; m. Rose Mary Tudyk, Sept. 1, 1942; children—William Hubert, Rosemary Claire, Mary Angela, Dawn Elizabeth. Research and editorial specialist, USAF Air U., Maxwell Field, Ala., 1949-57, asst. prof. meteorology, 1952-55, asso. prof., 1955-57; editor U.S. nat. com. Internat. Geophys. Year, Washington, 1957-58; systems analyst Inst. Def. Analysis, Washington, 1958-59; with NASA, Washington and Moffett Field, Cal., 1959—, systems analyst, Washington, 1969-72, dir. Congl. inquiries, 1972—. Served to lt. col. USAAC, 1937-39, 41-45. Mem. Internat. Acad. Astronautics (corr.), A.A.A.S., World Future Soc., Am. Optical Soc. Author: (with P.H. Nesbitt and A.W. Pond) The Survival Book, 1959. Editor: Dictionary of Technical Terms for Aerospace Use, 1965; International Academy of Astronautics Multilingual Dictionary, 1969. Home: 5024 Garfield St NW Washington DC 20016 Office: NASA Office Legis Affairs Washington DC 20546

ALLEN, WILLIAM SAMUEL, agrl. engr.; b. Watertown, Tenn., Nov. 23, 1919; s. Matt Martin and Mamie (Routin) A.; B.S, U. Tenn., 1947; M.S., Tex. A and M U., 1964; m. Betty Eng, Aug. 31, 1946; children—Lisbeth Elaine, Baldwin Kaye. Extension agrl. engr. Tex. A. and M U., College Station, 1947-50, 52—, tchr. adult edn.; dir., officer H& A Constrn. Co., Bryan, Tex., 1954-72; grain storage operator Mid-Brazos Valley Industries, Inc., Bryan, 1959-70; officer, dir. Crimpomatic Mill & Equipment Co., 1961—; pres. Lynndale Acres, Inc., 1966—. Cons. agrl. engr., 1960—. Served from pvt. to capt. AUS, 1943-46 from capt to maj., 1950-52; now col. Res. Decorated Bronze Star medal with oak leaf cluster. Mem. Am. Soc. Agr. Engrs., Nat., Tex. socs. profl. engrs., Tex. Agr. Workers Assn., Profl. Engrs. in Pvt. Practice, Res. Officers Assn. Baptist. Mason. (Shriner). Contbr. articles to profl. jours. Home: 521 Moran St Bryan TX 77801 Office: Box 304 Tex A and M U College Station TX 77840

ALLERS, JOHN CHRISTIAN, broadcasting co. exec.; b. New Milford, N.J., Jan. 15,, 1918; s. John Christian and Edna Susan (Reeve) A.; student N.C. State Coll., 1936-38; certificate N.Y. State U., Morrisville, 1939; m. Lorraine Humphrey, July 7, 1942; children—Katherine Lee, Susan Carol (Mrs. Paul Frizell Miller). Salesman, Copeland &Thompson, Inc., N.Y.C., 1939-41, Manhattan Soap Co., Raleigh, 1952-53; asst. mgr. Kimbrell's Furniture Co., Raleigh, N.C., 1945-50; sales mgr. Capital Broadcasting Co., Raleigh, 1960-68; with Durham Life Broadcasting Service, Raleigh, 1968—, gen. sales mgr., 1969—. Pres. P.T.A., 1963-65; chmn. Millbrook Adv. Council, 1964-69. Bd. dirs. Wake Found Inc., pres. 1969—. Served to 1st lt. AUS, 1941-45. Mem. Assn. Nat. Farm Broadcasters, Nat. Agrl. Advt. and Marketing Assn., Sales and Marketing Execs. Club, Raleigh Advt. Club (sec. 1971-72). Baptist (deacon 1969-71). Clubs: Raleigh Sports (dir. 1970-73), Civitan (Raleigh). Home: 3315 Baugh St Raleigh NC 27604 Office: 410 S Salisbury St Raleigh NC 29602

ALLEY, J. T., JR., city ofcl.; b. Lubbock, Tex., June 26, 1923; s. J.T. and Edna Ann (Mullins) A.; student FBI Nat. Acad., 1952, Tex. Technol. U., 1955-56, U. Okla., 1962, U. Louisville, 1963, U. Tex., 1967; m. Dorris D'Arlene Reed, Jan. 8, 1944; children—Mary Ann (Mrs. David Andy Wilkinson), Patricia K., Billie D'Arlene, Jaye Tori. Patrolman, Lubbock Police Dept., 1946-47, Sgt., 1947-51, capt., 1951-57, chief of police 1957—. Served with USMCR, 1942-46. Mem. Am. Fedn. Police, Internat. Assn. Chiefs of Police (chmn. emergency planning com. 1972—). Methodist. Rotarian (dir. 1968-70). Home: 4207 39th St Lubbock TX 79413 Office: Box 2000 Lubbock TX 79457

ALLGEIER, ROBERT KEITH, aerospace engr.; b. Albany, Ga., Oct. 14, 1941; s. Robert Keith and Mary Ann (Johnson) A.; student Adams State Coll., Colo., 1959-60; B.S., N.M. State U., 1964; M.S., U. Houston, 1973. Aerospace engr., contract adminstr. NASA, Johnson Space Center, Houston, 1964—. Recipient Apollo Achievement award, Apollo Group Achievement award NASA, 1969; NASA Patent award, 1970. Registered profl. engr., Tex. Mem. Pi Tau Sigma, Sigma Tau. Republican. Author: The Development of Cryogenic Storage Systems for Spaceflight, 1971. Patentee in field. Home: 2001 San Sebastian Ct Houston TX 77058 Office: 2101 Nasa Blvd Houston TX 77058

ALLIN, JOHN MAURY, clergyman; b. Helena, Ark., Apr. 22, 1921; s. Richard and Dora (Harper) A.; B.A., U. South, 1943, B.D., 1945; M.Ed., Miss. Coll., 1960; m. Frances Ann Kelly, Oct. 18, 1949; children—Martha May, John Maury, Kelly Ann, Frances Elizabeth. Ordained to ministry Protestant Episcopal Ch.; vicar St. Peter's Mission, Conway, Ark., vicar of chs., Harrison, Euraka Springs, Russellville (all Ark.), 1945-49; curate St. Andrews Ch., New Orleans, 1950-52; rector Grace Ch., Monroe, La., 1952-58; pres., rector All Saints' Jr. Coll., Vicksburg, Miss., 1958-61; consecrated bishop coadjutor Episcopal Diocese Miss., 1961-66, diocesan bishop, 1966—, presiding bishop, 1973—. Chmn. dept. Christian edn. Diocese La.; v.p. dept. Christian edn. Province of Sewanee; mem. joint com. on ecumenical relations; adv. com. on deaconesses House of Bishops; pres. Com. of Concern, 1966-67. Bd. regents U. South; trustee All Saints' Sch.; chmn. bd. dirs. Sewanee Summer Tng. Sch. Mem. Newcomen Soc., St. Luke's Alumni Assn. U. South, Kappa Sigma. Home: 3775 Old Canton Rd Jackson MS 39216 Office: 112 S West St Jackson MS 39201

ALLISON, FRED, JR., physician, educator; b. Abingdon, Va., Sept. 8, 1922; s. Fred and Elizabeth Harriet (Kelly) A.; B.S., Ala. Poly. Inst., 1944; M.D., Vanderbilt U., 1946; m. Clara Knox, Oct. 18, 1949; children—Rebecca (Mrs. Henry Nutt Parsley), Martha, Fred, Robert Gardiner. Intern Vanderbilt Hosp., Nashville, 1946-47; resident Peter Bent Brigham Hosp., Boston, 1949-50; practice medicine, specializing in internal medicine, 1946—; asst. prof. medicine Washington U., St. Louis, 1955; prof. medicine, head infectious disease dept. U. Miss., Jackson, 1955-68; prof. medicine, head dept. medicine La. State U., New Orleans, 1968—; head La. State U. div. Charity Hosp., 1968—. Served with AUS, 1943-46, 47-49. Diplomate Am. Bd. Internal Medicine. Home: 7821 Freret St New Orleans LA 70118 Office: 1542 Tulane Av New Orleans LA 70112

ALLISON, HANSELL JACK, educator; b. Baton Rouge, Jan. 16, 1938; s. Hanselle Jullian and Nonnie (Young) A.; B.S. in Elec. Engring., La. State U., 1959; M.S. in Elec. Engring., 1961; Ph.D. in Elec. Engring., Okla. State U., 1966; postgrad., 1966-68; m. Carol Lynn Chase, Oct. 11, 1971; 1 son, Jeremy Hale. Draftsman and design engr. Gen. Dynamics, Ft. Worth, 1957-59; design engr. Tex. Instruments, Dallas, 1959-61; prof. engring. Okla. State U., Stillwater, 1961—. Registered profl. engr., Okla. Mem. I.E.E.E., Am. Soc. Elec. Engrs., Okla. Soc. Profl. Engrs. (Outstanding Engring. Achievement in Okla. award 1972). Triangle (faculty adviser 1963—), Sigma Xi, Tau Beta Pi, Phi Mu Epsilon, Pi Eta Sigma, Sigma Tau (faculty advisor 1966-68). Contbr. articles to profl. jours. Patentee in energy conversion and storage. Home: 1006 Ridge Rd Stillwater OK 74079

ALLISON, IRL, pianist, music educator; b. Warren, Tex., Apr. 8, 1896; s. John Van and Mary Cleona (Richardson) A.; A.B., Baylor U., 1915, A.M., 1922; D.Mus. (hon.), Southwestern Conservatory, Dallas, 1947; LL.D., Hardin-Simmons U., 1954; attended Chgo. Mus. Coll., summer 1919, Columbia U., 1920-21, summers 1942, U. Tex., 1943; Dr. Music (hon.), Houston Conservatory, 1954; piano study Ezra Rachlin, Rudolph Hoffman, Josef Evans, Percy Grainger, Ernest Hutcheson, Harold von Mickwitz, Walter Gilewicz; m. Jessie Johnson, July 3, 1918; children—Mary J. (dec.), John (dec.), Irl, Lucille (Mrs. Therl Ockey). Dean music, Rusk Coll., 1918-19; instr. piano Baylor Coll. Women, 1921-23; dean fine arts Montezuma Coll., 1923-27; dean music Hardin-Simmons Univ., 1927-34. Founder, pres. Nat. Guild Piano Tchrs.; pres. Am. Coll. Musicians, 1934-60; founder Golden Rule Peace Movement and originator World Peace Programs (radio), 1948; mgr. Nat. Piano-Playing Auditions (founder), 1929-60; editor Piano Guild Notes, 1951-60. Mem. Music Tchrs. Nat. Assn., Music Educators Nat. Conf., Nat. Music Council, Author: Through the Years; Our George. Compiler editor Irl Allison Piano Library, 33 vols. Contbr. to newspapers, music publications. Co-founder, donor grand prize Van Cliburn Internat. Quadrennial Piano Competition. Home: 1500 Murray Lane Austin TX 78703

ALLISON, JULIAN TRACY, real estate broker; b. Greer, S.C., Dec. 24, 1934; s. Tracy H. and Nell (Whitlock) A.; B.S., U.S.C., 1959; postgrad. U. Tenn., 1959-61; m. Kaye Turbyfill, Sept. 1, 1956 (div. 1973); children—Julian Tracy II, Jason Whitlock. Real estate broker, 1962—; organizer United State Acres, Ltd., 1964; organizer, chmn. bd. Security Fed. Savs. & Loan Assn., Alcoa, Tenn., 1967—; owner Julian T. Allison Enterprises, Maryville, Tenn., 1964—; organizer, pres. Allied Realty, Inc., Lakeside Park, Inc., Maryville; organizer, partner John Sevier Townhouses, Maryville; partner Smoky Mountain Trailer Sales; chmn. bd. Concepts, Inc., Kingsport, Tenn.; gen. partner Concepts, Ltd., Kingsport; pres. Sexton Enterprises, Inc., Bristol, Tenn. Served with USNR, 1952-55. Mem. Maryville-Alcoa (past pres.), Knoxville (past dir.) homebuilders assns., Maryville Bd. Realtors (past v.p., dir.). Address: Alcoa Hwy at Lakemont Box 1026 Maryville TN 37801

ALLISON, MARSHALL L., lawyer; b. Lavonia, Ga., Mar. 3, 1897; s. Thomas F. and Gertrude (Bost) A.; B.S., Young Harris Coll., 1915-3m. Marion W. Willbanks, Aug. 27, 1919; 1 dau., Julia Carolyn (Mrs. Robert J. Urick). Admitted to Ga. bar, 1926, practiced in Lavonia, 1926-36, city atty., 1926-36; asst. atty. gen. of Ga., Atlanta, 1937-38, 1938-41, 1943-45; judge No. Jud. Circuit of Ga., Lavonia, 1938; law asst. to chief justice of Ga. Supreme Court, 1941-42; pvt. practice of law under own name, Atlanta, 1945-53; in law practice, Lavonia, Ga., 1953—; apptd. mem. Jud. Council Ga., 1962-64. U.S. Supreme Court, 1936. Trustee Young Harris Coll., 1942—. Served with F.A., U.S. Army, World War I. Mem. Am., Ga. bar assns., Bar Assn. No. Jud. Circuit Ga., Am. Legion (1st comdr.). Methodist (steward). Lion (1st pres.). Author: Compiled Opinions of Attorney General of Georgia, 1939-41, 1941-43. Address: 55 Bowman St Lavonia GA 30553

ALLISON, WILLIAM ADOLPHUS, assn. exec.; b. Asheville, N.C., Sept. 1, 1911; s. Floss and Geneva Burnice (Honeycutt) A.; B.A., Erskine Coll., 1937; m. Dorothy Robinson, Aug. 14, 1941; children—Adrienne Louise (Mrs. Phillip L. Egler), William Arthur, John Robert. Boys work dir. YMCA, Spartanburg, S.C., 1937-42; youth dir., phys. dir. YMCA, Roanoke, Va., 1942-52; exec. sec. West Fulton br. YMCA, Atlanta, 1952-57; exec. dir. YMCA, Clearwater, Fla., 1957-67, YMCA of Pickens County, Easley, S.C., 1967—. Mem. Nat. Council YMCAs, 1958-61. Scout master Boy Scouts Am., 1935-37; active A.R.C., Camp Fire Girls. Bd. dirs. YMCA Blue Ridge Assembly, 1963-65. Served with USNR, 1943-45. Presbyn. (elder). Lion. Home: 405 Laurel Rd Easley SC 29640 Office: 201 Burns Rd Easley SC 29640

ALLISON, WILLIAM BURGESS, coal co. exec.; b. Monteray, Tenn., Sept. 5, 1925; s. Virgil Croft and Anna M. (Copeland) A.; student U. South, 1943-44, Princeton, 1944, Columbia, 1945; B.S. Tenn. Tech. U., 1948; m. Katy Helen Garner, Aug. 25, 1963; children—Ann Grier, William Kenneth, Mrs. Larry Wayne Thomas. Accountant, Central Coal Co., Monteray, Tenn., 1948-49; chief accountant, dept. mgr. Cumberland Elec. Membership Corp., 1949-50; U.S. govt. cost accountant Arnold Engring. Devel. Center, Tullahoma, Tenn., 1951; pub. accountant, Fayetteville, Tenn., 1951-54; owner, operator Largin Motor Inn and Restaurant, Fayetteville, 1954-60; exec. v.p. Tenn. Consol. Coal Co., ICC Internat., Nashville, Tracy City and Jasper, 1960—, also dir.; dir. cos. including Grundy Mining Co., Chestnut Coal Co., Va. Mining Co., Walnut Coal Co., Whitewell Coal Corp. Lectr., Austin Peay State Coll., Clarksburg, Tenn., 1949-50. Active various civic drives; mem. Marion County Indsl. Adv. Bd., Jasper, Tenn., 1968—. Served to lt. (j.g.) USNR, 1943-46; PTO. Mem. Lincoln County C. of C. (dir. 1953-57). Presbyn. (deacon 1952-61). Kiwanian. Home: PO Box 865 Victoria Av Jasper TN 37347 Office: PO Box 878 Betsy Pack Dr Jaser TN 37347

ALLMAN, ELAINE GIBBARD (MRS. MAURICE R. ALLMAN), lawyer; b. Sulphur, Okla., Mar. 14, 1945; d. Frank and Veva Jean (Rogers) Gibbard; student Swarthmore Coll., 1962-64; B.A., Okla. U., 1966, J.D., 1969; m. Maurice R. Allman, Nov. 25, 1967. Admitted to Okla. bar, 1969; mem. firm Gibbard, Allman & Allman, Sulphur, 1969—; U.S. magistrate, Eastern Dist. of Okla., 1971—. Pres. Murray County Women's Democratic Club, 1972—; 1st alternate del. to Dem. Nat. Conv., 1972. Mem. Order of the Coif, Am. Bar Assn., Okla. Bar. Assn. (civil rights com. 1971), Okla. Trial Lawyers Assn., Am. Civil Liberties Union, Phi Alpha Delta. Home: PO Box 624 Sulphur OK 73086 Office: PO Box 436 Sulphur OK 73086

ALLRED, DEWITT TALMAGE, physician; b. Caseyville, Miss., July 27, 1890; s. John Sylvester and Alla (McLaurin) A.; B.S., U. Miss., 1916; M.D., Tulane U., 1918; m. Velma Ann Watkins, Dec. 1, 1920; children—DeWitt Talmage, Doris Mae (Mrs. C.E. Bane, Jr.), Anne (Mrs. G.H. Bethea). Intern, Charity Hosp., New Orleans, 1918-19; practice medicine, Collins, Miss., 1919—. Examiner, SSS, 1940—. Served with USNR, 1918-20. Recipient Presdl. citation for 30 years service to SSS, 1970. Mem. A.M.A., Miss. Med. Assn., S. Miss. Med. Soc. Mason, Rotarian. Address: PO O Box 302 Collins MS 39428

ALLSBROOK, OGDEN OLMSTEAD, JR., educator; b. Wilmington, N.C., July 1, 1940; s. Ogden Olmstead and Elizabeth Barringer (Warren) A.; A.B., Wake Forest U., 1962; Ph.D., U. Va., 1966. Asst. prof. econs. U. Miami, Coral Gables, Fla., 1965-66; operations research analyst U.S. Dept. Def., Washington, 1966-68; asst. prof. econs. U. Ga., Athens, 1968-73, asso. prof. econs., 1973—. Lectr. U. Md., College Park, 1967-68. Served to capt. AUS, 1966-68. Decorated Army Commendation medal. Mem. Am., So., Western econs. assns., Pub. Choice Soc., A.A.A.S., Royal Econs. Soc., Atlanta Econs. Club, Omicron Delta Epsilon, Lambda Chi Alpha. Lutheran. Author: The Utilization of Military Resources, 1968; A Survey of Army Automated Cost Models, 1968. Home: 107 Ashley Circle Apt 6 Athens GA 30601

ALLUISI, EARL ARTHUR, psychologist, educator; b. Richmond, Va., June 11, 1927; s. Humbert Peter and Elizabeth Mary (Dini) A.; B.S., Coll. William and Mary, 1949; M.A., Ohio State U., 1950, Ph.D., 1954; m. Mary Jane Boyle, Dec. 16, 1954; children—John, Jean, Paul, Janet. Research psychologist Army Med. Research Lab., Ft. Knox, 1951-52; vis. instr. psychology dept. Coll. William and Mary, summers 1953-54; research asso., lectr. Ohio State U., 1954-57; head environmental factors sect. U.S. Army Med. Research Lab., 1957-58; head engring. psychology Stanford Research Inst., 1958-59; from asst. prof. to asso. prof. psychology Emory U., 1959-61; asso. scientist human factors research lab. Lockheed-Ga. Co., 1961-63; lectr. Ga. Inst. Tech., 1962-63; prof. psychology U. Louisville, 1963-74, asst. dean Grad. Sch., 1966-67, exec. officer for planning and devel., 1967-69, asso. dean Grad. Sch., 1970-71, dir. performance research lab., 1968-72, research prof. 1968-74, v.p. planning and instl. research 1971-74; univ. prof. Old Dominion U., 1974—; with I.D.A., 1969-70. Served as capt. AUS, 1944-47, 50-52, 57-58. Fellow Am. (div. pres. 1973-74), Ky. (pres. 1966-67) psychol. assns., A.A.A.S.; mem. Psychonomic Soc., Psychometric Soc., So. Soc. Philosophy and Psychology (sec. 1962-65, councilman 1965-66, pres. 1967-68), Ky. Acad. Sci. (chmn. psychol. sect. 1964-65), Am. Assn. U. Profs., Am. Council for Higher Edn., Ky. Humanities Council (pres., chmn. bd. 1972-73), Human Factors Soc., Ky. Civil Liberties Union (dir. 1964-74, chmn. 1972-74), Phi Beta Kappa, Sigma Xi, Psi Chi, Alpha Psi Delta, Phi Kappa Phi. Home: 1421 Rylands Rd Virginia Beach VA 23455

ALLYN, KENNETH HERSCHEL, city ofcl.; b. Elyria, O., Feb. 17, 1912; s. Richard H. and Frances Hanna (Briggs) A.; student U. Mich., 1930-32, LaSalle U., 1938-40; m. Mabel Christine Walsh, July 25, 1938;children—John Kenneth, Joyce (Mrs. Robert E. Coleman). Accountant, City of Coral Gables (Fla.), 1935-40, purchasing agt., 1940-45, chief accountant, 1945-56, asst. finance dir., 1956-59, finance dir., 1959—. Recipient Good Government award Jr. C. of C., 1968-69. Mem. Municipal Finance Officers Assn. U.S. and Can. (Fla. chpt. pres. 1954-55, Fla. chmn. 1956-71, exec. bd. 1971-73, dir. 1971, mem. Hall of Fame), Fla. Soc. Ins. Buyers (pres. 1966-67). Office: PO Drawer 1549 Coral Gables FL 33134

ALMACK, DON LEE, banker; b. Tonkawa, Okla., July 7, 1927; s. Dennis F. and Juanita (McBride) A.; grad. high sch.; m. Beryle D. Dingler, July 12, 1947; 1 son, Glenn A. Loan officer First Nat. Bank & Trust Co., Oklahoma City, 1947-55; v.p. Capitol Hill State Bank, Oklahoma City, 1955-63, 64—; pres. Grant Sq. Bank & Trust Co.,

Oklahoma City, 1963-64. Sec., v.p., bd. dirs. Okla. Goodwill Industries. Served with USAAF, 1945-46, USAF, 1951-52. Mem. Christian Ch. Club: Capitol Hill Sertoma (sec., past chmn. bd., pres.). Home: 2109 SW 71st St Oklahoma City OK 73159 Office: 700 SW 29th St Oklahoma City OK 73109

ALMAND, BOND, ret. judge; b. Lithonia, Ga., Jan. 13, 1894; s. Alexander James and Clara Emily (Bond) A.; Ph.B., Emory U., 1913; LL.B., Columbia, 1916, A.M., 1916; m. Helen Whitefoot Barnett, June 18, 1932; children—Helen (Mrs. Roy F. Morgan, Jr.), Bond. Admitted to Ga. bar, 1916; practiced in Atlanta, 1916-42; asst. city atty., 1939-42; judge Fulton County Superior Ct., 1942-43, 1945-49, asso. justice Supreme Ct. of Ga., 1949-69; chief justice Supreme Ct. of Ga., 1969—; solicitor Criminal Ct. Fulton County, 1939-42; lectr. Emory U. Sch. Law, 1951-72. Rep. Ga. Gen. Assembly, 1935-38. Served as 1st lt., Inf., U.S. Army, with 82d and 9th divs., A.E.F., World War I. Mem. Am. Bar Assn., Inst. Jud. Adminstrn., Phi Beta Kappa, Sigma Nu, Phi Alpha Delta, Omicron Delta Kappa. Episcopalian. Home: 3291 Rilman Rd NW Atlanta GA 30327

ALMON, ROBERT NATHANIEL, civil engr.; b. Selma, Ala., May 3, 1933; s. Nathaniel and Mary (Johnson) A.; B.S., U. Ala., 1955, M.S., 1964; m. Marion H. Skinner, Sept. 10, 1955; children—Mary Julia, Robert Nathaniel. Engr., Alsey C. Parker & Son, Tuscaloosa, Ala., 1958-69, pres., sr. partner, 1969-73; pres., sr. partner Almon & Assos. Inc. cons. engrs., Tuscaloosa, 1973—. Pres., dir. Tuscaloosa Testing Lab. Inc., 1970—. Leader, Black Warrior council Boy Scouts Am., 1964-68. Served to comdr. C.E., AUS, 1955-57. Registered profl. engr. Ala. Mem. Cons. Engrs. Council Ala. (state treas. and dir., 1970-72), Am. Soc. C.E., Am. Water Works Assn., Nat. Soc. Profl. Engrs., Am. Cons. Engrs. Council, Tuscaloosa C. of C., Kappa Alpha. Presbyn. Rotarian. Home: 723 Canyon Rd Tuscaloosa AL 35401 Office: 1312 24th Av Tuscaloosa AL 35401

ALMOND, VANCE DELMA, engr.; b. Albemarle, N.C., July 17, 1912; s. John Albert and Nora Magdoline (Sides) A.; B.S., N.C. State U., 1937; m. Harriett Yolande Welch, May 23, 1941; 1 dau., Harriett Elizabeth. Engr. Carolina Power & Light Co., Raleigh, N.C., 1937-41, TVA, Nashville, 1946-60, Muscle Shoals, Ala., 1960—. Served with AUS, 1941-46. Decorated Bronze Star medal. Mason. Club: Golf and Country (Florence, Ala.). Home: 1930 Fairfax Dr Florence AL 35630 Office: 522 First Fed Bldg Florence AL 35630

ALPERT, ESTHER SHIRLEY OFFERMAN (MRS. BARNETT ALPERT), civic worker; b. N.Y.C.; d. Samuel and Sadie (Meyers) Offerman; B.A., Hunter Coll., 1930, postgrad., 1933-36; m. Barnett Alpert, June 17, 1932; children—Michael Allen, Judith Ruth. Substitute tchr. N.Y.C. Sch. System, 1940-45; caseworker Dept. Welfare, N.Y.C., 1933-38. Vice-pres. Mental Health Assn. Broward County, Fla., 1961, pres., 1962-65; coordinator vol. services South Fla. State Hosp., 1963-65; mem. Coummunity Mental Health Planning Com., 1964-69, 73—; chmn. South br. Broward County Med. Aux., 1965-66; state chmn. mental health Fla. Med. Aux., 1966-68; v.p. Henderson Clinic Broward County, 1965-66, pres., 1966-67, corr. sec., 1967-68, bd. dirs., 1971—, rec. sec., 1973—; mem. exec. com. N.Y. Philanthropic League, N.Y.C., 1952-56; rec. sec. Fla. Adv. Council on Mental Health, 1968-69, vice chmn., 1969—; mem. Com. on Aging, 1964-65; founder, adviser Mental Health Forum, Broward County, 1961—. Recipient Bronze plaque for services rendered to mentally ill Mental Health Assn. Fla., 1965. Mem. Nat. Council Jewish Women (exec. com. 1958-60), Hadassah (pres. United Order True Sisters 1950-51), Hunter Coll. Alumni Assn., Am. Jewish Congress. Jewish religion. Home: 1135 N North Lake Dr Hollywood FL 33020

ALSOBROOK, JAMES SAMUEL, JR., interior designer; b. Rossville, Ga., June 21, 1918; s. James S. and Ettie (Hullender) A.; B.S., U. Chattanooga, 1939; postgrad. U. Ga., U. Ala., N.Y. Sch. Interior Design; m. Alice E. Jobron, July 15, 1945; 1 dau., Lynn. Gen. practice interior design, Chattanooga, 1948—; pres. Alsobrook Decor, Chattanooga, 1953—; chmn. bd. ADX Corp., 1966—; design. cons. to bd. Caldsted Found. Bd. dirs. Houston Mus. Served with USAAF, 1942-45. Fellow Inst. Profl. Designers London; mem. Am. Inst. Interior Designers (state bd. dirs.), Pi Kappa Alpha, Gamma Sigma Epsilon, Phi Chi. Presbyn. Patentee in field. Home: 1619 Fairydell Trail Lookout Mountain TN 37350 Office: 900 Mcalle Av Chattanooga TN 37403

ALSTON, CLARENCE WYATT, banker; b. Richmond, Va., June 12, 1926; s. Joseph John and Elizabeth (Alston) A.; student U. Richmond, 1943-44, 46-47; B.B.A., Emory U., 1949; m. Anne Elizabeth Simpson, Aug. 21, 1954; children—Allen Davies, Charles Wyatt, Joanne Elizabeth, Susan Douglas. Supr., Miller & Rhoads, Richmond, 1949-50; asst. cashier Bank Va., Richmond, 1950-60, sr. v.p., 1962—; bank examiner U.S. Treasury Dept., Charlotte, N.C., 1960-62. Pres. Richmond chpt. Easter Seal Soc., 1965-67. Served with USNR, 1944-45. Mem. Richmond C. of C., Va. C. of C., Am. Inst. Banking (pres. Richmond chpt. 1956-57, mem. adv. bd.), Va. (chmn. installment credit com. 1965-67), Am. (adv. bd. installment credit com. 1967—), consumer (gov. 1972—) bankers assns., Alpha Kappa Psi, Phi Gamma Delta. Republican. Presbyn. Clubs: Civitan (pres. Richmond 1968-69), Bull and Bear; Salisbury Country. Home: 2436 Chancellor Rd Richmond VA 23235 Office: 800 E Main St Richmond VA 23214

ALTER, RONALD, educator; b. N.Y.C., Mar. 27, 1939; s. Manny and Charlotte (Harris) A.; B.S., City Coll. N.Y., 1960; M.A. (Teaching fellow 1960-62; NSF Summer fellow 1962), U. Pa., 1962, Ph.D. (Research fellow 1962-64), 1965; m. Arlene Barbara London, Nov. 16, 1963; children—Roy Samuel, Robin Damian, Tao Daniel. Asst. prof. math. U. Cal., Los Angeles, 1964-67; math. analyst Litton Systems, Inc., Beverly Hills, Cal., 1966; asso. research scientist System Devel. Corp., Santa Monica, Cal., 1968-69; asst. prof. math. and computer sci. U. Ky., Lexington, 1970-71, asso. prof. computer sci., 1971—, dir. grad. studies dept. computer sci., 1973—. Recipient postdoctoral Research fellowship U. Pa., 1967-68. Mem. Am. Math. Soc., Math. Assn. Am., Assn. for Computing Machinery. Contbr. articles to profl. jours. Home: 521 N Broadway Lexington KY 40508

ALTOFT, MURLIN WILLIAM, retail trade exec., clergyman; b. Rochester, N.Y., July 8, 1940; s. Orlo Bertram and Jeannie Wilhelm Altoft; B.S., Evangel Coll., 1964; postgrad. Wesley Theol. Sem., 1965-66, Am. U., 1969-71; m. Marilyn Jean Kimel, June 10, 1961; children—Carmella Jean, Christina Jo. Treas., Kimels Furniture, Inc., Arlington, Va., 1968-71, v.p., 1971—; ordained minister Assembly of God, 1973; pastor Key to Life ch., McLean, Va., 1972—. Home: 1030 Dead Run Dr McLean VA 22101 Office: 4040 Four Mile Run Dr Arlington VA 22206

ALTOUNEY, EDWARD GREGORY, civil engr.; b. N.Y.C., June 1, 1933; s. Edward Gregory and Jeanne (Baladi) A.; Dipl. Civil Engr. magna cum laude, M.S. in Physics, U. Lyon, 1955; postgrad. Mass. Inst. Tech., 1956-57; Ph.D. in Civil Engring., Stanford, 1963. Research engr. Gen. Electric Co., 1955-56; research asst. hydrodynamic lab. Mass. Inst. Tech., Cambridge, 1956-57; asso. engr. Boeing Airplane Co., Washington, 1957-58; asst. hydraulic engr. Dept. Water Resources, State Cal., Sacramento, 1958-60, asso. engr., 1960-63, sr. engr., program mgr. water resources, 1963-64; systems analyst Stanford Research Inst., Menlo Park, Cal., 1964-65, engr.-economist, 1965-67; phys. scientist Office Water Resources Research, U.S. Dept. Interior, Washington, 1967-71, sci. tech. research mgr., 1971-72; staff asst. Office of Asst. Sec., U.S. Dept. Interior, Washington, 1972-73; sr. specialist in engring. and pub. works Congl. Research Service, Library of Congress, Washington, 1973—. Research fellow engring. U. Cal., Los Angeles, 1964; guest lectr. U. Cal., 1969, U. Ill., 1971, Okla. State U., 1971, N.C. State U., 1973; cons. water resources project U.S. engring. firms, 1963-67. Registered profl. engr., Cal. Mem. Am. Geophys. Union, Am. Soc. C.E., Am. Water Resources Assn. Home: 1400 S Joyce St Arlington VA 22202 Office: Library of Congress Washington DC 20540

ALTSCHUL, AARON MAYER, educator, govt. ofcl.; b. Chgo., Mar. 13, 1914; s. Philip and Sophie (Fox) A.; B.S., U. Chgo., 1934, Ph.D. in Phys. Chemistry, 1937; m. Ruth Braude, Oct. 24, 1937; children—Sandra (Mrs. M. Frank Norman), Judith (Mrs. David Bonderman). Mem. spectroscopic biol. investigation unit dept. chemistry U. Chgo., 1937-41; mem. staff So. Regional Research Lab., U.S. Dept. Agr., New Orleans, 1941-67, head protein and carbohydrate div., 1949-52, head oilseed sect., 1952-58, chief research chemist Seed Protein Pioneering Research Lab., 1958-66; spl. asst. to sec. agr., Washington, 1966; spl. asst. for internat. nutrition improvement Internat. Agrl. Devel. Service, cons. to sec. agr., 1967-69; spl. asst. to sec. for nutrition improvement, 1969-1971; prof. dept. community medicine and internat. health Georgetown U. Sch. Medicine, Washington, 1971—. Prof. dept. chemistry, lectr. dept. biochemistry, Tulane, 1943-66; lectr. dept. nutrition and food sci. Mass. Inst. Tech., 1951-70. Mem. sub-panel on increasing high quality protein Pres.'s Sci. Adv. Com., 1968; adv. com. Inst. Nutrition Central Am., Panama, 1964; research cons. Nat. Cottonseed Products Assn., 1954-63; mem. panel on nutrition U.S.-Japan Coop. Med. Research Program, 1966-70. Mem. agrl. bd. Nat. Acad. Scis.-NRC, 1969-72; mem. nat. adv. council Monell Chem. Senses Center, U. Pa., 1968-72; mem. select com. GRAS substances Am. Soc. Exptl. Biology, 1972-73. Mem. Am. Soc. Biol. Chemists, Am. Chem. Soc., Inst. Food Technologists, Am. Inst. Nutrition, Phi Beta Kappa, Sigma Xi, Phi Tau Sigma. Author: Proteins, Their Chemistry and Politics, 1965. Editor: Processed Plant Protein Foodstuffs, 1958; New Protein Foods, Vol. 1A Technology, 1974. Editorial bd. Econ. Botany, Plant Foods for Human Nutrition; editorial adv. bd. Chem. and Engring. News. Contbr. numerous articles to profl. publs. Patentee in field. Home: 700 New Hampshire Av NW Washington DC 20037

ALVARADO-TIZOL, HECTOR MANUEL, oral surgeon, lawyer; b. Carolina, P.R., Mar. 26, 1935; s. Antonio Benito and Amina (Tizol) Alvarado; B.S., The Citadel Mil. Coll. S.C., 1956; D.M.D., U. P.R., 1961; J.D., Interam. U., 1974; m. Carmen Theresa Munoz, Dec. 28, 1957; children—Maria Victoria, Antonio Ramon, Carmen Teresa, Marta Larissa. Research asso. Univ. Hosp., San Juan, P.R., 1963-64; resident oral surgery San Juan Municipal Hosp., 1964-67, attending oral surgeon, 1967—. Served to capt. AUS, 1961-63. Mem. Am. Dental Assn., P.R. Soc. Oral Surgeons, Phi Delta Gamma. Democrat. Roman Catholic. Club: Exchange (pres. 1969—) (San Francisco); Santa Maria (Rio Piedras, P.R.). Contbr. articles to profl. jours. Home: Beverly Hills Bo Río Guaynabo PR 00657 Office: RFD No 3243K Rio Piedras PR 00928

ALVERSON, LUTHER, superior ct. judge; b. East Point, Ga., Aug. 13, 1907; s. James Carroll and Minnie (Flemning)A.; student Emory U., LL.B., Atlanta Law Sch. 1941; m. Ruth Long, Mar. 21, 1942; children—Elizabeth (Mrs. Richard P. Heist), Patricia (Mrs. Robert M. Kelly). Admitted to Ga. bar, 1941; practiced in Atlanta, 1941-52; mem. firms Hooper, Hooper & Miller, 1941-43, Woodruff, Alverson & O'Neal, 1946-48; mem. Ga. Ho. of Reps., 1948-52; judge Fulton County Criminal Ct., Ga., 1952-56, Atlanta Jud. Circuit Superior Ct., 1957—. Bd. dirs., pres. YMCA; bd. dirs. Community Council, Ga. Assn. Mental Health, Family Service Soc., Atlanta; mem. exec. com. Joint Information Service; chmn. joint information service Am. Psychiat. Assn. and Nat. Assn. for Mental Health. Chmn. bd. dirs., exec. com. Nat. Assn. for Mental Health, 1953-60, pres., 1957-59, bd. dirs., 1966-69, 69-72, v.p. region, 1967-69. Served from pvt. to 1st lt., AUS, 1943-45. Mem. Ga. Council Superior Ct. Judges (pres. 1965-66), Am. Ga., Atlanta bar assns., Atlanta Lawyers Club, Delta Theta Phi (dean alumni senate). Democrat. Baptist. Clubs: Atlanta Athletic, Buckhead Civitan, Piedmont Driving, Druid Hills Golf (Atlanta). Home: 3635 Rembrandt Rd Atlanta GA 30327 Office: Fulton County Ct House Atlanta GA 30303

ALVES, REX DOUGLAS, accountant, educator; b. Tampa, Fla., Aug. 7, 1935; s. Clifford and Alma Lucile (Peters) A.; B.S., Fla. So. Coll., 1958; M.C.S., Rollins Coll., 1970; m. Joan Costen Edwards, June 29, 1961 (div. Mar. 1971). Internal revenue agt. Internal Revenue Service, Orlando, Fla., 1960-71; partner Stanaland & Alves, C.P.A.'s, Orlando, 1971-72; practice accounting, Orlando, 1972—. Adj. instr. Rollins Coll., Winter Park, Fla., 1970—. C.P.A., Fla. Mem. Am. Inst. C.P.A.'s, Fla. Inst. C.P.A.'s, Pi Kappa Phi, Delta Sigma Pi. Home: 690 Osceola Av Apt 210 Winter Park FL 32789 Office: PO Box 1545 Winter Park FL 32789

ALVIS, JAMES CHESTER, former ednl. adminstr.; b. Thomas, Okla., July 29, 1903; s. William Elmer and Effie (Falen) A.; grad. Southwestern State Tchrs. Coll., 1928; M.A., N. Tex. State Coll., 1943; m. Fairy Jewel McCain, July 20, 1928; 1 dau., Chestella Ann (Mrs. William A. Hudel). Athletic coach, tchr., Crescent, Okla., 1926-27, 28-29, Weatherford, Okla., 1927-28; prin. high sch., Temple, Okla., 1929-39; supt. schs., Byers, 1939-43, Springlake, 1943-45, Bandera, 1945-57, Nordheim, 1957-68 (all Tex.), ret., 1968; dir. Dist. III Soil and Water Conservation. Mayor, Nordheim, Tex. Active Boy Scouts; life mem. Parent Tchrs. Assn. Mem. N.E.A., Am., Tex assns. sch. adminstrs. Lion, Mason; mem. Order Eastern Star. Home: PO Box 158 Nordheim TX 78141 Office: 500 N Broadway Nordheim TX 78141

AMACKER, DAVID MUIR, educator, planter; b. East Carroll Parish, La., Feb. 26, 1897; s. Amos Kent and Elizabeth Chalmers (Muir) A.; student Miss. Coll., 1912-13; A.B., Princeton, 1917; B.A. (Rhodes scholar), Oxford U., 1922, M.A., 1927. YMCA relief worker, Germany, summer 1920; researcher Inquiry; N.Y.C., spring 1923; instr. Culver (Ind.) Mil. Acad., 1923-26; instr. polit. sci. Dartmouth, 1926-30, asst. prof., 1930-36; asso. prof. history La. Poly. Inst., 1927-28; prof. polit. sci. Southwestern U. at Memphis, 1936-67, emeritus, 1967—, vis. prof., 1967-69; pres., dir. Hollybrook Land Co., Inc., Lake Providence, La., 1947—. Mem. secretariat Am. Commn. to Negotiate Peace, Paris, 1919; interpreter League of Nations Commn., Paris, 1919. Dir. La. Delta Council, 1949-50; mem. Beltwide Cotton Acreage Conf., 1949. Alt. N.H. del. Dem. Nat. Conv., 1936. Served with ACF, 1917-19. Mem. Phi Beta Kappa. Methodist. Home: 600 1st St Lake Providence LA 71254 Office: Hollybrook Land Co Lake Providence LA 71254

AMADEO, JOSE H., physician, educator; b. N.Y.C., July 16, 1928; s. H. R. and Carmen (Nigaglioni) A.; B.Sc., Ursinus Coll., 1948; M.D., Jefferson Med. Coll., 1952; m. Patricia Carron; children—Jose F. Javier, Luis Robert; children (by previous marriage)—Mary Martha, Jose H., John Michael, Jennifer. Intern Jefferson Med. Coll. Hosp., Phila., 1952-53, resident surgery, 1953-57, Am. Cancer Soc. fellow, 1956-57; instr. surgery Jefferson Med. Coll., 1959-61; chief surg. service San Juan (P.R.) VA Hosp., 1961—, prof. surgery U. P.R. Sch. Medicine, San Juan, 1961—. Mem. Phila. Dist. Health and Welfare Council, 1960-61. Served to capt. M.C., USAF, 1957-59; now lt. col. Res.; med. adviser to state dir. Selective Service. Diplomate Am. Bd. Surgery, Am. Bd. Thoracic Surgery, Nat. Bd. Med. Examiners. Fellow A.C.S., Internat. Soc. Surgery; mem. A.M.A., Pan Am. Med. Assn., Soc. Thoracic Surgery, Assn. Mil. Surgeons U.S., Am. Fedn. Clin. Research, Res. Officers Assn., Alpha Omega Alpha, Alpha Kappa Kappa. Republican. Roman Catholic. Contbr. articles to med. and surg. publs. Home: PO Box 10837 Caparra Heights PR 00922 Office: VA Hospital San Juan PR 00936

AMADOR, FRANCISCO ALBERTO, dentist; b. Quebradillas, P.R., Dec. 6, 1935; s. Alberto and Carmen Luisa (Rodriguez) A.; A.A., Sunflower Jr. Coll., 1953-55; predental student U. Md., 1955-57; D.M.D., U. P.R., 1961; m. Xochitl G. Aznar, June 20, 1959; children—Marissa C., Francisco A., Jorge A., Xochitl G. Individual practice dentistry, Camuy, P.R., 1964—; No. regional dir. Oral Health, Arecibo, P.R., 1963—. Mem. dental com. State Health Bd. P.R. Served with USAF, 1961-63, now maj. Res. Fellow Am. Pub. Health Assn.; mem. Colegio de Cirujanos Dentistas de P.R. (auditor 1969), Asociacion Dentistas Salud Publica de P.R. (pres. 1966-68), Am. Dental Assn., Am. Acad. Gen. Dentistry, Phi Eta Mu. Rotarian (pres. 1969-70), Lion (v.p. 1970-71). Home: Bo Terranova Quebradillas PR 00742 Office: District Hospital Arecibo PR 00612

AMBLER, ERNEST, govt. ofcl.; b. Bradford, Eng., Nov. 20, 1923; s. William and Sarah Alice (Binns) A.; B.A., New Coll., Oxford, Eng., 1945, M.A., 1946, Ph.D., 1952; m. Alice Virginia Seiler, Nov. 19, 1955; children—Christopher William, Jonathan Ernest. Came to U.S., 1953, naturalized, 1958. Physicist, Armstrong Siddeley Motors, Ltd., Coventry, Eng., 1944-48; Nuffield research fellow, Oxford, Eng., 1953; with Nat. Bur. Standards, Washington, 1953—, dep. dir., 1973—. U.S. rep. Internat. Conf. Weights and Measures. Nuffield fellow Oxford U., 1953; John Simon Guggenheim Meml. Found. fellow 1963. Recipient Gold medal Dept. Commerce, 1957; Arthur S. Flemming award Jr. C. of C., 1961; John Price Wetherill medal Franklin Inst., 1962; Stratton award Nat. Bur. Standards, 1964. Mem. Washington Acad. Scis. (award 1957), Fed. Profl. Assn. Patentee in field. Home: 6920 Blaisdell Rd Bethesda MD 20034 Office: Adminstrn Bldg Nat Bur Standards Washington DC 20234

AMBROSE, CHARLES EDWARD, artist, educator; b. Memphis, Jan. 6, 1922; s. William Thomas and Minnie (Langdon) A.; B.F.A., U. Ala., 1949, M.A., 1950; m. Betty Carol Rainer, Oct. 21, 1950; children—Charles Edward, Michael Rainer, Marc Carroll, Jamie Elizabeth. Prof. art, resident artist U. So. Miss. at Hattiesburg, 1950-70; chmn. art dept. Miss. U. for Women, 1970—; exhibited in major cities of south; art cons. U.S. Govt. programs. Pres., S. Miss. Art Assn.; mem. gov.'s staff State of Miss., 1969—; mem. adv. com. Miss. Art Assn.; trustee Hattiesburg Acad. Served with USMCR, 1941-45. Mem. Miss. Edn. Assn., La. Watercolor Soc., Internat. Platform Assn., S.E. Coll. Art Conf., So. Assn. Sculptors, Civitan Internat. (dist. gov. 1967-68). Elk. Home: 1125 7th St N Columbus MS 39701 Office: Box 70 MSCW Columbus MS 39701

AMBURN, LUTHER FRANKLIN, JR., publisher; b. Boonville, N.C., Sept. 10, 1932; s. L. F. and Martha (Oakley) A.; grad. Mitchell Coll., 1952; postgrad. U. N.C., 1952-53; m. Emily Ann Greer, June 1, 1957; children—Martha Ruth, Melissa, Luther Franklin III, Paul, Emily. Rural carrier, circulation dept. Statesville Record Landmark, 1950-53, reporter, 1953-58, news editor, 1958-62; pres., gen. mgr., pub. Chowan Herald, Inc., 1965—; exec. dir. Edenton Housing Authority, 1968—; pres. Eden Press, Inc., Cape Colony Haven, Inc.; editor, pub. New East mag.; co-mgr. Vance Motor Inn: 1962-64. Apptd. U.S. commr. Statesville div. Western Dist. Ct. of N.C., 1953-64; founder, 1st pres. Statesville Town Affiliation Council, 1961-62; sec.-treas. Iredell County Jr. Dept. Sheriff's League; pres. lo-County Albemarle Area Devel. Assn., 1972-73. Served with AUS, 1954-56. Mem. Edenton C. of C., Eastern N.C. Press Assn. (pres. 1971-72), Pi Kappa Phi. Democrat. Methodist. Elk. Clubs: Statesville City, Civitan (past pres.); Chowan Golf and Country. Home: 104 W Gale St Edenton NC 27932 Office: 421-425 S Broad St Edenton NC 27932

AMERMAN, ALMERON EARL, JR., lawyer; b. Houston, Oct. 16, 1911; s. Almeron Earl and Cordelia (Bostick) A.; B.A., Rice U., 1932; LL.B., Tex. U., 1935; m. Dorothy Blackburn Kenyon, May 27, 1936; children—Cora (Mrs. Robert Blackbird), Mary (Mrs. George Walteon Weir), June (Mrs. Frank Jeff Dyke Jr.), Dorothy. Admitted to Tex. bar, 1935, since practiced in Houston; mem. firm Fouts, Amerman and Moore, 1935-51. Served with USNR, 1943-45. Mem. Am., Houston, Tex. bar assns., Delta Kappa Epsilon. Democrat. Mem. Christian Ch. Home: 407 Pinghaven St Houston TX 77027 Office: 830 Bankers Mortgage Bldg Houston TX 77002

AMES, DONALD EUGENE, pub. relations adminstr.; b. Jacksonville, Fla., Aug. 18, 1936; s. Clarence Collins and Elizabeth Carolyn (Fountain) A.; B.S., Jacksonville U., 1959; postgrad., Boston U., 1963; m. Mary Olive Miles, Aug. 22, 1959; children—Mary Elizabeth, Sheryl Denise, Donna Lee, Travis Pendleton. Asst. to pres. Jacksonville U., 1959-60, dir. devel. 1960-65, dir. devel. and community relations, 1965—, exec. sec. univ. council, also exec. sec. devel. com. of bd. trustees, 1961—. Mem. Jacksonville Sesquicentennial Commn. Mem. Jacksonville Area C. of C., Jacksonville U. Alumni Assn. (dir. 1962-63), Am. Coll. Pub. Relations Assn., Am. Alumni Council. Toastmaster (pres. 1958-59), Kiwanian (dir. 1970-71, v.p. 1973). Home: 2976 Oak St Jacksonville FL 32205

AMES, EDWARD ALMER, JR., banker; b. Onley, Va., Jan. 22, 1903; s. Edward Almer and Lena (Trower) A.; student Randolph Macon Coll., 1919-21; A.B., Washington and Lee U., 1924; LL.B., 1925; m. Elizabeth Johnson Melson, Jan. 8, 1936; 1 son, Edward Almer III. Admitted to Va. bar, 1924, since practiced in Accomack County; commonwealth's atty., Accomack County, 1943-55; dir. First Nat. Bank, Onanock, Va., 1953—, v.p., 1956-69, pres., 1969—. Mem. Va. Senate, 1956-68; chmn. Accomack County Democratic Com., 1948-69; mem. State Central Dem. Com. Va., 1956-72. Mem. Am., Va., Accomack County (pres. 1956-57) bar assns., Order of Coif, Phi Beta Kappa, Phi Delta Phi. Democrat. Presbyn. Mason, Rotarian. Clubs; Ruritan; Eastern Shore Yacht and Country; Downtown of Richmond. Home: Accomac VA 23301 Office: Onancock VA 23417

AMES, EDWARD ALMER III, lawyer; b. Nassawadox, Va., Feb. 26, 1939; s. Edward Almer and Elizabeth Johnson (Melson) A.; B.A., Washington and Lee U., 1961, J.D., 1964; m. Elizabeth Henry Mumford, Sept. 9, 1967; children—Elizabeth Kenly, Katherine Henry. Admitted to Va. bar, 1964, since practiced in Onancock, 1964—; mem. firm Ames & Ames, 1965—. Dir. First Nat. Bank, Onancock. Mem. Accomack County Democratic Com., 1969—. Bd. dirs. Accomack County A.R.C., Eastern Shore Heart Assn. Mem. Am., Va., Accomack County (sec. treas. 1969-73) bar assns., Va. State Bar, Eastern Shore Jr. C. of C. (v.p. 1968), Omicron Delta Kappa, Phi Delta Phi, Delta Tau Delta, Pi Sigma Alpha. Presbyn. (trustee). Club:

Eastern Shore Yacht and Country. Home: Bayly Farm Onancock VA 23417 Office: Ames Bldg PO Box 177 Onancock VA 23417

AMICK, HUBERT RAY, sanitation systems co. exec.; b. Saluda County, S.C., May 16, 1918; s. Silas Effie and Blanche (Parrott) A.; student Newberry Coll., 1936-39; m. Sarah Eleanor Johnson, Oct. 23, 1940; children—Rosalyn (Mrs. John R. Carson), Harriett (Mrs. Allen P. Anderson), William Ray, Miriam Ellen. Bookkeeper, asst. cashier S.C. Nat. Bank Br., Leesville, 1940-44, asst. cashier, 1945-46, mgr., 1946; office mgr., bookkeeper State Machinery & Supply Co., West Columbia, S.C., 1946-49, exec. v.p., gen. mgr., 1949-58; organizer Amick Equipment Co., Inc., West Columbia, 1959, pres., 1959—. Mem. Gov.'s Task force on Solid Waste Mgmt. for S.C., 1972. Served with USAAF, 1944-45. Lutheran (pres. Luth. Men 1941-42, mem. ch. council 1946-49, 56-60, 72—). Rotarian (charter mem.). Club: Congaree County (charter mem. West Columbia, pres. 1953-54). Patentee fishing boat steering device. Home: 1331 Guignard Av West Columbia SC 29169 Office: Box 401 West Columbia SC 29169

AMICK, STANLEY EUGENE, elec. engr.; b. Scottsburg, Ind., Oct. 12, 1936; s. Willoughby F. and Vera Maxine (Peacock) A.; B.S., Rose-Hulman Inst. Tech., 1959; m. Karen Yvonne Miller, Oct. 2, 1960; 1 son, Scott Eugene. Electronic engr. advanced devel. sect. Magnavox Co., Ft. Wayne, Ind., 1959; instrumentation engr. Pine Bluff (Ark.) Arsenal, 1960-62; elec. engr. missiles Little Rock AFB, Jacksonville, Ark., 1962, base elec. engr., 1962-68, chief constrn. mgmt. sect., 1971—; staff elec. engr. Fuchu Air Sta., Japan, 1968-71. Served with AUS, 1959-62. Registered profl. engr., Ark. Home: 5186 N Cedar St North Little Rock AR 72116 Office: 314CES Little Rock AFB Jacksonville AR 72076

AMIR-MOEZ, ALI REZA, mathematician, educator; b. Teheran, Iran, Apr. 7, 1919; s. Mohammad and Fatema (Gorgestani)A-M.; B.A., U. Teheran, 1942; M.A., U. Cal. at Los Angeles, 1951, Ph.D., 1955. Came to U.S., 1947, naturalized, 1961. Instr. math. Teheran Tech. Coll., 1942-46; asst. prof. math. U. Ida., 1955-56, Queens Coll., N.Y.C., 1956-60, Purdue U., 1960-61; asso. prof. U. Fla., Gainesville, 1961-63; prof. math. Clarkson Coll., Potsdam, N.Y., 1963-65; prof. math. Texas Tech U., Lubbock; 1965—. Served to 2d lt. Persian Army, 1936-38. Decorated Honor emblem Persian Royal Ct. Mem. Am. Math. Soc., Math. Assn. Am., Soc. Indsl. and Applied Math., Sigma Xi, Pi Mu Epsilon. Author: Elements of Linear Space, 1961; (play) Kaleeheh & Demneh, 1962; Three Persian Tales, 1961, Matrix Techniques Trigonometry and Analytic Geometry, 1964; Mathematics and String Figures, 1966; Classes Residues et Figures ovec Fuelle, 1968; Extreme Properties of Linear Transformations and Geometry in Unitary Spaces, 1971; Elements of Multilinear Algebra, 1971; Linear Algebra of the Plane, 1973. Contbr. articles to math. jours. on proper and singular values of linear operators and matrices. Office: Dept Math Texas Tech U Lubbock TX 79409 Dept Math Texas Tech U Lubbock TX 79409

AMIS, GUY BALLARD, banker; b. Juno, Tenn., Dec. 11, 1897; s. August Joseph and Bettie (Ballard) A.; student W. Tenn. Tchrs. Coll., 1921, Union U., 1930-33; m. Dora Alberta Holmes, Dec. 24, 1923; 1 dau., Carol Ann (Mrs. William Thomas Stone). Tchr. and ins. salesman, 1921-30; supt. Lexington City Schs., 1933-41; cashier Central State Bank, 1941-62, pres., 1962—; pres. Lexington Broadcasting Service, 1957-71, dir., 1957—; pres. Amis & Stone, Inc., 1960—. Bd. dirs. Lexington Indsl. Improvement Assn., Inc., 1946—, pres., 1970—; bd. dirs. Henderson County Fair Assn., 1960—; chmn. bd. dirs., v.p. W. Tenn. Indsl. Assn., Inc., 1956-62; chmn. Lexington Indsl. Com., 1941—; mem. Tenn. Indsl. and Agrl. Devel. Commn., 1967-71; mem. bd. Lexington Municipal Gas System. Served with Tenn. State Guard, 1941-45. Named Rotarian of Yr., 1969. Mem. Am., Tenn. (mem. legislative com. 1961-69, mem. exec. council 1964-67) bankers assns., Am. Judicature Soc. Democrat. Methodist. Rotarian (dir. 1955-56, 61-62). Club: Pine Tree Country. Home: 208 Monroe St Lexington TN 38351 Office: Church and Monroe St Lexington TN 38351

AMLEY, EDWARD ARNOLD, dentist; b. Portland, Me., July 6, 1942; s. Arnold O. and Beth M. (Kehler) A.; B.A. in History, Duke, 1963; D.D.S., Emory U., 1967; certificate in orthodontics U. Pa., 1968; m. Margaret M. Shedd, June 18, 1966; children—Edward A., Hollis Marie. Pvt. practice orthodontics, St. Petersburg, Fla., 1969—. Chmn. orthodontic sect. Pinellas County Dental Research Clinic, 1970-71; lectr. practice mgmt. U. Pa., 1971-72, Emory U., 1971-72. Chmn. Children Dental Health Week Com., 1971. Mem. C. of C. (mem. leadership seminar 1971-72), Pinellas County Dental Soc. (chmn. dental health edn. adv. com. 1973), Emory U. Alumni Soc. (pres. Pinellas County chpt. 1969-70). Conglist. Home: 1771 Serpentine Dr St Petersburg FL 33712 Office: 1751 66th St N St Petersburg FL 33710

AMMERMANN, ERNEST GIFFORD, physician; b. Morristown, N.J., Apr. 11, 1934; s. Ernest Henry and Lillian Christine (Hatje) A.; B.S., Manchester Coll., 1956; M.R.E., Bethany Theol. Sem., 1958, B.D., 1959; postgrad. Western Ill. U., 1960-61; M.D., Northwestern U., 1965; m. Eleanor Ruth Furry, June 16, 1957; children—Phillip, Peter, Pamela Sue, Todd, Heather. Ordained to ministry Brethren Ch.; pastor Woodland Ch. of the Brethren, 1959-60; intern Chgo. Wesley Meml. Hosp., 1965-66, resident, 1966-69; fellow Oak Ridge Asso. Univs., 1969-70; asst. pathologist U. Tenn. Hosp., Knoxville, 1970-72, asst. prof. pathology and nuclear medicine, 1970-72; chief nuclear medicine VA Hosp., Salem, Va., 1972—; asst. prof. radiology U. Va., 1973—. Diplomate Am. Bd. Pathology, Am. Bd. Nuclear Medicine. Fellow Oak Ridge Asso. Univs.; mem. Am. Soc. Clin. Pathologists, Soc. Nuclear Medicine, Coll. Am. Pathologists, Roanoke Acad. Medicine, U.S. Power Squadron. Home: 5323 North Lakes Dr NW Roanoke VA 24019 Office: VA Hosp Salem VA 24153

AMONTREE, EDWARD JOSHUA, dentist; b. N.Y.C., May 2, 1919; s. Max and Elaine (Neger) Mandelbaum; A.B., Columbia Coll., 1941; A.B., Columbia Sch. of Dental and Oral Surgery; D.D.S., U. Chgo., 1944-45; m. Eva Johanna Hagenstein, July 17, 1955; children—Michael Joshua, Madelaine, Thomas Samuel. Practice of dentistry, N.Y.C., 1945-52; Sarasota, Fla., 1954—; mem. staff Sarasota Meml. Hosp.; pres. Shamont Corp.; dental dir., trustee Environmental Health and Light Inst. Bd. dirs. South Gate Assn. Served to capt., Dental Corps, AUS, 1942-44, 52-54. Mem. Fla., West Coast Dist., Manatee-Sarasota dental socs., First Dist. Dental Soc. of N.Y. Sarasota Power Squadron, Am. Soc. Photobiology. Elk. Clubs: Ivy League, Bath and Racquet (Sarasota). Home: 3850 Tangier Terrace Sarasota FL 33579 Office: 3100 South Gate Circle Sarasota FL 33579

AMOS, ROBERT FRANCIS, mech. engr.; b. Mobile, Ala., Aug. 15, 1934; s. Arthur James and Willie May (Delchamps) A.; student Spring Hill Coll., 1952-53; B.S. in Mech. Engring., U. Ala., 1956, M.S. in Mech. Engring., 1957; m. Elizabeth Sharon Wall, Apr. 30, 1966; children—Robert F., Carolyn, Michael, Madeline. Asso. engr. Internat. Paper Co., Mobile, 1957-59, project engr., Pine Bluff, Ark., other locations, 1959-69, asst. plant engr., Bastrop, La., 1969-70, plant engr., 1970-73, supt. tech. and engring. services, 1973—. Served with AUS, 1958. Registered profl. engr., Ala. Mem. Am. Soc. M.E., Tau Beta Pi, Pi Tau Sigma. Roman Catholic. Home: 2007 Saturn Dr Bastrop LA 71220 Office: Box 312 Bastrop LA 71220

AMSDEN, ROBERT GOODRICH, electronics engr., govt. ofcl., b. Poughkeepsie, N.Y., July 24, 1925; s. Burton Robert and Ella May (Smith) A.; B.S. in Elec. Engring., Worcester Poly. Inst., 1949; m. Martha Granum, Dec. 25, 1948 (dec.). Elec. engr. Naval Station, Newport, R.I., 1954-61, Naval Air Sta., Quonset Point, R.I., 1961-66, naval electronics systems command, Washington, 1966—. Registered profl. engr., R.I. Mem. I.E.E.E., Order of Patrons of Husbandry, Smithsonian Assos. Methodist. Clubs: Chantilly National Golf and Country, Playboy. Home: 1245 4th St SW Apt E 808 Washington DC 20024 Office: U S Naval Electronic Systems Command Washington Navy Yard Washington DC 20374

AMSLER, HENRY MOORE, banker, business exec.; b. Marienville, Pa., Mar. 20, 1896; s. Cornelius Washington and Ida (Moore) A.; student U. Pa., 1915; m. Jean Wilson, Sept, 27, 1918 (dec.); children—Henry C., E. Wilson; m. 2d, Hannah Goheen, Aug. 4, 1967. Mgr. New Wellsboro Store, Tioga W. Va., 1917 asst. supt., Birch Valley Lumber Co., 1918-19; supt. mgr., dir., pres. Hamler Coal Co., Inc. and affiliated cos., Clarion, Pa., 1919-37; dir. emeritus First Seneca Bank & Trust Co., Oil City, Pa., 1932—; dir. Alta Co., Inc., Clarion, Pa.; owner Amsler Co., Clarion; partner Fishwell Co., Clarion, H &H Co., St. Petersburg, Fla. Mem. Clarion Town Council, 1930-42, pres., 1934-42. Trustee Polk State Sch., 1938-42, Clarion State Coll., 1946-58. Served as lt. comdr. USCG Res., World War II, dist. officer 7th Naval Dist., USCG Aux., 1942-45. Mem. St. Petersburg Power Squadron (comdr. 1944-46), Delta Phi Delta, Phi Sigma Kappa. Presbyn. (trustee). Mason. Clubs: St. Petersburg Yacht (Fla.); Oil City (Pa.); Classics Car Club Am.; Antique Automobile Am., Auburn Cord Duesenberg, Inc. Cal. Home: 707 Main St Clarion PA 16214 also 105 2d St N St Petersburg FL 33701 Office: 2 Grant St Clarion PA 16214 also 103 2d St N St Petersburg FL 33701

AMSTER, ADOLPH BERNARD, govt. ofcl.; b. N.Y.C., Nov. 22, 1924; s. Milton Melvin and Jennie (Feigin) A.; B.S., Coll. City N.Y., 1943; M.A., Columbia, 1947; Ph.D., Ohio State U., 1951; m. Ruth Irene Mittelman, June 1, 1953; 1 son, Kenneth. Chemist, Nat. Bur. Standards, Washington, 1951-53; supervisory chemist Naval Ordnance Lab., Silver Spring, Md., 1953-60; mem. tech. staff United Tech. Center, Sunnyvale, Cal., 1960-61; chmn. dept. phys. and inorganic chemistry Stanford Research Inst., Menlo Park, Cal., 1961-68; head explosives and pyrotechnics br. USN, Washington, 1968—. Served to 1st lt. AUS, 1943-45. Decorated Purple Heart, Bronze Star with cluster, Belgian Unit Citation. Recipient USN Meritorious Civilian Service award, 1960. Mem. Phi Lambda Upsilon. Club: Sierra (chmn. Potomac chpt. 1973). Contbr. articles to profl. jours. Home: 1205 Edgevale Rd Silver Spring MD 20910 Office: ORD-0332 USN Washington DC 20360

ANDERS, BRAXTON DANIEL, accountant; b. Malakoff, Tex., May 12, 1931; s. Braxton and Rosa Marie (Frosch) A.; B.S.C., Tex. Christian U., 1957; m. Peggy Joan Mace, Sept. 20, 1958. Accountant, Estate of Milton Daniel, Breckenridge, Tex., 1957-59; partner LaRue, Lawrence, Wood & Kelley, Ft. Worth, 1959—. Served with USAF, 1948-52. C.P.A., Tex. Mem. Am. Inst. C.P.A.'s, Tex. Soc. C.P.A.'s. Home: 2323 Ridgmar Blvd Fort Worth TX 76116 Office: 9th Floor WT Waggoner Bldg Fort Worth TX 76102

ANDERS, GEORGE WILBUR, gas transmission co. exec.; b. Pine Bluff, Ark., Sept. 29, 1923; s. George Washington and Nora Ellen (Frye) A.; B.S. in Econs., State Coll. Ark., 1947; M.S. in Bus. Adminstrn., U. Ark., 1948; m. Rita Dean Haynes, Aug. 16, 1946; children—Lauren (Mrs. Edward Wilmsherr), George Stephen. Laborer, Interstate Oil Pipeline Co., 1948; safety engr., mgr. pub. relations Tex. Eastern Transmission Corp., Houston, 1949-56; dir. pub. relations, asst. to pres. Tex. Gas Transmission Corp., Owensboro, Ky., 1956-66, v.p., 1966—; instr. econs. State Coll. Ark., 1948. Regional dir. Nat. Jr. Achievement; v.p., treas., bd. dirs. Jr. Achievement Owensboro and Daviess County; trustee Potter Orphan Home, Bowling Green, Ky. Served with USNR, 1942-44. Recipient awards Jr. Achievement, 1971, Boy Scouts Am., 1973. Mem. Pub. Relations Soc. Am., N.A.M., Am. Gas Assn., Ind. Gas Assn. Am., Owensboro C. of C. Mem. Ch. of Christ (elder). Clubs: Owensboro Country, Campbell. Home: 508 Wesleyan Pl Owensboro KY 42301 Office: 3800 Frederica St Owensboro KY 42301

ANDERS, SARAH FRANCES, educator; b. Monroe, La.; d. Edward Eugene and Malda M. (Elliott) Anders; A.B., La. Poly. Inst., 1945; M.R.E., So. Bapt. Theol. Sem., 1948; M.A., Fla. State U., 1952, Ph.D., 1955; postdoctoral Rensselaer Poly Inst., 1965, U. N.H., 1968. Ednl. dir. 1st Bapt. chs., Quincy, Fla., 1948-52, Gadsden, Ala., 1952-53; asst. dir. research lab. Fla. State U., Tallahassee, 1953-55; faculty, chmn. sociology dept. Mary Hardin Baylor Coll., Belton, Tex., 1955-62; prof. sociology, head dept. La. Coll., Pineville, 1962—, acting dean, 1972-73; vis. prof. So. Meth. U., summer 1961. Mem. Tex. Gov.'s Com. on Children and Youth, 1959; treas. La. Council Family Relations. Bd. dirs. Children's Receiving Center, Girl Scout Regional Council, Drug Council, Family Service Agy., Child Guidance Center. Named Piper prof., State of Tex., 1959; NSF fellow, 1965, 1968. Mem. Am. Assn. U. Women, Southwestern Religious Research Assn. (past pres.), Nat., Tex. (past pres.) councils on family relations, Southwestern Social Sci. Assn., Am. Sociol. Assn. Author book, numberous articles. Home: 111 Mary St Pineville LA 71360

ANDERSEN, ALICE EVELYN KLOPSTAD (MRS. DANIEL JOHANNES ANDERSEN), govt. ofcl.; b. nr. Elk Point, S.D., Apr. 12, 1912; d. Samuel Andreas and Anna Marie (Larson) Klopstad; A.B., George Washington U., 1941; m. Daniel Johannes Andersen, June 28, 1937; one dau., Dianne Marie (Mrs. Paul L. Tecklenberg). With Prudential Life Ins. Co. Am., Sioux Falls, S.D., 1930-31, Wilson Transp. Co., Sioux Falls, 1931-33, Home Owner's Loan Corp., Sioux Falls, 1933-34; sec. to U.S. Senator William J. Bulow, S.D., clk. to Senate Civil Service Com., 1934-43; exec. sec. Religious Heritage Am., Washington, 1961-64; govt. adminstrn. asst. U.S. Ho. Reps., Washington, 1966—. Co-chmn. Am. Cancer Crusade, 1958-59; pres. Wesley Heights circle Florence Crittenton Home and Hosp., 1954-58, v.p., mem. bd. mgrs., Washington, 1958-60, pres., 1960-62; mem. women's bd. George Washington U. Hosp., 1962—; vol. gift shop, 1962-63, v.p. bd. mgrs., 1963-64. Recipient Alumni Service award George Washington U. Assn., 1963. Mem. Kappa Kappa Gamma. Lutheran. Clubs: American Newspaper Women's (Washington), Friday Morning Music (Washington), Chevy Chase. Home: 4441 Lowell St NW Washington DC 20016 Office: Longworth Office Bldg Washington DC 20515

ANDERSEN, DANIEL JOHANNES, lawyer; b. Jamestown, N.Y., Nov. 3, 1909; s. Christian J. and Maria (Hansen) A.; A.B., George Washington U., 1937, J.D., 1940; postgrad. Army War Coll., 1965; m. Alice Klopstad, June 29, 1937; 1 dau., Dianne Marie (Mrs. Paul L. Tecklenberg). With U.S. Dept. Labor, Washington, 1933-37; statis, clk., procedures analyst-job analyst Social Security Adminstrn., U.S. Employment Service, Washington, 1937-40; admitted to D.C., U.S. Supreme Ct. bars, 1940; mem. firm Baker, Beedy & Magee, Washington, 1940-42, Magee, Bulow & Andersen, Washington, 1946-58; individual practice law, Washington, 1958—. Mem. men's bd. Florence Crittenton Home and Hosp., 1963—. Bd. dirs. Gettysburg Coll., 1963—, chmn. devel. com., mem. exec. com., 1965—; bd. dirs., pres. Dr. O.E. Howe Found. Served with USAAF, 1941-46; ETO, MTO. Mem. Judge Advs. Assn. (pres.), Delta Phi Epsilon, Sigma Chi. Clubs: Newcomers (Washington); Chevy Chase (Md.); Nat. Lawyers, Nat. Press. Author: Job Descriptions and Code Manual, 1937. Home: 4441 Lowell St NW Washington DC 20016 Office: Woodward Bldg Washington DC 20005

ANDERSEN, ERIK CHRISTIAN, reporter, news anchorman; b. Balt., May 15, 1944; s. Theo Charles and Anne (Loeber) A.; B.A. in Journalism, Washington and Lee U., 1966; m. Janet Capps. Reporter, announcer radio sta. WREL, Lexington, Va., 1964-66; reporter, news anchorman WTLV-TV, Jacksonville, Fla., 1969—. Bd. dirs. Navy Recruiting Dist. Adv. Council. Served to lt. USNR, 1967-69. Recipient Outstanding Service award Cystic Fibrosis Found., 1972. Producer A.P. Best Documentary Fla., 1971. Mem. Kappa Sigma. Episcopalian. Home: PO Box 51175 Jacksonville Beach FL 32250 Office: PO Box 1212 Jacksonville FL 32201

ANDERSON, AMOS MILLEDGE, judge; b. Houston County, Ga., Dec. 7, 1908; s. Amos Milledge and Irene (Phillips) A.; student Emory U., 1926-28; J.D., Mercer (now Walter F. George) Sch. Law; 1932; m. Laura Killen Gilbert, July 18, 1930; children—Angela (Mrs. Fred M. Hasty), Laura Killen (Mrs. Laura A. Hedgepeth), Phyllis Irene (Mrs. Irvin G. Bullock), Amos Milledge III. Admitted to Ga. bar, 1931; practiced in Perry, 1931-39; Ga. dir. penal adminstrn., 1938-39; judge Superior Cts., Macon Jud. Circuit, 1939-44, 46-61, now emeritus; practiced law in Perry and Macon, 1945-46; v.p., trust officer The 1st Nat. Bank & Trust Co., Macon, 1961-71. Mem. Jud. Council Ga., 1956-72; mem. rules com. Ga. Supreme Ct., 1954—. Mayor, Perry, 1934-39. Bd. dirs. Ga. Municipal Assn., 1936-39; trustee Mercer U., 1950-71, Ga. Indsl. Home; bd. govs. Stratford Acad. Chmn. Houston County Democratic Exec. Com., 1934-39. Served from apprentice seaman to lt. USNR, 1944-45. Mem. Am., Ga., Macon bar assns., Ga. Council Superior Ct. Judges, Am. Judicature Soc., Inst. Jud. Adminstrn. Rotarian. Home 1293 S Jackson Springs Rd Macon GA 31201

ANDERSON, CHARLES DARWIN, newspaper editor; b. Lakeville, Minn., Sept. 6, 1916; s. Paul H. and Mabel G. (Johnson) A.; student Ft. Dodge Jr. Coll., 1934-36; B.A., State U. Ia., 1938; m. Louise Elisabeth Wigdahl, Dec. 14, 1942. News editor Pierre (S.D.) Daily Capital Journal, 1938-52, Iowa City (Ia.) Press-Citizen, 1952-54; editorial asso. Sioux City (Ia.) Journal, 1954-60, Sunday editor, 1960-68; Sunday editor Dallas Morning News, 1968—. Served to lt. comdr., USNR, 1942-46, 50-51. Mem. S.D. Jr. C. of C. (nat. dir. 1950-51), Navy League, Retired Officers Assn. Elk. Office: Dallas Morning News Communications Center Dallas TX 75222

ANDERSON, CHARLES HILL, govt. ofcl.; b. Chattanooga, June 16, 1930; s. Ray and Lois (Entrekin) A.; J.D., U. Tenn., 1953; m. Virginia R. Baker, May 5, 1956; children—Eric Scott, Alicia Lea, Burton Hill. Admitted to Tenn. bar, 1953; practice law, Chattanooga, 1953-60; asso. gen. counsel Life & Casualty Ins. Co. Tenn., Nashville, 1960-69; U.S. atty. Middle Dist. of Tenn., Nashville, 1969—. Del. Tenn. Constl. Conv., 1965; chmn. Davidson County, (Tenn.) Republican party, 1965-66; mgr., Nixon-Agnew Campaign, Davidson County, 1968. Served to maj. AUS. Mem. Am., Tenn., Nashville bar assns., Assn. Life Ins. Counsel, Phi Delta Phi, Phi Kappa Phi. Republican. Presbyn. Editor: Tenn. Law Rev., 1951-53. Home: 4704 Granny White Pike Nashville TN 37220 Office: Room 879 US Courthouse Nashville TN 37203

ANDERSON, CHARLES WESLEY, JR., food broker; b. Tupelo, Miss., July 18, 1914; s. Charles Wesley and Helen (Baker) A.; student Union U.; m. Maureen Barksdale, June 5, 1938; children—Charles Wesley III, Sheron Lee. Salesman, Del Monte Corp., Jackson, Miss., 1938-45; owner Anderson Brokerage Co., Jackson, 1945-48, merged with A.W. Duperier to become Duperier and Anderson, Inc., 1948—, now pres. Active in civic activities. Served to lt., AUS, 1942-45. Mem. Nat. Food Brokers Assn., Jackson Food Brokers. Republican. Presbyn. Club: Country of Jackson. Home: 2238 Greenbriar Dr Jackson MS 39211 Office: 245 W Lorenz Blvd Jackson MS 39213 also PO Box 4766 Fondren Sta Jackson MS 39216

ANDERSON, CLARENCE ALFRED, II, coll. dean; b. Randolph, N.Y., Oct. 14, 1921; s. Clarence Alfred and Grace (Vanderhoof) A.; B.A., St. John's Coll., Annapolis, Md., 1949; M.A. in Philosophy, U. Va., 1951; m. Irene Eleanor Webb, June 21, 1945; children—Erik V., Reilly R., John V., Dorothy Jo. Accountant, Kesler & Robinson, C.P.A.'s, Charlottesville, Va., 1953-58; accountant U. Va., Charlottesville, 1958-67; chief bus. officer, asst. prof. philosophy Patrick Henry Coll., U. Va., 1967-71; dean financial and adminstrv. services, asso. prof. Patrick Henry Community Coll., Martinsville, Va., 1971—. Scuba leader examiner YMCA, 1970—; scuba diver Nat. Assn. Underwater Instrs., 1967—; water safety instr. A.R.C., 1960—. Served to 1st lt. USAAF, 1942-45; MTO; ETO. Decorated Air medal with 1 silver and 4 bronze oak leaf clusters. Originator coll. seminar in creative morality. Home: 724 Beechnut Lane Martinsville VA 24112

ANDERSON, CLAYTON EARLE, constrn. exec.; b. Leavenworth, Kan., Feb. 16, 1932; s. Herbert Thomas and Kathryn Francis (Walter) A.; B.S., U. Kan., 1954; m. Carolyn Jan Bryant, Feb. 3, 1961; children—Jan Cecile, Michael William, John Clayton, Eric Lee. Resident engr. Cities Service Oil Co., Bartlesville, Okla., 1954-61; constrn. engr., supt. R.L. Frailey, Inc., Perry, Okla., 1961-65; sr. resident engr. Gen. Electric Co., RECO, Schenectady, 1965-69; dir. constrn. Walt Disney World, Buena Vista Land Co., Orlando, Fla., 1969-73; dir. engring. and constrn. Ringling Brothers Barnum & Bailey Circus World, Orlando, 1973—. Tribal chief YMCA Indian Guides, 1971; umpire Rolling Hills Little League, 1972-73. Served to 1st lt. USAF, 1954-56. Named Ky. Col. Registered profl. engr., Okla. Mem. Am. Soc. C.E., Home Builders Assn. Home: 5620 Hollow Oak Rd Orlando FL 32808 Office: PO Box 2006 Haines City FL 33844

ANDERSON, CONWELL AXEL, coll. pres.; b. Sister Bay, Wis., May 24, 1926; s. Arthur J. and Amy (Seaquist) A.; grad. Bethel Jr. Coll., 1947; B.A., U. Ala., 1949, M.A., 1950, Ph.D.,1954; m. Marjorie Jean Erickson, Aug. 29, 1947; children—Sheryl A. Craig, Susan Lynn, Steven Conwell. Mem. faculty U. Ala., 1950-54; dean of coll., prof. history Mary Hardin-Baylor Coll., Belton, Tex., 1954-60; pres. Judson Coll., Marion, Ala., 1960-65; asso. dir. Inst. Higher Edn., U. Ga., Athens, 1966; pres. Averett Coll., Danville, Va., 1966—. Mem. City Sch. Bd., Marion, Ala., 1965; Va. mem. membership council Regional Edn. Lab. for Carolinas and Va., 1968-71; pres. Danville Theatre Prodns., Inc., 1967-69; bd. dirs. Nat. Tobacco-Textile Mus., 1971—; bd. dirs. Danville YMCA, 1968-73, pres., 1970-71; mem. edn. and culture com. Citizens Adv. Com., 1968-69; budget and planning com. Danville United Fund, 1968-73, bd. dirs., 1974—; mem. City Beautiful Com., 1970—. Served with USNR, 1944-46. Decorated Purple Heart. Mem. Assn. So. Bapt. Colls. and Schs., Latin Am. Conf., So. Assn. Colls. for Women (pres. 1963-64), Ala. Edn. Assn. (pres. div. higher edn. 1963-64), Ala. Assn. Coll. Adminstrs. (pres. 1965), Ala. Assn. Ind. Colls. (v.p. 1963-65), Danville Hist. Soc., Newcomen Soc. N.Am., Phi Alpha Theta, Sigma Delta Pi, Phi Delta Kappa.

Baptist (deacon). Mason, Lion (dir. 1955-56, 59-60, tail twister 1963), Rotarian (dir. 1970—, v.p. 1973-74). Contbr. articles periodicals. Home: 174 Mountain View Av Danville VA 24541

ANDERSON, DELIA MAY CASH (MRS. MACK HARVIE ANDERSON), ret. librarian; b. Collins, Ark.; d. Hogan Allen and Carrie (Oliver) Cash; A.B., Ark. A. and M. Coll., 1938; M.S., U. Ark. 1952, La. State U., 1955; m. Mack Harvie Anderson, June 20, 1925; children—Mack Hogan, Alice Carolyn (Mrs. Earl Craig Beard). Tchr., DeSota Sch., Arkansas City, Ark., 1923-24, Yancopin Sch., Watson, Ark., 1924-26, Neal Sch., McGehee, Ark., 1926-27, 31-35, McGehee Pub. Schs., 1938-46; tchr.-librarian Desha Central Sch., Rowher, Ark., 1946-54; librarian Delhi (La.) High Sch., 1954-70, Dermott (Ark.) Pub. Schs., 1970-74; vis. librarian, cataloger Ark. State U., summer 1964; instr. N.E. La State U., summer 1965-68. Mem. N.E.A., Ark. Library Assn., Ark. Classroom Tchrs., Ark. Tchrs. Assn., Ark. Sch. Librarians Assn., Am. Assn. U. Women, Bus. and Profl. Women's Club (pres. 1948-49), Kappa Delta Pi, Delta Kappa Gamma. Baptist. Mem. Order Eastern Star. Home: RFD 1 Box 61 McGehee AR 71654

ANDERSON, DONALD MORGAN, entomologist; b. Washington, Dec. 27, 1930; s. John Kenneth and Alice Cornelia (Morgan) A.; B.A., Miami U., Oxford, O., 1953; Ph.D., Cornell U., 1958. Grad. teaching asst. Cornell U., 1954-57; asst. prof. sci. State U. N.Y. Coll., Buffalo, 1959-60, research fellow, 1960; research entomologist Dept. Agr., Washington, 1960—. Sigma Xi grantee, 1959. Mem. Entomol. Soc. Washington (corr. sec. 1963-65), Entomol. Soc. Am., Soc. Systematic Zoology, Coleopterists Soc., A.A.A.S., Am. Inst. Biol. Scis., Sigma Xi, Phi Kappa Phi. Contbr. articles profl. jours. Home: 2929 Connecticut Av NW Washington DC 20008 Office: Systematic Entomology Lab Dept Agr c/o US Nat Mus Washington DC 20560

ANDERSON, DOUGLAS RICHARD, ophthalmologist, educator; b. Memphis, Apr. 7, 1938; s. William Arnold Douglas and Harriott Isabelle (Gates) A.; B.A. magna cum laude, U. Miami Coll. Arts and Scis., 1968; M.D., Washington U., 1962; m. Wirtley Anne Raine, Nov. 28, 1964; children—John Douglas, Wendy Anne, Michael Allen Scott. Rotating intern U. Hosps. Cleve., 1962-63; resident ophthalmology U. Cal. Med. Center, San Francisco, 1965-68; research fellow Howe Lab. Ophthalmology, Boston, 1968-69; staff asso. Lab. Viral Oncology, Nat. Cancer Inst., Bethesda, Md., 1963-65; practice medicine specializing in ophthalmology, Miami, Fla., 1969—; mem. staffs Jackson Meml. Hosp., Highland Park Gen. Hosp.; mem. faculty U. Miami Sch. Medicine, 1969—, asst. prof. dept. ophthalmology, 1969—. Served with USPHS, 1963-65. Diplomate Am. Bd. Ophthalmology. Mem. Am. Acad. Ophthalmology and Otolaryngology, Assn. for Research in Vision and Ophthalmology, Miami Ophthalmologic Soc., Dade County Med. Assn. Office: 1638 NW 10th Av Miami FL 33152

ANDERSON, EDWARD EUGENE, physician; b. Jackson, Miss., Sept. 19, 1936; s. William Eugene and Mabel (Koenig) A.; B.A., Vanderbilt U., 1957, M.D., 1961; m. Kay Klemens Kratz, June 14, 1969. Intern, resident in internal medicine Vanderbilt U. Hosp., 1961-63, clin. instr., 1971—; fellow in cardiology U. Va. Hosp., 1966-69; dir. coronary care unit St. Thomas Hosp., Nashville, 1969-71, cardiologist cardiovascular lab., 1969—; dir. cardiology Westside Hosp., Nashville, 1972—; cons. disability determination sect. Social Security Adminstrn. Served with USNR and USMC, 1963-66. Mem. Aerospace Med. Assn., Am. Heart Assn., Phi Beta Kappa, Alpha Tau Omega. Roman Catholic. Home: 3503 Woodmont Lane Nashville TN 37215 Office: 21st and Hayes Med Bldg Nashville TN 37203

ANDERSON, EDWARD RILEY, lawyer; b. Chattanooga, Aug. 10, 1932; s. Carl Lester and Mary Catherine (Tillery) A.; B.S., U. Tenn., 1955, LL.B., J.D., 1957; m. Laura Mae Barton, Dec. 27, 1962; children—Colin, Karin, Scott, Blake. Admitted to Tenn. bar, 1957; asso. Joyce & Wilson, Oak Ridge, 1957-61; partner Joyce, Anderson, Wood & Meredith, Oak Ridge, 1961—. Chmn., March Dimes drive, Anderson County, 1961. Bd. dirs. Roane Anderson Mental Health Found.; bd. dirs. YMCA, 1962-64, pres., 1964. Mem. C. of C. (v.p. 1973), Anderson County (pres. 1961), Tenn. (bd. dels. 1972—) bar assns., Anderson County U. Tenn. Alumni Assn. (pres. 1967), Phi Gamma Delta, Phi Delta Phi. Methodist. Rotarian. Club: Oak Ridge Country (v.p. 1970-71). Home: 119 Wendover Circle Oak Ridge TN 37830 Office: Town Hall Bldg Kentucky Av Oak Ridge TN 37830

ANDERSON, FLOYD EDMOND, educator; b. Racine, Wis., Oct. 16, 1915; s. Bert Floyd and Margaret Ella (Prengel) A.; B.S., U. Wis., 1939; M.S., U. Mich., 1946, Ph.D., 1949; m. Elizabeth Marie Perkins, Jan. 31, 1947; 1 dau., Christine L. Chem. analyst Ditzler Color Co., Detroit, 1939-40; organic research chemist Lakeside Labs., Inc., Milw., 1940-44; research engr. Battelle Meml. Inst., Columbus, O., 1944-45; asst. prof. chemistry W.Va. U., Morgantown, 1948-49; sr. organic research chemist Nepera Chem. Co., Yonkers, N.Y., 1949-50, dir. organic chem. research, 1951-57; sr. research asso. Warner Lambert Research Inst., Morris Plains, N.J., 1957-60; head organic research and devel. pharm. div. Wallace & Tiernan, Inc., Belleville, N.J., 1960-63; asso. prof. medicinal chemistry Coll. Pharmacy, Northeastern U., Boston, 1963-66; prof. chemistry Luther Rice Coll., Alexandria, Va., 1966-70, chmn. dept. chemistry, 1967—, prof. chemistry, chmn. div. sci., 1970—; supervisory chemist FDA div. neuropharmacological drugs, Washington, 1966-70; chief drug information br., program mgr. Early Warning and Drug Information System, Bur. Narcotics and Dangerous Drugs, Dept. Justice, Washington, 1970-74, chief chem.-biol. coordination, spl. programs div. Drug Enforcement Agy., 1974—. W.S. Merrell research fellow, 1945-48. Mem. A.A.A.S., Am. (dir. N.Y. sect. 1957-59, nat. chmn. membership com. 1967-68), Westchester (chmn. 1955-56) chem. socs., N.Y. Acad. Scis., Gideons Internat., Sons of Norway, Sigma Xi, Rho Chi, Phi Lambda Upsilon. Baptist. Contbr. articles profl. jours. Patentee in field. Home: 2500 N Van Dorn St Alexandria VA 22302 Office: 1405 Eye St NW Washington DC 20537

ANDERSON, FRANK JOHN, librarian; b. Chgo., Jan. 29, 1919; s. Charles Emil and Alida (Solomon) A.; student U. Conn., 1947-48; A.B., Ind. U., 1950; M.S., Syracuse U., 1951; m. Jeanette Irene Rioux, Feb. 17, 1944; 1 dau., Maria Alida. Librarian, Kan. Wesleyan U., 1952-56; br. head East Chicago (Ind.) Pub. Library, 1956-57; dir. Submarine Library, Groton, Conn., 1957-60; librarian Kan. Wesleyan U., Salina, 1960-66, Wofford Coll., Spartanburg, S.C., 1966—. Owner, mgr. Kitemaug Books, Spartanburg, 1959—, Kitemaug Press, 1965—. Served with submarine service USNR, 1943-45, 51-52. Mem. Spl. Libraries Assn., Southeastern, S.C. (chmn. coll. and univ. sect. 1970-72) library assns., Am. Assn. Univ. Prof. (chpt. sec. 1968—), Am. Civil Liberties Union, U.S. Naval Inst., Amalgamated Printers Assn. Author: Submarines, Submariners and Submarining, 1963; Private Presses in the Southeastern United States, 1973. Book reviewer Library Jour., 1954—. Contbr. articles to profl. publs. Home: 229 Mohawk Dr Spartanburg SC 29301

ANDERSON, FREDRICK EBEN, electronic engr.; b. Covina, Cal., May 6, 1938; s. Harold Fredrick and Esther May (Eaton) A.; B.S. in Elec. Engring., State U. Ia., 1961; postgrad. U. Ala., 1965-71; m. Carolyn Jean Miller, Feb. 19, 1967; children—Esther Inez, Elizabeth Naomi. With U.S. Army Missile Command, Redstone Arsenal, Ala., 1962—, electronic engr., 1966—. Mem. I.E.E.E., Inst. Environmental Scis. Methodist. Home: 618 Hemlock Dr SE Huntsville AL 35803 Office: US Army Missile Command Redstone Arsenal AL 35809

ANDERSON, FRITHIOF BERTRAM, communications engr.; b. Phila., Dec. 27, 1903; s. George and Louise (Michaelis) A.; B.S., in Elec. Engring., U. Pa., 1926, E.E., 1934; m. Dorothy Harp Smalley, Apr. 4, 1931; (dec. 1967); 1 dau., Ruth (Mrs. Arthur Andrew Trimble); m. 2d, Flora Truett Ross, Oct. 23, 1971. Mem. tech. staff Bell Telephone Labs., Inc., N.Y.C., 1926-64, communications engr. Bradenton, Ga., 1964-67, Chamblee, Ga., 1967—; newspaper columnist, 1970—. Mem. Mensa, Atlanta Writers Club, Dixie Council Authors and Journalists, Theosophical Soc., Eta Kappa Nu. Mason. Author: Upsidown, 1966; Stay A Notion Ahead:, 1967—; Jesus Started Something:, 1969. Home: 3361 Chamblee-Tucker Rd Chamblee GA 30341

ANDERSON, HOWARD WAYNE, chem. engr.; b. Cin., Feb. 18, 1934; s. Fred A. and Irene M. (Andersen) A.; B. in Chem. Engring., U. Del., 1956; M.S. (NSF fellow), U. Cal. at Berkeley, 1958; m. Eleanor L. Diener, June 7, 1958; children—Stephen Eric, Karen Louise. Research engr. DuPont, Wilmington, Del., 1958-68, sr. engr., Victoria, Tex., 1969—. Mem. Am. Inst. Chem. Engrs., Am. Chem. Soc., Phi Kappa Tau. Home: 410 Salisbury Lane Victoria TX 77901 Office: Plastics Dept EI Du Pont De Nemours & Co Victoria TX 77901

ANDERSON, HUBERT MAXWELL, JR., mfrs. rep.; b. Brewster, Fla., Mar. 12, 1939; s. Hubert Maxwell and Louise (Whidden) A.; B.E.E., U. Fla., 1963; postgrad. Alexander Hamilton Inst. Bus., 1969-70; m. Marie Lou Franceschini, Feb. 18, 1967; children—Allan Max, Maurice Enrique. Design engr. Internat. Tel. & Tel. Research and Devel. Lab., San Juan, P.R., 1964-66; engr. RCA Information System div., West Palm Beach, Fla., 1967-68; v.p. E. Franceschini Assos., Santurce, P.R., 1968—. Served with AUS, 1959. Mem. I.E.E.E., Mfrs. Agts. Nat. Assn., Armed Forces Communications Assn. Club: Caribe Hilton Swimming and Tennis (San Juan, P.R.). Home: 187 Jose Padin St Hato Rey PR 00918 Office: Box 7068 Bo Obrero Sta Santurce PR 00916

ANDERSON, JACK NORTHMAN, newspaper columnist; b. Long Beach, Cal., Oct. 19, 1922; s. Orlando N. and Agnes (Mortensen) A.; student U. Utah, 1940-41, Georgetown U., 1947-48, George Washington U., 1948; m. Olivia Farley, Aug. 10, 1949; children—Cheri, Lance F., Laurie, Tina, Kevin N., Randy, Tanya, Rodney, Bryan. Reporter, Salt Lake Tribune, 1939-41; war corr. Deseret News, 1945; reporter Washington Merry-go-Round, 1947—, partner, 1965—; Washington editor Parade mag., 1954-68, bur. chief, 1968—. Missionary in So. states for Church of Jesus Christ of Latter Day Saints, 1941-44; sec., trustee Chinese Refugee Relief, 1962—. Served with U.S. Mcht. Marine, 1944-45; with AUS, 1946-47. Mem. White House Corr. Assn. Club: Nat. Press (Washington). Author: (with Ronald May) McCarthy the Man, the Senator, the Ism, 1952; (with Fred Blumenthal) The Kefauver Story, 1956; (with Drew Pearson) U.S.A. Second Class Power?, 1958; Washington Expose, 1966; (with Pearson) The Case Against Congress, 1968; The Anderson Papers, 1973. Home: 7300 Burdette Ct Bethesda MD 20034 Office: 1612 K St NW Washington DC 20006

ANDERSON, JERRY DEAN, basketball coach; b. Lexington, Okla., Dec. 2, 1927; s. Perry D. and Grace (King) A.; B.S., E. Central State Coll., Ada, Okla., 1951; M.S., Okla. U., 1955; m. Letitia M. Swoap, Jan. 20, 1950; children—Michael David, Ronald Kent. Basketball coach Stratford (Okla.) High Sch., 1951-52, Blackwell (Okla.) High Sch., 1952-56, Panhandle State Coll., Goodwell, Okla., 1956-67; basketball coach E. Central State Coll., Ada, 1967—. Active various civic and ch. groups. Served with AUS, 1946-47. Recipient Outstanding Citizen award C. of C., 1967. Mem. Nat. Basketball Coaches Assn., Okla. Tchrs. Assn., Okla. Coaches Assn. Democrat. Methodist. Elk, Kiwanian. Home: 1600 S Broadway Blvd Ada OK 74820

ANDERSON, JOHN EDWIN, JR., coll. adminstr.; b. Akron, O., Jan. 26, 1932; s. John Edwin and Ella (Kennedy) A.; B.A., U. Akron, 1953; Ph.D., Ohio State U., 1957; m. Joyce E. Querry, June 11, 1956; children—Christie Lynn, John Edwin III, Karen Joyce. Instr. Rochester Inst. Tech., 1957-58; asst. to asso. prof. psychology Fla. State U., 1958-63; prof. psychology, dean of coll. Columbus (Ga.) Coll., 1963—. Chmn. bd. dirs. Brookstone Sch.; adv. com. div. vocational rehab. Ga. Dept. Edn. Registered psychologist, Ga.; certified psychologist, Fla. Mem. Am. Psychol. Assn. Rotarian. Home: 3411 Cambridge Dr Columbus GA 31906 Office: Columbus College Columbus GA 31907

ANDERSON, JOHN (LARRY) WASHINGTON III, accountant; b. Borger, Tex., Apr. 7, 1942; s. John Washington and Ann Ayleez (Hill) A.; B.S. in Edn., Tex. Technol. U., 1967; m. Betty Helen Womble, Aug. 19, 1966; children—Christopher Todd, Randal Ty. Accountant, Ernst & Ernst, Lubbock, Tex., 1967-71, Mason, Nickels & Warner, 1971—. Pres., Lubbock Juvenile Rehab. Center, 1971—. Bd. dirs. Tex. Boys Ranch. C.P.A., Tex. Mem. Am. Inst. C.P.A.s, Tex. Soc. C.P.A.s, Lubbock Jr. C. of C. (treas. 1971-73). Mason (Shriner). Home: 5501 78th St Lubbock TX 79424 Office: Tower of Plains 5010 University Av Lubbock TX 79401

ANDERSON, JOHN PALMER, coll. adminstr.; b. New Orleans, Mar. 27, 1939; s. William Wyatt and Lottie Palmer (Johnson) A.; B.S., Ga. Inst. Tech., 1961, M.S. in Engring. Mechanics, 1963, M.S. in Math., 1964, Ph.D., 1966; m. Mary Agnes Harris, June 16, 1962; children—Deborah Louisa, Michael Gary, William Benjamin, James Scott. Asst. prof. Ga. Inst. Tech., Atlanta, 1965-66; asst. prof. U.S. Air Force Acad., Colorado Springs, Colo., 1966-67, asso. prof., 1967-68; asso. prof. engring. and math. U. Ala., Birmingham, 1968-71, asst. to v.p., 1971—, prof. engring., dir. financial planning, 1973—. Served to capt., AUS, 1966-68. Mem. Am. Soc. M.E., Am. Soc. C.E., Am. Soc. Engring. Edn. (sec. mechanics div. 1968—), Sigma Xi, Tau Beta Pi, Pi Mu Epsilon, Phi Kappa Phi. Methodist. Home: 3424 Brookwood Rd Mount Brook AL 35223 Office: Office Financial Planning U Alabama Birmingham AL 35294

ANDERSON, JOHN QUINCY, educator; b. Wheeler, Tex., May 30, 1916; s. Albert Slayton and Emily (Grant) A.; B.A., Okla. State U., 1939; M.A., La. State U., 1948; Ph.D., U.N.C., 1952; m. Marie Loraine Epps, Aug. 24, 1946. Asst. prof. McNeese State Coll., 1952-53; faculty Tex. A. and M. U., College Station, 1953-66, prof. English, 1959-66, head dept., 1962-66; prof. English, U. Houston, 1966—. Served to capt. AUS, 1940-46. Decorated French Medaille de la Reconnaissance. Mem. Modern Lang. Assn., S. Central Modern Lang. Assn., Am. Studies Assn. Tex. (pres. 1963-64), Am. Studies Assn. (exec. council 1964-67), Southwestern (editor 1970—), Western Am. lit. assns., Am., Tex. (pres. 1955-56) folklore socs. Author: Brokenburn: The Journal of Kate Stone, 1955; A Texas Surgeon in the C.S.A., 1957; Louisiana Swamp Doctor: The Life and Writings of Henry Clay Lewis, 1962; Tales of Frontier Texas, 1966; Campaigning with Parsons' Texas Cavalry, C.S.A., 1967; John C. Duval, First Texas Man of Letters, 1967; With the Bark On: Popular Humor of the Old South, 1967; Texas Folk Medicine, 1970; The Liberating Gods: Emerson on Poets and Poetry, 1971. Mem. editorial bd. Miss Quar., 1963—; Computer Studies in Verbal Behavior and the Humanities, 1966—, Paisano Books, Tex. Folklore Soc., 1968—. Contbr. numerous articles to profl. jours. Home: 11327 Gaymoor St Houston TX 77035

ANDERSON, LEO JOSEPH, mfg. co. exec.; b. Lecompton, Kan., Aug. 15, 1921; s. Michael Alexander and Helen Marie (O'Brien) A.; student U. Kan.; m. Henrietta Slavens, Oct. 20, 1943; children—Leo Joseph II, Kathleen Lynn. With Kan. Hwy. Commn., 1946-49; elec. engr. Army C.E., Pickstown, S.D., 1950-52; chief engr., constrn. div. Hdqrs., SAC, USAF, Air Force, Omaha, 1952-59; chief regional engr., region 10, U.S. Postal Service, Wichita, Kan., 1959-62, dir. engring. and facilities div., region 10, 1962-67, asst. dir. design, constrn. engring. Bur. Research and Engring., 1967-69, dir. process engring., Bur. Research and Engring., 1969-71; exec. v.p. Hendrickson Anderson, Inc., McLean, Va., 1971-72; v.p. Rohr Plessey Corp., Rockville, Md., 1972—; chmn. bd. Kendale, Inc., mech. contractors, Arlington, Va., 1972—. Served to capt. C.E., AUS, 1942-46; ETO. Registered profl. engr. Mem. Nat., D.C. socs. profl. engrs. Home: 2111 Jefferson Davis St Apt 403N Arlington VA 22202

ANDERSON, LEROY FREDERIC, educator; b. Charleston, S.C., Nov. 30, 1917; s. James William and Anna (Pettigrew) A.; B.A., Fisk U., 1939, M.A., 1948; Ed.D., U. Ky., 1962; m. Melicent Marie Olphin, May 14, 1951; children—Karen Lisa, Anna Maeria, Olphine Leroy. Tchr., Simonton Elementary Sch., Charleston, S.C., 1939-41, guidance counselor Burke High Sch., Charleston, 1948-53; prin. W. Gresham Meggett Sch., James Island, S.C., 1953-60; prof. S.C. State Coll. at Orangeburg, 1962-63, chmn. edn. and psychology dept., 1963-67, dir. instl. research, 1967-69; asso. prof. psychology Med. U. S.C., also project dir. Franklin C. Fetter Family Health Center, Charleston, 1969—. Mem. Nat. Adv. Council Edn. of Disadvantaged; cons. staff orientation programs Project Headstart; dir. Guidance and Counseling Insts., Nat. Def. Edn. Act (summers); dir. Tchr. Corp Pre-Service and In-Service Tng. Commr. Charleston Community Mental Health Bd.; chmn. Health Forum, Comprehensive Health Planning. Bd. dirs. Charleston Area Mental Health Assn., Horizon House. Served from sgt. to maj. with AUS, 1941-46. Mem. N.E.A. (TEPS task force), Inst. Services to Edn., Phi Delta Kappa, Alpha Delta Kappa, Alpha Phi Alpha. Episcopalian. Home: 189 Sans Souci St Charleston SC 29403 Office: 417-419 Meeting St Charleston SC 29403

ANDERSON, LEWIS DANIEL, orthopaedic surgeon, univ. adminstr.; b. Greensboro, Ala., Oct. 13, 1930; s. Thomas Jefferson and Frances (Daniel) A.; student Emory U., 1947-50; M.D., U. Pa., 1953; M.S. in Orthopaedic Surgery, U. Tenn., 1960; m. Stella Stickney Cobbs, July 6, 1951; children—Evelyn (Mrs. William B. McGehee, III), Lewis Daniel, Tunstall C., Lida T. Intern, Hosp. U. Pa., Phila., 1953-54, resident, 1954, 56-57; resident Campbell Clinic, Memphis, 1957-60; practice medicine specializing in orthopaedic surgery, Memphis, 1960—; chief staff William F. Bowld Hosp., Memphis, 1965-73; faculty U. Tenn., Memphis, 1960—, prof. orthopaedic surgery, 1971—, asso. dean for hosp. affairs, 1972—, chmn. surg. council, 1973—; med. dir. City Memphis Hosp., 1972—. Served with USNR, 1954-56. Am.-Brit.-Canadian traveling fellow Gt. Britain, 1967. Mem. Am. Acad. Orthopedic Surgeons. Episcopalian. Clubs: University, Faculty (Memphis). Contbr. numerous articles to profl. jours. Home: 636 East Dr Memphis TN 38112 Office: 858 Madison Av Memphis TN 38103

ANDERSON, MABLE BELL, educator; b. Birmingham, Ala., Sept. 7, 1930; d. I.C. and Beatrice (Craddock) Bell; B.S. (inst. scholar), Tuskegee Inst., 1950; M.A. (univ. scholar), Mich. State U., 1952; Ed.D., Pa. State U., 1965; postgrad. Grambling Coll., summer 1960, Bank St. Coll. Edn., summer 1967, Yeshiva U., summer 1967; m. Furman C. Anderson, June 9, 1958 (div. May 1965). Instr. home econs. and health Fayette County Tng. Sch., Fayette, Ala., 1950-51; tchr.-trainer in home econs. edn. and child devel. Grambling Coll., 1952-54; mem. faculty child devel. and family relationships Miles Coll., Birmingham, 1954-60; presch. asst. tchr. Pa. State U., 1961-62; dir. Migrant Day Care Center, Dept. Child and Family Welfare, Harrisburg, Pa., summer 1961, social caseworker, summer 1962; prof. child devel., chmn. grad. studies in home econs. Tenn. A. and I. State U., 1963-66; prof. elementary edn. Western Ky. U., Bowling Green, 1966-69, supr. student tchrs. in elementary edn., 1966; prof. Center for Early Childhood Personnel Devel., State Coll. Ark., Conway, 1969-70; prof. edn., coordinator early childhood edn., 1970—, asso. dir. tchr. corps. Albany (Ga.) State Coll., 1970-72. Instr., guest lectr. Head Start Tchr. Tng. programs George Peabody Coll., Pa. State U., 1965; workshop leader TACUS tchrs., Chattanooga and Knoxville, Tenn., 1966, 67; rep. Ky. Com. on Early Childhood Edn., 1966-70; adviser, cons. kindergartens, day care centers, Bowling Green, 1967-70; mem. com. Ga. Comprehensive Early Childhood Devel. programs; chmn. Dougherty County Task Force in comprehensive Early Childhood Devel. programs cons. Warren County-Bowling Green Assn. Mental Retardation, 1966-70, Coll. of Ozarks, Clarksville, 1969-70; lectr., cons. P.R. Dept. Edn., San Juan; mem. Ark. Gov.'s Task Force Com. on Early Childhood, 1969-70, Citizen's Adv. Com., Albany; bd. dirs., tech. adv. . So. Ky. Econ. Opportunity Council, 1967-70, Child Devel. Asso. Consortium, 1972—, Ga. Accreditation Commn., 1972—. Research in Child Devel., Assn. Childhood Edn. Internat. (dir. 1970-73), Nat. Council Family Relations (dir. 1969-73), Ky. Edn. Assn., Nursery-Kindergarten Nat. Edn. Assn., Am. Home Econs. Assn., Am. Assn. U. Women, Am. Assn. U. Profs., Groves Conf. Family Life. Home: PO Box 876 Albany GA 31702

ANDERSON, MARIAN MCCUTCHEN (MRS. WILLIAM WHITE ANDERSON), hosp. adminstr.; b. Bishopville, S.C., June 2, 1913; d. Robert Othello and Florence (Jenkins) McCutchen; student U. S.C., 1930-32, 36; grad. Draughan's Bus. Coll. 1936; m. William White Anderson, May 30, 1941 (dec. May 1949);children—Susan Anderson (Mrs. Donald Eugene Mathis), McCutchen Brooks. Chief clk. Selective Service Bd., 1941-42; sec.-bookkeeper Ashwood Area Vocational Sch., Bishopville, 1949-50; bookkeeper Lee County Meml. Hosp., Bishopville, 1950-58, adminstr., 1958—. Mem. Santee-Wateree Health Planning Council. Bd. dirs. Lee County Mental Health Assn., Lee County chpt. A.R.C., Mem. Am., S.C. hosp. assns., Hosp. Financial Mgmt. Assn. (Follmer award for outstanding service S.C. chpt. 1966, sec. 1966—), Internat. Platform Assn., French Huguenot Soc., Soc. Magna Charta Dames. Presbyn. Home: 211 S Heyward St Bishopville SC 29010 Office: Church St Extension Bishopville SC 29010

ANDERSON, MILES EDWARD, univ. adminstr.; b. Fort Worth, Dec. 13, 1926; s. Dewitt Phillip and Mary (Wise) A.; B.S., North Tex. State U., 1949, M.S., 1950; Ph.D., Stanford, 1963; m. Harlene Gaston, Jan. 31, 1948; children—Gail, Barbara Ann, David Philip. Research asst. U. Mich. Willow Run Research Center, Ypsilanti, 1952-54; mem. faculty North Tex. State U., Denton, 1954—, prof., 1960—, asso. v.p. for acad. affairs, 1969—. Vis. lectr. Washington U., St. Louis, 1962-63. Mem. physics subcom. Com. on Edn. in Agr. and Natural Resources, Nat. Acad. Scis., 1968-70. Served with USNR, 1944-46. NSF Sci. Faculty fellow, 1957-58, 1958-59; Danforth Found. grantee, 1956-57.

Mem. Am. Phys. Soc., Am. Assn. Physics Tchrs., Am. Assn. for Higher Edn. Home: 529 Mimosa St Denton TX 76201 Office: Box 5371 Denton TX 76203

ANDERSON, PAUL SIGFRIED, JR., epidemiologist, educator; b. New Haven, June 10, 1927; s. Paul Sigfried and Gladys G. (Shufelt) A.; B.A., Wesleyan U., Middletown, Conn., 1950; M.S., Yale, 1951, Ph.D., 1957; m. K. Joyce Miller, June 22, 1950; children—Paul Sigfried III, Kurt D., Nancy G. Instr. dept. epidemiology and pub. health Yale Med. Sch., 1951-54, asst. prof., 1957-60, asso. prof., 1962-68; prof., chmn. dept. biostatistics and epidemiology Coll. Health, U. Okla. Health Scis. Center, Oklahoma City, 1968—; statistician Atomic Bomb Casualty Commn., Hiroshima and Nagasaki, Japan, 1960-61. Cons., Nat. Center for Health Statistics, Washington, Research Triangle Park, N.C., FDA, Washington, FAA, Oklahoma City; mem. adv. com. NIH, Bethesda, Md.; mem. Lipid Research Center Com., Nat. Heart and Lung Inst., Bethesda. Served with USNR, 1945-46. Fellow Am. Pub. Health Assn.; mem. Am. Statis. Assn. (pres. Conn. chpt. 1965-67), Assn. Tchrs. Preventive Medicine, Soc. Epidemiologic Research, Biometric Soc., A.A.A.S., N.Y. Acad. Sci., Sigma Xi. Home: 2612 Cambridge Ct Oklahoma City OK 73116 Office: U Okla Health Scis Center PO Box 26901 Oklahoma City OK 73190

ANDERSON, R. BRUCE W., educator; b. Evanston, Ill., Oct. 10, 1938; s. Edward Ralph and Ruth E. (Wilmot) A.; A.B., Stanford, 1961; M.A., Northwestern U., 1965; Ph.D. (Nat. Inst. Mental Health fellow), Duke, 1970; m. Birgit Vendelbo, June 21, 1963; children—Britt V., Belinda E., Bodil J. Asst. prof. sociology Carroll Coll., Waukesha, Wis., 1965-67, U. Man. (Can.) Winnipeg, 1971-73; asso. prof. U. Tex. at Arlington, 1973—. Bd. dirs. Winnipeg Pollution Probe, 1971-72. Postdoctoral fellow Center Study Aging and Human Devel., Duke, 1969-71. Mem. Am., Internat. sociol. assns., So. Sociol. Soc., Am. Statis. Assn., Alpha Kappa Delta, Alpha Delta Sigma. Office: Dept Sociology U Texas Arlington TX 76019

ANDERSON, RICHARD MAURICE, mech. engr.; b. Galesburg, Ill., Sept. 6, 1930; s. Maurice and Eldora (Wilson) A.; student U. Ill., 1946-48, U. Wis., 1952-53, U. Tenn., 1969-70; m. Celeste Joan Bolger, Dec. 15, 1953; children—Selene, Elizabeth, Richard, Eldora, Antonia. Estimator, Clark Palmer Co., Galesburg, 1954-55; service mgr. Wolfer Refrigeration Co., Pekin, Ill., 1955-56; jr. engr. Mitchell Mfg. Co., Chgo., 1956-58; engr. Addison Products Co. (Mich.), 1958-64; chief engr. air conditioning Heil Quaker Corp., Nashville, 1964—. Served with USNR, 1951-53; Korea. Recipient Sci. award Bausch & Lomb, 1948. Club: Bass Anglers Sportsman Society (Smyrna, Tenn.). Patentee in field. Home: 208 Cumberland Dr Smyrna TN 37169 Office: 647 Thompson Lane Nashville TN 37204

ANDERSON, ROBERT LANIER, JR., lawyer; b. Macon, Ga., Aug. 3, 1899; s. Robert Lanier and Gertrude Snider (Roberts) A.; B.A., U. Ga., 1920; LL.B. cum laude, 1922; m. Helen Caroline Waterbury, Oct. 3, 1931; children—Helen (Mrs. Sydney Balsbaugh), Robert Lanier, III. Admitted to Ga. bar, 1922; partner Anderson, Walker & Reichert, Macon, 1928—. Dir. CMP Drug Co., Macon. Served as 1st lt. AUS, 1918-19. Mem. Macon Circuit Bar Assn. (pres. 1938-39), Ga. Bar Assn. (sec. 1944-47), Phi Delta Theta, Phi Delta Phi. Presbyn. Rotarian. Clubs: Exchange (pres. 1932-33), Idle Hour Country (pres. 1932-33) (Macon). Home: 475 Vista Circle Macon GA 31204 Office: 404 First Nat Bank Bldg Macon GA 31201

ANDERSON, SAMUEL ARMISTEAD, III, architect; b. Richmond, Va., Dec. 18, 1933; s. Samuel and Frances Gertrude (Webster) A.; B.A., U. Va., 1955; B.Arch., U. Pa., 1961; m. Alice Gordon Childs, Mar. 24, 1956; children—Sarah Gordon, Ann Starling, Lucy Daniel, Susannah Webster. Designer, Venturi & Rauch, Phila., 1962; project designer Ballinger Co., Phila., 1963, Harbeson, Hough, Livingston, Larsen, Phila., 1964; project design coordinator Llewelyn-Davies Weeks & Partners, London, Eng., 1965-66; staff architect Rawlings & Wilson, Richmond, Va., 1967-68; partner Glave Newman Anderson, Richmond, 1969—. Lectr. Bartlett Sch. Arch., Univ. Coll. U. London, 1965; pres. Richmond Community Design Center Inc., 1972-74. Chmn., Chesterfield County A.R.C., 1971-72. Mem. Va. Democratic Central Com. Bd. dirs. Richmond Scenic James Council, 1971-73, Richmond Urban League, 1973—, Fans of the James Com., 1973—. Served to lt. USNR, 1955-58. Mem. A.I.A. (pres. Richmond sect. 1970, dir. Va. chpt. 1974—), Am. Inst. Planners (asso. mem.), Council Ednl. Facilities Planners, Central Richmond Assn., Zeta Psi. Clubs: Country Virginia, Engineers (Richmond). Architect Basingstoke (Eng.) Town Center Redevel., 1964-66, Va. Commonwealth U. Master Plan, 1970. Home: 8511 Ben Nevis Dr Bon Air VA 23235 Office: 209 W Franklin St Richmond VA 23220

ANDERSON, STANLEY JAMES, city ofcl.; b. Washington, Sept. 24, 1927; s. James Edward and Ethel Anderson; B.S., Howard U., 1948, postgrad. Sch. Social Work, 1965-67; m. Virginia Alice Ingram, Jan. 12, 1950; children—Stanice Lucretia, Stanley James. With D.C. Recreation Dept., 1946-67, dir. roving leader program, 1961-66, dep. dir. neighborhood centers div., 1966-67; mem. D.C. City Council, 1967-73; mem. Washington Met. Transit Authority, 1970-73, chmn., 1973—. Cons. youth, transp. Pres., Hillsdale Civic Assn., 1959-63. Bd. dirs. S.E. Community Hosp., Washington, Eugene and Agnes Meyer Found., Washington Met. Transit Authority Retirement Trust, Samuel Stern Family Fund, United Givers Fund. Recipient Melvin C. Hazen award outstanding D.C. govt. service, 1963; Fellowship award Nat. Recreation and Park Assn., 1963. Mem. Am. Recreation Assn. Contbr. articles to profl. jours. Home: 2604 Stanton Rd SE Washington DC 20020 Office: 601 D St SW Washington DC 20201

ANDERSON, W. E. (ANDY), writer, film producer; b. Carlinville, Ill., Dec. 2, 1903; s. Crittenden Henry Crawford and Nellie (Patchen) A.; ed. Tex. A. and M. Coll.; m. Mabel Mae Rooks, Nov. 15, 1930. With Nat. Life & Accident Ins. Co., Dallas, 1933-54; gen. partner Adventurers Assos., producer hunting films; producer, narrator, participant Hollywood prodn. Big Game Hunting in North America; dir., producer, narrator Wildlife and mem. hunting film Big Game Trails, 1973. Leader's Round Table of Tex., 8 yrs. Past bd. dirs. YMCA, West Dallas Social Center. Mem. S.A.R. Methodist (mem. adminstrv. bd., finance com., chmn. new pledge com., stewardship com.). Clubs: Oak Cliff Lions (past chmn. membership com., health and welfare com., civic com., interstate and internat. pub. relations com., Achievement award 1962, Monarch award 1964), Oak Cliff Country (charter), Dallas Woods and Water (charter; 1st chmn. big game hunting com.). Author poem: The Hunter's Dream; stories: Bushytails of the Llano; Duke, the Story of a Bird Dog; with Deep in the Heart of Texas; Johnnie's Lucky Day, with illustrations; Skyline Meadows, 1954; King Caribou, 1954; Sleek and Glossy, 1954; A Texan Meets a Silvertip, 1957; Five from Which to Choose, 1957. Contbr. articles to Sports Afield, Sports Afield Hunting Ann., Am. Hunter, Tex. Game & Fish, Guns mag., Alaskan Sportsman, Am. Rifleman, Field and Stream, Outdoor Life mag. Home: 955 Sam Dealey Dr Dallas TX 75208

ANDERSON, WALLACE LEE, elec. engr., educator; b. Adams, N.D., Dec. 2, 1922; s. Holger Ferdinand and Helen Marie (Lala) A.; B.S. in Elec. Engring., U. N.D., 1948; M.A. in Physics (grad. scholar), Rice U., 1957; Sc.D., U. N.M., 1961; m. Kimberly Ruth Wheaton, Feb. 4, 1956 (div. July 1969); children—Julie Jeanne, Cristina Lee; m. Claire Worth Corley, Apr. 21, 1973. Operator, McCollum Exploration Co., Houston, 1948-50, party mgr., 1950-51, research engr., 1954-55; research asso. U. N.M., Albuquerque, 1957-59, teaching asso., 1959-60, lectr., 1960-61; asso. prof. elec. engring. dept. N.Y. U., N.Y.C., 1961-64; sr. research engr. S.W. Research Inst., San Antonio, 1964-68, staff scientist, 1968-69; asso. prof. physics dept. Trinity U., San Antonio, 1965-69; prof. elec. engring. dept. U. Houston, 1969-72, chmn. elec. engring. dept., 1972—. Cons. Smithsonian Inst., Washington, 1969-70, Gaertner Sci. Co., Chgo., 1968-69. Served to 1st lt. USAAF, 1943-46. Nat. Inst. Gen. Med. Scis. grantee, 1966, 67, 68, 71, 72, 73; NSF grantee, 1971-73. Mem. I.E.E.E., Am. Phys. Soc., Optical Soc. Am., A.A.A.S., Soc. Photog. and Instrumentation Engrs., Houston Engring. and Sci. Soc., Sigma Xi, Sigma Tau, Sigma Pi Sigma, Kappa Mu Epsilon. Republican. Unitarian. Contbr. articles to profl. jours. Inventor of high resolution lensless holographic microscopy. Home: 2102 Morse St Houston TX 77019

ANDERSON, WILLARD WOODBURY, govt. research instn. engr.; b. Boston, July 22, 1939; s. Robert Adams and Sylvia Margaret (Peterson) A.; B.S., Northeastern U., 1962; M.S., Mass. Inst. Tech., 1964, Sc.D., 1967; m. Jane Louise Ballard, Oct. 18, 1957; children—Dennis Robert, Kimberly Jane, Nicolle Woodbury, John Willard. Research asst. Mass. Inst. Tech., Cambridge, 1962-65; sr. engr. Cohoon and Heasley, Inc., Cambridge, 1964-66; head Stability and Control br. NASA-Langley Research Center, Hampton, Va., 1968—. Served to capt., C.E., AUS, 1966-68. Mem. Sigma Xi, Tau Beta Pi, Pi Tau Sigma. Co-inventor of Annular Momentum Control Device for Space Vehicle Control. Contbr. articles to profl. jours. Home: 333 Moore House Rd Yorktown VA 23690 Office: NASA-Langley Research Center Hampton VA 23601

ANDERSON, WILLIAM HINTON WILDER, assn. exec.; b. Washington, Nov. 27, 1914; s. Parker Richardson and Katharine Wilder (Fort) A.; A.B., U. N.C., 1936; M.S., Columbia, 1937; m. Mary Elizabeth Ferguson, July 5, 1939; children—William Hinton Wilder, Jr., Margaret (Mrs. John Harrelson McGee), David Ira Fort. Reporter, Washington Daily News, 1937-38; reporter, copy editor News and Observer, 1938-42; night editor Asso. Press, 1946-48; copy editor Richmond Times Dispatch, 1948-50; information officer Va. Dept. Hwys., 1950-53; dir. pub. relations and travel promotion Va. State C. of C., 1953-57; mng. dir., exec. sec. treas. Tobacco Growers' Information Com., Raleigh, N.C., 1957—. Mem. Gov's. Adv. Com. Jamestown (Va.) Festival, 1956-57. Trustee, v.p. Va. Episcopal Sch., 1960-66. Served with USNR, 1942-46; lt. comdr. ret. Mem. Pub. Relations Soc. Am., Richmond (pres. 1956-57), Raleigh (pres. 1970) pub. relations assns., Raleigh C. of C., Va. Soc., S.A.R., Sigma Nu. Democrat. Episcopalian. Clubs: Carolina Country, City (Raleigh, N.C.). Editor: Virginia Highway Needs During the National Defense Era, 1952; First American Heritage, 1959; Pride of Kentucky, 1965. Home: 2607 St Marys St Raleigh NC 27609 Office: PO Box 12046 Raleigh NC 27605 also 2016 Cameron St Raleigh NC 27605

ANDERT, RICHARD ALLEN, broadcasting exec.; b. Chanute, Kan., Mar. 10, 1945; s. Henry John and Elma Lenore (Irwin) A.; A.A., Tulsa Jr. Coll., 1973; m. Mary Helen Myers, Mar. 24, 1973. Announcer, asst. news dir. WTMA Radio, Charleston, S.C., 1966-67; announcer, prodn. dir. KELI Radio, Tulsa, 1967-68; announcer KRMG Radio, Tulsa, 1968, prodn. dir., 1968-73, music dir., 1973—. Free-lance radio-TV-newspaper advt. announcer and actor, model. Bd. dirs., chmn. publicity com. Tulsa Little Theatre, 1973—. Served with USNR, 1964-66. Mem. Tulsa Advt. Club (Addy award for outstanding radio comml. prodn. 1969). Lutheran. Republican. Home: 4155 E Skelly Dr Tulsa OK 74135 Office: KRMG 1502 S Boulder St Tulsa OK 74119

ANDRADE, LUCIANO PEDRO, computer systems analyst; b. Fall River, Mass., Aug. 22, 1918; s. Joseph Pedro and Mary (Mello) A.; grad. high sch.; m. Millicent Ferreira, June 16, 1947; children—Joyce (Mrs. Kevin Thomas McLaughlin), Joan Mercedes. Computer programmer Internal Revenue Service, Washington, 1962-68, Dept. Housing and Urban Devel., Washington, 1968-71; systems analyst Internal Revenue Service, Washington, 1971—. Served with USN, 1942-62. Decorated Sec. of Navy Commendation for Achievement award, Purple Heart, Presidential Unit Citation. Mem. Am. Mgmt. Assn., Assn. for Systems Mgmt. Democrat. Roman Catholic. K.C. Home: 6419 Maplewood Dr Falls Church VA 22041 Office: Internal Revenue Service Statistics Div 1111 Constitution Av NW Washington DC 20224

ANDRE, WILLIAM JOSEPH, carpet mfg. co. exec.; b. Croghan, N.Y., Aug. 4, 1926; s. E. A. and Madeline Cecilia (Clark) A.; B.S. in Mgmt. Engring., Rensselaer Poly. Inst., 1950; m. Vesta Helen Powers, Nov. 12, 1949; children—Judith (Mrs. Dwight Gatlin), Janet, Robert, Nancy, Sarah, Mary, William. Tech. asst. Mohawk Carpet Mills, Amsterdam, N.Y., 1950-58; asst. plant supt. Mohasco Industries, Inc., Amsterdam, 1959-62, asst. gen. mgr., Laurens, S.C., 1962-64, gen. mgr., 1964-65, gen. mgr., Dublin, Ga., 1965—. Pres. Dublin Central P.T.A., 1968. Bd. dirs. A.R.C., 1968-69. Served with USNR, 1944-46, 50-51. Mem. Ga. Textile Mfrs. Assn., Ga., Dublin (v.p.) chambers commerce, Epsilon Delta Sigma. Democrat. Roman Catholic. Rotarian (pres. 1970), Elk. Club: Dublin Country (pres. 1969). Home: 1705 Meadowdale Dr Dublin GA 31021 Office: PO Box 430 Dublin GA 31021

ANDREW, WILLIAM FRANK, mgmt. cons.; b. Manitowoc, Wis., Jan. 9, 1929; s. Edward Frank and Evelyn R. (Bouril) A.; B.S., Marquette U., 1952; M.Engring., U. South Fla., 1969; m. Carol Marie Brilliant, Aug. 22, 1951; children—Glenn, Neil. Indsl. engr. Mirro Aluminum Co., Manitowoc, Wis., 1953-60; sr. indsl. and systems engr. Internat. Minerals and Chem. Corp., Bartow, Fla., 1960-67, Skokie, Ill., 1967-68; dir. mgmt. engring. Lakeland (Fla.) Gen. Hosp., 1968-70; pres. William F. Andrew & Assos., Winter Haven, Fla., 1970—, Vacation Information & Planning Corp., Winter Haven, 1973—. Served with USN, 1946-48. Named Outstanding Indsl. engr. Southeastern Region, Am. Inst. Indsl. Engrs., 1970. Registered profl. engr., Fla. Mem. Am. Inst. Indsl. Engrs. (chpt. pres. 1963-64), Am. Hosp. Assn., Hosp. Mgmt. Systems Soc. Republican. Roman Catholic. K.C. (4 deg.). Address: PO Box 9226 Winter Haven FL 33880

ANDREWS, ALFRED STOKES, bus. exec.; b. Dayton, O., Jan. 16, 1903; s. Harry Caho and Clare Margaruite (Stokes) A.; B.S., Carnegie Inst. Tech., 1926; postgrad. Cleve. Marshall Law Sch., 1929-30; m. Estelle Garibaldi, Sept. 2, 1926. Supt., Walker & Weeks, Architects, Cleve., 1926-28; dist. engr. for N.E. Ohio, U.S. Fidelity & Guaranty Co., Cleve., 1929-34; pres. Great Lakes Box Co. (now St. Regis subsidiary), Cleve., 1934-38; owner Am. Flag & Decorating Co., also gen. mgr. Cleve. Aircraft Products Co., 1940-45; pres. Andrews-Bartlett & Assos., Inc., Cleve., 1945-68, chmn. bd., 1968—. Cons. 15 bldg. supply dealers, Cleve. area, 1940-42. Chmn., Ohio City Planning Sponsors and Near West Devel. Assn., 1958-67; v.p. West Side Civic Council, 1960-66; chmn. vis. com. Margaret Morrison Coll., 1960-68; pres., exec. dir. Cuyahoga County Assn. for Retarded, 1965-67. Trustee, Carnegie Mellon U., 1960, life trustee, 1969—; trustee Luth. Hosp., Cleve., 1960-68, adv. bd., 1968—. Recipient Raphael award for work with retarded Cleve. Raphael Soc., 1967, Distinguished Service award Carnegie-Mellon, 1968. Mem. Am. Soc. C.E. (life), Cleve. C. of C. (chmn. lakefront com. 1954-58), Cleve. Engring. Soc., Cleve. Advt. Club, Area Council Cleve. Welfare Assn., Carnegie Tech. Alumni (pres. fedn. 1960), Sigma Alpha Epsilon. Presbyn. (trustee). Club: Clifton (Lakewood, O.). Author: Carnegie Song Book, 1924; Andrews-Wright Genealogy, 1970. Home: Marine Tower 2500 E Las Olas Fort Lauderdale FL 33301 Office: 1849 W 24th St Cleveland OH 44113

ANDREWS, HARVEY WELLINGTON, med. lab. exec.; b. Stowe Twp., Pa., Sept. 9, 1928; s. Robert W. and Theresa R. (Reis) A.; B.B.A. cum laude, U. Pitts., 1952; M.B.A., Harvard, 1957; m. Jane Garland, Aug. 9, 1969; children—Marcia Lynne, Glynis Susann. With Gen. Electric Co., Syracuse, N.Y., 1952-55, Scovill Mfg. Co., Waterbury, Conn., 1957; comptroller Alcon Labs., Inc., Ft. Worth, 1958-61, comptroller, treas., 1961-65, v.p. finance, 1964-68; pres. Medimation, Inc., Ft. Worth, 1968—, also dir.; dir. Med. Scis. Computer Corp., First's Clin. Labs., Hereford Med. Labs., Dalworth Med. Labs., Union Bank of Ft. Worth. Mem. Tarrant County Health Planning Council. Bd. dirs., mem. exec. com. Fort Worth Opera Assn. Served with AUS, 1946-48. Mem. A.A.A.S., Am. Acad. Polit. and Social Scis., Soc. Advancement Mgmt., Order Artus, Scabbard and Blade, Sigma Alpha Epsilon. Republican. Lutheran. Mason (32 deg.). Clubs: Fort Worth Boat, Colonial Country, Century II. Home: PO Box 1786 3124 Chaparral Lane Fort Worth TX 76101 Office: 714 Main St Fort Worth TX 76102

ANDREWS, HENRY G., JR., lawyer; b. Stamford, Tex., Mar. 5, 1922; s. Henry G. and Gladys (Ledbetter) A.; B.B.A., U. Tex., 1943, LL.B., 1947; m. Alice Tatum, May 31, 1947; children—Lisa, Diane. Admitted to Tex. bar, 1947; practiced in Stamford, 1948-54, 64—, Anson, 1955-63; mem. firm Andrews & Andrews, 1948—. Dir. Stamford Fed. Savs. & Loan Assn., R. D. Bandeen Co., Inc., San Antonio. County judge, Jones County, Tex., 1955-63; mayor City of Stamford, 1965-68. Bd. dirs. Tex. Motor Vehicle Commn., 1971-72, Tex. Dept. Pub. Welfare, 1972—; dist. lay leader N.W. Tex. Annual Conf., 1970-73; trustee King's Manor, Hereford, Tex., 1970—. Served with USAAC, 1943-46. Mem. Am., Tex. bar assns., Chi Phi. Democrat. Methodist (chmn. adminstrv. bd. 1959-63). Rotarian. Club: Stamford (pres. 1963-64). Home: 1413 Hudson Rd Stamford TX 79553 Office: 117 S Wetherbee St Stamford TX 79553

ANDREWS, IKE F., congressman; b. Bonlee, N.C., Sept. 2, 1925; s. Archie F. and Ina Azalene (Dunlap) A.; B.S., U. N.C., 1950, J.D., 1952; married; children—Alice (Mrs. John J. Hackney), Nina Patricia. Admitted to N.C. bar; practiced law, Siler City, N.C., 1952-72; mem. 93d Congress from 4th N.C. dist. Mem. N.C. Gov.'s Commn. Restructuring Higher Edn. Mem. N.C. Senate, 1959-61; mem. N.C. Ho. of Reps., 1961-63, 67-71, Democratic majority leader, speaker pro-tem, 1971. Bd. govs. U. N.C., 1972. Served with AUS, 1943-45. Decorated Bronze Star, Purple Heart. Baptist (chmn. bd. deacons, Sunday Sch. tchr.). Mason. Home: Pine Forest Dr Siler City NC 27344 Office: 501 Cannon House Office Bldg Washington DC 20515

ANDREWS, JAMES CLAIRE, physician; b. Pleasant Plain, Ia., Mar. 7, 1921; s. Claire H. and Lola E. (Crew) A.; student Upper Ia. U., 1940-42; B.S., U. Notre Dame, 1945; M.D., U. Mich., 1949; m. Katherine P. McGinnis, June 21, 1947; 1 son, John C. Intern, St. Joseph's Hosp., Lexington, Ky., 1949-50; resident U. Va. Hosp., 1950, 52-55; practice medicine, specializing in dermatology, Charlottesville, Va., 1955—, mem. staff Martha Jefferson Hosp., Charlottesville. Served with USNR, 1942-46; as capt. M.C., USAF, 1950-52. Mem. A.A.A.S., Am. Acad. Dermatology, Am., So. med. assns., Washington Dermatol. Assn., Va., Albemarle County med. socs., Soc. Investigative Dermatology, Internat. Soc. Tropical Dermatology, Am. Assn. Automotive Assn., Va. Dermatol. Soc. Presbyn. (elder). Home: Woodland RFD 6 Box 303 Charlottesville VA 22901 Office: Doctor's Bldg 801 E High St Charlottesville VA 22901

ANDREWS, JAMES LEWIS, army officer, oral surgeon; b. Canton, O., June 7, 1929; s. Lloyd F. and Gertrude (Griggs) A.; D.D.S. cum laude, Ohio State U., 1953; postgrad. Northwestern U., 1961-62; m. Joanne Mary Jenkins, Aug. 2, 1952; children—Susan L., Ellen J., David L. Intern oral surgery Univ. Hosps., Columbus, O., 1953-54; commd. 1st lt. U.S. Army, 1954, advanced through grades to col. 1971; stationed Ft. Knox, Ky., 1954-57; oral surgeon U.S. Army Hosp., Berlin, Germany, 1958-61; resident oral surgeon Letterman Gen. Hosp., San Francisco, 1962-64, asst. chief oral surgery, 1965-66, chief oral surgery, 1966-68; chief dental services 106th Gen. Hosp., 1968-70; chief clinician dental clinic Camp Zama, Japan, 1970-71; oral surgeon Darnall Army Hosp., Ft. Hood, Tex., 1971—. Diplomate Am. Bd. Oral Surgery. Fellow Am. Coll. Dentists; mem. Am. Soc. Oral Surgeons, Am. Acad. Oral Pathology, Am. Dental Assn., Omicron Kappa Upsilon. Mason. Contbr. articles to profl. jours. Address: Darnall Army Hosp Fort Hood TX 76544

ANDREWS, JOE WILLIAM, JR., assn. exec.; b. Blanton, Ala., Feb. 14, 1926; s. J.W. and Charlie Belle (Williams) A.; A.B., Mercer U., 1948, postgrad., 1949-50; student Southeastern Inst. Comml. Orgn. Execs., 1955-56; m. Virginia Garland, Apr. 22, 1951; children—Joe W. III, Laura. Editorial dept. Macon (Ga.) Telegraph & News, 1943-49; dir. pub. relations S.C. Farm Bur., Anderson, 1949-51, WMAZ Radio and TV, Macon, 1951-62; pres. So. Assn. Services, Inc., Macon, also Southeastern Services, Inc., Macon, 1963—; owner J & L Prodns.; pres. Builders Mortgage Corp.; dir. Carlisle Investment Co., Inc., Train, Inc. Served as lt. inf. AUS, World War II. Mem. Am. Soc. Assn. Execs., Multiple Assn. Mgmt. Assn., Sales Execs. Club Macon (pres. 1959), Distributive Edn. Club Am. (hon. life), Sigma Delta Chi, Phi Delta Theta. Baptist. Clubs: Macon Farmers (pres. 1958), Kiwanis (Macon). Home: 720 Forest Ridge Dr W Macon GA 31208 Office: 1239 2d St Macon GA 31202

ANDREWS, JOHN HOLT, banker; b. Dallas, Dec. 30, 1908; s. Allen Llewlyn a and Hassie (Martin) A.; student Ala. Poly. Inst., 1926, Southwestern U., 1927; m. Tommy Lou Robertson, July 2, 1932; 1 dau., Barbara Ruth (Mrs. John Fredrick Kopsky). With Frost Nat. Bank, San Antonio, 1928-42, 46-50; asst. cashier First State Bank, Bishop, Tex., 1950-51; asst. v.p. First State Bank, Memphis, Tex., 1952; asst. cashier Nat. Bank of Fort Sam Houston (Tex.), 1953-55, asst. v.p., 1955-60, v.p., 1960-65, sr. v.p., 1965-70, exec. v.p., 1970-72, pres., 1972—, also dir. Served to 1st lt. arty. AUS, 1942-46. Mem. Am. Inst. Banking (pres. San Antonio chpt. 1962-63), San Antonio C. of C., Am. Logistics Assn., Assn. U.S. Army. Sigma Phi Epsilon. Methodist. Mason, Optimist. Home: 411 Beverly Dr San Antonio TX 78228 Office: 1422 E Grayson St San Antonio TX 78208

ANDREWS, RAWLE, physician; b. Grenada, W.I., Feb. 4, 1929; s. Lawrence and Adina (Gibbes) A.; came to U.S., 1952, naturalized, 1969; B.S. with honors, Hampton Inst., 1956; postgrad. U. R.I., U. Mich., 1956-58; M.D., Meharry Med. Coll., 1963; m. Naomi Cox, Aug. 17, 1963; children—Rawle, Rhetta, Ronald. Intern Los Angeles County Gen. Hosp., 1963-64; gen. practice medicine, Houston, 1964—. Sch. physician Charles R. Drew Sch., Houston, 1964, William Jr.-Sr. High, Houston, 1965-67; mem. adv. bd. Riverside Nat. Bank, Houston. Pres., Houston Med. Forum, 1970, 71-72; v.p. Acres Home Citizens Council, 1969-70, pres., 1970-72. Bd. dirs. Operation

Breadbasket, co-chmn. task task force com. Houston Galveston Area council, 1970—; bd. dirs. So. Christian Leadership conf.; mem. adv. bd. Eliza Johnson Center for Aged, Martin Luther King Center; v.p., trustee Montessori Sch., Houston, 1970-71. Recipient Humanitarian award Antioch Bapt. Ch., 1969. Mem. A.M.A., Royal Soc. Health, Nat. Med. Assn. (chmn. bd. trustees, bd. dirs.). Mason (med. dir. lodge). Home: 5325 Blythewood Houston TX 77021 Office: 7901 W Montgomery Rd Houston TX 77088

ANDREWS, WILLIAM FREDERICK, mfg. co. exec.; b. Easton, Pa., Oct. 7, 1931; s. William Frederick and Lydia Nielson (Cross) A.; B.S., U. Md., 1953; M.B.A., Seton Hall U., 1961; m. Carol Meadow Beaman, Feb. 8, 1962; children—William, Whitney, Carter, Clayton, Sloane. Mgmt. trainee W.R. Grace & Co., N.Y.C., 1956-57; salesman Kaiser Aluminum Co., N.J., 1957-58; salesman Scovill Mfg. Co., Mills div., N.Y. and N.C., 1958-62, dist. mgr., Southeast, 1962-65; product mgr. rod and wire, Waterbury, Conn., 1965-68, gen. mgr. fluid power div., Raleigh, N.C., 1968-72, group v.p. automotive and fluid power group, Nashville, 1973—; dir. occidental Life Ins. Co., Raleigh, Peden Steel Co., Raleigh, Peninsular Life Ins. Co., Jacksonville, Fla., McMillan Corp., Jacksonville, Valves & Produits, Pontarlier, France, Schrader Scovill Duncan Ltd., Bombay, India, Schrader Scovill Brazil, Schrader Scovill Japan, Schrader Scovill Australia. Bd. dirs. Middle Tenn. Council Boy Scouts Am. Served to capt. USAF, 1953-56. Mem. Nat. Fluid Power Assn. (v.p., bd. dirs. 1970—), Machinery and Allied Products Inst. (marketing council 1969—), Fluid Power Found. (bd. trustees 1970—, v.p. 1971—), Sigma Chi, Gate and Key. Republican. Episcopalian. Clubs: Carolina Country (Raleigh), Hillwood Country. Home: Rolling River Farm Old Hillsboro Rd Franklin TN 37064 Office: 2000 Richard Jones Rd Nashville TN 37215

ANDUJAR, JOHN J., physician; b. Chgo., Jan. 26, 1912; s. M.A. and Lily (Kurzenknabe) A.; B.S., Pa. State Univ., 1930; M.D., Temple U., 1934; postgrad. Union U., 1935-36, Cornell U., 1942; m. Elizabeth Richards, Aug. 16, 1935; children—Betty Jo, Linda Lee. Intern Harrisburg Gen. Hosp., 1934-35, Memorial Hosp., N.Y. C., 1942-43, Bender Hygienic Lab., Albany, N.Y., 1935-36; asso. prof. U. Ark., 1937-38; practice of medicine, Ft. Worth, 1938—; prof. med. technology Tex. Christian U., 1938-50; dir. Ft. Worth Med. Labs., Doctors Hosp. Labs., Ft. Worth Dept. Health Labs., Texas Dept. Health Regional Labs.; cons. pathologist USPHS, John Peter Smith hosps., Carswell AFB Sta. Hosp. Past pres. Tarrant County Crime Commn. Past. pres. Am Pathology Found.; pres. World Pathology Found. Diplomate Nat. Bd. Med. Examiners, Am. Bd. Pathology (past pres.). Fellow Am. Soc. Clin. Pathologists (past. pres.), A.C.P., Coll. Am. Pathologists (founder); mem. A.A.A.S., A.M.A., Am. Assn. Blood Banks (founder), Am. Assn. Phys. and Surg., Am. Cancer Soc., Soc. Am. Bacteriologists, Pan-Am. Tex. Acad. Internal Medicine, Assn. Mil. Surgeons U.S., Internat. Acad. Pathology, Am. Public Health Assn., Tex. Acad. Sci., Tex. Hosp. Assn., Tex. Pub Health Assn., Tex. Soc. Pathologists (past pres.), Tarrant County Med. Soc. (past pres.), Internat. Council Soc. Pathology, Royal Soc. Health, World Assn. Soc. Pathology (pres. 1969-72), Tarrant County Mental Health Soc., Phi Beta Pi. Presbyterian. Clubs: Fort Worth Boat, Peninsula Country, Torch. Address: PO Box 1118 Fort Worth TX 76101

ANGELE, GUSTAVE JOHN, SR., civil engr.; b. Balt., Mar. 30, 1906; s. John and Emma Anna (Wirth) A.; student Internat. Corr. Schs., 1920-24, Johns Hopkins, 1927-30; m. Myrtle Marie Sauer, June 19, 1935; 1 son, Gustave John, Jr. Sr. design engr. Union Carbide Nuclear div. Union Carbide Corp., Oak Ridge, 1944-71; plant san. engr., Oak Ridge, 1971. Chmn. bd. plumbing examiners City Oak Ridge, 1961-71; mem. U.S. Power Squadron, 1947—. Registered profl. engr., Tenn. Mem. Am. Water Works Assn. (chmn. backflow com.; moderator cross connection control seminars), Am. Soc. San. Engrs., Am. Soc. C.E. Mason. Contbr. articles to profl. jours. Home: 120 Porter Rd Oak Ridge TN 37830 Office: PO Box 237 Oak Ridge TN 37830

ANGER, CHARLES LEROY, educator; b. Balt., May 13, 1912; s. Charles P. and Catherine (Kemp) A.; B.S., U. Va., 1932, M.S., 1933, Ph.D., 1940; m. Elizabeth Abbey Foy, Oct. 4, 1963. Asst. prof. The Citadel, Charleston, S.C., 1941-44. asso. prof., 1946-55. prof., head dept. history, 1955—. Chmn., S.C. Commn. Archives and History, 1965—, S.C. bd. review Nat. Register Historic Places, 1969—; mem. S.C. Am. Revolution Bicentennial Commn., 1971—. Mem. Am. (life), S.C. (pres. 1959-61), So. hist. assns. Episcopalian. Clubs: Carolina Yacht, Charleston. Home: 843 Sheldon Rd Charleston SC 29407

ANGLIN, W(ILLIAM) E(NGLISH), judge; b. Burnsville, N.C., Oct. 24, 1907; s. Geo. W. and Carrie (English) A.; B.S., U. N.C., 1934, LL.B. 1934. Admitted to N.C. bar, 1934, practiced under own name in Burnsville, 1934-42, 46-65; resident superior ct. judge, 1965—. Served to comdr. USNR, 1942-46; PTO. Mem. N.C. Bar Assn., Theta Chi, Phi Delta Phi. Office: PO Box 217 Burnsville NC 28714

ANGUIZOLA, GUSTAVE ANTONIO, educator; b. Panama City, Panama, Feb. 28, 1927; s. Antonio Anguizola and Melida Guerra (Kern) Parma; B.S., Panama Instituto Nacional, 1944; B.A. (U.S. Jr. C. of C. scholar), U. Evansville, 1948; M.A. (fellow), Ind. U., 1950, Ph.D., 1953; M.S., Mich. State U., 1953; postgrad. Am. Sch. Classics and Archaeology, Athens, Greece, 1964; m. Elizabeth Gavin, Feb. 28, 1952 (div. (Apr. 1955)); 1 son, Jerome Anthony. Personal sec. to Antonio Anguizola, 1939-44; lab. technologist Bird & Son, Gary, Ind., 1956-61, sr. chem. tester, 1958-60; prof. econs. and govt., chmn. dept. Morris (S.C.) Coll., 1960-61; prof. Latin Am. history and govt. N.C. State U., Elizabeth City, 1961-62, chmn. dept., 1962-63; vis. prof. Latin Am. instns. N.Y. State U., 1962, 63; asst. prof. history polit. sci. Purdue U., Lafayette, Ind., 1963-66; asso. prof. history polit. sci. Chgo. State U., 1967-68; asst. prof. history polit. sci. U. Tex., Arlington, 1966—. Spl. asst. to mayor of Chgo. for Pan Am. Games, 1959; cons. Hispanic Am. Hist. Rev., 1970, Panama's Treatymaking commn., 1964-65, 67-68, Wax Mus., Dallas, 1973—. Served with AUS, 1942-44. Recipient grand prize, gold medal Sesquicentennial Commn. for Panama Canal, 1953; Hays-Mundt award, 1953, Fulbright-Hays award, 1964-65. U. Tex. grantee, 1973, 74. Mem. Am., So., European, Nat., hist. assns., Am. Assn. U. Profs., Conf. Latin Am., Renaissance Soc. Am., Community Coll. Social Sci. Assn., Rocky Mountain Social Sci. Assn. Clubs: Westerners (Ft. Worth); Playboy (Chgo.); Newman (Arlington, Tex.). Author: The Taft Convention, 1955. Home: 920 Appleton St Arlington TX 76010 also 2909 W Logan Blvd Chicago IL 60647 Office: Box 19488 University of Texas Station Arlington TX 76019 also PO Box 2138 Panama City Panama

ANKRUM, WARD ELWOOD, educator; b. Danville, Ill., Mar. 2, 1910; s. Wesley Jay and Margaret Elizabeth (Ward) A.; student Wabash Coll., 1929-32; B.S. in Edn., U. Ill., 1934, M.S. in Edn., 1941; student U. Denver, 1942-43; Ed.D., U. Mo., 1951; m. Wilma Mooney Walloch, May 30, 1965. Instr. speech and English, Danville High Sch., 1938-42; ednl. specialist, div. instr. tng. USAAF, 1942-44; instr. speech and English, U. Denver, 1943-44; chmn. English dept. Coronado (Cal.) High Sch., 1944-45; instr. div. communications Stephens Coll., Columbia, Mo., 1945-52, dir. audio-visual library, 1952-57; asso. prof., dir. audio-visual edn. Henderson State Tchrs. Coll., Arkadelphia, Ark., 1957-63, prof., dir. audio visual edn., 1963—; Ford Found. lectr. Ark. A. and M. Coll., 1953; co-dir. Grad. and Undergrad. Credit Workshop, Northeast Mo. State Tchrs. Coll., Kirksville, 1954-58, 62, 64, 66; asst. dir. Ednl. Media Inst. Ark. State Coll., summer 1967; spl. research influence selected TV programs on preservice tchrs. fundamental factors in reading rate acceleration. Charter pres. Columbia (Mo.) Art Theatre Adv. Council, 1955-58; chmn. audiovisual services Mo. P.T.A., 1955-58; del. from Mo. nat. conv. P.T.A., 1957; chmn. audio-visual services Ark. P.T.A., 1958-61; pres. dept. audio visual services Mo. Tchrs. Assn., 1955-56; juror Golden Reel Film Festival, N.Y.C., 1955, juror, chmn. motion pictures in edn., 1956. Mem. Clark County Health Adv. Bd., 1972—. Mem. adv. bd. Wonderland Sch., Arkadelphia. Mem. Nat. (parliamentarian dept. audio visual instrn. 1960—), Ark. (pres. Ark. audio visual assn. 1959-61, treas. 1971—, pres. unit 1973—) edn. assns., Ark. Ednl. TV Assn. (v.p. 1961—, Phi Delta Kappa, Tau Kappa Epsilon. Republican. Presbyn. Mason. Co-author: Utilization of Audio-Materials in Missouri, 1955. Contbr. articles to profl. jours. Home: 309 Riverside Dr Arkadelphia AR 71923

ANSLEY, JOSEPH ALBERT, banker; b. Americus, Ga., Feb. 24, 1906; s. Joseph A. and Jessie (Whitaker) A.; student Stetson U., 1925-26, Am. Inst. Banking, 1948, Sch. Financial Pub. Relations, Northwestern U., 1950, Grad. Sch. Banking, Rutgers, The State U., 1953; m. Barbara Jean Holmes, Nov. 13, 1943; children—Barbara Jean, Mary Elizabeth. Advt. dir. Ft. Myers News-Press, 1927-42; with Lee County Bank, Ft. Myers, Fla., 1945—, pres., 1966—, chmn. bd., 1967—.*Pres., Lee Meml. Hosp., Ft. Myers, Fla., 1963-65, bd. dirs., 1947—. Served with USNR, 1942-45. Recipient citations Bankings Forum in Print, 1951, 52, 53. Mem. Am. Inst. Mgmt. (fellow pres.'s council 1967—), Am. Bankers Assn. (mem. exec. council 1970-71), Fla. Bankers Assn. (pres. 1957), Financial Pub. Relations Assn., 40 and 8, Am. Legion (comdr. 1947), Fla., Ft. Myers chambers commerce; Am. Orchid Soc. Presbyn. Mason. Clubs: Kiwanis (pres. 1937), Royal Palm Yacht (commodore 1966). Home: 441 Keenan Av Fort Myers FL 33901 Office: 1st and Monroe Sts Fort Myers FL 33902

ANSPACH, THOMAS EARL, computer engr., b. Sterling, Ill., Apr. 15, 1933; s. Floyd Melvin and Clarisse Marion (Jones) A.; B.S. in Elec. Engring., Milw. Sch. Engring., 1959; m. Helmi Gawboy, Sept. 21, 1957 (div. Aug. 1970); children—Marie Ellen, Thomas Alan, Jeffry Eugene, Bruce Wayne. Design engr. Bell Labs., Whippany, N.J., 1959-63; design engr. Honeywell, Inc., St. Petersburg, Fla., 1963-69, project engr., 1969—. Served with USN, 1952-56. Mem. I.E.E.E. Largo/Clearwater Jaycees (sec. 1964-65, v.p. 1966-67, dir.). Mason. Home: 710 Beach Trail Indian Rocks Beach FL 33535 Office: 13350 US Hwy 19 St Petersburg FL 35733

ANTHONY, JACK RAMON, mech. engr.; b. Hobbs, N.M., Dec. 9, 1932; s. Wadie Fowler and Zelma (Allen) A.; B.S., U. N.M., 1959; postgrad. Tex. Tech. U., 1969—; m. Peggy Lou Berryhill, July 17, 1953; children—Vera Lynn, Michael Ray. Engr. Controls Co. Am., Santa Fe, 1959-61; project engr. Eberline Instrument Corp., Santa Fe, 1961-63; engr. space div. Chrysler Corp., New Orleans, 1963-65; design engr. Dresser Co., Houston, 1965-67; project engr. Mason & Hanger, Amarillo, Tex., 1967—. Mem. Sheriff's Posse Hutchison County, 1968—. Served with AUS, 1953-55. Registered profl. engr., Tex. Mem. Tex. Soc. Profl. Engrs., Pi Tau Sigma. Toastmaster. Home: PO Box 3389 Borger TX 79007 Office: PO Box 647 Amarillo TX 79105

ANTHONY, LONNIE LESLIE, JR., elec. engr.; b. Wilson, Okla., May 20, 1922; s. Lonnie Leslie and Mabel Oneta (Bell) A. B.S. in Elec. Engring., U. Tex., 1943; M.S. in Elec. Engring., U. Tenn., 1967; m. Annie Justine Naiser, Apr. 28, 1943; children—Barbara (Mrs. Everett Hampton Lowe), Lynn (Mrs. Kenneth Spake), Mary, Karen, Richard. Test engr. Gen. Elec. Co., Schenectady, 1943-44; vacuum test engr. Kellex Corp., N.Y.C., 1944, Oak Ridge, 1944; engr. Union Carbide Corp., Oak Ridge, 1944, operations supr., 1945-54, shift supt., 1954-63, dept. head, 1967—. Registered profl. engr., Tenn. Mem. I.E.E.E. (chmn. Oak Ridge sect. 1961-62), Assn. for Computing Machinery, Eta Kappa Nu, Tau Beta Pi, Kappa Kappa Psi. Kiwanian (pres. 1964). Home: 104 Enfield Lane Oak Ridge TN 37830 Office: PO Box P Oak Ridge TN 37830

ANTON, PAUL NAJIB, engr.; b. Jerusalem, Palestine, Dec. 19, 1934; s. Nicola Najib and Mary Michail (Salama) A.; diploma St. George's Coll., Heliopolis, Egypt, 1951; B.A., U. Tex., 1960; postgrad. St. Mary's U., San Antonio, 1960-62; m. Alida Ihle Anton, Aug. 11, 1973; 1 dau. by previous marriage, Cybele Najib. Came to U.S., 1954, naturalized, 1962. Various banking duties Alamo Nat. Bank, San Antonio, 1959-61; sci. programming analyst Lockheed Missiles and Space Co., Sunnyvale, Cal., 1962-70; devel. project engr. Well Services div. Schlumberger Tech. Corp., Houston, 1970—. Mem. Assn. Computing Machinery. Republican. Home: 13290 Trail Hollow Houston TX 77024 Office: PO Box 2175 Houston TX 77001

APEL, JOHN RALPH, physicist; b. Absecon, N.J., June 14, 1930; s. Ezio A. and Grace A. (Rose) Baltera; B.S., U. Md., 1957, M.S., 1961; Ph.D. (William S. Parsons fellow), Johns Hopkins, 1970; m. Martha Eleise Davis, Sept. 8, 1956; children—Denise Allison, Jacqueline Jeanne. With applied physics lab. Johns Hopkins U., Silver Spring, Md., 1957-70, sr. physicist, 1961-70, asst. group supr., 1966-70; dir. for ocean remote sensing lab., Atlantic oceanographic and meteorol. labs. Nat. Oceanic and Atmospheric Adminstrn., Miami, Fla., 1970—. Adj. prof. physics U. Miami, 1970—; cons., NASA, 1971—. Served with USNR, 1951-52. Mem. Am. Phys. Soc., Philos. Soc. Washington, N.Y. Acad. Scis., Am. Geophys. Union, Sigma Xi, Sigma Pi Sigma, Phi Delta Theta. Club: Country Coral Gables. Contbg. author: Advances in Geophysics, Vol. 9, 1962. Contbr. to profl. jours. Home: 3266 Riviera Dr Coral Gables FL 33134 Office: 15 Rickenbacker Causeway Virginia Key Miami FL 33149

APFFEL, ERVIN AUGUST, JR., lawyer; b. Galveston, Tex., Aug. 9, 1929; s. Ervin A. and Angie (Coselli) A.; B.S., St. Edward's U., 1951; LL.B., St. Mary's U., 1957; m. Christine Matthews, June 4, 1955; children—Jeanie Marie, Ervin III, Patricia Ann, Pamela Ann, Darrell Anthony, Christi Carol. Admitted to Tex. bar, 1957; asst. dist. atty., Galveston County, Tex., 1957-61; asst. city atty. City Galveston, 1961-64, city atty., 1964, acting city mgr., 1964; partner firm McLeo, Alexander, Powel & Apffel, Inc., Galveston, 1965—. Served with AUS, 1951-53. Tex. Bar Found. fellow, 1968—. Mem. C. of C. (dir. 1969-71), Galveston County Bar Assn. (pres. 1972-73, dir.), Bar Assn. State Tex., Tex. Assn. Def. Counsel, Phi Delta Phi. Home: 1006 Airway Lane Galveston TX 77550 Office: 200 University Blvd PO Box 629 Galveston TX 77550

APINIS, JOHN, chemist; b. Katvari, Latvia, Mar. 20, 1933; s. Augusts and Marta (Gravelsins) A.; B.S., Clemson U., 1960; m. Johnnie Verena Burden, Feb. 6, 1960. Came to U.S., 1949, naturalized, 1954. Apprentice, Am. Thread Co., Willimantic, Conn., 1951-52, Leiss Velvet Mfg. Co., Willimantic, 1952-53; asst. plant chemist Burlington Industries, Wake Finishing Co., Raleigh, N.C., 1960-65, plant chemist, 1965—. Served with AUS, 1953-55. Mem. Am. Assn. Textile Chemists and Colorists. Elk, Rotarian (v.p. 1963-64, pres. 1964-65, dir. 1963-66). Research in textile color computer and chromosorter. Home: 2205 Millbrook Rd Raleigh NC 27604 Office: Box 2748 Raleigh NC 27602

APONTE-PEREZ, FRANCISCO, labor lawyer; b. Barranquitas, P.R., Sept. 17, 1928; s. Delfin and Catalina (Perez) Aponte; B.A. magna cum laude, U. P.R., 1950; LL.B., U. Kan., 1958; m. Ana C. Alices, Oct. 27, 1957; children—Liza, Maria, Emma. Admitted to P.R. bar; adminstrv. tech. staff P.R. Bur. Budget, San Juan, 1951-53; labor mediator and arbitrator P.R. Dept. Labor, San Juan, 1953-58; trial examiner P.R. Labor Relations Bd., San Juan, 1958-60; practiced labor law, Santurce, P.R., 1960—. Lectr. U. P.R., mem. bd. bar examiners P.R. Supreme Ct. Pres. P.R. Civil Service Commn.; mem. P.R. Pub. Housing Reform Com., P.R. Labor Law Reform Commn. Served as 1st lt. AUS. Recipient citations Interam. U., Govt. of V.I., Am. Trial Lawyers Assn. Mem. P.R. (pres. 1970—), Interam. (pres. law commn.), Am. (mem. pres.'s conf.) bar assns. Columnist San Juan Star, El Mundo. Contbr. articles to law revs. Home: A-1 Montebello Gardens Hills PR 00619 Office: 607 Condado Av Santurce PR 00908

APPEL, WILLIAM GEORGE, assn. exec.; b. Pitts., Dec. 13, 1925; s. Ellwood and Charlotte (Wiertheimer) A.; student Inst. Orgn. Mgmt., Mich. State U., 1968-70; div.; 1 son, Robert William. Shipping clk. Paramount Pictures, Pitts., 1948-50, booker, Atlanta, 1950-51; booker Universal Pictures, Atlanta, 1951-54, salesman, Cin., 1954-57; sales engr. Shower Door Co. Am., Atlanta, 1958-61; v.p. sales A-B Real Estate & Constrn. Co., Smyrna, Ga., 1961-63; gen. sales mgr. King-Williams Land Co., Smyrna, 1963-64; asst. v.p. Potter & Co., Smyrna, 1964-66; exec. dir. Ga. Automotive Wholesalers Assn., Atlanta, 1966—. Mem. Heart Assn. Fund, 1965. Served with AUS, 1944-46; ETO. Recipient Distinguished Service award So. Automotive Show, 1969, 74. Mem. Automotive Wholesalers Assn. Execs. (chmn. liaison com. 1971-74, chmn. edn. com. 1970—, sec. 1969-70, v.p. 1970-71, pres. 1971-72), Ga. Soc. Assn. Execs. (sec. treas. 1968-71, sec. 1973-74, v.p. 1974—, exec. com.), Automotive Booster Club, Am. Soc. Assn. Execs., Internat. Platform Assn., Airline Passengers Assn. Contbg. columist Automotive Aftermarket News, 1971-72, Cotton Pickers jour. Atlanta Automotive Boosters, 1970—. Home: 3838-C Brockett Trail Clarkston GA 30021 Office: 8 LaVista Perimeter Office Park Tucker GA 30084

APPLE, MELVIN J., optometrist; b. Charleston, W.Va., Oct. 9, 1940; s. Gerald and Dora (Cohen) A.; student W.Va. U., 1955-58; D.Optometry, Ill. Coll. Optometry, 1961; m. Ursula Frances Hand, June 3, 1963; children—Marc, Michele. Individual practice optometry, Boca Raton, Fla., 1968—. Cons. visually related learning disabilities to various schs. Div. Children's Med. Services. Mem. adv. bd. Gables Acad. and Learning Success Center, 1970—. Served to capt. USAF, 1961-68. Fellow Am. Acad. Optometry, Coll. Optometrists in Vision Devel.; mem. Am., Fla., Palm Beach County (v.p. 1973-74) optometric assns. Kiwanian. Home: 719 Elm Tree Lane Boca Raton FL 33432 Office: 152 S Federal Hwy Boca Raton FL 33432

APPLE, WILLIAM SHOULDEN, assn. exec. b. Spokane, Wash., July 28, 1918; s. Harry and Ann (Chon) A.; student Wayne State U., 1945-46; B.S. in Pharmacy, U. Wis., 1949, M.B.A., 1951, Ph.D., 1954; D.Sc. (hon.), U. L.I., 1966, Union U., 1969; m. Lucille Harriet Josephs, May 3, 1942; children—Chandra Eden, Hugh Charles. Instr. pharmacy U. Wis., 1951-53, asst. prof., 1953-56, asso. prof., chmn. dept. pharmacy adminstrn., 1956-58; asst. sec. Am. Pharm. Assn., Washington, 1958-59, sec., gen. mgr., 1959, exec. dir., 1959—. Del. U.S. Pharmacopeial Conv., Washington, 1960; mem. Com. 100 for Nat. Health Ins. Charter bd. dirs. Community Health Inc.; bd. dirs. Am. Assn. World Health Inc., U.S. com. for WHO. Served to maj. AUS, 1941-46; lt. col. Res. Named Am. Druggist of Yr., 1961, 67, Rho Pi Phi Man of Yr., 1961; recipient J. Leon Lascoff Meml. award, 1961, Wayne State U. Distinguished Service award, 1962, Hugo H. Schaefer medal, 1966, Remington Honor medal, 1967; Colegio de Quimico Farmaceuticos de Chili, 1961; U. Wis. citation, 1965. Fellow A.A.A.S., Am. Soc. Hosp. Pharmacists; mem. National Drug Trade Conf. (sec.-treas., pres. 1970), Am., Wis. (pres. 1956-57, chmn. bd. 1957-58) pharm. assns., Am. Council Pharm. Edn. (past pres.), Internat. Pharm. Fedn. (U.S. rep.), N.Y. Acad. Scis., Japan Pharm. Assn. (hon.), Rho Chi, Phi Lambda Upsilon, Phi Kappa Phi. Home: 6423 Crosswoods Dr Falls Church VA 22044 Office: 2215 Constitution Av NW Washington DC 20037

APPLEGATE, CHARLES STANLEY, JR., physician; b. Fort Smith, Ark., June 23, 1920; s. Charles Stanley and Helen Louise (Parmelee) A.; B.S., U. Ark., 1942, M.D., 1945; m. Annabel Applegate, Apr. 3, 1954; children—Jo Anne (Mrs. Chester Vogt), Charles Stanley III. Intern, Univ. Hosp., Little Rock, 1945-46; gen. practice medicine, Springdale, Ark., 1949—. Pres., dir. Springdale Savs. & Loan Assn., 1960—. Chmn. adv. com. to mayor of Springdale, 1969—. Chmn. Springdale Housing Authority, 1967—. Served with M.C., AUS, 1946-48. Mem. A.M.A., Ark. (pres. 1971-72), Washington County med. socs., Am. Assn. Family Practice, Springdale C. of C. (pres. 1969-70, chmn. indsl. com. 1966—). Home: 322 S Pleasant St Springdale AR 72764 Office: 220 Meadow Av Springdale AR 72764

APPLESTEIN, ALLAN HAMBURGER, food co. exec.; b. Balt., Jan. 16, 1932; s. Aaron S. and Rose (Hamburger) A.; B.A. magna cum laude, Brandeis U., 1953; M.S. in Biochemistry, Harvard, 1955, D.J.S. summa cum laude, 1956; m. Judith Gould, Nov. 4, 1961; children—Abbie Jo, Andie Jane, Amie Jill. Chmn. bd. Basic Food Industries, Inc. and subsidiaries, South Miami, Fla., 1959—; dir. numerous pvt. cos. Bd. overseers World Bank; prof. U. Miami Grad. Sch. Law and Biochemistry. Bd. dirs. Brandeis U., Boston Coll., Miami Mus. Sci., U. Miami, Citizens League; bd. dirs., 1st chmn. Coral Gables Cult Series; trustee Temple Judea, Miami Philharmonic Orch. Served to lt. gen. U.S. Army, 1954. Decorated Purple Heart with 4 oak leaf clusters, D.S.C. with oak leaf cluster. Mem. Am. Bar Assn., Internat. Platform Assn., MENSA, Phi Beta Kappa. Clubs: Bankers, Harvard (Miami); Branfiff International Council (Dallas); National High Sch. and Coll. Hall of Fame (Ohio). Author: The Labyrinth of Life, 1950; Bentham and Utilitarianism, 1953; Constitution of State of Israel, 1952; Charter International Monetary Fund, 1956. Home: 130 Casuarian Concourse Coral Gables FL 33143 Office: 7600 Red Rd South Miami FL 33143

APRIL, GARY CHARLES, chem. engr., educator; b. New Orleans, Jan. 5, 1940; s. Walter Clarence and Audrey Mae (Marks) A.; B.S., La. State U., 1962, M.S., 1968, Ph.D., 1969; m. Lynne Claire Slocovich, June 23, 1962; children—Andrew Gavin, Brian Richard, Elizabeth Lynne. Engr. Research and Devel. E. I. duPont deNemours Co., Orange, Tex., 1962-66; grad. research asst. La. State U., Baton Rouge, 1966-69, grad. teaching asst., 1968; asst. prof. chem. engring. U. Ala., Tuscaloosa, 1969-70, asso. prof., 1970—. Cons. Chem. Process Industries. Registered profl. engr., Ala. Mem. Am. Inst. Chem. Engrs. (chmn. sect. 1972-73), Sigma Xi (Ala. chpt. treas. 1973—), Phi Lambda Upsilon, Tau Beta Pi, Omega Chi Epsilon. Research in removal of ammonia from coke oven gases, math. modeling reacting flow systems, estuarine modeling. Home: 5719 Kew Lane Tuscaloosa AL 35401 Office: PO Box 6312 Univ AL 35486

APTON, RALPH JULIUS, govt. ofcl.; b. Cologne, Germany, Oct. 16, 1930; s. Adolph A. and Erna (Neu) A.; brought to U.S. 1935, naturalized, 1940; B.A., U. Chgo., 1950, M.B.A., 1954; m. Renate Sickinger, Dec. 30, 1959; 1 dau., Kory Kim. Fgn. trade and investment asst. AID, Washington, 1954; asst. indsl. analyst, New Delhi, India, 1955-57; dep. regional tech. aids coordinator for Latin Am., Mexico City, 1957-59; dep. exec. sec. Pres. Task Force for Fgn. Econ. Assistance, Washington, 1960-61; chief mgmt. analysis br. Bur. for Latin Am. Affairs, Washington, 1962; devel. loan officer, Quito, Ecuador, 1963-65, AID del. to Ecuadorian Hwy. Transp. Com., 1963-65; chief preinvestment loans Inter-Am. Bank, Washington, 1966—; real estate operator. Cons. Amigo Industries. Trustee Stonewall Dairy Farm. Mem. Am. Finance Assn., Am. Marketing Assn., Psi Upsilon. Clubs: U. Chgo. of Washington (dir.), River Bend Country (Va.), Quito Golf and Tennis. Home: 9610 Beach Mill Rd Great Falls VA 22066 Office: 808 17th St NW Washington DC 20577

ARANGO, JORGE SANIN, architect; b. Bogota, Colombia, Nov. 29, 1916; s. Fernando Arango and Maria Sanin; student Sch. Architecture, Universidad Catolica de Chile, 1935-42; postgrad. Harvard Grad. Sch. Design, 1942-43; m. Judith Wolpert, Dec. 14, 1952; children—Richard, Virginia; 1 son, Pedro (by previous marriage). Came to U.S., 1957, naturalized, 1963. Practice architecture, Bogota, 1945-57, Caracas, Venezuela, 1957-59, Miami, Fla., 1959—. Prof. archtl. design Nat. U. Colombia, 1946-48; vis. lectr. Coll. Architecture, U. Cal. at Berkeley, 1954,56. Adminstr. pub. bldgs. Colombia, 1948-49 U.S. Dept. State, N.Y. Mus. Modern Art guest to U.S., 1943-44. Mem. A.I.A. Author: The Urbanization of the Earth, 1971; (with C. Martinez) Architecture in Colombia, 1952. Home: 3920 Wood Av Miami FL 33133 Office: 3141 Commodore Plaza Miami FL 33133

ARAUJO, OSCAR EDUARDO, pharmacist, educator; b. Rio Grande do Sul, Brazil, June 2, 1927; s. Olavo and Rita (Parr) A.; came to U.S., 1947, naturalized, 1955; B.S., Purdue U., 1954, M.S. in Pharmacy, 1955, Ph.D., 1957; m. Betty Lou Duncan, Sept. 30, 1950; children—Linda Kay, Stephen Michael. Grad. asst. Purdue U., Lafayette, Ind., 1954; asst. prof. pharmacy Ohio No. U., Ada, 1957-62; asst. prof. U. Fla. Coll. Pharmacy, Gainesville, 1962-68, asso. prof., 1968—. Mem. Alachua County Pharm. Assn. (pres. 1972), Sigma Xi, Rho Chi (pres. 1955), Phi Lambda Upsilon, Phi Delta Chi. Research in rheology of pharm. systems. Home: 406 SW 40th Terrace Gainesville FL 32607

ARAYA, PEDRO ALFONSO, cons.; b. Valparaiso, Chile, Jan. 19, 1922; s. Francisco Araya and Nella Proromant; B.S. in Mech. Engring., Chilean Naval Coll., 1943; B.A., U. Chile, 1945; M.S. in Indsl. and Mgmt. Engring., Columbia, 1963; m. Esther Emma Roussillion, Apr. 17, 1957; 1 dau., Carla Francesca. Came to U.S., 1955, naturalized, 1963. Various positions with rubber and plastics industry, 1949-59; gen. mgr. Coca-Cola Export Corp., Venezuela, 1959-61; indsl. mgmt. cons., Mexico and C. Am., 1961-63; asst. area mgr. Coca-Cola Export Corp., Middle East, North Africa and South West Asia, 1963-67, marketing mgr., S.Am., 1968-69; corporate cons. prodn. and operations Coca-Cola Co., Atlanta, 1970—; pres. Global Growth and Devel. Co., Wilmington, Del., 1973—. Served to lt. Chilean Navy, 1943-45. Mem. A.A.A.S., Am. Inst. Indsl. Engrs., Inst. Environmental Scis., Am. Soc. M.E., Soc. Naval Architects and Marine Engrs., Marine Tech. Soc., Am. Chem. Soc., Am. Soc. Quality Control, I.E.E.E., Illuminating Engrs. Soc., Am. Inst. Plant Engrs., Soc. Advancement Mgmt., Assn. Iron and Steel Engrs., Operations Research Soc. Am., Operations Research Soc. Japan, Acad. Applied Sci., Nat. Soc. Corporate Planning, Am. Phys. Soc., Soc. Packaging and Handling Engrs., Nat. Council Phys. Distbn. Mgmt., Soc. Gen. Systems Research, Am. Marketing Assn., Am. Soc. Agrl. Engrs., Inst. Food Technologists, Am. Agrl. Econs. Assn., Internat. Cargo Handling and Coordination Assn. (Eng.), Colo. Sci. Soc., Ga. Engring. and Archtl. Soc., Assn. Computing Machinery, Am. Geophys. Union, Forage Grass Council (Australia). Clubs: American, Lawn (Buenos Aires); Union (Santiago, Chile). Contbr. articles to profl. jours. Home: 710 Peachtree St NE Atlanta GA 30308 Office: 310 N Av NW Atlanta GA 30301

ARBIB, JOHN A., constrn. co. exec.; b. Lawrence, N.Y., Sept. 18, 1924; s. Robert Simeon and Edna (Henry) A.; student Pa. State Coll., 1942-43, Ala. Polytech. Inst., 1943, Columbia U., 1946-47; m. Leonore Grandlinger, June 5, 1949; children—John Paul, Peter Laurence, Diane Lynn. Partner, Robert S. Arbib & Co., N.Y.C., 1946-57; pres. Arbib Building Corp., Margate, Fla., 1958-62; pres. Custom Craft Homes of So. Fla., Inc., Boca Raton, 1962-65; v.p. VR Corp., Hallandale, Fla., 1965-68; v.p. Royal Palm Beach Colony Inc., Hallandale, 1968-72, St. Petersburg, Fla., 1971-72; v.p. Pinebrook Bldg. Corp., Pembroke Pines, Fla., 1972—, dir., 1972—. Pres., Lakeville Estates, N.Y. Civic Assn., 1953-54; mem. Fla. Condominium Commn., 1972—. Bd. dirs. Progress for Dade County, Fla., 1973—. Served with AUS, 1943-46; E.T.O. Named Builder of Month, Gen. Electric Corp., Oct., 1971. Mem. Builders Assn. of S. Fla. (pres. 1973), Fla. Home Builders Assn. (area v.p. 1973), Nat. Assn. Home Builders (dir. 1970—, vice chmn. bus. mgmt. com. 1974). Democrat. Unitarian (dir. 1965-70). Home: 5561 SW 8th St Plantation FL 33317 Office: PO Box 3746 Hollywood FL 33023

ARBOLEYA QUIROS, CARLOS J., banker; b. Havana, Cuba, Feb. 1, 1929; s. Fermin and Ana (Quiros) Arboleya; ed. Havana U.; advanced courses Systems and Research, Mgmt., Personnel; hon. doctorates Universidad Internat. Montexuma, Paris, U. Internat. Guillermo Marconi, Rome, U. Leonardo da Vinci, Italy, U. Mexico; m. Martha Quintana, Aug. 29, 1954; 1 son, Carlos. Came to U.S., 1960, naturalized, 1969. With 1st Nat. City Bank of N.Y., Havana, 1946-57, advancing to asst. head collection dept.; asst. mgr. trust and securities dept. Trust Co. of Cuba, Havana, 1957-59, also examiner and auditor, now mem. Employees in Exile Assn.; chief auditor controller's div. Banco Continental Cubano, Havana, 1959-60; from clk. to office mgr. and controller Allure Shoe Corp., Miami, Fla., 1960-62; v.p. operations and personnel, cashier, sec. Blvd. Nat. Bank Miami, 1962-66; exec. v.p., chief exec. officer, sec. Fidelity Nat. Bank South Miami (Fla.), 1966-69, pres., vice chmn. bd., chief exec. officer, 1969-74, also dir.; pres., chief exec. officer Flagler Bank, Miami, 1974—. Tchr. banking operations Am. Inst. Banking, Miami, Bank Adminstrn. Inst., City Bank Club, Havana; econ. adviser Latin C. of C.; adv. bd. Small Bus. Adminstrn.; mem. Nat. Adv. Council on Econ. Opportunity. Acting pres. Sts. Peter and Paul Parents Assn., Miami; co-chmn. Latin-Am. div. United Fund; adviser Greater Miami Jr. Achievement; mem. Latin Am. Affairs Commn. of Fla., Fla. Council Internat. Devel.; mem. internat. affairs action com. City of Miami; mem. citizens adv. planning com. City of South Miami; mem. nat. bd., archdiocesan chmn. Cath. Com. on Scouting; asst. council commr., exec. bd. Boy Scouts Am. Bd. dirs. Cuban Little League, Miami, YMCA, Miami; exec. bd. nat. council Invest in Am. Recipient Diploma of Honor Lincoln-Marti, Fed. Govt., George Washington honor medal Freedoms Found. at Valley Forge, Am. Eagle award Invest in Am., numerous awards for work in community and civic affairs. Mem. Bank Adminstrn. Inst. (pres. 1967-68, dir.; pres. S. Fla. chpt., ofcl. rep. from Fidelity Nat. Bank South Miami; recipient Distinguished Service award S. Fla., 1965), Am. Inst. Banking (v.p. and gov. Miami), Nat. Amateur Athletic Union Havana (past dir.), Quivican Amateur Athletic Union Havana (past bd. dirs.), Nat. Softball Assn. (past del.), Havana U. Honor Athletes Assn., Inter-Am. Assn. Bus. Men in Miami, Latin C. of C. (pres. banker's adv. bd.), Dade County (mem. bd.), Fla. (econ. devel. council) bankers assns., Hispanic Am. Council Fla. (treas.). Kiwanian. Clubs: City Bank (past pres., past sports commr., past dir.) (Havana); Bankers (past dir., past del. Cuban Olympic Com., past sports commr.) (Havana). Home: 1941 SW 23d St Miami FL 33145 Office: Flagler Bank 3737 NW 7th St Miami FL 33126

ARBURN, ROBERT WILLIAM, architect; b. Pueblo, Colo., June 10, 1933; s. Darwin William and Ethel Marie (Lamb) A.; student (scholar) Denver U., 1951-52; B.Arch. (Univ. scholar 1955-56), U. Tex., 1956; m. Lavonne Leatrice Kennedy, Sept. 14, 1955; children—Donald Joseph, Ginger Ann. Architect Dean Eichelberger, Houston, 1956; designer Monroe Licht & Higgins, El Paso, Tex., 1957; architect Davis-Foster & Thorp, El Paso, 1958, Carroll & Daueblo, El Paso, 1959-61, Bartlett Cocke & Assos., El Paso, also San Antonio, 1961-71; pvt. practice architecture, 1971-73; architect Robert Arburn & Assos., San Antonio, Arburn-Reitzer & Assos., San Antonio, 1973—. Architect Randolph-Brooks Fed. Credit Union, Randolph AFB, 1973. Recipient Malon D. & Luna M. Thatcher Found. award, 1956. Mem. Tex. Soc. Architects (mem. criminal justice com.), Am. Inst. Architects, Constrn. Specifications Inst. Mason (Shriner). Clubs: Optimist, Toastmaster (pres. 1971-72) (both San Antonio). Home: 122 Dogwood St San Antonio TX 78213 Office: 8400 Data Point St San Antonio TX 78229 also 3211 Nacogdochesrd St San Antonio TX 78217

ARCENEAUX, GEORGE, JR., lawyer; b. New Orleans, May 17, 1928; s. George and Louise (Austin) A.; B.A., La. State U., 1949; LL.B., Am. U., 1957; m. Mary Elizabeth Martin, Aug. 17, 1954; children—Mary Elizabeth, George III, Robert Martin. Program dir. Radio Sta. KCIL, Houma, La., 1949; state editor Daily Advertiser, Lafayette, 1949-50; legislative asst. Senator Allen J. Ellender, Washington, 1952-56, adminstrv. asst., 1957-60; admitted to La. bar, 1959; practiced in Houma, 1960—; mem. firm Duval, Arceneaux, Lewis & Gaidry, 1960—. Chmn., Houma-Terrebonne Regional Planning Commn., 1963—. Served with AUS, 1950-51. Mem. Am., La., Terrebonne Parish (pres. 1964-65) bar assns., C. of C. (dir. 1963, pres. 1966-67). Methodist. Clubs: Plimsoll, International House (New Orleans); University (Washington); Rotary (dir. 1963, pres. 1966, dist. gov. 1971-72). Home: 2 El Paso Dr Houma LA 70360 Office: 504 Belanger St PO Box 1568 Houma LA 70360

ARCHBOLD, BENDER LAWTON, ch. exec.; b. Providencia Isla, Colombia, June 12, 1908; s. Sheridan Tyler and Matilda (Robinson) A.; student La Sierra Coll., 1932; B.A., Pacific Union Coll., 1935; M.A., Andrews U., 1961; m. Frances Victoria Burke, Nov. 24, 1936; children—Elizabeth Joy (Mrs. John Philbert McDonald), Ruth Frances (Mrs. Enoch Sherman). Came to U.S., 1960, naturalized, 1965; Ordained to ministry Seventh-Day Adventist Ch., 1943; tchr. elementary sch., 1928-30; dean men, dept. English, West Indies Coll., Mandeville, Jamaica, 1935-1; youth leader, sec. edn. Panama Conf., 1941-46; prin. Panama Acad., Pedregal, Republic of Panama, 1946-49; pres. Caribbean Union Coll., Trinidad, 1957-62; mem. staff Seventh-Day Adventist Ch., various locations, 1928-30, 35-62, sec. lay activities Gen. Conf., Coral Gables, Fla., 1962-66, exec. sec., 1966-70; v.p. gen. conf. for Inter-Am. div., 1970—, mem. exec. com. 1962—. Bd. dirs. Pacific Press Pub. Assn., Mountain View, Cal., chmn. coordinating com., 1972—. Home: 6540 SW 28th St Miami FL 33155 Office: 760 Ponce de Leon Blvd Coral Gables FL 33134

ARCHER, ALFORD, geographer; b. Garrettsville, O., Apr. 11, 1908; s. John Clark and Cathaline (Alford) A.; student Hiram Coll., 1925-26, Carnegie Inst. Tech., 1927-29; B.S., Columbia, 1935, M.S., 1936; Ph.D., Ohio State U., 1962; m. Barbara Kathleen Dietrich, Oct. 14, 1938; children—John Clark, Joan Elizabeth. Asst. dept. geography Ohio State U., 1936-41; instr. geology and geography Ind. State Tchrs. Coll., 1941-42; asst. prof. commerce and geography, Toledo U., 1942-46, asst. dir. summer session, 1946; with U.S. Bur. Census, 1946—, geographer geography div., 1946-49, 55-59, 68-71, chief cartographic methods br., 1959-61, Internat. Statis. Programs as census geography adviser Republics of Panama, 1949-50, Bolivia, 1950, Honduras, 1951-55, 60, Costa Rica, 1952-54, El Salvador, 1953-55, 61, Thailand, 1961-63, Iran, 1966-68, Argentina, 1969, Paraguay, 1971-72, chief fgn. census research br., 1963-66, prof. geographer, 1972—. Occasional instr. George Washington U., Am. U. Mem. adv. com. to Pan-Am. Inst. Geography and History, Nat. Acad. Scis., 1959-62. Pres. Rolling Terrace Civic Assn., Silver Spring, 1958-59, 64-65. Recipient Meritorious Service award from sec. commerce, 1956. Mem. Assn. Am. Geographers, Congress on Surveying and Mapping, Population Assn., Am. Statis. Assn. Home: 711 Forston Dr Takoma Park MD 20012 Office: Internat Statis Programs Center Bur of Census Washington DC 20233

ARCHER, CASS LOUIS, educator; b. nr. Spearman, Tex., June 1, 1924; s. Charles Otis and Jessie (Karr) A.; B.S., U. Tex., 1950, M.Ed., 1954, M.A., 1959, Ph.D., 1967; m. Irma Ruth Fulbright, July 25, 1953; children—Laura, Deborah, Timothy. High sch. tchr. Beeville (Tex.) Pub. Schs., 1950-51, Seminole (Tex.) Pub. Schs., 1951-58; prof., chmn. math. dept. Angelo State U., San Angelo, Tex., 1959—. Cons. math. Tex. Edn. Agy., 1962-64; speaker Conf. Advancement Math. Teaching, 1966, 67. Vice pres. P.T.A., 1967-68, pres., 1966-67. Served with USAAF, 1943-46. NSF fellow, 1958-59. Mem. Math. Assn. Am. (rep.), Tex. Assn. Coll. Tchrs., Nat. Council Tchrs. Math., Am. Math. Soc., Seminole Jr. C. of C. (past dir.), Phi Delta Kappa (pres. 1970-71), Pi Mu Epsilon, Rotary Internat. Home: 2810 Vista del Arroyo San Angelo TX 76901

ARCHER, DAVID R., judge; b. Huntsville, Ala., Nov. 20, 1917; s. Henry Lee and Martha Ellen (Throneberry) A.; A.B., U. Ala., 1949, LL.B., 1951; grad. Nat. Coll. State Trial Judges, 1968; m. Lillian Knight, Oct. 23, 1943; 1 dau., Patti Nell. Laborer, Huntsville Mfg. Co., 1934-39; mgr. Variety Store, Joe Bradley Sch., Huntsville, 1939-41, salesman Joe Bradley Sch., 1945-46; admitted to Ala. bar, 1951; practiced in Huntsville, 1953-61; circuit judge 23rd jud. circuit Ala., Huntsville, 1961—. Mem. Ethics Commn. State Ala., Huntsville, 1971—. Mem. Ala. Senate, 1958-61; mem. So. Region Edn. Bd., 1959-62, 72—. Served with USNR, 1941-45, 51-52. Mem. Fed., Ala., Madison County bar assns., Am. Judicature Assn., Ala. Circuit Judges Assn., Ala. Cattlemen's Assn., Assn. U.S. Army, Am. Legion, V.F.W., World Peace thru Law. Democrat. Methodist. Mason (Shriner). Home: 3002 Barcody Rd SE Huntsville AL 35802 Office: Courthouse Huntsville AL 35801

ARCHER, STANLEY LOUIS, educator; b. Tyler, Tex., Apr. 6, 1935; s. James Carl and Lena (Linnstaedter) A.; B.A., Tex. A. and M. U., 1959; M.A. (Nat. Def. Edn. Act. fellow), U. Miss., 1961, Ph.D., 1965; m. Mary Christine Korkmas, July 12, 1955; 1 dau., Kerstin Ann. Tchr. English, Three Rivers (Tex.) High Sch., 1959; teaching asst. U. Miss., Oxford, 1961; faculty English, Tex. A and M U., College Station, 1962—, prof. English, 1970—. Dir. Region VI, Tex. Joint English Com., 1972—; reader ETS Advanced Placement Program, 1966—. Mem. Modern Lang. Assn., Nat. Council Tchrs. English, S.Central Modern Lang. Assn., Tex. Ornithol. Soc., Conf. Coll. Tchrs. of English. Contbr. articles to profl. jours. Home: 1219 Westover St College Station TX 77840

ARCHER, WILLIAM REYNOLDS, JR., congressman; b. Houston, Mar. 22, 1928; s. William Reynolds and Eleanor (Miller) A.; student Rice U., 1945-46; B.B.A., U. Tex., 1949, LL.B., 1951; m. Patricia Moore, Nov. 21, 1953; children—William Reynolds III, Richard Moore, Sharon Leigh, Elizabeth Ann, Barbara Elise. Admitted to Tex. bar; pres. Uncle Johnny Mill, Inc., Houston, 1953-61, W.R. Archer, Inc., 1961—; partner firm Harris, Archer Parks & Graul, 1967-72; dir. Heights State Bank, 1967-71; mem. 92d-93d congresses from 7th Tex. Dist., mem. ways and means com. Councilman, mayor pro-tem City of Hunters Creek Village, Tex., 1955-62. Bd. dirs. Houston Soc. for Prevention of Cruelty to Animals. Served from pvt. to 1st lt., USAF, 1951-53; capt. Res. Recipient Man of Yr. award Sigma Alpha Epsilon, 1968, Outstanding Alumnus award St. Thomas High Sch., 1971; Man of Year award Dist. 7 B'nai B'rith, 1973. Mem. Houston Bar Assn., State Bar Tex., Phi Delta Phi. Republican. Roman Catholic. Home: 3127 Avalon St Houston TX 77019

ARD, JACK TAMMANY, elec. engr., city utility adminstr.; b. Ft. Worth, Nov. 14, 1927; s. Garland B. and Iva L. (Riffle) A.; B.S. in Elec. Engring., U. Tex., Austin, 1955; m. Mary Nell Battershell, Apr. 12, 1952; children—Catherine Ann, Elizabeth Lynn, Robert Jack. Engr., Electric Dept., City of Austin, Tex., 1950-62; dir. electric utilities City of Greenville, Tex., 1962—. Mem. Hunt County Mental Health Bd., 1970-72. Bd. dirs. YMCA, 1970—. Served with USNR, 1945-46; PTO. Registered profl. engr., Tex. Mem. I.E.E.E. (com. chmn. 1953—), Tex. Municipal Utilities League (pres. 1972—), Greenville C. of C. (pres. 1973), Tex. Soc. Profl. Engrs. (pres. East Tex. chpt. 1958—). Baptist (deacon 1960—, com. chmn. 1958—). Rotarian (pres. 1968-69). Home: 5600 New Haven St Greenville TX 75401 Office: PO Box 1049 Greenville TX 75401

ARENSON, NATHAN, radiologist; b. N.Y.C., Mar. 27, 1912; s. Morris Louis and Rose (Aronson) A.; B.S., Coll. City N.Y., 1933; M.D., N.Y. Med. Coll., 1937; m. Alice Gilbert, Dec. 24, 1936; children—Michael Allan, Ronald Lee. Intern Met. Hosp., N.Y.C., 1937-39; postgrad. VA facility, Hines, Ill., 1940; med. officer VA, Augusta, 1941; asst. radiologist Watts Hosp., Durham, N.C., 1945-47; asso. radiologist Touro Infirmary, New Orleans, 1947-48; head dept. radiology Sacred Heart Hosp., Pensacola, Fla., 1948—, also chief radiology Med. Center Clinic, Pensacola. Cons. radiology Naval Air Station, Pensacola, 1950-65, Eglin AFB, Fla., 1951-65. Served with M.C., AUS, 1942-45: ETO. Decorated Bronze Star. Recipient Sportsman of Year award Pensacola Sports Assn., 1970. Diplomate Am. Bd. Radiology. Mem. Am. Coll. Radiology, Radiol. Soc. N.Am., So. Radiol. Conf., Escambia County Med. Soc., Fla. Radiol. Soc., Fla. Med. Assn., A.M.A., Pan Am. Med. Assn. (hon. life), Am. Coll. Nuclear Medicine, Nat. Rifle Assn. (dir.). Clubs: Florida Pistol Assn., Pensacola Rifle and Pistol Club, Fla. Sportsmens Assn., Pensacola Sports Assn., Gulf Breeze Sports Assn. Home: 312 N Sunset Blvd Gulf Breeze FL 32561 Office: 1750 N Palafox St Pensacola FL 32501

ARGANBRIGHT, ROBERT PHILIP, chemist; b. Ft. Leavenworth, Kan., Nov. 7, 1923; s. Frank and Alice (O'Brien) A.; B.S., U. Kan., 1950; Ph.D., U. Colo., 1956; m. Marie M. Garrett, Aug. 24, 1957; children—Ann Cecelia, Philip James. Research chemist Continental Oil Co., Ponca City, Okla., 1950-52; research specialist Monsanto Co., Texas City, 1956-63, St. Louis, 1963-67; research asso. Petro-Tex Chem. Corp., Houston, 1967—. Served with AUS, 1943-46. Mem. Am. Chem. Soc., S.W. Catalysis Soc. (chmn. 1972-73). Contbr. articles to profl. jours. Patentee in field. Home: 814 Devonport St Seabrook TX 77586 Office: 8600 Park Place Blvd Houston TX 77017

ARGYLL, MARION H. G., real estate broker; b. New Orleans, Jan 29, 1912; d. Franklin Johns and Sarah (Henry) Gustine; ; attended pvt. schs.; widow 1 son, James E. Med. records librarian Doctors Hosp., Washington, 1944-47; asst. to neurosurgeon VA, Washington, 1948-51; electro-encephalographic tech. service NIH, 1952-55; tchr. real estate Washington Real Estate and Ins. Sch., 1958-60; real estate broker, Washington, 1958—, Va., 1958—, Md., 1959—. Recipient award in recognition of services to Nation, Pres. U.S., 1940, award for vol. work with United China Relief, 1942. Mem. So. Electro-encephaolography Soc. Club: Kenwood Golf and Country (Bethesda, Md.). Author: Moonlight Poems; also scenarios under pseudonym Julie de Quistine. Patentee san. disposable baby bottle, payroll safety box, adjustable automobile seat, protective garment. Creator Argyll mortgage plan. Home: 15 E Irving St Chevy Chase Village MD 20015 Office: 810 18th St Washington DC 20015

ARKIN, L. JULES, lawyer; b. N.Y.C., Mar. 19, 1929; s. Joseph L. and Mildred (Neidenberg) A.; Student Emory U., 1946-48; LL.B., U. Miami, 1952; m. Sandra Rauthbord, Mar. 24, 1957; children—Richard, Gary. Admitted to Fla. bar, 1952, since practiced in Miami Beach; asso. firm Meyer, Weiss, Rose, and Arkin, 1954—, partner, 1963—. Dir. Financial Fed. Savs. and Loan Assn. of Dade County, Arkin Constrn. Co., Inc., Century U.S.A. Corp. Mem. City of Miami Beach Social Services Adv. Bd., 1963—, chmn., 1966-71. Bd. dirs. Mt. Sinai Med. Center of Greater Miami, Am.-Jewish Joint Distrbn. Com. Served to lt. comdr. USNR, 1952-54. Named Civic Leader of Year, Miami Beach Civic League, 1971; recipient Young Leadership award, Greater Miami Jewish Fedn., 1969. Mem. The Fla. Bar, Dade County, Miami Beach bar assns., Alpha Epsilon Pi. Mason, Kiwanian (pres. 1966-67). Office: 407 Lincoln Rd Miami Beach FL 33139

ARMAN, ARA, educator; b. Istanbul, Turkey, Sept. 12, 1930; s. Hayg and Marie (Papazian) A.; B.S. in Civil Engring., Robert Coll. (Istanbul), 1955; M.S., U. Tex., 1956; m. Claudia Catherine Carr, Nov. 31, 1963; children—Eric Hayg, Michelle Marie. Came to U.S., 1955, naturalized, 1961. With La. Dept. Hwys., Baton Rouge, 1956-63, dist. lab. engr., 1958-61, soils-design engr., 1961-63; mem. faculty La. State U., Baton Rouge, 1963—, asso. prof. civil engring., 1967-70, prof., 1970—, asst. dir. div. engring. research, 1965—. Vice pres. Shelltech Engrs., Baton Rouge, 1964-68, Systems Analysis & Design Optimization, Inc., Baton Rouge, 1968—; cons. civil engring., 1963—. Mem. Nat. Acad. Scis. (mem. maintenance bituminous pavements com. 1965—, soil cement stblzn. com. 1966—), Am. Road Builders Assn. (v.p. nat. edn. div. 1970, pres. nat. edn. div. 1972-73, mem. mass transp. com. 1973-74), Hwy. Research Bd., Am. Soc. C.E., Internat. Soc. Soil Mechanics and Found., Am. Soc. Engring. Edn., Am. Soc. Testing and Materials, Internat. Peat Soc. Club: Piedmont (Baton Rouge). Contbr. profl. jours. Home: 1148 Verdun Dr Baton Rouge LA 70810

ARMBRECHT, WILLIAM HENRY, lawyer; b. Mobile, Ala., Nov. 1, 1908; s. William Henry and Anna Bell (Peterson) A.; student Spring Hill Coll., 1927-29; LL.B., U. Ala., 1932; m. Katherine Little, Oct. 8, 1927; children—William Henry III, Elizabeth A. (Mrs. J.D. Brown), Anna Bell (Mrs. William Bru), Conrad P. II, Clara L. Admitted to Ala. bar, 1932; since practiced in Mobile; partner firm Armbrecht, Jackson & DeMouy; gen. counsel McLean Industries; chmn. bd., dir. 1st Nat. Bank, Mobile; dir. Title Ins. Co. Mobile, So. Industries Corp., Grand Hotel Co., Diamond Head Corp. Mem. Mobile Indsl. Devel. Bd. Bd. dirs. Found. for Pub. Higher Edn.; bd. regents Spring Hill Coll. Mem. Am., Ala., Mobile (pres. 1954) bar assns., Phi Delta Phi, Alpha Tau Omega. Episcopalian. Kiwanian. Clubs: Lakewood Country (Point Clear, Ala.); Mobile Country, Athelsten, Bienville, Internat. Trade,

Propeller; Lunch (N.Y.C.). Home: 112 Pinebrook West Mobile AL 36608 Office: 1101 Mchts Bank Bldg Mobile AL 36602

ARMBRECHT, WILLIAM HENRY, III, lawyer; b. Mobile, Ala., Jan. 13, 1929; s. William Henry and Katherine (Little) A.; B.S., U. Ala., 1950, J.D., 1952; m. Dorothy Jean Taylor, Sept. 1, 1951; children—Katherine Handley, William Taylor, Alexander Paterson. Admitted to Ala. bar, 1952; asso. firm Inge, Twitty, Armbrecht & Jackson, Mobile, 1952-56; partner Armbrecht, Jackson, McConnell & DeMouy, Mobile, 1956-65, Armbrecht, Jackson & DeMouy, Mobile, 1965—; dir., v.p. Landel, Inc. Served to 1st lt. AUS, 1952-54. Mem. Am., Ala. (mem. exec. council jr. bar sect. 1957-58, mem. grievance com. 1970—, chmn. 1973—, exec. council corp., partnership and bus. law sect. 1972—), Mobile (mem. exec. council 1960, pres. jr. bar sect. 1960), bar assns., Mobile C. of C. (vice chmn. community planning com. 1969-70), Southeastern Corporate Law Inst. (mem. planning com.), Phi Delta Phi, Delta Kappa Epsilon. Episcopalian. Clubs: Mobile Country, Athelstan, International Trade (Mobile). Home: 600 Fairfax Rd East Mobile AL 36608 Office: 1101 Mchts Nat Bank Bldg 61 St Joseph St Mobile AL 36601

ARMENDAREZ, PETER X., educator; b. San Pedro, Cal., Sept. 7, 1930; s. Pedro M. and Carmen (Miranda) A.; B.S., Loyola U. of Los Angeles, 1952; M.S., Washington U., 1954; Ph.D., U. Ariz., 1963; m. Charlene Towery, Oct. 23, 1954; children—Mary Agnes, Peter, Patrick, Philip, John, Lawrence, William. Instr. Odessa Coll., 1958-59; asst. prof. U. Tenn. at Martin, 1963-65, Brescia Coll., Owensboro, Ky., 1965-67; prof., chmn. dept. physics Brescia Coll., 1968—; research asso. Ill. Inst. Tech., summers 1964-66. Served as capt., USAF, 1954-57. Mem. Am. Chem. Soc., Am. Crystallog. Assn. Research and publs. on molecular spectroscopy and structure of inorganic complexes. Home: 1224 Parrish Av Owensboro KY 42301 Office: Brescia College Owensboro KY 42301

ARMOUR, ROLLIN STELY, educator; b. Miami, Fla., Dec. 5, 1929; s. Thomas and Frankie Ella (Calhoun) A.; B.A., Baylor U., 1950; B.D., So. Bapt. Theol. Sem., 1953; S.T.M., Harvard, 1956, Th.D., 1963; m. Mary Anne Crum, May 30, 1957; children—Ellen True, Rollin Stely, Stephen Frank. Asst. prof. religion Stetson U., DeLand, Fla., 1960-65, asso. prof. religion, 1965-67, prof. religion, 1967-73; prof., head dept. religion Auburn (Ala.) U., 1973—. Served to 1st lt., chaplain AUS, 1953-55. Soc. for Religion in Higher Edn. fellow study Asian religions, 1968-69. Mem. Am. Soc. Ch. History, Am. Acad. Religion (regional pres. 1972-73), So. Bapt. Hist. Soc. (pres. 1972-73), Fla. Bapt. Hist. Soc. (curator 1962-73), Democrat. Baptist. Rotarian. Author: Anabaptist Baptism: A Representative Study, 1966. Home: 913 Cherokee Rd Auburn AL 36830

ARMOUR, THOMAS SCOTT, JR., elec. engr.; b. Columbia, S.C., Mar. 24, 1923; s. Thomas Scott and Elisabeth (Rivers) A.; B.E.E., Clemson U., 1947; M.S., La. State U., 1950; m. Irene Blair Watson, Feb. 14, 1947; children—Irene Elisabeth, Thomas Scott III. Elec. engr. Plantation Pipe Line Co., Atlanta, Baton Rouge, 1947-49; teaching fellow La. State U., 1949-50; engr. Patchen & Zimmerman, engrs., Augusta, Ga., 1950-53; engr. Lyles, Bissett, Carlisle & Wolff, architects and engrs., 1953-63; v.p., dir., gen. mgr. operations Jones & Assos., Augusta, then Jones & Fellers, architects, engrs. and planners, Augusta and Savannah, Ga., Columbia, S.C., 1963-70; self-employed as elec. design cons., Columbia, S.C. and Augusta, Ga., 1970—. Pres. Sr. Citizens Council of Augusta and Richmond County. Served with AUS, World War II. Registered profl. engr., S.C., Ga., Tex., N.C. Mem. Nat., Ga., S.C. socs. profl. engrs., Constrn. Specifications Inst. (past. chpt. pres.), Soc. Mil. Engrs., Assn. U.S. Army, Illuminating Engring. Soc., Congaree Power Squadron. Episcopalian. Elk. Club: Augusta Country. Home: 2166 Shady Lane Columbia SC 29206 Office: 4445 Devine St Columbia SC 29205

ARMSTRONG, A(LBERT) FRED, JR., ins. exec.; b. Dallas, Apr. 21, 1918; s. A. F. and Mayme (Miller) A.; student So. Meth. U., 1935-36; m. Ernestine Dublin, Aug. 17, 1940; 1 dau., Tina. With Employers Casualty Co., Dallas and Houston, 1935-43, gen. agt., Houston, 1946-54; pres., dir. Am. Capitol Ins. Co., 1954—; dir. Nat. Assn. of Life Cos., Chem. Bank, Houston. Served with USAAF, 1943-46. Mem. Tex. Legal Res. Ofcls. Assn. (dir., past pres.). Methodist. Mason. Home: 10603 Gawain St Houston TX 77024 Office: 3839 Buffalo Speedway Houston TX 77006

ARMSTRONG, ARTHUR ALEXANDER, chem. engr., educator; b. Gastonia, N.C., July 13, 1921; s. Arthur Alexander and Julia T. (Compton) A.; student Belmont Abbey Coll., 1938-40; B.Chem. Engring., N.C. State U., 1947, M.S., 1949, Ph.D., 1957; m. Helene Adele Payet, June 15, 1956; children—Alexander Charles, Richard George. Chem. engr. Gen. Electric Co., Pittsfield, Mass., 1947, Duke Power Co., Charlotte, N.C., 1949-50, Chemstrand Corp., Pensacola, Fla., 1953-54; tech. supt. Celanese Corp., Rock Hill, S.C., 1954-58; asso. prof. U. S.C., Columbia, 1958-59, N.C. State U., Raleigh, 1959-65, U. N.M., Albuquerque, 1965-68; engring. fellow Chemstrand Research Center, Inc., Durham, N.C., 1968—; cons. chem. engr., 1959—. Served to 1st lt. USAAF, 1943-45. Mem. Am. Inst. Chem. Engrs., Am. Soc. for Engring. Edn., Sigma Xi. Home: 219 Rose St Cary NC 27511 Office: PO Box 731 Durham NC 27702

ARMSTRONG, DICKWIN DILL, assn. exec.; b. Muncie, Ind., Aug. 18, 1934; s. Colby C. and Elizabeth A. (Houck) A.; B.S., Ind. U., 1956; m. Janice Flora, June 2, 1957; children—Brent D., Stacey J. Mgr., Madison (Ind.) C. of C., 1959-61; exec. v.p. Frankford (Ind.) C. of C., 1961-63, Marion (Ind.) C. of C., 1963-66, Lakeland (Fla.) C. of C., 1966—. Served with AUS, 1957-59. Mem. Ind. Exec. Assn. (v.p. 1966), Fla. C. of C. Execs. (pres. 1972—), Ind. U. Alumni Assn. Methodist. Rotarian. Home: Route 1 Box 355 Lakeland FL 33803 Office: 35 Lake Morton Dr Lakeland FL 33801

ARMSTRONG, EDWARD RODNEY, telephone co. engr.; b. Columbus, O., June 13, 1919; s. Elliott Barlow and Grace (Ottman) A.; student U. S.C., 1946; m. Lexine Roberts, Nov. 22, 1972; 1 stepson, Danny C. Reeves. With So. Bell Telephone Co., Columbia, S.C., 1941—, supervisory engr., 1965—. Served with AUS, 1941-45, 50-52. Mem. I.E.E.E. (treas. Columbia sect. 1973). Home: 1522 Fairhaven Dr Columbia SC 29210 Office: PO Box 752 Columbia SC 29202

ARMSTRONG, ELMER E., accountant; b. Monmouth, Ill., Dec. 20, 1904; s. Elmer Ellsworth and Alice (Logan) A.; A.A., Kansas City Jr. Coll., 1921; postgrad. Centenary Coll., 1942-43; m. Ruth Marie Dale, July 25, 1925; children—Dale E., Lenora Ann (Mrs. Steven Cowel). Mem. editorial staff Kansas City Jour., 1920-22, Kansas City Kansan, 1922-25; editor Alva Record, Okla., 1922; account specialist Burroughs Adding Machine Co., 1925-45; with Smith, Cole, Saur & Armstrong, and predecessor firm, C.P.A.'s, Shreveport, La., 1945—, sr. partner, 1952—; treas. Honor Oil Co., Inc., Shreveport, 1951—. Lectr. advanced accounting Centenary Coll. of La., 1950-52, So. States Accounting Conf., Savannah, Ga., Conf. Lawyers and C.P.A.'s, U. Miss. at Hattiesburg, 1951; dean Shreveport Sch. Theology, 1968—. Mem. Nat. Conf. Christians and Jews, Shreveport, 1968—, dir. Speakers Bur., 1969—, chmn. Brotherhood Week, 1972; chmn. Shreveport Housing Authority, 1967—. C.P.A., La., Tex. Mem. Soc. La. C.P.A.'s (pres. Shreveport 1967-68), Am. Inst. C.P.A.'s, Shreveport C. of C., Internat. Platform Assn., Am. (dist. treas.), Shreveport (v.p. 1970-71) rose socs. Methodist (steward; dir. adult tchrs. 1963-66; dist. dir. adult ministries Shreveport dist. 1968—). Kiwanian (treas. 1952-56, bd. dirs. 1969-71, Shreveport), Toastmaster (dist. gov. 1952). Clubs: Shreveport Petroleum, Metropolitan Dinner. Home: 1402 Audubon Pl Shreveport LA 71105 Office: Smith Cole Saur & Armstrong Pioneer Center 1400 Line Av Shreveport LA 71101

ARMSTRONG, GEORGE GLAUCUS, JR., physician; b. Houston, Miss., Feb. 28, 1924; s. George Glaucus and Lelia Estelle (Riddick) A.; B.A. in Physics, U. Miss., 1948, M.S. in Physiology, 1950; B.S. in Medicine, 1952, Med. Certificate, 1954; M.D., U. Ill., 1956; m. Doris Belle Moore, Dec. 26, 1948; children—Jennifer Ann, Marcia Gale. Rotating intern U. Miss. Med. Center, 1956-57; asso. prof. physiology U. Miss., 1957-64; research med. office NASA, Johnson Space Center, Houston, 1964-72, chief health services div., 1972—. Served with USNR, 1943-47. Fellow A.A.A.S.; mem. Am. Physiol. Soc., Soc. Exptl. Biology and Medicine, Aerospace Med. Assn., Undersea Med. Soc., I.E.E.E., N.Y. Acad. Sci., U.S. Power Squadron. Contbr. chpts. to Shock and Hypotension, 1965, Progress in Surgery, 1964. Home: 4106 Clovernook Lane Seabrook TX 77586 Office: NASA 1 Houston TX 77058

ARMSTRONG, GEORGE THOMSON, phys. chemist; b. Castor, Alta., Can., Dec. 8, 1916; s. George Alexander and Margaret (Faris) Armstrong; (parents Am. citizens); B.S. U. Fla., 1939, M.S., 1943; Ph.D., Johns Hopkins U., 1948; m. Patricia Eliza Cadigan, June 16, 1945; children—Margaret Lucille (Mrs. Francis M. Chapman, Jr.), Michael Faris. Scientist radiation lab. Mass. Inst. Tech., Cambridge, 1942-45; instr. chemistry Yale U., New Haven, 1948-51; scientist U.S. Nat. Bur. Standards, Washington, 1951—, chief thermo-chemistry sect., 1968—. Lectr., Boston U., 1950, 51; cons., 1973—. Mem. Woodside Park Civic Assn., 1960—. Recipient Silver medal U.S. Dept. Commerce, 1967. Fellow Am. Phys. Soc., Washington Acad. Sci.; mem. Am. Chem. Soc., U.S. Calorimetry Conf. (dir. 1961-66, chmn. 1963-64), Philos. Soc. Washington (mem. council 1973—), Chem. Soc. Washington, N.Y. Acad. Scis., Am. Soc. Testing Materials (mem. tech. coms. 1958—, chmn. com. gaseous fuels 1974—), Potomac Appalachian Trail Club. Mem. United Ch. Christ. Club: Cosmos (Washington). Home: 1401 Dale Dr Silver Spring MD 20910 Office: US National Bureau Standards Washington DC 20234

ARMSTRONG, JACKSON LAVONE, food processing co. exec.; b. nr. Headland, Ala., Aug. 9, 1924; s. Jackson M. and Johnnie (Radney) A.; student Auburn U., 1944, Troy State Radio Sch., 1944-45; m. Irene Woodham, July 13, 1945; children—Donna (Mrs. Michael Forest Curl), Jacqueline, Keith. With Colonial Baking Co. div. Campbell Taggart, Inc., Atlanta, 1951—, Campbell Taggart, Inc., Dallas, 1966, v.p. Colonial Baking Co., Atlanta, 1968, pres., 1968—. Mem. DeKalb C. of C., So. Bakers Assn., Atlanta Bakers' Club (pres.). Home: 1312 Hidden Hills Pkwy Stone Mountain GA 30083 Office: 211 Moreland Av NE Atlanta GA 30307

ARMSTRONG, JAMES CLYDE, civil engr., engring. co. exec.; b. Wheelock, Tex., Dec. 23, 1933; s. James Benjamin and Leafy Menla (Lightsey) A.; B.S. in Agronomy, Tex. A. and M. U., 1955, B.S. in Civil Engring., 1961, M.S. in Civil Engring., 1962, Ph.D., 1966; m. Cecil Ann Hudette, Apr. 5, 1958; children—William Henry, Larry Wayne, Rebecca Ann. Asst. research engr. Tex. Transp. Inst., College Station, 1962-66; asst. prof. civil engring. U. Mo., Rolla, 1966-69; asso. prof. civil engring. U. Ark., 1969-71; dir. engring. operations Southwestern Labs., Arlington, Tex., 1971-72; sr. cons. engr., pres. Soil Cons., Inc. Arlington, 1972—. Adj. lectr. civil engring. U. Tex., Arlington, 1972—. Served with USAF, 1957. NSF Research fellow U. Mo., 1968-69. Mem. Internat. Soc. Soil Mechanics and Found. Engring., Am. Soc. C.E., Tex. Soc. Profl. Engrs., Ft. Worth Geol. Soc. Home: 423 Southmoor Dr Arlington TX 76010 Office: PO Box 6224 Arlington TX 76011

ARMSTRONG, SINCLAIR WALKER, banker; b. Okemah, Okla., Aug. 1, 1905; s. Robert Walker and Margaret June (Edmundson) A.; student Okla. U., 1926-27; m. Lola Irene Aston, June 9, 1929; children—Ann (Mrs. Archie Farmer), Robert A., Sinclair Walker. With Vian State Bank (Okla.), 1922—, pres., 1965—. Trustee City of Vian, 1933—, mayor, 1950—. Chmn., Sequoyah County Democratic central com., 1945-47. Trustee Cookson Hills Electric Co-op. Baptist. Mason (32 deg., Shriner, Jester). Address: Vian OK 74962

ARMSTRONG, THOMAS HARPER, dentist; b. Mesa, Ariz., June 12, 1912; s. Thomas Ackerman and Mabel (Harper) A.; student Eldorado Coll., 1931-32; D.D.S., Northwestern U., 1942; postgrad. Harvard, 1942-43; m. Vara Marie Freeman, Sept. 5, 1935; children—Thomas W., John Harper. Individual practice dentistry, Lebanon, Tenn., 1945—; prof., chmn. dept. aux. personnel U. Tenn. Sch. Dentistry, 1969—. Active orgn. Little League Softball, Lebanon, 1955; active vocational guidance program for high sch. Served to capt. Dental Corps, AUS, 1943-45. Recipient Fellowship Key Outstanding Dentist Tenn., 1965; award Ohio Sch. Journalism for Sci. Writing, 1970. Fellow Am. Coll. Dentists (council 1959), Internat. Coll. Dentists; mem. Am. Dental Assn. (council journalism 1970—), Tenn. Dental Assn., Am. Assn. Dental Editors (pres. 1965; Man of Year award 1970), Pierre Fauchard Acad., Omicron Kappa Upsilon. Baptist (deacon 1949—, past chmn. and co-chmn.). Kiwanian (pres. 1954-55). Club: Exchange (pres. 1946). Editor: Tenn. Dental Assn. 1955—. Home: 220 S McLean St Memphis TN 38104 Office: 847 Monroe St Memphis TN 38103

ARMSTRONG, WALLACE FARIS, chem. co. exec.; b. Castor, Alta., Can., Apr. 26, 1915; s. George A. and Margaret (Faris) A.; U.S. citizen, came to U.S., 1922; B.S., U. Fla., 1938, M.S., 1940; postgrad. Harvard, 1954; m. Eileen Ratterree, Aug. 15, 1941; children—Betty Eileen (Mrs. Michael E. Kirby), George Alexander, Robert Calvin, William Wallace. With Ethyl Corp., Baton Rouge, 1939—, resident mgr., 1956-66, gen. mgr. mfg., 1966, v.p., gen. mgr. mfg., 1967—. Pres. United Givers Fund; mem. adv. council La. State U. Coll. Bus. Adminstrn. Bd. dirs., council trustees Gulf South Research Inst.; bd. dirs. Pub. Affairs Research Council La., Council for A Better La. Mem. Am. Chem. Soc., Am. Inst. Chem. Engrs., Am. Petroleum Inst., Chlorine Inst., Baton Rouge C. of C., Phi Kappa Phi, Sigma Tau, Gamma Sigma Epsilon. Presbyn. (elder). Rotarian. Clubs: Country, City, Camelot (Baton Rouge). Home: 7622 Bocage Blvd Baton Rouge LA 70809 Office: Ethyl Corp 451 Florida Baton Rouge LA 70801

ARMSTRONG, WALTER PRESTON, JR., lawyer; b. Memphis, Oct. 4, 1916; s. Walter Preston and Irma Lewis (Waddell) A.; grad. Choate Sch., Wallingford, Conn., 1934; A.B., Harvard, 1938, J.D., 1941; D.C.L. (hon.), Southwestern at Memphis, 1961; m. Alice Kavanaugh McKee, Nov. 3, 1949; children—Alice Kavanaugh, Walter Preston III. Admitted to Tenn. bar, 1940, practiced in Memphis, 1941—; asso. Armstrong, Allen, Braden, Goodman, McBride & Prewitt, and predecessor law firms, Memphis, 1941—, partner, 1948—. Commr. for Promotion Uniformity of Legislation in U.S. for Tenn., 1947-67 mem. Tenn. Hist. Commn., 1969— pres. bd. edn. Memphis City Schs., 1956-61; mem. Tenn. Higher Edn. Commn., 1967—. Served from pvt. to maj. AUS, 1941-46. Fellow Am. Bar Found. (sec. 1960-62), Am. Coll. Trial Lawyers; mem. Am. (mem. ho. of dels.), Tenn. (pres. 1972-73), Memphis and Shelby County, Inter-Am., Internat. bar assns., Assn. Bar City N.Y., Am. Law Inst., Am. Judicature Soc., Nat. Conf. Commns. on Uniform State Laws (pres. 1961-63), Harvard Law Sch. Assn., Order of Coif, Scribes (pres. 1960-61), Omicron Delta Kappa. Author articles in field. Home: 1530 Carr Av Memphis TN 38104 Office: One Commerce Sq Memphis TN 38103

ARNESON, ANNE M. (MRS. R. GORDON ARNESON), social scientist; b. Monticello, Ark.; d. Walter Fagan and Alma (Shadow) McClerkin; B.A., Mary Washington Coll. of U. Va., 1951; postgrad. Am. U., 1952, 63—; m. Jack H. Jonas, Nov. 5, 1952 (dec. Aug. 1968); m. 2d, R. Gordon Arneson, June 10, 1972. Producer ednl. radio program Careers in New Orleans, 1950; social sci. research and propaganda analysis Rand Corp., Washington, 1951-61; profl. staff Weapons Systems Evaluation Div., Inst. Def. Analyses, Washington, 1961-65; polit. scientist Strategic Studies Center, Stanford Research Inst., Washington, 1965-67, editor Cameo of Zeta Phi Eta, 1958-59; cons., author politico-mil. affairs, conservation of natural resources, 1968—. Instr. swimming and water safety A.R.C., 1946-51. Mem. Am. Assn. Advancement Slavic Studies, Acad. Polit. Sci., Am. Acad. Polit. and Social Sci., D.A.R., Reston Garden Club (rec. sec. 1973-74), Zeta Phi Eta (pres. D.C. Alumnae chpt. 1953-54, nat. officer 1958-59, alumnae adviser Alpha Mu chpt. 1961-70). Democrat. Author articles in field. Address: 11803 Breton Ct Reston VA 22091

ARNETT, DONALD EDWARD, elec. engr.; b. Orlando, Fla., May 15, 1941; s. J.D. and Mary Jane (O'Cain) A.; B.E.E., Auburn U., 1964; M.B.A., Stetson U., 1972; m. Alice Anne Sasser, July 9, 1962; 1 dau., Pamela. With Fla. Power & Light Co., Daytona Beach, 1964—, engr., 1969—, power sales engr., 1971—. Served with AUS, 1965-67. Mem. Fla. Engring. Soc. (v.p.), I.E.E.E., A.A.A.S., Nat. Soc. Profl. Engrs., Daytona Beach C. of C., V.F.W. Mason, Kiwanian (treas.). Home: 24 Oakmont Circle Ormond Beach FL 32074 Office: PO Box 1978 Daytona Beach FL 32015

ARNETT, EUGENE BRITTON, JR., dentist; b. Lexington, Ky., Nov. 1, 1929; s. Eugene and Frances (Kirk) A.; B.S., Georgetown Coll., 1951; D.M.D., U. Louisville, 1956; m. Sharkey Utley, Oct. 31, 1953; children—Eugene Britton III, Allison Sharkey, Claire Elisabeth. Pvt. practice dentistry, Louisville, 1956-60, Owens Med. Center, 1960—. Mem. Ky. Bd. Dental Examiners; v.p. Ky. State Bd. Dentistry, 1971, pres., 1972. Served from A/b to A/2c, USAF, 1951-52. Mem. Louisville Dist., Ky., Am. dental socs., Order Ky. Colonels, Pierre Fauchard Acad., Kappa Alpha (life), Delta Sigma Delta (life), Phi Delta. Democrat. Baptist (deacon). Clubs: Hurstbourne Country; Lions. Charter mem. Ky. Athletic Hall of Fame. Home: 2802 Lime Kiln Lane Louisville KY 40222 Office: 4122 Shelbyville Rd Louisville KY 40207

ARNETT, HALBURN CLINTON, dentist; b. Mayfield, Ky., May 29, 1928; s. Samuel Clinton and Lola Belle (Allen) A.; student U. Louisville, 1947-49, D.M.D., 1954; B.S., Western Ky. U., 1950; m. Theresa Ann Kuhn, June 28, 1952; children—Karen Lynn, Martin Allen, Bryan Clinton. Intern Walter Reed Hosp., Washington, 1954-55; gen. practice dentistry, Louisville, 1957—; dir. Nat. Chem. Corp., Louisville, Dart Industries, Morganfield, Ky., Ky. Resorts, Inc., Louisville. Served with USAF, 1954-57. Mem. Louisville Dental Soc., Ky., Am. dental assns., Lambda Chi Alpha, Delta Sigma Delta, Omicron Delta Kappa, Phi Delta. Mason, Kiwanian. Club: Louisville Boat. Home: 3409 Nandina Dr Louisville KY 40222 Office: Starks Bldg Louisville KY 40202

ARNETT, JOHN LESLIE, lawyer, city ofcl.; b. Paintsville, Ky., Feb. 3, 1936; s. Eugene Britton and Frances (Kirk) A.; B.A., U. Ky., 1959; J.D., U. Louisville, 1963; m. Annette Violet Pemberton, May 4, 1956; children—Deborah Lynn, Timothy Lee. Admitted to Ky. bar, 1963; with FBI, Washington, 1954-56; partner Collier, Arnett, Coleman & Cooper, Elizabethtown, Ky., 1963—; city atty. City of Elizabethtown, 1967—. Instr. U. Ky. Community Coll., Elizabethtown, 1964-66. Leader Boy Scouts Am., Elizabethtown, 1967-69; chmn. Hardin County (Ky.) Blood Program, 1966-68. Precinct chmn. Democratic Party County Com., 1964-68, sec. 26th legislative dist. of Ky., 1964-68; vice chmn. Young Democrats, 1966-69. Mem. Am., Ky. (ho. dels. 1973—), Hardin County (pres. 1972-74) bar assns., Elizabethtown-Hardin County C. of C. (bd. dirs. 1966-69), Omicron Delta Kappa. Methodist. Club: Lions (pres. Elizabethtown, dep. dist. gov. 1973). Home: 622 El Dorado Dr Elizabethtown KY 42701 Office: 128 W Dixie Av Elizabethtown KY 42701

ARNHOLT, WALDON SYLVESTER, artist; b. Nankin, O., Jan. 1, 1909; student C. Fritz Hoelzer, N.Y.C., 1932-38; m. Helen Mayflower Howman, Sept. 6, 1938. Pvt. art tchr., O., N.Y., 1929-61, Clearwater, Fla.; artist-lithographer A.L. Garber Co., Ashland, O., 1931-61; one-man shows in Ashland, Cleve., Parthenon Gallery, Nashville, Municipal Gallery, Tampa, Fla., Fla. Fedn. Arts Hdqrs. and Mus., DuBarry, Tampa, Clearwater, Lakeland, St. Petersburg, Dunedin, Fla.; exhibited in group shows in Ashland, Mansfield, O., Tampa, Clearwater, Lakeland, St. Petersburg, Dunedin; cons. Mus. Sci. and Natural History, Tampa. represented in permanent collections Mus. Sci. and Natural History, also various chs. Recipient ribbons, medals, certificates for art. Mem. Ohio, Fla. fedns. art. Home and studio: 1224 Sunset Point Rd Clearwater FL 33515

ARNOLD, DAVID SCOTT, editor; b. Findlay, O., Aug. 16, 1920; s. Ed Samuel and Florence (Adams) A.; A.B., Lafayette Coll., 1942; M.S., Syracuse U., 1943; m. Catherine Rose Fury, Apr. 18, 1953; children—Susan Scott, David Fury. Field cons. Pub. Adminstrn. Service, Chgo., 1943-49; staff mem., asst. dir. publications Internat. City Mgmt. Assn., Washington, 1949—. Mem. Am. Soc. for Pub. Adminstrn. (chpt. pres. 1961-62). Home: 3303 Brandy Ct Falls Church VA 22042 Office: 1140 Connecticut Av NW Washington DC 20036

ARNOLD, DAVID WALKER, chem. corp. exec.; b. Dundee, Miss., Dec. 6, 1936; s. Jesse Braxton and Irene Myrtle (Mitchell) A.; B.S. in Chem. Engring., U. Miss., 1958; M.S., Ia. State U., 1963, Ph.D., 1966; m. Barbara Ann Daves, Jan. 10, 1958; 1 dau., Janet Gracen. Jr. engr. Inst. for Atomic Research, Ia. State U., Ames, 1963-66; dir. engring. Miss. Chem. Corp., Yazoo City, 1966—. Sec., Jr. Achievement Yazoo City, 1969-70, treas., 1970-72, v.p., 1972-73, pres., 1973—; mem., sec. Yazoo City Planning and Zoning Commn., 1970—. Chmn. Yazoo County (Miss.) Republican party, 1970-72; del. State Conv., 1972. Bd. dirs. U. Miss. Alumni Assn. Served with USNR, 1958-63. Registered profl. engr., Miss. Mem. Am. Inst. Chem. Engrs., Am. Mgmt. Assn., Beta Theta Pi, Phi Lambda Upsilon, Gamma Sigma Epsilon. Republican. Episcopalian. Club: Yazoo Country. Home: 2026 Country Club Dr Yazoo City MS 39194 Office: PO Box 388 Yazoo City MS 39194

ARNOLD, EDGAR FRANK, JR., real estate broker; b. Madisonville, Ky., Sept. 29, 1925; s. Edgar F. and Caroline (Long) A.; student Kan. State Tchrs. Coll., 1943-44, U. Ky., 1946-47; m. Ruby Jarvis Mitchell, June 20, 1948 (div. June 1965); children—Frank Edgar, Gillis Mitchell, Brian Bowen; m. Jeanne Campbell Hannah, Mar. 11, 1966. With Madisonville (Ky.) Messenger, 1946-70, editor, pres. Madisonville Pub. Co., 1963-70; past editor Ky. State Democrat; real estate broker, Madisonville, 1970—. Mem. Ky. Athletic Commn., 1964-68. Sec. Madisonville Coll. Found., Hopkins County-Madisonville Hosp. Corp. Dep. sheriff Hopkins County, 1954-58; mem. Ky. Ho. of Reps., 1958-59; mem. Ky. Democratic Exec. Com., 1966-72. Served from pvt. to flight officer USAAC, 1943-45. Mem. Madisonville Bd. Realtors, C. of C. (pres. 1970). Home: 62 E Broadway St Madisonville KY 42431 Office: 246 Country Club Lane Madisonville KY 42431

ARNOLD, GENE ROSS, announcer, program mgr.; b. Houston, Nov. 16, 1935; s. Frank and Buelah (Frierson) A.; B.F.A., U. Houston, 1959; m. Laurel Ann Ricke, Apr. 4, 1964; children—Mark, Dan. Announcer, KWTX Radio and TV, Waco, Tex., 1959-63; dir. news, sports dept. radio sta. KODA, Houston, 1963—; corr. Houston, World of Sports, ABC radio, 1966-72; announcer S.W. Coll. Football Network, 1968—. Home: 2234 South Blvd Houston TX 77006 Office: 4808 San Felipe St Houston TX 77027

ARNOLD, HAROLD DONALD, bus. information service exec.; b. Enid, Okla., Sept. 2, 1925; s. William Perry and Hattie Alley (Dull) A.; B.A., Phillips U., 1948; M.A., U. Okla., 1951; m. Jean Hyland, July 6, 1945; 1 dau., Paula Jean. With Retail Credit Co., Atlanta, 1952—, head Communications Div., 1960-65, dir. advt. and publicity, 1965-68, dir. spl. programs, 1968-71, dir. advt. and pub. relations, 1971—. Served with USNR, 1943-45, 51-52. Mem. Am. Advt. Fedn., Pub. Relations Soc. Am., Newcomen Soc. Am., Assn. Indsl. Advertisers (v.p. 1973—). Club: Atlanta Press. Home: 3935 Chamblee Dunwoody Rd Chamblee GA 30341 Office: PO Box 4081 Atlanta GA 30302

ARNOLD, IRA LEE, ophthalmologist; b. Owenton, Ky., Sept. 20, 1918; s. Ira Lee and Ruth (Reeves) A.; B.S., U. Ky., 1940; M.D., U. Louisville, 1943; postgrad. Northwestern U., 1946; m. Beatrice Welch, June 26, 1943; children—Coleman Lee, Jane Carol (Mrs. Edward Barnhill). Intern U.S. Marine Hosp., Statten Island, N.Y., 1943-44; resident Memphis Eye, Ear, Nose & Throat Hosp., 1947-49; practice medicine specializing in ophthalmology, Chattanooga, 1949—; chief staff Baroness Erlanger Hosp., Chattanooga, 1968-70, chief dept. ophthalmology, 1970-72; mem. staffs Erlanger Meml., Parkridge hosps. Bd. dirs. Bethel Bible Sch., Chattanooga, 1968—; bd. trustees Tenn. Bapt. Childrens Home, Chattanooga, 1968—; pres. Chattanooga Ophthalmol. Found., 1968—. Served with USCG, and USPHS, 1944-46. Diplomate Am. Bd. Ophthalmology. Mem. A.C.S., A.M.A., Tenn. Acad. Ophthalmology and Otolaryngology (pres. 1967), Hamilton County Med. Soc. (pres. 1974—), Phi Beta Pi. Home: 10 N Lynncrest St Chattanooga TN 37411 Office: 203 Medical Arts Bldg Chattanooga TN 37402

ARNOLD, JESSE CHARLES, educator; b. Bowie, Tex., Sept. 28, 1937; s. Jesse Conolly and Lillie (Stark) A.; B.S., Southeastern State Coll., 1960; M.S., Fla. State U., 1965, Ph.D., 1967; m. Peggy Lou Peveto, Aug. 23, 1959; children—Christa Louise, Jesse Charles. Asst. prof. dept. edn., research, testing Fla. State U., Tallahassee, 1967-68; asst. prof. dept. statistics Va. Poly. Inst. and State U., Blacksburg, 1968-70, asso. prof., 1970-73, prof., 1974—, chmn. dept., 1973—. Bd. dirs. Wesley Found., Va. Poly. Inst. and State U. Served with USPHS, 1961-63. NIH fellow, 1963-67; Va. Water Control Bd. grantee, 1969-70. Mem. Am. Statis. Assn. (sec. Va. 1969-70), Va. Acad. Sci. (sec. statistics sect. 1969-70), Biometric Soc., Pi Mu Epsilon, Blue Key, Kappa Delta Pi. Independent. Methodist. Contbr. profl. jours. Home: 916 Buchanan Dr Blacksburg VA 24060 Office: Dept Statistics Va Poly Inst State Univ Blacksburg VA 24061

ARNOLD, LEONARD EUGENE, civil engr., constrn. co. exec.; b. Smithville, Tenn., Sept. 4, 1941; s. Samuel Eugene and Katherine Rose (Foster) A.; B.S. in Civil Engring., Tenn. Tech. U., 1964; m. Shirley Ann Mason, Aug. 25, 1961; children—Leonard, Cara Ann, Tracy Diana. Sr. engr. Met. Pub. Work Dept., Nashville, 1964-69; pres., civil engr., contractor Arnold & Rice Constrn. Co., Madison, Tenn., 1969-73; pres. Arnold Constrn. Co., Inc., Madison, 1973—. Active Boy Scouts Am. Registered profl. engr., Tenn. Mem. Tenn. Soc. Profl. Engrs. Baptist (dir. young adults dept. 1972-73, youth dir. 1969-71). Home: 817 N Summerfield Dr Madison TN 37115

ARNOLD, LYNWOOD FREDERICK, real estate broker, state senator; b. Jacksonville, Fla., Oct. 6, 1916; s. Columbus Washington and Margaret (Lee) A.; B.A., Stetson U., 1941; postgrad. Princeton, 1942; m. Elsie Ferguson, May 30, 1947; children—Lynwood Frederick, Pamela Hope. Real estate broker; pres. Statewide Sales & Services, Jacksonville; mem. Fla. Ho. of Reps., 1963-70, Fla. Senate, 1971—. Served to lt. USNR, 1941-46; PTO. Mem. Southside, Northside bus. men's clubs, Sigma Nu. Episcopalian. Mason (Shriner), Elk, Lion. Home: 1504 Harbor Oaks Rd Jacksonville FL 32207 Office: PO Box 5062 Jacksonville FL 32207*

ARNOLD, PHILIP MILLS, chem. engr.; b. Springfield, Mo., Feb. 9, 1911; s. Anthony L. and Mary Genevieve (Hodnett) A.; B.S., Washington U., 1932, Chem. E., 1941; Chem. engr. research div. Phillips Petroleum Co., 1937-48, asst. mgr. chem. dept., 1948-50, mgr. research and devel. dept., 1950-64, v.p. research and devel., 1964—. Fellow Am. Inst. Chemists; mem. NRC (div. chemistry and chem. tech. 1959-68, div. engring. and indsl. research 1965-68), Indsl. Research Inst. (pres. 1964-65), Am. Inst. Chem. Engrs., Am. Chem. Soc., A.A.A.S., Coordinating Research Council (dir. 1964—, pres. 1969-71), Internat. Union Pure and Applied Chemistry (chmn. finance com. 1963-71, mem. bur. 1969—, exec. com. 1971—), World Petroleum Congress (mem. permanent council 1965-71), Am. Petroleum Inst., Am. Soc. Testing and Materials, Atomic Industrial Forum (dir. 1966-69), Soc. Chem. Industry (mem. exec. com. 1967-70), Nat. Acad. Engring., Tau Beta Pi, Alpha Chi Sigma, Sigma Chi. Republican. Home: Box 1457 Bartlesville OK 74003 Office: Phillips Petroleum Co Bartlesville OK 74004

ARNOLD, ROGER MURRAY, tool co. exec.; b. Glastonbury, Conn., Feb. 3, 1934; s. William Milton and Evelyn (Mahorney) A.; B.S., U. Houston, 1959; m. Wanda Ruth Webb, Feb. 13, 1953; children—Wanda Sue, Roger David, William Clyde. Asst. to v.p. mfg. and engring. Mission Mfg. Co., Houston, 1957-60; cons. Bonner & Moore Engring. Assos., 1960; pres. Diatron Electronics Corp., Houston, 1961; mgr. information systems Hughes Tool Co., Houston, 1964-69, group mgr. diversified prodn., 1969-73, mgr. maj. projects, 1973—. Standard Oil Acad. scholar U. Houston, 1957-58; Franklin Found. fellow U. Houston, 1955-56. Mem. Assn. for Systems Mgmt. (dir. 1967, 68), Systems and Procedures Assn. (dir. 1965, 66), Am. Mgmt. Assn. (mem. continuing systems seminar; mem. exec. com.). Home: 15721 Juneau Lane Houston TX 77040 Office: 5425 Polk Av Houston TX 77001

ARNOLD, WILLIAM BUCK, lawyer; b. Houston, Nov. 18, 1919; s. Thomas J. and Georgia (Buck) A.; B.B.A., U. Tex., 1942, LL.B., 1949; m. Lucy Gray, May 30, 1948; children—Lucinda Gray, Georgia Anne, Mary Virginia. Admitted to Tex. bar, 1949; mem. law firm Vinson, Elkins, Weems and Searls, Houston, 1949—. Dir. South Main Bank, Tex. Electric Steel Casting Co., Quintana Petroleum Corp. (Houston), A-V Corp. Chmn. bd. trustees Kinkaid Sch. Served as pvt. AUS; then to lt. comdr., USNR, 1942-46. Mem. Am., Tex., Harris County bar assns., Am. Judicature Soc., Order of Coif, Phi Delta Phi, Phi Gamma Delta. Methodist. Clubs: Houston Country (dir.); Ramada. Home: 3440 Ella Lee Lane Houston TX 77027 Office: First City Nat Bank Bldg Houston TX 77002

ARNOLD, WILLIAM H., JR., lawyer; b. Texarkana, Ark., Jan. 30, 1893; grad. Phillips Exeter (N.H.) Acad.; A.B., Harvard, 1914; M.A. (Rhodes scholar), Oxford (Eng.) U., 1918. Admitted to Ark. bar, 1916, La. bar, 1932, Tex. bar, 1937, U.S. Supreme Ct. bar, 1928; mem. firm Arnold, Arnold & Lavender, Ltd., Texarkana. Mem. Am., Ark. bar assns., State Bar Tex. Office: 507 Hickory St Texarkana AR 75501

ARNOLDY, ROMAN F., corp. exec.; b. Clements, Minn., Aug. 5, 1911; s. Frank Joseph and Magdalen (Zettel) A.; student St. Thomas Coll., 1928-30; M.E., U. Minn., 1933; m. Lillian Ethyl Joint, May 2, 1947; children—John, Susan. Salesman, Standard Oil Co. (Ind.), Mason City, Ia., 1933-34; self employed oil refining, Savage, Minn., 1934-36; supt. ind. survey U. Minn., 1936; devel. engr. Union Carbide Corp., Newark, 1936-39, dist. engr., Houston, 1939-44; founder, pres. Houston Heat Treating Co., 1944-46; founder, v.p. Houston Grinding & Mfg. Co., 1944-46; founder, pres. Tex. Alloy Products, Houston, 1946—. Mem. C. of C., Am. Welding Soc. (dir.), Am. Soc. for Engring. Edn., N.A.M., Tex. Mfrs. Assn., Breakfast Assn. Clubs: Rotary, Warwick, Lakeside Country, University. Contbr. articles to profl. jours. Inventor Bulkweld Process. Home: 225 Millbrook Lane Houston TX 77024 Office: 1403 N Post Oak Rd Houston TX 77055

ARNOTT, HOWARD JOSEPH, educator; b. Los Angeles, Mar. 9, 1928; s. Andrew Hugh and Evelyn Leonore (Donelly) A.; A.B., U. So. Cal., 1952, M.S., 1953; Ph.D., U. Cal. at Berkeley, 1958; m. Wanda Jean Cross, Jan. 28, 1950; children—John Joseph, Catherine Jean, Susan Leonore, Virginia Anne. Asst. prof. biology Northwestern U., Evanston, Ill., 1958-64; asso. prof. dept. botany U. Tex., Austin, 1965-68, prof., 1968-72, acting chmn. dept., 1970-71; prof., chmn. dept. biology U. So. Fla., Tampa, 1972—. Cons. Ency. Brit. Films, NASA. Served with USNR, 1946-48. NSF grantee, 1963-65; NIH postdoctoral fellow U. Tex., 1964-65. Mem. Bot. Soc. Am., Am. Soc. Cell Biology, Soc. Invertebrate Pathology, Am. Microscopical Soc., A.A.A.S., Sigma Xi, Psi Sigma. Club: Carrollwood Village Country (Tampa). Contbr. articles, abstracts to sci. jours., chpts. to books. Home: 13301 Golf Crest Circle Tampa FL 33624

ARNOUX, PATRICK CAMPBELL, TV exec.; b. Hot Springs, Ark., Nov. 16, 1927; s. Given Campbell and Natalie Adeline (Brigham) A.; student George Sch., Newtown, Pa., 1943-46, Norfolk div. William and Mary, Va. Poly. Inst., 1947; m. Gale Priscilla Coffin, Sept. 21, 1963; children—Amy Suzanne, Given Campbell. Radio-TV engr. WTAR, Norfolk, Va., 1947-52, dir., 1952-57, TV prodn. mgr., 1957-62; TV program dir. WSPA-TV, Spartanburg, S.C., 1962-63; TV program mgr. WNBE-TV, New Bern, N.C., 1963-64; TV program mgr. Hampton Rds. Ednl. TV Assn. WHRO-TV, Norfolk, 1965—. Served with N.G., 1948-55. Recipient George Foster Peabody award for overall instructional programming, 1973. Mem. Mayflower Soc. Presbyn. Rotarian. Home: 1364 Monterey Av Norfolk VA 23508 Office: 5200 Hampton Blvd Norfolk VA 23508

ARNTSON, PETER ANDREW, lawyer; b. Washington, May 23, 1938; s. Paul Lee and Mary Ellen (Garrigan) A.; B.A., U. Va., 1960, J.D., 1965; LL.M. in Taxation, Georgetown U., 1971; m. Colette Odile Rousseau, July 11, 1962; 1 son, Eric Paul. Admitted to Va. bar, 1965, U.S. Supreme Ct. bar, 1973; practiced in Arlington, 1965—; asso., partner firm Phillips, Kendrick, Gearheart and Aylor, 1965—. Lectr. fed. taxation Va. State Bar Continuing Legal Edn. Seminars, 1972-73. Mem. Arlington County Commn. Human Resources, 1973-74, Legislative Adv. Com. to Arlington Sch. Bd., 1972—. Bd. dirs. Heart Assn. No. Va., Inc. Served to 1st lt. AUS, 1960-62. Recipient Outstanding Service award Heart Assn. No. Va., Inc., 1972. Mem. Am., Va. (com. on taxation 1973—), Arlington County bar assns., No. Va. Jr. Bar (v.p. 1966), Arlington C. of C., Res. Officers Assn., TILKA, Nat. Assn. for Retarded Children, Sigma Nu, Phi Alpha Delta. Rotarian (dir. 1974-75). Contbr. articles on taxation to profl. publs. Home: 5127 N 38th St Arlington VA 22207 Office: Suite 400 2009 N 14th St Arlington VA 22201

ARON, WILLIAM, oceanographer, marine biologist; b. Bklyn., June 26, 1930; s. Jack J. and Rose (Heidekel) A.; B.S., Bklyn. Coll., 1952; M.S., U. Wash., 1957, Ph.D., 1960; m. Helen Wozniak, Dec. 23, 1961; children—Thomas Lee, Jane Ann. Research asst. prof. U. Wash., Seattle, 1956-61; head biol. oceanography group Gen. Motors Def. Research Labs., Goleta, Cal., 1961-67; head oceanography and limnology program Smithsonian Instn., Washington, 1967-71; dir. Office Ecology and Environmental Conservation Nat. Oceanic and Atmospheric Adminstrn., Washington, 1971—. Served with AUS, 1954-56. Mem. A.A.A.S., Am. Inst. Biol. Scis., Marine Tech. Soc., Sigma Xi. Contbr. articles to sci. jours. Home: 6822 Sorrell St McLean VA 22101 Office: 5813 Dept Commerce 14th and Constitution NW Washington DC 20230

ARONOV, AARON MORRIS, real estate exec.; b. Montgomery, Ala., Dec. 22, 1919; s. Jake and Nora (Varlow) A.; B.S., U. Ala., Coll. Commerce, 1941; m. Marjorie Schoenbaum, Sept. 2, 1945; children—Jake Frank, Teri Helene (Mrs. Sam Diamond), Owen William. Pres. Aronov Realty Co., Inc., Montgomery, Ala., 1952—. Dir. Peoples Bank & Trust Co., Montgomery, Ala., St. Jude Cath. Hosp., Montgomery, WYEA TV, Columbus, Ga., 1969—, WHNT-TV, Huntsville, Ala., Nat. Conf. Christians and Jews, Inc., Birmingham, Warner Nat. Corp., Cin. Bd. dirs. YMCA, Montgomery, Ala., 1973—; mem. Montgomery Indsl. Devel. Bd., 1966—; bd. controls Men of Montgomery, 1973—; mem. bd. St. Jude Cath. Hosp., Montgomery, 1971—; mem. bd. visitors Huntingdon Coll., Montgomery, 1973—; pres. Internat. Council Shopping Centers, 1966-67. Named Montgomery's Boss of Year Nat. Secs. Assn., 1963; Montgomery's Man of Year C. of C., 1966. Mem. Montgomery C. of C. (pres. 1961-62). Jewish religion. Club: Standard Country (Montgomery, Ala.). Home: 2088 Myrtlewood Dr Montgomery AL 36111 Office: 520 S Court St Montgomery AL 36104

ARPER, WILLIAM BURNSIDE, educator; b. Duluth, Minn., Dec. 10, 1915; s. William B. and Alice (Webster) A.; B.S., U. Okla., 1940, M.S., 1942; Ph.D., U. Kan., 1953; m. Elizabeth Jane Pearce, Nov. 6, 1942. Geologist, Phillips Petroleum Co., Shreveport, La., 1946-48; asst. instr. U. Kan., 1948-50; instr. U. Mo., 1950-53; asst. prof. geology Tex. Technol. U., Lubbock, 1953-56, asso. prof., 1956-60, prof., 1960—. Served with C.E., AUS, 1943-45. Fellow Geol. Soc. Am.; mem. Am. Assn. Petroleum Geologists, Soc. Econ. Paleontologists and Mineralogists, A.A.A.S., Am. Chem. Soc., Geo-chem. Soc., Southwestern Fedn. Geol. Socs. (sec.-treas. 1965-66), Lubbock Geol. Soc. (pres. 1967-68), Nat. Assn. Geology Tchrs., Sigma Xi. Home: 2117 31st St Lubbock TX 79411

ARQUEMBOURG, PIERRE CHARLES, physician; b. Lille, France, Nov. 15, 1919; s. Leon Emile and Medeleine Marie (Bossu) A.; B.S., Pasteur Inst., 1939, certificate, 1940, degree in clin. pathology, 1951; M.D., Lille U., 1951; m. Zahra Homa Sadrai, June 23, 1966; 1 dau., Kathy Huguette (Mrs. Donald McDonald). Came to U.S., 1960, naturalized, 1965. First class asst. Pasteur Inst., Lille, 1946-51; WHO lab. expert, Tunisia, Iran and Geneva, 1954-59; research asst. Pvt. Found. U.S.A., 1960, Tulane U., 1962, La. State U. Med. Center, 1963-72; immunology research A. Ochsner Found. Hosp., New Orleans, 1973—. Trustee, La. chpt. Leukemia Soc. Served with Brit. Liberation Army, World War II. Mason. Author: Primer of Immunoelectrophoresis, 1970. Patentee in field. Home: 758 Glencove Lane Gretna LA 70053 Office: 1520 Jefferson Hwy New Orleans LA 70121

ARREOLA, RAOUL ALBERT, ednl. adminstr.; b. Laredo, Tex., Sept. 18, 1943; s. Paul Peter and Olivia (Roderiguez) A.; B.A., Ariz. State U., 1965, M.A., 1968, Ph.D., 1969; m. Mona Jean Gravel, May 12, 1973. Asst. prof. Fla. State U., Tallahassee, 1969—, research asso. div. instructional research, 1969-70, dir. Office Evaluation Services, 1970—. Spl. cons. tests and measurement to select subcom. Commerce Com., Fla. Ho. of Reps., 1973-74. Mem. Am. Psychol. Assn., Am. Ednl. Research Assn., Am. Assn. Higher Edn., Am. Assn. U. Profs., A.A.A.S. Republican. Lutheran. Home: 237 Westridge Dr Tallahassee FL 32304

ARRINGDALE, WALLACE JOHN, physician; b. Boone, Ia., Oct. 31, 1937; s. John Bertrum and Carolyn Anna (Leininger) A.; B.S., Ia. State U., 1960, postgrad., 1960-61; M.D., U. Neb., 1965. Intern Immanuel Deaconess Inst., Omaha, 1965-66; gen. surgery resident St. Joseph's Hosp., Houston, 1968-72; resident thoracic and cardiovascular surgery St. Luke's Hosp., Tex. Heart Inst., Houston, 1972—; dir. med. edn. Career Acad., Houston, 1969-71. Served with M.C., AUS, 1966-68. Mem. Phi Rho Sigma. Home: 2200 Fountainview 49 Houston TX 77027 Office: Texas Heart Inst Houston TX 77501

ARRINGTON, ALYNE ROGERS (MRS. JAMES D. ARRINGTON), newspaper editor; b. Collins, Miss., Feb. 9, 1911; d. Thomas Carter and D. L. O. (Buchanan) Rogers; student pub. schs.; m. James D. Arrington, Oct. 8, 1931 (dec. 1957); children—Analyn (Mrs. James Rogers Goff), Carol Jeanne (Mrs. Albert Sidney Gooch, Jr.), James D. Asst. editor The News Commercial, 1931-57, editor, owner, 1957—; owner, editor-Mt. Olive Tribune, weekly, 1960—; owner comml. printing plant. Active A.R.C., Am. Heart Assn., Mental Health Assn., Nat. Found., Easter Seal group. Sec. Covington County Democratic exec. com., 1950—. Mem. Miss. Press Women (v.p. 1956-57, 65—), D.A.R. (treas. 1962-70), Nat. Fedn. Press Women, Nat. Editorial Assn., Miss. Press Assn., C. of C., Nat. Soc. Colonial Dames XVII Century. Baptist. Address: Collins MS 39428

ARRINGTON, JOHN LESLIE, JR., lawyer; b. Pawhuska, Okla., Oct. 15, 1931; s. John Leslie and Grace Louise (Moore) A.; grad. Lawrenceville Sch., 1949; A.B., Princeton, 1953; LL.B., Harvard, 1956, LL.M., 1957; m. Elizabeth Anne Waddington, July 21, 1956 (div. Jan. 1972); children—Elizabeth Anne, John Leslie III, Winifred Louise, Katherine Moore; m. 2d, Linda Vance Mullendore, 1972. Admitted to Okla. bar, 1956; with Huffman, Arrington, Scheurich & Kihle and predecessor firms, Tulsa 1957—, partner, 1961—. Bd. dirs. Tulsa Charity Horse Show, Family and Children's Service, Tulsa; trustee Holland Hall Sch., Tulsa. Recipient Jr. award for service to profession Tulsa County Bar Assn., 1962; named Outstanding Young Man, Tulsa Jr. C. of C., 1963. Mem. Okla., Tulsa County (pres. 1970), Am. Fed. Power bar assns., Am. Soc. Internat. Law, Harvard Law Sch. Assn. Okla (pres. 1961) Phi Beta Kappa. Republican. Episcopalian (vestryman). Clubs: Tulsa, Southern Hills Country, Princeton (pres. 1964-65) (Tulsa). Home: 2219 E 45th Pl Tulsa OK 74105 Office: Okla Natural Bldg Tulsa OK 74119

ARTHUR, SUSAN, librarian; b. nr. Pineville, Ky.; d. John M. and Lettie (McKeehan) Arthur; student Cumberland Coll., 1932-34, A.B. Berea Coll., 1936; B.S. in L.S., U. Ky., 1948. High sch. tchr. English and social studies, Pineville, 1937-41; high sch. librarian, 1941-48; asst. librarian Henderson State Tchrs. Coll., Arkadelphia, Ark., 1951-52; asst. librarian Union Coll., Barbourville, Ky., 1952-54; tchr. English, Barbourville High Sch., 1954-56; serials librarian, instr. library sci. Berea Coll., 1956-60; classified librarian in tech. manuals Transp. Research Center, U.S. Army, Ft. Eustis, Va., 1960-61; librarian, Barbourville City Schools, 1969—. Mem. pub. library bd. for Knox County, 1953-55. Mem. Am. Assn. U. Women (local br. pres. 1965-67), Am. Assn. U. Profs. Mem. Disciples of Christ Ch. Club: Barbourville, Garden (pres. 1969—). Home: 601 N Main St Barbourville KY 40906

ARYA, VIJAY KUMAR, geophysicist; b. Malout, Punjab, India, Aug. 21, 1939; s. Prabh Dayal and Budh (Chawla) A.; B.Engring. with honors, Birla Engring. Coll. (Pilani, India), 1960, M.Engring., 1961; Ph.D. in Elec. Engring., Ohio State U., 1967; m. Karen Elizabeth Thomas, June 17, 1967; 1 son, Sunjay. Came to U.S., 1963, naturalized, 1974. Asst. prof. dept. elec. engring. Birla Engring. Coll., 1961-63; research engr. Shell Oil Co., Shell Devel. Co., Deer Park, Tex., 1967-72, sr. research geophysicist, Houston, 1972—. Recipient Gold Medal awards highest honors Birla Engring. Coll., 1960, 61. Mem. I.E.E.E. (chmn.), Control Systems Soc., Sigma Xi. Contbr. articles to profl. jours. Home: 10821 Sandpiper Dr Houston TX 77035 Office: PO Box 481 Houston TX 77001

ASAL, NABIH RAFIA, educator; b. Haifa, Israel, Dec. 21, 1938; s. Rafia Saleem and Mary (Naser) A.; A.A., Hannibal LaGrange Coll., 1961; A.B., Jewell Coll., 1963; M.S., Mo. U., 1965; Ph.D., Okla. U., 1968; m. Jan Marie Schrik, June 4, 1966; 1 son, Rafia Bryan. Came to U.S., 1959, naturalized, 1972. Instr., U. Okla. Health Scis. Center, Oklahoma City, 1968-69, asst. prof. epidemiology, 1969-72, asso. prof., 1973—. Dir. Smoking Cessation Clinics Am. Cancer Soc., 1973—. Mem. Am. Pub. Health Assn., Soc. Epidemiologic Research, N.Y. Acad. Sci., Sigma Xi, Sigma Nu. Republican. Baptist (Sunday sch. tchr.) (finance com. ch. 1971—). Contbr. articles to profl. jours. Home: 1805 NW 42nd St Oklahoma City OK 73118

ASAM, JULIA MCCAIN LAMPKIN (MRS. JOSEPH ASAM), cancer research scientist; b. Tuscaloosa, Ala., Feb. 27, 1931; d. Charles Barnett and Julia (McCain) Lampkin; B.S., U. Ala., 1952; M.S., George Washington U., 1954, Ph.D. (NSF fellow), 1958; m. Joseph Asam, Apr. 7, 1971. Founder, 1st pres. Lampkin-Asam Cancer Inst., Perrine, Fla., 1965-66, mem. sci. staff, sci. dir., 1966—. Instr., U. Tampa Extension, Homestead AFB, Fla., 1970—. Corr. sec. South Dade County Democratic Club Women, 1969. Am. Cancer Soc. grantee, 1963-66. Mem. Am. Assn. Cancer Research. Baptist. Author: Lymphomas: Regression, Carcinogenesis and Prevention, 1966; Malignant Intrigue, 1973. Address: PO Box 252 Perrine FL 33157

ASBILL, JIMMIE SHEARRON, petroleum engr.; b. Tipton, Okla., May 6, 1934; s. Smith Langford and Lois (Gilliland) A.; B.S., Tex. Technol. Coll., 1956; m. Marilyn Jean Campbell, Sept. 11, 1954; children—Jimmie Kyle, Kimberly Marie, Darin William. With Cities Service Oil Co., various locations, 1956—, petroleum engr., Bartlesville, Okla., 1961-69, region reservoir engr., Jackson, 1969-73, exploitation mgr., Jackson, 1973—. Served with AUS, 1956-58. Registered profl. engr., Okla. Mem. Soc. Petroleum Engrs. (sect. vice chmn. 1968-69), Am. Petroleum Inst., Tau Beta Pi, Pi Epsilon Tau. Mem. Ch. of Christ (deacon). Home: 6166 Whitestone Rd Jackson MS 39206 Office: PO Box 12026 Jackson MS 39211

ASBILL, PAULINE PORTER (MRS. DAVID ST. PIERRE ASBILL), office mgr.; b. Royston, Ga., Sept. 19, 1906; d. James Alexander and Ophelia Kathryn (Fowler) Porter; R.N., Med. Coll. S.C. Sch. Nursing, 1926; m. David St. Pierre Asbill, Feb. 9, 1928; 1 son, David St. Pierre. Nurse charge pediatrics dept. Roper Hosp., Charleston, S.C., 1926-28; nurse obstet. dept. N.Y. Polyclinic Med. Sch. and Hosp., N.Y.C., 1928-29; mgr. physician's office, Columbia, S.C., 1934—. State of S.C. Civil Def. nurse in Richland County Civil Def. Council, 1953—. Mem. Woman's Aux. Assn. Surgeons So. Ry. and S.A.L. R.R. Systems, Woman's Aux. Columbia Med. Soc. (chmn. decorations 1948-55, v.p. 1942), Woman's Aux. S.C. Med. Assn. (charge decoration 1952-55), Internat. Platform Assn., Intercontinental Biog. Assn., Columbia Art Assn. (mem. art com. 1935-36), Delphian Soc. Episcopalian. Clubs: Columbia Woman's (publicity chmn. 1940; decorations com. 1939), Altrusa, Summit, Forest Lake Country (Columbia). Home: Senate Plaza 1520 Senate St Columbia SC 29201 Office: 1417 Barnwell St Columbia SC 29201

ASBILL, SMITH LANGFORD, JR., physician, anesthesia assn. exec.; b. Tipton, Okla., Oct. 10, 1931; s. Smith Langford and Lois (Gilliland) A.; B.A. in Chemistry, Tex. Technol. U., 1957; M.D., U. Tex. Southwestern Med. Sch., 1961; m. Marjorie Ann Smith, Mar. 23, 1951;children—Lisa Ann, Leslie Annette, Robert Lawrence, Lea Anne, Laurel Allison. Intern Meth. Hosp., Dallas, 1962-64; resident Parkland Meml. Hosp., Dallas; individual practice medicine specializing in anesthesiology, Lubbock, Tex., 1964—; with Lubbock Anesthesia Assos., Lubbock, 1964—, v.p., bus. mgr., 1970-72; mem. staff Meth. Meml. Hosp., Lubbock, chief anesthesia, 1968-69, 73-74. Cartoonist Tex. Soc. Anesthesiologist Newsletter, 1970—. Served with USN, 1951-54. Decorated Korean Presidential Unit Citation, Korean Service Ribbon with star. Mem. Am., Tex. socs. anesthesiologists, Phi Rho Sigma, Alpha Epsilon Delta. Methodist (mem. adminstrv. bd., chmn. social concerns commn.). Home: 4418 10th St Lubbock TX 79416 Office: 3516 22d Pl Lubbock TX 79410

ASBURY, KENNETH PERRY, lawyer; b. Wise, Va., Oct. 25, 1922; s. Reecy Thomas and Julia (Craft) A.; LL.B., Washington and Lee U.; m. Velma Irene Lee, Oct. 19, 1956; 1 dau., Lorna Dawn. Admitted to Va. bar, 1949; practiced in Wise, 1950—. Vice pres. Clinch Haven Farms, Big Stone Gap, Va., 1972-73, Marco Coal Co., Wise, 1973—; dir. Wise County Nat. Banks. Pres. Gladeville Housing Authority, Ltd.; adv. council Clinch Valley Coll. U. Va., 1956-58. Mayor, Wise, 1952-56; Commonwealth's atty. Wise County, Va., 1956-72; mem. Va. Democratic State Central Com., 1972—. Trustee Appalachian Regional Hosp., Inc., Lexington, Ky., S.W. Va. Community Health Services; bd. dirs. Va.-Appalachian Regional Health Services. Served with AUS, 1942-46. Name Wise County Citizen of Yr., 1965. Mem. Va. State Bar (council 1972-73), Wise County Bar Assn. (pres. 1966), Wise County C. of C. (pres. 1964-65), V.F.W. (comdr. 1956-72). Mason, Kiwanian (pres. Wise Club 1962). Club: Lonesome Pine Country (Wise). Home: 122 Valley St Wise VA 24293 Office: 128 Main St Wise VA 24293

ASCHER, BERNARD, govt. economist; b. Bklyn., Dec. 7, 1933; s. Nelson Nathan and Ida (Buchwald) A.; B.A., Bklyn. Coll., 1956; M.B.A., City Coll. N.Y., 1962; m. Elinor Hirsch, Aug. 12, 1956; children—Scott, Ruth, Mark. With Aero Sea Shipping Corp., export-import, N.Y.C., 1950-57, Continental Grain Co., 1959-60, Jack Liss & Sons Co., exporters, textiles and fashions, 1960-62; commodity analyst U.S. Tariff Commn., Washington, 1962-65; sr. economist, dir. import policy staff and legislation and tariff analysis div. Bur. Internat. Commerce, U.S. Dept. Commerce, 1965-71, dir. Indsl. Products div. Office Import Programs, Washington, 1971—. Instr. Econs. U. Balt., 1966-70; credit analyst R.H. Macy & Co., N.Y.C., 1960-62; v.p. Forest Knolls Pool, Silver Spring, Md., 1970, pres., 1971. Active Forest Knolls Boys Club. Served with AUS, 1957-59. Recipient medallion Am. Marketing Assn., 1962. Mem. Am. Econ. Assn., City Coll. N.Y. Alumni Assn., Bklyn. Coll. Alumni Assn., Beta Gamma Sigma. Contbr. articles to profl. pubs. Home: 811 Caddington Av Silver Spring MD 20901 Office: Main Commerce Bldg Washington DC 20230

ASELTINE, HERSCHEL EDWARD, educator; b. Richford, Vt., Dec. 28, 1915; s. William Henry Edward and Lucy (Fuller) A.; B.A. McMaster U., 1951, B.D., 1952; M.A., U. Chgo., 1955; Ph.D., So. Ill. U., 1963; m. Gwendolyn Ruth Pamenter, June 11, 1948; children—Edward George, Richard Malin, Alice Lynne. Ordained to ministry Baptist Ch., 1949; pastor various chs., 1945-56; asst. prof. sociology Elmhurst Coll., 1958-61; mem. faculty So. Ill. U., 1961-63, U. So. Fla., 1963-67; prof. sociology Middle Tenn. State U., Murfreesboro, 1967—, chmn. sociology, 1967-70. Served with RCAF, 1940-45. Mem. So. Sociol. Soc. Home: 1919 Riverview Dr Murfreesboro TN 37130

ASH, ROY LAWRENCE, govt. ofcl; b. Los Angeles, Oct. 20, 1918; s. Charles K. and Fay E. (Dickinson) A.; M.B.A. Harvard, 1947; m. Lila M. Hornbek, Nov. 13, 1943; children—Loretta (Mrs. Truman T. Ackerson), James, Marilyn (Mrs. R. Stanley Hodge), Robert, Charles. With Bank of Am., 1936-42, 47-49; chief financial officer, Hughes Aircraft Co., 1949-53; co-founder Litton Industries, Inc., Beverly Hills, Cal., 1953-72, dir., 1953-72, pres., 1961-72; dir. Bank Am. Corp., 1968-72; dir., mem. exec. and trust coms. Bank of Am., 1964-72, Global Marine, Inc., 1965-72, Pacific Mut. Life Ins. Co., 1965-72; asst. to Pres., dir. Office Mgmt. and Budget, Washington, 1972—. Chmn. Pres.'s Adv. Council on Exec. Orgn., 1969-71; co-chmn. Japan-Cal. Assn., 1965-72. Trustee Cal. Inst. Tech., 1967-72; Com. for Econ. Devel., 1970-72, Urban Inst., 1971-72; bd. dirs. Los Angeles World Affairs Council, 1968-72, pres., 1970-72. Mem. Am. Mgmt. Assn., Financial Execs. Inst. Clubs: Bel Air Country, Harvard (Los Angeles). Home: 655 Funchal Rd Los Angeles CA 90024 Office: The White House Washington DC 20037

ASHBROOK, ARTHUR GARWOOD, JR., economist; b. Pitts., Jan. 30, 1921; s. Arthur Garwood and Theodora (Hoerle) A.; B.S., Haverford Coll., 1941; Ph.D., Mass. Inst. Tech., 1947; m. Cecilia Garcia, June 20, 1964; children—Marina-Yolanda, Alexandra. Asst. prof. econs. Duke, 1947-51, Carnegie Inst. Tech., 1953-54; economist U.S. Govt., Washington, 1954—. Served with USAAF, 1943-45. Research on Chinese Communist economy. Home: 2925 39th St NW Washington DC 20016 Office: Central Intelligence Agy Washington DC 20505

ASHE, ARTHUR, tennis player; b. Richmond Va., 1943; grad. U. Cal. at Los Angeles, 1966. Winner two U.S. Inter-collegiate championships during coll.; winner U.S. Men's Hard Court Championship, 1963, U.S. Amateur title, 1968, U.S. Open championship, 1968; now mem. U.S. Davis Cup Team; Australian open winner U.S. Men's Clay Ct., 1967; pres. Players Enterprises, Inc., Washington. Served with AUS. Address: 888 17th St NW Washington DC 20006

ASHE, DAVID CROCKETT, lumber co. exec.; b. Oak Hill, Fla., July 27, 1925; s. Haven M. and Maude (Ritchie) A.; student Broward Bus. Coll., 1950; m. Betty Jo Whiddon, Sept. 15, 1950; children—Sharon (Mrs. John M. Springman), Joel David. With Causeway Lumber Co., Boca Raton, Inc., Boca Raton, Fla., 1950—, v.p., mgr., 1951—. Bd. dirs. Fla. Lumber & Bldg. Material Dealers, Inc., Orlando, 1973-74. Chmn. YMCA, Boca Raton, 1970-72. Councilman City Boca Raton, Fla., 1973—. Served with USNR, 1942-46. Named Man of Year C. of C., 1971. Mem. C. of C. (dir. 1968-70, 72-75), Am. Legion. Baptist (bd. trustees 1972-74). Elk, Lion (pres. 1965). Clubs: Gold Coast Dinner (pres. 1971), Bankers, Boca Raton. Home: 420 Coconut Palm Rd Boca Raton FL 33432 Office: PO Box 248 400 NW 2d Av Boca Raton FL 33432

ASHER, DAVID COLSON, physician; b. Pineville, Ky., Feb. 1, 1927; s. Thomas Jefferson and Effie Catherine (Colson) A.; B.S., U. Ky., 1948; M.D., U. Louisville, 1953; m. Marjorie Ann Smith, May 28, 1965; children—David Michael, Georgianna, Sharon Louise, Byron Patrick. Intern Good Samaritan Hosp., Lexington, Ky., 1953-54, resident in surgery, 1954-55; practice medicine specializing in gen. medicine and surgery, Pineville, Ky., 1955—; staff Pineville Community Hosp., 1955—, chief of surgery, 1955-73, chief staff, 1974—, also bd. dirs., 1955—. Vice pres. Colonel Drive Inn, Richmond, Ky., 1959—; dir. First State Bank, Pineville. Mem. Pineville Sch. Bd., 1963—; chmn. sch. bd. Pineville Ind. Sch., 1969—; mem. Ky. State Bd. Edn., 1973—. Served with USNR, 1945. Mem. Pineville Jr. C. of C. (pres. 1959), Ky. C. of C. (state health chmn. 1961), Jr. C. of C. of U.S. (internat. senator 1960—), Bell County Med. Soc. (pres. 1958), A.M.A., Ky. Med. Assn., Alpha Kappa Alpha. Club: Pineville Athletic Boosters (pres. 1961-63). Presbyn. (deacon 1968—; elder 1972). Home: Box 507 Pineville KY 40977 Office: 850 Riverview Av Pineville KY 40977

ASHFORD, THEODORE ASKOUNES, chemist, educator; b. Greece, Feb. 27, 1908 (came to U.S. 1922, naturalized 1930); s. Nicholas and Catherine (Togias) Askounes; B.S., U. Chgo., 1932, M.S., 1934, Ph.D., 1936; m. Venette Tomaras, Sept. 3, 1933; children—Nicholas, Theodore II, Robert. Tchr. math., chemistry and physics Chgo. pub. schs., 1932-36; instr., then asst. prof. chemistry U. Chgo., 1936-50; asso. prof., then prof. chemistry St. Louis U., 1950-60; prof. chemistry U. So. Fla., Tampa, 1960—, dir. div. natural scis. and math., 1960-66, asso. dean Coll. Liberal Arts, 1966-71, dean Coll. Natural Sci., 1971-73. Mem. Bd. Basic Scis., State of Fla., 1963-69; UNESCO cons. to Syria, 1966, Ceylon, 1968, Poland, Greece, 1973; NSF cons. to India, 1968, 70. Bd. dirs. Fla. Found. Future Scientists. Recipient citation Nat. Sci. Tchrs. Assn., 1971. Fellow A.A.A.S.; mem. Am. Chem. Soc. (chmn. exams. com. 1946—; recipient award chem. edn. 1965), N.E.A., Fla. Edn. Assn., Am. Assn. U. Profs., Am. Assn. Higher Edn., Fla. Acad. Sci., Sigma Xi, Sigma Pi Sigma. Author: From Atoms to Stars, 1960; The Structure of the Atom, the Mystery of Matter, 1965; The Physical Sciences, 1967. Editor numerous tests Am. Chem. Soc., U.S. Armed Forces Inst. Contbr. articles to profl. jours. Home: 1832 Bearss Av Tampa FL 33612

ASHLER, PHILIP FREDERIC, ednl. adminstr.; b. N.Y.C., Oct. 15, 1914; s. Philip and Charlotte (Barth) A.; B.B.A. cum laude, St. John's Coll., 1935; M.B.A., Harvard, 1937; postgrad. Indsl. Coll. Armed Forces, 1956; Sc.D., Fla. Inst. Tech., 1969; LL.D., U. W.Fla., 1969; m. Jane Porter, Mar. 4, 1942 (dec. 1968); children—Philip Frederic, Robert Porter, Richard Harrison; m.2d, Elise Barrett Duvall, June 21, 1969; stepchildren—Richard Edward Duvall, Jeffries Harding Duvall. Enlisted USMCR, 1932; commd. ensign U.S. Navy, 1938, advanced through grades to rear adm., 1959; dir. Office of Small Bus. Dept. Def., Washington, 1948-51; mem. joint staff Joint Chiefs of Staff, Washington, 1957-59; ret., 1959; dir. devel. Pensacola Jr. Coll., 1960-68; vice chancellor adminstrn. State U. System Fla., Tallahassee, 1968-70, exec. vice chancellor, 1970—. Mem. Fla. Edn. Council, 1967-68; commr. from Fla., Edn. Commn. of States, 1967-68; mem. legislative adv. council So. Regional Edn. Bd., 1966-68; chmn. Fla. Civil Def. Adv. Council, 1966-69; mem. State Bd. Ind. Colls. and Univs. Fla.; mem. Select Council on Post-High Sch. Edn., 1967-68; mem. Fla. Council Internat. Devel. Mem. Fla. Ho. of Reps., 1963-68. Bd. dirs. Fla. Heart Assn., 1963—, chmn., 1969-71; bd. dirs. Am. Heart Assn., LeMoyne Art Found., Tallahassee, Tallahassee Meml. Hosp. Decorated Bronze Star medal with Combat V; recipient Kiwanis Internat. Distinguished Service award, 1965, Am. Heart Assn. Distinguished Service award, 1965, 71, St. Petersburg Times Legislative award, 1967. Mem. Kappa Delta Pi. Democrat. Episcopalian (lay reader). Mason (32 deg., Shriner), Rotarian. Clubs: National Sojourners, Capital City Country, Capital City Tiger Bay (v.p.) (Tallahassee). Home: 1506 Argonne Rd Tallahassee FL 32303 also 11 Riad Sultan Kasbah Tangier Morocco Office: Bd Regents 107 W Gaines St Tallahassee FL 32304

ASHLEY, CONNELL DEWITT, lawyer; b. SanSaba, Tex., Oct. 28, 1927; s. Reuben DeWitt and Jamye (Campbell) A.; B.A., U. Tex., 1949, LL.B., 1951; m. Janet Reaves, May 31, 1959; children—Gregory, Stephen, Mark. Admitted to Tex. bar, 1951, practiced in Ft. Stockton, 1951-62, Odessa, 1962—; city atty. Ft. Stockton, 1953-55; dist. atty. 112th Jud. Dist., 1955-62; asso. firm Shafer, Gilliland, Davis, Bunton and McCollum, Odessa, 1962—. Mem. Pecos County (pres. 1960-61), Trans Pecos bar assns., Odessa C. of C., Ft. Stockton Jaycees (pres. 1959—). Lion. Home: 3202 Blossom Lane Odessa TX 79760 Office: PO Box 1552 Odessa TX 79760

ASHLEY, EDWARD EVERETT, III, economist; b. Palisade, N.J., Apr. 27, 1906; s. Edward Everett, Jr. and Lillian (Shaw) A.; Ph.B., Yale, 1929; M.B.A. with distinction, Harvard, 1931; m. Mary Josephine Callahan, Apr. 3, 1965; children—Susan Joyce (Mrs. David A. Rounds), Peter Shaw. Constrn. economist Tri Continental Corp., N.Y.C., 1931-41; chief cons. to Def. Housing Coordinator, Washington, 1941-42; dir. statistics and reports Nat. Housing Agy., Washington, 1942-46; dir. econ. research Housing and Home Finance Agy., Washington, 1947-54, dir. statis. reports and analysis, 1954-65; dir. statis. reports and devel. Dept. Housing and Urban Affairs, Washington, 1965-68; exec. asst. Health and Welfare Council, Washington, 1968-69; self employed as cons. economist, Arlington, Va., 1969—; mem. housing adv. com. Arlington, (Va.) Bd. of Suprs., 1971—. Vis. lectr. housing and urban devel. U. Mich., 1960—, Howard U., 1958—. Pres. Nat. Capital Area council Girl Scouts Am., 1962-64, Arlington Community Chest and Council, 1963-65; chmn. Arlington Health and Welfare Council, 1963-65; v.p. Health and Welfare Council Greater Washington, 1963-65; bd. dirs. Health and Welfare Council of Nat. Capital Area, 1963-67, mem. membership and budget com., 1973—. Mem. A.A.A.S., Gerontol. Soc., Com. of 100, Order of Chamaro (Guam), Alpha Sigma Phi. Clubs: Torch, Yale (Washington); Harvard Business School. Author books including: A Happy Home for the Later Years, 1962; How and Where to Live When You Retire, 1971; Choosing the Right Housing Arrangements for the Later Years, 1972; The Right House After You Retire, 1973. Home: 2604 Arlington Blvd Arlington VA 22204 Office: 2604 Arlington Blvd Arlington VA 22204 also Box 442 Indian Lake NY 12842

ASHLEY, JERRY SHELTON, automobile dealer, state legislator; b. nr. Orr, Okla., Jan. 20, 1906; s. Jerry and Ida Pearl (Cobb) A.; student Cameron Coll., 1923, Okla. State U., 1924-25; m. Thelma Townsend, June 25, 1932. Tchr. pub. schs., Bea, Okla., 1922; clk. Peden Iron & Steel Co., San Antonio, 1926; territorial mgr. Rayvac Co., 1927-30; dist. mgr. Chevrolet Motor div. Gen. Motors Corp., 1931-34, sales promotion mgr., 1935-36, divisional used car mgr., 1937; owner, pres. Jerry Ashley Chevrolet, Inc., Crowley, La., 1938—; pres. Rice Bolt Ins. Co., Crowley, 1946—, Ashley Oil Co., Crowley, 1957—; treas. Republic Wholesale Parts Co., Crowley, 1945—; mem. La. Ho. of Reps., 1960—. Mem. La. Bd. Nuclear Energy, 1962-63. Finance officer Crowley Little Theatre, 1947—; pres. Internat. Rice Festival, 1941, 46; chmn. Crowley Indsl. Devel. Bd., 1963; mem. Acadia Parish Sch. Bd., 1952-56; mem. automobile dealers planning com. Chevrolet div. Gen. Motors Co., 1954-60. Bd. dirs. Found. of La. State U. Served to lt. col. AUS, 1942-45; ETO. Recipient 25 year Plaque Chevrolet Motor Div., 1963. Mem. Nat., La. (pres. 1963-64) automobile dealers assns., Am. Legion (La. legislative chmn.), Crowley C. of C. (pres. 1948-49). Democrat. Mem. Disciples of Christ Ch. (chmn. bd. deacons and elders). Mason (Shriner). Club: Crowley Business (pres. 1941). Home: 1701 N Parkerson Av Crowley LA 70526 Office: 919 W 2d St Crowley LA 70526

ASHLEY, THELMA TOWNSEND (MRS. JERRY ASHLEY), club woman; b. Frederick, Okla., Nov. 10, 1904; d. Jay E. and Anna (McGuire) Townsend; B.S., U. Okla., 1927; postgrad. U. Colo., summer 1928; m. Jerry S. Ashley, June 25, 1932. Tchr. home econs. high schs., Temple, Walters and Lawton, Okla., 1923-24, 28-32; mgr. Jerry Ashley Chevrolet, Inc., Crowley, La., 1941-47, now v.p. Pres. Crowley Little Theater, 1949; v.p. Community Concert, 1950; asso. dir. Girls State of La., Inc., 1972, bd. dirs., 1972—. Mem. Am. Legion Aux. (nat. exec. committeewoman 1955, nat. v.p. 1957, nat. vice chmn. nat. security 1959-61, nat. chmn. edn. scholarships 1962, state historian 1951, 1st v.p. 1952, 2d v.p. 1953, pres. 1954, state asso. dir. La. Girls State 1954—, state finance chmn. 1960—, mem. joint child welfare com. 1953—, regional chmn. legislation 1958, nat. div. chmn. nat. civil def.), Crowley Bus. and Profl. Women (pres. 1958), Delta Zeta (province dir. 1951, 52). Democrat. Mem. Christian Ch. Home: 11601 N Parkerson Av Crowley LA 70526

ASHLEY, WILLIAM MOSES, san. engr.; b. Hazlehurst, Miss., Nov. 27, 1928; s. Ailous Simon and Josephine Joretha (Thompson) A.; B.S., Miss. Coll., 1949; M.S., Purdue U., 1951; postgrad. U. Cal. at Los Angeles, 1965-69; m. Harriet Louisa Smith, Jan. 1, 1954; children—David William, Dralene Marie, Donna Lee. Teaching fellow Purdue U., Lafayette, Ind., 1949-51; with Douglas Aircraft Co., Santa Monica, Cal., 1951-59; Titan missile project engr. TRW Systems, Redondo Beach, 1959-64, guidance system engr., 1964-67, missile and space systems engr., 1967-70; statistician Volkswagen Pacific, Culver City, 1971; san. engr. City of Jackson (Miss.), 1971—. Instr. math. Purdue U., 1949-51; instr. math., acting head dept. Los Angeles Bapt. Coll., 1960-66; tchr. Jackson Adult Edn. Program, 1973—. Pres. Santa Monica City Choir, 1952-54. Trustee Los Angeles Bapt. Coll., 1958-74, sec., 1959-66, chmn. acad. com., 1966-71. Registered profl. engr., Cal., Miss. Mem. Am. Pub. Works Assn., Miss. Water Pollution Control Operators Assn., Water Pollution Control Fedn., Am. Soc. C.E., Nat. Soc. Profl. Engrs., Miss. Engring. Soc. (chmn. scholarship and edn. com. 1972-74). Baptist (deacon 1952-56, 59-65, trustee 1958-59, treas. 1973-74). Home: 5938 Baxter Dr Jackson MS 39211 Office: PO Box 17 Jackson MS 39205

ASHMAN, LEE EARLE, computer co. exec.; b. Norwalk, Conn., Sept. 27, 1929; s. William Earle and Lucy Smith (Hall) A.; B.S., U.S. Naval Acad., 1952, postgrad., 1958-59; m. Rita Marie Todd, July 4, 1958; children—Therese, Rita, William, Michael, Mary, Christina. Commd. ensign USN, 1952, advanced through grades to lt. comdr., 1962; served in USS Remey, 1952-56, USS Pursuit, 1956-57; with Office Chief Naval Operations, 1959-60; served in USS Dealey, 1961-62, USS Dash, 1962-63; with Naval Command Systems Support Activity, 1963-67; engring. mgr. Logicon, Inc., Falls Church, Va., 1968-71; dist. marketing mgr. System Devel. Corp., Falls Church, 1972-73; dir. corporate devel. Techplan Corp., Falls Church, 1973—. Mem. I.E.E.E., Assn. for Computing Machinery, Assn. Old Crows, Mensa, D.C. Road Runners. Contbr. articles profl. jours. Home: 10311 Confederate Lane Fairfax VA 22030 Office: 5205 Leesburg Pike Falls Church VA 22041

ASHMORE, WILLIAM THOMAS, JR., candy mfr.; b. Batesburg, S.C., Feb. 14, 1912; s. William Thomas and Carrie Bryson (Glenn) A.; grad. Jr. Coll. of Augusta, 1932; A.B., LL.B., Mercer U., 1935, J.D., 1970; m. Sara Marbut Zealy, Dec. 17, 1942; children—Sara (Mrs. Kenneth W. Parrish), Martha (Mrs. John H. Burton), Elizabeth (Mrs. John P. Turner, Jr.). Editor alumni mag. Mercer U., 1935-37; asst. trust dept. 1st Nat. Bank of Macon, 1937-41; v.p., sec., dir. Fine Products Co., Inc., Augusta, Ga., 1944—; dir. Richmond Bonded Warehouse Co., Inc. Dir. Augusta-Richmond County Pub. Library, 1961-70, pres. bd., 1966-68; dir. A.R.C., 1961-67; dir. Augusta Opera Assn., Augusta Symphony League. Mem. Augusta City Council, 1959-63, 68—. Mem. Ga. Bar Assn., Augusta Coll. Alumni Assn. (pres. 1965-66), Mercer U. Alumni Assn. (dir.), Phi Alpha Delta, Alpha Tau Omega. Clubs: Exchange (pres. 1958), Augusta Country, Pinnacle (Augusta). Home: 2429 McDowell St Augusta GA 30904 Office: 833 Telfair St Augusta GA 30903

ASHTON, ALBERT A., mech. engr.; b. Adana, Turkey, Feb. 16, 1908; s. Hampar H. and Esther (Haleblian) Ashjian; student Am. U. Beirut, 1924-26, Los Angeles Poly. U., 1926-30; m. Elizabeth Carson Leland, May 16, 1934; children—Denis Leland, Bruce Leland. Engr., Hallet Mfg. Co., Los Angeles, 1930-32; engr. Emsco Derrick & Equipment Co., Los Angeles, 1936-52; chief engr. Emsco Mfg. Co., Houston, 1942-52; dir. engring. Continental-Emsco, Dallas, 1952-73, cons., 1973—. Lectr. oilwell drilling machinery U. Tex. Extension Div., 1952-56, Tex. A. and M. U., 1961-62. Recipient Spl. Citation for Meritorious Service, Am. Petroleum Inst., 1961. Mem. Am. Soc. M.E. (named engr. of year N.Tex. sect. 1973), Am. Gear Mfg. Assn. (chmn. oilfield gears com. 1958-66), Am. Petroleum Inst. (chmn. mfrs. sub.-com. 1954-68), Am. Inst. Mining, Metall. and Petroleum Engrs., Am. Ordnance Assn., Am. Inst. Aeros. and Astronautics, Am. Soc. Metals (Quarter Century of Service award 1970). Republican. Conglist. Patentee in field. Home: 6920 Midbury Dr Dallas TX 75230 Office: Box 359 Dallas TX 75221

ASKEW, HUBERT CARL, dentist; b. Houston, Sept. 30, 1939; s. Hubert Carl and Mary Eugiene (Philip) A.; B.S., U. Tex., 1962, D.D.S., 1966; m. Rebecca Ann Beckering, June 15, 1963. Individual practice dentistry, Houston, 1968—; asst. Meml. Bapt. Hosp., 1969—; mem. staff Meml. City Hosp.; cons. VA Hosp., Houston, 1969—. Served to capt., Dental Corps, AUS, 1966-68. Recipient children's dental health week citation USPHS, 1969. Mem. Am., Tex. dental assns., Xi Psi Phi, Phi Sigma Kappa. Home: 14527 Kellywood St Houston TX 77024 Office: 902 Frostwood St Houston TX 77024

ASKEW, REUBIN O'DONOVAN, gov. of Fla.; b. Muskogee, Okla., Sept. 11, 1928; s. Leo Goldberg and Alberta Nora (O'Donovan) A.; B.S. in Pub. Adminstrn., Fla. State U., 1951; LL.B., U. Fla., 1956; postgrad. Denver U.; LL.D. (hon.), Fla. So. Coll., Lakeland, 1972, U. Notre Dame, 1973; D.P.A. (hon.), Rollins Coll., Winter Park, Fla., 1972; L.H.D., Stetson U., Deland, Fla., 1973; m. Donna Lou Harper, Aug. 11, 1956; children—Angela Adair, Kevin O'Donovan. Admitted to Fla. bar, 1956; practice law, Pensacola, Fla., 1956-70; partner firm Levin, Askew, Warfield, Graff and Mabie, Pensacola, 1956-70; asst. county solicitor Escambia County (Fla.), 1956-58; gov. of Fla., 1971—. Chmn. Edn. Commn. of States, 1973—; vice chmn. So. Govs.' Conf., 1973—. Past pres. Western div. Children's Home Soc. Fla.,

Pensacola Oratorio Soc., Pensacola chpt. City of Hope; past mem. state exec. com. Fla. Tb and Health Assn. Mem. Fla. Ho. of Reps., 1958-62; mem. Fla. Senate, 1962-70, pres. pro tem, 1969, 70; keynote speaker Democratic Nat. Conv., 1972. Past pres. bd. dirs., past mem. state exec. com. Fla. Assn. for Retarded Children; past bd. dirs. Pensacola YMCA, United Fund, Heart Assn. Served with AUS, 1946-48, to capt. USAF, 1951-53. Recipient John F. Kennedy Profiles in Courage award B'nai B'rith, 1971; Nat. Wildlife Fedn. award, 1972; Outstanding Conservationist of Yr. award Fla. Audubon Soc., 1972; Herbert H. Lehman Ethics award, 1973; John F. Kennedy award Nat. Council Jewish Women, 1973. Mem. Am. Bar Assn., Fla. Bar, Am. Legion, Phi Alpha Delta, Delta Tau Delta, Alpha Phi Omega. Democrat. Presbyn. (elder). Mason (Shriner), Rotarian. Home: 700 N Adams St Tallahassee FL 32303 Office: The Capitol Tallahassee FL 32304

ASKINS, KNOX WINFRED, lawyer; b. Houston, July 19, 1937; s. Elgie Joseph and Geneva (Rulison) A.; B.F.A., U. Houston, 1958, J.D., 1962; student Blinn Jr. Coll., 1955-56; m. Augusta Ann Thomas, Sept. 13, 1958; children—Diane, Suzanne, Sally Ann, James, Paul, Clark. Admitted to Tex. bar, U.S. Dist. Ct. bar, 1962, U.S. Supreme Ct. bar, 1970; practice law, La Porte, Tex., 1962—; gen. counsel, dir. Bayshore Nat. Bank of La Porte, 1966—; city atty., City of La Porte, 1965—; govt. appeal agt. Selective Service Local Bd., 1970-72; dir. Houston Area Rapid Transit Authority, 1973—. Mem. Am., Tex., Houston bar assns., Am. Judicature Soc., Texas City Atty.'s Assn., Nat. Inst. Municipal Legal Officers, Order of the Barons, Mensa, Delta Theta Phi. Club: Houston Yacht. Office: 122 S Broadway La Porte TX 77571 Home: 1010 S Country Club Dr La Porte TX 77571

ASPLEY, DONALD BRUCE, physician; b. Glasgow, Ky., Dec. 24, 1935; s. Joe William and Buela (Cornelius) A.; A.B., Transylvania Coll., 1957; M.D., U. Louisville, 1961; m. Patricia Gail Monroe, Sept. 7, 1957; children—Donald Bruce Jr., James William, Rebecca Ann. Intern Med. Center, Columbus, Ga., 1961-62; practice gen. medicine, Glasgow, 1962-69; staff physician Tenn. Eastman Co., Kinsport, 1969—; mem. staff Holston Valley Community Hosp., Kingsport. Mem. Sullivan-Johnson County, Tenn., So., Indsl. med. assns., Phi Delta Theta. Eagle, Moose. Home: 208 Claymore Dr Kingsport TN 37663 Office: Tenn Eastman Co Kingsport TN 37662

ASPLUND, ELMER M., civil engr.; b. nr. Loomis, Neb., Mar. 17, 1907; s. Charles Arvin and Hilma (Ekstrom) A.; grad. high sch.; m. Berty D. Baker, Dec. 24, 1934; 1 dau., Phyllis Jean. Detail draftsman Cessna Aircraft Co., Wichita, Kan., 1928-29; chief draftsman Lenert Aircraft Co., Pentwater, Mich., 1929-30; chief engr. Johnstown Aircraft Co. (Pa.), 1930-31; aero. engr. United Airlines, Cheyenne, Wyo., 1933-34; pvt. practice civil, structural and hydraulic engring., 1934-42; structures engr. Consol. Aricraft Corp., San Diego and Ft. Worth, 1942-53; group engr. Bell Helicopter Co., Ft. Worth, 1953-71, cons. engr., 1972; pvt. practice cons. engr., Ft. Worth, 1972—. Instr. engring. war tng. program Tex. A. and M. Coll., World War II; engring. rep. CAA, 1954-71, FAA, 1971—. Served with USAAC, 1926-27. Registered profl. engr., Okla. Home: 2719 Scott Av Fort Worth TX 76103

ASTLER, VERNON BENSON, physician; b. Wyoming, O., Sept. 5, 1925; s. Vernon Wolfert and Blanche (Benson) A.; student Miami U., 1943-45; M.D., Temple U., 1949; M.S., U. Mich., 1953; m. Louise Menge, Aug. 9, 1949 (div.); children—Kim Louise, Kristy Lee, Douglas Vernon; m. 2d, Diane Rosacker, Dec. 31, 1969. Intern Univ. Hosp., Ann Arbor, Mich., 1949-50, resident, 1950-57; practice medicine, specializing in surgery, Boynton Beach, Fla., 1958—; mem. staff Bethesda Hosp., Boca Raton Hosp., Doctors Hosp., Lake Worth, Fla. Mem. Fla. State Bd. Med. Examiners (pres. 1971-73). Served with M.C., AUS, 1953-55. Diplomate Am. Bd. Surgery. Fellow A.C.S., Southeastern Surg. Congress; mem. Am. Hosp. Assn. (com. on physicians 1973), Fla. Med. Assn. (gov. 1971—), Frederick A. Coller Surg. Soc., A.M.A., Delray Beach C. of C., Sigma Nu, Phi Chi. Mason (Shriner), Kiwanian. Home: 3268 N Ocean Blvd Gulfstream FL 33444 Office: Med Arts Center 2800 S Seacrest Blvd Boynton Beach FL 33435

ASTON, FLOYD DWIGHT, oil co. exec.; b. Sherman, Tex., Nov. 20, 1905; s. John Elmore and Permelia (Outhouse) A.; B.A., Austin Coll., 1927; C.P.A., LaSalle Extension U., 1935; m. Marguerite Stuart Stokes, June 23, 1951; 1 son, Dwight Stuart; 1 stepson, Joseph Morgan Stokes, Jr. Accountant, traveling auditor Tex. Power & Light Co., Dallas, 1927-36; accountant Haskins & Sells, Dallas, 1936, Houston, 1937-40; sec., chief accountant Berkshire Oil Co., Houston, 1940-62; chief accountant Frankel Oil & Gas Co., Houston, 1963—; sec. Cove Oil, Inc., Houston, 1966—, also dir. Sec.-treas. Maurice Frankel Found., 1963—. Mem. Am. Inst. C.P.A.'s, Tex. Soc. C.P.A.'s, Am. Accounting Assn., Petroleum Accountants Soc. Houston. Methodist. Club: Valley Lodge (Simonton, Tex.). Home: 3301 Bluebonnet St Houston TX 77025 Office: 815 Walker St Houston TX 77002

ASTON, JAMES W(ILLIAM), banker; b. Farmersville, Tex., Oct. 6, 1911; s. Joe A. and Jimmie Gertrude (Jackson) A.; B.S. in C.E., A & M. Coll. Tex., 1933; m. Sarah Camilla Orth, June 29, 1935; 1 son, James William. Asst. city mgr., Dallas, 1935-39, city mgr., 1939-41; city mgr., Bryan, Tex., 1939; v.p. Republic Nat. Bank of Dallas 1945-55, exec. v.p., 1955-57, dir., pres., 1957-65, chmn., chief exec. officer, dir., 1965—; dir. Am. Airlines, Inc., Lone Star Steel Co., Gen. Portland Cement Co., Times Mirror Co., Zale Corp., Group Hosp. Service, Inc., Group Med. & Surg. Service, Group Life & Health Ins. Co., Neuhoff Brothers Packers, Dallas Times Herald. Mem. Greater Dallas Planning Council; treas. City of Dallas. Trustee Tex. Research Found., Southwestern Med. Found., Southwest Research Inst., Wadley Inst. of Molecular Medicine, S.W. Legal Found., Hoblitzelle Found.; bd. dirs. State Fair Texas; bd. govs. So. Meth. U., United Way of Am. Served from lt. to col. USAAF, 1941-45. Decorated D.S.M., Legion of Merit. Registered profl. engr. Mem. Assn. Res. City Bankers, Trinity Improvement Assn. (v.p.), Internat. C. of C. (dir. U.S. council), Newcomen Soc. N. Am., Am. (exec. council 1965-68), Tex. bankers assns., Tau Beta Phi. Mem. Christian Ch. Clubs: City, Dallas, Northwood Country, Athletic, Petroleum Country, Dallas Country (Dallas); Army-Navy Country (Washington); Brook, Marco Polo (N.Y.C.); Tres Vidas (Acapulco, Mexico); Chaparral, Southwest; Cherokke Lancers; Las Colinas Country; Preston Trail Golf. Home: PO Box 5961 Dallas TX 75222

ASTROP, WILLIAM BOWEN, investment counsel; b. Charleston, S.C., Sept. 22, 1929; s. Robert Collins and Arretha Robertson (Bowen) A.; B.A., U. Richmond, 1950, M.B.A. (J. Spencer Love fellow), Harvard, 1953; m. Jean Anne Trimmer, Sept. 28, 1963; children—William B., Douglas Du B. Vice pres. Fla. Capital Corp., Palm Beach, 1960-63, Stone & Webster Securities, N.Y.C., 1963-68, UniCapital Corp., Atlanta, 1968-70; chmn. bd. Post & Astrop, investment counsel, Atlanta, 1970—; dir. Kem Mfg. Corp., Atlanta, Founders Corp., Palm Beach, Cavalier Corp., Chattanooga, Am. Agy. Life Ins., Atlanta, Am. Agy. Financial Corp. Instr. U. Richmond, eves. 1958-60. Mem. Com. of 100, Emory U., 1971—; financial v.p. High Mus., Atlanta. Served with USNR, 1953-56; lt. comdr. Res. (ret.). Chartered financial analyst. Mem. N.Y., Atlanta socs. security analysts, Clubs: Harvard (Atlanta, Palm Beach); Commerce, Piedmont Driving (Atlanta); Everglades (Palm Beach). Home: 2415 Hanover W Lane N W Atlanta GA 30327 Office: 134 Peachtree St Atlanta GA 30303

ASTUDILLO SANDOVAL, HOMERO, lawyer, Mexican govt. ofcl.; b. Mexico, D.F., Mexico, 1940; Atty. at Law, Nat. Autonomous U. Mexico; Diploma in Social Policy, Inst. Social Studies, The Hague; Diploma in Pvt. Internat. Law, Internat. Ct. Justice; Diploma, Inst. Labor Studies, Geneva, Switzerland. Admitted to Mexico bar, 1962; asst. chief social security dept. Labor Union of Mexican Republic, Mexico D.F. Mem. Studies Assn. Mexican Social Security (pres. 1971). Address: Paseo de la Reforma 116-404 Mexico DF Mexico

ASUNCION, JUAN SANTOS, physician; b. Philippines, June 12, 1932; s. Eustaquio Mateo and Leoncia (Santos) A.; A.A., Manila Central U., 1953, M.D., 1958; m. Margaret Ann James, Oct. 1, 1960; children—Kimberly, Terri, Alesia, Christine. Intern Sts. Mary & Elizabeth Hosp., Louisville, 1958-59, dir. house physicians, 1971-72, med. dir. inhalation therapy, 1969-73, chmn. dept. anesthesia, 1969-73; resident in surgery Norton Meml. Infirmary, Louisville, 1959-63; resident in anesthesia Balt. City Hosps., 1964-67, asst. chief anesthesiologist, 1967-68; instr. anesthesiology Johns Hopkins Med. Sch., 1967-68, U. Md. Sch. Medicine, 1967-68. Mem. ch. council Our Lady Mt. Carmel Cath. Ch., Louisville, 1971-73. Mem. A.M.A., Am. Soc. Anesthesiologists, Ky. Med. Assn., Med. and Chirurgical Soc. Md., Jefferson County Med. Soc. Louisville, Louisville, Ky. Socs. anesthesiologists. Home: 501 Wilderness Rd Louisville KY 40214 Office: 4602 Southern Pkwy Louisville KY 40214

ATCHLEY, DANIEL GENE, investment co. exec.; b. Fort Worth, Tex., Oct. 29, 1942; s. Emory Elmer and Edith Blanche (Stanley) A.; B.A., U. Houston, 1967, D.C.L. (hon.), 1973; m. Judith Holke, Nov. 15, 1967; children—John, Natalie, David, Adrianne Edith. Programmer Black, Sivalls & Bryson, Oklahoma City, 1961-62; systems analyst U.S. P.O., Houston, 1962-64; mgr. data processing Delta Engring., Houston, 1964-67; dir. computer services Pace Co., Houston, 1967-71; pres. Gallery Printing Co., Houston, 1971—, A/G Property Mgmt., Houston, 1971—, JAKCO Investments, Houston, 1971—; chmn. bd. G/A Investments, Houston, Media Trend Prodns., Houston; partner Lafayette Ltd., Houston, Whispering Pines, Ltd. Mgr., Little League Baseball, 1969-73; leader Sam Houston area council Boy Scouts Am., 1971-73. Trustee Atchley Family Trust, 1970—, Adrianne Edith Atchley Trust, 1971—. Kiwanis grantee, 1961-64. Mem. Data Processing Mgmt. Assn., Adminstrv. Mgmt. Soc., Civil Engring. Programming Assn., Assn. Computing Machinery. Lion. Home: 3427 Del Monte Dr Houston TX 77019 Office: Lafayette Bldg #1 701 N Post Oak Rd Houston TX 77024

ATCHLEY, EDWARD NOAH, boat mfg. co. exec.; b. Knoxville, Tenn., Mar. 27, 1935; s. Curtis Bentley and Alma Ada (Wells) A.; B.B.A., U. Tenn., 1956; m. Sharon Ester Thompson, Aug. 16, 1963; children—Teresa Lynne, Edward Scott, Stanley Dean. Dist. mgr. McCulloch Corp., Los Angeles, 1958-63; v.p., gen. mgr. Stowaway Marinas Inc., St. Petersburg, Fla., 1963-67; field salesman Cobia Boats, Inc. div. Ashland Oil Co., Inc., Sanford, Fla., 1967-69, v.p. marketing, 1969-73, exec. v.p., gen. mgr., 1973—. Bd. dirs. St. Petersburg Boat Show, 1964-67. Served with USNR, 1953-61. Mem. Boating Industry Assos., Nat. Assn. Engine and Boat Mfrs., St. Petersburg Beach C. of C. (chmn. marine com. 1964-67). Home: 516 Tivoli Ct Altamonte Springs FL 32701 Office: 100 Silver Lake Rd Sanford FL 32771

ATCHLEY, FIELDING HURST, lawyer; b. Chattanooga, Mar. 8, 1916; s. James Franklin and Kate (McGill) A.; student U. Chattanooga, 1933; LL.B., Chattanooga Coll. Law, 1936; m. Anna Mary Pierce, Nov. 2, 1941; 1 son, Fielding Hurst, Jr. Admitted to Tenn. bar, 1936; with Atchley & Atchley, Chattanooga, 1936-42, jr. partner, 1936-65; sr. partner Atchley, Atchley & Cox, Chattanooga, 1965—. Dir. Standard Appliances, Inc., Chattanooga, Tenn. Pres. YMCA Men's Club, Chattanooga, 1947-49; pres. Chattanooga Little Theater, 1949-50, 1962-63, dir., 1940-73. Served to capt. USAF, 1942-46; served with USAF Reserves, 1946-62. Mem. Am. (gov. 1962-65, chmn. comml. tort sect. 1973), Tenn., Chattanooga (pres. 1967) trial lawyers assns. Mem. Christian Ch. (mem. bd. 1948-73). Club: Golf and Country (Chattanooga). Home: 1502 Mississippi Av Chattanooga TN 37405 Office: 540 Pioneer Bldg Chattanooga TN 37402

ATHANASAKOS, ELIZABETH, judge; b. Bklyn.; d. Clement and Irene (Vrettakos) Athanasakos; B.A., St. John's U., 1948, LL.B., 1956. Marketing research work Psychol. Corp., A.C. Nielsen Co., N.Y.C., 1948-56; claims adjuster Allstate Ins. Co., Bklyn., 1956-57; admitted to N.Y. bar, 1956, Fla. bar, 1957; partner Alexas & Athanasakos, Fort Lauderdale, Fla., 1958-61; gen. practice, Fort Lauderdale, 1961—; municipal judge City of Wilton Manors, Fla., 1964; asso. municipal judge City of Oakland Park, Fla., 1968—. Mem. Pres.' Task Force on Women's Rights and Responsibilities, 1969; chairperson adv. com. on women's rights and responsibilities Dept. Health, Edn. and Welfare, 1972-73. Pres. Womens Republican Club Broward County, 1967-69; bd. dirs. Nat. Fedn. Rep. Women, 1968-71, vice chmn. nationalities com., chmn. women's rights and responsibilities; mem. nat. adv. com. Women for Nixon-Agnew, 1968; mem. nat. adv. com. for re-election Pres., 1972. Bd. dirs. United Way, Broward County, 1973-75. Mem. Fla., Broward County bar assns., Fla. Assn. Women Lawyers, Broward County Municipal Judges, N.Am. Judges Assn., Nat. Assn. Women Lawyers, League Women Voters, Bus. and Profl. Women (woman of achievement dist. 10, 1969-70, 73, asst. dir. dist. 10, 1972-73, dist. dir. 1973-75, pres. Ft. Lauderdale 1970-72), Am. Assn. U. Women (legislative chmn. Ft. Lauderdale br. 1971-73), Fla. Women's Polit. Caucas Council Phi Delta Delta. Republican. Mem. Greek Orthodox Ch. Mem. Order Eastern Star (past matron), Daus. of Penelope (grand pres. 1965-66). Clubs: Ft. Lauderdale Womens; Women's Civic; Broward Women's Breakfast (past pres.); Zonta (corr. sec. 1971-73; chmn. dist. XI Status Women Com. 1972—; mem. internat. by-laws com. 1972—). Home: 2113 NE 16th Av Fort Lauderdale FL 33305 Office: 2633 N Federal Hwy Fort Lauderdale FL 33306

ATHANASIOU, BETTYE, pub. relations exec., editor; b. Dallas, June 15, 1923; d. J.L. and Edythe (Stewart) Raiden; student Massey Bus. Sch., 1947 div.; children—Rolanette Mackie, Susan Saul. Pvt. sec. to sec.-treas. Mission Mfg. Co., Houston, 1947-49; pvt. sec. to pres. Marine Exploration Co., Houston, 1949-52; sec., editor, pub. relations Robert H. Ray Co., Houston, 1952-56; mgr. pub. relations, editor Geo. Space Corp., Houston, 1963-73; mgr. pub. relations Walker-Hall-Sears, Inc., 1973—, also editor co. mag. Co-chmn. publicity 36th, 40th Ann. Internat. Soc. Exploration Geophysicists Meetings, 1966. Gen. chmn. Gov. Bill Daniels Ann. Crippled Childrens Party, 1956-69; capt. Pin Oaks Charity Horse Show, 1959-64. Pres. Hedgecroft Hosp. Aux., President's Council Houston Hosp. Aux.; bd. dirs. Tex. Hosp. Auxs. Recipient Service award Geophys. Soc. Houston, 1968. Mem. Am. Bus. Womens Assn. (charter pres. Houston), Soc. Exploration Geophysicists (tech. program com. 5th, 6th ann. offshore tech. confs.), Geophys. Soc. Houston (publicity chmn. 1971—), Internat. Council Indsl. Editors, Internat. Assn. Bus. Communicators, Am. Soc. for Oceanography, European Assn. Exploration Geologists, Houston C. of C. (mem. communications and information com. 1972—), Asociacion Mexicana de Geofisicos de Exploracion. Home: 3102 Suffolk St Houston TX 77027 Office: 8400 Westpark Dr Houston TX 77042

ATHERTON, HOLT, machinery co. exec.; b. Stockton, Cal., Sept. 8, 1920; s. Warren Hendry and Ann (Holt) A.; B.A., U. Cal. at Berkeley, 1941; m. Flora Cameron Kampmann, Sept. 28, 1970; children—Holt, Jr., Steve, Geary, Megan. Check pilot Pan Am. World Airways, San Francisco, 1946-52; with Holt Machinery Co., San Antonio, 1952—, pres., 1963—. Partner Holt Oaks Land Devel., Cal., 1946—, Marina West, Stockton. Pres. San Antonio Safety Council, 1958. Bd. trustees Southwest Research Center, San Antonio, 1960-66. Served as brig. gen. USAAF, 1941-46, res., 1946-64. Mem. San Antonio C. of C. (dir. 1961-67), Daedalians. Clubs: Bohemian (San Francisco); Outrigger Canoe (Honolulu). Home: 315 Westover Rd San Antonio TX 78209 Office: PO Box 658 San Antonio TX 78293

ATHERTON, JAMES CHRISTIAN, educator; b. Bolivar, La., Aug. 4, 1915; s. James G. and Mary (Matthews) A.; B.S., La. State U., 1935, M.S., 1947; Ed.M., U. Ill., 1949, Ed.D., 1950; m. Ruth Victoria Cash, Nov. 26, 1937; children—James Christian, George A., Ruth V. Tchr., Loranger (La.) High Sch., 1935-42, 45-46, prin., 1946-48; prof. agrl. edn. U. Ark., Fayetteville, 1950-65, La. State U., Baton Rouge, 1965—. Pres. tchr. tng. sect. So. Regional Conf. Agrl. Edn., 1957-58. Vice pres. So. Agrl. Edn. Conf., 1971-72. Served to lt. col. AUS, 1942-45. Recipient Distinguished Service award in agrl. edn. So. Regional Conf. Agrl. Edn., 1962; outstanding service citation, Nat. Vocational Agrl. Tchrs. Assn., 1968; hon. state farmer degree, Ark., La. Future Farmers Am., 1955, 67. Mem. Am. Vocational Assn., Nat. Vocational Agr. Tchrs. Assn., Am. Assn. Tchr. Educators in Agr. editor Jour. 1966-70, Alpha Tau Alpha (nat. 1st v.p. 1965-69), Phi Kappa Phi, Alpha Zeta, Gamma Sigma Delta, Phi Delta Kappa. Democrat. So. Baptist. Co-author: Essential Aspects of Career Planning and Development, 1969. Editor Ark. Service Bull., 1955-65; regional editor Agrl. Edn. mag., 1955-62, 64—. Contbr. articles to profl. jours. Home: 6099 S Pollard Pkwy Baton Rouge LA 70808

ATHEY, THOMAS WINFIELD, judge; b. Thacker Mines, W.Va., Sept. 5, 1923; s. Winfield Thomas and Leota Carrington (Quinn) A.; B.A., Coll. of William and Mary, 1948, B.C.L., 1954; m. Mary Beth Wooldridge, Oct. 19, 1957; children—Thomas Edloe, Mary Beth, Susan Irella. Admitted to Va. bar, 1954; partner Watkins & Athey, Yorktown, Va., 1954-59; claim rep. State Farm Mut. Automobile Ins. Co., Newport News, Va., 1959-61; asso. Carneal, Smith & Anderson, Williamsburg, Va., 1961-65; partner Carneal, Smith & Athey, Williamsburg, 1965—; substitute judge Gen. Dist. Ct. and Juvenile and Domestic Relations Dist. Ct. York County, Yorktown, 1964-68, judge, 1969—. Legal cons. Contact Peninsula, Newport News, 1973—. Bd. dirs. Jamestown Acad., Williamsburg, Va. Served with USAAF, 1943-45. Mem. Phi Kappa Tau (nat. field sec. 1948-51). Methodist (lay leader 1973—). Lion. Editor: William and Mary Law Rev., 1954. Home: 502 York-Warwick Dr Yorktown VA 23690 Office: Box 440 Williamsburg VA 23185

ATKIN, JOHN THATCHER, retail sales co. exec.; b. Georgetown, Tex., Apr. 21, 1904; s. Samuel Thatcher and Sallie (Mason) A.; A.B., Southwestern U., Georgetown, 1925; M.A., U. Tex., Austin, 1930; m. Genevieve Critz, June 11, 1931; children—Richard T., John M. Tchr. math. Southwestern U., 1926, 37-38; tchr. math. U. Miss., 1927-29, U. Tex., 1930; instr. U.S. Treasury Dept., San Antonio, 1935; auditor U.S. Dept. Labor, Georgetown, 1936; with S.T. Atkin Furniture Co., Georgetown, 1931-35, 37—, now owner, mgr.; dir. Georgetown Savs. & Loan Assn. Chmn. United Fund Drive, Georgetown, 1967. Mem. City Council, mayor, Georgetown, 1947-58; mem. Gov.'s Statewide Water Com., 1952-57; precinct chmn. Williamson County Democratic Exec. Com., 1950—. Pres., bd. dirs. Williamson County Tb. Assn., Georgetown Library; bd. dirs. Tex. United Fund. Served with Tex. N.G., 1941-47. Recipient Silver Beaver award Boy Scouts Am., 1962, Most Worthy Citizen award, Georgetown, 1971. Mem. Tex. Retail Furniture Assn., Georgetown C. of C. (dir.), Williamson County Sheriffs Posse (hon. life), Pi Kappa Alpha. Methodist. Mason (Shriner), Rotarian. Club: Georgetown Country (dir.). Home: 1108 Church St Georgetown TX 78626 Office: 701-05 Main St Georgetown TX 78626

ATKINS, HARDIN LOUIS, JR., agriculturist; b. Asheville, N.C., Nov. 7, 1898; s. Hardin Louis and Elizabeth (Whitaker) A.; B.S. in Animal Husbandry, Tex. A. and M. Coll., 1922; m. Elizabeth Buford Beasley, Mar. 18, 1926; children—Hardin Louis III, Joseph Noble, Elizabeth (Mrs. Charles Alan Bray), Lydia (Mrs. Lydia L. Canterbury). Asst. in cane cultivation Russell & Co., Fortuna, P.R., 1922-23; country agrl. agt. Mitchell County, Colorado City, Tex., 1924-26, Midland County, Tex., 1926-28; asso. editor Progressive Farmer, Dallas, 1928-32; field agt. emergency feed and seed loans U.S. Dept. Agr., Dallas, 1932-33; county agrl. agt. for Andrews, Crane, Ector counties, Odessa, Tex., 1933-48; div. mgr., dir. McElroy Ranch Co., Midland, Tex., 1949-54; mgr. personal investments oil royalties, ins. stocks, 1954—. Founding incorporator San Hills Hereford Show, Odessa. Past dir. Black Gold dist. Boy Scouts Am. Mem. Selective Service Bd., 1961-72. Mem. Odessa C. of C. (past dir.), Tex. County Agts. Assn. (pres. 1941). Methodist (ofcl. bd. 1933—). Mason (32 deg., K.T.), Rotarian (pres. Odessa 1947-48). Home: 1409 Byron Av Odessa TX 79760

ATKINS, JAMES HOMER, engring. co. exec.; b. Jacksonville, Fla., Dec. 28, 1929; s. Edwin Francis and Dorothy (Rockhold) A.; B.S. in Mech. Engring., B.S. in Indsl. Engring., U. Fla., 1952; m. Eloise Toole, Mar. 4, 1955; children—Melinda Diane, James Homer. Engr., Gen. Elec. Co., Lynn, Mass., 1952; sales engr. Ceco Corp., Jacksonville, 1954-58, regional mgr., Miami, Fla., 1958-72; pres. J.H. Atkins & Assos., Inc., Miami, 1972—. Served to 1st lt. USAF, 1952-54. Registered profl. engr., Fla. Mem. Nat. Soc. Profl. Engrs., Fla. Engring. Soc., Sigma Chi. Democrat. Baptist. Clubs: Riviera Country, Rod and Reel. Home: 3121 Anderson Rd Coral Gables FL 33134 Office: 9655 S Dixie Hwy Miami FL 33134

ATKINS, MARVIN CLEVELAND, govt. ofcl.; b. Ballinger, Tex., July 30, 1931; s. Marvin Cleveland and Mary Reid (Murchison) A.; B.S., Tex. A. and M. U., 1952; M.S., U. Ill., 1953; Ph.D., U. Mich., 1961; m. Lois M. Doescher, June 11, 1955; children—David M., Nancy E. Commd. lt. USAF, 1952, advanced through grades to maj., 1964; project officer Air Force Materials Lab., Dayton, O., 1953-57; br. chief Air Force Weapons Lab., Albuquerque, 1960-64; asst. mgr. materials sci., mgr. engring. tech., dir. environmental sci. and tech. AVCO Corp., Wilmington, Mass., 1964-67, Lowell, Mass., 1967-70; asst. to dept. dir. Def. Nuclear Agy., Washington, 1970—. Mem. Am. Nuclear Soc., Sigma Xi. Episcopalian. Home: 3103 Cunningham Dr Alexandria VA 22309 Office: Def Nuclear Agy Washington DC 20305

ATKINS, ORIN ELLSWORTH, oil co. exec.; b. Pitts., June 6, 1924; s. Orin E. and Dorothy (Whittaker) A.; student Marshall U., Huntington, W.Va., 1942-43, 46-47, LL.D., 1970; student U. Pa., 1943-44; LL.B., U. Va., 1950; m. Kathryn Agee, Nov. 25, 1950; children—Randall, Charles. Admitted to W. Va. bar, 1950, Ky. bar, 1952; with Ashland Oil & Refining Co. (Ky.), 1950—, exec. asst., 1956-59, adminstrv. v.p., 1959-65, pres., chief exec. officer, 1965-72, chmn. bd., chief exec. officer, 1972—, dir.; dir. Cin. br. Fed. Res. Bank Cleve., 1968-71. Mem. Nat. Pub. Adv. Com. on Regional Econ. Devel., 1970—; mem. Nat. Indsl. Pollution Control Council; mem. Nat. Petroleum Council Ky., chmn. com. on factors affecting U.S. refining, 1972—; mem. Council Econ. Advisers. Chmn. bd. advisers Marshall U. Served with AUS, 1942-46. Mem. Am., W.Va., Ky. bar assns., Conf. Bd. Presbyn. Home: 602 Amanda Dr Bellefonte Ashland KY 41101 Office: PO Box 391 Ashland KY 41101

ATKINS, ROBERT MARSH, dentist, county ofcl.; b. Tampa, Fla., June 28, 1939; s. Cedric Donald and Martha Kathryn (Marsh) A.; student Emory U., 1957, 58, U. Fla., 1958, 59; D.D.S., Emory U., 1963; now postgrad. M.P.H., U. N.C., 1974; m. Janis Amanda Dodson, Nov. 27, 1961; children—James Donald, Linda Kay, Kenneth Edwin. Individual practice dentistry, Frostproof, Fla., 1963-69; dental dir. Palm Beach County Health Dept., West Palm Beach, Fla., 1969—. Dental cons. Palm Beach County Home and Gen. Care Facility, Palm Beach County Bd. Pub. Instrn.; asso. prof. dept. community dentistry U. Fla. Spl. dep. sheriff Palm Beach and Polk counties. Mem. Am. Dental Assn., Fla., Am. pub. health assns., Am. Assn. Pub. Health Dentists, Fla. Pub. Health Assn., Fla. Dental Assn., Am. Profl. Practice Assn., Atlantic Coast Dist., Palm Beach County dental socs., Xi Psi Phi. Home: 7715 St Andrews Dr Lake Worth FL 33460 Office: 826 Evernia St West Palm Beach FL 33402

ATKINSON, CARROL HOLLOWAY, educator; b. Fairbury, Neb., Oct. 24, 1896; s. Charles Raymond and Florence (Bennie) Atkinson; A.B., Lawrence Coll., 1920; student U. Grenoble (France), 1919, Pacific U., 1922, U. Ore., 1922, U. Wash., 1923, U. Cal. at Los Angeles, 1926, U. Tex., 1937; M.A., U. So. Cal., 1929; Ph.D., George Peabody Coll. for Tchrs., 1938; m. Ruby Baker, Aug. 23, 1921 (dec. 1925) children—Yvonne Dorothy, Carroll Holloway; m. 2d, Mary Hansen, 1926 (dec. 1941); m. 3d, Carol Mary Gonzales, 1959; children—Ardith Anne, Alicia Arthurita, Arthur Amigo. Jr. clerk Met. Life Ins. Co., 1915-16; steno. Sheridan (Wyo.) Iron Works, 1917-18; statistician Kimberly-Clark Paper Co., Wis., 1920-21; athletic coach Lawrence Coll., 1915-17 and 1919-21; prof. and athletic coach Coll. of Ida., 1921-22; prin. and coach, Forest Grove, Ore., 1922-23, Thorp, Wash., 1923-24, North Bend. Ore., 1924-25; salesman Acme Fast Freight Service, 1925-26; tchr. Pasadena Pub. Schs., 1926-30; prin. and coach San Luis Obispo, Cal., 1930-35; ednl. advisor CCC, 1935-36; asso. prof. N. Tex. State Tchrs. Coll., 1936-37, Edinboro (Pa.) State Tchrs. Coll., 1938-39; asso. prof. and dir. radio Jersey City and Newark State Tchrs. colls., 1939-41; dir. Nelson and McLucas Meml. Libraries, Detroit, 1941-45; pub. relations dept. Key System, Oakland, Cal., 1945-46; columnist Honolulu Star-Bulletin and radio producer, 1946-47; columnist Santa Fe New Mexican, 1951-52; dean men Southwestern U., 1947-49; dir. tchr. tng. Dakota Wesleyan U., 1949-51; lectr. St. Michaels Coll., Santa Fe, 1951-54, also summer; supervising prin. pub. schs., Pojoaque, N.M.; tchr. summer sch. U. Wash., 1940, U. Wyo., No. Mont. Coll. and Eastern Mont. State Normal Sch., 1941, U. Utah, 1943, N.M. Highlands U., 1949, supervising prin. Belen (N.M.) Pub. Schs., 1954-57; tchr. pub. schs., Grants, N.M., 1957-60; prof. edn. and psychology Tex. Luth. Coll., Sequin, Tex., 1960-61; chmn. psychology dept. Pacific U., 1961-64; vis. prof. history Fla. Meml. Coll., 1964-66; asso. prof. edn. Bethune-Cookman Coll., 1966-72, Extension staff faculty N.M. Western Coll., 1954-57; radio producer, 1931—; promotion mgr. The Three Young Atkinsons, 1967—. Mem. exec. com. Boy Scouts Am. Served with A.E.F., World War I. Life mem. N.E.A.; mem. A.A.A.S., Tex. Acad. Scis., Texas Psychol. Assn., Am. Assn. Sch. Adminstrs., Soc. Advancement Learning, Am. Legion, Acad. Polit. Sci., United Comml. Travelers, Portland Psychol. Assn., Am. Assn. of Croix de Guerre, Vets. Fgn. Wars, Am. Assn. U. Profs., Daytona Beach Psychol. Assn., Advt. Club, Vets. Bus. Mens Assn., C. of C., Jr. C. of C. (asso.). Methodist. Author 19 books, 1928—, including: Intellectual Tramp, 1955; Story of Education, 2d edit., 1965; True Confessions of a Ph.D., 1938. Home: 3021 N Oleander Av Daytona Beach FL 32018

ATKINSON, EDWARD RUDOLPH, pediatrician; b. Clarksville, Tenn., May 4, 1916; s. Edward and Karlene Hoy (Rudolph) A.; student Austin Peay State U., 1933-34; B.S., Southwestern U., 1938; M.D., U. Tenn., 1940; m. Anna Kathryn Wall, May 26, 1942; children—Edward Rudolph, Elizabeth (Mrs. William F. Summers, Jr.), William Hunter. Intern, John Gaston Hosp., Memphis, 1940-42; practice medicine, specializing in pediatrics, Clarksville, 1946—; mem. staff Meml. Hosp., Clarksville. Mem. Montgomery County Bd. Health, 1958—; mem. adv. bd. Youth Challenge Inc., 1972—. Served to maj. M.C., AUS, 1942-46. Mem. A.M.A., Tenn., Montgomery County med. socs., Alpha Tau Omega, Phi Chi, Alpha Omega Alpha. Presbyn. (trustee). Clubs: Tower (Clarksville); Century (Knoxville). Home: 1440 Golf Club Lane Clarksville TN 37040

ATKINSON, EVELYN ROREX, architect; b. Panhandle, Tex., Dec. 29, 1931; d. Joe and Lydia (Lill) Rorex; student West Tex. State Coll., 1949-50; B.Arch., Tex. Technol. Coll., 1955. Draftsman, designer to campus landscape architect Tex. Technol. Coll., 1953-55; draftsman, designer Parks and Recreation Dept., Lubbock, Tex., 1953-55, Atcheson, Atkinson and Cartwright, architects and engrs., Lubbock, 1955-71; partner Atcheson, Atkinson, Cartwright and Rorex, architects and engrs., Lubbock, 1971—. Registered architect, Tex. Mem. A.I.A. (corporate; Outstanding Grad. Student award Panhandle chpt. 1955, treas. 1970), Alpha Chi. Democrat. Methodist. Home: 3201 29th St Lubbock TX 79410 Office: 1214 14th St Lubbock TX 79401

ATKINSON, GENE, univ. dean, educator; b. Houston, June 20, 1925; s. Smith Bachman and Nellie Marie (Shaffer) A.; B.A., Rice U., 1947; M.Ed., U. Houston, 1951, Ed.D., 1957; m. Claudene Douglas, Jan. 25, 1947; 1 son, Mark Douglas. Tchr., Brazosport Schs., Freeport, Tex., 1948-51, 53-55; asst. prof. dept. physics Cal. State U. at Long Beach, 1957-60, asso. prof., 1960-64, prof., asso. dean instrn., 1964-66; asso. prof. edn. U. Houston, 1966-70, prof., 1970—, asso. dean Coll. Edn., 1967-70, asst. dean Faculties, 1970—. Served to ensign, USNR, 1945-46, to lt., 1951-53; comdr. Res. ret. Fellow A.A.A.S.; mem. Am. Assn. for Higher Edn., Am. Assn. U. Profs., Sigma Pi Sigma. Home: 8015 Glen Valley Dr Houston TX 77017

ATKINSON, HENRY ALEXIS, II, dentist; b. Belvidere, Tenn., Nov. 11, 1919; s. Henry Alexis and Nelle Gray (Mason) A.; B.S., U. of the South, 1943; D.D.S., U. Tenn., 1947; m. Elizabeth Frances Ruch, June 30, 1946; children—Henry Alexis III, Bette Nelle, Richard Samuel. Individual practice gen. dentistry, Winchester, Tenn., 1948-51, 53—. Mem. Tenn. Dental Health Council, 1963-69. Trustee Franklin County Resource Devel. Assn., Maxwell Cemetary. Served with Dental Corp AUS, 1951-53. Mem. 4th Dist. Dental Soc. (pres. 1960-61), Pierre Fauchard Acad. Baptist (deacon 1971). Lion (pres. 1950). Club: Maxwell Community (pres. 1962-63). Home: 2 RFD Belvidere TN 37306 Office: 214 1st Av S E Winchester TN 37398

ATKINSON, JAMES HAROLD, coll. pres.; b. Liberty Hill, Tex., Feb. 22, 1918; s. Harold and Olivia Mae (Powell) A.; B.A. cum laude, Southwestern U., 1938; M.Ed., U. Houston, 1948; postgrad. A. and M. U. Tex., U. Tex.; Litt.D., Houston Bapt. Coll., 1970; m. Katherine Louise Smith, Aug. 25, 1945 (dec.); children—James Durham, David Harold; m. 2d, Eva Medoris Beazley, May 25, 1973. High sch. coach, tchr., La Grange, Tex., 1939-41, Llano, Tex., 1941-42; prin. high sch. Cypress-Fairbanks High Sch., Cypress, Tex., 1946-47; athletic dir., head coach Blinn Coll., Brenham, Tex., 1947-49, dean, 1949-57, pres., 1957—. Dir. Consol. Funds of Washington County, Tex., 1957—, pres., 1965-71; chmn. City Brenham Planning and Zoning Com. Served from pvt. to lt. col. USAAF, 1942-46; ETO. Mem. Tex. Jr. Coll. Athletic Assn. (pres. 1954-55, 58-59), Tex. Jr. Coll. Football Fedn. (pres.), Washington County Tchrs. Assn. (pres. 1958-59), Am. Legion (comdr. 1949), Southwestern Sci. Soc., C. of C., V.F.W., Tex. Jr. Coll. Agrl. Assn. (hon.), Alpha Chi, Phi Delta Kappa, Phi Theta Kappa Frats. Methodist (chmn. ofcl. bd. 1959-60). Mason, Rotarian, Lion. Club: The Red Red Rose. Home: 906 Green St Brenham TX 77833

ATKINSON, JAMES THOMAS, pedodontist; b. Six Mile, S.C., July 25, 1937; s. Thomas Benson and Jessie Mae (Sullivan) A.; B.S., Furman U., 1958; D.D.S., Med. Coll. Va., 1962, postgrad. pedodontics, 1962; resident pedodontics Children's Hosp., Washington, 1964-65; m. Sherry Jones Atkinson, Aug. 23, 1958; children—James Thomas, Tara Leslie, Paul Benson. Pvt. practice specializing pedodontics, Greenville, S.C., 1962—. Dental dir. United Fund of Greenville County, 1968; dir. Citizens for Community Action Council, 1968—. Recipient Spoke award, U.S. Jr. C. of C., 1964, award for service to mankind, Sertoma, 1968. Mem. Pedodontic Assos. Profl. Assn. (pres.), Am. Dental Assn., Greenville County, S.C. dental socs., Am., S.C. socs. dentistry for children, Piedmont Dist. Dental Soc., Am., Internat. acads. orthodontics, Begg Study Group, Alpha Epsilon Delta, Xi Psi Phi. Clubs: Paladin of Furman University (dir.), Gamecock (Greenville County). Home: 1201 Parkins Mill Rd Greenville SC 29607 Office: 410 Pelham Rd Greenville SC 29607

ATKINSON, JOHN LITTLETON BOONE, educator; b. Vance, Miss., May 11, 1918; s. Thomas Robinson and Sallie (Prescott) A.; B.A., La State U., 1939, M.A., 1941; Ph.D., U. Pa., 1951; m. Gloria Jean Lewis, July 20, 1965; children by previous marriage—Judith, Prescott, John, William. Prof. history Air U., 1949-62; prof. internat. affairs, dir. George Washington U. Center, 1962-67; chmn. dept. history Miss. State U. for Women, Columbus, 1967—. Lectr., European history, 1952-57. Served with USAAF, 1942-46. Mem. Am. Hist. Assn., Soc. French Hist. Studies. Home: 905 6th Av S Columbus MS 39701

ATKINSON, MALLORY COOK, ret. lawyer, jurist, educator; b. Newnan, Ga., Feb. 23, 1906; s. Theodore Ellis and Mary Lou (Cook) A.; Ph.B., Emory U., 1926, LL.B., 1930; m. Gertrude Gist-Gee, June 9, 1928; children—Bettie A. (Mrs. James D. Lawrence), Jane A. (Mrs. Henry Middlebrooks), Mallory Cook. Admitted to Ga. bar, 1930; practiced law in Macon, 1930-44, 55-74; lectr. Walter F. George Sch. Law, Mercer U., Macon, 1954, prof., 1955-68; gen. counsel State Bar Ga., 1965-72; judge Superior Cts., Macon Circuit, 1944-54. Mem., v.p., past sec. Bibb County Bd. Edn., Macon, 1944-67. Bd. dirs., past pres. Macon YMCA. Mem. Am., Ga., Macon bar assns., Am. Judicature Soc., Sigma Alpha Epsilon. Democrat. Methodist (chmn. bd. trustees, past chmn. adminstrv. bd. local church). Mason, Lion (past pres., past sec.). Home: 294 Corbin Av Macon GA 31204

ATKINSON, THOMAS SCOTT, communications engr.; b. Houston, Mar. 3, 1938; s. Patrick Joseph and Florence (Scott) A.; B.S. in Physics, Tex. A. and I. U., 1961; postgrad. Air Force Communications Officers Sch., 1961-62; m. Margaret Ann Young, Aug. 26, 1961; children—Margaret Elizabeth, Charlotte Elaine. Communications systems engr. NASA Apollo project Lockheed Electronics Co., 1967-68; communications cons. Executone of Houston, 1968-70; cons. Atkinson & Assos., Houston, 1970-71; sr. communications engr. Tenneco, Inc., Houston, 1971—; communications cons. Houston, 1971—. Served to capt. USAF, 1961-67; maj. Res. Mem. I.E.E.E., Armed Forces Communications and Electronics Assn. (pres.), Houston Engring. and Sci. Soc. Methodist. Optimist. Home: 1131 Montour Dr Houston TX 77058 Office: 1433 W Loop S Houston TX 77027

ATKINSON, WILLIAM ROBERT, ednl. adminstr.; b. Wilson County, N.C., July 16, 1939; s. Walter Clifton and Mary (Ellis) A.; B.S., Atlantic Christian Coll., 1961; M.A., E. Carolina U., 1965; m. Mary Jo Daniel, Dec. 22, 1963; 1 son, William Robert. Tchr., Norfolk (Va.) City Schs., 1961-62, Wayne County Schs., Goldsboro, N.C., 1962-67; asst. prin. Wilson (N.C.) City Schs., 1967-69; with Richard T. Fountain Sch., Rocky Mount, N.C., 1969—, sch. dir., 1971—. Presbyn. Club. Optimist (dir. Rocky Mount). Address: Richard T Fountain Sch Rocky Mount NC 27801

ATLAS, MORRIS, lawyer; b. Houston, Dec. 25, 1926; s. Sam and Bluma (Cohen) A.; B.B.A., Tex. U., 1948, LL.B., 1950; m. Rita Jean Willner, Aug. 31, 1947; children—Scott J., Debra Lynne, Lauren Teri, Lisa Gayle. Admitted to Tex. bar, 1950, since practiced in McAllen; sr. partner, mng. partner Atlas, Hall, Schwarz, Mills, Gurwitz & Bland, 1953—. Pres., dir. Frontier Devel. Co., El Padre, Inc.; sec., dir. Tide Products, Inc., La Casita Farms, Inc.; dir. Jefferson Savs. & Loan Assn. Chmn. Cancer Drive, 1960; state chmn. Anti-Defamation League B'nai B'rith, 1963-64. Chmn. Hidalgo County Democratic Exec. Com., 1968—; del. Dem. Nat. Convs., 1968, 72. Chmn. bd. regents Pan Am. U.; mem. adv. bd. Latin Am. Inst.; mem. exec. com. Tex. Council for Higher Edn., 1968; mem. Gulf Coast Adv. Council on Water Resources. Served with USNR, 1942-46. Fellow Tex. Bar Found.; mem. Am., Tex., Hidalgo County (pres. 1961) bar assns., Tex. Assn. Def. Counsel (dir. 1967), Assn. Ins. Attys., Rio Grand Valley (dir. 1955), McAllen (dir. 1956) chambers commerce, Phi Delta Phi. Jewish religion (past pres. congregation). Club: McAllen Country (dir., past pres.). Home: 1600 Iris St McAllen TX 78501 Office: PO Drawer 1870 McAllen TX 78501

ATRIA, NICHOLAS FRED, physician; b. West Orange, N.J., Dec. 1, 1906; s. James V. and Catherine D. (Stefano) A.; B.A., Washington and Lee U., 1928; M.D., Tulane U., 1932; m. Ethel Davis, May 21, 1937; children—James Adrian, Nicholas Davis, Mark Stewart. Intern, Med. Center, Jersey City, 1932-33, resident, 1933-35; commd. 1st lt. USAF, 1936, advanced through ranks to col.; grad. Army Med. Field Service Sch., Carlisle Barracks, Pa., 1937-38, USAF Sch. Aerospace Medicine, Randolph Field, Tex., 1942; instr. physiology Tulane Sch. Medicine, 1947-48; instr. mil. medicine USAF Sch. Aerospace Medicine, 1948-49; asst. air attache US embassy and exchange officer, London, 1949-51; ret., 1959; dep. commr. mental health Tenn., 1959-63; supr. Kan. Neur. Inst., Topeka, 1963-64; chief med.-surg. service Crafts-Farrow State Hosp., Columbia, S.C., 1964—. Decorated Bronze Star medal with six battle stars; recipient Arrow Head A.M.A., 1936. Diplomate Am. Bd. Preventive Medicine. Mem. Am. Pub. Health Assn., Aerospace Med. Assn., Am. Coll. Preventive Medicine, Am. Geriatrics Soc., Royal Soc. Health, Phi Rho Sigma. Home: 3160 Travis Ct Columbia SC 29204 Office: Craft-Farrow State Hosp Columbia SC 29203

ATTAWAY, FRED JOHN, JR., aero. engr.; b. Sterling, Okla., July 27, 1932; s. Fred John and Minnie Ora (Yandell) A.; B.S. in Aero. Engring., U. Okla., 1960, postgrad., 1960-61; postgrad. Fla. Inst. Tech., 1964-66, U. Fla., 1967, 70-71; m. Audrey F. Jacques, June 25, 1955; children—David M., Mark J., Dianna M. Aero. engr. Aero Comdr., Norman, Okla., 1960-61; sr. flight test engr. Gen. Dynamics Co., Kennedy Space Center, Fla., 1961-67; sr. flight test engr., asst. spacecraft mgr. Rockwell Internat. Corp., Kennedy Space Center, 1967-71, safety supr., 1972—. Served with USNR, 1953-54, as capt. USMC, 1954-57. Registered profl. engr., Fla. Mem. Sigma Gamma Tau. Clubs: Indian River Yacht (Cocoa, Fla.); North American Rockwell Management (Kennedy Space Center, Fla.). Home: 1722 Hubbard Dr Rockledge FL 32955 Office: Rockwell Internat Corp Kennedy Space Center FL 32905

ATTAWAY, HUGH ELDON, orthodontist; b. Aransas Pass, Tex., Jan. 5, 1931; s. Hugh Milton and Lela Evelyn (Chambers) A.; student Tex. A. and I. U., 1948-50; D.D.S., Baylor U., 1954; M.S.D., U. Neb., 1961; m. Joan Elizabeth Evans, Sept. 17, 1955; children—Leigh, Linda, Douglas. Instr. crown and bridge Baylor U. Coll. Dentistry, 1958-59; pvt. practice orthodontics, Irving, Tex., 1961—. Asso. prof. orthodontics Baylor Coll. Dentistry, 1962—. Served with Dental Corps, AUS, 1954-58. Diplomate Am. Bd. Orthodontics. Mem. Am. Assn. Orthodontists, Am., Tex. dental assns., Dallas County Dental Soc., Charles H. Tweed Tex. Orthodontic Study Group (C. T. Roland award 1965). Rotarian. Home: 2909 Pacific Ct Irving TX 75062 Office: 801 N O'Connor Rd Irving TX 75061

ATTERIDG, PAUL THEODORE, chem. engr.; b. Summit, N.J., Nov. 1, 1924; s. George Stockton and Lida Higginson (Wolcott) A.; B.S. in Chem. E., Cornell, 1945, B.Ch.E., 1947; m. Louise Van Nederynen, July 3, 1948; children—Ellen (Mrs. Thomas G. Watkins IV), Paul Theodore, John Wolcott, Susan Joanne and Barbara Joan (twins), James Andrew. With M.W. Kellogg Co., Houston, 1947—, mgr. comml. devel. and analysis, 1970-72, mgr. comml. proposals, 1972—. Chmn. Sch. Budget Study Com., Montclair, N.J., 1966-67. Bd. advisers Vols. of Am., Houston, 1972—; bd. dirs. East Harlem Protestant Parish, N.Y.C., 1969-70. Served to lt. (j.g.) USNR, 1943-46. Mem. N.Y. Acad. Sci., Am. Inst. Chem. Engrs., N. Am. Soc. Corp. Planning, Cornell Soc. N.Y., Sci. Research Soc. Am. (br. pres. 1953-54), Phi Kappa Psi. Conglist. (trustee). Patentee in petroleum processing. Contbr. articles to profl. jours. Home: 123 Plantation Rd Houston TX 77024 Office: 1300 Three Greenway Plaza E Houston TX 77046

ATWATER, JOHN SPENCER, physician; b. Cin., Oct. 12, 1913; s. Carleton William and May (Spencer) A.; student Western Res. U., 1931-32; A.B., Denison U., 1935; student Ind. U. Sch. Medicine, 1934-36; M.D., Johns Hopkins, 1939; M.S. in Medicine, U. Minn., 1944; m. Laura Virginia Zipplies, July 29, 1939; children—John Spencer, Paul Carleton, Elizabeth Baron. Intern medicine U. Chgo. Clinics, 1939-40, asst. resident medicine, 1940-41; fellow Mayo Found., 1941-44, 1st asst. medicine Mayo Clinic, Rochester, Minn., 1943-44; practice medicine specializing in internal medicine and gastroenterology, Atlanta, 1946—; mem. staffs Ga. Bapt. Hosp., Crawford W. Long Meml. Hosp., Atlanta Hosp.; asso. chief medicine Ga. Bapt. Hosp., 1948-57, acting chief medicine, 1958-60, chief medicine, 1973—, pres. staff, 1962, mem. exec. com., 1961-64, chmn. exec. com., 1963, chief gastroent. sect., 1948—; chief dept. medicine Atlanta Hosp., 1968-69, chief medicine, 1969-72, mem. exec. com., 1968-72, chmn. credentials com., 1968-69, mem. utilization rev. com., 1968-69, mem. med. recs. com., 1968, mem. joint conf. com., 1970-72; cons. in gastroenterology Robert T. Jones Meml. Hosp., Canton, Ga., 1962—, Cobb Gen. Hosp., Austell, Ga., 1968-73; instr. in medicine U. Minn., 1943-44; instr. in medicine Emory U., 1946-54, asso. in medicine, 1954-65; cons. internal medicine VA, Ga. Dept. Edn., Fgn. Mission Bd. So. Bapt. Conv., U.S. Dept. State. Chmn. Atlanta Grad. Med. Assembly, 1958-59, exhibit chmn., 1960, mem. adv. com., 1961, mem. emergency care service com., 1964-65; mem. Gov.'s Commn. on Aging, 1959-62, chmn. health com., 1959-62; del. White House Conf. on Aging, 1961; chmn. Gov.'s Conf. on Aging, 1960, Ga. Joint Council to Improve Health Care of Aged, 1959—; mem. health adv. com. Ga. Commn. on Aging, 1964—; mem. clin. lab., blood bank and tissue bank com. Ga. Dept. Pub. Health, 1971—. Partner, Caduceus Properties, 1969—; dir. So. Gen. Ins. Co., Stuyvesant Ins. Co., Stuyvesant Life Ins. Co., Jersey Ins. Co. N.Y., 1st Ga. Bank, Peoples Am. Bank Atlanta. Bd. dirs. Atlanta Boys Club, med. dir., 1953-65, mem. endowment com., 1970-72; bd. dirs. Atlanta Girls Club, vice chmn., 1957-58, chmn. bd. 1958-59, 3d v.p., 1960. Served as lt. M.C., USNR, 1944-46. Recipient Certificate of Appreciation, Fulton County Med. Soc., 1960, 63; Aven Citizenship award, 1961; Award of Recognition, Atlanta Boys Club, 1966; Keystone Bronze award Boys Clubs Am., 1968; Letter of Appreciation, Med. Assn. Ga., 1969, Certificate of Appreciation, 1970. Diplomate Am. Bd. Internal Medicine, Am. Bd. Gastroenterology. Fellow A.C.P., Am. Geriatrics Soc.; mem. A.M.A. (cons. council med. services 1960—, chmn. reference com. med. edn. 1969, mem. reference com. financing med. care 1967, mem. reference com. ins. and med. services 1971), Med. Assn. Ga. (chmn. bd. spl. activities 1961—, treas. 1962—, mem. publs. com. jour. 1962—, mem. exec. com. 1962—, mem. finance com. 1962—, mem. spl. finance, central billing, hdqrs. expansion and bldg. coms., chmn. awards com.), Fulton County (chmn. com. on aging 1959, 60, 61), 5th Dist. med. socs., So. Med. Assn. (past chmn.), Am. Gastroent. Assn., Am. Gastroscopic Soc., Am. Soc. for Gastrointestinal Endoscopy, World Congress Gastroenterology, N.Y. Acad. Scis., Am. Heart Assn., Alumni Assn. Mayo Found. Med. Edn. and Research, Mayo Gastrointestinal Alumni Assn., Johns Hopkins Med. and Surg. Soc., U. Chgo. Med. Alumni Assn. Am., Ga. socs. internal medicine. Johns Hopkins Alumni Assn. (past pres. Ga. soc., past nat. v.p.), Atlanta C. of C., S.A.R., Phoenix Soc., Phi Gamma Delta, Nu Sigma Nu, Baptist. Kiwanian (mem. boys and girls work com. 1966-70, fund-raising com. 1969-70, vocational guidance com. 1969, operation drug alert com. 1970-71. Clubs: Commerce, Atlanta City (charter mem.). Author numerous articles in field; sci. exhibits at med. meetings (with others); films, TV demonstrations in field. Home: 2625 Howell Mill Rd NW Atlanta GA 30327 Office: 478 Peachtree St NE Atlanta GA 30308

ATWOOD, JOHN HORTON, offshore drilling contractor; b. Janesville, Wis., Jan. 27, 1923; s. Leo Holmes and Besse Beatrice (Burch) A.; student U. Wis., 1940-42; B.S., Purdue U., 1951; m. Janet Ione Morrissey, Jan. 8, 1949; children—John Holmes, Marjorie Jane, Kathryn Joan, Susan Carol, Michael Patrick, Patrick Kevin. Halfback, N.Y. Football Giants, 1948-49; engr. Standard Oil Co. of Ohio, Ill., 1951-52, drilling engr., Okla., 1952-56; chief engr. Warren-Bradshaw Exploration Co., 1956-57; offshore mgr. Standard Oil Co. of Ohio, New Orleans, 1957-58, asst. Gulf Coast prodn. mgr., Houston, 1958-60, chief drilling supt., Oklahoma City, 1960-61; Gulf Coast mgr. Global Marine, Inc., Houston, 1961-62, v.p., 1962-66, exec. v.p., 1966-68; founder Atwood Oceanics, Inc., Houston, 1968, chmn. bd., pres., chief exec. officer, 1968—; dir. Travis Body & Trailer, Inc., Houston, Randazzo, Inc., Dallas, Invespian Inc., Madrid, Spain. Served with USMCR, 1942-45. Decorated Purple Heart. Mem. Am. Petroleum Inst., Internat. Assn. Oilwell Drilling Contractors (dir.), Am. Mining and Petroleum Engrs., Nat. Oceanographic Assn., Petroleum Club. Clubs: Houston, Lakeside Country, Houston, Warwick. Home: 347 Fawnlake St Houston TX 77024 Office: 10555 Katy Freeway Town and Country Office Park Houston TX 77024

AUFORTH, FRED CORTLANDT, lawyer; b. Pasadena, Cal., June 19, 1927; s. F. Cortland and Lela Laura (Lockhart) A.; B.A., Stanford, 1950; LL.B., U. Tex., 1954; m. Mary Ann McLandrich, June 14, 1952;

children—Frederic Cortlandt III, Karen Kay, Claire Ann. Admitted to Tex. bar, 1954; partner Park, Hemphill & Auforth, Snyder, Tex., 1954-59, Auforth & Nehrat and predecessor firms, Corpus Christi, 1959—. Asst. dist. atty. Nueces County, 1961-63. Served with USNR, 1945-46. Mem. Am., Tex., Nueces County bar assns. Episcopalian. Mason (32 deg., Shriner). Home: 345 Palmetto St Corpus Christi TX 78401 Office: 3318 S Alameda St Corpus Christi TX 78411

AUG, ROBERT GAENGE, educator, psychiatrist; b. Cin., Sept. 13, 1930; s. George Christian and Gertrude (Gaenge) A.; student U. Cin., 1947-49, M.D., 1955; A.B. magna cum laude, Whitman Coll., 1951; m. Lois Marie Edelen, Jan. 14, 1956; children—Lisa Marie, Suzanne Yvette. Intern Cin. Gen. Hosp., 1955-56; resident psychiatry U. Cin., 1956-58, fellow child psychiatry, 1958-60; asst. prof. psychiatry U. Ky. Med. Center, 1962-64; asso. clin. prof. psychiatry Marquette U. Med. Sch., 1964-68; dir. tng. child psychiatry Milw. County Mental Health Center, 1964-68, dir. children's inpatient service, 1967-68; asso. prof. psychiatry U. Ky. Med. Center, Lexington, 1968-72, prof. psychiatry, 1972—, dir. div. child psychiatry, 1968—; mem. staff University Hosp. Founder, organizer, first dir. grad. and undergrad. tng. programs child psychiatry Milw. County Mental Health Center, 1965. Served to capt. M.C., 1960-62. Diplomate in psychiatry and child psychiatry Am. Bd. Psychiatry and Neurology (examiner in child psychiatry 1969—). Fellow Am. Acad. Child Psychiatry; mem. Am. Psychiat. Assn., A.M.A., Milw. (co-founder 1965, pres. 1966-67), Cin. councils child psychiatry, Phi Beta Kappa, Delta Tau Delta, Phi Chi. Presbyn. Home: Route 4 Groggins Ferry Rd Nicholasville KY 40356 Office: U Ky Med Center Lexington KY 40506

AUGSBURGER, MYRON SHENK, clergyman, educator, coll. pres.; b. Elida, O., Aug. 20, 1929; s. Clarence Aaron and Estella (Shenk) A.; B.A., Eastern Mennonite Coll., 1955, Th.B., 1958; B.D., Goshen Coll., 1959; Th.M., Th.D., Union Theol. Sem., 1964; postgrad. George Washington U., 1964-65; m. Esther Louise Kniss, Nov. 28, 1950; children—John, Michael, Marcia. Ordained to ministry Mennonite Ch., 1951; pastor of students Eastern Mennonite Coll., Harrisonburg, Va., 1953-54, asst. prof. theology, 1962-65, prof. theology, pres., 1965—. Dir., Valley Nat. Bank, Harrisonburg, Shenandoah Valley Ednl. TV. Corp. Mem. council Mennonite Colls.; bd. dirs. Council for Advancement Small Colls. Mem. Nat. Assn. Evangelicals (bd. adminstrn. 1969-73). Author: Called to Maturity, 1963; Quench Not the Spirit, 1964; Plus Living, 1965; Invitation to Discipleship, 1966; Principles of Biblical Interpretation, 1966; Pilgrim Aflame, 1967; Faith for a Secular World, 1968; The Broken Chalice, 1971; The Expanded Life, 1972. Home: 1545 Hillcrest St Harrisonburg VA 22801

AUGUSTINE, NORMAN RALPH, govt. ofcl.; b. Denver, July 27, 1935; s. Ralph Harvey and Freda Irene (Immenga) A.; B.S., Princeton, 1957, M.S., 1959; postgrad. Columbia, 1958, U. Cal. at Los Angeles, 1958, 60, U. So. Cal., 1960; m. Margareta Engman, Jan. 20, 1962; children—Gregory Eugen, René Irene. Research asst. Princeton, 1957-58; chief engr. Douglas Aircraft Co., Inc., Santa Monica, Cal., 1958-65; asst. dir. def. research and engring. Office Sec. Def., Washington, 1965-70, cons., 1971-73; v.p. advanced systems, missiles and space div. LTV Aerospace Corp., Dallas, 1970-73; asst. sec. Army, The Pentagon, Washington, 1973—. Cons. Exec. Office of Pres., 1971-73; mem. research and tech. adv. com. NASA, mem. research and devel. adv. council; mem. policy council Def. Systems Mgmt. Sch. Fund raiser YMCA, Arlington, Tex., 1971-72; chmn. pack com. Boy Scouts Am., Arlington, 1972-73. Recipient Sec. Def. Meritorious Service medal, 1970. Asso. fellow Inst. Aeros. and Astronautics; mem. Am. Def. Preparedness Assn. (chpt. dir.), Am. Helicopter Soc. (dir.), Phi Beta Kappa, Sigma Xi, Tau Beta Pi. Presbyn. Kiwanian. Mem. adv. bd. Jour. Def. Research, 1970—. Contbr. articles to profl. jours. Home: 1329 Merrie Ridge Rd McLean VA 22101 Office: Pentagon Washington DC 20310

AUSBAND, JOHN RUFUS, physician; b. Winston-Salem, N.C., Oct. 14, 1920; s. Charles Clarence and Estelle (Crowell) A.; B.A., Asbury Coll., 1940; M.D., Bowman Gray Sch., Wake Forest Coll., 1943; m. Geraldine Belva Trent, June 25, 1949; children—Leigh Trent, Elinor Ann. Intern, Hartford (Conn.) Hosp., 1944; resident N.C. Bapt. Hosp., Winston-Salem, 1944-46, 49-52, now mem. staff; practice medicine, specializing in otolaryngology, Winston-Salem, 1952—; instr., asst. prof., asso. prof. otolaryngology Bowman Gray Sch. Medicine, 1952-67, prof., 1967—. Trustee Med. Found. N.C. Bapt. Hosp., Bowman Gray Sch. Medicine. Served from 1st lt. to capt. M.C., AUS, 1946-48. Diplomate Am. Bd. Otolaryngology. Mem. N.C. Soc. Ophthalmology and Otolaryngology (past pres.), Am. Broncho Esophagological Assn. (pres. 1971), A.M.A., Med. Soc. State N.C., Internat. Broncho Esophagological Soc., Am. Acad. Ophthalmology and Otolaryngology, Am. Laryngol., Rhinological and Otological Soc., Am. Laryngol. Assn., Forsyth County Med. Soc., Phi Rho Sigma (grand chpt. pres. 1966-70). Home: 909 Goodwood Rd Winston-Salem NC 27106 Office: Bowman Gray Sch Medicine Winston-Salem NC 27103

AUSERE, JOE MORRIS, food co. exec.; b. Miami, Ariz., Sept. 29, 1929; s. Joe P. and Josephine (Sanez) A.; student Phoenix Jr. Coll., 1948, U. So. Cal., 1949; B.S. in Indsl. Engring., Ariz. State U., 1951; m. Elizabeth Ann Oxford, Dec. 19, 1959; children—Melinda Jo, Leigh Ann, Michael Joseph. Sales and prodn. supr. Rainbo Baking Co., Phoenix, 1941-51; prodn. and engring. cons. Campbell-Taggart Asso. Bakeries, Dallas, 1951-60; v.p. mfg. and sales Am. Foods, Inc., Atlanta, 1960-65; exec. v.p., dir. Merico, Inc., Dallas 1965-70, pres., dir., 1970—; v.p. Campbell Taggart, 1973—. Served with AUS, 1955-58. Mem. Phi Sigma Kappa. Republican. Baptist. Home: 4415 Myerwood Lane Dallas TX 75234 Office: 1820 N Josey Lane Dallas TX 75234

AUSTIN, CLARENCE WESLEY, JR., metallurgist; b. Amsterdam, N.Y., Nov. 29, 1935; s. Clarence W. and Beulah (Weaver) A.; B.Metall. Engring., Rensselaer Poly. Inst., 1957. Materials research engr. U.S. Army Ballistic Missile Agy., Redstone Arsenal, Ala., 1957-60; research asso. metallurgy Am. Dental Assn. research div. Nat. Bur. Standards, Washington, 1960; sr. research phys. metallurgist, phys. scis. lab. U.S. Army Missile Command, Redstone Arsenal, Ala., 1961—. Mem. Am. Soc. Metals, Am. Soc. Testing and Materials, Internat. Metallographic Soc., Electron Probe Analysis Soc. Am. Contbr. articles to profl. jours. Home: 404 Hillmont Circle NW Huntsville AL 35805 Office: US Army Missile Command Redstone Arsenal AL 35809

AUSTIN, ELEANOR LOUISE SEGO (MRS. JAMES LLOYD AUSTIN), club woman; b. Florence, Ala., Nov. 16, 1911; d. John Thomas and Lillie (Blair) Sego; grad. S.W. Bapt. Coll., 1931-33; student Florence State Coll., 1934-35; m. James Lloyd Austin, May 6, 1934; 1 son, James Lloyd. Tchr. Lauderdale County Schs., Ala., 1935-43. Mem. women's com. Birmingham Symphony; vol. Bapt. Med. Center, Montclair; patron Civic Ballet; mem. womans aux. Salvation Army. Mem. Montgomery Fedn. Women's Clubs (publicity chmn. 1957-59, asst. treas. 1959-60), Arlington Hist. Assn., Birmingham Mus. Art, Mothers Circle of Montgomery (mem. exec. bd. 1959-65, corr. sec. 1959-61, prospectus chmn. 1960-61, fedn. dir. 1961-63, pres. 1963-65), Samford U. Aux. (corr. sec.). Baptist. Democrat. Clubs: Woman's Civic (exec. bd., bd. dirs. 1972-76, v.p., corr. sec.) (Birmingham); Normandale Garden (rec. sec. 1964-65). Home: 3744 Crestbrook Rd Birmingham AL 35223

AUSTIN, J(AMES) LLOYD, ins. exec.; b. Cloverdale, Ala., Oct. 7, 1909; s. James R. and Minnie (Koonce) A.; student Florence State Tchrs. Coll., 1932-33; m. Eleanor Sego, May 6, 1934; 1 son, James Lloyd. With Lauderdale Country Bd. Edn., 1932-37; agt. So. Life & Health Ins. Co., Florence, Ala., 1937-39, asst. mgr., 1939-41, auditor, insp., 1941-45, mgr. Jacksonville (Fla.) dist., 1945-55, div. mgr., 1955-65, agy. sec., 1965-70, field v.p., 1970—, also trustee profit sharing. Mem. adv. bd. Bapt. Home for Children, Jacksonville; trustee So. Life and Health Ins. Co. Mem. Jacksonville Life Underwriters Assn. (past pres.), Gen. Agts. and Mgrs. Assn. (pres.), C. of C., Jacksonville Civil Round Table, Nat. Assn. Life Underwriters (charter builder, com. 100, bd. dirs.), Baptist (deacon, supt. Sunday Sch., pres. Men's Fellowship). Democrat. Clubs: South Montgomery Exchange (bd. dirs.); Ponte Vedra; So. Montgomery Exchange (pres.); Executive (Birmingham). Home: 3744 Crestbrook Rd Mountain Brook Birmingham AL 35223 Office: 2121 Highland Av Birmingham AL 35205

AUSTIN, JAMES WESCOAT, dentist; b. Cottage Grove, Tenn., Aug. 20, 1920; s. Dudley Emerson and Sally Maggie (Wescoat) A.; B.S., Abilene Christian Coll., 1946; D.D.S., Tex. U., 1950; m. Julia Hill, Feb. 22, 1946; children—Miriam, Alan, Ray. Individual practice dentistry, Corpus Christi, Tex., 1952—. Mem. adv. bd. Abilene Christian Coll., 1970—. Served to capt., Dental Corps, AUS, 1950-52. Mem. Am., Tex. dental assns., Nueces Valley Dist. Dental Soc. (pres. 1970-71). Kiwanian. Home: 433 Cape Henry Corpus Christi TX 78412 Office: 4141 Gollihar St Corpus Christi TX 78411

AUSTIN, THOMAS LEROY, mathematician; b. Memphis, Sept. 8, 1929; s. Thomas LeRoy and Vela Mae (Davis) A.; B.B.A., U. Ga., 1951, M.A., 1954; m. Phyllis Jean Bundy, Aug. 19, 1955; 1 dau., Rebecca Leslie. Mathematician, Nat. Security Agy., Washington, 1955-60; sr. analyst combat operations Research Group, Ft. Monroe, Va., 1960; mgr. operations research lab. Am. Systems, Inc., 1961-62; research specialist Gen. Dynamics, Pomona, Cal., 1962-64; sr. tech. specialist Autonetics div. N.Am. Rockwell, Anaheim, Cal., 1964-66, tech. adviser, 1966-70; mathematician Def. Communications Agy., Washington, 1970—. Research asso. U. N.C., 1957-58; lectr. George Washington U., 1960. Served to lt. AUS, 1951-53. Nat. Security Agy. fellow, 1956-57. Mem. Am. Math. Soc., Inst. Math. Statistics, Am. Ordnance Assn., Phi Kappa Phi, Beta Gamma Sigma, Delta Tau Delta. Contbr. articles profl. jours. Home: 1768 Ivy Oak Sq Reston VA 22090

AUTEN, PAUL PAGE, gas co. exec.; b. Collinsville, Okla., Apr. 9, 1918; s. Robert Franklin and Lenora Mae (Taylor) A.; student East Central State Coll., 1935-37; m. Myrtle Wray Underwood, Oct. 29, 1937; children—Barbara (Mrs. William B. Shives), Carol (Mrs. A. W. Hampf), Paul Wayne. Asst. circulation mgr. Tulsa Daily World, 1933-37; asst. circulation mgr. Ada (Okla.) Evening News, 1937-39; plant operations Carbide Carbon & Chem. Co., 1940-44; pres. Automatic Butane Gas Co., Houston, 1946—; dir., chmn. bd. Pinemont Bank. Mem. fire prevention com., City of Houston, 1969—, mem. transp. study com., 1971—. Served with inf., AUS, 1944-45. Decorated Purple Heart. Mem. Tex. LP Gas Assn. (v.p. 1958). Club: Racquet. Office: 451 Hunterwood St Houston TX 77024

AUTER, HENRY FENIMORE, govt. ofcl.; b. Vicksburg, Miss., Sept. 26, 1924; s. Henry Fenimore and Florence Virginia (Furr) A.; B.S. in E.E., Miss. State U., 1949; certificate Fed. Exec. Inst., 1972; m. Miriam Frances Noble, July 4, 1948; children—Alan Henry, Kenneth Noble, Amy Lorelle. Br. chief Missile Research and Devel., Army Ballistic Missile Agy., Huntsville, Ala., 1953-64; dep. dir. Miss. Test Facility, NASA, Bay St. Louis, Miss., 1964—. Treas., Friends of Library, Picayune, Miss., 1971—; pres. Council of Orgns., Picayune, 1969-70; mem. Pineburr Area council Boy Scouts Am., 1968—, chmn. long range planning com., 1970—, dist. chmn., 1967-69. Served with AUS, 1943-46, with USAF, 1951-53. Recipient Distinguished Service medal NASA, 1970; named Citizen of Year, Picayune, 1969. Registered profl. engr., Ala. Mem. Lambda Chi Alpha. Presbyn. (elder 1960—; clk. of session 1971—). Home: 1200 2d Av Picayune MS 39466 Office: Miss Test Facility Bay St Louis MS 39520

AUTHEMENT, RAY, coll. pres.; b. Chauvin, La., Nov. 19, 1929; s. Elias Lawrence and Elphia (Duplantis) A.; B.S., U. Southwestern La., 1950; M.S., La. State U., 1952, Ph.D., 1956; m. Barbara B. Braud, June 1, 1950; children—Kathleen Elizabeth, Julie Ann. Instr. La. State U., Baton Rouge, 1952-56; asso. prof. McNeese State Coll., Lake Charles, La., 1956-57; asso. prof. U. Southwestern La., 1957-59, prof. math., 1957—, acad. v.p., 1966-73, pres., 1973—; vis. prof. U. N.C. at Chapel Hill, 1962-63. Mem. Downtown Devel. Com. Lafayette, 1972—; mem. La. Bicentennial Commn., 1973, Lafayettee Bicentennial Commn., 1973; mem. Econ. Devel. Com., Lafayette, 1973; mem. Sch. bd. Fatima Parish, Lafayette, 1963-65. Bd. dirs. United Way, Lafayette, 1973, U. Southwestern La. Found., 1967; mem. bd. advisers St. Joseph Sem., 1967. Mem. Math. Assn. Am., Blue Key, A.A.A.S., Phi Kappa Phi, Kappa Mu Epsilon, Sigma Pi Sigma, Phi Kappa Theta. Roman Catholic. Rotarian. Home: 609 Landry Dr Lafayette LA 70501

AUTRY, MAYME BLANKINSHIP (MRS. DAVID EDGAR AUTRY), personnel exec.; b. Stephenville, Tex., Nov. 2, 1896; d. Martin Dawson and Dora Leona (Hickey) Blankinship; student Brantley Draughon Coll., 1916; m. David Edgar Autry, Jan. 20, 1917 (dec. 1944). Tchr. pub. schs., 1914-16; editor Hartley County News, Channing, Tex., 1926-37; bus. mgr., advt. mgr. Dalhart Pub. Co. (Tex.), Dalhart Texan, 1926-37; advt. mgr. Liberal (Kan.) News, 1937-39, Ochiltree County Herald, Perryton, Tex., 1937-39; owner, mgr. Autry Co., advt., Ft. Worth, 1939-45; owner, mgr. Autry Employment Service, Ft. Worth, 1943-72, mgr., Dallas, 1956-65; v.p. Acme-Autry Personnel Service, Ft. Worth, 1972—; pres. Mayme B. Autry, Inc., 1972—; owner, pub. Mansfield (Tex.) News, 1940-45; mgr. Kelly Services, Inc., Ft. Worth, Tex., 1955—, Dallas, 1956-66. Dir., Nat. Employment Bd., 1959-60. Pres. Women's Civic Club Council, Ft. Worth, 1950; chmn. Bus. Owners Group, 1947; commr. Tex. Centennial of Statehood, 1945; mem. Ft. Worth Mayor's Com. on Status of Women, 1971—, also chmn. speakers bur.; mem. Pan Am. Round Table No. 1. Recipient Pub. Relations award Kelly Girl Service, Inc., 1960, Silver medal award, Citizen of Year, 1961, 72. Mem. Assn. pvt. Employment Services (pres. Ft. Worth 1960-61), S.W. Employment Bd. (pres. 1958-59, editor Tall Tales 1963-64, Outstanding Service award 1959), Internat. Platform Assn., Adminstrv. Mgmt. Soc. (dir. 1959-60, 63-64, chmn. 5-state conf. 1963), Nat. Employment Assn., Tex., Fort Worth pvt. employment assns., Better Bus. Bur. (chmn. woman's div. 1957, Distinguished Service award 1957), Ft. Worth C. of C., Retail Mchts. Assn., Ft. Worth Bus. and Profl. Women's Club (dir. 1946), Alpha Iota. Mem. Order Eastern Star. Clubs: Woman's Zonta (pres. 1947-50, dir. 1963-65, 71—) (Ft. Worth). Home: 2014 6th Av Fort Worth TX 76110 Office: Sinclair Bldg Fort Worth TX 76102

AUTRY, OTWA TILDEN, supt. schs.; b. Gracemont, Okla., Jan. 7, 1910; s. Samuel Tilden and Sarah Jane (Mays) A.; B.A., Phillips U., 1932, M.A., 1935, LL.D., 1965; m. Esther Alma Bank, Jan. 9, 1932; children—Barbara Jo (Mrs. Floyd Stroup), Richard Bank, Steven Tilden. Instr., Phillips U., 1932-34; tchr., coach Emerson Jr. High Sch., 1934-35, prin., 1953-59; tchr., coach Enid (Okla.) High Sch., 1935-40, 45-53, prin. 1959-64; supt. Enid Pub. Schs., 1964—. Served with AUS, 1940-45, 50-52. Decorated Silver Star, Bronze Star medal with oak leaf cluster. Mem. N.G. Assn. (div. pres. 1946-47), N.E.A., Am., Okla. assns. sch. adminstrs., Okla., Enid edn. assns. Presbyn. (deacon 1934-51, elder 1953-62, trustee 1969-72). Lion. Home: 1310 Ramona Dr Enid OK 73701 Office: 500 S Independence St Enid OK 73701

AUXIER, JOHN ALDEN, research co. exec.; b. Paintsville, Ky., Oct. 7, 1925; s. John Brown and Stella (Robinson) A.; B.S., Berea Coll., 1951; M.S., Vanderbilt U., 1952; Ph.D., Ga. Inst. Tech., 1972; m. Opal Wright, Feb. 21, 1948; children—Rebecca Gay, Barbara Gale. Mem. staff U. Tex. Primate Lab., Houston, 1952-55; with Oak Ridge Nat. Lab., 1955—, mem. staff health physics div., 1955-63, sect. chief health physics div., 1963-72, dir. health physics div., 1972—. Recipient Nat. Preparedness award Nat. Inst. Disaster Mobilization, 1962. Mem. Health Physics Soc. (Elda E. Anderson award 1963), A.A.A.S., Am. Phys. Soc., Scientists and Engrs. for Appalachia (1st pres. 1969-70). Home: 109 Wimberly Lane Oak Ridge TN 37830 Office: PO Box X Oak Ridge TN 37830

AVANT, WILLIAM EARL, dentist; b. Georgetown, S.C., Aug. 28, 1919; s. Landy Wood and Mary Ella (Grier) A.; A.B., Duke, 1954; student U. Ga., 1955-56; B.S., Med. Coll. Va. (A.D. Williams scholarship award; NIH student fellow), 1959, D.D.S., 1960; M.S. (and certificate prosthodontics), Ohio State U., 1967; m. Annie Eleanor Duke, June 2, 1951; children—Alan Barry, David Keith. Dental intern USPHS Hosp., Balt., 1960-61; gen. practice dentistry, Georgetown, Columbia, S.C., Union, S.C., 1961-64; instr. prosthodontics U. Md. Sch. Dentistry, 1964-65; grad. research asst., tchr. Ohio State U. Coll. Dentistry, 1965-67; individual practice orthodonitcs, Columbia, S.C., 1967—. Served with USNR, 1940-45. Tng. fellow Nat. Inst. Dental Research, 1965-67. Mem. Am. Assn. Orthodontists (certificate 1970), Am., S.C., Greater Columbia dental assns., So. Soc. Orthodontists, S.C. Orthodontic Assn., Central Dist. Dental Soc., Phi Beta Kappa, Omicron Kappa Upsilon, Sigma Zeta, Alpha Sigma Chi. Methodist. Contbr. articles to profl. jours. Home: 8004 Pinelake Rd Columbia SC 29204 Office: 2827 Millwood Av Columbia SC 29205

AVEN, ALEXANDER PHIPPS, mgmt. cons. exec.; b. San Antonio, Aug. 23, 1929; s. William Ralph and Rhoma (Phipps) A.; B.S., U. Okla., 1951; M.B.A., Harvard, 1955; m. Camilla Lytle, Dec. 26, 1951; children—William Cobb, Margaret Farrar. Geologist, Brit. Am. Oil Producing Co., Denver, Casper, Wyo., 1951-55, Continental Oil Co., 1955-57; v.p., dir. Eason Oil Co., Oklahoma City, 1957-64; petroleum cons., 1964-69; sr. partner Resource Analysis & Mgmt. Group, Oklahoma City, 1969—; dir. Hugh Breeding, Inc., Computer Mgmt. Corp., Bandera, Inc., Internat. Pacific Exploration Co. Ltd., Tolbert Co. Asso. bus. Oklahoma City U., 1964-71; cons. to adminstr. NASA, 1966-70; vice chmn. Okla. Energy Adv. Council; gov.'s rep. Nat. Energy Symposium. Mem. alumni adv. council Sch. Geology and Geophysics, U. Okla. Served with USAF, 1955-57. Mem. Am. Assn. Petroleum Geologists, Am. Assn. Petroleum Landmen, Am. Soc. Photogrammetry. Democrat. Episcopalian. Clubs: Economic of Okla. (pres. 1973-74), Men's Dinner, Beacon, Harvard Business School Oklahoma (pres. 1965; dir. 1964-67) Oklahoma City Golf and Country; University (Washington). Home: 1213 Larchmont Lane Oklahoma City OK 73116 Office: First Nat Center Oklahoma City OK 73201

AVEN, HILREY LEON, agrl. co. exec.; b. Plainview, Tex., Sept. 13, 1920; s. Alonzo Lester and Mabel Estell (King) A.; B.S., West Tex. State U., 1943; m. Mary Lou Allmon, June 26, 1949; children—Richard D., Hilrey Lewis, Michael Alan, Joycelyn. Sec., treas. Big T Pump Co., Inc., Hereford, Tex., 1956-66, pres., 1966—; sec. Big Tex Cattle & Grain Inc., Hereford, 1969—. Pres., Hereford Sch. Bd., 1971-72, mem., 1972-73, sec., 1973. Served from ensign to lt. comdr., USNR, 1943-46. Decorated Bronze Star. Named Hon. Farmer of Yr. Hereford chpt. Future Farmers Am., 1972. Mem. Hereford C. of C. (v.p. 1966-67). Lion (1st v.p. Hereford Club 1967-68). Home: 230 Ranger St Hereford TX 79045 Office: New York St Hereford TX 79045

AVERA, DAVID SANDER, JR., mech. engr.; b. Winston-Salem, N.C., Feb. 24, 1931; s. David Sander and Jessie (Davis) A.; student N.C. State U., 1949-50; B.S., Duke, 1954; m. Margaret Elaine Williams, Oct. 3, 1953; children—Sarah Elizabeth, Nancy Sander, Mary Caroline. Pres., owner Candor Co., Inc., Myrtle Beach, S.C., 1950—. Served to 1st lt. USAF, 1954-56. Mem. I.E.E.E., Nat. Soc. Profl. Engrs., Electronic Reps. Assn., Mfrs. Agts. Nat. Assn. Home: Box 447 Mt Gilead Murrells Inlet SC 29576 Office: PO Box 2220 Myrtle Beach SC 29577

AVERILL, JOHN MONTAGUE, aerospace and mech. engr., farmer; b. Columbus, Ga., Apr. 9, 1937; s. John Sylvester and Lula Moore (Hester) A.; B.S. in Mech. Engring., Auburn U., 1959; m. Sally Virginia Saliba, Dec. 22, 1961; children—John Montague, Julianna Saliba. Mech. engr. service engring. div. Warner Robins Air Logistics Center, Robins AFB, Ga., 1959-63, aerospace engr., 1963—, air force chief structural engr. for C-130 aircraft, 1967—. Owner, operator Averill Farms, Dooly County, Ga., 1962—. Served with C.E., AUS, 1959-60. Registered profl. engr., Ala. Mem. Pi Tau Sigma, Sigma Pi. Methodist. Home: Drayton Rd Byromville GA 31007 Office: WRALC/MMEAI Robins AFB GA 31098

AVERITT, FRANKLIN MURPHY, lawyer; b. Fayetteville, N.C., Dec. 12, 1911; s. Herschel Strange and Cornelia (Culbreth) A.; B.A., Wake Forest Coll., 1932, LL.B., 1936; m. Carolyn Wooten Council, Feb. 1, 1936; children—Cornelia A. (Mrs. Charles Sugg Fox), Franklin M., Carolyn Council. Tchr. pub. schs. Columbus County (N.C.), 1932-34; admitted to N.C. bar, 1936; gen. practice law Fayetteville, 1936—. Mem. Gen. Assembly of N.C., 1945-49. Mem. Am., N.C. bar assns. Democrat. Episcopalian. Club: Highland Country. Home: 303 Sylvan Rd Fayetteville NC 28305

AVERRE, CHARLES WILSON III, plant pathologist; b. Castilla, Honduras, June 3, 1932 (parents Am. citizens); s. Charles Wilson, Jr. and Margaret Elizabeth (Frazier) A.; B.S., N.C. State U., 1955, M.S., 1960; Ph.D., Purdue U., 1963; m. Bess Lenora Peeler, Aug. 20, 1955; children—Charles Wilson IV, Alice Louise. Research dept. Standard Fruit Co., Honduras, 1955-56; research, asst. prof. plant pathology U. Fla., Homestead, 1963-66, U. Ga., Griffin, 1967-68; asso. prof. plant pathology N.C. State U., Raleigh, 1968—. Pres., Internat. Biol. Services, Inc., 1970-73. Chmn., Pre-Sch. Center for Retarded Children, 1966. Served with AUS, 1956-58. Mem. Am. Phytopath. Soc., N.C. Acad. Scis., Blue Key, Gamma Sigma Delta. Presbyn. (deacon, elder). Asso. editor Phytopathology, 1973—; sect. editor Fungicide-Nematicide Tests, 1971—. Home: 1205 Imperial Rd Cary NC 27511 Office: Dept Plant Pathology NC State U Raleigh NC 27607

AVERY, FREDERICK FIFIELD, beverage co. exec.; b. Peoria, Ill., Oct. 8, 1930; s. N. Kirk and Elisabeth (Fifield) A.; B.A. in Econs., Williams Coll., 1952; M.B.A. in Marketing, U. Wis., 1953; m. Joan Abbey Oldberg, Sept. 7, 1956; children—Cynthia, Kirk, Karen. Group mgr. Marshall Field & Co., Chgo., 1953-57; various brand mgr. positions Procter & Gamble Co., Cin., 1957-65; mgr. marketing Folger Coffee Co., Kansas City, Mo., 1965-69; pres. ENRG Internat., Mpls., 1969-70; v.p., gen. mgr. Dr. Pepper Corp. Bottling Plants, Dallas, 1970-73; exec. v.p. Dr. Pepper Co., Dallas, 1973—; dir. Dr. Pepper Bottling Co. (Dallas, Waco, Tex., Ft. Worth, San Antonio), S.W. Fountain Supply Co. (Dallas). Chmn. gov.'s invitation com. Dallas Salute to Vietnam Vets., 1973—. Mem. Aerobics Inst., Beta Theta Pi. Presbyn. Rotarian. Clubs: Sales and Marketing Executives (dir.), Dallas Athletic, Lancers, Willow Bend (Dallas). Home: 4407 Melissa Lane Dallas TX 75229 Office: Dr Pepper Co 5523 E Mockingbird Lane Dallas TX 75222

AVERY, GORDON BENNETT, pediatrician, neonatologist, educator; b. Beirut, Lebanon, Dec. 10, 1931 (parents Am. citizens); s. Bennett Franklin and Margaret Anne (Scales) A.; grad. Phillips Acad., 1949; A.B. cum laude, Harvard, 1953; M.D., U. Pa., 1958, Ph.D., 1959; m. Ruth Elizabeth Butler, June 12, 1954; children—Melody Anne, Wendy Jean, Heidi Elizabeth. Intern, U.S. Naval Hosp., Bethesda, Md., 1958-59; resident, 1959-61; chief pediatrics U.S. Naval Hosp., Quantico, Va., 1962-63; dir. newborn service Children's Hosp., Washington, 1963—, chief embryology lab., 1963—; prof. child health and devel. George Washington U. Sch. Medicine, 1971—. Cons. Howard U., Nat. Inst. Child Health and Devel., Walter Reed Army Hosp., Holy Cross Hosp. Mem. mental retardation research and tng. com. Nat. Inst. Child Health and Human Devel., 1968-71. Served with M.C. USNR, 1958-63. Recipient Lederle Research award, 1954; Rose Meadow Leavensen prize in cancer research, 1957; O.H. Perry Pepper prize for clin. and research achievement, 1958. Diplomate Am. Bd. Pediatrics. Mem. Soc. for Pediatric Research, Am. Acad. Pediatrics (vice chmn. Washington chpt. 1971-73, nat. com. on disaster and emergency medicine 1973—), Dist. Med. Soc. (child welfare com. 1969, chmn. 1970), Alpha Omega Alpha. Editorial reviewer Pediatrics, 1968—. Home: 7801 Winterberry Pl Bethesda MD 20034 Office: Children's Hosp 2125 13th St NW Washington DC 20009

AVERY, PARNELL NAPOLEON, surgeon; b. Henderson, N.C., Feb. 18, 1931; s. Napoleon and Hazel (Bing) A.; B.S., Va. State Coll., 1952, M.S., 1958; M.D., Meharry Med. Coll., 1962; m. Gloria Magdalene Reid, July 12, 1954; children—Natalie Sherena, Sibyl Charlene, Vida Letitia. Tchr. biology Burley High Sch., Charlottesville, Va., 1954-56, Carver High Sch., Chesterfield, Va., 1957; intern Hubbard Hosp. of Meharry Med. Coll., Nashville 1962-63, extern, summer 1965, resident surgery, 1966-70; extern Walter Reed Army Hosp., summer 1964; resident surgery USPHS Hosp., Seattle, 1967-68; clin. instr. Meharry Med. Coll., 1969-71; chief dept. surgery Riverside Gen. Hosp., Houston; mem. staff hosps., Houston. Served as capt. M.C., AUS, 1952-54. Decorated Bronze Star. Fellow Am. Geriatric Soc., Am. Soc. Abdominal Surgeons, Internat. Acad. Proctology, Am. Coll. Emergency Physicians; mem. A.M.A., Nat. Med. Assn., Harris County, Old North State, R.F. Boyd med. socs., Houston Med. Forum, Internat. Platform Assn., Omega Psi Phi, Omega Psi Phi. Contbr. arcitles to profl. jours. Home: 4014 Woodmont Dr Houston TX 77045 Office: 8109 Cullen Blvd Houston TX 77051

AVERY, ROBERT BRUCE, physician; b. Alamo, Tenn., June 14, 1938; s. Harry Smith and Rebecca Sue (Fleming) A.; B.S., U. Tenn., 1959, M.D., 1962; m. Shirley Bannister, June 18, 1960; children—David, Andrew, Daniel. Rotating intern U. Mich. Med. Center, 1962-63, resident internal medicine, 1963-66, hematology-oncology fellow, 1966-68; instr. medicine U. Mich., 1967-68; practice medicine, specializing in hematology and oncology, Knoxville, Tenn., 1970—; asso. prof. medicine U. Tenn. Meml. Research Center; mem. staff U. Tenn. Hosp., St. Marys Meml. Hosp., Ft. Sanders Profl. Hosp., E. Tenn. Baptist Hosp., E. Tenn. Childrens Hosp. Served to maj. USAF, 1968-70. Mem. A.C.P., Am. Soc. Hematology, A.M.A., Tenn. Med. Assn., Knoxville Acad. Medicine, Am. Soc. Clin. Oncology, Am. Cancer Soc., Phi Kappa Phi, Alpha Omega Alpha. Home: 822 Westborough Dr Knoxville TN 37919 Office: 717 W Cumberland Av Knoxville TN 37902

AVILA, NEFTALI EHLERS, engring. cons.; b. Queretaro, Mexico, Mar. 6, 1912; s. Sixto and Raquel (Ehlers) A.; degree in Elec. and Mech. Engring., E.S.I.M.E., 1936, later postgrad.; m. Josefina Gomez Jurado, Dec. 28, 1940; children—Graciela (Mrs. Eduardo Castro), Efrain, Alicia (Mrs. Everardo Villalobos), Olivia, Lucrecia. Asst. engr. AEG Elec. Co., Mexico City, Mexico, 1936; elec. supr. Am. Smelting & Refining Co., Parral, Chihuahua, Mexico, 1937-43, Santa Barbara, Chihuahua, 1943-47, electromech. supr., Taxco, Guerrero, Mexico, 1954-63; master mechanic Industria Electrica de Mexico, Mexico City, 1948; chief electro-mech. inspection dept. Mexican Secretariat Hydraulic Resources, Mexico City, 1948-51, cons. engr. to dir. studies and projects, 1965-67; chief projects engr. Incontri, S.A. Contractor Co., Mexico City, 1951-54; asst. dir. Centros de Capacitacion para Trabajo Industrial Pub. Edn. Secretariat, Mexico City, 1963-64, dir., 1964-65, cons., 1965-67; mech. and elec. engr. Asarco Mexicana, S.A., Baja California Mexico, 1966-68, chief engr., 1968-71, cons. engr., 1971—. Registered profl. engr., Mexico. Mem. Mexican Assn. Elec. and Mech. Engrs., Coll. Mech. and Elec. Engrs., I.E.E.E. (sr. mem.). Home: 597 Mitla Mexico City DF 13 Mexico Office: 200 Baja California Mexico City DF 7 Mexico

AVINGER, WILLIAM HERSCHEL, coll. ofcl.; b. Brownwood, Tex., Aug. 6, 1915; s. Willie Barnard and Dora Ethel (Hutcherson) A.; B.A., Howard Payne Coll., 1937; M.A., U. Tex., 1943; Ed.D., Tex. Technol. U., 1965; m. Ora Juanita Hunt, Aug. 26, 1939; children—James Hershel, John Ross. Tchr., prin., Coleman, Tex., 1937-45; prin. high sch., Marfa, Tex., 1945-47; prin., supt., Electra, Tex., 1947-49; supt. schs., Plainview, Tex., 1949-53; dir. pupil personnel services, Lubbock, Tex., 1953-65; dir. grad. studies in edn. Abilene (Tex.) Christian Coll., 1965—. Dir. Lubbock Child Guidance Clinic, 1962-65; mem. Lubbock Community Planning Council, 1960-65. Mem. Am., West Tex. (pres. 1951-52) assns. sch. adminstrs., Internat. Assn. Pupil Personnel Workers (dir. 1964-65), Lubbock C. of C., Phi Delta Kappa. Mem. Ch. of Christ. Kiwanian (pres. Lubbock 1962). Home: 910 Harwell St Abilene TX 79601

AVIS, KENNETH EDWARD, educator; b. Elmer, N.J., June 3, 1918; s. Clinton F. and Clara U. (Urion) A.; B.S., Phila. Coll. Pharmacy and Sci., 1942, M.S., 1947, D.Sc., 1956; postgrad. U. Pa., 1950-52; m. Irma Jeanette Hildreth, Feb. 19, 1943; children—Carolyn Ruth (Mrs. Patrick P. Porter), John Neil, Beverly Jean. Asst., Phila. Coll. Pharmacy and Sci., 1946-48, instr., 1948-56, asst. prof., 1956-57, asso. prof., 1957-61; asso. prof. Coll. Pharmacy, U. Tenn. Med. Units, 1961-72, prof., dir. div. parenteral medications, dept. medicinal chemistry, 1972—. Cons., Jefferson Med. Coll. Hosp., 1948-61, Carron Products Co., Phila., 1958-67, VA Hosp., Memphis, 1962—, Dept. Health, Edn. and Welfare, Nat. Cancer Inst., 1966-68, FDA, 1968—. Mem. Nat. Formulary Com. on Specifications, 1970—. Pres. bd. trustees Evang. Christian Sch. Served with Hosp. Corps, USNR, 1942-45. Lederle Grad. Research fellow, 1945. Fellow Acad. Pharm. Scis.; mem. Am., Tenn., Mexican (hon.) pharm. assns., Memphis and Shelby County Pharm. Soc., Am. Soc. Hosp. Pharmacists, Parenteral Drug Assn. (dir., past pres.), Am. Assn. Colls. Pharmacy (Conf. Tchrs.), Rho Chi. Author: Parenteral Dosage Forms, An Annotated Bibliography for 1959-1963, 64-67, 69, 72. Contbr. chpts. to Remington's Pharmaceutical Sciences, 1965, 70; The Theory and Practice of Industrial Pharmacy, 1970. Home: 1312 Carol Dr Memphis TN 38116 Office: 26 S Dunlap St Memphis TN 38103

AWAD, JOHN MICHAEL, mental health adminstr.; b. Jackson, Miss., Jan. 4, 1934; s. Samuel and Lena (Katool) A.; B.A., Millsaps Coll., 1956; M.S.W., Tulane U., 1961; Ph.D., Fla. State U., 1972. Child welfare worker Miss. Dept. Pub. Welfare, Greenville, 1959-60; caseworker Family Counseling Center, Mobile, Ala., 1961-63; asst. planning coordinator Miss. Mental Health and Retardation Planning Program, Jackson, 1963-66; chief social work cons. Fla. Div. Mental Health, 1966-68, adminstr. mental health program grants, 1968-70, dep. dir., 1970—; cons. in field. Served with AUS, 1956-58. Mem. Nat. Assn. Social Workers, Acad. Certified Social Workers, Millsaps Coll. Alumni Assn., (dir. 1962-64, v.p. 1965-66), Kappa Sigma. Episcopalian. Home: 410 Victory Garden Dr Tallahassee FL 32301 Office: 1323 Winewood Blvd Tallahassee FL 32301

AXBERG, DONALD EDWARD, food co. exec.; b. Lincoln, Neb., Dec. 21, 1932; s. George Theodore and Alta Margaret (Butts) A.; B.S. in Bus. Adminstrn., U. Neb., 1958, M.B.A. (Regents scholar), 1959; postgrad. Northwestern U., 1961-62, Purdue U., 1962-64, U. Minn., 1967-69; m. Mary Lou Richie, June 30, 1957; children—William Christopher, Thomas Charles, John R. Auditor, Gen. Mills, Inc., Chgo., 1959-61, plant personnel mgr., Chgo., 1961-65, div. tng. mgr., Mpls., 1965-66, personnel mgr. mfg. div., 1966-68, div. controller, 1968-69, v.p. finance and personnel Goodmark div., Raleigh, N.C., 1969—. Instr. econs. U. Neb., 1958-59; partner Reynco Assos., Raleigh, 1972—; dir., sec. United Investors of Chapel Hill, Inc. (N.C.), 1971—. Chmn., Crusade of Mercy, South Chgo., 1965. Active Young Republicans of Ill., 1960-64; block capt. Rep. party, Minn., 1966, 67. Bd. dirs. Jr. Achievement. Served with AUS, 1951-54. Mem. Raleigh C. of C., Delta Sigma Pi. Roman Catholic. Kiwanian, K.C., Lion. Club: Raleigh Racquet. Author tech. and tng. manuals for employer. Home: 1008 Pebblebrook Dr Raleigh NC 27609 Office: 3825 Barrett Dr Raleigh NC 27609

AXEL, JAMES FREDERICK, JR., TV news broadcaster; b. Grand Haven, Mich., Oct. 31, 1934; s. James Frederick and Violet (Reitz) A.; grad. Brown Inst., 1957; m. Leota Mildred Carter, Dec. 28, 1955; children—Jeff, Bobby, Jason. Announcer, chief engr. radio sta. WCHK, Canton, Ga., 1957-59; news editor radio sta WSB, Atlanta, 1959-62; with WAGA TV, Atlanta, 1962—, news anchorman, 1962-73, news broadcaster, comml. and narrative prodns., 1962—. Pres., Axel Diversified Services, 1962—. Trustee Protestant Radio and TV Center, Atlanta, 1971—. Served wit USNR, 1952-55. Recipient Quill award Sigma Delta Chi, 1971, A.P. awards for news Superiority, 1960-62, 65-69, 71. Mem. AFTRA (pres. 1967—), Sigma Delta Chi. Lutheran. Home: 2593 Flemington Rd NE Atlanta GA 30345 Office: 1551 Briarcliff Rd Box 4207 Atlanta GA 30302

AXTON, WILLIAM FITCH, educator; b. Louisville, Sept. 24, 1926; s. Edwin Dymond and Blanche Thompson (Miller) A.; B.A., Yale, 1948; M.A., U. Louisville, 1951; Ph.D., Princeton, 1961; m. Joanne Virginia Lewis, June 23, 1951 (dec. Aug. 1965); children—Blanche Miller, Lucy Riggs, Belle Sherlock; m. 2d, Anne Elizabeth Millard, Aug. 5, 1967. Instr. Brown U., Providence, 1957-61; asst. prof. U. Ky., Lexington, 1961-66, asso. prof. English, 1966-67; asso. U. Louisville, 1967-68, prof. English, 1968—, chmn. dept., 1971. Served with USNR, 1944-46, 51-53. Mem. Modern Lang. Assn., Victorian Soc., Victorian Soc. in Am. (adviser 1971-72), Dickens Soc. (pres. 1972), Tennyson Soc., Browning Soc., Browning Inst., Byron Soc., Ky. Hist. Soc. Clubs: Polo (Lexington); Harmony Landing Country, Filson (Louisville). Editor: Melmoth the Wanderer (C.R. Maturin), 1961; Circle of Fire: Dickens' Vision and Style and the Nineteenth Century Theater (W.F. Axton), 1966; asso. editor Dickens Studies Annual, 1969—; rev. editor Dickens Newsletter, 1969-72. Home: 2421 Cherokee Pkwy Louisville KY 40204

AYCOCK, BENJAMIN FRANKLIN, chemist; b. Washington, May 18, 1922; s. Benjamin Franklin and Lucy Belle (Robertson) A.; B.S., U. N.C. at Chapel Hill, 1942, M.S., U. Ill., 1945, Ph.D., 1947; m. Jane Chandler Williams, Sept. 6, 1948; children—Benjamin F., William D., Charles R., Thomas H., David F. Asst. prof. chemistry U. Wis.-Madison, 1947-50; with Rohm & Haas, Phila. and Huntsville, Ala., 1950-69, lab. head, Phila., 1952-59, sect. head, Huntsville, 1959-69; head chemistry dept., sr. research scientist Burlington Industries, Greensboro, N.C., 1969—. Asst. prof. U. Minn., summer 1950. Mem. Am., Swiss chem. socs., Phi Beta Kappa, Sigma Xi, Pi Mu Epsilon, Phi Lamba Upsilon, Alpha Chi Sigma. Patentee in field. Home: 2310 N Elm St Greensboro NC 27408 Office: Burlington Industries PO Box 21327 Greensboro NC 27420

AYCOCK, EZRA KENNETH, physician, state ofcl.; b. Pinewood, S.C., Mar. 23, 1927; s. Robert James and Helen B. (Geddings) A.; A.B., Duke, 1950; M.D., S.C. Med. Coll., 1954; M.P.H., Harvard, 1964; m. Mary Echo Cook, June 4, 1954; children—Doris Dawson, Ezra Kenneth. Intern Columbia (S.C.) Hosp., 1954-55; resident in pediatrics Childrens Hosp., Los Angeles, 1955-56, S.C. Med. Coll. Hosp., Charleston, 1956-57; practice medicine, specializing in pediatrics, Columbia, 1957-63; chief pediatrics depts. Baptist, Hosp., Columbia Hosp., Providence Hosp., 1957-63; asst. dir. Maternal and Child Health div. S.C. Bd. Health, 1963-65, also dir. Child Evaluation Clinics; dir. Charleston County Health Dept., 1965-66, S.C. health officer, 1967-73; commr. S.C. Dept. Health and Environmental Control, 1973—. Chmn. S.C. Child Devel. Council, 1971—. Served with USNR, 1944-46. Diplomate Am. Bd. Preventive Medicine, Am. Acad. Pediatrics (mem. S.C. chpt.). Fellow Am. Coll. Preventive Medicine; mem. Am., S.C. med. assns., Columbia, Charleston med. socs., S.C. Pediatric Assn., Am. (pres. so. br. 1972-73), S.C. (pres. 1970) pub. health assns., S.C. Mental Health Assn. (dir.), Assn. State and Territorial Health Officers (exec. com. 1970, sec. 1971-73, pres.-elect 1973-74), S.C. Assn. Retarded Children (dir.), State Employees Assn. (pres. Charleston County chpt. 1966-67), Alpha Omega Alpha. Episcopalian. Rotarian. Contbr. articles profl. jours. Home: 1401 Kathwood Dr Columbia SC 29206 Office: SC Dept Health and Environmental Control Columbia SC 29201

AYCOCK, WILLIAM FRANK, JR., newspaper pub. co. exec.; b. Selma, Ala., Jan. 6, 1909; s. William Frank and Mamie (Finlayson) A.; B.S., Sanford U., 1930; m. Margaret O'Dell, June 15, 1935; 1 dau., Peggy (Mrs. Malcolm L. Prewitt, Jr.). With Birmingham News Co. (Ala.), 1937-56; v.p., asst. to gen. mgr. Memphis Pub. Co., 1956-57, pres., bus. mgr., 1957—. Mem. exec. com. Future Memphis. Bd. dirs. Danny Thomas Memphis Classic Golf Tournament, Memphis Cotton Carnival Assn., Mid-South Fair, Better Bus. Bur.; adv. com. Baptist Meml. Hosp., Memphis; trustee So. Newspaper Pub. Assn. Found. Served as lt. comdr. USNR, World War II. Decorated Legion of Merit with V device, Air medal with gold star, Purple Heart. Mem. So. Newspaper Pubs. Assn. (past pres.), Navy League of Memphis (dir., life mem.), Pi Kappa Alpha. Baptist. Rotarian. Home: 50 Cherry Rd Memphis TN 38117 Office: 495 Union Av Memphis TN 38101

AYCOCK, WILLIAM JASPER, physician; b. Phoebe, Miss., Oct. 8, 1888; s. William Jefferson and Rosie (Wooten) A.; student Miss. Coll., 1906-07; M.D., U. Tenn., 1912; postgrad. Postgrad. Sch. N.Y., 1919, Tulane U., 1938; m. Marian Denley, June 12, 1919; children—Josephine (Mrs. R. E. Anderson), Bobbie Ruth (Mrs. Bernard Senter), Willie Rose (Mrs. R. L. Liddell), Nancy (Mrs. R. P. Rogers). Individual practice gen. medicine, Smithville, Miss., 1912-16, Derma, Miss., 1919-34, Calhoun City, Miss., 1934—. Pres. Sch. Bd., Agrl. Sch., Derma, Miss., 1924-34, Calhoun City Pub. Schs., 1934-47; col. Gov.'s Staff, 1942-50. Mem. Bd. of Aldermen, 1920-34. Trustee Houston Hosp., 1924-42. Served with inf. U.S. Army, 1917-18. Recipient Robins award Miss. Med. Soc., 1970. Mem. N.E. Miss. Med. Soc. (pres. 1928, 43). Baptist (deacon). Mason (32 degree, Shriner), Rotarian. Club: Country (Calhoun City). Home: Calhoun City MS 38916

AYENSU, EDWARD SOLOMON, plant biologist; b. Sekondi, Ghana, Aug. 28, 1935; B.A. (Ghana Govt. scholar), Miami U., Oxford, O., 1961; M.Sc. (Ghana Govt. scholar), George Washington U., 1963; Ph.D. (Ghana Govt. scholar), U. London, 1966; postgrad. on bot. histo-chemistry U. Cal. at Berkeley, 1967; m. Dinah Ameley. Asso. curator dept. botany Smithsonian Instn., Washington, 1966-69, curator, 1970—, chmn. dept. botany, 1970—. Vis. prof. U. Ghana, 1969—; mem. adv. panel for systematic biology NSF; mem. U.S. com. Internat. Union Biol. Scis. Trustee, InterFuture, N.Y.C. Fellow Ghana Acad. Arts Scis., Linnean Soc. London, Washington Acad. Scis.; mem. Bot. Soc. Am., Internat. Assn. Plant Taxonomy, West African, Ghana sci. assns., A.A.A.S., Am. Inst. Biol. Scis., Assn. for Tropical Biology (exec. dir. 1969-71), Bot. Soc. Wash., Internat. Soc. Tropical Ecology, Internat. Assn. Wood Anatomists, Assn. for Advancement Agrl. Scis. in Africa. Club: Cosmos (Washington). Author: Anatomy of the Monocotyledons, Dioscoreales, 1972; co-author Tropical Ecosystems in Africa and South America: A Comparative Review, 1973. Contbr. articles to profl. jours. Research on comparative anatomy and phylogeny of angiosperms, vascular architecture and histology of monocotyledons, tropical biology, behavior of fruit-eating bats. Home: 103 G St SW Washington DC 20024 Office: Nat Museum of Natural History Constitution at 10th St Washington DC 20560*

AYER, ANTHONY JENNEY, real estate broker; b. N.Y.C., Jan. 15, 1937; s. Frederick and Betty (Jenney) A.; B.A., Cornell, 1960; m. Roberta Still, Aug. 15, 1959 (div. Nov. 13, 1973); 1 dau., Jenney Cathern. Founder, partner Richard & Ayer Assos., Realtors, Frederiksted, St. Croix, 1960—. Mem. V.I. Real Estate Commn., 1969—, chmn., 1972, 73; treas. pres. V.I. Territorial Bd. Realtors, 1961-74, St. Croix Bd. Realtors, 1961-74. Vice pres., co-founder Frederiksted Civic Assn., 1966-74; pres. St. Croix Horse Show Assn., 1969; mem. V.I. Bd. Edn., 1970. Pres. bd. dirs. Estate Carlton Home Owners Assn., 1971-74; pres., chmn. bd. trustees Good Hope Sch., Frederiksted, 1966-74. Mem. Nat. Assn. Real Estate License Law Ofcls., St. Croix C. of C. (dir. 1972-74), St. Croix Orchid Soc. (pres. 1965), Sigma Alpha Epsilon. Rotarian. Home: 53 Prince St Frederiksted St Croix VI 00840 Office: 12 Strand St PO Box 754 Frederiksted St Croix VA 00840

AYERS, GAYLORD LEW, broadcast exec.; b. Madison, S.D., July 11, 1935; s. Milton Bernard and Virginia Dare (Thompson) A.; B.A., U. S.D., 1965, M.A., 1969; m. Brenda Gale Primm, June 20, 1970. Announcer, KYNT Radio, Yankton, S.D., 1956-57; continuity dir. KROX-TV, Rochester, Minn., 1957-58, KAYS-TV, Hays, Kan., 1958-59; prodn. dir. KORN-TV, Mitchell, S.D., 1959-64; producer-dir., operations dir. KUSD-TV, U. S.D., Vermillion, 1964-69; prodn. mgr. WDCN-TV, Nashville, 1969-70, program mgr., 1970—. Mem. So. Ednl. Communications Assn. (vice chmn. pub. television council). Club: University Flying (pres. Vermillion 1968-69). Home: 4900 Trousdale St Nashville TN 37220 Office: PO Box 12555 Nashville TN 37212

AYERS, JUDSON FREEMAN, lawyer; b. Greenwood, S.C., Mar. 17, 1933; s. Judson Freeman and Viola Malissa (Pitts) A.; A.B., U. S.C., 1954; J.D., U. Va., 1959; m. Mildred Ann Smith, Apr. 23, 1963; children—Jill Malissa, Heidi Lee, Judson Freeman. Admitted to Tenn. bar, 1959, S.C. bar, 1960; practiced in Chattanooga, 1959-60, in Greenwood, S.C., 1960—; mem. firm Watson, Ayers & Shaw, 1961—; magistrate Greenwood County, 1961-64. Mem. City Council, Greenwood, 1960-61; mem. S.C. Legislature, 1965-69; mem. S.C. Constl. Revision Study Com., 1968-69. Served with USNR, 1954-56. Mem. Am., S.C., Greenwood County bar assns., S.C., Am. trial lawyers assns. Democrat. Baptist. Mason, Moose, Lion. Home: North Hill Rd Chinquapin Greenwood SC Office: PO Drawer 799 Greenwood SC 29646

AYRES, LAURENCE THOMASON, urban planner; b. Aransas Pass, Tex., Dec. 4, 1913; s. Laurence Thomason and Priscilla Douglass (Lovell) A.; student U. Tex., 1934, U. N.C., 1957-59; B. Gen. Edn., U. Neb. at Omaha, 1960; m. Virginia Leisering, Feb. 10, 1938; children—Carol (Mrs. William Lawrence), Ann L., Nancy (Mrs. Nancy A. Rose). Distbr. Gulf Oil Co., Aransas Pass, 1936-40; asst. cashier, dir. First State Bank, Aransas Pass, 1940-42; commd. lt. U.S. Army, 1942, advanced through grades to col., 1960, ret., 1963; inf. comdr. Korea, 1954-55; dir. instrn., asst. commdt. Spl. Warfare Sch., Fort Bragg, N.C., 1956-60; adviser Capital Republic of Korea Div., Chor Won, 1961-62; exec. asst. emergency resources planning com. State of Tex., Austin, 1964-66, cons. state shelter planning, 1966—. Decorated Legion of Merit. Home: 3000 Susquehanna Lane Austin TX 78723 Office: Disaster Emergency Services Dept Pub Safety 5805 N Lamar St Austin TX 78773

AYRES, RICHARD, mech. engr.; b. England, Ark., Mar. 17, 1915; s. Gold and Georgia (Walker) A.; B.S. in Mech. Engring., U. Ark., 1936; married. Engr., Fuel Process Co., South Charleston, W.Va., 1937-40, E.I. du Pont de Nemours & Co., Inc., Charleston, 1940-42, Magnolia Petroleum Co., Dallas, 1942-46; engring. mgr. Rohm & Haas Co., Houston, 1946—. Councilman, City of West University Place (Tex.), 1961-65. Registered profl. engr., Tex. Mem. Nat., Tex. (state chmn. employment practices com. 1958-59, ins. adv. com. 1971-73) socs. profl. engrs., C. of C. Houston (water conservation com. 1969-70, 71-72, 73-74), Sigma Chi. Republican. Presbyn. Home: 2723 University Blvd Houston TX 77005 Office: PO Box 672 Deer Park TX 77536

AYSCUE, BILLY NEWCOMB, agrl. research adminstr.; b. Vance County, N.C., Jan. 29, 1937; s. Ira Morris and Virgie (Abbott) A.; B.S. in Agrl. Edn., N.C. State U., 1959; m. Nancy Ruth Mustian, July 16, 1960; children—Cynthia Lynn, William Randall. Tchr. vocational agr. South Edgecombe Sch., Pinetops, N.C., 1963-64; adminstrv. officer div. research stas. N.C. Dept. Agr., Raleigh, 1964-67; supt. Oxford (N.C.) Tobacco Research Sta., 1967-73; supt. Hort. Crops Research Sta., Clinton, N.C., 1973—. Mem. Oxford Zoning Bd., 1971-72. Served with USNR, 1959-63. Mem. N.C. Soc. Farm Mgrs. and Rural Appraisers, N.C. Employees Assn. Baptist. Lion (dir. 1970-72). Home: Route 5 Box 43 Clinton NC 28328 Office: Horticultural Crops Research Sta Route 5 Box 43 Clinton NC 28328

AZAR, KAY LOUIS, hearing aid co. exec.; b. Harrisburgh, Ill., May 23, 1927; s. Charles and Mary A. (Homsey) A.; student U. Ill., 1950; m. Elsie Wojtowicz, Nov. 23, 1961; children—Mark, Carla, Jason. In import-export bus., San Francisco, 1955-57, ins., Chgo., 1958-61; sales mgr. Beltone Hearing Aids Corp., Huntsville, Ala., 1962—; dir. Minicomp Corp. Vice chmn. Ala. Bd. Hearing Aid Dealers. Mem. Pres.'s Council on Handicapped, 1970—; mem. Area Council Handicapped, 1970—; chmn. Honor Am. Day with Gov. Wallace, 1973—. Served with USNR, 1945-46; with USAF, 1950-54. Recipient Pres.'s Cup, Beltone Electronic Corp., 1973. Mem. Ala. Hearing Aid Dealers (past pres., past dir.), Sertoma Speech and Hearing Assn. (chmn. 1969—), Theta Chi. Elk. Clubs: Sertoma (past dir., com. chmn.), Whitesburg Boat and Yacht (fleet capt., commodore, dir.). Home: 2305 Sockwell Dr Huntsville AL 35805 Office: 302 E Clinton Av Huntsville AL 35801

BABB, BARBARA CAROLINE, state bar exec.; b. Fountain Inn, S.C., Dec. 16, 1933; d. Victor Morgan, Jr. and Ida Kate (Morrison) Babb; student Sweet Briar Coll., 1951-53; B.A., U. N.C., 1959, postgrad., 1963, J.D., 1968. Admitted to S.C. bar, 1968, also Fed. Dist. Ct. bar; sec. Woodside div. Dan River Mills, Greenville, S.C., 1954-58, 60-65, indsl. and pub. relations artist, 1954-70; spl. instr. for prospective legal secs. Greenville Tech. Inst., 1969-70; exec. dir. S.C. Bar Assn., Columbia, 1970-71; exec. sec.-treas. S.C. State Bar, Columbia, 1970—; pvt. practice law, Fountain Inn, 1972—. Spl. cons. Appalachian Regional Commn., Greenville, 1970; mem. Chief Justice's Com. to Study S.C. Ct. System, 1970-71. Mem. Am. (real property sect.), S.C. bar assns., S.C. State Bar (com. to establish statewide lawyer referral service), Am. Judicature Soc., Nat. Assn. Bar Execs., Am. Hort. Soc., Met. Opera Guild, Smithsonian Instn. Presbyn. Home: 407 S Main St Fountain Inn SC 29644 Office: South Carolina Supreme Court Bldg PO Box 11297 Capitol Station Columbia SC 29211

BABB, HERBERT EUGENE, coll. dean; b. McDonough, Ga., Aug. 25, 1922; s. Archie Tye and Maud Alma (Foster) B.; student West Ga. Coll., 1939-41; B.A., Emory U., 1943; M.S., Ph.D., U. Ky., 1955; m. Evelyn Marie Riley, Oct. 30, 1948; children—Franklin Tye, Mary Riley. Claims adjuster Liberty Mut. Ins. Co., Roanoke, Va., 1947-50; sr. psychologist Milledgeville (Ga.) State Hosp., 1955-57; instr. U. Ky., Lexington, 1959; asst. prof. Queens Coll., Charlotte, N.C., 1957-58, asso. prof., head dept., 1958-61, prof., dean coll., 1961-70; dir. programs N.C. Leadership Inst., Greensboro, 1970-71, v.p., 1971-73; vis. prof. Guilford Coll., Greensboro, part-time, 1971-72; dean of faculty Coker Coll., Hartsville, S.C., 1973—. Recipient scholarship K.T., Masonic Order, 1941. Mem. Am. Psychol. Assn., Zeta Sigma Pi, Pi Sigma Alpha. Democrat. Methodist. Rotarian (bd. dirs. 1967-70). Home: Route 2 Box 432G Hartsville SC 29550

BABBITT, MILTON FREDERICK, architect; b. Aberdeen, S.D., Sept. 4, 1940; s. Harry Z. and Alice P. (Pederson) B.; B.Arch. with honors, U. Tex., 1963; m. Judith L. Knecht, Mar. 6, 1965. Architect, Ford, Powell & Carson, San Antonio, 1965—, prin., 1972—. Bd. dirs. Friends of McNay, McNay Art Inst., San Antonio. Mem. A.I.A., Tau Sigma Delta. Prin. archtl. works include Lamplighter Sch., Dallas, Brown Wing, McNay Art Inst., San Antonio, Site Planning and Devel., U. Tex., San Antonio, Lang Galleries, McNay Art Inst., San Antonio. Home: 205 Redwood St San Antonio TX 78209 Office: 528 King William St San Antonio TX 78204

BABCOCK, ROBERT EARL, coll. dean; b. Chgo., Oct. 10, 1937; s. Earl and Elizabeth Ruth (Wilson) B.; B.S., U. Okla., 1959, M.S., 1962, Ph.D., 1964; m. Grace Elizabeth Harmon, June 11, 1959; children—Robert Earl, John Brook (dec.), David Benjamin. Sr. research engr. Esso Prodn. Research Co., Houston, 1964-65; faculty U. Ark., Fayetteville, 1965—, asso. prof. chem. engring., 1968—, asst. dean for research, dir. water resources research center, 1971—. Juvenile probation officer, 1969—; chmn. Washington County Community Foods Program, 1970-73; mem. adv. bd. Salvation Army, 1972—. Mem. Am. Inst. Chem. Engrs., Soc. Petroleum Engrs., Am. Water Resources Assn. (pres. Ark. sect. 1972-73). Home: 2100 Manor Dr Route 9 Fayetteville AR 72701

BABELAY, EDWIN FRANK, engr.; b. Knoxville, Tenn., June 6, 1916; s. Vincent (dec.) and Cleo (Adair) B.; B.S. in Agr., U. Tenn., 1939; m. Mary Whitehead Babelay, Mar. 13, 1945; children—Mary Elizabeth (Mrs. Robert Nicholas), Cleo Margaret, Edwin Frank. Engr., Tri-County Electric Membership Corp., Lafayette, Tenn., 1939-40; instr. U. Tenn., Knoxville, 1940-41; sanitation engr. City Knoxville, 1941-42; with Union Carbide Corp., Oak Ridge, Tenn., 1944—, devel. engr., 1950-54, sr. devel. engr., 1954-60, dept. head, 1960-70, asso. div. dir., 1970—. Served with USAF, 1942-44. Registered profl. engr., Tenn. Mem. Tenn. Soc. Profl. Engrs. Home: Route 27 Knoxville TN 37918 Office: PO Box P Oak Ridge TN 37830

BABER, JAMES PENDLETON, lawyer; b. Columbia, Va., July 29, 1936; s. Frank Howard and Mary Tyler (Baker) B.; B.A., U. Richmond, 1958; LL.B., U. Va., 1961; m. Carolyn Rudd Stonnell, June 14, 1958; children—Clayton Anderson, Catherine Shepherd, Courtenay James. Admitted to Va. bar, 1961; practiced in Cumberland, Va., 1961—; commonwealth's atty., Cumberland County, Va., 1968—; dir. Bank Powhatan, S. B. Cox, Inc. Pres. Central Va. chpt. Va. Mus. Fine Arts, 1968—. Bd. dirs. Va. Horse Shows Assn., 1961-64. Mem. Am. Bar Assn., Va. State Bar (mem. 4th dist. ethics com. 1970-71), Commonwealths Attys. Assn. Va., Fifth Judicial Circuit Bar Assn. (pres. 1968-70), Phi Delta Theta, Phi Delta Phi. Democrat. Methodist. Club: Wedgewood Country (Farmville, Va.). Home: Doubletree Farm Cumberland VA 23040 Office: Box 63 Cumberland VA 23040

BACHI, MICHAEL MARIO, artist, educator; b. Genoa, Italy, Mar. 1, 1920 (parents Am. citizens); s. Angelo Luigi and Alcisa (Cardinale) B.; B.A., Oklahoma City U., 1951; M.F.A., U. Okla., 1953, postgrad., 1953; postgrad. Southeastern State Coll., Durant, Okla., 1954, Instituto de Allende, San Miguel De Allende, Gt., Mexico, 1964; m. Mable Naomi Baker, Apr. 5, 1947. Tchr. art McAlester (Okla.) Jr. and Sr. High Schs., 1953-56; prof., head dept. art Rio Grande (O.) Coll., 1956-57; asst. prof. art Wis. State Coll., Superior, 1957-60; asst. prof. art Chadron (Neb.) State Coll., 1960-62; asso. prof. art Central State U., Edmond, Okla., 1962—, mem. faculty governance com., 1968-69, senator Faculty Senate, 1969-70; exhibited in one man shows Henson Gallery, Yukon, Okla., 1966, Ballet Theatre Sch., Oklahoma City, St. Pauls Cathedral, Oklahoma City, 1968; exhibited in group shows Philbrook Mus., Tulsa, 1953, Okla. U. Show at Forum Gallery, N.Y.C., 1954, Tweed Gallery, Duluth, Minn., 1959, galleries Superior, Wis., 1958, Norman, Okla., 1963, Yukon, 1966, Oklahoma City, 1967. Faculty Show, Okla. Sci. and Arts Found., 1965, Okla. Painting and Sculpture Biennial, 1971, Balcony Art Gallery, Oklahoma City, 1971; executed mural Midland Coop. Supermarket, Superior, 1959; tchr. water color Okla. Sci. and Art Found. Faculty, 1965-66. Mem. Gov.'s Council on Arts and Humanities, 1966. Served with USAAF, 1941-45. Decorated Bronze Star medal with five clusters. Mem. Contemporary Art Found. of Oklahoma City, Am. Assn. U. Profs. (exec. com. local chpt.), Kappa Pi, Delta Phi Delta. Democrat. Home: 3700 Mason Hills Dr Edmond OK 73034

BACHMAN, MELVIN NORMAN EMIL, electronic engr.; b. Belleville, Ill., Apr. 23, 1925; s. Henry Charles and Frances Elizabeth (Kehrer) B.; student Utah State U., 1943, Regis Coll., Denver, 1958, U. Ariz., 1957-58, U. Ala., 1962-64; m. Dorothy Elizabeth Fields, Apr. 30, 1972; children—Norman E., Patrick M., Dianne; stepchildren—Cynthia M. (Mrs. Jeffery Cowan), George F., Susan M. Electronic engr. Frederick Research Corp., Bethesda, Md., 1954-58; group engr. Martin Co., Denver, 1958-62; gen. engr., supervisory electronic engr. Dept. Army, Redstone Arsenal, Ala., 1962-73, on spl. assignment Hdqrs. U.S. Army in Europe, Heidelberg, Germany, 1973—; owner, mgr. Bachman Television Co., Silver Spring, Md., 1948-54. Dist. commr. Tennessee Valley council Boy Scouts Am., 1970-71. Served with USMCR, 1942-48; PTO. Mem. I.E.E.E. Contbr. articles to tech. jours. Home: Box 256 Madison AL 35758 Office: Hdqrs US Army Europe ODCSI PDN APO NY 09403

BACK, WILLIAM TECUMSEH, hydrogeologist; b. East St. Louis, Ill., Aug. 9, 1925; s. Normal Earl and March May (McReynolds) B.; A.B., U. Ill., 1948; postgrad. U. Colo., 1948-49; M.S., U. Cal. at Berkeley, 1956; M.P.A. (Ford Found. fellow), Harvard, 1957; Ph.D., U. Nev., 1969; m. Constance Albaugh, June 15, 1950; children—William Scott, Peter Wade, David Bishop, Nancy Daniels. Geologist U.S. Geol. Survey, Sacramento, 1950-54, research hydrogeologist, Washington, 1954—. Lectr. Am. U., Washington, 1957-59; cons. FAO to Israel, 1964; adviser US-AID to Pakistan, 1971, UN devel. program, Costa Rica, 1971. Fellow Geol. Soc. Am. (O.E. Meinzer award 1973); mem. Geochem. Soc., Am. Geophys. Union, A.A.A.S. Club: Cosmas (Washington). Contbr. articles and chpts. to profl. jours. and books. Home: 4100 Nelly Custis Dr Arlington VA 22207 Office: US Geol Survey Reston VA 22092

BACKER, WARREN HOWARD ALONZO, food co. exec.; b. New Orleans, Jan. 22, 1930; s. Albert Fredrick and Leota Emily (Alonzo) B.; student Soule Coll., 1946-47; B.A., Tulane U., 1951; m. Jean C. Smith, Sept. 18, 1954; children—Karen E., Cheryl E., Warren Howard Alonzo. Pres., Backer-LeJeune, Inc., New Orleans, 1972—, also dir.; dir. Nat. Bank Commn., Backer Realty Co. Mem. grad. sch. adv. bd. Tulane U., 1972—; mem. bd. City Park, New Orleans, 1965—. Served with USAF, 1950-52. Mem. Nat. (nat. dir. 1964-67), New Orleans (pres. 1968) food brokers assns. Rotarian. Home: 7441 Canal Blvd New Orleans LA 70124 Office: PO Box 9279 Metairie LA 70055

BACKSTROM, MARTHA CAROLYN MURPHREE (MRS. JAMES WALTON BACKSTROM), educator; b. Pittsboro, Miss., Aug. 20, 1916; d. Stanley Thomas and June Elizabeth (Byars) Murphree; B.A. cum laude, Miss. State Coll. for Women, 1937; m. James Walton Backstrom, May 22, 1938; 1 son, James Walton. Tchr. pub. schs., Greene County, Miss., 1937-64; coordinator Elementary and Secondary Edn. Act. Program, Greene County Sch. Dist., Leakesville 1966—. Sec., Backstrom Timber Co. Mem. fund raising coms. Nat. Found., Cancer Fund, A.R.C., Tb Soc.; mem. Leakesville Beautification Com., 1966; mem. Inter-Alumni Council for Instns. Higher Learning in Miss. Mem. D.A.R. (chpt. chmn. 1963-71, state chmn. 1965-68, sec. 1966-69, chpt. vice regent 1969-71, chpt. regent 1971—), Miss State Coll. for Women Alumnae Assn. (dir. 1967-69), Murphree Geneal. Soc., Miss., Calhoun County hist. socs., Miss., Nat. edn. assns., Pi Gamma Mu. Methodist; also active Baptist Ch. Clubs: Three Arts (pres. 1941-42, 65-66)(Leakesville). Home: PO Box 108 Leakesville MS 39451 Office: Dept Edn Greene County Sch Dist Leakesville MS 39451

BACON, DONALD CONRAD, journalist; b. Jacksonville, Fla., Jan. 15, 1935; s. Francis H. and Myrtis (Gunter) B.; B.S. in Journalism, U. Fla., 1957 ; m. Barbara Lee Barnwell, June 22, 1957; 1 dau., Elizabeth. Staff writer Wall St. Jour., 1957-61; Ford Found. Congl. fellow, 1961-62; with Washington Evening Star, 1962-63; congl. corr. Newhouse Nat. News Service, Washington 1963-68, White House corr., 1968—, sr. corr., 1971—. Congl. fellow Am. Polit. Sci. Assn.; mem. White House Corrs. Assn., Fla. Blue Key, Beta Theta Pi, Sigma Delta Chi. Club: Internat. Author: Congress and You, 1969; (with others) The New Millionaires, 1961. Home: 3514 Livingston St NW Washington DC 20015 Office: 1750 Pennsylvania Av NW Washington DC 20006

BACON, DONALD WALTER, bus. exec.; b. Cin., Aug 28, 1914; s. Frank B. and Laura (Claassen) B.; A.B., Antioch Coll., 1939; m. Lois Neuhart, June 8, 1946; children—Janet, Anne, David, Susan. With Lybrand, Ross Bros. & Montgomery, C.P.A.'s, Chgo., 1939-40; asst. budget dir. Studebaker Corp., South Bend, Ind., 1940-42; staff Office Comptroller Gen., Washington, 1946-53, Dept. Army, Washington, 1953-54; with Internal Revenue Service, 1954-71, regional commr., 1956-62, asst. commr., 1962-71; dir. taxes Gulf & Western Industries, Inc., Washington, 1971—. Served as lt. comdr. USNR, 1942-46. Mem. Am. Inst. C.P.A.'s, Mass. Soc. C.P.A.'s, Fed. Govt. Accountants Assn. (nat. pres. 1962-63), D.C. Inst. C.P.A.'s, Tax Execs. Inst., Internat. Fiscal Assn. Club: Internat. (Washington). Home: 1440 Cola Dr McLean VA 22101 Office: Gulf & Western Industries Inc Room 920 600 New Hampshire Av NW Washington DC

BACON, FRANKLIN CAMP, mining co. exec.; b. White Springs, Fla., July 30, 1919; s. Nathaniel Hunter and Elizabeth Brett (Camp) B.; A.B in Journalism, U. Ga., 1940; m. Marjorie Edna Caldwell, Feb. 28, 1942; children—Franklin Camp, Paul Caldwell, John Lee. Editorial asst. Douglas (Ga.) Enterprise, 1940; city reporter Columbus (Ga.) Enquirer, 1940-41; commd. 2d lt. USMC, 1941, advanced through grades to col., 1962; ret., 1967; mgr. pub. relations Freeport Sulphur Co., New Orleans, 1968—. Mem. Devel. Council, Sara Mayo Hosp., 1970-71. Bd. dirs., treas. La. Assn. for Mental Health, 1972-74. Decorated Legion of Merit, Bronze Star medal, Purple Heart. Mem. La. Assn. Broadcasters (asso. mem., dir. 1971—), Marine Corps Res. Assn. (pres. 1971-72, chmn. bd. New Orleans chpt.), Press Club New Orleans (v.p. 1969-70), Mil. Order World Wars (comdr. chpt. 1973-74). Home: 2725 Prancer St New Orleans LA 70114 Office: Box 61520 New Orleans LA 70161

BACON, JAMES LANGSTON, mech. engr.; b. Camden, Ark., Dec. 17, 1938; s. Edmond James and Annie Belle (Walker) B.; student So. State Coll., Magnolia, Ark., 1955-57; B.S., U. Ark., 1959, postgrad., 1972; m. Marsha Diane Winans, Dec. 28, 1962; 1 dau., Lori Beth. Engr., Pine Bluff (Ark.) Arsenal, 1960-61, 62-73; engr. Army Materiel Command program mgr. for demilitarization chem. materiel, Aberdeen Proving Ground, Md., 1973—. Bd. dirs., sec.-treas. Watson Chapel (Ark.) Water Assn., 1967-71. Served with AUS, 1961-62. Registered profl. engr., Ark. Mem. Am. Soc. M.E. (Ark. pres., 1968-69, certificate appreciation 1970, 71), Nat. Soc. Profl. Engrs., Am. Ordnance Assn., Am. Farm Bur., U. Ark. Alumni Assn. Home: Route 1 105 Suburbia Pine Bluff AR 71601 Office: Office of Program Mgr for Demilitarization Chem Materiel Attn AMX DC-T Aberdeen Proving Ground MD 21010

BACON, PHILLIP, geographer, educator, author; b. Cleve., July 10, 1922; s. Hollis Phillip and Emma (Schneider) B.; student The Citadel, 1940-41; A.B., U. Miami, 1946; M.A., George Peabody Coll. for Tchrs., 1951, Ed.D., 1955; m. Dorothy Willey; children—Laura Jane (Mrs. Robert C. Fraser), Phillip Everett. Tchr. social studies Castle Heights Mil. Acad., Lebanon, Tenn., 1946-47, Army and Navy Acad., Carlsbad, Cal., 1948-53; grad. asst. geography George Peabody Coll. for Tchrs., 1953-55, dean Grad. Sch. 1963-64; asst. prof. geography U. Pitts., 1955-57; vis. asst. prof. geography Columbia Tchrs. Coll., 1956-57, asso. prof., 1957-60, prof., 1960-63, 64-66; prof. geography U. Wash., Seattle, 1966-71, co-dir. tri-univ. project in elementary edn., 1967-71; prof. geography U. Houston, 1971—, chmn. dept. geography and anthropology, 1973—. Vis. prof. geography U. Colo., summer 1961, N.C. Central U., spring 1966, U. Tex., summer 1966; NSF vis. scientist, 1969-71. Mem. editorial adv. bd. World Book Ency., 1965—; bd. cons. World Book Atlas, 1965-70, chmn. area studies com., 1969—; cons. editor Golden Press, 1958-61; cons. book div. Time, Inc., 1960-69; cons. social sci. project Ednl. Research Council Am., 1962-70; mem. steering com. High Sch. Geography Project, 1965-70; cons. U.S. Office Edn., 1964—; mem. Wash. Social Studies Adv. Commn., 1968-71; curriculum cons. Served with USNR, 1942-45. Fellow Royal Geog. Soc., Am. Geog. Soc. N.Y.; mem. Assn. Am. Geographers, Nat. Council for Geog. Edn. (pres. 1966, Distinguished Service award 1974), N.E.A., Am. Assn. Higher Edn., Assn. Pacific Coast Geographers, Nat., Tex. councils social studies, Sigma Xi, Sigma Alpha Epsilon, Phi Delta Kappa, Kappa Delta Pi, Pi Gamma Mu. Presbyn. Clubs: Men's Faculty of Columbia; Mercer Island Country; Bay Area Racket. Author: Australia, Oceania, and the Polar Lands, 1961, North America, 1961; Golden Book Picture Atlas of the World, 6 vols., 1961; Children's Picture Atlas of the World, 1966; Children's Picture Atlas in Colour, 1966; (with Norman Carls and Frank E. Sorenson) Knowing Our Neighbors in the United States, 1966; Knowing Our Neighbors in the United States and Canada, 1966; Regions Around The World, 1970; (with R.R. Boyce) Towns and Cities, 1970; (with others) The United States and Canada, 1970; (with P.V. Greco) The Story of Latin America, 1970; Field Media Kit series, 1973; (with T.F. McGann and P.R. Rivera) People of the Americas, 1974. Editor: Focus on Geography, Key Concepts and Teaching Strategies, 1970; co-editor: Foundations of World Regional Geography Series, 1970—. Cons. editor Life Pictorial Atlas of the World, 1961, Jour. of Geography, 1967-70, Where and Why?, 1972. Co-dir. Field Elementary Social Studies Series. Contbr. chpts. to books and yearbooks, articles to profl. jours. Home: 1827 Saxony Ct Nassau Bay Houston TX 77058

BACON, WILLIAM ARTHUR, lawyer; b. Durant, Miss., Feb. 8, 1912; s. James Webster and Zouella (Guess) B.; LL.B., U. Miss., 1935; m. Carolee Meyer Pratt, Mar. 15, 1941; 1 son, William A. Admitted to Miss. bar, 1935; city atty., Durant, Miss., 1935-40; asst. U.S. dist. atty., So. Dist., Miss., 1942, 46; state bond atty., Miss., 1951—. Mem. Miss. Ho. of Reps., 1936-40. Pres. Crestview Home, 1957-64; pres. Miss. Children's Home Soc, 1964—; pres. Jackson YMCA 1963-64. Served as lt. USNR, 1942-46. Mem. Am., Miss., Hinds County (pres. 1959-60) bar assns., Jackson Photog. Soc. (pres 1957), Miss. State Bar (pres. 1970-71), Fed. Bar Assn., Am. Judicature Soc. Democrat. Episcopalian (vestryman). Clubs: Gulf States Camera (pres. council), Men's Y (pres. 1947); Kiwanis (pres. 1956), Jackson Country, River Hills (dir.). Home: 3909 Pinewood Dr Jackson MS 39211 Office: Bankers Trust Plaza Bldg PO Box 15 Jackson MS 39205

BADDERS, HURLEY EDMUND, hist. agy. dir.; b. Cedartown, Ga., June 21, 1931; s. Herald Edmund and Parilee (Parker) B.; grad. pub. high sch.; m. Barbara Ann Storey, Nov. 12, 1955; children—Barbara April, Parker Lanier. Asst. state news editor Anderson (S.C.) Ind., 1957-61, news dir., 1961-68; exec. dir. Pendleton Dist. Hist. and Recreational Commn., 1968—. Cons. several comml. firms. Mem. So. Travel Dirs. Council, 1970—; exec. bd. S.C. Fedn. Museums, 1971—; chmn. Appalachian Council Govts. Leisure Resources Com., 1972—. Bd. dirs. S.C. Travel Council; trustee Anderson Heritage, Inc. Served with USNR, 1951-53. Recipient award for news reporting S.C. Press Assn., 1960, award for in-depth reporting, 1963. Mem. Anderson Area C. of C. (tourism chmn. 1970), Am. Assn. Museums, Nat. Trust Hist. Preservation, Assn. State and Local History, Am. Booksellers Assn. Baptist. Elk. Author: Pendleton Historic District, 1973. Home: 2517 Lindale Rd Anderson SC 29621 Office: 125 E Queen St Pendleton SC 29670

BADER, FRANZ, gallery dir.; b. Vienna, Austria, Sept. 19, 1903; s. David and Elsa (Steindler) B.; ed. Vienna; m. Antonia Blaustein, Dec.2, 1928; m. 2d, Virginia Forman, July 31, 1971. Owner, Wallishausser Book Shop, Vienna; v.p., gen. mgr. Whyte Gallery, Washington, 1939-53;, pres. Franz Bader Gallery, Washington, 1953—; cons. for collectors, art appraisals for mus. and pvt. collectors. Mem. Print Council Am., Am. Book Sellers Assn., Friends of Music at Dumbarton Oaks, Mus. of Modern Art. Decorated Goldene Ehrenzeichen fuer Verdienste (Austria); Verdienstkreuz Erster Klasse (Germany). Club: George Washington Univ. Home: 2242 48th St NW Washington DC 20007 Office: 2124 Pennsylvania Av NW Washington DC 20037

BADKE, FRANK CHARLES, JR., equipment mfg. co. exec.; b. Cleve., Dec. 10, 1922; s. Frank Charles and Alta (Jordan) B.; student Ohio State U., 1940-42; B.S., Cleve. State U., 1949; m. Mary LaDonna Alexander, Aug. 5, 1944; children—Gregory Charles, Carol Gene. Asst. plant engr. Reliance Electric & Engring. Co., Cleve., 1941-44; plant engr. Universal Wire Spring Co., Bedford, O., 1949-58; asst. plant mgr. Hoover Ball & Bearing Co., Bedford, 1958-61; ind. indsl. cons., Cleve., 1961-65; v.p., gen. mgr. Victor Equipment Co., Denton, Tex., 1965—. Republican campaign organizer, 1964. Served with C.E., AUS, 1944-46. Registered profl. engr., Ohio, Tex. Mem. Dental Indsl. Assn. (chmn. 1968—), Cleve. Engring. Soc., Profl. Engring. Soc. Episcopalian. Contbr. articles to profl. jours. Patentee in field. Home: 1314 Mistywood Lane Denton TX 76201 Office: Airport Rd Denton TX 76201

BAER, ALFRED, physician; b. Strasbourg, France, Mar. 15, 1917; s. Arthur and Frances (Cohn) B.; student Sorbonne, U. Paris, 1937-39; A.B., Ohio State U., 1942; M.D., Johns Hopkins, 1945; m. Eva Rosenberg, Aug. 28, 1949; children—Barbary, Alan. Came to U.S., 1939, naturalized, 1946. Intern pathology Montefiore Hosp., N.Y.C., 1946; intern Lincoln Hosp., N.Y.C., 1945-46, resident, 1948-50; practice medicine, specializing in internal medicine and rheumatology, Washington, 1950—; mem. staffs George Washington U. Med. Center, Washington Hosp. Center; asso. clin. prof. medicine George Washington U. Sch. Medicine, Washington, 1966—. Bd. dirs., mem. med. adv. com. various times Arthritis and Rheumatism Assn. Met. Washington. Diplomate Am. Bd. Internal Medicine. Fellow A.C.P.; mem. A.M.A., Am. Rheumatism Assn., Am. Heart Assn., N.Y. Acad. Scis., Phi Beta Kappa. Home: 4400 Springdale St NW Washington DC 20016 Office: 730 24th St NW Washington DC 20037

BAER, CHARLES MICHAEL, exec. elec. engr.; b. Balt., Oct. 20, 1909; s. Charles Edward and Dorothy (Fuchs) B.; B.S. in Mil. Engring., U.S. Mil. Acad., 1932; grad. Nat. War Coll., 1950; m. Esther Debelius, Nov. 1, 1932; children—Charles Michael, Alan LeRoy, Esther Sandra (Mrs. Thomas R. Savoie). Commd. 2d lt. Signal Corps, U.S. Army, 1932, advanced through grades to brig. gen., 1957; signal officer 2d Army, Ft. Meade, Md., 1953-56; chmn. European mil. communications coordinating com., chmn. civil emergency communications planning com. NATO, Paris, 1956-59; comdt. U.S. Army Signal Sch. and comdg. gen. Ft. Monmouth, N.J., 1959-62; retired, 1962; European rep. G.T.&E. Co., 1962-64; with State Dept., 1965; asst. chief scientist Communications Satellite Corp., Washington, 1966—. Bd. dirs. Am. Club, Paris, 1963-64. Decorated Legion of Merit with oak leaf cluster. Sr. mem. I.E.E.E.; charter mem.

Armed Forces Communications Electronics Assn. Mason (Shriner). Club: Army-Navy (Washington). Home: 3864 N Chesterbrook Rd Arlington VA 22207 Office: 950 L'Enfant Plaza SW Washington DC 20024

BAER, GEORGE MARTIN, veterinarian; b. London, Eng., Jan. 12, 1936; s. Curtis Otto and Katherine Gertrude (Meyer) B.; came to U.S., 1940, naturalized, 1946; D.V.M., Cornell U., 1959; M.P.H., U. Mich., 1961; m. Maria Olga Lara, July 2, 1960; children—Katherine, Yvette, Isabella. Individual practice vet. medicine, Beaumont, Cal., 1959-60; with N.Y. State Dept. Health, 1961-63; acting chief Rabies Investigations Lab., Atlanta, 1963-64; chief Southwest Rabies Investigations Sta., Las Cruces, N.M., 1964-66; cons. Nat. Communicable Disease Center, Pan Am. Health Orgn., Mexico, 1966-69; chief lab. investigations sect. Viral Zoonoses br. Viral Diseases div. Bur. Epidemiology, Center Disease Control, Lawrenceville, Ga., 1969—. Mem. N.Y. Acad. Sci., Am. Pub. Health Assn. Home: 5462 Rosser Rd Stone Mountain GA 30083 Office: Box 363 Communicable Disease Center Lawrenceville GA 30245

BAER, HENRY, lawyer; b. Wissen a/Sieg, Germany, Dec. 30, 1930; s. Ernest and Anneliese (Bernstein) B.; came to U.S., 1940, naturalized, 1946; B.A., So. Meth. U., 1952, LL.B., 1955; m. Anne Marie Sanders, June 16, 1966; children—Lisa Ann, Henry Douglas. Admitted to Tex. bar, 1955; practiced in Dallas, 1957—; mem. firm Wynne & Wynne, Attys., 1957-60, Wynne, McKenzie, Jaffe & Tinsley, Attys., 1960-62, McKenzie & Baer, Attys., 1963— (all Dallas); theatrical agt. Don Meredith Prodns., Dallas, 1970—. Mem. Am., Tex., Dallas bar assns., Am. Contract Bridge Assn. (exec. sec., dir. dist. 16), Phi Beta Kappa. Home: 5512 Royal Crest Dallas TX 75201 Office: McKenzie & Baer 2222 LTV Tower Dallas TX 75201

BAER, MAX FRANK, charitable orgn. exec.; b. Frankfurt, Germany, Nov. 10, 1912; s. Bernard and Erna (Pollak) B.; came to U.S., 1921, naturalized, 1926; LL.B., Creighton U., Omaha, 1937, J.D., 1970; M.A., Columbia, 1942; Ed.D., George Washington U., 1947; m. Gertrude Smith, Feb. 14, 1967. Asst. exec. sec. Aleph Zadik Aleph, B'nai B'rith, 1934-37; nat. dir. B'nai B'rith Vocational Service, 1938-54; internat. dir. B'nai B'rith Youth Orgn., Washington, 1948—. Vis. lectr. Catholic U., George Washington U., Bucknell U., Marquette U. Mem. fed. adv. council Bur. Employment Security, 1948-58, cons., 1963-66; cons. Bur. Hearings and Appeals, Social Security Adminstrn., 1963-66, Dr. Max Baer Cultural Centre, Druze Village, Ussifiyeh, Israel. Mem. exec. com. World Consultative Com. on Jewish Youth Orgns. Mem. Am. Psychol. Assn., Nat. Assn. Social Workers, Acad. Certified Social Workers, Am. Guidance and Personnel Assn., Nat. Vocational Guidance Assn. (pres. 1950-51), Nat. Orgn. Children and Youth (vice chmn. council 1969-71), Phi Delta Kappa. Author: (with Edward C. Roeber) Occupational Information, 1951, 57, 64. Founding editor: Vocational Guidance Quar., 1951. Contbr. articles to profl. jours. Home: 4201 Cathedral Av NW Washington DC 20016 Office: 1640 Rhode Island Av NW Washington DC 20036

BAETZ, ERNEST ARTHUR, banker; b. San Antonio, Feb. 28, 1898; s. Max and Clara (Giesen) B.; student Wharton Sch. Finance and Commerce, U. Pa., 1916-17; m. Frances Helen Lucas, June 28, 1921; children—Dorothy (Mrs. Kenneth E. Jackson), Ernest Arthur, Jr., Barbara. Asst. cashier Bexar County Nat. Bank, San Antonio, chmn. bd., 1968—, pres., 1946—. Chmn. bd. San Antonio Portland Cement Co., 1968—, also dir.; dir. Roegelein Provision Co., San Antonio. Served with U.S. Army, 1917-18. Recipient Silver Beaver award Boy Scouts Am., 1955; citation Nat. Conf. Christians and Jews, 1967. Mem. San Antonio Zool. Soc. (sec. 1960). Mason (33 deg., Shriner), Kiwanian. Club: San Antonio Country. Home: 524 Tuxedo Av San Antonio TX 78209 Office: Travis and St Marys San Antonio TX 78291

BAFALIS, LOUIS ARTHUR, congressman; b. Boston, Sept. 28, 1929; s. Louis J. and Veska (Reenstierna) B.; A.B., St. Anselm's Coll., 1952; m. Mary Elizabeth Lund, Feb. 18, 1956; children—Renee Louise, Gregory Louis. Partner firm Kirk & Co., investment bankers, Palm Beach, Fla., 1970—; mem. Fla. Ho. Reps., 1964-66, Senate, 1966-70; mem. 93d Congress, 10th Dist. Fla. Vice-chmn. Palm Beach County A.R.C., 1963-67; hon. dir. South Fla. Fair and Expn., 1965-70; county chmn. Muscular Dystrophy Assn., 1970. Candidate for Gov. Fla., 1970; chmn. Republican Nat. Gov.'s Conf., 1968. Served to capt. AUS; Korea. Mem. North Palm Beach C. of C., Palm Beach Gardens Jaycees. Mason. Home: Cresciente 401 S 7150 Estero Blvd Fort Myers Beach FL 33931 Office: 1713 Longworth Bldg Washington DC 20515

BAGBY, WILLIAM RARDIN, lawyer; b. Grayson, Ky., Feb. 19, 1910; s. John Albert and Nano (Rardin) B.; A.B., Cornell U., 1933; LL.B., U. Mich., 1936; postgrad. Northwestern U., 1946-47; m. Mary Carpenter, Sept. 4, 1939; 1 son, John Robert. Admitted to Ky. bar, 1937, Ohio bar, 1952; practiced in Grayson, 1937-43; city atty., Grayson, 1939-41, judge, 1941-43; counsel U.S. Treasury, 1946-54; practiced law, Lexington, Ky., 1954—. Prof. law U. Ky., 1956-57; pub. Enquirer, Grayson, 1937-43. Mem. Lexington-Fayette County Bd. Adjustment, 1965—. Trustee Bagby Music Lovers' Found., N.Y.C.; bd. dirs. Blue Grass Trust for Historic Preservation. Served as lt. USNR, 1944-46. Mem. Am., Ky., Ohio, Fed. bar assns., Kappa Sigma, Democrat, Episcopalian, Rotarian. Club: Spindletop. Home: 228 Market St Lexington KY 40508 Office: First Nat Bldg Lexington KY 40507

BAGG, JAMES ERSKINE, JR., mag. editor; b. New Orleans, July 28, 1942; s. James Erskine and Odile Hood (Holland) B.; A.B. cum laude, Coll. William and Mary, 1964; M.A., Tufts U., 1968. Advt. copywriter Prentice-Hall, Englewood Cliffs, N.J., 1965-66; John Wiley & Sons, N.Y.C., 1966-67; teaching asst. English U. Tex. at Austin, 1968-70; advt. copywriter Winn-McLane Advt., Austin, 1970-71; editor, dir. advt. Tex. Pub. Employee, Austin, 1971-73; mng. editor Library Chronicle, Austin, 1973—. Mem. Internat. Assn. Bus. Communicators (v.p. programs 1972-73). Home: 2311 Wilke Dr Austin TX 78701 Office: Humanities Research Center U Tex Austin TX 78711

BAGGA, DAVINDERJIT KAUR, microbiologist; b. Amritsar, Punjab, India, Dec. 14, 1939; d. Jiwan Singh and Mahinder Kaur (Chhabra) Tucker; B.Sc. with honors, Punjab U., Chandighar, Punjab, India, 1959, M.Sc. with honors, 1961; M.S., U. Wis., Madison, 1963, Ph.D., 1968; m. Harmahinder Singh Bagga, Mar. 5, 1961; children—Smita, Ranjit Singh. Came to U.S., 1961, naturalized, 1973. Grad. research asst. dept. plant pathology U. Wis., Madison, 1964-68; asso. plant pathologist Delta br. Miss. Agrl. and Forestry Expt. Sta., Stoneville, 1968-71; bacteriologist Delta Health Center, Mound Bayou, Miss., 1972-73; vice pres. Soil Enterprise, Inc., Stoneville, Miss., 1973—. Founder, pres. India Women Club, Madison, Wis., 1963. Mem. Am. Phytopathol. Soc., Sigma Xi. Mem. Sikh religion. Home: 201 Lakeview Dr Leland MS 38756 Office: Soil Enterprise Inc Stoneville MS 38776

BAGGA, HARMAHINDER SINGH, plant pathologist; b. Amritsar, Punjab, India, Sept. 24, 1936; s. Karam Singh and Harbhajan (Sethi) B.; F.Sc. in Agrl. Sci., Punjab U., Chandigarh, India, 1954, B.Sc. in Agr., 1957, postgrad., 1957-59, Indian Council Agrl. Research fellow, 1958-60; Ph.D., U. Wis. at Madison, 1966; m. Davinderjit Kaur Tucker, Mar. 5, 1961; children—Smita, Ranjit Singh. Came to U.S., 1961, naturalized, 1974. Insp., Dept. Agr., Punjab, India, 1960-61; asso. plant pathologist Delta br. Miss. Agrl. and Forestry Expt. Sta., Stoneville, 1966-68, plant pathologist, 1968—. Pres., Messrs. H.S. Bagga & Brother, Importers and Exporters, Majith Mandi, Amritsar, 1967—, Bagga Foods Inc., Leland, Miss., 1972—, Fareast Co., Leland, 1972—. Mess mgr., common room sec. Hostel, Punjab Agrl. Univ., Ludhiana, India, 1957-59. Mem. Am. Phytopathol. Soc., Nat. Cotton Disease Council, Miss. Acad. Scis., So. Phytopathological Soc., Sigma Xi. Mem. Sikh religion. Contbr. profl. jours. Home: 201 Lakeview Dr Leland MS 38756 Office: Delta Branch Miss Agrl and Forestry Experiment Sta Stoneville MS 38776

BAGGETT, AGNES, state ofcl.; b. Columbus, Ga.; d. John R. and Leila (Thomason) Beahn; student pub. schs., Columbus, Ga., Jones Law Sch., Montgomery, Ala.; m. George Lamar Baggett, Oct. 14, 1926 (dec. 1949). With L.& N. R.R., 1925-27; various positions sec. state's office, Montgomery, 1927-46, sec. state, 1951-55, 63-67, state auditor, 1955-58, state treas., 1959-63, 67-70, 71—. Mem. Am. Legion Aux. (chmn. Girls State, Ala.; state legislative chmn.), Bus. and Profl. Women's Club (past state pres.). Mem. Order Eastern Star. Club: Altrusa (pres.). Home: 3202 Montezuma Rd Montgomery AL 36106 Office: State Capitol Montgomery AL 36104

BAGGETT, BRYCE ALLEN, lawyer, former state senator; b. Oklahoma City, June 4, 1932; s. James Everett and Esther (Tippens) B.; A.B., U. Okla., 1954, LL.B., 1956; m. Barbara Jean Bolton, Dec. 21, 1953; children—Bryce Allen, Breene Everett, Barbara Lynn. Admitted to Okla. bar, 1956, since practiced in Oklahoma City; mem. Okla. Ho. of Reps., 1958-64; mem. Okla. Senate, 1964-72. Dir., Capitol Hill State Bank & Trust Co. Okla. commr. Nat. Conf. Commrs. Uniform State Laws; mem. steering com. Edn. Commn. States. Named Outstanding Young Man of Okla., Okla. Jr. C. of C., 1961, Outstanding Young Man Oklahoma City, Oklahoma City Jr. C. of C., 1967. Mem. Am., Okla., Oklahoma County (dir. 1974—) bar assns. Home: 804 Westridge Terrace Norman OK 73069 Office: 1st Nat Bldg Oklahoma City OK 73102

BAGGETT, MONTE RAY, accountant; b. Gotebo, Okla., Sept. 23, 1931; s. Boney and Bessie (Warren) B.; A.A., Kilgore Jr. Coll., 1956; B.B.A., U. Tex., 1957. Mgr., Peat, Marwick, Mitchell & Co., Houston, 1958-67; partner Coopers & Lybrand, Tulsa, 1968—. Served with USNR, 1951-54. Mem. Am. Inst. C.P.A.'s, Tulsa C. of C. Club: Toastmasters Internat. Home: 1642 E 36th St Tulsa OK 74105 Office: Philtower Bldg Tulsa OK 74103

BAGGS, LEAH L. BATES (MRS. LINTON DANIEL BAGGS, JR.), social leader; b. Franklinville, N.Y.; d. William Henry and Arlie Mae (Bozworth) Bates; A.B., Barnard Coll., 1922; student spl. courses various univs.; m. Linton Daniel Baggs, Jr., Oct. 1, 1926; children—Joan Bates (Mrs. Herbert A. McKenzie, Jr.), Linton Daniel III. Hon. bd. dirs. Macon Community Concert Assn., 1968—, pres., 1959-64; bd. dirs. Middle Ga. Camellia Soc., v.p. Macon Grand Opera Assn., 1954—; vice regent Ga. div. Magna Charta Dames, 1968-70, regent, 1970-72; hon. state regent Daus. Am. Colonists, 1962, nat. chmn. colonial heritage com., 1962-64; com. chmn. Ga. br. Sons and Daus. of Pilgrims Soc., 1954-55. Mem. Am. Assn. U. Women, Ga. Soc. Mayflower Descs. (corr. sec. 1960-62), Pilgrim John Howland Soc., D.A.R., Middle Ga. Hist. Soc. (charter mem.). Am., Ga., middle Ga., SC. camellia socs., Nat. Trust for Historic Preservation, Sigma Alpha Iota. Presbyn. Clubs: Barnard College (Atlanta, v.p. 1967-72). Morning Music (pres. 1951-53), Atlanta Music, Capitol City Atlanta, Idle Hour Country (Macon, Ga.). Home: 1137 N Jackson Springs Rd Macon GA 31201

BAGGS, LINTON DANIEL, JR., corp. exec.; b. Bainbridge, Ga., Dec. 27, 1902; s. Dr. Linton Daniel and Madge Ione (Morgan) B.; student Mercer U., 1920-21, Pace Inst., 1921-22; m. Leah Bates, Oct. 1, 1926; children—Linton Daniel III, Joan Bates (Mrs. Herbert Alonzo McKenzie, Jr.). Accountant, L. D.Baggs & Co., Macon, Ga., 1923-46; v.p. Jacksonville Broadcasting Co. (Fla.), 1942-52; pres. Community Broadcasting Co., Asheville, N.C., 1946-49, Bibb Transit Co., Macon, 1949-67, Coca Cola Bottling Co., Hannibal, Mo., Coca Cola Bottling Co., Kankakee, Ill., Coca Cola Bottling Co., Dubuque, Ia., all until 1967; sec.-treas. Brower-Baggs Press, Inc., North Miami; Fla., 1967—; dir. Ga. Bank & Trust Co., Macon, Peeler Hardware Co. Mem. Ga. Bd Accountants, 1953-58. Bd. regents Univ. System of Ga. C.P.A., Ga. Mem. Ga. Soc. C.P.A.'s, Am. Inst. C.P.A.'s, Am., Middle Ga. (pres. 1961-62, dir. 1968—) camellia socs., Sigma Nu. Presbyn. Mason, Rotarian (pres. 1957-58), Elk. Clubs: Idle Hour (Macon); Capitol City (Atlanta). Home: 1137 N Jackson Springs Rd Macon GA 31201 Office: 1137 N Jackson Springs Rd Macon GA 31201 also 12365 W Dixie Hwy North Miami FL 33161

BAGWELL, CHARLES MALCOLM, civil engr.; b. Lawrenceville, Ga., May 25, 1934; s. John Danial and Julia Ellen (Morcock) B.; B.C.E., Ga. Inst. Tech., 1959; m. Susan Grovia Brender, Nov. 8, 1964; children—Jennifer Ann, Tyler Ernst. Civil engr. Ga. Hwy. Dept., Atlanta, 1959-63, Dept. Housing and Urban Devel., Atlanta, 1963-65; civil engr. Urban Renewal, Atlanta, 1965-67; civil engr., planner Dept. Health, Edn. and Welfare, Constrn. Services, Office of Edn., Atlanta, 1967-71; civil engr. Fac. Engring. Constrn. Agy., Dept Health, Edn. and Welfare, Atlanta, 1971—. Registered prof. engr., Ga. Served with AUS, 1954-56. Mem. Am. Soc. C.E. Home: 137 Lancelot Way Lawrenceville GA 30245

BAGWELL, JESSE CLINTON, investment co. exec.; b. Atlanta, May 18, 1917; s. Jesse Clinton and Dorothy Drew (Smith) B.; student Ga. Inst. Tech., 1940; m. Frances Rozelle Roderick, Apr. 3, 1964; 1 son, Jesse Clinton III. With Times Enterprises, Inc., subsidiary El Paso Times, Inc. (Tex.), 1965—, pres. 1970—; v.p. Mesa Vista, Inc., El Paso, 1971-73. Bd. dirs. Roderick Found., Inc., El Paso, 1966-74. Served to lt. comdr. USNR, 1941-46. Mem. Quiet Birdman, Phi Delta Theta, El Paso C. of C. Episcopalian. Kiwanian. Club: Coronado Country (El Paso). Home: 909 Cherry Hills Lane El Paso TX 79912 Office: PO Drawer 20 El Paso TX 79999

BAHN, GILBERT SCHUYLER, mech. engr.; b. Syracuse, N.Y., Apr. 25, 1922; s. Chester Bert and Irene Eliza (Schuyler) B.; B.S., Columbia, 1943; M.S. in Mech. Engring., Rensselaer Poly. Inst., 1965; 1 son, Gilbert Kennedy. Chem. engr., Gen. Electric Co., Pittsfield, Mass., 1946-48, devel. engr., Schenectady, 1948-53; sr. thermodynamics engr. Marquardt Co., Van Nuys, Cal., 1953-54, research scientist, 1954-64, research cons., 1964-70; engring. specialist LTV Aerospace Corp., Hampton, Va., 1970—. Mem. JANNAF Performance Standardization Working Group, 1966—, thermochemistry working group, 1967-72; proprietor, Schuyler Tech. Library, 1952—. Active Boy Scouts Am. Served to capt. USAAF, 1943-46. Recipient Silver Beaver award Boy Scouts Am., 1970. Registered profl. engr., N.Y., Cal. Asso. fellow Am. Inst. Aeros. and Astronautics; mem. Am. Soc. M.E., Am. Inst. Chem. Engrs., Am. Chem. Soc., Spl. Libraries Assn., Combustion Inst. (sec. western states sect. 1957-71). Democrat. Episcopalian (vestryman 1968-70). Author: Reaction Rate Compilation for the H-O-N System, 1968. Founding editor Pyrodynamics, 1963-69; proceedings editor Kinetics, Equilibria and Performance of High Temperature Systems, 1960, 63, 67. Contbr. articles to profl. jours. Home: 615 Brandywine Dr Newport News VA 23602 Office: 3221 N Armistead Av Hampton VA 23666

BAHNER, THOMAS MAXFIELD, lawyer; b. Little Rock, Nov. 26, 1933; s. Carl Tabb and Catharine (Garrott) B.; B.S., Carson Newman Coll., 1954; B.D., So. Bapt. Theol. Sem., 1957; LL.B., U. Va., 1960; m. Sara Minta McIntyre, Sept. 28, 1957; children—Maxfield Tabb, Minta Susan, Margaret Catharine. Admitted to Va., Tenn. bars, 1960, asso. firm Kefauver, Duggan and McDonald, Chattanooga, 1960-62; partner firm Duggan, McDonald and Bahner, Chattanooga, 1962-64, firm Chambliss, Bahner and Crawford, Chattanooga, 1964—. Pres. United Cerebral Palsy Greater Chattanooga, 1966-67; mem. allocations steering com. United Fund Greater Chattanooga, 1970—, vice chmn. com., 1972-73. Bd. dirs. Chattanooga Council Alcoholism, 1964-65, Team Evaluation Center Inc., Chattanooga, 1965-70, bd. dirs. Orange Grove Sch. and Center for Retarded, Chattanooga, 1962—, pres., 1973—; mem. Hamilton County Sch. Bd., 1969—; mem. adv. bd. Carson-Newman Coll., Jefferson City, Tenn., 1969—; mem. Tenn. and Am. Sch. Bds. Assn. Mem. Chattanooga (pres. 1969-70), Tenn. (lectr. 1965, bd. govs. local bar conf. 1969-71, chmn. legal aid and referral com. 1971-72), Am. bar assns., Va. State Bar, Am. Judicature Soc., Estate Planning Council (bd. dirs. 1971-72), Baptist (deacon). Club: Mountain City (Chattanooga). Home and office: Maclellan Bldg 721 Broad St Chattanooga TN 37402

BAHNMAN, HELMUT WILLIAM, realtor; b. Waldheim, Sask., Can., Dec. 15, 1908; s. N.W. and Meta (Regier) B.; brought to U.S., 1922, naturalized, 1937; ed. pub. high schs.; m. Alma F. Kobs, May 31, 1931; children—Marvin, Leah (Mrs. Zellard Brooks), Lynnette (Mrs. Don Wilson). Owner, Bahnman Chevrolet Co., Meade and Plains, Kan., 1931-41, Bahnman Aviation Co., Commerce, Tex., 1945-51; owner, prin. Bahnman Realty Co., Harlingen, Tex., 1952—. Mem. Capital Improvement Bd., Harlingen, 1958-66, Municipal Airport Bd., 1957-66, Tex. Aviation Adv. Council, 1956-64; chmn. Harlingen chpt. United Fund, 1963. Served with USAAF, 1942-45. Named col. Confederate Air Force, 1972, admiral Neb. Navy, 1972, Ark. traveler, 1972. Mem. Nat. (regional v.p. 1972), Tex. (pres. 1966) assns. realtors, Soc. Real Estate Appraisers (pres. 1960-61), Inst. Real Estate Mgmt. (certified property mgr.), Harlingen C. of C. (pres. 1962-63). Methodist. Mason (32 deg., Shriner), Elk, Lion. Home: 1217 E Bowie Av Harlingen TX 78550 Office: 503 E Harrison Av Harlingen TX 78550

BAIER, A. LEIGH, bus. exec.; b. White Plains, N.Y., July 1, 1941; grad. Taft Sch., Watertown, Conn., 1959; B.A. in Polit. Economy, Williams Coll., 1963; LL.B., Duke, 1966; m. Alyse Gautier Lucas Corcoran. Admitted to Ga. bar; with firm Hansell, Post, Brandon &Dorsey, Atlanta, 1966-69; now pres., chmn. bd. Baier Corp., Atlanta; chmn. bd. First Atlanta Equity Corp., Restoration Atlanta, Inc. Bd. dirs. Atlanta Council Internat. Visitors; bd. sponsors Atlanta Symphony Orch. Mem. Atlanta Arts Alliance, Atlanta, Ga. bar assns., Atlanta Music Club (mem. men's adv. com.), Atlanta C. of C., Central Atlanta Progress. Kiwanian. Clubs: Atlanta Polo, Commerce, Capital City, Lawyers (Atlanta); Carolina Yacht (Charleston, S.C.). Home: Glenwoods 1632 Ponce de Leon Av NE Atlanta GA 30307 Office: Baier Corp Equitable Bldg 100 Peachtree St NW Atlanta GA 30303

BAILEY, ALDEN ORVILLE, motel exec.; b. Pasadena, Tex., Aug. 17, 1924; s. William Bennie and Addie (Brown) B.; B.S., Sam Houston State Coll., 1947; M.Ed., U. Houston, 1955; student Southwestern La. Inst. 1943-44; m. Dorothy Jane Roberts, Jan. 12, 1949; children—Alden Olin, Deborah Jane, Ronald W. Band dir. Cedar Bayou (Tex.) High Sch., 1947-54; pres. Frontier Ranch Motel, Inc. (now Rodeway Inn), Pasadena, gen. mgr., 1954-73; owner Alden's Restaurant, 1956-73; owner Tex. Mex Brick & Import Co., Pasadena, 1963-64. Mem. Pasadena Sch. Bd., 1965-68, v.p., 1969; mem-at-large Sam Houston Area Council, Boy Scouts of Am., 1965—; chmn. San Jacinto dist. 1970—. Mem. Pasadena Rodeo Assn., 1954—, dir., 1959. Served with USMC, 1942-46, 51-52. Mem. Houston Motel Assn. (pres. 1956-59), Tex. Motel Assn. (dir. 1957-59), C. of C. (pres. 1959, dir. 1955-60, 69), USMC Res. Officers Assn. (nat. dir. 1965-68). Methodist (trustee). Mason (Shriner), Rotarian (pres. 1965-66, dist. treas. 1969-70, dist. gov. 1968-69). Home: 721 Perla St Pasadena TX 77502 Office: 114 S Richey St Pasadena TX 77502

BAILEY, AMOS PURNELL, clergyman; b. Grotons, Va., May 2, 1918; s. Louis William and Evelyn (Charnock) B.; B.A., Randolph-Macon Coll., 1942, D.D., 1956; B.D., Duke, 1948; Th.M., Union Theol. Sem., 1957; m. Ruth Martin Hill, Aug. 22, 1942; children—Eleanor Carol (Mrs. Thomas T. Harriman), Anne Ruth (Mrs. Peter S. Page), Joyce Elizabeth, Jeanne Purnell. Ordained to ministry United Methodist Ch., 1942; student pastor, Emporia, Va., 1938; pastor Richmond (Va.), 1938-43, New Kent (Va.) Circuit, 1943-44, Oak Grove Ch., Norfolk, Va., 1948-50, Grace Ch., Newport News, Va., 1950-54, Centenary Ch., Richmond, 1954-61; dist. supt. Richmond dist. Meth. Ch., 1961-67; sr. minister Reveille Ch., Richmond, 1967-70; exec. sec. Commn. on Chaplains, United Meth. Ch., Washington, 1970—. Mem. Meth. Commn. Higher Edn. 1960—, v.p. 1961; mem. Meth. Interbd. Council, 1960-70, Meth. Chaplains Commn., 1964—; mem. World Meth. Council; del. S.E. Jurisdictional Confs. Methodist Ch., 1964, 68; mem. Gen. Conf., 1964, 66, 68, 70, World Meth. Conf., London, Eng., 1966, Denver, 1971; mem. com. pastoral care, com. on ministry to servicemen Nat. Council Chs.; pres. joint radio com. S.E. Jurisdiction and S.C. Jurisdiction, 1968—, S.E. Jurisdiction Communications Commn., 1968—; mem. program and coordinating councils United Meth. Ch.; mem. family life com. Meth. Hist. Soc., mem. Council of secs.; dir. Interpretation, Interagy. Staff Com. on Research. Mem. adv. bd. VA Chaplaincy; mem. Armed Forces chaplains Bd.; trustee, mem. exec. com. trustees Randolph-Macon Coll.; trustee, mem. exec. com. So. Sem.; bd. dirs. Va. Meth. Advocate, 1952-66; bd. visitors Duke Div. Sch., 1962-68; bd. mgrs. Richmond YMCA. Served with Chaplain Corps, AUS, 1945-47. Mem. Duke Div. Alumni Assn. (past pres.), Coll. Chaplains, Assn. Mental Health Chaplains. Kiwanian. Author: syndicated column Bread of Life, 1945—; syndicated radio devotional Daily Bread, 1945—; The Night Pastor, religious counseling radio stas., 1955-69, Sunshine and Shadows, 1967-70. Meth. speaker on The Protestant Hour, 1962, 71. Contbr. articles to profl. publs. in U.S., Can., Eng., Australia, Japan; contbr. to Ency. of World Methodism. Home: 7815 Falstaff Rd McLean VA 22101 Office: 3900 Wisconsin Av NW Washington DC 20016

BAILEY, BYRON JAMES, otolaryngologist, educator; b. Oklahoma City, Apr. 5, 1934; s. Jay Gordon and Christine Fredericka (Koehn) B.; B.A., U. Okla., 1955; M.D., U. Okla. Sch. Medicine, 1959; m. Margaret Ann Whale, June 6, 1957; children—Michael Jon, Debra Lynn, James Grant, Jennifer Leigh, John Albert. Intern U. Cal. Los Angeles Med. Center also resident; practice medicine specializing in otolaryngology, Los Angeles, 1964-68, Galveston, Tex., 1968—; mem. staffs U. Tex. Med. Br. hosps., USPHS Hosp., Galveston; asst. prof. surgery U. Cal. Med. Center/Harbor Gen. Hosp., Los Angeles, 1964-68; mem. faculty U. Tex. Med. Br., Galveston, 1968—, prof. otolaryngology, 1968—, chmn. dept. otolaryngology, 1968—. Cons. U.S. Pub. Health Service, Galveston, 1969, Brooke Army Med. Center, San Antonio, 1971. Chmn. com. emergency tng. A.R.C.,

Galveston, Tex., 1970. Bd. dirs. Soc. U. Otolaryngologists, 1971, Am. Council Otolaryngology, 1973, Am. Acad. Facial Plastic and Reconstructive Surgery, 1971-73. Recipient Mosher award Am. Laryngology, Rhinology and Otolaryngology Soc., 1971; Honor award Am. Acad. Ophthalmology and Otolaryngology, 1972. Presbyn. Republican. Rotarian. Contbr. articles to sci. publs. Home: 2954 Dominique Galveston TX 77550 Office: Univ Tex Med Br Galveston TX 77550

BAILEY, CHARLES LYLE, mfg. co. exec.; b. Old Washington, Tex., Oct. 15, 1934; s. Robert F. and Opal (Lyle) B.; B.B.A., U. Tex., 1957; m. Gayle Marie Fread, Oct. 19, 1957; children—Michele Renee, Craig Lyle, Julie Ann. With Tenn. Life Ins. Co., Houston, 1959-68, asst. mgr., 1963-64, mgr.. 1964-68; asst. sec. Tenneco Inc., Houston, 1968-70, v.p., 1971—; asst. sec. Tenneco Chems. Inc., Tenneco Oil Co., 1970; dir. Oil Ins. Ltd.; pres., dir. Eastern Ins. Co. Ltd., Hamilton, Bermuda, 1971—. Served with AUS, 1957-59. Mem. Houston Soc. Ins. Mgmt. (pres. 1967-68), Houston C. of C. (mem. ins. com. 1967-69). Office: PO Box 2511 Houston TX 77001

BAILEY, DONALD ETHERIDGE, univ. dean; b. nr. Moore County, N.C., May 4, 1931; s. Etheridge Shelton and Lena Alice (Nall) B.; B.S., U. N.C., 1953, M.Ed., 1958, Ed.D., 1962; m. Betty Lou Dyson, Dec. 24, 1954; children—Donald Etheridge, Elizabeth. Tchr. sci. Charlotte (N.C.) City Schs., 1953-54, 56-57, Chapel Hill (N.C.) City Schs., 1958-60; prof. sci. edn. E. Carolina U., Greenville, N.C., 1961—, dean Gen. Coll., 1969—. Served with AUS, 1954-56. Mem. Nat. Sci. Tchrs. Assn., Phi Delta Kappa. Democrat. Presbyn. (elder). Kiwanian. Club: Brook Valley Country. Author: An Analysis of Science Misconceptions Held by Secondary School Pupils in North Carolina, 1962. Home: 214 York Rd Greenville NC 27834

BAILEY, DURYL MIDDLETON, civil engr.; b. Belton, Tex., Jan. 2, 1935; s. Ardian Leonald and Pauline Margeret (Justice) B.; B.S., U. Tex. at Austin, 1958, M.S., 1968; postgrad. U. Fla., 1962-65; m. Delores Herring, June 10, 1957; children—Keith Middleton, Boyce Craig, Doak Herring, Regina Diane. Asst. engr. bridge div. Tex. Hwy. Dept., 1958-62; project engr. soils div. U.S. Army Waterways Expt. Sta., 1965-66; asst. prof. civil engring. U. Tex. at Arlington, 1966-73; prin. Paul Louis and Haberman and Duryl Middleton Bailey, Irving, Tex., 1973-74; pres. Duryl M. Bailey Cons. Engr., Inc., Arlington, Tex., 1974—. Ford Found. fellow, 1962-64; named outstanding tchr. U. Tex. at Arlington, 1970-71. Mem. Am. Soc. C.E., Am. Concrete Inst., Am. Soc. Testing and Materials, Nat. Soc. Profl. Engrs., Chi Epsilon, Tau Beta Pi. Contbr. articles to profl. jours. Address: 1603 Forest Glen Ct Arlington TX 76013

BAILEY, GEORGE OSGOOD, physician; b. Sheboygan, Wis., Mar. 6, 1932; s. Morton Stevens and Fern Jeanette (Snow) B.; B.S., Furman U., 1956; M.D., Med. Coll. S.C., 1959; m. Joan Beverly Powell, Feb. 21, 1953; children—Dawn Marie, Steven Powell, George Osgood. Intern Greenville (S.C.) Gen. Hosp., 1959-60; gen. practice medicine, Greenville, 1960—; chmn. family practice dept. Greenville Gen. Hosp., 1969—. Served with USNR, 1951-53. Diplomate Am. Bd. Family Practice. Mem. Am. Acad. Family Practice, A.M.A., So., S.C. med. assns., Greenville County Med. Soc., Assn. Am. Physicians and Surgeons, Greenville Jr. C. of C., Phi Rho Sigma, Chi Delta Phi. Rotarian. Home: 17E Tallulah Dr Greenville SC 29605 Office: 12 Greenacre Rd Greenville SC 29607

BAILEY, GUY VERNIE, transp. co. exec.; b. Alexander, N.C., Aug. 7, 1929; s. Allen Lee and Lydia (Bradshaw) B.; A.A., Asheville-Biltmore Coll., 1954; B.S., U. Tenn., 1957; m. Weyburn Lewis Reid, Aug. 6, 1955; children—Kay Lynn, Barry Douglas, Mgmt. trainee R. C. Motor Lines, Jacksonville, Fla., 1957-60; v.p. Valley Transfer, Inc., Lenoir, N.C., 1960-66, pres., 1966—, chmn. bd. dirs., 1966-69. Precinct chmn. Republican Party, 1967. Served with AUS, 1951-53. Mem. N.C. Motor Carriers Assn. Baptist (trustee, deacon). Republican. Rotarian (pres. 1965-66, dist. chmn. 1969-70, dist. gov.-elect 1972-73). Home: Moore-Lan Park PO Box 88 Granite Falls NC 28630 Office: 233 Country Side Dr PO Box 26 Lenoir NC 28645

BAILEY, HARRY HUDSON, educator; b. Burkeville, Va., Jan. 22, 1921; s. Bertie Everett and Annie Lou (Dunnavant) B.; B.S., Va. Poly. Inst., 1942; M.S., Mich. State U., 1949, Ph.D., 1956; m. Ethyl Phylis Childs, Sept. 1, 1948; children—Linda, Lee, Ruth. Soil surveyor Va. Agr. Expt. Sta., 1946; soil scientist Dept. Agr., Va., N.H. and Mich., 1946-55; asst. prof., asso. prof., prof. dept. agronomy U. Ky., Lexington, 1955—; mem. Ky. contract team Faculty Agr., U. Indonesia, Bogor, 1959-61. Pres., bd. dirs. Big Bros. of Lexington. Served with AUS, 1942-46, 51-52; col. Res., ret. Mem. Am. Soc. Agronomy, Soil Sci. Soc. Am., Soil Conservation Soc. Am., Internat. Soil Sci. Soc., Clay Minerals Soc., Sigma Xi, Gamma Sigma Delta. Kiwanian. Home: 501 Ridge Rd Lexington KY 40503

BAILEY, HERBERT JOHN, banker; b. Anderson, Ala., Oct. 4, 1907; s. Henry Dee and Edna Frances (Dunkle) B.; grad. high sch.; m. Mabel Anne Jordan, Mar. 3, 1934. Asst. mgr. Planters & Mchts. Bank, Minor Hill, Tenn., 1928-31; cashier, dir. East Lauderdale Banking Co., Rogersville, Ala., 1932-42; v.p., cashier, dir. Parker Bank & Trust Co., Cullman, Ala., 1946-74, exec. v.p., 1974—. Registered Angus cattle breeder, Cullman, 1961—. Served with AUS, 1942-45. Named County Key Banker, Ala. Bankers Assn., 1970. Mem. Ala. Bankers Assn. (group chmn. 1969—), Am. (conv. del. 1970), Ala. angus assns. Presbyn. Club: Civitan (v.p. 1936). Address: PO Box 615 Cullman AL 35055

BAILEY, JAMES EDWARD, architect; b. Birmingham, Ala., Jan. 7, 1932; s. Clifton Owen and Ila Browning (Ayers) B.; B.Arch., Auburn U., 1955; m. Myrtle Elizabeth Jones, Sept. 8, 1951; 1 son, Daniel Edwin. Architect, Charles McCauly, 1957-58; with H.S. Long, Architect, Birmingham, 1958-65; practice architecture, Birmingham, 1965—. Architect Birmingham Internat. Fair, 1973. Bd. dirs., mem. exec. com. Birmingham Festival Arts, 1972-73. Served with AUS, 1955-57. Mem. A.I.A. Baptist (deacon). Civitan (pres. Green Acres club 1958-59), Rotarian. Home: 3324 Stoneridge Dr Birmingham AL 35223 Office: 400 Office Park Dr Birmingham AL 35223

BAILEY, JAMES HINTON POU, judge; b. Balt., Aug. 14, 1917; s. Josiah W. and Edith (Pou) B.; grad. Woodberry Forest Sch., 1935; A.B., U. N.C., 1940, J.D., 1941; m. Marie Fiquet Pate, Aug. 1, 1945 (dec. Oct. 1968); children—James H. Pou, Edwin Pate; m. 2d, Ann T. 1972; practiced in Raleigh, N.C., 1946-65; mem. firm Bailey & Bason, 1954-62, Bailey & Ragsdale, 1962-65; resident judge Superior Ct., 10th Jud. Dist., 1965—; gen. counsel N.C. Bankers Assn., 1953-65; spl. agt. Washington, FBI, 1941; mem. faculty Nat. Coll. State Trial Judges, 1968. Active, Occoneeche council Boy Scouts Am., 1953-60; chmn. Raleigh Traffic Safety Council; chmn. N.C. Media-Adminstrn. of Justice Council, 1972-73. Mem. N.C. State Senate, 1950-54; mem. N.C. Gen. Statutes Commn., 1953-59; chmn. Senate Judiciary Com., 1953. Served from pvt. to capt. AUS, 1942-46. Mem. Am., N.C., Wake County (mem. exec. com 1947-49), 10th Dist. (pres. 1963-64) bar assns., C. of C. (mem. exec. com. 1952-53)., Nat. Rifle Assn. (life), US Power Squadrons (rear comdr. 1971—), Nat. Conf. State Trial Judges (chmn. com. on bench-press relations 1973-74), Alpha Tau Omega. Democrat. Presbyn. Home: 1509 Chester Rd Raleigh NC 27608 Office: Wake County Court House Raleigh NC 27602

BAILEY, JAMES LOVELL, state ofcl.; b. Portland, Tenn., Dec. 18, 1907; s. James Johnson and Annie May (Lovell) B.; student Bowling Green U., 1925, Middle Tenn. State Tchrs. Coll., 1926-29, Western Ky. State Coll., 1929-30, George Washington U., 1931-33, U. Tenn., 1938-41; m. Fairrelle Brown, June 1, 1940; 1 dau., Annie Elizabeth. With U.S. Bur. of Census, 1930-32, U.S. Dept. of Agr., 1933-37; with Tenn. Dept. Conservation, Nashville 1937—, dir. ednl. service, 1957—. Pres. Davidson County (Tenn.) chpt. Muscular Dystrophy Assn., 1957. Mem. edn. com. Tenn. Bot. Gardens and Fine Arts Center, Nashville, 1969—. Trustee Southeastern Indian Antiquities Survey; charter mem., bd. dirs. Tenn. Environmental Council, 1970— Tenn. Beautiful, 1972—. Served with USNR, 1942-45. Recipient awards including Cartter Patten award Tenn. Conservation League, 1963, Key Man award Conservation Edn. Assn., 1967, Gov.'s Conservationist of Year award, 1971, silver seal Nat. Council State Garden Clubs, 1973. Fellow Soil Conservation Soc. Am. (pres. Tenn council chpts. 1961); mem. Middle Tenn. Conservancy Council, E. Tenn. Edn. Assn., Nat. Assn. Conservation Edn. and Publicity, Conservation Edn. Assn., Keep Tenn. Green Assn., Tenn. Hist. Soc., Nat. Wildlife Fedn., Tenn. Assn. Preservation Antiquities, Tenn. Fedn. Garden Clubs Inc. (life). Club: Nashville Torch (pres. 1963-64). Author: Our Land and Our Living, 1940. Asso. editor Tenn. Conservationist, 1959-72, editor-in-chief, 1972—. Home: 450 Moss Trail Goodlettsville TN 37072 Office: 2611 West End Av Nashville TN 37203

BAILEY, JOE HARDEN, librarian; b. Dallas, Jan. 16, 1918; s. David Joseph and Minnie Belle (Perry) B.; B.A., N. Tex. State Coll., 1938, M.A., 1941; B.S., George Peabody Coll. for Tchrs., 1946, postgrad., 1951-53; m. Elizabeth Lloyd DeBrohun, July 26, 1946; children—Elizabeth Lloyd, Margaret Anne. Prin. Carrollton Elementary Sch., 1939-41; librarian Union Grove High Sch., Gladewater, Tex., 1941-42; periodicals and ref. librarian So. Meth. U., 1946-47; librarian, head library sch. Murray State Coll., 1947-51; grad. asst. library sch. George Peabody Coll. for Tchrs., 1951-53; librarian W. Tex. State Coll., Canyon, 1953-57, N. Tex. State U., Denton, 1957—. Served as sgt. M.C., AUS, 1942-45. Mem. A.L.A., Southwestern (treas.), Ky. (dir. 1949-51), Tex. library assns., Western Ky. Ednl. Assn., Tex. Edn. Assn., Tex. Panhandle Audubon Soc. (pres. 1955, dir. 1956), Am. Ornithologist Union, Pi Delta Kappa, Kappa Delta Phi. Author: (with Elizabeth L. Bailey) Checklist of the Birds of the Panhandle of Texas, 1956. Contbr. to library lit. Home: 2010 N Locust St Denton TX 76201

BAILEY, JOHN ALBERT, educator; b. Liverpool, Eng., June 8, 1937; s. John Albert and Phylis Caterine (Monk) B.; B.Sc., Birmingham (Eng.) Coll. Advanced Technology, 1957; B.Sc. in Metallurgy, Univ. Coll. Swansea (Eng.), 1960, Ph.D., 1963; m. Anne Thomas, May 7, 1963. Came to U.S., 1963, naturalized, 1973. Asso. prof. Ga. Inst. Tech., Atlanta, 1963-67; mem. faculty N.C. State U., Raleigh, 1967—, prof. 1970—. Cons. Celanese Fibers Co., Charlotte. Recipient research grants NSF, 1964, 66, 72, NASA, 1964, 72. Mem. Iron & Steel Inst., Inst. Metals, Soc. Mfg. Engrs. Contbr. profl. jours. Home: 6029 Caledonia St Raleigh NC 27609 Office: Dept Mechanical and Aerospace Engring NC State Univ Raleigh NC 27607

BAILEY, JOHN MARTYN, educator; b. Chester, Eng., May 13, 1929; s. Leonard and Bertha Matilda (Jones) B.; B.Sc., U. Wales, 1949, Ph.D., 1952, D.Sc., 1970; m. Barbara Schroeder, July 16, 1963; children—Maureen-Lynn, Beverley-Kim, John Leonard. Came to U.S., 1954, naturalized, 1960. Fellow Canadian Nat. Research Council, 1952-54; research asso. Ia. State U., 1954-55; fellow Johns Hopkins Med. Sch., 1955-59; asst. prof. George Washington Med. Sch., Washington, 1959-62, asso. prof., 1962-69, prof., biochemistry, 1969—. Cons. biochemistry Holy Cross and Cafritz Hosps., Washington, 1969—; vis. prof. U. Miami, 1971. Recipient Career award USPHS, Nat. Cancer Inst., 1967. Mem. Am. Soc. Biol. Chemistry, Am. Inst. Nutrition, Am. Heart Assn., Am. Geophys. Union, Am. Soc. Microbiology, Soc. Exptl. Biology and Medicine (chmn. Washington sect. 1968-69). Home: 4921 Seminary Rd Alexandria VA 22311 Office: George Washington U Med Sch Washington DC 20037

BAILEY, JOSEPH THOMAS, ceramic engr.; b. Clemson, S.C., Oct. 16, 1937; s. Carl Columbus and Gertrude Malinda (Ramsay) B.; B.S., Clemson U., 1959, M.S. (Phi Kappa Phi fellow), 1960; Ph.D. (research fellow 1964-66), Ohio State U., 1966; m. Cora Faye Hanback, June 2, 1962; children—Anne Elizabeth, Michael Thomas. Project engr. Tech. Ceramic Product div. 3M Co., Chattanooga, 1962, research mgr., 1966—. Mem. troop com. Cherokee Council Boy Scouts Am., 1970—; mem. YMCA, 1970—. Vice chmn. Dupont precinct Republican party, 1969-71, mem. 7th Dist. Coordinating Com., 1970-72. Trustee Highland Plaza United Methodist Presch. Center, 1969—. Served to 1st lt. AUS, 1960-62. Mem. Am. Ceramic Soc. (nat. sec. electronics div. 1973-74), Nat. Inst. Ceramic Engrs., Keramos, Sigma Xi, Tau Beta Pi. Methodist. Patentee in field. Contbr. articles to profl. jours. Home: 6413 Point Pleasant Hixson TN 37343 Office: Tech Ceramic Products Div 3M Co Cherokee Blvd Chattanooga TN 37405

BAILEY, KINCHEON HUBERT, JR., educator; b. Zebulon, N.C., Dec. 21, 1921; s. Kincheon Hubert and Ellen Florence (Williams) B.; student Lake Forest Coll., 1941; B.S., U.S. Mil. Acad., 1945; M.Ed. (NSF fellow), Pa. State U., 1967; postgrad. N.C. State U., 1967—; m. Tommye Lou Williams, Dec. 18, 1948; children—Kincheon Hubert III, Linda Lou (Mrs. William Hux), Beth Ellen, Laura Jane, Nancy Margaret. Commd. 2d lt. U.S. Army, 1945, advanced through grades to lt. col., 1963, ret., 1966; dir. tech. edn. Holding Tech. Inst., Raleigh, N.C., 1967-72, instr. electronics, 1972—. Adviser, John Wiley & Sons, N.Y.C., 1972—. Emergency coordinator Am. Radio Relay League, Wake County, Raleigh, 1971—; mem. Radio Amateur Civil Emergency Service, 1971—; Mem. Raleigh Amateur Radio Soc., I.E.E.E. (chmn. membership and transfers com. 1970—), Holding Tech. Inst. Amateur Radio Soc. (trustee 1970—), Pa. State U. Alumni Assn., Am. Security Council, Citizens for Decent Lit., Friends of Library N.C. State U., Kappa Sigma. Club: Northbrook Country (Raleigh). Home: 701 Currituck Dr Raleigh NC 27609

BAILEY, LLOYD WHITFIELD, physician; b. Phila., Mar. 24, 1928; s. Clarence Whitfield and Olive (Magnusson) B.; B.S., Wake Forest Coll., 1949; M.D., Jefferson Med. Coll. Phila., 1953; postgrad. U. Pa., 1957-58; m. Ann Witherspoon Lewis, July 29, 1955; children—Lloyd Whitfield, Linda Lee, Joan Lewis. Intern, Jefferson Med. Coll. Hosp., Phila., 1953-54; resident Wills Eye Hosp., Phila., 1958-60; practice medicine, specializing in ophthalmology, Rocky Mount, N.C., 1960—; mem. staff Nash Gen. Hosp., Rocky Mount Sanatorium. Chmn. disaster com. A.R.C., Rocky Mount, 1963-69; mem. Nash County Republican Exec. Com., 1966-68; Presdl. elector for 2d Congl. Dist. N.C., 1968; mem. exec. com. Am. party of N.C., 1970-71. Served with USAF, 1955-57. Recipient Liberty award Congress of Freedom, 1969. Mem. So. Med. Assn. (life), Med. Soc. State N.C., N.C. (com. on eye care and eye banks 1963—, ho. of dels. 1969-73), Nash County med. socs., Am. Assn. Ophthalmology, Wills Eye Hosp. Soc., N.C. Soc. Ophthalmology and Otolaryngology, Assn. Am. Physicians and Surgeons, U.S. Power Squadron, Ducks Unltd., John Birch Soc. (life), Kappa Alpha, Phi Chi. Baptist. Home: 3813 Hawthorne Rd Rocky Mount NC 27801 Office: 109 Foy Dr Rocky Mount NC 27801

BAILEY, LOWELL FREDRICK, educator; b. Holton, Kan., June 15, 1911; s. William Marshall and Daisy May (Shirey) B.; B.Edn., So. Ill. U., 1932; M.S., U. Mich., 1935, Ph.D., 1938; m. Alice Eleanor Draper, June 23, 1937; 1 son, John Marshall. Instr. Grand Rapids (Mich.) Jr. Coll., 1938-42; plant chemist Ky. Agrl. Expt. Sta., Lexington, 1942-44; wood chemist TVA, Norris, Tenn., 1944-47; asst. prof. botany U. Tenn., Knoxville, 1947-51; asso. prof. plant physiology U. Ark., Fayetteville, 1951-56, prof., 1956—, chmn. dept., 1964—. Fellow A.A.A.S.; mem. Bot. Soc. Am., Am. Soc. Plant Physiologists, Societas Physiologiae Scandinavica, Ark. Acad. Sci., Sigma Xi. Contbr. profl. jours. Home: 1513 Markham Rd Fayetteville AR 72701 Office: Dept Botany Univ Ark Fayetteville AR 72701

BAILEY, PAUL EDWIN, dentist; b. nr. Huntington, Ind., Apr. 14, 1912; s. George Albert and Elmina (Myers) B.; B.S., Marion Coll., 1933, A.B., 1934; D.D.S., Ind. U., 1950; m. Mildred Elizabeth Gillis, Jan. 23, 1943; children—James Malcolm, Paul Edwin, Robert Eugene. Chemist Anaconda Wire & Cable Co., 1935-41; gen. practice dentistry, Hattiesburg, Miss., 1950—; mem. staff Meth. Hosp. Mem. adv. bd. Salvation Army; committeeman Boy Scouts Am. Sec. Forrest County Republican Exec. Com., chmn., 1972—. Served with AUS, 1941-46. Fellow Internat. Coll. Dentists; mem. Am., Miss. (trustee) dental assns., Forrest County, East Dist. dental socs., Assn. Am. Dentists, Acad. Gen. Dentistry, Am. Profl. Practice Assn., Am. Legion (comdr. post), V.F.W., Am. Numismatic Assn., Hattiesburg C. of C., Delta Sigma Delta. Presbyn. Elk. Home: 122 Short Bay St Hattiesburg MS 39401 Office: 509 Main St Hattiesburg MS 39401

BAILEY, ROBERT WILSON, county agrl. agt.; b. Greer, S.C., Sept. 23, 1915; s. James Robert and Tishie (Moore) B.; B.S., Clemson U., 1939; postgrad. Cornell U., 1953-54, U. Wis., 1956-58; m. LaVerne Eva Crain, Dec. 25, 1937; children—Judith (Mrs. Norman B. Turkett), Rebekah. County agt. Clemson U. Agrl. Extension Service, Columbia, S.C., 1944—; agrl. editor radio sta. WIS, 1944—, WIS-TV, 1953—. Tchr. Richland County Civil Def. Bd., 1950-72; mem. bldg. com. Columbia Hosp., 1965-70; dir. Richland-Lexington Manpower Commn. Dir. Midlands Planning Commn., Richland County Planning Bd., County Beautification and Community Devel. Bd. Bd. dirs. S.C. chpt. Am. Cancer Soc., Columbia chpt. Am. Heart Assn., S.C. Mental Health Assn., 1960-74. Recipient Distinguished Service award S.C. County Agts. Assn., 1954; Conservation award Columbia Masons, 1960; Wildlife Conservation award S.C. Wildlife Assn., 1970. Mem. Columbia C. of C. (ambassador 1973), Alpha Tau Alpha, Sigma Tau Epsilon. Methodist (chmn. ch. adminstrv. bd. 1972-73). Mason, Rotarian (pres. 1942-44). Clubs: Ruritan (pres. Union club 1940), Transportation (Columbia). Home: Route 1 Box 166 Columbia SC 29203 Office: 2020 Hampton St Columbia SC 29201

BAILEY, SCOTT FIELD, bishop; b. Houston, Oct. 7, 1916; s. William Stuart and Tallulah (Smith) B.; B.A., Rice U., 1938; student U. Tex. Law Sch., 1938-39; B.D., Va. Theol. Sem., 1942, D.D., 1965; D.D., U. of South, 1965; m. Evelyn Williams, Dec. 11, 1943; children—Louise (Mrs. Allen C. Taylor), Nicholas, Scott Field, Sarah. Ordained to ministry Episcopalian Ch., 1942; pastor in Waco, Lampasas, Nacogdoches, San Augustine and Austin, Tex., 1942-61; asst. to bishop of Tex., 1961-64; suffragan bishop of Tex., 1964—. Sec. house of bishops Episcopal Ch., 1967—, exec. officer Gen. Conv., 1974—. Served as chaplain USNR, World War II. Fellow Coll. Preachers; mem. Phi Delta Theta. Home: 5309 Mandell St Houston TX 77005 Office: 520 San Jacinto Houston TX 77002

BAILEY, THOMAS EDWARD, state ofcl.; b. Milw., Oct. 25, 1930; s. Thomas Johnson and Adele Louise (Doering) B.; B.S., Northwestern U., 1953; m. Betty Lou Wells, Sept. 21, 1957; children—Thomas Mark, Thomas Alan, Thomas Lynn. Test engr. Soil Testing Services, Inc., Chgo., 1953, 56; structural engr. Stearns Roger Mfg. Co., Denver, 1956-58; with Reed-Mullins & Assos., architects and engrs., Fayetteville, Tenn., 1958-72, v.p., 1969-72; with Teledyne Engring. Co., Huntsville, Ala., 1972-73; program mgr. Top Ala. Regional Council Govts., Huntsville, 1973—. Task force chmn. Elk River Devel. Assn., 1970-71; chmn. Fayetteville Regional Planning Commn., 1963-69, sec., 1970-72; mem. Fayetteville Gas Bd., 1970-72. Vice chmn. bd. dirs. Multi County Mental Health Center, Tullahoma, Tenn., 1969-72. Served with AUS, 1953-55. Recipient poetry prize Tenn. Poetry Contest, 1970. Mem. Am. Soc. C.E., Nat. Model R.R. Assn. (regional pres. 1973-74, various awards 1964-70). Presbyn. (mem. session 1967-72). Home: Route 1 Fayetteville TN 37334 Office: Suite 350 Cental Bank Bldg Huntsville AL 35801

BAILEY, WILLIAM DAVID, orgn. exec.; b. Jackson, Miss., Oct. 30, 1935; s. Charles E. and Emmie (Roberts) B.; student Millsaps Coll., 1953-55, U. Houston, summers 1961-66; m. Sylvia Royce Golmon, July 18, 1956; 1 son, Charles Alan. Instr. choral music Jackson Pub. Sch. System, 1956-57; adminstrv. asst. IBM Corp., Jackson, 1957-59; dir. pub. relations and advt. 1st Miss. Corp., Jackson, 1959-60; asso. dir. pub. relations Lamar Life Ins. Co., Jackson, 1960-61; exec. v.p. Pascagoula (Miss.) C. of C., 1961-69; exec. v.p. Dothan (Ala.) C. of C., 1969-72; cons. Tri-Rivers Devel. Assn., 1972-73; exec. officer Home Builders Assn. Miss., 1973—. sec., Pascagoula Planning Commn., 1964-66; chmn. water safety com. Jackson County chpt. A.R.C., 1962, asso. chmn., disaster com., 1963-67. Mem. Am., Miss. (pres. 1967-68), So. (dir. 1964-66) assns. chamber commerce execs. Home: 108 Robinhood Rd Jackson MS 39206 Office: PO Box 20407 Jackson MS 39209

BAILEY, WILLIAM S., elec. contracting exec.; b. Calvert, Tex., Aug. 13, 1907; s. William S. and Tallulah (Smith) B.; B.A., Rice U., 1930; m. Jessie Jones, Oct. 1, 1931; children—William S., Margaret Elizabeth. With Jesse Jones Interests, Tex., 1930-42; v.p. corporate sales client devel. program dir. Fischbach & Moore, Inc., Houston, 1946-69, sr. v.p., 1969—; dir. MacGregor Park Nat. Bank. Bd. dirs. Air Force Acad. Served with USAAF, 1942-46. Episcopalian. Clubs: Houston, Petroleum, Old Capitol, Fort Worth, University, Lakeside Country. Home: 5552 Tupper Lake Rd Houston TX 77027 Office: Gulf Bldg Houston TX 77002

BAILEY, WILSON MONROE, mfg. co. exec.; b. Altha, Fla., Mar. 1, 1897; s. David Samuel and Elle M. (Coxwell) B.; student pub. schs.; m. Thelma Clary, May 22, 1919; children—Inez (Mrs. M.C. Eldridge), Wilson L., Betty Jo (Mrs. Tommy Miller). Pres., Coastal Variety Works, Inc., Blountstown, Fla., 1960—. Dir. Calhoun County Indsl. Commn., county commr., 1939-52. Mason (Shriner), Lion. Home: 1106 S Pearl St Blountstown FL 32424 Office: 2 1/2 MS Hwy 71 Blountstown FL 32424

BAILIE, ROBERT EDWARD, cons. mech. engr.; b. N.Y.C., Sept. 3, 1935; s. Robert James and Olive Louise (Bailie) B.; B.S., Rutgers U., 1961; m. Patricia Ruth Oelschlager, June 12, 1958; children—Charles Robert, Diane Michelle. Asso. project engr. AMF, Waterford, Conn., 1961-65; supr. project engr. Westinghouse Electric Corp., Lester, Pa., 1965-67; plant mgr. Key West Desalting Plant (Fla.), 1967-68; founder, v.p., treas. Desalting Systems & Services,

Inc. (named changed to DSS Engrs. Inc. 1972), Fort Lauderdale, 1968-73; pvt. cons. seawater desalination, 1973—. Served with AUS, 1958-60. Registered profl. engr. Mem. Nat. Water Supply Improvement Assn. (charter; dir., treas. 1973-74), Am. Soc. Mech. Engrs., Am. Water Works Assn., Cons. Engrs. Council Fla., U.S. Club: Gulfstream Sailing. Address: 38 Pelican Isle Fort Lauderdale FL 33301

BAIN, CECIL WILLIAM, lawyer; b. San Antonio, June 22, 1943; s. Cecil William and Mary Virginia (Thompson) B.; B.B.A., U. Tex., 1965, J.D., 1968; m. Linda Lee Dullye, Aug. 22, 1964; children—Cecil William, Scott Christopher. Admitted to Tex. bar, 1968, since practiced in San Antonio; mem. firm Nicholas and Barrera, 1968-73; partner firm Cobb, Thurmond & Bain, 1973—. Mem. legal and judiciary com. Drug Abuse Central, San Antonio, 1973-74. Mem. State Bar Tex., San Antonio Jr. (dir. 1970-71, sec.-treas. 1972-73, pres. 1974-75), San Antonio (sec. criminal law and procedure com. 1973-74), Am. bar assns., State Jr. Bar Tex. (mem. drug abuse program com. 1972-73, chmn. ann. meeting com. 1973-74), Tex. Criminal Def. Lawyers Assn., Nat. Assn. Criminal Def. Lawyers, San Antonio Trial Lawyers Assn., Assn. Trial Lawyers Am., Am. Judicature Soc., Comml. Law League, San Antonio Bus. Econ. Soc. (pres. 1973-74), Phi Alpha Delta, Order of DeMolay (chmn. adv. council San Antonio chpt. 1973-74), Baptist. Mason (32 deg., Shriner). Home: 5419 Billington St San Antonio TX 78230 Office: 1665 Frost Bank Tower San Antonio TX 78205

BAINBRIDGE, THOMAS RUTHERFORD, textile mfg. exec.; b. Savannah, Ga., May 22, 1917; s. Herbert Bartholomew and Edith Davis (Nichols) B.; B.S., Clemson Coll., 1939; m. Clyde Hellen Schuler, Sept. 15, 1940; children—Carl Davis, Steven Nichols. With acetate yarn div. Tenn. Eastman Co., Kingsport, 1939—, lab. supr., 1947-48, supr. quality inspection, 1948-53, asst. supt. quality and standards, 1953-62, supt. quality and standards, 1962—. Moderator Holston Prebytery, Presbyn. Ch., 1969, central treas. benevolences Holsten Presbytery, 1958-63, chmn. com. on women's work, 1968, chmn. com. on stewardship, 1969, chmn. com. on restudy and reorgn., 1969-71, chmn. com. on crisis, 1971. Trustee Presbyn. Sch. of Christian Edn. Served to maj. AUS, 1942-46. Recipient Braumbaugh award Am. Soc. for Quality Control, 1966. Fellow Am. Soc. Quality Control, Am. Soc. Testing and Materials (Merit award 1973); mem. Phi Kappa Phi, Alpha Chi Sigma. Home: 4527 Timberlake Lane Kingsport TN 37664 Office: Tenn Eastman Co Kingsport TN 37662

BAINE, JOHN RAYMOND, found, exec.; b. Paragould, Ark., Nov. 20, 1909; s. Albert and Willie T. (Hay) B.; B.A., Ouachita Coll., 1930; m. Alice May Brennan, Oct. 24, 1936; 1 son, William Brennan. Pub. sch. prin., Columbus, Ark., 1931-32; employee U.S. Ho. of Reps., Washington, 1932-38; singer, N.Y.C., 1938-42; polit. officer U.S. Dept. State, Washington, Milan and Rome, Italy, and Lisbon, Portugal, 1945-69; treas. Waterford (Va.) Found., 1970-71, pres., 1972-73. Pres., Va. Mus. Fine Arts, Loudoun County, 1972—. Served to capt., AUS, 1942-45. Clubs: Waterford Players (dir.); Leesburg (Va.) Bridge (pres.). Home: Meeting House Waterford VA 22190 Office: Waterford Found Waterford VA 22190

BAIRD, DALE SEYMOUR, indsl. engr.; b. Guthrie, Okla., Feb. 9, 1930; s. Ralph Edward and Joya Lucille (Bowen) B.; B.S. in Gen. Engring., Okla. State U., 1953, M.S., 1958; m. Betty Vionia Lowe, Aug. 31, 1952; children—Betty Jane, Terry Lynn, Judy Gale, Martha Kay. Materials engr. Phillips Petroleum Co., Bartlesville, Okla., 1953-62, sr. mech. design engr., 1962-68, mgmt. analyst, 1968-71, indsl. engring. coordinator, 1971—. Pres. Sixth and Osage, Inc.; dir. Osage Rentals, Inc. Chmn. profl. devel. com., mem. steering com. Bartlesville Edn. Council, 1971—; mem. adv. bd. Okla. State U. Registered profl. engr., Okla. Mem. Am. Inst. Indsl. Engrs., Okla. Soc. Profl. Engrs., U.S. (nat. dir. 1965-66), Okla. (v.p. 1964-65, chmn. govtl. affairs 1962-64) jaycees, Jr. Chamber Internat. Mem. Ch. Christ (deacon 1969—, chmn. benevolent com. 1970—). Contbr. articles on indsl. engring. to tech. and profl. publs. Home: 4710 Brookline Dr Bartlesville OK 74003 Office: 7PB Phillips Petroleum Co Bartlesville OK 74004

BAIRD, EDWARD ALLEN, basso, educator; b. Kansas City, Mo., Mar. 18, 1933; s. Edward Allen and Mary Sue (Bradley) B.; B.A., U. Mo. at Kansas City, 1955, M.A., 1957; D.Mus. Arts, U. Mich., 1962; m. Shirley Jean Vedder, June 29, 1952; 1 son, Keith Allen. Supr. music recreation div. of Kansas City (Mo.) Welfare Dept., 1954-56; instr. music Midland Coll., Fremont, Neb., 1956-59, asst. prof. music, 1959-60, chmn. dept. fine arts, 1957-60; grad. teaching fellow U. Mich., 1960-62; instr. voice Nat. Music Camp, Interlochen, Mich., 1962; asst. prof. music North Tex. State U., Denton, 1962-64, asso. prof., 1964-68, prof., 1968—. Basso with orchs., operas, recitals including Houston Grand Opera, San Diego Opera, Kansas City Lyric Opera, Fort Worth Opera, St. Louis Opera Theater, Corpus Christi Opera, New Orleans Opera, Beaumont Opera; guest soloist Dallas, Chgo. symphonies, Kansas City Philharmonic, New Orleans Symphony, San Angelo (Tex.) Symphony, Corpus Christi Symphony. Mem. Am. Assn. U. Profs., Tex. Music Educators Assn., Tex. Assn. Coll. Tchrs., Nat. Assn. Tchrs. Singing (gov. Southwestern region 1970-73), Am. Choral Dirs. Assn., Tex. Choral Dirs. Assn. Pi Kappa Lambda, Omicron Delta Kappa, Phi Mu Alpha, Tau Kappa Epsilon. Presbyn. Home: 2602 Woodhaven Dr Denton TX 76201

BAIRD, JACK VERNON, educator; b. Grand Island, Neb., July 7, 1928; s. Absolom Cash and Eileen P. (Poore) B.; B.S., U. Neb., 1949, M.S., 1951; Ph.D., Wash. State U., 1955; m. Leota P. Rawlings, June 5, 1949; children—Warren, Byron, Craig. Asst. prof. agronomy U. Ill., Urbana, 1958-60; asso. agronomist, prof. Kan. State U., Manhattan, 1960-64; prof. soil sci. N.C. State U., Raleigh, 1964—. Mem. Sigma Xi, Gamma Sigma Delta, Alpha Zeta, Epsilon Sigma Xi, FarmHouse. Methodist. Home: 3730 Swift Dr Raleigh NC 27606

BAIRD, JAMES ADAM, JR., research corp. exec.; b. Montgomery, Ala., Aug. 10, 1935; s. James Adam and Martha (Grantham) B.; B.S. in Mech. Engring., U. Ala., 1958, M.S. in Engring. Mechanics, 1962, Ph.D., 1966; m. Alexandra Graves, Aug. 24, 1957; children—Martha Kathrine, Linda Adair, Molly Ann, Patricia Alexandra. Mgr. systems engring. dept. Teledyne-Brown Engring. Co., Huntsville, Ala., 1963-70; dep. dir. site def. project office Safeguard System Command, Huntsville, 1970-73; dir. So. operations Gen. Research Corp., Huntsville, 1973—. Asst. prof. engring. U. Ala. at Huntsville, 1966—. Served to capt. USAF, 1958-61. NSF fellow, 1965. Registered profl. engr., Ala. Mem. Assn. U.S. Army, Am. Inst. Aeros. and Astronautics, Huntsville C. of C., Tau Beta Pi, Pi Tau Sigma, Phi Gamma Delta. Club: ACME (pres. 1969) (Huntsville). Home: 2223 Briarcliff Rd Huntsville AL 35801 Office: 307 Wynn Dr Huntsville AL 35807

BAIRD, JAMES OSCAR, coll. pres.; b. Lebanon, Tenn., Jan. 16, 1920; s. James O. and Harriet (Morrow) B.; student Freed-Hardeman Coll., Henderson, Tenn., 1938-40; B.A., George Peabody Coll. for Tchrs., 1941, M.A., 1942, Ph.D., 1948; student Princeton Theol. Sem., 1943-44, Rutgers U., 1940-41; LL.D., George Pepperdine Coll., 1966; m. Mary Avanelle Elliott, May 31, 1946; children—Harriet Adelle, Lynn M., Elisa F., James, Morrow Beth. Prof. Bible and sociology David Lipscomb Coll., Nashville, 1944-50; dean Okla. Christian Coll., Oklahoma City, 1950-54, pres., 1954—; staff The Ministers Monthly, 20th Century Christian, Teenage Christian; speaker, lecturer. Pres. Council for Advancement Small Colls., 1970-72. Recipient George Washington Honor medal Freedoms Found., Valley Forge, Pa., 1967; Gold Good Citizenship medal Nat. Assn. S.A.R., 1972; Outstanding Alumnus of Year award Freed-Hardeman Coll., 1974. Mem. N.E.A., Newcomen Soc., C. of C., Phi Delta Kappa, Kappa Delta Pi, Kappa Delta Kappa, Pi Gamma Mu. Kiwanian. Author: The Life and Times of Charles Edgar Little, 1948. Contbr. articles religious jours. Home: 2108 Smiling Hill Blvd Edmond OK 73034

BAIRD, RALPH OWEN, JR., trading stamp co. exec.; b. Milw., Jan. 29, 1920; s. Ralph Owen and Marian Agnes (Burgoyne) B.; student Ill. State U., 1940-44; m. Helen Louise Bayless, Feb. 13, 1943; children—Judith Lynne, Sandra Kathleen (Mrs. Ralph Burnett), Mary Jennifer (Mrs. Richard Mohl), Margaret Ellen (Mrs. Dwight Branvold), Ralph Owen III, Douglas Scott. Newspaper writer, editor Bloomington (Ill.) Pantagraph, 1936-44, St. Louis Globe-Democrat, 1944-49, St. Louis Post-Dispatch, 1949-50; publicity mgr. St. Louis-San Francisco Ry., 1950-55; regional pub. relations mgr. Pa. R.R., Indpls., 1955-56, Cin., 1956-60; regional govt. relations mgr. Sperry & Hutchinson Co., Cin., 1960-65, asst. dir. govt. relations, N.Y.C., 1965-70, dir. fed. affairs, Washington, 1970—; instr. journalism Webster Coll., Webster Grove, Mo., 1948. Dir. Norwood C. of C., 1963-65; chmn. Citizens Sch. Com., Norwood, O., 1964-65. Mem. Pub. Relations Soc. Am. (three Presdl. citations, dist. chmn., past. chpt. pres.), U.S. C. of C., N.A.M., Pub. Affairs Council. Democrat. Conglist. (chmn. bd. trustees). Clubs: Capitol Hill, National Press, GIO (Washington). Home: 8202 Briar Creek Dr Annandale VA 22003 Office: 425 13th St NW Washington DC 20004

BAKER, BENJAMIN RIVES, dentist; b. Durham, N.C., July 25, 1928; s. Newell Edward and Edith (Rives) B.; A.B., Guilford Coll., 1951; M.Ed., U. N.C., 1952, D.D.S., 1961, M.S., 1964; m. Mary Elizabeth Barney, July 30, 1949; children—Drury Penn, Mary Bennett. Coach, tchr. Liberty (N.C.) High Sch., 1952-53; recreation dir., Liberty, 1952-53; coach, instr. phys. edn. Guilford Coll., 1953-57; instr. pedodontics U. N.C., Chapel Hill, 1961-62, asst. prof. pedodontics, 1964-68, dir. dental aux. tchr. edn., 1966-68; pvt. practice pedodontics, Kinston, N.C., 1968—. Served with M.C., AUS, 1945-47. Recipient Nat. Sci. Writing award for corr. textbooks, 1969. Mem. N.C. State Bd. Dental Examiners, 1973. NIH fellow Lancaster Cleft Palate Clinic, 1964. Mem. Am. Acad. Pedodontics, Am. Dental Assn., Royal Soc. Health, N.C. Dental Soc., N.C. Soc. Dentistry for Children (pres. 1970-71), Southeastern, N.C. socs. pedodontics, Econodontic Study Club, Demerit Study Club, Yaupon Soc., C. of C., Xi Psi Phi, Phi Delta Kappa. Rotarian. Clubs: Kinston (dir. 1970—), Kinston (N.C.) Country. Co-author: (textbooks) Clinical Sciences, 1970, Clinical Application, 1970; contbg. author Dental Assistant, 1970. Editor N.C. Dental Jour., 1969-72. Home: 1709 Cambridge Dr Kinston NC 28501 Office: 2101 N Herritage St Kinston NC 28501

BAKER, BILL BERT, coll. adminstr.; b. Gilbert, Ark., July 19, 1932; s. Noel Riley and Lucille (Moore) B.; B.S., Ark. Tech., 1953; M.S., U. Ark., 1954, Ed.D., 1962; m. Bonnie Jean King, July 13, 1953; children—Bill Bert II, Joe Brian, Julia Jane. Coach, West Fork (Ark.) High Sch., 1953-54; asst. coach, instr. Ark. Tech., Russellville, 1957-59, dir. pub. relations, 1960-68, dean students, athletic dir., 1968—. Cons. Ark. Sch. Bd. Assn. Mem. Gov's. Adv. Council on Childhood Edn., 1967—; v.p. West Ark. council Boy Scouts of Am., 1967-69. Bd. dirs. Wesley Found., Ark. Jr. Miss. Served with AUS, 1955-57. Mem. Nat. Assn. Student Personnel Adminstrs., N.E.A., Ark. Edn. Assn., Ark. Sch. Adminstrs. Assn., Nat. Assn. Coll. Athletic Dirs., Ark. High Sch. Coaches Assn., Phi Delta Kappa. Methodist. Mason (32 deg.); mem. Order Eastern Star (past patron). Home: 1414 W 2d Pl Russellville AR 72801

BAKER, BROUGHTON LEONARD, educator; b. Columbia, S.C., July 26, 1912; s. Andrew Charles and Lilliam (Yarbrough) B.; B.S. in Chem. Engring., U.S.C., 1933 Ph.D. in Chem. Engring., N.C. State Coll., 1955; m. Mary Rawls, Oct. 22, 1952; children—Thomas, Julianne. Chem. engr. Gen. Chem. Co., 1935-40, C.W.S., 1940-42; plant mgr. Naylee Chem. Co., 1942-44; sec. Elliott Labs., Inc., 1944-46; with U. S.C., Columbia, 1946—, successively asso. prof. chmn. div. chem. engring, 1946-56, prof., head dept. chem. engring., 1956-68, prof. engring., 1968—; research participant Oak Ridge Inst. Nuclear Studies, 1951. Mem. S.C. Bd. Engring. Examiners. Registered profl. engr., S.C. Mem. Am. Inst. Chem. Engrs., Am. Chem. Soc., Am. Soc. for Engring. Edn., Nat. Soc. Profl. Engrs., S.C. Soc. Engrs. (pres. 1965), S.C. Acad. Scis., Sigma Xi, Tau Beta Pi, Omicron Delta Kappa. Baptist. Kiwanian. Address: 819 Burwell Lane Columbia SC 29205

BAKER, BRUCE ROBERT, elec. engr.; b. Passaic, N.J., Oct. 31, 1946; s. Byard Leonard and Florence Johanne (Hoegel) B.; B.S., U. Wash., 1968; postgrad. U. Fla., 1969-71. Elec. engr., NASA, Kennedy Space Center, Fla., 1968—, mem. launch team Apollo 8, 10, 12-17, Skylab 1-3, Apollo-Soyuz test project. Mem. I.E.E.E., Titusville (sec. 1970-71), Mims-Scottsmoor (treas. 1971-72, state dir. 1972-73) jr. chambers commerce. Home: 5400 Kathy Dr Titusville FL 32780 Office: LS ENG 51 Kennedy Space Center FL 32899

BAKER, BRYAN, JR., educator; b. Grenada, Miss., Feb. 24, 1923; s. Bryan and Evie (Hall) B.; B.S., Miss. State U., 1947, B.S. in Edn., 1948, M.S., 1952; Ph.D., U. Ill., 1955; m. Nona Jumper, Mar. 1, 1946; 1 dau., Suzanne. Asso. prof. Va. Poly. Inst., Blacksburg, 1955-56; mem. faculty Miss. State U., Mississippi State, 1956—, asso. prof. animal sci., 1956-59, prof., 1960—. Served with AUS, 1943-46. Mem. Soc. Study Reproduction, Am. Soc. Animal Sci., Sigma Xi, Alpha Tau Alpha, Gamma Sigma Delta. Methodist. Kiwanian. Home: Route 2 11 Tallyho Dr Starkville MS 39759 Office: Box 5228 Dept Animal Science Mississippi State Univ Mississippi State MS 39762

BAKER, CARLETON HAROLD, educator; b. Utica, N.Y., Aug. 2, 1930; s. Harold George and Loretta (Darling) B.; B.A., Utica Coll., Syracuse U., 1952; M.A., Princeton, 1954, Ph.D., 1955; m. Sara Johnson, July 20, 1963; children—Elizabeth Ann, Janet Lee. Asst. prof. to prof. Med. Coll. Ga., 1955-67; prof. physiology U. Louisville Coll. Medicine, 1967-71; prof., chmn. dept. physiology U. South Fla. Coll. Medicine, Tampa, 1971—. Bd. dirs. research com. Fla. Heart Assn., Hillsborough County Heart Assn. Research grantee NIH, Heart Assns. Mem. Am. Physiol. Soc., Am. Heart Assn., Soc. Exptl. Biology and Medicine, Microcirculatory Soc., Sigma Xi. Club: Carrollwood Village Golf and Tennis. Contbr. articles profl. jours. Home: 4305 Golf Crest Ct Tampa FL 33624 Office: Dept Physiology U S Fla Coll Medicine Tampa FL 33620

BAKER, CHARLES BELK, structural engr.; b. Sumter, S.C., Aug. 4, 1933; s. John Henry and Charlotte M. (Belk) B.; B.S., The Citadel, 1955; m. Stephanie Jeanne Counts, Oct. 28, 1962; children—Charles Belk II, John Steven, Charlotte Suzanne, Shannon Elizabeth. Design engr., civil engring. dept., dept. pub. works U.S.N., Charleston, S.C., 1955-58; chief engr., prodn. supr. Perma-Stress, Inc., Daytona Beach, Fla., 1958-62; asst. chief engr. So. Prestressed Concrete, Inc., Pensacola, Fla., 1963-71, chief structural devel. engr., 1971-73; chief engr. Dura-Stress, Inc., Leesburg, Fla., 1973—. Served to 1st lt. C.E., AUS, 1955-57. Registered profl. engr., Ala., Fla. Mem. Nat. Soc. Profl. Engrs., Fla. Engring. Soc. (chpt. pres. 1969; outstanding mem. award 1967), Prestressed Concrete Inst. Baptist. Kiwanian (pres. 1971—). Home: 404 S 12th St Leesburg FL 32748

BAKER, CLIFFORD HOWARD, marketing research co. exec.; b. Paoli, Ind., Oct. 14, 1932; s. James A. and Alice (Limeberry) B.; B.S., U.S. Mil. Acad., 1956; M.S., Purdue U., 1965; Ph.D. in Econs., Statistics and Indsl. Psychology, N.C. State U., 1972; Ph.D. in Bus. Adminstrn. (hon.), Colo. State Christian Coll., 1972; m. Joan B. Meyer, Feb. 4, 1958; children—Steven Conrad, Bradford Nelson, Paul Milton, Jeffrey Todd, Douglas Ross. Indsl. marketing exec. Tex. Instruments, Dallas, 1959-61; market research exec. Gen. Motors Corp., Kokomo, Ind., 1961-65; supr. market analysis Corning Glass Works, Raleigh, N.C., 1965-70; pres. Indsl. Edn. Inst., Raleigh, 1970—. Served with AUS, 1956-59. Recipient Nat. Def. Service medal West Point, 1956. Mem. I.E.E.E., Assn. Grads. West Point, Adminstrv. Mgmt. Soc. Mem. Ch. of Christ. Home: 4816 Deerwood Dr Raleigh NC 27612 Office: 4505 Creedmoor St Raleigh NC 27612

BAKER, DANIEL RICHARD, systems analyst; b. nr. Rostock, Denmark, Mar. 19, 1932; s. Arthur and Molly (Needman) B.; Came to U.S., 1936, naturalized, 1945; student Tufts Coll., 1949-51; B.A., Bklyn. Coll., 1957; m. June Ellin Nebenzahl, Oct. 2, 1960; children—David Charles, Jill Alison. Math tchr. Bd. Edn., N.Y.C., 1958-59; computer programmer Systems Devel. Corp., Paramus, N.J., 1959-61; programmer analyst I.T&T., Paramus, 1961-64; sr. mathematician Melpar, Falls Church, Va., 1964-65; systems analyst Wolf Research & Devel. Corp., Bladensburg, Md., 1965-66, ARIES Corp., McLean, Va., 1966-68; sr. systems analyst N. Am. Rockwell Corp., Roslyn, Va., 1968-70; pres. Baker & Baker Data Assos., North Springfield, Va., 1970—. Served with AUS, 1954-55. Mem. Am. Math. Soc., Math. Assn. Am., Soc. Indsl. and Applied Math., Am. Soc. Cybernetics. Home: 5624 Heming Av Springfield VA 22151 Office: Baker & Baker Data Assos North Springfield VA 22150

BAKER, DAVID, architect; b. Chgo., Feb. 7, 1917; s. A. Josiah and Sarah (Gross) B.; B.S., Ill. Inst. Tech., 1938; postgrad. (scholar), Ill. Inst. Tech. 1938-39; M. Arch. (Kendall grad. scholar), Harvard, 1942; diploma ship constrn., George Washington U., 1943; m. Beverly L. Brody, Nov. 25, 1951; children—Jonathan Brody, Stuart Glenn. Researcher in historic Am. bldg. for Earl Reed, architect, Chgo.; archtl. designer Alphonso Iannelli, sculptor and indsl. designer, Park Ridge; archtl. designer Thomas Shaver, engr. Chgo., Samuel A. Marx, architect; urban planner Chgo. Housing Authority, 1936-40; asst. field rep. architect's supt. James Gamble Rogers, architect, N.Y.C., architect Neiler, Rich & Bladen, engrs., Chgo., 1940-41; archtl. designer Shaw, Naess & Murphy, Chgo., 1941-42; Walter Bogner, Cambridge, Mass., 1942; archtl. and engring. designer Naval Ordnance Lab., Washington, 1942-43; naval architect, engr. Bur. Ships, Navy Dept., 1943-45; architect for electronics div. Dept. Navy, 1945-49, for Hdqrs. Command USAF, 1950-51; architect Solar-Space House, built and exhibited, Washington, 1952; cons. architect 1952—. Trustee Boys Club Greater Washington. Registered architect, Ill., Mass., D.C., Md., Va.; registered profl. engr. Ill.; Nat. Council Archtl. Registration Bds., 1948. Recipient 1st Medals Beaux Arts Inst. Design Competitions, 1937, 38; prize Insulux Glass Block Competition, 1939; beneficial tech. award Bur. Ships, USN, 1945; A.I.A. award for Scholarship; Charles L. Hutchinson medal for highest record in archtl. design; award of merit Georgetown Progressive Citizens Assn., 1954; plaque for design Pres.'s Com. on Beautification of Nation's Capitol, 1966. Mem. Ill. Inst. Technology Alumni Association. (pres. chpt. 1961), A.I.A. (corporate mem.; chmn. pub. relations com. Washington-Met. 1950). Club: Harvard (Washington). Contbr. articles to profl. jours. Office: 2141 Sudbury Pl Washington DC 20012

BAKER, DAVID LLOYD, univ. adminstr.; b. Louisville, Nov. 23, 1940; s. David Lloyd and Evelyn Diana (Beville) B.; B.A., U. Louisville, 1964, J.D., 1969; m. Mary Anne King, Sept. 4, 1962; 1 son, David Lloyd III. Dir. news bur. U. Louisville, 1962-64, asst. dir. pub. information, 1964-65, dir. pub. information, 1965-72, legal affairs officer, 1972-73, dir. pub. relations, 1973—. Sec. Toward Greater Quality Com., 1969-71. Mem. Pub. Relations Soc. Am., Am. Coll. Pub. Relations Assn., Am., Ky., Louisville bar assns., Ky. Civil Liberties Union, Anti-Slavery Soc. Democrat. Baptist. Home: 1837 Lauderdale Rd Louisville KY 40205

BAKER, DAVID LOUIS, accountant; b. Clarendon, Tex., Nov. 6, 1946; s. Louis Truman and Miriam Nell (Waters) B.; A.A., Frank Phillips Jr. Coll., 1967; B.B.A. with highest honors, U. Tex. at Austin, 1969; m. Vicki Lynn Bell, Jan. 26, 1968; 1 son, David Aaron. Accountant, Peat, Marwick, Mitchell & Co., C.P.A.'s, Amarillo, Tex., 1969-73, supr., 1973—. Mem. Tex. Soc. C.P.A.'s, Am. Inst. C.P.A.'s, Beta Alpha Psi, Beta Gamma Sigma, Phi Theta Kappa, Phi Kappa Phi. Republican. Baptist. Club: Amarillo. Home: 7008 Dreyfuss Rd Amarillo TX 79106 Office: 1510 American Nat Bank Bldg Amarillo TX 79101

BAKER, DILLARD WOODWARD, lawyer; b. Coleman, Tex., Oct. 7, 1912; s. Jesse Kirkland and Willie (Woodward) B.; J.D., U. Tex., 1936; m. Mary Margaret Thomas, Jan. 30, 1938; children—Jesse Kirkland, Roger Thomas. Admitted to Tex. bar, 1936; gen. atty. Humble Oil & Refining Co. (now Exxon Co. U.S.A.), Houston, 1956—. City councilman, Bunker Hill Village, Tex., 1955-57. Fellow Am. Coll. Trial Lawyers; mem. Am., Houston bar assns., State Bar of Tex., Houston C. of C., Kappa Sigma. Methodist. Clubs: Houston Hereford (pres.), World Trade, Houston (Houston); Austin. Home: 4 Pine Forest Circle Houston TX 77027 Office: PO Box 2180 Houston TX 77001

BAKER, DONALD JERRY, ins. co. exec.; b. Austin, Tex. Apr. 1, 1940; s. Loie Goldman and Kittie Lou (Herring) B.; B.B.A., Baylor U., 1962, LL.B., 1964; LL.M., N.Y. U., 1965; m. Charlette Ann Price, Dec. 23, 1966; children—Scott Douglas, Stacey Dawn. Admitted to Tex. bar, 1964; atty. firm Naman, Howell, Smith & Chase, Waco, Tex., 1965-70; pres., atty. Dependable Life Ins. Co., Waco, 1970—. Bd. dirs. Bayler-Waco Found. C.P.A., Tex. Mem. Gen. Agts. and Mgrs. Conf., Nat., Waco (dir. 1971-72) assns. life underwriters, Tex. Soc. C.P.A.'s, Tex., Waco-McLennan County bar assns., Waco C. of C. Club: Civitan (Waco). Home: 2920 Austin Av Waco TX 76710 Office: PO Box 1459 Waco TX 76710

BAKER, DONALD LEE, civil engr.; b. Sealy, Tex., Aug. 16, 1930; s. Thomas John and Alma (Hartmann) B.; B.S., Tex. A. and M. Coll., 1960; m. Mary Beth Gregory, May 22, 1963; children—John Donald, Wilber Lee, Thomas Edgar. Engring. asst. Tex. Hwy. Dept., Houston, 1960-64, designing engr., 1964—. Served with AUS, 1953-55. Mem. Am. Soc. C.E., Am. Soc. Testing and Materials, Tau Beta Pi, Phi Kappa Phi. Lutheran. Home: Route 1 Box 177E Brookshire TX 77423 Office: Box 656 Bellville TX 77418

BAKER, EVERARD GREEN, chem engr., educator; b. Natchez, Miss., Feb. 19, 1922; s. Everard Green and Josephine (Balfour) B.; B.S., Miss. State U., 1943, postgrad., 1948-49; M. Chem. Engring. (Inst. Indsl. Research fellow), U. Louisville, 1949; m. Lillian Louise Wheeler, Nov. 23, 1947; children—Everard Green III, Francis Lee. Jr. chemist Miss. State Chem. Lab., State College, 1943-44, asso.

chemist, 1950-53, chemist, instr. chemistry and chem. engring., 1953-60, chemist, asst. prof., 1960-63, asso. prof. chem. engring., 1963-73, asst. statis. chemist, 1973—, dir. Petroleum Products Lab., 1973—; research engr. U. Louisville, 1949-50. Tchr., Natchez High Sch., 1946-48; cons. Humble Oil & Refining, S.E. Esso region, summer 1963. Served with AUS, 1944-46; lt. col. USPHS Res. NASA-Am. Soc. Engring. Edn. fellow Marshall Space Flight Center, summer 1965, 66. Registered profl. engr., Miss., Ala., La. Mem. Am. Inst. Chem. Engrs., Am. Chem. Soc. (past sec. Miss. sect.), Nat., Miss. (past pres. Tombigbee chpt.) socs. profl. engrs., Tombigbee Chem. Engr. Club (past pres.), Tau Beta Pi. Presbyn. Home: 205 White Dr Starkville MS 39759

BAKER, FRANCIS WILLIAM, lawyer; b. Victoria, Tex., May 30, 1924; s. William Westhoff and Marguerite (Golke) B.; B.S. in Commerce with high honors, St. Mary's U., San Antonio, 1948, J.D. with highest honors, 1949; m. Mary Johnson, May 3, 1952; children—Susan Judith, Stephen Francis, Patricia Ann, Matthew William. Admitted to Tex. bar, 1949; asst. criminal dist. atty. San Antonio, 1950-51; with Eaton & Huddle, C.P.A.'s, San Antonio, 1952-55; partner law firm Matthews, Nowlin, Macfarlane & Barrett, San Antonio, 1956—. Lectr., St. Mary's U. Law Sch., 1956-63; dir. Southwell Co., San Antonio. Served with AUS, World War II; now col. USAFR. Decorated Bronze Star medal. Mem. Am., San Antonio (pres. 1971-72) bar assns., State Bar Tex., Order of Alhambra, St. Mary's U. Alumni Assn. (pres. 1973), Delta Theta Phi. Democrat. Roman Catholic. K.C. (state adv. 1965-67). Home: 323 Royal Oaks Dr San Antonio TX 78209 Office: Alamo Nat Bldg San Antonio TX 78205

BAKER, GEORGE WILBER, curator; b. Lansing, Mich., Apr. 21, 1927; s. Donald Howard and Harriett (Root) B.; B.A. in Landscape Architecture, Mich. State U., 1949; m. Ara Marie Schultz, Sept. 1, 1961. Partner, Lakeview Garden Center, landscape nursery, Ypsilanti, Mich., 1953-57; supr. maintenance Dearborn campus U. Mich., 1957-65; curator Norfolk (Va.) Bot. Gardens, 1965—; garden columnist Virginian-Pilot newspaper, 1967-71; tchr. gardening adult edn. Old Dominion U., 1967—. Served with AUS, 1945. Mem. Am. Bonsai Soc. (pres. 1971-72). Rotarian. Home: 2407 Blueberry Rd Norfolk VA 23518 Office: Norfolk Botanical Gardens Airport Rd Norfolk VA 23518

BAKER, HOUSTON ALFRED, hosp. adminstr.; b. Louisville, May 6, 1908; s. Harry W. and Susie (Talley) B.; B.S. in Bus. Adminstrn., W.Va. State Coll., 1931; M.B.A., U. Pa. Wharton Sch. Finance, 1937; M.H.A., Northwestern U., 1948; m. Viola Smith, June 11, 1938; children—John, Houston Alfred, William. Tchr. Louisville pub. schs., 1933-44; adminstr. Red Cross Hosp., Louisville, 1944-52; asst. supt. Freedman's Hosp., Washington, 1953, 61-66, dep. supt., 1966-70, acting hosp. dir., 1970-71, asso. hosp. dir., 1971—; dir. personnel Mammoth Life Ins. Co., Louisville, 1954, adminstrv. asst. to pres., 1955-56. Chmn. Vocational Ednl. Adv. Council to Bd. Edn., Washington, 1967-69. Mem. Democratic affirmative action com. Home Rule D.C. Trustee 12th St. YMCA, Washington, 1962-65. Named Indsl. Man of Year, Vocational Ednl. Adv. Council to Washington Bd. Edn., 1969. Mem. Assn. Asst. Adminstrs. Nat. Capital Area, Boule. Presbyn. (mem. dept. ministerial relations). Home: 1441 Manchester Lane NW Washington DC 20011 Office: Freedman's Hospital 6th and Bryant Sts NW Washington DC 20001

BAKER, HOWARD HENRY, JR., U.S. senator, lawyer; b. Huntsville, Tenn., Nov. 15, 1925; s. Howard Henry and Dora (Ladd) B.; grad. McCallie Sch., 1943; student U. of South, Tulane U.; J.D., U. Tenn., 1949; LL.D., Tusculum Coll.; D.C.L., Southwestern U., Memphis; m. Joy Dirksen, Dec. 22, 1951; children—Darek, Cynthia. Practice law, Knoxville, Tenn.; formerly partner firm Baker, Worthington, Barnett & Crossley; formerly chmn. bd. First Nat. Bank, Oneida, Tenn.; U.S. senator from Tenn., 1966—. Served to lt. (j.g.) USNR, 1943-46. Chmn. Tenn. delegation Republican Nat. Conv., 1968. Mem. Am., Knoxville, Scott County bar assns., Bar Assn. Tenn., Scarabbean Soc., Phi Delta Phi, Pi Kappa Phi. Presbyn. Home: Huntsville TN 37756 Office: Huntsville TN also US Senate Washington DC 20510

BAKER, IRA LEE, educator; b. Fairwood, Va., Sept. 5, 1915; s. Joseph Franklin and Celia (Blackburn) B.; B.A., Wake Forest Coll., 1936; M.A., Columbia, 1952; postgrad. U. Ill., U. Wis., U. Tenn., Syracuse U.; M.Sc. in Journalism, U. Ill., 1963. Instr. English, N.C. State Coll., Raleigh, 1946-50, asst. extension editor State Coll. Extension Service and mng. editor Extension Farm-News, 1950-51; head journalism dept. Furman U., Greenville, S.C., 1951-65; asso. prof. journalism and English, High Point (N.C.) Coll., 1965-68; prof. journalism East Carolina U., Greenville, 1968—. Corr. for the Religion News Service, 1953—. Publicity chmn. Wake County council N.C. Symphony Orch., 1947-51; permanent advisor S.C. Collegiate Press Assn.; active Raleigh Music Club, Raleigh Little Theatre, 1946-51, Greenville Little Theater, 1951—; mem. alumni council Wake Forest Coll., 1964. Del., S.C. Republican Conv., 1958. Served with USAAF, 1942-44. Recipient Scholastic Pioneer award Nat. Scholastic Press Assn., 1970. Mem. Am. Assn. Coll. and U. Profs. (v.p. Furman U. chpt.), Am. Assn. Tchrs. Religious Journalism, Assn. Ednl. Journalism, S.C. Press Assn., Nat. Council Coll. Publs. Advisers (membership chmn. dist. III 1967-68), S.C. Assn. Coll. Publs. Advisers (pres. 1957—), South Atlantic Modern Lang. Assn., Pitt County (N.C.) Hist. Soc., (publicity chmn.) S.A.R., Sigma Delta Chi, Tau Kappa Epsilon, Alpha Phi Gamma (nat. pres. 1968-70). Baptist. Co-author: Modern Journalism, 1961. Mem. adv. bd. Student Writer; chmn. adv. bd. Cerebral Palsy News of S.C.; mem. bd. editors Scholastic Mag.; mem. book reviewing staff Greensboro News, 1960; editor The Collegiate Journalist. Contbr. book revs. to Raleigh News and Observer, 1968—, articles to Ency. So. Bapts., 1958. Address: Box 2707 East Carolina U Greenville NC 27834

BAKER, JEFFERSON TASWELL, JR., lawyer, real estate broker; b. Cedar Hill, Tex., Mar. 25, 1900; s. Jefferson T. and Georgia Thalle (Strauss) B.; student North Tex. Agrl. Coll., 1925-26, S.W. Tex. Tchrs. Coll., 1926-27, Jefferson U. Law Sch., 1928-30, U. Houston, 1940-41; J.D., Dixie U., 1932; B.S., Northwestern U., 1945; m. Doris Mae Upton, Oct. 10, 1921 (dec. 1945); 1 son, Reginald Gordon; m. 2d, Claribel Victoria Vinas, Oct. 15, 1941; children—Charlotte Diane (Mrs. Nathan Camarda), Jefferson Taswell III. Mem. faculty various schs., 1932-44; instr. USN Radio Sch., Northwestern U., 1944-45; admitted to Ark. bar, 1933; practiced in Texarkana, Ark., 1933; real estate and mortgage loan broker Baker Real Estate & Mortgage Co., Pasadena, Tex., 1933—; chmn. bd. Alcanus, Inc., 1959—, McSalb, Inc., 1959—. Mem. City Charter Com., Pasadena, 1952. Served to capt. AUS, 1933-34. Named Ky. col., 1971, adm. Tex. Navy, 1972. Fellow Internat. Acad. Forensic Psychology; mem. Alpha Beta Sigma (charter mem., chancellor 1928—, pres. 1968—). Roman Catholic. Club: Sports Car of Am. (competition driver 1958-71). Address: 713 Armor Av Pasadena TX 77502

BAKER, JOANNE THERESE KAYE (MRS. HOWARD MICHAEL BAKER), librarian; b. Chgo., July 21, 1927; d. Thomas and Cecilia (Keil) Kaye; B.A. DePaul U., 1962; A.M. in L.S. Rosary Coll., 1964; m. Howard Michael Baker, Nov. 30, 1963; 1 dau., Cecilia Mary. Tchr. pub. schs., Chgo., 1948-61; librarian, Oak Lawn, Ill., 1961-63; head librarian St. Joseph's Coll., East Chicago, Ind., 1963-65, Upper Ia. Coll., Fayette, 1965-68, Lea Coll. on Lake Chapeau, Albert Lea, Minn., 1968-70, Pikeville (Ky.), 1970—. Vol., A.R.C. Mem. A.L.A., Ill library assns. Home: PO Box 196 Pikeville Coll Pikeville KY 41501

BAKER, JOHN GORDON, devel. enterprises exec.; b. Boyce, La., Apr. 20, 1916; s. Benjamin H. and Lucy Texada (Robert) B.; student Northwestern State U., 1938-40; m. Patricia Armand Meredith, Dec. 29, 1942; children—John Gordon, David Gregory, Martha Patricia, Jane Elizabeth. Asst. mgr. F.W. Woolworth, Alexandria 1933-36; oil field worker, 1935-38; owner, operator flight sch., Alexandria, La., 1946-57; pres., chmn. bd. So. Ventures Corp., dir. So. Motor Lodges of Alexandria. Mgr. Little League Baseball Team, 1957-58; cubmaster Attakapas council Boy Scouts Am., 1955-59. Mem.-at-large, chmn. Rapides Parish Democratic Exec. Com., 1964—; chmn. ethics com. Rapides Parish Police Jury. Pres. Greater MacArthur Dr. Assn. Served with USAAF, 1941-42. Recipient Optimist of Year award and plaque, 1960. Roman Catholic. Club: Downtown Optimist (past pres. com. chmn.) Alexandria. Home: 1231 Heyman Lane Alexandria LA 71301 Office: 736 MacArthur Dr Alexandria LA 71031

BAKER, JOHN WESLEY, educator; b. Austin, Tex., Aug. 6, 1920; s. William Loyd and Edith (Mosher) B.; B.A., U. Tex., 1942; Ph.D. in Polit. Sci., U. Cal. at Berkeley, 1953; m. Mary Ethel Posey, Jan. 8, 1943; children—Robert Shelton, Frederick, Brian, John Preston. Instr., Trinity U., 1947-49, asso. prof. polit. sci., 1951; asst. prof. polit. sci. U. Fla., 1952-53; asso. prof. polit. sci. Humboldt State Coll., 1953-58; prof., chmn. dept. polit. sci. Coll. Wooster, 1958-69; asso. exec. dir., dir. research Bapt. Joint Com. on Pub. Affairs, Washington, 1969—; vis. scholar U. Cal. at Berkeley, 1962-63, vis. prof., summer 1966; vis. scholar Brookings Instn., Washington, 1967-68; vis. prof. Am. U., 1968, 69—. Mem. Democratic Central Com., Humboldt County, Cal., 1954-58. Served from pfc. to maj. USMCR, 1942-46. Decorated Purple Heart. Mem. Am., So. polit. sci. assns., Am. Acad. Polit. and Social Sci., A.A.A.S., Acad. Polit. Sci., Am. Soc. Pub. Adminstrn., Pi Sigma Alpha. Baptist. Author: (with Clem Miller) Member of the House, 1962; author monograph. Editor: Dissent in Church and State, 1970; Religious Liberty and the Bill of Rights, 1972. Contbr. articles to profl. jours. Home: 6414 Crane Terrace Bethesda MD 20034 Office: 200 Maryland Av NE Washington DC 20002

BAKER, KYLE ALAN, banker; b. Waco, Tex., Aug. 10, 1945; s. Orvis Kyle and Katherine (Montgomery) B.; B.B.A., North Tex. State U., 1968; m. Linda Ann Kattness, Sept. 2, 1967; 1 son, Christopher Kyle. Sr. accountant Main Lafrentz & Co., Austin, Tex., 1968-71; asst. controller Am. Bank, Austin, 1971—. C.P.A., Tex. Mem. Am. Inst. C.P.A.'s, Tex. Soc. C.P.A.'s, Austin Chpt. C.P.A.'s, Nat. Assn. Accountants, Beta Alpha Psi. Home: 1704 Raven Dr Austin TX 78752 Office: 6th and Colorado Austin TX 78780

BAKER, LAMAR, congressman; b. Chattanooga, Dec. 29, 1915; student David Lipscomb Coll.; B.S., Harding Coll., 1940; m. Sue Batey; children—Edward L., Susan. Owner Comml. Janitors, Inc., Floormaster Rug Cleaning Co.; mem. 92d Congress from 3d Tenn. dist. Mem. Chattanooga Safety Council, Chattanooga Citizens' Good Govt. League. Formerly mem. Tenn. Ho. of Reps., Tenn. Senate. Bd. dirs. U. Tenn. at Chattanooga Christian Student Center; trustee Boyd Buchana Sch. Mem. Greater Chattanooga C. of C., Am. Legion. Republican. Club: Civitan. Home: 2324 Roosevelt Blvd Chattanooga TN 37412

BAKER, LEONARD STANLEY, author; b. Pitts., Jan. 24, 1931; s. Charles and Bess (Schwartz) B.; B.A., U. Pitts., 1952; M.S., Columbia, 1955; m. Liva Weil, Aug. 1, 1958; children—David, Sara. Reporter, St. Louis Globe-Democrat, 1955-56, Newsday, L.I., N.Y., 1956-65; author: The Johnson Eclipse, 1966; Back to Back, 1967; The Guaranteed Society, 1968; Roosevelt and Pearl Harbor, 1970; Brahmin in Revolt, 1972; John Marshall-A Life in Law, 1974. Served with AUS, 1952-54. Address: 606 4th Pl SW Washington DC 20024

BAKER, LEROY SUMMERS, JR., elec. engr.; b. Harrisburg, Pa., Oct. 1, 1936; s. LeRoy Summers and Daisy (Wells) B.; A.A. (Iota Sigma scholar), Phoenix Coll., 1958; B.S. in Elec. Engring. (Phelps Dodge scholar), Ariz. State U., 1960, M.S., 1961; m. Bettina Yvonne Harris, June 3, 1961; children—Denise Yvonne, Donna Leigh, Karen Lynn. Engr. Aeronautics Corp., Newport Beach, Cal., 1961-62, Nortronics Corp., Anaheim, Cal., 1962-65; project engr. Astrodata Corp., Anaheim, 1965-68; sr. engr. Anaconda Electronics Corp., Anaheim, 1965-69, sect. mgr., 1969-72, mgr. engring., 1972; mgr. elec. design Continental Telephone Electronics Corp., Euless, Tex., 1972—. Mem. I.E.E.E., Phi Kappa Phi, Pi Beta Tau. Republican. Baptist (deacon). Home: Route 2 Box 224-L Grapevine TX 76051 Office: 1001 Pamala St Euless TX 76039

BAKER, MARGARET V., librarian; b. Savannah, Ga.; d. Clarence Edwin and Carrye (Keller) Baker; student Randolph-Macon Womens Coll., 1929-31; A.B., Valdosta State Coll., 1933; A.B. in L.S., U. N.C., 1939. Librarian, Valdosta (Ga.) High Sch., 1934-40; cataloger reference div. Gen. Library, U. Ga., Athens, 1940-43; librarian Washington Sem., Atlanta, 1943-45; with reference dept. main library U. Fla. at Gainesville, 1946; librarian Emory Jr. Coll., Valdosta, 1946-48; dir. S. Ga. Regional Library, Valdosta, 1948-71; library cons. South Ga. Med. Center, Valdosta, 1972—. Bd. dirs. Civic Music Assn., 1955-60. Mem. Ga., Southeastern library assns., Lowndes County Hist. Assn. (bd. dirs. 1967-72), Am. Assn. U. Women, D.A.R. (auditor 1957-62, sec. 1973—), Delta Kappa Gamma, Phi Mu. Club: Valdosta. Home: 1017 Slater St Valdosta GA 31601 Office: South Ga Med Center Valdosta GA 31601

BAKER, MARILYN JEANINE MILLER (MRS. ALLYN LEE BAKER), journalist, editor; b. Chickasha, Okla., July 13, 1934; d. Basil Eugene and Vivian (Townsend) Miller; A.A., Tex. Southmost Coll., 1954; B.J., U. Tex., 1956; m. Allyn Lee Baker, Aug. 31, 1956; children—Lisa Denise, Darryl Allyn. Reporter, Brownsville Herald, 1956-57; women's editor Denton (Tex.) Record-Chronicle, 1956-57; asst. editor Tex. Press Messenger, Tex. Press Assn., 1959-60; asst. editor Tex. State Jour. Medicine, Tex. Med. Assn., 1960-62; mng. editor Tex. State Jour. Medicine, 1962—. Mem. Internat. Assn. Bus. Communicators (pres. 1971), Theta Sigma Phi. Methodist. Home: 8904 Currywood Dr Austin TX 78759 Office: 1801 N Lamar Blvd Austin TX 78701

BAKER, MELVIN HOWARD, govt. ofcl.; b. Mason City, Ia., Jan. 17, 1920; s. Charles Edgar and Grace Ada (Miner) B.; student Ia. State Tchrs. Coll., 1939-42; B.Sc., State U. Ia., 1948, M.B.A., 1950; m. Hazel Mae Kjarsgaard, June 25, 1944; children—Steven Kent, Vicki Lee. Faculty, State U. Ia., 1948-50; practice pub. accounting San Antonio, 1951; auditor USAF, 1952-58; audit/financial mgmt. exec., 1958-61; budgeting ofcl. to asst. sec. Dept. Def., comptroller, 1961-68, comptroller Def. Supply Agy., Fairfax, Va., 1968-73, dep. asst. sec. def. mgmt. systems, 1973—; dir. Pentagon Fed. Credit Union. First v.p. Cub Scouts Am., Fairfax, 1955-56. Served to capt. USAAF, 1944-46, USAF, 1951-54. Decorated Air medal. Recipient Def. Distinguished Civilian Service award Dept. Def., 1972; Exceptional Civilian award Def. Supply Agy., 1970, 73. C.P.A., Tex. Mem. Am. Inst. C.P.A.'s, Am. Soc. Mil. Comptrollers (v.p. chpt. 1972), Phi Mu Alpha. Baptist (deacon, moderator). Contbr. articles to profl. jours. Home: 3303 Mantua Dr Fairfax VA 22030 Office: Pentagon Alexandria VA

BAKER, MICHAEL ALAN, lawyer; b. Shreveport, La., Sept. 27, 1945; s. Troy L. and Ethel M. (Harmon) B.; B.B.A., U. Houston, 1968, J.D. cum laude, 1971; m. Susanne E. Walker, June 8, 1968; 1 son, Dwight Alan. Accountant, J.K. Lasser & Co., Houston, 1968-71; admitted to Tex. bar, 1971; mem. firm Fulbright, Crooker & Jaworski, Houston, 1971-72; atty. Browning-Ferris Industries, Inc., Houston, 1972—. Adj. prof. law Bates Coll. Law U. Houston, 1971—. Vol. for Vols. in Tech. Assistance. Served to 1st lt. Finance Corps, AUS, 1971. Houston Inst. for Urban Studies fellow, 1970-71; Bates Coll. Law Teaching fellow, 1970. Mem. Tex. Soc. C.P.A.'s, Tex. State Bar, Houston, Am. bar assns., Phi Sigma Kappa, Alpha Phi Omega, Phi Delta Phi. Editor: Houston Law Rev., 1970-71. Home: 10802 Wickersham Houston TX 77042 Office: Fannin Bank Bldg Houston TX 77025

BAKER, OLLIE MARIE OSBORN (MRS. RUSSELL MONTEZ BAKER, SR.), civic worker; b. Texarkana, Ark., Feb. 13, 1909; d. Charles Westly and Harriett V. (Raney) Osborn; student Celeste Morton Sch. Voice, 1926-27; m. Russell Montez Baker, Aug. 26, 1927; children—Harriett Kay (Mrs. William Frank Bain), Russell Montez. Dir. Blue Birds Bradfield Sch., Dallas, 1943-44, room mother, 1944-45; den mother Shady Brook Manor Sch. Cub Scouts Am., Dallas, 1945-46; capt. polio dr., Dallas, 1950, block worker, 1950—, chmn. rummage sale Cosmo-Pal Club, 1951-52, pres. 1952; v.p. Gamma Phi Beta Mother's Club, 1953-54; mem. White Contemporary Group, 1958-63; vol. worker Thrift House and Altar Guild. Ch. of Incarnation; corr. sec. Tuesday study dept. Dallas Woman's Forum, 1960; block worker Heart Dr., Cancer Dr., Muscular Distrophy Dr., 1955—. Mem. Dalla Lawyer's Wives Club, Laurel Book Club, Women's Aux. Nat. Assn. Claimants' Counsel of Am., Dallas Theatre Guild State Fair Tex. Clubs: Dallas Athletic Club, Dallas Athletic Country Club. Home: 6256 Lupton Dr Dallas TX 75225

BAKER, REGINALD BARNES, elec. engr.; b. Winchester, Va., June 4, 1941; s. Charles Barnes and Mary Genevieve (Sullivan) B.; B.E.E., U. Va., 1963, postgrad., 1965; m. Elva Francis McCauley, Apr. 18, 1960; children—Karen Yvonne, Eric Barnes. Designer, Reynolds Metals Co., Richmond, Va., 1963-66; elec. engr. research and devel. Doubleday & Co., Berryville, Va., 1966-68; v.p. Baker & Anderson Electric Co., Inc., Winchester, Va., 1968—; partner Baker Assos., cons. engrs. Fallout shelter analyst Dept. Def. Registered profl. engr., Va., W.Va. Mem. Nat., Va. (Bull Run chpt.) socs. profl. engrs. Club: Mountain Falls Hunt. Home: Route 6 Box 353-1A Winchester VA 22601 Office: 27 N Braddock St Winchester VA 22601

BAKER, RUSSELL MONTEZ, lawyer; b. Celeste, Tex., Mar. 11, 1906; s. William Perry and Kathleen (Bolte) B.; grad. So. Meth. U., 1928; m. Ollie Marie Dedman, Aug. 26, 1927; children—Harriet Kay, Russell Montez. Admitted Tex. bar, 1929, asso. Caldwell, Gillen, Francis & Gallagher, Dallas, 1929-32; jr. partner Caldwell, Gillen, Francis & Gallagher, 1932-38; mem. firm Caldwell, Baker &Jordan, Dallas, 1938-59; now sr. mem. firm Baker & Foreman. Research fellow Southwestern Legal Found. Fellow Am. Coll. Trial Lawyers, Tex. Bar Found.; mem. Assn. Trial Lawyers Am.) Am. Judicature Soc., Law Science Acad., Law Sci. Found. of Am., Internat. Acad. Trial Lawyers, Tex. Assn. Plaintiff Attys. (pres.), Internat. (patron), Am. (nuclear energy com. 1971-73), Tex., Dallas bar assns., Am. Bd. Trial Advocates, Internat. Soc. Barristers, Delta Chi. Clubs: Dallas Athletic. Dallas Athletic Country, Cosmopolitan (internat. pres. 1950-51). Editor Am. Trial Lawyers Assn. Law Jour. Home: 6256 Lupton Dr Dallas TX 75225 Office: 1907 Elm St Dallas TX 75201

BAKER, THOMPSON SIMKINS, mining exec.; b. Jacksonville, Fla., Aug. 25, 1905; s. John Daniel and Julia Church (Simkins) B.; grad. Ga. Mil. Acad., 1922; B.S., Davidson Coll., 1926; m. Cynthia L'Engle, Nov. 23, 1931 (dec.); children—Sarah Church (Mrs. Philip J. Porter), Edward L., John Daniel II; m. 2d, Sarah Burroughs Savitz, Apr. 12, 1970. Chmn. bd. Fla. Rock Industries, Inc. (name formerly Shands & Baker, Inc.), Jacksonville, 1929—; dir. State Bank of Jacksonville, State Bank of North Jacksonville, Fla. Pub. Co., Barnett Mortgage Trust. Mem. Fla. Council of 100; v.p. North Fla. council Boy Scouts Am.; mem. Gator Bowl Assn.; pres. Evergreen Cemetery Assn.; mem. Duval County Adv. Com.; chmn. devel. com. Jacksonville Port Authority; mem. devel. council Bapt. Meml. Hosp. Bd. dirs. YMCA, United Fund, Jacksonville Zool. Soc., St. Luke's Hosp.; trustee Jacksonville U.; bd. visitors Davidson Coll. Served to lt. col., USMCR, 1942-45. Decorated Legion of Merit, Bronze star, Purple Heart. Mem. Jacksonville Area C. of C. (Com. of 100), Sigma Alpha Epsilon. Presbyn. Rotarian (dir.). Clubs: Fla. Yacht, Friars, Timuquana Country, Seminole, Ponte Vedra, River, University (Jacksonville). Home: 3761 Ortega Blvd Jacksonville FL 32210 Office: PO Box 4667 Jacksonville FL 32201

BAKER, WILLIAM ROBERT, judge; b. Nashville, Apr. 30, 1932; s. William Gilbert and Jane Elizabeth (Petty) B.; grad. McCallie Sch., 1949; B.A., Vanderbilt U., 1953, J.D., 1956; postgrad. Emory U., 1954; m. Glover Dale Tarver, June 9, 1956; children—Jane Clopton, John Sims Tarver. Fgn. service officer U.S. Dept. State, 1956-59; U.S. vice consul, Belém, Pará, Brazil, 1956-58; admitted to Tenn. bar, 1956; practiced in Ashland City, Tenn., 1959-73; gen. sessions judge Cheatham County, 1966—. Dir. Ashland City Bank and Trust Co. Mem. Ashland City Planning Commn., 1967—, Cheatham County Planning Commn., 1969—; sec.-treas. Tenn. Gen. Sessions Judges Conf., 1968-73; chmn. Cheatham County Indls. Devel. Bd., 1968—; del. to 1965 Tenn. Constnl. Conv. Bd. dirs. St. Augustine's Student Center Vanderbilt U., Nashville. Mem. Ashland City C. of C. (pres. 1961-63), Am., Tenn. bar assns. Republican. Episcopalian (vestryman, sr. warden 1966-68, 71; del. to Tenn. Diocesan Conv. 1959—; layreader 1956—). Home: 308 S Main St Ashland City TN 37015 Office: 205 N Main St Ashland City TN 37015

BAKKE, BURTON FRED, periodontist; b. Montevideo, Minn., Apr. 19, 1923; s. Fred Oscar and Hilda Victoria (Anderson) B.; student Hamline U., 1941-42; D.D.S., U. Minn., 1951; m. Mona Ann Simpson, Sept. 17, 1949; children—Denise, Susan, Bart. Gen. practice dentistry, Brownton, Minn., 1951-54; staff dentist VA Hosp., Excelsior Springs, Mo., 1954-57; resident in periodontics VA Hosp., N.Y.C., also N.Y. U., 1957-59; staff dentist Syracuse (N.Y.) VA Hosp., 1959-65; chief dental service VA Hosp., Washington, 1965—; asso. prof. periodontics Howard U. Coll. Dentistry, 1966—. Mem. adv. bd. Prince Georges Community Coll. Served to 1st lt. USAAF, 1943-46. Decorated Air Medal. Fellow Internat. Coll. Dentists; mem. Am. Dental Assn., Am. Acad. Periodontists, N.E. Soc. Periodontists, Greater Washington Soc. Periodontics, Omicron Kappa Upsilon. Home: 9804 Arbor Hill Dr Silver Spring MD 20903 Office: VA Hosp 50 Irving St NW Washington DC 20422

BALD, MARGARET, librarian; b. Pitts., Sept. 3, 1913; d. Edmond James and Margaret (Siemon) Bald; A.B., Asbury Coll., 1934; B.S., Carnegie Inst. Tech., 1935. Asst. Carnegie Library, Pitts., 1935-37; asst. librarian Carnegie Steel Corp., 1937-40; asst. Pasadena Pub.

Library, 1940-44; various positions U.S. Navy Dept., 1944-48; librarian Bob Jones U., Greenville, 1948—. Mem, Am., S.C. library assns. Home: Bob Jones Univ Greenville SC 29614

BALDERRAMA, FRANCISCO ENCINAS, physician, med. service adminstr.; b. Mexico City, Mexico, Aug. 12, 1928; s. Roman B. and Guadalupe G. (Encinas) B.; M.D., Nat. Sch. Medicine, U. Mexico, 1952; diploma fgn. asst. Sorbonne U., Paris, France, 1954; postgrad. Nat. Inst. Nutrition, 1955-58. Intern, Gen. Hosp., Mexico, 1950; practice medicine, specializing in gastroenterology and internal medicine, Mexico City, 1957-63; asst. med. dir. Syntex Labs., Palo Alto, Cal., 1962-65; asst. med. dir. clin. research birth control Syntex Internacional, Mexico City, 1966-72, med. dir., 1972—. Mem. Family Planning Assn. Ams., Mexican Soc. Gastroenterology, Am. Assn. Planned Parenthood Physicians, Am. Fertility Soc. Home: A-13 1004 Torres de Mixcoac Mexico 19 DF Mexico Office: 2822 Carretera Mexico Toluca Mexico 10 DF Mexico

BALDINGER, STANLEY, govt. ofcl.; b. St. Paul, Jan. 11, 1932; s. Samuel Charles and Ethel Sylvia (Yaffe) B.; B.A., U. Minn., 1953, M.A., 1956; M.S., Columbia, 1969; m. Judith Gittl Altman, Dec. 20, 1970. Fgn. service officer State Dept., Washington, Rome, Italy, 1957-64; program organizer for fgn. govt. ofcls. Social Security Adminstrn., Washington, 1964-66; adminstrv. asst. to dept. dir. Nat. Capital Planning Commn., Washington, 1966-67; chief overall program design D.C. Office Planning and Mgmt., Washington, 1970—. Recipient Merit award D.C. Office Planning and Mgmt., 1972. Towser Found. fellow, 1956, William Kinne Fellows fellow, 1968. Mem. Am. Acad. Polit. and Social Sci., World Future Soc., Nat. Trust for Historic Preservation, Smithsonian Instn. Author: Planning and Governing the Metropolis: The Twin Cities Experience, 1971. Home: 2939 Van Ness St NW Washington DC 20008 Office: 1325 E St NW Washington DC 20004

BALDRIDGE, WILLIAM KARNES, lawyer, county judge; b. Bartlett, Tex., Aug. 13, 1908; s. William and Cora (Karnes) B.; student N. Tex. State U., 1929-31; LL.B., So. Methodist U., 1942; m. Catherine Martin, Apr. 10, 1930; children—Betty, Barbara (Mrs. C.E. Hesse). Admitted to Tex. bar, 1940; pvt. practice, Denton, 1940—; asst. dist. atty., 1941-45, dist. atty., 1945-51, county judge, 1955-69, judge county ct. at law, 1969-71. Mem. C. of C., State Bar Tex., Denton County Bar Assn. Kiwanian. Home: 2015 Locksley Lane Denton TX 76201 Office: 326 E McKinney St Denton TX 76201

BALDWIN, BENJAMIN ARMISTEAD, rice mill exec.; b. Dallas, Aug. 30, 1916; s. Bernard Benjamin and Aline Willett (Leache) B.; B.S. in Mech. Engring., Tex. A. and M. U., 1939; m. Violet Elizabeth Hill, Oct. 6, 1940; children—Benjamin Armistead, Alan Carter. Spl. rep. Timken Roller Bearing Co., Dallas, 1940; purchasing agt. Uncle Ben's Inc., Houston, 1946-53, marketing asst., 1954-57, export sales dir., 1958-67, v.p. export and comml. operations, 1968—. Served to maj. CAC, AUS, 1941-46. Mem. Houston (internat. com. 1964—), Am. Arab (dir. 1969—) chambers commerce, Rice Millers Assn. (dir. 1964-72, pres. 1973), Rice Council Assn. (dir. 1968—), Rotarian. Clubs: Memorial Drive Country, University (Houston). Home: 11915 Broken Bough St Houston TX 77024 Office: 13000 Westheimer St Houston TX 77042

BALDWIN, DONALD EARL, veterinarian; b. Kansas City, Mo., Jan. 25, 1930; s. Charles Joseph and Bertha (Schweddi) B.; student Kansas City Jr. Coll., 1952-53; B.D., D.V.M., Kansas State U., 1958; M.S. in Microbiology, Ohio State U., 1962; m. Gloria Ermatinger, Apr. 26, 1952; children—Deborah, Eric, Marianne. Animal disease research U.S. Dept. Agr., Plum Island, N.Y., 1958-60; instr. Ohio State U., 1960-62; animal disease research U.S. Dept. Agr., Ames, Ia., 1962-65; tech. dir. research and prodn. Affiliated Labs., White Hall, Ill., 1965-71; tech. adviser Ft. Dodge-Nova Lab., Mexico City, Mexico, 1971-72; dir. bio prodn. Fort Dodge (Ia.) Labs., 1972—. Served with USCG, 1948-52. Mem. Am. Vet. Med. Assn., Am. Soc. Microbiology, Tissue Culture Assn., Am. Legion, Phi Zeta. Lion. Address: Fort Dodge-Nova Lab Mexico City DF Mexico

BALDWIN, E. JOAN BOLLING (MRS. DONALD WINSTON BALDWIN), govt. ofcl.; b. Norton, Va., Aug. 31, 1930; d. Henry Cecil and Nelle (Mann) Bolling; A.B., Hollins Coll., 1953; M.A., U. Va., 1955; m. Donald Winston Baldwin, Nov. 16, 1957; children—Winston Monroe, Elizabeth Bolling, Alan Henry. Adminstrv. sec. to asst. register of copyrights Library of Congress, 1955-59; profl. staff mem. U.S. Senate Republican Policy Com., 1959-62; press and research asst. to U.S. Senator Len B. Jordan, 1962-64; polit. analyst, researcher Rep. Nat. Com., 1964; polit. researcher James N. Juliana & Assos., Washington, 1964-69; legislative asst. to U.S. Senator James B. Pearson, Washington, 1969-71; spl. asst. to asst. sec. for community and field services Dept. Health, Edn. and Welfare, Washington, 1971-73; profl. mem. staff for legislation U.S. Senate Rep. Policy Com., 1973—. Treas. Twig, Alexandria, Va., 1968—. Pres. Alexandria Rep. Women's Club, 1965-66. Mem. D.A.R. (chpt. provisional mem.), Chi Omega Alumnae No. Va., Hollins Coll. Alumnae No. Va. Episcopalian. Clubs: Belle Haven Country (Alexandria), Capitol Hill (Washington). Home: 1309 Trinity Dr Alexandria VA 22314 Office: 330 Independence Av SW Washington DC 20201

BALDWIN, ESTHER LILLIAN, pianist, composer; b. Chgo.; d. George and Minnie (Neidigh) Baldwin; pvt. study Dr. Francis Hemington, Chgo.; Mus. B., Columbia Sch. Music and Art, in 1946; Mus. D.; widow. Tchr., dir. Baldwin Music Studios, Columbia, S.C., 1927—, concert pianist, 1946—; composer Sonata in C Major; Sonata in D Major. Mem. faculty Nat. Guild Piano Tchrs. Adjudicator Nat. Guild Piano Tchrs. Bd. govs. Exec. and Profl. Hall of Fame. Fellow Internat. Inst. Arts and Letters; mem. Internat. Pianist's Guild, Nat. Guild Piano Tchrs. (chmn. Columbia, S.C. chpt.), Am. Coll. Musicians, Internat. Platform Assn., Musicians Club Am. Home: Box 114 Apt 118 Davis Hotel Columbia SC 29202 Studio: 1712 Sumter St Columbia SC 29201

BALDWIN, GARZA, JR., lawyer; b. Litchfield, Ill., Mar. 10, 1921; s. Garza and Hazel (Satterlee) B.; student Vincennes U., 1938-39; B.S., Ind. U., 1942, J.D., 1948; m. Margaret Jean Skinner, Sept. 7, 1946; children—Deborah Allen (Mrs. Ellsworth Rutherford Lyman, Jr.), Garza III, Mary Beth, Daniel David, Benjamin Willis. Admitted to Ind. bar, 1948, U.S. Supreme Ct. bar, 1956, N.C. bar, 1959; practiced in Sullivan, Ind., Indpls., 1948-57; city atty. Sullivan, 1951-55; asso. counsel Olin Mathieson Chem. Corp. (name changed to Olin Corp.), Pisgah Forest, N.C., 1957-58, div. counsel, 1958-63, sr. counsel, 1963-69, group v.p., 1969-71, group pres., 1971—; dir. Asheville office Wachovia Bank & Trust Co. Dir. Pub. Works and Safety, Sullivan, 1951-55; trustee, sec. Sullivan Sch. Bd. 1956-57; pres. N.C. Indsl. Council, 1965-67; dir. Ednl. Found., Commerce and Industry N.C., Inc., 1965—; mem. N.C. Gov.'s Council Econ. Devel., 1967-68; mem. N.C. Gov.'s Efficiency Study Commn., 1973—. Trustee Transylvania Community Hosp.; bd. dirs., v.p., mem. exec. com. N.C. Citizens Assn., pres., 1974; bd. dirs. U. N.C. at Asheville Found., N.C. Engring. Found.; trustee U. N.C. at Asheville. Served to lt. (j.g.) USNR, 1942-45. Mem. Am., Ind., N.C. State bar assns., Western Carolina Mfrs. Assn. (pres. 1962-71), Am. Judicature Soc., Order of Coif, Am. Legion, Kappa Sigma, Phi Delta Phi. Republican. Presbyn. Mason (32 deg.), Elk. Clubs: Asheville (N.C.) Country (bd. govs.), Asheville City, Biltmore Forest Country. Home: 18 Beaverdam Knoll Asheville NC 28804 Office: PO Box 200 Pisgah Forest NC 28768

BALDWIN, JACK NORMAN, educator; b. Nephi, Utah, Dec. 6, 1919; s. Ernest Frank and Eva (Christison) B.; B.A., U. Utah, 1942, M.A., 1947; Ph.D., Purdue U., 1950; m. Adell Cheney, Sept. 6, 1946; children—Marian (Mrs. Bruce Broadhead), Jack Norman, Jr., Eva Lee. Asst. prof., asso. prof., then prof. microbiology Ohio State U., Columbus, 1950-63; prof. microbiology U. Ky., Lexington, 1963-67; research prof. microbiology U. Ga., Athens, 1967—. Served with M.C., AUS, 1942-45. Mem. Am. Soc. Microbiology, Am. Acad. Microbiology, Soc. for Gen. Microbiology, A.A.A.S., Soc. Exptl. Biology, Sigma Xi, Phi Lambda Upsilon. Home: 185 Pendleton Dr Athens GA 30601 Office: Dept Microbiology U Ga Athens GA 30601

BALINT, FRANCIS JOSEPH, govt. ofcl.; b. Johnstown, Pa., Mar. 2, 1932; s. William Stephen and Mary Myrtle (Beaujon) B.; B.S., Ind. U., 1954; M.S., U. Pitts., 1959; postgrad. Am. U., 1967-68; m. Barbara Jean Eggleston, Apr. 7, 1956; children—Franics Joseph, Stephen, Kathleen, Aimee, Thomas, Patricia. Customer engr. IBM, Pitts., 1955-56; sr. project engr. Gulf Research & Devel. Co., Pitts., 1956-65; supr. phys. sci. U.S. Weather Bur., Washington, 1965-69; chief mgmt. systems div. Nat. Oceanic and Atmospheric Adminstrn., Washington, 1969-72, dep. dir. Office Mgmt. and Computer Systems, 1972—. Lectr., Am. U., Civic Service Inst.; nat. lectr. Assn. for Computing Machinery. Bd. dirs. Internat. U. U.S.A. Recipient U.S. Dept. Commerce Suggestion of Year award, 1970; U.S. Dept. Commerce Silver medal, 1971. Mem. Assn. for Computing Machinery, N.Y. Acad. Sci., Kappa Delta Pi, Sigma Phi Epsilon. Roman Catholic. K.C. Home: 2400 Jackson Pkwy Vienna VA 22180 Office: AD3 NOAA Rockville MD 20852

BALL, CHARLES DENVER, supt. schs.; b. Mattie, Ky., May 16, 1917; s. Greenville and Virginia (Moore) B.; B.S., Morehead State U., 1946; M.A., Marshall U., 1959; postgrad., U. Ky., 1965-67; m. Kathryn Wolford, Dec. 4, 1937; children—Denny James, Jenny (Mrs. Buford Crager). Tchr. math. and physics pub. schs., Russell, Ky.; 1946-47; Raceland, Ky., 1947-48; Ashland, Ky., 1949-51; dean boys Ashland High Sch., 1954-55; prin. Raceland High Sch., 1954-58; supt. schs. Fairview Ind. Schs., Ashland, 1959—. Mem. Ashland Bd. Edn., 1952-53. Mem. N.E.A., Ky. Edn. Assn. (dir. 1973—), Am., Ky. assns. sch. adminstrs., Nat. Assn. Sch. Execs. (acad. leader 1969-71, 73-74). Home: 1428 Wurts Av Ashland KY 41101 Office: Fairview Schools Ashland KY 41101

BALL, CLAYTON GARRETT, JR., physician; b. Evanston, Ill., June 28, 1939; s. Clayton Garrett and Una L. (Brown) B.; B.S., Yale, 1961; M.D., Northwestern U., 1965; m. Anne F. Morrison, June 27, 1962; children—Martha Anne, Clayton Garrett III, Jennifer Corrine. Intern, Evanston Hosp., 1965-66; resident anesthesiology U. Va. Med. Center, Charlottesville, 1968-71; asst. prof. anesthesiology, 1971—. Served with USNR, 1966-68. Diplomate Am. Bd. Anesthesiology. Fellow Am. Coll. Anesthesiology; mem. Va., Albermarle County med. socs., Am., Va. socs. anesthesiologists. Home: 632 Preston Pl Charlottesville VA 22903

BALL, EDWARD, chmn., dir. Fla. East Coast Ry. Co.; pres., dir. Jacksonville Properties, Inc., St. Joseph Tel. & Tel. Co., Port St. Joe Dock & Terminal Ry., Apalachicola No. R.R., St. Joseph Land and Devel. Co., Keystone Sand Co., Ballynahinch Castle, Inc., Jacksonville Properties, Inc., Wakulla Silver Springs Co., Gen. Die & Mfg. Corp., Fla. Fibre Box Co., New Eng. Container Co., Talisman Sugar Corp., Fla. Sugar Corp., West Fla. Properties, Am. Tangier Trading & Devel. Co., Tangier Benevolent Co., Nat. Bd. & Paper Mills, Dublin, Ireland, others; chmn. exec. com., pres., dir. St. Joe Paper Co., Jacksonville. Pres., treas., dir. Nemours Found.; bd. dirs. Alfred I. DuPont Found. Cons. Edward Ball Wildlife Found. Office: 803 Fla Nat Bank Bldg Box 1380 Jacksonville FL 32202

BALL, GENE V., physician, educator; b. Rivesville, W. Va., June 28, 1931; s. John Franklin and Rebecca E. (Rush) B.; M.D., Vanderbilt U., 1959; m. Sara Jane Clark, June 6, 1959; children—Rebecca Anne, Hilary Elizabeth. Intern Cin. Gen. Hosp., 1959-60; resident U. Pa. Hosp., Phila., 1960-61, U. Miami-Jackson Meml. Hosp., 1961-65; instr. U. Ala. Sch. Medicine, 1965-66, asst. prof., 1966-68, asso. prof., 1968-71, prof. internal medicine, 1971—. Pres. Ala. chpt. Arthritis Found., 1969-71. Served with AUS, 1952-54. Diplomate Am. Bd. Rheumatology. Fellow A.C.P.; mem. Ala. Zool. Soc. (v.p. 1969-71). Republican. Episcopalian. Clubs: Mt. Brook Swim and Tennis, Relay House (Birmingham). Home: 3516 Springvalley Ct Birmingham AL 35223 Office: 1919 7th Ave S Birmingham AL 35223

BALL, IVAN ESTUS, utility co. exec.; b. Ages, Ky., July 5, 1923; s. Alex and Maude (Crider) B.; student Eastern Ky. State Tchrs. Coll., 1939-41; B.S. in Accounting, Bowling Green Coll. Commerce, 1948; m. Madaline Cornett, Oct. 18, 1946 (div. 1952); 1 dau., Lynn Estes (Mrs. George John Hume); m. 2d, Mona Elizabeth Gilbert, Sept. 25, 1954; 1 stepdau., Penelope Elizabeth (Mrs. Burton G. Goldstein). With Peoples Water & Gas Co., Miami Beach, Fla., 1948-58, financial v.p., 1957-58; with Tampa Gas Co. (Fla.), 1955-57, financial v.p., 1957; controller So. Gulf Utilities, 1959-60; controller City Gas Co. Fla., Hialeah, 1961, financial v.p., asst. sec., asst. treas., 1966—; v.p. finance, asst. sec., asst. treas., dir. Essel Corp., 1973—; mgmt. cons. Stone & Webster Service Corp., 1962-65. Served with USAAF, 1941-45. Decorated Bronze Star medal. Mem. Gas Inst. Greater Miami, Am. Gas Assn., C. of C., Beta Pi. Democrat. Clubs: Miami Shores Country, Basset Hound (Am.), South Fla. Basset Hound, Greater Miami Dog. Home: 800 NE 97th St Miami Shores FL 33138 Office: 955 E 25th St Hialeah FL 33013

BALL, JAMES AUGUSTUS, educator; b. Bessemer, Ala., Mar. 19, 1922; s. William Franklin and May Belle (McKinney) B.; B.S., Auburn U., 1950, M.S., 1960; m. Helen Florence Whitehead, Feb. 21, 1943; children—May Belle (Mrs. Michael Teeters), Kathleene (Mrs. John Bolles), Jane (Mrs. Norris Vaughan). With U.S. Steel Corp., 1940; profl. baseball player and mgr., 1946-55; tchr., athletic dir. Baker High Sch., Columbus, Ga., 1950-66; athletic dir. Gainesville (Ga.) Jr. Coll., 1967—, chmn. dept. phys. edn., 1967—. Speaker coaching clinics and banquets, 1946—. Served with USNR, 1942-46. Recipient Freedom Found. award, 1962; Outstanding Educator award, 1970; Coach of Year award City of Columbus, Ga., 1954-56, 59-60, 66, State of Ga., 1955. Mem. Nat., Ga. edn. assns., Ga. Athletic Coaches Assn., Ga. Assn. Health and Phys. Edn., A.A.H.P.E.R. Baptist. Home: Rt 1 Oakwood GA 30566

BALL, LEWIS EDWIN II, diesel and turbine generator sets co. exec.; b. Huntsville, Tex., July 1, 1931; s. William Perry and Mary Ethel (Osborne) B.; B.B.A., U. Tex., Austin, 1952; m. Marion Buchanan, June 5, 1954. Mgr., Ernst & Ernst, C.P.A.'s, Houston, 1952-71; v.p., controller Stewart & Stevenson Services, Inc., Houston, 1971—, also dir.; v.p., treas. C. Jim Stewart & Stevenson, Inc., Houston, 1971—, Machinery Acceptance Corp., Houston, 1971—. Vice pres., bd. dirs. Soc. for Performing Arts; asst. treas. bd. dirs. Childrens Mental Health Services, Houston; asst. treas., trustee Houston Mus. Natural Sci. C.P.A., Tex. Mem. Am. Inst. C.P.A.'s, Tex. Soc. C.P.A.'s (dir.), Nat. Assn. Accountants, Financial Execs. Inst., Am. Soc. Ins. Mgmt., Houston C. of C. Methodist (vice chmn. adminstrn. bd.). Club: Ramada, Garden of the Gods. Home: 6122 Valley Forge Houston TX 77027 Office: Box 1637 Houston TX 77001

BALL, MAHLON MARSH, geophysicist, educator; b. Lawrence, Kan., Apr. 7, 1931; s. Mahlon Cyrus and Leona Ruth (Marsh) B.; B.S., Kan. U., 1953, M.S. in Geology, 1957, Ph.D., 1959; M.Sc. in Geophysics, U. Birmingham, Eng., 1958; m. Marilyn Ringler, Aug. 10, 1953; children—Jon, Jeffrey. Research geologist Shell Devel. Co., Miami, Fla., 1959-63, mgr. prodn. research, Houston, 1965-67; div. geologist Shell Oil Co., Houston, 1963-65; prof. geophysics U. Miami Rosenstiel Sch. Marine and Atmospheric Sci., 1967—. Cons. geophysicist Amoco, City Service, Shell, Siebens, Union oil cos., Gulf U. Research Corp., Joint Oceanographic Instn. Mem. geol. adv. bd. U. Kan. Served to lt. (j.g.) USNR, 1953-56. Grantee, Office Naval Research, 1967-73, Nat. Geog. Soc., 1971-73, NSF, 1967—. Recipient Best Paper award Soc. Econ. Paleontologists and Mineralogists, 1967; Eramus Haworth award U. Kan., 1952. Mem. Geol. Soc. Am., Am. Assn. Petroleum Geologists (Best Paper award 1962), Soc. Exploration Geophysicists, European Soc. Exploration Geophysics, Am. Geophys. Union, Kan. U. Alumni Assn. (pres. Miami chpt.), Miami Geol. Soc. (pres.), Tau Beta Pi, Sigma Chi, Sigma Tau, Sigma Gamma Epsilon, Omicron Delta Kappa. Club: Kansas (v.p.). Contbr. articles to profl. jours. Home: 3903 Granada Blvd Coral Gables FL 33134 Office: 13 Rickenbacker Causeway Miami FL 33149

BALL, MICHAEL FRANCIS, JR., med. educator, assn. exec.; b. N.Y.C. Dec. 27, 1933; s. Michael Francis and Rita Patricia (Klipper) B.; B.S. St. Peter's Coll., 1955; M.D., Georgetown U., 1959; m. Janet Margaret deGroot, June 18, 1960; children—Michael F., Frederick A., Margaret J., Joseph A., Patricia K., Edward C. Intern Georgetown U. Hosp., Washington, 1959-60; resident Duke Med. Center, Durham, N.C., 1960-62, fellow, 1962-63; research fellow Georgetown U., Washington, 1963-64, instr. dept. medicine, 1964-67, asst. prof., 1967-72, asso. prof., 1972—; dir. biomed. research and faculty devel. Assn. Am. Med. Colls., Washington, 1972—. Established investigator Am. Heart Assn., 1968-72. Recipient Research and Devel. award Am. Diabetic Assn., 1966-67. Fellow A.C.P.; mem. Am. Fedn. Clin. Research (pres. 1972-73), Am. Diabetic Assn., Endocrine Soc., So. Soc. Clin. Investigation. Editor Clin. Research, 1969-71. Home: 6201 Kellogg Dr McLean VA 22101 Office: Assn Am Med Colls 1 Du Pont Circle Washington DC 20036

BALL, RUSSELL MARTIN, elec. engr.; b. Chgo., Oct. 28, 1927; s. William Ashby and Florence Charlotte (Weiner) B.; B.S., U. Ill., 1949, M.S., 1950; Ph.D., U. Va., 1970; m. Ruth Lois Halvorsen, Apr. 23, 1955; children—Russell Martin, Thomas Alan, Sarah Ruth. Chief engr., Nuclear Chgo., 1950-54; lab. mgr. Babcock & Wilcox, Lynchburg, Va., 1956—. Pres., Lynchburg Guidance Center, 1962-68; mem. curriculum cum. Central Va. Community Coll., Lynchburg, 1969—. Served with inf., AUS, 1945-46. AEC fellow, Reactor Sch., 1954, nuclear fellow, 1966. Mem. Am. Nuclear Soc., I.E.E.E. Elk. Home: 1620 Belfield Pl Lynchburg VA 24503 Office: PO Box 1260 Lynchburg VA 24505

BALL, THEODORE MACKLIN, JR., civil engr.; b. Worcester, Mass., Aug. 26, 1929; s. Theodore Macklin and Ella (Gerow) B.; B.S. in C.E., Va. Mil. Inst., 1952; M.S. in Indsl. Engring., Purdue U., 1962; m. Katherine Wells, Dec. 27, 1952; children—Ted, John. Commd. 2d lt. USAF, 1952, advanced through grades to maj., 1964; pilot, 1952-67; honorable discharge, 1967; aerospace environmental test facility constn. engr. USAF, Arnold Air Force Sta., Tenn., 1967—. Decorated D.F.C., Bronze Star medal, Air medal with 12 oak leaf clusters. Mem. Soc. Am. Mil. Engrs. Mason. Home: 405 Lannom Circle Tullahoma TN 37388 Office: AEDC (DEL) Arnold Air Force Station TN 37388

BALLANTYNE, ROBERT HUBBARD, educator; b. Kansas City, Mo., Aug. 2, 1932; s. Robert Law and Ruth (Hubbard) B.; B.A., U. Ia., 1954, M.A., 1958; Ed.D., Wash. State U., 1962; m. Mary Ann Olsen, Sept. 30, 1956; children—Shelli Ann, Kerri Lynn, Robbi Kay, Brian Robert. Instr. edn. Wash. State U., 1961-62; faculty edn. Duke, 1962, sr. counselor, 1962-64, coordinator instl. studies, 1964-66, asst. to pres., 1966-67, dir. admissions, 1967-73, asso. prof. edn., 1967—, asst. to provost, 1973—. Served with USAF, 1954-57. Fulbright lectr. and cons., Cyprus, 1973-74. Mem. Am. Psychol. Assn., Am. Personnel and Guidance Assn. Presbyn. (elder). Home: 2510 Wrightwood St Durham NC 27705

BALLARD, CHARLES LEE, utilities co. exec.; b. Kannapolis, N.C., July 13, 1933; s. Homer Lee and Luella (Reynolds) B.; B.S. in E.E., Duke, 1958; M.B.A., U. Miami, 1969; m. Cynthia Elizabeth McAden, Apr. 12, 1957; children—Robert Scott, Lee McAden, LuAnn Marie. Planning engr. Fla. Power & Light Co., Miami, 1958-67, computer systems analyst, 1967-68, sr. analyst, 1968-69, dir. computer systems and programming, 1969-73, exec. asst., 1973—. Troop com. mem. S. Fla. council Boy Scouts Am., 1973-74; pres., Mangowood Estates Civic Assn., 1971-72, also bd. dirs. Served with Signal Corp, AUS, 1953-55. Registered profl. engr., Fla. Mem. I.E.E.E., Phi Delta Theta. Democrat. Methodist (mem. pastor-parrish relations com. 1972-73). Clubs: Toastmasters (pres. Miami 1965). Home: 8265 SW 151st St Miami FL 33158 Office: 4200 W Flagler St Miami FL 33158

BALLARD, DAVID GEORGE, lawyer; b. Maryville, Tenn., July 17, 1934; s. Fred Raymond and Georgia (Dykes) B.; B.A., Eastern Ky. State U., 1960; LL.B., U. Tenn., 1962; m. Judith Jones, Oct. 17, 1964; children—David George, Steven Glenn. Adjuster State Farm Mutual Ins. Co., Nashville, 1962-63; admitted to Tenn. bar, 1962; practiced in Maryville, Tenn., 1964—; mem. firms Bird, Navratil, Ballard & Tate, 1964—. Chmn. Blount County Democratic Exec. Com., 1966-70; co-chmn. Blount County Citizens for Humphrey-Musky, 1968. Served with USNR, 1955-59. Kiwanian. Home: Route 8 Luther Dr Maryville TN 37801 Office: 100 N Court St Maryville TN 37801

BALLARD, EDWIN DAVIDSON, state ofcl.; b. Lancaster, Ky., Aug. 17, 1917; s. George Thomas and Elizabeth (Buchanan) B.; student U. Ky., 1938-39; m. Mary Nancy Gray, Sept. 19, 1942; children—Patricia Carol, Elizabeth Ann. Civilian flight instr. USAAF Res., 1942-45; comml. pilot, 1945-47; bur. mgr. Van Winkle & Arhold, auto agy., Lancaster, Ky., 1947-50; with Ky. Dept. Revenue, Frankfort, 1950—, supr., 1956-60, asst. dir., 1960-62, dir. tax div., 1962—. Instr., Internat. Assn. Assessing Officers, 1960—; Latin Am. tax assistance res. Internal Revenue Service, 1963—. Recipient Donohoo essay award Internat. Assn. Assessing Officers, 1966. Mem. Internat. Assn. Assessing Officers (editorial bd. 1968-70; presdl. citation 1972), Soc. Real Estate Appraisers (past pres. Lexington, dir.). Democrat. Author: Manual on Tax Maps, 1960; Property Tax Administration Manual, 1957; Real Property Appraisal Manual, 1962. Home: 235 Pepper Dr Lexington KY 40505 Office: Capitol Annex Frankfort KY 40601

BALLARD, GEORGE SPEIGHTS, JR., bldg. materials co. exec.; b. Monticello, Ga., July 27, 1919; s. George Speights and Willie Maude (Benton) B.; grad. McCallie Sch., Chattanooga, 1936; A.B., Emory U., Atlanta, 1940; M.B.A., Harvard, 1942; m. Marguerite Louisa Candler, Feb. 3, 1973. With Coca-Cola Co., Atlanta, 1947-52; mgr. corporate finance Underwood, Neuhaus & Co., Houston, 1953-64; spl. asst. Small Bus. Assn., Washington, 1965-66; asso. dir. devel. Emory U., Atlanta, 1966-68; v.p. finance West Lumber Co. and subsidiary Asso. Distbrs., Inc., Atlanta, 1968—. Served to capt. USNR, 1942-46. Mem. Phi Beta Kappa, Omicron Delta Kappa. Episcopalian. Author: Long-Term Financing for Retailers, 1962. Home: 3092 Argonne Dr NW Atlanta GA 30305 Office: 1491 Piedmont Dr Atlanta GA 30309

BALLARD, HAROLD NOBLE, physicist; b. Little Rock, Feb. 11, 1919; s. John Alexander and Gladys Georgina (Booker) B.; B.S., U. Tex., 1948; M.S., Tex. A. and M. U., 1950; postgrad. (NSF fellow) N.M. State U., 1960-61, Advanced Study Inst. Aurora and Airglow, U. Keele (Eng.), 1966, Advanced Study Inst. for Physics and Chemistry of Atmospheres, 1972; m. Bo Clay Ballard, May 22, 1969. Faculty, U. Tex., El Paso, 1950-54, asso. prof., 1957-64; physicist Los Alamos Sci. Lab., 1954-57; physicist upper atmosphere research atmospheric scis. lab. White Sands Missile Range, 1964—. Served with AUS, 1941-45. Recipient NSF certificate for contbns. to 1966 U.S. solar eclipse expdns.; 14 awards for contbns. to research programs Dept. Army, 1964-72. Mem. Am. Phys. Soc., Am. Meteorol. Soc., Am. Geophys. Union, A.A.A.S., Sigma Xi, Sigma Pi Sigma, Phi Kappa Phi, Alpha Chi. Co-author book, 1960; author monograph, 1964. Contbr. articles to profl. jours. Patentee in field. Home: 239 El Puente St El Paso TX 79912 Office: Atmospheric Scis Lab White Sands Missile Range NM 88002

BALLARD, NANCY LEE (MRS. W. MICHAEL WALSH), librarian; b. Bedford, Va., Aug. 25, 1927; d. Henderson Suter and Ethel Blanche (Davis) Ballard; B.A. in Edn., Madison Coll., 1948; postgrad. Am. U., 1966-68; m. W. Michael Walsh, Mar. 3, 1973. Tchr. pub. schs., Bassett, Va., 1948-56; reference librarian Office Chief of Engrs. Library, U.S. Army, Washington, 1956-60; chief pub. services sect. Indsl. Coll. Armed Forces Library, Washington, 1960-64, asst. librarian, 1964-66, library dir., 1966—. Mem. Spl. Libraries Assn. (sec.-treas. mil. librarian's div. 1969-70), Am. D.C. library assns., D.A.R., U.D.C., Beta Sigma Phi. Episcopalian. Home: 4306 S 8th St Arlington VA 22204 Office: Industrial College of Armed Forces Library Fort Lesley J McNair Washington DC 20315

BALLARD, ROBERT EARL, lawyer; b. Center, Tex., Feb. 27, 1936; s. Wayman E. and Effie M. (Wheeler) B.; B.B.A., U. Houston, 1960, LL.B., 1967; m. Eva Oakley, Dec. 23, 1960; children—Lewis, Laura. Admitted to Tex. bar, 1965; mem. firm Kronzer Abraham & Watkins, Houston, 1962—, pres., 1969—. Served with USMC, 1960-65. C.P.A., Tex. Home: 41 Carolane St Houston TX 77024 Office: 711 Fannin St Houston TX 77002

BALLARD, WILEY PERRY, JR., petroleum co. exec.; b. Birmingham, Ala., Oct. 23, 1922; s. Wiley Perry and Helen (McCary) B.; student U. N.C., 1940-43; m. Anne Hart Equen, Sept. 12, 1947; children—Anne McCary, Wiley Perry. Pres. Ballard Corp., Atlanta, 1948—, Ballard & Curren Corp., Atlanta, 1948—, Ballard & Cordell Corp., Atlanta, 1958—; dir. Phenix Supply Co., Atlanta, Phenix Supply Co., Tampa, Fla., W.P. Ballard Co., Greensboro, N.C. and Washington, Phenix Supply, Birmingham. Mem. Mineral Leasing Commn. Ga., 1968-71. Served with USAAF, 1943-45. Mem. Oil Investment Inst. (gov.), Phi Delta Theta. Episcopalian. Clubs: Atlanta Country, Peachtree Golf, Commerce, Piedmont Driving, Capital City (Atlanta). Home: 2576 Howell Mill Rd NW Atlanta GA 30327 Office: 1608 Peachtree Center Towers 230 Peachtree St NW Atlanta GA 30303

BALLARD, WILLIAM THOMAS, chem. engr.; b. Mt. Pleasant, Tex., Dec. 22, 1923; s. William T. and Jeanie (Jackson) B.; B.S., U. Tex., 1946; M.S., Ga. Inst. Tech., 1950; m. Marian LaVerne Ehlers, May 3, 1947; children—William Brian, Bruce Thomas, Barbara Ann. Dist. engr. Tex. Dept. Health, Tyler, 1946-58; process engr. LaGloria Oil & Gas Co., Tyler, 1958-65, chief engr., 1965-69, gen. supt., 1969-70; regional dir. environmental health Tex. Dept. Health, Tyler, 1970—. Fellow Tex. Pub. Health Assn. (pres. 1956-57); mem. Nat., Tex. socs. profl. engrs. Mason (Shriner). Club: Optimist. Home: 1015 N Azalea Dr Tyler TX 75701 Office: PO Box 2003 Tyler TX 75701

BALLEW, LOWELL NAMON, ednl. adminstr.; b. Oak Grove, Tex., Nov. 21, 1929; s. James Arvel and Fannie Ann (Richardson) B.; Asso. Sci., Texarkana Coll., 1957; B.S., E. Tex. State U., 1958, postgrad., 1968-72; M.S., Tex. Inst. Technol., 1961; postgrad. Tex. A. and M. U., 1962; m. Paula Pearson, Jan. 22, 1970; children—Michelle, William. Head dept. math. and engring. Frank Phillips Coll., Borger, Tex., 1958-64; sr. programmer, analyst McDonnell Douglas Aircraft, St. Louis, 1965-66; instr. computer sci. E. Tex. State U., Commerce, 1966-69, dir. computer center, 1969—. Served with USAF, 1948-52. Faculty research grantee, 1968-70. Mem. Tex. Assn. Ednl. Data Systems (mem. bd. 1972—), Phi Delta Kappa. Home: 201 Brookhaven Terrace Commerce TX 75428

BALLINGER, CHARLES L., med. assn. ofcl., osteo. physician; b. East Liberty, O., Aug. 20, 1899; s. Amer Jesse and Anna (Morse) B.; B.A., Ohio Wesleyan U., 1922; D.O., Kirksville Coll. Osteo. Medicine, 1925; m. Mildred Elizabeth Bowling, Sept. 2, 1922; children—Richard, Bowling, Robert Morse, Lucy Ann (Mrs. Robert Craig), Larson. Intern Delaware Springs Hosp., Delaware, O., 1925-26, gen. practice of osteo. medicine and surgery, Medina, O., 1926-35, Akron, O., 1935-43, Toledo, 1943-59. Trustee Parkview Hosp., Toledo, 1939—, sec., treas., 1943—. Fellow Am. Coll. Osteo. Surgeons (gov. 1942-58, sec. 1953—, exec. sec. 1960—, pres. 1950—, Orel F. Martin medal 1968), Ohio Assn. Osteo. Physicians and Surgeons (pres. 1948—). Methodist (trustee 1930-49). Kiwanian (pres. 1936). Home: Apt 302 6815 Edgewater Dr East Coral Gables FL 33133 Office: Suite 21 4601 Ponce de Leon Blvd Coral Gables FL 33146

BALLINGER, JAMES N., rancher; b. Hanna, Okla., Apr. 1, 1914; s. George H. and Millie J. (McClain) B.; B.S. in Agr., Okla. State U., 1937; m. Mary Katherine Henson, Jan. 1, 1938; children—Barbara (Mrs. Paul Moore), James N., George C., Amelia Kay (Mrs. James Pearce). Asst., county supr. Farm Security Adminstrn. (now Farmers Home Adminstrn.), Okla., 1937-43; farmer, Eufaula, Okla., 1943—; dairy farmer, 1953-66; tchr. vets. agr. Eufaula Sch. System, 1946-57; land appraiser Eufaula Lake Project, 1958-60; mem. Okla. Bd. Agr., Oklahoma City, 1964—, pres., 1966-71; mem. Okla. Agrl. Stablzn. and Conservation Com., 1973—; dir. Canadian Valley Elec. Co-op. Mem. McIntosh County Republican Com., 1960—. Chmn. bd. dirs. Eufaula Indsl. Found.; McIntosh County Soil and Water Conservations Dists. Named Hon. State Farmer, County 4-H Club. Mem. Farm Bur., Eufaula C. of C. (dir.), McIntosh County Dairy Herd Improvement Assn. (sec.-treas.), Alpha Zeta. Baptist (deacon). Lion (dir.). Home: Route 3 Eufaula OK 74432

BALLINGER, ZOMA CHARLES, petroleum engr.; b. Traverse City, Mich., Mar. 19, 1916; s. Charles Clinton and Ruth (Schumburgh) B.; B.S. in Chem. Engring., Okla. State U., 1940; m. Minnie Lois Wagnon, Nov. 11, 1941. Engr., chemist Halliburton Services, Flora, Ill., 1940-42; asso. engr. Office Chief of Ordnance, Detroit, 1942-44; area engr. Gulf Oil Co., Houston, 1944-65; sr. engr. Skelly Oil Co., Oklahoma City, 1966—. Instr., Our Am. Bus. System; cons. corrosion supr. Monsanto Chocolate Bayou Chem. Plant; chmn. Hobbs (N.M.) Petroleum Industries Com., 1962—. Mem. Am. Petroleum Inst. (chmn. Duncan, Okla. chpt.), Soc. Petroleum Engrs. Mason. Home: 2303 Country Club Rd Duncan OK 73533 Office: Skelly Oil Co 1001 Beech OK 73533

BALMAN, SIDNEY, constrn. co. exec.; b. Mpls., Mar. 19, 1919; s. Max and Lea (Goodman) B.; student U. Minn., 1937-40; B.B.A., So. Meth. U., 1952; m. Patricia Ann Papert, Nov. 29, 1952; children—Beth Leigh, Sidney, Jr. Owner, chief exec. officer Tex. Builders Devel. Co., Dallas, 1950-67; owner, pres. Sidney Balman, Inc., Dallas, 1965—; gen. partner Sidney Balman, Ltd., Dallas, 1965—; mem. nat. operators marketing com. Howard Johnson Co., 1970—; partner, operations exec. Preston Alpha Properties. Capt., Presbyn. Hosp. Bldg. Drive, 1962; vol. solicitor United Fund, 1960; mem. jr. bd. Jewish Welfare Assn., 1955-56; mem. Cotton Bowl Council, Dallas, 1969-73; hon. councilman Circle 10 council Boy Scouts Am., 1972—; asso. bd. mem. Girl's Town U.S.A., Austin, 1972—; active fund-raising Nat. Jewish Hosp., Denver, 1960-72, Children's Med. Center, Dallas, 1965—, Dallas Symphony Assn., 1970-71, Dallas Civic Opera Assn., 1970, 71; orgn. worker N. Tex. Devel. Council, 1971—. Trustee St. Mark's Sch., Dallas, pres. Dads Club, 1968-69. Served with USAAF, 1941-45; ETO. Decorated Air medal with 4 oak leaf clusters, D.F.C. Mem. N. Dallas C. of C. (pres. 1973), Hotel Sales Mgmt. Assn., So. Meth. U. Alumni Assn., Nat., Tex. hotel-motel assns., UN Assn. U.S. (mem. UN Day com.). Jewish religion (trustee temple). Mason (Shriner). Clubs: T Bar M Tennis, Dallas Tennis, Sportsmen's of Tex., Dallas Woods and Water (Dallas). Home: 4645 Park Lane Dallas TX 75220 Office: 10333 N Central Expy Dallas TX 75231

BALMER, GLENN GRAVES, scientist; b. Woodston, Kan., Dec. 24, 1914; s. Clarence A. and Myrtle W. (Graves) B.; A.B., Ft. Hays Kan. State Coll., 1937; M.S., State U. Ia., 1939; postgrad. U. Mich., Summer 1940, U. Colo., evenings 1950-54, Northwestern U., evenings 1955-56; m. Mary F. Neely, Dec. 25, 1942; children—Darrell G., Glenn B. Grad. asst. State U. Ia., Iowa City, 1937-39; tchr. Estherville (Ia.) Jr. Coll., 1939-41; physicist engring., research lab. Bur. Reclamation, Denver, 1945-54; sr. devel. engr. research, devel. lab., Portland Cement Assn., Skokie, Ill., 1955-66, highway research engr., Fed. Hwy. Adminstrn., Washington, 1966—. Served with AUS 1941-45; PTO; lt. col. Res. Decorated Air medal. Mem. Nat. Safety Council (com. on winter driving hazards), Am. Soc. Testing Materials, Am. Concrete Inst., Transp. Research Bd., Sigma Xi, Delta Epsilon. Contbr. articles tech. lit. Home: 11128 Hunt Club Dr Potomac MD 20854 Office: Fed Hwy Adminstrn Washington DC 20590

BALNICKY, ROBERT GABRIEL, clergyman; b. Elizabeth, N.J., Apr. 18, 1922; s. Harry and Irene (Sawicky) B.; student Pensacola Jr. Coll., 1949, Emory U., 1950. Columbia Theol. Sem., Decatur, Ga., 1952; m. Elizabeth Marie Hartenstein, Apr. 18, 1943; children—Richard Ozzie, Barbara Gail. With Merck & Co., Rahway, N.J., 1939-42; pastor Troy (N.C.) Presbyn. Ch., 1952-55, 1st Presbyn. Ch., Ocean Drive Beach, S.C., 1955-56, McCutchen Meml. Ch., Union, S.C., 1956-60, Fairfield Presbyn. Ch., Pensacola, Fla., 1960-64; founder, pastor Trinity Bible Ch., Pensacola, 1964-70; pastor Inskip Presbyn. Ch., Knoxville, Tenn., 1970-72, Grace Presbyn. Ch., Knoxville, 1973—; chaplain Pay Cash Wholesale Grocery, 1972—; pres. Robert G. Balnicky Evang. Assn., Inc., Pensacola. Pres. Union County (S.C.) Ministers Assn., 1957; chmn. Enoree Presbytery Com. Evangelism, 1956-60; mem. com. evangelism S.C. Synod, 1956-60; chmn. bd. dirs. Pensacola Youth for Christ; bd. dirs. Fla. Alcohol-Narcotics, Inc., Fla. United Christian Action, Inc.; mem. adv. bd. Community Action Program, Am. Security Council. Lt. col., chaplain Fla. Civil Air Patrol, 1965-70; dep. wing chaplain Tenn. Civil Air Patrol 1970—. Served as aviation machinist's mate, flight engr. 1st class USN, 1942-49. Recipient Four Chaplains citation Chapel Four Chaplains, Phila., 1960, Meritorious Service award Civil Air Patrol, 1973. Mem. Am. Legion (state chaplain S.C. 1956-58, post comdr. 1953-54; grad. Am. Legion Coll., Indpls. 1954; mem. nat. press assn.; chmn. S.C. religious emphasis com. 1956-58, mem. nat. comdr.'s flying squadron; mem. Century Club 1954-55), 40 and 8 (grand aumonier S.C.; state chaplain 1957-59, aumonier nat., nat. chaplain 1959-60; local chaplain 1961-70), Navy League, World Ministry Fellowship (pres. 1966-68), Nat. Assn. Evangs., Internat. Order St. Luke the physician. Mason (32 deg.). Office: PO Box 12228 Knoxville TN 37912

BALOSSI, JOHN FRANCESCO, artist, educator; b. S.I., N.Y., May 28, 1931; s. Francesco and Anunziata (Venditti) B.; B.F.A., Columbia, 1956, M.A., 1960; m. Yolanda Lopez, Apr. 26, 1953; children—John Alexander, Albert, Yolanda Yvette. One man shows at U. P.R. Mus., San Juan, 1961, Casa del Arte, San Juan, 1963, Galeria Colibri, San Juan, 1963-65, Ruth White Gallery, N.Y.C., 1966, 68, 71, Galerie Jacques Perrin, Paris, France, 1968, Galeria Santiago, San Juan, 1968-72, Galleria San Marco, Genoa, Italy, 1966, J. Walter Thompson Gallery, N.Y.C., 1966-68. Sculpture represented in pub. collections at U. P.R. Mus., Rio Piedras, Mus. Modern Art, N.Y.C., Museo de P.R., San Juan, Chase-Manhattan, N.Y., Ponce (P.R.) Mus., Finch Coll., N.Y.C.; executed murals at U. P.R., Corp. Renovación Urbana y Vivienda, Manati, P.R. Asst. prof. fine arts U. P.R., 1962—, also dir. extension gallery, 1968-70, design center, 1972-73. Served with USMCR, 1948-52; Korea. Home: 725 Cafeto St Rio Piedras PR 00924

BALOWS, ALBERT, microbiologist; b. Denver, Jan. 3, 1921; s. Lazerus and Anna (Kleiner) B.; B.A. in Biology (Lowell scholar), Colo. Coll., 1942; M.S. in Microbiology, Syracuse U., 1948; Ph.D. in Microbiology (Haggin fellow), U. Ky., 1952; m. Patricia Ann Barker, Oct. 7, 1956; children—Eve Ellen, Daniel Scott. Microbiologist St. Joseph Hosp., Lexington Clinic, Lexington, Ky., 1952-69; chief bacteriology br. Center Disease Control, USPHS, Atlanta, 1969—; asst. prof. U. Ky. Med. Center, Lexington, 1960-63, asso. prof. medicine, cell biology, 1963-69; asso. prof. pathology Emory U. Med. Sch., 1970—; prof. biology Ga. State U., Atlanta, 1970—; cons. clin. microbiology VA Hosp., Good Samaritan Hosp., both Lexington, 1965-69, Med. Service Corps, U.S. Dept. Army, 1973—. Bd. dirs. Nat. Conf. Christians and Jews, Lexington, 1960-64. Served with M.C., AUS, 1943-45. Diplomate Am. Bd. Microbiology. Fellow Am. Acad. Microbiology (bd. govs. 1973—), N.Y. Acad. Scis., A.A.A.S., Am. Pub. Health Assn.; mem. Am. Soc. Microbiology, Am. Soc. Clin. Pathology, Soc. Gen. Microbiology, Am. Assn. U. Profs., Med. Mycol. Soc. Ams., Soc. Applied Bacteriology, Assn. Schs. Allied Health Professions, Am. Venereal Disease Assn., Sci. Writers Guild, Blue Key, Sigma Xi, Tau Kappa Alpha. Mem. B'nai B'rith. Editor: Applied Microbiology, 1965—, C.C. Thomas series Medical Microbiology of books, 1964—. Home: 7640 Ryefield Dr NE Atlanta GA 30338 Office: Center Disease Control 1600 Clifton Rd NE Atlanta GA 30333

BALSLEY, HOWARD LLOYD, educator; b. Chgo., Dec. 3, 1913; s. Elmer Lloyd and Katherine (McGlashing) B.; A.B., Ind. U., 1946, M.A., 1947, Ph.D., 1950; postgrad. John Hopkins, 1947-48, U. Chgo., summer 1948; m. Irol Verneth Whitmore, Aug. 24, 1947. Asst. prof. econs. U. Utah, Salt Lake City, 1949-50; asso. prof. econs., dir. Sch. Bus., Russell Sage Coll., Troy, N.Y., 1950-52; asso. prof. econs. Washington and Lee U., Lexington, Va., 1952-54; prof. bus. statistics, head dept. bus. and econ. research La. Tech. U., Ruston, 1954-65; prof. bus. adminstrn. and statistics Tex. Tech. U., Lubbock, 1965—. Served with USAAF, 1943-46. Mem. Am. Econ. Assn., Am. Statis. Assn., Southwestern Social Sci. Assn., Am. Inst. Decision Scis. Club: Lubbock (Tex.) Country. Author: (with James Gemmell) Principles of Economics, 1953; Readings in Economic Doctrines, vols. 1 and 2, 1961; Introduction to Statistical Method, 1964; Quantitative Research Methods for Business & Economics, 1970; (with Vernon Clover) Business Research, 1974. Home: 2609 Ridge Rd Lubbock TX 79409

BALSLEY, IROL WHITMORE (MRS. HOWARD L. BALSLEY), educator; b. Venus, Neb., Aug. 22, 1912; d. Sylvanus Bertrand and Nanna (Carson) Whitmore; B.A., Neb. State Coll., Wayne, 1933; M.S., U. Tenn., 1940; Ed.D., Ind. U., 1952; m. Howard Lloyd Balsley, Aug. 24, 1947. Tchr. high schs., Osmond and Walthill, Neb., 1934-37; asst. prof., Ind. U., 1942-49; lectr. U. Utah, 1949-50, Russell Sage Coll., 1953-54; prof. office adminstrn. La. Tech. U., 1954-65, also head dept. office adminstrn., 1963-65; prof. bus. edn. Tex. Tech. U., 1965-72, prof. edn., 1972—; coordinator of USAF clk.-typist tng. program Pa. State U., 1951, inst., head office tng. sect. TVA, 1941-42; editorial asst. South-Western Pub. Co., 1940-41. Mem. Nat. Bus. Edn. Assn. (past pres. research found.), Nat. Assn. for Bus. Tchr. Edn., Adminstrv. Mgmt. Soc., N.E.A., Nat. Collegiate Assn. Secs. (co-founder, past pres.), Pi Lambda Theta, Delta Pi Epsilon (past nat. sec.), Beta Gamma Sigma, Pi Omega Pi, Sigma Tau Delta, Alpha Psi Omega. Author: (with Wanous) Shorthand Transcription Studies, 1968; (with Robinson) Integrated Secretarial Studies, 1963; (with Wood and Whitmore) Homestyle Baking, 1973. Home: 2609 Ridge Rd Lubbock TX 79403

BAMBER, JOHN IRVING, city ofcl.; b. Plaucheville, La., Aug. 20, 1921; s. James Deway and Mary Madeline (Ducote) B.; student La. State U., 1939-41, Internat. Corr. Schs., 1960; m. Arclie Phrozine McMaster, Nov. 9, 1941; 1 son, Deway James. Forms rep. Economy Forms Corp., Des Moines, 1941-45; with Stearns Rogers Co., Denver, 1945-50; heavy constrn. supt. R.P. Farnsworth, New Orleans, 1950-56; asst. city engr., Marshall, Tex., 1956-67; dir. pub. works, Nederland, Tex., 1967—. Profl. handwriting analyst; personnel cons., marriage and teaching counselor; tchr. Am. Banking Inst., Lamar U., 1971-72. Mem. Internat. Graphoanalysis Soc., Inst. Certification Engring. Technicians, Am. Water Works Assn., Am., Tex. (membership com. 1967-74) pub. works assns. Episcopalian. Mason (Shriner); mem. Order Eastern Star. Home: 1420 Chicago Av Nederland TX 77627 Office: PO Box 967 Nederland TX 77627

BAMFORTH, STUART SHOOSMITH, educator; b. White Plains, N.Y., Oct. 23, 1926; s. Arthur and Eva Madeleine (Shoosmith) B.; A.B., Temple U., 1951; M.A., U. Pa., 1954, Ph.D., 1957; m. Olivia Mary Birdsell, July 8, 1952; children—John, Marjory. Mem. faculty biology Newcomb Coll. of Tulane U., New Orleans, 1957—, asso. prof., 1964-72, prof., 1972—. Cons. protozoologist Phila. Acad. Natural Scis., summers 1956, 60, 63, 68, 73. Mem. A.A.A.S., Soc. Protozoologists (exec. com.), Ecol. Soc. Am., Am. Soc. Limnology and Oceanography, London Zool. Soc., Groupement des Protistologues de Langue Francais. Home: 2512 Pine St New Orleans LA 70125

BANDELIN, FREDERICK JOHN, pharm. co. exec.; b. Cin., Mar. 24, 1913; s. Frederick and Lillian (Sebald) B.; B.S., U. Cin., 1936, B.A., 1939; postgrad. Antioch Coll., 1940-42, Stevens Inst. Tech., 1943-45, U. Ill., 1947-49, Western Res. U., 1958-61, U. Tenn. at Memphis, 1965-68, U. Wis. seminar, 1965, St. Louis Coll. Pharmacy, 1968-69, Sadler Inst., 1968, U. Tenn., 1968; m. Mary Margaret Johnson, May 29, 1940; children—MaryJean, Fred John. Chemist, William S. Merrell Co., Cin., 1936-41; chemist Fidelity Med. Supply Co., Dayton, 1941-42; pharm. chemist Vick Chem. Co., N.Y.C., 1942-46; tech. dir. Flint, Easton & Co., Decatur, Ill., 1946-58; dir. pharm. research Strong, Cobb & Co., Cleve., 1958-60; v.p., dir. research Strong, Cobb, Arner, Inc., Cleve., 1960-63; dir. lab. control and devel. Plough Inc., Memphis, 1963-68, dir. labs. research and devel., 1968—. Adviser, U.S. Pharmacopoeia Com., 1950—; instr. med. units U. Tenn., 1965-72, asst. prof., 1972; mem. Nat. Formulary Com., 1950—. Pres., Brierwood Assn., Memphis, 1965-66. William S. Merrell fellow, 1936-37. Fellow A.A.A.S., Am. Inst. Chemist; mem. Am. Pharm. Assn. (chmn. sci. sect., 1949-50, 52-53), Am. Chem. Soc. (chmn. 1954-55), N.Y. Acad. Scis., Soc. Cosmetic Chemists, Am. Inst. Engrs., Walter Reed Soc. Contbr. articles to profl. jours. Home: 253 Brierview St Memphis TN 38138 Office: 3030 Jackson Av Memphis TN 38112

BANDERA OLAVARRIA, JOSE, lawyer; b. Mexico City, Mexico, July 7, 1931; s. Jose and Virginia (Olavarria) Bandera; student Escue la Libre de Derecho, 1948-53, Lawyer Degree, 1954; Dr. Degree, U. Paris, 1955; m. Maria Teresa Quijano, May 8, 1962; children—Maria Teresa, Jose, Matilde. Admitted to Mexico bar, 1954; mem. firm Hardin Hess Santos Galindo & Hanhausen, Mexico City, 1951—. Clubs: Campestre de la Ciudad de Mexico, Bankers (Mexico City). Home: 13 Montes de Oca Mexico City 11 Mexico Office: 1-401 Lopez Mexico City 1 Mexico

BANDROFCHECK, JOSEPH, mfg. co. exec.; b. Hunker, Pa., Sept. 1, 1920; s. Paul and Catherine (Kukla) B.; student Internat. Accountants Soc., 1948-53, U. Pitts. Extension, 1950-54; m. Mary Kay Wesbecher, Oct. 27, 1951; children—Charles Paul, Susan Kathleen, Mark Joseph. Accountant, Robertshaw Controls Co., Youngwood, Pa., 1941-57, Richmond, Va., 1957-59, asst. controller, 1959-68, asst. treas., 1968-69, treas. 1969—. Served with USNR, 1944-46. Mem. Nat. Assn. Accountants (pres. Richmond chpt. 1967-68), Financial Execs. Inst., Planning Execs. Inst. (pres. Richmond chpt. 1964-65), West Richmond Bus. Men's Assn. Home: 3705 Shore Dr Richmond VA 23225 Office: 1701 Byrd Av Richmond VA 23261

BANDY, WILLIAM HENRY, physician; b. Maiden, N.C., July 25, 1917; s. William Gaither and Myrtle (Daniel) B.; B.S., Appalachian State U., 1937; M.D., Med. Coll. Va., 1941; M.P.H., Johns Hopkins, 1952; m. Pauline Pope, June 21, 1941; children—Margaret Elizabeth (Mrs. Albert Barnes Marshall), William Hollis. Intern, City Hosp., Winston Salem, 1941-42; resident Watts Hosp., Durham, N.C., 1946-49; practice medicine, specializing in preventive medicine, Georgetown, Del., 1949-56, Hickory, N.C., 1956-66, Williamsburg, Va., 1966-71, Hampton, Va., 1972—; dep. state health dir., Georgetown, 1949-56; dist. health dir., Hickory, 1956-66; dir. pub. health Colonial Health Dist., 1966-71; dir. Hampton Health Dept., 1972—. Served from 1st lt. to maj. M.C., AUS, 1942-46. Diplomate Am. Bd. Preventive Medicine. Fellow Am. Coll. Preventive Medicine; mem. A.M.A., Va., Hampton med. socs. Am. Pub. Health Assn. Home: 207 Watkins Dr Hampton VA 23669 Office: 3130 Victoria Blvd Hampton VA 23661

BANG, GARY RACH, dentist; b. Chgo., July 19, 1941; s. Olaf Edward and Orpha Agatha (Hulteen) B.; A.B., U. Richmond, 1963; D.D.S., Med. Coll. Va., 1967; m. Susan Stitley Block, Aug. 14, 1965; children—Michael Edward, Eric Riley. Pvt. practice dentistry, Staunton, Va., 1969—; mem. dental staff Kings Daus. Hosp., Staunton, 1969—, sec., 1971-72. Bd. dirs. Staunton-West Augusta

County unit Am. Cancer Soc. Served with Dental Corps, AUS, 1967-69. Mem. Am., Va. dental assns., Va. Gun Owners and Sportsmens Alliance (dir. 1972—), Nat. Rifle Assn. (life), Amateur Trapshooting Assn., N.G. Assn. U.S., Alumni Assn. Med. Coll. Va., Delta Sigma Delta (life), Sigma Alpha Epsilon. Presbyn. (dir. ch.). Mason (32 deg., Shriner), Elk, Kiwanian (dir.). Clubs: Stonewall Rifle and Pistol (sec. 1970-71), Rockbridge Baths Hunt, Westside Swim. Home: 502 Robin St Staunton VA 24401 Office: Profl Bldg W Frederick St Staunton VA 24401

BANISTER, JOHN ROBERT, librarian; b. Saginaw, Mich., Feb. 5, 1912; s. John Lansing and Agnes (Bell) B.; A.A., Bay City (Mich.) Jr. Coll., 1934; A.B., U. Mich., 1936; B.S. in L.S., U. Ill., 1937; m. Nancy Simpson, Sept. 9, 1944; 1 dau., Nancy Anne (Mrs. Edmund Alan Attebury, Jr.). Asst. reference librarian Mich. State Library, Lansing 1936-41; order librarian, tech. library TVA, 1942-44; extension librarian Lansing Pub. Library, 1944-46; regional librarian Ill. State Library, Mt. Carmel, 1946-48; pub. library cons. gen. extension div. U. Fla., 1948-50; dir. libraries Chattahoochee Valley Regional Library, Columbus, Ga., 1951—; cons. in field, 1960—. Del. Assembly Libraries of Ams., 1946; chmn. jr. mems. round table Mich. Library Assn., 1941, Ill. Library Assn., 1946. Chmn. Muscogee County (Ga.) chpt. Am. Heart Assn., 1952, Community Services Assn. Columbus, 1956-58; bd. dirs. Columbus Symphony Guild, 1962—, Columbus United Givers, 1957-59. Mem. Am. (council 1940-41, chmn. jr. mems. round table 1946), Ga. (v.p. 1960), Southeastern (chmn. pub. libraries sect. 1948) library assns. Presbyn. Rotarian (dir. Columbus 1963—), Club: Columbus Country. Editor: The Junior Librarian, 1939-41; The Florida Public Library News-Letter, 1948-50. Contbr. articles to profl. jours. Home: 2952 Roswell Lane Columbus GA 31906 Office: W C Bradley Mem Library Columbus GA 31906

BANKS, DAVID LEE, personnel exec.; b. Lynchburg, Va., Mar. 8, 1925; s. Lonnie T. and Mamie L. (Singleton) B.; B.S., Bluefield State Coll., 1948; M.S., W.Va. U., 1950; m. Ophelia E. Thompson, Apr. 17, 1954. Faculty, Bluefield State Coll., 1952-69, asso. prof., 1967-69; employment rep. Babcock & Wilcox Co., Lynchburg, 1969-70, employee relations rep., 1970-73, mgr. employee relations, 1973—. Mem. Sch. Bd., Lynchburg, 1971—. Served with AUS, 1943-46; ETO. Mem. Am. Soc. Personnel Adminstrn., W.Va. Acad. Sci. (life), Alpha Phi Alpha. Home: 4606 Hilltop Dr Lynchburg VA 24502 Office: PO Box 785 Lynchburg VA 24505

BANKS, HARVEY W., educator, astrophysicist; b. Atlantic City, N.J., Feb. 7, 1923; s. Harvey W. and Nettie Lee (Jackson) B.; B.S. in Physics, Howard U., 1946, M.S. in Physics, 1948; Ph.D. in Astronomy, Georgetown U., 1963; m. Ernestine Boykin, Aug. 20, 1951; children—Harvey Washington, III, Deborah, Dwann, Darryle. Research asso. Howard U., Washington, 1948-50; electronic engr. Nat. Electronics, Washington, 1952-54; research asso. Georgetown U., 1955-63; prof. dept. physics and astronomy Howard U., Washington, 1968—. Active Boy Scouts Am. Mem. Am. Astron. Soc., Am. Optical Soc., Am. Phys. Soc., Sigma Xi, Beta Kappa Chi, Sigma Pi Sigma. Club: Golf (Arlington, Va.). Home: 6233 N 23d St Arlington VA 22205

BANKS, RICHARD GRIFFIN, army officer, ednl. adminstr.; b. Montgomery, Ala., Oct. 12, 1912; s. Richard Griffin and Blanche (Cartter) B.; B.A.E., U. Fla., 1934; M.A., U. Va., 1949; m. Isabel Gwendolyn Day, July 26, 1942; children—Ann Cartter, Barbara Jane. Tchr. pub. schs., Fla., 1935-40; commd. 1st lt. U.S. Army, 1940, advanced through grades to col., 1960; dir. instrn. Arty. Sch., 1954-57, polit. rep. U.S. Forces Germany to German Govt., 1958-61, prof. mil. sci. U. Miami, 1964-67, ret. 1967; research scientist U. Miami, Coral Gables, Fla., 1967-71, asst. dean Coll. Arts and Scis., 1971—. Decorated Legion of Merit, Bronze Star with oak leaf cluster, Purple Heart; Order of Ulchi (Korean). Mem. Delta Tau Delta, Phi Kappa Phi, Kappa Delta Pi, Phi Delta Kappa, Pi Delta Epsilon. Democrat. Episcopalian. Club: Army Navy of Coral Gables. Co-author articles pattern analysis of disturbed coll. students. Home: 14320 SW 86th Av Miami FL 33158 Office: U Miami Coral Gables FL 33146

BANKS, ROBERT BLACKBURN, found. exec.; b. Wichita, Kan., Oct. 12, 1922; s. Bernard T. and Georgia (Corley) B.; B.S., Northwestern U., 1947, M.S., 1948; Ph.D. (Hilp fellow), U. Cal., 1951; D.I.C., U. London, 1952; m. Gunta Matisons, Dec. 25, 1960 children—Steven, Erik. Research engr. U. Cal., 1949-51, Infilco, Inc., Tucson, 1952-54; asso. prof. civil engring., Northwestern U., 1954-59, chmn. sci.-engring. com., 1955-57, chmn. dept. civil engring., 1956-59, asst. dean research and grad. studies, prof. engring. sci., 1959-61; dean engring. U. Ill., Chgo., 1963-67; adviser sci. and engring. Ford Found., Mexico and C.Am., 1967—; vis. prof. Grad. Sch. Engring., Nat. Univ. of Mexico, 1967—; dir. of research SEATO Grad. Sch. Engring., Bangkok, Thailand, 1961-63. Cons., McDonnell Aircraft Corp., 1958, Space Tech. Labs, Inc., 1960. Served from ensign to lt. (j.g.), USNR, 1943-46. Fulbright fellow, 1951-52. Mem. Am. Inst. Aeros. and Astronautics, Am. Soc. C.E., Internat. Hydraulics Research Assn., A.A.A.S., Am. Geophys. Union, Am. Soc. Engring. Edn., Sigma Xi, Tau Beta Pi, Pi Mu Epsilon, Delta Nu Alpha, Sigma Chi. Home: Meseta 111 Pedregal Mexico City 20 Mexico Office: Ford Found Alejandro Dumas 42 Mexico City 5 Mexico

BANKS, THOMAS GRAY, civil engr.; b. Nelsonville, Tex., Aug. 1, 1887; s. Francis Marion and Hermine (Schaefer) B.; certificate in civil engring. Internat. Corr. Schs., 1906-13; m. Sallie Florida Haralson, May 4, 1909; children—Thomas Gray Jr., Sarah May (Mrs. Alex W. Leslie), Lucy Mildred (Mrs. Robert M. Van de Pas), James Robert, William Ross. With M.K.T. Ry., Tex. and Okla., 1906-30; asst. city engr. Okla. City, 1930-32, supt., engr. water dept., 1932-37; sole practice cons. engring., Oklahoma City, 1937-39, Woodville, Tex., 1950-54; with Corps Engrs. U.S. Army, various locations, 1939-44, chief installations, utility operations, 1944-50; civil engr. firm C.H. Guernsey & Co., Oklahoma City, 1956—. Served to capt. C.E., U.S. Army, 1918-19; ETO. Registered profl. engr., Okla., Tex. Fellow Am. Soc. C.E.; mem. Okla. Geneal. Soc., S.A.R., Ret. Officers Assn., Am. Decs. Knights Garter, Barons Magna Charta, Banks Assn. and Related Families. Mason, Rotarian. Club: Oklahoma City Boat. Home: 716 NE 21st St Oklahoma City OK 73105 Office: 2701 N Oklahoma St Oklahoma City OK 73105

BANKSTON, JESSE H., state ofcl., cons.; b. Mt. Hermon, La.; B.A., La. State U., also M.A. in Pub. Adminstrn.; Ph.D., U. N.C.; m. Ruth Paine; 4 children. Formerly cons. Griffenhagen and Assos., Chgo.; research supr. La. Dept. Revenue, Baton Rouge; adminstrv. asst. La. Dept. Civil Service, Baton Rouge; exec. asst. La. Dept. Instns., then dir.; dir. La. Hosp Bd.; exec. sec. La. Hosp Assn.; dir. La. Dept. Hosps., Baton Rouge; now mem. La. Bd. Edn. Sec.-treas. Bankston Enterprises, Inc.; now prin. Bankston Assos.; dir. Baton Rouge Bank and Trust Co. Formerly pres. YMCA, Baton Rouge, chmn. fund-raising com.; chmn. fund-raising com. Baton Rouge Gen. Hosp.; mem. fund-raising coms. Our Lady of the Lake Hosp., Salvation Army; mem. White House Conf. Children and Youth, 1950, 60, 70, White House Conf. on Aging, 1960-61. Mem. La. Democratic central com., now also sec. Mem. Assn. for Mental Health (dir.), La., Am. hosps assns., Am. Soc. Pub. Adminstrn., Acad. Hosp. Counselors, Internat. inst. Hosp. Cons. Baptist (trustee). Mason (Shriner). Home: 9526 Southmoor Dr Baton Rouge LA 70815 Office: 5700 Florida Blvd Suite 206 Baton Rouge LA 70806

BANUELOS, ROMANA ACOSTA (MRS. ALEJANDRO BANUELOS), banker; b. Miami, Ariz., Mar. 20, 1925; d. Juan Francisco and Teresa (Lugo) Acosta; ed. elementary sch., Mexico; m. Alejandro Banuelos, Dec. 31, 1949; children—Martin Torres, Carlos Torres, Ramona. Founder, Ramona's Mexican Food Products, Inc., Los Angeles, 1949; founding dir. Pan Am. Nat. Bank, East Los Angeles, Cal., 1964, chmn. bd. dirs., 1969—; treas. U.S., Washington, 1971-74. Founder, Ramona's Mexican Food Products Scholarship Found., Inc., 1970. Active Nat. Fedn. Republican Women, Women's Nat. Rep. Club N.Y., Griffith Park Hills Rep. Assembly Los Angeles, League Rep. Women D.C. Named Outstanding Businesswoman of Year Mayor of Los Angeles, 1969; recipient Commendation award Bd. Suprs. County Los Angeles, 1971; Nat. award achievement Office Minority Bus. Enterprise, U.S. Dept. Commerce, 1972. Clubs: Capitol Hill (Washington); International Friendship (San Diego). Home: 2500 Virginia Av Washington DC 20037 Office: Treasury Dept Office of Treasurer Washington DC 20220

BARAFF, ALVIN SIDNEY, clin. psychologist; b. Washington, Apr. 22, 1935; s. Abraham and Betty (Zuckerman) B.; B.A., U. Md., 1957; M.S., U. Miami (Fla.), 1959; Ph.D., U. Ky., 1963 children—Ramie Lynn, Todd Mitchell. Clin. trainee VA Hosps., Lexington, Ky., Cin., 1960-63; child psychologist Woods Schs., Langhorne, Pa., 1959; asst. prof. Emory U., Atlanta, 1963-66; clin. psychotherapist, Atlanta, 1966-69; supervisory clin. psychologist Rehab. Center for Alcoholics, Occoquan, Va., 1969—; pvt. practice psychotherapy, Washington, 1969—. Pres., dir. Career Planning, Inc., Atlanta, 1967—; bd. dirs. Gestalt Inst., Washington, 1971—. Mem. Am., Ga., D.C., Va., Md., assns. Home: 1400 S Joyce St Arlington VA 22202 Office: 2430 Pennsylvania Av NW Washington DC 20037

BARANCO, RAPHAEL ALVIN, dentist; b. Baton Rouge, Nov. 19, 1932; s. Beverly Victor and Evelyn Gertrude (Edmond) B.; B.S. in Biology, Xavier U., 1956; D.D.S., Meharry Med. Coll., 1961; m. Terry Bryant, June 10, 1961; children—Angela, Rachel, Raphael. Intern, Jersey City Med. Center, 1961-62; pvt. practice dentistry, Baton Rouge, 1962-63; instr. prosthetic dentistry Meharry Med. Coll., Nashville, 1963-64; dir. clin. dentistry VA Hosp., Tuskegee, Ala., 1964-68; individual practice dentistry, Lafayette, La., 1968—. Mem. Lafayette Council on Human Relations, 1968—; chmn. Lafayette Parish Community Action Council, 1971-72; mem. Lafayette Parish Sch. Bd., Lafayette Parish Council of Govt. Mem. Sheriffs' Adv. Commn., 1968—. Bd. dirs. Tri-Parish Community Action Agy., United Givers Fund; pres., bd. dirs. Holy Family Sch., 1971—. Served with AUS, 1953-55. Mem. N.A.A.C.P. (chmn. housing com.), Am. Dental Assn., C. of C., Alpha Phi Alpha, Alpha Phi Omega, Chi Delta Mu. Democrat. Roman Catholic. Home: 200 Alfred St Lafayette LA 70501 Office: 120 Louisiana Av Lafayette LA 70501

BARANOWSKI, RICHARD MATTHEW, educator; b. Utica, N.Y., Mar. 1, 1928; s. Walter and Agnes (Krug) B.; B.A., Syracuse U., 1951; M.S., U. Conn., 1953, Ph.D., 1959; m. Helen B. Venn, June 16, 1951; children—Gena, Alison, Lisa. Research asst. U. Conn., 1953-56; asst. prof. U. Fla. Agrl. Research and Edn. Center at Homestead, 1956-63, asso. prof., 1963-67, prof. entomology, 1967—. Recipient Fla. Plant Protection award of Eminence, 1973; several grants U.S. Dept. Agr. Mem. Entomol. Soc. Am., Fla. Entomol. Soc., Fla. Hort. Soc., Sigma Xi, Gamma Sigma Delta. Author: Golden Book of Insects, 1964. Home: 26000 SW 197th Av Homestead FL 33030

BARB, MARIAN LESTER, assn. exec.; b. Los Angeles, June 13, 1925; d. Peter Keyes and Marian (Chace) Shafer; A.B., Am. U., 1958, grad. certificate, 1969; m. John Charles Barb, Sept. 1945 (div. 1948); 1 dau., Jeannette (Mrs. Robert Edward Hurley). Partner, Jeanne Viner Assos. pub. relations, Washington, 1960-63; asso. dir. pub. relations United Givers Fund, Washington, 1963-66; dir. alumni relations Am. U., Washington, 1966-70; dir. ann. fund, 1970-72; press sec. to U.S. Rep. Lawrence J. Hogan, Washington, 1972-74; dir. devel. Nat. Capital Area YWCA, 1974—. Mem. Pub. Relations Soc. Am., Women In Communications, Am. Women in Radio and TV, Am. Assn. U. Women, Phi Delta Gamma. Home: 4707 Connecticut Av NW Apt 616 Washington DC 20008

BARBAY, FLOYD LOUIS, elec. engr.; b. St. Rose, La., Oct. 15, 1929; s. Harry Louis and Eunice Marie (Zeringue) B.; B.S., La. State U., 1956, M.E.E., 1962; m. Dolly Ann Bergeron, Mar. 10, 1951; children—Randy, Donna, Tammy. Elec. engr. Metrailer & Ingram, cons. engrs., Baton Rouge, 1956-59; chief elec. engr. Albert Switzer & Assos., 1959-61; partner Ray E. Ingram & Assos., 1962, Ingram-Barbay, Inc., 1962-68; pres. Barbay Engrs., Inc., Baton Rouge, 1968—. Served with USAF, 1951-54. Mem. I.E.E.E., La. Engring. Soc., Cons. Engrs. Council, Baton Rouge Elec. League. Home: 3032 Elgin St Baton Rouge LA 70805 Office: PO Box 66424 6942 Titian St Baton Rouge LA 70806

BARBEE, LINTON ELZIE, lawyer; b. Big Spring, Tex., Sept. 1, 1938; s. Gary Wilson and Opal Pearl (Fallin) B.; student N. Tex. State U., 1961-63; LL.B. with honors, U. Tex., 1966; m. Joan Barbara Furr, Sept. 2, 1961; children—Michael, Angela. Admitted to Tex. bar, 1966; asso. firm Coke & Coke, Dallas, 1966-70; partner firm Hewett Johnson Swanson & Barbee, Dallas, 1970—. Served with USN, 1957-61. Mem. Am., Dallas, bar assns., State Bar Tex., Order of Coif, Phi Delta Phi, Phi Kappa Phi. Asso. editor, revs. editor Tex. Law Rev., 1964-66. Home: 3617 Granada Dallas TX 75205 Office: 211 North Ervay Bldg Dallas TX 75201

BARBER, CLYDE HARWELL, mfg. co. exec.; b. Weatherford, Tex., Apr. 12, 1926; s. Clyde Clinton and Rita (Williams) B.; B.S., Tex. A. and M. U., 1949; m. Carolyn Ruth Grisham, July 8, 1950; children—Stephen, Callie. With Rita Barber, Inc., Abilene, Tex., 1949—, exec. v.p., 1962—. Dir. Citizens Nat. Bank, Abilene, Tex., First Security Savs. Assn., Abilene. Pres. United Way, Abilene, 1967; pres. Abilene Council on Alcoholism, 1971-72; v.p. YMCA, 1970. Trustee, Rita Barber Inc. Employees Profit Sharing Trust, 1962—, Barber Found., 1968—; mem. investment Com. West Tex. Rehab. Center Found., 1969—. Councilman, Abilene, 1974—. Served with USNR, 1944-46. Recipient Outstanding salesman award for funeral industry in N.M., N.M. Sales Club, 1956, in Tex. Tex. Funeral Supply Sales Club, 1957. Mem. Abilene C. of C. (v.p. 1970). Episcopalian. Mason (Shriner). Clubs: A and M (pres. 1962-63); Exchange (v.p. 1965); Abilene (Tex.) Country. Home: 1501 Woodridge St Abilene TX 79605 Office: 518 Butternut Abilene TX 79602

BARBER, JOHN CLARK, govt. ofcl.; b. Liberty, N.C., Jan. 6, 1925; s. Yates Middleton and Emily Lucille (Clark) B.; B.S. in Forestry, N.C. State U., 1950, M.S. in Forestry, 1951; Ph.D., U. Minn., 1961; m. Francene King, June 16, 1951; children—John Clark, Lewis Williams. With Forest Service, U.S. Dept. Agr., 1951—, project leader seed, nursery, genetics research, 1957-64, project leader Inst. Forest Genetics, Gulfport, Miss., 1964-67, br. chief timber mgmt. research, Washington, 1967-71, asst. to dep. chief research, 1971-72; dir. So. Forest Expt. Sta., New Orleans, 1972—. Served with AUS, 1943-46; ETO. Mem. A.A.A.S., Am. Forestry Assn., Forest Farmers Assn., Soc. Am. Foresters (award Gulf State sect. 1967), Internat. Union Forestry Research Orgns., N.Am. Forestry Commn., Internat. Poplar Commn., Sigma Xi. Home: 2136 Octavia St New Orleans LA 70115 Office: 701 Loyola Av New Orleans LA 70113

BARBER, LLOYD ERNEST, pub. co. exec.; b. Oakland, Cal., Feb. 17, 1921; s. William Ernest and Irene Josephine (Speck) B.; student LaSierra Coll., 1947; B.S., Pacific Union Coll., 1950; m. Maidelle Dozier, Mar. 12, 1944; children—Lloyd Wayne, Gary Steven. Mgr. Acad. Press, Honolulu, 1950-59, Indonesia Publishing House Bandung, Java, Indonesia, 1959-70; estimator So. Publishing Assn., Nashville, 1970-71, supt., 1971—. Served with AUS, 1942-46. Seventh-day Adventist (deacon 1970—). Home: 1232 Shawnee Rd Madison TN 37115 Office: PO Box 59 Nashville TN 37202

BARBER, MONTY CLYDE, cosmetic co. exec.; b. Rockdale, Tex., Jan. 12, 1931; s. Clyde and Hattie Estelle (Montague) B.; B.B.A., LL.B., U. Tex., 1955; m. Kay Wallace, June 29, 1963; children—Kelty Lynn, Brandon Chase. Admitted to Tex. bar, 1955; mem. firm Biggers, Baker, Lloyd & Carver, Dallas, 1957-67; v.p. Liquid Paper Corp., Dallas, 1967; v.p., sec., gen. counsel Mary Kay Cosmetics, Inc., Dallas, 1968—. Bd. mgrs. The Mary Kay Found. Served with AUS, 1955-57. Mem. Silver Spurs, Phi Delta Phi, Alpha Tau Omega. Home: 3508 Crescent St Dallas TX 75205 Office: 8900 Carpenter Freeway Dallas TX 75247

BARBER, WILLIAM GILBRETH, III, lawyer; b. Austin, Tex., Dec. 14, 1931; s. William Gilbreth and Mildred (Williams) B.; B.A., U. Tex., 1954; LL.B., Harvard, 1957; m. Patricia Leonore Wallum, June 28, 1958; children—Mary Elizabeth, William Gilbreth, John Patrick, Katherine Marie. Admitted to Tex. bar, 1958; briefing atty. Supreme Ct. Tex., Austin, 1958-59; practice law firm Brown, Maroney, Rose, Baker & Barber, Austin, 1959—. Mem. Citywide Com. Human Rights, Austin, 1970—. Served with AUS, 1957. Mem. State Bar Tex., Travis County Bar Assn., Tex. Assn. Def. Counsel, Fedn. Ins. Counsel, Am. Arbitration Assn., Def. Research Inst., Lay Cath. Speakers Guild, Austin Deanery Council Cath. Men, Phi Beta Kappa, Phi Eta Sigma, Beta Theta Pi. Rotarian. Contbr. articles legal jours. Home: 3200 Maywood Av Austin TX 78703 Office: 900 Brown Bldg Austin TX 78701

BARBER, WILLIAM JOSEPH, SR., clergyman; b. Jamesville, N.C., Mar. 21, 1927; s. Benjamin Luther and Lettice Ann (Keyes) B.; B.S., St. Augustine Coll., 1949; M.S., Butler U., 1959; B.D., Christian Theol. Sem., 1959; certificate in adult edn. Ind. U., 1965; m. Eleanor Lucille Patterson, Nov. 25, 1961; children—William Joseph II, Charles Edgar. Tchr. Warrenton (Ga.) High Sch., 1949-52; counselor Eastside Christian Center, Indpls., 1952-53; staff asst., cannery and gardens Flanner House, Indpls., 1954-59, work camp dir. 1954-59; field worker Disciples of Christ, 1954-59; social case worker Marion County Dept. Pub. Welfare, Indpls., 1955-57; ordained to ministry Christian Ch., 1956; student pastor Market St. Christian Ch., Carthage, Ind., 1954-57, High St. Christian Ch., Carlisle, Ky., also 2d Christian Ch., North Middletown, Ky., 1959-60; pastor, dir. Hillside Christian Center, Indpls., 1962-65; tchr. sci. and math. Booker T. Washington Jr. High Sch., Indpls., 1960-63; asso. campus minister, instr. dept. humanities Jarvis Christian Coll., Hawkins, Tex., 1965-66; field worker Tex. Christian Missionary Fellowship, Hawkins, 1955-66; interim pastor 2d Christian Ch., Farmville, N.C., 1968-70; tchr. math. and sci. Washington County (N.C.) schs., 1966-70; coordinator agrl. coops. Martin County Community Action, Inc., Williamston, N.C., 1970, econ. developer, 1971-73; asso. econ. devel. coordinator, 1973—. Historian, Eastern Seaboard, Gen. Assembly, Chs. of Christ, Disciples of Christ, 1952—, cons. minister, ednl., polit. and socio-econ. affairs, Washington and Norfolk Dist. Assembly, 1968—, gen. evangelist, chmn. com. on evangelism Gen. Assembly, 1973—. Founding mem. bd. dirs. Washington County Civic and Charitable Assn., Martin County Coop. Assn., Inc., Rodgers Community Produce and Products Coop., Inc., Martin Indsl. Devel. Assn., Inc., N.C. Fedn. Chil Devel. Centers, Inc. Served with USNR, 1945-46. Mem. N.C. Folklore Soc., Disciples Christ Hist. Soc., Alpha Phi Alpha. Home: PO Box 66 Roper NC 27970 Office: Econ Devel Sect Martin County Community Action PO Box 806 Williamston NC 27892

BARBIERI, CHRISTOPHER ALDO, television sta. exec.; b. Dedham, Mass., Aug. 18, 1942; s. Aldo and Elizabeth (Christopher) B.; student U. Me., 1963; B.S., Boston U., 1964; m. Anne Helen Fattig, Nov. 13, 1966; 1 son, Christopher Aldo. Dir. pub. relations I.J. Filler, Inc., Atlanta, 1967; account exec. Batten, Barton, Durstine & Osborn, N.Y.C., 1967-68, adminstrv. asst. to exec. com., 1968-70; v.p. sales and programming WJCL-TV, Savannah, Ga., 1970—. Co-chmn. Christmas Seals, 1970; chmn. Savannah Italian Club, 1971—, also bd. govs.; gen. chmn. Peach Bowl Dist. 18B, Ga. Lions, 1973; pub. relations com. United Fund, 1973. Bd. dirs. Savannah Visitors Council, Inc., Cardio Vascular Council. Served as capt. Signal Corps, AUS, 1965-67. Named Boston U. Man of Year, 1964, Outstanding Man of Community, 1970. Mem. Catholic Apostulate Radio/Television and Advt., Pub. Relations Soc. Am., Ga. Pub. Relations Soc., Res. Officers Assn., Savannah Advt. Club (dir.). Lion. Clubs: Players, Soqui. Home: 3 Elder Ct Savannah GA 31406 Office: 10001 Abercorn Extension Savannah GA 31406

BARBLES, EUGENE ANTHONY, savs. and loan exec.; b. Houston, Nov. 24, 1922; s. Nick and Anna (Barretta) B.; student Tex. A. and M. Coll., 1939-40, U. Houston, 1941; m. Dorothy Cecile Block, Jan. 17, 1943; children—Gary Eugene, Larry Drew. Asst. chief engr. Rice Hotel, 1946-52; bldg. mgr. San Jacinto Bldg., 1952-60; bldg. mgr. Main Bldg., from 1960; partner, dir. Bonded Maintenance Co., Dallas, also Ft. Worth; partner B & D Laundromats; dir. Milam Co., Inc., N.G.L. Corp.; now v.p. Am. Savs. and Loan Assn., Houston; pres. Am. Place Land Co., also dir.; pres. ASLA, Inc., Gene Barbles and Assos.; sec., treas. Staff Inc., also dir.; dir. Main Bank Houston. Mem. Houston Examining Bd. for Stationary Engrs., 1958—, Houston Code Com., 1958—; founder Stationary Engrs. Apprenticeship Tng. Sch., 1956, chmn., 1956—. Served from ensign to lt. (j.g.), U.S. Maritime Service, 1942-45. Mem. Internat. (1st v.p. 1973—), Nat., Tex. (past pres.), Houston (past pres.) Southwest conf. (v.p.) assns. bldg. owners and mgrs. Club: Maxims. Home: 5034 Tangle Lane Houston TX Office: 3120 South West Freeway Houston TX 77006

BARBOT, JULIAN AUGUSTUS, JR., civil engr.; b. Wilmington, N.C., Apr. 9, 1928; s. Julian Augustus and Vera Gladys (Hawes) B.; B.S., U. N.C., 1952; postgrad. U.S. Army Engr. Sch., 1957-60, Fla. Jr. Coll., 1968-69; m. Eunice M. North, Aug. 28, 1954. With U.S. Army C.E., various locations, 1952—, civil engr., Jacksonville, Fla., 1955-56, supr. civil engr., 1956—. Mem. S.C. Hist. Soc., 1971—. Served with AUS, 1946-47; Korea. Mem. Soc. Mil. Engrs., Heraldry Soc. (London), Mil. Heraldry Soc. (Britain), Soc. Mil Insignia Collectors, Sigma Gamma Epsilon. Home: 5455 Selton Av Jacksonville FL 32211 Office: PO Box 4970 Jacksonville FL 32201

BARBOUR, OFFIE ALMON, JR., publicist; b. Benson, N.C., Sept. 20, 1916; s. Offie Almon and Emily (Canaday) B.; student Boiling Springs Jr. Coll., 1934, U. N.C., 1935-39; m. Frances Margaret Lewis, Feb. 9, 1957; children—Frances Lewis, Nancy Spence, Aubrey Elizabeth, Margaret Adams, Emily Sharon. Reporter, staff writer The Raleigh (N.C.) Times, 1941; pub. affairs dir. N.C. Dept. of Labor,

Raleigh, 1942—. Served with USNR, 1944-46. Mem. Oratorio Soc. (past pres.), Raleigh Pub. Relations Soc. (past treas.). Club: Wake County Young Democrat. Editor North Carolina Labor and Industry, monthly bull., 1941—. Home: 2710 Kittrell Dr Raleigh NC 27608 Office: Box 27407 Raleigh NC 27611

BARBOUR, ROGER WILLIAM, educator; b. Morehead, Ky., Apr. 5, 1919; s. John William and Laura (Hall) B.; B.S., Morehead State U., 1938; M.S., Cornell U., 1939, Ph.D., 1949; m. Bernice Anne Lewis, Dec. 28, 1938; children—Marsha Anne (Mrs. E.C. Hale, Jr.), Roger William, James Lewis. Mem. faculty U. Ky. at Lexington, 1950—, prof., 1968—. Served with AUS, 1945-46. Mem. A.A.A.S., Am. Soc. Mammalogists, Am. Soc. Ichthyologists and Herpetologists, Am. Ornithologists Union, Wildlife Soc., Sigma Xi. Author: (with W.H. Davis) Bats of America, 1969; Amphibians and Reptiles of Kentucky, 1971; (with M.E. Wharton) A Guide to Wildflowers and Ferns of Kentucky, 1971; (with Peterson and others) Kentucky Birds, 1973; (with C.H. Ernst) Turtles of the U.S., 1972. Home: Route 1 Tates Creek Rd Lexington KY 40503 Office: Dept Biology Univ Ky Lexington KY 40506

BARBOW, GORDON-HURST, clergyman; b. Louisville, Jan. 5, 1915; s. Emerson Gordon and Allene (Brown) B.; B.A., U. La., 1940; M.Div., Yale, 1943; postgrad. N.Y. State Tchrs. Coll., 1946-49, U. Chgo., 1951-52, Columbia, 1952-53; m. Josephine Condict Bierhaus, Aug. 25, 1954; children—Elizabeth Gordon, John Condict-Hurst, Edward Graham-Hurst, Amanda McLaughlin. Ordained priest, Episcopal Ch., 1943; canon precentor, Albany, N.Y., 1945-51, Chgo., 1951-58; dir. religious edn., Indpls., 1958-63, Tulsa, 1963—. James Mills fellow, 1972-73. Club: Indianapolis Athletic. Developer standard Sunday Sch. curriculum for U.S., pre-sch. through 9th grade, 1958-72. Home: PO Box 2871 Tulsa OK 74101 Office: PO Box 7749 Tulsa OK 74105

BARCLAY, CARL ARCHIE, physician; b. Nanticoke, Md., July 30, 1922; s. Souvenir Archie and Viola Victoria (Elsey) B.; B.S., Hampton Isnt., 1942; M.D., Howard U., 1947; m. Mae Neece Hodge, June 4, 1949; children—Carl Archie, Kenneth Dale. Teaching asst. Hampton Inst., 1942-44; intern Homer G. Phillips Hosp., St. Louis, 1947-48; house physician Edwards Meml. Hosp., Oklahoma City, 1948-51; sch. physician Oklahoma City Bd. Edn., 1949-59; gen. practice, Oklahoma City, 1951—; physician Guthrie (Okla.) Job Corps Center for Women, 1971—. Dir., treas., mng. officer M-D-P Investment Fund, Inc. Chmn. met. outreach dept. Greater Oklahoma City YMCA, 1971—. Mem. Nat. Med. Assn., Oklahoma City Med-De-Phar Soc. (pres. 1962-65), Okla. Med., Dental and Pharm. Assn. (pres. 1965-66), Oklahoma City Urban League, N.A.A.C.P. (life). Democrat. Mem. A.M.E. Ch. Home: 2813 NE 19th St Oklahoma City OK 73111 Office: 215 N Walnut Av Oklahoma City OK 73104

BARCLAY, HERSCHEL LEE, banker; b. Chester, Tex., Feb. 5, 1923; s. Clarence Albert and Ettie Rose (Hardy) B.; grad. La. State U., Sch. Banking, 1970; m. Joyce M. Sturrock, Apr. 8, 1952; 1 dau., Beverly Kim Barclay. Asst. cashier Chester State Bank, 1944-56; v.p. Am. Nat. Bank of Beaumont (Tex.), 1956—. Exec. sec. Tex. Rice Festival, 1972-73. Mem. Am. Inst. Banking (pres. 1966-67), Beaumont C. of C. (chmn. A9RT bus. com. 1967-69), Beaumont Farm and Ranch Club (pres. 1965-66). Baptist. Lion. Home: 980 23d St Beaumont TX 77706 Office: Box 2751 Beaumont TX 77704

BARCZAK, VIRGIL JOSEPH, mineralogist; b. Toledo, O., Nov. 29, 1931; s. Joseph Anthony and Rosalie (Obarski) B.; B.S., U. Mich., 1958, M.S., 1959; M.B.A. in Indsl. Mgmt., Okla. City U., 1966; m. Patricia Kathleen Sullivan, June 6, 1959; children—Kathleen, Steven, David, Thomas. Research petrographer ceramic div. Champion Spark Plug Co., Detroit, 1959-64; research mineralogist Kerr-McGee Corp., Oklahoma City, 1964—. Served with USMC, 1952-55. Fellow Geol. Soc. Am.; mem. Mineralogical Soc. Am., Mineralogical Assn. Can., Am. Ceramic Soc. (co-recipient Ross Coffin Purdy award 1966), Am. Inst. Ceramic Engrs. Contbr. articles to profl. jours. Home: 2500 NW 109th St Oklahoma City OK 73120 Office: Kerr-McGee Corp Tech Center Oklahoma City OK 73102

BARD, EDWIN JAY, dentist; b. Mpls., Apr. 6, 1924; s. Samuel David and Edith Sophia (Carlson) B.; student Washington U., St. Louis, 1943; B.S., U. Minn., 1950, D.D.S., 1952; m. Barbara Jeanne Hultgren, Mar. 17, 1949; children—Ann Elizabeth (Mrs. Charles Oswald), Nancy Leigh, Brian Jay, Irene Dell, David Jay, Barbara Claire, James Jay, April Jeanne. Dentist, State Bd. Health Dental Services, Jacksonville, Fla., 1952; pvt. practice dentistry, Jacksonville, 1952—; dir. Hayes Oil & Gas Co. Active Am. Cancer Soc. Trustee Trinity Rescue Mission, Jacksonville. Served with USAAF, 1943-46. Decorated D.F.C., Purple Heart (5), Air medal. Mem. Am. Dental Assn., N.E., Jacksonville dental socs., D.A.V., Parington Study Group, Psi Omega. Democrat. Baptist (deacon 1967—, trustee 1967-72). Mason (Shriner). Home: 8568 San Jose Blvd Jacksonville FL 32217 Office: 50 W 8th St Jacksonville FL 32206

BARDIN, JESSE REDWIN, artist, educator; b. Elloree, S.C., Mar. 26, 1923; s. Jesse Redwin and Ethel (Etheredge) B.; A.B., U.S.C., 1951; grad. Art Students League of N.Y., 1953; children from previous marriage—J. Redwin III, Allen, Philip Bardwin. Mem. faculty Richland Art Sch., Columbia (S.C.) Mus. of Art, 1955—, supr., 1960—; exhibited in one-man shows at Mint Mus., Charlotte, N.C., The Gallery, Ft. Lauderdale, Fla., N.C. State U., Raleigh, Hunter Gallery of Art, Chattanooga, Oak Ridge Art Center, Gibbes Art Gallery, Charleston, S.C., Columbia (S.C.) Coll., Blacksburg (Va.) Regional Art Festival, Artists Assos. Gallery, Atlanta, Arnold Finkel Gallery, Phila.; exhibited in numerous group shows in U.S., fgn. countries; represented in permanent collections at Mint Mus., Williams Coll., Pa. State U., Columbia Mus. Art, N.C. Mus., La. State U., U.S.C., Gibbes Art Gallery, Hunter Gallery of Art, Furman U., U. S. Fla., Blacksburg (Va.) Art Assn.; various pvt. collections in fgn. countries. Home: 1723 Devine St Columbia SC 29201 Office: Columbia Museum of Art and Science 1112 Bull St Columbia SC 29201

BARGEON, HERBERT ALEXANDER, JR., lawyer; b. Fayetteville, N.C., May 23, 1934; s. Herbert Alexander and Violet (Geilfuss) B.; B.S. in Bus. Adminstrn., U. Va., 1956; LL.B., U. Fla., 1968; m. Gail Freer, Mar. 14, 1963; children—Brett Elizabeth (by previous marriage), Herbert Alexander III, Violet Gail. Admitted to Fla. bar; partner firm Anderson & Rush, Orlando. Vice pres. bd. trustees Orlando Pub. Library; pres., chmn. bd. Royal Poinciana Playhouse, Palm Beach, Fla. Served to 2d lt. AUS, 1957. Mem. Am. Bar Assn., Orlando C. of C. Republican. Presbyn. Club: Poinciana (Palm Beach). Home: 1314 Chichester Rd Orlando FL 32803 Office: 322 E Central Blvd Orlando FL 32801

BARGER, ALPHONSO SLEDGE, lawyer; b. York, Ala., May 6, 1908; s. Eugene E. and Frances (Jackson) B.; B.S., Howard Coll., 1932; LL.B., George Washington U., 1939; m. Edith Christine Smith, Dec. 25, 1935; children—Alphonso S., Ken, Edith Ann. Admitted to D.C. bar, 1938, Tenn. bar, 1948; scientist Bur. Ordnance, U.S. Navy, 1934-39; atty. Social Security Bd., 1939-41; commr. U.S. Conciliation Service, 1946-48; pvt. practice, Chattanooga, 1948—; asst. city atty., 1962—. Active Boy Scouts Am.; sec. Hamilton County Election Commn., 1952-58. Served as maj. AUS, 1941-46. Decorated Victory medal. Mem. Fed., Am., D.C., Tenn., Chattanooga bar assns., V.F.W. (trustee 1948-60, state judge advocate 1957-58). Democrat. Presbyn. Mason (Shriner; merit award 1967). Club: Yacht (dir. 1967). Home: 401 Talley Rd Chattanooga TN 37411 Office: Hamilton Bank Bldg Chattanooga TN 37402

BARGFREDE, JAMES ALLEN, lawyer; b. Seguin, Tex., Sept. 10, 1928; s. Herman Fred and Elsie (Vorpahl) B.; B.S., Tex. A. and M. U., 1950; postgrad. Ohio State U., 1952-53; J.D., St. Mary's U., 1957; m. Virginia Felts, Nov. 27, 1970. Engr., Signal Corps, San Antonio, 1950-52; elec. engr. San Antonio Pub. Service Bd., 1953-58; admitted to Tex. bar, 1957; patent counsel Hubbard & Co., Chgo., 1958-59; practiced in Chgo., 1959-60, Houston, 1960—; mem. firm Butler, Binion, Rice, Cook & Knapp, 1960-68; pvt. practice law, 1968-74; with Bargfrede & Thompson, 1974—. Served with USAF, 1952-53. Mem. Am., Houston (chmn. automated equipment com. 1971-73) bar assns., State Bar of Tex., Houston Patent Law Assn., Former Students Tex. A. and M. U., Am. Patent Law Assn., Houston Livestock Show and Rodeo, Delta Theta Phi. Baptist. Home: 5649 Piping Rock Lane Houston TX 77027 Office: 1800 St James Pl Houston TX 77027

BARHAM, CHARLES, ret. found. exec.; b. Nashville, Oct. 18, 1903; s. Charles and Mary Hannah (Wilkinson) B.; B.A., Vanderbilt U., 1924; m. Emmalou Wheeler, Oct. 10, 1928; children—Frank Wheeler, Charles III. Teller Fourth & First Nat. Bank, Nashville, 1924-31, br. mgr., 1931-32; sec.-treas. Modern Bread Co., Nashville, 1932-40; owner Radio Sta. WCHV, Charlottesville, Va., 1940-59; developer Bellair Estates, Charlottesville, Va., 1946—; pres. Thomas Jefferson Meml. Found., Charlottesville, 1966-74; hon. dir. Va. Nat. Bank, Norfolk. Pres. beautification com., Charlottesville, 1962; chmn. Albemarle Planning Com. Mem. C. of C. (pres. 1946). Club: Farmington Country (Charlottesville). Home: 3 Lake Rd Charlottesville VA 22903

BARHAM, MACK ELWIN, judge, justice; b. Bastrop, La., June 18, 1924; s. Henry A. and Lockie (Harper) B.; J.D., La. State U., 1946; postgrad. U. Colo., 1966; m. Ann LeVois, June 3, 1946; children—Bret, Megan (Mrs. Thomas Richard). Admitted to La. bar, 1946; practiced in Bastrop; judge Bastrop City Ct., 1949-61, Fourth Jud. Dist. Ct., 1961-68, 2d Circuit Ct. Appeal, 1967-68; asso. justice La. Supreme Ct., New Orleans, 1968—. Mem. faculty Am. Acad. Jud. Edn., U. Ala., 1968-73; vis. prof. La. State U. Mem. White House Conf. on Youth, 1960; chmn. Boy Scouts Am., Bastrop, 1950—. Vice pres., dir. S. Central Region Edn. Lab., Ark., La., Miss., Kan., Okla., 1966-68. Recipient award Freedoms Found. at Valley Forge, 1969. Mem. La. Juvenile Ct. Judges Assn. (past pres.), Am., Fourth Dist., La. State bar assns., La. Law Inst. Council, Am. Judicature Soc., Order of Coif, Blue Key, Phi Alpha Delta, Lambda Chi Alpha, Omicron Delta Kappa, Phi Delta Phi. Kiwanian. Home: 5837 Bellaire Dr New Orleans LA 70124 Office: 301 Loyola Av New Orleans LA 70112

BARHYDT, EMILY TARBELL (MRS. RAYMOND BARHYDT), educator; b. Milford, N.H., May 13, 1896; d. George and Elizabeth (Bennett) Tarbell; A.B., Syracuse U., 1916; B. Oral English, 1924, M.A., 1954; postgrad. U. Havana (Cuba), 1953; m. Raymond S. Barhydt, July 29, 1949. Tchr. Odessa (N.Y.) High Sch., 1916-18, Syracuse (N.Y.) Vocational High Sch., 1918-60, adult evening sch., 1960-71. Mem. Everson Museum Fine Arts; chmn. film festival N.Y. State Fair, 1955. Trustee Robert R. Decormier Rehab. Found. Recipient Gov. Averell Harriman tchr. award, 1956. Mem. N.E.A. (exec. com. 1942-46, pres. dept. classroom tchrs. 1937-38, eastern regional dir. 1934-37, editor News-Bull. 1938-39, mem. ednl. policies comm. 1939-44), Am. Assn. U. Women (pres. dist. 1934-36), Nat. League Tchrs. Assns. (eastern v.p. 1953-56), N.Y. State (dir. 1948-56), Syracuse (editor bull. 1932-53), tchrs. assns., Tchrs. Welfare League N.Y., State Ret. Tchrs. Assn. (2d v.p. 1958-73), Nat. Parliamentarians Assn., N.Y. State Council State Commn. Human Rights, Am. Acad. Polit. and Social Sci., Am. Assn. Ret. Persons (nat. legislative counsel), Onondaga Hist. Assn., Syracuse Profl. Women's League, League Women Voters, Alpha Omicron Pi, Pi Lambda Theta. Author: (with others) Teacher and Public, 1934. Contbr. articles to profl. jours. Home: Regency House 33 W Adams St Jacksonville FL 32202

BARKAS, EDWARD, mfg. co. exec.; b. Atlanta, July 26, 1925; s. Alexander and Marie (Dreyfus) B.; B.S., The Citadel, 1950; m. Kathleen Prolman, Aug. 3, 1951; children—Marilyn, Daniel. Salesman, Morgan Mfg. Co., Chattanooga, 1951-55; sales mgr. Lindheimer Mfg. Co., Hillsborough, N.C., 1955-58, v.p. sales, 1958—. Active Boy Scouts Am. Trustee Central Bapt. Hosp. Served with AUS, 1941-45; ETO. Decorated Purple Heart. Mem. Hillsborough C. of C., N.A.M., Nat. Assn. Sales Execs. Democrat. Home: Box 365-A Route 3 Hillsborough NC 27278

BARKELEW, CHANDLER HARRISON, chem. engr.; b. Fresno, Cal., Oct. 12, 1919; s. Verne and Helen Pond (Harrison) B.; B.A., Pomona Coll., 1941, Ph.D., U. Cal. at Berkeley, 1944; m. Virginia May Koorn, Apr. 12, 1947; children—Claire, James, Julia. Chemist, Manhattan Project, Berkeley, Cal., 1944-45; chem. engr. Shell Devel. Co., Emeryville, Cal., 1945-72, Houston, 1972—. Lectr. chem. engring. U. Cal., Berkeley, 1971. Mem. A.A.A.S., Am. Chem. Soc., Am. Inst. Chemists, Am. Inst. Chem. Engrs., Instrument Soc. Am. Home: 13607 Queensbury St Houston TX 77024 Office: PO Box 481 Houston TX 77001

BARKER, BRADLEY SINCLAIR, coll. adminstr.; b. Lexington, Mass., June 17, 1932; s. Paul Nicholas and Eve (Woodbine) B.; B.A., Duke, 1954; M.A., U. Tex., 1960; m. Maxine Allen, Aug. 25, 1956; children—Jennifer Lynn, Bradley Sinclair. Asst. to city mgr., Durham, N.C., 1960-65, city mgr., Concord, N.C., 1965-68; cons. Republic Liberia, West Africa, 1968-70; dir. office urban affairs U. Tenn., Chattanooga, 1971—. Mem. Human Services Adv. Bd. Chattanooga, 1973—; chmn. Urban Forum, Chattanooga, 1973. Bd. dirs. Adult Edn. Council. Served to capt. USAF, 1954-57. Grantee Scottish Rite Found., 1959. Mem. Internat. City Mgmt. Assn. Home: 206 Richardson St Lookout Mountain TN 37350 Office: Office Urban Affairs Univ Tenn Chattanooga TN 37401

BARKER, EDWARD LEO, govt. ofcl.; b. Washington, Nov. 19, 1919; s. Walter Leo and Nanncye Edwards (Tinsley) B.; cartographic engring. certificate George Washington U., 1942; B.A., U. Md., 1947; postgrad. U.S. Naval War Coll., 1959-60, St. John's Coll., Oxford, Eng., 1962; m. Pauline Francis Clark, Oct. 22, 1949; children—Russell E., Christopher T. Cartographic engr. Coast and Geodetic Survey, Washington, 1941-47; intelligence analyst Office Naval Intelligence, 1949-59; polit./def. analyst U.S. embassy, London, Eng., 1960-64; tech. dir. Naval Intelligence Processing Systematic Support Activity, Washington, 1964—. Served to lt. USNR, 1942-46; now capt. Res. Mem. U.S. Naval Inst., Nat. Geog. Soc. Club: Kenwood Country (Washington). Author: Naval Air Intelligence Manual, 1949; Aircraft Recognition Manual, 1951-59. Contbr. numerous articles to profl. jours. Home: 5104 Brookeway Dr Washington DC 20016 Office: 2461 Eisenhower Av Alexandria VA 22331

BARKER, KENNETH REECE, nematologist, educator; b. Benham, N.C., Feb. 1, 1932; s. Benjamin Harrison and Bertha Angeline (Pruitt) B.; B.S. in Agronomy, N.C. State U., 1956, M.S. in Plant Pathology, 1959; Ph.D. in Plant Pathology, U. Wis., 1961; m. Betty Marie Flynt, Dec. 21, 1958; children—Elizabeth Marie, Nicole Jane. Asst. prof. plant pathology U. Wis., 1961-66; asso. prof. plant pathology N.C. State U., Raleigh, 1966-71, prof., 1971—. Served with U.S. Army, 1957. Mem. Am. Phytopathological Soc., Soc. Nematologists. Contbr. articles profl. jours. Home: 1515 Delmont Dr Raleigh NC 27607

BARKER, RICHARD MICHAEL, ednl. adminstr.; b. Humboldt, Tenn., Aug. 30, 1939; s. Montie C. and Ida Beatrice (Hendrix) B.; B.S., U. Tenn., 1961; M.A., George Peabody Coll., 1964; m. Martha Carol Taylor, Aug. 12, 1961; children—John Richard, Carol Anne. Tchr. sci. Humboldt High Sch., 1961-64; prin. Humboldt Elementary Sch., 1964-66; sci. supr. Tenn. Dept. Edn., Martin, 1966-69, dir. instrn., 1969-73, coordinator curriculum, 1973—. Mem. Humboldt Utility Bd. Named Humboldt Tchr. of Year, 1961. Mem. Tenn. Edn. Assn., Tenn. Acad. Sci., Phi Delta Kappa. Methodist. Club: Humboldt Exchange (treas., dir.). Home: 1402 Bradford Dr Humboldt TN 38343 Office: U Tenn Martin TN 38237

BARKLEY, FRED ALEXANDER, educator; b. Hobart, Okla., Nov. 4, 1908; s. Alexander and Maie (Webster) B.; A.B., Okla. U., 1930, M.S., 1932; Ph.D., Washington U., St. Louis, 1937; m. Elizabeth Anne Ducker, Aug. 14, 1930; children—Robert Wheeler, William Hugh, Anne (Mrs. Thomas J. Powers), Jorge Aracue M. Prin. high sch., Mayesville, Okla., 1930-31; instr. botany U. Mont., 1937-42; tchr. biology Austin (Tex.) High Sch., 1942-43; instr. botany U. Tex., 1943-45, asst. prof., curator herbarium, 1945-47; State Dept. vis. prof., prof. Jefe Faculted Nacional de Agonoria Medeilin, Colombia, 1947-49; prof. extrordianrio Fundacion Miguel Lillo, Nat. U. Tucuman (Argentina), 1949-51; virologist Haktoon inst., Chgo., 1951-52; dir. research microbiology Nepera Chem. Co., Yonkers, N.Y., 1952-57; sr. research asso. Warner Lambert Research Inst., Morris Plains, N.J., 1957-61; Fulbright prof. Coll. Agr., U. Baghdad (Iraq), 1961-65, chmn. dept. botany, 1963-65; prof. biology Northeastern U., Boston, 1965-74, prof. emeritus, 1974—; prof. botany faculty agr. U. Khartoum (Sudan), 1974—. Fulbright vis. prof. Jafa de Biologla y el Instituto de Investigaciones de founa y Flora, Nat. U. Autonoma de Henduras, Tagucigalpa, 1969-70. Mem. Phi Sigma (nat. vice chancellor 1939-47). Contbr. numerous articles to tech. jours. Bot. collections from U.S.A., Mexico, Colombia, Argentina, Iraq, Honduras. Home: 104 E Highland St Tecumseh OK Office: PO Box 32 Khartoum North Sudan

BARKLEY, ROBERT EMMANUEL, city ofcl.; b. Cleve., Sept. 24, 1927; s. E. Ray and Nelle(Doke) B.; B.S. in Civil Engring. with honors, Case Inst. Tech., 1949; M.S. in Civil Engring., Purdue U., 1950; certificate in hwy. transp., Yale, 1951; m. Brenda Voit, Aug. 14, 1954; children—Bryan, Bradford. Prin. asso. Wilbur Smith & Assos., New Haven, 1951-54; asst. dir. City-County Planning Bd., Winston-Salem, N.C., 1954-56; dir. Urban Renewal, Chattanooga, 1956-58; exec. dir. Redevel. Commn. Greensboro (N.C.), 1958—. Sec.-treas. Cumberland Cts., Inc., Greensboro, 1962—; chmn. legislative com. Carolinas Council Housing and Redevel. Ofcls. Hon. trustee Old Salem (North Carolina) Restoration Project. Recipient Outstanding Service award Phi Beta Sigma, 1966. Registered profl. engr., Ohio, N.C. Mem. Am. Soc. C.E. (sect. v.p. 1967—), Sigma Xi. Baptist (mem. finance com. 1967-69). Author: Origin-Destination Surveys and Traffic, 1951. Contbr. articles profl. publs. Home: 3314 Northampton Dr Greensboro NC 27401 Office: 311 Municipal Bldg Greensboro NC 27401

BARKSDALE, JAMES BRYAN, JR., educator; b. Blytheville, Ark., Dec. 29, 1940; s. James Bryan and Vera (Worthy) B.; B.A., U. Ark., 1964, M.S., 1966, Ph.D., 1969; m. Edith Adele Ellis, June 6, 1972. Tchr. math., Blytheville (Ark.) High Sch., 1963-64; asso. prof. math. Western Ky. U., Bowling Green, 1968—. Vis. lectr. jr. high and high sch. math clubs, 1971—; lectr. Mu Alpha Theta nat. high sch. and jr. coll. math. club, 1970—. Mem. Math. Assn. Am., Am. Math. Soc., Pi Mu Epsilon, Sigma Pi Sigma. Home: 2702 Industrial Dr Bowling Green KY 42101 Office: Dept Math Western Kentucky Univ Bowling Green KY 42101

BARKSDALE, JAMES DEWRING, structural engr.; b. Memphis, Aug. 10, 1921; s. Evert Earl and Bessie Lee (Millwood) B.; spl. student engring. U. Tenn., 1947-50, Christian Bros. Sch., 1963-65; m. Lupe Marie Bezzrial, Oct. 5, 1940; children—James, Vincent, Robert, Donald. Design engr. Choctaw, Inc., Memphis, 1950—, Montgomery, Ala., Jackson, Miss., Little Rock, 1951—. Cons. U.S. Forest Service, Miss., Miss. State Hwy. Dept.; tchr. bridge design U.S. Forest Service Concrete Sch., Jackson, 1961—. Pres., Kingsbury High Sch. Boosters, 1954-55. Served with AUS, 1939-45. Decorated Purple Heart. Registered profl. engr., Miss. Mem. Am. Concrete Inst., Nat., Miss. socs. profl. engrs., Soc. Am. Mil. Engrs. Address: 316 Vescovo Dr Memphis TN 38117

BARLEY, GEORGE EMERSON MCKIM, fertilizer co. exec.; b. Manassas, Va., Oct. 23, 1904; s. John McKim and Lida Estelle (Finch) B.; grad. high sch.; m. Mary Elizabeth Daly, Oct. 29, 1929; children—Charles McKim, George Emerson McKim, Elizabeth Anne, John David. Office boy R. G. Dun & Co., Jacksonville, Fla., 1918-21; asst. bookkeeper Nitrate Agys. Co., 1925-35; sec. Atlantic & Gulf Fertilizer Co., 1935-39; with Am. Potash & Chem. Corp., Travelling, Fla., 1939-41; Fla. rep. Ashcraft-Wilkinson Co., Atlanta, 1941-48; asst. mgr. Wheeler Fertilizer Co., Oviedo, Fla., 1948-50; v.p., mgr. Diamond R. Fertilizer Co., Winter Garden, Fla., 1950—. Chmn. council local govts. Orange County, Fla., 1970-71. Commr. City of Winter Garden, Fla., 1952-58, mayor, 1967-73, mem. water adv. bd., 1968-69. Mem. Fla. Agrl. Research Inst. (pres. 1971-72). Episcopalian (treas. 1961-72). Elk, Rotarian (pres. 1962). Clubs: Orlando Press, University (Orlando, Fla.); West Orange Country (Winter Garden, Fla.). Home: 115 Temple Grove Dr Winter Garden FL 32787 Office: Hennis Rd PO Box 1137 Winter Garden FL 32787

BARLOW, THOMAS JAMES, indsl. corp. exec.; b. Houston, June 22, 1922; s. Thomas Jefferson and Dorothy (James) B.; B.S., Tex. A. and M. Coll., 1943; postgrad. Harvard, 1962; m. Billye Louise Sears, May 31, 1944; children—Lance, Lynne. Trainee, Western Cottonoil Co., Abilene, Tex., 1946-47, asst. gen. mgr., 1958-59; constrn. engr. San Joaquin Cottonoil Co., Bakersfield, Cal., 1948; supt. Western Cotton Products Co., Phoenix, 1949-50; prodn. mgr. Nile Ginning Co., Minia, Egypt, 1951-55; process engr. Anderson, Clayton & Co., Houston, 1956-57, now pres., dir.; dir. Pan Am. Ins. Cos., Anderson, Clay & Hunt Pty., Ltd., Houston br. Fed. Res. Bank Dallas, Central & S.W. Corp., Ranger Ins. Co. Mem. Chgo. Bd. Trade, N.Y. Produce Exchange, Memphis Bd. Trade. Mem. Houston C. of C. (dir.), Newcomen Soc. N.Am., Tex. Research League (dir.). Home: 35 Willowend St Houston TX 77024 Office: Box 2538 Houston TX 77001

BARMETTLER, RICHARD OTTO, JR., petroleum co. exec.; b. Omaha, Nov. 28, 1928; s. Richard Otto and Jane (Harvey) B.; student Springhill Coll., 1946-47; B.S., Auburn U., 1950; m. Joyce McCrory, Apr. 15, 1955; 1 dau. Valerie Anne. Sales engr. Chevron Asphalt Co., Mobile, Ala., 1953-64, sales mgr., 1964-69; v.p., sales mgr. Seminole Asphalt Refining Co., St. Marks, Fla., 1969—. Bd. dirs. Asphalt Inst. Served with AUS, 1950-52. Mem. Am. Soc. C. E., Soc. Am. Mil. Engrs., Kappa Alpha. Democrat. Roman Catholic. Elk. Home: 2808

Roscommon Dr Tallahassee FL 32303 Office: Seminole Asphalt Refining Co Main Hwy St Marks FL 32355

BARNARD, BILLINGS, editor; b. Abilene, Tex., Apr. 30, 1926; s. Bernie D. and Lora (Billings) B.; B.A., U. Tex., 1952, B.J., 1952, M.A., 1959; m. Billie Kathryn Roche, July 28, 1947; 1 dau., Kathryn Annabel. Editor Alice (Tex.) News, 1952-54, Gulf Pub. Co., Houston, 1954-56, Martin-Marietta Corp., Denver, 1958-60, Gen. Dynamics Co., San Diego, 1960-65; editor Stanford Research Inst., Menlo Park, Cal., 1965-67; editor, economist Fed. Res. Bank of Chgo., 1967-69; sr. editor, economist Fed. Res. Bank of Dallas, 1969—; cons. Gulf Pub. Co., Houston, 1956-57. Served with USNR, 1944-46. Mem. Am. Econ. Assn., A.A.A.S. Democrat. Contbr. articles to profl. jours. Home: 1636 Russell Glen Lane Dallas TX 75232 Office: Fed Reserve Bank of Dallas Station K Dallas TX 75202

BARNARD, JAMES WILLIAM, psychologist; b. N.Y.C., June 11, 1932; s. James Henry and Frances Louise (Moch) B.; A.B., Middlebury Coll., 1955; M.A., U. Vt., 1958; M.A., Yale, 1960, Ph.D., 1963; m. Caroline Genovese, Oct. 24, 1968; children—Carrie Louise, Pamela Mae, James Henry. Asst. prof. child psychology U. Minn., Mpls., 1962-64; asso. prof. psychology George Peabody Coll., Nashville, 1964-68; research asso. prof. ednl. research U. S. Fla., Tampa, 1968—, dir. Inst. on Exceptional Children and Adults, 1970—. Kennedy Found. vis. prof. Peabody Coll., 1964-65; psychol. cons. Tenn. Dept. Mental Health, 1965-66; field reader U.S. Office Edn., 1970-73; teaching cons. Hillsborough Community Coll., Tampa, 1968-72. Mem. Community Coordinating Council, Tampa, 1971-73. USPHS tng. fellow, 1958-62; Office Edn. grantee, 1969-71. Mem. Am. Psychol. Assn., Am. Assn. Mental Deficiency, Soc. Research Child Devel., Am. Ednl. Research Assn., Council for Exceptional Children, Sigma Xi. Contbr. articles to profl. jours. Home: 2912 Forest Circle Seffner FL 33584 Office: Dept Spl Edn U S Fla Tampa FL 33620

BARNARD, LESLIE RAYDENE, gas co. exec.; b. Mitchellville, Tenn., Apr. 24, 1929; s. Marvin S. and Tallie Mai (McCombs) B.; B.S., U. Tenn., 1959; m. Pauline Sue Paul, Dec. 26, 1952; children—Paulla Rei, Melody Ann, Roma Leigh, Jeffrey. With East Tenn. Natural Gas. Co., Knoxville, 1955-68, chief engr., 1964-68; gen. mgr. Natural Gas Utility Dist., Rogersville, Tenn., 1968—. Served with AUS, 1951-53. Mem. Am. Soc. C.E., Nat. Soc. Profl. Engrs., Rogersville Area C. of C. (pres. 1971—). Rotarian (Rogersville pres. 1969-70). Home: PO Box 128 Rogersville TN 37857 Office: 850 W Main St Rogersville TN 37857

BARNES, AL-G, elec. engr.; b. Ponca City, Okla., Dec. 19, 1937; s. Lester Herbert and Blanche Alberta (Crockett) B.; B.S. in Elec. Engring., Okla. State U., 1961; m. Chloe Dell Williams, Jan. 10, 1970; children—Kelli Leigh, Lawson Layne. With Continental Oil Co., Westlake, La., 1961—, insp., 1961-66, elec. foreman, 1966-67, warehouse supt. in-charge setting up IBM, machine and fortran, 1967-68, supr. power plant in-charge steam, elec. generating facilities, 1968—. Mem. La. Mgmt. Assn. Inventor measuring thickness device. Home: PO Box 2226 Maplewood LA 70663 Office: PO Box 37 Westlake LA 70669

BARNES, BEN F., constrn. co. exec., former state ofcl.; b. Gorman, Tex., Apr. 17, 1938; s. B.F. Barnes; student Tarleton State Coll., Tex. Christian U., U. Tex. at Austin; LL.D., McMurry Coll., Tex. Tech U., St. Edwards U.; m. Nancy Sayers; children—Greg, Amy, Scott, Brian. Lt. gov. State of Tex., 1969-73; owner Herman Bennett Co., Brownwood, Tex., 1973—. Mem. Tex. Ho. of Reps., 1960-68, chmn. rules com., 1963, speaker, 1965-68. Chmn. Tex. legislative council and legislative budget bd., 1969-73; chmn. So. conf. Council State Govts., 1967-68, mem. exec. com., 1968-70; pres. Nat. Legislative Conf., 1968-69. Named one of 10 outstanding young men in U.S., U.S. Jr. C. of C., 1970. Mem. Tex. Jr. C. of C. (one of 5 outstanding young Texans 1965), S.W. Cattle Growers Assn. Methodist. Elk. Home: Brownwood TX 76801 Office: Herman Bennett Co Brownwood TX 76801

BARNES, BENNY BLAIR, educator, elec. engr.; b. Gadsden, Ala., Mar. 7, 1935; s. Newton Eldridge and Sara (Roach) B.; student Jacksonville (Ala.) State U., 1952-53; B.S., Ala. Poly. Inst., 1956; M.S., U. Ala., 1962; Ph.D., Auburn U., 1965; m. Patsy Harris Barnes, June 3, 1956; 1 son, Douglas. Design engr. Chance Vought Aircraft, Dallas, 1956-57; instrument engr. E. I. duPont de Nemours, Aiken, S.C., 1957-59; aerospace technologist NASA, Huntsville, Ala., 1959-63; instr. elec. engring. Auburn (Ala.) U., 1963-65, asso. prof., 1970—, dir. computer center, 1970—; asst. prof. Va. Poly. Inst., 1965-66; mgr. simulation dept. Computer Scis. Corp., Huntsville, 1966-67; asso. prof. elec. engring., U. Tenn., Knoxville, 1967-70, asso. prof. computer sci., 1969-70, asst. dean Coll. Engring., 1967-69. Served with AUS, 1957. Registered profl engr., Tenn., Ala. Mem. I.E.E.E., A.A.A.S., Soc. Computer Simulation, Assn. for Computing Machinery, Tau Beta Pi, Eta Kappa Nu, Pi Mu Epsilon, Sigma Pi Sigma. Home: 130 Talheim Dr Auburn AL 36830

BARNES, CHARLES MILLER, med. physicist; b. Rising Star, Tex., July 21, 1922; s. George Thomas and Erie Inez (Rich) B.; D.V.M., Tex. A. & M. U., 1944; Ph.D., U. Cal. at Davis, 1957; m. Anna Loyce Rose, Dec. 23, 1943; children—Polly (Mrs. Douglas Blankenship), Molly (Mrs. Daryl Pizanie), John, James. Individual practice vet. medicine, Cisco, Tex., 1944-47; field veterinarian U.S. Dept. Agr., Mexico, 1947-50; commd. capt. USAF, 1950, advanced through grades to col., 1968, ret., 1970; with NASA, Houston, 1970—, mgr. health applications office, 1972—. Prof. comparative pathology U. Tex. Sch. Pub. Health and Grad. Sch. Biomed. Scis., Houston, 1970—. Dist. chmn. Boy Scouts Am., Bayshore dist., 1973. Chmn. bd. Internat. Vet. Med. Found., Houston, 1973—. Recipient Silver Beaver award Boy Scouts Am. Mem. Am. Vet. Med. Assn., Health Physics Soc. Contbr. articles to profl. jours. Home: 1710 Booth Bay Dr Houston TX 77058 Office: Mail Code DD12 NASA Houston TX 77058

BARNES, FANNIE BURRELL (MRS. RICHARD ALEXANDER BARNES), librarian; b. New Orleans; d. Alexander and Lorenza (Nicholas) Burrell; A.B., Dillard U., 1945; M.S., Atlanta U., 1950; m. Roscoe Ross, May 18, 1962 (div.); children—Erica Arnetta, Maria Monique; m. 2d, Richard Alexander Barnes, May 29, 1968. Tchr. English, Gilbert Acad., New Orleans, 1945-49; asst. librarian Atlanta U., summer 1950, 57-61, 67; head librarian Claflin Coll., Orangeburg, S.C., 1950-54; head librarian Clark Coll., Atlanta, 1954—, tchr. children's lit., 1957—; childrens librarian Atlanta Pub. Library Bookmobile, summer 1961. Mem. A.L.A., N.E.A., N.A.A.C.P., Alpha Kappa Alpha. Baptist. Home: 1981 Valley Ridge Dr SW Atlanta GA 30331 Office: 240 Chestnut St SW Atlanta GA 30314

BARNES, HERSCHIEL SEVIER, lawyer; b. Cookeville, Tenn., Dec. 19, 1919; s. Herschiel Sevier and Susan Gertrude (Tinnon) B.; B.S., George Peabody Coll., 1940; J.D., Vanderbilt U., 1948; m. Vivian Jean Hicks, Dec. 22, 1950; children—Amy (Mrs. John H. Gibson, Jr.), Joel, Thomas. Tchr. pub. schs., St. Petersburg, Fla., 1939-40; admitted to Tenn. bar, 1947; practiced in Cookeville, Tenn., 1948—; mem. firm Crawford & Barnes, 1949-71, Crawford, Barnes & Acuff, 1971—. Dir. Crest Lawn Meml. Cemetery, Cookeville Sheet Metal Works. City atty., Cookeville, 1948-52; referee in bankruptcy Northeastern div. Middle Dist. Tenn., 1954-58. Chmn. bd. Cookeville Gen. Hosp., 1948-72, trustee, 1964-72. Served with AUS, 1941-45; ETO. Decorated Purple Heart. Mem. Phi Delta Phi, Order of Coif. Democrat. Methodist (chmn. adminstrv. bd. 1971; lay leader 1972). Home: 957 Sunset Dr Cookeville TN 38501 Office: 101 S Jefferson Av Cookeville TN 38501

BARNES, JOHN EVAN, JR., clergyman; b. Pratt City, Ala., July 9, 1911; s. John Evan and Hattie (Pollard) B.; A.B., Samford U., 1934; Th.M., So. Bapt. Theol. Sem., 1937; D.D., Miss. Coll., 1948; m. Maron Stallworth, Aug. 25, 1936; children—Frances Marilyn, John Evan III, Elizabeth Carson. Ordained to ministry Bapt. Ch., 1932; pastor 1st Bapt. Ch., Atmore, Ala., 1937-42, West Point, Miss., 1942-44, Main St. Bapt. Ch., Hattiesburg, Miss., 1944—. Pres. Miss. Bapt. Conv., 1953-54, chmn. edn. commn., 1965—, chmn. commn. on bds., 1956—; pres. So. Bapt. Sunday Sch. Bd., 1964—; pres. bd. dirs. So. Bapt. Hosp. Commn., 1957—. Co-chmn. United Gives Fund, Hattiesburg, 1955—. Kiwanian (dir. 1946). Writer tract, Is it Right, 1951; also articles. Home: 1000 Estelle St Hattiesburg MS 39401 Office: 1101 Main St Hattiesburg MS 39401

BARNES, JOHN VANDERSLICE, JR., steel co. exec.; b. Roanoke, Va., Oct. 6, 1923; s. John Vanderslice and Anna Lee (Branscome) B.; B.S. in Indsl. Engring., Va. Poly. Inst., 1948; m. Mary Augusta Cox, Mar. 20, 1948; 1 son, John Vanderslice III. Asst. plant mgr. Am. Bridge div. U.S. Steel Corp., Birmingham, Ala., 1948-63; plant mgr. Ingalls Iron Works, Birmingham, 1963-70; v.p. prodn. steel fabrication Bristol Steel & Iron Works (Va.), 1970—. Chmn. troop com. Boy Scouts Am., Birmingham, 1966-70. Served as pilot USAAF, 1942-45. Decorated Air medal. Registered profl. engr., Ala. Mem. C. of C. Kiwanian, Optimist. Presbyn. (elder). Club: Country of Bristol. Home: 212 Forest Hills Dr Bristol TN 37620 Office: 420 Piedmont Av Bristol VA 24201

BARNES, RUDOLPH COUNTS, JR., lawyer; b. Columbia, S.C., Sept. 16, 1942; s. Rudolph C. and Ella Caroline (Carson) B.; A.B. with honors in Polit. Sci., The Citadel, 1964; J.D., U. S.C., 1967; m. Jeanette Neville Wall, Aug. 29, 1964; children—Tracie Neville, Rudolph Counts, III, Ashley Carson. Admitted to S.C. bar, 1967; asst. atty. gen. S.C. Tax Commn., Columbia, 1967; partner firm Barnes, Austin & Ellison, Attys. at Law, Columbia, 1971—. Dir. Bank of Commerce. Instr. bus. law U. Md., Far East Div., 1969-70. Pres., dir. Richland-Lexington Council on Aging, 1973—; v.p., dir. Jr. Achievement Greater Columbia, 1972—; dir., chmn. Devel. Council Columbia Urban Service Center, 1973—; chmn. law enforcement subcom. Greater Columbia Community Relations Council, 1971—. Served with Judge Advocate Gen.'s Corps AUS, 1967-71. Mem. Am., S.C., Richland County, Okinawa bar assns., S.C. Income Property Assn., Am. Judicature Soc., World Peace Thru Law Soc., Greater Columbia C. of C. (chmn. com. to assist relocation Ugandan refugees 1973—). Methodist (lay mem. urban work com. S.C. Conf. 1971—; chmn. pastor-parish relations com. 1973—). Club: Columbia Luncheon. Home: 2400 Wheat St Columbia SC 29210 Office: Bankers Trust Tower PO Box 11921 Columbia SC 29211

BARNES, WILLIAM ROY, lawyer; b. Houston, Sept. 11, 1923; s. Roy Owen and Florine (King) B.; B.B.A., U. Tex., 1950, J.D., 1951; m. Dorothy Louise Stephenson, Mar. 22, 1946; children—Michael Allen, Patrick Louis, William Roy, Stephanie Ann (Mrs. John Langford). Admitted to Tex. bar, 1951, practiced in Odessa, 1952—; mem. firm Mason & Barnes, 1952-55, John J. Watts, 1955-59, Milburn, Bell, Knight & Barnes, 1959-64; individual practice, 1964—. Served with USNR, 1943-47, 50-51. Mem. Tex. Bar Assn., Tex., Am. trial lawyers assns., Fellows Tex. Bar Found., Phi Alpha Delta. Office: Suite 510 American Bank Bldg Odessa TX 79761

BARNESS, LEWIS ABRAHAM, physician; b. Atlantic City, N.J., July 31, 1921; s. Joseph and Mary (Silverstein) B.; A.B., Harvard, 1941, M.D., 1944; M.A. (hon.), U. Pa., 1971; m. Elaine Berger, June 14, 1953; children—Carol, Laura, Joseph. Intern Phila. Gen. Hosp., 1944-45; resident Children's Med. Center, Boston, 1947-50; asst. chief, then chief dept. pediatrics Phila. Gen. Hosp., 1951-72; vis. physician U. Pa. Hosp., 1952-57, acting chief, then chief, 1957-72; mem. faculty U. Pa. Sch. Medicine, 1951-72, prof. pediatrics, 1964-72; prof. pediatrics, chmn. dept. U. So. Fla. Med. Sch., Tampa, 1972—. Served to capt. AUS, 1945-46. Recipient Lindback Teaching award U. Pa., 1963; Borden award nutrition, 1972. Mem. Am. Pediatric Soc. (recorder-editor 1964—), Soc. Pediatric Research, Am. Inst. Nutrition, A.A.A.S., Sigma Xi, Alpha Omega Alpha. Author: Pediatric Physical Diagnosis Yearbook, edits. 1-4, 1957—. Home: 548 W Davis Blvd Tampa FL 33606

BARNETT, BENJAMIN LEWIS, JR., physician; b. Woodruff, S.C., July 22, 1926; s. Benjamin Lewis and Mattie Bernice (Skinner) B.; B.S., Furman U., 1946; M.D., U. S.C., 1949; m. Annalyne Louise Hall, Oct. 25, 1958; children—Benjamin Lewis III, Jane Kristen. Intern, Protestant Episcopal Hosp., Phila., 1949-50; pvt. practice gen. medicine, Woodruff, 1950-70; asso. prof. family practice Med. U. S.C., Charleston, 1970—, asst. dir. family practice residency program, 1970—, vice chmn. dept. family practice, 1973—; mem. clin. staff Med. U. Hosp., Charleston County Hosp., 1970—; chief of staff Woodruff Hosp., 1966-69. Health officer Town of Woodruff, 1950-54. Mem. Spartanburg County Bd. Edn., 1968-70, sec., 1969-70; mem. drug adv. council S.C. Dept. Social Services, 1973—. Trustee, Bethea Bapt. Home for Aged, Darlington, S.C., 1972-73. Served with USNR, 1954-56. Named Citizen of Year, Woodmen of World, 1968; recipient Golden Apple award Student A.M.A., 1973. Diplomate Am. Bd. Family Practice. Mem. A.M.A., So., S.C. med. assns., Charleston County Med. Soc., Soc. Tchrs. Family Practice, Am. Acad. Family Practice, Spartanburg County Med. Soc. (v.p. 1968), Am. Philatelic Soc., Am. Manuscript Soc., Furman U. Alumni Assn. (dir.), Alpha Omega Alpha (faculty councilor), Alpha Kappa Kappa, Kappa Alpha. Baptist (deacon, chmn. bd.). Mason (32 degree). Editor S.C. Family Physician, 1973—. Contbr. articles to med. jours. Home: 673 Pawley Rd Mount Pleasant SC 29464

BARNETT, BERNARD HARRY, lawyer; b. Helena, Ark., July 13, 1916; s. Harry and Rebecca (Grossman) B.; student U. Mich., 1934-36; J.D., Vanderbilt U., 1940 ; m. Marian Spiesberger, Apr. 9, 1949; 1 son, Charles Dawson. Admitted to Ky. bar, 1940; pvt. practice, Louisville, 1940-42; asso. Woodward, Dawson, Hobson & Fulton, 1946-48; partner Bulitt, Dawson & Tarrant, 1948-52, Greenebaum, Barnett, Wood & Doll, 1952-70; partner Barnett & McConnell, 1972, Barnett, Greenebaum, Martin & McConnell, 1972—. Chmn. exec. com., dir. Nat. Industries, Inc.; dir. Bank of Louisville, Madison Fund, Inc., Paz Oil Co., Ltd. Mem. adv. group Joint Com. on Internal Revenue Taxation, U.S. Congress, 1953-55, Com. on Ways and Means, U.S. Ho. of Reps. 1956-58. Chmn. Louisville Fund, 1952-53; mem. nat. exec. com., nat. campaign cabinet United Jewish Appeal, 1959—, nat. chmn., 1967-71; chmn. Louisville United Jewish Appeal, 1968-69. Mem. Louisville and Jefferson County Republican Exec. Com., 1954-60; chmn. Ky. Rep. Finance Com., 1955-60. Served as lt. USNR, 1942-45. Mem. Am., Ky., Louisville bar assns. Home: Apt 1024 Glenview East 5100 Brownsboro Rd Louisville KY 40222 Office: 614 Kentucky Home Life Bldg Louisville KY 40202

BARNETT, CRAWFORD FANNIN, JR., physician; b. Atlanta, May 11, 1938; s. Crawford Fannin and Penelope Hollinshead (Brown) B.; student Taft Sch., 1953-56, U. Minn., 1957; A.B. magna cum laude, Yale, 1960; postgrad. (Davison scholar) Oxford (Eng.) U., 1963; M.D. (Trent scholar), Duke, 1964; m. Elizabeth McCarthy Hale, June 6, 1964; children—Crawford Fannin III, Robert Hale. Intern internal medicine Duke U. Med. Center, Durham, N.C., 1964-65, resident, 1965; resident internal medicine Wilmington (Del.) Med. Center, 1965-66; dir. Tenn. Heart Disease Control Program, Nashville, 1966-68; practice medicine, specializing in internal medicine, Atlanta, 1968—; mem. staff Crawford Long, Northside, Ga. Bapt., Grady Meml., Jessie Parker Williams, Doctors Meml., West Paces Ferry, Bolton Rd., Piedmont, Atlanta hosps. (all Atlanta); mem. teaching staff Vanderbilt Med. Center, Nashville, 1966-68, Crawford Long Meml. Hosp., 1969—; clin. instr. internal medicine, dept. medicine Emory U. Med. Sch., Atlanta, 1969—. Vice pres., dir. Preferred Equities Corp., 1970—. Mem. Good Govt. Atlanta. Bd. govs. Doctors Meml. Hosp., 1971-73. Served as surgeon USPHS, 1966-68. Fellow Am. Geog. Soc.; mem. Am. Fedn. Clin. Research, Council Clin. Cardiology, A.A.A.S., Am., Ga., Atlanta med. assns., Am., Ga. heart assns., Am., Ga. socs. internal medicine, Am. Assn. History Medicine, Ga., Atlanta hist. socs., Nat. Trust for Historic Preservation, Internat. Hippocratic Found. Soc. (Greece), Faculty of History of Medicine and Pharmacy Worshipful Soc. Apothecaries of London (Eng.), Atlanta Com. on Fgn. Relations (chmn. exec. com.), So. Council on Internat. and Pub. Affairs, Newcomen Soc., Atlanta Clin. Soc., Victorian Soc. Am. (bd. advisers Atlanta chpt. 1971—), Internat. Platform Assn. Mensa, Gridiron, Phi Beta Kappa. Episcopalian. Clubs: Piedmont Driving, Yale (dir. 1970—), Nine O'Clocks (Atlanta); Pan Am. Doctors (Hidalgo, Mexico). Contbr. articles to profl. publs. Home: 2739 Ramsgate Ct NW Atlanta GA 30305 Office: 3250 Howell Mill Rd NW Atlanta GA 30327

BARNETT, GERALD PAUL, real estate exec.; b. Lynnwood, Cal., Sept. 1, 1929; s. Claude Willard and Myrtle Fern (Loop) B.; B.A., U.S. Naval Postgrad. Sch., 1963, M.S., 1963; m. Lola M. Myers, Jan. 18, 1952; children—Richard Allen, Elizabeth Anne, George William, Deborah Lee, Gerald Paul III. Commd. ensign U.S. Navy, 1950, advanced through grades to comdr., 1965; ret., 1970; v.p. Internat. Realty & Wilderness Battlefield Park, Alexandria, Va., 1970-71, exec. v.p., 1971—; exec. v.p. Presdl. Lakes Devel. Co., Inc.; instr. U. Va., George Washington U., Old Dominion Coll., 1963-64. Decorated Silver Star medal, Air medal, Naval Commendation medal. Mem. Am. Assn. Exptl. Test Pilots. Mason (32 deg.). Contbr. articles to profl. jours. Home: 4738 Lafitte Ct Alexandria VA 22312 Office: 4660 Kenmore Av Alexandria VA 22304

BARNETT, HENRY D., business exec.; b. Sumter, S.C., May 29, 1919; B.S. in Bus. Adminstrn., The Citadel, 1941; m. Patricia Levi, Dec. 1950; children—Patricia Loryea, Henry D., Wendell L. Owner, pres., gen. mgr. B.J. Barnett, Inc., Sumter; partner, mgr. Barnett Farms; pres., mgr., an owner Barnett Canning Assn.; partner Barnett-Moses Real Estate; dir. Palmetto Fire Ins. Co.; sec., co-owner Dalzell Gin Co.; treas., co-owner Ag-Rotov, Inc. Pres., S.C. Peach Council and Promotion Bd.; chmn. Sumter County Commn. for Higher Edn.; chmn. Sumter Soil and Water Conservation Commn. Served from 2d lt. to lt. col. USAF, World War II. Mem. Sumter Agrl. Soc. (past pres.), Sumter C. of C. (chmn. agr. com.), Sumter Prodn. Credit Assn., Am. Legion, V.F.W. Kiwanian, Elk. Clubs: Sunset Country, Cotillion, Trian, Assembly (pres.). Office: Box 276 9 E Liberty St Sumter SC 29150

BARNETT, JAMES ARDEN, lawyer, judge; b. Miss., Aug. 4, 1924; s. Arden and Vera (Turner) B.; B.B.A., U. Miss., 1948, LL.B., 1949; m. Lucy Lee Owen, Mar. 4, 1945; children—Ruth Elizabeth, James Arden, Vera Susan. Admitted to Miss. bar, 1949; mem. firm Barnett, Montgomery, McClintock and Cunningham, Jackson, 1949-65; partner Barnett & Barnett, Jackson, 1965-70; individual practice, 1970-71; mem. Miss. Ho. of Reps., 1964-68; mem. Miss. Senate, 1968-71; chancery judge, Jackson, 1971—. Mem. Hinds County Sch. Bd., 1954-64. Served with USNR, 1943-45. Decorated D.F.C., Air medal. Mem. Am., Miss., Hinds County bar assns. Baptist. Republican. Lion (past pres.). Home: 710 E Leake Clinton MS 39056 Office: Chancery Ct Jackson MS 39201

BARNETT, JAMES E., sch. supt.; b. Flo, Tex., Apr. 26, 1927; s. William Wade and Sally (Owens) B.; B.S., Sam Houston State U., 1949, M.Ed., 1958; m. Joann Cecelia Perryman, Jan. 18, 1951; children—Barry, Kevin. Tchr. coach Oakwood (Tex.) Ind. Sch. Dist., 1949-51, Woodhouse Sch., 1951-60; supt. Leverett Chapel schs., Overton, Tex., 1960—. Served with USNR, 1945-46; PTO. Mem. Am., Tex. assns. sch. adminstrs., N.E.A., Tex. Tchrs. Assn. Rotarian. Home and office: Route 2 Overton TX 75684

BARNETT, JIMMY LYLE, elec. engr.; b. nr. Medina, Tenn., Oct. 2, 1938; s. Lyle Stanford and Ruby Lucille (Goodrich) B.; B.S., U. Tenn., 1961, postgrad., 1972—; m. Etta Louise Futrell, July 9, 1961; children—Jeffery Lynn, Tracy Lee. Chief engr. in charge engring. and constrn., electric dept. Jackson Utility Div., 1961—. Served with Tenn. N.G., 1961-67. Mem. I.E.E.E. (pres. Jackson chpt.), Nat., Tenn. socs. profl. engrs., Tenn. Electric Municipal Power Assn. (chmn. engring. and operations sect.). Baptist (chmn. bd. deacons). Club: Hub City Toastmasters (pres., past sec., v.p.). Home: 82 Timberhill Dr Jackson TN 38301 Office: 119 E College St Jackson TN 38301

BARNETT, JUANITA MCMILLAN, librarian; b. Hope, Ark., May 3, 1915; d. David Williams and Leila Belle (Allen) McMillan; B.A., Ouachita Bapt. U., 1936; B.S. in L.S., George Peabody Coll. Tchrs., 1937; m. James Russell Barnett, Aug. 14, 1938 (dec. July 1954); children—Judy (Mrs. William Robert Jennings), Barbara (Mrs. Richard Galbraith). Librarian, Ouachita Bapt. U., Arkadelphia, Ark., 1936-40, 56—. Mem. Arkadelphia Woman's Library Assn., Am. (state membership com. 1964), Southwestern, Ark. (2d v.p. 1964, chmn. coll. sect. 1959-60) library assns., Ark. Found. Asso. Colls. (sec. com. librarians 1966-67, pres. com. librarians 1970), Clark County Hist. Assn. (charter, asst. exec. sec. 1972—). Presbyn. (sec. 1954-56, deacon 1971—). Editor: 2d edit. Periodical Holdings in the Ark. Found. Asso. Colls., 1963. Home: 610 Pine St Arkadelphia AR 71923 Office: Riley Library Ouachita Bapt U Arkadelphia AR 71923

BARNETT, ROBERT JAMES, ballet sch. exec.; b. Okanogan, Wash., May 6, 1925; s. James Garfield and Vera (Berry) B.; dance tng. with Bronislava Nijinska, Lubov Egorova, Olga Preobrajenska, Sch. Am. Ballet; m. Virginia Gleaves Rich, July 20, 1967; children—Robert James, David Michael. With Original Ballet Russe, Europe, 1948-49, N.Y.C. Ballet, 1950-58; dir. Atlanta Ballet Inc., 1958—; part owner, co. exec. Atlanta Sch. Ballet, 1969—. Served with USNR, 1943-46. Mem. South Eastern Regional Ballet Assn. (coordinator), Nat. Assn. for Regional Ballet, Inc. (v.p.), Pacific Regional Ballet Assn. (ajudicator), South West Regional Festival Assn. Choreographer: The Nutcracker, La Valse, Fate, Pas de Trois, Quatre Vignettes, Suite Brilliante, Waltz Pas de Deux, Divertimento. Ballet master: Swan Lake, Sleeping Beauty, Giselle. Home: 27 W Andrews Dr NW Atlanta GA 30305 Office: 3215 Cains Hill Pl NW Atlanta GA 30305

BARNETT, SAMUEL CLARENCE, educator; b. Chatsworth, Ga., May 10, 1922; s. Jesse Ragon and Marguerite (Heartsell) B.; B. Indsl. Engring., Ga. Inst. Tech., 1948, M.S., 1956, Ph.D., 1962; m. Dorothy Rhea Willett, Nov. 25, 1950; 1 son, Daniel Ragon. Mem. faculty Ga. Inst. Tech., Atlanta, 1952—, prof. mech. engring., 1955—, asso. dean undergrad. div., 1968-72, head dept. indsl. engring. technology, 1972—. Pres., Piedmont Heights Divic Club, 1966-67. Served with AUS, 1942-45. Mem. Am. Soc. Mech. Engrs. (chmn. 1965-66. Mason (Shriner, 32 deg.). Club: Ansley Golf. Home: 1938 Gotham Way NE Atlanta GA 30324 Office: Dept Indsl Engineering Tech Ga Inst Tech Atlanta GA 30332

BARNETT, TALMADGE LORENZO, correctional adminstr.; b. Winston-Salem, N.C., July 28, 1935; s. Robert L. and Thelma (Moore) B.; B.S., N.C. Agrl. and Tech. U., 1957; m. Rosa Marie Peacock, Apr. 4, 1958; children—Talmadge, Rodney. Youth rehab. counselor Goldsboro (N.C.) Youth Center, 1959-69; prison rehab. supr. Eastern area N.C. Dept. Correction, 1969-70, regional supr., 1970-73, correctional adminstr., Greenville, 1973—. Sec. bd. dirs. E.A. House Boys Club, Goldsboro, 1965-66. Mem. Am. Correction Assn., N.C. Law Enforcement Assn., Alpha Phi Alpha. Methodist. Home: 1106 Branch St Goldsboro NC 27530 Office: PO Drawer 5044 Greenville NC 27834

BARNETT, WILLIAM HALBERT, architect; b. Lewisburg, Tenn., July 11, 1915; s. William Lee and Erma (Halbert) B.; B.S. in Architecture, Ga. Inst. Tech., 1940, B.Arch., 1941; m. Norma Cook, June 12, 1942; children—Thomas Vance, Andrew Preston, Mary Cecile. With Burge &Stevens, Atlanta, 1938-40, Perkins & Will, Chgo., 1946; with Stevens & Wilkinson, architects & engrs., planners, Atlanta, 1947—, pres., 1972—. Served with USNR, 1941-46; comdr. ret. Mem. A.I.A. Club: Cherokee Town & Country (Atlanta). Home: 5550 Dupree Dr NW Atlanta GA 30327 Office: 100 Peachtree St NW Atlanta GA 30303

BARNETT, WILLIAM WOODSON, JR., ednl. adminstr.; b. Lexington, Mo., Oct. 23, 1920; s. William Woodson and Elizabeth (Slusher) B.; A.A., Wentworth Mil. Acad., 1939; B.S., U. Mo., 1941, M.A., 1949; m. Ann Mahler, Oct. 29, 1946; 1 son, Theodore Mahler. Accounting clk. Gen. Electric Co., Bridgeport, Conn., 1941-42; commd. 2d lt. U.S. Army, 1942, advanced through grades to lt. col., 1954, ret., 1965; instr. Wentworth Mil. Acad., Lexington, 1965-67; dir. publicity and student publs. Schreiner Coll., Kerrville, Tex., 1967—, asso. prof. journalism, 1967—. Chmn. service unit Salvation Army, 1970-72. Decorated Bronze Star medal with oak leaf cluster; recipient George C. Marshall medal Command and Gen. Staff Coll., 1961. Presbyn. (elder). Kiwanian (dir. 1970-72). Home: Schreiner Campus Kerrville TX 78028 Office: Schreiner Coll Kerrville TX 78028

BARNHARDT, WILLIAM MCLAUGHLIN, textile co. exec.; b. Latrobe, Pa., July 29, 1928; s. William Horace and Margaret (McLaughlin) B.; grad. Woodberry Forest Sch., 1946; student Princeton, 1947; B.S., N.C. State U., 1950; m. Harriet Oehler Bangle, Sept. 7, 1949; children—William Bangle, Richard Alan, Steven Fredric. With textile fibers dept. E. I. duPont de Nemours & Co., Wilmington, Del., 1950-52; v.p. Barnhardt Elastic Corp., Charlotte, N.C., 1952-58, area sales mgr., 1958-66, v.p. sales, 1967—; pres. So. Webbing Mills, 1974—; v.p., dir. Am. Textile Corp., Barnhardt Bros. Co., Tryon Processing Co.; dir. Riverview Acres. Pres. Blue Ridge Assembly, YMCA, 1969—, v.p. nat. council YMCAs, 1973—. Commr. Charlotte (N.C.) Housing Authority, 1968-73. Bd. dirs. Charlotte YMCA, 1966—; nat. bd. dirs. YMCA, 1970—; mem. exec. bd. Mecklenburg council Boy Scouts Am., 1960—; mem. adv. bd. Salvation Army, 1964-67; bd. mgrs. Camp Thunderbird, 1954—; bd. dirs. Found. U. N.C. at Charlotte, 1973—; bd. dirs. Mecklenburg chpt. A.R.C., 1962-65, Greater Charlotte Found., Charlotte Choral Soc., 1966-71; bd. dirs., v.p. Barnhardt Found.; bd. visitors Davidson Coll.; trustee Presbyn. Hosp. Recipient Silver Beaver award Boy Scouts Am., 1966. Mem. Internat. Brotherhood Magicians, Soc. Am. Magicians, Charlotte Textile Club (dir. 1956-57), Charlotte C. of C. (dir. 1965-67), Newcomen Soc. N.Am. Rotarian (dir. 1972—). Clubs: Quail Hollow Country, City (Charlotte, N.C.). Home: 3921 Arborway St Charlotte NC 28211 Office: NC Nat Bank Bldg Charlotte NC 28202

BARNHART, HARRY BASCOMB, JR., ind. oil producer; b. Austin, Tex., Aug. 9, 1911; s. Harry Bascomb and Nelle (Sterzing) B.; student U. Tex., 1929-32. Self employed as investor, independent oil and gas producer, 1948—. Mem. Mus. of Fine Arts, Houston Symphony Soc. Served from pvt. to 1st lt., AUS, 1942-45; PTO. Mem. Am. Petroleum Inst., Ind. Petroleum Assn. Am., Tex. Mid-Continent Oil and Gas Assn., Sigma Nu. Presbyn. Clubs: Petroleum, River Oaks Country. Office: Post Oak Bank Bldg Houston TX 77027

BARNHART, PAUL FRED, ind. oil producer; b. Austin, Tex., Nov. 23, 1913; s. Harry Bascomb and Nelle (Sterzing) B.; B.S., Okla. U., 1937; m. Katherine Pillot Lee, Feb. 12, 1972; children by previous marriage—Leslie Irvin, Velda (Mrs. James P. Wyche), Paul Fred. With Barnsdall Oil Co., Victoria, Tex., 1936-42, div. petroleum engr., asst. div. prodn. mgr., 1937-42; gen. mgr. operations Frank & George Frankel, oil co., Houston, 1942-50; petroleum engr., ind. oil producer, rancher, 1950—; chmn. bd. Barnhart Co., Houston, 1962—, BBM Drilling Co., 1949—; dir., mem. exec. com. Continental Bank of Tex., Houston. Mem. exec. com. Sam Houston Area council Boy Scouts Am., 1957—. Chmn. bd. trustees Kinkaid Sch., Houston, 1970-72; trustee, mem. exec. com. chancellor's council U. Tex., 1972—. Mem. Ind. Petroleum Assn. Am. (past v.p., dir.), Tex. Mid-Continent Oil and Gas Assn. (past dir.), Am. Inst. Mining, Metall. and Petroleum Engrs., Rice Assos. Presbyn. Club: Ramada (past sec., dir.) (Houston). Home: 3358 Inwood Dr Houston TX 77109 Office: 600 Post Oak Bank Bldg Houston TX 77027

BARNS, PAUL DRYDEN, JR., lawyer; b. Miami, Fla., Feb. 17, 1924; s. Paul D. and Victoria (Coleman) B.; B.S. in Bus. Adminstrn., Washington and Lee U., 1944; LL.B., U. Fla., 1948; m. Kathline Ghislane Hall, Jan. 26, 1961 (dec. Nov. 1967); m. 2d, Carol Ann Powelson, June 13, 1970. Admitted to Fla. bar, 1948; individual practice law, Miami, 1948-49; v.p., trust officer Security Trust Co., Miami, 1949-65; partner firm, Salley, Barns & Pajon, Miami, 1965—, Dir. Paek, Madrid, Spain. Served to lt. USNR, 1944-46. Mem. Am., Dade County bar assns., Fla. Bar (chmn. state tax com. 1969-71). Democrat. Presbyn. Home: 3941 Park Av Miami FL 33133 Office: 100 Biscayne Tower Miami FL 33132

BARNSTEIN, CHARLES HANSEN, sci. adminstr., editor; b. Newton, Wis., June 25, 1925; s. Charles Herman and Alma Catherine (Hansen) B.; B.S., U. Wis., 1952, M.S., 1955, Ph.D., 1960; m. Beatrice Lylabelle Kimber, Jan. 30, 1954; children—Brian Otis, Eric Charles, Chris John. Instr., Ida. State U., 1956-60, asst. prof., 1960-62, asso. prof., 1962-63; asso. prof. U. Wis., Milw., 1963-70; asst. dir. Nat. Formulary, Washington, 1970, asso. dir., 1970—, sec. bd., editor, 1970—. Cons. profl. services VA, 1967-69. Vocational guidance speaker Milw. Kiwanis Club, 1964-69. Mem. Am. Pharm. Assn., Acad. Pharm. Scis. (sec. sect. on pharm. analysis and control), Am. Chem. Soc., A.A.A.S., Sigma Xi, Phi Delta Chi, Rho Chi, Phi Lambda Upsilon, Phi Sigma. Contbr. articles to profl. jours. Home: 2411 Cavendish Dr Alexandria VA 22308 Office: 2215 Constitution Av NW Washington DC 20037

BARON, FREDERICK MARTIN, lawyer; b. Cedar Rapids, Ia., June 20, 1947; s. Abraham and Rose (Levin) B.; B.A., U. Tex. at Austin, 1968, J.D., 1971; m. Wendy Flatow, June 9, 1968; children—Andrew Michael, Courtney Melaine. Law clk. U.S. Commn. on Civil Rights, Washington, 1970; admitted to Tex. bar, 1971; mem. firm Mullinax, Wells, Mauzy & Baab, Inc., Dallas, 1971—. Mem. Tex. Law Rev. Ex-editors Assn. Home: 7015 Lakewood Blvd Dallas TX 75214 Office: 8204 Elmbrook Dr Dallas TX 75247

BARON, HOWARD NAFTALI, citrus fruit co. exec.; b. Berlin, Germany, June 16, 1922; s. Leon Y. and Friede (Kohane) B.; student U. London, Eng., 1936-39; m. Rebecca Zimerman, Dec. 5, 1950; children—Allen, Martin, Michael-Lesley. Came to U.S., 1954, naturalized, 1960. Vice pres. internat. Fla. Citrus Exchange (now known as Seald-Sweet Growers, Inc.), Tampa, Fla., 1954—; consul of Finland, 1966—. Sr. v.p. Tampa World Trade Council. Vice pres. Tampa Consular Corps, 1967-70, now v.p. Served with Israeli Army, 1947-49. Decorated Officier de Merit Agricole (France). Mem. Tampa Greater C. of C. Clubs: Commerce, University, Palma Golf and Country (Tampa); Tower. Contbr. articles to profl. jours. Home: 2303 Bendelovy Trail Tampa FL 33609 Office: Florida and Oak Av Tampa FL 33602

BARONDESS, STUART HENRY, radio sta. exec.; b. N.Y.C., Apr. 1, 1927; s. William H. and Belle (Toplitz) B.; B.A. cum laude, Norwich U., 1949; m. Shirley Spiegel, Apr. 1, 1955; children—David Paul, Mark Adam. Publicity, sales promotion, TV prodn. WTVJ, Miami, Fla., 1950-57; script writer for Gabriel Heatter, Mut. Network, 1951; sta. mgr. KCUL Radio, Ft. Worth, 1957-58; account exec. WNJR Radio, gen. sales mgr. WRAP Radio, Rollins, Inc., Norfolk, Va., 1959—. Active Point O'View P.T.A. Served with inf., AUS, 1945-46; ETO. Honored by Womens Aux. Norfolk Community Hosp. for efforts in promoting broadcast campaign for heart machine, 1973. Home: 100 Conference Ct Virginia Beach VA 23462 Office: WRAP Radio PO Box 598 Norfolk VA 23501

BARQUÍN, RAMÓN CARLOS -II, systems engr.; b. La Habana, Cuba, Aug. 8, 1942; s. Ramón María and Hilda Graciela (Cantero) B.; came to U.S., 1960; student U. Ala., 1961; B.S., U. P.R., 1965, B.S. in Elec. Engring., 1966, M.S. in Math., 1969; E.E., Mass. Inst. Tech., 1972, Ph.D., 1974; m. Rebecca Torres Guzman, Sept. 10, 1972; 1 son, Ramón Carlos III. Systems engr. IBM, Santurce, P.R., 1966-68, systems instr., 1969, systems engr. data processing, 1973—; research asso. Project Mac, Mass. Inst. Tech., 1970-71. Bd. dirs. Am. Mil. Acad. P.R. Resident study grantee IBM, 1970-73. Mem. I.E.E.E., Am. Fedn. Information Processing Socs., U. P.R. Alumni Assn., Mass. Inst. Tech. Alumni Assn., Internat. Judo Fedn. (dir.), Sigma Chi, Tau Beta Pi. Club: San Juan Judo. Author: Annotations for the History of Mathematics in Cuba, 1969; The Statistics of Judo, 1973. Home: Los Robles 7K Rio Piedras PR 00918 Office: IBM Co 1605 Kings Ct Santurce PR 00914

BARR, FRED SPROLES, microbiologist; b. Benhams, Va., Jan. 22, 1926; s. William Alexandria and Thelma Lamata (Sproles) B.; B.S., U. Tenn., 1952, postgrad., 1960; M.A., East Tenn. State U., 1957; m. Wilma Jean Qualls, Apr. 7, 1950; children—Freda Rene, Tony Alan. With Beecham-Massengill Pharm. Co. (formerly S.E. Massengill Co.), Bristol, Tenn., 1952—, research asso., 1960-69, sect. mgr. microbiology, 1970—. Mem. Bristol (Va.) City Council, 1962-71, Bristol Dept. Pub. Welfare Bd., 1967-71, Bristol Sch. Bd., 1971—. Served with USNR, 1943-48. Decorated Purple Heart. Mem. Am. Soc. Microbiology, Am. Chem. Soc., Sigma Xi. Mason (K.T.). Contbr. articles to profl. jours. Patentee in field antimicrobial agts. and antibiotics. Home: 500 Carter St Bristol VA 24201 Office: 501 5th St Bristol TN 37620

BARR, GLADYS H. HUTCHISON (MRS. THOMAS C. BARR), author; b. Butte, Mont., Dec. 19, 1904; d. David and Laura (Mooney) Hutchison; student State U. N.Y., 1924-25; LL.B., Albany Law Sch., 1926; m. Thomas C. Barr, Oct. 27, 1928; children—Thomas C., Ann (Mrs. Donald A. Weems), Jane, William Hune. Admitted to N.Y. bar, 1927; practiced in N.Y.C., 1926-29. Lectr. schs., colls., womens clubs, others. Vice chmn. bd. Pub. Libraries of Met. Govt. of Nashville and Davidson County, Tenn., 1959—. Mem. Am., Tenn., Southeastern library assns., Women's-Nat. Book Assn., Authors Guild, Authors League of Am., English Speaking Union. Democrat. Presbyn. Clubs: Centennial, Ladies of Richland Country. Author: Monk in Armour, 1950; Cross, Sword and Arrow, 1955; Master of Geneva and the Tinker's Armor, 1961; The Pilgrim Prince, 1963; Famous Witches and Ghost Series, 1969; The Bell Witch at Adams, 1969; The Ghost at Epworth Rectory, 1970; various stories and articles. Home: 110 Jefferson Sq 5039 Hillsboro Rd Nashville TN 37215 Office: Box 706 Nashville TN 37215

BARR, JAY DAVID ADELSTON, retail store exec.; b. Norfolk, Va., Nov. 30, 1936; s. Phillip and Dena (Adelston) Barr; B.A., U. Va., 1958, LL.B., 1964; M.A., U. London, 1961; m. Clay Hofheimer, Dec. 21, 1962; children—Philippa Elise, Elena Ann Hofheimer. Asso., Etheridge Baylor Hofheimer, Inc., Norfolk, Va., 1963-69; sec.-treas. Barr Corp., real estate devel., 1963—; pres. Cofers, Inc., interior design studios, 1969—; dir. Barr Bros., Inc., jewelers, 1966—. Bd. dirs. Feldman Chamber Music Soc. Served to lt. USNR, 1958-60. Republican. Clubs: Harbor (Norfolk, Va.); Raffles (N.Y.C.); St. James (London, Eng.). Home: Meadowbrook Point Norfolk VA 23505 Office: 1611 Colley Av Norfolk VA 23517

BARR, JESSE ALFRED, banker; b. Cleveland, Miss., Dec. 19, 1936; s. Jesse Coleman and Arlene (Shaffer) B.; B.S., Delta State Coll., 1959; M.B.A., Rutgers U., 1973; m. Connie Buckels, Jan. 24, 1960; children—Anne Louise, Sarah Catherine. With Union Planters Nat. Bank, Memphis, Tenn., 1961—, sr. v.p., sr. loan officer, 1970-73, exec. v.p., 1973—. Tchr., Am. Inst. Banking, 1966-67. Mem. Memphis Cotton Carnival Assn., 1967-68; treas. Citizens-Police Community Relations Com., 1968-69. Bd. dirs. Chickasaw Council Boy Scouts Am., dist. chmn., 1966-67, commr., 1963-66; bd. dirs. Delta State Coll. Found. Served with AUS, 1959-61. Recipient Distinguished Service award Memphis Jr. C. of C., 1965. Mem. Am. Inst. Banking (consul 1966-68), Nat. Assn. Credit Men, Robert Morris Assos., Delta State Coll. Alumni Assn. (pres. 1971—). Home: 6227 Quince St Memphis TN 38117 Office: 67 Madison St Memphis TN 38103

BARR, JOHN MONROE, broadcasting co. exec.; b. Smithville, Tex., Oct. 29, 1938; s. John Monroe and Matilda Helena (Raemsch) B.; B.B.A., U. Tex., 1961; m. Helen Grace Burns, Sept. 3, 1960; children—Lisa, Sherri, John. Agt., Internal Revenue Service, Houston, 1961-70, dist. conferee, 1970-71; v.p. finance Tex. Broadcasting Corp., Austin, 1971—; dir. Citizens Nat. Bank, Austin, City Nat. Bank. Sec. treas. Lyndon Baines Johnson Found., 1971—. C.P.A., Tex. Mem. Tex. Soc. C.P.A.'s (sec. 1969-70). Rotarian. Clubs: Austin, Headliners. Home: 4300 Woodway St Austin TX 78731 Office: PO Box 1209 Austin TX 78767

BARR, STANLEY GRAVES, JR., lawyer; b. Norfolk, Va., July 29, 1939; s. Stanley Graves and Edith Marjorie (Black) B.; student Old Dominion U., 1958-61; B.A., William and Mary Law Sch., 1962, LL.B., 1966; m. Anne Elizabeth Haynes, Apr. 6, 1963; children—Peter Marshall, Matthew Thornton. Admitted to Va. bar, 1966; practiced in Norfolk, Va., 1966—; partner firm Canoles, Mastracco, Martone, Barr & Russell, 1971—. Instr. in labor relations and indsl. relations U. Va., Norfolk, 1972-73; labor relations cons. Active Norfolk Housing Devel. Corp. Bd. dirs. Norfolk Free Clinic, Norfolk Drug Focus Com. Mem. Am., Va., Norfolk-Portsmouth (chmn. young lawyers sect. 1972) bar assns., Va. State Bar. Democrat. Methodist. Club: Harbor (Norfolk). Home: 416 Fairfax Av Norfolk VA 23507 Office: 1620 Virginia Nat Bank Bldg Norfolk VA 23510

BARRANGER, DALTON JOSEPH, lawyer; b. Houma, La., Feb. 6, 1901; s. Harry and Mathilde (Dupuis) B.; student Coll. S.W. La., 1915-17; J.D., Loyola U. (New Orleans), 1927; m. Miriam Ruth Garic, Sept. 12, 1928; 1 son, Garic Kenneth. Admitted to La. bar, 1927; practiced in New Orleans, 1927-37, Covington, 1937—; mem. firm. Ellis & Ellis, Ellis & Barranger, Ellis, Barranger & Suthon, 1937-47, D. J. Barranger, 1947-62, Barranger, Barranger, Jones & Fussell, 1962—. Dir. Comml. Bank & Trust Co. City atty., Covington, La., 1949—; town atty., Mandeville, La., 1962—; chmn. St. Tammany Parish chpt dr. A.R.C., 1957; govt. appeal atty. St. Tammany Parish (La.) Draft Bd., 1941—. Dir. Playmakers, Inc., 1962-68. Mem. Am., La., St. Tammany Parish bar assns., Delta Theta Phi. Democrat. Mason (32 deg.). Clubs: Covington Country (dir. 1958-62), Lion (pres. 1959). Home: Folsom Rd PO Box 1268 Covington LA 70433

BARRANGER, MIRIAM RUTH GARIC (MRS. DALTON JOSEPH BARRANGER), artist, craftsman; b. New Orleans; d. Henry Lawson and Lilly (Guedry) Garic; student Tulane U., 1927-28, 62-63; m. Dalton Joseph Barranger, Sept. 12, 1928; 1 son, Garic Kenneth. Exhibited one-man shows Isaac Delgado Mus. Art, New Orleans, 1951, Carl Barnetts, Inc., Dallas, 1952, La. Art Commn. Gallery, 1952, Mus. Art, Columbia, S.C., 1953, 331 Gallery, New Orleans, 1959, St. Tammany Art Assn., Covington, La., 1964, Foster Art Gallery, Baton Rouge, 1965, La. Crafts Council, New Orleans, 1970; exhibited in numerous shows, New Orleans, 1970; exhibited in numerous group shows including La. Art Commn. Galleries, Baton Rouge, 1953, 63, 65, 66, Isaac Delgado Mus., 1950-53, 58, New Orleans Downtown Gallery, 1961-63, Mint Mus. Art, Charlotte, N.C., 1966, 67 (hon. mention 1966), Mus. Contemporary Crafts, N.Y.C., 1963, N.C. Mus. Art, Raleigh, 1963, 66, Brooks Meml. Art Gallery, Memphis, 1965, La. Craft Council Gallery, New Orleans, 1965, Cabild. Presbytere, New Orleans, 1966. Chmn., St. Tammany Parish Welfare Bd., 1943-48; mem. adv. bd. La. Mental Health, 1959-61; chmn. home nursing, supr. surg. dressings groups A.R.C., 1942-45; vol. occupational therapist S.E. La. Hosp., Mandeville, La., 1962-63; membership chmn., editor Newsletter, La. Assos. Acad. Religion and Mental Health, 1962-65; chmn. St. Tammany Parish (La.) Tb Assn., 1942-48. Bd. dirs. New Orleans Tourist and Conv. Commn.; mem. nat. adv. com. Am. Crafts Council Devel. Fund. Recipient 1st prize in crafts New Orleans Art Assn., 1951; hon. mention Ann. Juried Show, La. Crafts Council, New Orleans, 1969, 70, 1st prize jewelry, 1972; 1st prize crafts Hodges Gardens Art Festival. Dir., v.p. Playmaker's Inc., Covington, 1966-67. Mem. St. Tammany Art Assn. (1st prize crafts 1971, (founder, past pres.) Am. Craftsmen's Council (La. rep. S.E. region; mem. internat. com. 1974), La. Craft Council (bd. mem., chmn. pub. relations 1966-70), Theosophical Soc. (past pres. Covington lodge). Designed, executed murals Comml. Bank and Trust Co., Covington, La., 1962. Address: Red Bluff Box 1268 Covington LA 70433

BARRETT, BRUCE RAY, govt. ofcl.; b. Ardmore, Okla., Apr. 8, 1938; s. Ray Andrew and Verna Lucille (Ray) B.; B.S., Okla. State U., 1961, M.S., 1962; m. Nancy Sue Warden, Nov. 21, 1959; children—Eugene Ray, Thomas Warden, James Andrew. San. engr. Cal Regional Water Quality Control Bd., Sacramento, 1962-66; with Environmental Protection Agy., Ada, Okla., 1966-72; water pollution control engr. U.S. Dept. Commerce, Washington, 1972—. USPHS trainee, 1961-62. Registered profl. engr., Cal., Okla., Tex. Mem. Cal. Water Pollution Control Fedn. (chmn. Sacramento area sect. 1965), Water Pollution Control Fedn., Am. Water Works Assn. Republican. Methodist. Contbr. articles to profl. jours. Research on aeobic sewage sludge digestion. Home: 9510 Wythal Lane Burke VA 22015 Office: US Department of Commerce Washington DC 20230

BARRETT, CHARLES BUTLER, lawyer; b. Roanoke Rapids, N.C., Oct. 8, 1942; s. Thedro Jefferson and Naomi (Butler) B.; B.A. in Am. History, U. Va., 1965; J.D., Coll. William and Mary, 1968; m. Betty Ann Sabo, June 17, 1966; children—Kathryn Arden, Anne Elizabeth. Admitted to Va. bar, 1968; asso. mem. firm Harrell & Hendrick, Emporia, Va., 1968-70; partner firm Warriner & Outten, Emporia, 1970—; asso. judge Greensville County Ct., 1969—. Co-chmn. Com. to Re-elect Pres., Greensville County, 1972. Chmn. bd. dirs. Western dist., mem. exec. bd. Old Dominion Area council Boy Scouts Am., 1970—. Mem. 4th Dist. (sec. ethics com.), Va., Am. bar assns., Emporia Jr. C. of C. (past sec.). Republican. Lutheran (steward). Mason, Rotarian. Club: Ruritan (Greensville). Home: 627 Tillar Av Emporia VA 23847 Office: 314 S Main St Emporia VA 23847

BARRETT, CHARLES HENRY, transp. co. exec.; b. N.Y.C., June 7, 1914; s. Charles H. and Isabelle (Lee) B.; student Trenton Bus. Coll., 1932-34; Sparton Sch. Engring., 1942-43; grad. Drake U., 1947; m. Ruth Mary McClean, Sept. 13, 1947; children—Victoria Marie, Charles Michael, Robert McClean, Thomas Henry. Pres., Refrigerated Motor Carrier Tank Transp. System, 1934-42; pres., owner White Line A Motor Carrier, 1946-52; founder, pres., owner Van-Pak Inc., 1952-64; pres., dir., owner U.S. Van Line, Washington, 1964—; pres. Ind. Uniment, Inc., Mishawaka, 1972—; dir. Manley Industries, Areon Corp. Financial cons. motor carriers, 1960—. Served with USAF, 1942-46; CBI. Decorated Legion of Merit. Mem. House Hold Goods Forwarded Assn. (dir. 1963-66), Movers and Warehouse Assn. Am. (1964—, dir.), Am. Movers Conf. (dir. 1968—), Internat. Gold Flow Com. (dir. 1964-66), Movers Tarriff Com. (dir. 1965—). Home: 51312 Mayflower Rd South Bend IN 46628 Office: 1523 L St NW Washington DC 20026

BARRETT, DAVID LAUN, physician; b. Louisville, Mar. 7, 1931; s. Howard Eldridge and Rosa Elizabeth (Laun) B.; B.A., U. Louisville, 1953, M.D., 1957; m. Carol A. Reider, July 9, 1970. Intern U.S. Naval Hosp., Pensacola, Fla., 1957-58; resident in pathology Cleve. Clinic, 1960-64; practice medicine specializing in pathology, Euclid, O., 1964-70, Murray, Ky., 1970—; co-dir. pathology Euclid (O.) Gen. Hosp., clin. instr. pathology Case-Western Res. U., Cleve., 1964-70; dir. labs. Murray (Ky.)-Calloway County Hosp., 1970—. Served to lt. comdr. M.C., USNR, 1957-60. Fellow Am. Coll. Pathologists; mem. Am., Ky. med. assns., Ky. Soc. Pathologists, Am. Soc. Clin. Pathologists. Home: 1203 Peggy Ann Dr Murray KY 42071 Office: 803 Poplar St Murray KY 42071

BARRETT, GEORGE DICKEY, architect; b. Cornelia, Ga., Jan. 25, 1910; s. George W. and Nellie (Fox) B.; B.S. with honors in Architecture, Ga. Inst. Tech., 1931, postgrad. in engring.; m. Mary Carolyn Burns, July 27, 1935; children—Elizabeth, Richard Fox. Engr. and architect Cooper & Cooper, architects, 1936-42, Corps

Engrs., War Dept., 1942-44; v.p., dir. Cooper, Bond & Cooper, Atlanta, architects and engrs., 1945-52; exec. v.p., dir. Cooper, Barrett, Skinner, Woodbury & Cooper, Inc., architects and engr., Atlanta, 1952-64, pres., 1964—. Mem. A.I.A., Am. Concrete Inst. Kiwanian. Principal archtl. works include Coll. Vet. Medicine. U. Ga., 1948. Atlanta Masonic Temple, 1959. Home: 885 St Charles Av NE Atlanta GA 30306 Office: Carnegie Bldg Atlanta GA 30303

BARRETT, HENRY CHARLES, educator; b. Birmingham, Ala., Mar. 2, 1923; s. Henry Clifford and Marcia Powers (White) B.; B.S., U. Ala., 1950, M.A., 1950; postgrad. Columbia, Juilliard Sch. Music; m. Betsy Joann Mason, July 23, 1955; children—John Mason, Marcia Helen, Mildred White. Porf. music U. Ala., 1950—; violist Cadek Quartet, 1950—; viola soloist 12 symphony orchs. Southeast U.S.; artist, mem. faculty Brevard Music Center, 1953, Sewanee Music Center, 1958-60, 63-65; mem. Aspen (Colo.) Festival Orch., 1961, 62; prin. violist Birmingham Symphony Orch., 1950-60; participant numerous workshops and clinics for tchrs. and performers of stringed instruments; lectr. performer nat. convs. music tchrs., Chgo., St. Louis, Kansas City, New Orleans, Jacksonville, Fla.; dir. research projects sponsored U. Ala., Nat. Endowment for Arts and Humanities; sponsored in concert Elizabeth Sprague Coolidge Found., Young Audiences, Inc., Am. Assn. Colls.; recordings Am. Assn. U. Broadcasters. Served with USNR. Mem. Ala. Music Tchrs. Assn. (chmn. string div.), Ala. Music Educators Assn. (chmn. string div. 1966-72), Am. Assn. U. Profs., Am. String Tchrs. Assn., Music Educators Nat. Conf., Music. Tchrs. Nat. Assn., Pi Kappa Lambda (pres. Alpha Pi chpt. 1972-74. Author: The Viola: Complete Guide for Teachers and Students, 1972. Contbr. articles to profl. jours. Home: 6 Fairmount Dr Tuscaloosa AL 35401 Office: Box 2886 University AL 35486

BARRETT, JOHN WILLIAM, educator; b. Columbus, O., July 27, 1913; s. John Francis and Mamie Frances (Whaley) B.; B.S., U. Mich., 1937, M.F., 1947; Ph.D., State U. Coll. Forestry, 1953; m. Vivian Carolyn Hammond, July 23, 1934; children—Sheila Carolyn (Mrs. Joseph James Mueller), John Michael. Forestry foreman Soil Erosion Service, 1933-35; logging engr. Long-Bell Lumber Co., Wash., 1937-40, Ore., 1945-46; instr. Coll. Forestry, Syracuse, N.Y., 1947-50, asst. prof., 1951-53, asso. prof., 1954-63, prof., 1963-64; prof., head dept. forestry U. Tenn., Knoxville, 1964—. Served to col. AUS, 1940-45. Recipient Sr. Vis. Fellowship, Orgn. European Econ. Coop., 1963. Mem. Soc. Am. Foresters (mem. nat. council 1966-67, 70-71), Soil Conservation Soc., Sigma Xi, Xi Sigma Pi, Alpha Gamma Delta, Alpha Xi Sigma. Lion. Editor: Regional Silviculture of the United States, 1962. Home: 9413 Needles Dr Knoxville TN 37919

BARRETT, LAWRENCE JAMES, JR., banker; b. Butler, Okla., Oct. 25, 1923; s. Lawrence James and Olive (Bovey) B.; B.S., U. Okla., 1947; m. Marion Eleanor Law, Aug. 4, 1956; children—Diane, Judy, Randy. With Watonga (Okla.) State Bank, 1947—, pres., chmn., 1963—. Served to 1st lt. USAAF, 1942-45. Decorated Air medal, D.F.C. Mem. C. of C. (past pres.). Home: 1005 N Forrest St Watonga OK 73772 Office: 101 W Main St Watonga OK 73772

BARRETT, O'NEILL, JR., physician, ret. army officer; b. Baton Rouge, Mar. 21, 1929; s. O'Neill and Hazel (Lauman) B.; B.S., La. State U., 1949, M.D., 1953; M.Sc., Baylor U., 1958; m. Joycelyn Clements, June 7, 1952; children—Deborah, Michael, William. Commd. 1st lt. U.S. Army, 1953, advanced through grades to col., 1973; intern Brooke Gen. Hosp., San Antonio, Tex., 1953-54, resident in internal medicine, 1955-58; asst. chief hematology service, asst. dir. basic scis. course Walter Reed Army Inst. Research, Washington, 1959-60; chief gen. med. services, hematology-oncology service, tng. officer dept. medicine Madigan Gen. Hosp., Tacoma, Wash., 1960-62; asst. chief dept. medicine, chief hematology-oncology service Letterman Gen. Hosp., San Francisco, 1963-68; chief dept. medicine Tripler Gen. Hosp., Honolulu, mem. staff, teaching cons. internal medicine, hematology Queen's Med. Center, Honolulu, clin. prof. medicine U. Hawaii Sch. Medicine at Honolulu, 1968-71; chief dept. medicine Walter Reed Gen. Hosp., clin. prof. medicine Georgetown U. Sch. Medicine, Washington, 1971-73; chief med. service VA Hosp., Tampa, Fla., prof., vice chmn. dept. medicine U. S.Fla., Tampa, 1973—; asst. clin. prof. medicine U. Cal. Sch. Medicine, San Francisco, 1964-68; mem. staff U. Cal. Moffett Hosp., San Francisco, San Francisco County Hosp., 1963-68. Diplomate Am. Bd. Internal Medicine with subsplty. in med. oncology. Fellow A.C.P., Am. Coll. Clin. Pharmacology; mem. Cal. Acad. Medicine, N.Y. Acad. Scis., A.M.A., Am. Soc. Hematology, Am. Soc. Clin. Oncology, Western Soc. Clin. Research, Am. Soc. Clin. Pharmacology and Therapeutics, Soc. Nuclear Medicine, Am. Fedn. Clin. Research. Contbr. articles to profl. jours. Home: Route #2 Box 1390 Lutz FL 33549 Office: 13000 N 30th St Tampa FL 33612

BARRETT, RICHARD, publisher; b. N.Y.C., Feb. 18, 1943; s. Anthony Joseph and Eleanor Louise (Kanouse) B.; B.A., Rutgers U., 1964. Pres. Barrett & Co., Jackson, Miss., 1967—; pres. Dixie D Co.; editor Jackson Citizen-Observer. Exec. dir. S.C. Ind. Party, summer 1968; del. Regular Miss. Dem. Party, 1971. Chmn. bd. trustees America's Found., 1971—. Served with inf., AUS, 1964-66. Decorated Purple Heart (U.S.), Rep. of Vietnam Commendation; recipient freedom award, Sertoma Internat., 1966, merit award, Lions Internat., 1969. Mem. Vets. Fgn. Wars. So. Baptist. Home: 154 S Sunset Terrace Jackson MS 39207 Office: 3030 N State St Jackson MS 39207

BARRETT, ROBERT EARL, rubber co. exec.; b. Wooster, O., Mar. 8, 1923; s. Clarence Dale and Cathryn Ann (DeChant) B.; B.S., Mich. State U., 1947; M.S., Ohio State U., Ph.D., 1951; m. Dorothy Jean Brown, Mar. 27, 1944; children—Steven, Cathy, Michael, Susan, Peggy. Prin. chemist Visking Corp., Chgo., 1951-52; prin. chemist Battelle Meml. Inst., Columbus, O., 1952-57; supr., asst. to v.p. research and devel. Copolymer Rubber & Chem. Corp., Baton Rouge, 1957-74, research mgr., 1974—. Scoutmaster Boy Scouts Am., Baton Rouge, 1958—; mem. Broadmoor Citizens Assn., 1965-66. Served with AUS, 1943-46. Recipient Silver Beaver award Boy Scouts Am., 1970. Mem. Am. Chem. Soc. Presbyn. (deacon, elder). Patentee in field. Home: 9545 Southmoor Dr Baton Rouge LA 70815 Office: PO Box 2591 Baton Rouge LA 70821

BARRETT, ROLIN FARRAR, ednl. adminstr.; b. White Sulphur Springs, W.Va., Aug. 25, 1937; s. Leonard Ward and Edna Coble (Farrar) B.; B.S. in Mech. Engring., N.C. State U., 1959, M.S. in Mech. Engring., 1962, Ph.D. (Shell Oil Co. fellow) in Mech. Engring., 1965; m. Dixie Linda Hobbs, Sept. 10, 1960; children—Rolin Farrar, Claire Hobbs. Instr. mech. and aerospace engring. dept. N.C. State U., Raleigh, 1962-65, asst. prof., 1965-68, asso. prof., 1968-73, prof., 1973—, asst. adminstrv. dean for research, 1973—. Cons. to legal and ins. professions, pvt. industry, govt. agys.; lectr. in indsl. safety, product liability, biomech. interests, auto safety. Recipient numerous grants for research, 1965—. Mem. Am. Inst. Aeros. and Astronautics (chmn. Carolina sect. 1969-70), Am. Soc. M.E. (treas. Eastern N.C. sect. 1973-74), Soc. Automotive Engrs., Sigma Xi, Phi Kappa Tau. Home: 3404 Huckabay Circle Raleigh NC 27612

BARRETT, RUSSELL HUNTER, educator; b. Cottonwood Falls, Kan., Dec. 30, 1919; s. Raymond John and Mabel Adele (Hunter) B.; B.A., U. Kan., 1946, M.A., 1947; Ph.D., U. Melbourne, 1952; postgrad. (East Asian Studies fellow) Harvard, 1958-59; m. Alamada Orpha Bollier, June 17, 1947; children—Valerie Sue, Pamela Anne. Instr., U. Kan. at Lawrence, 1947-50, U. Cal. at Berkeley, 1952-53, San Francisco State Coll., 1953-54; asst. prof. polit. sci. U. Miss., University, 1954-57, asso. prof., 1957-61, prof., 1961—. Mem. Miss. adv. com. U.S. Commn. on Civil Rights, 1965-66. Served with USAAF, 1942-45. Rockefeller Found. Travel grantee, 1966; Social Sci. Research Council Research grantee, 1964. Mem. Am. Assn. U. Profs. (mem. nat. council 1965-67), Am., So. polit. sci. assns., Phi Beta Kappa, Pi Sigma Alpha, Phi Kappa Phi. Author: Integration at Ole Miss, 1965; Promises and Performances in Australian Politics, 1959, rev. edit., 1963. Home: 544 N 9th St Oxford MS 38655 Office: Deupree Hall University MS 38677

BARRETT, WILLIAM ARVEL, hosp. exec.,; b. Bluefield, W.Va., Aug. 16, 1919; s. Lawrence Witten and Beatrice (Massey) B.; B.B.A., Ga. State Coll., 1957; m. Dorothy Clements, Sept. 21, 1947 (div); children—William Arvel III (dec.), Johnny, Perry, Joy; m. 2d, Frances S. Whitley, Oct. 24, 1970. Asst. adminstr. Ga. Bapt. Hosp., Atlanta, 1955-58; adminstr. Athens (Ga.) Gen. Hosp., 1958-72; pres. Heritage Nursing & Convalescent Center, Inc., 1965—, Barrett Convalescent Center, Inc., 1966, Spring Valley Convalescent Center, Elberton, Ga.; cons. Internat. Med. Industries, Inc., Atlanta. Partner B & G Farm. Past trustee Ga. Hosp. Assn. Served with Med. Service Corps, AUS, 1943-46, 51-54. Mem. Am. Coll. Hosp. Adminstrs., Ga. Hosp. Service Assn. (past (trustee Columbus), Am. (chmn. regional conf.), Ga. (dir.) nursing home adminstrs. Baptist. Home: 515 Highland Av Athens GA 30601 Office: 797 Cobb St Athens GA 30601

BARRINGER, PAUL BRANDON, lumber co. exec.; b. Sumter, S.C., Aug. 22, 1930; s. Victor Clay and Gertrude (Hampton) B.; B.S., U. Va., 1952; student George Washington U., 1954; m. Merrill Underwood, May 27, 1957; children—Merrill U., Victor Clay, Ann Hampton. With Human Relations Lab., Washington, 1954; with Coastal Lumber Co., Weldon, N.C., 1954—, pres., treas., dir., 1967—; pres., treas., dir. Dubarco Lumber Co., Havana, Fla., 1967—; 1st v.p., dir., exec. com. State Record Co., Columbia, S.C., 1966—, Gulf Pub. Co., Biloxi, Miss., 1967; dir. Bestway Express, Sun Publishing Co., State Printing Co., Caro Craft, Inc., Columbia Newspapers, Inc., State Telecasting Co. Inc. Regional fund chmn. A.R.C., 1960, dir., 1962-66; chmn. bd. visitors Louisburg Coll. Pres., trustee Enfield Acad.; trustee Brandon Ednl. Found. Served with USAF, 1952-54. Mem. Eastern N.C. Lumber Mfg. Assn. (sec.-treas. 1957—), Nat. Assns. Mfrs., Nat. Lumber Mfrs. Assn., Zeta Psi, Sigma Delta Psi, Lambda Chi. Episcopalian. Clubs: Clockoyotte Country, Farmington Country, Downtown. Home: Country Club Rd Weldon NC 27809 Office: PO Box 231 Weldon NC 27890

BARROLL, JOHN LEEDS, educator; b. Lausanne, Switzerland, July 20, 1928 (parents Am. citizens); s. John Leeds and Mary Hargrove (Bellamy) B.; A.B. cum laude, Harvard, 1950; M.A., Princeton, 1955, Ph.D., 1956; m. Rayna Sue Klatzkin, Mar. 17, 1951; children—John Leeds, James Edmondson, Ellen. Asst. prof. English, U. Tex., Austin, 1956-60; asso. prof. U. Cin., 1960-64, prof., 1964-67, asst. dean Grad. Sch., 1965-66, asso. dean Grad. Sch., 1966-67; vis. prof. English lit. U. Newcastle upon Tyne (Eng.), 1967-68; prof. English, Vanderbilt U., Nashville, 1968-69; dean arts and scis. William Paterson Coll., Wayne, N.J., 1969-70; prof. English lit. U. S.C., Columbia, 1970—, also dir. center for Shakespeare studies. Served with AUS, 1946-48. Huntington Library fellow, 1957, 59, Folger Shakespeare Library fellow, 1958; recipient Sachs award Cin. Inst. Fine Arts, 1966. Mem. Shakespeare Assn. Am. (exec. sec., trustee), Modern Lang. Assn., Malone Soc., Internat. Assn. U. Profs., Modern Humanities Research Assn. Episcopalian. Clubs: D.U., Hasty Pudding (Harvard). Author: (with Austin Wright) The Art of the Short Story, 1969; Artificial Persons, 1973; (with Bentley and Hosley) History of the Drama in the English Language, 1974. Editor: Shakespeare Studies, ann., 1965—; Shakespeare Studies Monograph Series, 1969—; The Blackfriars Shakespeare, 1969—; gen. editor: The South Carolina Shakespeare, 1972—. Home: 2024 Quail Run Columbia SC 29206

BARRON, DEMPSEY J., state senator; b. Andalusia, Ala., Mar. 5, 1922; s. Jessie Carl Dempsey and Minnie (Brown) B.; B.S., Fla. State U.; LL.B., U. Fla.; m. Louverne Hall, Jan. 27, 1952; children—Stephen C., Stuart J. Atty. firm Barron, Redding, Boggs & Hughes, 1954—; owner D Bar Ranch; mem. Fla. Ho. of Reps., 1956-60; mem. Fla. senate, 1960—, pres. pro tem, 1967—. Dir. Panama City and Bay Co. Chmn. Panama City (Fla.) Heart Fund Drive, United Fund, Bd. Dirs. Boys Club Am. Served with USNR, 1942-47; PTO, ETO. Named one of 10 outstanding mems. Fla. legislature by press, 1957—, one of 2 outstanding mems. Fla. senate, 1965. Mem. Panama City C. of C. (bd. dirs). Methodist. Home: 224 Woodlawn Dr Panama City FL 32406 Office: Box 1638 Panama City FL 32401

BARRON, ORAN JAMES, JR., rancher; b. Athens, Tex., May 29, 1916; s. Oran James and Mavit (Hardin) B.; student U. Ariz., 1933, Tex. Western U,, 1934-35; m. Eleonora Prudence Swenson, Feb. 20, 1942; children—Oran James III, Helen Mavit, Amanda Hope. Owner Spur Hdqrs. Ranch, Spur Tex., 1946—; pres. Caprock Telephone Co. Inc., Spur 1955—; dir. Swenson Land & Cattle Co., N.Y.C., 1959—. Mem. Tex. Water Resources Research Adv. Com., 1968-71; mem. Tex. Brush and Range Improvement Com., 1969—; mem. Tex. Agrl. Water Com., 1972—. Chmn. Dickens County (Tex.) bd. edn., 1956—; pres. Dickens County Water Control and Improvement Dist. 1, 1962-70. Dir. Tex. Exptl. Ranch Com., 1958—. Served to maj. AUS, 1941-45. Decorated Bronze Star with oak leaf cluster. Mem. Am. Soc. Animal Sci., Am. Soc. Range Mgmt., Tex. Cattle Feeders Assn. (dir. 1967—, treas. 1972—). Methodist. Address: Route 1 Spur TX 79370

BARRON, ROGER L., research co. exec.; b. Washington, Nov. 22, 1934; s. Bryton and Ella Rosalie (Lillibridge) B.; B.S., Princeton, 1955; postgrad. (NSF fellow) Cambridge (Eng.) U., 1955-56; M.S. (Sperry Gyroscope fellow), Mass. Inst. Tech., 1957; m. Virginia Gayle Young, Sept. 11, 1956; children—Rowena L., Andrew Roger, Jenifer Gayle, David William. Engr., Nat. Bur. Standards, Washington, 1954-57; v.p. Dodco, Inc., Princeton, N.J., 1957-60, mem. tech. staff Melpar, Inc., Falls Church, Va., 1960-61; pres. Adaptronics, Inc., McLean, Va., 1961—. Treas. Turnpike Baseball League, 1973. Holder 4 nat. records, also numerous maj. awards in model aviation competition. Mem. Am. Inst. Aeros. and Astronautics, I.E.E.E. (nat. vice chmn. Systems, Man and Cybernetics Soc. div. 1970), Instrument Soc. Am. (sr.), Acad. Model Aeros. (leader), Am. Radio Relay League. Contbr. numerous tech. publs., articles on adaptive control, advanced computation techniques, aerospace trajectory mechanics to profl. jours. Patentee in field. Home: 8605 Ardfour Lane Annandale VA 22003 Office: Adaptronics Inc 7700 Old Springhouse Rd McLean VA 22101

BARROSO, LUIS QUINTIN, dir. children's theatre, actor; b. Havana, Cuba, Oct. 31, 1944; s. Felipe Neri and Guillerma Yolanda (Hernandez) B.; came to U.S., 1955, naturalized, 1965; B.A., Rollins Coll., 1966; postgrad. Tulane U., 1966-68. Dir. children's theatre, tech. dir. Gallery Circle Theatre, 1968-70; dir. children's theatre Le Petit Theatre du Vieux Carre's Children's Corner, New Orleans, 1970—; actor appearing at Merry-Go-Round Playhouse, Miami, Fla., Tulane U., LePetit Theatre, Gallery Circle Theatre, People Playhouse, Tulane Summer Lyric Theatre, Ballet Hysell, Puppet Playhouse, NORD Opera. Recipient Zeta Phi Eta award for excellence in theatre for children, 1973. Mem. Am., Children's Am. Community theatre assns., S.W. Theatre Conf., Theatres of La., Theta Alpha Phi. Home: 932 St Peter St New Orleans LA 70116 Office: 616 St Peter St New Orleans LA 70116

BARROW, DAVID BROWN, JR., architect; b. Austin, Tex., June 28, 1931; s. David Brown and Nelle Imogene (Harmon) B.; B.B.A., B.Arch., U. Tex., 1955; m. LuAnn Saage, Dec. 7, 1956; children—David Brown III, Thomas Edward. Asso. architect Harwell Harris, Dallas, 1958-61; with Barrow & Stahl, Austin, 1961—. Pres., dir. N.W. Savs. Assn. Austin, 1972—; v.p. Austin Corp., 1962—. Mem. City Planning Commn., 1971-73. Served to capt. USAF, 1955-58. Episcopalian. Clubs: Headliners, Baccones Country, Great Hills Country. Home: 6201 Cat Mountain Cove Austin TX 78731 Office: 3637 Far West Blvd Austin TX 78731

BARROW, JOHN PARHAM, JR., printing co. exec.; b. Lexington, Ky., July 18, 1931; s. John Parham and Caroline Cassidy (Steese) B.; B.S., U. Ky., 1952; m. Virginia Tilton, Dec. 21, 1951; children—Caroline, Lucy, Mary. With Transylvania Printing Co., Lexington, 1949—, v.p., treas., 1963—; dir. Bank Lexington, Caluma, Inc., Lexington, Wildwood Corp., Burgin, Ky. Mem. Ky. Council Higher Pub. Edn., 1970. Chmn., Fayette County Republican party, 1962-66, Sayre Sch. Bd. Trustees, 1960-68, Lexington Planning Commn., 1966-70; mem. bd. Lexington Met. Airport Bd., 1974. Bd. dirs. Good Samaritan Hosp., Shakertown, Lexington Sch., Blue Grass Trust Historic Preservation. Served with AUS, 1952-54. Mem. Aircraft Owners and Pilots Assn., Printing Industries Tech. Inst. (chmn. 1969-72), Printing Industries Central Ky., Ky., Am., So. Graphic Arts Assn. (pres. 1969-72), Lexington C. of C., Phi Delta Theta. Rotarian. Home: Box 272 Newtown Pike Lexington KY 40505

BARRY, GUY THOMAS, govt. ofcl.; b. Montreal, Que., Can., Apr. 14, 1920; s. Thomas and Leonie (Prevost) B.; B.Sc., Sir George William Coll., 1942; Ph.D., McGill U., 1946; children—Raymond Barry, Janet (Mrs. Mitchell Hackel). Asso. prof. Rockefeller U., N.Y.C., 1946-58; research prof. U. Tenn. Meml. Research Center and Hosp., Knoxville, 1958-65; dir. biochemistry E.R. Squibb & Sons, New Brunswick, N.J., 1965-68; dep. dir. tech. service U.S. Customs Service, Washington, 1968—. Cons. E. Tenn. Bapt. Hosp., Knoxville, 1959-65; asst., Rockefeller U., 1950-56, asso., 1956-58. Spl. fellow NIH, 1946-48; Am. Cancer Soc. fellow, 1948-50; grantee NIH, 1958-65, NSF, 1962-65. Mem. Am. Soc. Biol. Chemists, Am. Chem. Soc. Contbr. articles to profl. jours. Home: 3044 Oliver St NW Washington DC 20015 Office: 2100 K St NW Washington DC 20229

BARRY, JAMES JOSEPH, retail business exec.; b. Charleston, S.C., Sept. 25, 1907; s. James Thomas and Charlotte (Thweatt) B.; student pub. schs.; m. Katherine Mims, Jan. 8, 1936; children—James Joseph, Katherine Mims. Owner, Barry's Dept. Store, St. Stephen, S.C., 1929—; pres. Berkeley Radio & Furniture Co., St. Stephen, 1936—; pres. Indsl. Devel. Corp., St. Stephen, L. Mendel Rivers Indsl. Park, Inc.; mem. adv. bd. S.C. Nat. Bank, Moncks Corner. Mem. South Carolina Hwy. Commn. from 9th Dist. 1946-50; 54-58.; adv. com. Charleston Area Comprehensive Health Planning; mem. Berkeley County Bd. Edn., Monoks Corner, S.C., 1958—; mem. Berkeley-Charleston-Dorchester Regional Planning Council, 1973. Bd. dirs. Berkeley County Hosp. Mem. Hibernian Soc., S.C. C. of C. (dir. 1959-60). Roman Catholic. Lion (charter pres. St. Stephen 1958-59). Address: PO Box 606 St Stephen SC 29479

BARRY, WILLIAM LOGAN, lawyer, ex-state legislator; b. Lexington, Tenn., Feb 9, 1926; s. Henry Daniel and Mary (Logan) B.; B.A., Vanderbilt U., 1947; LL.B., 1950; M. Joanne Coffman, 1966. Admitted to Tenn. bar, 1950; practiced in Lexington; mem. firm Barry & Walker; mem. Tenn. Ho. of Reps., 1955-67, speaker, 1963-67; exec. asst. to gov. Tenn., 1967-71; asst. atty. gen. State of Tenn., Nashville, 1971—. Chmn. Tenn. Legislative Council, 1965-67; chmn. Tenn. Am. Revolution Bicentennial Commn., 1972—. Served as 1st lt. AUS, 1951-53. Mem. Am. Legion, V.F.W. Democrat. Baptist. Lion. Elk, K.P. Home: RFD 1 Lexington TN 38351 Office: Supreme Ct Bldg Nashville TN

BARTA, REGINALD DUNBAR, govt. ofcl.; b. New Rockford, N.D., July 20, 1912; s. Albert A. and Ellen M. (Dunbar) B.; B.A., George Washington U., 1957, M.A., 1965; m. Virginia A. Paulsen, Dec. 30, 1950. Mgmt. analyst Hdqrs. USAF, Washington, 1953-61; adminstr. Dept. Army, Washington, Charlottesville, Va., 1962—. Lectr., George Washington U., 1968—. Bd. govs. YMCA, Washington. Served with USAAF, 1943-46, USAF, 1950-51. Mem. Assn. Computing Machinery, Data Processing Mgmt. Assn., George Washington U. Alumni Assn. (mem. bd. govs. 1958—). Club: George Washington University (D.C.). Home: 7623 Mendota Pl Springfield VA 22150 Office: 220 NE 7th St Charlottesville VA 22901

BARTEL, WALTER ALLEN, mfg. co. exec.; b. Isabella, Okla., Jan. 3, 1926; s. Peter V. and Bienna (Kliewer) B.; grad. high sch.; m. Glendora June Fast, Aug. 26, 1948; children—Lonnie Allen, Jay Lynn. Welder, Smith Machine Shop, Fairview, Okla., 1948-52; co-owner, mgr. Bartel Bros. Welding, Fairview, 1952-55; farmer, 1956; partner Fairview Pipe & Supply, 1957-59, v.p., 1959-64; v.p. Waldon Inc., Fairview, 1964-66, pres., 1966—; dir. Farmers and Mchts. Bank Fairview. Mem. C. of C. Rotarian (pres. 1970-71). Mennonite. Home: 801 Highland Dr Fairview OK 73737 Office: 201 W Oklahoma St Fairview OK 73737

BARTELLA, ROBERT MARK, finance co. exec.; b. Escanaba, Mich., Mar. 16, 1916; s. John Joseph and Meta Alice (Wickert) B.; student Lawrence U., 1933-37; children—Judy, Cathy. Exec. v.p. Ky. Finance Co., Inc., Lexington, 1951—. Home: 55 Lexington Hill 2150 Richmond Rd Lexington KY 40507 Office: 200 E Main St Lexington KY 40507

BARTH, ALF OTTO, architect; b. Risor, Norway, Aug. 5, 1921; s. Haakon Hjalmar and Emilie (Gisslerud) B.; came to U.S., 1929, naturalized, 1943; B.Arch. with honors, U. Fla., 1953; m. Mary Jayne Ingram, Apr. 28, 1951; children—Kathleen Elizabeth, Paul Haakon. Architect, dir. sch. planning Polk County, Fla., 1956-60; asso. dir. sch. planning Dade County, Fla., 1960-64; coordinating architect Orange County (Fla.) schs., 1964-65; architect in charge Charles W. Cole & Son, South Bend, Ind., 1966; chief architect Dade County, 1968—; cons. architect, 1956—; prin. works include Oakland Elementary Sch., Haines City, Fla., 1960; Sanctuary for Grace Lutheran Ch., Winter Haven, Fla., 1960, ednl. bldg., 1967; addition Redeemer Luth. Ch., Miami Shores, Fla., 1961; Immanuel Luth. Ch., Tavernier, Fla., 1967; ednl. bldg. Concordia Luth. Ch., Miami, 1966. Chmn. Dade County Archtl. Selection Com., 1968—. Bd. dirs. Eastridge Retirement Village, Miami, 1963-64. Served with USNR, 1943-46; AUS, 1947-50. Mem. A.I.A. (dir. local chpt. 1964), Nat. Council Archtl. Registration Bds., Am. Arbitration Assn., Am. Pub. Works Assn., Gargoyle (historian), Phi Kappa Phi. Lutheran (chmn. trustees 1961-65). Mason, Odd Fellow. Home: 7581 SW 58th St Miami FL 33143 Office: 1351 NW 12th St Miami FL 3125

BARTHA, LOUIS ALEXANDER, accountant; b. Toledo, June 18, 1917; s. Stephen Joseph and Susan (Piszkaly) B.; student Berea Coll., 1935-36, Ohio State U., 1936, U. Ill., 1936-39, 40; m. Ruth Kathryn Woodson, May 18, 1942; 1 son, Gregory Woodson. Accountant Louis A. Bartha C.P.A., Midland, Tex., 1945—; sec.-treas., dir. Palafox Exploration Co., Midland, 1957—; v.p., dir. Scharbauer Cattle Co., Midland, 1958—; sec.-treas., dir. Scharbauer Bros. & Co., 1958—, Alamositas Cattle Co., 1958—; sec., dir. Ranching Enterprises, Inc., 1966-70. Mem. Tex. State Bd. Pub. Accountancy, 1958-67. Chmn. Midland County Democratic Exec. Com., 1948-52. Sec., dir. Midland Fair, Inc., 1950-65; treas., dir. Midland Indsl. Plan, Inc., 1954-65; sec., dir. Prairie Found., Midland, Tex., 1957—; chmn. Midland County Draft Bd., 1966—. C.P.A., Tex. Trustee Midland Ind. Sch. Dist., 1957-63, sec., 1959-63. Served to capt. USAAF, 1941-45. C.P.A., Tex. Mem. Am. Inst. C.P.A.'s, Tex. Soc. C.P.A.'s, Accounting Research Assn., Financial Mgmt. Assn., Am. Accounting Assn. Rotarian. Home: 905 Bedford Dr Midland TX 79701 Office: 1st Nat Bank Bldg Midland TX 79701

BARTKY, IAN ROBERTSON, govt. scientist; b. Chgo., Mar. 15, 1934; s. Walter and Elizabeth Inrig (Robertson) B.; B.S. in Chemistry, Ill. Inst. Tech., 1955; Ph.D. in Chemistry, U. Cal. at Berkeley, 1962; m. Elizabeth Louise Hodgins, July 30, 1960; children—David John, Anne Robertson. Research chemist Nat. Bur. Standards, Washington, 1961-68, sci. asst. to dir. Inst. for Basic Standards, 1968-71, Inst. for Applied Tech., 1971—. Dept. Commerce Sci. fellow, 1973. Recipient Mid-Career award Nat. Inst. Pub. Affairs, 1968. Mem. Am. Chem. Soc., A.A.A.S., Sigma Xi. Home: 7804 Custer Rd Bethesda MD 20014 Office: Nat Bur Standards Washington DC 20234

BARTLETT, ANTHONY JACKSON, II, utility exec.; b. New Orleans, Jan. 18, 1926; s. Anthony Jackson and Corinne (Dabezies) B.; B.S. in Elec. Engring., Tulane U., 1949; m. Leona Marie Bauer, July 3, 1952; children—Anthony J. III, George R., Robert D., Thomas W. With New Orleans Pub. Service Inc., 1950-67, delay communications engr., 1952-60, asst. mgr. results div., 1960-67; gen. engr., mgr. system planning Middle South Services, Inc., New Orleans, 1967—. Served with USNR, 1945-47. Registered profl. engr., La., Ark. Mem. I.E.E.E., La. Engring. Soc., Nat. Soc. Profl. Engrs., Edison Elec. Inst., Mason. Club: Timerlane Country (Gretna, La.). Home: 4005 Delgado Av New Orleans LA 70119 Office: PO Box 61000 New Orleans LA 70160

BARTLETT, CHARLES LEFFINGWELL, newspaperman; b. Chgo., Aug. 14, 1921; s. Valentine C. and Marie (Frost) B.; student St. Mark's Sch., Southboro, Mass., 1934-39; A.B., Yale, 1943; m. Josephine Martha Buck, Dec. 16, 1950; children—Peter B., Michael V., Robert S., Helen B. Reporter Chattanooga Times, 1946-63, Washington corr., 1948-63; editor News Focus Service, 1958-63; columnist Chgo. Sun-Times, 1963—. Served as lt. USNR, 1943-46. Recipient Pulitizer prize for nat. reporting, 1955. Roman Catholic. Clubs: National Press, Gridiron, Federal City. Author: (with Edward Weintal) Facing the Brink, 1957. Home: 4615 W St NW Washington DC 20007 Office: 1717 Pennsylvania Av NW Washington DC 20006

BARTLETT, DEWEY FOLLETT, senator; b. Marietta, O., Mar. 28, 1919; s. David A. and Jessie (Follett) B.; grad. Lawrenceville (N.J.) Sch., 1938; B.S. in Geol. Engring., Princeton, 1942; m. Ann C. Smith, Apr. 2, 1945; children—Dewey Follett, Joan, Mike. Partner, Keener Oil Co., Tulsa, 1951—; pres. Dewey Supply Co. (Okla), 1953-56; owner-operator ranch in Wagoner County, Okla., 1958-64, in Delaware County, 1958—. Mem. Okla. Senate from Tulsa County, 1962-66; gov. of Okla, 1967-73; U.S. senator from Okla., 1973—. State chmn. Ozarks Regional Commn., 1968-69; chmn. Interstate Oil Compact Commn., 1970—. Bd. dirs. Tulsa County chpt. A.R.C. Served as pilot USMCR, World War II. Decorated Air medal. Mem. Ind. Petroleum Assn. Am. (dir.), Okla. Ind. Producers Assn. (dir.). Republican. Roman Catholic. Home: 2462 E 30th St Tulsa OK 74114 Office: National Bank of Tulsa Bldg Tulsa OK 74103

BARTLETT, DOROTHY LUCILLE WOOD (MRS. KENNETH FRANKLIN BARTLETT), librarian; b. Richmond, Va.; d. Wilfred Walton and Maude (Robins) Wood; B.A., Randolph-Macon Woman's Coll., 1932; B.A. in L.S., Emory U., 1933; m. Kenneth Franklin Bartlett, Oct. 20, 1945. Library asst., head children's dept. Richmond Pub. Library, 1933-40; map asst., archives div. Va. State Library, Richmond, 1940-42; chief circulation dept. City Library Assn., Springfield, Mass., 1942-43; map curator Nat. Archives, Washington, 1943-44; map analyst, chief map research sect. Fgn. Econ. Adminstrn., Washington, 1944-45; map analyst Dept. Agr., Beltsville, Md., 1946; chief reference sect., map library Dept. State, Washington, 1946-47; map librarian CIA, Washington 1948-61; head reference and bibliography sect., geography and map div. Library Congress, Washington, 1962-70, bibliographer of div., 1970—. Mem. Spl. Libraries Assn. (chpt. vice chmn. geography and map group 1964-66, chmn. 1966-67, nominating com. 1967), Jamestowne Soc., U. D.C., Assn. Am. Geographers, Am. Assn. U. Women, Assn. Preservation Va. Antiquities, Carto-Philatelists, Va. Mus. Fine Arts, Library of Congress Profl. Assn., Va. Library Assn. Methodist. Contbr. articles to profl. jours. Home: 1713 Wainwright Dr Reston VA 22090 Office: Library Congress Washington DC 20540

BARTLETT, JACK ARNOLD, real estate exec.; b. Dallas, May 23, 1947; s. Roger Frost and Dorothy Louise (Loop) B., Jr.; B.B.A., North Tex. State U., 1969, M.B.A., 1971; postgrad (teaching fellow) Mich. State U., 1971-72; m. Barbara Faye Niemeier, Aug. 29, 1971. Teaching fellow North Tex. State U., Denton, 1969-71; auditor Arthur Andersen & Co., Dallas, 1969, 72-73; asst. v.p., controller Cowbridge Cos., Dallas, 1973—. C.P.A., Tex. Mem. Tex. Soc. C.P.A.'s, Am. Accounting Assn., Real Estate Financial Execs. Assn., Tex. Hist. Soc., Blue Key, Beta Gamma Sigma, Beta Alpha Psi, Alpha Chi. Home: 3906 Harvest Hill Rd Dallas TX 75234 Office: 2301 Fidelity Union Tower Dallas TX 75201

BARTLETT, WILLIAM MARCUS, broadcasting co. exec.; b. Richland, Ga., Aug. 19, 1910; s. William Mercer and Eula Mae (Bell) B.; A.B. in Journalism, Emory U., 1939; m. Mamie Ruth Baggott, Dec. 18, 1943; children—Ann (Mrs. Cecil Cannon), Bill, Bruce, Blair, Brian. Announcer, musician, sportscaster, musical dir., prodn. mgr., program dir. radio sta. WSB, Atlanta, 1930-48; program dir., sta. mgr., gen. mgr. WSB-TV, 1948-64; v.p. Cox Broadcasting Co., Atlanta, 1964-69, exec. v.p., 1969—; dir. United Tech. Publs., Cox Cable Communications, Bing Crosby Prodns., Manheim Services Corp. Lectr. Emory U., 1941-42, 46. Bd. dels. NBC-TV Affiliates, 1959-63, sec.-treas., 1963. Chmn. bd. visitors Emory U., 1969-70; mem. adv. bd. Atlanta Salvation Army; bd. dirs. Fulton-Dekalb County chpt. Nat. Found. Served to lt. USNR, 1943-45. Mem. Nat. Cable Television Assn. (sec. 1969-70), Ga. Assn. Broadcasters (v.p. for TV 1961-62, dir. 1960-61), Phi Beta Kappa, Sigma Chi, Omicron Delta Kappa, Di Gamma Kappa (named Broadcast Pioneer of Year 1965), Sigma Delta Chi. Baptist (ch. organist 1960—). Kiwanian. Clubs: Cherokee Town and Country, Commerce (Atlanta). Home: 4694 Tall Pines Dr NW Atlanta GA 30327 Office: 1601 W Peachtree St NE Atlanta GA 30309

BARTLEY, ERNEST R., educator, urban planning cons.; b. Lincoln, Neb., May 11, 1919; s. James Earl and Neva Leona (McNiel) B.; A.B. with distinction, Neb. Wesleyan U., 1940; M.A., U. Neb., 1941; Ph.D., U. Cal. at Berkeley, 1948; m. Ruth Arline Nielsen, Apr. 17, 1942; children—Susan Kay, Deborah Dell. Instr. polit. sci. Ore. State Coll., 1948-49; instr. polit. sci. U. Fla., 1949-51, asso. prof., 1951-55, prof. 1955—; acting dir. U. Fla. Pub Adminstrn. Clearing Service, 1950, dir., 1957-58; adviser com. adminstr. law and procedure Fla. Bar Assn., 1952-58; lectr. legal insts. Fla. Bar Assn., 1952-58; fellow Fund Advancement Edn., 1954-55; cons. Alaska Statehood Com., Pub. Adminstrn. Service on Alaska Constl. Conv., 1955; cons. numerous cities and counties; dir. research Fla. Constl. Adv. Commn., 1955-56. Served from 2d lt. to maj. 21st Bomber Command, USAAF, 1941-45. Decorated 3 battle stars, Air medal; recipient Freedom Found. award, 1956. Mem. Am. Inst. of Planners (pres. Fla. chpt. 1972—), Am. So. polit. soi. assns., Am. Soc. Planning Ofcls., Fla. Planning and Zoning Assn. (pres. 1970-71), Am. Assn. U. Profs., Pi Sigma Alpha, Pi Kappa Delta, Pi Gamma Mu, Phi Kappa Phi, Phi Kappa Tau. Democrat. Methodist. Mason. Author: Municipal Zoning: Florida Law and Practice (with William W. Boyer, Jr.), 1950; Principles and Problems of American National Government (with John M. Swarthout), 1951; The Tidelands Oil Controversy, 1952; Principles and Problems of State and Local Govt. (with John M. Swarthout), 1958; A Model Zoning Ordinance for Small and Medium-Sized Cities (with Fred H. Bair, Jr.), 1958, rev. edit., 1965, 3d edit., 1967; Mobile Home Parks and Comprehensive Planning (with Fred H. Bair, Jr.), 1961. Editor: Materials on American National Government (with John M. Swarthout), 1952; Papers on Florida Administrative Law, 1952. Contbr. profl. jours. Home: 1050 SW 11th St Gainesville FL 32601

BARTLEY, JERALD HOWARD, oil co. exec.; b. Springtown, Tex., Nov. 25, 1913; s. Hugh Thomas and Emma (Johnson) B.; B.S. in Geology, U. Tex., 1937; m. Bernice O. Lonsdorf, Jan. 19, 1946; children—Bruce Howard, Steven Charles, Ann Marie. Geologist, U.S. Geol. Survey, 1937-38, Tex. U. Lands, Midland, 1938-49; cons. geologist, ind. oil operator, Midland, 1949—; exec. v.p., chief geologist Tex. Am. Oil Corp., Midland, 1955-66; partner Autograph Driltime Corp., Midland, 1961-66, Broxson-Bartley Ins. Agy., Midland, 1966-69; v.p., dir. Pacific Union Gas Co., Midland, 1961-66, Western Oil Shale Corp., Midland, 1964—. Served to lt. USNR, 1942-46. Mem. Geol. Soc. Am., Am. Assn. Petroleum Geologists, Soc. Ind. Profl. Earth Scientists (dir.), Ind. Petroleum Assn. Am., Mid-Continenta Oil and Gas Assn., Tex. Ind. Producers and Royalty Owners Assn., Tex. Acad. Sci. Roman Catholic. Elk. Author Bulls. Patentee in field. Home: 1705 W Illinois St Midland TX 79701 Office: 300 W Wall St Midland TX 79701

BARTLEY, JOHN WILLIAM, assn. exec.; b. Toledo, June 30, 1923; s. Clark Merle and Alma (Kaeser) B.; student U. Toledo, 1941-43, 46-47; B.S. in Phys. Edn., George Williams Coll., 1949; m. Joanne Louise Budd, June 7, 1946; children—Byron Allen, Barbara Ann, (Mrs. Larkin Mead), Kathy Louise. Phys. edn. dir., various YMCA's, Chgo., 1947-55, Dallas, 1955-59; exec. dir. YMCA, Ardmore, Okla., 1959-64, Wichita Falls, Tex., 1964—. U.S. rep. Internat. Sports Sch., Paris, France, 1957. Served with 607th F.A., AUS, 1943-46; ETO. Recipient outstanding phys. dir. award Ill., 1955, S.W., 1959. Mem. Nat. Phys. Edn. Soc. (past v.p.), Assn. Phys. Dirs. YMCA. Rotarian. Methodist. Home: 4811 Danberry Pl Wichita Falls TX 76308 Office: 1010 9th St Wichita Falls TX 76301

BARTOLO, ADOLPH MARION, food co. exec.; b. Cairo, Egypt, Apr. 12, 1929; s. Edgar Charles and Emma C. (Borrelli) B.; came to U.S., 1947, naturalized, 1953; B.S. in Chem. Engring., La. State U., 1950; m. Joycelyn Mary Bergeron, June 7, 1950; children—Pamela Bridget, Edgar Charles II, Janice Ann, Mary Elizabeth. From chem. engr. to asst. supt. Southdown Sugar, Inc., Houma, La., 1951-58; with Imperial Sugar Co., Sugarland, Tex., 1958—, v.p. refinery operations, 1968—, also dir.; dir. Cane Sugar Refiners Research Project, 1965—; dir., mem. exec. com. Sugar Industry Technologists, Inc. Mem. La. State U. Found., 1966-68. Mem. Am. Inst. Chem. Engrs., Internat. Sugar Research Found. (dir.), U.S. Nat. Com. Sugar Anaylsis. Roman Catholic. Lion (pres. Sugarland 1960-61). Clubs: Exchange (Fort Bend); Riverbend Country (Sugarland). Home: 303 S Belknap St Sugarland TX 77478 Office: PO Box 9 Sugarland TX 77478

BARTON, ALEXANDER JAMES, ecologist, educator; b. Mt. Pleasant, Pa., May 9, 1924; s. Paul Carnahan and Barbara (Eggers) B.; B.S., Franklin and Marshall Coll., 1946; M.S., U. Pitts., 1957; m. Arlene Florence Arment, Oct. 6, 1945; children—Sandra, Lynne, Alexander James III. Herpetologist, Highland Park Zool. Gardens, Pitts., 1946-52; instr. biology Stony Brook (N.Y.) Sch., 1952-63, dir. admissions and financial aid, 1957-63; profl. asst. NSF, Washington, 1963-65, profl. asso., 1965-70, program dir., 1970-73, program mgr. student-oriented program, 1973—. Adj. asst. prof. biology C.W. Post Coll., Brookville, N.Y., 1961-63; dir. Savannah (Ga.) Natural History Mus., 1957; cons. sci. books Doubleday & Co., 1962-64. Scoutmaster Allegheny County council Boy Scouts Am., Pitts., 1947-52, mem. nat. adv. com., 1950-54, mem. exec. council Suffolk County council, 1957-63; mem. Internat. Com. on Endangered Reptiles and Amphibians, 1967—. Pres., Arlington Rose Found., 1970-71. Served to comdr. USNR, 1943-45. Mem. Potomac Rose Soc. (1st v.p. 1972-73, pres. 1974—), Am. Rose Soc. (vice chmn. Colonial dist. 1971-72, cons. rosarian 1970—, chmn. nat. long-range planning com., mem. nat. bd. 1973—; accredited rose show judge 1970—), Assn. Admissions Officer Ind. Secondary Schs. (pres. 1959-62), A.A.A.S., Am. Inst. Biol. Sci., Ecol. Soc. Am., others. Presbyn. (deacon 1946—, lay preacher 1954-65, tchr. adult bible class 1964-68). Home: 3818 N Vernon St Arlington VA 22207

BARTON, DAVID, educator, psychiatrist; b. Selma, Ala., Dec. 3, 1936; s. Morris and Fannie Leone (Gusdorf) B.; B.S., U. Ala., 1958; M.D., Tulane U., 1962; m. Lynn Ina Palmer, Aug. 16, 1961; children—David Kirk, Amy Lynn, Daniel Frederick. Intern, Ochsner Found. Hosp., 1962-63; resident, dept. psychiatry Tulane U. Med. Sch. and affiliated hosps., 1963-66; practice medicine specializing in psychiatry, Ft. Hood, Tex., 1966-68, Charlottesville, Va., 1968-70, Nashville, Tenn., 1971—; mem. staff Vanderbilt Hosp., Nashville; asst. prof. psychiatry U. Va. Sch. Medicine, 1968-70; asst. prof. psychiatry Vanderbilt Med. Center, Nashville, 1971-72; asso. prof., 1972-73, asso. clin. prof., 1973—, acting asst. dean, 1972-73. Served to capt., M.C., AUS, 1966-68. Decorated Army Commendation medal. Mem. A.M.A., Am. Psychiat. Assn., Am. Psychosomatic Soc., Phi Beta Kappa, Alpha Omega Alpha. Home: 6559 Jocelyn Hollow Rd Nashville TN 37205

BARTON, DON FREDERICK, advt. agy. exec.; b. Anderson, S.C., Aug. 19, 1924; s. David J. and Harriet (Crouch) B.; A.B., U. S.C., 1949; m. Betty Kneece, Aug 7, 1955; 1 dau., Mary Elizabeth. Pub. relations U. S.C., Columbia, 1950-56, 58-60; sports editor Columbia (S.C.) Record, 1949, 56-58; sec. Rodgers-Newman-Barton Advt., Columbia, 1960-62; dir. pub. relations WIS-TV, Columbia, 1963-65; pres. Barton-Blair-Coreton Advt. Agy., Columbia, 1965—. Chpt. chmn. A.R.C., Richland County, S.C., 1966-67; chmn. Riverbanks Park Commn., 1969—. Pres., S.C. Speech and Hearing Clinic, 1969-70. Served with USAAF, 1943-45. Mem. Alpha Delta Sigma, C. of C. Presbyn. Clubs: Forest Lake Country, Columbia Touchdown (pres. 1963), Sertoma (pres. 1968-69), Columbia Sales and Marketing Execs. (dir. 1973-74). Author: The Carolina-Clemson Game-1896-1966, 1967. Home: 117 Spring Lake Rd Columbia SC 29206 Office: 2512 Devine St Columbia SC 29206

BARTON, ELEANOR KEESE (MRS. WILLIAM P. BARTON), newspaperwoman; b. Walhalla, S.C., May 31, 1901; d. John Perry and Soula T. (Reeder) Keese; B.A., Greenville Woman's Coll., 1921; postgrad. Cornell U., 1923; m. William P. Barton, July 19, 1924; 1 dau., Eleanor Sue (Mrs. John O. Allen). Instr. Greenville Woman's Coll., 1921-24, pub. relations work, 1921-29; woman's editor Greenville (S.C.) Piedmont, 1929-51, columnist, 1951—; feature writer, 1951—; radio news commentator, 1956-62. Pres., Crescent Music Club, 1939-41, now hon. life mem., pres. Community Concert Assn., 1953-55; mem. vol. corps U.S.O., 1951-63, chmn., 1959-61; chmn. Greenville County chpt. A.R.C., 1956-57; pres. Crescent Community Club, 1953-55; v.p. Better Govt. Assn., 1956-57; mem. Greenville Symphony Assn., 1949-65; mem. Greenville County Heart Council; adv. bd. S.C. div. Nat. Found.; bd. dirs. S.C. div. Am. Cancer Soc.; pres. Crescent Literary Club, 1961-63; v.p. Greenville County Fedn. Women's Clubs, 1965-66, chmn. Diamond Jubilee, Gen. Fedn. Women's Clubs; helped establish S.C. Commn. on Aging; pres. Myrtle Hall Fund for Scholarships; adv. com. Palmetto Outdoor Hist. Drama Assn.; mem. S.C. Tricennial Adv. Com. Recipient Nat. Bus. and Profl. Women's Club award, 1932; Certificate Appreciation, Boys' Club Am., 1956; Nat. Recreation Assn. citation, 1961; Plaque from Greenville Symphony Assn., 1966. Gen., and State Fedns. Women's Clubs citation, 1955-56; Nat. Community Achievement citation, 1956. Mem. Furman U. Alumni Council, Hand and Torch, Nat. Fedn. Music Clubs (hon. life), Sigma Iota Chi. Democrat. Baptist. Club: Woman's (dir. 1951-61, 63—). Author: History of the Crescent Music Club. 1956; History of Greenville Woman's Club, 1960—; also papers, reports, brochures. Editor: U.S.O. Volunteer, 1959-61. Home: 208 McIver St Greenville SC 29601 Office: The Greenville Piedmont PO Box 1688 Greenville SC 29602

BARTON, FRANK LEWIS, agrl. banker; b. Tigerville, S.C., Feb. 9, 1917; s. Hovey Goodist and Anne (McKinney) B.; B.S., Berea Coll., 1937; postgrad. U. Ky., 1937, Clemson U., 1940, 50; M.Ed., U. S.C., 1952; m. Margaret Ettie Coggins, June 5, 1939; children—Lollie, Frank Lewis, Nancy. Tchr. agr. Spartanburg County (S.C.), 1937-48; supr. agrl. edn. S.C. Dept. Edn., 1948-59; dir. information Farm Credit Banks, Columbia, 1959-66; v.p. Fed. Land Bank, Columbia, 1966-69, v.p., sec., 1969-72; v.p., sec. Fed. Land Bank and Fed. Intermediate Credit Bank, 1972—. Mem. exec. com., sec.-treas., trustee Am. Inst. Coop. Recipient awards including Hon. Degree of Am. Farmer Future Farmers Am., 1960. Mem. Pub. Relations Soc. Am. (pres. S.C. chpt. 1970, assembly del. 1968-73), S.C. Vocational Assn., S.C. Farm Bur. Fedn., Am. Berkshire Assn. (pres. 1954-56), S.C. Livestock Assn. (sec. 1950-56), S.C. Livestock Council (sec. 1956-61), S.C. Agrl. Council (sec. 1968), Block and Bridle. Baptist. Rotarian. Clubs: Columbia, Chester, Woodruff. Contbr. articles to publs. Home: 2119 Dalloz Rd Columbia SC 29204 Office: 1401 Hampton St Columbia SC 29202

BARTON, HARVEY EUGENE, educator, entomologist; b. Couch, Mo., Aug. 26, 1936; s. Harvey Mansfield and Ruth Helen (Wheeler) B.; B.S., Ark. State U., 1962, M.S., 1963; Ph.D., Ia. State U., 1967; m. Margaret Alene Clark, Dec. 31, 1954; children—Richard, Larry, Peggy, Jeffrey, Susan. Research asso. Ia. State U., 1964-67; asst. prof. zoology Ark. State U., 1967-70, asso. prof., 1970—. Served with AUS, 1954-58. Eagle. Home: 909 Chestnut St Jonesboro AR 72467 Office: Box 501 State University AR 72467

BARTON, JACK QUINN, lawyer, instr., police chief; b. Denison, Tex., Nov. 27, 1932; s. Joseph R.T. and Marion (Quinn) B.; B.A., U. Tex., 1960, J.D., 1962; m. Jane Thomas, Aug. 30, 1958; children—Robert Barry, Catherine Eileen, Joseph Lawrence, Raymond Edward, Jerry Quinn. With Corpus Christi (Tex.) Police Force, 1956-57; admitted to Tex. bar, 1962; practiced in San Francisco, 1962-63; law book editor Matthew Bender Co.; city atty. Denton, Tex., 1963-72; instr., dir. police N. Tex. State U., Denton, 1972—, legal adviser, 1973—. Cons. municipal law to various cities. Mem. Decisions for Denton Com., 1969—; chmn. Denton March of Dimes, 1969. Trustee Optimist Meml. Found., Fairhaven Home for Aged, Denton; bd. dirs., chmn. finance com. Cross Timbers council Girl Scouts Am. Served with AC, USNR, 1951-55. Mem. Am., Tex., Denton County bar assns., Tex. Trial Lawyers Assn. K.C. Club: Breakfast Optimist (pres. 1972-73). Home: 124 Mill Pond Rd Denton TX 76201 Office: 1603 W Hickory St Denton TX 76203

BARTON, JAMES HOWARD, physician; b. Murphy, N.C., Apr. 14, 1931; s. Guy Arvil and Esta (Swaim) B.; B.A., U. N.C., 1953, M.S. in Pub. Health, 1958; M.D., Med. Coll. Ga., 1962; m. Barbara Nell Brown, June 18, 1957; children—Gregory Jay, Steven Lyle, Leslie Kay. Intern, Spartanburg Gen. Hosp., 1962-63; gen. practice medicine, Social Circle, Ga., 1963—. Mem. Walton County Bd. Health, Walton County Hosp. Bd. Authority, Social Circle Bd. Edn. Served with AUS, 1954-56. Mem. Am., Ga. med. assns. Methodist (trustee 1970). Lion (pres. Social Circle 1965). Home: 356 N Cherokee St Social Circle GA 30279 Office: PO Box 468 Social Circle GA 30279

BARTON, WILLIAM BRYAN, JR., educator; b. Oklahoma City, Oct. 6, 1923; s. William Bryan and Alma (Brundege) B.; B.A. cum laude, Abilene Christian Coll., 1944; B. Systematic Theology, Harvard, 1947, M. Systematic Theology, 1948, Ph.D., 1955; m. Mary Elizabeth Sturgeon, Aug. 11, 1946; children—John Bryan, Laura Alison, Rebecca Ann, Sylvia Jeanne. Instr., Cath. U. Am., Washington, 1948-49, Simmons, Coll., Boston, 1949-50; asso. prof. Harding Grad. Sch., Memphis, 1955-57; prof., philosophy Memphis State U., 1958—, chmn. dept., 1958-73. Bd. dirs. Barth House (Episcopal), 1964-67, 73—. Mem. Am. Philos. Assn., So. Soc. Philosophy and Psychology, Metaphys. Soc. Am., Internat. Soc. Phenomenological Research. Democrat. Episcopalian (bd. edn. Diocese Tenn. 1965-67). Author: Emerson's Method as a Philosopher, 1971; co-translator, author intro. to What is a Thing? (Martin Heidegger), 1973. Founder, editor So. Jour. Philosophy, 1963-73. Editor: Emerson's Unpublished Sermons, 1971—. Home: 7532 Nohapa Cove Germantown TN 38138

BARTON, WILLIAM LAWRENCE, physician; b. Macon, Ga., Nov. 16, 1909; s. William and Mary (Cherry) B.; B.S., Mercer U., 1932; M.D., Med. Coll. Ga., 1935; m. Rebecca Griffin, June 20, 1942 (dec. Dec. 1954); 1 dau., Mary Lynn; m. 2d, Carol Balkcom, Oct. 8, 1955; 1 son, William Lawrence. Intern Macon City Hosp., 1935-36; resident Columbia-Presbyn. Med. Center, N.Y.C., 1936-39; practice medicine specializing otolaryngology, Macon, 1940—; attending Middle Ga. Hosp., Coliseum Park Hosp.; cons. Med. Center Central Ga. Served as maj. Ga. State Guard, World War II, Recipient award for outstanding service YMCA, 1954. Diplomate Am. Bd. Served as maj. Ga. State Guard, World War II. Recipient Otolaryngology. Fellow A.C.S., Internat. Coll. Surgeons; mem. A.M.A., So., Ga., 6th Dist., Bibb County med. socs., Am. Acad. Otolaryngology and Ophthalmology, Pan-Am. Assn. Otorhinolaryngology and Bronchoesophagology, Alpha Omega Alpha. Methodist. Mason (Shriner, 32 deg.), Elk, Moose, Kiwanian. Clubs: Idle Hour Golf and

Country, Macon Touchdown, Centurion. Home: 1588 Waverland Dr Macon GA 31201 Office: 744 1st St Macon GA 31201

BARTSCHT, HERI BERT, sculptor, educator; b. Breslau, Germany, Aug. 30, 1919; s. Richard and Emma (Philipp) B.; student Acad. Fine Arts, Munich, Germany, 1946-52; m. Waltraud Erika Gutensohn, Mar. 31, 1950; 1 son, Martin Donald. Came to U.S., 1952, naturalized, 1959. Prof. sculpture, U. Dallas, 1961—, head div. art, music, speech and drama, 1965—. One-man shows, including Dallas, Oklahoma City, Austin, Tex.; exhibited in group shows, 1951—, including Ball State Tchrs. Coll. Muncie, Ind., 1959, U. Ill., 1961, Cranbrook Acad. Art, Mich., 1969; important works include Pieta, Ch. in Munich, 1952, Stas. of Cross, Jesuit High Sch., Dallas, 1963, library sculpture The Graduate, Tex. A. and M. U., 1968, sanctuary embellishment First Meth. Ch., Alexandria, La. Mem. Council for German Day in Tex., 1963; mem. condrs. com. Dallas Symphony, 1963. Pres., Dallas Goethe Center, 1971—. Served with German Army, 1939-45. Mem. Am. Soc. Ch. Architecture, Nat. Art Edn. Assn., Ch. Archtl. Guild, Dallas Fine Arts Assn., Dallas Soc. Contemporary Arts (founder, dir., trustee 1955-61), Guild Religious Architecture. Author: Twenty Years of My Sculpture, 1969, Research on Bronze Casting. Home and studio: 1125 N Canterbury Ct Dallas TX 75208

BARZE, KEITH EGBERT, television exec.; b. Winter Park, Fla., Feb. 19, 1928; s. Roland Detling and Marguerite (Enlow) B.; A.B., U. Ala., 1950, M.A., 1956; m. Nancy Ruth Hendrix, Oct. 11, 1953; children—Sandra Suzanne, Beverly Roxanne, Stacy Yvonne. Announcer, engr., various radio stas., 1947-54; instr. dept. radio-TV U. Ala., 1950-52, vis. lectr., 1970-71; engr. WBRC-TV, Birmingham, Ala., 1954-57, program dir., head program prodn. depts., 1957—. Mem. pub. relations council A.R.C., 1963-65; dir. Festival of Arts, 1964-65; mem. Jefferson County Radio and TV Council, 1957—; treas. Bd. of Missions, Ala., Fla, Miss. Synod, Cumberland Presbyn. Ch.; adviser Jr. Achievement Co., 1966—. Served with AUS, 1946-47. Mem. Ala. Broadcasters Assn. (dir. 1963-67, v.p. TV 1966-67, chmn. edn. com. 1971-72), Birmingham Advt. Fedn., Birmingham C. of C., Nat. Assn. TV Program Execs., Faith and Patiotism Soc. Am. (exec. council 1970—), Delta Chi, Alpha Epsilon Rho. Republican. Presbyn. (elder, dir. Birmingham council Christian edn. 1968—). Kiwanian (pres. Birmingham 1971-72). Clubs: Mountain Brook Swim and Tennis, Birmingham Press, Birmingham Amateur Radio. Home: 3581 Spring Valley Rd Birmingham AL 35223 Office: PO Box 6 Birmingham AL 35201

BASH, JAMES HAVENS, educator; b. Fort Wayne, Ind., June 28, 1924; s. Carl Edward and Maud (Trabue) B.; student Pa. State U., 1941; B.S., U. Va., 1949, M.Ed., 1953, Ed.D., 1960; m. Jean McNett, Aug. 13, 1946; children—Bonnie Jean, Michael McNett. Tchr., Lane High Sch., Charlottesville, Va., 1949; prin. Highland View Elementary Sch., Bristol, Va., 1949-52, Brosville Sch., Pittsylvania County, Va., 1952-54, Farmville (Va.) High Sch., 1954-55; instr. edn. U. Va., Charlottesville, 1956-60, asst. prof., 1960-62, asso. prof. edn., 1964-69, prof., 1969—, dir. office tchr. placement, 1956-62, coordinator grad. edn. in extension, 1958-62, asso. dir. div. tchr. placement and field services, 1963-64, asso. dir. Office Instnl. Analysis, 1964-65, dir. div. field services Sch. Edn., 1966-70, dir. Consultative Resource Center on Sch. Desegregation, 1967-72; program asso. So. Regional Edn. Bd. Atlanta, 1962-63; exec. sec. Assn. Sch. Coll. and Univ. Staffing, 1959-64; cons. Spong Commn. on Pub. Edn. in Va., 1959-62. Served with USNR, 1942-46. Recipient U. Va. Phi Delta Kappa award, 1962. Mem. Va. Edn. Assn., Phi Delta Kappa (mem. commn. edn., human rights and responsibilities 1962-69), Nat., Va. Assns. secondary sch. prins. Researcher sch. desegregation, 1965-66. Home: 1508 Jamestown Dr Charlottesville VA 22901 Office: Sch Edn U Va Charlottesville VA 22903

BASHAM, JACK DAVIS, savs. and loan exec.; b. Morrilton, Ark., Jan. 17, 1929; s. Albert and Audra (Ross) B.; B.S.E., State Coll. Ark., Conway, 1951; postgrad. U. Ark., 1951-53; m. Ann Louise Clemmons, June 22, 1957; children—Leslie, Camille, Karen. With First Fed. Savs. & Loan Assn., Pine Bluff, Ark., 1954-58, Leader Fed. Savs. & Loan Assn., Memphis, 1958-59; pres., mng. officer Ark. Savs. & Loan Assn., North Little Rock, 1960—; high sch. tchr., 1952-54. Dist. chmn. Thunderbird dist. Boy Scouts Am., 1968-69, commr. Quapaw Area council, 1970-72; pres. North Little Rock Boys Club, 1972. Bd. dirs. Pulaski County March of Dimes, United Way, Youth Home. Served with USNR, 1946-48. Recipient Silver Beaver award Boy Scouts Am., 1970; Man and Boy award N. Little Rock Boys Club, 1973; named North Little Rock Jaycees Boss of Year, 1968, Ark. Jaycees Boss of Year, 1968. Mem. U.S., Ark. (v.p.) savs. and loan leagues, North Little Rock C. of C. (1st v.p., dir.). Methodist. Mason, Rotarian (pres. 1972-73). Club: North Hills Country. Home: 3404 Sevier Dr North Little Rock AR 72116 Office: 2525 Main St North Little Rock AR 72114

BASHAW, ELEXIS COOK, educator, geneticist; b. Mt. Juliet, Tenn., July 21, 1923; s. Lex C. and Mabel C. (Wright) B.; B.S., Purdue U., 1947, M.S., 1948; Ph.D., Tex. A. and M. U., 1954; m. Bettye Louise Wood, Feb. 19, 1945; children—Jane (Mrs. George W. Kyle), Cheryl. Agronomist, La. Agrl. Expt. Sta., Baton Rouge, 1948-50; asst. prof. agronomy Tex. Agrl. Expt. Sta., College Station, 1951-56; research geneticist U.S. Dept. Agr., mem. grad. faculty dept. soil and crop scis. Tex. A. and M. U., College Station, 1956—. Cons. AID, Guyana, 1970. Served to lt. USNR, 1943-46. Recipient Superior Service award U.S. Dept. Agr., 1971, Outstanding Service award, 1964. Fellow Am. Soc. Agronomy; mem. A.A.A.S., Crop Sci. Soc. Am., Sigma Xi, Gamma Sigma Delta, Alpha Zeta. Contbr. articles to profl. jours. Home: 1208 Ashburn St College Station TX 77840

BASHFUL, EMMETT WILFORT, ednl. adminstr.; b. New Roads, La., Mar. 12, 1917; s. Charles and Mary (Walker) B.; student Leland Coll., 1936-37; B.S., So. U., 1940; M.A., U. Ill., 1947, Ph.D., 1955; m. Juanita Jones, Aug. 16, 1941; 1 dau., Cornell (Mrs. Charles Nugent). Tchr. Allen Parish (La.) Sch., 1940-41; asst. mgr. Keystone Co., 1941-42; mem. faculty Fla. A. and M. U., 1948-58, prof. polit. sci., 1955-58, head dept., 1950-58; prof. polit. sci. So. U., Baton Rouge, 1958-59; dean So. U., New Orleans, 1959-69, v.p., 1969—. Chmn. John Albert dist. Boy Scouts Am., New Orleans., 1965-67, mem. exec. bd., 1965—; mem. La. Youth Commn., 1965—. Bd. dirs. Community Relations Council, New Orleans, Frey Found. Served to 1st lt. AUS, 1942-46. Recipient Silver Beaver award Boy Scouts Am., 1967; Ford Found. fellow, 1954-55. Mem. Am., So. polit. sci. assns., Assn. Social Sci. Tchrs., Alpha Phi Alpha, Alpha Pi Omega, Sigma Rho Sigma, Pi Gamma Mu. Author: The Florida Supreme Court: A Study in Judicial Selection, 1958. Home: 5808 Lafaye St New Orleans LA 70122

BASHIR, NASIR AHMAD, physiologist, educator; b. Punjab, Pakistan, Jan. 9, 1935; s. Bashir Ahmad Khan and Rasul Begum Sivia; B.S., Forman Christian Coll., 1953; M.S., U. Punjab, 1956; Ph.D., Tulane U., 1967; postgrad. Meharry Med. Coll., 1970—; m. Lynne Lennox, Sept. 8, 1960; children—Shaan Jehan, Kirin Rahat. Came to U.S., 1958. Head dept. biology Talimul Islam Coll., Pakistan, 1956-58; chmn. dept. physiology Sch. Dentistry, Loyola U., New Orleans, 1966-68; asst. prof. physiology Meharry Med. Coll., Nashville, 1968—. Vis. lectr., cons. VA Hosp., Tuskegee, Ala., Pres., Pakistan Assn., New Orleans, 1966-68. Fulbright scholar, 1958-60; USPHS fellow, 1963-66. Mem. Am. Assn. U. Profs., Am. Soc. Zoologists, Am. Physiol. Soc. (asso.). Islam, Unitarian (bd. dirs. 1969-70, co-chmn. social responsibility com. 1969-70). Club: Chess (Lahore, Pakistan). Home: 3625 Rainbow Pl Nashville TN 37204 Office: 1005 18th Av N Nashville TN 37208

BASHORE, BOYD TRUMAN, govt. ofcl.; b. Washington, June 7, 1925; s. Wilbur Elsworth and Mabel (Truman) B.; B.S., U.S. Mil. Acad., 1950; grad. Army War Coll., 1968; m. Judy Campbell, Sept. 12, 1951; children—Brian, Stephen, Elizabeth, Laura, Charles. Enlisted U.S. Army, 1943, advanced through grades to col., 1971; command staff, sch. assignments; adminstrv. asst. Congressman John M. Murphy, Washington, 1972—; dir. Financial & Loan Corp., Alexandria, Va. Decorated Legion of Merit with oak leaf cluster, Bronze Star medal, Air medal, Army Commendation medal. Contbr. articles to profl. jours. Home: 6510 Lakeview Dr Falls Church VA 22041 Office: Reyburn House Office Bldg Washington DC 20515

BASINGER, JAMES MAYHEW, advt. agy. exec.; b. Aliceville, Ala., July 26, 1923; s. Albert Hunter and Mary (Mayhew) B.; B.S., U. Ala., 1949, postgrad., 1949-50; m. Ruth Wilson, Dec. 27, 1954; children—James M., Brian Hunter. Quality control engr. Westinghouse Electric Corp., Reform, Ala., 1951-53; dir. advt. U.S. Pipe & Foundry Co., Birmingham, Ala., 1954-65; pres. Basinger & Assos., Inc., Birmingham, 1966—. Served with AUS, 1942-45. Mem. Chi Phi. Methodist. Clubs: Downtown, Altadena Valley Country. Home: 2707 Lakeland Trail Birmingham AL 35243 Office: 13 Office Park Circle Birmingham AL 35243

BASKETT, WILLIAM CAROL, lawyer; b. Richmond, Va., Apr. 19, 1931; s. Elmo and Grace Evelyn (Tignor) B.; B.A., Coll. William and Mary, 1954; J.D., Marshall-Wythe Sch. Law, 1955; m. Harriett Lucille Rasmussen, Feb. 27, 1954; children—Cynthia, Virginia, William Carol. Admitted to Va. bar, 1955; trial atty., U.S. Treasury Dept., Phila., 1955-59; practiced in Norfolk, Va., 1959—. Lectr., U. Va. Extension, 1961-62. Served with USMCR, 1951. Lutheran (dir. southeastern dist. 1972—). Home: 5233 Fairfield Blvd Virginia Beach VA 23462 Office: Suite 1655 One Commercial Place Norfolk VA 23510

BASKIN, CLARENCE LEE, dentist; b. Apopka, Fla., Feb. 27, 1927; s. Horace and Carrie Belle (Weathers) B.; B.S., Morehouse Coll., 1948; D.D.S., Howard U., 1953; m. Thelma Erline Cobb, July 21, 1956; 1 son, Clarence Lee. Individual practice dentistry, Atlanta, 1954-56, Columbus, Ga., 1957—. Chmn. adv. bd. Washington Shores Fed. Savs. & Loan Assn., Orlando, Fla. Served with USNR, 1945-46. Mem. Am., Nat., Ga. dental assns., Western Dist. Dental Soc., Kappa Alpha Psi. Mem. A.M.E. Ch. (trustee). Home: 4539 Kerz Court Columbus GA 31907 Office: 500 1/2 9th St Columbus GA 31901

BASKIN, EVERETT ROY, advt. exec.; b. McAlester, Okla., Oct. 21, 1927; s. Everett Edmond and Lottie (Hattery) B.; B.S., Southeastern State Coll., 1952; m. Wanda Joy Major, Feb. 19, 1949; children—Rhonda Lea, Janice Lynn. Dept. head J. C. Penny Co., McAlester, Durant, Okla., 1943-50; asst. mgr. Duke & Ayres, Inc., Durant, 1950-54; account exec. McAlester News Capital, 1954-59; real advt. mgr. Donrey Operating Co., Ft. Smith, Ark., 1959-60, advt. and acting plant mgr., Okmulgee, Okla., 1960-61, plant mgr., Rogers, Ark., 1961-62; sales mgr. Mena (Ark.) Star, 1963-64; store mgr. Montgomery Ward & Co., Ft. Smith, 1964-66; advt. mgr. McAlester Democrat, New Offset Daily, 1966—. Served with USNR, 1945-46. Mem. Red Red Rose, Kappa Delta Pi, Sigma Tau Gamma, Pi Omega Pi. Democrat. Presbyn. Mason, Eagle. Home: 201 W Madison St McAlester OK 74501 Office: 106 E Cherokee St McAlester OK 74501

BASKIN, WILLIAM P., lawyer, banker; b. Bishopville, S.C., Apr. 27, 1904; s. William P. and Esther (Fleming) B.; A.B., U. S.C., 1925, LL.B., 1927; m. Margaret E. Pittman, June 14, 1932; children—William P., Emsley P., Sylvia Elaine. Admitted to S.C. bar, 1927, since practiced in Bishopville; sr. member Baskin & Baskin; former chmn. bd., pres., dir., gen. counsel Peoples Bank; state counsel Nat. Assn. Ind. Insureres; dir. Home Fed. Savs. & Loan Assn., Bishopville. Mem. S.C. Senate from Lee County, 1938-58. Mem. Lee County, S.C. State, Am. bar assns., S.C. Bankers Assn. (pres. 1965-66). Democrat (state chmn. 1947-52). Home: 330 S Main St Bishopville SC 29010 Office: Farmers Trust Bldg Bishopville SC 29010

BASMAJIAN, JOHN VAROUJAN, coll. adminstr.; b. Constantinople, Turkey, June 21, 1921; s. Mihran and Mary (Evalian) B.; diploma Brantford Collegiate Inst., 1940; M.D., U. Toronto, 1945; m. Dora Lucas, Oct. 4, 1947; children—Haig, Nancy, Sally. Canadian citizen, 1927. Faculty, U. Toronto, 1949-57, prof. anatomy, 1956; head dept. anatomy Queen's U., Kingston, Ont., 1957-69; dir. Rehab. Research and Tng. Center Emory U., Atlanta, 1969—. Mem. Bd. Edn. City Kingston, 1960-68. Chmn. bd. St. Lawrence Coll., Kingston, 1966-69. Served with M.C., Canadian Army, 1943-46. Recipient numerous govt. research grants. Mem. Internat. Soc. Electromyographic Kinesiology (founding pres. 1968-72), others. Mason. Author: Primary Anatomy, 6th edit., 1970; Grant's Method of Anatomy, 8th edit., 1971; (with M.A. MacConaill) Muscles and Movements, 1969; Muscles Alive, 3d edit., 1974; (with M. Smorto) Clinical Electroneurography, 1972; (with others) Computers in Electromyography, 1974. Home: 2617 Woodwardia Rd Atlanta GA 30345 Office: Ga Mental Health Inst 1256 Briarcliff Rd NE Atlanta GA 30306

BASS, BOB EUGENE, basketball coach; b. Big Spring, Tex., Jan. 28, 1929; s. William A. and Dovie (Law) B.; B.S., Okla. Bapt. U., 1950; M.P.E., Okla. U., 1954; m. Billie Pat Phelps, Aug. 6, 1950; children—Kelly E., Kip E. Athletic dir., basketball coach Okla. Bapt. U., Shawnee, 1952-67; head basketball coach Denver Rockets, Am. Basketball Assn., 1967-69, Tex. Tech. U., Lubbock, 1969-71; coach, gen. mgr. Floridians of Am. Basketball Assn., Miami, 1971—. Named Coach of Year, Nat. Assn. Inter-collegiate Athletics, 1967. Home: 13200 Coronado Lane North Miami FL 33161 Office: Miami Floridians 1175 NE 125th St North Miami FL 33161

BASS, CLARENCE CALVIN, corrosion engr.; b. Marvell, Ark., Apr. 7, 1928; s. James H. and Norah Ann (Tawney) B.; student Trinity U., 1952; B.S., Tulsa U., 1954; m. Lillian Steiner, Sept. 11, 1955; children—James T., Susan A. Prodn. foreman, petroleum engr. Atlantic Refining Co., Tex., 1954-62; corrosion engr. Olive Corrosion Control, Shreveport, La., 1962-64, Schmoldt Engring. Services Co., Bartlesville, Okla., 1965-67; pres. Bass Engring. Co., Longview, Tex., 1967—. Com. chmn. E. Tex. area Boy Scouts Am., 1969—. Served with USAF, 1946-49. Registered profl. engr., Tex., Okla. Mem. Am. Inst. Mining, Metall. and Petroleum Engrs., Am. Petroleum Inst. Home: 1702 Clinton St Longview TX 75601 Office: PO Box 5279 Longview TX 75601

BASS, CORNELIUS GRAHAM, oil jobber exec.; b. Latta, S.C., May 28, 1918; s. Howard H. and Sarah (Carmichael) B.; B.S. in Bus. Adminstrn., U. S.C., 1940; m. Ann Blair, May 23, 1942 children—Ann Blair (Mrs. James E. Crowder, III), AND Cornelius Graham. With The Latta Cotton Co., 1940-41; asst. mgr. Dilmar Oil Co., Latta, 1941-42; mgr. Santee Oil Co., 1945-47, sec.-treas., 1947-71, v.p., 1971—, gen. mgr., 1947—; partner, gen. mgr. S & P Tire Co., Kingstree, S.C., 1949—; sec.-treas., gen. mgr. Services, Inc., Kingstree, 1950-71; pres. Warsaw Mfg. Co., Kingstree, 1958-63: pres. Bass Farms, Inc., Latta. 1963—, pres. Santee Broadcasting Co., Inc. (radio sta. WDKD), 1965-69, treas., 1970—; pres. Kingstree Indsl. Devel. Corp., 1958—; sec.-treas. King's Tree Inn, Inc., 1967-70. Mem. Williamsburg Planning Commn., 1967—; chmn. Williamsburg County Bd. Edn., 1957-62. Served with AUS, World War II. Decorated Bronze Star. Mem. Kingstree C. of C. (v.p. 1956-58), S.C. Oil Jobbers Assn. (pres. 1954-55). Moose (past gov. Kingstree). Clubs: Kingstree Country (pres.), Optimist (past pres.), Lions (past pres.). Home: 1601 Fulton Av Kingstree SC 29556 Office: Santee Oil Co Inc Hwy 52 N Kingstree SC 29556

BASS, JACK SOLOMON, journalist, author; b. Columbia, S.C., June 24, 1934; s. Nathan and Esther (Cohen) B.; A.B., U. S.C., 1956; Nieman fellow Harvard, 1966; m. Carolyn Elizabeth McClung, Mar. 3, 1957; children—Kenneth Nathan, David Louis, Elizabeth Rose. Copy editor News & Courier, Charleston, S.C., 1960-61; editor, pub. West Ashley Jour., Charleston, 1961-63; govtl. affairs reporter, editor State-Record Co., Columbia, 1963-66; Columbia bur. chief Charlotte Observer, 1966-73. Lectr., U. S.C. Coll. Journalism part-time 1967-73; research fellow Inst. Policy Scis. and Pub. Affairs Duke, 1973—. Served to lt. (j.g.) USNR, 1956-60. Mem. Soc. Nieman Fellows, Sigma Delta Chi (Journalist of Year in S.C. 1968, 72). Jewish religion. Mem. B'nai B'rith. Author: (with Jack Nelson) The Orangeburg Massacre, 1970; Porgy Comes Home, 1972. Contbg. author You Can't Eat Magnolias, 1972. Home: 3508 Fox Hall Rd Columbia SC 29204 Office: 4875 Duke Sta Durham NC 27706

BASS, JOSEPH ALONZO, microbiologist; b. Eagle Pass, Tex., Aug. 14, 1918; s. Frederick Ernest and Helen Mae (Tell) B.; student S.W. Tex. State U., 1946-47; B.A., U. Tex., Austin, 1949; M.S., Ohio State U., 1951, Ph.D., 1953; m. Maria del Socorro Cortes, Sept. 9, 1952; children—Joseph Edward, Margaret Helen. Research fellow dept. internal medicine Ohio State U., 1951-53; prof. dept. microbiology U. Tex. Med. Br., Galveston, 1953-70, dir. bacteriology research lab., div. plastic and maxillofacial surgery, 1953-64; prof. dept. biol. scis. N.Tex. State U., 1970-73; prof. dept. microbiology U. Tex. Health Sci. Center, San Antonio, 1973—; chief div. microbiology Shriners Burns Inst., Galveston, 1967-70; regional biology cons. NSF/BSCS/U.S. AID Program with Central Am. univs., 1964-65; cons. Biological Sciences Curriculum Study, 1965-68, NASA, 1969-71, Edn. and World Affairs, 1965-67. Chmn. Internat. Cooperation Com., Biol. Scis. Curriculum Study, 1968-69. Pres. Band Parents Club, O'Connell High Sch., Galveston, 1967-69, bd. dirs. P.T.A., 1969-70. Pres., bd. dirs. U. Tex. Med. Br. Coop. Soc., 1960-63, 69-70. Served with AUS, 1941-45. Recipient grants and research contracts Dept. Health, Edn. and Welfare, 1960-70, U.S. Army, 1954-64, USAF, 1954-56. McLaughlin fellow U. Tex. Med. Br., 1955. Fellow Royal Soc. Tropical Medicine, Am. Pub. Health Assn., Tex. Acad. Sci.; mem. Am. Soc. Microbiology (pres. Tex. br. 1960-61), Am. Acad. Microbiology (chmn. com. vis. profs. for Latin Am.), A.A.A.S., N.Y. Acad. Scis., Tissue Culture Assn., Reticulo-Endothelial Soc., Internat. Soc. for Burn Injuries, Am. Burn Assn., Sigma Xi, Theta Kappa Psi. Roman Catholic. Editor: Tex. Reports on Biology and Medicine, 1960-64. Contbr. articles profl. jours. Home: 2141 W Gramercy Pl San Antonio TX 78201 Office: 7703 Floyd Curl Dr San Antonio TX 78229

BASS, MILTON GERSON, revenue ofcl.; b. Phila., Jan. 8, 1914; s. Joseph H. and Ruth (Back) B.; student Drexel Inst. Engring., 1931-32; B.C.S., Benjamin Franklin U., 1941, M.C.S., 1942; postgrad. George Washington U., 1942-43, U. Hawaii, 1944-45; m. Ernestine Shute, Aug. 14, 1946; 1 dau., June Yvonne. Various positions Fed. Govt., 1935-55; supr. Internal Revenue Service, Baton Rouge, 1955-58, chief rev. staff, New Orleans, 1958—. Served with USNR, 1942-45. C.P.A., Md., La. Mem. Am. Inst. C.P.A.'s, La. Soc. C.P.A.'s, Am. Legion. Baptist. Mason (32 deg.). Home: 17 Tennyson Pl New Orleans LA 70114 Office: Fed Bldg 600 South St New Orleans LA 70130

BASS, NORMAN HERBERT, physician, educator; b. N.Y.C., July 10, 1936; s. Julius and Celia (Annex) B.; B.A. (Ford Found. scholar 1953; N.Y. State Bd. Regents scholar 1954), Swarthmore Coll., 1958; M.D., Yale, 1962; m. Martha McKean, Aug. 10, 1961; children—Joel Martin, Rebecca Pier, Robert Farrell. Intern U. Wash. Hosp., Seattle, 1962-63; resident U. Va. Hosp., Charlottesville, 1963-65, Mass. Gen. Hosp., Boston, 1965-67; NIH postdoctoral fellow Harvard Med. Sch., Boston, 1965-67; asst. prof. div. neurology Med. Sch., U. Va., Charlottesville, 1967-70, asso. prof., 1970-73, prof., 1974—; vis. prof. dept. pharmacology U. Göteborg (Sweden), 1972; mem. staff U. Va. Hosp., Charlottesville. Served with M.C., AUS, 1963-69. Recipient S. Weir Mitchell research award Am. Acad. Neurology, 1967; John and Mary Markle scholar in acad. medicine, 1969—; research career devel. award grantee USPHS, 1971—; prin. investigator USPHS, 1967-71, NSF, 1971-73. Diplomate Am. Acad. Neurology. Mem. A.A.A.S., Am. Soc. Neurochemistry, Soc. Neurosci., Internat. Soc. Neurochemistry, Am. Assn. Anatomists. Contbr. articles to profl. jours. Home: 110 Buckingham Rd Charlottesville VA 22901 Office: Dept Neurology Box 147 Med Sch Univ Va Charlottesville VA 22901

BASS, RAY DEAN, state hwy. dir.; b. Slocomb, Ala., Dec. 19, 1933; s. Alexander Bell and Ellie Mac (Warr) B.; B.S., Auburn U., 1959; m. Clara Nell Smith, Dec. 22, 1957; children—Elizabeth Ellen, Thomas Ray, Joan Louise. With Ala. Hwy. Dept., Montgomery, 1959-60; engr. Lowndes County, 1960-65; county engr. W.O. Smith Contractors, Burkville, Ala., 1965-67; engr. Montgomery County, 1967-71; asst. hwy. dir. Ala. Hwy. Dept., Montgomery, 1971-72, dir. hwys., 1972—. Coordinator Lowndes County for George Wallace, 1967-70. Pres. bd. trustees Lowndes Acad., 1965-71; mem. Engring. Council Auburn (Ala.) U., 1972. Served with USNR, 1951-54. Mem. Nat. Soc. Profl. Engrs., Am. Rd. Builders, Nat. Assn. County Engrs., Ala. Assn. Pvt. Schs. (pres. 1967-69). Home: Route 2 Box 424 AA Montgomery AL 36108 Office: 11 S Union St Montgomery AL

BASS, ROY BYRN, lawyer; b. Waco, Tex., Oct. 31, 1918; s. Ivan McCullough and Carrie Hunt (Byrn) B.; A.B., Baylor U., 1938, LL.B., 1940; m. Anita Seay, Mar. 28, 1942; children—Roy Byrn, David Dewey, Mark Ivan. Admitted to Tex. bar, 1940; practiced in Lubbock, Tex., 1940-41, 46—; mem. firm Bass & Hobbs, 1959—. Tchr. bus. law and govt. Tex. Tech. U., Lubbock, part-time, 1946-54. Mem. exec. bd. Bapt. Gen. Conv. Tex., 1965-68. Pres. trustees Lubbock Symphony Orch., 1947. Trustee Baylor U., Waco, 1962-71, 72—. Served to lt. comdr. USNR, 1941-45. Named Outstanding Young Man of Lubbock Jaycees, 1952. Mem. Am., Lubbock County bar assns., State Bar Tex. (dir. 1971—), Lubbock C. of C. Kiwanian (pres. Lubbock Club 1950; lt. gov. internat. 1951). Home: 2514 57th St Lubbock TX 79413 Office: 18 Briercroft Office Park Lubbock TX 79412

BASS, SAMUEL EARL, banker; b. Mount Calm, Tex., Mar. 23, 1930; s. Wayne Earl and Alyne (Ferguson) B.; B.B.A., Baylor U., 1951; M. Profl. Accounting, U. Tex., 1961; LL.B., So. Meth. U., 1964; postgrad. Southwestern Grad. Sch. Banking, 1969; m. Vilma A. Vieira, Feb. 25, 1965; children—Vivienne Kay, Rochelle Andrea. Bldg. contractor, 1951-56; with Hunt Oil Co., 1958-62, Haskins & Sells, C.P.A.'s, 1962-63, Mobil Oil Co., 1963-64; admitted to Tex. bar, 1964; with First Nat. Bank, Dallas, 1964—, v.p., trust officer, 1964—.

C.P.A., Tex. Mem. Tex. Soc. C.P.A.'s, Am., Tex., Dallas bar assns., Southwestern Legal Found., Am. Inst. C.P.A.'s, Dallas Estate Council, Tex. Bankers Assn. (legislative com.), Delta Theta Phi. Clubs: Dallas Baylor, German-American (Dallas). Home: Apt 112 4716 Homer St Dallas TX 75204 Office: Room 673 First Nat Bank Bldg Dallas TX 75222

BASS, THOMAS HUTCHESON, III, educator; b. Houston, Jan. 11, 1927; s. Thomas Hutcheson and Mary Lee (Scoggins) B.; B.A., U. Tex. 1950; M.Ed., U. Houston, 1954, postgrad., 1959—; m. Mary Ann King, Sept. 2, 1950; children—Patricia, Martin, Paul, Rita, Amy, Victoria, Robert, Daniel, Laura, David. Retail store mgr. Western Auto Supply Co., Houston, 1951-52; tchr. Houston Ind. Sch. Dist., 1952-60; asst. prof. polit. sci. Sacred Heart Dominican Coll., Houston, 1960-67; prof. U. St. Thomas, Houston, 1967—, chmn. dept. polit. sci., 1968—; mem. Tex. Legislature from Harris County, 1963-72. Guest lectr. ednl. and religious instns. Chmn. social action dept. Tex. Cath. Conf.; mem. Cath. interracial com. and supervisory com. Houston Tchrs. Credit Union; Harris County commr. Commrs. Ct., 1973—. Served with AUS, 1945-47. Named Outstanding Religious Layman, Houston Jr. C. of C., 1961. Mem. Am. Polit. Sci. Assn., Am. Assn. U. Profs., Res. Officers Assn., Nat. Catholic Edn. Assn. (sec. adv. com. on history 1962-63), Phi Delta Kappa, Kappa Delta Pi. Democrat. Roman Catholic. Home: 3437 N Parkwood St Houston TX 77021 Office: Family Law Center 1115 Congress Av Houston TX 77002

BASSET, GENE, editorial cartoonist; b. Bklyn., July 24, 1927; student U. Mo., 1946-47, Cooper Union, 1947-50; B.A., Bklyn. Coll., 1950; student Pratt Inst., 1954, Art Students League N.Y., 1953-54; m. Charlotte Goldenberg, July 8, 1951; children—Darien, Roger, Brian. Sketch artist Indpls. Times, 1951-53; theatrical and sports cartoonist Bklyn. Eagle, 1953-54; sports cartoonist Boston Post, 1955-56; tchr. Famous Artists Sch., Westport, Conn., 1957-62; editorial cartoonist Honolulu Star-Bull., 1962, Scripps-Howard Newspapers, 1962—. Served with USCGR, 1944-46. Mem. Nat. Cartoonist Soc., Assn. Am. Editorial Cartoonists (pres.), Sigma Delta Chi. Home: 8106 Birnam Wood Dr McLean VA 22101 Office: 777 14th St NW Washington DC 20005

BASSETT, NORMAN, editor; b. Dover, N.J., Mar. 22, 1917; s. Edward T. and Edith (Tompkins) B.; A.B., U. Ala., 1940; m. Alva Hilbish, Dec. 25, 1940; children—Mary Alva (Mrs. Victor T. Stark), Howard, Elizabeth (Mrs. Drayton Weer), William, Charles. Reporter Lakeland News, Dover, 1940; telegraph editor Tuscaloosa (Ala.) News, 1940, Rome (Ga.) News-Tribune, 1940-41; telegraph editor, mng. editor, editor Tuscaloosa News, 1941-46; asso. dir., acting dir. U. Ala. News Bur., 1946-50; acting field mgr. Ala. Press Assn. 1949-50; mng. editor, editor, exec. editor, v.p. Tuscaloosa News, 1950—. Bus. mgr. Tuscaloosa Civic Chorus. Bd. dirs. Warrior-Tombigbee Devel. Assn., Ala. Press Assn. Journalism Found., 1974—. Recipient Freedoms Found. citation, 1956; named Lion of the Year, Tuscaloosa Lions Club, 1963; Layman of Year award Ala. Parks and Recreation Soc., 1973. Mem. Ala. AP Assn. (treas.), Tuscaloosa Civic Chorus (pres.), Tuscaloosa County Preservation Soc. (dir., v.p. 1971—). Club: Lions (dep. gov. internat. 1964-65). Office: 2001 6th St Tuscaloosa AL 35401 9 Forest Hill Tuscaloosa AL 35401

BASSETT, WALTER SARTIS, lawyer; b. McGee, Miss., Oct. 3, 1913; s. Walter Scott and Emma Francis (Craine) B.; B.A., Miss. Coll., 1934; J.D., La. State U., 1937; m. Maide Emily Chatman, Aug. 3, 1937 (div. Feb. 1945); m. 2d, Doris Marie Bradley, Mar. 13, 1965. Admitted to La. bar, 1937; practice in Oak Grove, 1937-41, 72—; insp. Dept. Labor, 1941-44; asst. dist. atty. 5th Jud. Dist. La., 1950-58, 60-72. Owner B & K Discount Grocery, Oak Grove, 1969—. Mem. Miss. N.G., 1932-34. Mem. 5th Dist. Bar Assn. (past pres.). Democrat. Baptist. Lion. Home: North St Oak Grove LA 71263 Office: Marietta St Oak Grove LA 71263

BASSETT, WILLIAM EARL, banker; b. Mobile, Ala., Apr. 18, 1936; s. George Richard and Bonnie Lynn (Joiner) B.; student La. Coll., 1958, La. State U., 1959; m. Jo Anne Reed, Feb. 3, 1962; children—Billy, Lowell, Shane. Asst. cashier Comml. Guaranty Bank, Mobile, 1965-69; asst. v.p. Comml. Nat. Bank, Pensacola, Fla., 1969-70; sr. v.p. Second Nat. Bank, Clearwater, Fla., 1970-71; pres., chief exec. officer, chmn. bd. Am. Nat. Bank (now S.E. Nat. Bank), St. Petersburg, Fla., 1971—. Case worker Fla. Parole and Probation Bd.; chmn. Pinellas Area council Boy Scouts Am., mem. exec. bd. Mem. A.I.M. (pres.'s council), Am. Mgmt. Assn., Am. Inst. Banking, Ind., Fla. (chmn. group 4) bankers assns., Newcomen Soc., Com. of 100, Fla., Pinellas County Area, St. Petersburg Beach, St. Petersburg Area, Madeira Beach chambers commerce, Fla. Sheriffs Assn. Clubs: Commerce, Cove Cay Country, Port-O-Call. Home: 1646 Belcher Rd S Clearwater FL 33516 Office: 1075 Pasadena Av S St Petersburg FL 33733

BATCHELDER, DAVID GEORGE, agrl. engr., educator; b. Hiawatha, Kan., Apr. 30, 1920; s. David Nelson and Annetta Mary (Hammond) B.; student Highland Jr. Coll., 1938-39; B.S. in Agrl. Engring., Kan. State U., 1955; M.S., Okla. State U., 1962; m. LaVeta Marie Clements, July 22, 1944; children—Michael, Barbara (Mrs. Harold Eugene Namminga), Phillip, David Scott. Farmer Doniphan County, Kan., 1946-53; instr. Okla. State U., Stillwater, 1955-62, asst. prof., 1962-70, asso. prof., 1970—. Cons. Office of Econ. Opportunity and Indsl. Devel. Commn. Merit Badge counselor Boy Scouts Am. Served to 2nd. lt., USAAF, World War II. Recipient Wonder of Engring. award Okla. Soc. Registered profl. engrs., 1968, 72. Registered profl. engr., Okla. Mem. Am. Soc. Agrl. Engrs. (mem. nat. coms. 1960—, chmn. research group 1973-74), Sigma Xi. Republican. Presbyn. (elder 1966—). Club: Okla. State U. Faculty (pres. 1971-72). Author: (with J.G. Porterfield) Textbook for Farm Machinery Course, 1971. Contbr. articles on agrl. engring. to profl. publs. Patentee thermal defoliator, 1969. Home: 1102 S Stanley St Stillwater OK 74074

BATCHELLER, DAVIS SPRINGSTEEN, lawyer; b. Miami, Fla., May 28, 1928; s. George Ellinwood and Ella (Springsteen) B.; LL.B., U. Fla., 1950; m. Joe Ann Deming, Aug. 8, 1957; children—David S., Elizabeth St. Claire, Osmer, John A. Admitted to Fla. bar, 1950, partner Smathers, Thompson. Mem. adv. bd. Pan Am. Bank of Miami; dir. Pan Am. Bank of Dade County (Fla.). Bd. dirs., Dade County chpt. A.R.C., chmn., 1971-72; bd. dirs. Miami Heart Inst. Mem. Fla. Bd. Pilot Commrs. and Port Wardens of Port Miami, 1956-64. Served with USNR. Mem. Am., Dade County (dir. 1957-60) bar assns., Fla. bar, Internat. Assn. Ins. Counsel, Maritime Law Assn., Phi Delta Phi. Episcopalian. Home: 4595 Sabal Palm Rd Bay Point Miami FL 33137 Office: DuPont Bldg Miami FL 33131

BATCHELLER, JOE ANN DEMING (MRS. DAVID SPRINGSTEEN BATCHELLER), business exec.; b. Jacksonville, Fla., Dec. 11, 1932; d. Osmer St. Clair and Lorena (Jones) Deming; A.A., Stephens Coll., 1952; B.A., U.N.C., 1955; m. David Springsteen Batcheller, Aug. 8, 1957; children—Elizabeth St. Clair, Osmer Deming, John Alden. Sec., Seminole Oil Co., Miami, 1957, pres., dir., 1961—; sec., dir. Blue Grass Plant Foods, Inc., Cynthiana, Ky., 1958; chmn. bd. dirs. Superior Plant Foods, Inc., Lakeland, Fla., 1958; v.p., dir. Pensacola Petroleum Co., Inc. (Fla.), 1961—, Top Power Stations, Inc., Miami, 1961—; chmn. bd. Blue Water Mobile Home Subdiv., Inc. Travernier, Fla., 1967—; pres. Blue Waters Mobile Home Sales, Inc. Bd. dirs. Miami Heart Inst., 1970—, v.p. aux., 1970—; trustee Miami Heart Inst., 1973—; adv. bd. Convent of Sacred Heart, 1973—. Mem. Young Patronesses of Opera, Symphony Club, Beaux Arts, Opera Guild, Vizcayans, D.A.R., Pi Beta Phi. Republican. Episcopalian. Home: 4595 Sabal Palm Rd Bay Point Miami FL 33137

BATEMAN, CLINTON FRANK, accounting firm exec.; b. Fort Worth, May 2, 1940; s. Leonard Clinton and Frances (Ramsey) B.; B.B.A., Baylor U., 1962; m. Susan Smith, June 16, 1962; children—Stacie, Robyn, Kara. Supr. audit staff firm Lybrand, Ross Bros. & Montgomery, Dallas, 1961-66; partner firm Myron Anderson & Co., Midland, Tex., 1966-67; pres. firm Bateman & Co., Inc., Houston, 1967—, also chmn. bd.; partner Wellington Group, real estate developers, Houston. Instr. dept. accounting So. Methodist U., 1966. Treas., mem. bd. dirs. Widowed, Inc., Houston, 1971—. Recipient Spl. Service award Vols. in Tech. Assistance, 1973. C.P.A., Tex. Mem. Am. Inst. C.P.A.'s, Tex. Soc. C.P.A.'s (dir.), Baylor U. Ex-students Assn. (dir.). Baptist. Home: 12319 Queensbury Houston TX 77024 Office: 4041 Richmond Av Houston TX 77027

BATEMAN, F. ELLIS, JR., state ofcl.; b. Atlanta, Feb. 5, 1942; s. Francis Ellis and Douglas (Cousins) B.; B.S. in Industrial Mgmt., Ga. Inst. Tech., 1964; M.B.A., Ga. State U., 1967; m. Rebecca Ann Collier, Feb. 17, 1962; children—James Ellis, Rebecca Kathleen. Personnel technician Ga. State Merit System, 1964-66; personnel mgmt. analyst Ga. Dept. Edn., Atlanta, 1966-67, mgmt. analyst, 1969—; asst. prof. data processing Chattanooga State Tech. Inst., 1967-69; cons. data processing systems Hamilton County Health Dept., Chattanooga, 1968-69. Mem. Sigma Nu. Office: Ga Dept Edn State Office Bldg Atlanta GA 30303

BATEMAN, ROBERT EDWARD, real estate broker; b. Wauchula, Fla., July 27, 1907; s. Wiley Wallace and Sophronia Cordelia (Heard) B.; B.S.A., U. Fla., 1929; m. Elizabeth Lane Bryan, June 11, 1938; children—Elizabeth Anne (Mrs. Ray Blesi West), Alice Cordelia (Mrs. Earl Clifford Catron), Virginia Jean (Mrs. Ronald Mack Sinderud). Insp., Mediterranean fruit fly eradication U.S. Dept. Agr., Fla., 1929-31; various capacities Fed. Land Bank of Columbia (S.C.), 1932-37; salesman Barrett div. Allied Chem. & Dye Corp., 1938-42; real estate broker, ins. agt., citrus grower, land developer, Pompano Beach, Fla., 1946—; developer Lighthouse Point and Coconut Creek subdivs., Pompano Beach; pres. Bateman & Co., Winter Haven Corp.; chmn. bd. Bateman, Gordon & Sands, Inc.; founder, dir. 1st Nat. Bank of North Broward County, 1st Nat. Bank of Margate, Beach 1st Nat. Bank of Pompano Beach, 1st Nat. Bankshares Fla. Inc. Served to lt. comdr. USNR, 1942-46; ETO. Mem. Pompano Beach C. of C. (past pres.), Alpha Zeta, Gamma Sigma Delta. Presbyn. Home: 935 Hillsboro Beach Pompano Beach FL 33062 Office: 2401 Atlantic Blvd Pompano Beach FL 33061

BATEMAN, ROBERT SPRING, landscape architect, city planner; b. Baton Rouge, Dec. 29, 1929; s. John Wesley and Bertha (Spring) B.; B.S., La. State U., 1952, M.S., 1956; City planner, Ala. Planning and Indsl. Devel. Bd., Montgomery, 1956-59; pres. Robert S. Bateman & Assos., Mobile, Ala., 1959—; dir. Icon Industries, Livingston. Pres., Environment, Inc., Mobile, 1972—. Mem. So. Ala. Regional Planning Com., Mobile, 1967—, Mobile Beautification Bd., 1968-73. Mem. Democratic Com. Mobile, 1962-66. Served with USAF, 1952-56; Korea; lt. col. Res. Mem. Am. Soc. Landscape Architects, Am. Soc. Cons. Planners, Am. Inst. Planners, Am. Soc. Planning Ofcls. Mason (Shriner). Office: 433 Bel Air Blvd Suite E Mobile AL 36606

BATEMAN, WILLIAM CAREY, JR., lawyer; b. Memphis, May 6, 1938; s. William Carey and Marjorie (Meeker) B.; student U. Tenn., 1956-57; J.D., Memphis State U., 1965; m. Margaret Condon, July 2, 1965; children—Newman, Lee, Carey. Admitted to Tenn. bar, 1965; Fed. Judicial System; practiced in Memphis, 1965—; asst. city atty., 1972—. Bd. dirs. Vis. Nurses Assn. Mem. Am., Tenn., Memphis, Shelby County bar assns. Club: University (Memphis). Home: 5419 Southwood Dr Memphis TN 38117 Office: 100 N Main Bldg Memphis TN 38103

BATES, ALFRED SCOTT, educator, poet; b. Evanston, Ill., June 13, 1923; s. Alfred R. and Eleanor (Fulchar) B.; B.A., Carleton Coll., 1947; M.A., U. Wis.-Madison, 1948, Ph.D., 1954; m. Phoebe Strehlow, Apr. 17, 1948; children—Robin Ricker, Jonathan Reed, David Scott, Samuel Jackson. Prof. French, U. of the South, Sewanee, Tenn., 1954—. Chmn. bd. dirs. Highland Center, Knoxville, Tenn., 1968—. Served with AUS, 1943-46. Fulbright scholar, 1951-53. Mem. Modern Lang. Assn., Am. Assn. U. Profs., Am. Assn. Tchrs. French. Author: Guillaume Apollinaire, 1967; Poems of War Resistance, 1969. Contbr. poems to various jours. and mags. Home: Sewanee TN 37375

BATES, BURWELL MILLARD, mining co. exec.; b. Konawa, Okla., Jan. 18, 1921; s. Samuel Walter and Bertha (Rudell) B.; B.A., U. Okla., 1942; m. Elaine Lucas, Dec. 11, 1943; children—Craig Laird, Carla (Mrs. Leaford L. Blevins III). Owner, pres. Johnson-Bates Drilling Co., Konawa, Okla., 1953—; owner Bates Limousin Ranch, 1948—; dir. Fed. Nat. Bank, Shawnee, Okla., Okla. State Bank, Konawa. Mem. Sch. Bd., Konawa, 1948-60; active Boy Scouts Am., Future Farmers Am., P.T.A. Bd. dirs. North Am. Limousin Found., 1969-74, pres., 1972-73. Served to lt. (j.g.) USNR, 1942-45. Mem. Okla. Limousin Breeders (pres. 1970—), Petroleum Club, Am. Legion, Pi Delta Theta. Baptist. Mason, Lion (pres. 1949-50). Clubs: Tulsa, South Hills Country (Tulsa). Home: Route 2 Konawa OK 74849 Office: 107 S Broadway Box 55 Konawa OK 74849

BATES, CATHERINE WEST, educator; b. Greenville, S.C., Oct. 6, 1914; d. William Austin and Sara Elizabeth (West) Bates; A.B., Agnes Scott Coll., 1936; M.R.E., Woman's Missionary U. Tng. Sch. of So. Bapt. Theol. Sem., Louisville, 1943; profl. diploma in guidance and student personnel adminstrn. Columbia, 1957, Ed.D., 1965. Dir. religious edn. First Bapt. Ch., Norfolk, Va., 1936-38, La Grange, Ga., 1938-39; state rep. Sunday Sch. dept. Ga. Bapt. Conv., 1939-40; dir. religious edn. St. John's Bapt. Ch., Charlotte, N.C., 1943-45; asst. prof. religion Judson Coll., Marion, Ala., 1945-48; dean women William Jewell Coll., 1948-65; dean women, asso. prof. edn. Georgetown (Ky.) Coll., 1965—. Sr. lectr. psychology Hong Kong Bapt. Coll., 1970-71. Del. World Bapt. Youth Congress, Zurich, Switzerland, 1937, Bapt. World Alliance, Atlanta, 1939, Copenhagen, Denmark, 1947, N. Am. Bapt. Women's Union (exec. com. 1972—). Bapt. Women N.A., Columbus, 1953. Mem. Nat., Mo. (pres. 1963-65), Ky. (pres. 1969-70), So. Bapt. (pres.), assns. women deans and counselors, Religious Edn. Assn., Assn. Higher Edn., Am. Assn. U. Women (pres. br. 1972—), Kansas City Browning Soc., No. Assn. Social Welfare, Am. Coll. Personnel Assn., Nat. Vocational Guidance Assn., Georgetown Coll. Club (pres. 1966-67), P.E.O., Delta Kappa Gamma, Alpha Lambda Delta, Kappa Delta Pi, Eta Sigma Phi, Beta Sigma. Club: Fortnightly Study. Home: 508 E Main St Georgetown KY 40324

BATES, CHARLES EARL, metallurgist; b. Wilsonville, Ala., May 24, 1941; s. Robert C. and Maurine (Dobbs) B.; B.S., U. Ala., 1963; M.S., Case Inst. Tech., 1965; Ph.D., 1967; m. Lois E. Strickland, June 23, 1963; children—Katherine, Ellen, Evan. Technician, engine and foundry div. Ford Motor Co., Sheffield, Ala., 1962-63; grad. research asst. Case Inst. Tech., Cleve., 1963-67; research metallurgist So. Research Inst., Birmingham, Ala., 1967-70, head metallurgy sect., 1970—. Mem. grad. faculty Auburn (Ala.) U., 1973—. Bd. dirs. Health Talents Inc., Birmingham. Mem. Am. Soc. Metals (vice chmn. 1972-73), Am. Foundrymen's Soc., Am. Inst. Metall. Engrs. Author: (with J.F. Wallace, P.F. Wieser) Solidification of Iron-Carbon-Silicon Alloys, 1966. Editorial bd. Cast Metals Research Jour., 1972—. Home: 116 Venetian Way Birmingham AL 35209 Office: 2000 9th Av S Birmingham AL 35205

BATES, CLYDE THOMAS, educator; b. Sadieville, Ky., June 6, 1933; s. Thomas Marion and Carrie Josephine (Gillespie) B.; B.S., U. Ky., 1960, M.S. 1961, Ph. D., (Water Resources Inst. grantee), 1969; m. Frances Ruth Phillips, July 10, 1956; children—Bobby Gene, Calvin Thomas. Instr. econs. Western Ky. Coll., Bowling Green, 1961-63; research asst. U. Ky., Lexington, 1964; asso. prof. econs. Georgetown Coll., 1965—. Served with AUS, 1954-56. Mem. Appalachian Finance Assn., So. Econ. Assn., Omicron Delta Epsilon, Beta Gamma Sigma, Lambda Chi Alpha (hon.). Mem. Church of Christ (elder). Club: Optimist (pres. 1970-71) (Georgetown). Home: 1112 Inca Trail Georgetown KY 40324

BATES, HAROLD MARTIN, lawyer; b. Glamorgan, Va., Mar. 11, 1928; s. William Jennings and Reba (Williams) B.; B.A., Coll. William and Mary, 1952; LL.B., Washington and Lee U., 1961; m. Audrey Rose Doll, Nov. 1, 1952; children—Linda, Carl. Spl. agt. FBI, Newark, N.Y.C., 1952-56; tech. sales rep. Hercules Powder Co., Wilmington, Del., 1956-58; admitted to Ky. bar, 1961; practiced in Louisville, 1961-62; sec.-treas., house counsel Life Ins. Co. of Ky., Louisville, 1962-67, also dir.; pvt. practice law, Roanoke, Va., 1967—; mem. firm Bates, Cruey & Lee. Served with AUS, 1946-47. Mem. Va., Roanoke bar assns., Phi Alpha Delta, Sigma Nu. Presbyn. Kiwanian. Club: Hidden Valley Country. Home: 2602 Sharmar Rd SW Roanoke VA 24018 Office: Shenandoah Bldg Roanoke VA 24011

BATES, HARRY EUGENE, physicist; b. Orlando, Fla., Dec. 9, 1938; s. Harry George Aquilla and Elizabeth Platt (Sperry) B.; B.S., Auburn U., 1962; M.S., Rollins Coll., 1965; Ph.D., U. Fla., 1969; m. Carolyn Ann Hall, May 2, 1959; 1 son, Harry Eugene. Research scientist Martin Marietta Aerospace Corp., Orlando, Fla., 1969—. Cons. optical physics; adj. asst. prof. Rollins Coll., Winter Park, Fla., 1969—. Mem. Optical Soc. Am. (pres. Fla. sect. 1972-73), Am. Assn. Physics Tchrs., Am. Phys. Soc., Sigma Xi, Sigma Pi Sigma. Patentee optical devices. Home: 240 E Ridgewood St Orlando FL 32801 Office: PO Box 5837 MP 276 Orlando FL 32805

BATES, J(AMES) EDWARD, architect; b. Oklahoma City, July 5, 1939; s. James Clement and Mary Juanita (Jones) B.; B.Arch. (Phi Beta Kappa Alumni Assn. scholar, A.I.A. scholar), U. Okla., 1962; m. Joann Rodden, Aug. 12, 1961; 1 dau., Jamie Lynn. Staff architect Thomas M. Rogers, Architects, Enid, Okla., 1965-68; partner Rogers & Bates, A.I.A. Architects, Enid, 1968-69; asso. Thomas E. Stanley, Architects & Engrs., Dallas, 1969—. Pres. Northside Elementary Sch. P.T.A., 1972-73. Served to 1st lt. AUS, 1963-65. Mem. A.I.A., Nat. Council Archtl. Registration Bd., Tex. Soc. Architects, Tau Beta Pi, Sigma Tau. Republican. Baptist. Clubs: Internat. Toastmasters (pres. chpt. 728 1966-67); Am. Business (dir. 1968-69) (Enid). Home: 408 Lakewood Dr DeSoto TX 75115 Office: PO Box 1554 Dallas TX 75221

BATES, JOHN WALTER, trans. planner; b. Bainbridge, Ga., Sept. 24, 1939; s. Clarence Floyd and Lillian (Drake) B.; B.C.E., Ga. Inst. Tech., 1962; M.B.A., Ga. State U., 1967; m. Martha Harriet Smith, July 1, 1961; children—Andrew John, Robin Elizabeth. With Ga. State Hwy. Dept., Atlanta, 1962-71, successively trainee, hwy. planning engr., asst. chief of urban planning, 1962-68, chief planning and operations research, 1968-71; sr. transp. planner, acting dir. planning Met. Atlanta Rapid Transit Authority, 1971-73, mgr. research and devel., 1973—. Prin., Transp. Hwy. Econ. Planning Assos., Inc., Atlanta, 1967—. Sec.-treas. Alpha Nu Home Owning Corp., 1964-66, 68-70, chmn. bd., 1967. Registered profl. engr., Ga., Fla. Mem. Am. Soc. C.E. (sect. dir. 1969, 72), Am. Inst. Planners (asso.), Inst. Traffic Engrs. (sec.-treas. Ga. div. 1972), Phi Kappa Sigma. Presbyn. Mason (K.T.). Home: 4303 Rocking Chair Lane Stone Mountain GA 30083 Office: Suite 1300 100 Peachtree St NW Atlanta GA 30303

BATES, JOSEPH HENRY, physician; b. Little Rock, Sept. 19, 1933; s. Henry Ermer and Susan Elizabeth (Wallis) B.; B.S., U. Ark., 1954, M.D., 1957, M.S., 1963; m. Patsy McGinnis, Aug. 5, 1955; children—Patricia, Susan Elizabeth, Joseph Henry III, Elisabeth Lee. Intern, U. Ark. Med. Center, Little Rock, 1957-58, resident, 1958-61; instr. dept. medicine U. Ark., 1961-63, asst. prof., 1963-68, asso. prof., 1968-71, prof. medicine microbiology, 1971—; chief medicine VA Hosp., Little Rock, 1967—. Cons. Ark. State Health Dept., 1965—; mem. com. for phage typing mycobacteria WHO, 1965—. Royal Coll. Physicians (London) fellow, 1971. Fellow A.C.P., Am. Coll. Chest Physicians; mem. Infectious Disease Soc., So. Soc. Clin. Investigation, Pulaski County Tb and Respiratory Disease Assn. (pres. 1968-71). Club: Racquet (Little Rock). Home: 5 Glenridge Rd Little Rock AR 72207 Office: 300 E Roosevelt Rd Little Rock AR 72206

BATES, ROBERT LEWIS, mathematician; b. Mt. Carmel, Ill., July 29, 1930; s. Scott Edward and Rosalind Anne (Wise) B.; B.A., Gallaudet Coll., 1955; postgrad. Am. U., 1955—; m. Joan Margaret Macaluso, July 23, 1955; children—Richard, Robert Lewis, Randolph, Roger. Mathematician, programmer U.S. Dept. Navy, Bur. Aeronautics, 1955-59; mathematician, head sci. programming sect. Bur. Naval Weapons, 1959-61, mathematician, system analyst Navy Information Center, 1961, mathematician, project leader Naval Command Systems Support Activity, Washington, 1961—. First v.p. Va. Assn. Deaf, 1973; pres., Internat. Cath. Deaf Assn., 1973-75; treas., Council Orgns. Serving Deaf, 1972-74. Recipient Internat. award Kiwanis Club, 1950, Letters of Commendation USN, 1962. Mem. Am. Inst. Parliamentarians, Assn. Computing Machinery (vice-chmn. 1971-73), Nat. Fraternal Soc. Deaf, Spl. Interest Group for Deaf, Gallaudet Coll. Alumni Assn. Lion. Home: 8419 Wesleyan St Vienna VA 22180 Office: Washington Navy Yard NAVCOSSACT Bldg 196 Code 03 Washington DC 20390

BATES, THOMAS ISAAC, JR., civil engr.; b. Charleston, Tenn., June 29, 1913; s. Thomas I. and Margaret (Bates) B.; B.C.E., Tenn. Tech. U., 1936; grad., U. Tenn., 1948; postgrad. Mass. Inst. Tech., 1961. Engr. aid Soil Conservation Service, U.S. Dept. Agr., 1938; with Bur. Pub. Rds., various states, 1938-43; sr. engr. Dept. Commerce. Civil Aeros. Adminstrn., 1943-47; with Republic Steel Corp., 1947-54; with Fla. Dept. Transp., Tallahassee, 1954—, asst. state traffic and planning engr., 1955—. Pres. Young Democrats of Tenn., 1936—. Registered profl. engr., Fla. Mem. Am. Soc. C.E., Nat. Soc. Profl. Engrs., Fla. Engring. Soc., Inst. Traffic Engrs., Engrs. Joint Council. Episcopalian. Mason, Kiwanian (hon.). Home: PO Box 1321 Tallahassee FL 32302 Office: Dot Bldg Tallahassee FL 32304

BATES, WILL LEWIS, realtor; b. Corpus Christi, Tex., Aug. 8, 1923; s. Will Lewis and Agnes (McAllister) B.; student pub. schs.; m. Cherry Dugger, July 6, 1943; children—William Glenn, Dan Mac, Mary Ann, Terri Elizabeth. Pres., W.L. Bates Co., Inc., Six Hundred Corp., Met. Land Co., 1969—, Coastal Bend Oil Co., 1960—, Bacor, Inc., 1967—. Past dir., v.p. Goodwill Industries; bd. dirs. Better Bus. Bur. Served with USNR, 1941-45. Mem. Soc. Indsl. Realtors, Tex. Assn. Realtors, Urban Land Inst., Corpus Christi Bd. Realtors (past pres.), Tex. Indsl. Council, C. of C., Am. Orchid Soc. (trustee). Mem. Christian Ch. Mason (32 deg., Shriner). Club: Corpus Christi Country. Home: 238 Cape Cod Corpus Christi TX 78412 Office: Suite 1800 600 Bldg Corpus Christi TX 78403

BATES, WILLIAM KERVIN, educator, biochemist; b. Houston, Nov. 16, 1936; s. Wilbur Leon and Elsie Marie (Neeley) B.; B.A., Rice Inst., 1959, Ph.D., 1963; m. Wilma Kathryn Hettler, May 31, 1959; children—Loretta Lynn, Paul William. NIH postdoctoral trainee Stanford, 1963-66; asst. prof. biology U. N.C., Greensboro, 1966-69, asso. prof., 1969-74, prof., 1974—. Research grantee NSF, 1966. Research Council U. N.C., Greensboro, 1969-72, N.C. Ednl. Computing Service, 1971, N.C. Bd. Sci. and Tech., 1972. Mem. Am. Chem. Soc., N.C. Acad. Sci., Genetics Soc. Am., Am. Soc. Microbiology, A.A.A.S., Sigma Xi. Contbr. articles to profl. jours. Home: 3004D Overton Dr Greensboro NC 27408

BATES, WILLIAM LEROY, JR., land devel. co. exec.; b. Columbia, S.C., Mar. 8, 1921; s. William LeRoy and Ruth (Hawley) B.; B.B.A., Emory U., 1941; postgrad. U. Pa., 1941; m. Valerie Ogden Bates, Jan. 5, 1946 (div. Jan. 1965); 1 dau., Catherine (Mrs. Akin); m. 2d, Charlotte Louise Starr Bagley, Jan. 1970; 1 dau., Claire Starr Bagley (Mrs. Ramers). Commd. 2d lt. USMC, 1941, advanced through grades to col., 1962; comdg. officer Marine detachment U.S.S. Lexington, 1944-45; co. comdr. 1st Marine Div., Korean War; strategic planner U.S. European Command, 1952-54; head Marine Corps tng., 1954-58; acad. head Amphibious Warfare Coll., 1960-62; bn. comdr. Parris Island, S.C., 1962-63; controller Parris Island, 1964-65; ret., 1965; v.p. Gen. Am. Devel. Corp., Atlanta, 1970—; pres. Bates Bldg. Supply Co., Atlanta, 1972—; sr. v.p. Asso. Distbrs. Inc., Atlanta, 1965-70. Decorated Silver Star medal, Bronze Star medal, Air medal, Navy Commendation medal, Presdl. Unit citation. Mem. Mil. Order World Wars, Am. Legion, Kappa Alpha, Alpha Kappa Psi. Republican. Episcopalian. Kiwanian. Home: 3155 Verdun Rd NW Atlanta GA 30305 Office: PO Box 12004 Atlanta GA 30305

BATSON, FRANK OTERI, JR., dentist; b. Greenville, Miss., Sept. 27, 1940; s. Frank Oteri and Hoyett (Wheat) B.; student U. Miss., 1958-60; D.D.S., Loyola U., New Orleans, 1964; m. Katherine Crosson Downing, Nov. 24, 1961; children—Megan Michelle, Allyson Leigh. Pvt. practice dentistry, Laurel, Miss., 1966, Columbus, Miss., 1966—; mem. dental staff Lowndes Gen. Hosp., Columbus Hosp., dental cons. Columbus Med. Center. Dir. Piedmont Investment Securities, Inc. City councilman, Columbus, 1969-73. Bd. dirs. Miss. Elected Rep. Assn., 1971. Served with USAF, 1964-66. Recipient Certificate of Recognition, Am. Acad. Roentgenology, 1964; Distinguished Service award, Columbus Man of Year award Columbus Jr. C. of C., 1971. Mem. Columbus C. of C., Am., Miss. Northeast Miss. dental assns., Am. Acad. Gen. Dentistry, Ducks Unltd., Phi Delta Theta, Delta Sigma Delta. Republican. Methodist (steward 1968-71, 73—). Kiwanian (chmn. operation drug alert 1971-72). Club: Columbus (Miss.) Country. Home: 337 Williamsburg Rd Columbus MS 39701 Office: 425 Hospital Dr Columbus MS 39701

BATSON, HOKE WADDY, pub. relations exec.; b. Greenville, S.C., June 10, 1936; s. Waddy Smith and Edna (McAlister) B.; B.A., Clemson Coll., 1958; postgrad. Furman U., 1958-59, Fla. Inst. Tech., 1962-63; m. Nelle Hill, June 12, 1959; 1 son, Kevin Tallysmith. With Dun & Bradstreet, Jacksonville, Fla., 1959-60, Ciba Pharm. Co., Montgomery, Ala., 1960-64, Spitz Electric Co., Melbourne, Fla., 1964-68; partner Allen-Batson, Melbourne, 1968-69; elec. mfg. rep., asso. Glenn Assos., Fla., Brandon, 1969—. Sec. Day-Nite Flyers, Inc., Melbourne, 1966—. Founder Brevard County Fair, 1968, v.p., 1967—; founder Indian River County Fair, 1969. Mem. City Council, Melbourne, 1968—; mayor City of West Melbourne, 1969-71. Trustee Melbourne Teen Town; bd. dirs. Brevard County Mental Health Assn. Served with AUS, 1959-60. Named U.S. Jaycee Ambassador, 1967. Mem. Fla. Pub. Relations Assn., Illuminating Engring. Soc., Fla. League Municipalities, Jr. C. of C. (local pres. 1966—, nat. dir.). Democrat. Baptist. Elk, Kiwanian. Home: 716 Debra Lynn Dr Brandon FL 33511 Office: Suite 207 Liberty Fed Bldg 1111 N Westshore Blvd Tampa FL 33607

BATSON, JAMES LUCIAN, mech. engr.; b. Steubenville, O., Feb. 13, 1936; s. James Lucian and Bertha Mae (Cummings) B.; B.S. in Aero. Engring., Ala. Poly. Inst., 1959; M.S., Auburn U., 1967; Ph.D., U. Tex., 1972; m. Sara Blake Bryant, Apr. 2, 1960; children—Sara Beth, James Lucian III. Coop. aero. engr. student trainee Redstone Arsenal, Ala. Poly. Inst., 1955-59; missile test engr., Redstone Arsenal, 1959-63; meteorol. rocket devel. mgr. U.S. Army, Redstone Arsenal, Ala., 1963-71, mech. engr. Missile Command, 1971—. Active Boy Scouts Am. Registered profl. engr., Ala. Mem. Am. Inst. Aeros. and Astronautics, Phi Kappa Phi, Sigma Gamma Tau. Methodist. Clubs: Optimist (pres. 1971-72) (Huntsville, Ala.); Browns Creek Sailing Association (Guntersville, Ala.). Home: 5607 Panorama Dr Huntsville AL 35801 Office: US Army Missile Command Redstone Arsenal AL 35809

BATTAGLIA, GASPARE FRANCIS, JR., agr. bus. exec.; b. Troy, N.Y., Mar. 1, 1910; s. Gaspare and Antonina (Caruso) B.; student Syracuse U., 1929; m. Catherine Wherrett, June 15, 1935; children—Gaspare Francis III, Catherine (Mrs. John Haley), Robert, Christine (Mrs. William Macchia), Mary (Mrs. James Welborn), Julia, Paul. Pres., Krisp-Pak Co., Inc., Norfolk, Va., 1954—, Battaglia Produce Shippers, Inc., Norfolk, 1955—, Farmers Potato Distbg. Co., Inc., Norfolk, 1958—. Mem. Va. State Commn. of Industry of Agr., 1964—, Va. Bd. Agr. and Commerce, 1967—, Va. Seed Potato Commn., 1960—. Bd. dirs. Norfolk Little Theatre, 1938—, pres., 1957; bd. dirs. Tidewater Regional Health Planning Council, v.p., 1973; bd. dirs. Health, Welfare, Recreation Planning Council, 1960—, Southeastern Tidewater Opportunity Poverty Project, 1966—, Commn. on Social Devel. of Diocese of Richmond, Catholic Family and Childrens Services, United Community Fund; bd. dirs. St. Marys Infant Home, pres., 1973; trustee De Paul Hosp.; pres., 1963, meml. lay bd., 1954—. Mem. Va. Assn. Vegetable and Potato Growers (pres. 1962). Roman Catholic. Home: 1331 Willowood Dr Norfolk VA 23509 Office: PO Box 1852 Norfolk VA 23501

BATTE, JAMES HERBERT, state ofcl.; b. Concord, N.C., July 8, 1913; s. George Albert and Fannie (Mallory) B.; B.S., Davidson Coll., 1935; student U.S. Mil. Acad., 1935-36; M.B.A., Harvard, 1950; m. Elenita Dyer, June 17, 1948. Commd. 2d lt. U.S. Army, 1940, advanced through grades to brig. gen., 1966; faculty Indsl. Coll. Armed Forces, 1958-61; spl. asst. congl. affairs Army Materiel Command, Washington, 1962-64; comdr. Edgewood (Md.) Arsenal Complex, 1965-66; sr. logistics adviser to Korean Army, 1967-68; asst. chief logistics Hdqrs. Continental Army Command, 1969-70; ret., 1970; exec. asst. to gen. mgr., dir. adminstrn. S.C. Pub. Service Authority, Moncks Corner, 1970—. Decorated D.S.M., Silver Star, Legion of Merit with 2 oak leaf clusters, Bronze Star with cluster, Purple Heart (U.S.); Fourragere (France). Mem. Interserv Financial Assn. (dir. 1970-72), Am. Pub. Power Assn. (chmn. fuels com. 1973—), Am. Soc. Mil. Comptrollers, Kappa Alpha, Gamma Sigma Epsilon. Home: 115 Briarwood Lane Summerville SC 29483 Office: South Carolina Public Service Authority Moncks Corner SC 29461

BATTELL, WILLIAM PUTNAM, ret. marine corps officer; b. Mediapolis, Ia., Dec. 26, 1906; s. Frederick Louis and Harriet Elizabeth (Chapman) B.; student Ia. State Coll., 1924-27, also marine corps, army and navy profl. schs.; m. Esther Lillian Martin, Feb. 15, 1930. Enlisted in USMC, 1927, commd. 2d lt., 1930, advanced through grades to maj. gen.; assigned communications and electronics, 1927-48, supply, 1948-65; Q. M. Gen. Marine Corps, 1963-65; ret., 1965; pres., dir. Sun City Center Bank (Fla.), 1971-72, chmn. bd., 1972—. Mem. corp. Nat. Capitol USO Club. Organizer, pres. S.W. Ga. Cerebral Palsy Assn.; mem. adv. com. Hillsborough County Charter Commn., v.p. Sun City Center Civic Assn., 1969-70, pres. 1971. Mem. Nat. Def. Transp. Assn. (v.p.), Def. Supply Assn. (hon. pres.), Armed Forces Mgmt. Assns. (bd. govs.), Am. Legion, Ret. Officers Assn., Old Timer Communicators of So. Cal., Am. Inst. Banking, Vet. Wireless Operators Assn., Southwest Fla. Srs. Golf Assn., Marine Corps Combat Corrs. Assn. Rotarian. Club: Sun City Center Men's (pres.). Home: 401 Blackhawk Circle Sun City Center FL 33570

BATTELSTEIN, BARRY LIVINGSTON, banker, real estate developer; b. Houston, Feb. 12, 1939; s. Ben D. and Virginia (Livingston) B.; B.B.A., Tulane U., 1960; M.A., N.Y. U., 1961; m. Roslyn Frohman, July 25, 1960; children—David, Philip, Nancy. Vice pres. Battelstein's, Inc., 1961-64; pres., West Dallas Distbg. Co., 1961-64; pres. Mortgage Co. Am., Houston, 1965-69, 73—, chmn., 1973—, dir., 1965—; vice chmn. Citizens Bank, 1968-69, co-chmn., 1969-70; vice chmn. La. Bank & Trust Co., Shreveport, 1969-70; chmn. exec. com., dir. Peden Industries, Inc., Houston, after 1970, now co-chmn.; chmn. bd. Properties Internat., Inc. (formerly Wheel Inn, Inc.), Houston, 1970—; dir. Oak Forest Bank, 1967—, co-chmn., 1969-71. Recipient Wall St. Jour. award in finance Tulane U., 1960. Clubs: Petroleum, University, Westwood Country (Houston). Jewish religion. Home: 3908 Del Monte Houston TX 77019 Office: 1333 W Loop S Houston TX 77027

BATTEN, JAMES WILLIAM, educator; b. Goldsboro, N.C., Aug. 5, 1919; s. Albert LeMay and Lydia Annie (Davis) B.; A.B., U. N.C., 1940, M.A., 1947, Ed.D., 1960: postgrad. Columbia, 1942; m. Sara Magdalene Storey, June 1, 1945. Tchr., Glendale High Sch., Kenly, N.C., 1940-41, Wilmington Jr. Coll., 1946-47; tchr., coach Princeton (N.C.) High Sch., 1947-50; prin. Micro (N.C.) High Sch., 1950-58; teaching fellow, narrator Morehead Planetarium, Chapel Hill, N.C., 1958-60; asso. prof. E. Carolina U., Greenville, N.C., 1960-62, prof. edn., 1962—, chmn. dept. secondary edn., 1967—, also asst. dean Sch. Edn. Active in civic affairs. Served to lt. comdr. USNR, 1941-46. Mem. N.E.A., N.C. Assn. Educators (chpt. pres. 1961-62), Nat. Sci. Tchrs. Assn., Assn. for Supervision and Curriculum Devel., Phi Delta Kappa (pres. 1961-62), Horace Mann League, Nat. Soc. Study of Edn., Am. Ednl. Research Assn., N.C. Lit. and History Assn., Kappa Delta Pi (counselor 1967—). Democrat. Baptist (deacon). Lion (pres. 1949-51). Author: Our Neighbors in Space, 1962, rev. edit., 1969; Research as a Tool for Understanding, 1965; Stars, Atoms, and God, 1968; (with J. Sullivan Gibson) Soils, 1970; Understanding Research, 1970, rev. edit., 1972; (with Sister Mary Waddell) Human Perspectives in Educational Research, 1973. Contbr. numerous articles profl. jours. Home: 1014 E Wright Rd Greenville NC 27835

BATTEN, SARA STOREY (MRS. JAMES WILLIAM BATTEN), librarian; b. Murfreesboro, N.C., Nov. 6, 1915; d. Gladstone Bunn and Eldorado (Whitley) Storey; A.B., Chowan Coll., 1936; M.S. in L.S., U. N.C., 1960; m. James William Batten, June 1, 1945. Tchr. pub. high sch., Enfield, N.C., 1937; tchr., librarian Glendale Sch., Kenly, 1937-45, Micro, N.C., 1945-46; tchr. high sch. New Hanover Sch., Wilmington, 1946-47; tchr., librarian, Micro, 1947-48; cataloger Joyner Library, East Carolina U., Greenville, N.C., 1960—. Established Hugo E. Miller scholarships East Carolina U., 1963. Mem. N.C., Southeastern library assns., N.C. Assn. Educators, East Carolina U. Women's Club, Beta Phi Mu. Baptist. Home: 1014 E Wright Rd Greenville NC 27834

BATTIGELLI, MARIO CESARE, educator; b. Florence, Italy, Dec. 18, 1927; s. Enrico and Maria Elena (Vigo) B.; M.D., U. Florence (Italy), 1951; M.P.H., U. Pitts., 1957; m. Giovanna Torri, May 31, 1958; children—Ann Frances, Lisa, David, John. Came to U.S., 1958, naturalized, 1964. Intern, Ospedali S. Maria Nuova, U. Florence, 1950-51; resident Istituti Clinici Perfezionamento, U. Milan (Italy), 1952-54, St. Francis Gen. Hosp., Pitts., 1956-57; practice medicine, specializing in internal medicine and toxicology, Milan, 1957-58, Pitts., 1958-65, Chapel Hill, N.C., 1966—; mem. staff N.C. Meml. Hosp., Chapel Hill, Watts Hosp., Durham, N.C.; house staff, instr. Clinica Del Lavoro, U. Milan, 1952-58; mem. faculty Schs. Pub. Health and Medicine, U. Pitts., 1958-65; asso. prof. medicine Schs. Medicine and Pub. Health, U. N.C., Chapel Hill, 1965—. Cons. U.S. Dept. Army, Edgewood Arsenal, Md., 1968—; dir. med. service N.C. State Hwy. Patrol, 1968—. Spl. fellow Istituto Nazionale Infortuni Lavoro (Italy), 1955, Nat. Inst. Occupational Safety and Health, 1971. Mem. A.M.A. (mem. council on environmental, occupational and pub. health 1973), Am. Thoracic Soc., Am. Assn. U. Profs., Am. Coll. Preventive Medicine, Am. Acad. Occupational Medicine, A.A.A.S. N.Y. Acad. Scis. Home: 1307 Wildwood Dr Chapel Hill NC 27514

BATTIN, ROBT DAVIS, clergyman; b. Mpls., Oct. 8, 1929; s. Robert Davis and Harriot Ada (MacMurray) B.; B.S., U. Ala., 1953; M.Div., Episcopal Sem. S.W., 1956; M.Ed., Miss. Coll., 1973; m. Charlotte Alice Wilson, Feb. 7, 1953; children—Barbara, Deborah, Brenda, Leslie, Nancy. Ordained to ministry Episcopal Ch., 1956; rector, Calvary Ch., Americus, Ga., 1958-62, St. Agustine Ch., Augusta, Ga., 1962-66; asso. rector, headmaster Ch. of Advent, Birmingham, Ala., 1966-70; headmaster St. Andrew's Sch., Jackson, Miss., 1970-73; rector, headmaster Holy Nativity Ch. and Sch., Panama City, Fla., 1973—. Served with AUS, 1956-58. Fellow in Celtic ch. history, 1961. Mem. Nat. Assn. Episcopal Schs. (elementary bd. 1973—), Kappa Delta Pi. Home: 125 N Lakewood St Panama City FL 32401 Office: 1005 Second Plaza Panama City FL 32401

BATTISTE, MERLE ANDREW, educator; b. Mobile, Ala., July 22, 1933; s. David Theodore and Flossie (Older) B.; B.S., The Citadel, 1954; M.S., La. State U., 1956; Ph.D., Columbia, 1959; m. Anita Elaine Luise, Mar. 12, 1960; children—Mark Andrew, John Lawrence. Research asso. U. Cal. at Los Angeles, 1959-60; asst. prof. U. Fla., Gainesville, 1961-66, asso. prof., 1966-70, prof. chemistry, 1970—. Served to 2d lt. AUS, 1961. Alfred P. Sloan Research fellow, 1967-69; Fulbright-Hays Research sr. scholar, 1974. Mem. Am. Chem. Soc., Chem. Soc. (London), Alpha Chi Sigma, Phi Lambda Upsilon. Contbr. articles in field organic chemistry to scientific jours. Home: 427 SW 41st St Gainesville FL 32601

BATTLE, MAX GEORGE, city ofcl.; b. St. Petersburg, Fla., Nov. 9, 1925; s. Jesse Brown and Clara Louise (Cherbonneaux) B.; student Fla. State U., 1948-50; B.C.E., U. Fla., 1952; m. Marguerite Josephine Thibadeau, June 14, 1952; children—Max George, John. Water and waste engr. E.I. duPont de Nemours & Co., Inc., Camden, S.C., 1952-53; with engring. dept. City Tampa (Fla.), 1953-56; project mgr. subdiv. plans Rader & Assos., St. Petersburg, Fla., 1956-59; partner, airport cons. Harold A. Wilde & Assos., St. Petersburg, 1959-62; dir. pub. works City Clearwater, Fla., 1962—. Pres., treas. Cons. Engrs., Inc., Clearwater, 1962—. Served with USMCR, 1942, USAAF, 1943-45. Registered prof. engr., Fla., N.C. Mem. Am. Soc. C.E., Fla. Engring. Soc., Nat. Soc. Profl. Engrs., Am. Pub. Works Assn., Tampa Bay Soc. Registered Land Surveyors, Fla. Bd. Profl. Engrs. and Land Surveyors, Sigma Tau. Elk. Home: Clearwater FL 33516 Office: PO Box 4748 Clearwater FL 33518

BATTLE, TURNER WESTRAY, assn. exec., cons.; b. Rocky Mount, N.C. Nov. 30, 1921; s. Turner Westray and Helen (Staats) B.; B.S. in Engring., U.S. Naval Acad., 1942; m. Francesca Barksdale Shackelford, June 22, 1942; children—Turner Westray, Stephen Shackelford, Richard Staats. Pres., North State Constrn. Co., Inc, Rocky Mount, 1948-65; exec. dir. N.C. Wildlife Fedn., 1959-74, cons., 1974—; v.p. Westwood Lumber Co., Inc., 1951-71, N.C. rep. to Nat. Wildlife Fedn., 1958-72, nat. dir., 1972-74, v.p., 1974—; mem. N.C. Aquatic Recreation Study Commn., 1963, Gov.'s Com. on Water Safety, 1965; vice chmn. Pesticide Adv. Com., mem. spl. adv. bd. N.C. Dept. Natural and Econ. Resources; mem. adv. bd. Water Resource Inst., U. N.C.; pres. Nat. Wild Turkey Fedn., 1974—. Mem. nat. council Boy Scouts Am. Pres., chmn. bd. Rocky Mount Acad., 1968—; trustee, sec. N.C. Conservation Edn. Found.; adv. bd. N.C. Zool. Authority, 1971—. Served with USN, 1942-46; PTO. Recipient Silver Beaver award Boy Scouts Am., 1964; Distinguished Conservation Service award Nat. Wildlife Fedn., 1965, spl. award, 1974; Nat. Conservation award Am. Motors Corp., 1971; Conservationist of year award N.C. Wildlife Fedn., 1974. named Ky. col, Hon. Citizen of Tex. Mem. Nat. Rifle Assn. (life), Am. Philatelic Soc. (life), Outdoor Writers of Am., Wilderness Soc., Nat. Audubon Soc., Nat., N.C. wildlife fedns., Southeastern, Tar Heel outdoor press assn., Am. Forestry Assn., Trout Unltd., Ducks Unltd., Save-the-Redwood League (life), U.S. Naval Acad. Alumni Assn. (life). Democrat. Episcopalian. Clubs: Jones Hill Gun, Roanoke and Tar River Gun, Benvenue Country. Kiwanian. Editor: Friend of Wildlife, 1959—. Home: 1633 Pinecrest Rd Rocky Mount NC 27801 Office: 109 S Main St Rocky Mount NC 27801

BATTLE, WILLIAM RAINEY, ins. co. exec.; b. Santa Anna, Tex., July 10, 1924; s. Fred and Margaret (Rainey) B.; student U. Tex. at El Paso, 1941-43; B.A., U. Ia., 1947, M.S., 1948; m. Jane Nichol Brown, Jan. 6, 1951; children—Rebecca Brown, William Lee. Mgr. actuarial dept. Nat. Life & Accident Ins. Co., Nashville, 1948-51; asso. actuary Southwestern Life Ins. Co., Dallas, 1951-58; actuary Shenandoah Life Ins. Co., Roanoke, Va., 1959-62, v.p., actuary, 1962-70, v.p. financial operations, 1970-71, exec. v.p., 1971-72, pres., 1972—, also dir.; dir. Am. Nat. Bank Roanoke Chmn. bd. trustees Employees Retirement System, City of Roanoke; mem. adv. bd. Salvation Army; mem. adv. council Va. Poly. Inst. & State U. Served to 1st lt. USAAF, 1943-46. Fellow Soc. Actuaries; mem. Middle Atlantic Actuarial Club (pres. 1967), Am. Acad. Actuaries, Newcomen Soc., Roanoke Valley C. of C. (pres. 1973). Home: 3221 Fordham Rd Roanoke VA 24014 Office: 2301 Brambleton Av SW Roanoke VA 24015

BATTLES, JOHN WADE, steamship co. exec.; b. Cleve., Apr. 2, 1924; s. Myron Edward and Jessie Wade (MacMaster) B.; B.A., Denison U., 1948; m. Barbara Joyce Weis, Dec. 2, 1960. Regional mgr. Reinhold Pub. Corp., N.Y.C., 1949-56; pres. Chester Blackburn & Roder Ltd., St. Thomas, V.I., 1961—; tchr. Antilles Sch. Flotilla comdr., div. vice capt. USCG Aux., P.R. and V.I., 1963-73. Served with USNR, 1942-46. Rotarian. Clubs: St. Thomas Yacht (commodore 1970-72), V.I. Game Fishing (dir. 1964-66). Home: 17 Windward Way Cowpet Bay Village St Thomas VI 00801 Office: PO Box 5227 St Thomas VI 00801

BATTS, B.F. (JERRY), city ofcl.; b. St. Louis, July 11, 1921; s. Bascom Franklin and Lila May (Bartlett) B.; B.S., U. Mo., 1942; postgrad., Harvard, Mass. Inst. Tech.; m. Edna Helen Vahrenkamp, Sept. 1, 1951. Edn. dir. Tex. Coll. Tech., San Antonio, 1948-51; sr. research engr. Southwest Research Inst., San Antonio, 1951-55, mgr., 1955-58; sect. head Motorola Inc., Phoenix, 1958-60; program mgr. LTV Continental Electronics, Dallas, 1960-65, F&M Systems Co., Dallas, 1965-68 dir., systems engring. div., Def. Electronics, Inc., Rockville, Md., 1968-69; v.p. systems Nat. Data Controls, Inc., Dallas, 1969-70; tech. and research coordinator City of Dallas, 1971—. Served to 1st lt. Signal Corp, AUS, 1942-46: ETO. Registered profl. engr., Tex. Mem. Nat., Tex. socs. profl. engrs., I.E.E.E., Eta Kappa Nu, Pi Mu Epsilon, Phi Kappa Psi. Kiwanian. Home: 9308 Vinewood Dr Dallas TX 75228 Office: 1500 W Mockingbird Lane Dallas TX 75247

BAUCOM, MARGARET DEAN (MRS. H. BASCOM BAUCOM), newspaper worker, feature writer, poet; b. Charlotte, N.C., Sept. 25, 1909; d. John Calvin and Lelia (Robinson) Dean; student pub. schs.; m. Hiram Bascom Baucom, Sept. 20, 1927 (dec.); 1 dau., Joan (Mrs. James Preston Brown, Jr.). Automobile dealer B & M Motor Co., Monroe, N.C., 1950-53; now free lance writer for newspapers and others; soc. editor The Monroe Enquirer. Bd. dirs. Mecklenburg-Union Tb and Respiratory Disease Assn. Founder Marshville Pub. Library. Recipient Etta Caldwell Harris Poetry award; 1st prize Ill. Poetry Soc., 1972. Mem. N.C. Hist. Soc., U.D.C. (pres. 1956-58, state chmn. patriotic service), Colonial Dames 17th Century, D.A.R. (publicity chmn.), Union County Hist. Soc., Little Theatre (v.p. and role participant), Women's Golf Assn., Monroe Opera Guild (charter), Carolinas Geneal. Soc. (co-editor bull.), Daus. Am. Colonists, Huguenot Soc., Internat. Platform Assn. (mem. publicity com. 1966—), Nat. Fedn. Press Women, N.C. Press Women, Nat. League Am. Pen Women, Cal. Fedn. Chaparral Poets, Ill. Poetry Soc., World Poetry Soc. Internat., Am. Poets Fellowship Soc. Presbyn. Clubs: Monroe Woman's Golf (charter mem., past pres.), Monroe Woman's (past pres.), Monroe Garden (past pres.), Monroe Music (past pres.), N.C. Press Woman's (dist. chmn. 1965-66), Silhoutte Dance. Author: Mood Poetry, A Book of Contemporary Poetry. Contbr. to poetry mags. Address: 710 S Hayne Monroe NC 28110

BAUCUM, DON MICHAEL, lawyer; b. Charleston, Miss., Mar. 25, 1946; s. William A. and Charlsie (Brunson) B.; B.A., S.W. Tex. State Coll., J.D., St. Mary's Law Sch. Admitted to Tex. bar; partner firm King, Joseph & Baucum, San Antonio, 1971—. Bd. dirs. Am. Materials Industries, Inc., Lawns of Beauty, Inc. Mem. San Antonio Bar Assn. (mem. com. 1972-73), Tex. Bar Assn., Phi Kappa Tau, Alpha Chi, Phi Delta Theta. Home: 303 Basswood St San Antonio TX 78213 Office: 204 C Central Park San Antonio TX 78216

BAUER, HENRY HERMANN, educator; b. Vienna, Austria, Nov. 16, 1931; s. Martin Josef and Anna (Rafael) B.; B.Sc. with 1st class honors, U. Sydney (Australia), 1951, M.Sc., 1952, Ph.D., 1956; m. Myra Lee Levin, June 28, 1958; children—Helen Suzanne, Judith

Ann. Came to U.S., 1965, naturalized, 1969. Fulbright postdoctoral research asso. U. Mich. at Ann Arbor, 1956-58, Fulbright vis. scientist, 1965-66; lectr. U. Sydney, 1958-62, sr. lectr., 1962-66; asso. prof. dept. chemistry U. Ky., Lexington, 1966-69, prof., 1969—; vis. prof. U. Southampton (Eng.), 1972-73. Mem. Electrochemical Soc., Am. Chem. Soc., Internat. Soc. Electrochemistry, Am. Assn. U. Profs. Author: Alternating Current Polarography and Tensammetry, 1963; Electrodics, 1972. Contbr. profl. jours. Home: 736 Glendover St Lexington KY 40502 Office: Dept Chemistry Univ Ky Lexington KY 40506

BAUER, JOHN HENRY, accountant; b. Evansville, Ind., Dec. 23, 1940; s. Joseph S. and Estelle J. (Corressell) B.; B.S., St. Edward's U., 1962; postgrad. South Tex. Coll. Law, 1966; m. Junia Lee Oakleaf, Sept. 24, 1966; children—Julie Ann, Jill Jaye, John Joseph. Staff accountant Coopers & Lybrand, C.P.A.'s, Houston, 1962-73, partner, 1973—. Instr. accounting St. Thomas U., 1969. Trustee St. Edwards U., Austin, Tex. Served with AUS, 1962. Recipient Coronat award St. Edward's U., 1972. C.P.A., Tex. Mem. Am. Inst. C.P.A.'s, Tex. Soc. C.P.A.'s, Houston Jr. C. of C. (dir. 1968-69). Republican. Roman Catholic. Home: 10727 Lynbrook Dr Houston TX 77042 Office: 1010 Jefferson St Houston TX 77001

BAUER, ROBERT EDWARD, aluminum co. exec.; b. Buffalo, Sept. 13, 1924; s. Edward Louis and Eleanor Louise (Ziegler) B.; B.E.E., U. Detroit, 1951; m. Mary L. Bean, Sept. 24, 1955; children—Robert, Donald, Michael, Susan, Thomas, Maureen. Elec. engr. Lake Erie Engring. Co., Buffalo, 1951-52; electro-hydraulic engr. Gen. Riveters, Inc., Buffalo, 1952-53; elec. engr. Anaconda Am. Brass, 1953-61; plant engr. Foster-Wheeler, Mountaintop, Pa., 1961-63; engring. mgr. Wall Rope Co., Beverly, N.J., 1963-64; engring. mgr. Masonite Corp., Towanda, Pa., 1964-66; asst. dir. corporate engring. Anaconda Aluminum Co., Louisville, 1966-73; v.p. engring. Russell Anaconda Aluminum, Inc., Miami, Fla., 1973—; v.p. Bluegrass Bus. Forms, Louisville. Mem. Louisville Environmental Control Com., 1971-72. Served with USMCR, 1943-46; PTO. Recipient Buckskin award Boy Scouts Am., 1973, Adviser award Jr. Achievement, 1973. Mem. Kentuckiana Constrn. Users Council, Am. Inst. Plant Engrs., I.E.E.E. Home: 7480 NW 6th Ct Plantation FL 33317 Office: 5700 NW 37th St Miami FL 33142

BAUGH, ANNETTA BERNICE, educator; b. Beaumont, Tex., June 29, 1911; d. John Milford and Carrie (Hatter) B.; A.B., Fisk U., 1932, M.A., 1939; postgrad. Tex. So. U., 1963, U. Wis., 1964, Lamar State Coll. Tech., summers 1965-70. Tchr. pub. schs. Beaumont, Tex., 1932-43; tchr. Lab. Sch., Ala. State U., Montgomery, 1943-64, instr. univ. math. dept. 1943-57, 64—. Chmn. adult program com. YMCA, 1950—. Recipient Meritorious Service awards YMCA, 1952-56; Service award Zeta Phi Beta, 1960; Service award Delta Sigma Theta, 1958; Distinguished Alumni award Fisk U., 1969; Distinguished Service award Ala. State U., 1974. Mem. Nat. Inst. Sci., Am. Assn. U. Profs., Math. Soc. Am., Ala. Edn. Assn., Ala. Assn. Student Councils (exec. sec. 1960-65), Am. Assn. U. Women, Gen. Alumni Assn. Fisk U. (v.p. S.E. region), Beta Kappa Chi (nat. sec. 1948-52), Delta Sigma Theta (life), Alpha Kappa Mu (regional dir.). Methodist. Clubs: University Women, Tuesday Players Bridge (Montgomery). Home: 1400 Deer St Montgomery AL 36106 Office: 829 S Jackson St Montgomery AL 36101

BAUGH, JOHN BERNARD, tobacco co. exec.; b. Clinton, Ind., July 11, 1915; s. George W. and Ivah Mae (Morgan) B.; grad. high sch.; m. Marjorie Agnes Fontana, June 28, 1941. Stock boy, floorman S.S. Kresge Co., Louisville, 1934-36; sec. to mgr. Montgomery Ward & Co., Louisville, 1936-37; stenographer produce and soap divs. Armour & Co., Indpls., 1937-38; sec. to TBA mgr. Standard Oil of Ky., Louisville, 1938-40; sec. to purchasing agt., asst. prodn. supr. Ferguson-Sherman Mfg. Co. (Harry Ferguson, Inc.), Detroit, 1940-43; office mgr., traffic mgr., export mgr., corporate sec. Hail & Cotton, Inc., Louisville, 1943—; dir. Internat. Tobacco Co., Inc., Greenville, N.C. Pres., bd. dirs. Success, 1964-67. Chmn. adv. bd. Salvation Army, 1971-72. Mem. Assn. Dark Leaf Tobacco Dealers (sec. 1962), Burley Leaf Tobacco Dealers Assn. (sec.-treas. 1966-67). Kiwanian. Home: 1207 Falcon Dr Louisville KY 40213 Office: 100 N 6th St Louisville KY 40202

BAUGHMAN, SAMUEL NATHAN, JR., instrumentation designer; b. St. Petersburg, Fla., Dec. 3, 1926; s. Samuel Nathan and Alice Henrietta (Eastman) B.; B.A., U. Fla., 1958; m. Joyce Elaine Wallis, Aug. 22, 1948; children—Jeff Nathan, Gail Lynn. Elec. systems designer Fla. Power Corp., St. Petersburg, 1946-53; elec. designer Ebaugh & Goethe Cons. Engrs., Gainesville, Fla., 1953-56; elec. instrumentation and mech. systems designer Black, Crow and Eidsness, Inc., Gainesville, 1958—. Mason. Home: Route 5 Box 484 Gainesville FL 32601 Office: PO Drawer 1647 Gainesville FL 32601

BAUKNIGHT, CLARENCE BROCK, wholesale, retail co. exec.; b. Anderson, S.C., May 14, 1936; s. John Edward and Theodosia (Brock) B.; m. Harriet League, June 29, 1959; children—Harriet League, Clarence Brock. Dist. mgr. Wickes Corp. (and predecessor), Atlanta, 1960-65; exec. v.p. Builder Marts of Am., Inc., Greenville, S.C., 1965-70, pres., 1970—, also dir.; dir. Citizens Builder Marts, Frank Ulmer Lumber Co. (both Greenville), Parks Lumber Co. (Gainesville, Ga.), Westwood Lumber Co. (Rocky Mount, N.C.). Mem. Indsl. Mgmt. Soc., Young Presidents Orgn., Phi Delta Theta. Methodist (adminstrv. bd.). Mason (Shriner). Clubs: Green Valley Country, Greenville Country, Poinsett (Greenville); Wildcat Cliffs (Highlands, N.C.). Home: 22 La Vista Ct Greenville SC 29601 Office: Builder Marts of Am Daniel Bldg Greenville SC 29602

BAUM, GEORGE FREDERICK, JR., investment co. exec.; b. Corsicana, Tex., Dec. 17, 1932; s. George Frederick and Priscilla Camille (Hartzell) B.; grad. Phillips Exeter Acad., 1951; student Oxford U., Eng., 1953; A.B., Harvard, 1955; LL.B., So. Meth. U., 1963; m. Catherine Margaret McLemore, May 1, 1965; children—George Frederick III, Mary Katherine, Edward McLemore, Elizabeth Hartzell. Partner, Baum Properties, 1957—; admitted to Tex. bar, 1963; enforcement atty. SEC, Fort Worth, 1963-64; estate tax atty. U.S. Treasury Dept., Dallas, 1964-66; practiced law, Dallas, 1966-69; sec., gen. counsel Capital S.W. Corp., Dallas, 1969—. Served with USAF, 1955-57. Mem. Am., Tex., Dallas bar assns., S.W. Legal Found., U.S. (nat. dir. 1963), Tex. (v.p. 1963) jr. chambers commerce, Sons Republic Tex. (1st v.p. Dallas chpt. 1973, pres. 1974), Mil. Order World Wars. Mem. Christian Ch. Club: Harvard co-chmn. schs. com. 1966-68, (Dallas). Home: 4331 Lorraine St Dallas TX 75205 Office: Merc Dallas Bldg Dallas TX 75201

BAUMBACH, DONALD OTTO, educator; b. Oil City, Pa., June 25, 1926; s. Otto Ernest and Erna Eva (Zielke) B.; B.S., Syracuse U., 1954; M.S., Pa. State U., 1959, Ph.D., 1962; m. Leona May Anderson, Oct. 26, 1962; 1 son, Timothy Donald. Chemist, Solvay Process div., Allied Chem. Corp., Moundsville, W.Va., 1954-56; research chemist Lord Mfg. Corp., Erie, Pa., 1962-65; sr. research chemist Tex. U.S. Chem. Co., Parsippany, N.J., 1965-68; asst. prof. chemistry St. Paul's Coll., Lawrenceville, Va., 1970—. Served with Signal Corps, AUS, 1944-46, 47-50; ETO. Allied Chem. Corp. fellow, Pa. State U., 1959. Mem. Sigma Xi, Phi Lambda Upsilon, Sigma Gamma Epsilon. Presbyn. (deacon 1966). Address: Box 752 St Paul's Coll Lawrenceville VA 23868

BAUMBERGER, THEODORE SHRIVER, state agy. exec.; b. Glasgow, Ky., Aug. 28, 1925; s. Perry Alvin and Helen (Shriver) B.; B.A., U. Louisville, 1949, M.A., 1950; Ph.D., U. Okla., 1961; m. JoAnn Dodson, Apr. 12, 1948; children—Erick Theodore, Andrea Leigh, Brent Lane. Exec. sec. Ky. Com. for Children and Youth, Mid-Century White House Conf., Louisville, 1950-51; adminstrv. asst., acting dir. div. sch. health Ky. Dept. Health, Louisville, 1951-52; supr. psychol. unit Okla. Dept. Instns., Social and Rehab. Services, 1954-59, supr. div. state homes and schs., 1960-68, acting supr. psychol. unit, 1960-68, adminstrv. asst., 1968-69, project dir. Juvenile Delinquency Planning Unit, Council Juvenile Delinquency, 1969—; practicum supr. Psychol. Clinic, U. Okla., 1953-54, 58-68, staff psychologist Guidance Service, 1959-60, cons. Psychol. Clinic, 1961-68, adj. asst. prof., 1963-68; individual practice psychotherapy, Norman, Okla., 1963-70; cons. psychologist Okla. Bd. Pub. Affairs, 1956-59, Peace Corps Tng. Program, U. Okla., 1965-67, Oklahoma City Bd. Edn., 1966-69, Griffin Meml. Central State Hosp., 1968—, Fed. Bur. Prisons, El Reno Reformatory 1969—, Dept. Health, Edn. and Welfare, 1971—, others; mem. profl. adv. bd. North Oklahoma City Mental Health Center. Sec. Okla. Bd. Examiners Psychologists, 1965-67, chmn., 1967-68. Mem. Okla. Gov.'s Com. on Vocational Rehab., 1966-67, Correctional Task Force, 1973—; vice-chmn. therapeutic adv. council drug abuse and alcoholism Okla. Dept. Mental Health, 1972—; mem. adv. com. Okla. Commr. Narcotics and Dangerous Drugs Control, adv. task force criminal process edn. Okla. State Regents Higher Edn., 1973, numerous others. Served with USAAF, 1943-45. Mem Am., Southwestern, Okla. (past pres.) psychol. assns., Am. Acad. Psychotherapists, Am. Group Psychotherapy Assn., Southwestern Group Psychotherapy Soc., Am. Pub. Welfare Assn., Nat. Assn. Tng. Schs. and Juvenile Agys., Nat., Okla. (mem. adv. com.) councils on crime and delinquency, Okla. Psychiat. Soc., Okla. Group Process Soc., Okla. Health and Welfare Assn., Sigma Chi Sigma, Delta Upsilon, Psi Chi, Delta Phi Alpha. Democrat. Methodist. Home: 616 NW 41st St Oklahoma City OK 73118 Office: PO Box 25352 Oklahoma City OK 73125

BAUMGARTNER, ERNEST ALLEN, relay engr., utility co. exec.; b. Houston, May 15, 1923; s. Ernest Andrew and Inez Eleanor (Dunkerley) B.; B.S. in Elec. Engring., Rice U., 1949; m. Barbara Ellen Bell, Apr. 28, 1944. Supr. relay design and coordination Gulf States Utilities Co., Beaumont, Tex., 1949-56, relay engr., 1956-65, supr. relay design, 1965—. Mem. Planning Com. Tex. A. and M. Relay Conf., 1959—. Served with USAAF, 1943-46. Registered profl. engr. Tex. Mem. I.E.E.E. (chmn. Beaumont sect. 1958-59, mem. power systems relaying com. 1965—, vice chmn. relaying practices subcom. 1969-73). Club: Pinewood Country. Contbr. articles on relay engring. to tech. mags. and publs. Home: 2875 Lakeview Circle Beaumont TX 77703 Office: PO Box 2951 Beaumont TX 77704

BAUMGARTNER, FREDERICK NEIL, mfg. co. exec.; b. Bluffton, O., June 4, 1920; s. Lysle Frederick and Eddyth Ruby (Bogart) B.; A.B., Miami U. at Oxford, O., 1942; Ph.D., U. Ill., 1948; m. Mary Pauline Wolfe, June 10, 1944; children—Sarah (Mrs. Glenn Thurow), Stephen Lysle, Richard Neil. Research chemist Esso Research & Engring. Co., Linden, N.J., 1948-57, sect. head, 1957-61, chem. tech. service adviser Esso Internat., N.Y.C., 1961, head market research, chem. dept., 1961-63, mgr. market research Esso Chem. Co., Inc., N.Y.C., 1963-65, mgr. market research Esso Chem. S.A., Brussels, Belgium, 1965-68, sr. adviser, market planning Esso Chem. Co., Inc., N.Y.C., 1968-70, mgr. corp. new ventures Enjay Chem. Co., N.Y.C., 1970-71, mgr. market research, 1971-73, mgr. market research Exxon Chem. Co., Houston, 1973—. Served to 1st lt. USAAF, 1942-46: PTO. Fellow Am. Inst. Chemists; mem. Chem. Marketing Research Assn., Am. Chem. Soc., Phi Beta Kappa, Delta Tau Delta. Presbyn. Patentee detergents, metal soaps. Home: 7525 Chevy Chase Dr Houston TX 77042 Office: 1333 W Loop S Houston TX 77001

BAUR, JOSEPH RALPH, plant physiologist; b. Indpls., May 27, 1938; s. Francis Adolph and Margaret Jane (Overman) B.; B.S., Purdue U., 1960, M.Sc., 1963; Ph.D., Tex. A. and M. U., 1967; m. Jeanette Arcaro, Jan. 14, 1961; children—Matthew James, Andrea Lynne. Weed scientist, brush control and plant growth regulators U.S. Dept. Agr., College Station, Tex., 1967—. Distbr., Amway Corp., College Station, 1969—; dir. Eljean Properties, real estate devel., College Station. Mem. Planning and Zoning Bd. College Station, 1969-70. NASA trainee, 1967-69. Mem. N.Y. Acad. Sci., Am. Soc. Plant Physiologists, Scandinavian Soc. Plant Plysiology, Soc. Exptl. Biology, Weed Sci. Soc. Am., Sigma Xi, Gamma Sigma Delta. Contbr. articles to profl. jours. Episcopalian. Home: 1100 Westover St College Station TX 77840 Office: Dept Range Sci Tex A and M Univ College Station TX 77843

BAUSSUS VON LUETZOW, HANS GERHARD, govt. scientist; b. Nortorf in Holstein, Germany, Feb. 13, 1921; s. Fritz and Dora Katharina (Hostrup) B.; came to U.S., 1956, naturalized, 1961; B.S., M.S., U. Kiel, 1949; postgrad. in econs., U. Cologne, 1953-55; Sc.D., U. Kiel, 1963; m. Helga Baroness von Luetzow, Oct. 30, 1952; children—Ulrike, Wernher, Ingo. Unit chief, dept. sect. chief, dept. br. chief Aeroballistics Lab., Army Ballistic Missile Agy., Redstone Arsenal, Ala., 1956-60; sci. adviser to dir. Aeroballistics Lab. Marshall Space Flight Center, Huntsville, Ala., 1960-62; tech. chief systems div. U.S. Army Strategy and Tactics Analysis Group, Bethesda, Md., 1962-63; prin. scientist math. and mechs. advanced programs Gen. Precision Co., Wayne, N.J., 1963-64; referent div. mil. tech. Fed. Ministry of Def., Bonn, Germany, 1964-66; sr. scientist C.E., U.S. Army, Ft. Belvoir, Va., 1966—. Cons. global atmospheric research program World Meteorological Orgn. Served to lt. German Air Force, 1940-45. Asso. fellow Am. Inst. Aeros. and Astronautics; mem. Am. Astronautical Soc. (sr.), N.Y. Acad. Scis., Am. Geophys. Union, Am. Statistic Assn. Lutheran. Home: 8021 Garlot Dr Annandale VA 22003 Office: 701 Prince St Alexandria VA 22314

BAWER, ROBERT, electronic co. exec.; b. Ellenville, N.Y., Feb. 12, 1925; s Abraham and Minnie (Slutsky) B.; B.E.E., U. Fla., 1947; M.S., Mass. Inst. Tech., 1949; postgrad. George Washington U., 1956-61; m. Norma Haas, Sept. 11, 1949; children—Joyce, Kenneth, Paula. Project engr. Melpar, Inc., Falls Church, Va., 1949-56; prin. engr. Emerson Research Labs., Washington, 1956-58; asst. dir. research Aero Geo Astro Corp., Alexandria, Va., 1958-60; with Radiation Systems, Inc., McLean, Va., 1960—, pres., 1963—. Mem. I.E.E.E., Electronic Industries Assn., Sigma Tau, Phi Kappa Phi, Sigma Xi. Home: 3529 Glenbrook Rd Fairfax VA 22030 Office: 1755 Old Meadow Rd McLean VA 22101

BAXLEY, WILLIAM ALLISON, cardiologist, educator; b. Washington, May 10, 1933; s. Haughton Whithridge and Maureen (Orr) B.; B.S., Duke, 1955, M.D., 1962; m. Mary Lynn Williams, July 15, 1956; children—Christian, David, Joseph. Intern Duke Hosp., Durham, N.C., 1962-63; resident U. Wash., Seattle; practice medicine specializing in cardiology, Birmingham, 1966-70, 72—, Albuquerque, 1970-72; asst. prof. Med. Faculty U. Ala., Birmingham, 1966-70, asso. prof., 1972—; asso. prof. Med. Faculty U. N.M., 1970-72. Served with USMCR, 1955-57. Fellow Am. Coll. Physicians, Am. Coll. Cardiology. Contbr. articles to med. jours. Home: 3848 N Woodridge Rd Birmingham AL 35223 Office: Dept of Medicine Univ Hospital Birmingham AL 35233

BAXTER, ALLIN PRESTON, lawyer; b. Sanitary Springs, N.Y., May. 1, 1929; s. Preston Lee and Violette Cordella (Regal) B.; B.A., U. Va., 1952; LL.B., George Washington U., 1957; m. Diana Hopkins, Nov. 26, 1953; children—Audrey McNair, David Hopkins. Admitted to U.S. Dist. Ct. bar, 1957, U.S. Ct. Appeals bar, 1965; atty. SEC, Washington, 1957-61; v.p., sec. Steadman Security Corp., Aberdeen Mgmt. Corp., Asso. Fund Mgmt. Corp., Asso. Mut. Funds, Washington, 1961-70; partner Jones, Baxter & Ansary, Attys., Washington, 1970—; pres. Baxter, Blyden, Selheimer & Co., Inc., Washington, 1970-73; dir. Bronwen Corp., Communications Unltd., Inc.; sec. Gold & Minerals Co., Inc. Seminar speaker Mut. Fund Seminar Assos., 1971. Served to 1st lt. AUS, 1952-54. Mem. Fed., D.C. bar assns., Nat. Lawyers Club. Clubs: Metropolitan (Washington); Monterey Country (pres. 1970-72) (Blue Ridge Summit, Pa.). Home: 4643 Kenmore Dr NW Washington DC 20007 also Monterey Circle Blue Ridge Summit PA Office: 1775 K St NW Washington DC 20006

BAXTER, GEORGE WILLIAM, JR., educator; b. Moresville, Tenn., Oct. 8, 1925; s. George William and Lenora (Long) B.; A.B., Emory U., 1946; M. Div. cum laude, Yale, 1951; M.A., George Peabody Coll., 1968, Ph.D., 1969; m. Jane Elizabeth Farrar, Aug. 28, 1959; children—George William III, Elizabeth Lynne. Instr. religion Fla. So. Coll., Lakeland, 1959-60, asst. acad. dean, registrar, 1960-66; prof., chmn. dept. psychology King Coll., Bristol, Tenn., 1969—, Mary Reynolds Babcock prof. psychology, 1970—, chmn. div. social scis., 1970—. Served with USNR, 1943-45. Mem. Am. Assn. Higher Edn., Am. Assn. U. Profs., Am., Southeast psychol. assns., Soc. Psychol. Study Social Issues, Soc. Scientific Study Religion, Va. Archeol. Assn., Phi Beta Kappa. Methodist (adminstrv. bd. 1970—). Contbr. articles to profl. publs. Home: 928 Florida Av Bristol TN 37620

BAXTER, HARRY STEVENS, lawyer; b. Ashburn, Ga., Aug. 25, 1915; s. James Hubert and Anna (Stevens) B.; A.B. summa cum laude, U. Ga., 1936, LL.B. summa cum laude, 1939; postgrad. Yale, 1939-40; m. Edith Ann Teasley, Apr. 4, 1943; children—Anna Katherine (Mrs. Paul Worley) (dec.), Nancy Julia (Mrs. John Adams Sibley III). Admitted to Ga. bar, 1941; instr. U. Ga. Law Sch., Athens, 1941; asso. Smith Kilpatrick, Cody, Rogers & McClatchey, Atlanta, 1942-51; partner Kilpatrick, Cody, Rogers, McClatchey & Regenstein, Atlanta, 1951—. Mem. State Bd. Bar Examiners Ga., 1960-66, chmn., 1961-66. Dir. Latex Contrns. Co., Atlanta. Pres., Atlanta Community Chest, 1963; mem. bd. visitors U. Ga. Law Sch., 1965-68, chmn., 1965-66, chmn. alumni adv. com. on reorgn., 1962-64; chmn. chancellor's alumni adv. com. on selection of pres. U. Ga., 1966-67; gen. co-chmn. Joint Ga. Tech.-Ga. Devel. Fund, 1967, mem. exec. com., 1968—. Trustee U. Ga. Found., chmn., 1973—; trustee William E. Honey Found. Served with AUS, 1942-45. Recipient Distinguished Alumnus award U. Ga. Law Sch., 1967. Fellow Am. Bar Found.; mem. Am. Law Inst., Am., Ga., Atlanta bar assns., Atlanta C. of C. (dir. 1959-62), Atlanta Legal Aid Soc. (pres. 1956-57), U. Ga. Alumni Soc., Phi Beta Kappa, Phi Beta Kappa Assos., Phi Kappa Phi, Omicron Delta Kappa, Phi Delta Phi, Clubs: Capital City (pres. 1965-67), Lawyers (pres. 1958-59), Piedmont Driving, Commerce, University Yacht, Atlanta City (Atlanta). Home: 3197 Chatham Rd NW Atlanta GA 30305 Office: Equitable Bldg 100 Peachtree St NW Atlanta GA 30303

BAXTER, RICHARD DUNCAN, purchasing exec.; b. Fort Payne, Ala., May 6, 1918; s. Stephen Elisha and Jessie (Duncan) B; student pub. schs.; m. Viola Nancy Ellis, Mar. 11, 1947; children—Ellis Fielding, Stephen Tyrus. Clk., So. Ry., 1936-54; traffic mgr. Kingsberry Homes Corp., 1954-56, purchasing agt., traffic mgr., 1956-64, v.p., purchasing and traffic, 1964-67; dir. purchasing and traffic Kingsberry Homes div. Boise Cascade Corp., 1967. Councilman, Fort Payne, 1948-52. Mem. DeKalb County (Ala.) Democratic Exec. Com., 1950-63, vice chmn., 1956-60. Served with USNR, 1941-46. Baptist. Author: A History of the Baxter Family of DeKalb County, Alabama, 1957; Annals of Fort Payne Baptist Church, 1964. Home: 1890 Gainsborough Dr Atlanta GA 30341 Office: 61 Perimeter Park E Atlanta GA 30341

BAY, KENNETH KING, elec. engr.; b. St. Louis, July 17, 1926; s. Lovell and June (King) B.; grad. Phillips Exeter Acad., 1944; B.S. in Physics, U. Mich., 1950; m. Jane Evertson Phillips, Oct. 24, 1951; children—Keith Alden, Deborah Lovell. Engr. Ferroxcube Corp., Am., Saugerties, N.Y., 1950-51; elec. engr. Gen. Electric Co., Syracuse, N.Y., 1951-59, Lynchburg, Va., 1959-60, project engr. Phila., 1960-62, elec. engr., Lynchburg, 1962—. Mem. Nat. Industry Adv. Com. to Fed. Communications Commn., 1967—. Mem. Lynchburg City Republican Com., 1964-70. Served with USNR, 1944-46. Mem. I.E.E.E., Am. Radio Relay League, North Am. Yacht Racing Union, Tau Beta Pi, Delta Tau Delta. Club: Va. Inland Sailing Assn. Home: 1924 Parkland Dr Lynchburg VA 24503 Office: General Electric Co Lynchburg VA 24502

BAYER, ALVIN, III, dentist; b. Jacksonville, Fla., Dec. 31, 1935; s. Alvin and Margaret (Patterson) B.; A.A., Jacksonville U., 1957; D.D.S., Emory U., 1962; student U. Fla., 1957-58; m. Renia Catherine Poe, June 17, 1961; children—Michael Alvin, Allison Marie, Renia Catherine. Practice dentistry, Fernandina Beach, Fla., 1964—; mem. staff Humphreys Meml. Hosp. Pres., Nassau Food Services, Inc., Fernandina Beach, 1965-72. Asst. fund dr. chmn. Nassau County Cancer Soc., 1968, dir., 1967-69; co-chmn. Nassau County United Fund, 1971. Served to lt. Dental Corps, USNR, 1962-64. Mem. Acad. Gen. Dentistry (Fla. pres. 1969-70, Fla. v.p. 1973-74, pres. elect 1974-75), Am., Fla., N.E. Dist. (sec.-treas. 1973-74, 2d v.p. 1974-75), Jacksonville dental assns., Am. Soc. Dentistry for Children, Am. Analgesia Soc., Am. Soc. for Preventive Dentistry, Internat. Assn. for Orthodontics, Fernandina Beach Golf Assn. (v.p. 1970, sec. 1971, dir. 1969-70), Psi Omega. Democrat, Rotarian (dir., sec.-treas. 1973-74, pres. 1974-75). Home: 1803 Parkway Fernandina Beach FL 32034 Office: 1325 Atlantic Av Fernandina Beach FL 32034

BAYLEN, JOSEPH OSCAR, educator; b. Chgo., Feb. 12, 1920; s. Leo and Mary (Lakin) B.; A.A., Wright Coll., 1939; B.E., No. Ill. U., 1941; M.A., Emory U., 1947; Ph.D., U. N.M., 1949; m. Martha Louis Pharr, Mar. 27, 1943; 1 son, James Leo. Instr. history U. N.M., 1948-49; asst. prof. history N.M. Highlands U., Las Vegas, 1950-52, asso. prof., 1952-54; prof. history, chmn. div. social sci. Delta State Tchrs. Coll., 1954-57; prof. history Miss. State U., 1957-61; prof. history U. Miss., 1961-66, chmn., 1963-66; Regents' prof., chmn. dept. history Ga. State U., 1966—; vis. asst. prof. U. Md. Overseas Program, Europe, 1952-53; vis. asso. prof. Agnes Scott Coll., 1953; vis. prof. summers, Emory U., 1952, U. Ala., 1960, Georgetown U., 1964, 1965, Tulane U., 1966, 68; Fulbright-Hays lectr. Univ. Coll. of Wales, 1961-62, U. York, 1972-73. Mem. Miss. Hist. Commn., 1954-57, 63-66; vice chmn. So. Humanities Conf., 1964-65, chmn., 1965-66; mem. Nat. Fulbright Adv. Screening Com., 1962-64, chmn., 1964-65; cons. Nat. Endowment for Humanities, 1969—; mem. Fed. Govt. Regional Archives Com., 1971—. Trustee Victorian Periodicals Research Soc. Served from pvt. to capt. AUS, 1941-45. Guggenheim fellow, 1958-59; Fulbright lectr. U.K., 1961-62, 72-73; research fellow

Inst. Advanced Studies, Princeton, 1966; summer fellowships and awards include So. Fellowship Found., 1955; Am. Philos. Soc., 1956, 65, Am. Council Learned Socs., 1961-62. Fellow Royal Hist. Soc.; mem. Am. (mem. exec. council 1972—), So. (chmn. European history sect. 1972-73) hist. assns., Conf. Brit. Studies, So. Humanities Conf., Popular Culture Assn., Am. Assn. U. Profs., Phi Kappa Phi, Omicron Delta Kappa, Phi Alpha Theta, Pi Gamma Nu, Kappa Delta Pi, Phi Kappa Tau. Author monographs: Mme. Juliette Adam, Gambetta, and the Idea of a Franco-Russian Alliance, 1960; Lord Kitchener and the Viceroyalty of India, 1910, 1965; Soldier-Surgeon; The Crimean War Letters of Dr. D.A. Reid, 1855-1856, 1968; W.T. Stead And The Russian Revolution of 1905, 1969; (with O.S. Pidhainy) East-European and Russian Studies in the American South, 1972. Bd. editors So. Humanities Rev., Miss. Quar. Contbr. articles to profl. jours. Home: 916 Barton Woods Rd NE Atlanta GA 30307

BAYLESS, JON WILLIAM, govt. scientist; b. Cordell, Okla., Apr. 17, 1940; s. Ovid Luer and Frances Ella (Adams) B.; B.S. in Elec. Engring., U. Okla., 1964; M.S. in Elec. Engring., U. Ala., 1964; Ph.D. in Engring., Ariz. State U., 1967; m. Wanda Sue Schwieter, Nov. 17, 1956; children—Jon William, Jeanne Anne. Sr. engr. govt. electronics div. Motorola Co., Scottsdale, Ariz., 1964-67; sr. specialist govt. electronic systems E Systems, Inc., Greenville, Tex., 1967-68; asst. prof. Inst. Tech., So. Meth. U., Dallas, 1968-70; tech. dir. DCA Hybrid Simulation Center, Def. Communications Agy., Reston, Va., 1970—. Adj. prof. Va. Poly. Inst. and State U., Reston Extension Campus. Pres., Moneys Corner Assn., Fairfax County, Va. Served with USAF, 1956-60. Mem. I.E.E.E., N.Y. Acad. Scis., Acoustical Soc. Am., Tau Beta Pi, Eta Kappa Nu, Sigma Tau, Phi Eta Sigma. Rotarian. Author: (with others) Circuit Analysis: With Emphasis on Computer Usage, 1972. Home: 12307 Delevan Dr Herndon VA 22070 Office: Def Communications Engring Center 1860 Wiehle Av Reston VA 22090

BAYLESS, ROBERT PAUL, civil engr.; b. Cullman, Ala., Feb. 3, 1932; s. Clarence M. and Myrtle (Silvey) B.; B.C.E., U. Fla., 1959; m. Florence Emily Pace, Dec. 24, 1954; children—Catherine Jane, Stephanie Jo. with Rader & Asso. Engrs., St. Petersburg, Fla., 1959-61, Misener Marine Constrn., Inc., St. Petersburg, 1961-62; project engr. Black, Crow & Eidsness Assos., Engrs., Clearwater, Fla., 1962-65; designer, project engr. Misener Marine Constrn., Inc., St. Petersburg Beach, 1965-69, v.p. engring. and sales, 1969-72; pres. Gulf Found., Inc., St. Petersburg, 1972—. Served with USNR, 1951-55. Registered profl. engr., Fla., Ga., Tex. Mem. Am. Soc. C.E., Nat. Soc. Profl. Engrs., Fla. Engring. Soc. Democrat. Baptist. Kiwanian. Office: 500 64th St S St Petersburg FL 33707

BAYLIN, GEORGE JAY, educator, radiologist; b. Balt., May 15, 1911; s. Morris Jacob and Pauline (Shulman) B.; A.B., Johns Hopkins, 1931; M.D., Duke, 1937; m. Sarah Hartman, July 10, 1938; children—Stephen Bruce, Jon Frank, Eric. Intern surgery Sinai Hosp., Balt., 1937-38; fellow pathology Guys Hosp., London, Eng., 1938-39; resident radiology Duke Med. Sch., 1939-41, instr., 1941-43, asst. prof., 1943-46, asso. prof., 1946-50, prof. radiology, 1950-74, prof. otolaryngology, 1974—; practice medicine specializing in radiology, Durham, N.C.; chief ear, nose and throat div. radiology Duke Hosp., 1973—; cons. radiologist VA, 1960—. Chmn. Duke div. United Community Fund, 1958—; mem. exec. bd. United Med. Services, Durham, 1965-70. Bd. dirs. Cancer Com., Duke Med. Sch., 1950-54. Recipient Gold Medal award for research N.C. Med. Soc., 1955, Golden Apple award for teaching Student A.M.A., 1968. Fellow Am. Coll. Radiologists; mem. Am. Coll. Radiology, N.C. Radiology Soc. (chmn. 1958), So. Med. Soc., Sigma Xi, Alpha Omega Alpha. Contbr. articles to profl. jours. Home: 2535 Wrightwood Av Durham NC 27705

BAYNE, JAMES MANUEL, architect; b. Piggott, Ark., Dec. 24, 1928; s. Manley Earl and Mabel (Hodges) B.; B.S. in Archtl. Engring., U. Ill., 1951; postgrad. U. Miami, 1955, Lawrence Inst. Tech., 1955; A.M.P., Harvard, 1971; m. Melba Lois Beckmeyer, June 5, 1951; children—Melanie Lee, Melissa Ann. Structural engr. Smith, Hinchman & Grylls, Detroit, 1951-53, architect 1955-61; architect, chief of planning and design Manned Spacecraft Center., NASA, Houston, 1961-66, architect, chief of constrn. Electronics Research Center, NASA, Cambridge, Mass., 1967-70, dir. design and constrn. NASA, Washington, 1970-71, dir. programs and engring., 1971—. Instr. archtl. design and art Detroit Inst. Tech., 1956-61. Served with C.E., AUS, 1953-55. Mem. A.I.A., Tex. Soc. Architects, Mich. Assn. Professions, Pi Kappa Phi. Clubs: Illini, Harvard Business School (Washington). Home: 4902 Tarheel Way Annandale VA 22003 Office: 600 Independence Av SW Washington DC 20546

BAZELON, DAVID LIONEL, judge; b. Superior, Wis., Sept. 3, 1909; s. Israel and Lena (Krasnovsky) B.; student U. Ill., 1928-29; B.S. in Law, Northwestern U., 1931; LL.D., Colby Coll., 1966; LL.D., Boston U., 1969, Albert Einstein Coll. Medicine, Yeshiva U., 1972; m. Miriam M. Kellner, June 7, 1936; children—James A., Richard Lee. Admitted to Ill. bar, 1932, practiced law, 1932-35; asst. U.S. atty. No. Dist. Ill., in charge fed. tax matters, 1935-40; sr. mem. firm Gottlieb & Schwartz, 1940-46; asst. atty. gen. U.S. Lands Div., 1946-47, Office of Allen Property, 1947-49; judge U.S. Ct. of Appeals for D.C. Circuit, 1949—, chief judge, 1962—. Lectr. law and psychiatry U. Pa. Law Sch., 1957-58, 58-59; Sloan vis. prof. Menninger Found., Topeka, 1961-62; Regent's lectr. U. Cal., Los Angeles, 1964; mem. faculty dept. psychiatry Johns Hopkins U. Sch. Medicine, 1964—; clin. prof. psychiatry George Washington U., 1966—. Chmn. task force on law President's Panel on Mental Retardation; cons. to HEW on guidelines for sterilization of minors and legally incompetent individuals, 1973—; chmn. adv. com., model sch. div. D.C. Pub. Schs., 1964-66; mem. adv. com. Harvard U. Program Tech. and Soc., 1966-71; nat. adv. mental health council USPHS, 1967-71; bd. dirs. Joint Commn. Mental Health Children, Inc., 1965-70; mem. nat. adv. com. John F. Kennedy Center Research Edn. and Human Devel., 1968—; mem. com. on ethics Am. Heart Assn., 1968—; mem. Battelle-N.W. Behavioral and Social Sci. Cons. Panel, 1970; chmn. adv. bd. Boston U. Center for Law and Life Scis., 1970—; bd. dirs. Citizens Bd. Inquiry into Health Services for Ams., Washington, 1969-71; mem. adv. com. on child devel. Nat. Research Council of Nat. Acad. Scis., 1971—; mem. Twentieth Century Fund Task Force on Working Women, 1970—; mem. U.S. Mission on Mental Health to USSR, 1967. Bd. overseers Brandeis U. Center for Study of Violence; trustee Salk Inst. Biol. Studies. Recipient Isaac Ray award Am. Psychiat. Assn., 1960. Fellow Am. Psychiat. Assn. (hon.), Am. Acad. Arts and Scis.; mem. Am. Orthopsychiat. Assn. (pres.), Am. (commn. on mentally disabled 1973-74), Fed. bar assns., Bar Assn. D.C., Nat. Assn. State Mental Health Program Dirs. (adv. council), Am. Psychol. Assn. Democrat. Jewish religion. Club: Cosmos. Home: 2700 Virginia Av NW Washington DC 20037 Office: US Ct House Washington DC 20001

BEACH, DERYL ERWIN, accountant; b. Pearsall, Tex., Jan. 12, 1924; s. Elmer Clare and Nell (Little) B.; student Trinity U., 1946-47; B.B.A., S.W. Tex. State Tchrs. Coll., 1949; m. Charlyne Barrett, Dec. 21, 1946; children—Bradley Deryl, Barrett Allen. With Aikman & Aikman, Accountants, San Antonio, 1949, Internal Revenue Service, Corpus Christi and Kerrville, Tex., 1950-56, W.L. Robinson, Accountant, Kerrville, 1956, Ziegler, Weiner & Gill, C.P.A.'s, Dallas, 1957; practice accounting, Kerrville, 1957—. Mem. Kerrville Ind. Sch. Dist. Bd., 1973—. Served with USAAF, 1942-45; ETO. Decorated Purple Heart, Air Medal. Mem. Tex. Soc. C.P.A.'s. Mason. Home: Rt 1 Box 238 Kerrville TX 78028 Office: PO Box 1444 Kerrville TX 78028

BEACH, LEWIS CONNER, oil co. exec.; b. Lansing, Mich., Aug. 21, 1933; s. David E. and Elda (Anderson) B.; student Okla. Mil. Acad., 1951-53; B.S. in Geology, U. Tulsa, 1956; m. Billie Joan Campbell, Mar. 4, 1972. Div. mgr. Great Lakes Petroleum Service, Oklahoma City, 1964-66; mgr. prodn. Pawnee Petroleum Co., Tulsa, 1966-67; geol. engr. KWB Corp., Tulsa, 1967-68; pres. Beach Operating Co., Tulsa, 1968—. Served with AUS, 1957-59. Registered profl. engr., Okla. Mem. Soc. Petroleum Engrs., Okla. Ind. Petroleum Assn., Nat., Okla. socs. profl. engrs., Ind. Petroleum Assn. Am., Oklahoma City Geol. Soc., Sigma Gamma Epsilon. Republican. Club: Petroleum (Tulsa). Home: 505 Meadowood Dr Broken Arrow OK 74012 Office: Mayo Bldg Tulsa OK 74103

BEACH, LOUIS ANDREW, physicist; b. Greenville, Ind., June 2, 1925; s. George Covert and Clara (Kiesler) B.; B.S., Ind. U., 1944, M.S., 1947, Ph.D., 1949; m. Virginia Ann McHugh, Oct. 20, 1956; children—Andrew, Ann Marie, Ruth Christine, Covert John. Research asso. Lab. Nuclear Studies, Cornell U., 1949-51; physicist Naval Research Lab., Washington, 1951—, head shielding sect., 1953-55, head nuclear reactions br., 1955-66, head physics I sect., cyclotron br., 1966-71, head nuclear physics sect., 1971—. Lectr. grad. program nuclear engring. Catholic U. Am., 1960-66. Served with AUS, 1944-46. Fellow Washington Acad. Sci.; mem. Am. Phys. Soc., A.A.A.S., Philos. Soc. Wash. Democrat. Roman Catholic. Home: 1200 Waynewood Blvd Alexandria VA 22308 Office: Code 6611 Naval Research Lab Washington DC 20375

BEACH, ROBERT OLIVER, computer exec.; b. Washington, June 25, 1932; s. Oliver Fairmont and Aldora (Stone) B.; student George Washington U., 1950-51, 57-62; m. Patricia Carrington, May 9, 1952 (div.); children—Patricia Ann, Robert Edward, Michael Oliver, John Roger. With Engring. Research Corp., 1951-52; design engr. Nems-Clarke, 1952-55; project engr. Frederick Research Corp., 1955-59; project mgr. Am. Machine & Foundry Co., 1959-62; pres., founder SAID, Inc., Falls Church, Va., 1962—; pres. Quick Copy, Inc., 1972—; real estate broker; comml. airplane pilot; cons. marketing and finance; v.p. Interstate Service Corp.; high sch. faculty adviser devel. data processing curriculum, 1971. Mem. Data Processing Mgmt. Assn., UNIVAC Users Assn., Aircraft Owners and Pilots Assn. Home: 500 N Roosevelt Blvd Falls Church VA 22044 Office: 1243 W Broad St Falls Church VA 22046

BEACH, WALTER EGGERT, assn. exec.; b. North Adams, Mass., Aug. 24, 1934; s. W. Edwards and Liselotte Josephine Sophie (von Usedom) B.; B.A., Dickinson Coll., 1956; M.A., George Washington U., 1961. Staff asso. Am. Polit. Sci. Assn., Washington, 1965-68, asst. dir., 1968—, editor PS, 1970—. Bd. dirs. Mt. Vernon Coll., Washington; trustee Prevention of Blindness Soc. Met. Washington. Served with AUS, 1956-58. Home: 5719 Chevy Chase Pkwy NW Washington DC 20015 Office: 1527 New Hampshire Av NW Washington DC 20036

BEACHAM, WOODARD DAVIS, physician; b. McComb, Miss., Apr. 10, 1911; s. Woodard D. and Ida (Felder) B.; B.A., U. Miss., 1932; B.S. 1933; M.D., Tulane U., 1935. Intern Charity Hosp. of La., New Orleans, resident obstetrics and gynecology; now sr. vis. surgeon; prof. clin. gynecology and obstetrics Tulane U. Sch. Medicine, 1949—; obstetrician and gynecologist So. Bapt. Hosp., pres. staff, 1961; past pres. surg. staff Charity Hosp., New Orleans; cons. Beacham Meml. Hosp. Magnolia, Miss., Hotel Dieu Sisters Hosp., New Orleans, Methodist Hosp., New Orleans; practice medicine specializing in obstetrics and gynecology, 1940—; Pres. Beacham Corp. Recipient A.C.S. medical records prize, 1943. Diplomate Am. Bd. Obstetrics and Gynecology. Fellow A.C.S. (gov. as rep. obstet., gynecol. sect. A.M.A. 1955-60, gov. as rep. Am. Gynecol. Soc. 1961-63; adv. council gynecology and obstetrics 1963-67, chmn. council 1967, past pres. La. chpt., 2d v.p. 1972-73), Am. Gynecol. Soc. (council 1959, 60), Am. Assn. Obstetricians and Gynecologists (com. on material welfare 1960, v.p. 1970-71), Am. Coll. Obstetricians and Gynecologists (first pres., nominating com. 1972, liaison com. with Internat. Fedn. Gynecology and Obstetrics 1973—); mem. So. Gynecol. and Obstet. Soc. (pres. 1967), Am. (chmn. sect. obstetrics and gynecology 1957-58), So. (chmn. sect. on obstetrics 1949, mem. council 1961-63, gen. chmn. arrangements ann. meeting 1972, 2d v.p. 1972, 1st v.p. 1973) med. assns., Internat. House (founder; dir. 1974), Internat. Trade Mart, C. of C., La., Orleans Parish med. socs., New Orleans Grad. Med. Assembly (past pres.), New Orleans Gynecol. and Obstet. Soc. (past pres.), Conrad G. Collins Obstetric and Gynecologic Soc. Tulane U. (1st pres.), Central Assn. Obstetricians and Gynecologists (exec. com. 1948-52), Am. Assn. Med. Colls., U. Miss. Alumni Assn. (dir. 1962-65, past pres. New Orleans), Philippine Obstet. and Gynecol. Soc. (hon.), A.A.A.S., Assn. Profs. Gynecology and Obstetrics, Peruvian (hon.), Paraguayan (hon.) obstet. and gynecol. socs., Tulane Med. Alumni Assn. (sec. 1971-73, v.p. 1974—), Sigma XI, Alpha Omega Alpha, Phi Chi (grand presiding sr., nat. pres. 1970-73, trustee 1973—), Beta Theta Pi. Methodist (trustee, mem. adminstrv. bd.) Clubs: Plimsoll, New Orleans Country. Author: (with Robert J. Crossen and Dan W. Beacham) Synopsis of Gynecology (5th edit.), (with Dan W. Beacham) 6th edit., 1963, 7th edit., 1967, 8th edit., 1972. Editor for gynecology and obstetrics Stedman's Med. Dictionary, 23d edit. Contbr. to publs. in field. Home: 1527 S Carrollton Av New Orleans LA 70118 Office: 4240 Magnolia at General Pershing St New Orleans LA 70115

BEACOM, JOHN PATRICK, broadcasting exec., mayor; b. St. Joseph, Mo., May 27, 1905; s. Timothy Patrick and Mary (Davies) B.; student Omaha U., 1923-25, U. Tulsa, 1925-27; B.A., Marshall Coll., 1930; m. Emily May Peed, July 15, 1955; children—Mary Davies, George Patrick. U.S. Army Sch. Mil. Govt., Charlottesville, Va., 1942—; pres., owner Beacom Broadcasting Enterprises, WDTV, Fairmont, W. Va., WTVX, Ft. Pierce, Fla., WVVW, Grafton, W. Va., WETZ, New Martinsville, W. Va., WBUT AM-FM, Butler, Pa., WAC-Y, Kissimee, Fla.; pub. pres. Mannington (W. Va.) Times. Mem. W.Va. Ho. of Reps., 1933-35, W.Va. Senate 1935-40; city dir., mayor, Fairmont, 1955-60; mayor City of St. Lucie (Fla.), 1965—. Mem. W. Va. Athletic Commn., 1950-53. Chmn., St. Lucie County Republican Exec. Com., 1970—. Mem. C. of C. (dir.). Clubs: University Nat. Broadcasters (Washington); Variety (Pitts.); Pelican Yacht, St. Lucie Country (Ft. Pierce). Home: 2811 N Indian River Dr St Lucie FL 33450 Office: Beacom Bldg 101 Atlantic Av Fort Pierce FL 33450

BEADLES, ARLON GLENN, educator; b. Sulphur Springs, Tex., Jan. 6, 1941; s. Arlon Woodrow and Ruth Marie (Hoover) B.; A.A., Southwestern Coll., Oklahoma City, 1962; B.S., Bethany Nazarene Coll., 1964; M.Teaching, Central State U., Edmond, Okla., 1966; m. Patricia Ann Tignor, May 30, 1964; children—Gregory Glenn, Traci Gail. Tchr., coach Southwestern High Sch., Oklahoma City, 1966-64; mem. faculty coach basketball Oklahoma City Southwestern Jr. Coll., 1966-69, dean student affairs, 1970, head dept. health and phys. edn., coach basketball, athletic dir., 1971—. Recipient Outstanding Faculty award Oklahoma City Southwestern Jr. Coll., 1968, Merit award, 1971. Mem. Nat., Okla. edn. assns., Nat. Jr. Coll. Coach Assn., Okla. Coach Assn. Democrat. Mem. Pentecostal Ch. (deacon, lay pastor, dir. lifeliners 1971—). Home: Route 2 Tuttle OK 73089

BEADLES, BOYD JAMES, food broker co. exec.; b. Vicksburg, Miss., July 17, 1920; s. Charles Calloway and Carrie Elizabeth (Browder) B.; student N.E. La. Jr. Coll., 1938-39; m. Beverley Jean Folmar, Jan. 23, 1940; children—Larry, Steve, Linda (Mrs. Fred Traylor), James. Salesman, Borden Co., Houston, 1940-42; sales mgr. Wright & Co., Inc., Shreveport, La., 1946-58; pres., Beadles & Wright, Inc., Shreveport, La., 1958—; dir. Shreve Mortgage Corp. Served with AUS, 1943-45. Decorated Purple Heart. Mem. Am. Legion, Shreveport Food Brokers Assn. (pres. 1956), Shreveport Allied Food Club (pres. 1963, chmn. scholarship com. 1970—), C. of C. (chmn. distbn. com. 1973—), Shreveport Sports Found. Methodist. Mason, Elk. Club: Petroleum (Shreveport). Home: 3825 Truett Blvd Shreveport LA 71107 Office: 1132 Silverlake Dr Shreveport LA 71101

BEAIRD, CHARLES T., machinery co. exec., educator; b. Shreveport, La., July 17, 1922; s. James Benjamin and Mattie Connell (Fort) B.; B.A., Centenary Coll., 1966; Ph.D. in Philosophy Columbia, 1972; m. Carolyn Williams, Feb. 6, 1943; children—Susan (Mrs. George M. McCormick), Marjorie (Mrs. M. Buie Seawell, Jr.), John B. Vice pres., gen. mgr. J.B. Beaird Corp., Shreveport, 1946-57; self employed in oil and investments, Shreveport, 1957-59; pres. Beaird-Poulan Inc., Shreveport, 1959-73; chmn. bd. Beaird-Poulan div. Emerson Electric Co., 1973—; dir. Westport Devel. Corp.; dir. Fed. Res. Bd. Dallas, 1972—, dep. chmn., 1973—. Asst. prof. Centenary Coll., Shreveport, 1969—. Chmn. United Fund Campaign, 1962; mem. Caddo Parish Police Jury, 1956-60. Chmn. Caddo Parish Republican Exec. Com., 1952-56; del. Rep. Nat. Conv., 1956. Pres. Charles T. Beaird Found. Served to capt. USMCR, 1943-46. Decorated D.F.C., Air medal. Mem. C. of C. (v.p. 1965-66). Clubs: Shreveport, Shreveport Country, Demolselle (Shreveport). Home: 7030 E Ridge Dr Shreveport LA 71106 Office: PO Box 9329 Shreveport LA 71109

BEAL, ERNEST OSCAR, educator; b. Lancaster, Ill., Mar. 7, 1928; s. Oscar Elmer and Ruth Ethel (Smith) B.; B.A., N. Central Coll., 1950; M.S., State U. Ia., 1952, Ph.D., 1955; m. Sara Lou Fromm, Aug. 30, 1946; children—Ann Louise, Thomas Loren, Kenneth Ernest. Asst. prof. N.C. State U., Raleigh, 1954-60, asso. prof., 1960-65, prof. botany, 1965-69; head dept. biology Western Ky. U., Bowling Green, 1968—. Mem. Rural Ky. Med. Scholarship Fund., 1971—. Recipient Research award Assn. Southeastern Biologists, 1966, Outstanding Tchr. award N.C. State U., 1968. Fellow A.A.A.S.; mem. Ecol. Soc. Am., Bot. Soc. Am., Am. Assn. Plant Taxonomists, Internat. Assn. Plant Taxonomy, Am. Inst. Biol. Scis., A.A.A.S., Assn. Southeastern Biologists. Home: 1023 Highland Dr Bowling Green KY 42101

BEALE, HOBART H., physician; b. Martin, Tenn., Sept. 19, 1936; s. Harry Hobart and Helen Deborah (Brooks) B.; student U. Miss., 1954-55; D.D.S., U. Tenn., 1959, M.D., 1967; m. Patsy Ann Nanney, June 1, 1957; children—Julie Ann, Bonnie Lynn. Pvt. practice dentistry, Albertville, Ala., 1962-64; intern Tampa (Fla.) Gen. Hosp., 1967-68; practice medicine Martin, Tenn., 1968—; mem. staff Volunteer Gen. Hosp., Martin. Dir. student health U. Tenn. at Martin, 1968-70; city health officer Martin, 1970-73. Served to capt. AUS, 1960-62. Mem. N.W. Tenn., Tenn. med. assns., A.M.A., Delta Sigma Delta, Sigma Nu. Baptist. Mason. Home: Hawks Rd Martin TN 38237 Office: Kennedy Dr Martin TN 38237

BEALE, ROBERT VINCENT, lawyer; b. Norfolk, Va., Jan. 10, 1936; s. Robert Harrison and Ella Virginia (Vincent) B.; student Med. Coll. of Va. Pharmacy Sch., 1955-56; B.S. in Bus. Adminstrn., U. Richmond, 1961, J.D., 1964; m. Joan Marilyn Turner, Feb. 15, 1959; 1 son, Mark Douglas. Clk. accounting dept. Seaboard R.R., 1956-59; admitted to Va. bar, 1964; asst. city atty. Newport News, Va., 1964-68, city atty., legal adviser City Council, City Mgr. and all dept. heads, 1968-70; partner firm Bateman, West & Beale, Newport News, 1970—. Bd. dirs. Newport News Econ. Opportunity Com., 1967-68; counsel Newport News Sch. Bd., 1968—; mem. Newport News Council com. on disposition, devel. pub. property, 1968-70, Oyster Point com. plan, devel. 632A publicly owned property for research, 1968-70; commr. Peninsular Ports Authority of Va., 1972—. Mem. Va., Newport News bar assns., Va. Trial Lawyers Assn., Nat. Sch. Bd. Assn. Council Sch. Bd. Attys. Lion. Clubs: Peninsula Executives, Warwick Yacht and Country (both Newport News). Home: 26 Hilton Terrace Newport News VA 23601 Office: 11048 Warwick Blvd Newport News VA 23601

BEALLE, JOHN RUFUS, lawyer, univ. ofcl.; b. Tuscaloosa, Ala., May 6, 1918; s. John Rufus and Josie (Bell) B.; A.B., U. Ala., 1940, J.D., 1942; m. Elizabeth Ann Turner, Oct. 26, 1948; children—John Rufus, Sally Hays. Admitted to Ala. bar, 1942, partner firm Davis and Bealle, Tuscaloosa, 1946-49; county solicitor, Tuscaloosa County, 1949-51; city atty., Northport, Ala., 1952-54; atty., land commr., sec. bd. trustees U. Ala., 1953-69, sec. bd. trustees, gen. counsel, 1969—, v.p., 1974—. Supr. in bankruptcy Western div. No. Dist. Ala., 1946-48. Past chmn. Tuscaloosa County Bd. Pub. Welfare. Pres. Black Warrior council Boy Scouts Am., 1961; v.p. Tuscaloosa County United Fund, 1962. Mem. exec. com., Tuscaloosa County Democratic Com., 1946-60, sec., 1947-60, chmn., 1946-47. Treas. U. Ala. Law Sch. Found. Served from 2d lt. to maj. A.A.A., AUS, 1942-46: now col. Res. ret. Past chmn. Ala. Jr. Bar Assn. Mem. Nat. Assn. Coll. and Univ. Attys. (dir. 1962-72, v.p. 1966, pres. 1969-70), U. Ala. Law Sch. Alumni Assn. (sec., treas. 1949). Res. Officers Assn. (pres. Tuscaloosa 1947, pres. Ala. dept. 1962), Am. Bar Assn., Newcomen Soc. N. Am., Omicron Delta Kappa, Pi Kappa Alpha, Phi Delta Phi. Presbyn. (elder). Home: 194 The Highlands Tuscaloosa AL 35401 Office: U Ala University AL 35486

BEAMAN, LESTER HENRY, clergyman; b. Enid, Okla., Dec. 8, 1936; s. Henry Virgil and Evelyn (Setchell) B.; B.Th., N.W. Christian Coll., 1966; M.Div., Lexington Theol. Sem., 1969; m. Lois Evan Barnard, Feb. 6, 1959; children—Bonnie Lee, Cheri Lynn. Ordained to ministry Christian Ch., 1966; minister Irving Ch., Eugene, Ore., 1964-66, Somerset Ch., Mt. Sterling, Ky., 1966-68, Chaplin Ch. (Ky.), 1968-69, 1st Chs., Forrest City, Ark., 1969-71, Searcy, Ark., 1971—. Youth camp dir., Ark., 1970, 72, 73; condr. Christian edn. workshops various chs., 1970, 73; tchr. classes for ministers on consultation on ch. unity, Forrest City; chmn. regional dept. ministry and worship Christian Ch. in Ark., 1971—, mem. dept. Christian edn. and dept. financial promotion and interpretation, 1969-71. Religious awards chmn. White River Dist. Boy Scouts Am., 1973; mem. exec. bd. White County Mental Health Assn., 1972—. Served with AUS, 1954-57. Recipient commendation Forrest City Human Relations Council, 1971. Mem. Searcy Area Ministerial Alliance (pres. 1973). Home: 311 E Center St Searcy AR 72143 Office: Main and Market Sts Searcy AR 72143

BEAMAN, NATHANIEL, III, banker; b. Norfolk, Va., Apr. 29, 1925; s. Robert P. and Salome (Slingluff) B.; A.B. Duke, 1945, J.D., 1949; m. Elizabeth Middleton Dashiell, Dec. 28, 1950;

children—Nathaniel IV, Elizabeth Johns, William Prentis. Admitted to Va. bar, 1949; practiced in Norfolk, 1949-50, 62-66, asso. firm Breeden & Hoffman, 1949-50; asso. trust officer First Citizens Bank & Trust Co., Raleigh, N.C., 1952-54; v.p., trust officer So. Bank of Norfolk, 1955-62; v.p., trust officer First & Mchts. Nat. Bank, Norfolk, 1966—, dir. Norfolk adv. bd. 1967-73; pres., dir. So. Ins. Agy. Treas. DePaul Hosp. Bldg. Fund; bd. dirs. Tidewater (Va.) Heart Assn.; trustee Norfolk Found., Portsmouth Community Trust; vice chmn. bd. Norfolk City Employees Retirement Trust, 1970-74; exec. com. Tidewater Estate Planning Council. Served to lt. USNR, 1943-46, 50-52. Mem. Tidewater Duke Alumni Assn. (v.p.), Am., Va., Norfolk-Portsmouth bar assns., Va. Bankers Assn., Norfolk Assembly, Navy League, English Speaking Union, Kappa Alpha, Phi Delta Phi. Episcopalian. Clubs: Norfolk German (sec.), Norfolk Yacht and Country, Harbor (Norfolk). Home: 5220 Edgewater Dr Norfolk VA 23508 Office: One Bank St Norfolk VA 23510

BEAMES, CALVIN GREENWOOD, JR., educator; b. Kingston, Okla., Oct. 29, 1930; s. Calvin Greenwood and Grace Loree (Chesnut) B.; A.B., (Cancer Soc. Research fellow), N.M. Highlands U., 1955, M.S., 1956; Ph.D., U. Okla., 1961; m. Joyce Charlene Smith, June 1, 1952; children—Deborah Lee, Calvin Greenwood III, Rebecca Ann. Tchr. high sch. biology Santa Fe, 1956-57; mem. faculty Okla. State U., Stillwater, 1962—, asso. prof. physiology, 1963-70, prof., 1970—. Served with 45th Inf. Div., AUS, 1950-52. NIH postdoctoral fellow, Rice U., Houston, 1961-62, traineeship, 1960-61, recipient NIH research grants, 1964—. Mem. Am. Physiol. Soc., A.A.A.S., Am. Soc. Zoologists, Am. Chem. Soc., Am. Soc. Parasitologists, Okla. Acad. Sci., Sigma Xi, Phi Sigma, Phi Lambda Upsilon, Phi Zeta. Home: 2222 Glenwood Dr Stillwater OK 74074 Office: Dept Physiological Sciences Okla State Univ Stillwater OK 74074

BEAMS, JESSE WAKEFIELD, educator; b. Belle Plaine, Kan., Dec. 25, 1898; s. Jesse Wakefield and Kathryn (Wylie) B.; A.B., Fairmount (Kan.) Coll., 1921; M.A., U. Wis., 1922; Ph.D., U. Va., 1925; Sc.D., William and Mary Coll., 1941; Sc.D., U. N.C., 1946; Sc.D., Washington and Lee U., 1949; Sc.D., Fla. Inst. Tech., 1969; m. Maxine Sutherland, June 16, 1931. Instr. physics and math. Ala. Poly. Inst., 1922-23; Nat. Research fellow U. Va., 1925-26, Yale, 1926-27; instr. physics Yale, 1927-28; asso. prof. physics U. Va., Charlottesville, 1928-30, prof., 1930-69, prof. emeritus, 1969—, Francis H. Smith prof. physics, chmn. dept. physics, 1948-62. Recipient Potts medal Franklin Inst., 1942; John Scott award, 1956; Alumni Achievement award U. Wichita; Thomas Jefferson award, Nat. medal Sci., 1967. Fellow Am. Phys. Soc. (pres. 1958-59), A.A.A.S. (chmn. sect. B., 1943); mem. Am. Acad. Arts and Scis., Am. Philos. Soc. (Lewis award 1958, v.p. 1960-62), Am. Optical Soc., Va. Acad. Sci. (pres. 1947), Am. Physics Tchrs. Assn., Am. Assn. U. Profs., Nat. Acad. Scis., Phi Beta Kappa, Sigma Xi, Sigma Pi Sigma (hon.), Raven Soc. Club: Colonnade. Contbr. numerous articles to profl. jours. Home: 1705 Kenwood Lane Charlottesville VA 22901

BEAN, ALAN L., astronaut; b. Wheeler, Tex., Mar. 15, 1932; s. Arnold H. Bean; B.S. in Aero. Engring., U. Tex., 1955; grad. U.S. Navy Test Pilot Sch.; postgrad. U. So. Cal. Sch. Aviation Safety; m. Sue Ragsdale; children—Clay, Amy Sue. Commd. ensign U.S. Navy, 1955, advanced through grades to capt.; project officer various aircraft for preliminary evaluation, initial trials, final bd. inspection and survey trials. Patuxent, Md., 1960-63; replacement pilot Attack Squadron 44, Cecil Field, Fla., 1963, then Attack Squadron 172; astronaut with Manned Spacecraft Center, NASA, 1963—; lunar module pilot Apollo XII flight to moon, 1969; spacecraft comdr. Skylab Mission II, 1973. Decorated D.S.M.; recipient Distinguished Service medal NASA, Man of Year award Tex. Press Assn., 1969, Rear Adm. William S. Parsons award for sci. and tech. progress, 1970; Distinguished Grad. award U. Tex., 1970, Distinguished Alumnus award, 1970; Godfrey L. Cabot award, 1970, Spl. Trustees award Nat. Acad. TV Arts and Scis., 1970. Fellow Am. Astronautical Soc.; mem. Soc. Exptl. Test Pilots, Delta Kappa Epsilon. Home: 18706 Point Lookout Dr Houston TX 77058 Office: Johnson Space Center NASA Houston TX 77058

BEAN, CHARLES FOLSOM, educator; b. Bellwood, Ill., Sept. 13, 1926; s. Folsom Spencer and Eleanor Ann (Oliver) B.; Ph.B., Northwestern U., 1959; M.Engring., U. So. Fla., 1968; m. Ellen Dora Airey, Feb. 21, 1953; children—Laura Ellen, Jason Douglas. With Internat. Minerals & Chem. Corp., Chgo. and Fla., 1943-68, process engr., 1956-62, prodn. control supr., 1962-68; asst. prof. U. So. Fla., Tampa, 1968—. Registered profl. engr., Fla. Mem. World Future Soc., Operations Research Soc. Am., Am. Inst. Indsl. Engrs. (chpt. pres. 1973-74). Clubs: Torch, Nat. Rifle Assn. Home: Route 1 Box 127 Land O'Lakes FL 33539 Office: College Engineering Univ So Fla Tampa FL 33620

BEAN, LORENZO LEE, JR., lawyer; b. Fort Meade, Fla., Mar. 10, 1916; s. Lorenzo Lee and Adelaide (Dortch) B.; student Hampden-Sydney Coll., 1934-35, 37-38; LL.B., U. Va., 1941; m. Maxine Lucy Hay, June 18, 1949; children—Rebecca Ann, Lorenzo Lee III, Meredith Lee. Admitted to Va. bar, 1940; atty. Rural Electrification Adminstrn., Washington, also St. Louis, 1941-47; practice law, Arlington, Va., 1947—. Adv. Bd. Washington & Lee Savs. & Loan Assn., 1972—. Chmn. Infantile Paralysis Found., Arlington, 1956-59; pres. Nat. Orthopaedic and Rehab. Hosp., Arlington, 1958-64, legal adv., 1964-72; vice chmn. Arlington chpt. Boy Scouts Am., 1957-58. Chmn. Bd. Zoning Appeals Arlington County, 1954-57; vice chmn. Juvenile Detention Commn. No. Va., 1957; mem. Arlington County Sch. Bd., 1958-61, chmn., 1959-60. Trustee, legal advisor Methodist Bd. Missions and Ch. Extension, 1951—, Methodist Bd. Edn., 1956—; mem. No. Va. Adv. Bd. Hermitage, 1960—; bd. dirs., vice chmn. Arlington YMCA, 1958—; mem. bd. vis. Radford (Va.) Coll., 1963-71. Named Outstanding Young Man of Va., Va. Jr. C. of C., 1950, Profl. Man of the Year Arlington C. of C., 1958, Boss of the Year Arlington Jaycees, 1971. Mem. Am., Va. State, Arlington County (pres. 1961-62) bar assns., Va. State Bar, Am. Trial Lawyers Assn. (dir. 1962—, pres. 1966-67), Va. (pres. 1951), Arlington (pres. 1950) jr. chambers of commerce, Arlington Council Chs. (dir., pres. 1956-57), Am. Automobile Assn. (No. Va. adv. bd. 1955—, chmn. 1955-57, 74—), Omicron Delta Kappa, Phi Alpha Delta, Chi Phi, Hampden-Sydney Circle. Methodist. Home: 3820 N 37th St Arlington VA 22207 Office: 2045 15th St N Arlington VA 22201

BEANE, JOHN WALTERS, dentist; b. Lake Worth, Fla., Dec. 4, 1928; s. Edgar Graham and Virginia Kathryn (Priddy) B.; B.S., Fla. So. Coll., 1951; D.D.S. (Research fellow), Emory U., 1957; m. Mary Sue Weathersbee, Nov. 18, 1950; children—Alden Graham, John Dale. Tchr. Northside High, Atlanta, 1951-52; teaching fellow in biochemistry Emory U., 1954-55; practice of dentistry, Lake Worth, Fla., 1957—; dir. Fed. Savs. and Loan Assn. Mgr. Youth Baseball Assn., 1968—; pres. R. Kent Smith Meml. Scholarship Fund, 1968—. Served with AUS, 1946-48. Mem. Am., Fla., Palm Beach County (treas. 1971-72, sec. 1972-73, v.p. 1973-74, pres. 1974-75) dental assns., S.A.R., Atlantic Coast Dental Research Clinic (charter mem.), C. of C. Presbyn. Rotarian (treas. 1965-66, v.p. 1972-73, pres. 1973-74). Home: 2301 N Federal Hwy Lake Worth FL 33460 Office: 509 Lake Av Lake Worth FL 33460

BEANE, THOMAS ORVILLE, lawyer; b. Manassas, Va., Aug. 8, 1931; s. Ardie Orville and Josephine Alice (Huffman) B.; B.A., U. Richmond, 1953; M.A., U. Va., 1957; J.D. (T.C. Williams law scholar), U. Richmond, 1960; m. Ensa Elizabeth Bright, June 19, 1955; children—Elizabeth Anne Beane, Victoria Leigh, Samuel Thomas. Admitted to Va. bar, 1960; practiced in Richmond, 1960-64, Manassas, 1964—; spl. counsel Va. Employment Commn., Richmond, 1960-64; partner, Owens, Underwood & Beane, Manassas, Va., 1964—. Commr. in chancery Circuit Ct. Prince William County, Va., 1966—. Manassas (Va.) residential chmn. Am. Cancer Soc., 1967. Mem. Prince William County Sch. Bd., 1968—, vice-chmn., 1972—. Served with AUS, 1953-56. Recipient award Albemarle County Hist. Soc., 1967. Mem. Am., Va., Prince William County (treas. 1966) bar assns., Va. State Bar, Va. Sch. Bd. Assn. (no. region sec. 1970, state bd. dirs. 1973—), McNeil Law Soc., Lamda Chi Alpha. Baptist (deacon 1967-70). Kiwanian (past pres.). Home: PO Box 167 Manassas VA 22110 Office: 9403A Grant Av Manassas VA 22110

BEARD, ALICE GAMBLE (MRS. OWEN WAYNE BEARD), physician, educator; b. Rochester, Minn., Aug. 29, 1919; d. Joseph William and Isable Florence (Huggins) Gamble; B.S., U. Minn., 1942, M.D., 1944; m. Owen Wayne Beard, Apr. 9, 1944; children—Margaret (Mrs. Gary Wayne Cage), William King, Barbara Jo. Intern U. Tex. at Galveston, 1945-47, resident pediatrics, 1945-47; asst. prof. pediatrics U. Ark. Med. Center, Little Rock, 1948-58, asso. prof., 1958-70, prof., 1970—. Mem. Am. Acad. Pediatrics (com. fetus and newborn 1965-68), Alpha Omega Alpha. Contbr. articles to profl. jours. Home: 7008 Rockwood Rd Little Rock AR 72206

BEARD, BOB J., petroleum co. exec.; b. El Paso, Tex., Feb. 8, 1932; s. Raymond and Thera Ersa (Hughes) B.; B.S. (Franklin Found. scholar), U. Houston, 1956; m. Emmajean Ewald, Nov. 2, 1951; children—Bradley Kent, Donald Ray, Lana Jean, Robert J. Mgr. natural gas dept. Delhi-Taylor Oil Corp., Dallas, also v.p. subsidiaries Delhi Pipeline Corp., Natural Gas Gathering Corp., 1956-60; exec. v.p. Gulf Energy & Devel. Corp., San Antonio, 1960-63, pres., dir., 1963—. Trustee Northside Ind. Sch. Dist., San Antonio, 1967-74, pres., 1971-73. Methodist (chmn. commn. on edn. 1965-66). Home: 21120 Babcock Rd Route 15 Box 237D San Antonio TX 78228 Office: 7th Floor Petroleum Bldg 8626 Tesoro Dr San Antonio TX 78209

BEARD, MARION FOREE, physician; b. Shelbyville, Ky., Nov. 29, 1905; s. Samuel Lowery and Jessie L. (McClure) B.; A.B., U. Louisville, 1927, M.D., 1930; m. Margaret Jefferson, Dec. 26, 1930. Intern, then resident pathology Louisville Gen. Hosp., 1930-32; instr. pathology U. Louisville, 1932-34, asso. prof. medicine, 1953-65, clin. prof., 1965—; practice medicine specializing in internal medicine, Louisville, 1935-40, specializing in hematology, Louisville, 1941—; instr. research hematology Ohio State U., 1940-41; pres. staff Ky. Bapt. Hosp., 1967. Recipient Gold medal Am. Soc. Clin. Pathologists, 1940; citation Transylvania Coll., 1956, U. Louisville, 1956. Fellow A.C.P., Internat. Soc. Hematology; mem. Am. Fedn. Clin. Research, N.Y. Acad. Scis., A.A.A.S., Am. Soc. Hematology, Sigma Xi, Alpha Omega Alpha. Clubs: Louisville Boat, Pendennis (Louisville). Home: 9 Woodhill Rd Louisville KY 40207 Office: 814 Medical Towers Louisville KY 40202

BEARD, OWEN WAYNE, physician; b. Wattensaw, Ark., Nov. 15, 1916; s. Walter King and Esther Minnie (Northcutt) B.; student Okla. State U., 1937-39; B.S., U. Ark., 1943, M.D., 1943; m. Alice Hawthorne Gamble, Apr. 9, 1944; children—Margaret (Mrs. Gary Wayne Cage), William King, Barbara Jo. Intern, John Sealy Hosp., Galveston, 1943-44; resident, 1944-45; practice medicine specializing in internal medicine, cardiology; instr. medicine U. Tex. Med. Br., Galveston, 1945-47; asst. prof. medicine U. Ark. Sch. Medicine, Little Rock, 1947-52, asso. prof., 1952-70, prof., 1970—; asst. chief med. service Little Rock VA Hosp., 1956—; cons. cardiology State Hosp. Nervous Diseases, 1947-53, Little Rock VA Hosp., 1951-53. Served with USAF, 1953-55. Recipient Faculty Key, U. Ark., 1943. Mem. A.M.A., Am. Assn. U. Profs., A.C.P., Am. Coll. Cardiologists, Am. Bd. Internal Medicine, Am., Ark. (bd. mem. 1948—, pres. 1972-74) heart assns., Ark., Pulaski med. socs., Phi Eta Sigma, Alpha Omega Alpha. Contbr. articles to profl. jours. Home: 7008 Rockwood Rd Little Rock AR 72207 Office: 300 E Roosevelt Rd Little Rock AR 72206

BEARD, ROBIN, congressman; b. Knoxville, Tenn., Aug. 21, 1939; grad. Montgomery Bell Acad., Nashville, 1957; B.A., Vanderbilt U., 1961; m. Catherine Rieniets, 1963; children—Robin John, Lisa Paige. State commnr. personnel, 1970-72; mem. 93d Congress from Tenn. Served to capt. USMCR, 1962-65. Club: Nashville Exchange. Office: 124 Cannon Office Bldg Washington DC 20515

BEARDEN, HARLIE, physician; b. Claremore, Okla., Sept. 3, 1924; s. Buchanon H. and Rilla (Newport) B.; B.S., Centenary Coll., 1953; M.D., La. State U., 1957; m. Mary Jane Marine, Dec. 23, 1947; children—William H., Robin Jean. Intern USPHS Hosp., New Orleans, 1957-58; gen. practice resident Charity Hosp., Lafayette, La., 1958; pvt. practice medicine, specializing in family practice, Jennings, La., 1958—; mem. staff Am. Legion Hosp., Jennings; clin. instr. La. State U. Med. Sch., Charity Hosp., Lake Charles; med. examiner FAA. Pres., bd. dirs. Southwest La. Tb-RD Assn., 1968—. Served with USAF, 1943-50; PTO. Recipient Air medal with three oak leaf clusters; recipient 12 Battle Stars. Diplomate Am. Bd. Family Practice. Mem. Am. Acad. Family Practice, Alpha Omega Alpha, Phi Kappa Phi, Omicron Delta Kappa, Alpha Sigma Chi, Lambda Chi Alpha. Kiwanian (pres. 1967). Home: 410 Decker St Jennings LA 70546 Office: 711 N Main St Jennings LA 70546

BEASLEY, CHARLES ARTHUR, banker, lawyer; b. Garland, Ark., Mar. 13, 1918; s. Charles Arthur and Susie (Moore) B.; student Ouachita Coll., 1935-37; J.D., U. Ark., 1940; m. Mary Frances Romaine, Jan. 11, 1942; children—Charles Arthur, Robert Burke, John Romaine. Admitted to Ark. bar, 1940; practiced in Texarkana, Ark., 1940-41; asst. U.S. atty., Fort Smith, Ark., 1941-53; practiced in Fort Smith, Ark., 1953-62; v.p., trust officer 1st Nat. Bank Fort Smith; 1962—; dir. 1st Fed. Savs. and Loan Assn. Fort Smith, Bank of Mulberry. Bd. dirs. Fort Smith Pub. Library, Salvation Army, Bost Sch. for Limited Children, Inc., Harbor House, Inc., A.R.C. Served with USNR, 1942-46. Mem. C. of C., Kappa Sigma. Methodist (chmn. bd. 1966-67, dist. lay leader, 1963-65). Mason (32 degree). Club: Exchange (Fort Smith). Home: 613 Clifton Ct Fort Smith AR 72901 Office: 6th and Garrison Sts Fort Smith AR 72901

BEASLEY, CLARK WAYNE, educator; b. Pittsburg, Kan., June 6, 1942; s. Keith Paul and Laura Mae (Johnson) B.; B.S., Kan. State Coll. Pittsburg, 1964; Ph.D. (NSF fellow 1964-66), U. Okla., 1968; m. Barbara Sue Allman, May 29, 1965; 1 son, Craig Clark. Instr. biology Mo. So. Coll., Joplin, 1968-69; asst. prof. biology McMurry Coll., Abilene, Tex., 1969-72, asso. prof. biology, 1972—, head biology dept., 1973—; instr. biology Kan. State Coll. Pittsburg, summer 1969. Mem. Sigma Xi, Beta Beta Beta, Phi Sigma, Omicron Delta Kappa. Home: 1626 Yorktown Abilene TX 79603

BEASLEY, CLOYD ORRIS, JR., physicist; b. Florence, Ala., July 9, 1933; s. Cloyd Orris and Olga (Zaunner) B.; B.A., Vanderbilt U., 1955, M.A., 1957; Ph.D., U. Wis., 1962. Physicist, Oak Ridge Nat. Lab., 1962—. Culham research asso. Culham Lab., U.K. Atomic Energy Agy., 1966-67; Scoutmaster, Gt. Smoky Mountain council Boy Scouts Am., 1963—; pres. Oak Ridge Indsl. Airport Com., 1965-66; with Oak Ridge Civic Orch., 1967—, pres., 1971-72, bd. dirs., 1972-73, treas., 1973—; A.R.C. 1st aid instr., 1968—; patrol leader Nat. Ski Patrol System, 1969-71, divisional jr. adviser, 1971—. Served with AUS, 1958. Mem. Am. Phys. Soc. (plasma physics div.). Mem. Ch. of Christ. Club: Concord Yacht (fleet capt.). Contbr. articles to profl. jours. Home: 110 S Purdue Av Oak Ridge TN 37830 Office: Oak Ridge Nat Lab Oak Ridge TN 37830

BEASLEY, JERE LOCKE, lt. gov. Ala.; b. Tyler, Tex., Dec. 12, 1935; s. Browder L. and Florence (Camp) B.; B.S., Auburn U., 1959; LL.B., U. Ala., 1962; m. Sara Baker, Mar. 15, 1958; children—Jere Locke, Julia Anne, Linda Lee. Admitted to Ala. bar, 1962; practice in Tuscaloosa, 1962-64, Clayton, 1964-71; mem. firm Beasley, Williams & Robertson, 1969-71; dir., legal counsel Bank of Commerce, Clayton; lt. gov., Ala., 1971—. Mem. Am., Ala., Barbour County (past pres.) bar assns., Am. Trial Lawyers Assns., Clayton C. of C. (past pres.). Lion (past pres. Clayton). Home: 301 N Midway St Clayton AL 36016 Office: 104 Court Sq Clayton AL 36016 also 125 S Orange St Eufaula AL 36027

BEASLEY, JOHN SNODGRASS, II, lawyer, banker; b. Franklin, Tenn., Oct. 2, 1930; s. Thomas Earl and Elsie (Eggleston) B.; B.A., Vanderbilt U., 1952, J.D., 1954; m. Mary D. Allison Tidman, Sept. 4, 1958; children—John Snodgrass III, Eleanor Christensen. Admitted to Tenn. bar, 1954; practiced in Franklin, 1957-58; exec. sec. Vanderbilt U. Alumni Assn., 1958-62; asst. dean, asst. prof. law Vanderbilt U. Law Sch., Nashville, 1962-64, asso. dean, asst. prof. law, 1964-66, asso. dean, asso. prof. law, 1966-69, asso. dean, prof. law, 1970-71; sr. v.p., head trust and investment div. Commerce Union Bank, Nashville, 1971—; pres., dir. Pebblestone Ct., Inc., Franklin; sec., dir. Cumberland Machinery Co.; bd. dirs. Nashville. Mem. bd. Franklin Spl. Sch. Dist. Trustee Battle Ground Acad.; bd. dirs. Tenn. Bot. Gardens and Fine Arts Center, pres., 1973; pres. Coverdale Scholarship Found., 1965-67. Bd. dirs. Nashville Symphony Assn., 1959-65, pres., 1962-64; bd. dirs. Heritage Found. of Franklin and Williamson County, pres., 1968; bd. dirs. Met. YMCA, Salvation Army, Historic Site Found. Served with USNR, 1954-57. Mem. Am., Tenn. bar assns., Assn. Preservation Tenn. Antiquities (trustee 1962-70), Order of Coif, Phi Beta Kappa, Omicron Delta Kappa, Sigma Chi, Pi Delta Epsilon, Phi Delta Phi. Republican. Episcopalian. Clubs: Carnton (Franklin); Belle Meade Country; University, Nashville City, Cumberland (Nashville). Home: 335 4th Av S Franklin TN 37064 Office: Commerce Union Bank 400 Union St Nashville TN 37219

BEASLEY, PERCY EUGENE, supt. schs.; b. Rocky Ford, Ga., Oct. 23, 1913; s. Stephen Enoch and Lillia Jane (Fennell) B.; A.B., Furman U., 1938; M.Ed., U. S.C., 1947; m. Amelia Evangeline Schroder, May 31, 1938; children—Stephen Tully, Frederick Alexander, James Fennell. Prin., coach Springfield (S.C.) High Sch., 1938-42; supt. schs., Salley, S.C., 1943-50; supt. Salley and Windsor Area Schs., 1950-54; supervisory prin. elementary schs., Aiken, S.C., 1954-58, supt. schs. adminstrv. area 1, Aiken, 1968—. Mem. state Com. Accreditation Elementary Schs., 1948-49. Served as lt. (j.g.) USNR, 1943-46. Mem. Nat., S.C., Aiken County (pres. 1948) edn. assns., Am., S.C. assns. sch. adminstrs. Mason, Lion. Home: 205 Barnard Av SE Aiken SC 29801 Office: Box 657 Aiken SC 29801

BEASLEY, PHILIP GENE, educator; b. Harrisburg, Ill., Dec. 22, 1927; s. L.M. and Blanche (Hilliard) B.; B.A., Washington U., St. Louis, 1949; M.S., Auburn U., 1962, Ph.D., 1966; m. Alice Joan Lang, Apr. 19, 1952. Lab. asst., spl. agt. FBI, 1950-59; grad. asst., instr. Auburn U., 1960-66; asst. prof. U. Montevallo (Ala.), 1966-69, asso. prof., 1969-71, prof., chmn. dept. biology, 1971—. Mem. N.Y. Acad. Scis., Sigma Xi, Phi Kappa Phi, Gamma Sigma Delta. Mason, Rotarian. Home: 124 Shoshone St Montevallo AL 35115

BEASLEY, WILLIAM ROBERT, dentist; b. Richmond, Va., Aug. 22, 1927; s. Joseph Dewitt and Jenneill (Allison) B.; B.S., U. Richmond, 1953; D.D.S., Med. Coll. Va., 1957; m. Betty Bolling Hurt, Dec. 27, 1952; children—Mark Dewitt, Jenneill Allison, John Stringfellow, James Thornton. Intern oral surgery Med. Coll. Va. Hosp., 1957-58; resident oral surgery U. Ia. Hosp., 1958-60, asst. prof. oral surgery, 1960-64; pvt. practice dentistry, specializing in oral surgery, Harrisonburg, Va., 1964—; cons. oral surgery VA Hosp., Iowa City, Ia., 1960-64. Pres. local unit Am. Cancer Soc., 1971-72; pres. Shenandoah Valley Choral Soc., 1970-73; pres. Valley Players, 1967-68; scoutmaster Cub Scouts Am., 1967-68. Bd. dirs. Shenandoah Valley Music Festival, 1970-71. Served with USN, 1945-48. Diplomate Am. Bd. Oral Surgery. Mem. Am., Southeastern, Va. (pres. 1971-72) socs. oral surgeons. Elk, Rotarian. Contbr. articles to dental jours. Home: Route 1 Forest Hills Harrisonburg VA 22801 Office: 725 S Mason St Harrisonburg VA 22801

BEATTIE, JACK ROBERT, dentist; b. Bay City, Mich., Oct 2, 1934; s. Aaron Joseph and Sadie Evelyn (Young) B.; B.A., Mich. State U., 1956; D.D.S., U. Mich., 1960; M.S., Western Reserve U., 1963; m. Ernestine Linda Johnson, June 27, 1959; children—John Robert, Jeffrey Lind, Kimberly Young, Beattie. Orthodontist, Orlando, Fla., 1963—. Guest lectr. Internat. Acad. Stomatology, Lima, Peru, 1965. Chmn. Orange County (Fla.) Republican Exec. Com., 1968—; mem. Fla. delegation Rep. Nat. Conv., 1968, 72. Recipient Milo Hellman Research award Am. Assn. Orthodontists, 1964. Mem. Am., Fla., Central Dist., Orange County dental assns., Fla. Orthodontic Soc., Am. Assn. Orthodontists, So. Soc. Orthodontists. Mem. All-Am. Collegiate Swimming Team, 1955. Home: 561 Via Lugano Winter Park FL 32789 Office: 618 E South St Orlando FL 32801

BEATTY, BEULAH LEE COOPER (MRS. JOHN DAY BEATTY), club woman; b. Louisburg, N.C., May 28, 1901; d. Willie Jackson and Annie Laura (Bowden) Cooper; student Louisburg Coll., 1918-19, 25-26; m. John Day Beatty, July 14, 1926; children—Laura Day (Mrs. Clyde Buchanan Rosser), Beulah (Mrs. Andrews), Neill McLaurin. Genealogist, 1959—. Historian, Bladen County Hist. Soc., 1963—; pres. Bladen Stars chpt. U.D.C., 1961-64, N.C. div. v.p., 1964-66, treas. N.C. div., 1966-68; dir. dist. 3, Wilmington Presbytery Women Ch., 1966-68; pres. Lord Craven chpt. Colonial Dames 17th Century, 1964-66, registrar, 1966-72. Mem. Daus. Founders and Patriots Am. (registrar N.C. Soc. 1970—). D.A.R. (regent Battle of Elizabethtown chpt. 1971-73, vice dist. dir. 1973—), Huguenot Soc. S.C., Nat. Geneal. Soc., New Eng. Historic Geneal. Soc. N.C. Soc. County and Local Historians. Democrat. Presbyn. Home: PO Box 905 Elizabethtown NC 28337

BEATTY, JAMES TULLY, land devel. co. exec., state legislator; b. N.Y.C., Oct. 28, 1934; s.; Henry Elder and Mary (Guccione) B.; A.B., U. N.C., 1957; m. Barbara Ann Harmon, Feb. 20, 1960; children—James Tully, Mary Kathleen. With Ervin Co., Charlotte, N.C.; mem. N.C. Ho. of Reps., 1966—. Guest commentator ABC-TV Wide World of Sports, 1964—; mem. U.S. Olympic Com., 1965—; alumni rep. U. N.C. Athletic Council, 1967—. Served with AUS, 1957-58. Recipient Sullivan award as Am.'s amateur athlete of year Amateur Athletic Union U.S., 1962; named one of Am.'s Ten Outstanding Young Men of Year U.S. Jr. C. of C., 1962; charter mem.

N.C. Sports Hall of Fame, 1963. Democrat. Roman Catholic. Home: 1609 Scotland Av Charlotte NC 28207 Office: Tega Cay Fort Mill SC 29715

BEATUS, BENJAMIN LOUIS, JR., psychiatrist; b. Memphis, Sept. 21, 1936; s. Benjamin Louis and Celeste (Borodofsky) B.; student Tulane U., 1954-57; M.D., U. Tenn., 1960; m. Sandra Louise Loskovitz, Dec. 21, 1958; children—Mitchell, Todd. Intern St. Joseph's Hosp., Memphis, 1961; resident in psychiatry U. Kan. Med. Center, Kansas City, 1962-64; staff psychiatrist Tenn. Psychiat. Hosp. and Inst., Memphis, 1967-69; practice medicine specializing in psychiatry, Memphis, 1969—; instr. U. Tenn. Med. Sch., Memphis, 1967-71, asst. prof. psychiatry, 1971—; mem. staff Baptist Meml., Meth., St. Joseph, Americare Psychiat. hosps. Bd. dirs. Jewish Community Center, Memphis. Served with M.C., USAF, 1965-67. Mem. A.M.A., Am. Psychiat. Assn., Am. Bd. Psychiatry and Neurology. Club: Ridgeway Country (Memphis, Tenn.). Home: 6669 Corsica St Memphis TN 38138 Office: 969 Madison St Memphis TN 38104

BEAUCHAMP, CARROLL LEE, optometrist; b. Washington, Aug. 1, 1908; s. Ellis Franklin and Vera Etta (Menefee) B.; student Va. Inst. Tech., 1929-30, Atlantic U., 1930-31, Pa. Coll. Optometry, 1932-33; D.Optometry, Ill. Coll. Optometry, 1933; m. Garnet Payne, Nov. 3, 1946; 1 son, Barry. Resident, Chgo. Eye, Ear & Throat Hosp., 1938; pvt. practice optometry, Norfolk, Va., 1944-48, Covington, Va., 1948—. Mem. med. adv. bd. Va. Dept. Motor Vehicles; mem. Va. Gov.'s Adv. Bd. To Improve Safety Standards on Hwys., 1961-63. Bd. dirs. A.R.C., 1963-65. Named Optometrist of Year, State of Va., 1963. Mem. Va. (chmn. motorist vision and hwy. safety com. 1964-72), Western (pres. 1960-62) optometric assns., Covington Safety Council. Mason, Moose (gov. 1959-60), Lion (dir. 1953-54). Club: Alleghany Country (Covington). Home: Oakwood Forest Covington VA 24426 Office: Peoples Bank Bldg Covington VA 24426

BEAUCHAMP, JOHN HERNDON, wholesale produce co. exec.; b. Greenville, Tex., Sept. 5, 1911; s. John Bryan and Lena (Herndon) B.; student Wesley Coll., Greenville, 1929-31; B.A., B.B.A., Tex. Technol. U., 1933; m. Agnes Jones, Feb. 4, 1939; children—Jeanne (Mrs. John Lew Rumley), Nancy Ellen. Salesman, Williams-Eubank Wholesale Grocery, 1933-38, br. mgr., Ardmore, Okla., 1938-50; br. mgr. Ben E. Keith Co., Longview, Tex., 1950-52, Dallas, 1952-60, Ft. Worth, 1960-65, v.p. sales, 1965-74, pres., 1974—, also dir.; dir. Panhandle Fruit Co., Amarillo, Tex.; v.p., dir. Dillaha Fruit Co., Little Rock. Mem. United Fresh Fruit and Vegetable Assn. Washington (dir. adv. bd. 1970-72, pres. 1974-75), United Merchandising and Mgmt. Inst. Washington (chmn. bd. 1967). Kiwanian. Club: Ridglea Country. Home: 4108 Clayton Rd W Fort Worth TX 76116 Office: 9th and Pecan Sts Fort Worth TX 76102

BEAUCHAMP, RAYMOND ORVAL, dentist; b. Monett, Mo., July 26, 1906; s. William Harry and Annie Maude (Bell) B.; B.S., U. Ark., 1929; D.D.S., U. Mo., 1935; m. Helen Ruth Pennington, Mar. 12, 1938; 1 son, James Harry. Student asst. biology U. Mo. Dental Coll., Kansas City, 1932-34; pvt. practice dentistry, Broken Bow, Okla., 1935-38, Stillwater, 1938-43, 46—. Bd. dirs. YMCA, 1969-70, Partners in Prayer. Served with AUS, 1943-46; lt. col. ret. Mem. Am., Okla. (ho. dels. 1966-68) dental assns., Payne County Dental Soc. (pres. 1946-47), Delta Sigma Delta, Sigma Nu. Presbyn. (elder). Elk, Kiwanian (pres. 1957). Club: Stillwater Golf and Country. Home: 4824 Woodland Dr Stillwater OK 74074 Office: 119 W 7th St Stillwater OK 74074

BEAUDREAU, THELMA FAY JACKSON (MRS. NED BEAUDREAU), musician, club woman; b. Kiowa, Okla., Nov. 12, 1907; d. George Edmond and Leona May (Harris) Jackson; student San Antonio Coll. Music, 1926-27, Kansas City Conservatory Music, 1929-30, San Angelo Coll., 1948, Tex. Coll. Arts and Industries, 1957-58, 60-61; m. Ned Willard Beaudreau, June 6, 1931; children—Vance Jackson, Marilyn Anne (Mrs. David B. Coulson). Dir., music instr., Lamesa (Tex.) High School Orch., 1925-1926; music instr., Big Spring, Tex., 1927-29, 31-34, Corpus Christi (Tex.) pub. schs., 1948-50; tchr. Presbyn. Day Sch., 1952, charter mem. Corpus Christi Symphony, 1945, mem. string sect., 1945—; mem. Jackson-Wade Trio, Dallas, fall 1930; mem. String Ensemble Driscoll Hotel, Corpus Christi, 1941-42. Rec. sec. Harmony Music Club, 1945-47, pres., 1949-51; jr. scrapbook chmn. 5th Dist. Fedn. Music Clubs, Tex., 1956-57; patron Thursday Music Club, Corpus Christi; rec. sec. Corpus Christi chpt. D.A.R., 1955-57, regent, 1958-60, parliamentarian, 1960-62; chmn. Am. Music com. Tex. Soc. D.A.R., 1961-64, chaplain Regents Club, 1964-66. Recipient 25 year award Corpus Christi Symphony. Mem. Internat. Platform Assn., Nueces County Hist. Survey Com., Nueces County Hist. Soc., Nat. Assn. Music Tchrs., Corpus Christi Symphony Guild, Corpus Christi Music Tchrs. Assn., Episcopalian. Clubs: Harmony Music (corr. sec. 1965-67, v.p. 1972—); Thursday Music. Address: 109 E Vanderbilt St Corpus Christi TX 78415

BEAVER, PAUL CHESTER, educator; b. Glenwood, Ind., Mar. 10, 1905; s. John Chester and Blanche Emma (Murphy) B.; A.B., Wabash Coll., 1928, D.Sc. (hon.), 1963; M.S., U. Ill., 1929, Ph.D., 1935; m. Lela E. West, Oct. 16, 1931; 1 dau., Paula Jean (Mrs. David Ross Chipman). Asst. in zoology U. Ill., 1928-29, 31-34; instr. zoology U. Wyo., 1929-31; instr. biology Oak Park Jr. Coll., 1934-37; asst. prof. biology Lawrence Coll., 1937-42; biologist Ga. Dept. Pub. Health, 1942-45; asst. prof. parasitology Tulane U. Med. Sch., 1945-47, asso. prof., 1947-52, prof., 1952—, head dept. parasitology, 1956—, William Vincent prof. tropical diseases and hygiene, 1958—, dir. Internat. Center for Med. Research and Tng., Colombia, 1967—; vis. prof. Eastern Mont. Normal Sch., summers 1935-37, Colo. State Coll., 1941, U. Mich., 1954-56, 58, U. Natal Med. Sch., Durban, South Africa, 1957; hon. vis. prof. U. del Valle, Cali, Colombia, 1970—. Cons. Ga. Dept. Pub. Health, 1946-53, USPHS Hosp., New Orleans, 1949—, WHO, 1960—; mem. com. standards and exams. Am. Bd. Microbiology, 1960-67; mem. commn. parasitic diseases Armed Forces Epidemiological Bd., 1953-73, dir. commn. on parasitic diseases, 1967-73; mem. Am. Found. for Tropical Medicine, 1960-66; microbiology fellowships rev. panel NIH, 1960-63; mem. WHO expert com. on intestinal helminths, 1963, also WHO expert panel on parasitic diseases, 1963—; bd. sci. counselors Nat. Inst. Allergy and Infectious Diseases, NIH, 1966-68, mem. NIH parasitic diseases panel U.S.-Japan Cooperative Med. Sci. program, 1965-69; mem. adv. sci. bd. Gorgas Meml. Inst. Tropical and Preventive Medicine, 1970—. Diplomate Am. Bd. Microbiology. Fellow Am. Acad. Microbiology (gov. 1966—), A.A.A.S., Am. Soc. Tropical Medicine and Hygiene (councilor 1956-57, v.p. 1958, pres. 1969); mem. Internat. Filariasis Assn., Royal Soc. Tropical Medicine and Hygiene, Am. Soc. Parasitologists (councilor 1952-54, 56-59, pres. 1968), Am. Micros. Soc. (v.p. 1953, exec. com. 1955-59, 61-62), Am. Pub. Health Assn., Soc. Exptl. Biology and Medicine, Societe Belge de Medicine Tropicale de Parasitologie et de Micologie, Sociedad Mexicana de Parasitologia (hon.), New Orleans Acad. Sci., Societe de Pathologie Exotique France (hon.), Brazilian Soc. Tropical Medicine (hon.), Sigma Xi, Alpha Omega Alpha (hon.), Delta Omega. Clubs: Internat. House, Round Table (New Orleans). Co-author: Faust's Animal Agents and Vectors of Human Disease, rev. edit. Contbg. author: Mitchell-Nelson's Pediatrics, Control of Communicable Diseases of Man. Mem. editorial bd. Am. Jour. Tropical Medicine and Hygiene, 1958-60, 67-70, editor-in-chief, 1960-66, 72—; asso. editor Am. Jour. Hygiene, 1961-64, Jour. Parasitology, 1965—, Am. Jour. Epidemiology, 1966—; editorial bd. Trans. Am. Micros. Soc., 1966—, Ceskoslovenska Parasitologie, 1966—, Author sci. papers. Home: 1416 Cadiz St New Orleans LA 70115 Office: 1430 Tulane Av New Orleans LA 70112

BEAVERS, MORRIS EUGENE, utilities co. exec.; b. Avoca, Ind., Aug. 20, 1924; s. Smith E. and Mabel E. (Geyger) B.; student U. Wis., 1942-43; B.S. in E.E., Purdue U., 1949; postgrad. U. Tenn., 1950-51; m. Marjorie Helen Huber, June 27, 1945; children—John Thomas, Carol (Mrs. William Skolfield, Jr.), Marge Ann. Distbn. engr. Chattanooga Electric Power Bd., 1949-55; field engr. Line Material Industries, Knoxville, Tenn., 1955-61; chief engr. Cleveland Electric System (Tex.), 1961-65, gen. mgr., 1965—. Chmn., United Fund, 1966, Ocoee council Boy Scouts Am., 1968-69. Served with Signal Corps, AUS, 1943-45. Mem. I.E.E.E., Central Service Assn. (pres. 1971—), Tenn. Municipal Electric Power Assn. (dir.), Cleveland C. of C. (chmn. 1970), Am. Legion. Lutheran. Kiwanian. Club: Country (Cleveland). Home: 2221 Glenwood Dr Cleveland TN 37311 Office: 2450 Guthrie Dr Cleveland TN 37311

BEAZLEY, JON STANTON, civil engr.; b. Social Circle, Ga., July 11, 1915; s. Ruben Rogers and Abigail (Stanton) B.; student No. Ga. Coll., 1932-35; C.E., Internat. Corr. Schs., 1938; m. Hazel Solomon, Nov. 15, 1941; children—Hazel, Teresa, Abigail, Jon Stanton. Asst. engr. govt. surveys Eastern and So. U.S., 1935-40; project engr. U.S. mil. bases, 1940-42; photogrammetric engr. Fla. State Rd. Dept., Tallahassee, 1946-55, div. engr., 1955-70, state topographic engr., 1971—; cons. aerial surveys. Mem. Fla. Math. Textbook Com., Tallahassee, 1953-65; pres. North Fla. Ga. Tech. Alumni Assn., 1965-66. Served with AUS, 1942-45. Mem. Am. Congress Surveying and Mapping (dir. 1962-65), Fla. Engring. Soc. (dir. 1963-65, sr. v.p. 1972), Am. Assn. State Hwy. Ofcls., Am. Soc. C.E., Am. Soc. Photogrammetry (dir. 1974—), Nat. Soc. Profl. Engrs., Am. Geophys. Union. Contbr. articles to profl. jours. Patentee in field. Home: 330 Ponce St Tallahassee FL 32303 Office: Florida State Dept Transp Tallahassee FL 32304

BECHTEL, ROBERT WARREN, banker; b. Slaton, Tex., July 29, 1933; s. Robert B. and Esther (Heatherly) B.; B.S., Okla. U., 1957, LL.B., 1961; m. Joan Morrison, Jan. 28, 1955; children—Susan, Amy. Field engr. Halliburton Co., Midland, Tex., 1957-58; admitted to Tex. bar, 1961; title analyst Shell Oil Co., Midland, 1961-62; trust officer First Nat. Bank of Midland, 1962-68, head financial and planning dept., 1969—; pres. Eagle Computing Corp., 1970-73, chmn. exec. com., 1973—, also dir. Bd. dirs. Chapparal dist. Boy Scouts Am. Beal Found. Potts & Sibley Found. Served with AUS, 1955-56. Mem. Midland, Tex., Am. bar assns., Delta Theta Phi. Author: Uniform Commercial Code in Texas, 1966. Home: 10 Cambridge Ct Midland TX 79701 Office: 303 Wall St Midland TX 79701

BECK, ARTHUR CHARLES, JR., ednl. adminstr.; b. Richmond, Va., May 4, 1921; s. Arthur C. and Adelaide H. (Alvis) B.; B.S. in Bus. Adminstrn., U. Richmond, 1940; M.B.A., U. Pa., 1941; m. Sudie Elizabeth Yager, Sept. 6, 1947; children—Rosemary (Mrs. Richard F.D. Martin), Janet, Sarah. Partner, Lindsey & Co., Richmond, 1946-55; pres. Diggs & Beadles Seed Co., Richmond, 1955-61; marketing mgr. Smith Douglas Co., Norfolk, Va., 1961-63; advt. mgr. So. Planter, 1963-64; asso. dir. U. Richmond Inst. for Bus. and Community Devel., 1964—. Served with USNR, 1942-46. Mem. Am. Marketing Assn. (pres. Va. chpt. 1966-67), Am. Soc. for Tng. and Devel. (dir. Va. chpt.), Richmond (pres. 1953-54), Va. (v.p. 1954-55) jr. chambers commerce, Lambda Chi Alpha. Roman Catholic. Club: Virginia First. Author: (with Ellis D. Hillmar) A Practical Approach to Organization Development Through Management by Objectives, 1972; Decision Making for Local Parish Leaders, 1973. Home: 327 Albemarle Av Richmond VA 23226

BECK, DORRIS DILLS, librarian, media specialist; b. Cullowhee, N.C., Jan. 18, 1933; d. Jesse Grady and Gracie Ellen (Green) Dills; B.S. in Edn., Western Carolina U., 1955, M.S. in Edn. in Audiovisual, 1972; m. Samuel F. Beck, Dec. 19, 1953; children—Teresa Kay, Susan Lynn. Circulation librarian, asst. librarian Western Carolina U., 1955-65; counselor, dep. dir. Neighborhood Youth Corps, Sylva, N.C., 1966-68; librarian Southwestern Tech. Inst., Sylva, 1968-71, dir. Learning Resource Center at inst., 1971-73; media specialist Fairview Elementary Sch., Sylva, 1973—. Pres. Sylva Elementary Sch. P.T.A., 1970-72. Mem. Southeastern, N.C. library assns., Community Coll. Ednl. Media Assn., N.E.A., Classroom Tchrs. Assn., Phi Kappa Phi. Baptist. Compiler manuals. Home: 126 Old Dillsboro Rd Sylva NC 28779 Office: Fairview Elementary Sch Sylva NC 28779

BECK, EMIL FREDERICK, III, savs. and loan exec.; b. Houston, May 27, 1924; s. Emil Frederick II and Hertha Clara (Willig) B.; student San Angelo Jr. Coll., 1941-43, Knox Coll., 1943-44; B.B.A., Tex. Tech. U., 1950; postgrad. Ind. U., 1971-73; m. Norma Dale Reagan, Sept. 29, 1947; children—Karen Ann, Janine Carrie, Reagan Emil, Leslie Pamela. Salesman Spaulding Co., Odessa, Tex., 1950-54; v.p. Key Investment Co., Odessa, Tex., 1954-58; exec. v.p. First Savs. & Loan, Odessa, Tex., 1958—. Mem. city planning bd., Odessa, Tex., 1955-65; mem. dist. adv. council Small Bus. Adminstrn., 1970-73; pres., United Fund, 1967. Served with AUS, 1943-46; ETO. Mem. Tex. Savings & Loan League (dir. 1972-75), Odessa Meteoritical Soc. (dir. 1955-73), Soc. Real Estate Appraisers, Odessa C. of C. (pres. 1966), Odessa Bd. Realtors (pres. 1970). Presbyn. (elder 1955-75). Lion. Home: 1430 Verde St Odessa TX 79761 Office: 110 E 7th St Odessa TX 79761

BECK, GEORGE PRESTON, physician; b. Wichita Falls, Tex., Oct. 21, 1930; s. George P. and Amanda (Wilbanks) B.; B.S., Midwestern U., 1951; M.D., U. Tex., 1955; m. Constance Carolyn Krog, Dec. 22, 1953; children—Carla Elizabeth, George P., Howard W. Intern, John Sealy Hosp., 1955-56; resident anesthesiology Parkland Meml. Hosp., Dallas, 1959-62, vis. staff, 1964—; practice medicine, specializing in anesthesiology, Lubbock, Tex., 1964—; chief staff Meth. Hosp., Lubbock, 1967-68; asst. prof. anesthesiology Southwestern Med. Sch., Dallas, 1962-64, asst. clin. prof., 1964-71, asso. clin. prof. anesthesiology U. Tex. Med. Br. at Galveston, 1971—. Owner, Gt. Plain Ballistics Corp., 1967—. Pres. found. bd. Tex. Tech U., 1972—. Served with USAF, 1956-59. Diplomate Am. Bd. Anesthesiology. Fellow Am. Coll. Anesthetists; mem. Am., Tex. (pres. 1974) socs. anesthesiologists, Tex. Med. Assn., Lubbock County Med. Soc., Lubbock Surg. Soc. Lutheran (pres. ch. council 1965-66, pres. congregation 1965-66). Author: The Ideal Anesthesiologist, 1960; Mnemonics as an Aid to the Anesthesiologist, 1961; Anterior Approach to Sciatic Nerve Block, 1962. Home: 4601 W 18th St Lubbock TX 79416 Office: PO Box 16385 Lubbock TX 79490

BECK, HUBERT FREDERICK, clergyman; b. Duquoin, Ill., July 21, 1931; s. Louis Carl and Martina Clara (Dierks) B.; B.A., Concordia Sem., St. Louis, 1953, M.Div., 1956; postgrad. Luth. Sch. Theology, 1966-67; m. Betty Lee Beaver, Oct. 6, 1956; children—Kathleen Ann, Cynthia Sue, Mary Lee, John Mark. Ordained to ministry Luth. Ch., 1956; pastor St. John Luth. Ch., Topeka, Ill., 1956-58, Immanuel Luth. Ch., Charleston, Ill., 1958-65, Immanuel Luth. Ch., Des Plaines, Ill., 1965-67, Univ. Luth. Chapel, College Station, Tex., 1968—. Kiwanian. Author: The Christian Encounters the Age of Technology, 1970; The Way of God and the Ways of Man, 1972; Thoughts for Today, 1972; Why Can't the Church be Like This?, 1973. Home: 1405 Francis St College Station TX 77840 Office: 315 Main St College Station TX 77840

BECK, NANCY MANN MCCONNICO (MRS. EARL C. BECK, JR.), distbg. co. exec.; b. Memphis, Aug. 31, 1930; d. John Davis and Pauline (Hilton) McConnico; grad. So. Sem. and Jr. Coll., 1949; m. Dean Carlton Dubois, Aug. 19, 1950 (div. Nov. 1963); children—Denise Hilton, Dean Carlton; m. 2d, Earl C. Beck, Jr., Jan. 31, 1971; 1 son, John Harrington. Asst. buyer, sportswear John Gerber Co., Memphis, 1949-50; fashion coordinator J. Hilton McConnico, Designer, Memphis, 1963-65; buyer, mgr. Bridal Salon, Goldsmiths, Memphis, 1965-70, French Room, 1970-71; v.p. Beck Distbg. Co., 1970—. Press relations Hunter Lane for mayor, 1967. Mem. Memphis Arts Council, Internat. Platform Assn., Memphis Symphony League. Episcopalian. Home: Casa Lorraine Plantation Hughes AR 72348

BECK, RALPH ARTHUR, ednl. adminstr.; b. N.Y.C., Mar. 22, 1922; s. Ralph Fernando and Ethel Victoria (Aplustille) B.; B.A., Fordham U., 1943; m. Gwendolyn Farrar, Sept. 20, 1947; 1 dau., Suzanne Farrar. Advt. mgr. Thalhimers Dept. Store, Richmond, Va., 1946-51; sales promotion dir. Mabley & Carew, Dept. store, Cin., 1957-59; v.p. sales promotion Davison's Dept. Store Atlanta, 1959-71; asst. v.p. devel. Ga. State U., Atlanta, 1971—. Vice-pres., Atlanta Community Chest, 1964. Mem. exec. bd. Atlanta Area council Boy Scouts Am., commr., 1971—, nat. bd., 1971—; bd. dirs. Atlanta chpt. A.R.C., Community Council Atlanta; bd. sponsors Atlanta Art Sch.; sec. Ga. State U. Found., Inc., 1971—. Served with AUS, 1942-46, 51-52. Decorated Bronze Star; recipient Silver Beaver award Boy Scouts Am., 1966, Outstanding Pub. Service award Ga. Pub. Relations Soc. Am., 1969. Mem. Atlanta C. of C. Home: 4350 Harris Valley Rd Atlanta GA 30327

BECK, RAYMOND WARREN, educator; b. New Smyrna, Fla., Oct. 20, 1925; s. George Arliss and Sara Kathryn (Hightower) B.; B.S., U. Fla., 1949, M.S., 1952; Ph.D., U. Wis., 1956; m. Charlotte Ann Hudgens, Aug. 23, 1958; children—Warren Findlay, Andrew Hudgens. Teaching asst. dept. bacteriology U. Fla., 1950-52; research asst. dept. bacteriology U. Wis., 1952-55; asst. prof. dept. microbiology U. Tenn., Knoxville, 1955-60, asso. prof., 1960-71, prof., 1971—. Cons., Cumberland View Farms, Clinton, Tenn., 1960—. Served with USNR, 1943-46. Mem. Am. Soc. Microbiology (pres. Ky.-Tenn. br. 1963), Sigma Xi, Phi Kappa Phi. Home: 2509 Lakemoor Dr Knoxville TN 37920

BECK, SISTER RICHARD MARIE, coll. adminstr.; b. N.Y.C., May 19, 1935; d. Richard Joseph and Mary (Cody) Beck; B.A., Marymount Manhattan Coll., 1956; M.A., Marquette U., 1961. Registrar, dir. admissions Marymount Coll., Arlington, Va., 1958-60; tchr. Marymount Coll., Quebec, Que., Can., 1961-62; dir. admissions Marymount Coll., Tarrytown, N.Y., 1962-66; acad. dean Marymount Coll., N.Y.C., 1966-67; dean of admissions Marymount Coll., Boca Raton, Fla., 1967—. Mem. Coll. Entrance Exam. Bd. Mem. Fla. Personnel Guidance Assn., Assn. Coll. Admission Counselors, Am. Assn. Collegiate Registrars and Admission Officers. Address: Marymount Coll Boca Raton FL 33432

BECK, RONALD JERRY, lawyer; b. Kingsport, Tenn., Sept. 22, 1941; s. Victor Ritzendollar and Anna (Ratliffe) B.; B.A., Emory and Henry Coll., 1965; postgrad. Emory U., 1965-66; J.D., U. Tenn., 1968; m. Lillian Louise Bundy, Oct. 11, 1970; children—Robyn, Gabriel. Admitted to Tenn. bar, 1969; mem. firm Mitchell & Beck, 1970—. Asst. dist. atty. 26th Judicial Dist. Tenn., 1972-73. Mem. Am., Kingsport, bar assns., Am., Tenn. trial lawyers assns. Moose, Eagle. Home: Route 13 Oldstage Rd Kingsport TN 37664 Office: 222 E Center St Kingsport TN 37660

BECKER, ARTHUR MARVIN, lawyer; b. N.Y.C., Aug. 30, 1908; s. Charles and Frances (Blumberg) B.; student Fordham U., 1925-26; B.A., N.Y.U., 1929; J.D., Columbia U., 1931; m. Faye Elizabeth Samples, Nov. 20, 1953; 1 son, Francis Evans. Admitted to N.Y. State bar, 1932, D.C., bar, 1946; practiced in N.Y.C., 1932-35, Washington, 1946—; sr. atty. U.S. Dept. Agr., 1935-41; prin. atty. WPB, 1941-42; asst. gen. counsel War Shipping Adminstrn., 1942; sr. asst. gen. counsel U.S. Maritime Commn., 1945-46; partner firm Mudge, Rose, Guthrie and Alexander, and predecessors, N.Y.C., Washington and Paris, 1964—. Mem. Pres.'s Commn. Am. Shipbldg., 1970-73. Bd. dirs. Washington Internat. Horse Show. Served to comdr. USNR, 1942-45. Mem. Am., Fed. bar assns., Bar Assn. D.C. Clubs: Propeller, Nat. Lawyers, Army-Navy, Columbia University, International, 1925 F St (Washington); Potomac Hunt; India House (N.Y.C.). Home: 8800 Bradley Blvd Bethesda MD 20034 Office: Paris France also 20 Broad St New York City 10005 also 1701 Pennsylvania Av NW Washington DC 20006

BECKER, CHARLES LEE, supermarket exec.; b. Cheyenne, Wyo., Oct. 1, 1919; s. A. L. and Adele (Moussier) B.; student U. Tex.; m. Peggy Friedrich, Dec. 2, 1950; 1 dau., Peggy Lee; 1 stepson, George Karutz. With Handy-Andy, Inc., 1937—, v.p., 1950-54, pres., chmn. bd., 1964—, also dir.; gen. partner Community Realty Co.; dir. San Antonio Savs. Assn., San Antonio Belt & Terminal Ry. Co., Great So. Life Ins. Co. Trustee Handy-Andy Found. Tex., Handy-Andy Employees Profit Sharing Trust. Served to 1st lt. USAAF, 1941-45. Mem. San Antonio C. of C. (dir. 1967-69), Tex. Cavaliers, Order of Alamo. Club: San Antonio German. Home: 8715 Starcrest San Antonio TX 78219 Office: 3000 E Houston St San Antonio TX 78206

BECKER, JOHN VERNON, govt. ofcl.; b. Albany, N.Y., Aug. 18, 1913; s. Vernon Hyney and Elma Frances (Fuller) B.; B.S., N.Y. U., 1935, M.S., 1936; m. Rowena Fleming Daniel, May 4, 1946; children—Mary (Mrs. Julian Rosser Adams), Nancy, John. Designer, Naval Aircraft Factory, 1936; aero. researcher NACA, Hampton, Va., 1936-58, chief hypersonic vehicles div. NASA, 1958—; dir. Travel Assos. Ltd., Newport News, Va. Fellow Am. Inst. Aeros. and Astronautics (Sylvanus Reed award 1960); Sanger Meml. lectr. 1968. Clubs: Hampton Yacht; Engineers (Hampton). Contbr. articles to profl. jours. Home: 28 Oakland Dr Newport News VA 23601 Office: NASA Langley Research Center Hampton VA 23665

BECKHAM, JOE WARREN, engring exec.; b. Brownwood, Tex., Mar. 31, 1922; s. Ernest A. and Mae (Blair) B.; B.A., Daniel Baker Coll., 1943; B.S. in Civil Engring., Tex. U., 1948; m. Marjorie Ann Chambers, Oct. 23, 1948; children—Carol G., Blair W., Phillip C. Asst. research engr. Tex. Foundries, Inc., Lufkin, 1948-52, design engr., 1952-55, product devel. engr., 1955-58, research and design supt., 1958—, also dir.; dir. Am. Pole Structures Corp. Mem. finance com. Diocese Tex. (Episcopal Ch.), 1966-69. Bd. dirs. Wilson McKewen Treatment Center, St. Cyprians Sch. Served to 1st lt. USAAF, 1942-45; PTO. Mem. Soc. for Exptl. Stress Analysis, Am. Soc. for Testing and Materials, Am. Foundrymen's Soc. (dir. Tex. chpt. 1962-67, 70—, internat. dir. 1967-70), Phi Gamma Delta, Chi Epsilon. Clubs: Lufkin (dir.), Lufkin Country. Patentee in field. Home:

2210 Copeland St Lufkin TX 75901 Office: PO Box 1608 Lufkin TX 75902

BECKHAM, LACY CALDWELL, periodontist; b. Abilene, Tex., Jan. 30, 1930; s. Lacy Hiram and Agnes (Caldwell) B.; B.A., Hardin-Simmons U., 1951; D.D.S., Baylor U., 1955; certificate Periodontology, Columbia, 1959; postgrad. in periodontics Boston U., 1965, 66, 67, 71, 73; m. Joanne Blunk, June 18, 1952; children—Mildred Karen, Steven Caldwell. Practice limited to periodontics, Amarillo, Tex.; asst. clin. prof. periodontics Coll. Dentistry, Baylor U., Dallas; lectr., clin. instr. Amarillo Coll. Cons. Amarillo AFB. Bd. dirs. United Fund Amarillo. Served to capt., Dental Corps, USAF, 1955-57. Fellow Acad. Internat. Dentistry, Royal Soc. Health; mem. Am. Acad. Periodontology, Am. Dental Assn., Am. Soc. Periodontology (charter), S.W. Soc. Periodontics (sec.-treas.), Psi Omega. Presbyn. (elder). Rotarian. Contbr. articles to profl. publs. Home: 3003 Harmony St Amarillo TX 79101 Office: 1422 Tyler St Amarillo TX 79101

BECKJORD, PHILIP RAINS, educator, physician; b. Manila, Philippine Islands, Jan. 9, 1914; s. Harry Lyman and Helen Gertrude (Rains) B.; B.S., U. Minn., 1935, M.B., 1937, M.D., 1938, M.P.H., 1949; Dr. P.H., Johns Hopkins, 1957; m. Margaret McGilvray, Oct. 17, 1937; children—Cedric Jon, Pamela Margaret, Peter Rains, Ross Forrester. Surg. intern U. Minn. Hosps., Mpls., 1937-38; gen. practice medicine, Willmar, Minn., 1938-40; prof., chmn. dept. health services adminstrn. Sch. Pub. Health and Tropical Medicine, Tulane U., New Orleans, 1960—. Fulbright prof. U. Hamburg, 1966-67; vis. prof. Am. U. Beirut, 1966, U. Edinburgh, 1967; mem. pub. health research study sect. NIH, Washington, 1957-59; mem. nat. community health research training com. USPHS, 1965-68; cons. La. State Health Dept., 1968—. Served to col., M.C., AUS, 1940-60. Recipient Fellowships, La. State U./USPHS, 1961, WHO/Inst. Nutrition For Central Am. and Pan Am., 1962, WHO, 1963-64; decorated Bronze Star medal. Diplomate Am. Bd. Preventive Medicine. Fellow Am. Coll. Preventive Medicine (v.p. 1965), Am. Pub. Health Assn.; mem. A.M.A., Assn. Tchrs. Preventive Medicine, Am. Soc. Tropical Medicine and Hygiene, Orleans Parish Med. Soc., U.S.-Mexico Border Pub. Health Soc., La. Pub. Health Assn., N.Y. Soc. Tropical Medicine, Delta Omega Pub. Health Soc., Phi Rho Sigma. Home: 2529 Jefferson Av New Orleans LA 70115 Office: 1430 Tulane Av New Orleans LA 70112

BECKMAN, GAIL MCKNIGHT, educator; b. N.Y.C., Apr. 8, 1938; d. Irland McKnight and Elizabeth (Hurlock) Beckman; grad. Baldwin Sch., 1955; B.A., Bryn Mawr Coll., 1959; J.D., Yale, 1963; diploma (Fulbright scholar), U. Tubingen (Germany), 1960; M.A., U. Pa., 1966. Admitted to Pa. bar, 1964, Ga. bar, 1972, D.C. bar, 1964, U.S. Supreme Ct. bar, 1968; counsel Legal Aid Soc. Phila., 1961; asso. firm Morgan, Lewis, Bockius, Phila., 1963-66; lectr. law U. Glasgow (Scotland), 1967-71; asso. prof. law Ga. State U., Atlanta, 1971—. Research asso. Am. Philos. Soc., 1966-69. Mem. Phila., Atlanta, Ga., Am. (chmn. com. internat. ct. of justice, 1968—), Internat. bar assns., Am. Assn. U. Women, Jr. League Atlanta, Nat. Soc. Colonial Dames Am., Yale Club Atlanta, Bryn Mawr Club Phila., St. Andrew's Soc. Atlanta (co-founder, sec., 1971), Presbyn. Soroptimist. Club: Yale. Contbr. articles to profl. jours. Home: 1270 W Peachtree St Atlanta GA 30309

BECKMANN, GEORGE CLAUS, JR., hosp. adminstr.; b. Savannah, Ga., Aug. 16, 1922; s. George Claus and Lucile (North) B.; B.S., Ga. Inst. Tech., 1951; m. Mary Helen Scranton, Sept. 19, 1944; children—Barbara Ann, Nancy Ann. Marine draftsman Savannah Machine & Foundry, 1945-46; asst. to exec. dir. Elks Aidmore Inc., Atlanta, 1947-50; asst. adminstr. Emory U. Hosp., Atlanta, 1951-53; adminstr. med. services Ga. Warm Springs Found., 1953-66, adminstr., 1967—. Guest lectr., preceptor grad. program in hosp. and health adminstrn. U. Fla., 1967—; mem. Ga. Joint Council To Improve Health Care for Aged; mem. Ga. Gov.'s Com. on Arthritis, Com. on Employment of Handicapped, 1970—. Trustee Nat. Amputee Golf Scholarship Fund. Served with USAAF, 1942-45. Mem. Am. Coll. Hosp. Adminstrs., Am. Acad. Health Adminstrs., Am. (alternate del. 1972—, chmn. governing council sect. for rehab. and chronic disease hosps. 1971, council financing), Ga. (treas. 1970-71) hosp. assns., West Central Ga. Hosp. Council (pres. 1958), Ga. Gerontology Soc. (v.p. 1965-66), Ga. Hosp. Service Assn. (trustee 1963—), Assn. Rehab. Centers, Nat., Ga. (pres. 1961) rehab. assns. Nat. Amputee Golf Assn. (trustee). Rotarian (pres. 1956). Home: 22 S Cromwell Rd Savannah GA 31404 Office: Candler Gen Hosp PO Box 9787 Savannah GA 31402

BECKNER, DAVID STUART, banker; b. Roanoke, Va., Sept. 5, 1911; s. Alexander Lyle and Ida Belle (Davis) B.; grad. Sch. Banking U. Wis., summer, 1960; m. Dorothy Gertrude Rhodes, Oct. 15, 1938; children—Dorothy (Mrs. James A. McClung), David Stuart. With Va. Nat. Bank, Norfolk, 1930-45, bookkeeper, 1940-43; chief clk., 1940-45; with Bank of Va., Norfolk, 1945—, asst. v.p., 1959-67, v.p. 1967—. Mem. Norfolk, Norfolk Jr. (past pres.) chambers commerce, Am. Inst. Banking, Hampton Roads Maritime Assn., Hampton Roads Fgn. Commerce Club. Baptist (deacon). Kiwanian. Home: 3715 Wedgefield Av Norfolk VA 23502 Office: 500 Plume St E Norfolk VA 23501

BEDFORD, MADELEINE ALANN PECKHAM (MRS. CHARLES FRANCIS BEDFORD), civic worker; b. Ontario, Cal., Jan. 25, 1910; d. Allen Lewis and Madeleine (Elliott) Peckham; A.B., U. Cal. at Berkeley, 1930, M.A., 1937; LL.D., Tex. Christian U., 1973; m. Charles Francis Bedford, Dec. 30, 1930; children—Madeleine Alann, Frances Ellen, Charlotte Jean. Supr. tchr. tng. and counseling, in charge testing Univ. High Sch., U. Cal. at Berkeley, 1931-38; tchr. English to fgn. born San Leandro (Cal.) Evening Schs., 1931-38. Treas., Tarrant County Day Care Assn., 1953-54; pres. Ft. Worth and Tarrant County council Camp Fire Girls, 1961-63, pres. nat. council, 1965-68; pres. Ft. Worth Lit. Council, 1963-65; v.p. Tarrant County United Fund and Community Council, 1963-66, mem. exec. com. bd. dirs., 1963—, chmn. speakers tours film div. United Way Met. Tarrant County, 1973; pres. Ft. Worth chpt. Am. Field Service, 1964-66; chmn. budget sub-com. United Fund, 1959-68; sec. Tex. United Community Services, 1968-70, v.p., 1970-73, pres., 1973—; mem. Mid-Am. Regional Vol. Task Force United Way Am. Tex. rep. for UNICEF, 1969—; mem. gov.'s steering com. White House Conf. on Children and Youth, 1970, chmn. task force com. for Tex. on internat. relations, 1970; chmn. Met. div. Crusade of Hope campaign; chmn. Mayor's Council Youth Opportunity, Fort Worth, 1971—; chmn. Tarrant County Task Force Aging, 1972—. Bd. dirs. Tarrant County chpt. A.R.C. united Cerebral Palsy, Tarrant County Community Action Agy., Tarrant County Community Council, Tex. Social Welfare Assn.; trustee Assn. for Grad. Edn. and Research North Tex., 1971—; bd. visitors Add-Ran Coll., Tex. Christian U., 1971—. Recipient Gulick award Camp Fire Girls, 1961, Wo-He-Lo award 1968; award of Excellence for Outstanding Leadership and Service Tarrant Co. Community Council, 1964, Civic award First Lady Ft. Worth Altrusa, 1966. Mem. Ft. Worth Lecture Found., Mortar Board, Phi Beta Kappa (pres. Ft. Worth 1958-59), Alpha Chi Omega, Pi Sigma Alpha. Episcopalian. Club: Ft. Worth Woman's (past pres. history sect.). Home: 7 Westover Rd Fort Worth TX 76107

BEDGOOD, DALE RAY, mathematician, educator; b. Saltillo, Tex., Aug. 10, 1932; s. William M. and Martha L. (Alcorn) B.; B.S., E. Tex. State U., 1954; M.A., U. Ark., 1959; Ed.D., Okla. State U., 1964; m. Betty Langford, Aug. 15, 1959; children—Jennifer, Scott Langford. Instr., N.E. La. State U., Monroe, 1960-62, asso. prof., head dept. math., 1964-67; prof., head dept. math. E. Tex. State U., Commerce, 1967—. Served with USAF, 1954-58. Mem. Math. Assn. Am., Am. Math. Soc., Nat. Council Tchrs. Math. Home: 2817 McCarley St Commerce TX 75428

BEDNAR, DICK DOWNEY, mech. engr.; b. Grand Island, Neb., Dec. 28, 1917; s. Gerald and Annie Gertrude (Carr) B.; B.S. in Mech. Engring., U. Okla., 1949; m. Nevada Ishmael Wilkinson, June 13, 1942; children—Dick Downey, Charles Dean. Installations engr. U.S. Air Force, U.S., Scotland, 1951-58; instr. U. Okla. Coll. Engring., 1958-60; mem. staff Hudgens, Thompson, Ball & Asso., Architects-Engrs., Oklahoma City, 1965-69; supt. utilities, pumping div. Oklahoma City Water Dept., 1969—, project engr. Stars and Stripes Park-Lake Hefner, 1969-71. Served with USAAF, 1941-46, USAF, 51-53. Decorated Air Medal. Registered profl. engr., Okla. Mem. Am. Water Works Assn. Democrat. Baptist. Home: 129 SW 62d St Oklahoma City OK 73139 Office: Oklahoma City Water Dept 200 N Walker Oklahoma City OK 73102

BEDWELL, EDWARD ELISHA, lawyer; b. Ft. Smith, Ark., Jan. 21, 1921; s. Maurice D. and Edna (Carver) B.; B.A., U. Okla., 1941; J.D., U. Ark., 1948; m. Eloise Stuckey, Aug. 29, 1946; children—Anne, Barbara, Edward Elisha, Elise. Admitted to Ark. bar, 1948; since practiced in Ft. Smith; asst. pros. atty., 1948-50; pvt. practice, 1951—. Dir. City Nat. Bank, Ft. Smith. Served to capt. USAAF, 1943-45. Mem. Sebastian County Bar Assn. (pres. 1957), Phi Delta Theta, Omicron Delta Kappa. Presbyn. (elder). Rotarian. Home: 2200 S 46th St Fort Smith AR 72901 Office: 24 N 7th St Fort Smith AR 72901

BEEBE, BURTON ELDRED, elec. engr.; b. Kansas City, Mo., May 31, 1914; s. Leo Edwin and Minnie J. (Eldred) B.; B.S., John Brown U., Siloam Springs, Ark., 1936; m. Mary Belle Vestal, Feb. 20, 1936; children—William E., Richard E., Charles B., Jo Ann (Mrs. Tony R. Gilliam). Instr. elec. engring. John Brown U., 1935-39; elec. engr. comml. dept. Kansas City Power & Light Co., 1939-41; elec. engr. Evans Elec. Constrn. Co., Kansas City, 1941-42, J.F. Pritchard & Co., Kansas City, 1942-43, N.Am. Aviation, Inc., Kansas City, Kan., Dallas, 1943-45; elec. engr. drafting div. engring. dept. Tex. Power & Light Co., Dallas, 1946-51, mech. engr., 1951-54, elec. engr. Spl. Engring. Services div., 1954—. Mem. I.E.E.E., Am. Soc. Heating, Refrigerating and Air Conditioning Engrs., Dallas Elec. Club. Baptist (deacon). Home: 611 Greenleaf Dr Richardson TX 75080 Office: PO Box 6331 Dallas TX 75222

BEEBE, WILLIAM DOW, utility ofcl.; b. Bridgeport, Conn., Dec. 7, 1917; s. Ira Dow and Mary Margaret (Bell) B.; student George Washington U.; m. Hazel Emma Fowler, Apr. 2, 1954; children—William Dow, Donald James, Barbara Ann, Margaret Frances. With Potomac Elec. Power Co., Washington, 1937—, relay tester high voltage power apparatus, 1949-53, foreman of substa. test dept., 1953—. First aid instr. A.R.C.; mem. adv. com. United Fund; pres. Friends of Woodrow Wilson Library; v.p., trustee Barcroft Terrace Citizens Assn.; mem. exec. com. P.T.A., 1957-58, 72-73. Served with Signal Corps, AUS, 1943-46; PTO. Recipient Silver Beaver award Boy Scouts Am., 1958. Mem. I.E.E.E., PEPCO Engrs. Assn. (past sec.), UN Assn. Methodist. Mason. Home: 6227 Parkhill Dr Alexandria VA 22312 Office: 1900 Pennsylvania Av NW Washington DC 20006

BEENE, WOODIE EUGENE, supt. schs.; b. Hillsboro, Tex., Aug. 16, 1916; s. Wood and Jessie (Hunt) B.; A.A., Hill Jr. Coll., 1935; B.S., North Tex. State U., 1938; M.Ed., West Tex. State U., 1950; m. Corrie Luzelle Bryan, June 1, 1954; children—Richard Eugene, Judith Ann. Tchr. pub. schs. Sunray, Tex., 1938-41, supt., 1941-45; tchr. pub. schs. Panhandle, Tex., 1946; program sec. YMCA, Amarillo, Tex., 1946-47; ednl. therapist VA Hosp., Amarillo, 1947-50; prin. pub. schs., Claude, Tex., 1950-51, supt., 1951-55; supt schs., Canadian, Tex., 1955-66, Stamford, Tex., 1966—. Mem. Am., Tex. assns. sch. adminstrs., Tex. Tchrs. Assn., Panhandle Sch. Leaders Assn. (past pres.), Red Red Rose. Mason. Lion. Home: 1406 Bartley St Stamford TX 79553 Office: PO Box 1238 Stamford TX 79553

BEERS, CHARLES ANDREW, govt. ofcl.; b. Emporia, Fla., Apr. 15, 1924; s. John Lenord and Rebecca Jane (St. Clare) B.; B.S. in E.E., U. Kan., 1950; m. Lois Lee Soctt, July 30, 1945; children—Charles Jimmy, Patricia Ann, Sharon Lee, Susan Lyn. Electronics engr. AEC div. Bendix Corp., 1953-55, project engr. radio div., 1959-62; mfg. engr. aviation gas turbine div. Westinghouse Electric Corp., 1955-57; cons. engr. Allstates Design & Devel. Corp., 1958-59; chief operations analysis br., tech. asst. flight control div. NASA, Johnson Space Center, Houston, 1962—. Served with USNR, 1942-45. Registered profl. engr., Kan. Home: 707 Huntington St Friendswood TX 77546 Office: NASA Johnson Space Center Houston TX 77058

BEERS, HOWARD WAYLAND, ret. educator; b. Gouverneur, N.Y., Apr. 14, 1905; s. Wayland Lewis and Elizabeth Cordelia (Beardsley) B.; B.S., Cornell U., 1929, M.S., 1930, Ph.D., 1935; postgrad. U. Chgo., 1930-31; m. Sara Bernice VanSickle, Mar. 31, 1929; children—Marilyn Ruth Lynn, Rowland V., Julia (Mrs. Ronald C. George). Asso. prof. rural sociology Rutgers U., New Brunswick, N.J., 1936-38; prof. rural sociology U. Ky., Lexington, 1939-74, head dept., 1948-59, head dept. sociology, 1951-59, dir. Center for Developmental Change, 1967-74, asso. dean grad. sch., 1973-74, emeritus prof., 1974—. N.J. State leader 4-H Club Work, New Brunswick, 1937-38; Fulbright prof. Coll. Agr., Athens, Greece, 1949-50; expert in community devel. UN, 1952; expert in evaluation European Productivity Agy., Paris, France, 1955-56; cons. Ford Found., India, 1958-59; asso. Agr. Devel. Council, Indonesia, 1960-65; chief of party U. Ky./AID Contract Team, Bogor, Indonesia, 1962-66. Trustee Ky. Welfare Found., 1950-58. Mem. Am., So. (pres. 1943), Rural (pres. 1953) sociol. socs., Ky. Welfare Assn. (pres. 1943, 49). Author: An American Experience in Indonesia, 1971; also articles. Editor: Kentucky: Designs for Her Future, 1945; Indonesian Resources and Their Technological Development, 1970. Editor Rural Sociology, 1945-48. Home: 774 Sherwood Dr Lexington KY 40502

BEESON, CLARENCE EARL, wholesale distbg. co. exec.; b. Winston-Salem, N.C., June 14, 1901; s. Charles H. and Zena (Berrier) B.; grad. Evans Bus. Coll., Winston-Salem, 1921; m. Ruth V. Ransom, Mar. 21, 1945; children—Clarence Earl, Carolyn Ruth. Owner, City Retreading and Vulcanizing Co., N. Wilkesboro, N.C., 1918-20; bookkeeper So. Bearings and Parts Co., Inc., Charlotte, N.C., 1922-26, sec., treas., 1927-40, v.p., treas., 1940-48, pres., 1948-72, chmn. bd., chief exec. officer, 1972—; pres. Charlotte Appliance Service, Inc., 1948-73, Carolina Nurseries, Inc., Charlotte, 1950-65; dir. N.C. Nat. Bank. Mem. Masons, 1928—, pres. Masonic Fellowship Luncheon Club (Charlotte) 1949-50; mem. Shriners, 1929—; gen. chmn. Shrine Bowl of Carolinas, Inc., 1944-45, pres., 1946-47, chmn. bd., 1957-73, emeritus, 1973—; potentate Oasis Temple of Shrine, Charlotte, 1956, chmn. bd. trustees, 1956; bd. govs. Shriners Hosp. Crippled Children, 1958-73, emeritus, 1973—; mem. Jesters, formerly dir. Trustee Charlotte Rehab. Hosp., Pfeiffer Coll., Misenheimer, N.C. Mem. Southeastern Parts Jobbers Assn. (sec., treas. 1927-29), Va.-Carolinas Wholesalers Assn. (past dir.), Motor and Equipment Wholesalers Assn. (past dir.), Charlotte C. of C. (past dir.). Methodist (trustee). Lion. Clubs: Myers Park Country (dir., pres.) Red Fez Country (Charlotte); Country of N.C. (Pinehurst, N.C.) Grandfather Golf and Country (charter mem.) (Linville, N.C.). Home: 2400 Woodhaven Rd Charlotte NC 28211 Office: 219 E 8th St Charlotte NC 28201

BEESON, WILLARD HUGH, ins. co. exec.; b. Panama City, Panama, Sept. 8, 1935; s. Charles L. and Florence (Wilkinson) B.; student Hotchkiss Sch., 1950-53; B.A., Duke U., 1957; m. Yvonne Paulet, Oct. 19, 1957; children—Catherine, Jeffrey, Patricia, Gary. With Chase Manhattan Bank, 1957-64, Mexican rep., Mexico City, 1962-64; v.p. Deltec Banking Corp., also Banco de la Ciudad de México, Mexico City, 1965-68; v.p., treas. Restaurantes Polinesios, Mexico City, 1968—; mng. dir. Pan American de México, Compañía de Suguros, S.A., Mexico City, 1970—; pres. Maia, Mexico City, 1973—. Trustee, U. of Americas, Puebla, Mexico. Mem. Am. Soc. (pres. 1968), Am. C. of C., Asociación Méxicana de Instituciones de Seguros, Asociación para Evitar la Ceguera en México. Clubs: University, Chapultepec Golf, Reforma Athletic, American (pres. 1966-68). Home: Fernando Alén Caster 245 México DF 10 México Office: 355 Paseo de la Reforma México DF 5 México

BEEUWKES, LAMBERT BAER, broadcast sta. mgmt. cons.; b. Balt., May 6, 1907; s. John Christian and Elizabeth (Baer) B.; grad. Balt. Poly. Inst., 1926; student Johns Hopkins, 1926-28; m. M. Eleanor Byerly, Oct. 14, 1936; 1 son, Foster L. Aero. Constrn. and exptl. design aircraft Ford-Stout, Fokker, Glenn L. Martin, 1928-35; radio sta. mgmt. and constrn. stas. KYW, WXYZ, WROV, WDAS, Mich. Radio Network WLAW, MBS, NBC, 1936-70; sales dir. NBC Radio Network, 1970-72; personal mgr. The Lone Ranger, 1942-45. Inventor retractable wing, boundary layer laminar flow control; pioneer broadcast techniques such as telephone giveaway, continuous news program, guarantee sales compensation. Address: 4596 Mountain Creek Dr Roswell GA 30075

BEGLEY, MICHAEL J., clergyman. Ordained priest Roman Catholic Ch., 1934; apptd. bishop, Charlotte, N.C., 1971, consecrated, 1972. Address: Rectory St Peter's Cath Ch 507 S Tryon St Charlotte NC 28202*

BEGLEY, ROBERT JENNINGS, drug chain exec.; b. Richmond, Ky., Dec. 11, 1938; s. Robert Bruce and Vera Elizabeth (Jennings) B.; student U. Ky., 1956-58, Sch. Pharmacy U. Cin., 1958-61; m. Suzan Gail Scrivner, June 3, 1967; children—Leigh Jennings, Ashley Marcum. Clk. Begley Drug Co., Richmond, 1954, mdse. mgr., Lexington, Ky., 1956-58, mdse. mgr. 5 stores, Lexington, after 1963, warehouse mgr., seasonal and promotional buyer, 1967, dir. mdse., 1967, dist. store supr., Lexington, 1967, v.p. drug operations, 1968-72, v.p. advt., merchandising and mdse. distbn., 1972—, also dir.; dir. Affiliated Drug Stores, N.Y.C. Vice pres., mem. council Blue Grass council Boy Scouts Am. Bd. dirs. Blue Grass Regional Health Planning Council, Inc. Named Outstanding Young Man Am., 1972. Mem. Ky. Retail Fedn. (pres., dir.), Nat. Assn. Chain Drug Stores (mem. small chain com.), Ky. C. of C. (mem. Econ. Devel. Council), Sigma Alpha Epsilon. Mem. Christian Ch. (deacon). Home: Route #7 Walnut Hill Rd Richmond KY 40475 Office: Eastern Ky U By-Pass Richmond KY 40475

BEJAR, FELICIANO, sculptor, painter, printmaker, state designer; b. Jiquilpan, Mexico, July 14, 1920; s. Feliciano Bejar-Moncada and Juana Ruiz Guizar; student Salesian Coll., Guadalajara, Mexico, 1932-34. Sculptor, painter, printmaker; one-man shows in Mexico, U.S., Canada, France, Eng., Norway, Poland, Austria, others; works rep. in permanent collections Fine Arts Mus., Toronto, Ont., Can., Castle Mus., Norwich, Museo de Arte Moderno, Mexico, City Mus., Birmingham, Eng., Lowe Art Mus., Coral Gables, Fla., others; stage designer many theatres including Ballet Folklorico de Mexico; built small village in San Angel suburb of Mexico City, 1951-67; commd. by J. Walter Thompson Co., N.Y.C., 1970, Carborundum Co., Niagara Falls, 1971, Banco do Brasil, Mexico, 1973. Recipient 1st Sculpture prize Nat. Inst. Fine Arts, Mexico, 1973. Inventor type of sculpture (Magiscopes) using lenses of crystal or plastic to produce optical effects. Home: Antiguo Camino a Acapulco 369 San Angel Inn Mexico City 20 DF Mexico Office: Apartado Postal 20 029 Mexico 20 DF Mexico

BELCHER, JEWELL GREEN, JR., mech. engr.; b. El Dorado, Ark., May 19, 1934; s. Jewell Green and Lera (Allman) B.; B.M.E., Auburn U., 1959; m. Barbara Ann Mears, Sept. 5, 1955; children—Deborah Diane, Geri Lynn. Design draftsman Tenn. Coal and Iron div. U.S. Steel Corp., Fairfield, Ala., 1960; jr. engr. Ala. Power Co., Birmingham, 1960-63; sr. project engr. Brown Engring., Teledyne Co., Huntsville, Ala., 1963-68; mech. engr. U.S. Army Corps Engrs., Huntsville div., 1968-69; aerospace engr. NASA, Marshall Space Flight Center, Ala., 1969—. Served with AUS, 1954-56. Mem. Nat., Ala. socs. profl. engrs., Am. Soc. M.E., (chmn. North Ala. sect. 1969-70), Ala. Inventors Assn. Baptist. Home: 3609 Wilbur Av Huntsville AL 35810 Office: NASA George C Marshall Space Flight Center AL 35812

BELCHER, WILLIAM ALVIS, rancher, veterinarian; b. Del Rio, Tex., Aug. 25, 1918; s. Clifton C. and Willie (Cochran) B.; D.V.M., Tex. A. and M. U., 1943; postgrad. Mich. State U., Colo. State U.; m. Hazel Arledge, Sept. 8, 1937; children—Willie Ellen (Mrs. Lindsay L. Langham), Madge Elizabeth (Mrs. Samuel M. Rhoades). Gen. practice vet. medicine, Crystal City, Tex., 1943-46; rancher, Brackettsville, Tex., 1946—; owner, operator Shirley Comm. Co.-Ft. Worth Stockyard 1956-59; area veterinarian Tex. Animal Health Commn., 1965—; 1st v.p. Del Rio Wool and Mohair Co., 1950—; chmn. bd. dirs. San Antonio br. Dallas Fed. Res. Bank. County chmn. Screw Worm Eradication Program, 1961—; veterinarian in charge Tex. Screw Worm Program; Mem. Am. Vet. Med. Assn., Tex., S.W. cattle raiser's assn., Tex. Sheep and Goat Raiser's Assn. (dir.), Tex. Angus Assn. (dir.). Address: Box 588 Bracketville TX 78832

BELK, IRWIN, mcht., former state senator; b. Charlotte, N.C., April 4, 1922; s. William Henry and Mary Leonora (Irwin) B. ; student Davidson Coll., U. N.C., 1946; m. Carol Grotnes, Sept. 11, 1948; children—William, Irene, Marilyn, Carl. Trained in mdse. field since childhood; chmn. bd. Monroe Hardware Co.; pres. Belk Enterprises, Inc.; v.p., dir. Belk Group of Stores, Charlotte, P.M.C., Inc., Raleigh, N.C.; exec. v.p. finance Belk Stores Services, Inc., Charlotte; dir. First Union Nat. Bank, Stonecutter Mills, Spindale, N.C., Fidelity Bankers Life Ins. Co., Richmond, Va., Henry River Mills Co., Adams-Millis Corp., Lumbermen's Mut. Casualty Co. Chmn. bd. Belk Found. Mem. N.C. Ho. of Reps., 1959-60, 61-62; N.C. state senator, 1960-61, 63-66; mem. N.C. Lesgislative Council, 1963-64, Legislative Research Commn., 1965-66; del. Nat. Democratic Conv., 1956, 60, 64, 68, 72; Democratic nat. committeeman, 1969-72. Mem. finance com., trustee U. N.C., Charlotte; trustee, mem. finance com. Queens Coll.; dir. Bus. Found. N.C.; local dir. Am. Heart Assn.; mem. ho. of dels., local dir. Am. Cancer Soc.; bd. dirs. N.C. Med. Adv. Council U. N.C.; mem. Gov.'s Commn. to Study Cause and Control Cancer; co-chmn. Edenton and Chowan County Historic Commn.; past pres. Carolinas

Carrousel; bd. dirs. Charlotte Opera Assn. (mem. finance bd.), Hist. Found. Presbyn. and Reformed Chs.; bd. assos. Mars Hill Coll., Campbell Coll.; bd. advisers Chowan Coll.; mem. adv. council Wingate Coll.; bd. visitors Appalachian State Tchrs. Coll.; bd. assos. Meredith Coll.; bd. counselors Erskine Coll.; bd. dirs., past pres. N.C. Soc. Prevention Blindness; bd. dirs. Bus. Found. N.C., Ednl. Found., Inc. (both Chapel Hill); mem. bd. Wake Forest U. Sch. Bus. Served as sgt., 8th Air Force, World War II. Named One of 10 Outstanding Young Men in Charlotte, 1954, 55, 56, 57. Mem. N.C. Mchts. Assn. (past pres., state dir.), C. of C. (dir.), Charlotte Mchts. Assn., Kappa Alpha, Delta Sigma Pi. Presbyn. (deacon; past pres. men's council Synod of N.C.). Mason (shriner), Lion (past dist. gov.). Clubs: Executives (dir., past pres.), Charlotte Country, Myers Park Country, Charlotte City (Charlotte); Raleigh City; Sky (N.Y.C.). Home: 400 Eastover Rd Charlotte NC 28207 Office: 308 E 5th St Charlotte NC 28201

BELK, JOHN MONTGOMERY, dept. store exec., mayor; b. Charlotte, N.C., Mar. 29, 1920; s. William Henry and Mary (Irwin) B.; B.S. in Econs., Davidson Coll., 1941; m. Claudia Watkins, Feb. 20, 1971. With Belk Stores Services, Inc., Charlotte, 1941—, pres., 1955—, also dir; dir. Wachovia Bank & Trust Co., Charlotte, Winston-Salem, N.C., Integon Inc., Winston-Salem. Mem. exec. bd. Southeast region Boy Scouts Am., 1958—. Mayor of Charlotte, 1969—. Past trustee Davidson Coll., now bd. visitors; bd. dirs. Found. U. N.C., Charlotte, N.C. Research Triangle Found., Tom Haggai & Assos. Found., N.C. Sports Hall Fame, Mint Mus. Served to capt. AUS, 1943-45. Recipient Silver Beaver award Boy Scouts Am., 1955, Silver Antelope award, 1962. Mem. Charlotte C. of C. (pres. 1964), Am. Mgmt. Assn. (dir.), Nat. Retail Mchts. Assn. (chmn. 1974), World Bus. Council, Omicron Delta Kappa, Mason (Shriner). Home: 2318 Beverly Dr Charlotte NC 28207 Office: 308 E 5th St Charlotte NC 28234

BELK, THOMAS MILBURN, dept. store exec.; b. Charlotte, N.C., Feb. 6, 1925; s. William Henry and Mary (Irwin) B.; student Davidson Coll., 1942-43; B.S. in Marketing and Commerce, U. N.C., Chapel Hill, 1948; m. Katherine Whitner McKay, May 19, 1953; children—Katherine Whitner, Thomas Milburn, Hamilton McKay, John Robert. With Belk Stores Services Inc., Charlotte, 1948—, 1st exec. v.p., 1971—; dir. N.C. Nat. Bank, Mut. Savs. & Loan Assn., Bus. Devel. Corp. N.C. Pres. United Community Services, 1963, dir., 1959-70; pres. Central Charlotte Assn., 1965, 66; mem. exec. bd. Boy Scouts Am., 1970-73. Trustee Presbyn. Hosp., Crossnore Sch.; chmn. bd. St. Andrews Presbyn. Coll., 1968-72; bd. visitors Davidson Coll., Presbyn. Coll.; bd. dirs. YMCA. Served to lt. (j.g.) USNR, 1943-46; PTO. Named Jaycee's Young Man of Yr., 1960; Charlotte News Young Man of Yr., 1962; Delta Sigma Pi Man of Yr., 1962; Raleigh News & Observer Tarheel of Week, May 12, 1964. Mem. Newcomen Soc. N.A., N.C. Citizens Assn. (pres. 1973). Presbyn. (elder 1964—). Mason (32 deg., Shriner). Home: 2441 Lemon Tree Lane Charlotte NC 28211 Office: 308 E 5th St Charlotte NC 28201

BELKIN, ARNOLD, painter; b. Can.; student Nat. Poly. Inst., Mexico City, Mexico. Asst. prof. mural techniques, U. of Ams., Mexico City, 1953-60; prof. theatre design U. Motolinia, Mexico City, 1954-60; guest instr. painting Pratt Inst., N.Y.C., 1967-71. One-man shows, 1952—, latest being Phoenix Art Mus., 1967, Ankrum Gallery, Los Angeles, 1967, Galeria Jack Misrachi, Mexico City, 1969, 10 Downtown, N.Y.C., 1970, Jack Misrachi Gallery, N.Y.C., 1970, London Arts, Detroit, 1971, Galeria Pecanins, Mexico City, 1971, Midtown Gallery, Atlanta, 1971, Lerner-Misrachi Gallery, N.Y.C., 1972; exhibited in numerous group shows, 1959—, latest being Expo '67, Montreal, Que., Can., 1967, U. Tex. Art Mus., Ausitn, 1967, Hemisfair '68, San Antonio, 1968, I Salon de Independientes, Mexico City, 1968, IX Internat. Arts Festival, Cali, Colombia, 1969, Internat. Graphics Biennale, San Juan, P.R., 1969, I Panam. Biennale Graphics, Cali, 1970, Lerner-Misrachi Gallery, N.Y.C., 1971, 72, II Latin Am. Graphics Biennale, San Juan, 1971, Bienal de Arte Coltejer, Medellin, Colombia, 1972; murals executed at Nat. Poly. Inst., Mexico City, 1952, Continental Hilton Hotel, Mexico City, 1956, Casa de Piedra, Cuernavaca, Mexico, 1957, Jewish Community Center, Vancouver, B.C., Can., 1959, Fed. Penitentiary, Mexico City, 1961, Sch. for Rehab. Handicapped Children, Mexico City, 1963, Jewish Cultural Center, Mexico City, 1967, Mexican Pavillion, Expo '67, Hemisfair '68, Lock Haven (Pa.) State Coll., 1971; represented in permanent collections Mus. Modern Art, Mexico City, Phoenix Art Mus., Betzalel Nat. Mus., Jerusalem, Israel, Los Angeles County Mus., Mass. Inst. Tech., Gen. Motors Collection Mexican Graphics, Austin, Club de Industriales, Mexico City, Queens Coll., Des Moines Mus., Nat. Mus., New Delhi, India, Pitts. Mus., USIS, Kresge Internat. Collection, Detroit, Bank of Chgo. Lectr. on Mexican art in Can., U.S., Mexico, to museums and cultural insts., on radio and TV. Recipient purchase prize II Latin Am. Graphics Bienal, San Juan, 1971. Founder, co-editor Neuva Presencia, 1961-64. Contbr. numerous articles on Mexican artists of 5th generation to profl. publs. Address: Pecanins Gallery Mexico City DF Mexico*

BELKNAP, PAUL ALCON, rubber co. exec.; b. Sherrodsville, O., Sept. 13, 1916; s. Emmet Ellsworth and Catherine Inez (Tombaugh) B.; student Coll. Wooster, 1934-35; B.S., Ohio U., 1938; M.S., Ia. State U., 1941; m. Barbara Silver, Apr. 12, 1941; children—Jeff, Greg. Research chemist Nat. Adhesives Corp., N.Y.C., 1941-42; chief chemist Surety Rubber Co., Carrollton, O., 1942-48; founder Charleston Rubber Co. (S.C.), 1948—, pres., 1959—. Cons. rubber protective equipment Edison Electric Inst., 1959—; dir. Burris Chem. Co., Charleston, S.C. Nat. Bank, Charleston. Mem. exec. bd. United Fund Charleston County, 1952-55, mem. budget com., 1952—, council commr., 1957, dist. chmn., 1958; pres. YMCA, Charleston, 1970—. Bd. dirs. Carolina Art Assn., 1955-65, treas., 1960-62; bd. dirs. YMCA, Jr. Achievement. Recipient citation of merit Q.M.C., 1945; Silver Beaver award Boy Scouts Am., 1969. Mem. Am. Chem. Soc., N.A.M., U.S. Indsl. Council (pres. 1974—), Nat. Alliance Businessmen (metro chmn. 1969), Agrl. Soc. S.C., Charleston Mfrs. Club, Greater Charleston C. of C. (v.p. 1959, 61-67). Rotarian. Clubs: Charleston, Carolina Yacht (Charleston). Patentee in field. Office: 3370 Rivers Av Charleston Heights SC 29405 Home: 13 Meeting St Charleston SC 29401

BELL, AUBREY BLAN, reprodn. co. exec.; b. Center, Tex., May 26, 1909; s. Dan Marion and Edna (Adams) B.; B.S., U. Tex., 1938; m. Vera Catherine McDaniel, Nov. 22, 1928 (dec. July 1971); m. 2d, Mary Jane Dulaney Shultz, May 1, 1972. Rodman, then asst. engr. City of Abilene (Tex.), 1928-31; prin. asst. H.L. Thackwell, cons. engr., Longview, Tex., 1938-39; sales engr. Keuffell & Esser Co., Austin, Tex., 1939-42; cons. Bell Reprodn. Co., Ft. Worth, 1946—. Alderman, Village of Edgecliff, 1974—. Served from 1st lt. to maj. San. Corps, AUS, 1942-46. Decorated Bronze Star; named Boss of Year, Exec. Secs., Ft. Worth, 1966; Engring. Friend of U., Sch. Engring. U. Tex. at Arlington, 1973. Registered profl. engr., Tex. Mem. Nat., Tex. (past pres. Ft. Worth, Richard Van Trump award 1972, Engr. of Yr. award Ft. Worth chpt. 1974) socs. profl. engrs., South Mid Continent Blue Print Assn. (past pres.), Am. Soc. C.E. (pres. Ft. Worth 1951), Internat. Soc. Blue Print and Allied Industries (dir. 1956-59). Home: 37 Brenton Rd Fort Worth TX 76134 Office: 907 Throckmorton St Fort Worth TX 76102

BELL, BRYAN, real estate, oil investment exec., educator; b. New Orleans, Dec. 15, 1918; s. Bryan and Sarah (Perry) B.; B.A., Woodrow Wilson Sch. Pub. and Internat. Affairs, Princeton, 1941; M.A., Tulane U., 1962; m. Rubie S. Crosby, July 15, 1950; children—Rubie Perry, Helen Elizabeth, Bryan, Beverly Saunders, Barbara Crosby. Pres., Tasso Plantation Foods, Inc., New Orleans, 1945-66; partner Bell Oil Cos., New Orleans, 1962—, Greenwood Villa Apts., Lafayette, La., 1965—, Forest Royale Apts., Hattiesburg, Miss., 1968—, Park Villa Apts., Shreveport, La., 1968—, Meadowdale Apts., Marrero, La., 1967—, Bienville Apts., Natchez, Miss., 1968—, Lafayette Royale Apts., 1969—, Huntington Arms Apts., Pensacola, Fla., 1970—, Suffolk Manor Apts., Lake Charles, La., 1971—, The Bell-Drumm Co., New Orleans, 1970—; pres. Bell & Assos., Inc., New Orleans, 1970—; dir. Royal St. Louis, Inc., New Orleans, New Orleans Armature Works, Inc., Louisiana Electric Coil, Inc., Creative Prodns. and Displays, Inc., Marine Concrete Structures, Inc. Instr. econs. of real estate devel. Sch. Architecture, Tulane U., New Orleans, 1967—. Mem. Garden Dist. Assn., 1964—; bd. dirs. United Fund for Greater New Orleans Area, 1964-71, pres., 1968-69; chmn. Human Talent Bank Com., New Orleans, 1969—. Mem. City Planning Commn., New Orleans, 1956-58; mem. bd. Met. Area Com., 1968—, Bur. Govtl. Research, 1966—, pres., 1971—; chmn. com. Met. Leadership Forum, 1969—; mem. bd. New Orleans Area Health Council, 1966-70. Bd. dirs. Tulane-Lyceum, 1947-51, Family Service Soc., 1951-58, pres., 1956-58; bd. dirs. St. Martin's Protestant Episcopal Sch., 1964-68, Metairie Park Country Day Sch., 1967-71; bd. dirs. Trinity Episcopal Sch., chmn., 1958-68. Served to 1st lt. AUS, World War II. Mem. New Orleans C. of C., Princeton Alumni Assn. La. (pres. 1962-63), Fgn. Relations Assn. Democrat. Episcopalian (vestry 1960—, jr. warden 1968-70, sr. warden 1970-72). Clubs: Internat. House, Boston, New Orleans Lawn Tennis, Wyvern, Lakeshore, Pickwick, Pendennis. Address: 1331 Third St New Orleans LA 70130

BELL, CRAIG THOMAS, pulp and paper co. exec.; b. Easthampton, N.Y., Oct. 8, 1929; s. Willard Conklin and Eleanor (Thomas) B.; B.S., Syracuse U., 1953; m. Patricia Bushnell Bates, Jan. 30, 1951 children—Willard B., Serena B., Stephanie T. Forester N.C. Forest Service, Newton, 1953-55, Canal Wood Corp., Conway, S.C., 1955-57, Elizabethtown, N.C., 1957-58; area rep, Container Corp. Am., Kissimmee, Fla., 1958—. Active Boy Scouts Am.; dir. Osceola County United Appeal, 1966-67; chmn. Osceola County Recreation Commn., 1966; mem. Gov's. Task Force on Recreation, 1969; mem. Osceola County Bd. Edn., 1971—. County campaign mgr. Gov. Haydon Burns, 1964-66, U.S. Senator Edward Gurney, 1968. Served with USMCR, 1950-52. Recipient Silver Beaver award Boy Scouts Am., 1964, 25-year vet. award, 1973. Mem. Soc. Am. Foresters (Fla. sect. chmn. 1966), Nat. Recreation and Parks Assn. (Fla. rep. to nat. citizens com. 1969), Fla. Bd. Forestry (pres. 1968-70, 72-73), Fla. Forestry Assn. (dist. dir. 1964—), Fla. Conservation Council (mem. exec. com. 1968—), Fla. Audubon Soc. (v.p. Kissimmee Valley chpt. 1968), Fla. Conservation, Beta Theta Pi. Republican. Methodist. Kiwanian. Home: PO Drawer 640 Kissimmee FL 32741 Office: N 8th St Fernandina Beach FL 32034

BELL, DANIEL JOSEPH, JR., food co. exec.; b. Corsicana, Tex., Mar. 7, 1914; s. Daniel Joseph and Mary (Rucker) B.; student U. Wash., 1945, So. Methodist U., 1966; m. Ella Ruth Sims, July 19, 1937; children—Betty Jo, Ruth Ann. Accountant, Am. Well & Prospecting Co., Corsicana, 1933-41; insp. U.S. Dept. Labor, Little Rock, 1941-44; with Gen. Accounting Office, U.S. Navy, Seattle, 1944-46; plant mgr. Wolf Brand Products, Inc., Corsicana, 1948—. Chmn. City Beautification, 1965-67; chmn. Corsicana Citizen Com., 1965-67; mem. adv. bd. Salvation Army, 1971—. Commr. City of Corsicana, 1967—. Served with USNR, 1944-46. Recipient Pub. Service award City of Corsicana, 1968. Mem. Nat. Inst. Food Technologists, Nat. Canners Assn., Tex. Mfrs. Assn., Tex. Food Processors Assn. Methodist. Club: Corsicana Country (dir.). Home: 1704 Sycamore St Corsicana TX 75110 Office: 416 S Main St Corsicana TX 75110

BELL, FRANCIS LANEY, textile exec.; b. Lancaster, S.C., May 20, 1917; s. John Ulysse and Mayme (Gregory) B.; B.S., Clemson U., 1938; student exec. program U. N.C., 1961-62; m. Mary Alice Jones, Jan. 12, 1942; children—Francis Laney, Ira Jones. Instr. chemistry Clemson U., 1938-39; with Springs Mills, Inc., Ft. Mill, S.C., 1939—, now v.p. personnel adminstrn.; dir. Leroy Springs & Co., Inc. Mem. businessmen's adv. bd. Coll. Bus. Adminstrn. U. S.C.; mem. adv. com. S.C. Dept. Corrections. Served to capt. USAAF, 1941-46. Mem. Am. Legion, Scabbard and Blade, 40 and 8, Blue Key, Sigma Tau Epsilon. Mem. Asso. Ref. Presbyn. Ch. Moose. Home: 614 W Barr St Lancaster SC 29720 Office: Springs Mills Inc White St Fort Mill SC 29715

BELL, JAMES LAMAR, SR., real estate broker; b. Noma, Fla., Oct. 2, 1917; s. G. B. and Mae (Skinner) B.; m. Phyllis Frances Kelly, Sept. 4, 1969. Owner, James L. Bell & Assos., Engrs., Overland Park, Kan., Denver, 1945-63; self employed real estate investor, 1963-69; self-employed as real estate broker, Naples, Fla., 1969—; pres., Gulf So. Realty, Inc., Naples, Fla., 1969—. Ofcl. U.S. rep. Fedn. Internat. de Geometres, Vienna, Austria, 1962. Mem. zoning bd. and bd. appeals, Naples, Fla., 1963-66; mem. Collier County (Fla.) Zoning Bd. and Coastal Planning Bd., 1964-68. Registered profl. engr., Kan. Mem. Am. Congress on Surveying and Mapping (pres. survey sect. 1955, dir. 1962), Kan. Soc. Land Surveyors (pres. 1961). Office: 1156 3d St S Naples FL 33940

BELL, JAMES M., museum ofcl.; b. Texarkana, Tex., Sept. 1, 1943; s. Clarence Malcolm and Eliose Francis (Jefferson) B.; B.S., North Tex. State U., 1965; M.A., Stephen F. Austin Coll., 1968; m. Janet C. Caddenhead, May 28, 1966 (div. Dec. 1972); 1 son, Jamie Marcus. Supr. art pub. schs., Texarkana, Tex., 1966-68; asst. edn. curator Wichita (Kan.) Art Mus., 1968-70; dir. Abilene (Tex.) Fine Arts Museum, 1970-73; dir. Tampa (Fla.) Bay Art Center, 1973—. Mem. art juror com. Gasparilla Sidewalk Art Show, 1973-74. Bd. dirs. Tampa Community Concert Assn., 1973-74. Mem. Am. Assn. Museums, Coll. Art Assn., Fla. Art Mus. Dirs. Assn. Club: Westwood, Abilene, Tex. Home: 1515 S Howard St Tampa FL 33614 Office: 320 North Blvd Tampa FL 33606

BELL, JAMES MICHAEL, dentist; b. Fond du Lac, Wis., Apr. 9, 1943; s. James Walter and Irene Pauline (Roraff) B.; D.D.S., Marquette U., 1967; m. Karen Joan Bellman, Aug. 20, 1966; children—James Michael II, Jeffrey G. Research asst. dept. pathology Marquette U., 1965-67; practice dentistry, St. Thomas, V.I., 1969—. Acting cons. Title XIX, V.I. Dept. Social Welfare, 1973—. Served to capt. Dental Corps, USAF, 1967-69; PTO. Mem. V.I. (sec. 1970-73, pres. elect 1973), Am. (alternate del. 1972-73) dental assns., Acad. Gen. Dentistry, Federation Dentaire Internationale, Am. Acad. Oral Medicine, Am. Soc. Preventive Dentistry. K.C. Home: PO Box 3928 St Thomas VI 00801 Office: St Thomas Garden Mall St Thomas VI 00801

BELL, JOHN ALTON, dentist; b. Roanoke, Va., May 20, 1909; s. John Henry and Madie (Likens) B.; student Emory and Henry U., 1929-32; M.C.S., Benjamin Franklin U., 1939; postgrad. George Washington U., 1942; D.D.S., Georgetown U., 1946; m. Mary Lou Ruth, July 15, 1939; children—Susan, John Alton. Practice gen. dentistry, Arlington, Va., 1946—; asso. prof. operative dentistry Georgetown U., Washington, 1947-51, 53-57. Mem. Va. Bd. Dental Examiners, 1971—. Mem. Arlington County Youth Commn., 1967-69. Bd. dirs. Mt. Olivet Found. Fund. Served to capt. USAAF, 1951-53. Fellow Internat. Coll. Dentists, Va. State Dental Assn.; mem. Am., Va. dental assns., No. Va. Dental Soc. (pres. 1965-66), Georgetown Alumni Assn., Pan Am. Med. Soc., Old Dominion Study Club, Arlington C. of C., Omicron Kappa Upsilon, Psi Omega. Methodist (mem. adminstrv. bd.). Mason, Kiwanian (pres. 1962). Clubs: Washington Golf and Country; Northern Virginia Acquatic, Better Sports (pres. 1968-69) (Arlington). Home: 4710 N 33d St Arlington VA 22207 Office: 4625 Old Dominion Dr Arlington VA 22207

BELL, JULIAN BAKER, civil engr.; b. Newport News, Va., Sept. 29, 1940; s. Julian Baker and Bessie (Salmons) B.; B.C.E., Va. Poly. Inst., 1973; m. Carola Gean Gullum, Apr. 29, 1961; children—Julian Baker, Jon Burl, Jay W. Area engr. E.I. duPont de Nemours & Co., Martinsville, Va., 1962-65; engr. Ford Pile Founds., Virginia Beach, Va., 1965; engr. E.I. duPont de Nemours & Co., Chattanooga, 1965-71; v.p. Perry Smith Co., Chattanooga, 1971—. Asst. city engr., Chattanooga, 1972—. Cubmaster pack 3030 Boy Scouts Am., 1973—. Mem. Am. Soc. for Testing Materials, Am. Soc. C.E., Am. Pub. Works Assn., Chattanooga Engrs. Club. Methodist. Home: 407 Lark Lane Chattanooga TN 37415

BELL, KENNETH JOHN, chem. engr., educator; b. Cleve., Mar. 1, 1930; s. Harold Henry and Alma Wilma (Southwick) B.; B.S. in Chem. Engring., Case Inst. Tech., 1951; M. Chem. Engring., U. Del., 1953, Ph.D., 1955; m. Karen Yvonne McLemore, June 23, 1956; children—Lorna Lyn, Tamra Ann, Craig Ian, Ellen Kym. Engr. Gen. Electric Co., Richland, Wash., 1955-56; asst. prof. chem. engring. Case Inst. Tech., Cleve., 1956-61; asso. prof. chem. engring. Okla. State U., Stillwater, 1961-67, prof., 1967—; sr. research engr. Heat Transfer Research Inc., Alhambra, Cal., 1968-69. Cons. Phillips Petroleum Co., Falcon Research and Devel. Co.; vis. prof. Oak Ridge Sch. Reactor Tech., 1958. Mem. Sci. Com. Internat. Centre for Heat and Mass Transfer, Belgrade; U.S. del. to assembly for Internat. Heat Transfer confs. Registered profl. engr., Okla. Mem. Am. Inst. Chem. Engrs., Nat. Soc. Profl. Engrs., Am. Soc. Engring. Edn., Soc. History Tech. Republican. Contbr. articles on fluid mechanics and heat transfer to sci. jours. Home: 2801 Fox Ledge Route 5 Stillwater OK 74074

BELL, PAUL BUCKNER, lawyer; b. Charlotte, N.C., July 29, 1922; s. George Fisher and Carrie (Savage) B.; B.S., Wake Forest U., 1947, J.D. cum laude, 1948; m. Betty Sue Trulock, May 3, 1952; children—Paul B., Morris Trulock, Betty Fisher, Douglas Savage. Admitted to N.C. bar, 1948; patent atty.; pres. firm Parrott, Bell, Seltzer, Park & Gibson, Charlotte, 1948—. Dir. Pilot Research Corp., Southland Investors, Inc., Idlewild Farms, Inc., Charpat Investment Corp. Trustee Mecklenbury Presbytery, Alexander Children's Center, Presbyn. Home of Charlotte, Mountain Retreat Assn. Served as 1st lt. USAAF, 1943-46. Mem. Am. N.C., Mecklenburg bar assns., Am. Patent Law Assn., Licensing Execs. Soc., Sigma Phi Epsilon, Phi Alpha Delta. Presbyn. (elder). Clubs: Charlotte City, Charlotte Country, Charlotte Textile (past pres.), Grandfather Golf and Country; Union League (N.Y.C.). Home: 4001 Foxcroft Rd Charlotte NC 28211 Office: 1211 E Morehead St PO Box 10337 Charlotte NC 28201

BELL, RONDAL EDWARD, educator; b. Kennett, Mo., Dec. 29, 1933; s. Cecil Edward and Lola Nadine (Cumpton) B.; B.A., William Jewell Coll., 1955; M.S., U. N.M., 1960; Ph.D., U. Miss., 1971; m. Phyllis Anne Rose, July 23, 1954; children—Blake Allen, Tracy Lynne. Asst. prof. biology Millsaps Coll., Jackson, Miss., 1960-64, prof. biology, chmn. dept., 1964—, dir. environmental studies program, 1967—. Dir. Miss. Council Environmental Edn., 1969-73. Served with AUS, 1955-57. Mem. Miss. (pres. 1968-69), N.Y. acads. scis., A.A.A.S., Miss. Sci. Tchrs. Assn. (pres. 1970-71), Soc. Mammalogy, Am. Microbiology Soc., Sigma Xi. Contbr. articles profl. jours. Home: 5135 Shirlwood Dr Jackson MS 39211

BELL, WARREN EARL, lodge and country club exec.; b. Findlay, O., Jan. 26, 1922; s. Charles Omar and Mearl Marie (Alheim) B.; student Ohio State U., 1941-42; m. Peggy Kirk, Aug. 18, 1953; children—Bonnie, Peggy Ann, Kirk. Distbr. salesman Krantz Brewing Corp., Findlay, 1944-49; with sales and promotion dept. A. G. Spalding & Bros., Chgo., 1949-53; designer, builder, owner, operator Pine Needles Lodges and Country Club, Southern Pines, N.C., 1953—. Served with AUS, 1942-43. Elk. Home: Grove Dr Southern Pines NC 28387 Office: Midland Rd Southern Pines NC 28387

BELL, WILLIAM JACK, educator; b. nr. Norcatur, Kan., Nov. 1, 1915; s. James S. and Ruth (Diefendorf) B.; B.A., B.S., Emporia Kan. State Tchrs. Coll., 1937, M.S, 1940; Ph. D., U. Mo., 1949; m. Marjorie May Andrews, May 9, 1942. Tchr. high sch., Colby, Kan., 1937-42; reporter-editor Colby Free Press-Tribune, 1937-42; grad. asst., instr. U. Mo. Sch. Journalism, 1946-49; asst. prof. U. Okla. Sch. Journalism, 1949-51; photographer Daily Oklahoman, Oklahoma City, summer 1951; prof. journalism, head journalism and graphic arts dept. East Tex. State U., Commerce, 1951—. City commr., Commerce, 1960-64, mayor pro-tem, 1964-66, 74—, mayor, 1967-70; chmn. Airport Adv. Bd., 1971-74. Bd. dirs. Sulphur River Municipal Water Dist., 1971-72. Mem. exec. com. NetSeO Trails council Boy Scouts Am., 1953-57. Served with USNR, 1942-45. Mem. Am. Soc. Journalism Sch. Adminstrs., Sports Information Dirs. (coordinator 68—; nat. pres. 1965-67) Nat. Assn. Intercollegiate Athletics (Hall of Fame 1970), C. of C. (dir. 1955-57, 59-62; 69-72), Tex. Journalism Edn. Council (exec. com. 1972-73), Phi Delta Kappa (historian 1957-69), Sigma Delta Chi. Lion (pres. 1959-60, dep. dist. gov. 1962-64). Home: 2500 Washington St Commerce TX 75428

BELL, WILLIAM WOODWARD, lawyer; b. Brownwood, Tex., May 15, 1938; s. Charles Smith and Jane Mae (Woodward) B.; B.B.A., Baylor U., 1960, J.D., 1965; m. Mary Elizabeth Beniteau, May 31, 1969. Admitted to Tex. bar, 1965; practiced in Waco, 1965-68, Brownwood, 1968—; partner Sleeper, Boynton, Burleson, Williams & Johnston, Waco, 1965-68, Holloway, Slagle & Bell, Brownwood, 1969-72, Johnson, Slagle & Bell, Brownwood, 1972—; municipal judge City of Brownwood, 1968—; v.p. Bell Mortgage & Investment Co., 1962—; sec., dir. Mould-N-Mount, Inc., (both Brownwood). Chmn. Brownwood chpt. A.R.C., 1972-74. Bd. dirs. Brownwood Indsl. Found., Boy's Club, Mental Health Mentally Retarded Workshop. Served as capt. USMCR, 1960-63. Mem. Am., Tex., Brown County bar assns., Am. Judicature Soc., Assn. Trial Lawyers Am., Brownwood C. of C. (dir. 1971-74). Rotarian. Home: 1810 Durham St Brownwood TX 76801 Office: Johnson Slagle & Bell First Nat Office Bldg Brownwood TX 76801

BELLAH, CHARLIE LEWIS, architect, structural engr.; b. Corpus Christi, Tex., Feb. 26, 1937; s. Doy B. and Pearl (Boswell) B.; B. Arch., Tex. Technol. Coll., 1961; postgrad. in planning, structural, civil and soil engring.; m. Dixie Darlyne Hulsey, Jan. 29, 1960; children—Anthony Todd, Barry Kip. Asso. R.S. Colley & Assos., Corpus Christi, 1961-69; partner Valentine & Bellah, architects, engrs., Corpus Christi, 1969-70; owner, prin. Charlie L. Bellah, architects, engrs., planners, Corpus Christie, 1970—. Mem. A.I.A. adv. com. to Del Mar Technol. Sch., Corpus Christi, 1968—, guest lectr., instr., spring 1971. Bd. dirs. Redevel. Assistance Center. Registered architect, Tex., Okla. Mem. A.I.A. (chpt. pres. 1973-74; mem. bd. 1974-75), Tex. Soc. Architects (mem. ins., sureties com., profl. devel. com.), Constrn. Specification Inst. (chpt. v.p. 1969-70 pres., chmn. bd. dirs. 1970-71), Soc. Am. Mil. Engrs. (pres. 1972-73), Nat., Tex. (Young Engr. of Year Nueces chpt. 1972) socs. profl. engrs. Home: 7141 Pharoah Dr Corpus Christi TX 78412 Office: 4517 S Staples St Woodbury Sq Corpus Christi TX 78411

BELLENGER, JAMES FARIS, physician; b. Birmingham, Ala., Feb. 22, 1932; s. James Oscar and Lola Mae (Faris) B.; A.B., Harvard, 1953; M.D., Northwestern U., 1960; m. Joyce Edlarose Sand, June 30, 1956; children—James Keith, Kathleen Anne, Michelle Lenore, Maria Rose. Intern Akron (O.) Gen. Hosp., 1960-61; resident in gen. practice U. Tenn. Research Center and Hosp., 1961-62; gen. practice medicine specializing in hypnoanalysis, Clarksville, Tenn., 1962—; mem. faculty Am. Inst. Hypnosis, part-time 1973—. Mem. Civitan Club, Clarksville, Tenn., 1962—. Served with AUS, 1955-57. Mem. A.M.A., Tenn. Med. Assn., Tenn. Acad. Gen. Practice, Am. Acad. Gen. Practice, Am. Inst. Hypnosis. Home: 556 Chesterfield Dr Clarksville TN 37040 Office: 625 Riverside Dr Clarksville TN 37040

BELLINGER, EDGAR THOMSON, lawyer; b. N.Y.C., Sept. 23, 1929; s. John B. and Margaret (Thomson) B.; B.A., Haverford Coll., 1951; J.D., George Washington U., 1955; m. Adrian J. Dunn, Nov. 23, 1957; children—Edgar, Robert, Margaret. Admitted D.C., Md. bars, 1955; law clk. to chief judge U.S. Dist. Ct. for D.C., 1955-57; asst. U.S. atty. for D.C., 1957-59; partner firm Pope Ballard and Loos, Washington, 1959—. Chmn. unauthorized practice of law com. D.C. Ct. of Appeals. Bd. dirs. DC chpt. A.R.C., Children's Hosp D.C., Mem. Am., D.C., Md., Montgomery County bar assns., The Barristers, Phi Alpha Delta. Episcopalian. Clubs: Chevy Chase (dir.), Metropolitan. Home: 28 Quincy St Chevy Chase MD 20015 Office: 888 17th St NW Washington DC 20006

BELLMON, HENRY, U.S. senator; b. Tonkawa, Okla., Sept. 3, 1921; s. George and Edith (Caskey) B.; B.S. in Agr., Okla. State U., Stillwater, 1942; m. Shirley Osborn, Jan. 24, 1947; children—Patricia, Gail, Ann. Engaged in farming, Billings, Okla., 1946—; mem. Okla. Ho. of Reps. from Noble County, 1946-48; gov. State of Okla., 1962-66; U.S. senator from Okla., 1968—. Past chmn. Interstate Oil Compact Commn.; past mem. exec. com. Nat. Gov.'s Conf. Chmn. Okla. Republican Com., 1960-62; past nat. chmn. Nixon-for-Pres. Com. Served with USMCR, 1942-46. Presbyn. Home: Route 1 Red Rock OK 74651

BELLOMY, BRUCE BEN, pathologist; b. La Feria, Tex., Sept. 28, 1927; s. Frank Ray and Grace (Ashworth) B.; student U. Cal. at Berkeley, 1945-48; M.D., George Washington U., 1952; m. Eleanor Marie Tiley, May 29, 1952; children—Ray Michael, Barbara Ann, Rex Robert. Intern, Vanderbilt U. Hosp., Nashville, 1952-53; USPHS Hosp., Seattle, 1953-54; fellow in pathology U. Va., 1954-55; resident in pathology Clin. Center, NIH, Bethesda, Md., 1955-57; sr. surgeon USPHS, 1956-58; asso. pathologist Bapt. Hosp., Nashville, 1958-61; chief of pathology Ft. Sanders Presbyn. Hosp., Knoxville, Tenn., 1961—, East Tenn. Children's Hosp., Knoxville, 1961—. Instr. pathology U. Tenn., Knoxville, 1963—; dir. Knoxville City Sch. System Sch. of Certified Lab. Assts., 1968—. Pres. bd. Helen Ross McNabb Mental Health Center, Knoxville, 1969—. Served with USPHS, 1956-58; now comdr. Res. Mem. A.M.A., Tenn. Med. Assn., Coll. Am. Pathologists, Am. Soc. Clin. Pathologists, Knoxville Acad. Medicine, Tenn. Soc. Pathologists. Home: 3600 Montlake Dr Knoxville TN 37920 Office: 1909 W Clinch Av Knoxville TN 37916

BELLOS, JACK FRANK, dentist; b. San Antonio, Aug. 20, 1939; s. Photios Peter and Aphrodite (Varessis) B.; B.S., U. Tex. at Austin, 1962; D.D.S., U. Tex. at Houston, 1969; m. Mary Jane Beck, July 26, 1969; 1 son, Gregory. Pharmacist, Sommers Drug Stores, San Antonio, 1962-63, Univ. Drug Store, San Antonio, 1963-65; practicing dentist, San Antonio, 1969—. Mem. Psi Omega, Kappa Psi. Mem. Greek Orthodox Ch. (v.p. bd. dirs.). Mem. Order DeMolay. Home: 415 Rockhill St San Antonio TX 78209 Office: 7411 Broadway PO Box 6574 San Antonio TX 78209

BELLOWS, THOMAS JOHN, educator; b. Chgo., Aug. 15, 1935; s. Charles Everett and Dorothy (Morrison) B.; student Am. U., 1956, U. Cal. at Los Angeles, 1956-57; B.A., Augustana Coll., 1957; M.A., U. Fla., 1958; M.A., Yale, 1960, Ph.D., 1968; m. Mellie Joyce Spencer, July 12, 1956; children—Roderick Alan, Adrienne Marie, Jeannine Louise, Derek John. Asst. prof. polit. sci. West Ga. Coll., Carrollton, 1962-64, 66; asst. to asso. prof. polit. sci. U. Ark., Fayetteville, 1967—, chmn. dept., 1971—. Vis. lectr. depts. history, polit. sci. Nanyang U., Singapore, 1965. Bd. dirs. Southwest Conf. Asian Studies. Mem. Am., Southwestern (exec. council) polit. sci. assns., Assn. Asian Studies, Phi Beta Kappa, Phi Alpha Theta. Methodist. Author: (with S. Erikson and H. Winter) Political Science: Introductory Essays and Readings, 1971; The People's Action Party of Singapore: Emergence of a Dominant Party System, 1970. Home: 2327 Berry St Fayetteville AR 72701

BELOTE, PHILIP WILLIAM, auto repair shop propr.; b. Tarrytown, N.Y., June 1, 1920; s. James Clifton and Sara Jane (Teetsell) B.; grad. Morrisville (N.Y.) Agrl. and Tech. Inst., 1942; m. Leona R.S. Miller, May 18, 1958; 1 son, Robert C. Mechanic, Bridgeport Packard (Conn.), 1946-47, Hayne Chrysler, 1948; owner Belote's Garage, Dunedin, Fla., 1949—. Served with AUS, 1943-46; ETO. Decorated Purple Heart. Mem. Ind. Garage Owners of Fla. (3d v.p.), Automotive Service Council, Nat. Fedn. Independent Bus., Nat. Safety Council (Pinellas, Fla. chpt.), Car Care Council, Automotive Information Council, Dunedin Civic Assn., Dunedin Hist. Soc., Antique Automobile Club Am., Marmon Owners Club, Vet. Motor Car Club Am. (dir. Southeastern region 1968-69), Classic Car Club Am. (dir. Fla. region), D.A.V. (chaplain Dunedin chpt.), N.Y. U. Alumni Assn. Democrat. Presbyn. Elk. Home: 629 Orangewood St Dunedin FL 33528 Office: 949 Broadway Dunedin FL 33528

BELSER, CAROLINE DICK MCKISSICK, civic worker; b. Sumter, S.C., July 15, 1900; d. George William and Caroline (Hutchison) Dick; B.A., Winthrop Coll., 1921; postgrad. U. Wis., summer 1928-29, U. S.C., summer 1939-40; LL.B. (hon.), U. S.C., 1969; m. J. Rion McKissick, May 18, 1927 (dec. Sept. 1944); m. 2d, Irvin Furman Belser, June 21, 1947 (dec. Aug. 1969). Tchr., High Point (N.C.) Grammar Sch., 1921-23, Greenville (S.C.) High Sch., 1923-24, Sumter High Sch., 1924-26. Dir., Alice Mfg. Co., 1945—. Mem. Columbia Jr. League, 1929-40, sustaining mem., 1940—, founder Jr. League Book Club; pres. Dept. S.C., Am. Legion Aux., 1946-47, founder Palmetto Girls' State, 1947, pres. unit to Post 6, 1950-51, nat. v.p. So. div., 1953-54, only life mem. of Girls' State Com.; v.p. Garden Club S.C., 1956-59, chmn. Gardening Symposium, 1960-65. Vice chmn. Democratic Com. S.C., 1960-64. Charter mem. bd. assos. Converse Coll., 1962—; rep. Diocese Upper S.C., Nat. Cathedral Assn., 1962-65; mem. U. S.C. Found., Found. Chair Club; pres. U. S.C. Caroliniana Soc., 1954-60; chmn. bd. women visitors U. S.C., 1960—; mem. S.C. Am. Mother's Com. Recipient Algernon Sidney Sullivan award, 1951; Hon. S.C. State Mother award, 1968; past col. Gov.'s Staff; Distinguished Alumnus award U. S.C., 1972. Mem. English Speaking Union, Mus. of Art, Richland County, Sumter County hist. socs., League Women Voters; hon. mem. S.C. Press Assn. (pres. womens div. 1968-69), U. S.C. Aux., Mortar Board, Tau Kappa Alpha. Episcopalian (pres. Daus. of Holy Cross 1957-59). Clubs: Fortnightly Book (pres. 1944-45), New Century Book, Evening Music. Home: 15 Heathwood Circle Columbia SC 29205

BELSER, HARVIE JORDAN, lawyer, restaurant exec.; b. Leonia, Fla., June 3, 1917; s. Theodore Lamar and Abbie Lee (Gillis) B.; student Cambell's Bus. Col., 1938, George Washington U., 1938-39; L.B., Nat. U., 1947; m. Nancy Carolina Granade, June 22, 1951; children—Jennie Catherine, Nancy Granade, Harvie Jordan, Holly Elizabeth, Chauncey Lee. Admitted to D.C., Fla. bar, 1948; law practice, Bonifay, Fla.; county atty., county pros. atty., Holmes County, Fla., 1951-56; atty. Bonifay Sch. Bd., 1956-57; atty. Bd. Pub. Instrn., Holmes County, 1957—; owner Belser's, Bonifay, 1964—. Mem. Fla. Ho. of Reps., Holmes County, 1951-52, 55-56, Fla. Senate, 3rd dist., 1956-60; candidate for gov. 1960. Govt. appeal agt. Selective Service Bd., Holmes County, 1949—; sheriff, Holmes County, 1969—. Served to capt., USAAF, 1941-46; Decorated French Croix de Guerre avec Palme. Mem. Am., 14th Jud. Circuit (pres. 1953-54). Fla. (gov. 1949-50) bar assns., Phi Beta Gamma. Baptist. Home: 608 N Waukesba St Bonifay FL 32425 Office: 211 N Oklahoma St Bonifay FL 32425

BELSER, TOWNSEND MIKELL, JR., lawyer; b. Columbia, S.C., Apr. 30, 1937; s. Townsend Mikell and Pamela Cunningham (Burney) B.; B.S. in Chem. Engring., Ga. Inst. Tech., 1958; certificate Bettis Reactor Engring. Sch., AEC, Pitts., 1960; LL.B., George Washington U., 1965; m. Virginia Davis Lutz, May 5, 1962; children—William Burney, Elizabeth Davis. With Cushman, Darby & Cushman, Washington, 1962-65; admitted to S.C. bar, 1965, S.C. Supreme Ct., U.S. Patent Office, U.S. Supreme Ct. bars; asso. Belser, Belser, Baker & Barwick, Columbia, 1965-67, partner, 1968—. Real estate broker; instr. law U. S.C. Served to lt. comdr. USNR, 1958-62. Mem. Am., S.C., Richland County bar assns., Am. Patent Law Assn., Delta Theta Phi. Episcopalian. Kiwanian. Clubs: Columbia Sailing (sec. 1969-71, rear commodore 1972), Palmetto, Summit, Columbia Ski, Tarantella Dance. Home: 1135 Sunnyside Dr Columbia SC 29204 Office: 1213 Lady St Columbia SC 29211

BELSHAW, GEORGE WILLIAM, lead thermal systems engr.; b. Buffalo, Oct. 16, 1940; s. Derwin George and Mary Elizabeth (Russell) B.; B.S. in Aerospace Engring., Auburn U., 1963; m. Kathleen Powers Howard, Dec. 21, 1962; children—George William, Scott Howard. Sr. thermal design engr. Brown Engring. Co., Huntsville, Ala., 1963-68; lead thermal systems engr. Gen. Electric Co., Houston, 1968—. Recipient Presdl. Medal of Freedom award for work done to save Apollo 13 Spacecraft, 1970. Registered profl. engr., Ala., Tex. Mem. Delta Chi (alumni adviser 1971—). Home: 15807 LaCabana Dr Houston TX 77058 Office: 1830 NASA Rd 1 Houston TX 77058

BELSHEIM, ROBERT OSCAR, mech. engr.; b. Leland, Ia., Aug. 26, 1924; s. G. Oscar and Ida Sophia (Kessey) B.; student Waldorf Coll., 1940-41; B.S. in Mech. Engring., Ia. State U., 1944; M.S. in Mech. Engring., Purdue U., 1948, Ph.D., 1953. Engr. Naval Research Lab., Washington, 1944-45; research asso. Purdue U., Lafayette, Ind., 1946-50; engr. Naval Research Lab., Washington, 1950-58, head structures br., 1958-69, cons., 1969-72, dir. Shock and Vibration Information Center, 1972-74, cons., 1974—. Tchr. Purdue U., 1948-50. Served with USNR, 1944-45. Mem. Am. Soc. M.E. (tech. achievement award 1963; treas. 1959-61, vice chmn. 1961-62, chmn. Washington sect. 1962-63), Soc. Exptl. Stress Analysis (treas. Washington sect. 1956-57, v.p. 1957-58, pres. 1958-59; dir. nat. soc. 1960-62), Research Soc. Am., Acoustical Soc. Am., Washington Soc. Engrs., Philos. Soc. Washington, Washington Acad. Scis., Sigma Xi. Home: 2475 Virginia Av NW Washington DC 20037 Office: Naval Research Lab Code 8403 Washington DC 20375

BELTRAN-FORTUNY, RAFAEL, chemist; b. Jalapa, Veracruz, Mexico, Oct. 29, 1928; s. Jose M. Beltran and Carmen V. Fortuny, B.; B.S., U. Cal. at Berkeley, 1955; m. Maria Cristina Rivera, Feb. 14, 1959; children—Claudia Cristina, Rafael, Carlos Jose, Luis Roberto. Trainee for research engr. Electric Auto-Lite Co., Oakland, Cal. and Owoosso, Mich., 1953-54; research chemist Cal. Packing Corp., San Francisco, 1955-57; research chemist Stauffer Chem. Co., Richmond, Cal., 1957-58; chief chemist Monsanto Mexicana SA, Lecheria, Mexico, 1958-63; quality control mgr. Avon Cosmetics SA Mexico City, 1963-64; with Uhthoff, Gomez Vega & Uhthoff, Mexico City, Mexico, 1964—, dir. internat. patent matters, 1968—. Mem. Asociacion Mexicana de la Propiedad Industrial AC, Association Internationale pour la Protection de la Propriete Industrielle, Instituto Mexicano de Ingenieros Quimicos AC, Asociacion Nacional de la Industria Quimica AC. Club: Reforma Athletic. Home: 47 Juan Escutia Circle Heroes Satelite Edo de Mexico Mexico Office: 260 Hamburgo Mexico DF 6 Mexico

BELZILE, JOSEPH DANIEL, dentist, army officer; b. Van Buren, Me., May 9, 1930; s. Joseph Paul and Anne Elizabeth (Cyr) B.; B.S., Coll. Holy Cross, Worcester, Mass., 1953; D.D.S., U. Pa., 1957; Ph.D., Georgetown U., 1965; m. Beverly Renee Bernier, Aug. 10, 1963; children—Joseph Daniel, Michael William, Mark Gregory. Commd. 2d lt. U.S. Army, 1956, advanced through ranks to col., 1972; intern Tripler U.S. Army Hosp., Honolulu, 1957-58; periodontist 25th Inf. div. Schofield Barracks, Hawaii, 1958-60; post dental surgeon U.S. Army Garrison, Fort Totten, N.Y., 1960-62; resident pathology Armed Forces Inst. Pathology, Washington, 1965-66; researcher U.S. Army Inst. Dental Research, Washington, 1966-69; oral pathologist Ireland Army Hosp., Ft. Knox, Ky., 1969-73, Brooke Army Med. Center, San Antonio, 1973—. Asst. prof. oral pathology Georgetown U., 1965-71; cons. oral pathology 1st Army Dental Surgeon, Reynolds Army Hosp., Ft. Sill, Okla., U.S. Army Hosp., Ft. Campbell, Ky., U.S. Army Hosp., Ft. Jackson, S.C., Darnall U.S. Army Hosp., Ft. Hood, Tex. Diplomate Am. Bd. Oral Pathology, Am. Bd. Oral Medicine. Fellow Am. Acad. Oral Pathology; mem. Am. Dental Assn., Psi Omega. Roman Catholic. Home: 1008 Gorgas Circle Fort Sam Houston TX 78234 Office: Brooke Army Med Center Fort Sam Houston TX 78234

BENAVIDES, JAIME MIGUEL, physician; b. Chuquicamata, Chile, Oct. 20, 1923; s. Jaime and Elena (Spikula) B.; came to U.S., 1926, naturalized, 1934; A.B., Duke, 1943; M.D., U. Pa., 1947; m. Nela Montejo, May 14, 1947 children—Suzanne, Maria, Jaime Manuel. Intern, resident Lutheran Hosp., Cleve., 1947-49; resident orthopaedics U.S. Naval Hosp., Phila., 1953-55, asst. chief orthopedics, Newport, R.I., 1955-56; resident Newington (Conn.) Hosp. Crippled Children, 1957; asst. chief orthopedics U.S. Navy Hosp., Phila., 1958-61, chief orthopaedics, Key West, Fla., 1961-66; ret. as capt. USN, 1966; chief of staff Monroe Gen. Hosp., Key West, 1966-70; chief staff, chief surgery Fla. Keys Meml. Hosp., 1971—; chmn. bd. Lower Fla. Keys Hosp. Dist., 1970-71, mem. med. adv. council Fla. Easter Seal Soc. Bd. dirs. Monroe County Health Planning Council. Diplomate Am. Bd. Orthopedic Surgeons. Fellow A.C.S., Am. Acad. Orthopedic Surgeons, Internat. Coll. Surgeons, Am. Orthopedic Foot Soc., N.Y. Acad. Scis.; mem. Monroe County Med. Soc. (pres. 1971), Fla., Miami, Eastern orthopedic socs., A.M.A., So., Fla. med. assns., Coll. Sports Medicine, Am. Fracture Assn., U.S. Power Squadron, Internat. Platform Assn., Greater Key West C. of C. (dir. 1970-73), Kappa Sigma, Phi Rho Sigma. Roman Catholic. Home: PO Box 1240/13 Hilton Haven Key West FL 33040 Office: 638 United St Key West FL 33040

BENCHOFF, EDMUND FREDERIC, lawyer; b. McNary, Ariz., Sept. 23, 1929; s. Albert Joseph and Elizabeth Lillian (Cox) B.; B.B.A., U. Tex., Austin, 1952, LL.B. (J.D.), 1954; m. Sara Ann McAlister, May 29, 1954; children—Edmund McAlister, Sara Elizabeth. Asst. examiner Tex. State Bd. Water Engrs., 1953-54; admitted to Tex. bar, 1954; U.S. Supreme Ct., U.S. Ct. of Appeals 5th Circuit, U.S. Dist. Ct. Eastern Dist. Tex.; partner McAlister & Benchoff, Nacogdoches, 1955-61; pvt. practice law, 1966-70; partner Benchoff & Guidry, Nacogdoches, 1970—. County atty., Nacogdoches County, 1961-66. Chmn. Bd. of Adjustment, Nacogdoches, 1970-71. Bd. dirs. Nacogdoches County Hosp. Dist.; bd. dirs. Nacogdoches Baseball Assn., 1966-69, pres., 1968-69. Served with USNR, 1948-49; to capt. USAF Res., 1952-67. Mem. Am., Tex. (chmn. grievance com.), E.Tex. (dir. 1961-63), Nacogdoches County (pres. 1961-63) bar assns., Am. Judicature Soc., Arnold Air Soc., Nacogdoches C. of C., Kappa Alpha. Episcopalian. Club: Piney Woods Country. Home: 1800 E Starr St Nacogdoches TX 75961 Office: 316 University Dr Nacogdoches TX 75961

BENDA, CHARLES JEFFERSON, JR., architect; b. Hilo, Hawaii, Feb. 16, 1927; s. Charles Jefferson and Eleanor (Rose) B.; B.A., Fla. State U., 1952; m. Nancy Carlton Tribble, Aug. 19, 1950. Cons., architect Fla. Dept. Edn., Tallahassee, 1960-66; architect firm Charles J. Benda, Tallahassee, 1966-69, Odom Benda Assos., Tallahassee, after 1969; now owner Charles Benda Assos., Tallahassee. Cons. architect U.S. AID, Survey of Njala U. Coll., Sierra Leone, West Africa. Mem. Council Ednl. Facility Planners, 1969. Served with AUS, 1945-47. Mem. Nat. Council Schoolhouse Constrn., Bldg. Research Inst., A.I.A., Sigma Nu. Democrat. Elk. Clubs: St. Mark's Yacht, Apalachee Bay Yacht. Home: 1700 Kathryn Dr Tallahassee FL 32303 Office: Charles Benda Assos Architects 710 Barnett Bank Bldg Tallahassee FL 32301

BENDER, JAMES ARTHUR, govt. adminstr.; b. Webster, S.D., Nov. 27, 1923; s. Lynn Orson and Elsie Gertrude (Priebe) B.; B.A., U. S.D., 1947, M.A., 1948; M.S., Rensselaer Poly. Inst., 1968; m. Beverly Ann Brooks, June 26, 1948; children—Gary Arthur, Barry Arden, Bruce Alan. Research scientist, snow, ice and permafrost research establishment U.S. Army, Wilmette, Ill., 1950-61, chief research div., cold regions research and engring. lab., Hanover, N.J., 1961-68, phys. sci. adminstr. U.S. Army Materiel Command, Washington, 1968—. Served with AUS, 1943-45. Mem. Am. Inst. Physics, Glaciological Soc., Am. Geophys. Union, A.A.A.S. Contbr. profl. jours. Home: 1016 Aponi Rd SE Vienna VA 22180 Office: 5001 Eisenhower Av Alexandria VA 22304

BENDER, ROGER STILLMAN, educator; b. Cresson, Pa., Aug. 20, 1915; s. Samuel Louis and Freda (Stillman) B.; B.S., Yale, 1936; Ph.D., Harvard, 1945; m. Margaret Krivonak, June 17, 1960; children—Michele Eve, Christopher Stillman. Chmn. physics dept. Mass. Inst. Tech. Radiation Lab., 1941-45; research asst. U. Wis., 1945-48; asso. prof. U. Pitts., 1948-57; physicist, Oak Ridge Nat. Lab., 1957-66; prof. physics The Citadel, Charleston, S.C., 1966—, dept. chmn., 1969—. Cons. physicist Radiation Biology Group, Med. U. Va., 1968-72. Mem. Am. Phys. Soc., S.C. Acad. Scis. Contbr. articles to profl. jours. Address: The Citadel Charleston SC 29409

BENDER, WALLACE HINCKELY, JR., civil engr.; b. Phila., Sept. 3, 1921; s. Wallace Hinckely and Marian (Lohr) B.; B.S., Okla. State U., 1952; m. Hildegard Hamprecht, Nov. 7, 1961; 1 dau., Patricia Ann. With Okla. State Hwy. Dept., Oklahoma City, 1952-54; chief structural engr., plant engr. Douglas Aircraft Co., Tulsa, 1954-56; various assignments USAF, U.S. and Europe, 1960-71. Served with AUS, 1940-49. Mem. Nat. Soc. Profl. Engrs., D.C., Columbia chpts. profl. engrs. Republican. Baptist. Mason (Shriner). Home: 4331 Cederlake Ct Alexandria VA 22309

BENDHEIM, LEROY S., lawyer, state senator; b. Alexandria, Va., Feb. 12, 1906; s. Charles and Edith (Schwarz) B.; A.B., George Washington U., 1928, J.D., 1929; grad. Provost Marshall Gen. Sch. for Mil. Govt., 1944; m. Ethel Colman, June 10, 1934. Admitted to D.C., Va. bars, 1929; pvt. practice law, 1929—; mem. firm Bendheim & Ratner; instr. George Washington U., 1949-50; mem. Va. Senate, 1963—. dir. 1st Fed. Savs. & Loan Assn. of Alexandria, Park & Shop, Alexandria Corp., Downtown Garage, Inc., Columbia Bldg. Products Co., Inc., 1st Va. Bank. Mem. Alexandria Bd. Edn., 1934-43, chmn., 1934-40; mem. city council 1948-61; vice mayor 1952-55, mayor, 1955-61. Former bd. dirs. Alexandria dist. Boy Scouts Am., Nat. Capital area council; dir. B'nai B'rith Found., United Jewish Appeal; mem. adv. council Nat. Community Relations; hon. chmn. Jewish Welfare Bd. Asso. adv. mem. Alexandria Selective Service Bd., 1934-43; asst. staff member NRA Rev. Bd., 1935-36. Served with AUS, 1943-45. Mem. Am., Alexandria (pres. 1951-52), Va. bar assns., Bar Assn. D.C., C. of C., V.F.W. (past dept. comdr. Va.), Am. Legion, Nat. Assn. of Army (adv. com. George Washington chpt.). Jewish religion (hon. pres. Beth El congregation). Mason, Elk, Odd Fellow (grand master Va., 1955-56), Eagle, Lion. Contbg. editor Probate Law Digest for State Va. Home: 309 Mansion Dr Alexandria VA 22302 Office: 718 Jefferson St Alexandria VA 22314

BENEDICT, JOHN LOUIS, elec. engr.; b. Miami, Fla., Oct. 28, 1952; s. Ralph Henry and Gloria Theresa (Garcia) B.; B.S. in Elec. Engring. cum laude, U. Miami, 1971; M.E.E., Rensselaer Poly. Inst., 1973. Asst. engr. Central Office equipment maintenance engring. So. Bell Tel. & Tel. Co., Miami, 1972—. Instr. for profl. engr. examination rev. course U. Miami, part-time 1972—. Mem. Fla. Engring. Soc. (pres. student chpt. 1969-70), I.E.E.E., Am. Inst. Aeros. and Astronautics (treas. student chpt. 1971), Iron Arrow Honor Soc. (sec.-treas. 1973—), Omicron Delta Kappa (alumni bd. mem. 1973—; charter mem. Miami Alumni Circle), Tau Beta Pi (pres. 1970, 71-72, v.p. 1970-71), Eta Kappa Nu (nat. corr. 1970-71, initiations dir. 1971-72), Phi Eta Sigma (sec. hist. 1969-70, sr. adviser 1970-71). K.C. Home: 6425 SW 93d Pl Miami FL 33143 Office: 666 NW 79th Av Miami FL 33126

BENEDICT, WALTER HANFORD, ophthalmologist; b. Rochester, Minn., Dec. 28, 1921; s. William Lemuel and Edith Henrietta (Betz) B.; student Carleton Coll., 1940-43; M.D., U. Mich., 1946; M.Sc., Mayo Clinic, 1952; m. Burnette Bolin Benedict, July 10, 1965; children—John W., Walter Hanford. Intern, Johns Hopkins Hosp., 1947-48, resident, 1948-50; resident Mayo Clinic, 1950-52; practice medicine specializing in ophthalmology, Knoxville, Tenn., 1952—; chief staff E. Tenn. Bapt. Hosp., 1969. Mem. A.M.A., Am. Ophthal. Soc., Eye Study Club, Tenn. Med. Assn., Knoxville Acad. Medicine (pres. 1970). Home: 5516 Riverbend Dr Knoxville TN 37919 Office: 505 Blount Profl Bldg Knoxville TN 37920

BENEFIELD, JUNE, newspaper columnist; b. Gorman, Tex., 1921; student U. Tex. News reporter Houston Press; columnist Houston Chronicle, 1956—. Recipient Matrix award, Houston, 1965, News award Tex. Bar Assn., 1971, Houston Bar Assn., 1971. Mem. Women in Communications. Author: Laughing To Keep From Crying, 1972. Office: 512-30 Travis St Houston TX 77002

BENENATI, JOSEPH ANGELO, physician; b. Bklyn., Nov. 4, 1920; s. Francis and Margaret (Leonardi) B.; B.S., Fordham U., 1941; M.D., U. State N.Y. at Bklyn., 1950; m. Virginia Angela Scileppi, July 11, 1953; children—Joseph Michael, James Francis, Margaret Anne, Laura Marie. Intern, St. Vincent's Hosp., N.Y.C., 1950-51, resident, 1951-52; pvt. practice medicine, specializing in family medicine, Massapequa, N.Y., 1952-66, Ft. Lauderdale, Fla., 1966—; med. dir. Grumman Aerospace Corp., Bethpage, N.Y., 1955-66; attending physician Holy Cross Hosp., Ft. Lauderdale, Fla. Served with AUS, 1942-46. Diplomate Nat. Bd. Med. Examiners; charter diplomate Am. Bd. Family Practice. Fellow Indsl. Med. Assn.; mem. Am. Acad. Family Practice, A.M.A., Fla., Broward County med. assns., Phi Chi. Office: 2940 E Commercial Blvd Fort Lauderdale FL 33308

BENESI, HANS ARPAD, chemist; b. Graz, Austria, Sept. 27, 1921; s. Leo and Valerie M. (Benesi) Mittelmeier; B.S., U. Pitts., 1942, M.S., 1943; M.A., Princeton, 1944, Ph.D., 1946; m. Alice Joy Ebert, Mar. 27, 1948; children—Alan James, Steven Craig. Postdoctoral fellow U. Cal. at Berkeley, 1947-50; asst. prof. chemistry U. Conn. at Storrs, 1950-51; research chemist Shell Devel. Co., Emeryville, Cal., 1951-72, Deer Park, Tex., 1972—. Chmn. Gordon Research Conf. on Catalysis, 1966. Served with AUS, 1944-46. Mem. Am. Chem. Soc., A.A.A.S., Sigma Xi. Contbr. articles to profl. publs. Patentee in field. Home: 803 Baronridge Dr Seabrook TX 77586 Office: PO Box 100 Deer Park TX 77536

BENGOA-TORO, JOSE, lawyer; b. San Juan, P.R., Mar. 29, 1940; s. Jose E. and Gloria Maria (Toro) Bengoa; grad. Massanutten Mil. Acad., Va. 1958; B.A., U. P.R., 1958, B.L., 1966; m. Gilda Teresa Bonnet, Nov. 19, 1966; children—Gildren, Vanessa, Maria Elean. Admitted to P.R. bar, 1966; resident counsel El Mundo newspaper, 1966-67; asst. atty. firm McConnell Valdes Kelley Sifre Griggs & Ruiz-Suria, San Juan, 1967—. Mem. Am., P.R. bar assns. Home: 1693 Juan Kepler St Urbanización Tulipan Cupey Bajo Rio Pedras PR Office: GPO Box 4225 San Juan PR 00936

BENGSTON, GARY LYNN, lawyer; b. Rockford, Ill., Feb. 17, 1938; s. Tagee S. and Vayda C. (Boyd) B.; B.S., So. Ill. U., 1960; J.D., U. Chgo., 1963; m. Gail Kopp, Aug. 27, 1960; children—Adelle, Karen, Jennifer. Spl. agt. FBI, 1964-68; admitted to Va. bar, 1968; practiced in Danville, Va., 1968—; mem. firms Koplen & Bengston, 1968-72; individual practice, 1972—; pres., Westover Cartage, Ltd., 1972—. Del. nat. conv. Republican party, 1972; chmn. fifth congl. dist. Va. Rep. com., 1972—. Bd. dirs. Big Bros. Danville, Va. Mem. Small Bus. Adminstrn. (mem. regional adv. council 1969—), Va. Council Criminal Justice. Lutheran (chmn. exec. bldg. com.). Lion. Club: Toastmasters (pres. 1970-71) (Danville, Va.). Home: 284 W Main St Danville VA 24541 Office: PO Box 2135 Danville VA 24541

BENINTENDE, ALFRED JOSEPH, JR., communications co. exec.; b. New Orleans, Apr. 9, 1936; s. Alfred Joseph and Anna Elizabeth (Becker) B.; B.S., La. State U., 1962; postgrad. Bell System Communications Engring. Sch., Clemson U., 1963-64; m. Virginia Lucean Rhudy, July 27, 1957; children—Alfred Joseph III, Cheryl Suzanne. Student engr. So. Bell Telephone Co., Baton Rouge, 1962-65, engr., New Orleans, 1965-67; project engr. So. Central Bell Telephone Co., Birmingham, Ala., 1967-70, audit supr. accounting, 1970-71, Bell-ind. relations mgr., New Orleans, 1971—; v.p. City News, Kenner, La.; 1972—. Pres. Birmingham Interclub Council, 1970-71; vice chmn. County Cancer Crusade, 1970. Bd. dirs. Operation New Birmingham, 1969-71, Birmingham Jaycee Found., 1969-71. Served with USAF, 1954-58. Named Gold Key Man, New Orleans Jr. C. of C., 1967, Jaycee of Yr., Birmingham Jr. C. of C., 1970, Outstanding Local Jaycee Pres. in Dist., Ala. Jr. C. of C., 1970. Registered profl. engr., Ala., La. mem. I.E.E.E. (vice chmn. New Orleans communicaton tech. group 1966-67), La. Telephone Assn. (dir. 1971—). Home: Box 131 Military Rd Covington LA 70433 Office: 1215 Prytania St New Orleans LA 70140

BENITEZ, JAIME, govt. ofcl.; b. Vieques, P.R., Oct. 29, 1908; s. Luis and Candida (Rexach) B.; LL.B., Georgetown U., 1930, LL.M., 1931; A.M., U. Chgo., 1939; LL.D., Poly. Inst., P.R., 1950, N.Y.U., 1960, Fairleigh Dickinson U., 1961, Cath. U. P.R., 1965, U. West Indies, 1969, U. Miami, 1970; Litt.D., Temple U., 1969; m. Luz A. Martinez, Aug. 15, 1941; children—Clotilde, Jaime N., Margarita. Instr. polit. sci. U. P.R., 1931-41, asso. prof., 1941-42, chancellor univ., 1942-66, pres., 1966-73; resident commr. from P.R. in U.S., 1973—. Head hearings officer Nat. War Labor Bd., Washington. Del. to Gen. Conf. UNESCO, Paris, 1951; mem. U.S. Nat. Commn. UNESCO, 1951-55; pres. com. of Bill of Rights, P.R. Constl. Conv., 1951; U.S. del. Conf. of Univs., Utrecht, Holland, 1948; mem. adv. com. on coll. housing program Housing and Home Agy., 1957; co-chmn. Caribbean Conf. P.R., 1960; pres. Assn. Caribbean Univs., 1969; mem. 2d Ad Hoc Adv. Group on P.R., 1973. Named Citizen of Year, Inst. of P.R. in N.Y., 1958; Distinguished Citizen award Soc. Knights of St. John, Chgo., 1959. Mem. Am. Acad. Arts and Scis., P.R. Tchrs. Assn., Nat. Assn. State Univs. (pres. 1958), Georgetown U., U. Chgo. alumni assns., Am. Acad. Polit. and Social Scis., Fed. Bar Assn., Colegio de Abogados de Puerto Rico, Assn., Insular Employees. Clubs: Cosmos (Washington); Berwind's Country; Bankers (San Juan). Author: The Concept of the Family in Roman and Common Law Jurisprudence, 1931; Political and Philosophical Theories of Jose Ortega Y Gasset, 1939; Reflexiones Sobre el Presente, 1950; La Iniciacion Universitaria Y las Ciencias Sociales, 1952; The United States, Cuba and Latin America, 1961; Junto a La Torre, 1963; La Universidad del Futuro, 1964; Sobre el Futuro Cultural y Politico de Puerto Rico, 1965; 25 Anos de Direccion Universitario, 1967; Crisis en el Mundo y en La Educacion, 1968; with the Odds Against Us, 1969; Los Colegios Regionales en La Vida Universitaria, 1969; Where is Our Courage? 1970. Home: Condominio Lakeshore Apt 4-A 1 Madrid St Miramar Santurce PR 00907

BENITO, LOUIS, advt. agy. exec.; b. Tampa, Fla., Nov. 23, 1914; s. Luis and Concha (Bonera) B.; grad. high sch.; m. Helen Canedo, Nov. 19, 1944; children—John, Mary Charles, Cristina, Conchita, Louis, Olga, Davian. With R.E. McCarthy Advt. Agy., 1934-54; chmn. bd. Louis Benito Advt. Agy., Inc., Tampa, 1954—. Sr. v.p. Tampa World Trade Council; pres. Fla. Travel council; mem. marketing/distributive edn. adv. bd. Hillsborough Community Coll. Trustee, Tampa Childrens Home; bd. counselors U. Tampa; bd. dirs. Tampa Pub. Library; adv. com. Curtis Hixon Rehab. Center. Served with AUS, 1942-46. Recipient Top Mgmt. award Sales and Marketing Execs., 1965; named Tampa Advt. Man of Year, 1954, 59. Mem. Am. Assn. Advt. Agys. (past sec.-treas.), Affiliated Advt. Agys. Internat., Fla. (sec.), Greater Tampa (gov.) chambers commerce, Tampa Advt. Fedn. Roman Catholic. Rotarian. Clubs: Palma Ceia Golf and Country, Tampa Yacht and Country, Tower, University (Tampa). Home: 200 Corsica St Tampa FL 33606 Office: PO Box 3382 915 Ashley Dr Tampa FL 33602

BENJAMIN, BLANCHE STERNBERGER, civic worker; b. Mayesville, S.C., May 15, 1901; d. Emanuel and Bertha (Strauss) Sternberger; student Wellesley Coll., 1920-21; m. Edward B. Benjamin, Oct. 19, 1921; children—Edward B., W. Mente, Jonathan S. Vice pres. Starmount Co., Greensboro, N.C. 1930-67, Friendly Center, Inc., Greensboro, 1955-67; dir. Benjamin Minerals, Inc., New Orleans, 1947—. Vice pres. New Orleans Garden Soc., 1927-30, New Orleans Philharmonic Soc., 1928-51; mem. orgn. com. Newcomb Presch. and Metairie Park Country Day Sch.; bd. dirs. Isaac Delgado Museum, New Orleans, 1958-72; v.p. Benjamin Fund, New Orleans Symphony Soc.; co-founder (with husband) Sternberger Hosp., Starmount Forest Country Club; co-founder Emanuel Sternberger Ednl. Fund, Greensboro. Mem. Jr. League. Clubs: Orleans (corr. sec. 1947-49), Garden Soc., New Orleans Country, Southern Yacht (New Orleans); Greensboro Country, Assembly, Dogwood Garden (Greensboro); Saratoga Golf (Saratoga Springs, N.Y.). Address: 383 Walnut St New Orleans LA 70118

BENJAMIN, EDWARD B., corp. exec.; b. New Orleans, Nov. 18, 1897; s. Emanuel Victor and Rachel (Goldsmith) B.; A.B. magna cum laude, Harvard, 1918; D.H.L., U. Rochester, 1960; m. Blanche Sternberger, Oct. 19, 1921; children—Edward Bernard Jr., William Mente Sternberger, Jonathan Sternberger. Began with family interests, 1919; v.p. E.V. Benjamin Co., Inc., 1919-29, pres., 1939-47; pres. Bay Chem. Co., 1938-47, Myles Salt Co., 1940-47; pres. Starmount Co., 1929-67, Friendly Center, Inc., 1953-67, Benjamin Minerals Co. Bd. dirs. U.S. Coast Guard Acad. Found., 1969-71, Grayson Found; pres. Benjamin Fund. Donor Benjamin Awards for Restful Music. Trustee, founder (with Mrs. Benjamin) Sternberger Children's Hosp., Greensboro, N.C.; mem. vis. com. dept. biology Harvard, 1953-59; export adv. com. U.S. Dept. Commerce, 1946; orgn. com. New Orleans Community Chest, New Orleans Welfare Com., 1930-32; bd. dirs., v.p. New Orleans Opera House Assn.; bd. dirs. Human Betterment League; chmn. organizing com., 1st pres. Cultural Attractions Fund Greater New Orleans, 1960-61; pres. Community Concert Assn. New Orleans, 1960-68. Served with Harvard ROTC, 1917, Camp Lee, Va., 1918. Clubs: Round Table, Southern Yacht (New Orleans); Merchants and Manufacturers (Greensboro); Turf and Field; Bankers (N.Y.C.); New Orleans Country; Greensboro Country; Saratoga Golf; Royal Thames Yacht (London, Eng.). Author: The Larger Liberalism, 1918. Contbr. articles to mags. Home: 383 Walnut St New Orleans LA 70118 Office: Whitney Bldg New Orleans LA 70130

BENJAMIN, EDWARD BERNARD, JR., lawyer; b. New Orleans, Feb. 11, 1923; s. Edward Bernard and Blanche (Sternberger) B.; B.S., Yale, 1944; LL.M., Tulane U., 1952; m. Adelaide Wisdom, May 11, 1957; children—Edward Wisdom, Mary Dabney, Ann Leith, Stuart Minor. Admitted to La. Bar, 1952, since practiced in New Orleans; now partner firm Jones, Walker, Waechter, Poitevent, Carrere & Denegre. Chmn. bd. Starmount Co., Greensboro, N.C. Lectr. fed. taxation Tulane Tax Inst., N.Y.U. Inst. Fed. Taxation, others. Trustee Hollins Coll.; vice chmn. bd. Southwestern Legal Found. Research Fellows, Bur. Govtl. Research New Orleans. Served to 1st lt. AUS, 1943-47. Mem. Am. (sec. sect. taxation 1967-69), La. (chmn. sect. taxation 1959-60), New Orleans bar assns., Am., La. law insts. Episcopalian (vestryman, chancellor). Clubs: New Orleans Country, New Orleans Lawn Tennis, Greensboro City, Greensboro Country, Southern Yacht, Plimsoll, Petroleum, Internat. House. Home: 1837 Palmer Av New Orleans LA 70118 Office: 225 Baronne St New Orleans LA 70112

BENJAMIN, FRED BERTHOLD, physiologist; b. Darmstadt, Germany, Oct. 24, 1912; s. Karl Joseph and Clara (Stern) B.; D.M.D., Bonn (Germany) U., 1935; M.S., U. Ill., 1950; Ph.D., Loyola U., Chgo., 1953; m. Rita Mullerheim, Mar. 22, 1942; children—Peter, Ronald. Came to U.S., 1946, naturalized, 1951. Practice dentistry, Kashmir, Pakistan, 1935-46; med. researcher U. Ill., Chgo., 1949-53, U. Pa., Phila., 1953-60; sr. research coordinator Republic Aviation, L.I., N.Y., 1960-64; sr. research physiologist space med. research NASA, Washington, 1964-70; sr. staff physiologist med. research Dept. of Transp. Washington, 1970—. Chmn. biology dept. Washington Saturday Coll., 1970—. bd. govs., 1970—. Bd. govs. Am. Assn. Community Edn., 1970—. Mem. Am. Physiol. Soc., A.A.A.S. Co-editor Excerpta Medica, 1952—, Science, 1972—. Contbr. to books and profl. jours. Home: 11115 Easecrest Dr Silver Spring MD 20902 Office: Dept Transportation N43-40 Washington DC 20590

BENJAMIN, PAUL RAYMOND, sales exec.; b. Wellsboro, Pa., Nov. 24, 1914; s. Raymond Mortica and Neva (Jackson) B.; grad. high sch.; m. Sarah Ellen Williamson, Dec. 21, 1947; children—Paul Raymond, Ellen Blair. With Dept. Mil. Affairs, State of Pa., 1936-41; owner Paul R. Benjamin Assos., advt., 1951-66; account exec., 1969—; account exec. First Financial Marketing Group, 1966-67, Bankers Systems, Memphis, 1967—. Mem. bd. dirs. Memphis & Shelby County A.C.S., 1973—. Served with AUS, 1941-47. Decorated Bronze Star medal with oak leaf pendulant. Methodist (steward, adminstrv. bd.). Club: Lost Chord (dir. 1960-62, pres. 1962—). Address: 1759 Eastmoreland St Memphis TN 38104

BENNER, CLAUDE JACOB, aerospace co. exec.; b. Wilkes-Barre, Pa., Sept. 16, 1917; s. Rollie O. and Blanche (Engler) B.; certificate in aero. engring. Casey Jones Sch. Aero., 1940; m. Marie M. Meaney, June 14, 1947; children—Susan (Mrs. Michael E. O'Neill), Linda Joy (Mrs. John Benjamin), Patricia Lee. With LTV Aerospace Corp., Dallas, 1940—, dir. adminstrn., 1965-68, v.p. adminstrn., 1968-73; pres. Vought Helicopter Corp., 1973—. Bd. dirs. Jr. Achievement, Dallas. Mem. Am. Inst. Aeros. and Astronautics. Club: Royal Oaks Country (Dallas). Home: 4535 Mill Creek Rd Dallas TX 75234 Office: 1701 W Marshall Dr Grand Prairie TX 75050

BENNETT, ALLYN CHARLES, civil engr.; b. Mart, Tex., Jan. 6, 1916; s. Luther Estes and Arlye (Allen)B.; B.S., Tex. A. and M. U., 1939; m. Margaret Thurston, Jan. 22, 1943; children—Allyn C., James T., Stephen E., Kenneth R., Margaret K. Engr., Soil Conservation Service, Tex., 1939-42, civil engr., 1945—. Served to lt. col. USAAF 1942-45. Decorated Air Medal with oak leaf cluster, D.F.C. Registered profl. engr., Tex. Mem. Nat., Tex. socs. profl. engrs., Am. Soc. Agrl. Engrs. (nat. drainage com.), Soil Conservation Soc. Am., Air Force Assn. Am. Heritage Soc. Episcopalian. Home: 2 East Walker Temple TX 76501 Office: PO Box 95 Temple TX 76501

BENNETT, ARTHUR GORDON, educator; b. Jackson, Mich., Jan. 2, 1929; s. Arthur Gordon and Colletta Jeanette (McEachern) B.; B.S., U. Mich., 1951; M.S., Purdue U., 1958, Ph.D., 1964; m. Virginia Vogelsang, May 23, 1959; children—John, Barbara. Engr., ARO, Inc., Tullahoma, Tenn., 1951-53; project engr. Brown Engring. Co., Huntsville, Ala., 1953-55; instr. engring. sci. dept. Purdue U., Lafayette, Ind., 1955-64; supr. engring. research Boeing Co., Seattle, 1964-65, Huntsville, Ala., 1965-68; asso. prof. aerospace engring. Auburn (Ala.) U., 1968—. NSF grantee 1962, 63; recipient New Tech. award NASA, 1968, awards for tech. briefs, 1968, 69, 71. Registered profl. engr., Ala. Mem. Am. Astronautical Soc. (sr. mem.; mem. nat. bd. 1969-71, vice chmn. S.E. sect. 1968—), Ala. Acad. Sci. (v.p. engring. 1968-69). Home: 543 Auburn Dr Auburn AL 36830

BENNETT, CARROLL HINES, elec. engr.; b. Waycross, Ga., July 9, 1925; s. Lester Lee and Rose Ella (Eason) B.; B.E.E., Ga. Inst. Tech., 1951; m. Mary Agnew, Apr. 23, 1967; children—Carroll Ann, Elaine Cole. Jr. electronic engr. Warner Robbins Air Material Area, 1951-57, chief electronics engr. outside plant communications. With Tampa Electric Co., 1957—, mgr. system operation and communication, 1965—. Served with USAAF, 1944-45. Decorated Air medal with five oak leaf clusters. Mem. I.E.E.E., Fla. Engring. Soc. Home: 11114 N 21st St Tampa FL 33612 Office: PO Box 111 Tampa FL 33601

BENNETT, CHARLES EDWARD, congressman; b. Canton, N.Y., Dec. 2, 1910; s. Walter James and Roberta Augusta (Broadhurst) B.; A.B., U. Fla., 1934, J.D., 1934; H.H.D., U. Tampa, 1950; LL.D. (hon.), Jacksonville U., 1972; m. Jean Bennett; children—Bruce, Charles, James, Lucinda. Admitted to Fla. bar, 1934, practiced in Jacksonville, until 1949; mem. 81st-93d congresses from 3d Fla. Dist., mem. armed services com., chmn. seapower subcom. Mem. Fla. Ho. of Reps., 1941. Bd. dirs. Boys' Home, A.R.C., Tb Assn. Council Social Agys., Multiple Sclerosis Assn.; trustee Lynchburg Coll. Served from pvt. to capt., inf., AUS, 1942-47; New Guinea and Philippines, including guerrilla fighting in Luzon. Decorated Silver Star, Bronze Star: Phillippine Legion of Honor and Gold Cross; recipient Certificate of Merit, Freedoms Found., 1951, 56, Good Govt. award, Jr. C. of C., 1952, Good Citizenship gold medal Nat. S.A.R., 1959. Mem. D.A.V., V.F.W., Fla. Bar. Am. Legion, Fleet Res. Assn. (hon.), Jacksonville Bar Assn., Jr. C. of C. (pres. 1939). Democrat. Mem. Disciples of Christ Ch. (elder). Mason. Author: Laudonniere, 1964; Settlement of Florida, 1967; also hist. papers. Home: 2130 Riverside Av Jacksonville FL 32204 Office: Rayburn House Office Bldg Washington DC 20515

BENNETT, CLARENCE EUGENE, structural engr.; b. Idamay, W.Va., Oct. 11, 1936; s. Clarence and Bonnie (Husk) B.; B.S. in Civil Engring., W.Va. U., 1958; J.D. (scholar award 1972), YMCA Coll., Nashville, 1972; m. Mary Lou Reece, Dec. 5, 1959; children—Susan Lynn, Julie Ann. Bridge design engr. W.Va. Dept. Hwys., Charleston, 1958-63; bridge engr. Fed. Highway Adminstrn., Arlington, Va., 1963-65, asst. div. structural engr., Trenton, N.J., 1965-67, div. structural engr., Nashville, 1967—; admitted to Tenn. bar, 1972. Served with AUS, 1959. Registered profl. engr., W.Va. Mem. Tenn. Bar Assn., Am. Soc. C.E., Tau Beta Pi, Chi Epsilon. Methodist. Home: 2830 Rural Hill Circle Nashville TN 37217 Office: 4004 Hillsboro Rd Nashville TN 37215

BENNETT, CLARENCE HENRY, assn. exec.; b. Pittstown, N.J., Mar. 23, 1906; s. Charles Henry and Elizabeth (Brier) B.; A.B., Western Md. Coll., 1928; postgrad. in law U. Balt., 1929-30, George Washington U., 1932-33; m. Dorothy Gilligan, Dec. 25, 1930; 1 dau., Peggy Susan (Mrs. Robert Howard Lipsitz). Sr. interviewer personnel dept. Balt. Gas & Elec. Co., 1929-32; tchr. pub. speaking and English, McKinley High Sch., Washington, 1933-34; sr. interviewer to acting dir. D.C. Employment Center, 1934-43; asst. to v.p. Commerce Clearing House, 1943-46; pres. Nat. Standards Assn., Inc., Washington, 1946—; pres. Nat. Contract Bridge Inst., Inc.; v.p., dir. Source Chem. Industries, Inc.; editor, pub. tech. manuals, symposia, looseleaf-standards services, bulls., sources of supply. Trustee Western Md. Coll. Named Alumnus of Year, Western Md. Coll., 1971. Mem. Western Md. Coll. Alumni Assn. (pres. 1964-66). Democrat. Methodist (adminstrv. bd.). Clubs: University, Nat. Aviation (Washington); Columbia (Md.) Country. Home: 5202 Falmouth Rd Washington DC 20016 Office: 1321 14th St NW Washington DC 20005

BENNETT, DONALD WAYNE, lawyer, govt. ofcl.; b. Columbus, O., May 7, 1930; s. Benjamin Edward and Marjorie Beatrice (Brown) B.; B.S. in Bus. Adminstrn., Ohio State U., 1951, J.D., 1956; m. Joan Elaine Riedel, Dec. 28, 1957; children—Susan, Stephen, David. Admitted to Ohio bar, 1956, practiced in Cleve., 1960-72; atty. N.Y.C. R.R., Co., Cleve., 1956-60; mem. firm Heiss, Day and Bennett, 1960-69, Ross, Kraushaar and Bennett, 1969-72; chief counsel Fed. R.R. Adminstrn. Dept. Transp., Washington, 1972—. Served with USMCR, 1951-53. Mem. Am., Ohio, Fed. bar assns., Sigma Nu. Episcopalian. Home: 6226 Nelway Dr McLean VA 22101 Office: Federal Railroad Administration Dept of Transportation Washington DC 20590

BENNETT, FRANKLIN DAVIS, hardware co. exec.; b. Sanford, Fla., Jan. 25, 1916; s. John Croswell and Mary Anne (Wall) B.; B.S. in Bus. Adminstrn., U. Fla., 1937; m. Ann Wells, Aug. 21, 1941 (div. 1961); children—John Franklin, William Wall. Comptroller Race & Race, Inc., aluminum irrigation, Winter Haven, Fla., 1945-46; with Baird Hardware Co., wholesalers, Gainesville, 1946—; treas., 1948—, v.p., 1950—, dir., 1948—. Served with AUS, 1941-45. Mem. Phi Kappa Tau. Democrat. Kiwanian (treas. 1955-73). Home: 1014 NE 3d St Gainesville FL 32601 Office: PO Drawer B Gainesville FL 32601

BENNETT, GARLAND BRAXTON, clergyman; b. Greensboro, N.C., Aug. 25, 1929; s. George Robert and Thama (Carter) B.; B.A., Elon Coll., 1958; B.D., Duke U., 1963; m. Peggy Matherly, Mar. 25, 1949; children—Cindy (Mrs. Brantley Powell), Lynn (Mrs. Charles Mangum), Robin, Susan. Called to ministry Christian Ch., 1953; pastor Zion Christian Ch., Burlington, N.C., 1954-55, Ramseur (N.C.) Christian Ch., 1955-62, Great Bridge Christian Ch., Chesapeake, Va., 1962-66, Wake Chapel Christian Ch., Fuquay-Varina, N.C., 1966—. Tchr. 7th grade pub. sch., Franklinville, N.C., 1957-58, Police Sch., Chesapeake. Mem. fund-raising team Duke U., 1965-69, Elon Coll., 1970. Mason (Shriner). Home: Wake Chapel Rd Fuquay-Varina NC 27526 Office: Box 307 Fuquay-Varina NC 27526

BENNETT, GERARD JOSEPH, pharm. mfg. co. exec.; b. N.Y.C., May 27, 1930; s. Arthur John and Agnes Cecilia (Sheehan) B.; B.A., St. John's U., 1955; postgrad. N. Y. U., 1957-60; M.B.A., St. Mary's U., 1967; m. Barbara A. Howlana, Aug. 3, 1951 (div. 1973); children—Daniel, Jean (Mrs. Cary C. Laster), Carolyn, Elaine, Amy, Virginia. Product mgr. Pfizer, Inc., N.Y.C., 1960-65; sales promotion Dorsey Labs., 1965-67; marketing research supr. Tex. Pharmacal Co., San Antonio, 1967—. Lectr. econs. Our Lady of the Lake Coll.; instr. bus. St. Philipis Coll. Served with USAF, 1951-55. Mem. Am. Marketing Assn. (pres. San Antonio chpt. 1971-73), San Antonio Advt. Fedn. (dir. 1972-73), Eastern Pharm. Marketing Research Group, Zeta Sigma Pi. Club: Harmony Hills Cabana of San Antonio (dir. 1962-63). Home: 115 NW Loop 410 San Antonio TX 78216 Office: 307 E Josephine St San Antonio TX 78296

BENNETT, GORDON DANIEL, govt. scientist; b. Elmira, N.Y., Oct. 5, 1931; s. William Stanislaus and Mary Catherine (Mack) B.; B.S. in Geology, U. Notre Dame, 1956; M.S. in Geophysics, Pa. State U., 1961; postgrad. Poly. Inst. Bklyn., 1968-69; m. Patricia Ann Collins, Oct. 25, 1958; children—Alice Patricia, Margaret Mary, Christopher Joseph. Geophysicist, U.S. Geol. Survey, Harrisburg and Greenville, Pa., 1957-61, hydrologist, Mineola, L.I., 1966-68, San Juan, P.R., 1969-72, Washington, 1972—; tech. adviser AID, Lahore, Pakistan, 1962-66. External examiner, lectr. U. Punjab, Lahore, 1963-66; mem. Yauco Valley Water Control Com., San Juan, 1972. Served with AUS, 1951-53. NSF fellow, 1957-58. Recipient Superior Honor award Dept. State, 1966. Author: Ground Water Hydraulics—

A Programmed Text for Self Instruction, 1974. Contbr. articles to profl. jours. Home: 9810 Barlow Rd Fairfax VA 22030 Office: US Geol Survey Washington DC 20242

BENNETT, HENRY HOBSON, accountant; b. Grand Rivers, Ky., Dec. 17, 1898; s. Alfred Roland and Mary Ellen (Jones) B.; B.C.S., Bowling Green Bus. U., 1920, M.A., 1922; postgrad. Sch. Commerce Northwestern U., 1926, 27; m. Leora Wallace, Aug. 9, 1927; children—Alfred Judson, Wallace John, Alben Trice. Chief bookkeeper So. Bell Tel. Co., Jackson, Miss., 1919-20; jr. accountant John Creech & Co., C.P.A., Harlan, Ky., 1923-34; chief accountant Harlan Central Coal Co. (Ky.), 1934-50; owner H.H. Bennett C.P.A., Harlan, 1950—. Prin. elementary sch. Livingston County, Ky., 1917-18. C.P.A., Ky. Mem. Commerce Club Northwestern. Mason. Home: Route 1 Salem KY 42078 Office: Howard Bldg Salem KY 42078

BENNETT, HOWARD ALLEN, physician; b. Mt. Vernon, Ia., Jan. 1, 1919; s. Joseph and Belle A. (Turner) B.; B.A., Cornell Coll., Mt. Vernon, 1941; M.D., U. Ia., 1943; m. Margaret A. Christensen, Apr. 10, 1943; children—Howard Allen, Barbara Lynn (Mrs. Henry Eddins), Nancy Gayle (Mrs. Gerald W. Shonkwiler). Intern, Louisville Gen. Hosp., 1943-44; resident anesthesiology U. Ia. Hosp., Iowa City, 1946-48; prof., chmn. dept. anesthesiology U. Okla. Sch. Medicine and Univ. Hosp., Oklahoma City, 1948-55, clin. prof. anesthesiology Sch. Medicine, Tulsa, 1955-73; chmn. anesthesia sect. Jane Phillips Meml. Hosp. and Med. Center, Bartlesville. Served to maj. M.C., AUS, 1944-46; ETO. Mem. Am. (dir. 1950-73), Okla. (founding pres. 1949, pres. 1952) socs. anesthesiologists, Okla. Med. Assn., Washington County Med. Soc. Alpha Omega Alpha, Phi Beta Pi. Republican. Methodist. Elk. Club: Hillcrest Country (Bartlesville, Okla.). Home: 2824 Redhawe Ct Bartlesville OK 74003 Office: 3325 E Frank Phillips Blvd Bartlesville OK 74003

BENNETT, HUBERT DOUGLAS, state ofcl.; b. nr. Danville, Va., Nov. 18, 1906; s. Coleman Douglas and Sallie (Hogan) B.; B.S., U. Va., 1933, LL.B., 1938; m. Georgean Cameron Phillips, Dec. 30, 1938. Tchr. pub. schs., Pittsylvania County, Va., 1931-33; mem. Va. Ho. of Dels., 1934-36; admitted to Va. bar, 1937; judge Pittsylvania County C., Chatham, Va., 1938-52; exec. sec. Supreme Ct. Appeals of Va., Richmond, 1952—. Served with USNR, 1942-45. Mem. Am., Va. bar assns., Nat. Conf. Ct. Administrv. Officers. Methodist. Home: 38 Locke Lane Richmond VA 23226 Office: Supreme Ct Bldg 11th and Broad Sts Richmond VA 23219

BENNETT, JAMES BAXTER, geologist; b. Houston, Jan. 5, 1935; s. James Benjamin and Mary (Baxter) Mauldin; B.S., U. Tex., 1961; m. Kathryn Adele Giddens, Jan. 28, 1961; children—Kathryne Alison, Wiley Baxter. Oil scout Tex. Eastern Transmission Corp., Shreveport, La., 1960-63, exploration geologists, 1964-67; exploration petroleum geologist Skelly Oil Co., Shreveport, 1967-70; area geologist Champlin Petroleum Co., Shreveport, 1970, Houston, 1970-72; area geologist Belco Petroleum Corp., Houston, 1972—. Served with AUS, 1957-59. Mem. Am. Assn. Petroleum Geologists, Shreveport (2d. v.p. 1969-70), Houston geol. socs., Sigma Nu. Republican. Home: 10930 Burgoyne St Houston TX 77042 Office: 8707 Katy Freeway Houston TX 77024

BENNETT, JAMES GORDON, JR., ship bldg. co. exec.; b. Wilkinsburg, Pa., Dec. 5, 1921; s. James Gordon and Evalina Parks (Miller) B.; B.A., Westminster Coll., 1947; m. Marjorie Ruth Beck, Mar. 20, 1948; children—Karen Holly, Janine Gordon. Instr., Westminster Coll., New Wilmington, Pa., 1947; chief accountant McCrady-Rogers, Pitts., 1948-52; office mgr. Rinker Materials, West Palm Beach, Fla., 1953-54; v.p. finance Spencer Boat Co., West Palm Beach, 1955—, dir., 1956—. Served with USNR, 1942-46; now comdr. Res. ret. Mem. Navy League U.S. (founding council pres. 1966-67), Soc. Preservation and Encouragement Barber Shop Quartet Singing in Am., Am. Legion, Nat. Office Mgmt. Assn., Alpha Sigma Phi. Presbyn. (elder 1971-73). Lion (dep. dist. gov. 1963-64). Home: 1569 40th St West Palm Beach FL 33407 Office: 4000 N Dixie St West Palm Beach FL 33407

BENNETT, (JAMES) JEFFERSON, univ. pres.; b. Owensboro, Ky., June 8, 1920; s. James Henry and Amelia (Brownfield) B.; B.S., U. Ala., 1941, LL.B., 1948, LL.D., 1966; m. Christine Thaxton, Oct. 21, 1941; 1 son, James Jefferson. Admitted to Ala. bar, 1948; practiced in Birmingham, 1948, Fairhope, 1948-50; asst. prof. U. Ala. Sch. Law, University, 1950-52, asso. prof., 1952-53, asst. to dean, 1952-54, prof., 1953-69, asst. to pres. for devel. U. Ala., 1954-56, adminstrv. asst. to pres., 1956-60, adminstrv. v.p., 1960-68, provost, 1968; asst. adminstr. for legislation and pub. policy, health service and mental health adminstrn. U.S. Dept. Health, Edn. and Welfare, 1968-69; exec. dir. Health Edn. Authority of La., New Orleans, 1969-71; vice chancellor, pres. U. of South, Sewanee, Tenn., 1971—. Dir. City Nat. Bank, Tuscaloosa, Ala., 1962-68. Chmn. bd. dirs. Assn. Epis. Colls., 1973—. Served to maj. USMCR, 1942-46; maj. Res. Recipient Algernon Syndey Sullivan award, 1964. Mem. Farrah Order Jurisprudence, Sigma Chi, Omicron Delta Kappa, Phi Delta Phi. Episcopalian (sec. standing com. Ala. Diocese 1958-65, pres. Episcopal Churchmen Ala. 1955-67). Club: AEDC (Tullahoma, Tenn.). Home: Fulford Hall Sewanee TN 37375

BENNETT, JAMES THOMAS, cons. statistician, educator; b. Memphis, Oct. 19, 1942; s. Louie Edward and Carrie (Tunnell) B.; B.S., Case Inst. Tech., 1964, M.S., 1966, Ph.D., 1970; m. Sara Ellen Dorman, Sept. 2, 1967. Operations research analyst, finance central staff Ford Motor Co., Dearborn, Mich., 1964-65; cons. econ. statistician Chesapeake & Ohio Ry. Co., 1966-70; research asso. Case Inst. Tech., 1965-67; asst. prof. indsl. mgmt. Cleve. State U., 1967-70; asst. prof. econs. George Washington U., 1970—, also sr. staff scientist program in logistics; cons. Cleve. Transit System. Trustee Ohio Epsilon Corp. Research fellow Fed. Res. Bank Cleve., 1969-70. Mem. Am. Econ. Assn., Am. Statis. Assn., Econometric Soc., Phi Kappa Psi, Tau Beta Pi. Democrat. Presbyn. Home: 8702 Bluedale St Alexandria VA 22308 Office: George Washington Univ Washington DC 20006

BENNETT, JOHN CARLYLE, accountant; b. Doyle, Tenn., Sept. 11, 1910; s. John P. and Florence (Parker) B.; student Duke, 1929-31, Cecil's Bus. Coll., Ashville, N.C., 1932-33, corr. course I.A.S., 1934-40; m. Betty E. Strunk, Dec. 1, 1943; children—Gloria Louise, John Richard, William Gordon, Charlotte Emily. Accountant, So. Dairies, Inc., Asheville, N.C., 1933-35; head accounting 15th Naval Dist., Panama C.Z., 1938-39, auditor Panama Canal, constrn. foreman Army Engrs., 1939-42; accountant, auditor, mem. staff Ernst & Ernst, C.P.A.'s, Detroit, 1943-45; chief accountant Alexander Tool & Mfg. Co., Detroit, 1945; internal revenue agt., 1945-48; practice as C.P.A., 1948—. Played with Ringling Bros. Circus Band; mem. Charlotte Symphony Orch.; bus. mgr. Charlotte Community Band Assn. Served with AUS, 1935-38, USNR, 1943. Mem. Am. Fedn. Musicians, Nat. Small Business Assn. Mason (32 deg., Shriner). Club: Red Fez Country. Author: Book of Income Tax Rates, Federal Income Tax Calculator (pub. annually); Outlaws in Swivel Chairs, 1958; also articles and legal actions on polit sci. under Article III of Constn. Address: 2245 Chambwood Dr Charlotte NC 28205

BENNETT, JOHN DANIEL, cons. engr.; b. Spartanburg, S.C., Nov. 1, 1941; s. Clyde Edward and Dorothy Love (Hubbard) B.; B.S., Clemson U., 1963; M.S., U. Tenn., 1968; m. Charlene Fay Grant, Jan. 26, 1964; children—Brian Edward, Alan Wayne. Design engr. Hensley Schmidt, Inc., Cons. Engrs., Chattanooga, 1968-71; design engr. LBC&W-Harwood Beebe Co., Cons. Engrs., Spartanburg, S.C., 1971, project engr., 1972, project mgr., 1973—. State dir. U.S. Jaycees, Chattanooga, 1969-70. Served to 1st lt. Ordnance Corps, AUS, 1964-66. Registered profl. engr., Tenn., S.C. Mem. Am. Soc. C.E., Water Pollution Control Assn., Nat. Soc. Profl. Engrs., Christian Bus. Men's Com. Home: 431 Farnsworth Rd Spartanburg SC 29301 Office: PO Box 2646 Spartanburg SC 29302

BENNETT, LAWRENCE HERMAN, physicist; b. Bklyn., Oct. 17, 1930; s. Harold and Irene (Kamel) B.; B.A. cum laude, Bklyn. Coll., 1951; M.S., U. Md., 1955; Ph.D. (research fellow), Rutgers U., 1958; m. Devora Mae Spintman, Mar. 22, 1953; children—Claire A., Charles L., Craig David. Physicist, U.S. Naval Ordnance Lab., Silver Spring, Md., 1950-55; physicist Nat. Bur. Standards, Gaithersburg, Md., 1958-63, chief alloy physics sect. 1963—. Asso. prof. dept. physics and astronomy U. Md., part-time 1960—. Served with AUS, 1953-55. Recipient Gold medal U.S. Dept. Commerce, 1972. Fellow Am. Phys. Soc., Washington Acad. Scis.; mem. Am. Soc. Metals (Burgess Meml. award 1974), Am. Inst. Mining, Metall. and Petroleum Engrs., Phi Beta Kappa. Editor: (with J. Waber) Energy Bands in Metals and Alloys, 1968; Electronic Density of States, 1971; (with R. Willens) Charge Transfer/Electronic Structure of Alloys, 1974. Home: 6524 E Halbert Rd Bethesda MD 20034 Office: Nat Bur Standards Washington DC 20234

BENNETT, LESLIE HERMAN, newspaper exec.; b. Monroe, La., Oct. 20, 1925; s. Leslie Herman and Mildred (Howell) B.; B.A., La. State U., 1948; m. Margaret Ann Chiaborel, Apr. 14, 1946; 1 son, Bruce. Reporter, Galveston (Tex.) News, 1948-49; news editor New Orleans Item, 1950-57; with Houston Chronicle, 1957—, city editor, 1963-71, sr. asso. editor, 1972—. Served with USAAF, 1943-46. Mem. Sigma Delta Chi. Methodist. Club: Houston Press. Home: 9011 Bintliff Houston TX 77036 Office: 512 Travis St Houston TX 77001

BENNETT, LUTHER ESTES, JR., banker; b. Mart, Tex., Feb. 17, 1919; s. Luther Estes and Arlye (Allen) B.; student Tex. A. and M. U., 1937-38, 40-42, Westminster Jr. Coll., 1939-40, Okla. Baptist U., 1942, U. Paris, 1946; grad. Southwestern Sch. Banking, So. Methodist U., 1965; m. Frances Grace Gregory, Oct. 30, 1948; children—Beverly Earl, Bradley Estes. Farmer, rancher, Groesbeck, Tex., 1947—; wholesale consignee Mobil Oil Co., 1954-60; v.p. Farmers State Bank, Groesbeck, 1959—. Chmn. bd. dirs. Soil Conservation Dist. of Limestone-Falls County, Groesbeck Housing Authority. Served with USAAF, 1942-47. Decorated Air medal with seven oak leaf clusters. Mem. Groesbeck C. of C. (pres. 1964). Mason, Lion (pres. 1969). Home: 501 E Farrar St Groesbeck TX 76642 Office: 201 N Ellis St Groesbeck TX 76642

BENNETT, MAX LEON, lawyer; b. Kingsville, Tex., May 6, 1938; s. Roy Chilton and Zachie Ford (Dunahay) B.; student Tex. A. and I. U., 1956-57; B.A., Baylor U., 1960, J.D., 1962; m. Betty Joyce Trapp, Dec. 23, 1961; children—Catherine, Susan. Admitted to Tex. bar, 1962; atty. Humble Oil and Refining Co., Corpus Christi, Tex., 1962-65; practiced in Corpus Christi, 1965—; partner firm Howard, McDowell, Bennett and Cartwright, 1973—; judge-elect Nueces County Ct. at Law. Instr. in law adult edn. Del Mar Coll., Corpus Christi, 1971-72. Bd. dirs. Corpus Christi Boys Club, 1973—; mem. devel. council Baylor U., 1973—. Mem. Tex., Nueces County (pres. 1968-69) trial lawyers assns., Nueces County Bar Assn. (dir. 1972-74), Assn. Trial Lawyers Am., Coastal Bend Baylor Alumni Club (pres. 1972-73). Home: 602 Chamberlain Corpus Christi TX 78404 Office: 315 United Savs Bldg Corpus Christi TX 78411

BENNETT, RICHARD HOWELL, JR., sales exec.; b. Chgo., Aug. 10, 1916; s. Richard Howell and Beatrice (Schieberl) B.; student U. Ill., 1935-37; m. Dorothy Caroline Brain, Dec. 28, 1940; children—Carol Ann (Mrs. Robert V. Matenaer), Richard Edwin, Dorothy Marion (Mrs. Bruce V. Shope). Buyer coll. textbook dept. Wilcox & Follett, Chgo., 1937-42; salesman Bauer-Black, Oshkosh, Wis., Detroit, 1942-47; salesman, dist. mgr., regional mgr., nat. sales mgr. U.S. Time Corp., N.Y.C., 1947-54; gen. sales mgr. Amity Leather Products, West Bend, Wis., 1954-64; mdse. coordinator Am. Optical Co., Boston, 1964-65; nat. sales mgr. Bentley Lighter Corp., N.Y.C., 1965-69; Fla. regional mgr. Garrity Industries, Inc., Stamford, Conn., 1969—; chmn. bd. Bennett Industries, Inc., Naples, Fla., 1969—. Mem. Fed. Wholesale Druggists Assn., Nat. Assn. Tobacco Distbrs., Nat. Assn. Chain Drug Stores, Mawanda Assn. of U. Ill., Delta Alpha Epsilon. Clubs: Boston Skating, Glades Country (Naples). Home: 626 Park Shore Dr Naples FL 33940

BENNETT, SARA SHAW (MRS. CLYDE CICERO BENNETT), civic worker; b. Quincy, Fla.; d. Charles Richard and Olive (Sampson) Shaw; student Lucy Cobb Inst., 1922-23, Converse Coll., 1923-24, Fla. State U., 1924-25; m. Alexander Love Wilson, June 14, 1928 (dec. Oct. 1951); children—Alexandra Love (Mrs. Emmett Edward Johnson), Olive Shaw (Mrs. Roby Robinson, Jr.); m. 2d, Clyde Cicero Bennett, June 18, 1954. Vice pres. Women's Aux. Fish Meml. Hosp., DeLand, Fla., 1961-64; charter mem. Quincy Civic Music, 1952—; disaster chmn. Gadsden County chpt. A.R.C., 1951-53; mem. adv. com. Patriotic Edn. Inc., DeLand, 1956-66. Mem. founding group DeLand chpt. Democratic Women's Club, 1957—, social chmn., . 1957-58. Mem. D.A.R. (founders group), Ams. Royal Descent, Royal Order of Garter, Magna Charta Dames, Plantagenet Soc., Hemerocallis Soc., Nat. League Am. Pen Women, Fla. Hist. Soc. (charter mem.), Alpha Delta Pi. Clubs: Garden, Yacht, Country. Exhibited photography DeLand Mus. Art, 1965, oil paintings Volusia County Artists Exhbn., Stetson U., 1970, 71; exhibited Lock Haven Art Center, 1972; represented in permanent collection West Volusia Meml. Hosp., DeLand. Recipient merit award DeLand Sidewalk Show 1972. Home: 601 N Boston Av DeLand FL 32720

BENNETT, WORD BROWN, JR., tobacco co. exec.; b. Nashville, Oct. 24, 1915; s. Word B. and Cora (Sanford) B.; B.A., Vanderbilt U., 1939, M.S., 1940; m. Lera Polk, Dec. 22, 1939; children—Thomas W., Ruth (Mrs. Frank Bauch), Clifford, Nancy. Chief chemist U.S. Tobacco Co., Nashville, 1940-50, research dir., 1950-66, v.p. research and devel., 1966—, also dir. Bd. dirs. David Lipscomb Coll., Lake Shore Home. Home: 2700 Overhill Dr Nashville TN 37214 Office: 905 Harrison St Nashville TN 37202

BENNIGHT, J D, elec. engr.; b. Steepcreek, Tex., Oct. 14, 1920; s. Jerome Willie and Allie Faye (Coats) B.; B.S., Rice U., 1943; m. Gaye Charlene Whitaker, Sept. 17, 1943; children—James Dennis, Susan Winnette, Deborah Gay. Elec. engr. Reed Roller Bit Co., Houston, 1946-47; field engr. Schlumberger Well Surveying Corp., Houston, Liberty, Tex., 1947-49; sales engr. Gulf Coast Electronics, Houston, 1949-50; elec. engr. Red River Arsenal, Texarkana, Tex., 1950-54, Redstone Arsenal, Huntsville, Ala., 1954-56; supervisory elec. engr. Army Ballistic Missile Agy., Huntsville, 1956-60; br. chief Marshall Space Flight Center, NASA, Huntsville, 1960—. Mem. com. Boy Scouts Am., 1965-67. Served to 1st lt. Signal Corps, AUS, 1943-46. Registered profl. engr., Ala. Methodist (asso. dist. lay leader; chmn. adminstrv. bd.). Home: 3904 Thomas Rd SW Huntsville AL 35805 Office: Marshall Space Flight Center Huntsville AL 35812

BENNING, CARL JOSHUA, JR., electronics engr.; b. Springfield, Mo., Dec. 4, 1930; s. Carl Joshua and Catherine (Dicks) B.; B.S., U.S. Naval Acad., 1953; M.S. in E.E., U. N.M., 1964; postgrad. U. Tex., 1965-66; m. Jacqueline F. Fournier, Oct. 1, 1955; 1 son, James D. Staff mem. Sandia Corp., Albuquerque, 1957-62, 63-64; research asst. U. N.M., 1962-63; sr. engr. Braddock, Dunn & McDonald, El Paso, Tex., 1964-65; sr. scientist Tracor, Inc., Austin, Tex., 1965-67; sr. staff mem. Tex. Instruments, Inc., Dallas, 1967—. Mem. spl. test and evaluation task force Defense Sci. Bd., 1973. Served to lt. USNR, 1953-57. Mem. I.E.E.E. Republican. Home: 905 Sandalwood St Richardson TX 97080 Office: 13500 N Central Expressway Dallas TX 75222

BENOLKEN, ROBERT MARSHALL, educator; b. St. Paul, May 11, 1932; s. Robert Herman and Marion Hazel (Eisenhardt) B.; B.S., Marquette U., 1954; Ph.D., Johns Hopkins, 1959; m. Lucretia Ann Stafford, Sept. 21, 1957; children—Ann Louise, Gretchen Amy, Eric Jon, Martha Susan, Sara Jean, Edith Mary. Asst. prof. U. Minn., Mpls., 1959-64, asso. prof., 1964-68; prof. neural scis. U. Tex., Houston, 1968—; adj. prof. physiological optics Baylor Coll. Medicine, Houston, 1968—. Recipient Grants, NSF, NIH, 1960-74. Fellow A.A.A.S.; mem. Soc. Neuro. Scis., Soc. Gen. Physiology, Biophysical Soc. Home: Route 2 Box 1377 Magnolia TX 77355 Office: 6420 Lamar Fleming Houston TX 77025

BENSON, HAROLD AUGUSTUS, JR., social worker; b. Poughkeepsie, N.Y., Aug. 19, 1933; s. Harold Augustus and Helen (Cole) B.; A.B., Colgate U., 1955; postgrad. Syracuse U., 1956; M.S., Columbia, 1957. Social worker Travelers Aid Soc. N.Y., 1957-60; psychiat. social worker Yale, 1960-63; chief social worker Child Guidance Clinic, Winston-Salem, N.C., 1963-64, dir., 1966-69; clinic coordinator Clinic for Retarded, East Orange, N.J., 1964-66; asst. commr. N.C. Dept. Mental Health, Raleigh, 1969-72, dep. commr. children and youth, 1972-73; state program cons. United Cerebral Palsy, Washington, 1973—; counseling cons. Geneva Sch. Bus., N.Y.C. Mem. Gov.'s Adv. Council Mental Health, 1966-69, N.C. Child Day Care Licensing Bd., 1971-73, Gov.'s Adv. Commn. on Children and Youth, 1972-74. Mem. Nat. Assn. Social Workers, Am. Orthopsychiat. Assn., Am. Group Psychotherapy Assn., Am. Assn. for Mental Deficiency, Am. Pub. Health Assn., Assn. Mental Health Clinics N.C. (pres.), Columbia U. Sch. Social Work Alumni Assn. (dir. 1972-73). Home: 204 G St SW Washington DC 20024 Office: 15 E St NW Washington DC 20001

BENSON, HARRY DONALD, lumber co. exec.; b. Pawhuska, Okla., Mar. 1, 1931; s. Harry Garfield and Louella (Parrott) B.; B.S. in Commerce, Okla. A. & M. Coll., 1953; m. Mary Karen Emery, Sept. 19, 1953; children—Harry Emery, Anne Elizabeth, Ruth Louise, Catherine Lou, Nancy. Vice pres. Benson Lumber Co., Pawhuska, 1953-69, pres., 1969—. Served to lt. USAF, 1955-57. Mem. Okla., Kan., Southwestern lumbermens assns. Am. Legion, Pawhuska C. of C., Sigma Chi, Alpha Kappa Psi. Democrat. Presbyn. Mason, Rotarian (pres. 1962-63). Home: Route 1 Pawhuska OK 74056 Office: 5th and Osage Sts Pawhuska OK 74056

BENSON, JOHN, JR., ins. co. exec.; b. Durant, Okla., Sept. 14, 1918; s. Tom and Eunice (Boston) B.; B.S. in Econs., U. Pa., M.B.A. in Accounting, U. Tex., 1947; grad. Advanced Mgmt. Program, Harvard, 1957; m. Betty Mitchell, Apr. 4, 1942; children—John III, Sally, Elizabeth. Supr. prodn. control Lockheed Aircraft Co., Burbank, Cal., 1940-41; instr. U. Tex., Austin, 1946-48; mgr. Tenn. Life Ins. Co., Houston, 1948-56, dir. ins., 1956-59, v.p., 1959-61, sr. v.p., 1961—. Served to capt. USAF, 1941-46. C.P.A., Tex., Okla., C.L.U. Fellow Life Office Mgmt. Assn. Presbyn. (elder 1965-68). Rotarian. Club: Racquet (Houston). Home: 11111 Wickway St Houston TX 77024 Office: 8th Floor Chamber of Commerce Bldg Houston TX 77001

BENSON, KENNETH EDWARD, indsl. research exec.; b. DeKalb, Ill., Sept. 6, 1911; s. John Edward and Mary (Johnson) B.; student U. Akron, 1934-37; m. Anita Mae Foust, Jan. 15, 1939; children—Kenneth Edward, Anita Joan (Mrs. Wade Phillips Young, Jr.), Mary Andrea (Mrs. Joel Douglas Eaton), Barbara Jean (Mrs. Kermit Stuart Taylor); m. 2d, Leona Schaefer Smith, Aug. 2, 1968. Mgr. dept. Akron (O.) C. of C., 1937-39; sales mgr. Textilite Corp., 1939-41; owner Benson Fotocopist Co., Orlando, Fla., 1941-42; 1st lt. intelligence officer Civil Air Patrol, Coastal Patrol, Sarasota, Fla., 1942-43; sales engr. Communications Co., Inc., Coral Gables, Fla., 1944-45; dept. mgr. Ackerman Ins. Co., Miami Fla., 1946-52; exec. v.p. Nat. Union Life Ins. Co., 1953-56; real estate broker Benson & Smith Realty, 1956-64; bus. cons. aviation industry, 1965-72; exec. v.p. Energy Research, Inc., Coral Gables, 1964-71; dir. Riddle Airlines 1953-57. So. Region v.p. NAA, Washington, 1963-71; citizens aviation adv. bd. Dade County Port Authority, 1957-65. Lt. col., Fla. Wing. Civil Air Patrol, 1967-71. Recipient Dedicated Service award City of Miami, 1961, certificate of honor Nat. Aero. Assn., 1964, Distinguished Service award Greater Miami Aviation Assn., 1970. Mem. Greater Miami Aviation Assn. (pres. 1954-71, life pres. emeritus 1970—), Air Force Assn., Am. Inst. Aeros. and Astronautics, Nat. Aerospace Edn. Council, Aircraft Owners and Pilots Assn., Internat. Platform Assn., Miami Bookfellows, Nat. Hist. Soc., Smithsonian Assos., Silver Wings Fraternity, Solar Energy Soc. Mason (32 deg., Shriner, K.T.). Clubs: Ambassadors, Admiral, Clipper, Three Coast, Florida Alligator, Birmingham Aero, OX5; LaGorce Country; Miami Beach Rod and Reel; Miami Acacia, Miami Millionaires, Around the World, Circus Saints and Sinners. Home: 9064 Garland Av Surfside FL 33154 Office: PO Box 6641 Surfside FL 33154

BENSON, PAUL HARRISON, JR., radio station exec.; b. Simpsonville, S.C., Apr. 18, 1915; s. Paul Harrison and Lucile (Woodside) B.; student U. S.C., 1932-33; A.A., Anderson Coll., 1934; student High Mus. Sch. Art (Atlanta), 1934-36; m. Sara D'Oyley Croft, Nov. 6, 1937; children—Paul Harrison III, George Laurence, Sara Legere, Peter Woodside. Mgr., partner Atlantic Outdoor Advt. Co., Florence, S.C., 1936-47; mng. dir. Radio Sta. WJMX, Florence, 1948—; sec.-treas. Atlantic Broadcasting Co., 1947—; dir. Darlington Raceway Radio Network. Mem. Florence County Selective Service Bd., 1946-49, chmn. bd., 1948-49. Bd. dirs. Florence County chpt. A.R.C., 1974, Florence Boys Club; dir.-at-large Pee Dee council Boy Scouts Am., 1971-73. Served with USNR, 1945. Recipient Honor Certificate for editorial comment Freedoms Found. at Valley Forge, 1966; George Washington Honor medal, 1967, Honor certificate, 1968, 69. Mem. Florence C. of C. (dir. 1960-63), Assn. of Broadcasters (charter), S.C. Broadcasters Assn. (dir. 1970-72). Rotarian (sec. Florence 1942-44). Home: Black Creek Rd Florence SC 29501 Office: PO Box 1211 Florence SC 29501

BENSON, ROBERT DALE, financial exec.; b. Little River, Kan., June 4, 1912; s. Leslie Robert and Vernena (Sherer) B.; grad. Hutchinson Jr. Coll., 1932; student Northwestern U., 1939-40; grad. Army Indsl. Coll., 1944; m. Nelle Malick Payne, Dec. 23, 1933 (dec.); children—Robert Payne, Robin Sherwood. Chief accountant The Asso. Dairies Wichita, Kan., 1933-34; accountant Steffen Ice & Ice Cream Corp., Wichita, 1933-36, comptroller, 1936; with Spurrier &

Wood, C.P.A.'s, Wichita, 1936-37; partner Spurrier, Wood & Benson, accountants and auditors, Hutchinson, Kan.; 1941-43; with P.H. Willems & Co., accountants and auditors, MacPherson, Kan., 1937; partner Willems & Benson, accountants and auditors, McPherson, 1937-43; chief fixed price audits br., also chief termination audits br. Hdqrs., USAAF, 1943-46; chief spl. audits br. Army Audit Agy., 1946-48; dep. auditor gen. Hdqrs., USAF, 1948-53; dep. for accounting and financial mgmt. to asst. sec. air force, Washington, 1953-58, dep. asst. sec. air force, 1958-71; now chmn. bd. Internat. Finance and Mgmt. Corp.; guest lectr. George Washington U., 1953-56. Mem. bd. U.S. Civil Service Examiners, 1955-71. Recipient Air Force Decoration for Exceptional Civilian Service, 1953, 55, 69-71; named Outstanding Young Man Kan., 1942. Mem. U.S. Jr. (v.p. 1943-44, treas. 1943-44, dir. 1941-45). Kan. (dir. 1942-43), Kan. Jr. (pres. 1942-43) chambers commerce, Fed. Govt. Accountants Assn., Kan. State Soc. Municipal Pub. Accountants, Am. Accounting Assn. Clubs: Kenwood Golf and Country, Army-Navy (Washington). Ordre des Compagnons du Bontemps-Medoc (Bordeaux, France), Internat. Wine and Food Soc., Les Amisdu Vin, Kan. State Soc. Asso. editor Future Magazine, 1944. Home: 3506 Manor Rd Chevy Chase MD 20015

BENSON, STANLEY HUGH, librarian; b. Sparta, Ill., Oct. 1, 1930; s. Edward Hugh and Laurence (Sanders) B.; B.S., So. Ill. U., 1951; B.D., Southwestern Bapt. Theol. Sem., 1956, Th.D., 1964; M.L.S., U. Tex. at Austin, 1965; m. Sara Elizabeth Collins, Dec. 28, 1959; children—Andrew, Raymond. Library asst. Tex. Christian U., 1959-61; head librarian Ky. So. Coll., 1964-68, Gardner-Webb Coll., 1968-69, Berry Coll., 1969-71, Okla. Bapt. U., Shawnee, 1971—. Instr. library sci. and religion, part-time 1964—. Lilly Endowment fellow Am. Theol. Library Assn., 1963. Mem. A.L.A., Am. Theol. Library Assn., Okla. Library Assn. Baptist. Home: 2706 Frank Buck Dr Shawnee OK 74801 Office: Oklahoma Baptist University Library Shawnee OK 74801

BENSON, WALTER RUSSELL, pathologist; b. Tamaqua, Pa., July 27, 1920; s. John Berier and Mary (Green) B.; student Duke, 1938-41, M.D., 1944; m. Ruth Velva Cogan, Dec. 9, 1950 (dec. Dec. 1972); children—John, Christina, Eric, Carl. Intern Duke Hosp., 1944-45; resident VA Hosp., Ft. Howard, Md., 1947-51; resident in pathology Duke Sch. Medicine, 1951-54, asso. pathologist, 1954-55; chief lab. VA Hosp., Louisville, 1955-56; asst. prof. pathology U. Louisville, 1955-56; asst. prof. pathology U. N.C. Sch. Medicine, Chapel Hill, 1956-60, asso. prof. pathology, 1960-67, prof. pathology, 1967—; cons. in pathology Watts Hosp., Durham, N.C., 1959—. Served with AUS, 1945-47. Diplomate Am. Bd. Pathology. Mem. Internat. Acad. Pathology, Am. Assn. Pathologists and Bacteriologists, Am. Soc. Exptl. Pathology, Soc. for Exptl. Biology and Medicine, Phi Beta Kappa, Sigma Xi, Phi Eta Sigma. Mason. Home: 910 Coker Dr Chapel Hill NC 27514

BENT, DOROTHY FLORENCE (MRS. ALLEN EMERY BENT), home economist; b. Whitingham, Vt., June 1, 1920; d. Harold Edgar and Florence Vernette (Hicks) Plumb; B.S. (Cotting Meml. scholar), U. Mass., 1942; M.A. in Teaching, U. Vt., 1968; m. Allen Emery Bent, Nov. 11, 1944; children—Kim Allen, David Emery, Douglas Gene, Robert Arnold, Cynthia Lee. County 4-H club agt. Chittenden County, Burlington, Vt., 1942-43, Orange County, Middletown, N.Y., 1943-44; acting county club agt. Orange County, Chelsea, Vt., 1954; tchr. Whitcomb High Sch., Bethel, Vt., 1960-67; county extension agt. Windsor County, Woodstock, Vt., 1967-72; now home economist, real estate salesman. Cons., instr. handicapped homemakers. Adviser Windsor, Springfield family centers; mem. tech. adv. com. Health Care and Rehab. Services Southeastern Vt., Inc., 1970—; Orange County rep. to Vt. 4-H Club Found., 1952-53; mem. Orange County Extension Adv. Bd., 1965-67; mem. sub-com. on edn. Gov.'s Com. on Children and Youth, 1971-72; den. mother Cub Scouts, 1957-58; pres. Randolph Unit P.T.A., 1961-63; mem. Vt. Inter-Agy. Council on Smoking and Health, 1971-72, Vt. Preschool Planning Com., 1971—; del. White House Conf. on Children, 1970. Town auditor Town of Braintree (Vt.), 1950-55; mem. Orange County Republican Com., 1961-62. Trustee Downer 4-H Camp; bd. dirs. Central Vt. Community Action Council, First Chance Project of Pre-Sch. Edn. Centers, Windsor County and Vt. Community Coordinated Child Care Com.; named Mrs. Vt. of 1963, Mrs. America Homemakers Council. Mem. Nat., Vt. edn. assns., Nat. Congress Parents and Tchrs. (life mem.; mem. health and welfare commn. 1969-72, mem. nat. bd. mgrs. 1969-72), Vt. P.T.A. (pres. 1969-73), Nat. Rehab. Assn., Nat. Assn. Extension Home Economists, New Eng. Assn. Extension Home Economists (sec. 1969-71), Vt. Home Econs. Assn., Nat. Home Econs. Assn., Winter Haven Bd. Realtors, Nat. Assn. Real Estate Bds., Am. Assn. U. Women, Braintree Hist. Soc. (charter mem.), Orange County 4-H Leaders Assn. (pres. 1952-53), Vt. 4-H Hon. Soc., Mass. All-Stars 4-H Hon. Soc., Vt. Assn. Extension Home Economists (v.p. 1969-71), League Vt. Writers. Conglist. Clubs: White Water Wheelers (Rochester, Vt.); Hearth and Heath Extension Homemakers (charter mem.) (Braintree, Vt.); Metropolitan Dinner. Home: 1310 Lake Elbert Dr SE Winter Haven FL 33880

BENTLEY, CLARENCE EDWARD, savs. and loan exec.; b. Ranger, Tex., Oct. 9, 1921; s. Clarence E. and Rosa Estell (Bryant) B.; student McMurry Coll., 1939-42; m. Gloria Gill, Oct. 9, 1943; children—Jon, Kitty, Perry. With Abilene (Tex.) Savs. Assn., 1943—, exec. v.p., 1950-60, pres., 1960—, also dir.; dir., chmn. exec. com. Southwestern Group Investors, Houston, 1973—; dir. Mutual Savs., Fort Worth. Pres., Abilene (Tex.) United Fund, 1963; pres., Abilene (Tex.) Indsl. Found., 1972; mem. Tex. State Hosp. Bd., 1962-63; mem. Finance Commn. Tex., 1963-73, chmn., 1970. Trustee McMurry Coll. Served with USAAF, 1942-45. Named Outstanding Citizen, C. of C., 1965; recipient Distinguished Alumnus award McMurry Coll., 1972. Mem. Nat. League Insured Savs. Assns. (pres. 1970), Tex. Savs. and Loan League (pres. 1970), Abilene C. of C. (pres. 1964-65). Clubs: Preston Trails Gulf (Dallas); Country (Abilene, Tex.). Home: 3565 Hunters Glen Abilene TX 79603 Office: 402 Cedar St Abilene TX 79604

BENTLEY, FRED BLAKE, coll. pres.; b. Roanoke, Va., Sept. 11, 1935; s. William Louis and Haleene Virginia (Wilson) B.; B.A., Baylor U., 1958; M. R.E., So. Bapt. Theol. Sem., 1960; studied at Nat. Pedagogical Inst., Paris, 1961; Ed.D. (Univ. fellow), Ind. U., 1962; m. Doris Virginia Phillips, June 29, 1956; children—Stephen Blake, Philip Alan, Rhonda Lyn. Ednl. dir., internat. contract programs Ind. U., Bloomington, 1962-64; asst. dean coll. arts and scis. U. Louisville, 1964-66; pres. Mars Hill (N.C.) Coll., 1966—. Cons., So. Assn. Colls. and Schs., 1967—. Bd. dirs. Asheville (N.C.) Art Mus., 1967-71, St. Joseph's Hosp., 1971—. Mem. Soc. Advancement Mgmt., Am. Assn. Health Edn., Phi Mu Alpha, Phi Delta Kappa. Baptist (deacon). Club: Civitan. Home and office: Box 398 Mars Hill NC 28754

BENTLEY, JAMES ROBERT, assn. curator; b. Louisville, Feb. 14, 1942; s. Francis Getty and Katharine Elizabeth (Wescott) B.; B.A., Centre Coll. Ky., 1964; M.A., Coll. William and Mary, 1971. Research asst. Colonial Williamsburg (Va.), 1966-68; asst. to curator Filson Club, Louisville, 1964-65, curator, 1968—, sec., 1972—. Dir. G.R. Clark Press, Louisville. Mem. adv. com. to photograph archives U. Louisville, 1971-72. Mem. Louisville Bicentennial Com., 1973—, Hist. Zoning Task Force Louisville and Jefferson County, 1971-73; mem. historic protection and preservation com. Bd. Alderman Louisville, 1972-73; commr. Historic Landmarks and Preservation Dists. Commn., Louisville, 1973—. Mem. S.A.R. (registrar 1970—), Ky. Soc. Mayflower Descs. (historian, librarian 1970—), Ky. Soc. Colonial Wars (councillor 1971—), Jeffersontown Hist. Soc. (dir. 1972-73, v.p. 1974—), Soc. Am. Archivists, Manuscript Soc., Ky. Civil War Round Table, Historic Homes Found. Louisville, Vt. Hist. Soc. (life), Bennington (Vt.) Mus., Vt. Geneal. Soc., Conn. Soc. Genealogists, Vt. Old Cemetery Assn., Alden Kindred Am., Soc. Stukely Westcott Descs., Edmund Rice 1638 Assn., Soc. Descs. Robert Bartlett of Plymouth Colony, St. Albans (Vt.) Hist. Soc., Order Ky. Cols. Club: Pendennis (Louisville). Home: 9708 Old Six Mile Lane Jeffersontown KY 40299 Office: 118 W Breckinridge St Louisville KY 40203

BENTLEY, JOHN BRADLEY, soft drink co. exec.; b. Whitesburg, Ky., Sept. 15, 1915; s. Ewen and Bertha (Collins) B.; grad. high sch.; m. Dixie J. Skaggs, Sept. 13, 1936; children—Ronald, Barbara (Mrs. Mike Krupp). With Bentley & Son, truck hauling, Whitesburg, 1935-44; owner, operator Big Block Coal Co., 1944-49; pres. R.C. Cola Co., Whitesburg, 1949—. Ky. Col. Mem. Ky. Sheriffs Assn., U.S., Whitesburg Area chambers commerce. Address: Route 119 at Bradstreet Whitesburg KY 41858

BENTLEY, KENTON EARL, chemist; b. Detroit, June 1, 1927; s. Kenneth and Marion (Tillman) B.; B.S., U. Mich., 1950, Ph.D., U. N.M., 1959; m. Elizabeth Montrose, Apr. 18, 1953. Research phys. chemist Consol. Electro-dynamics Corp., Pasadena, Cal., 1956-57; ind. cons. chemist, Albuquerque, 1957-59; vis. prof. Highlands U., Las Vegas, N.M., 1959; asst. prof. chemistry Am. U. Beirut Lebanon, 1959-61; research scientist Lockheed Cal. Co., Burbank, 1962-63; scientist, task leader Jet Propulsion Lab. Cal. Inst. Tech., Pasadena, 1963-65; head electrochemistry group Hughes Aircraft Co., Culver City, Cal., 1965-67; dir. sci. and applications br. Lockheed Electronics Co., Inc., Houston, 1967—. Served with USNR, 1945-46. Los Alamos research fellow, U. N.M., 1954-56. Mem. Am. Chem. Soc., A.A.A.S. (lofe), Am. Assn. U. Profs., Am. Astronautical Soc. (sr. mem., dir. 1969-73), Nat. Mgmt. Assn., Sigma Xi (life), Alpha Chi Sigma. Contbr. to profl. jours. Home: 18100 Nassau Bay Dr Houston TX 77058 Office: 16811 El Camino Real Houston TX 77058

BENTLEY, RICHARD RAYMOND, educator; b. Polo, Ill., Apr. 7, 1920; s. Everette E. and Helen L. (Buck) B.; B.M.E., Cornell Coll., 1946; Mus.M., Northwestern U., 1947; Ed.D., U. So. Cal., 1955; m. Marjorie Helen Tullis, June 14, 1947; children—Richard R., Beth Ann, Martha Jane. Supr. music Redfield (S.D.) City Schs., 1947-50; gen. secondary substitute tchr. Los Angeles City Schs., 1950-54; asso. prof. music edn. Southwestern Coll., Winfield, Kan., 1954-55; instrumental music tchr. Napa (Cal.) City Schs., 1955-65; asso. prof. music edn. Tex. Womans U., Denton, after 1965, now prof. Bd. dirs. Denton County Tchrs. Fed. Credit Union, Community Concert Assn. Served with AUS, 1941-45. Mem. N.E.A., Music Educators Nat. Conf., Am. Assn. U. Profs., Nat. Council on Measurement in Edn., Tex. Music Educators Assn., Phi Mu Alpha Sinfonia. Methodist. Home: 2907 Foxcroft Circle Denton TX 76201

BENTON, BENJAMIN FREDERICK (JACK), surgeon; b. Jonesboro, Ark., Jan. 10, 1924; s. Ellsworth Eugene and Freda Ellen (Wening) B.; B.S., U. Mo., 1944; M.D., U. Tenn., 1946; children—Kathleen Ann, James Mark, Steven Carl. Intern, St. Vincent's Hosp., Bridgeport, Conn., 1946-47; resident surgery U. Tenn.-Bapt. Meml. Hosp., Memphis, 1949-53; practice medicine specializing in gen. surgery Bapt. Meml. Hosp., Memphis, 1953—; asso. prof. dept. surgery Coll. Medicine, U. Tenn., 1970—, prof., sec. dept., 1970—; mem. cons. staff St. Josephs Hosp.; cons. staff, past pres. surg. staff Baptist Hosp., LeBonheur Childrens Hosp.; cons. staff Methodist Hosp.; mem. attending staff City of Memphis Hosp. Served to capt. AUS, 1943-46, 47-49. Diplomate Am. Bd. Surgery. Fellow A.C.S. (past pres. Tenn. chpt.); mem. A.M.A., Tenn., Shelby County, Memphis med. assns., Southeastern Surg. Congress, Memphis Surg. Soc. Club: University (Memphis). Contbr. articles profl. jours. Home: 2948 Southern St Memphis TN 38111 Office: 20 S Dudley St Memphis TN 38103

BENTON, DEMPSEY EUGENE, JR., city ofcl.; b. Elizabeth City, N.C., Mar. 2, 1945; s. Dempsey Eugene and Atwood (Sutton) B.; B.A., U. N.C., 1967, M.P.A., 1972; m. Barbara Thornton, Aug. 20, 1966. Asst. to city mgr. Rocky Mount, 1968-69, finance dir., city clk., 1969-71; city mgr. Elizabeth City, N.C., 1971—. Sec.-treas. ElectriCities N.C., 1972—. Mem. budget com. United Fund Rocky Mount, 1970, Elizabeth City, 1972, 73; sec. Central Regional Planning Commn., 1969-70. Mem. N.C. League Municipalities (resolutions com., dir.), Phi Beta Kappa, Pi Alpha Theta. Rotarian. Home: 1515 Crescent Dr Elizabeth City NC 27909 Office: 300 E Colonial Av E Elizabeth City NC 27909

BENTON, DUANE MARSHALL, environmental scientist; b. Savannah, O., Nov. 1, 1933; s. William Marshall and Mary Frances (Lashley) B.; B.A. in Chemistry, Ashland Coll., 1955; B.S. in Meteorology, U. Utah, 1958; M.S. in Analytical Chemistry, Ohio State U., 1964; M.S. in Bus. Adminstrn., George Washington U., 1967; m. Carolyn Kay Hutchison, Jan. 29, 1960; children—Mary Kaye, Kristy Anne, Michael Duane. Asst. analytical research chemist Hess & Clark, Inc., Ashland, O., 1954-56, 58-59; faculty Ashland Coll., 1959-60, 62-73, asso. prof. phys. sci., 1969-73, faculty welfare com., 1967-71, chmn., 1970-71; environmental engr. Dept. Army, Washington, 1973—. Commd. 2d lt. Ohio Air N.G., 1956, advanced through grades to lt. col., 1972; comdr. 164th Weather Flight, Mansfield Lahm Airport, O., 1971—; capt. Berlin Crisis, Etain, France, 1961-62; lt. col. USAF Air War Coll., Montgomery, Ala., 1972-73. Civil def. nuclear radiation fallout monitor Ashland County, O., 1967-73. Mem. Am. Meteorol. Soc., Am. Assn. Physics Tchrs., Am. Inst. Physics, Am. Assn. U. Profs. (chpt. pres. 1971). Club: 179th Tactical Fighter Group Officers (Mansfield Lahm Airport). Home: 5000 King Richard Dr Annandale VA 22003 Office: Dept Army DCSLOG Environmental Office Pentagon Washington DC 20310

BENTON, EVELYN FLEMING, librarian; b. Ponchatoula, La., Aug. 10, 1921; d. Walter Raleigh and Mabel Magdalene (Varnado) Fleming; B.F.A. with high distinction and spl. mention in music, Okla. State U., 1943; student U. Tex. Grad. Sch. Library Sci., 1959-60; m. Douglas C. Benton, Aug. 25, 1942; children—Walter Bradford, Christopher Paul. Circulation asst. Tulsa Pub. Library, 1944, 1st asst. tech. dept., 1945; reference asst. Okla. State U., Stillwater, 1946-48, jr. reference librarian, 1948-50; piano tchr., Baytown, Tex., 1958-60; asst. librarian Lee Coll., Baytown, 1960-66; library dir. Deer Park (Tex.) Pub. Library, 1967—. Pres. San Jacinto Music Tchrs. Assn., 1960. Pres. Baytown Unitarian Fellowship, 1965. Mem. Am., Tex. (chmn. nominating com. 1971-72, chmn. reference roundtable 1972-73, sec. dist. V, 1969, treas. dist. VIII, 1971), Southwestern (conf. program com. 1974), Pub. (editorial com.) library assns., Tex. Municipal Librarians Assn., Internat. Platform Assn., Houston Library Club, Phi Kappa Phi, Sigma Alpha Iota (treas. Iota Alpha chpt. 1942-43). Unitarian. Home: 3401 Woodcrest St Baytown TX 77520 Office: 3009 Center St Deer Park TX 77536

BENTON, GEORGE OLIVER, lawyer; b. Jackson, Tenn., June 22, 1915; s. Oliver and Luey Burkett (Wilkerson) B.; B.A., Vanderbilt U., 1938, J.D., 1940; m. Theresa Ray Anderson, Nov. 6, 1943; children—Jane A., George Oliver, Hu A. Admitted to Tenn. bar, 1940; partner atty. Moss & Benton, Jackson, 1940-41, 45—; dir. Nat. Bank Commerce, Jackson. Mem. Tenn. Senate, 1947-51; mem. state exec. com. Democratic party, 1954-72; mem. Madison County (Tenn.) Election Commn., 1953-71. Served with USMCR, 1941-45. Fellow Am. Coll. Trial Lawyers, Internat. Acad. Trial Lawyers; mem. Def. Research Inst., Sigma Chi. Episcopalian (mem. vestry 1973). Elk. Clubs: Golf and Country (Jackson); Summit (Memphis). Home: 101 Oakslea Pl Jackson TN 38301 Office: First Nat Bank Bldg Jackson TN 38301

BENTON, ISHMAEL CLAUD, educator; b. Romance, Ark., Oct. 16, 1920; s. Claud Leland and Ida Viola (Pearson) B.; student U. Md., 1954-57, Kan. State U., 1957-58, Purdue, 1958-59, Ind. U., 1959-60; B.S., U. Ark., 1962, M.Ed., 1964, Ed.D., 1970; m. Alice Elizabeth Stottle, Dec. 11, 1946; children—Beverly Ann, Robert Shearer. Commd. 2d lt., U.S. Army, advanced through grades to maj., 1960; ret., 1960; tchr. Fayetteville (Ark.) High Sch., 1962-65; adminstr. community service U. Ark., 1965-70, asst. dean, 1970-71, asst. provost, 1971-72, asst. prof., chmn. ind. study dept. U. S.C., 1972—. Amateur radio operator, mem. Mil. Affiliate Radio System. Mem. Fayetteville C. of C.; Phi Delta Kappa. Methodist. Mason. Clubs: Fayetteville Kiwanis (dir.); Fort Jackson (S.C.) Officer and Golf. Home: 5500 Sylvan Dr Columbia SC 29206

BENTON, JOHN WILLIAM, JR., physician; b. Enterprise, Ala., July 3, 1930; s. John William and Martha (Bain) B.; B.S., U. Ala., 1951; M.D., Med. Coll. Ala., 1955; m. Ann Abernathy, Dec. 17, 1955; children—John, Keith, Beth. Intern University Hosp., Birmingham, Ala., 1955-56; resident in pediatrics Salt Lake County Hosp., 1956-57, U. Minn. Hosp., 1959-60; NIH trainee neurology U. Ala. Med. Coll. at Birmingham, 1960-62; NIH fellow neurology Mass. Gen. Hosp., Harvard Med. Sch., Boston, 1964-66; practice medicine specializing in pediatric neurology, Birmingham, 1966—; instr. pediatric dept. Med. Coll. Ala. at Birmingham, 1960-62, asst. prof. dept. pediatrics-neurology, 1962-66, asso. prof. dept. pediatrics, 1966-69, interim chmn. dept. pediatrics, 1968-69, dir. Center Developmental and Learning Disorders, 1962-68; asso. prof. div. neurology U. Ala. Sch. Medicine at Birmingham, 1966—, prof., chmn. dept. pediatrics, dir. Children's Hosp., 1969—. Served to capt., AUS, 1957-59. Mem. Am. Acad. Neurology, Am. Acad. Pediatrics, Med. Assn. Ala., So. Soc. Pediatric Research, Am., Jefferson County pediatric socs. Home: 3008 Brook Hollow Lane Birmingham AL 35243 Office: 1601 6th Av S Birmingham AL 35233

BENTON, WILLIAM JOSEPH, constrn. co. exec.; b. Verbena, Ala., Dec. 29, 1921; s. William Joseph and Lovie (Holdbrooks) B.; student Marion Inst., 1948-50; m. Baroness Waldtraut Hilda Von Den Brincken, Dec. 19, 1959. Various engring. positions, constrn. div. E.I. duPont de Nemours & Co., Inc., Ala., Wash. and Tex., 1941-48; various mgmt. positions to v.p. fgn. subsidiaries heavy marine constrn. J. Ray McDermott & Co., Inc., La. and Netherlands, 1950-64; with Ingram Corp., Harvey, La., 1964—, sr. v.p., 1969—, chief operating officer world constrns. operations, 1966—, corp. dir., 1967—, exec. v.p. various operating subsidiaries, 1966—, also dir. subsidiaries. Trustee Tommy C. Turner Meml. Found. Served with AUS, 1943-45. Decorated Purple Heart, Bronze Star medal, Silver Star. Life fellow Internat. Oceanographic Found.; mem. A.I.M., Am. Soc. Agrl. Engrs., Am. Topical Assn., German, Am. (life) philatelic socs. New Orleans C. of C. Clubs: Timberlane Country (Gretna, La.); International House (New Orleans). Office: 4100 One Shell Sq New Orleans LA 70139

BENTSEN, LLOYD MILLARD, JR., U.S. senator; b. Mission, Tex., Feb. 11, 1921; s. Lloyd M. and Edna Ruth (Colbath) B.; LL.B., U. Tex., 1942; m. Beryl Ann Longino, Nov. 27, 1943; children—Lloyd M. III, Lan, Tina (Mrs. Eric Maedgen). Admitted to Tex. bar, 1942; practice law, McAllen, Tex., 1945-48; judge Hidalgo County, Tex., hdqrs. Edinburg, 1946-48; mem. 80th to 83d congresses from 15th Tex. Dist.; pres. Lincoln Consol., Houston, 1955—; U.S. Senator from Tex., 1971—. Mem. finance, pub. works and joint econs. coms., chmn. transp. sub-com.; chmn. NATO sub-com. mut. and balanced force reduction. Gov., Soc. Performing Arts, Houston, United Fund Houston and Harris County. Trustee Tex. Presbyn. Found., U. Tex. Devel. Bd. Served to lt. col. AUS, 1942-45. Decorated D.F.C., Air Medal with 3 oak leaf clusters. Home: 3435 Westheimer St Houston TX 77027 Office: Senate Office Bldg Washington DC 20510

BENTZ, JOHN JENNINGS, furniture co. exec.; b. Naperville, Ill., July 4, 1900; s. John and Anna Elizabeth (Baumgartner) B.; corr. student Walton Sch. Commerce, Chgo., 1920-21, So. Meth. U., evenings 1942-43; m. Lolita M. Koob, Sept. 3, 1932; children—John D., Barbara (Mrs. Bill B. Dendy). Jr. accountant J.B. Cook & Co., Chgo., 1921-23; with Kroehler Mfg. Co., Naperville, Dallas, 1923-46; plant mgr. Rowe Furniture Corp., Roanoke and Salem, Va., 1946-50; plant mgr. Jackson Mfg. Co., Chattanooga, 1950-55, exec. v.p., Houston, Miss., 1955-69; vice chmn. bd. Shannon Chair Co., Houston, 1969—. Mayor, Houston, 1970-73. Mem. revenue and finance com. Congress of Cities, Nat. League Cities, Washington, 1971-73; v.p. N.E. Devel. Assn. Miss., Hope Hwys. Our Pressing Emergency State of Miss. Bd. dirs. Miss. Municipal Assn., Jackson, Prairie council Girl Scouts U.S.A. Mem. Miss. Mfrs. Assn. (past chmn. bd.). Presbyn. (deacon). Mason (32 degree, Shriner). Clubs: Houston Exchange (past dist. gov.), Houston Country (past pres.). Address: PO Box 506 Houston MS 38851

BENZ, GEORGE ALBERT, educator; b. St. Louis, Feb. 21, 1926; s. George and Genevieve B. (Klueg) B.; B.B.A., N. Tex. State U., 1953, M.S., 1955; Ph.D., U. Okla., 1969; m. D. Jean Tabor, Apr. 14, 1951; 1 dau., Lynda Kaye. Grad. asst. U. Okla., 1957-59; asst. prof. Central State U., 1959-66; asso. prof., chmn. dept. econs. St. Mary's U., San Antonio, 1969-71, acting dir. U. Research Center, 1971—, chmn. urban studies dept., 1972—. Cons. several poverty projects. Chmn., San Antonio Civil Liberties Union, 1970-71; mem. Tex. State adv. com. U.S. Civil Rights Comm., 1969—. Served with Paratroops 11th Airborne Div., AUS, 1943-49. Decorated Bronze Star medal. Mem. Assn. of U. Profs. (v.p. Tex. chpt. 1970-71), Am., So. econ. assns., Southwest Social Science Assn. Home: 206 E Sunshine Dr San Antonio TX 78228 Office: 2700 Cincinnati St San Antonio TX 78284

BERAZA, FELIPE GARCIA, orgn. exec.; b. Cuernavaca, Morelos, Mexico, May 1, 1920; s. Fructuoso Garcia Campos and Maria Eugenia Beraza y Ruiz de Valesco; student history Facultad de Filosofia y Letras, U. Nat. Autonoma Mexico, 1938-40, Letras Inglesas, Facultad y Letras, 1942. Exec. sec. Mexican Writing Center, 1951—; instr. Spanish summer sch. Nat. U. Mexico, 1946-68, instr. extension courses of univ. at San Antonio, 1947-69; instr. Spanish Smith Coll. group El Colegio de Mexico, 1947-50; registrar fgn. students Nat. U. Mexico, 1947-69; press adviser Mexican-Am. Cultural Inst., 1966-73, dir. cultural activities, 1973—; founder Soc. Defensora del Tesoro Artistico de Mexico, 1958; co-founder Soc. para Proteccion del Paralitico Cerebral, 1974. Decorated Cruz del Bien Comun (France); Cruz del la Orden de Petion y Bolivar (Haiti). Editor El Informador Economico, 1952-53, Recent Books in Rev., 1964.

Collator encys., books. Contbr. numerous articles to profl. jours. Home: 28-8 Lerma Mexico 5 DF Mexico Office: 115 Hamburgo Mexico 6 DF Mexico

BERDJIS, CHARLES CHOAIB, pathologist; b. Kashan, Iran, July 1, 1918; s. Yagoub and Hosni (Fakimi) B.; M.D., U. Paris, 1947; M.D., U. Geneva, Switzerland, 1945; m. Odette R. Bezzola, Mar. 12, 1941; children—Mariam (Mrs. Stefan Burgener), Mary F. came to U.S., 1953, naturalized, 1958. Intern, State Hosp., Geneva, Switzerland, 1940-41, resident, 1941-45; asst., State Hosp. and Inst. Pathology, Sch. Medicine, Geneva, Switzerland, 1940-45, Anticancer Center, Paris, France, 1946-49; dir., Anticancer Center, Red Cross Hosp., Tehran, 1950-53; asst., lectr. pathology AEC and Sch. Medicine, U. Cal. at San Francisco, 1954-57; commd. maj. U.S. Army, 1957, advanced through grades to col., 1967; chief pathology, sr. pathologist U.S. Army installations, 1957-69; pathologist, Armed Forces Inst. Pathology, Washington, 1969—. Mem. Am. Soc. Exptl. Pathology, Am. Soc. Experimental Pathology, Radiation Research Soc., A.M.A., Assn. Mil. Surgeons U.S., Am. Chem. Soc., Royal Soc. Medicine (London), Internat. Soc. Sci. and Arts, Divers Internat. Congress. Author: Pathology of Irradiation, 1971; Behavioral Sciences, 1966; Human Parathyroids, 1946. Contbr. articles to profl. jours. Home: 1701 Holly St Washington DC 20012 Office: Armed Forces Inst Pathology Washington DC 20306

BERENSON, GERALD SANDERS, physician; b. Bogalusa, La., Sept. 19, 1922; s. Meyer A. and Eva (Singerman) B.; B.S., Tulane U., 1943, M.D., 1945; m. Joan Seidenbach, Mar. 7, 1951; children—Leslie, Ann, Robert, Laurie. Intern, US Navy Hosp., Great Lakes, Ill., 1945-46; practice medicine specializing in cardiology, New Orleans; mem. staff Charity Hosp., Crippled Children's Hosp.; instr. dept. medicine Tulane U., 1949-52; asst. prof. dept. medicine La. State U. Sch. Medicine, 1954-58, asso. prof., 1958-63, prof., 1963—; dir. Specialized Center Research-Arteriosclerosis, New Orleans, 1972—; sr. vis. physician Charity Hosp. La., New Orleans, 1948—; cons., Touro Infirmary, 1967—; cons. medicine Hotel Dieu, 1962—. Served with USNR, 1945-48. USPHS fellow U. Chgo., 1952-54. Mem. So. Soc. Clin. Investigation (pres. 1969), La. Heart Assn. (pres. 1971), New Orleans Acad. Internatl. Medicine (pres. 1966), Sigma Xi, Alpha Omega Alpha. Contbr. articles to profl. jours. Home: 505 Northline St Metairie LA 70005 Office: Dept Medicine La State U Med Center New Orleans LA 70112

BERES, RUDY JOHN, cons. engr.; b. Hurley, Wis., Feb. 18, 1937; s. Rudolph Joseph and Mary Helen (Kopacz) B.; B.C.E., Mich. Coll. Mining and Tech., 1959; postgrad. U. Colo., 1965; m. Margaret Helen Johnson, Feb. 23, 1963; children—Anne, Eva. Civil engr. asst. Los Angeles County Rd. Dept., Los Angeles, 1959-63; design engr. Ken R. White Co. Cons. Engrs., Denver, 1963-67, sr. engr., Honolulu, 1967-68, chief engr., Miami, Fla., 1968-72, mgr., Miami, 1973—. Served with AUS, 1960. Registered profl. engr., Ga., Colo., Hawaii, Fla., Tenn. Mem. Nat. Soc. Profl. Engrs., Am. Soc. C.E., South Fla. Emerald Soc. Home: 13425 SW 102d Av Miami FL 33156 Office: 7331 Coral Way Miami FL 33155

BERESFORD, JOHN CLINTON, information industry exec.; b. St. Paul, Mar. 11, 1930; s. Howard Clinton and Vivian (Brand) B.; B.A., Antioch Coll., 1951; M.A., U. Mich., 1953; m. Nancy Harris, Mar. 29, 1951; children—Alison, John Roderic. Market research asst. Nat. Cash Register Co., Dayton, O., 1949-50; factory sales engr. Gates Rubber Co., Denver, 1950-51; teaching fellow, research asst. U. Mich., Ann Arbor, 1955-58; fertility specialist Bur. of Census, Washington, 1959, household statistics specialist, 1960-63, staff asst. population div., 1964-66, spl. asst. to asso. dir., 1967, chief data access and use lab., 1967-69; pres. Data Use and Access Labs., Inc., Washington, 1969—. Served with AUS, 1953-55. Mem. Am. Statis. Assn., Am. Sociol. Assn., Population Assn. Am., Council Social Sci. Data Archives, Am. Soc. Information Scis.; Urban and Regional Information Systems Assn. (pres. 1971-72), Internat. Union Sci. Study Population. Home: 1317 Alexandria Av Alexandria VA 22308 Office: 1601 N Kent St Suite 900 Arlington VA 22209

BERG, HAROLD FREDRIC, surgeon; b. Bklyn., May 22, 1918; s. David and Rachel (Graf) B.; B.A., U. Louisville, 1939, M.D., 1942; m. Pearl Greenberg, Sept. 5, 1953; children—Amy Lisa, Dena Alison, Karen Aviva, Lauren Andrea. Intern, Louisville Gen. Hosp., 1942-43, resident in surgery, 1946-51; practice medicine specializing in surgery, Louisville, 1952—; chief surgery Jewish Hosp., Louisville, 1966-68; asst. prof. surgery U. Louisville, 1951—. Cons. Oak Ridge Inst. Nuclear Studies, 1948-62. Researcher, Damon Runyon Fund, 1950-53. Bd. dirs. Arthritis Found., Jewish Community Center, Bur. Jewish Edn. Served to maj., M.C., AUS, 1943-46. Decorated Purple Heart. Jewish religion (chmn. adult edn. com. 1966-71, dir. temple). Home: 608 Jarvis Lane Louisville KY 40207 Office: Med Towers Louisville KY 40207

BERGE, TRUMAN KENT, air force officer; b. Erskine, Minn., Sept. 2, 1922; s. Thor Knute and Pauline (Larson) B.; student U. Minn., 1939-42; B.S., U.S. Mil. Acad., 1946; M.S., Purdue U., 1952; m. Genevieve Medlin, May 15, 1948; children—Karen, Pamela, Thomas Kent, David Medlin, Heidi Ann. Commd. 2d lt. U.S. Army, 1946, advanced through grades to col., U.S. Air Force, 1968; reconnaissance pilot, flight test maintenance officer Brooks AFB, Tex., Langley AFB, Va., Yokota AFB, Japan, Itazuke AFB, Japan, Taegu, Korea, 1946-50; instr., asst. prof. physics U.S. Mil. Acad., West Point, N.Y., 1952-55; research and devel. administr., Brussels, Belgium, 1955-58; asst. prof., asso. prof. physics U.S. Air Force Acad., Colorado Springs, Colo., 1958-61; student Armed Forces Staff Coll., 1962; physicist, research and devel. administr. Patrick AFB, Fla., 1962-65; dep. dir. Tactical Operations, Air Forces Korea, 314th Air Div., 1965; dep. comdr. 343d Fighter Group, Duluth, Minn., 1965-66; student Air War Coll., 1966-67; flight comdr. 361st Tactical Electronic Warfare Squadron, Nha Trang, Vietnam, 1967-68; staff scientist and dir. analysis and modeling Data Services Center, Hdqrs. U.S. Air Force, Washington, 1968-72; comdr. Fed. Computer Performance Evaluation and Simulation Center, 1972—. Decorated D.F.C. with oak leaf cluster, Air medal with ten oak leaf clusters. Fellow Brit. Phys. Soc.; mem. Am. Phys. Soc., Am. Soc. Physics Tchrs., A.A.A.S. Assn. Grads. U.S. Mil. Acad., Sigma Xi (asso.), Sigma Pi Sigma. Lutheran. Home: 4610 Mansfield Manor Dr Washington DC 20022 Office: FEDSIM 5240 Port Royal Rd Springfield VA 22151

BERGEAUX, PHILIP JAMES, educator; b. Eunice, La., May 1, 1918; s. Velmont Laurence and Lydia (Guillory) B.; B.S., Southwestern La. U., 1940; postgrad. N.C. State U., 1946-47; M.S., U. Ga., 1960, postgrad., 1970—; m. Gertrude Arlene Scholl, Jan. 15, 1943; children—Philip James, Lois Arlene. Sales agronomist Tenn. Corp., Atlanta, 1947-56; extension agronomist U. Ga., Athens, 1956—. Cons. to Lowe & Stephens, Atlanta, 1966-70. Served to lt. comdr. USNR, 1944-46. Decorated Bronze Star. Mem. Am. Soc. Agronomy, County Agts. Assn., Ga. Plant Food Ednl. Soc. (hon. life; ednl. adviser), Phi Kappa Phi. Lutheran. Home: 125 Sharon Circle Athens GA 30601

BERGEN, JOSEPH BODELL, Lawyer; b. Savannah, Ga., Mar. 12, 1925; s. Cletus William and Hildegarde (Blake) B.; student Mich. State Coll., 1943, Ga. Inst. Tech., 1945-48; J.D., U. Ga., 1950; m. Shirley Shearouse, Feb. 2, 1952; children—Elizabeth Blitch, Virginia Blake, Frederick Shearouse. Admitted to Ga. bar, 1951, D.C. bar, 1960; asst. U.S. atty. So. Dist. Ga., 1953-57, U.S. commr., 1959-63; practiced in Savannah, 1951—. Served to lt. col., judge adv. USAF, 1943-45, 51-52. Mem. Savannah Area C. of C., Civitan Club, Am. Legion, Mil. Order World Wars, S.A.R., Holland Soc. (N.Y.C.), Hibernian Soc., Am., Fed. (pres. Savannah chpt. 1967-68), Ga., Savannah bar assns., Am. Judicature Soc., Judge Advs. Assn., Sigma Alpha Epsilon, Delta Theta Phi. Elk. K.C. Clubs: University of Ga., Savannah Yacht and Country, Savannah Golf, Forest City Gun. Home: 3 E 49th St Savannah GA 31405 Office: 125 Habersham St Savannah GA 31401

BERGER, BRUCE, land investment co. exec.; b. Omaha, June 10, 1939; s. Alvin Sanford and Marjorie (Frieden) B.; B.S., U. Pa., 1961; J.D., Harvard, 1964; m. Jean Karen Levendula, Sept. 9, 1961;1 dau., Lauren Beth. Admitted to Ohio bar, 1964, D.C. bar, 1968; atty.-adviser to judge Tax Ct. U.S., Washington, 1964-66; atty. Office Tax Legislative Counsel, U.S. Treasury Dept., Washington, 1966-68; sec.-treas., chmn. bd. Network Mgmt. Corp., Washington Investment Network, Inc., 1968-73; pres., treas. U.S. Land Resources, Inc., Washington, 1971—. C.P.A., Md. Mem. Am. Bar Assn. Democrat. Jewish religion. Home: 1721 Chesterford Way McLean VA 22101 Office: 1700 K St NW Washington DC 20006

BERGER, NORMAN JACK, dentist; b. Mobile, Ala., Jan. 19, 1929; s. Nathan and Leah (Mattes) B.; B.S., Spring Hill Coll., 1950; M.S., U. Ala., 1952; D.D.S., Loyola U., New Orleans, 1957; m. Ruth Miriam Rosen, Aug. 10, 1952; children—Karen, Harry David. Tchr., Vigor High Sch., Prichard, Ala., 1952-53; gen. practice dentistry, Mobile, Ala., 1959—. Second v.p. Mobile Mental Health Assn., 1971. Mem. Mobile County Sch. Bd., 1970—, v.p. bd. sch. commrs. Bd. dirs. Fonde Sch. P.T.A., 1959-63, pres., 1961-62; bd. dirs. Mobile area Pub. Higher Edn. Found., Inc., Mobile County Found. Pub. Higher Edn. Served with USPHS, 1957-59. Mem. Am., Ala. dental assns., Am. Soc. Dentistry for Children, Mobile C. of C., U. Ala. Alumni Assn. (dir.), Ala. Sch. Bd. Assn. Blue Key, Omicron Kappa Upsilon, Xi Psi Phi, Zeta Beta Tau. Clubs: Mobile Touchdown, Civitan (dir. 1960-65). Home: 4454 Airport Blvd Mobile AL 36608 Office: 266 S McGregor Av Mobile AL 36608

BERGER, RICHARD STEIL, synthetic fiber co. exec.; b. Bklyn., Apr. 28, 1929; s. Elmer Steil and Elsie (Feinberg) B.; B.S. in Chemistry, Stanford, 1950; M.S., U. Wis., 1954, Ph.D. in Organic Chemistry, 1954; m. Freeda Schatzberg, Aug. 15, 1954; children—Eugene, Steven. Chemist, Shell Devel. Co., Emeryville, Cal., 1956-65; mgr. fiber chemistry br. Phillips Petroleum Co., Bartlesville, Okla., 1965-70; dir. research projects Phillips Fibers Corp., Greenville, S.C., 1970-73, dir. long range planning, 1973—. Chmn., Salute to Edn. in Greenville County, 1973. Served with AUS, 1954-56. Mem. Sigma Xi, Alpha Chi Sigma (pres. Alpha chpt. 1952), Tau Beta Pi, Phi Lambda Upsilon. Elk. Contbr. articles to sci. jours. Patentee in field. Home: 26 Stillwood Dr Greenville SC 29607 Office: PO Box 66 Greenville SC 29602

BERGER, WILLIAM ERNEST, newspaper pub.; b. Ferris, Ill., June 6, 1918; s. William George and Ethel (Nelson) B.; student Carthage Coll., 1935-38; m. Jerry June Barnes, Feb. 26, 1943; children—William Edward, Barbara, John Jeffrey. Newspaper editor and pub., Hondo, Tex., 1946-65; commr. Tex. Water Rights Commn., Austin, 1965-69; pres. Asso. Tex. Newspapers, Inc., 1957—; v.p. Tex. Offset Printing Service, Inc., Seguin, 1966—; owner radio sta. KRME Hondo 1969—; co-founder Tex. Star, 1970—. Treas., Medina Meml. Hosp., Hondo, 1962-64. Del., Tex. Democratic Conv., 1962, 64, 66, 68, Nat. Dem. Conv., 1968. Served with AUS, 1942-46. Mem. Tex. (pres. 1963), South Tex. (pres. 1954) press assns., Sigma Delta Chi (chpt. treas. 1967-69). Methodist. Lion (Hondo past pres.). Clubs: Headliners Westwood Country (Austin). Home: 1801 Exposition Blvd Austin TX 78703 Office: 1801 Exposition Blvd Austin TX 78703

BERGERON, CLAUDE ERNEST, JR., accountant; b. New Orleans, July 16, 1941; s. Claude Ernest and Mary Lee (Richard) B.; B.S., Nicholls State U., 1963; M.S., La. State U., 1965; m. Kathleen Ann Noel, Jan. 29, 1966; children—Michael, Kristen, Mary Grace. With Peat, Marwick, Mitchell & Co., 1965-73, sr. accountant, New Orleans, 1966-69, supr., 1969-70, mgr., Houston, 1970-73; with Clement & Bergeron, Houma, La., 1973—. Mem. Bd. Tax Equalization in Water Dist. 91, 1973—. C.P.A., La., Tex. Mem. Am. Inst. C.P.A.'s, Tex., La. socs. C.P.A.'s. Home: 803 Chene Dr Houma LA 70360 Office: PO Box 403 Houma LA 70360

BERGERON, CLYDE JOSEPH, JR., educator; b. New Orleans, July 2, 1932; s. Clyde J. and Ethel J. (Fernandez) B.; B.S., Loyola U. South, 1955; Ph.D., La. State U., 1959; m. Argelia Marcela Alvarez, Aug. 25, 1956; children—Stephen Paul, Jeffery Mark, Christopher Michael. Research asso. La. State U., Baton Rouge, 1959, asst. prof., New Orleans, 1960-63, asso. prof., 1963-68, prof. physics, 1968—. Cons. electronuclear div. Oak Ridge Nat. Lab., 1961-66. Recipient Distinguished Faculty Service award La. State Alumni Fedns., 1971. Club: Beach (Metairie, La.). Home: 4808 Green Acres Ct Metairie LA 70003 Office: Physics Dept La State U Lakefront New Orleans LA 70122

BERGERON, WILTON LEE, physician; b. Scott, La., Feb. 13, 1933; s. Lee and Ida Ruby (Duhon) B.; B.S., U. Southwestern La., 1956; M.D., La. State U., 1958; m. Juanita Marie Landry, Aug. 3, 1957; children—David, Marcel, Rene, Jeanne. Intern, Confederate Meml. Med. Center, 1959; resident Lafayette Charity Hosp., 1959-60; gen. practice medicine, Scott, La., 1960-68; Mead Johnson fellow in allergy Tulane Med. Center, 1968-69; practice medicine, specializing in allergy and related skin diseases, Lafayette, La., 1969—; cons., dir. allergy clinic Lafayette (La.) Charity Hosp., 1969—. Mem. A.M.A., Am. Cath. Physicians, Am. Coll. Allergists, Am. Acad. Family Practice, So. Med. Assns., La. State Med. Soc., Cursillio in Christianity. Roman Catholic. Lion. Home: PO Box 98 Scott LA 70583 Office: 105 St Joseph St Lafayette LA 70501

BERGIDA, HAL, writer; b. N.Y.C., June 25, 1922; s. William and Dorothy (White) B.; B.A., in Journalism, U. Miami, 1952.; m. Jessica R. Reynolds, 1966. Pub. relations cons. 1st motion picture unit USAAF, Culver Cal., 1942-44; free lance writer, 1944-48; editor Tamiami News, Miami, Fla., 1953-54, mem. staff Miami Beach Daily Sun, 1954-55; exec. sec. Greater Miami Beach Motel Assn., 1955-59; editorial rep. nat. mags., 1960—; daily columnist Miami Review, 1965—; polit. commentator sta. WINZ. Lobbyist foreign aid bill, 1961. Served with USAAF, 1942-44. Mem. Am. Legion, Internat. Platform Assn., D.A.V., Sigma Delta Chi. Clubs: Toastmasters, Tiger Bay (exec. sec.). Home: 3301 NE 5th Av Miami FL 33137 Office: 2975 SW 8th St Miami FL 33135

BERGIN, MARION JOSEPH, geologist; b. Lavoye, Wyo., May 2, 1927; s. Martin Joseph and Pearl Marie (Brighton) B.; B.S., U. Wyo., 1951; m. JoAnne Olds Falkenburg, Dec. 27, 1958; children—Martin H., Kevin W., David J. Geologist, U.S. Geol. Survey, Reston, Va., 1951—. Served with AUS, 1945-47. Mem. Geol. Soc. Am., Geol. Soc. Washington. Home: 100 Yeonas Dr SW Vienna VA 22180 Office: US Geol Survey Nat Center 956 1220 Sunrise Valley Dr Reston VA 22092

BERGSTROM, CLINTON NEIL, govt. ofcl.; b. Detroit, Jan. 23, 1935; s. Victor Gustave and Hazel Lillian (Pierce) B.; B. Applied Sci., U. Houston, 1966; postgrad. George Washington U., 1968-69. With Naval Electronics Systems Command, Washington, 1966—, project engr., 1968—. Served with AUS, 1957-58. Recipient Spl. Achievement award Navelex, 1970. Mem. A.A.A.S., Am. Forestry Assn., I.E.E.E., Marine Tech. Soc., Profl. Assn. Naval Electronic Engrs. and Scientists. Home: Rural Route 3 Box 494 Front Royal VA 22630 Office: Naval Electronic Systems Command Code 51023 Washington DC 20360

BERINATI, VINCENT JAMES, system engr.; b. Bklyn., Nov. 24, 1917; s. Vincent James and Kathryn Veronica (McCann) B.; B.Aero. Engring., N.Y. U., 1939; M. Aero. Engring., Cath. U., 1951, D.Engring., 1957; m. Ruth Margaret Fitzpatrick, Apr. 25, 1942; children—Judith (Mrs. Allan Baillie), Donald. Asso. gen. mgr. tech. div. Aerospace Corp., San Bernadino, Cal., 1961-69; research staff mem. Inst. Defense Analyses, Arlington, Va., 1969—. Fellow Am. Inst. Aeros. and Astronautics. Roman Catholic. Home: 2000 S Eads St Apt 1232 Arlington VA 22202 Office: 400 Army-Navy Dr Arlington VA 22202

BERING, CONRAD, realtor; b. Houston, Dec. 20, 1895; s. August C. and Josephine (Pauska) B.; student U. Tex., 1914-17; m. Lorene Rogers, July 8, 1920 (dec. Nov. 1965); children—Conrad, Donald Rogers, Barbara (Mrs. Garrett S. Dundas). Owner, operator Conrad Bering Co., Houston, 1922—; pres. Longwoods Corp., Houston, 1952-72, chmn. bd., 1972—; sec.-treas. Bering Realty Corp., Houston, 1952—, Rogers Investment, Inc., Austin, Tex. Life mem. bd. Methodist Hosp., Houston; founder mem. Naval War Coll. Found., Inc., U.S. Naval War Coll., Newport, R.I. Mem. Houston Bd. Realtors, Tex. Real Estate Assn., Navy League U.S. (hon. life pres. Houston council), Nat. Assn. Real Estate Bds., Houston C. of C. (mil. affairs com.). Methodist (mem. bd.). Clubs: Houston, Kiwanis (Houston). Home: 306 Fall River Ct Houston TX 77024 also Box 108 Route 5 Long Island Dr Lake Hamilton Hot Springs AR Office: Conrad Bering Co Suite 121 2221 S Voss Rd Houston TX 77027

BERKE, LEONARD MOSES, govt. ofcl.; b. N.Y.C., Nov. 21, 1917; s. Gershon and Helen (Rogoff) B.; A.B., Bklyn. Coll., 1940; M.A., George Washington U., 1948; m. Ruth Kobre, Aug. 18, 1946; children—Allison, Jennifer, Richard L. Econ. adviser anti-trust div. U.S. Dept. Justice, Washington, 1948—. Served with USAAF, 1943-46; col. USAF Res. Mem. Am. Econ. Assn., Soc. Govt. Economists, Air Force Assn., Res. Officers Assn. Home: 6524 Elgin Lane Bethesda MD 20034 Office: US Dept Justice Washington DC 20530

BERKELEY, FRANCIS LEWIS, JR., archivist, univ. adminstr.; b. Albemarle County, Va., Apr. 9, 1911; s. Francis Lewis and Ethel (Crissey) B.; B.S., U. Va., 1934, M.A., 1940; m. Helen Wayland Sutherland, June 12, 1937. Tchr. Va. pub. schs., 1934-38; asst. In charge manuscripts U. Va. Library, Charlottesville, 1938-41, curator manuscripts and univ. archivist, 1946-63, asso. librarian, 1957-63, sec. of Rector and Visitors, 1953-58, exec. asst. to pres., 1963—; council Inst. Early Am. History and Culture. Fulbright research fellow U. Edinburgh, 1952; Guggenheim fellow U. London, Eng., 1961-62; sec. of navy adv. com. on naval history, 1958—. Vice pres. Thomas Jefferson Meml. Found.; mem. adv. com. Papers of Thomas Jefferson; mem. Va. Com. on Colonial Records, 1955—. Served with USNR, 1942-46. Fellow Soc. Am. Archivists; mem. Am. Artiquarian Soc., Mass., Va., (v.p. 1970—), and other hist. socs., Colonial Soc. Mass., Walpole Soc., Raven Soc., Phi Beta Kappa, Omicron Delta Kappa. Democrat. Episcopalian. Clubs: Colonnade (Charlottesville); Century (N.Y.). Editor and compiler: Dunmore's Proclamation of Emancipation, 1941; Annual Reports on Historical Collections, University of Virginia Library, 1945— with cumulative indexes, 1945, 50); Jefferson Papers of the University of Virginia, 1950; Papers of John Randolph of Roanoke, 1950; John Rolfe's True Relation. 1951; Introduction to Thomas Jefferson's Farm Book, 1953. Editorial bd. Va. Quarterly Review, 1961—. Contbr.: Dictionary of Biography, Ency. Brit., Collier's Nat. Am. Cyclopedia; and other reference works. Home: 1927 Thomson Rd Charlottesville VA 22903

BERKMAN, DAVE, educator, govt. ofcl.; b. Bklyn., May 6, 1934; s. Henry and Edna (Berkowitz) B.; B.A., cum laude, L.I. U., 1955; M.S., Syracuse U., 1956; Ed.D., N.Y. U., 1963; m. Jo Castellucci, June 29, 1963; children—Linda, Elena, Neil. Producer, dir. WHIZ-TV, Zanesville O., 1956-57, ednl. TV sta. WTVS, Detroit, 1957-59, instr. radio-TV, N.Y. Inst. Tech., 1960-61; tchr. N.Y.C. High Sch., 1961-63; pub. relations and edn. dir. Dist. 65, AFL-CIO, N.Y.C., 1963-64; asst. prof. speech Nassau (N.Y.) Community Coll., 1964-65; communications media coordinator Kingsborough Community Coll. City U. N.Y., 1966-67; sr. media systems specialist, edn. div. Xerox Corp., 1967-68; edn. systems cons. Xerox Edn. Group Hdqrs., Stamford, Conn., 1968-70; v.p. Ergonomics, Inc., 1970; asso. prof. mass communication Am. U., 1970-71, adj. prof. mass communication, 1972—; TV specialist U.S. Office Edn., 1971—. Mem. Am. Civil Liberties Union; bd. mem. Fairfield County Civil Liberties Union; state bd. Conn. Civil Liberties Union, 1969-70. Mem. Nat. Assn. Ednl. Broadcasters, Nat. Acad. TV Arts and Scis., Am. Assn. U. Profs., Am. Fedn. Tchrs., Am. Fedn. Govt. Employees, Authors League of Am., N.Y. State Ednl. Radio-TV Assn. Club: Roosevelt Reform Democratic Party of Bklyn. (past pres.). Cons. editor: Ednl. Television mag., 1968-70. Contbr. articles in field to profl. jours. Home: 2019 Golf Course Dr Reston VA 22091 Office: Nat Center Ednl Tech US Office Edn Washington DC 20202

BERKSON, JAMES HAROLD, research and computer software corp. exec.; b. Kansas City, Mo., Nov. 5, 1920; s. Harry and Mary (Applebaum) B.; B.M.E., U. Kan., 1942; J.D., Pacific Coast U., 1955; postgrad. U. Cal. at Los Angeles, 1958. Admitted to Cal. bar, 1965, D.C. bar, 1973, U.S. Supreme Ct. bar, 1973; with U.S. Govt., 1946-56; adminstrv. contracting officer Hughes Aircraft Co., 1955-56; contract and fiscal adminstr., SDD, The Rand Corp., Santa Monica, Cal., 1956-57; treas. System Devel. Corp., Santa Monica, 1957-64; mgmt. cons., practice of law, Los Angeles, 1964—, Washington, 1971—; head corporate projects Aerospace Corp., El Segundo, Cal., 1965-66; sr. v.p. dir., CACI, Inc., 1966—; dir. Asso. Computing Services, Inc., Canoga Park, Cal., 1969—; dir. Advanced Software Resources, Inc., Arlington, Va., 1971—. Served with U.S. Army, 1942-46. Mem. Nat. Contract Mgmt. Assn. (dir. 1962—, nat. treas. 1963-65, nat. v.p. 1965-66), Am., Cal., D.C. bar assns., Am. Judicature Soc., U. Cal. at Los Angeles Exec. Assn. Home: Watergate South Apts 700 New Hampshire Av NW Washington DC 20037 Office: 1815 N Fort Myer Dr Arlington VA 22209 also 12011 San Vicente Blvd Los Angeles CA 90049

BERLE, ANTON ALOIS, editor; b. Switzerland, Dec. 26, 1919; s. John Emille and Mary (Steckenbiller) B.; B.A., U. Conn., 1945; M.A., N.Y. U., 1948; postgrad. Johns Hopkins, 1948-50; m. Beatrice Conrath, Feb. 17, 1945; children—Margaret (Mrs. Stefan Dasho),

Isobel (Mrs. Joseph Wiggs), Jenifer, David. Asso. prof. U. Balt., 1947-50; writer, editor Civic Edn. Service, Washington, 1950-69, editor Civic Leader mag., 1965-69; editor Civic Leader mag. Scholastic Mags., Inc., N.Y.C., 1969—; prof. govt. and econs. Benjamin Franklin U., Washington, 1951—. Ednl. cons.-writer Changing Times Edn. Service, Washington, 1970-72, mem. editorial bd., 1970-72. Recipient Vigilant Patriot award All-Am. Conf. to Combat Communisn, 1963; Eleanor Fishburn award Ednl. Press Assn. 1969. Mem. Nat. Council for Social Studies, Ednl. Press Assn., Am. Hist. Assn., Am. Polit. Sci. Assn. Contbr. to Am. Observer. Address: 4201 Duncan Dr Annandale VA 22003

BERLIN, JERRY DEAN, cell biologist, educator; b. Trenton, Mo., Aug. 28, 1934; s. Ben F. and Clara E. (Gabrielson) B.; B.S., Mo. U., 1960, M.A., 1961; Ph.D., Ia. State U., 1964; m. Ellen J. Fairchild, Aug. 17, 1958; children—Brenda, Paula, Dana. Sr. research scientist Battelle N.W., Richland, Wash., 1964-68; asso. prof. biology Tex. Tech U., Lubbock, 1968-73, prof. biology, 1973—. Served with USAF, 1954-58. Mem. A.A.A.S., Am. Soc. Cell Biology, Bot. Soc. for Am., Electron Microscope Soc. Am., Tex. Soc. for Electron Microscopy (sec. 1973—). Home: 7922 Joliet Lubbock TX 79423

BERLY, ROBERT HERMAN, JR., elec. engr.; b. Elloree, S.C., Oct. 20, 1924; s. Robert Herman and Cecile Claudius (Adams) B.; B.S., Clemson U., 1948; m. Opal Newkirk Buie, Aug. 20, 1947; children—Barbara, Kathryn. Dist. engr. Carolina Power & Light Co., Marion, S.C., 1948-51, dist. engr., Sumter, S.C., 1951-65, sr. engr. div. office, Wilmington, N.C., 1965-67, sr. engr. planning and gen. engring. sect., Raleigh, N.C., 1967-68, distbn. planning engr., Raleigh, 1968-72, prin. engr. distbn. planning, Raleigh, 1972—. Mem. adv. bd. Salvation Army, Sumter, 1963-66. Served with USAAF, 1942-45; now lt. col. USAF Res. ret. Named Sumter Man of Yr., Civitan Club, 1962. Registered profl. engr., N.C., S.C. Mem. Raleigh Engrs. Club. Presbyn. (deacon 1966-67, elder 1971-74). Club: Civitan (pres. Sumter club 1960-61, zone lt. gov. 1960-61, dir. membership S.C. club 1961-62, dir. Wilmington, N.C. club 1966-67) (Raleigh, N.C.). Home: 4104 Southall Rd Raleigh NC 27604 Office: Box 1551 Raleigh NC 27602

BERMAN, DONALD ABEL, physician; b. Wildwood, N.J., Oct. 23, 1932; s. Louis and Isabel (Dresnick) B.; B.S. cum laude, U. Miami, 1953; M.D., Tulane U., 1957; m. Frona Lee Sherman, Aug. 15, 1954; children—Lynn Daryl, Marla Sharon, Jill Mallorie. Intern, Walter Reed Army Med. Center, 1957-58; practice medicine, specializing in family practice, Hollywood, Fla., 1961—; mem. staff Hollywood Meml. Hosp., chmn. dept. family practice, 1973—; med. dir. Med. Exam. Centers, Inc., 1971—, Nat. Acupuncture Centers, Inc., 1973—; clin. instr. U. Fla. Sch. Medicine, 1971—. Served with AUS, 1957-61. Diplomate Am. Bd. Family Practice. Mem. A.M.A., Am., Fla. acads. gen. practice, So., Fla. med. assns., Broward County Med. Assn., Hollywood Hills Homeowners Assn., Phi Delta Epsilon, Alpha Epsilon Pi. Mason (32 deg.). Club: Graduate. Author: Masada, 1973. Home: 2941 Fairway Dr Hollywood FL 33021 Office: 3301 Johnson St Hollywood FL 33021

BERMAN, DONALD CHARLES, indsl. engr.lb. N.Y.C., May 18, 1931; s.; Sol and Sue (Orzach) B.; student Carnegie Inst. Tech., 1949-53; B.S., N.Y.U., 1958; m. Harriet Hope Waldbaum, Sept. 13, 1958; children—David Shawn, Daniel Ross. Project engr. Artisan Electronics, Morristown, N.J., 1953-54; indsl. engr. Emerson Radio, Jersey City, 1954; mgr. engring. quality control Polarad Electronics, L.I., N.Y., 1956-59; head reliability assurance dept. Olympic div. Siegler Corp., L.I., 1959; reliability project engr. Astrionics div. Fairchild Stratas Corp., L.I., 1959-61; supr. components and standards Aeronutronics div. Philco Corp., Newport Beach, Cal., 1961-63; chief components and standards Northrop Space Labs, Hawthorne, Cal., 1963-64; head vendor reliability control TRW Systems, Redondo Beach, Cal., 1964-66, engring. sect. head, reliability and systems assurance, 1966-68; dir. product assurance TRACOR, Inc., Austin, Tex., 1968—. Chmn. Austin regional group Sierra Club; program chmn., mem. exec. com. Tex. Environmental Coalition; mem. Austin Town Lake Beautification Com.; mem. com. Chmn. Citizens Evironmental Bd., City of Austin. Bd. govs. Environmental Action for Tex. Served with AUS, 1954-56. Mem. Am. Soc. Quality Control. Contbr. articles in field to profl. jours. Home: 7608 Rustling Rd Austin TX 78731 Office: 6500 Tracor Lane Austin TX 78721

BERMAN, HAROLD BERNARD, lawyer; b. Sweetwater, Tex., June 4, 1926; s. Hyman I. and Alice Rachel (Shapiro) B.; B.A., U. Tex., 1947; spl. study in Japanese, U. Chgo., 1944-45; LL.B., Harvard, 1950; m. Shirley Cotlar, June 1, 1969; children—Alvin Katz, Toni Hilary Berman, Brenda Katz, Bruce Katz. Admitted to Tex. bar, 1950; practiced in Dallas, 1950—; mem. firms Corenbleth, Thuss & Jaffe, 1950-51, Berman, Fitchner & Mitchell, 1967—; individual practice, 1951-67. Lectr. Southwestern Med. Sch., Nat. Interfraternity Conf. Dir. various corps. Pres. Julius Schepps Jewish Community Center, Dallas, 1972-74. Served with AUS, 1944-46. Mem. Am., Tex., Dallas bar assns., Am. Trial Lawyers Assn., Dallas Assn. Trial Lawyers, Harvard Law Sch. Assn. Tex. (pres. 1964-65), King's Bench Harvard Law Sch., Alpha Epsilon Pi (nat. pres. 1968-69). Mason (Shriner); mem. B'nai B'rith (state pres. 1962). Club: Columbian Country (v.p. 1973) (Dallas). Home: 5330 Tanbark Dallas TX 75229 Office: 2650 LTV Tower Dallas TX 75201

BERMAN, HOWARD BENJAMIN, dentist; b. N.Y.C., Jan. 8, 1939; s. Hyman and Evelyne Pearl (Bernstein) B.; student Emory U., 1956-57, U. Miami, 1957-58; D.D.S., U. Md., 1962; M.S., Georgetown U., 1967; m. Drazia Schacter, June 11, 1961; children—Marcie, Robin, Steven Barry. Intern Jackson Meml. Hosp., Miami, Fla., 1962-63, chief resident oral surgery, 1963-64; pvt. practice oral surgery, Hollywood, Fla., 1967—; mem. Dade County Dental Research Clinic, Miami, Fla., 1967-71; lectr. Miami-Dade Jr. Coll. Sch. Dental Hygiene, 1971-72; sr. attending oral surgeon Meml. Hosp., Hollywood, Fla., 1967—, chief dept. oral and maxillofacial surgery, 1973-74; mem. staff Doctors' Hosp., Golden Isles Hosp., Community Hosp. South Broward; pres. Ambulatory Surg. Facility Hollywood, 1973—. Chmn. bd. Profl. Mgmt. Cons., 1972—. Served to capt. AUS, 1964-66. Mem. Fla. (del. 1971-72), East Coast Dist. (exec. bd. 1971-72), Greater Hollywood (pres. 1971-72) dental socs., Am., Fla. socs. oral surgeons, Am. Soc. Dental Anesthesiology, Young Leadership Group Jewish Welfare Fedn. (adviser 1971-72). Jewish religion (bd. dirs. temple 1971-72). Home: 3500 N 33d Terrace Hollywood FL 33021 Office: 4410 Sheridan St Hollywood FL 33021

BERMAN, MILTON S., mcht.; b. Rochester, N.Y., Sept. 29, 1907; s. Julius and Annie (Schooler) B.; ed. U. Rochester, 1929, Harvard, 1931; m. Ruth Kasdan, Jan. 17, 1936; children—William, Susan, David. With Jordan Marsh Co., Boston, 1931-45, successively trainee, buyer, divisional mdse. mgr.; with Abraham & Straus, Bklyn., 1945-64, successively divisional mdse. mgr., merchandising v.p., v.p., gen. mdse. mgr.; pres. Foley's Houston, (became div. Federated Dept. Stores, Inc., 1945), chmn. bd., 1967—, also v.p., dir. parent co. Bd. dirs. Assn. Community TV (Channel 8), Houston Housing Devel. Corp., Houston Symphony Soc., Tex. Bill of Rights Found., Asso. Credit Services, Inc.; trustee Bus. Resource Devel. Center; founding dir. Soc. Performing Arts; patron Mus. Fine Arts Houston, Houston Contemporary Arts Mus., Alley theatre. Mem. Am. Civil Liberties Union. Clubs: Houston, Houston Racquet (dir.), Houston Yacht, Harvard of Houston. Home: 1400 Hermann Apt # 16G Houston TX 77007 Office: 1110 Main St Houston TX 77001

BERMAN, SIDNEY ARTHUR, social worker; b. Chgo., June 18, 1924; s. Joseph A. and Nettie (Roth) B.; B.S., DePaul U., 1949; M.A., U. Fla., 1951; M.S., U. Tenn., 1958; student Tulane U., 1955-56; m. Carol Siegel, July 20, 1956; children—Steven, Adrian, Welfare visitor Fla. Dept. Pub. Welfare, Jacksonville, 1952-55, unit supr., Ft. Pierce, 1956-57; psychiat. social worker Nashville Mental Health Center, 1958-61; chief social worker Bristol (Va.) Mental Health Clinic, 1961-64; dir. profl. service Peninsula Family Service & Travel Aid, Newport News, Va., 1964-70; exec. dir. No. Va. Family Service, Falls Church, 1970—. Instr. U. Va. Extension, 1968-69. Pres., Bristol Mental Health Assn., 1963, Va. Council on Social Welfare, 1966-67, Peninsula Council on Human Relations, 1967, Reston Community Assn., 1971, Reston chpt. Va. Mus. Fine Arts, 1972-73. First v.p. Nat. Conf. Christians and Jews, 1968-69. Served to 2d lt. USAAF, 1944-45. Mem. Nat. Assn. Social Workers, Am. Orthopsychiat. Assn. Democrat. Home: 1721 Wainwright Dr Reston VA 22070 Office: 803 W Broad St Falls Church VA 22046

BERNAL Y GARCIA PIMENTEL, IGNACIO, archaeologist; b. Paris, Feb. 13, 1910; s. Rafael Bernal and Rafaela Garcia Pimentel; M.A. in Anthropology, Escuela Nacional de Antropologia, 1946; Ph.D. in Archaeology, U. Nacional Autonoma de Mexico, 1949; L.H.D. (hon.), U. Am., 1967; L.H.D., U. Cal. at Berkeley, 1969; LL.D., St. Mary's U., 1970; m. Sofia Verea Corcuera, Oct. 14, 1944; children—Ignacio, Rafaela, Carlos, Concepcion. Prof. U. Nacional Autonoma de Mexico, 1948—; dir. anthropology Mexico City Coll., 1948-59; cultural attache Mexican embassy, Paris, 1955-56, also permanent del. Mexico to UNESCO; mem. Internat. Commn. Monuments, UNESCO, 1956—; dir. Teotihuacan Project, 1962-64, Nat. Museum Anthropology, 1962-68; pres. Soc. Am. Archaeology, 1969-70; dir. gen. Inst. Nacional de Antropologia e Historia, 1968-70; dir. Nat. Museum Anthropology, 1970—. Decorated officer Royal Order Orange-Nassau (Netherlands); officer Legion of Honor (France); comdr. Order of Merit (Italy); officer Order of Crown (Belgium); comdr. Order of Merit (Germany); officer Royal Order Danebrog (Denmark); recipient Nat. Sci. award Mexico, 1969, Theodore Brent award, New Orleans, 1970, Lotos Club medal, 1970, Drexel medal, Phila., 1971. Fellow Am. Anthrop. Assn., Am. Acad. Arts and Scis.; regular mem. Mexican Acad. History; mem. Colegio Nacional (Mexico), Brit. Acad., Soc. Am. Archaeology, Acad. Nacional de Ciencias, Soc. des Americanistes de Paris, Soc. Mexicana de Antropologia, Acad. Nacional de la Investigacion Cientifica. Author: (with Alfonso Caso) Urnas de Oaxaca, 1952; Bibliografia de Arqueologia y Etnografia, Mesoamerica y Norte de Mexico, 1514-1960, 1962; La Ceramica de Monte Alban, 1967; El Museo Nacional de Antropologia, 1967; El Mundo Olmeca, 1968; Ancient Mexico in Colour, 1968; The Olmec World, 1969. Home: 65 Tres Picos Mexico 5 DF Mexico Office: Nat Museum Anthropology Mexico 5 DF Mexico

BERNARD, CHARLES TAYLOR, dry cleaning co. exec., farmer; b. Helena, Ark., Sept. 10, 1927; s. Charles L. and Sallie (Eakin) B.; B.A., Baylor U., 1950; LL.B. (hon.), Shorter Coll., Little Rock, 1969; m. Betty Ann Hill, Nov. 26, 1953; children—Sallie Hill, Mary Troy, Charles Taylor, David Wesley, John Harbert. Self employed in field agr., cotton ginning and elevator operation, 1950—; owner, operator Bernard Manor One Hour Dry Cleaning Chain, Erle, Ark., 1957—; dir. Earle State Bank; rancher, builder, land developer. Del. to Nat. Cotton Council, 1971—. Mem. Ark. Bank Commn., 1969—, chmn., 1971; mem. adv. com. to Small Bus. Adminstrn., 1973; mem. S.W. regional adv. com. Nat. Park Service. Vice pres., mem. exec. bd. Eastern Ark. Area council Boy Scouts Am., mem. exec. com., chmn. finance com. Region 5, also mem. Nat. Council; mem. exec. com. Ark. region Nat. Conf. Christians and Jews, also dir.; Ark. fund raising chmn. Nat. Cystic Fibrosis Research Found., 1970. Mem. Earle City Council, 1956-62; chmn. Crittenden County Republican Party, 1966-67, treas., 1967-68; finance chmn., vice chmn., 1969-70, chmn., 1970-72; Rep. candidate U.S. Senate, 1968; mem. Rep. Nat. Com.; chmn. Ark. delegation to Rep. Nat. Conv., 1972; mem. Ark. Electoral Coll., 1972. Bd. dirs. Ark. Chpt. Nat. Cystic Fibrosis Research Found., Memphis Area chpt. A.R.C.; past sec. bd. trustees So. Bapt. Coll., now hon. trustee; mem. exec. bd. Bapt. State Conv. Ark.; trustee Shorter Coll. Served with USNR, 1944-45. Recipient Silver Beaver and Silver Antelope awards Boy Scouts Am. Mem. Ark.-Mo. Ginners Assn. (past pres.), So. Cotton Ginners Assn. (past pres.), Delta Sigma Pi. Baptist (deacon, chmn. deacon bd., mem. exec. conv. Ark.). Mason (32 deg., Shriner), Rotarian. Home: Bernard Farms Earle AR 72331 Office: 1000 Main St Earle AR 72331

BERNARD, HAROLD GRADY, state ofcl.; b. Jamestown, Ky., Apr. 3, 1938; s. Byron H. and Creola (Foley) B.; B.S., Eastern Ky. State Coll., 1962; div.; children—Lisa Jean, Andrew Coleman. Auditor, Ky. Dept. Revenue, Bowling Green, 1962-66, audit supr., 1966-68; dir. div. rates and services, rate specialist Ky. Dept. Motor Transp., Frankfort, 1968-73, dir. div. motor carriers, 1973—. Served with AUS 1955-58. Mem. V.F.W. Episcopalian. Home: Route 7 Frankfort KY 40601 Office: New State Office Bldg Frankfort KY 40601

BERNARD, LOUIS JOSEPH, surgeon, educator; b. LaPlace, La., Aug. 19, 1925; s. Edward and Jeanne (Vinet) B.; B.A., Dillard U., 1946; M.D., Meharry Med. Coll., 1950; m. Gladys Mae Williams, June 3, 1948; children—Marie (Mrs. Leroy T. Jenkins), Phyllis Elaine. Intern, Hubbard Hosp., Nashville, 1950-51, resident, 1954-56, 57-58; resident Meml. Center, N.Y.C., 1956-57; practice medicine specializing in surgery, Oklahoma City, Okla., 1959-69, Nashville, 1969—; mem. staffs Hubbard, Riverside hosps. (both Nashville); clin. asso. prof. surgery U. Okla., Oklahoma City, 1959-69; asso. prof., vice chmn. surgery dept. Meharry Med. Coll., Nashville, 1969-73, prof., chmn. surgery dept., 1973—, asso. dean Sch. Medicine, 1974—. Served to 1st lt. USMCR, 1951-53. Nat. Cancer Inst. research fellow, 1953-54; Am. Cancer Soc. clin. fellow, 1958-59. Fellow Am. Coll. Surgeons; mem. Southeastern Surgical Congress, Nashville Acad. Medicine, Tenn., Nat. med. assns., Alpha Omega Alpha, Alpha Phi Alpha, Sigma Pi Phi. Home: 4000 Anderson Rd Nashville TN 37217 Office: 105 18th Av N Nashville TN 37208

BERNARD, ROY JAMES, data processing specialist, educator; b. Effie, La., Aug. 25, 1925; B.A., La. Coll., 1950; postgrad. La. State U., 1951-53; M.S., Northwestern State U., 1961; postgrad. U. Southwestern La., 1959, 65, Okla. State U., 1965, Southeastern La. U., 1972; m. Doris Lea Gilliam, Oct. 10, 1944; children—Gary James, Debra Elaine, Karen Sue, Kristie Lynn. Tchr. math. Lafargue (La.) High Sch., 1951, 57-61, Bolton High Sch., Alexandria, La., 1961-63; asst. prof. math. La. Coll., Pineville, 1961-66; asso. prof. math. and computer sci., dir. Computing Center, Southeastern La. U., Hammond, 1966—, cons. data processing, 1968—. Chmn. adminstrv. network com., mem. personnel needs com. La. Dept. Edn. Pres., Lakewood Recreation Corp., 1973. Served with AUS, 1943-46. Mem. Nat. Council Tchrs. Math., Alpha Chi, Pi Mu Epsilon, others. Baptist (Sunday sch. supt. 1967-71, pastor's adv. council 1967-71, chmn. finance, budget planning and promotion 1967—, deacon 1968—, chmn. concerned citizens for moral decency). Kiwanian (dir. Hammond 1966-73, treas. 1967, pres. 1969-71, div. lt. gov.-elect 1973). Home: 606 Jodi Dr Hammond LA 70401

BERNAT, HARRY, govt. ofcl.; b. St. Paul, May 16, 1924; s. Maier and Bertha (Weiss) B.; student Reed Coll., 1944, Harvard, 1945; B. Elec. Engring. with distinction, U. Minn., 1949, B.B.A. with distinction, 1949, M.A. in Pub. Adminstrn., 1951; postgrad. polit. sci. Johns Hopkins, 1951-53, Naval Postgrad. Sch., 1973; m. Frances Lorraine Simon, Sept. 2, 1951; children—Renae Ellyn, Corey Mitchell, Donna Jeanne. Tech. plans, program officer hdqrs. Air Research and Devel. Command, U.S. Air Force, Balt., 1951-58, mgmt. systems engr. Air Force Systems Command, Andrews AFB, Md., 1958-63; research and devel. program mgr. Def. Communications Agy., Dept. Def., Washington, 1963-73, asst. to chief scientist for research and devel., 1973—. Vice pres., account exec., ins. agt. Manna Financial Planning Corp., Falls Church, Va., 1962—, also dir.; dir. Manna Equities Corp., Falls Ch.; instr. adult edn. program Prince George's County, Md., 1970—. Mem. Greater S.E. Community Hosp. Found., Inc., Washington, 1960—; treas. Troop 705, Nat. Capital council Boy Scouts Am., 1966-68. Bd. dirs. River Ridge Recreation Council, Oxon Hill, Md., (pres. 1971). Served with AUS, 1943-46. Congl. fellow Am. Polit. Sci. Assn., 1968-69. Mem. Am. Polit. Sci. Assn., Eta Kappa Nu, Tau Beta Pi, Beta Gamma Sigma, Sigma Alpha Sigma. Toastmaster (distinguished award 1972). Home: 7202 Cloverdale Dr Oxon Hill MD 20021 Office: Asst to Chief Scientist for Research and Devel (Code 101R) Def Communications Agy Dept Def Washington DC 20305

BERNER, ARNOLD ALFRED, farm orgn. exec.; b. Kress, Tex., Nov. 27, 1921; s. Alfred William and Minnie Marie (Buhrkuhl) B.; B.S., U. Ark., 1949; m. Lois Katherine Scheele, July 5, 1944; children—Steve, Dennis, Charlene (Mrs. Stanley Eldon Reed). Asst. county agt., Sebastian County, Ark., 1949-50; county agt., Pope County, Ark., 1951-52; dist. dir. field services Ark. Farm Bur. Fedn., Little Rock, 1953-60, dir. pub. relations, 1960-68, asst. v.p., 1968-71, exec. v.p., 1971—; dir. Union Nat. Bank, Little Rock, Ark. Blue Cross and Blue Shield, Inc., Miss. Chem. Corp., Yazoo City, So. Farm Bur. Casualty Ins. Co., Jackson, Miss., So. Farm Bur. Life Ins. Co., Jackson, Asso. Industries of Ark., Inc., Little Rock. Pres. Ark. County Agts. Found.; mem. Ark. Future Farmers Am. Found.; bd. dirs. Ark. Careers. Served with USNR, 1943-46. Decorated Bronze Star medal with 5 oak leaf clusters. Mem. Gamma Sigma Delta. Lutheran (pres. 1971-72). Rotarian. Home: 4 Leawood Circle Little Rock AR 72205 Office: 7th at High St Little Rock AR 72203

BERNER, ARTHUR SAMUEL, oil co. exec.; b. N.Y.C., Nov. 12, 1943; s. Hyman and Sylvia (Shlakman) B.; B.A., Coll. City N.Y., 1964; J.D. cum laude, N.Y. U., 1967; m. Roberta Anne Sinnreich, June 20, 1964; children—Jocelyn Meryl, Evan David. Admitted to N.Y. bar, 1967, U.S. Supreme Ct. bar, 1973; asso. mem. firm Cahill, Gordon Sonnett, Reindel & Ohl, N.Y.C., 1967-70; v.p., gen. counsel, sec. Inexco Oil Co., Houston, 1970—. Pomeroy scholar, 1965-67. Mem. Am., Fed. bar assns., Bar City N.Y., Order Coif, Phi Delta Phi. Jewish religion (trustee congregation). Research editor N.Y. U. Law Rev., 1966-67. Home: 2215 Parana Dr Houston TX 77055 Office: Houston Club Bldg Houston TX 77002

BERNSTEIN, IRWIN SAMUEL, educator, primatologist; b. Bklyn., July 11, 1933; s. Nathan and Ida (Garber) B.; B.A., Cornell U., 1954; M.A., U. Chgo., 1955, Ph.D., 1959; m. Susan Duvall, July 16, 1972; children—Celeste, Brad, Tao, Evan. Primatologist Yerkes Labs. Primate Biology (now Yerkes Regional Primate Research Center Emory U., 1960—; prof. dept. psychology U. Ga., Athens, part-time 1968-71, full time 1971—. Served to lt. USAF, 1955-57. Grantee NSF, Nat. Inst. Mental Health, U.S. Army Surgeon Gen.'s Office, Wenner Cren Found. Mem. Animal Behavior Soc. (exec. com. 1970-74), Internat. Soc. Study Aggression, Internat. Primatol. Soc., A.A.A.S., Am. Psychol. Assn., Sigma Xi. Contbr. articles to books and sci. jours. Home: 4245 Old Lexington Rd Athens GA 30601

BERNSTEIN, JOSEPH, lawyer; b. New Orleans, Feb. 12, 1930; s. Eugene Julian and Lola (Schlemoff) B.; B.S., U. Ala., 1952; LL.B., Tulane U., 1957; m. Phyllis Maxine Askanase, Sept. 4, 1955; children—Jill, Barbara, Elizabeth R., Jonathan Joseph. Clk. to Justice E. Howard McCaleb of La. Supreme Court, 1957; admitted to La. bar, 1957; asso. firm Jones, Walker, Waechter, Poitevent, Carrere & Denegre, 1957-60, partner, 1960-65; gen. practice New Orleans, 1965—. Pres. CATV Systems of Jefferson, Inc.; pres. Turci's Inc. Past pres., New Orleans Jewish Community Center. Served to 2d lt. AUS, 1952-54. Mem. Am., La., New Orleans bar assns., Phi Delta Phi, Zeta Beta Tau. Democrat. Jewish religion. Home: 5705 St Charles Av New Orleans LA 70115 Office: 310 Security Homestead Bldg Veterans Blvd Metairie LA 70002

BERRY, BOB D., assn. exec.; b. Duncan, Okla., July 9, 1937; s. Robert I. and Annie H. (Dean) B.; ed. Southeastern State Coll.; m. Patricia Griffith; children—Paula, Robert, Margaret, Chris. Exec. dir. Atoka County (Okla.) Indsl. Devel. Assn., 1959-60; mgr. Wewoka (Okla.) C. of C., 1960-62; asst. mgr. Duncan C. of C., 1962-64; asst. exec. dir. Tenn. Med. Assn., 1964-66; mgr. Wharton C. of C., 1966-69; exec. dir. Okla. Dental Assn., Oklahoma City, 1969—; exec. sec. Okla. Dental Found. Research and Edn.; organizer, incorporator, dir., sec.-treas. Okla. Dental Service Corp. Mem. Okla. Regional Med. Program, now dir. Organizer Okla. Dental Polit. Action com. Served with Armed Forces, 1961. Mem. Okla. Soc. Assn. Execs., Okla. Heart Assn., Oklahoma City, Okla., U.S. chambers commerce, Blue Key, Tau Kappa Epsilon. Methodist. Lion. Home: 1209 N Utah St Oklahoma City OK 73107 Office: 629 Northwest Expressway Oklahoma City OK 73118

BERRY, BURT, lawyer; b. Killeen, Tex., Sept. 17, 1926; s. William Henry and Jessie (Williams) B.; B.B.A., So. Meth. U., 1953, LL.B., 1958; m. Barbara Keenan, Dec. 24, 1954. Admitted to Tex. bar, 1958; since practiced in Dallas; mem. firm Berry, Fisher & Brown. Mem. Am., Tex. (dir. 1972—), Dallas (pres. 1971) trial lawyers assns., Am., Dallas bar assns., State Bar Tex. Home: 2913 Fondren St Dallas TX 75205 Office: 601 Mercantile Securities Bldg Dallas TX 75201

BERRY, CHARLES EDWARD, trust co. exec., state legislator; b. Columbus, Ga., July 16, 1908; s. Turner E. and Annie Belle (Lynch) B.; B.A., U. of South, 1929; m. Martha L. Bartlett, Apr. 28, 1933 (dec. Nov. 1967); children—Charles Edward, William, Mary; m. 2d, Mildred H. Holleman, Oct. 13, 1968; stepchildren—Ralph M., Mildred (Mrs. J. M. Dean). Basement mdse. mgr. J.A. Kirven Co., Columbus, 1931-41, asst. mgr., 1941-44; partner and office mgr. Columbus Fixture Mfg. Co., 1944-68, was v.p. and sec., now ret.; v.p. Trust Co. Columbus, 1969—; mem. Ga. Ho. of Reps., 1966—. Dir. Gulf States Mortgage Co. Past mem. City-County Bd., Columbus Water Bd. Trustee Ga. Hosp. Service Assn. Mem. City-County Planning Bd., Columbus Water Bd., 1955, mem. city council, 1954-60, mayor, 1955; mem. Ga. Democratic Exec. Com., 1966-70; mem. exec. bd. emeritus City of Columbus; lt. col. Gov.'s Staff; mem. gov.'s staff Ga. and Ala. Dir. United Cerebral Palsy Muscogge County; bd. mgmt. Armed Services YMCA, chmn., 1955; past bd. dirs. Chattahoochee Valley Fair Assn.; vice chmn. Ga. Commn. Devel. Chattahoochee River Basin, 1967-71. Mem. Ga. Sheriff's Assn. (hon.), Ga. State

Patrol (hon.), Nat. Soc. State Legislators, Third Congl. Legislative Assn., 40 and 8, Am. Legion (comdr. 3d dist. 1950; life mem.; Ga. legislative chmn.), Assn. U.S. Army, Am. Ch. Union, Am. Numis. Assns., Columbus C. of C. (past dir.), Asso. Industries of Ga., Ga. Municipal Assn. (hon. life), Delta Tau Delta. Episcopalian (vestryman 1952-55, jr. warden 1954-55). Mason, Moose, Elk, Lion (past dir., Key mem.). Club: The '49 Er. Home: 2516 Harding Dr Columbus GA 31906 Office: Trust Co of Columbus PO Box 57 Columbus GA 31902

BERRY, DALE, machinery co. exec.; b. Mesquite, Tex., Sept. 3, 1928; s. Roscoe Shelby and Ida Myrl (Ellis) B.; student Draugons Bus. Coll., 1948; m. Dorothy Louise Lewis, Jan. 25, 1946; children—Susan Dee, Robin Dale, Mark Wayne. Country Western radio star, touring U.S. with Grand Ol' Opry, 1945-48; performed as singer, guitarist, actor in motion pictures, including Hidden Valley Days, 1946; Free White and 21, 1960; TV appearances include Route 66 series, 1966; exec. v.p. Transcontinental Artists Corp., 1962-71, Berry Bros. Machinery, Inc., Mesquite, Tex. 1971—. Home: 2655 Lanecrest St Dallas TX 75228 Office: 2615 Big Town Blvd Mesquite TX 75223

BERRY, FRANK LAFAYETTE, bank exec.; b. Columbia, Miss., Jan. 11, 1899; s. James Russell and Mollie Elmira (Riley) B.; student U. Miss., 1916-17; grad. pharmacist Atlanta Coll. Pharmacy, 1919-21; m. Pearl Chesnut, July 22, 1961; 1 stepdau., Cheryl Miller Guynn. Owner Berry's Drug Stores, Gaffney, S.C., 1922-27; salesman E.R. Squibb & Sons, N.Y.C., 1928-58; owner Real Estate Investments, 1958—; organizer, dir. Citizens and So. Bank Chamblee (Ga.), 1968—; dir. Chamblee (Ga.) Nat. Bank. Tchr. chemistry Atlanta Sch. Pharmacy, 1920-21. Served with AEF, 1917-19. Mem. Ga. Pharm. Assn. (pres. traveling men's aux. 1948-49), DeKalb C. of C., DeKalb Hist. Soc., Chamblee-Doraville Bus. Men's Assn., English Speaking Union U.S. Democrat. Methodist (chmn. bd. trustees 1969-70). Mason, Rotarian. Club: Dunwoody (Atlanta). Home: 1734 Dunridge Ct Atlanta GA 30338 Office: PO Box 80424 Atlanta GA 30341

BERRY, GENE ALLEN, petroleum co. exec.; b. Stillwater, Okla., Aug. 20, 1923; s. Raymond Bryan and Daisy Leon (Lane) B.; student Clemson U.; B.S., Okla. State U., 1947; m. Joan O'Mealey, Apr. 15, 1945; children—Raymond, J. Steven. Asst. engr., asst. city mgr. City Bartlesville, Okla., 1947-51; with Phillips Petroleum Co., Bartlesville, 1951—, sr. design engr., 1959-61, staff engr., 1961-67, 71-72, adminstrv. asst., 1967-71, mgr. operations and maintenance, 1973—. Served with AUS, 1942-46. Registered profl. engr., Okla. Republican. Methodist. Mason (Shriner). Home: 1112 Brookside Pkwy Bartlesville OK 74003 Office: Adams Bldg Bartlesville OK 74004

BERRY, JAMES D., banker; b. Sapulpa, Okla., June 23, 1921; s. James D. and Gertrue (Morrow) B.; B.S., U. Okla., 1943; grad. Rutgers U. Grad. Sch. Banking, 1959; grad. Advanced Mgmt. Program, Harvard, 1963; m. Mary Evelyn Irby, Oct. 16, 1946; children—Beverly, James D., Robert Neil. With Am. Nat. Bank, Sapulpa, 1932-50, asst. v.p., 1948-50; with Republic Nat. Bank, Dallas, 1950—, sr. v.p., 1961-63, exec. v.p., now vice chmn. bd.; partner I-B Cattle Co. Bd. dirs. Dallas County chpt. A.R.C., Dallas Crime Commn., Dallas Better Bus. Bur., Dallas Heart Assn., Dallas Summer Musicals, Dallas Theatre Center, Goodwill Industries Dallas. Served to capt. AUS, 1943-46. Mem. Inter-frat. Council, Scabbard and Blade, Beta Theta Pi, Mason (32, Shriner). Clubs: Dallas (dir.), Chaparral (Dallas); Coterie; Northwood. Home: 3901 Lovers Lane Dallas TX 75225 Office: PO Box 5961 Dallas TX 75222

BERRY, JAMES RUSSELL, civil engr.; b. Franklin, Ark., Nov. 10, 1933; s. David Ewell and Zelphia (Ellis) B.; B.S. in C.E., U. Ark., 1960; m. Leila Privet Moore, Sept. 2, 1956; children—James Russell, Brenda Carol. Engr. in tng. Ark. Hwy. Commn., 1960; engr. McNutt-Schneller, Inc., Little Rock, 1960-62; engr. Garver & Garver, Inc., Little Rock, 1962—, sr. asso. engr., 1973—. Served with USNR, 1951-52. Registered profl. engr., Ark. Mem. Am. Soc. C.E., Am., Ark. socs. profl. engrs. Optimist (past pres.). Home: 3509 Dunkeld Dr North Little Rock AR 72116 Office: 11th and Battery Sts Little Rock AR 72202

BERRY, LEWIS EDWARD, editor; b. Crystal Springs, Ark., Sept. 11, 1914; s. Charles Lucien and Minerva (Lewis) B.; student Southeastern U., 1935-37; m. Gertrude Louise Allen, May 23, 1942; children—Zora Margaret (Mrs. Richard R. Wilcoxen), Lewis Edward, Susan Elizabeth (Mrs. William J. Matthews), Patricia Ann (Mrs. William Harmon Simmons, Jr.). Hwy. patrolman Tex. Dept. Pub. Safety, 1941-42, pub. information officer, 1949-52, 1952-57; detective Met. Police Dept., Washington, 1942-48; officer regional police coordinator Fed. Civil Def. Adminstrn., 1952; editor Tex. Lawman, 1956—; exec. sec. Sheriffs' Assn. of Tex., 1957-72. Served with USMC, 1934-37; asso. editor Leatherneck Mag.; col. Tex. State Guard, 1950—. Recipient Tex. Medal of Merit, 1965. Mem. Sigma Delta Chi. Mason, K.P. Home: 5501 Caprice Dr Austin TX 78731 Office: 5520 N Lamar Blvd Austin TX 78751

BERRY, LOIS THARRINGTON, libarian; b. Charlotte County, Va., July 19, 1914; d. Floyd Brooks and Irene Bertha (Hudson) Tharrington; profl. certificate State Tchrs. Coll., Farmville, Va., 1931-33; B.S. with high honors, Longwood Coll., Farmville, 1951; M.S. in L.S., U. N.C. at Chapel Hill, 1966; m. Paul Douglas Berry, June 1, 1938 (dec. 1958); children—Paul Douglas, Earl Tharrington. Elementary sch. tchr., Charlotte County, Va., 1935-36, 47-50, Mecklenburg County, Va., 1950-51; elementary sch. prin., Charlotte County, 1936-38; elementary and high sch. librarian, Mecklenburg County, 1951-66, Chesterfield County, Va., 1966-67; asst. prof. library sci. East Carolina U., Greenville, 1967-73; librarian, Chesterfield County, Va., 1973—. Mem. Am., Southeastern, N.C. library assns., Am., N.C. assns. sch. librarians, Am. Assn. U. Profs., Am. Assn. Library Schs., Chesterfield County, Va. edn. assns., Longwood Coll. Alumnae Assn., Ruffner Lit. Soc., Alpha Beta Alpha, Kappa Delta Pi. Baptist. Home: 7260 Beach Rd Chesterfield VA 23832

BERRY, LOREN MURPHY, business exec.; b. Wabash, Ind., July 24, 1888; s. Charles D. and Elizabeth (Murphy) B.; student Northwestern U., 1909-10; LL.D., Rio Grande (Ohio) Coll.; m. Lucile Kneipple, June 9, 1909 (dec.); children—Loren Murphy, Martha Sue Fraim, John William, Elizabeth Anne Gray; m. 2d, Helen Anderson Henry, Aug. 28, 1938; 1 son, Leland. Newspaper reporter, Wabash, Ind., Joliet, Ill., Chgo.; sold telephone directory advt., Marion, Ind., 1910, St. Louis, Louisville, Indpls., which developed into nat. sales orgn. of L. M. Berry & Co., main office, Dayton, O., now vice chmn. bd.; dir. emeritus United Telecommunications, Inc., Kansas City, Mo., 3d Nat. Bank & Trust, Dayton; dir. Mut. Broadcasting Corp., N.Y.C., Super Food Services, Inc., Dayton, Fla. Telephone Corp., Ocala, Laughter Corp., Dayton, Hulman Realty Co., Dayton, Edison Nat. Bank, Ft. Myers, Fla. Mem. Republican Nat. Finance Com., Washington. Bd. dirs. Jr. Achievement, Dayton; trustee Rio Grande Coll. Mem. U.S. Ind. Telephone Pioneers (pres. 1938-39), Bell Telephone Pioneers Assn. (v.p. N.C. Kingsbury chpt. 1939-40). Republican. Episcopalian. Mason (32 deg., Shriner). Clubs: Dayton City, Engineers, Kiwanis, Dayton Country, Moraine Country, Bicycle (Dayton); Surf (gov.), Committee of 100, Indian Creek (Miami Beach, Fla.); Bohemian (San Francisco); Capitol Hill (Washington). Home: 1155 Ridgeway Rd Dayton OH 45419 also Surf Club Apts 9133 Collins Av Miami Beach FL 33154 Office: 3170 Kettering Blvd PO Box 6000 Dayton OH 45401 also 3818 Bay Vista Av Tampa FL 33611

BERRY, ROBERT DOUGLAS, constrn. co. exec.; b. Columbus, Ga., Nov. 24, 1925; s. George Oliver and Lottie Lanier (Echols) B.; B.S., Auburn U., 1949; m. Mary Eleanor Kent, Mar. 2, 1951; children—Barbara L., Robert Douglas, David K. With Wright Contracting Co., Columbus, 1949—, asst. treas., 1954-71, treas., dir., 1971-73, sec.-treas., dir., 1973—; dir. Wright Assos., Inc., 1966-72. Served with USAAF, 1944-45. Decorated Air medal with 7 oak leaf clusters. Mem. Phi Delta Theta. Episcopalian. Kiwanian. Clubs: Country, Columbus Auburn Alumni (pres. 1973). Home: 2579 Fremont Av Columbus GA 31906 Office: PO Box 1580 Columbus GA 31902

BERRY, ROY ALFRED, JR., educator; b. New Hebron, Miss., Dec. 11, 1933; s. Roy Alfred and Fannie Belle (Newsome) B.; B.S., Miss. Coll., 1956; Ph.D., U. N.C., 1962; m. Marian Jean Hord, June 6, 1957; children—Roy Alfred III, Jefferson Hord. Grad. asst. dept. chemistry U. N.C., 1956-59, R.J. Reynolds Tobacco Research fellow, 1959-60, Petroleum Research Fund fellow, 1960-61; postdoctoral research fellow dept. chemistry U. Fla., 1961-62; asst. prof. dept. chemistry Millsaps Coll., Jackson, Miss., 1962-65, acting chmn. dept. chemistry, 1966-67, asso. prof., 1965-68, prof., 1969—, chmn. dept., 1971—; vis. prof. dept. pharmacology U. Miss. Med. Center, 1968-69. Recipient Barnhill Chemistry award Miss. Coll., 1956; Research award Miss. Acad. Scis., 1963. Mem. Am. Chem. Soc. (treas. Miss. sect. 1965-71), Am. Meteorol. Soc., Am. Assn. U. Profs. (pres. Millsaps chpt. 1971-72), Sigma Xi. Club: Northside Civitan (pres. 1969-70) (Jackson). Home: 644 Elmwood Circle Jackson MS 39206

BERRY, WILLIAM AYLOR, asso. justice Okla. Supreme Ct.; b. Ripley, Okla., Dec. 28, 1915; s. Thomas Nelson and Harriett Virginia (Patton) B.; B.A., Okla. State U., 1939; LL.B., Okla. U., 1940; m. Carolyn Burwell, Jan. 2, 1947; children—Elizabeth Patton, Nichols Burwell. Admitted to Okla. bar, 1940; county atty. Payne County, 1940-41; asst. U.S. dist. atty. for Western Dist., Oklahoma City, 1947-50; Oklahoma County judge, Oklahoma City, 1953-59; asso. justice of Supreme Ct. of Oklahoma, 1959—, vice chief justice, 1967-70, chief justice, 1971-72. Nat. comdr. Am. Ex-Prisoners of War, Inc., 1953, nat. judge advocate, 1955—; chmn. com. on cooperation between state and fed. judges, 1960. Bd. dirs. Oklahoma County chpt. A.R.C., 1956-60; bd. dirs. Salvation Army. Served from ensign to lt. comdr. USNR, 1941-46. Decorated Purple Heart. Mem. Am. Bar Assn. (chmn. com. coop. between state and fed. judges), Okla. C. of C. (dir.), Sigma Nu, Phi Delta Phi. Home: 1706 Wilshire Blvd Oklahoma City OK 73116 Office: State Capitol-Supreme Ct Oklahoma City OK 73105

BERRYHILL, HENRY LEE, JR., govt. geologist; b. Charlotte, N. C., Nov. 6, 1921; s. Henry Lee and Viola Estelle (Johnston) B.; B.S., U. N.C., 1947, M.S. in Geology, 1949; m. Louise Randall Russell, Sept. 13, 1947; children—Stuart Randall, Keith Courtney. With U.S. Geol. Survey, 1948—, chief publs. officer, Denver, 1963-65, research marine geologist, 1965-66, chief marine geology Gulf of Mexico-Caribbean region office, Corpus Christi, Tex., 1967-70, chief Office Marine Geology, Washington, 1970-73, sr. research marine geologist, Corpus Christi, 1973—. Tech. adviser offshore prospecting com. ECAFE, 1972-73; Dept. Interior rep. Fed. Intragy. Com. on Marine Sci. and Engring., 1970-73. Served with USAAF, 1942-45. Decorated D.F.C., Air medal with 3 oak leaf clusters Recipient Outstanding Performance award U.S. Geol. Survey, 1969. Fellow Geol. Soc. Am.; mem. Am. Assn. Petroleum Geologists, Soc. Econ. Paleontologists and Mineralogists, A.A.A.S., Sigma Xi. Author: Geology and Coal Resources of Belmont County, Ohio, 1963; Geology of the Ciales Area, Puerto Rico, 1965; Coal-Bearing Upper Pennsylvanian and Lower Permian Rocks, Washington Area, Pennsylvania, 1971; The Worldwide Search for Petroleum Offshore-A Status Report for the Quarter Century 1947-72, 1974. Contbr. articles to sci. publs. Home: 231 Rosebud St Corpus Christi TX 78404 Office: US Geol Survey Office Marine Geology PO Box 6732 Corpus Christi TX 78411

BERRYMAN, JACK HOLMES, govt. ofcl.; b. Salt Lake City, July 28, 1921; s. Richard G. and Theo (Anderson) B.; A.A. with honors, Westminster Coll., 1940; B.S., U. Utah, 1941, M.S. with honors, 1947; m. Juanita Nussbaum, Aug. 9, 1941; children—Marjorie Sharon, Richard Gordon. Research and devel. staff Utah Dept. Fish and Game, 1947-50; asst. regional supr. U.S. Fish and Wildlife Service, Albuquerque, 1950-53, Mpls., 1953-59, chief div. wildlife services Bur. Sport Fisheries and Wildlife, Washington, 1965—; asso. prof. wildlife scis. Utah State U., 1959-65; cons. U.S. Sec. Interior, 1960-64, Shade Rivers Wonderland, O., 1964-65; participant White House Conf. Conservation, 1962, Nat. Acad. Sci. Symposium Pesticides, 1963, Agrl.-Wildlife Relationships, 1965—; chmn. legislative com. Utah Wildlife Fedn., 1963-65. Served with USMC, 1941-45. Decorated Silver Star, Purple Heart; recipient Minn. award outstanding service wildlife, 1960. Mem. Wildlife Soc. (pres. 1964-65), Washington Biologists Field Club, N.Y. Acad. Scis., Sigma Xi, Xi Sigma Pi. Presbyn. (mem. ministerial com.). Contbr. articles to profl. jours. Home: 10503 Linfield St Fairfax VA 22030 Office: Dept Interior Washington DC 20240

BERRYMAN, MACON MOORE, welfare agy. ofci.; b. Lexington, Ky., Feb. 17, 1908; s. James Henry and Elizabeth (Bridges) B.; B.A., Lincoln U., 1930, postgrad., 1931, D.C.L., 1967; grad. Atlanta U. Sch. Social Work, 1933; m. Dortha Alice Hackett, June 19, 1943; 1 son, James Henry. Investigator, Emergency Relief Adminstrn., Burlington County, N.J., 1933-34, dist. adminstr., case supr., 1934-36; social worker, parole officer N.Y. State Tng. Sch. Boys, N.Y.C., 1936-45; exec. dir. Sunnycrest Farm for Boys, Cheyney, Pa., 1945-50; dir. insular div. child welfare Dept. Social Welfare, St. Thomas, V.I., 1950-58, acting commr. social welfare, 1958-59, commr., 1959-74. An organizer, chmn. bd. People's Bank of V.I., 1971—. Cons. V.I. Commn. on Aging, 1959-67, V.I. Commn. on Children and Youth, 1950-67. Chmn. Gov.'s Com. on Employment Handicapped, 1959-67; vice chmn. Gov.'s Commn. Human Resources, 1964-69; mem. local bd. no. 1 SSS, 1964-73; mem. V.I. dist. com. Boy Scouts Am., 1964-66, pres. V.I. council, 1966-69, Nat. council rep., 1964-67, 69—, mem. Region II com., 1968— (all St. Thomas). Bd. dirs. St. Thomas chpt. Hands Across Sea Scholarship Com. (treas. 1955-60), St. Thomas Community Chest (treas. 1955), St. Thomas U.S.O. Recipient Alumni award Lincoln U., 1954. Mem. Am. Pub. Welfare Assn. (welfare policy com. 1959-62, nat. membership com. and chmn. V.I. membership com. 1959-68), Nat. Assn. Social Workers (mem. cabinet div. social policy and action 1967-68), Acad. Certified Social Workers, Lincoln U. Alumni Assn. (pres. V.I. chpt. 1964-67), Alpha Phi Alpha. Anglican. Mason, Rotarian (pres. St. Thomas 1966-67). Home: 26 AC Lindberg Bay St Thomas VI 00801 Office: Peoples Bank St Thomas VI 00801

BERRYMAN, ROBERT LEE, drilling co. exec.; b. nr. Palestine, Tex., Oct. 11, 1899; s. Lee J. and Cora (Hathcock) B.; student Washington and Lee U., 1919-20, Tex. U., 1920-21; m. Juanita McPherson, Sept. 26, 1955; children—John Robert, Hugh Lee, Lee Howard. With Wheless Drilling Co., Shreveport, La., 1925—, sec.-treas., 1941—, dir., 1941—. Trustee, treas. Southfield Sch., Shreveport, 1936-46. Served with U.S. Army, 1918-19. Clubs: Shreveport, Shreveport Country. Home: 532 Monrovia St Shreveport LA 71106 Office: 920 Commercial Nat Bank Bldg Shreveport LA 71166

BERSCH, ROBERT SHERRILL, lawyer; b. Lynchburg, Va., Aug. 29, 1935; s. Benjamin Ernest and Mary Elizabeth (Dalton) B.; B.S., U. Va., 1957, LL.B., 1960; LL.M., Coll. William and Mary, 1961; m. Helen Kytha Padgett, June 18, 1960. Admitted to Va. bar, 1960, D.C. bar, 1965, U.S. Supreme Ct. bar, 1963; tax atty., office chief counsel IRS, Washington, 1961-65; tax atty. firm Haynes & Miller, Washington, 1965-70; partner firm Eggleston & Glenn, Roanoke, 1970—. Tchr. income taxation Am. Coll. C.L.U.'s, Roanoke; tax aspects of real estate adult div. City Schs. Roanoke, 1971—. Mem. Am., Va., Roanoke, D.C. bar assns., Va. State Bar (gov. tax sect. 1971—), Raven Soc., Beta Gamma Sigma, Phi Eta Sigma, Theta Delta Chi. Baptist (deacon). Clubs: Shenandoah. Lake of the Woods Golf and Country. Home: 1921 Braeburn Dr Salem VA 24153 Office: Shenandoah Bldg PO Box 2887 Roanoke VA 24001

BERT, CHARLES WESLEY, univ. adminstr., educator; b. Chambersburg, Pa., Nov. 11, 1929; s. Charles Wesley and Gladys Adelle (Raff) B.; B.S. in Mech. Engring., Pa. State U., 1951, M.S. in Mech. Engring., 1956; Ph.D., in Engring. Mechanics, Ohio State U., 1961; m. Charlotte Elizabeth Davis, June 29, 1957; children—Charles Wesley IV, David Raff. Jr. design engr. Am. Flexible Coupling Co., State Coll., Pa., 1951-52; aero. design engr. Fairchild Aircraft div. Fairchild Engine and Airplane Corp., Hagerstown, Md., 1954-56; prin. M.E. Battelle Inst., Columbus, O., 1956-61, sr. research engr., 1961-62, program dir., solid and structural Mechanics Research, 1962-63, cons., 1964-65; asso. prof. U. Okla., Norman, 1963-66, prof., 1966—, dir. Sch. Aerospace, Mech. and Nuclear Engring., 1972—; instr. engring. mechanics, Ohio State U., Columbus, 1959-61; cons. mgmt. services div. Lear Siegler, Inc., Oklahoma City, 1973—. Active Norman Council Boy Scouts Am. Bd. dirs. Midwestern Mechanics Conf., 1971—. Served from 2d lt. to 1st lt. USAF, 1952-54. Registered profl. engr., Pa., Okla Asso. fellow Am. Inst. Aeronautics and Astronautics (mem. nat. tech. com. on structures 1969-72, vice chmn. Central Okla. sect. 1965-66, chmn. 1966-67); mem. Am. Acad. Mechanics (founder), Am. Soc. for Engring. Edn., Am. Soc. M.E. (Central Okla. sect. exec. com. 1973—, Region X mech. engring. dept. heads com. 1972—), Aerospace Dept. Chairmen Assn., Assn. Chairmen Depts. Mechanics, N.Y., Okla. acads. scis., Nat., Okla. socs. profl. engrs., Soc. for Experimental Stress Analysis (membership com. Kan. sect. 1973-74, sec. mid-Ohio sect. 1958-59, chmn. 1959-60, adv. bd. mem. 1960-63), Scabbard and Blade, Sigma Xi, Sigma Tau, Pi Tau Sigma, Sigma Gamma Tau, (Distinguished Engr. award), Tau Beta Pi (Distinguished Engr. award). Contbr. chpts. to books, articles and papers to profl. jours. and publs. Home: 2516 Butler Dr Norman OK 73069 Office: Sch Aerospace Mech and Nuclear Engring U Okla 865 Asp Av Norman OK 73069

BERTRAN, CARLOS ENRIQUE, physician; b. Santurce, P.R., July 4, 1926; s. Juan Manuel and Pilar (Margarida) B.; B.A., Cornell U., 1945, M.D., 1948; m. Patrice Minette Neve, Sept. 6, 1952; children—Patrice Minette, Muriel Pilar, Carlos Enrique, Michele, Alexandra, John, Charlotte. Intern, Lincoln Hosp., N.Y.C., 1948-49; resident in medicine Bellevue Hosp., N.Y.C., 1949-52; clin. asst. in medicine N.Y.U. Postgrad. Med. Sch., 1951-52; asst. prof. medicine U. P.R., 1952-56, asst. clin. prof. medicine Sch. Medicine, 1958-66, Sch. Dentistry, 1959—; practice medicine, specializing in internal medicine, cardiology, Santurce, 1958—; asst. clin. prof. medicine U. P.R., 1958—; dir. Cardiac Clinic, Rio Piedras Municipal Hosp., 1958-66; mem. staff Presbyn. Hosp., 1961—, dir. cardiac clinic, 1966—, dir. coronary care unit, 1967—; mem. staff Doctors, Auxilio Mutuo, San Juan City hosps. Mem. P.R. Bd. Med. Examiners, 1961-66. Bd. dirs. P.R. Heart Assn., 1960—, chmn. com. research, postgrad. edn., 1960-62, pres., 1965-66; trustee Presbyn. Hosp., Santurce. Served as maj. M.C., USAF, 1956-58. Diplomate Am. Bd. Internal Medicine. Fellow A.C.P., Am. Coll. Cardiology; mem. A.M.A., Am. Heart Assn., P.R. Med. Assn. (chmn. sci. council; pres. 1963-64). Research in gastrointestinal bleeding, chronic ulcerative colitis, hepatitis, cardiac arrhythmias. Home: 1468 Ashford Av Santurce PR 00907 Office: Ashford Med Center San Juan PR 00907

BERTRAND, JOHN AVERY, supt. schs.; b. Corsicana, Tex., Oct. 27, 1925; s. Joseph Avery and Anaise (Boone) B.; B.A. summa cum laude, U. Southwestern La., 1950; M.S., La. State U., 1952; Ph.D., U. Tex., 1966; m. Ella Mae Simar, June 1, 1946; children—Ronald Joseph, Linda Gail (Mrs. John Steib, Jr.), Darlene Frances, Angela Michelle. Tchr. pub. schs., Acadia Parish, La., 1950-52, Calcasieu Parish, La., 1952-53; prin. Starks (La.) High Sch., 1953-56; prin. College Oaks Elementary Sch., Lake Charles, La., 1956-58, F.K. White Jr. High, Lake Charles, 1958-65; supt. schs. Acadia Parish, Crowley, La., 1965—. Asst. prof. U. Southwestern La., Lafayette, summer, 1954; dir. So. Educators Corp., Baton Rouge. Served with USCGR, 1943-46; ETO; PTO. Mem. Crowley Commerce and Agr. Chamber (dir. 1968—), La. Tchrs. Assn., La. Supts. Assn., Am. Assn. Sch. Adminstrs., N.E.A., Kappa Delta Pi, Pi Gamma Mu, Phi Delta Kappa. Roman Catholic. K.C. Home: 1505 North Av D Crowley LA 70526 Office: PO Box 309 Crowley LA 70526

BERZAK, WILLIAM PETER, govt. ofcl.; b. Czechoslovakia, Mar. 23, 1914; s. Michael F. and Anna (Matlon) B.; came to U.S., 1920; B.S.L., U. Minn., 1938, J.D., 1940; M.P.A., St. Louis U., 1960; m. Maurine McCaskill, Jan. 4, 1947: children—Susan, William, Frank. Admitted to Minn. bar, 1940, also U. S. Supreme Ct. bar; with U. S. Civil Service Commn., 1946—. dep. chmn. Bd. Appeals and Review, Internat. Orgns. Employees Loyalty Bd., 1966, chmn., 1966—. Served to capt. AUS, 1941-46. Mem. Minn., Fed. bar assns., Bar Assn. D.C., Nat. Civil Service League, Internat. Personnel Mgmt. Assn., Am. Legion, Delta Theta Phi. Contbr. articles to law jours. Home: 1416 Carrington Lane Vienna VA 22180 Office: 1900 E St NW Washington DC 20415

BESEMANN, EBERHARD FRANZ, physician; b. Wolfen, Germany, May 2, 1923; s. Franz and Luzie (Schmidt) B.; M.D., U. Frankfort (Germany), 1952; m. Johanna M. Giorgi, Oct. 26, 1955; children—Hans, Klaus. Came to U.S., 1954. Intern, St. Mary's Hosp., East St. Louis, Ill., 1954-55; resident Mo. Pacific Hosp., St. Louis, 1955-57, St. Louis City Hosp., 1957-60; practice medicine, specializing in radiology, Bellevue, Wash., 1960-63, Chattanooga, 1963—; mem. staff Erlanger Hosp., acting chief radiol. services, 1973—. Served with M.C., German Army, 1940-45. Diplomate Am. Bd. Radiology. Mem. East Tenn. Radiol. Soc. (sec.-treas. 1968-70). Lutheran. Translator, editor profl. books from German into English. Contbr. articles to profl. jours. Home: 41 Carriage Hill Signal Mountain TN 37377 Office: Erlanger Hosp Chattanooga TN 37403

BESS, WILLIAM LAFAYETTE, JR., architect; b. El Paso, Tex., Oct. 22, 1927; s. William Lafayette and Rose (Backler) B.; m. Ridla French, June 21, 1948; 1 dau., Lisa Denise. Draftsman C.E., U.S. Army, 1948-49; designer NASA, 1949-51; chief draftsman aviation and meteorology Dept. Army, 1951-53; C.E. Armstrong, architects, Fort Worth, 1953-56; chief designer R.L. Brown, architects, Roanoke, Va., 1956-59; asso. Preston M. Geren, architects and engrs., Fort Worth, 1959-69, project architect, 1969-72; partner Dockstader &

Partners, Architects and Planners, Ft. Worth, 1972-73; asso. Growald and Schutts, architects, Ft. Worth, 1973—. Mem. bldg. code bd. appeals, Fort Worth, 1971-73. Bd. dirs. Fort Worth Community Theatre. Served with USMC, 1946-47. Mem. A.I.A. (treas. Fort Worth chpt. 1968-69, sec. 1972), Nat. Council Archtl. Registration Bds., Tex. Christian U. Alumni Assn., English Speaking Union. Republican. Episcopalian (mem. com. on ch. architecture and applied arts 1971-73). Rotarian. Home: 3574 Dryden Rd Fort Worth TX 76109 Office: Fort Worth Nat Bank Bldg Fort Worth TX 76102

BEST, FRANK MILTON, publisher; b. N.Y.C., Dec. 26, 1930; s. Frank M. and Mary (Leitner) B.; B.A., Cath. U. Am., 1952, M.S., 1957, postgrad., 1957-58; m. Princess Susanne Schachowskoi, Dec. 29, 1971. Staff, Nat. Cath. Welfare Conf. News Service 1951-54; staff Army-Navy Jour./Jour. Armed Forces, 1957-65, asso. editor, 1962-65; pub. U.S. Medicine, Washington, 1965—, U.S. Transport, Washington, 1966-69; pres. Profl. Lithography, Inc., Washington, 1967—. Served with AUS, 1955-56. Mem. Am. Med. Writers Assn., Nat. Press Club, Phi Beta Kappa. Address: 2310 California St NW Washington DC 20008

BEST, HERMAN EUGENE, city ofcl.; b. Maryville, Tenn., May 4, 1930; s. George D. and Sina E. (Fields) B.; B.S., U. Tenn., 1960; m. Betty June Boone, Sept. 4, 1959; children—Elaine Rae, Sarah Kathryn. Farmer, Blount County, Tenn., 1948-53; instrumentman Batson & Himes, engrs., Knoxville, Tenn., 1959; asst. city engr. City of Maryville, 1960-61, city engr., dir. pub. works, 1961—. Served with AUS, 1953-55. Registered profl. engr., Tenn.; registered land surveyor, Tenn. Mem. Am. Soc. C.E., Chi Epsilon. Baptist (deacon 1963—). Mason. Club: Civitan (Maryville-Alcoa). Home: Route 10 Peterson Lane Maryville TN 37801 Office: 400 W Broadway Av Maryville TN 37801

BEST, STEPHEN ERNEST III, banker; b. Austin, Tex., Sept. 10, 1936; s. Ernest and Margaret (Knippa) B.; B.B.A., U. Tex., 1958; m. Kathryn F. Forrest, May 23, 1959; children—Shari, Stephen, Carrington. Vice pres. Steck-Warlick Co., Austin, 1959-73; v.p. advt. and marketing Austin Nat. Bank, 1973—. Treas., Child and Family Services, 1973; United Fund, 1974. Served with USAF Res., 1958-64. Mem. Bank Marketing Assn. Presbyn. Rotarian. Home: 4214 Deepwoods Dr Austin TX 78731 Office: PO Box 908 Austin TX 78781

BEST, WINFIELD JUDSON, writer, pub. relations cons., ednl. agy. exec.; b. Dillon, Mont., Oct., 1919; s. Floyd and Margaret (Pearson) B.; B.S. summa cum laude, Northwestern U., 1943; m. Lois Gustafson, 1948; children—Charles, Mark, Constance. Editorial asso. Pub. Adminstrn. Clearing House, Chgo., 1946-48; dir. pub. relations Am. Municipal Assn., 1948-50; dir. research publs. HHFA, Washington, 1951-52; pub. relations dir. Planned Parenthood Fedn. Am., 1952-63; exec. v.p. Planned Parenthood-World Population, N.Y.C., 1963-69; exec. dir. Businessmen's Ednl. Fund, 1969-72; dir. communications and planning Carolina Population Center U.N.C. at Chapel Hill, 1972—; freelance writer. Served with AUS, 1943-46. Mem. Nat. Assn. Sci. Writers, Am. Pub. Relations Soc., Phi Beta Kappa. Episcopalian. Author: (with Alan F. Guttmacher and Frederick S. Jaffe) The Complete Book of Birth Control, 1962, Planning Your Family, 1964; Birth Control and Love, 1969. Contbr. numerous articles in fields of population, sex conservation, social action in bus. to nat. mags.; contbr. to Ency. Brit. Home: Jones Ferry Rd Route 5 Box 212 Chapel Hill NC 27514 Office: Carolina Poplation Center U NC Chapel Hill NC 27514

BETHEA, BARRON, lawyer, state legislator, elec. hardware mfr.; b. Birmingham, Ala., May 20, 1929; s. Malcolm and Wilma (Edwards) B.; student U. of South, 1948-50; B.S., U. Ala., 1952, LL.B., 1953. Admitted Ala. bar, 1953; practiced in Birmingham, 1953-54; founder Barron Bethea Co., Inc., elec. hardware mfrs., Birmingham, 1957, pres., sec., treas. 1957—. Mem. Ala. Democratic Exec. Com., 1958-62—; mem. Ala. Ho. of Reps., 1962—. Mem. mgmt. bd. Five Points YMCA, 1962—. Served as 1st lt. USAF, 1954-56. Mem. Ala. State Bar, Birmingham Bar Assn., Asso. Industries Ala., Birmingham C. of C., Scabbard and Blade, Phi Gamma Delta, Phi Alpha Delta. Methodist. Elk. Home: PO Box 2202 Birmingham AL 35201 Office: 1625 Carolina Av Bessemer AL 35020

BETHEA, JOHN BUELL, JR., ry. co. pres.; b. Columbia, Miss., Oct. 20, 1924; s. John B. and Mamie (Freeman) B.; student Miss. State U., 1942-43; B.S., U. Tenn., 1950; postgrad. exec. program U. N.C., 1965; m. Joyce Annette Crawford, June 29, 1945; children—John Audis, Janice Lu. Gen. sales mgr. Dixie Hwy. Express, Meridian, Miss., 1950-61; dir. traffic and transp. Springs Mills, Inc., Lancaster, S.C., 1961-70; v.p., Lancaster & Chester Ry. Co., 1962-72, pres., 1973—. Served as pilot AUS, 1943-47; ETO. Decorated Air medal with 4 bronze clusters. Mem. Am. Trucking Assn. (dir. sales council 1955-60), So. Traffic League (pres. 1970-71), Delta Sigma Pi, Delta Nu Alpha, Delta Tau Delta. Baptist (deacon). Rotarian (pres. 1973). Home: 131 Sherwood Circle Lancaster SC 29720 Office: 512 S Main St Lancaster SC 29720

BETHEA, WILLIAM LAMAR, JR., lawyer; b. Dillon, S.C., June 2, 1940; s. William Lamar and Lillie Harding (Hotchkiss) B.; A.B. in English, Newberry Coll., 1962; J.D., U. S.C., 1969; m. Margaret M. McInnis, June 23, 1962; 1 son, William Lamar, III. Admitted to S.C. bar, 1969; partner firm Harvery, Battey Macloskie & Bethea, Beaufort and Hilton Head Island, S.C., 1969—. Bd. dirs. Hilton Head Med. Services, Inc.; bd. regents Beaufort County Meml. Hosp. Served with USMCR, 1962-66. Recipient Claud N. Sapp award faculty and students U. S.C., 1969. Mem. Am., S.C., Beaufort County bar assns., Hilton Head Island C. of C. (dir.), Phi Alpha Delta (Outstanding Scholastic Achievement award 1969), Order Wig and Robe. Episcopalian. Mason, Lion (sec. 1973, dir. 1973—). Editorial bd. S.C. Law Rev., 1968-69. Home: #9 Port Tack Palmetto Dunes Hilton Head Island SC 29928 Office: Peoples Bank Bldg Pope Av Hilton Head Island SC 29928

BETHEL, MILLARD BAIMBRIDGE, physician; b. Elizabethtown, Ky., Apr. 12, 1911; s. William Robert and Rebecca (Jenkins) B.; student Vanderbilt U., 1930-33; M.D., U. Tenn., 1936; M.P.H. U. N.C., 1941; m. Elizabeth Newell Roach, May 10, 1938; children—Brenda Gwynn, Rebecca, Thomas. Dir. Mecklenburg County Health Dept., Charlotte, N.C., 1945-59; prof. pub. health adminstrn., asst. dean Sch. Pub. Health, U. N.C., Chapel Hill, 1959-62; dir. dept. environmental health A.M.A., Chgo., 1962-64; dir. Wake County Health Dept., Raleigh, N.C., 1964—. Fellow Am. Pub. Health Assn., Am. Acad. Preventive Medicine and Pub. Health; mem. A.M.A. Home: 2231 Whitman Rd Raleigh NC 27607 Office: 3010 New Bern Av Raleigh NC 27610

BETHEL, PAUL DUANE, broadcasting exec.; b. Churchill, Ida., July 30, 1919; s. John Harrison and Dora (Evans) B.; B.A., Stanford, 1948, postgrad., 1949, student Columbia, 1945-46; children by previous marriage—J. David, Paulette R.; m. 2d, Diana E. Gonzalez, Nov. 22, 1967; 1 son, Erik Paul. Writer continuity Ameche Enterprises, N.Y.C., 1945-46; with U.S. Fgn. Service, 1949-61, adminstrv. asst. office sec., 1949-50, resident officer U.S. High Commn., Germany, 1950-53; vice consul, Pao, Nagoya, Japan, 1953-56; press officer Am. Embassy, Tokyo, Japan, 1956-57; press attache Am. Embassy, Havana Cuba, 1958-61; v.p. Copri Films, Miami, Fla., 1961-63; fgn. corr. Mutual News, Dominican Republic, 1965; asso. editor The Reporter mag., N.Y.C., 1965-68; pres. Villa Broadcasting Co., Miami, Fla., 1973—; gen. mgr. Radiocentro WRIZ, Miami, 1973—. Pres. Citizens Com. for a Free Cuba, 1964-72; cons. USIA. 1970-72. Republican candidate Fla. 13th Dist. to U.S. Ho. of Reps., 1972. Served with AUS, 1941-45. Nominated for Pulitzer prize, 1970, 72. Clubs: Nat. Press, Overseas Press. Author; Cuba y Los Estados Unidos, 1962; O Trabaljo Em Cuba, 1966; The Losers, 1969. Home: 2379 SW 28th St Miami FL 33133 Office: 420 SW 8th Av Miami FL 33130

BETHEL, SHELBA JEAN, physician; b. Gans, Okla., Sept. 8, 1937; d. Earl Wilson and Pearl Juanita (Brunk) Henry; B.S., Northeastern State Coll., Tahlequah, Okla., 1960; M.D., U. Okla., 1965; m. Lander Bethel, June 2, 1955; children—Lander Louis, Lesa Jean, Steven Henry. Intern, St. Anthony Hosp., Oklahoma City, 1965-66, resident pathology, 1966-67, resident obstetrics and gynecology, 1967-70; practice medicine, specializing in obstetrics and gynecology, Norman, Okla., 1970—; mem. staff Norman Municipal Hosp.; cons. Purcell (Okla.) Hosp., Moorse (Okla.) Municipal Hosp., Westinghouse Hosp., Norman, Cleveland County Health Dept. Jr. fellow Am. Fertility Soc., Am. Coll. Obstetrics and Gynecology; mem. Am. (Achievement award 1970), So., Okla. med. assns., Okla., Cleveland-McClain County med. socs., Oklahoma City Obstetrics and Gynecology Soc., Am. Med. Womens Assn., League Women Voters, Oklahoma U., Okla. U. Med. Sch. med. assns. Address: 500 E Robinson St Norman OK 73069

BETTERSWORTH, JOHN K(NOX), educator; b. Jackson, Miss., Oct. 4, 1909; s. Horace Greely and Annie McConnell (Murphey) B.; B.A. magna cum laude. Millsaps Coll., 1929; Ph.D. (grad. fellow), Duke, 1937; m. Ann L. Stephens, Oct. 28, 1943; 1 dau., Nancy Elizabeth. Tchr., Jackson Central High Sch., 1930-35; vis. prof. Duke, summer 1940; vis. instr. Asheville (N.C.) Normal, summer 1937; instr. history Miss. State U., State College, 1937, asst. prof., 1938-42, asso. prof., 1945-48, prof., 1948—, head dept. history and govt., 1948-61, dir. Social Sci. Research Center, 1950-60, asso. dean liberal arts, Coll. Arts and Sci., 1956-61, acad. v.p., 1961—, dean faculty, 1966—; text editor Miss. Hist. Commn., 1948-68. Chmn. Miss. Research Clearing House, 1953-55; pres. Mississippians for Ednl. Television, 1971-72. Trustee Miss. State Dept. Archives and History, 1955—. Served as lt. (j.g.) USNR, 1942-45; instr. Naval Indoctrination Sch., Tucson. Mem. Miss. Hist. Soc. (dir. 1963—, pres. 1963-64), Orgn. Am. Historians., Am., So. hist. assns., Phi Beta Kappa, Phi Kappa Phi, Phi Alpha Theta, Alpha Tau Omega, Omicron Delta Kappa. Democrat. Episcopalian. Rotarian (pres. Starkville 1951-52). Author: Confederate Mississippi, The People and Policies of a Cotton State in Wartime 1943; People's College: A History of Mississippi State, 1953; Mississippi: A History, 1959; Mississippi in the Confederacy, vol. 1, 1967; co-author South of Appomattox, 1959; Your Old World Past, 1961; Mississippi Yesterday and Today, 1964; co-author This Land of Ours. 1965; New World Heritage, 1969. Contbr. articles prof. publs. Home: 401 Broad St Starkville MS 39759 Office: Drawer B Mississippi State MS 39762

BETTIS, JOHN RANDOLPH, city ofcl.; b. Greenville, S.C., Aug. 20, 1917; s. Zeb Vance and Alice (Reamey) B.; B.S. in M.E., Clemson U., 1940; m. Louise Murray Cauthen, June 17, 1941; children—Anne Louise, John R., Vance Jackson, Susan Cauthen. With Commrs. Pub. Works, Charleston, S.C., 1940—, asst. mgr., engr., 1947-54, chief exec. officer, 1954—. Chmn. adv. bd. Salvation Army, Charleston, 1968-72. Bd. dirs. Water Pollution Control Fedn., 1967-70. Served with AUS, 1942-46; ETO. Mem. Am. Water Works Assn. (chmn. Southeastern sect. 1959; recipient Water Utility Man Year award 1961, Herman F. Wiedeman award 1965), St. Andrews Soc., Mech. Engs. Club Charleston (past chmn.). Methodist (past chmn. bd. trustees). Rotarian. Contbr. profl. jours. Home: 179 3d Av Charleston SC 29403 Office: 14 George St Charleston SC 29402

BETTS, CHARLES O., judge; b. Centenary, S.C., Aug. 17, 1907; s. William A. and Lula Frances (Young) B.; student Schreiner Inst., 1925-27, U. Tex., 1927-32, Cumberland U., 1932-33; m. Eula Lea Kohn, Oct. 6, 1934; children—Charles Adolph, Cheryl Frances. Admitted to Tex. bar, 1933, practiced in Austin, 1934-41; judge County Ct., 1941-46, Dist. Ct., 1946—. Bd. dirs. Tex. Inst. Children and Youth; mem. bd. Travis County Child Welfare Unit; dir. Tex. Inst. Children and Youth, chmn., 1960; mem. adv. council judges Nat. Council Crime and Delinquency; chmn. lay adv. bd. Seton Hosp., Austin; chmn. com. on adjudication and appeals So. Dist. Am. Lutheran Ch., mem. bd. theol. edn. 1968—; mem. Central Tex. Comprehensive Health Planning Commn., 1969—. Bd. dirs. Capital Area Radiation and Research Found. Served with AUS, 1944-45. Mem. Am., Travis County (past pres.) bar assns., State Bar Tex. (chmn. com. on adoption, family law sect.), Am. Judicature Soc., Nat. Council Juvenile Ct. Judges, Tex. Probation and Parole Assn. (exec. com.), Nat. Assn. State Trial Judges, Tex. Juvenile Officers Assn., Tex. Social Welfare Assn., Am. Legion, C. of C., Tex. State Guard Assn., Delta Theta Phi. Lutheran. Mason (32 deg., Shriner), K.P. Home: 5422 Shoalwood Av Austin TX 78756 Office: Travis County Courthouse PO Box 1748 Austin TX 78767

BETTS, DWIGHT BARTON, constrn. co. exec.; b. Raleigh, N.C., Dec. 22, 1919; s. Dwight Fairfax and Dessie (Wellons) B.; B.S. in Civil Engring., N.C. State U., 1940; m. Frances Ray Williams, June 8, 1942; children—Donald Barton, Marianne Fairfax, Richard Wellons, Katherine Ray. With J.A. Jones Constrn. Co., Charlotte, N.C., 1940—, v.p., 1967—; v.p., dir. constrn. firm, Teheran, Iran, 1960-61. Bd. dirs. N.C. State U., 1958-59. Served to lt. col. AUS, 1942-46. Mem. C. of C., Execs. Club, Newcomen Soc., Knights of Carrousel, Mil. Order World Wars, Soc. Am. Mil. Engrs. Democrat. Baptist (deacon). Mason, Lion. Club: Myers Park Country. Home: 4108 Foxcroft Rd Charlotte NC 28211 Office: 521 E Morehead St Charlotte NC 28201

BETZ, DANIEL OLIVER, JR., nematologist, entomologist, plant pathologist; b. Ada, O., Sept. 15, 1916; s. Daniel Oliver and Alice G. (Mohler) B.; student Ohio Northern U., 1934-37, Bowling Green State U., 1937-38; B.Sc., Ohio State U., 1947, M.S., 1947; m. Janet W. Loegler, Oct. 12, 1945; children—Daniel, James, Jane. Agt.-insp. U.S. Dept. Agr.-Agrl. Research Service, Golden Nematode Project, Hicksville, N.Y., 1948-49, control supr., 1949-56, supervisory insp. plant pest control div., 1956-59, asst. chief staff officer pesticides regulation div., Washington, 1959-70; head tech. sect. Environmental Protection Agy., Washington, 1970—. Served with AUS, 1942-45. Decorated Bronze Star, Purple Heart with 2 oak leaf clusters. Recipient certificate of merit U.S. Dept. Agr., 1963. Mem. Soc. Nematologists. Home: 8405 Wagon Wheel Rd Alexandria VA 22309 Office: South Agrl Bldg Washington DC 20250

BEVER, CHRISTOPHER THEODORE, psychiatrist; b. Munich, Germany, Mar. 12, 1919; s. Rudolf Paul and Maria (Bever) Berliner; A.B., Harvard, 1940, M.D., 1943; diploma Wash. Sch. Psychiatry, 1952; postgrad. Wash. Psychoanalytic Inst., 1947-53; m. Josephine Jordan Morton, Mar. 12, 1944; children—Christopher Theodore, Caroline Stackpole, Edward Watts M., Sarah Sayward. Intern, Hartford (Conn.) Hosp., 1944; resident in psychiatry St. Elizabeths Hosp., Washington, 1947-48, psychiatrist, 1948-50; psychiatrist Washington Inst. Mental Hygiene, 1950-51; dir. Montgomery County (Md.) Mental Hygiene Clinic, 1951-54; asso. prof. Med. Sch., U. N.C., Chapel Hill, 1954-56; practice medicine, specializing in psychiatry and psychoanalysis, Washington, 1956—; mem. staff George Washington U. Hosp., 1956—; mem. faculty Wash. Psychoanalytic Inst., 1954—, Washington Sch. Psychiatry, 1956—; mem. faculty Med. Sch., George Washington U., 1957—, asso. clin. prof., 1965—; cons. Walter Reed Hosp., 1972—. Bd. dirs. Community Psychiat. Clinic, 1958—, pres., 1973—; bd. dirs. D.C. Inst. Mental Hygiene, 1966-73, pres., 1966-68, trustee, 1973—. Served to capt. M.C. Aus, 1944-47. Diplomate Am. Bd. Psychiatry. Fellow Am. Psychiat. Assn., Am. Acad. Psychoanalysis, Am. Orthopsychiat. Assn.; mem. Am. Psychoanalytic Assn. Club: University (Washington). Home: 6812 Connecticut Av Chevy Chase MD 20015 Office: 2141 K St NW Washington DC 20037

BEVERIDGE, THEODORE MELVIN, ecologist; b. Oklahoma City, Mar. 9, 1919; s. Charles Granville and Ida Pearl (Field) B.; student U. Okla., 1937-40; diploma Command and Gen. Staff Coll., 1944; B.S., U. Neb., 1961; M.A., U. Tex., Arlington, 1972, 74; postgrad. N. Tex. State U., 1973; m. Eileen Davis, Nov. 30, 1970; 1 dau., Steffani (Mrs. Amin Hakim Davoud). Commd. 2d lt. Mil. Intelligence, U.S. Army, 1940, advanced through grades to lt. col., 1958; mil. asst. to U.S. rep. in conclusion Austrian State Treaty and Treaty of Triest, 1953-56; asst. mil. attache, Vienna, Rome, 1961-62; ret., 1966; pres. Beveridge Constrn. Co., Oklahoma City, 1946-52; pollution control officer State of Tex., 1968-71; cons. profl. ecologist with commerce and industry, Ft. Worth, 1971—. Recipient German Red Cross Silver medal (Bavarian), 1963; German-Am. Friendship award, 1964. Mem. S.A.R., Intercontinent Biog. Assn., Internat. Platform Assn., Ret. Officers Assn., Tex. Pub. Health Assn., Tex. Sanitarians Assn., Asso. Gen. Contractors Am., Scabbard and Blade, Soc. Pen and Sword, Sigma Chi. Mason. Club: Playboy International. Address: 1617 Oakland Blvd Fort Worth TX 76103

BEVERINA, FRANCIS FELICE, project engr.; b. Montpelier, Vt., Jan. 1, 1936; s. Romolo Angelo and Rose (Ricciarelli) B.; B.C.E., U. Vt., 1959; student George Washington U., 1960-66; m. Ruth Marie Kinder, Apr. 15, 1961; children—Vincent Angelo, Anthony Francis, Andrew Kinder. Project engr. U.S. Army Engring. Research and Devel. Lab., Ft. Belvoir, Va., 1959-66; supervisory project engr., research and devel. Naval Ship Systems Command, Washington, 1966—. Chmn. planning and zoning Kings Park Civic Assn., 1971-72; mem. Annandale dist. steering com. Fairfax County Devel. Plan, 1972. Served with USAF, 1961-62. Mem. Am. Soc. C.E. (mem. com. on lightweight alloys 1968-70). Roman Catholic (mem. parish council 1972-73). Contbr. numerous articles to tech. symposiums. Home: 8414 Derby Ct Springfield VA 22151 Office: Naval Ship Systems Comd Washington DC 20362

BEVERLEY, WILLIAM, lawyer; b. San Juan, P.R., May 20, 1930; s. James Rumsey and Mary (Jarmon) B.; grad. Choate Sch., 1948; B.S., William and Mary Coll., 1952; J.D., U. Va., 1956; m. Marcela Blanco, Dec. 19, 1959; children—William, Henry, Robert. Admitted to P.R. bar, 1957; since practiced in San Juan; mem. firm Beverley, Pesquera & Lluberas-Kells, San Juan, 1967—. Pres. bd. trustees San Juan YMCA. Home: B-4 Meadow Lane Urb Garden Hills Guaynabo PR 00916 Office: 150 Tetuan St San Juan PR 00905

BEVILL, TOM, lawyer, congressman; b. Townley, Ala., Mar. 27, 1921; s. Herman and Fannie Lou (Fike) B.; B.S., U. Ala., 1943, LL.B., 1948; m. Lou Betts, June 24, 1943; children—Susan B., Donald H., Patricia Lou. Admitted to Ala. bar, 1949; practiced in Jasper, Ala., 1949-1967; past mem. Ala. Ho. of Reps.; mem. 90th-93d congresses from 4th Ala. Dist. Mem. Am., Ala., Walker County (pres. 1954-55) bar assns., Am. Judicature Soc. Home: 1600 Alabama Av Jasper AL 35501 Office: Longworth House Office Bldg Washington DC 20515

BEYER, ARTHUR FREDERICK, educator; b. Toledo, O., Mar. 13, 1922; s. Arthur F. and Emma M. (Eriksen) B.; B.Sc., Ohio U., 1943, M.Sc., 1945; Ph.D., U. Cin., 1950; m. Ruth Inez Long, Sept. 18, 1943; children—Bradley A., Bryan A. Instr. biology Case Western Res. U., Cleve., 1948-50; prof. biology Midwestern U., Wichita Falls, Tex., 1950—, chmn. dept. biology, 1960—. Chmn. citizen's adv. commn. City of Wichita Falls (Tex.), 1968—; chmn. Wichita County chpt. A.R.C., 1972-73; chmn. Goals for Tex. Study, 1969. Served with AUS, 1942-43. Recipient Americanism award Lion's Club, 1968; Liberty Bell award Bar Assn., 1967; Service to Mankind award Sertoma Club, 1966; Sci. Fair award Midwestern U. Students, 1969; Vol. Leadership award Nat. Found. March of Dimes, 1969-72; Citizen's Aide award State Tex., 1967. Fellow Tex. Acad. Scis.; mem. Bot. Soc. Am., A.A.A.S., Tex. Coll. Tchrs. Assn., Beta Beta Beta. Club: Knife and Fork (pres. 1972-73) (Wichita Falls). Home: 3208 Milby Av Wichita Falls TX 76308 Office: Midwestern U Wichita Falls TX 76308

BEYERS, BERNICE WEST (MRS. ROBERT A. BEYERS), sculptor; b. N.Y.C., Apr. 26, 1906; d. E. Lovette and Bess (Palmer) West; A.A. in Fine Arts and Drama, Bennett Coll., 1925; pupil Alexander Archipenko, Edmond Amateis, Lu Duble, William Zorach, Winold Reiss, 1926-28, 1929, 1921-25, 1930; m. Robert A. Beyers, Mar. 2, 1940 (dec. Feb. 1962); children—Robert West, Arthur L. Exhibited one-woman shows Contemporary Arts Gallery, N.Y.C., 1931, Feragil Galleries, N.Y.C., 1933, Mid-Town Gallery, N.Y.C., 1932, Mint Mus., Charlotte, N.C., 1941, other galleries in South and Southwestern U.S.; group exhbns. include So. Vt. Art Center, Manchester, 1929-71, Mt. Dora (Fla.) Art League, 1935-40, Tex. Ann. and Dallas County Ann., 1946-67, Dallas Mus. Fine Arts, 1946-67, numerous others; represented in permanent collections including monument at Silver Springs, Fla., displays at Mead Bot. Gardens, Winter Park, Fla., Venice-Nokomis, Fla., Wadsworth Athenaeum, Hartford, Conn., Swarthmore Coll., Mint Mus. Mem. women's com. Dallas Theater Center; mem. Dallas Art Mus. League. Bd. dirs. Dallas Symphony Orch. League, Dallas Civic Opera Guild; trustee Dallas Civic Ballet Soc. (Trustee) Dallas Symphony Assn., Dallas Civic Opera, So. Vt. Artists, Inc. Awarded 1st prize sculpture So. States Art League, 1940, Conn. Acad. Fine Arts, 1943; recipient Medal of Honor Nat. Assn. Women Artists, 1932. Mem. Craft Guild Dallas, Print Soc. Dallas, Dallas Hist. Soc., Local History and Geneal. Soc., So. Vt. Artists, (dir.), D.A.R., Soc. Mayflower Descs., Nat. Soc. Magna Carta Dames, Colonial Order of Crown, Soc. Descs. Most Noble Order Knights of Garter, Plantegenet Soc., Sovereign Colonial Soc., Ams. Royal Descent, Nat. Soc. Women Descs. of Ancient and Hon. Arty. Co., Soc. Old Plymouth Colony Descendants, Nat. Soc. Colonial Dames Am., Nat. Soc. New Eng. Women, Order Descs. Colonial Govs., Nat. Soc. Daus. Am. Colonists, Nat. Soc. Daus. Founders and Patriots Am., Order of Washington, Soc. Daus. Colonial Wars. Episcopalian. Clubs: Garden, Woman's Brook Hollow Golf (all Dallas); Pen and Brush, Ekwanok Country (Vt.). Address: 10008 Meadowbrook Dr Dallas TX 75229

BHASKAR, SURINDAR NATH, dentist; b. Rasul, India, Jan. 7, 1923; s. Jagan Nath and Maya D. (Devasar) B.; came to U.S., 1944, naturalized, 1954; D.D.S., Northwestern U., 1946; M.S., U. Ill., 1948, Ph.D., 1951; m. Norma Ziegle, Jan. 7, 1950; children—William

Carlos, Philip Brian, Thomas Adrian. Asso. prof. pathology U. Ill. Dental Sch., 1951-55; chief oral tumors br. Armed Forces Inst. Pathology, Washington, 1955-61; chief dept. oral pathology Walter Reed Army Inst. Research, 1961-62; chief div. oral pathology U.S. Army Inst. Dental Research, Walter Reed Army Med. Center, 1962-70, dir. inst., 1970-73; dir. personnel Army Surgeon Gen., 1973—. Registrar, U.S. Army Registry Clin. Oral Pathology, 1961—; cons. oral pathology to Asst. Surgeon Gen. and Chief Dental Corps, U.S. Army, 1960—; prof. Georgetown U. Med. and Dental Sch., 1964—. Mem. profl. edn. com. Am. Cancer Soc., Washington, 1962—. Diplomate Am. Bd. Oral Pathology, Am. Bd. Oral Medicine. Fellow A.A.A.S., Am. Acad. Oral Pathology (fellowship com.); mem. Am. Dental Assn., Internat. Assn. Dental Research, Internat. Acad. Oral Pathology, Am. Acad. Oral Medicine, Sigma Xi, Delta Sigma Delta. Author books including: Synopsis of Oral Histology, 1962; Roentgenographict Interpretation for the Dentist, 1970; Oral Histology and Embryology, 1972; Synopsis of Oral Pathology, 1973. Contbr. numerous articles to profl. publs. Home: 8201 Kenfield Ct Bethesda MD 20034 Office: Office Surgeon Gen US Army Forrestal Bldg Washington DC 20012

BIANCHI, AL, basketball coach; b. Long Island City, N.Y., Mar. 26, 1932; s. Alfred and Rose (Sciallo) B.; grad. Bowling Green State U., 1954; children—Mark, Al, Shireen, Carol, Leah. Player basketball Syracuse (N.Y.) Nats., 1956-63, Phila. 76ers, 1963-66; asst. coach Chgo. Bulls, 1966-67; coach Seattle Supersonics, 1967-69, Washington Caps, 1969-70, Va. Squires, 1970—. Served with M.C., AUS, 1954-56. Named to Bowling Green State U. Hall of Fame, 1965. Mem. Sigma Alpha Epsilon. Roman Catholic. Office: 300 Boush St Norfolk VA 23510

BIASCO, FRANK, educator, social worker, psychologist; b. Chgo., Jan 15, 1928; s. Joseph and Mary (Pernini) B.; A.B., Wheaton Coll., 1953; M.S.W., Loyola U., 1956; Ed.D., Ind. U., 1965; m. Nancy Ellen Oplinger, Jan. 30, 1953; children—Richard Alan, James Randal, Constance Marie, Thomas Edward, Gary David. Tchr., counselor Park Forest (Ill.) Pub. Schs., 1959-64; asst. prof. dept. counseling and guidance Ind. U., Bloomington, 1964-66; asso. prof. psychology State U. N.Y. at Oswego, 1966-68; asso. prof. Fla. State U., Tallahassee, 1968-70; dir. pupil personnel services Jacksonville (Fla.) Pub. Schs., 1970-71; coordinator counselor edn. U. West Fla., Pensacola, 1971—. Cons. U.S. Office of Edn., State Dept. Edn., Leon County Pub. Schs. Served with USNR, World War II, Korea. Mem. Nat. Assn. Social Workers, N.E.A., Am. Assn. U. Profs., Council Social Work Edn., Am. Psychol. Assn., Am. Personnel and Guidance Assn., Am. Ednl. Research Assn., Am. Rehab. Counseling Assn., Southeastern, Fla. psychol. assns., Am. Orthopsychiat. Assn., Am. Legion, Pi Gamma Mu, Phi Delta Kappa. Home: 9759 Pickwood Dr Pensacola FL 32504

BIBB, THOMAS FARRIS, mfg. co. exec.; b. Murfreesboro, Tenn., July 26, 1943; s. Charles McLean and Ann Larue (Farris) B.; B.S., La. State U. at New Orleans, 1964; m. Barbara Eliasen, Nov. 14, 1964; children—Patrick, Michael, John. Accountant, Ernst & Ernst, New Orleans, 1964-67, San Antonio, 1967-69; controller Conroy, Inc., San Antonio, 1969—. C.P.A., Tex., La. Mem. Am. Inst. C.P.A.'s, Nat. Assn. Accountants. Democrat. Roman Catholic. Home: 3743 Chartwell St San Antonio TX 78230 Office: 1100 Alamo National Bldg San Antonio TX 78205

BIBB, WILLIAM COLWELL, judge; b. Montgomery, Ala., Nov. 13, 1914; s. John Dandridge and Phebe Mosgrove (Colwell) B.; A.B., U. Ala., 1937, LL.B., 1937; m. Mary Jeanette Humphrey, Sept. 18, 1943; 1 son, David Humphrey. Admitted to Ala. bar, 1937; practiced in Anniston, 1937-61; atty. OPA Rent Office, 1944-45; mem. firms Bibb & Bibb, 1945-51, Bibb & Hemphill, 1951-57, Bibb, Hemphill & Casey, 1957-59, Bibb & Casey, 1959-61; circuit judge, Anniston, 1961—. Mem. Ala. State, Calhoun County bar assns., Ala. Assn. Circuit Judges. Episcopalian. Home: 816 Coleman Dr Anniston AL 36201 Office: Courthouse Anniston AL 36201

BICE, RICHARD NOLAN, broadcasting co. exec.; b. Ft. Worth, Feb. 17, 1926; s. Asbury and Hazel Elizabeth (Harwell) B.; student Tex. Christian U., 1950-51; m. Charlene W. Waller, Apr. 6, 1947; children—Charles. Richard Craig. Sr. fleet service clk. Am. Airlines, 1943-50; stage mgr. WBAP-TV, Ft. Worth, 1952-69, producer-dir., prodn. supr., 1969—; owner Scand Design, Ft. Worth, 1973—. Served with USNR, 1943-46. Mason. Home: 4771 Martha Lane Fort Worth TX 76103 Office: 1900 Barnett St Fort Worth TX 76103

BICKERSTAFF, HOPE ELIZABETH (MRS. JOHN MARSHALL BICKERSTAFF), real estate broker; b. Providence, R.I., Feb. 17, 1928; d. Henry and Elizabeth Josephine (Coopy) Taylor; student Pembroke Coll., 1945-46; m. Lawrence Wells Lawton, Feb. 7, 1948 (div. Jan. 1965); children—Linda Jane (Mrs. Linda Jane Glick), Lawrence Wells, Lance Taylor, Louise Ann; m. 2d, John Marshall Bickerstaff, Aug. 14, 1969. Profl. figure skater Ice Follies, 1946-47; tchr. figure skating Ohio State U., Columbus, 1961-62, Coliseum, Jacksonville, Fla., 1968-70; salesperson Frank W. Brown & Asso., Orange Park, Fla., 1965—, real estate broker, 1970—. Mem. Council of 500, Duval County Republican Com., 1973-74. Mem. Nat. Inst. Real Estate Brokers, Nat., Fla. assns. of realtors, Clay-Bradford County Bd. Realtors (pres. 1974—), Fla. Women's State Golf Assn. (dir., sec. 1973—), Jacksonville Womens Golf Assn. (treas. 1973, v.p. 1974). Episcopalian (mem. Atlar Guild). Club: Timuquana Country (Jacksonville). Home: 4703 Queen Lane Jacksonville FL 32210 Office: PO Box 215 Orange Park FL 32073

BICKERTON, REECE ISAAC, govt. ofcl.; b. Monessen, Pa., June 15, 1916; s. George Alben and Hallie Elizabeth (Isaac) B.; student U. Pitts. extension, 1940-41, Pa. State U., 1949-50; m. Margaret E. Koehl, Jan. 24, 1942; 1 son, Charles Darrell. Supt., Ragner Bros., gen. contractors. Pitts., 1945-47; field engr., supt machinery div. Dravo Corp., Pitts., 1948-55; field engr., project engr. Russell & Axon, Daytona Beach, Fla., 1955-57; dir. pub. works City Ocala (Fla.), 1957-68; supt. pub. works City West Palm Beach (Fla.), 1968—. Served with USNR, 1942-45: PTO. Mem. Am. Pub. Works Assn. Republican. Methodist. Home: 1447 42d St West Palm Beach FL 33407 Office: 844 Newark St West Palm Beach FL 33401

BICKHAM, LUZINE BENJAMIN, univ. dean; b. New Orleans, Mar. 2, 1923; s. Benjamin L. and Ruby L. (Higginbotham) B.; B.B.A., U. Mich., 1947, M.B.A., 1948; Ph.D., U. Tex., 1965; m. Dorothy B. Williams, Aug. 24, 1949; children—Luzine Benjamin, Nedra Eileen. Jr. Accountant T.A. Jones & Co., Chgo., 1948-49; instr. bus. adminstrn. Dillard U., New Orleans, 1949-50; sec. Watchtower Life Ins. Co., Houston, 1950-52; prof. bus. adminstrn. Tex. S. U., Houston, 1952-69, dean, prof. Sch. Bus., 1969—. Dir. Tex. So. Finance Corp., Standard Savs. & Loan Assn. Served with USAAF, 1943-45. So. fellowships fellow, 1963. Mem. Am. Marketing Assn., Alpha Phi Alpha, Beta Alpha Psi, Beta Gamma Sigma. Republican. Conglist. Home: 3422 S MacGregor Way Houston TX 77021

BICKLEY, N. ALEX, city ofcl.; b. Abilene, Tex., Mar. 7, 1918; s. W.C. and Frankie (Alexander) B.; student McMurry Coll., 1935-38; LL.B., U. Tex., 1941; m. Dorothy Hennegas, Feb. 12, 1943; children—Barbara Ann, Lynn Denise, Neil Alexander. Asso. firm Smith, Eplen & Bickley Attys., Abilene, 1946-50; city atty., Abilene, 1955-58; then mem. firm Smith, Bickley & Pope, Attys., Abilene, 1st asst. city atty., Dallas, 1958-65, city atty., 1965—. Prof. oil and gas legislation McMurry Coll., 1956-57; chmn. Inst. Condemnation S.W. Legal Found., 1964; prof. law Acad. Am. and Internat. Law So. Meth. U. Council commr. Circle Ten council Boy Scouts Am., 1956-57; pres. YMCA, Abilene, 1957. Legislation liaison City of Dallas with Tex. Legislature. Trustee, Southwestern Legal Found. Served with USN, 1941-46, 50-51. Decorated Bronze Star. Named Outstanding Man of Abilene, 1947. Mem. Nat. Inst. Municipal Law Officers (2d v.p., dir.), Tex. City Attys. Assn. (pres. 1965-66). Democrat. Methodist (chmn. bd. stewards; mem. Dallas Council Ch. Bds.). Mason (32 deg.). Contbr. articles to profl. jours. Home: 3437 Webb Garden Dr Dallas TX 75229 Office: 501 City Hall Dallas TX 75201

BICKNELL, SIDNEY LANE, urologic surgeon; b. Memphis, Feb. 13, 1934; s. Quentin Parrish and Sally Rebecah (Lane) B.; student Memphis State U., 1953-57; M.D., U. Tenn., 1960; m. Doris Annette Schaeffer, Nov. 14, 1964; children—Summer Lynn, Holly Ruth. Intern, Methodist Hosp., Memphis, 1960-61, resident in gen. surgery, 1963-66; resident in urology John Gaston Hosp., Memphis, 1966-69; practice medicine, specializing in urologic surgery, Jackson, Tenn., 1969—; mem. staff urology dept. Jackson Clinic, 1969—, also bd. dirs. Med. adviser Madison County chpt. Am. Cancer Soc. Served with USAF, 1961-63. Fellow A.C.S.; mem. A.M.A., Tenn. Med. Assn. (del.), Am. Urol. Assn. (Southeastern sect.), U. Tenn. Alumni Assn. (pres. Madison County), Consol. Med. Assembly W. Tenn. (sec.). Home: 1021 N Parkway Jackson TN 38301 Office: 616 W Forest Av Jackson TN 38301

BIELEY, PEGGY MOSES, economist; b. N.Y.C., June 5, 1929; d. Louis and Bella (Kenarik) Moses; B.S. magna cum laude, N.Y.U. Sch. Commerce, 1950; M.A., Stanford U., 1953; student Columbia, 1952-53; m. Alfred D. Bieley, Dec. 25, 1953; children—Harlan C., Lily Beth. Economist Nat. Indsl. Conf. Bd., N.Y.C., 1949; economist Jules Backman Asso., N.Y.C., 1949-50; teaching fellow Stanford, 1950-51; economist Nat. Manpower Council, Columbia, 1951-53; instr. econs. U. Miami, 1954-55; v.p., chief economist Julian Langner Research, Inc., Miami, 1955-60; pres., chief economist Bieley, Wagner & Assos., Miami, 1960-70, Econ. Data Bank, Inc., Miami, 1970-73; economist 1st Fed. Savs. and Loan Assn., Tampa, Fla., 1973—; cons. economist savs. and loan assns., comml. banks. Mem. Am. Econ. Assn., Am. Statis. Assn., Econ. Soc. So. Fla., Beta Gamma Sigma, Contbr. articles to tech. jours., nat. mags. Home: 11601 SW 64 Av Miami FL 33156

BIENVENU, LIONEL JOSEPH, govt. park ofcl.; b. Opelousas, La., Mar. 9, 1931; s. Lionel Joseph and Carrie Gillis (Rogers) B.; student premed. Tulane U., 1948-51, postgrad., 1955; B.A., U. So. La., 1953; certificate humanities U. London (Eng.), 1953; postgrad. La. State U. Med. Sch., 1954; m. Patricia Collins, June 30, 1956; children—Patricia, Lionel, Louise, William. With Pan Am. Petroleum Co.- New Orleans, 1954-55, Sun Life Ins. Co. Can., New Orleans, 1956-58; with Nat. Park Service, various locations, 1958—, chief historian, Cabrillo and Channel Islands, Cal., 1964-67, supt. Pea Ridge (Ark.) Mil. Park, 1967—. Mem. Pi Gamma Mu, Pi Alpha Theta. Rotarian. Club: St. Vincent de Paul Men's. Address: Pea Ridge Nat Mil Park Pea Ridge AR 72751

BIERY, JOHN CARLTON, educator; b. Jackson, Mich., Oct. 8, 1927; s. John Mahlon and Dorothy Christine (Schaibly) B.; B.S., U. Mich., 1951; Ph.D. (NSF fellow), Ia. State U., 1961; postgrad. U. Wis., 1962; m. Glee Dudgeon, Dec. 23, 1950; children—Gay Maurene, John Dudgeon. Mem. staff, alternate group leader Los Alamos (N.M.) Sci. Lab., 1962-70, cons., 1971—; asst. group leader, research and devel. engr. Dow Chem. Co., Denver, 1951-58; postdoctoral fellow U. Wis., 1962; asso. prof. chem. engring. U. Ariz., 1970-71; prof., chmn. dept. chem. engring. U. Fla., Gainesville, 1971—. Cons. Argonne Nat. Lab., 1970-71. Served with AUS, 1946-47. Alumni Achievement Fund fellow 1958. Mem. Am. Inst. Chem. Engrs., Am. Inst. Chemists, N.Y. Acad. Scis., Sigma Xi. Unitarian (pres. 1968-69, dir. summer camp 1969). Home: 5010-128 NE Waldo Rd Gainesville FL 32601

BIESER, ALBERT HOWARD, computer mfg. co. exec.; b. Steamboat Springs, Colo., Jan. 31, 1932; s. Frank William and Besse Iola (Cram) B.; B.S. in Bus. Adminstrn., Colo. U., 1953, B.S. in Elec. Engring., 1959; M.S., So. Methodist U., 1961; m. Barbara Louise Strate, Nov. 11, 1955; children—Scott Howard, Frank William III. With Recognition Equipment Inc., Dallas, 1961-68, dir. European operations, 1965-66, dir. market research and devel., 1967-68; pres., chief exec. officer Gen. Computer Systems Corp., Dallas, 1968-72; chmn. bd., chief exec. officer B E Industries, Dallas, 1972—; partner Isle TV Internat., Nassau, Bahamas, 1973—, Televideo Co., Nassau, 1973—. Mem. Kappa Mu Epsilon, Delta Sigma Pi. Mason (Shriner). Home: 609 Carroll Dr Garland TX 75041 Office: 505 N Ervay St Dallas TX 75201

BIGBY, MARY FRANCES WILSON (MRS. LUTHER S. BIGBY), county ofcl., civic worker; b. Williamston, S.C.; d. James G. and Mary (Cason) Wilson; B.S., Greenville Woman's Coll., 1932; m. Luther S. Bigby, Oct. 12, 1935; children—Luther, James. Tchr. pub. sch., Pelzer, S.C., 1932-33; saleslady J. C. Penney Co., Greenville, 1933-34; caseworker Emergency Relief Adminstrn., Greenville, 1934-42; dept. head Greenville Army Air Base, 1942-45; retirement clk. Greenville County Dept. Edn., 1946-53; 1st clk. Office County Supr., Greenville, 1953-74, adminstrv. asst., 1974—. Corr. sec. S.C. Conf. on Status of Women, 1964-66, chmn. nominating com., 1966—, treas., 1969-70, 2d v.p., 1970-72, 1st v.p., 1972-74, pres., 1974—; mem. S.C. Council for Common Good, 1960—, chmn. nominating com., 1974; mem. S.C. Gov.'s Commn. on Status of Women, 1965-70; membership chmn. Greenville Forum on World Affairs, 1967—; residential chmn. Cancer Crusade, 1969; chmn. camp com. Salvation Army Aux., 1st v.p., 1974—; mem. County Home Aux., Greenville County Mental Health, Friends of Library. Named Woman of Yr., Greenville Bus. and Profl. Woman's Club, 1968. Mem. Greater Greenville Women's Div. of C. of C. (1st v.p. 1965, pres. 1966), Order Eastern Star, S.C. Fedn. Bus. and Profl. Women's Clubs (corr. sec. 1959-61, rec. sec. 1961-62, 2d v.p. 1962-64, 1st v.p. 1964-66, pres. 1966-68, nat. contact. chmn. 1959-60, nat. bd. 1966-68, parliamentarian 1970-74; dir. Edn. Found. 1970, pres. 1972-73), Greenville Bus. and Profl. Women's Club (pres. 1958-59, chmn. nominating com. 1970-72), Nat. Secs. Assn. (local coms.). Baptist (pres. Sunday Sch. class). Clubs: Altrusa (pres. 1970-72, mem. bd.), Blue Ridge (presiding partner 1971-72). Home: 9 W Augusta Pl Greenville SC 29605 Office: Courthouse Greenville SC 29601

BIGGERS, NEAL BROOKS, JR., lawyer; b. Corinth, Miss., July 1, 1935; s. Neal B. and Sara (Cunningham) B.; B.A., Millsaps Coll., 1957; LL.B., U. Miss., 1963; Admitted to Miss. bar, 1963; pvt. practice, Corinth, 1963—; county atty. Alcorn County, 1964-68; dist. atty. 1st Judicial Dist. Miss., 1968—. Served to lt. comdr. USNR, 1957-60. Mem. Miss., Am. bar assns., Nat. Dist. Atty. Assn. Home: 818 Shilon Rd Corinth MS 38824 Office: 402 Franklin St Corinth MS 38824

BIGGS, E. GLENN, banker; b. San Angelo, Tex., June 10, 1933; s. Bennie Austin and Clara (Stucke) B.; B.A., Baylor U., 1956; m. Ann Carolyn Dendy, July 29, 1955; children—Barry, Brian. Partner, real estate ins. firm, Abilene, Tex., 1956-65; exec. aide to speaker Tex. Ho. Reps., 1965-67; pres. Nat. Western Life Ins., Austin, Tex., 1968-70, also dir.; chmn. bd. Stockman Nat. Life, Rapid City, 1968-70; pres. Aberdeen Petroleum Inc., Tulsa, 1968-70, also dir.; pres., dir. 1st Nat. Bank, San Antonio; dir. Signal Life Ins. Co., San Antonio. Mem. Gov.'s Com. on Lang. Disabilities, 1968—; chmn. Tex. Conservation Found. Bd. dirs. Harry Jersig Lang. Center, San Antonio; trustee Hendrick Meml. Hosp., Abilene, Hardin-Simmons U., Abilene, Tex. State Hist. Found.; chmn. bd. dirs. Met. Gen. Hosp., San Antonio. Home: 603 Cave Lane San Antonio TX 78209 Office: 231 E Travis St San Antonio TX 78205

BILBREY, WALTER GREEN, JR., ins. exec.; b. Lima, O., June 17, 1926; s. Walter Green and Cecile Hannah (Bowers) B.; B.S., Manchester Coll., 1949; m. Helen Jane Peterson, Dec. 24, 1964; children—Mark William, Scott Ashley. Sr. cons. Life Ins. Agy. Mgmt. Assn., Hartford, Conn., 1960-64; v.p. sales, marketing Provident Life Ins. Co., Bismarck, N.D., 1964-71, now dir.; pres. Marketing Services Internat., Inc., 1971—. Served with USNR, 1944-46; comdr. Res. ret. C.L.U. Mem. Nat. Assn. Life Underwriters, Am. Coll. Life Underwriters, Nat. Pilots Assn., Nat. Rifle Assn., Amateur Trapshooting Assn. Republican. Lutheran. Elk. Home: 707 E 6th St Cookeville TN 38501 Office: Box 234 Cookeville TN 38501

BILES, WILLIAM ROY, cons. chem. engr.; b. Cin., Dec. 20, 1923; s. Roy E. and Mary (Roll) B.; B.S., U. Cin., 1949; M.S., Pa. State U., 1952, Ph.D., 1954; m. Elizabeth Kaufman, Sept. 10, 1945 (div. Feb. 1970); children—Robert, Barbara, Jonathon, Michele, Nancy, Randall; m. 2d, Marilyn A. Marta, Nov. 10, 1972. Prodn. supr. Am. Cyanamid Co., Bound Brook, N.J., 1949-51; with Shell Oil Co., Houston, 1954-60, research engr., 1954-56, group leader engring. research, 1956-58, group leader math. and computing, 1958-60, sr. engr., N.Y.C., 1962-64, mgr. research and devel., 1964-69; exchange scientist Royal Dutch Shell Group, Amsterdam, Netherlands, 1960-61; v.p. process control Davis Computer Systems, N.Y.C., 1969-70; pres. Biles & Assos., Houston, 1970—. Served to 1st lt. USAAF, 1942-45. Decorated D.F.C., Air medal with 3 oak leaf clusters. Registered profl. engr., Tex., Ohio. Mem. Am. Chem. Soc., Canadian Inst. Chemists, Am. Inst. Chem. Engrs., I.E.E.E., Instrument Soc. Am., Sigma Xi, Phi Lambda Upsilon, Alpha Chi Sigma. Home: 13915 Perthshire St Houston TX 77024 Office: PO Box 26125 Houston TX 77032

BILL, DORA COX, govt. ofcl., civic worker; b. Knoxville, Tenn., Apr. 18, 1911; d.Charles Fred and Imogene (Masters) Cox; student LaGrange Coll., 1928, 29; flower show judging degree U. Ga., 1950; m. C. R. Dodson, May 1930; m. 2d, Clayton Justin Cosse, Apr. 9, 1950; 1 dau., Jeanie Cox (Mrs. Albert A. Price, Jr.); m. 3d, Russell W. Bill, June 20, 1969. Gen. mgr. So. office J. H. McGillvra Co. of N.Y., Atlanta, 1948-49; formed Dora Dodson Radio Rep. Agy., 1949, So. mgr. Forjoe Co., Atlanta, 1949; formed Dora-Clayton Agy., Inc., 1950, v.p., treas., 1950-68; pub. information specialist S.E. regional office Econ. Opportunity, Atlanta, 1968-71; pub. information officer ACTION, Atlanta, 1971—. Active in Cerebral Palsy, A.R.C. drives; pres. Civitan Aux., 1955-56; mem. Atlanta Symphony Guild, Atlanta Opera Guild, So. Council Internat. and Pub. Affairs; nat. bd. Heart Assn. Recipient silver medal Printers Ink, 1968. Mem. Am. Women in Radio and Television (nat. local boards, chpt. pres., nat. pres. 1965-66; trustee Ednl. Found. 1966-72), Broadcast Execs. Club, Internat. Platform Assn., Internat. Soc. Radio and Television, C. of C., Am. Fedn. Advt. Clubs, Atlanta Advt. Club, League of Women Voters. English-Speaking Union, Atlanta Art Assn., Am. Soc. for Pub. Adminstrn., Am. Acad. Polit. and Social Sci., Presidents Council Atlanta, UN Council. Episcopalian. Clubs: Atlanta Press, Atlanta Women's Golf Assn., East Lake Golf Assn. (sec. 1956-58), Atlanta Variety (women's com.), Parkwood Garden (sec.), Atlanta Athletic, East Lake Country (all Ga.); Ponte Vedra (Fla.) Country; Highlands (N.C.) Country. Home: 6851 Roswell Rd Apt B14 Atlanta GA 30328 Office: ACTION 730 Peachtree St Atlanta GA 30308

BILLIG, OTTO, psychiatrist; b. Vienna, Austria, Aug. 10, 1910; s. Neure and Ottilie (Butschowitz) B.; B.A., Fed. Realschule (Austria), 1929; M.D., U. Vienna, 1937;; m. Sebby Orr, Oct. 5, 1943; 1 dau., Martha Gwen. Came to U.S., 1939, naturalized, 1944. Intern, U. Vienna Hosp., 1934-36, resident, 1936-38; asst. neurology Rothschild Hosp., Vienna, 1938-39; clin. dir. Highland Hosp., Asheville, N.C., 1939-46; instr. psychiatry Duke, 1941-43, asso. psychiatry Duke Univ., 1943-46, asst. prof. neuropsychiatry, 1946-48; dir. mental health clinic Vanderbilt U. Hosp., Nashville, 1948-60, asso. prof., 1952-69, clin. prof. psychiatry, 1969—; acting chmn. dept. psychiatry Meharry Med. Coll., Nashville, 1952-66, prof. clin. psychiatry, 1967—. Lectr., U. Tenn. Sch. Social Work, Nashville, 1952—, VA Hosp., Murfreesboro, Tenn., 1949—; vice chmn. Met. Bd. Health Nashville-Davidson County, 1963-69, chmn., 1969-73. Pres., Nashville Art Council, 1961-63. Bd. dirs. Peabody Coll. Art Mus., Nashville. Diplomate Am. Bd. Psychiatry and Neurology. Fellow Royal Soc. Health; mem. A.M.A., Am. Psychiat. Assn., Internat. Soc. Psychopath. Expression, (hon., mem. council), Soc. Projective Techniques, World Congress Psychiatry. Contbr. articles to profl. jours. Home: 1050 Overton Lea Rd Nashville TN 37220 Office: 2011 Ashland Av Nashville TN 37212

BILLINGS, EARL REXFORD, ednl. adminstr.; b. Kendall, N.Y., Mar. 7, 1917; s. Earl C. and Edna M. (Blake) B.; A.A., Rochester Inst. Tech., 1932; A.B., Cornell U., 1934; Ed.M., State U. N.Y. at Buffalo, 1957; m. Lu M. Kilgore. Chemist, E.I. duPont de Nemours & Co., Inc., 1932-36; tchr. Bd. Edn. Niagara Falls, N.Y., 1936-46; acad. dean Erie County Tech. Inst., Buffalo, 1946-70; adviser tech. edn. Govt. of Pakistan, 1965-67; gen. mgr. James Connolly Campus, Tex. State Tech. Inst., Waco, 1970—. Mem. Am. Chem. Soc., Am. Tech. Edn. Assn., Am. Vocational Assn., Am. Soc. for Engring. Edn. Home: 7610 Bosque Blvd Waco TX 76710

BILLINGS, FRANK EDWARD, lawyer; b. San Antonio, Dec. 24, 1936; s. Norman A. and Cora Vivian (Henderson) B.; B.B.A., U. Tex. at Austin, 1960, J.D., 1966; m. Theo M. Minturn, Dec. 17, 1965; children—Frank Edward, Tracey. Admitted to Tex. bar, 1966; since practiced in Houston; mem. firm Hinds & Meyer, Houston, 1966—. Served with USNR, 1960-63. Mem. Am. Bar Assn., State Bar Tex., Houston Bar Assn., Maritime Law Assn. U.S. Methodist. Clubs: Propeller U.S., Houston Mariners, Toastmasters. Home: 3123 Sunset St Houston TX 77005 Office: 704 Capital Nat Bank Bldg Houston TX 77002

BILLINGS, PAUL BARRETT, food co. exec.; b. Memphis, Feb. 4, 1931; s. Paul Alexander and Besse Lee (Barrett) B.; B.A., Vanderbilt U., 1953; m. Karen Young, Nov. 30, 1957; children—Paul Barrett, B. Welby, Bardford. Sales rep. Crown Zellerbach Corp., Memphis, 1956-62; sales mgr. Osceola Foods, Inc. (Ark.), 1962-67, v.p. sales, 1967-69, pres., 1969—; dir. Planters Bank, Osceola. Served with AUS, 1954-56. Mem. Nat. Assn. Margarine Mfrs. (dir. 1970), Osceola C. of C. (dir.). Republican. Mem. Christian Ch. (dir.). Home: 1005 W Hale St Osceola AR 72370 Office: PO Box 368 Osceola AR 72370

BILLINGS, RAY HENRY, elec. engr.; b. Vernon, Tex., Jan. 30, 1922; s. Melford Ray and Louise Dorothy (Frank) B.; B.E.E., Ga. Inst. Tech., 1949; m. Elizabeth Truitt; children—Truitt Ray, Maria Frieda, Henry Lee, Raynette Leila. Power plant electrician Ford Motor Co.,

Hapeville, Ga., 1950-51; communication technician, City Atlanta, 1951—. Served with USAAF, 1940-45. Decorated Bronze Star medals; recipient Silver Beaver award Boy Scouts Am., 1973. Mem. I.E.E.E., Am. Radio Relay League, Asso. Pub. Safety Communication Officers, Inc. (v.p. 1971-73), Radio Club Am. Baptist. Home: 1948 W Mercer Av College Park GA 30337 Office: 175 Decatur St SE Atlanta GA 30303

BILLINGSLEY, DAVID LEWIS, internat. petroleum cons.; co. exec.; b. Houston, Nov. 8, 1935; s. Louis Samuel and Mary Hazel (Bufkin) B.; B.S. in Petroleum Engring. (Socony Mobil scholar), U. Tex., 1957, M.S. in Petroleum Engring. (Pan Am. Petroleum Corp. fellow), 1958; m. Madora Mae Baker, Feb. 20, 1954; children—David Lewis, Carl Russ, John Thomas, Madora. Jr. petroleum engr. Pan Am. Petroleum Corp., Andrews, Tex., 1958-59; partner, cons. petroleum engr. Kirkpatrick & Assos., Shreveport, La., 1959; chief engr. Caddo Oil Co., Shreveport, 1959-63; organizer, owner Billingsley Engring. Co., Shreveport, 1963—; dir. Engineered Property Mgmt., Inc., Power Cons., Inc., Billingsley Engring. Co., Billingsley Environmental Control, Inc., Explofunds, Inc., Billingsley Multinat., Inc. Co-chmn. area fund campaign Boy Scouts Am., 1965, 66; chmn. profl. petroleum engrs. div. United Fund Drive, 1972. Registered profl. engr., Ark., La., Okla., Tex. Mem. Am. Petroleum Inst., Am. Assn. Petroleum Engrs., Am. Assn. Petroleum Geologists, Internat. Oil Scouts Assn., Ind. Petroleum Assn. Am., Tex. Ex-Students Assn. (pres. N.W. La. chpt. 1969), Soc. Petroleum Engrs. (chmn. La.-Ark. sect. 1963-64, dir. 1964-65), Soc. Petroleum Evaluation Engrs., Nat. Soc. Petroleum Engrs., La. Engring. Soc., Shreveport Geol. Soc., Shreveport C. of C., Pub. Affairs Research Council La., Historic Preservation of Shreveport, La. Forestry Assn., Aircraft Owners and Pilots Assn., La. Quarter Horse Breeders Assn., La. Cattlemen's Assn., Am. Quarter Horse Assn., Am. Hereford Assn., Nat. Cutting Horse Assn., Nat. Rifle Assn., Sigma Gamma Epsilon, Tau Beta Pi. Episcopalian. Clubs: Petroleum of Shreveport, Shreveport Country Ark-La.-Tex. Ambassadors, Gulf Coast Big Game Hunters, Safari Internat. Contbr. articles to profl. jours. Home: Route 1 Keithville LA 71047 Office: 2000 Fairfield Av Shreveport LA 71104

BILLINGSLEY, HASCAL SANDERS, beverage co. exec.; b. Wylie, Tex., Dec. 26, 1905; s. James Clement and Eva (Sanders) B.; student Advanced Accounting Sch., U. Tex., 1926-27; m. Mary Louise Bruss, Nov. 15, 1935;children—Hascal Bruss, Martha Joan (Mrs. Ralph D. Bowman). Accountant, Peat, Marwick, Mitchell & Co., C.P.A.'s. Dallas, 1927-30; with Dr. Pepper Co., Dallas, 1931—, pres., 1966-69, chmn. bd., 1969—. Mem. Salesmanship Club Dallas (bd. dirs. 1953-54, sec. 1953-54), All Sports Assn., Beta Alpha Psi. Club: Dallas City. Home: 4818 Melissa Lane Dallas TX 75229 Office: 5523 E Mockingbird Lane Dallas TX 75222

BILLINGTON, TED FRANKLIN, cons. engr.; b. Almo, Ky., Now. 22, 1938; s. Eldred Guy and Lurline (Morris) B.; student Murray State U., 1956-59; B.S. in C.E., U. Ky., 1961; m. Joan Patricia Baker, Apr. 25, 1961; children—Julia Kathryn, Claudia Joan, Cheryl. Assn. resident engr. Ky. Dept. Hwy., Ashland, 1961-62; chief structural engr. Lee Potter Smith & Assos., architects, Paducah, Ky., 1962-67; cons. engr. Ted F. Billington, Murray, Ky., 1967—, prin. cons. services civil and structural engring., land surveying. Registered land surveyor, Ky.; registered profl. engr., Tenn., Ky., Ind. Mem. Am. Soc. C.E., Nat. Soc. Profl. Engrs., Am. Soc. Testing Materials, Am. Concrete Int., Ky. Soc. Profl. Engrs. Baptist. Rotarian. Home: 505 Whitnell St Murray KY 42071 Office: Johnson Blvd Box 422 Murray KY 42071

BILLIONS, GERALD FREEMAN, dentist; b. Memphis, Oct. 14, 1939; s. Robert Edward and Rosa Louise (Humphries) B.; student Memphis State U., 1957-61; D.D.S., U. Tenn., 1965; m. Barbara Ann Robins, Nov. 25, 1961; children—Jeffrey Lowell, David Andrew. Asso. O.C. Faulkner, Memphis, 1968; instr. operative dentistry U. Tenn., 1969-70; pvt. practice, Memphis, 1970—. Served to capt. AUS, 1965-67. Mem. Memphis, Tenn. dental socs., Am. Dental Assn., Memphis Dental Legion, Delta Sigma Delta. Republican. Baptist. Club: Optimist (Memphis). Home: 2702 Kelmscott Cove Germantown TN 38138 Office: 4676A Knight Arnold Rd Memphis TN 38118

BINDER, LEONARD JAMES, editor; b. Jackson, Mich., June 21, 1926; s. Leonard George and Ethel Cecille (Lilly) B.; B.S., Central Mich. U., 1952; m. Margery Elizabeth Rose, Sept. 7, 1950; children—Timothy James, Michael Paul, Douglas Harold. Editor Wingfoot Clan, Goodyear Tire & Rubber Co., Jackson, 1952-54; editor-in-chief Wayne (Mich.) Eagle, 1954-55; news editor Pontiac (Mich.) Press, 1955-57; editor AP, Detroit, 1957-60; state editor Detroit News, 1960-67; editor-in-chief Army Mag., Washington, 1967—. Spl. writer, book reviewer Nat. Observer, 1967-70. Bd. dirs. Central Mich. U. Devel. Fund. Served with USNR, 1944-46. Mem. Central Mich. U. Alumni Assn. (v.p. Detroit chpt. 1966-67). Methodist (adminstrv. bd. 1969—). Clubs: Nat. Press, Detroit Press. Home: 304 Lewis St Vienna VA 22180 Office: 1529 18th St NW Washington DC 20036

BINGHAM, BARRY, editor; b. Louisville, Feb. 10, 1906; s. Robert Worth and Eleanor (Miller) B.; student Middlesex Sch., Concord, Mass., 1921-23; A.B. magna cum laude, Harvard, 1928; LL.D., U. Ky., Kenyon Coll., Centre Coll.; Litt.D., U. Louisville, U. Cin., Edgecliff Coll., Alfred U.; m. Mary Clifford Caperton, June 9, 1931; children—Worth (dec.), Barry, Sarah (Mrs. Micheal Iovenko), Eleanor. With Courier-Jour. and Louisville Times Co., 1930—, reporter, sec., asso. pub., pub., 1930-45, editor, pub., until 1971, now chmn. bd.; chmn. bd. WHAS, Inc., Standard Gravure Corp. Chmn. bd. dirs. Historic Homes Found.; chmn. bd. trustees Berea Coll.; trustee Pine Mountain Settlement Sch.; overseer U. Louisville; bd. dirs. Asia Found.; past chmn. Internat. Press Inst., Am. Press Inst. Chief of mission to France, ECA, 1949-50. Nat. chmn. Vols. for Stevenson-Kefauver, 1956. Served with USNR, 1941-45; comdr., 1945; ETO, PTO. Decorated comdr. Order Brit. Empire, comdr. Legion of Honor; recipient Sullivan award U. Ky. Mem. Sigma Delta Chi (hon. nat. chmn.). Democrat. Episcopalian. Clubs: Jefferson, River Valley, Wynn-Stay, Louisville Country (Louisville); Century Assn. Home: Glenview KY 40025 Office: Courier-Journal and Times Louisville KY 40202

BINGHAM, JOHN JAY, assn. exec.; b. Vilas, N.C., Aug. 20, 1929; s. Thomas McCoy and Kenova Virginia (Morrell) B.; B.S., Appalachian State U., 1956; m. Joan Edna Phillips, May 21, 1954; children—Kirk, Brent. Phys. dir. Wilkes YMCA, North Wilkesboro, N.C., 1956-61; head phys. dept. Cannon Meml. YMCA, Kannapolis, N.C., 1961-68; exec. dir. Greater Clinton (S.C.) YMCA, 1968—. Mem. Carolinas Phys. Edn. Com., 1959-72; adviser to John R. Mott, Internat. Y's Mens Club, 1963-68. Served with AUS, 1951-53. Recipient Distinguished Service award Jr. C. of C., 1969, S.C. Phys. Fitness award, 1970. Mem. Assn. Profl. YMCA Dirs. (pres. S.C. chpt. 1971-72). Methodist. Rotarian. Home: 504 Chestnut St Clinton SC 29325 Office: PO Drawer 329 Clinton SC 29325

BINGHAM, MARY CAPERTON (MRS. BARRY BINGHAM), newspaper exec.; b. Richmond, Va., Dec. 24, 1904; d. Clifford R. and Helena (Lefroy) Caperton; B.A., Radcliffe Coll., 1928; postgrad. (Charles Eliot Norton fellow) Am. Sch. Classical Studies, Athens, 1929; D.Litt., U. Louisville, 1954; m. Barry Bingham, June 9, 1931; children—Robert W. (dec.), G. Barry, Sarah (Mrs. Michael Iovenko), Jonathan W. (dec.), Eleanor M. Vice pres., dir. Courier-Jour. and Louisville Times, WHAS, Inc., 1942—; editor World of Books column Louisville Courier Jour., 1943-67. Bd. dirs. Council Basic Edn., Washington, Nature Conservancy, Washington. Recipient Margaret Douglas Conservation award Garden Club Am., 1972. Mem. Colonial Dames. Clubs: River Valley, Louisville Country (Louisville); Cosmopolitan (N.Y.C.); Glenview (Ky.) Garden. Home: Glenview KY 40025 Office: 525 W Broadway Louisville KY 40202

BINGHAM, ROBERT J., food co. exec.; b. Blackfoot, Ida., Feb. 17, 1932; s. Wintle Albern and Lavell (Jones) B.; student Ricks Coll., 1951-53; B.S., Utah State U., 1959; M.S., U. Wis., 1960, Ph.D., 1963; m. Lynetta Kunz, June 26, 1959; children—Lynn Robert, Lisa Kae, LuAnne, Allen Kunz, Scott Robert, Amy. Asst. prof. N.C. State U., Raleigh, 1963-68; mgr. agri-products div. research Beatrice Foods Co., Chgo., 1968-70; v.p. Nutrico food research, devel., mfg., Tulsa, 1970—, also dir.; dir. Banfield, Tulsa. Served with USNR, 1955-56. Mem. Inst. Food Technologists, Am. Inst. Chemists, Am. Chem. Soc., Sigma Xi, Phi Lambda Upsilon, Alpha Zeta. Mem. Ch. of Jesus Christ of Latter-day Saints (bishop Tulsa ward). Club: Summit (Tulsa). Contbr. articles to profl. jours. Patentee in field. Home: 5505 E 64th St Tulsa OK 74136 Office: Nutrico 7636 E 46th St Tulsa OK 74146

BINION, STANLEY BOND, lawyer; b. Brownwood, Tex., Nov. 9, 1936; s. James Milton and Mildred (Bond) B.; B.B.A., U. Houston, 1960, J.D., 1962; m. Martha Linda Pendarvis, July 12, 1958; children—Parker Bond, Elizabeth Ann. Admitted to Tex. bar, 1962; law clk. to chief judge U.S. Dist. Ct. for So. Tex., Houston, 1962-64; asso. mem. firm Bracewell, Reynolds & Patterson, Houston, 1964-66; partner firm Reynolds, White, Allen & Cook, Houston, 1966—; judge Municipal Ct. City of West University Place, Houston, 1966-68. Lectr. corporate law Practice Skills Inst., State Bar Tex., 1971—. Mem. Am. Judicature Soc., Bar Assn. Tex., Houston Bar Assn., U. Houston Law Alumni Assn. (dir.), Phi Delta Phi. Home: 11907 Broken Bough St Houston TX 77024 Office: 1100 Milam Bldg Houston TX 77002

BINKLEY, JOE PITTS, JR., lawyer; b. Nashville, June 13, 1944; s. Joe Pitts and Martha John (Ormes) B.; B.A., Vanderbilt U., 1966, J.D., 1969; m. Suzanne Gay Griffith, June 16, 1967; children—Joe Pitts III, Louise Holland. Admitted to Tenn. bar, 1969; since practiced in Nashville; mem. firm Binkley & Binkley. Mem. chancellor's council Vanderbilt U. Law Sch., 1973-74. Bd. dirs Nashville Hemophilia Soc. Mem. Am., Nashville (sec. 1970-74) trial lawyers assns., Am., Tenn., Nashville (dir.) bar assns., Phi Delta Theta, Phi Delta Phi. Home: 1715 Kingsbury Dr Nashville TN 37215 Office: 1601 Parkway Towers Nashville TN 37219

BINNING, BETTE FINESE (MRS. GENE HEDGCOCK BINNING), athletic assn. ofcl.; b. Brandon, Man., Can., Sept. 20, 1927 (father Am. citizen); d. Henry Josiah and Beatrice Victoria (Harrop) Ames; grad. Brandon Collegiate, 1944; student Brandon, U., 1944-46; m. Gene Hedgcock Binning, May 3, 1952; children—Gene Barton, Barbara Jo, Bradford Jay. Exec. sec. to mgr. Gardner-Denver Co., Denver, 1950-52; mem. age group swimming com. Amateur Athletic Union U.S., 1966-68, 70-72, women's swimming com., 1968-69, 72-75, age group swimming objectives subcom., 1970-71, del. conv., 1971, 72, 73, 74; Okla. state chmn. age group swimming Amateur Athletic Union, 1966-68, 70-72, chmn. women's swimming com., 1968-69, 72-75, mem. Okla. exec. bd. for all amateur sports, also registration com., 1971-75; mem. U.S. Olympic com., 1972-75; nat. dir. swimming records, 1972-75. Team capt. YMCA fund drives, 1966—; active Community Chest, Cancer, Muscular Dystrophy fund drives, Okla. Horse Shows, Presbyn. Mem. Kiwanis Ladies, Youth Study Club (treas. 1971-72). Presbyn. Clubs: Kerr-Mcgee Swim (dir. 1968—), Quail Creek Golf and Country, Oklahoma City Ski (Oklahoma City). Home: 3101 Rolling Stone Rd Oklahoma City OK 73120

BINNING, GENE HEDGCOCK, air conditioning co. exec.; b. Casper, Wyo., Oct. 28, 1927; s. Lloyd Cecil and Vera (Rhodes) B.; B.S., U. Wyo., 1949; postgrad. Oklahoma City U., 1959, U. Okla., 1963-64; m. Bette Fenis Ames, May 3, 1952; children—Gene Barton, Barbara Jo, Bradford Jay. Sales engr. Trane Co., Denver, 1950-58, mgr. Okla. dist., Oklahoma City, 1958—; pres. Gene H. Binning Co., Inc., Comml. Devel. Co.; mgr. Binning Oil & Gas Investment & Devel. Co. Served with AUS, 1946-47. Recipient Heating and Air Conditioning Seminar Course awards, 1966. Registered profl. engr., Okla. Mem. Am. Soc. Heating and Air Conditioning Engrs. (dir.), Oklahoma City C. of C., Sigma Nu. Presbyn. (elder). Mason (Shriner), Kiwanian. Club: Quail Creek Golf and Country. Home: 3101 Rollingstone Rd Oklahoma City OK 73120 Office: 3800 Willowsprings Rd Oklahoma City OK 73112

BINSTOCK, MARTIN HAROLD, nuclear mfg. co. exec.; b. N.Y.C., Jan. 16, 1922; B.S., Rensselaer Poly. Inst., 1942, M.Metall. Engring., 1948; m. Adelaide Solomon, Aug. 31, 1947; children—Cathy, Peter, James. Factory mgr. Am. Electro Metal Corp., 1948-50; group leader Westinghouse Electric Corp., 1950-53; sect. head nuclear div. Sylvania Electric Products, 1953-56; dept. head nuclear div. Rockwell Internat., 1956-69; project and operations mgr. nuclear div. Kerr-McGee Corp., Oklahoma City, 1969—. Instr. metallurgy U. Cal. at Los Angeles, 1966-69. Served to lt. (j.g.) USNR, 1944-46. Mem. Am. Soc. Metals, Am. Nuclear Soc. Patentee in field. Home: 1216 NE 55th St Oklahoma City OK 73111 Office: PO Box 315 Crescent OK 73028

BINYON, NICHOLAS CROMWELL, JR., accountant; b. Shreveport, La., Dec. 13, 1941; s. Nicholas Cromwell and Heloise Evelyn (Brown) B.; student Odessa Jr. Coll., 1960-62; B.B.A. with honors, U. Tex., 1966; m. Saranel Brewer, May 16, 1959; children—Laura Joy, William Keith. Mem. staff accounting dept. El Paso Natural Gas Products Co., Odessa and El Paso, Tex., 1960-64; sr. accountant Bixler, Carlton, Dickinson & Rister, C.P.A.'s, El Paso, 1964-69; practice accounting, El Paso, 1969-73; partner Binyon & Stone, El Paso, 1973—; dir. Pan Am. Optical Co., Inc., El Paso, H.W. Enterprises, Inc., Ruidoso, N.M., Tools Export, Inc., El Paso. Instr. accounting El Paso Community Coll., 1971, 72. Mem. Tex. United Community Services, 1970—; chmn. C.P.A.'s for U. Tex. at El Paso Excellence Fund Drive, 1972; adv. council Salvation Army Booth Meml. Home. Mem. Am. Inst. C.P.A.'s, Tex. Soc. C.P.A.'s, Delta Sigma Pi, Alpha Chi. Mason (Shriner), Lion (dir. El Paso 1969—). Home: 820 Melrose St El Paso TX 79932 Office: Binyon & Stone CPA's 6400 Convair Rd El Paso TX 79925

BIRD, DANIEL DAVID, constrn. co. exec.; b. Kansas City, Mo., Apr. 22, 1941; s. Charles Daniel and Mary (Gould) B.; B.S. in Civil Engring. (Kan. Contractors scholar), U. Kan., 1963; m. Mildred Louise Barr, Aug. 16, 1959; children—Cory David, Derek Daniel, Wendy Danielle. Engr., Martin K. Eby Constrn. Co., various locations, 1963-64, chief engr., 1964-66; chief engr. Henry C. Beck Co., Dallas, 1966, chief regional field engr., 1966-68, project mgr., supr., 1968; supt. projects Hensel Phelps Constrn. Co., Los Alamos, N.M., 1968-70; constrn. mgr. Forum Builders, Inc., Dallas, 1970-71; sr. project mgr. Charter Builders, Inc., Dallas, 1971-72; v.p. Cimarron Constrn. Co., Dallas, 1972; owner, mgr. Bird Constrn. Co., Dandan Engring., Dallas, 1972—. Registered profl. engr., Kan. Mem. Nat. Soc. Profl. Engrs., Am. Soc. C.E., Constrn. Specifications Inst. Home: 3137 Jubilee Trail Dallas TX 75229 Office: 2860 Walnut Hill Lane Suite 115 Dallas TX 75220

BIRD, DANIEL WOODROW, JR., lawyer; b. Bland, Va., Dec. 26, 1938; s. Daniel Woodrow and Elizabeth Kegley (Dunn) B.; B.S., Va. Poly. Inst., 1960; LL.B., Washington and Lee U., 1966; m. Barbra Joan McEldowney, June 17, 1967; children—Virginia Elizabeth, Daniel Woodrow III, James Banjamin. Admitted to Va. bar, 1966; counsel office Va. Atty. Gen., Richmond, 1965-66; mem. firm Gleaves, Bird & Boyd, Wytheville, Va., 1966—. Pres. Mountain Security Savs. & Loan Assn., Wytheville, 1972-75. Pres. Wythe County United Fund, Wytheville, 1970-71; chmn. Wythe County 4-H Com., 1972-73. Sec. Wythe County Dems., 1973-74. Served with AUS, 1960-61. Mem. Am., Va., Wythe County bar assns., Va. Tech. Alumni Assn. (dir. 1970-76). Lion (pres. 1974-75), Elk. Home: 1620 W Main St Wytheville VA 24382 Office: 208 W Main St Wytheville VA 24382

BIRD, FRANCIS MARION, lawyer; b. Comer, Ga., Sept. 4, 1902; s. Henry Madison and Minnie Lee (McConnell) B.; A.B., U. Ga., 1922, LL.B., 1924; LL.M., George Washington U., 1925; m. Mary Adair Howell, Jan. 30, 1935; children—Francis Marion, Mary Adair, Elizabeth Howell, George Arthur. Admitted to Ga. bar, 1924, D.C. bar, 1925, since practiced in Atlanta; with U.S. Senator Hoke Smith, 1925, pvt. practice, 1930-45, Bird & Howell, 1945-59, now Jones, Bird & Howell; served as part-time U.S. referee in bankruptcy, 1945-54; spl. asst. to U.S. atty. gen. as hearings officer Nat. Selective Service Act. Mem. commn. for preparation plan of govt. City of Atlanta and county in which located; mem. permanent rules com. Ga. Supreme Ct.; chmn. Met. Atlanta Commn. on Crime and Juvenile Delinquency, 1969-70; Ga. co-chmn. Tech-Ga. Devel. Fund. Trustee Young Harris Coll., U. Ga. Found., Atlanta Lawyers Found., Interdenominational Theol. Center; trustee, past mem. exec. com. Emory U. Chmn. Ga. Bd. Bar Examiners, 1954-61; mem. Permanent Editorial Bd. Uniform Comml. Code, Fed. Jud. Conf., 5th Circuit. Recipient Distinguished Service citation U. Ga. Law Sch., Alumni Achievement award George Washington U., 1965. Fellow Am. Bar Found.; mem. Am. Judicature Soc. (past dir.) Am. Law Inst. (council 1949—), Am., Ga. (past pres.), Atlanta (past pres.) bar assns., Assn. Bar City N.Y., Atlanta C. of C. (past pres., Atlanta Civic Service award 1957), U. Ga. Alumni Assn. (past pres., Certificate merit 1952), Sigma Chi, Phi Kappa Phi, Phi Delta Phi. Meth. Clubs: Peachtree Golf, Piedmont Driving, Capitol City, Lawyers of Atlanta (past pres.), Atlanta Athletic (past pres.), Kiwanis (Atlanta); Augusta (Ga.) Nat. Golf. Home: 89 Brighton Rd NE Atlanta GA 30309 Office: Haas-Howell Bldg Atlanta GA 30303

BIRD, FRANK BABINGTON, lawyer; b. nr. Athens, Tenn., Mar. 12, 1917; s. James Turner and Emily Jane (Merrill) B.; LL.B., U. Tenn., 1941; m. Agnes Clair Thornton, Mar. 10, 1946; 1 dau., Patricia Anne. Admitted to Tenn. bar, 1941; practiced in Maryville, 1946—; abstractor TVA, 1941-42; price atty. OPA, 1942, 46. Dir. Maryville Savs. & Loan Corp. Gen. counsel Democratic County Exec. Com., 1963—. Bd. dirs. More Blount Jobs, Inc., Indsl. Devel. Bd. Blount County. Served with USAAF, 1942-46. Democrat. Unitarian. Home: Cold Springs Rd Maryville TN 37801 Office: Box 647 Maryville TN 37801

BIRD, GEORGE TILLOTSON, cons. elec. engr.; b. Sherman, N.Y., Apr. 6, 1916; s. Alton Roy and Liela Leola (Tillotson) B.; B.S. in E.E., Tex. A. and M. Coll., 1940; m. Katie Maureen McClure, Mar. 14, 1941; children—Evelyn Kay, Carolyn Joyce, George Tillotson. Geophysicist, Carter Oil Co., Tulsa, 1940; asso. prof. elec. engring. U. Houston, 1946-51; engr. Arinc Research Corp., Washington, 1953-59; pres. Bird Engring. Research Assos., Inc., Vienna, Va., 1959—. Served with USAAF, 1941-46; to lt. col. USAF, 1951-53. Registered profl. engr., D.C., Va., Tex., Md. Mem. I.E.E.E., Nat. Soc. Profl. Engrs., Internat. Assn. Chiefs Police. Home: 2100 Whippoorwill Rd Vienna VA 22180 Office: PO Box 37 Vienna VA 22180

BIRDSONG, ANDREW WILLIS, JR., juvenile judge; b. LaGrange, Ga., Jan. 30, 1925; s. Andrew Woodie and Bessie (Cofield) B.; J.D., U. Ga., 1951; m. Sarah Elizabeth Cliatt, Sept. 16, 1948; children—Nancy Leslie, Sarah Elizabeth, Katherine Guinn. Admitted to Ga. bar, 1950; practiced in LaGrange, 1951-55; partner firm Richter & Birdsong, LaGrange, 1955—; Troup County (Ga.) juvenile judge, 1958—. Organizer, dir., sec. RSB Fiberglass Forms, Inc.; partner K & B Farms; pres. Lakeshore Properties, Inc.; organizer, dir., mem. exec. com. Peoples Bank of LaGrange. Sec. Devel. Authority, LaGrange. Chmn. Troup County Democratic Com., 1962. Trustee Camp Viola, La Grange. Served with AUS, 1943-47. Mem. Am., Ga. hereford assns., Am. Judicature Soc., Am., Ga. bar assns., Assn. Ins. Attys., Phi Delta Theta, Phi Alpha Delta. Baptist (chmn. bd. deacons). Moose, Elk, Lion (pres. LaGrange 1965-66). Club: Highland Country (pres., gov.). Home: Lakeshore Dr LaGrange GA 30240 Office: 306 N Lewis St LaGrange GA 30240

BIRDSONG, MCLEMORE, physician, educator; b. Suffolk, Va., Dec. 11, 1911; s. Thomas Henry and Martha Lewis (McLemore) B.; student Randolph Macon Coll., 1930-33; M.D., U. Va., 1937; m. Charlotte Clark Spain, Oct. 18, 1941; children—McLemore, James Spencer, Harvard Russell II. Intern, U. Va. Hosp., 1937-38, resident, 1938-40; resident Boston Children's Hosp., 1940-41; practice medicine, specializing in pediatrics, Charlottesville, Va., 1941—; asst. prof. pediatrics U. Va., 1941-46, asso. prof., 1946-55, prof., 1955—, chmn. dept. pediatrics, 1960-64. Dir. Citizens Bank & Trust Co.; v.p., dir. Citizens Commonwealth Corp.; cons. rheumatic fever div. Va. Crippled Childrens Bur. Mem. Albemarle County Planning Commn., 1948-62; mem. Charlottesville Planning Commn., 1963-68, chmn., 1967-68. Bd. dirs., mem. exec. com. U. Va. Med. Sch. Found. Diplomate Am. Bd. Pediatrics. Fellow Am. Acad. Pediatrics; mem. So., Va. (past pres.), Albemarle County (past pres.) med. socs., Va. Pediatric Soc. (past pres.), So. Soc. Pediatric Research, Alpha Omega Alpha, Omega Delta Kappa. Methodist (trustee). Contbr. articles to profl. jours. Home: 2021 Spotswood Rd Charlottesville VA 22903 Office: U Va Med Center Charlottesville VA 22901

BIRD-SOTO, HECTOR MANUEL, physician; b. Santurce, P.R., Apr. 21, 1928; s. Modesto Bird and Agustina Soto; B.A., Emory U., 1949; M.T., P.R. Sch. Medicine, 1951; M.D., U. de Zaragoza, Spain, 1961; m. Iraida Hernandez Terreforte, Aug. 29, 1954; children—Hector Manuel, Alberto Modesto, Mirena Maria, Jose Agustin, Juan Carlos. Intern, Arecibo Dist. Hosp., 1961-62; physician Dorado Health Center, 1962-63; house physician Hosp. Pavia, 1963; physician Bayamon Health Center, 1964-67, U. Dist. Hosp., 1967-69; physician family planning project U. P.R. Sch. Medicine, 1969-70, instr. family planning, 1970; resident in neuropsychiatry VA Hosp., San Juan, P.R., 1971—; mem. faculty Pub. Health Sch., Dept. Human Devel., U. P.R., 1971. Roman Catholic. Elk. Club: Casa de Espana de P.R. (San Juan, P.R.). Home: 1-15 Hucare Caparra Hills San Juan PR 00920 Office: VA Hosp Rio Piedras PR 00936

BIRDWELL, BEN JASON, physician; b. Whitleyville, Tenn., Aug. 20, 1937; s. Paul Edwin and Mary Jo (Meadows) B.; B.S., Tenn. Tech U., 1958; M.D., U. Tenn., 1961; m. Peggy Ann Brown, May 21, 1955; children—Alison Lee, Ben Jason. Intern, St. Thomas Hosp., Nashville, 1962-63, resident in internal medicine, 1963-65, chief resident internal medicine, 1965-66; practice medicine specializing in internal medicine, Nashville, 1966—; mem. staff St. Thomas, Baptist, Park View, Donelson, Met. Gen. hosps. Bd. dirs. Donelson Child Devel. Center for Retarded Children. Served to capt., M.C., AUS, 1966-68. Decorated Bronze Star medal. Mem. A.M.A., So. Med. Assn., Tenn. Heart Assn., Tenn. Med. Assn., Nashville Acad. Medicine, Nashville Area C. of C., Alpha Omega Alpha, Phi Chi. Mem. Ch. of Christ. Home: 3143 Hunters Hill Rd Nashville TN 37214 Office: 2531 Park Dr Nashville TN 37214

BIRKE, RONALD LEWIS, educator, chemist; b. St. Louis, Jan. 4, 1939; s. Jack Morris and Sylvia (Schumitzky) B.; B.S., U. N.C., 1961; Ph.D. (Monsanto fellow), Mass. Inst. Tech., 1965; m. Yanina F. Shimanski, Aug. 26, 1962 (dec.); children—Susan Ann, Mimi Beth. Postdoctoral fellow U. Brussels (Belgium), 1966; instr. Harvard, 1966-69; asso. prof. chemistry U. South Fla., Tampa, 1969—. Vis. acad. scientist U.S. Army Office Sci. Research, 1968-69; v.p. Chemsultants, Inc., 1970—. Bd. dirs. Hillel Sch., Tampa. NIH grantee for research, 1970—; Belgium-Am. Ednl. Found. Adv. fellow, 1966. Mem. Am. Chem. Soc., A.A.A.S., Electrochem. Soc., N.Y. Acad. Sci., Sigma Xi, Alpha Chi Sigma, Tau Epsilon Phi. Jewish religion (dir. synogogue). Contbr. articles to profl. jours.

BIRKENWALD, EMIL S., civil engr.; b. Milw., May 30, 1901; s. Edward Bernard and Clara (Silber) B.; B.S. in Civil Engring., U. Wis., 1922; S.M., Mass. Inst. Tech., 1923; m. Edith Fauerbach, Sept. 29, 1925. With So. Ry. Co., various locations, 1924-67, bridge engr., 1946-64, asst. chief bridge engr., Atlanta, 1964-67; sole practice ry. bridge cons. engring., Atlanta, 1968—. Fellow Am. Soc. Civil Engrs. (life mem.); mem. Am. Ry. Engring. Assn. (life mem.), Am. Soc. Testing Materials. Republican. Episcopalian. Mason (32 deg.). Address: 4011 Roswell Rd NE Apt F3 Atlanta GA 30342

BIRMINGHAM, EUGENE, food technologist; b. White Hall, Md., Aug. 29, 1927; s. Ralph and Hila Blanche (Gemmill) B.; B.S., U. Md., 1950; M.S., U. Mo., 1954, Ph.D., 1960; m. Barbara Ann Carpenter, Feb. 10, 1951; children—Hila Jean, Robert Meredith. Meat scientist U.S. Dept. Agr., Beltsville, Md., 1950-52; meat instr. U. Mo., Columbia, 1952-60; head cured meats research Swift & Co., Chgo., 1960-66; dir. research and devel./quality assurance Deltec Internat. Ltd., Coral Gables, Fla., 1966—. Mem. staff research to pres. Swift Argentina-Buenos Aires div. Deltec, 1968. Mem. Am. Meat Sci. Assn., A.A.A.S., Am. Soc. Animal Sci., Inst. Food Technologists, Am. Chem. Soc., Sigma Xi, Gamma Alpha, Gamma Sigma Delta. Contbr. articles in field to profl. jours. Home: 7180 SW 64th St Miami FL 33143 Office: 2801 Ponce de Leon Blvd Coral Gables FL 33134

BIRNBAUM, OWEN, govt. atty.; b. N.Y.C., Mar. 1, 1925; s. Alvin Jerome and Mildred (Safferstone) B.; A.B., Cornell U., 1945; LL.B., Yale, 1947; m. Claire Weil, Oct. 14, 1950; children—Jane Ellen, Andrew Jon. Admitted to N.Y. State bar, 1948, D.C. bar; practiced in N.Y.C., 1948-51; atty. govt. contracts Dept. Army, 1951-59; with Office of Gen. Counsel, FAA, 1960—, asso. gen. counsel, 1968—. Mem. Yale Law Sch. Alumni Assn., Fed. Bar Assn. (chmn. civil rights com. 1964-66; chmn. govt. contracts com. 1962-64), Scribes, Assn. Bar City N.Y., Beta Sigma Rho. Club: Yale (Washington). Contbr. articles to profl. jours. Home: 6431 Bannockburn Dr Bethesda MD 20034 Office: Fed Aviation Agy Washington DC 20590

BIRTEL, FRANK THOMAS, educator; b. New Orleans, Apr. 4, 1932; s. Frank and Virginia (Petrie) B.; B.S., Loyola U. South, New Orleans, 1952; M.S., U. Notre Dame, 1953, Ph.D., 1960; m. JaneElla Moriarty, Sept. 16, 1964; children—Rebecca Anne, Michael Teilhard. Asst. prof. dept. math. Ohio State U., Columbus, 1960-62; Office Naval Research postdoctoral fellow Yale, New Haven, Conn., 1961-62; mem. faculty Tulane U., New Orleans, 1962—, asso. prof., 1964-67, prof., 1967—, head dept. math., 1970-73, chmn. dept., 1973—, faculty rep. to bd. adminstrs. ednl. fund, 1972—; prof. Catholic U. of Nijmegen (Netherlands), 1968-69. Served to lt. USNR, 1953-57. NSF research grantee, 1962—. Mem. Math. Assn. Am., Am. Math. Soc., Alpha Sigma Nu, Omicron Delta Kappa, Delta Epsilon Sigma, Sigma Chi. Roman Catholic. Author: Geometric Analysis on Differentiable Manifolds, 1966; Elementary Complex Analysis from a Several Variable Viewpoint, 1971; Algebras of Holomorphic Functions, 1972. Editor: Function Algebras, 1966. Contbr. articles to profl. jours. Home: 1229 Cadiz St New Orleans LA 70115 Office: Dept Math Tulane Univ New Orleans LA 70118

BISH, HUGH WILLIS, supt. schs.; b. Okeene, Okla., Dec. 15, 1911; s. Robert Conrad and Laura (Willis) B.; student Okla. State U., 1930-31; A.B., N.M. Highlands U., 1934, M.A., 1941; m. Marion Elizabeth Knox, Nov. 6, 1937; 1 dau., Billie Ruth (Mrs. Wilson David Fargo). Tchr., Wheatland High Sch., Cameron, N.M., 1934-35; prin. high sch., Nara Visa, N.M., 1935-38, supt. schs., 1938-42; tchr. Lawton (Okla.) Pub. Schs., 1945-46, prin. jr. high sch., 1946-47, prin. high sch., 1947-62, asst. supt. schs., 1962-66, supt. schs., 1966—. vice pres. YMCA, Lawton, 1952—. Served with USNR, 1942-45. Mem. Nat., Lawton edn. assns., Nat., Okla. assns. sch. adminstrs., Assn. Supervision and Curriculum Devel. (state pres. 1965-66), Secondary Sch. Prins. Assn. (state pres. 1954-55), Okla. North Central Assn. (state exec. com. 1964-70), C. of C. (bd. dirs. 1969-70). Mason, Lion (pres. 1956-57). Home: 1008 Kingswood Rd Lawton OK 73501 Office: 753 Fort Sill Blvd Lawton OK 73501

BISHOP, ARCHER WORTMAN, physician; b. Bristol, Tenn., Oct. 22, 1911; s. Archer and Edna Burdette (Wortman) B.; B.S., U. Tenn., 1932, M.D., 1936; m. Mary Ellen Baker, June 18, 1938; children—Archer Wortman, Mary Ellen (Mrs. Herbert D. Kimmel). Intern, St. Vincent Hosp., S.I., N.Y., 1936-37; gen. practice medicine, Clinton, Tenn., 1937—. Dir. Union Peoples Bank, Clinton. Mem. Am., Tenn. med. assns. Club: Cherokee Country. Home: 501 Eagle Bend St Clinton TN 37716 Office: 122 Broad St Clinton TN 37716

BISHOP, BARRY LEE, journalist; b. Floresville, Tex., Oct. 7, 1906; s. Charles Milton and Zella (Riggs) B.; student U. Tex., 1923-28; m. Josephine Foester, Dec. 1, 1929 1 son, Barry Louis (dec.). Asst. state house corr. Dallas Morning News, 1926-29, reporter, staff writer, corr. specializing city planning and racial integration progress, 1929-45, Latin Am. corr., 1945-50, staff corr. Washington bur., 1951; press-information officer Am. embassy, Mexico City, 1951-54; chief Latin Am. press service USIA, Washington, 1955-58; information officer Am. embassy, Buenos Aires, Argentina, 1958-59; pub. affairs officer-attache Am. embassy, La Paz, Bolivia, 1959-62; attache Am. embassy, Madrid, Spain, 1962; Latin Am. corr. Chgo. Tribune Press Service, Mexico City, 1967—. Mem. Sigma Delta Chi. Mason (Shriner). Clubs: Overseas Press (N.Y.C.); Nat. Press (Washington); American (Buenos Aires). Office: care Chgo Tribune Press Service 435 N Michigan Av Chicago IL 60611 also Paseo de la Reforma 46-6 Mexico City 1 Mexico

BISHOP, CARRIE LEE (MRS. JOHN G. BISHOP), ednl. adminstr.; b. Port Lavaca, Tex., May 10, 1907; d. James Monroe and Ida (Dobbins) Carruth; student Tex. Tech. Coll., 1925-26, B.S., 1941, M.S., 1949; m. John Gaston Bishop, July 24, 1928; children—Cara Juan (Mrs. Jack Schuster), James Gaston. Tchr. elementary edn., Fairview, Tex., 1927-28, Circle Back, Tex., 1936-37, Longview, Tex., 1937-40; vocational home econs. tchr. Roaring Springs, Tex., 1941-42; Seagraves, Tex., 1942-45, Lubbock, Tex., 1945-50; counselor Lubbock pub. schs. and housing authority, 1945-49; area supr. vocational home econs. Tex. Edn. Agy., Kingsville, 1950-51; dean women Tex. Coll. Arts and Industries, 1951—. Mem. exec. com. Kenedy Kleberg County Tb Assn., 1951-56. Mem. Am. Assn. U. Women (local pres. 1954-56, mem. state legislative com. 1956-57), Nat., Tex. (sec. 1956-58) assns. women deans and counselors, Tex. Tchrs. Assn., Delta Kappa Gamma. Baptist. Contbr. to Forecast for Home Economics. Home: 526 William St Kingsville TX 78363

BISHOP, GEORGE F.L., oil co. exec.; b. Panhandle, Tex., Oct. 9, 1913; s. George F.L. and Floyda Margaret (Hickox) B.; B.S. in Chemistry, West Tex. State U., 1935; m. Sarah Virginia McGowen, June 6, 1941; children—George F.L. III, Nicholas F., Sarah Margaret. Laborer, Phillips Petroleum Co., 1935-37, chief chemist, Borger Refinery (Tex.), 1939-41; on loan to Aviation Gasoline Adv. Com., N.Y.C., 1943-44; asst. to mgr., Alamo Refining Corp., Houston, 1947-49; mgr. Phillips Petroleum Co., Okmulgee Refinery, Okmulgee, Okla., 1949-54, Northwest Refining Div., Salt Lake City, 1954-57; mgr. mfg. Pacific Petroleums, Ltd., Fort Saint John, B.C., and Calgary, Alta., Can., 1957-59, mgr., mfg. dept., West Coast Operations, Martinez, Cal., 1970-71; corporate v.p. Phillips Petroleum Co., Bartlesville, Okla., 1971—. Bd. dirs. Indsl. Uranium Co., Indsl. Western, Inc., Maple Hills, Inc., Osage Western, Inc. Bd. dirs. Davis County Community Hosp., 1965-70; bd. dirs. Utah Tech. Coll., 1969-70; mem. Utah Air Conservation Com., 1966-70. Served to sgt., Tex. Nat. Guard, U.S. Army, 1931-35. Recipient Young Man of the Year award, Borger, Jr. C. of C., 1944. Methodist. Lion (pres. local club 1942-43), Rotarian (pres. local clubs 1953-54, 63-64). Patentee in field. Home: 2421 Locust Rd Bartlesville OK 74003 Office: Phillips Bldg Bartlesville OK 74003

BISHOP, JIM, author; b. Jersey City, Nov. 21, 1907; s. John Michael and Jenny Josephine (Tier) B.; student Drakes Secretarial Coll., 1923; Litt.D., St. Bonaventure U., 1958, Belmont Abbey Coll., 1968; m. Elinor Margaret Dunning, June 14, 1930 (dec. Oct. 1957); children—Virginia Lee, Gayle Peggy; m. 2d, Elizabeth Kelly Stone, May 1961; children—Karen, Kathleen. Copy boy N.Y. News, 1929-30; reporter N.Y. Daily Mirror, 1930-32, asst. to Mark Hellinger, columnist, 1932-34, rewrite man feature writer Daily Mirror, 1934-43; asso. editor Colliers mag., 1943-44, war editor, 1944-45; exec. editor Liberty mag., 1945-47; dir. lit. dept. Music Corp. Am., 1947-49; founding editor Gold Medal Books, 1949-51; exec. editor Catholic Digest, founding editor Catholic Digest Book Club, 1954-55. Author: The Glass Crutch, 1945; The Mark Hellinger Story, 1952; Parish Priest, 1953; The Girl in Poison Cottage, 1953; The Making of a Priest, 1954; The Day Lincoln Was Shot, 1955; The Golden Ham, 1956; The Day Christ Died, 1957; Go With God, 1958; Some of My Very Best; 1960; The Day Christ Was Born, 1960; The Murder Trial of Judge Peel, 1962; Honeymoon Diary, 1963; A Day in the Life of President Kennedy, 1964; Jim Bishop: Reporter, 1965; A Day in the Life of President Johnson, 1967; The Day Kennedy was Shot, 1968; The Days of Martin Luther King, Jr., 1971. Columnist, King Features Syndicate. Contbr. to nat. mags. Home: Golden Isles Hallandale FL 33009

BISHOP, MINNIE SLADE (MRS. SANFORD DIXON BISHOP), librarian; b. East Spencer, N.C., May 15, 1915; d. John Robert and Lossie Annie (Jones) Slade; A.B., Shaw U., 1936; postgrad. Columbia, summer 1937; B.S. in L.S., Hampton Inst., 1939; m. Sanford Dixon Bishop, Aug. 18, 1942; 1 son, Sanford Dixon. Tchr., librarian Ellerbe (N.C.) High Sch., 1936-38; librarian Cherry St. br. Evansville (Ind.) Pub. Library, 1939-40; librarian Ark. Agrl., Mech. and Normal Coll., Pine Bluff, 1940-41; organizer, librarian Mobile center Ala. State Coll., 1943-65; librarian S.D. Bishop State Jr. Coll., Mobile, 1965—. Mem. Am. Southeastern, Ala., Bay Area library assns., Ala. Council on Higher Edn., Ala. Assn. Jr. Colls., Ala. Jr. Coll. Library Assn., Nat. Faculty Assn., Nat., Ala. edn. assns., Community Coll. Assn. Instrn. and Tech., League Women Voters, Delta Sigma Theta. Baptist. Mem. Order Eastern Star. Home: 2413 Ridge Rd Mobile AL 36617 Office: 351 North Broad St Mobile AL 36603

BISHOP, MORRIS FRANKLIN, city ofcl.; b. Chriesman, Tex., July 15, 1934; s. Houston Franklin and Ethel Mae (Simonton) B.; student civil engring. Internat. Corr. Schs., 1953-56; m. Evonne Del Clark, Feb. 11, 1952; children—Michael, Steven, Lawrence, Christopher, Dana. With City Dallas, 1952—, supt. san. services, 1963-72, asst. dir. st. and san. services, 1972—. Cons. sanitation operations and mgmt. Home: 10028 Milltrail Dallas TX 75238 Office: 2721 Municipal Dallas TX 75215

BISHOP, ROBERT JEFFERSON, lawyer, public relations cons, state ofcl.; b. Bishopville, Fla., Mar. 25, 1913; s. Stephen Ward and Archie (Mills) B.; B.S.A., U. Fla., 1935, LL.B., 1943; m. Edna Yacobian, June 1, 1939; children—Carol (Mrs. John J. Phifer), Judith (Mrs. Errol L. Greene). Admitted to Fla. bar, 1943, practiced law before state and fed. cts., 1943—; pub. relations counsel to chain store industry, Fla., 1944-48; exec. sec. Lawyers Title Guaranty Fund, 1948-49; exec. dir. Atlantic Union Com., Inc., 1949-50, bd. govs., 1950; dir. consumer services State of Fla.; exec. sec. Fla. Consumers Council. Chmn. Fla. Scholarship and Loan Commn. Designated One of 5 Outstanding Young Men in Fla., 1948. Mem. Am. Bar Assn., Fla. Bar, Am. Judicature Soc., Am. Acad. Polit. Sci., Tallahassee Jr., Fla. Jr. (pres. 1946-47), U.S. Jr. (v.p. 1947-48), Internat. Jr. (treas. 1948-49) chambers commerce, U. Fla. Alumni Assn. (v.p. 1943-52, pres., 1952), Fla. Blue Key, Alpha Gamma Rho. Alpha Zeta, Phi Alpha Delta. Democrat. Episcopalian. Mason (Shriner), Elk. Club: Rio Pinar Country. Home: 1215 Munster Av Orlando FL 32803 Office: State Capitol Tallahassee FL 32304

BISHOP, THOMAS RAY, mech. engr.; b. Hutchinson, Kan., Oct. 26, 1925; s. Orren E. and Myrtle (Dale) Bish; student California (Pa.) State Tchrs. Coll., 1947-48; B.S., U. Houston, 1953; postgrad. U. Wash., 1960-61; grad. Alexander Hamilton Bus. Inst., 1972; m. Mary Lou Nesmith, Sept. 1, 1951 children—Thomas Ray II, Frances Joann. Research engr. Boeing Co., Seattle, 1953-69, research engr. Apollo program, 1964-69; asst. chief engr. Product div. Bowen Tools, Inc., Houston, 1969—; pres. Bishop & Assos., mech. engring. consultants, Houston, 1970—. Precinct committeeman King County Democratic Com., 1960. Served with USMCR, 1944-46. Decorated Purple Heart; named Engr. of Year, Boeing Aerospace Co., 1966. Registered profl. engr., Ala., La., Tex. Mem. Tex. Soc. Profl. Engrs. Democrat. Unitarian. Mason. Contbr. articles to profl. jours. Home: 8411 Delwin St Houston TX 77034 Office: 2429 Crockett St Houston TX 77001

BISHOP, WILLIAM ERNEST, constrn. co. exec.; b. Melrose, Mass., July 24, 1910; s. Jerden Everett and Annie Blanche (Quimby) B.; B.S., Northeastern U., 1934; m. Kathryn M. Lane, Jan. 28, 1944; children—William L., Jerden A., Michael D., Thomas E., Kathryn A. Constrn. engr. Tidewater Constrn. Co., Norfolk, Va., 1935-46; dist. mgr. Texas Constrn. Co., Dallas, 1946-52; v.p., partner Gulf States Marine Constrn. Co., Beaumont, Tex., 1952-65; v.p. Tellepsen Constrn. Co., Houston, 1965, also dir. Instl. dir. Neches council Boy Scouts Am., 1961-64; mgr. Little League, Beaumont, 1962. Served with USNR, 1942-46. Mem. Am. Soc. C.E. (state bd. dirs. 1962, 64). Methodist. Home: 10934 Creektree Rd Houston TX 77070 Office: 1710 Telephone Rd Houston TX 77001

BISHOP, WILLIAM MERCER, cons. engr.; b. Quincy, Fla., Sept. 9, 1923; s. Nichols Mercer and Lessie (May) B.; B.C.E. cum laude, U. Fla., 1952; m. Martha Jean Thomas, Jan. 22, 1950; 1 dau., Jan Carole. Asst. resident engr. Fla. State U., Tallahassee, 1952, 53-55; asst. project engr. Cobb Constrn. Co., Tampa, 1953, Bishop & Coloney, Tallahassee, 1955-56; partner Barrett, Daffin & Bishop, Tallahassee, 1957-66; owner William M. Bishop Cons. Engrs., Tallahassee, 1966—. Sec.-treas. Fla. Bd. Profl. Engrs. and Land Surveyors, 1973—. Served to 1st sgt. F.A. AUS, 1943-46. Decorated Bronze Star. Mem. Fla. Engring. Soc. (pres. 1972-73), Cons. Engrs. Fla. (chmn. 1968-69), Am. Water Works Assn., Water Pollution Control Fedn., Am. Pub. Health Assn., Phi Kappa Phi, Chi Epsilon. Elk. Office: PO Box 3407 Tallahassee FL 32303

BISNO, ALAN LESTER, physician; b. Memphis, Sept. 28, 1936; s. Ralph and Rosella (Katz) B.; B.A., Princeton, 1958; M.D., Washington U., St. Louis, 1962; m. Barbara Klearman, Aug. 11, 1963; children—Susan Naomi, Neal Joseph. Intern Vanderbilt U. Hosp., Nashville, 1962-63, resident in internal medicine, 1963-65; fellow in infectious diseases dept. medicine U. Tenn., Memphis, 1968-69, asst. prof. medicine, 1969-71, asso. prof. medicine, 1971—, chief sect. infectious diseases, 1969—; attending staff City Memphis Hosps.; cons. staff Bapt. Meml. Hosp., Memphis. Served with Epidemic Intelligence Service, USPHS, 1965-68. Diplomate Am. Bd. Med. Examiners, Am. Bd. Internal Medicine (subsplty. infectious diseases). Fellow A.C.P. (teaching and research scholar 1969-72); mem. Infectious Diseases Soc. Am., Central Soc. for Clin. Research, So. Soc. for Clin. Investigation, Memphis and Mid-South Med. Soc., Tenn. Med. Assn., Phi Beta Kappa. Contbr. articles to med. jours.; also chpts. to text-books. Home: 4483 Charleswood Rd Memphis TN 38117 Office: 951 Court Av Room 241-D Memphis TN 38163

BISPLINGHOFF, DONALD MORRIS, metals co. exec.; b. Orlando, Fla., Feb. 20, 1935; s. Henry Sun and Alma Irene (Mathis) B.; student U. Fla., 1953-55; m. Cynthia Ann Ziock, Sept. 1, 1956; children—Ann, Donald Morris, Lyn, Robert E., Dave. Touring golf profl., 1958-63; research and devel. dir. Tremont Corp., Atlanta, Covington, La., 1963-68; pres., chief operating officer Adcom Metals Co., Container Wire Products Co., Jacksonville, Fla., 1968—. Served with AUS. Mem. Ind. Wire Drawer Assn. Am. (sr. v.p. 1973—), Am. Wire Assn. (regional bd. mem. 1970-73), U. Fla. Alumni Assn. Republican. Clubs: Hidden Hills Country, Ponte Vedra Country (Jacksonville, Fla.). Home: 7258 Trails End Jacksonville FL 32211 Office: 925 N Lane Av Jacksonville FL 32211

BISSET, NORMA BLAKELY (MRS. JOHN BISSET), dept. store exec.; b. Joliet, Ill., Jan. 12, 1924; d. King and Florence (Samuelson) Salle; degree, Joliet Jr. Coll., 1942; degree, Northwestern Bus. Coll., 1944; m. John W. Bisset, Dec. 12, 1965; 1 dau. (by previous marriage), Billie Blakely (Mrs. Harvey L. Miller). Buyer, Davison Paxon Dept. Store, Atlanta, 1950-53; buyer, mgr. Boston Store, Joliet, Ill., 1953-56; owner Blakely's Dept. Stores, Taylorville, Ill. and Ft. Pierce, Fla., 1956—; pres. Blakewood Realty Corp., Chgo., 1961—; pres. Blake-Bisset Corp., Chgo. Trustee George O. Blakely Trust. Episcopalian. Mem. Order Eastern Star. Clubs: Lighthouse Point Yacht and Tennis (Pompano Beach, Fla.), Boca Raton (Fla.) Hotel. Home: 2204 Bay Dr Pompano Beach FL 33062 Office: 124 N 2d St Ft Pierce FL 33450

BISSON, WHEELOCK ALEXANDER, physician; b. Key West, Fla., 1898; s. George Henry and Sarah Jane (Kemp) B.; B.S., Fla. A. and M.U., 1922; M.D., Meharry Med. Coll., 1929; m. Maude Lee Voorhies, June 2, 1930. Intern, Royal Circle Hosp., Memphis, 1931-33; gen. practice, Memphis, 1931—; clinician Memphis and Shelby County Health Dept., 1932—. Named Tenn. Doctor of the year by Vol. State Med. Assn., 1962, 63; recipient Citation, Key to City, Memphis and Shelby County Health Dept., 1965; practioner of yr. award Nat. Med. Assn., 1967. Fellow Royal Soc. Health; mem. Am. Thoracic Soc., A.A.A.S., Nat. Pub. Health Assn., Nat. Rehab. Assn., N.A.A.C.P. (life), Internat. Platform Assn., Tenn. Acad. Sci., Am., Tenn. State, Nat. (2d v.p. 1966-68, nat. sickle cellanemia com.), The Vol. State (1st v.p. 1965) med. assns., Bluff City (sec.), Memphis and Shelby County med. socs. Elk (past state pres.). Address: 2312 Park Av Memphis TN 38114

BITNER, GEORGE E., lawyer; b. Fort Harrison, Ind., Sept. 16, 1939; s. Robert Eugene and Anna Jane (Stephen) B.; A.B., Ohio Wesleyan U., 1961; J.D., George Washington U., 1964; m. Sally Ann Overly, June 16, 1962; children—James Edward, Julia Ann. Admitted to Va. bar, 1964, D.C. bar, 1965; asso. mem. firm Kinney, Smith & Barham, Arlington, Va., 1964-67, partner, 1967—. Mem. Falls Church (pres. 1968-69, chmn. bd. 1969-70), Va. (life) jr. chambers commerce, Phi Alpha Theta, Phi Kappa Psi. Presbyn. (deacon). Home: 10421 Adel Rd Oakton VA 22124 Office: 6521 Arlington Blvd PO Box 2137 Falls Church VA 22042

BIVANS, RICHARD WILLIAM, govt. ofcl.; b. Ft. Lauderdale, Fla., July 3, 1929; s. William Weaver and Effa Beth (Brendla) B.; B.E.E., U. Fla., 1955; m. Helen C. Tudder, Mar. 5, 1955; children—Richard William, Carolyn, Roger. Electronics engr. Radiation, Inc., Melbourne, Fla., 1955-62; with NASA, Kennedy Space Center, Fla., 1962—, chief telemetry br., 1972—. Served with AUS, 1951-52. Mem. I.E.E.E. Home: 2290 Grove St Titusville FL 32780 Office: In-Tel-1 NASA Kennedy Space Center FL 32899

BIVINS, DANIEL EUGENE, III, univ. adminstr.; b. Monroe, La., July 14, 1932; s. Daniel Eugene and Carmen (Anderson) B.; B.A., La. State U., 1954, postgrad., 1957, 60; postgrad. U. Chgo., 1955; m. Claudia Faye Atkins, Feb. 5, 1971; children (by previous marriage)—Barbara, Stephan, Lawrence; stepchildren—Jeffrey, Christie. Reporter, Monroe Morning World, 1956, Baton Rouge Morning Adv., 1957; with sales promotion dept. Caterpillar Tractor Co., Peoria, Ill., 1957; sales promotion mgr. Boyce-Harvey Machinery, Inc., Baton Rouge, 1958; asst. dir. alumni affairs La. State U., Baton Rouge, 1959-67, dir. alumni affairs, 1968-72, dir. univ. relations, 1972—, sec. La. State U. Found., 1972—; exec. dir. La. State U. Alumni Fedn., 1968-72. Bd. dirs. A.R.C., 1965-72, chmn. pub. information, 1965-66, treas., 1968-69; bd. dirs. Greater Baton Rouge Safety Council, 1966-69. Served with AUS, 1954-56. Recipient editorial awards Am. Alumni Council, 1962, 64, 65, 67, Alumni Adminstr. Yr. award 1972. Mem. Sigma Delta Chi, Omicron Delta Kappa (dir. alumni 1969-71), Phi Kappa Phi, Sigma Chi, Phi Sigma Iota, Pi Alpha Mu. Roman Catholic. Rotarian (chmn. Rotaract 1969-70, chmn. Rotary Found. 1972-73). Home: 10869 Goodwood Blvd Ct Baton Rouge LA 70815

BIXBY, TAMS, III, publishing co. exec.; b. Muskogee, Okla., Dec. 10, 1918; s. Tams and Esther (Bailey) B.; student U. Pa., 1938; m. Oleta Belle Roller, Jan. 21, 1962; 1 son, Tams IV. With Okla. Press

Pub. Co., Muskogee, 1946—, gen. mgr., 1955-70, pres., 1970—; with Springfield Newspapers, Inc., 1949—, v.p., 1970—, gen. mgr., 1970—, dir., 1941— dir. Okla. Printing Co., 1942-71, pres., 1970-71; dir. Phoenix Improvement Co., 1942—, pres., 1970—; dir. Springfield TV. Co., 1st Nat. Bank. Chmn. Muskogee Met. Area Planning Commn., 1960-63; pres. Muskogee County Polio Found., 1949-59; chmn. Muskogee County chpt. A.R.C., 1956-58, Nat. vice-chmn., 1959; gen. chmn. Muskogee United Fund, 1955; chmn. Urban Renewal, 1969—. Bd. dirs. Okla. Med. Research Found., Okla. Crippled Childrens Soc. Served with USAAF, 1941-45. Mem. A.P., So. Newspaper Pubs. Assn. (dir. 1967-69, pres. 1973-74), Am. Newspaper Pubs. Assn., Muskogee C. of C. (dir. 1961-69), Newcomen Soc., Am. Legion, V.F.W. Republican. Episcopalian (warden 1971-72). Kiwanian. Clubs: Muskogee Country (pres. 1971-73), Southern Hills Country (Tulsa); Hickory Hills Country (Springfield, Mo.). Home: Route 3 Box 129 Muskogee OK 74401 Office: PO Box 1968 Muskogee OK 74401

BJELETICH, DAN, helicopter co. exec.; b. Bileca, Yugoslavia, Jan. 29, 1925; s. George Peter and Angea (Lalich) B.; B.B.A., U. Okla., 1953; m. Marguerite M.E. Gauthier, Apr. 20, 1946; 1 dau., Cheryl Lynn. Civilian personnel adminstr. Rhein-Main AFB, Frankfort, Germany, 1946-50; sr. accountant Arthur Andersen & Co., 1953-59; mgr. budgets and finance Bell Helicopter Co., Fort Worth, 1959—. Served to 1st lt. AUS, 1943-46. C.P.A., Tex., Okla. Mem. Planning Execs. Inst., Beta Gamma Sigma, Phi Eta Sigma, Delta Sigma Pi. Republican. Presbyn. (elder 1958—, deacon 1958—). Home: 1501 Shady Creek Euless TX 76039 Office: PO Box 482 Fort Worth TX 76101

BJORK, PAUL ANDREW, hosp. adminstr.; b. Sterling, Ill., Mar. 1, 1919; s. Otto Victor and Julia (Buckley) B.; student Milw. State Tchrs. Coll., 1939-40; B.S., Marquette U., 1949; m. Laura Jean Scovel, Dec. 23, 1942; children—Donald, Laura, Barbara, Cynthia. Asst. adminstr. Kenosha (Wis.) Hosp., 1949-52; adminstr. Community Gen. Hosp., Sterling, Ill., 1952-59; exec. dir. Oak Ridge Hosp. of Methodist Ch., 1959-67, Methodist Hosp., New Orleans, 1967—. Adj. asst. prof., dept. health services Tulane U.; pres. New Orleans Hosp. Council. Trustee New Orleans Hosp. Service Assn. (Blue Cross). Preceptor George Washington U. Served to 1st lt. AUS, 1941-46. Fellow Am. Coll. Hosp. Adminstrs., Royal Soc. Health-Eng.; mem. Tenn. (dir. 1965-67), Ill. (dir. 1957-59), La. (dir.) hosp. assns. Home: 13018 Deauville Ct New Orleans LA 70129 Office: 5620 Read Blvd New Orleans LA 70127

BLACH, HAROLD BOWMAN, JR., retail exec.; b. Birmingham, Ala., Oct. 29, 1931; s. Harold Bowman and Alice (Wilzin) B.; B.A., U. Ala., 1955; m. Joan Adah Baim, Mar. 24, 1956. With J. Blach & Sons, Inc.; dir. 1st Fed. Savs. & Loan Ala., Mid-South Co., Inc., Birmingham; mem. adv. bd. So. area 1st Nat. Bank Birmingham, 1967—. Bd. visitors U. Ala. Coll. Commerce and Bus. Adminstrn. U. Ala., 1972—. Bd. dirs. Birmingham Bapt. Hosps. Found., Arthritis and Rheumatism Found., Spastic Aid Ala., Jewish Community Center, Operation New Birmingham, Birmingham Better Bus. Bur. Served to capt. USAF, 1955-57. Mem. U. Ala. Alumni Assn. (exec. com. 1962—), Newcomen Soc., Zeta Beta Tau. Kiwanian. Jewish religion. Clubs: Monday Morning Quarterback, Touchdown, Club, Relay House, Downtown, Pine Tree Golf and Country. Home: 3931 Knollwood Dr Birmingham AL 35243 Office: 1928 3d Av N Birmingham AL 35203

BLACK, ALBERT SCOTT, advt. agy. exec.; b. Bryan, Tex., Oct. 8, 1923; s. John William and Mattie Belle (Scott) B.; student U. Ga., 1942-43, Tex. A. and M. U., 1941-46; m. Marilyn Hammer, Sept. 7, 1944; children—Barbara, Scott, Patricia. Prodn. mgr. Geizendanner Co., 1946-48; account exec. Wallace Davis & Co., 1948-49; pres. A.S. Black & Co., Inc., 1949-62; v.p. Glenn Advt., Inc., Houston, 1963-69; pres. First Marketing Group, Inc., 1969—. Trustee St. Stephens Episcopal Sch., Austin, Tex.; bd. dirs. Harris County A.R.C. Served with USNR, 1943-45. Decorated D.F.C., Air medal with 2 oak leaf clusters. Mem. Am. Assn. Advt. Agys. (gov. central region 1962-65), Houston C. of C. (chmn. aviation com.). Episcopalian (sr. warden). Mason. Club: Memorial Drive Country (pres. 1961-62). Home: 7603 Del Monte St Houston TX 77042 Office: 1535 W. Loop South Houston TX 77027

BLACK, BARBARA ONDERCHEK (MRS. FRANK SNYDER BLACK), urologist; b. Jamaica, N.Y., Oct. 24, 1940; d. George Stephen and Irene Elizabeth (Gaydos) Onderchek; B.A., Trinity Coll., 1962; M.D., Georgetown U., 1966; m. Frank Snyder Black, Jr., July 12, 1969; 1 son, Frank Snyder III. Intern, Georgetown U. Hosp., Washington, 1966-67, resident in gen. surgery, 1967-68, resident in urology, 1968-71; clin. instr. urology George Washington Med. Center, Washington, 1971—. Mem. A.A.A.S., Am. Med. Women's Assn., Am. Assn. U. Women, D.C. Med. Soc., Washington Urol. Soc. Republican. Roman Catholic. Home: 5603 Durbin Rd Bethesda MD 20014 Office: 4900 Massachusetts Av NW Washington DC 20016

BLACK, BRUCE JEFFRIES, elec. engr.; b. Orange, N.J., July 6, 1936; s. John Eldridge and Helen (Bode) B.; B.E.E., U. Fla., 1964, postgrad. Holland Law Center, 1971-72; m. Mary Preston Gray, Aug. 15, 1963; children—Bruce Jeffries, Mary Katherine. Engr., RCA Missile Test Project, Patrick AFB, Fla., 1964-66; engr. Louis A. King, Cons. Engrs., Bristol, Tenn., 1966-67; design engr. Gen. Space Systems, Tampa, Fla., 1967-71; sr. engr. Electronic Communications, Inc., St. Petersburg, Fla., 1972—. Chmn., Largo adv. com. Tampa Bay Regional Planning Council, 1973—. Served with U.S. Army, 1958-60. Mem. I.E.E.E., Am. Radio Relay League, Phi Alpha Delta. Republican. Presbyn. (elder). Home: 1860 Harmony Dr Clearwater FL 33516 Office: 1501 72d St N St Petersburg FL 33733

BLACK, CHARLES ALVIN, cons. engr.; b. Gainesville, Fla., July 7, 1920; s. Alvin Percy and Lillian Barnes (Russell) B.; B.S., U. Fla., 1947; m. Elizabeth Beck, Sept. 12, 1943; children—Charles Russell, Elizabeth Ann. Pres. Black, Crow and Eidsness of Ga.; sr. v.p. Black, Crow & Eidness, Inc., 1950—. San. engr. USPHS, 1959—; mem. Fla. Gov.'s Task Force for Water, Minerals and Solid Fuels for Civil. Served AUS, 1944-45. Recipient U.S.A. citation for outstanding pub. service. Registered profl. engr., Fla., Ga., S.C., Ala., Kan. Diplomate Am. Acad. Environmental Engrs. Mem. Am. Water Works Assn. (chmn. purification div. 1951, chmn. Fla. sect. 1962; George Warren Fuller award 1961, nat. dir. 1966—, nat. v.p. 1969-70, nat. pres. 1971-72), Cons. Engrs. Council, Cons. Engrs. Fla., Am. Soc. C.E., Royal Soc. Health, Nat. Soc. Profl. Engrs., Am. Pub. Health Assn., Internat. Water Supply Assn., Internat. Assn. Water Pollution Research, Fla. Pollution Control Assn., Soc. Am. Mil. Engrs., Alpha Tau Omega. Episcopalian. Elk. Contbr. articles to profl. jours. Home: 2941 NW 21st Av Gainesville FL 32601 Office: SE 3d St Gainesville FL 32601

BLACK, CLARENCE ERVIN, physician; b. Bamberg, S.C., Sept. 25, 1915; s. Clarence Ervin and Leonard (Folk) B.; B.S., The Citadel, 1936; A.B., Mercer U., 1939; M.D., U. Ga., 1943; m. Carol Moore, Jan. 5, 1944; 1 dau., Carolyn. Intern, USPHS Hosp., New Orleans, 1943; resident in radiology Ochsner Found., New Orleans, 1947-50; practice medicine specializing in radiology, New Orleans, 1943—; dir. dept. radiology and nuclear medicine West Jefferson Gen. Hosp., Marrero, La.; vis. faculty Tulane U. Med. Sch., New Orleans. Served with M.C., AUS, World War II. Diplomate Am. Bd. Radiology. Mem. A.M.A., Am. Coll. Radiologists, La., Jefferson Parish med. socs., Alpha Kappa Kappa, Kappa Alpha. Club: Southern Yacht (bd. dirs.) (New Orleans). Home: 434 Pine St New Orleans LA 70118 Office: 4520 Wichers Dr Marrero LA 70072

BLACK, CRAIG CALL, museum dir., educator; b. Peking, China, May 28, 1932 (parents U.S. citizens); s. Arthur Proctor and Mary (Nichols) B.; grad. Kent Sch., 1950; A.B., Amherst Coll., 1954, A.M., 1957; postgrad. (Simpson fellow) Johns Hopkins, 1954-55; Ph.D. (Kellog fellow, NIH fellow), Harvard, 1962; m. Constance Elizabeth Hockenberry, May 26, 1967; children—Lorna Varn, Christopher Arthur. Geologist, Okla. Geol. Survey, Norman, summer 1956; asso. curator vertebrate fossils Carnegie Mus., Pitts., 1960-62, curator, 1962-70; asso. prof. dept. systematics and ecology U. Kan., Lawrence, 1970-72; mus. dir., prof. geoscis. Tex. Technol. U., Lubbock, 1972—. Mem. mus. adv. panel Tex. Arts and Humanities Council, 1973—. NSF grantee 1963-73; Gulf Oil Corp., 1963-70; Nat. Geog. Soc. grantee, 1973-74. Fellow Geol. Soc. Am., Linnaen Soc. London; mem. Am. Soc. Mammalogists, Soc. for Study Evolution, Soc. Vertebrate Paleontology (sec.-treas. 1967-69, v.p. 1969-70, pres. 1970-71), Soc. Systematic Zoologists, Ranch Hdqrs. Assn. (dir.), W. Tex. Mus. Assn. (dir.), Sigma Xi. Contbr. articles to profl. jours. Home: 4502 15th St Lubbock TX 79416

BLACK, DAVID LUTHER, research inst. exec.; b. Plainview, Tex., Apr. 3, 1934; s. Mac Truman and Wilma Louise (Bailey) B.; A.B., Baylor U., 1954; postgrad. U. Tex., 1956-59; m. Julia Virginia Williams, Nov. 17, 1956; stepchildren—Barry Snell, Whitfield Snell; 1 son, R. David. Asso. dir. exec. devel. program U. Tex., 1957-59; asst. dir. pub. relations S.W. Research Inst., San Antonio, 1959-64, dir. spl. programs, 1967-72, dir. spl. programs, also asst. to the pres., 1972—; dir. pub. relations HemisFair 1968, 1964-65; pres. David Black & Assos., 1965-67. Cons. UN Indsl. Devel. Orgn., Vienna, Austria, 1971—, UNESCO, 1974—; mem. UN mission to Latin Am., 1972—. Bd. dirs. Planned Parenthood Assn., 1966-69; bd. dirs. San Antonio Chamber Music Soc., pres., 1972—; bd. dirs. First Repertory Theater, San Antonio. Mem. A.A.A.S., Am. Soc. for Metals, Nat. Assn. Sci. Writers. Episcopalian. Contbr. articles to profl. jours. Home: 213 Allen St San Antonio TX 78209 Office: Box 28510 San Antonio TX 78284

BLACK, INA GRIFFITH, pharmacist, educator; b. Mulvane, Kan., Jan. 30, 1906; d. George Clarence and Pearl (Shade) Griffith; Ph.C., U. Okla., 1927, B.S., 1930, M.S., 1931; m. Joseph Brundidge Black, Nov. 8, 1944 (dec. June 1966). Tchr. Sch. Pharmacy, U. Okla., Norman, 1929-44; pharmacist Liberty Drug Store, Chickasha, Okla., 1945-50, Owl Pharmacy, Chickasha, 1950-54, Green's Prescription Shop, Chickasha, 1954-61; asso. prof. pharmacy Southwestern State Coll. Sch. Pharmacy, Weatherford, 1961—, asso. dean Sch. Pharmacy, 1970—. Co-chmn. pharmacists fund-raising campaign for Okla. Med. Research, 1952. Recipient award for service to pharmacy Okla. U. Alumni Assn., 1959, Grad. award Kappa Psi. Mem. Okla. Pharm. Assn. (exec. council), P.E.O., Sigma Xi, Rho Chi (past nat. sec.), Iota Sigma Pi, Phi Sigma, Lambda Kappa Sigma, Alpha Xi Delta. Methodist (ofcl. bd.). Contbr. articles to profl. jours. Home: 715 Eureka St Weatherford OK 73096

BLACK, JAMES MILTON, lawyer; b. Port Arthur, Tex., Apr. 13, 1942; s. Earl Milton and Lola Mae (Fuller) B.; B.A., U. Tex., 1964, LL.B., 1967; m. Judith Nan Oxford, Feb. 4, 1967; children—William Oxford, James Robert, John Milton. Admitted to Tex. bar, 1966; law clk. to judge U.S. Dist. Ct. for Eastern Tex., 1966-67; practiced in Port Arthur, 1967—; mem. firm Black & Black, 1969—. Dir. First Savs. Assn., Port Neches, Tex. Bd. dirs. South Jefferson County Civic Center Authority and Community Concert Assn., South Jefferson County unit Am. Cancer Soc. Mem. Am., Port Arthur (pres. 1971), Jefferson County (dir. 1970) bar assns., State Bar Tex., Am. Judicature Soc., Phi Gamma Delta. Episcopalian. Rotarian (dir. North Port Arthur 1973—). Club: Port Arthur. Home: 4250 Forest Dr Port Arthur TX 77640 Office: PO Box 3286 Port Arthur TX 77640

BLACK, JOE WILLIAM, JR., physician; b. Knoxville, Tenn., Nov. 29, 1933; s. Joe William and Jeannette (Armstrong) B.; M.D., U. Tenn., 1957; m. Shirley Jean Tindell, June 8, 1954; children—Jan Marie, Joe William III, Steven Edward, David Thomas. Intern, U. Tenn. Meml. Research Center and Hosp., 1958, resident in pediatrics, 1960; resident in pediatrics Tobey Children's Hosp., 1959; practice medicine specializing in pediatrics, Knoxville, 1963—; mem. staff, asso. prof. pediatrics U. Tenn. Med. Research Center and Hosp. at Knoxville, 1963—; mem. staff St. Mary's, Ft. Sanders Presbyn., Children's hosps. Served with USAF, 1960-62. Fellow Am. Acad. Pediatrics; mem. A.M.A., Knoxville Acad. Medicine, Tenn. Pediatric Soc., U. Tenn. Pres.'s Club. Home: 2945 Walkup Dr Knoxville TN 37918 Office: 4741 N Broadway Knoxville TN 37918

BLACK, JOHN ALEXANDER III, accountant; b. Washington, July 28, 1946; s. John Alexander, Jr. and Gladys (Champe) B.; B.B.A., U. Houston, 1969; m. Carolyn Louise Bergen, May 29, 1970. Accountant, G.C. Branom & Co., C.P.A.'s, Houston, 1969-71, Masquelette, Bruhl & Co., C.P.A.'s, Houston, 1971-72, Coopers & Lybrand, C.P.A.'s, Houston, 1972—. Served with AUS, 1964. Mem. Am. Inst. C.P.A.'s, Tex. Soc. C.P.A.'s (Houston chpt.). Home: 5754 Firenza St Houston TX 77035 Office: 1010 Jefferson St Houston TX 77002

BLACK, RALPH, ballet mgr.; b. Knoxville, Tenn., July 11, 1919; s. Ernest Watson and Margaret Marie (Caston) B.; B.S., Houghton Coll., 1941; m. Eva Landsberger, Aug. 1, 1950; children—Johana, Eric, Ralph, Dean. Gen. mgr. Chattanooga Symphony, 1950-51, Buffalo Philharmonic, 1951-55, Nat. Symphony, 1955-60, Balt. Symphony, 1960-63, Nat. Ballet, Washington, 1963-73; exec. dir. Am. Symphony Orch. League, Vienna, Va., 1973—. Mem. Am. Symphony Orch. League (v.p. 1954-60), N.Am. Ballet Assn. (pres. 1963-73), Assn. Am. Dance Cos. (founding chmn. 1965), Major Dance Cos. Conf. (chmn. 1972-73), Am. Guild Mus. Artists (trustee). Club: Congressional Country (Bethesda, Md.). Home: 7005 Winslow St Bethesda MD 20034 Office: Box 66 Vienna VA 22180

BLACK, RALPH POWELL, city mgr.; b. Pulaski, Va., July 20, 1921; s. Ernst Glen and Jennie Lewis (Powell) B.; student pub. schs., Nat. Bus. Coll. Internat. City Mgmt. Assn.; m. Mildred Virginia Webster, Aug. 4, 1942; children—Ralph Powell, Susan Patricia, Maud Ellen, Caroline Lee, Kathryn Page. Mgr. Vets. Housing Authority, Roanoke, Va., 1946-50; asst. to city mgr. Alexandria, Va., 1950; city mgr. Jasper, Ala., 1951-53, Athens, Tenn., 1953-55, Aiken, S.C., 1955-58, Dothan, Ala., 1958-60, Florence, S.C., 1960-73, Sumter, S.C., 1973—. Mem. Smoky Mountain council Boy Scouts Am. Served as comdr. USNR. Mem. Christian Bus. Men's Com. (past chmn.), Internat. (past pres.) city mgrs. assns., Am. Acad. Polit. and Social Sci., Nat. Inst. Govt. Purchasing, Municipal Finance Officers Assn., A.I.M., S.C. Municipal League, Jr. C. of C. (past pres.), Res. Officers Assn. U.S. (pres. S.C. dept. 1972-73, mem. nat. council 1973-74). Baptist. Rotarian. Mem. editorial bd. Am. Security Council. Home: 737 Ingram St Sumter SC 29150 Office: City Hall Sumter SC 29150

BLACK, RICHARD LAWRENCE, county ofcl.; b. Butler, Pa., Dec. 22, 1919; s. Chester Leroy and Hazel (Thompson) B.; student U. Pitts., 1949; A.B., Grove City Coll., 1948; M.G.A., U. Pa., 1950; m. Dorothy Isobel Rumbaugh, Aug. 31, 1943; children—Lawrence Elliott, Richard Gregory, Virginia Louise. Asst. to county mgr. Montgomery County, Rockville, Md., 1949-51; village adminstr., Bronxville, N.Y., 1951-54; city adminstr., Englewood, N.J., 1954-61; city mgr. Webster Groves, Mo., 1961-68; county mgr. Charleston County, Charleston, S.C., 1968—. Served to capt. USAAF, 1942-46. Mem. Internat. City Mgmt. Assn., Municipal Finance Officers Assn., Am. Soc. Pub. Adminstrs. Home: 113 Manchester Rd Charleston SC 29407 Office: 2 Courthouse Square Charleston SC 29401

BLACK, ROY WILLIS, clergyman, navy chaplain; b. ElDorado, Okla., Oct. 31, 1928; s. Charles Gustif and Mary Alice (Bandy) B.; A.A., Altus Coll., 1949; Th.B., Th.M., Am. Bible Coll., 1951, Th.D., 1956; B.A., Okla. Bapt. U., 1953; B.D., Central Bapt. Sem., 1958; M.A., Goddard Coll., 1972; m. Dorothy Edna Driggers, Dec. 14, 1947; children—Deborah, Carrie, Jennifer. Ordained to ministry Bapt. Ch., 1947; pastor Southside Bapt. Ch., Altus, Okla., 1947-49, Olive Bapt. Ch., Drumright, Okla., 1949-51; social worker Juvenile Detention Home, Kansas City, Kan., 1954-56; pastor First Bapt. Ch., Gallatin, Mo., 1956-59, St. James Episcopal Ch., Springfield, Mo., 1959-61, Ch. of Good Shepherd, Kansas City, Mo., 1961-64; commd. lt. USN, 1964, advanced through grades to lt. comdr., 1966; chaplain Destroyer Squadron 23, 1964-66, Hdqrs. USMC, 1966-68, Vietnam, 1969; ministry to bereaved families and burials Arlington Nat. Cemetery, 1970-72; chaplain, psychologist Navy Alcohol Rehab. Center, Norfolk, Va., 1972—. Decorated Vietnamese Cross of Gallantry. Mem. Acad. Certified Social Workers, Am. Assn. Marriage and Family Counselors, Soc. for Sci. Study Sex, Inst. Bio-energetic Analysis, Nat. Assn. Social Workers, Assn. for Humanistic Psychology, Bio-feedback Research Soc., Internat. Soc. for Profl. Hypnosis. Home: 549 Longfellow Av Virginia Beach VA 23462 Office: Naval Rehab Center Bldg J50 Naval Sta Norfolk VA 23511

BLACK, SHELTON GLENN, chem. co. exec.; b. Greggton, Tex., Dec. 24, 1931; s. Grandison Dee and Faira Jewel (Weldon) B.; B.S. in Agr., Tex. A. and M. U., 1953, M.S. in Agronomy, 1958; m. Ethel Marie Fountain, June 20, 1953; children—Teresa Lynn, Doyle Glenn, Keith Layne. Agronomist, Tex. A. and M. U., 1958-61; v.p. sales Am. Humates, Inc., Dallas, 1962-66; with Allied Chem. Corp., Houston, 1966—; now asst. gen. mgr. Texgas Corp. subsidiary, Sarasota, Fla. Served to capt. AUS, 1953-55. Mason. Home: 2908 Post Rd Sarasota FL 33581 Office: PO Box 1658 Sarasota FL 33578

BLACK, WILLIAM ELMER, economist; b. Moxahala, O., June 3, 1915; s. Frank and Barbara (Komyate) B.; student Cleve. Coll., 1934; B.S., Ohio State U., 1938; M.S., Cornell U., 1940, Ph.D., 1942; m. Olive Rose Bischoff, June 26, 1948; children—Jeffrey, Jennifer, Randal, Renee. Gen. mgr. Cash Crops Co-op., Wis., 1949-51; gen. mgr. Fla. Tomato Com., 1955-59; dir. econ. and marketing research Fla. Citrus Commn., 1959-67; economist marketing and policy Tex. Agr. Extension Service, Tex. A. and M. U., College Station, 1967—. Asso. coordinator Tex. Agrl. Marketing Research and Devel. Center; grad. faculty Tex. A. and M. U. Chmn. So. Extension marketing com. Tex. Agrl. Extension Marketing Staff, So. Regional Agrl. Outlook Workshop. Bd. dirs. Brazos County Fed. Employees Credit Union. Served to capt. AUS, World War II; to maj., Korean War. Danforth fellow, 1937. Mem. Am. Agrl. Economists Assn., So. Economists Assn., Am. Marketing Assn., Found. for Econ. Edn., Alpha Zeta, Gamma Sigma Delta, Phi Kappa Phi. Presbyn. (deacon, elder). Club: Sertoma (Lakeland, Fla.). Editor-in-chief Ag Student, 1937-38. Contbr. articles to profl. jours. Home: 3805 Courtney Circle Bryan TX 77801 Office: 107B Agr Bldg Tex A and M U College Station TX 77843

BLACKARD, WILLIAM GRIFFITH, physician; b. Balt., July 14, 1933; s. Embree Hoss and Margaret Lounsbury (Griffith) B.; M.D., Duke, 1957; m. Attelia Shealy, Oct. 1, 1960; children—Harriet Attelia, William Griffith, Kirland Lounsbury. Intern, N.Y. Hosp., N.Y.C., 1957-58, resident, 1958-59; resident fellow Duke Med. Center, 1960-64; instr. La. State U. Med. Center, New Orleans, 1964-65, asst. prof., 1965-68, asso. prof., 1968-72, prof., 1972—. Vis. prof U. Geneva, 1971-72. Served with USPHS, 1961-63. Markle Found. scholar, 1968—; Sinsheimer Found. award, 1971—; NIH fellow, 1971. Mem. Am. Soc. Clin. Investigation, Am. Fedn. Clin. Research (pres. So. sect. 1973-74), So. Soc. Clin. Investigations, Endocrine Soc., Am. Diabetes Assn., Sigma Xi, Kappa Alpha. New Orleans Lawn Tennis Assn. Methodist. Contbr. articles and reviewer numerous sci. jours. Home: 1309 Cadiz St New Orleans LA 70115

BLACKBURN, BENJAMIN BENTLEY, III, congressman; b. Atlanta, Feb. 14, 1927; s. Benjamin Bentley, Jr. and Sara (Medlock) B.; B.A., U. N.C., 1947; LL.B., Emory U., 1954; m. Mary A. Pandora, 1952; children—Michael, Robert, Kathryn, David. Admitted to Ga. bar, 1954; practiced in Atlanta, 1956-66; mem. staff Atty. Gen. Ga., 1955-56; partner firm Peck, Whaley & Blackburn, 1963-66; mem. 90th-93d congresses from 4th Dist. Ga., 1966—. Mem. DeKalb County Republican Exec. Com., 1964-67; sec. 4th Congl. Dist. Rep. Exec. Com., 1966-67. Served with USNR, 1944-46, 50-52. Mem. Am. Ga., Atlanta bar assns., Phi Delta Phi. Episcopalian. Optimist. Club: Lawyers (Atlanta). Home: 9603 Hillridge Dr Kensington MD 20795 Office: Longworth House Office Bldg Washington DC 20515

BLACKBURN, EULESS BERTRAM, JR., educator; b. Decatur, Tex., Aug. 4, 1919; s. Euless Bertram and Annie (Baughier) B.; student Decatur Bapt. Coll., 1937-39; B.S., N. Tex. State U., 1941; M.Ed., Hardin-Simmons U., 1952; Ed.D., U. Colo., 1962; m. Verginia Scruggs, Nov. 19, 1941; children—Velva Ruth, Bert. Tchr. Blooming Grove (Tex.) Ind. Sch. Dist., 1941-42; elementary prin. Forsan (Tex.) Ind. Sch. Dist., 1942-43; civilian mgr. Post Exchange, Big Spring (Tex.) Bombardier Sch., 1943-46; chief clk. Kimball-Midland (Tex.) Co. 1946-47; prin. supr. Big Spring (Tex.) Ind. Sch. Dist., 1947-49, Ballinger (Tex.) Ind. Sch. Dist., 1949-62; prof. edn. Lamar U., Beaumont, Tex., 1962-69, dean Coll. Grad. Studies, 1969—. Cons. remedial reading program S. Park Ind. Sch. Dist., Beaumont, 1966—, Silsbee (Tex.) Ind. Sch. Dist., 1966—. Mem. Tex. Soc. Coll. Profs. Edn., Tex. Assn. Coll. Tchrs. (chpt. pres. 1967-68), Tex. Elementary Prin. and Suprs. Assn., Tex. Assn. for improvement of Reading, Kappa Delta Pi, Phi Delta Kappa. Home: 6350 Arrowhead Dr Beaumont TX 77707

BLACKBURN, JOHN GILL, neurophysiologist; b. Lake Charles, La., June 25, 1935; s. Frank Canfield and Catherine Jewel (Gill) B.; B.S., Tulane U., 1959, Ph.D., 1965; m. Shirley Dee Bradford, June 29, 1956; children—John Bradford, Steven Canfield. Instr. in physiology Med. U. S.C., Charleston, 1964-67, asso. in physiology, 1967-68, asst. prof. physiology, 1968—. Committeeman, Boy Scouts Am., 1970-73; mem. Civil Air Patrol, 1967-73. NIH pre-doctoral fellow, 1962-64; NSF summer fellow, 1967; recipient several research grants. Mem. A.A.A.S., S.C. Acad. Sci., Digital Equipment Computers Users Soc., Am. Assn. U. Profs., Sigma Xi. Episcopalian. Contbr. articles to sci. jours. Home: 707 London Dr Charleston SC 29412

BLACKBURN, MELVILLE CAMPBELLE, lawyer; b. Junction, Tex., Mar. 3, 1911; s. Marvin Ellis and Retta Ann (Daugherty) B.; student San Antonio Coll., 1931-32; m. Geraldine Fite, Dec. 23, 1935; children—Melville Campbelle, William Keaton, Mary Ruth, Barry. Apprentice law offices Judge M.E. Blackburn, Junction, Tex., 1932-38; admitted to Tex. bar, 1936, U.S. 5th Ct. of Appeals bar, 1966, U.S. Supreme Ct. bar, 1967, Fed. Dist. Ct. bar, 1967; practiced in Kimble County, (Tex.), 1937-42, Junction, Tex., 1950—; county atty. Kimble County, 1942-43, county judge, 1947-50; pres. Blackburn Abstract Co., Junction, 1936—; atty. Rural Electrification Adminstrn., Junction, 1964-71. Mem. draft bd. Selective Service Bd., Junction, 1959-61; mem. Kimble County Hist. Survey Com., 1964—. Chmn. Kimble County Democratic Com., 1966. Served with USNR, 1943-45. Mem. State Bar Tex. (mem. grievance com. 1962), Hill Country Bar Assn. (pres. 1954), Am. Judiciary Soc., V.F.W. (post comdr. 1965—), Junction C. of C. (pres. 1963). Methodist (chmn. adminstrv. bd. 1970—). Mason (Shriner); mem. Order Eastern Star. Home: 209 N 9th St Junction TX 76849 Office: PO Box 444 Junction TX 76849

BLACKBURN, ROBERT THOMAS, JR., lawyer; b. Boston, Apr. 30, 1945; s. Robert Thomas and Arma Ruth (Whitlow) B.; B.S. in Accounting, U. Ky., 1967; J.D., Vanderbilt U., 1971; m. Jennifer Wright, Aug. 24, 1966; children—Robert Thomas III, Stephanie Wright. Accountant, Price Waterhouse & Co., Nashville, 1967-69; admitted to Ky. bar, 1971; practiced in Louisville, 1971—; mem. firm Ewen, MacKenzie & Peden, Louisville, 1972—. Instr. law U. Louisville Sch. Law, 1971—. C.P.A., Ky. Mem. Am. (subcom. comml. comml. banking 1971—), Ky., Louisville (tax com. 1973—) bar assns. Baptist. Home: 2110 Mammoth Way Louisville KY 40299 Office: Commonwealth Bldg Louisville KY 40202

BLACKLEDGE, HAROLD JOYCE, hosp. adminstr.; b. Laurel, Miss., Sept. 7, 1927; s. Henry B. and Nellie (Mitchell) B.; student Jones County Jr. Coll., 1948-49; B.S., U. Miss., 1951; postgrad. U. So. Miss., 1964; m. Dorothy Anita Sanders, June 6, 1948; children—Rebecca Ann, Debra Lynn. Pharmacist, Wiggins Drug Co., Pascagoula, Miss., 1951; pharmacist Jones County Community Hosp., Laurel, 1952, purchasing agt., 1953, office mgr., 1954-57, asst. adminstr., 1957-63, adminstr., 1963-67, adminstr. Hancock General Hosp., Bay St. Louis, Miss., 1967-72; adminstr. Laird Hosp. and Clinic, Union, Miss., 1973—. Pres., Laurel Safety Council, 1963; chmn. prospect devel. com. Laurel Indsl. Com. of 100, 1966; mem. adv. bd. Hearthside Haven Convalescent and Retirement Home, Laurel, 1964-66; past pres. Laurel Teen Center, Inc., established 1st Poison Control Center in Miss., 1960, Jones County Community Nursing Sch. 1964, Sch. Radiol. Tech., 1965, Practical Nurses Tng. Program, 1965. Bd. dirs. Am. Cancer Soc., Jones County Nurses Scholarship Fund. Served with USMCR, 1945-46. Mem. Am. Coll. Hosp. Adminstrs., Am., Miss. hosp. assns., Miss. Pharm. Assn., Southeastern Miss. Hosp. Council, U. Miss. Alumni Assn., Am. Legion, V.F.W. Lion (pres. 1965-66). Home: 216 Peachtree St Union MS 39365 Office: Laird Hosp and Clinic Peachtree St Union MS 39365

BLACKMAN, BRUCE ALLEN, elec. engr.; b. Weleetka, Okla., Dec. 21, 1919; s. George C. and Ruby (Hamilton) B.; B.S., Okla. State U., 1941, M.S., 1955; m. Dorothy Atterberry, July 1, 1945; children—Barry, Susan. Instr. mech. engring. Okla. State U., Stillwater, 1946-48; research engr. Dowell Inc., Tulsa, 1948-53, Well Surveys, Inc., Tulsa, 1953-60; project engr. Otis Engring. Corp., Dallas, 1960-62; devel. engr., sect. leader Halliburton Co., Duncan, Okla., 1962-69, sect. supr., 1969—. Served to 1st lt. Signal Corps AUS, 1941-46, to capt., 1950-52. Registered profl. engr., Okla. Mem. I.E.E.E., Soc. Petroleum Engrs., Eta Kappa Nu. Home: 1924 Parkview St Duncan OK 73533 Office: Research Center Duncan OK 53533

BLACKMAN, MURRAY, rabbi; b. N.Y.C., Nov. 18, 1920; s. Maxwell and Sarah (Levy) B.; B.S.S., Coll. City N.Y., 1940; B.H.L., Hebrew Union Coll., 1945, M.H.L., 1949, D.D., 1974; postgrad. Columbia, 1954-56, U. Cin., 1960-63; doctoral fellow Walden U., 1973—; m. Martha Dora Mecklenburger, Aug. 31, 1947; children—Michael Simon, Margaret Jo, Barbara Sarah. Rabbi, 1949; asst. rabbi Temple B'nai Jeshurun, Newark, 1949-50; rabbi Temple Concord, Binghamton, N.Y., 1950-51, Barnert Temple, Patterson, N.J., 1953-56; sr. rabbi Rockdale Temple, Cin., 1956-67; rabbi St. Thomas (V.I.) Synagogue, 1967-70, Temple Sinai, New Orleans, 1970—. Spl. lectr. edn. Hebrew Union Coll., Cin., 1962-67; instr. comparative religion Coll. of V.I., 1967-70; spl. lectr. history La. State U., Baton Rouge, 1971—. Chmn. Cin. Jewish Community Relations Com., 1966-67; interfaith chmn. Greater New Orleans United Fund, 1971; mem. adv. council New Orleans council Boy Scouts Am., 1971—; mem. Mayor's Job Force for Vets. Com., 1970-72; mem. exec. bd. Community Health and Welfare Council, Cin. Community Chest, Mayor's Friendly Relations Com. Mem. Am. Jewish Com., Central Conf. Am. Rabbis, Jewish Family Service Bur.; chmn. community relations com. Jewish Welfare Fedn., New Orleans, 1971—; pres. New Orleans Rabbinical Council, 1973—; mem. joint commn. on interfaith activities Central Conf. Am. Rabbis-Union Am. Hebrew Congregations, 1973—. Served with USNR, 1951-53. Mem. Adult Edn. Assn. U.S., Soc. Israel Philatelists, Phi Delta Kappa. Rotarian. Home: 1408 Frankfort St New Orleans LA 70122 Office: 6227 St Charles Av New Orleans LA 70118

BLACKMON, BILLY JACK, bus. exec.; b. Vernon, Tex., Dec. 28, 1927; s. Charlie Culberson and Stella Mae (Shirley) B.; A.A., Odessa Coll., 1950; m. Edith Hilda Hezel, Sept. 4, 1949; children—Mark, Brent, Sherrie, Janie, B'Jaye. Pres., Bob's Casing Crews, Inc., Odessa, Tex., 1955—; chmn. bd. Emco Machine Works Co., Odessa, 1969—; pres. Ector County Ranch & Cattle Co., Odessa, 1965—; owner Letter b Ranch, McCamey, Tex.; dir. Nat. Bank Odessa. Sponsor, Troop 876 Buffalo Trail council Boy Scouts Am., 1964—. Bd. dirs. Indsl. Founds., 1960-70, pres., 1964. Served with USNR, 1945-47. Baptist. Inventor pipe racker. Home: Route 3 Box 1000 Odessa TX 79760 Office: PO Box 2412 Odessa TX 79760

BLACKMON, JACK RUSSELL, judge; b. Leesville, La., Feb. 5, 1918; s. Robert Franklin and Mamie Edna (Wisenbaker) B.; A.A., Wesley Coll., 1936; LL.B., So. Meth. U., 1939; m. Margaret Lucinda McGlain, July 14, 1940; children—Robert M., Margaret Diane (Mrs. David Barfield), Deborah Claire (Mrs. A.E. Cox). Admitted to Tex. bar, 1939; partner firm Berger, Swearingen, Wade & Blackmon, Corpus Christi, Tex., 1946-49, North, Blackmon & White, Corpus Christi, 1949-72; dist. judge 117th Jud. Dist. Tex., Corpus Christi, 1973—. Sec.-treas. NBW Bldg. Corp., Corpus Christi, 1956—; pres. Mcpl. Gas Corp., Corpus Christi, 1967-71. Gen. chmn. Sister City Com. Corpus Christi, 1972-73. Mem. Tex. Democratic Exec. com., 1954-58; mem. City Council, Corpus Christi, 1963-65, mayor pro tem, 1965-67, mayor, 1967-71. Trustee U. Corpus Christi, 1969—, chmn. 1971—. Served with USNR, World War II. Named Outstanding Citizen Corpus Christi by Bd. Realtors, 1973. Mem. Nueces County Bar Assn. (past pres.), Res. Officers Assn. (past pres.), Naval Res. Lawyers Assn. (dir. 1972-73), Phi Alpha Delta. Mason (Shriner, 32 deg.). Clubs: (v.p. zone 8 1973-75). Home: 101 Alta Plaza Corpus Christi TX 78411 Office: Courthouse Corpus Christi TX 78401

BLACKMORE, JAMES HERRALL, clergyman, ednl. adminstr.; b. Warsaw, N.C., Feb. 15, 1916; s. Willie Richard and Martha Janie (Sansbury) B.; B.A. cum laude, Wake Forest Coll., 1937; B.D. (Rauschenbusch scholar, Colgate-Rochester scholar), Colgate-Rochester Div. Sch., 1940; postgrad. Duke, 1940-41, U. Ia., 1949; Ph.D., U. Edinburgh (Scotland), 1951; m. Ruth May Lillick, Jan. 26, 1945;children—Julia, John. Dir. religious edn. Parsells Av. Bapt. Ch., Rochester, N.Y., 1938-40; ordained to ministry Baptist Ch., 1940; pastor King (N.C.) Bapt. Ch., 1941-43, Masonboro Bapt. Ch., Wilmington, 1947-49, First Bapt. Ch., Spring Hope, 1951-61; dir. pub. relations Southeastern Bapt. Theol. Sem., Wake Forest, N.C., 1963-69, dir. publs., spl. instr., 1969—, editor Outlook, sem. mag., 1963—. Pres. Wilmington Ministerial Conf., 1948-49; moderator Tar River Bapt. Assn., 1960-61; sec. bd. dirs. Bibl. Recorder, 1959-62; chmn. hist. com. Bapt. State Conv., N.C., 1970-72. Served to maj. AUS, 1943-46. Mem. Bapt. Pub. Relations Assn., Kappa Delta Alpha, Chi Eta Tau. Lion. Author: The Cullom Lantern, A Biography of W.R. Cullom, 1963; A Preacher's Temptations, 1966; A Reticle, A Collection of Short Stories and Essays, 1969. Contbr. to various religious and learned jours., also encys. Home: 315 S Wingate St Wake Forest NC 27587

BLACKMUN, HARRY ANDREW, justice U.S. Supreme Ct.; b. Nashville, Ill., Nov. 12, 1908; s. Corwin Manning and Theo H. (Reuter) B.; A.B. summa cum laude, Harvard, 1929, LL.B., 1932; LL.D. (hon.), DePauw U., 1971, Hamline U., 1971, Ohio Wesleyan U., 1971, Morningside Coll., 1972, Wilson Coll., 1972, Dickinson Sch. Law, 1973; D.P.S., Ohio No. U., 1973; m. Dorothy E. Clark, June 21, 1941; children—Nancy (Mrs. Coniaris), Sally Ann, Susan Manning. Admitted to Minn. bar, 1932; law clk. for John B. Sanborn, judge 8th circuit, U.S. Ct. of Appeals, St. Paul, 1932-33; asso. Dorsey, Colman, Barker, Scott & Barber, Mpls., 1934-38, jr. partner, 1939-42, gen. partner, 1943-50; instr. St. Paul Coll. Law, 1935-41, U. Minn. Law Sch., 1945-47; resident counsel Mayo Clinic, Mayo Assn., Rochester, 1950-59, mem. sect. adminstrn., 1950-59; judge 8th Cir., U.S. Ct. of Appeals, 1959-70; asso. justice U.S. Supreme Ct., 1970—. Sec., mem. bd. members Mayo Assn., Rochester, 1953-60; bd. dirs., mem. exec. com. Rochester Methodist Hosp., 1954-70. Trustee Hamline Univ., William Mitchell Coll. Law. Mem. Am., Minn., Olmsted County, 3d Jud. Dist. bar assns., Phi Beta Kappa. Methodist. Clubs: Harvard of Minn. (pres. 1940); Rotary (pres. Rochester 1955-56); Minneapolis, Univ. Rochester. Contbr. profl. articles to legal, med. jours. Office: US Supreme Ct Bldg 1 1st St NE Washington DC 20543

BLACKSHEAR, AUGUSTUS TROY, JR., lawyer; b. Dallas, July 5, 1942; s. Augustus Troy and Janie Louise (Florey) B.; B.B.A. cum laude, Baylor U., 1964, LL.B. cum laude, 1968; m. Patty D. Milner, Aug. 9, 1973. With Arthur Andersen & Co., Dallas, 1964-66; admitted to Tex. bar, 1968; since practiced in Houston; asso. firm Fulbright & Crooker, Houston, 1969—. Lectr. McLennan Community Coll., 1968-69. Mem. Am. Bar Assn. (tax sect.), State Bar Tex. (tax sect.; chmn. com. on exempt orgns.). Home: 6473 Bayou Glen Houston TX 77027 Office: 800 Bank Southwest Bldg Houston TX 77002

BLACKSTOCK, LEROY, lawyer; b. El Reno, Okla., Apr. 19, 1914; s. Herbert Austin and Ethel Mae (Gwin) B.; grad. Draughon's Bus. Inst., Tulsa, 1933; LL.B., U. Tulsa, 1938; m. Virginia Lee Lowman, Dec. 29, 1939; children—Craig, Priscilla, Birch, Lore, Trena. Admitted to Okla. bar, 1938; practice law, Tulsa, 1941—; sr. partner firm Blackstock, Joyce, Pollard & McInerney; with Phillips Petroleum Co., Tulsa, 1933-41, asst. credit mgr., 1939-41. Dir. First Bank, Owasso, 1967-70, Fourth Nat. Bank of Tulsa; pres. Gt. Western Investments Trust, Skelly Stadium Corp.; dir., gen. counsel Tulsa Home Builders Assn., 1959-68; lectr. econs. and mgmt. Pres., Tulsa County Legal Aid Soc., 1961-62, bd. dirs., 1958-66; pres. bd. dirs. Tulsa County Bar Found., 1968-71; chmn. Citizen's Adv. Com. County Commrs., 1963-66; pres. Tulsa Bapt. Laymen's Corp., 1962-66; mem. Mayor's Adv. Com. Community Problems, 1957-58; mem. Gov.'s Acad. State Govt., 1966-68; pres. Tulsa Campire Council, 1971-72; chmn. U. Tulsa Alumni Loyalty Fund, 1969-70. Bd. dirs. Tulsa County Mental Health Assn., 1963-68, Tulsa Psychiat. Found., 1964-67, Jud. Reform Okla., Tulsa Sci. Center, Inc.; mem. nat. adv. council Practising Law Inst. Served with USNR, 1943-46. Recipient Distinguished Citizens award Okla. Psychol. Assn., 1963. Mem. Am. (ho. dels. 1965-67, mem. com. nat. coordination of disciplinary enforcement, standing com. profl. discipline), Okla. (pres. 1966), Tulsa County (pres. 1962; Outstanding Atty. award 1961) bar assns. Republican. Baptist (chmn. deacons 1962, chmn. bldg. com. 1951-66). Clubs: Petroleum, Summit. Author: Paper Dolls; Lawyers' Fees. Home: 3740 Terwillleger St Tulsa OK 74105 Office: 1304 Petroleum Club Bldg Tulsa OK 74119

BLACKSTOCK, VIRGINIA LEE LOWMAN (MRS. LEROY BLACKSTOCK), civic worker; b. Bixby, Okla., July 2, 1917; d. Joseph Arthur and Winifred (Lundy) Lowman; student Tulsa Coll. Bus., 1935-37; m. Leroy Blackstock, Dec. 29, 1939; children—Vincent Craig, Priscilla Gay (Mrs. Richard S. Kurz), Birch Lee, Lore Anne, Trena Jan. Legal sec. law firm, Tulsa, 1937-41. Chmn. program Internat. Students in Tulsa, 1955-65; mem. Tulsa Council Camp Fire Girls, 1963-66; mem. youth com. Tulsa Philharmonic Soc., 1969-70; now mem. women's assn.; pres. Eliot Elementary P.T.A., 1961-62, Edison High Sch. P.T.A., 1971-72; mem. Tulsa Opera Guild. Co-chmn. Democratic precinct No. 132, 1960-67. Mem. Tulsa County Bar Aux. (pres. 1954-55, sec. 1962-63, chaplain 1966-67). Baptist. Clubs: Summit, Petroleum. Home: 3740 Terwilleger Blvd Tulsa OK 74105

BLACKWELDER, CHESTER ARTHUR, apparel mfg. co. exec.; b. nr. Taylorsville, N.C., July 9, 1904; s. Carl Columbus and Emma Mae (Campbell) B.; ed. pub. schs.; m. Ruby Lee Adams, Feb. 23, 1929; 1 dau., Venita Lee (Mrs. Billy Lee Dwiggins). With Cannon Mills, Kannapolis, N.C., 1920-22, Dillon-Vitt Underwear Co., Statesville, N.C., 1926-30; plant supt. McNeer-Dillon Co., Statesville, 1930-32; mgr. Marathon Underwear Co., 1933-36; plant mgr. Carolina Underwear Co., Thomasville, 1937-46; organizer, chief exec. officer Monleigh Garment Co., Thomasville, 1946-48, Mocksville, 1948—; organizer, chief exec. officer Blackwelder Mfg. Co., Inc., Mocksville, 1956—, Carolina Mfg. Co., Inc., Mocksville, 1957—, Piedmont Garment Co., Inc., Harmony, N.C., 1961—; Harmony Sportswear Co., Inc., Mocksville, 1961—, B & F Mfg. Co., Inc., Mocksville, 1952—, Edgewood Shirtmakers Ltd., Mocksville, 1970—; dir. Branch Banking and Trust Co., Mocksville. Baptist. (trustee 1967—). Rotarian (pres. 1969-70). Address: Box 808 Mocksville NC 27028

BLACKWELL, ANNA MARGARET THOMPSON (MRS. DAMIAN LEE BLACKWELL, JR.), orgn. exec.; b. Ewing, Ill., Aug. 29, 1905; d. Edmund Lee and Effie (Moss) Thompson; student U. Ala., 1926, Watkins Inst., 1936-37, 38; m. Damian Lee Blackwell, Jr., May 22, 1926 (dec. Jan. 1967); children—Evelyn (Mrs. Marvin E. Loney), Sarah (Mrs. Hollis O. Birdwell), Barbara (Mrs. Harold W. Atkinson). Recreation dir. Morgan County, Somerville, Ala., 1938-41; order office mgr. Sears, Roebuck & Co., Decatur, Ala., 1941-53; cashier White Way Pure Milk Co., Decatur, 1953-57; asso. dir. Morgan County United Fund, Decatur, 1957—. Mem. Community Services Planning Council, 1957—, pres., 1962-63, 67. Mem. Ala. Assn. Retarded Children, Morgan County Assn. for Mental Health, Morgan County Soc. Crippled Children and Adults, Internat. Platform Assn., Am. Bus. Women's Assn. (treas., pres. 1972-73), Wesleyan Service Guild (pres. 1964-68). Methodist. Club: Pilot (treas. Decatur 1971-72). Home: Route 1 Box 294 Somerville AL 35670 Office: PO Box 1058 Decatur AL 35601

BLACKWELL, GORDON WILLIAMS, univ. pres.; b. Timmonsville, S.C., Apr. 27, 1911; s. Benjamin L. and Amelia (Williams) B.; A.B., Furman U., 1932, LL.D., 1958; M.A., U. N.C., 1933, LL.D., 1967; A.M., Harvard, 1937, Ph.D., 1940; D.H.L., Rollins Coll., 1961; LL.D., U. Miami (Fla.), 1964, The Citadel, 1968, William Jewell Coll, 1968; m. Elizabeth Blair Lyles, Aug. 21, 1937; children—Gordon Lyles, Randolph Williams, Elizabeth Blair, Amelia Mayo. Research asst. U. N.C., 1932-33; research N.C. Emergency Relief Adminstrn., 1933-34, W.P.A., 1935-36; fellow Harvard, 1936-37; prof. and head dept. sociology Furman U., Greenville, S.C., 1937-41, pres., 1965—; asso. prof. sociology and research asso. Inst. for Research in Social Sci. U. N.C., 1941, study of community understanding in teacher edn. Com. on Tchr. Edn. 1942, dir. Inst. for Research in Social Sci., and research prof. sociology U. N.C., 1944-57, became Kenan prof. sociology, 1955, chancellor Woman's Coll., U. N.C., 1957-60; pres. Fla. State U., 1960-65. Field instr. Columbia, summers, 1939-41, vis. prof., summers 1948, 49. Mem. So. Regional Edn. Bd., 1969—. Staff, Greenville County Council for Community Devel., 1937-41; chief, tng. sect. and community problems sect. Civilian War Services br. Office Civilian Def., 1942-43; mem. adv. com. on computing activities NSF, 1968-72. Trustee Eckerd Coll. Named Greenville Man of Yr., Soc. Advancement Mgmt., 1968. Mem. Am., So. (chmn. com. on research 1946; 1st v.p. 1947), Rural (chmn. com. on research 1945, com. on extension 1948, 49, v.p. 1948) sociol. socs., So. Univ. Conf. (pres. 1973-74), Assn. So. Baptist Colls. (pres. 1971-72), Am. Assn. U. Profs., Phi Beta Kappa, Phi Kappa Phi, Omicron Delta Kappa, Alpha Phi Omega, Kappa Sigma, Alpha Kappa Delta, Pi Gamma Mu, Alpha Kappa Psi. Baptist. Clubs: Quaternion, Poinsett, Green Valley, The Mountains. Author: (with L.M. Brooks and S.H. Hobbs, Jr.) Church and Community in the South, 1949; (with R.F. Gould) Future Citizens All, 1952; (with G. E. Nicholson) Game Theory and Defense Against Community Disaster, 1954; Addresses of Gordon W. Blackwell, 1965. Dir. Study Coll. Teaching of Social Sci. in South, So. Assn. Colls. and Secondary Schs., 1944-48; dir., editor Studies of So. Resources, for So. Assn. Sci. and Industry, 1943-50; library adv. bd. Air U., 1951-54; editor Social Forces, 1954-57; asst. editor Am. Sociol. Rev., 1946-50; com. on adminstrv. affairs Am. Council on Edn., 1962-63, com. on plans and objectives for higher edn., 1965-67; mem. com. coll. adminstrn. Am. Assn. Colls., 1965-67; pres. S.C. Assn. Colls., 1968-69; adv. bd. Ency. Internat., 1962-65. Contbr. articles to profl. publs. Home: 68 Kensington Rd Greenville SC 29609

BLACKWELL, LUCY WHITE, ret. govt. ofcl.; b. Jackson, Tenn., Apr. 22, 1912; d. William Francis and Ethel (White) Blackwell; A.B., Lambuth Coll., 1933; postgrad. West Tenn. Bus. Coll., 1934-35. Stenographer Tenn. Emergency Relief Adminstrn., Jackson, 1935; accounting clk. FSA, Jackson, Brownsville, Tenn., 1936-39; stenographer Tenn. Dept. Pub. Welfare, Jackson, 1939-40; clk., interviewer, local office mgr. Tenn. Dept. Employment Security, Jackson, 1940-73. Comdr. Am. Cancer Soc., Madison County, Tenn., 1943-54, dist. comdr. West Tenn., 1947-48; rec. sec. Tenn. div., 1954-56, bd. dirs., 1945—, organizer Madison County unit, 1954, pres., 1954-55; bd. dirs. Jackson Community Chest, 1955-57; pres. League Women Voters, 1951. Treas., chmn. bd. trustees Jackson Free Library, 1948-57. Recipient R.E. Womack Alumni Achievement award Lambuth Coll. Alumni Assn., 1956; named Jackson-Madison Woman of Year, 1955. Mem. Internat. Assn. Personnel Emloyment Security (pres. Jackson 1956), Lambuth Coll. Alumni Assn. (pres. 1962-63). Presbyn. Clubs: Pilot (past pres. Jackson, dist. gov. Tenn., internat. dir. exec. com.), Altrusa (chmn.). Home: 111 Cherokee Dr Jackson TN 38301

BLACKWELL, REBEL EUGENE, JR., marketing exec.; b. Dallas, Jan. 28, 1935; s. Rebel Eugene and Mary Mildred (Foster) B.; B.S., U. Tex., 1957, B.B.A., 1960; m. Phyllis Jean Pryor, Aug. 16, 1958; children—Rebel Eugene, H. Pryor, Frances Foster. Trainee Graybar Electric Co., Dallas, 1959-60; sales rep. IBM, Dallas, 1960-65; registered rep. Rauscher Pierce Securities Corp., Midland, Tex., 1965-69, v.p. mut. fund sales, 1970-72, sr. v.p. marketing, 1972—. Active Circle Ten council Boy Scouts Am., 1971—. Bd. dirs. YMCA, Midland, 1968-69, United Fund of Midland, 1968-69. Mem. Sigma Phi Epsilon. Republican. Baptist (Sunday sch. tchr. 1963—). Home: 3129 Bryn Mawr St Dallas TX 75225 Office: 900 Mercantile Dallas Bldg Dallas TX 75201

BLACKWELL, WILLIAM HAYDEN, lawyer; b. Pacolet, S.C., Nov. 12, 1916; s. William Joseph and Eva (Genoble) B.; A.B., Wofford Coll., 1938; LL.B., U. S.C., 1939; m. Helene Hickson Carpenter, Nov. 16, 1946; children—Helene Anne, Elizabeth Hayden. Admitted to S.C. bar, 1939; practiced in Florence, S.C., 1939-41, 46—; mem. firm Wright, Scott, Blackwell & Powers, 1959—. Vice pres., dir. Security Savs. & Loan Assn., Florence, 1967—. Served from pvt. to maj., USAAF, 1942-46. Mem. Am., S.C., Florence bar assns., Jud. Council S.C., C. of C. (pres. 1952), Blue Key, Phi Beta Kappa. Clubs: Kiwanis (pres. 1958), Florence Country (dir., sec. bd. 1966-67). Home: 617 Rosewood Av Florence SC 29501 Office: 234 W Cheves St Florence SC 29501

BLACKWELL, WILLIAM MARSHALL, lawyer, textile co. exec.; b. Richmond, Va., Oct. 22, 1911; s. Benjamin T. and Lola B. (Gary) B.; B.S., U. Va., 1932; J.D., U. Richmond, 1935; m. Helen L. Dodd, Apr. 22, 1965. Admitted to Va. bar, 1933; partner firm Shewmake & Gary, Richmond, 1937-70, firm Cutchins, Wallinger, Christian & House, Richmond, 1971—. Vice pres. Brooks Warehouse Corp., 1945—; gen. counsel, asst. sec. Ga. Bonded Fibers, Inc., Newark and Buena Vista, Va., 1954—; sec., gen. counsel Henry W. Woody, Inc., Richmond, 1968—; gen. counsel Overnite Transp. Co., Richmond; instr. U. Richmond, 1947-48. Spl. asst. city atty., Richmond, 1938-39; chmn. Bd. Zoning Appeals, Richmond, 1948-52. Trustee Stonewall Found., 1972—. Served to capt., AUS, 1942-46. Mem. Am., Richmond (pres. 1961-62), Va. State bar assns., Phi Beta Kappa, Delta Sigma Phi, Delta Theta Phi. Baptist. Clubs: Bull and Bear, Country of Virginia (Richmond); Farmington Country (Charlottesville, Va.). Home: 9300 Cragmont Dr Richmond VA 23229 Office: Mutual Bldg Richmond VA 23219

BLADES, CARLTON JENSEN, utility co. exec.; b. Walkerville, Mich., June 11, 1912; s. Garfield and Mary (Jensen) B.; B.S. in Agr., Western Mich. U., 1934; M.S. in Forestry, U. Mich., 1936; m. Helen Brookshire Phifer, Jan. 16, 1942; children—John Carl, Carla Jean, Mary Helen. Forester, Duke U., Durham, N.C., 1936-39; chief forester Duke Power Co., Charlotte, N.C., 1939-58, mgr. real estate, 1958-70, v.p. real estate, 1970—. Served to capt., AUS, 1942-45; ETO. Mem. Soc. Am. Foresters. Home: 521 Lansdowne Rd Charlotte NC 28211 Office: PO Box 2178 Charlotte NC 28201

BLAIR, DON J., med. assn. adminstr.; b. Enid, Okla., July 1, 1929; s. Ralph J. and Pauline A. (Wynes) B.; B.A., U. Okla., 1953; m. Julianne James, Jan. 17, 1958; children—Linda Carol, Elisabeth Anne. Asso. exec. dir. Okla. State Med. Assn., Oklahoma City, 1955-62, exec. dir., 1962—. Exec. v.p. Okla. Found. for Peer Rev.,

Oklahoma City, 1972—; mem. regional policyowners council Mass. Mut. Life Ins. Co., Springfield, 1973—; mem. adv. group Regional Med. Program, Oklahoma City, 1966—. Served to 1st lt. arty. AUS, 1953-55; Korea. Mem. Am. Assn. Med. Soc. Execs., Am., Okla. socs. assn. execs. Club: Beacon. Home: 11312 Leaning Elm Rd Oklahoma City OK 73120 Office: 601 NW Expressway Oklahoma City OK 73118

BLAIR, FORBES WESLEY, lawyer; b. Chester, W.Va., Dec. 17, 1926; s. Andrew Clark and Edna (McHenry) B. A.B., W.Va. U. 1950; LL.B., 1952;; m Hilma Deem Robbins, June 20, 1954; children—Kristin Robbins, Forbes Robbins. Admitted to W.Va. bar, 1952; law clk. Adminstrv. Office U.S. Cts., Washington, 1952; law clk. to U.S. Atty. for D.C., 1953-54; asst. U.S. atty. for D.C., 1955-57; asso. firm Welch & Morgan, Washington, 1957-66, partner, 1966-69; partner firm Bilger & Blair, 1970—. Mem. Montgomery County (Md.) Charter Revision Commn., 1968. Regional chmn. Montgomery County Republican Com., 1967—; bd. govs. Montgomery County Men's Rep. Club, 1970—, pres., 1972. Asso. mem. W.Va. U. Found., 1967-71. Served with USNR, 1944-46. Mem. Am. Judicature Soc., Am. Fed., Fed. Communication bar assns., W.Va. U. Alumni Assn. (pres. D.C. chpt. 1960), W.Va. Soc. Washington (bd. govs. 1973—), Phi Alpha Delta. Republican. Presbyn. Mason (32 deg.). Editor: Civitan Bull., Washington, 1965-70. Contbr. articles to profl. jours. Home: 13826 Overton Lane Silver Spring MD 20904 Office: 1730 M St NW Washington DC 20036

BLAIR, HENRY CLAY, lawyer; b. nr. Granite Falls, N.C., Feb. 18, 1913; s. William H. and Mary Lou (Satterwhite) B.; A.B., U. N.C., 1938, J.D. 1941; m. Shirley Miller, Nov. 21, 1945; children—Lucille (Mrs. Clifford L. Coultes), William H. Admitted to N.C. bar, 1941; since practiced in Fayetteville. Mem. Am., N.C. bar assns., N.C. State Bar. Home: 2211 Meadow Wood Rd Fayetteville NC 28301 Office: 120 Gillespie St Fayetteville NC 28301

BLAIR, ROGER LEE, forest geneticist; b. Sterling, Ill., Sept. 6, 1941; s. Orville Louis and Elsie May (Thome) B.; student Ill. Wesleyan U., 1959-62; B.S., U. Ill., 1964; M.F., Yale, 1965; Ph.D., N.C. State U., 1970; m. Patricia Jean Wilson, June 15, 1963; children—Douglas, Kristin. Biometrician, Internat. Paper Co., Bainbridge, Ga., 1968-70, research forester, Southlands Expt. Forest, 1970—. Adj. prof. N.C. State U., Raleigh, 1972—. Recipient Demmon Research award N.C. State U., 1970. Home: Route 1 Bainbridge GA 31717 Office: Southlands Expt Forest Bainbridge GA 31717

BLAISDELL, GLENN CHAMBERLAIN, county ofcl.; b. Boston, Mar. 31, 1927; s. Clifford C. and Marguerite (Burbank) B.; B.C.S., Ga. State U., 1952; LL.B., Woodrow Wilson Coll. Law, 1956; m. Frances Lucy Cone, Mar. 31, 1966; children—Mark, Constance, Catherine. Various accounting positions, Atlanta, 1946-53; admitted to Ga. bar, 1956; sr. accountant Mount & Carter C.P.A., Atlanta, 1953-59; pvt. financial cons., Lewiston, Me., 1959-60; partner Westberry & Blaisdell C.P.A.'s, Atlanta, 1960-61; dir. finance Dekalb County, Decatur, Ga., 1962-67, Mecklenburg County, Charlott, N.C., 1967-70; asst. county mgr. Mecklenburg County, 1970, county mgr., 1970—. Bd. dirs. United Community Services, Goodwill Industries. Served with USNR, 1944-46. C.P.A., Ga. Mem. N.C. Assn. City and County Mgrs., Nat. Assn. County Ofcls., Internat. City Mgrs. Assn., Am. Inst. C.P.A.'s, Blue Key, Delta Sigma Pi. Presbyn. (deacon). Home: 1115 Linda Lane Charlotte NC 28211 Office: 720 E 4th St Charlotte NC 28202

BLAKE, GARTH KERMIT, educator; b. Larned, Kan., Dec. 24, 1919; s. Loyd C. and Velma (Rex Road) B.; student Wheaton Coll., 1937, John Brown U., 1938-39; B.M.E., Okla. State U., 1946; M.Ed., U. Tulsa, 1951, Ed. D., 1956; m. Bonnie Jean Fretwell, Aug.8, 1941; 1 son, Richard G. Music tchr. Strang, Jefferson, Nowata, Okla., 1940-42; dir. music, Sapulpa, Okla., 1946-53, prin. high sch., 1953-57, supt. schs., 1957; asso. prof. edn. Fla. State U., Tallahassee, 1957-59, prof., head dept. student teaching, 1959-67, asst. dean Coll. Edn., 1967-72, asso. dean, 1972—. Served with USNR, 1944-46. Mem. Nat., Fla. edn. assns., Nat. Assn. for Student Teaching, Phi Kappa Phi, Phi Delta Kappa, Phi Beta Mu, Kappa Delta Pi. Rotarian. Home: 902 N Ride Tallahassee FL 32301

BLAKE, HU AL, surgeon, educator; b. Ervin, Tenn., Apr. 20, 1922; s. Howard Ernest and Dora (White) B.; M.D., Jefferson Med. Coll., Phila., 1946; m. Louise Coffrath, Sept. 25, 1945; children—Hu, Randall, Andrew. Intern, Jefferson Med. Coll., 1946-47; resident Fitzsimmons Army Hosp., Denver, 1950-54; commd. 1st lt. M.C., U.S. Army, 1948, advanced through grades to col., 1964; heart surgeon Fitzsimmons Army Hosp., 1950-54, Walter Reed Army Hosp., 1954-62, Brooke Gen. Hosp., 1962-67; ret., 1967; prof., chmn. dept. surgery U. Tenn. Meml. Hosp., Knoxville, 1968—. Vice pres. Phys. Med. Edn. and Research Found., 1968—. Decorated Legion of Merit. Diplomate Am. Bd. Surgery, Am. Bd. Thoracic and Cardiovascular Surgery. Fellow A.C.S. Contbr. articles to med. and surg. jours. Home: 7765 Devonshire Dr Knoxville TN 37919

BLAKELEY, ROBERT PHILIP, real estate co. exec.; b. Hampton, Ky., Jan. 3, 1917; s. William Roney and Gladys Mae (Styers) B.; student Dyke Sch. Commerce, 1936-38; m. Evelyn Diane White, Apr. 19, 1941; children—Brent Philip, Diana Gaye. Asst. office mgr. Chandler Products Co., Cleve., 1941-48; sec.-treas., gen. mgr. Plantation Farms, Inc., Plantation, Fla., 1949—; pres., dir. Old Plantation Water Control Dist., 1958—; chmn. governing bd. Central & So. Fla. Flood Control Dist.; dir. Farsouth Growers Coop. Assn., Tropical Agr. Coop. Assn., Plantation 1st Nat. Bank, Security 1st Nat. Bank. Fire chief Plantation Vol. Fire Dept., 1960-62; Mem. Broward County Water Resources Adv. Bd. Bd. dirs. Broward County Indsl. Devel. Bd., 1965-66; co-trustee Plantation Land Trust, 1964-66; dir. Broward County chpt. A.R.C. Mem. C. of C. (dir. 1962-66, past pres.), Aquatic Weed Sci. Soc. (dir.), Hyacinth Control Soc. (dir.), Weed Sci. Soc. Am., So. Weed Soc. Kiwanian. Home: 320 E Tropical Way Plantation FL 33314 Office: 7049 NW 4th St Plantation FL 33313

BLAKEY, LESLIE WINFIELD, neurologist; b. Hardyville, Ky., Sept. 29, 1917; s. James Winfield and Verda Eugenia (King) B.; B.S., Western Ky. State Tchrs. Coll., 1939; M.D., U. Louisville, 1947; m. Freda B. Yonce, Sept. 15, 1943; 1 dau., Martha Ann. Grad. asst. in zoology U. Ky. Grad. Sch., 1940-41; rotating intern Indpls. Gen. Hosp., 1948-49; resident, fellow in internal medicine Mayo Found. for Med. Edn. and Research, 1956, fellow in neurology, 1957-59; gen. practice medicine, Hopkinsville, Ky., 1949-55, Cadiz, Ky., 1949-55; head sect. neurology Lexington (Ky.) Clinic, 1960—; mem. staff St. Joseph Hosp., Lexington; mem. courtesy staff Good Samaritan Hosp., Central Baptist Hosp.; cons. neurology Shriners Hosp. for Crippled Children, 1960—, Nat. Insts. Mental Health Clin. Research Center, 1969-73; asso. prof. clin. neurology U. Ky., Lexington, 1966—. Trustee Hunter Found. Health Care, Inc., Lexington, 1972-73. Diplomate Am. Bd. Psychiatry and Neurology. Fellow Am. Acad. Neurology; mem. A.C.P., A.M.A., Ky. Med. Assn. (del. 1966—), Fayette County Med. Soc. (pres. 1971-72), Alpha Omega Alpha, Omicron Delta Kappa, Phi Kappa Phi. Home: 672 Mt Vernon Dr Lexington KY 40502 Office: 1221 S Broadway Lexington KY 40504

BLALOCK, DANIEL BRAXTON, JR., constrn. machinery co. exec.; b. Atlanta, July 22, 1912; s. Daniel Braxton and Estelle (Zellars) B.; B.S., Ga. Inst. Tech., 1934; m. Dorothy Eleanor Pettus, Nov. 12, 1945; children—Mary Estelle, Daniel Braxton III, William Pettus. With Austin Western Machinery Co., Harvey, Ill., 1934-35; with Blalock Machinery & Equipment Co., Atlanta, 1935-41, 46—, salesman, partner, v.p., 1935-61, pres., 1961—. Mem. Ga. Democratic Exec. Com., 1951-54, 59-62. Served to lt. col. C.E., AUS, 1941-46. Mem. Ga. Bus. and Industry Assn. (vice chmn. 1969-70), Ga. Inst. Tech. Nat. Alumni Assn. (pres. 1969-70), Asso. Equipment Distbrs. (nat. pres. 1962), Kappa Alpha. Episcopalian. Clubs: Capitol City, Piedmont Driving, Commerce, Cherokee Town and Country, Atlanta Country. Home: 1224 Johnson Ferry Rd NE Atlanta GA 30319 Office: 225 Forsyth St SW Atlanta GA 30302

BLALOCK, JOHN VERNON, tobacco co. exec.; b. Durham, N.C., Aug. 1, 1921; s. Reuben Allen and Lelia Pearl (Goss) B.; B.A., Duke, 1944; m. Kathleen Glymph, Apr. 6, 1947; children—Kathleen (Mrs. Alexander Prescott IV), Barry Vernon. Various positions Durham Morning-Herald, 1942-48; asst. dir. pub. relations Seaboard R.R., Norfolk, Va., 1948-49; asst. v.p. advt. and pub. relations Liberty Life Ins. Co., Greenville, S.C., 1949-61; dir. pub. relations Brown & Williamson Tobacco Corp., Louisville, 1961—. Guest lectr. U. Louisville. Active United Way, Louisville Devel. Com.; commr. Commonwealth of Ky. Hist. Commn. Bd. dirs. Louisville Fund, Greater Louisville Conv. Assn., Parkhill Community Council, Sts. Mary and Elizabeth Hosp., Louisville Med. Research Found. and Family Health Center. Recipient medal of honor Freedoms Found., 1954, medal of merit Jewish War Vets. U.S., 1971, Human Relations Leadership award Am. Jewish Com., 1971. Mem. Pub. Relations Soc. Am. (local pres., del. nat. assembly), Louisville Area C. of C., Phi Kappa Sigma. Presbyn. Clubs: Jefferson, Hurstbourne Country, Filson, Louisville Executives (Louisville). Home: 4907 Clovernook Rd Louisville KY 40207 Office: 1600 W Hill St Louisville KY 40201

BLALOCK, THOMAS CARLTON, univ. adminstr.; b. Lucama, N.C., Oct. 6, 1924; s. Walter Henry and Pearl Lee (Barnes) B.; B.S., N.C. State U., 1948, M.S., 1952; Ph.D. (Kellogg fellow), U. Wis., 1963; m. Alva Cornelia Peacock, June 8, 1947; children—Thomas Carlton, Walter Douglass, Phyllis Leigh. Instr., N.C. State U., Raleigh, 1949-50, extension specialist, 1951-59, specialist in charge, 1959-63, dist. agt., 1963-64, asst. dir. 4-H, 1964-70, asst. dir. adminstrn., 1970-72, asso. dir., 1972—; mgr. Wis. Sci. Breeding Inst., 1950-51. Cons. Peruvian Govt. on Yough Programs, 1966; chmn. Nat. 4-H Sub-Com. of Extension Com. on Organization and Policy, Mem. adv. council N.C. Gov's. Com. for Children and Youth, 1968-70. Served with Signal Corps, AUS, 1943-46. Mem. Assn. So. Agrl. Workers (pres. youth sect. 1968-69), N.C. Adult Edn. Assn., N.C. Rural Safety Council (award chmn. 1970-72), Epsilon Sigma Phi, Alpha Zeta. Baptist (deacon 1962-65, 67-70). Club: Faculty (v.p. 1966-67). Home: 1315 Brooks Av Raleigh NC 27607

BLANCETT, KENNETH SIDNEY, petroleum engr.; b. Trousdale, Okla., Dec. 13, 1924; s. Ralph and Ethel (York) B.; B.S., U. Okla., 1952; m. Iris L. Ferguson, Apr. 3, 1953; children—Craig A., John C., Kevin M., K. Scott, Sara V. With Kewanee Oil Co., 1952-71, chief evaluation engr., mgr. property acquisition, 1965-71; v.p. evaluation engr. Hudson Cons., Inc., Tulsa, 1971—; dir. Terrane Corp., Tulsa, 1971-73. Scoutmaster Tulsa council Boy Scouts Am., 1972-74, finance chmn. Eagle dist., 1972-74. Served with USNR, 1943-46. Mem. Am. Inst. Mining, Metall. and Petroleum Engrs., Acacia. Mason. Clubs: Petroleum, Harvard (Tulsa). Home: 6024 E 57th St Tulsa OK 74135 Office: 300 Thompson Bldg Tulsa OK 74103

BLANCHARD, CAREY EDWARD, hosp. adminstr.; b. Boyce, La., Aug. 24, 1917; s. Carey Edward and Perla Greenville (Carter) B.; student Charity Hosp., New Orleans, 1946, Gradwohls Sch., 1947, U. Ala., 1971; m. Evelyn Louise Corley, Oct. 25, 1945 (div.) 1 son, Carey Edward IV; m. 2d, Virginia F. Sadler. Dir., lab. x-ray technician, anesthetist Broyles Hosp., Leesville, La., 1948-50, Carthage (Tex.) Panola Clinic, 1950-68; adminstr. Hartner Med. Center, Urania, La., 1968-69, Merryville (La.) Gen. Hosp., 1970-73; adminstr. Blvd. Hosp., Ft. Worth, 1973—; dir. Respiratory Service, Inc., Merryville; pres. Merryville Indsl. Corp., 1971-73. Served with inf., M.C., AUS, 1940-45. Fellow Am. Coll. Med. Technicians; mem. Am. Acad. Hosp. Adminstrs., Am. Radiol. Technicians. Methodist (dir. 1970-71). Mason (Shriner, K.T.); mem. Order Eastern Star, Lion. Address: 3705 Camp Bowie Fort Worth TX 76107

BLANCHARD, HUBERT HOWARD, edn. assn. exec.; b. Sulphur Rock, Ark., July 21, 1920; s. Hubert H. and Van (Martin) B.; B.S., U. Ark., 1943, M.S., 1951, diploma Sch. Adminstrn., 1966; m. Janive Segraves, June 14, 1946; children—Warren Martin, Charles Howard. High sch. tchr., Strawberry, Ark., 1946-51; supt. schs., Strawberry, 1951-54; supr. schs., Lawrence County, 1954-59; asst. exec. sec. Ark. Edn. Assn., Little Rock, 1959—. Mem. White House Conf. Edn., 1960; treas. Ark. Com. for Pub. Schs., 1962—; mem. Ark. Polit. Action Com. for Edn. Lawrence County chmn. March of Dimes, 1958. Served with USNR, 1943-46. Mem. Ark. Edn. Assn., N.E.A., Am. Assn. Sch. Adminstrs., Phi Delta Kappa. Democrat. Methodist (chmn. ofcl. bd. 1957-59, chmn. com. edn. 1967-70). Mason (32 deg.). Home: 3417 Pope Av North Little Rock AR 72116 Office: 1500 W 4th St Little Rock AR 72201

BLANCHARD, PHYLLIS EDRA WALTERS, foods co. exec.; b. Dallas, Sept. 29, 1914; d. Edward D. and Rhoda (Dennison) Walters; student U. Houston, 1931-32, evenings 1947-49; LaSalle Extension U., 1944-46; m. Hillis Robert Blanchard, Mar. 16, 1935 (dec. 1957). With Herrin Transp. Co., Houston, 1932-38; with Maxwell House div. Gen. Foods Corp., Houston, 1938—, traffic mgr., 1948—. Named Woman of Year in Transp., Traffic Club Houston, Houston Freight Carriers Assn., Women's Traffic Club Houston, 1960. Mem. Traffic Club Houston (dir. 1952-53, 54), Women's Traffic Club Houston (pres. 1952-53), Houston Freight Carriers (assoc.), S.W. Shippers (adv. bd.), Bus. and Profl. Women's Club Houston (pres. 1964-65). Mem. Order Eastern Star. Club: Flagg (v.p. Houston 1964-65). Home: 3224 Amherst St Houston TX 77005 Office: 3900 Harrisburg Blvd Houston TX 77001

BLANDIN, TAYLOR WADE, mortgage banker; b. Dallas, July 22, 1918; s. Wade A. and Phoeba H. (Taylor) B.; student Dallas Pub. Coll., 1937-39, So. Meth. U., 1956-60; m. Katherine Kingsley, June 25, 1943; 1 son, Donald W. Mgr., Crystal Ice Co., Dallas, 1936-43; sec.-treas. S.W. Title Ins. Co., Dallas, 1946-55; asst. dist. supr., regional investment office Nat. Life Ins. Co., Dallas, 1955-69; sr. v.p., sec. So. Trust & Mortgage Co., Dallas, 1969—. Troop committeeman Circle Ten council Boy Scouts Am., 1964-67. Served with AUS, 1943-46. Decorated Bronze Star medal with 2 oak leaf clusters. Mem. Dallas Mortgage Bankers Servicing Assn. (past pres.), Mortgage Bankers Assn. Am., Tex. Mortgage Bankers Assn. Presbyn. Home: 1019 DeWitt Circle Dallas TX 75224 Office: 2355 Stemmons Freeway Dallas TX 75207

BLANDING, WARREN, publishing exec.; b. Providence, Dec. 9, 1921; s. Percy Howard and Helen (Eddy) B.; grad. Phillips Acad., Andover, Mass., 1939; A.B. cum laude, Harvard, 1943; m. Betty Estelle Lightfoot, Nov. 27, 1947 (div. 1965); children—India, Brett (dec.). Pres. Wayward Printers, Inc., Washington, 1947-51; asst. to pres. Directorios Publicitarios, Mexico, 1951-52; asst. to pres., dir. marketing, editor and asso. pub. Traffic Service Corp., Washington 1953-65; exec. v.p. Marketing Publs., Inc., Washington, 1965-67, pres., 1967—; v.p. Schuyler Hopper Co., N.Y. Mem. U.S. Dept. Agr. Market Research Adv. Com., 1965—. Served with AUS, 1943-46. Clubs: Nat. Press, Harvard of N.Y.C. Contbr. articles to profl. jours. Home: 1829 Parkside Dr NW Washington DC 20012 Office: Nat Press Bldg Washington DC 20004

BLANK, CARL HERBERT, microbiologist; b. Toledo, Mar. 16, 1927; s. Carl Herman and Edna Ellen (Burmeister) B.; B.S., Toledo U., 1950; M.S., Utah State U., 1957; M.P.H., U. N.C., 1965, D.P.H., 1967; m. Audrey Margaret Krohn, June 21, 1950; 1 son, Eric. With Utah Dept. Health, Salt Lake City, 1951-72, dept. microbiologist, 1961-67, dep. dir. bur. labs., 1967-72; chief exam. and documentation sect., lab. licensure and proficiency testing br. Center for Disease Control, Atlanta, 1973—. Clin. instr. med. tech. and microbiology U. Utah, Salt Lake City, 1968-72. Served with USAAF, 1946. Fellow Am. Pub. Health Assn. (sec. lab. sect. 1971—), Am. Acad. Microbiology; mem. Am. Soc. Microbiology (pres. intermountain br. 1971), Utah Pub. Health Assn. (pres. 1972), Conf. Pub. Health Lab. Dirs., Sigma Xi, Phi Kappa Phi, Delta Omega. Lutheran. Home: 1351 Jody Lane NE Atlanta GA 30329 Office: 1600 Clifton Rd Atlanta GA 30333

BLANK, RALPH JOHN, JR., banker, lawyer; b. Lake City, Fla., Apr. 2, 1922; s. Ralph John and Stella Pauline (Kleinbeck) B.; B.S., B.A., U. Fla., 1942, J.D., 1948; m. Merry Lake, May 17, 1952; children—Pamela Hellin, Liisa Pauline, Michelle Susan. Admitted to Fla. bar, 1948; asso. mem. firm Moorehead, Pallot, Smith, Green & Phillips, Miami, 1948-49; home office counsel Am. Fire & Casualty Co., Orlando, Fla., 1950-51; individual practice law, West Palm Beach, Fla., 1952-72; sr. partner firm Blank, Williams & Benn, West Palm Beach, 1972—; chmn. bd. Citizens Bank Palm Beach County, West Palm Beach, 1963—. Mem. Fla. Ho. of Reps., 1956-60, Fla. Senate, 1960-64; mem. Civil Service Bd. West Palm Beach, 1965—. Trustee Fla. Atlantic U. Endowment Corp., Boca Raton, 1960—. Served with Arty., AUS, 1942-45; ETO; CIC, 1951-52; lt. col. Res. ret. Decorated Air medal with 5 oak leaf clusters. Presbyn. Home: 122 Forest Hill Blvd West Palm Beach FL 33405 Office: 316 Pan American Bldg West Palm Beach FL 33401

BLANKENSHIP, ASA LEE, JR., banker; b. Amarillo, Tex., July 27, 1926; s. Asa Lee and Beatrice (Shore) B.; A.A., Amarillo Jr. Coll., 1948; B.A., U. Tex., 1950, M.A., 1952; m. Bonnie Hinson, Nov. 27, 1947; 1 dau., Ellen Sue. With Skelly Oil Co., Abilene, Tex., 1952-61, Allstate Ins., Amarillo, Tex., 1961-63; account exec. H. Hentz & Co., Amarillo, 1963-65; trust investment officer First Hutchings-Sealy Nat. Bank, Galveston, Tex., 1965-68; v.p., trust investment officer Houston Nat. Bank, 1968—; dir. Smith Transport Ltd., Toronto, Ontario, Canada. Served with AUS, 1944-46. Mem. Houston Soc. Financial Analysts, Financial Analyst Fedn. Mem. Ch. of Christ (bd. elders 1971—). Home: 7519 Jason St Houston TX 77036 Office: PO Box 2518 Houston TX 77001

BLANKENSHIP, JACOB WATSON, educator; b. Denison, Tex., Mar. 6, 1933; s. Lee Harold and Christine (Wiest) B.; B.S., Southeastern State Coll., 1957; M.Ed., East Tex. State U., 1960; Ph.D., U. Tex. at Austin, 1964; m. Helen Louise McDonald, Oct. 8, 1954; children—Helen Ann, Jacob Watson, Susan Diane. Tchr. chemistry and physics Denison (Tex.) Sr. High Sch., 1957-61; asst. prof. Okla. State U., Stillwater, 1964-66, asso. prof., 1966-69; prof., chmn. dept. curriculum and instrn. U. Houston, 1969—. Program planning specialist Southwest Edn. Devel. Lab., 1967. Served with AUS, 1953-55. Fellow A.A.A.S.; mem. Assn. for Edn. Tchrs. in Sci. (nat. sec.-treas. 1971-74), Nat. Assn. for Research in Sci. Teaching, Nat. Sci. Tchrs. Assn., Kappa Delta Pi, Phi Delta Kappa. Contbr. articles to profl. jours. Home: 815 Greenbelt Houston TX 77024

BLANKENSHIP, JAMES EMERY, neurophysiologist; b. Sherman, Tex., Mar. 19, 1941; s. Walter A. and Georgia (Reynolds) B.; B.A., Austin Coll., 1963; M.S., Yale, 1965, Ph.D. (NSF fellow), 1967; m. Leota Blanche Atkinson, May 7, 1960; children—J. Patrick, John A. Research scientist Marine Biomedical Inst., U. Tex. Med. Sch., Galveston, 1970—, also asst. prof. physiology. Postdoctoral fellow N.Y. U., 1967-69, Nat. Inst. Mental Health, Bethesda, Md., 1969-70; recipient Career Devel. award NIH, 1973—. Mem. Am. Physiol. Soc., Soc. Neurosci., N.Y. Acad. Sci., Internat. Oceanographic Found., Sigma Xi. Office: Marine Biomedical Inst Univ Tex Med Sch Galveston TX 77550

BLANKENSHIP, LILLIAN BARTLETT (MRS. HARVEY TAYLOR BLANKENSHIP), social worker; b. Dallas, Jan. 20, 1932; d. James Lloyd and Grace (McCormack) Naylor; student Blinn Coll., 1949-51; A.B., U. Houston, 1953; M.S.W., La. State U., 1959; m. Harvey Taylor Blankenship, May 20, 1968. Psychiat. social worker Child Guidance Clinic of Fort Worth and Tarrant County, 1959-65, Child Guidance Center, Houston, 1965-66; asso. dir. Child Guidance Clinic of Ft. Worth and Tarrant County, 1966—; field instr. U. Tex. Sch. Social Work; pvt. practice social work Psychotherapy Inst. of Ft. Worth. Recipient Outstanding Scholastic Achievement award La. State U., 1959. Mem. La. State U. Alumni Council, Acad. Certified Social Workers, Am. Orthopsychiat. Assn., Nat. Assn. Social Workers (sec. Fort Worth 1962-63), Am. Assn. Marriage and Family Counselors, Tex. Social Welfare Assn., Nat. Conf. on Social Work, Council on Social Work Edn., Tarrant County Assn. for Mental Health (com. on childhood mental illness, sec. 1963-65), Tex. Soc. Clin. Social Workers. Episcopalian. Club: Fort Worth Skiers. Home: PO Box 17101 Fort Worth TX 76102 Office: 927 8th Av Fort Worth TX 76104

BLANKMAN, RICHARD HARVEY, architect; b. Winthrop, Mass., Jan. 19, 1940; s. Max and Evelyn (Rosenberg) B.; student San Antonio Coll., 1958-60; B.Arch., Tex. A. and M. U., 1963; m. Linda Sisson, Jan. 25, 1974. Intern, Noonan & Krocker, San Antonio, 1963-64, Hesson & May, San Antonio, 1964-65, Arthur Dykes, 1965-67; architect, Johnson & Dempsey, San Antonio, 1967-72, Lloyd Jary, San Antonio, 1973; owner, Richard Blankman & Assos., architects, San Antonio, 1973—. Served with USCGR, 1963-69. Mem. A.I.A. Republican. Home: 3253 Hillcrest St Apt 133 San Antonio TX 78201 Office: 3211 Nacogdoches St San Antonio TX 78217

BLANKS, CHARLES PRESTON, JR., state ofcl.; b. Meridian, Miss., June 27, 1913; s. Charles Preston and Mary Eleanor (Pumphrey) B.; B.S. Miss. State Coll., 1940 M.S. Harvard, 1947; M.P.H., U. N.C., 1957; m. Shirley Rue Dumas, Aug. 20, 1932. Chief, pub. health div. AID, Nicaragua, 1960-63, chief pub. health div., Columbia, 1963-65, chief malaria adviser, Pakistan, 1965-67; health planning adminstr. Ala. Dept. Pub. Health, Montgomery, 1968—. Served with AUS, 1942-46. Mem. Nat. Soc. Profl. Engrs., Harvard Soc. Engrs. and Scientists, Inter-Am. Soc. San. Engrs., Tau Beta Pi, Delta Omega. Home: 3315 Walton Dr Montgomery AL 36102 Office: State Office Bldg Montgomery AL 36104

BLANKS, JAMES BAILEY, educator; b. Clarksville, Va., Aug. 6, 1903; s. Lyddall Bailey and Isabelle (McBriety) B.; B.B.A., U. Richmond, 1926; M.A., Wake Forest (N.C.) Coll., 1929; postgrad. guidance, Columbia; m. Margaret Earle, Sept. 10, 1932; children—Margaret Elizabeth, Mary Isabelle (Mrs. Aubrey A. West). Prin. schs., Va. 1925-27; prof. edn. and acting dean Boiling Springs Jr. Coll., 1929-30; asso. prof. edn. and psychology Limestone Coll., 1930-31; prof. edn. and psychology La Grange (Ga.) Coll., 1932-57, prof. psychology and social sci., 1957-71, prof. emeritus, 1971—, chmn. dept. psychology 1957-67, chief examiner grad. record examination, 1949-57; individual practice psychol. counseling, lectr. history and econs., 1943; guidance and mental hygiene cons., 1937; dir. Vets. Guidance Center, Furman U., Greenville, S.C., 1945-47; vis. prof. U. Ga. Off-Campus Center, Columbus, 1947-57, Carson-Newman Coll., Summers 1956, 57; cons. Troup County Family and Children Services, Ga. Dept. Edn. Mem. Ga. Mental Health Assn., Ga. Psychol. Assn. (chmn. legal affairs com.), So. Council on Tchr. Edn., Am. Acad. Polit. and Social Sci., Ga. Edn. Assn., N.E.A., Southeastern Assn. Geographers, Pi Gamma Mu (sec.) Democrat. Baptist. Mason. Licensed to practice applied psychology Ga. Bd. Examiners of Psychologists, 1951. Surveyor ednl. systems, both plant and curriculum, Ga. Contbr. psychol. articles to newspapers and other publs. Home: 114 College Av LaGrange GA 30240 Office: LaGrange Coll LaGrange GA 30240

BLANKS, JAMES RIGHTMAN, mech. engr.; b. Hohenwald, Tenn., Mar. 21, 1937; s. William Ezekiel and Lillie Norine (Harrell) B.; B.S. in Mech. Engring., U. Tenn., Knoxville, 1960; M.S., U. Tenn. Space Inst., Tullahoma, 1968; m. Janice Dean Webb, Sept. 13, 1959; children—Lisa Karen, James Harrell, Laura Leigh. Asso. mech. devel. engr. Union Carbide Nuclear Co., Oak Ridge, Tenn., 1960-62; aeroballistic range and installation engr. ARO Inc., Arnold Engring. Devel. Center, Arnold AFB, Tenn., 1962—. Registered profl. engr., Tenn. Mem. Pi Tau Sigma, Tau Beta Pi, Phi Kappa Phi, Pi Kappa Alpha. Mem. Ch. of Christ. Home: 304 Heights Av Tullahoma TN 37388

BLANNING, ROBERT BRESSLER, elec. engr.; b. Williamstown, Pa., Jan. 7, 1920; s. Charles Franklin and Carol Merle (Bressler) B.; B.S., Pa. State U., 1941; m. Estelle Marcelle Adams, Jan. 12, 1946; children—Kenneth, Virginia, Lisa, Linda. Engr., Gen. Electric Co., Schenectady, 1946-54; supervisory engr. Ordnance Dept. U.S. Army, WSPG, N.M., 1954-56; tech. specialist TEMCO, Dallas, 1956-61; prin. staff engr. Martin Marietta Corp., Orlando, Fla., 1961—. Served to capt. C.E., AUS, 1941-46. Registered profl. engr., N.Y. Asso. fellow Am. Inst. Aeros. and Astronautics; sr. mem. I.E.E.E. Home: 5120 Dorian Av Orlando FL 32809 Office: Sand Lake Rd Orlando FL 32805

BLANTON, HOOVER CLARENCE, lawyer; b. Green Sea, S.C., Oct. 13, 1925; s. Clarence Leo and Margaret (Hoover) S.; J.D., U. S.C., 1953; m. Cecilia Lopez, July 31, 1949; children—Lawson Hoover, Michael Lopez. Admitted to S.C. bar, 1953; since practiced in Columbia; mem. firm Whaley & McCutchen, 1953-66, Whaley, McCutchen, Blanton & Richardson, 1967-72, Whaley, McCutchen, Blanton & Dent, 1973—. Dir. Legal Aid Service Agy., Columbia, chmn., 1972-73. Gen. counsel S.C. Republican Com., 1963-66; pres. Richland County Rep. Conv., 1962; del. Rep. State Convs., 1962, 64, 66, 68, 70, 74. Bd. dirs. Midlands Community Action Agy., Columbia, vice chmn., 1972-73. Served with USNR, 1942-46, 50-52. Mem. Am., S.C., Richland County bar assns., S.C. State Bar (historian 1969—), S.C. Def. Attys. Assn., Assn. Ins. Attys. (state chmn. 1971—), Phi Delta Phi. Baptist. Clubs: Toastmasters (pres. 1959), Columbia Young Lawyers. Home: 3655 Deerfield Dr Columbia SC 29204 Office: 1414 Lady St Columbia SC 29201

BLANTON, JAMES LAMAR, supermarket exec.; b. Pelham, Ga., Dec. 21, 1923; s. Joseph James and Mary (Kemp) B.; ed. pub. schs.; m. Frances Catherine Woodward, May 12, 1941; children— Franklin Lamar, James Roger, Janice (Mrs. Franklin D. Anglin), David Kemp, Charles Carey. With Publix Super Markets, Lakeland, Fla., 1940—, v.p. meat operations, 1969—. Served with AUS, World War II. Named Hon. Future Farmer Am., 1965. Mem. Lakeland C. of C. Baptist. Mason. Home: 1603 Leighton Av Lakeland FL 33803 Office: 1936 New Tampa Hwy Lakeland FL 33802

BLANTON, TED CARROLL, JR., indsl. elec. contracting co. exec.; b. Pasadena, Tex., Oct. 27, 1943; s. Ted Carroll and Marguerite (Williams) B.; B.S., Sam Houston U., 1966; m. Paula Gunter, Oct. 14, 1972; children by previous marriage—Tonya Lee, Tiffany Kay; 1 stepdau., Stacy Anne Shaw. With Blanton Electric Co., Inc., Beaumont, Tex., 1966—, v.p., 1967-71, pres., 1971-72, chmn. bd., 1972—; organizer, 1968, since pres., chmn. bd. Nat. Indsl. Electric Co., Beaumont; owner Cardinal Equipment Co., Beaumont, 1970—, Cardinal Devel. Co., Beaumont, 1970—. Mem. Nat. Elec. Contractors Assn. (dir. S.E. Tex. chpt., bd. dirs. joint apprentice and tng. fund 1969—), Beaumont C. of C., Young Men's Bus. League, Pi Kappa Alpha. Methodist (dir., mem. finance com.). Home: 5995 Tangledahl Lane Beaumont TX 77706 Office: PO Box 789 Beaumont TX 77704

BLASDELL, JONATHAN HIRAM, electric co. exec.; b. Kyle, Tex., Jan. 30, 1905; s. Jonathan Hiram and Martha Rose (Capers) B.; student U. Houston, 1936; m. Gladys Viola Fruzia, May 21, 1927; children—Jonathan Hiram, James Edward, Taneen (Mrs. Arlie Bentrup). Engr., Houston Electronics, 1925; contractor Compton Electric, 1926-27, Caywood Electric, 1935-41; v.p. Fisk Electric Co., contractors, engrs., Houston, 1942—. Mem. Ch. of Christ (elder 1950—). Club: Atascocito Country (Houston). Home: 312 Eleanor St Houston TX 77009 Office: 3102 Milam St Houston TX 77006

BLAU, GEORGE GAFFORD, III, social worker; b. Columbus, Ga., Apr. 10, 1936; s. George Gafford, Jr. and Elese (Cornett) B.; B.S. in Edn., U. Ga., 1958; M.Div., Vanderbilt U., 1961; postgrad. Ind. U., 1964-65; m. Janet Gray, Feb. 15, 1971; 1 dau., Margaret Linn. Ordained to ministry Christian Ch. (Disciples of Christ), 1961; minister edn. Glen Oak Christian Ch., Peoria, Ill., 1961-64; dir. Atlanta Lay Sch. Theology, 1965-72; investigator Fulton County Juvenile Ct., Atlanta, 1972—. Bd. sponsors Atlanta Interfaith Broadcasters, 1969-70; producer radio program Turn-On, 1969-70, TV program Reflections, 1970; cons. TV program Sound of Youth, 1970-71. Mem. Am. Civil Liberties Union, Atlanta Council in Internat. Visitors. Treas., Georgians for McCarthy, 1968; Ga. del. Nat. Democratic Conv., 1968. Pres., Dir.'s sect. Peoria Area Council Chs., 1963; chmn. Atlantans for Peace, 1967-68; mem. exec. bd. Christian Council Met. Atlanta, 1967-71. Mem. Atlanta Disciple Ministers Assn. (v.p. 1967-68), Soc. for Bibl. Lit., Assn. Recorded Sound Collections, Automatic Mus. Instruments Collectors Assn. Contbr. articles to profl. jours. Home: 5555 Roswell Rd NE Atlanta GA 30342 Office: 445 Capitol Av SE Atlanta GA 30312

BLAUSTEIN, SAUL J., economist; b. N.Y.C., July 30, 1924; B.S., City Coll. N.Y., 1948 postgrad. U. So. Cal., 1948-50, George Washington U., 1951-53. Price and cost living economist Bur. Labor Statistics, U.S. Dept. Labor, Washington, 1951-55, dir. unemployment ins. program research Bur. Employment Security, 1955-67; sr. staff economist unemployment and related manpower research W.E. Upjohn Inst. for Employment Research, Washington, 1967—. Tchr. econs. George Washington U., 1953-55. Served with USAAF, 1943-45. Recipient Meritorious Service award U.S. Dept. Labor, 1959. Mem. Indsl. Relations Research Assn., Am. Econ. Assn., Phi Beta Kappa. Home: 9308 Compton St Silver Spring MD 20901 Office: 1101 17th St NW Washington DC 20036

BLAZER, DAN GERMAN, II, physician; b. Nashville, Feb. 23, 1944; s. Dan German and Mary Elizabeth (Owsley) B.; B.A., Vanderbilt U., 1965; postgrad. Harding Grad. Sch., 1966; M.D., U. Tenn., 1969; m. Sherrill Walls, Aug. 19, 1966; children—Dan German III, Natasha Leigh. Intern, City Memphis Hosps., 1970; med. dir. Christian Mobile Clinic, Kumba, United Republic Cameroon, 1971, 72; resident physician in psychiatry Duke U. Med. Center, Durham, N.C., 1973—, teaching fellow dept. psychiatry, 1973—; mem. staff Central State Psychiat. Hosp., Nashville, 1972—. Mem. Christian Med. Soc., Alpha Phi Omega. Mem. Ch. of Christ (tchr. Bible sch. classes). Home: 5102 Longleaf Dr Durham NC 27705 Office: Duke U Med Center Box 2995 Durham NC 27710

BLAZER, JOHN ALLISON, clin. psychologist; b. Nashville, Apr. 18, 1930; s. John Payne and Henryetta (Rowland) B.; B.A., Andrew Jackson U., 1954; A.B., Cumberland U., 1958; B.S., Coll. William and Mary, 1959; M.S., 1960; Ph.D., Episcopal U., 1962; Sc.D., Burton Coll., 1965; postgrad. U. Tenn., 1958, Vanderbilt U., 1960; U. Miami, 1961, U. London, 1962, Sorbonne, U. Paris, 1962; Ph.D. (hon.), Ohio Christian Coll., 1970; m. Judith Kristine Rosen, Mar. 28, 1964; 1 dau., Allison Kristine. Individual practice psychology, Dallas, 1962; staff psychologist Bristol Mental Health Clin., Meml. Hosp. Bristol, Va.-Tenn., 1963-64; dir. Bristol (Va.) Family Guidance Center, 1964; clin. psychologist mental health clin. Chatham County Health Dept., Savannah, Ga., 1964—, acting dir., 1971; pres. Psychol. Press, Savannah, 1962—; sch. psychologist Bristol (Tenn.) Bd. Edn., 1963-64; cons. Bayview Psychol. Services, Portsmouth, Va., 1964—; instr. Am. U. Savannah, 1966—, Med. Coll. Ga. Savannah, 1966; dir. Children's Learning Center, 1969—, Savannah Reading Center, 1970—; personnel dir. Wachtel's Physician Supply Co., 1968-69; personnel cons. Candler Gen. Hosp., 1969-70; asso. psychologist Marion F. Smith and Assos., psychol. consultants, 1969—. Served with USMCR, 1948-53. Decorated Purple Heart. Mem. Am. Assn. for Humanistic Psychology, Am. Sociol Assn., Am. Assn. Criminology (chmn. Com. crime prevention, psychology criminality 1964—, v.p. Ga. chpt. 1966—), Ga. mental health sect. (chmn. 1967-68) Ga. Pub. Health Assn., Ga. Psychol. Assn., Nat. Council Family Relations, Am. Assn. Sex Educators and Counselors, Am. Assn. Suicidology, Am. Counselors Soc., Am. Personnel and Guidance Assn., Ga. Sch. Psychol. Services Assn., Internat. Assn. Hypnotists, Nat. Assn. Sch. Psychologists, Nat. Assn. Social Workers, Soc. for Sci. Study Sex, Am. Acad. Mental Health Technicians, Southeastern Council on Family Relations. Luthern. Editor Psychology—A Journal of Human Behavior, 1963; editorial adviser Edn., 1970; cons. editor Psychologists and Educators Press, 1970. Contbr. articles to profl. jours, poems to lit. mags. Home: 308 Kensington Dr Savannah GA 31405 Office: Chatham County Health Dept Savannah GA 31405

BLAZER, REXFORD S(YDNEY), oil exec.; b. Aledo, Ill., Sept. 1, 1907; s. Frederick B. and Elizabeth E. (Niederlander) B.; A.B., U. Ill., 1928; D.Sc., (hon.), Pikeville Coll., 1969; hon. degree in Bus. Adminstrn., Morehead State U., 1973; m. Mary Elizabeth Vary, 1935 (dec.); 1 dau., Mary Linda; m. 2d, Frances Montross Green, 1942 (div.); 1 son, Richard M.; m. 3d, Lucile Thornton Scott, 1954; 1 son, Rexford Sydney; stepchildren—Dan W. Scott III, W. Thornton Scott. Joined Allied Oil Co., Inc., Cleve., 1928, dir., 1935-59, v.p., 1938, pres., 1948-59; dir. Ashland Oil, Inc. (Ky.) (formerly Ashland Oil & Refining Co.), 1949-73, pres., 1951-57, chmn. bd. 1957-72, chmn. exec. com., 1972-73; dir. 3d Nat. Bank of Ashland. Bd. dirs. U. Ill. Found.; mem. exec. com. U. Ky. Devel. Council; trustee Ky. Ind. Coll. Found., 1952-64; past regent, trustee U. of South; bd. dirs. Spindletop Research Center. Mem. Ky. Indsl. Devel. Bd., 1956-69, East Ky. Regional Planning Commn., 1960-64 chmn. adv. council Ohio Valley Improvement Assn.; mem. adv. com. Nat. Waterways Conf. Recipient Illini Achievement award U. Ill., 1968; named fellow, hon. alumnus U. Ky. Mem. Nat. Petroleum Assn. (past pres.), Western Petroleum Refiners Assn. (v.p. 1957-61), Nat. Petroleum Refiners Assn. (dir., mem. exec. and finance coms. 1960-70), Am. Petroleum Inst. (v.p. transp. 1971-72, exec. com., dir. 1957-73), Asphalt Inst. (dir. 1960-68), 25 Year Club of Petroleum Industry (past pres.), Hwy. Users Fedn. for Safety and Mobility, (past chmn.), Ky. (pres. 1955-56), Ohio (dir. 1960-68) chambers commerce, Ky. Oil and Gas Assn. (dir.), Psi Upsilon (chmn. bd. govs. Omicron chpt., past v.p. exec. council). Episcopalian (sr. warden Ashland 1959, 73; mem. exec. council Lexington Diocese 1958-62). Rotarian. Clubs: Bellefonte Country (Ashland); Idle Hour Country (Lexington); Westwood Country (Cleve.); Pendennis (Louisville); Filson. Home: 2711 Seminole Av Ashland KY 41101 Office: 1409 Winchester Av Ashland KY 41101 Died Jan. 2, 1974.

BLAZQUEZ Y SERVIN, CARLOS HUMBERTO, pathologist; b. Mexico City, Mexico, Oct. 9, 1926; s. Carlos Luis Blazquez Duran and Lucia Maria Servin-Arias Caballero; A.A., Chaffey Coll., 1952; B.S., U. Cal. at Davis, 1955; M.S. U. Fla., 1957, Ph.D., 1959; m. Annelise Jeanne Van Royen, Jan. 23, 1965; children—Maria-Isabel, Carlos Adrian. Came to U.S., 1942, naturalized, 1945. Plant pathologist Firestone Plantations Co., Liberia, West Africa, and Itubera, Brazil, 1959-61; asst. plant pathologist United Fruit Co., La Lima, Honduras, 1961-63; plant pathologist-in-charge Citrus Research U. West Indies, Jamaica, 1964-66; asst. plant pathologist South Fla. Field Lab., U. Fla., Immokalee, 1966-72, asso. plant pathologist, 1972—, prin. investigator Internat. Fedn. Aquarium Socs.-NASA Earth Resources Tech. Satellite program, 1973—; project leader weather and disease surveillance project S.W. Fla., 1973—. Cons. L. & Rose Co., Dominica, West Indies, 1964-66, Micronairs, Ltd., Isle of Wight, Eng., 1970, Nat. Aerial Application Assn., Loveland, Colo., 1970. Mem. bd. Lehigh Acres Community Day Care Center, 1971, pres., 1972. Served with USNR, 1944-46, USCG, 1946-50. Recipient Project Leader Aerial Application grant U. Fla., 1969-70. Mem. Am. Phytopathological Soc. (mem. com. 1972—), Mycol. Soc. Am., Am. Soc. Photogrametry, Assn. Applied Biologists, Am. Chem. Soc., Fla. State Hort. Soc., Am. Assn. Hort. Sci. Home: 1422 Huntdale St Lehigh Acres FL 33936 Office: Agr Research Route 1 Box 2 G Immokalee FL 33934

BLECKNER, EDWARD, JR., data communications co. exec.; b. Pompano, Fla., June 30, 1933; s. Edward and Emma (DeLozier) B.; B.E.E., U. Fla., 1954; m. Sondra Marie Roush, June 25, 1954; children—Karen Marie, Laura Louise. Sr. engr. Melpar Inc., Falls Church, Va., 1956-59; staff engr. Aero Geo Astro Corp., Alexandria, Va., 1959; with Milgo Electronic Corp., Miami, 1960—, mgr. Data Communications div., 1966-67, v.p., 1970—, also dir., pres. subsidiary Internat. Communications Corp., Miami, 1967—; pres. Milgo-IDAB Corp., Miami, 1966-67; dir. Racal-Milgo Ltd., Reading, Berkshire, Eng. Served with USAF, 1954-56. Mem. Sigma Chi. Republican. Methodist. Patentee in field. Office: 7620 NW 36th Av Miami FL 33147

BLESSEY, WALTER JEROME, IV, investment co. exec.; b. Biloxi, Miss., Apr. 17, 1939; s. Walter James and Geraldine Ann (Fountain) B.; B.B.A. in Accounting, U. Miss., 1961, J.D., 1964; m. Mary Alice Wingo, Dec. 18, 1960 (div. Aug. 1968); children—Walter John V; m. 2d, Beverly Wartenbach Johnson, Sept. 29, 1968; stepchildren—Mitzi Lynn, Michael Louis. Instr. accounting U. Miss., 1962-64; admitted to Miss. bar, 1964; tax accountant Arthur Andersen & Co., Houston, 1966-69; controller, partner John E. Kilgore & Co., Houston, 1969—; v.p. Indianola Co., Houston, 1971—; sec., treas., dir. Cambridge Royalty Co., Houston. Served to 1st lt., AUS, 1964-66. C.P.A., Tex. Mem. Am. Inst. C.P.A.'s, Am., Miss. bar assns., Tex. Soc. C.P.A.'s, Am. Legion, Delta Sigma Pi, Beta Alpha Psi, Phi Alpha Delta. Episcopalian (vestryman 1970-72). Clubs: University, Plaza (Houston). Home: 27222 Lana Lane Conroe TX 77301 Office: John E Kilgore & Co San Jacinto Bldg Houston TX 77002

BLEVINS, BRYAN O'DONNELL, dentist; b. Baytown, Tex., July 19, 1939; s. Arthur Buster and Ollie Marie (Norris) B.; student Panola Coll., 1957-59, Northeast State U., 1959-61; B.S., D.D.S., Baylor U., 1965; m. Doris Jeanne Vaughn, Feb. 15, 1964; children—Bryan O'Donnell, Jamie D'Lea. Pvt. practice dentistry, Lufkin, Tex., 1965—. Mem. Am. Acad. Gold Foil Operators, Am., Tex. dental assns., East Tex. Dental Soc., Am. Acad. Gen. Dentistry, Am. Soc. Preventive Dentistry, Internat. Acad. Orthodontics, Jr. C. of C., C. of C., Psi Omega. Baptist. Home: 1407 Oak Hill St Lufkin TX 75901 Office: 105 E Bremond St Lufkin TX 75901

BLEWER, GLENDA GLORIA (MRS. ALTON GEORGE BLEWER), banker; b. Higgins, Tex.; Mar. 2, 1927; d. Lee Roy and Lillie Mae (Reimer) Goettsche; student Draughon's Bus. Coll., 1944-45, Tex. Tech U., 1952; m. Alton George Blewer, Apr. 7, 1946; 1 dau., Alison (Mrs. David Little King). Tchr. typing and machine practice Draughon's Bus. Coll., Lubbock, Tex., 1945; billing clerk Lubbock Sash and Door Co., 1946; bookkeeper First Nat. Bank, Lubbock, 1948-49, teller, 1950-55, asst. cashier, 1965-71, asst. v.p., 1972—. Vice pres. Lubbock P.T.A., 1957-58; electoral mem. YWCA, 1959—; life mem. Tex. Congress Parents and Tchrs., 1959—. Mem. Nat. Assn. Bank Women, Inc., Am. Inst. Banking (sec. 1965), Bank Adminstrn. Inst. Baptist. Home: 2308 53d St Lubbock TX 79412 Office: 1500 Broadway St Lubbock TX 79401

BLEWER, JOHN RANDALL, gas pipeline co. exec.; b. Shreveport, La., Sept. 9, 1929; s. Edwin Laurine and Mildred (Sewall) B.; B.S., La. State U., 1950; m. Nancy Harper, Feb. 28, 1959; children—John Randall, Susan Elizabeth. Mgr. community and stockholder relations Tex. Eastern Transp. Corp., Shreveport, 1952-59; mgr. financial relations Bozell & Jacobs, Inc., N.Y.C., 1959-60; dir. pub. relations Tex. Gas Transmission Corp., Owensboro, Ky., 1960-71, v.p. pub. relations, financial relations and advt., 1971—. Mem. adv. bd. Salvation Army, chmn. 1971-73; mem. adv. bd. Jr. Service League; bd. dirs., mem. exec. com. United Way. Served to capt. AUS, 1951-52. Mem. Am., So. gas assns., Ind. Natural Gas Assn., Mid-Continent, Ky. Oil and gas assns., Ohio Valley Improvement Assn., U.S. Indsl. Council, Pub. Relations Soc. Am., Assn. Petroleum Writers. Clubs: Campbell (dir. 1969-72, pres. 1970), Owensboro Country (Owensboro). Home: 1805 Littlewood Dr Owensboro KY 42301 Office: 3800 Frederica St Owensboro KY 42301

BLISS, DONALD TIFFANY, JR., govt. ofcl.; b. Norwalk, Conn., Nov. 24, 1941; s. Donald Tiffany and Marina (Popova) B.; B.A. with highest honors, Principia Coll., 1963; J.D. cum laude, Harvard, 1966. Admitted to N.Y. State bar, 1966, also D.C. bar, Trust Terr. of Pacific Islands bar; vol. Peace Corps, Micronesia, 1966-68; asso. firm LeBoeuf, Lamb, Laeby and MacRae, N.Y.C.; now asst. to sec., exec. sec. Dept. Health, Edn. and Welfare, Washington. Recipient Spl. citation Sec. Health, Edn. and Welfare. Mem. Fed. Bar Assn., Rippon Soc. Co-editor: Trust Territory Reporter, vol. I-III, 1968; editor: Micronesia Advocate, 1966-68. Home: 727A Delaware St SW Washington DC 20024 Office: Room 5239 Dept Health Edn and Welfare 330 Independence Av Washington DC 20201

BLISS, WHITNEY CARLETON, JR., city ofcl., civil engr.; b. Miami, Fla., Sept. 9, 1923; s. Whitney Carleton and Louvenia (Crews) B.; B.C.E., U. Fla., 1949; postgrad. Northeastern U., 1964; m. E. Wynonah Zetroun, Nov. 1, 1953; children—David Alan, Donald Carleton. Project engr. DeLeuw, Cather & Brill, 1953-58; partner Kratzert & Bliss, Engrs., Sanford, Fla., 1958-60; county engr. Seminole County, Sanford, Fla., 1960-62; asst. v.p., chief engr. DeLeuw, Cather & Co., Newark, Boston, 1962-70; city engr., Ocala, Fla., 1970-73, city mgr., 1973—. Served to lt. col. USAAF, 1942-46; ETO. Registered profl. engr., 17 states, D.C. Fellow Am. Soc. C.E.; mem. Inst. Traffic Engrs., Fla. Engring. Soc. (pres. Forest chpt.). Baptist (deacon). Kiwanian. Home: 1735 SE 6th Av Ocala FL 32670 Office: PO Box 1270 Ocala FL 32670

BLOCH, JULES, JR., oil co. exec.; b. Oklahoma City, July 15, 1915; s. Jules and Josie (Hirsch) B.; B.S., U. Okla., 1937; B.A., Oklahoma City U., 1954; m. Xenia C. Bank, June 5, 1963. Ind. geologist and oil operator, 1946—; pres., dir. Torii Co., Oklahoma City, 1961—. Served with USNR, 1940-46. Decorated Order of the Fatherland War (U.S.S.R.); recipient commendation U.S. sec. of navy, 1942. Mem. Am. Assn. Petroleum Geologists, Oklahoma City Geologic Soc. Clubs; Oklahoma City Golf and Country, Embassy, Colony. Home: 700 Yukon Av Yukon OK 73099 Office: First Nat Bank Bldg Oklahoma City OK 73102

BLOCK, (EDWARD) BATES, lawyer; b. Atlanta, Aug. 16, 1918; s. E. Bates and Julia (Porter) B.; A.B., Emory U., 1940 LL.B., U. Ga., 1942; m. Margaret Ann Davison, Dec. 18, 1956; foster children—Julia, Baxter, Douglas Jones. Admitted to Ga. bar, 1942; partner firm Hansell, Post, Brandon & Dorsey, Atlanta; sec., dir. So. Syndicate, Inc., 1962-73, Ga. Capital Corp.; pres., dir. Valley Devel. Corp., 1954-71, Woodlands, Inc. Mem. Ga. Student Loan Commn., 1964-70. Trustee Chi Phi Ednl. Trust. Mem. Ga. Geneal. Soc. (pres. 1965-66), Atlanta Hist. Assn., Atlanta Art Assn., Ga., Atlanta (sec. 1943-49) bar assns., Atlanta Lawyers Club, Motor Carrier Lawyers Assn., Phi Beta Kappa, Omicron Delta Kappa, Chi Phi (nat. v.p.). Presbyn. Clubs: University Yacht; Capital City, Nine O'Clocks, Piedmont Driving (Atlanta). Editor: Atlanta Lawyer, 1956-62, Ga. Bar News, 1963-64. Home: 25 Valley Rd NW Atlanta GA 30305 Office: First Nat Bank Bldg Atlanta GA 30303

BLOCK, HERBERT LAWRENCE (HERBLOCK), editorial cartoonist; b. Chgo., Oct. 13, 1909; s. David Julian and Tessie (Lupe) B.; student Lake Forest (Ill.) Coll., 1927-29, L.L.D. (hon.), 1957; student Art Inst. Chgo. (part time classes); unmarried. Editorial cartoonist Chgo. Daily News, 1929-33, NEA Service, 1933-43, U.S. Army, 1943-45; editorial cartoonist The Washington Post, 1946—. Recipient Pulitzer prize, 1942, 54; Am. Newspaper Guild award, 1948; Heywood Broun award, 1950; Sigma Delta Chi Nat. Editorial Awards, 1949, 50, 52, 57; Sidney Hillman award (for book), 1953; Reuben award Nat. Cartoonists Soc., 1957; Lauterbach award for civil liberties union, 1960; Distinguished Service Journalism award U. Mo., 1961. Fellow Am. Acad. Arts and Scis. Club: Cosmos (Washington). Author: The Herblock Book, 1952; Herblock's Here and Now, 1955; Herblock's Special for Today, 1958. Address: The Washington Post 1515 L St NW Washington DC 20005

BLOCK, WILLIAM JOSEPH, JR., physician; b. San Antonio, Oct. 3, 1921; s. William Joseph and Mary Irene (McNelly) B.; B.A., St. Mary's U., San Antonio, 1942; M.D., U. Tex. at Galveston, 1945; M.S., U. Minn., 1952; m. Margaret Patricia O'Daniel, Aug. 18, 1949; children—Patricia Irene, Susan Kearney, Mary Kathleen, Martha Terry, Sharon Ann, William Joseph III, Michael Alfred. Intern Robert B. Green Hosp., San Antonio, 1945-46; resident medicine Boston City Hosp., 1948-49, Mayo Clinic, 1949-52; practice medicine, specializing in cardiology, San Antonio, 1952—; clin. prof. medicine U. Tex. at San Antonio; cons. cardiology to Surgeon Gen.; mem. staff Nix Meml., Robert B. Green Meml., Bexar County Teaching hosps.; mem. courtesy staff S.W. Tex. Meth., Bapt. Meml., Santa Rose, St. Benedict's, Grace Gen. hosps.; cons. cardiology San Antonio State Tb Hosp. Active San Antonio A.R.C. Bd. dirs. Travelers Aid Soc.; trustee S.W. Research Found. Served with AUS, 1946-48. Diplomate Am. Bd. Internal Medicine. Fellow A.C.P., Am. Heart Assn., Am. Coll. Chest Physicians, Am. Coll. Cardiology (past gov.); mem. Tex. (past pres.), San Antonio (past pres.) heart assns., Tex. Acad. Internal Medicine (past pres.), Tex. Club Cardiologists (past pres.), San Antonio Club Internal Medicine (past pres.), Tex. Soc. Internal Medicine (past dir.), San Antonio C. of C., Sigma Xi, Alpha Omega Alpha. Rotarian (dir.). Clubs: Christmas Cotillion, Town, German, Order of Alamo, Texas Cavaliers, San Antonio Country, Argyle, University, St. Anthony (San Antonio). Home: 407 Elizabeth Rd San Antonio TX 78209 Office: Nix Professional Bldg San Antonio TX 78205

BLOMME, CARLYLE WHITNEY, JR., educator; b. Wilmington, N.C., Oct. 14, 1933; s. Carlyle Whitney and Vivian Inez (Darden) B.; A.A., Wilmington Jr. Coll., 1957; B.A., U. N.C., 1971; m. Dorothy Blount Anderson, June 8, 1960; 1 son, Carlyle Anderson. Chief survey party John B. Davis, Jr., surveyor, Wilmington, 1956-57; partner Davis & Blomme Surveying Co., Wilmington, 1957-59; owner Blomme Surveying Co., Wilmington, 1959-68; instr. engring. tech., chmn. civil tech. div. Coastal Carolina Community Coll., Jacksonville, 1969—; instr., Cape Fear Tech. Inst., Wilmington, 1965-67. Engring. adviser to exec. com. Wilmington Presbytery, Presbyn. Ch., Synod N.C., 1967—. Served with USCGR, 1952-55. Mem. Am. Congress Surveying and Mapping, Am. Soc. Engring. Edn., N.C. Soc. Surveyors (chpt. pres. 1962, chmn. edn. com. 1972), V.F.W. Democrat. Presbyn. (deacon). Home: Route 3 Box 282 Richlands NC 28574 Office: 222 Georgetown Rd Jacksonville NC 28540

BLOMSTROM, DAVID BENJAMIN, accountant; b. Houston, June 22, 1936; s. Gunnar and Rosanna Reeves (Hirsch) B.; B.B.A., U. Houson, 1961; m. Eugenia Martha Ybanez, Oct. 27, 1963; children—Deborah Beth, Denise Bernadette. Auditor, Main & Co. C.P.A.'s, Houston, 1961-63; asst. to treas. Tex. 1st Mortgage Co., Houston, 1963-64; controller George Consol. gen. contractor, Houston and New Orleans, 1964-65, Rosewood Gen. Hosp., Houston, 1965-67; owner David B. Blomstrom C.P.A., Houston, 1968—; sec.-treas., dir. J & B Enterprises, Inc., restaurants, Houston, 1969—. Bd. dirs. City of Cities Municipal Utility Dist., Fort Bend County, Tex., 1973—. Served with USNR, 1954-57; Korea. C.P.A., Tex., La. Mem. Am. Inst. C.P.A.'s, Tex., La., Houston socs. c.p.a.'s. Baptist. Clubs: Fort Bend County Exchange, Lions of Sugar Land, Sugar Creek Country. Home: 2707 Fairway St Sugar Land TX 77478 Office: 6300 Hillcroft St Houston TX 77036

BLOODWORTH, JAMES NELSON, justice; b. Decatur, Ala., Jan 21, 1921; s. Benjamin M. and Marguerite (Nelson) B.; student Athens Coll., 1938-39; B.S., U. Ala. Sch. Commerce, 1942; LL.B., U. Ala., 1947; m. Mary Jean Gregg, Sept. 27, 1963; children—Catherine, Sandra, Jean Marguerite. Admitted to Ala. bar, 1947; mem. firm Calvin & Bloodworth, Decatur, 1947-58; judge, Recorder's Ct., Decatur, 1948-51; solicitor Morgan County, Decatur, 1951; judge Circuit Ct. Ala., 8th Jud. Circuit, Decatur, 1959-68; asso. justice Ala. Supreme Ct., 1968—. Co-chmn. Circuit Judges' Seminars Ala., 1960-66; lectr. before judges, solicitors assns., seminars, 1963—; chmn. Ala. Pattern Jury Instr. Com., 1966-68. Pres. Morgan County Jury Com., 1966-68. Pres. Decatur Boys Club, 1951; moderator North Ala. Presbytery, 1965; mem. bd. Morgan County chpt. A.R.C., 1959-60. Mem. Bd. Pardons and Paroles Ala., 1951-52; chmn. Ala. Democratic campaign steering com., 1961-63; faculty adviser Nat. Coll. State Trial Judges, 1967, 71; faculty Am. Acad. Jud. Edn., 1970—; lectr. Ala. Police Acad., 1969—. Served from pvt. to capt. AUS. Decorated Bronze Star medal, Combat Infantry badge. Mem. Ala. Res. Officers Assn. (pres. chpt. 1959), Morgan County Bar Assn. (pres. 1955), Decatur C. of C., Ala. Bar Assn., Phi Delta Phi, Kappa Alpha Order, Omicron Delta Kappa. Presbyn. (elder). Mason (K.T., Shriner), Rotarian (pres. 1953-54). Home: 3221 Bankhead Av Montgomery AL 36106 Office: Judicial Bldg Capitol Montgomery AL 36104

BLOSKAS, JOHN D., editor, pub. relations dir.; b. Waco, Tex., July 13, 1928; s. George and Alvina (Schrader) B.; B.A., Baylor U., 1953; m. Anna Louise Nelson, Feb. 7, 1955; children—Suzanne, John D., Kenneth Douglas. Exec. sec. Waco Jr. C. of C., 1953-55; asso. editor Mexia (Tex.) Daily News, 1955-56; dir. publicity Valley C. of C., Weslaco, Tex., 1956-57; religion editor Houston Chronicle, 1957-58; v.p. pub. relations annuity bd. So. Bapt. Conv., Dallas, 1958—. Served with USNR, 1945-49, 50-51. Mem. So. Bapt. (past pres.), Tex. Bapt. (past pres.) pub. relations assns., Pub. Relations Soc. Am. (accredited), Religious Pub. Relations Council, Fellowship of Christians in Arts, Media and Entertainment. Editor: The Years Ahead. Home: 5816 Clendenin Dallas TX 75228 Office: 511 N Akard Bldg Dallas TX 75201

BLOSSER, DALE ALAN, architect; b. Brussels, Belgium, Oct. 3, 1927; s. (father Am. citizen) Rolland Ernest Blosser and Josephine (My) B.; student Carnegie Inst. Tech., 1947-49; B.Arch., N.C. State Coll., 1956; m. Louise Ann Schultz Pinkerton, May 25, 1967; stepchildren—Stephen R., Susan L., Timothy J., Don Charles, Lizabeth Ann. Architect, Geodesics, Inc., Raleigh, N.C., 1957-60, John D. Latimer & Asso., Durham, N.C., 1960-62, Synergetics, Inc., Raleigh, 1962-65, Dale Blosser & Assos., archtl. constrn. administrn., Raleigh, 1966-72; partner Blosser, Boone & Assos., 1972—. Lectr. profl. practice dept. architecture Sch. Design, N.C. State U. Served with AUS, 1945-47. Registered architect, N.C., S.C., Va. Mem. Am. Soc. Testing Materials (councilor Carolinas dist.), A.I.A. (office procedures com. N.C. 1966—, sec. Raleigh sect. 1970-71), Constrn. Specification Inst. (Raleigh-Durham chpt. pres. 1967-68, tech. chmn. 1968-69, 73-74), Bldg. Research Inst. (chmn. sect 5.05 constrn. techniques subcom. of Div. V constrn. mgmt. 1969-71), N.C. Assn. Professions, Am. Concrete Inst., Am. Inst. Steel Constrn. Unitarian-Universalist (pres. Thomas Jefferson dist. 1968-69). Works include Library-Student Union Complex; U. N.C., Chapel Hill, 1968, St. James United Meth. Ch., Raleigh, 1970. Home: 3008 Ruffin St Raleigh NC 27607 Office: 2008 Hillsborough St Raleigh NC 27605

BLOUNT, FLOYD EUGENE, chem. engr.; b. Dallas, Dec. 11, 1922; s. Hal Holt and Ina Adelia (Fagala) B.; B.S. in Chemistry, East Tex. State U., 1943; postgrad. U. Tex., 1946-47; m. Easter Lue McGowan, Apr. 6, 1968. With Mobil Research and Devel. Corp., 1947—, research chemist, Paulsboro, N.J., 1947-52, sr. research chemist, Dallas, 1952-64, engring. asso., 1964—. Served with USNR, 1943-46, 1950-52. Decorated Navy Commendation medal. Mem. Soc. Petroleum Engrs., Nat. Assn. Corrosion Engrs., Am. Chem. Soc., Research Soc. Am., Am. Inst. Chem. Engrs. Patentee in field. Home: 5909 Burgundy St Dallas TX 75230 Office: 3600 Duncanville Rd Dallas TX 75211

BLOUSE, LOUIS ERNEST, JR., microbiologist, epidemiologist; b. San Antonio, Nov. 29, 1931; s. Louis and Otilia (Mireles) B.; B.A., U. Tex., 1953, M.A., 1955; Ph.D., La. State U., 1971; m. Jeannie Dodds, June 6, 1958; children—Gary, Tracy, Elaine. Asst. immunologist Tex. State Dept. Health, Austin, 1954-55; lab. dir. El Paso (Tex.) City Health Dept., 1957-59; med. microbiologist USAF Epidemiol. Lab., San Antonio, 1959-68; chief disease surveillance/epidemiology div. Sch. Aerospace Medicine, San Antonio, 1971—. Cons. microbiology Meth. Hosp., New Orleans, 1971; mem. adv. com. NIH Grant for Minority Schs. Biomed. Research Program, United Cath. Colls. San Antonio, 1972-73. Mem. Indian Guides, Longhouse council YMCA, San Antonio, 1971-72. Served with USNR, 1955-57. Recipient Outstanding awards USAF, 1964, 67, 68; Certificate of Merit, USAF Systems Command, 1966; USAF Career Devel. award La. State U. Sch. Medicine, 1969-71, Fisher Sci. award, 1972. Mem. Electron Microscopy Soc. Am., Am. Soc. Microbiology, A.A.A.S., Soc. Air Force Lab. Scientists, Sigma Xi. Home: 5414 El Tejano St San Antonio TX 78233 Office: USAF Sch Aerospace Medicine Epidemiology Div Brooks AFB TX 78235

BLUE, HERBERT CLIFTON, newspaper publisher, state legislator; b. nr. Vass, N.C., Aug. 28, 1910; s. John Patrick and Christian Ann (Stewart) B.; student pub. schs., Vass; m. Gala Lee Nunnery, July 4, 1937; children—Patricia Joyce (Mrs. David E. Bailey), Herbert Clifton, John Lee, Elizabeth Ann. Founder, owner, pub. The Captain (consol. with Sandhill Citizen 1934), Vass. 1932-36, Aberdeen, N.C., 1936—; owner, pub. Robbins (N.C.) Record, 1958—; dir. Carolina Bank, Pinehurst, N.C., Montgomery Herald, Troy, N.C.; mem. N.C. Ho. of Reps., 1947—, speaker, 1963-64. Pres., N.C. Young Democratic Clubs, 1948-49; sec. N.C. Dem. Exec. Com., 1949-52. Bd. dirs. N.C. Cancer Inst., 1961-64, N.C. Soc. for Crippled Children and Adults; chmn. N.C. Cancer Crusade Campaign, 1966; pres. N.C. div. Am. Cancer Soc., 1968; chmn. bd. trustees Sandhills Community Coll. Mem. N.C. Weekly Newspaper Assn. (pres. 1951-52), N.C. Press Assn. (dir. pres.), N.C. Community Coll. Trustees Assn. (pres. 1971-72), Assn. Community Coll. Trustees (state chmn. 1973), Woodmen of World. Democrat. Presbyn. (elder, trustee). Mason, Lion. Home: 800 N Poplar St Aberdeen NC 28315 Office: 202 N Sandhills Blvd Aberdeen NC 28315

BLUM, ETHEL WIDLUS (MRS. MILTON R. BLUM), editor; b. Cleve., Aug. 16, 1921; d. Abe and Minnie (Cherlin) Widlus; student Ohio State U., 1942; m. Milton R. Blum, Feb. 23, 1942 children—Carol Lynn (Mrs. Gould), Jeffrey D., Roger. Editor for Gen. MacArthur, Japan, 1947-50; free lance travel writer, 1950—; travel editor, women's editor Miami Beach (Fla.) Daily Sun, 1964-69, asso. editor, 1969-71; editor Travel Publs., Inc., Miami Beach, Fla., 1970—; travel editor Miami Mag., 1972—, Gold Coast Pictorial, 1972—; editor Cruise Guides, 1971—; broadcaster WKAT, Miami. Pres., Cancer Inst. Miami. Mem. Dade County Democratic Exec. Com., 1972—. Recipient Fla. Press Womens award for best series articles written by a woman, 1966, 67, 68. Mem. Fla. Press Womens Assn., Soc. Am. Travel Writers (chmn. Southeastern U.S.-Caribbean chpt.). Author, editor: Travel Guides, 1970; author: The Total Traveler; syndicated column Traveline. Home: Apt 10B 5838 Collins Av Miami Beach FL 33140 Office: One Lincoln Rd Miami Beach FL 33139

BLUM, HERMAN, cons. engring. co. exec.; b. New Orleans, May 12, 1914; s. Herman and Abbie (Jacobs) B.; B.S. in Mech. Engring., Tulane U., 1938; m. Jeanne Branshaw Glass, July 25, 1973; children—Andrew Jay, Denise Frances, Jeffery Jay, Michael Eugene Glass. Engr., estimator, field supr. C. Wallace Plumbing Co., Dallas, 1938-45; pres. Herman Blum Cons. Engrs., Inc., Dallas, 1945—; a founder APEC (Automated Procedures for Engring. Consultants), 1966, pres., 1966-67. Recipient Constrn. Industry Brotherhood citation, 1965. Registered profl. engr., Tex., Ariz., Ark., Colo., Conn., D.C., Ga., Ill., Ind., Kan., Ky., La., Miss., Mo., N.M., Ohio, Okla., Oreg., Pa., Tenn., Va., Wash., Wis., Wyo. Mem. Nat. Bur. Engring., Cons. Engrs. Council Tex., Nat., Tex. socs. profl. engrs., Am. Soc. Heating, Refrigeration and Air Conditioning Engrs. (pres. Dallas chpt. 1950). Clubs: City, Columbian, Chapparal, Lancers, Engineers. Designer World's 1st computer-controlled bldg. system, 1968. Home: 4730 Bobbitt Dr Dallas TX 75229 Office: 1015 Elm St Dallas TX 75202

BLUM, MAURICE DAULTON, interior designer; b. San Francisco, July 27, 1925; s. Julian Jack and Juliette Vivian (Cohen) B.; B.S., U. Cal. at Los Angeles, 1945; postgrad. Rudolph Schaeffer Sch. Design, 1950. Vice-pres. John J. Greer-Maurice D. Blum Assos., Inc., Washington, 1947—; pres. Interior Design Cons., 1955—. Founder mem. Friends of Kennedy Center. Served with USNR, 1942-45, 47-49. Mem. Am. Inst. Interior Designers, Zeta Beta Tau. Clubs: Arts, Black Tie (Washington). Address: 2108 Bancroft Pl NW Washington DC 20008

BLUM, ROBERT ALLAN, psychiatrist, educator; b. Phila., May 16, 1938; s. Frank A. and Sara (James) B.; B.S., Mass. Inst. Tech., 1959, M.S. (NSF fellow), 1960; M.D., U. Pa., 1964; postgrad. Balt.-Dist. Columbia Inst. for Psychoanalysis, 1969—; m. Irene Harriet Segal, Aug. 2, 1959; children—Lisa, Lora. Engr. Gen. Atronics Corp., Wyndmoor, Pa., 1958-61; intern Meml. Hosp., Long Beach, Cal., 1964-65; resident in psychiatry Mass. Mental Health Center, Boston, 1965-67; practice medicine specializing in psychiatry and psychoanalysis, Washington, 1969—; chief clin. research center Mass. Mental Health Center, Boston, 1966-67; staff asso. Nat. Inst. Mental Health, Washington, 1967-69, research psychiatrist, 1969-70; research psychiatrist Nat. Inst. on Alcohol Abuse and Alcoholism, Washington, 1970—; teaching fellow Harvard Med. Sch., 1965-67; instr. in psychiatry Johns Hopkins U., 1969—; instr. in psychiatry George Washington U., 1969—; clin. asst. prof. psychiatry Georgetown U., 1972—. Served to lt. comdr. USPHS, 1967-69. Diplomate Am. Bd. Psychiatry and Neurology. Mem. A.A.A.S., Am. Psychiat. Assn., Am. Psychoanalytical Assn., Montgomery County Med. Soc., Soc. for Gen. Systems Research, Washington Psychiat. Soc., Sigma Xi, Alpha Omega Alpha, Eta Kappa Nu, Tau Beta Pi. Contbr. articles to profl. jours. Home: 9819 Hill St Kensington MD 20795 Office: 3000 Connecticut Ave NW Washington DC 20008

BLUM, WILLIAM, JR., lawyer, corp. exec.; b. Washington, July 6, 1911; s. William and Willetta C. (Baylis) B.; student Swarthmore Coll.; B.S. cum laude, U. Pa., 1932; J.D., Georgetown U., 1942; postgrad. George Washington U., Catholic U., Am. U.; m. Virginia Henry, May 30, 1945 (dec. 1964); children—Margaret L., William M. H.; m. 2d, Ruth M. Truitt, Apr. 9, 1966. With Riggs Nat. Bank, Washington, 1932-34, E.I. du Pont de Nemours & Co., Wilmington, Del., 1934, investment dept. Nat. Savs. & Trust Co., Washington, 1934-40; admitted to D.C. bar, 1942; practiced in Washington, 1945—; mem. firm Blum, Lindsey & Powell, Blum, Olson & Oulihan. Dir., sec. Fed. Bar Building Corp., Washington, 1959-67; mem. council Fed. Bar, 1967—. Bd. dirs., gen. counsel Episcopal House of Mercy, 1947-63; pres., gen. counsel, dir. Columbia Hosp., 1955-65. Trustee D.C. chpt. A.R.C.; bd. dirs. Episcopal Home for Children. Served to lt. comdr. USNR, 1940-45. Mem. Fed., D.C., Am., N.Y. State assns. Episcopalian. Clubs: Nat. Lawyers, University, Metropolitan (Washington); Chevy Chase (Md.); Jefferson Islands (Md.); North Springs (W.Va.); Rolls Royce Owners. Home: 4301 Massachusetts Av NW Washington DC 20016 Office: Fed Bar Bldg 1815 H St NW Washington DC 20006

BLUMBERG, MARVIN, broadcasting engring. cons.; b. Atlantic City, N.J., Aug. 6, 1924; s. Abe and Elizabeth (Cohen) B.; B.S. in Elec. Engring., George Washington U., 1950; postgrad. U. Pa., 1950-51; m. Charlotte Maletz, Apr. 11, 1954 (dec.); children—Joan and Laura (twins). Electronic equipment devel. Philco Corp., Phila., 1950-51; partner A.D. Ring & Assos., Washington, 1951—; treas.-sec. Dataworld, Inc., 1971—. Served with AUS, 1942-46; ETO, PTO. Mem. Assn. Fed. Communications Cons. Engrs. (sec. 1967, treas. 1968). Jewish religion (dir. temple). Contbr. articles to profl. publs. Home: 6912 Heatherhill Rd Bethesda MD 20034 Office: 1771 N St NW Washington DC 20036

BLUMENTHAL, HERBERT, toxicologist; b. N.Y.C., May 1, 1925; s. Isaac and Celia (Levine) B.; B.S., Coll. City N.Y., 1948; Ph.D., U. So. Cal., 1955; m. Diane Korten, June 25, 1950; children—Matthew David, Debra Ann. Acting chief pharmacodynamics br. FDA, Washington, 1955-58, asst. to chief toxicity br., 1958-61, chief petitions rev. br., 1964-70, dep. dir. div. toxicology, 1971—. A prin. investigator NIH, Nat. Inst. Dental Research, Bethesda, Md., 1958-61. Armed Forces Epidemological Bd. fellow, 1951-55. Recipient award of Merit, FDA, 1972. Fellow A.A.A.S.; mem. Soc. Toxicology, Environmental Mutagen Soc., Soc. Environmental Geochemistry and Health, Soc. Exptl. Biology and Medicine, N.Y. Acad. Scis., Sigma Xi, Phi Lambda Upsilon. Mem. editorial bd. Toxicology, 1972—. Home: 13215 Holdridge Rd Silver Spring MD 20906 Office: 200 C St SW Washington DC 20204

BLUMRICH, HENRY CHRYSOLOGUS, dept. store exec.; b. Lockhart, Tex., Sept. 7, 1913; s. Henry Chrysologus and Wiley (Williamson) B.; B.B.A., U. Tex., Austin, 1948; m. Marey Dunlap, Sept. 2, 1939 children—Brenda Nell, Donald Dunlap. Clk., Lockhart Post Office, 1933-43; store controller Sears, Roebuck & Co., Galveston, Tex., 1949, Houston, 1950-56, Pasadena, Tex., 1956—. Served with USCGR, 1943-45. C.P.A. Mem. Am., Tex. socs. C.P.A.'s. Home: 8535 Dover St Houston TX 77017 Office: 1107 S Shaver St Pasadena TX 77502

BLYTH, JOSEPH AVERITT, cons. firm exec., Democratic nat. committeeman; b. Raleigh, N.C., Mar. 18, 1930; s. George L. and Ruby (Averitt) B.; B.A., U. Ariz., 1953; postgrad. Gen. Motors Inst., 1973, Sales Analysis Inst., 1973, Northwood Inst., 1974; m. Margaret Swain, Mar. 16, 1968; 1 dau., Rachael Irene. Actor, 1953-54; exec. asst. Muller Bros., Oldsmobile dealership, Hollywood, Cal., 1954-57; service supr., expeditor Z. Frank, Chevrolet dealership, Chgo., 1958-61; customer relations rep. Cadillac Motor div. Gen. Motors Corp., Chgo., 1961-62; nat. cons. to retail automotive trade, Raleigh, 1963-72; pres. Automotive Research Assos. and Automotive Research Inst., Raleigh, 1973—; v.p., co-owner Wangers Chevrolet, Milw., 1973—; dir. Briggs Chevrolet, Inc., South Amboy, N.J., Palisades Chevrolet, Inc., Santa Monica, Cal. Exec. instr. Sales Analysis Inst., Oak Brook, Ill. Mem. Dem. Nat. Com. from N.C. 1972—. Mem. Nat. Automobile Dealers Assn., Automotive Orgn. Team, Internat. Platform Assn., U.S. Capitol Hist. Soc., Smithsonian Instn., N.C. Hist. Assn., Am. Civil Liberties Union, Common Cause, Wilderness Soc., Fortune Soc., Ams. for Dem. Action. Baptist. Author: Retail Automotive Service Marketing; Retail Automotive Service Management; Retail Automotive Parts Management, 1974. Contbr. to automotive trade mags. Home: 1235 Onslow Rd Raleigh NC 27606 Office: 16 N Dawson St Raleigh NC 27605

BOAL, JAN LIST, educator; b. Canton, O., Oct. 20, 1930; s. Jan and May Ann (List) B.; B.M.E., Ga. Inst. Tech., 1953, M.S. (Gerard Swope Grad. fellow), 1954; Ph.D., Mass. Inst. Tech., 1959; m. Bobby Snow, Mar. 21, 1953; children—Robert Kelly, Emily Ann, Virginia List. Instr. math. Mass. Inst. Tech., Cambridge, 1959-60; asst. prof. U. S.C., Columbia, 1960-62, asso. prof., 1962-69; prof., chmn. dept. math. Ga. State U., Atlanta, 1969—. Danforth grad. fellow, 1953-59, Danforth Asso., 1970—. Mem. Am. Math. Soc., Math. Assn. Am., Soc. Indsl. and Applied Math., Am. Sci. Affiliation. Baptist (deacon 1964-68, 73—). Home: 1126 Clifton Rd NE Atlanta GA 30307

BOARDMAN, WILLARD HARLOW, physician; b. Dundee, N.Y., Jan. 6, 1922; s. Warren Milton and Lulu B. (Covert) B.; M.D., U. Buffalo, 1944; m. Jean Elizabeth Moore, Oct. 13, 1956; children—Lori Ann, Lisa Allyn, Lynn Amy. Intern, E.J. Meyer Meml. Hosp., Buffalo, 1944-45, resident, 1945-46, 49-50; fellow in cardiology-vascular diseases U. Buffalo, 1951-52; practice medicine, specializing in cardiology, Lancaster, N.Y., 1953-56, Orlando, Fla., 1956—; mem. staffs Orange Meml. Hosp., Orlando, Fla. Hosp., Orlando, Winter Park (Fla.) Hosp.; pres. staff Fla. Hosp., 1963, chief dept. cardiology, 1971—; v.p. Evans Central Fla. Cardiology Group, 1969—. Bd. dirs. Fla. Heart Assn.; bd. dirs. Central Fla. Heart Assn., pres., 1962. Served with M.C., AUS, 1946-48, 53. Diplomate Am. Bd. Internal Medicine. Fellow Am. Coll. Cardiology and Chest Physicians, A.C.P.; mem. A.M.A., Am. Heart Assn. Presbyn. Clubs: Citrus, Committee of One Hundred (Orlando, Fla.). Home: 701 Balmoral Rd Winter Park FL 32789 Office: 500 E Colonial Dr Orlando FL 32803

BOATNER, LYNN ALLEN, physicist; b. Clarksville, Tex., Aug. 3, 1938; s. Fred Leroy and Nila Avanell (Allen) B.; B.S., Tex. Tech. Coll., 1960, M.S., 1961; Ph.D., Vanderbilt U., 1966; m. Martha Alice Goodwin, Sept. 5, 1961; children—Mark Jesse, Ivan Aaron, Philip Gordon. Research scientist LTV Research Center, Dallas, 1966-70; prin. scientist Advanced Tech. Center, Inc., Dallas, 1970-72, program mgr. for sensors, 1972—. Vis. prof. Inst. Physics, Nat. U. Mexico City, 1970. Oak Ridge Asso. Univs. travel grantee, 1966. Mem. Am. Phys. Soc., N.Y. Acad. Sci., A.A.A.S., Nat. Rifle Assn., Sigma Xi, Sigma Pi Sigma, Phi Eta Sigma, Pi Kappa Alpha. Patentee in field. Home: 1010 Greenwood Pl Duncanville TX 75116 Office: PO Box 6144 Dallas TX 75222

BOAZ, LONNIE ROY, JR., physician; b. Hampton, Va., Nov. 29, 1926; s. Lonnie Roy and Hattie W. (Winston) B.; B.S., Hampton Inst., 1951; M.D., Howard U., 1955; m. Aurellia E. Mitchell, Aug. 13, 1949; children—Valerie, Lonnie Roy III, Andre. Intern, Kate Bittings Reynolds Hosp., Winston-Salem, N.C., 1955-56; practice medicine specializing in family practice, Chattanooga, 1956—; mem. staff Parkridge, Meml., Erlanger hosps. Mem. exec. com. Baroness Erlanger Hosp., 1971-73. Served with AUS, 1945-46. Mem. Kappa Alpha Psi. Home: 5330 Lee Av Chattanooga TN 37408 Office: 1620 S Market St Chattanooga TN 37408

BOBBITT, WILLIAM HAYWOOD, state supreme ct. justice; b. Raleigh, N.C., Oct. 18, 1900; s. James Henry and Eliza May (Burkhead) B.; A.B., U. N.C., 1921, LL.D., 1957; LL.D., Davidson Coll., 1953; m. Sarah Buford Dunlap, Feb. 28, 1924 (dec. Oct. 1965); children—Sarah (Mrs. John W. Carter), William Haywood (dec.), Buford (Mrs. Ekkehart Sachtler), Harriet (Mrs. Dan S. Moss).

Admitted to N.C. bar, 1922; practiced in Charlotte, N.C., 1922-38; judge Superior Ct., 14th Jud. Dist., 1939-54; asso. justice Supreme Court of N.C., Raleigh, 1954-69, chief justice, 1969—. Mem. N.C. Jud. Council, 1949-54, chmn., 1966-69. Trustee Brevard (N.C.) Coll., 1933-52. Mem. Am., N.C. bar assns., Am. Judicature Soc., Gen. Alumni Assn. U. N.C. (pres. 1954-55). Methodist. Club: Civitan (past pres. Charlotte). Home: Boylan Apts Raleigh NC 27603 Office: Justice Bldg Raleigh NC 27602

BOBKO, KAROL J., astronaut; b. N.Y.C., Dec. 23, 1937; s. Charles P. and Veronica (Sagatis) B.; B.S., U.S. Air Force Acad., 1959; grad. USAF Aerospace Research Pilot Sch., 1966; M.S., U. So. Cal., 1970; m. Frances Dianne Welsh, Feb. 11, 1961; children—Michelle Ann, Paul Joseph. Commd. officer U.S. Air Force, advanced through grades to lt. col.; pilot trainee, 1959-61; F-100 tactical fighter pilot, 1961-63; F-105 tactical fighter pilot, 1963-65, test pilot, 1965-67, astronaut, 1967—. Roman Catholic. Office: NASA Johnson Space Center 2101 NASA Blvd Houston TX 77012

BOBLITT, ROBERT LEROY, educator, univ. adminstr.; b. Springfield, O., Nov. 1, 1925; s. Lloyd LeRoy and Helen (Jobe) B.; student Ohio State U., 1942-43; B.S., Ohio No. U., 1948; Ph.D. (Samuel Melendy fellow), U. Minn., 1953; m. Leita Elizabeth Eaton, Sept. 16, 1944; children—Barbara (Mrs. Joseph Blasberg), Deborah Lee, Pamela (Mrs. Bradley Kent), Robert LeRoy. Asst. prof. dept. pharm. chemistry U. Houston, 1953-56, asso. prof., 1956-70, prof., 1970—, asst. dean Coll. Pharmacy, 1973—. Insp., Tex. Bd. Pharmacy Internship, 1970—. Mem. Harris County Health Careers Recruiting Council, 1972—. Served with USMCR, 1943-45. Recipient Teaching Excellence award U. Houston, 1973. HEW grantee, 1972. Mem. Am. Chem. Soc., Am., Harris County, Tex. pharm. assns., Sigma Xi, Delta Sigma Phi, Phi Delta Chi. Home: 7622 Montglen St Houston TX 77017

BOCKIAN, HERBERT HAROLD, psychiatrist; b. Jersey City, Oct. 14, 1927; s. Abraham and Eva (Skner) B.; A.B., Columbia, 1950; M.A. in Modern Langs., U. Miami (Fla.), 1955; M.D., U. Tenn., 1960; m. Natalie Paula Fink, Aug. 15, 1958; children—Phyllis Ann, David Alan, Barry Israel, Steven Teo. Intern, St. Thomas Hosp., Nashville, 1960-61; resident adult psychiatry Vanderbilt U. Hosp., 1961-63, child psychiatry, 1963-65; dir. adolescent service Central State Hosp., Nashville, 1965-67; staff child psychiatrist Children's Psychiat. Center Miami, Inc., Coral Gables, Fla., 1967—; practice medicine, specializing in psychiatry, Coral Gables, 1967-73; clin. dir. Bristol (Tenn.) Regional Health Center, 1974—; instr. modern langs. Memphis State U., 1956-60; instr. psychiatry Vanderbilt U., Nashville, 1962-65; clin. instr. psychiatry U. Miami, Coral Gables, 1967-70, clin. asst. prof., 1970-73; adj. clin. prof. psychopathology Grad. Sch. Social Work, Barry Coll., Miami Shores, Fla., 1972-73; mem. staff Jackson Meml. Hosp., Highland Park Gen. Hosp., Variety Children's Hosp., Miami, 1968-73, Bristol Meml. Hosp., 1973—. Mem. Children's Com., Nashville, 1965-67; chmn. small craft safety com., instr.-trainer water safety Dade County chpt. A.R.C., 1950—. Served with USNR, 1946-47. USPHS research fellow, 1958-59; recipient Charles C. Verstaendig award U. Tenn., 1960. Diplomate Am. Bd. Psychiatry and Neurology. Mem. Am., S. Fla. psychiat. assns., So., Fla., Date County med. assns., Alpha Kappa Kappa. Jewish religion. Address: Bristol Regional Mental Health Center 26 Midway St Bristol TN 37620

BODDEKER, EDWARD WILLIAM, III, architect, govt. ofcl.; b. Houston, Mar. 22, 1929; s. Edward William and Ruth Margaret (Cook) B.; B.Arch., Tex. A. and M. U., 1951; 1 son, Mark Montagne. Architect, MacKie & Kamrath, architects, Houston, 1960-63; architect Manned Spacecraft Center, NASA, Clear Lake, Tex., 1963—, project design mgr., 1963-65, master planner, 1965-67, head master planning sect., 1967-68, head archtl. civil sect., engring. div., 1968—. Bd. dirs., treas. Clear Creek Basin Authority, 1972-74. Served to 1st lt. Army Security Agy., AUS, 1953-54. Recipient Apollo Achievement award NASA, also NASA Gemini, Apollo, Skylab group achievement awards. Registered architect, Tex. Mem. A.I.A., Tex. Soc. Architects. Unitarian. Home: 2004 San Sebastion Ct No 313 Houston TX 77058 Office: NASA Johnson Space Center Clear Lake TX 77058

BODEY, GERALD PAUL, physician; b. Hazleton, Pa., May 22, 1934; s. Allen Zartman and Marie Frances (Smith) B.; A.B. magna cum laude, Lafayette Coll., 1956; M.D. (Henry Strong Denison fellow), Johns Hopkins, 1960; m. Nancy Louise Wiegner, Aug. 25, 1956; children—Robin Gayle, Gerald Paul, Sharon Dawn. Intern, Osler Med. Service, Johns Hopkins, Balt., 1960-61, resident, 1961-62; clin. asso. Nat. Cancer Inst., NIH, Bethesda, Md., 1962-65; resident U. Wash., Seattle, 1965-66; asso. internist, asso. prof. medicine U. Tex.-M.D. Anderson Hosp. and Tumor Inst., Houston, 1966—; adj. asso. prof. microbiology, asso. clin. prof. medicine Baylor Coll. Medicine, Houston, 1969—; cons. Brooke Gen. Hosp., Brooke Army Med. Center, Fort Sam Houston, Tex., 1971—. Leukemia Soc. scholar, 1969-74; NIH grantee, 1966—. Diplomate Nat. Bd. Med. Examiners, Am. Bd. Internal Medicine. Fellow A.C.P.; mem. A.M.A., Am. Assn. Cancer Research, Am. Soc. Clin. Oncology, Am. Soc. Hematology, Am. Soc. Microbiology, Infectious Diseases Soc. Am., Royal Soc. Promotion Health, Sigma Xi, Phi Beta Kappa. Presbyn. Contbr. articles to profl. jours. Home: 5023 Glenmeadow St Houston TX 77035 Office: MD Anderson Hosp 6723 Bertner St Houston TX 77025

BODNAR, STEPHEN JOHN, chem. co. exec.; b. Carteret, N.J., July 6, 1925; s. Stephen and Helen (Sadowski) B.; B.A., Lafayette Coll., 1951; Ph.D., U. Ill., 1954; m. Louise C. Brechka, Sept. 20, 1947; children—Alison B. (Mrs. Dwight Auckland), Patrice L., Kristin M. Chem. engr. Esso Standard Oil Co., Baton Rouge, La., 1954-60; mgr. process engring. section Tex. U.S. Chem. Co., Port Neches, Tex., 1960—. Served with AUS, 1943-46. Decorated Purple Heart, Metz medal. Mem. Am. Chem. Soc., So. Rubber Group, 95th Inf. Div. Assn., Alpha Chi Sigma, Phi Lambda Upsilon. Patentee in field. Home: 6320 Pansy Dr Beaumont TX 77706 Office: PO Box 846 Port Neches TX 77651

BODRE, ROBERT JOSEPH, research chemist; b. Phila., Mar. 6, 1921; s. Andrew and Anna (Fischler) B.; B.S., St. Joseph's Coll., 1943; Ph.D., U. Louisville, 1961; m. Irene Fike, June 23, 1945. Chemist, Publicker Industries, Phila., 1943-45; research chemist Whitaker Co., Phila., 1945-47, Chemetron Corp., Louisville, 1947-57; process specialist Monsanto Co., Texas City, Tex., 1960—. Research asso. U. Louisville, 1957-60. AEC research grantee, 1957-60. Mem. Am. Chem. Soc., Am. Inst. Chemists, Sigma Xi. Club: Amateur Organist Assn. Internat. Contbr. articles to chem. jours. Patentee in field. Home: 2501 Meadow Lane La Marque TX 77568 Office: Box 1311 Texas City TX 77591

BOECKMAN, DUNCAN E., lawyer; b. Houston, Sept. 17, 1926; B.B.A., U. Tex., 1948, LL.B., 1951. Admitted to Tex. bar, 1951; now mem. firm Golden, Potts, Boeckman & Wilson, Dallas. Gen. counsel Tex. Republican Exec. Com., 1964—. Mem. Am., Dallas bar assns., State Bar Tex., Phi Delta Phi. Office: 2300 Republic Nat Bank Bldg Dallas TX 75201*

BOEGLEN, DURWOOD LOUIS, bldg. supply co. exec.; b. Albany, Ala., Jan. 4, 1917; s. Louis Edward and Vernon Irene (Murphree) B.; student Southwestern U. Accounting, Washington, 1935-37; m. Margaret Cordelia Herron, Nov. 14, 1941; children—Katharine (Mrs. James C. Chapin), Bonnie (Mrs. Gary L. DiGirolamo), Jay Louis. With United Clay Products Co., Washington, 1934-47; with Cushwa Brick & Bldg. Supply Co., Washington, 1947—, pres., 1965—; exec. v.p. Compackager Corp., Washington, 1969—; adv. bd. Suburban Trust Co., Hyattsville, Md., 1959—. Trustee, Nat. Jewish Hosp., Denver, Boys Clubs D.C. Mem. Masonry Isnt. (pres. 1955), Nat. Assn. Distbrs. and Dealers Structural Clay Products (pres. 1957-58), Home Builders Assn. D.C. (pres. 1966-70), Home Builders Met. Washington Found. (pres. 1967—), Washington Bldg. Congress (treas. 1968-69), Met. Washington Builders Assn. (pres. 1972). Methodist. Mason (Shriner), Kiwanian. Clubs: Columbia Country (Chevy Chase, Md.); University (Washington); Congressional Country (pres. 1968-69) (Potomac, Md). Home: 4807 Enfield Rd Bethesda MD 20014 Office: 137 Ingraham St NE Washington DC 20011

BOEHNE, JOHN WILLIAM, III, govt. ofcl.; b. Evansville, Ind., Feb. 6, 1921; s. John William and Selma O. (Heitmuller) B.; B.S., Ind. U., 1942; postgrad. Western Res. U., 1948-50; m. Audrey S. Sattler, Aug. 10, 1946; children—Gregg William, Lynne Andre. Chemist Lederle Labs., Pearl River, N.Y., 1946-48; research asst. Western Res. U., Cleve., 1950-57; with Div. Nutrition, FDA, Dept. Heath, Edn. and Welfare, Washington, 1957—. Instr. human ecology U. Md., College Park, part-time, 1969-70. Served with USNR, 1942-46. Recipient Award of Merit FDA, 1971, 73. Mem. Am. Inst. Nutrition, Alpha Chi Sigma, Phi Gamma Delta. Lutheran. Contbr. articles to various jours. Home: 10763 Kinloch Rd Silver Spring MD 20903 Office: 200 C St SW Washington DC 20204

BÖER, GERMAIN BONIFACE, educator; b. Rockne, Tex., Nov. 19, 1937; s. August Henry and Lena (Bartsch) B.; B.S., St. Edward's U., Austin, Tex., 1960; M.B.A., Tex. Tech U., 1961; Ph.D., La. State U., 1964; m. Elinor Charles O'Brien, Jan. 25, 1964; children—Kathleen Marie, Robert James. Asso. prof. dept. accounting, acting asst. dean Coll. Bus. Adminstrn. Tex. Tech U., Lubbock, 1964-66; faculty resident Arthur Andersen & Co., Chgo., 1966-67; project mgr. Nat. Assn. Accountants, N.Y.C., 1968-70; asso. prof. dept. accounting Okla. State U., Stillwater, 1968—. Cons. Nat. Assn. Accountants, Hosp. Financial Mgmt. Edn. Found. C.P.A., Tex. Mem. Nat. Assn. Accountants (nat. dir.), Am. Inst. C.P.A.'s, Beta Alpha Psi, Beta Gamma Sigma. Author: (with others) Automation and Management in the Clinical Laboratory, 1972. Home: 1002 Liberty Lane Stillwater OK 74074 Office: Dept Accounting Coll Bus Adminstrn Okla State Univ Stillwater OK 74074

BOERCKER, FRED DONALD, educator; b. St. Louis, July 16, 1924; S. Fred William and Della May (Butemeyer) B.; A.B., U. Cal. at Berkeley, 1945; M.A., Washington U. at St. Louis, 1948, Ph.D. (NSF fellow), 1960; m. Marguerite Jeanne Steelhammer, July 10, 1948; children—David Bryan, Geoffrey Keith, Martha Elizabeth. Asst. prof. physics Western Ky. U., Bowling Green, 1960-62; dir. manpower studies Am. Inst. Physics, N.Y.C., 1962-63; asso. prof. physics Georgetown (Ky.) Coll., 1964-66; dir. edn. and employment studies Nat. Acad. Scis., Washington, 1966-70; prof. physics Austin Peay State U., Clarksville, Tenn., 1970—. Chmn. adv. com. manpower studies Am. Inst. Physics, 1971—. Served with USNR, 1943-46. Ednl. Testing Service summer asso. in sci., 1959. Mem. Clarksville-Montgomery County C. of C., Assn. U.S. Army, Manpower Analysis and Planning Soc. Washington, Ky., Tenn. acad. scis., Am. Phys. Soc., Am. Assn. Physics Tchrs., Sigma Pi Sigma. Author: Physics Manpower and Education Statistics, 1962; Physics Education, Employment and Financial Support, 1964; Doctorate Recipients From U.S. Universities, 1967; Effects of NIGMS Training Programs on Graduate Education in Biomedical Sciences, 1969; Education and Employment Patterns of Bioscientists, 1971. Home: 361 Fairway Dr Clarksville TN 37040 Office: Dept Physics Austin Peay State Univ Clarksville TN 37040

BOETHEL, CAREY BUCHANAN, lawyer; b. Hallettsville, Tex., Sept. 24, 1941; s. Paul Carl and Frances Claire (Christian) B.; A.A., Victoria Coll., 1962; B.S., U. Houston, 1965; J.D., Tex. Tech. U., 1970; m. Joan Myrle Garlichs Sept. 9, 1967; children—Carey Paul, James Blanton. With FBI, Washington, 1960; admitted to Tex. bar, 1970; practice law, Giddings, Tex., 1970—. Pres., Lee County Recreation, 1972-73. Mem. Am., Lee County (pres. 1971-72) bar assns., State Bar Tex., Tex. Trial Lawyers Assn., Phi Alpha Delta. Democrat. Presbyn. Club: Cummins Creek Country (Giddings). Home: 295 Woodland St Giddings TX 78942 Office: 268 E Austin St Giddings TX 78942

BOGARD, ROY WARD, JR., architect; b. Fort Worth, Jan. 3, 1940; s. Roy Ward and Doris (Shrewder) B.; B.Arch., Tex. Tech. Coll., 1963; m. Charlotte Elaine Ensley, Apr. 17, 1971. Draftsman firm Maples-Jones Assos., Fort Worth, 1963-64, firm Wilson, Morris, Crain & Anderson, Houston, 1964-65; project architect firm Kneer & Hamm, Fort Worth, 1965-68; partner firm Wooten & Bogard, Fort Worth, 1968—. Mem. A.I.A., Tex. Soc. Architects, Sigma Nu. Home: 724 Little Horse Trail Fort Worth TX 76108 Office: 1319 Ballinger St Fort Worth TX 76102

BOGGESS, JOHN P., elec. engr.; b. Demopolis, Ala., Oct. 19, 1914; s. Norman West and Katherine (Thompson) B.; B.S., U. Ala., 1938; m. Dorothy Gaynelle McClusky, Apr. 2, 1941; children—Dorothy Gaynelle, (Mrs. Henry Owen Wharton), Tina Marie. Engr. asst. sub-sta. constrn. Ala. Power Co., Birmingham, 1937-38; operations and maintenance engr. Lakeland (Fla.) Light & Water Plant, 1939-40; owner, mgr. Boggess Florist & Nursery, Demopolis, 1946-52; chief coordinator Vets. Tng. for Marengo County, Linden, Ala., 1946-51; asst. plant engr. Beaunit Mills, Inc., Childersburg, Ala., 1952-60; elec./aerospace engr. Marshall Space Flight Center (Ala.), 1960—. Dir. girls activities Continental Athletic Assn., Huntsville, 1972-73. Served as capt. C.E., AUS, 1940-46; ETO, PTO. Mem. Nat., Ala. (chpt. and state dir. 1963—), Huntsville socs. profl. engrs. Presbyn. Club: Ten/Twenty Stock (pres. 1967-72). Home: 6311 Sheri Dr NW Huntsville AL 35806 Office: S&E-Qual-E Marshall Space Flight Center AL 35812

BOGGS, CHESTER L., cotton coop. exec.; b. Myra, Tex., Jan. 15, 1934; s. Harvey A. and Flora M. (Whitley) B.; student Tex. Tech. U., 1956-60; m. Juanita Ann Alford, Dec. 13, 1963; children—Lynn, Rhonda Bob Francis, Karen, Denise. Automobile mechanic George Calvert's Garage, 1952-55; police officer, City of Lubbock, Tex., 1955-56; accounting clk. Ralph Penny Chevrolet, 1956; jr. and sr. accountant Edwin E. Merriman & Co., C.P.A.'s, 1956-61, partner, 1961-65; partner Berry, Morton & Boggs, C.P.A.'s, 1965-66; office mgr. Plains Cotton Coop., Lubbock, Tex., 1966-67, asst. gen. mgr., 1967—; dir. H & H Feed Lot, Inc., Roscoe, Tex. Mem. community planning council United Fund, Lubbock, Tex., 1967-69, mem. speaker's bur., 1969—, sec.-treas. exec. com., 1971-72; pres., Rush Elementary Sch. P.T.A., 1971-72; mem. Speakers Bur., Lubbock (Tex.) Com. 70, 1970-71. Mem. bd. commrs. Urban Renewal, Lubbock. Bd. dirs. A.R.C., Lubbock, Tex., 1969-70. Recipient Distinguished Pub. Service award Tex. Soc. C.P.A.'s, 1972. Mem. Tex. Soc. C.P.A.'s (mem. exec. com. 1970-71, dir. 1967-68, pres. Lubbock chpt. 1967-68), Lubbock C. of C. (mem. internat. trade com. 1970—). Democrat. Mem. Ch. of Christ (mem. budget and finance com. 1969-71). Kiwanian, Rotarian, Toastmaster (pres. 1967). Club: Lubbock Country (dir. 1971—). Home: 4604 9th St Lubbock TX 79408 Office: PO Box 2827 Lubbock TX 79416

BOGGS, CORINNE C., congresswoman; b. Brunswick Plantation, La.; grad. Sophie Newcomb Coll.; m. Thomas Hale Boggs (dec.); children—Barbara (Mrs. Paul Sigmund), Thomas Hale, Corinne (Mrs. Steven V. Roberts). Active numerous civic activities; elected to 93d congress from 2d La. dist. in spl. election to fill vacancy caused by death of husband, 1973; mem. Banking and Currency Com. Past pres. Women's Nat. Democratic Club, Dem. Congl. Wives' Forum, Congl. Club; active numerous Dem. events including inaugural balls Pres. Kennedy and Pres. Johnson. Bd. dirs. La. Council Music and Performing Arts. Mem. Nat. Soc. Colonial Dames, League Women Voters. Roman Catholic. Address: U S Congress Washington DC 20515*

BOGGS, GAIL EVERETT, communications co. exec.; b. Chgo., Apr. 22, 1921; s. Walter H.C. and Margaret (Alberts) B.; B.E.E., George Washington U., 1948; M.S., U. Md., 1952; m. Mary Evelyn Elsea, Nov. 17, 1945; 1 son, Wayne Everett. With Nat. Bur. Standards, Washington, 1948-56; v.p., dir. research and devel. Page Communications Engrs. Inc., Vienna, Va., 1956-63; sr. v.p. Telcom, Inc., McLean, Va., 1963—, also chmn. bd.; mem. adv. bd. Fairfax County Nat. Bank, Falls Church, Va., 1972—. Served with AUS, 1943-46. Mem. I.E.E.E. Methodist. Patentee in field. Home: 4126 N Randolph St Arlington VA 22207 Office: 8027 Leesburg Pike McLean VA 22101

BOGGS, JAMES BISHOP, architect; b. Fort Worth, Jan. 21, 1936; s. Harry Hobart and W. Vera (Bishop) B.; student U. Miami (Fla.), 1954-55; B.Arch., Tex. Tech. U., 1962; m. Martha Juanita Dodson, Sept. 10, 1957; children—Pamela E., James Michael, Patricia Elaine, Paula Elisa. Designer firm Smyth & Smyth, architects, Corpus Christi, Tex., 1963-68; pvt. practice, Corpus Christi, 1968-70; sec.-treas. firm Environmental Disciplines Inc., Corpus Christi, 1970-71; prin. firm James B. Boggs, A.I.A., Corpus Christi, 1972—. Chmn. dept. architecture DelMar Coll., Corpus Christi, 1970—. Chmn. projects com. Municipal Arts Commn., Corpus Christi, 1969-73. Founding mem. bd. dirs. Redevel. Assistance Center, 1970-72; bd. dirs Beautify Corpus Christi Assn., Community Devel. Corp. Served with USAF, 1954-62. Recipient certificate Nat. Council Archtl. Registration Bds., 1970; mem. 1st class Leadership Corpus Christi, 1973; Tex. Edn. Agy. grantee, 1971-72. Mem. A.I.A. (corporate mem.), Corpus Christi, Jr. (dir. 1967-72) chambers commerce, Tex. Tech. Ex-Students Assn. (dist. rep.), Tex. Soc. Architects, Tex. State Jr. Colls. Tchrs. Assn., Theta Chi, Alpha Phi Omega. Methodist (mem. ch. adminstrv. bd.). Clubs: Conquistadors, League of United Latin American Citizens (Corpus Christi). Home: 4701 Donegal St Corpus Christi TX 78413 Office: 1806 S Alameda St Corpus Christi TX 78404 also Dept Architecture and Drafting Tech Del Mar Coll Baldwin and Ayers Sts Corpus Christi TX 78404

BOGGS, JAMES ERNEST, educator; b. Cleve., June 9, 1921; s. Ernest Beckett and Emily (Reid) B.; A.B., Oberlin Coll., 1943; M.S. in Chemistry, U. Mich., 1944, Ph.D., 1953; m. Ruth Ann Rogers, June 22, 1948; children—Carol (Mrs. Harwell Edgar Norris III), Ann, Lynne. Asst. prof. dept. chemistry Eastern Mich. U., Ypsilanti, 1949-52; instr. U. Mich. at Ann Arbor, 1952-53; mem. faculty dept. chemistry U. Tex. at Austin, 1953—, asso. prof., 1958-66, prof., 1966—. Mem. Am. Chem. Soc., Am. Phys. Soc., Sigma Xi, Phi Beta Kappa, Phi Lambda Upsilon, Gamma Alpha. Contbr. articles to profl. jours. Home: 4603 Balcones Dr Austin TX 78731

BOGGS, JEAN CASTERTON BULETTE (MRS. LAWRENCE K. BOGGS), civic worker; b. York, Pa.; d. Warren Clifton and Ruth (Casterton) Bulette; B.A., Coll. William and Mary, 1944; m. Lawrence K. Boggs, Oct. 15, 1949; children—Randall and David (twins), Elizabeth. Editorial dept., caption title and subtitle writer Sat. Eve. Post, 1945-50; with research dept. Holiday Mag., 1950-51, asst. editor, 1951-52. Mem. residence com. YWCA, 1958-67; mem. aux. bd. Presbyn. Hosp., 1959-60; sect. chmn. United Appeal, 1962; treas. Med. Aux., 1965-66; co-chmn. Culture Week for State N.C., 1968; publicity chmn. Met. Opera Benefit Concert, 1969; active Myers Park Homeowners Assn. Bd. dirs. Latta Pl., Inc., 1972—, Presbyn. Home Charlotte, 1974—. Mem. Soc. for Preservation Antiquities N.C., D.A.R. (regent 1966-68), Mecklenburg County Hist. Assn. (rec. sec. 1973—), Delta Delta Delta. Republican. Presbyn. (pres. Women of Ch. 1973-74). Clubs: Queen of Spades Garden (pres. Charlotte, N.C. 1965-66), Fortnightly Book (pres. 1967-68), Charlotte Guild Debutante (mem. bd. 1969-70, pres. 1971-72), Charlotte Country, N.C. Golddiggers Investment (Charlotte). Address: 2208 Wellesley Av Charlotte NC 28207

BOGGS, LAWRENCE KENNEDY, physician; b. Birmingham, Ala., Feb. 13, 1925; s. Ralph Erwin and Meta (Long) B.; student Davidson Coll., 1943, Duke, 1943-45; M.D., Jefferson Med. Coll., 1949; m. Jean Casterton Bulette, Oct. 15, 1949; children—Randall, David, Elizabeth. Intern, Phila. Gen. Hosp., 1949-51; resident urology Charlotte (N.C.) Meml. Hosp., 1953-56; practice medicine specializing in urology, Charlotte, 1956—; chief staff dept. urology Presbyn. Hosp., v.p. med. staff, 1966-67, pres. med. staff, 1967; mem. teaching staff dept. urology Charlotte Meml. Hosp., dir. med. assistance, 1960—. Vice chmn. local Boy Scouts Am., dist. chmn., 1963. Bd. dirs. Mecklenburg unit Am. Cancer Soc., Arts Council; mem. adv. bd. Planned Parenthood; coordinator 1968 Culture Week, State of N.C. Republican precinct chmn., 1957-58. Served with USNR, 1943-46, as 1st lt. AUS, 1951-53. Hartford Found. fellow, 1954-55, 55-56. Diplomate Am. Bd. Urology. Fellow A.C.S.; mem. Am. (S.E. sect.), N.C. urologic assns., Mechlenburg County Med. Soc. (pres. 1970), Mechlenburg Hist. Assn. (dir.), C. of C. Presbyn. (elder 1967). Rotarian (pres. 1961—, dir. 1959-61). Clubs: Executives, Goodfellows, London Dinner (pres. 1966-67), Charlotte Country (Charlotte); St. Andrews. Home: 2208 Wellesley Av Charlotte NC 28205 Office: Doctors Bldg Charlotte NC 28801

BOGITSH, BURTON JEROME, educator; b. Bklyn., Feb. 9, 1929; s. Leonard and Anna (Beatus) B.; A.B., N.Y. U., 1949; M.A., Baylor U., 1954; Ph.D. (DuPont fellow), U. Va., 1957; m. D. Mafoi Carlisle, June 6, 1951; children—Rhonda Lea, Glenn Carlisle, Adrian Hunter, Priscilla Dru. Asst. prof. biology Ga. So. Coll., 1957-59, asso. prof. biology, 1959-62, prof. biology, 1962-63; asst. program dir. NSF, Washington, 1963-64; asso. prof. biology Vanderbilt U., Nashville, 1964-71, prof. biology, 1971—, chmn. dept. biology, 1972—. Cons. NSF, 1964-70. Served with AUS, 1952-54. Spl. research fellow NIH, 1973; NIH research grantee, NSF research grantee, Dept. Army research grantee. Mem. Am. Assn. Parasitologists, Am. Microscopial Soc., Histochem. Soc., Assn. S.E. Biologists (exec. com. 1967-70, v.p. 1972-73), S.E. Soc. Parasitology (pres. 1971). Editorial bd. Exptl. Parasitology, 1969-73, Jour. Parasitology, 1971—. Bd. reviewers Trans. Am. Microscop. Soc., 1968—. Home: 6615 Ormond Dr Nashville TN 37205

BOGLE, ERNEST VERLE, civil engr.; b. Pittsburg, Kan., Sept. 27, 1910; s. Frank White and Ina Asenith (Smith) B.; B.S. in C.E., Kan. State U., 1933; m. Jane Orr, Nov. 11, 1935; children—Robert (dec.), Janet. Asso. engr. Kan. State Hwy. Commn., Chanute, 1935-39; engring. inspector Kan. Pub. Works Adminstrn., Kansas City, 1939-40; resident engr. TVA, Knoxville, Tenn., 1940-44; constrn. engr. Tenn. Eastman Corp., Oak Ridge, 1944-47, Union Carbide Corp., Oak Ridge, 1947—. Registered profl. engr., Kan. Club: Oak Ridge Country. Home: 100 Union Rd Oak Ridge TN 37830 Office: Box P Oak Ridge TN 37830

BOGUE, MALEN DEVON, san. engr.; b. Pomona, Fla., Nov. 20, 1924; s. William Orange and Stella (Harrison) B.; student John B. Stetson U., 1944; B.Civil Engring., Ga. Inst. Tech., 1950; M.P.H., U. Cal. at Berkeley, 1953; m. Antonetta Connaughton, July 6, 1964; children—DeVon Jr., Stephen Arno, Pamela Marie, Lisa Dian. With USPHS, various locations, 1950-71, dir. Fla. Aedes Aegypti Eradication program, Jacksonville, Fla., 1965, dir. Solid Waste Mgmt. Program Region IV, Atlanta, 1966-69, environmental control dir., Region IV, Atlanta, 1970, dir. Mission 5000 program Environmental Protection Agy., Region IV, 1971; v.p. environmental engring. Anson Grove Haak & Assos., Fort Lauderdale, Fla., also sr. engr., mgr. Atlanta office Engring.-Sci. Inc., 1972-74, tech. dir. solid waste mgmt., 1974—. Served with USNR, 1944-46; PTO. Mem. Am. Pub. Works Assn., Inst. Solid Wastes. Home: 2407 Windon Ct Doraville GA 30340 Office: 1423 Perimeter Center E Atlanta GA 30346

BOHAN, ROBERT WALTER, savs. and loan exec.; b. Houlton, Me., Sept. 27, 1930; s. Walter T. and Hazel F. (Cordrey) B.; B.B.A., U. Me., 1952; m. Shirley M. Marchion, Nov. 28, 1953; children—Brent Alan, Marc Robert, Damon Eugene. Teller, internal auditor Chase Fed. Savs. & Loan, Miami Beach, Fla., 1954; auditor Washington Fed. Savs. & Loan, Miami Beach, 1957-59, asst. treas., 1959-61, asst. v.p., 1961-63, v.p., 1963—. Mem. Greater Miami (Fla.) Community Relations Bd., 1963. Dir. Pan-Am. Hosp., Miami, 1966-72. Served with USMC, 1952-54. Mem. Fla., Greater Miami chambers commerce. Home: 785 NW 168th Terrace North Miami FL 33169 Office: 1701 Meridian Av Miami Beach FL 33139

BOHANAN, JAMES OVERSTREET, state ofcl.; b. Louisville, June 11, 1935; s. James Otis and Mary Margaret (Overstreet) B.; A.B., Centre Coll. Ky., 1956; M.B.A., Columbia, 1961; m. Jane Georgeann Morris, May 17, 1969; children—Scott James, Amy Jane. Financial analyst Rohm & Haas Co., chem. co., 1961-62; research analyst, Ky. Dept. Commerce, State Indsl. Devel. Agy., Frankfort, 1963-65, dir. research, 1965-67; asst. Ga. field dir. Coastal Plains Regional Commn., Multi-State Regional Planning Agy., Atlanta, 1968-70; dir. research Ga. Dept. Industry and Trade, State Indsl. Devel. Agy., Atlanta, 1970-72; asst. dep. commr. Ga. Dept. Community Devel., State Econ. Devel. Agy., Atlanta, 1972—. Mem. Ga. Adv. Council on Vocational Edn., 1973—. Served to lt. USNR, 1956-60. Mem. Am., So. indsl. devel. councils, Ga. Indsl. Developers Assn., Ga. Planning Assn., Sigma Alpha Epsilon. Presbyn. Club: Toastmasters. Home: 1028 W Nancy Creek Dr NE Atlanta GA 30319 Office: 270 Washington St SW PO Box 38097 Atlanta GA 30334

BOHANNON, MARSHALL TOPPING, JR., lawyer; b. Norfolk, Va., Aug. 22, 1930; s. Marshall Topping and Grace (Bargamin) B.; B.A., U. Va., 1952, LL.B., 1954; m. Ruth Constance Page, July 12, 1955; children—Page, Marshall Topping III. Admitted to Va. bar, 1953; since practices in Norfolk; partner firm Herbert & Bohannon, Norfolk, 1958—. Served with USNR, 1955-58. Mem. Am., Va., Norfolk bar assns. Kiwanian. Home: 1661 Sheppard Av Norfolk VA 23518 Office: Suite 402 Plaza One Norfolk VA 23510

BOHANNON, ROBERT LAPOINTE, lawyer; b. Norfolk, Va., Nov. 27, 1934; s. Marshall Topping and Grace (Bargamin) B.; B.A., U. Va., 1956, LL.B., 1959; m. Ann Boggs, Mar. 25, 1961; children—Grace Leigh, Catherine LaPointe. Admitted to Va. bar, 1959; since practiced in Norfolk; partner firm Herbert & Bohannon, Norfolk, 1959—. Mem. Am., Va. State, Norfolk/Portsmouth bar assns. North South Skirmish Assn., Hampton One Design Sailing Assn. Club: Optimist (pres.) (Norfolk). Home: 7468 N Shore Rd Norfolk VA 23505 Office: 402 Plaza One Norfolk VA 23510

BOHANNON, TROY BUTLER, physician; b. Cookeville, Tenn., Oct. 18, 1934; s. Oliver Troy and Ila (Butler) B.; B.S., Tenn. Tech. U., 1955; M.D., U. Tenn., 1958; m. Mary Evelyn Weatherly, June 1, 1957; children—Richard Troy, Michael Kevin. Intern Hillcrest Med. Center, Tulsa, 1959; resident Nashville Gen. Hosp., 1960-63; practice medicine specializing in obstetrics and gynecology, Tuscumbia, Ala., 1963—; mem. staff Colbert County, Shoals, Eliza Coffee Meml., Colonial Manor hosps.; trustee Shoals Hosp., Sheffield, Ala., chief of staff, 1972—. Diplomate Am. Bd. Obstetrics and Gynecology. Fellow Am. Coll. Obstetrics and Gynecology; mem. A.M.A., So., Ala. med. assns., Colbert County Med. Soc., Ala. Obstetrics and Gynecology Assn., Am. Fertility Soc., Phi Rho Sigma. Baptist (deacon). Home: 405 Meadow Hill Rd Sheffield AL 35660 Office: 120 E 5th St Tuscumbia AL 35674

BOHLER, CLORINDA SCARPA-SMITH (MRS. T. GORDON BOHLER), physician; b. Buenos Aires, Argentina; d. Jose and Maria (Smith) Scarpa; M. Teaching, Ministerio Nacional de Educacion de la Nacion (Buenos Aires), 1941, B.A., 1942; M.D., U. Buenos Aires, 1949; m. T. Gordon Bohler, Jan. 4, 1959. Intern Hosp. Argerich Buenos Aires, 1946-47, resident 1948-51; instr. anatomy U. Buenos Aires, 1946-47, asst. physician, dept. medicine, 1949-57; chief of colpocitology sect. Instituto Nacional de Endocrinologia, Nat. Ministry of Health, Buenos Aires, 1950-56; prof. spltys, of medicine Red Cross Sch. for Nurses, Buenos Aires, 1952-56; practice medicine, specializing in endocrinology, Buenos Aires, 1950-56; asst. physician Dr. Fred A. Simmons, Mass. Gen. Hosp., Harvard Med. Sch., Boston, 1957; clin. and research fellow Mass. Gen. Hosp., 1957; head sect. of Gonads and infertility NIH, Buenos Aires, Argentina, 1958; research fellow, dept. endocrinology Med. Coll. Ga., Augusta, 1958; cardiovascular research, 1959-60, research asso., 1960-63; research asso., dept. physiology and hemodynamic unit, dept. medicine Eugene Talmadge Meml. Hosp., Med. Coll. Ga., Augusta, 1963-65, asst. prof., dept. obstetrics-gynecology, instr. dept. physiology, 1965-70; research fellow endocrinology Med. Coll. Ga., 1970-71; practice medicine, specializing in endocrinology and metabolism, Augusta, 1971—; clin. tchr. Med. Coll. Ga., 1972—. NIH and Ga. Heart Assn. grantee, 1966-69. Baptist. Author: Nociones de Especialidades Medicas para Enfermeras, 1954. Contbr. articles in field to profl. jours. Home: 2279 Wrightsborough Rd Augusta GA 30904

BOHORFOUSH, JOSEPH GEORGE, physician; b. Birmingham, Ala., Dec. 20, 1907; s. George and Susan (Joseph) B.; A.B., Vanderbilt U., 1929, M.D., 1933; m. Bliss Paige, Feb. 17, 1960; children—David, William, Eugenia Paige Hoffman (Mrs. R. S. Sayers). Intern Hillman Hosp., Birmingham, 1933-34; resident Waverly Hills (Ky.) Sanatorium, 1934-35; asst. med. dir. Lake View Sanatorium, Madison, Wis., 1936-41; med. dir. Jefferson Sanatorium, Birmingham, 1946-47; instr. medicine U. Ala. Med. Coll., 1946-48; chief profl. services VA Hosp., Memphis, 1947-51; asst. prof. medicine U. Tenn., Memphis, 1947, 51; clin. prof. medicine Med. Coll. Ga., 1951-60; chief medicine VA Hosp, Augusta, Ga., 1951-60; dir. phys. health services Central State Hosp., Milledgeville, Ga., 1960-69; dir. Jones Hosp., Milledgeville, 1969-72. Dir. Bohorfoush Corp. Served as maj. M.C., AUS, 1941-45; col. M.C. ret. Diplomate Am. Bd. Internal Medicine, Am. Bd. Pulmonary Diseases. Fellow A.C.P., Am. Coll. Chest Physicians, Am. Fedn. Clin. Research; asso. Royal Soc. Medicine; mem. A.M.A., Med. Assn. Ga., Baldwin County, 10th Dist. med. socs., Am., Ga. thoracic socs., Pan Am., So. med. assns., Ga. Acad. Sci., Ga. Heart Assn., Ret. Officers Assn., Internat. Soc. Internal Medicine. Kiwanian. Club: Milledgeville Country. Home: 1862 Tanglewood Rd Milledgeville GA 31061 Office: 811 N Cobb St Milledgeville GA 31061

BOHORFOUSH, ROBERT LOUIS, real estate developer. b. Birmingham, Ala., Jan. 11, 1946; s. Louis Charles and Ruth (Davis) B.; B.A., Birmingham So. Coll., 1967; m. Martha Carol Minor, Dec. 20, 1969. Sales coordinator Saunders Leasing System, Inc., Birmingham, 1967-69; co-founder, adminstrv. v.p. Met. Properties, Inc., Birmingham, 1969—. Co-chmn. Downtown Birmingham Clean-Up Drive, 1970. Mem. Nat. Inst. Real Estate Bds. (certified comml. investment mem.) Birmingham Bd. Realtors (dir.), Nat. Inst. Real Estate Brokers. Club: The Club (Birmingham). Home: 3421 Mountainside Rd Birmingham AL 35243 Office: Title Bldg Birmingham AL 35203

BOHUSLAV, ELLA LILLIAN STRATMAN (MRS. GEORGE F. BOHUSLAV), civic worker; b. Giddings, Tex., Nov. 8, 1911; d. Charles Bernard and Minnie (Schlottman) Stratman; student Tex. Christian U., 1929-31; B.A., S.W. Tex. State U., 1940; m. George F. Bohuslav, July 27, 1935; children—Jacquelyn Sue (Mrs. Neville B. Graham, Jr.), Georgia Ellan (Mrs. Willie N. Raven). Tchr. speech Giddings High Sch., 1931-33, Shiner High Sch., St. Ludmilla's Acad., 1933-35; tchr. English, prin. Midfields Jr. High Sch., 1936-39; tchr. English-speech Lockhart High Sch., 1940-42; tchr. English, Baker Jr. High Sch., Austin, Tex., 1942. Sec., Austin Dist. Dental Aux., 1947-48, pres., 1948-49; treas. Casis P.T.A., Austin, 1959-60; women's chmn. March of Dimes, Travis County, Tex., 1964; pres. O'Henry Band Boosters' Club, 1962-63, Lady Lion's Club, 1972-73; dir. jr. vols. Seton Hosp., Austin, 1965-66, pres. Aux., 1966-67, treas., 1967-70; leader Girl Scouts U.S.A., 1951-57, Y-Teens, 1960-63; v.p. Alpha Phi Mothers' Club, 1969-70; pres. Alpha Chi Omega Mother's Club, 1969-70. Lady, Equestrian Order Holy Sepulchre. Mem. Internat. Platform Assn. Roman Catholic (pres. parish council 1955-57, parish guild 1971-72). Clubs: Westwood Country, Austin Woman's (financial com.) (Austin). Home: 2706 Scenic Dr Austin TX 78703

BOHUSLAV, GEORGE FRANK, dentist; b. Hallettsville, Tex., Sept. 16, 1909; s. Adolph Frank and Lillie Matilda (Hajek) B.; B.S., S.W. Tex. State U., 1935; D.D.S., U. Tex., 1942; postgrad. Coll. Physicians and Surgeons, Sch. Dentistry, San Francisco, 1947, U. Mich., 1949, U. Ala., 1959, Boston U., 1969; m. Ella Lillian Stratman, July 27, 1935; children—Jacquelyn Sue (Mrs. Neville B. Graham), Georgia Ellan (Mrs. Willie N. Raven). Prin. Midfields (Tex.) High Sch., 1936-38; cons. dental health edn. Dental div. Tex. Dept. Health, Austin, 1942-46; pvt. practice dentistry, specializing in pedodontics, Austin, 1946—. Chmn. dental div. United Funds, 1969. Named papal knight Temple of Jerusalem, Knight Equestrian Order Holy Sepulchre. Fellow Am. Acad. Pedodontists; goodfellow Tex. Dental Assn.; mem. Austin Dist. Dental Soc. (pres. 1949-50), Tex. Soc. Dentistry for Children (pres. 1944-46), Southwestern Soc. Pedodontists (pres. 1952), U. Tex. Ex-Student's Assn., Pierre Fauchard Acad., Xi Psi Phi. Roman Catholic. K.C. (4 deg.), Lion. Clubs: Serra (pres. 1956-58), Longhorn, Westwood Country (Austin). Home: 2706 Scenic Dr Austin TX 78703 Office: 715 W 34th St Austin TX 78705

BOIKESS, OLGA SHNIPER, lawyer; b. Jamaica, N.Y., Dec. 25, 1938; d. Robert and Bella (Jarus) Shniper; B.A., Barnard Coll., 1960; J.D., U. Cal. at Los Angeles, 1964. Admitted to Cal. bar, 1964, D.C. bar, 1969; law clk. U.S. Dist. Ct. for So. Dist. Cal., 1964-65; atty. gen. counsel's office, Office Econ. Opportunity, Exec. Office Pres., Washington, 1965-68; asso. Galland, Kharasch, Calkins & Brown, Washington, 1968—. Cons. in health services and econ. devel. for fed. agys. and govt. contractors, 1968—. Mem. Am. Civil Liberties Union (vol. atty. 1968—), Health and Welfare Council (mem. nat. capital area membership com. 1970-73, budget com. 1970-73, Sierra Club (vol. atty. 1970—). Office: 1054 31st St NW Washington DC 20007

BOINODIRIS, STAVROS, electronic systems engr.; b. Drama, Greece, Nov. 15, 1943; s. Antonios and Elizabeth (Aslanoglou) B.; came to U.S., 1961; B.S., U. Fla., 1967, M.E., 1968; m. Despina Kokinos, Sept. 2, 1967; 1 dau., Phaedra. Jr. engr. IBM, Boca Raton, Fla., 1969, asso. engr., 1969-71, sr. asso. engr., 1971—, also sub-system group leader. Recipient outstanding performance award IBM. Mem. Instrument Soc. Am. Patentee isolated digital to analog converter. Home: 4915 NW 5th Av Boca Raton FL 33432 Office: PO Box 1328 Boca Raton FL 33432

BOLAND, THOMAS EDWIN, banker; b. Columbus, Ga., July 8, 1934; s. Clifford E. and Helen M. (Robinson) B.; student Emory U., 1952-54; B.B.A., Ga. State U., 1957; postgrad. Stonier Grad. Sch. Banking, Rutgers U., 1964-66; m. Beth Ann Campbell, May 23, 1959; children—Susan Ann, Thomas E., Jr. With First Nat. Bank Atlanta, 1954—, v.p., 1968-73, group v.p., 1973—; dir. Aunt Fanny's Baking Co., Atlanta. Trustee Atlanta Baptist Coll., 1970-73. Served with AUS, 1957. Named Salesmen of Year, Atlanta Sales and Marketing Execs. Club, 1969. Mem. Am. Bankers Assn. (bank card com. 1964-66). Kiwanian. Club: Cherokee Town and Country (Atlanta). Home: 3603 Embry Circle Atlanta GA 30341 Office: PO Box 4148 Atlanta GA 30302

BOLDEN, JOHN HENRY, educator; b. River Junction, Fla., Jan. 10, 1922; s. Idell and Eddie L. (Jackson) B.; B.S., Fla. Meml. Coll., 1950; M.S., Fla. A. and M. U., 1952, M.Ed., 1963; Ed. S., Ind. U., 1966, Ed.D., 1968; m. Bertha M. Johnson, Sept. 5, 1942; 1 son, Richard L. Pres., Bolden's Coll. Music, Jacksonville, Fla., 1958-67, chmn. bd. dirs., 1958—; research asst. Ind. U., 1967-68; dean tchr. edn. Cheyney (Pa.) State Coll., 1968-69; area dir. elementary edn. Duval County Schs., Jacksonville, 1969-73; asso. prof. adminstrn. and supervision Fla. State U., Tallahassee, 1973—. Vis. lectr. Jacksonville U., Fla. A. and M. U.; vis. dir. bands Edward Waters Coll. Bd. dirs. Johnson br. YMCA, 1950—. Served with USNR, 1942-45. Recipient Nathan W. Collier Meritorious Service award Fla. Meml. Coll., Miami, 1968. Mem. Am. Assn. Sch. Adminstrs. (Acad. Profl. Devel. award), Nat., Fla. edn. assns., N.A.A.C.P., Jacksonville Urban League, Phi Delta Kappa, Kappa Delta Pi. Author: Systematic Approach to School Management, 1972; Curriculum Development Module: Designing an Instructional Management System, 1972. Home: 2922 Pearce St Jacksonville FL 32209

BOLDEN, THEODORE EDWARD, dentist, educator; b. Middleburg, Va., Apr. 19, 1920; s. Theodore D. and Mary E. (Jackson) B.; A.B., Lincoln U., 1941; D.D.S., Meharry Med. Coll., 1947; M.S., U. Ill., 1951, Ph.D., 1958; m. Dorothy M. Forde, June 17, 1952. Asso. prof. oral diagnosis and pathology Seton Hall Coll., 1960-62; prof. dentistry, chmn. dept. oral pathology and oral medicine, dir. research Meharry Med. Coll., 1962-69, prof. dentistry, chmn. dept. oral pathology, dir. research, 1969-71, asso. dean Sch. of Dentistry, 1967-73. Chmn. health com. Montclair (N.J.) Health Dept., 1959-60; abstractor N.Y. State Dental Jour., 1960; mem. dental edn. rev. com. Dept. Health, Edn. and Welfare, 1969—; cons. dentistry VA Hosps., Tuskegee, Ala., and Nashville. Served with Dental Corps, AUS, 1951-52. Diplomate Am. Bd. Oral Medicine. Fellow Am. Acad. Oral Pathology; mem. Ewell Neil Dental Soc., Nat. Dental Assn., Capital City, Lincoln dental socs., Internat. Assn. Dental Research, Northeastern Soc. Periodontists, N.Y. Acad. Scis., Omega Psi Phi. Baptist. Author: (with J. Manhold) Outline of Pathology, 1960; (with E. L. Mobley and E. S. Chandler) Dental Hygiene Examination Review Book, Vol. I, Edit. 3, 1973. Contbr. articles profl. jours. and books. Home: 3404 Panorama Rd Nashville TN 37218 Office: 1005 18th Av N Nashville TN 37208

BOLDT, ALBERT WALTER, govt. ofcl.; b. Altoona, Pa., Aug. 28, 1904; s. John Henry and Bertha (Seig) B.; B.S., Gettysburg Coll., 1927; M.A., Lehigh U., 1938; Ed. D., U. Fla., 1958; married; children—Jacqueline (Mrs. Robert C. Poor), Sandra (Mrs. Samuel Bockman). Instr. Reading (Pa.) Sch. Dist., 1930-42; chief Vocational Rehab. and Edn. div. VA, Reading, 1945-48; asst. dean men U. Fla., Gainesville, 1948-58; dean students Am U., Washington, 1958-60; dir. div. higher edn. Dept. Health, Edn. and Welfare Region IV, U.S. Office Edn., Atlanta, 1960—. Cons. evaluation sch. dists. Atlanta, Jacksonville, DeLand and Ocala, Fla., 1950-58. Served to lt. comdr. USNR, 1942-45. Mem. Am. Coll. Personnel Assn., Nat. Assn. Student Personnel Adminstrs., Nat. Assn. Sch. and Coll. Placement, N.E.A., Assn. Higher Edn., Nat. Assn. Deans and Advisers Men, Phi Delta Kappa, Phi Kappa Phi, Kappa Delta Pi. Author: Objective Tests in American History, 1940; History of the Schools of Reading from 1748 to 1859, 1938; The Leadership Fraternity in American Society—A Study of the Florida Blue Key, 1956. Editor: Gator Guide. Home: 3804 Briarcliff Rd NE Atlanta GA 30329 Office: 50 7th St NE Atlanta GA 30323

BOLEN, BENJAMIN HOMER, park adminstr.; b. Fancy Gap, Va., Sept. 16, 1917; s. Marcus Moore and Myrtle Francis (Snow) B.; B.A., Emory and Henry Coll., 1938; m. Edith Neblett Cahill, June 4, 1955; 1 son, Marcus William. State hwy. engr. Commonwealth of Va., 1938-50, asst. commr. state parks, 1960-61, commr. state parks, 1961—; supt. Claytor Lake State Park, Dublin, Va., 1950-60. Chmn. Breaks Interstate Park Commn., 1966-74. Recipient Gov.'s State Conservation award, 1970; Silver Cornelius Amory Puglsey award Am. Scenic and Historic Preservation Soc., 1970; Meritorious Service award Nat. Conf. on State Parks, 1973. Mem. Nat. Recreation and Park Assn. (trustee 1970-74), Va. Recreation and Park Soc. (dir. 1970-74), Nat. Conf. on State Parks (pres. 1970-72), Nat. State Park Dirs. Assn., Southeastern State Park Dirs. Assn. Mason, Elk, Moose. Home: 2609 Lancers Blvd Richmond VA 23224 Office: 1201 State Office Bldg Capitol Square Richmond VA 23219

BOLEN, ERIC GEORGE, educator, conservationist; b. Plainfield, N.J., Nov. 24, 1937; s. Wilbur Fraser and Doris June (Wicks) B.; B.S., U. Me., 1959; M.S., Utah State U., 1962, Ph.D., 1967; m. Rebecca Ann Woodhull, Aug. 12, 1967; 1 son, Brent Fraser. Asst. biologist Vt. Fish and Game Dept., Addison, 1957, 58, 62; refuge biologist U.S. Fish and Wildlife Service, Fish Springs, Utah, 1959-61; instr. biology dept. Tex. A. and I. U., Kingsville, 1965-66, adj. prof. Corpus Christi campus, 1974—; asst. prof. Tex. Tech U., Lubbock, 1966-69, asso. prof., 1969-73, prof., 1973; asst. dir. Welder Wildlife Found., Sinton, Tex., 1973—. Cons. U.S. Parks Service, U.S. Dept. Agr. Faculty research fellow Tex. Tech U. Mem. Wildlife Soc. (pres. Tex. chpt. 1974-75), Cooper Ornithol. Soc., Am. Ornithologists Union, Ecol. Soc., Brit. Ornithologists' Union, Wilson Ornithologists' Union (life), Southwestern Naturalists (sec. 1973, bd. govs. 1972-73), Am. Soc. Mammalogists. Rotarian. Clubs: Toastmasters (pres. 1970-71) (Lubbock); Ducks Unltd. (pres. W. Tex. chpt. 1972-73). Home: Drawer 1400 Sinton TX 78387

BOLEN, HAROLD JEAN, lectr., writer, ret. coll. pres.; b. Wildersville, Tenn., July 3, 1901; s. William R. and Florence (Parish) B.; A.B., Cumberland U., 1925, LL.B., 1926; B.C.S., Am. Bus. U., 1928; B.C.Ed., Haddock Bus. U., 1932; M.S., Cal. Coll. Commerce, 1952, LL.D., 1953; Ph.D., U. of West, 1957; Ed.D., Burton Coll., 1961; m. Lucy Jane Huggins, Aug. 28, 1926; children—Hannah Jean (Mrs. Martin L. Bridges), Martha Jane (Mrs. Charles David Moore), William Harold. Vice-prin. Jasper (Fla.) High Sch., 1928-33; v.p., prin. Draughon's Bus. Coll., Savannah, Ga., 1933-40, pres., 1940-52; pres. Bolen-Draughon Coll., Savannah, 1952-69. Bd. dirs. Savannah YMCA; trustee Brewton-Parker Coll., Mt. Vernon, Ga. Mem. So. Bus. Edn. Assn., Nat. Bus. Edn. Assn., Southeastern Bus. Coll. Assn. (pres.), Am. Assn. Comml. Colls. (dir.), Savannah C. of C., Nat. Sales Execs. Club, Pi Rho Zeta. Club: Exchange (Savannah). Home: 3605 Bull St Savannah GA 31405

BOLENE, MARGARET ROSALIE STEELE (MRS. ROBERT V. BOLENE), bacteriologist, civic worker; b. Kingfisher, Okla., July 11, 1923; d. Clarence R. and Harriet (White) Steele; student Ore. State U., 1943-44; B.S., U. Okla., 1946; m. Robert V. Bolene, Feb. 6, 1948; children—Judith Kay, John Eric, Sally Sue, Janice Lynn, Daniel William. Technician bacteriology dept. Okla. Dept. Health, Oklahoma City, 1946-48; asst. bacteriologist Henry Ford Hosp., Detroit, 1948-49; bacteriological cons., also asst. bus. mgr. Ponca Gynecology and Obstetrics, Inc., 1956—. Organizing dir. Bi-Racial Council, 1963; lay adviser Home Nursing Service, 1967-68; mem. exec. bd. P.T.A., 1956-71; active various community drives; sponsor Am. Field Service; patron Ponca Playhouse. Precinct organizer Republican party, 1960. Mem. Am. Assn. U. Women (treas. 1964-66), D.A.R. (sec.-treas. 1961-67, first vice regent 1972-74), Kay-Noble County Med. Aux. (treas. 1957-58, 66-67), Ponca City Art Assn., Lambda Tau, Phi Sigma, Alpha Lambda Delta. Presbyn. Club: Ponca City Country. Home: 2116 Juanito St Ponca City OK 74601

BOLENE, ROBERT VICTOR, physician; b. Enid, Okla., Aug. 31, 1925; s. Victor Emanuel and Alna (Brown) B.; student Phillips U., 1942-43; Northwestern U., 1943, U. N.H., 1943-44; M.D., U. Okla., 1948; m. Margaret Rosalie Steele, Feb. 6, 1948; children—Judith Kay, John Eric, Sally Sue, Janice Lynn, Daniel William. Surg. intern Henry Ford Hosp., Detroit, 1948-49; county health dir. Garvin and Murray County, Okla., 1949-50; chief surgery VA Hosp., Sulphur, Okla. 1950, 1952-53; resident obstetrics and gynecology U. Okla. Med. Center, Oklahoma City, 1953-56, asso. instr., chief resident faculty Sch. Medicine, 1955-56; practice medicine specializing in obstetrics and gynecology, Ponca City, Okla., 1956—; mem. staff Ponca City Hosp., chief dept. obstetrics and gynecology, pres.-elect, 1971, chief staff, 1972; mem. staff Fairfax Hosp. Committeeman, Boy Scouts Am., patron Ponca City Playhouse; sponsor YMCA, 1960-61; rep. Cub Scouts Am., 1959-61. Served from pvt. to pfc Inf., AUS, 1942-46; served from 1st lt. to capt. M.C., USAF, 1950-52. Diplomate Am. Bd. Obstetrics and Gynecology. Fellow A.C.S., Am. Coll. Obstetricians and Gynecologists, Am. Geriatric Soc.; mem. Am. Soc. Study Sterility, Internat. Fertility Assn., Tulsa Obstetrics and Gynecology Soc., A.M.A., Okla., Kay Noble County (pres. 1969) med. socs., C. of C., New Hosp. Devel. Orgn., Phi Chi. Republican. Presbyn. Club: Ponca City Country. Home: 2116 Juanito St Ponca City OK 74601 Office: Ponca Med Arts 1215 E Hartford St Ponca City OK 74601

BOLES, CLYDA GRACE (MRS. GEORGE WAYLAND BOLES), chem. mfg. co. exec.; b. Mansfield, Ark., June 15, 1912; d. Richard Thomas and Eva Viola (Carter) Hodges; m. George Wayland Boles, Feb. 15, 1936; children—Sharon Kay (Mrs. Michael Earl Batchelder), Marcia Beth (Mrs. Jim Alan Patterson), Barbara Ann. Exec. sec. to pres. Square Deal Film Exchange, Oklahoma City, 1934-38; partner Sani-Wax Co., Dallas, 1939-45, 52—; co-pub, co-editor Scene, Mag. of the Southwest, Dallas, 1946-48; sec.-treas. Trojan Foundries, Inc., Dallas, 1950-54, partner, 1954—; sec.-treas. Plantation Press, Inc., Dallas, 1969—. Contbr. articles, stories and poems to various publs. Composer; I'm Still Here, 1950; Why Didn't I Know, 1950; lyricist We All Wish You All Merry Christmas, 1949. Home: 5210 Meaders Lane Dallas TX 75229 Office: 1500 Plantation Rd Dallas TX 75235

BOLES, PAUL DARCY, author; b. Auburn, Ind., Mar. 5, 1919; s. Ernest A. and Gwendolyn (Cowan) B.; student pub. schs.; m. Dorothy Kathleen Flory, Dec. 25, 1941; children—Shawn Michael, Terence Ross, Patric Laurence. Recipient Friends of Am. Writers Medal and $1,000 award, 1958; fiction gold medal Ga. Writers Assn., 1969; award U. Ind., 1969. Author: The Streak, 1953; The Beggars in The Sun, 1954; Glenport, Illinois, 1956; Deadline, 1957; Parton's Island, 1958; A Million Guitars, 1968 (Ind. U. Writers Conf. award 1969); I Thought You Were a Unicorn, 1971; The Limner, 1974; Contbr. The Living Novel, 1957. Contbr. numerous short stories to maj. mags. Home: 4009 Wieuca Rd NE Atlanta GA 30305

BOLEY, ROBERT EUGENE, assn. exec.; b. Washington, Nov. 25, 1925; s. Charles Taylor and Viva (Weightman) B.; A.B., George Washington U., 1953 M.A., 1958; m. Janet Elizabeth McCarty, May 26, 1950; 1 stepson, Stephen C. Sole. Geographer Fed. Govt., 1953-54; research asso. George Washington U., 1954-56; dir. Indsl. Devel. Com. of Prince George County (Md.), 1956-57; with Urban Land Inst., Washington, 1957-73, exec. dir., 1968-73; cons. Soc. Indsl. Realtors, 1973, exec. v.p., 1974—. Bd. dirs. Urban Land Research Found. Served with AUS, 1943-46. Decorated Air medal. Mem. Assn. Am. Geographers, Am. Indsl. Devel. Council (chmn. research edn. and cons. com. 1969-73), Lambda Alpha, Pi Gamma Mu. Contbr. indsl. sect. of Community Builders Handbook, 1969. Home: 3430 N Randolph St Arlington VA 22207 Office: 925 15th St NW Washington DC 20005

BOLGER, ROBERT JOSEPH, trade assn. exec.; b. Phila., Aug. 9, 1922; s. Harold Stephen and Edna (Adams) B.; B.S., Villanova U., 1943; postgrad. Northwestern U., 1945-46, U. Pa., 1946-47, U. Geneva (Switzerland), 1948-49; m. Helen Siegfried, May 22, 1954; children—Robert, Mary T., Cynthia A., Ann M., Catherine B., David A. Salesman, Container Corp., Phila., 1946; sales supr. Kraft Food Co., Phila., 1949-52; overseas mgr., dir. retail relations Smith, Kline & French Labs., Phila., 1952-62; exec. v.p. Nat. Assn. Chain Drug Stores, Inc., Arlington, Va., 1962-72, pres., 1972—. Bd. dirs. Am. Found. Pharm. Edn.; bd. dirs. Nat. Drug Trade Conf., pres., 1974—. Served to lt. comdr., USNR; PTO. Decorated Air medal; named Man of Year Cosmetic and Toiletry Sect. United Jewish Appeal, 1972. Mem. Am. Pharm. Assn., Nat. Assn. Retail Druggists. Clubs: Belle Haven Country (Alexandria); Canadian (N.Y.C.); Army-Navy, Capitol Hill (Washington); Germantown Cricket (Phila.). Contbr. articles to trade publs. Home: 906 Dalebrook Dr Alexandria VA 22308 Office: 1911 Jefferson Davis Hwy Arlington VA 22202

BOLIN, RICHARD ARNOLD, city ofcl.; b. York, S.C., Dec. 24, 1935; s. John Henry and Cora (Clinton) B.; B.S., Appalachian State Tchrs. Coll., 1958; m. Glenda Kay Tucker, Aug. 1, 1964; children—John Patrick, Margaret Lynne. Budget and personnel officer, asst. to city mgr. City of Greenville, S.C., 1962-64; dir. finance City of Brunswick (Ga.), 1964-65; town mgr. Town of Canton (N.C.), 1965-68; city mgr. City of Anderson (S.C.), 1968-70, City of Newnan (Ga.), 1970—. Pres., Canton (N.C.) Bethel-Clyde United Fund, 1968, drive chmn., 1968; 3d v.p. Newnan United Fund, 1972. Bd. dirs. Canton chpt. A.R.C., 1967, Newnan chpt., 1972—, Chat-Flint Area Planning and Devel. Commn., 1971-74. Served to lt. (j.g.) USNR, 1959-62. Mem. Internat. City Mgmt. Assn., Ga. City-County Mgrs. Assn. (sec.-treas. 1971-72, pres. 1973-74), Ga. Municipal Assn. (dir. 1973-74), Am. Judicature Soc. Methodist. Lion. Home: 4 Mansour Circle Newnan GA 30263 Office: 25 Jefferson St Newnan GA 30263

BOLING, EDWARD JOSEPH, univ. adminstr.; b. Sevier County, Tenn., Feb. 19, 1922; s. Sam R. and Nerissa (Clark) B.; B.S. in Accounting, U. Tenn., 1948, M.S. in Statistics, 1950; Ed.D. in Ednl. Adminstrn., George Peabody Coll. Tchrs., 1961; m. Carolyn Pierce, Aug. 8, 1950; children—Mark Edward, Brian Marshall, Stephen Clark. With Wilby-Kinsy Theatre Corp., Knoxville, Tenn., 1940-41, Aluminum Co. Am., 1941-42; instr. statistics U. Tenn., 1948-50; research statistician Carbide & Carbon Chem. Corp., Oak Ridge, 1950, supr. source and fissionable materials accounting K-25 plant, 1951-54; budget dir. Tenn., 1955-59, commr. finance and adminstrn., 1959-61; v.p. U. Tenn., 1961-70, pres., 1970—. Dir. Nashville br. Fed. Res. Bank of Atlanta, Benco Plastics, Inc., Swan Bros., Magnavox Corp. Mem. So. Regional Edn. Bd., 1957-61, 71—; mem. Nat. Govs. Conf. Good Will Tour to Brazil and Argentina, 1960; chmn. Tenn. Tax Modernization and Reform Commn.; mem. task force coordination, goverance and structure postsecondary edn. Edn. Commn. States. Bd. dirs. Knoxville United Fund, East Tenn. Speech and Hearing Assn., Bill Wilkerson Speech and Hearing Center, Nashville. Served with AUS, 1943-46; ETO. Mem. Am. Statis. Assn., Assn. Higher Edn., Am. Council Edn. (com. taxation commn. fed. relations), Nat. Assn. Land-Grant Colls., Am. Coll. Pub. Relations Assn. (trustee, chmn. com. on taxation and philanthropy, mem. exec. council pub. affairs com.), Am. Alumni Council, Knoxville C. of C. (v.p.), Am. Legion, L.Q.C. Lamar Soc., Phi Kappa Phi (Scholarship award 1948), Beta Gamma Sigma (charter pres. Alpha chpt. 1948), Phi Delta Kappa. Democrat. Author: (with D. A. Gardiner) Forecasting University Enrollment, 1952. Home: 940 Cherokee Blvd Knoxville TN 37914

BOLING, JEWELL, govt. ofcl.; b. Randleman, N.C., Sept. 26, 1907; d. John Emmitt and Carrie (Ballard) Boling; student Women's Coll., U. N.C., 1926; Am. U., 1942, 51-52. Interviewer, N.C. Employment Service, Winston-Salem, Asheboro, 1937-41; occupational analyst US. Dept. Labor, Washington, 1943-57, placement officer, 1957-58, employment service adviser, 1959-61, occupational analyst, 1962, employment service specialist counseling and testing, 1963-69, manpower devel. specialist, 1969—. Recipient Meritorious Achievement award Dept. Labor, 1972. Mem. A.A.A.S., Am. Personnel and Guidance Assn. (profl. mem. nat. vocational guidance assn.). Am. Rehab. Counselling Assn. (archivist 1964-67), Assn. Measurement and Evaluation in Guidance, Internat. Assn. Personnel in Employment Security, Am. Assn. Humanistic Psychology, Smithsonians, Audubon/Naturalist Soc., Nat. Capital Astronomers (editor Star Dust 1949-58), Internat. Platform Assn., Sierra Club, Defenders of Wildlife. Author: Counselor's Handbook, Interviewing Guides in Individual Appraisal, 1967; Counselor's Desk Aid, Eighteen Basic Vocational Directions, 1967; Handbook for New Careerists in Employment Security, 1971. Contbr. articles to profl. publs. Home: 1514 17th St NW Washington DC 20036 Office: 601 D St NW Washington DC 20004

BOLINGER, JOHN MICHAEL, veterinarian; b. E. Dare and Rina (Morrison) B.; student Wofford Coll., 1959-62, Clemson U., 1962-63; D.V.M., Coll. Vet. Medicine, U. Ga., 1963-67; m. E. Marcella Meredith, Nov. 10, 1962 (div.); children—Jara, Joy, Jony, Ann, Mike. Veterinarian, Central Soya Co., Decatur, Ind., 1967-69; pvt. practice vet. medicine, Gaffney, S.C., 1969—. Mem. Gaffney Jr. C. of C., Cherokee Sertoma, Am., S.C. vet. med. assns., Gaffney C. of C., Parents Without Partners, Gaffney YMCA, Alpha Zeta. Home: 308 W Race St Gaffney SC 29340 Office: PO Box 1333 S Granard St Gaffney SC 29340

BOLLENBACHER, DONALD RICHARD, chem. engr.; b. Toledo, Mar. 2, 1936; s. Otto and Martha Rose (Slupecki) B.; B.S. in Chem. Engring., U. Toledo, 1959; postgrad. U. Ala., 1965, U. Okla., 1969-73; m. Judith Anne O'Callaghan, June 13, 1959; children—Jeffrey Arthur, Timothy Otto, Heidi Marie. Process engr. Hercules Powder Co., Radford, Va., 1959-63; engr. on Pershing and Shillelagh missile systems U.S. Army Missile Command, Redstone Arsenal, Ala., 1963—, product assurance dir., 1971—. Pres. Huntsville Community Chorus Assn., 1970-71. Registered profl. engr., Ala. Mem. Tau Kappa Epsilon (historian 1957-59). Lutheran (choir dir. 1959—). Kiwanian. Home: 3916 Richland Rd Huntsville AL 35810 Office: AMSMI-QPO Redstone Arsenal AL 35809

BOLLET, ALFRED JAY, educator, physician; b. N.Y.C., July 15, 1926; s. Maurice and Sorrell (Ross) B.; B.S., N.Y. U., 1944, M.S., 1948; m. Audrey K. Brown, June 20, 1954; 1 son, Jeffrey Brown. Intern Mt. Sinai Hosp., N.Y.C., 1948-49, asst. resident physician in medicine, 1951, chief resident physician in medicine, 1952-53; ward surgeon Neponsit Marine Hosp., 1949; resident physician chest service Bellevue Hosp., N.Y.C., 1950, asst. resident physician in medicine, 1952; clin. research asso. Nat. Inst. Arthritis and Metabolic Diseases, 1953-55; asst. in medicine Johns Hopkins, 1954-55; asso. physician Detroit Receiving and Wayne County Gen. Hosps., 1955-59; asst. prof. medicine Wayne State U. Coll. Medicine, 1955-59; asso. prof. internal medicine and preventive medicine U. Va. Sch. Medicine, Charlottesville, 1959-65, prof. internal medicine and preventive medicine, 1965-66; dir. rheumatic disease research and tng. program and chronic disease unit U. Va., 1959-66; prof., chmn. dept. medicine Med. Coll. Ga. Sch. Medicine, Augusta, 1966—. Vis. prof. Robert Breck Brigham and Peter Bent Brigham Hosps. Harvard, 1964, U. Miss. Sch. Medicine, 1966, 69, U. Tenn. Sch. Medicine, 1967, Emory U. Sch. Medicine, 1967, Brazilian Congress Rheumatology, Curitiba, Brazil, 1972, Assn. for Rheumatologic Investigation, Buenos Aires, Argentina, 1972, State U. N.Y. Downstate Med. Center, Bklyn., 1972, U. Ky. Coll. Medicine, 1973. Mem. gen. medicine study sect. NIH, 1961-65, chmn., 1965-66; mem. arthritis tng. grants com. Nat. Inst. Arthritis and Metabolic Diseases, 1966-70, mem. career devel. awards com., 1970-73; mem. endocrinology and metabolism research evaluation com. VA, 1968-69; mem. continuing edn. task force Ga. Regional Med. Programs, 1967-68, chmn. steering com., 1970—, mem. regional adv. group, 1970—; program cons. Nat. Found., 1960-64, Arthritis Found., 1965-66; cons. to U.S. Army Specialized Treatment Center, Ft. Gordon, Ga., 1966—, to Surgeon Gen. U.S. Army, 1970. Served with USPHS, 1949, 53-55. Recipient Wortis award in medicine, neurology and psychiatry N.Y. U. Coll. Medicine, 1948; Markle scholar in med. scis., 1956-61. Diplomate Nat. Bd. Med. Examiners, Am. Bd. Internal Medicine. Fellow A.C.P.; mem. A.M.A., Richmond County Med. Soc., Med. Assn. Ga., Am. Soc. Internal Medicine, Am. Assn. U. Profs., A.A.A.S., Am. Rheumatism Assn., Am. Fedn. for Clin. Research (pres. 1963-64), Central Soc. for Clin. Research, Soc. for Exptl. Biology and Medicine, Am. Soc. for Clin. Investigation, So. Soc. for Clin. Investigation (pres. 1973-74), Am. Physiol. Soc., Assn. Am. Physicians, Assn. Profs. Medicine, Am. Clin. and Climatol. Assn., Sigma Xi, Alpha Omega Alpha. Editorial bd. Arthritis and Rheumatism, 1966-73, Am. Jour. Med. Scis., 1966—, Am. Bd. Internal Medicine, 1971—. Contbr. chpts. and articles to numerous med. jours., also abstracts. Home: 1314 Comfort Rd Augusta GA 30904

BOLLET, AUDREY KATHLEEN BROWN (MRS. ALFRED JAY BOLLET), physician; b. N.Y.C.; d. Joseph Henry and Ann J. (Nemec) Brown; B.A. summa cum laude, Barnard Coll., 1944; M.D., Columbia, 1945; m. Alfred Jay Bollet, June 20, 1954; 1 son, Jeffrey. Intern, 1st Med. Service Columbia Div., Bellevue Hosp., N.Y.C., 1950-51; resident Bellevue Hosp., 1951-53; fellow Babies's Hosp., N.Y.C., 1953-54; civilian pediatrician Walter Reed Army Hosp., Washington, 1954-55; research asso. Child Research Center, Detroit, 1955-59; asst. prof., asso. prof. pediatrics U. Va., Charlottesville, 1959-66; prof. pediatrics Med. Coll. Ga., Augusta, 1966-68, acting chmn. pediatrics, 1969—. Mem. com. phototherapy Nat. Acad. Sci.; mem. com. on human embryology and developmental study sect. NIH. Recipient Bicentennial Commemorative medallion Columbia. Bd. dirs. Augusta Civic Ballet, Augusta Hist. Soc. Fellow Am. Acad. Pediatrics; mem. Soc. Pediatric Research (past v.p.), So. Soc. Pediatric Research, Royal Soc. Health, Royal Soc. Medicine, Augusta Pediatric Soc., Pan Am. Med. Assn., Am. Hematologic Soc., A.A.A.S., N.Y. Acad. Sci., Sigma Xi. Contbr. articles in field to profl. jours. Home: 1314 Comfort Rd Augusta GA 30902 Office: 15th and Gwinett St Augusta GA 30904

BOLON, LESLIE WILSON, ret. structural engr.; b. Smithfield, Ill., Dec. 10, 1918; s. Charles Henry and Bertha (Helle) B.; B.S., Auburn U., 1942; diesel/elec. engring. certificate Purdue U., 1943; postgrad. in law Emory. U., 1948-51; m. Mildred Cosper, Jan. 23, 1942; children—Leslie (Mrs. Carl H. Wagle), Carl Bradley. Instr. celestial nav. Ga. Inst. Tech., Atlanta, 1952; asst. dep. mgr. Pan Am. World Airways Eastern Guided Missile Test Range, Patrick AFB, Fla., 1958-59, supt. quality control, 1959-63; planning and programming engr. Cape Kennedy, Patrick AFB, 1963-65; regional site engr. FHA, Washington, 1965-66; gen. engr. AEC, Oak Ridge, 1966-74; ret., 1974—. City commr., Melbourne, Fla., 1960-63. Served with USN, 1942-45, 48-53; comdr. Res. (ret.). Decorated 2 Bronze Stars with Combat V. Registered profl. engr., Ga., Ala. Mason (32 deg.). Home and office: 718 Espanola Way W Melbourne FL 32901

BOLTON, ELLIS TRUESDALE, research lab. exec.; b. Linden, N.J., May 4, 1922; s. Elliott L. and Elizabeth (Lindsay) B.; B.S., Rutgers U., 1943, Ph.D. in Zoology, 1950; postgrad. Harvard-Mass. Inst. Tech. Radar Sch., 1943-44; m. V. Elaine Alber, Sept. 11, 1943; children—Roger T., Craig E. Instr. zoology Rutgers U., 1946-49; mem. staff Dept. Terrestrial Magnetism, Carnegie Instn., Washington, 1951-64, chmn. biophysics sect., 1961-66, asso. dir., 1964-66, dir., 1966—; vis. investigator Rocky Mountain Lab., NIH, 1956, 57, U. Auckland, New Zealand, 1960-61. Mem. internat. fellowship award panel USPHS, 1964-68. Served to capt. USMCR, World War II. Recipient Washington Acad. Sci. award, 1959. Carnegie Instn. fellow, 1949-51. Mem. A.A.A.S., Biophysics Soc. (council 1964-66), Am. Geophys. Union, Sigma Xi. Club: Cosmos (Washington). Research in devel. of agar technique to immobilize single strands of DNA for studies of hybridezation reactions; pioneer in developing new techniques in field of molecular biology. Home: 1 Briggs Ct Foxhall Silver Spring MD 20906 Office: Dept Terrestrial Magnetism Carnegie Instn 5241 Broad Branch Rd NW Washington DC 20015

BOLYARD, ROCHELLE HARRISON (MRS. MARION BURL BOLYARD), assn. exec.; b. Clayton, N.C., Nov. 6, 1921; d. Brenton and Bettie (Coates) Harrison; student various bus. schs. and colls.; m. Marion Burl Bolyard, Apr. 5, 1947; children—Robert Burl, Richard Harrison. With Glenn L. Martin Co., Balt., 1946-47, N.C. Revenue Dept., Raleigh, 1946-47, Budd Co., Detroit, 1947-55, Electric Storage Battery Co., Raleigh, 1964-65, Investors Diversified Services, Raleigh, 1965-66; state sec. N.C. Pork Producers Assn., Raleigh, 1967-68; sec. to owners R. & R. Brokerage Co., Raleigh, 1969; exec. sec. Clayton (N.C.) C. of C., 1970—. Exec. sec. Human Relations Council Clayton, 1971—; pres. So. Belles chpt. Clayton Centennial, 1969; mem. Clayton Community Improvement Council, 1971—. Recipient Pres.'s plaque Clayton C. of C., 1971, 73, Gov.'s award, 1972. Mem. Clayton C. of C. (mem. exec. bd. 1970—). Home: Route 2 Box 274 Clayton NC 27520 Office: PO Box 246 Clayton NC 27520

BOMAR, HORACE LELAND, lawyer; b.Spartanburg, S.C., May 20, 1912; s. Horace Leland and Mallie (Brown) B.; A.B., Furman U., 1933; LL.B., Duke, 1936; m. Martha Grier, Mar. 20, 1947; children—Horace Leland III, James Grier, Martha Elizabeth. Admitted to S.C. bar, 1936; asso. firm Chadbourne, Wallace, Parke & Whiteside, N.Y.C., 1936-37; practiced in Spartanburg, 1937-42; asst. U.S. atty., 1940-42; partner firm Holcombe, Bomar & Cureton, Spartanburg, 1946—. Pres., Spartanburg Legal Aid Soc., 1967-68; mem. S.C. Bd. Edn., 1968—. Past trustee Furman U.; trustee Spartanburg Jr. Coll., Kennedy Library. Served with USNR, 1942-46. Mem. Am., Spartanburg (pres. 1965—), S.C. (v.p. 1967—), bar assns., Spartanburg C. of C (pres. 1960-61), Order of Coif. Presbyn. Home: 1019 Andrews Farm Rd Spartanburg SC 29302 Office: 305 Montgomery Bldg Spartanburg SC 29301

BOMBA, JOHN GILBERT, civil engr.; b. Yorktown, Tex., Feb. 8, 1932; s. Vincent Englebert and Regina (Ibrom) B.; student St. Mary's U., San Antonio, 1949-51; B.S. in Petroleum Engring., Tex. A. and M. U., 1954; m. Jane Killingsworth, June 9, 1958; children—Anne Killingsworth, Marian Regina , Beatrice Joan, Norma Jane. Civil engr. Collins Constrn. Co., Port Lavaca, Tex., 1954-61, Sigler, Clark & Assos., Cons. Engrs., Weslaco, Tex., 1961-64; sr. marine engr. Williams Bros. Engring. Co., Tulsa, 1964-71, mgr. marine engring., 1972—. Served with Signal Corps, AUS, 1954-56. Registered profl. engr., Tex., Okla. Mem. Nat., Tex., Okla. socs. profl. engrs., Am. Soc. C.E. (various coms.), Marine Tech. Soc. Toastmaster. Home: 4354 E 57th St Tulsa OK 74135 Office: Resource Scis Center 321 S Boston Av Tulsa OK 74103

BOMSE, FREDERICK MARTIN, scientist; b. N.Y.C., Jan. 24, 1939; s. Edward L. and Iris (Goodman) B.; B.S. in Physics, Antioch Coll., 1961; Ph.D. in Physics, 1965; m. Barbara Jean Benedict, Sept. 18, 1965; children—Mark, Monique, Michele. Asst. prof. Vanderbilt U., Nashville, 1966-70; physicist/operations analyst Center for Naval Analyses, Arlington, Va., 1970—. Mem. Am. Phys. Soc. Home: 10334 Nightmist Ct Columbia MD 21044 Office: 1401 Wilson Blvd Arlington VA 22209

BON, JAMES WILLARD, mech. engr.; b. Washington, Feb. 18, 1942; s. Lewis Willard and Lois Audrey (Darnell) B.; B.S. in M.E., U. Fla., 1966; m. Carolyn Sue Quick, Dec. 23, 1964; children—Troy Michael, Russell Allen. Mech. engr., test coordinator and supr. Dept. Navy, Indianhead, Md., 1966-68; mech. engr. U.S. Naval Ship Research & Devel. Center, Cardarock, Md., 1968-69; mech. engr., coordinator mech. test technology IBM Corp., Boca Raton, Fla., 1969—. Engring. asso., cons. Talbott Realty Co., Boca Raton, 1972-73. Mem. Cocoanut Creek (Fla.) Police Dept. Aux., 1973. Registered profl. engr., Fla. Mason. Patentee in field. Home: 2123 NW 63d Av Margate FL 33063 Office: PO Box 1328 Dept. 95H/002-1 Boca Raton FL 33432

BOND, ALMON DEWEY, trade assn. exec.; b. Willoughby, O., Jan. 3, 1923; s. Forrest H. and Lennah (Battles) B.; B.S., Ohio State U., 1947; M.S., Cornell U., 1948; Ph.D., Mich. State U., 1953; m. Ruth Collar, June 13, 1953; children—Philinda, Laurel, Carolyn, Sylvia. Asst. dir., fruit and vegetable dept. Am. Farm Bur. Fedn., Washington, 1948-50; asst. dir. marketing dept. Am. Meat Inst., Chgo., 1953-56, dir., Washington office, 1956-74, v.p., 1974—; exec. sec. Nat. Meat Canners Assn., Washington, 1962—. Mem. adv. com. hog cholera U.S. Sec. Agr. Served with USNR, 1943-46. Mem. Washington Soc. Assn. Execs. (pres. 1971-72), Am. Agrl. Econs. Assn. Clubs: Nat. Press, Nat. Economists. Home: 458 River Bend Rd Great Falls VA 22066 Office: PO Box 3556 Washington DC 20004

BOND, BERNARD BATSON, materials engr.; b. Wiggins, Miss., Mar. 28, 1906; s. Willard Faroe and Susie (Graham) B.; B.A. in Chemistry, Miss. Coll., 1926; m. Laura Lee Traylor, Dec. 24, 1931 (div.); 1 dau., Myrna Rose; m. 2d, Elizabeth Elmore Fisher, July 17, 1953. Chemist testing div. Miss. Hwy. Dept., Jackson, 1936-42; materials engring. supt. overhaul and repair dept. U.S. Naval Air Sta., Pensacola, Fla., 1942-67, dir. materials engring. div. Naval Air Rework Facility, 1967-71; dir. Tech. Support Center, Dept. Def. Equipment Oil Analysis Program, 1971-72; cons. spectrometric wear metal analysis, Warrington, Fla., 1972—. Fellow Am. Inst. Chemists, A.A.A.S.; mem. N.Y. Acad. scis., Am. Chem. Soc., Am. Inst. Aeros. and Astronautics, Navy League U.S., Am. Camelia Soc. Baptist. Mason. Home: 308 E Sunset Av Warrington FL 32507 Office: 308 E Sunset Av Warrington FL 32507

BOND, DANIEL WEBSTER, JR., chem. co. exec.; b. Leesville, La., July 15, 1926; s. Daniel Webster and Alice Belle (McRae) B.; B.S., La. State U., 1950; m. Elaine Vandigriff, Aug. 30, 1947; children—Daniel, James, Suzanne. Various engring. and plant mgmt. positions Cabot Corp., Ville Platte, La., 1950-59, various personnel and labor relations mgmt. positions, Pampa, Tex., 1959—, dir. personnel and indsl. relations, 1965—. Mem. adv. bd. Salvation Army, 1968-74; mem. adv. bd. Adobe Walls council Boy Scouts Am., 1973—. Bd. dirs. Gray County Hosp., 1969-73, pres. 1971—. Served with USNR, 1944-46. Mem. Panhandle Personnel Assn. (pres. 1965), Bur. Nat. Affairs Personnel Policy Forum. Republican. Presbyn. (elder 1966—). Mason, Kiwanian (pres. 1971). Home: 2228 Aspen St Pampa TX 79065 Office: Cabot Corp PO Box 1101 Pampa TX 79065

BOND, GEORGE DOHERTY, educator; b. Hillsboro, Tex., Oct. 23, 1903; s. George Doherty and May (Wigley) B.; A.B., So. Meth. U., 1924, M.A., 1937; Ph.D., U. Mich., 1947; m. Mildred Elizabeth Martin, Sept. 6, 1922; children—Margaret Burke (Mrs. James T. Richmond), Robert Doherty. Instr. English So. Meth. U., 1924-27, 35-41, asst. prof., 1941-47, asso. prof., 1947-50, prof., 1950-69, chmn. dept., 1953-57, chmn. faculty Senate, 1957-58. Mem. Democratic Organizing Com. of Dallas County, Tex., 1953-57, mem. Modern Lang. Assn., Linguistic Soc. Am., Coll. English Assn., Am. Assn. U. Profs., Tex. Conf. Coll. Tchrs. English (v.p. 1954, pres. 1965-66), Poetry Soc. Tex. (v.p. 1963-66), Tex. Inst. of Letters, Phi Beta Kappa, Kappa Sigma. Methodist. Author: (with J.B. Hubbell and M.D. Hemke) Prairie Pegasus, 1924; (with J.W. Bowyer, J.L. Brooks, and I.H. Herron) Better College English, 1950. Editor: Inter-American Publs., 1941-45. Editor Southwest Review. 1925-27, 44-45, contbg. editor, 1946-63. Home: 3460 Mockingbird Lane Dallas TX 75205

BOND, JOHN RUSSELL, dentist; b. Roseland, La., May 28, 1918; s. Rufus and Mollie Mae (Russell) B.; B.S., Northwestern State U., 1940; postgrad. Tulane U., 1944-45; D.D.S. cum laude, Loyola U., New Orleans, 1950; m. Lillian Alice Bernadas, Jan. 15, 1944 (dec. July 1962); children—Hester Lyn, John Russell; m. 2d, Ramona Ellen Goff, May 21, 1966; 1 son, Jonathan Scott. With Burroughs Adding Machine Co., New Orleans, 1950-51; pvt. practice dentistry, New Orleans, 1950—. Instr. bus. adminstrn. Loyola U. of the South; mem. teaching staff La. State U. Sch. Dentistry; instr. oral surgery Charity Hosp., New Orleans; mem. staff So. Bapt. Hosp., Ear, Nose, and Throat Hosp. Sec., Young Men's Bus. Club, New Orleans, 1940-42; chmn. dental div. United Fund, 1952-57. Served with USNR, 1942-45. Fellow Internat. Coll. Dentists, Acad. Gen. Dentistry; mem. Royal Soc. St. George, Soc. of War of 1812, New Orleans C. of C., New Orleans Postgrad. Dental Group (pres. 1968-69), Alpha Sigma Nu, Omicron Kappa Upsilon, C. Victor Vignes Soc. Baptist (chmn. bd. deacons 1970). Club: Timberlane Country. Contbr. articles to profl. pubs. Home: 49 Stilt St New Orleans LA 70124 Office: 1035 Maison Blanche Bldg New Orleans LA 70112

BOND, JULIAN, politician, civil rights leader; b. Nashville, Jan. 14, 1940; s. Horace Mann and Julia Agnes (Washington) B.; B.A., Morehouse Coll., 1971; m. Alice Louise Clopton, July 28, 1961; children—Phyllis Jane, Horace Mann, Michael Julian, Jeffrey Alvin, Julia. A founder Com. Appeal for Human Rights, 1960, exec. sec., 1961; a founder Student Nonviolent Coordinating Com., 1960, communications dir., 1961-66; reporter, feature writer Atlanta Inquirer, 1960-61, mng. editor, 1963; mem. Ga. Ho. of Reps. from Fulton County, 1965—; barred from house because of Vietnam statements, 1966; U.S. Supreme Ct. ruled his Constl. rights were violated, 1966. Bd. dirs. So. Conf. Edn. Fund; mem. Robert Kennedy Meml. Fund, Highland Research and Edn. Center. Mem. So. Corr. Reporting Racial Equality Wars, Phi Kappa (hon.). Author poems, articles. Address: 361 Westview Dr SW Atlanta GA 30310

BOND, LOUIS DEAN, mfg. co. exec.; b. Valliant, Okla., Jan. 26, 1940; s. Joe Wheeler and Dorothy Inez (Wiggington) B.; B.A., Harding Coll., 1967; m. Judith Maye Limburg, July 31, 1965; children—Shawn RaeAnn, Eric Scott. Sr. accountant Peat, Marwick, Mitchell & Co., Dallas, 1967-70, sr. auditor, Louisville, 1970-71; controller Servomation-Williams, Inc., Louisville, 1971-73; credit mgr., office mgr. Haas Cabinet Co., Inc., Sellersburg, Ind., 1973—. Mem. pres.'s devel. council Harding Coll. Served with USN, 1959-63. C.P.A., Ky., Tex. Mem. Am. Inst. C.P.A.'s, Ky. Soc. C.P.A.'s, Nat. Assn. Accountants, Ky. Hist. Soc. Republican. Mem. Ch. of Christ (treas. 1971—, deacon 1972—, dir. adult edn. 1972—). Home: 9109 Danby Ct Fern Creek KY 40291 Office: 613 W Utica St Sellersburg IN 47172

BOND, ROBERT LEVI, educator; b. Ozark, Ark., Feb. 23, 1940; s. Robert Hasque and Lettie Mae (Williams) B.; B.S., State Coll. Ark., 1961; M.S., U. Ark., 1964, Ph.D., 1968. Sr. research physicist S.W. Research Inst., San Antonio, 1968-71; asst. prof. electronics and instrumentation Grad. Inst. Tech., U. Ark., Little Rock, 1971-74, asso. prof., 1974—. Cons. Avco Corp., Tulsa, 1966-68, Blount & George, Inc., Jacksonville, Ark., 1973—. Mem. A.A.A.S., I.E.E.E., Instrument Soc. Am., Optical Soc. Am., Sci. Research Soc. Am., Sigma Xi, Phi Kappa Phi, Sigma Tau Gamma, Alpha Chi. Republican. Mem. Ch. of Nazarene. Mason. Sci. exhbn. Laser 10, Smithsonian Instn., 1970. Contbr. profl. jours. Home: 215 Normandy Rd Little Rock AR 72207 Office: PO Box 3017 Little Rock AR 72207

BOND, ROLAND S., corp. exec.; b. Van Alstyne, Tex., Dec. 5, 1898; s. Richard Walden and Laura Pauline (Shenley) B.; ed. So. Methodist U., U. Tex.; m. Sadie Adrienne Adickes, Aug. 20, 1925; children—Roland Selik, James Herbert. Ind. oil producer, 1919—; organizer several cos. including Pan Am. Sulphur Co., Renwar Oil Corp., Bond Oil Corp. Bd. dirs. Dallas Symphony, Dallas Museum Art; trustee Presbyn. Hosp., St. Stephen's Episcopal Schg., Austin, Tex. Served to lt. col. AUS, World War II. Mason. Clubs: Dallas, Dallas Petroleum; Brookhollow Golf; Northwood; Eldorado Country. Home: 4600 Brookview Dr Dallas TX 75220 Office: 2600 Republic Nat Bank Bldg Dallas TX 75201

BOND, THOMAS RIDGELY, civil engr.; b. Little Rock, Mar. 16, 1938; s. Morris Thomas and Martha (Bell) B.; B.S., U. Ark., 1961; m. Patricia Lee Parker, Aug. 12, 1960; children—Melissa, Kathryn Kelly, Thomas William. With tng. program Ark. Hwy. Dept., Little Rock, 1961-62; city engr. City of West Memphis, Ark., 1962-64; design engr. Ray H. Russell, Cons. Engr., Little Rock, 1964-66; mgr., engr. Organized Bond Cons. Engrs., Jacksonville, Ark., 1966—. Registered profl. engr., Ark. Mem. Am. Water Works Assn., Ark. Soc. Profl. Engrs., Cons. Engrs. Council of Ark., Aircraft Owners and Pilots Assn., Jacksonville C. of C. (dir. 1969-71, com. chmn. 1967-72). Methodist (chmn. bd. trustees 1968). Club: Sertoma (dist. sec., treas. 1969-70) (Jacksonville). Home: 2807 Gray Fox Jacksonville AR 72076 Office: 1000 School Dr Jacksonville AR 72076

BONDARENKO, WILLIAM, urban planner; b. Detroit, Mar. 6, 1930; s. Sam Peter and Martha (Ahonen) B.; student Mich. Coll. Mining and Tech., 1949; B.S., Mich. State U., 1953; postgrad. Wayne State U., 1957, U. So. Cal., 1963; certificate transp. planning (fellow), Carnegie-Mellon U., 1973; m. Hesperia Louis, Dec. 28, 1950; children—Marc, Fernande, Leif. Planning cons., prin. Munson Assos., Detroit, 1955-60; planning engr. U.S. Navy Dept., China Lake, Cal., 1960-63; sr. planner NASA, Huntsville, Ala., 1963-64; with Birmingham (Ala.) Regional Planning Commn., 1965—, exec. dir., 1971—. Mem. adv. com. Center for Urban Studies, U. Ala., Birmingham, 1971—; co-chmn. phys. design task force Goals for Birmingham Program, 1969-70; mem. exec. com. Regional Health Planning Commn.-Community Services Council, 1973-74; mem. health research com. Community Service Council, 1971—. Served as 1st lt. M.P., AUS, 1953-55. Mem. Am. Inst. Planners (dir. Ala. sect. 1969-70, chpt. pres. 1971-72), Am. Soc. Landscape Architects (sec.-treas. Mich. 1960), Am. Soc. Planning Ofcls., Young Men's Bus. Club Birmingham (exec. v.p. 1970), Pinson Valley Assn. Mason. Home: 3232 Tyrol Rd Birmingham AL 35216 Office: Suite 220 2112 11th Av S Birmingham AL 35205

BONDS, FRANK LANIER, banker; b. Fairfield, Ala., May 25, 1930; s. Erskine Webster and Lois E. (Graham) B.; B.A., Auburn U., 1955; m. Lavada M. Reese, Sept. 28, 1951 children—Cheryl Ann, Frank Lanier, Brian David. Jr. analyst U.S. Steel Corp., Fairfield, Ala., 1955-58, asst. analyst, 1958-61, analyst, 1961-64; dir. market research Birmingham (Ala.) Trust Nat. Bank, 1964-68, v.p., dir. marketing, 1968—. Served with AUS, 1948-49, 50-51. Recipient Most Valuable Member award Birmingham chpt. Am. Marketing Assn., 1968. Mem. Am. Marketing Assn. (pres. 1968-69), Ala. Bus. Research Council (treas. 1964-67), Birmingham C. of C. (chmn. research com. 1968). Kiwanian. Clubs: Birmingham (Ala.) Advertising (dir. 1969); Green Valley Country. Home: 1831 Thornton Pl Birmingham AL 35226 Office: 112 N 20th Birmingham AL 35202

BONDURANT, GORDON EMERSON, sch. pres.; b. Winston-Salem, N.C., Jan. 13, 1935; s. Stuart O. and Dorothy Louise (Siewers) B.; A.B., Davidson Coll.; postgrad. U. N.C.; M.A., U. Chattanooga; m. Linda Jane Reeves, Aug. 16, 1964; children—Robert Emerson, William Gordon. Tchr. McCallie Sch., Chattanooga, 1957-60, 62-66, asst. dean, 1964-66; dir. camps, confs. and youth work Moravian Ch. Am., Winston-Salem, 1960-62; dir. admissions and records U. Chattanooga, 1967-68, also chmn. scholarship com.; pres. Darlington Sch., Rome, Ga., 1968—. Mem. Rome coordinating com. Project Concern, Inc.; mem. state adv. council Title III. Past bd. dirs. United Fund; lay v.p., bd. dirs. Am. Cancer Soc.; bd. dirs. Rome Community Concert Assn.; pres. Ga. Found. Ind. Schs. Mem. Nat., Ga., 7th Dist. assns. high sch. prins., Ga. Assn. Ind. Schs. (past pres.), Rome Area C. of C. (dir.). Presbyn. (mem. ch. session). Rotarian (past dir., trustee student fund). Address: Darlington Sch Rome GA 30161

BONE, ALAN CLARKE, clergyman; b. Galesburg, Ill., Mar. 11, 1938; s. Thomas LeRoy and Sylvia Christine (Gilliland) B.; B.A., Eureka Coll., 1960; B.D., Lexington Theol. Sem., 1963; postgrad. U. Ky., 1961; m. Joan Ruth Arenberg, Aug. 7, 1968; children—Cynthia Darlene, Eric David. Ordained to ministry Christian Ch., 1963; pastor Luray (S.C.) Ch., 1963-66; state camp dir., youth dir. Christian Chs. of S.C., 1965-66; asso. pastor 1st Ch., Parkersburg, W.Va., 1966-67, Central Ch., Marietta, O., 1967-72, Forest Ch., Jacksonville, Fla., 1972—. Dist. youth work chmn. Ohio Christian Chs., 1967-72, Fla., 1972—; co-chmn. steering com. Eastside Christian Ch., 1973—. Mem. Marietta Human Rights Commn., 1967-68. Mem. Hampton County (pres. 1965-66), Greater Marietta (pres. 1971-72), Jacksonville ministerial assns., S.P.E.B.S.Q.S.A. Home: 2452 Gayland Rd Jacksonville FL 32218 Office: 3134 Trout River Blvd Jacksonville FL 32208

BONE, CHARLES WILLIAM, lawyer; b. Nashville, Tenn., Sept. 25, 1946; s. William L. and Lulu Nokes (Moss) B.; B.A. in Econs., Vanderbilt U., 1967; J.D., U. Tenn., 1970; m. Baylor Anne McKay, June 18, 1971. Admitted to Tenn. bar, 1971; practiced in Gallatin, 1971—; partner Goodall & Bone, Gallatin, Tenn., 1972—. Dir. Bank of Gallatin, Tenn., Bank of Kingston Springs, (Tenn.), Carroll County Bank, Huntingdon, Tenn.; instr. bus. law and polit. sci. Vol. State Community Coll., Gallatin, 1972-73; county atty. Sumner County, 1972—. Dir., pres. Sumner County Guidance Center, Gallatin, 1971-73; dir. Sumner County unit Am. Cancer Soc., Inc., 1972. Served to 1st lt. AUS, 1972. Named Outstanding Young Man of Year Gallatin Jr. C. of C. Mem. Am., Tenn. (sec., treas. young lawyers conf. 1973—), Sumner County (v.p. 1973, pres. 1974) bar assns., Gallatin C. of C. (dir. 1972), Assn. for Guidance, Aid, Placement and Empathy (mem. com. 1973), Phi Delta Phi. Mem. Ch. of Christ. Home: 211 Island Dr Hendersonville TN 37075 Office: Goodall and Bone Ct Square Gallatin TN 37066

BONE, LARRY EARL, librarian; b. Memphis, Oct. 31, 1932; s. Blondell Foster and Thelma Catherine (Crouch) B.; B.A., Southwestern at Memphis, 1954; M.S. in L.S., Western Res. U., 1955. Asst. reference librarian San Francisco State Coll., summer 1955; br. librarian Memphis Pub. Library, 1955-57, asst. dir. libraries for pub. services, 1970—; asst. head govt. sect. Library of Congress, Washington, 1958; librarian George Mason Coll. U. Va., 1958-59; head librarian Avon Lake (O.) Pub. Library, 1959-62; dir. Mentor (O.) Pub. Library, 1962-63; county librarian Shelby County (Tenn.) Libraries, 1963-66; asst. dir., asst. prof. Grad. Sch. Library Sci. U. Ill., 1966-70. Vis. asst. prof. librarianship U. Wash., summer 1968; dep. librarian Am. Library, Paris, France, 1968-69; vis. asst. prof. George Peabody Coll. Tchrs., summer 1970; vis. prof. Columbia Sch. Library Service, summer 1972; vis. instr. Memphis State U., 1973-74. Mem. staff A.L.A. Library/USA exhibit N.Y. World's Fair, summer 1965; chmn. Memphis Librarian Council, 1965. Council on Library Resources fellow, 1974-75. Mem. A.L.A. (council 1972—, reference and subscription books com. 1969-72), Ohio, Tenn. librarians assns., Phi Beta Kappa, Beta Phi Mu. Author: Library Education: An International Survey, 1968; Library School Teaching Methods, 1969. Home: 1277 S Highland St Memphis TN 38111

BONEY, DURHAM SAWYER, JR., savs. and loan exec.; b. Ridgeway, S.C., Nov. 16, 1933; s. Durham Sawyer and Elizabeth Ann (Kelly) B.; student U. Ga., 1973; m. Elsie Celeste Park, June 19, 1954; children—Debra E., Cynthia E. With Citizens & So. Nat. Bank, Columbia, S.C., 1951-64; v.p. Home Fed. Savs. & Loan Assn., Columbia, 1964—. Instr. Am. Savs. & Loan Inst. Chmn. Indsl. Com., City of Cayce, 1964, Granby Dist. Boy Scouts Am., 1964-65, Lexington County United Fund Drive, 1964; pres. S.C. Savs. and Loan Jr. Execs. Conf., 1971; treas., Fellowship of Christian Athletics. Served with AUS, 1956-58. Mem. Am. Savs. and Loan Inst. (pres. Columbia chpt.), Am. Savs. and Loan Assn., Greater Columbia (past dir.), West Columbia-Cayce (past pres.) chambers commerce, Columbia Sales, Marketing and Execs. Club (dir., v.p.), Am. Legion. Presbyn. (chmn. bd. deacons, elder). Rotarian (dir., past pres.). Clubs: Columbia Country, Hidden Valley Country, Palmetto. Home: 2733 Stepp Dr Columbia SC 29204 Office: 2200 Beltline Blvd Columbia SC 29204

BONEY, WALTER THOMAS, city ofcl.; b. Savannah, Ga., May 6, 1937; s. Clark Howell and Evelyn (Anderson) B.; B.S., Jacksonville U., 1963; A.A., S. Ga. Coll., 1957; m. Mickey Ogden, July 12, 1958; children—Cheryl Lynn, Walter T., William Henry. Dir. recreation and parks dept. Duval County, Jacksonville, Fla., 1960-68; supt. recreation and pub. affairs dept. Consol. City of Jacksonville, 1968—. Pres., chmn. bd. Pastime Enterprises, Inc., 1969—; v.p., dir. Jacksonville Developers, Inc., 1969—; gen. agt. Springfield Life Ins. Co., 1970—. Chmn. Cancer Crusade, Duval County Employees, 1966-67; mem. Community Planning Council, 1968-69, dir., 1968-69. Commr., Pop Warner Football Conf., 1962-69. Bd. dirs. Greater Jacksonville Econ. Opportunity, Inc., 1972—. Fellow Fla., Assn. for Health, Phys. Edn. and Recreation, Fla. Inst. Park Personnel; mem. Fla. Assn. County Park and Recreation Execs. (dir. 1964-69), Nat. Parks and Recreation Assn., Fla. Recreation Assn., Amateur Softball Assn. Am. (dist. commr. 1965-69), Nat. Assn. County Park and Recreation Execs., C. of C. Methodist. Mason (32 deg.). Club: Quarterback (dir. 1968). Home: Route 1 Box 289E Keystone Heights FL 32656 Office: 1245 E Adams St Jacksonville FL 32202

BONEY, WILLIAM JERRY, educator; b. N.Y.C., Nov. 20, 1930; s. Cecil DeWitt and Myrtle Elizabeth (Cox) B.; A.B., Princeton, 1952; B.D., Union Theol. Sem., 1955; postgrad. U. Tubingen, Germany, 1961-62; Ph.D., Drew U., 1963; m. Nancy Jane Dyck, Aug. 23, 1958; children—Elizabeth Jane, William Thomas, Paul DeWitt. Ordained to ministry Presbyn. Ch., 1955; minister to students Blacksburg (Va.) Presbyn. Ch., 1955-58; lectr. religion Douglass Coll., Rutgers U., New Brunswick, N.J., 1962-63; prof. theology Sch. Theology, Va. Union U., Richmond, 1963—. Minister, Hanover Presbytery, Presbyn. Ch., U.S., 1965—, inter-church relations com., 1971-73; Protestant cons. to Ecumenical Affairs Commn., Roman Cath. Diocese of Richmond, 1966—; Presbyn. Ch. U.S. del. to Consultation on Ch. Union, 1973—. Am. Assn. Theol. Schs. fellow, 1968-69. Fellow Inst. Ecumenical and Cultural Research; mem. Am. Acad. Religion, N.Am. Acad. Ecumenists (sec.-treas. 1972—). Democrat. Club: Princeton (N.J.) Quadrangle. Editor: (with L.E. Molumby) The New Day: Catholic Theologians of the Renewal, 1968; (with P.A. Crow, Jr.) Church Union at Mid-Point, 1972. Home: 2904 Noble Av Richmond VA 23222

BONHAM, HOWARD BRYAN, JR., security analyst; b. Tulsa, Dec. 21, 1928; s. Howard Bryan and Aubrey Estelle (Combs) B.; B.A. in Econs., U. Va., 1952; postgrad. Grad. Sch. Bus. U. Okla., 1955-57; m. Nancy Luella Furr, Aug. 23, 1958; children—Holly Adair, Howard Bryan, III, Alison York. With Shell Pipe Line Corp., Houston, 1957-60; pub. investment materials and editor Brookmire Investment Reports, Memphis, 1961-65; investment officer Life & Casualty Ins. Co. Tenn., Nashville, 1965-69; trust officer Republic Nat. Bank Dallas, 1969-73; sr. analyst Rauscher Pierce Securities Corp., Dallas, 1973—. Lectr. in corporate finance Fisk U., Nashville. Bd. dirs. Good Shepherd Episcopal Sch., Dallas. Served with AUS, 1952-54. Recipient Graham-Dodd award Financial Analyst Fedn., 1969. C.F.A. Mem. Inst. Chartered Financial Analysts, Dallas Soc. Investment Analysts, Am. Finance Assn., Am. Econ. Assn., Financial Analysts Fedn., U. Va. Alumni Assn., Soc. Mayflower Descs., Sigma Nu. Episcopalian. Author: Ticker Talk, 1960. Contbr. to CFA Readings in Investment Analysis, Financial Analysts Jour., Stock Market Handbook. Home: 3747 Alta Vista Lane Dallas TX 75229 Office: 1200 Mercantile Dallas Bldg Dallas TX 75201

BONIN, JOSEPH MAURICE, educator; b. LeRoy, La., Mar. 21, 1930; s. E. Whitney and Rita (Villien) B.; B.S., Spring Hill Coll., 1950; M.A., La. State U., 1952, Ph.D., 1960; m. Margie Ann Johnson, Dec. 22, 1956; children—Catherine, Theresa, Elizabeth, Susan, Judith, John, Rita. Instr., La. State U., 1957-58, asst. prof., 1959-60; asst. prof. U. Ark., 1958-59; asso. prof. Auburn U., 1960-63, prof., 1963-66; prof. econs. U. Ga., Athens, 1966—. Research analyst Soc. Security Adminstrn., Washington, 1964-65. Served to lt. (j.g.), USNR, 1952-55. Earhart Found. fellow, 1956-57; NSF grantee, 1969-71. Mem. Nat. Tax Assn., Am., So. econ. assns., Am. Finance Assn., Am. Statis. Assn., Pi Gamma Mu, Beta Gamma Sigma. Roman Catholic. Editor Jour. Bus. Research, 1972—. Contbr. articles to profl. jours. Home: 170 Hunnicutt Dr Athens GA 30601

BONNELL, WILLIAM FREDERIC, dentist; b. Fort Worth, Oct. 28, 1940; s. William Fearnley and Jean (Booth) B.; B.A., Okla. U., 1961; D.D.S., Baylor U., 1965; m. D'Ann Elisabeth Walsh, June 17, 1965; children—William Frederic, Laura Elisabeth, Jonathan Richard. Pvt. practice dentistry, Fort Worth, 1965-66, 68—. Chmn., Tarrant County chpt. Nat. Children's Dental Health, 1970-72. Served with Dental Corps, AUS, 1966-68. Recipient award of merit Fort Worth Dist. Dental Soc., 1971. Mem. Am., Tex. dental assns., Fort Worth Dist. Dental Soc., Phi Delta Theta. Clubs: Canterbury, Steeplechase. Home: 6120 Curzon St Fort Worth TX 76116 Office: 3403 Hulen St Fort Worth TX 76107

BONNER, ALLAN BAKER, dentist; b. Aurora, N.C., Oct. 28, 1912; s. George Irving and Vesta Catherine (Mooring) B.; student U. N.C., 1933-36, 37-39; D.D.S., U. Tenn., 1943; m. Sally Ballou Jordan, Aug. 14, 1940; children—Allan Baker, Kathryn (Mrs. Robert Levin Reese), James J., Charles M. Pvt. practice dentistry, Hertford, N.C., 1943—. Chmn., Perquimans County Morehead Found.; chmn. Alcoholic Beverage Control Bd., Town of Hertford, 1961-63; chmn. Perquimans County Sch. Bd., 1963-69. Mem. Am., N.C. dental assns., Phi Chi. Democrat. Episcopalian (sr. warden 1965-66). Mason (Shriner), Rotarian (past pres.). Home: Route 1 Box 284D Hertford NC 27944 Office: 111 Market St Hertford NC 27944

BONNER, EDWIN EUGENE, ednl. adminstr.; b. Dalton, Ga., Sept. 16, 1926; s. Fred Allen and Agnes (Mullinax) B.; A.B., Mercer U., 1951; M.Ed., U. Tenn., 1960; Ed.S., U. Ga., 1963; m. Priscilla A. Sample, Jan. 15, 1974; children from previous marriage—Gregory Allen, Frances Lynn. Tchr., Whitfield County (Ga.) Bd. Edn., 1951-54, tchr., asst. prin., 1954-60, prin., 1961—. Served with USNR, 1944-46. Coe Found. Am. Studies grantee, summers 1958, 59; Freedom Found. grantee, summer 1971. Mem. Nat. (life), Ga. edn. assns., 7th Dist. Prin. Assn. (sec. 1967-74), Nat. Assn. Secondary Sch. Prins., Nat. Assn. Elementary Prins. Democrat. Baptist (minister of music 1951—). Club: Ruritan. Home: Route 3 Dalton GA 30720 Office: 2818 Airport Rd Dalton GA 30720

BONNER, JAMES CALVIN, educator, author; b. nr. Carrollton, Ga., June 16, 1904; s. William Allen and Sara (Moore) B.; A.B., U. Ga., 1926, M.A., 1936; Ph.D., U. N.C., 1943; m. Ida Gayle Munro, Nov. 23, 1937; children—Page Munro (Mrs. Wm. Warren Craghead), James Calvin, William Allen II. Instr., asst. prof. social sci. W. Ga. Coll., 1933-41; adj. prof. history Randolph-Macon Womans Coll., 1942-44; prof. history Ga. Coll., Milledgeville, 1944—, chmn. dept. social studies, faculty research and grad. study, 1948-65. Mem. Ga. Hist. Commn., 1965—. Trustee, sec.-treas. Lockerly Arboretum Found., Elizabeth, N.J., 1965—. Mem. Am., Ga., So. (editorial bd. jour. 1950-54) hist. assns., Agrl. History Soc. (editorial bd. jour. 1963-67). Author: Studies in Georgia History and Government, 1940; The Georgia Story, 1958; A History of Georgia Agriculture, 1964; The Journal of a Milledgeville Girl, 1861-67; Georgians in Profile, 1957, (with others) Writing Southern History, 1965; Georgia's Last Frontier, 1971; numerous articles profl. jours. Home: 120 S Jackson St Milledgeville GA 31061

BONNER, JOHN F., bus. exec.; b. Chgo., 1922; ed. Harvard. Vice pres. Deltona Corp., Miami, Fla.; v.p. Marco Island Devel. Corp.; pres., dir. Pacific Gas & Electric Co. Home: 3830 Alhambra Ct Coral Gables FL 33134 Office: 3250 SW 3d Av Miami FL 33129*

BONNER, WILLIAM PAUL, educator; b. Bowdon, Ga., July 7, 1931; s. William Arthur and Avis Pearl (Treadaway) B.; B.S., U. Ga., 1952; M.S., U. Fla., 1965, Ph.D., 1967; m. Marjorie Ethel Rice, Aug. 4, 1956; children—Bruce William, Brent Howard, Brenda Ann. Chemist Union Carbide Corp., Oak Ridge, 1952-54, devel. engr., 1956-62; research staff mem. Oak Ridge Nat. Lab., 1962-64, 1967-71; prof. civil engring. Tenn. Technol. U., Cookeville, 1972—, chmn. Coll. Engring. research group, 1972—. Cons. Oak Ridge Nat. Lab., 1972-73; dir. research grant Office Water Resources Research, 1972-73; co-dir. Environmental Protection Agy. Tng. Grant, 1973. Mem. bd. edn. Clinton (Tenn.) City Schs., 1970-72. Served with Chem. Corps AUS, 1954-56. Recipient USPHS fellowship, 1964-67; Research grant Office Water Resources Research, 1972-73; Faculty Research grant Tenn. Tech. U., 1972. Mem. Water Pollution Control Fedn., Am. Chem. Soc., Am. Water Resources Assn., Sigma Xi. Baptist (mem. com. 1972-74; deacon 1961-71; Sunday Sch. supt. 1961-64). Rotarian. Contbr. articles to various publs. Home: Buck Mountain Rd Cookeville TN 38501

BONNETTE, IRLEY ABREY, lawyer; b. Elmer, La., May 2, 1920; s. David Editor and Polly (Braddy) B.; student Lamar Jr. Coll., 1939-41; LL.B., U. Tex., Austin, 1948; m. Hazel Yeatts, June 4, 1965; children (by previous marriage)—Bonnie, Gail, Gary. Admitted to Tex. bar, 1948; practiced in Alice and Houston, 1948-56; gen. atty. Ambassador Oil Corp., Ft. Worth, 1956-65; gen. atty., sec. Anadarko Prodn. Co., Ft. Worth, 1965—; sec., gen. atty. Anadarko Petroleum Can. Ltd., Calgary, Alta., Can., 1965—; sec., gen. atty., dir. Anadarko Espana, Inc., Ft. Worth, 1972—, Anadarko Malagasy, Inc., Ft. Worth, 1973—; sec., dir. Anadarko Oil and Gas Co., Ft. Worth, 1965—. Served to capt. F.A. AUS, 1941-46. Decorated Bronze Star, Four Combat Stars, European African Middle Eastern Campaign Medal with 4 stars, World War II Victory medal. Mem. Am., Tex., Ft. Worth-Tarrant County bar assns., Phi Delta Phi. Methodist. Clubs:

Ridglea Country, Petroleum (Ft. Worth). Home: 5417 El Dorado Fort Worth TX 76107 Office: 3109 Winthrop Fort Worth TX 76116

BONNEY, EDWARD LEWIS, cons. mech. engr.; b. Malden, Mass., Oct. 25, 1912; s. Frank Sleep and Minnie Roie (Powell) B.; B.S. in M.E., U. Fla., 1938; m. Lorraine Burroughs, Dec. 20, 1940; children—Sharon Lorraine, Frank Elton. Draftsman Internat. Paper Co., Panama City, Fla., 1941-42, asst. plant engr., 1945-46; draftsman U.S. Air Force, Tyndall Field, Fla., 1946-48; engr. Navy Mine Countermeasures Sta., Panama City, 1948-51, 53-56; engr. U.S. Air Force, Eglin AFB, Fla., 1956-70; cons. engr., Fort Walton Beach, Fla., 1970—; pres., treas., dir. South Shore Assos., Inc., elec., mech. and san. engrs., Fort Walton, 1972—. Mem. engring. adv. council U. Fla., 1971, joint alumni faculty com., 1969—. Served with AUS, 1938-39, 40-41, USAAF, 1942-45, USAF, 1951-53. Registered profl. engr., Fla., Ga. Mem. Am. Soc. Heating, Refrigerating and Air Conditioning Engrs., Nat., Fla. (pres. 1970) socs. profl. engrs., Fla. Pollution Control Assn. Baptist (deacon). Lion. Home: 219 Sotir St Fort Walton Beach FL 32548 Office: 2 Maples St NW Fort Walton Beach FL 32548

BONNEY, HAL JAMES, JR., lawyer, judge; b. Norfolk, Va., Aug. 27, 1929; s. Hal J. and Mary (Shackelford) B.; B.A., U. Richmond, 1951, M.A., 1953; J.D., Coll. William and Mary, 1969; m. Marie McBee, July 4, 1963; children—David James, John Wesley. Instr. Norfolk pub. schs., 1951-61; supt. Douglas MacArthur Acad., 1961-67; practiced law, 1969-71; law clk. U.S. Dist. Ct., 1969; prof. U. Va., 1964-71, Coll. William and Mary, 1969-71; U.S. bankruptcy judge, Norfolk, 1971—. WTAR radio tchr. Wesleymen Bible class, 1962—. Treas., Wesleymen Found., Inc.; v.p. Va. Methodist Children's Home. Mem. Am., So. hist. assns., Phi Alpha Theta, Pi Sigma Alpha, Phi Alpha Delta. Methodist. Mason (Shriner). Home: 1357 Windsor Point Rd Norfolk VA 23509 Office: 408 US Court House Norfolk VA 23501

BONNEY, JOSEPH JAMES, lawyer; b. Dallas, Mar. 10, 1943; s. Herbert Staats and Anna Margaret (Hudnall) B.; B.A., Austin Coll., 1965; J.D., St. Mary's U., 1968; m. Kathylyn Heidrich, Nov. 27, 1972. Admitted to Tex. bar, 1969; partner firm Bonney, Wade & Stripling, Dallas, 1969—. Trustee Bonney Trusts, 1969—. Served with Tex. Air, N.G., 1968-74. Mem. Tex., Dallas bar assns. Club: Dallas Country. Home: 3223 Blackburn Dallas TX 75206 Office: 1822 Fidelity Union Tower Dallas TX 75201

BONNEY, SAMUEL ROBERT, lawyer; b. Dallas, Mar. 10, 1943; s. Herbert Staats and Anna Margaret (Hudnall) B.; B.A., Austin Coll., 1965; LL.B., U. Tex., 1968; m. Emily Ellen Cox, Dec. 5, 1970; children—Samuel Robert II, Heather Noel. Admitted to Tex. bar, 1968; partner firm Bonney, Wade & Stripling, Dallas, 1968—. Trustee Bonney Trusts, 1969—. Served with AUS, 1969—. Mem. Tex., Dallas bar assns., Estate Planning Council. Club: Dallas Country. Home: 3206 Cornell Dallas TX 75205 Office: 1822 Fidelity Union Tower Dallas TX 75201

BOOG, JANET MARGARET, physician; b. Cin., Mar. 4, 1913; d. Fredrick Anthony and Gertrude (Petit) Boog; student U. Cin., 1931-33; M.D., N.Y. Med. Coll., 1939. Intern, Good Samaritan Hosp., Cin., 1939-40; resident N.Y. Infirmary for Women and Children, N.Y.C., 1940-41, Margaret Hague Hosp., Jersey City, 1942-43, Univ. Hosp., Ann Arbor, Mich., 1943-44, Omaha, 1945-46; cons. obstetrics Dept. of Health, Honolulu, 1946-48; practice medicine specializing in gynecology and obstetrics, Lawrence, Mass., 1949-52, Detroit, 1953-57; resident neuropsychiatry VA Hosp., N.Y.C., 1959-62; staff psychiatrist Longview State Hosp., Cin., 1962-66; unit chief psychiatry VA Hosp., Lexington, Ky., 1966—; clin. instr. psychiatry U. Ky., 1968—. Diplomate Am. Bd. Obstetrics and Gynecology. Fellow Am. Coll. Obstetrics and Gynecology; mem. Am. Psychiat. Assn., Cin. Soc. Neurology and Psychiatry, Wilderness Soc. Club: Sierra. Contbr. articles in field to profl. jours. Home: 1545 Alexandria Dr Lexington KY 40504 Office: Leestown Pike Lexington KY 40507

BOOHER, JAMES FINICE, architect; b. Wichita Falls, Tex., June 5, 1936; s. William Finice and Jewell (Bates) B.; B.Arch., Tex. Tech U., 1964; m. Patti Helen Neill, Aug. 3, 1957; children—Russell, Steven, Kelli, Andrew. Job capt. Ralph D. Spencer, Lubbock, Tex., 1964-67; prin. Spencer, Woukman & Booher, Lubbock, 1967-69; project mgr. Harrell & Hamilton, Dallas, 1969-70; pres. Booher & Assos., Inc., Dallas, 1970—. Mem. A.I.A., Tex. Soc. Architects, Dallas Chpt. Architects, Oak Cliff C. of C. Baptist (deacon). Home: 115 Willowbrook St Duncanville TX 75116 Office: 5301 S Westmoreland St Dallas TX 75237

BOOHER, ROBERT WAYNE, aerospace engr.; b. Mishawaka, Ind., May 22, 1923; s. Encil Darwin and Georgia May (Jaqua) B.; B.Indsl. Engring., Gen. Motors Inst., 1947; M.S., U. Notre Dame, 1949; m. Norma Jean Whetstone, Mar. 4, 1956; 1 dau., Kathi Jo. Project engr. Bendix Corp., South Bend, Ind., 1949-63; prin. engr. Teledyne, Huntsville, Ala., 1963-71; aerospace engr. Army Missile Command, Huntsville, 1971—. Served with AUS, 1945-46. Registered profl. engr., Ala., Ind. Mem. Nat. Mgmt. Assn., Am. Radio Relay League, Tau Beta Pi. Mem. Christian Ch. Home: 1009 Dellwood Rd SE Huntsville AL 35802 Office: AMSMI-RGP Redstone Arsenal AL 35809

BOOKATZ, SAMUEL, artist; b. Phila., Oct. 3, 1910; s. Barnett and Anna (Cohen) B.; student John Huntington Poly. Inst., Cleve., 1928-31, Cleve. Mus. Inst. Art, 1931-35, Boston Mus. Sch. Fine Arts, 1935-37, Harvard, 1935-37, Slade Art Inst., London U., Eng., 1937-38, Grande Chaumiere, Paris, France, 1938, Collorossi, Paris, 1939, Am. Acad. in Rome, Italy, 1938-41; m. Helen Meyer, Oct. 12, 1963. One man shows at Smithsonian Instn., Nat. Mus., Washington, 1950, Corcoran Gallery Art, Washington, 1948, Am. Acad., Rome, 1938, Paris, 1939, Cleve. Inst. Art, 1940, I.F.A. Gallery, Washington, 1952, Artist Mart, Washington, 1950-60, Monede Gallery, N.Y.C., 1962-63; exhibited in group shows at Inst. Contemporary Art, Washington, 1955, Corcoran Gallery Art, 1948-63, Pa. Acad. Fine Arts, Phila., 1947-60, Va. Mus. Art, Richmond, 1940, Ill. State Fair, Springfield, 1948, Phillips Gallery, Washington, 1954, Butler Art Inst., Youngstown, O., 1958, Cleve. Mus. Art, 1938-50, A.M.A., Phila., 1942, Cal., 1946, Creative Arts Gallery, N.Y.C., 1953, Terry Art Inst., Miami, Fla., 1952, Milw. Art Inst., 1956, Library of Congress, 1953-56, Mus. Fine Arts, Birmingham, Ala., 1956, Rochester (N.Y.) Mus. Art, 1964, Balt. Mus. Art, 1955, U. Ill., 1953, John Russell Mitchell Found. Mus., Mt. Vernon, Ill., 1965, Amherst (Mass.) Coll. Gallery, 1965, Wilderstein & Co. Gallery, N.Y.C., 1952, Salmagundi Gallery, N.Y.C., 1967, Crystal House Gallery, Miami Beach, 1968, Safri Gallery, Jerusalem, Israel, 1968, Agra Gallery, Washington, 1971; represented in numerous permanent collections. White House artist under Roosevelt adminstrn. Served to comdr. USNR, 1942-45. Recipient numerous awards, including Ford Found. grant in humanities, 1962. Cleve. Inst. Art scholar, 1931-35, Boston Mus. Sch. Art scholar, 1935-37. Club: Salamagundi (N.Y.C.). Address: 2700 Que St NW Washington DC 20007 also 9719 Leesburg Pike Vienna VA 22180

BOOKER, DOYLE RAY, mfg. co. exec.; b. Mangum, Okla., Nov. 26, 1934; s. Raymond Leslie and Geneva Estelle (Tyson) B.; B.S. in Aero. Engring., Okla. State U., 1957; M.S. in Meteorology, Pa. State U., 1962, Ph.D., 1965; m. Martha Earlene Hobbs, Mar. 18, 1955; children—Karen Lynn, Larry Wayne, Garry Lee, Renee Michelle. Weather forecaster TV sta. KWTV, Oklahoma City, 1960-61; research asst. Pa. State U., 1961-65; pres. Weather Sci. Inc., Norman, Okla., 1965—. Adj. asst. prof. Okla. U., 1968—. Served with USAF, 1958-60. Mem. Am. Meteorol. Soc. (chmn. bd. profl. ethics 1962—). Developed numerous meteorol. and aircraft instruments. Home: 1920 Logan Dr Norman OK 73069

BOOKER, HENRY MARSHALL, educator; b. Newport News, Va., Jan. 12, 1935; s. William Henry and Mary Evelyn (Wheeler) B.; B.S. cum laude, Lynchburg Coll., 1959; Ph.D., U. Va., 1965; m. Sarah Porter Cheatwood Phillips, June 22, 1963; children—Mary DeMott, Sharon. Sinclair, Paige Meriwether. Teller, Bank Hampton Rds., Hampton, Va., 1951-53; instr. econs. Salem Coll., Winston-Salem, N.C., 1962-64; asst. prof. econs. Frederick Coll., Portsmouth, Va., 1964-65; asso. prof., dir. grad. studies in econs. Old Dominion U., Norfolk, Va., 1965-69; dean faculty Christopher Newport Coll., Newport News, 1969-73, prof. econs., 1969—. Cons. Bank Hampton Rds., W. A. Norris, Portsmouth, George Washington U., NASA, Langley Field, C. of C., Newport News, Indsl. Coll. Armed Forces. Civilian with USAF, 1953-55. E. I. duPont Nat. fellow U. Va., 1959; Nat. Defense fellow, U. Va., 1959-62; Am. Soc. Engring. Edn. Summer Faculty fellowship NASA, 1968, 69; recipient Achievement award in finance Wall St. Jour., 1959. Mem. Am. Acad. Polit. and Social Sci., Am., So. econs. assns., S.A.R. (pres. Thomas Nelson chpt. 1971-73), Omicron Blue Key, Alpha Kappa Psi. Episcopalian (mem. vestry 1970-73). Contbr. articles to profl. jours. Home: 31 Indian Springs Dr Newport News VA 23606 Office: PO Box 6070 Hidenwood Sta Newport News VA 23606

BOOKER, JOHN PARKS, physician; b. Charlotte, N.C., Dec. 3, 1910; s. James Carter and Belle (Rowland) B.; student Duke, 1929-32; M.D., S.C. Med. U., 1936; m. Frances Louise Schumacher, June 17, 1940;children—John Parks, Robert Leonard, Edward Henry. Intern and resident Gen. Hosp., Greenville, S.C., 1936-38; practice medicine specializing in surgery, Walhalla, S.C., 1938—; former chief staff, Oconee Meml. Hosp., also chief surgery. Chmn. Oconee County Aeros. Commn. Mayor pro tem Walhalla, Bd. dirs. S.C. Blue Shield, S.C. Regional Med. Program, Appalachian Regional Health Policy and Planning Council; trustee Wickcliffe Fund. Served to col. AUS, World War II. Mem. Oconee County Med. Soc. (past pres.) S.C. Med. Assn. (chmn. council 1968-69, pres. 1971-72), Sigma Phi Epsilon, Phi Rho Sigma. Methodist (ch. bd.). Mason. Home: 315 Church St Walhalla SC 29691 Office: Broad and Church Sts Walhalla SC 29691

BOOKMAN, RONALD WESTMORELAND, JR., editor; b. Houston, July 7, 1941; s. Ronald W. and Martha (Bown) B.; B.A., Tex A. and M. Coll., 1963; m. Sylvia Ann Ideus, Sept. 23, 1961; children—Ronald W. III, William Daniel. Reporter, copy editor Houston Press, 1962-64; reporter Houston Post, 1964; reporter, make-up editor, exec. sports editor Memphis Press-Scimitar, 1964-68; pub. relations dir., profl. tennis tour, 1968-72; asso. publisher, editor World Tennis mag., 1972-73, editor, 1973—. Mem. U.S. Tennis Writers Assn. (1st v.p. 1972—), Sigma Delta Chi. Episcopalian. Club: Houston Press. Home: 18014 Bambriar St Houston TX 77090 Office: 8100 Westglen St Houston TX 77042

BOOKSTAVER, ALEXANDER, mortgage banker; b. Sag Harbor, N.Y., Apr. 11, 1911; s. Samuel and Jennie (Lekus) B.; student Coll. City N.Y., 1929-32; student bus. adminstrn., N.Y.U., 1933-34; grad. Am. Inst. Banking, 1936; m. Dorothy Ravitt, Sept. 3, 1936; 1 son, Richard. With trust dept. Hanover Bank, N.Y.C., 1930-41; with comptroller's dept. Schroder Trust Co., N.Y.C., 1941-46; v.p., comptroller Amalgamated Bank N.Y., 1946-56; controller, dir. investment dept. Internat. Ladies Garment Workers Union, N.Y.C., 1956-61; dir. investment dept. AFL-CIO, Washington, 1961-68; v.p. instl. relations Anchor Corp., Elizabeth, N.J., 1968-71; sr. v.p. investor liasion Heritage Corp. South Fla., Miami, 1971-73; v.p., sr. mortgage loan officer Midwest Mortgage Co., Miami, 1973—; dir. Peoples Nat. Bank of Md., Suitland. Mem. adv. com. housing and urban devel. AID, 1963-68; mem. adv. bd. Nat. Found. Health, Welfare and Pension Plans, 1963-68. Bd. dirs. Hebrew Inst. of L.I. Editorial adv. bd. Pension and Welfare News. Home: 20 Island Av Belle Isle Miami Beach FL 33139 Office: 120 NE 9th St Miami FL 33132

BOOMERSHINE, WALTER MCKINLEY, JR., automobile dealer; b. Charlotte, N.C., July 20, 1929; s. Walter McKinley and Nellie (McConnell) B.; B.S., Ga. Inst. Tech., 1951; postgrad. Harvard Bus. Sch., 1973; m. Winifred Forbes, Sept. 9, 1950; children—Linsay Ann, Kathy Renee, Jacquelyn Gay, Joanne Patrice, Walter McKinley III. With Boomershine Pontiac, Inc., Atlanta, 1946—, v.p., gen. mgr., 1959-65, pres. 1965—; pres., dir. Alexander Williams Co., Inc., Atlanta, 1960—; pres. Boomershine Agy., Inc., ins. and leasing, 1968—, Boomershine Life Ins. Co., 1970—; dir. Citizens & So. Nat. Bank, Atlanta. Served with USAF, 1951-53. Mem. Atlanta (pres., dir.), Ga. (dir.) automobile dealer assns., Atlanta C. of C. (tax com.), Chi Phi. Presbyn. (elder). Kiwanian (dir.). Home: 4636 Powers Rd Marietta GA 30060 Office: 390 Spring St Atlanta GA 30308

BOONE, SISTER JOSEPH ANGELA, educator; b. New Haven, Ky.; d. William Joseph and Mary Josephine (Greenwell) Boone; B.A., Brescia Coll., 1961; M.S., Cath. U. Am., 1963; postgrad. Tulane U., 1965. Tchr. jr. high parochial schs., Owensboro and Louisville, 1949-61; tchr. math. Brescia Coll., Owensboro, Ky., 1963—, mem. adminstrv. bd., dean of women, 1966-70; treas. Mt. St. Joseph Ursuline Sisters, 1970—. Mem. Nat. Council Tchrs. Math., Math. Assn. Am., Assn. Physics Tchrs. Home: Maple Mount KY 42356

BOONE, KYLE CLAYTON, architect; b. Washington, Dec. 16, 1932; s. William Kyle and Irvel Elizabeth (Lowry) B.; student Emory and Henry Coll., 1956-58; B.Arch., Va. Poly. Inst., 1962; m. Helen Emmett Kirk, May 5, 1956; children—Kyla Alexis, Helen Elizabeth, Kirk Clayton, Kathleen Clair. Architect, Echols-Sparger & Assos., Marion, Va., 1962-63, Six Assos., Inc., Asheville, N.C., 1963-68; pvt. practice architecture, Weaverville, N.C., 1968—. Chmn., United Fund, North Buncombe, 1971; vol. Heart Fund, 1970; mem. North Buncombe Boosters Club, 1971—, Weaverville P.T.A., 1963—, North Buncombe Banaiders Assn., 1971—, Weaverville Recreation Commn., 1972—. Election judge Republican Party, 1967-72. Served with AUS, 1953-56. Recipient Design award Lincoln Arc Welding Found., 1961, Reynolds Aluminum prize for archtl. students, 1962. Mem. A.I.A. Methodist. Mason (32 deg., K.T.), Lion (pres. 1970-73). Home: PO Box 425 Weaverville NC 28787 Office: PO Box 577 Weaverville NC 28787

BOONE, MICHAEL MAULDIN, lawyer; b. Henderson, Tenn., Jan. 31, 1941; s. Daniel Lacey and LaNelle Ruby (Stovall) B.; B.B.A., So. Meth. U., 1963, J.D., 1967; m. Marla Hays, Aug. 2, 1969. Admitted to Tex. bar, 1967; since practiced in Dallas; asso. mem. firm Richard D. Haynes, Dallas, 1967-68; partner Haynes & Boone, Dallas, 1969—. Lectr. securities regulation So. MMth. U. Sch. Law, 1971-73. Mem. 500, Inc., service orgn., Dallas, 1971—. Mem. Am., Tex., Dallas bar assns., Phi Gamma Delta, Phi Delta Phi. Mem. Ch. of Christ. Club: Calyx. Home: 3516 University Blvd Dallas TX 75205 Office: 2900 LTV Tower Dallas TX 75201

BOONE, SHELLEY SHELTON, ednl. adminstr.; b. Wauchula, Fla., May 7, 1922; s. Falcon B. and Ethel (Clardy) B.; B.S. in Econs., Fla. So. Coll., 1947, M.A., in Pub. Sch. Adminstrn. and Supervision, 1949; postgrad. U. Fla., 1949-52; m. Facheon Lee Kirby, Apr. 6, 1947; children—Shelley S. II, James A., William David. Tchr. pub. schs., Auburndale, Fla., 1948-51; prin. Haines City (Fla.) High Sch., 1951-57, Lakeland High Sch., 1957-58; supervising prin. Winter Haven (Fla.) area schs., 1958-60; dir. personnel Polk County (Fla.) Sch. Bd., Bartow, Fla., 1960-61; supt. pub. instrn. Polk County Schs., 1961-68; exec. dir. div. jr. colls. Dept. Edn., State of Fla., 1968-69, dir. div. elementary and secondary edn., 1969-72; dep. commr. edn. State of Fla., 1972—. County supt., Polk County, 1961-68. Served as lt. comdr. USNR, 1942-46. Mem. N.E.A., Fla. Edn. Assn. (past dir.), Fla. Assn. Secondary Sch. Prins. (past dir., pres.), Fla. Congress Parent-Tchrs. Assn. (past v.p.), Kappa Sigma. Democrat. Methodist. Rotarian. Clubs: Haines City (pres.); Lakeland (Fla.) (dir.). Home: 901 Chestwood Av Tallahassee FL 32303 Office: Room 115 Capitol Bldg Dept Edn Tallahassee FL 32304

BOONE, SYDNEY KENTON, JR., controller; b. Shreveport, La., Apr. 13. 1945; s. Sydney Kenton and Betty Matilda (Anderson) B.; B.S. in Accounting, La. Tech. U., 1967; postgrad. South Tex. Coll. Law, 1972—; m. Carolyn Houston, Jan. 26, 1966. Asst. auditor Arthur Andersen & Co., Houston, 1967-69, semi-sr., 1969-70, sr. auditor, 1970-72; controller Wolff, Morgan & Co., Houston, 1972—. Mgr. Little League, Houston, 1969-72; coach Little League Football, Houston, 1971. C.P.A., Tex. Mem. Am. Inst. C.P.A.'s, Tex. Soc. C.P.A.'s, Delta Sigma Pi, Kappa Alpha (pres. 1966-67). Home: 10031 Overbrook St Houston TX 77042 Office: 20 Briar Hollow Houston TX 77027

BOORAS, THEODORE PETER, banker; b. Pensacola, Fla., July 13, 1918; s. Peter Nick and Melpomeni (Poulos) B.; student La. State U., 1968-70; m. Marion Lois Taranto, Apr. 22, 1941; children—Constance (Mrs. Conrad Borzych), Patricia (Mrs. James Morrison), Theodore Peter. Co-owner Booras & Weidlich, Pensacola, Fla., 1946-56; sales rep. Grice Electronics, Inc., Pensacola, Fla., 1956-65; v.p. First Nat. Bank, Ft. Walton Beach, Fla., 1965—. Committeeman Gulf Coast council Boy Scouts Am., 1966—. Bd. dirs. United Fund, 1967-68, A.R.C. Served with USNR, 1942-46, 51-52. Mason (32 deg., Shriner), Rotarian. Home: 735 Revere Av Fort Walton Beach FL 32548 Office: PO Drawer 1327 Fort Walton Beach FL 32548

BOORSTIN, DANIEL J., author, historian Smithsonian Instn.; b. Atlanta, Oct. 1, 1914; s. Samuel and Dora (Olsan) B.; A.B. summa cum laude, Harvard, 1934; B.A. with 1st class honors (Rhodes scholar), Balliol Coll., Oxford (Eng.) U., 1936, B.C.L. with 1st class honors, 1937; postgrad. in law Inner Temple, London, 1934-37; J.S.D. (Sterling fellow), Yale, 1940; Litt.D., Cambridge (Eng.) U., 1967; m. Ruth Carolyn Frankel, Apr. 9, 1941; children—Paul Terry, Jonathan, David West. Admitted as barrister-at-law to Inner Temple, 1937, Mass. bar, 1942; instr., tutor history and lit. Harvard and Radcliffe Coll., 1938-42, also lectr. legal history Law Sch., Harvard, 1939-42; sr. atty. Office Lend Lease Adminstr., Washington, 1942-43, Office Asst. Solicitor Gen. U.S., 1942-43; asst. prof. history Swarthmore Coll., 1942-44; asst. prof. U. Chgo., 1944-49, asso. prof., 1949-56, Preston and Sterling Morton Distinguished prof. Am. history, 1956-69; dir. Nat. Mus. History and Tech., Smithsonian Instn., Washington, 1969-73, sr. historian, 1973—. Fulbright vis. lectr. Am. history U. Rome (Italy), 1950-51, Kyoto (Japan) U., 1957; cons. social sci. research center U. P.R., 1955; lectr. for State Dept. in Turkey, Iran, Nepal, India, Ceylon, 1959-60, Indonesia, Australia, New Zealand, Fiji Islands, 1968; 1st incumbent of chair Am. history and instns. U. Paris, 1961-62; Pitt prof. Am. history and instns. Cambridge U., also fellow Trinity Coll., 1964-65; fellow Huntington Library, 1969. Mem. Am. Revolution Bicentennial Commn., 1966-71. Mem. bd. visitors U.S. Air Force Acad., 1968-70. Mem. Colonial Soc. Mass., Am. Acad. Arts and Scis., Am. Antiquarian Soc., Am. Studies Assn. (pres. 1969-71), Internat. House Japan, Am., Miss. Valley, So. hist. assns., Phi Beta Kappa. Jewish religion. Clubs: Cosmos, Nat. Press (Washington); Elizabethan (Yale). Author: The Mysterious Science of the Law, 1941, Delaware Cases, 1792-1830 (3 vols.), 1943; The Lost World of Thomas Jefferson, 1948; The Genius of American Politics, 1953; The Americans: The Colonial Experience, 1958 (Bancroft award 1959); America and the Image of Europe, 1960, The Image or What Happened to the American Dream, 1962; The Americans; The National Experience, 1965 (Francis Parkman prize 1966); The Landmark History of the American People, 2 vols., 1968, 70; The Decline of Radicalism, 1969; The Sociology of the Absurd, 1970; The Americans: The Democratic Experience, 1973; Democracy and Its Contents, 1974. Editor: Chicago History of American Civilization, 30 vols., 1951—; An American Primer, 1966; American Civilization, 1972. editor for Am. history Ency. Brit., 1951-55. Contbr. articles, book revs. to profl. jours. Home: 3541 Ordway St NW Washington DC 20016 Office: Nat Museum History and Technology Smithsonian Instn Washington DC 20025

BOOSALIS, JAMES JOHN, food co. exec.; b. Mpls., May 27, 1924; s. John James and Stamata (Villas) B.; B.A., U. Minn., 1947; m. Inga Margarita Swanson, Aug. 5, 1941; children—Joanne, John, Julie, Jimmy, Janet. Sales mgr. John Morrell Co., Chgo., 1948-61; dir. sales Am. Bakeries, Chgo., 1961-66; v.p. sales Jeno's, Inc., Duluth, Minn., 1966-69; v.p. marketing sales United Foods, Inc., Memphis, 1969-72, also dir.; v.p. Standard Brands Foods, N.Y.C.; sr. v.p. in charge Fleischmann div. Standard Brands Inc., N.Y.C., 1972—; dir. John Ingles Frozen Food Co. Served with AUS, 1941-45. Club: Colonial (Memphis). Home: 6180 Heather Dr Memphis TN 38138 Office: 625 Madison Av New York City NY 10022

BOOTH, ARCH NEWELL, orgn. exec.; b. Wichita, Kan., July 9, 1906; s. Winfield Milton and Laura Belle (Parker) B.; A.B., Wichita State U., 1927; Nat. Inst. Comml. and Trade Orgn. Exec., Northwestern U., 1932-43; LL.D., Hillsdale (Mich.) Coll., 1953; m. Wilma Grace Harrison, Feb. 2, 1929; children—Joan, Robert Harrison, Donald A. Spl. rep. Wheeler-Kelley-Hagney Trust Co., Wichita, 1927-29; asst. mgr. Wichita C. of C., 1929-38, gen. mgr., 1938-43; asst. gen. mgr. U.S. C. of C., 1943-47, mgr., 1947-50, exec. v.p., 1950-74, chief staff officer, spokesman, 1970-74, pres., 1974—, pub. Nations Bus. Mag., 1950—; dir., mem. exec. com. Union Trust Co., Washington; dir. Financial Gen. Corp. Mem. Indsl. Pollution Control Council. Bd. dirs. U.S.-USSR Trade and Economic Council, Nat. Center for Voluntary Action. Recipient gold medal Freedoms Found., 1952, Spl. Freedom Leadership award, 1963; named Vol. Leader of Year, Am. Assn. Orgn. Execs., 1960; Bus. Man of Yr., Christian Heritage Found., 1973. Mem. Pi Kappa Delta. Methodist (trustee). Mason (Shriner). Club: Metropolitan (Washington). Home: 3520 Overlook Lane NW Washington DC 20016 Office: 1615 H St Washington DC 20006

BOOTH, CHARLES FITZPATRICK, cons. engr.; b. Prattville, Ala., Nov. 29, 1902; s. Charles and Sarah Lou (Fitzpatrick) B.; B.S. in Chem. Engring., U. Ala., 1921, M.S., 1922, Chem. Engr., 1924; m.

Weenona Hansen Peck, May 24, 1927; children—Emily Fitzpatrick (Mrs. Hugh Dubose Maulden), Sarah Elmore (Mrs. William Sim Mooneyham), Margaret Caoffey (Mrs. Norman E. Horton). Chem. engr., research group leader Swann Chem. Co., Anniston, Ala., 1922-36; research group leader, prin. chemist, sr. technologist Monsanto Chem. Co., Clinton Labs. AEC, Anniston, Oak Ridge, and Dayton, O., 1936-50; pres. Covington Fertilizer Co., Andalusia, Ala., 1950-57; then sect. leader, asso. dir. research and devel. V-C Chem. Co., 1957-63; asso. dir. research and devel. indsl. chem. div. Mobil Oil Co., Richmond, Va., 1963-67; owner C.F. Booth Cons. Engr., Elmore, Ala., 1967—. Cons. Ala. Gas Def., World War II. Served with SATC, World War I. Registered profl. engr., Ala. Mem. Am. Inst. Chem. Engrs., Air Pollution Control Assn. Methodist. Rotarian. Contbr. numerous articles to profl. jours. Patentee in field. Address; PO Box 68 Elmore AL 36025

BOOTH, EDEN COMFORT, ret. exec.; b. Cedar Springs, Mich., Feb. 21, 1900; s. Fremont D. and Ida Jane (Gates) B.; LL.B., Peoples Coll., Ft. Scott, Kan., 1922; m. Lucy C. Temple, May 2, 1922 (dec. Mar. 1966); 1 dau., Elizabeth Jane (Mrs. William L. Frakes); m. 2d Mozelle Murray, Jan. 13, 1968. Founder, chmn. bd. Colonial Poultry Farms, Inc., Pleasant Hill, Mo., 1922-55; pres. Mo., Poultry Expt. Sta., Mt. Grove, 1934-43; pres. Pleasant Hill Bank, 1940-51. Pres. bd. edn., Pleasant Hill, 1930-48, mayor, 1956-58. Trustee Patriotic Edn., Inc., 1963—. Mem. S.A.R. (pres. DeLand chpt. 1962-63, state registrar 1963-68). Democrat. Presbyn. Mason (Shriner), Lion, Odd Fellow. Publisher: Standard Poultry Jour., 1925-31 Genealogy of the Booth family, 1956. Home and Office: 806 W Howry Av DeLand FL 32720

BOOTH, EDGAR CHARLES, lawyer; b. Gainesville, Fla., July 13, 1934; s.Clyde V. and Bertha (Hutchison) B.; B.S., U. Fla., 1956, LL.B., 1962; m. Anne Payne Cawthon, Sept. 6, 1958; children—Rainey Cawthon, Jonn Edgar. Research asst. to G. Harold Carswell, U.S. Dist. Ct., Tallahassee, 1962-63; admitted to Fla. bar, 1962; practiced in Tallahassee, 1963—; mem. firm W. Dexter Douglass, 1963-65, Douglass and Booth, 1965-70; judge Small Claims Ct., Leon County, Fla., 1964-65; municipal judge City of Tallahassee, 1965-71. Chmn. March of Dimes, Tallahassee, 1965; pres. Sigma Nu House Corp.; regional dir. Fla. Drug Abuse Program, 1972—. Sec., bd. dirs. Fla. Heritage Found. Served from 1st lt. to capt., USAF, 1957-60. Mem. Am., Tallahassee (sec.-treas. 1971-72) bar assns., Fla. Bar. Democrat. Episcopalian. Club: Exchange. Home: 907 High Rd Tallahassee FL 32301 Office: PO Box 1388 Tallahassee FL 32302

BOOTH, JOHN CARROLL, JR., accountant; b. Folsom, La., Aug. 11, 1919; s. John Carroll and Ollie Belle (Laird) B.; B.S. in Accounting, La. State U., 1948; m. Kathleen Lois Burns, Feb. 24, 1944; 1 son, James Michael. Staff accountant Magnolia Petroleum Co. subsidiary Mobil Oil Corp., Dallas, 1948-54, mgr. methods research, 1954-60; comptroller Rio Grande Valley Gas Co., Brownsville, Tex., 1960; cons., mgr. Peat, Marwick, Mitchell & Co., Dallas, 1961-64, partner, Houston and Paris, France, 1964—; dir. Pinter's Mens Wear, Inc., Houston. Served with AUS, 1942-45, 52-53; ETO. C.P.A., Tex., La. Mem. Am. Inst. C.P.A.'s, Tex. Soc. C.P.A.'s. Clubs: Houston, Lakeside Country (Houston). Home: 217 Kensington Ct Houston TX 77024 Office: 4300 One Shell Plaza Houston TX 77002

BOOTH, JOSEPH WARD, city ofcl.; b. Johnson City, Tenn., Dec. 5, 1939; s. Clay Evans and Gladys (Crussell) B.; B.S., E. Tenn. State U., 1965; postgrad. U. Ga., 1971, U. Tenn., 1972; m. Emily S. Lyons, May 27, 1965; children—Joseph Ward II, James Warner. Co-owner Patrick-Booth Enterprise, Johnson City, 1965-67; asst. city mgr. City of Johnson City, 1967-73; city mgr. City of Gatlinburg (Tenn.), 1973—. Vice pres. Tenn. 4-H Clubs, 1957; mem. Washington County Alcohol and Drug Commn., 1972-73, Mayne-Williams Library Bd., Johnson City, 1969-73. William H. Danforth scholar, 1968. Mem. Internat., Tenn. city mgrs. assns., Am. Pub. Works Assn., Pi Kappa Alpha. Elk. Clubs: Johnson City (Tenn.) Country; Gatlinburg Country, Gatlinburg Ski, Sooner. Home: Alpendorf Rd Gatlinburg TN 37738 Office: Office of City Manager Gatlinburg TN 37738

BOOTH, STUART EDGAR, chem. co. exec.; b. Summit, N.J., Nov. 9, 1939; s. John Stuart and Eleanor Frances (Edgar) B.; B.S. in Zoology, Duke, 1962; m. Carol Spence, Sept. 29, 1962; children—Barry Craig, Kimberly Carol. Sales rep. Kerr McGee Chem. Co., Atlanta, 1968-69, mgr. sales adminstrn., Oklahoma City, 1970—. Adviser Jr. Achievement, 1972-73. Bd. dirs. YMCA, Oklahoma City, 1971. Served to lt. USNR, 1962-68. Mem. Oklahoma City Jr. C. of C., Alpha Tau Omega. Home: 11333 N May Av Oklahoma City OK 73120 Office: Kerr McGee Tower 1503 PO Box 25861 Oklahoma City OK 73125

BOOTH, WILLIAM EDWARD, ins. holding co. exec.; b. Owensboro, Ky., Jan. 8, 1920; s. Henry Overstreet and Elizabeth Rogers (Sweeney) B.; B.A., Vanderbilt U., 1941; m. Jessie Gardner McCracken, Dec. 13, 1941; children—Elizabeth Anne (Mrs. B. Taylor Bennett III), Susan McCracken, Lucinda Forrest. Sales engr. IBM, 1941-46; 1st v.p., co-founder Cherokee Ins. Co., Nashville, 1946-64; co-founder v.p., sec. Forrest Life Ins. Co., Nashville, 1964-69; v.p., sec. Synercon Corp., Nashville, 1969-73. Pres., Vanderbilt Alumni Panhellenic Council, 1954-56; bd. dirs. Nashville Police Assistance League, 1965-73, Nashville Mental Health Assn., 1971-73, Davidson County Anti Tb. Assn., 1957-62. Served to maj. AUS, 1942-46. Decorated Legion of Merit; recipient Presdl. award Insurors of Tenn., 1961. Mem. Soc. Chartered Property and Casualty Underwriters (past nat. v.p., chpt. pres.), S.A.R., Phi Beta Kappa, Sigma Nu (past pres., alumni adviser), Omicron Delta Kappa, Omicron Delta Gamma. Club: Wildwood Country. Home: 4315 Beekman Dr Nashville TN 37215 Office: 301 Plus Park Blvd Nashville TN 37202 Died Dec. 25, 1973.

BOOTLE, WILLIAM AUGUSTUS, judge; b. Colleton County, S.C., Aug. 19, 1902; s. Philip Lorraine and Laura Lilla (Benton) B.; A.B., Mercer U., Macon, Ga., 1924, LL.B., 1925; m. Virginia Childs, Nov. 24, 1928; children-William Augustus, Anne (Mrs. Ellsworth Hall III), James C. Admitted to Ga. bar, 1925; practiced in Macon, 1925-29; mem. firm Carlisle & Bootle, 1933-54; U.S. dist. atty. Middle Dist. Ga., 1929-33; acting dean Law Sch., Mercer U., 1933-37, prof. law, part-time, 1926-37; U.S. dist. judge, 1954—. Trustee, Mercer U., 1933—, chmn. exec. com., 1941-46; trustee Walter F. George Sch. Law Found., 1961—, v.p., 1963-65, pres., 1965-66. Recipient Distinguished Alumnus award Mercer U., 1961. Mem. Phi Alpha Delta, Phi Delta Theta. Republican. Baptist. Mason (33 deg., Shriner). Clubs: Civitan (pres. 1936), Idle Hour Country. Home: 365 Old Club Rd Macon GA 31204 Office: PO Box 26 Macon GA 31204

BOPP, CHARLES DAN, chem. engr.; b. Decatur, Ill., Feb. 4, 1923; s. Charles Dan and Edna (Rybolt) B.; B.S. in Chem. Engring., Purdue U., 1944; m. Mary Elizabeth McLeod, Mar. 13, 1971. Chemist Y-12 Plant Oak Ridge, 1944-47; devel. engr. Oak Ridge Nat. Lab., 1947—. Fellow Am. Inst. Chemists; mem. Am. Chem. Soc., Am. Ceramic Soc., Am. Nuclear Soc., Am. Inst. Chem. Engrs. (asso.), A.A.A.S., Research Soc. Am., N.Y. Acad. Scis. Home: 306 Virginia Rd Oak Ridge TN 37830 Office: Oak Ridge Nat Lab PO Box X Oak Ridge TN 37830

BORDELON, DONALD RAY, dept. store exec.; b. Marksville, La., Jan. 26, 1933; s. Hilton and Mary Jane (Bielkiewicz) B.; student La. State U., 1951-52; B.S., U. Southwestern La., 1956; m. Martha H. Campbell, Apr. 23, 1960; children—Donna, Celia, Daryl. Accountant, P. G. Bell, Inc., Houston, 1956; salesman accounting systems Nat. Cash Register, Shreveport, La., 1967; accountant W. F. Beall Co., Shreveport, 1958, Dealers Truck Equipment, Shreveport, 1959; accountant, asst. mgr. Shreveport Cigar & Tobacco Co., Inc., 1960-64; controller Master Packaging, Inc., Shreveport, 1965-70; v.p., controller Palais Royal, Inc., Shreveport, 1970—; pres., dir. Custom Labels, Inc. Mem. steering com. Gillis Long for Gov. Democratic campaign, 1971. Bd. dirs. promotion com. Downtown Shreveport Unltd. Baptist. Mason (32 deg., Shriner). Home: 6036 Dillingham St Shreveport LA 71106 Office: 600 Milam St Shreveport LA 71120

BORDENCA, CHARLES MICHAEL, dentist; b. Birmingham, Ala., Sept. 14, 1943; s. Vincent Joseph and Lena Louise (Latham) B.; student St. Bernard Coll., 1961-63; B.A., Samford U., 1965; D.M.D., U. Ala., 1969; m. Marie Elizabeth Giardina, July 27, 1968; 1 son, Mark Adam. Intern, resident pediatric dentistry U. Ala. Sch. Dentistry and Children's Hosp., Birmingham, 1971-73. Served with USPHS, 1969-71. Recipient Bill Jensen award for outstanding acad. achievement, 1967. Mem. Am. Dental Assn., Am. Acad. Pedodontics, Am. Soc. Dentistry for Children, Ala. Dental Assn. Contbr. articles to profl. jours. Home: 1536 Crest Hill Rd Birmingham AL 35213 Office: 129 1st St Alabaster AL 35007

BORDERS, ROBERT WILLIAM, physician; b. Stratton, Colo., Nov. 17, 1925; s. Herschel C. and Hazel Mae (Harrison) B.; B.S., La. Tech. U., 1949; M.D., Kan. U., 1949; m. Emma Jean Sewell, Oct. 17, 1969; children—Robert, Thomas, Anne, Blaine. Intern New Orleans Charity, 1949-50; resident Duke, 1952-54; pvt. practice medicine, specializing in anesthesiology, Shreveport, La., 1954-66; dir. dept. anesthesiology Bossier City (La.) City Gen. Hosp., 1966—; mem. staff Schumpert Meml. Hosp., Confederate Meml. Hosp., Doctor's Hosp., Willis Knighton Hosp., Highland Hosp., Brentwood Hosp. (all Shreveport); clin. asst. prof. anesthesiology Sch. Med., La. State U., Shreveport. Pres. La. Tennis Assn., 1963-64. Served with USNR, 1943-46, 1950-52. Diplomate Am. Bd. Anesthesiology. Fellow Am. Coll. Anesthesiology; mem. La., Shreveport, 4th Dist. (v.p. 1969) med. socs., Am. Soc. Anesthesiologists, Internat. Anesthesia Soc. Home: 2977 Risinger St Shreveport LA 71109 Office: 2105 Airline St Bossier City LA 71010

BORDERS, WILLIAM D., bishop; b. Washington, Ind., Oct. 9, 1913; ed. St. Meinrad Sem., Notre Dame Sem., U. Notre Dame. Ordained priest Roman Catholic Ch., 1940; rector St. Joseph Cathedral, Baton Rouge; bishop of Orlando (Fla.), 1968—. Address: PO Box 3069 Orlando FL 32802

BORDNER, JON BENTON, educator; b. Massillon, O., Jan. 25, 1940; s. Delmar B. and Martina (Brenner) B.; B.S., Case Inst., 1962; Ph.D. (NIH fellow), U. Cal. at Berkeley, 1966; m. Lois Eleanor Baird, Dec. 26, 1969; 1 dau., Kimberly Ellanor. Asso. prof. chemistry N.C. State U. at Raleigh, 1969—, chmn. organic div. dept. chemistry, 1971—. Dreyfus tchr.-scholar, 1972—; Cal. Inst. Tech. postdoctoral fellow, 1966-69; NSF research grantee, 1972. Mem. Am. Crystallographic Assn., Am. Chem. Soc., Sigma Xi, Alpha Chi Sigma, Tau Beta Pi. Contbr. articles to profl. jours. Home: 1302 Salterton Ct Raleigh NC 27608 Office: Dept Chemistry NC State Univ Raleigh NC 27607

BOREN, DAVID LYLE, lawyer, state legislator; b. Washington, Apr. 21, 1941; s. Lyle H. and Christine (McKown) B.; B.A. summa cum laude, Yale, 1963; M.A. (Rhodes scholar), Oxford (Eng.) U., 1965; J.D. with honors, U. Okla. 1968; m. Janna Lou Little, Sept. 7, 1968; children—Carrie Christine, David Daniel. Resident counsellor U. Okla., Norman, 1965-66; practiced in Wewoka and Seminole, Okla., 1968—; prof. polit. sci., chmn. div. social scis., Okla. Baptist U., Shawnee, 1969—; mem. Okla. Ho. of Reps. 1966—. Propaganda analyst USIA, Washington, 1962—; asst. to liaison dir. OCDM, Washington, 1961. Mem. Okla. Gov.'s Task Force on Tech. Edn., 1967—. Named Outstanding Young Oklahoman, Okla. Jr. C. of C., 1969. Mem. Am., Okla. (vice chmn. law schs. com.) bar assns., Am. Assn. Rhodes Scholars, Seminole, Wewoka, Seminole Jr. Chambers commerce, Order of Coif, Phi Beta Kappa, Phi Delta Phi. Democrat. Methodist. Clubs: Yale (Western Okla.); Seminole Sportsman's. Home: 917 Wilson St Seminola OK 74868 Office: State Capitol Oklahoma City OK 73105

BORENSTEIN, EMANUEL, social worker; b. Manchester, N.H., Apr. 11, 1904; s. Solomon and Etta (Salzberg) B.; student Harvard, 1921-22; B.A., Coll. City N.Y., 1925; M.S. in Social Work, Boston U., 1942; m. Gertrude Perlman, Dec. 8; 1 dau., Selma (Mrs. Alvin Milchen). Exec. dir. Montreal (Que., Can.) Hebrew Orphan Home, 1929-30; parole supr. Mass. Dept. Pub. Welfare, Boston, 1931-43; asst. chief Fgn. Inquiry unit A.R.C., Washington, 1943-44; mem. staff War Refugee bd., Washington, 1944; exec. dir. New Eng. Zionist Region, Boston, 1944-48; dir. for Brazil Am. Jewish Joint Distbn. Com., San Paulo, Brazil, 1948-49; chief mission for CARE, Israel, 1949-50; area dir. Israel Bond Orgn., Indpls., Harrisburg, Pa., Boston, 1951-54; exec. dir. Neustadter Convalescent Center, Yonkers, N.Y., 1955-56; psychiat. social worker pub. schs., Wantagh, N.Y., 1958-61; exec. dir. Pride Judea Children's Services, Bklyn., 1961-62; asst. dir., clinic adminstr. Infants Home Bklyn., 1962-64; adminstr. Hempstead (N.Y.) Consultation Service; supr. home health care services Greenpoint Hosp., Bklyn., 1965-67; adminstr. Glen Oaks Nursing Home, 1967-68; social work cons., N.Y., Fla., 1968-71; dir. dept. social work Meml. Hosp., Hollywood, Fla., 1968-72; regional dir. social work Am. Medicorp. Inc., Dr.'s Hosp., Hollywood, 1972—; instr. Boston U., 1935-42, Endicott Jr. Coll., 1946-47; Adelphi Coll. 1957-61. Vice pres. Broward County (Fla.) Service Agy. Sr. Citizens; chmn. adv. bd. Broward County Ret. Sr. Vol. program; v.p. Jewish Family Service Broward County. Mem. Democratic exec. com., Broward County. Bd. dirs. Am. Civil Liberties Union Broward County; bd. dirs., pres. Broward Community Concerts Assn. Mem. Nat. Assn. Social Workers (former chmn. L.I. chpt., Soc. Hosp. Social Work Dirs. (past chmn. Fla. chpt.), Am. Hosp. Assn. Club: Harvard (Broward County). Home: 1701 S Ocean Dr Apt 902 Hollywood FL 33020 Office: Drs Hosp 1859 Van Buren St Hollywood FL 33020

BORG, JOSEPH FRANKLIN, physician; b. St. Paul, Aug. 27, 1898; s. Samuel Andrews and Dorothea Sophia (Youngberg) B.; student MacAlester Coll., 1916-18; B.S., U. Minn., 1920, M.B., 1922, M.D., 1923; m. Esther Lane, Sept. 14, 1948. Intern, Aucker Hosp., St. Paul, 1922, resident, 1923-24; intern City Hosp., Cleve., 1923; practice medicine specializing in cardiology, St. Paul, 1924-66, Tryon, N.C., 1966—; electrocardiographer Bethesda Hosp., St. Paul, 1930-68; clin. asso. prof. internal medicine U. Minn., 1942-68. Served to col. AUS, 1941-46. Decorated Bronze Star medal. Mem. A.M.A., A.C.P., Am. Therapeutic Soc. (pres. 1945), Am. Heart Assn., Ramsey County Med. Soc. (pres. 1941). Rotarian. Home: Box 306 Tryon NC 28782 Office: 100 Jervey Rd Tryon NC 28782

BORGET, LLOYD GEORGE, architect; b. Winnipeg, Man., Can., May 25, 1913, (parents Am. citizens); s. Henry John and Mabel Ann (Duval) B.; B.Arch., U. Minn., 1937. Mem. staff Stanley Bliss, Architect, Corpus Christi, Tex., 1937-42, Alden B. Dow, Inc., Architect, Houston, 1942-46, Lloyd & Morgan, Architects, Houston, 1947, Rather, Moore & Asso., Houston, 1948; partner Mackie & Kamrath, A.I.A., Architects, Houston, 1949—. Mem. A.I.A., Tex. Soc. Architects, Scarab, Sigma Nu. Prin. works include M.D. Anderson Hosp., Houston, 1954—; U. Houston Sci. and Research Bldg., 1968; City of Houston Health Adminstrn. Bldg., 1966. Home: 4519 W Alabama St Houston TX 77027 Office: 2713 Ferndale Pl Houston TX 77006

BORING, GEORGE WALLACE, JR., dentist; b. Arcadia, Fla., Jan. 9, 1939; s. George Wallace and Pearl Lois (Johnston) B.; student Presbyn. Coll., 1957-58; B.S., Fla. State U., 1962; D.M.D., U. Louisville, 1966; m. Nancy Marie Migliore, Dec. 16, 1956; children—Deborah Marie, George Wallace III, Nancy Elizabeth, Mary Ann. Pvt. practice dentistry, Brooksville, Fla., 1966—; mem. staff Lykes Meml. Hosp. Dir. Hernando State Bank, Hernando Indsl. Corp. Bd. dirs. Hernando County Guidance Center. Mem. Am., Fla., Withiacoochee (pres. 1970-71) dental assns., Acad. Gen. Dentistry, Am. Soc. Preventive Dentistry, Hernando County C. of C. (dir. 1968-71), Psi Omega. Presbyn. (deacon). Kiwanian (pres. 1972-73). Home: 750 Fernwood Dr Brooksville FL 33512 Office: 609 Lamar Av Brooksville FL 33512

BORN, SIDNEY, chem. engr.; b. N.Y.C., June 12, 1889; s. Jacob and Emilie (Saalfeld) B.; B.S., Columbia, 1910, Ph.D., 1913; m. Suzanne Vleck, May 1, 1914; 1 son, Harold J. Chief chemist Rittman Process Corp., Pitts., 1915; mgr. tech. div. Empire Refinery, Inc., also Empire Gas & Fuel Co., 1916-20; asst. gen. supt. Transcontinental Oil Co. (now Marathon Oil Co.), 1920-31; prof. petroleum research U. Tulsa, 1931-46; sr. partner Born Engring. Co., Tulsa, 1946—; v.p. Gen. Steel Fabricating, Inc., Tulsa. dir. Born Internat. Anstalt, Liechtenstein, Societe des Fours Born France, Paris, Born Africa (Pty.) Ltd., Johannesburg, Societa Italian Forni Born S.R.L., Milan, Born Heaters Ltd., Brighton, Eng. Trustee Philbrook Art Center. Named to U. Tulsa Hall of Fame. Registered profl. engr. Okla. Mem. Am. Inst. Chemists, Am. Soc. Testing Materials, Tulsa Engrs. Club, Sigma Xi, Phi Lambda Upsilon. Clubs: Tulsa, Tulsa Fin and Feather. Contbr. articles to profl. jours. Patentee in field. Home: 4241 S Victor St Tulsa OK 74105 Office: 408 N Boston St Tulsa OK 74103

BORNE, RONALD FRANCIS, educator; b. New Orleans, Nov. 17, 1938; s. Adelard Francis and Leonie (Bonnet) B.; student La. State U., 1956-57; B.S. in Chemistry, Loyola U. New Orleans, 1960; M.S. in Organic Chemistry, Tulane U., 1962; Ph.D. (NIH fellow) in Medicinal Chemistry, U. Kan., 1967; m. Kathleen Taylor, May 30, 1959; children—Debra Ann, Michael Jude, Merribeth. Research asst. Ochsner Research Found., New Orleans, 1956-62; research chemist C.J. Patterson Co., Kansas City, Mo., 1962-63, Mallinckrodt Chem. Works, St. Louis, 1967-68; teaching asst. Tulane U., New Orleans, 1961-62; asst. prof. medicinal chemistry U. Miss. at University, 1968-70, asso. prof., 1970-73, prof., 1973—. Recipient Outstanding Tchr. award U. Miss., 1972, Outstanding Educator award, 1973. Mem. Acad. Pharm. Scis., Miss. Pharm. Assn., Am. Chem. Soc., Internat. Soc. Heterocyclic Chemistry, Sigma Xi, Rho Chi, Phi Delta Chi. Contbr. articles to profl. jours. Home: 101 Clubview Rd Oxford MS 38655

BOROCHOFF, CHARLES ZACHARY, mfg. co. owner; b. Atlanta, Apr. 11, 1921; s. Isadore and Pauline (Reisman) B.; LL.B., Atlanta Law Sch., 1941; m. Ida Dorothy Sloan, Jan. 11, 1942; children—Lynn (Mrs. Myles Jarrett Gould), Toby Ann (Mrs. Stanley Edison Galkin), Jean Sue, Lance Mark. Exec v.p. So. Wire & Iron Works, Atlanta, 1936-63; pres. Borochoff Properties, Inc., real estate, Atlanta, 1954—, Designs Unlimited, Inc., Atlanta, 1964—, Scottdale Enterprises, Atlanta, 1972—. Mem. High Museum of Art, 1955—, Nat. Conf. Christians and Jews, 1967—, Planned Parenthood, 1970—. Trustee Atlanta Playhouse, 1971—. Mem. Nat. Retail Wholesale Furniture Assn., Internat. Home and Furniture Reps. Assn. Jewish religion (trustee synagogue). Mason (Shriner, 32 deg.); mem. B'nai B'rith. Clubs: Atlanta Music, Progressive. Home: 3450 Old Plantation Rd NW Atlanta GA 30327 Office: 795 Glendale Rd Scottdale GA 30079

BOROD, RONALD SAM, lawyer; b. Memphis, Aug. 9, 1941; s. Marx J. and Margaret (Morris) B.; A.B., magna cum laude, Princeton, 1963; J.D., Harvard, 1966; LL.M. (Research fellow), N.Y. U., 1967; m. Nan Dattel, June 26, 1965; children—Margaret Gail, Emily Rose. Admitted to Tenn. bar, 1966; since practiced in Memphis; mem. firm Rosenfield, Borod, Bogatin & Kremer, Memphis, 1967—, partner, 1970—, mng. partner, 1972—. Lectr. taxation and constl. law Memphis State U. Law Sch., 1967—. Acting pres. Memphis and Shelby County Legal Services Assn., 1973—. Mem. Shelby County Democratic Exec. Com., 1970-72; chmn. rules com. Tenn. Dem. Conv., 1972; mem. Tenn. Dem. Exec. Com., 1973—. Bd. dirs. Jewish Service Agy., 1970—, Jewish Children's Regional Service, 1970—. Mem. Memphis and Shelby County, Tenn., Am. bar assns., L.Q.C. Lamar Soc., Harvard Law Assn., Princeton Alumni Club, Phi Beta Kappa. Club: Harvard (Memphis). Contbr. chpt. You Can't Eat Magnolias, 1972. Contbr. profl. and polit. jours. Home: 1509 Carr Av Memphis TN 38104 Office: 1105 Union Planters Bldg Memphis TN 38103

BORSCHOW, RON CLARKE, statis. cons.; b. Houston, Feb. 8, 1933; s. Reuben and Hazel I. (Beatty) B.; B.B.A., U. Houston, 1958 M.B.A., So. Methodist U., 1960; postgrad. Ohio State U., 1958, U. Chgo., 1960-61, U. Houston, 1964—. Market research analyst Toni Co., Chgo., 1960-61; research mgr. Product Acceptance & Research, Evansville, Ind., 1961-63; founder, pres. R. Borschow & Assos., statis. and market research consultants, Houston, 1963—; statis. cons. Houston Health Dept., 1964—. Mem. Am. Marketing Assn., Am. Statis. Assn., Tex. Pub. Health Assn., Houston Symphony Soc., Houston Grand Opera Assn., Phi Theta Kappa. Home: 2422 Albans St Houston TX 77005 Office: 1115 N MacGregor St Houston TX 77025

BORSI, PETER N., govt. ofcl., engr.; b. Altoona, Pa., May 2, 1916; s. Joseph and Theresa (Henninger) B.; student U. Wis., 1934, Fenn Coll., 1942-43, Northwestern U. Technol. Inst., 1948-53. Communications specialist Signal Corps, U.S. Army, 1935-38; aviation radio communications specialist AAC, 1938-39; asst. airways keeper, radio operator CAA, Dept. Commerce, 1939-44; radio insp., radio—electronics engr., supr. Field Engring. and Monitoring Bur., FCC, 1944-65, supervisory electronics engr. Office Emergency Communications, Washington, 1965—. Cons., exhibitor USIA show Photography-USA, 1974—. Activity mgr. Sterling Park Recreation Center, chmn. sports program, 1971-72, instr. tennis, 1965-74; mem. Sterling Park Civic Assn., Sterling Area P.T.A.; leader, instr. Boy Scouts Am.; asst. adviser Boys Clubs Am.; cons., adviser Smithsonian Assos. Named hon. citizen Boystown U.S.A. Mem. Am. Legion, 4-H Clubs Am., FCC Communicators Club (charter mem. radio intelligence div.), Morse Telegraph Club Am. (life), Antique Wireless Assn., Am. Radio Relay League, I.E.E.E., Loudoun Area Radio Klub (charter mem., founder), Sterling Park Radio Club, Broadcast Pioneers, Nat. Rifle Assn., Am. Legion, D.A.V. (life), others. Roman Catholic (mem. council, edn. exec. bd., asso. editor newsletter). Toastmaster. Author instrs. rig. aids, morse code and tennis courses. Address: 111 N Alder Av Sterling VA 22170

BORUM, OLIN HENRY, govt. adminstr.; b. Spencer, N.C., Nov. 3, 1917; s. Oscar Henry and Marjorie Mae (Leigh) B.; B.S., U. N.C., 1938, M.A., 1947, Ph.D., 1949; postgrad., teaching fellow, U. Md., 1940-41; m. Beatrice Star Comulada, Nov. 14, 1944; children—Pamela Leigh, Robin Olin, Denis Richard. Research chemist E.I. duPont de Nemours & Co., Phila. Lab., 1949-50; interim research asst. prof. Cancer Research Lab., U. Fla., 1950; instr., asst. prof. chemistry U.S. Mil. Acad., 1952-55; research adminstr. U.S. Army Chem. Corps Research and Devel. Command, Washington, 1956-60; research adminstr. U.S. Army Material Command, Washington, 1964—; tchr. chemistry U. Va., Arlington, 1966-68; teaching fellow U. Md., 1940-41; grad. asst., teaching fellow U. N.C., 1946-49. Adult scouter Nat. Capital Area council Boy Scouts Am., 1964, unit commr., 1968—; sec. Mt. Vernon (Va.) Civic Assn., 1965-66; mem. Com. of 33 (nat. adv. groups Nat. Sojourners, Inc.), 1962-71, chmn., 1969-71. Nat. trustee Nat. Sojourners, Inc. Served from 2d lt. to maj., AUS, 1941-46; as maj. USAF, 1951-56, lt. col., 1960-64. Recipient Certificate of Achievement Dept. Army, 1971. Fellow Am. Inst. Chemists; mem. Am. Chem. Soc., Phi Beta Kappa, Sigma Xi. Presbyn. Mason (K.T., Shriner). Contbr. articles profl. jours. Home: 9002 Volunteer Dr Alexandria VA 22309 Office: Research Div Hdqrs Army Materiel Command Alexandria VA 22304

BORUM, RODNEY LEE, corp. exec.; b. nr. High Point, N.C., Sept. 30, 1929; s. Carl Macy and Etta (Sullivan) B.; student U. N.C., 1947-49; B.S., U.S. Naval Acad., 1953; m. Helen Marie Rigby, June 27, 1953; children—Richard Harlan, Sarah Elizabeth. Design-devel. engr. Gen. Electric Co., Syracuse, N.Y., Cape Kennedy, Fla., 1956-58, missile test condr., Cape Kennedy, 1958-60, mgr., ground equipment engr., 1960-61, mgr. Eastern Test Range Engring., 1961-65; adminstr. Bus. and Def. Services Adminstrn. U.S. Dept. Commerce, 1966-69; pres. Printing Industries of Am., Inc., 1969—. Dir. Strangers Cay, Ltd. Dir. United Fund, Brevard County, Fla., 1963—, v.p., 1964-65; exec. council Cub Scouts Am., 1965; dir. Brevard Beaches Concert Assn., 1964. Republican candidate Fla. Ho. of Reps., 1960. Served to 1st lt. USAF, 1953-56. Named Boss of Yr., Jr. C. of C., 1965; recipient Bausch and Lomb sci. award; award Am. Legion. Mem. U.S. Naval Inst., U.S. Naval Acad. Alumni Assn., Phi Eta Sigma. Methodist. Clubs: Columbia Country, City Tavern. Home: 4008 Glenrose St Kensington MD 20795 Office: 1730 N Lynn St Arlington VA 22209

BORZELLECA, JOSEPH FRANCIS, educator; b. Norristown, Pa., Oct. 3, 1930; s. Peter and Madeline (Fiorillo) B.; B.S., St. Joseph's Coll., 1952; M.S., Thomas Jefferson U., 1954, Ph.D., 1956; m. Mary Elizabeth Ford, Jan. 8, 1955; children—Joseph, Paul, David, Michael, Therese Marie, Mark. Instr. pharmacology Women's Med. Coll. Pa., Phila., 1956-59; asst. prof. Med. Coll. Va., Richmond, 1959-62, asso. prof., 1962-67, prof., 1967—. Cons. Nat. Inst. Mental Health, Food and Drug Adminstrn., U.S. Army, Nat. Acad. Sci.-NRC, Certified Colors Mfrs. Assn. USPHS, research grantee. Mem. Soc. Toxicology (pres. 1973-74), Am. Soc. Pharmacology and Exptl. Therapeutics, A.A.A.S., Am. Soc. Chem., Soc. Exptl. Biology Medicine. K.C. Home: 8718 September Dr Richmond VA 23229 Office: Med College Va Dept Pharmacology Richmond VA 23298

BOS, WILLIAM GLEN, educator; b. Chgo., Jan. 18, 1937; s. Bernard and Alice (Talsma) B.; A.B., Calvin Coll., 1958; Ph.D., Wayne State U., 1963; m. Ruth Elaine VanArkel, June 13, 1958; children—Sheryl Lynn, James William, Krista Jean, Steven David. Research asso. U. Ill., Urbana, 1963-64; asst. prof. dept. chemistry U. Louisville, 1964-68, asso. prof., 1968-72, prof., 1972—, faculty research participant Oak Ridge Nat. Lab. Mem. NSF Proposal Rev. Panel Instructional Sci. Equipment Program. Bd. dirs., vice chmn. Presbyn. Community Center, Louisville. NSF grad. teaching fellow Wayne State U., 1962. Mem. Am. Chem. Soc. (chmn. Louisville sect. 1970-71), Sigma Xi, Phi Lambda Upsilon. Presbyn. Contbr. articles to profl. jours. Home: 2411 Broadmeade Rd Louisville KY 40205

BOSCHMA, WILLIAM JOSEPH, retail exec.; b. Vincennes, Ind., Oct. 30, 1936; s. Riniji Dootsie and Dorothy Evelyn (Case) B.; B.A., Mich. State U., 1962; m. Betty Louise De Hart, Sept. 11, 1964; children—Bradley, Brett. Staff accountant Price Waterhouse & Co., C.P.A.'s, Houston, 1962-65, mgr. audit, 1969-73; controller Steve Kruchko Co. mech. contractor, Drayton Plains, Mich., 1965-69; v.p. finance Wicks N Sticks Inc., candle retailers, Houston, 1973—. Mem. Am. Inst. C.P.A.'s, Tex. Soc. C.P.A.'s. Toastmaster. Home: 13923 Britoak St Houston TX 77024 Office: Wicks N Sticks PO Box 40307 Houston TX 77040

BOSHELL, BURIS RAYE, physician, educator; b. nr. Phil Campbell, Ala., Oct. 9, 1926; s. Harvey M. and Lela (Alexander) B.; B.S., Ala. Polytech. Inst., 1947, postgrad., 1947-49; postgrad. Med. Coll. Ala., 1949-51; M.D., Harvard, 1953; m. Martha Sue Johnson, June 4, 1951; children—Patty, Thomas Eppinger. Intern, Peter Bent Brigham Hosp., Boston, 1953-54, resident, 1954-59; practice medicine, specializing in internal medicine, Birmingham, Ala., 1959; mem. staff U. Ala. Hosps. and Clinics; instr. Harvard, 1956-58, asst. in medicine, 1958-59; asst. prof. medicine Med. Coll. Ala, 1959-62, asso. prof., 1962-64, prof., 1964-67, Ruth Lawson Hanson prof. medicine, 1967—, asst. dir., dept. medicine, 1963-69, dir. div. diabetes, endocrinology and related disorders, 1970—; med. dir. Diabetes Research and Edn. Hosp.; dir. div. endocrinology and metabolism U. Ala. Sch. Medicine, Birmingham. Pres. bd. dirs. Diabetes Trust Fund of Ala.; bd. dirs. Diabetes Research Lab. Diplomate Am. Bd. Internal Medicine. Fellow A.C.P., Am. Coll. Clin. Pharmacology and Chemotherapy; mem. A.M.A., Ala., Jefferson County med. assns., Am. Assn. U. Profs., Birmingham Acad. Medicine, Ala. Acad. Sci., Am., New Eng., N.Y., Ala. diabetes assns., Endocrine Soc., Am. Fedn. for Clin. Research, So. Soc. for Clin. Investigation, Sigma Xi, Omicron Delta Kappa, Phi Kappa Phi, Gamma Sigma Delta, Tau Kappa, Alpha Omega Alpha. Contbr. articles to profl. jours. Home: 3017 Old Ivy Rd Birmingham AL 35210 Office: 1808 7th Av S PO Box 3371-A Birmingham AL 35294

BOSLEY, DAVID EMERSON, textile co. chemist; b. Lundale, W. Va., Dec. 16, 1927; s. Thomas Richard and Bess Dale (Corey) B.; B.S. in Chemistry, W. Va. U., 1950; Ph.D. in Phys. Chemistry, Mass. Inst. Tech., 1954; m. Ann Wheeler, May 31, 1952; children—Rebecca, Matthew, Linus, Patience. Research asso. Dacron tech. sect. E. I. du Pont de Nemours & Co., Kinston, N.C., 1956—. Commr. Grifton, N. C., 1967-69; mayor, Grifton, 1969—. Served with AUS, 1954-56. Mem. Phi Beta Kappa, Sigma Xi. Home: PO Box 531 Grifton NC 28530

BOSS, HAROLD FRANCIS, life ins. exec.; b. Washington, July 10, 1903; s. Joseph Centennial and Lillie (Bowdler) B.; student Okla. U., 1922-23; B.S., U. Va., 1926; m. Josephine Brodnax, Sept. 17, 1928; children—Bruce Whitaker, Gregory Brodnax. Securities and wholesale glass bus., Va., 1929-33; agt. Universal Life & Accident Ins. Co., Dallas, 1934-35, div. mgr., San Antonio, 1935-43, v.p., Dallas, 1935-68, dir., 1943-68; dir. Southwestern Gen. Life Ins. Co., 1969—; columnist Life Insurer mag. Dir. Dallas Area unit Am. Lung Assn., 1958—, pres., 1962-64; bd. dirs. Am. Lung Assn. Tex., S.W. Area YMCA; bd. dirs. Dallas Services for Blind Children, pres., 1967-69; bd. dirs. Met. YMCA, 1956-70, mem. internat. com., 1959—, mem. exec. com., 1969—, chmn. internat. bldg. and capital needs com., 1969—; pres. Dallas Health and Sci. Mus., 1958-60, trustee, 1946—. Recipient Distinguished Service award S.W. Area YMCA, 1967. Mem. Ins. Club (dir.), Lightning Class Assn. (dist. commodore 1959), Phi Beta Kappa, Delta Upsilon. Methodist. Clubs: Corinthian Sailing, Reaugh Art (Dallas). Author: Prospecting—the Fountain of Success, 1946. Home: 3405 Southwestern Blvd Dallas TX 75225 Office: Ross and Akard Sts Dallas TX 75221

BOSSIER, ALBERT LOUIS, JR., shipbuilding co. exec.; b. Gramercy, La., Nov. 29, 1932; s. Albert Louis and Alba Marie (Dufrense) B.; B.S., La. State U., 1954, B.S. in Elec. Engring., 1956; J.D., Loyola U., New Orleans, 1971; m. Jo Ann Decedue, Jan. 11, 1958; children—Albert Louis III, Brian, Donna, Steven. With Avondale Shipyards, Inc., New Orleans, 1957—, gen. plant supt., 1967-69, v.p. prodn. operations, 1969-72, exec. v.p., 1972—, also dir. Chmn., La. Democratic Exec. Com., 1972. Served to 1st lt., Signal Corps, U.S. Army, 1957. Mem. Am. Soc. E.E., Am. Welding Soc., Am., La., Jefferson Parish bar assns. K.C. Clubs: Marine, Propeller (New Orleans). Home: 4904 Henican Pl Metairie LA 70003 Office: PO Box 50280 New Orleans LA 70150

BOST, ARMON HENRY, constrn. equipment exec.; b. Alva, Okla., May 18, 1909; s. Henry A. and Jessie O. (Thatcher) B.; B.S., Okla. State U., 1933; student Indsl. War Coll., 1950; m. Jeanine A. Fabian, Aug. 26, 1931; children—Cheryl (Mrs. Richard Cline), Robert F., James A., Beverly E. (Mrs. Thomas Golden), Merrilee J. Jr. engr. Cities Service Oil Co., East Chicago, Ind., 1931-33, No. Ind. Pub. Service Co., Hammond, 1933-36; accountant Gulf Oil Corp., Tulsa, 1936-41; v.p. Midwestern Engring. and Equipment Co., Inc., Tulsa, 1946-60; pres., 1960—; pres. Midwestern Pipe Line Products Co., 1955—, Midwestern Mfg. Co., 1955—, Rix Equipment Co., San Leandro, Cal., 1971—, Hi-Way Equipment Co., Houston, 1972—, Midwesco Industries, Inc., Tulsa, 1973—. Mem. Tulsa Bd. Edn., 1953-61, pres., 1959-61; active in Community Chest, Boy Scouts Am.; pres. Tulsa Boys Home, 1947-63; mem. adv. bd. YMCA, 1955-62. Bd. regents Okla. State U., Okla. A. and M. Colls., 1969—, now chmn. bd regents. Mem. Okla. Commn. Edn., 1969. Served from 1st lt. to col., AUS, 1941-46, as col., 1950-51. Mem. Am. Gas Assn., Nat. Assn. Corrosion Engrs., Pipe Line Contractors Assn., Distbn. Contractors Assn., Asso. Equipment Distbrs., C. of C., Newcomen Soc. Democrat. Methodist (mem. exec. com. 1969). Mason (Shriner, Jester), Rotarian. Clubs: Tulsa, Summit. Home: 7334 Sleepy Hollow Dr Tulsa OK 74135 Office: 4645 Southwest Blvd Tulsa OK 74101

BOST, ROGER BROWNING, pediatrician, state ofcl.; b. Clarksville, Ark., Oct. 28, 1921; s. Roger Samuel and Fae (Browning) B.; student Okla. State Coll., 1939-40, Coll. of Ozarks, 1941-42; M.D., U. Ark., 1945; m. Kathryn Elizabeth King, June 23, 1944; children—Roger Kingsley, Rebecca, Margaret, Virginia. Intern Santa Rosa Hosp., San Antonio, 1945-46; asst. resident, chief resident pediatrics Duke Hosp., Durham, N.C., 1948-51; practice medicine specializing in pediatrics, Ft. Smith, Ark., 1954-65; instr. pediatrics Duke Sch. Medicine, Durham, N.C., 1950-51, Tulane U. Sch. Medicine, New Orleans, 1951-52, asst. prof. pediatrics, 1952-54; pediatrician Ochsner Clinic and Oschner Found. Hosp., New Orleans, 1951-54; pediatric cons. Crippled Children's Program Ark., 1954-65, Ark. Tb Sanitorium, Booneville, 1954-65, project head start for Ark, Ark. Mental Retardation Planning Project, 1964-66; dir. birth defects center U. Ark. Med. Center, Little Rock, 1965-70, dir. cystic fibrosis center, 1965-70, acting chmn. dept. pediatrics, prof. pediatrics, 1970-71; dir. Ark. Dept. Social and Rehab. Services, Little Rock, 1971—. Coordinator Ark. Regional Med. Program, 1967-69. Served with M.C., USNR, 1946-48. Diplomate Am. Bd. Pediatrics. Fellow Am. Acad. Pediatrics; mem. A.M.A., So. Soc. for Pediatric Research, Central Ark. Pediatric Soc., Ark. Med. Soc. Methodist. Home: 12 Patricia Lane Little Rock AR 72205

BOSTIC, ORAN MONTGOMERY, govt. ofcl.; b. Biscoe, N.C., Nov. 25, 1938; s. Dewey Vann and Myrtle (McDonald) B.; A.A. in Bus. Adminstrn., Anson Tech. Inst., 1973; certificate correctional adminstrn. E. Carolina U., 1973; m. Betty Jane Hardy, Jan. 8, 1965; 1 dau., Rhonda Jane. With N.C. Dept. Corrections, Monroe, 1959—, capt., 1971-72, supt., 1972—. Instr. Montgomery Tech. Inst., 1964—. Pres. Montgomery County Softball League, 1966-71. Served with AUS, 1957-59. Mem. N.C. Law Enforcement Officers Assn. Democrat. Baptist. Home: Route 4 Box 75 Monroe NC 28110 Office: 200 Sutherland Av Monroe NC 28110

BOSWELL, FRED CARLEN, educator; b. Monterey, Tenn., Aug. 20, 1930; s. F.C. and Julia (Speck) B.; B.S., Tenn. Tech. U., 1954; M.S., U. Tenn., 1956; Ph.D., Pa. State U., 1960; m. Marjorie Brown, Sept. 3, 1954; children—Elaine, Julia. Asst. agronomist U. Tenn., Knoxville, 1955-56; asst. agronomist Ga. Expt. Sta., 1956-57; grad. tching. asst. Pa. State U., University Park, 1958-60; asst. soil chemist, asso. prof. soil chemistry and soil fertility U. Ga., Athens, 1960-71, prof., 1971—. Served with AUS, 1951-53. Mem. Am. Soc. Agronomy, Soil Sci. Soc. Am., Internat. Soil Sci. Soc., Sigma Xi, Phi Kappa Phi, Gamma Sigma Delta. Research in soil fertility and chemistry. Home: 1125 Skyline Dr Griffin GA 30223 Office: University of Georgia Georgia Sta Experiment GA 30212

BOSWELL, GARY TAGGART, electronics co. exec.; b. Ft. Worth, Dec. 24, 1937; s. David W. and Marjory (Taggart) B.; B.A., Tex. Christian U., 1958, M.S., 1965; postgrad. San Diego State Coll., 1960-61; m. Margaret Ruth Yelvington, Sept. 8, 1957; children—Michael David, Margaret McQuiston, Susannah Ruth. Scientist U.S. Govt., White Sands (N.M.) Missile Range, 1958-59; research engr. Gen. Dynamics, San Diego, 1959-60; programmer Bell Helicopter, Hurst, Tex., 1960-63; sect. head Collins Radio Co., Dallas, 1963-68; mgr. software devel. Tex. Instruments, Inc., Austin, 1968-72; mem. ASC Marketing, 1973—. Mem. Am. Nat. Fortran Standards Com., 1970—. Mem. Assn. Computing Machinery, Snipe Class Internat. Racing Assn. (internat. rules com.). Republican. Episcopalian. Clubs: Austin Yacht; Austin Sailing. Designer several Fortran Compliers. Winner Western Hemisphere Snipe championship, 1970, also other maj. regattas. Home: 4205 Woodway Dr Austin TX 78731 Office: PO Box 2909 Austin TX 78767

BOSWELL, GEORGE MARION, JR., surgeon; b. Grand Prairie, Tex., May 12, 1920; s. George Marion and Viola (Scarbrough) B.; B.S., Tex. Tech. Coll., 1940; M.D., U. Tex., 1950; m. Veta M. Fuller, Oct. 30, 1958; children—Brianna Fuller, Kama, Maia. Intern, Parkland Hosp., Dallas, 1950-51; resident surgery and orthopaedic surgery Parkland, Baylor U. Med. Center, and Scottish Rite Hosps., Dallas, 1950-55; practice medicine specializing in surgery, Dallas, 1955—; instr. anatomy U. Tex. Southwestern Med. Sch., 1955—; chief surg. service Garland Hosp., 1960-61; attending staff Baylor U. Med. Center and Doctors Hosp., 1955—. Served from ensign to lt. comdr., USNR, 1940-45. Diplomate Am. Bd. Orthopaedic Surgery. Fellow A.C.S.; mem. Tex., Western orthopaedic assns., Am. Acad. Orthopaedic Surgeons, Tex., Dallas County med. assns., Am. Coll. Traumatology, Tex. Soc. Traumatology, Flying Physicians Assn. (pres. Tex. chpt. 1959, nat. dir.), U. Tex. Southwestern Med. Sch. Alumni Assn. (pres.), Phi Chi. Republican. Methodist (chmn. ofcl. bd., charge lay leader, trustee, del. Gen. Conf. Home: 7249 Wabash St Dallas TX 75214 Office: 4849 W Lawther Dr Dallas TX 75218

BOSWELL, JAMES MALCOLM, coll. pres.; b. Cynthiana, Ky., Jan. 26, 1906; s. Joseph and Fannie (Thomason) B.; A.B., Georgetown Coll., 1928, LL.D., 1949; M.A., U. Ky., 1931, postgrad. in Math., summers 1937, 38, 40, 41, 1938-39, U. Mich., summer 1930; m. Mary Susan Dudley, Jan. 23, 1932; children—James Malcolm, Frances Louise (Mrs. Hershel Tipton). Instr. math. Georgetown Coll., 1928-31, U. Ky., 1938-39; with Cumberland Coll., Williamsburg, Ky., 1931-38, 40-42, 45—, dean adminstrn., 1945, acting pres., 1946-47, pres., 1947—. Served from lt. to lt. comdr. USNR, 1942-45. Mem. Am. Math. Assn., Ky. Assn. Colls. and Secondary Schs. (past v.p.), So. Assn. Bapt. Colls (past pres.), So. Assn. Jr. Colls. (past pres.). Baptist. Rotarian. Home: 804 Main St Williamsburg KY 40769

BOSWELL, JOHN HOWARD, lawyer; b. Houston, Mar. 22, 1932; s. Henry Oliver and Opal Everest (Wineberg) B.; B.B.A., U. Houston, 1954, J.D., 1963; m. Sharon Lee Ueckert, Dec. 19, 1959; children—John Brooke, Mark Richard. Admitted to Tex. bar, 1963; sr. partner Boswell, O'Toole, Davis & Pickering, Houston, 1962—. Dir. Union Bank, Houston, 1969—; adv. dir. Am. Bank & Trust Co., Houston, 1966—. Served with USNR, 1955-58. Mem. Am., Tex., Houston bar assns., Tex. Assn. Def. Counsel, Sigma Nu, Delta Theta Phi. Home: 10811 Pine Bayou Houston TX 77024 Office: 2400 Two Shell Plaza Houston TX 77002

BOTSKO, GEORGE EDWARD, newspaper exec.; b. Ambridge, Pa., Dec. 14, 1931; s. Joseph Stephen and Mary (Zilka) B.; B.S. in Indsl. Engring., Geneva Coll., 1958; m. Marjorie R. Miller, Sept. 1, 1955; children—Roy E., Nancy R., Jennifer L. Printer, Daily Citizen, Ambridge, 1949-58; composing foreman Beaver County Times, Beaver, Pa., 1958-61; prodn. mgr. South Dade News Leader, Homestead, Fla., 1961-68, gen. mgr., 1968—; v.p., dir. Homestead News Inc. Bd. dirs. Homestead Little League, 1970—, pres., 1971-72. Served with AUS, 1952-54. Mem. Homestead C. of C. (v.p. 1970-72). Republican. Methodist (ofcl. bd. 1966-67). Rotarian. Club: Civitan (sec. 1964-65) (Homestead, Fla.). Home: 19201 SW 312th St Homestead FL 33030 Office: 15-17 NE 1st Rd Homestead FL 33030

BOTTOMLEY, RICHARD HAROLD, oncologist; b. Arkansas City, Kan., Nov. 24, 1933; s. Harold and Frances Eva (Herbert) B.; B.S. in Zoology, U. Okla., 1954; M.D., U. Okla. Sch. Medicine, 1958; m. Sylvia Stakle, June 5, 1958; children—Astrid Elizabeth, Ian Phillip. Intern, U. Utah Coll. Medicine, Salt Lake City, 1958-59; resident internal medicine U. Okla. Sch. Medicine, Oklahoma City, 1959-61, instr., 1964-67, asst. prof., 1967-71, asst. prof. research biochemistry, 1965-68, asso. prof. research biochemistry, 1968—, asso. prof. medicine, 1971—, chief oncology div. dept. medicine, 1972—; fellow oncology McArdle Meml. Lab., Madison, Wis., 1961-62, Okla. Med. Research Found. Oklahoma City, 1962-63; sr. investigator cancer sect. Okla. Med. Research Found., Oklahoma City, 1964-65, asst. head cancer sect., 1965-71, asso. mem., 1965—; mem. staff various hosps. Recipient Roche award, 1956. Diplomate Am. Bd. Internal Medicine. Fellow A.C.P.; mem. Central Soc. Clin. Research, Am. Assn. Cancer Research, So. Soc. Clin. Research, Am. Soc. Clin. Oncology, N.Y. Acad. Sci., Am. Soc. Hematology, Phi Beta Kappa. Home: 1325 NE 54th St Oklahoma City OK 73111 Office: 825 NE 13th St Oklahoma City OK 73104

BOTTOMS, CHARLES BENSON, JR., food co. exec.; b. Atlanta, Nov. 11, 1928; s. Charles Benson and Wylena Claire (Hutchinson) B.; B.S., Ga. Inst. Tech., 1950, Ala. Poly. Inst., 1950; M.A., Randolph Coll., 1951, M.B.A., 1952; Ph.D., Hamilton State U., 1953; m. Sandra Hardin, July 8, 1954; children—Charles Benson III, Andrea Hardin. With Coca Cola U.S.A., Atlanta, 1954—, nat. merchandising mgr., 1974—. Pres. McClatchey Sch. P.T.A., Atlanta, 1968-69; chmn. Eagle bd. rev. Atlanta Area council Boy Scouts Am., 1973-74. Bd. dirs. YMCA, 1966-69, Ga. Land Devel. Assn., 1969-73; trustee Mt. Vernon Christian Acad., 1974—. Served to 1st lt. AUS, 1952-53. Recipient Silver Beaver award Boy Scouts Am., 1973. Mem. Am. Mgmt. Assn., Tenn. Squires, Sales Promotion Execs. Assn., Sigma Alpha Epsilon Alumni Assn. (nat. employment bd.), Epsilon Delta Chi, Alpha Phi Omega, Sigma Alpha Epsilon. Home: 4174 McClatchey Circle Atlanta GA 30342 Office: PO Box 1734 Atlanta GA 30301

BOTTOMS, WILLIAM RALPH, physician; b. nr. Cumming, Ga., Jan. 14, 1914; s. George Washington and Maude Emily (Hughes) B.; student North Ga. Coll., 1933-34, 39; B.A. cum laude, Mercer U., 1955; M.D., Med. Coll. Ga., 1959; m. Mildred Mae Heard, May 21, 1935; children—Nancy (Mrs. Donald Ray Jordan), Carol (Mrs. Robert Warren Richter), William Ralph, Jr. Tchr. Forsyth County (Ga.) Sch., 1935-41; methods engr. Sears Roebuck & Co., Atlanta, 1941-43; indsl. engring. dept. Bell Aircraft Corp., Marietta, Ga., 1943-44; indsl. engr. Firestone Tire and Rubber Co., Atlanta, 1944-45; head indsl. engring. dept. Chevrolet plant Gen. Motors Corp., Atlanta, 1945-53; ordained to Ministry Bapt. Ch., 1954; pastor Camak (Ga.) Bapt. Ch., 1953, Haddock (Ga.) Bapt. Ch., 1954-55; intern Midstate Bapt. Hosp., Nashville, 1959-60; practice medicine specializing in family practice, Cumming, Ga., 1960-70, Blairsville, Ga., 1970-72; chief of staff Union Gen. Hosp., Blairsville, 71—. Med. examiner Union County, 1970—. Med. v.p. Union County Cancer Fund, 1970—; mem. Ga. Heart Assn. Founder Wm. Ralph Bottoms Missionary Ednl. Fund. Mem. A.M.A., Med. Assn. Ga., Hall County, 9th Dist. med. assns., Am. Acad. Family Practice. Democrat. Baptist. Kiwanian. Address: 601 US Hwy 19N Cummings GA 30130

BOUCHARD, ANDRÉ, pipe coating co. exec.; b. Austin, Tex., Nov. 15, 1936; s. Harry Alfred and Hazel (Hancock) B.; B.B.A. with honors, U. Tex., 1960, M.B.A., 1963; m. Betty Ann Moore, Aug. 29, 1959; children—Cyrene Michelle, Andre Charles. Staff accountant Haskins & Sells, Houston, 1963-67, mgmt. cons., Houston, Chgo., 1967-70; treas. Geocom, Inc., Houston, 1970-71; v.p. finance Surfcote, Inc., 1971-72, Surfcote Pipe Coating Inc., Houston, 1972—. Pres., Thornwood Sch. P.T.A., Houston, 1973—. Served as lt. AUS, 1960-62. C.P.A., Tex. Mem. Houston C. of C., Tex. Soc. C.P.A.'s, Am. Inst. C.P.A.'s, Planning Execs. Inst. (pres. Houston chpt. 1971-72), U. Tex. Ex-Students Assn. (life) U. Tex. Grad. Bus. Sch. Club, U. Tex. T Assn., Beta Gamma Sigma. Office: 2929 Richmond Av Houston TX 77006

BOUDREAUX, BERNARD EDWARD, JR., lawyer; b. Berwick, La., May 20, 1937; s. B. Edward and Martha (Chapron) B.; B.A., U. Southwestern La., 1960; LL.B., La. State U., 1961; m. Patricia Fitzgerald, Aug. 26, 1961; children—Cynthia Leigh, Jennifer Kay, Bernard Edward III. Admitted to La. bar, 1961; asso. firm M.J. McNulty, Jr., Franklin, La., 1961, Bauer, Darnall, Fleming & McNulty, Franklin, 1964-67; partner firm Bauer, Darnall, McNulty & Boudreaux, Franklin, 1967—; asst. dist. atty. 16th Jud. Dist. La., 1966—; atty. City of Franklin, 1968—. Dir., Franklin Nursing Center, Inc. (La.), Louisa Sugar Coop, Inc., J.C.B. Devel. Corp., Inc., Teche Corp., Inc., Bayou Sale Corp., Inc. (all Franklin). Served to capt., Judge Adv. Gen's Corps, USAF, 1961-64. Mem. Am., La. State bar assns., Franklin C. of C. (v.p. 1966-68), Kappa Sigma, Gamma Eta Gamma. Rotarian. Home: 117 Eastwood Dr Franklin LA 70538 Office: Lawless Bldg Franklin LA 70538

BOUDREAUX, EDMOND, univ. adminstr.; b. Carencro, La., Oct. 25, 1930; s. Walter and Evelia (Richard) B.; B.S., La. State U., 1953, M.S., 1966, postgrad., 1969—; postgrad. U. Tenn., 1963, U.Chgo., 1964; m. Bonnie Ruth Hunter, June 12, 1953; children—Amy, Edmond Steven, Walter Barry, Glenn Robert, Madelyn Kay. Farm mgr. Greenwell Spring (La.) Hosp., 1954-56; personnel technician La. Dept. Civil Service, Baton Rouge, 1956-57; coordinator short courses and confs. La. State U., Baton Rouge, 1957—. Lectr., U. Ala. Med. Sch., Birmingham, 1971-72; vis. prof. So. U., Baton Rouge, i967-68; co-owner Nat. Edn. and Exam. Devel. Service, Shreveport, La., 1970—; chmn. La. Bd. Examiners for Nursing Home Adminstrs., 1970, 71, 74, vice chmn., 1973; cons. nursing home adminstrn. Mem. Nat. Assn. Bds. Examiners Nursing Home Adminstrs. (chmn. edn. com. 1970-72), Soc. Advancement Mgmt. (pres. Baton Rouge chpt. 1961-62, gov. 1962-63), Royal Soc. Health (Eng.). Club: Civitan Internat. Contbr. articles to profl. jours. Home: Route 7 Box 202 Gibben Rd Baton Rouge LA 70807 Office: PO Box 21341 Louisiana State Univ Station Baton Rouge LA 70803

BOUDREAUX, EDWARD ANTHONY, educator; b. New Orleans, Oct. 30, 1933; s. Frank Anthony and Margurite Ann (Robert) B.; B.S., Loyola at New Orleans, 1956; M.S., Tulane, 1959, Ph.D., 1962; m. Carolyn Rose Amato, Feb. 19, 1955; children—Edward Anthony, Margaret, Yvette, Robert. Research scientist Kalvar Corp., New Orleans, 1956-62, cons., 1962-64; asst. prof. chemistry La. State U., New Orleans, 1962-64, asso. prof., 1964—. Cons., U.S. Dept. Agr., New Orleans, 1968-70. Treas., Cub Scouts, New Orleans, 1963-72. Served to capt., Signal Corps, AUS, 1962-63. Fulbright fellow, 1970-71; recipient research grants Petroleum Research Fund, 1964-66, Greater New Orleans Cancer Assn., i966, NSF, 1967. Fellow Chem. Soc. London; mem. Am. Chem. Soc., Sigma Xi. Author: Noble-Gas Compounds, 1963; Modern Aspects of Diffuse Reflectance Spectroscopy, 1968. Editor: Theory, Principles and Application of Magnetochemistry, 3 vols., 1973; editorial adv. bd. Inorganica Chimica Acta, 1967, Inorganica Chimica Acta Revs., 1967. Contbr. profl. jours. Home: 432 12th St New Orleans LA 70124

BOUDREAUX, WARREN LOUIS, bishop; b. Berwick, La., Jan. 25, 1918; s. Alphonse Louis and Loretta Marie (Senac) B.; student St. Joseph's Sem., Benedict, La., 1931-36; student Notre Dame Sem., New Orleans, 1937, 42, LL.D., 1963; student Grand Sem. de St. Sulpice, Paris, France, 1938-39; J.C.D., Catholic U. Am., 1946; D.D., Pope John XXIII, 1962. Ordained priest Roman Catholic Ch., 1942; asst. pastor, Crowley, La., 1942-43; vice chancellor Diocese Lafayette, La., 1946-54, officialis, 1949-54; pastor St. Peter's Ch., New Iberia, La., 1954-71; vicar gen. Diocese Lafayette, 1957-71, also diocesan consultor; dean New Iberia Deanery, 1954-71; apptd. aux. bishop Diocese of Lafayette, 1962, bishop Diocese of Beaumont (Tex.), 1971—. Mem. Bishops Com. on Liturgy, Nat. Conf. of Catholic Bishops, 1966-70, mem. Louvain com., 1971—; mem. U.S. Cath. Conf. Adv. Council, 1969—; chmn. liaison com. Nat. Conf. Cath. Bishops-U.S. Cath. Conf., 1972—. Vice pres. S.W. La. Register Newspaper, 1957—. Mem. New Iberia Community Relations Council, 1963—. Bd. dirs. Iberia Paris Youth Home, Consolata Home for Aged, New Iberia, Southwest Ednl. Devel. Lab. Pres. Archdiocesan Conf. Chancery Ofcls., Archdiocese New Orleans, 1950-51, bd. dirs., 1952-55. Address: 703 Archie St Beaumont TX 77701

BOUGHTON, JAMES KENNETH, tire and rubber co. exec.; b. Akron, O., Mar. 22, 1922; s. James Arthur and Louise (Smith) B.; student U. Akron, 1940-42; B.S. in Elec. Engring., Ill. Inst. Tech., 1944; M.S., Lamar Coll. Tech., 1968; m. Evelyn Frances Robottom, Feb. 10, 1945; children—Steven Kent, Susan Lynn, Lisa Jean, Jeffrey Leigh. With Goodyear Tire and Rubber Co., 1942—, machine designer, Akron, 1951, atomic supt. elec. and instrument maintenance, 1953-60, mgr. engring., Beaumont, Tex., 1960—. Instr. U. Akron, 1947-49. Mem. cultural affairs com. Lamar U., 1968—; active Beaumont Symphony, Lamar Philharmonic Orch. Served to lt. comdr. USNR, 1942-45, 51-53; PTO. Registered profl. engr., Ohio. Mem. I.E.E.E., Beaumont C. of C. Republican. Episcopalian (sr. warden 1970-71). Club: Pinewood Country (Pinewood Estates, Tex.). Patentee tire bldg. machines, prodn. counters and controls. Home: Route 1 Box 260 Beaumont TX 77706 Office: Box 3687 Beaumont TX 77704

BOULMAY, GARDNER CASTANEDO, motel exec.; b. New Orleans, Dec. 15, 1916; s. Lionel Soniat and Isabell Marie (Castanedo) B.; grad. high sch.; m. Leanora Ann Tedesco, July 1, 1942; children—Gardner Francis, Gregory, Geoffrey, Gerald, Grant, Gigi. Owner, Boulmay's Service Sta., New Orleans, 1935-39; parts mgr. Bert Wells Nash Co., New Orleans, 1939-42; owner Gentilly Appliance Co., New Orleans, 1943-45; self-employed as gen. contractor, 1945-63; mgr., owner Vieux Carre Motor Lodge, New Orleans, 1964—. Mem. Vieux Carre Action Assn. Bd., 1969-72, Vieux Carre Property Owners Bd., 1968-72, Greater New Orleans Tourist and Conv. Bd., 1971-72, New Orleans Food Fest Bd., 1969-71; mem. Super Bowl Task Force, 1970-72. Bd. dirs. La. Tb and Respiratory Disease Assn. Served with AUS, 1942-43. Mem. Greater New Orleans Hotel Motel Assn. (chmn. bd. 1972). Clubs: Krewe of Bacchus (New Orleans); Country (Covington, La.). Home: 187 Country Club Dr Covington LA 70433 Office: 920 N Rampart St New Orleans LA 70116

BOUNDS, LAURENCE HAROLD, gas co. exec.; b. Newcastle, Wyo., Feb. 15, 1922; s. James Henry and Blanche Agnes (McKay) B.; B.S., Simpson Coll., 1943; postgrad. Columbia, 1943; m. Dorothy May Bostrom, Nov. 20, 1965. With comptroller dept. Kemper Ins., Chgo., 1947-51; sec.-treas. W & J Constrn. Co., 1951-64; auditor, Roosevelt Hotel, Jacksonville, Fla., 1964-66; v.p., sec., dir. Western Natural Gas Co., Jacksonville, 1966—. Served to lt. USNR, 1942-46. Mem. Adminstrv. Mgmt. Soc. (asst. treas. 1971), Navy League, Alpha Tau Omega. Episcopalian. Club: Willow Lakes Golf and Country. Home: 1929 Constant Dr Jacksonville FL 32210 Office: 2960 Strickland St Jacksonville FL 32205

BOUNDS, SAM, JR., mech. engr.; b. Florence, Ala., June 23, 1924; s. Sam and Pearl (Huepel) B.; B.M.E., Auburn U., 1948; postgrad. U. Houston, 1949-50, U. Cal. at Los Angeles, 1962, U. Tex. extension, 1952; m. Julia Dixon, Oct. 27, 1951; children—Molly, Beverly, Sarah, Timothy Dixon. Engr. Stanolind Oil & Gas Co., Okla. and Tex., 1948-52, Carter Oil Co., Okla, 1952-54; designer Douglas Aircraft Co., Tulsa, 1954-60; mech. engr. U.S. Army Missile Command, Redstone Arsenal, Ala., 1960—. Served AUS, 1943-45. Decorated Purple Heart. Registered profl. engr. Ala. Mem. Am. Soc. M.E., Am. Legion, Pi Tau Sigma, Tau Beta Pi. Presbyn. (elder 1953, deacon 1968). Club: Burningtree Country. Home: 2507 College St SE Decatur AL 35601 Office: Bldg 5400 Redstone Arsenal AL 35809

BOUOREAUX, HENRY BRUCE, educator; b. Scott, La., Nov. 12, 1914; s. Joseph and Emelie (Broussard) B.; B.S., U. S.W. La., 1936; M.S., La. State U., 1939, Ph.D., 1946; m. Rose Mae Guidroz, Aug. 12, 1941; 1 son, John Philip. Asst. prof. U. S.W. La., Lafayette, 1936-47; mem. faculty La. State U., Baton Rouge, 1947—, asso. prof. entomology, 1952-60, prof., 1960—. Fellow A.A.A.S.; mem. Entomol. Soc. Am., La. Entomol. Soc., Assn. S.E. Biologists, La. Acad. Sci., Acarological Soc. Am. (1st pres. 1971-73), Sigma Xi, Phi Kappa Phi. Contbr. articles to profl. jours. Research in aphid and mite taxonomy, biology and morphology. Home: 555 Ursuline Dr Baton Rouge LA 70808

BOURASSA, RONALD RAY, educator; b. Oklahoma City, Sept. 7, 1940; s. Raymond Andrew and Mildred Helen (Rawlings) B.; B.A., Rice U., 1962; M.S., U. Ill. at Urbana, 1964, Ph.D. in Physics, 1967; m. Patricia Suzanne Hayes, June 9, 1962; children—Leslie Ann, Amy Lynn, Brevin Andrew. Sr. Research physicist Battelle-Northwest, Richland, Wash., 1967-68; asst. prof. physics U. Okla. at Norman, 1968-73, asso. prof, physics, 1973—. Coordinator Common Cause, Okla. 4th Congl. Dist., 1972—. Chmn. precinct Democratic Party, 1970—. Mem. Am. Phys. Soc., Sigma Xi. Presbyn. (elder). Contbr. articles to profl. jours. Home: 544 Shawnee St Norman OK 73069

BOURGOYNE, JULIOUS ROY, dentist; b. Beaumont, Tex., Nov. 13, 1914; s. Rene Jules and Ora Lee (Norton) B.; student Tulane U., 1933-34; B.S., Sam Houston Coll., 1936; D.D.S., Loyola U., New Orleans, 1941; m. Helen Ruth Bass, Mar. 15, 1947; children—Ruth Elaine, Lisa Helen, Rene Stephen, Laura Jean. Intern oral surgery Charity Hosp., New Orleans, 1941-42, resident, 1942-44; fellow in pathology Tufts Coll. Dental Sch., Boston, 1944; chief div. oral surgery and anesthesia U. Tenn. Coll. Dentistry, Memphis, 1944-59; individual practice oral surgery, Memphis, 1947—; mem. staff Memphis hosps. Cons. oral surgery VA, USPHS hosps., Memphis, U.S. Naval Air Sta. Hosp., Millington; chmn. Tenn. Hosp. Dental Service Com. Diplomate Am. Bd. Oral Surgery. Mem. Am. Soc. Oral Surgeons, Am. Dental Assn., Memphis Dental Soc. (pres. 1973-74), Southeastern Soc. Oral Surgeons, Pierre Fauchard Acad., Dean Odontol. Soc. (charter), Delta Sigma Delta, Omicron Kappa Upsilon. Baptist. Club: Chickasaw Country (Memphis). Author: Surgery of the Mouth and Jaws, 1949, Oral Cancer, 1954; (with Nevin) Conduction, Infiltration and General Anesthesia in Dentistry, 1959, also articles. Home: 310 S Perkins Rd Memphis TN 38117 Office: 1422 Lamar Av Memphis TN 38104

BOURNE, GEOFFREY HOWARD, educator; b. Perth, Western Australia, Nov. 17, 1909; s. Walter Howard and Mary Ann (Mellon) B.; B.S. (hon.), U. Western Australia, 1931, M.S., 1932, D.Sc., 1935; Dr. Phil., Oxford (Eng.) U., 1943; m. Gwen Jones, Dec. 31, 1935 (div. Feb. 1964); children—Peter, Mervyn; m. 2d, Maria Nelly Golarz, Oct. 31, 1964. Biologist Australian Inst. Anatomy, Canberra, 1934-36; biochemist adv. council on nutrition Commonwealth of Australia, 1936-38; Beit Meml. fellow for med. research Oxford (Eng.) U., 1938-41, dept. demonstrator in physiology, 1938-43; Machenzie-Mackinnon research fellow Royal Coll. Surgeons, Royal Coll. Physicians, 1941-43; maj. in charge research and devel. Spl. Forces, S.E. Asia, biology and medicine, Eng., 1943-45; lt. col. and nutritional adv. Brit. Mil. Adminstrn., Malaya, 1945-46; reader histology U. London, 1947-57; chmn. dept. anatomy Emory U., Atlanta, 1957-62, dir. Yerkes Regional Primate Research Center, 1962—. Served to lt. col. Brit. Army, 1943. Fellow Royal Soc. Medicine, Zool. Soc. London, Brit. Interplanetary Soc., Inst. Biology, Am. Gerontological Soc.; mem. Sigma Xi. Author or editor numerous books including: Structure and Function of Muscle, 1963, 2d edit., 1972; Biochemistry and Physiology of Bone, 1956, 2d edit., 1972; Muscular Dystrophy in Man and Animals, 1963. Editor: Internat. Rev. of Cytology, 1950—, World Rev. of Nutrition and Dietetics, 1959—, Structure and Function of Nervous Tissue, 1969, Vols. 4-6, 1972; The Ape People, 1971; Primates in Biomedical Research, 1972; Primate Odyssey, 1974. Home: 849 Lullwater Pkwy Atlanta GA 30307 Office: Yerkes Regional Primate Center Emory Univ Atlanta GA 30322

BOUSQUET, THOMAS GOURRIER, lawyer; b. Houston, Oct. 18, 1934; s. John A. and Ophelia Ann (Tucker) B.; B.A., U. Tex. at Austin, 1956, J.D., 1958; m. Katherine Lynn Cummings, Aug. 22, 1959 (div. Feb. 1970); children—Thomas Gourrier, Robert Brant, Katherine Lynn; m. 2d, Duke Ellen Taylor, Nov. 27, 1970 (div. Feb. 1973). Admitted to Tex. bar, 1958, U.S. Supreme Ct. bar, 1971; practiced in Houston, 1958—; partner firm Wandel, Bousquet, McPherson and Berke; dir. Electronic Data Labs., Inc., Houston, Paloma Devel. Co., Houston, Figure World Internat., Houston. Served to maj. USAF, 1958-64; maj. Res. Mem. Houston Bar Assn. (sec. 1960, v.p. 1961), Lawyers Soc. Houston (pres. 1973), Tex. Assn. Def. Counsel, Order Stars and Bars, S.A.R. (chancellor 1966), Sons Confederate Vets, Houston Heritage Soc., Spain and Tex. Soc., Phi Alpha Delta. Clubs: Cadre, Houston. Author: Become an Effective Player at Casino Craps, 1973. Home: 5330 Beverly Hill Lane Houston TX 77027 Office: Suite 745 1010 Louisiana St Houston TX 77002

BOUTALL, JOHN CHARLES, judge; b. Jefferson Parish, La., Sept. 28, 1920; s. Charles A. and Lillian (Bruning) B.; B.A., Tulane U., 1940, LL.B., 1946; m. Marilyn Margaret Bartol, Mar. 31, 1945; children—Richard John, Katherine E., William C., Charles A. Admitted to La. bar, 1946; practiced in Jefferson Parish, 1946-55; judge 24th Jud. Dist. Ct., Jefferson Parish, 1955-70, Ct. Appeals, 4th Circuit La., New Orleans, 1970—. Past mem. Jud. Council, State of La. Served to lt. USNR, 1942-45. Mem. La., Jefferson Parish bar assns., La., Am. Judicature Soc., Internat. Acad. Law and Sci., Dist. Judges Assn. (pres.). Lion. Home: 1521 Lakeshore Dr Metairie LA 70005 Office: 210 Civil Courts Bldg 421 Loyola Av New Orleans LA 70112

BOUVIER, HELEN SCHAEFER (MRS. JOHN A. BOUVIER, JR.), leasing co. exec.; b. McAlester, Okla., Sept. 11, 1910; d. William John and Anna (Perrin) Schaefer; student U. Fla., 1928-29, Northwestern U., 1929-30; m. John A. Bouvier, Jr., June 6, 1928; children—Helen Elizabeth (Mrs. William Spencer), John A. III, Thomas R. Sec., Sunset Rock & Sand Co., Miami, Fla., 1939-45, Coral Rock & San Co., 1945-48; now chmn. Nat. Leasing, Inc.; pres., dir. Knight Manor, Inc., Miami, Miami Service Co., South Central Manor Inc. West Kingsway, Inc., Miami, East Kingsway, Inc., Miami, South Kingsway, Inc., Miami, Fiftieth St. Heights, Inc., Miami, Karen Garden, Inc. Ft. Lauderway, Inc., Fiftieth St. Heights, Inc., Miami and N.Y.C.; also mgmt; cons., Miami, N.Y.C., 1945—. Dir., v.p. Ella R. Bouvier Found. Presbyn. (pres. womens aux., pres. womens aux. synod). Clubs: Corinthian (Syracuse, N.Y.); Skaneateles (N.Y.) Country; Riveria County (Coral Gables, Fla.), (Surfside, Fla.); Beach Colony (Miami Bleach, Fla.). Home: 2756 NE 17th St Fort Lauderdale FL 33305 Office: Blowing Rock NC also 6888 NW 7th Av Miami FL 33150

BOUVIER, JOHN ANDRE, JR., lawyer, corp. exec.; b. nr. Ocala, Fla., May 16, 1903; s. John Andre and Ella (Richardson) B.; student Davidson Coll., 1922-24; A.B., U. Fla., 1926, LL.B., 1929; M.B.A., Northwestern U., 1930; m. Helen A. Schaefer, June 6, 1928; children—Helen Elizabeth (Mrs. William Spencer), John Andre III, Thomas Richardson. Admitted to Fla. bar, 1929, pvt. practice, Gainesville, 1929, Miami, 1930—, specialist corp., real estate and probate law, cons. atty.; gen. counsel Patterson and Maloney. attys. chmn. exec. com. Permutit Co.; chmn. bd. Prosperity Co. div. vice chmn. bd. Ward Industries Corp., 1958; chmn. bd., pres. Pantex Mfg. Corp., 1958—, Nat. Leasing Inc., Miami; chmn. bd. Knaust Bros., Inc., K-B Products Corp., Iron Mountain Atomic Storage Vaults, Inc., Miami Service Co., Knight Manor 1, Inc., South Central Manor, Inc.; sec. West Kingsway, Inc., East Kingsway, Inc., South Kingsway, Inc., Fiftieth Street Hts., Inc., Dade Constrn. Co., Farm Industries, Inc., Iron Mountain Atomic Storage Vaults, Inc. (all Miami), Karen Club Apt. Hotel, Ft. Lauderdale; pres. Knaust Bros., Inc., West Coxsackie, N.Y., 1960-64, chmn., 1964—; pres. K-B Products Corp., Hudson, N.Y., 1960-61, chmn., 1964—; dir. Ocean First Nat. Bank, Farquhar Machinery Co., Landmark Banking Corp. Commr. Dade County council Boy Scouts Am.; chmn. Malecon Com. Dade County; dir. Syracuse Govtl. Research Bur., Inc.; mem. Nat. Def. Exec. Res. planning council Zoning Bd. Miami; chmn. Coxsackie-Athens Area Redev. Com.; vice chmn. Nat. Parkinson Found. Trustee Parkinson Rehab., Diagnostic and Research Inst., Windham Coll.; adv. bd. Fla. Meml. Coll.; bd. dirs. Boys Club Broward; pres., dir. Ella R. Bouvier Found. Mem. Internat. Platform Assn. N.A.M. (conservation renewable natural resources com.) Mfrs. Assn. Syracuse (dir.), Miami, Auburn civic music assns. Cayuga Mus. History and Art, Am. Acad. Polit. Sci., Am. Judicature Soc., Am., Fla., Broward County, Dade County bar associations, Chamber of Commerce, Sigma Chi. Presbyn. (chmn. bd. trustees). Mason (Shriner), Elk, Rotarian. Clubs: Miami Beach Rod and Reel, Surf, Riveria Country, Skaneateles Country; Ponte Verde; Washington Lawyers; Civitan (dir.). Author monographs, newspaper articles in field. Home: 2756 NE 17th St Fort Lauderdale FL 33305 also Box 14 Climax NY 12042 Office: 6888 NW 7th Av Miami FL 33150 also Kenann Bldg Fort Lauderdale FL 33306 also Blowing Rock NC 28605

BOVEY, RODNEY WILLIAM, govt. ofcl.; b. Craigmont, Ida., July 17, 1934; s. William August and Elnora Lucile (Click) B.; B.S. (Sears Roebuck scholar), U. Ida., 1956, M.S., 1959; Ph.D., U. Neb., 1964; m. Shirley E. Deffenbaugh, Mar. 3, 1956; children—Seth, Todd, Shawn, Cary. Research fellow U. Ida., 1956-59; instr. U. Neb., 1959-64; research agronomist U.S. Dept. Agr., Tex. A. and M. U., College Station, 1964-67, project leader Agr. Research Service, 1968-72, research leader, 1972—, project leader Fed. Expt. Sta., Mayaguez, P.R., 1967-68. Mem. Weed Sci. Soc. Am., So. Weed Sci. Soc., Tex. Weed Workers Conf. (pres. 1973—), Sigma Xi. Methodist (past supt. youth div., bd. ofls., pastor-parish relations com. 1972—, nominations com. 1973—; commr. on missions, 1973—). Contbr. numerous articles to profl. jours. Home: 1014 Walton Dr College Station TX 77840 Office: US Dept Agr Tex A and M U College Station TX 77843

BOVIS, HENRY EUGENE, govt. ofcl.; b. Kenansville, Fla., Mar. 31, 1928; s. Henry P. and Vassie Curtis (Wright) B.; B.A. cum laude, U. Fla., 1948, M.A., 1950; certificats d' etudes francaises, ler et 2e degres, U. Grenoble, France, 1951; Ph.D., Am. U., 1968; m. Beatrice Louise Wilfong, June 24, 1958; 1 son, Henry Eugene. Arabic lang. and area trainee U.S. Fgn. Service, Beirut, 1953-54; research analyst Dept. State, 1954-57, Hebrew lang. trainee U. Pa., 1957-58, 2d sec. Am. embassy Tel Aviv, 1958-60, consul, Haifa, 1960-63, polit./econ. officer Dept. State, 1963-69, 2d sec. U.S. interests sect. Spanish embassy, Cairo, 1969-71; vis. lectr., asst. prof. polit. sci. USAF Acad., 1971-73; coordinator polit. studies Dept. State Fgn. Service Inst., Washington, 1973—. Sec. sch. bd. Cairo (Egypt) Am. Coll., 1970-71; mem. sch. bd. Schutz Sch., Alexandria, Egypt, 1969-71. Rotary Found. fellow, 1950-51. Mem. Internat. Studies Assn., Am. Fgn. Service Assn., Am. Polit. Sci. Assn., Middle East Studies Assn., Middle East Inst., Phi Beta Kappa. Author: The Jerusalem Question, 1971. Home: 10461 Courthouse Dr Fairfax VA 22030 Office: Fgn Service Inst Dept State Washington DC 20520

BOW, RUSSELL LEON, clergyman; b. Bow, Ky., Jan. 23, 1925; s. Stephen Tyler and Lula (King) B.; A.A., Lindsey Wilson Coll., 1944; student Union Coll., 1945-46; A.B., Ky. Wesleyan Coll., 1949; B.D., Emory U., 1952; m. Roxie Marie Minton, Sept. 15, 1945; children—Michael, Beverly. Ordained to ministry Methodist Ch., 1952; asst. pastor Settle Meml. Meth. Ch., Owensboro, Ky., 1952-56; pastor, Woodlawn Meth. Ch., Owensboro, 1956-61, Preston Hwy. Meth. Ch., Louisville, 1961-67, United Meth. Temple, Russellville, Ky., 1967-71, Ogden Meml. United Meth. Ch., Princeton, Ky., 1971—. Mem. bd. finance and adminstrn. Louisville conf. United Meth. Ch. Bd. dirs. Welsey Found., U. Ky. Mason. Club: Civitan (pres. 1954) (Owensboro). Home: 304 Hospital Dr Princeton KY 42445 Office: W Main at Cave Sts Princeton KY 42445

BOWDEN, GEORGE EDWIN, govt. ofcl.; b. Norfolk, Va., July 26, 1924; s. Lemuel and Mary Gilbert (Broughton) B.; B.S., Duke, 1945; M.S., Cornell U., 1948; m. Grace Louise Scovill, June 16, 1951; children—George Edwin III, Ellen Evangeline, Paul Lemuel. Devel. engr. Gen. Electric Co., Schenectady, 1951-53; sr. mathematician Vitro Corp., Eglin AFB, Fla., 1953-55; supr. applied math. United Aircraft Co., East Hartford, Conn., 1957-58; scientist Booz-Allen Applied Research, Bethesda, Md., 1959-62; sr. engring. specialist Philco-Ford Corp., Arlington, Va., 1963-68; mem. profl. staff Center for Naval Analyses, Arlington, 1968-70; operations research analyst U.S. Army, Washington, 1971—. Tchr. grad. extension courses U. Fla., 1954-55; cons., 1970-71. Fellow A.A.A.S.; mem. Operations Research Soc. Am., Math. Assn. Am., Am. Ordnance Assn. (dir. 1954-55), Forty-Plus of Washington (sr.), Pi Mu Epsilon, Sigma Pi Sigma. Patentee missile homing guidance system. Home: 5907 Greenlawn Dr Bethesda MD 20014 Office: Hdqrs Dept of Army Washington DC 20314

BOWDEN, OSSIE HANSON, corp. exec.; b. Cullman, Ala., Jan 1, 1918; s. Richard E. and Stella (Allgood) B.; grad. with honors Auburn U., 1941; m. Julia Batastini, Dec. 20, 1941; 1 dau., Sara Beatrice. County agt. Ala. Agrl. Extension Service, 1941-44; farm products marketing agt. T.C.I. div. U.S. Steel Corp., Birmingham, Ala., 1944-54; gen. mgr. Farmers Marketing and Exchange Assn., Montgomery, Ala., 1954-60; v.p. Gold Kist, Inc. (formerly Cotton Producers Assn.), Atlanta, 1960—. Bd. govs. St. Bernard Coll.; bd. dirs. Asso. Coops., Ala. Farmers Coop.; pres. Ga. Council of Farmers Coop. Mem. Atlanta C. of C., Am. Inst. Coops. (trustee), Ga. Bus. and Industry Assn. (bd. govs.), Internat. Platform Assn., Nat. Coop. Council, Phi Kappa Phi, Gamma Sigma Delta, Kappa Delta Phi. Baptist. Mason. Club: Chattahoochee Plantation. Home: 4686 Brinkley Lane NE Atlanta GA 30342 Office: 3348 Peachtree Rd NE Atlanta GA 30326

BOWDEN, WILLIAM ANTON, JR., architect; b. Memphis, Feb. 25, 1930; s. William Anton and Sybil Naomi (Arnold) B.; B.A., Southwestern U., 1951; B.Arch. with high honor, Auburn U., 1957; m. Janice Swanson Livingston, Mar. 17, 1962; children—Carolyn, Bill (children from previous marriage), Livingston, Max. Apprentice, A.L. Aydelott & Assos., Memphis, 1957-58, Lawrence S. Whitten, Birmingham, Ala., 1958-59, Mann & Harrover, Memphis, 1959-60; jr. mem. firm Eason, Anthony, McKinnie, & Cox, Inc., architects, Memphis, 1960-63; asso. firm Buchmueller, Whitworth, & Assos., Sikeston, Mo., 1963-64; prin. Fischer-Bowden, Inc., Carbondale, Ill., 1964-68; asso. univ. architect Duke U., Durham, N.C., 1968-71; pres., exec. dir. LBC &W Assos. N.C., Inc., Greensboro, 1971—. Active campaign United Fund; mem. Carbondale Pub. Bldgs. Com., 1966-68, sidewalk adv. com., 1966-68, profl. engr. selection com., 1966-68. Served with USMCR, 1947-49, 52-53; now lt. col. Res. ret. Mem. A.I.A., Constrn. Specifications Inst., Nat. Panel Arbitrators, Am. Arbitration Assn., Marine Corps League, Marine Corps Res. Officers Assn., Scarab, Phi Kappa Phi, Sigma Nu, C. of C. (bd. dirs. 1965-68). Episcopalian. Elk. Club: Tennessee (Memphis). Home: 3008

Greenbrook Dr Greensboro NC 27408 Office: care LBC & W PO Box 9576 Greensboro NC 27408

BOWDOIN, WILLIAM REDDING, banker; b. Atlanta, July 21, 1913; s. William Henry and Pauline (Collins) B.; LL.B., U. Ga., 1933; LL.D., Emory U., 1970; m. Margaret Stoddard, July 30, 1942; children—William Redding, John Collins. Admitted to Ga. bar, 1934; with Peoples Bank, Winder, Ga., 1936-41; pres. First Nat. Bank, East Point, Ga., 1946-48; with Trust Co. Ga., Atlanta, 1948—, vice chmn. bd., 1964—, also dir.; chmn., pres. Trust Co. Ga. Assos., 1964—; dir. First Nat. Bank & Trust Co., Augusta, Fourth Nat. Bank, Columbus, First Nat. Bank & Trust Co., Macon, First Nat. Bank, Rome, Liberty Nat. Bank & Trust Co., Savannah. Chmn. Ga. Ports Authority, 1953-55, Gov. Ga. Commn. Efficiency and Improvement, 1963-64; supr. purchases Ga., 1959; co-chmn. Atlanta Meml. Cultural Center campaign, 1964; treas. Ga. Assn. Crippled Children, 1964; adv. com. Ga. Vocational Assn., 1963-64. Trustee Emory U., Ga. Found. Ind. Colls.; trustee, vice-chmn. adminstrn. Atlanta Arts Alliance; vice chmn. bd. Berry Schs. Served to maj. AUS, 1941-46. Recipient Ga. Citizen of Year award Ga. Assn. County Commrs., 1963, Nat. Citizenship award Future Farmers Am., 1964; named to Officer Candidate Sch. Hall of Fame, Ft. Benning, Ga., 1970; recipient Pres.'s award Assn. Pvt. Colls. and Univs. in Ga., 1972. Mem. Gridiron Secret Soc. (U. Ga.) (hon.), Beta Gamma Sigma, Sigma Alpha Epsilon. Episcopalian. Home: 3845 Club Dr NE Atlanta GA 30319 Office: Trust Co of Georgia Atlanta GA 30302

BOWDRE, CARL EUGENE, banker; b. Champaign, Ill., Oct. 5, 1930; s. Harold Alonzo and Euncie (Perkins) B.; student U. Tex., 1953, 54, Am. Inst. Banking, 1959, 60, 63; m. Mary Virginia Franklin, June 24, 1951; children—Pamela Glen, Stephen Franklin, Linda Ann. With Nat. Bank Monticello (Ill.), 1956-57; with Peoples Group Nat. Banks, Dade County, Fla., 1957-70, pres., North Miami Beach, Fla., until 1970; sr. v.p. Pan Am. Bank of Dade County, North Miami Beach, 1970-74; pres. Pan Am. Bank, Ormond Beach, Fla., 1974—. Adviser, Sch. Banking Dade County Jr. Coll., Miami, 1968—. Served with USAF, 1950-54. Mem. North Miami Beach C. of C. (pres. 1968-69), Bank Adminstrn. Inst. S. Fla. (bd. dirs.). Republican. Mem. Ch. of Jesus Christ Latter-day Saints. Kiwanian (pres. 1972-73). Home: 10 Pine Valley Circle Ormond Beach FL 32074 Office: Box 528 Ormond Beach FL 32074

BOWE, ROBERT LOOBY, med. scientist, educator; b. Worcester, Mass., Jan. 25, 1925; s. Jeffrey John and Agnes Dorothea (Looby) B.; grad. Boston Latin Sch., 1943; certificate Mus. Sch. Fine Arts, 1943; B.S., Boston Coll., 1950, M.S., 1956; Ph.D., U. Tenn., 1960; m. Mary Ellen Wagner, June 15, 1957; children—Robert, Karyl Leigh, Stephen, Kristine. Lectr. clin. physiology and pathophysiology U. Tenn., 1958-60; asst. prof. clin. pharmacology and therapeutics Med. Coll. S.C., Charleston, 1960-64; asst. prof. pharmacology Med. Coll. Va. of Va. Commonwealth U., Richmond, 1964-65, asso. prof., 1964—. Vis. prof. psychophysiology and psychopharmacology S.C. State Hosp., Columbia, 1961-64; lectr. Council on Drug Abuse Control, 1970—; lectr. on continuing edn.; speaker workshops on drug abuse. Scoutmaster, Cub Scouts, 1964-67; asst. scout leader Robert E. Lee council Boy Scouts Am., 1967—, mem. council, 1971—; med. program adviser Explorer Scouts, 1971-73; v.p. P.T.A. Ruby F. Carver Sch., Richmond, 1966-68. Served with 97th Inf., AUS, 1942-46. Recipient Outstanding Tchr. award Sch. Med. Va., 1970, 71, Appreciation awards Boy Scouts Am., 1967, 70, 73. Fellow A.A.A.S.; mem. Am. Chem. Soc., Am. Assn. Dental Schs., Am. Assn. U. Profs., N.Y., Va. acads. sci. Contbr. articles to profl. jours.; coordinator, lectr. TV edn. series on pathophysiology of human body, 1968-70. Research on cardiovascular and renal physiology and pharmacology, psychophysiology and psychopharmacology. Home: 11305 Wimberly Dr Richmond VA 23223 Office: Dept Pharmacology Medical College Virginia Richmond VA 23219

BOWEN, A'DELBERT, lawyer; b. Tuscumbia, Ala., Nov. 13, 1919; s. A'Delbert and Gertrude (Willett) B.; student State Tchrs. Coll., Florence, Ala., 1936-38; LL.B., Atlanta Law Sch., 1954; m. Rebecca Montez Proctor, July 27, 1945; children—A'Delbert III, Lanny Proctor, Montez Elizabeth. Gen. ins. agt. Proctor Ins. Agy., Cuthbert, Ga., 1950—; admitted to Ga. bar, 1954, since practiced in Cuthbert; atty. City of Shellman (Ga.), City of Georgetown (Ga.); county atty. Randolph County, Ga., 1960-71, Quitman County, Ga., 1966—. Mem. Ga. Gen. Assembly, 1959-64. Sec., bd. dirs. Randolph Devel. Corp.; trustee Andrew Coll. Served to maj. USAAF, 1941-47. Decorated Air medal with five oak leaf clusters. Mem. Am., Ga. bar assns., Am. Legion. Republican. Methodist (trustee). Mason. Home: 118 W Harris St Cuthbert GA 31740 Office: 111 Court St Cuthbert GA 31740

BOWEN, CHARLES ELBERT, supt. schs.; b. Austell, Ga., May 10, 1913; s. Urben and Mattie Jane (Bolding) B.; A.B., U. Ga., 1934, M.A., 1939; postgrad. Peabody Coll. for Tchrs.; m. Irene Elizabeth Cooper, June 6, 1942; children—Peggy Ann (Mrs. Charles Green), Charles Elbert. Prin., Weston (Ga.) Sch., 1934-36; asst. prin. Fitzgerald (Ga.) High Sch., 1936-38; asst. math. dept. U. Ga., 1938-39; asst. prin. Sandersville (Ga.) High Sch., 1939-40; prin. Ft. Hill Jr. High Sch., Dalton, Ga., 1940-43; instr. math. Ga. Inst. Tech., 1946; prin. Dalton High Sch., 1946-68; asst. supt. Dalton Pub. Schs., 1968-69, supt., 1969—. Mem., past chmn. N.W. Ga. YMCA; mem. adv. council Cherokee dist. Boy Scouts Am. Chmn. Dalton Planning and Zoning Commn., 1962-67. Bd. dirs. Big Bros. Served to lt. (j.g.), USNR, 1943-46. Mem. N.E.A., Ga., Dalton assns. educators, Ga. Assn. Sch. Supts. (past chmn.), Nat., Ga. assns. secondary sch. prins., So. Assn. Colls. and Schs. (past chmn. Ga. com.), Pi Mu Epsilon (charter). Baptist (deacon). Rotarian (past pres. Dalton). Home: 906 Hillcrest Dr Dalton GA 30720 Office: PO Box 1408 Dalton GA 30720

BOWEN, CORNELIUS MONROE, health adminstr.; b. Jersey City, Nov. 6, 1912; s. Cornelius William and Isabel (Monroe) B.; M.P.A., N.Y. U., 1958; m. Catherine Stecker Neal, Feb. 19, 1966. Regional health officer Bergen County, N.J., 1937-48; with USPHS, N.Y.C., 1948—, asst. regional health dir., 1969—. Instr. human biology Fairleigh Dickinson U., Rutherford, N.J., 1952-63; chmn. Bd. Health New Providence, N.J., 1935-37, Bd. Health Montclair, N.J., 1963-65. Fellow Royal Soc. Health, Am. Pub. Health Assn. Home: 319 Sunset Dr N St Petersburg FL 33710 Office: Federal Plaza New York City NY 10007

BOWEN, DAVID REECE, congressman; b. Houston, Miss., Oct. 21, 1932; s. David Reece and Lera (Pinnix) B.; student U. Mo., 1950-52; A.B., Harvard, 1954; M.A., Oxford U., 1957. Asst. prof. polit sci. and history Miss. Coll., 1958-59; prof. polit. sci. Millsaps Coll., 1959-64; coordinator S.E. region Office of Econ. Opportunity, Washington, 1966-67; staff asso. for edn. U.S. C. of C., Washington, 1967-68; spl. asst. to gov., coordinator Fed.-State programs State of Miss., 1968-72; mem. 93d Congress from Miss. Served with AUS, 1957-58. Mem. Kappa Alpha Order. Democrat. Home: Route 1 Box 137 Cleveland MS 38732 Office: 1207 Longworth House Office Bldg Washington DC 20515

BOWEN, DOYLE BRUCE, govt. ofcl.; b. Pickens, S.C., Sept. 24, 1925; s. Robert Pickens and Janie (Chastain) B.; B.E.E., Clemson U., 1950; m. Frances Knox, Sept. 29, 1951; children—Linda, Jeanie, Nancy, Lisa. Test. engr. Gen. Electric Co., Lynn, Mass., 1950-51; elec. engr. Miller Electric Co., Aiken, S.C., 1951-52; with TVA, Knoxville, 1952—, asst. design project mgr., 1973—. Served with USNR, 1943-46. Mem. I.E.E.E., Knoxville Tech. Soc. Baptist. Mason. Home: 4417 Larigo Dr Knoxville TN 37914 Office: 314 LB TVA Knoxville TN 37902

BOWEN, FRANK WESTON, physician; b. Memphis, May 5, 1921; s. George Samuel and Virgie (Hamill) B.; B.A., U., Miss., 1948, B.S. 1949; M.D., U. Tenn., 1951; m. Bobbie Elizabeth McPhail, May 1, 1943; 1 son, Frank Weston. Intern, Methodist Hosp., Memphis, 1951-52; practice family medicine, Walnut Grove, Miss., 1952-57, Carthage, Miss., 1957—; chief of staff Leake County Meml. Hosp., Carthage, 1961, 72. Served from pvt. to 2nd lt., MAC, AUS, 1942-46. Diplomate Am. Bd. Family Practice. Fellow Am. Geriatrics Soc., mem. Am. Heart Assn., A.M.A., Am. Acad. Family Practice, Miss. Med. Assn., Central Med. Soc. (pres. 1969), C. of C., N.Y. Acad. Scis., Leake County Hist. Soc., Phi Chi. Methodist. Home: 700 N Pearl St Carthage MS 39051 Office: 303 W Franklin St Carthage MS 39051

BOWEN, JAMES MILTON, virologist, educator; b. Graham, Tex., Feb. 1, 1935; s. James Raymond and Denzel Dora (Roberts) B.; B.S., Midwestern U., Wichita Falls, Tex., 1955; M.S., Ore. State Coll., 1958, Ph.D., 1961; m. Lucy Jane Rohovec; children—Sheryl Rae, Kimberley Ann, Bradley James. Student asst. biology Midwestern U., 1953-55; grad. research asst. virology Ore. State Coll., 1957-59, instr. microbiology, 1959-61; USPHS postdoctoral research fellow U. Tex. M.D. Anderson Hosp. and Tumor Inst., 1961-62, asst. virologist, 1964, asst. prof. virology, 1965-69, chief sect. molecular virology, 1968, asso. prof. virology, 1969, virologist, prof. virology, chief sect. viral immunology, chief sect. molecular virology, dept. virology, 1973—; asso. research biologist Sterling-Winthrop Research Inst., Rensselaer, N.Y., 1962-64; asso. mem. Grad. Sch. Biomed. Scis., U. Tex., Houston, 1966, asso. prof. virology, mem. grad. faculty 1970, prof. virology, 1973—. Invited participant various confs., 1971—. Recipient Outstanding Ex-Student award Midwestern U., 1968. Mem. Am. Assn. for Cancer Research, Am. Soc. Microbiology, Sigma Xi. Contbr. articles to profl. jours. Office: MD Anderson Hosp and Tumor Inst U Tex Houston TX 77025

BOWEN, RAY MORRIS, educator; b. Fort Worth, Mar. 30, 1936; s. Winford Herbert and Elizabeth (Williams) B.; B.S. in Mech. Engring., Tex. A. and M. U., 1958, Ph.D., 196i; M.S., Cal. Inst. Tech., 1959; m. Sally Elizabeth Gibbons, July 5, 1958; children—Ray Jr., Beth. Postdoctoral fellow Johns Hopkins, Balt., 1964-65; asso. prof. dept. engring. mechanics La. State U., Baton Rouge, 1965-67; mem. faculty dept. mech. engring. Rice U., Houston, 1967—, asso. prof., 1969-73, prof., 1973—, also chmn. dept., 1972—. Cons. Sandia Corp., Albuquerque, 1970—. Served with USAF, 1961-64. Mem. Houston Philos. Soc., Soc. Natural Philosophy, Soc. Scholars (Johns Hopkins U.), Sigma Xi, Phi Kappa Phi, Tau Beta Pi. Contbr. articles to profl. jours. Home: 3720 Olympia St Houston TX 77019

BOWEN, WILLIAM WARD, physician; b. Grenada, Miss., Nov. 11, 1927; s. Hugh and Myrtle (Stevens) B.; B.S., La. State U., 1950, M.D., 1954; m. Betsy Ann Green, June 29, 1950; children—Charlotte Ann, Cynthia Louise, William Ward, Melinda Rose, Elizabeth Emily, Frederick Carl. Intern, McLeod Infirmary, Florence, S.C., 1954-55; practice gen. medicine, Hartsville, S.C., 1955—; owner Hartsville Hosp., 1956—; founder, pres. Hartsville Convalescent and Nursing Home, 1968—. Mem. Hartsville Bd. Health, 1961—; v.p. S.C. Health Care Plan, 1970-72; mem. S.C. Bd. Examiners for Nursing Home Adminstrs., 1971-74. Vice pres. Hartsville Area Council for Retarded, 1968; bd. dirs., 1st vice chmn. Hartsville A.R.C.; pres. Pee Dee Found. for Handicapped, 1968-71; mem. steering com. White House Conf. on Children and Youth, 1970. Served with USNR, 1945. Named Civitan of Year, Hartsville, S.C. 1967; Honor medal S.C. Civitan Club, 1968; Annual award for outstanding community service, Hartsville, 1969. Mem. Am., So., S.C. med. assns., S.C. Nursing Home Assn. (treas. 1971-74), Darlington County (pres. 1958), Pee Dee (pres. 1962) med. socs., Flying Physicians Med. Assn., S.C. Assn. for Retarded Children (dir.), Nat. Assn. Bds. Examiners for Nursing Home Adminstrs. (dir. 1971-72), Am. Assn. of Mental Deficiency, Kappa Sigma, Nu Sigma Nu. Democrat. Methodist (trustee). Clubs: Hartsville Red Fox (pres. 1960), Hartsville Civitan (v.p. 1959-60). Home: 507 Carolina Av Hartsville SC 29550 Office: 412 Home Av Hartsville SC 29550

BOWERS, CLAYTON DANIEL, elec. engr.; b. Beaumont, Tex., Dec. 5, 1934; s. Rastas Clayton and Agnes (Blackmon) B.; student Abilene Christian Coll., 1953-54; B.S. in Elec. Engring., Lamar State U., 1958; m. Gay Sue Willis, Dec. 18, 1954; children—Clayton Daniel, Connie, Tammye, Randal. Plant elec. engr. U.S. Gypsum Co., New Orleans, 1958-62; sr. design engr. Boeing Co., New Orleans, 1962-65; plant engr. Western Electric Co., Shreveport, La., 1965—. Bd. dirs., charter mem. Christian Acad. Shreveport, 1970-72; chmn. bd. trustees, charter mem. La. Child Care and Placement Services, Inc., Shreveport, 1966—. Recipient spl. achievement award civic service Western Electric Co., 1972. Registered profl. engr., La. Mem. I.E.E.E. Mem. Ch. of Christ (elder). Republican. Home: 2731 Hoyte Dr Shreveport LA 71108 Office: 9595 Mansfield Rd Shreveport LA 71130

BOWERS, JOHN LOWRY, educator; b. Troy, Tex., Nov. 9, 1915; s. John Frederick and Leonora (Nix) B.; B.S., Tex. A. and M. Coll., 1937; M.S., U. Md., 1939, Ph.D., 1950; m. Virginia Eleanor Thomas, June 28, 1940. Instr. horticulture U. Ark., Fayetteville, 1940-44, asso. prof. horticulture, prof. horticulture, 1956—; asso. prof. horticulture Miss. State Coll., State College, 1944-48, 1949-51; grad. asst. U. Md., 1948-49. Fellow Am. Soc. Hort. Sci.; mem. Am. Soc. Hort. Sci., Internat. Hort. Soc., Sigma Xi, Gamma Sigma Delta, Alpha Zeta. Episcopalian. Lion. Home: 1907 Garland St Fayetteville AR 72701

BOWERS, QUINTON ROOSEVELT, lawyer, state legislator; b. Samson, Ala., Mar. 20, 1921; s. William E. and Mary (Alpin) B.; B.S., U. Ala., 1949; J.D., Birmingham Sch. Law, 1955; m. Betty Mathews, Dec. 5, 1953; one dau., Lita Kay. Salesman, Goodyear Service Store, Gadsden, Ala., 1950-51; adjuster Universal C.I.T. Credit Corp., Birmingham, Ala., 1951-52, Am. Fore Ins. Group, 1953-57; admitted to Ala. bar, 1960; practiced in Birmingham, 1957—; spl. asst. atty. gen. State of Ala., 1967—; mem. Ala. Ho. of Reps., 1962—, mem. com. on local legislation number 2, mem. judiciary com., chmn. com. mil. affairs. Chmn. exec. com. Old Age Pension Inst. of Ala., Birmingham, 1958-59; mem. Ala. Vets.' Affairs Com., 1965-69; mem. Gov.'s Com. Employment of the Physically Handicapped, State of Ala.; mem. permanent study comn. Ala. Judicial Commn., 1971—, chmn. subcom to study coroner system; mem. Continuing Women's Commn. Ala., 1971. Served with USMC, 1939-45. Mem. Am., Ala., Birmingham bar assns., State Ala. Employees Assn., Ala. League Aging Citizens (life), Ala. Peace Officers Assn., Jefferson County Sportsmen's Assn., C. of C., Am. Legion, V.F.W. (comdr. dept. Ala. 1963-64, comdr. Kelly Ingram post 1961-62, mem. all-Am. team of state comdrs. 1964, state comdr. of yr. award 1964, vice chmn. nat. legislative com. 1964-66), Sigma Delta Kappa. Democrat. Methodist. Mason (32 deg., Shriner), Eagle. Club: Civitan. Home: 1528 Shades Crest Rd Birmingham AL 35226 Office: Frank Nelson Bldg Birmingham AL 35203

BOWERS, RONALD WILLIAM, dentist; b. St. Louis, Dec. 10, 1941; s. Paul William and Dorothy Geraldine (Barton) B.; D.D.S., Emory U., 1965; m. Nancy Lee Heath, Apr. 29, 1960; children—Ronald William, Amy Elizabeth, Barton Bentley. Intern Fla. Instnl. Dental Service, 1965-66; pvt. practice dentistry, 1966-70, mem. profl. corp., Augusta, Ga., 1970—; dir. Bowers Finance Co. Chmn. adv. bd. Salvation Army; chmn. profl. div. Am. Cancer Soc.; chmn. budget panel United Way. Mem. AUS Res. Mem. Augusta Dental Soc. (pres.), Am., Ga. dental assns., Xi Psi Phi. Methodist. Elk. Clubs: Augusta Country, Augusta Sailing, Highgate Green and Tennis. Home: 810 Windsor Ct Augusta GA 30904 Office: 3643 Walton Way Extension Augusta GA 30904

BOWKLEY, HERBERT LOUIS, educator; b. Pittston, Pa., July 9, 1921; s. Raymond Edward and Sarah Louise (Lewis) B.; student Mo. Sch. Mines, 1946-47, M.S., 1951; B.S., U. Mich., 1950; Ph.D., Pa. State U., 1955; m. Betty Adele Morrow, Aug. 23, 1947; children—Raymond Edward, Andrea Lynn, Susan Marie. Research chemist Nat. Lead Co., South Amboy, N.J., 1951-52; group leader Pitts. Plate Glass, 1956-57; sr. research chemist Olin Mathieson, New Haven, 1957-58, Thiokol Chem., Elkton, Md., 1964-65; group leader Am. Cyanamid, New Castle, Pa., 1960-63; asso. prof. Appalachian State U., Boone, N.C., 1966—, prof. chemistry, 1968—. Served with AUS, 1942-46. Mem. Am. Forestry Assn., Sigma Xi, Phi Lambda Upsilon, Sigma Pi Sigma, Alpha Chi Sigma. Republican. Unitarian. Home: 104 Edora Rd Boone NC 28607

BOWLER, F. WALLACE, finance co. executive; b. Norfolk, Va., Dec. 31, 1923; s. Ernest R. and Jonnie (Walters) B.; grad. Coll. Hampton Roads, 1942; m. Julia C. O'Farrell, May 24, 1952; children—Frank Wallace, Julia O'Farrell. Pres., Eastern Finance Corp., Norfolk Eastern Credit Corp., Norfolk, 1942—, United Corp. Am., United Oil & Gas Co., Wilmington, Del., Norfolk; chmn. bd. Mut. Bankers Ins. Co., Richmond, Fidelity Trust Co., Atlanta; chmn., pres. First City Bank pres. Home Mortgage Corp.; chmn. bd. Overnite Inns, Inc.; dir. Williamsburg Corp. Mem. Navy League U.S., Young Pres.'s Orgn., Am. Legion. Mason (Shriner), Elk. Clubs: Surf (Miami); Norfolk Yacht and Country, Harbor (Norfolk); Cedar Point (Crittenden, Va.); Green Boundry (Aiken, S.C.); Williamsburg Country. Home: 1546 Blanford Circle Norfolk VA 23505 Office: 1 Koger Exec Center Suite 209 Norfolk VA 23502

BOWLES, EDWARD JAMES, pollution control co. pres.; b. Temple Tex., Sept. 12, 1912; s. John Henry and Coleta (Estes) B.; B.S., So. Meth. U., 1935; m. Elsie Lois Novey, Mar. 29, 1937; children—Lois Jane (Mrs. Richard A. Means), James Bradley. Mgr. pump and elec. dept. Fairbanks, Morse & Co., Dallas, 1935-42; engr., Koch & Fowler, cons. engrs., Dallas, Myers, Noyes & Lemmon, cons. engrs., Dallas, Brown & Root, Inc., contractors, San Angelo, Tex., W.G. Cullum & Co., contractors, Temple, Tex., 1942-44; v.p. Bowles & Edens Corp., Dallas, 1945-72; pres. Bowles & Edens div. Certain-Teed Products, Corp., Dallas, 1972—. Recipient Dad of year award Central Dad's Club Tex., 1950, Silver Beaver award Boy Scouts Am., 1958. Registered profl. engr., Tex., Ark., Okla., La. Mem. Dallas C. of C., So. Meth. U. Ex-Students Assn. (past pres.), Tex. Soc. Profl. Engrs. (state dir. 1973—), Nat. Soc. Profl. Engrs., Municipal Contractors Assn. (asso.), Tex. Water Utilities Assn., Am. Water Works Assn., Tex. and Fed. Water Pollution Control Assn., Tech. Club Dallas, Engrs. Club Dallas, Circle Ten Council (exec. bd. 1957—), Alpha Tau Omega. Methodist. Clubs: Shawnee Trail Assn., Salt Grass Trail Assn., Am. Quarter Horse Assn. Contbr. articles to profl. jours. Home: 7109 Kenny Lane Dallas TX 75230 Office: PO Box 47085 Dallas TX 75247

BOWLING, ROBERT EDWARD, JR., microbiologist, educator; b. Pauls Valley, Okla., Aug. 9, 1926; s. Robert Edward and Clara Ellen (Merkle) B.; B.S., U. Okla., 1948, M.S., 1950, Ph.D., 1957; m. Dorothy Ann Clark, Mar. 12, 1955; children—Ann Elizabeth, John Robert, Susan Ellen, Mary Merkle, Paul Edward. Asst. microbiologist Okla. Health Dept., 1950-51; instr. dept. microbiology U. Ark. Med. Center, Little Rock, 1957-59, asst. prof., 1959-68, asso. prof. microbiology, 1968—, asst. dean Sch. Medicine, 1973—. Mem. Am. Soc. Microbiology, Soc. for Gen. Microbiology (Gt. Britain), Am. Inst. Biol. Scis., Soc. for Cryobiology, Soc. for Exptl. Biology and Medicine, Ark. Acad. Sci., Sigma Xi. Episcopalian. Home: 4400 I St Little Rock AR 72205

BOWLING, WILLIAM EDGAR, elec. engr.; b. Dunbar, W.Va., Sept. 25, 1941; s. William Green and Pearl (Hartley) B., Jr.; B.S. in Elec. Engring., W.Va. U., 1964; postgrad U. Ala., 1965-71; m. Katherine Ann Erwin, Aug. 21, 1965; 1 dau., Karen Ann. Jr. engr. IBM, Owego, N.Y., 1964-65, asso. engr., Huntsville, Ala., 1966-68, sr. asso. engr., 1968-71, staff engr., 1971—. Instr. IBM Vol. Edn. Porgram, Huntsville, 1973-74. Registered profl. engr. Mem. I.E.E.E., Eta Kappa Nu, Pi Kappa Alpha. Baptist. Club: Sherwood Swim. Home: 506 Seaborn Dr Huntsville AL 35806 Office: 150 Sparkman Dr Huntsville AL 35805

BOWMAN, EDMUND DELONG, distillery exec.; b. Lexington, Ky., Sept. 13, 1911; s. Abram Smith and Katherine Lyttleton (DeLong) B.; B.A., Princeton, 1934; m. Helen Caldwell Potts, Feb. 17, 1942; children—Katherine (Mrs. W. Frederic Burton, Jr.), Nena (Mrs. John B. Adams, Jr.). Gen. mgr. Sunset Hills (Va.) Farm, 1930-62; gen. mgr. A. Smith Bowman Distillery, Sunset Hills, 1935-49, v.p., 1949-52, pres., 1952—. Trustee Fauquier Hosp., Warrenton, Va., Oatlands, Nat. Trust for Historic Preservation; trustee, v.p. Bowman Found., Inc. Mem. Va. Mfrs. Assn. (dir. 1964-67, 72—). Clubs: Society of Cincinnati (Washington); Chevy Chase, Nat. Lawyers (Chevy Chase, Md.); Commonwealth, Downtown (Richmond, Va.); Fauquier (Warrenton, Va.); Nassau; Princeton (N.Y.C.); Orange County Hunt, Fairfax Hunt, Thoroughbred Am., Press of Va.; Evergreen Country (Haymarket, Va.). Home: Belvoir Farm The Plains VA 22171 Office: A Smith Bowman Distillery Sunset Hills VA 22070

BOWMAN, JOHN FRANCIS, educator; b. Saranac Lake, N.Y., Oct. 24, 1916; s. William Conroy and Mary Belle (Durgan) B.; student St. Lawrence U., 1934-37; D.M.D., Tufts U., 1941, certificate oral prosthetics, 1954; certificate prosthetic dentistry U.S. Navy Dental Sch., 1947; m. Elinore May Whitney, Sept. 25, 1941; children—Dale Anne (Mrs. Frank Laumer), Rhoda (Mrs. Douglas Sheppard Lynn), Penelope Jean (Mrs. Edward Kosheba), Patricia Jane. Asso. prof. Sch. Dental Medicine, U. Pitts., 1963-69; prof. Coll. Dentistry, U. Fla. at Gainesville, 1969—, chmn. div. complete denture prosthodontics, 1969—. Cons. central office VA, various VA Hosps., U.S. Navy Hosp. Diplomate Am. Bd. Prosthodontics. Fellow Am. Coll. Prosthodontists, Am. Coll. Dentists, Internat. Coll. Dentists; mem. Am. Prosthodontic Soc., Am. Assn. U. Profs., Omicron Kappa Upsilon. Author: (with others) Removable Partial Prosthodontics Clinical Procedures and Technology, 1965. Home: 4510 NW 13th Av Gainesville FL 32601

BOWMAN, LINDEN ALLEN, aerospace components mfr.; b. Timberville, Va., Mar. 22, 1932; s. Vernon Erasmus and Cora Ellen (Fansler) B.; student Berea Coll., 1949-50; B.S., Va. Poly. Inst., 1958; m. Marilyn Blankenship, Dec. 15, 1973; children by previous marriage—Steve Allan, Barry Marvin. With Poly-Sci. div. Litton Industries, Inc., Blacksburg, Va., 1956—, div. pres., 1970—; dir. North br. Nat. Bank of Blacksburg. Bd. dirs. Blacksburg United Fund, Showalter Meml. Hosp. Served with USNR, 1950-54. Mem. Am. Mgmt. Assn., Va. Mfrs. Assn. (taxation com.), U.S., Va. chambers commerce. Republican. Lutheran. Home: 1412 Palmer Dr Blacksburg VA 24060 Office: 1213 N Main St Blacksburg VA 24060

BOWMAN, NEWELL STEDMAN, educator; b. Rocky Ford, Colo., Sept. 4, 1924; s. Newell Leroy and Lillian Marguerite (Stedman) B.; B.S., U.S. Naval Acad., 1946; B.S., U. Md., 1951; M.A. (Allied Chem. and Dye fellow), Princeton, 1954, Ph.D., 1955; m. Pearl Laveda Cox, Nov. 1, 1946; children—Charlene Roxane, Donald Duane, Aaron Leroy. Post-doctoral fellow Purdue U., Lafayette, Ind., 1954-56; mem. faculty U. Tenn., Knoxville, 1956—, prof. chemistry, 1969—. Fulbright lectr. Karlsruhe (Germany) U., 1969-70. Served with USN, 1943-49. Mem. Am. Chem. Soc., Sigma Xi. Author: (With J.H. Wood, C.W. Keenan, W.E. Bull) Fundamentals of College Chemistry, 1964. Editor: (with C.J. Collins) Isotope Effects in Chemical Reactions, 1970. Home: 2516 Lakemoor Dr Knoxville TN 37920

BOWMAN, RALPH JEROME, city ofcl.; b. Valeda, Kan., Sept. 27, 1925; s. Glenn T. and Vida (Neidigh) B.; B.S. in Bus., U. Kan., 1950; m. Retha J. Burns, Aug. 14, 1953. Cost accountant Carl Bjorkman, C.P.A., Topeka, 1951-52, C. Robert Belt, C.P.A., Coffeyville, Kan., 1952-54: city office mgr., Ponca City, Okla., 1954-59, city treas., 1959—. Served with USNR, 1943-46. C.P.A., Okla. Mem. Am. Inst. C.P.A.'s, Okla. Soc. C.P.A.'s, Am. Legion. Home: 613 E Emporia Av Ponca City OK 74601 Office: 516 E Grand Av Ponca City OK 74601

BOWMAN, SAMUEL LEONARDO, clergyman; b. Benton, Miss., Feb. 19, 1933; s. Warren and Nora (Johnson) B.; B.S., Natchez (Miss.) Coll., 1950, Th.D. (hon.), 1972; Th.B., Miss. Baptist Sem., 1960; m. Willie M. Jackson, June 30, 1957; children—Gwendolyn, Jacqueline. Ordained to ministry Bapt. Ch., 1952; pastor, Mt. Olive, Miss., 1956-65, Greater Clark St. Bapt. Ch., Jackson, Miss., 1965—; prof. O.T., Miss. Bapt. Sem., 1961—. Bd. dirs. Jackson Urban League, 1969-72; chmn. bd. mgrs. Farish St. br. YMCA, Jackson, 1970-72. Recipient Outstanding Citizenship award Mich. State Legislature, 1972. Mem. Bapt. Ministers Union Jackson (pres. 1968—). Mason. Author: Black Sons of Thunder, 1973. Home: 3761 Terrell Av Jackson MS 39213 Office: 415 N Gallatin St Jackson MS 39203

BOWMAN, WALLACE DEAL, govt. ofcl.; b. Jacksonville, Ill., Dec. 10, 1926; s. Robert William and Minnie (Fowler) B.; A.B. in Biology, Washington U., St. Louis, 1949, M.S. in Exptl. Psychoacoustics, 1953; M.A., Yale, 1956; Schoen-Renne Fellow, U. Mich., 1958-59; m. Kira Zelljadt, Nov. 4, 1961; children—Ingrid, Alexander, Margaret. Resource planner Office Gov. Alaska, 1961-62; exec. officer Conservation Found., N.Y.C., 1962-64; sr. reports officer UN Devel. Fund, N.Y.C., 1964-67; sr. specialist, chief environmental policy div. Congl. Research Service, Library of Congress, Washington, 1967—. Sci. adviser Conservation Found., Washington. Trustee Conservation and Research Found., New London, Conn. Served with USNR, 1944-46. Mem. Internat. Council Environmental Law, Nat. Inst. Ecology. Club: Yale (N.Y.C.). Author: Alaska's Recreation Potential, 1961; Research on Natural Resources, 1962; Congressional White Paper on Environmental Policy, 1968; others. Home: 6232 Lakeview Dr Falls Church VA 22041 Office: Library of Congress Washington DC 20540

BOWMER, JIM DEWITT, lawyer; b. Temple, Tex., May 4, 1919; s. DeWitt and Linnie B. (Morgan) B.; A.A., Temple Jr. Coll., 1938; B.A. cum laude, Baylor U., 1940, LL.B. cum laude, 1942;; m. Daurice Spoonts, Mar. 26, 1961; children—Bonnie Nell (Mrs. David Dan Simmonds), Mary Helen. Admitted to Tex. bar, 1942; county atty. Bell County, Tex., 1946-47; lectr. law Baylor U. Law Sch., 1949-50, 56-57; mem. firm Bowmer, Courtney, Burleson & Pemberton, 1964—. Bd. dirs. Nat. Park Found., 1968-69. Served with AUS, 1942-46. Mem. Am. Law Inst., Am. Judicature Soc., Tex. Assn. Def. Counsel, Temple C. of C. (past pres.), Baylor Law Alumni Assn. (past pres.), Bell-Lampasas-Mills Counties Bar Assn. (past pres.), State Bar Tex. (dir. 1968-71, chmn. bd. 1970-71, pres. 1972-73), Phi Alpha Delta. Democrat. Baptist. Mason (K.T.), K.P. (past grand chancellor Tex.), Kiwanian. Contbr. articles to profl. jours. Home: Bowmer's Ranch Route 2 Killeen TX 76541 Office: First Fed Savings & Loan Bldg Temple TX 76501

BOXELL, JOHN FREDERICK, otolaryngologist; b. Marion, Ind., Nov. 19, 1939; s. Walton W. and Hazel M. (Brooks) B.; A.B. in Zoology, Ind. U., 1961; M.D., 1965; m. Marilyn Kay Smith, June 3, 1962; children—Elizabeth Ann, Brian Frederick. Intern, Methodist Hosp., Indpls., 1965-66; resident in otolaryngology Ind. U. Med. Sch., 1966-71; practice medicine, specializing in otolaryngology, Chattanooga, 1971—. Diplomate Am. Bd. Otolaryngology. Fellow A.C.S.; mem. A.M.A., Hamilton County, Tenn. State med. socs., Chi Phi. Club: Centurian. Home: 813 Brynewood Park Lane Chattanooga TN 37415 Office: 1000 E 3d St Chattanooga TN 37405

BOXER, ROBERT JACOB, educator; b. Bklyn., Apr. 9, 1935; s. Nathan and Frieda (Walkin) B.; B.S., Brooklyn Coll., 1956; Ph.D., Rutgers U., 1961; m. Riette Hirsch, Nov. 28, 1963; children—Mark, Deborah. Asst. prof. chemistry Oglethorpe Coll., Atlanta, 1961-62, asso. prof., 1962-64; asso. prof. chemistry Ga. So. Coll., Statesboro, 1964-72, prof., 1972—. Vis. lectr. secondary schs., 1965-66. Mem. Am. Chem. Soc., Ga. Acad. Scis. Jewish religion. Home: 211 Henderson St Statesboro GA 30458

BOYARSKY, LOUIS LESTER, neurophysiologist, educator; b. Jersey City, Sept. 5, 1919; s. Samuel and Emma (Newman) B.; B.S., Coll. City N.Y., 1941; M.S., Purdue, 1945; Ph.D., U. Chgo., 1948; m. Lila Harriet Benjamin, Dec. 25, 1941; children—Amy, Gregory. Psychophysiologist, Inst. for Juvenile Research, Chgo., 1949-50; asst. prof. neurophysiology U. Ky., Lexington, 1950-52, asso. prof., 1952-58, prof., 1959—; vis. prof. U. Hawaii, Honolulu, 1968-69. Served with USAAF, 1941-43. Recipient Alumni research award U. Ky., 1959; Fulbright fellow U. Milan, 1958. Mem. Am. Physiol. Soc., Biophysics Soc., Soc. Exptl. Biol. Medicine, Phi Beta Kappa, Sigma Xi. Editor: Physiological Basis of Medical Practice (Best and Taylor). Contbr. articles to profl. jours. Home: 1729 Traveller Rd Lexington KY 40504

BOYCE, EDWARD WAYNE, JR., lawyer; b. Tuckerman, Ark., June 20, 1926; s. Edward Wayne and Sylla (Harvey) B.; student The Citadel, 1943-44; A.B., U. Ark., 1950, LL.B., 1951; m. Phyllis Elayne Williams, Oct. 29, 1951; children—Martha Elayne, Edward Wayne III. Admitted to Ark. bar, 1951; asso. firm Pickens & Pickens, 1951-54; practiced law, 1954-59; mem. firm Pickens, Boyce, McLarty & Watson, and predecessor, Newport, Ark., 1959—. Dep. pros. atty., 1951-56, pros. atty., 3d Jud. Circuit, 1957-60. Mem. Ark. Penitentiary Study Commn. Chmn., Jackson County chpt. Nat. Found., 1965-69. Served with 31st Inf. Div., AUS, 1944-47. Mem. Am. (bd. gen. practice sect.), Ark. (exec. com. 1968-71), Jackson County (pres. 1954, 62), 8th Chancery (v.p. 1973) bar assns., Ark. Legal Edn. Council, Am. Law Inst., Am. Judicature Soc., Phi Alpha Theta, Phi Delta Theta. Episcopalian (mem. exec. council Diocese of Ark. 1970-73). Chmn. editorial adv. bd. Law Notes for the general practitioner. Home: 7 Pickens St Newport AR 72112 Office: 209 Walnut St Newport AR 72112

BOYCE, WILLIAM HENRY, physician; b. Ansonville, N.C., Sept. 22, 1918; s. William Henry and Louise (Gaddy) B.; B.S., Davidson Coll., 1940; M.D., Vanderbilt U., 1944; m. Anna Doris Shore, June 5, 1948; children—William Lockhart, Catharine Louise, Anna Barbara, Frederick Shore. Intern, Bowman Gray Sch. Medicine and N.C. Baptist Hosp., Winston-Salem, 1944-45, resident, 1947; resident N.Y. Hosp., Cornell U. Med. Center, N.Y.C., 1948-49, U. Va. Hosp., Charlottesville, 1950-52; practice medicine, specializing in urology, Winston-Salem, 1952—; mem. staff N.C. Bapt. Hosp., Forsyth Meml. Hosp.; mem. faculty dept. urology Bowman-Gray Sch. Medicine, Winston-Salem, 1952—, asso. prof., 1958-60, prof., chmn. dept. 1960—. Served to capt. M.C., AUS, 1945-47; ETO. Recipient annual award Am. Urological Assn., 6 times. Diplomate Am. Bd. Urology. Fellow A.C.S.; mem. Am., N.C. urol. assns., Am. Assn. Genitourinary Surgeons, Clin. Soc. Genitourinary Surgeons, Internat. Urol. Soc., A.A.A.S., N.Y. Acad. Scis., So. Soc. Clin. Research, Soc. Exptl. Biology and Medicine, N.C. Med. Soc., Soc. Univ. Surgeons, Soc. Univ. Urologists, Sigma Xi, Alpha Omega Alpha. Contbr. articles to profl. jours. Producer several motion pictures med. topics. Editor: (with J.S. King Jr.) High Molecular Weight Substances in Human Urine, 1963; (with J.F. Glenn) Urologic Surgery, 1969. Home: 1970 Georgia Av NW Winston-Salem NC 27104 Office: Dept Urology 300 Hawthorne Rd SW Winston-Salem NC 27103

BOYD, ANN LOUISE STRIPLING, realtor; b. Bonaire, Ga., Apr. 1, 1917; d. John Robert and Estelle (Greene) Stripling; student Piedmont Coll., 1936-40, U. Miami, 1961; grad. Fla. State U.; m. Joseph A. Boyd, Jr., June 6, 1938; children—Joanne, Betty Jean, Joseph, James, Jane. Asst. city clk., Hialeah, Fla., 1945-46; realtor Hialeah, 1947—. Sec., bd. dirs. Hialeah-Miami Springs YMCA, 1958-59, chmn.; bd. dirs. Tallahassee Easter Seal Center. Mem. Hialeah-Miami Springs Bd. Realtors (dir., treas., past pres.), Fla. Assn. Realtors (dist. v.p. 1967), Hialeah-Miami Springs C. of C. (treas., dir., v.p.), Am. Legion Aux. (past pres., dist. pres.), Dade County Women's Democratic Club. Clubs: Pilot, 8 and 40 (pres. Fla. Chapeau), Bus. and Profl. Women's (past pres., dist. sec.), Womens, Garden (treas.) (Tallahassee). Home: 2210 Monaghan Dr Tallahassee FL 32303 Office: 168 Hialeah Dr Hialeah FL 33010

BOYD, CLARENCE ELMO, surgeon; b. Leesville, La., Nov. 2, 1911; s. Isaac C. and Ada Lee (Stakes) B.; B.A., U. Tex., 1933, M.D., 1935; m. Emma Sims, Aug. 13, 1937; children—Charles E., Marjorie E., Frances A., James E. Intern, Charity Hosp., New Orleans, 1935-36; resident North La. San. (now Doctors Hosp.), Shreveport, La., 1936-37; gen. practice medicine, Shreveport, 1937-42, specializing in gen. surgery, 1942—; founder, sr. mem. C.E. Boyd Clinic, Shreveport, 1942—; vis. surgeon Doctors Hosp., Shreveport, 1937—; jr. vis. surgeon Charity Hosp. (now Confederate Meml. Hosp.), 1937-42; sr. vis. surgeon Confederate Meml. Hosp., Shreveport, 1944—; clin. asst. prof. surgery La. State U. Postgrad. Sch. Medicine, 1957-67, La. State U. Sch. of Medicine, Shreveport, 1967—; teaching faculty Am. Bd. Abdominal Surgeons, 1967; chief surgeon La. and Ark. Ry. Co. Employees' Hosp. Assn. to 1967. Founding dir. Shreveport Bank & Trust Co., 1954—, chmn. investment com., 1954—, chmn. bd. dirs., 1961—. Sponsors com. Shreveport United Fund, 1962-66. Dir. Vols. Am., 1950-58, pres. bd., 1955-57; trustee Pub. Affairs Rev. Council, Shreveport, 1959—; chmn. exec. com., chmn. bd. dirs. Doctors Hosp. and Research Found., Shreveport, 1959—. Fellow A.C.S., Internat. Coll. Surgs., Southwestern Surg. Congress, Am. Soc. Abdominal Surgeons (chmn. com. preparing audio-visual postgrad. program on diseases of gall bladder); mem. A.M.A. (chmn. surg. sect. 1967-68, alternate del. sect. council on surgery 1972—, mem. surg. council 1972—), La. (chmn. pub. policy and legislative com. 1954-57, 4th dist. councilor 1959-66, del. 1945-59, v.p. 1967-68), Shreveport (pres. 1956) med. socs., Am. Cancer Soc. (dir. Caddo br. 1952-58), Surg. Assn. La., So. Med. Assn. (asso. Councilor), Assn. Abdominal Surgeons (founding mem.; pres. 1966-67), Am. Assn. Physicians and Surgeons (del., mem. chmn., pres. La. chpt. 1972). Rotarian (pres. Cedar Grove, Shreveport, 1940-41, founder and chmn. com. of student loan fund), Mason (32 deg., Shriner). Contbr. articles to profl. jours. Research on operative cholangiography, local hernioplasty with immediate ambulation; producer color film on cholangiogram, 1954, 60. Home: 401 Delaware St Shreveport LA 71106 Office: 6815 Southern Av Shreveport LA 71106

BOYD, CROSBY NOYES, newspaper exec.; b. Phila., Jan. 2, 1903; s. George W. and Miranda C. (Noyes) B.; grad. St. George's Sch., Newport, R.I., 1920; A.B., Princeton, 1924; m. Elizabeth Utz, Jan. 2, 1932; children—Elizabeth Noyes, Crosby Noyes, Susan Ann. Asst. advt. mgr. Evening Star Newspaper Co., Washington, 1938-44, asst. bus. mgr., 1944-49, also asst. sec.-treas., 1941-49, bus. mgr., treas., 1949-63, exec. v.p., 1955-63, pres., 1963-68, chmn. bd., 1968—, also dir.; dir. Evening Star Broadcasting Co., Washington Star Communications, Inc., Nat. Bank of Washington. Bd. dirs. Bur. Advt. Served to capt. USAAF, 1942-45. Clubs: Metropolitan, Chevy Chase (Washington); Court (Princeton, N.J.). Home: 2801 New Mexico Av NW Washington DC 20007 Office: 225 Virginia Av SE Washington DC 20003

BOYD, DANIEL FRANKLIN, mfg. co. exec.; b. Farrell, Miss., Aug. 29, 1922; s. William Franklin and Lola (McDonald) B.; student Johns Hopkins U., 1941-42, Aero Indsl. Tech. Inst., 1943; m. Mary Virginia DuBose, Mar. 5, 1944; children—Daniel Franklin II, Sarah DuBose (Mrs. Shaw). Salesman Tuckers Sporting Goods, Sarasota, Fla., 1945-50; sales mgr. So. Mill Creek Products, Tampa, Fla., 1950-53; nat. sales mgr. Silver Creek (N.Y.) Precision, 1953-55, Curtis Automotive Devices, Bedford, Ind., 1955-56, Manatee Corp., Tampa, Fla., 1956-59; v.p. sales Lowndes Engring., Valdosta, Ga., 1960—. Served USAAF, World War II. Recipient award Chem. Specialties Mfrs. Assn., 1972. Mem. Fla. Entomol. Soc., Am. (chmn. comml. com., 1964, 1966), Fla. (chmn. comml. dept. 1963-66) mosquito control assns. Baptist (deacon 1961-67, asst. supt. Sunday sch., 1962-65). Mason (Shriner). Patentee in field. Research thermal aerosol equipment; designed electronic liquid formulating equipment, insecticide dispersant. Home: 203 Avondale Av Temple Terrace FL 33617 Office: 125 Blanchard St Valdosta GA 31601

BOYD, DANIEL REID, judge; b. Montgomery, Ala., Oct. 1, 1903; s. Clary Lynn and Willie Lee (Crow) B.; student Auburn U., 1921-22; J.D., U. Ala., 1927; m. Gladys Baxter, May 27, 1930; 1 dau., Catherine Curry (Mrs. William Reeves Johnson). Admitted to Ala. bar, 1927, since practiced in Roanoke; mem. firm Vann-Boyd, 1927-32; city atty., Roanoke, 1930-36; mem. Ala. Senate, 1939-43; dist. atty. Ala. 5th Circuit, 1947-55, circuit judge, 1960—. County chmn. A.R.C., 1955-56; mem. area council Boy Scouts Am., 1934-36. Mem. Judges Assn. Ala., Ala. Bar Assn., Sigma Chi, Sigma Delta Kappa. Baptist (deacon 1932—, Sunday sch. tchr. and supt. intermittently 1930-60). Mason (Shriner), Lion (pres. 1931-32). Home: 406 West Point St Roanoke AL 32674 Office: Leader Bldg Roanoke AL 36274

BOYD, DONALD EDWARD, engr., educator; b. Aruba, W.I., Jan. 12, 1933 (parents Am. citizens); s. Ralph William and Eva Faye (Bartley) B.; B.S., in Aerospace Engring., U. Okla., 1960; M.S. in Aerospace Engring., U. Colo., 1963, Ph.D. in Civil Engring., 1965; m. Linda Louise Morris, Dec. 14, 1956; children—Donna, Bartley, Bradley, Darla. Asst. engr. Douglas Aircraft Co., Tulsa, 1956; structures engr. Aero Comdr., Inc., Bethany, Okla., 1956-60; design specialist Martin-Marietta Co., Denver, 1960-65; mgr. design dept. Brunswick Corp., Marion, Va., 1965; asst. prof. civil engring., Okla. State U., Stillwater, 1965-67, asso. prof., 1968, asso. prof. mech. and aerospace engring., 1968-73, prof., 1973—. Served with AUS, 1953-55. Registered profl. engr., Okla. Mem. Am. Inst. Aero. and Astronautics (sec. Central Okla. sect. 1970, v.p. 1971, pres. 1972, nat. tech. com. on structures 1973, nat. student activities com. 1972, 73), Am. Soc. Engring. Edn., Am. Acad. Mechanics (founding mem.). Contbr. articles to profl. jours. Home: Route 3 Stillwater OK 74074

BOYD, HELEN MCPHERSON (MRS. DEWARD GASTON BOYD, JR.), mathematician; b. Marks, Miss., Jan. 27, 1937; d. William Joseph and Miriam (Till) McPherson; student Miss. State Coll. Women, 1954-55; B.A. with distinction, U. Miss., 1958, M.A., 1959; postgrad. U. Ala., 1967; m. Deward Gaston Boyd, Jr., June 1, 1963. Instr. math Miss. State U., State College, 1959-64; asst. prof., 1964-65; release chemist Baxter Labs, Mountain Home, Ark., 1965; mathematician Army Missile Command, Redstone Arsenal, Ala., 1967—. Mem. Southeast Huntsville Civic Assn., 1972—; vol. mem. Madison County Local Govt. Study Commn., 1972—. Recipient Taylor medal math. U. Miss., 1958; So. Fellowships Fund fellow, 1958-59. Mem. Math. Assn. Am., Assn. U.S. Army, Am. Meteorol. Soc., Assn. Women in Math., Federally Employed Women, Phi Kappa Phi, Gamma Sigma Epsilon. Presbyn. Toastmistress. Home: 703 Dellwood Rd SE Huntsville AL 35802 Office: US Army Missile Command AMSMI-RRA Redstone Arsenal AL 35809

BOYD, HERMAN WAYNE, educator; b. Murfreesboro, Tenn., Aug. 22, 1935; s. Herman Roy and Fanny Tennessee (Davis) B.; A.B., Middle Tenn. State U., 1957; M.A., Vanderbilt U., 1959, Ph.D., 1964; m. Mary Cannon Tucker, June 2, 1966; children—Richard Alan, Russell Lane, Sarah Helen. Instr. physics Middle Tenn. State U., 1959-63; asso. prof. W.Ga. Coll., Carrollton, 1963-68, head dept. physics, 1965, prof. physics, 1968—. AEC radiol. physics fellow Vanderbilt U., 1958; research participant Oak Ridge Nat. Lab., 1964; vis. prof. physics N.M. State U., 1966, NSF Insts., 1971-73. Mem. Am. Phys. Soc., Am. Assn. Physics Tchrs., Sigma Xi. Home: 262 Colonial Dr Route 10 Carrollton GA 30117

BOYD, HOWARD, gas co. exec.; b. Woodside, Md., 1909; A.B., Georgetown U., 1932, J.D., 1935. Chmn. bd., chief exec. officer El Paso Natural Gas Co., Houston; chmn. Geonuclear Nobel-Paso, S.A.; dir. Beaunit Corp., Phillips Pacific Chem. Co., El Paso Products Co., Greyhound Corp., Armour and Co., Tex. Commerce Bank N.A., Houston. Mem. Nat. Petroleum Council, Am. Gas Assn., Ind. Natural Gas Assn. Am. (dir.). Home: 6042 Crab Orchard Houston TX 77027 Office: 2727 Allen Pkwy Houston TX 77019

BOYD, JOSEPH ARTHUR, JR., justice Fla. Supreme Ct.; b. Hoschton, Ga., Nov. 16, 1916; s. Joseph Arthur and Esther (Puckett) B.; grad. Piedmont Coll., LL.D., 1963; J.D., U. Miami, 1948; m. Ann Stripling, June 6, 1938 children—Joanne (Mrs. Robert Goldman), Betty Jean (Mrs. David Jala), Joseph, James, Jane. City atty., Hialeah, Fla., 1951-58; commr. Dade County, 1958-68, vice mayor, 1967; chmn. Dade County Commn., 1963; dir. Fla. Assn. County Commrs., 1964-68; justice Fla. Supreme Ct., Tallahassee, 1969—. Trustee Piedmont Coll. Served with USMCR, 1943-46; PTO. Decorated Japanese Occupation medal with one star; recipient Top Hat award for advancing status of women Nat. Bus. and Profl. Women's Clubs, 1967. Mem. Am. Fla., Dade County, Hialeah-Miami Springs (pres. 1955) bar assns., Hialeah-Miami Springs C. of C. (pres. 1956), Am. Legion (state comdr. 1953), V.F.W., Soc. of Wig and Robe, Pi Kappa Psi, Phi Alpha Delta. Baptist. Mason (Shriner), Lion, Elk, Moose. Home: 2210 Monaghan Dr Tallahassee FL 32303 Office: Supreme Ct Bldg Tallahassee FL 32304

BOYD, LENORE FRANCES ANGLIN, psychologist; b. Tahoka, Tex., Dec. 3, 1923; d. Walter S. and Fannie (Teague) Anglin; B.A. with honors, Tex. Technol. Coll., 1948; postgrad. Los Angeles State Coll., spring 1951; M.A., N.E. Mo. State Tchrs. Coll., 1955; postgrad. U. Tex., summer 1960, 64-65, Tex. A. and M. U., 1972; m. John H. Boyd, Aug. 18, 1944 (div. Feb. 1970); children—John H. III, Alan R., J. Robin. Tchr. sci. and math. pub. schs., Brownfield, Tex., 1942-43, Uvalde, Tex., 1943-44, Louise, Tex., 1946, 55-57, Wolforth, Tex., 1946-48, Galveston, Tex., 1948-49, Flomot, Tex., 1949-50, Kirksville, Mo., 1951-55; coop. county unit counselor Wharton County Schs., Louise, East Bernard, Hungerford, Tex., 1957-70; spl. edn. counselor, psychologist Lamar Consol. Ind. Sch. Dist., Rosenberg, Tex., 1970—; counselor East Bernard, Tex., 1965-66. Mem. Am., Tex. personnel and guidance assns., Nat. Vocational Guidance Assn., Am. Sch. Counselors Assn. (life), N.E.A. (life), Bus. and Profl. Women's Club (pres. Louise 1969-70), Tex. Tchrs. Assn. (pres. Wharton County 1963-64), Nat. Assn. Sch. Psychologists; Tex. Assn. Osteo. Physicians and Surgeons Aux. (pres. dist. 9, 1957-58, state treas. 1959-61, pres. 1962-63), Am., Tex. psychol. assns., Mensa, Kappa Delta Pi. Episcopalian. Home: 101 2111 Thompson Rd Richmond TX 77469 Office: Adminstrn Bldg Lamar Consol Ind Sch Dist Rosenberg TX 77471

BOYD, LOUIS JEFFERSON, educator; b. Lynn Grove, Ky., Mar. 14, 1928; s. Bernice B. and Ethel Belle (Turnbow) B.; B.S., U. Ky., 1950, M.S., 1951; Ph.D., U. Ill., 1956; m. Rebecca Charlotte Conner, June 12, 1948; children—Beverly (Mrs. Timothy T. Gallagher), Beda, Garth, Bettina. Extension specialist U. Ky., Lexington, 1951-53; research asso. U. Ill., Urbana, 1953-56; asso. prof. U. Tenn., Knoxville, 1956-62; prof. Mich. State U., East Lansing, 1963-72; prof., chmn. div. animal sci. U. Ga., Athens, 1972—. Researcher, Inst. Research on Animal Diseases, Agrl. Research Council, Compton, Eng., 1970-71. Served with AUS, 1946-47. Recipient Outstanding Adviser award Am. Dairy Sci. Assn., 1966, Outstanding Extension Specialist award Mich. State U., 1971, NSF travel grant, France, 1968. Mem. Soc. Study Reproduction, Am. Soc. Animal Sci., Am. Dairy Sci. Assn., Soc. Study Fertility, A.A.A.S., Farm House (nat. dir. 1960-64), Sigma Xi, Gamma Sigma Delta, Sigma Phi. Presbyn. (elder). Optimist (v.p. 1961). Breeding columnist Hoard's Dairyman mag., 1967-72. Patentee process to improve fertility of animal semen. Home: 106 St James Ct Athens GA 30601 Office: Div Animal Science Univ Georgia Athens GA 30602

BOYD, ROBERT FRIEND, lawyer; b. Richmond, Va., May 11, 1927; s. Oscar L. and Ruby (Friend) B.; A.B., Coll. William and Mary, 1950, J.D., 1952; m. Sara Grace Miller, Sept. 20, 1952; children—Robert Friend, David Miller, Mary Elizabeth, James Matheson. Admitted to Va. bar, 1952; practiced in Norfolk, 1955—; sr. partner firm Boyd, Davis & Payne, 1957—; commr. Chancery for Circuit Ct., Norfolk, Circuit Ct., Chesapeake, Va., 1967—. Dir., Santee Portland Cement Corp., Cementon, S.C., Holly Hill Lumber

Co. (S.C.); treas., dir. Stewart Sandwiches, Inc. (Va.). Bd. dirs. Union Mission, Am. Heart Assn., Fraternal Order Police Assns.; mem. adv. com. Norfolk city council, 1966-71. Trustee, treas., mem. exec. com. Va. Wesleyan Coll.; trustee, v.p. Randolph-Macon Acad.; bd. dirs. Coll. William and Mary Law Sch., Norfolk Municipal Hosp.; chmn. bd. Va. Cultural Found.; mem. pres.'s council Coll. William and Mary. Served to capt. USMC, 1952-54. Named Outstanding Young Man of City, Norfolk Jr. C. of C., 1958. Mem. Nat. Assn. Coll. and U. Attys., Va. Trial Lawyers Assn. (v.p.), Tau Kappa Alpha. (chmn. ofcl. bd.). Methodist. Mason (Shriner), Kiwanian (dir., pres. Norfolk). Clubs: Harbor, Norfolk Yacht and Country. Home: 912 Hanover Av Norfolk VA 23508 Office: Va Nat Bank Bldg Norfolk VA 23510

BOYD, ROLAND WELDON, lawyer; b. Lavon, Tex., Sept. 10, 1908; s. William F. and Fannie Belle (Stimson) B.; B.A., U. Tex., 1931; LL.B., So. Methodist U., 1933; m. Nanette Gay, Sept. 6, 1935; children—William Maston, Betty (Mrs. Jim Skelton). Admitted to Tex. bar, 1933; criminal dist. atty. Collin County, Tex., 1939-42; practice law, McKinney, Tex., 1942—; now sr. mem. firm Boyd, Veigel & Gay, attys. at law. Chmn. bd. Central Nat. Bank, McKinney, 1970—. Research fellow Southwest Legal Center, So. Meth. U.; cons. U. Wis. Condemnation Research Project, 1966; mem. Presdl. Emergency Bd. to mediate L.I.R.R. dispute, N.Y., 1967. Past county chmn. Cancer Crusade; organizer, past pres. East Fork Watershed Assn.; v.p., chmn. air route com. North Tex. Commn., Dallas and Ft. Worth, 1972—. Pub. del. UN Econ. and Social Council, Geneva, Switzerland, 1967. Recipient Unselfish Service award in Soil and Water Conservation Collin County, 1964, 66; Unselfish Service in Soil Conservation award Soil Conservation Soc. Am., 1950; Regional Unselfish service award 170 Counties Tex., 1966; named East Texan of Month, Apr. 1971, McKinney Most Outstanding Citizen, 1972; Tex. Conservation award Ft. Worth Area C. of C., 1973. Fellow Am. Coll. Probate Counsel, Tex. Bar Found.; mem. Am. (past chmn. condemnation law com., mem. faculty nat. inst. on eminent domain), Tex., North Tex., Collin County bar assns., Am. Judicature Soc., Collin County Hist. Survey Com. (chmn.), E. Tex. C. of C. (pres. 1972). Baptist. Address: 218 E Louisiana St McKinney TX 75069

BOYD, V(AUGHAN) FRANK, JR., agrl. products co. exec.; b. Raleigh, N.C., July 2, 1924; s. Vaughan F. and Willa (Gray) B.; B.S., Va. Poly. Inst., 1949, M.S., 1952; postgrad. U. Md., 1952-53; Ph.D. in Biochemistry, Tex. A. and M. U., 1959; m. Virginia Mae Bradley, May 28, 1960; children—Deborah, Richard, Laura, Philip, Michael, Bradley. Research chemist Am. Cyanamid, Princeton, N.J., 1960-63; dir. chemistry AME Assos., Princeton, 1963-65; residue, metabolism leader CIBA Agrochem. Co., Vero Beach, Fla., 1965-71; mgr. chemistry regulatory dept. Sandoz-Wander, Inc., Homestead, Fla., 1972—. Mem. exec. com. Hopewell (N.J.) Democratic party, 1963-65. Pres., P.T.A., Homestead, 1972—. Served with AUS, 1944-46. Mem. Am. Chem. Soc. (sec. treas. pesticide div. 1970-72), Sigma Xi, Phi Sigma. Presbyn. Mason, Lion. Home: 948 NW 10th St Homestead FL 33030 Office: 311 8th St NW Homestead FL 33030

BOYD, WAYMON LEWIS, pipeline constrn. co. exec.; b. nr. Port Lavaca, Tex., Sept. 2, 1933; s. Arbie Lewis and Ruby (Elswick) B.; grad. pub. high sch.; m. Ann Fisher, July 8, 1956; children—Wayne Allen, Randy Lynn. With King Fisher Marine Service, Inc., Port Lavaca, 1956—, pipeline foreman, 1958-67, v.p. constrn., 1967—; pres. Bafco, Inc., Port Lavaca, 1971—. Leader 4-H Club, Port Lavaca, 1969—. Served with AUS, 1954-56. Home: 2304 Larry St Port Lavaca TX 77979 Office: PO Box 108 Port Lavaca TX 77979

BOYDSTON, EDWARD ARMOND, petroleum co. exec.; b. Edmond, Okla., June 6, 1923; s. Samuel Edward and Mary Katherine (Moyer) B.; B.S. in Bus. Adminstrn., Oklahoma City U., 1949; grad. Naval War Coll., 1971; m. Iris Josephine Jack, Nov. 28, 1948; children—Brenda Gayle (Mrs. Jeff Chatham), Rhonda Joline, Mona Rena. Clk., Office of Gov. State of Okla., Oklahoma City, 1947-49; mem. staff land and prodn. dept. Harper Oil Co., 1949-70, v.p., 1970—, mem. adv. bd. profit sharing plan, 1970—. Mem. council Evangel Coll., Springfield, Mo., 1970—. Served with USNR, World War II; capt. Res. Mem. Am., Oklahoma City assns. petroleum landmen, Naval Res. Assn., U.S. Naval Inst., Navy League, Res. Officers Assn. (pres. Adm. Marc Mitcher chpt., mem. nominating com.), Am. Legion. Mem. Assembly of God Ch. (deacon, tchr. Sunday sch.). Club: Petroleum (Oklahoma City). Home: 3005 SE Hidden Valley Road Edmond OK 73034 Office: 904 Hightower Bldg Oklahoma City OK 73102

BOYDSTUN, JACKSON BENJAMIN, architect; b. Natchitoches, La., Feb. 5, 1908; s. Benjamin Kendall and Eunice Augusta (Hargis) B.; grad. high sch.; m. Bernice Erline Hill, Apr. 19, 1930; children—Nelwyn (Mrs. Dan W. Poole, Jr.), Betty Sue (Mrs. Stuart Carpenter), Jackson Benjamin, David H. Constrn. supervising engr. constrn. firms, 1936-46; archtl. asso. Barron, Hienberg & Brocato, architects, Alexandria, La., 1947-50; self-employed as architect, Natchitoches, 1960—; dir., chmn. bd. J. B. Boydstun & Assos., Inc. Mem. Constrn. Legislative Council La., 1970-72. Served with AUS, World War II. Mem. A.I.A., Am. Legion (comdr. 1945-46), La. Architects Assn. Democrat. Methodist. Mason (Shriner). Prin. archtl. works include Marthaville Phys. Edn. and Auditorium, St. Matthew High Sch., Elementary Sch. Library, Allen High Sch. Classroom Bldg., Goldonna High Sch. Auditorium and Classroom Bldg., Robeline Phys. Edn. and Classroom Bldg. Home and office: 410 Stephens Av Natchitoches LA 71457

BOYE, CHARLES ANDREW, JR., physicist; b. Appalachia, Va., Nov. 15, 1928; s. Charles Andrew and Laura Mazola (Henly) B.; m. Mary Kathryn Steffey, Dec. 20, 1950; children—Clinton Andrew, Daniel Matthew. Tchr. pub. schs., Giles County, Va., 1953-54; asst. prof. physics E. Tenn. State U., Johnson City, 1956-57; research physicist Tenn. Eastman Co., Kingsport, Tenn., 1956-59, sr. research physicist, 1959-70, research asso., 1970—. Served with AUS, 1951-52. Mem. Am. Phys. Soc., Am. Chem. Soc., Tenn. Acad. Sci., Sigma Xi. Clubs: Civitan (dir.), So. Appalachian (pres. 1974—). Home: 2355 Mountain Dr Kingsport TN 37664 Office: Research Labs Tenn Eastman Co Kingsport TN 37662

BOYER, LESTER LEROY, JR., archtl. engr., educator; b. Hanover, Pa., Apr. 6, 1937; s. Lester Leroy and Ruth Florence (Kessler) B.; B. Archtl. Engring., Pa. State U., 1960, M.S., 1964; postgrad. in Architecture, U. Cal. at Berkeley, 1973—; m. Patricia Barbara Hayes, Dec. 28, 1958; children—Douglas Lester, Blane Edward, Darla Mae. Instr. archtl. engring. Pa. State U., 1960-64; research engr. Armstrong Cork Co., Lancaster, Pa., 1964-68; sr. cons. acoustics and noise control Bolt Beranek and Newman, Inc., Cambridge, Mass., 1968-70; asso. prof. architecture Okla. State U., Stillwater, 1970—; cons. acoustics and environmental comfort, 1970—. Active Will Rogers council Boy Scouts Am. Named Explorer Adviser of Year, Lancaster (Pa.) Council, 1967. Registered profl. engr., Pa., Mass., Okla. Am. Iron and Steel Inst. grantee, 1972. Mem. Acoustical Soc. Am., Illuminating Engring. Soc., Am. Soc. Heating, Refrigerating and Air Conditioning Engrs., Nat. Soc. Profl. Engrs. (course dir. 1964—), Am. Soc. Engring. Edn., Sigma Tau, Scarab, Alpha Rho Chi, Theta Xi. Democrat. Lutheran. Editor: Design for Environmental Hazards (Dept. of Defense), 1973. Author articles on comfort, acoustics, lighting, thermal control, to tech. jours. Home: PO Box 205 Stillwater OK 74074 Office: School of Architecture Oklahoma State University Stillwater OK 74074

BOYERS, ROBERT CYRUS, dentist, army officer; b. Morgantown, W.Va., Nov. 15, 1924; s. Fred Earl and Imogene Mary (Harkness) B.; student Duke, 1944-45, W.Va. U., 1947-48; D.D.S., U. Pitts., 1952; M.S., Georgetown U., 1961; m. Nina Helen Ullery, July 26, 1947; children—Barbara (Mrs. Ralph Young), Laura (Mrs. Larry Burt), Janet (Mrs. James Crum), Beverly (Mrs. Stephen Kefalas), Nanette. Commd. 1st lt., Dental Corps, U.S. Army, 1954, advanced through grades to col., 1971; chief dept. pathology Walter Reed Army Inst. Research, 1961; cons. oral pathology to dental surgeon U.S. Army, Europe, 1963-66; asst. chief dept. oral pathology U.S. Army Inst. Dental Research, Walter Reed Army Med. Center, Washington, 1966-69, chief dental and oral pathology div., Armed Forces Inst. Pathology, 1969—, course dir. oral and forensic pathology, 1969—; lectr. oral pathology Sch. Dentistry, W.Va. U., 1968-70; prof. oral pathology Sch. Dentistry, Howard U., 1971; asso. prof. oral pathology Georgetown U., 1968—; asst. prof. George Washington U. Grad. Sch., 1972. Recipient Surgeon Gen.'s award for profl. superiority, 1971. Diplomate Am. Bd. Oral Medicine, Am. Bd. Oral Pathology. Fellow Am. Acad. Pathology (v.p.); mem. Am. Dental Assn., Am. Soc. Forensic Odontology (pres.), Internat. Acad. Law and Scis., Capitol Order Oral Pathologists (founder 1970). Mason (Shriner). Contbr. articles to profl. jours. Home: 4601 Harling Lane Bethesda MD 20014 Office: Armed Forces Inst Pathology Washington DC 20306

BOYERS, THOMAS, IV, lawyer; b. McAllen, Tex., Mar. 18, 1927; s. Thomas and Johnnie May (Harkey) B.; student Vanderbilt U., 1947-49, Middle Tenn. State U., 1949-50; LL.B., George Washington U., 1955; m. Elizabeth Butler, May 3, 1958; children—Thomas, Tracey Elizabeth. Clerical asst. to U.S. senator from Tenn., 1952-53; admitted to Tenn. bar, 1956, since practiced in Gallatin; city atty. Gallatin, Tenn., 1965—. Mem. Tenn. Ho. of Reps., 1956-58, Tenn. Senate, 1958-64. Trustee for Preservation of Tenn. Antiquities, Cragfont. Served with AUS, 1945-47. Mem. Am., Tenn., Sumner County bar assns., Am. Legion, V.F.W., Kappa Alpha. Presbyn. (deacon 1971—). Home: 909 Lakeshore Dr Gallatin TN 37066 Office: 102 Public Square Gallatin TN 37066

BOYKINS, ERNEST A., JR., coll. pres.; b. Vicksburg, Miss., Sept. 5, 1931; s. Ernest A. and Georgia (Allen) B.; B.S., Xavier U., 1953; M.S., Tex. So. U., 1958; Ph.D., Mich. State U., 1964; postgrad. U. Conn., 1960; m. Beverly Malveaux, Aug. 17, 1955; children—Darryl, Rhea, Constance, Karen. Instr. Alcorn A. and M. Coll., 1954-57, acting head sci. dept., 1958-59, prof., 1964-71, dir. div. arts and scis., 1970-71; pres. Miss. Valley State Coll., Itta Bena, 1971—. Mem. selection panel Inter-Instl. Coop. Program for Coll. and Pub. Sch. Tchrs. of Disadvantaged Youth, NSF, 1968; mem. regional older persons adv. com. Office Equal Opportunity, 1972—; mem. adv. group Miss. Regional Med. Program, 1970—; mem. Miss. Manpower Program, 1971—, Miss. Devel. Econ. Council, 1973—, Miss. Conservation Ednl. Adv. Council. Mem. Am. Council Edn., Am. Inst. Biol. Scis., Sigma Xi, Beta Kappa Chi, Omega Psi Phi. Research with effect of DDT on birds. Office: President's Office Mississippi Valley State College Itta Bena MS 38941

BOYLAND, HERBERT LAYTON, lawyer; b. Dallas, Jan. 2, 1927; s. Herbert Layton and Bessie (Jones) B.; student U. Ark., 1944-45, Kilgore Coll., 1947, East Tex. Bapt. Coll., 1947-48; LL.B., Baylor U., 1950; m. Peggy Jane Porter, Mar. 5, 1949; children—Rex, Laurie, Kurt, Sharon. Admitted to Tex. bar., 1950; partner firm Kenley, Boyland, Hawthorn, Starr & Coghlan, Longview, Tex., 1950—. Dir. Gregg County Savs. & Loan Assn., 1968-73, chmn. bd., 1974—. Pres., Longview Symphony League, 1969-70, then dir.; pres. Longview Parents League, 1970-71. Chmn., Democratic Precinct Com., 1970—. Bd. dirs. Baylor Stadium Corp. Served with AUS, 1945-47. Mem. Gregg County (pres. 1969), Tex. (fellow Bar Found.), Am. bar assns., Tex. Assn. Def. Counsel (dir. 1968-70), Internat. Assn. Ins. Counsel, Fedn. Ins. Counsel, Am. Judicature Soc., Assn. Ins. Attys. Mem. Ch. of Christ. Rotarian, Mason (32 degree, Shriner). Home: 2009 Smallwood St Longview TX 75601 Office: Petroleum Bldg Longview TX 75601

BOYLE, JOHN FRANCIS, lawyer; b. Chgo., Mar. 29, 1935; s. John F. and Margaret (Lawless) B.; B.S. in Commerce, Tex. Christian U., 1958; LL.B., U. Tex., 1961; m. Marion Katherine Murphy, Feb. 23, 1962; children—Fitz, Ben, Eileen, Rebecca, Matthew. Admitted to Tex. bar, 1961, practiced in Dallas, 1961-64, Irving, 1964—; asst. dist. atty. Dallas County, 1961; asst. city atty. City of Dallas, 1962-64; city atty. City of Irving, 1964-70; mem. firm English, Deatherage and Boyle, Irving, 1970—. Vice pres. Irving Symphony, 1973. Mem. Tex. Ho. of Reps. from Dallas County, 1971-72. Mem. State Bar Tex., Dallas County, Irving (v.p. 1973) bar assns., Irving C. of C. (dir. 1968-72). Rotarian, K.C. (advocate 1973). Home: 1405 Oak Lea Irving TX 75061 Office: 304 Southwest Bank Bldg Irving TX 75060

BOYLE, JOHN HARTFORD, electronics co. exec.; b. Chattanooga, July 6, 1918; s. Hartford D. and Clementine (Zimmerman) B.; B.B.A., U. Chattanooga, 1941; m. Paty Spearman, Mar. 23, 1946; children—John Michael, Robert Hartford, Patrick Joseph, Timothy Richard, Sharon Paty. Football coach U. Chattanooga, 1940-41; pilot European operations Am. Overseas Airlines, 1946-49; pilot, mgr. European operations Pan Am. World Airways, 1949-52; v.p. corporate marketing Collins Radio Co., Dallas, 1952—. Served to maj. USAAF, 1941-46. Home: Box 87 Route 1 Allen TX 75002 Office: Collins Radio Co Dallas TX 75207

BOYLE, VIRGINIA HILL (MRS. FRANK GORDON BOYLE), banker; b. Tishomingo, Okla., Nov. 6, 1942; d. Johnie Lee and Rose (Stewart) Hairell; grad. high sch.; m. Frank Gordon Boyle, Aug. 6, 1966. Sec., Pacific Finance, Wichita Falls, Tex., 1961-64; sec. Meml. Bank, Houston, 1964-67, asst. cashier, 1967-69, asst. v.p., 1969-74; retail loan officer Corpus Christi State Nat. Bank (Tex.), 1974—. Mem. Meml.-Spring Branch C. of C. (dir. 1972—), Nat. Assn. Bank Women, Am. Inst. Banking, Bank Adminstrv. Inst. Club: Bank Women's (project chmn. 1969-70, publicity chmn. 1970-71, by-laws chmn. 1971-72, v.p. 1972, pres. 1973). Home: 6822 Sahara St Corpus Christi TX 78412 Office: PO Box 301 Corpus Christi TX 78403

BOYLES, CARL LEROY, dentist; b. Hubbard, Tex., July 29, 1924; s. Carl and Eiliese (McWilliams) B.; student Baylor U., 1941-43; D.D.S., U. Tex., 1946; m. Lucy Marie Wiggins, Apr. 21, 1970; children (by previous marriage)—Harriet (Mrs. Leon Berry), Carl Leroy, Elizabeth, William Gilbert, Christopher David. Pvt. practice dentistry, Houston, 1949—; mem. staff Bapt. Meml. Hosp. Postgrad. instr. U. Tex. Dental Sch., 1951-57. Scoutmaster Sam Houston area council Boy Scouts Am., 1950-53; chmn. dental health sub-com. Houston Ind. Sch. Dist., 1970-72. Served to capt. Dental Corps, AUS, 1946-48. Recipient award of merit Houston Ind. Sch. Dist., 1972. Mem. Am. Soc. Preventive Dentistry, Am. Acad. Gold Foil Operators, Am., Tex. dental assns., S.W. Soc. Dental Medicine (pres. 1958-59), Acad. Gen. Dentistry, Houston Dist. Dental Soc. (chmn. preventive dentistry com. 1970-72). Baptist. Home: 4023 Gulf St Houston TX 77017 Office: 8060 Moline St Houston TX 77017

BOYLES, HARLAN EDWARD, SR., state ofcl.; b. Vale, N.C., May 6, 1929; s. Curtis E. and Kate (Scronce) B.; student U. Ga., 1947-48; B.S., U. N.C., 1951; m. Frances Wilder, Feb. 29, 1928; children—Lynn, Harlan Edward. Auditor, N.C. Dept. Revenue, 1951-56; exec. sec. N.C. Tax Rev. Bd., 1956-60; dep. treas. State of N.C., Raleigh, 1960—, sec. N.C. Local Govt. Commn., 1960—. C.P.A., N.C. Mem. N.C. Assn. C.P.A.'s. Presbyn. (elder). Rotarian. Home: 1924 Fairfield Dr Raleigh NC 27608 Office: Albemarle Bldg Raleigh NC 27611

BOYLES, JAMES EDWARD, indsl. engr.; b. Houston, Aug. 15, 1929; s. Lester Tucker and Hazel Viola (Montgomery) B.; B.S., Tex. A. and M. U., 1951; m. Martha Faye Brannen, Oct. 20, 1961; children—Johnna, William. Home builder, Houston, 1955; indsl. engr. Reed Roller Bit Co., 1956-60; indsl. engr. W.K.M. Valve div. A.C.F. Industries, Houston, 1960-66, head indsl. engring. dept., 1966-69, mgr. indsl. engring., 1970-73, mgr. mfg. engring., 1973—; lectr. U. Houston. Served from lt. to capt. USAF, 1952-54, now lt. col. Res. Registered profl. engr., Tex. Mem. Am. Inst. Indsl. Engrs. (pres.; nat. gen. conf. chmn. 1969), Res. Officers Assn., Air Force Assn., Armed Forces Communications and Electronics Assn., Tex. Soc. Profl. Engrs., Nat. Mgmt. Assn. Home: 4415 Woodvalley Dr Houston TX 77035 Office: PO Box 2117 Houston TX 77001

BOYLSTON, SAMUEL LIONEL, assn. exec.; b. Springfield, S.C., May 8, 1923; s. Raymond Powell and Lillie Victoria (Boylston) B.; LL.B., U. S.C., 1950; m. June Christine Busbee, July 3, 1957; stepchildren—Robin Virginia Cheatham, Norma June Cheatham. Admitted to S.C. bar, 1950; atty. City of Springfield, 1950-56; dir. Warehouse div. S.C. Dept. Agr., Columbia, 1956-62; gen. mgr. Motor Transp. Assn. S.C., Columbia, 1963—. Mem. S.C. Ho. of Reps., 1951-56. Served with USAAF, 1943-46. Mem. S.C. Hwy. Users Conf. (pres. 1969), S.C. Soc. Assn. Execs. (pres. 1970). Democrat. Rotarian. Home: 3201 Stepp Dr Columbia SC 29205 Office: 2425 Devine St Columbia SC 29204

BOYNTON, JOHN HILL, JR., mfg. co. exec.; b. Palmetto, Ga., Feb. 24, 1924; s. John Hill and Marie Ethel (Collins) B.; B.S., U. Ga., 1954; M.S., Rollins Coll., 1969; m. Martha Murray, Aug. 7, 1950; children—Gary, Barbara. Test and engring. mgr. Fla. operations apparatus service div. Gen. Electric Co., Tampa, 1947-64; v.p. Orlando Armature Works (Fla.), 1964—, Superior Armature Works, Ft. Lauderdale, Fla., Electric Constrn. Co., Orlando; sec.-treas. Rowand Electric, Lakeland, Fla.; pres. Boynton & Assos., Orlando; v.p. Caldwell, Boynton & Asso., Ft. Lauderdale. Served with USNR, 1942-46. Registered profl. engr., Fla. Mem. Nat. Soc. Profl. Engrs., I.E.E.E., Fla. Engring. Soc., C. of C. Baptist. Mason, Rotarian. Home: 1301 Glastonberry Rd Maitland FL 32780 Office: 600 W Central Blvd Orlando FL 32802

BRACHMAN, SOLOMON, business exec.; b. Jacobstadt, Latvia, Dec. 15, 1896; s. Marcus and Mindel (Vershok) B.; m. Etta L. Katzenstein, Oct. 31, 1921; children—Malcolm K., Marilyn. Came to U.S., 1905, naturalized, 1918. With Producers Supply & Tool Co., Marietta, O., 1918-19. Ft. Worth, 1919—, officer and dir., 1920—, pres., 1934—; vice chmn. bd. Pioneer Am. Ins. Co., Ft. Worth, 1948—. Trustee Tex. Christian U., Harris Hosp. Mem. Am. Petroleum Inst. Jewish religion. Mason. Clubs: Ft. Worth, Shady Oak, Columbian, Colonial, Petroleum, Ridglea, Dallas. Office: Trans Am Bldg Fort Worth TX 76102

BRACK, EDYTHE ELLA MULVEYHILL (MRS. REGINALD BRACK), civic worker; b. Kansas City, Kan.; d. William Edward and Easter (Loftus) Mulveyhill; A.B., U. Kan., 1934; m. Reginald Brack, July 28, 1934; children—Reginald, William Dennis, Linda (Mrs. John Samuel McFarland). Bd. mem. Dallas Day Nursery Assn., 1961—, sec. bd., 1967; co-chmn. Southwestern bd. Met. Opera, 1963-69, chmn., 1969—; area adviser Nat. Panhellenic Conf., 1964-69; mem. Caruth Rehab. Center Aux., Dallas. Internat. v.p. Pi Beta Phi, 1964-67, mem. nat. bd. dirs. grand council 1961-67. Mem. Nat. Assn. Women Deans and Counselors, Dallas Art Assn., Art Mus. League. Episcopalian (directress altar guild 1954—, mem. St. Simons day care bd. 1954-62). Clubs: Dallas Woman's (bd. govs. 1970—), Dallas Garden (membership chmn. 1968—), Colony. Home: 6043 Walnut Hill Lane Dallas TX 75230

BRACKEN, WILLIAM EARL, JR., lawyer, city ofcl.; b. Phila., Jan. 25, 1934; s. William Earl and Alabell (Terry) B.; B.B.A., Baylor U., 1956, J.D., 1958; m. Sarah Lou Graves, May 31, 1958; children—Elizabeth Louise, Terry Suzanne, Sarah Lynn. Admitted to Tex. bar, 1958; asso. Bryan, Maxwell, Wilson & Olson, Waco, Tex., 1961-63; asst. city atty. City of Waco, 1963-67, city atty., 1967—. Loan exec. United Fund, 1965—; bd. dirs. Lake Air Little League, 1964-69; pres. Meml. Little League, 1964-66; active various fund-raising drives. Served with USAF, 1958-61. Mem. State Bar Tex., Waco-McLennan County Bar Assn. (sec. treas. 1963), Tex. City Attys. Assn. (pres. 1970-71, dir. 1971-72), Waco-McLennan County Jr. Bd. Assn. (pres. 1969). Baptist. Home: 5000 Ridgeview Waco TX 76710 Office: City Hall PO Box 1370 Waco TX 76703

BRADBURY, ROBERT WESLEY, economist, educator; b. Louisville, Jan. 3, 1905; s. Herbert Roberts and Kate (Fitch) B.; A.B., Albion Coll., 1926; M.A., U. Mich., 1927, Ph.D., 1937; m. Elizabeth C. Kukst, Jan. 30, 1948; children—Joan Elizabeth, Robert Douglas. Instr. U. Mich., 1927-31; asst. prof. La. State U., 1931-37, asso. prof., 1939-41, prof., dir. div. Latin Am. studies, 1941-42; dir. Bur. Research and Statistics, La. Dept. Labor, 1937-39; econ. attache Am. embassy, Panama City, Panama, 1942-44, attache, Mexico City, 1945-46; polit. economist Dept. State, 1944-45; dean Am. Inst. Fgn. Trade, 1946-47; spl. exec. rep. Pan Am. Airways, 1947-50; prof. econs. U. Fla., Gainesville, 1950—; Am. consul, Sao Paulo, Brazil, 1952-53. Hon. prof. U. Asuncion (Paraguay), U. San Andres, La Paz, Bolivia. Mem. Am., So. econ. assns., Phi Beta Kappa, Sigma Nu. Author: Water-Borne Commerce of New Orleans, 1937; El Comercio Internacional, 1959. Editor: Bolivian Economic Seminar, also Second Bolivian Economic Seminar, 1959-60. Home: 501 SW 21st Av Gainesville FL 32601

BRADEN, PATRICK O'CONNOR, univ. pres., clergyman; b. Houston, Feb. 1, 1924; s. Albert Henry and Kathleen Veronica (O'Connor) B.; B.S., Rice U., 1944; M.S., U. Tex., 1954, Ph.D., 1961. Instr. Rice U., Houston, 1946-47; joined Congregation St. Basil, 1947; ordained priest Roman Cath. Ch., 1952; instr. math., physics St. Michael's Coll., Toronto, Ont., Can., 1949-53; prof. physics U. St. Thomas, Houston, 1954—, pres., 1967—. Bd. dirs. Nat. Space Hall of Fame; trustee Inst. Storm Research, Houston, 1966—. Served with USNR, 1944-46. NSF Research grantee, 1965; Tex. A. and M. U. grantee, 1966. Mem. Houston C. of C. (edn. com. 1970—), Am. Assn. Physics Tchrs., Sigma Xi, Tau Beta Pi, Pi Tau Sigma. Research in heat transfer, utilization of solar heat. Home: 3812 Montrose Blvd Houston TX 77006

BRADEN, ROY EDISON, civil engr.; b. Beaver Falls, Pa., Apr. 2, 1918; s. Ross Edison and Edith Fern (Strohacker) B.; student Geneva Coll., 1947-48, Internat. Corr. Schs., 1951-55; m. Wanda Bembnowski, Feb. 20, 1941; 1 son, Roy E. Process engr. Curtiss-Wright Corp., 1940-42; systems engr. Koppers Co., 1942-50;

v.p. Michael Baker, Jr., Inc., Rochester, Pa., 1951-68; engr., sales rep. West Coast Industries, Inc., Ft. Myers, Fla., 1969—. Cons. to engring. cos. in Far East. Served with USMCR, 1943-46, 50-51. Registered profl. engr., Fla., Pa. Mem. Nat., Pa. socs. profl. engrs., Fla. Engring. Soc. Home: 106 SE Colonial Blvd Port Charlotte FL 33952 Office: 520 King St Punta Gorda FL 33950

BRADEN, WALDO W., educator; b. Ottumwa, Ia., Mar. 7, 1911; s. Wilbern C. and Stella (Warder) B.; B.A., Penn Coll., 1932; M.A., U. Ia., 1938, Ph.D., 1942; m. Dana Crane, Aug. 18, 1938; 1 dau., Helen Dana. Tchr., Fremont (Ia.) High Sch., 1933-35, Mt. Pleasant High Sch., 1935-38; tchr. speech Ia. Wesleyan Coll., 1938-40, dean of students, 1942-43, 45-46; asso. prof. speech La. State U., Baton Rouge, U., 1946-51, prof., 1951-73, Boyd prof., 1973—, chmn., 1958—. Vis. prof. Washington U., summer 1952, Mich. State U., summer 1953, U. Pacific, summer 1965, Cal. State Coll., Fullerton, summer 1969. Served with AUS, 1943-45. Mem. Speech Assn. Am. (council 1954—, exec. sec. 1954-57, pres. 1962), So. Speech Assn. (pres. 1969-70), Am. Studies Assn., Pi Kappa Delta, Delta Sigma Rho, Tau Kappa Alpha, Omicron Delta Kappa. Methodist. Author: (with Gray) Public Speaking, 1951, rev. 1963; (with Brandenburg) Oral Decision-Making, 1955; (with Gehring) Speech Practices, 1958; Public Speaking: Essentials, 1966; (with Pennybacker) Broadcasting and the Public Interest, 1969; (with Thonssen and Baird) Speech Criticism, 1970. Editor: Speech Methods and Resources, 1961; revised, 1972; The Speech Teacher, 1967-69; Oratory in the Old South, 1970; Representative American Speeches, 1971, 72, 73. Contbr. articles speech, hist. jours. Home: 535 Ursuline Dr Baton Rouge LA 70808

BRADFIELD, WILLIAM HENRY, JR., publisher; b. Dallas, May 3, 1927; s. William Henry and Lillialma (Boswell) B.; student U. Tex., 1943-45; B.S. in Journalism, So. Meth. U., 1949; m. Clarice Eloise Sargent, Apr. 20, 1952; one son, Clayton Ross. Editor Garland (Tex.) Daily News, 1952-58, Tex. Mesquiter, Mesquite, 1957-61, pub., 1962-65; pub. Financial Trend, 1970—; chmn. bd. Equity Media Inc.; dir. Garland Bank & Trust. Served with USAAF, World War II. Mem. Sigma Delta Chi. Mem. Ch. of Christ. Rotarian. Home: 7588 Benedict Dr Dallas TX 75214 Office: 7616 LB Johnson Freeway Dallas TX 75240

BRADFORD, ADDISON MORTON, JR., lawyer, corp. exec.; b. Lee County, Ark., Jan. 2, 1918; s. Addison Morton and Olivette (Bonner) B.; B.A., Ark. State U., 1939; postgrad. So. Meth. U., 1940-41, J.D., 1948; m. Peggy Caraway, June 18, 1942; children—Paul Randolph, Patricia Gay, Timothy Caraway. Admitted to Tex. bar, 1948, U.S. Supreme Ct.; practiced in Dallas, 1948—; partner firm Bradford & Pritchard, Dallas, 1953-68, Anderson, Henley, Shields, Bradford & Pritchard, 1968—; dir. Central Bank & Trust Co., R.B. Wilber Co.; v.p., dir. Town & Country Vending Service, Inc.; sec., dir. O.E.M. Industries, Inc., Tex. Sign Supply Co.; sec., dir. Tex. Screen Process, Inc.; v.p., dir. Mahard Pullet Farms, Inc.; dir. J.T. Chapman Co.; v.p., dir. Mahard Egg Farm, Inc., Mahard Egg Co., Mahard Feed Mill, Inc., S.L. Ewing Co., Inc. Served as finance officer, capt. AUS, 1943-46. Mem. Am., Dallas bar assns., State Bar Tex., Am. Judicature Soc., Delta Theta Phi. Democrat. Methodist. Mason (32 degree, K.T., Shriner). Clubs: Lancers, Knife and Fork (Dallas); Brookhaven Country. Home: 5339 Royal Crest Dallas TX 75229 Office: Fidelity Union Tower Dallas TX 75201

BRADFORD, TUTT S., publisher; b. Columbia, S.C., Apr. 30, 1917; s. Tutt S. and Zula (Bowen) B.; student Wofford Coll., 1934; m. Elizabeth Hendley, June 30, 1941; children—Nancy, Debbie. Pub. Cleve. Daily Banner, 1948-51; asst. to pres. Gen. Newspapers, 1951; pub. Bristol (Va.) Herald Courier, 1951-55, Maryville (Tenn.) Alcoa Daily Times, 1955—; dir. Cairo (Ill.) Tribune. Pres. Blount County Indsl. Devel. Bd., 1970-72. Mem. bd. Audit Bur. Circulations, 1967-72. Served with AUS, 1943-45; ETO. Recipient Distinguished Service award Bristol Jr. C. of C., 1952, Maryville-Alcoa Jr. C. of C., 1958. Mem. So. Newspaper Pubs. Assn. (dir. 1968-70), Blount County C. of C. (pres. 1960), Tennessee River Valley Assn. (dir.), Sigma Delta Chi. Kiwanian (pres. Maryville 1967). Home: 1901 Westwood St W Maryville TN 37801 Office: 307 E Harper St Maryville TN 37801

BRADLEY, (CHARLES) NORMAN, newspaper editor; b. Flora, Miss., Aug. 7, 1913; s. William Hampton and Annie (Lee) B.; B.S. summa cum laude, Millsaps Coll., 1934; m. Mary Frances Weems, June 29, 1936 children—Caroline, William. Reporter Jackson (Miss.) Clarion Ledger, 1934-37; corr. A.P., 1937-47; editorial writer Chattanooga Times, 1947-54; exec. news editor, 1956-57, asso. editor, 1958-71, editor, 1971—; editor-in-chief Jackson State Times, 1954-55, Pres., bd. dirs. Family Service Agy.; charter pres. Adult Edn. Council, 1952; charter dir. Chattanooga Area Literacy Movement, 1960; mem. bd., pres. Chattanooga Symphony; bd. dirs. Chattanooga Art Assn.; trustee Found. World Literary. Mem. Am. Soc. Newspaper Editors, Kappa Alpha, Sigma Delta Chi. Democrat. Methodist. Clubs: Kiwanis, Lookout Mountain Fairyland. Home: 309 W Brow Rd Lookout Mountain TN 37350 Office: 117 E 10th St Chattanooga TN 37402

BRADLEY, FLORENE JORDAN (MRS. STEVE BRADLEY), librarian; b. Magnolia, Ark., Aug. 18, 1917; d. Thomas Scott and Nellie (Nipper) Jordan; student So. State Coll., Ark., 1935-37; B.A., Henderson State Tchrs. Coll., 1939; B.S. in L.S., George Peabody Coll., 1947; m. Steve Bradley, Nov. 23, 1966. Librarian, tchr. Burdette High Sch., 1939-42, Calhoun High Sch., 1942-43, Magnolia High Sch., 1943-51; regional librarian Columbia-Lafayette-Ouachita-Calhoun Regional Library, Magnolia, 1951—. Sec. City Planning Commn., Columbia County Fair Bd. Recipient Ark. Community Devel. Leadership award, 1969; named Magnolia Woman of the Year service and civic clubs, 1963; Citizen of Yr., 1968. Mem. Magnolia Bus. and Profl. Women's Club, Am. Assn. U. Women, Magnolia League Women Voters, Ark. (past pres.), Southwestern (past chmn. pub. library div.) library assns., A.L.A. (mem. notable books council adult services div. 1962-64), Magnolia-Columbia County C. of C. (past pres.; leadership award), Delta Kappa Gamma. Methodist. Club: Quota. Home: 405 Calhoun St Magnolia AR 71753 Office: 220 E Main St Magnolia AR 71753

BRADLEY, GEORGE ALEXANDER, educator; b. Staunton, Va., Dec. 4, 1926; s. Frank Davis and Alverta (Shull) B.; B.S. in Horticulture with distinction, U. Del., 1951; M.S., Cornell U., 1953, Ph.D., 1955; m. Freda L. Matthews, May 23, 1959; children—Steven George, Susan Virginia. Mem. faculty dept. horticulture U. Ark., Fayetteville, 1955—, asso. prof., 1958-63, prof., 1963—, chmn. dept. horticulture and forestry, 1968—. Served with AUS, 1945-47. Alpha Zeta Meml. fellow, 1951. Fellow A.A.A.S.; mem. Am. Soc. Hort. Sci. (nat. chmn. vegetable sect. 1971-72), Sigma Xi, Alpha Zeta, Gamma Sigma Delta, Phi Kappa Phi. Democrat. Methodist. Contbr. articles to profl. jours. Home: 1700 Viewpoint St Fayetteville AR 72701

BRADLEY, JAMES HYETTE, cast iron pipe co. exec.; b. Livingston, Ala., Feb. 20, 1941; s. Floyd Jackson and Ruth (Maddox) B.; student Howard Coll., 1962, Jefferson State Jr. Coll., 1965, U. Ala., 1966, Sanford U., 1968-69; m. Elizabeth Diane Hening, Jan. 23, 1960; children—Michael Cory, Beth Anne. With Clow Corp., Birmingham, Ala., 1959—, materials mgr., 1971—. Mem. Am. Prodn. Inventory Control, Birmingham Traffic Transp. Mason (Shriner). Home: Rural Route 3 Box 485-D Pinson AL 35126 Office: PO Box 6226 Birmingham AL 35217

BRADLEY, JOHN SAMUEL, geologist; b. Oklahoma City, Feb. 23, 1923; s. John Samuel and Charleen (Holloway) B.; Geol. Engr. Colorado Sch. Mines, 1948; Ph.D., U. Washington, 1952; m. Janet Madeline Rich, Nov. 24, 1951; children—Anne, Elizabeth, James. Research geologist Humble Oil & Refining Co., Houston, 1950-54; marine geologist U. Tex., Port Aransas, 1954-56; research geologist Atlantic Refining Co., Dallas, 1956-64, Amoco Prodn. Co., Tulsa, 1964—. Sector rep. Vision 2000, Tulsa, 1972-73; asst. dist. chmn. Greater Tulsa Council, 1973—. Precinct co-chmn. Democratic party, 1966—. Served with C.E., AUS, 1943-46. Mem. Geol. Soc. Am., Am. Assn. Petroleum Geologists, Am. Geophys. Union, Tulsa Geol. Soc., Soc. Econ. Paleontologists and Mineralogists, Sigma Xi, Sigma Gamma Epsilon. Democrat. Unitarian (trustee). Contbr. articles to sci. publs. Patentee in field. Home: 3355 S Braden St Tulsa OK 74135 Office: Box 591 Tulsa OK 74102

BRADLEY, JOHN SPURGEON, educator; b. Gulfport, Miss., Jan. 28, 1934; s. A.E. and Rae E. (Ball) B.; B.S., U. So. Miss., 1955; M.A. (Carnegie fellow), George Peabody Coll., 1956; Ph.D., U. Ia., 1964; m. Beverley J. Roberts, July 16, 1958; children—Karen, Douglas, Lisa. Instr. U. So. Miss., Hattiesburg, 1956-57, Peabody Coll., Nashville, 1959-60; asst. prof. math. U. Tenn., Knoxville, 1964-68, asso. prof., 1968-72, prof., 1972—; vis. prof. U. Dundee (Scotland), 1971-72. Served to 1st lt. AUS, 1957-59. NASA research grantee, 1967; NSF research grantee, 1969. Mem. Am. Math. Soc., Math. Assn. Am., Edinburgh Math. Soc., Sigma Xi, Omicron Delta Kappa. Author: (with J.H. Barrett) Ordinary Differential Equations, 1972. Home: 6904 Quail Dr Knoxville TN 37919

BRADLEY, LEJEUNE PLATTNER, educator; b. Auburn, Ga., Nov. 22, 1921; s. Thomas Monroe and Daisy (Williams) B.; student Ga. State U., 1940-42, Wabash Coll., 1945; A.B. in Journalism, U. Ga., 1947; M.S., Ind. U., 1948; Ed.D., 1951; m. Doris Marie Mitchell, June 3, 1961; children—Indy Maria, Dawn Michelle, Tammie Doris, Sandra Leanne. Adminstrv. asst. Atlanta Gen. Depot, U.S. Army, Conley, Ga., 1940-42; asst. to dean Sch. Edn., counselor Ind. U., 1948-49; dean men Auburn (Ala.) U., 1949-50; asst. prof. bus. adminstrn. U. Ga., Atlanta div., 1951-56, dir. guidance 1951-67, asso. prof. bus. edn., 1956-65; prof. bus. edn. Ga. State U., Atlanta, 1965—. Con. Ward Found., reading techniques; instr. Am. Inst. Banking 1967—; profl. genealogist; bus. communications cons. U.S. Govt., Industry and Commerce, 1965—; condr. seminars in reading improvement U.S. Internal Revenue Service, 1966, 68. Officer in charge Naval Intelligence Unit Atlanta, 1969-71. Mem. bd. founders George M. Sparks Scholarship Fund, 1957—, chmn., 1962-63; mem. high. sch. accrediting com. Atlanta Pub. Schs.; profl. adv. com. Met. Atlanta Mental Health Assn. Served with USNR 1942-46; PTO; comdr. Res. Recipient Cross of Mil. Service; award Sigma Kappa Chi, 1955; citation U.D.C., 1960; Most Outstanding Intelligence Officer award 6th Naval Dist., 1964; Silver Beaver award, outstanding achievement WSB Radio-TV, Atlanta, 1965; distinguished alumni award Indiana Univ., 1969, Outstanding Service award Ga. Dept. Bus. and Office Edn., 1972, others. Fellow A.A.A.S.; founding asso. Nat. Hist. Soc.; mem. Am. Personnel and Guidance Assn., Am. (state membership chmn. 1956-59), So. coll. personnel assns., Nat. Vocational Guidance Assn. (state membership chmn. 1952-56), Am. Ga., Southeastern psychol. assns., Am. Assn. U. Profs., Adult Edn. Assn., Am., Ga. vocational, assns. Nat., Ga. edn. assns., Nat. Assn. Guidance Suprs., Sales and Marketing Execs. Atlanta, Nat. So., Ga. (editor armchair bull, 1968-70) bus. edn. association, New York Academy of Sciences, International Platform Association, Navy League U.S. (pres. Met. Atlanta council 1971-72), (chmn. edn. com. 1968-69), Naval Inst., Naval Res. Assn., Am. Mus. Natural History, Wabash Coll., Ind. U. (pres. Ga. 1967-69) alumni assns., Sigma Chi, Kappa Sigma (hon.), Sigma Delta Chi, Phi Delta Kappa, Delta Sigma Pi, Alpha Delta Sigma, Kappa Phi Kappa, Alpha Delta (hon.), Sigma Tau Delta. Alpha Psi Omega, Alpha Phi Omega, Sigma Kappa Chi (hon.), Chi Gamma Iota, Pi Sigma Epsilon (hon.), Delta Pi Epsilon. Baptist. Elk, Optimist (lt. gov. Ga. dist.). Club: Optimist (br. pres. 1966-67, dir. 1966-68). Co-author: The American Business Education Yearbook, Vol. XI, 1954; Adult Reading Techniques, 1965 to profl. jours. Home: 2525 Wilson Woods Dr Decatur GA 30033 Office: Ga State U University Plaza Atlanta GA 30303

BRADLEY, MARTHA WASHINGTON NUTTER (MRS. GEORGE WASHINGTON BRADLEY), educator; b. East St. Louis, Ill.; d. Cecil Grafton and Mabel (Hunt) Nutter; B.S. in Edn., U. Va., 1951, M.Ed., 1960; diplome de la langue Francaise, Alliance Francaise, Paris, 1958; Ph.D. (Nat. Def. Edn. Act fellow), Syracuse U., 1967; m. George Washington Bradley, Feb. 20, 1960. Tchr. elementary sch., East St. Louis, 1951-53, Long Beach, Cal., 1953-54, U.S. Army Dependent Schs., Europe, 1954-59, 60-61; reading cons. pub. schs., Fredericksburg, Va., 1961-62; instr. U. Va. Sch. Gen. Studies, 1962-63; asst. prof. edn. East Tenn. State U., Johnson City, 1967-70, asso. prof. edn., 1970—, faculty adviser Student N.E.A., 1968-71. Trustee George and Martha Washington Bradley Found., Johnson City; bd. dirs. People to People, Johnson City, 1971, 2d v.p., 1972—. Mem. Nat. (life), Tenn., East Tenn. edn. assns., Conf. English Edn. evaluator com. to evaluate documents 1968—), Nat. Council Tchrs. English, D.A.R. (chmn. service for vet. patients Tenn. 1971-74, chpt. vice regent 1974—), Daus. Am. Colonists (rec. sec. 1973-76), Internat. Reading Assn. (upper East Tenn. council research chmn. 1969-70), Bus. and Profl. Womens Club (chmn. personal devel. com. 1969-70, pres. 1971-72, 2d v.p. 1972-73; chmn. by-laws com. 1973-74), Am. Ednl. Research Assn., Nat. Soc. Study of Edn., Am. Assn. U. Women (publicity chmn. 1968-70), Am. Assn. U. Profs., Unaka Rock and Mineral Soc. (pres. 1969-70), Friends of the Reece Mus. (mem. edn. com. 1973—), Phi Kappa Phi (charter pres. East Tenn. State U. chpt. 1970-72), Kappa Delta Pi (counselor Zeta Iota chpt. 1968—), Delta Kappa Gamma (1st v.p. 1972-74). Mem. Christian Ch. (pres. Women's council 1970-72, dir. Bible sch. 1971-73). Clubs: Wednesday Morning Music (yearbook com. 1971-74), East Tenn. State U. Women's Faculty (co-chmn. book com. 1969-70), v.p. 1971-72, pres. 1972-73). Office: Box 2757 East Tenn State U Johnson City TN 37601

BRADLEY, NOLEN EUGENE, JR., coll. dean; b. Memphis, Nov. 29, 1925; s. Nolen Eugene and Anice Pearl (Luther) B.; B.S., Memphis State U., 1951, M.A., 1952; Ed.D., U. Tenn., 1966; m. Eloise Mullins, Jan. 7, 1947; children—Sharon (Mrs. Leonard A. Brabson), Diana (Mrs. Wiley M. Rutledge), Nolen Eugene III, David Lee. Instr. polit. sci. Memphis State U., 1951-52; tchr. English, Messick High Sch., Memphis, 1952-56; asst. dean admissions Memphis State U., 1956-64; dir. State Agy. for Title I, Higher Edn. Act 1965, Div. Continuing Edn., U. Tenn., 1966-70; dean instrn. Vol. State Community Coll., Gallatin, Tenn., 1970—. Served with AUS, 1944-46. Mem. Am. Assn. Sch. Adminstrs., Tenn. Adult Edn. Assn., Tenn. Edn. Assn., Omicron Delta Kappa, Pi Delta Epsilon, Phi Delta Kappa, Phi Kappa Phi. Baptist (deacon 1966—). Lion. Home: 907 Harris Dr Gallatin TN 37066

BRADLEY, ROBERT JAMES, physician, ret. army officer; b. Milw., June 11, 1922; s. Harold A. and Hazel (Bautz) B.; B.S., U. Wis., 1943, M.D., 1945; M.H.A., Baylor U., 1966; m. Charlotte Marie Cornett, Aug. 9, 1947; children—Barbara Janet, Elizabeth Louise. Commd. lt. M.C., U.S. Army, 1946; intern Med. Coll. Va., Richmond, 1945-46; resident internal medicine Fitzsimons Gen. Hosp., Denver, 1947-50; resident hosp. adminstrn. Army-Baylor Program U.S. Army Med. Field Service Sch., San Antonio, 1965-66; chief med. service 34th Gen. Hosp., La Chapelle, St. Mesmin, France, 1953-56, Irwin Army Hosp., Ft. Riley, Kan., 1956-61, Ryukyus Army Hosp., Okinawa, 1961-64; comdg. officer U.S. Army Hosp., Ft. Huachuca, Ariz., 1965-67; dir. Coco Solo Hosp., C.Z., 1967-70; army surgeon N.G. Bur., Washington, 1970-74, ret., 1974; asst. prof. medicine U. Va., 1973—. Mem. A.M.A., Assn. Mil. Surgeons U.S., Med. Assn. Isthmian C.Z., Baylor U.-Army Hosp. Adminstrn. Alumni Assn., U. Wis. Med. Alumni Assn., Res. Officers Assn., Ret. Officers Assn., Interallied Confedn. Res. Med. Officers, Am. Numis. Assn., Phi Beta Kappa, Phi Eta Sigma, Alpha Omega Alpha. Methodist (elder). Home: 303 Gloucester Rd Charlottesville VA 22901

BRADLEY, TERRY WADE, lawyer; b. Vernon, Tex., Aug. 2, 1934; s. Montrise Garland and Naomi (Canafax) B.; B.A., Am. Internat. Coll., 1959; LL.B., Tulane U., 1963; m. Clara Jean Nickelson, Nov. 17, 1959; children—Michael Keith and Cheryl Lynn (twins), Sara Ann. Admitted to Tex. bar, 1963; asso. atty. firm Walker, Baker & Altaras, Cleburne, Tex., 1964-68; sole practice, Cleburne, 1969—. Trustee Cleburne Ind. Sch. Dist. Served with AUS, 1953-55. Republican. Methodist (trustee 1970). Home: 1210 Surry Pl Cleburne TX 76031 Office: 107 E Henderson St Cleburne TX 76031

BRADSHAW, HERBERT CLARENCE, newspaperman; b. Rice, Va., Nov. 7, 1908; s. Herbert Leslie and Dell Garnett (Weaver) B.; A.B., Hampden-Sydney Coll., 1930, Litt.D., 1967; M.A., U. Va., 1933; m. Mildred Elizabeth Cunningham, June 20, 1936; children—Kate Weaver (Mrs. Charles William Cloninger), Herbert Cunningham, Elizabeth Scott. Instr., McGuire's U. Sch., 1930-32; prin. Darlington Heights (Va.) High Sch., 1933-38; instr. English Hampden-Sydney Coll. summer sessions, 1937,38; prin. Emporia (Va.) pub. schs., 1938-49; Sunday feature editor Durham (N.C.) Morning Herald, 1949-50, asso. editor, 1951-64, editor editorial page, 1964-74; spl. lectr. N.C. State U., 1974; contbg. editor Winston-Salem (N.C.) Jour., 1974—. Mem. N.C. Commn. for Blind, 1952-70; pres. N.C. Council World Affairs, 1961-63; mem. N.C. Adv. Commn. to Peace Corps, 1963-65; mem. Gov.'s Study Com. in Vocational Rehab., 1967-68; pres. N.C. Soc. for Prevention of Blindness, 1967-69, treas., 1969-71; moderator Yates Bapt. Assn., 1957-59; mem. N.C. Adv. Council on Comprehensive Health Planning, 1968-70; mem. Nat. Policy and Performance Council Rehab. Services Adminstrn., 1968-72; v.p. Tobacco History Corp., Durham, 1972-73; mem. Durham Redevel. Commn., 1974—. Bd. dirs. Nat. Soc. for Prevention Blindness, 1967-73, Found. for Research on Nature of Man. Recipient Distinguished Service award. N.C. Rehab. Assn., 1967. Mem. S.A.R. (pres. N.C.), N.C. Lit. and Hist. Assn. (past v.p.) Huguenot Soc. N.C. (past pres.), Am. Clan Gregor Soc., Va. Hist. Soc., Va. Bapt. Hist. Soc., Phi Beta Kappa, Omicron Delta Kappa, Sigma Upsilon. Democrat. Baptist. Lion (pres.; dist. gov. 1969-70, chmn. state council 1969-70). Author: History of Prince Edward County, Virginia, 1936, rev. edit., 1955; History of Farmville, Va. 1948; Toward the Dawn: History of the First Quarter Century of the N.C. State Assn. for the Blind. 1961. Contbr. articles to mags. Home: 1107 Vickers Av Durham NC 27707

BRADSHAW, LILLIAN MOORE, librarian; b. Hagerstown, Md., Jan. 10, 1915; d. Harry M. and Mabel E. (Kretzer) Moore; B.A., Western Md. Coll., 1937; B.L.S., Drexel U., 1938; m. William Theodore Bradshaw, May 19, 1946. Asst. adult circulation dept. Utica (N.Y.) Pub. Library 1938-41, asst. head, 1941-43; adult librarian Enoch Pratt Free Library, Balt., 1943-44, asst. coordinator work with young adults, 1944-46; br. librarian Dallas Pub. Library, 1946-47, readers adviser, 1947-52, head dept. circulation, 1952-55, coordinator work with adults, 1955-58, asst. dir., 1958-62, dir., 1962—. Mem. steering com. Nat. Library Week; bd. dirs. Dallas County Community Action Program; mem. profl. adv. com. Greater Dallas Community Relations Commn.; mem. adv. bd. Friends Tex. Libraries; conferee, asst. task force leader Goals for Dallas, So. Methodist U. Bd. Publs., 1970-73, vice chmn. goals achievement com. for continuing edn., 1971-72, chmn., 1972—; mem. Com. to Plan Future of Goals for Dallas, 1973—; mem. Gov.'s Commn. on Status of Women; mem. adv. com. U. Tex. at Dallas; library edn. adv. com. Tex. Coll. and U. System Coordinating Bd.; mem. U.S. Com. for Am. Library in Paris, 1970-71; mem. friendship mission to France, 1970; mem. Nat. Reading Council, 1970-73. Bd. dirs. Hoblitzelle Found. Named Tex. Librarian of Yr. 1961; recipient Distinguished Alumnus award Drexel Library Sch., 1970, Titche's Arete award, 1970. Mem. A.L.A. (dir. adult services div. 1962-65, pres. adult services div. 1967-68, dir. exec. com. pub. relations sect., library adminstrn. div. 1964-66, chmn. membership com. 1973-74, chmn. nominating com. 1966-67, mem. council 1968-69, mem. pub. library study com. 1968-69, pres. 1970-71, bd. dirs. Freedom To Read Found. 1969-71), Internat. Fedn. Library Assns. (rep. to revise standards for pub. libraries 1970-72), Tex. Library Assn. (pres. 1964-65, chmn. pub. libraries div., chmn. awards com. 1973-74), Am. Assn. U. Women, Tex. Municipal League (dir. 1966-68, com. of future 1971—), Assn. Grad. Edn. and Research North Tex. (adv. council bd. trustees), League Women Voters, Beta Phi Mu. Club: Zonta. Bd. cons. Library Jour., 1962-63. Contbr. articles to profl. jours. Home: 6318 E Lovers Lane Dallas TX 75214 Office: 1954 Commerce St Dallas TX 75201

BRADSHAW, LUCY HYMAN (MRS. JOSEPH ELTON BRADSHAW), librarian; b. Clinton, N.C., July 20, 1922; d. Zachariah Henry and Laura (McCorkle) Hyman; B.S., Winston-Salem State Coll., 1943, B.S. in L.S., Atlanta U., 1946, M.S., 1955; m. Joseph Elton Bradshaw, Dec. 24, 1946; children—Cheryl Yvonne, Joseph Elton. Library asst. Winston-Salem Tchrs. Coll., 1943-45, asst. librarian, 1946-61, acting librarian, 1961-62, librarian, 1962—. Mem. A.L.A., N.C., Southeastern library assns., Urban League Guild, Am. Assn. U. Women, Winston-Salem Symphony Guild, Beta Phi Mu. Baptist. Home: 442 26th St NW Winston-Salem NC 27105

BRADY, EDWARD LEWIS, govt. ofcl.; b. Charleston, S.C., Apr. 21, 1919; s. Aaron W. and Theresa (Morgenstern) B.; B.A., U. Cal. at Los Angeles, 1940, M.A., 1942; Ph.D., Mass. Inst. Tech., 1948; m. Evelyn G. Padway, Aug. 22, 1944. Research asst. metall. lab. U. Chgo., 1942-43; research asso. Clinton Labs., Oak Ridge, 1943-46, Gen. Electric Research Lab., Schenectady, 1948-55; mgr. coolant chemistry Knolls Atomic Power Lab., Schenectady, 1955-56, mgr. exptl. equipment devel., 1958-59; U.S. rep. AEC, London, Eng., 1956-58; sci. adv. U.S. mission to IAEA, Vienna, Austria, 1959-61; asst. chmn. chemistry dept. Gen. Atomic div. Gen. Dynamics Corp., San Diego, 1961-63; chief Office of Standard Reference Data, Nat. Bur. Standards, Washington, 1963-69, asso. dir. for information programs, 1969—. Mem. Am. Chem. Soc., Am. Phys. Soc., Am. Nuclear Soc., A.A.A.S., Phi Beta Kappa, Sigma Xi. Home: 4620 N Park Av Chevy Chase MD 20015 Office: Nat Bureau of Standards Washington DC 20234

BRADY, JAMES HARRY, indsl. exec. mgmt. cons., syndicated columnist; b. Cleveland, Tenn., June 4, 1924; s. Harry Lee and Edith (Rutherford) B.; grad. Fork Union (Va.) Mil. Acad.; student Am. U. Assigned to Manhattan Engring. Dist., Oak Ridge (where atom bomb was produced), 1943-44; Navy reporter, Army and Navy Jour., 1944-45; reporter for Yankee Network and Indpls. Star, 1944-45; with Mil. News Service, 1944, Washington editor, 1945-56; asso. Army and Navy Pub. Co. and Washington Press Service, 1945-47; author columns Inside Washington, Washington Newsletter, bus. columns, reporting events on Capitol Hill, White House, etc.; asst. to pres. Lancaster Engring. Corp., Daffin Mfg. Co., Lancaster, 1949-54; now owner James H. Brady Enterprises, Knoxville, Tenn.; exec. com., dir. pub. relations Zimmerman Equipment Co., Inc., Nashville; pres. Motel Mgmt., Inc., Knoxville; dir. several corps.; merchandising cons. Enterprise Paint Mfg. Company, Chgo., Inertol Co., Inc., Newark, promotion mgr., Knoxville News Sentinel 1948-49; prepared and issued first satis. findings on cost of World War II, 1945; served as pub. relations asso., Soc. for Advancement Mgmt., 1945; pub. relations asso. Washington Coll. Law, 1945. Named col. staff Gov. of Tenn. Officer. Chmn. exec. com. Serene Manor Med. Center. Mem. White House Corrs. Assn. Republican. Methodist. Mason (K.T., Kiwanian. Clubs: Nat. Press, Variety of Am. (Washington); Deane Hill Country, Senator, Elks (Knoxville); Lancaster County Riding (Lancaster). Contbr. articles to ednl. and sci. jours. Address: 3236 Fairmont Blvd Knoxville TN 37917 also Nat Press Club Washington DC 20004

BRADY, RUFUS HOLLAND, JR., architect; b. Tryon, N.C., June 21, 1925; s. Rufus Holland and Julia Fort (Carroll) B.; student Clemson U., 1942-43; B.Arch., U. Mich., 1950; m. Carolyn Flynn, May 12, 1951; children—Marcus Fort, Alison Stuart. Instr. architecture U. Mich., 1950; vis. instr. architecture Clemson U., S.C., 1955-57; asso. Shannon Meriwether, architect, Tryon, 1951-53; pvt. practice Holland Brady, Jr., architect, Tryon, 1953-70; sr. partner Brady & Brannon, Architects, 1970—; dir. The Northwestern Bank, Tryon. Pres., Lanier Library Assn., Tryon, 1965; chmn. Tryon Planning Bd., 1968; chmn. Local Selective Service Bd., 1958—. Served with AUS, 1943-46; ETO. Decorated Purple Heart. Mem. A.I.A., Alpha Rho Chi. Democrat. Conglist. Clubs: Red Fox Country, Tryon (N.C.) Country; Michigan Union (Ann Arbor). Major archtl. works include Presbyn. Ch., Tryon, 1958, parish house Ch. of St. John in Wilderness, Flat Rock, N.C., 1967. Home: Horseshoe Curve Rd Tryon NC 28782 Office: PO Box 1362 114A N Trade St Tryon NC 28782

BRADY, RUPERT JOSEPH, lawyer; b. Washington, Jan. 24, 1932; s. John Bernard and Mary (Rupert) B.; B.E.E., Catholic U. Am., 1953; LL.B., J.D., Georgetown U., 1959; m. Maureen Mary MacIntosh, Apr. 20, 1954; children—Rupert Joseph, Laureen, Kevin, Warren, Jeannine, Jacqueline, Brian, Barton. Elec. engr. Sperry Gyroscope Co., L.I., N.Y., 1953-56; patent specification writer John B. Brady, patent atty., 1956-59; patent agt. B. P. Fishburne, Jr., patent atty., Washington, 1959-61; pvt. practice patent agt., Washington, 1961, patent atty., 1961-63; sr. partner firm Brady, O'Boyle & Gates, specializing in domestic and internat. patent, trademark, copyright law, Washington, 1963—; admitted to U.S. Ct. Customs and Patent Appeals, 1961, U.S. Supreme Ct., 1969. Mem. Am., Md., D.C. bar assns., Am. Patent Law Assn., Senators Club Alumni. Patentee. Home: 7201 Pyle Rd Bethesda MD 20034 Office: 920 Chevy Chase Bldg 5530 Wisconson Av Washington DC 20015

BRAIBANTI, RALPH JOHN, educator; b. Danbury, Conn., June 29, 1920; s. Daniel V. and Jane (Helena) B.; B.S., Western Conn. State Coll., 1941; A.M., Syracuse U., 1947, Ph.D., 1949; m. Lucy Kauffman, Feb. 19, 1943; children—Claire (Mrs. Lex Larson), Ralph L. Faculty, Kenyon Coll., Gambier, O., 1949-53; faculty Duke, 1953—, James B. Duke prof. polit. sci., 1969—. Cons. U.S. AID, Pakistan, 1960-62, Ford Found., Saudi Arabia, 1972, U.S. Army, Ryukyu Islands, 1950, UN, Malaysia, 1974. Served with AUS, 1942-47. Decorated Commendation medal. Social Sci. Research Council fellow, 1953; Ford Found. fellow, 1953. Mem. Am. Inst. Pakistan Studies (founding pres. 1973—), Internat. Studies Assn. (pres. 1971-72). Author: Research on the Bureaucracy of Pakistan; Asian Bureaucratic Systems Emergent from the British Imperial Tradition; Tradition, Values and Socio-economic Development. Contbr. articles to profl. jours. Club: Cosmos (Washington). Home: 3805 Darby Rd Durham NC 27707

BRAIDO, ROBERT HAROLD, architect-planner; b. New Brunswick, N.J., Oct. 1, 1926; s. Amerigo John and Rozilia (Wantuck) B.; student Palm Beach Jr. Coll., 1948, U. Fla., 1953; m. Alice Lorraine MacDonald, Dec. 27, 1950; children—Robert H., Scott Stephen. Chief draftsman to architect Geo. I. Votaw, 1953; asst. zoning dir. Palm Beach County, 1957-59; chief estimator Wiggs & Maale Constrn. Co., W. Palm Beach, Fla., 1959-67; gen. practice Lake Pk., Fla., 1958-67; owner Jones & Braido, Inc., Naples, Fla., 1957-;. Chmn. adv. com. sch. plant planning, Palm Beach County, 1967, chmn. Lake Park zoning commn., 1965; mem. Naples Planning and Zoning Bd., 1968—. Bd. dirs. United Fund, 1972—. Served USNR, 1944-46. Mem. A.I.A., Naples C. of C. (v.p. 1973-74). Democrat. K.C. (4th deg.) Rotarian. Club: Royal Poinciana Golf. Home: 1565 Crayton Rd Naples FL 33940 Office: 291 Broad Av S Naples FL 33940

BRAILSFORD, JAMES MONCRIEF, state justice; b. Orangeburg, S.C., July 3, 1910; s. James Moncrief and Mary Elizabeth (Bates) B.; A.B., U. S.C., 1932, LL.B., 1934; m. Louise Rook Tompkins, Nov. 5, 1938 (dec. Aug. 1962) children—James Moncrief, Daniel Tompkins, Amelia Tompkins, Martha Aldrich; m. Joan Ward Culler, June 19, 1971. Admitted to S.C. bar, 1934; practiced in Orangeburg, 1934-49; circuit judge S.C., 1949-62; asso. justice Supreme Ct. S.C., 1962—. Mem. S.C. Ho. of Reps. from Orangeburg County, 1939-42, 47-49. Served with AUS, World War II. Mem. Phi Beta Kappa. Address: PO Box 386 Orangeburg SC 29115

BRAINARD, JAYNE DAWSON (MRS. ERNEST SCOTT BRAINARD), club woman; b. Amarillo, Tex., Nov. 1; d. Bill Cross and Evelyn (McLane) Dawson; A.B., Oklahoma City U., 1950; m. Ernest Scott Brainard, Nov. 26, 1950; children—Sydney Jane, Bill Dawson. Guardian Camp Fire Assn., 1960-65; vol. N.W. Tex. Hosp. Aux., 1960-63; state chmn. Am. Heritage, D.A.R., 1963-67, vice regent chpt. 1963-66, regent, 1966-68, state historian Tex. soc., 1967-70, state chmn. marshalls Tex. soc., 1967-70, nat. vice chmn. marshal com., 1969-74, Tex. rec. sec., 1970-73, mem. state organizing com., 1967-70, nat. vice chmn. motion picture commn., 1971-74, Tex. chmn. State Regents Project, 1973—, State vice chmn. nat. def., 1973—, also organizing pres. Children of Am. Revolution, 1963-66, state chmn.; organizing regent Daus. Am. Colonists, 1972; br. pres. Am. Assn. U. Women, 1963-65, mem. state library com., 1967-69; sec.-treas. group League of Democratic Women, 1964; pres. Amarillo Rep. Women's Club, 1968, v.p., 1972, pres., 1973; pres. Panhandle Geol. Soc. Aux., 1959; pres. Speaking of Living Study Club, 1962-63; pres. Starlighters Dance Club, 1963-64; bd. dirs., chmn. pub. relations Amarillo Little Theater; chmn. Leaders Assn. Amarillo Camp Fire Council, 1964-69; mem. steering com. Nat. Library Week, Amarillo, 1964-68; bd. dirs. Amarillo Fine Arts Council, 1966-68, Amarillo Heart Assn., 1972-73; pres. Amarillo Little Theatre, 1968-69; mem. Revitalize Amarillo Com. Mem. U.D.C., Internat. Platform Assn. Editor: Texas Society D.A.R. Cookbook, 1972. Home: 2119 S Lipscomb St Amarillo TX 79109 Office: Box 1101 Amarillo TX 79105

BRAMAN, LEONARD, superior ct. judge; b. Phila., Aug. 21, 1925; s. Harry and Katie (Rappaport) B.; B.S., Temple U., 1949; LL.B., U. Va., 1952; m. Joyce J. Roberts, June 22, 1952; children—David Henry, Barrett Andrew. Admitted to D.C. bar, 1952; law clk. U.S. Ct. Appeals for D.C., Washington, 1952-53; asst. U.S. atty. criminal div. D.C., Washington, 1953-54; Bigelow teaching fellow U. Chgo. Law Sch., 1954-55; mem. firms Newmyer & Bress, Washington, 1955-61, David G. Bress, 1961-64, Bress, Braman & Hilmer, 1964-65, Surrey, Karasik, Greene & Hill, 1965-70; asso. judge Superior Ct. D.C., Washington, 1970—. Served with USAAF, 1943-45. Mem. Am., D.C. bar assns., Internat. Platform Assn., Order of Coif. Editorial bd. U. Va. Law Sch., 1952. Home: 12600 Springloch Ct Silver Spring MD 20904 Office: 440 G St NW Washington DC 20001

BRAMBLE, RONALD LEE, educator; b. Pauls Valley, Okla., Sept. 9, 1937; s. Homer Lee and Ethyl Juanita (Stephens) B.; A.A., San Antonio Coll., 1957; B.S., Trinity U., 1959, M.S., 1964; postgrad. St. Mary's Univ. Sch. Law, 1969-71; LL.D., Pacific Western Coll., 1970; D.B.A., Ind. No. U., 1973; m. Kathryn Louise Seiler, July 2, 1960; 1 dau., Julia Dawn. Mgr., buyer Fed-Mart, Inc., San Antonio, 1959-61; tchr. bus. San Antonio Ind. Sch. Dist., 1961-65, edn. coordinator, bus. tng. specialist, 1965-67; asso. prof., chmn. dept. mgmt. San Antonio Coll., 1967-73. Prin. Ron Bramble Assos., San Antonio, 1967—; lectr. bus., edn. and ch. groups, 1965—; cons. editor Prentice-Hall, Inc., Englewood Cliffs, N.J., 1969-71. Served with AUS, 1959. Recipient Wall Street Jour. award Trinity U., 1959; Distinguished Salesman award Sales and Marketing Execs., 1967; Merit award Adminstrv. Mgmt. Soc., 1968. Mem. San Antonio C. of C. (mem. com. 1967—), Adminstrv. Mgmt. Soc. (pres. 1966-68), Bus. Edn. Tchrs. Assn. (pres. 1964), Sales and Marketing Execs. San Antonio (dir. 1967—), Phi Delta Phi. Republican. Methodist. Lion. Club: San Antonio Advertising. Contbr. articles to profl. jours. Home: 127 Palo Duro San Antonio TX 78216

BRAME, DURWARD BELMONT, gen. engr., govt. ofcl.; b. Sherman, Tex., Apr. 20, 1914; s. James Richard and Mary Ann (Fields) B.; student U. Tulsa, 1935-36, So. Meth. U., 1941-42, various service schs.; m. Doris June Hibbard, Sept. 1, 1967; children by previous marriage—Dulcie Anne (Mrs. Lyndell N. Sumner), Nancy Lynn (Mrs. Richard D. Landes). Inspection and quality engr. USAF, 1941-57; aerospace engr. NASA, 1961-67; developer quality systems, mgr. quality programs for Apollo/Saturn hardward Dept. of Def., Tulsa, 1967-71; mgr. indsl. resources services div. Def. Contract Adminstrn., Dallas, 1971—. Mem. Stone Ridge Home Owners Assn., Irving Fire Fighters, Internat. Circus Fund Underprivileged Children, Tarrant County Police Benefit Assn. Mem. Am. Soc. Metals, Am. Soc. Quality Control. Republican. Presbyn. Mason (32 deg., Shriner). Author: Quality Assurance Familiarization Manual, 1943; Instruction Manual Midwestern Procurement District Functions, 1944. Home: 2510 Richmond Dr Arlington TX 76014 Office: 500 S Ervay St Dallas TX 75201

BRAMLETT, JOHN KENNETH, educator; b. Jefferson, Tex., June 1, 1934; s. John Grady and Nellie Adele (Cloninger) B.; A.S., Perkinston Jr. Coll., 1954; B.S., Miss. Coll., 1956, M.Ed., 1959; m. Nancy Elizabeth Stringer, May 7, 1954; children—Pamela Elizabeth, John Kenneth. Asst. coach Clinton (Miss.) High Sch., 1956-57, Miss. Coll., Clinton, 1961-63; head coach Forest (Miss.) High Sch., 1957-61, 66-70, Prentiss (Miss.) High Sch., 1963-66; athletic dir., head football coach N.W. Miss. Jr. Coll., Senatobia, 1970—. Recipient Coach of Year awards Little Dixie Conf., Jackson Touchdown Club, 1959, 64, 69. Mem. Nat. Jr. Coll. Athletic Assn., Miss. Edn. Assn., Miss. Assn. Coaches. Baptist. Mason, Rotarian. Home: 108 McClure St Senatobia MS 38668

BRAMLETTE, SELMA GEORGIA MITCHELL (MRS. JAMES D. BRAMLETTE), librarian; b. Centerhill, Ark., July 22, 1893; d. Virgil B. and Sarah L. (Adams) Mitchell; B.A., Tex. Coll. Arts and Industries, 1930; B.S. in L.S., Tex. Woman's U., 1946, M.L.S., 1950; m. James D. Bramlette, July 24, 1912 (dec. Oct. 1967); children—Sarah J. (Mrs. C. A. Buenning), James D., Mary Jane (Mrs. W. D. Hughart). Social studies tchr., Stephenville, Tex., 1924, Waco State Home, 1943-46, Sinton, Tex., 1945-46; librarian Sinton (Tex.) High Sch., 1946-49; supr. libraries Sinton Ind. Sch. Dist., 1949-62; librarian Refugio County Pub. Library, Refugio, Tex., 1962—. Recipient certificate of merit Sinton Pub. Schs., 1962. Mem. N.E.A. (life), Tex. State, Coastal Bend (pres. 1952-53) library assns., Alumni Assn. Tex. Coll. Arts and Industries, Delta Kappa Gamma, Alpha Beta Alpha. (life). Clubs: Sinton Faculty; Century (Stephenville). Democrat. Baptist. Home: 214 W Heard St Refugio TX 78377 Office: 815 S Commerce St Refugio TX 78377

BRAMMER, KARL EDMUND, purchasing agt.; b. Lake Charles, La., Sept. 5, 1920; s. Peter Bernhardt and Edith Martha (Bailey) B.; ed. Vincent Bus. Coll., Sowela Tech. Sch., Lake Charles, U. Fla., Gainesville; m. Janice Normand, Dec. 19, 1945; children—Cynthia Hughes, Martha, Peter, Elizabeth. Purchasing agt. Olin Mathieson Chem. Corp., Lake Charles, 1945-57; purchasing agt., traffic mgr. Ormet Corp., Burnside, La., 1957—. Served with AUS, 1938-45. Lutheran. Home: Route 4 Box 458 Gonzales LA 70737 Office: PO Box 15 Burnside LA 70738

BRANCH, DAN PAULK, architect; b. Fitzgerald, Ga., Mar. 3, 1931; s. Felix W. and Mavis P. (Paulk) B.; B.Arch., U. Fla., 1954; M.S. in Architecture, Columbia, 1956; certificate tropical architecture Archtl. Assn., London, Eng., 1956; m. Sonya Meyer, Dec. 10, 1960; children—Thomas A., Martin A. Practice architecture, 1959—; partner C.R. Wedding & Assos., St. Petersburg, Fla., 1972—; mem. faculty U. Fla., 1961-73, asso. prof. architecture, 1966-73; vis. prof. U. Miami, 1972—. W.K. Fellows fellow, 1956-57, Perking-Boring fellow, 1963. Mem. Archtl. Assn. London, A.I.A. (treas. No. Fla. chpt. 1965). Club: Treasure Island (Fla.) Yacht and Tennis. Author: Folk Architecture of the East Mediterranean, 1966; also articles. Home: 3800 Bayshore Blvd St Petersburg FL 33703 Office: 2901 58th Av N St Petersburg FL 33714

BRANCH, LEE WADSWORTH, accountant; b. Dallas, Aug. 6, 1906; s. James Lee and Maude (Darrow) B.; B.B.A., U. Tex., 1928; m. Helen Othel Bauman, May 12, 1934; children—Paula Tobin, Charles, Ellen (Mrs. Stephen A. Wakefield). Practice accounting, Dallas, 1935-60; partner Branch & Orcutt, C.P.A.s, Dallas, 1960—. C.P.A., Tex. Mem. Tex. Soc. C.P.A.s (dir. 1954, 60, 68), Nat. Assn. Investment Clubs (dir. 1973—). Methodist (steward 1955—). Mason, Kiwanian (dir. 1955). Club: Dallas Country. Home: 3310 Fairmount St Dallas TX 75201 Office: 750 One Main Pl Dallas TX 75250

BRAND, JOHN, state ofcl.; b. St. Louis, Apr. 30, 1923; s. William Herman and Mabel Edith (Wimbush) B.; B.S. in Mech. Engring., Mo. Sch. Mines and Metallurgy, 1944; M.Div., Louisville Presbyn. Theol. Sem., 1964; postgrad. U. Ky., 1969-70; m. Virginia May Haggard, Dec. 24, 1970; children—Christy (Mrs. David M. Lashbrook), Ronald C. Rainey, Donald C., Stephanie L. Rainey Virginia (Mrs. Larry Baker), Robin Rainey, Elizabeth Carol. Plant engr. Krummrick plant Monsanto Chem. Corp., East St. Louis, Ill., 1944-46, Queeny plant, East St. Louis, 1946-53, mech. standards engr. organic div., St. Louis, 1953-55, mgr. mech. standardization, research and engring. div., world hqrs., St. Louis, 1955-58; ordained to ministry Presbyn. Ch. U.S., 1964 (transferred to Christian Ch. 1970); pastor South Presbyn. Ch., Louisville, 1958-60, Eastminster Presbyn. Ch., Lexington, Ky., 1960-69; cons. services adminstr. Ky. Dept. Child Welfare, Frankfort, 1970-72; asst. dir. office occupational programs, bur. health services Dept. for Human Resources, Frankfort, 1972—. Part time pastor Berea Christian Ch., Henry County, Ky., 1970—. Bd. deacons Westminster Presbyn. Ch., St. Louis. Mem. Mfg. Chemists Assn. (chmn. mech. tech. com.), Am. Standards Assn., Lexington Assn. Social Professions, Lexington Ministers Assn., Engrs. Club St. Louis, Kappa Sigma. Rotarian. Home: 107 Reservoir Rd Frankfort KY 40601 Office: Dept for Human Resources Bldg Frankfort KY 40601

BRAND, PAUL WILSON, surgeon; b. India, July 17, 1914; s. Jesse Mann and Evelyn Constance (Harris) B.; student Univ. Coll. Sch., London, Eng., 1933; M.B., B.S., Univ. Coll. Hosp., London, 1943; LL.D., Wheaton Coll., 1971.; m. Margaret Elizabeth Berry, May 29, 1943; children—Christopher W., Jean M., Constance M., Estelle F., Patricia N., Pauline F. Intern Univ. Coll. Hosp., 1943-44, resident, 1944-45; resident Hosp. for Sick Children, London, 1945-46; tchr. orthopaedic surgery Christian Med. Coll., Vellore, India, 1946-64, prof. surgery, 1954-64, also past pres.; chief rehab. br. USPHS Hosp., Carville, La., 1966—; clin. prof. surgery La. State U. Med. Sch., 1966—; spl. research to correct deformity in leprosy, 1947—; past chmn. world com. Leprosy rehab. Internat. Soc. Rehab. Disabled, 1962-70; Hunterian prof. (reconstructive surgery in leprosy), Royal Coll. Surgeons, 1952, 62. Recipient Lasker award for distinguished services field rehab., 1958, medal Am. Assn. Plastic Surgeons, 1966; decorated comdr. Order Brit. Empire; medal Merit Swedish Red Cross. Fellow Royal Coll. Surgeons, Royal Soc. Medicine, Brit. Orthopaedic Assn., Am. Surg. Assn. (hon.), A.C.S.; hon. mem. Am. Soc. Surgery Hand; corr. mem. Am. Assn. Plastic and Reconstructive Surgery. Address: USPHS Hospital Carville LA 70721

BRAND, VANCE DEVOE, astronaut; b. Longmont, Colo., May 9, 1931; s. Rudolph William and Donna (DeVoe) B.; B.S. in Bus., U. Colo., 1953, B.S. in Aero. Engring., 1960; M.B.A., U. Cal. at Los Angeles, 1964; grad. U.S. Naval Test Pilot Sch., Patuxent River, Md., 1963; m. Joan Virginia Weninger, July 25, 1953; children—Susan Nancy, Stephanie, Patrick Richard, Kevin Stephen. With Lockheed-Cal. Co., Burbank, 1960-66, flight test engr., 1961-62, traveling engr. rep., 1962-63, engring. test pilot, 1963-66; astronaut NASA Manned Spacecraft Center, Houston, 1966—, mem. crew for Joint U.S./USSR Mission, 1973—. Served with USMC, 1953-57. Mem. Soc. Exptl. Test Pilots, Am. Inst. Aeros. and Astronautics. Home: 18607 Martinique Houston TX 77058 Office: NASA Manned Spacecraft Center Houston TX 77058

BRANDENBERGER, STANLEY GEORGE, research chem. supr.; b. Houston, Jan. 18, 1930; s. Stanley Sylvester and Evelyn Ella (Duke) B.; B.A., Rice U., 1952; Ph.D., U. Tex., 1956; m. Betty Lea McCauley, June 17, 1967; 1 son by previous marriage, Joel Harris; 1 dau., Evelyn Lea. Research chemist Houston Research Lab., Shell Oil Co., 1956-64, supr., 1964-68, 69-72, sect. head Royal Dutch Shell Lab., Amsterdam, 1968-69; staff research chemist, supr. Houston Research Center, Shell Devel. Co., 1972—. Mem. Am. Chem. Soc., Catalysis Soc. Am., S.W. Catalysis Soc., Sigma Xi, Phi Lambda Upsilon, Alpha Chi Sigma. Presbyn. (deacon). Contbr. articles profl. jours. Patentee in field. Home: 5726 Kuldell St Houston TX 77035 Office: PO Box 481 Houston TX 77001

BRANDENBURG, E. CRAIG, clergyman; b. Corydon, Ind., Aug. 26, 1907; s. William S. and Brittie (Breeden) B.; B.A., Ind. Central Coll., 1930, D.D., 1945; B.D., United Theol. Sem., 1935, M.Div., 1972; m. Eva Traylor, Aug. 20, 1933; 1 son, Calvin. Ordained to ministry Evang. U.B. Ch., 1930; pastor First Ch., Evansville, Ind., 1935-44; supt. Ind. Conf., Bedford, Ind., 1944-55; exec. sec. Nat. Bd. Christian Edn., Evang. U.B. Ch., Dayton, O., 1955-68; asso. gen. sec. Bd. Edn., United Meth. Ch., Nashville, 1968-72, asst. gen. sec. Bd. Higher Edn. and Ministry, 1973—. Trustee Ind. Central Coll., 1947—, United Theol. Sem., Dayton, O., 1955—, Evang. Theol. Sem., 1955-71. Mem. Nat. Council Chs., Trinium, and Div. of Christian Edn., World Council Christian Edn., 1955-68. Home: 55 Williamsburg Circle Brentwood TN 37027 Office: 1001 19th Av S Nashville TN 37202

BRANDLI, JEAN S., telephone co. ofcl.; b. New Haven, Sept. 13, 1918; d. Arthur J. and Beatrice (Murray) Smith; student So. Sem., Jr. Coll.; grad. mgmt. devel. program U. Kan., 1966; grad. engring. mgmt. course U. Mich., 1967; m. 3d, Henry E. Brandli, Jr., June 28, 1964. Treas., Lexington Telephone Co., 1951-54, pres., 1954-58; pres. Coosa Valley Telephone Co., Pell City, Ala., 1955—, No. Ind. Telephone Co., Wawaka, Ind., 1959-67. Mem. Southeastern telephone exec. delegation to Russia, 1966; leader People to People travel to Russia, 1969; sec. Rural Telephone Bank Bd. Mem. Ala. Bd. Pensions and Security, 1972. Named Ala. Telephone Woman of Yr., 1966; recipient Pacesetter award 1973). Mem. C. of C. Greater Pell City (pres.), Orgn. for Protection and Advancement Small Telephone Cos. (dir.), Ala.-Miss. Telephone Assn. (dir., pres.), Ind. Telephone Pioneers Am., So. Sem. Alumnae Assn. (pres.), Bus. and Profl. Women's Clubs (pres. Pell City). Clubs: The Club; Relay House; Pine Harbor Country; Downtown (Birmingham, Ala.). Home: Abbot Dr Rivere Estates Pell City AL 35125 Office: 1700 Cogswell Av Pell City AL 35125

BRANDON, HEMBREE BEDELL, newspaper editor; b. New Albany, Miss., July 11, 1936; s. Roy Bedell and Pearl (Miller) B.; A.A., N.E. Miss., 1956; m. Gloria Jean Floyd, June 22, 1961; children—Stephen Alan, Lisa Carole. Pub. relations dir. No. dist. Miss. Hwy. Dept., Tupelo, 1956-62; editor Winona (Miss.) Times, 1962-73; exec. editor Delta Farm Press, Clarksdale, Miss., 1974—. Mem. Miss. Press Assn., Profl. Photographers Assn. Am., Profl. Photographers Assn. Miss.-Ala., Sigma Delta Chi. Methodist. Rotarian. Home: 1204 Park Lane Clarksdale MS 38614 Office: Hwy 61N Box 998 Clarksdale MS 38614

BRANDON, WALTER WILEY, JR., physicist; b. Gainesville, Ga., Dec. 1, 1929; s. Walter Wiley and Nancy Katherine (Logan) B.; diploma Emory Jr. Coll., 1950; B.A., Emory U., 1952, M.S. (fellow), 1953; m. Patricia H. Donham, May 18, 1957; children—Dean Corbly, Miles Logan, Nancy Lynn. Physicist, tech. staff Redstone research labs. Rohm & Haas Co., Huntsville, Ala., 1953-65, 67-71; physicist, tech. staff space div. Boeing Co., Huntsville, 1965-67; tchr. pub. schs., Huntsville, 1971-72; instr. Calhoun Jr. Coll. extension, Huntsville, 1972; physicist U.S. Army Missile Command, Huntsville, 1972—. Fellow Am. Inst. Aeros. and Astronautics (asso.); Mem. Am. Phys. Soc. (S.E. Sec.), Assn. U.S. Army, Sigma Xi (asso.), Sigma Pi Sigma. Home: 1902 Colice Rd SE Huntsville AL 35801 Office: US Army Missile Command Redstone Arsenal AL 35809

BRANDT, GEORGE FRED, JR., civil engr.; b. Wetumpka, Ala., July 14, 1927; s. George Fred and Alpha (Leonard) B.; student U. Tenn., 1946-48; B.C.E., Clemson Coll., 1951; m. Jo Frances Oulla, June 9, 1951; children—David George, Donna Jo. Constrn. engr. E. I. Dupont Co., Savannah River (S.C.) Plant, S.C., 1951-54, prodn.

supr., 1954-59; plant engr. Merry Bros. Brick & Tile Co., Augusta, Ga., 1959-62; head civil engring. dept. Jones & Fellers, Augusta, 1962-66; owner Brandt & Assos., cons. engrs., North Augusta, S.C., 1966—. Served with USNR, 1945-46. Registered profl. engr., Ga., S.C., N.C., Tenn., Fla. Mem. Am. Soc. C.E., S.C. Water and Pollution Control Assn., Nat., Ga. socs. profl. engrs. Baptist. Home: 516 Tanager Rd North Augusta SC 29841 Office: Brandt & Assos 516 Tanager Rd North Augusta SC 29841

BRANDT, HARRY, economist; b. Dresden, Germany, Apr. 13, 1925; s. George and Margarethe (Hamburger) B.; came to U.S., 1938; B.A., U. Wash., 1947; M.S., Columbia, 1949, Ph.D., 1954; m. Frances M. Jacobson, Oct. 29, 1950; children—Stephen J., Douglas M., Sandra J. Instr., Rutgers U., 1949-52, City Coll. N.Y., summer 1951, Ga. State Coll., Atlanta, 1955-59; asst. economist Fed. Res. Bank of Atlanta, 1954, asso. economist, 1955-58, economist, 1958-59, sr. economist, 1959-60, asst. cashier, 1961, asst. v.p., 1962-65, v.p. research, 1965-74, v.p., dir. research, 1974—. Served with AUS, 1944-46. Mem. Am., So. econ. assns., Am., So. (pres. 1971-72) finance assns. Home: 2722 Foster Ridge Rd NE Atlanta GA 30345 Office: 104 Marietta St NW Atlanta GA 30303

BRANNEN, WENDALL E., architect; b. Charleston, Me., Mar. 20, 1934; s. William Durval and Carrie Flayvilla (Robbins) B.; student McNeese State Coll., Lake Charles, La., 1957-58; m. Berlyn Rae DuBose, June 30, 1956; children—Polly, Judy. Archtl. draftsman So. Constrn. Corp., Lake Charles, 1957-59, Paul F. Thompson, architect, Lake Charles, 1959-60, Robert L. Miller, architect, Lake Charles, 1960, Platt & Rice, architect-engr., Lake Charles, 1960-62, Austin Co., engrs.-builders, Houston, 1962-64, 65-66, McGinty Partnership, architects, Houston, 1964-65, Roger Rasbach, designer, Houston, 1966-67; project mgr. Neuhaus & Taylor, architects, Houston, 1967-69, 69-72; prodn. mgr. Hoff-Blackston-Strode, architects, Houston, 1969, Simpson Assos. Inc., architects, Austin, Tex., 1972-73; project architect Page, Southerland and Page, architects, Austin, 1973—. Hon. dep. sheriff Harris County (Tex.), 1969-72. Served with USAF, 1953-57. Mem. A.I.A. (mem. pub. relations com. Houston chpt. 1971-72), Tex. Soc. Architects. Prin. works: home office bldg. Am. Nat. Ins. Co., Galveston, Tex., 1967-69; Dresser Tower, Houston, 1970-72, Dresser Garage, Houston, 1970-72, No. 2 Toll Bldg., Austin, 1972-73, Stark Museum, Orange, Tex., 1973-74. Home: 8201 Mowinkle Dr Austin TX 78746 Office: 602 West Av Austin TX 78767

BRANNIAN, ROSS EDWIN, geophysicist; b. Randolph, Ia., Nov. 9, 1925; s. Harold Benjamin and Edna (Fichter) B.; student Ia. State U., 1943-45; B.S. in Geophysical Engring., U. Tulsa, 1948. With Geophys. Service, Inc., Dallas, 1948-67, party chief, 1952-65, sr. seismologist, 1965-67; ind. geophys. and geol. cons., 1968—. Precinct chmn. Dallas County Republican party, 1969—; regional chmn. Legis. Dist. 33-C, 1972—. Bd. dirs. Oak Lawn Preservation Soc. Mem. Dallas Geophysical Soc. (sec.), Soc. Exploration Geophysicists, Am. Assn. Petroleum Geologists, Canadian Soc. Petroleum Geologists, Dallas Geol. Soc. Home and office: PO Box 45011 3260 N Hall St Dallas TX 75235

BRANNON, JAMESTON REZIN, JR., educator; b. Shreveport, La., June 3, 1935; s. Jameston Rezin and Emma (Collins) B.; Med. Technologist, Radiography Technologist, Gradwohl Sch. Lab. and X-Ray Technique, St. Louis, 1955; B.S., Stephen F. Austin State U., 1959, M.A., 1960. Dir. lab. Beall-Pennington Clinic, Nacogdoches, Tex., 1957-59; teaching asst. La. State U., Baton Rouge, 1960-62; prof. biology, chmn. dept. Panola Jr. Coll., Carthage, Tex., 1963—. Mem. Am. Inst. Biol. Scis., Tex. Acad. Sci., Nat. Assn. Biology Tchrs., Am. Assn. U. Profs., N.E.A., Tex. Jr. Coll. Tchrs. Assn., Stephen F. Austin Alumni Assn. (life), Am. Radiography Technologists (charter), Nature Conservancy (trustee 1968—, sec. Tex. 1967), Ozark Soc., Nat. Rifle Assn. (life), Magna Charta Barons, Soc. Descs. Knights of Garter, Ams. Royal Descent, Panola County Hist. Soc. (dir. 1967, pres. 1968), Panola County C. of C., Panola County Jaycees (2d v.p. 1967), Phi Delta Kappa, Kappa Delta Pi. Lion (chmn. ednl. com. 1967). Home: 1012 College Circle Carthage TX 75633

BRANNON, JOAN CAGE (MRS. WILLIAM LOVE BRANNON), oil operator; b. Sinton, Tex., Oct. 12, 1930; d. James Bailess and Leola (Moss) Cage; student Southwestern U., 1947-48; B.A., U. Tex., 1951; m. William Love Brannon, Oct. 5, 1963; children—William Love, Lea. Legal sec. Shell Oil Co., Corpus Christi, Tex., 1953-56, Am. Petrofina Oil Co., Dallas, 1956-58, Union Oil Co. of Cal., Houston, 1958-63; oil operator Cage Prodn. Co., Taft, Tex., 1958—; dir. State Bank Taft. Rancher and farmer, nr. Taft and Llano, Tex., 1958—. Home: 11511 Raindrop Dr San Antonio TX 78216 Office: care William Carter 1835 W Hunt St McKinney TX 75609

BRANSON, GENE NEWLAND, therapist; b. Higginsville, Mo., Sept. 30, 1926; s. John Lloyd and Lottie Belle (Newland) B.; B.A., Phillips U., 1951; B.D., Vanderbilt U., 1955; certificate Nat. Center for Mental Health Services, Washington, 1971; m. Muriel Danese Plotner, Aug. 16, 1947; children—Joyce (Mrs. Charles David Ferguson), Carolyn. Ordained to ministry Christian Ch. (Disciples of Christ), 1951; pastor First Christian Ch., Plattsburg, Mo., 1957-63; asso. pastor/campus pastor First Christian Ch., Kirksville, Mo., 1963-65; pastor Miami Shores Christian Ch., Miami, Fla., 1965-66, First Christian Ch., Benton, Ky., 1966-70; chaplain intern St. Elizabeths Hosp., Washington, 1970-71; adminstr., supr., therapist Bluegrass East Comprehensive Care Center, Winchester, Ky., 1971—; exec. sec. Land Between the Lakes Area Ministry, Benton, 1967-70. Served with AUS, 1945-46. Commd. instl. chaplain Christian Ch., 1972. Democrat. Author: Joy Beyond Sorrow, 1962. Contbr. articles to profl. jours. Home: 32 Lisle Lane Winchester KY 40391 Office: 217 S Main St Winchester KY 40391

BRANSON, ROBERT EARL, market research economist; b. Dallas, Dec. 3, 1918; s. Earl and Gertrude (Smith) B.; B.S. in Bus. Adminstrn., So. Meth. U., 1941; M.A. in Econs., Harvard, 1949, M.A. in Pub. Adminstrn., 1948, Ph.D. in Econs., 1954; m. Ruth Parker, May 18, 1945; children—Donald Elliott, Richard Parker. Economist, U.S. Dept. Agr., 1941-47; asso. dir. market research U. P.R., 1949-50; statistician U.S. Dept. Agr., 1950, economist, 1951-54; prof. econs., chmn. market devel. research, dept. agrl. econs. and sociology Tex. A and M. U., also dir. consumer market research Tex. Agrl. Expt. St., 1954-69, coordinator Tex. Agrl. Market Research and Devel. Center, 1969—; pres. Branson & Assos., Inc.; cons. economist U.S. AID, Argentina, 1962. Chmn. Bryan City Planning Commn., 1970-72. Served as economist OSS, Hdqr. Detachment, U.S. Army, Washington, World War II. Mem. Am. Marketing Assn., Am. Econ. Assn., Am. Farm Econs. Assn. Democrat. Methodist (bd. dirs). Kiwanian. Author: (with others) Marketing Efficiency in Puerto Rico, 1955. Contbr. articles on consumer marketing. Home: 2511 Broadmoor St Bryan TX 77801 Office: Agrl Market Research and Devel Center Tex A and M Univ College Station TX 77840

BRANTLEY, ALICE VIRGINIA SINGER (MRS. EDWARD FITZROY BRANTLEY), civic worker; b. Muncie, Ind.; d. Harry Dwight and Dessa (Slater) Singer; student Muncie Conservatory Music, 1912-20, Met. Sch. Music, 1920-22; studied harp with Louise Schelschmidt Koehne, Indpls., 1917-22, Henriette Renie, Paris, France, 1922-26, 50; m. Edward Fitzroy Brantley, Sept. 19, 1956. Concert debut, Paris, 1925; mem. Septuor Renie, 1923-26; concerts in Paris, N.Y.C., Chgo., Ft. Wayne, Indpls., St. Petersburg, Fla., 1920-63, with Alice Singer Trio, St. Petersburg, 1933-56; performed with St. Petersburg Symphony, Jacksonville (Fla.) Symphony, Tampa (Fla.) Philharmonic, Fla. Philharmonic, 1950-66; radio program WSUN, St. Petersburg, 1933. Ambassador, People-to-People Goodwill Mission from St. Petersburg to Europe and Middle East, 1960, to Soviet Union and satellites, 1965; mem. Fla. Art Commn., 1964-67; v.p. Suncoast Goodwill Industries, 1965-69, v.p. Aux. Guild, 1965-66; mem. St. Anthony's Hosp. Guild, 1961—, Children's Home Soc., 1963—, Suncoast Heart Assn., 1966; chmn. Queen of Hearts Ball, St. Petersburg, 1968; Heart Sunday chmn., 1963. Bd. dirs. Pinellas County Mental Health Assn., Mound Park Hosp. Aux., All Children's Hosp. Guild. Recipient Renie Harp award Paris, 1926, citation Radio Sta. WDAE, Tampa, 1965; named Princess of Royal Ct., St. Petersburg Heart Assn., 1963, Queen of Hearts, 1967; Contessa of Yr., Suncoast Opera Guild, 1970. Mem. Fla. Philharmonic Soc. (charter pres. 1954), Chamber Music Soc. (charter pres. 1966-68), Bel Canto (charter 1956), St. Petersburg opera assns., Fla. Art Council (charter 1963), Lions Club Aux. (past pres.), Soroptimist Internat. (pres. St. Petersburg 1962-63), St. Petersburg Hist. Soc., Mus. Fine Arts. Home: 1910 Brightwaters Blvd NE St Petersburg FL 33704

BRANTLEY, BILLY BURDETTE, supt. schs.; b. McLean, Tex., Nov. 20, 1925; s. Thaddius Frederick and Ada Fern (Robinson) B.; A.B., Panhandle State Coll., 1949; M.Ed., West Tex. State U., 1955; postgrad. U. Tex. 1957-58; m. Margaret Irene Hood, Aug. 7, 1949; children—Janelle, Billy Burdette, Jacalyn, Jerri. Dir. guidance Dumas (Tex.) Ind. Sch. Dist., 1949-64; supt., Claude (Tex.) Ind. Sch. Dist., 1964-68, Kilgore (Tex.) Ind. Sch. Dist., 1968—. Served with USNR, 1944-46. Mem. Am., Tex. assns. sch. adminstrs., N.E.A. (life), Tex. Tchrs. Assn. (life), Kilgore C. of C. (dir. 1969-72), Phi Delta Kappa. Democrat. Baptist (deacon 1960-72). Lion, Rotarian. Home: 500 Bean St Kilgore TX 75662 Office: PO Box 1541 Kilgore TX 75662

BRANTLEY, MICHAEL WILEY, museum ofcl.; b. Troy, Ala., Aug. 11, 1938; s. Oliver Wiley and Betty (Gaston) B.; B.A., U. Ala., 1959, M.A., 1962; Fulbright fellow Edinburgh U., 1962-63; postgrad. La. State U., 1963-65. Grad. teaching asst. La. State U., 1963-65; instr., asst. prof. U. N.C., Charlotte, 1965-67; asst. prof. Spring Hill Coll., Mobile, Ala., 1967-71; dir. Tryon Palace Restoration Complex, New Bern, N.C., 1971—. Pres., Mobile Historic Devel. Commn., 1970-71; mem. Historic New Bern Found., 1971—, New Bern Revolutionary Bicentennial Commn., 1973-74. Bd. dirs. New Bern Hist. Soc. Nat. Trust for Historic Preservation grantee William and Mary Coll., 1970. Mem. Nat. Trust for Historic Preservation, Am. Assn. State and Local History, Am. Assn. Museums, N.C. Museums Council, Delta Kappa Epsilon, Phi Alpha Theta. Home: 614 Middle St New Bern NC 28560 Office: 613 Pollock St New Bern NC 28560

BRANUM, LOWELL EDWIN, drilling co. exec.; b. Memphis, Tex., Oct. 24, 1913; s. Ben Alvin and Eula Jean (Davenport) B.; B.S., Sul Ross State U., 1940; J.D., Georgetown U., 1949; m. Ruth L. Chambers, Dec. 14, 1940 (div. Nov. 1957); 1 dau., Helen Lowella (Mrs. Robert Ellenger). Admitted to D.C. bar, 1949, Tex. bar, 1953; with U.S. Civil Service Commn., Washington, 1948-52, U.S. Dept. Justice, Washington, 1948-52; partner McCormick, Branum, Jennings, Cason, Midland, 1952-55; with Tri-Service Drilling Co., Midland, 1952—, sec.-treas., 1955—. Served with USMCR, 1943-45. Mem. Marine Corps Res. Officer Assn. (Midland pres. 1969-70), Res. Officers Assn. U.S. (v.p. marines 1971—). Eagle. Home: 2200 N D St Midland TX 79701 Office: First Nat Bank Bldg Midland TX 79701

BRASHEAR, ARTHUR PRICE, mfg. co. exec.; b. Gatesville, Tex., June 9, 1918; s. Arthur Price and Lois L. (Ward) B.; student Tex. Mil. Coll., 1936-38, Temple Jr. Coll., 1939-40; also U. Wis.; m. Marjory M. Miller, Oct. 15, 1939; children—Arthur Price III, Saranne McCalley Randle. Pres. Am. Desk Mfg. Co., Temple, 1949-51; pres. Taylor Mfg. Co. (Tex.), 1954-59; v.p. Globe Mfg. Co., Amarillo, Tex., 1953-59; v.p. Am. Rental & Storage, Temple, 1949-59; v.p. Amarillo (Tex.) Rental & Storage, 1953-59; pres. HRB&Y Theatres, Temple, 1951-56; v.p. BY&H Theatres, Temple, 1949-56; dir. Ralph Wilson Plastics Corp., Temple; with Tex-O-Cal Hardwoods, Temple, 1961—, now pres., chmn. Pres. Bell County Chpt. A.R.C., Temple, 1950-51; organizer, pres. Bell County Council on Alcoholism, Temple, 1963-64. Trustee Kings Daus. Hosp., 1964—, Mary Hardin Baylor Coll., 1951-52, Christian Farms, 1970—, Kimsolving Canyon Lodge, 1970-71; bd. dirs. Bell County Cripple Soc., 1949-50, Temple Boys Club, 1955-56. Mem. Tex. Mfrs. Assn. (dir.), Temple C. of C. (pres. 1954-55). Home: 1112 N 8th St Temple TX 76501 Office: Industrial Blvd Temple TX 76501

BRASWELL, EDWIN MAURICE, judge; b. Rocky Mount, N.C., Dec. 16, 1922; s. Walter R. and Ella (Denson) B.; LL.B., U. N.C., 1950; student Nat. Coll. State Trial Judges, U. Colo., 1966; m. Ruth Cox, Jan. 19, 1945; children—Susan, Edwin, Mark. Admitted to N.C. bar, 1950; practiced in Fayetteville, N.C., 1950-62; solicitor 9th Dist., Fayetteville, 1955-62; judge Superior Ct., 12th Jud. Dist., Fayetteville, 1963—. Faculty adviser Nat. Coll. State Trial Judges, U. Nev., 1970. Served with USAAF, 1942-45. Decorated Air medal with three oak leaf clusters, Purple Heart. Democrat. Methodist. Author: Voir Dire-Use and Abuse, 1970; (with Elmer R. Oettinger) Color Me Straight, 1972, Truths and Consequences, 1972. Home: 333 Devane St Fayetteville NC 28305

BRATAGER, PETE (ELLSWORTH), newspaper exec.; b. Miami, Fla., Oct. 11, 1928; s. Ellsworth Victor and Garnet (Severin) B.; B.A., U. Miami, 1951; m. Alicia Helen Radulski, Jan. 10, 1953; children—Stephen Ellis, Daniel Victor, Donald Pete, James Edward, Reid Thomas. Sports writer Miami Herald, 1946-59, night sports slot, 1959-64, Fla. state news editor, 1964-69, photo editor, 1969—. Served with AUS, 1951-53. Home: 245 E 34th St Hialeah FL 33012 Office: 1 Herald Plaza Miami FL 33101

BRATTON, FRANK N., lawyer; b. Cowan, Tenn., Dec. 29, 1908; student U. of South, U. Tenn.; LL.B., Cumberland U., 1933. Admitted to Tenn. bar, 1934; practiced in Athens, Tenn. Fellow Am. Bar Found., Am. Coll. Trial Lawyers, Am. Coll. Probate Counsel; mem. Am. (ho. of dels. 1960—, chmn. com. on lay assts. gen. practice sect. 1968-72, chmn. late reports com. of Ho. of Dels. 1970-71, mem. council gen. practice sect. 1971—, mem. adv. com. continuing legal edn. of bar com. from Tenn. 1969-70, chmn. com. on state orgn. of gen. practice sect. 1972-74), Internat., Tenn. (central council 1950-52, v.p. 1953-54, chmn. joint com. on ct. modernization 1965-69, pres. 1971-72, award of merit 1967), McMinn County bar assns., Nat. Assn. R.R. Trial Counsel, Am. Judicature Soc. (dir. 1967-71), Inst. Jud. Adminstrn., Internat. Soc. Barristers, Scribes, World Peace through Law Center (charter). Office: 121 N Jackson St Athens TN 37303*

BRATTON, JAMES HENRY, JR., lawyer; b. Pulaski, Tenn., Oct. 9, 1931; s. James Henry and Mabel (Shelley) B.; B.A., U. of South, 1952 B.A. Oxford U. (Eng.), 1954; LL.B., Yale, 1956; m. Alleen Sharp Davis, Oct. 15, 1960; children—Susan Shelley, James Henry III, Margaret Alleen. Admitted Tenn. bar, 1956, Ga. bar, 1957; practice in Atlanta, 1956—; mem. firm Gambrell, Russell, Moye, Killorin, 1956—. Vis. lectr. law U. Ga., 1967—. Bd. dirs. Protestant Welfare and Social Service, Atlanta, 1960—; mem. council Christian Council of Met. Atlanta, 1966—. Mem. Am., Ga., Atlanta bar assns., Am. Judicature Soc., Gridiron Secret Soc., Phi Beta Kappa. Democrat. Methodist. Clubs: Lawyers, Burns (both Atlanta). Contbr. articles to profl. jours. Home: 63 N Muscogee Av NW Atlanta GA 30305 Office: 1st Nat Bank Tower Atlanta GA 30303

BRATTON, SAMUEL ISAAC, supt. schs.; b. Grenada, Miss., Jan. 7, 1911; s. Amos Gwyn and Minnie Augusta (Harper) B.; B.A., Hendrix Coll., 1933; M.A., George Peabody Coll., 1941; diploma advanced study U. Ark., 1965; m. Pauline Kilgore, May 24, 1940; children—Samuel Isaac, George. Tchr., Earle (Ark.) High Sch., 1933-39, prin., 1939-42, 46-47; supt. Earle Pub. Schs., 1947—. Served with AUS, 1942-46. Mem. Ark. Sch. Adminstrs. Assn. (pres. 1966-67, Ark. Edn. Assn. (pres. supt. sect. 1973-74). Methodist. Rotarian (past pres. Earle). Home: 808 5th Av Earle AR 72331 Office: 1425 2d St Earle AR 72331

BRAUER, ALFRED T(HEODOR), educator; b. Berlin, Germany, Apr. 9, 1894; s. Max and Caroline Lilly (Jacob) B.; student U. Heidelberg, 1913; Ph.D., U. Berlin, 1928; LL.D. (hon.), U.N.C., 1972; m. Hildegard Franziska Wolf, Sept. 4, 1934; children—Ellen Evelyn (Mrs. Berton H. Kaplan), Carolyn Toni (Mrs. Richard H. Hudson). Came to U.S. 1939, naturalized, 1944. Asst., U. Berlin, 1926-35, privatdocent, 1932-35; asst. Inst. for Advanced Study, Princeton, N.J., 1939-42; lectr. N.Y. U., 1940-42; instr. U. N.C., 1942, asst. prof., 1942-43, asso. prof., 1943-47, prof. 1947-59, Kenan prof., 1959-66; vis. prof. U. Colo., summer 1962, 67, Wake Forest U., Winston-Salem, N.C., 1965—. Served with German Army, 1914-19. Recipient Sci. Research award for significant contbns. to sci. in South, Oak Ridge Inst. Nuclear Studies, 1948; Hegel medal Humboldt U., Berlin, 1971. Mem. Am. Math. Soc., Math. Assn. of Am., N.C. Acad. Sci., Elisha Mitchell Sci. Soc., Sigma Xi. Home: 300 Woodhaven Rd Chapel Hill NC 27514

BRAUER, GEORGE CHARLES, JR., educator; b. Cleve., Aug. 7, 1925; s. George Charles and Hazel (Batig) B.; B.A., Princeton, 1947; M.A., 1949; Ph.D., 1952. Instr. English, U. Tex., Austin, 1952-56; asst. prof. English, U. S.C., Columbia, 1956-60, asso. prof., 1960-69, prof., 1969—. Recipient Russell award for creative research U. S.C. Mem. Modern Lang. Assn., Istituto di Studi Romani, Am. Schs. Oriental Research, Princeton Alumni Assn., Phi Beta Kappa, Omicron Delta Kappa (faculty adviser 1963-67), Chi Psi (faculty adviser 1964—). Republican. Lutheran. Club: Campus (Princeton). Author: The Education of a Gentleman: Theories of Gentlemanly Education in England, 1660-1775, 1959; The Young Emperors: Rome, A.D. 193-244, 1967; Judaea Weeping, 1970. Home: Cornell Arms Apts Columbia SC 29201

BRAUER, HARROL ANDREW, JR., TV sta. exec.; b. Richmond, Va., Oct. 17, 1920; s. Harrol Andrew and Bertie (Gregory) B.; B.A., U. Richmond, 1942; m. Elizabeth Anne Hill, May 18, 1946; children—Harrol Andrew III, William Lanier, Gregory Hill. Chief announcer, program dir., account exec. various radio stas. in Va. 1939-42, 45-49; asso. WVEC radio, Hampton, Va. 1949—; v.p., dir. sales WVEC-TV, Hampton, 1953—; v.p. Peninsula Cable Corp., 1966—; dir. Peninsula Broadcasting Corp. Mem. Hampton Sch. Bd., 1963—, vice chmn., 1964-67, chmn., 1967—. Trustee, Hampton Roads Ednl. TV Assn., chmn. bd. trustees, 1965—. Pres. Hampton Community Chest, 1951-52; dir. Peninsula unit Am. Cancer Soc., mem. hist. and cultural com. City of Hampton; vice chmn. pres.'s adv. council Christopher Newport Coll., 1973—. Dir. YMCA, Va. U.S.O. Served from midshipman to lt., USNR, 1942-45. Mem. Broadcast Pioneers, Hampton Retail Mchts. Assn. (past pres., dir.), Peninsula C. of C. (dir. 1964—), Jamestowne Soc., Sigma Alpha Epsilon. Episcopalian. Clubs: Peninsula Executive's (past pres., dir.), Kiwanis (past dir., pres., lt. gov.), James River Country; Harbor; Huntington. Home: 35 N Boxwood St Hampton VA 23669 Office: 1930 E Pembroke Av Hampton VA 23663

BRAUGHLER, GUY ERNST, non-powder guns and ammunition mfg. co. exec.; b. Punxsutawney, Pa., Aug. 31, 1932; s. Ernst C. and Wilma (Bortnik) B.; Asso. Mech. Engr., U. Pa., 1958; student Internat. Corr. Schs., 1963, Alexander Hamilton Inst., 1970; m. Alice M. Bretz, July 5, 1958; children—Bonnie Sue, Beth Ann, Amy Marie. Employed various gun shops, Washington, 1951-55; with U. Pa., 1955-58; engr. Crosman Arms Co., Fairport, N.Y., 1958-61; engr. Daisy-Heddon Co., Rogers, Ark., 1961-64, engring. mgr., 1964—. Served with AUS, 1953-55. Certified Mfg. engr. Mem. Soc. Mfg. Engrs. (chpt. chartering chmn. 1968-70). Home: 1003 S Lakeview Dr Rogers AR 72756 Office: PO Box 220 Rogers AR 72756

BRAUN, JOHN WALTER, ret. govt. ofcl., educator; b. Two Rivers, Wis., Oct. 18, 1907; s. Paul and Metta L. (Cole) B.; B.C.S., Benjamin Franklin U., 1943, M.C.S., 1946; J.D., Am. U., 1960; m. Lary H. Dalton, Oct. 31, 1941; children—John F., Gerry C., Lary Ann. With Benjamin Franklin U., 1960—; with Treasury Dept, Washington, 1949-73, Bur. of Mint, 1949-56, Bur. of Accounts, 1956-67, comptroller of currency, 1967-73. Served with A.R.C., 1943-45. C.P.A., D.C. Mem. Am. Inst. C.P.A.'s. Elks. Home: 2239 N Underwood St Falls Church VA 22043

BRAUN, WARREN L(OYD), radio engr.; b. Postville, Ia., Aug. 11, 1922; s. Karl William and Cornela (Muller) B.; student Valparaiso Tech. Inst., 1940-41, Capitol Engring. Inst., 1946; m. Lillian Carol Stone, May 24, 1942; children—Warren (dec.), Dikki Carol. Chief engr. WKEY, 1941, WSVA, 1941; E.S.M.W.T.P. sect. head, 1942-45; charge installation stas. WSIR, WTOW, WSVA-FM, WJMA, TV stas. WAAM and WSVA-TV, Blue Ridge TV cable facilities, 1945-65; pres. Com Sonics, Inc., Research and Devel. Labs., Warren Braun, cons. engrs. Panel 44 mem. TV allocations study orgn.; v.p. Market Dimensions, Inc. Bd. dirs. Salvation Army, 1961—. Chmn. Harrisonburg-Rockingham County Recreation Study Commn.; mem., sec. Va. Air Pollution Control Bd., 1966-73; pres. Shenandoah Valley Devel. Corp.; mem. Va. Citizens Com. for Va. Outdoor Planning; chmn. Upper Valley Regional Park Authority, 1966-69, dir., 1969—; mem. Regional Export Expansion Council; mem. Va. Far East Trade Mission, 1972; mem. bd. Tb and Thoracic Soc., Va. state seal chmn., 1967—. Registered profl. engr. Va. Chmn. bus. relations com. Harrisburg C. of C. 1959-61, mem. bd., 1961-66, pres., 1964. Recipient Jefferson Davis medal U.D.C. 1961; named outstanding engr. of yr. Va. Soc. Profl. Engrs., 1965; man of yr. Harrisonburg and Rockingham County; nat. award, Am. Soc. Engring., 1969, Internat. award, 1969; Rietzke Nat. award, 1972. Fellow Audio Engring. Soc. (membership chmn. 1963-64), Internat. Consular Acad.; mem. I.E.E.E., Soc. Motion Picture and TV Engrs., Acoustical Soc. Am., Nat. Va. (mem. bd. and exec. com. 1963-64, chpt. pres. 1963-64, Distinguished Service award 1973) socs. profl. engrs., Va. Assn. Professions (charter, regional v.p. 1971-73, pres. designate 1973-74), Nat. Assn. Broadcasters, Va. C. of C. (chmn. world trade conf. 1968, chmn. world trade com. 1968—, dir. 1973, v.p. 1974—). Lutheran (deacon). Elk. Club: Engineers (Richmond, Va.). Address: 680 New York Av Harrisonburg VA 22801

BRAWLEY, JOEL VINCENT, JR., educator; b. Mooresville, N.C., Feb. 2, 1938; s. Joel Vincent and Dorothy (Cavin) B.; B.S. in Engring. Math., N.C. State U., 1960, M.S. in Math., 1962, Ph.D., (Ford Found. fellow), 1964; m. Frances Owen, Aug. 22, 1959; children—Albert Vincent, Daniel Owen, Frances Ann. Instr. N.C. State U., Raleigh, 1964-65, vis. asso. prof., 1971-72; mem. faculty dept. math. Clemson (S.C.) U., 1965—, asso. prof., 1968-72, prof., 1972—. Reviewer Zentralblatt fur Mathematik jour., 1968—. Mem. Am. Math. Soc., Math. Assn. Am. (mem. vis. lectrs. panel), Phi Kappa Phi, Pi Mu Epsilon, Tau Beta Pi. Contbr. profl. jours. Home: 105 Lakeview Circle Clemson SC 29631

BRAWNER, LEE BASIL, librarian; b. Seguin, Tex., May 1, 1935; s. Lee Basil and Thelma (Davenport) B.; student Tex. A. and M. U., 1953-55; B.A., N. Tex. State U., 1957; M.A., George Peabody Coll. Tchrs., 1960; m. Nancy Jayne Wallis, Dec. 6, 1958; children—Betsy Lynn, Allen Lee. Head popular library and circulation dept. Dallas Pub. Library, 1958-60, head Lakewood br., 1961-62, chief br. services, 1964-67; dir. Waco (Tex.) Pub. Library, 1962-64; asst. state librarian Tex. State Library, 1967-71; dir. Oklahoma County Libraries System, Oklahoma City, 1971—. Chmn. Southwestern Library Interstate Library Coop. Endeavor Project, 1971-72. Served with AUS, 1957-58. Mem. Am., Okla., Southwestern (pres. 1971-72) library assns., Am. Library Trustee Assn. (2d v.p. 1973-74), Okla. C. of C., Sigma Phi Epsilon. Contbr. articles to profl. jours. Home: 5013 NW 61st Pl Oklahoma City OK 73122 Office: 131 NW 3d St Oklahoma City OK 73102

BRAXTON, HERMAN HARRISON, physician; b. Almanance County, N.C., Nov. 13, 1906; s. James Guy and Nette E. (Guthrie) B.; A.B., U. N.C., 1928; M.D., Johns Hopkins, 1932; m. Anne Norfolk Grimm, June 22, 1935; children—Herman Harrison II, Elizabeth Anne. Mem. house staff Duke Hosp., 1932-33, White Plains (N.Y.) Hosp., 1933-34; gen. practice medicine, Chase City, Va., 1934—; mem. staffs Community Meml. Hosp., South Hill, Va., Southside Community Hosp. Farmville, Va., local med. dir. Nat. Found.; med. examiner Mecklenburg County, 1947—; surgeon So. R.R. Bd. dirs. Chase City Indsl. Devel. Corp.; mem. adv. bd. Fidelity Nat. Bank. Mem. local bi-racial commn., 1965—. Mem. Chase City Town Council, 1955-63. Mem. Va. Med. Soc., A.M.A., Am. Acad. Gen. Practice, Chase City C. of C. (past pres.), Phi Beta Kappa. Episcopalian (sr. warden). Clubs: Lions (past pres., zone chmn.); Mecklenburg Country (past pres.). Home: 440 Walker St Chase City VA 23924 Office: 4th and Main Sts Chase City VA 23924

BRAXTON, HERMAN HARRISON, JR., lawyer; b. Durham, N.C., May 15, 1936; s. Herman Harrison and Anne (Grimm) B.; A.B. in Polit. Sci., U. N.C., 1958; J.D., U. Va., 1961; m. Patricia Gail Galway, June 26, 1965; children—Herman Harrison III, Grace Anne. Admitted to Va. bar, 1961; partner firm Willis, Garnett & Braxton, Fredericksburg, 1965—; commonwealth atty. City Fredericksburg, 1974—. Pres. Fredericksburg chpt. Va. Mus. Fine Arts, 1970-72. Served to capt. Judge Advocate Gen. Corps, USAF, 1961-64. Recipient distinguished service award Fredericksburg Jr. C. of C. Mem. Fredericksburg C. of C., Va., 15th Judicial Circuit bar assns., Pi Kappa Alpha, Phi Alpha Delta. Episcopalian. Kiwanian. Home: 1204 Charles St Fredericksburg VA 22401 Office: 1013 Princess Anne St Fredericksburg VA 22401

BRAYNON, EDWARD JOSEPH, JR., dentist; b. Miami, Fla., Jan 15, 1928; s. Edward Joseph and May Dell (Jackson) B.; B.S., Howard U., 1949; D.D.S., 1954; student Fisk U., 1945-47; m. Ann Carey, July 24, 1954; children—Edward Joseph III, Keith Warren. Practice dentistry, Miami. Mem. Dade County Youth Adv. Bd. Dir. YMCA, 1957-61. Served as capt., Dental Corps, USAF, 1954-56. Mem. Dade County Acad. Medicine, Am. Dental Soc. Anesthesiology, Fla. Med., Dental and Pharm. Assn., Nat. Dental Assn., Am., East Coast dental assns., Fla., North Dade, South Dade dental socs., Howard U. Alumni Assn. (pres. Miami 1968—), Omega Psi Phi (meritorious service award 1963, 7th Dist. Man of Year 1970, 7th dist. rep.), Chi Delta Mu, Omega Psi Phi. Methodist. Club: Century. Home: 2271 NE 191st St North Miami Beach FL 33160 Office: 5594 NW 17th Av Miami FL 33142

BRAZELTON, JAMES MELVILLE, clergyman; b. Quincy, Ill., May 30, 1911; s. Roy Melville and Leta Ethel (Cannon) B.; B.A., Tex. Christian U., 1965, M.Div., 1969; m. Cathryn Viola Dawson, July 18, 1940; children—Sue (Mrs. Allen White), Lee-Ann (Mrs. Stanley Shipman), Roy William. Singer, NBC Radio, Chgo., Chgo. Acapella Choir, Chgo. Fine Arts Opera Co., 1930-36; indsl. engr. N.Am. Aviation Corp., Ford Motor Co., Chance Vought Aircraft, Inc., Dallas, 1937-60, supr. indsl. engring., 1950-60; ordained to ministry Christian Ch. (Disciples of Christ), 1969; minister First Christian Chs., Grapeland, Tex., 1961-64, Kaufman, Tex., 1965-69, Antioch Christian Ch., Hooks, Tex., 1969-71, First Christian Ch., DeQueen, Ark., 1971—. Pres., DeQueen Ministerial Alliance, Dist. C Christian Chs. in Ark.; mem. gen. bd. Christian Ch. in. Ark. Parliamentarian, Dallas County Republican party, Dallas, 1952-57. Mem. Ill. N.G., 1937-40. Mason (32 degree, K.T., Shriner). Club: Senate (past pres. Dallas). Home: 417 W Stilwell Av DeQueen AR 71832

BREAUX, JOHN B., congressman; b. Crowley, La., Mar. 1, 1944; s. Ezra H., Jr. and Katherine (Berlinger) B.; B.A. in Polit. Sci., U. Southwestern La., 1965; J.D., La. State U., 1967; m. Lois Gail Daigle, Aug. 1, 1964; children—John B., William Lloyd, Elizabeth Andre. Admitted to La. bar, 1967; partner Brown, McKernan, Ingram & Breaux, 1967-68; legislative asst. to Congressman Edwin W. Edwards, 1968-69, dist. asst., 1969-72; mem. 92d-93d Congresses from 7th Dist. La. Recipient Am. Legion award. Moot Ct. finalist La. State U., 1966. Mem. La., Acadia Parish bar assns., Internat. Rice Festival Assn. (dir.), Crowley Jr. C. of C., La. Jr. C. of C., Pi Lambda Beta, Phi Alpha Delta, Lambda Chi Alpha. Democrat. Office: 319 Cannon House Office Bldg Washington DC 20515

BREAZEALE, WILLIAM HORACE, JR., chemist, educator; b. Breensboro, N.C., Aug. 30, 1938; s. William Horace and Ruby (Grant) B.; B.S., U. S.C., 1961; Ph.D., 1965; m. Madeleine Hamilton Bradley, Aug. 30, 1963; children—William James, Grant Hamilton. Asst. prof. chemistry Winthrop Coll., Rock Hill, S.C., 1965-70; prof. chemistry Francis Marion Coll., Florence, S.C., 1970—, also chmn. dept. chemistry, asso. dean of Coll., 1973—. Mem. Am. Chem. Soc., S.C. Acad. Sci., Sigma Xi, Phi Kappa Phi. Mason. Home: 1859 Devonshire St Florence SC 29501 Office: Francis Marion College Florence SC 29501

BREBBIA, JOHN HENRY, lawyer; b. Boston, Feb. 16, 1932; s. Joseph Dante and Gertrude (Hogan) B.; A.B., Stonehill Coll., 1953; LL.B., Boston Coll., 1956; m. Patricia Mary Burke, Jan. 9, 1967. Admitted to Mass. bar, 1957, D.C. bar, 1965; practiced in Boston, 1960-61; trial atty. FTC, Bur. Restraint of Trade, 1961-64; asso. Davies, Richberg, Tydings, Lamda & Duff, Washington, 1965-67; partner Alston, Miller & Gaines, Washington and Atlanta, 1967—, mng. partner Washington office, 1971—; dir., v.p. and gen. counsel First Western Financial Corp., Las Vegas, 1966-67, 69—, pres., dir., 1967-69; dir. First Western Savings & Loan Assn., Las Vegas, 1966—. Mem. atomic safety and licensing bd. U.S. AEC, 1972—. Mem. campaign staff Senator Robert F. Kennedy, 1964. Served from 1st lt. to capt. Judge Adv. Gen. Corps, AUS, 1957-60. Mem. Am., Fed. bar assns., Bar Assn. D.C. Home: 3232 Kingle Rd NW Washington DC 20008 Office: 1776 K St NW Washington DC 20006

BRECHNER, BEVERLY LORRAINE, educator; b. N.Y.C., May 27, 1936; d. Herman and Goldie (Zimmerman) Brechner; B.S., U. Miami, 1957, M.S., 1959; Ph.D., La. State U., 1964. Instr. La. State U., New Orleans, 1962-64, asst. prof., 1964-68; asst. prof. U. Fla., Gainesville, 1968-71, asso. prof. math., 1971—. Vis. lectr. La. Acad. Sci., 1967-68; reviewer Zentralblatt Fur Maths., 1968—, Math. Reviews, 1971—; mem. Inst. Advanced Grad. Students Topology, U. Ga., Athens, 1961, Topology Manifolds Inst., 1961. Mem. Am. Math. Soc., Math. Assn. Am., A.A.A.S., Fla. Found. Future Scientists (dir. 1970-73), Sigma Xi. Democrat. Jewish religion. Office: Dept Math Univ Fla Gainesville FL 32611

BRECK, LOUIS WILLIAM, physician, orthopaedic surgeon; b. El Paso, Mar. 24, 1909; s. Louis M. and Olive Jane (Roblee) B.; B.S., Northwestern U., 1930, M.D., 1933; m. Julia S. North, June 11, 1932; children—Louis W., Julia A., Alan N., Susan M. Rotating intern Mary's Help Hosp., 1932-33, gen. resident, 1933-35; spl. tng. orthopaedic surgery Mayo Clinic, 1935-37; practice medicine, specializing in orthopaedic surgery, El Paso, 1937—; mem. staff Hotel Dieu Sisters Hosp., chief of staff, 1955; cons. Thomason Gen. Hosp., Carrie Tingley Hosp. for Crippled Children; civilian cons. to William Beaumont Gen. Hosp.; orthopaedic cons. S.P. R.R., Tex. Crippled Children's Div., New Mexico Crippled Children's Hosp. Mem. med. adv. bd. Tex. Rehab. Commn. Served from capt. to lt. col. AUS, 1942-46; chief orthopaedic sect. Regional Hosp., Camp Swift, Tex. Recipient Legion of Honor Order of DeMolay, 1953; Outstanding Civilian Service award Surgeon gen. U.S. Army; Order of Phoenix, others. Fellow A.C.S., Am. Writers Assn.; mem. Am., Tex. State, S.W. (pres. 1950-51) med. assns., El Paso County Med. Soc. (pres. 1961), Am. Acad. Orthopaedic Surgeons, Assn. Bone Joint Surgeons (pres. 1955), Western (pres. N.M. chapt. 1958), Texas (pres. 1950) orthopaedic assns., Societe Internationale de Chirurgie et de Traumatologie, Tex. Soc. Athletic Team Physicians (pres. 1965), Tex. Traumatic Surg. Soc. (pres. 1967), Tex. Rehab. Assn. (pres. 1968), Sigma Alpha Epsilon, Phi Beta Pi (Arnold-Surman lectr. U. Tex. 1951). Mason (32 deg., Shriner), Kiwanian. Author: Atlas of the Osteochondroses. Editorial bd. Clin. Orthopaedics, Jour. Indsl. Medicine. Contbr. articles to profl. jours. Home: 1207 N Kansas St El Paso TX 79902 Office: 1300 N Stanton St El Paso TX 79902

BRECKINRIDGE, CHARLES EDWARD, JR., educator; b. Louisville, June 21, 1923; s. Charles Edward and Elizabeth Clark (Kendall) B.; B.S. with distinction, U. Ky., 1953; M.S., Purdue U., 1959, Ph.D. (NIH fellow), 1960; m. Doris Jean Smith, June 25, 1955; children—Charles Edward III, Debbie Jean, Richard Glenn. Instr., U. Ky., Lexington, 1954-57; instr. Purdue U., Lafayette, Ind., 1957-59, prof., 1964; sr. health physicist Oak Ridge Nat. Lab., 1960-63; sr. scientist Hanford Labs., Richland, Wash., 1963; prof. environmental health scis. Sch. Pharmacy, U. Ark. Med. Center, Little Rock, 1965—, chmn. dept., 1965—, dir. radiol. health tng. program, 1965—. Mem. Am. Pharm. Assn., A.A.A.S., Ark. Pharm. Assn., Pulaski County Pharm. Assn., Sigma Xi, Rho Chi, Phi Delta Chi. Asst. editor: Nuclear Safety, 1962-63. Contbr. articles to profl. jours. Home: 11601 Southridge Dr Little Rock AR 72207

BRECKINRIDGE, JOHN BAYNE, congressman; b. Washington, Nov. 29, 1913; s. Dr. Scott Dudley and Gertrude (Ashby-Bayne) B.; A.B., U. Ky., 1937, LL.B., 1939; m. Helen Congleton; children—Knight, John Bayne. Admitted to Ky. bar, 1940; atty. anti-trust div. Dept. Justice, 1940-41; pvt. practice law, 1946—; mem. Ky. Ho. of Reps., 1956-59; atty. gen. of Ky., 1960-64, 67-73; mem. 93d Congress from Ky.; corp. counsel for the City of Lexington (Ky.), 1964. Del. to White House Conf. on Children and Youth, 1960; mem. adv. com. state ofcls. AEC; vice chmn. So. Interstate Nuclear Bd.; chmn. Ky. Adv. Com. Nuclear Energy, 1960-64; chmn. Ky. Inter-Agy. Legislative Program Com., 1960-64; trustee Frontier Nursing Service; commr. Nat. Conf. Commns. on Uniform State Laws, 1960-64; mem. Ky. Constn. Rev. Com., 1960-62; counsel Ky. Citizens for Child Welfare, 1956-59. Past vice chmn. Ky. Welfare Assn., v.p. 1962-63; chmn. So. Interstate Nuclear Bd.; vice chmn. Ky. Social Welfare Found.; chmn. Ky. Sci. and Tech. Adv. Council; mem. Ky. Commn. on Children and Youth, 1966—, Ky. Crime Commn., 1967—; chmn. Ky. Water Pollution Control Commn., 1968—; v.p., mem. operating bd. officers, exec. com. United Cerebral Palsy Assn.; past asst. v.p. So. region, past pres. United Cerebral Palsy of Ky., United Cerebral Palsy of Bluegrass. Del., Democratic Nat. Conv., mem. rules com., Los Angeles, 1960. Served from 1st lt. to col. AUS 1941-46; chief projects and indsl. licensing div. Bd. Econ. Warfare, 1941-42, asst. chief internat. div. USAFIME Hdqrs., comdg. officer Mil. Liaison Hdqrs., Albania. Mem. Am. Council for Community (past mem. exec. com., dir.), Am., Ky., Fayette County bar assns., Am. Judicature Soc. (dir. Ky.), Ky. Hist. Soc. (pres. 1962-64), Atlantic Union Com. (pres. Ky. chpt. mem. council), Kentucky Peace officers' Standards and Tng. Council, Kappa Alpha (pres. Theta chpt. 1936-37). Democrat Contbr. articles to legal jours. Home: 1100 Fincastle Rd Frankfort KY 40601 Office: Office of Atty Gen State Capitol Frankfort KY 40601

BREEDIN, B. BRENT, ednl. adminstr.; b. Beaufort, S.C., Nov. 3, 1925; s. Berryman Brent and Jane (Dixon) B.; B.A., Washington and Lee U., 1947; m. Louise Allain Crenshaw, Sept. 10, 1959; children—David Singleton, Sarah duBois, Amelia Knowles. Reporter, Corpus Christi (Tex.) Caller, 1947; sports editor Anderson (S.C.) Daily Mail, 1949-52; dir. sports publicity Clemson U., 1952-55, univ. editor, 1964-66; resident mgr. Hunt Internat. Petroleum Co., Pakistan, 1955-58; press and research asst. U.S. Senator Strom Thurmond of S.C., 1958-59; pub. relations DuPont Co., 1960-63; editor-pub. South Carolinian, 1963-64; editor Coll. and Univ. Jour., 1966-71; asso. dir. ERIC/Higher Edn., 1971-72; dir. publs. Council on Library Resources, 1972—. Served with USNR, 1944-45. Mem. Am. Coll. Pub. Relations Assn., Ednl. Press Assn., Am. Acad. Polit. and Social Sci., Sigma Delta Chi, Sigma Alpha Epsilon. Episcopalian. Rotarian. Club: Nat. Press. Home: 5419 41st St NW Washington DC 20015 Office: 1 Dupont Circle NW Washington DC 20036

BREEDLOVE, JAMES GERALD, bus. exec.; b. Opp, Ala., Nov. 7, 1920; s. E. Marvin and Mary (Jeffcoat) B.; B. Ceramic Engring., Ga. Inst. Tech., 1950; m. Carolyn Elizabeth Archer, Nov. 27, 1947; children—Mary Carolyn (Mrs. P. J. Peacock), Sally Elizabeth, Donna Ellen. Ceramic engr. Am. Lava Corp., Chattanooga, 1950-53, mgr. Titania div. lab., 1953-63, mgr. new product devel. lab., 1963-68, research supr., 1968—. Chief aux. police, Signal Mountain, Tenn., 1964—. Served to sgt. AUS, 1941-45. Recipient Distinguished Community Service award Signal Mountain Lions Club, 1968. Mem. Am. Ceramic Soc., Inst. Ceramic Engrs., Chattanooga C. of C., Signal Mountain Sportsman's Assn., Nat. Rifle Assn. Democrat. Episcopalian. Patents and publs. in fields tech. ceramics, dielectrics, procelain enamels. Inventor composite armor plate (ceramic-glass fiber). Home: 804 James Blvd Signal Mountain TN 37377 Office: Am Lava Corp Cherokee Blvd Chattanooga TN 37405

BREEDLOVE, WILLIAM ALFORD, banker; b. nr. Nashville, N.C., May 13, 1928; s. James William and Ellen Louise (Harris) B.; student N.C. State U., 1945-46, Campbell Coll., 1948-49, Smithdeal Massey Bus. Coll., 1949-50, Stonier Grad. Sch. Banking, 1965-68, Nat. Comml. Lending Sch., 1970; m. Bettye Catherine Evans, Dec. 20, 1952; children—William Alford, Laura Lynne. Credit mgr. Universal C.I.T. Corp., Charlotte, N.C., 1951-53, mgr., Fayetteville, N.C., 1953-55; with Planters Nat. Bank and Trust Co., Rocky Mount, N.C., 1955—, sr. v.p., 1970—, sr. v.p., city exec. br. bank, Mt. Airy, N.C., 1971—. Sec., Rocky Mount Human Relations Commn., 1968. Served with USAAF, 1946-47. Mem. Am. Inst. Banking (pres. 1961-62), Bank Adminstrn. Inst. (pres. 1966-67, dir. 1967-71). Democrat. Baptist (deacon 1955—). Elk, Rotarian (dir. 1969-70). Club: Mt. Airy Country. Home: 664 Knollwood Dr Mount Airy NC 27030 Office: 501 N Main St Mount Airy NC 27030

BREELAND, JEWELL JEROME, JR., physician; b. Tylertown, Miss., Jan. 13, 1930; s. Jewell J. and Tressa (Istvan) B.; B.A., U. So. Miss., 1951; M.D., U. Miss., 1960; m. Jane Manning, June 14, 1953; children—Marjorie, Durwood, Jeri, Peggy. Intern Chatham County Hosp., Savannah, Ga., 1960-61; pvt. practice medicine in gen. practice and obstetrics, Brookhaven, Miss., 1961—; mem. staff Kings Daus. Hosp., Brookhaven. Served with USAF, 1951-55. Mem. Lincoln County Cancer Soc. (pres. 1968-70), A.M.A., South Central County Med. Assn., Miss. Med. Assn. Presbyn. Home: S Church Extension Brookhaven MS 39601 Office: 439 N Jackson St Brookhaven MS 39601

BREEN, JAMES LOWELL, educator; b. Charleston, Ill., May 14, 1921; s. Charles C. and Myrtle (Potts) B.; B.S., Eastern Ill. U., 1948; M.S., U. Ill., 1949, Ph.D., 1959; m. Juanita June Chesser, June 6, 1943; children—Suanne, Pamela (Mrs. Henry Koch), Janette Deane, Barbara Jo. Mem. faculty, U. Ill., 1948-57; dir. research Chgo. Nat. League Baseball Club, Inc., 1957-58; faculty Tulane U., 1959-69, head dept. phys. edn., 1960-69; chmn. dept. phys. edn. George Washington U., Washington, 1969—. Cons. Balt. Orioles Baseball Club, 1972-73. Co-chmn., mem. exec. com. Greater New Orleans March of Dimes, 1965-67; mem. exec. com. Mus. Therapy Assn., New Orleans, 1968. Served to lt. USNR, 1942-45. Mem. Am. Coll. Sports Medicine, Am. Personnel and Guidance Assn., Am. Assn. U. Profs., Am. (chmn. phys. fitness sect. 1965-66), La. assns. health, phys. edn. and recreation. Republican. Methodist. Contbr. articles to publs. Producer, dir. ednl. film. Home: 2611 Lemontree Lane Vienna VA 22180 Office: Phys Edn Dept George Washington 817 23d St NW Washington DC 20006

BREEN, JOHN EDWARD, educator; b. Buffalo, May 1, 1932; s. Timothy J. and Alice C. (Keenan) B.; B.C.E., Marquette U., 1953; M.S., U. Mo., 1957; Ph.D., U. Tex., 1962; m. Marian T. Killian, June 20, 1953; children—Mary L., Michael T., Dennis P., Sheila A., Sean E., Kerry T., Christopher D. Structural designer Harnischfeger Corp., Milw., 1952-53; asst. prof. civil engring. U. Mo., Columbia, 1957-59; instr. civil engring. U. Tex., Austin, 1959-62, asst. prof., 1962-65, asso. prof., 1965-68, prof., 1969—. Engring. cons., 1957-59, 63—; cons. Constructional Chems., Inc., Nat. Bur. Standards, also various legal firms. Served to lt. C.E., USNR, 1953-56. Recipient Teaching Excellence award U. Tex. Student Assn., 1963, Standard Oil of Ind., 1968, Gen. Dynamics, 1971; Wason medal Am. Concrete Inst., 1972, Raymond C. Reese research medal, 1972. Registered profl. engr., Tex., Mo. Mem. Am. Soc. C.E., Am. Concrete Inst. (dir. 1974—), Prestressed Concrete Inst. Democrat. Roman Catholic. Home: 8603 Azalea Trail Austin TX 78759

BREESKIN, BARNETT, orch. condr.; studied with Leon Barzin, Hans Kindler, Pierre Monteux. Solo violinist; with various symphony orchs.; condr., dir., mgr. Miami Beach (Fla.) Symphony, 1955—. Home: 5301 Alton Rd Miami Beach FL 33140 Office: 420 Lincoln Rd Mall Suite 401 Miami Beach FL 33139

BREHM, THOMAS WALTER, educator; b. Columbus, O., Oct. 14, 1924; s. Walter E. and Helen Lucille (Fountain) B.; student Ohio State U., 1942-44; D.D.S., Ohio State Dental Coll., 1949; postgrad. U. So. Cal., 1955-56; m. Reva Ruth Libby, July 3, 1949; children—Pamela (Mrs. Richard Cheeks), Timothy, Bruce. Dental intern, Walter Reed Gen. Hosp., 1949-50; commd. 1st lt. Dental Corps, AUS, 1948, advanced through grades to col., 1967; dental officer Pentagon Dispensary, Washington, 1950-52, SHAPE, Paris, France, 1952-55; asso. prof., dir. fixed prosthodontics U. Ky. Coll. Dentistry, Lexington, 1969—. Chief fixed prosthodontics Brooke Gen. Hosp., 1956-62, Darnall Gen. Hosp., 1962-66, Tripler Gen. Hosp., 1966-69. Sponsor, Leilehua Choir, Oahu, Hawaii, 1968-69; active P.T.A. Decorated Army Commendation medal, Meritorious service medal. Diplomate Am. Bd. Prosthodontics. Fellow Am. Coll. Dentistry; mem. Am. Dental Assn., Am. Assn. Dental Schs., Am. Coll. Prosthodontics, Internat. Assn. Dental Research, Blue Grass Dental Soc., Psi Omega, Beta Theta Pi, Phi Eta Sigma, Omicron Kappa Upsilon. Methodist. Home: 3145 Lamar Dr Lexington KY 40502

BREIG, ERNEST RICHARD, architect; b. San Antonio, Nov. 25, 1937; s. Ernest George and Diamantina Esquivel (Carranza) B.; student San Antonio Jr. Coll., 1955, 57, 58; B. Arch., U. Tex., 1966; postgrad. Tex. Agrl. and Mech. U., 1969; m. Yvette Jeane Von Toussaint, Aug. 15, 1964; 1 son, Ernest Richard II. Architect, Brooks Martin, architect, San Antonio, 1966, Roberts, Allen & Helmke, architects, 1966-68, Joseph Hans, architect, Corpus Christi, Tex., 1968-70, Peter Callins & Asso., architect, San Antonio, 1970-73; partner Breig & Asso.-Architect, San Antonio, 1973—. Instr., San Antonio Jr. Coll., 1971—. Registered profl. architect, Tex. Mem. A.I.A. Roman Catholic. Lion (dir. 1968). Home: 17010 Mt Everest St San Antonio TX 78216 Office: 7701 Broadway St San Antonio TX 78209

BREITHAUPT, HELEN DIANE BUTEUX (MRS. JAMES FREDERICK BREITHAUPT), lawyer; b. Ithaca, N.Y., Dec. 7, 1941; d. Edwin Henry and Helen Booth (Jewhurst) Buteux; A.B., Mt. Holyoke Coll., 1963; postgrad. Syracuse U., 1963-65; J.D., N.Y. U., 1966; m. James Frederick Breithaupt, Sept. 5, 1964; 1 son, William Brandon. Admitted to Fla. bar, 1967, U.S. Ct. Appeals for 5th Circuit, 1967, U.S. Dist. Ct. for Middle Dist. Fla., 1967, for No. Dist. Fla., 1971; intern Internat. Labor Standards div. ILO, Geneva, Switzerland, 1962; law clk. and atty. Carlton, Fields, Ward, Emmanuel, Smith & Cutler, Tampa, Fla., 1966-70; practice in Gainesville, Fla., 1971—. Mem. com. on specialization Fla. bar, 1971—. Admissions rep. Mt. Holyoke Coll., Gainesville. Mem. Am., Fla., 8th Jud. Circuit bar assns., Am. Arbitration Assn. Democrat. Presbyn. Contbr. articles to legal publs. Home: 3462 NW 36th Pl Gainesville FL 32605 Office: 1208 NW 23d Av Gainesville FL 32601

BRELAND, JABE ARMISTEAD, physician; b. Memphis, Dec. 1, 1924; s. Loren Dewey and Gladys Louise (Davenport) B.; M.D., La. State U., 1948; m. Betty Jane Baker, Sept. 16, 1948; children—Jabe Armistead, Thomas Lynn, Margaret Elaine, Henry Baker, Anna Elizabeth. Intern, John Sealy Hosp., U. Tex. Med. Br., Galveston, 1948-49; resident El Paso (Tex.) Gen. Hosp., 1949-50; practice medicine, specializing in family practice, Marianna, Fla., 1950—; chief profl. staff Jackson Hosp., 1971-72; chmn. cons. med. staff Marianna Convalescent Center, 1971-72; pres. Camp Seclusion, Inc.,

1966—; mem. Gov.'s Spl. Edn. Task Force Com., 1972—. Chmn. Selective Service Appeal Bd., No. Fed. Jud. Dist. Fla., 1968—. Served with AUS, 1942-43. Diplomate Am. Bd. Family Practice, 1970. Mem. So., Fla. med. assns., Am., Fla. acads. family practice. Episcopalian (licensed lay reader 1963—). Mason (32 deg., Shriner), Elk. Club: Marianna (Fla.) Country. Home: Country Club Hills Marianna FL 32446 Office: 709 3d Av Marianna FL 32446

BRELSFORD, GEORGE WILLIAM, V, fiberglass co. exec.; b. Bridgeton, N.J., Oct. 5, 1927; s. George William and Jeanette (Brockway) B.; A.B., Vanderbilt U., 1949; m. Patricia Murphy, Oct. 15, 1949; children—George William VI, Kathleen, Robin, Jean Ann, Debbie. Personnel staff asst. Owens-Ill., Bridgeton, N.J., 1949-59, employment mgr., Barrington, N.J., 1959-60, corporate communications supr., Toledo, 1960-63; personnel dir. Owens-Corning Fiberglas Corp., Aiken, S.C., 1963—. Adj. prof. U. S.C., Columbia, 1971—. Pres. Aiken County United Fund, 1970. Bd. dirs. Community Action Commn.; trustee Hopelands Meml. Park; adv. bd. Salvation Army. Recipient communications award for mgmt. publs. Internat. Council Indsl. Editors, 1961, 62. Mem. Am. Assn. Indsl. Editors (dir. 1962, 63), Am. Soc. Tng. and Devel., S.C. (chmn. human relations com.), Aiken (dir.) chambers commerce, Kiwanian (pres. 1974). Clubs: Pinnacle (Augusta, Ga.); Palmetto Golf, Midland Valley Country, Green Boundary, Fermata (Aiken). Home: 807 Calhoun St Aiken SC 29801 Office: PO Box 499 Aiken SC 29801

BRENER, MILTON ERNEST, lawyer; b. New Orleans, Jan. 11, 1930; s. Sol and Rose (Feldman) B.; LL.B., Tulane U., 1952; m. Isabel Fedlstein, Nov. 16, 1952; children—Lisa, Ann, Neil, Matthew. Admitted to La. bar, 1952; asst. dist. atty. Orleans Parish, 1956-58, 62-63; partner firm Garon, Brener & McNeely, New Orleans, 1958—. Served to 1st lt. Judge Adv. Gen. Corps, AUS, 1953-56. Mem. La., New Orleans, bar assns. Author: The Garrison Case-A Study in the Abuse of Power, 1969. Home: 6038 St Charles Av New Orleans LA 70118 Office: First Nat Bank of Commerce Bldg New Orleans LA 70112

BRENNAN, GERALD JOHN, mining co. exec.; b. N.Y.C., June 15, 1938; s. Timothy Brenden and Catherine (Judge) B.; B.B.A., St. John's U., 1960; M.B.A., City U. N.Y., 1970; m. Theresa Ann Leonard, May 11, 1963; children—Stephen, Barbara, Paul, Kenneth, John. Sr. accountant RCA, N.Y.C., 1963-67; chief accountant Rosario Resources Co., N.Y.C., 1967-71; controller, asst. sec., trustee pension plan Dixie Lime & Stone Co. Ocala, Fla. 1971—, asst. treas., dir. Marion AG, Hauling Inc. div., 1972—. Served with AUS, 1960, 61-62. Mem. Ocala C. of C. K.C. Home: 513 SE 18th St Ocala FL 32670 Office: PO Box 910 Ocala FL 32670

BRENNAN, JOHN FREDERICK, mfg. co. exec.; b. Whitman, Mass., Sept. 6, 1932; s. William Edward and Mabel Anix (Corcoran) B.; B.A., Williams Coll., 1954; M.B.A., Harvard, 1958; m. Dianne Snow, Oct. 11, 1958; children—Kevin, Tracy, Kerry, Sean, Shannon. Mgmt. cons. Bromfield Assos., Boston, 1958-61; pres. Oak Ridge Atom Industries, Inc., 1962-66; pres. Chem. Separations Corp., Oak Ridge, 1966—; chmn. bd. Tennecomp Systems, Inc., Oak Ridge; dir. Tennelec, Inc., Hamilton First Nat. Bank, Clinton, Tenn., Grove Devel. Corp., Oak Ridge. Chmn. bd. commrs. Oak Ridge Utility Dist., 1970—, sec., 1972-73. Bd. dirs. Oak Ridge Civic Music Assn., 1963-65, treas., 1965; bd. dirs. Oak Ridge Boys Club, 1968-73, v.p., 1971-73. Served to capt. USAF, 1955-57. Recipient Rensellaer medal Rensellaer Poly. Tech., 1950; named Outstanding Young Man in Oak Ridge, Jaycees, 1967, Outstanding Young Man in Tenn., Tenn. Jaycees. Mem. Am. Water Works Assn., Oak Ridge C. of C. (pres. 1967), Delta Upsilon. Roman Catholic. Clubs: Oak Ridge Country; Fox Den Country (Knoxville, Tenn.); Carolina Caribbean (Banner Elk, N.C.). Home: 2660 Oak Ridge Turnpike Oak Ridge TN 37830 Office: 795 Oak Ridge Turnpike Oak Ridge TN 37830

BRENNAN, WILLIAM J(OSEPH), JR., U.S. Supreme Ct. justice; b. Newark, Apr. 25, 1906; s. William J. and Agnes (McDermott) B.; B.S., U. Pa., 1928; LL.B., Harvard, 1931; m. Marjorie Leonard, May 5, 1928; children—William Joseph, Hugh Leonard, Nancy. Admitted to N.J. bar, 1931, practiced in Newark, 1931-49, mem. Pitney, Hardin, Ward & Brennan; superior ct. judge, 1949-50; appellate div. judge, 1950-52; justice Supreme Ct. N.J., 1952-56; asso. justice U.S. Supreme Ct., 1956—. Served with Gen. Staff Corps, U.S. Army, World War II. Decorated Legion of Merit. Office: Supreme Ct Bldg Washington DC 20004

BRENNER, EDGAR H(IRSCH), lawyer; b. N.Y.C., Jan. 4, 1930; s. Louis and Bertha (Guttman) B.; B.A., Carleton Coll., 1951; J.D., Yale, 1954; m. Phyllis Rudstrom, June 2, 1952; children—Charles Sand, David McCaskie, Paul Rudstrom. Admitted to D.C. bar, 1954; mem. legal task force staff Second Hoover Commn., 1954; trial atty. U.S. Dept. Justice, 1954-57; mem. firm Arnold & Porter, Washington, 1957—. Commr. Fairfax County (Va.) Econ. Devel. Authority, 1963—, chmn., 1964-66, 70-73. Bd. dirs. Stella and Charles Guttman Found.; trustee Inst. for Behavioral Research; co-dir. Behavioral Law Center, 1974—. Recipient citation of merit Fairfax County C. of C., 1966. Mem Am., Fed. (chmn. ct. of claims com. 1957) bar assns., Bar Assn. D.C. Home: 2205 Marthas Rd Alexandria VA 22307 Office: 1229 19th St NW Washington DC 20036

BRENT, J. ALLEN, beverage co. exec.; b. Carmi, Ill., Nov. 21, 1921; s. J. A. and Mabel C. (Rvg) B.; B.S., Eastern Ill. U., 1943; Ph.D., U. Fla., 1949; m. Norma U. Miller, Jan. 8, 1946; children—Mark Allen, Robert Lee, Karen Ann, William Michael. Chemist Manhattan Project, Tonawanda, N.Y., 1943-46; naval stores research asst. U. Fla., Gainesville, 1946-49; head chemistry dept. Jacksonville U., 1949-51; chief chemistry sect. research and devel. Minute Maid Co. div. Coca-Cola Co., Plymouth, Fla., 1951-62, asso. dir. research, 1962-64, dir. research and devel. carbonated beverages Coca-Cola Co., Atlanta, 1956—; v.p. Coca-Cola U.S.A., 1968—. Mem. Am. Chem. Soc. (chmn. Fla. sect.), A.A.A.S., Inst. Food Technologists. Sigma Xi, Gamma Sigma Epsilon. Roman Catholic. K.C. (4th deg.). Rotarian. Patentee in field. Home: 8900 Huntcliff Trace Atlanta GA 30328 Office: The Coca-Cola Co Atlanta GA 30304

BRESNAHAN, JOHN FRANCIS, librarian; b. Medford, Mass., Sept. 29, 1918; s. Michael J. and Margaret (Campbell) B.; A.B., Villanova, 1942, M.S. in L.S., 1953, M.A., 1961. Ordained as priest Roman Catholic Ch., 1961; librarian Villanova Prep. Sch., Ojai, Cal., 1944-57; asst. librarian Augustinian Coll., Wash., 1958-60, Msgr. Bonner High Sch., Drexel Hill, Pa., 1961-62; librarian Biscayne Coll., Miami, Fla., 1962—. Mem. Dade dist. com. Fla. Library Devel. Council. Trustee South Fla. Econ. Opportunity Devel. Council. Mem. Am., S.E., Fla., Cath. library assns. Home: 16400 NW 32d Av Miami FL 33054

BRESNAHAN, WILLIAM ALMAN, trade assn. exec.; b. Washington, July 5, 1915; s. William Lloyd and Vivien (Whelan) B.; m. Lillian Anita Springmann, Jan. 8, 1937; children—William Byron, Daniel Alman, Patricia Erin. With A.P., Washington, 1935-37; editor Am. Trucking Assns., Inc., Washington, 1938-43, research dir., 1944-53, dir. interstate cooperation, 1954-56, asst. mng. dir., 1961-64, mng. dir., 1964-70, pres., 1970—; gen. mgr. Nat. Automobile Transporters Assn., Washington, 1957-60. Home: 10110 Chickadee Lane Adelphi Forest MD 20783 Office: Am Trucking Assn Inc 1616 P St NW Washington DC 20036

BRETT, CHARLES EVERETT, ednl. adminstr.; b. Nebraska City, Neb., June 1, 1932; s. Charles Henry and Melba Delores (Durst) B.; B.S., Okla. A. and M. Coll., 1953; M.S., U. N.C., Ph.D., 1963; m. Glenna Dean Smith, June 21, 1953; children—Bonnie Lynn, Barry Charles. Research asso. Humble Research Center, Houston, 1963-64; offshore exploration micropaleontologist Humble Oil & Refining Co., New Orleans, 1964-66; asst. prof. geology U. Ala., University, 1966-69, interim dir. Marine Sci. Inst., 1969-71, dir. Natural Resources Center and Marine Sci. Programs, Tuscaloosa, 1973—; coordinator Ala. Marine Environmental Scis. Consortium, Dauphin Island, Ala., 1971-73. Served with C.E., AUS, 1953-55. Mem. Am. Assn. Petroleum Geologists, Ala. Geol. Soc., Soc. Econ. Paleontologists and Mineralogists, Sigma Xi. Home: 1020 52d St E Tuscaloosa AL 35401 Office: U Ala Natural Resources Center Box 6282 University AL 35486

BREWER, CLYDE SAVAGE (MRS. CLAUDE A. BREWER), educator, civic worker; b. Whitewright, Tex.; d. Charles Edward and Flora Belle (Payne) Savage; grad. North Tex. State U., 1917; B.S., So. Meth. U., 1951; m. Claude A. Brewer, Jan. 13, 1918; children—Bette Belle (Mrs. Carl H. Ingwer, Jr.), James Ashley II, Claude A. Tchr., Jefferson, 1914-15, Sherman, Tex., 1917-18, Dublin, Tex., 1920-21, Ranger, Tex., 1921-22, Big Springs, Tex., 1922-23, Cumby, Tex., 1925-27, Dallas, 1935-38, 1943-44, Dallas Pub. Schs., 1942-54; substitute tchr. Dallas Schs., 1967—. Publicity chmn. Dallas Woman's Forum, 1967—; mem. Local History and Geneal. Soc.-Dallas Pub. Library, 1955—, dir., 1963-69; pres. Clionean Study Club, 1964-65, v.p., 1973-74; del. State Federated Clubs, 1915-17; pres. Christian Woman's Fellowship Fowler Homes, 1966-67, 1967-68; mem. P.T.A., Robert E. Lee Elementary Sch., 1927-43, J. L. Long Jr. High Sch., 1933-35, Woodrow Wilson High Sch., 1932-40, Spence Jr. High Sch., 1941-45, North Dallas High Sch., 1946-50; active various fund drives. Mem. D.A.R. (house chmn. 1965-69), Nat. Soc. China Painters, So. Meml. Assn. (v.p. 1973-74). Mem. Christian Ch. (pres. Lida C. Walls Bible Class 1956, corr. sec. Christian Women's Fellowship 1969-70). Clubs: Palm (pres. 1956-57) Mary Arden. Address: 6824 Dalhart Lane Dallas TX 75214

BREWER, EUGENE WILLIAMS, lumber and bldg. materials co. exec.; b. New Castle, Ky., Sept. 29, 1929; s. Eugene Strother and Dora (Williams) B.; B.S., U. Ky., 1952; m. Juanita Lee Tingle, Sept. 13, 1950; children—Eugene Allan, Stephen Leslie. Dist. mgr. Massey Ferguson, Indpls., 1952-55; field sales engr. Brandeis Machine Co., Louisville, 1956-60; sales mgr. Wilson Machinery Co., Lexington, Ky., 1960-62; pres. Brewer Lumber Co., New Castle, Ky., 1962-71; pres., chmn. bd. Weir Magic Pit Corp., New Castle, 1971—. Chmn. Com. on Health Facilities Planning, Louisville, 1968—; chmn. Municipal Housing Commn., New Castle, 1965—. Pres. Henry County Fair Bd., HOST Community Action, Indsl. Devel. Found. New Castle; v.p. Community Coll. Com. Henry County; bd. dirs. Falls Region Health Council, Louisville. Ky. Col. Methodist (trustee). Home: PO Box 28 New Castle KY 40050 Office: PO Box 296 New Castle KY 40050

BREWER, GEORGE MADISON, hosp. adminstr.; b. Glazier, Tex., Jan. 4, 1916; s. Robert Edward and Blanche Julia (Palmer) B.; B.S., U. Colo., 1947; M.S., Northwestern U., 1957; L.H.D., McMurry Coll., 1964. Mgr., Indsl. Clinic, Pampa, Tex., 1937-42; merchandiser Montgomery Ward & Co., Oakland, Cal., 1947-49; adminstr. Hansford Hosp., Spearman, Tex., 1949-50, Roosevelt Gen. Hosp., Portales, N.M., 1950-55, Los Alamos (N.M.) Med. Center, 1955-56; asst. adminstr. Presbyn. Hosp. Center, Albuquerque, 1957-58; dir. Louisville Gen. Hosp., 1958-61; adminstr. Meth. Hosp., Lubbock, Tex., 1961-72, pres., 1972—. Prof. hosp., clinic adminstrn. U. Louisville, 1958-61. Dir. N.M. Blue Cross Plan, 1953-56; mem. Tex. Radiation Adv. Bd., 1970-76. Served to lt. (j.g.) USNR, 1942-45. Fellow Am. Coll. Hosp. Admnstrs.; mem. Am., Tex. (chmn. council on profl. service 1964-66; trustee 1966-69, 72—) hosp. assns. Rotarian. Home: 5305 43d St Lubbock TX 79414 Office: 3615 19th St Lubbock TX 79410

BREWER, JACK ALAN, religious orgn. exec.; b. Elmore City, Okla., Apr. 13, 1933; s. Jesse Elijah and Opal Mae (Brookshire) B.; B.A., E. Central State Coll., 1958; M. Religious Edn., Southwestern Bapt. Theol. Sem., 1960; m. Carolyn Sue Wright, Mar. 15, 1953; children—Lee, Lisa, Lynn. Merchandising rep. Spokane (Wash.) Daily Chronicle; ordained to ministry Baptist Ch., 1970; minister youth First Bapt. Ch., Tulia, Tex., 1960-62, Springfield, Mo., 1962-65, Texarkana, Tex., 1965-67, Tallowood Bapt. Ch., 1967-70; exec. dir. Boys Country, Houston, 1970—, mem. exec. bd. 1971—. Founder Youth Ecol. Soc., Houston, 1971. Active Pres. Youth Employment Campaign, 1966. Served with USAF, 1951-55. Named Outstanding Man of Yr., Airline Optimist Club, 1973. Mem. Southwestern Bapt. Religious Edn. Assn. Democrat. Author: Fellowships From A-Z, 1967; Serving In My Community, 1970. Contbr. articles to profl. jours. Home: 12718 Dermott St Houston TX 77065 Office: 18806 Roberts Rd Hockley TX 77447

BREWER, JAMES MALCOLM, dentist; b. Leesburg, Ala., June 24, 1914; s. Murt and Mary Emma (Cartlidge) B.; student High Point Coll., 1939; B.S., Jacksonville State U., 1937; D.D.S., Emory U., 1943; m. Maureen Roberts, Jan. 24, 1969; children by previous marriage—Stephen J., Anne Elizabeth (Mrs. Ray Selvage). Tchr. pub. schs., 1935-38; gen. practice dentistry, Ft. Payne, Ala., 1946—; dir. 1st Fed. Savs. & Loan Assn. Chmn. A.R.C. Bd. dirs. Mountain Manor Nursing Home. Served with AUS, 1943-46. Fellow Internat. Coll. Dentists; mem. Am., Ala. (pres. 1972) dental assns., 5th Dist., Chgo. dental socs., Am. Soc. Dentistry for Children, So. Acad. Oral Surgery, Am. Legion (comdr.). Baptist. Mason (Shriner). Home: 300 16th St NW Fort Payne AL 35967 Office: PO Box 428 Fort Payne AL 35967

BREWER, MICHAEL FRASER, social scientist; b. N.Y.C., May 9, 1929; s.George E. and Ann (Fraser) B.; B.S., Yale, 1953; M.S., U. Mich., 1955; Ph.D., U. Cal. at Berkeley, 1959; m. Charlotte J. Kidder, June 11, 1955; children—Henry, Fraser, Mika, Polly. Asst. prof. U. Cal. at Berkeley, 1959-62; staff economist Council of Econ. Advisers, Exec. Office of Pres., Washington, 1962-63; dir. Natural Resources Policy Center, George Washington U., 1965-67; v.p. Resources for the Future, Inc., Washington, 1967-71; pres. Population Reference Bur., Washington, 1971-74. Mem. Am. Econ. Assn., Am. Agrl. Econ. Assn., Student Conservation Assn. (dir. 1969—). Served with AUS, 1950-52. Home: 6817 Connecticut Av Chevy Chase MD 20015

BREWER, NORMAN C(RAIG), JR., lawyer, city judge; b. Black Hawk, Miss., Oct. 4, 1913; s. Norman C. and Ella Hunter (Jumper) B.; A.B., U. Miss., 1935, LL.B., 1937; m. Martha Manly. Apr. 12, 1946; children—Martha, Norman III. Admitted to Miss. bar, 1937, since practiced Greenwood; sr. mem. firm Brewer, Deaton & Evans; city judge, 1939-43; 47-57. Commr. Yazoo-Miss. Delta Levee Dist. Mem. adv. bd. Mt. Buelah Christian Center, Edwards, Miss.; treas. Nat. Found. Infantile Paralysis, Inc., Le Flore County, 1948—; state pres. Conv. Christian Chs.; dir. Girl Scout Campers; chmn. bd. Miss. Christian Missionary Soc. Served as lt. comdr. USNR, 1942-46; overseas, 1943-45, comdr., 1953—. La. colonel, 1948-52, Miss., 1952—. Chmn. Bd. Bar Admissions, Miss., 1958-60. Named Ky. Col. Mem. Am. Coll. Probate Counsel, V.F.W., S.A.R. (state pres.), Am. Legion (past comdr.), Internat. Assn. Ins. Counsel, Am., Leflore County (pres.) bar assns., Miss. Assn. Def. Lawyers, Miss. State Bar, C. of C. (mem. exec. com.), Soc. Colonial Wars (gov.), Sigma Chi (nat. pres.), Omicron Delta Kappa, Phi Delta Phi. Mem. Christian Ch. (chmn. ofcl. bd.). Elk. Clubs: Batteaux Bay (Tobago, B.W.I.); Greenwood (Miss.) Country; Summit (Memphis). Home: W River Rd Greenwood MS 38930 Office: 107 W Market St Greenwood MS 38930

BREWER, PHILIP WARREN, civil engr.; b. Hagerstown, Md., Dec. 18, 1923; s. J. Chester and Ruth (Emmert) B.; B.S., U. Md., 1945; m. Elizabeth Marvel Wynn, Aug. 29, 1947; children—Dorothy Wynn, Bruce Douglas. Hydraulic engr. Water Resources Br., U.S. Geol. Survey, College Park, Md. 1945-47; designing engr. Wash. Suburban San. Commn., Hyattsville, Md., 1947-53; san. engr., civil engr. Bur. of Yards and Docks, Dept. Navy, Washington, 1953-68, head spl. design Naval Facilities Engring. Command, 1968-73, chief civil engr., 1973—. Registered profl. engr. Mem. Am. Soc. C.E., Soc. Am. Mil. Engrs. Episcopalian. Home: 12545 Two Farm Dr Silver Spring MD 20904 Office: Code 0415 Naval Facilities Engring Command 200 Stovall St Alexandria VA 22332

BREWER, RALPH WRIGHT, JR., lawyer; b. Alexandria, La., Jan. 9, 1928; s. Ralph Wright and Margot (Riviere) B.; B.J., La. State U., 1950, J.D., 1955 ; m. Peggy Knapps; 1 dau., Margo Beatrice; children (by previous marriage)—David, Daniel, Ralph Wright III, William. Admitted to La. bar, 1955; practice law, Baton Rouge, 1955—. Served with USNR, 1946-48, 1950-52. Mem. Am., La., Baton Rouge bar assns., V.F.W., Amvets, Am., La. trial lawyers assns., Nat. Defender and Legal Aid Assn., Sigma Delta Chi, Sigma Alpha Epsilon. Democrat. Presbyn. (elder). Home: 1023 Waverly Dr Baton Rouge LA 70806 Office: 200 Government St Baton Rouge LA 70802

BREWER, RICHARD HARDING, educator; b. San Diego, Aug. 12, 1921; s. Herbert William and Grace (Foncanon) B.; B.A. in Music, San Jose State Coll., 1943; postgrad. Columbia, 1943, Westminster Choir Coll., 1952-53, U. Cal. at Los Angeles (Atwater Kent fellow), 1955-59; M.Mus., Ind. U., 1949, D.M.A. with honors, U. So. Cal., 1965; m. Eileen Lysne, Aug. 18, 1951; children—Cora Lynne, Andrew Lyon. Asst. prof. dept. music Minot (N.D.) State Coll., 1949-51, Omaha U., 1952-55; minister music Wilshire Meth. Ch., Los Angeles, 1960-62; prof. music, head dept., chmn. div. fine arts Pfeiffer Coll., Misenheimer, N.C., 1962—. Served with USNR, 1943-48. Mem. Am. Choral Dirs. Assn., Music Educators Nat. Conf., Coll. Music Soc., Nat. Assn. Tchrs. Singing, Phi Mu Alpha. Methodist. Kiwanian. Composer: 6 choral works. Home: Box K Misenheimer NC 28109

BREWER, ROY VINCENT, educator; b. Cisco, Ga., Feb. 4, 1908; s. John Taylor and Mary Jane Gocia (Cockburn) B.; B.S. in Elec. Engring., Ga. Inst. Tech., 1932; M.A., Oglethorpe U., 1938; m. Martha Elizabeth Birchmore, Oct. 5, 1935; children—John Edwin, Martha Ann (Mrs. Marion Wesley Owen), Bettie Jean. Tchr., coach track and basketball Avondale High Sch., Avondale Estates, Ga., 1935-36; tchr. Hapeville (Ga.) High Sch., 1936-73, head sci. dept., 1940-73, head football coach, 1936-62, dir. Athletics, 1936-73. Served to lt. comdr. USNR, 1943-46. Named Star Tchr., Ga. State C. of C., 1963, 69. Mem. N.E.A., Nat. Intercollegiate Soc. of Spiked Shoes, Ga. Football Coaches Assn., Ga. Acad. Sci., Ga. Assn. Educators, Kappa Phi Kappa. Baptist (deacon 1935-73). Mason. Clubs: Civitan, Optimist (Hapeville). Home: 1868 Linwood Av East Point GA 30344

BREWSTER, DANIEL FERGERSON, clergyman; b. Newnan, Ga., Dec. 23, 1916; s. Daniel Fergerson and Sara (Stevens) B.; B.A., Emory U., 1945; M.Div., Candler Sch. Theology, 1948; D.D., LaGrange Coll., 1966; m. Helen Howe Glawson, June 7, 1943. Ordained to ministry Meth. Ch., 1948; minister, Lithia Springs, Ga., 1943-48, Dallas, Ga., 1948-52, Barnesville, Ga., 1953-57, Thomson, Ga., 1957-61, Newnan, 1961-64; exec. dir. Ga. Meth. Commn. Higher Edn., Atlanta, 1964—. Treas., Ga. Pastor's Sch., 1953-56, chmn. bd. dirs., 1956-60, dean, 1960-64; sec. N.Ga. Conf. Meth. Bd. Edn., 1952-56, N. Ga. Conf. Promotion, Cultivation, 1960-66. Dist. commr. Atlanta Area council Boy Scouts Am., 1967; mem. Emory U. Alumni Council, 1953—. Trustee LaGrange (Ga.) Coll., Reinhardt Coll., Waleska, Ga. Recipient Meritorious Service award Ga. Meth. Admission Dirs., 1971. Mem. Soc. Advancement Continuing Edn. Ministry, Council Religion and Internat. Affairs, World Meth. Council. Editor: North Georgia Handbook, 1962-70. Home: 1727 Clairmont Way NE Atlanta GA 30329 Office: 159 Forrest Av NE Atlanta GA 30303

BREWTON, CHARLES SIDNEY, lawyer; b. Larkinsville, Ala., Nov. 9, 1913; s. Charles Spurgeon and Ora (Smith) B.; student Birmingham-So. Coll., 1932-35; J.D., U. Ala., 1938; m. Jewell Wann, Oct. 12, 1940; children—Carol Ann, Charles Sidney III. Admitted to Ala. bar, 1938; practice in Scottsboro, Ala., as partner Brewton & Jones, 1938-40; spl. asst. to U.S. atty. gen., 1940-43; staff dir. U.S. Senate Com. Expenditure in Exec. Depts., 1943-44; adminstrv. asst. to U.S. Senator Lister Hill, 1943-56; asso. dir. law and legislation Joint Commn. Mental Illness and Health, Cambridge, Mass., 1956-59; gen. counsel Senate Com. Small Bus., 1959-61; asst. dir. Office Emergency Preparedness Exec. Office President, 1961-69; gen. counsel Joint Com. Def. Prodn., 1969-73; with Charles S. Brewton Law Assos., 1973—. Chmn. com. arrangements Nat. Conf. Nat. Def. Exec. Res., 1965. Asst. campaign mgr. presdl. nominee Adlai E. Stevenson, 1952, 56; asst. to chmn. Presdl. Inaugural Com., 1965. Mem. Assn. Senate Adminstrv. Assts. and Exec. Secs. (past pres.), Nat. Grange, Sigma Alpha Epsilon. Clubs: President's; Nat. Capitol Democratic. Author: (with others) Action for Mental Health, 1961. Home: Moody Ridge Scottsboro AL 35768 Office: 114 E Willow St Scottsboro AL 35768

BREWTON, RALEIGH GERALD, trucking co. exec.; b. Ocala, Fla., May 5, 1943; s. Curtis Edward and Orpah (Cribb) B.; B.A. in Psychology, Jacksonville U., 1972; m. Bessie Wanda Caldwell, Nov. 14, 1970. Mgr. Foundry Press Inc., Orangeburg, S.C., 1966-69; office mgr. Am. Council Christian Chs., Atlanta, 1969-71; comptroller Barton Internat. Inc., Jacksonville, Fla., 1971—. John Wesley fellow, 1970. Mem. Francis Asbury Soc. Ministers, Nat. Thespian Assn. Writer, producer program Children's Story Hour, WJAX radio, Jacksonville, 1961. Home: 2852 Yellow Pine Dr Jacksonville FL 32211 Office: PO Box 37029 Jacksonville FL 32205

BREWTON, WILLIAM FRANKLIN, lawyer; b. New Port Richey, Fla., Sept. 5, 1932; s. Wade Hampton and Jewell (McLean) B.; B.A., Emory U., 1954; LL.B., U. Fla., 1957; m. Patricia M. Brewton, 1970; 1 son, Derek H. Admitted to Fla. bar, 1957; partner Brewton and Brewton, Dade City, 1958-65, owner, 1965-73; partner Brewton & Council, 1973—; municipal judge City of Dade City, Fla. Mem. Pasco County Farm Bur. Served with AUS, 1957-58. Mem. Fla. Bar, Am., Pasco County (pres. 1964) bar assns., Am. Judicature Soc., Fla. Heart Assn. (parliamentarian for bd. dirs., del. to Am. Heart Conv.), Pasco County Cattlemen's Assn., Sertoma, Sigma Nu, Phi Delta Phi, Pi Sigma Alpha. Democrat. Methodist. Mason (Shriner). Clubs: Dade City Rod and Gun; Zephyrville Shrine. Home: 1501 W Missouri Av Dade City FL 33525 Office: 708 E Meridian Av Dade City FL 33525

BREYERE, EDWARD JOSEPH, biologist, educator; b. Washington, Apr. 25, 1927; s. Edward Joseph and Mollie (Swing) B.; B.S., U. Md., 1951; M.S., U. Md., 1954, Ph.D., 1957; m. Marjorie Louise Gillet, June 16, 1951; 1 son, Edward John. Teaching asst. U. Md., 1954-55; research fellow Nat. Cancer Inst., 1955-57, 57-61; asso. prof. Am. U., Washington, 1961-67, prof. biology, 1967—, dir. Leukemia Research Fund, 1966—; dir. Immunogenetics Lab., Sibley Meml. Hosp., Washington. Served with AUS, 1945-46. Mem. Transplantation Soc., Am. Assn. Cancer Research, A.A.A.S., Am. Inst. Biol. Scis., Am. Genetics Assn., Sigma Xi, Phi Kappa Phi. Contbr. Articles profl. jours. Home: 6707 Sulky Lane Rockville MD 20852 Office: 5255 Loughboro Rd NW Washington DC 20016

BRIAN, ALEXIS MORGAN, JR., lawyer; b. New Orleans, Oct. 4, 1928; s. Alexis Morgan and Evelyn (Thibaut) B.; B.A. in Sociology, La. State U., 1949, J.D., 1956; M.S. in Psychology, Trinity U., 1954; m. Elizabeth Louise Graham, Mar. 17, 1951; children—Robert Morgan, Ellen Graham. Admitted to La. bar, 1956; asso firm Deutsch, Kerrigan & Stiles, New Orleans, 1956-60, partner, 1961—. Mem. com. on bds. So. Bapt. Conv., 1969, mem. exec. bd. New Orleans Bapt. Assn., 1958-63, sec. trustees, 1967-70. Asst. scoutmaster local troop Boy Scouts Am., 1963-70. Trustee New Orleans Bapt. Theol. Sem., 1961-74, v.p., 1966-68, pres., 1968-74; bd. dirs. Goodwill Industries, 1968—, New Orleans Bapt. Theol. Sem. Found., 1972—. Served with USAF, 1951-55. Named Boss of Year, New Orleans Legal Secs. Assn., 1966. Mem. Am., La., New Orleans bar assns., Internat. Assn. Ins. Counsel, La. Assn. Def. Counsel, Def. Research Inst., Am. Arbitration Assn. (panel of arbitrators 1970—); Phi Delta Phi, Theta Xi. Baptist (deacon; trustee; tchr.; lay preacher). Home: 1738 S Carrollton Av New Orleans LA 70118 Office: One Shell Sq New Orleans LA 70139

BRIANS, AUDREY LEE, architect; b. Corsicana, Tex., Aug. 23, 1934; d. Robin Hood and Audrey Mae (Harris) Brians; B.Arch., U. Tex., 1956, postgrad. community and regional planning, 1971—. With Nat. Park Service, Phila., 1956; with York & Sawyer, N.Y.C., 1958, Internat. Basic Economy Corp., N.Y.C., 1959-64; with Daniel, Mann, Johnson, & Mendenhall, Madrid, Spain, 1964-68; partner Lammers & Brians, Austin, Tex., 1968-71; individual practice architecture, Austin, 1971-72; dir. design Lundgren & Maurer, Architect, Austin, 1972-73; architect in charge C.I.T.E.C., Mexico City, Mexico, 1973; now prin. Brians & Assos., Inc., supervising architect Langson Bros. Constrn. Co., Houston. Mem. Community Devel. Corp., Austin, 1969, Laguna Gloria Mus., Austin; commr. Austin Tomorrow projects. Bd. dirs. Zachary Scott Civic Theatre, Austin, 1968-69. Registered landscape architect. Mem. A.I.A., Constrn. Specifications Inst., Women's Equity Action League (pres. Austin chpt.), Am. Assn. U. Women., League Women Voters, Alpha Alpha Gamma, Alpha Delta Pi. Home: 14800 Memorial Dr Apt 143 Houston TX 77024 Office: 1111 Upland Dr Houston TX 77043

BRICE, LAURIE SIMONTON, educator; b. Winnsboro, S.C., Apr. 18, 1916; s. Eugene Douglas and Laura Lee (Jamison) B.; A.B., Erskine Coll., 1937; certificate in personnel psychology U. Pitts., 1943; M.Ed., U. S.C., 1948; m. Margaret Mae Hemminger, Sept. 7, 1943; children—Laurie Simonton, James Douglas, Carolyn Ann. Prin. Johnsonville (S.C.) Pub. Schs., 1937-40, Calhoun Falls (S.C.) Pub. Schs., 1940-42; supt. Indiantown Schs., Williamsburg County, S.C., 1946-49; prin., dir. edn. John de la Howe Sch., McCormick, S.C., 1949-67, supt., treas., 1967—. Sec-treas. McCormick County Devel. Bd., 1964-68; mem. commn. Piedmont Tech. Coll. Bd. dirs. Area 6 S.C. Lung Assn. Served with AUS, 1942-46, PTO, 1944-46. Mem. N.E.A. (life), McCormick County Edn. Assn., S.C. Hist. Soc. Democrat. Presbyn. (elder). Lion (pres. 1961-62). Home: McCormick SC 29835 Office: John de la Howe Sch McCormick SC 29835

BRICE, LUTHER KENNEDY, JR., educator; b. Spartanburg, S.C., Jan. 29, 1928; s. Luther Kennedy and Frances (Boggs) B.; B.A., Harvard, 1949; M.A., Dartmouth, 1951; Ph.D., Duke, 1955. Mem. faculty dept. chemistry Va. Poly. Inst. and State U., Blacksburg, 1954—, asso. prof., 1957-65, prof., 1965—; vis. prof. Duke U., Durham, N.C., 1956, U. Va., Charlottesville, 1957; research participant Oak Ridge Nat. Lab., 1954. Recipient Outstanding Teaching award Va. Poly. Inst. and State U., 1960, 65; NSF grantee, 1965-70, Am. Chem. Soc. grantee, 1965-66. Mem. Am. Chem. Soc., A.A.A.S., Sigma Xi, Omicron Delta Kappa, Phi Lambda Upsilon. Contbr. articles to profl. jours. Home: 101 Sherwood Ct Blacksburg VA 24060

BRICK, IRVING BENJAMIN, physician, educator; b. Oakland, Cal., Apr. 24, 1914; s. Harry and Gertrude (Gibbs) B.; A.B., George Washington U., 1937, M.D., 1941. Intern, Gallinger Municipal Hosp., Washington, 1941-42; resident Tufts Med. Service, Boston City Hosp., 1942-43, 46-47; instr. gastroenterology Georgetown U., Washington, 1947-50, asst. prof., 1950-54, asso. prof., 1955-61, prof., 1961—, acting chmn. dept. medicine, 1968-72. Sr. med. cons. Nat. Vets. Affairs and Rehab. Commn., 1948—. Served with AUS, 1943-46. Diplomate in gastroenterology Am. Bd: Internal Medicine. Mem. Am. Gastroenterology Assn., So. Soc. Clin. Investigation, Harveian Soc., London, Am. socs. gastrointestinal endoscopy, A.C.P., Am. Fedn. Clin. Research. Contbr. articles in field to profl. jours. Home: 3616 Suitland Rd SE Washington DC 20020

BRICKER, SHIRLEY ZUBRADT, advt. agy. exec.; b. Alta, Ia., Jan. 10, 1927; d. Theodore William and Mabel (Peterson) Zubradt; grad. high sch. 1 dau., Linda M. Asst. prodn. mgr. Cabell Eanes, Inc., Richmond, Va., 1954-57; v.p., prodn. mgr. Advt. Assos., Inc., Richmond, 1957-60; asst. mgr. research dept. U.S. Fed. Res. Bank, Richmond, 1960-62; media supr. Cargill, Wilson & Acree, Inc., Richmond, 1962-70, advt. cons., 1970; media dir. Lin Lockhart Advt., Inc., 1970-71; media dir. Clinton E. Frank, Inc., 1971—. Mem. Advt. Club Richmond (dir. 1965-68, treas. 1968-69, sec. 1969-70). Club: Press (hon.) (Va.) Address: 501 N Daisy Av Highland Springs VA 23075

BRICKEY, JACK MARTIN, elec. engr.; b. Kingsport, Tenn., June 30, 1944; s. Emerson Lee and Ima (McConnell) B.; student (Elk scholar) East Tenn. State U., 1962-64; B.S., U. Tenn., 1967; m. Sharon Ruth Hartley, Feb. 14, 1970. Elec. engr. Tenn. Eastman Co., Kingsport, 1967—. Registered profl. engr., Tenn. Mem. Tenn. Soc. Profl. Engrs. (membership chmn.), I.E.E.E. (pres.), Intrument Soc. Am. (chmn. publs. 1971), Am. Automobile Assn. Methodist. Elk, Moose. Club: Cedar Hills Country (Lee County, Va.). Home: 1809 Birchwood Rd Kingsport TN 37660 Office: Eastman Rd Kingsport TN 37662

BRIDGE, HOWARD ANTHONY, JR., broadcasting exec.; b. Dallas, Dec. 17, 1931; s. Howard Anthony and Ruth (Pitchford) B.; B.S., So. Meth. U., 1953; m. JoAnn Odom, June 28, 1954; children—Howard Anthony III, Victoria Caswell, James Martin. News editor WFAA, Dallas, 1953; program dir., KBEL, Idabel, Okla., 1953; dir. programming WBOF, Virginia Beach, 1954-55; pres. KAHT; v.p. KMHT. Marshall, 1955—; v.p. KLUE AM-FM. Longview, after 1959, now pres.; v.p. Outdoor Marshall, Inc., 1965—. Served with USNR, 1955-57. Mem. Tex. Assn. Broadcasters (past pres.), Marshall C. of C. (dir.), Outdoor Advt. Assn. Tex. (dir.), Phi Delta Theta. Episcopalian. Mason (32 deg., Shriner). Home: 2504 Arlington Rd Marshall TX 75670 Office: 4 Garden Ct Marshall TX 75670

BRIDGE, WILLIAM JOHN, govt. ofcl.; b. Ft. Wayne, Ind., Jan. 22, 1942; s. Charles Dwight and Berniece (Hershberger) B.; student Purdue U., 1962-64; A.B. with high distinction, Ind. U., 1967. Planning asst. Model City Program, Norfolk, Va., 1967-69, planning specialist, 1969-70, dir. planning, 1970; economist Norfolk (Va.) Redevel. and Housing Authority, 1970-71, dir. program devel., 1971—. Served with USNR, 1960-62. Mem. Am. Econ. Assn., Am. Soc. Planning Ofcls., Nat. Assn. Housing and Redevel. Ofcls., Phi Beta Kappa. Home: 535 Washington Park Norfolk VA 23517 Office: PO Box 968 Norfolk VA 23501

BRIDGEMAN, BEN DALY, lawyer; b. New Orleans, Nov. 29, 1932; s. Sidney and A. Irene (Daly) B.; B.B.A., Loyola U., New Orleans, 1954; LL.B., Tulane U., 1961; m. Dorothy E. Brennan, Sept. 4, 1954; children—D. Brennan, B. Daly, Bradford D. Admitted to La. bar, since practice in New Orleans; mem. firm Bridgeman & Conway; chmn. bd. Merc. Bank & Trust Co., Gretna, La., Security Broadcasting, Inc., New Orleans, Beverly Dinner Playhouse, Inc., New Orleans and Shreveport, La., So. Bankers Life Ins. Co., New Orleans, Granada Constrn. Co., Inc., Metairie, La.; partner Claiborne Co., New Orleans; dir. Peoples Bank and Trust Co., Chalmette, La., Liberty Bank and Trust Co., New Orleans. Bd. dirs. Vols. Am., New Orleans. Served to 1st lt. AUS, 1954-56. Club: Metairie Country. Home: 105 Mulberry Dr Metairie LA 70005 Office: 6th Floor Metairie Tower Office Bldg 433 Metairie Rd Metairie LA 70005

BRIDGER, JAMES ALBERT, JR., civil engr.; b. Bladenboro, N.C., Jan. 28, 1931; s. James Albert and Elise Fogle (Matthews) B.; student U. N.C., 1946-50, certificate in municipal adminstrn., 1962; B.S., N.C. State U., 1959; m. June Morris, Dec. 19, 1953; children—James Albert III, Matthew Anthony, M. Randall, R. Cameron. Office mgr., estimator Crowell Constrn. Co., Fayetteville, N.C., 1959, gen. supt., field engr., 1959-60; chief inspection div. City of Raleigh, N.C., 1960-64; resident engr. William C. Olsen & Assos., Raleigh, 1964-69; owner J. A. Bridger, Jr., cons. engrs., Raleigh, 1969—; pres., dir. Bridger Motor Co.; v.p., dir. Crowell Constructors; sec., dir. Pait Transfer Co., Kelly Supply Co., So. Builders Equipment Co.; dir. Bank of Bladenboro, Bladenboro Cotton Mills, Bridger Corp. Dist. commr. Boy Scouts Am., 1964. Served to 1st lt. USAF, 1951-56. Mem. Raleigh Engrs. Club, Am. Water Works Assn., N.C. Soc. Engrs. Baptist. Home: Route 1 Apex NC 27502 Office: 3917 Western Blvd Raleigh NC 27606

BRIDGERS, WILLIAM FRANK, neuroscientist, univ. dean; b. Asheville, N.C., July 26, 1932; s. John Dixon and Ruth (Norberg) B.; B.A., U. South, 1954; postgrad. (fellow in biochemistry), Duke, 1954-55; M.D. cum laude, Washington U., St. Louis, 1959; m. Anne Jenkins, Feb. 10, 1955; children—Jeffrey Wright, William David, Daniel Lawson. Intern Barnes Hosp., St. Louis, 1959-60, resident, 1962-63; asst. prof. medicine Washington U., St. Louis, 1963-66; asso. prof. medicine U. Miami (Fla.), 1966-68; prof. psychiatry U. Ala., Birmingham, 1968-72, dir. neuroscis. program, dir. sponsored programs, asso. dean Schs. Medicine and Dentistry, 1972—; staff officer com. health care resources in VA, Nat. Acad. Scis.-NRC, 1974-75. Served with USPHS, 1960-62. United Health Found. fellow, 1963-65; NIH grantee, 1963-73. Mem. Am. Soc. Biol. Chemistry, Am. Soc. for Neurochemistry, Am. Soc. Clin. Nutrition, Am. Inst. Nutrition, Sigma Xi, Phi Beta Kappa, Alpha Tau Omega. Democrat. Asso. editor Nutrition Revs., 1963-68, Internat. Rev. Neurobiology, 1972—. Contbr. articles to profl. jours. Home: 2825 Montevallo Rd Birmingham AL 35233 Office: U Ala Birmingham University Station AL 35294

BRIDGES, ALBERT FOSTER, banker, ret. sch. athletics adminstr.; b. Athens, La., Mar. 17, 1905; s. Milton L. and Minnie Florence (Word) B.; student Bryson Coll., 1922-25; B.S., George Peabody Coll., 1926, M.A., 1932; m. Margaret Burrow, June 2, 1931. Tchr., coach Peabody High Sch., Trenton, Tenn., 1926-30, Milan (Tenn.) High Sch., 1930-31; tchr. Chester County High Sch., Henderson, Tenn., 1931-35, Byars Hall High Sch., Covington, Tenn., 1935-36; supt. Trenton Pub. Schs., 1936-43; supt. Covington City Schs., 1943-46; exec. sec. Tenn. Secondary Sch. Athletic Assn., Trenton, 1946-72; v.p. Bank of Trenton, Trenton Trust Co. Sec.-treas. Girls Nat. Basketball Rules Com., 1952-69. Treas. Laura Harlan Mack Morris Home for Aged. Inducted into Tenn. Sports Hall of Fame, 1971. Mem. Tenn. Pub. Sch. Officers Assn. (pres. 1945-46), Gibson County Edn. Assn. (pres. 1936-37). Methodist. Rotarian. Home: 210 10th St Trenton TN 38382 Office: Box 67 Trenton TN 38382

BRIDGES, WORTH TALMADGE, JR., dentist; b. Hickory, N.C., May 29, 1928; s. Worth Talmadge and Florrie Jane (Jeffcoate) B.; B.S., Wake Forest U., 1954; D.M.D., U. Louisville, 1959; m. Ethel Lawing, Aug. 23, 1953; children—Melissa Kay, Sherri Leigh. Pvt. practice dentistry, Shelby, N.C., 1959, Mooresville, N.C., 1960—. Dep. Sheriff Iredel County. Bd. dirs. Lowrance Hosp., Mooresville. Served with USNR, 1946-51. Mem. Am. Dental Assn., Iredel County Dental Soc. (sec.-treas. 1962-63, pres. 1972), N.C. Dental Soc., Southeast Analgesia Soc. (charter, chmn. N.C. chpt. 1972), Am. Fedn. Police, Alpha Sigma Phi, Delta Sigma Delta. Republican. Baptist. Mason, Elk. Home: 781 Pinewood Circle Mooresville NC 28115 Office: 213 S Broad St Mooresville NC 28115

BRIEVE, FREDERICK JAY, univ. adminstr.; b. Holland, Mich., Aug. 17, 1928; s. Frank and Alice (Gebben) B.; A.B., Hope Coll., 1950; M.A., Mich. State U., 1956, Ed.D., 1963; m. Joyce Elane Baker, Aug. 11, 1950; children—Tom, Betsy. Tchr., Grand Ledge, Mich., 1950-53; high sch. prin., North Muskegon, Mich., 1955-60; supt. schs., Muskegon, Mich., 1960-63; adminstr. Mich. State U., 1963-64; adminstr. Dept. State, 1964-65; v.p. Kettering Found., Dayton, O., 1966-68; dept. chmn. U. Houston Sch. Adminstrn., 1968-70; asso. supt. schs., Dallas, 1970-71; head div. adminstrn. and ednl. services Va. Tech. U., Blacksburg, 1971—. Served with USNR, 1953-55. Mem. N.E.A. (life), Am., Tex. assns. sch. adminstrs., Am. Soc. Curriculum Devel., Council Ednl. Facilities Planners, Phi Delta Kappa. Elk. Home: 12 Shawnee Trail RFD 1 Blacksburg VA 24060

BRIGGLE, ANTHONY NOEL, splty. store exec.; b. Dallas, Nov. 30, 1937; s. William James and Virginia (Aechternacht) B.; B.A., So. Meth. U., 1959; m. Evelyn Carroll Cary, June 29, 1963; children—Evelyn Cary-Elisa, Georgie Fonda Schneider, Frances Caroline Curtis. Dir. pub. relations and spl. events Neiman-Marcus Co., Dallas, 1965—; asst. to v.p. sales promotion Tex. United Fund, 1963-65. Corr., Archtl. Digest, 1971. Chmn. men's div. TACA, 1970; v.p. Dallas Symphony Orch. Guild, 1971—; mem. adv. com. Jr. Players Guild, 1969—. Trustee U.S. Film Festival So. Meth. U. Sch. Fine Arts, 1971—; bd. dirs. Theatre Three, Dallas Civic Ballet Soc., Irish Georgian Soc. Mem. Pub. Relations Soc. Am., So. Meth. U. Alumni Assn., Kappa Alpha. Clubs: Mustang, Terpsichorean (Dallas). Home: 5711 Redwood Lane Dallas TX 75209 Office: Main and Ervay Sts Dallas TX 75201

BRIGGS, BRUCE BURRY, judge; b. Mars Hill, N.C., June 20, 1937; s. Clarence W. and Eula (Burry) B.; A.A., Mars Hill Coll., 1958; J.D., Wake Forest U., 1962; student Western Caroline U., 1958-59; m. Jean Elizabeth Miller, Nov. 26, 1967; 1 dau., Elizabeth Ashley. Admitted to N.C. bar, 1962; practiced in Asheville, N.C., 1962-69; mem. firm Riddle & Briggs, 1963-69; atty., Madison County, 1968-69; asst. U.S. atty., Asheville, 1969-72; now judge N.C. Dist. Ct. Mem. N.C. Senate, 1966-69; chmn. Madison County Republican Com., 1964-66; 11th dist. congl. chmn., 1966—; mem. N.C. Rep. Exec. and Central Coms., 1964-69; vice chmn. Young Rep. Club, 1966. Bd. advisers Western Carolina U., Bus. Assn. Mars Hill Coll. Served with AUS, 1962. Mem. Am. Trial Lawyers Assn., N.C., Buncombe County, Madison County, Fed. bar assns., Am. Judicature Assn., Phi Alpha Delta. Baptist (deacon). Home: 135 Mountainview Dr Mars Hill NC 28754 Office: Main St PO Box 81 Mars Hill NC 28754

BRIGGS, DALE JEROME, lawyer; b. Sand Springs, Okla., Feb. 4, 1926; s. Fred Gerome and Willie (Wood) B.; LL.B., U. Tulsa, 1950; student Central Mo. State Tchrs. Coll., 1944-45; m. Dorothy Jean Cardwell, Aug. 1, 1945; children—William Dale (dec.), Patricia, Judith Lynn, Robert Steven. Admitted to Okla. bar, 1950, since practiced in Tulsa; mem. firm Berringer, Patterson & Briggs, Tulsa, 1950—; judge Ct. of Common Pleas, Tulsa County, Okla., 1955-59. Mem. Okla. Ho. of Reps., 1950-52; pres., bd. dirs. Okla. for Constl. Rep. and Citizens for Constl. Reapportionment, 1954-62; pres. Tulsa Council, Camp Fire Girls, 1962-64. Served with USNR, 1944-46. Mem. Am., Okla. (dir.; pres. 1969) trial lawyers assns., Am., Okla., Tulsa County bar assns., Am. Judicature Soc., Delta Theta Phi. Republican. Mason. Club: The Summit. Home: 5928 S 72d E Av Tulsa OK 74145 Office: Beacon Bldg Tulsa OK 74103

BRIGGS, FRED NORMAN, physiologist, educator; b. Oakland, Cal., Sept. 12, 1924; s. Fred and Dorothy Elizabeth (Crane) B.; A.B., U. Cal. at Berkeley, 1947, M.A., 1948, Ph.D., 1953; m. Geneva Ozall Yates, Apr. 11, 1949; 1 dau., Laura Elizabeth. Radiologist, U.S. Naval Radiol. Lab., San Francisco, 1948-49; instr. pharmacology Harvard, Boston, 1952-55, asso. pharmacology, 1956-58; asst. prof. Tufts U., Boston, 1958-61; research fellow Max-Planck Institut for Medezinische Forschung, Heidelberg, Germany, 1955-56; asso. prof. physiology Tufts U., Boston, 1961; prof. physiology U. Pitts., 1961-71; prof., chmn. dept. physiology Va. Commonwealth U., Richmond, 1971—. Mem. basic sci. com. Am. Heart Assn., 1963-65; mem. study sect. physiol. tng. program USPHS, 1967-70. Recipient Established Investigator award Am. Heart Assn., 1960-64, USPHS Research Career award Nat. Heart Inst., 1964-71. Mem. Am. Physiol. Soc. (edn. com. 1971—), Cardiac Muscle Soc., Biophys. Soc., Internat. Study Group for Research in Cardiac Metabolism. Contbr. articles to profl. jours. Co-editor: Am. Jour. Physiol., 1970—, Jour. Applied Physiol. Home: 401 Lakeway Dr Richmond VA 23229

BRIGGS, JOHN CARMON, ednl. adminstr., biologist; b. Portlan Ore., Apr. 9, 1920; s. Revoe Carlisle and Jessie May (Carmon) b.; B.. Ore. State U., 1943; M.A., Stanford, 1947, Ph.D., 195. children—Linda (Mrs. Richard L. Smith), David, Daniel, Carleton, Douglas, Katherine, Samuel, Elizabeth, Margaret; m. 3d, Eila A. Hanni, Mar. 9, 1973. Aquatic biologist U.S. Fish and Wildlife Service, Corvallis, Ore., 1945-46, biologist Cal div., Orick, 1950-51; research asso. Natural History Mus. Stanford 1952-54; instr. U. Fla., Gainesville, 1954-56, asst. prof. 1956-58; asst. prof. U. B.C., Vancouver, Can., 1958-61; research scientist U. Tex., Port Aransas, 1961-64; prof. zoology U. South Fla., Tampa, 1964-71, chmn. dept. zoology, dir. div. grad. studies, 1971—. Cons. Fisheries Research Bd. Can., Fla. Inst. Oceanography. Mem. exec. com. Conf. So. Grad. Schs., 1971-72. Trustee Fla. Defenders of Environment. Served with USAAF, 1943-45. Easter Seal Found. grantee, 1957-58; NRC Can. grantee, 1958-61; NSF grantee, 1962-70. Mem. Am. Soc. Ichthyologists and Herpetologists (bd. govs. 1969-73), Soc. for Study Evolution (council mem. 1969-73), Sigma Xi, Gamma Alpha, Phi Sigma, Phi Gamma Delta. Author: Monograph of the Clingfishes, 1955, Marine Zoogeography, 1974. Contbr. articles to sci. jours Home: 209 S Gardenia Av Tampa FL 33609

BRIGGS, RICHARD EVERETT, assn. exec.; b. Amesbury, Mass., Dec. 26, 1938; s. Richard Clark and Marjorie (Lloyd) B.; A.B. summa cum laude, Princeton, 1960; postgrad. Harvard, 1960-61; m. Cecilia M. McDonald (div. June 1971); 1 son, Richard E. II. Spl. asst. to commr. ICC, Washington, 1962-64, spl. asst. to chmn., 1965-69; dir. research N.J. Democratic Com., Trenton, 1964-65; exec. dir. Am. Sound Transp. Rev. Orgn., Washington, 1970-72; asst. to pres., dir. office information, pub. affairs Assn. Am. R.R.'s, Washington, 1972—. Woodrow Wilson fellow, 1960-61. Mem. Met. Washington Bd. Trade, Nat. Def. Transp. Assn., Traffic Club Washington, Advt. Club Washington, Phi Beta Kappa. Democrat. Mem. United Ch. Christ. Clubs: Internat., Nat. Press (Washington); River Bend Golf and Country (Great Falls, Va.). Author: (with others) The American Railroad Industry: A Prospectus, 1970. Contbr. articles to profl. jours. Home: 121 North Carolina Av Washington DC 20003 Office: 1920 L St NW Washington DC 20036

BRIGHAM, BESMILR (MRS. ROY C. BRIGHAM), poet; b. Pace, Miss., Sept. 28, 1923; d. Monroe I. and Bessye (Emmons) Moore; B.Journalism, Mary Hardin-Baylor Coll., 1945; postgrad. New Sch. Social Research, 1954-56; m. Roy C. Brigham, Apr. 12, 1941; 1 dau., Heloise (Mrs. Keith C. Wilson). Author poetry collections: Agony Dance: Death of the Dancing Dolls, 1969; Heaved from the Earth, 1971; poetry included in numerous anthologies of modern poetry, 1969—; contbr. fiction, poetry to numerous jours., mags., 1966—. Nat. Endowment Arts fellow, 1970; P.E.N. Emergency grantee, 1972. Home and office: Route 1 Horatio AR 71842

BRIGHT, EDGAR ALLEN GORDON, banker; b. New Orleans, May 15, 1895; s. Edgar H. and Ella (Mehle) B.; grad. Westminster Sch., 1913; Ph.B., Sheffield Sci. Sch., Yale, 1916; m. Ethel Fox, Nov. 29, 1927: children—Edgar A.G., Jane (Mrs. Maunsel Hickey). Partner, Tullis, Craig & Bright, cotton mchts., New Orleans, 1923-56; ltd. partner Merrill Lynch, Pierce, Fenner & Smith, N.Y.C., 1957-59; chmn. bd. Standard Mortgage Corp., New Orleans, 1964—; pres. Phoenix Devel. Corp.; dir. Maison Blanche, New Orleans, 1921—, Royal St. Louis, Inc., New Orleans, 1957—, Internat. Trade Mart, 1966—, Internat. House, New Orleans, 1966-69, Urban Corp., 1968—; pres. Vermillion Irrigation, New Orleans, 1959—, New Orleans Cotton Exchange, 1948-50; pres. Acadia Vermillion Rice Irrigation, 1970—; v.p. Information Council Am., 1964—. Pres. United Fund Greater New Orleans, 1960-61, treas. Community Chest, 1965-74, chmn., 1974—; bd. commrs. Port New Orleans, 1952-58, pres., 1956-57. Bd. dirs. Flint Goodridge Hosp., 1958—; pres. Cottage Sch. Deaf Children, 1958-70. Served to 1st lt. with U.S. Army, 1917-19, to lt. col. with AUS, 1942-45; PTO. Named Rex King of Carnival, New Orleans, 1956; recipient Loving Cup, Times-Picayune, 1966. Mem. Tennis Patrons Assn. Greater New Orleans (pres. 1960-64), Yale Alumni Assn. La. (pres. 1924-28, 47-54), St. Elmo Soc., Delta Phi. Episcopalian. Home: 421 Audubon St New Orleans LA 70118 Office: 1 Shell Sq New Orleans LA 70139

BRIGHTMAN, SAMUEL CHARLES, pub. affairs and pub. relations cons.; b. Lancaster, Mo., June 22, 1911; s. Samuel Charles and Alberta (Steele) B.; A.B., Washington U., St. Louis, 1932; B.J., U. Mo., 1933; grad. Tank Destroyer Officers Candidate Sch., 1943; m. Lucy Kirk Cleaver, July 26, 1947; children—Samuel Charles, Elizabeth, George, David. Reporter, St. Louis Star-Times, 1933-35;

copy editor Cin. Post, 1935-36, chief copy editor, asst. news editor, 1937-40; news editor radio sta. KSD, St. Louis, 1937; copy editor, spl. writer, Washington corr. Louisville Courier Jour., 1940-42, 47; dep. asst. adminstr. Surplus Property Adminstrn., Washington, 1945-46; spl. asst. to Housing Expediter, 1946; asst. dir. publicity Democratic Nat. Com., 1947-52, dir. publicity, 1952-57, dep. chmn. pub. affairs, 1957-65; pub. affairs and pub. relations cons., Washington, 1965—; editor Adult and Continuing Edn. Today, Today Publs., Washington, 1970—. Cons. ABC News, 1966-73, CBS News, 1972. Served to capt. AUS, 1942-45. Mem. Sigma Delta Chi, Alpha Tau Omega. Democrat. Episcopalian. Clubs: National Press (Washington); Kenwood (Md.) Golf. Mng. editor Dem. Digest, 1953-57, editor, 1957-60. Home: 6308 Crathie Lane Washington DC 20016 Office: Today Publs Nat Press Bldg Washington DC 20004

BRIGHTMIRE, PAUL WILLIAM, judge; b. Washington, Mo., June 12, 1924; s. Quinton C. and Alvena (Wehr) B.; B.A., U. Tulsa, 1949, J.D., 1951; m. Lorene E. Edwards, Nov. 7, 1952; children—Deborah Sue, William Paul, John Edward, Christiana Ann, Thomas Edward. Admitted to Okla. bar, 1951, since practiced in Tulsa; now judge Okla. Ct. Appeals, presiding judge, 1971—. Served with USNR, 1943-46. Mem. Am., Okla., Tulsa County (exec. com.) bar assns., Am. (state committeeman) Okla. (pres.), Tulsa (pres.) trial lawyers assns., Kappa Sigma. Episcopalian. Mason (32 deg., Shriner). Home: 4041 S Birmingham Tulsa OK 74105 Office: 402 Center Bldg Tulsa OK 74127

BRIGHTWELL, JUANITA SUMMER (MRS. LOUIE BRIGHTWELL), librarian; b. Sylvester, Ga., Jan. 4, 1918; d. Robert Beauregard and Lottie (Davis) Sumner; tchrs. certificate in piano Kate Land Sch. Mus., 1935; normal diploma Ga. Southwestern Coll., Americus, Ga., 1936; B.S. in Edn., Woman's Coll. Ga., 1938; M.Librarianship, Emory U., 1965; m. Louie Brightwell, June 30, 1938; 1 dau., Claire (Mrs. Charles W. Shaeffer, Jr.). Tchr. Weston (Ga.) High Sch., 1937-38; tchr. English, also librarian Smithville (Ga.) High Sch., 1941-42, Americus High Sch., 1942-43; operator Brightwell's Nursery, Americus, 1946-52; asst. librarian Lake Blackshear Regional Library (formerly Americus Carnegie Library), 1952-55, dir. library services in Sumter County, 1962—, Crisp County, 1964—, Schley County and Dooly County, 1970—; tchr. New Era Elementary Sch., Americus, 1955-56; tchr. English, also library asst. Americus High Sch., 1956-62. Vol. worker Camp Fire Girls, Americus, 1944-45; vol. chmn. Sumter County Tb Assn., 1952. Tchr. Merit scholar program Ga. Dept. Edn., 1962-65. Mem. Am., Southeastern, Ga. (children's and young people's div. v.p. 1963-65, chmn. pub. library sect. 1969-71) library assns., Ga. Library Assts. Assn., Am. Assn. U. Women, D.A.R., Am. Camellia Soc., Azalea Garden Club (pres. 1955), S.W. Ga. Camellia Soc., Federated Garden Clubs Ga. (del. 1951-52), Woman's Coll. Ga. Alumnae Assn. (dist. dir. 1965-67), U.D.C., Bus. and Profl. Woman's Club (pres. 1968-69; Woman of Year 1968), Ga. Fedn. Bus. and Profl. Women's Clubs, Inc. (chmn. Nike Samothrace com.), Alpha Chi Omega, Delta Kappa Gamma. Baptist (tchr. Sunday sch.). Home: 1307 Hancock Dr Americus GA 31709 Office: 111 S Jackson St Americus GA 31709

BRILEY, CLIFTON BEVERLY, mayor; b. Nashville, Jan. 11, 1914; s. Clifton W. and Willie (Vaughan) B.; student Vanderbilt Sch. Engring., 1930; LL.B., Cumberland U., 1932; m. Dorothy Gordon, July 3, 1934; children—Clifton Beverly, Martha Diane (Mrs. P.R. Easterling). Admitted to Tenn. bar, 1932, practiced in Nashville, 1932-43, 45-50; judge Davidson County, Tenn., 1950-62; mayor Met. Nashville and Davidson County, 1962—. Pres., Nat. Assn. Counties, 1962-63, Tenn. County Services Assn., 1955—; pres. Tenn. Municipal League, 1966—; mem. joint com. Am. Assn. Hwy. Commrs.-Nat. League Cities-Fed. Hosp. Council, 1963—; chmn. com. law enforcement Nat. League Cities; chmn. Urban County Congress, 1959; mem. human relations com. U.S. Conf. Mayors, 1964—, also mem. exec. com.; mem. Presdl. Adv. Commn. Intergovernmental Relations, 1973—, Nat. Commn. Productivity, 1973—; pres. elect Mid-Cumberland Council Govts., 1975. lectr. on govtl. structure. Vice pres. Middle Tenn. council Boy Scouts Am., 1956—. Mem. Tenn. Democratic Com., 1948-52. Served with USNR, 1943-45; PTO. Mem. Tenn., Nashville bar assns., Nat. League Cities (dir.), Pi Kappa Alpha. Mason (Shriner). Club: Blue Grass Country (Hendersonville, Tenn.). Contbr. articles on govt. to various publs. Home: 1406 Windingway Rd Nashville TN 37216 Office: Metropolitan Courthouse Nashville TN 37201

BRILL, DAVID H., JR., lawyer; b. Chgo., 1927; Ph.B., U. Chgo., 1945; B.A., U. Wis., 1949; J.D., Harvard, 1952; Mexican law degree Nat. U. Nuevo Leon Law Sch., Monterrey, Mexico. Admitted to Mexico bar; mem. firm Goodrich, Dalton, Little & Riquelme, Mexico D.F., Mexico; conseil juridique Tribunal del Grande Instance de Paris. Address: Paseo de la Reforma 355 Mexico DF Mexico

BRINDLEY, CLYDE OWENS, physician; b. Temple, Tex., Feb. 17, 1917; s. George Valter and Martha Arabella (Owens) B.; A.B., U. Tex., 1938; M.D., Duke, 1943; M.A., U. Minn., 1954; m. Gwendolyn M. Weber, Sept. 14, 1952. Intern, Mass. Gen. Hosp., 1949-50; resident Mayo Clinic, 1950-54; practice medicine and surgery specializing in oncology, Bethesda, Md., 1955-62, Johnson City, Tenn., 1962—; surgeon Nat. Cancer Inst., USPHS, Bethesda, Md., 1955-62; staff physician VA Center, Mountain Home, Johnson City, 1962—. Owner, mgr. farm and ranch Falls County (Tex.), 1948—. Mem. VA Lung Cancer Study Group, 1965—. Served with M.C., AUS, 1944-46. Mass. Inst. Tech. fellow, 1946-48. Diplomate Am. Bd. Internal Medicine. Mem. A.M.A., Am. Soc. Clin. Oncology, Phi Beta Kappa. Republican. Baptist. Research in evaluation of drugs in cancer patients. Home: 1208 Seminole Dr Johnson City TN 37601 Office: VA Center Mountain Home Johnson City TN 37684

BRINEGAR, CLAUDE STOUT, govt. ofcl.; b. Rockport, Cal., Dec. 16, 1926; s. Claude Leroy and Lyle (Rawies) Stout; B.A. in Econs., Stanford 1950, M.S. in Math. Statistics, 1951, Ph.D. in Econs., 1954; m. Elva Jackson, July 1, 1950; children—Claudia, Meredith, Thomas. Research asst. Food Research Inst., Stanford, Cal., 1950-53; econ. cons. Emporium-Capwell Corp., San Francisco, 1950-53; with Union Oil Co. Cal., 1953-73, mgr. econs. and corp. planning, 1962-65, v.p. econs. and corp. planning, 1965-66, pres. div. Pure Oil Co., 1965-68; pres. Pure Transp. Co., 1966-72, Union 76 div., Los Angeles, 1968-73, also sr. v.p., mem. exec. com., dir., 1968-73; dir. Internat. Speedway Corp., Daytona Beach, Fla., 1966-73; U.S. sec. transp., Washington, 1973—. Extension instr. U. Cal. at Los Angeles, 1955-60, Cal. Inst. Tech., 1957, Whittier Coll., 1956. Bd. dirs. Los Angeles County Mental Health Assn., 1964-65, Am. Petroleum Inst., 1970-73. Served with USAAF, 1945-47. Mem. Young Presidents Orgn., Am. Statis. Assn., Phi Beta Kappa, Sigma Xi. Club: California (Los Angeles). Contbr. articles to profl. jours. Home: 4056 41st St N Arlington VA 22207 Office: Dept of Transp 400 7th St NW Washington DC 20590

BRINKER, NORMAN EUGENE, restaurant exec.; b. Denver, June 3, 1931; s. Eugene C. and Katheryn Bess (Payne) B.; B.A., San Diego State Coll., 1957; m. Magrit Fendt, Mar. 27, 1971; children—Cynthia Ann, Brenda Lee, Christina Magrit. With Foodmaker Co., San Diego, 1957-69, regional dir., 1960-64; pres. Steak & Ale Restaurants, Dallas, 1964—; dir. 1st Nat. Bank, Dallas. Trustee So. Methodist U., 1970—, mem. asso. bd. Sch. Bus. Adminstrn., 1972—; trustee St. Paul's Hosp., 1973—; bd. dirs. Dallas Civic Opera, 1972—, Dallas Symphony, 1972—, Greenhill Sch., 1974—, Dallas Assembly, 1972—. Served with USNR, 1951-54. Named Outstanding Restauranteur, Dallas, Tex. Restaurant Assns., 1972. Mem. Young President's Orgn., Dallas C. of C. (dir.), Dallas Symphony Guild. Club: Willow Bend Polo and Hunt (Dallas). Home: 3727 Frontier Dallas TX 75214 Office: 12890 Hillcrest PO Box 22102 Dallas TX 75222

BRINKLEY, JACK THOMAS, congressman, lawyer; b. Faceville, Ga., Dec. 22, 1930; s. Lonnie Elester and Pauline (Spearman) B.; student Young Harris Coll., 1947-49, Okla A. and M., 1952; LL.B. cum laude, U. Ga., 1959; m. Alma Lois Kite, May 29, 1955; children—Jack Thomas, Fred Alen II. Admitted to Ga. bar, 1958; asso. mem. firm Young, Hollis and Moseley, 1959-61; partner Coffin and Brinkley, 1961-66; part-time tchr. Columbus Coll., 1964; mem. Ga. Ho. of Reps., 1965-66; mem. 90th-93d congresses from 3d Ga. Dist., mem. armed service com. Pres. Reese Rd. P.T.A., 1963-64. Chmn. fund raising and Ga. state chmn. Nat. Found., 1966. Judge adv. South Ga. Dist. Civitan Internat., 1964-65. Served to 1st lt., pilot, USAF, 1951-56. Mem. Am., Ga., Columbus bar assns., Am. Legion, Blue Key, Phi Alpha Delta. Democrat. Baptist (supt. Sunday Sch. 1962-64). Mason. Home: 4108 Appalachian Way Columbus GA 31907 Office: Cannon Bldg Washington DC 20515

BRINKLEY, PARKE CULVER, assn. exec.; b. Suffolk, Va., July 31, 1915; s. Fairlie Flavius and Mary (Culver) B.; B.S., Va. Poly. Inst., 1937; m. Dorothy Holland, Nov. 5, 1938; children—Kaye (Mrs. Henry Cannon Spalding Jr.), Richard Fairlie. Farmer, Nansemond County, Va., 1937-50, also county agrl. agt., 1941-46; exec. sec. Va. Assn. Peanut and Hog Growers, 1947-50; commr. agr. State Va., Richmond, 1950-62; pres. Nat. Agrl. Chems. Assn., Washington, 1962—. Vice pres. Holland Peanut Co. (Va.), 1947-48, Bank Whaleyville (Va.), 1940-50. Mem. Va. Amateur Field Trial Assn. (pres. 1968—), Nat. Open Shooting Dig Championship (pres. 1958-68) Mason. Clubs: Metropolitan, Capitol Hill (Washington); Commonwealth (Richmond); Washington Golf and Country (Arlington, Va.). Home: 1131 Litton Lane McLean VA 22101 Office: 1155 15th St NW Washington DC 20005

BRINKLEY, RONALD EUGENE, state ofcl.; b. Columbus, Ga., July 5, 1911; B.S., Murray State U., 1934; M.A., George Peabody Coll., 1946; m.; 2 children. Tchr., Clinton (ky.) High Sch., 1935-37, Dupont High Sch., Davidson County, Tenn., 1938-39, Cumberland High Sch., 1940-43; prin. Bellevue High Sch., 1943-46, Dupont High Sch., 1946-49; state supr. Mid-Tenn. State U., 1949-55; dir. spl. edn. Tenn. Dept. Edn., Nashville, 1955-59, exec. asst. to commr., 1959-63, dep. commr., 1963—. Mem. nat. adv. edn. council Appalachian Regional Commn. Mem. Nat., Tenn. (state coordinator) assns. secondary sch. prins., Tenn. Edn. Assn., Tenn. Prin. Studies Council (exec. sec.), Council Chief State Sch. Ofcls. (nat. planning com.). Home: Lake Ct Brentwood TN 37027 Office: 100-C Cordell Hull Bldg Nashville TN 37219

BRINKLEY, WILLIAM LAMBRETH, JR., ednl. adminstr.; b. Richmond, Va., Apr. 3, 1923; s. William L. and Elizabeth (Payne) B.; A.B., Duke, 1944; M.Personnel Service, U. Colo., 1954. Asst. to sec. Duke, 1944-46, field sec. admissions, 1946-48, asst. dir. admissions, 1948-51, asst. registrar, asso. registrar, 1951-61, then dir. under-grad. admissions; dir. admissions Johns Hopkins; v.p. for student affairs Coll. of Charleston (S.C.); 1970—. Trustee Coll. Charleston Found. Served with AUS, 1941. Mem. S.C. Coll. Personnel Assn., Nat. Assn. Student Personnel Adminstrs., Am. Assn. Collegiate Registrars and Admissions Officers, Nat. Trust Historic Preservation, Preservation Soc. Charleston, Alliance Francaise, Pi Kappa Phi (nat. sec.), Omicron Delta Kappa. Democrat. Methodist. Lion. Clubs: ToBac (Durham); John Hopkins (Balt.). Home: 22 Limehouse St Charleston SC 29401

BRINSON, ROBERT EDWARD, r.r. exec.; b. Arapahoe, N.C., Feb. 7, 1922; s. Jarvis Vendrick and Bessie (Yates) B.; adminstrv. certificate Miss. So. Coll., 1943; grad. Utilities Engring. Inst., Chgo., 1948; m. Olive Juanita Jones, Oct. 27, 1945; children—Glenda (Mrs. Otis William Seward), Patricia (Mrs. Jerry Max Breen), Robert, Keith, Gregory. Sales control Am. News Co., Orlando, Fla., 1939; mechanic Va. Chem. Co., Portsmouth, 1940; mgr. Western Auto Supply Co., 1947-50; salesman Higgins Realty Co., Virginia Beach, Va., 1964-72; asst. corp. sec. Norfolk & Portsmouth Belt Line R.R., Norfolk, 1942—, treas., agt., 1972—; real estate sales cons., 1964-72. Area chmn. Am. Heart Assn., 1960-71; chmn. Recreation Commn., Portsmouth, 1961-64; mem. Portsmouth City Sch. Bd., 1961-64, 70-73; pres. Little League Baseball, 1958-64. Served with AUS, 1942-46. Mem. Am. Assn. R.R.s (co-chmn. 2d congl. dist. 1971-73), Va. Claims Conf., Va., Portsmouth chambers commerce. Baptist (chmn. finance com. deacon 1970—, trustee. Rotarian. Clubs: Norfolk and Portsmouth Traffic, Virginia. Home: 14 Maupin Av Portsmouth VA 23702 Office: Law Bldg Norfolk VA 23510

BRINTON, EDGAR HARRY, librarian; b. Kansas City, Mo., July 5, 1916; s. Edgar Parrish and Juanita Irene (Swarner) B.; A.B., U. Denver, 1938; M.S., Columbia, 1957; m. Jane O. Dallimore, Apr. 23, 1944 (dec. Aug. 1967); 1 son, William David; m. 2d, Ann Furlong Marron, June 12, 1971. Govt. documents librarian Okla. A. and M. Coll., 1938-39, U. Kansas City (Mo.), summers 1939, 40; librarian Topeka High Sch., 1939-40; catalogue and mgr. traveling libraries Mo. Library Commn., 1940-41; seccessively chief order dept., chief extension dept., acting librarian, adminstrv. asst. Kansas City (Mo.) Pub. Library, 1941-59; dir. Jacksonville (Fla.) Pub. Library, 1959—; cons. in field, 1960—. Mem. Am. (council 1948-52), Mo. (pres. 1957-58), Fla. (pres. 1964-65) library assns., Jacksonville Area C. of C. Clubs: University, Jacksonville Civitan. Contbr. articles to profl. jours. Editor Mo. Library Assn. Quar., 1955-57. Home: 1721 Dogwood Pl Jacksonville FL 32210 Office: 122 N Ocean St Jacksonville FL 32202

BRISCOE, DOLPH, JR., gov. Tex. Past mem. Tex., Legislature; gov. Tex., 1973—. Democrat. Office: The Capitol Austin TX 78711*

BRISCOE, HERSCHELL ROBERT, JR., elec. engr.; b. Chattanooga, Dec. 26, 1925; s. Herschell Robert and Styrline (Dabbs) B.; student (Adolph S. Ochs Meml. scholar), U. Chattanooga, 1943-47; m. Evelyn P. Toomey, July 25, 1965; stepchildren—Glenn D. Wallace, James David Wallace. With WDEF Broadcasting Co., Chattanooga, 1942-68, chief engr. studio facilities, 1957-68; with WTCI-TV, Tenn. Dept. Edn., Chattanooga, 1969—, chief engr., 1969—. Served with Signal Corps, AUS, 1944-46, 51-52, now lt. col. Res. Decorated Bronze Star, Purple Heart. Mem. Soc. of Motion Picture and TV Engrs., I.E.E.E., Sigma Pi Sigma. Methodist. Home: 3537 Valley High Chattanooga TN 37415 Office: 4411 Amnicola Hwy Chattanooga TN 37406

BRISKY, MARY OWEN, city ofcl.; b. Anniston, Ala., May 19, 1930; d. Ozie Whitton and Melinda Everlina (Welchel) Owen; grad. high sch.; div.; 1 son, James Elic. Asst. to city clk. City of Anniston, 1956-62, dep. city clk., 1962-66, city clk., 1966—. Recipient Municipal Accounting award Ala. Soc. C.P.A.'s, 1963. Baptist. Home: 1520 E 10th St Anniston AL 36201 Office: PO Box 670 Anniston AL 36201

BRISTER, BILL H., lawyer; b. Sieper, La., Mar. 5, 1930; s. Clayton Houston and Era (Price) B.; B.S. in Chemistry, Northwestern State U. (La.), 1949; J.D., U. Tex., 1958; m. Carolyn Lea McDowell, June 11, 1955; children—Jeffrey, Laurie, Julie. Admitted to Tex. bar, 1957; asst. dist. atty. Lubbock County, Lubbock, Tex., 1958-59; pvt. practice law, Lubbock, 1960—; U.S. magistrate, Lubbock, 1971—. Served with USMCR, 1951-52. Home: 3302 58th St Lubbock TX 79413 Office: Lubbock Nat Bank Bldg Lubbock TX 79401

BRISTOW, MABEL MORROW, mfg. co. exec.; b. Roland, N.C., Feb. 25, 1914; d. Marion C. and Alice Lucile (Curlee) Bristow; grad. high sch., Lakeland Bus. Coll. Supr. applications crop subsidy Agrl. Dept., Florence, S.C., 1940-42; civilian supr. property and accounting Chief Clk. Base Supply, Florence AFB, 1942-46; gen. office mgr. Vulcraft, steel joists mfg., Florence, S.C., 1947-52; civilian supr. monetary accounting and appropriation accounting, dir., sec. credit union Shaw AFB, S.C., 1953-57; controller, Vulcraft div. Nucor Corp., Florence, 1957—, asst. sec. home office. Charlotte, 1962—. Recipient Civilian Worker award U.S. Air Force, 1956, award of excellent efficiency rating, 1943-46, Meritorious Service award, 1945, spl. commendation and award, 1955. Mem. Florence C. of C. (sec. woman's div. 1964). Baptist. Club: Business and Professional Womens. Home: 1810 Marsh Av Florence SC 29501 Office: PO Box 3009 Florence SC 29501

BRISTOW, WALTER JAMES, JR., lawyer, state senator; b. Columbia, S.C., Oct. 14, 1924; s. Walter James and Caroline (Melton) B.; student Va. Mil. Inst., 1941-43; A.B., U. N.C., 1947; LL.B. cum laude, U. S.C., 1949; LL.M., Harvard, 1950; m. Katherine Stewart Mullins, Sept. 12, 1952; children—Katherine Mullins, Walter James III. Admitted to S.C. bar, 1950; practiced in Columbia, S.C.; mem. firm Marchant, Bristow & Bates, 1953—; mem. S.C. Ho. of Reps., 1956-58; mem. S.C. Senate, 1958—. Nat. asso. Boys Clubs of Am., 1958—; past council commr. Central S.C. council Boy Scouts of Am.; past pres. Carolina Carillon; trustee Elvira Wright Fund for Crippled Children. Served with AUS, 1943-45. Mem. Alpha Tau Omega, Wig and Robe, Pi Gamma Mu. Democrat. Presbyn. (deacon). Elks. Home: 4149 W Buchanan Dr Columbia SC 29206 Office: 830 Laurel St Columbia SC 29201

BRITO, JULIO, broadcast engr.; b. Havana, Cuba, Nov. 28, 1935; s. Juan and Mercedes (Fernandez) B.; B.S., Instituto de la Habana, 1950, U. Havana, 1954; m. Vivian Yankovich, Aug. 29, 1969. Came to P.R., 1954, naturalized, 1958. Audio engr. Hammond Organ Co., Chgo., 1955; television engr. WOLE-TV, P.R., 1959-60, chief engr., 1960-62; dir. engring. WAPA-TV, San Juan, P.R., 1962—; cons. engr.; pvt. practice hypnology, 1971—. Served with USAF, 1955-59. Mem. Sociedad de Hipnologos Clinicos y Experimentales de P.R. (pres.), Rosicrucian Order, Soc. Motion Picture and Television Engrs., Internat. Soc. Profl. Hypnosis. Club: Circulo Cubano de Puerto Rico (San Juan). Home: Calle 9 F 4 Tontillo Gardens Guaynobo PR 00619 Office: GPO Box 2050 San Juan PR 00936

BRITO MORENO, MANUEL, lawyer; b. Mexico D.F., Mexico, Nov. 6, 1934; student Nat. Autonomous U. Mexico Law Sch. Admitted to Mexican bar, 1960; mem. firm Brito Foucher y Brito Moreno, Mexico D.F. Mem. Bar Assn. Mexico, Mexican Acad. Space Law. Author: The Value of Human Life in Mexican Law, 1961. Office: Avenida San Juan de Letran 11 Mexico 1 DF Mexico

BRITT, ALBERT SIDNEY, JR., soc. exec.; b. Nashville, June 18, 1908; s. Albert Sidney and Anne Elizabeth (Dennedy) B.; B.S. in E.E., Va. Mil. Inst., 1930; postgrad. Brit. Army Staff Coll., Camberley, Eng., 1948, Indsl. Coll. Armed Forces, 1954-55; m. Anne Lawton McIntosh, June 15, 1935; chilren—Albert Sidney III, William Olin, Jane McIntosh. Commd. 2d lt. F.A., U.S. Army, 1930, advanced through grades to col., 1950; comdr. 863d F.A. Bn., 63d Inf. Div., Camp Van Dorn, Miss., ETO, 1943-45, instr. Command and Gen. Staff Coll., Fort Leavenworth, Kan., 1949-51; dep. chief of staff for adminstrn. 7th U.S. Army, Germany, 1952-54; comdr. 52d F.A. Group, Ft. Sill, Okla., 1955-56; dir. dept. publs. and nonresident tng. Arty. and Guided Missile Sch., Fort Sill, 1956-57; chief of staff mil. Assistance Adv. Group., Taiwan, 1957-59; dep. chief staff 5th Army, Chgo., 1959-60, chief of staff, 1961; ret., 1962; cons. econs. Savannah Port Authority, 1963-66; hist. research cons. So. Natural Gas Co., Savannah, and Superior Ct. Chatham County, Ga., 1969-72; pres. bd. curators Ga. Hist. Soc., Savannah, 1970—. Bd. dirs. Savannah Sci. Mus. 1964-67. Decorated Legion Merit, Bronze Star medal with oak leaf cluster; Croix de Guerre with silver gilt star (France). Mem. Soc. Cin. (state pres. 1969-72, nat. dir. 1971—), Ga. Soc. Colonial Wars (historian 1968—), St. Andrews Soc. Savannah (archivist 1973—), Savannah Area Ret. Officers Assn. (pres. 1964-65). Clubs: Savannah Yacht, Oglethorpe. Editor: (with Lilla M. Hawes) The MacKenzie Papers, 1973. Home: 602 E 58th St Savannah GA 31405 Office: 501 Whitaker St Savannah GA 31401

BRITT, CHESTER OLEN, elec. engr.; b. Hughes Springs, Tex., July 2, 1920; s. Beverly A. and Ida Emma (Martin) B.; student Texarkana Jr. Coll., 1938-40; B.S., U. Tex., 1949, M.S., 1951; Ph.D., 1962; m. Patricia Ashworth, Jan. 4, 1946. Research engr. Elec. Engring. Research Lab., Austin, Tex., 1951-56, systems devel. specialist, 1956-61; systems devel. specialist U. Tex. at Austin, 1961-62, research scientist dept. chemistry, 1962—. Served with USAAF, 1941-46. Decorated D.F.C., Air Medal with oak leaf clusters. Registered profl. engr., Tex. Mem. I.E.E.E. (sr.), A.A.A.S., Am. Phys. Soc. Home: 2708 Rae Dell Av Austin TX 78704

BRITT, CLAUDE HENRY, JR., educator; b. St. Pauls, N.C., Sept. 18, 1929; s. Claude Henry and Tera (Godwin) B.; B.A., Wake Forest Coll., 1951; M.A., U. Ala., 1953; Ph.D., Northwestern U., 1966. Tchr. Spanish and history A. L. Brown High Sch., Kannapolis, N.C., 1955-56; asst. prof. Spanish, Gardner-Webb Coll., 1956-57; instr. French, Stetson U., 1959-60; asst. prof. Spanish, Mercer U., 1960-62; asst. prof. Spanish, Ga. So. Coll., Statesboro, 1963-67, asso. prof., 1967—. Served with U.S. Army, 1953-55. Mem. Am. Assn. Tchrs. Spanish and Portuguese, Modern Lang. Assn., South Atlantic Modern Lang. Assn., Am. Assn. U. Profs., Sigma Delta Pi, Sigma Pi Alpha. Address: PO Box 1836 Ga So Coll Statesboro GA 30458

BRITT, ELIZABETH LETITIA SMITH, corp. exec.; b. Medon, Tenn.; d. Samuel Edward and Rosalee (Kinney) Smith; student Union U., 1927-29, Norton Bus. Coll., 1942. Cemeterian-sec. Forest Park Cemetery, Inc., Shreveport, La., 1942—, sec.-treas., 1957—, dir., 1957—. Mem. Nat. Secs. Assn., Internat. Platform Assn., Zonta (mgr. Shreveport Antique Show). Baptist. Home: 3820 Fairfield Av Shreveport LA 71104 Office: PO Box 1764 Shreveport LA 71102

BRITT, HENRY GRADY, biologist, educator; b. Colerain, N.C., Apr. 24, 1915; s. John Monroe and Mary Geneva (Mitchell) B.; B.S., Wake Forest Coll., 1936, M.A., 1938; Ph.D. (duPont Research fellow), U. Va., 1944. Inst. biology Wake Forest Coll., Winston Salem, N.C., 1938-40, asst. prof., 1947-52, asso. prof., 1952-60, prof., 1960-64; asst. prof. Mary Washington Coll., Fredericksburg, Va., 1944-47; asso. prof. biology La. State U., Alexandria, 1964-72, prof., 1972—. Vis. prof. zoology U. N.C., Chapel Hill, 1946-47. NSF fellow, 1961, 63, 64. Mem. La. Acad. Scis., Assn. Southeastern Biologists, Sigma Xi, Phi Beta Kappa. Democrat. Baptist. Contbr. articles on cytotaxonomy and helminthology to sci. publs. Home: 5616 Hall St Alexandria LA 71301

BRITTAIN, JACK OLIVER, lawyer; b. Greenwood, La., Sept. 24, 1928; s. Clarence L. and Irene (Humphries) B.; B.S., La. Poly. Inst., 1949; LL.D., La. State U., 1957; m. Ann Marie Williams, Nov. 25, 1955; children—Jack Oliver, Marguerite Ann, Rebecca Ann, Lala Beth, Eliza Ann, John A., Mary Jane Ann. Land man Magnolia Petroleum Co., Midland Tex., 1953-54; admitted to La. bar, 1957; practiced in Natchitoches, 1957—; mem. firm Brittain & Williams. Owner, Crown Colony Antiques, Crown Colony Canines; dir. Pak-A-Sak, Inc., Grand Ecore Preservation, Inc., CBS Mobile Homes, Inc., Evans-Brittain, Inc. Bd. dirs. Natchitoches Youth Assn., Inc. Served to maj. AUS, 1951-53. Named Outstanding Man Natchitoches Parish, 1959; recipient Distinguished Service award Jr. C. of C., 1958. Mem. Natchitoches Parish C. of C. (pres. 1961), U.S. Jr. C. of C. (nat. dir. 1962). Am., La., Natchitoches Parish bar assns., Fedn. Ins. Counsel, Am. Legion, Omicron Delta Kappa, Lambda Chi Alpha, Phi Delta Phi. Democrat. Methodist (bd. stewards; chmn. adminstrv. bd. 1969; lay leader; chmn. drug abuse com.). Mason, Rotarian. Home: 919 Parkway Dr Natchitoches LA 71457 Office: 111-113 E 5th St St Natchitoches LA 71457

BRITTAIN, JOHN ORIN, bus. exec.; b. South Pittsburgh, Tenn., June 12, 1902; s. Reuben E. and Martha (Jenkins) B.; A.B., U. Okla., 1926; m. Mary Elizabeth Hill, Dec. 27, 1928; 1 dau., Sally Adair (Mrs. Robert C. Saunders). Chmn. bd. Brittain Bros., 1942—, chief exec. officer, 1973—; dir. City Nat. Bank and Trust Co. Mem. Nat. Automotive Parts Assn. (dir.), Nat., Oklahoma City chambers commerce, Alpha Tau Omega, Alpha Kappa Psi. Republican. Mem. Christian Ch. Clubs: Oklahoma City Men's Dinner, Oklahoma City Golf and Country, Beacon, Whitehall. Home: 1708 Randel Rd Oklahoma City OK 73116 Office: 700 S Western Av Oklahoma City OK 73125

BRITTIN, GEOFFREY MELLOR, physician, educator; b. Syracuse, N.Y., Oct. 1, 1934; s. Norman Aylesworth and Florence Sykes (Mellor) B.; grad. Phillips Andover Acad., 1952; B.A., Columbia, 1956, M.D., 1959; m. Suzanne Benay Miller, Oct. 3, 1964; children—Paul H., Alice A., Christopher N., David G. Intern, Johns Hopkins Hosp., Balt., 1959-60; resident in clin. pathology Clinic Center NIH, Bethesda, Md., 1960-62; resident in anatomical pathology U. Minn. Hosp., Mpls., 1962-63; asst. hematologist Clin. Center, NIH, Bethesda, 1963-65; clin. pathologist Madison Gen. Hosp., also clin. asst. prof. pathology U. Wis., 1965-67; pathologist St. Mary's Hosp., Columbus, Wis., 1966-67; dir. program for certified lab. assts. Madison Vocational, Tech. and Adult Schs., 1966-67; vice chmn., chief hematology sect., dir. blood bank div. clin. pathology and lab. medicine, asst. prof. clin. pathology and lab. medicine U. Cal. Med. Center, 1967-69; asso. prof. pathology U. Tex., M.D. Anderson Hosp. and Tumor Inst., Houston, 1969-72, chmn. dept. clin. pathology, 1969—, prof., 1972—. Served with USPHS, 1960-65. Mem. Soc. Exptl. Biology and Medicine, Am. Soc. Hematology, Am. Soc. Clin. Pathologists, Am. Assn. Pathologists and Bacteriologists, Am. Soc. Exptl. Pathology, Am. Soc. Clin. Research, Acad. Clin. Lab. Physicians and Scientists, Houston Soc. Clin. Pathologists, A.M.A., Tex. Med. Assn., Houston Med. Soc. Editor: Automation and Data Processing in the Clinical Laboratory, 1970. Editorial bd. Blood, Jour. of Hematology, 1972—, Pathology A Study Sect., NIH, 1973—. Research on automation in hematology, regulation of intestinal iron absorption. Home: 2388 Bluebonnet St Houston TX 77025 Office: 6723 Bertner St Houston TX 77025

BRITTON, JAMES JUDSON, assn. ofcl.; b. Montgomery, Ala., July 23, 1913; s. William Brown and Ruth (Abbott) B.; LL.B., Jones Law U., U. Ala., 1936; m. Dorothy Bennett, Feb. 4, 1939; children—Karen (Mrs. John B. Johnson), Nancy (Mrs. Garry Guilloud). Salesman and treas. Interstate Oil Co., Montgomery, 1943-50; dir. Ala. Petroleum Council, 1950-66; exec. v.p. Ala. State C. of C., 1966—. Chmn. Ala. Cancer Crusade, 1965; mem. Ala. Rural Devel. Adv. Council. Bd. dirs. Ala. Council on Econ. Edn.; bd. visitors U. Ala. Sch. Commerce and Bus. Adminstrn. Served with AUS, 1943-47, 51-52. Mem. The 13, Newcomen Soc., Ala. Hist. Soc., Ala. Export Council, C. of C. Execs. Assn. Ala., Nat. Council C. of C., U.S. C. of C. (mem. natural resources com.), Pi Kappa Alpha, U. Ala. Alumni Assn. Clubs: Country (Montgomery); Internat. (Mobile); Downtown (Birmingham). Episcopalian. Rotarian. Home: 1222 Augusta St Montgomery AL 36111 Office: PO Box 76 Montgomery AL 36101

BROACH, BILLY GENE, electronics engr.; b. Wadley, Ala., Mar. 24, 1939; s. Willie Felton and Emma Jean (Kilgore) B.; B.E.E. (Lee Moody scholar), Auburn U., 1961; postgrad. U. Ala., 1970; m. Paula Nan Clapp, Dec. 21, 1958; children—Jeffrey David, Timothy Michael. Elec. engr. Chrysler Corp., Huntsville, Ala., 1962-64, Heat Tech., Inc., 1964-66; pres. Huntsville Investors, Inc., rental property devel., 1967—; pres. Engrs. Unltd., Inc., nat. engring. placement firm, 1965—; pres. Broach Labs., Inc., med. instrumentation devel., 1963—; electronics engr. U.S. Army Missile Command, Redstone Arsenal, 1968—. Campaign mgr. Republican candidate for sheriff of Madison County, Ala. Presbyn. Club: Sertoma (Huntsville, Ala.). Patentee in field. Home: 3610 Pulaski Pike St Huntsville AL 35810 Office: US Army Missile Command AMSMI RCR Redstone Arsenal AL 35808

BROACH, WILSON JAMES, univ. dean; b. Atkins, Ark., Aug. 14, 1915; s. William James and Margaret Victoria (Pettit) B.; student Ark. Tech. Jr. Coll., 1933-35; B.A., Henderson State Coll., 1937; M.S., U. Ark., 1948, Ph.D., 1952; m. Billie E. Godbey, Aug. 22, 1942; children—Mary (Mrs. Leonard Scott Jr.), James R., Robert W., Vicky J. Instr., Little Rock Jr. Coll., 1946-48, U. Ark. at Fayetteville, 1948-52, So. State Coll., Magnolia, Ark., 1952-54; asso. prof. Northwestern State U. La., Natchitoches, 1954-57; asso. prof. dept. chemistry U. Ark., Little Rock, 1957-60, prof., 1960—, chmn. phys. sci., math. div., 1960-72, dean phys. scis., math., 1973—. Served to lt. comdr. USNR, 1943-46. Mem. Am. Chem. Soc. (counselor 1963—), A.A.A.S., Ark. Acad. Sci., Sigma Psi. Contbr. articles to profl. jours. Home: 5511 Stonewall Rd Little Rock AR 72207

BROAD, RICHARD, shipbuilding co. exec.; b. Newport News, Va., Oct. 1, 1921; s. Richard and Hazel (Congdon) B.; B.S. Engring. in Naval Architecture, U. Mich., 1949, M.S. in Marine Engring., 1950; postgrad. Oak Ridge Sch. Reactor Tech., 1952-53; m. Janet Gwendolyn Hubbard, Apr. 22, 1944; children—Jennifer Lou, Debora Mae, Richard III, David Wingfield, Janice Carol. With Newport News Shipbuilding Dry Dock Co. 1938—, chief nuclear engring. operations, 1963-70, v.p. nuclear engring., 1970—. Soc. Naval Architects and Marine Engrs. scholar, 1949-50. Mem. Am. Soc. Naval Engrs., Navy League U.S., Va. State C. of C., Soc. Naval Architects and Marine Engrs. (chmn. 1966-67). Clubs: James River Country, Huntington (Newport News). Home: 809 Riverside Dr Newport News VA 23606 Office: Washington and 41st Sts Newport News VA 23607

BROADDUS, HOWARD THOMAS, dept. store exec.; b. Amarillo, Tex., Oct. 4, 1918; s. Julian Askin and Violet Pearl (Howard) B.; student Amarillo Coll., 1936-38, West Tex. State U., 1953-59; m. Margaret Alice Bussey, June 5, 1947; children—Alice Dianne (Mrs. Larry Wayne Smith), Howard Thomas, Julian Landrum. With White & Kirk, Inc., Amarillo, 1936-69, controller, operations mgr., 1961-69; with Sakowitz, Inc. of Houston, 1969—, v.p., dir. operations, 1971—; dir. Fashion Fabrics Center, Inc., Albuquerque. Guest instr. West Tex. U., Canyon, 1961. Served to capt. AUS, 1941-46, 51-52. Decorated Bronze Star medal. C.P.A., Tex. Mem. Tex. Soc. C.P.A.'s, C. of C., Downtown Mchts. Assn. (pres. 1961-62, treas. 1963). Democrat. Baptist. Kiwanian. Home: 3427 E Sells Dr Phoenix AZ 85018 Office: PO Box 1207 Scottsdale AZ 85252

BROADHEAD, SAMUEL L., JR., electronic engr.; b. Clanton, Ala., Jan. 26, 1916; s. Samuel L. and Roberta (Culp) B.; ed. U. Chgo., U. Ia.; m. Opie Merritt, Mar. 23, 1940. Civilian radar instr. U.S. Army. World War II; electronic engr. Communications Co., Coral Gables, Fla., 1946-47, Eastern Air Lines, 1947-51, Wilcox Electric Co., Kansas City, Mo., 1951-52, Collins Radio Co., Cedar Rapids, 1952-65; sr. staff engr. SCI Electronics, Huntsville, Ala., 1965—. Sr. mem. I.E.E.E. Contbr. articles in field of advanced avionics equipment. Patentee in field. Research med.-elec. equipment. Home: 9800 Wallwood Rd SE Huntsville AL 35803 Office: 8620 Memorial Pkwy SW Huntsville AL 35802

BROADY, ROBERT ALEXANDER, physician; b. Forest Hill, Ind., June 5, 1903; s. William Cowan and Nancy Katharine (Hartman) B.; B.A., Maryville Coll., 1925; M.D., U. Pa., 1930; postgrad. Coll. Chinese Studies, Peiping, 1932-33; m. Ellen Elizabeth Cox, June 14, 1930; children—Robert (dec.), William S., John Cox (dec.), JoAnn, Joe, Barbara. Intern Presbyn. Hosp., Phila., 1930-32; missionary doctor, China, 1932-37; dir. hosp., Hunan, China, 1934-37; practice medicine specializing in family practice, Sevierville, Tenn., 1938—; operator Broady Hosp., 1940-65; mem. staff Sevier County Hosp., 1965—. Owner dairy farm, Sevierville, 1943-69. Mem. city council, Sevierville, 1958-62, vice mayor, 1960-62. Named Sevierville Man of Year, Lions 1970. Mem. Am. Physicians and Surgeons Assn., A.M.A., Tenn., Sevier County (pres. 1956-57) med. assns. Presbyn. (elder 1960-69). Rotarian (pres. club 1972-73). Home: 223 Bruce St Sevierville TN 37862 Office: 217 Bruce St Sevierville TN 37862

BROBST, DONALD ALBERT, govt. ofcl.; b. Allentown, Pa., May 8, 1925; s. Harold Jacob and Florence Evelyn (Baer) B.; A.B., Muhlenberg Coll., 1947; Ph.D., U. Minn., 1953; m. Marie Weir Katz, Dec. 16, 1950; 1 dau., Alice Marie. With U.S. Geol. Survey, 1948—, geologist Minerals Deposit Br., Denver, 1955-73, dept. chief Office Mineral Resources, Reston, Va., 1973—. Served with AUS, 1944-46. Decorated Bronze Star medal. Fellow Geol. Soc. Am.; mem. Am. Inst. Mining, Metall. and Petroleum Engrs., A.A.A.S., Soc. Econ. Geologists, Am. Mineral. Soc. Contbr. articles to tech. lit. Home: 2483 Pyrenees Ct Reston VA 22091 Office: Office Mineral Resources US Geol Survey Reston VA 22902

BROCATO, ANTHONY GERARD, lawyer; b. Beaumont, Tex., Dec. 6, 1932; s. Tony A. and Lena (Fertitta) B.; B.B.A., U. Tex., 1954, J.D., 1958; m. Myrna Loy Johnson; children—Jeanne Marie, Anthony G., Walter C., James M., Elizabeth. Admitted to Tex. bar, 1958, since practiced in Beaumont; asst. city atty. City of Beaumont, 1958-64, city atty., 1967-69; mem. firm Adams and Brocato, 1965-66; mem. firm Weller, Wheelus, Green and Brocato, 1970-72, Crutchfield, DeCordova and Brocato, 1973—. Co-chmn. City Charter Amendment Rev. Com., 1972, Southeast Tex. Citizen's Adv. Com. to Tex. Constl. Revision Commn., 1973. Served to lt. USAF, 1954-56. Mem. Tex., Jefferson County bar assns. Roman Catholic. Home: 195 Ridgeland St Beaumont TX 77706 Office: 1210 Petroleum Bldg Beaumont TX 77701

BROCK, CARLTON ELBERT, wholesale co. exec.; b. Oklahoma City, Sept. 29, 1932; s. Elbert Doyle and Agnes (Lorenzen) B.; B.S., Central State U., 1960; m. Natalie Jo McDivitt, Aug. 31, 1952; children—Brenda Gaye, Bruce Elbert. With T G & Y Stores Co., Shreveport, La., 1961—, br. office and traffic mgr., 1971—. Served with USAF, 1952-55. Home: 209 Peyton Colquitt Pl Shreveport LA 71105 Office: 6701 Sippel Shreveport LA 71130

BROCK, EUGENE CASEY, city planner, landscape architect; b. Sylvester, Ga., Dec. 16, 1926; s. Henry Newton and Katherine Louise (Casey) B.; B. Landscape Architecture, U. Ga., 1952; m. Joann Bird Brock, Mar. 28, 1954; children—Tasha Ann, Eugene Casey II. Landscape architect Nat. Park Service, Tupelo, Miss., 1952-55; dir. planning So. Ala., Ala. Devel. Office, Montgomery, 1955-58; owner, pres., Urban Cons., Inc., Montgomery, 1958—, Casey Realty, 1971—. Served with AUS, 1946-48. Mem. Am. Soc. Cons. Planners (nat. dir. 1971-73), Am. Inst. Planners, S.E. Soc. Landscape Architects (pres. 1971-73), Am. Soc. Planning Ofcls., Nat. Assn. Housing and Redevel. Ofcls., Urban Land Inst. Baptist. Mason (Shriner). Clubs: Montgomery Country, The Club, Birmingham. Home: 3526 Landsdowne Dr Montgomery AL 36111 Office: 908 S Hull St Montgomery AL 36104

BROCK, FRANK EDGAR, diversified Industry exec.; b. Houston, Jan. 7, 1932 ; s. Robert Frank and Alma (Sealock) B.; B.B.A., U. Tex., 1955; m. Rebecca Ann Morgan, Feb. 28, 1953; children—Randal Eugene, Lynne Anne. Accountant Pan Am. Petroleum Corp., Ft. Worth, 1955-64; chief accountant Loma Products div. Vistran Corp., mfg. fabricated household plastic goods, Ft. Worth, 1964-65, controller, 1965-68; sec., treas., controller Universal Sheet Metal Co., Ft. Worth, 1968-70; v.p. adminstrn., sec-treas. Broyles & Broyles, Inc., mech. contract constrn., 1970—, dir., 1970—; sec.-treas., dir. Universal Performance, Universal Fabrication, Mech. Contracting Services, Inc.; v.p., Universal Insulation Co., Inc. Active children programs YMCA. Sponsoring com. Tex. Christian U. Research Found. Served to 1st lt. USAF, 1957-59. Mem. Nat. Assn. Accountants, Arnold Air Soc. Clubs: Colonial Country (Ft. Worth); DeCordva Bend Estates Country (Granbury, Tex.). Home: 2316 Lynn Haven St Fort Worth TX 76103 Office: Box 11067 305 W Arlington St Fort Worth TX 76110

BROCK, JAMES RUSH, educator; b. McAllen, Tex., Dec. 30, 1931; s. Jerome Dalton and Bess (Beeler) B.; B.A., Rice U., 1952, B.S., 1953; M.S., U. Wis., 1954, Ph.D., 1960; m. Mary Lou Waghorn, July 4, 1964; children—Ianthe Joy, Stella Elizabeth Alison. NSF postdoctoral fellow Free U. Brussels, 1962-63; mem. faculty dept. chem. engring. U. Tex. at Austin, 1960—, asso. prof., 1965-69, prof., 1969—; vis. prof. U. Paris (France), 1973. Mem. various state and fed. govtl. adv. coms. NSF grantee, 1961, 65, 67, 69; Environmental Protection Agy. grantee, 1965—. Mem. Am. Chem. Soc., Am. Inst. Chem. Engrs., A.A.A.S., Am. Inst. Chemists, others. Author: The Dynamics of Aerocollodial Systems, 1971. Co-editor: Current Topics in Aerosol Science, vol. 1, 1972, vol. II, 1973. Editor Internat. Revs. in Aerosol Physics and Chemistry, 1967—; asso. editor Environmental Letters; editorial adv. bd. Jour. Colloid Sci., 1967-68. Home: 2518 Tanglewood Trail Austin TX 78703

BROCK, WILLIAM ELIHU, univ. dean; b. Blackwell, Okla., Aug. 10, 1914; s. Zedakiah Clark and Bertha (King) B.; student Park Coll., 1933-35; A.B., Wichita State U., 1937; D.V.M., Kan. State U., 1944; M.S., Okla. State U., 1955, Ph.D., 1958; Dr. honoris causa, San Carlos U. (Guatemala), 1967; m. Alice Lee Massey, Sept. 30, 1939; 1 dau., Lina Lee. Practice vet. medicine, Oregon City, Ore., 1944-49; faculty Okla. State U. Coll. Vet. Medicine, 1949—, asso. prof., 1955-59, prof., 1959—, dean coll., 1969—. Chief party AID project, Guatemala, 1965-67. Recipient service citation Okla. Senate, 1965; service award Okla. Cattlemen's Assn., 1970. Mem. Okla. (award merit 1966), Am. vet. med. assns., Research Workers Animal Disease Soc., U.S. Animal Health Assn., Am. Soc. Vet. Clin. Pathologists, Am. Soc. Vet. Parasitologists, Sigma Xi, Phi Zeta, Gamma Sigma Delta. Patentee in field. Contbr. articles to profl. jours. Home: 102 Georgia St Stillwater OK 74074

BROCK, WILLIAM EMERSON, III, senator; b. Chattanooga, Nov. 23, 1930; s. William Emerson and Myra (Krusei) B.; grad. McCallie Sch., 1949; B.S. in Commerce, Washington and Lee U., 1953; m. Laura Handly, Jan. 11, 1957; children—William Emerson IV, Oscar Handly, Laura, John Kruesi. With Brock Candy Co., Chattanooga, 1956-63; mem. 88th-91st Congresses from 3d Tenn. dist., mem. com. on banking and currency, mem. joint econ. com.; U.S. senator from Tenn., 1970—, mem. Banking, Housing and Urban Affairs Com., Com. on Govt. Operations. Served as lt. (j.g.) USNR, 1953-56; lt. Res. Named Outstanding Young Man Tenn. Jaycees, 1964, Outstanding Young Man Young Republicans, 1964. Mem. Sigma Alpha Epsilon. Presbyn. Home: Dogwood Dr Lookout Mountain TN 37350 Office: 254 Senate Office Bldg Washington DC 20515

BROCKMAN, EDWARD WILSON, JR., lawyer; b. Pine Bluff, Ark., July 2, 1921; s. Edward Wilson and Mildred (Westmoreland) B.; student Washington and Lee U., 1938-40; B.A., U. Ark., 1942, LL.B., 1948. Admitted to Ark. bar, 1948, since practiced in Pine Bluff; pros. atty. Jefferson County, 1957-64. Mem. Ark. Gen. Assembly, 1947-55. Served with AUS, 1942-46. Mem. Am., Ark. bar assns. Presbyn. Mason (Shriner). Home: 1300 W 17th St Pine Bluff AR 71601 Office: Simmons Bldg Pine Bluff AR 71601

BROCKMAN, THOMAS, concert pianist, educator; b. Greer, S.C., Jan. 12, 1922; s. W. Thomas and Bernice (Wood) B.; student Curtis Inst. Music, 1937-40; B.S., Juilliard Sch., 1948; pupil Edwin Fischer, Robert Casadesus, Nadia Boulanger (Europe), 1952-53. Concert pianist, European tours, 1953, 55, 56, 59; appearances with maj. symphony orchs. U.S.; vis. lectr. U. Ia., Iowa City, 1961; artist, lectr. So. Meth. U., 1961-62; asso. prof. piano Rollins Coll., Winter Park, Fla., 1962—. Served from pvt. to 1st lt. AUS, 1942-46. Mem. Pi Kappa Lambda (chpt. pres. 1967-69). Episcopalian. Home: 271 Virginia Dr Winter Park FL 32789

BROCKWAY, ALLAN REITZ, editor; b. Hutchinson, Kan., Mar. 22, 1932; s. Horace Austin and Esther Jane (Reitz) B.; B.A., Hendrix Coll., 1954; B.D., So. Meth. U., 1957; M.A., U. Chgo., 1963; m. Martha Lou King, Aug. 28, 1956; children—Paul, Scot, Dan, Benjamin. Ordained to ministry Methodist Ch., 1957; campus minister West Tex. State U., Canyon, 1957-59; editor Christian Faith and Life Community, Austin, Tex., 1959-61; asst. editor The Kiwanis Mag., Chgo., 1962-63; editor Concern, Gen. Bd. Ch. and Soc., Washington, 1963-68, editor Engage, 1968-72, Engage/Social Action, 1973—. Danforth Campus Ministry grantee, 1961, 63. Mem. Northwest Tex. Ann. Conf. United Meth. Ch. Author: The Secular Saint, 1968, Uncertain Men and Certain Change, 1970. Home: 3 Park Valley Rd Silver Spring MD 20910 Office: 100 Maryland Av NE Washington DC 20002

BRODBECK, EDWARD JAMES, marketing research exec.; b. Swanton, O., July 5, 1933; s. Ernest and Oral (Myers) B.; B.S., Bowling Green State U., 1958; postgrad. La. State U., 1959-64; m. Elisa J. Portela Lavastida, Aug. 16, 1938; children—Ana Maria, Susana Elisa, Jennifer Cristina. Field marketing Dun & Bradstreet, Inc., Toledo, 1958; market research A. C. Nielsen Co., Chgo., 1958-59; market-sales analyst Copolymer Rubber & Chem. Corp., Baton Rouge, 1959-61, customer service, 1961-63, marketing research analyst, 1963-68, market devel. mgr., 1968-70, mgr. marketing research and planning, 1971—. Neighborhood group leader Republican party, 1966, 68, 70, 72. Served with AUS, 1953-55. Mem. Am. Marketing Assn., Chem. Marketing Research Assn., Am. Chem. Soc., European Assn. Indsl. Marketing Research. Methodist. Home: 7005 Whitlow Dr Baton Rouge LA 70808 Office: PO Box 2591 Baton Rouge LA 70821

BRODE, MARVIN JAY, lawyer, former state legislator; b. Memphis, Aug. 26, 1931; s. Howard M. and Erneice J. (Jacob) B.; B.A., Vanderbilt U., 1953, LL.B., 1954; m. Freda Cohn, June 24, 1965; children—William Howard, Robert Mark. Admitted to Tenn. bar, 1955, since practiced in Memphis; mem. firm Brode and Fisher, 1958-65, Brode & Dunlap, 1965-70, Brode & Smith, 1970-72, Brode & Sugg, 1973—; spl. judge City Ct., Memphis, 1957-63; Mem. Pres.'s Nat. Traffic Adv. Com., 1963-64; mem. Tenn. Art Commn., 1965-72; mem. Mayor's Community Action Com., 1965; hon. col. on staff Tenn. gov., 1967—. Del. So. Regional Edn. Conf., 1964, 1965, 1966. Mem. Tenn. Ho. of Reps., 1962-65; asst. city atty. City of Memphis, 1965-68; mem. Shelby County Democratic Exec. Com., 1966—. Bd. dirs. West Tenn. chpt. Arthritis and Rheumatism Found. Mem. Am., Shelby County, Memphis bar assns., Bar Assn. Tenn., Memphis Arts Council, Phi Alpha Delta. Jewish religion (dir. Temple Brotherhood). Mason (32 deg., Shriner). Co-editor: Memphis Municipal Code. Home: 4841 Walnut Grove Rd Memphis TN 38111 Office: Suite 3116 100 N Main Memphis TN 38103

BRODE, WILLIAM EDWARD, educator; b. Athens, Tenn., Dec. 17, 1929; s. Edward John and Aline (Crowe) B.; student Millsaps Coll., 1950-51; B.S., Miss. So. Coll., 1952; M.A., U. So. Miss., 1954, Ph.D., 1969; postdoctoral Highlands (N.C.) Biol. Sta., 1971; m. Nancy LaVerne Caplenor, Sept. 2, 1960; children—William Edward Jr., John Sidney, Paul Kirk, David Andrew. Instr., Copiah Lincoln Jr. Coll., Wesson, Miss., 1954-57; tchr. Columbia (Miss.) High Sch., 1962-65; prof. dept. biology Wesleyan Coll., Macon, Ga., from 1969; now with Tenn. Dept. Transp., Environmental Planning and Research, Nashville; mem. research staff Gulf Coast Research Lab., Ocean Springs, Miss., summers 1957-64. Adviser environmental affairs Macon Mus. Arts and Scis., 1970—. Recipient honors award Nat. Assn. Biology Tchrs., 1965; NSF grantee, 1957-64; Tb and Respiratory Diseases grantee, 1973—. Mem. Am. Inst. Biol. Sci., A.A.A.S., Assn. Southeastern Biologists, Am. Soc. Ichthyologists and Herpetologists, Am. Midland Naturalist Soc. Home: 917 Shauna Drive Nashville TN 37214 Office: Tennessee Dept Transportation Environmental Planning and Research 512 Doctor's Bldg Nashville TN 37203

BRODIE, RALPH GRAY, lawyer; b. Marshall, Ark., Mar. 24, 1940; s. Frank Theodore and Hazel (Gray) B.; B.S. in Indsl. Engring., U. Ark., 1963, J.D., 1966; LL.M. in Taxation, N.Y.U., 1973. Admitted to Ark. bar, 1966; law clk. for Chief Justice Carleton Harris, Ark. Supreme Ct., 1966-67; asst. atty. gen. State of Ark., Little Rock, 1967-69; financial planner also house counsel Diversified Financial Services Internat., 1969-72; tax atty., Little Rock, 1973—. Served with AUS, 1963-64; capt. Res. ret. Mem. Am., Ark., Pulaski County bar assns., Little Rock Jr. C. of C. (v.p. 1968-69). Democrat. Baptist. Home: 6714 Greenwood Rd Little Rock AR 72207 Office: 1540 Worthen Bank Little Rock AR 72201

BROEMER, WALTER WILLIAM, state ofcl.; b. San Antonio, Sept. 11, 1924; s. Charles Paul and Margarethe Elfriede (Frouboes) B.; B.S., U. Tex., 1952; M.Ed., Sul Ross State U., 1954; m. Frances Anne Roberts, Aug. 5, 1948; children—Walter Robert, Cynthia (Mrs. Billy Joe Brakel), William Fulton. Dir. outdoor edn. Austin Pub. Schs., 1952-57; supt. Alabama Coushatta Indian Reservation, Livingston, Tex., 1957-71, exec. dir., 1972—. Adminstr., H.E. Butt Found. Camp, Leakey, Tex., 1955-57; chmn. econ. devel. com. Gov.'s Interstate Indian Council, 1971-73, council chmn., 1965, also mem. bd. dirs. Pres. Polk County Planning Com., 1970-71. Served with inf. AUS, 1944-46; PTO. Decorated Purple Heart. Named Outstanding scoutmaster Three River council Boy Scouts Am., 1961, hon. mem. Ala. Coushatta Indian Tribes, 1967, SBA man of year, Houston regional area, 1968, Polk County man of year, 1970; recipient Spl. award for outstanding devotion to Indian people, Gov. of Tex., 1972. Mem. Tex. Forestry Assn., Big Thicket Assn., Polk County C. of C., Discover Tex. Assn. (dir.). Methodist (dir.). Lion. Club: T Assn. (U. Tex.). Home: 1007 Alston St Livingston TX 77351 Office: Alabama Coushatta Indian Reservation Livingston TX 77351

BROIN, THAYNE LEO, geologist; b. Kenyon, Minn., Sept. 18, 1922; s. Oscar Arthur and Ella (Hoff) B.; B.S., St. Cloud State Coll., 1943; M.A., U. Colo., 1952; Ph.D. (Regents fellow), U. Colo., 1957; m. Beverly Johnson, Dec. 21, 1949; children—Martin, Dana, Valerie. Instr., Colo. State U., Ft. Collins, 1950-54, asst. prof., 1956-57; research geologist Cities Service Research & Devel. Co., Tulsa, 1957-58, tech. group leader, 1958-60, head geol. research, 1960-65; research coordinator Cities Service Oil Co., Tulsa, 1965-72, chief computer geologist, 1972—. Served to capt. USAAF, 1943-48. Mem. Am. Assn. Petroleum Geologists, Geol. Soc. Am., Soc. Econ. Paleontologists and Mineralogists, Tulsa Geol. Soc. (pres. 1972-73), Sigma Xi. Home: 5719 E 64th St Tulsa OK 74136 Office: Cities Service Oil Co Box 300 Tulsa OK 74102

BROKAW, CHARLES FORREST, JR., broadcasting co. exec.; b. Shawnee, Okla., Sept. 5, 1928; s. Charles Forrest and Bernice Evelyn (Scott) B.; B. Journalism, Woodbury Coll., Los Angeles, 1949; m. JoNell Louise Foster, Aug. 27, 1950; children—Charles Forrest III, Nancy Beth, Linda Susan. News dir. radio-TV sta. KVOO, Tulsa, 1956-61; city hall reporter Tulsa Tribune, 1954; news dir. radio sta. KELI, Tulsa, 1961-65, account exec., 1965-68, news dir., 1968-72; gen. mgr. sta. KIXZ, Amarillo, Tex., 1972—. Mem. Amarillo Bd. Convs. and Visitor Activities. Served with AUS, 1946-48. Mem. Sigma Delta Chi (pres. Tulsa chpt. 1960). Clubs: Tulsa Press (pres. 1972); Amarillo Advertising (dir.). Home: 2236 Laurel St Amarillo TX 79109 Office: 1702 Avondale St Amarillo TX 79106

BROKAW, DEAN EDWARD, county ofcl.; b. Lookeba, Okla., Apr. 22, 1927; s. Frank Morgan and Addie (McGlothin) B.; student Southwestern State Coll., Weatherford, Okla., 1944-45; m. Julia Joan Jones, Apr. 7, 1956; children—Gary Wayne, Linda (Mrs. Charles Coe), Kenneth Alan, Nancy Ann. Farmer, Caddo County, Okla., 1948-54; projects engr. Lippert Constrn. Co., Oklahoma City, 1954-58; supt. Anchor Constrn. Co., 1958-62; self-employed contractor, 1962-68; field engr. CMI Corp., Oklahoma City, 1969-70; project mgr. Haskell Lemon Constrn. Co., Oklahoma City, 1970-71; foreman Westinghouse and Embassy West Projects, Norman, Okla., also Oklahoma City, 1970-71; mgr. Arbuckle Regional Devel. Authority, multicountry solid waste collection and disposal, Ardmore, Okla., 1971—. Mgmt. cons., So. Okla. Waste Disposal Authority, Ardmore Airpark, 1973-74. Scoutmaster, later neighborhood commr. Last Frontier council Boy Scouts Am., 1966-68; mem. exec. com. Girl Scouts U.S., 1966-68. Recipient Service Appreciation awards Boy Scouts Am., 1967-68. Mem. Am. Pub. Works Assn., Inst. Solid Wastes, Nat. Solid Wastes Mgmt. Assn. Odd Fellow. Contbr. articles to mags. Home: 125 Meadowbrook St Ardmore OK 73401 Office: Arbuckle Regional Devel Authority Box 3125 Ardmore OK 73401

BROLLIAR, HAROLD LEE, constrn. co. exec.; b. Sigourney, Ia., Apr. 14, 1898; s. Charles and Barbara (Weber) B.; diploma Sch. Commerce Northwestern U., 1935; m. Agnes V. McSpadden, Aug. 27, 1923; 1 son, Lamont Gene. Store mgr. Reisman Co., Oskaloosa, Ia., 1923-25, W. V. Shipley Co., Mason City, Ia., 1926-29; City, Ia., 1926-29; hotel mgr. Westmoorland Hotels, Chgo., 1930-41; office mgr. C.R. Daniels Co., Chgo., 1941-43; asst. auditor Chgo. Motor Club, 1943-48; pres., chmn. bd. Brolliar Constrn. Co., Ft. Lauderdale, Fla., 1949-59; pres., chmn. bd. Fla. Palm Aire, Inc., Pompano Beach, 1959-65, chief exec. officer, chmn. bd., 1965—. Pres. Joe E. Brown Tent Circus Sts. and Sinners, 1963, chmn. heart com., 1966. Dir. North Broward Republican Club, 1958-62. Served with SAC, 1918. Address; 2400 NE 46th St Lighthouse Point FL 33064

BROMBERG, ALAN ROBERT, lawyer, educator, writer; b. Dallas, Nov. 24, 1928; s. Alfred L. and Juanita (Kramer) B.; A.B., Harvard, 1949; J.D., Yale, 1952; m. Anne Ruggles, July 26, 1959. Admitted to Tex. bar, 1952, U.S. Tax Ct. bar, 1959; asso. firm Carrington, Gowan, Johnson, Bromberg and Leeds, Dallas, 1952-56; atty. and cons., 1956—; part-time lectr. Law Sch., So. Methodist U., Dallas, 1955-56, vis. asst. prof. law, 1956-57, asst. prof. law, 1957-58, asso. prof., 1958-62, prof. law, 1962—, chmn. law curriculum com., 1961-72, trustee retirement plan, 1967-70, faculty rep. bd. trustees, 1969-70, mem. exec. com. faculty senate, 1968-70, mem. presdl. search group, 1971-72; faculty adviser Southwestern Law Jour., 1958-65; sr. fellow Yale Law Faculty, 1966-67; vis. prof. Stanford Law Sch., 1972-73; lectr. in field. Counsel Internat. Data Systems, Inc., 1961-65, sec., dir. 1963-65; mem. Tex. Legislative Council Bus. and Commerce Code Adv. Com., 1966-67. Sec., mem. bd. dirs. Community Arts Fund, 1963-73; gen. atty. Dallas Mus. Contemporary Arts, 1956-63. Bd. dirs. Dallas Theater Center, 1955—, sec., 1957-66, finance com., 1957-65, mem. exec. com., 1957-70, life mem., 1973—. Served as cpl. M.I., AUS, 1952-54. Mem. Am. Bar Assn. (mem. com. partnerships; mem. com. fed. regulation of securities), Dallas Bar Assn. (chmn. com. on uniform partnership act 1959-61), State Bar Tex. (mem. com. on corporate law revision 1957—, mem. com. on securities and investment banking 1957—, chmn. 1965-69, mem. com. on information of corp. banking and bus. law sect. 1961-69, mem. council of sect. 1963-69, vice chmn. 1965-67, chmn. 1967-68, reporter com. on revision of penal code 1967-70), Am. Law Inst., Southwestern Legal Found., Am., Assn. U. Profs. (exec. com. So. Methodist U. chpt. 1962-63; chmn. acad. freedom and tenure com. 1968-70, 71-72), Assn. Am. Law Schs. (mem. coms.), Nat. Tax Assn. Author: (with Byron D. Sher) Cases and Materials on Texas Partnerships, 1958, supplemented 1960; Supplementary Materials on Texas Corporations, 1959, rev. 1965, 71; Partnership Primer—Problems and Planning, 1961; Materials on Corporate Securities and Finance—A Growing Company's Search for Funds, 1962, rev. 1965; Securities Law-Fraud-Sec Rule 10b-5, Vol. 1, 1967, Vol. 2, 1970, Vol. 3, 1973, supplements pub. annually; Crane and Bromberg on Partnership, 1968. Contbr. numerous articles and revs. to law and bar jours. Adv. editor Rev. Securities Regulation, 1969—, Securities Regulation Law Jour., 1973. Office: So Meth U Law Sch Dallas TX 75275

BROMBERG, MILTON JAY, chem. exec., b. Bklyn., Sept. 15, 1923; s. David Ezra and Esther Yetta (LeVine) B.; B.S., Coll. City N.Y., 1943; M.S., Columbia, 1948; m. Marie Louise Van Der Hoeven, June 15, 1945; 1 dau., Jacqueline (Mrs. John Etienne Abadie). Asst. research chemist Columbia, 1943; chief chemist H.A. Brassert Co., Washington, Conn., 1948-51; tech. mgr. explosive div. Olin Corp., Newport, Ind., 1951-57, mgr. quality control high energy fuels div., Niagara Falls, N.Y., 1957-60, staff cons. organics div., New Haven, 1960-62, mgr. quality assurance Doe Run plant, Brandenbeurg, Ky., 1962-72, mgr. quality assurance, Lake Charles, La., 1972—. Active Terre Haute (Ind.) Community Theatre, 1953-56. Served with AUS, 1944-46. Ky. col. Fellow Am. Inst. Chemists; mem. Am. Chem. Soc., Am. Soc. Quality Control, N.Y. Acad. Scis., Am. Ordnance Assn., Lake Charles C. of C., Chemist Club N.Y. Mason (Shriner). Research on nitramine explosives, fluoroaromatics, TDI, polyols. Home: PO Box 5274 Lake Charles LA 70601 Office: PO Box 2896 Lake Charles LA 70601

BRONAUGH, EDWIN LEE, elec. engr.; b. Salina, Kan., July 22, 1932; s. Edwin and Violet (Dryden) B.; B.A. in Physics and Math., East Tex. State U., 1955, postgrad., 1955; diploma Air U., 1960; m. Geraldine Kelley, Dec. 10, 1955; children—Cecilia Ann, Dana Lea. Commd. 2d lt. U.S. Air Force, 1955, advanced through grades to maj., 1968; instr. U.S. Air Force Pre-Flight Tng. Sch., Lackland AFB, San Antonio, 1956-58; pilot 2d Air Div., Dhahran, Saudi Arabia, 1959-60, 11th Aeromed. Transport Squadron, Scott AFB, Ill., 1960-66, Aerospace Rescue and Recovery Service, Da-Nang, Vietnam, Kansas City, Mo., 1966-68; ret., 1968; research engr. electronics div. S.W. Research Inst., San Antonio, 1968-69, sr. research engr., 1969—. Decorated Bronze Star, Air Force Commendation medal. Mem. I.E.E.E. (chmn. electromagnetic compatibility group Central Tex. 1971-72), Am. Radio Relay League, Alpha Phi Omega. Republican. Presbyn. Kiwanian. Home: 6024 Cammie Way San Antonio TX 78238 Office: 8500 Culebra Rd San Antonio TX 78284

BROOKBANK, JOHN WARREN, educator; b. Seattle, Wash., Apr. 3, 1927; s. Earl Bruce and Louise (Stoecker) B.; B.A., U. Wash. at Seattle, 1949, M.S., 1953; Ph.D., Cal. Inst. Tech., 1955; m. Marcia Quam Ireland, Sept. 16, 1950; children—Ursula, John Jr., Phoebe. Mem. faculty U. Fla., Gainesville, 1955—, asso. prof. zoology, 1958-68, prof., 1968-71, prof. zoology, microbiology, 1971—, chmn. faculty cellular biology, 1971—. USPHS grantee, 1957-69, NSF grantee, 1970-72. Mem. Soc. Developmental Biology, Am. Soc. Zoologists, Sigma Xi. Contbr. articles to profl. jours. Home: 1521 NW 31st St Gainesville FL 32601

BROOKE, GEORGE MERCER, JR., educator; b. Tokyo, Japan, Oct. 21, 1914 (parents Am. citizens); s. George Mercer and Isabel (Tilton) B.; B.A., Va. Mil. Inst., 1936; M.A., Wash. and Lee U., 1942; Ph.D., U. N.C., 1955; m. Frances Fleming Bailey, June 13, 1942; children—George Mercer III, Marion Bailey (Mrs. John Robert Philpott, Jr.). Spl. agt. Md. Casualty Co., Newark, 1937-41; instr. history Va. Mil. Inst., Lexington, 1942-43, asst prof., 1948-55, asso. prof., 1955-58, prof. history, 1958—, head dept. history, 1965-70; instr. Washington and Lee U., 1946-47, 70. Fulbright research scholar Keio U., Tokyo, 1962-63; Fulbright lectr. Am. history, Nat. Taiwan U., Taipei, 1963. Pres. Stonewall Jackson Area Council Boy Scouts Am., 1964-67, exec. bd., 1958—. Bd. dirs. United Fund, 1965—. Served with AUS, 1943-46. Recipient Silver Beaver award Boy Scouts Am., 1967. Mem. Am., Rockbridge (pres. 1960-62) hist. socs., Assn. Asian Studies, Internat. House of Japan, Soc. of Cin., Phi Beta Kappa, Kappa Alpha. Episcopalian (lay dep. to the gen. convention 1969-70). Author: Collected Documents of Japanese Mission to America, Vol. V, 1961. Contbr. to Ency. Brit. Home: 405 Jackson Av Lexington VA 24450

BROOKE, JOHN LEWIS CHRISTY, chem. co. exec.; b. Gulfport, Miss., July 13, 1917; s. James Christy and Iva (Lewis) B.; B.S., Temple U., 1938; m. Eleanor Adams, Dec. 4, 1948 (dec. Dec. 1964); children—Karen (Mrs. Gerry Gividen), Kathy (Mrs. John Martin), Karla; m. 2d, Eve E. Steven, Nov. 12, 1971. With DuPont, Wilmington, Del., 1941-66, asst. dir. marketing, 1960-66; v.p. Celanese Coatings Co., Louisville, 1966-67; v.p. Kerr McGee Chem. Corp., Oklahoma City, 1967—. Mem. Nat. Paint and Coatings Assn. (dir. 1969-72). Episcopalian. Club: New York Athletic. Died Apr. 12, 1974. Office: McGee Tower Oklahoma City OK 73102

BROOKER, FRANCIS MILTON, chem. co. exec.; b. Utica, Ill., May 7, 1915; s. Claud W. and Lucy (Munro) B.; B.S., Monmouth Coll., 1938; M.S., Washington U., St. Louis, 1940; m. Geneva Morton, Oct. 31, 1942; children—Linda (Mrs. David M. Welch), Francis Allen, Gail Ellen. Chief chemist B. T. Fooks Mfg. Co., Camden, Ark., 1940-42; v.p., dir. research, devel., quality control Grapette Co., Inc., Camden, 1946—. Served to 1st lt. AUS, 1942-46. Mem. Soc. Soft Drink Technologists, Inst. Food Technologists. Presbyn. (deacon, elder). Rotarian. Home: 1033 Westwood St Camden AR 71701 Office: 157 Grinstead St Camden AR 71701

BROOKINGS, HENRY NASON KINNEY, petroleum geologist; b. San Francisco, May 25, 1917; s. Walter DuBois and Marian (Kinney) B.; grad. Phillips Exeter Acad., 1935; A.B., Princeton, 1939; m. Frances Ellis Winter, Nov. 18, 1944; children—Deborah DuBois, Henry Nason Kinney (dec.), David Winter, Jeffrey Baker. Sr. geologist Phillips Petroleum Co., El Dorado, Ark., Oklahoma City, Shreveport, La., 1939-53; ind. cons. geologist, Shreveport, 1953-58; partner, geologist Brookings, Moffatt & Waddle, oil and gas cons., Shreveport, 1958—. Swimming meet coordinator Am. Amateur Union. Mem. Shreveport Park and Recreation Council. Served with USNR, 1941-45. Mem. Certified Petroleum Geologists Am., Assn. Petroleum Geologists, Shreveport Geol. Soc., Res. Officers Assn., Ret. Officers Assn., Am. Legion, V.F.W. Democrat. Methodist. Club: North Shreveport Swimming (pres. 1956-62). Home: 3701 Eddy Pl Shreveport LA 71107 Office: 1902 Beck Bldg Shreveport LA 71101

BROOKS, A. GORDON, educator; b. Mathews, Va., June 21, 1914; s. Rodney L. and Ida (Hudgins) B.; B.A., Randolph-Macon Coll., 1938; LL.D. (hon.), 1969; M.Ed., U. Va., 1950; postgrad. (John Hay fellow), Colo. Coll., summer 1965; m. Polly Teretta, Oct. 30, 1942; 1 dau., Betsy Gordon (Mrs. Thomas E. Carr). Tchr., dean boys Ferrum Jr. Coll., West Point (Va.) High Sch., 1938-41; supr. vocational rehab. Va. State Bd. Edn., 1945-47; prin. sch. divs. Nansemond County, Campbell County, and Roanoke, 1947-57; supt. schs. Bottetourt County (Va.), 1957-59; supr., dir. secondary edn. Va. Dept. Edn., Richmond, 1959-62, dir. div. tchr. edn., 1962-73, asst. supt. profl. and ednl. support services, 1973—. Mem. Va. State Library Bd.; exec. sec. Va. com. So. Assn. Colls. and Schs., 1959-62; a.d.c. Staff Gov. Va., 1968. Bd. dirs. Roanoke Cancer Soc., Family Service Assn. Served to lt. (s.g.) USN, 1941-45; PTO. Mem. Nat. Assn. State Dirs. Tchr. Edn. and Certification (v.p. So. region), Am. Assn. Sch. Adminstrs., Nat., Va. edn. assns., Phi Delta Kappa, Sigma Phi Epsilon. Home: 202 Portland Pl Richmond VA 23221 Office: State Dept Edn Richmond VA 23216

BROOKS, CYRUS LEE, city ofcl.; b. nr. Monroe, N.C., Jan. 19, 1933; s. Judge Ellis and Hennrietta Drucella (Griffin) B.; A.B., U. N.C., 1955; postgrad. U. Alaska, 1959-60; M. Govtl. Adminstrn., U. Pa., 1962; m. Madria Sue Cumby, June 6, 1953; 1 son, Cyrus Lee. Adminstrv. asst. to city mgr., Charlotte, N.C., 1961-62; city mgr. Town of Mooresville, 1963-66, City of Morganton, N.C., 1966-73; city mgr., Rocky Mount, N.C., 1973—. Chmn. Regional Solid Waste Commn., Morganton, 1971-72. Served to 1st lt. USAF, 1955-60. Mem. Am. Soc. Pub. Adminstrn., Internat. City Mgmt. Assn., Pub. Personnel Assn. Baptist (ordained deacon). Elk, Rotarian (dir. 1968-69, 72-73). Home: 3600 Mansfield Dr Rocky Mount NC 28701 Office: PO Drawer 1180 Rocky Mount NC 28701

BROOKS, ELSTON HARWOOD, newspaper columnist; b. Kansas City, Mo., Feb. 18, 1930; s. Amos Elston and Dorthy Miller (Gale) B.; student night sch. Tex. Christian U., 1957-58; m. Mary Lee O'Brien, Sept. 5, 1953; 1 son, David Bryan. Reporter, Ft. Worth Press, 1947-48; amusements editor Ft. Worth Star-Telegram, 1948—, columnist The Elston Brooks Column, 1949—. Star radio program Ballads by Brooks, stas. KXOL, WBAP, Ft. Worth, 1947-50, The Elston Brooks Show, sta. WBAP, 1965—. Served with AUS, 1950-52. Recipient numerous awards for reporting from A.P., Sigma Delta Chi, State Headliners, Big Story award. Mem. Sigma Delta Chi. Home: 1951 Shelman Trail Fort Worth TX 76112 Office: Star-Telegram Ft Worth TX 76112

BROOKS, FREDERIC LENNOX, broadcasting exec.; b. Bemis, Tenn., June 10, 1935; s. Roy Lennox and Mable (Mullis) B.; student Pathfinder Radio and TV Sch., Washington, 1953-54; m. Delois Earlene Bell, Oct. 13, 1962; children—Frederic Glenn, Freida Dawn. Newscaster dir. news dept. KFDX-TV, Wichita Falls, Tex., 1959-64; reporter, newscaster KPRC-TV, Houston, 1964-65; news dir., newscaster WBRZ-TV, Baton Rouge, La., 1966—. Recipient Best Newsfilm award U.P.I.-Tex., 1964; Merit citation La. Bar Assn., 1972; News Media award La. Tchrs. Assn., 1973; Community Service award, 1974; others. Mem. Radio-TV News Dirs. Assn., Nat. Rifle Assn., Pelican Arms Collectors Assn. (dir. pub. relations), S.C.V. Clubs: Baton Rouge Pistol, Civil War Roundtable Baton Rouge Press (Baton Rouge). Home: 2100 College Dr #98 Baton Rouge LA 70808 Office: 1650 Highland Rd Box 2906 Baton Rouge LA 70821

BROOKS, FREDERICK PHILLIPS, JR., educator; b. Durham, N.C., Apr. 19, 1931; s. Frederick Philips and Octavia (Broome) B.; B.A., Duke U., 1953; S.M. in Applied Math., Harvard, 1955, Ph.D., 1956; m. Nancy L. Greenwood, June 16, 1956; children—Kenneth Phillips, Roger Greenwood, Barbara Suzanne. With IBM Corp., Poughkeepsie, N.Y., 1956-65, corporate process mgr. System/360 computer devel., 1961-64; mgr. operating System/360, 1964-65; prof., chmn. dept. computer sci. U. N.C., Chapel Hill, 1964—; adj. asst. prof. Columbia, N.Y.C., 1960-61; vis. prof. Twente Tech. U., Enschede, The Netherlands, 1970. Dir. N.C. Ednl. Computing Service, Raleigh, 1964—, Triangle Univs. Computation Center, Research Triangle Park, N.C., 1965—; mem. nat. computer scis. research adv. com. AEC, 1967-72; cons. Orgn. Econ. Coop. Devel., 1967-68; mem. computer sci. panel NSF, 1966-70; mem. exec. com. div. math. scis. NRC, 1967-70; mem. adv. council Computer Center, Princeton U., 1969-72; mem. adv. com. computing activities NSF, 1972-73, Stanford U., 1972—. Recipient Man of Year award Data Processing Mgmt. Assn., 1970. Guggenheim fellow, 1974-75. Fellow I.E.E.E. (McDowell award computer group 1970); mem. Assn. Computing Machinery (mem.-at-large nat. council 1966-70), A.A.A.S., Assn. Computational Linguistics, Ergonomics Research Soc., Sigma Xi, Phi Beta Kappa. Author: (with K.E. Iverson) Automatic Data Processing, 1963; (with K.E. Iverson) Automatic Data Processing, System/360 edit., 1969; The Mythical Man-Month: Essays on Software Engineering, 1974. Contbr. articles to prof. jours. Home: 413 Granville Rd Chapel Hill NC 27514 Office: Dept Computer Sci New West Hall Univ NC Chapel Hill NC 27514

BROOKS, GARY DONALD, ednl. adminstr.; b. Ogden, Utah, Sept. 3, 1942; s. William Monroe and Aline (Smith) B.; Mus.B. Edn., Millikin U., 1964; M.S. in Edn., Ind. U., 1966, Ed.D., 1967; m. Donna Kathlene Riley, Jan. 28, 1972. Dean men Millikin U., Decatur, Ill., 1967-68; mem. staff U. Tex., El Paso, 1968, v.p. student affairs, 1971-73, chmn. dept. ednl. adminstrn. and supervision, 1973—. Mem. Am. Assn. Higher Edn., Am. Personnel and Guidance Assn., Nat. Assn. Student Personnel Adminstrs., Am. Assn. Sch. Adminstrs., Phi Delta Kappa. Author: (with Bonnie S. Brooks) The Literature on Student Unrest, 1970. Editor (with Richard W. Burns) Curriculum Design in Changeing Society, 1970. Contbr. articles to profl. jours. Home: 252 Shadow Mountain E-4 El Paso TX 79912 Office: U Tex El Paso TX 79968

BROOKS, GEORGE DANIEL, ins. exec.; b. Martin, Tenn., Oct. 13, 1907; s. George Martin and Mayme (Mathis) B.; student Vanderbilt U., 1924-48; m. Julia Evans Clements, Apr. 23, 1929; children—Frances Moore (Mrs. Michael Corzine), Julia Clements (Mrs. Clarke T. Reed). Employed Caldwell & Co., investment bankers, Nashville, 1928-30, Third Nat. Bank, Nashville, 1930-31; joined Nat. Life & Accident Ins. Co., Nashville, 1931, mgr. investment dept., after 1939, v.p., 1950-59, treas., 1953-59, financial v.p., 1959-63, sr. v.p., chmn. finance com., 1963-64, exec. v.p. 1964-65, pres., 1965-67, chmn. bd., chief exec. officer, 1967-72), also dir.; past chmn. bd., now dir. WSM, Inc., NLT Corp.; trustee U.S. Trust Co. N.Y.; mem. trust bd. 3d Nat. Bank, Nashville; dir. 1st Tenn. Nat. Corp., Memphis. Financial adviser of Old Woman's Home, Nashville; mem. adv. com. Jr. League, Nashville. Served as lt. comdr. USNR, 1942-45. Decorated Commendation medal (Navy). Mem. Mortgage Bankers Assn. Am. (gov.), Life Ins. Assn. Am. (dir.), Vanderbilt U. Alumni Assn. (past pres.), Sigma Nu. Presbyn. Clubs: Cumberland, Belle Meade Country (Nashville); National Golf (Augusta, Ga.); The Links (N.Y.C.). Home: 113 Clarendon Av Nashville TN 37205 Office: Nat Life Center Nashville TN 37203

BROOKS, GEORGE WILLIAM, educator; b. Macon, Ga., June 7, 1918; s. John William and Lois (Henderson) B.; B.S., Ind. U., 1941; M.S., 1942, Ed.D., 1955; LL.B., LaSalle Extension U., 1947; m. Fannie E. Crafton, May 25, 1945; 1 son, George W. (dec.). Instr. Voorhees Jr. Coll., 1942-43; asst. prof. social studies Prairie View A. and M. Coll. of Tex., 1943-53; prof. social studies and edn. S.C. State Coll., Orangeburg, 1955-59, chmn. dept. social studies, 1959-60, dean Sch. Grad. Studies, 1960—. Mem. council on coop. coll. projects TVA, 1963—. Mem. Am. Assn. Sch. Adminstrs., N.E.A., Nat. Council for Social Studies, S.C. Psychol. Assn., Palmetto Edn. Assn. (parliamentarian ho. of dels. 1959—), Kappa Alpha Psi, Phi Delta Kappa, Phi Alpha Theta. Mason (Shriner). Home: State Coll Orangeburg SC 29115

BROOKS, HENRY PHELPS, JR., banker; b. Balt., Jan. 12, 1918; s. Henry Phelps and Evaline Clapp (Boggs) B.; student The Citadel, 1934-37, La. State U., 1941-43; m. Lillian Verne Smith, Jan. 1, 1941; children—Lillian F. (Mrs. Forrest C. Wilkerson), Henry Phelps III. With Farrell-Birmingham Co., Buffalo, 1937, Life Ins. Co. of Va., Greenville, S.C., 1938-38; Rock Hill Printing & Finishing Co. (S.C.), 1940, Comml. Bank, Chester, S.C., 1941-46; asst. cashier The Peoples Nat. Bank of Chester, 1946-51, dir., 1948—, v.p., 1951-59, pres., trust officer, 1959—; dir. Charlotte br. Fed. Res. Bank, Spratt Savs. & Loan Assn., Chester, Investors Nat. Life Ins. Co., Columbia, S.C. Pres. Chester County Bd. Commerce and Devel., 1960-61; pres. Chester area United Fund, 1963-64. Chmn. bd. dirs. The Children's Bur. S.C., 1965-67. Mem. S.C. Bankers Assn. (pres. 1968-69), Ind. Bankers S.C. (pres. 1964-65). Rotarian (pres. 1948-49). Home: 157 Walnut St Chester SC 29706 Office: 120 Church St Chester SC 29706

BROOKS, JACK, congressman; b. Dec. 18, 1922; s. Edward Chachere and Grace Marie (Pipes) B.; m. Charlotte Collins; children—Jack Edward, Katherine Inez, Kimberly Grace. Admitted to Tex. bar, 1949; mem. Tex. Legislature, 1946-50; mem. 83d-93d Congresses from 9th Tex. dist. Col. USMCR ret. Home: 1029 East Dr Beaumont TX 77706 Office: House Office Bldg Washington DC 20515

BROOKS, JAMES CARLTON, JR., physician; b. Baldwin County, Ga., June 22, 1940; s. James Carlton and Mildred (Rozar) B.; B.A. summa cum laude, Mercer U., 1962; M.D. (Avolon fellow), Med. Coll. Ga., 1966. Rotating intern Macon (Ga.) Hosp., 1966-67, med. resident, 1967-68; med. resident Tex. Med. Center, Houston, 1968-70; mem. staffs Tanner Meml. Hosp., Carrollton, Ga., Heard Meml. Hosp., Franklin, Ga. Mem. S. Fla. Conservancy Commn., 1962-72; Tex. coastal dir. environmental protection, 1968-70. Served to maj. M.C., AUS, 1970-72. Mem. A.M.A., Med. Assn. Ga., Sigma Xi, Beta Beta Beta, Phi Eta Sigma, Sigma Mu, Alpha Omega Alpha. Roman Catholic. Contbg. author Butterflies of Georgia, 1972. Contbr. papers on ecology, lepidopterology and botany. Home: Box 368 Franklin GA 30217 Office: Country Plaza Med Group Franklin GA 30217

BROOKS, JERRY CLAUDE, food co. exec.; b. College Park, Ga., Apr. 23, 1936; s. John Bennett and Mattie Mae (Timms) B.; B.S., Ga. Inst. Tech., 1958; m. Peggy Sue Thornton, Feb. 26, 1961; children—Apryll Denise, Jerry Claude, Susan Vereen. Safety engr. Cotton Producers Assn., Atlanta, Ga., 1959-64, dir. safety and loss control 1964-70; dir. corporate protection Gold Kist, Inc., Atlanta, 1970—. Instr., Ga. Safety Inst., Athens, Ga., 1971—. Bd. dirs. Ga. Safety Council, Ga. Soc. Prevention of Blindness. Served with AUS, 1958-59. Mem. Am. Soc. Safety Engrs. (chpt. pres. 1968-69), Nat. Safety Council (gen. chmn. fertilizer sect. 1969-70), So. Safety Conf. (pres. 1973), Am. Soc. Indsl. Security. Mason, Rosicrucian. Club: Exchange (pres. 1969-70) (Lithonia, Ga.). Home: 6411 Evans Mill Way Lithonia GA 30058 Office: 3348 Peachtree Rd Atlanta GA 30326

BROOKS, MARION JACKSON, physician; b. Fort Worth, Feb. 15, 1920; s. Roy Edwin and Eula Mae (Jackson) Brooks; B.S., Prairie View A. and M. Coll., 1940; M.D., Howard U., 1951; m. Marie Louise Norris, Dec. 25, 1945; children—Marian (Mrs. William C. Bryant), Carol Eleanor (Mrs. Ira A. Stroughter), Roy Charles, Clarence Jackson, Marie Anne. Intern Freedmen's Hosp., Washington, 1951-52; gen. practice medicine, Fort Worth, 1952—; mem. staff St. Joseph Hosp., Harris Hosp., All Saints Hosp.; dir. Great Liberty Life Ins. Co., Dallas. Pres. Neighborhood Action, Inc., 1967-68; chmn. Sickle Cell Anemia Assn. Tex., 1971—; active Fort Worth Symphony Assn., Community Action Agy., Fort Worth-Tarrant County, Tex. Mem. Fort Worth City Park and Recreation Bd., 1963-67. Bd. dirs. Tarrant County Precinct Workers Council. Served to 1st lt. AUS, 1942-47; ETO. Mem. Tex. Council Voters (dir. 1961—), Alpha Phi Alpha. Methodist (trustee 1963—). Mason (Shriner). Home: 2451 Evans Av Fort Worth TX 76104 Office: 2200 Evans Av Fort Worth TX 76104

BROOKS, MILDRED STALNAKER (MRS. J. RICHARD BROOKS), lawyer, former judge; b. Ft. Valley, Ga., Dec. 11, 1908; d. James William and Minnie Lee (Fountain) Stalnaker; student Mchts. and Bankers Bus. Coll., N.Y., 1935; LL.B., U. Miami, 1955; m. Frank Bruce Akerman, Dec. 24, 1955 (dec.); m. 2d, J. Richard Brooks, Apr. 29, 1972. Comptroller Loudee Iron & Metal Co., Ltd., N.Y.C., 1938-40; office mgr. Hubbard & Carr, attys., also Sen. Claude Pepper, Miami, Fla., 1940-52; admitted to Fla. bar; asst. atty. gen. to atty. gen. of Fla., 1955-57, also atty. to 8 state agys.; judge Small Claims Ct., Broward County, Fla., 1959-71; practice law, Tavernier, Fla., 1971—. Mem. Fla. Gov.'s Commn. on Status of Women. Bd. dirs. A.R.C. Recipient certificate of service State of Fla.; certificate of service to law sch. U. Miami. Mem. Am., Broward County bar assns., Fla. Bar, Am. Judicature Soc., Internat., Nat., Fla. (pres. 1957-58) assns. women lawyers, Bus. and Profl. Womens Clubs, Am. Assn. U. Women, Kappa Beta Pi (past pres. local chpt.). Conglist. Clubs: Soroptimist, Isla morada Fishing. Home: PO Box 38-446 Upper Key Largo FL 33037 Office: Profl Bldg Tavernier FL 33070

BROOKS, PAUL ALLISON, supt. schs.; b. Joy, Tex., Mar. 31, 1918; s. Isham A. and Alma E. (Hargrove) B.; B.S., North Tex. State U., 1942, M.B.A., 1949, Ed.D., 1957; m. Rhoda A. Brooks, May 18, 1940; children—Gary, Sandra, Joe M. Supt. schs., Stoneburg, Tex., 1948-53, Cedar Hill, Tex., 1953—. Served with AUS, 1943-46. Mem. N.E.A., Am., Tex. assns. sch. adminstrs., Tex. Tchrs. Assn., Dallas County Sch. Adminstrs. (pres. 1957-58), Cedar Hill C. of C. (dir. 1962-65, 68-71). Mason, Lion. Home: 425 Lee St Cedar Hill TX 75104 Office: 333 S Hwy 67 Cedar Hill TX 75104

BROOKS, ROBERT FRANKLIN, educator, entomologist; b. Columbus, O., Mar. 17, 1928; s. Lawrence Traynor and Beatrice Eva (Eberts) B.; B.S., Ohio State U., 1954, M.S., 1955; Ph.D., U. Wis., 1960; m. Harriet Marie Huntington, Oct. 31, 1959; 1 son, Lawrence Bertram. Research asst. Ohio State U., 1954-55; research asst. U. Wis., 1956-58, project asso., 1958-59, instr., 1959; faculty U. Fla., Lake Alfred, 1960—, prof. entomology, 1970—. Citrus cons. Standard Fruit Co., La Ceiba, Honduras. Mem. adv. bd. Polk County Juvenile Ct. Served with USNR, 1946-48, 50-52. NSF grantee, 1972. Mem. Entomol. Soc. Am., Fla. Entomol. Soc., Fla. Hort. Soc., Internat. Orgn. for Biol. Control, Sigma Xi. Contbr. articles to profl. jours. Home: 660 W Orange St Lake Alfred FL 33850

BROOKS, SAM ALLEN, JR., hosp. operating co. exec.; b. Waco, Tex., Jan. 31, 1939; s. Sam Allen and Norma (Reynolds) B.; B.B.A., Baylor U., 1962; m. Linda Daniel; children—Wendy, Daniel. Audit mgr. firm Ernst & Ernst, Dallas, 1962-69; treas. Hosp. Corp. Am., Nashville, 1969—. Treas., bd. dirs. Davidson County Assn. Retarded Children, Tng. and Rehab. Center; bd. drs. Bill Wilkerson Hearing and Speech Center, all Nashville. Home: 529 Clematis Dr Nashville TN 37205 Office: PO Box 550 Nashville TN 37202

BROOM, PERRY MORRIS, educator; b. Effingham, Ill., Aug. 7, 1908; s. Charles A. and Lillian (Cohea) B.; B.S., Sam Houston State Coll., 1936; M.Ed., U. Tex., 1938; D.Ed. (Univ. fellow), 1942; M.B.A., East Tex. State Coll., 1953; m. Inez Miller, 1947 (div. 1950); 1 dau., Brenda Karen. Tchr. pub. schs., Hebbronville, Tex., 1936-37; prin. high sch., San Diego, Tex., 1937-40; instr. U. Tex., 1945-46, 50-51; asso. prof. Howard Coll., 1946-47; prof. edn. Franklin Coll., 1947-49; asso. prof. bus. adminstrn. East Tex. State Coll., 1951-60, prof. bus. adminstrn., 1960—. Served to lt., USNR, 1942-45; PTO, Phillipines. Mem. N.E.A., Am. Statis. Assn., Am. Inst. Mgmt., C. of C., Phi Alpha Theta, Alpha Chi, Phi Delta Kappa, Sigma Iota Epsilon, Delta Sigma Pi, Kappa Delta Pi, Pi Gamma Mu, Pi Omega Pi, Kappa Phi Kappa, Psi Chi. Baptist. Rotarian. Author: Simplified Business Statistics, 1955. Editor: (with M. Decherd) Commerce Curriculum Bull., Tex. Dept. Edn., 1938. Home: 90 ET PO Sta Commerce TX 75428

BROOME, DOUGLAS RALPH, JR., restaurant owner, mgmt. cons.; b. Columbia, S.C., Nov. 30, 1936; s. Douglas Ralph and Olive (Odom) B.; B.S. in Elec. Engring., The Citadel, 1959; m. Shirly Ruth Blizzard, Dec. 28, 1956 (dec. Apr. 1969); children—Douglas R. III, Morris L.; m. 2d, Janice Rose Laski, Oct. 4, 1969; children—David T. Laski, Pamela J. Laski. Communications engr. NASA, 1959-61, with Apollo Spacecraft Program Office, Houston, 1961—, chief project engr. Apollo Block II, Command and Service Modules, 1965-67, chief project engr. Apollo Block I and II Command and Service Modules, 1967-68, asst. chief CSM project engring. div., 1968-70; asst. program mgr. lunar surface elec. properties expt. program Raytheon Co., Sudbury, Mass., 1970-72; v.p. DRB Systems, Columbia, S.C., 1972-73; now owner restaurant, mgmt. cons. Served to 2d lt. AUS, 1959-60, Mem. Mensa, I.E.E.E. (subgroups on tech. mgmt., information systems), Nat. Rifle Assn., The Citadel Alumni Club. Office: 2501 N Main St Columbia SC 29206

BROPHY, JOSEPH DANIEL, accountant; b. Dallas, Sept. 16, 1946; s. James J. and Mary (Kromand) B.; B.B.A. with honors, N. Tex. State U., 1970, M.B.A., 1971. Teaching asst. U. Tex. at Austin, 1971; practice accounting, Dallas, 1972—; dir., treas. Dallas Land Investors, Inc., 1971—. Instr., U. Tex. at Arlington, 1972—. Bd. dirs., treas. Royal Central Condominium Assn., Dallas, 1973—. N. Tex. State U. scholar, 1970-71; Inst. Internal Auditors scholar, 1970; Price Waterhouse fellow, 1971-72. C.P.A., Tex. Mem. Am. Inst. C.P.A.'s, Tex. Soc. C.P.A.'s, Blue Key, Beta Gamma Sigma, Beta Alpha Psi. Home: 7926 Royal Lane Dallas TX 75231 Office: 3611 Oak Lawn Av Dallas TX 75219

BROSS, JOHN ADAMS, environmental center exec.; b. Chgo., Jan. 17, 1911; s. Mason and Isabel Foster (Adams) B.; student Chgo. Latin Sch., Groton Sch.; A.B., Harvard, 1933, LL.B., 1936; m. Priscilla Prince, June 1936; children—Wendy, John, Justine; m. 2d, Joanne Bass, Oct. 28, 1947; 1 son, Peter F. Admitted to N.Y. State bar, 1938; practiced in N.Y.C., 1936-42; asso. Parker & Duryee, N.Y.C., 1936-49, mem. firm, 1942-49; asst. gen. counsel U.S. High Commr. to Germany, 1949-51; U.S. govt. cons. fgn. affairs, 1951-57, 60-63; spl. adviser, coordinator Am. embassy, Bonn, Germany, 1957-60; dep. to dir. Central Intelligence for Nat. Intelligence Programs Evaluation, 1963-71; chmn. bd. dirs. Central Atlantic Environment Center, 1971—. Mem. staff task force on nat. mil. establishment Hoover Commn., 1948. Served from 2d lt. to col., USAAF, 1942-46. Decorated Legion of Merit, Bronze Star; Order Brit. Empire; King Christian X Medal of Liberty. Mem. Assn. Bar City N.Y. (chmn. com. state legislation 1946-49), Council on Fgn. Relations N.Y. Clubs: River, Harvard (N.Y.C.). Home: 4501 Crest Lane McLean VA 22101

BROTHERS, CASSIE MARIE CAMPBELL (MRS. WILLIAM JOHN BROTHERS, JR.), librarian; b. Wabash, Ark., Oct. 20, 1928; d. John Calvin and Marie (Parker) Campbell; B.S., U. Ark., 1951; M.L.S., U. Miss., 1962; m. William John Brothers, Jr., Apr. 23, 1950; children—William John III, Brooke Ann. Librarian, Helena-West, Helena Sch. System, Helena, Ark., 1952—, now library coordinator, supr. Mem. Phillips County Hist. Assn., Phillips County Library Assn., Am., Ark. library assns., N.E.A., Ark. Edn. Assn., Assn. Childhood Edn. (chpt. past pres.), Classroom Tchrs. Assn. (chpt. past pres.), Delta Kappa Gamma (pres. local chpt.), Sigma Alpha Iota, Zeta Tau Alpha. Democrat. Home: 123 Summit Dr Helena AR 72342 Office: Helena-West Helena Sch System Helena AR 72343

BROTHERS, WILLIAM JOHN, JR., agrl. warehousing firm exec.; b. Shelby, Miss., Mar. 11, 1920; s. William John and Anne (Kingston) B.; student Christian Bros. Coll., 1938-40, Memphis State U., 1940-41; m. Cassie Marie Campbell, Apr. 23, 1950; children—William John III, Brooke Ann. Plant mgr. Helena Chem. Co. (Ark.), 1957-69, v.p. mfg., 1969-72; pres. Blackhawk Warehouse & Leasing Co., Helena, 1970—. Commr. State Police, State of Ark., 1971—; mem. Civil Service Commn., 1966—, Helena Welfare Bd., 1968-70. Bd. dirs. Phillips County Community Coll., Helena. Served with USAAF, 1941-45; ETO, PTO. Mem. Helena C. of C. Democrat. Roman Catholic. K.C. Home: 123 Summit Dr Helena AR 72342 Office: PO Box 809 Helena AR 72342

BROTT, CLIFFORD JOHN, securities co. exec.; b. Crawford, Neb., June 12, 1925; s. Harry V. and Viola (Auer) B.; A.B., Providence Coll., 1950; M.A., Boston U., 1953; m. Martha Fisette, June 12, 1945; children—Martha Louise (Mrs. Marvin R. Mikeska), Clifford John, Susan Genevieve, Claudette Marie (Mrs. Beverly Hall), Elizabeth Ann, Edwin T., William G., Robert J. Asst. prof. econs. Providence Coll., 1950-55; with Merrill Lynch, Pierce, Fenner & Smith, Dallas, 1955-63, Goodbody & Co., Inc., Dallas, 1963-64, Shearson Hammill, Inc., Dallas, 1964-68; sr. v.p. Weber, Hall, Cobb & Caudle, Inc., Dallas, 1968—. Lectr. finance Dallas Coll., 1958-64, So. Methodist U., Dallas, 1958-74, Baylor U., Waco, Tex., 1969-70. Served with USNR, 1943-46. Home: 6737 Briar Cove Dallas TX 75240 Office: 1800 LTV Tower Dallas TX 75201

BROTTON, WILLIAM GLEASON, wood preserving co. exec.; b. Eufaula, Okla., Jan. 29, 1922; s. Thomas Edwin and Rowena (Gleason) B.; student Okla. A. and M. Coll., 1939-41; m. Elizabeth Moran, May 22, 1943; children—William Danile, Sally Ann, Rebecca Jane. Lumber insp. Halsey Hardwood Co., Edenton, N.C., 1947-49; ind. lumber buyer Eastern N.C., 1949-52; pres. Milwork Lumber, Inc., Scotland Neck, N.C., 1952-64; pres. Carolina Wood Preserving Co., Scotland Neck, 1960—, also dir. Served with USMCR, 1942-43, USNR, 1943-45. Decorated Air medal. Mem. Soc. Wood Preservers Am., N.C. (pres. 1967) Wood Preservers assns., V.F.W., Am. Legion, Scotland Neck Bus. Bur. Republican. Baptist. Club: Scotfield Country (Scotland Neck). Home: 814 Church St Scotland Neck NC 27874 Office: E 17th St Scotland Neck NC 27874

BROUILLETTE, BILL, motel exec.; b. New York Mills, N.Y., June 22, 1930; s. Everett Andrew and Delores Margaret (Martin) B.; grad. high sch.; m. Mary Ruth Freeman, Dec. 12, 1965; children—Bill, Roy Andrew, Brandee Rene. Chef, Madison Co., Rome, N.Y., 1950-55; salesman Continental Baking Co., Utica, N.Y., 1955-59; motel mgr. Helmsley Spear Hospitality Cons. Div., N.Y.C., 1959-70; v.p., gen. mgr. Sheraton Motor Inn, Fort Myers, Fla., 1970—, owner, 1972—; v.p. Pate Industries, Fort Myers, 1971—; v.p. Am. Motor Inns, 1969—. Cons. motel multiple property supervision. Mem. Tex. Tourist Council, 1970; mem. adv. council Edison Community Coll. Served with USMCR, 1948-50. Named mgr. year Helmsley Spear Hospitality Cons. Div., 1969-70. Mem. Fla., Lee County (pres. 1973-74) hotel motel assns., Hotel Sales Mgrs. Assn., C. of C. (tourist com. 1961-63), Nat. Def. Transp. Assn., Bons Vi Vant, Sales and Marketing Exec. Elk. Clubs: El Antonio Country, Business and Professional Mens, University (San Antonio). Home: 2248 Crystal St Fort Myers FL 33901 Office: 8900 S Tamiami Trail Fort Myers FL 33901

BROUSSARD, CHARLES ELLIOT, rancher; b. Vermilion Parish, La., Jan. 9, 1925; s. Alphe A. and Odile (Cade) B.; student La. State U., 1942-43, U. Southwestern La., 1946-49; m. Rose Ashy, Mar. 30, 1948; children—Richard C., Yvonne (Mrs. Conrad A. Simon), Alan J., Hal J. Farmer, rancher, Kaplan, 1951—; pres., mgr. Flying J Ranch, Inc., Kaplan, La., 1968—; owner Broussard Ins. Agy., Lafayette, La., 1947-51, Teche Collection Agy., Lafayette, 1947-51, Flying J Ranch Land Inc., Kaplan, 1968—, Broussard Real Estate Agy., 1972—. Commr., La. Coastal Commn., 1972—; pres. Isle Marone Draining Dist., 1959-60; v.p., mem. exec. com. La. Intra Coastal Seway Assn., 1972—; mem. Pub. Affairs Research Council La., 1970—. Chmn. campaigns various candidates state, national office, 1950—. Bd. dirs. Vermilion Parish Farm Bur., 1966-67, Internat. Relationship Assn., Lafayette, Mermentare Basin Assn., La. Served with USAAF, 1944-46. Mem. Vermilion Parish (pres. 1965-68), Nat. (pres. 1965-69) rice growers assns., Vermilion Parish Cattlemans Assn. (pres. 1968), S.W. La. Water Control Assn. (pres.), Greater Kaplan C. of C. (dir.), La. Charolais Breeders Assn. (v.p. 1968-71), Charolais Herd Breeders Internat. (dir.), Am. Brahman Breeders Assn., Am. Internat. Charolais Assn., Am. Chianina Assn., Charolais Herdbook Internat., Agri-Bus. Council La. (dir.), Am. Legion. Democrat. Roman Catholic. Address: Flying J Ranch Kaplan LA 70548

BROUSSARD, JAY R., state ofcl.; b. New Iberia, La., Dec. 22, 1920; ed. La. State U., U. Southwestern La.; m. Emma Joan Landry; 3 children. Dir. La. Dept. Art, Hist. and Cultural Preservation, Baton Rouge, 1947—; also painter; works exhibited Corcoran Gallery Art, Washington, Pa. Acad. Design, Butler Art Museum, Youngstown, O., Denver Art Mus., High Mus. Art, Atlanta, Isaac Delgado, others. Served with USAAF, World War II. Mem. Am. Assn. Museums, Am. Fedn. Arts, Nat. Trust Historic Preservation, Mus. Modern Art N.Y., La. Crafts Council, Baton Rouge Art League (hon.), La. Art and Artists Guild (hon.), La Watercolor Soc. (hon.), Gulf State Camera Clubs (hon.). Address: la Dept Art Hist and Cultural Preservation Old State Capitol Baton Rouge LA 70801

BROUSSARD, JOEL EARL, JR., dentist; b. Houston, July 29, 1938; s. Joel Earl and Hazel Virginia (Brisbois) B.; B.S., U. Tex., 1961, D.D.S., 1967; M.S. in Orthodontics, U. Tenn., 1969; m. Anita Louise McFarland, Sept. 4, 1959; children—Anissa Lynn, Joel Evan. Research chemist Pitts. Plate Glass, Corpus Christi, Tex., 1961-63; gen. practice dentistry, Memphis, 1967-69; gen. practice orthodontics, Austin, 1969—. Mem. Am. Dental Assn., Am. Assn. Orthodontists, Southwest Soc. Orthodontists, Omicron Kappa Upsilon, Delta Sigma Delta. Baptist. Rotarian. Home: 4603 Arapahoe Trail Austin TX 78745 Office: 2222 Western Trails Blvd Austin TX 78745

BROWDER, ROBERT MICHAEL, utility co. exec.; b. Birmingham, Ala., Apr. 20, 1943; s. Robert and Runette (Hardin) B.; B.E.E., Auburn U., 1966; M.Adminstrv. Sci., U. Ala., 1973; m. Catherine Naugher, Mar. 16, 1963; children—Robert Michael, Lisa Annette. Engr., J.F. Bevis Co., Gadsden, Ala., 1965-67; supt. engring. Huntsville Utilities (Ala.), 1967-72; supt. operations and engring. Bristol Electric System (Tenn.), 1972—. Football coach Little League, 1972-73, basketball coach, 1971. Registered profl. engr., Ala., Tenn. Mem. I.E.E.E., Am. Mgmt. Assn., Am. Pub. Power Assn. (engring. and operating com. 1973—). Mason, Rotarian (youth com. 1973). Home: 451 Brookwood Dr Bristol TN 37620 Office: 37 4th St Bristol TN 37620

BROWER, JOHN HAROLD, educator; b. Augusta, Me., June 8, 1940; s. Auburn E. and Lurana C. (Van Doren) B.; B.S., U. Me., 1962; M.S., U. Mass., 1964, Ph.D., 1965; m. Moonyean A. Smallidge, Sept. 1960; children—Ian T., Brook D. Vis. research asso. Brookhaven Nat. Lab., Upton, N.Y., 1961-65; research entomologist Agrl. Research Sta., U.S. Dept. Agr., Savannah, Ga., 1965—; asst. prof. entomology U. Ga., Athens, 1971-74; prof. biology Armstrong State Coll., Savannah, 1965-71. Winner Me. Westinghouse Sci. Talent Search, 1958. Mem. Entomol. Soc. Am., Canadian, Ga. entomol. socs., Ecol. Soc. Am., Radiation Research Soc. Club: Savannah Stamp. Home: 3 Althea Pkwy Savannah GA 31405 Office: PO Box 5125 Savannah GA 31403

BROWER, WALTER JORDAN, physician; b. Birmingham, Ala., Feb. 5, 1921; s. Walter Scott and Elizabeth (Jordan) B.; B.A., U. Ala., 1942; M.D., Duke, 1947; m. Miriam Timmons, Jan. 20, 1949; children—William Jordan, Carl Timmons, Caroline Elizabeth, Franklin Perry. Rotating intern at Jefferson-Hillman Hosp., 1947-48, resident in radiology, 1948-51; instr. radiology Med. Coll. Ala., 1948-51; practice medicine specializing in radiology, Birmingham, 1955—; dir. dept. radiology VA Hosp., 1956-57; cons. radiologist Cullman, Blount Meml., Chilton hosps.; also clin. asst. prof. Med. Coll. Ala., 1957—. Served with Med. Dept., AUS, 1944-46; from lt. to capt. M.C., USAF, 1951-55. Fellow Am. Coll. Radiology (chpt. pres. 1969-70; councillor 1971—), Radiol. Soc. of N.Am., So. Radiol. Conf. (charter; chmn. 1974-75), Am., So. med. assns., Ala., Cullman County med. socs., Ala. Cattleman's Assn., Nat. Skeet Shooting Assn. (life), Arlington Hist. Assn., So. Commemorative Soc., Sons Confederate Vets., Soc. War 1812, Nat. Rifle Assn., Delta Kappa Epsilon, Alpha Kappa Kappa. Episcopalian. Mason (Shriner). Home: Hayden Route 2 Bangor AL 35079 Office: Downtown Plaza Cullman AL 35055

BROWN, AARON CLIFTON, lawyer, chancellor; b. Murray, Ky., Oct. 16, 1911; s. Ed and Minnie (Cotham) B.; student U. Tenn., 1931-32; LL.B., Cumberland U., 1936; m. Viria Alice Bell, Mar. 11, 1939; children—Aaron Clifton, Gerald Bell. Admitted to Tenn. bar, 1936; since practiced in Paris, Tenn.; master chancery ct. 1946-52; mayor, Paris, 1955-59; founder firm Brown, Brown & Guinn, 1965—; chancellor 8th chancery Div. Tenn., 1968—. Pres., Tenn. Constl. Conv., 1965; chmn. Draft Bd. Henry County, 1946—. Mem. Tenn. Senate, 1966-68. Served with USNR, 1964-66. Mem. Bar Assn. Tenn., Am., Paris-Henry County bar assns., Am. Judicature Soc., Am. Trial Lawyers Assn., V.F.W. Methodist. Lion (Paris pres. 1957). Home: 1212 Chickasaw St Paris TN 38242 Office: 302 Commercial Bank Bldg Paris TN 38242

BROWN, ALBERT WOODROW, accountant; b. Pottsboro, Tex., July 1, 1918; s. Albert Sidney and Sallie Goode (Cowherd) B.; grad. Hill's Bus. U., 1941; m. Viola Jones, Sept. 29, 1942; children—Albert George, Carol (Mrs. Colin Light). Prin., Albert W. Brown, C.P.A., Sherman, Tex., 1950-71; pres. Albert Brown, Jackson & Co., C.P.A.'s, Sherman, 1971—; dir. Grayson County State Bank, Sherman, other diversified cos. Pres., Goodwill Industries North Tex., 1970-73; treas. Tex. Lions Crippled Children's Camp, Kerrville, 1973-74. Mem. Am. Inst. C.P.A.'s, Tex. Soc. C.P.A.'s, Dallas Estate Council. Baptist (deacon). Lion (dist. gov. 1972-73). Home: 900 S Maurice Av Denison TX 75020 Office: PO Box 940 Sherman TX 75090

BROWN, ALEX SMITH, JR., indsl. engr.; b. Tennille, Ga., Nov. 23, 1922; s. Alex Smith and Lillian (Daley) B.; B.S., The Citadel, 1947; grad. exec. program U. N.C. Sch. Bus. Adminstrn., 1971; m. Nancy Cockman, Dec. 4, 1965; 1 dau., Ellen Daley. Indsl. engr. Dan River Mills, Danville, Va., 1947-49; field engr. Am. Asso. Cons., 1949-56, chief engr., 1956-58, v.p., chief engr., dir., 1958-60; chief indsl. engr. Burlington Industries, Inc. Greensboro, N.C., 1960—. Trustee Davison Sch., Atlanta. Served to capt. AUS, 1943-46. Mem. Soc. for Advancement of Mgmt. (past pres., v.p.), Am. Inst. Indsl. Engrs., Assn. Citadel Men (dir. 1969-70). Republican. Baptist. Club: Greensboro Country. Home: 2307 Danbury Rd Greensboro NC 27408 Office: 3330 W Friendly Av Greensboro NC 27402

BROWN, ALGIE DEE, lawyer; b. Waldo, Ark., Mar. 8, 1910; s. John Spence and Lodie (Bryan) B.; A.B., Centenary Coll., 1934; student Tex. U., 1932, La. State U. Law Sch., 1935-36; m. Hazel Turner, Dec. 27, 1947; children—Bryan Turner, Curtis Siebert. Admitted to La. bar, 1937, since practiced in Shreveport. Mem. La. Ho. of Reps.,

1948-72; mem. Shreveport Democratic Exec. Com., 1939—. Served as lt. USNR, 1943-46. Mem. Am., La., Shreveport bar assn., Am. Judicature Soc., Am. Legion, V.F.W. Baptist (bd. dirs.). Elk. Home: 331 McCormick Pl Shreveport LA 71104 Office: Lane Bldg Shreveport LA 71101

BROWN, ANN ROREM, educator; b. Des Moines, Sept. 30, 1924; d. Mark and Hazel Jeannette (Gronsdahl) Rorem; B.S., Okla. State U., 1946, Ed.D. 1965; M.A., U. No. Colo., 1955; m. Vincent Watts, Jr., July 6, 1946 (div. 1952); 1 dau., Sara Kathryn Watts; m. 2d, Robert Wilson Brown, Jr., Dec. 31, 1966. Tchr., prin. pub. schs., Oklahoma City, 1948-59; instr. U. Okla., 1959-62; asso. prof. edn. Oklahoma City U., 1962—. Cons. Mark Twain Child Devel. Center, Oklahoma City, 1969—. Bd. dirs. Spottswood Child Devel. Center, Oklahoma City, 1969—, New World Sch., Oklahoma City, 1972—. Mem. Delta Gamma, Alpha Lambda Delta, Kappa Delta Pi, Pi Lambda Theta, Delta Kappa Gamma. Democrat. Methodist. Home: 12001 Quail Creek Rd Oklahoma City OK 73120

BROWN, AUGUSTUS BART, geologist, rancher; b. Coconut Grove, Fla., Apr. 3, 1914; s. Jamot and Margaret Bart (Berger) B.; B.S., Yale, 1937; m. Jenilee Knight, July 14, 1938; children—Bart Berger, Jennifer Knight Alexander. Field geologist Hudnall & Pirtle, Tyler, Tex., 1937-38; geologist Mudge Oil Co., Dallas, 1938-40, chief geologist, 1940-42; mng. partner Hudnall, Pirtle & Brown, Dallas and San Antonio, 1946-54; engaged in petroleum exploration & investment, also ranching, Dallas, 1954—; asso. Bass & Vessels, Bass, Vessels & Brown, McAllen, Tex. and Denver, 1954-57; asso. Wood Bros. & Langham, Wood Bros., Mission, Tex., 1957-68; v.p. Berger Land Co., Denver, 1968—; dir. Millican Oil Co., Tyler, Tex.; dir. The Importers Wine & Spirits, Inc., Dallas. Served to lt. USNR, 1942-46. Mem. Am. Assn. Petroleum Geologists, Am. Inst. Mining, Metall. and Petroleum Engrs., Dallas Geol. Soc. Clubs: Dallas Petroleum, Northwood. Home: 8801 Briarwood Lane Dallas TX 75209 Office: 8801 Briarwood Lane Dallas TX 75209

BROWN, BARRY WILSON, biomathematician; b. Buffalo, Dec. 20, 1939; s. George Wilson and Iva (Roberts) B.; B.S., U. Chgo., 1959; M.A., U. Cal. at Berkeley, 1961, Ph.D., 1963; m. Diane J. Prasil, Jan. 27, 1963; children—Sheryl J., Marion L., Lisa E. Asst. prof. U. Chgo., 1963-68; asso. prof. dept. biomath. U. Tex., Houston and M.D. Anderson Hosp., 1968—; chief computer scis. sect. M.D. Anderson Hosp., 1971—; adj. asso. prof. Rice U., Houston, 1971—. Mem. Am. Statis. Assn., Biometics Soc., Assn. Computing Machinery, A.A.A.S. Contbr. articles to profl. jours. Home: 5830 Yarwell St Houston TX 77035 Office: 6723 Bertner St Houston TX 77025

BROWN, BEVAN WOOD, JR., civil engr., pub. utilities exec.; b. Starr, S.C., Oct. 19, 1928; s. Bevan Wood and Nelle (Smith) B.; B.S., Clemson U., 1949, M.S., 1950; M.S. in Civil Engring., Stanford, 1968; m. Sarah Franes Hill, Aug. 22, 1952; children—Bevan W., Jeffrey Hill, Myra Lynelle. Civil engr. Flood control br. TVA, Knoxville, Tenn., 1950-61, head project studies sect., 1961-64, asst. br. chief, 1964-72, asst. to dir. div. water control planning, 1973—. Lectr. dept. civil engring. U. Tenn., 1968—. Registered profl. engr., Tenn. Mem. Am. Soc. C.E. (nat. dir. 1973-76), Nat. Soc. Profl. Engrs., Internat. Assn. Hydraulic Research, Am. Soc. Engring. Edn. Home: 9508 Briarwood Blvd Knoxville TN 37919 Office: 445 Evans Bldg Care of TVA Knoxville TN 37902

BROWN, BRADFORD S(TEARNS), statis. cons.; b. Newton, Mass., Jan. 16, 1931; s. John Fiske and Dorothy (Dudley) B.; A.B., Harvard, 1953; M.S., U. Ill., 1954; children—Rachel Elizabeth, Abigail Cathryn, Oliver Fiske. Asso. service engr. E. I. duPont de Nemours & Co., Niagara Falls, N.Y., 1956-59, statistician, Newark, 1959-63, sr. statistician, Newark, Del. and Old Hickory, Tenn., 1963-68, cons., Old Hickory, 1968—. Pres., Fairfield Crest Civic Assn., Newark, Del., 1964. Democratic committeeman, Newark, Del., 1963-66; sec.-treas. Tenn. Conf. Unitarian Universalists, 1972—. Served with AUS, 1954-56. Mem. Am. Statis. Assn. (pres. chpt. 1972-73), Am. Soc. Quality Control (local chmn. 1971-72), Mensa. Unitarian-Universalist (pres. ch.). Home: 1508 Grandview Dr Nashville TN 37215 Office: ESD Computer Group DuPont Co Old Hickory TN 37138

BROWN, CALVIN ANDERSON, JR., physician; b. Athens, Ga., Sept. 13, 1931; s. Calvin Anderson and Ruth (Haynes) B.; B.S., Morehouse Coll., 1952; M.D., Meharry Med. Coll., 1958; m. Joy San Walker, Dec. 31, 1953; children—Joi Sanne, Sanna Gai. Intern Hubbard Hosp., Nashville, 1958-59; practice medicine specializing in family practice, Atlanta, 1959—; dir. Atlanta Southside Comprehensive Health Center, 1968; med. dir. Pineview Convalescent Center, Atlanta, 1968—; mem. staff Holy Family Hosp., Atlanta, Hughes Spalding Hosp., Atlanta; chief staff Martin Luther King, Jr. Nursing Center, Atlanta, 1971-73; chief physician Fulton County Jails, Atlanta, 1971; asst. prof. dept. preventive medicine Med. Sch., Emory U., 1968-69. Mem. task force on cardio-vascular disease, hypertension and diabetes Ga. Regional Med. Program, 1971. Pres. Nat. Alumni Assn. Morehouse Coll., 1962—; trustee Morehouse Coll. Served with AUS, 1952-54. Mem. Atlanta Med. Assn. (pres. 1968), Alpha Phi Alpha. Baptist (trustee 1969—). Home: 2947 Oldknow Dr NW Atlanta GA 30318 Office: 1475 Pryor Rd SW Atlanta GA 30315

BROWN, CHARLES QUENTIN, coll. adminstr.; b. Roanoke Rapids, N.C., Sept. 12, 1928; s. James Wallace and Dessie Elizabeth (Bell) B.; B.S., U. N.C., 1951, M.S., 1953; Ph.D., Va. Poly. Inst., 1959; m. Barbara Jean Hedgepeth, June 4, 1950; children—Elizabeth Leigh, Charles Quentin. Tchr. sci. Chapel Hill (N.C.) High Sch., 1953-54; asso. prof. geology Clemson (S.C.) U., 1954-66; faculty E. Carolina U., Greenville, N.C., 1966—, prof. geology, 1967—, chmn. dept., 1967-69, dir. instl. devel., 1969—. Mem. N.C. Marine Sci. Council, 1970—. Bd. dirs. Wesley Found. Greenville, Served with AUS, 1946-48. Mem. E. Carolina U. Alumni Assn. (dir.), Geol. Soc. Am., Soc. Econ. Paleontologists and Mineralogists, Am. Coll. Pub. Relations Assn., Am. Alumni Council, Sigma Xi. Home: 1307 N Overlook Dr Greenville NC 27834

BROWN, C(LAUDE) HAROLD, lawyer; b. Mendenhall, Miss., July 28, 1931; s. Claude S. and Mildred (Bush) B.; B.B.A., Vanderbilt U., 1957; LL.B., U. Tex., 1960; m. Carol Wynn, June 14, 1957; children—Tracey Gwen, Terry Lynne, Allison Anne, Harold Allen. Admitted to Tex. bar, 1960; partner firm Wynn, Irby, Brown, McConnico & Mack, Ft. Worth, 1960—. Dir. Clardy Mfg. Co., Ft. Worth, Kinro Industries, Inc., Ft. Worth. Bd. dirs. A.J. and Jessie Duncan Found., Ft. Worth, Edna Gladney Home, Ft. Worth. Served with AUS, 1953-55. Mem. State Bar Tex., Am., Ft. Worth-Tarrant County (pres. 1962) bar assns., Alpha Tau Omega, Phi Delta Phi. Republican. Mem. Disciples of Christ (dir.). Mason (Shriner), Rotarian. Clubs: Fort Worth Vanderbilt (pres. 1966), American Brittany (dir.). Home: 3470 Sagerest Terrace Fort Worth TX 76109 Office: 1300 Schick Bldg Fort Worth TX 76102

BROWN, CLAUDE LAMAR, physician; b. Mobile, Ala., Mar. 12, 1923; s. Claude Lamar and Pauline (Johanna) B.; B.S., Tulane U., 1943, M.D., 1945; m. Vernice Brown, Aug. 16, 1968; children (by previous marriage)—Claude Lamar III, Paul William, Christianna Lori. Intern City Hosp., Mobile, Ala., 1945-46; resident psychiatry Menninger Found. Sch. Psychiatry, Topeka, 1948-51; practice medicine specializing in psychiatry, Mobile, 1951—; mem. staff Mobile Infirmary, Providence, Gen. Drs. hosps., Mobile; asso. prof. psychiatry U. South Ala. Cons., USPHS, 1951, Ala. Rehab. and Crippled Children Service, 1951—; chmn. Ala. State Mental Health Bd., 1967-69. Served to lt. (j.g.) M.C., USNR, 1946-48. Diplomate psychiatry Am. Bd. Psychiatry and Neurology. Fellow Am., So. psychiat. assns.; mem. A.M.A., Ala. State, So., Pan Am. med. assns., Ala. Acad. Psychiatry and Neurology, Mobile County Med. Soc. (pres. 1962). Rotarian. Home: 4951 Winslow Dr Mobile AL 36608 Office: 176 Louiselle St Mobile AL 36607

BROWN, CONRAD NAGEL, architect; b. Bartlesville, Okla., Mar. 28, 1934; s. Conrad Nagel and Leiah Lucille (Lawless) B.; student Okla. State U., 1952-53; B.S., U. Kan., 1958; m. Angelica Velilla Robertin, June 12, 1959; children—Conrad Nagel III, Ana Melisa, David. Individual archtl. practice, Tulsa, 1962-63, Guayama, P.R., 1968-70; with Phillips Petroleum Co., Bartlesville, 1963-68; gen. mgr. Modular Bldg. Systems Corp., Salinas, P.R., 1971-72; mgr. Scovil, Brown & Assos., Architects & Engrs., San Juan, P.R., 1973—. Served to lt. (j.g.) USNR, 1958-62. Mem. A.I.A. Address: GPO Box 3028 San Juan PR 00936

BROWN, DENNISON ROBERT, educator; b. New Orleans, May 17, 1934; s. Elihu Thomson and Floy Clements (Edwards) B.; B.S., Duke, 1955; M.S., La. State U., 1960, Ph.D., 1963; m. Janet Madden, June 9, 1956; children—Robert Leslie, Alan Madden. Instr., La. State U., New Orleans, 1958-61, Baton Rouge, 1962-63; asst. prof. U. Tenn., Knoxville, 1963-65, asso. prof., 1965-67; asso. prof. U. Houston, 1967-70, prof. math., 1970—, departmental dir. grad. studies, 1969-72. Vis. lectr. Math. Assn. Am., 1965-72; cons. Com. on Undergrad. Program in Math., 1972—. Mgr. Little League, 1964—. Served to lt. USN, 1955-58. NSF grantee, 1965-69. Mem. Am. Math. Soc., Math. Assn. Am., Sigma Xi, Kappa Sigma. Methodist. Editor, Semigroup Forum, 1970—. Contbr. articles to profl. jours. Home: 8411 Langdon Lane Houston TX 77036 Office: Dept Math U Houston Houston TX 77004

BROWN, DOROTHY LAVINIA, physician; b. Phila., Jan. 7, 1919; d. Frank Brown and Emma Brown Bates, foster d. Samuel Wesley and Lola Redmon; B.A., Bennett Coll., Greensboro, N.C., 1941; M.D., Meharry Med. Coll., Nashville, 1948; 1 adopted dau., Lola Denise. Intern Harlem Hosp., N.Y.C., 1948-49; surg. residency Hubbard Hosp., Nashville, 1949-54; clin. prof. surgery Meharry Med. Coll.; chief surgery Riverside Hosp.; attending surgeon George Hubbard, Gen., Nashville hosps. Mem. Tenn. Ho. Reps. Trustee Bennett Coll. Fellow A.C.S.; mem. A.M.A., Am. Assn. U. Profs., Nat. Council Negro Women, Nashville Acad. Medicine, R. F. Boyd Med. Soc., Nat. Med. Assn., Assn. Am. Med. Colls., Negro Bus. and Profl. Women's Clubs, Internat. Platform Assn., N.A.A.C.P., Delta Sigma Theta, Kappa Delta Pi. Home: 3109 Centennial Blvd Nashville TN 37209

BROWN, DUANE HOUGHTON, financial exec.; b. Washington, Sept. 14, 1933; s. Frank Stern, Jr. and Ella (Ayers) B.; A.A., Mars Hill Coll., 1952; B.S., U. Richmond, 1954; m. Barbara Kimes Smith, Jan. 25, 1958; children—Kimberly Ann, Lynn Houghton. Sr. accountant Price Waterhouse & Co., Washington, 1957-63, A. M. Pullen & Co., Washington, 1963-64; financial asst. to exec. v.p. Barber & Ross Co., Washington, 1964-65; bus. mgr. Washington Ednl. TV Assn., Washington, 1965-68; asst. controller Leasco Systems & Research Corp., 1968-69; adminstrv. mgr. Peat, Marwick, Mitchell & Co., Washington, 1969-70; sr. accountant, mem. treas.'s staff IMF, Washington, 1970—. Cons. Washington Journalism Center, Translation Cons. Ltd., Arlington, Va. Mem. City of Alexandria (Va.) Adv. Tax Commn., 1967-68; mem. Alexandria Adv. Planning Commn., 1969-72. Republican candidate city councilman, Alexandria, 1967. Bd. dirs. Alexandria Hosp., Children and Youth Confs. Served with AUS, 1954-57. Mem. Am., D.C. insts. C.P.A.'s, Nat. Assn. Accountants. Baptist (deacon). Mason. Home: 5124 Clinton Rd Alexandria VA 22312 Office: 19th and H Sts NW Washington DC 20431

BROWN, DUWARD, realtor, ins. agt.; b., Ala., Dec. 24, 1929; s. James Rias and Martha Sedera (McCarley) B.; B.S., Miss. State U., 1958; grad. Realtors Inst., 1973; m. Peggy Ann Richardson, Aug. 28, 1952; children—Teresa Ann, Sedera Elizabeth, Jeffrey Lloyd, Robert Gregory, Duward Stacy. Agy., Standard Life Ins. Co., Jackson, Miss., 1958-63; v.p., sec. Winston-Savelle Agy., Inc., Columbus, Miss., 1963—; v.p. T. & M. Steel Erectors, Inc. Sec.-treas. Columbus Bd. Realtors, 1970-71, v.p., 1971-72, pres., 1972—. Served with USN, 1950-54. Named Realtor of Year, Columbus Bd. Realtors, 1973. Mem. Columbus-Lowndes C. of C. (com. chmn.), Miss. State U. Alumni Assn. Baptist. Home: 404 Idlewild Rd Columbus MS 39701 Office: PO Box 485 Columbus MS 39701

BROWN, EARL APPLETON, JR., lawyer; b. Tulsa, Oct. 20, 1917; s. Earl Appleton and Ellen Augusta (Works) B.; B.A., U. Okla., 1938, LL.B., 1940; LL.M., U. Tex., 1941; m. Betty Jane Galt, July 20, 1943; 1 dau., Susan (Mrs. Susan Brown Barry). Admitted to Okla. bar, 1940, Tex. bar, 1941, Mont. bar, 1953, U.S. Supreme Ct. bar, 1954, N.Y. bar, 1957; gen. counsel, dir. Mobil Producing Co., Billings, Mont., 1953-56; pres. Mobil Latin Am., N.Y.C., 1959-62; sr. exec. bus. devel. Socony Mobil Corp., N.Y.C., 1962-65; partner firm Anderson, Brown, Orn & Jones, Houston, 1966—. Served to lt. comdr. USNR, 1942-45. Mem. Phi Beta Kappa, Phi Delta Phi. Clubs: Union League (N.Y.C.); Houston Country, Petroleum (Houston). Home: 3711 San Felipe St Houston TX 77027 Office: 1122 SW Tower Houston TX 77002

BROWN, EDGAR ALLAN, lawyer, state senator; b. nr. Aiken, S.C., July 11, 1888; s. Augustus Abraham and Elizabeth (Howard) B.; student Graniteville Acad., 1902-06; LL.B. (hon.), Clemson U., 1955; L.H.D., Med. U. S.C., 1964; LL.D., U.S.C., 1972; m. Annie Love Sitgreaves, Dec. 30, 1913; 1 dau., Emily McBurney (Mrs. Richard M. Jeffries, Jr.). Ct. reporter 2d S.C. Circuit, 1908-18; admitted to S.C. bar, 1910; sr. mem. Brown, Jefferies & Boulware, Barnwell, S.C.; dir. Bankers Trust of S.C. Mem., past chmn. bd. mgrs. Council of State Govts.; chmn., gen. counsel Clark's Hill Authority of S.C.; mem. State Budget and Control Bd. Del.-at-large Nat. Democratic Conv., N.Y.C., 1924, Phila., 1948, Chgo., 1952, 56, 68, Los Angeles, 1960, Atlantic City, 1964; candidate for U.S. Senate, 1926, 38; mem. nat. exec. com. Dem. Party of S.C., 1953-70; chmn. county Dem. exec. com., mem. state Dem. exec. com., 1914—; mem. Ho. of Reps., S.C., 1921-26, speaker, 1925-26; mem. S.C. Senate, 1929—, pres. pro tem, also chmn. senate finance com., 1942-71). Life mem., pres. bd. trustees Clemson U. Mem. Am., S.C. (former pres.) bar assns., Carolina Motor Club (former chmn. bd.). Methodist (trustee). Mason (Shriner). Home: Main St Barnwell SC 29812 Office: Bankers Trust Bldg Barnwell SC 29812

BROWN, EDGAR WILLIAM, JR., banker, industrialist; b. Orange, Tex., Feb. 10, 1894; s. Edgar William and Carrie (Lutcher) B.; ed. pvt. schs.; m. Gladys Slade, July 23, 1915 (dec. Sept. 1959); children—Edgar William III, John S., L. Slade, Charles E.; m. 2d, Helen Elizabeth Smith, Nov. 20, 1960. With Lutcher & Moore Cypress Lumber Co., Ltd. (La.), 1917-73, pres., 1946-64, chmn. bd., 1964—, also dir.; chmn. bd., pres. v.p., dir. Dibert, Stark & Brown Cypress Lumber Co., Donner, La., 1920-38, liquidator, 1938—; pres., dir. Higman Towing Co., Orange, 1922-59, Levingston Shipbldg. Co., Orange, 1933-46; v.p., dir. Vinton Petroleum Co., Orange, 1925-67; chmn. bd., pres., v.p., dir. Brown Paper Mill Co., Inc., Monroe, La., 1922-55; chmn. bd., pres., dir. Orange Nat. Bank, 1928-64; organizer, chmn. bd., dir. County Nat. Bank, Orange, 1959—; chmn. bd., dir. Gulfport Shipbldg. Co., Port Arthur, Tex., 1963-70. Chmn., sec., purchasing agt., commr. Orange Wharf and Dock Commn., 1928-47; founder, dir. Orange Indsl. Devel. Com., 1946-52; mem. adv. bd., dir. Houston Livestock Show and Rodeo; chmn. bd., pres., gen. chmn., dir. Bill Williams Charity Capon Dinner Assn.; councilor Tex. A. and M. U. Research Found.; chmn., life mem. bd. dirs. Orange County chpt. A.R.C.; life mem. Orange County Meml. Hosp. Trustee Linden Fund com. Meth. Homes for Older People, Orange; mem. Intracoastal Canal Assn. La. and Tex. Methodist (trustee, trustor Slade Meml. Found.). Home: Linden-Pinehurst Ranch Orange TX 77630 Office: County Nat Bank Bldg PO Box 400 Orange TX 77630

BROWN, EDWARD BYNUM, lumber co. exec.; b. Asheville, N.C., Aug. 12, 1925; s. Albert Mack and Nell Bell (Belote) B.; B.S. in Mech. Engring., Ga. Sch. Tech.; m. Helene Whiddon, Sept. 16, 1946; children—Carol, Mack, Dan. With Crossett Lumber Co. (Ark.), 1947-57, plant engr., 1955, chief engr., purchasing agt., 1956-57; with Kirby Lumber Corp., Silsbee, Tex., 1957-71, plant mgr., 1968-70, lumber mgr., 1970-71, dir. product devel., 1971; v.p. Birmingham Forest Products, Jasper, Ala., 1971—. Served with USNR, 1943-47. Mem. Forest Products Research Soc. Lion, Kiwanian, Rotarian. Home: 1301 6th Av Jasper AL 35501 Office: PO Drawer H Cordova AL 35550

BROWN, EDWARD MCLAIN, JR., lawyer; b. Balt., Apr. 26, 1929; s. Edward McLain and Rita Virginia (House) B.; student U. Pa., 1946-47; B.B.A., U. Tex., 1958, LL.B., 1960; m. Patsy Sue Millikan, Jan. 28, 1956; children—Carol Lorraine, Ruth Virginia, David William. Admitted to Tex. bar, 1960; practiced in Lamesa, 1960-62, Dallas, 1962—; asso. firm Karl Cayton, 1960-62, Lyne, Blanchette, Smith and Shelton, 1962-65; mem. firm Brown, Elliott, Brown, 1965-70, Brown & Moore, 1970—. Sec., dir. Fas-Pak, Inc., 1971—, Pat Jetton, Inc., 1971—; pres., dir. Joppe Co., 1972—; dir. Regal Real Estate Co., Metro Investment Co., Jerry W. Parks Builders, Inc., Dal-Capri, Inc., since 19—, Vari-Universal, Inc. Mem. Dallas Estate Planning Council, Greater Dallas Planning Council, 1965-69, Farmers Branch Charter Com., 1967-70, chmn. 1969-70; mem. Farmers Branch Indsl. Devel. Com., 1971. Bd. dirs. Farmers Branch Library, 1964-67, chmn., 1967-68. Served with USAF, 1950-56. Mem. Lamesa (sec. treas. 1961-62), Dallas (legal ethics com. 1972-73) bar assns., State Bar Tex., Farmers Branch-Carrollton Lawyers Assn. (pres. 1973). Episcopalian (sr. warden 1967). Lion (treas. 1961-62), Rotarian. Home: 3212 Rolling Knoll Pl Dallas TX 75234 Office: 2711 Valley View Lane Suite 101 Dallas TX 75234

BROWN, EDWIN RANDOLPH, editor, trade assn. exec.; b. Page, W.Va., Jan. 21, 1917; s. Chilton Eustace and Effie (Hill) B.; A.B., Marshall U., 1941; m. Helen Lucile Gravis, Apr. 9, 1944; children—Edwin Randolph, Sarah Lou, Elizabeth Gravis. Reporter, editor Huntington (W.Va.), Pub. Co., 1938-41; reporter, radio news editor, copy editor WORZ, also Orlando (Fla.) Sentinel, 1946-49; mng. editor Orlando Star, 1949-53; exec. sec. Central Fla. chpt. Asso. Gen. Contractors, Orlando, 1954-72; free-lance writer, editor, 1954—; pub. Fla. Ind. Automobile Dealers Assn. Jours., Orlando, 1960—; mgr. Fla. Ind. Automobile Dealers Assn., Orlando, 1960—. Bd. dirs. Fla. Lung Assn. (formerly Tb Assn.), 1949—; pres. Orange County Tb Assn., 1965; trustee Central Fla. Tb and Respiratory Disease, Assn., 1966—. Served with USAAF, 1942-45. Mem. Fla. Soc. Assn. Execs., Alpha Psi Omega. Democrat. Episcopalian (mem. Central Fla. deanery council 1973—). Home: 22 E Vanderbilt St Orlando FL 32804

BROWN, FARRELL BLENN, educator; b. Mount Ulla, N.C., Nov. 29, 1934; s. William Blenn and Helen (Karriker) B.; B.S., Lenoir-Rhyne Coll., 1957; M.S., U. Tenn. at Knoxville, 1959, Ph.D., 1962; m. Elma Ann Isenhour, Aug. 17, 1958; children—Russell Andrew, Sharon Elaine. Robert A. Welch postdoctoral fellow Tex. A. and M. U., College Station, 1962-63; mem. faculty dept. chemistry Clemson (S.C.) U., 1963—, asso. prof., 1967-73, prof., 1973—, asst. to grad. dean, 1972—. Mem. Am. Chem. Soc., Am. Cryptogram Assn., S.C. Acad. Sci., Sigma Xi. Home: 206 Willow St Clemson SC 29631

BROWN, FREDERICK RAYMOND, govt. ofcl.; b. Peoria, Ill., Feb. 15, 1912; s. Lyman Harrison and Mary Ann (Weber) B.; B.S. in Civil Engring., U. Ill., 1934; m. Louise Ferry, June 10, 1936; children—Sandra (Mrs. Thomas N. Swilley), Frederick Raymond, Roger Alan. Chief hydrodynamics br. Waterways Expt. Sta., Vicksburg, Miss., 1934-61, chief nuclear effects div., 1961-63, asst. tech. dir., 1963-69, tech. dir., 1969—. Chmn. Vicksburg City Planning Commn., 1963—. Recipient Meritorious Civilian Service award Dept. Army, 1947, 69, exceptional civilian service award, 1973. Registered profl. engr., Miss. Mem. Am. Soc. C.E., Nat. Soc. Profl. Engrs., Soc. Am. Mil. Engrs. Rotarian. Home: 105 Stonewall Rd Vicksburg MS 39180 Office: PO Box 631 Vicksburg MS 39180

BROWN, GAITHOR WRIGHT, JR., retail co. exec.; b. Chattanooga, June 9, 1926; s. Gaithor Wright and Mattie Sue (Lowry) B.; student U. Tenn., 1947, Tenn. Poly. Inst., 1948, Harvard Bus. Sch., 1965; m. Gloria Jean Collignon, June 11, 1948; children—Sharon Kathleen (Mrs. Walter Winfield Miller III), Gaithor Wright III. With Bondurant Bros., Knoxville, Tenn., 1948-51; with Free Service Tire Co., 1952—, exec. v.p., Johnson City, Tenn., 1971—. Served with USNR, 1944-46. Republican. Methodist. Home: 1607 Fairway Dr Johnson City TN 37601 Office: 126 Buffalo St Johnson City TN 37601

BROWN, HARLEY PROCTER, educator; b. Uniontown, Ala., Jan. 13, 1921; s. Harley Procter and Martha (McGinniss) B.; A.B., Miami (O.) U., 1942, A.M. (Miami U. fellow), 1942; Ph.D. (Ohio State U. fellow), Ohio State U., 1945; m. Laura Clifford Williams, June 1, 1942; 1 dau., Mary (Mrs. Gary Wayne Catron). Mem. faculty dept. zoology U. Okla., Norman, 1948—, asso. prof., 1952-62, prof., 1962—; vis. research prof. Ohio State U., Columbus, 1949. Active Last Frontier council Boy Scouts Am., 1949—. Mem. Miami Univ. Speakers Bur., Sigma Xi, Phi Beta Kappa, Delta Phi Alpha, Phi Eta Sigma, others. Democrat. Presbyn. (elder). Club: Cleveland County Bird. Author: Aquatic Dryopoid Beetles of the U.S., 1972. Editor zoology sect. Proc. Okla. Acad. Scis., 1960—. Contbr. articles to profl. jours. Home: 529 Dakota St Norman OK 73069 Office: 730 Van Vleet Oval Norman OK 73069

BROWN, HARVEY CHESTER, clergyman; b. Camp Hill, Ala., Oct. 30, 1892; s. Daniel Chester and Ella (Thompson) B.; A.B., Birmingham So. Coll., 1917, D.D., 1957; B.D., Emory U., 1920; Th.M., Drew U., 1923, Th.D., 1925; m. Angela Rayburn Hamilton, June 28, 1923; children—Harvey Chester, Angela. Ordained to ministry Methodist Ch., 1920; minister Methodist chs., Warrior, Ala., 1920-22, Vienna, N.J., 1922-25; Wesley Found. dir. and dean Sch. Religion, U. Tenn., 1927-32; head dept. religion Huntingdon Coll.,

Montgomery, Ala., 1932-33; dir. Meth. Student Movement, Gen. Bd. Christian Edn. M.E. Ch. South, 1933-40; dir. edn. Wesley Found., Meth. student movement, Meth. Ch., Nashville, 1940—; vis. prof. summers, Candler Sch. Theology, Emory U., Atlanta, 1942-52. Mem. World Student Christian Fedn., Nat. Student Christian Fedn., So. Soc. Philosophy, Theta Phi. Mason. Afounder Motive mag. Contbr. articles to profl. jours. Home: 115 Woodmont Blvd Nashville TN 37205

BROWN, HENRY, chem. co. exec.; b. Charleston, S.C., Jan. 25, 1909; s. Charles and Clara (Rashbaum) B.; student U. N.C., 1928-30; m. Juanita Beatrice Burnstein, July 14, 1946; children—Henry Stephen, Charles Roger. Asst. store mgr. Furchgott's Dept. Store, Charleston, 1930-36; asst. store mgr. Kline's Dept. Store, Atlanta, 1936-41; state sales mgr. Am. Beauty Products Co., Richmond, Va., 1946-47; mgr., partner Va. Jewelry Store, Richmond, 1947-49; sr. v.p. sales Momar, Inc., Atlanta, 1949—, also dir. Bd. dirs. YMCA, 1957; founder, bd. dirs. Atlanta chpt. Muscular Dystrophy Assn., nat. v.p., 1953-63. Served with AUS, 1942-46; ETO. Decorated Bronze Star medal. Named Salesman of Year, Momar, Inc., 1966; recipient Sales Exec. Trophy, 1972, Exec. Sales award of Quarter Century, 1972. Mem. Res. Officers Assn., Ret. Officers Assn., The Temple, Northside Bus. Assn. (dir. 1971, pres. 1972-73). Clubs: Sertoma (v.p. 1957), Standard, Fort McPherson Officers (Atlanta). Home: 4407 Jett Rd NW Atlanta GA 30327 Office: 1830 Ellsworth Dr NW Atlanta GA 30318

BROWN, HENRY EDWARD, JR., wholesale co. exec.; b. Bishopville, S.C., Dec. 20, 1935; s. Henry Edward and Lougenia (Mathis) B.; student The Citadel, 1967, Bapt. Coll. (Charleston, S.C.), 1970; m. Artie Winifred Beaver, Jan. 15, 1956; children—James Edward, Catherine Elizabeth, Debra Lynn. With Charleston Naval Shipyard, 1954-57; dir. data processing Piggly Wiggly Carolina, Charleston, S.C., 1958—, v.p. operations Low Country Investment Co., Charleston, 1968—, also dir. Tchr., Tech. Edn. Center, Berkeley-Dorchester-Charleston, 1966-67. Mem. Citizens Adv. Council N. Charleston, 1973-74; chmn. Grievance Task Force, 1973-74; pres. J.H. Berry Sch. P.T.A., 1971, 73-74. Mem. Data Processing Mgmt. Assn. (treas.). Baptist (deacon). Mason. Club: Civic. Home: 5200 Princeton St North Charleston SC 29406 Office: PO Box 10447 Charleston SC 29411

BROWN, HOYT WILLIAM, JR., engring. co. exec.; b. Brunswick, Ga., Apr. 8, 1923; s. Hoyt William and Frances Rebecca (Symons) B.; B.S., U.S. Mcht. Marine Acad., 1949; B.S. in Mech. Engring., U. Wis. 1949; m. Sylvia Joyce Dickerson, Oct. 26, 1963; children—Kim (Mrs. Mark F. Shogren), Hoyt W. III, Terry D., Kelly Lee, Stacey Lynn. With Combustion div. Combustion Engring., Inc., New Orleans, 1949—, dist. mgr. 1959—. Served with USNR, 1943-46. Registered profl. engr., La., Ala. Mem. Am. Soc. M.E. (chpt. v.p. Ala., Miss. 1959), Nat. Soc. Profl. Engrs., La. Engring. Soc. (state dir. 1969, pres. 1972-73), Am. Nuclear Soc. Home: 3759 Pin Oak St New Orleans LA 70114 Office: 505 K & B Plaza New Orleans LA 70130

BROWN, HYDER JOSEPH, JR., architect; b. Hillsboro, Tex., Oct. 16, 1925; s. Hyder Joseph and Rosalie (Wilkinson) B.; B.Arch., U. Tex., 1951. Cons. sch. architecture Tex. Edn. Agy., Austin, 1951-57; with Paderewski, Dean & Assos., architects, San Diego, 1957-62; architect partner Livingstone & Brown, La Jolla, Cal., 1962-67; project architect firm Jessen Assos., Inc. Architects and Planners, Austin, Tex., 1967-72, asso., dir. programming and devel., 1972—. Mem. adv. bd. Austin (Tex.) Pre-Sch. Hearing Center, 1955-56; mem. Council Ednl. Facility Planning, 1954—; mem. Planning and Zoning Commn., West Lake Hills, Tex., 1971-72, chmn., 1972-73. Trustee Woodall-Bowden Trusts 1 and 2; patron Laguna Gloria Art Museum, Austin. Served with USNR, 1943-46. Mem. Tex. Soc. Architects (mem. resolutions com. 1973), A.I.A. (chpt. chmn. commn. on edn. and research 1966; chmn. chpt. activities 1971, chpt. chmn. pub. affairs commn. 1972-73, pres.-elect chpt. 1974; recipient outstanding service award San Diego chpt. 1962; corporate mem.), Austin Symphony Assn., Tex. Fine Arts Soc. Episcopalian (lay reader). Contbr. to profl. jours. Prin. works include schs., pub. housing, residences, instns., apts., comml. bldgs. Home: 1512 Hardouin Av Austin TX 78703 Office: 700 Am Bank Tower Austin TX 78701

BROWN, ISAAC DALE, physician; b. Mosheim, Tenn., Jan. 26, 1915; s. Walter C. and Matilda (Hartman) B.; B.A., B.S., Carson-Newman Coll., 1937; M.D., U. Tenn., 1941; m. Kathryn Jones, June 14, 1942; children—Gale Ann (Mrs. Lynn Baumgartner), Dale. Intern, Nashville Gen. Hosp., 1942; practice medicine, Mosheim, 1943—; mem. staff Greeneville, Laughlin, Takoma hosps. Mem. Am. Acad. Family Physicians, A.M.A., World, So., Tenn., Greene County (pres. 1944-52) med. assns. Republican. Mason (32 deg., Shriner). Address: Box 38 Mosheim TN 37818

BROWN, J. QUANTIN, stockbroker; b. Balt.; LL.B., U. Denver; m. Dolores J. Brown; children—Mark J., Beverly J., Jonathan W. Buyer Martin Co., 1957-62; founder Logictron, Inc., electronics co.; chmn. bd. J. Brown Corp., Denver, 1960-70; prof. econs. and history Denver Community Coll., 1968-70; mgr. Sooner Securities, Inc., financial cons., mgmt. cons., 1970—. Bd. dirs. Tulsa Urban League, 1971—. Mem. Mayor's Com. for Econ. Planning and Manpower, Tulsa. Candidate for Colo. Ho. of Reps., 1968. Recipient citation Mayor of Denver, 1965; named Outstanding Citizen in Denver, 1969. Mem. Mensa, Nat. Assn. Securities Dealers. Author: The Black Sucker. Home: 1737 W Fairview St Tulsa OK 74127 Office: PO Box 6034 Tulsa OK 74106

BROWN, JAMES CURTISS, judge; b. Burkett, Tex., Oct. 4, 1921; s. Aubrey Murphy and Eva (Thate) B.; student Tarleton State U., 1938-40; LL.B. (James Lockhart Aubrey scholar), U. Tex. at Austin, 1943; m. Catherine Ann Davis, Jan. 27, 1948 (div. Apr. 1952); children—J. Curtiss Jr., Catherine Ann, William Aubrey; m. 2d, Lovice Constance Switzer, Aug. 11, 1960. Admitted to Tex. bar, 1943; asso. firm Baker, Botts, Andrews & Wharton, Houston, 1943-52; partner firm Brown, Kronzer, Abraham, Watkins & Steely, Houston, 1952-73; asso. justice 14th Ct. Civil Appeals, Houston, 1973—. Dir. Colonial Savs. Assn., Houston. Instr. S. Tex. Coll. Law, Houston, 1945-50, Sch. Law, U. Houston, 1950-52. Trustee Houston Legal Found., 1965-71, Tex. Bar Found., 1966-70. Fellow Internat. Soc. Barristers, Am. Coll. Trial Lawyers; mem. State Bar Tex. (chmn. bd. dirs. 1969-70), Order Coif, Phi Delta Phi, Sigma Nu Phi, Chancellors. Clubs: Century, Malacca, Forest (Houston). Editor-in-chief Tex. Law Rev., 1943. Home: 523 Bolton Pl Houston TX 77024 Office: 105 Civil Cts Bldg 301 Fannin St Houston TX 77002

BROWN, JAMES DOUGLAS, lawyer; b. Ozark, Ala., Feb. 14, 1912; s. W. A. and Pearl (Hicks) B.; student Southwestern U., 1929, Auburn U., 1930-32; LL.B., U. Ala., 1935; postgrad. Georgetown U., 1936; m. Kathryne Parker, Nov. 1, 1944; children—Kathryne (dec.), Patricia, Clementine. Admitted to Ala. bar, 1935, practiced in Athens, 1936-38, Ozark, 1938—; pres., dir. Ozark Broadcasting Corp., 1953—; pres., owner Douglas Brown Ins. Agy., Inc., owner Brown Real Estate Co.; pres. Brown Devel. Co., Enterprise, Ala.; owner Donnell Blvd. Shopping Center, Daleville, Ala.; dir. Comml. Bank of Ozark, Enterprise Motel Co., Inc., Frit Industries, Inc., Ozark. Chmn. Ala. Adv. Com. on Civil Rights, 1959-60, Dale County Hosp. Assn., Dale County Mental Retardation Bd. Mem. Ala. Senate, 1942-46; mayor of Ozark, 1948-60, 64-68; chmn. Pub. Bldg. Authority City of Ozark; mem. Utilities Bd. City Ozark. Bd. dirs. Army Aviation Museum Assn. Served from pvt. to sgt. USAAF, 1943-44. Recipient Most Outstanding Alumnus award U. Ala. Law Sch., 1971. Mem. Am., Ala. bar assns., ICC Practitioners, Law Sci. Acad., Am. Judicature Soc., Kappa Alpha, Phi Alpha Delta. Democrat. Presbyn. (deacon). Mason (Shriner), Rotarian. Clubs: Ozark Country; Dothan Country; Willow Oaks Country. Home: 737 E Broad St Ozark AL 36360 Office: 35 S Court Sq Ozark AL 36360

BROWN, JAMES HENRY, psychiatrist; b. Rossville, Ga., Dec. 27, 1923; s. Henry LaFayette and Madge (Blaylock) B.; student U. Chattanooga, 1942, DePauw U., 1943; M.D., Med. Coll. Ga., 1948; m. Carol Olson, Feb. 13, 1954; children—Diane Elizabeth, Thomas Walter III, James Henry, Jr. Intern, Erlanger Hosp., Chattanooga, 1948-49; resident Vanderbilt U. Hosp., Nashville, 1949-50, Inst. Living, Hartford, 1950-51, Bethesda (Md.) Naval Hosp., 1951-52, Neurol. Inst., Columbia, 1953-54; resident in psychoanalytic medicine Tulane U., New Orleans, 1954-56; practice medicine specializing in psychiatry, New Orleans, 1956—; mem. staff DePaul Hosp., pres. staff, 1962-63; mem. staff, chmn. dept. psychiatry So. Baptist Hosp.; asso. prof. Sch. Medicine, Tulane U., 1965—. Pres. I.J. Realty Co., Inc., New Orleans, 1958—. Served to lt. M.C., USNR, 1942-44, 51-53. Diplomate Am. Bd. Psychiatry and Neurology. Home: 370 Broadway St New Orleans LA 70118 Office: 2731 Napolean Av New Orleans LA 70115

BROWN, JAMES POPE, savs. and loan exec.; b. Hawkinsville, Ga., Sept. 1, 1911; s. Stephen William and Elizabeth Calhoun (Bivins) B.; diploma Ga. Mil. Coll., 1930; certificate Grad. Sch. Savs. and Loan, Ind. U., 1961; m. Josephine Sibley Jennings, June 17, 1939; 1 son, James Pope. With Rankin-Whitten Realty Co., Atlanta, 1937-41, Fulton Fed. Savs. & Loan Assn., Atlanta, 1947-60; v.p. advt. and pub. relations Atlanta Fed. Savs. & Loan Assn., 1960—. Tchr., Am. Savs. and Loan Inst., 1960-65. Mem. Atlanta Citizens Crime Com., 1958-61, Atlanta Civic Design Com., 1969-72; pres. Grand Jurors Assn. Fulton County, 1967; treas. Met. Atlanta Rapid Transit Authority, 1970-72. Served as lt. col. C.E., AUS, 1941-46. Mem. Am. Marketing Assn., Am. Legion, Savs. Instns. Marketing Soc. Am. Presbyn. (elder). Contbr. articles to profl. jours. Home: 33 Beverly Rd NE Atlanta GA 30309 Office: 20 Marietta St NW Atlanta GA 30303

BROWN, JAMES WINSOR, banker; b. Ford City, Pa., May 24, 1929; s. Winsor William and Almira (Callen) B.; B.B.A., U. Pitts., 1951, postgrad., 1952-58; postgrad. Stonier Grad. Sch. of Banking, Rutgers U., 1968; m. Gertrude Colwell, Feb. 3, 1951; children—Alan, Susan, David, Leanne. Asst. cashier, mgr. credit dept. Pitts. Nat. Bank, 1951-59; v.p. comml. loans Dania Bank, (Fla.), 1959-67; v.p. comml. loans Coral Ridge Nat. Bank, Ft. Lauderdale, 1967; exec. v.p., cashier Guaranty First Nat. Bank, 1967-71; pres., chmn. bd. S.E. Bank of Deerfield Beach, Fla., 1971—. Mem. Robert Morris Assos. Kiwanian. Club: Lighthouse Point (Fla.) Yacht and Tennis. Home: 1331 SE 14th Ct Deerfield Beach FL 33441 Office: 1007 South Federal Hwy Deerfield Beach FL 33441

BROWN, JESSE GLENN, hosp. adminstr.; b. Marshall County, Ala., July 15, 1930; s. John Henry and Mary Ethel (Womack) B.; A.A., Snead Coll., 1959; student Jacksonville State U., 1960-62; grad. sch. Community and Allied Health Resources U. Ala., 1972; m. Eloise Strickland, Apr. 19, 1953; children—Jesse Glenn, Terry Lynn. Mgr. jewelry store, 1953-55; adminstrv. asst. U.S. Army Res., Decatur, Ala., 1955-57, bus. mgr. Boaz (Ala.)-Albertville, 1957-62; adminstr. Arab (Ala.) Hosp., 1962—. Chmn. fund raising United Givers Fund, Arab, 1966-67, pres., 1968-69; publicity chmn. Marshall County chpt. A.R.C., 1968-69, chpt. bd. dirs., 1966-73; mem. adv. com. home health services Ala. Dept. Health, 1969—; chmn. adv. com. Ret. Sr. Vol. program, Marshall County, 1972—. Served with AUS, 1948-53. Mem. Ala. Hosp. Assn. (chmn. personnel practices com. 1968-70; chmn. profl. standards and services com. 1971), Northeast Ala. Hosp. Council (pres. 1966-67), Res. Officers Assn., Airborne Assn., Am. Coll. Hosp. Adminstrs., Ala. Assn. Hosp. Execs. Baptist (deacon, supt. Sunday sch. 1965-68). Mason. Home: 403 6th St Arab AL 35016 Office: 200 S Main St Arab AL 35016

BROWN, JOE JERALD, apparel products co. exec.; b. Dallas, Apr. 15, 1946; s. George Jerald and Julia Josephine (Haswell) B.; B.S. in Mech. Engring. So. Methodist U., 1969, M.B.A. (Univ. fellow), 1971; m. Mary Francine Rice, Nov. 24, 1968. Mech. engr. Tex. Instruments Co., Dallas, 1969-70; pres. Ripley Shirt Co., Dallas, 1971—. Campaign worker Heart Fund Drive, 1973, Del. to 8th Republic. Senatorial Dist. Conv., 1970. Mem. Nat. Fedn. Ind. Bus., Dallas C. of C., Tex. Soc. Profl. Engrs. (Jr.), Alpha Tau Omega (Thomas Arkle Clark award 1968), Sigma Tau, Pi Tau Sigma (pres. 1968-69). Methodist. Home: 3408 Stanford St Dallas TX 75225 Office: 1717 N Beckley St Dallas TX 75203

BROWN, JOHN CALVIN, banker; b. Goree, Tex., Nov. 30, 1930; s. Harvey Alexander and Annie Lee (West) Brown; student U. Tex., 1948, Tex. Wesleyan Coll., 1955-58; grad. Nat. Mortgage Sch., Ohio State U., 1967; m. Nelda Jo Hinkle, Apr. 22, 1950; children—Donna Ruth, Lindsey Paul. With Ft. Worth Nat. Bank, 1950-52, 54—, asst. cashier, 1962-64, mgr. real estate and mortgage loan dept., 1964—, asst. v.p., 1964-66, v.p., 1966, mem. bank discount com., 1966-72, mgr. comml. loan dept., 1972—, chmn. bank discount com., 1972—, head div. comml. banking, 1973—, mem. bank mgmt. com., 1973—, sr. v.p., 1973—. Mem. faculty Southwestern Grad. Sch. Banking, 1967-69. Chmn. West Side br. Ft. Worth YMCA; treas., bd. dirs. Tarrant County chpt. A.R.C., Panther Boys Club. Served with AUS, 1952-54. Mem. Nat. Assn. Homebuilders (dir. Ft. Worth chpt. 1970-71), Tex. Bankers Assn. (mortgage finance com. 1969), Tex., Ft. Worth mortgage bankers assns. Baptist (minister music 1959-72). Clubs: Petroleum, Shady Oaks Country, Century II (Ft. Worth). Home: 4116 Winding Way Fort Worth TX 76126 Office: 501 Throckmorton St Fort Worth TX 76101

BROWN, JOHN HALL, JR., architect; b. Houston, Tex., Dec. 27, 1937; s. John Hall and Hilda (Hardy) B.; B.Arch., Tex. A. and M. U., 1961; postgrad. Air Force Inst. Tech., 1961; m. Marna Lynn Johnson, Apr. 8, 1963; children—John Hardy, Daren Thomas. Constrn. supr. firm Brown & Keller, Richardson, Tex., 1964-68; partner firm Brown, Moore & Brown, Sherman, Tex., and Dallas, 1968-71, firm Brown & Brown, Dallas, 1971—. Dir. Laffette Resort, Inc., Gray Eagle, Minn.; partner Capital Syndications, Dallas. Served to 1st lt. USAF, 1961-64. Mem. A.I.A., Tex. Soc. Architects, Constrn. Specifications Inst. Presbyn. (deacon 1969-72). Toastmaster. Home: 808 Woodland Way Richardson TX 75080 Office: 13333 N Central Expressway Dallas TX 75231

BROWN, JOHN WESLEY, univ. dean, educator; b. Chgo., Dec. 2, 1925; s. Earl Jackson and Myrtle (Bailey) B.; B.S., Elmhurst Coll., 1950; M.S., U. Ill., 1953, Ph.D., 1956; m. Lois Joy Smith, Aug. 12, 1950; children—Suzanne, Janice, Paul. Tech. rep. E. I. DuPont de Nemours & Co., Inc., Wilmington, Del., 1956-57; asst. prof. biochemistry U. Louisville, 1957-63, asso. prof., 1963-67, curriculum dir., 1963-64, asst. dean, 1964-65, asso. dean Med. Sch., 1965-67, asst. dean Grad. Sch., 1967-68, prof. chemistry, 1969—, asso. dean Grad. Sch., 1972—. Served with inf. AUS, 1944-46. Decorated Purple Heart. Recipient Faculty Sci. Achievement award Ky. State Med. Assn., 1964. Mem. Am. Chem. Soc. Am. Soc. Biol. Chemists, A.A.A.S. Contbr. articles to sci. jours. Home: 1960 Meadowcreek Dr Louisville KY 40218

BROWN, KATHERINE TSANOFF (MRS. H. FLETCHER BROWN), educator. Mem. faculty art dept. Rice U., Houston, also dean undergrad. affairs. Recipient George R. Brown award superior teaching, 1970, also George R. Brown prize excellence in teaching. Address: Dept Art Rice U Houston TX 77001

BROWN, KENNETH HAROLD, appliance mfg. exec.; b. Cleveland, Tenn., May 31, 1914; s. Grover Cleveland and Lizzie (Harrison) B.; student Tulane U., 1933-35, McKenzie Bus. Coll., 1935-36; m. Miriam Palmer Ash, June 5, 1935; children—Kenneth Harrison, Rachel Burwell. Treas., Brown Stove Works, Inc., Cleveland, 1942-43, sec.-treas., 1943-61, exec. v.p., 1961-63, pres., 1963—; pres. Brown Realty Corp., Cleveland, 1956—; dir. Cleveland Nat. Bank, 1972—. Pres. Jr. Achievement Bradley County, Inc., 1967-68; pres. Cleveland Asso. Industries, 1970-72; pres. Cleveland Community Chest, 1959-60; pres. Tri-States Assn. for Cripples, 1958-59; mem. U. Tenn. Devel. Council, 1971—; mem. exec. bd. Cherokee council Boy Scouts Am. Mem. Cleveland Sch. Bd., 1950-61, chmn., 1957-59. Bd. dirs. Hosp. for Crippled Adults, Memphis, 1958-61; trustee Cleveland Day Sch., 1964—, treas., 1968—. Mem. Inst. Appliance Mfrs. (trustee 1945-53), Gas Appliance Mfrs. Assn. (dir. 1970-72), Alpha Tau Omega. Republican. Presbyn. (chmn. bd. deacons 1959-63). Rotarian (past dist. gov.), Elk (past exalted ruler). Clubs: Cleveland Golf and Country; Atlanta Athletic. Home: Annandale Park Cleveland TN 37311 Office: Carolina and 15th Sts Cleveland TN 37311

BROWN, KENNETH HARRISON, range mfg. co. exec.; b. Cleveland, Tenn., Mar. 15, 1941; s. Kenneth Harold and Miriam (Ash) B.; B. Indsl. Engring., Ga. Inst. Tech., 1964; certificate Exec. Devel. Program, U. Tenn., 1972; m. Barbara Lindon Kagey, June 15, 1963; children—Matthew Harrison, Louise Palmer. Safety dir., traffic mgr. Brown Stove Works, Inc., Cleveland, Tenn., 1963-64, sec., 1964—, also dir. Justice Peace Bradley County, 1970—. Mem. Bradley County Regional Planning Commn., 1972—. Treas. Bradley County Young Republican Club, 1971-72. Bd. dirs. March Dimes, Bradley County, 1969-72, Citizens Scholarship Found., 1970-72. Mem. Bradley County C. of C. Rep. Presbyn. (trustee, deacon). Elk (exalted ruler 1969-70), Rotarian (pres. local club 1973-74). Home: PO Box 325 Cleveland TN 37311 Office: PO Box 490 Cleveland TN 37311

BROWN, LOWELL ELMER, mill mgr.; b. Burns Fiat, Okla., July 2, 1936; s. Jesse Thomas and Buena (Carpenter) B.; grad. high sch.; m. Dorothy Jolene Simmons, Aug. 25, 1956; children—Lowell David, Joel Brett, Virginia Lyn. With Clinton Cotton Oil Mill (Okla.), 1956—, office mgr., 1965-69, mill mgr., 1969—. Bd. dirs. Okla. Cotton Research Found. Mem. Nat. Cotton Council (alt. del. 1970-72), Burns Flat Alumni Assn. (pres. 1970-72). Baptist. Lion. Home: 1426 Pine St Clinton OK 73601 Office: 200 E Frisco St Clinton OK 73601

BROWN, LYLE, justice Ark. Supreme Ct.; b., 1908; A.B., Henderson State Coll.; M.A., So. Meth. U. Admitted to Ark. bar, 1935; now asso. justice Ark. Supreme Ct., Little Rock. Office: Ark Supreme Ct Little Rock AR 72201

BROWN, MALCOLM HENDRICKS, lawyer; b. Fort Worth, Tex., July 7, 1903; s. J. Malcolm and Minerva (Hendricks) B.; LL.B., U. Tex., 1926; m. Ruth Bartels Stovall, June 1, 1929; children—Charlotte B. (Mrs. Charlotte Brown Carter), Mary Lou (Mrs. W.J. Rapson Jr.). Admitted to Tex. bar, 1926; sr. partner firm Brown, Crowley, Simon & Peebles and predecessor firms, Fort Worth, 1945—; asst. dist. atty. Tarrant County, Tex., 1929-30, 1st asst. dist. atty., 1939-44. Fellow Tex. Bar Found.; mem. Am., Tex., Fort Worth-Tarrant County (recipient Blackstone award 1972) bar assns., Tex. Def. Attys. Assn. (dir. 1972). Home: 1363 Roaring Springs Rd Fort Worth TX 76114 Office: 1200 Continental National Bank Bldg Fort Worth TX 76102

BROWN, MARCUS GORDON, ret. educator; b. Miami, Fla., Mar. 14, 1908; s. David Chappel and Lula (Bell) B.; A.B., Washington Missionary Coll., 1927; M.A., Emory U., 1936; Docteur es Lettres, U. Dijon (France), 1939; Doctor en Filosofia y Letras, U. Madrid (Spain), 1940. Tchr. fgn. langs. high sch., Jacksonville, Fla., 1927-30, Boys' High Sch., Atlanta, 1930-36; instr. English and French, U. Fla., 1936-38; asst. prof. fgn. langs. Ga. Inst. Tech., Atlanta, 1940-42, asso. prof., 1942-43, prof., 1943-50; specialist U.S. Office Edn., 1944-46; cultural attache Am. embassy, Bogota, Colombia, 1950-52, Rio de Janeiro, Brazil, 1952-54; asst. chancellor Univ. System Ga., Atlanta, 1954-57; fgn. lang. coordinator Ga. State Dept. Edn., Atlanta, 1957-62; asso. prof. Romance langs. Memphis State U., 1963-67, prof., 1967-71, prof. modern langs., 1971-73. Recipient Anchieta medal Municipality of Rio de Janeiro, Brazil, 1954; medals for excellence in French lang. and lit. French Govt., 1936. Mem. Sociedad Bolivariana de Colombia, Am. Assn. Tchrs. Spanish and Portuguese, Am. Assn. Tchrs. French, Am. Assn. Tchrs. Italian, Am. Assn. Tchrs. German, Am. Assn. U. Profs., Modern Lang. Assn. Am., South Central Modern Lang. Assn., Tenn. Edn. Assn., Tenn. Philol. Assn. Author: Les Idees Politiques et Religieuses de Stendhal, 1939; La Vida y Las Novelas de Emilia Pardo Bazan, 1940; (with J. Russell) Bibliography for the Teaching of English to Foreigners, 1947. Address: 4182 Faronia Rd Apt 6 Memphis TN 38116

BROWN, MARK, educator; b. Miami, Fla., Dec. 31, 1925; s. Leo and May (Marmur) B.; B.S., U. Miami, 1946; M.D., Vanderbilt U., 1950; m. Julia Dudley Hudson, Jan. 24, 1953; children—Karen Lynn, Lisa Ann, Leslie Carol. Intern, Vanderbilt U. Hosp., 1950-51; asst. resident surgeon U. Miami Sch. Medicine, 1955-56; resident radiology Mallinckrodt Inst. Radiology, Barnes Hosp.-Washington U. Med. Center, St. Louis, 1956-59; research asso. anatomy Vanderbilt U. Sch. Medicine, Nashville, 1951-52; instr. radiology Washington U. Sch. Medicine, St. Louis, 1959-60; mem. faculty Med. Coll. Ga., Augusta, 1963—, prof. radiology, 1963—, chmn. dept. radiology, 1963—, chief sect. nuclear medicine, 1971—; cons. radiology VA Hosp., Augusta, Ga., 1963—, Eisenhower Med. Center, Fort Gordon, Ga., 1964—, Gracewood (Ga.) State Hosp., 1964—; adj. prof. Ga. Tech., Atlanta, 1968—. Trustee Am. Registry of Radiol. Technologists, 1969—. Served to capt. USAF, 1953-55. Diplomate Am. Bd. Radiology, Am. Bd. Nuclear Medicine. Fellow Am. Coll. Radiology. Home: 809 Windsor Ct Augusta GA 30904 Office: Nuclear Medicine Sect Med Coll Ga Augusta GA 30902

BROWN, MARTIN LEVI, bank exec.; b. Lexington, S.C., June 10, 1928; s. Martin Levi and Regenner Gertrude (Shumpert) B.; B.S., Newberry Coll., 1949; certificate Dale Carnegie Inst., 1953, Am. Inst. Banking, 1954, La. State U., 1961, Harvard, 1971; m. Mary Lenora Long, Dec. 2, 1969; 1 dau., Mary Jo. With Comml. Bank & Trust, Columbia, S.C., 1950-54; sr. examiner S.C. State Bd. of Bank Control, Columbia, 1954-70; with First Peoples Nat. Bank of S.C., Hartsville, 1970—, pres., 1974—, also dir. Pres., chmn. bd., chief operating officer Motco, Inc., Hartsville, 1974—; mgr. Brown Bros. Enterprises, Columbia, 1954—. Dir. Hartsville Indsl. Bd., 1972; chmn. pub. service com. United Way, 1972, dir., 1973-75; mem. adv. council Boy Scouts Am., 1973-74. Mem. Hartsville C. of C. (pres. 1973). Methodist (chmn. bd. trustees 1973). Club: Civitan (pres. 1973, lt. gov. 1974) (Hartsville). Moose. Home: 109 Yaupon Dr Hartsville SC 29550 Office: PO Box 40 Hartsville SC 29550

BROWN, NANCY POLLARD, educator; b. Newton Abbot, Devon, Eng., Mar. 16, 1921; d. Nicholas Alfred and Mary (Panniers) Grose; B.A., U. London (Eng.), 1942, M.A., 1948; m. Samuel Ernest Brown, June 30, 1952. Came to U.S., 1952. Tchr. English, The Ladies' Coll., Cheltenham, Eng., 1948-50; instr. English, Trinity Coll., Washington, 1959, asst. prof., 1960-62, asso. prof., 1962-66, prof., 1966—, chmn. dept. English, 1968-70, 73—. Served to capt. Brit. Army, 1942-46. Commonwealth Fund fellow, Yale, 1950-51; Folger Shakespeare Library fellow, summer 1954, summer-fall 1955; E. Harris Harbison fellow Danforth Found., 1966; Huntington Library summer fellow, 1971; Am. Council Learned Socs. grantee, 1971-72. Mem. Modern Lang. Assn., Am. Assn. U. Profs., Shakespeare Assn., Renaissance Soc. Am., Amici Thomae Mori, Phi Beta Kappa. Editor: (with James H. McDonald) The Poems of Robert Southwell, 1967; Robert Southwell, Two Letters and Short Rules of a Good Life, 1973. Contbr. articles to profl. jours. Home: 12 Green Knolls Pl Greenbelt MD 20770 Office: Dept English Trinity Coll Washington DC 20017

BROWN, RAY STEPHEN, constrn. co. exec.; b. Roanoke, Va., July 7, 1942; s. Ray Calvin and Willie Edna (Lawhorn) B.; A.A., Roanoke Tech. Inst., 1964; B.S., Va. Poly. Inst., 1968; m. Ann Graves Cundiff, June 26, 1965; children—Stephanie Rae, Stacie. Mgr., Drapers Meadow Apts., Blacksburg, Va., 1964-68; sec.-treas. W. E. Cundiff Co., Inc., Vinton, Va., 1968—, Hollins Hardware Co., Inc., 1968—, v.p. Bowles-Cundiff, Inc., Vero Beach, Fla., 1971—. Mem. Local Selective Service Bd., 1972. Mem. Roanoke County Democratic Com., 1969-72. Bd. dirs. Roanoke Valley Apt. Council, 1970; bd. dirs., pres. Vinton (Va.) Dogwood Festival. Mem. Roanoke Valley Homebuilders Assn., Southampton Homeowners Assn., Inc. (dir. 1970), Vinton Jr. C. of C. Methodist. Mason (Shriner), Moose, Lion. Club: Vico Investment (Vinton, Va.). Home: 714 Dillon Dr Vinton VA 24179 Office: 118 S Pollard St Vinton VA 24179

BROWN, RAYMOND JOSEPH, financial service co. exec.; b. Burlington, Vt., May 10, 1923; s. John Francis and Elizabeth (Lovejoy) B.; student U.S. Govt. Insts., U. Vienna, 1947-48, 53-54; m. Judith Laszlo, May 20, 1948; children—Gloria C., Raymond P., Michael S., Leslie Ann. Spl. agt. fgn. service U.S. Dept. Army, 1945-50, CIA, 1950-53 Dept. state, 1953-58; with Washington (D.C.) Planning Corp., 1958-60; exec. v.p., gen. sales mgr. Registered Funds, Inc., Charlotte, N.C., 1960-65; sr. v.p. Financial Service Corp., Atlanta, Ga., 1965-71; pres. B & S Financial Services, Inc., Charlotte, 1971—. Served with AUS, 1942-46. Mem. Internat. Assn. Financial Planners. Club: Carmel Country (Charlotte, N.C.). Contbr. articles to profl. pubs. Home: 2330 Thornridge Rd Charlotte NC 28211 Office: 4108 Park Rd Charlotte NC 28209

BROWN, RICHARD CHRISTOPHER, physician; b. Gainesville, Fla., Jan. 16, 1932; s. Joseph Pell and Mildred (Smith) B.; A.B., Western Res. U., 1953; M.D., U. Fla., 1962; M.P.H., U. Cal. at Berkeley, 1967; m. Linda Jeanne Dickinson, July 2, 1960; children—Douglas Randolph, Jennifer Anne. Intern, Virginia Mason Hosp., Seattle, 1962-63; resident VA Hosp., Portland, Ore., 1964-66; practice medicine specializing in geriatrics and gen. medicine, Clearwater, Fla., 1968—; mem. staff Morton Plant Hosp., Clearwater. Epidemiology cons. USPHS for Navajo Indian Reservation, 1967-68; instr. dept. preventive medicine U. Okla. Med. Center, 1967-68. Served with AUS, 1954-56. Mem. Am. Pub. Health Assn., Fla. Med. Assn., Fla. Soc. Preventive Medicine (sec.-treas. 1971-72; pres. 1974), Delta Tau Delta. Home: 415 Jasmine Way Clearwater FL 33516 Office: 1887 W Bay Dr Largo FL 33540

BROWN, RICHARD FARGO, found. exec.; b. N.Y.C., Sept. 20, 1916; s. Percy Melville and Hazel (Wyatte) B.; A.B., Bucknell U., 1940; postgrad. N.Y. U., 1940-42; M.A., Harvard, 1948, Ph.D., 1952; m. Polly Story, Dec. 19, 1941; 1 son, Michael Fargo; m. 2d, Jane Hoag, 1968; children—Richard B., Tracy E.M. Teaching fellow Harvard, 1947-49, vis. prof. fine arts, 1954; research scholar, lectr. Frick Collection, N.Y.C., 1949-54; chief curator Los Angeles County Mus., 1955-62; dir. Los Angeles County Mus. Art, 1962-66, also trustee; head dept. art County Los Angeles, 1961-66; dir. Kimbell Art Found., Ft. Worth, 1966—. Trustee Mus. Western Art, Ft. Worth. Mem. Cal. Arts Commn. Served with USNR, 1942-46. Decorated Order Arts and Letters (France). Bacon-Rich travelling fellow Harvard, 1949. Mem. Coll. Art Assn. Am. (pres., dir.), Am. Assn. Art Mus. Dirs. (sec.-treas, exec. com., pres. 1970-71), Am. Assn. Museums (council), Western Assn. Museums (pres.), Nat. Council on Arts, Phi Beta Kappa. Home: 4001 Edgehill Rd Fort Worth TX 76116 Office: Kimbell Art Museum Fort Worth TX 76107

BROWN, ROBERT KEVIN, real estate cons.; b. Teaneck, N.J., July 3, 1930; s. Walter Lydecker and Elizabeth Rose (Eagan) B.; B.S., Johns Hopkins, 1952; M.A., U. Pitts., 1954, Ph.D., 1958; m. Joanne Lee Pople, Aug. 16, 1952; children—Robert Kevin, Joanne Lee. Prof., Ga. State U., Atlanta, 1956-67, chmn. dept. real estate and urban affairs, 1956-67; prof. real estate U. S.C., Columbia, 1967-69; prof. U. Pitts., 1969, asso. dean grad. sch. bus., 1969; v.p. Lyles Bissett Carlisle & Wof, Inc., Columbia, S.C., 1970-73, dir. research, 1970-73; pres. Robert Kevin Brown Assos., Columbia, 1973—. Pres., Research Inc., Atlanta, 1960—; chmn. bd. dirs., Foster & Burton Co., Atlanta, 1967—, dir. Roy D. Warren Co., Atlanta, 1962—. Mem. Forward Atlanta Com. of 100, 1960-66; pres. Ga. Urban Design Com., 1965-67. Mem. Mortgage Bankers Assn. (fellow at Stanford U. 1966), Atlanta Jr. C. of C. (named Outstanding Young Man in Edn. 1966), Am. Inst. Planners, Soc. Real Estate Appraisers, Columbia Bd. Realtors, Am. Real Estate and Urban Econs. Assn., Real Estate Edn. Found. (dir. 1960—), Lambda Alpha, Omicron Delta Epsilon, Delta Sigma Pi, Alpha Epsilon Pi. Author: Public Housing in Action, 1958; Public Housing Progam in the U.S., 1960; Real Estate Primer, 1960; The Ideal City, 1964; Real Estate Economics, 1965; Essentials of Real Estate, 1969; A Primer on Real Estate Development, 1972. Editor for McGraw-Hill, 1964-68, Prentice-Hall, 1965-73, Houghton-Mifflin Co., 1965-73. Contbr. articles to profl. jours. Home: 3454 Northshore Rd Columbia SC 29206 Office: Forest Plaza 5115 Forest Dr Columbia SC 29206

BROWN, ROBERT THOMAS, textile co. exec.; b. Paterson, N.J., July 16, 1929; s. Robert Power and Elizabeth (Nino) B.; B.S., Phila. Textile Inst., 1951; m. Helen Patricia Wilson, Apr. 11, 1953; children—Robert, Thomas, Patricia, Mary, Barbara, Margaret, Joan. Asst. supt. weaving Hill-Brown, Clifton, N.J., 1951-53; mfg. supt. Celanese Corp., Narrows, Va., 1953-67; with Cone Mills Corp., Greensboro, N.C. and Whitmire, S.C., 1967—, asst. to dir. consumer product mfg., 1967, staff asst. to pres., 1968, gen. mgr. Cone Knits Plant, 1969—. Bd. dirs. Newberry County United Fund. Mem. Am. Assn. Textile Tech. Roman Catholic. K.C. Home: 2105 Woodland Way Newberry SC 29108 Office: PO Box 31 Whitmire SC 29178

BROWN, ROBERT WADE, engring. exec.; b. Dallas, June 2, 1933; s. Jones Lemoyne and Blanche (Webb) B.; B.A., North Tex. State Coll., 1955, M.S., 1955; m. Nelva Mozelle Rawson, July 2, 1954; children—Robert Lemoyne, Cindy, Candy, Cathy. Student instr., grad. tutor North Tex. State Coll., 1951-55; process analyst Temco, Grand Prairie, Tex., 1955-56; research chemist Western Co., Ft. Worth, 1956-59, chem. engring. group supr., 1959-60, research supr., 1960-63; mgr. indsl. div. of Westco Research div. Western Co. N.A., 1963-64; pres., gen. mgr. BPR Constrn. & Engring. Inc., Dallas, 1964-71; pres., chmn. Webb Properties, Inc., 1968—; chmn. bd. Eddies' Pit Barbecue, Inc., 1966-71; pres., chmn. Brown Found. Repair & Cons., Inc., 1971—; pres., chmn. Brown Fence Installation, Inc., 1973—; partner Brown Bag Restaurant, 1974—. Instr. Odessa (Tex.) Jr. Coll., 1958-59, Kilgore Coll., API Sch. Prodn. Tech., 1960-64. Mem. Soc. Petroleum Engrs. Am. Inst. Mining Metall. and Petroleum Engrs., Am. Chem. Soc., Am. Soc. C.E., Alpha Chi Sigma. Contbr. to profl. publs. Patentee in field. Home: 7605 Meadowhaven Dallas TX 75240 Office: 1907 Rhome St Dallas TX 75229

BROWN, ROBERT WILSON, JR., ednl. adminstr.; b. Cordele, Ga., Sept. 18, 1922; s. Robert Wilson and Carolyn (Van Devender) B.; B.A. in Physics, Oklahoma City U., 1958, M.A.T., 1970; m. Ann Rorem, Dec. 31, 1966; children—Sara Watts, Ronald A. With FAA Acad., Oklahoma City, 1951—, chief data processing sect., 1974—. Cons., adviser Civil Aviation Dept., Argentina, 1961-62. Served with USNR, 1944-46. Registered profl. engr., Okla. Mem. I.E.E.E. (sr.). Home: 12001 Quail Creek Rd Oklahoma City OK 73120

BROWN, RODGER ALAN, research meteorolgist; b. Ellicottville, N.Y., Mar. 24, 1937; s. Ellsworth LeRoy and Gladys Lucille (Brown) B.; B.S., Antioch Coll., 1960; M.S., U. Chgo., 1962; postgrad. U. Chgo., 1962-65, U. Okla., 1971—; m. Diane Priscilla McLeod, June 27, 1959; children—Christopher, Elizabeth, Katherine. Weather observer Mt. Washington Obs., Gorham, N.H., 1955-56, Blue Hill Meteorol. Obs., Harvard, 1956; sci. aide U.S. Weather Bur., Washington, 1957, observer, Little Am. V., Antarctica, 1957-59; research asst. U. Chgo., 1960-65; research meteorologist Cornell Aero. Lab., Buffalo, 1965-70, Environmental Sci. Services Adminstrn., Wave Propagation Lab., Boulder, Colo., 1970, Nat. Oceanic and Atmospheric Adminstrn., Nat. Severe Storms Lab., Norman, Okla., 1970—. Antioch Coll. Alumni sch. rep.; troop instnl. rep., dist. com. mem. Boy Scouts Am. Mem. Am., Canadian, Royal meteorol. socs., Meteorol. Soc. Japan, Am. Geophys. Union, Sigma Xi. Contbr. articles to profl. jours. Home: 2232 Crestmont St Norman OK 73069 Office: 1313 Halley Circle Norman OK 73069

BROWN, RODGERS N., food chain exec.; b. Columbia, Tenn., Jan. 3, 1911; s. William Albert and Bessie Belle Brown; grad. Inst. Mgmt., Northwestern U.; m. Mary Elizabeth Cook, Apr. 1, 1934; children—Mary Elizabeth (Mrs. James B. Green), Patricia Diane (Mrs. Louis P. Mattis), Deborah Cook Hill. With Kroger Co., 1928-57, v.p., dir. subsidiary Wesco Foods Co., 1951-57; pres., dir. Mohican Co., 1957-59; v.p., dir. Nat. Food Stores La., Inc., 1961—; v.p. Nat. Tea Co., 1965—, regional v.p., 1967-69. Active local Community Chest, 1950, 59, 60, 64. Home: 45 Farnham Pl Metairie LA 70005

BROWN, ROGER HENRY, hwy. constrn. co. exec.; b. Helena, Ga., Nov. 22, 1921; s. William Sloan and Daisy (Blann) B.; B.C.E., Ga. Inst. Tech., 1952; m. Carolyn Moore, June 28, 1952; 1 son, Roger Henry. Hwy. constrn. engr. Ga. Hwy. Dept., 1952-62; pres. Southeastern Hwy. Constrn. Co., Gainesville, Ga., 1962—. Vice chmn. Hall County Devel. Authority, 1971; mem. exec. bd. Boy Scouts Am., 1971. Served with USNR, 1942-45. Registered profl. engr., Ga. Fellow Am. Soc. C.E.; mem. Nat. Soc. Profl. Engrs., Ga. Hwy. Contractors Assn. (pres.), Atlanta C. of C. (dir.), Nat. Alumni Ga. Inst. Tech. (trustee), V.F.W., Am. Legion, Sigma Nu. Episcopalian. Elk. Club: Chattahooches Country (pres.). Home: 3501 Edgewood Circle Gainesville GA 30501

BROWN, RUTH CUNNINGHAM (MRS. WILLIAM RUSSELL BROWN), club woman; b. Brooksville, Miss., Jan. 6, 1914; d. George William and Ruth (Hambrick) Cunningham; student Sophie Newcombe Coll., 1933-34, U. Tex., 1934-36; m. William Russell Brown, Apr. 19, 1941; children—Betsy (Mrs. Thomas M. Smith III), Virginia (Mrs. Fred E. Riddle, Jr.), Russell. Bd. dirs. Houston Community Council, 1962-63, mem. women's aux. Houston Bar Assn., 1956; bd. dirs., horticulture chmn. Garden Club of Houston, 1955-57; bd. visitors Sullins Coll., Bristol, Va., 1966-67, 69—. Mem. D.A.R. (dir. John-McKnitt chpt. 1963), Kappa Kappa Gamma (v.p. Houston alumnae assn. 1961). Republican. Episcopalian. Clubs: Houston, Houston Country. Address: 5816 Bayou Glen Rd Houston TX 77027

BROWN, S. SPENCER NEVILLE, banker; b. Meridian, Miss., Dec. 29, 1920; s. Stanton and Maria F. (Neville) B.; B.B.A., Baylor U., 1942; m. Margaret Cannon Boyce, Mar. 31, 1951; children—Spencer, Jr., Margaret, Maria Stanton, Stanton Boyce. With Exporters & Traders Compress &Warehouse Co., Waco, Tex., 1946—, pres., chief exec. officer, 1959—; chmn. bd., chief exec. officer First Nat. Bank, Temple, Tex., 1970—; chmn. bd., chief exec. office Superior Tech Mark, Dallas, 1967—; pres. Nat. Diversified, Waco, Tex., 1947—; dir. Rogers Delinted Cottonseed Co., Waco. Pres. United Fund, 1963-64; gen. chmn. Providence Hosp. Drive, Waco, 1964-65. Trustee Episcopal Theol. Sem. Southwest, 1954, Woodberry Forest Sch., 1961-67; mem. exec. com. bd. trustees Kings Daus. Hosp., 1970—. Served with AUS, 1942-46; PTO. Mem. Nat. Cotton Compress and Cotton Warehouse Assn. (pres. 1960-61, dir. 1953-70), Waco C. of C. (dir. 1952-54, 69-71), Waco Library Assn. Episcopalian (sr. warden 1953). Rotarian (pres. 1970-71). Author: Christian Answers to Teenage Sex Questions, 1970. Home: 2620 MacArthur Dr Waco TX 76708 Office: PO Drawer 1339 Waco TX 76703

BROWN, SAMUEL LOVITT, economist; b. Topeka, Feb. 8, 1915; s. Ira William and Ruth (Lovitt) B.; Ph.B., Rockhurst Coll., 1936; M.A., Georgetown U., 1939, Ph.D., 1951; m. Martha Murray, June 15, 1946; children—Michael, Christopher, Stephen, Timothy. Instr., Coll. Arts and Scis. Georgetown U., 1947-50, asst. prof., 1950-51, lectr., 1962—; economist Chrysler Corp., Detroit, 1951-57; sr. staff mem. Council Econ. Advisers, Exec. Office Pres., Washington, 1957-61; sr. econ. statistician Bur. Census, 1961-64; research economist, statistician CAB, Washington, 1964-73, asst. dir. Bur. Accounts and Statistics, 1973—. Mem. Am. Statis. Assn. (past mem. council), Am. Econ. Assn. Roman Catholic. K.C. (4 deg.). Author: Price Variation in New Houses, 1964; The Demand for Air Travel, 1968. Home: 1525 44th St Washington DC 20007 Office: 1825 Connecticut Av Washington DC 20428

BROWN, SARAH COLE (MRS. STERLING F. BROWN), librarian; b. Conway, Ark.; d. Russell T. and Mary (Craig) Cole; B.A., Hendrix Coll., 1934; B.S. in Library Sci., U. Ill., 1939; m. Sterling F. Brown, Oct. 25, 1941 (dec. Sept. 1970); 1 son, Sterling Russell. Asst. librarian Ala. Coll., 1939-41, Air Corps Tactical Sch., 1941-43; cataloger, asso. librarian U. Ala. Med. Center, 1949-55, librarian, 1955—, now dir. Lister Hill Library Health Scis., also prof. library sci. Chmn. liaison com. Nat. Library Medicine-Med. Library Assn. Mem. Med. Library Assn. (dir.; pres. 1973-74), Spl. Libraries Assn., Am. Assn. Med. Colls., Am. Assn. Dental Schs. (chmn. sect. learning resources 1970-71), Am. Assn. History Medicine, Am. Acad. Dental History, Am., Ala. (pres. 1969-70) library assns. Home: 2100 Mountain View Dr Birmingham AL 35216 Office: Lister Hill Library of Health Scis U Ala Univ Station Birmingham AL 35294

BROWN, SCOTT NEWTON, real estate, ins. cons.; b. Chattanooga, May 3, 1909; s. C. Victor and Catherine (Colburn) B.; student Davidson Coll., 1926-28; B.S. in Commerce, U. Tenn., 1930; student Am. Inst. Banking, 1931; spl. courses Am. Inst. Real Estate Appraisers, 1947, 68; grad. Law Sch., LaSalle Extension U.; m. Margaret Frierson Williamson, Dec. 2, 1939; children—Scott Newton, George W. Clk., Provident Life & Accident Ins. Co., 1930-31, Hamilton Nat. Bank, 1931-32; with Peerless Woolen Mills, 1932-33; property mgr. C. V. Brown & Bro., 1933-39; pres. Real Estate Mgmt., Inc., 1939-62, 1st Trust Co., 1950-62, Glenwood Park Co., 1951-62, Chattanooga Realty Co., 1940-62, Signal Properties, Inc., 1961—, Scott N. Brown Co. Real estate commr. State of Tenn., 1959-62. Vice chmn. City Planning Commn., 1940-42; dir. Chattanooga Safety Council, 1950-51; commr. Walden's Ridge Utility Dist., 1948-53, Chattanooga-Hamilton County Hist. Commn., 1953. Trustee, sec. McCallie Sch. Alumni Endowment Fund, Inc. Mem. Am. Finance Assn., Nat. Assn. Real Estate Appraisers, Nat. Apt. Assn., Chattanooga Bd. Realtors (pres. 1948, 62), Chattanooga C. of C. (pres. 1958), Insurors of Chattanooga (pres. 1949), Delta Sigma Pi, Pi Kappa Phi. Presbyn. (past elder). Lion (past sec. Chattanooga). Home: 401 Crewdson St Chattanooga TN 37405 Office: James Bldg Chattanooga TN 37402

BROWN, STANLEY WINFORD, dentist; b. Mexico, Mo., Nov. 11, 1913; s. Arthur Merritt and Callie Braxton (Gritton) B.; student Central Coll., Fayette, Mo., 1929-30; D.D.S., Washington U., 1934; postgrad. U.S. Naval Dental Sch., 1950, Mayo Found., 1945; m. Dorus Louise Moser, July 14, 1935 (div. Dec. 1968); children—David Arthur, Stanley Mason. Individual practice dentistry, Jefferson City, Mo., 1934-36; Jacksonville Beaches, Fla., 1959-68, Sarasota, 1968-69, Jacksonville, 1969—. Mem. Neptune Beach (Fla.) Zoning Bd. Appeals, 1967. Served to capt. USN, 1936-59. Recipient Alumni award Washington U. Dental Sch., 1934. Mem. Am., Fla., Northeast dental assns., Jacksonville Dental Soc., Navy League, Omicron Kappa Upsilon, Delta Sigma Delta. Episcopalian. Mason. Clubs: Ponte Vedra (Fla.); Selva Marina (Atlantic Beach, Fla.). Home: 8105 Jamaica Rd North Jacksonville FL 32216 Office: 3263 Southside Blvd Jacksonville FL 32216

BROWN, THOMAS AUGUSTINE, lawyer; b. Galveston, Tex., Oct. 10, 1932; s. Thomas Augustine and Louise Katherine (Mayfield) B.; A.A., Alvin Jr. Coll., 1951; B.A., U. Tex., 1953, J.D. with honors, 1957; m. Carolyn Janice Heasley, June 12, 1959; children—Thomas Reed, Frank Heasley, Christopher Mayfield. Admitted to Tex. bar, 1957, since practiced in Houston; asso. firm Fulbright, Crooker, Freeman, Bates & Jaworski, 1957-67; mem. firm Brown & Sims, 1967-70, Brown & Teed, 1970—. Served with USNR, 1953-55. Mem. Am., Tex., Houston bar assns., Maritime Law Assn. U.S., Assn. Average Adjusters U.S., Houston Mariners Club (skipper 1969), Phi Delta Phi (historian Roberts Inn 1957). Republican. Episcopalian. Club: Houston Propeller (legislative com. chmn. 1966). Home: 5218 Green Tree St Houston TX 77027 Office: 2323 Caroline St Houston TX 77004

BROWN, TOULMIN HUNTER, newspaper exec.; b. New Orleans, Sept. 9, 1925; s. Edmund Graves and Esther (Ewing) B.; student La. State U., 1946-47, Tulane U., 1947-48, Soule Bus. Coll., 1948; m. Cynthia Ann Parker, Oct. 27, 1954; children—Toulmin Hunter, Walter Parker, Alexander Pike. With Time Pub. Co., Ltd., Shreveport, La., 1950—, v.p., 1968—, also dir. Bd. dirs. Shreveport Symphony Soc., 1965-69. Served with USAAF, 1944-46. Decorated Air medal with 3 clusters. Mem. Air Force Assn. (La. pres. 1970-71). Clubs: Shreveport Country, Shreveport, Petroleum. Home: 6931 East Ridge Dr Shreveport LA 71106 Office: 222 Lake St Shreveport LA 71102

BROWN, WALTER LEE, educator, historian; b. Gatesville, Tex., June 13, 1924; s. Franklin Jeremiah and Alice Belle (Berry) B.; B.A., Tex. A. and M. Coll., 1949; M.A., U. Tex., 1950, Ph.D., 1955; m. Jane Eleanor Richart, Aug. 11, 1950; children—Michael Morgan, Janet Lee (dec.), Phillip Richart. Tchr. history Pampa (Tex.) High Sch., 1950-51; mem. faculty U. Ark., 1954—, prof. history, 1967—. Mem. Ark. Pub. Records Law Study Com., 1969-71. Mem. Fayetteville City Planning Commn., 1967-73; mem. Washington County Democratic Central Com., 1964—. Served with USAAF, 1943-46. Mem. Ark. Hist. Assn. (sec.-treas. 1955—, editor quar. 1958—, J. Howard Stebbins prize 1956), Am., So. hist. assns., Orgn. Am. Historians. Episcopalian (vestry 1966-68). Mason. Author: Our Arkansas, 3d edit., 1969; Teacher's Guidebook: Our Arkansas, 1968. Home: 1138 N Vandeventer St Fayetteville AR 72701 Office: History Dept U Ark Fayetteville AR 72701

BROWN, WALTER LOUIS, educator; b. Elmira, N.Y., July 8, 1919; s. Louis H. and Bertha A. (Kowalska) B.; B.S. in Chemistry, W.Va. Wesleyan U., 1941; postgrad. Ithaca Coll., 1951, Cornell U., 1951, Buffalo U., 1968, U. S.C., 1969; M.S. in Edn., Ind. U., 1953, Ed.D., 1956; m. Gene Meek, Mar. 27, 1943; children—David Meek, Carol Gene. Engr. Bendix Co., 1941; research chemist Corning Glass Corp. (N.Y.), 1941-43; research asso. Ind. U., Bloomington, 1953-65; prof. East Tex. U., Commerce, 1956-58; prof., head media center Minn. State Coll., Moorhead, 1958-65; prof. asso. acad. dean W.Va. Wesleyan U., Buckhannon, 1965-71; prof. Ga. So. Coll., Statesboro, 1971—, head instructional media center, 1971—. Ednl. cons., fed. grant coordinator; indsl. adviser to sch. systems, bus. and industry, state ednl. depts. Active Boy Scouts Am. Bd. dirs. United Fund, Nova Acad. NSF grantee, 1970. Mem. Am. Assn. U. Profs., Assn. Acad. Deans, Am. Assn. Univ. Adminstrs., Assn. Edn., Communication and Tech., Phi Delta Kappa. Rotarian. Author: Selected Readings in Educational media, 1968. Contbr. articles to ednl. jours. Home: 25 Golf Club Circle Statesboro GA 30458

BROWN, WILLARD RICHARD, lawyer, banker; b. Scipio, Utah, July 25, 1909; s. George Ernest and Susan (Yates) B.; A.B., U. Utah, 1934; LL.B., Columbia, 1937; m. Mary Scull Jacoby, Nov. 24, 1948; children—Bowman, Barton, James Ralph, John Scull, Katharine Creevey. Admitted to N.Y. bar, 1938, Fla. bar, 1950; asso. Shearman & Sterling, N.Y.C., 1939-44; trust officer Chem. Bank & Trust Co., N.Y.C., 1944-50; v.p., sr. trust officer First Nat. Bank, Miami, Fla., 1950-61; partner Shutts & Bowen, attys., Miami, 1961—; dir. Westchester Nat. Bank, Miami, Midway Nat. Bank of Dade County. Pres., S.E. Fla. Estate Planning Council, 1959-60; guest lectr. U. Miami Law Sch. Enrollment rep. Columbia U., South Fla. Trustee J. D. Shatford Meml. Trust Assn., Halifax, N.S., Can. Mem. Am., Fla., bar assns., Bar City N.Y., Corporate Fiduciaries Assn. (pres. S.E. Fla. 1957), Fla. Bankers Assn. (past chmn. trust div., founder, trustee, instr. trust tng. sch., mem. legislative com. trust div.), Kappa Sigma, Phi Alpha Delta. Episcopalian. Kiwanian. Clubs: Church, The Pilgrims (N.Y.C.); Rivera Country, Century (Coral Gables, Fla); Naples (Fla.) Yacht. Contbr. articles to law jours. Home: 3720 Harlano St Coral Gables FL 33134 Office: First Nat Bank Bldg Miami FL 33131

BROWN, WILLIAM ARTHUR, JR., physician; b. Wildsville, La., July 17, 1930; s. William Arthur and Eula (Martin) B.; B.S., Miss. Coll., 1953; M.D., U. Miss., 1957; m. Margaret Imogene Oglesby,

Aug. 19, 1954. Intern Ark. Baptist Hosp., Little Rock, 1957-58; practice gen. medicine, Mathiston, Miss., 1958—; owner Mathison Clinic, 1968—; mem. staff Houston (Miss.) Hosp. Founding pres. bd. Vadalia (La.) Furniture Mart, Inc., 1969—; partner Furniture Mart, Mathiston, 1970—; Founding bd. dirs. Chief Econo Inc., Columbus, Miss. Fellow Am. Acad. Family Practice; mem. profl. sect. Am. Diabetes Assn., North Central (pres. 1970-71), Miss., Am. med. assns., Miss. Acad. Family Practice, Am. Geriatrics Soc., Am. Inst. Hypnosis, Alpha Kappa Kappa. Baptist. Mason. Contbr. articles to profl. jours. Home: Church St Mathiston MS 39752 Office: Box 211 Mathiston Clinic Mathiston MS 39752

BROWN, WILLIAM ERNEST, univ. dean; b. Benton Harbor, Mich., Aug. 29, 1922; s. William Ernest and Gertrude (Elliot) B.; D.D.S., U. Mich., 1945, M.S., 1947; m. Theo Nesbitt McDonold, Oct. 21, 1944 (dec. July 16, 1969); children—Judith (Mrs. David Allen Smith), Wendy (Mrs. Robert Kerschbaum, Jr.), Terrence Nesbitt; m. 2d, Eula Mae Ditmore, Sept. 11, 1970. Individual practice dentistry, specializing in pedodontics, Ann Arbor, Mich., 1947-61; instr. pedodontics U. Mich., 1947-61, asso. dir. W. K. Kellogg Found. Inst. Grad. and Postgrad. Dentistry, 1961-69; dean Sch. Dentistry, U. Okla., Oklahoma City, 1969—, acting provost Health Scis. Center, 1973—. Cons. Council on Dental Edn., 1967-73, mem. Council Dental Edn., 1974—; mem. Dental Health Research and Edn. Adv. Com. USPHS, 1966-71; mem. dental edn. rev. com. NIH, 1971-73. Mem. Human Relations Commn., Ann Arbor, 1960-66, chmn., 1965-66; chmn. U. Mich. Senate Adv. Com. on Univ. Affairs, 1966-67. Recipient Gies Editorial award, 1965, 67. Diplomate Am. Bd. Pedodontics (chmn. examining bd. 1964-65). Mem. Am. Acad. Pedontics (pres. 1963-64), Am. Soc. Dentistry for Children (pres. 1959-60), Am. Coll. Dentists (pres. 1971-72), Am., Mich. (pres. 1968-69) dental assns. Rotarian. Editor Jour. Mich. State Dental Assn., 1959-67, U. Mich. Dental Alumni Bull., 1966-69. Home: 24 S Easy St Edmond OK 73034

BROWN, WILLIAM HENRY, elec. engr.; b. Goldsboro, N.C., Jan. 12, 1924; s. Leslie Thomas and Mildred Wilhelmina (Pearson) B.; student N.C. State U., 1941-44; A.B., E. Carolina U., 1949, postgrad., 1949-50; postgrad. Fla. Inst. Tech., 1958-59; m. Enola Mae Vail, July 6, 1951; children—Billie Kaye, Shirley Vail. Radio engr. to 1950; with Philco Corp., 1950-51, Western Electric Co., 1951-56, Convair, 1956-60, RCA, 1960-62, Gen. Electric Co., 1962-64; sr. project engr. NASA, Johnson Space Center, Tex., 1964—. Dir. Tech. Enterprises, Inc., Astro Enterprises, Inc.; owner WOGO and WWBC. Served with USNR, 1944-46. Mem. I.E.E.E., Sigma Chi. Club: New Smyrna Beach Yacht. Patentee in field. Home: 109 Claridge St Satellite Beach FL 32937 Office: Kennedy Space Center FL 32899

BROWN, WILLIAM NOBLE, radio sta. exec.; b. Washington, May 25, 1950; s. Raymond Robert and Hulit (Wiley) B.; B.A. in Broadcast and Psychology, Am. U., 1971. With WAMU-FM, Washington, 1970—, prodn. mgr., 1971-73, program dir., 1973—. Teaching asso. dept. communication Am. U., Washington, 1973. Judge regional Emmy Awards competition Nat. Acad. TV Arts and Scis., 1971. Recipient meritorious achievement award Sinking Creek Nat. Film Competition, Greenville, Tenn., 1970. Home: 4425 Greenwich Pkwy NW Washington DC 20007 Office: 4451 Massachusetts Av NW Washington DC 20016

BROWN, WILLIAM PERRY, SR., investment banker, financial cons.; b. New Orleans, Apr. 19, 1899; s. William Perry and Marguerite (Braughn) B.; student Tulane U., 1919; m. Yvonne Elder, June 20, 1923 (dec. June 1966); children—William Perry III, Henry Elder, Yvonne Marguerite (Mrs. John Marshall Collier). With Shepard & Gluck, 1919-22, H.W. Fitzpatrick & Co., 1923-26, Perry Brown & Co., 1927-32, Woolfolk, Huggins & Shober, 1933-35, Newman Harris & Co., 1935-39; partner Newman, Brown & Co., 1940-66; sr. partner Kohlmeyer & Co., 1966-73; v.p. Thomson, McKinnon, Archenklos, Kohlmeyer, Inc., 1973-74; financial cons., 1974— (all New Orleans). Mem. faculty Loyola U. of South, New Orleans, 1932-33, Chmn., U.S. Treas. War and Savs. Bond Program, 1941-74. Recipient Patriotic Service 25 yr. award U.S. Treasury, 1966, Patriotic Service award, 1971-72. Mem. Nat. (pres. 1943-44), New Orleans (past pres.) security traders assns., New Orleans Bond Club (dir.), La. Securities Assn. (v.p. 1966-72), Investment Bankers Assn. Am., Internat. House, New Orleans, Pass Christian chambers of commerce, Gulf Yachting Assn. (commodore 1970-71), Miss. Coast Yachting Assn. (past pres.), Municipal Forum N.Y., Delta Kappa Epsilon. Clubs: City of Baton Rouge; Plimsoll (New Orleans); Ponte Verdra of Fla.; Pass Christian (Miss.) Yacht (past commorore, vice commodore 1965—). Home and office: 4520 Francesco Rd Venetian Isles New Orleans LA 70129

BROWN, WILLIAM RUSSELL, lawyer; b. Holly Springs, Miss., July 5, 1914; s. Horace Brightberry and Aileen (Blackburn) B.; B.B.A., LL.B., U. Tex., 1937; m. Ruth Cunningham, Apr. 19, 1941; children—Betsy (Mrs. Thomas M. Smith III), Virginia, Russell. Admitted to Tex. bar, 1937, since practiced in Houston; asso. firm Baker, Botts, Andrews & Wharton (now Baker & Botts), 1937—, partner, 1948—; gen. counsel, dir. Houston Lighting & Power Co. Served as lt. USNR, 1943-45. Decorated Bronze Star. Mem. Am., Tex., Houston bar assns. Democrat. Episcopalian. Clubs: Houston, Houston Country. Home: 5816 Bayou Glen Rd Houston TX 77027 Office: 29th Floor 1 Shell Plaza Houston TX 77002

BROWNE, EPPES WAYLES, JR., cons.; b. Shreveport, La., Nov. 1, 1909; s. Eppes Wayles and Grace Hall (Long) B.; A.A., N.M. Mil. Inst., 1927; B.A., Stanford, 1929; M.B.A., Harvard, 1932, M.P.A., 1948, M.A., 1949, Ph.D., 1955; m. Virginia Senders, Nov. 24, 1934; children—Eppes Wayles III, Martha Finch; m. 2d, Barbara Moulton, Mar. 30, 1962. Economist, statistician U.S. Dept. Agr., 1934-39; economist Dept. Commerce, 1939-41, Nat. Housing Agy., Washington, 1941-47, Nat. Security Resources Bd. and Def. Prodn. Adminstrs., 1948-51; expert Pres.'s Materials Policy Commn., 1951-52, Dept. of Interior, 1952-54; economist Banking and Currency Com., U.S. Senate, 1955, chief statistician Privileges and Elections Subcom., 1956-57, economist Antitrust and Monopoly Subcom., 1957-65, 67-71; economist Office Econ. Opportunity, 1965-66; sr. economist Econ. Assos., Inc., Washington, 1966-67; pvt. cons. econs., Garden Grove, Cal., 1972—. Bd. dirs. Potomac Basin Fedn., W.Va., 1967—; bd. dirs. Nat. Consumers League, 1961—; nat. bd. dirs. Am. Vets. Com., 1963-74. Served to maj. AUS, 1931-60. Club: National Democratic (Washington). Home: 3700 Oliver St NW Washington DC 20015 Office: 8100 Garden Grove Blvd Garden Grove CA 92644

BROWNELL, JAMES HENRY, mgmt. cons.; b. Burlington, Vt., Dec. 3, 1937; s. Allan Thomas and Elizabeth (Emery) B.; B.S., Norwich U., 1959; m. Martha Merselis, Jan. 21, 1967; children—Marion Elizabeth, Barbara. Civil engr. State of Vt., 1959-63; civil engr. Paul Hardeman, Cape Kennedy, Fla., 1963-65; mgmt. cons. Meridian Engrs., Columbia, Md., 1965-68; v.p. Griffith Services, Charlotte, N.C., 1968; mgmt. cons. DBA Systems, Indialantic, Fla., 1969—. Served with C.E., AUS, 1960-63. Registered profl. engr., Vt. Mem. Am. Inst. Indsl. Engrs., Am. Soc. C.E. (pres. local chpt. 1973), Soc. Am. Mil. Engrs., Soc. Advancement Mgmt., Nat. Soc. Profl. Engrs., Fla. Engrs. Soc. (exec. v.p. Indian River chpt. 1973). Club: Florida Norwich University Alumni (pres. 1973). Home: 300 Cocoa Av Indialantic FL 32903 Office: 325 Fifth Av Indialantic FL 32901

BROWNING, BERNARD S., bus. counseling co. exec.; b. Browning, Mo., Nov. 7, 1923; s. John Howard and Alma Elaine (Lawrence) B.; student N.E. Mo. State Tchrs. Coll., 1939-41, Georgetown U., 1942, U. Richmond, 1943; M.B.A., Harvard, 1947; postgrad. N.Y.U., 1947-50; m. Adeline Townsend Rogers, Aug. 6, 1955; children—Frances Elaine, Virginia Diane, John Scott, Lawrence Rogers. Dir. customer relations Frederick Research Corp., Bethesda, Md., 1954-56; ind. bus. cons., Bethesda, 1956-62; pres. Gen. Bus. Services, Inc., Washington, 1962—. Lectr. money and banking Fisher Sch., Boston, 1947-58; lectr. marketing Am. U., Washington, 1955-56. Bd. govs. Boston Coll. Center for Small Bus.; trustee Boy's Club Washington. Served with USN, 1944-54; now rear adm. Supply Corps, Res. Mem. President's Assn., Internat. Franchise Assn. (dir. 1971—), Navy Supply Corps Sch. Alumni Assn. (dir. 1971-73). Clubs: Army-Navy Country (Arlington, Va.); Lakewood Country (Rockville, Md.). Home: 9825 Belhaven Rd Bethesda MD 20034 Office: 7401 Wisconsin Av Washington DC 20014

BROWNING, CHARLES BENTON, educator; b. Houston, Sept. 16, 1931; s. Earl William and Emma (Sumerlin) B.; B.S., Tex. Technol. Coll., 1955; M.S., Kan. State U., 1956, Ph.D., 1958; m. Magda Luest, Jan. 14, 1956; children—Susan, Charles Benton, Steven, Karen, Heidi, Gary. Research fellow Kan. State U., 1955-58; asst. prof. Miss. State U., 1958-60, asso. prof., 1960-64, prof., 1964-66; chmn. dairy sci. dept. U. Fla., Gainesville, 1966-69, prof., 1966—, dean Coll. Agr. 1969—, also dean resident instrn. Inst. Food and Agrl. Scis. Mem. Am. Dairy Sci. Assn., Am. Soc. Animal Sci., Sigma Xi, Alpha Zeta, Gamma Sigma Delta. Kiwanian. Contbr. articles to profl. jours. Home: 5610 NW 4th Pl Gainesville FL 32601

BROWNING, HARLEY LINWOOD, educator; b. Akron, O., Mar. 28, 1927; s. Ernest Grafton and Dolcie (Lashley) B.; B.A., Kent State U., 1949; Ph.D., U. Cal. at Berkeley, 1962; m. Waltraut Feindt, Mar. 6, 1960; children—Erik, Tulio. Mem. faculty dept. sociology U. Tex. at Austin, 1962—, asso. prof., 1965-70, prof., 1971—, dir. Population Research Center, 1963—. Mem. Am. Sociol. Assn., Population Assn. Am., Internat. Union Sci. Study Population. Author: Men in a Developing Society: Geographic and Social Mobility in Monterrey, Mexico, 1973. Home: 2701 Pecos St Austin TX 78703 Office: 200 E 26 1/2 Austin TX 78712

BROWNING, HARRELL ZEEKIE, lawyer; b. Corpus Christi, Tex., Aug. 17, 1939; s. Joe Drumgold and Ruby (Harrell) B.; B.S. in Agr. Bus., Tex. A. and I. U., 1963; LL.B., U. Tex., 1966; m. Lila Jean Holcomb, June 24, 1962; children—Polly Ann, James Thomas. Admitted to Tex. bar, 1966; since practiced in Corpus Christi; atty. firm Fischer, Wood, Burney & Nesbitt, Corpus Christi, 1969-70; partner firm Harris, Cook, Browning & Barker, Corpus Christi, 1971—. Chmn. Nueces County Republican Com., 1971—. Served with USAF, 1966-69. Home: 349 Palmetto St Corpus Christi TX 78412 Office: 1717 Bank and Trust Tower Corpus Christi TX 78403

BROWNING, JAMES ROBERT, accountant; b. San Antonio, Tex., Sept. 30, 1944; s. Clyde Barcus and Jac (King) B.; B.A., Tex. Tech. U., 1967; m. Susan Alexis Gully, May 31, 1969; 1 son, Michael Robert. Audit mgr., Arthur Andersen & Co., Dallas, 1967-73; v.p. finance Alan I. Jones Companies, Inc., Dallas, 1973—; also dir. C.P.A., Tex. Mem. Am. Inst. C.P.A.'s, Tex. Soc. C.P.A.'s. Mem. Christian Ch. Home: 8741 Mediterranean Dr Dallas TX 75238 Office: 3128 Lemmon Av E Dallas TX 75204

BROWNING, JAMES SCOTT, research metallurgist; b. Booth, Ala., Apr. 24, 1920; s. Floyd Morrison and Arvazena (Smith) B.; B.S., U. Ala., 1947, Engr. of Mines, 1955; M.S., U. Ida., 1948; m. Lorene May, June 4, 1946; children—Cynthia Jeanne, Timothy Scott. Research fellow, Ida. Bur. Mines, Moscow, 1947-48; metalfurgist U.S. Bur. Mines, Tuscaloosa, Ala., 1949-56, supr. metallurgist, 1956-62, project coordinator, 1962-70, chief of lab., 1970-73, indsl. minerals cons., 1973—. Served with USMCR, 1941-46. Decorated Purple Heart medal, Presidential Unit citation; recipient Meritorious Service award, U.S. Dept. Interior, 1968, Certificate of Merit, U.S. Bur. Mines, 1964. Registered profl. engr., Ala. Mem. Am. Ex-prisoners of War (nat. comdr. 1954-55, nat. legislative officer 1955-60, nat. judge advocate 1953-54, nat. dir. 1952-59), Am. Inst. Mining and Metal. Engrs., Ala. Acad. Sci., Sigma Xi, Sigma Gamma Epsilon. Contbr. articles to profl. jours. Patentee in field. Address: 2536 14th St E Tuscaloosa AL 35401

BROWNING, ROBERT COOPER, cons. engr.; b. Balt., Oct. 31, 1919; s. Romanus Getty and Bertha (Cooper) B.; B.C.E., N.C. State Coll., 1941; m. Mary Frances Gerding, May 9, 1942; children—Robert Cooper, Lawrence Michael, Ann Frances. Field engr., v.p. Loftis Co., contractors and cons. U.S. mil. bases, 1940-41; engr. J. E. Sirrine, cons. engrs., 1941; civilian san. engr. U.S. Navy, Camp Lejeune, N.C., 1941-42; cons. mech. and elec. engr. William C. Olsen, cons. engr., 1946-50; cons. engr., Raleigh, N.C., 1950—; v.p., dir. engring. Modular Industries, Inc., 1972—; v.p., dir. engring. Med. Environment Corp. Am., 1972—; mech. and elec. engring. cons. Chmn. cons. engring. Profl. Engrs. N.C., 1962, bd. dirs. Central Carolina chpt., 1962-63, state dir., 1963-66, pres., 1969-70; sec., treas. Tarheel sect. Illuminating Engr. Soc., 1963; lt. comdr., edn. officer U.S. Power Squadron, Raleigh, 1963-65; comdr. Raleigh Power Squadron, 1965-66; chmn. bd. rev. Boy Scouts Am., 1963-66. Served as lt. and capt. C.E., AUS, 1942-45; ETO. Registered profl. engr., Md., D.C., Va., N.C., S.C., Ga., Tenn., Tex., Miss. Mem. N.C. Soc. Engrs., Profl. Engrs. N.C., Internat. Assn. Structural and Bridge Engrs., Am. Soc. Heating, Refrigeration and Air-Conditioning Engrs., Am. Radio Relay League, Royal Soc. Health (London), Triangle Internat. Trade Assn. (pres. 1972-74), N.C. Assn. Professions (dir. 1970-74), Inst. Environmental Scis. (dir. 1973-74). Contbr. articles to profl. jours. Home: 829 Bryan St Raleigh NC 27605 Office: 510 St Marys St Raleigh NC 27605

BROWNLEE, DONALD SHAW, mech. engr.; b. Charlton, Ia., Oct. 8, 1928; s. Leland Cain and Ethel Garland (Shaw) B.; B.S. in Mech. Engring., Ia. State Coll., 1953; m. Mary Janice Zimmerlee, Jan. 8, 1949; children—Margaret Ann, Donald Shaw, Michael David. Project engr., asst. plant engr. Rayonier Paper Mill, Fernandina Beach, Fla., 1958-67; sr. design engr. Rust Engring. Co., Cleveland, Tenn., 1967-70; asst. plant engr. St. Regis Paper Co., Monticello, Miss., 1970—. Pres. Lucas County (Ia.) 4-H Club; v.p. Ia. Future Farmers Am., 1946; pres. Rayonier Employees Credit Union, 1966. Served with USMCR, 1946-49. Registered profl. engr., Tenn. Presbyn. (chmn. bd. deacons 1965, treas. 1963, 65). Co-inventor single point hitch for Internat. Harvester Cub Tractor, 1954. Home: 426 W Chickasaw St Brookhaven MS 39601 Office: St Regis Paper Co Monticello MS 39654

BROWNLEE, WILLIAM RUSSELL, orgn. exec.; b. Cleveland, Tenn., Dec. 1, 1905; s. Colin C. and Jessie Louisa (Hazelton) B.; B.S., U. Ariz., 1927, E.E., 1954; m. Elizabeth Cecil Marquet, June 18, 1932; 1 dau., Jane (Mrs. Cooper G. Hazelrig). Applications engr. Westinghouse, East Pitts., 1927-28; test engr. Tenn. Electric Power Co., Chattanooga, 1929-39; planning engr. Commonwealth & So. Corp., Jackson, Mich., 1939-49; supr., power systems engr. Commonwealth Assn., Inc., Jackson, 1949-51; chief systems studies engr. So. Services, Inc., Birmingham, Ala., 1951-57, system planning engr., 1957-59, power pool mgr., 1959-64, v.p., 1964-66, exec. v.p., 1966-67, pres., 1967-69, chmn., 1969-71; v.p. engring., dir. So. Co., 1968-71; dir. So. Electric Generating Co., 1968-71; adminstrv. mgr. Southeastern Electric Reliability Council, Birmingham, 1971—. Dept. dir. Ala. Electric Power Agy., 1967-72. Named Birmingham (Ala.) Engr. of Year, Birmingham Engring. Council, 1968. Fellow I.E.E.E. (Outstanding Engr. 1970); mem. Tau Beta Pi, Phi Kappa Phi. Clubs: Downtown, The Club (Birmingham). Contbr. articles in field to profl. jours. Patentee in field. Home: 780 Montgomery Dr Birmingham AL 35213 Office: 15 S 20th St Birmingham AL 35233

BROWNSON, ANNA LOUISE HARSHMAN (MRS. CHARLES B. BROWNSON), editor; b. Indpls., May 4, 1926; d. Walter W. and Jennie Andrea (Jensen) Harshman; B.A., Butler U., 1949, postgrad., 1950-51; m. Charles B. Brownson, Nov. 23, 1966; children—Dwight, Bruce, David, Catharine, Scott. Asst. biochemistry lab. Ind. U. Med. Sch., Indpls., 1944-47; grad. asst. Butler U., Indpls., 1949-51; adminstrv. asst. to U.S. congressman from 11th Dist. Ind., Indpls., 1951-58; asso. editor, treas. Congl. Staff Directory, Washington, 1959—; asso. Charles Brownson Assos., govtl. and assn. counselors, Washington, 1959—; pub., owner, editor (with husband) Advance Locator for Capitol Hill, 1963—, Election Index, 1966-;. Patron Corcoran Art Gallery. Mem. Ind. Soc. Washington, Smithsonian Assos., Nat. Historic Trust Preservation, Internat. Oceanographic Found. Washington Butler Alumni, Kappa Alpha Theta. Presbyn. Home and Office: 4748 Neptune Dr Alexandria VA 22309

BROYHILL, JAMES THOMAS, congressman; b. Lenoir, N.C., Aug. 19, 1927; s. James Edgar and Satie (Hunt) B.; B.S., U. N.C., 1950; m. Louise Robbins, June 2, 1951; children—Marilyn L., James Edgar II, Philip R. Mem. 88th-93d Congresses, 10th dist. N.C. Recipient Young Man of Year award City of Lenoir, 1957. Republican. Baptist (Sunday sch. tchr.). Mason (Shriner). Office 2159 Rayburn House Office Bldg Washington DC 20515 Home: Lenoir NC 28645

BROYHILL, JOEL THOMAS, congressman; b. Hopewell, Va., Nov. 4, 1919; s. Marvin Talmage and Nellie Magdalene (Brewer) B.; student Fork Union (Va.) Mil. Acad., George Washington U., 1939-41; m. Jane Marshall Bragg, May 17, 1942; children—Nancy, Jane-Anne, Jeanne Marie. Mem. 83d-93d U.S. Congresses from 10th Dist. Va. Chmn. planning commn., mem. sch. bd. constrn. adv. council, fiscal affairs adv. council, bd. trustees community fund council Arlington County; finance chmn. Arlington-Fairfax Heart Assn., 1951-52; bd. dirs. Arlington County Hosp. Fund Dr., 1951, Cancer Fund Dr.; mem. disaster com. A.R.C. Mem. County Republican Exec. Com., 1949-53, pres., 1950-51; Va. State Rep. Finance Com., 1952—. Trustee Fork Union Mil. Acad. Served as capt. 106th Inf. AUS, World War II. Mem. Va. State, Arlington County (pres., dir.) chambers commerce, Nat. Assn. Home Builders, Home Builders Assn. Met. Wash., Wash. Bldg. Congress, No. Va. Home Builders Assn., Washington Bd. Trade, Alexandria-Arlington Fairfax Real Estate Bd. (past sec.), Am. Legion, Res. Officers Assn. U.S., V.F.W., 40 and 8, D.A.V., Kappa Alpha Alumni Assn. Republican. Lutheran (ch. council). Mason (K.T., Shriner), Tall Cedars of Lebanon, Moose, Eagle; Optimist (dir., past pres., sec.). Home: 4845 Old Dominion Drive Arlington VA 22207

BROYLES, ARTHUR AUGUSTUS, educator, physicist; b. Atlanta, May 16, 1923; s. Richard Johnson and Mary Ruth (Jones) B.; B.S. with high honors, U. Fla., 1942; Ph.D., Yale, 1949; m. Jenna Anne Schneider, Dec. 25, 1943; children—Rhea Diane, David Charne, Bonnie Sue, Frances Eileen. Asst. prof. physics U. Fla., Gainesville, 1949-50; research physicist Los Alamos Sci. Lab., 1950-53 sr. physicist Rand Corp., Santa Monica, Cal., 1953-59; prof. physics U. Fla., 1959—. Pres., Assn. for Community Wide Protection from Nuclear Attack, 1964-71; mem. Fla. Civil Def. Adv. Bd., 1965-68. Served with USNR, 1942-45. Fellow Am. Phys. Soc.; mem. Sigma Xi, Phi Beta Kappa, Phi Eta Sigma, Phi Kappa Phi, Alpha Tau Omega. Contbr. articles to sci. jours. Home: 3716 SW 6th Place Gainesville FL 32601

BROYLES, FARRELL RUDOLPH, banker; b. Madison County, Ind., Feb. 26, 1932; s. Rudolph Farrell and Daisey Madge (Adams) B.; grad. Sch. Consumer Banking, U. Va., 1966; m. Alice Rosalyn Darter, Aug. 5, 1951 (div. Dec. 1970); children—Gregory Farrell, Jeanette Lynn. Apprentice, Del. Printing & Lithograph Co., Muncie, Ind., 1951-52; sales mgr. Goff Jewelry, Ft. Myers, Fla., 1952; with First Nat. Bank, Ft. Myers, 1953—, sr. v.p., dir., 1969—. Treas., United Fund Lee County, 1950. Mem. Am. Inst. Banking, Lee County Credit Assn., Fla. Bankers Assn. (installment credit com. 1971-72). Elk, Civitan. Home: 2120 Hanson St Fort Myers FL 33901 Office: PO Box 130 Fort Myers FL 33902

BRUBAKER, PAUL EUGENE, II, biologist; b. Indiana, Pa., Dec. 31, 1934; s. Paul Eugene and Harriett (Ludwig) B.; B.A., St. Vincents Coll. (Latrobe, Pa.), 1959; M.S., Catholic U. Am., 1965, Ph.D. (NASA fellow 1967), 1968; m. Joanne Catherine Quinn, July 11, 1965; children—Paul Eugene III, Joseph Justin. Lectr. dept. biology Immaculata Coll. Washington, 1963-68; faculty teaching asst. George Washington U., 1963-68; staff fellow NIH, Research Triangle Park, N.C., 1968-70, sr. staff fellow, 1970-72; research biologist human studies lab. Environmental Protection Agy., Research Triangle Park, N.C., 1972-73, chief molecular biology br., 1972-74, mem. spl. studies staff nat. and internat. environmental affairs Office of Dir., 1974—. Mem. Nat. Air Pollution Research Adv. Com., 1972—, Interagency Panel on Environmental Mutagenesis. Served with AUS, 1960-62. Mem. A.A.A.S., Am. Soc. Cell Biologists, Tissue Culture Assn., Environmental Mutagen Soc., Am. Petroleum Inst. (mem. coordinating research council), Sigma Xi. Democrat. Contbr. profl. jours. Home: 1010 Cuscowilla Dr Cary NC 27511 Office: Nat Environmental Research Center Environmental Protection Agy Research Triangle Park NC 27711

BRUCCOLI, MATTHEW JOSEPH, educator; b. N.Y.C., Aug. 21, 1931; s. Joseph M. and Mary (Gervasi) B.; A.B., Yale, 1953 M.A., U. Va., 1956, Ph.D., 1961; m. Arlyn Firkins, Oct. 5, 1957; children—Mary, Joseph Matthew, Josephine, Arlyn. Instr. English U. Va., 1958-59; asst. prof. Ohio State U., 1961-64, asso. prof., 1965, prof., 1965-69; prof. English, U. S.C., 1969—; dir. Center Editions Am. Authors, Modern Lang. Assn., 1969—; cons. So. Ill. U. Press, 1965—, U. Pitts. Press, 1966—; founding partner Bruccoli Clark Publishers. Guggenheim fellow, 1971. Club: Grolier. Author: Composition of Tender is the Night, 1962; Ernest Hemingway's Cub Reporter, 1970; Ernest Hemingway's Apprenticeship, 1971; F. Scott Fitzgerald in His Own Time, 1971; As Ever, Scott Fitz, 1972; Kenneth Millar/Ross Macdonald, 1971; John O'Hara: A Checklist, 1972, F. Scott Fitzgerald: A Descriptive Bibliography, 1972; Bit of Paradise, 1973; F. Scott Fitzgerald Ledger, 1973; The Great Gatsby: A Facsimile of the Manuscript, 1973; (with Clark) Hemingway at Auction, 1973. Editor: Bruccoli Clark Books, Fitzgerald Newsletter, 1958-68, Fitzgerald/Hemingway Annual, 1969—; The Pittsburgh Series Bibliography. Home: 31 Heathwood Circle Columbia SC 29205

BRUCE, CLEMONT HUGHES, geologist; b. nr. Central City, Ky., Sept. 5, 1921; s. Ezra Clemont and Nancy (Woodson) B.; B.S., U. Ky., 1948, M.S., 1949; m. Bettie J. Kemp, June 11, 1949; children—Donna Lynette, Byron Hughes. Geologist, Mobil Oil Corp., Mt. Vernon, Ill., 1949-53, Dallas, 1953-55, sr. exploration geologist, Jackson, Miss., 1955-65, asso. exploration geologist, Corpus Christi, Tex., 1965-68, geol. specialist, 1968-72, geologist specialist so. region, Houston, 1972—. Served with USAAF, 1942-45. Mem. Am. Assn. Petroleum Geologists (distinguished lectr. 1973-74), Geol. Soc. Am., Houston Geol. Soc., Sigma Xi, Sigma Gamma Epsilon. Baptist (deacon). Contbr. articles to profl. jours. Home: 830 Thread Needle 235 Houston TX 77024 Office: Suite 800 3 Greenway Plaza East Houston TX 77046

BRUCE, ELMER IVAN, physician; b. Center, Tex., Aug. 20, 1917; s. E. Ivan and Eddie (Sanders) B.; A.A., U. Cal. at Los Angeles, 1938; M.D., U. Tex., 1942; m. Reba Lami, June 8, 1946; children—Patricia, Elizabeth, Barry. Intern U. Wis. Gen. Hosp., Madison, 1942-43; resident U. Tex. Med. Br. Hosp., Galveston, 1946-49, now mem. staff; practice medicine specializing in psychiatry, Galveston, 1946—; instr. U. Tex. Med. Br., 1949, asst. prof., 1949-54, asso. prof., 1954-65, prof., 1965—. Served to lt. M.C., USNR, 1944-46. Fellow Am. Psychiat. Assn., A.A.A.S., Am. Coll. Psychiatrists; mem. Am., Tex., Galveston County med. assns., Am. Assn. U. Profs., Central Neuropsychiat. Assn., Phi Rho Sigma. Episcopalian. Clubs: Doctors, Galveston Artillery. Contbr. articles to profl. jours. Home: 1901 Carter Lane La Marque TX 77568 Office: 1014 Texas Av Galveston TX 77550

BRUCE, ROBERT BLACK, chem. products co. exec.; b. Bamberg, S.C., Feb. 18, 1918; s. Roy Marion and Mary Belle (Berry) B.; B.S., Coll. Charleston, 1941; Ph.D. (Research fellow), U. N.C., 1951; m. Margaret Matilda Darrough, Sept. 7, 1947; children—Robert Darrough, John Berry, Roy Carver. Chemist, Va. Carolina Chem. Co., Charleston, S.C., 1941-42; biochemist Jr. League Blood Center, Milw., 1951-53; bioanalyst Hazleton Labs., Falls Church, Va., 1953-57, Radioisotope Sch., Oak Ridge, 1957; Palo Alto, Cal., 1957-60; U. Cal., Berkeley, 1958; dir. drug metabolism A.H. Robins Co., Inc., Richmond, Va., 1960—. Served with AUS, 1942-45. Recipient S. Keith Johnson medal Coll. Charleston, 1941. Mem. A.A.A.S., Va. Acad. Sci., Am. Chem. Soc., Nat. Geog. Soc., Va. Mus. Fine Arts. Contbr. articles to sci. jours. Home: 3612 Seminary Av Richmond VA 23227 Office: 1211 Sherwood Av Richmond VA 23220

BRUCE, ROBERT NOLAN, JR., educator; b. Melville, La., Oct. 11, 1930; s. Robert Nolan and Frances (Patterson) B.; B.S., Tulane U., 1952, M.S., 1953; postgrad. (Fulbright scholar), U. Ghent (Belgium), 1955-56; Ph.D., U. Ill. at Urbana, 1962; m. Catherine Eleanor Colquitt, May 3, 1958 (div. Feb. 1969); children—Sarah Johnson, Robert McKinnon. Engr.-in-charge Gulf of Mexico area Raymond Internat. Inc., 1953-60; mem. faculty dept. civil engring. Tulane U., New Orleans, 1961—, asso. prof., 1961-67, prof., 1964—. Cons. industry, Dept. Def., Civil Service Commn., Fed. Hwy. Adminstrn., State La. La. Dept. Hwys.-Fed. Hwy. Adminstrn. grantee, 1971; Dept. Def. grantee, 1971. Mem. Am. Soc. C.E. (pres. La. chpt. 1970), Am. Concrete Inst. Club: Southern Yacht (New Orleans). Contbr. articles to profl. jours. Home: 2420 Camp St New Orleans LA 70130

BRUCE, WILLIAM RANKIN, ins. co. exec.; b. Columbia, S.C., Oct. 18, 1915; s. Charles Joy and Anna (Rankin) B.; B.S. in Commerce, U. S.C., 1937; m. Jane Parsley Emerson, Jan. 12, 1946; children—William Rankin, Jane Emerson, Charles Joy. With Seibels Bruce & Co., Columbia, 1937—, v.p., 1958-66, pres., 1966—, also dir.; pres., dir. S.C. Ins. Co., Consol. Am. Ins. Co., Catawba Ins. Co., Argus Life Ins. Co., Premium Service Corp. Columbia, 1966—; dir. Home Fed. Savs. & Loan Assn., Columbia, First Service Corp. S.C., Nylene Corp., Investors Nat. Life Ins. Co. Mem. Columbia adv. bd. S.C. Nat. Bank. Served to lt. comdr. USNR, 1941-45. Mem. Columbia C. of C., Columbia Ball Soc. (pres. 1963). Clubs: Forest Lake (pres. 1967-68), Palmetto, Summit. Home: 4367 Chicora St Columbia SC 29206 Office: 1501 Lady St Columbia SC 29201

BRUCKMAN, THOMAS RICHARD, banker; b. Altoona, Pa., June 6, 1936; s. Jack Richard and Geraldine (Hoover) B.; B.S., Fla. State U., 1958; J.D., Stetson U., 1964. Vice pres., trust Investment officer 1st Nat. Bank, Clearwater, Fla., 1964-70; v.p., sr. trust officer Pinellas Central Bank and Trust Co., Largo, Fla., 1970—, also dir. Chmn. uniform probate com. Fla. Bankers Assn., 1973-74. Chmn. bd. dirs., treas. Play Parc Sch. for Retarded Children, 1968-73, chmn., Largo Recreation Complex & Park Devel., 1968-74; 1st v.p. Upper Pinellas Assn. Retarded Children, 1973—; bd. govs. Suncoast Sci. Center, St. Petersburg, Fla., 1971-72; trustee Suncoast Hosp., 1971-73. Mem. Largo Charter Revision commn., 1973-74. Served with USNR, 1958-61. Mem. Am., Fla., Clearwater Mid-County (pres. 1973) bar assns., Clearwater Jaycees (dir. 1967), Kappa Sigma (did grand master Fla., 1967-71), Phi Delta Phi, Phi Eta Sigma, Club: Sertoma (pres. 1967-68, dist. gov. 1968-70, internat. dir. 1970-72, internat. v.p. 1972-73, internat. pres. elect 1973-74). Home: 908 S Highland Av Clearwater FL 33516 Office: West Bay Dr Largo FL 33540

BRULEY, DUANE FREDERICK, educator; b. Chippewa Falls, Wis., Aug. 3, 1933; s. Casper and Hazel (Kuehn) B.; B.S., U. Wis., 1956; M.S. (AEC fellow), Stanford, 1959; Ph.D. (Texaco Found. fellow, Shell Found. fellow), U. Tenn., 1962; m. Suzanne Bigler, June 14, 1959; children—Scott Bruley, Randy, Mark. Research and devel. engr. Union Carbide Nuclear Corp., Oak Ridge, 1956-58; head varsity tennis coach U. Tenn., 1961-62; asso. prof. chem. engring. Clemson (S.C.) U., 1962-70, prof., 1970-74, head varsity coach, 1962-73; adj. prof., 1974—; head dept. chem. engring. Tulane U., New Orleans, 1974—, asst. varsity tennis coach, 1973—. Vis. prof. Princeton, 1970; referee In Sunshine Cup Tennis Matches, Miami, 1968, 69; rep. Wilson Sporting Goods, Clemson area, 1965-73, Gretna, La., 1973—; cons. W.Va. Pulp & Paper Co., 1964-67, dept. anatomy Med. Coll. S.C., 1963—, vis. prof. systems physiology, 1973—. Oak Ridge Sch. Reactor Tech. fellow, 1956-57; Universal Oil Products scholar, 1955-56; travel grantee NRC, 1967, NIH, 1967—, NSF, 1964-66, travel, 1972, Ford Found., summer 1965, 68. Recipient 1st pl. research award Am. Soc. Engring. Edn., 1967. Mem. Analog/Hybrid Computer Ednl. Users Group (nat. dir.), Internat. Soc. Oxygen Transport to Tissue, Am. Chem. Soc., Internat. Platform Assn., European Soc. Micro Circulation, Am. Inst. Chem. Engr., U.S., U.S. Profl. lawn tennis assns., Inter Collegiate Tennis Coaches Assn., Sigma Xi, Tau Beta Pi. Clubs: Gatlinburg (Tenn.) Skiing; Timberlane Country (resident tennis profl.) (Gretna). Editor: Oxygen Supply, 1973; Oxygen Transport to Tissue, 1973. Contbr. articles to profl. jours. Home: 513 Fairfield Av Gretna LA 70053 Office: Dept Chem Engring Tulane U New Orleans LA 70118

BRUMBACK, CHARLES TIEDTKE, newspaper exec.; b. Toledo, Sept. 27, 1928; s. John Sanford and Frances Hannah (Tiedtke) B.; B.A., Princeton, 1950; postgrad U. Toledo, 1953-54; m. Mary Louise Howe, July 7, 1951; children—Charles Tiedtke, Anne V., Wesley W., Ellen P. With Arthur Young & Co., C.P.A.'s, 1950-57; with Sentinel Star Co., Orlando, Fla., 1957—; v.p., dir., Sentinel Star Express Co.; asst. sec. Fla. Forms, Inc.; asst. sec. Fla. Sunpapers Inc. Treas., United Appeal Orange County, Fla., also mem. exec. com.; treas., dir. Sentinel Star Community Assn. Mem. Orlando Municipal Planning Bd., 1958-63. Bd. trustees Orlando Pub. Library, 1958-63; treas. bd. govs. Orange Meml. Hosp. Served to 1st lt. AUS, 1951-53. Decorated Bronze Star medal. C.P.A., Ohio, Fla. Mem. Ohio, Fla. socs. C.P.A.'s, Am. Inst. C.P.A.'s, Orlando Area C. of C. (dir., v.p.), Fla. Press Assn. (treas. 1969—), Inst. Newspaper Controllers and Finance Officers, Financial Execs. Inst. (sec. local chpt. 1970—), Rotarian. Clubs: Orlando Country, University. Home: 911 Seville Pl Orlando FL 32804 Office: 633 N Orange Av Orlando FL 32802

BRUMBY, PAUL BINGHAM, physician; b. Goodman, Miss., Sept. 28, 1902; s. Walter Eldridge and Mattie Theodora (Alexander) B.; M.D., U. Tex., 1929; postgrad. N.Y. Polyclinic, 1935, Harvard, 1939; m. Linda Fay Patton, June 25, 1935; children—Paul Bingham, Linda (Mrs. James Donald Holder). Intern, Shreveport (La.) Charity Hosp., 1929-30; pvt. practice gen. medicine, Lexington, Miss., 1930—; chief of staff Holmes County Community Hosp., Lexington, 1946—. Bd. dirs. Miss. Found. for Med. Care., 1970—. Served with AUS, 1943-46. Decorated Bronze Star medal. Mem. North Central Miss. Med. Soc. (pres. 1954), Miss. Acad. Family Practice (v.p. 1958), Miss. State Med. Assn. (pres. 1971; trustee 1971). Presbyn. (elder 1966—). Mason (32 deg., Shriner), Rotarian. Home: 102 Westwood Av Lexington MS 39095 Office: 102 N Carrollton St Lexington MS 39095

BRUMBY, SEWELL MARION, librarian; b. Cedartown, Ga., May 20, 1911; s. Charles Rush and Annie Lee (Sewell) B.; B.S., U.S. Mil. Acad., 1932 M.S., Columbia, 1961; J.D., U. Ga., 1964; m. Mary Kent Hart, Sept. 28, 1935; children—Marianne Curran, Mira Lee Sewell, Sewell Robeson Brainerd. Commd. 2d lt. U.S. Army, 1932, advanced through grades to col., 1954; assult bn. comdr. 4th Inf. div. D-Day, Normandy; comdr. Camp Fuji, Japan, 1954; sec. U.S.-Japan Joint Com., 1955-57; ret., 1960; law librarian U. Ga., Athens, 1961—. Mem. Am. Assn. Law Libraries. Home: 350 Glenwood Dr Athens GA 30601 Office: Law Library U Ga Athens GA 30602

BRUNEAU, L(ESLIE) HERBERT, educator; b. Cornwall, Ont., Can., Nov. 28, 1928; s. Victor Herbert and Linda (Leslie) B.; B.Sc., McGill U., 1950; M.A., U. Tex., 1952, Ph.D., 1956; m. Betty Jane Leifheit, Aug. 1, 1953; children—Carol Lorraine, David Emmeit Herbert. Came to U.S., 1950, naturalized, 1959. Mem. faculty Okla. State U., Stillwater, 1955—, asso. prof., 1960-66, prof., 1966—, chmn. dept. biol. sci., 1960—. Active Will Rogers council Boy Scouts Am., 1968—, dist. chmn., 1972—. Bd. dirs. Stillwater chpt. United Fund. Recipient Outstanding Tchr. award Coll. Arts & Scis., Student Council, Okla. State U., 1968. Mem. Soc. Study Evolution, Stillwater C. of C., Sigma Xi. Home: 2140 W Admiral Av Stillwater OK 74074

BRUNER, QUINTON DOSSIE, r.r. exec.; b. Dothan, Ala., June 28, 1921; s. Charlie Crozier and Annie Mae (Williams) B.; m. Mary Ellen Slusher, June 23, 1946; children—Charles Stephen, Martha (Mrs. Wayne Burdette), Mary Quinn (Mrs. James E. Couch). Sec. to auditor-treas. Atlanta & St. Andrews Bay Ry. Co., Dothan, 1939-40, sec. to asst. gen. mgr., 1940-42, sec. to pres. and gen. mgr., 1945-46, comml. agt., 1946-60, gen. agt., 1960-63, asst. gen. freight agt., 1963-68, traffic mgr., 1968-72, chief traffic officer, asst. sec., 1972—, also dir., mem. exec. com. Sec. chpt. A.R.C., 1967-68. Bd. dirs. United Fund. Served with USAAF, World War II; PTO. Mem. Assn. U.S. Army, So. Freight Assn. (mem. exec. com. 1968—), So. Ports Fgn. Freight Com. (gen. com. 1968—), C. of C. (dir. 1961-63), Com. 100. Baptist (deacon 1958—). Kiwanian (pres. 1957). Editor, The Bay Liner, 1963-69. Home: 207 Sequoyah Dr Dothan AL 36301 Office: 514 E Main St Dothan AL 36301

BRUNER, RUTH AVALINA, educator; b. Chickasha, Okla., Nov. 12, 1912; d. Peter N. and Cora (May) Bruner; B.S., Memphis State U., 1934; M.A., Northwestern U., 1946, Ph.D., 1959, La. State U. Tchr., Whitehaven (Tenn.) High Sch., 1937-40; sec. to Commr. Finance, City of Memphis, 1934-36; exec. sec. to asst. to pres. Todd-Houston Shipbldg. Corp., Houston, 1941-44; asst. prof. Northwestern State Coll., Natchitoches, La., 1946-56, asso. prof., 1956-59, prof., 1960-64; prof., head dept. office adminstrn. Northeast La. U., Monroe, 1964-73; vis. prof. Coll. Bus., Ariz. State U., Tempe, 1972-73. Communications cons. State Farm Ins., Monroe, La., 1971—, Internat. Tel. & Tel., Monroe, 1970—. Named Distinguished Tchr. of Year, Northeast La. U., 1972. Mem. Am. Assn. U. Women, Am. Assn. U. Profs., Nat. So., La. bus. edn. assns., Am. Bus. Women's Assn., Delta Kappa Gamma, Delta Pi Epsilon, Phi Kappa Psi (chpt. pres. 1962-63). Contbr. articles to bus. edn. jours. Home: 31 Fair Oaks Monroe LA 71201

BRUNGARDT, ADOLPH JOHN, dentist; b. Morland, Kan., Jan. 20, 1909; s. John M. and Catherine (Bach) B.; student St. Benedict's Coll., 1929-31; D.D.S., Creighton U., 1935; m. Mildred Cates, May 27, 1940; children—Maurice Philip, Adolphine (Mrs. Richard D. Shaw), James M., Joseph A., Charles E., Mary Ann. Pvt. practice dentistry, Lindsay, Okla., 1935—. Vice pres. Garvin County Library Bd., 1969-72; mem. Lindsay Indsl. Found. Mem. Am., Okla., South Central Dist. dental assns., C. of C. Democrat. Roman Catholic (mem. ch. com. 1950-53). Rotarian (past pres.). Home: 210 Willians St Maysville OK 73057 Office: 2 W Chickasaw St Lindsay OK 73052

BRUNINGA, WILLIAM HENRY, restaurant exec.; b. Peoria, Ill., Oct. 4, 1927; s. William John (dec.) and Helen Arlouine (Loucks) B.; student DePauw U., 1947-48; B.S., U. Ill., 1950; m. Beverly Anne Ward, July 5, 1952; children—John, Stephen, Susan. Accounting supr. Maule Industries, Inc., Miami, Fla., 1952-59; controller Velda Dairies, Miami, 1959-62, Burger King Corp., Miami, 1963-66; operator Burger King Restaurant, Des Moines, 1967-68; sec., treas. Shoney's Big Boy Enterprises, Nashville, 1969—. Adviser Jr. Achievement, 1957-59, 1964. Served with USAAF, 1945-47. Episcopalian. Home: 2140 Timberwood Dr Nashville TN 37215 Office: 1727 Elm Hill Pike Nashville TN 37210

BRUNINI, JOSEPH BERNARD, bishop; b. Vicksburg, Miss., July 24, 1909; s. John and Blanche (Stein) B.; A.B., Georgetown U., 1930, LL.D., 1957; S.T.D., North Am. Coll., Rome, 1933; J.C.D., Cath. U., Washington, 1937. Ordained priest Roman Catholic Ch., 1933; rector Cathedral, Natchez, Miss., 1943-44; chancellor Natchez Diocese, 1941-49; pastor St. Peter's Co-Cathedral, Jackson, Miss., 1949-62; vicar gen. of Diocese, 1951-66, aux. bishop Natchez-Jackson Diocese, 1957-66, apostolic adminstr., 1966-67, bishop, 1967—. Recipient John Carroll award Georgetown U. Mem. Cath. Hosp. Assn. U.S. and Can. (past pres.), Fed. Hosp. Council, Am. Hosp. Assn. (trustee). K.C. (4 deg.). Home: 123 N West St Jackson MS 39201 Office: Box 2248 Jackson MS 39205

BRUNSON, BOB CURRAN, JR., mech. engr.; b. Charleston, S.C., May 31, 1921; s. Bob Curran and Switzer (Hiers) B.; B.S. in Mech. Engring., Ga. Inst. Tech., 1943; M.Automotive Engring., Chrysler Inst. Tech., 1945; m. Virginia Lee Campbell, Feb. 14, 1944 (div. Feb. 1966); 1 dau., Karen Dagmar (Mrs. Robert Margolis); m. 2d, Beatrice Darden Trevathan, Dec. 17, 1966. With Connell Assos. Inc., Miami, 1948—, v.p., gen. mgr., 1970-72, pres., chief exec. officer, 1972—; partner firm Connell, Pierce, Garland & Friedman, Miami, 1960—. Registered profl. engr., Fla. Mem. Fla. Engring. Soc., Nat. Soc. Profl. Engrs., Am. Soc. Mech. Engrs., Am. Soc. for Testing and Materials, Nat. Fire Protection Assn., Alpha Tau Omega, Tau Beta Pi, Phi Eta Sigma. Methodist. Kiwanian. Clubs: Key Biscayne (Fla.) Yacht; Country (Coral Gables, Fla.); Miami, Bankers (Miami). Home: 1125 Alhambra Circle Coral Gables FL 33134 Office: 1320 S Dixie Hwy Coral Gables FL 33146

BRUNSON, DONALD LYONS, dentist; b. Houston, June 13, 1922; s. Howard Edward and Ouida (Lyons) B.; B.B.A., U. Tex. at Austin, 1944, D.D.S., 1950; m. Elayne Hope Duke, Aug. 18, 1942; 1 dau., Cassandra. Gen. practice dentistry, Baytown, Tex., 1950—; dir. Citizens Nat. Bank & Trust Co. Mem. Tex. Bd. Dental Examiners. Former chmn. Baytown Civil Service Commn. Trustee San Jacinto Meth. Hosp.; bd. regents Lee Coll. Served with Dental Corps, USAF, 1953-55. Fellow Am., Internat. colls. dentists; mem. Baytown Dental Study Club (pres. 1971-72), Am., Tex. dental assns., Houston Dist. Dental Soc., U. Tex. Ex-Students Assn. (life), Am. Acad. Gen. Dentistry, Baytown C. of C. (dir.), Psi Omega, Delta Chi. Methodist (adminstrv. bd., trustee). Club: Baytown Rotary (v.p. 1962). Home: 1803 Southwood Dr Baytown TX 77520 Office: 1105 E James St Baytown TX 77520

BRUNSON, JOEL GARRETT, physician, educator; b. Greenville, S.C., Apr. 22, 1923; s. James Edwin and Leila (Ballenger) B.; student Furman U., 1940-43, Miss. State Coll., 1943; M.D., U. Buffalo, 1950. Intern, U. Ala. Med. Center, 1950-51; resident pathology U. Minn. Hosps., 1951-55; Am. Cancer Soc. fellow U. Minn., 1951-55, instr., pathology Med. Sch., 1955-57, sr. research fellow USPHS, also asst. prof. pathology, 1957-59; prof. pathology, chmn. dept. U. Miss. Med. Center, Jackson, 1959—; cons. VA Hosp., Jackson; cons. pathology A study sect. USPHS; mem. VA Instl. Research Programs Evaluation Com. Served with AUS, 1943-46. Diplomate Nat. Bd. Med. Examiners, Am. Bd. Pathology. Mem. Am. Assn. Pathologists and Bacteriologists, Internat. Acad. Pathology, Am. Soc. Exptl. Pathology, Am. Nuclear Soc., A.A.A.S., Soc. Research Reticuloendothelial System, Nat. Assn. Standard Med. Vocabulary, N.Y. Acad. Scis., Miss. Assn. Pathologists, Am. Heart Assn., Am. Assn. U. Profs., Am. Soc. Nephrology, Assn. Pathology Chmn. (sec.-treas. 1967-70, v.p. 1971, pres. 1972), Cryobiology Soc., Sigma Xi, Nu Sigma Nu. Co-editor: Concepts of Disease, 1971. Contbr. articles med. jours. Mem. editorial bd. Am. Jour. Pathology. Home: RFD 2 Terry MS 39170 Office: Univ Med Center Jackson MS 39216

BRUNSON, JOHN SOLES, lawyer; b. Houston, Tex., Jan. 8, 1934; s. Nathan Bryant and Jonnie E. (Sanders) B.; B.B.A., Baylor U., 1956, LL.B., J.D., 1958; m. Joan Erwin, Dec. 26, 1953; children—Wilson Mark, Dana Ruth. Admitted to Tex. bar, 1958; asso. Dillingham & Schleider, 1958-63; partner Brunson & Brill and predecessor firms, 1964-69; v.p., gen. counsel Contran Corp., 1969-70, partner law firm Baker, Heard & Brunson, Houston, 1970-72; dir. J.S. Williams & Co., McNair Trucklease Inc. Mem. Tex. Dem. Exec. Com., 1968—. Mem. Pres. Council, Houston Baptist Coll., 1966—. Mem. State Bar Tex., Houston, Am. bar assns. Club: Houston. Home: 10307 Greentree St Houston TX 77042 Office: 1440 One Allen Center Houston TX 77002

BRUNSON, PIERCE BUTLER, sch. adminstr.; b. Macon, Ga., Sept. 7, 1917; s. Zack A. and Hattie (Jackson) B.; student Albany State Coll. 1934-35; B.A., Morris Brown Coll. 1938; M.A., Atlanta U. 1955, postgrad. 1962-64; m. Brunetta F. Jacobs, June 19, 1946; children—Frank Bernard, Yolande Iris. Tchr., Austell (Ga.) Elementary Sch., 1938-39; ins. salesman Pilgrim Health and Life Ins. Co., Waycross, Ga., 1939-41; tchr. social sci. Hudson High Sch., Macon, Ga., 1947-49; tchr. social sci. Ballard-Hudson Sr. High Sch., 1949-65, chmn. dept. social sci., 1958-65; prin. Maude C. Pye Elementary Sch., 1965—. Bd. dirs. Macon Tchrs. Fed. Credit Union, 1966-68. Served as 1st lt. Transp. Corps, AUS, 1941-45; now capt. Res. ret. Mem. N.E.A., Ga. Assn. Educators, Ga. Elementary Prins. Assn., Bibb Elementary Prins. Assn. (v.p. 1971-72, pres. 1972-73), Omega Psi Phi. Baptist (deacon 1968—). Home: 1994 Vining Circle Macon GA 31204 Office: 855 Anthony Rd Macon GA 31204

BRUNTON, JOHN GEORGE, steel co. exec.; b. San Diego, Oct. 17, 1912; s. George and Agnes McKellar (Rankin) B.; B.S., U. Cal. at Berkeley, 1934; m. Vera M. Ukeneskey, June 12, 1936; children—Nancy (Mrs. Robert H. Cox, Jr.), Robert C. Sales mgr. Pennsalt Chems. Co., 1939-49; v.p. Kolker Chem. Corp., 1949-63; mgr. crop protection chems. USS Agri-Chems. div. U.S. Steel Corp., Atlanta, 1963—. Agrl. chem. industry adviser WPB, War Food Adminstrn., 1943-46. Club: Country (Atlanta). Home: 545 Riverside Pkwy NW Atlanta GA 30328 Office: 30 Pryor St SW Atlanta GA 30301

BRUSCA, DONALD RICHARD, pharm. co. exec.; b. Syracuse, N.Y., June 6, 1939; s. Donald Dominick and Dorothy (Schmidt) B.; B.S. in Chemistry, Rensselaer Poly. Inst., 1960; postgrad. Kan. State U., 1960-63; Ph.D. (Lotta M. Crabtree fellow), U. Mass., 1964; m. Ellen Mary Buzick, Sept. 2, 1961; children—Ann Marie, Lisa Michele. Sr. investigator Pacific NW Research Found., Seattle, 1964-66; asso. dir. lab. Schick Pharm. Corp., Seattle, 1966-69; head bioscis. research Corp. Research Labs., Esso Research & Engring. Co., Linden, N.J., 1969-70; v.p. health services div. USV Pharm. Corp., Arlington, Va., 1971—. Co-chmn. enzyme engring. conf. Engring. Found., 1971. Mem. Am. Assn. Bioanalysts (sci. program chmn. nat. meeting 1974, eastern regional dir.), N.Y. Acad. Scis., Soc. for Study Reprodn., Am. Assn. Clin. Chemists, Am. Chem. Soc., Pacific Coast Fertility Soc., Sigma Xi, Phi Kappa Tau. Club: Westwood Country. Patentee in field. Contbr. articles to profl. jours. Home: 2429 Sunny Meadow Lane Vienna VA 22180 Office: 653 N Glebe Rd Arlington VA 22203

BRUSEWITZ, CALVIN EMANUEL, civil engr.; b. Green Bay, Wis., June 11, 1930; s. Walter Christian and Emma (Schrader) B.; Asso. Sci., Weber Coll., 1951; B.S. in Civil Engring., Utah State Coll., 1956; m. Doris E. Bronson, June 25, 1957; children—Ann, Nancy, Susan. Spl. studies engr. Gen. Telephone Co., Spokane, Wash., 1957-62; bridge engr. Spokane County Engring. Dept., 1962-63; sr. structural engr. McDonnell-Douglas Aircraft Corp., Tulsa, 1963-67, mgr. facilities engring. br., 1967—. Served with AUS, 1951-53. Registered profl. engr., Okla., Wash. Mem. Okla. Soc. Profl. Engrs., Am. Soc. C.E., Nat. Mgmt. Club. Home: 5532 E 62d St Tulsa OK 74136 Office: 2000 N Memorial Dr Tulsa OK 74115

BRUSEWITZ, GERALD HENRY, educator, agrl. engr.; b. Green Bay, Wis., June 1, 1942; s. Henry Jackson and Wardeen Mae (Thiel) B.; B.S. in Agr., U. Wis., 1964, B.S. in Mech. Engring., 1965, M.S. in Agrl. Engring., 1966; Ph.D. (Nat. Def. Edn. Act fellow), Mich. State U., 1969; m. Susan Gayle Caine, Aug. 21, 1965; children—Kelly Katherine, Nicole Joanna. Asst. prof. agrl. engring. Okla. State U., Stillwater, 1969—. Active Big Bros. Lansing. Mem. Am. Soc. Engring. Edn., Am. Soc. Agrl. Engrs. (co-editor Food Engring. newsletter 1973-74), Inst. Food Tech., Sigma Xi, Pi Tau Sigma, Alpha Zeta. Methodist (Mem. finance com. 1972-74. Sunday sch. tchr. 1968, 72, 74, mem. adminstrv. bd. 1971-73). Home: 29 Summit Circle Stillwater OK 74074

BRUSILOW, ANSHEL, conductor; b. Phila., Aug. 14, 1928; s. Leon and Dora (Epstein) B.; grad. Curtis Inst. Music, 1943; Artist's diploma, Phila. Mus. Acad., 1947; m. Marilyn Rae Dow, Dec. 23, 1951; children—David, Jennie, Melinda. Concertmaster, asst. condr. New Orleans Symphony, 1954-55; asso. concertmaster Cleve. Orch.,

1955-59; concertmaster Phila. Orch., 1959-66; founder, condr. Phila. Chamber Orch., 1961-65, Chamber Symphony Phila., 1966-68; condr., music dir. Dallas Symphony Orch., 1970-73; vis. prof. N. Tex. State U., 1973—. Host TV program Portraits in Music, Sta. WRCV, 1961-63. Bd dirs. Ednl. TV Council. Named Outstanding Young Man of Year, Phila. C. of C., 1963. Home: 4545 Laren Lane Orchestra Dallas TX 75234

BRUSSO, FRANK STEPHEN, mech. engr.; b. Elmira, N.Y., Apr. 16, 1922; s. John Joseph and Minerva (Rathbun) B.; B.S., Okla. State U., 1953; m. Blanche Evangeline Brown, Jan. 31, 1947; children—Frank Stephen, Sandra Lee (Mrs. Michael Eugene Bauer), Denise (Stephen Jay Isley). Mech. engr. Dresser Engring. Co., Tulsa, 1953-55; resident engr. firm Owen, Mansur, & Steele, Tulsa, 1955-57; gen. mgr. Woods Constrn. Co., Tulsa, 1957-60; design engr. Williams Bros. Engring. Co., Tulsa, 1960-61, firm Fell & Wheeler, Tulsa, 1961-65; partner firm Fell Brusso Bruton, Inc., Tulsa, 1966—, also dir. Served with USAAF, 1942-45. Registered profl. engr., Okla., Tex. Mem. Nat. Soc. Profl. Engrs., Am. Water Works Assn., Okla. Soc. Prof. Engrs., Am. Congress Surveying and Mapping, Pi Tau Sigma. Baptist (deacon). Home: 1219 E 8th St Sand Springs OK 74063 Office: 6311 E Tecumseh St Tulsa OK 74151

BRUSTAD, WESLEY OTTO, state ofcl.; b. Fergus Falls, Minn., Aug. 16, 1943; s. Otto Waldemar and Doris Mina (Holoien) B.; B.A. cum laude (NSF scholar, Alcoa scholar), U. Wash., 1964, M.A., 1970; m. Karla Kay Stratford, Dec. 23, 1970; children (by previous marriage)—Robert Wesley, Jason Michael. Adviser, publicity dir. U. Wash., 1969-70; communications coordinator Friends of Youth (social agy.), Seattle, 1970; asst. dir. Ohio Arts Council, Columbus, 1970-71; exec. dir. S.C. Arts Commn., Columbia, 1971—. Cons. various theatre projects, art forms. Served with USAF, 1965-69. Mem. Am. Theatre Assn., numerous assns. arts Presbyn. Designed and conceived theatrical concept spatial theatre. Mailing address: 1708 York Dr Columbia SC 29204

BRUTON, EMMA QUINTILLA GEER (MRS. JAMES DEWITT BRUTON, JR.), civic worker; b. Walton, Ky., Dec. 16, 1907; d. James Arthur and Celia Exular (Wooten) Geer; student pub. schs.; m. James DeWitt Bruton, Jr., June 11, 1932. Bookkeeper, stenographer mfg. firm, Tampa, Fla., 1927-29; clerical worker Standard Oil of Ky., 1929-31; bookkeeper, stenographer Plant City (Fla.) Courier, Wayne Thomas, Pub., 1932-34, Wayne Thomas, Real Estate and Bond Broker, 1934-41; legal stenographer, 1943-44. Vice chmn. Fla. State Library Adv. Council, 1969-71; bd. dirs., exec. com. Hillsborough County Tb and Health Assn., 1960-67, v.p., 1964-66, life mem., 1967; rep. bd. dirs. Fla. Tb and Health Assn., Jacksonville, 1964; bd. Plant City Library, 1959-73, chmn., 1959-67; mem. County Adv. Library Com. 1961—, chmn., 1961-72; mem. Fla. State Library Bd., 1961-63, chmn., 1962-63; mem. Fla. Library and Hist. Commn., 1963-69, chmn., 1967-68; mem. Fla. Library Study Commn., 1970-73; mem. Council Fla. Archives, 1964-65. Mem. Am., Fla., Hillsborough County library assns., Am., Fla. (v.p. 1961-63) library trustee assns., Am. Assn. State Libraries, Hillsborough County Friends of Library (dir. 1960-73, pres. 1967-68), Fla. Audubon Soc. (life), Nature Conservancy, Mus. Sci. and Natural History, Brandon (Fla.) friends of library, Ruskin Library Assn., Tampa Execs. Club, Aux. to Bar Assn. of Tampa and Hillsborough County. Democrat. Methodist. Clubs: Plant City Golf and Country, Plant City Garden (v.p. 1966-68), Women's (Plant City); Tampa Bird. Home: 910 Roux St Plant City FL 33566

BRUTON, JAMES DE WITT, JR., judge; b. Magazine, Ark., Feb. 2, 1908; s. James David and Pattie Lee (Bruton) B.; LL.B., U. Fla., 1931, J.D., 1967; m. Quintilla Geer, June 11, 1932. Admitted to Fla. bar, 1931, since practiced at Plant City; asst. criminal court solicitor, Tampa, 1934-37; elected to Fla. Ho. of Reps., 1935-36; municipal judge, Plant City, 1937-57; corp. and civil lawyer, 1931-61; former probate judge Hillsborough County, Fla.; now circuit judge, Tampa. Dir. Tampa Abstract & Title Ins. Co., Hillsboro Bank, Plant City. Mem. Fla. Bd. Law Examiners, Tampa Mental Health Assn., Tampa A.R.C., Inter-Profl. Family Council, Suicide Prevention Center of Hillsborough County; establisher, owner Bruton's Audubon Acres Bird Sanctuary, Plant City. Fellow Am. Bar Found.; mem. Fla. Municipal Judges Assn. (pres. 1956-57), Com. of 100, C. of C. Plant City (bd. dirs.), Plant City Civic Music Assn. (pres.), Jr. C. of C. (pres. 1940), U. Fla. Alumni Assn. (v.p.), Fla. (gov. 1949-50; chmn. bd. editors Jour. 1950-52; chmn. com. Am. citizenship 1952-53; chmn. com. on world peace through law 1959-61), Am. (ho. of dels. 1951-58), Tampa bar assns., Am. Coll. Probate Counsel (jud. fellow), County Judges Assn. Fla. (v.p.), Am. Judicature Soc. (dir.), Audubon Soc., Fla. Cattle Assn., Tampa Humane Soc. (life), Selden Soc. London, Am. Ornithologists Union (life), Fla. Hist. Soc. (life mem., dir.), Chi Phi. Democrat. Methodist. Elk, Kiwanian (past lt. gov.; dir. Plant City). Clubs: Plant City Golf and Country; Tampa Executives (pres. 1951-52, dir.), Tampa Bird. Home: 910 Roux St Plant City FL 33566 Office: County Courthouse Tampa FL 33602

BRYAN, BART EBERT, assn. exec.; b. Johnstown, Pa., May 5, 1894; s. Bart and Carrie (Ebert) B.; student U. Mass., 1913-14, Cornell U., 1914-15; m. Marie Elizabeth Genung, Mar. 28, 1921; children—John B., William Joseph. Directory publisher, Asbury Park, N.J. 1923-24; salesman display advt. St. Petersburg (Fla.) Times, 1927-34, advt. mgr., 1934-44, pub. relation dir., 1944-59; pub. St. Petersburg Visitors News, 1944-46; pres. St. Petersburg Motor Club (A.A.A.), 1960-65, treas., 1965-70, dir., 1947—. Pres. St. Petersburg Inter Civic Council, 1942; chief fire watcher Civilian Def., 1943; treas. St. Petersburg Civic Music Assn., 1962-69; life mem. bd. Pinellas Area council Boy Scouts Am. Served with AEF, 1917-19. Recipient Mr. Citizen award, 1958; Silver citation First Fed. Savs. & Loan Assn., 1958. Mem. Am. Legion, V.F.W., Pinellas County Com. 100. Episcopalian (sec. vestry 1960-62). Clubs: St. Petersburg Yacht, Advertising (life mem.) (St. Petersburg). Editor: You Can Sell Newspaper Advertising, 1941. Address: 2616 48th St S St Petersburg FL 33711 2616 48th St S St Petersburg FL 33711

BRYAN, DAVID TENNANT, newspaper pub.; b. Richmond, Va., Aug. 3, 1906; s. John Stewart and Anne Eliza (Tennant) B.; student U. Va., 1925-28; LL.D., U. Richmond, 1973; m. Mary Harkness Davidson, May 11, 1932. Chmn. bd., dir. Media Gen., Inc.; pub. Richmond Times-Dispatch and Richmond News Leader; dir. Asso. Press, So. Ry. Co. Vice chmn., trustee Richmond Meml. Hosp.; bd. assos. U. Richmond; bd. overseers Hoover Instn. War, Revolution, Peace. Active USNR, 1942-46. Recipient Thomas Jefferson award for pub. service Richmond chpt. Pub. Relations Soc. Am., 1965. Mem. Am. Newspaper Pubs. Assn. (pres. 1958-60), Soc. of Cincinnati, S.A.R., S.R., Va. Hist. Soc. (mem. exec. com.), Soc. Colonial Wars, Sigma Delta Chi. Clubs: Commonwealth, Country of Va. (Richmond); Farmington Country (Charlottesville); St. Anthony, Union (N.Y.C.); National Press, Alfalfa (Washington); Bohemian (San Francisco). Home: Ampthill Rd Richmond VA 23226 Office: 333 E Grace St Richmond VA 23219

BRYAN, FRANK LEON, microbiologist; b. Indpls., Aug. 29, 1930; s. Frank Leslie and Marie (Vogt) B.; B.S., Ind. U., 1953; M.P.H., U. Mich., 1956; Ph.D., Ia. State U., 1965; m. Ruth Ann McDonald, Aug. 30, 1952; children—Steven Harris, Sharryl Ann. Tng. officer New Eng. Field Tng. Sta., USPHS, Amherst, Mass., 1956-58, tng. officer environmental health sect. tng. program Communicable Disease Center, Atlanta, 1958-63, scientist-dir., chief foodborne disease activity Center Disease Control, 1965—. Served to 1st.lt. Med. Service Corps, AUS, 1953-55. Mem. Am. Soc. Microbiology, Inst. Food Technologists, N.Y. Acad. Scis., Internat. Assn. Milk, Food, Environmental Sanitarians (mem. edit. bd.), USPHS Commd. Officers Assn. (sec. 1972-73), Sigma Xi (chpt. v.p. 1974), Delta Omega, Phi Tau Sigma, Gamma Sigma Delta. Contbr. to books, articles to profl. jours. Home: 2022 LaVista Circle Tucker GA 30084 Office: Center Disease Control Atlanta GA 30333

BRYAN, JACK YEAMAN, author, photographer, ret. fgn. service officer; b. Peoria, Ill., Sept. 24, 1907; s. James Yeaman and Regina (Gibson) B.; student U. Chgo., 1925-27; fellow philosophy, Duke, 1933-35; B.A. with high distinction, U. Ariz., 1932, M.A., 1933; Ph.D., U. Ia., 1939; m. Margaret Gardner, June 21, 1934 children—Joel Yeaman, Guy Kelsey, Donna Gardner (Mrs. Robert Warren Welch), Kirsten Stuart (Mrs. Sidney Bruce Kelley, Jr.). Research analyst Fed. Emergency Relief Adminstrn., Washington, 1935-36; from instr. English to prof., chmn. dept. journalism, U. Md., 1936-48; pub. relations adviser OCD, 1942-43; dir. pub. information Welfare Fedn. Cleve., 1943-45; pub. information officer UNRRA, 1945-46; cultural attache Am. embassy, Manila, Philippines, 1948-51; chief program planning Internat. Exchange Service, Dept. State, 1951-53; pub. affairs officer USIS, Bombay, India, 1953-54, Bangalore, India, 1954-55; cultural affairs officer Am. embassy, Cairo, Egypt, 1956, Tehran, Iran, 1956-58; cultural attache, chief cultural affairs officer Am. embassy, Karachi, Pakistan, 1958-63; chief personnel officer for Africa, USIA, 1964-65; officer in charge Project AIM, U.S. Dept. State, Washington, 1965-67; chief cultural affairs adviser USIA, 1968; lectr. creative photography U. Cal. at Riverside, 1968—. Chmn. publs. bd. U. Md., 1946-48; chmn. bd. dirs. U.S. Ednl. Found. in Philippines, 1949-51, U.S. Ednl. Found. in Pakistan, 1958-63; exec. dir. Iran-Am. Soc. in Tehran, 1956-58; founder, exec. dir. Pakistan-Am. Cultural Center, 1959-60, 62, 63. Recipient ann. prize for best fiction Tex. Inst. Letters, 1964, Summerfield Roberts award, 1964. Mem. Tex. Inst. Letters, Tex. Hist. Assn., Am. Mus. Natural History, Am. Soc. Mag. Photographers, Am. Acad. Polit. and Social Scis., Am. Fgn. Service Assn., Phi Delta Theta, Kappa Alpha Mu, Pi Delta Epsilon. Club: Faculty (U. Cal. at Riverside). Author: (novel) Come to the Bower, 1963. Contbr. short stories, articles and photographs to various mags., anthologies, textbooks, including Sunset book on Mexico, 1972. One-man exhibit of photos of Asia touring U.S. colls. and univs.; one-man photo exhibits in India, Pakistan, Washington. Home: 3594 Ramona Dr Riverside CA 92506 also 4107 Van Buren St University Park MD

BRYAN, JACOB FRANKLIN, III, ins. co. exec.; b. Jacksonville, Fla., Feb. 26, 1908; s. Jacob Franklin and Olive (Gibson) B. II; grad. Fla. Bus. U., 1932; LL.D., Bethune-Cookman Coll., 1965; m. Josephine Christian Hendley, May 25, 1935; children—Jacob Franklin IV, Carter Byrd, Kendall Gibson. With Ind. Life & Accident Ins. Co., Jacksonville, Fla., 1927—, exec. v.p., 1954-56, pres., 1957—, also chmn. bd.; pres., chmn. bd. Herald Life Ins. Co., Jacksonville, 1960—; dir., mem. trust com. Fla. Nat. Bank, Jacksonville, 1957—; dir. Security Fed. Savs. & Loan, Jacksonville, 1957—, S.C. Life & Health Inst. Guaranty Assn. Columbia, S.C., 1972—. Mem. White House Com. Fund Raising Fed. Employees, 1953-61, White House Com. Employment Handicapped, 1962—; pres. Jacksonville Symphony Assn., 1968-70, now bd. dirs.; state chmn. fund dr. Fla. Heart Assn., 1970, Fla. Arts Commn., 1961-65, Health Planning Council Jacksonville Area, 1964-70; v.p. Fla. div. Am. Cancer Soc.; state v.p., mem. exec. com., bd. dirs. So. States Indsl. Council, 1970—; v.p. Cathedral Cound. Jacksonville, 1963-72; exec. adviser N. Fla. Council Boy Scouts Am., 1961—; former chmn. Citizens Com. Juvenile Ct., sec., mem. bd. dirs. Fla. Devel. Commn., 1961-65; mem. Fla. Council 100, 1962—, State Ins. Adv. Com., 1960-70, contact com. HUD, 1970—, adv. bd. Jacksonville Art Mus., 1959, nat. adv. council SBA, 1970, Commn. Quality Edn., 1967, lay adv. bd. St. Vincent's Med. Center, 1972—. Mem. Fla. Pub. Sch. Bd., 1968-69; chmn. 3d Congl. Dist., Nixon-Agnew campaign, 1972. Bd. dirs. Indsl. Am. Corp., Jacksonville, Jr. Achievement, March Dimes, Girls' Club Jacksonville, Child Guidance Clinic, Childrens Home Soc. Fla., Jacksonville Downtown Devel. Authority, Community Planning Council Jacksonville Area, Inc., United Negro Coll. Fund, and several others; trustee Jacksonville U. (also mem. operations com., bd. devel.), Baptist Meml. Hosp., Bethune-Cookman Coll.; founding trustee Jacksonville Episcopal High Sch.; mem. bd. fellow U. Tampa (Fla.). Recipient Champions Higher Ind. Edn. Fla. award Ind. Colls., Univs. Fla. Assn., 1971. Mem. Fla. (dir.-at-large), Jacksonville Area (mem. adv. com. Com. 100) chambers commerce, Internat. Platform Assn., Fla. Life Ins. Cos. Assn. (pres.), Newcomen Soc. Fla., Nat. Orchid Soc., (pres.), S.A.R., Huxford Genealogical Soc. Inc., Fla., Jacksonville hist. socs., Nat. Trust Hist. Preservation, Order Stars and Bars, English Speaking Union (dir.), Sons Confederate Vets. Episcopalian. Clubs: Florida Yacht, Timuquana Country, River, Seminole, Ye Majestic Revellers (all Jacksonville); Ponte Vedra (Fla.). Home: 4255 Yacht Club Rd Jacksonville FL 32210 Office: 233 W Duval St Jacksonville FL 32202

BRYAN, JAMES CLARENCE, chem. engr.; b. Munford, Tenn., Jan. 26, 1923; s. Clarence Talmadge and Ruby (Flaniken) B.; B.S. in Chem. Engring., U. Tenn., 1948, M.S., 1952, Ph.D. (DuPont fellow), 1954; m. Helen Louise Sehorn, Oct. 9, 1948; children—James Flaniken, Helen Sehorn, With E.I. DuPont de Nemours & Co., Chatanooga, 1954-61, Waynesboro, Va., 1961-65, Camden, S.C., 1965—, process supr., 1965-69, sr. research engr., 1969—. Served with AUS, 1943-45; PTO. Mem. Am. Chem. Soc., Am. Inst. Chem. Engrs. (chmn. 1972-73), Sigma Xi. Episcopalian. Patentee in field. Home: 1900 Brook Dr Camden SC 29020 Office: E I DuPont de Nemours & Co Camden SC 29020

BRYAN, JOHN HENRY DONALD, zoologist, educator; b. London, Eng., Sept. 18, 1926; s. John and Mary (Barnes) B.; came to U.S., 1947, naturalized, 1957; B.Sc., U. Sheffield, Eng., 1947; M.A., Columbia, 1949, Ph.D. (McCallum Found. fellow), 1952; m. Janet Goff, Aug. 23, 1952; children—Mary Elizabeth, Melissa Loring. Instr. biology Mass. Inst. Tech., Cambridge, 1951-54; asst. prof. genetics Ia. State U., Ames, 1954-60, asst. prof. zoology, 1960-62, asso. prof., 1962-67, chmn. cell biology com., 1962-67; prof. zoology U. Ga., Athens, 1967—. Cons. to NSF, AID, Indian Edn. Program, New Delhi and Bombay, 1968-69. Fellow A.A.A.S., Am. Inst. Biol. Scis.; mem. Am. Soc. Cell Biology, Am. Soc. Naturalists, Am. Soc. Zoologists, N.Y. Acad. Scis., Soc. Devel. Biology, Sigma Xi. Club: Torch. Contbr. articles on zoology and biology to sci. jours. Office: Dept Zoology 703 Biol Scis Bldg Univ Ga Athens GA 30602

BRYAN, LOREN ALDRO, chemist; b. Emporia, Kan., Feb. 4, 1916; s. Earl Austin and Anna (Spencer) B.; A.B. Emporia State Tchrs. Coll., 1937, B.S., 1937; M.S., Kan. State U., 1939; Ph.D., Northwestern U., 1944; postdoctoral study Rutgers U., 1959; m. Mabel Corine Norris, June 7, 1952; 1 dau., Ann Corine. Research asso. Miner Labs., Chgo., 1943-53; project engr. Melpar Inc., Alexandria, Va., 1953-54, sr. mem. chem. research, devel. sect., 1954; sr. chemist FMC Corp., Carteret, N.J., 1954-60; head organic chem. sect. Great Lake Carbon Corp., Morton Grove, Ill., 1960-62; sr. chemist Great Lakes Research Corp., Elizabethton, Tenn., 1962—. Instr. first aid, mem. blood bank com. Carter County (Tenn.) unit A.R.C., 1970—; pres. Expt. in Internat. Living, Elizabethton, 1973—. Fellow Am. Inst. Chemists, A.A.A.S.; mem. Am. Chem. Soc., N.Y. Acad. Scis., Sigma Xi, Kappa Mu Epsilon, Pi Mu Epsilon, Phi Lambda Upsilon, Lambda Delta Lambda, Kappa Delta Pi, Alpha Chi Sigma. Presbyn. (elder). Patentee in field. Home: 1206 Michigan St Elizabethton TN 37643 Office: PO Box 1031 Elizabethton TN 37643

BRYAN, LYMAN LOWELL, govt. ofcl.; b. Newcastle, Okla., Dec. 8, 1924; s. Albert Roy and Florence (Bowlan) B.; B.A. in Journalism (Kayser scholar 1948), U. Okla., 1948; m. Alice Louise Modlin, Dec. 31, 1944; children—Lowell, Lisa, Laurel, Layne. Asst. dir. pub. relations Pan American Petroleum Co., Texas City, Tex., 1949-50; dir. information Independent Petroleum Assn. Am., Washington, 1951-54; mgr. community relations Chrysler Corp., Detroit, 1954-56; dir. Washington div. Am. Inst. C.P.A.'s, Washington, 1957-73, also Washington editor Jour. of Accountancy, 1957-73; dir. pub. and congl. affairs office Minority Bus. Enterprise, Commerce Dept., 1973—; guest lectr. U. Okla., Mich. State U., Southeastern U. Participant White House Conf. Bus. Editors, 1962; mem. U.S. Savs. Bonds nat. orgn. com. Treasury Dept.; del. ann. meetings U.S. C. of C., 1959-65; mem. U.S. C. of C.'s Assn. Council on Pensions. Bd. dirs. Arlington (Va.) Better Sports Club, 1963-67; mem. Com. County Expenditures, Arlington County; mem. Arlington Youth Found. Served with USAAF, 1943-45. Recipient Patriotic Civilian Service award U.S. Army Audit Agy., 1963. Mem. A.A.A.S., Fed. Govt. Accountants Assn. (mem. publs. com.), Am. Soc. Pub. Adminstrn., Am. Soc. Assn. Execs., Am. Acad. Polit. and Social Sci., Am. Judicature Soc., U. Okla. Journalism Sch. Alumni Assn. (regional v.p. Washington), Sigma Delta Chi. Baptist. Clubs: Nat. Press, University (Washington). Contbr. numerous articles to nat. farm, bus., accounting mags. Home: 2900 N Greencastle St Arlington VA 22207 Office: Main Commerce Bldg 14th and E Sts Washington DC 20230

BRYAN, MALVERN THORNTON, physician; b. Memphis, Aug. 30, 1912; s. John Gano and Myrtle (Thornton) B.; B.A., U. Tenn., 1934; M.D., Washington U., St. Louis, 1938; M.P.H. (USPHS fellow), U. Cal. at Berkeley, 1967; m. Ione Ruth Grace Freund, May 20, 1941; children—John G., Mary Ellen (Mrs. Jose A Goenaga), Kathleen (Mrs. Robert McCrory), Sally Ann, Ruth M. Intern, St. Louis City Hosp., 1938-39, Mo. Pacific Hosp., St. Louis, 1939-40; resident in obstetrics and gynecology John Gaston Hosp., Memphis, 1947-48, Bapt. Meml. Hosp., Memphis, 1948-50; practice medicine, specializing in obstetrics and gynecology, Memphis, 1954—; mem. staff Bapt. Meml., Meth., City of Memphis, St. Joseph's hosps. (all Memphis); asst. in gynecology and obstetrics Sch. Medicine, U. Tenn., Memphis, 1954—; asst. dir. div. maternal and child health W. Va. Dept. Pub. Health, 1968. Served with M.C., AUS, 1940-46, 50-53. Fellow Am. Coll. Obstetricians and Gynecologists; mem. Memphis-Shelby County, Tenn. obstetrics and gynecology socs. Home and office: 1366 Carr Av Memphis TN 38104

BRYAN, MIRIAM GERTRUDE MAY (MRS. JAMES E. BRYAN), educator; b. P.E.I., Can., Feb. 1, 1908 (parents Am. citizens); d. George William and Emma (Lawless) May; B.S. in Edn., Bridgewater (Mass.) State Coll., 1929; postgrad. Boston U., 1929-30, Yale, 1935-36, U. Cal. at Los Angeles, 1937, U. Colo., 1938; M.A., N.Y.U., 1940; m. James E. Bryan, Oct. 31, 1941. Tchr., Howard High Sch., West Bridgewater, Mass., 1929-35, Hamden (Conn.) High Sch., 1935-36, East Haven (Conn.) High Sch., 1936-40, Hastings on Hudson (N.Y.) High Sch., 1941-43; head adv. service Coop. Test Service, N.Y.C., 1943-45, adminstrv. asst., 1945-46, editor, 1947-48; editor-in-chief Coop. Test div. and nat. tchr. exams. Ednl. Testing Service, N.Y.C., 1948-49; asst. editor Silver Burdett Co., N.Y.C., 1949-55; test specialist Psychol. Corp., N.Y.C., 1955-56; asst. prof. edn. Rutgers U., New Brunswick, N.J., 1958-60, co-adjutant staff mem., 1956-58; sr. asso. in test devel. Ednl. Testing Service, Princeton, N.J., 1960-61, asso. dir. test devel., 1961-67, sr. editor and asso. dir. Coop. Test Div., 1967-68, cons. elementary and secondary sch. testing program, 1968-72, asso. dir. Atlanta office, 1972—. Test editor, cons. Ia. testing programs State U. Ia., Iowa City, 1950-56; test cons. ednl. div. Reader's Digest Services, Inc. 1955-58; research cons. N.Y. State Dept. Edn., 1962-68; cons. U. N.H., WNH-TV, 1966-67, 70-71; lectr. Mich. State U., summer 1970. Sec., West Bridgewater Republican Town Com., 1934-35. Mem. Am. Ednl. Research Assn., Internat. Reading. Assn., Nat. Council on Measurements in Edn., N.E.A., Am. Assn. U. Profs., Am. Assn. U. Women, N.Y.U., Bridgewater State Coll. (Nicholas Tillinghast award 1970) alumni assns., Nat. Council Tchrs. English, Am. Personnel and Guidance Assn., Assn. for Measurement and Evaluation in Guidance, USPHS Wives, Kappa Delta Pi, Pi Lambda Theta (pres. Rho chpt. 1957-58, editor nat. publs. 1961-64, 71—, chmn. nat. fellowship awards com. 1961-64, cons. 1964-65, nat. pres. 1965-69, cons. 1969). Editorial asso., contbr. 4th Mental Measurements Yearbook, 1952-53, 5th, 1957-59, 6th, 1964, 7th, 1972. Contbr. numerous articles to profl. publs. Author various tests. Home: 4978 Vernon Springs Dr Atlanta GA 30338 Office: Educational Testing Service 17 Executive Park Dr NE Atlanta GA 30329

BRYAN, RICHARD WALKER, educator; b. Dalton, Ga., Nov. 10, 1892; s. William Edward and Alice (Lyle) B.; Ph.B., Emory U., 1916; M.S., N.Y.U., 1924, Ph.D., 1949; student Ga. Inst. Tech., 1920-21, Columbia, summers 1921, 38; m. Ellen L. Fenstermacher, Sept. 28, 1927; 1 son, Richard Walker. Asso. prof. Auburn (Ala.) U., 1934-35; head dept. bus. adminstrn. U. Tampa, Fla., 1935-40; head dept. commerce U. Bridgeport, Conn., 1940-46, Catawba Coll., Salisbury, N.C., 1946-47; prof. econs. and finance La. Poly. Inst. (now La. Tech. U.), Ruston, 1947-58; head div. bus. adminstrn. Athens (Ala.) Coll., 1958-67, prof. econs. and finance, 1969—; prof. econs. and bus. adminstrn. Martin Coll., Pulaski, Tenn., 1967-69. Mem. Am. Legion, Delta Sigma Pi, Eta Mu Pi, Delta Pi Epsilon, Delta Mu Delta. Democrat. Methodist. Mason. Home: 206 N Madison St Athens AL 35611 Office: Athens Coll Athens AL 35611

BRYAN, ROSS HENRY, cons. structural engr.; b. nr. Ellsworth, Kan., Apr. 16, 1910; s. James E. and Jenny (Henry) B.; B.S., U. Kan., 1933; m. Josephine Kandt, May 30, 1936 (dec. 1968); 1 dau., Penelope (Mrs. Gerald W. Kriegel); m. 2d, Irene Hodgden Simpson, July 26, 1969. Bridge designer Kan. Hwy. Dept., Topeka, 1933-40; structural designer Panama Canal Dept., Office Engr. Div., 1940-43; structural engr. Marr & Holman, Architects, Nashville, 1946-49; partner Bryan & Dozier, Cons. Engrs., Nashville, 1949—; pres. Ross H. Bryan Inc., Cons. Engrs., Nashville, 1952—. Bd. dirs. Salvation Army. Served to lt. USNR, 1943-46. Fellow Am. Soc. C.E.; mem. Nat. Soc. Profl. Engrs., Am. Concrete Inst., Prestressed Concrete Inst., Cons. Engrs. Council, Am. Inst. Cons. Engrs., Sigma Chi, Theta Tau. Kiwanian. (pres. 1968). Home: Harbor Island Old Hickory TN 37138 Office: 3d Nat Bank Bldg Nashville TN 37219

BRYANT, A(LTON) BYRNES, JR., savs. and loan exec.; b. Graniteville, S.C., Oct. 23, 1929; s. Alton B. and Roxie (Duffie) B.; B.S., U. S.C., 1955; postgrad. U.S.C., 1955, Grad. Sch. Savs. and Loan, Ind. U., 1967-69; m. Anna May Marcella, Oct. 1, 1950; children—Michael Byrnes, Karen Sue. Asst. v.p., asst. treas., loan officer Home Fed. Savs. & Loan, 1955-61; asst. v.p. Security Fed. Savs. & Loan, Columbia, S.C., 1961-63; sr. v.p. Home Fed. Savs. &

Loan Assn., Columbia, 1963—. Mem. Richland County Rural Recreation Commn.; mem. finance com. Columbia Sch. Bd. Pres., Columbia Savs. and Loan League, 1969, 74; chmn. legislative com. S.C. Savs. and Loan League, circuit chmn., 1970, county chmn., 1969, 71, chmn. com., 1974. Bd. dirs. United Community Services. Served with USN, 1948-52. Mem. Columbia C. of C., S.C. C. of C., Am. Savs. and Loan Inst., Assn. U.S. Army, Alpha Kappa Psi. Clubs: Forest Lake Country, Sertoma, Palmetto. Home: 187 Arcadia Springs Circle Columbia SC 29206 Office: 1500 Hampton St Columbia SC 29201

BRYANT, BEAUFORD H., educator; b. Chatham, Va., June 8, 1923; s. B. Dudley and Nannie M. (Bolling) B.; B.A., Johnson Bible Coll., 1943; B.D., Phillips U., 1946, M.A., 1944; M.Th., Princeton Theol. Sem., 1948; Ph.D., U. Edinburgh (Scotland), 1957; m. Dorothy Jane Larson, July 11, 1965; children—Susan, John Paul. Prof. Bible, Phillips U., 1945-56; prof. Bible, Milligan Coll. (Tenn.), 1956-65, prof., chmn. area N.T., Emmanuel Sch. Religion, 1965—; Welsheimer lectr., Johnson Bible Coll., 1963; ann. lectr. Maritime Christian Coll., Can., 1968; alumni lectr. Ky. Christian Coll., 1971. Mem. Christian Ch. Address: Box 222 Milligan College TN 37682

BRYANT, BRITAIN HAMILTON, state senator; b. Louisville, Mar. 21, 1940; s. William Hamilton and Virginia (Throgmorton) B.; student Centre Coll. Ky., 1958-59; B.S. in Law, U. Louisville, 1962, J.D., 1964; postgrad. Sch. Law, Washington and Lee U., 1963; m. Peyton Gresham, Apr. 24, 1965; children—Anne Hamilton, Stewart Wells. Admitted to Ky. bar, 1965, V.I. bar, 1965, U.S. Supreme Ct. bar, 1972; partner firm Bryant, Costello & Burke, Christiansted, St. Croix, V.I., 1970—; mem. V.I. Senate, 1973—. Bd. dirs. St. Croix chpt. A.R.C. Mem. V.I. (sec. 1969-71, v.p. 1972), Am. bar assns., St. Croix C. of C. (sec. 1969-72), Am. Trial Lawyers Assn., World Peace through Law Assn., V.I. Jud. Council, Beta Theta Pi, Phi Delta Phi. Home: 3 Betsy's Jewel Christiansted St Croix VI 00820 Office: 7 King St Christiansted St Croix VI 00820

BRYANT, CELIA MAE SMALL, educator; b. Porum, Okla., Aug. 11, 1913; d. George Milton and Elsie (Sigmon) Small; Mus.B. in Piano, U. Okla., 1947, Mus.M., 1948; pvt. study Frank Mannheimer; m. William Cullen Bryant III, Oct. 3, 1932 (div. May 1945); children—Ann (Mrs. Robert L. Trent), Mary Carol (Mrs. Robert Fritchof Hansen), Culleen (Mrs. Ronald George Tobin). Mem. faculty U. Okla., Norman, 1948—, prof. music, 1967—; vis. prof. Interlochen Music Acad., summers 1972-73. Appeared as pianist numerous recitals; music adjudicator, clinician; mem. Okla. Commn. Tchr. Edn. and Profl. Standards, 1962-63. Mem. exec. bd. Camp Fire Girls, Norman, 1950-54; bd. dirs. Nat. Music Council, 1971—, Music Tchrs. Nat. Assn. Scholarship Found., 1972—. Named one of Nine Outstanding Music Educators in Nation, Mu Phi Epsilon, 1962, Outstanding Okla. Musician, 1972; nat. citation Phi Mu Alpha, 1972. Mem. Music Tchrs. Nat. Assn. (life mem., div. pres. 1956-58, nat. pres. 1969-73), Am. Music Scholarship Assn. (adv. bd. 1972—), Okla. Music Tchrs. Assn. (pres. 1962-66), U. Okla. Tchr. Edn. Council (chmn. 1958-62), Alpha Chi Omega Alumnae Assn. (state pres. 1950-51), Editor piano pedagogy dept. Clavier Mag., 1961—, writer series Music Lesson, 1963—. Contbr. articles to publs. Home: 614 E Okmulgee St Norman OK 73069

BRYANT, CHALMERS, mayor; b. Dozier, Ala., Oct. 18, 1922; s. James L. and Bertha (Colvin) B.; B.S., Auburn U., 1945; postgrad. U. Ga., 1947, 48; m. Edith Telintelo, Jan. 26, 1951; children—Marilyn H. (Mrs. Stephen Wright), Kim Alan, Keith Evan, Bruce Thomas. Sales rep. Creamery Package Mfg. Co., Atlanta, 1948-54; with Covington Creamery, Inc., Andalusia, Ala., 1954-68, mgr., 1954-68, treas., 1954-68 mayor, Andalusia, 1968—. Dir. Ala. Electric Coop., Andalusia; owner CB's Pit Barbecue, Andalusia, 1969—. Chmn. Covington County Blood Program A.R.C., 1961-68; capt. Andalusia Rescue Squad, 1965-68. Served with AUS, 1945-46. Named Andalusia Man of Year, Andalusia Kiwanis Club, 1966. Mem. Andalusia Mchts. Assn. (pres. 1960), Andalusia C. of C. (v.p. 1966-67). Mem. Ch. of Christ (deacon). Rotarian (pres. Andalusia club 1965-66). Home: 301 3d Av Andalusia AL 36420 Office: PO Box 292 Andalusia AL 36420

BRYANT, CYRIL ERIC, JR., ch. assn. adminstr.; b. Booneville, Ark., Aug. 8, 1917; s. Cyril Eric and Ruth Elizabeth (Best) B.; student Ouachita Coll., 1934-36; A.B., Baylor U., 1939; postgrad. So. Bapt. Theol. Sem., 1942-43; Litt.D., Ouachita Bapt. U., 1971; m. Flossie Juanita Wells, Apr. 29, 1943; children—James Edwin, Mary Elizabeth (Mrs. Leland R. Smith). Dir. news Baylor U., 1939-42, dir. pub. relations, 1949-57; editor Ark. Baptist News Mag., 1943-47; dir. publicity So. Bapt. Conv., 1947-49; dir. publs. Bapt. World Alliance, Washington, 1957-71, asso. sec., 1971—. Mem. Asso. Ch. Press, Religious Pub. Relations Council. Am. Bible Soc. (adv. council 1965—), Sigma Delta Chi. Club: Nat. Press. Author: Operation Brother's Brother, 1968. Editor Bapt. World, 1957—. Contbr. articles to profl. jours. Home: 1628 16th St NW Washington DC 20009 Office: 1628 16th St NW Washington DC 20009

BRYANT, GEORGE BADGER, III, newspaper editor; b. Washington, Dec. 7, 1938; s. George Badger and Elsie Freeman (Spenny) B.; A.B. in Journalism, U. N.C.; m. Mardge Etta Lupton, July 22, 1961; 1 son, George Badger IV. Reporter U.P.I., 1960; sports editor Daily Reflector, Greenville, N.C., 1961-63; reporter Virginian-Pilot, Norfolk, Va., 1963-68, city editor, 1968—. Mem. U.S. Power Squadron, Virginia Beach, Va. Home: 2320 Dodd Dr Virginia Beach VA 23454 Office: 150 W Brambleton Av Norfolk VA 23501

BRYANT, RICHARD MILES, clin. psychologist; b. Princeton, Ill., June 6, 1932; s. Miles William and Amanda (Kaar) B.; B.A., Washington U. (St. Louis), 1954; Ph.D., U. Tex., 1958; student U. Ia., 1954-55; m. Patricia Ruth Patton, Aug. 20, 1955; children—Richard Miles, William Patton, Melissa Ruth. Chief clin. psychology sect. Mental Hygiene Consultation Service, Ft. Leonard Wood, Mo., 1958-60; supr. psychol. services Juvenile Residential Treatment Program, State Hosp., Fulton, Mo., 1960-63; asst. prof. part-time Lincoln U., Jefferson City, Mo., 1960-63; spl. lectr. Wm. Woods Coll., Fulton, Mo., 1960-63; sr. clin. psychologist Children's Med. Center, Tulsa, 1963-64, dir. psychol. services, 1964—; pvt. practice clin. psychology, Tulsa, 1964—. Past chmn. Okla. State Bd. Examiners of Psychologists. Diplomate Am. Bd. Profl. Psychology. Mem. Am., Midwestern, Southwestern, Okla. (sec.-treas. 1969-71, pres. 1972-73) psychol. assns., Am. Soc. Clin. Hypnosis, A.A.A.S., Sigma Xi, Kappa Alpha, Tulsa Psychol. Assn. (past pres.). Home: 5353 S Joplin Av Tulsa OK 74135 Office: 4818 S Lewis Av Tulsa OK 74105

BRYANT, THOMAS FLOYD, JR., physician; b. Wellington, Tex., July 17, 1937; s. Thomas Floyd and Tiny Willie (Glasgow) B.; B.A., North Tex. State U., 1959; M.D., U. Tex., 1963; m. Beryl U. Dickens, Aug. 15, 1970; children (by previous marriage)—Thomas Floyd III, Enid Tina. Intern St. Joseph Hosp., Ft. Worth, 1963-64; resident U. Tex. Med. Br. Hosps., 1966-68; resident in pediatric anesthesiology Children's Hosp., Los Angeles, 1968-69; practice medicine specializing in anesthesiology, Galveston, Tex., 1969—; former mem. staffs U. Tex. Med. Br. Hosps., John Sealy Hosp.; asst. prof. anesthesiology U. Tex. Med. Br., Galveston, 1971—; asso. clin. prof. anethesiology Tex. Tech U. Sch. Medicine. Served with AUS, 1964-66. Diplomate Am. Bd. Anesthesiology. Fellow Am. Coll. Anesthesiologists; affiliate fellow Am. Acad. Pediatrics; mem. A.M.A., Am., Atlantic (hon.), Tex. socs. anesthesiologists, Randall-Potter County Med. Soc. Home: 3510 Langtry St Amarillo TX 79109 Office: 3309 Bedford St Amarillo TX 79106

BRYANT, WILLIAM ARTHUR, physician; b. Pensacola, Fla., Sept. 1, 1919; s. James Edward and Nora (Donaldson) B.; B.S., Madison Coll., 1942; M.D., Loma Linda U., 1947; m. Vesta Elnora Dunn, June 22, 1941; children—Rodney Craig, Gary Barton, Nancy Ellen. Intern, Nashville Gen. Hosp., 1946-47; resident Madison (Tenn.) Hosp., 1947-48; practice gen. medicine, Woodbury, Tenn., 1950—; mem. staff Good Samaritan Hosp., Woodbury. Med. examiner Cannon County, Tenn., 1965—; dir. Peoples Bank, Woodbury. Bd. dirs., v.p. Found. for Rehab. of Emotionally Handicapped; mem. exec. bd. Middle Tenn. council Boy Scouts Am. Served to capt. M.C., AUS, 1948-50. Mem. Am., Tenn., So., Woodbury (pres. 1956-57) med. assns., Am. Acad. Gen. Practice, Rutherford County and Stones River Acad. Medicine (sec.-treas. 1972-73, pres. 1973). Mem. Seventh-day Adventist Ch. (elder). Lion (past pres.). Home: Hollis Creek Rd Woodbury TN 37190 Office: 301 Main St Woodbury TN 37190

BRYANT, WILLIAM RANDOLPH, lawyer; b. Sherman, Tex., Jan. 22, 1919; s. Randolph and Julia (Hoard) B.; B.B.A., U. Tex., 1939, LL.B., 1946; m. Kathleen Brill, May 23, 1942; children—Beverly Ann, Julia Kathleen, Rebecca Jane. Admitted to Tex. Bar, 1946; partner firm Henderson, Bryant & Wolfe, Sherman, 1946—. Republican candidate for Gov. Tex., 1952. Trustee Wilson N. Jones Meml. Hosp., Sherman. Served to capt. USAAF, 1941-45. Rotarian. Home: 1231 Washington St Sherman TX 75090 Office: Box 239 Sherman TX 75090

BRYCE-LAPORTE, ROY SIMON, sociologist; b. Ancon, C.Z., Panama, Sept. 7, 1933; s. Simon J. and Myra Celestina (Laporte) Bryce; A.A., C.Z. Coll. with honors, 1954; B.S. (Honor Found. scholar 1959-61), U. Neb., 1960, M.A., 1961; advanced certificate (Pan-Am. Union Found. fellow) U. P.R., 1962; Ph.D. with deptl. distinction (Regents fellow 1966-67), U. Cal. at Los Angeles, 1968; m. Dorotea Lowe, Apr. 21, 1956; children—Robertino Omar, Camila Roxanne, Rene Bernardino. Came to U.S., 1959. Tchr. Latin Am. schs., C.Z., 1954-59; instr. U. So. Cal., 1964-66; lectr. edn. and sociology Syracuse U., 1966-68; asst. prof. sociology Hunter Coll., N.Y.C., 1968-69; asso. prof. sociology, dir. Afro-Am. studies Yale, 1969-72; dir. Research Inst. Immigration and Ethnic Studies Smithsonian Instn., Washington, 1973—; vis. prof. sociology U. Pa., 1973—; sr. field researcher P.R. Dept. Health, 1963; bibliographer, rappoteur Mexican-Am. study U. Cal. at Los Angeles, 1964; sr. research analyst Econ. and Youth Opportunities Agy., Los Angeles, 1966; cons. in field. Chmn. com. Afro-Am. Socs. and Culture Social Sci. Research Council, 1971—; mem. task force ethnic studies Ford Found., 1973—; reviewer UNESCO, 1967-70, CHOICE, 1970—, NSF, 1973-74. Asso. Inst. Black World, Atlanta, Center African and Afro-Am. Studies Atlanta U., 1969. Danforth Found. fellow, 1971; fellow Woodrow Wilson Center Scholar, 1971; fellow, vis. scientist Nat. Inst. Mental Health, 1972-73; Council Overseas Liaison com. Am. Council Edn., 1974—; cons. in field. Mem. Am. (mem. com. pub. information), Eastern, D.C., Internat. sociol. assns., Internat. Studies Assn., Caucus Black Sociologists, Alpha Kappa Delta, Pi Gamma Mu, Phi Delta Kappa, Mu Epsilon Nu, Phi Sigma Iota, Alpha Phi Alpha. Author: Black Captivity: Sociology of a Plantation Past, 1974. Co-editor Contemporary Alienation. Editorial adv. bd. Jour. Black Studies, 1970—, editor spl. issue, 1972. Contbr. numerous articles to profl. jours. Home: 1413 Floral St NW Washington DC 20012 Office: L'Enfant Plaza Astral Bldg North Suite 3500 SW Washington DC 20020

BRYDON, NATHANIEL COLEMAN, ins. co. exec.; b. Morgantown, W.Va., Dec. 12, 1910; s. George MacLaren and Nathalie Page (Coleman) B.; B.S., U. Va., 1933; m. Grace Langhorne Slater, June 26, 1937; children—Nathaniel Coleman, Jr., George MacLaren III, Sally Slater. Clk. actuarial dept. Life Ins. Co. Va., Richmond, 1936-40, clk. underwriting dept., 1940-46; dept. head VA Ins. Service, 1946-51; mgr. actuarial and underwriting depts. Richmond (Va.) Life Ins. Co., 1952-56; actuary Fidelity Bankers Life Ins. Co., Richmond, 1956-62, v.p. operations, 1962—. Bd. dirs. Jr. Achievement Richmond. Served with USNR, 1942-45; lt. comdr. Res. ret. Mem. Middle Atlantic Actuarial Club. Episcopalian (vestryman 1949-50, 56-58). Club: Bull and Bear (Richmond). Home: 7405 Three Chopt Rd Richmond VA 23226 Office: 9th and Main Sts Richmond VA 23219

BRYMER, ROBERT LEWIS, advt. exec.; b. Muskogee, Okla., Mar. 7, 1932; s. Winston Edward and Lois Ross (Nash) B.; B.A., U. Colo., 1954; postgrad. U. Chgo., 1958, Northwestern U., 1957; m. Natalie Ruth Snell, June 26, 1954; children—Kathleen, Robert, Charles, William. With Young & Rubicam Advt., Chgo., 1954; dir. marketing services Borg-Warner Internat. Corp., 1956-59; account exec., sr. v.p., dir. Zimmer, McClaskey, Lewis Inc., Louisville, 1959—. Served with USAF, 1954-56. Decorated Commendation Medal. Mem. Pub. Relations Soc. Am., Ky. Indsl. Advt. Assn. (pres. 1972-73). Club: Pendennis (Louisville). Home: 525 Country Lane Louisville KY 40207 Office: 1469 S 4th St Louisville KY 40208

BRYSON, JAMES MARION, city ofcl.; b. Owings, S.C., Oct. 25, 1922; s. James Marion and Nannie (Cox) B.; B.S. in Civil Engring., U. S.C., 1943; m. Helen Wallace Bobo, Nov. 8, 1947; children—Martha (Mrs. William H. Rhodes), Sara Bobo (Mrs. William Theodore Smith). County engr., Laurens County, S.C., 1949-55; bldg. ofcl. City of Spartanburg (S.C.), 1955-58, dir. pub. works and urban renewal, 1958-72, dir. community devel., asst. city mgr., 1972—. Served with USAAF, 1943-46. Recipient award of excellence for community service Spartanburg Council of Architects, 1968. Mem. Am. Pub. Works Assn., Nat. Assn. Housing and Redevel. Ofcls. (pres. Carolinas council 1969-70), award for program contbg. most to city-wide housing improvement Southeastern regional council 1965. Presbyn. (elder 1966—). Home: 315 Holly Dr Spartanburg SC 29301 Office: PO Box 1749 Spartanburg SC 29301

BUBIER, ROBERT HARVEY, city ofcl.; b. Hartford, Conn., June 12, 1927; s. Sylvester Breed and Ruth (Harvey) B.; A.B. in Journalism, U. Miami, 1951; m. Rosemary Theresa Brogan, July 26, 1951; children—Debra Ruth, Michelle. Personnel technician City of Ft. Lauderdale (Fla.), 1956-59, acting dir. recreation, also asst. city mgr., 1961-62, city mgr., 1963—. Dir. Civil Def., Ft. Lauderdale, 1964—. Bd. dirs. United Fund, YMCA, Swimming Hall of Fame, A.R.C., Broward County Jr. Achievement. Served with USNR, 1943-46, USAF, 1951-53, 61-62; lt. col. Res. Recipient Good Govt. award Ft. Lauderdale Jr. C. of C., 1967. Mem. Internat. City Mgrs. Assn. (v.p. S.E. region), Fla. (dir.), Broward County (past pres.) leagues of municipalities, Florida City and County Mgmt. Assn. (past pres.), Air Force Assn. (pres. Gold Coast chpt.), Am. Legion, Sigma Delta Chi, Simga Chi. Episcopalian (vestryman). Rotarian. Elk. Home: 300 Lido Dr Fort Lauderdale FL 33301 Office: 100 N Andrews Av Fort Lauderdale FL 33302

BUCHANAN, EMMETT LASCAR, JR., sales exec.; b. Detroit, Feb. 1, 1920; s. Emmett Lascar and Lillian (Kreekun) B.; student U. Mo., 1938-39; m. Betty Jean Pounders, June 30, 1951; children—Shirley Jean, Nancy Joyce. Salesman Bankers Life Ins. Co., John Hancock Ins. Co., Proctor & Gamble, 1940-42; salesman Health-Mor, Chgo., 1942-45; with Cooper U.S.A., Research Triangle Park, N.C., 1946—, salesman, regional mgr. So. region, 1946—. Served with AUS, 1942-45; PTO. Mem. Entomology Soc. Am., Tex. Producers Vet. Supplies (v.p. 1960). Methodist. Club: San Antonio Golf Assn. Home: Apt 75 6106 Vance Jackson St San Antonio TX 78230 Office: PO Box 12338 Research Triangle Park NC 27709

BUCHANAN, GERALD, librarian; b. Forrest County, Miss., July 26, 1937; s. W. L. and Melba (Griffith) B.; B.A., William Carey Coll., 1957; M.S., U. So. Miss., 1965; m. Dottie Renick, May 16, 1960; children—Kay, Donna, Cynthia. English tchr. Okolona (Miss.) Pub. Schs., 1957-59, Perkinston (Miss.) Jr. Coll., 1959-62; asst. librarian Perkinston Jr. Coll., 1962-65; librarian Perkinston campus Mississippi Gulf Coast Jr. Coll., 1965-73; asst. dir. library operations Miss. Library Commn., 1973—. Mem. Am., Southeastern, Miss. library assns., Miss. Edn. Assn. Baptist. Home: 711 Bellvue St Clinton MS 39056

BUCHANAN, HERSHEL, furniture mfg. co. exec.; b. Morristown, Tenn., July 31, 1918; s. James and Jane (Howard) B.; student U. Tenn., 1953; m. Mary Gertrude Horner, Sept. 30, 1939; children—Stephen Clay, Frances Sue, John Paul, Wanda Janelle. Supr. shipping Interwoven Stocking Co., Morristown, Tenn., 1940-43; gen. mill overseer Belding Heminway Co., Morristown, 1946-61; purchasing agt. Forest Products Corp., Morristown, 1961—. Served with AUS, 1943-45. Mem. V.F.W., Am. Legion. Woodman World, Mason (Shriner). Republican. Baptist. Home: Route 6 Morristown TN 37814 Office: 1010 Cherokee Dr Morristown TN 37814

BUCHANAN, JAMES JUNKIN, educator; b. Pitts., Mar. 7, 1925; s. John Grier and Charity (Packer) B.; A.B., Princeton, 1946, Ph.D., 1954; M.B.A., Harvard, 1948; m. Joanne Harriett Cherrington, Mar. 31, 1951; children—Susan Grier, Edison Cherrington, Constance Packer, James Junkin, Charles Sturm. Mem. staff investment adv. dept. 1st Boston Corp., N.Y.C., Pitts., 1948-51; instr. classics Princeton, 1953-56, asst. prof., 1956-60; chmn. depts. Latin and Greek, So. Meth. U., 1960-62, dean Coll. Arts and Scis., 1962-63; chmn. dept. classics Trinity U., San Antonio, 1963-64; prof. classical langs. Tulane U., New Orleans, 1964—. Treas., U. League Nursery Sch., Princeton, 1957-59. Bd. mgrs. Am. Sch. Classical Studies, Athens, Greece. Served with USNR, 1942-43. Mem. classical Assn. Midwest and S., Classical Assn. Eng., Am. Philol. Assn., Archaeol. Inst. Am., Princeton Alumni Council (exec. council), Phi Beta Kappa. Democrat. Episcopalian. Clubs: Essex (New Orleans); Princeton (N.Y.C.). Author: Boethius: Consolation of Philosophy, 1957, Theorika, 1962, Zosimus: Historia Nova, 1967. Contbr. to Ency. Americana, various jours. Home: 1542 Calhoun St New Orleans LA 70118

BUCHANAN, JAMES MCGILL, JR., economist, educator; b. Murfreesboro, Tenn., Oct. 2, 1919; s. James McGill and Lila (Scott) B.; B.S., Middle Tenn. State Coll., 1940; M.A., U. Tenn., 1941; Ph.D., U. Chgo., 1948; m. Anne Bakke, Oct. 5, 1945. Prof. econs U. Tenn., 1950-51; prof. econs. Fla. State U., 1951-54, prof., chmn. dept., 1954-56; prof. econs., U. Va., 1956-62, Paul G. McIntyre prof. econs., 1962-68, chmn. dept., 1956-62; prof. econs. U. Cal. Los Angeles, 1968-69; prof. econs. Va. Polytech. Inst., 1969—; dir. Center for Pub. Choice, 1969— Fulbright research scholar, Italy, 1955-56; Ford Faculty research fellow, 1959-60; Fulbright vis. prof. Cambridge U., 1961-62. Served as lt. USNR, 1941-46. Decorated Bronze Star medal. Mem. Am. (exec. com. 1966-69, v.p. 1971), So. (pres. 1963) econ. assns., Royal Econ. Soc. Author: (with C.L. Allen and M.R. Colberg) Prices, Income and Public Policy, 1954; Public Principles of Public Debt, 1958; The Public Finances, 1960; Fiscal Theory and Political Economy, 1960; The Calculus of Consent (with G. Tullock), 1962; Public Finance in Democratic Process, 1966; The Demand and Supply of Public Goods, 1968; Cost and Choice, 1969; (with N. Devletoglou) Academia in Anarchy, 1970; (with R. Tollison) Theory of Public Choice, 1972. Co-editor: LSE Essays on Cost, 1973. Contbr. profl. jours. Home: 504 South Gate Dr Blacksburg VA 24060

BUCHANAN, JOHN HALL, JR., congressman; b. Paris, Tenn., Mar. 19, 1928; s. John Hall and Ruby (Lowrey) B.; A.B., Howard Coll., 1949; grad. student U. Va., 1950-51; Th.B., So. Bapt. Theol. Sem., 1957; LL.D., Samford U., 1967; m. 2d, Elizabeth Moore, May 9, 1961; children—Elizabeth Jakes, Lynn Lowrey. Ordained to ministry Baptist Ch., 1952; pastor in Glasgow, Va., 1952-53, Hartsville, Tenn., 1955-56, Birmingham, Ala., 1957-62; minister edn. Southside Bapt. Ch., Birmingham, 1953-54; speaker, lectr. in Ala., also interim and supply pastor, 1962-64; mem. 89th-93d Congress from 6th Dist. Ala. Mem. U.S. delegation to UN, 1973, also spl. session, 1974. Chmn. Jefferson County Republican Com., 1964—; pres. Rep. Workshops Ala., 1963-64; mem. exec. com., dir. finance Ala. Rep. Com., 1963-64. Served with USNR, 1945-46. Mem. Pi Kappa Alpha. Mason, Kiwanian. Home: 2909 Highland Av S Birmingham AL 35205 Office: Longworth House Office Bldg Washington DC 20515

BUCHANAN, WILLIAM THOMAS, aero. engr., govt. ofcl.; b. Nashville, June 10, 1940; s. Charles Bingley and Bessie Mai (Cummings) B.; B.S. in Mech. Engring., U. Tenn., 1962, M.S., m. Mary Sue Hardy, Apr. 14, 1960; children—Cheri Lynn, Kimberly Gail. Engr., ARO, Inc., Arnold Air Force Sta., Tenn., 1962—. Cons. engring., 1970—. Registered profl. engr., Tenn. Home: 315 Crestwood Dr Tullahoma TN 37388 Office: PWT TO ARO Inc Arnold Air Force Station TN 37389

BUCHER, DONALD ROY, hosp. adminstr.; b. St. Louis, Nov. 17, 1927; s. George Henry and Leonora Frances (Arms) B.; B.S., St. Louis U., 1949; m. Patricia Lakebrink, May 18, 1958; children—Amy, Anna. Accounting dept. mgr. Butler Bros.-City Products Corp., St. Louis and Kansas City, Mo., 1953-63; internal auditor Consumers Coop. Assn., Kansas City, Mo., 1963-65; controller Baugh Wiley Smith Hosp., Decatur, Ala., 1965-68, adminstr., 1968—. Active Morgan County chpt. Nat. Cystic Fibrosis Research. Served with USNR, 1944-46, AUS, 1951-53. Mem. Ala. Hosp. Execs., Ala. Hosp. Financial Mgmt. Assn. (dir. 1969-70), Ala. Hosp. Assn. (trustee 1973-74), N. Ala. Hosp. Council (pres. 1973). Club: St. Louis University Alumni (St. Louis). Home: 1208 Noble St SW Decatur AL 35601 Office: 222 Gordon Dr SE Decatur AL 35601

BUCHHOLZ, ALBERT EDWARD, dentist; b. Pigeon, Mich., Apr. 27, 1916; s. Herman and Anna (Schuette) B.; B.S., Mich. State U., 1939; D.D.S., U. Mich., 1943; m. Margaret Olivia Petersen, June 19, 1943; children—William Arthur, Robert Alan, Mark Steven. Pvt. practice dentistry, St. Louis, Mich., 1946-54, Ft. Lauderdale, Fla., 1954—. Chmn., United Fund, 1948, 49; coach Little League Baseball and Football, 1958-66. Served to capt. Dental Corps, AUS, 1943-46; ETO. Mem. Broward County Dental Soc., Exec. Assn. Ft. Lauderdale (bd. dirs. 1964-65), Am. Legion, Broward County U. Mich. Alumni Assn. (pres. 1971-72), Tri County Dental Soc. (pres. 1947-48), Delta Sigma Delta. Republican. Presbyn. (deacon 1962-65). Mason, Rotarian. Clubs: Tennis, Touchdown (Ft. Lauderdale, Fla.). Home: 2549 Middle River Dr Fort Lauderdale FL 33305 Office: 852 NE 20th Av Fort Lauderdale FL 33304

BUCHHOLZ, DONALD ALDEN, stock brokerage co. exec.; b. LaPorte, Tex., Mar. 10, 1929; s. Fred T. and Chrystine (McCombs) B.; B.B.A., North Tex., U., 1952; m. Ruth Vernon, May 17, 1958; children—Robert, Chrystine Louise. Accountant, staff auditor Peat Marwick Mitchell, Dallas, 1952-54; asst. sec.-treas, chief accountant ICT Discount Corp., 1954-56; comptroller Eppler-Guerin & Turner, Inc., 1956-59; partner Cheshier-Buchholz, pub. accountants, 1959-60; comptroller, sec. Parker Ford, Inc., stock brokers, Dallas, 1960-63, also dir., 1962-63; v.p. Weber Hall, Cobb & Caudle, Inc., Dallas, 1963-72, also sec., dir.; v.p., partner MidSouthwest Securities, Inc., Dallas, 1972—; dir. Tucker Electronics Co., Garland Bank & Trust (Tex.), Gainsworth Devel. Co., Hedgfan Petroleum Co. Tchr., N.Y. Inst. Finance. Bd. govs. N.Y. Stock Exchange, 1969-72; mem. Bd. Trade City Chgo., 1963-72, Midwest Stock Exchange, 1963-72. Trustee Garland Ind. Sch. Dist., 1971—, pres. bd., 1973—. Served with USAAF, 1946-49. C.P.A., Tex. Mem. Dallas Security Dealers Assn. (sec. 1961). Baptist. Kiwanian (Garland v.p. 1959, pres. 1968). Home: 3627 Glenbrook Ct Garland TX 75041 Office: Mercantile Bank Bldg Dallas TX 75201

BUCHMAN, PAUL SIDNEY, lawyer, govt. ofcl.; b. Tampa, Fla., June 5, 1923; s. Julius M. and Lillian (Neuwirth) B.; LL.B., U. Fla., 1948; m. Beryle Solomon, Feb. 7, 1950; children—Julius Miles, Kenneth William. Admitted to Fla. bar, 1948; pvt. practice law, Plant City, Fla., 1948—; city atty. Plant City, 1949—; atty., exec. dir. Plant City Housing Authority, 1956—; atty., exec. dir. Plant City Urban Renewal Agy., 1961—. Chmn. Fla. Conf. of City Attys., 1960; pres. Ridge League of Municipalities, 1958. Served from pvt. to cpl. AUS, 1943-45, ETO. Decorated Purple Heart; recipient Distinguished Service award U.S. Jr. C. of C., 1961. Mem. Am. Bar Assn., Am. Judicature Soc., Nat. Inst. Municipal Law Officers, Fla. Bar (chmn. local govt. com. 1972-73, chmn. local govt. sect. 1973—), Fla. Assn. Housing and Redevel. Ofcls. (pres. 1968), Fla. Blue Key, Am. Legion, 40 and 8, Phi Alpha Delta, Pi Lambda Phi. Mason. Club: Lions. Home: 1010 N Knight St Plant City FL 33566 Office: 212 N Collins St Plant City FL 33566

BUCHTLER, HAROLD RICHARD, petrochem. co. exec.; b. Galveston, Tex., June 8, 1920; s. Walter and Nina Dorothy (Robinson) B.; B.B.A., U. Houston, 1952; m. Ula Palestine Owen, Nov. 22, 1945; children—Virginia (Mrs. Lawrence Randolph Sherfy), Harold Richard. Timekeeper, Todd Galveston Dry Dock, 1938-42; with Sinclair Rubber Inc., Houston, 1945-47, 50-55, McCarthy Chem. Co., Houston, 1947-50; cost accountant Petro-Tex Chem. Corp., Houston, 1955-57, budget analyst, 1957-63, budget dir. 1963-65, treas., 1967—. Merit Badge Counselor Sam Houston council Boy Scouts Am., 1963-65; adviser Jr. Achievement, 1957-60. Del. Republican County Conv., 1960. Served with USMC, 1942-45. Mem. Nat. Assn. Accountants. Episcopalian (mem. vestry 1964-66). Home: 1422 Pirates Cove Nassau Bay TX 77058 Office: 8600 Park Place Blvd Houston TX 77017

BUCHWALD, ART, columnist; b. Mt. Vernon, N.Y., Oct. 20, 1925; s. Joseph and Helen (Kleinberger) B.; student U. So. Cal., 1945-48; m. Anne McGarry, Oct. 11, 1952; children—Joel, Conchita Mathilde, Jennifer. Syndicated columnist, newspapers throughout world; columnist N.Y. Herald Tribune, 1948—. Served with USMCR, 1942-45. Clubs: Anglo-American Press (Paris); National Press (Washington). Author: Paris After Dark, 1950; Art Buchwald's Paris, 1954; The Brave Coward, 1957; A Gift From the Boys; More Caviar; Un Cadeau Pur Le Patronn (Prix de la Bonne Humeur, 1958); Don't Forget to Write, 1960; Art Buchwald's Secret List to Paris, 1961; How Much is That in Dollars, 1961; Is It Safe to Drink the Water?, 1962; I Chose Capital Punishment, 1963; And Then I Told the President, 1965; Son of the Great Society, 1966; Have I Ever Lied To You, 1968. Home: 4327 Hawthorne St NW Washington DC 20020 Office: 1750 Pennsylvania Av NW Washington DC 20006

BUCK, GEORGE HERMAN, JR., radio and TV sta. exec.; b. Elizabeth, N.J., Dec. 22, 1928; s. George Herman and Loretta (Reavey) B.; B.A., Lynchburg Coll., 1951; m. Eleanor Lipson, Dec. 22, 1969; children—Eve Gobey, George Simpson. Owner, pres. sta. WCOS-AM-FM, Columbia, S.C., 1958—, sta. WHVN, Charlotte, N.C., 1971—, sta. WQAK, Decatur, Ga., 1973—; producer, owner Jazzology-GHB Records; owner Big Horn Jazz Club, Underground Atlanta; writer, pub. Jazzology, quar. jazz mag. Founder, Carolina Jazz Festival, Columbia; past pres. Columbia Jazz Soc. Mem. Atlanta Jazz Soc., Potomac River Jazz Club (hon.). Home: 3008 Wadsworth Mill Ct Decatur GA 30032 Office: PO Box 32186 Decatur GA 30032

BUCK, LUCIUS A(DOLPHUS), lawyer; b. Abingdon, Va., July 3, 1905; s. E. C. and Mary (Lee) B.; student Emory and Henry Coll., Emory, Va., 1923-24; J.D., U. Va., 1929; m. Margaret Winters, Mar. 29, 1935; 1 son, David Mason V. Admitted to Va. bar, 1928, Fla. bar, 1929, N.Y. bar, 1940; practice law, West Palm Beach, Fla., 1929-34; spl. asst. to U.S. Atty. Gen., 1934-38; sr. tax asso. Davis, Polk Wardwell Sunderland & Kiendl, N.Y.C., 1938-42, 45-48; practice in Jacksonville, Fla., 1948—; sr. partner Buck, Drew & Glocker, 1954—; pres., dir. Sky-Tige, Inc., Chattanooga. Chmn. com. fiscal policies govt. Fla., 1955; chmn. Jacksonville Expressway Authority 1955-61. Bd. dirs. Cathedral Found., Inc., Jacksonville, 1966-70; trustee Frank Lubbock Miller Ednl. Found., 1958—, Jacksonville Episcopal High Sch., 1966-74; founding mem., dir. gen. So. Acad. Letters, Arts and Scis., 1971—. Served as capt. and maj. AUS, 1942-45; ETO, PTO, MTO. Decorated Bronze Star. Mem. Am., Jacksonville bar assns., Fla. bar (chmn. tax. sect. 1955-56), Order of Coif, Raven Soc., Phi Alpha Delta, Theta Chi. Episcopalian (sr. warden 1960-61, chmn. parish day sch. div. Diocese of Fla. 1959-62, chmn. bd. regents parish and diocesan schs. Diocese Fla. 1962-67, mem. restructure commn. 1971-72). Clubs: University, River (Jacksonville). Home: 326 Ocean Blvd Atlantic Beach FL 32233 summer Hot Ashes Dahlonega GA 30533 Office: 1120 Fla Title Bldg Jacksonville FL 32202

BUCK, RICHARD FREDERICK, container mfg. co. pres.; b. West Collingswood, N.J., Dec. 4, 1917; s. Delos Marvin and Beatrice Amy (Bigelow) B.; student Brown U., 1937-40; m. Evelyn Winifred Dugdale, Nov. 27, 1941; children—Geraldine (Mrs. Robert P. Price), Douglas M., Jeffrey H., Charles F. Salesman, Dictaphone Corp., Hartford, Conn., 1940; partner Barre Plywood Co. (Vt.), 1940-51; plant mgr. Atlas Plywood Corp., Boston, 1951-59; gen. mgr. U.S., Korboard Corp., High Point, N.C., 1959-67; gen. mgr., pres. Chattanooga Container Corp., 1967—. Served with USAAF, 1943-46. Lion, K.C. Home: 718 Bacon Trail Chattanooga TN 37412 Office: PO Box 350 Chattanooga TN 37401

BUCK, ROBERT FLETCHER, optometrist; b. Trenton, N.J., May 7, 1918; s. Ellard A. and Sue (Fletcher) B.; D. Optometry, Pa. Coll. Optometry, 1940; m. Ellen Marr Truax, May 14, 1943; children—Gwendolyn Sue, Penelope Jo. Individual practice optometry, Hackettstown, N.J., 1946-53, Dallas, 1954-55, Corpus Christi, Tex., 1955-56, San Antonio, 1956—. Bd. dirs. S.E. YMCA, San Antonio. Mem. Tex. Optometric Assn. (dir.), Bexar County Optometric Soc. (pres. 1964-66). Mason, Rotarian (pres. local chpt. 1960-61). Home: 11123 Ballet Dr San Antonio TX 78216 Office: 3310 E Southcross Blvd San Antonio TX 78223

BUCK, WILLIAM LEONARD, educator; b. Gotebo, Okla., July 27, 1926; s. William Leonard and Margaret (Rogers) B.; B.S., U. Okla., 1951; Ed.M. (NSF summer scholar) U. Fla., 1964, postgrad. (Nat. Sanitation Found. scholar), 68-70; m. Elizabeth Lucile Tuten, Nov. 16, 1952; children—Sharon Elizabeth, Gladys Margaret, Jacqueline Lucile, Carolyn Kinsley. Resident engr. J.E. Sirrine Co., Greenville, S.C. 1951-54; designer Lockheed Aircraft Marietta, Ga., 1954-55, Dunedin, Fla., 1956-57; designer Fairchild Aircraft, St. Augustine, Fla., 1956; engring. trainee, designer Fla. Rd. Dept., Lake City, 1958-60; math., sci. tchr. Hastings (Fla.) High Sch., 1960-61; math. tchr. Palatka (Fla.) Jr. High Sch., 1961-65; instr. engring. tech. St. Johns River Jr. Coll., Palatka, Fla., 1965—. Asso. trustee Briarwood Sch., Palatka. Served with F.A., AUS, 1945-46. Registered profl. engr., also registered land surveyor, Fla. Mem. Am. Soc. C.E., Nat. Soc. Profl. Engrs. Fla. Engring. Soc. (sr.), Am. Soc. Engring. Edn., Fla. Assn. Community Colls., Water Pollution Control Fedn. Democrat. Presbyn. (elder 1971—). Mason, Kiwanian (pres. 1955). Home: 602 S 14th St Palatka FL 32077

BUCKBERG, ALBERT, economist; b. Bklyn., Aug. 25, 1922; s. Isidor Paul and Anna (Litwack) B.; B.A., George Washington U., 1947; M.A., U. Mich., 1954, Ph.D., 1960; m. Gloria Bean, Feb. 26, 1967; 1 dau., Elaine Karen. Indsl. relations analyst WSB, Washington, 1951-52; instr. econs. dept. U. Mich., 1955-57; instr., asst. prof. Ia. State U., 1957-62; economist Bur. Budget, Exec. Office of Pres., Washington, 1962-66; economist Joint Com. Internal Revenue Taxation, U.S. Congress, Washington, 1966—; mem. review and evaluation team, tax administrn. assistance program AID and Internal Revenue Service, 1966; staff dir. spl. com. on social scis. NSF, 1968. Served with AUS, 1943-46. Decorated Bronze Star medal. Home: 5906 Maiden Lane Bethesda MD 20034 Office: Longworth House Office Bldg Washington DC 20515

BUCKLEW, (WILLIAM) HENRY, editor, publisher; b. Maxie, Miss., Apr. 10, 1925; s. Henry and Eunice (Clark) B.; student Jones County Jr. Coll., 1942-43, Tex. State Tchrs. Coll., 1945—; B.A., Miss. Coll., 1957; LL.B., Jackson Sch. Law, 1962; m. Euna Fern Varner, Aug. 21, 1945; children—Cheryl Darlene, Twyla Renae. Editor, pub., owner So. Bapt. News, Laurel, Miss., 1945—. Mayor, Laurel, Miss., 1965-66; active Gov. Wallace presdl. campaign, 1964. Founder, bd. dirs. Magnolia Boys Town. Served with AUS, 1943-45. Mem. V.F.W. (Miss. Distinguished Citizen award 1960, Humanitarian award 1962, Lit. Achievement award 1963, nat. chaplain 1965-66), Am. Legion, Dixie Golf Assn. (founder, pres. 1961-62), 40 and 8, Mil. Order Cooties (nat. chaplain 1972-74). Baptist. Woodman of World, Moose, Lion. Club: Laurel Sports (past pres.). Author: Your Daily Dozen Spiritial Vitamins, 1963. Home: 753 8th Av Laurel MS 39440 Office: PO Box 608 Front & 7th St Laurel MS 39440

BUCKLEY, EMERSON, music dir., condr.; b. N.Y.C., Apr. 14, 1916; s. Wendell and Minnie (Buckley) B.; B.A., Columbia, 1936; L.H.D., U. Denver, 1959; m. Mary Henderson, May 27, 1948; children—Robert Allen, Richard Edward. Music dir. Columbia Grand Opera, 1936-38, Palm Beach (Fla.) Symphony and Chorus, 1938-41, N.Y.C., Symphony, 1941-42, San Carlo Opera, 1943-45, WOR-MBS, N.Y.C., 1945-54, Marquis de Cuevas Ballet, 1950, Mendelssohn Glee Club, N.Y.C., 1954-63, P.R. Opera Festival, 1954-58, Symphony of the Air, also Empire State Mus. Festival, 1955, Tagarazuka Dance Theatre, also Greek Theatre, Los Angeles, 1958, Chautauqua Festival, N.Y., 1960, Temple U. Music Festival and Inst., 1970; music dir. Miami (Fla.) Opera Guild, 1950—; artistic dir. Greater Miami Opera Assn., 1973—; music dir. Central City (Colo.) Opera, 1956-69, Ft. Lauderdale (Fla.) Symphony, 1963—, Seattle Opera, 1964-74; condr. N.Y.C. Opera, 1955-69, New Orleans, Balt., Cin., Duluth (Minn.) operas, 1970—. Guest appearances with various orchs., including Toronto (Ont., Can.) Philharmonic, Mpls. Symphony, Miami Symphony; mem. faculty U. Denver, 1956, Columbia, 1957-58, Manhattan Sch. Music, 1958-70; dir. world premiers of Am. operas including The Ballad of Baby Doe, 1956, Gallantry, 1958, He Who Gets Slapped, 1959, The Crucible, 1961, Gentlemen Be Seated, 1963, Lady from Colorado, 1964; recordings for M-G-M, Columbia, Composers Records Inc., Heliodor. Recipient Fox prize Columbia Coll., 1936; Alice M. Ditson Conductor's award, 1964; Colo. Ambassadors Sash, 1965; Gold Chair award Central City Opera, 1965; Am. Patriot award state of Fla., 1971; decorated Chevalier des Arts et Lettres (France). Mem. Nat. Assn. Am. Composers and Condrs. Mason (Shriner). Home: 2271 NE 61st Ct Imperial Point Fort Lauderdale FL 33308 Office: 450 E Las Olas Blvd Fort Lauderdale FL 33301 also 1200 Coral Way Miami FL 33145

BUCKLEY, J. PAUL, civil engr.; b. Utica, N.Y., June 10, 1909; s. John M. and Katherine (McDonald) B.; B.C.E., U. Mich., 1932, M.C.E., 1933; m. Lucille E. Blaess, Apr. 15, 1931; 1 son, James Edmund. Asst. civil engr. City of Detroit, 1933; with Mich. Hwy. Dept., Lansing, 1934-42, project engr., 1934-37, statis. engr., 1938-39, asst. dir. planning and traffic div., 1939-42; cons. Cal. Legislature, 1946; engr., dir. Mich. Road Fedn., Lansing, 1947; chief engr. Automotive Safety Found., Washington, 1948-69; dir. tech. services div. Hwy. Users Fedn., Washington, 1970—. Served to maj. AUS, 1943-45. Fellow Am. Soc. Civil Engrs.; mem. Inst. Traffic Engrs., Mich. Engring. Soc., Nat. Assn. County Engrs. Home: 305 Ellsworth Dr Silver Spring MD 20910 Office: 1776 Massachusetts Av NW Washington DC 20036

BUCKLEY, THOMAS HUGH, historian, educator; b. Elkhart, Ind., Sept. 11, 1932; s. Bernard L. and Martha B. (Swoveland) B.; student Northwestern U., 1950-53; A.B., Ind. U., 1955, M.A., 1956, Ph.D., 1961; postgrad. Stanford, 1968; m. Patricia Cox, 1968; children—Christopher, Kathryn, Elizabeth, Thomas, Barbara. Instr. history U. S.D., Vermillion, 1961, asst. prof., 1961-64, asso. prof., 1964-68, prof., 1968-69; vis. prof. Ind. U., Bloomington, 1969-71; prof. history U. Tulsa, 1971—, chmn. dept., 1971—. Recipient citation for Best First Book by Historian, Phi Alpha Theta, 1971. Fulbright fellow, 1962. Mem. Orgn. Am. Historians, Phi Alpha Theta. Author: The United States and the Washington Conference, 1921-1922, 1970. Home: 4756 S Harvard St Tulsa OK 74129

BUCKLEY, THOMAS PATRICK, pathologist; b. Reading, Pa., Mar. 9, 1929; s. John Carroll and Sara Ann (Garst) B.; D.S.C., Chgo. Coll. Chiropody and Pedic Surgery, 1949; student La. State U., 1951-53, Tufts U., 1953-55; B.S., Hahnemann Med. Coll., 1959; m. Ann Gallen, Aug. 23, 1958; children—Sara Ann, Thomas M., John Carroll, Mary Kate, Joseph P., Julia Ellen, James Daniel. Rotating intern St. Joseph's Hosp., Reading, Pa., 1959-60; resident internal medicine, 1960, resident pathology, 1962-63; gen. practice medicine, Reading, 1960-62; lab. dir. Good Samaritan Hosp., Pottsville, Pa., 1966-70, Locust Mountain State Gen. Hosp., Shenandoah, Pa., 1966-70, Shamokin (Pa.) State Gen. Hosp., 1966-70, Southeastern Ky. Bapt. Hosp., Corbin, Ky., 1970—, Scott County Hosp., Oneida, Tenn., 1971, Meml. Hosp., Manchester, Ky., 1972, Knox County Hosp., Barbourville, Ky., 1971; clin. asst. prof. pathology Hahnemann Med. Coll. and Hosp., Phila., 1965-71; instr. chemistry St. Camillus Acad., Corbin, Ky., 1973—. Mem. exec. com. Northeastern Area Susquehanna Valley Regional Med. Program, 1966-70, mem. regional adv. group, 1966-70, mem. council on cancer Northeastern area, 1967-70; med. dir. certified lab. asst. program U. Ky., 1971-72, med. lab. technician program Cumberland Coll., 1972—. Bd. dirs. Montessori Children's House Reading, Inc., 1963-71, Quality Control Labs., Inc., Reading, 1965-70, Keystone Community Blood Bank, Inc., 1968-70. Served with AUS, 1951-53. Mem. A.M.A., Pa., Ky., Tenn. med. assns., Berks County Med. Soc., Schuylkill County, Whitley County, Scott County, Clay County, Knox County med. socs., Coll. Am. Pathologists, Am. Soc. Clin. Pathologists, Pa. Assn. Clin. Pathologists, Ky. Soc. Pathologists, Am., Pa., Ky. assns. blood banks, Phila. Pathol. Soc., Am. Assn. Clin. Chemists, Internat. Assn. Coroners and Med. Examiners, Internat. Acad. Pathology, N.Y. Acad. Sci., Assn. Clin. Scientists, South Central Assn. Clin. Microbiology. Home: 1202 Forest Circle Dr Corbin KY 40701 Office: Southeastern Ky Bapt Hosp Corbin KY 40701

BUDENSTEIN, PAUL PHILIP, educator, physicist; b. Phila., June 27, 1928; s. Samuel and Stella Betsy (Friend) B.; B.A., Temple U., 1949; M.S., Lehigh U., 1951, Ph.D., 1957; m. Jane Mitchell Gabler, Dec. 14, 1957; children—Steven Earl, Samuel Allen, David Franklin, Rebecca Ruth, Jennifer Alice. Mem. tech. staff Bell Telephone Labs., Holmdel, N.J., 1957-58; asst. prof. physics dept. Auburn (Ala.) U., 1959-62, asso. prof., 1962—. Cons. U.S. Army Missile Command, 1969—. Pres., Auburn U. Fed. Credit Union, 1972-73, Auburn High Sch. P.T.A., 1973—. Mem. Am. Phys. Soc., Am. Assn. Physics Tchrs., Am. Vacuum Soc., Electrochem. Soc., Am. Assn. U. Profs. (sec.-treas. Ala. Conf.). Jewish religion. Club: Civitan. Editor, contbr. Digest of Literature on Dielectrics, vol. 35, 1973, vol. 36, 1974. Home: 370 Bowden Dr Auburn AL 36830

BUECHNER, HELMUT KARL, ecologist; b. Scotia, N.Y., Aug. 5, 1918; s. Guenther Abraham and Helene (Nitz) B.: B.S. magna cum laude, N.Y. State U., 1941; M.S., Tex. A. and M. U., 1943; Ph.D., Okla. State U., 1949; m. Jimmie Irene Hatton, July 18, 1942; children—Nancy Carol (Mrs. James C. Crane), Hannele. Faculty, Wash. State U., Pullman, 1948-65, prof. zoology, 1963-65; head office Ecology, Smithsonian Inst., Washington, 1965-69, sr. ecologist, Office of Environmental Scis., 1969-72, sr. ecologist Nat. Zool. Park, 1972—. Served with USAF, 1943-45. Decorated D.F.C., Air medal with 5 oak leaf clusters. Fulbright research scholar, 1956-58; NSF grantee, 1959, 62-63; NASA grantee, 1969—. Fellow A.A.A.S.; mem. Am. Inst. Biol. Scis., Am. Soc. Mammalogists, Am. Soc. Zoologists, Internat. Assn. for Ecology, Animal Behavior Soc., Assn. for Tropical Biology, Brit. Ecol. Soc., Ecol. Soc. Am., Fauna Preservation Soc., Wilderness Soc., Wildlife Soc., World Acad. Arts and Scis., Sigma Xi. Rev. editor: Bird Banding, 1950-56, Jour. Wildlife Mgmt., 1959-61; editor: Northwest Sci., 1950-57. Contbr. articles to profl. jours. Home: 1863 N Patrick Henry Dr Arlington VA 22205 Office: Nat Zool Park Smithsonian Instn Washington DC 20009

BUECHNER, HOWARD ALBERT, physician; b. New Orleans, Feb. 1, 1919; s. Daniel and Grace (McCrackan) B.; B.S., Tulane U., 1939; M.D., La. State U., 1943; m. Emajean Vivian Jordan, May 18, 1947. Intern, Los Angeles County Gen. Hosp., 1943-44; resident VA Hosp., New Orleans, 1947-50, chief pulmonary disease sect., 1950-56, chief med. service, 1956-74; practice medicine specializing in pulmonary diseases, New Orleans, 1950—; faculty medicine Tulane U., 1950—, La. State U. Sch. Medicine, 1973—; sr. vis. physician Charity Hosp. La., 1958—; cons. pulmonary diseases USPHS Hosp., New Orleans. Bd. dirs. La. Tb Assn. Served to capt. M.C., AUS, 1944-47, to col. 1961-62. Decorated Bronze Star medal. Diplomate Am. Bd. Internal Medicine. Fellow A.C.P., Am. Coll. Chest Physicians (pres. So. chpt. 1965-66, gov. La. 1963—); mem. Am. (bd. councilors 1971—), So. (pres. 1961-62) Thoracic Socs., Phi Beta Kappa. Sr. editor med. jour. chest, 1968-72. Contbr. numerous articles to profl. jours. Research Tb, lung cancer, fungus diseases of lungs. Home: 300 Cuddihy Dr Metairie LA 70005 Office: 1542 Tulane Av New Orleans LA 70112

BUEHLER, JOE, mfg. co. exec.; b. Schenectady, May 28, 1928; s. Arthur G. and Eileen M (Sullivan) B.; B.B.A., Sienna Coll., 1953; m. Shirley E. Sinsig, Nov. 21, 1953; children—Katherine, Susan, Mark. Chief cost accountant Nat. Automotive Fibers Corp., Cohoes, N.Y., 1953-58; asst. controller Barclay Home Products, Cohoes, 1958-60; treas. Thermo Dynamics Inc., subsidiary Foster Refrigerator Co., Hudson, N.Y., 1960-67; controller Launch Support div. Bendix Corp., Cocoa Beach, Fla., 1967—. Served with USAAF, 1945-48. Mem. Fed. Gov. Accountants Assn. (chpt. dir. 1970-74), Nat. Assn. Accountants, U.S. Volleyball Assn. Home: 205 York Dr Cocoa FL 32922 Office: 1355 N Atlantic Av Cocoa Beach FL 32931

BUEHLER, JOHN ADOLPH, educator, minister; b. Phila., Nov. 17, 1916; s. Charles and Caroline Wilhelmiene (Kramer) B.; B.A. (scholar), U. Pa., 1939; B.Th., Anderson Coll. and Theol. Sem., 1944; Ph.D. (Eli Lilly fellow), Ind. U., 1949; m. Josie Dell Trigleth, Aug. 16, 1945; children—Harold Eugene, Donald Dean, Jane Marie. Chemist, Barrett Coal Tar Co., Phila., 1939-40, Midvale Steel, Phila., 1940-41; foreman Empire Ordinance, Phila., 1941-43; inspector Guide Lamp Co., Anderson, Ind., 1943-44; lab. asst. Ind. U., Bloomington, 1944-47; asst. prof. chemistry Anderson Coll., 1947-52; asso. prof., 1952-56, prof., 1956-60, chmn. dept. chemistry and div. of natural sci. and math., 1948-60; instr. chemistry Ind. U. Adult Center, Indpls., 1950-60; prof. chemistry, chmn. dept. LeMoyne-Owen Coll., Memphis, 1960—, div. chmn. div. of natural sci. and math., 1973—. Cons. Midwest Chem. Consultants, 1950-65; water cons. to Rome City, Ind., 1954-60. Pastor, Ch. of God, Memphis, 1960—; dean, Bay Ridge Christian Coll., 1960-70; ordained to ministry Ch. of God, 1962. Adviser to mayor, Anderson, 1956-60; chmn. 4-C's, Memphis 1968-69. Trustee Bay Ridge Christian Coll., Fellow A.A.A.S.; mem. Am. Sci. Affiliate, Am. Chem. Soc., Sigma Xi, Sigma Gamma Epsilon, Sigma Zeta, Alpha Chi Sigma. Contbr. articles to profl. jours. Home: 2276 Redwood Memphis TN 38108

BUEHLER, MARTIN STOWELL, physician; b. Omaha, Oct. 23, 1910; s. Martin Anton and Lucinda (Stowell) B.; B.S., U. Minn., 1936, B.M., 1938, M.D., 1939, M.S. in Medicine, 1941; m. Fern Scott, May 13, 1944; children—Lucinda Stowell, Martin Stowell, James Stowell. Intern, Abbott Hosp., Mpls., 1937-38; rotating intern Gallinger Municipal Hosp., Washington, 1938-39; resident Mpls. Gen. Hosp., 1939-41, teaching fellow in medicine, 1939-42, chief med. residents, 1941-42; teaching fellow in medicine U. Minn., Mpls., 1939-42, clin. asst., asst. to prof. medicine, 1941; practice medicine specializing in internal medicine and cardiology, Dallas, 1946—; attending physician in medicine Parkland City County Hosp., Dallas, 1945—, VA Hosp., McKinney Tex., 1950-60, VA Hosp., Dallas, 1950—, Presbyn. Hosp., Dallas, 1966—; mem. staff, attending physician Baylor U. Hosp., Dallas, 1946—; mem. clin. staff Episcopal Hosp., Caruth Meml. Rehab. Center, Wadley Insts. Molecular Medicine, Granville C. Morton Cancer and Research Hosp., all Dallas; mem. courtesy staff St. Paul's Meth. Gaston hosps., all Dallas, 1946—; asst. clin. prof. Southwestern Med. Coll. U. Tex., 1946-74; chest and cardiac cons. VA, Dallas, 1946-52; cons. physician Poliomyelitis Service, Dallas City County Hosp., 1950-53; internal medicine cons. Caruth Meml. Rehab. Center, Dallas, Wadley Insts. Molecular Medicine, 1968—; Met. Life Ins. Co., 1973—; cons. Humble Oil Co., Am. Airlines, Tex. Instruments, Ling-Temco-Vought Co., Kaiser Industries, Schenley Distillers Co.; guest lectr. numerous med. schs., med. socs.; med. dir., v.p., dir. Am. Investors Life Ins. Col., Dallas, 1953-56; med. dir. Res. Life Ins. Co., Dallas, 1956-58; med. dir., v.p. Am. Life Ins. Co., Dallas, 1962-65. Internal medicine mem. U.S. Govt. Commn. to investigate health of Navajo and Hopi Indians, 1948; guest honor Congress Medicine, Guadalajara, Mexico, 1952, 60. Mem. White House Com. on Aging, 1962-65; founder, 1st pres. Internat. Good Neighbor Council, Tex. chpt., co-chmn. internat. health com., 1965-67. Hon. bd. dirs. Muguerza Hosp., Monterrey, Mexico; mem. adv. council Dallas Community Chest Trust Fund. Served from lt. (j.g.) to comdr. M.C., USNR, 1942-66; PTO. Decorated Bronze Star medal; Legion of Merit with combat star; comdr. Legion of Honor (P.I.). Diplomate Am. Bd. Internal Medicine. Fellow A.C.P., Am. Coll. Nuclear Medicine, Am. Coll. Angiology; mem. Internat. Soc. Internal Medicine, Am. Heart Assn., World, So. med. assns., Tex. Geriatrics Soc. (founder, past pres.), Tex. Acad. Internal Medicine (founder, past pres.), Royal Soc. Health London, Soc. Nuclear Medicine, Pan Am. Med. Assn. Council Sect. on Internal Medicine, Res. Officers Assn. (nat. surgeon gen. 1952-53). Clubs: Dallas Gun, Lancers (Dallas). Contbr. numerous papers, articles to profl. publs. Home: 5616 Yolanda Circle Dallas TX 75229 Office: 3225 Turtle Creek Blvd Dallas TX 75219

BUENGER, DANIEL LEE, banker; b. Shiner, Tex., Feb. 1, 1925; s. Lee Edward and Mary Augustine (Engbrock) B.; grad. high sch.; m. Alma Marie Zahn, Sept. 29, 1947; children—Sandra, Daniel Lee, Thomas, Ann. With Security Bank & Trust Co., Wharton, Tex., 1948—, cashier, 1960-71, v.p., 1971—, also dir. Treas., Wharton (Tex.) Little League, 1962-64, E. Wharton County (Tex.) March of Dimes, 1964-69, Wharton P.T.A. Assn., 1967-69, Wharton County chpt. Am. Cancer Soc., 1973—; pres. E. Wharton County (Tex.) United Fund, 1970. Bd. dirs. E. Wharton County chpt. A.R.C. Served with AUS, 1945-46. Democrat. Roman Catholic (dir. 1965-71). K.C., Lion. Home: PO Box 604 Wharton TX 77488 Office: PO Box 1150 Wharton TX 77488

BUESCHER, BRENT JOSEPH, physicist; b. Galesburg, Ill., Sept. 15, 1940; s. Frank Joseph and Francis (Shaner) B.; B.S., U. N.C., 1962; Ph.D., U. Ariz., 1969; m. Katherine Louise Christy, Aug. 14, 1965; children—Brent Joseph, Andrew Eli. Postdoctoral asso. Rensselaer Poly. Inst., 1969-71; postdoctoral research appointment Argonne Nat. Lab., Argonne, Ill., 1971-73; physicist nuclear power generation div. Babcock & Wilcox, Lynchburg, Va., 1973—. Mem. Am. Phys. Soc., A.A.A.S., Sigma Pi Sigma. Contbr. articles to profl. jours. Home: 1519 E Overbrook Dr Lynchburg VA 24505 Office: Babcock & Wilcox PO Box 1260 Lynchburg VA 24505

BUESCHER, EDWARD LOUIS, physician; b. Cin., July 24, 1925; s. Edwin B. and Geneva C. (Summe) B.; B.S., U. Dayton, O., 1945; M.D., U. Cin., 1948; m. Elizabeth Louise Fincel, June 19, 1947; children—M. Christine (Mrs. Medard R. Lutmerding), E. Stephen, Michael D., Monica A., Teresa M. Intern, Cin. Gen. Hosp., 1948-49; resident Children's Hosp. Cin., 1948-50; commd. capt. M.C., U.S. Army, 1950, advanced through grades to col., 1966; chief dept. virus and rickettsial diseases Far East Med. Research Unit, Tokyo, 1951-54; asst. chief dept. virus diseases Walter Reed Army Inst. Research, Washington, 1954-56, chief, 1956-68, dir. div. communicable diseases and immunology, 1967-70, dep. dir. Walter Reed Army Inst. Research, 1969-71, dir., 1971—; clin. asso. prof. pediatrics Georgetown U. Med. Sch., 1963-69, clin. prof. pediatrics, 1970—. Cons. Surg. Gen. U.S. Army, 1960—, WHO Study Group, 1960, USPHS study sect., 1960-69, 70—, mem. panel for microbiology Office Sci. and Tech., Exec. Office of Pres., 1964; mem. Commn. on Virus Infections, asso. mem. commn. on Influenza, Armed Forces Epidemiological Bd., 1965—; mem. vaccine devel. com. Nat. Inst. Allergy and Infectious Diseases, NIH, 1967-69; cons. infectious diseases br., 1971—. Decorated Bronze Star medal, Gorgas medal, Legion of Merit. Diplomate Am. Bd. Microbiology. Fellow Am. Acad. Microbiology; mem. A.M.A., Am. Fedn. Clin. Research, Am. Soc. Microbiology, Am. Assn. Immunologists, Am. Epidemiological Soc., Infectious Disease Soc. Am., Nat. Wildlife Assn., Wilderness Soc., Nat. Geog. Soc. Contbr. articles to profl. jours. Home: 9213 Midwood Rd Silver Spring MD 20910 Office: Walter Reed Army Inst Research Washington DC 20012

BUFFINGTON, WILLIAM EDGAR, builder, investor; b. Pryor, Okla., Oct. 22, 1930; s. Charles Ross and Mary (Kelso) B.; B.A. in Archtl. Engring., Okla. State U., 1953; postgrad. U. Md. Extension, Ruislip, Eng., 1956-57, London Poly Tech. Inst., 1957; m. Donna Lee Vandever, May 1, 1954; children—William Douglas, Craig Michael. Vice pres. Mansur-Steel Assos., Tulsa, 1954-64; pres. Star Builders, Inc. of Tulsa, 1956—; partner Buffington-Smith Enterprises, Tulsa, 1960—; pres. Starlane Corp., Tulsa, 1965; prin. William E. Buffington Enterprises, Tulsa, 1965—; chmn. bd. Star Builders, Inc., Oklahoma City, 1969—. Mem. Gov.'s Reapportionment Com., 1959. Served to capt. USAF, 1956-58. Registered profl. engr., Okla. Mem. Okla. Soc. Profl. Engrs., Tulsa Home Builders, Tulsa Constrn. Specifications Inst. (v.p. 1969, chmn. metal bldgs. specifications com. 1970), Metal Bldgs. Dealers Assn. (pres. 1969), Tulsa Jr. C. of C. (dir. civic affairs com. 1959, Key Man award 1960, bd. dirs. 1960), Theta Chi. Kiwanian. Home: 5615 S Trenton Tulsa OK 74105 Office: 2930 E 51 St Tulsa OK 74105

BUFFUM, ELIZABETH WHITNEY (MRS. WHITNEY BUFFUM), club woman; b. Pitts.; d. Frederick Delano and Helen (Kerruish) Buffum; A.B., Vassar Coll.; m. John Erwin Beaumont II (div.); children—John Erwin III, Peter Whitney; m. 2d, Theodore Jack Vaitses (div.). Mem. D.A.R. (dir. Lucy Jackson chpt. 1959-65), Buffum Miami Jr. League, New Eng. Hist. and Geneal. Soc., Bostonian Soc. Episcopalian. Clubs: Surf, Vassar (Miami, Fla.). Home: Miami Beach FL 33154

BUFKIN, ERNEST RALPH, banker; b. Atlanta, Nov. 27, 1931; s. Ernest Ralph and Chrystene Mercer (Cox) B.; B.S., U. Md., 1955; children—Ernest Ralph, Mark L., Kathryn A. Staff accountant Ernst & Ernst, C.P.A.'s, Atlanta, 1955-57; partner DeLoach & Bufkin, C.P.A.'s, Brunswick, Ga., 1957-63; pres. Coastal Bank of Ga., St. Simons Island, 1963—, also dir.; dir. Golden Isles Aviation, Inc. Bd. dirs. Boys Club Glynn, Inc., Salvation Army, United Community Fund, Coastal Hwy. Commn., Ft. Frederica Found., Brunswick Coll. Found., St. Simons Library Bd., Okefenokee Area council Boy Scouts Am. Served as lt. Supply Corps, USNR. C.P.A., Ga. Mem. Ind., Am., Ga. bankers assns., Ga. Soc. C.P.A.'s, Coastal Ga. Hist. Soc. (dir. 1969—), Navy League (dir. 1967—), St. Simons C. of C. (dir. 1964—). Rotarian. Home: 100 Mallory St Simons Island GA 31522 Office: Box 818 St Simons Island GA 31522

BUFORD, FREDERICK SEYMOUR, architect; b. Dallas, Oct. 10, 1909; s. Frederick Seymour and Bennie (Meadows) B.; B.S., Tex. A. and M. Coll., 1931; m. Merlene Mamie Vaughn, Oct. 26, 1935; children—John Frederic, George Meadows, Harriet Frances (Mrs. Zivko Ristevski). Supt., J. Floyd Malcom Co., gen. contractors, Abilene, Tex., 1933-36; owner Fred Buford & Co., Architects-Engrs., Abilene, 1936-40; specification writer Wyatt C. Hedrick Co., Architects-Engrs., N.Y.C., 1940-43, office mgr., Dallas, 1946-48; partner Buford & Feinberg, Architects-Engrs., Dallas, 1948-54; owner Fred Buford & Assos., Architects-Engrs., Dallas, 1954-67, pres., 1967—. Mem. adv. council Coll. Architecture, Tex. A. and M. U.; mem. adv. com. to bd. dirs. Christian Schs., Inc., Dallas. Served to capt. USMCR, 1944-45; PTO. Recipient Meritorious Civilian award Chief, Bur. Yards and Docks, Navy Dept., 1942. Mem. A.I.A., Tex. Soc. Architects, Nat., Tex. socs. profl. engrs., Engrs. Club of Dallas (chmn. bd. 1965). Clubs: City, Brook Hollow Golf (Dallas); Canyon Creek Country (Richardson, Tex.). Important archtl. works include Central Tex. Coll. Campus, Killeen, Richardson, J.J. Pearce, Lloyd V. Berkner and Lake Highlands high schs., Richardson, Kimball High Sch. and Loos Stadium and Field House, Dallas, Waples Meth. Ch., Denison, Houston County Hosp., Crockett, Richardson Gen. Hosp., Purchasing and Stores Bldg., Tex. A. and M. U., others. Home: 4801 N Lindhurst Av Dallas TX 75229 Office: 1505 Federal St Dallas TX 75201

BUFORD, THOMAS CARNES, farmer; b. Memphis, Dec. 8, 1919; s. Thomas Carnes and Lillian Lee (Sturdivant) B.; student U. Miss., 1937-39; B.S., Washington and Lee U., 1941; M.B.A., Harvard, 1943; m. Ada Gwin Pryor, July 16, 1955; children—Lillian Lee, Gwin Pryor, Sarah Gil, Donna Mills. Partner Buford Plantations, Glendora, Miss., 1946-59, owner, 1959—; chmn. bd. Bell Mfg. Co., Inverness, Miss.; dir. Shrimp Boats, Inc., Macon, Ga. Chmn. Tallahatchie County (Miss.) Agrl. Stblzn. and Conservation Com., 1969-72. Mem. County Republican Exec. Com., 1960-72. Served to capt. Transp. Corps, AUS, 1943-46. Mem. Phi Delta Theta. Episcopalian. (jr. warden 1969-72). Clubs: Beulah Island Hunting (pres. 1962—) (Deshea County, Ark.); Moisie Salmon (Quebec, Can.); Memphis Country, Memphis University (Memphis). Home: Buford Hall Glendora MS 38928 Office: Route 1 Glendora MS 38928

BUFORD, THOMAS OLIVER, educator; b. Overton, Tex., Nov. 17, 1932; s. Oliver Parker and Annie Doris (Smith) B.; B.A., N. Tex. State U., 1955; B.D., Southwestern Bapt. Theol. Sem., 1958; Ph.D., Boston U., 1965; m. Delores Jean Phife, Dec. 27, 1954; children—Russell Warren, Robert Carl, Anna Louise. Faculty, Ky. So. Coll., Louisville, 1962-68; asso. prof. N. Tex. State U., Denton, 1968-69, Furman U., Greenville, S.C., 1969—. Bd. dirs. United Fund for Furman U. Nat. Endowment for the Humanities fellow, 1972. Mem. Am. Philos. Assn., So. Soc. for Philosophy and Psychology, S.C. Soc. for Philosophy (sec. treas. 1972-73). Editor: Toward a Philosophy of Education 1969; Essays on Other Minds, 1970. Home: 104 Abingdon Way Greenville SC 29613

BUGGS, JOHN ALLEN, govt. ofcl.; b. Bruswick, Ga., Nov. 20, 1915; s. John Wesley and Leonora (Clark) B.; A.B., Dillard U., 1939; M.A. in Sociology, Fisk U., 1941; D.Hum., Chapman Coll., 1972; m. Mary Gale Brown, Feb. 28, 1943; children—Zara Gale, Diane Dorinda. Dir. Fessenden Acad., Ocala, Fla., 1942-51; dep. probation officer, Los Angeles County, 1952-54; exec. sec. Los Angeles County Commn. Human Relations, Los Angeles, 1954-63, exec. dir., 1963-67; dep. dir. Model Cities Adminstrn., U.S. Dept. Housing and Urban Devel., 1967-69; v.p. Nat. Urban Coalition, 1969-71; dep. staff dir. U.S. Commn. Civil Rights, Washington, 1971-72, staff dir., 1972—. Bd. dirs. Vols. for Internat. Tech. Assistance, 1972—. Mem. Nat. Assn. Intergroup Relations Ofcls. (dir. 1963—, nat. pres. 1966-67), N.A.A.C.P. (sec. Fla. conf. 1945-49), Nat. Legal Aid and Defenders Assn. (exec. com. 1968-71), Episcopal Soc. Cultural and Racial Unity (dir. 1960-64), Am. Arbitration Assn. (dir.), Alpha Phi Alpha. Episcopalian. Home: 2805 Village Lane Wheaton MD 20906 Office: 1121 Vermont Av NW Washington DC

BUIE, EUGENE CLOY, govt. ofcl.; b. Stamford, Tex., Jan. 24, 1912; s. John Cloy and Pearl Eugenia (Hamm) C.; B.S. in Agrl. Engring., Tex. A. and M. U., 1933; M.S., U. Mich., 1964; m. Lucile Stocks, Mar. 31, 1934; children—Eugene Cloy, Judith Ann, Johnny Merle Price. Asst. prof. Tex. Tech Coll., Lubbock, 1934-35; asst. regional engr. Soil Conservation Service, U.S. Dept. Agr., Amarillo, Tex., 1935-41, zone engr., Ft. Worth, 1946-53, asst. watershed planning specialist, 1954-56, watershed planning specialist, Spartanburg, S.C., 1956-63; asst. dir. Watershed Planning div., Washington, 1963-65, dir. River Basins div., 1965-70, asst. dep. adminstr., 1970—. Served with AUS, 1941-46. Recipient Superior Service award U.S. Dept. Agr. 1962. Registered profl. engr., Tex. Mem. Am. Soc. Agrl. Engrs., Soil Conservation Soc. Am. Baptist. Home: 9005 Stratford Lane Alexandria VA 22308 Office: Soil Conservation Service Washington DC 20250

BULBER, FRANCIS GERARD, educator; b. New Orleans, Mar. 7, 1909; s. Eugene W. and Mathilda (Noullet) B.; Mus.B., La. State U., 1935, Mus.M., 1937, B.A., 1941; postgrad. Northwestern U., summer 1935; Ph.D., George Peabody Coll., 1948;; m. Mayola Desporte, Feb.2, 1930 (dec. Jan. 1954); 1 dau., Mary Frances (Mrs. John Vallie Reed); m. 2d, Patricia Cavell, May 31, 1960; children—Patricia Cecile, Gerard Sean, Colette Marie. Head dept. music Pearl River Coll., Poplarville, Miss., 1937-38; dir. community music project La. State U., Baton Rouge, 1938-40; prof. music, head dept. music, McNeese State Coll., Lake Charles, La., 1940-52, dean fine arts, 1952-56, academic dean coll., 1956-62, dir. grad. studies, 1961-62, dean fine arts, 1962—. Condr., Lake Charles Civic Symphony Orch., 1938-43, Lake Charles Messiah Chorus, 1940—. Pres. La. Coll. Conf., 1955-56; bd. dirs. Community Concerts Assn., 1942—. Mem. La. Music Educators Assn. (dir.), La. Tchrs. Assn., Music Educators Nat. Conf., La. Music Tchrs. Assn., Music Tchrs. Nat. Assn., Phi Kappa Phi, Phi Mu Alpha, Phi Delta Kappa. K.C. Club: Lions. Author: Teacher Activities of the Vocal School Music Program, 1948; articles pub. in profl. jours. Home: 819 Azalea St Lake Charles LA 70601

BULL, FRANK JAMES, architect; b. Chattanooga, June 25, 1922; s. Louis H. and Augusta (Clausius) B.; B.S., Ga. Inst. Tech., 1948, B. Arch., 1949; m. Betty Frances Graham, May 7, 1949; 1 son, Birney O'Brian. Pilot, Pan Am. Airways, 1942-46; architect Aeck Assos., 1949-57; partner Bull & Kenney, Architects, Atlanta, 1957—. Bd. dirs. Galloway Schs., Inc., 1969—, vice chmn., 1969-71, exec. com., 1971—; pres. Atlanta Spring, Inc., 1967—. Trustee Holy Innocents Parish Day Sch., Atlanta, 1962-68, chmn., 1966; bd. dirs. Architects and Engrs. Inst., Atlanta, 1964-68. Mem. A.I.A. (dir. Ga. assn. 1972—), Beta Theta Pi, Omicron Delta Kappa, Tau Beta Pi, Phi Eta Sigma, Phi Kappa Phi. Club: Cherokee Town and Country (Atlanta). Works include Sanctuary bldg. Holy Innocents Episcopal Ch., Atlanta; Speech Sch. and Clinic, Atlanta Speech Sch.; Hummel Hall, Episcopal High Sch.; Alexandria, Va.; Jekyll Island Golf Clubhouse, Ga.; McLarty Hall, Tull Hall, Turner Gymnasium, Westminster Schs., Atlanta. Contbr. articles to profl. jours. Home: 1795 Northridge Rd Atlanta GA 30338 Office: 1261 Spring St NW Atlanta GA 30309

BULLARD, EDGAR EARL, instrument co. exec.; b. El Campo, Tex., Mar. 2, 1933; s. Clifton and Helen (Amman) B.; student Tulsa Tech. Coll., 1957-59; m. Josiane Desbarbieux, July 13, 1957; children—Christine, Jill. Party mgr. Teledyne Co., 1956-68; v.p. Houston Atlas, Inc., 1968—. Served with AUS, 1953-55. Club: Fort Bend Country (Richmond, Tex.). Home: 1011 Blue Willow St Houston TX 77042 Office: 9441 Baythorne St Houston TX 77041

BULLARD, EDWIN ROSCOE, JR., geophysicist; b. El Paso, Tex., Dec. 15, 1921; s. Edwin Roscoe and May (Ober) B.; B.S. in Geology, Tex. Coll. Mines, 1949; B.S. in Physics, Tex. Western Coll., 1963; m. Norma Eileen Holford, Feb. 24, 1945; 1 son, Edwin Roscoe. Subsurface geologist Kerr McGee Oil Co., Midland, Tex., 1949-52, Ralph Lowe, Midland, 1958-62; research geophysicist U.S. Geol. Survey, Denver, 1963-65; research geophysicist Globe Universal Scis. Co., El Paso, 1965—, also dir. Cons. geologist, 1962—. Served with USNR, 1942-45. Mem. Am. Assn. Petroleum Geologists, Sigma Pi Sigma. Inventor method of tape rec. geophys. logs, indicator for aircraft instant rate of climb. Home: 724 Kern Dr El Paso TX 79902 Office: 201 W Baltimore El Paso TX 79902

BULLARD, JOHN MOORE, clergyman, educator; b. Winston-Salem, N.C., May 6, 1932; s. Hoke Vogler and May E. (Moore) B.; B.A., U. N.C., 1953, M.A., 1955; B.D., Yale, 1957, Ph.D., 1962. Instr., Yale Div. Sch., 1958-61; asst. prof. religion Wofford Coll., Spartanburg, S.C., 1961-65, chmn. dept. religion, 1962—, asso. prof., 1965-70, Albert C. Outler prof. religion, 1970—; minister music Hamden Plains Meth. Ch., New Haven, 1955-61, Central United Meth. Ch., Spartanburg, 1961-72, Bethel United Meth. Ch., 1972—; ordained elder Meth. Ch., 1962. Vis. prof. Bibl. lit. U. N.C. at Chapel Hill, 1966, 67. Mem. Am. Guild Organists (chpt. dean 1965-67), Am. Acad. Religion, Soc. Bibl. Lit. (pres. So. sect. 1967-68), Hymn Soc. Am., Am. Schs. Oriental Research, Am. Assn. U. Profs., Am. Oriental Soc., Inst. for Mediterranean Studies, Phi Mu Alpha. Home: 2123 Selwyn Av Charlotte NC 28207 Office: Main Hall Wofford Coll Spartanburg SC 29301

BULLARD, ROGER AUBREY, educator; b. Memphis, Aug. 1, 1937; s. Roger Maurice and Mable (Bennett) B.; B.A., Union U., 1958; M.A., U. Ky., 1959; B.D., Southeastern Bapt. Theol. Sem., 1962; Ph.D., Vanderbilt U., 1965; m. Carol Louise Hawthorne, May 21, 1961; children—Kenneth Maurice, Floyd Andrew. Mem. faculty Atlantic Christian Coll., Wilson, N.C., 1965—, prof. religion and philosophy, 1968—. Corr. mem. Inst. for Antiquity and Christianity of Claremont, Cal., 1966—. Recipient awards for summer study Am. Council Learned Socs., 1967, Nat. Found. Humanities, 1968. Mem. Soc. Bibl. Lit., Am. Acad. Religion, Am. Assn. U. Profs., So. Bapt. Hist. Soc., Am. Bible Soc. (mem. today's English version translations com. 1967—). Democrat. Baptist. Author: The Hypostasis of the Archons. 1970. Abstractor New Testament Abstracts, 1966-69. Office: Atlantic Christian Coll Wilson NC 27893

BULLEN, ADELAIDE KENDALL (MRS. RIPLEY PIERCE BULLEN), anthropologist; b. Worcester, Mass., Jan. 12, 1908; d. Oliver Sawyer and Grace (Marble) Kendall, III; A.B. cum laude, Radcliffe Coll., 1943; grad. study Harvard, 1943-48, 50; m. Ripley Pierce Bullen, July 25, 1929; children—Dana Ripley II, Pierce Kendall. Research anthropologist Health Center, Radcliffe Coll., 1943-44, Fatigue Lab., Harvard Grad. Sch. Bus. Adminstrn., 1944-46; civilian cons. in anthropology U.S. War Dept., 1946; anthropologist dept. anthropology, Peabody Mus., Harvard U., 1946-48, Fla. State Mus., 1949—. Fellow Am. Anthrop. Assn., A.A.A.S., Royal Anthrop. Inst., London, Soc. Applied Anthropology; mem. Am. Assn. Phys. Anthropologists, Am. Psychosomatic Soc., Am. Acad. Social and Polit. Sci., Soc. Research in Child Devel., World Fedn. for Mental Health, Sigma Xi. Clubs: Gainesville Garden, Gainesville Golf and Country, University Women's, Gainesville Woman's. Author: New Answers to the Fatigue Problem, 1956; also articles in field. Contbg. editor anthropology Handbook of Latin Am. Studies, Library of Congress, 1969-71. Home: 2720 SW 8th Dr Gainesville FL 32601 Office: Fla State Mus Univ Fla Gainesville FL 32611

BULLOCK, CHARLES SPENCER, JR., govt. ofcl.; b. Kansas City, Mo., Dec. 10, 1914; s. Charles Spencer and Maud (Pook) B.; A.A., Kansas City N.E. Jr. Coll., 1933; A.B., William Jewell Coll., 1940; M.A., Vanderbilt U., 1942; m. Eleanor Alice Davis, Aug. 2, 1941; children—Charles Spencer III, Robert Davis. Asso. prof. Mo. State Coll., 1946; sr. statistician Tenn. Dept. Employment Security, 1946-48; regional employemnt analyst U.S. Bur. Labor Statistics, Atlanta, 1949-60, asst. regional dir., 1960-71, dep. regional dir., 1971—; dir. Peachtree Fed. Credit Union. Served with AUS, 1943-46; CBI. Mem. Am. Statis. Assn. (chpt. pres. 1965), Atlanta Assn. Fed. Execs. (pres. 1971). Episcopalian (vestryman). Home: 4471 Cain Circle Tucker GA 30084 Office: 1371 Peachtree St NE Atlanta GA 30309

BULLOCK, JOSEPH PHILLIP, chem. co. exec.; b. Boston, Sept. 30, 1929; s. William John and Rose Ann (Boitano) B.; certificate indsl. chemistry Franklin Tech. Inst., 1950; Asso. Sci. in Chemistry, Lincoln Tech. Inst., 1956; B.B.A. in Sci. and Mgmt., Northeastern U., 1958, M.B.A., 1960; m. Helen Patricia Oakes, Sept. 26, 1948; children—Patricia (Mrs. Walter E. Farnsworth), Paula (Mrs. Richard D. Anderson), Joseph Steven, Eric Paul, Robin Eileen. Prodn. supr. Myerson Tooth Corp., Cambridge, Mass., 1950-52; prodn. supr. Am. Biltrite Rubber Co., Chelsea, Mass., 1952; chemist, prodn. supr. Carters Ink Co., Cambridge, 1952-58; chemist Boston Woven Hose & Rubber Co., Cambridge, 1958-60; sr. research chemist Naugatuck Chem. Co. (Conn.), 1960-61; tech. sales service UBS Chem. Co., Cambridge, 1961-63; tech. sales chem. div. Goodyear Corp., Boston, 1963-67; gen. sales mgr. Copolymer Rubber & Chem. Co., Baton Rouge, 1967—. Served with AUS, 1946-48. Mem. Am. Chem. Soc., V.F.W. Home: 12461 Parkwood Av Baton Rouge LA 70815 Office: Box 2591 Baton Rouge LA 70821

BUMGARDNER, DAVID WEBSTER, JR., mortician, state ofcl.; b. Belmont, N.C., Nov. 2, 1921; s. David Webster and Winnifred (Ballard) B.; student Belmont Abbey Jr. Coll., 1938-40, Gupton-Jones Coll. Mortuary Sci., 1941-42; m. Sara Margaret Jones, Aug, 14, 1948; children—Sharon Inez, Sandra Jo. Pres., treas. Bumgardner Funeral Home, Inc., Belmont, 1948—. Mem. N.C. Ho. of Reps., 1967, 69, 71, 73. Dir. Belmont Savs. and Loan Assn., N. State Gen. Ins. div. N.W. Security Life Ins. Co.; pres. Conf. Funeral Service Examining Bds. of U.S., 1955-56. Mem. adv. bd. Sacred Heart Coll., Belmont. Served with AUS, 1943-45. Named Man of Year Belmont C. of C., 1967. Fellow Dallas Inst. Mortuary Sci. Kiwanian (div. lt. gov. 1966). Home: 209 Peachtree St Belmont NC 28012 Office: PO Box 904 Belmont NC 28012

BUMPERS, BETTY LOU FLANAGAN (MRS. DALE BUMPERS), wife gov. Ark.; m. Dale Bumpers, Sept. 4, 1949; children—Dale Brent, William Mark, Margaret Brooke. Address: Charleston AR 72933*

BUMPERS, DALE, gov. Ark.; b. Charleston, Ark., Aug. 12, 1925; grad. U. Ark.; LL.B., Northwestern U., 1951; m. Betty Flanagan; children—Brent, Bill, Brooke. Owner Charleston Hardware and Furniture Co., 1951-66; admitted to Ark. bar, practiced in Charleston, 1951-70; owner cattle breeding farm, 1966-70; gov., Ark., 1971—. Past chmn. United Fund, Boy Scouts Am. Fund, Cancer Fund. Former city atty., Charleston; past pres. Charleston Sch. Bd. Served with USMC, World War II. Recipient C. of C. Citizen's award. Democrat. United Methodist. Office: State Capitol Little Rock AR 72201

BUNCE, JAMES FREDRICK, agrl. extension agt.; b. Cumberland County, N.C., Nov. 21, 1922; s. Empie Lee and Maggie Lee (Ellis) B.; A.A., Presbyn. Jr. Coll., 1943; B.S., N.C. State U., 1949, M.Ed., 1969; m. Alice Marie Parker, Aug. 6, 1950; 1 dau., Laura Kathryn. Clk. typist Civil Service, Fort Bragg, N.C., 1941-42; tchr. vocational agr. Onslow County Pub. Schs., Jacksonville, N.C., 1949-56; agr. extension agt. N.C. Agrl. Extension Service, Duplin County, Kenansville, N.C., 1956-68; county extension chmn. Carteret County, Beaufort, N.C., 1968—. Served with AUS, 1943-46; PTO. Mem. N.E.A., N.C. Tchrs. Assn. (v.p. agrl. edn. div. 1953), Nat.

(Distinguished Service award 1972); N.C., assns. county agrl. agts. Baptist (deacon 1961—). Mason, Rotarian, Lion (pres. 1959). Home: 207 Vine St Beaufort NC 28516 Office: Courthouse Annex Beaufort NC 28516

BUNCE, PAUL LESLIE, physician; b. Fargo, N.D., Sept. 24, 1916; s. Paul Fay and Harriet Elisabeth (Black) B.; A.B., Oberlin Coll., 1938; M.D., U. Chgo., 1942; m. Anne Hetherington Gregory, Nov. 26, 1945; children—Gregory Paul, Leslie Ann. Intern, U. Chgo. Billings Hosp., 1942-43; instr. pharmacology U. Pa., Phila., 1946-48; resident urology Johns Hopkins Hosp., Balt., 1948-51; practice medicine specializing in urol. surgery, Balt., 1951-52, Chapel Hill, N.C., 1952—; mem. staff N.C. Meml. Hosp., Chapel Hill, 1952—, chief urology, 1952-71; 1946-48; faculty U. N.C., Chapel Hill, 1952—, prof. surgery. Served with AUS, 1943-45. Mem. A.M.A., Am. Urologic Assn. Home: Rural Route 7 Box 646 Chapel Hill NC 27514 Office: NC Meml Hosp Chapel Hill NC 27514

BUNCE, WILLIAM DEAN, govt. ofcl.; b. Fayetteville, N.C., June 6, 1933; s. Purdue Frankle and Ethel Mae (Jackson) B.; student N.C. State Coll., 1959; m. Joanne Buie McGill, Aug. 12, 1956; children—Hilda Joanne, Amy Elizabeth, William Dean II, Alexander McGill. With N.C. Hwy. Commn., 1956—, field engr., Dunn, 1956-57, Fayetteville, 1959-64, div. staff engr., Fayetteville, 1964-69, asst. resident engr., Lumberton, N.C., 1969—. Tchr., N.C. Hwy. Commn., 1970—; designer various subdivs. N.C., 1960-71. Civil def. officer 5 N.C. counties, 1963—. Served with AUS, 1956-58. Mem. N.C. Soc. Engrs. (dir.), Cape Fear Engr. Club (sec.-treas.), N.C. Hwy. Assn. (sec.-treas.). Presbyn. (Sunday sch. supt. 1966-70, deacon, 1966, 70, 71—). Clubs: Ruritan (sec.-treas.), Green Valley Country (Fayetteville). Home: 5400 Jarvis St Fayetteville NC 28304 Office: 209 E 6th St Lumberton NC 28358

BUNCH, CHARLES, physician, ret. naval officer; b. Raleigh, N.C., Jan. 30, 1905; s. Charlie Christopher and Mattie (Hamer) B.; student U. N.C., 1924-27; M.D., Med. Coll. S.C., 1931; B.S. with honors, N.C. State Coll., 1958;; m. Dell Cahoon, Mar. 5th, 1955; children—Mary Elizabeth, Linda Ann. Intern Central Dispensary and Emergency Hosp., Washington, 1932-33; resident Childrens Hosp., Phila., 1934, N.Y. Polyclinic Hosp., 1934-35; commd. lt. (j.g.) USNR, 1933, advanced through grades to capt., 1955; practice medicine, specializing in gen. surgery, Charlotte, N.C., 1935-40, 46-49; surg. staff U.S. Naval Hosp., Parris Island, S.C., 1942; sr. med. officer U.S. Naval Air Sta., Antigua, B.W.I., 1942-43, Repair Facility, San Juan, P.R., 1943-44; staff Bainbridge (Md.) Naval Tng. Sta., 1944; head surg. team USS McCracken, 1944-66; asst. chief of surgery Naval Hosp., Charleston, S.C., 1949-52; surg. staff Naval Hosp., Yokosuka, Japan, 1952; mem. USN Adv. Group, sr. med. officer, fleet activities, Sasabo, Japan, 1952-53, Pusan, Korea, 1953; sr. med. officer naval recruiting, Raleigh, N.C., 1953-57; sr. med. officer U.S. Naval Shipyard, Portsmouth, Va., 1958-61; med. officer U.S. Naval Propellant Plant, Indian Head, Md., 1961-62; asst. dist. med. officer 5th Naval Dist., Portsmouth, 1962-66, ret., 1966; mem. staff U.S. Naval Hosp., Portsmouth; mem. active surg. staffs Mercy Hosp., 1935-39, Presbyn. Hosp., 1935-39, Good Samaritan Hosp., 1935-59 (all Charlotte), now mem. hon. surg. staffs; chief surg. service, med. dir. Warren Gen. Hosp., Warrenton, N.C.; local med. adviser SSS; local surgeon Seaboard Coast Line R.R. Mem. Warren County Bd. Edn. Commd. Ky. col. Diplomate Am. Bd. Abdominal Surgery. Fellow A.C.S.; mem. A.M.A., Med. Soc. State N.C. (ho. of dels.), Royal Soc. Health (London, Eng.), Warren County Med. Soc. (sec.), Internat. Coll. Surgeons, Seaboard Med. Assn., So. Med. Assn., Am. Acad. Occupational Medicine, Am. Assn. Ry. Surgeons, Am. Soc. Abdominal Surgeons (mem. edn. faculty), Am., N.C. pub. health assns., Nat. Rifle Assn. (patron), N.C. Rifle and Pistol Assn. (patron), Am. Med. Writers Assn., S.A.R., Sons Confederate Vets., Order Stars and Bars, Mil. Order World Wars, Am. Legion (past post comdr.), V.F.W. Episcopalian (vestryman). Mason (32 deg., Shriner, K.T., past master), Elk, Moose, Rotarian (dir.). Clubs: Midtown (charter) (Portsmouth, Va.); Red Fez (Charlotte); City (Raleigh, N.C.); Warrenton Country, Recreation (charter mem.) (Warrenton, N.C.). Contbr. to profl. jours. Home: 105 Halifax St Warrenton NC 27589 Office: Warren Gen Hosp Warrenton NC 27589

BUNCH, MARY ELIZABETH (MRS. JAMES HENDERSON LOVE), physician; b. Asheboro, N.C.; d. Walter Anderson and Pattie (Lowe) Bunch; student U. N.C., 1947; M.D., Bowman Gray Sch. Medicine, 1951; m. James Henderson Love, July 12, 1959; 1 son, James Henderson. Intern, N.C. Bapt. Hosp., Winston-Salem, N.C., 1951-52, asst. resident internal medicine, 1952-55; staff physician Western N.C. Sanatorium, Black Mountain, 1955-59; emergency room physician Meml. Mission Hosp., Asheville, N.C., 1969—. Served to 1st lt. Army Nurse Corps, 1943-46. Mem. Am. Med. Women's Assn., A.M.A., Am. Coll. Emergency Physicians (charter), N.C., Buncombe County med. socs., Am. Legion, V.F.W. Methodist. Home: 103 3d St Black Mountain NC 28711 Office: 509 Biltmore Av Asheville NC 28801

BUNDY, STEPHEN ANDREW, textile co. exec.; b. Jamestown, N.C., Oct. 17, 1917; s. Oscar Mayfield and Nettie Lisa (Johnson) B.; B.S., N.C. State U., 1941; grad. Exec. Mgmt. Course, Sch. Bus. Adminstrn. U. Va., 1968; m. Alice Baskerville Ligon, Dec. 6, 1941; children—Stephen Andrew, Henry Ligon. Supr. quality control Burlington Hosiery Co., 1946-53, plant mgr., 1953-61, v.p. new product devel., 1961-69; pres., chief exec. officer Morganton Hosiery Mills, Inc. div. Dan River, Inc., Morganton, N.C., 1969—. Chmn. indsl. div. United Fund for Burke County, 1971; chmn. Roan County (Tenn.), March of Dimes, 1948-53; chmn. county Smoky Mountain council, Boy Scouts Am., 1955-61. Trustee, Western Piedmont Community Coll., 1969-73; bd. dirs. MHD Found., 1969-73. Served with USAAF, 1941-45. Mem. Sigma Nu, Phi Psi. Rotarian. Home: 519 Riverside Dr Morganton NC 28655 Office: 101 Lenoir St Morganton NC 28655

BUNGE, CARL CRAIG, real estate broker; b. Tebetts, Mo., Mar. 11, 1933; s. Oscar Carl and Susanna Vivian (Cannell) B.; B.S., U. Mo., 1955; m. Phyllis Sue Proctor, Dec. 24, 1955; children—Craig, Cheryl. Self-employed real estate and mortgage brokerage bus., Fort Walton Beach, Fla., 1963—; dir. First City Bank, 1969—; pres. The Bunge Corp. Capt., Okaloosa County United Fund, 1969-71. Vice pres. bd. dirs. Fort Walton Beach Bd. Realtors, 1964—; bd. dirs. Salvation Army, 1968-70, Boys' Club, 1968-70, Jr. Achievement, 1967-69. Served with USAF, 1955-63. Mem. C. of C. (v.p. 1969-70), Kappa Alpha. Mason (32 deg., Shriner), Kiwanian (pres. 1968). Home: 560 Mooney Rd Fort Walton Beach FL 32548 Office: 200 Eglin Pkwy Fort Walton Beach FL 32548

BUNKER, GEORGE RAYMOND, educator, artist; b. Danver, May 27, 1923; s. Arthur Hugh and Frances (Wilkinson) B.; B.A., Yale, 1946; student Art Students League N.Y., 1946-48, Bklyn. Mus. Art Sch., 1948-49, Academie Julien, Paris, 1949; m. Constance Wilcock, Sept. 29, 1959; 1 dau., Katherine Olson. Instr. art Swarthmore (Pa.) Coll., 1955-57; mem. faculty Phila. Coll. Art, 1955-74, prof., 1966-74, dean faculty, 1965-72; chmn. dept. art U. Houston, 1974—; vis. prof. art U. N.M., Albuquerque, 1973-74; one man shows Phila. Art Alliance, 1957, Socrates Perakis Gallery, Phila., 1965, Print Club Phila., 1973; exhibited in group shows Silvermine Guild Artists, 1962, N.A.D., 1956, Prints of Two Workds/Stampe di Due Mondi, Phila., Rome, Italy, 1967, U.S. State Dept. traveling exhbn., Art for Embassies, 1964-66, Am. Color Print Soc., 1973; represented in permanent collection Am. Field Service, N.Y.C., Library Congress, Washington, Swarthmore Coll., Nat. Gallery Art, Phila. Mus. Art and others; mem. vis. com. Coll. Fine Arts Washington U., St. Louis, 1971-72. Bd. dirs. Old Town Hist. Soc., Phila., 1971-72. Served as ambulance driver Am. Field Service, World War II. Recipient Spl. award Phila. Coll. Art, 1958, Gold Star award, 1972; Lessing J. Rosenwald prize Print Club Phila., 1956, 57, 61, Consol. Drake Press Purchase award Am. Color Print Soc. 33 Nat. Exhbn., 1973, and others. Mem. Print Club Phila. (bd. govs. 1956-62, 72-74), Nat. Prints in Progress (dir. 1969-71), Artists Equity Assn. (pres. 1959-60), Am. Assn. U. Profs. (past sec.), Coll. Art Assn., Mus. Modern Art. Club: Peale (Phila). Guest artist Tamarind Inst., Albuquerque, 1973. Office: Dept Art U Houston Cullen Blvd Houston TX 77004

BUNKER, WILLIAM MARVIN, elec. engr.; b. Burkburnett, Tex., July 11, 1926; s. Maxwell Byron and Velma (VanLoh) B.; B.S. in Elec. Engring., U. Okla., 1951; M.Engring., U. Fla., 1966, Ph.D., 1969; m. Joan Aberle Newitt, Sept. 29, 1956; children—William Marvin Jr., David Byron. Elec. engr. Hughes Aircraft Co., Culver City, Cal., 1954-58; elec. engr. Gen. Electric Co., Syracuse, N.Y., 1958-60, cons. engr., Daytona Beach, Fla., 1963—; chief engr. Contronics, Inc., Boston, 1961-63. Instr. Northeastern U., Boston, 1962-63; adj. prof. U. Fla., Gainesville, 1969-72, Fla. Technol. U., Orlando, 1972—. Bd. visitors Embry-Riddle Aero. U., Daytona Beach, Fla. Served with USNR, 1943-46. Mem. I.E.E.E., Soc. Computer Simulation, Soc. Information Display, Tau Beta Pi, Eta Kappa Nu, Pi Mu Epsilon. Patentee in field. Contbr. to profl. jours. Home: 504 S Halifax Dr Ormond Beach FL 32074 Office: Gen Electric Co Box 2500 Daytona Beach FL 32015

BUNN, AUBREY OWEN, banker; b. Lake Village, Ark., July 25, 1938; s. Ides Byrl and Dorothy Lee (White) B.; B.B.A., Tulane U., 1960; m. Patricia Ann Haller, May 30, 1959; children—Deborah, Douglas Owen. With Hancock Bank, Gulfport, Miss., 1960—, v.p., mgr. data processing, 1973—. Mem. Data Processing Mgmt. Assn., Jr. C. of C. Baptist. Elk. Home: 33 55th St Gulfport MS 39501 Office: PO Box 4019 Gulfport MS 39501

BUNN, JOHN ROBERT, geologist, oil operator; b. Ardmore, Okla., June 17, 1900; s. Clinton Orin and Mattie (Pulliam) B.; B.S., U. Okla., 1923; m. Wilma Whatley, Apr. 11, 1925; children—Jeree (Mrs. J. L. Barnett), Jack. Petroleum engr. U.S. Bur. Mines, U.S. Geol. Survey, 1923-25; cons. geologist, 1925-33; drilling contractor Continental Oil Co. Mexico, 1933-38; oil and gas explorations; U.S.; 1938—; owner Bunn Hydraulic Rig Co., Tyler, Tex., 1950-72. Served with U.S. Army, 1918. Mem. Am. Assn. Petroleum Geologists, Am. Geophys. Union, Ind. Petroleum Assn. Am., Sigma Gamma Epsilon, Kappa Sigma. Mason, Rotarian. Writer geol. and engring. reports for state surveys Okla., Colo., Tex. Patentee in field, including 1st successful hydraulic drilling rig. Address: 325 W 4th St Tyler TX 75701

BUNN, JULIAN WILBUR, JR., instrument mfg. exec.; b. Raleigh, N.C., Mar 21, 1918; s. Julian Wilbur and Maude (Davis) B.; B.S., N.C. State U., 1941; m. Martha Ware Britt, June 1, 1946; children—Julian Wilbur III, John Britt, Thomas Ware. With advance engring. sect. Gen. Electric Co., Lynn, Mass., 1941-46; v.p., gen. mgr. Gen. Equipment Co., Raleigh, N.C., 1946-53; v.p., prodn. mgr. Aerotron Corp., Raleigh, 1953-56 prodn.-devel. engr. Aeroglide Corp., Raleigh, 1956-60, v.p. engring., 1960-73; exec. v.p. Trienco Inc., Raleigh, 1973—. Mem. Profl. Engrs. N.C. Club: Civitan (dir.). Home: 3005 Granville Dr Raleigh NC 27609 Office: 518 W Cabarrus St Raleigh NC 27603

BUNTING, DAVIS ELI JR., bank exec.; b. Washington, June 3, 1943; s. Davis Eli and Margaret Ann (Soper) B.; B.A., U. Louisville, 1965; J.D., Georgetown U., 1970; m. Patricia Ann Murphy, Dec. 27, 1968; 1 dau., Sarah Margaret. With Riggs Nat. Bank, Washington, 1965—, dir. investment research, 1973—. Bd. dirs., treas., Civic Assn., 1972-73. Mem. Washington Soc. Investment Analysts (asst. treas. 1971), D.C. Bankers Assn., Delta Theta Phi. Episcopalian. Home: 1510 Chatham Colony Court Reston VA 22090 Office: 800 17th St NW Washington DC 20013

BUNTING, J(AMES) WHITNEY, coll. pres.; b. Phila., Nov. 23, 1913; s. George Miller Lewis and Helen Elizabeth (Whitney) B.; B.S., U. Pa., 1934, M.A., 1936, M.B.A., 1937, Ph.D., 1946; student U. Louisville, 1938-39;; m. Mildred Eleanor Griscom, Oct. 14, 1939; 1 dau., Helen Whitney. Economist Pa. Planning Bd., Harrisburg, 1934-35; gen freight agt. Preston (Md.) Trucking Co., 1935-36; instr. econs., marketing finance Jr. Coll. Commerce, New Haven, 1937-39, coll. dean, 1949-50; asst. prof. bus. adminstrn. Hanover (Ind.) Coll., 1939-42, also dir. pub. relations; prof. applied econs. Hobart Coll., Geneva, N.Y., 1945-49, asso. and acting dean, 1946-48. dir. indsl. community program, 1947-48; asst. treas. Market Basket Corp., Geneva, 1948-49; prof. econs., chmn. dept. U. Ga., Atlanta, 1950-51, prof. econs., Athens, 1951-52, dir. bur. bus. research, 1951-52; exec. v.p. Oglethorpe U., 1952, pres., 1953-55; prof. finance N.Y. U., 1957-60; cons. higher edn. and research Gen. Electric Co., 1955-62; dean Coll. Bus. Adminstrn., U. Ga., 1962-68; pres Ga. Coll., Milledgeville, 1968—; cons. utility costs Ga. Pub. Service Commn. Economist WpB, Washington, 1942. Pres. Citizen's Com. for Rye Pub. Schs. Served as lt. Supply Corps, USNR, 1942-45. Life fellow Internat. Inst. Arts and Letters; mem. Nat. Invest in Am. Com. (bd. govs., eastern regional chmn., mem. exec. com., pres.), Am. Assn. State Colls. and Univs. (chmn. pub. affairs com. 1970—), Am. Econ. Assn., Am. Geog. Soc., Am. Marketing Assn., Am. Acad. Polit. and Social Sci., Nat. Sales Execs., So. Econ. Soc., Gamma Omicron Tau, Delta Sigma Pi, Delta Chi. Rotarian. Clubs: Milledgeville (Ga.) Country; Advertising (N.Y.C). Author: Effective Retail Selling, 1953; Ethics for Modern Business Practice, 1953; Higher Education, A Twenty Year Look Ahead, 1957; Your Share in America's Prosperity, 1960. Author, editor: Bus. Leaders in People's Capitalism, 1959. Editor of Atlanta Economic Review, 1950-51, Georgia Business, 1951-52; contbg. econs. editor Elec. South, 1952-70. Contbr. articles profl. jours. Home: The Mansion Milledgeville GA 31061 Office: Georgia Coll Milledgeville GA 31061

BUNTING, JOHN JAMES, physician; b. Sunbury, Pa., Nov. 7, 1913; s. James Henry and Doroa (Smith) B.; B.S., Lafayette Coll., 1934; M.D., U. Md., 1938; postgrad. U. Pa., 1945-46;; m. Katharyne Denton, Sept. 28, 1941; children—Beverly Sue (Mrs. Robert Austin Moor), John James, William D. Intern, resident U. Hosp., Balt., 1938-40; resident Jersey City Med. Center, 1940-41; practice medicine, specializing in internal medicine, Houston, 1946—; mem. staff Meml. Hosp., Methodist Hosp., St. Luke's Episcopal Hosp., Hermann Hosp., Jefferson Davis Hosp., St. Joseph Hosp., Diagnostic Hosp., Rosewood Hosp., Twelve Oaks Hosp., Ben Taub Hosp., Center Pavilion Hosp.; asso. prof. clin. medicine Baylor Med. Sch., 1947—; asso. in. medicine U. Tex., 1957—. Pres. Post Grad. Med. Assembly S. Tex. Adv. com. Civil Def., 1949-51. Served from 1st lt. to maj. USAAF, 1942-45. Diplomate Am. Bd. Internal Medicine. Fellow Am. Coll. Angiology, A.C.P., Am. Coll. Chest Physicians; mem. A.M.A., Am. Heart Assn., Am. Diabetes Assn., A.A.A.S., Am. Geriatrics Soc., NY. Acad. Sci., Tex. Acad. Internal Medicine, So. Med. Assn. Episcopalian. Asso. editor Medical Record and Annals; editorial bd., contbr. Book of Health, 3d edit. Contbr. articles to profl. jours. and articles on space medicine. Home: 6142 Bordley Dr Houston TX 77027 also Lazy-B Ranch Booth TX 7742 Office: 6436 Fannin Houston TX 77006

BUNTON, HENRY CLAY, bishop; b. nr. Coker, Ala., Oct. 19, 1903; s. Isaac Washington and Sarah Lue (Noland) B.; student Miles Coll., L.H.D., 1972; A.B., Fla. A. and M. Coll., 1941; Th.M., Iliff Sch. Theology, Denver, 1952; D.D. (hon.), Tex. Coll., 1955; m. Estell McKinney, Dec. 24, 1923 (dec.); children—Mattye Lue, Marjorie Patricia, Henry Clay, Joseph Carpenter; m. 2d, Alfreda Gibbs, Oct. 27, 1958. Ordained to ministry Christian M.E. Ch., 1930; pastor chs., Ala., 1927-35, Fla., 1935-42, Ark., 1942-43, Tex., 1945-48, Colo., 1948-52, Memphis, 1952-62; elected bishop, 1962, now presiding bishop East Coast dist., Washington; mem. Bd. Christian Edn., 1953-54, dir. Leadership Tng. Bd. Christian Edn., 1953-54; pres. Publishing dept. Christian M.E. Ch., 1964—. Pres. Ministers Alliance, Memphis and Shelby County, Tenn., 1956-62. Trustee Painee Coll., Augusta, Ga., Miles Coll., Birmingham. Served with U.S. Army, 1943-46, 48-50. Mem. N.A.A.C.P., So. Christian Leadership Conf. (charter), Phi Beta Sigma. Mason. Author: The Challenge to Become Involved, 1966. Contbg. editor: Christian Index Christian M.E. Ch. Home: 6524 16th St NW Washington DC 20012 Office: 557 Randolph St NW Washington DC 20012

BUNUEL, LUIS, film dir.; b., 1900. Films include: Un Chien Andalou, 1929; L'Age d'Or, 1930; Land without Bread, 1936; Los Olvidados, 1950; The Adventures of Robinson Crusoe, 1953; The Criminal Life of Archibald de la Cruz, 1955; La Mort en ce Jardin (Evil Eden), 1956; Nazarin, 1958; Le Fievre monte a El Pao, La Jeune Fille, 1959; The Republic of Sin, 1960; The Young One, 1960; Viridiana, 1961 (prize Cannes Festival); Island of Shame, 1961; El Angel Exterminador, 1962. Address: Ultramar Films Remorna 503 Mexico City Mexico

BURCH, ELZA FAIN, coal co. exec.; b. Nicholasville, Ky., Apr. 3, 1926; s. John G. and Bertha (Gabbard) B.; B. Minning Engring., U. Ky., 1950, M. Mining Engring., 1951; m. Dorothy Everman, Aug. 5, 1950; children—Jeffrey Neil, Carol. Research engr. U.S. Steel Corp., Fairfield, Ala. and Monroeville, Pa., 1951-53, 60-64; corporate mgr. of preparation Island Creek Coal Co., Cleve. (now Lexington, Ky.), 1953-60, 68—; sales engr. Elmco Corp., Pitts., 1964-68. Served with USNR, 1944-46; PTO. Registered profl. engr., Pa., Ky., W. Va. Mem. Am. Inst. Mining and Metall. Engrs., Order Ky. Cols., Tau Beta Pi. Republican. Methodist. Patentee in field. Contbr. articles to profl. jours. Home: 1516 Green Hills Rd Lexington KY 40505 Office: 465 E High St Lexington KY 40508

BURCH, GEORGE WILEY, computer co. exec.; b. Tsingtao, China, Sept. 12, 1937; s. Cecil Ray and Esther (Respess) B.; B.S., U.S. Air Force Acad., 1959; postgrad. (NSF fellow) Johns Hopkins U., 1966-69; m. Susan Lynn Weller, Nov. 26, 1960; children—Melissa Caitlin, Elena Kirsten, William Linnaeus. Mathematician, Center for Naval Analysis, Washington, 1963-68; pres. Computer Cartography, Inc., Silver Spring, Md., 1968—, also dir. Lectr. John Hopkins, 1967—; cons. math. urban environments. Served with USAF, 1955-63. Mem. Operations Research Soc. Am (sr., edn. com. 1968—). Founder Jour. Differential Games, 1967, editor, 1968. Home: Apt 105 2853 Ontario Rd NW Washington DC 20009 Office: 1111 Bonifant St Silver Spring MD 20910

BURCH, JOHN CHRISTOPHER, physician; b. Nashville, July 21, 1900; s. Lucius Edward and Sarah Polk (Cooper) B.; M.D., Vanderbilt U., 1923; m. Frances Vivian Harris, Nov. 11, 1938; children—John Christopher, Lucius Edward III. Intern Free Hosp. for Women, Brookline, Mass., 1923; house officer Bellevue Hosp., N.Y.C., 1924-25, resident, 1925-27; Rockefeller travelling fellow, 1927-28; practice medicine, specializing in gynecology, Nashville, 1926—; mem. staff St. Thomas Hosp., Vanderbilt Hosp. (both Nashville); dir. Burch Clinic Nashville, 1946—; mem. faculty dept. gynecology Vanderbilt U. Med. Sch., Nashville, 1926-65, prof., 1942-65, prof. emeritus, 1965—. Served to 2d lt. U.S. Army, 1917-19, to col. M.C., 1942-46. Decorated Legion Merit; recipient Founder's medal Vanderbilt U., 1923. Diplomate Am. Bd. Surgery, Am. Bd. Obstetrics and Gynecology. Fellow A.C.S. (pres. Tenn. 1960-61,; Distinguished Service award 1965), Am. Assn. Obstetrics and Gynecology (hon.); mem. Am. (past treas.), So. (past pres.), Nashville (past pres.) surg. assns., Soc. Pelvic Surgeons (past pres.), Tenn. (Physician Year of 1971), Davidson County (past pres.) med. assns., Nashville Acad. Medicine (past pres.), So. Soc. Clin. Surgeons (past pres.), Endocrine Soc. (past v.p.), James IV Surg. Soc., Halsted Club, Am. Cancer Soc. (dir. at large 1953-55), Vanderbilt Med. Alumni Assn. (past pres.) Sigma Xi, Beta Theta Pi, Slpha Omega Alpha. Episcopalian (past vestryman, jr. warden). Mason (Shriner, K.T.); mem. Order Cincinnati. Clubs: Belle Meade Country, Cumberland, Round Table (Nashville). Author: (with H.T. Lovely) Hysterectomy, 1954; gynecol. sect. Christopher's Surgery, 1957. Home: 4414 Tyne Blvd Nashville TN 37215 Office: 2112 W End Av Nashville TN 37203

BURCH, LOREN WILLIAM, educator, news editor, clergyman; b. Epsilon, Mich., Jan. 9, 1907; s. Henry Alonzo and Emma (Odebrecht) B.; B.A., Kalamazoo Coll., 1927; B.D., Colgate-Rochester Div. Sch., 1932; M.A., Cornell U., 1941;; m. Mary Etta Anspach 1931 (dec.); children—Phyllis (Mrs. Pernell O. Nix, dec.), Byron H., Marilyn (Mrs. John R. Swan), Loren William, James O.; m. 2d, Olive May Reed Holder, June 5, 1971; stepchildren—Jerry Holder, Raymond Holder. Ordained to ministry Bapt. Ch., 1927; pastor Manitou Beach (Mich.) Bapt. Ch., 1927-29, student pastor Riga (N.Y.) Congl. Ch., 1930-32, West Groton (N.Y.) Congl. Ch., 1932-36, New Haven (N.Y.) Congl. Ch., 1936-43, United Community Ch., Castile, N.Y., 1946-48; asso. pastor United Ch. Christ, Mascoutah, Ill., 1965-66; instr. sociology, German, history Piedmont Coll., Demorest, Ga., 1966-69; pastor Demorest Federated Ch., 1966-69, St. Paul United Ch. Christ, Marshall, 1970-72; news editor Southeast News, Tulsa, 1972—. Served to maj., chaplain USAF, 1943-46, 48-65. Recipient Freedom's Found. award, George Washington medal, 1961; Air Force Commendation medal, 1965. Kiwanian, Rotarian (dir. internat. relations 1965-66), Mason (32 deg., Shriner). Author: Little Lessons from Mighty Men, 1967; A Tale of Sixty Years, 1969. Home: 7406 E Third St Tulsa OK 74112

BURCH, ROBERT RAY, physician; b. Edgard, La., May 28, 1924; s. George Edward and Lottie (Monroe) B.; student U. Southwestern La., Coll. Engring., 1941-43, Dickinson Coll., 1943; B.S., Tulane U., 1947; M.D., Tulane U. Sch. Medicine, 1951; m. Lillie Margaret Daves, June 11, 1955; children—Robert Ray, Jr., Gayle Anne. Intern, Phila. Gen. Hosp., 1951-52; asst. resident medicine Duke U. Hosp., Durham, N.C., 1952-53; fellow internal medicine Tulane U. Sch. Medicine, 1953-54, Nat. Inst. trainee dept. medicine, 1954-55, fellow medicine, 1955-56; practice medicine, specializing in internal medicine, New Orleans, 1956—; mem. staff So. Bapt. Hosp., New Orleans, sec. dept. medicine, 1957-61, 71-72, treas., 1969-70, sec., 1971-72, v.p., 1973; sr. vis. physician Charity Hosp., New Orleans, 1963—; instr. Tulane U. Sch. Medicine, 1954-56, asst. prof., 1956-66, asso. prof., 1966-73, clin. prof. medicine, 1973—. Physician adviser pub. edn. com. Orleans Parish Heart Council, 1966-67. Asso. mem.

La. Wildlife Fedn., 1964, 72, 73, Nat. Wildlife Fedn., 1965—; mem. Orleans Parish Sch. Bd. Com. Athletics Safety, 1966-67; mem. regional adv. group La. Regional Med. Program, 1970-73; mem. adv. bd. Jesuit High Sch. Parents' Club, 1973, Mercantile Bank and Trust Co., 1970—. Served to capt. USAF, 1943-46. Decorated Air Medal. Diplomate Am. Bd. Internal Medicine. Fellow A.C.P.; mem. Orleans Parish, La. med. socs., A.M.A., N.Y. Acad. Sci., Am., La. heart assns., New Orleans Acad. Internal Medicine, Am. Geriatrics Soc., Am. Soc. Internal Medicine. Clubs: Le Samedi Gras, Aesculapians, Scatter Brain Bone Head, Pendennis, Thackery Soc., Royal Society of St. George (New Orleans). Home: 2514 Audubon St New Orleans LA 70125 Office: 4303 Magnolia St New Orleans LA 70115

BURCHAM, GWENDOLYN FRANCES PARKER (MRS. RALPH JACK BURCHAM), home economist; b. Drakes Creek, Ark., June 11, 1932; d. Nolan Henry and Leta Clair (Drake) Parker; student John Brown U., 1949-51; B.S., U. Ark., 1953, M.S., 1957; postgrad., 1961-62; postgrad. Wichita State U., 1957-58; m. Ralph Jack Burcham, Apr. 9, 1955; 1 dau., Thresa Clair. Tchr. home econs., high Schs. in Elkins, Ark., Decatur, Ark., Wichita, Kan., Mabelvale, Ark., 1953-61; extention home economist Pulaski County, Ark., 1961-62; dir. pub. relations Am. Dairy Assn., Ark., 1962-65; dir. Ark. Milk Promotion Com., Little Rock, 1965-66; exec. dir. Dairy Council Ark., Little Rock, 1966-68; program coordinator Dairy Council, Inc., Little Rock, 1968—. Cons., TV stas. in Little Rock, 1961—. Recipient Outstanding Service award Ark. Extention Homemakers Council, 1968. Mem. Am. recorder state pres. unit 1972), Ark. (v.p.1968-69, pres. 1971-72, membership chmn. 1967—) home econs. assns., Am., Ark. pub. health assns., Am. Bus. Womens Assn., Am., Ark. home economists in bus., Ark. Women's Com. on Pub. Affairs (past pres.), Ark. Interagy. Nutrition Com. (program com. 1969—, sec. 1971-72, Pulaski County 4-H Clubs (hon.), Ark. Geneal. Soc. Baptist. Clubs: Ark. Kennel (past sec. Little Rock), German Shepherd Dog of Little Rock (dir. 1972), Lakeside Country. Home: 3924 Base Line Rd Little Rock AR 72209 Office: 6423 Forbing Rd Little Rock AR 72209

BURCHAM, RALPH JACK, civil engr.; b. Ft. Scott, Kan., Feb. 13, 1931; s. Ralph and Ruby (Hays) B.; student Ft. Scott Kan. Jr. Coll., 1949-51; B.S., U. Ark., 1957; m. Gwendolyn Francaes Parker, Apr. 9, 1955. Stress analyst Boeing Airplane Co., Wichita, Kan., 1957-59; sr. resident engr. Ark. Hwy. Dept., Little Rock, 1959-63; owner Ralph J. Burcham, cons. engrs., Little Rock, 1963-70; pres. Found. Explorations, Inc., Little Rock, 1965-70; partner Assos. Engrs. & Land Surveyors, Little Rock, Ark., 1967-70; engr. Granite Mountain Quarries, Sweet Home, Ark., 1970—. Served to capt. AUS, 1951-53. Decorated Bronze Star medal. Mem. Central Ark., Am., Ark. socs. profl. engrs., Ark. Kennel Club (dir. 1966-70), German Shepherd Dog Club Little Rock (pres. 1972). Baptist. Home: 3924 Base Line Rd Little Rock AR 72209 Office: Shamburger Lane Sweet Home AR 72206

BURCHFIELD, HARRY PHINEAS, JR., research inst. adminstr.; b. Pitts., Dec. 22, 1915; s. Harry Phineas and Florence Faye (Fearl) B.; A.B., Columbia, 1938, M.A., 1938, Ph.D., 1956; m. Eleanor Emerett Storrs, Nov. 29, 1963; children—Sarah Storrs, Benjamin Hyde. Research scientist Uniroyal Corp., Naugatuck, Conn., 1940-50, dir. plantations research dept., Indonesia, 1951-52; asso. dir. Boyce Thompson Inst. for Plant Research, Yonkers, N.Y., 1952-61; inst. scientist, mgr. S.W. Research Inst., San Antonio, 1961-65; chief pesticides research lab. USPHS, Perrine, Fla., 1965-67; sci. dir. Gulf South Research Inst., New Iberia, La., 1967—; adj. prof. chemistry U. Southwestern La., 1967—. Trustee Gulf Univs. Research Consortium, 1971—; mem. Carcinogenesis Panel of Secs., Health Edn. and Welfare Commn. on Pesticides, 1969; mem. nat. tech. adv. com. pesticides Environmental Protection Agy., 1971-72, project reviewer research grants, 1972; cons. carcinogenesis Nat. Cancer Inst., 1965-67; treas. The Acadiana Internat. Relations Assos., 1972-73, dir., 1973-74. Recipient award Chgo. Rubber Group, 1946. Environmental Protection Agy. grantee 1969. Mem. Am. Chem. Soc., Soc. Toxicology, Am. Inst. Biol. Scis., A.A.A.S., Am. Phytopath. Soc., N.Y. Acad. Scis. Author: (with Eleanor E. Storrs) Biochemical Applications of Gas Chromatography, 1962; (with D.E. Johnson and Eleanor Storrs) Guide to the Analysis of Pesticide Residues, 1965. Contbr. articles to profl. jours. Home: 303 Duperier Av New Iberia LA 70560 Office: PO Box 1177 New Iberia LA 70560

BURDETT, THOMAS LEE, lawyer; b. Blanco, Tex., Oct. 12, 1942; s. Clarence Winston and Pansy Edith (Rollins) B.; B.B.A., U. Tex., 1965, J.D., 1967; m. Carlie Sue Hunter, June 3, 1966; children—Sharon Bliss, Shannon Todd. Admitted to Tex. bar, 1967; asso. Witherspoon, Aikin, Thomas & Langley, Hereford, Tex., 1967-71, partner, 1971-72; mem. firm Thomas & Burdett, Hereford, 1972—. Asst. county atty. Deaf Smith County, Hereford, 1967-69; sec. Texham Corp., Hereford, 1971—; sec., treas. Lucky Cattle Co., Inc., Hereford, 1968—, also v.p., dir. Blackstone Corp., Hereford, 1973—; sec., dir. JMZ Corp., Hereford, 1972—. Served with AUS, 1967-68. Mem. State Bar Tex., Am., Hereford, 69th Jud. Dist. (sec. 1971-72) bar assns., Deaf Smith County C. of C. (dir. 1972—), Delta Theta Phi. Mem. Ch. of Christ (deacon 1973—). Kiwanian (dir., v.p. 1970-72). Home: 312 Douglas Hereford TX 79045 Office: PO Box 1917 Hereford TX 79045

BURDICK, EVERETTE MARSHALL, cons. chemist; b. Champaign, Ill., Aug. 9, 1913; s. Pearl Oscar and Margaret Alice (Hyde) B.; B.S. cum laude, U. Miami, 1935; M.S., Purdue U., 1937, Ph.D., 1943;; m. Lois Aline Enyart, Nov. 13, 1937. Research chemist U.S. Dept. Agr., Northern Regional Research Lab., Peoria, Ill., 1941-45, U.S. Fruit & Vegetable Products Lab., Weslaco, Tex., 1945-46; dir. research Texsum Citrus Exchange, Weslaco, 1946-52; tech. cons. Rio Farms, Inc., Edcouch, Tex., 1949-52; tech. dir. Am. Chlorophyll, 1952-53; dir. labs. Am. Chlorophyll div. Strong-Cobb & Co., 1953; v.p., dir. research Strong Cobb & Co., Inc., 1953-54; pres. Am. Papain & Chem. Co., Inc., 1954-57; cons. Florida Citrus Mutual, 1957-58, Wallerstein Labs., Baxter Labs., Arbee Biochem. Corp., Resources Research, 1959-64; dir. research and devel. True Taste Corp., 1961-63. Fellow Am. Inst. Chemists (chmn. Fla. sect. 1962-63), A.A.A.S.; mem. Am. Chem. Soc. (emeritus), Fla. Hort. Soc., Inst. Food Technologists (emeritus), N.Y. Acad Scis., Sigma Xi, Phi Lambda Upsilon. Methodist. Mason. Co-author: Modern Chemical Processes, vols. I and IV; Fruit and Vegetable Juice Production. Contbr. to profl. jours. Patentee in field. Home: 4821 Ronda St Coral Gables FL 33146 Office: Coral Gables FL 33146

BURDICK, LARRY GENE, supt. schs.; b. Mooreland, Okla., Aug. 28, 1932; s. James Wilbur and Dorothy Dane (Wheeler) B.; B.S., Okla. State U., 1954, M.S., 1962, Ed.D., 1967; postgrad. U. Okla., 1962-63; m. Betty Lou Meyer, Sept. 6, 1953; children—Karen Ann, Kevin Lee, Keith Alan. Tchr. math., coach Garber (Okla.) Pub. Schs., 1956-61, high sch. prin., 1961-62, supt. schs., 1962-66; dir. tchr. edn. Phillips U., Enid, Okla., 1967-68; supt. schs. Pryor (Okla.) Pub. Schs., 1968—. Bd. dirs. Pryor United Fund. Served with USAF, 1954-56. Mem. N.E.A., Am., Okla. (v.p. 1971-72, pres. elect 1972-73, pres. 1973-74) assns. sch. adminstrs., Assn. Sch. Bus. Ofcls. Okla., Okla. Edn. Assn., Okla. Pub. Sch. Research Council (pres. 1969-70), Pryor C. of C. (dir. 1969-71). Methodist (bd. edn. Okla. Conf. 1968—). Rotarian. Home: 1008 SE 14th St Pryor OK 74361 Office: 521 SE 1st St Pryor OK 74361

BURDON, ARTHUR PEMBERTON, physician; b. St. Louis, Nov. 23, 1924; s. Kenneth L. and Estelle (Pemberton) B.; B.S., Tulane U., 1945, M.D., 1947; m. Jane Talmage, June 14, 1947;children—Paula, Lois, Susan, John. Intern, USPHS Hosp,, S.I., N.Y., 1947-48; resident psychiatry Harvard Med. Sch., 1948-49, research group psychotherapy, 1959-60; chief psychiatry Mt. Auburn Hosp., Cambridge, Mass., 1959-60; practice medicine, specializing in psychiatry, and psychoanalysis, New Orleans, 1960—; asso. prof. psychiatry La. State U. Med. Sch., 1960-71, prof., 1971—. Bd. dirs. La. Assn. Mental Health. Served with AUS, 1944-47, USPHS, 1947-48, 51-53. Fellow Am. Group Psychotherapy Assn., Am., So. psychiat. assns. Presbyn. (elder). Contbr. articles profl. jours. Home: 382 Broadway New Orleans LA 70118 Office: 3720 Prytania St New Orleans LA 70115

BURFORD, ROGER LEWIS, educator; b. Independence, Miss., Jan. 19, 1930; s. Roger W. and Christene (Lewis) B.; B,B,A., U. Miss., 1956 M.A., 1957; Ph.D., Ind. U., 1961; m. Bettye Jane Marshall, Nov. 25, 1948; children—Pamela Denise, Roger Marshall. Lectr. econs., statistics Ind. U., 1959-60; mem. faculty Ga. State Coll., 1960-63 mem. faculty La. State U., Baton Rouge, 1963—, dir. div. bus. research, 1969—. Vice pres. Econ. and Indsl. Research, Inc., Baton Rouge, 1967—. Chmn., La. Council Econ. Advisers, 1973—. Ford Found. Predoctoral fellow, 1957-59, Fulbright fellow, 1968-69. Mem. Am., So. econ. assns., Econometric Soc., Am. Statis. Assn., Western Regional Sci. Assn. Author: Introduction to Finite Probability, 1967; Statistics-A Computer Approach, 1968; Basic Statistics for Business and Economics-A Computer Oriented Text, 1970. Home: 590 Castle Kirk Av Baton Rouge LA 70808

BURFORD, SELWYN OILVER, oil co. exec.; b. Santa Anna, Tex., Sept. 16, 1899; s. William Baxter and Effie (Oliver) B.; B.A. in Geology, U. Tex. at Austin, 1927, M.A., 1928; m. Myrle Louise Walker, Nov. 23, 1927; children—Marylouise (Mrs. David Nord), Patsy (Mrs. William Roy Samuel), Robert Oliver. Geologist, Henry L. Doherty Oil Co., Coahuila, Mexico, 1925; Instr. geology U. Tex., 1927-29; with Humble Oil Co. various Gulf Coast locations, 1929-64, research geologist, Houston, 1940-41, sr. geologist, Tyler, Tex., 1941-64; pres. Somyrol, Inc., Tyler, 1964—. Served with U.S. Army, 1918. Mem. Am. Assn. Petroleum Geologists, East Tex. Geol. Soc., Internat. Platform Assn., Sigma Gamma Epsilon, Acacia. Mem. Christian Ch. Address: Rural Route 2 Box 531 Tyler TX 75701

BURGER, ROBERT MERCER, physicist; b. Frederick, Md., Feb. 14, 1927; s. William Leslie and Grace Allene (Mercer) B.; B.S., Coll. William and Mary, 1949; Sc.M, Brown U., 1953, Ph.D., 1955; m. Marian Elizabeth Abbott, Sept. 10, 1949; children—Sharon A., Lisa A., Robert M. Physicist, Dept. Def., Washington, 1955-59; fellow engr. Westinghouse Elec. Co., Balt., 1959-62; dir. Solid State Lab., Research Triangle Inst., N.C., 1962-67, dir. engring and environmental sci. div., 1967-71, chief scientist, 1971—. Research asso. physics U. Md., College Park, 1957-59; adj. asso. prof. elec. engring. Duke, Durham, N.C., 1962-69. Served with USNR, 1945-46. Recipient Bauch and Lamb Sci. award, 1944. Mem. Am. Phys. Soc., I.E.E.E., A.A.A.S., Am. Ordnance Assn., Sigma Xi. Republican. Presbyn. Editor: (with R.P. Donovan) Fundamentals of Silicon Integrated Device Technology, vol. 1, 1967 vol. 2, 1968. Home: 1506 Rosedale Ave Durham NC 27707 Office: PO Box 12194 Research Triangle Park NC 27709

BURGER, WARREN E(ARL), chief justice of U.S.; b. St. Paul, 1907; s. Charles Joseph and Katharine (Schnittger) B.; student U. Minn., 1925-27; LL.B. magna cum laude, St. Paul Coll. Law (now Mitchell Coll. Law), 1931; m. Elvera Stromberg, Nov. 8, 1933; children—Wade Allan, Margaret Elizabeth. Admitted to Minn. bar, 1931; partner Faricy, Burger, Moore & Costello (and predecessor firms), 1935-53; faculty Mitchell Coll. Law, 1931-48; asst. atty. gen. U.S., 1953-56; judge U.S. Ct. Appeals, Washington, 1956-69; chief justice U.S., 1969—. Hon. master bench Middle Temple, 1969; pres. Bentham Club, U. Coll. London, 1972-73; hon. chmn. Inst. Jud. Adminstrn., Am. Bar Assn. Project on Criminal Justice Standards. Chancellor, bd. regents Smithsonian Instn.; chmn. bd. trustees Nat. Gallery Art; trustee Mitchell Coll. Law; trustee emeritus Macalester Coll., St. Paul, Mayo Found., Rochester, Minn. Office: Supreme Court US Washington DC 20543

BURGESS, ARTHUR HARRY, accountant; b. Sharon, S.C., Oct. 25, 1903; s. Arthur Calhoun and Mary (Love) B.; student Furman U., 1921-23; m. Sara Elizabeth Doll, Nov. 30, 1933; children—Sara Elizabeth (Mrs. John Sidney Frazer), Arthur Harry. Public accountant, Hickory, N.C., 1928—; pres. Arthur H. Burgess and Co., Hickory; dir. Maxwell Royal Chair Co. Mem. adv. bd. trustees Queens Coll.; pres. Sharon Found. C.P.A., N.C. Mem. Am. Inst. C.P.A.'s N.C. Assn. C.P.A.'s. Presbyn. Rotarian. Clubs: Catawba (Newton, N.C.); Lake Hickory Country (Hickory). Home: 322 3d Av NE Hickory NC 28601 Office: First Security Bldg Hickory NC 28601

BURGESS, BRYAN ELIJAH, ednl. adminstr.; b. Sparta, Tenn., Oct. 27, 1937; s. Elijah Bryan and Pauline (Pennington) B.; B.S., Tenn. Tech. U., 1960; M.S., U. Ala., 1965, postgrad., 1971; m. Katherine Kirby, June 10, 1961 (div. Dec. 1971); children—Belinda, Susan, Paula. Design engr. Hayes Internat. Co., Huntsville, Ala., 1960-61, 63-64; systems analyst Brown Engring. Co., Huntsville, 1964-67; v.p. Nashville, Speedways, Inc., 1968-70; dir. research Motlow State Community Coll., Tullahoma, Tenn. 1970—. Served to capt. AUS, 1961-63. Registered profl. engr., Tenn. Mem. Nat., Tenn. soc. profl. engrs., Tenn. Edn. Assn., Phi Kappa Phi. Home: 706 Stone Blvd Tullahoma TN 37388

BURGESS, CHESTER FRANCIS, educator; b. Brockton, Mass., Oct. 30, 1922; s. Chester Francis and Mary Ann (Cronin) B.; B.A., Yale, 1945; M.A., U. Notre Dame, 1961, Ph.D., 1962; m. Betty Lou Reigan, Sept. 1, 1945; children—Chester F. III, Deborah Ann. Instr. English, Yale, 1946-48; mgr. retail automobile agy., Rifle, Colo., 1948-60; instr. English, U. Notre Dame, 1960-62, pub. relations asst., 1961; asst. prof. English, Va. Mil. Inst., Lexington, 1962-63, prof., 1967—. Reporter, A.P., 1939-40. Served to capt., USMCR, 1943-46, 51-52. Ford Found. fellow, 1965-66; Folger Library fellow, 1968; Am. Council Learned Socs. fellow, 1971; Am. Philos Soc. grantee, 1963, 64, 65, 68. Mem. Modern Lang. Assn. Am., Shakespeare Assn. Am., Phi Beta Kappa. Author: The Letters of John Gay, 1966; Gay's Beggar's Opera and Companion Pieces, 1966; also articles. Home: 305 Letcher Av Lexington VA 24450

BURGESS, JAMES ALFRED, dentist; b. Pecola, Okla., Apr. 13, 1931; s. James Alfred and Jewell Louise (Farrar) B.; A.A., Fort Smith Jr. Coll., 1951; student U. Ark., 1954-56; D.D.S., U. Kansas City, 1959; m. Myra J. Spearman, May 27, 1951; children—Rozanne, James Alfred III, Dane Alan, Suzanne. Pvt. practice of dentistry, Greenwood, Ark., 1959—. Chmn. Greenwood Housing Authority, 1968-71; chmn. Sebastian County Housing Corp., 1971—. Bd. dirs. Sebastian County Fair, 1962-71; adv. bd. Westark Jr. Coll., 1970-71. Served with USNR, 1951-54. Mem. C. of C. (pres. 1966-67), Ft. Smith, Ark. dental socs., Am. Dental Assn., South Sebastian County Indsl. and Devel. Assn. (sec. 1969-71). Lion. Club: Greenwood Round-up (pres. 1963). Home: Greenwood AR 72936 Office: PO Box 478 Greenwood AR 72936

BURGESS, JAMES ROWLAND, JR., ret. coll. pres.; b. Ashburn, Ga., Feb. 17, 1907; s. James Rowland and Aurena (Evans) B.; diploma Young Harris Coll., 1927; A.B., Emory U., 1931; M.Ed., Duke, 1936; LL.D., La Grange Coll., 1960; m. Martha Elizabeth Stallings, Aug. 13, 1932; children—James Rowland III, Martha S. (Mrs. James Monroe Thorn). Prin., Oak Grove Sch., 1927-28, Cataula (Ga.) High Sch., 1928-30, Pitts (Ga.) Consol. Sch., 1931-36; supt. Vienna (Ga.) Pub. Schs., 1936-41; prin. Blue Ridge (Ga.) Dist Schs., 1941-43; supt. Baxley (Ga.) Pub. Schs., 1943-44; pres. Reinhardt Coll., Waleska, Ga., 1944-73, pres. emeritus, 1973—, dir. devel., 1973-74. Bd. mgrs. Ga. Congress P.T.A. Mem. bd. edn. N. Ga. Conf., United Meth. Ch., 1956-66, del. gen. Conf., 1960, alternat. del., 1972, del. Jurisdictional Conf., 1952, 56, 60, 64, 68, 72. Mem. Ga. Assn. Jr. Colls. (past pres.), Nat. Assn. Meth. Colls. (past pres. jr. coll. sect.), Ga. Assn. Colls. (pres. 1965), Ga. Hort. Soc. (dir. 1966-68, v.p. 1971-73, pres. 1973—), Pvt. Colls. and Univs. Ga. (exec. com. 1968—), Ga. Conservancy (trustee 1968-70), P.T.A. (hon. life), Kappa Phi Kappa, Kappa Delta Pi, Pi Kappa Delta, Phi Theta Kappa. Lion (pres. Canton 1962). Home: 1858 Ridgewood Dr NE Atlanta GA 30307

BURGESS, JOHN FREDERICK, JR., ednl. adminstr.; b. Washington, Jan. 23, 1932; s. John Frederick and Thelma (Gray) B.; A.A., St. Petersburg Jr. Coll., 1956; B.S., Fla. State U., 1958, M.S., 1960, Ed.D., 1966; m Betty Margaret Cleveland, Sept. 12, 1959; children—John, Donald. Instr., dept. marketing Fla. State U., Tallahassee, 1959, research asst., tchr, Sch. Bus., 1960-62; asst. study dir. Fla. Devel. Commn., Tallahassee, 1959-60; chmn. bus. econs. dept., dir. Community Services, Columbus Coll., Ga., 1962-66, dir. community services continuing edn., 1966—. Served with AUS, 1952-54. Mem. Ga. Adult Edn. Council, Assn. Continuing Edn., Pub. Service Adminstrs. Club: Exchange (past pres.). Home: 4749 Shanandoah Dr Columbus GA 31907

BURGESS, OLIVER TAYLOR, hairstylist, cosmetologist; b. Dendron, Va.; Aug. 29, 1918; s. Herman Oliver and Virginia (Trueheart) B.; student Kirby's Beauty Sch., Norfolk, Va., 1948, Robert Fiance Hair Design Inst., N.Y.C., 1949;; m. Ida Madjestic Chester, Dec. 17, 1941; 1 son, Oliver Taylor. Owner beauty salon, Wakefield, Va., 1948-50; owner beauty salons, Norfolk, 1950—, as owner Taylor Burgess Hairstyling Salons, Inc., 1962—; guest stylist John H. Breck Co., in U.S. and Europe, 1957—; pres., chmn. bd., dir. Polychem, Inc. Bd. dirs. Girl's Club of Norfolk. Cons. com. cosmetology Norfolk Tech. Vocational Center, Norfolk. Served as cpl. 116th Inf., AUS, 1941-45; ETO. Decorated Purle Heart, Bronze Star. Mem. Nat. (hair fashion com.), Norfolk hairdressers assns., Internat. Platform Assn., Intercoiffure U.S., Va. Hairdressers and Cosmetologists Assn. (pres. 1965-66), Va. Allied Council Cosmetology (charter mem.), Norfolk C. of C., Wards Corner Bus. Men's Assn. Baptist (trustee). Mason (Shriner), Lion. Club: Lafayette Yacht (Norfolk, Va.). Home: 6435 Newport Av Norfolk VA 23505 Office: 7500 Granby St Wards Corner Norfolk VA 23505

BURGESS, ROBERT HERRMANN, museum curator; b. Balt., May 27, 1913; s. William Kirk and Lula Ann (Dixon) B.; grad. Balt. City Coll., 1931; m. Mabel Adele Plitt, Feb. 4, 1938; children—Robert Bruce, Janet (Mrs. Lyn E. Hippert). Mem. staff Mariners Museum, Newport News, Va., 1941—, curator exhibits, 1955-73, curator publs., 1973—. Mem. adv. bd. Va. Skin Divers Assn., 1963. Bd. govs. Chesapeake Bay Maritime Museums, 1968—; trustee Chesapeake Bay Found., Annapolis, 1968—. Served with USNR, 1943-45; PTO. Nat. Endowment for Humanities fellow, 1967. Mem. Steamship Hist. Soc. Am., Richmond Ship Model Soc. (hon.), Hampton Roads Ship Model Soc. (hon.). Author: This Was Chesapeake Bay, 1963; Chesapeake Circle, 1965; Sea, Sails and Shipwreck, 1970; (with H. Graham Wood) Steamboats Out of Baltimore, 1968; Chesapeake Sailing Craft, 1974. Editor: Coasting Captain (L.S. Tawes), 1967; Journal of H.M. Gregory, Voyage of clipper ship Sea Serpent, 1854-1855, 1974. Editorial adv. bd. American Neptune, 1964—. Home: 1504 Gatewood Rd Newport News VA 23601 Office: Museum Dr Newport News VA 23606

BURGESS, WILBUR HARLIN, writer; b. Monmouth, Ill., Aug. 15, 1914; s. Charles Oliver and Lura (Harlin) B.; student Monmouth Coll., 1929-33; m. Suzanne Marie McLean, Dec. 29, 1940; children—Lysbeth (Mrs. John A. Chuck), Duncan H. Commd. capt. U.S. Army, 1940, advanced through grades to col.; staff comd. coll., 1953. Artillery sch. faculty, 1953-56, 59-60; adviser Korean Army, 1956-57, ret., 1960; tech. writer Franklin Co.-Phila., Ft. Sill, Okla., 1962-64; curricula specialist U.S. Civil Service, Ft. Sill, 1964—. Pres. Inst. Gt. Plains. Decorated Army Commendation medal with oak leaf cluster. Mem. Nat. Trust for Historic Preservation, Inst. of Gt. Plains, Smithsonian Assos., Internat. Council Museums, Am. Assn. Museums (mus. trustees com.), Lawton C. of C. Home: 210 Mimosa Lane Lawton OK 73501

BURGET, CARL EDWARD, banker; b. Chandler, Okla., June 26, 1921; s. Everett Edward and Stella Lee (Hutchinson) B.; student Tonkawa Jr. Coll., 1939, Central State U., 1946-47; J.D., U. Okla., 1949; m. Mary Sue McMinimy, Nov. 25, 1946; 1 son, Mark Edward. Commd. capt. U.S. Air Force, 1947, advanced through grades to col., 1963; asst. staff judge adv. Lowry AFB, Denver, 1949-52, Hdqrs. USAFE, Wiesbaden, Germany, 1952-55, Hdqrs. Continental Mil. Air Transport Service, San Antonio, 1955-58; staff judge adv. Hdqrs. 30th Air Div., Detroit, 1958-59; asst. staff judge adv. and staff judge adv. Hdqrs. 30th Air Div., Madison, Wis., 1959-63; staff judge adv. 3320th Tech. Tng. Center, Amarillo, Tex., 1963-65; ret., 1965; admitted to Tex. bar, U.S. Supreme Ct. bar; sr. v.p., trust officer Am. Nat. Bank, Amarillo, 1965-72; sr. v.p., sr. trust officer City Nat. Bank & Trust Co., Oklahoma City, 1972—. Bd. dirs. Deaconess Hosp.; mem. fiscal bd. Oklahoma City Found. Mem. Bank Marketing Assn., V.F.W., Okla. Bar Assn., Phi Delta Phi. Mason (32 deg.). Club: Touchdown (Norman, Okla.). Home: 408 E 6th St Edmond OK 73034 Office: PO Box 25715 Oklahoma City OK 73125

BURGETT, MONTE IRA, JR., govt. ofcl.; b. Midland, Ark., Mar. 8, 1921; s. Monte Ira and Elizabeth (Burnett) B.; student Hendrix Coll., 1938-39; B.S. in Elec. Engring., Ga. Inst. Tech., 1943; M.S., U. Pa., 1951; m. Marion Meyer, Sept. 7, 1946; children—Melissa Ruth, Marcia Irene, Monte Robert. With Philco Corp., Phila., 1943-63, mgr. advanced systems devel., 1961-62, engring. program mgr., 1962-63; chief engring. div., nat. mil. command systems tech. support Def. Communications Agy., Washington, 1963—. Mem. Phila. Sci. Council, 1951-56. Recipient Pres.'s award Philco Corp., 1954, Outstanding Performance awards Def. Communications Agy., 1971, 73. Mem. I.E.E.E. (sr.). Baptist (deacon). Mason. Home: 3123 Plantation Pkwy Fairfax VA 22030 Office: Code 931 Def Communications Agy Washington DC 20305

BURGHER, EDMON, electric co. exec.; b. Clay City, Ky., June 11, 1896; s. John Everett and Denannie (McKinney) B.; grad. Mich. State Auto Sch., 1920; m. Ethel Delcinia Johnson, Oct. 10, 1921; children—Edmon, Lorraine, (Mrs. Max Ervin). Asst. editor Clay City Times, 1910-25; shop foreman Cynthiana (Ky.) Democrat, 1925-33; postmaster, Clay City, 1938-39; ry. postal clk. 1939-41; ry. clk., U.S. Postal Service, 1946-59; pub. Clay City Times, 1959-64; dir. Powell County Bank, Stanton, Ky., 1959-65, Clark Rural Electric Coop. Corp., Winchester, Ky., 1962—; charter mem. Estill Fed. Savs. &

Loan Assn., Irvine, Ky. Alternate del. Nat. Democratic Conv., 1960; mayor, Clay City, 1959-61. Served with USMCR, 1917-19, USAF, 1941-44, U.S. Mcht. Marines, 1945-46. Mem. S.A.R., Am. Legion (comdr. 1961), 40 and 8, Vets. World War I, Ky. Am. Legion Press Assn. (pres. 1965). Baptist. Mason, Lion. Home: Clay City KY 40312

BURKE, DENZER, dentist; b. Atlanta, Sept. 22, 1933; s. Dennis and Sarah (White) B.; B.S., U. Mich., 1956 D,D.S., Howard U., 1959, Practice dentistry, Texarkana, Tex., 1963—. Vice chmn. Tex. State Adv. Com. to U.S. Commn. on Civil Rights, 1968—; sec. exec. com. Bowie County Econ. Advancement Corp., 1964-68. Bd. dirs. Texarkana Community Chest, Bowie Orgn. Loyal Democrats, Texarkana Spl. Edn. Kindergarten and Sch., Texans for Ednl. Excellence. Served with USNR, 1959-63. Mem. Am., Nat., Texarkana dental assns., Texarkana Orgn., Kappa Alpha Psi (chpt. sec.-treas. 1967—). Presbyn. Home: 25 S Robison Rd Texarkana TX 75501 Office: 523 W 3d St Texarkana TX 75501

BURKE, EDWARD WALTER, JR., educator; b. Macon, Ga., Sept. 16, 1924; s. Edward Walter and Lora (Waterman) B.; student Newberry Coll., 1943-44; B.S. in Math., Presbyn. Coll., 1947; M.S. in Physics, U. Wis., 1949, Ph.D., 1954; m. Julia Tharpe Struby, June 22, 1946; children—Edward Walter III, Julia Riley. Asso. prof. dept. physics King Coll., Bristol, Tenn., 1949-54, prof., 1954—, chmn. div. natural scis., 1960—. Chmn. Mayor's Adv. Council, 1969. Served to engisn USNR, 1944-45. Fulbright lectr. U. Chile, 1959; NSF grantee, 1963-70, Research Corp. grantee, 1972—. Mem. Am. Phys. Soc. (George B. Peagram award Southeastern sect. 1973), Am. Assn. Physics Tchrs. (pres. elect Tenn. chpt.), Tenn. Acad. Sci., Sigma Xi. Lion. Contbr. articles profl. jours. Home: 1307 Rock Rose Rd Bristol TN 37620 Office: King Coll Bristol TN 37620

BURKE, FRANK GERARD, govt. ofcl.; b. Bklyn., Apr. 22, 1927; s. James Francis and Eleanor Josephine (Thomas) B.; student U. Alaska, 1952-55; M.A., U. Chgo., 1959, Ph.D., 1969; m. Hildegard Waltraud Arndt, Aug. 1, 1959; children—Margaret, Catherine, Christina, Thomas, Elisabeth. Asst. curator archives and manuscripts U. Chgo., 1962-64; head Preparation sect. Manuscript div. Library Congress, Washington, 1964-67; information retrieval specialist Nat. Archives and Record Service, Gen. Services Adminstrn., 1967-68, dir. ednl. programs, 1968-73, asst. archivist for ednl. programs, 1973—; cons. archival automation State of Me., 1968, 70. Served with USNR, 1945-46. Fellow Soc. Am. Archivists (chmn. com. on description archives); mem. Am. Hist. Assn. Contbr. articles to profl. jours. Home: 3401 Charleson St Annandale VA 22003 Office: National Archives 8th and Pennsylvania Av NW Washington DC 20408

BURKE, HENRY FRANCIS, physician; b. Lynn, Mass., Feb. 22, 1925; s. James Michael and Mary (Thomas) B.; student Harvard, 1942-44; M.D., Boston U., 1948; m. Dorothy Jane Egan, Sept. 6, 1949; children—Henry, Patricia, James, Jane, Michael, Maureen. Intern, Beverly (Mass.) Hosp., 1948-49; resident VA Hosp., Boston and West Roxbury, Mass., 1951-54; practice medicine, specializing in internal medicine, Lynn, Mass., 1954, 55, St. Johnsbury, Vt., 1957-58; teaching fellow medicine Tufts U., Boston, 1953-54; staff physician U. Fla., Gainesville, 1956-57; asst. chief med. service and chief cardiology sect. VA Hosp., Providence, R.I., 1958-65; chief med. service VA Center, Bay Pines, Fla., 1965-73, chief of staff, 1973—. Mem. med. sci. com. R.I. Arthritis and Rheumatism Found. Served to lt. M.C., USNR, 1949-51. Diplomate Am. Bd. Internal Medicine; mem. A.C.P., A.M.A., Am. Heart Assn., Mass., Vt. med. socs. Home: 8083 Stimie Av N St Petersburg FL 33710 Office: VA Hosp Bay Pines FL 33504

BURKE, J. HERBERT, congressman; b. Chgo., Jan. 14, 1913; s. Joseph Patrick and Catherine (Lobert) B.; student Northwestern U., 1934-35; A.A., Central YMCA Coll., 1936; J.D., Kent Coll. Law, 1940; L.H.D. (hon.), Drake Coll., 1967, Fort Lauderdale U., 1970; LL.D., Chgo. Coll. Law, 1969; m. Evelyn Rose Krumtinger, Sept. 4, 1946; children—Michele Kathleen, Kelly Ann. Admitted to Ill. bar, 1940, Fla. bar, 1949, U.S. Supreme Ct. bar, 1949; practiced in Chgo., 1940-49, Hollywood, Fla., 1949—; asso. firm Pam, Hurd & Reichmann, 1940-49; sr. partner Burke & McMorrough, 1957-59, Burke & Hoffman, 1959—; mem. 90th-92d Congresses from 10th Dist. Fla., 93d Congress from 12th Dist. Fla., mem. fgn. affairs com. Chmn. March of Dimes South Broward County, 1955, Broward County Heart Fund, 1957-58; mem. S.E. adv. bd. Small Bus. Adminstrn., 1956-60; adviser Nat. Rivers and Harbors Congress, 1958. Mem. Broward County Commn., 1952-66, chmn., 1956-58, dean, 1958-64; Republican state committeeman, 1954-59; del. Rep. Nat. Conv., 1968, 72, also mem. platform com.; mem. nat. exec. com. Rep. Congl. Com. Served to capt. inf. AUS, 1942-45; ETO. Decorated Purple Heart, Bronze Star medal; recipient Outstanding Service medal Nat. Heart Assn., 1957; Good Govt. award Hollywood Jr. C. of C., 1963; Outstanding Citizenship award Hollywood Civitan Club, 1964; Distinguished Service award Ams. for Constl. Action, 1967-72; Watchdog of Treasury award Nat. Assn. Businessmen, 1967-72, service to Israel award Zionist Orgn. Am., 1969; citation for meritorious service Nat. Assn. Ret. Civil Employees, 1971. Mem. Am. Legion (past post comdr.), Amvets (life, citation 1969), 40 and 8, V.F.W., D.A.V., Hollywood C. of C., Phi Delta Phi. Roman Catholic. Eagle, Elk, Moose, Kiwanian. Home: 1218 Hollywood Blvd Hollywood FL 33022 Office: Longworth Bldg US Ho of Reps Washington DC 20515

BURKE, JACK DALE, univ. adminstr.; b. Weiser, Ida., Feb. 6, 1929; s. Earl Edward and Almia Etta (Burns) B.; B.A., U. Ore., 1953; B.D., Fuller Theol. Sem., 1957, M.S., 1962; Ph.D., U. So. Cal., 1968; m. Darlys Ann Cowan, Jan. 29, 1955; children—Linda, David. Tchr., Azusa (Cal.) Unified Sch. Dist., 1957-62; dir. Office Internat. Services, U. Pa., Phila., 1963-66; dir. Office Internat. Student Services, U. Houston, 1968—. Educare fellow U. So. Cal., 1966-68. Mem. Am. Psychol. Assn., Nat. Assn. Fgn. Student Affairs (mem. exec. com. community sect. 1966-71, dir. 1969-70, exec. com. council advisers to fgn. students and scholars 1973—), Am. Personnel Guidance Assn. Home: 13714 Perthshire St Houston TX 77024

BURKE, JAMES OTEY, physician; b. Richmond, Va., May 20, 1912; s. Matt Otey and Elizabeth (Armistead) B.; B.S., Va. Mil. Inst., 1933; M.D., Med. Coll. Va., 1937; m. Alice Delancey Davis, May 2, 1942; children—James Otey Jr., Henry Davis, Anthony Armistead, Richard Lowndes. Intern, U. Wis. Gen. Hosp., Madison, 1937-38, resident, 1938-39; resident Med. Coll. Va., 1939-41; practice medicine specializing in internal medicine, Richmond, 1946—; mem. staff Med. Coll. Va. Hosp.; mem. faculty Med. Coll. Va., Richmond, 1941—, asso. prof., 1954-59, asso. clin. prof. medicine, 1959—; dir. preventive medicine A.H. Robins Co., Richmond, 1960—; cons. VA Hosp., Richmond, 1960—. Mem. adv. council, chmn. personal health services com. Capital Area Health Planning Council, Richmond, 1971-73, chmn. coordinating com. health survey, 1971-73. Bd. corporators Protestant Episcopal Ch. Home, Richmond. Served to maj. AUS, 1941-46. Diplomate Am. Bd. Internal Medicine. Fellow A.C.P.; mem. Am. Fedn. Clin. Research, Am. Gastroent. Assn., Indsl. Med. Assn. Club: Country of Virginia (Richmond). Home: 7 Glenbrooke Circle Richmond VA 23229 Office: 1407 Cummings Dr Richmond VA 23220

BURKE, JOHN WOOLFOLK, JR., lawyer, assn. exec.; b. Washington, Sept. 19, 1915; s. John Woolfolk and Elizabeth Mayo (Atkinson) B.; A.B., Princeton, 1937; LL.B., U.Va., 1941; m. Agnes Alexander Spencer, June 14, 1941; children—John Woolfolk III, Elizabeth Gordon (Mrs. Lewis J. Dale), Agnes Alexander Spencer. Pvt. practice law, 1941; dir. personnel and indsl. relations Capital Airlines, 1946-57; v.p., asst. to chmn. bd. Civil Air Transport, 1957-59; exec. dir. Bus. Council, Washington, 1959—; mem. br. adv. bd. Am. Security & Trust Co. Trustee Gunston Sch. Served from ensign to lt. comdr., USNR, World War II. Mem. Phi Delta Phi. Episcopalian (vestryman). Clubs: Chevy Chase (Md.); Metropolitan (Washington). Home: 5014 Glenbrook Rd Washington DC 20016 Office: 888 17th St Washington DC 20006

BURKE, ROY HAMPTON, JR., lawyer; b. Dooley, Va., June 10, 1923; s. Roy Hampton and Lettye (Berry) B.; A.B., Emory and Henry Coll., 1943; J.D., U. Va., 1948; m. Glenna Louise Dolinger, June 10, 1950; children—Peggy Jane (Mrs. Charles Warren BeVille), Ann Ellen. Admitted to Va. bar, 1948, Fla. bar, 1969, U.S. Dist. Ct., 1950, 4th Circuit Ct. Appeals U.S., 1964; practice law, Marion, Va., 1948—. Pres. Marion P.T.A., 1963—. Trustee Goolsby Ednl. Fund. Served with USNR, 1943-45. Mem. Smyth County (past pres.), Am. bar assns., Marion C. of C. (mem. legis. com.), Nat. Geographic Soc. Methodist. Home: 310 Panorama Dr Marion VA 24354 Office: Profl Bldg Marion VA 24354

BURKE, SAM FRANCIS, ednl. assn. exec.; b. Hampton, Va., Nov. 5, 1903; s. Walter H. and Ava (Cunningham) B.; student Coll. William and Mary, 1921-22, 24, U.S. Naval Acad., 1922-23; A.B., U. S.C., 1925, A.M., 1927; m. Lucy Mae Bragg, Aug. 31, 1930; 1 son, Samuel Francis. Coach, Albany (Ga.) High Sch., 1927-31; prin., coach Greensboro High Sch., 1931-39; prin. Robert E. Lee Inst., Thomaston, Ga., 1939-41; supt. Thomaston Pub. Schs., 1941-46; 1st exec. sec. Ga. High Sch. Assn., Thomaston, 1946—. Cons. atletic, internat. athletic relations U.S. Dept. State, 1965-72; chmn. Nat. High Sch. Football Rules Com., 1949—. Chmn., (Ga.) Bd. Tax Assessors, 1966—, Thomaston and Upson County Planning Commn., 1962—; mem. Chattoochee Area Planning Commn., 1967—. Recipient Spl. Distinguished award S.C. Ofcls. Assn., 1965; Distinguished Service award Nat. Athletic Coaches Assn., 1967; Tiffany award YMCA, 1967; spl. citation Nat. Fedn. State High Sch. Assns., 1972. Mem. Nat. Fedn. State High Sch. Athletic Assn. (pres. 1954-55, 61-71, mem. exec. com. 1944—), Ga. Sch. Bd. Assn., Ga. Athletic Coaches Assn., Omicron Delta Kappa. Mason (32 deg., Shriner), Kiwanian (div. lt. gov. 1950). Home: Trice Cemetery Rd Thomaston GA 30286 Office: 151 S Bethel St Thomaston GA 30286

BURKE, SAMUEL MOODY, elec. engr.; b. Marianna, Ark., Oct. 11, 1922; s. Cornelius Charleston and Margaret (Shortridge) B.; B.S. in Elec. Engring., Miss. State Coll., 1947; m. Mary R. Logan, May 25, 1953; children—Samuel M. Jr., Margaret E. With Ala. Power Co., Birmingham, 1947—, sr. engr., 1953-67, design engr. Birmingham div., 1967—. Sec. Huffman Civitan Club, 1962-64, 71-74. Bd. dirs. Ala. Power Co. Credit Union, pres., 1970-71. Served with USNR, 1943-46. Registered profl. engr., Ala. Mem. I.E.E.E. (sr. mem.), Power Investors Stock Club (pres. 1972-73). Episcopalian (vestryman, sr. warden). Home: 9821 Redcliff Rd Birmingham AL 35215 Office: 15 S 20th St Birmingham AL 35291

BURKE, THOMAS ROBERT, economist; b. Trenton, N.J., Dec. 20, 1938; s. John Thomas and Mary Cecilia (Ryan) B.; A.B. (scholar), LaSalle Coll., 1960; A.M. (Nat. Def. Edn. Act fellow), Boston Coll., 1962, postgrad., 1963; m. Sharon Lee Bucs, Aug. 18, 1962; children—Rosemary Alane, Brendan Thomas, Heather Mary. Lectr., LaSalle Coll., Phila., 1962; lectr. dept. econs. Augusta (Ga.) Coll., 1964-65, U. Ga., Augusta, 1964-65, Georgetown U., Washington, 1965-68; sr. systems economist Avco Econ. Systems Corp., Washington, 1968-70; lectr. No. Va. Coll., Annandale, 1970—; cons. Office Sec., Asst. Sec. for Planning and Evaluation, Dept. Health, Edn. and Welfare, Washington, 1970-71, sr. staff economist Office Adminstrn., asst. adminstr. planning and evaluation, Social and Rehab. Service, 1971-72; sr. staff economist Office Price Policy Exec. Office of Pres., 1972; spl. asst. to exec. dir. Com. on Health Services Industry, Exec. Office of Pres., 1972—. Mem. exec. bd. Arlingtonians for Better Community, 1970; chmn. No. Va. Community Service Com., 1969-70. Served with AUS, 1963-65. Recipient Outstanding Service award City Trenton, N.J., 1958. Mem. Am. Econ. Assn., Am. Statis. Assn., Econometric Soc., Nat. Economists Club, Royal Econ. Soc., Friendly Sons St. Patrick, Washington Statis. Soc., Alpha Epsilon. Republican. Roman Catholic. Elk. Club: University (Boston Coll., Chestnut Hill, Mass.). Home: 1947 N Vermont St Arlington VA 22207 Room 5308 2025 M St NW Washington DC 20507

BURKE, WALKER DARIN, lawyer; b. Glenville, Ga., Nov. 16, 1920; s. Hardy Walker and Eva (Starling) B.; LL.B., U. Ga., 1949, J.D., 1959; m. Doris Ruby Cox, Apr. 16, 1944; children—Ralph Walker, Edward Neadom, Tommie Richard, James Stanley. Admitted to Ga. bar, 1949, Ga. Supreme Ct. bar, 1950, Fed. Ct. bars, 1960; practice law, Jesup, Ga., 1949-58, Warner Robins, Ga., 1958—; U.S. postmaster, Jesup, 1954-58. Vice pres. United Finance and Devel. Co., Warner Robins, 1963-66; also dir. Judge, City Ct. Warner Robins, 1965-66; county atty., Houston County, 1963, 64, 69-73. Mem. Ga. Democratic exec. com., 1962-66. Served from pvt. to capt., AUS, 1942-46; ETO; 1951-52. Mem. Ga. gov.'s staff, 1962-66. Recipient 50 Year Humanitarian award Jesup and Ga. jr. chambers commerce, 1970. Mem. Jesup and Wayne County Bar Assn. (pres. 1954), Houston County Assn. (pres. 1962, 67). Baptist. Mason, Elk, Moose. Home: 117 Briardale Av Warner Robins GA 31093 Office: 1606 Watson Blvd Warner Robins GA 31093

BURKE, WILLIAM TEMPLE, JR., lawyer; b. San Antonio, Tex., Oct. 30, 1935; s. William Temple and Adelaide (Raba) B.; B.B.A., St. Mary's U. (San Antonio), 1961, J.D., 1961; m. Mary Sue Johnson, June 8, 1957; children—Patrick, Michael, Karen. Admitted to Tex. bar, 1961; since practiced in Dallas; asso. firm Rudolph Johnson, 1962-65; partner firm Palmer, Green, Palmer & Burke, 1965-66, Plamer, Palmer & Burke, 1967-71, Green, Gilmore, Crutcher, Rothpletz & Burke, 1971—. Dir. various corporations, Dallas area. Pres. bd. dirs. Dallas County Small Bus. Devel. Center, 1966-68; v.p. Dallas County Hist. Survey Com., 1966—; mem. Troop 719 Com., Boy Scouts Am., 1970—. Bd. dirs. Dallas County War on Poverty. Served to capt. AUS, 1957-59. Mem. Am., Dallas bar assns., State Bar Tex., Am. Judicature Soc., Am. Trial Lawyers Assn., Phi Delta Phi. Roman Catholic. Optimist, Toastmaster, K.C. (founding pres. Dallas assn.). Home: 9751 Larchcrest St Dallas TX 75238 Office: Suite 400 Hexter-Fair Bldg 1307 Pacific St Dallas TX 75202

BURKES, MARSHALL R., govt. ofcl.; b. Lindsay, Okla., Mar. 27, 1934; s. Charley McClelland and Lou Marie (Park) B.; B.S., Okla. State U., 1956; M.S., Purdue U., 1960; Ph.D., Ohio State U., 1962; m. Audrey Louise Turner, Aug. 31, 1963. Mgr., Burkes Family Ranch, 1953-56; economist agrl. finance First Western Bank and Trust Co., San Francisco, 1962-65; bus. analyst, then asst. treas. Berkeley Bank for Coops. (Cal.), 1965-69; asst. adminstr. Farmers Home Adminstrn., U.S. Dept. Agr., Washington, 1969-72; dep. dir. finance Fed. Home Loan Banks, Washington, 1972-73, dir. finance, 1973—. Cons. ranch budgets, cash flows, marketing, land use, land acquisition, 1965—; faculty Am. Inst. Banking, 1964-69, U. Cal. at Berkeley Extension, 1965-69. Active Boy Scouts Am., Shriner's Crippled Children's Hosp. Served with U.S. Army, 1956-58. Mem. Municipal Forum Washington, Am. Marketing Assn., Alpha Gamma Rho, Alpha Zeta. Contbr. articles to tech. jours. Home: 5001 Wyandot Ct Ft Sumner Hills MD 20016 Office: Office Finance Fed Home Loan Banks 101 Indiana Av Washington DC 20552

BURKETT, HELEN ROSE (MRS. CHARLES WILLIAM BURKETT, JR.), co. exec.; b. Cleve., Dec. 22, 1903; d. Frederick Holland and Mary Chloe (Upson) Rose; B.A., Mt. Holyoke Coll., 1925; m. Charles William Burkett, Jr., Feb. 12, 1927; children—Charles William III, Diana Rose (Mrs. Hugh Cleland Brewer, Jr.), Helen Upson (Mrs. Gilbert H. Stevens). Sec., treas. Burkett Assos., Miami, Fla., 1951—. Chmn. communications Dept. Nat. Def., Harrison, N.Y., 1941-45, chief block leader service, 1943-45; mem. Harrison War Council, 1941-45, Service Corps A.R.C., 1945-47. Mem. Harrison Republican Town Com., 1946-47; mem. Dade County Rep. Exec. Com., Fla., 1956-58. Mem. D.A.R. (Fla. chmn. radio and TV 1954-56, rec. sec. 1958-60, regent Biscayne chpt. 1956-58, regents' council 1956-60), Children Am. Revolution (sr. pres. Golden Sands soc. 1960-63, 70-74, sr. state v.p. 1972-74), Colonial Dames XVII Century (Fla. sec. 1957-59, treas. 1959-61, librarian gen. 1959-61, state 1st v.p. 1961-63, state pres. 1963-65, nat. curator gen. 1965-67, nat. pres.-gen. 1967-69, hon. life pres.-gen. 1969—), Colonial Dames Am. (chpt. scholarship com. 1959-61, dir. 1969-71), Cleve. Apt. Owners Assn., Nat. Assn. Parliamentarians, Daus. Am. Colonists (chpt. v.p. 1961-64), Women Descs. Ancient and Honorable Arty. Co., Daus. of 1812 (chpt. v.p. 1961-63), N.Y. Geneal. and Biog. Soc., N.E. Hist. and Geneal. Soc., Nat. Geneal. Soc., Ams. Royal Descent, Magna Charta Dames Fla. (corr. sec. 1960—). Clubs: Westchester Country (Rye, N.Y.); Greenwich (Conn.) Country; La Gorce Country, Surf, Indian Creek Country, Bath (Miami Beach, Fla.). Home: 5800 N Bay Rd Miami Beach FL 33140 Office: 8080 NE 2d Av Miami FL 33138

BURKETT, JESSE ELVIN, univ. ofcl.; b. nr. Noble, Okla., Oct. 8, 1915; s. James Marcus and Sarah Ann (McLean) B.; B.S., U. Okla., 1947, Ed.M., 1950, Ed.D., 1958; m. Wanda Lucille Stufflebean, June 3, 1939; children—James Ronald, Mark Edward. Tchr. elementary schs., Cleveland County, Okla., 1936-45; dir. Okla. Sch. of Air, U. Okla., Norman, 1947-57, asst. dir. broadcasting services, 1954-57, extension specialist in charge research, 1957-61, coordinator liberal studies, 1961-64, asst. dean Coll. Continuing Edn., 1964-68, asst. v.p. univ. projects, 1968-71, asst. v.p. continuing edn. and pub. service, 1971—. Coordinator Okla. com. White House Conf. Children and Youth, 1960; cons. to Okla. Gov's and Legislative Council Joint Com. on Higher Edn., 1961. Served with AUS, 1945-46. Recipient Jour. award Am. Soc. Tchr. Devel., 1963. Mem. N.E.A., Okla. Edn. Assn., Am. Ednl. Research Assn., Nat. History Edn. Soc., Phi Delta Kappa, Kappa Delta Pi. Author: (with Paul G. Ruggiers) Bachelor of Liberal Studies: Development of a Curriculum at the University of Oklahoma, 1965. Editor: Okla. Parent Tchr., 1963-68. Contbr. articles to profl. publs. Home: 1519 Hollywood St Norman OK 73069

BURKETT, THOMAS WILLIAM, wholesale-retail owner; b. Huntsville, Ala., July 18, 1923; s. Alva Wallace and Wanda Stone (Bobo) B.; B.S., Auburn U., 1948; m. Margaret Ann Wall, Dec. 20, 1947 children—Leslie Ann, David Wallace, Jean Ann. With U.S. Civil Service, Redstone Arsenal, Huntsville, Ala., 1941-42; asst. foreman Allis-Chalmers Mfg. Co., Gadsden, 1948-49; engr. Thiokol Corp., Huntsville, 1949-52, Marshall, Tex., 1952-56; partner Book Shop, Huntsville, 1956-59; founder Burkett Inc., Huntsville, 1959, v.p., 1959-73, pres., 1973—, also dir.; established Burkett Sch. Supply Co., Huntsville, 1959, gen. mgr., 1959—. Tchr. adult edn., Huntsville, 1949-51. Mem. com. mgmt. central br. YMCA, Huntsville, 1966—. Pres. Huntsville Youth Orch., 1969-70. Served with AUS, 1943-46. Mem. Nat. Audio-Visual Assn., Nat. Sch. Supply and Equipment Assn., Ala. Sch. Distbrs. Assn. (sec. 1968-69, treas. 1969-70, pres. 1970-71) Nat. Assn. Wholesalers, Auburn Alumni Assn., Am. Book Sellers Assn., Am. Ordnance Assn., Am. Legion, V.F.W., Huntsville-Madison County C. of C. (dir. 1973-74), Sigma Nu. Club: Whitesburg Boat and Yacht (commodore 1972-73). Home: 2302 Big Cove Rd SE Huntsville AL 35801 Office: 304 Governors Dr SW Huntsville AL 35801

BURKHALTER, DAVID A., city ofcl.; grad. Bethel Coll.; m. Nell Burkhalter; 1 dau. Diane. Formerly with TVA; city mgr., Elizabethton, Tenn., Johnson City, Tenn., Springfield, Mo.; now city mgr., Charlotte, N.C. Served with USN. Mem. N.C., Internat., (pres. 1970) city mgmt. assns. Presbyn. Rotarian. Address: Offices City Mgr City Hall Charlotte NC 28202*

BURKHALTER, KENNETH VENOY, JR., data processor; b. Oak Park, Ill., Nov. 24, 1943; s. Kenneth Venoy and Mary (Ludolph) B.; Asso. Sci., Texarkana Coll., 1964; student E. Tex. State U., 1968; m. Mable L. Reed, Dec. 18, 1970. Supr. data processing Wadley Hosp., Texarkana, Tex., 1964-66; dir. data processing Texarkana Coll., 1966—, instr., 1967—. Cons. in field. Justice peace, Bowie County, 1970—. Med. dir. Bowie County Civil Def. Unit, 1965—; mem. Bowie County Law Enforcement Adv. Com., 1971—. Mem. Tex. Jr. Coll. Tchrs. Assn. (membership chmn. Tex. 1972-73). Kiwanian. Home: Route 9 Texarkana TX 75501 Office: Data Processing Texarkana Coll Texarkana TX 75501

BURKHART, HAROLD EUGENE, educator; b. Wellington, Kan., Feb. 29, 1944; s. Walter Frank and Zelma (Lutz) B.; B.S., Okla. State U., 1965; M.S. (Woodrow Wilson grantee), U. Ga., 1967, Ph.D. (Alumni Found. fellow), 1969; m. Katherine Bradley West, June 12, 1971. Asst. prof. dept. forestry Va. Poly. Inst. and State U., 1969-73, asso. prof., 1973—. Recipient Outstanding Tchr. award Curriculum Clubs Div. Forestry and Wildlife Resources, 1972, Gamma Sigma Delta, 1972. Mem. Soc. Am. Foresters (chmn.), Biometrics Soc., A.A.A.S., Am. Forestry Assn., Am. Assn. U. Profs., Va. Forests, Inc., Va. Acad. Sci., Sigma Xi, Phi Kappa Phi, Xi Sigma Pi (nat. pres.), Phi Sigma, Alpha Zeta, Gamma Sigma Delta. Contbr. articles to profl. jours. Home: 1030 Chestnut Dr Christiansburg VA 24073 Office: Forestry and Wildlife Resources Va Poly Inst and State Univ Blacksburg VA 24061

BURKHART, NELSON EUGENE, shoe mfg. co. exec.; b. Dover, Tenn., Aug. 30, 1930; s. John Henry and Callie Mae (Calhoun) B.; student Andrew Jackson Bus. U., 1948-52; m. Mary Ann Morgan, Apr. 23, 1953 (dec.); children—Phyllis, Michael, Ann, John. With Boot-Ster Mfg. Co., Inc., Clarksville, Tenn., 1952—, controller, dir., 1962—. Treas. adv. bd. Salvation Army, Clarksville, 1970—; Pres. Babe Ruth Baseball, Inc., Clarksville, 1970—, Clarksville Sr. Citizens Adv. Bd., 1968—, Athletic Support Group, 1969—. Named Outstanding Young Man of Clarksville and Montgomery County, Clarksville Jr. C. of C., 1965. Mem. U.S. Jr. C. of C. (life), Jr. C. of C. (pres. 1963-64). Mem. Christian Ch. (elder 1972-73). Mason (Shriner), Eagle, Moose. Club: Clarksville Civitan. Home: 2108 Layton Rd Clarksville TN 37040 Office: Boot Ster Mfg Co Inc 121 S 1st St Clarksville TN 37040

BURKS, BARNARD DEWITT, entomologist; b. Las Vegas, N.M., Nov. 12, 1909; s. John Kyrle and Emily Gardner (DeWitt) B.; B.A., U. Ill., 1933, M.A., 1934, Ph.D., 1937; m. Frances Kellie O'Neill, Oct. 1, 1966. Entomologist, Ill. Natural History Survey, Urbana, 1937-42, 46-49; entomologist U.S. Dept. Agr., Washington, 1949—, head hymenoptera sect. Systematic Entomology Lab., 1965—. Served from 1st lt. to maj. Signal Corps, AUS, 1942-46. Fellow Entomol. Soc. Am.; mem. Am. Entomol. Soc., Entomol. Soc. Washington, Sigma Xi, Phi Beta Kappa. Club: Cosmos (Washington). Home: 9703 Saxony Rd Silver Spring MD 20910 Office: Natural History Bldg Washington DC 20560

BURKS, MACK SKAGGS, mfg. exec.; b. Dallas, May 14, 1924; s. Joseph Cooper and Grace (Skaggs) B.; student U. Okla., 1942-43; Ph.D. in Bus. Adminstrn., Colo. State Christian Coll., 1973; m. Peggy Crosswhite, Sept. 14, 1946; children—Cynthia (Mrs. Terrence Fortune), Susan, Carol (Mrs. Michael Hawk). Sec.-treas. Connolly's Inc., 1947-52; partner Burks & Smartt, 1952-56; pres. Burks, Inc., 1956-61; account exec. Glenn Advt., Inc., 1962-64; v.p., sec.-treas. Keystone Industries, 1965-67; v.p. marketing Harter Concrete Products Inc., 1967— (all Oklahoma City); pres. Heritage Concrete Products, Inc., 1971—; dir. Ims, Inc. Chmn., Okla. Plan and Resources Bd., 1959-63, mem. bd., 1963-65; mem. Okla. Lakes Redevel. Authority, 1961-63; chmn. pub. relations Govs. Com. on Pub. Safety, 1962-63; mem. Oklahoma City Community Council. Chmn., 5th Congl. Dist. Democratic Party Okla. Bd. dirs. Traveler's Aid Soc., 1964-65, 72—, v.p., 1965, treas., 1967. Served with USNR, 1943-46. Mem. Nat. Concrete Masonry Assn. (chmn. marketing com.), C. of C. (vice chmn. tourist and conv. div.), Phi Gamma Delta. Methodist. Home: 1712 Guilford Lane Oklahoma City OK 73120 Office: 1628 W Main St Oklahoma City OK 73106

BURLAGE, DONALD WILLIAM, electronics engr.; b. St. Louis, Oct. 12, 1939; s. William Harvey and Helen Dorothea (Francis) B.; B.S. in E.E. (St. Joseph Minerals Co. scholar), U. Mo., 1961; M.S. in E.E., U. Ala., 1968, M.A., 1969, Ph.D., 1972; m. Wynona Heath, Sept. 5, 1964. Systems engr. Westinghouse Electric Corp., Lima, O., 1961-62; research engr. Boeing Co., Huntsville, Ala., 1965; sr. staff engr. Sperry Rand Corp., Huntsville, 1965-67; research asso. U. Ala., Tuscaloosa, 1967-72, instr., 1968-70; electronics engr. U.S. Army, Redstone Arsenal, Huntsville, 1972—. Served as lt. AUS, 1962-65. Registered profl. engr., Ala. Mem. I.E.E.E., Eta Kappa Nu, Kappa Kappa Psi, Pi Mu Epsilon, Sigma Xi. Home: 823 Tannahill Dr SE Huntsville AL 35802 Office: US Army Redstone Arsenal AL 35809

BURLESON, OMAR, congressman; b. Anson, Tex., Mar. 19, 1906; s. Joseph and Bettie (Couch) B.; student Abilene (Tex.) Christian Coll., 1924-26, Hardin-Simmons U., 1926-27, Cumberland U., 1927-29; LL.D. Hardin-Simmons U., 1967;; m. Ruth DeWeese, Apr. 21, 1929. County atty., Jones County, Tex., 1931-35, county judge, 1935-41; spl. agent, F.B.I., 1940-41; sec. Congressman Sam Russell, 1941-42; gen. counsel Nat. Capitol Housing Authority, Washington, Jan.-Dec. 1942; mem. 80th to 93d U.S. Congresses from 17th Tex. Dist. Served as lt. comdr., U.S. Navy, 1942-46; PTO. Pres. Tex. Welfare Assn., 1936-38; pres. County Judges and Commrs. Assn. of Tex. Mem. Lions Internat.; dist. gov. Lions Clubs, 1937-38. Democrat. Mem. Church of Christ. Mason. Home: Anson TX 79501 Office: Rayburn House Office Bldg Washington DC 20515

BURLING, EDWARD, JR., lawyer; b. Chgo., Feb. 5, 1908; Ph.B., Yale, 1929; LL.B., Harvard, 1932. Admitted to D.C. bar, 1934; now mem. firm Covington & Burling, Washington. Home: 1339 29th St NW Washington DC 20007 Office: Covington & Burling 888 16th St Washington DC 20006

BURLINGAME, JAMES MONTGOMERY, lawyer; b. Great Falls, Mont., Dec. 25, 1926; s. James Montgomery and Eloise (Corbin) B.; B.A., Tulane U., 1949, J.D., 1950; m. Joella Claire Blache, June 15, 1950; children—James Montgomery IV, Ann Blache, John Marshall. Admitted to La. bar, 1950, U.S. Supreme Ct bar, 1961 practiced in Washington, 1950; partner Jones, Walker, Waechter, Poitevent, Carrere and Denegre, New Orleans, 1953—. Served to ensign U.S. Maritime Service, 1945-46; to capt. AUS, 1950-52. Trustee, St. Martin's Protestant Episcopal Sch., 1968—. Mem. Am., Fed., La. (chmn. mineral sect. 1971-72), New Orleans bar assns., Am. Judicature Soc., Beta Theta Pi. Episcopalian. Club: Petroleum, New Orleans Country, Pickwick, Stratford, International House (New Orleans). Home: 433 Iona St Metairie LA 70005 Office: 225 Baronne St New Orleans LA 70112

BURNET, THORNTON WEST, marketing exec.; b. Cin., Aug. 27, 1917; s. David and Agnes McClurg (West) B.; B.S. in Commerce, U. Va., 1940; m. Mary Elizabeth Charlton, Aug. 14, 1948; 1 son, Thornton West. Asst. treas. Lincoln Service Corp., Washington, 1941-50, v.p., sec., 1950-59; v.p. marketing Am. Finance Mgmt. Corp., Silver Spring, Md., 1959—; v.p., treas., dir. Monet Constrn. Co., Fairfax, Va., 1962—. Committeeman, Boy Scouts Am., 1945—. Pres. bd. trustees Fletcher Meml. Library. Served with AUS, 1940-43. Mem. Alpha Kappa Psi. Republican. Episcopalian (vestryman, past sr. warden). Home: 10800 Hunters Valley Rd Vienna VA 22180 Office: 1320 Fenwick Lane Silver Spring MD 20910

BURNETT, CAREY CORLEY, civil engr.; b. Montgomery, Ala., Nov. 26, 1915; s. James Leonard and Louise (Davis) B.; student U. Fla., 1934-35; B.S., U. Ga., 1938; postgrad. Ala. Poly. inst., 1939-40; m. Mary Elizabeth Parker, July 5, 1946; children—Mary Kay, Carey Parker. City engr., Newman, Ga., 1940-42, 45-46; city engr., asst. city mgr., Thomasville, Ga., 1946-47; city engr., acting city mgr. City of Valdosta, Ga., 1947-51; chief design engr. J.E. Crainer Co. on USMC Supply Center Project, 1951-54; city mgr. Albany, Ga., 1954-61, chmn. elec. bd., 1954-61; city mgr. Columbia, S.C., 1961-70; v.p. environmental and municipal engring. Wilbur Smith and Assos., cons. engrs. and planners, Columbia, 1970-73; with Wiedeman & Singleton, engrs., Atlanta, 1973—. Dir. Flint River Valley Devel. Assn. Chmn. plumbing code com. So. Bldg. Code Congress; mem. health bd., bd., Albany-Doughtery County, Albany Community Council; bd. dirs. United Community Services, chmn. pub. employees div. United Fund Dr.; mem. Columbia Central City Devel. Com.; exec. com. Congaree Nav. Study Com.; adv. com. Richland Tech. Edn. Center, 1968-72. Recipient Certificate Merit for Leadership, Am. City mag., 1964, 65. Served with USAAF, 1942-45; PTO. Registered profl. engr., Fla., Ga., S.C., Tenn. Mem. Nat., Ga. socs. profl. engrs., Internat. v.p. Southeastern region 1968-70), S.C. (state pres. 1968-69). Ga. (state pres. 1958-59) city mgrs. assns., Am. Pub. Works Assn., Nat. Planning Assn., Am. Waterworks Assn., Nat. Water Pollution Control Fedn., Greater Columbia C. of C. (indsl. devel. commn.), S.C. Soc. Engrs. (regional dir.), Nat. Soc. Municipal Engrs., Nat. Soc. San. Engrs. Presbyn. Contbr. articles profl. jour. and Am. City mag. Home: Route 6 Box 571 Roscoe Rd Newnan GA 30263 Office: Wiedeman & Singleton 1789 Peachtree St NE Atlanta GA 30309

BURNETT, COLLINS WALTER, educator; b. Anderson, Ind., Mar. 28, 1914; s. Charles and Bertha (Liget) B.; A.B., Ball State U., 1935 M.A., Ohio State U., 1940, Ph.D., 1948; m. Bernice Kathryn Kaufman, May 10, 1941; children—Arlita (Mrs. Robert W. Smith), Michael Collins. Asso. prof. Fresno State Coll., 1946-50; asst. dean Coll. Edn., prof. psychology Ohio State U., 1950-63; prof. higher edn., 1963-68; prof. higher edn. U. Ky., Lexington, 1968—. Cons., Morris Harvey Coll., Alice Lloyd Coll., U. Americas. Served to comdr. USNR, 1944-46. Recipient Distinguished Alumni Service award Ball State U., 1966. Mem. Am. Psychol. Assn., Am. Personnel and Guidance Assn., Student Personnel Assn. for Tchr. Edn. (pres. 1957-58), Am. Edn. Research Assn. Author: Introduction to Teaching, 1963, The Community Junior College: An Annotated Bibliography with Chapter Introductions, 1968. Home: 947 Edgewater Dr Lexington KY 40502

BURNETT, GEORGE WESLEY, coll. dean; b. Graham, Tex., Nov. 22, 1914; s. Felix Grundy and Susan Jane (McAllister) B.; B.A., Tex. Tech. Coll., 1937; M.A., U. Tex., 1940; D.D.S., Wash. U., 1943; Ph.D., U. Rochester, 1950; m. Mary Wilma Kimmel, June 11, 1943; children—George Wesley, Mary Susan (Mrs. Don Hunter). Commd. 1st lt. D.C., U.S. Army, 1943, advanced through grades to col., 1960, ret., 1968; dir. Inst. Dental Research Washington, 1950-68; faculty Med. Coll. Ga., Augusta, 1968—, asso. dean Sch. Dentistry, 1971—. Cons., Office Surgeon Gen., Dept. Army, 1960-69, Dental Research Adv. Com., 1950-68, dental study sect. USPHS, 1953-58, Dental Caries Task Force, 1969-72; cons. to dir. Nat. Inst. Dental Research, 1969-72. Decorated Legion of Merit. Diplomate Am. Bd. Microbiology. Fellow Am. Acad. Microbiology, A.A.A.S., Am. Coll. Dentists. Club: Faculty (Augusta). Author: Oral Microbiology and Infectious Disease, 1957, rev. edit., 1968; Pathogenic Microbiology, 1973; Review of Pathogenic Microbiology, 1974; also articles. Home: 817 Poindexter Dr Augusta GA 30904 Office: School of Dentistry Medical College Georgia Augusta GA 30902

BURNETT, HARRY CHARLTON, JR., metallurgist; b. N.Y.C., June 4, 1918; s. Harry Charlton and Medora (Sassaman) B.; student Bard Coll., 1936-38; m. Helen Elizabeth Middleton, Dec. 8, 1944; children—David Charlton, Jane Elizabeth. With Nat. Bur. Standards, Washington, 1947—, research metallurgist, 1947-61, asst. to chief metallurgy div., 1961—. Scoutmaster, Montgomery County (Md.) council Boy Scouts Am., 1961-62. Served with USNR, 1942-46; PTO. Recipient Certificate Commendation, Dept. Commerce, 1965, 69, Silver Medal award, 1973. Mem. Washington Acad. Scis., Am. Soc. Metals (chmn. 1961-62), Smithsonian Assos., Soc. Automotive Engrs. (mem. gen. standards council), Sigma Alpha Epsilon. Republican. Presbyn. Mason. Contbr. to profl. jours. Home: 4507 Dalton Rd Chevy Chase MD 20015 Office: Metall Div Nat Bur Standards Washington DC 20234

BURNETT, IRAVIS ELMON, pipeline co. exec.; b. Gap, Tex., Mar. 4, 1918; s. Thomas E. and Carolinee (Lee) B.; B.B.A. cum laude, Baylor U., 1947; LL.B., South Tex. Coll., 1960; m. Yvonne O. Thompson, Apr. 26, 1941; children—Iravonne (Mrs. James E. Crain), Donna Sue (Mrs. David Peck), Leanne. Accountant, Humble Oil & Refining Co., Katy, Tex., 1947-49, right of way and claims agt., Houston, 1949-56. mgr. right of way and claims dept., 1956-60, atty. law dept., 1960-65; asso. gen. counsel Humble Pipe Line Co., Houston, 1965—; corp. sec. Dixie Pipeline Co., Houston, 1965—, v.p., dir., 1972—; admitted to Tex. bar, 1960. Democratic precinct committeeman, Houston, 1956-61; del. county and Tex. State Dem. convs., 1964-68. Served to 2d lt. USAAF, 1942-46. Mem. Delta Sigma Phi, Delta Theta Phi. Home: 10310 Cliffwood St Houston TX 77035 Office: PO Box 2220 Houston TX 77001

BURNETT, WILLIAM FRANKLIN, surgeon; b. Mayfield, Ky., Dec. 21, 1931; s. Voris Hurt and Lucille Bruce (Tewmey) B.; B.S., Lambuth Coll., 1953; postgrad. Vanderbilt U., 1957-58; M.D., U. Va., 1962, postgrad., 1964; m. Laura Frances Ray, May 31, 1953; children—Jeffrey Bruce, Laura Elizabeth. Intern U. Va., 1962-63, resident, 1963-64, 65-68; chief surgery VA Hosp., Salem, Va., 1968-70, Jackson-Madison County Gen. Hosp., Jackson, Tenn., 1971-72; surgeon Jackson Clinic, 1970—; asst. prof. surgery U. Va., Charlottesville, 1968-70. Trustee Lambuth Coll., Jackson, 1973-75. Served with USAF, 1953-55. Am. Cancer Soc. grantee, 1964. Fellow A.C.S., Lambuth Alumni Assn., (pres. Jackson 1974-75), West Tenn. Consol. Med. Assembly, Tenn. Med. Assn., Am. Assn. Sports Medicine, A.C.S. Home: 49 Stonehaven Dr Jackson TN 38321 Office: 616 Forest Av Jackson TN 38301

BURNETTE, ELMER WIGGINS, JR., dentist; b. Odessa, Fla., Dec. 14, 1920; s. Elmer Wiggins and Mary (Pettigrew) Burnette; student Fla. So. Coll., 1937-38; B.A., Emory U., 1943, D.D.S., 1945; certificate U. Tex., 1960; m. Rebecca Anne Benton, Apr. 2, 1941; children—Patricia (Mrs. James Redfield), Dianne (Mrs. Melvin Starr, Jr.), Susan (Mrs. Gregory Nebel), Edith (Mrs. Thomas L. Bergeron, Jr.). Intern, Fla. State Hosp., 1945-46; pvt. practice dentistry, Clearwater, Fla., 1946-50; commd. capt. U.S. Air Force, 1951, advanced through grades to col., 1966; base dental surgeon Goodfellow AFB, Tex., 1954-59; resident periodontics Lackland AFB, Tex., 1960-61, staff dept. periodontics, 1961-66, dir. tng., 1964-66; periodontist, Ramstein, Germany, 1966-68, base dental surgeon, 1968-69; chmn. dept. periodontics Andrews AFB, Washington, 1969-70, dir. dental services, dir. intern and resident tng., dental surgeon Hdqrs. Command, 1970-72; ret., 1973; asso. prof. U. Tex. Dental Sch. at San Antonio, 1973—. Spl. cons. periodontics Surgeon Gen. U.S. Air Force, 1969-72. Diplomate Am. Bd. Periodontology. Fellow Am. Coll. Dentists; mem. Am. Dental Assn., Am. Acad. Periodontology, Southwestern Soc. Periodontists, Greater Washington Soc. Periodontology, West German Armed Forces Dental Soc. (life), Lambda Chi Alpha. Mason. Club: Exchange (pres. 1948-49) (Clearwater, Fla.). Home: 3206 Yorktown St San Antonio TX 78230 Office: 7703 Floyd Curl Dr San Antonio TX 78284

BURNETTE, JOE EDWARD, clergyman; b. Denison, Tex., Dec. 27, 1918; s. Joe Stevenson and Viola (Sisk) B.; A.B., Carson-Newman Coll., 1942 M.R.E., Southwestern Bapt. Sem., 1946; m. Betty Ann Huguley, Oct. 8, 1954; 1 dau., Joann. Ordained to ministry Bapt. Ch., 1941; minister edn. Immanuel Bapt. Ch., Tulsa, 1946-50, First Ch., Baton Rouge, 1950-52, First Ch., Columbia, S.C., 1952-61; supt. Bethea Bapt. Home for Aging, Darlington, 1961-63; minister edn. First Bapt. Ch., Charlotte, N.C., 1963—. Mem. gen. bd. N.C. Bapt. Conv. Del., White House Conf. on Aging, 1961. Bd. dirs. Charlotte Family Life Council, Brooklyn Day Care Center, Charlotte; trustee Southwestern Bapt. Theol. Sem., Fort Worth, N.C. Bapt. Homes for Aging. Mem. So. Bapt., Southeastern (pres. 1957—) religious edn. assns., Gator, Orange bowl assns. Clubs: Optimist, Eastern Religious Education. Contbr. articles to publs. Home: 4244 Wright Av Charlotte NC 28211 Office: 318 N Tryon St Charlotte NC 28202

BURNETTE, JOHN QUINCY, banker; b. Charlotte, N.C., June 22, 1924; s. John Quincy and Mary (Kiker) B.; student La. State U., 1961-65; m. Allie Burch, July 4, 1943; children—Diane (Mrs. Edward M. Gouge), Marie B. (Mrs. Robert Olen Deal). Vice pres., govtl. service officer N.C. Nat. Bank, Charlotte, 1946—. Treas., Men's Democrat Club, 1970-71. Bd. dirs. Caroline Carrousel, Piedmont Better Bus. Bur. Served to lt. col. AUS, 1943-45. Mem. Charlotte C. of C. Baptist. Lion. Home: 1101 Burtonwood Circle Charlotte NC 28212 Office: PO Box 120 Charlotte NC 28212

BURNHAM, ROBERT CHESTER, physician; b. Waterbury, Conn., July 5, 1915; A.B., Yale, 1936, M.D., N.Y. Med. Coll., 1941; m. Donna Cecelia Boyd, May 31, 1942; children—Jeffrey Boyd, Roger Morris, Timothy Donald Eugene, Janet Christina. Intern St. Elizabeth's Hosp., Washington, 1941-42, psychiat. trainee, USN, 1942-43; psychiat. trainee Washington (D.C.) Sch. Psychiatry, 1947-51; psychoanalytic trainee Washington (D.C.) Psychoanalytic Inst., 1947-53, tng. analyst, 1958—; dir. Arlington County Guidance Center, Arlington, Va., 1948-50; practice of medicine, specializing in psychiatry, psychoanalysis, Arlington, Va., 1948—; mem. staffs Fairfax Hosp., Falls Church, Va. Asso. clin. prof. psychiatry Georgetown U. Coll. Medicine, Washington, 1960—. Mem. Law Enforcement Adv. Commn., Falls Church, 1969—. Served to lt. comdr. M.C., USN, 1942-47. Fellow Am. Psychiat. Assn., Am. Acad. Psychoanalysis; mem. Washington Psychoanalytic Soc. (pres. 1965-67), Am. Psychoanalytic Assn., A.M.A., A.A.A.S., So. Med. Assn. Home: 207 E Columbia St Falls Church VA 22046 Office: 333 S Glebe Rd Arlington VA 22204

BURNS, ARTHUR F., economist, govt. ofcl., educator; b. Stanislau, Austria, Apr. 27, 1904; s. Nathan and Sarah (Juran) B.; A.B., Columbia, 1925, A.M., 1925, Ph.D., 1934, LL.D., 1970; LL.B., Lehigh U., 1952, Brown U., 1956, Dartmouth Coll., 1956, Oberlin Coll., 1956, Wesleyan U., 1958, Swarthmore Coll., 1958, L.I. U., 1960, U. Chgo., 1960, Rikkyo U., Tokyo, 1965, Fordham U., 1969, N.Y. U., 1970, U. Cal., 1970; D. Sc., U. Pa., 1958, U. Rochester, 1963; L.H.D., Rutgers U., 1955, Pepperdine Coll., 1970; D. Econ., Chung-ang U., Korea, 1970; D.Phil., Hebrew U., Israel, 1970; m. Helen Bernstein, Jan. 25, 1930; children—David, Joseph. Instr. econs. Rutgers U., 1927-30, asst. prof., 1930-33, asso. prof., 1933-43, prof., 1943-44; asst. statistics Columbia, 1926. Gilder fellow, 1926-27, vis. prof., 1941-44, prof., 1944-59, John Bates Clark prof., 1959-69; research asso. Nat. Bur. Econ. Research, 1930-31, mem. research staff, 1933-69, dir. research, 1945-53, pres., 1957-67, chmn., 1967-68, hon. chmn., 1968—; counselor to Pres. U.S., 1969-70; chmn. bd. govs. Fed. Res. System, Washington, 1970—. Miller lectr. Fordham U., 1957; Murray lectr. State U. Ia., 1964; Fairless lectr. Carnegie Inst. Tech., 1965; Moskowitz lectr. N.Y. U., 1967; vis. prof. econs. Stanford, spring 1968; trustee 20th Century Fund. Served chief statistician Ry. Emergency Bd., 1941; cons. various govtl. agys. and depts. Chmn. Pres.'s Council Econ. Advisers, 1953-56; chmn. Adv. Bd. on Econ. Growth and Stability, 1953-56; chmn. Cabinet Com. on Small Bus., 1956; mem. Pres.' Adv. Com. on Labor-Mgmt. Policy 1961-66; mem. Gov.'s Com. on Minimum Wage, 1964. Mem. research adv. bd. Rutgers U., 1947-61; adv. bd. Indsl. Coll. Armed Forces, 1953-64; bd. mgrs. Swarthmore Coll., 1959-62; trustee Tax Found., Inc., 1962-68, Freedom House, 1966-68; mem. U.S. Adv. Council on Social Security Financing, 1957-58, N.Y. Temp. State Commn. on Econ. Expansion, 1959-60. Recipient Alexander Hamilton medal Columbia U., 1969; Distinguished Pub. Service award Tax Found., 1969; Mugungwha decoration Korean govt., 1970. Fellow Am. Statis. Assn., Econometric Soc., Am. Acad. Arts and Scis.; mem. Pilgrims Soc., Am. Philos. Soc., Council Fgn. Relations, Am. Econ. Assn. (pres. 1959, distinguished fellow), Acad. Polit. Sci. (pres. 1961-68), Institut de Sci. Economique Appliques (corr.), Phi Beta Kappa. Clubs: Cosmos (Washington); Men's Faculty (Columbia U.), Century Assn. Author: Production Trends in the U.S. since 1870, 1934; Economic Research and the Kaynesian Thinking of Our Times, 1946; Frontiers of Economic Knowledge, 1954; Prosperity Without Inflation, 1957; (with W.C. Mitchell) Measuring Business Cycles, 1946; The Management of Prosperity, 1966; (with P.A. Samuelson) Full Employment, Guideposts and Economic Stability, 1967; (with Jacob Javits, Charles Hitch) The Defense Sector and the American Economy, 1968; The Business Cycle in a Changing World, 1969. Home: 2510 Virginia Av NW Washington DC 20037 Office: Federal Reserve Bldg Washington DC 20551

BURNS, EDWARD ALLEN, accountant; b. Carrizo Springs, Tex., Jan. 12, 1916; s. Edward Jackson and Margaret Kellogg (Vandervoort) B.; B.A., U. Tex., 1937, M.A. in Pub. Adminstrn., 1940; m. Margaret Elizabeth Moses, Feb. 5, 1938; children—Morris Edward, Frederick Grant, Robert Allen, Carrol Ross. Clk. pub. works dept. City Dallas, 1940-42; office mgr. L-H Drug Co., Odessa, Tex., 1942-43; office mgr. McKean Eilers Co., Austin, Tex., 1945-49, Holland Page, Austin, 1949-51; accountant Edward A. Burns, Austin, 1952-68; partner Burns & Williams, C.P.A.'s, Austin, 1968—. Mem. exec. com. Estate Planning Council, Austin, 1965-72, pres., 1970-71. Mem. budget com. United Fund, Austin, 1958—, trustee, 1961-63, mem. exec. com., 1967-68; mem. exec. bd. Capitol Area council Boy Scouts Am., 1964-70; bd. dirs. Tex. United Fund, Dallas, 1967-69, mem. financial review com., 1967-69; bd. dirs. Tex. United Community Services, 1969—, mem. financial review com., 1969—, chmn., 1972, mem. exec. com., 1972-73. C.P.A., Tex. Mem. Am. Inst. C.P.A.'s, Tex. Soc. C.P.A.'s (v.p. chpt. 1964-65). Baptist (deacon 1946—; treas. 1970—). Lion (dir. 1965-66). Home: 4114 Idlewild Rd Austin TX 78731 Office: 400 Jefferson Bldg 1600 W 38th St Austin TX 78731

BURNS, EDWARD CLYDE, JR., physician; b. Greenville, S.C., Nov. 20, 1923; s. Edward Clyde and Etta Victoria (Green) B.; B.A., Emory U., 1944, M.D., 1946; m. Sally Louise Horne, Oct. 20, 1945; children—Barbara (Mrs. James Prather), Edward Clyde III, Carol Anne (Mrs. Melvin Horne), Alan, Bruce Mallory. Intern, Univ. Hosp., Augusta, Ga., 1946-47, resident, 1949-51; resident Percy Jones Gen. Hosp., Battle Creek, Mich., 1947-49, Royal Infirmary, Edinburgh, Scotland, 1950-51; pvt. practice medicine, specializing in radiology, Lake Wales, Fla., 1951—; dir. dept. radiology Lake Wales Hosp., 1951—, Polk Gen. Hosp., Bartow, Fla., 1951—, Bartow Meml. Hosp., 1951—, Winter Haven (Fla.) Hosp., 1955—, Heart of Fla. Hosp., Haines City, 1965—, Morrow Meml. Hosp., Auburndale, Fla., 1966—, Walker Meml. Hosp., Avon Park, Fla., 1962—, Highlands Gen. Hosp., Sebring, Fla., 1965—; pres. Drs. Burns and Assocs., 1963—. Organizer, dir. 1st Nat. Bank, Lake Wales, 1960—. Served as capt. M.C., AUS, 1947-49. Diplomate Am. Bd. Radiology. Mem. Fla., Polk County (pres. 1966-67) med. assns., A.M.A., Am. Coll. Radiology. Baptist. Home: 960 Lakeshore Blvd Lake Wales FL 33853 Office: Lake Wales Hosp Lake Wales FL 33853 also Winter Haven Hosp Winter Haven FL 33880

BURNS, GERALD ROBERT, surgeon; b. Maryville, Tenn., May 1, 1942; s. Herbert Victor and Lurline (McFarland) B.; B.S., U. Tenn., 1963, M.D., 1966; m. Diane Johnson, June 7, 1963; children—Steven Andrew, Kenneth Robert. Intern U. Hosp., Knoxville, Tenn., 1966; resident in surgery City of Memphis Hosp., 1967-69, U. Hosp., Knoxville, 1970-72; practice medicine specializing in surgery, Donelson, Tenn., 1974—. Served with USAF, 1972-74. Diplomate Am. Bd. Surgery. Candidate A.C.S. Home: 4318 Shallow Water St San Antonio TX 78233 Office: Donelson Clinic Donelson TN 37214

BURNS, GROVER PRESTON, physicist, mathematician; b. nr. Hurricane, W.Va., Apr. 25, 1918; s. Joshua Alexander and Virgie (Meadows) B.; A.B., Marshall U., 1937; M.S., W.Va. U., 1941; student Duke, 1939-40, U. Md., 1946; D.Sc. (hon.), Colo. State Christian Coll., 1973; m. Julia Belle Foster, Nov. 4, 1941; children—Julia Corinne, Grover Preston. Tchr. high sch., W.Va., 1937-40; fellow W.Va., U., 1940-41; instr. physics U. Conn., 1941-42; asst. prof. Miss State Coll., 1942-44, acting head physics dept., 1944-45; asst. prof. physics Tex. Tech. Coll., 1946; asso. prof. math. Marshall U., 1946-47; research physicist Naval Research Lab., Washington, 1947-48; asst. prof., chmn. physics dept. Mary Washington Coll., 1948-68, asso.

prof., chmn., 1968-69; quality control supr. Am. Viscose div. FMC Corp., 1950-67; pres. Burns Enterprises, Inc., Fredericksburg, Va., 1958—; mathematician Naval Weapons Lab., 1967—. Served with AUS, 1945-46. Mem. Am. Phys. Soc., Am. Assn. Physics Tchrs., Fed. Profl. Assn., Brit. Computer Soc., Am. Assn. U. Profs., N.Y. Acad. Sci. Author various articles pub. in profl. jours. Patentee in field of thermometers, conductivity testers, star finders. Research in fields of superconductivity, synthetic div., thermoelectricity, numerical integration, exterior ballistics. Home: 600 Virginia Av Fredericksburg VA 22401 Office: Naval Weapons Lab Dahlgren VA 22448

BURNS, HAROLD DEWEY, engring. exec.; b. Birmingham, Ala., Jan. 3, 1926; s. Dewey Gurley and Lucy (Polk) B.; B.S., Am. Inst. Engring., 1952; grad. exec. devel. program, Columbia, 1968; M.B.A., U. West Fla., 1973; m. Jeanne Bernice Tuley, Mar. 7, 1951; children—Dave Allen, Joann Lynn, Terry Lee. Engr. Daystrom Instruments, Archbald, Pa., 1952-53; maintenance asst. Lone Star Steel, Daingerfield, Tex., 1953-55; engr. Vitro Corp., Eglin AFB, Fla., 1955-60, dept. head, 1960-65, asst. mgr., 1965-68; mgr. systems engring. Automation Industries, Ft. Walton Beach, Fla., 1968-70; head engring. dept. Vitro Services div. Automation Industries, Eglin AFB, 1970—. Chmn. adv. com. Okaloosa-Walton Jr. Coll., Niceville, Fla., 1965—. Served with USNR, 1943-48, 50-52. Mem. I.E.E.E. (sect. chmn. 1967), Am. Def. Prepardness Assn. (sec. dir. 1968), Assn. Old Crows, Methodist. Lion (pres. 1974-75). Home: 101 4th Av NE Fort Walton Beach FL 32548 Office: Eglin AFB FL 32542

BURNS, HARRY EDWARD JR., architect; b. Jacksonville, Fla., Apr. 18, 1924; s. Harry E. and Coralie (Simmons) B.; B.S., Tulane U., 1945; B.Arch., U.Fla., 1949; m. Elizabeth Williams, Mar. 7, 1948 (div. 1970); children—Harry III, Thomas, Kathryn, Jean; m. 2d, Etoile Grantham, 1971; step-children—Gaye, Betty-Carolyn, Charles, Ena. Chmn. bd. Harry Burns & Assos., Architects-Planners, Inc., Jacksonville and Tallahassee, 1951—. Architect. Fla. Hotel and Restaurant Commn., 1960-64; mem. Fla. Bd. Architecture, 1962—, pres., 1965-66. Mem. Neptune Beach (Fla.) City Council, 1954-64. Served to lt. (j.g.) USNR, 1942-45; PTO. Mem. Fla. Assn. Architects (past pres.), A.I.A., Nat. Council Archtl. Registration Bds. (past chmn. So. dist). Home: 1012 Dogwood Dr Quincy FL 32351 Office: 201 S Bronough St Tallahassee FL 32304

BURNS, HENRY KNOX, III, brick co. exec.; b. Macon, Ga., Apr. 2, 1941; s. Henry Knox and Anne (Holmes) B.; student Ga. Inst. Tech., 1959-64; m. Katharine Miller, Aug. 24, 1962; children—Henry Knox IV, Stuart, Hubert. Foreman, Burns Brick Co., Macon, Ga., 1964-69, plant mgr., 1969—, also dir., asst. sec., 1971—; pres. Burns Machinery Internat. Llc., 1973—, Burns Automation Inc., 1973—. Mem. Am. Ceramics Soc. Presbyn. (deacon 1970—). Elk. Home: 1830 Redwood Dr Macon GA 31201 Office: 711 10th St Macon GA 31208

BURNS, HOWARD DEWITT, aerospace engr.; b. Buhl, Ala., Dec. 11, 1921; s. Howard and Edna (Eaton) B.; B.S. in E.E., U. Ala., 1947, LL.B., 1950; m. Marcella Holland, June 15, 1957; children—Howard DeWitt, Katherine Joyce. Jr. engr. Ala. Power Co., 1947-48; Redstone project mgr. indsl. div. Army Ballistic Missile Agy., Redstone Arsenal, Ala., 1959-60, dep. dir. test, evaluation and firing lab., 1960-62; chief Systems Integration and Evaluation Office, Systems Engring., Office Manned Space Flight, 1962-63; chief Saturn V Test Mgmt. Office, Indsl. Operations, Marshall Space Flight Center, Huntsville, Ala., 1963-70, chief vehicle devel., devel. office Space Shuttle Task Team, 1970-72, chief devel. and prodn. br., engring. mgmt. Shuttle Projects Office, 1972—. Served with USAAF, 1944-45. Registered profl. engr., Ala. Mem. Ala. State Bar, Theta Tau. Methodist. Home: Rural Route 10 Box 61 Athens AL 35611 Office: Huntsville AL 35812

BURNS, HOWARD LAMAR, lawyer; b. Greenwood, S.C., Sept. 11, 1914; s. James Calhoun and Maude (Cromer) B.; A.B., U. S.C., 1936, J.D., 1938; LL.M., Harvard, 1939; m. Elizabeth Simons Lucas, Mar. 6, 1943 (dec. 1972); children—Elizabeth (Mrs. Eugene Gaillard Johnson III), Anna (Mrs. James Graham Padgett, Jr.). Admitted to S.C. bar, 1938; since practiced in Greenwood; sr. partner firm Burns, McDonald, Bradford, Erwin & Few, Greenwood, 1939—; dir. Bankers Trust S.C., Columbia; spl. circuit judge Richland County (S.C.), 1961. Mem. Supreme Ct. Commn. Grievances and Discipline, 1958-61, Judicial Council S.C., 1964—, S.C. Bd. Law Examiners, 1973—. Bd. visitors Clemson (S.C.) U., 1960. Trustee Lander Coll., Greenwood, 1948-62, Winthrop Coll., Rock Hill, S.C., 1962—. Served with Ordnance Corps, AUS, 1942-46. Mem. Am. Law Inst., 4th Circuit Judicial Conf., Am., S.C., Greenwood bar assns., Am. Judicature Soc., S.C. (pres. 1960-61), Greenwood (past pres.) chambers commerce, Phi Beta Kappa, Chief Justice Wig and Robe, Omicron Delta Kappa, Sigma Alpha Epsilon, Phi Delta Phi. Rotarian. Clubs: Greenwood Country; Augusta (Ga.) National Golf. Home: 603 Henrietta Av Greenwood SC 29646 Office: 200-230 Greenwood Bldg Greenwood SC 29646

BURNS, JIMMY CLAY, physician; b. Brownwood, Tex., July 16, 1935; B.S. (Julia Ball Lee fellow), Tex. A. and M. U., 1957; M.D., Baylor U., 1960; m. Patsy Ann Cowan, Aug. 13, 1956; children—Clay Brooks, Ty Rolland, Kaylynn, Guy Akin. Asst. circulation mgr. Sweetwater Reporter, 1950-53; clk., timekeeper Santa Fe R.R., 1953-56; radioisotope technician Methodist Hosp., Houston, 1956-60; intern Jefferson Davis Hosp., Houston, 1960-61; practice medicine, specializing in family practice, West Columbia, Tex., 1963—; owner Pecan Oaks Farm, West Columbia, 1968—; mem. staff Sweeny, Bay City, Deaton hosps.; chief of staff Sweeny Community Hosp., 1968-70. Dir. First Capitol Bank, West Columbia; cons. Columbia Brazoria Sch. Dist.; health officer City of West Columbia. Active Boy Scouts Am. Served with USNR, 1961-63. Named Outstanding Young Man of Am., U.S. Jaycees, 1967. Diplomate Am. Acad. Family Practice. Mem. West Columbia C. of C., A.M.A., Am., Tex. acads. family practice, Tex. Med. Assn., Brazoria County Med. Soc. (pres. 1973-74), Southwestern Cattleman, Am. Internat. Charolais Breeders, Phi Eta Sigma, Phi Kappa Phi. Rotarian. Home: Farm Rd 2852 West Columbia TX 77486 Office: Columbia Clinic 503 Dance Dr West Columbia TX 77486

BURNS, JOHN GLASGOW, elec. engr., patent agt.; b. Narberth, Pa., Mar. 3, 1919; s. Arthur Wellwood and Effie (MacNiven) B.; B.S. in Elec. Engring., Va. Poly. Inst., 1941; postgrad. U. Miami, 1963-64; m. Mary Sydnor Tait, Aug. 14, 1942; 1 son, John Glasgow. Student engr. Gen. Electric Co., Schenectady, 1941-42; elec. engr. Bur. Ships, Navy Dept., Washington, 1942-46; asst. patent examiner U.S. Patent Office, Washington, 1946-55; patent agt., Miami, Fla., 1955—; field engr. Fla. Power & Light Co., Miami, 1955-61, engr., 1961—. Mem. So. Fla. Corrosion Coordinating Com., sec., 1963-68, program chmn. Fla. Gen. Conf. Corrosion, 1965-73; com. mem. Fla. Gen. Conf. and Corrosion Short Course, 1958-64, chmn. program com., 1962, visual aids com., 1964. Asst. cub master Boy Scouts Am., Alexandria, Va., 1954, mem. cub pack com. South Miami, 1955. Recipient awards for orchids. Mem. Nat. Assn. Corrosion Engrs. (sec. teas. Miami sect. 1958, 62, 69-73, chmn. Miami sect. 1963), Am. Assn. Registered Patent Attys. and Agts., Nat. Geog. Soc., So. Fla. Orchid Soc., Golden Triangle, Am. Orchid Soc., Fla. Orchid Assn., Fla. Patent Law Assn. Democrat. Presbyn. (deacon 1962, 63, 65). Club: South Dade Amateur Orchid. Exhibited in Internat. Orchid Show, 1957-60, Ft. Lauderdale Orchid Show, 1959. Home: 1036 Sorolla Av Coral Gables FL 33134 Office: 2121 Ponce St Coral Gables Fl 33134

BURNS, KENNETH HAROLD, lawyer; b. Rockford, Ill., July 6, 1929; s. Harry Harold and Gladys (Rasmussen) B.; student U. Ill., 1947-51; B.S., Trinity U., 1954; J.D., St. Mary's U., 1958; m. Laura Mae Howe, Mar. 28, 1951; children—Coni Jo, Pamela Sue, Lori Lynn. Admitted to Tex. bar, 1958, U.S. Supreme Ct. bar, 1962, D.C. bar, 1968; asst. to dir. traffic ct. program Am. Bar Assn., Chgo., 1958-59; asst. atty. gen. Tex., Austin, 1959-60; adminstrv. asst. to U.S. rep. from Tex., Washington, 1960-61; practice law, Dallas, 1961-62; spl. asst. to adminstr. U.S. Maritime Adminstrn., Washington, 1962-65, dir. congl. and legal matters, spl. asst. to chmn. Fed. Maritime Commn. and Solicitor, Washington, 1965-70; practice law, Houston, Washington, 1970—. Pres., Gustafson P.T.A., 1958-59. Bd. dirs. Arthritis and Rheumatism Assn.; trustee Nat. Multiple Sclerosis Soc. Served with USNR, 1948-51, USAF, 1951-55. Named Hon. Citzen Tenn., Gov. of Tenn., 1958; adm. Tex. Navy, 1960; Ky. col., 1965. Mem. Nat., Fed. (bd. govs. 1969), Am. bar assns., Am. Legion, Delta Theta Phi (spl. asst. to the nat. chancellor), Pi Kappa Delta, Kappa Pi Sigma, Alpha Phi Omega. Methodist. Mason. Club: Texas Breakfast (pres.1968) (Washington). Contbr. articles to profl. jours. Home: 450 Wilchester Blvd Houston TX 77024 Office: 767 Main Bldg Houston TX 77002 also 2000 L St NW Washington DC 20036

BURNS, PAUL ARTHUR, lawyer; b. West Reading, Pa., Jan. 4, 1943; s. James Stanley and Ruth Arline (Fryer) B.; A.B. in History, Tex. A. and M. U., 1963; J.D., Coll. William and Mary, 1966; m. Jacqueline Wilson Bemis, Nov. 1, 1969. Admitted to Va. bar, 1968; asso. mem. firm Donovan, Turnbull, Brophy & Burns and predecessor firm, 1968-71, partner, 1971—. Served with USMCR, 1966-68; Vietnam. Mem. Am., Falls Church, Fairfax County, Va. bar assns., No. Va. Jr. Bar Assn., Catholic War Vets. (hon. mem.), Phi Delta Phi. Clubs: Basenji of Am.; Mid-Atlantic Basenji (Mt. Airy, Md.), Old Dominion Kennel No. Va. (Arlington). Home: 7316 Brad St Falls Church VA 22042 Office: 106 Little Falls St Falls Church VA 22046

BURNS, SALLY GIPE (MRS. LEONARD O. BURNS), bus. exec.; b. Moody, Tex., Jan. 17, 1925; d. William Franklin and Velma (Meador) Gipe; student Draughn Bus. Sch., 1942; m. Leonard Odell Burns, Nov. 15, 1942; children—James Odell, Alton Jay. Office mgr. Garland (Tex.) Daily News, 1952-54; with Eastern Hills Country Club, Garland, 1955—, office mgr., 1955-61, gen. mgr., 1961—. Pres. Altrusa Club Garland, 1967-68, P.T.A., 1965 (hon. life mem. 1966). Precinct chmn. Democratic Party, 1966. Named Altrusa Woman of Yr., 1971. Mem. Garland Fedn. Womans Clubs (sec.), Nat. Club Mgrs. Assn. (dir. at large, membership chmn. Lone Star chpt.), C. of C., Dallas-Fort Worth Club Mgrs., Am. Bus. Women. Baptist. Home: 1621 Apache Dr Garland TX 75040 Office: Country Club Rd Garland TX 75040

BURNSIDE, HAMILTON STANLEY NATHANIEL, life underwriter; b. Nassau, New Providence, Bahamas, Nov. 22, 1899; s. Herbert Nathaniel and Caroline (Poitier) B.; student Cambridge U.; m. Mary Elizabeth Haynes, July 6, 1940; 1 dau., Florence Caroline (Mrs. Mays). Baggage and checking room Fla. East Coast R.R., 1922-25; also part-time sales Afro-Am. Life Ins. Co., 1922-25; agt., asst. mgr., mgr., agy. asst. Nat. Benefit Life Ins. Co., 1925-33; organized Columbia Life Ins. Co., 1933-35; field supr., mgr. Pilgrim Health & Life Ins. Co., 1935-45, mgr., 1954-69, cons., 1969—; mgr., supr. Guaranty Life Ins. Co., 1945-50; mgr. Mammoth Life Ins. Co., 1951-54. Divisional chmn. Cherokee div. N.E. Ga. Boy Scouts Am., 1942-69; chmn. bd. mgmt. Samuel F. Harris YMCA, Athens 1956-69, chmn. emeritus, 1969—; chmn. co-chmn. campaigns A.R.C., Community Services, and others. Served as cpl. Royal British Army, 1916-19. Recipient Silver Beaver Award Boy Scouts Am., 1950. Episcopalian. Home: 191 Chicamauga Av SW Atlanta GA 30314 Office: 181 W Washington St Athens GA 30601

BUROW, RICHARD WILCOX, mech. engr.; b. Danville, Ill., Aug. 16, 1939; s. George Edward and Esther (Wilcox) B.; B.S. in Math., Ill. Wesleyan U., 1962; B.S. in Mech. Engring., Duke, 1962, M.S., 1964; m. Suzanne Lee Porter, Aug. 24, 1963; children—Craig Porter, David Wilcox. Mech. engr. Kodel devel. div. Tenn. Eastman Co., Kingsport, 1964—. Registered profl. engr., Tenn. Mem. Am. Soc. M.E. (chmn.), Nat. Soc. Profl. Engrs., Sigma Xi. Mason (32 degree), Moose. Club: Sertoma (Kingsport). Patentee in field. Home: 5316 Orebank Rd Kingsport TN 37664 Office: PO Box 511 Bldg 226 Kingsport TN 37662

BURR, SAMUEL ENGLE, JR., educator, historian; b. Bordentown, N.J., Dec. 6, 1897; s. Samuel Engle and Elizabeth (Thompson) B.; Litt.B., Rutgers U., 1919; M.A., U. Wis., 1925, Columbia, 1927; Ed.D., U. Cin., 1936; m. Alice Elizabeth Gratz, June 28, 1924; children—Evelyn (Mrs. Eugene Dorr Biddle) (dec.), Samuel Engle III. Supt. schs., New Castle, Del., 1934-39, Rye Neck, N.Y., Mamaroneck, N.Y., 1939-42; dir. Am. U. Inst. World Affairs, Washington, 1949-59, prof. edn., 1947-68, dean summer sessions, 1963-65, prof. emeritus, 1968—; vis. prof. history Weatherford (Tex.) Coll., 1969-72; mng. dir. Burr Pubs., Ltd., Ft. Worth and Linden, 1968—. Mem. textbook selection com. U.S. Air Force Inst., Washington, 1955-59; dir. Skyland Community Corp., Linden, Va. Served to 2d lt. U.S. Army, 1918, to lt. col. inf., AUS, 1942-47. Decorated Purple Heart; recipient awards from various fgn. countries; named Ky. col., 1965, Tenn. col., 1973, Tenn. adm., 1974. Mem. Fed. Schoolmen's Club (pres. 1967-68), New Edn. Fellowship (pres. chpt. 1960—), S. Atlantic Philosophy Edn. Aaron Burr Assn. (pres. gen. 1946—), Nat. Hist. Soc., Tex. Hist. Assn., 14th Air Force Assn., Phi Kappa Phi, Kappa Phi Kappa, Phi Delta Kappa, Kappa Delta Pi, Phi Theta Kappa. Republican. Episcopalian. Rotarian (hon.). Author: Napoleon's Dossier on Aaron Burr, 1969; An Introduction to Progressive Education, 1937; Small Town Merchant, 1957; Colonel Aaron Burr: The American Phoenix, 1963; Colonel Aaron Burr: The Misunderstood Man, 1967; The Burr-Hamilton Duel & Related Matters, 1971. Home and office: Tremont Inca Rd Linden VA 22642

BURR, THEODORE JACKSON, JR., lawyer; b. Richmond, Va., July 15, 1944; s. Theodore Jackson and Jesse Garland (Cocke) B.; B.A., Hampden-Sydney Coll., 1966; LL.B., U. Richmond, 1969; m. Harriet Southard Williamson, Oct. 17, 1970; children—Theodore Madison and William Blakeney (twins). Admitted to Va. bar, 1969; travel aide, advance man gubernatorial campaign of Linwood Holton, 1969; counsel gen. laws com. Va. Ho. of Dels., 1970; asso. firm Warriner, Outten, Slagle & Barrett, 1970; partner firm Warriner & Outten, Emporia, Va., 1971—. Mgr. bus. solicitations Emporia-Greensville Heart Fund, 1971-73. Chmn. Emporia Republican Com., 1972—; mem. Rep. State Central Com., 1973; state coordinator election day activities Rep. campaign for gov., lt. gov., atty. gen., 1973. Recipient Freedom Guard award Regional Jaycees, 1972; named an outstanding young man of Am., Jr. C. of C., 1973. Mem. Am., Va. bar assns., Am. Judicature Soc., Chi Phi, Phi Delta Phi. Episcopalian (treas., vestryman). Club: Emporia Chess. Home: 500 Jefferson St Emporia VA 23847 Office: 314 S Main St Emporia VA 23847

BURRELL, GEORGE CHARLES, sales co. exec.; b. Carbondale, Pa., Feb. 3, 1939; s. George Charles and Filipina (Bliesener) B.; B.S. in Mining Engring. and Engring. Geophysics, Lehigh U., 1960; M.S. in Engring. Adminstrn., So. Methodist U., 1966; m. Rose Ann Norris, Sept. 20, 1963; children—Shannon Renee, Dawn Michele. Project mgr. Tex. Instruments Inc., Dallas, 1961-67; pres. Associometrics Inc., Dallas, 1967-70; ind. practice as financial, mgmt. cons., Dallas, 1970-73; v.p. adminstrn. IMCO Trading Corp., Dallas, 1973—; sec., treas., dir. United S.W. Buyers' Corp., Dallas, 1971-72. Adviser, Jr. Achievement, Dallas, 1966-67. Texaco scholar, 1956-60. Registered profl. engr., Tex. Mem. Soc. Exploration Geophysicists, Soc. Preservation and Encouragement Barbershop Quartet Singing in Am. (sec. treas. 1972-73). Mem. Christian Ch. (chmn. bd. deacons). Club: Dallas Athletic. Home: 9741 Maplehill Dr Dallas TX 75238 Office: 1300 Expressway Tower Dallas TX 75206

BURROUGHS, EDWIN ELWELL, mech. engr.; b. N.Y.C., Feb. 6, 1903; s. George G. and Clara E. (Elwell) B.; student Cooper Union Coll., 1922; m. Edna C. Westby, Oct. 12, 1925; div.; children—Edwin E., Lois V. (Mrs. Don Crammond), George W.; m. 2d, Florence E. Tullar, June 4, 1946; 1 stepdau., Marilyn D. (Mrs. Keith T. Dempsey). Apprentice machinist H.W. Cotton Co., Bklyn., 1919-20; draftsman Potdevin Machine Co., Bklyn., 1920-29, chief engr., 1931-44; machine designer Internat. Paper Co., N.Y.C., 1929-31; asst. dir. engring. St. Regis Paper Co., Pensacola, Fla., 1944-65; pres. Speculators, 1957-65; cons. on paper converting equipment, 1965—; bd. dirs., treas. Harvestor Fed. Credit Union, Cantonment, Fla., 1962-68. Fellow Am. Soc. M.E. (chmn. N.W. Fla. 1956-58, chmn. civic affairs com. Region IV, 1959); mem. C. of C., Speculators Club (pres. 1957-60). Clubs: Pensacola Country, Pensacola Dinner (pres. 1957, dir. 1956); New York Athletic. Patentee in field. Address: 1916 E Scott St Pensacola FL 32503

BURROW, DAVID HUTCHISON, lawyer; b. Sweetwater, Tex., Sept. 12, 1936; s. David Hiram and Mary Sunshine (Eatwell) B.; B.S. magna cum laude, McMurry Coll., 1958; LL.B., U. Tex. 1961; LL.M., Georgetown U., 1965; m. DeLoyce Montgomery, Feb. 14, 1971; children—Bradley, Christy, Laura. Admitted to Tex. bar, 1961; prosecutor City Atty's Office, San Antonio, 1961-62; partner firm Helm, Jones & Pletcher, Houston, 1965—. Served to capt., Judge Adv. Gen. Corps, AUS, 1962-65. Mem. Am., Houston bar assns., State Bar Tex., Houston Trial Lawyers Assn. (dir. 1973—), Phi Gamma Delta, Delta Theta Phi. Home: 407 Caesar's Circle New Caney TX 77357 Office: 711 Fannin Bldg Suite 800 Houston TX 77002

BURRUS, GEORGE JOSEPH, III, govt. ofcl.; b. Columbus, Ga., July 17, 1914; s. George J. and Effie May (Pierce) B.; B.S. in M.E., Auburn U., 1937; m. Mary J. Leonard, Dec. 14, 1962. Test engr. B-47 and C-130 aircraft Lockheed Aircraft Co., Marietta, Ga., 1952-57; field test engr. Thor Missile, Douglas Aircraft, Cape Canaveral, Fla., 1957-58; sr. field test engr. missile nose cones Avco, Cape Canaveral, 1958-63; engring. project mgr. mobile service structure NASA, Kennedy Space Center, 1963—. Pres. G.J. Burrus Co., Cocoa Beach, Fla., 1959—; owner Burrus Bldg., 1959—, Cocoa Beach Shopping Center, 1963-68. Charter mem. Melbourne (Fla.) Municipal Band, 1964—. Served to maj. USAAF, 1942-46; now lt. col. Res. ret. Mem. Melbourne C. of C. (mem. mil. affairs com.), Air Force Assn. (state v.p. 1964-67, pres. Cape Canaveral chpt. 1971—), NASA Athletic and Recreation Soc. (sec. 1967-69), Alpha Tau Omega. Baptist. Club: Patrick AFB Officers. Home: 707 N Palm Av Indialantic FL 32903 Office: John F Kennedy Space Center FL 32899

BURRUS, JOHN NEWELL, educator; b. Gilmer, Tex., Jan. 23, 1920; s. Herman Clifford and Beulah (Blalack) B.; A.B., U. Miss., 1942; M.A., La. State U., 1944, Ph.D., 1950; postgrad. U. Minn., 1945-47, Vanderbilt U., 1948. Grad. fellow La. State U. 1942-44, 48-49, research asso., 1949-50; teaching fellow U. Minn., 1945-47; faculty U. Miss., 1943-45, Vanderbilt U., 1947-48, U. Fla., 1950-51; faculty, chmn. dept. sociology U. So. Miss., Hattiesburg, 1951-70, prof., 1957-70, Distinguished U. prof., 1970—, mem. Council U. Honors Program, 1959-67. Active A.R.C. Mem. Am. Sociol. Assn., So. (nomination com. 1966-68, sect. chmn. 1968, mem. exec. com. 1955-58), Rural sociol. socs., Sigma Chi, Alpha Kappa Delta, Pi Gamma Mu, Phi Kappa Phi. Kiwanian. Author: Life Opportunities: Differential Mortality in Mississippi, 1951; (with C.A. McMahan, R.H. Bradford) Manual to Accompany the Sociology of Urban Life, 1952; (with H.A. Pedersen, M.B. King) Mississippi Life Tables, 1954; Mississippi's People, 1950; (with others) Social Problems, 1955. Mem. editorial bd. So. Quar., 1962-70, chmn., 1967-68. Contbr. to A History of Mississippi, 1973; also articles, book revs. to profl. publs. Home: 213 Arlington Loop Hattiesburg MS 39401

BURRUS, SWAN THOMAS, lawyer; b. Boswell, Okla., Sept. 16, 1924; s. Sam and Lota (Cotten) B.; student Okla. State U., 1942-43, Tex. Christian U., 1943-44; LL.B., U. Tex., 1946-48; m. Ann Cunningham, Nov. 6, 1954; children—Martha Amanda, Mary Ellis. Admitted to Tex. bar, 1948, practiced in Dallas, 1949-52, Houston, 1952-58, New Braunfels, Tex., 1962—; mem. firm Allen Melton, 1949-52, Cutrer & Cook, 1952-58; asst. atty. gen. State of Tex., Austin, 1958-62; city atty. New Braunfels, Tex., 1967-72; mem. firm Bartram, Reagan & Burrus. Pres. Community Fund, 1966. Vice chmn. Good Govt. League of New Braunfels, 1966; founder Tex. Legislative seminar. Served with USNR, 1943-46. Mem. Am., Tex. bar assns., New Braunfels (pres. 1967-68), South Tex. (mem. exec. com. 1972—) chambers commerce, Phi Alpha Delta. Democrat. Episcopalian (chancellor 1963—). Lion (pres. 1968-69). Home: 617 Fredericksburg St New Braunfels TX 78130 Office: PO Box 69 New Braunfels TX 78130

BURSON, JOHN HENRY, III, educator; b. Carrollton, Ga., July 30, 1934; s. John Henry and Clara (Miles) B.; B.Chem. Engring., Ga. Inst. Tech., 1956, M.S. in Metallurgy, 1963, Ph.D. in Chem. Engring., 1964; m. Barbara Anne Vaughn, Dec. 18, 1955; children—Susan Elaine, Sandra Anne, John Henry IV, Thomas Edward. Chief chemist Testworth Labs., 1956-59; mem. faculty Ga. Inst. Tech., Atlanta, 1959—, sr. research engr., 1964—, asso. prof. chem. engring., 1969—. Served with AUS, 1957. Recipient Research award Sigma Xi, 1964. Registered profl. engr., Ga., Cal., Pa. Mem. Am. Chem. Soc., Nat. Soc. Profl. Engrs., Am. Inst. Chem. Engrs. (chpt. chmn. 1970-72), Res. Officers Assn. (chpt. sec.-treas. 1970—), Fine Particle Soc. (nat. pres. 1969-70), Ga. Football Ofcls. Assn. (v.p. 1971-72), Sigma Xi. Contbr. articles to publs. Home: 1198 Citadel Dr NE Atlanta GA 30324

BURSON, ROBERT ALLEN, physician; b. Cleveland, Tenn., Feb. 11, 1943; s. Felix Melton and Nestle Lee (Smith) B.; B.S., Tenn. Tech. U., 1965; M.D., U. Tenn., 1967; m. Sarah Patricia Emerson, July 6, 1963 (div.); 1 son, Jeffrey Mark. Intern, Meth. Hosp., Memphis, 1968; resident in internal medicine Emory U. Affiliated Hosps., 1971-73; fellow in hematology and oncology U. Tenn. Coll. Medicine-City of Memphis Hosp., 1973—. Served with USNR, 1968-71. Decorated Air medal with clusters (U.S.); Medal of Honor (South Vietnam). Mem. A.M.A. Independent. Episcopalian. Mason. Home: 759 Brookhaven Circle Memphis TN 38117 Office: City of Memphis Hospitals Madison Av Memphis TN 38103

BURTON, ANNIE UNA, ret. mfg. co. exec.; b. Thorton, R.I., Oct. 9, 1889; d. Joseph Godber and Annie (Severn) Burton; B.A., Randolph Macon Woman's Coll., 1912. Tchr. schs., Lynchburg, Va., 1912-16; sec., treas. Lynchburg Hosiery Mills, 1916-67, trustee, mem. bd. Mem. Am. Assn. U. Women, Bus. and Profl. Women's Club. Clubs: Lynchburg Art (treas.), Womans. Home: 3819 Fort Av Lynchburg VA 24502

BURTON, F. JOHN, JR., accountant; b. San Antonio, Sept. 30, 1940; s. Felix Johnathan and Willie Lee (Friday) B.; B.B.A., Tex. A. and M. U., 1962; J.D., U. Tex., 1965; m. Jenny Kathleen Marwil, Sept. 6, 1963; children—Beth, Jeanette. Admitted to Tex. bar, 1965; accountant Arthur Andersen & Co., Houston, 1965-69, Alexander Grant & Co., Houston, 1969-70; pres., dir. Burton & Miller, Inc., Houston, 1970—. Mem. fund drive South Tex. Jr. Coll., 1969—. C.P.A., Tex. Mem. Am. Inst. C.P.A.'s, Tex. Soc. C.P.A.'s, State Bar Tex., Houston Jr. Bar Assn. Clubs: Quail Valley Golf, Willowisp Country. Home: 2938 La Quinta Missouri City TX 77459 Office: 2600 Southwest Freeway Houston TX 77006

BURTON, GEORGE AUBREY, JR., accountant, city ofcl.; b. Texarkana, Ark., June 21, 1925; s. George Aubrey and Theo (Simmons) B.; B.S., Centenary Coll. La., 1951m. Joan Cunningham, July 31, 1947; children—George Aubrey III, Sandra. Sr. accountant Opferkuch & McGuirt, Shreveport, La., 1950-53; partner Opferkuch, McGuirt, Watts & West, Shreveport, La., 1953-54; accountant G. A. Burton, Jr., Shreveport, La., 1954-66; partner Burton & Penn, Shreveport, 1966—; commr. finance City of Shreveport, 1971—. Instr., Centenary Coll., 1957-59. Mem. Shreveport Housing Rehab. Bd., 1956-57; mem. Caddo Sch. Bd. Com. for Rapid Learners, 1957-59; mem. citizens adv. com. Caddo Police Jury, 1967-68. Mem. Republican State Central Com., 1964—, sec., 1972—; mem. Caddo Parish Rep. Exec. Com., 1954—, chmn., 1960—. Mem. La. Jaycees. Home: 770 Delaware Shreveport LA 71106 Office: 1234 Texas Av Shreveport LA 71101

BURTON, GEORGE HERMAN, lumber co. exec.; b. Norfolk, Va., Sept. 29, 1910; s. George Herman and Charlotte (Mizell) B.; B.S. in Mech. Engring., Va. Poly. Inst.. 1933, M.S., 1934; m. Clarice Batten, June 29, 1940; children—George Herman III, Charlotte Ghee. Supr. E.I. DuPont de Nemours & Co., Richmond, Va., 1937-44; with Burton Lumber Corp., Chesapeake, Va., 1946—, pres., 1952—. Mem. adv. bd. Salvation Army, Norfolk, since 19—. Bd. dirs. Norfolk chpt. Goodwill Assn. Served with AUS, 1936-37, to lt. USNR, 1944-46. Registered profl. engr., Va. Mem. Va. Bldg. Materials Dealers Assn. (pres. 1962), Builders and Contractors Exchange (past pres.), Archtl. Woodwork Inst. (past Va. pres.), Va. Lumber Mfrs. Assn. (past treas.), Nat. Lumber and Bldg. Materials Dealers Assn. (treas.), Norfolk Retail Merchants Assn. (dir.), Hampton Rds. Engrs. Club (past pres.), Norfolk Va. Poly. Inst. Alumni Assn. (past pres.). Tau Beta Pi. Baptist (deacon). Mason (32 deg., Shriner), Rotarian (gov. Dist. 760 1966-67). Home: 850 Linbay Dr Virginia Beach VA 23451 Office: 835 Wilson Rd Chesapeake VA 23324

BURTON, GEORGE WASHINGTON, educator; b. Brosville, Va., July 4, 1908; s. John William and Annie (Harvey) B.; B.S., U. Va., 1929, M.A., 1942; m. Sarah Dudley, Mar. 24, 1945; children—Sarah Elizabeth, Brown Dudley. Tchr. high sch., Henry County, Va., 1930-32, prin., 1932-42; supt. schs., Clarke County, Va., 1946-66; state dir. secondary edn. Dept. Edn., Richmond, Va., 1966-68, asst. state supt. for instrn., Richmond, 1968-72, asst. state supt. adminstrv. field services, 1972—. Served with AUS, 1942-46. Mem. Am., Va. assns. sch. adminstrs., Va. Edn. Assn., C. of C. (pres. 1957-58). Lion (pres. 1960-61). Home: Route 1 Berryville VA 22611 Office: State Dept Edn Richmond VA 23216

BURTON, JOSEPH JOHN, advt. exec.; b. Greensboro, N.C., Mar. 9, 1919; s. Hilary Goode and Sarah (Harriss) B.; student Guilford Coll., 1936-38; B.S. in Commerce, U. N.C., 1940; m. Virginia Garrison Williams, Feb. 5, 1944; children—Joseph John Jr., Robert Dalrymple. Asst. to pres., gen. advt. mgr. Colonial Stores Inc., Atlanta, 1949-59; v.p. firm Liller Neal Battle, Atlanta, 1959-65; pres. Burton-Campbell Inc., Atlanta, 1965—. Publicity chmn. Am. Heart Assn., Atlanta, 1969—. Bd. dirs. Goodwill Industries, Atlanta, St. Jude's House, Atlanta. Served with USNR, 1940-45. Mem. Phi Beta Kappa, Beta Gamma Sigma, Alpha Delta Sigma. Democrat. Episcopalian. Contbr. poetry mags. Home: 2879 Normandy Dr NW Atlanta GA 30305 Office: 1800 Peachtree Rd NW Atlanta GA 30305

BURTON, UVA MARIE LOFTIS (MRS. J. B. BURTON), lawyer, realtor; b. Mena, Ark., Nov. 21, 1911; d. Charles Lemuel and Brooke Corene (Wimberly) Loftis; student Tulane U., 1929-30; LL.B., So. Meth. U., 1942; m. Hal Erwin, Oct. 24, 1942 (dec. Mar. 1953); children—William Hal, Judith Marie; m. 2d, Jesse Byron Burton, July 25, 1959 (dec. Jan. 1962). Family caseworker United Charities, Dallas, 1930-33; personnel and legal worker Atlantic Refining Co., Dallas, 1933-43; admitted to Tex. bar, 1942; lawyer, Houston, 1956—; asso. realtor Saffold Realty Co., Houston, 1965. Parliamentarian, Lynn Park Civic Club, Houston, 1963—. Mem. State Bar Tex., Houston Bd. Realtors, Tex. Real Estate Assn., Nat. Assn. Real Estate Bds., Women's Assn., Alpha Omicron Pi, Kappa Beta Pi. Episcopalian. Home: 4019 Sul Ross St Houston TX 77027 Office: 1314 Texas Av Houston TX 77002

BURTS, BETTY HUNT, librarian; b. Savannah, Ga., Oct. 16, 1912; d. George Wellington and Julia Reese (Moorhead) Hunt; A.B., Wesleyan Coll., 1933; B.L.S., Emory U., 1934; A.M. in L.S., Fla. State U., 1971; m. Albert Willard Burts, June 6, 1936; children—Julie (Mrs. Alex Reynolds, Jr.), Inez (Mrs. John Spear Colley). Librarian Norman Jr. Coll., Norman Park, Ga., 1934-35; library supr. WPA, Macon Ga., 1936; children's librarian Macon Pub. Library, 1937; librarian Savanhhan High Sch., 1935-36, 42-46, Comml. High Sch., 1951-56, Jenkins High Sch., 1956—. Instr. library sci. U. Ga. extension at Armstrong, part time, 1965-70; tchr. French, Richard Arnold Jr. High Sch., Savannah. Mary Calder scholar, 1967; Delta Kappa Gamma scholar, 1967. Mem. So. Assn. Evaluating Coms., Ga. Edn. Assn., N.E.A., Ga., Southeastern library assns., Delta Kappa Gamma. Lutheran. Home: 2018 Speir St Savannah GA 31406 Office: 1800 E Derenne Av Savannah GA 31404

BURTT, CLYDE LAWRENCE, chem. co. exec.; b. Akron, O., Nov. 18, 1920; s. Guy Woodmansee and Alma Elaine (Stenger) B.; M.E., U. Cin., 1950; M.B.A., Western Mich. U., 1965; m. Selma Alleene Sinclair, Apr. 14, 1945; 1 son, Clyde Lawrence. Asst. chief engr. Clopay Corp., Cin., 1950-51; divisional sales rep. Jones-Dabney Co., Louisville, 1951-64; with Reliance Universal Inc., Louisville, 1964—, corporate v.p., gen. mgr., 1969—. Served with USAAF, 1942-45. Mem. Nat. (mgmt. information com. 1971—), Louisville (dir. Louisville chpt. 1971—) paint and coatings assns. Home: 570 Blankenbaker Lane Louisville KY 40207 Office: Suite 1600 Watterson 1900 Bishops Lane Towers Louisville KY 40218

BURWELL, CLAYTON L., lawyer; b. Charlotte, N.C. Oct. 29, 1910; B.S., U. of the South, 1932; B.A. in Jurisprudence (Rhodes scholar), Oxford (Eng.) U., 1935; LL.B., U. N.C., 1936. Admitted to N.C. bar, 1941, U.S. Supreme Ct. bar, 1942; gen. counsel, v.p. Resort Airlines, 1945-48; spl. asst. to sec. navy, 1948-50; gen. counsel Ind. Airlines Assn., 1958-59, pres., 1959-61; now mem. firm Burwell & Hansen, Washington. Mem. U.S. Travel Service adv. com., 1962. Served with USNR, 1941-45. Mem. Naval Res. Assn. (nat. pres. 1953), Va., Am. bar assns., Bar Assn. D.C. Home: 1348 Lynnbrook St Dr Arlington VA 22201 Office: Burwell & Hansen 700 Federal Bar Bldg West Washington DC 20006

BURWELL, (GEORGE) ERNEST, automobile dealer; b. Tarboro, N.C., July 22, 1897; s. George Ernest and Lilla Pugh (Bell) B.; ed. pub. schs., spl. courses; m. Ethel Marie McMurray, Mar. 4, 1946; children—Ernest Burwell III, Faith (Mrs. James Stewart-Gordon). Owner, partner Burwell-Parker Motor Co., Gastonia, N.C., 1920-22; owner, pres. Ernest Burwell, Inc., Spartanburg, S.C., 1922-27, 27-32, 32—; owner, pres. Burwell Chevrolet, Inc.; owner Burwell Ins., Ernest Burwell, Inc. Organizer Spartanburg Naval Armory, 1946; dir. Kiyosato Ednl. Expt. Project, Japan, 1950—. Bd. dirs. Mchts. Bur., United Fund, Salvation Army, Mental Health Clinic; active Spartanburg Found.; mem. bd. assos. Wofford Coll. Served to comdr. USNR, 1940-46. Recipient Dealer award for S.C., Time mag., 1970. Mem. Nat. (S.C. dir. 1937-53), S.C. (dir.) automobile dealers assns., Am. Camellia Soc., S.C. Camellia Soc. (exec. v.p., dir.), Spartanburg C. of C. Episcopalian (vestryman). Clubs: Tryon (N.C.) Country, Tryon Riding and Hunt; Piedmont (Spartanburg); Highland (N.C.) Country. Home: Warrior Dr Tryon NC 28782 Office: 265 N Church St Spartanburg NC 29301

BURZLAFF, DONALD FREDERICK, educator; b. Dodge Center, Minn., May 30, 1923; s. William August and Clara Dorothy (Schleeter) B.; B.S., U. Wyo., 1950, M.S., 1952; Ph.D., Utah State U., 1960; m. Luella Anne Wright, Aug. 16, 1948; children—Diane Claire, Dayle Yvonne. Extension agronomist U. Neb. at Lincoln, 1953-73, prof., 1967-73; prof., chmn. dept. range and wildlife mgr., dir. brush control Tex. Tech. U., Lubbock, 1973—. Served with AUS, 1945-46. Mem. Soc. Range Mgmt. (recipient Neb. range mgmt. award, 1969), Am. Soc. Agronomy, Am. Forage and Grassland Council (merit award 1973), Soil and Water Conservation Soc. Am. Kiwanian (pres., pres. elect 1970-72). Research with fertilizer on semi-arid grassland. Home: 1617 27th St Lubbock TX 79405 Office: Dept Range and Wildlife Mgmt Texas Tech Univ Lubbock TX 79409

BUSBEE, ELIZABETH DIVERS (MRS. CHARLES MANLY BUSBEE), county ofcl.; b. Roanoke, Va., May 15, 1912; d. Alfred and Mary Bessie (Ramsey) Divers; student Martha Washington Coll., 1928, Milligan (Tenn.) Coll., 1928-29; B.S., Radford (Va.) Coll., 1934; postgrad. U. N.C., 1944-45, U. Va., 1945-46, Coll. William and Mary, 1966; m. Charles M. Busbee, July 3, 1957. Instr., coach West Jefferson (N.C.) High Sch., 1935-37, Gretna (Va.) High Sch., 1937-38; social worker Franklin County Dept. Pub. Welfare, Rocky Mount, Va., 1938-42, supt., 1942—. Bd. dirs. S.W. Soc. for Crippled Children, 1944-50; treas. Franklin County chpt. Nat. Found. for Infantile Parlysis, 1938—; pres. Va. League Local Welfare Execs., 1956-58; rep. from 5th Congl. Dist. Va. on League Local Welfare Execs., 1950-54, 63-65. Organizer, Woman's Club Rocky Mount, 1945, pres., 1950-52, 71-73, organizer Jr. Woman's Club, 1949; pres. U.D.C., 1956—. Home: 114 Taliaferro Av Rocky Mount VA 24151 Office: Franklin County Dept Pub Welfare Rocky Mount VA 24151

BUSBY, JOHN ARTHUR, JR., architect; b. Charleston, S.C., Aug. 30, 1933; s. John Arthur and Mildred (Inabinett) B.; B.S., Ga. Inst. Tech., 1956, B.Arch., 1959; m. Mary Ann Cross, July 16, 1961; children—Clarissa Ann, Julia Cross. Architect firm Abreu & Robeson, Atlanta, 1959-64; asso. v.p. firm Heery & Heery, Atlanta, 1964-66; partner firm Jova/Daniels/Busby, Atlanta, 1966—. Asst. prof. Ga. Inst. Tech., Atlanta, 1970—. Program chmn. Leadership Atlanta, 1971-72, 73—; sponsor High Mus. Art, Atlanta, 1967; mem. Central Atlanta Progress, Inc. Bd. dirs. Morningside-Lenox Park Assn., Vis. Nurse Assn., Christian Coll. Ga., Athens. Served with AUS, 1956-58. Mem. A.I.A. (pres. elect), Atlanta C. of C. Contbr. articles to profl. jours. Office: 100 Colony Sq Atlanta GA 30361

BUSCH, EDWARD ROBERT, printing co. exec.; b. New Rochelle, N.Y., Dec. 4, 1936; s. George L. and Nettie (Leviason) B.; B.A. magna cum laude, Princeton, 1958; J.D., Harvard, 1962; m. Francine Grace Cone, June 1, 1958; 1 dau., Allison Jane. Admitted to Pa. bar, 1963; asst. to pres. Titan Industries, N.Y.C., 1965-66; exec. v.p., dir. Wessel Co., Inc., Chgo., 1967-72; pres. Valley Forge Web Offset Corp. (Pa.), 1972-73; exec. v.p. Fisher-Harrison Corp., Greensboro, N.C., 1973—. Served with AUS, 1958-59. Mem. Am. Bar Assn., Am. Inst. Mgmt. (mem. pres.'s council 1973-74), Phi Beta Kappa. Episcopalian. Club: Hot Springs (Va.) Golf and Tennis. Home: Valhalla Warm Springs VA 24484 Office: Fisher—Harrison Corp PO Box 20630 Greensboro NC 27420

BUSH, ALBERT ERNEST, corp. exec.; b. Cedar Falls, Ia., May 19, 1931; s. Ernest M. and Mary (Jackle) B.; student Open Bible Coll., 1954, Midland Coll., 1954, Drake U., 1955-57; B.A., Tulsa U., 1963; m. Marilyn Ruth Huffman, Jan. 30, 1953; children—Carol Marie, Marta Lynn. Dept. mgr. Oral Roberts Assn., Inc., Tulsa, 1957-60, asst. operations mgr., 1960-63, operations mgr., 1963-66, exec. v.p., 1966-69, pres., 1969-72, trustee, 1972—; bd. regents Oral Roberts U., 1969—; chmn., pres., chief exec. officer Mentor Corp., Tulsa, 1972—, also dir.; dir. Boulder Bank & Trust Co., Tulsa, United Bank, Tulsa. Bd. dirs. Arts Council Tulsa, Tulsa Housing Authority, University Village, Inc. Mem. Am. Mgmt. Assn., Young Pres. Orgn., Tulsa C. of C. Republican. Presbyn. Kiwanian. Clubs: Tulsa, Summit, Southern Hills Country. Home: 7512 S Evanston Av Tulsa OK 74136 Office: 10 E 3d St Tulsa OK 74103

BUSH, EUNICE CARROLL, ins. co. exec.; b. Merryville, La., Jan. 7, 1907; d. Guy and Jennie (Hargrove) Carroll; student La. State Coll., 1924; m. Harry F. Bush, Nov. 6, 1933 (dec. July 1951); 1 son, Robert A. Seals. With Mut. Life Ins. Co. of N.Y., Baton Rouge, 1931—, successively dist. mgr., supervisory asst., asst. mgr., Baton Rouge, 1938-58, tng. asst. home office, N.Y.C., 1958, mgr., 1958-1964, life underwriter, 1964—. Pres. bd. dirs. YWCA, Baton Rouge, 1951-52, mem. adv. bd., 1962-63; mem. adv. bd. Baton Rouge Gen. Hosp., 1952-57; bd. dirs. Community Chest and United Givers of Baton Rouge, 1954-55. C.L.U. Mem. Nat. Assn. Life Underwriters (trustee 1950, vice chmn. com. on assns. 1962-63), Baton Rouge Life Underwriters Assn. (pres. 1942-43), Mut. of N.Y. Hall of Fame, Beta Gamma Sigma (hon.). Club: Quota (charter, past pres. Baton Rouge, gov. 21st Dist.) Home: 9544 Goodwood Blvd Baton Rouge LA 70815 Office: 8754 Goodwood Av Baton Rouge LA 70806

BUSH, RONALD MITCHELL, veterinarian; b. Santa Ana, Cal., July 21, 1941; s. Ronald A. and Pauline (Calkins) B.; B.S. summa cum laude, U. Cal. at Davis, 1963, D.V.M. summa cum laude, 1965. Intern, then mem. staff Angell Meml. Animal Hosp., Boston, 1965-67; veterinarian Balt. Zoo, 1967-72; veterinarian div. animal health Nat. Zool. Park, Smithsonian Instn., Rock Creek Park, Washington, 1972—. Faculty, Johns Hopkins Med. Sch., Balt., 1967—, asst. prof. dept. animal medicine, 1969-71, dept. radiology, 1971—. Mem. Am. Vet. Med. Assn., Am. Animal Hosp. Assn., Vet. Radiol. Soc., Am. Assn. Zool. Veterinarians. Home: 3802 Yuma St NW Washington DC 20016 Office: Nat Zool Park Rock Creek Park Washington DC 20009

BUSH, WILLIAM EDWARD, civil engr.; b. Jackson, Tenn., Dec. 6, 1924; s. Cecil Warren and Chrystabel (Herrick) B.; student Memphis State U., 1942-43, Miss. Coll., 1943-44; B.S., U. Tenn., 1949; m. Gladys E. Parker, Sept. 17, 1953; children—Nancy C., William Scott. Hydraulic engr. U.S. Corps of Engrs., Vicksburg, Miss., 1949-50, constrn. engr., Memphis, 1952-53; hydraulic engr. Soil Conservation Service, U.S. Dept. Agr., Memphis, 1953-62, soil conservationist, 1962-72, urban engring. specialist, 1972-73; hydrologist City of Memphis, 1973—. Cons., Water Resource Devel. Served with USNR, 1943-46; served with AUS, 1950-52. Recipient Achievement award, 1962, Writers award, 1970, Spl. Achievement award Soil Conservation Service, U.S. Dept. Agr., 1971. Registered profl. engr., Tenn. Mem. Am. Soc. C.E., Am. Pub. Works Assn. Methodist. Contbr. profl. jours. Home: 2462 Inverary Dr Memphis TN 38138 Office: City Hall 125 N Main St Memphis TN 38103

BUSHA, CHARLES HENRY, librarian; b. Library, S.C., Dec. 14, 1931; s. James Henry and Rosa Anna (Anderson) B.; B.A., Furman U., 1958; M.L.S., Rutgers U., 1961; Ph.D., Ind. U., 1971. Tchr., Berea High Sch., Greenville, S.C., 1958; library intern Greenville County Library, 1958-60, head tech. services, 1961-62, reference librarian, 1963; reference cons. S.C. Library Bd., Columbia, 1963-67; fellow Grad. Library Sch., Ind. U., 1967-70, lectr. univ., 1970-71, asst. prof., 1971-73; asso. prof. U. South Fla., Tampa, 1973—. Served to 2d lt. AUS, 1951-54; served to capt. S.C. N.G., 1954-67. Mem. A.L.A., Bibliog. Soc. Am., Southeastern, Fla. library assns., Friends of Hillsborough County (Fla.) Library, Beta Phi Mu, Tau Kappa Epsilon. Democrat. Unitarian-Universalist. Author: Freedom versus Suppression and Censorship, 1972. Contbr. articles to profl. jours. Home: 8708 N 50th St Tampa FL 33617

BUSHELMAN, TED JOSEPH, airport exec.; b. Lakeside Park, Ky., Jan. 30, 1936; s. Steve William and Irene (Egnor) B.; E.E., Ohio Mechanics Inst., 1956; B.S. in Radio, TV Prodn., Cin. Coll. Conservatory Music, 1959; B.S. in Edn., U. Cin., 1958; m. Marlene Haskell Apr. 26, 1960 (div.); children—Kimberly TeDene, Ted J. III. Producer, dir. WKRC-TV Cin., 1956-60; v.p. engring. KIOO radio, Oklahoma City, 1960-63; gen. mgr. WKKY radio, Erlanger, Ky., 1963-67; dir. community relations Greater Cin. Airport, 1967—. Vice chmn. Transit Authority No. Ky., 1971—; chmn. Boone County Library Bd., 1973—; tng. officer No. Ky. chpt. United Appeal, 1972—. Bd. dirs., mem. adv. bd. No. Ky. Salvation Army, 1974—; bd. dirs. No. Ky. Conv. Bur., 1974—, Cin. chpt. A.R.C., 1974—. Named Outstanding Young Man No. Ky., Ky. Post & Time Star, 1968; One of Five Top Pub. Relations Mem Greater Cin., WKKY Radio, 1970. Mem. Greater Cin. (pub. relations com.) No. Ky. (pres. 1973, dir.), Ky. chambers commerce, Boone County (past pres.), Ky. jr. chambers commerce, Boone County Businessmen's Assn. (pres. 1974—), Airport Operations Council Internat. (chmn. pub. relations), Pub. Relations Soc. Am. (dir.). Home: 107 Jo Ann Dr Florence KY 41042 Office: PO Box 75000 Cincinatti OH 45275

BUSHEY, HAROLD LEROY, physician; b. Olivet, Ill., Oct. 15, 1927; s. Clinton J. and Lilliam (Skow) B.; A.B., U. Ill., 1950; M.D., U. Rochester, 1954; m. Eulene Bell, Aug. 24, 1949; children—Susan Kay, William J., Kathleen. Intern Crawford W. Long Meml. Hosp., Atlanta, 1954-55; resident Usvamtgh Hosp., Memphis, 1955-56, C.W. Long Meml. Hosp., Atlanta, 1956-58; practice medicine, specializing in internal medicine, Barbourville, Ky., 1958—; mem. staff Knox County Gen. Hosp. Mem. Knox County Bd. Health, 1962—. Bd. dirs. Daniel Boone Festival, Henderson Settlement, Frakes, Ky. Served with USNR, 1946-47. Recipient Outstanding Citizens award Knox County C. of C., 1973. Mem. Ky. Med. Assn. (trustee 15 dist.), A.M.A., Knox County C. of C., Nat. Rifle Assn., Ky. Long Riflemen, Am. Numis. Assn., Phi Beta Kappa. Lion. Club: Barbourville Garden. Home: Route 3 Box 13 Barbourville KY 40906 Office: PO Box 770 Barbourville KY 40906

BUSHNELL, DAVID SHERMAN, assn. exec.; b. Whittier, Cal., Jan. 7, 1927; s. David Sherman and Lillian (Dudley) B.; Ph.B., U. Chgo., 1947, M.A., 1950; postgrad. (Research fellow) U. Wash., 1951-53; m. Alice Mencher, Aug. 14, 1965; children—Beckie Lynn, Kimberlie Anne, Karin Jo. Asst. study dir. U. Mich. Survey Research Center, 1953-55; mgmt. communications cons., corporate staff IBM Corp., N.Y.C., 1955-61; research sociologist Stanford Research Inst., Menlo Park, Cal., 1961-64; research dir. U.S. Office Edn., 1964-69; advance study fellow Battelle Meml. Inst., Washington, 1969-70; research dir. Am. Assn. Jr. Colls., Washington, 1970-72; dir. program devel. Human Resources Research Orgn., Alexandria, Va., 1972—. Cons. local, state depts. edn., colls. and univs.; vis. lectr. U. Washington Sch. Bus. Adminstrn., summer 1955, vis. prof. Ohio State U. Grad. Sch. Edn., 1970. Chmn. UN Week, Rochester, Minn., 1957; chmn. edn. com., bd. dirs. Rochester Art Center, 1957-61; pres. Rochester Personnel Assn.; mem. adv. bd. Empire State Coll., Antioch Coll. Served with USNR, 1945-46. Fellow Am. Sociol. Soc.; mem. Am. Ednl. Research Assn., Am. Psychol. Assn., Am. Vocational Assn., A.A.A.S. Author: Planned Change in Education; Organizing for Change: New Priorities for Community Colleges. Editorial bd. Jour. Human Resources, 1966-71. Home: 9620 Hawick Lane Kensington MD 20795 Office: 300 N Washington St Alexandria VA 22314

BUSKUHL, CLIFFORD JOE, architect; b. Blackwell, Okla., Sept. 26, 1940; s. Henry Benjamin and Myrtle (Ingraham) B.; student No. Okla. Jr. Coll., 1958-59; B.Arch., Okla. U., 1964; m. Jayne Bellmon, Aug. 24, 1962; children—Jill Angela, Mark Harrison. Architect, firm Harwood K. Smith & Partners, Dallas, 1968—. Served to lt. C.E., AUS, 1966-68. Decorated Bronze Star medal. Mem. Christian Ch. Home: 6434 Tulip Lane Dallas TX 75230 Office: 2902 Southland Center Dallas TX 75201

BUSSARD, RICHARD EARL, newspaper editor; b. Jacksonville, Fla., Dec. 14, 1934; s. Ernest H. and Mary Gladys (Davis) B.; grad. high sch.; m. Billee A. Neumann, Aug. 6, 1967; children—Sheryl Anne, Clifford Ernest, Tiffany Louise. Sports editor Leesburg (Va.) Daily Commercial, 1953-54; editor, pub. weekly Ocean Beach Reporter, Jacksonville Beach, 1955-57; city editor Jacksonville Jour., 1961—; pres. Poor Richard's Restaurants, Inc., Jacksonville Beach; owner Holiday Shop, Jacksonville Beach. Home: 803 5th Av N Jacksonville Beach FL 32250 Office: One Riverside Av Jacksonville FL 32201

BUSSART, WALTER WOODS, lawyer; b. Lewisburg, Tenn., Apr. 16, 1942; s. Christopher Leo and Mary Gertrude (Woods) B.; B.S. in Bus. Adminstrn., U. Tenn., 1965; J.D., 1966; m. Linda Dell Bailey, June 10, 1965. Admitted to Tenn. bar, 1966; legal research asst. to justice Tenn. Supreme Ct., Nashville, 1966-67; partner Lloyd & Bussart, Lewisburg, 1967-73; pvt. practice Walter Woods Bussart, Lewisburg, 1973—. Mem. Tenn. Army N.G., 1966—. Mem. Am., Tenn. bar assns., Am., Tenn. trial lawyers assns., C. of C., Alpha Tau Omega, Phi Delta Phi. Elk, Rotarian. Home: 434 4th Av S Lewisburg TN 37091 Office: W Court Sq Lewisburg TN 37091

BUSSE, EWALD WILLIAM, psychiatrist; b. St. Louis, Aug. 18, 1917; s. Frederick Ewald and Emily Louise (Stroh) B.; A.B., Westminister Coll., 1938; M.D., Washington U., 1942; D.Sc., Westminster Coll. 1960;; m. Ortrude Helen Schnaedelbach, July 18,

1941; children—Ortrude Susan (Mrs. White), Barbara Ann, Ewald Richard, Deborah Emily. Intern St. Louis City Hosp., 1942-43; asst. neurology Washington U., 1942-43; chief resident Colo. Psychopathic Hosp., 1946-48; chief electroencephalography U. Colo. Med. Center, 1946-53, instr. U. Colo., 1946-47, asst. prof., 1947, asso. prof., 1948-50, prof., head psychosomatic medicine, 1950-53; didactic psychoanalysis, 1948-50; prof. Duke Sch. Medicine, 1953—. J.P. Gibbons prof. psychiatry 1966—, chmn. dept. psychiatry, 1953—, dir. Center for Study of Aging and Human Devel., 1957-70; chief staff Duke Hosp., 1972-74; cons. neuropsychiatry VA, AUS, USAF, USPHS. Served as maj. AUS, 1943-46, chief electroencephalography, asst. chief neuropsychiat. service. Recipient Edward Allen award Am. Geriatrics Soc., 1967; Strecker award Inst. Pa. Hosp., 1967; Robert Kleemeier research award, Gerontol. Soc., 1968; William C. Menninger Meml. award, 1971; Modern Medicine award 1972. Diplomate Am. Bd. Psychiatry and Neurology (dir., sec.-treas. 1961-69). Fellow A.C.P. (William C. Menninger award 1971), Am. Psychiat. Assn. (v.p. 1966-67; pres. 1971-72), Am. Coll. Psychiatrists, Gerontol. Soc. (pres. 1967); mem. Assn. Research in Mental and Nervous Diseases, Am. Psychopath. Assn., N.C. Neuropsychiat. Assn., Am. Geriatrics Soc. (pres. elect 1974-75), Am. Psychosomatic Soc., Am. Orthopsychiat. Assn., Eastern, Central electroencephalographic socs., A.M.A., So. Electronencephalographic Assn., Am. Assn. Chmn. Depts. Psychiatry (pres. 1973-74), So. Psychiat. Assn., Sigma Xi, Phi Delta Theta, Phi Beta Pi, Omicron Delta Kappa. Mason, Rotarian (pres. Durham club 1972-73). Contbr. sci. articles profl. publs. Home: 1132 Woodburn Rd Durham NC 27705 Office: Duke U Med Center Durham NC 27710

BUSSELL, OPP, JR., educator; b. Mt. Vernon, Ky., July 5, 1922; s. Opp and Mazy (McClure) B.; B.S., Eastern Ky. U., 1949, M.A., 1964, postgrad., 1966; postgrad. U. Ky., 1968. Capt., Millersburg Military Inst., Millersburg, Ky., 1950-54; prin. Williamstown Independent Sch., (Ky.), 1965-67; prin. Falmouth High Sch., 1967-68; instructional supr. Anderson County Schs., Lawrenceburg, Ky., 1968—. Chmn., Rockcastle County (Ky.) Heart Fund Assn., 1965; spl. adviser to mayor of City of Frankfort, Ky., 1971-74. Served with AUS, 1941-45. Named Ky. col., adm., commodore; Ark. Traveler; hon. citizen Tex., Tenn., W.Va., Mo., Md. Mem. Okla., Ky. (outstanding teaching award 1964) edn. assns., Mass. Order of Paul Revere Patriots, Brotherhood of Colo. Mountain Men, N.C. Order of Longleaf Pine, Ky. Hist. Soc., Ky. Civil War Round Table, Phi Delta Kappa. Mason (32 deg.), Rotarian. Author: The Boone Way Man, 1971. Home: Box 202 Mount Vernon KY 40456 Office: 202 E Woodford St Lawrenceburg KY 40342

BUSSEY, THOMAS PATRICK, state justice; b. Parksville, S.C., May 7, 1905; s. John Morgan and Lillie Mobley (Connor) B.; LL.B., U. S.C., 1927; m. Louise McKelvey Florence, Dec. 6, 1931; 1 dau., Patricia B. Wheeler; stepson, Quinton Florence Jr. Admitted to S.C. bar, 1927, and practiced in Charleston until 1958; judge 9th Jud. Circuit S.C., 1958-61; asso. justice Supreme Ct. S.C., 1961—. Mem. Am. Bar Assn. Episcopalian. Mason. Home: 8 Broughton Rd The Crescent Charleston SC 29407 Office: Charleston County Ct House PO Box 326 Charleston SC 29401

BUSTAMANTE, JORGE ISAAC, govt. cons.; b. Mexico City, Jan. 17, 1931; s. Isaac Jorge and Carmen (Ceballos) B.; C.E., UNAM, 1956; M.S. (State Dept. fellow), U. Ill., 1957, Ph.D., 1964; postgrad. Mass. Inst. Tech., 1962, U. Mich., 1967; U. Cal. at Los Angeles, 1964, m. Ana Maria Magaloni, May 4, 1962; children—Jorge Ignacio, Ana del Carmen, Clara Eugenia. Faculty, Nat. U. Mexico, 1952, 55, 57-68, head operations research dept., 1957-68; prof. U. Guanajuato, 1953-54; partner Peat, Marwick, Livingston & Co., Mexico, 1968-69; partner Peat, Marwick, Mitchell & Co., Mgmt. Cons. for Mexico, C.Am., Panama, 1969-73, partner charge govt. cons. for Latin Am., 1973—. U.S. Govt. fellow, summer 1964; Ford Found. fellow, 1965. Mem. Am. Soc. C.E., Operations Research Soc. Am., Inst. Mgmt. Scis., Sociedad Mexicana de Planificacion, Soc. for Long Range Planning, Sigma Xi. Contbr. articles to profl. jours. Home: 728 Agua St Mexico 20 DF Mexico Office: 51 Reforma Mexico 1 DF Mexico

BUSTAMANTE, RODRIGO ANTONIO, physician; b. Cienfuegos, Cuba, Oct. 21, 1921; s. Rodrigo Segundo and Caroline Dominga (Marcayda) B.; B.S., B.A., Cienfuegos Inst., 1938; M.D., Havana (Cuba) U. Sch. Medicine, 1944; m. Sara I. Vianello, July 19, 1953; children—Sara M., Carolina, Rodrigo R., Eduardo, Victor. Intern Havana U. Hosps., 1944-45, resident, 1945-47; practice medicine, specializing in cardiology, Havana, 1950-61, Miami, Fla., 1968—; dir. cardiology dept. Havanna U. Hosp., 1959-61; asst. prof. medicine Marquette U. Sch. Medicine, Milw., 1962-66; chief cardiology sect. Wood VA Hosp., Milw., 1963, Miami VA Hosp., 1966-68; clin. prof. medicine Miami U Sch. Medicine, 1968—. Mem. Fla. Health Planning Council, 1969-70, Fla. Regional Med. Program, 1970-72. Brit. Council scholar, 1947. Diplomate Am. Bd. Internal Medicine, Am. Bd. Cardiovascular Diseases. Fellow A.C.P., Am. Coll. Cardiology, Am. Coll. Chest Physicians; mem. Royal Coll. Physicians. Clubs: Key Biscayne (Fla.) Yacht; Big Five (Miami). Contbr. articles to profl. publs. Author: (with others) Primer of Cardiac Catherization, 1964. Home: 320 Harbor Ct Key Biscayne FL 33149 Office: 495 Biltmore Way Coral Gables FL 33134

BUSWELL, ARTHUR WILCOX, physician, surgeon; b. Oklahoma City, Jan. 6, 1926; s. Albert Currier and Enid May (Scott) B.; B.Sc., U. Okla., 1950, M.D., 1952; m. Loieta JoAnn Sherrill, June 11, 1950; children—Arthur Lee, Robert Joseph, Barbara JoAnn, Brian A., Gayla, Richard; m. 2d, Jane Marie Fuksa, Mar. 1, 1969. Intern Fitzsimons Army Hosp. Aurora, Colo., 1952-53; surg. resident Wesley Hosp., Oklahoma City, 1954-55; practice medicine and surgery, Hennessey, Okla., 1955-63; dep. surgeon, Fort Wainwright and Yukon Command, 1963-65; chief staff Kingfisher, (Okla.) Community Hosp., 1956-57; supt. health Kingfisher County, 1960-61; chief profl. service Bassett Army Hosp., 1963-65; div. surgeon 1st Armored Div., Ft. Hood, Tex., 1965-67, 1st Inf. Div., 1967-68; med. project officer U.S. Army Combat Devels. Command, Experimentation Command, Ft. Ord. Cal., 1968-72, also chief human factors div. and chief experimentation div. of experimentation command; chief profl. services Reynolds Army Hosp., Ft. Sill, Okla., 1972-73; comdr. med. dept. activities Ft. Stewart, Ga., 1973—; adj. asst. prof. med. scis. Baylor U., 1973—. Served with AUS, 1944-46, 1st lt. U.S. Army, 1952-54, maj. to col., 1961—. Decorated Legion of Merit with oak leaf cluster, Soldier's medal, Bronze Star for Valor with oak leaf cluster, Air medal with 3 oak leaf clusters, Army Commendation medal; Gallantry cross with palm, Honor medal 1st class (both Vietnam). Fellow Royal Soc. Health; mem. Am., Okla. State (mem. ho. dels), Aerospace, Army Aviation (charter) med. assns., Assn. Mil. Surgeons U.S., Garfield-Kingfisher County Med. Soc. Home: Route 5 Kingfisher OK 73750 also US Army Med Dept Activities Ft Stewart GA 31313

BUTCHER, JANET RUTH JASPER (MRS. NORMAN LEE BUTCHER), savs. and loan assn. exec.; b. Van Lear, Ky., Jan. 11, 1936; d. Charles H. and Mary Martha (Conley) Jasper; student Mayo Vocation Sch., 1953-54; m. Norman Lee Butcher, Aug. 11, 1960; 1 dau., Teri Leigh. With 1st Fed. Savs. & Loan Assn., Paintsville, Ky., 1954—, asst. sec., 1969—, asst. treas., head teller, 1973—. Owner Tiger Restaurant, Paintsville, 1972-73. Mem. Ch. of Christ. Home: PO Box 369 Paintsville KY 41240 Office: 103 Main St Paintsville KY 41240

BUTCHER, ROBERT KIMBERLIN, advt. exec.; b. Harrodsburg, Ind., Feb. 9, 1910; s. Ralph E. and Hattie (Kimberlin) B.; student Okla. A. and M. Coll., 1927-29; m. Joanna Van Smith, May 10, 1936; children—Phillip Hurxthal, John Kimberlin. Pres., Robert K. Butcher & Assos., Inc., Shreveport, La., 1952—. Mem. Pub. Relations Soc. Am., Am. Assn. Advt. Agys., Nat. Press Club, Am. Gas Assn., So. Gas Assn. Democrat. Episcopalian. Home: 921 Unadilla St Shreveport LA 71106 Office: PO Box 1 Slattery Bldg Shreveport LA 71161

BUTLER, BROADUS NATHANIEL, assn. exec.; b. Mobile, Ala., May 28, 1920; s. John Nathaniel and Mary Lillian (Broadus) B.: B.A., Talladega Coll., 1941; M.A., U. Mich., 1947, Ph.D., 1951; m. Lillian Rutherford, Dec. 27, 1947; children—Bruce Nathaniel, Janet Cecile. Instr., St. Augustine's Coll., Raleigh, N.C., 1953; dean guidance, asst. prof. humanities Talladega (Ala.) Coll., 1953-56; asst. to dean Wayne State U., Detroit, 1956-57, grad. officer, 1957-64, adminstr., 1968-69; asst. to U.S. commr. edn., also spl. asst. to asso. commr. for higher edn., Washington, 1964-67; dean Coll. Liberal Arts, Tex. So. U., Houston, 1969; pres. Dillard U., New Orleans, 1969-73; dir. Office Leadership Devel. in Higher Edn., Am. Council on Edn., Washington, 1974—. Dir. New Orleans br. Fed. Res. Bank. Mem. La. Mus. Commn., 1971-73, La. Ednl. Television Authority, 1970-74, La. Commn. on Performing Arts, 1970—, Mayors Com. on Internat. Trade Relations, 1971-73. Bd. dirs. Internat. Trade Mart, 1971—, New Orleans Symphony, 1970—, Nat. Merit Scholarship Corp., 1970—, Flint Goodrige Hosp., 1969-73, Gulf South Research Inst., 1969—, Cemrel, Inc., 1970—; chmn. bd. grad. advs. Meharry Med. Coll., Nashville, 1971—. Served with USAAF, 1942-45; MTO. Decorated grand comdr. Order Star of Africa (Liberia); recipient Hon. Citizen award City of New Orleans, 1970, City of Mobile, 1970. Mem. New Orleans C. of C. (dir. 1972—), Sigma Pi Phi, Omega Psi Phi. Club: Cosmos (Washington). Home: 10014 Branch View Ct Silver Spring MD 20903 Office: American Council on Education One Dupont Circle Washington DC 20036

BUTLER, BRUCE, JR., surgeon; b. Pitts., Aug. 4, 1929; s. Bruce and Elizabeth (Truitt) B.; B.S., Franklin and Marshall Coll., 1951; M.D., George Washington U., 1955; m. Mary Eleanor Osborn, Apr. 15, 1954; children—Judy Ann, Bruce Alan, Lawrence Todd, Daniel Leonard, James Steele, Mary Beth. Intern, orthopaedic resident Walter Reed Gen. Hosp., 1955-60, hand surgery residency, 1961, chief hand surgery, asst. chief orthopaedic surgery, 1964-67; asst. chief orthopaedic surgery Madigan Gen. Hosp., Tacoma, 1962-64; chief, hand surgery D.C. Gen. Hosp., 1967—; asso. prof. orthopaedic soc. Howard U., Washington, 1967—; cons. orthopaedic surgery VA Hosp., Washington, 1965—, USPHS, Washington, Surgeon Gen. U.S. Army, Kimbrough Army Hosp., Ft. Meade, Md.; attending surgeon hand surgery Arlington County Crippled Children's Clinic; team physician Washington Ambassadors Football Club, 1974—. Served with M.C., AUS, 1955-67. Diplomate Am. Bd. Orthopaedic Surgery. Fellow A.C.S.; mem. Am. Acad. Orthopaedic Surgeons, Am. Soc. for Surgery of Hand, Assn. Mil. Surgeons. Contbr. articles to profl. jours. Home: 2625 E Meridith Dr Vienna VA 22180 Office: 5021 Seminary Rd Alexandria VA 22311

BUTLER, EDWARD FRANKLYN, securities firm exec.; b. Memphis, July 1, 1937; s. Oliver John and Arlene (Lovelace) B.; B.A. in Polit. Sci., U. Miss., 1958; J.D. (Ford Found. scholar), Vanderbilt U., 1961; m. Donna Gay Cox, Jan. 29, 1965; children—Edward Franklyn II, Jeffrey Darrell. Admitted to Tenn. bar, 1961, Tex. bar, 1973; practice law, 1961-71; with law firm Nelson, Norvell, Wilson & Thomason, Memphis, 1961-63; partner Cobb & Butler, Memphis, 1963-67, Butler & McDowell, Memphis, 1967-72; sec., gen. counsel, exec. officer firm Hibbard, O'Connor & Weeks, Houston, 1971—, also dir.; gen. counsel Communications Assos., also Mid Am. Ins. Agy., Inc., both Houston, 1973—; officer, dir. Safety First Fire Control Co., Inc., Memphis, 1961—; partner Law Realty Co., Memphis, 1963—. Lectr. dept. polit. sci. Memphis State U., 1964-65; spl. judge City Memphis, 1965-72. Mem. Shelby County Sheriff's Adv. Com., 1965-72, Memphis Mayor's Adv. Com., 1965-72. Trustee Hibbard, O'Connor & Weeks Charitable Found. Served with USAF, Res., 1954-62; now lt. comdr. Res., USNR. Recipient Gold Key Man award Memphis Jr. C. of C. 1964, City Key, Memphis, 1973; named Ky. Col., 1971, Tenn. Col., 1968. Mem. Tex. State Bar (mem. exec. council mil. law), Am., Tenn., Houston, Memphis Jr.(past dir.) bar assns., Memphis Trial Lawyers Assn. (past dir.), Houston C. of C. (mil. affairs com., dep. chmn. for navy), Navy League, Navy Res. Assn., Res. Officers Assn. (v.p. chpt.), Mortgage Bankers Assn. Am., banking assns. Tex. and other states, Phi Delta Phi, Sigma Chi. Mason (Shriner). Clubs: Dad's YMCA (Houston). Home: 310 Gentilly Pl Houston TX 77024 Office: 1300 Main St Houston TX 77002

BUTLER, HERBERT HARRISS, govt. ofcl.; b. Ada, O., Oct. 11, 1906; s. Herbert R. and Orienne (Harriss) B.; A.B., Washington Lee U., 1928; postgrad. Johns Hopkins, 1931-32; m. Vera E. Buck, Dec. 31, 1932; children—Herbert H., Jon T. Mgr. brs. C & P Telephone Co., Washington, Balt., 1928-41; pres., gen. mgr. Ill. Telephone Co., Bloomington, 1946-53; v.p., gen. mgr. Commonwealth Telephone Co., Dallas, Pa., 1954-61; sec., dir. govt. relations U.S. Ind. Telephone Assn., Washington, 1962-72; adminstrv. asst. to Congressman Lawrence J. Hogan 5th dist. Md., 1972—. Served with AUS, 1941-45. Decorated Legion Merit. Mem. Ind. Telephone Pioneer Assn. (sec. 1964-72), Phi Beta Kappa, Delta Upsilon. Rotarian. Home: 1612 22d St S Arlington VA 22202 Office: 1204 Longworth House Office Bldg Washington DC 20515

BUTLER, JACK BANKS, banker; b. Corsicana, Tex., May 5, 1940; s. Clark Earl and Hatcher Floy (Banks) B.; B.A., Baylor U., 1962; postgrad. So. Meth. U., 1969; m. Sandra Kay Styles, Apr. 17, 1966; children—Brian Samuel, Kevin Matthew. Adminstrv. asst. Southwestern Life Ins. Co., Dallas, 1962-66; area life spl. agt. Floyd West & Co., Dallas, 1966-67; asst. cashier State Nat. Bank, Corsicana, Tex., 1967-69, v.p., 1969; v.p. Huntsville (Tex.) Nat. Bank, 1969—. Drive chmn. Heart Fund, 1968, Huntsville United Fund, 1971. Bd. dirs. Community Concert Bd., 1969, Huntsville Meml. Hosp., 1973. Named Jaycee of the Year, 1968. Mem. Am. Quarterhorse Assn. (life), Houston Livestock Show and Rodeo (life), Bank Marketing Assn., Huntsville C. of C. (pres. 1973). Baptist (ordained deacon 1969—). Mason (Shriner), Kiwanian. Home: Old Riverside Rd Huntsville TX 77340 Office: PO Box 272 Huntsville TX 77340

BUTLER, JACK LAWRENCE, newspaper editor; b. Seymour, Tex., Oct. 21, 1917; s. Wash Cain and Margaret (Lawrence) B.; B.J., U. Tex., 1939; m. Mary Louise Ford, Oct. 26, 1940; children—Lawrence Ford, Helen Lynn (Mrs. David Hays). Mng. editor Tyler (Tex.) Morning Telegraph, 1940, Gladewater (Tex.) Tribune, 1940-41; news editor Austin (Tex.) Tribune, 1942-43; with Ft. Worth Star-Telegram, 1943—, city editor, 1951-54, news editor, 1954-58, asst. mng. editor, 1958-63, editor, 1963—. Bd. dirs. Tex. Christian U. Research Found.; trustee So. Meth. U., 1972—. Served with USNR, 1944-45. Mem. Am. Soc. Newspaper Editors, Sigma Delta Chi (pres. Tex. Assn. 1956). Home: 1613 Scenery Hill Rd Fort Worth TX 76103 Office: 400 W 7th St Fort Worth TX 76102

BUTLER, JESSE WILLARD, lawyer; b. Telico Plains, Tenn., June 15, 1924; s. William M. and Clara R. (Payne) B.; J.D., U. Tenn., 1950; m. Betty M. Butler. Admitted to Tenn. bar, 1950; head legal drafting dept. Roane-Anderson Co., 1951-52; gen. practice law, 1953—; partner Greene & Butler, 1955—; municipal judge City of Knoxville, 1966—; sec. Cherokee Aviation Aircraft Co. Bd. dirs. Knoxville Area Council on Alcoholism, Municipal Court Com. on Alcohol, Gideon, M. Jellinek Center. Served with A.C., AUS, 1943-45. Decorated D.F.C., Air medal with three oak leaf clusters. Mem. N. Am. Judges Assn., Knox County Humane Soc., Tenn. Knoxville bar assns. Methodist. Home: 2338 Island Home Av Knoxville TN 37920 Office: 3601 Chapman Hwy Knoxville TN 37920

BUTLER, MANLEY CALDWELL, congressman; lawyer; b. Roanoke, Va., June 2, 1925; A.B., U. Richmond (Va.), 1948; LL.B., U. Va., 1950; m. June Nolde. Chmn. Roanoke City Rep. party, 1960-61; mem. Va. Ho. of Dels., 1962-72, minority leader, 1966-72; mem. 92d-93d Congresses from 6th Dist. Va., 1972—. Mem. Va. State Bar, Am., Roanoke bar assns., Raven Soc., Order of the Coif, Phi Beta Kappa, Tau Kappa Alpha, Omicron Delta Kappa, Phi Gamma Delta. Episcopalian (vestryman). Home: 845 Orchard Rd SW Roanoke VA 24014 Office: Cannon House Office Bldg Washington DC 20515

BUTLER, MARION TYUS, univ. adminstr.; b. Carrollton, Ga., Oct. 3, 1914; s. John Marion and Mary Emma (Tyus) B.; A.B. in Journalism, U. Ga., 1935; M.A., La. State U., 1939, postgrad. U. Wis., 1941; m. Laurie Engenia Walker Reade, Sept. 7, 1946; children—Marion Tyus, Thomas W.; 1 step-son, William W. Reade. Asso. editor Calhoun (Ga.) Times, 1936, Cedartown (Ga.) Standard, 1937; prof. journalism U. Ga., Athens, 1939—, dir. alumni relations, 1956—. Served with AUS, 1943-46; lt. col. Res., ret. Mem. Blue Key, Sphinx, Gridiron, Phi Kappa Phi, Omicron Delta Kappa, Phi Delta Theta, Phi Gamma Mu, Sigma Delta Chi. Editor: Ga. Local Govt. Jour., 1955-58, Ga. Alumni Rec., 1946-56. Home: 108 Inverness Rd Athens GA 30601

BUTLER, MARY LOUISE (MRS. DAVID PHILLIP EDWARDS, SR.), ret. educator; b. Goldsboro, N.C.; d. Alman Holmes and Gatsey Louise (Stanton) Butler; A.B., East Carolina U., 1940; M.Edn. in History, U. N.C. at Chapel Hill, 1961; postgrad. Columbia, 1950, U. Ga., 1965; m. David Phillip Edwards, Sr., June 12, 1973. Tchr. pub. schs., Burlington, N.C., 1941-44, Greensboro, N.C., 1944-46, Charlotte, N.C., 1946-71. Mem. N.C. Fedn. Music Clubs (sec.-treas. So. dist. 1963-67), Charlotte Music Club (chmn. scholarship com. 1957-63, scholarship loan com. 1958-64), D.A.R., Nat., N.C. edn. assns., Nat., N.C., Charlotte depts. of classroom tchrs., Nat., N.C. councils for social studies, Mecklenburg Hist. Assn. (charter mem.). Methodist. Author: A Butler Family History: William Butler, John W. Butler of Sampson County, North Carolina and Their Descendants, 1972. Commenting cons. Critical Incidents in Teaching (Carsini and Howard), 1964. Home: 2320 West Dale Dr Fayetteville NC 28303

BUTLER, PETER JOSEPH, photog. equipment mfg. co. exec.; b. Dublin, Ireland, July 28, 1925; s. Joseph and Ann (Hill) B.; student Glasgow (Scotland) Sch. Accountancy, London (Eng.) Sch. Accountancy, 1946-51; B.B.A., Iona Coll., New Rochelle, N.Y., 1963; certificate George Washington U. Coll. Gen. Studies, 1968; m. Evelyn Caldwell, Sept. 28, 1949; children—Cherly Ann, Peter Joseph, Patricia F. Came to U.S., 1953, naturalized, 1959. Asst. mgr. cost, planning Northam Warren Corp., Stamford, Conn., 1953-57; mgr. marketing adminstrn. AMF Corp., Greenwich, Conn., 1957-64, York, Pa., 1964-65; v.p., treas. LogEtronics Inc., Springfield, Va., 1965—. Sec. treas. Lakeland Hills Assn., Ridgefield, Conn., 1962-64, Pack 997 Cub Scouts Am., Mount Vernon, Va., 1969-71. Mem. Adminstrv. Mgmt. Soc., Nat. Contracts Mgmt. Assn., Am. Mgmt. Assn., Washington Bd. Trade, Fairfax County C. of C., Ancient Order Hiberians. K.C. Clubs: Irish American (Washington); Mansion House Yacht (treas., dir. 1970—) (Mount Vernon). Home: 9325 Maybrook Pl Alexandria VA 22309 Office: 7001 Loisdale Rd Springfield VA 22150

BUTLER, ROBERT NEIL, psychiatrist; b. N.Y.C., Jan. 21, 1927; s. Fred and Easter (Dikeman) B.; B.A., Columbia, 1949, M.D., 1953; m. Diane McLaughlin, Sept. 2, 1950; children—Ann Christine, Carole Melissa, Cynthia Lee. Intern St. Lukes Hosp., N.Y.C., 1953-54; resident U. Cal. Langley Porter Clinic, 1954-55, Nat. Inst. Mental Health, 1955-56; research psychiatrist Nat. Inst. Mental Health, USPHS, 1955-62; founder geriatric unit Chestnut Lodge, 1958, adminstr., 1958-59; research psychiatrist Washington (D.C.) Sch. Psychiatry, 1962—. Mem. faculty George Washington U. Med. Sch., Washington, 1962—, Howard U. Sch. Medicine; cons. Nat. Inst. Mental Health, 1967—, U.S. Senate Spl. Com. on Aging. Sec. Nat. Ballet of Washington, 1962—, trustee, 1962—; chmn. D.C. Adv. Commn. on Aging, 1969—; bd. dirs. Nat. Council on Aging. Served with U.S. Maritime Service, 1945-47. Fellow Am. Psychiat. Assn., Am. Geriatrics Soc.; mem. Group for Advancement Psychiatry (trustee), Gerontol. Soc. Club: Cosmos (Washington). Author: (with others) Human Aging, 1963; (with Myrna I. Lewis) Aging and Mental Health, 1973; Why Survive? Old Age in America, 1974. Mem. editorial bd. Jour. Geriatric Psychiatry Aging and Human Devel. Contbr. articles to publs. Address: 3815 Huntington St NW Washington DC 20015

BUTLER, WENDELL HARDING, dentist; b. Carthage, Tex., Oct. 12, 1924; s. Thomas Butler and Inez (Black) B.; student Prairie View Coll., 1941-44; D.D.S., Howard U., 1949; m. Susie Sparrow, June 18, 1949; children—Wanda Marie, Karen Diane, Carol Diane, Susan Jean. Instr. Howard U., Washington, 1950-51; pvt. practice dentistry, Roanoke, Va., 1953—. Dir., sec., treas. Northwest Roanoke Corp., 1965—. Bd. dirs. Hunton YMCA. Commr. Roanoke Redevel. and Housing Authority, 1968-70, Blue Ridge Ednl. TV Assn., 1973—; mem. Roanoke City Sch. Bd. 1970—, vice-chmn., 1973—. Roanoke City Democratic committeeman, 1970—; mem. Va. Dem. Central Com., 1972—. Served to capt. USAF, 1951-53. Mem. Am. Dental Assn., Omega Psi Phi. Mason. Home: 2118 Andrews Rd Roanoke VA 24017 Office: 721 11th St NW Roanoke VA 24017

BUTLER, WENDELL (PACE), state ofcl.; b. Sulphur Well, Ky., Dec. 18, 1912; s. Henry and Pearl (Pace) B.; A.B., Western Ky. State Coll., 1936; M.A., U. Ky., 1950, postgrad., 1951; m. Edna Ford, Jan. 15, 1947; children—Rendell and Kendell (twins), Wendell Ford. Tchr. pub. schs.—Metcalfe County, Ky., 1931-36, supt. schs., 1938-42; supt. pub. instrn., Ky. Dept. Edn., 1952-55, 60-63; commr. agr. Commonwealth of Ky., 1964-67, 72—, supt. pub. instrn., 1968-71. Pres., mgr. School Service Co., Frankfort, Ky. 1956-59. Mem. Ky. State Senate, 1947-51, mem. com. on edn., 1950. Served with USNR, World War II. Mem. Nat., Ky. edn. assns., Farm Bur., Am. Legion, V.F.W., Phi Delta Kappa, Kappa Delta Pi. Methodist. Mason. Home: 121 Crittendon Rd Frankfort KY 40601 Office: State Dept Agr Frankfort KY 40601

BUTRUILLE, DANIEL CLAUDE, chemist; educator; b. Reims, France, Oct. 8, 1944; s. Edmond Alexis and Louise Francoise (Ducancel) B.; Licence in Chemistry, U. Paris (France), 1964; Chem. Engring., E.S.C.O.M., Paris, 1961-65; Ph.D. (France-Que. fellow), Laval U., Quebec, Can., 1968; m. Virginia Martinez Torres, Jan. 29,

1970; children—Gabriela, Etienne. Prof. chemistry Instituto Technologico y de Estudios Superiores de Monterrey (Mexico), 1968—. Rep., French Sci. Center in Mexico, Monterrey. Mem. Mexican, French chem. socs., French Civil Engrs. Soc., Franco-Mexican Assn. Engrs. Editor: Revista lationo-americana de quimica, 1973—. Contbr. articles to profl. jours.

BUTSON, KEITH DARROW, climatologist, hydrologist; b. Geneva, Ia., Aug. 15, 1920; s. Percy Snow and Amelia W. (Laipple) B.; B.S., Upper Ia. U., 1941; M.S., Ia. State U., 1947; m. Margaret Alice Boggess, Sept. 2, 1950; children—Linda C., Marian A. Salesman, Rath Packing Co., Waterloo, Ia., 1941-43; climatologist U.S. Weather Bur., Washington, 1946-47, 55-56, hydrologist, Portland, Ore., 1947-55, climatologist, Gainesville, Fla., 1956-66; with Nat. Climatic Center, Asheville, N.C., 1966—, exec. officer, 1973—. Served with USAAF, 1942-47. Home: 141 Windsor Rd Asheville NC 28804 Office: Nat Climatic Center Fed Bldg Asheville NC 28801

BUTT, HOWARD EDWARD, supermarket exec.; b. Memphis, Apr. 9, 1895; s. Charles C. and Florence (Thornton) Butt; student pub. schs.; m. Mary Elizabeth Holdsworth, Dec. 5, 1924; children—Howard Edward, Charles C., Margaret Eleanor (Mrs. William H. Crook). Chmn. bd. H. E. Butt Grocery Co., Corpus Christi, Tex., 1920—; operator H.E.B. Food Stores, Tex., 1920—. Baptist. Mason (33 deg.). Home: 3700 Ocean Dr Corpus Christi TX 78411 Office: 807 N Broadway Corpus Christi TX 78408

BUTT, LILLIAN STUART, educator; b. nr. Abingdon, Va., Nov. 25, 1901; d. Charles Henry and Josephine (Bailey) Butt; student Martha Washington Coll., 1919-20, Va. Intermont Coll., 1920-21; B.S., U. Va., 1929, M.S., 1936; summer study U. Wash., 1939. Tchr., Abingdon, Va., 1921-36, Charlottesville, Va., 1936-68, supervising tchr. dept. edn. U. Va., 1950-68; now ret.; chmn. social studies dept. Lane High Sch., 1953-64. Sponsor Jr. Red Cross, 1940-59; mem. youth in govt. com. Va. dist. YMCA. Recipient Valley Forge Classroom Tchrs. medal, 1959; Jeweled Tri-Hi-Y pin, 1951, YMCA plaque for service to youth, 1956, 66. Mem. D.A.R., U.D.C., Washington County, Albermarle hist. socs., Va. Charlottesville (pres. 1955-57) edn. assns., Va. Council for Social Studies (exec. bd. mem.), English-Speaking Union, Johnston Meml. Hosp. Aux., Wesleyan Service Guild, Nat. Ret. Tchrs. Assn., Delta Kappa Gamma. Democrat. Methodist. Club: Booklovers. Home: 363 Bradley St Abingdon VA

BUTT, THOMAS FRANKLIN, judge; b. Eureka Springs, Ark., Mar. 26, 1917; s. Festus O. and Esther (Cox) B.; J.D., U. Ark., 1938; m. Cecilia King, Apr. 25, 1942; children—Thomas King, Martin Andrew, William Jackson II. Admitted to Ark. bar, 1938, U.S. Supreme Ct. bar, 1955, Ct. Mil. Appeals, 1968; practiced in Eureka Springs, 1938, Fayetteville, 1939-40, 46-50; title examiner land dept. Carter Oil Co., Mattoon, Ill., 1938-39; prof. law U. Ark., 1939-40; area rent dir., atty. OPA, Fayetteville, 1946-49; chancery and probate judge, Fayetteville, 1951—. Pres. Ark. Jud. Council, 1956-57; mem. West Ark. Area council Boy Scouts Am., 1955-56. Served with AUS, 1940-46; brig. gen. Res. Mem. Am., Ark. (exec. council 1972-74), Washington County bar assns., Res. Officers Assn., Mil. Govt. Assn., Judge Advocate Gen. Assn., C. of C. Methodist. Mason. Club: Fayetteville Country. Home: 1004 Rebecca St Fayetteville AR 72701 Office: Court House Fayetteville AR 72701

BUTTERWORTH, CHARLES EDWIN, JR., educator, physician; b. Lynchburg, Va., Mar. 11, 1923; s. Charles Edwin and Erma Marian (Henry) B.; B.A., U. Va., Charlottesville, 1944, M.D., 1948; m. Joyce Craig, June 20, 1946; children—Charles Edwin III, Jane C., Hugh Craig. Intern, resident Univ. Hosp., Birmingham, Ala., 1948-53; prof. medicine and pediatrics, dir. nutrition program U. Ala. Sch. Medicine, Birmingham, 1958—. Cons. NIH, WHO. Served from capt. to maj. M.C., AUS, 1953-58. Named Distinguished Alumnus U. Va., 1973. Mem. Am. Soc. Clin. Nutrition (pres.), A.M.A. (chmn. Council on Foods and Nutrition), Ala., Jefferson County nutrition councils. Mem. editorial adv. bd. Jour. A.M.A., Nutrition Today, 1973—. Contbr. articles to profl. jours. Home: 3203 Pine Ridge Rd Birmingham AL 35213

BUTTERWORTH, WILLIAM EDMUND, III, author; b. Newark, Nov. 10, 1929; s. William Edmund and Gladys (Schnable) B.; m. Emma Josefa Macalik, July 14, 1950; children—Patricia Olga (Mrs. John A. Hood), William Edmund IV, John Scholefield II. Author: Comfort Me with Love, 1959; Hot Seat, 1960; No French Leave, 1960; Where We Go From Here, 1961; The Love Go Round, 1962; The Loved and The Lost, 1962; Heartbreak Ridge, 1962; Courtmartial, 1962; Hell on Wheels, 1963; The Girl in the Black Bikini, 1963; The Wonders of Astronomy, 1964; Once More With Passion, 1964; Le Falot, 1964; Article 92, Murder-Rape, 1965; The Wonders of Rockets and Missiles, 1965; Doing What Comes Naturally, 1965; L'il Wildcat, 1965; Warrior's Way, 1965; Fast Green Car, 1966; Tiger Rookie, 1966; Make War in Madness, 1966; Stock Car Racer, 1966, Soldiers on Horseback, 1966; The Image Makers, 1967; Helicopter Pilot, 1967; Road Racer, 1967; Bryans' Dog, 1967; Hunger for Racing, 1967; Air Evac, 1967; Fastest Funny Car., 1967; Grand Prix Racing, 1968; Orders to Vietnam, 1968; Maverick on the Mound, 1968; Redline 7100, 1969; Stop and Search, 1969; Up to the Quarterdeck, 1969; The Wheel of a Fast Car, 1969; Racing to Glory, 1969; Stars and Planets, 1969; Grand Prix Driver, 1969; Susan and Her Classic Convertible, 1970; Yankee Boy, 1970; Marty and the Micro-Midgets, 1970; Fast and Smart, 1971; Moving West on 122, 1971; The 12-Cylinder Screamer, 1971; Crazy to Race, 1971; Drag Race Driver, 1971; My Father's Quite a Guy, 1971; Return to Racing, 1971; Wheels and Pistons, 1971; The High Wind, 1971; Flying Army, 1971; Gestern Wir Ich Noch Allein, 1971; Racing Mechanic, 1971; The Sex Traveller, 1971; Flat Out, 1971; Long Ride on a Cycle, 1972; Team Racer, 1972; Dateline: Talladega, 1972; the Race Driver, 1972; the Narc, 1972; Sky Jacked!, 1972; Race Car Team, 1973; Dave White and The Electric Wonder Car, 1974; Tires and Other Things, 1974, Oil!, 1974. Home: PO Drawer Al Fairhope AL 36532 Office: care Paul R Reynolds Inc 599 Fifth Av New York City NY 10017

BUTTON, ROBERT YOUNG, state govt. ofcl.; b. Culpeper, Va., Nov. 2, 1899; s. John Young and Margaret Agnes (Duncan) B.; LL.B., U. Va., 1922; m. Kathleen Mary Antoinette Cheape, Aug. 20, 1931; children—Kathleen Margaret (Mrs. L. H. Ginn), Robert Young. Admitted to Va. bar, 1922; practice in Culpeper, 1922-61, 70—; atty. gen. Va., 1962-70; Dir. Mut. Fire Ins. Co. Loudoun, Mchts. Grocery Co. Culpeper, 2d Nat. Bank Culpeper, Central Hardware Co. Mem. Va. Commns. Pub. Edn., 1954, 59, Potomac River Commn., 1958, Va. Bd. Edn., 1945-60, Va. Parole Bd., 1942-45. Mem. Va. Senate from 27th Dist., 1946-61. Trustee Jamestown Corp. Fellow Am. Coll. Trial Lawyers, Am. Judicature Soc., Va. State Bar (council 1950-56). Am., Va., Richmond City, Culpeper bar assns. Democrat. Baptist. Mason, Rotarian. Clubs: Culpeper Country, Commonwealth (Richmond). Home: Culpeper VA 22701 Office: 139 W Davis St Culpeper VA 22701

BUTTON, WILLIAM GARLAND, utility co. exec.; b. McKinney, Tex., Dec. 1, 1918; s. Augusta Garland and Verba (Jessee) B.; B.S., E. Tex. State U., 1938; postgrad. U. Tex., 1939, 42; m. Margaret Miller, June 1, 1942; children—Betty Jo, Robert and William (twins). Tchr. adminstrn. Lindale (Tex.) High Sch., 1938-41; head dept. bus. adminstrn., sr. counselor Gladewater (Tex.) High Sch., 1941-44; plant accountant Tex. Telephone Co., Sherman, Tex., 1944-45; clk.-asst. v.p. Tex. Power & Light Co., Dallas, 1945-54, Taylor dist. mgr., 1954-55, So. div. mgr., Waco, 1955-61, Eastern div. mgr., Tyler, 1961-64, dir. indsl. devel., Dallas, 1964-66, gen. mgr. operations, Dallas, 1966-67, v.p. in charge operations, 1967—. Chmn. bd. regents E. Tex. State U. Mem. Taylor C. of C., Inter-Univ. Council Dallas, S.A.R., Council Governing Bds. State U. Lambda Chi Alpha. Episcopalian (vestryman, sr. warden). Mason (Shriner). Rotarian. Home: 2121 Abshire Lane Dallas TX 75228 Office: 1511 Bryan St Dallas TX 75222

BUTTS, DAVID PHILLIP, educator; b. Rochester, N.Y., May 9, 1932; s. George A. and Susie B. (Hicks) B.; B.S. in Biol. Sci., Butler U., 1954; M.S. in Sci. Edn., U. Ill., 1960, Ph.D., 1962; m. Velma M. Walton, Aug. 2, 1958; children Carol Sue, Douglas Paul. Ins. cons., Urbana, Ill., 1954-62; faculty sci. edn. Olivet Nazarene Coll., Kankakee, Ill., 1961-62, U. Tex., Austin, 1962-74; chmn. dept. sci. edn. U. Ga., 1974—. Served to capt. USAF, 1954-57. Recipient Nat. Ednl. Testing Service award, 1973. Fellow A.A.A.S.; mem. Nat. Sci. Tchrs. Assn., Assn. Edn. Tchrs. in Sci. (pres. 1973-75). Author: Teaching Science in Elementary School, 1973; The Teaching of Science, A Self Directed Guide, 1974. Home: Deerfield Rd Bogart GA 30622 Office: Dept Sci Edn U Ga Athens GA 30601

BUTTS, JAMES ALLEN, physician; b. Gainesville, Ga., July 6, 1936; s. Hubert L. and Mary Louise (Starr) B.; M.D., Emory U., 1960, postgrad., 1960-61; m. Wynelle Lowery, Sept. 3, 1960; children—James Allen, Lawrence Eugene, Katherine Louise. Resident physician Atlanta VA Hosp., 1963-65; splty. tng. internal medicine Emory U. and Atlanta VA Hosps., 1963-65; fellow hematology and oncology Emory U. Hosp., Atlanta, 1965-66; practice medicine, specializing in internal medicine and hematology, Gainesville, Ga., 1966—; mem. staff Hall County Hosp., Gainesville, chief med. service, 1971-73. Served with USPHS, 1961-63. Diplomate Am. Bd. Internal Medicine, Am. Bd. Med. Oncology. Mem. A.M.A., A.C.P. (asso. mem.), Am. Soc. Hematology, Am. Heart Assn., Med. Assn. Ga. Home: 1732 Valley Rd Gainesville GA 30501 Office: 1114 Vine St Gainesville GA 30501

BUTTS, ULYS RENEAU, engr.; b. Miami, Ariz., Sept. 12, 1918; s. Ulysses Reneau and Zula Beatrice (Jones) B.; student Kilgore (Tex.) Jr. Coll., 1937-39, U. Ark., 1939-40, B.S. in Mech. Engring., U. Houston, 1950; m. Evelyn Glenora Turner, Feb. 19, 1955; 1 son, Richard Alan. Mech. engr. Ellington AFB, 1951-54; mech. engr. pub. works dept. U.S. Naval Air Sta., Corpus Christi, Tex. 1954-55; engring. div. dir., 1955—. Partner, Turner's Tall Fashions. Mem. Nat., Tex. socs. profl. engrs., Soc. Am. Mil. Engrs. Methodist. Home: 526 Catalina Pl Corpus Christi TX 78411 Office: US Naval Air Station Corpus Christi TX 78419

BUTZ, EARL LAUER, govt. ofcl.; b. Albion, Ind., July 3, 1909; s. Herman Lee and Ada Tillie (Lower) B.; B.S.A., Purdue U., 1932, Ph.D., 1937; postgrad. U. Chgo., summer 1936; m. Mary Emma Powell, Dec. 22, 1937; children—William Powell, Thomas Earl. Farmer, Noble County, Ind., 1933; grad. research asst. agrl. econs. Purdue U., Lafayette, Ind., 1934-35, instr. agrl. econs., 1937-39, asst. prof., 1939-43, asso. prof., 1943-46, prof., head agrl. econs. dept., 1946-54, dean agr., 1957-67, dean continuing edn., v.p. Research Found., 1968-71; U.S. sec. agr., 1971—. Research economist Fed. Land Bank, Louisville, 1935-36, Brookings Inst., 1944, 51; research staff Nat. Bur. Econ. Research, 1944-45, lectr. Sch. Banking, U. Wis., 1946-65, Rutgers U., 1950-58; asst. sec. Dept. Agr., 1954-57, dir. CCC. Dir. Standard Life Ins. Co. Ind., 1951-71, Stokely-Van Camp Co., Indpls., 1969-71, Ralston Purina Co., St. Louis, 1958-71, Internat. Minerals & Chem. Corp., Chgo., 1960-71. Chmn. U.S. delegation FAO, Rome, 1955, 57; mem. White House Task Force Fgn. Econ. Devel., 1969-70. Bd. dirs. Farm Found., Chgo., 1960-70, Found. Am. Agr., Washington, 1957-71; trustee Nutrition Found., N.Y.C., 1967-71. Mem. Am. Farm Econ. Assn. (v.p. 1948, sec. treas. 1953-54), Am. Soc. Farm Mgrs. and Rural Appraisers, Ind. Acad. Social Sci. (v.p. 1948), Canadian Am. Com., Internat. Conf. Agrl. Economists, Scabbard and Blade, Skull and Crescent, Sigma Xi, Alpha Gamma Rho (nat. pres. 1948-50), Sigma Delta Chi, Tau Kappa Alpha, Alpha Zeta. Kiwanian. Author: The Production Credit System for Farmers, 1944; various bulls. Address: Dept of Agriculture The Mall between 12th and 14th Sts SW Washington DC 20250

BUTZNER, JOHN DECKER, JR., U.S. circuit judge; b. Scranton, Pa., Oct. 2, 1917; s. John Decker and Bess Mary (Robison) B.; B.A., U. Scranton 1939; LL.B., U. Va., 1941; m. Viola Eleanor Peterson, May 25, 1946; 1 son, John Decker III. Admitted to Va. bar, 1941; practiced in Fredericksburg, 1941-58; judge 15th and 39th Jud. Circuit of Va., 1958-62; U.S. dist. judge Eastern Dist. Va., 1962-67; U.S. circuit judge 4th Circuit, 1967—. Served with USAAF, 1942-45. Home: 5507 Dorchester Rd Richmond VA 23225 Office: PO Box 2188 Richmond VA 23217

BUXBAUM, MARTIN, poet; b. Richmond, Va., June 27, 1912; s. David and Sadie (McGuffin) Noll; student Columbia Tech. Coll., 1934-38; m. Alice Lee Lyons, Sept. 4, 1938; children—Joan (Mrs. Robert Galope), Alice (Mrs. Daniel Dick), Rosemary (Mrs. Samuel D. Redding), Roberta (Mrs. Daniel Walker), Martha (Mrs. Thomas Newpher), Kathleen, Martin, William. Editor, Hechinger Co., Washington, 1933-38; timekeeper Diamond Constrn. Co., Washington, 1938-39; free lance writer, photographer, 1939-41; editor mags. Engring. and Research Corp., Riverdale, Md., 1941-45, So. Dairies, Inc., Washington, 1945-53; became editor Table Talk, Marriott Corp., Washington, 1953, also dir. communications. Recipient George Washington Medal of Honor, 1964, 70, 71, 72, 73; named Poet of Year, State of Md., 1967; Syracuse U. established Martin Buxbaum Manuscript Collection, 1960; Lizette Woodward Reese Poetry award Md. Poetry Soc., 1969; named Ky. col., 1971. Mem. Internat. Platform Assn., Md. Poetry Soc. Author: (poetry) Rivers of Thought, 1958, The Underside of Heaven, 1963; Table Talk for Family Fun, 2 vols., 1964, 73; The Unsung, 1964, vol. II, 1965; The Unbroken Circle, 1964; Whispers in the Wind, 1966; Around Our House, 1968; Once Upon a Dream (poetry), 1970; The Warm World of Martin Buxbaum, 1974; Sing a Song of Sexpence, 1974. Counselor: Sunshine mag., 1970—. Home: 7819 Custer Rd Bethesda MD 20014 Office: 5161 River Rd Washington DC 20016

BUXTON, JAY ALBERTO, educator; b. Carrara, Italy, May 29, 1919; s. Selby Grandfield and Edith Jane (MacNavy) B.; B.S., S.W. Tex. State Tchrs. Coll., 1948; M.A., U. Tex., 1950; Ph.D., Ohio State U., 1957; postgrad. NSF Summer Inst. U. N.C., 1968, U. P.R., 1970, U. Colo., 1973; m. Audrey Elaine Kennedy, Jan. 3, 1946; children—John T., Rebecca L., Cynthia M. Mem. staff Ohio State U. Research Found., Columbus, 1950-51; researcher Battelle Meml. Inst., Columbus, 1952-57; mem. faculty Tex. Coll. Arts and Industries, Kingsville, 1957-61, Clemson (S.C.) U., 1961-67; prof., chmn. dept. biology Catawba Coll., Salisbury, N.C., 1967—. Active Boy Scouts Am., Girl Scouts U.S.A. Served with Armed Forces, 1942-45; ETO. Decorated Air medal; recipient Algernon Sydney Sullivan award, 1973-74, Swink award outstanding teaching, 1973-74. Fellow Ohio Acad. Sci.; mem. Entomol. Soc. Am., Am. Inst. Biol. Scis., A.A.A.S., N.C. Acad. Sci., Am. Assn. U. Profs., Nat. Tchrs. Assn., Sigma Xi. Kiwanian. Research entomology specializing in fruit insects. Home: 204 Prescot Dr Salisbury NC 28144

BUYCK, FRANCES REEDY, civic leader; b. Columbia, S.C., Apr. 27, 1938; d. Francis Crittendon and Rose (Stroman) Reedy; B.A., Converse Coll., 1960; M.B.A., U. S.C., 1962; m. William O. Buyck, Aug. 30, 1967; children—Rose Reedy, William Otis. Mgr. gen. office First Nat. Bank of S.C., Columbia, 1962-64, personnel asst., 1964-66; office mgr., tchr. Wade Hampton Acad., Orangeburg, S.C., 1967-68; dean Sch. Bus., Orangeburg-Calhoun Tech. Edn. Center, 1968-70; dir. Bank of Clarendon, Manning. Chmn. Orangeburg March of Dimes, 1972; mem. Orangeburg Jr. Service League, 1970—, mem. exec. bd., 1972; chmn. S.C. Rose Festival Rose Show, 1972; co-founder puppet troop Creative Factory. Exhibited group art shows in Manning, Summerton, Columbia, Greenville and Spartanburg, S.C. Named an outstanding woman of year, Orangeburg, 1973. Mem. D.A.R., Am. Legion Aux. (girl's state counsellor 1967, 71, bus. mgr. 1972-73), Converse Coll. Alumnae Assn. (pres. Orangeburg 1967), Am. Assn. U. Women, Garden Club S.C. (treas. 1969-71, rec. sec. 1971-73, jr. chmn. 1973—), Orangeburg Council Garden Clubs (treas. 1972). Clubs: Mid-Carolina Gun (sec-treas. 1968-69); Orangeburg Garden (pres. 1972). Address: 1035 Middleton St Orangeburg SC 29115

BUYCK, MARK WILSON, JR., lawyer; b. Columbia, S.C., Dec. 25, 1934; s. Mark Wilson and Mary (Otis) B.; B.A. in Journalism, U. S.C., 1956, J.D., 1959; m. Julia Steele Willcox, June 11, 1960; children—Mark W., III, Julia Johnson, Hugh Willcox. Admitted to S.C. bar, 1959; mem. firm Willcox; Hardee, Palmer, O'Farrell, McLeod & Buyck, Florence, S.C., 1962—. Vis. prof. U. S.C., Florence, 1963-69; founder Florence Times, 1967. Chmn., Florence County Republican party, 1966-68; alternate del. nat. conv., 1968; mem. exec. com. S.C., 1968-72. Mem. adv. bd. John F. Kennedy Center, Washington, 1969—; pres. Florence Little Theatre, 1965-66; mem. state bd. Cancer and Heart Assn., 1965—. Mem. S.C. Bar Assn. (v.p. 1970—), Fedn. Ins. Council; U. S.C. Alumni Assn. (nat. pres. 1969). Rotarian. Home: 1439 Cherokee Rd Florence SC 29501 Office: 248 W Evans St Florence SC 29501

BUZLEA, ROMEY D., dentist; b. Coalwood, W.VA., Feb. 11, 1929; s. Juventino and Florence (Buzlea) B.; A.B., U. W.Va., 1950 D.D.S., Northwestern Dental Sch., 1955; m. Jane Walsh, May 11, 1963; 1 son, Richard Walsh. Pvt. dental practice, W.Va., 1957-58, Apopka, Fla., 1958-63, Winter Park, Fla., 1963—. Served from 1st lt. to capt. USAF, 1955-57. Mem. Acad. Gen. Dentistry, Federation Dentaire Internationale, G.V. Black Soc., Winter Park, Maitland chambers commerce, Am. Dental Assn., Fla. Dental Soc., Jr. C. of C. (v.p. 1961), Xi Psi Phi. Club: University (Winter Park). Home: 614 Thunder Trail Maitland FL 32751 Office: 1549 Lee Rd Winter Park FL 32789

BYARS, ILA PEARL, orgn. exec., civic worker; b. Travis, Tex., June 25, 1908; d. William Lafayette and Sibyl Allen (Massey) Byars; student pub. schs. With Mid-West States Telephone Co., Blanco, 1924-53; with Bigden Ins. and Real Estate, Tex., 1953-55; pvt. kindergarten tchr., Blanco, 1955-56; waitress various restaurants, 1956-62, 63-65; with Wall Furniture, also Wall Funeral Home, Blanco, 1952-53, 65-66; staff food dept. Blanco Mill Nursing Home, 1966—. County chmn. Am. Heart Assn., 1957-72, meml. and campaign mgr., 1957-72. Bd. dirs. Blanco County unit Am. Cancer Soc., 1959-72, unit sec., 1971—; trustee Blanco Library, 1950-53, librarian, 1952-53; bd. dir. Blanco County Tb Assn., 1951-53. Recipient Achievement citations Am. Heart Assn., 1970, 71, Am. Cancer Soc., 1971. Mem. Blanco C. of C. (sec. 1967-72, dir. 1967-71), Wesleyan Service Guild (co-founder 1952, pres. 1968—). Methodist. (dir. Vacation Bible Sch. 1968—, Sunday Sch. tchr. 1949—, now mem. pastoral com.) Mem. Order Eastern Star. Home: PO Box 256 Blanco TX 78606

BYERS, WILLIAM SEWELL, elec. engr.; b. Ironton, O., Oct. 3, 1922; s. William T. and Anna M. (Sewell) B.; B.E.E., Ohio State U., 1951; M.B.A., Rollins Coll., 1966; M.Engring., Pa. State U., 1969, M.Ed., 1972; postgrad. Nova U., 1974—; m. Marjorie E. Reidel, Dec. 26, 1946; children—Thomas William, Robert M., Catherine G. Broadcast engr. Crosley Broadcasting Corp., Columbus, O., 1949-51; dist. engr. Gen. Elec. Co., Syracuse, N.Y., 1951-55; staff engr. Martin Marietta Aerospace Corp., Orlando, Fla., 1955—. Adj. faculty Seminole Jr. Coll., Fla. So. Coll., Valencia Community Coll. Trustee Peninsula Ind. U. Served as chief petty officer, USNR, 1940-45; PTO. Nat. Sci. Found. grant, 1968-69. Registered profl. engr., Fla. Mem. Soc. Wireless Pioneers, Am. Def. Preparedness Assn., Mensa, Central Fla. Groundwave Club, Pa. State Amateur Radio Club (hon. life), Eta Kappa Nu. Home: 3232 Wickersham St Orlando FL 32806 Office: Box 5837 Orlando FL 32805

BYKOSKI, LOUIS MARION, social scientist; b. Cleve., Feb. 7, 1928; s. Stanley and Theresa (Sladewski) B.; B.S., Ohio State U., 1954, M.B.A., 1955; Ph.D., Western Res. U., 1965; m. Janet Elizabeth Davis, Oct. 15, 1955; children—Mark, Karen. Trainee employee relations program Gen. Electric Co., Ft. Wayne, Ind., Conneaut, O. and Schenectady, 1955-58, specialist personnel practices Knolls Atomic Power Lab., Schenectady, 1958-59, specialist personnel, orgn. and procedures, 1959-60; mgr. econ. planning program Spindletop Research Inc., Lexington, Ky., 1965-73; sr. program analyst Enviro-Med, Inc., Washington, 1973—. Adj. lectr. U. Ky. at Lexington, 1969. Served with USNR, 1946-48. Nat. Bank Cleve. Scholarship grantee, 1963-64. Mem. Assn. Am. Geographers, Am. Econ. Assn., Indsl. Relations Research Assn., Nat. Acad. Econs. and Polit. Sci., A.A.A.S., Soc. Internat. Devel., Gamma Theta Upsilon, Alpha Delta Sigma, Omicron Delta Epsilon, Beta Gamma Sigma, Pi Sigma Alpha. Home: 5623 Jordan Rd Washington DC 20016 Office: 1120 Connecticut Av NW Washington DC 20036

BYNUM, ARLEN DEAN, lawyer. b. Abilene, Tex., Aug. 25, 1935; s. Charles Preton and Alma (Key) B.; B.A., Abilene Christian Coll., 1958; J.D., Baylor U., 1963; m. Charlsie Murphey, Aug. 22, 1959; children—Amy Elizabeth, Angela Dean. Admitted to Tex. bar, 1963; since practiced in Dallas; mem. firm Bradshaw and Bynum; counselor Law Sch., Baylor U., Dallas, 1963—; lectr. El Centro Jr. Coll., 1972—, Sch. Law, So. Methodist U., 1973—. Active Golden Gloves, Dallas, 1950—; mem. Dallas Forty, 1969—. Active state and local Democratic orgns., 1958—. Served with AUS, 1953-62. Mem. Dallas, Tex., Am. bar assns., Am. Bd. Trial Advocates, Trial Attys. Am., Dallas Assn. Def. Counsel, Baylor Law Sch. Alumni Assn. (dir.). Home: 4325 San Carlos St Dallas TX 75225 Office: 2001 Bryan Tower Dallas TX 75201

BYNUM, RALEIGH WESLEY, optometrist; b. Jacksonville, Fla., May 27, 1936; s. John Thomas and Corene (Brown) B.; student Fla. A. and M. U., 1954-56, Roosevelt U., 1956; B.S., Ill. Coll. Optometry, 1959, D.Optometry, 1960; postgrad. Trenton State Coll., 1963-64, U. Vienna Med. Sch., Austria, 1966; m. Thelmetia Yvette Argrett, Aug. 10, 1963; children—Raleigh Wesley, Zerrick Argrett, Monjya Felisha. Optometrist with Dr. Lee Mandel, 1960-62; individual practice optometry, Charlotte, N.C., 1967—. Vision cons. U.S. Mil. Induction Center, Charlotte, 1967—; vision cons. Concentrated Employment

Program, Charlotte, 1968—, Fla. Steel Corp., Charlotte, 1969—. Bd. dirs., pres. Bethlehem Center, Charlotte. Served to capt. AUS, 1962-67. Fellow Am. Acad. Optometry; mem. Mecklenburg County Assn. Optometrists, Nat. Optometric Assn. (editor newsletter), N.C. State Optometric Soc., Charlotte C. of C. (law enforcement com.), Am. Optometric Assn. (dir. minority recruitment So. region), Alpha Phi Omega (adviser to J.C. Smith U. chpt. 1968—). Democrat. Baptist (pres. men's brotherhood 1968—). Mason, Toastmaster (pres. Bavarian chpt. 1966-67). Home: 6426 Heatherbrook Rd Charlotte NC 28213 Office: Independence Medical Center Suite 300 Independence and McDowell Sts Charlotte NC 28202

BYNUM, ROBERT EUGENE, social worker; b. Wilburton, Okla., May 23, 1930; s. Turner Coleman and Clara (Boggs) B.; B.S., Oklahoma City U., 1955 M.S.W., U. Okla., 1957; m. Frances Ruth Pace, July 29, 1950; children—Genece Jo, Donna Sue. Psychiat. social worker-supr. Central State Mental Hosp., Norman, Okla., 1957-62; coordinator USPHS Nursing Home Project in Okla., 1962-65; social work cons. Okla. Dept. Health Regional Guidance Center, McAlester, Okla., 1965-67; social work cons. Okla. Dept. Health, Oklahoma City, 1967—. Rep. from Okla., Leadership Tng. Program for Social Workers in Mental Health Field. Served with C.E., AUS, 1950-52. Mem. Acad. Certified Social Workers, Nat. Assn. Social Workers, Okla. Health and Welfare Assn. (mem. exec. bd.), Am., Okla. (pres.) pub. health assns. Home: 607 Jean-Marie Dr Norman OK 73069 Office: NE 10th and Stonewall Oklahoma City OK 73105

BYRD, BENJAMIN FRANKLIN, JR., surgeon, educator; b. Nashville, May 18, 1918; s. Benjamin Franklin and Ida (Brister) B.; A.B., Vanderbilt U., 1938, M.D., 1941; m. Allison Caldwell, Feb. 6, 1950; children—Benjamin Franklin III, Barney Duncan, Damon Winston, Andrew Wayne, Evelyn Brister, John W. Thomas. Intern Nashville Gen. Hosp., 1941-42, asst. resident, 1942; asst. resident Vanderbilt U. Hosp., 1945-47, resident, 1947-48; practice medicine specializing in surgery, Nashville, 1948—; chief surgery St. Thomas Hosp., 1964-70; mem. staff Baptist Hosp., VA Regional Hosp.; instr. surgery Vanderbilt U., Nashville, 1947-54, asso. clin. prof. surgery, 1954-71, clin. prof. surgery, 1971—; asso. clin. prof. surgery Meharry Med. Coll., Nashville, 1951-69, prof. clin. surgery, 1969—. Pres., Tenn. div. Am. Cancer Soc., 1963, nat. bd. dirs., 1965—, nat. exec. com., 1970—, chmn. med. and sci. exec. com., 1973—; pres., mem. exec. bd. Tenn. Bot. Gardens and Fine Arts Center, 1971-73; pres. M.B.A. Fathers Club. Bd. trustees Sr. Citizens; bd. dirs. Children's Museum. Served to lt. col. MC, AUS, 1941-45. Decorated Bronze Star with oak leaf cluster, Silver Star, Purple Heart. Fellow A.C.S. (gov. 1973—, chmn. commn. on cancer); mem. Am. Surg. Assn., So. Surg. Assn., Am. Thyroid Assn., Nashville Surg. Soc. (pres. 1962-63), James Ewing Soc., Tenn. (mem. council), So. (mem. council) med. assns., Southeastern Surg. Congress (mem. council, pres. 1968-69), Nashville C. of C. (mem. health and hosp. coms. bd. govs., v.p. 1970), Nashville Exchange Club (pres. 1965-66), Sigma Xi. Home: 400 Ellendale Dr Nashville TN 37205 Office: 2122 W End Av Nashville TN 31203

BYRD, DOROTHY FAY, educator; b. Brownwood, Tex., Dec. 23, 1927; d. Earl D. and Fay (Alexander) Byrd; B.A. in Econs., Tex. Woman's U., 1949, M.A. in Econs., 1966; student U. Colo., Hardin-Simmons U., Eastern N.M. U., Colo. State Coll.; postgrad. N. Tex. State U. Tchr. pub. schs., Hobbs, N.M., 1949-50, Andrews, Tex., 1950-57; real estate broker, Andrews, 1954-57; city sec., tax assessor-collector City of Andrews, 1957-66; teaching fellow Coll. Bus. Adminstrn., N. Tex. State U., Denton, 1967, 69-70, research asst. div. mgmt., 1969, research asso. Univ. Center Community Services, 1968-69, projects coordinator, 1968-70, dir. center, 1970—; pvt. bus. cons. govtl. systems. State del. White House Conf. on Aging, 1971. Mem. Tex. Assn. Community Services and Continuing Edn. (sec., dir.), Am. Assn. U. Women (dir. Andrews 1958-62, v.p. 1958-60; pres. 1964-65), Andrews Classroom Tchrs. Assn. (founding pres. 1955), Bus. and Profl. Women's Clubs, Assn. City Clks. and Secs. Tex. (sec.-treas. 1960-63, v.p. 1963-64, pres. 1964-65), Am. Acad. Polit. and Social Sci., Tex. Assn. Assessing Officers (dir. 1961-63), Am. Soc. Pub. Adminstrn., Sigma Iota Epsilon, Pi Sigma Alpha. Contbr. articles profl. jours. Episcopalian. Home: 1824 Ruddell Denton TX 76201 Office: PO Box 5344 NTSU Sta Denton TX 76203

BYRD, FRANK CHEARELLA, lawyer; b. Memphis, June 9, 1916; s. Frank Chearella and Elizabeth (McCadden) B.; LL.B., So. U., Memphis, 1940; LL.B., Memphis State U., 1967; m. Helen Chloe Fielder, Dec. 13, 1945; children—Frank C. Jr., Elizabeth (Mrs. C. Michael Greene), Lillian, John Marshall. Admitted to Tenn. bar, 1940; since practiced in Memphis; asst. county atty., 1946-48. Pres. Serra Club, Memphis, 1965-66, v.p. Serra Internat., 1969-70; v.p. Memphis Speech & Hearing Center, 1959-60; pres. Holy Name Soc., Memphis, 1950-51, Exchange Club East, Memphis, 1957-58. Bd. dirs. Sr. Citizens Services, Memphis, Josephine K. Lewis Sr. Citizen Center, Memphis Jr. Achievement. Served with AUS, 1941-46, with USAF, 1951-52; Korea. Mem. Memphis and Shelby County, Tenn., Am. bar assns., Am. Trial Lawyers Assn., Tenn. Res. Officers Assn. (past pres.), Roman Catholic. Clubs: Oak Grove Hunt (Germantown, Tenn.); Long Green Hunt (Rossville, Tenn.). Home: 1797 Carr Av Memphis TN 38104 Office: 12 Main St 745 Commerce Title Bldg Memphis TN 38103

BYRD, GRETCHEN THOMSON (MRS. HARRY FLOOD BYRD, JR.), wife Senator of Va.; b. New Orleans, Dec. 27, 1917; d. Paul J. and Gretchen (Bigelow) Thomson; m. Harry Flood Byrd, Jr. (U.S. senator from Va.), Aug. 9, 1941; children—Harry Flood III, Thomas Thomson, Beverley Bigelow (Mrs. George Greenhalgh III). Home: 411 Tennyson Av Winchester VA 22601

BYRD, HAL CLIFFORD, textile co. exec.; b. Bunnlevel, N.C., Aug. 25, 1918; s. James Caleb and Melinda Anne (Hobbs) B.; B.S., N.C. State U., 1940; m. Martha Lisabeth Harris, Mar. 17, 1943; children—Hal C., Martha Lisabeth, Melinda Anne. Sales engr. trainee Saco Lowell Shops, Biddeford, Me., 1940; partner Byrd & Vermont, Real Estate & Ins. Co., Spartanburg, S.C., 1946-48; vice pres. purchasing agt. Deering Milliken Service Corp., Spartanburg, S.C., 1948—. Vice chmn. Spartanburg County Devel. Commn., 1960—. Mem. Republican Nat. Com. for S.C., 1972—; mem. Nat. Rep. Finance Com. Trustee, Spartanburg Day Sch. Served to maj. AUS, 1940-45. Mem. Phi Kappa Tau, Phi Psi, Spartanburg C. of C. (dir. 1969—), S.C. C. of C. (dir. 1964-69). Clubs: Piedmont, Capitol Hill, Spartanburg Country, Cotillion and Beaux Arts. Home: 1009 Glendalyn Circle Spartanburg SC 29302 Office: PO Box 1926 Iron Ore Rd Spartanburg SC 29301

BYRD, HARRY FLOOD, JR., newspaper editor, U.S. senator; b. Winchester, Va., Dec. 20, 1914; s. Harry F. and Anne Douglas (Beverley) B.; student Va. Mil. Inst., 1931-33, U. Va., 1933-35; numerous hon. degrees; m. Gretchen B. Thomson, August 9, 1941; children—Harry Flood III, Thomas Thomson, Beverley Bigelow (Mrs. G. P. Greenhalgh III). Editor Winchester (Va.) Evening Star, 1935—; pub. Harrisonburg (Va.) Daily News-Record, 1937—; pres., dir. Rockingham Pub. Co., 1946—; dir. H. F. Byrd, Inc., 1948—; dir. Asso. Press, 1950-59, 61-66, v.p., mem. exec. com., mem. U.S. Senate from Va., 1965—; mem. Va. Senate, 1947-65, author state automatic tax reduction law. Mem. State Democratic Central Com., 1940-66. Served as lt. comdr. USNR, 1942-46, exec. officer Patrol bombing squadron, Pacific. Recipient Honor Medal Freedoms Found. Mem. V.F.W., Am. Legion. Clubs: Rotary (pres. Winchester 1940-41); Nat. Press, Army-Navy (Washington). Home: 411 Tennyson Av Winchester VA 22601 Office: Senate Office Bldg Washington DC 20510

BYRD, IDA FAY (MRS. KENNETH BYRD), librarian; b. nr. Harmony, N.C.; d. Nelson Hall and Tracy (Groce) Caudle; B.S., Appalacian State U., 1959, M.A., 1961, Ed.S., 1972; m. Kenneth Byrd, Aug. 27, 1959; children—Teressa Rene, Edwin Scott. Tchr., librarian Jonesville (N.C.) High Sch., 1959-61; librarian, audio-visual dir. Jonesville Sch., 1961-64; instr. library sci. Marshall U., 1964-66; dir. learning resource center Wilkes Community Coll., Wilkesboro, N.C., 1966-74. Mem. N.C., Southeastern, Community Coll. (dir. of west for N.C. 1967-68, 73-74) library assns., Learning Resources Assn., N.C. Ednl. Assn., Div. Audio-Visual Instrn., White Plains Ladies' Circle (pres. 1960-62, 64-65). Baptist (librarian 1968-70). Home: Route 1 Roaring River NC 28669 Office: Drawer 120 Wilkesboro NC 28697

BYRD, VEDA ENGLAND WOMACK (MRS. JUSTIN S. BYRD), ednl. adminstr.; b. Ramsey, Ill., Oct. 16, 1911; d. Andrew and Edith Cline (Augustine) England; B.A., U. Tampa, 1949; M.A., U. Fla., 1952; m. Tornie Womack, May 2, 1934 (div. June 1945); m. 2d, Justin S. Byrd, Dec. 22, 1945 (dec. 1971). Tchr. elementary sch., Ill., 1930-45, Tampa, Fla., 1945-50; tchr. Bayside Sch. Physically Handicapped, Tampa, 1950-55; prin. Henderson Sch. for Educable and Elementary, Tampa, 1955-57, LaVoy Sch. Trainable Mentally Retarded, Tampa, 1957—; mem. staff MacDonald Tng. Center. Vice pres. Hillsborough Assn. Retarded Children, 1964-65. Mem. Gov.'s State Adv. Council on Mental Retardation, 1967-72, Recipient Dr. Tom Dooley humanitarian award St. Patrick's Day Assn., 1962; citation MacDonald Tng. Center, 1966. Mem. Fla. Council Exceptional Edn. (past pres.), Tampa Bay Area Chpt. Exceptional Children (past pres.), Am. Assn. U. Women, Hillsborough County Assn. Adminstrs. and Suprs. (treas. 1971-73), Hillsborough Assn. Retarded Children (dir.), Fla., Tampa elementary prins. councils, Alpha Delta Kappa. Home: 113 Cedar Av Tampa FL 33606 Office: 4410 Main St Tamp FL 33607

BYRD, WILBERT PRESTON, educator; b. Burlington, N.C., July 7, 1926; s. Drewey Allen and Vera (Walker) B.; B.S., N.C. State U., 1949, M.S., 1952; Ph.D., Ia. State U., 1955; m. Dori Neal Butler, Sept. 18, 1947; 1 son, Michael Neal. Asst. prof. Ohio State U., Columbus, 1955-56; asso. prof. dept. exptl. statistics Clemson (S.C.) U., 1956-67, prof., chmn. dept., 1967—. Served with USNR, 1944-46. Mem. Am. Statis. Assn., Am. Soc. Agronomy. Methodist. Lion. Home: 101 Chattooga Lane Clemson SC 29631

BYRNE, ROBERT LEE, educator; b. East Liverpool, O., Feb. 22, 1931; s. Robert L. and Noal (Parsons) B.; B.S., Ohio U., 1952; M.A., Kent State U., 1957; Ed.D., George Peabody Coll., 1962; m. Shirley M. Smith, Sept. 9, 1951; children—Robert L. III, Susan Ann, Colleen Anne. Tchr., Madison Sch., Hamilton, O., 1952-56, Lakeview Sch., Lorain, O., 1956-59; coordinator remedial reading Child Study Center, George Peabody Coll., 1959-60; instr. speed reading U. Tenn., 1960; dir. Reading Clinic, U. Mass., 1960-65; dir. Reading Center, Eastern Ky. U., Richmond, 1965—, dir. undergrad. research tng. program, 1967; vis. prof. Appalachian State Coll., 1964-65, Kent State U., 1970-71. Cons. Asso. Cons., Inc. Mem. Am. Edn. Research Assn., Internat. Reading Assn. (Ky. pres. 1969-70), Nat. Reading Conf., Am. Assn. U. Profs., Kappa Delta Pi, Phi Delta Kappa. Mason. Author: Remedial Reading, 1968; Dictionary Skills, vol. I, vol. II, 1967. Home: 110 Westwood Dr Richmond KY 40475

BYRNSIDE, OSCAR JEHU, JR., assn. exec.; b. Huntington, W.Va., June 2, 1935; s. Oscar Jehu and Eula (Bayliss) B.; B.S., Concord Coll., 1960; M.S., Va. Poly. Inst. and State U., 1961; Ph.D., Ohio State U., 1968; m. Patricia Ann Oxley, Aug. 1, 1954; children—Barbara Ann, Brenda Gail, Bethany Lynne. Tchr. bus. Kanawha County (W.Va.) Schs., 1960; coordinator vocational office tng. Danville (Va.) Pub. Schs., 1961-63; asst. prof. bus. edn., dir. data processing center Longwood Coll., Farmville, Va., 1963-65; state dir. bus., office and distributive edn. W.Va. Bd. Edn., 1965-66; cons., research asso. program evaluation Center for Research and Leadership Devel. in Vocational and Tech. Edn., Ohio State U., 1966-68; exec. dir. Nat. Bus. Edn. Assn., Washington, 1968—, Future Bus. Leaders Am., 1968-73. Vis. prof. Va. Poly. Inst. and State U., Catholic U. Am.; cons. Ednl. Testing Service, Princeton, N.J.; bus. edn. equipment cons. for edn. projects World Bank; mgmt. cons. to bus. and industry. Bd. dirs. Outstanding Educators Am.; treas. Center for Ednl. Assns., Alliance Assns. for Advancement Edn. Served with USMCR, 1953-56. Recipient award Acad. Faculty of Vocational and Tech. Edn., Ohio State U., 1970. Mem. N.E.A., Am. Vocational Assn., Nat. Bus. Edn. Assn., Am. Assn. Sch. Adminstrs., Nat. Assn. Secondary Sch. Prins., Assn. Supervision Curriculum Devel., Internat. Soc. Bus. Edn., Blue Key (nat. v.p.), Phi Kappa Phi, Phi Delta Kappa, Pi Omega Pi, Delta Pi Epsilon, Kappa Delta Pi. Editor: Bus. Edn. Forum, 1968—. Home: 2053 Eakins Ct Reston VA 22091 Office: 1906 Association Drive Reston VA 22091

BYRON, JAMES ALOYSIUS, broadcasting exec.; b. Denver, Jan. 31, 1903; s. James Aloysius and Agnes Frances (Munday) B.; student St. Vincent Coll., 1918-19; student U. Mo., 1919-21; m. Ruth Trimble, June 3, 1940 (dec. Dec. 1947). Clk. Burlington R.R., Ft. Worth, 1922-33; with Ft. Worth Star-Telegram, 1933-44; with sta. WBAP, Ft. Worth, 1944—, dir. broadcsting, 1968—. Chmn. Tex. A. and M. U. Journalism Adv. Com., 1955-56; v.p. Casa Manana Civic Playhouse, Ft. Worth, 1967-68. Recipient Distinguished Journalism award Southwest Journalism Forum, 1956; Sigma Delta Chi Wells Meml. Key award, 1963, Distinguished Journalistic Achievement award, 1963. Mem. Radio-TV News Dirs. Assn. (pres. 1954), Better Bus. Bus. (dir. 1970-72), Tex. Assn. Broadcasters (dir. 1972—), Sigma Delta Chi (pres. 1959). Roman Catholic. Clubs: Colonial Country (bd. govs. 1972—); Ft. Worth; Century (Ft. Worth). Home: 3720 Bellaire Dr N Fort Worth TX 76109 Office: PO Box 1780 WBAP AM TV Fort Worth TX 76101

BYRUM, ALBERT GASKINS, JR., orthodontist; b. Edenton, N.C., Apr. 22, 1937; s. Albert G. and Ruth (Pruden) B.; B.S., U. N.C., 1959, D.D.S., 1963; M.S., Fairleigh Dickinson U., 1970; m. Patricia Beams, Aug. 23, 1958; children—Elizabeth Holt, Martha Ruth, Albert G. III. Pvt. practice dentistry, Martinsville, Va., 1966-70; pvt. practice orthodontics, 1970—. Served to capt. USAF, 1963-66. Mem. Am., Va., Patrick Henry (sec. 1970, pres. 1973—) dental socs., Am. Assn. Orthodontists, Zeta Psi, Delta Sigma Delta. Club: Chatmoss Country. Author: Evaluation of Anterior-Posterior and Vertical Skeletal Change Vs. Dental Change in Rapid Palatal Expansion Cases as studied by Latoral Cephalograms, 1970. Home: 906 Hunting Ridge Rd Martinsville VA 24112 Office: Box 3271 Martinsville VA 24112

CABANISS, CHARLES DAVIS, lawyer; b. Birmingham, Ala., Feb. 5, 1927; s. Walter Marcus and Inez (Eaton) C.; B.A. in Liberal Arts, Tex. A. and M. Coll., 1950; J.D., U. Tex., 1955; m. Mary Kathryn Landers, July 29, 1961; children—Kevin Charles, Kristin. Admitted to Tex. bar, 1955; asst. to Tex. legislator, Austin, 1955; news reporter The Garland (Tex.) Daily News, 1955; asst. dist. atty., Dallas County, 1955-58, asst. atty. gen. Tex., Austin, 1959-60; practiced in Dallas and Garland, 1960-62; editor Tex. Mesquiter, Mesquite, 1960-62; asst. U.S. atty. No. Dist. of Tex., 1962—. Bd. dirs. N. Tex. Municipal Water Dist.; bd. dirs. Delta Theta Phi Ednl. Found., sec.-treas., 1960-61; alternate mem. Dallas-Ft. Worth Fed. Exec. Bd.; bd. mgmt. White Rock YMCA, 1972-75; del. Nat. Jr. Bar Conf., 1960-61; adv. bd. Garland Parks and Recreation Dept. Served to 1st lt. AUS, 1945-47; 50-52. Decorated Bronze Star medal, Purple Heart. Mem. Am., Tex., Travis County, Dallas, Fed. (v.p. 5th circuit 1967-69, pres. Dallas 1970-71) bar assns., Dallas (pres. 1958), Austin (bd. dirs. 1959-60) jr. bar assns., Dallas Fed. Bus. Assn. (dir. 1968-74), Austin Alumni (senate dean 1959-60), Dallas Alumni Senate, Delta Theta Phi, Phi Kappa Phi, Phi Eta Sigma, Sigma Delta Chi. Democrat. Clubs: Kiwanis (pres. 1957-58, chmn. div. officers council 1958), Texas A. and M. (local pres. 1957-58) (Garland). Home: 9611 Trailview Dr Dallas TX 75238 Office: 16 G 28 US Courthouse Dallas TX 75202

CABANISS, JOSEPH WARREN, lawyer; b. Macon, Ga., July 12, 1924; s. Emory Winship and Sarah (Adams) C.; A.B., Coll. Charleston, 1947; LL.B., U. S.C., 1949; m. Alice Hammond Ray, Apr. 28, 1956; children—Stephen Emory, Thomas Ray, Henry Harrison. Admitted to S.C. bar, 1949; practice law, Charleston, S.C., 1949—; mem. law firm Grimball and Cabaniss, Charleston, S.C., 1964—; lectr. economics Charleston Coll., 1953-56. Chmn. Charleston Council on Human Relations, 1966-70; pres. Coastal Carolina Fair, 1967; trustee Moultrie Sch. Dist., 1968-69. Bd. dirs. St. John's Mission Center. Served to maj. USMCR, 1943-46, 1950-53. Mem. Wig and Robe. Episcopalian (vestryman 1958-71, S.C. Diocesan Devel. commn. 1967-69). Mason. Clubs: Carolina Yacht, Exchange Club of Charleston (pres. 1960). Home: 334 Molasses Lane Mount Pleasant SC 29464 Office: 39 Broad St Charleston SC 29401

CABELL, JOSEPH BRECKINRIDGE, JR., wholesale co. exec.; b. Jackson, Miss., Aug. 24, 1933; s. Joseph Breckinridge and Pearl Ophelia (Moak) C.; B.S., Tulane U., 1956; postgrad. U. Miss., Millsaps Coll.; m. Floy Elaine Cruthirds, Sept. 17, 1960; children—Andrew Elaine, Joseph Breckinridge III. With Cabell Electric Co., Jackson, 1956—, v.p., 1973—, mgr. utility products, 1962—, also dir. Mem. Andrew Jackson exec. council Boy Scouts Am., 1973-74; chmn. Tulane Alumni Conf., 1960. Mem. C. of C. (transp. com. 1972-74, distbn. com. 1972-74), Sigma Pi Sigma. Home: 5450 Briarfield St Jackson MS 39211 Office: 422 S Farish St Jackson MS 39206

CABELL, JOSEPH EDWARD, educator; b. Victoria de las Tunas, Cuba, Mar. 16, 1943; s. Tiofilo and Consorcia Paulina (Perez) Cabezas; came to U.S., 1948, naturalized, 1962; B.A., Wake Forest Coll., 1966; M.F.A., U. Ga., 1968; postgrad. Fla. State U., 1973-74. Asst. prof. speech and drama, dir. theatre Gainesville (Ga.) Jr. Coll., 1968—. Dir. Gainesville Civic Theatre, 1968-70, Gainesville Jr. Service League Children's Theatre, 1968-73, Helen (Ga.) Summer Stock Theatre, 1973; dir. summer theatre program Ga. Tng. and Devel. renter, 1972. Bd. dirs. Gainesville Arts Council, 1971-72. Recipient Gov.'s Award in Arts, 1973; named Outstanding Faculty Mem., Ga. Jr. Coll., 1973. Nat. Endowment for Humanities fellow, 1973-74. Mem. Am. Theatre Assn., Southeastern, Ga. (pres. 1972-73) theatre confs. Office: Gainesville Jr Coll Gainesville GA 30501

CABELL, ROYAL EUBANK, JR., lawyer; b. Richmond, Va., June 25, 1923; s. Royal Eubank and Lillian Hoge (Lorraine) C.; B.A., Hampden-Sydney Coll., 1943; LL.B., U. Va., 1948; m. Kathleen Shirley Buchanan, Oct. 30, 1948; children—Royal E. III, Charles Lorraine, Kathleen. Admitted to Va. bar, 1948; mem. law firm Moncure & Cabell (formerly Cabell & Cabell), Richmond, 1948—. Dir., C.F. Sauer Co., Richmond, C & T Refinery, Inc., Richmond, Dean Foods Co., Richmond, Owens, Minor & Bodeker, Inc., Richmond, Powers & Anderson, Inc., Richmond; pres. Dominion Leaf Tobacco Co., Inc., Richmond; pres. Sarawak Co. (1959) Sinderhian Berhad, Sarawak, Malaysia, Marks Surg. Supplies, Inc., Augusta, Ga., Richmond. Pres. Richmond Symphony, 1972—. Chmn. 3d Dist. Republican Com., 1956; Rep. candidate for Congress, 1956; mem. Henrico County Rep. Com., 1956—. Trustee, sec. William H., John G., Emma Scott Found., 1956; trustee Collegiate Schs., Richmond Meml. Hosp., Hanover Presbytery, Hampden-Sydney Coll.; bd. dirs. Richmond Cerebral Palsy Center. Served to lt. (j.g.) USNR, 1943-46. Mem. Am., Richmond bar assns., Va. State Bar Assn., Am. Judicature Soc., Va., Richmond chambers commerce, English Speaking Union (pres. Richmond br. 1968-70), Newcomen Soc. Presbyn. (mem. joint com. Ref. Ch. in Am. and Presbyn. Ch. U.S. 1962-69). Kiwanian. Clubs: Commonwealth, Country of Virginia, Downtown (pres. 1957-58) (Richmond). Home: 510 Sleepy Hollow Rd Richmond VA 23229 Office: 921 Ross Bldg Richmond VA 23211

CABIBI, CHARLES EDMOND, lawyer, notary public; b. New Orleans, Nov. 26, 1914; s. Frank and Alice (Driscoll) C.; J.D., Loyola U., 1936; m. Dorothy McWaters, May 28, 1937; 1 son, Charles Edmond. Admitted to La. bar, 1937; practiced in La., 1937—; asst. city atty., New Orleans, 1946-60; pres. Cabibi Title Ins. Agy., Inc., 1971—; sec., L. F. Gaubert & Co., Inc., Marine Indsl. Cable Corp., Michoud Indsl. Complex, Carmel-Holiday Inn, Carmel Devel. Corp. Atty., New Orleans R.R. Terminal Bd., 1950-60; bd. advisers Bank New Orleans and Trust Co.; notary pub. First Homestead & Savs. Assn., 1966—. Bd. dirs., chmn. bd., pres. St. Bernard Gen. Hosp. Mem. Am. Judicature Soc., Am., La., New Orleans bar assns. K.C. Clubs: Optimist, Young Men's Business (New Orleans). Office: Richards Bldg New Orleans LA 70112

CABRANES, MANUEL, educator, social worker; b. Toa Alta, P.R., Dec. 18, 1904; s. Manuel and Ana (Velilla) C.; diploma Sch. Social Service, Fordham U., 1933; B.A. in Edn., U. P.R., 1939; m. Carmen López-Rosa, Dec. 24, 1933; children—Manuel A., Jose A. Tchr. elementary sch., P.R., then prin., after 1923; exec. dir. Child Welfare Bd., to 1938; dir. div. probation and parole Dept. Justice; supr. social work Dept. Edn.; dir. Insl. Sch. for Boys, Mayaguez, P.R., 1938-41; chief U.S. probation and parole officer, San Juan, P.R., 1941-46; exec. dir. Melrose House Community Center, Bronx, N.Y., 1946-48; dir. N.Y. office P.R. Dept. Labor, 1948-51; asst. sec. N.Y.C. Commn. for Foster Care of Children, 1951-53; cons. N.Y.C. Commr. Welfare, 1953-66; instr. sociology Coll. of Sacred Heart, San Juan, 1967; cons. to exec. dir. P.R. Ports Authority, San Juan, 1969—. Founder, exec. sec. N.Y.-Puerto Rican Scholarship Fund, 1961-65. Recipient citations Melrose House Community Center, 1948, Alexander and Sarah Burger Found., 1955, Mayor Robert F. Wagner, N.Y.C., 1960, P.R. Writers and Journalists Assn., 1965, P.R. Tchrs. Assn., 1965. Mem. P.R. Tchrs. Assn., Am. Assn. Social Workers. Home: 2072 Espana St Santurce PR 00911 Office: Puerto Rico Ports Authority GPO Box 2829 San Juan PR 00936

CACE, JOHN STEPHAN, JR., restaurant exec.; b. New Orleans, Jan. 8, 1917; s. John and Anastasia (Evasovich) C.; student La. State U., 1933-35; m. Valerie Savony, Nov. 30, 1939; children—John Stephan III, Gerard C., Daniel G. Owner Johnny Cace's Seafood and Steak House, Longview, Tex., 1949—; dir. Longview Bank & Trust Co. Bd. dirs. United Fund. Served with USAAF, 1942-46. Named Restauranteur of Year State, Tex. Restaurant Assn., 1968, Man of the Month East Tex. C. of C., May 1967; recipient Silver Beaver award

Boy Scouts of Am., 1968. Mem. Tex. Restaurant Assn. (pres. 1966-67), Longview C. of C. (pres. 1967-68), East Tex. C. of C. Roman Catholic. K.C. (4 deg.). Clubs: Pinecrest Country, Cherokee Country, Civitan (v.p. 1969) Columbus (dir. 1964-71) (Longview). Home: 13 Normandy Circle Longview TX 75601 Office: 1501 E Marshall St Longview TX 75601

CACERES, CESAR AUGUSTO, physician, scientist; b. Honduras, Apr. 9, 1927; s. Julian R. and Mariana (Culotta) C.; B.S., Georgetown U., 1949, M.D., 1953. Research, George Washington U., 1956-60, asso. prof. medicine, 1964-69, prof., chmn. dept. clin. engring., med. center, 1969-71; chief med. systems devel. lab. USPHS, Washington, 1960-69. Mem. Assn. Computing Machinery, Am. Fedn. Clin. Research, Am. Pub. Health Assn., N.Y. Acad. Sci., Fed. Profl. Assn. (v.p.), Soc. Advanced Med. Systems (pres. 1969-70), Assn. Advancement Med. Instrumentation (pres. 1971-72), Internat. Health Evaluation Assn. (pres. 1972-74). Author: Electronic and Computer Assisted Studies of Bio-Medical Problems, 1964; BioMedical Telemetry, 1965; The Innocent Murmur, 1966; Diagnostic Computers, 1968; Clinical Electrocardiography and Computers, 1970. Editor: Clinical Engring. Newsletter, 1973—. Contbr. articles to profl. jours. Home: 2500 Virginia Av NW Washington DC 20037 Office: 1759 Q St NW Washington DC 20009

CADDEN, RODNEY CARLTON, JR., banker; b. Columbus, Miss., June 13, 1938; s. Rodney Carlton and Addine (Armstrong) C.; B.S. in Edn., Miss. State U., 1961; postgrad. U. Miss., 1971-72; m. Mary Lee Sansing, Aug. 8, 1965; children—Jerry Alan, Jennifer Lyn. With First Nat. Bank Monroe Country, Aberdeen, Miss., 1967—, cashier, 1971-73, asst. v.p., cashier, 1973-74, v.p., br. mgr., 1974—; dir. IGA Discounter Food Store, Aberdeen. Pres. adv. council South Monroe County chpt. 4-H, 1970—; v.p. Monroe County Jr. Livestock Assn., 1971—; pres. Aberdeen Civitan Club, 1972, dist. lt. gov., 1973—; mem. Monroe County Coordinating Com., 1973—. Bd. dirs. United Givers Fund South, South Monroe County, Aberdeen, 1970-72, U.S.O., Aberdeen, 1970. Served with AUS, 1961-64. Recipient Certificate Recognition award U.S.O., 1970. Mem. Aberdeen C. of C. (mem. planning, zoning commn., park, recreation commn.), Miss. Jr. Bankers Assn., Am. Legion, Miss. State U. Alumni Assn. Baptist (treas.). Home: PO Box 87 Aberdeen MS 39730 Office: PO Box 1 Hamilton MS 39746

CADENHEAD, ALFRED PAUL, lawyer; b. LaGrange, Ga., Oct. 14, 1926; s. Roy E. and Omie (Bishop) C.; jr. coll. certificate W. Ga. Coll., 1944; LL.B., Emory U., 1949; m. Sara Davenport, Oct. 14, 1945; children—Steven Paul, David James. Admitted to Ga. bar, 1949; with firm Nall, Miller and Cadenhead and predecessors, Atlanta, 1949—, partner, 1954—; dir. various corps. Pres., Atlanta Legal Aid Soc., 1957, Met. Atlanta Mental Health Assn., 1964-65, Ga. Assn. for Mental Health, 1968. Served with AUS, 1944-46. Fellow Am. Coll. Trial Lawyers, Internat. Soc. Barristers; mem. Atlanta Bar Assn. (spl. pros. 1958-60, pres. 1970-71). Presbyn. (elder 1954—, commr. to gen. assembly 1966). Home: 6305 Riverside Dr NW Atlanta GA 30328 Office: 1500 Equitable Bldg Atlanta GA 30303

CADLE, DEAN, educator; b. Middlesboro, Ky., Jan. 16, 1920; s. David Bert and Dora (Brooks) C.; B.A., Berea Coll., 1947; postgrad. Columbia, 1946, Stanford, 1947-49, U. Kan., 1949, U. Tenn., 1951; M.A., U. Ia., 1950; M.S. in Library Sci., U. Ky., 1957; m. Jo Lee Dannel, May 28, 1952. Lit. tchr. Union Coll., Barbourville, Ky., 1950-53, Detroit Inst. Tech., 1954-55; librarian Frankfort (Ky.) Dept. Libraries, 1957-59, U. Ky., 1959-60, U. Ky. Southeast Community Coll., Cumberland, 1960-66; asso. prof., asst. librarian U. N.C., Asheville, 1966—. Winner nat. short story contest sponsored by Tomorrow mag. and Creative Age Press, 1947; Wallace Stegner Creative Writing fellow Stanford, 1947-48; short stories listed on honor roll and distinctive lists of Best Am. Short Stories anns. Mem. N.C., Southeastern library assns. Editor: High Cost of Writing, 1965, Gambit, 1950-53; faculty adviser Images, 1966—; adv. and contbg. editor Appalachian Heritage mag., 1972—. Contbr. fiction and criticism to various mags. and jours. including Yale Rev., S.W. Rev., Tomorrow, Carolina Quar., N.M. Quar.. to anthologies Stanford Short Stories, 1949, Deep Summer, 1963. Home: 30 Valle Vista Dr Asheville NC 28804

CADWELL, GLENN ALBERTSON, clergyman; b. Valley Center, Kan., July 24, 1916; s. Frank Corydon and Mabel Lovina (Albertson) C.; B.A., Phillips U., 1939, B.D., 1948; postgrad. Edinburgh (Scotland) Div. Sch., 1946, U. Chgo. Theol. Sem., 1948-49; Mus.B., Drake U., 1969; m. Lena Elizabeth Thomas, May 26, 1940; children—Warren Lee, Glynda Sue (Mrs. Gerald Lester Peck). Ordained to ministry Christian Ch., 1939; minister Christian ch., Oakley, Kan., 1940-41, Atwood, Kan., 1941-44, Seminole, Okla., 1950-53, Fredonia, Kan., 1953-57, Kansas City, Mo., 1957-58, Creston, Ia., 1959-65; asso. minister First Christian Ch., El Paso, 1970-71, acting sr. minister, 1971-72; minister First Christian Ch., Osceola, Ark., 1972—. Mem. stewrdship com. Christian Chs. in Ark., 1972—. Winner area 5, dist. 19 speech contest Toastmasters Internat., 1962, recipient Cap Sias award as Toastmaster of Yr., Dist. 19, 1964. Mem. Hymn Soc. Am., Assn. Disciples Musicians, Ministerial Assn. Osceola (pres. 1972-73). Kiwanian (hon. mem.). Home: 108 Margaret St Box 521 Osceola AR 72370 Office: Ford and Ermen Lane Osceola AR 72370

CAFFEY, JOHN WILLIAM, JR., physician; b. Greensboro, N.C., Sept. 29, 1927; s. John William and Pattie (Brawley) C.; A.B., Duke, 1949, M.D., 1953; m. Clotiel F. Moody, Jan. 13, 1964; children—Katie Jean, John William III; 1 step-son, Daniel Claude McMillan. Intern, N.C. Meml. Hosp., Chapel Hill, 1953-54, resident surgery, 1954-56, resident anesthesia, 1956-58; practice medicine, specializing in anesthesiology, Jacksonville, Fla., 1958—; mem. staff Bapt. Meml., St. Vincents, Hope Haven, University, St. Lukes, Riverside, Beaches hosps., Meml. Hosp. Jacksonville. Served with AUS, 1944-46. Diplomate Nat. Bd. Med. Examiners; Am. Bd. Anesthesologists. Fellow Am. Coll. Anesthesiologists; mem. A.M.A., So., Fla., Duval county med. assns., Am., Fla. socs. anesthesiologists, Internat. Research Soc. Anesthesia. Republican. Presbyn. (deacon). Home: 6224 Kellow Dr Jacksonville FL 32216 Office: 800 Prudential Dr Jacksonville FL 32207

CAFFEY, WILLIAM STEWART, educator; b. Gorman, Tex., Dec. 10, 1939; s. William Burton and Ina (Stewart) C.; B.A., Howard Payne Coll., 1962, M.Ed., 1965; m. Donajean Smith, July 20, 1963; children—Shana Marie, Terri Leigh, Michael David. Ordained to ministry Methodist Ch., 1963; tchr. Peace Corps, Morocco, 1962-63; minister Comanche Circuit, Methodist Ch., Comanche, Tex., 1963-65; tchr. Abernathy (Tex.) Jr. High Sch., 1965—, Adult Edn. Program, Abernathy, 1968-72. Vice pres. Abernathy Community Action Program, 1969-70; sch. rep. Dist. 17 Drug Edn. Program, 1971-72. Bd. dirs. Central Plains Community Action Program, Inc., Hale County. Mem. Tex. State Tchrs. Assn. (life; chmn. Dist XVII necrology com. 1971-72), Tex. (charter life mem.; pres. 1970-71), Abernathy classroom tchrs. assns., Internat. Platform Assn. Democrat. Methodist. Author: Dialogs and Drills for Intermediate Students in English As a Foreign Language, 1963; Abernathy-Now and Then, 1969; The Sidney Community, Vol. 1; A Football Scoresheet 1940-70, 1971. Home: 1103 Av G Abernathy TX 79311 Office: 708 Av E Abernathy TX 79311

CAFFREY, WILLIAM DANIEL, lawyer; b. Morehead City, N.C., Nov. 5, 1928; s. Daniel F. and Audrey (Phillips) C.; B.S., Ind. State U., 1950; M.A., George Washington U., 1954; postgrad. U. N.C., 1954; J.D., Duke, 1958; m. Ona Faye Willis, June 3, 1952; children—William Daniel, Russell Howard. Tchr., asst. prin. Aycock Jr. High Sch., Greensboro, N.C., 1950-54; prin. David Caldwell Sch., 1954-55; admitted to N.C. bar, 1958; mem. firm Jordan, Wright, Nichols, Caffrey & Hill, and predecessor, 1958—; instr. Greensboro div. Guildford Coll., 1959—; adj. prof. law (civil trial practice and ins.) Duke Sch. Law, 1969—; mem. faculty Nat. Inst. Trial Advocacy Am. Bar Assn., 1973, 74. Former state chmn. Def. Research Inst.; pres. Greensboro Sports Council; chmn. United Forces for Edn.; past pres. Joyner Sch. P.T.A. Trustee Greensboro Coll. and Meth. Children's Home. Served with USAAF, 1946-48. Mem. Am., N.C., Greensboro bar assns., Am. Judicature Soc., Internat. Assn. Ins. Counsel, Duke Law Alumni Assn. (past nat. pres.), Am. Acad. Polit. and Social Sci., Acad. Polit. Sci., Order of Coif, Blue Key, Phi Delta Phi, Pi Gamma Mu, Kappa Delta Pi. Democrat. Methodist (bishop's lay adv. com.). Civitan. Home: 2902 Round Hill Rd Greensboro NC 27408 Office: 500 W Friendly Av Bldg Greensboro NC 27402

CAHILL, CARL HENRY, ins. co. exec.; b. Louisville, Ky., Dec. 18, 1931; s. Carl F. and Rosa (Eskridge) C.; m. Rachel Sue Whiteley, Mar. 2, 1951; children—Stephen Craig, Susan Gayle, Gregory Scott, David Carl. Regional dir. Okla. Belknap Hardware & Mfg. Co., 1953-60; div. mgr. also asst. state mgr. Nat. Investors Life Ins. Co., 1960-63; state mgr. Investors Equity Life Ins. Co., Hawaii, 1963-65; exec. v.p., dir., 1965-67; exec. v.p., dir. Investors Equity of the West, 1964-67; exec. v.p., dir. Great Atlantic Life Ins. Co., Orlando, Fla., 1967-70; regional v.p., dir. Nat. Investors Life Ins. Co. Ala., Nat. Investors Life Ins. Co. Ark., Nat. Investors Life Ins. Co. Ga. 1967-70; founder, pres., chmn. bd. Southland Equity Corp., 1970—; founder, chmn. bd., pres. SEC Life Ins. Co., Fla., 1971—; founder, chmn. bd. SECO Life Ins. Co. Ala., 1972—. Bd. dirs., treas. Mental Health Assn. Fla. Mem. Orlando, Winter Park chambers commerce, Com. of 200. Baptist (deacon). Home: 123 Oakleigh Lane Maitland FL 32751 Office: Crane's Roost Office Park PO Box 400 Orlando FL 32802

CAHN, EDGAR S., lawyer, b. 1935; B.A., Swarthmore Coll.; LL.B., Yale, M.A., 1957, Ph.D., 1960; m. Jean Cahn. Admitted to D.C. bar, 1963; dir. Citizens Advocate Center, co-dean Antioch Sch. of Law, Washington. Home: 5500 39th St NW Washington DC 20015 Office: 1624 Crescent Pl NW Washington DC 20009

CAHN, JEAN CAMPER, lawyer; b. Balt., May 26, 1935; d. John Emory-Toussaint and Florine (Thompson) Camper; B.A., Swathmore Coll., 1957; postgrad. Newnham Coll., Cambridge, 1958-59; LL.B., Yale, 1961; m. Edgar S. Cahn, Mar. 22, 1957; children—Jonathan, Reuben. Admitted to D.C. bar, Conn. bar; since practiced in Washington; founder, co-dean Antioch Sch. of Law, Washington; prof. law Howard U.; faculty, lectr. Yale Law Sch.; founder, mem. nat. adv. bd. Office Econ. Opportunity Nat. Legal Services Program; internat. atty., adviser on African affairs U.S. Dept. State; asso. counsel eminent domain procedure New Haven Redevel.; Dixwell neighborhood atty. Neighborhood Services Program, Community Progress, Inc.; dir. community orgn. staff Harlem Park Renewal Area, Balt. Urban Renewal and Housing Agy.; cons. Ford Found., Neumeyer Found.; chmn. Navajo Nation; bd. dirs. Southeastern Pa. Transp. Authority, Nat. Inst. for Consumer Justice; lectr. Expt. in Internat. Living, 1966-69. Mem. ad hoc adv. com. Center for Urban Edn.; mem. adv. bd. Reginald Heber Smith Fellowship Program; bd. dirs. Martin Luther King Center for Advanced Study Medicine; chmn. bd. dirs. Inst. for Polit. Service to Soc.; mem. adv. council Washington Inst. Met. Studies. Recipient award City Council D.C., Sigma Gamma Rho award. Nat. John Hay Whitney fellow, Benneke scholar, Yale Law Sch. fellow, Md. State scholar. Mem. Nat., Am., Washington, Conn. bar assns., Yale Alumni Assn. (mem. exec. com.), Black Am. Law Students Assn. (nat. bd.). Author: Red Tape, 1968. Contbr. articles to profl. jours. Home: 5500 39th St NW Washington DC 20015 Office: 1624 Crescent Pl NW Washington DC 20009

CAHUE, ANTONIO, physician; b. Ciego de Avila, Cuba, Mar. 9, 1926; s. Antonio Vicente and Gertrudis Engracia (Romero) C.; B.S. cum laude, Inst. Secondary Instruction, Ciego de Avila, Cuba, 1944; M.D., Havana U. Med. Sch., 1951; m. Candelaria Bernardo, May 11, 1957; children—Monica Gertrudis, Claudina Veronica, Antonio Bernardo, Judith Lillian, Teodoro Eugenio. Came to U.S., 1953, naturalized, 1961. Intern internal medicine U. Hosp., Calixto Garcia, Havana, Cuba, 1951-53; rotating intern Michael Reese Hosp., Chgo., 1953-54, fellow cardiovascular disease, 1954-55, resident internal medicine, 1956-57, clin. asst. thoracic medicine, 1958-61; resident VA Research Hosp., Chgo., 1957; med. dir. dept. inhalation therapy and pulmonary function lab. Methodist Hosp., Gary, Ind., 1965-68; practice medicine specializing in internal medicine, cardiology and pulmonary disease, Orlando, Fla., 1970—; mem. staff, pres. staff Mercy Hosp.; mem. staff Orange Meml. Hosp., Orlando, Fla.; mem. courtesy staff Fla. Hosp., Orlando, Fellow Am. Coll. Chest Physicians, Am. Coll. Cardiology; mem. A.M.A., Fla. Med. Assn., Orange County Med. Soc., A.C.P., Am. Heart Assn., Am. Thoracis Soc. Home: 1141 Covewood Trail Maitland FL 32751 Office: 331 N Maitland Av Maitland FL 32751

CAILLEAU, RELDA MARIE, biochemist; b. San Francisco, Feb. 1, 1909; d. Armand Michael and Rose (Adler) Cailleau; A.B., U. Cal. at Berkeley, 1930, M.A., 1932; D.Sc., U. Paris (France), 1937. French Nat. Research fellow Pasteur Inst., Paris, 1937-40; asst. microbiologist vitamin assays U. Cal. at Berkeley, 1941-43; asso. nutritionist, home economist U.S. Dept. Agr., Washington, 1943-46; charge de recherche Nat. Center Sci. Research, French Ministry Edn., 1947-49; jr. asst. research biochemist U. Cal. at Berkeley, 1950-53, asst. research biochemist tissue culture, 1953-55; research asso. oncology, asst. research biochemist Cancer Research Inst., U. Cal. Med. Sch. at San Francisco, 1955-59, asso. research biochemist, 1959-70; research asso. dept. medicine M.D. Anderson Hosp. Tumor Inst., Houston, 1970—. Mem. Tissue Culture Assn., Soc. Exptl. Biology and Medicine, N.Y. Acad. Scis., Assn. de Microbiologistes de la Langue Francaise, Soc. Cell Biology, Sigma Xi, Iota Sigma Pi. Home: 7232 Staffordshire St Houston TX 77025 Office: M D Anderson Hospital Tumor Institute Dept of Medicine Houston TX 77025

CAIN, BYRON WILSON, utility exec.; b. Quitman, Tex., Aug. 15, 1918; s. Clifford E. and Minnie (Cox) C.; B.B.A., U. Tex., 1939; M.B.A., Harvard, 1948; m. Celia Louise Tucker, June 18, 1949; children—Byron W., Melinda Lee. Asst. controller Continental Emsco, Dallas, 1949-50, controller, 1950-57; asst. controller Youngstown Sheet & Tubo Co. (O.), 1957-62; v.p., controller First Nat. Bank Dallas, 1962-65; with So. Union Gas Co., Dallas, 1965—, v.p. finance, 1968-72, exec. v.p., 1972—; dir. Information Processing Corp., Houston. Mem. adv. bd. Bus. Sch., U. Tex. at Austin, 1968-71. Served to maj. AAC, 1942-46; PTO. Mem. Fina'cial Execs. Inst. (past pres.), So. Gas. Assn. (treas.), Delta Tau Delta. Republican. Methodist. Clubs: Dallas Petroleum, Dallas Club, Northwood (Dallas). Home: 4112 Windsor Pkwy Dallas TX 75205 Office: 1533 Fidelity Union Tower Dallas TX 75201

CAIN, DONALD EZELL, lawyer, judge; b. San Marcos, Tex., Oct. 8, 1921; s. Erie Montclair and Betty (Howell) C.; Asso. Sci., Arlington State Coll., 1941; B.B.A., U. Tex., 1943, LL.B., 1948; m. Betty Anne Culberson, June 14, 1952; children—David, Dale, Donald Ezell, Randolph C. With contracts dept. Convair div. Gen. Dynamics Corp., 1948-50; admitted to Tex. bar, 1948; asso. Rogers & Thompson, Pampa, 1951-52, Curtis Douglass, 1952-53; pvt. practice, Pampa, 1954—; county atty. Gray County, 1955-69, county judge, 1971—. Bd. dirs. United Fund, 1956-60; pres. Adobe Walls council Boy Scouts Am. 1957-60. Served from ensign to lt. USNR, 1943-46, lt. 1950-51. Recipient Silver Beaver award Boy Scouts Am., 1958. Mem. Am., Gray County (pres. 1968) bar assns., State Bar Tex., C. of C. (dir. 1959-60), Am. Judicature Soc., Phi Alpha Delta. Democrat. Baptist. Rotarian (pres. 1958-59). Home: 1826 Williston St Pampa TX 79065 Office: Court House PO Box 2160 Pampa TX 79065

CAIN, JAMES BYERS, bus. exec.; b. Uniontown, Pa., June 25, 1922; s. John Smith and Margaret Eleanor (Byers) C.; grad. Schreiner Inst., 1940; B.B.A., So. Meth. U., 1942; m. Lillian Kilgore, Apr. 28, 1944; children—Margaret Elaine, John Charles. Pres. Austin Flying Service (Tex.), 1946-47; owner Aero-Tel Airport, Austin, 1947-51; owner Athens Laundry and Laundromatic Enterprises (Tex.), 1951-60; pres. Tex. Wholesale Supply Co., Athens, 1960-65; sec., treas., dir. Henderson County Savs. and Loan Assn., Athens, 1965-73; chmn. bd. First State Bank, Eustace; dir. 1st Nat. Bank, Athens. Chmn., City Indsl. Team, 1963—; pres. Athens Indsl. Found., 1965-72, Athens Cemetery Assn., 1968—. Trustee Athens Municipal Water Authority, Athens City Commn., Athens Ind. Sch. Dist., Lakewood Pvt. Sch.; bd. dirs. Schlesinger Home Nursing Service. Served with USNR, 1941-46. Recipient Achievement award Kiwanis Club, 1964, Athens Salesman award Athens Jr. C. of C., 1969; various indsl. devel. citations. Mem. Athens (pres., recipient Community Leadership award 1971), E. Tex. (dir.) chambers commerce, Kappa Alpha. Presbyn. Mason (Shriner). Home: 1012 E Tyler Athens TX 75751 Office: PO Box 29 Athens TX 75751

CAIN, LEONARD FRANCIS, ednl. adminstr.; b. Pottstown, Pa., Jan. 29, 1922; s. Leonard F. and Catherine E. (McEvoy) C,; A.B., St. Joseph's Coll., 1943; M.A., Cath. U. Am., 1947, Ph.D., 1966; postgrad. Georgetown U., 1943, U. Wis., 1948-49; m. Mary T. Townsend, Mar. 10, 1944; children—Michael, Sheila, Patrick, Eileen, Teresa, Kevin, Christopher, Monica, Brendan, Anthony, Deirdre. Mem. faculty Cath. U. Am., Washington, 1949—, dean Coll. Arts and Scis., 1966-74, asst. to pres., 1974—. Bd. dirs. nat. capital region Nat. Conf. Christians and Jews, 1965—; mem. Commn. on Christian Edn., Archdiocese of Washington, 1973—. Served with AUS, 1943-46. Mem. Am. Assn. U. Profs., Am. Conf. Acad. Deans, Am. Econ. Assn., Am. Polit. Sci. Assn., Indsl. Relations Research Assn., Econ. and Social Research Inst. (Dublin), Pi Gamma Mu, Alpha Sigma Nu, Delta Epsilon Sigma. Democrat. Roman Catholic. Home: 1026 Newton St NE Washington DC 20017

CAIN, STEPHEN MALCOLM, educator, physiologist; b. Lynn, Mass., Oct. 4, 1928; s. Herbert and Eva (Rowe) C.; B.S., Tufts U., 1949; postgrad. Johns Hopkins, 1956; Ph.D., U. Fla., 1959; m. Helen Gladys Allen, Sept. 14, 1951; children—Nancy Ellen, Carol Ann. Physiologist, U.S. Chem. Corps Med Labs., Edgewood Arsenal, Md., 1951-56, USAF Sch. Aerospace Medicine, Brooks AFB, Tex., 1959-71; physiologist, prof. physiology, asso. prof. medicine U. Ala. Med. Center, Birmingham, 1971—. Served with AUS, 1951-53. Mem. Am. Physiol. Soc., Soc. Exptl. Biology and Medicine (editorial bd. 1972—), Aerospace Med. Soc. Mason. Editorial bd. Jour. Applied Physiology, Am. Jour. Physiology, 1972—. Contbr. articles to sci. jours., chpts. to books. Home: 3752 Forest Run Rd Birmingham AL 35223

CALATAYUD, JUAN BAUTISTA, physician; b. Valencia, Spain, May 17, 1928; s. Agustin and Carmen (Llobat) C.; M.D., U. Valencia (Spain), 1952; m. Helen T. Lupton, July 2, 1960; children—Mary Carmen, Juan Cesar. Intern, Alexian Bros. Hosp., Elizabeth, N.J., 1955; resident St. Pauls Hosp., Dallas, 1956-57; fellow in medicine George Washington U. Hosp., Washington, 1957-60, asst. prof. medicine, 1962-69, asso. prof. medicine, 1969-70; asso. dir. med. edn. Doctors Hosp., Washington, 1970—; research asst. U. Montreal (Que., Can.), 1960; fellow medicine Montreal Gen. Hosp., 1961; house physician Deborah Hosp., Browns Mills, N.J., 1961-62; practice medicine specializing in cardiology, Washington, 1962—; cons. VA Center, Martinsburg, W.Va., 1965—. Mem. Am., Washington heart assns., Am. Fedn. Clin. Research (v.p. 1966-67, pres. 1967-68), Am. Coll. Angiology, D.C. Med. Soc., A.A.A.S., Pan Am. Med. Assn., Peruvian Cardiac Soc. (hon.), Peruvian Angiology Soc. (hon.). Contbr. articles in field to profl. jours. Home: 6217 Cheryl Dr Falls Church VA 22044 Office: 1835 I St NW Washington DC 20006

CALATHES, JOHN, aerospace co. exec.; b. N.Y.C., Aug. 29, 1925; s. William Thomas and Argiria Helen (Ellis) C.; B.S., N.Y.U., 1950; postgrad. Johns Hopkins, 1956-57; m. Eileen Mary Buckley, Oct. 7, 1951; children—John Patrick, Margaret Ann. With Martin Marietta Co., 1951—, mgr. propulsion, thermodynamics, and armament dept., Balt., 1961-67, mgr. propulsion, thermodynamics, and ordnance dept., mech. engring. div., Orlando, Fla., 1967-68, dir. mech. engring., 1968, dir. aero-mech. engring., 1968, dir. systems engring., dir. engring. 1968—. Mem. internal com. design criteria NASA. Served with USAAF, 1943-45. Decorated Air medal with 2 oak leaf clusters. Fellow Am. Inst. Aeros. and Astronautics; mem. Am. Ordnance Assn. (exec. v.p. 1963-64), Aerospace Industries Assn. Am. (mem. rocket propulsion com. 1967—, air breathing propulsion com. 1967—), Chem. Propulsion Information Agy. (mem. propulsion com. 1969-71), Am. Soc. M.E. Clubs: Martin Marietta Management (dir. 1969—); Winter Park Racquet. Home: 750 Pine Tree Rd Winter Park FL 32789 Office: Martin Marietta Corp PO Box 5837 MP 3 Orlando FL 32805

CALCOTE, AUCIE DANIEL, savs. and loan exec.; b. Shreveport, La., Aug. 26, 1909; s. Alonzo Washington and Annie Idell (Dennis) C.; student Centenary Coll. La., 1926-27, 29, La. State U., 1928; m. Patty Lewis Redditt, Oct. 23, 1932; 1 son, Alan Dean. Asst. to pres. Clacote-Shaw Oil Co., Shreveport, 1929-32; wholesale mgr. Sparco 707 Tire Service, Shreveport, 1932-38; cost accountant Tri-State Transit Co., also sec.-treas. Gt. So. Coaches, Inc., Shreveport, Jonesboro, Ark., 1938-42; dist. rationing officer Office Def. Transp. and OPA, Shreveport, 1942-46; sec.-treas. First Fed. Savs. & Loan Assn., Shreveport, La., 1946-50, v.p., dir., 1952—; asst. chief underwriter FHA, Shreveport, 1950-52. Methodist. Mason (32 deg., Shriner, K.T.). Club: East Ridge Country. Home: 6013 Annette St Shreveport LA Office: 2050 Line Av Shreveport LA 71104

CALDWELL, BETTYE (MCDONALD), psychologist, educator; b. Smithville, Tex., Dec. 24, 1924; d. Thomas Milton and Juanita (Mayes) McDonald; A.B., Baylor U., 1945; M.A., State U. Ia., 1947; Ph.D., Washington U., 1951; m. Fred Thomas Caldwell, Jr., 1947; children—Paul Frederick and Elizabeth Lanier (twins). Asst. in med. psychology Washington U. Sch. Medicine, 1947-50, instr. 1950-53, dir. child evaluation clinic, 1956-58; research asso., dept. pediatrics, Upstate Med. Center, Syracuse, N.Y., 1959-69, dir. Children's Center, 1966-69; asst. prof. psychology Northwestern U., 1953-55; Dual prof. child devel. and edn. Syracuse U., 1966-69; prof. edn. U.

Ark. at Fayetteville, 1969-74, dir. Center for Early Devel. and Edn., 1969—, prof. edn. U. Ark. at Little Rock, 1974—. Fellow Am. Psychol. Assn., Am. Orthopsychiat. Assn.; mem. Soc. Research in Child Devel., Nat. Assn. for Edn. Young Children, Assn. for Childhood Edn. Internat., N.E.A. Editor: Child Devel., 1968-71; co-editor Rev. Child Devel. Research. Home: 187 Pleasant Valley Dr Little Rock AR 72207 Office: 814 Sherman St Little Rock AR 72202

CALDWELL, CLAUD REID, lawyer; b. Augusta, Ga., Sept. 18, 1909; s. John Mars and Ethel (Bennett) C.; student Acad. Richmond County, 1922-26; m. Josephine F. Clarke, June 30, 1940; children—Claud R., Kathryn C., James W. Admitted to Ga. bar, 1932, practiced in Augusta, 1934—; judge Municipal Ct., City of Augusta, 1948-49. Pres., Richmond County Independent Party, 1950-51. Dir. Augusta chpt. A.R.C., YMCA; chmn. Augusta council Boy Scouts Am., 1949-50. Served with AUS, 1941-45; ETO. Recipient Distinguished Pistol Marksman award U.S. Army, 1965. Mem. Am., Ga. bar assns., Ga. Sport Shooting Assn. (dir., past pres.). Presbyn. (deacon). Mason (32 deg., Shriner). Home: 343 Hemlock Hill Rd Augusta GA 30904 Office: Southern Finance Bldg Augusta GA 30902

CALDWELL, FRED THOMAS, JR., surgeon, educator; b. Hot Springs, Ark., May 12, 1925; s. Fred Thomas and Margaret (Rodgers) C.; B.S., Baylor U., 1946; M.D., Washington U., St. Louis, 1950; m. Betty Ruth MacDonald, June 8, 1947; children—Paul, Elizabeth. Intern, Barnes Hosp., St. Louis, 1950-52, asst. resident, 1952-53, 55-56, resident, 1957-58; research fellow Washington U., 1956-57; instr. surgery State U. N.Y., Syracuse, 1958-61, asst. prof. surgery, 1961-64, asso. prof., 1964; prof. surgery U. Ark. Med. Center, Little Rock, 1967—. Collaborator, John B. Pierce Lab., 1962; participant operation Billabong in Australia, 1966. Served with M.C., AUS, 1953-55. Clin. fellow Am. Cancer Soc., 1957-58. Mem. A.C.S., Am. Assn. U. Profs., Soc. U. Surgeons, Am. Physiol. Soc., Internat. Soc. for Burn Injury, Soc. Surgery Alimentary Tract, A.A.A.S., Am. Assn. Cancer Edn., Am. Gastroent. Assn., Southwestern Surg. Congress, Am. Assn. for Surgery of Trauma, N.Y. Acad. Sci., Western Surg. Soc., Am. Burn Assn., So. Surg. Assn., Am. Trauma Soc., Sigma Xi, Alpha Omega Alpha. Contbr. articles to profl. jours. Home: 187 Pleasant Valley St Little Rock AR 72207 Office: 4301 W Markham St Little Rock AR 72201

CALDWELL, GEORGE BRUCE, hosp. exec.; b. St. Paul, June 16, 1930; s. Gerlad James and Hazel Ruth (Paulson) C.; B.A., Cornell Coll., Mt. Vernon, Ia., 1952; M.A. in Health and Hosp. Adminstrn., State U. Ia., 1955; m. Phoebe Jean Wendt, Sept. 1, 1951; children—Carrie Lynn, Gerlad James, Amy Jo, David Marshall. Adminstr. resident Rockford (Ill.) Meml. Hosp., then asst. dir., asso. dir., 1954-61; adminstr., exec. v.p. Lake Forest (Ill.) Hosp., 1961-73; pres. Morris Cafritz Meml. Hosp.-Washington, 1973—; pres. Greater S.E. Community Hosp. Found., Inc., Washington, 1973—. Pres. Coordinated Health Services; v.p. Hosp. Computer Services; vis. lectr. U. Chgo., State U. Ia.; lectr. in field. Bd. dirs. Chgo. Hosp. Council, Health Care at Home. Mem. Ill. (dist. pres., trustee), Am. (chmn. adv. panel manuals) hosp. assns., Am. Coll. Hosp. Adminstrs. Presbyn. Contbr. numerous articles to profl. jours. Home: 7307 Burtonwood Dr Alexandria VA 22307 Office: 1310 Southern Av SE Washington DC 20032

CALDWELL, HAROLD LEROY, petroleum engr.; b. Pawnee, Okla., Aug. 14, 1925; s. Harold Ralph and Eula P. (Buckner) C.; B.S. in Petroleum Engring., U. Tulsa, 1951; m. Patricia T. Poorman, Dec. 24, 1948; children—Michael Alan, Douglas Owen. Exploitation engr. Sunray Oil Co., 1951-55; chief engr. Keener Oil Co., Tulsa, 1955-59, gen. supt. prodn., 1959-62; cons. engr., 1962-63; drilling engr. Fenix & Scisson, Inc., Tulsa, 1963-65; gen. prodn. supt. K.W.B. Oil Property Mgmt., Inc., 1965—; engr. Williams Bros. Engring. Co., 1967-74; mgr. Perrault-Caldwell, Inc., Tulsa, 1974—. Served with AUS, 1943-46. Registered profl. engr., Okla. Mem. Am. Inst. Mining Engrs., Am. Petroleum Inst., Okla. State Profl. Engrs. Republican. Mem. Reorganized Ch. of Jesus Christ of Latter-day Saints. Home: 5129 S Richmond Tulsa OK 74135 Office: 310 Philtower Bldg Tulsa OK 74103

CALDWELL, HOWARD EUGENE, investment counselor; b. Jacksonville, Fla., Mar. 16, 1924; s. Howard Eugene and Marye Elzie (Manning) C.; B.B.A. with high distinction, Emory U., 1948; m. Martha Norton, July 25, 1970; 1 son, Orman Norton. Security analyst Trust Co. Ga., Atlanta, 1948-53; security analyst Montag & Caldwell, Inc., investment counsel, 1953-56, partner, 1956-68, pres., 1968-72, chmn. bd., 1973—; adv. dir. Mercantile Nat. Bank of Atlanta; sr. v.p., dir. Alpha Fund, Alpha Research, 1968—. Served with AUS, 1942-45. Decorated Purple Heart. Mem. Atlanta Soc. Financial Analysts (past pres.), Financial Analyst Fedn., Inst. Chartered Financial Analysts, Investment Counsel Assn. Am. (bd. govs. 1971). Methodist. Kiwanian. Clubs: University Yacht, Commerce (Atlanta). Home: 77 E Andrews Dr NW Atlanta GA 30305 Office: 2901 First National Bank Bldg Atlanta GA 30303

CALDWELL, JAMES NEELY, III, lawyer; b. Rock Hill, S.C., Nov. 26, 1926; s. James Neely and Ruby (Graham) C.; A.B., U.S.C., 1948, LL.B., 1950. Admitted to S.C. bar, 1950; atty. Nat. Inst. Municipal Law Ofcls., Washington, 1951; trial atty. U.S. Dept. Justice, Washington, 1951-55; atty. post office civil service com., judiciary com. U.S. Senate, 1955-57; legal counsel, asst. dir. Municipal Assn. S.C., 1957-60, exec. v.p., 1960-73; spl. asst. to S.C. Commr. for Health and Environmental Control, Columbia, 1974—. Bd. dirs. YMCA, Columbia, 1959-61; pres. bd. dirs. Columbia Symphony Orch., 1972-73. Served with AUS, 1945-47. Mem. Am., Fed., S.C., Richland County bar assns., Nat. League Cities, Phi Kappa Sigma, Phi Delta Phi, Omicron Delta Kappa, Kappa Sigma Kappa. Presbyn. (elder, deacon). Kiwanian. Home: 819 Albion Rd Columbia SC 29205 Office: PO Box 322 Columbia SC 29202

CALDWELL, MILLARD F., JR., judge; b. Knoxville, Tenn., Feb. 6, 1897; s. Millard Fillmore and Martha Jane (Clapp) C.; student Carson and Newman Coll., 1913-14, U. of Miss., 1917-18, U. Va., 1919-22; LL.D., Rollins Coll., U. Fla., Fla. So. U., Fla. State U.; m. Mary Rebecca Harwood, Feb. 14, 1925; children—Millard Fillmore III (dec.), Sally. Purkins McCord, Susan B. Dodd. Admitted to Tenn. bar 1922, Fla. bar, 1925; served as pros. atty. and county atty., Santa Rosa County, Fla., and city atty., Milton; elected to Fla. State Legislature, 1928 and 1930; mem. 73d to 76th Congresses (1933-41), 3d Fla. Dist.; voluntarily retired from Congress to resume practice of law at Milton and Tallahassee, Fla.; elected gov. of Florida for term 1945-49; Fed. Civil Def. adminstrator 1950-52; justice Florida Supreme Court 1962—, chief justice, 1967-70. Del. Interparliamentary Union. Chmn. Nat. Govs. Conf., 1946-47; pres. Council of State Govts., 1946-48; chmn. bd. of control S. Regional Edn., 1947-50; chmn. Fla. Commn. Constl. Govt., 1957-66. Served as pvt. and 2d lt., F.A., U.S. Army, World War I. Mem. Am. Judicature Soc., Newcomen Soc., Huguenot Soc., S.A.R., Alpha Kappa Psi, Blue Key, Kappa Sigma, Phi Alpha Delta. Democrat. Home: Harwood Plantation Old Bainbridge Rd Tallahassee FL 32301 Office: Forum Bldg Monroe St Tallahassee FL 32302

CALDWELL, NATHAN GREEN, reporter; b. St. Charles, Mo., July 16, 1912; s. Albert Green and Sara (Jetton) C.; student Southwestern Coll., 1933, Cumberland U., 1934; Nieman fellow Harvard, 1940; m. Camilla Frances Jonston, Nov. 16, 1936; 1 son, John Sam. Polit. writer Nashville Tennessean, 1934-56, econs. and regional resource devel. reporter, 1956—. Co-recipient Pulitzer prize for nat. affairs reporting, 1961. Rosenwald fellow, 1947. Author: The Cotton Picker Moves People, 1947; The Strange Romance of John L. Lewis and Cyrus Eaton, 1961. Home: 1216 Eastdale Av Nashville TN 37206 Office: 1100 Broad St Nashville TN 37203

CALDWELL, PAUL ALFRED, nuclear physicist; b. Mpls., Jan. 28, 1918; s. Paul Alfred and Anna James (Lattin) C.; B.A., U. Minn., 1943; postgrad. U. Md., 1945-50; m. Elizabeth E., Jan. 27, 1942 (div. Dec. 1970); children—Elizabeth Ann, Dorothy Louise. With Naval Research Lab., Washington, 1942-59; nuclear physicist Harry Diamond Labs., U.S. Army Materiel Command, Washington, 1959—, chief nuclear radiation simulation tech. br., 1971—, dir. Aurora facility, 1972—. Mem. Am. Phys. Soc., A.A.A.S., I.E.E.E., Sci. Research Soc. Am., Philos. Soc. Washington. Home: 9317 Sudbury Rd Silver Spring MD 20901 Office: Harry Diamond Labs Aurora Facility Washington DC 20438

CALDWELL, THOMAS JONES, JR., lawyer; b. New Orleans, Oct. 17, 1923; s. Thomas Jones and Ethel Marie (Lee) C.; B.S. in Mech. Engring., U. Tex., 1944, J.D., 1949; B.S. in Econs., U. Houston, 1969. Admitted to Tex. bar, 1949, since practiced in Houston; asso. George Red, 1949-50; asso. Fouts, Moore, Caldwell & Coleman and predecessor firm, 1950-52, mem. firm, 1952—. Sec., dir. Delta Engring. Corp., Houston, 1954-69. Treas., Houston Com. on Fgn. Relations, 1965-70, chmn., 1970-71. Bd. dirs. Tex. Assn. Mental Health, 1969—, v.p., 1970-73, pres., 1973—; bd. dirs. Mental Health Assn. Houston, 1968—, v.p., 1969-70; bd. dirs. Child Guidance Center, Houston, 1960-68, 69-72, pres., 1965-67. Served with USNR, 1943-46. Mem. Am., Tex., Houston bar assns., Am. Judicature Soc., Kappa Sigma, Phi Delta Phi, Tau Beta Pi, Pi Tau Sigma, Phi Kappa Phi. Club: Houston Country. Home: 2021 Westcreek Apt 24B Houston TX 77019 Office: 4600 Post Oak Pl Dr Suite 207 Houston TX 77027

CALHOON, JERRY LEE, lawyer; b. Eldorado, Ill., June 6, 1942; s. Robert Lee and Effie Mae (Hammett) C.; B.B.A., U. N.M., 1965; J.D. cum laude, Baylor U., 1970; m. Rita Gay Sanders, Sept. 7, 1963; children—Michael Lee, Mark Alan. Accountant, H.K. Axness, C.P.A., Albuquerque, 1964-65; office mgr. Real Dairy Milk Products Co., Albuquerque, 1965; auditor Zia Co., Los Alamos, 1965-67; dep. state treas. N.M., Santa Fe, 1967-68; admitted to Tex. bar, 1970; atty. Ramey, Brelsford, Flock, Hutchins & Carroll, Tyler, 1970-73; practice law McDonald & Calhoon, Palestine, 1973—. Instr. accounting McLennan Community Coll., Waco, 1970. Recipient Nat. Harris award, 1970. C.P.A., N.M., Tex. Mem. Tex., Anderson County bar assns., Tex., E.Tex. Chpt. socs. C.P.A.'s, Palestine C. of C. (future studies council), Tex. Trial Lawyers Assn. (award 1970). Baptist. Asso. editor: Baylor Law Rev., 1969, sect. editor, 1970. Home: 214 Sheridan St Palestine TX 75801 Office: Box 816 608 E Crawford Palestine TX 75801

CALHOUN, EVELYN WILLIAMS, social worker; b. Tyler, Tex., Sept. 12, 1921; d. James Stanley and Norma (Skelton) Williams; B.A., Baylor U., 1941; M.S.W., Worden Sch. Social Work, 1960; postgrad. U. Chgo., 1955-56; m. William Benjamin Calhoun, Jr., Mar. 15, 1942 (div. Mar. 1949); children—William Bejamin III, Anne Stanley (Mrs. Donald Elliot Loyd). Field worker Tex. Dept. Pub. Welfare, Tyler, 1953-55; field placement Salvation Army Family Service, Chgo., 1955-56; child welfare worker Tyler-Smith County Child Welfare Unit, 1957-59; field placement Tex. Inst. Rehab. and Research, Houston, 1959-60, med. social worker, 1960-64; research social worker pre-natal research project, dept. obstetrics, gynecology U. Tex. Med. Br. at Galveston, 1964-66, supr. social service, dept. obstetrics, gynecology, 1966—, cons. satellite clinics, 1967—, cons. family planning program, 1969—; field instr. U. Houston Grad. Sch. Social Work, 1968—. Bd. dirs. Galveston County Community Action Council, 1966-68. Mem. Tex. Social Welfare Assn., Nat. Assn. Social Workers (chmn. research council San Jacinto chpt. 1963-64, chmn. Galveston br. 1964-67, sec. 1967-68, group leader so. regional inst. 1966, Tex. del. 1969—, alternate del. Tex. state council 1967), Acad. Certified Social Workers, Am. Assn. U. Women, Order De Moley, Delta Alpha Pi. Episcopalian. Toastmistress. Home: 2408 Av O Galveston TX 77550

CALHOUN, FRANK WAYNE, lawyer, state legislator; b. Houston, Apr. 15, 1933; s. Wilmer Cecil and Ruby Edith (Willis) C.; B.A., Tex. Tech U., 1956; LL.B., U. Tex., 1959, J.D., 1969; m. Doris Lee Wampler, July 5, 1956 (div. Sept. 1973); children—Michael, David. Admitted to Tex. bar, 1959; partner Byrd, Shaw, Weeks & Calhoun, Abilene, Tex., 1959-73; asso. Liddell, Sapp, Zively & Brown, Houston, 1974—; mem. Tex. Ho. of Reps., 1966-74. Mem. Tex. Constl. Revision Conv., 1974. Mem. exec. bd. Chisholm Trail council Boy Scouts Am.; Bd. dirs. Abilene YMCA; trustee Tex. Tech Law Sch. Found. Served with USNR, 1951-53. Named Abilene's Outstanding Young Man, Jr. C. of C., 1968; Distinguished Service award State Bar Tex., 1969. Mem. Am., Tex. (past com. chmn.) bar assns., Abilene C. of C. (past dir.), Tex. Tech U. Ex-Students Assn. (past pres.), Nat. Soc. State Legislators (bd. govs., past program chmn., exec. com.), Tex. Archeol. Soc., Nat. Audubon Soc., Abilene Fine Arts Mus., Abilene Assn. for Mental Health, Sigma Alpha Epsilon, Alpha Kappa Psi. Democrat. Methodist. Rotarian. Club: Sierra. Contbg. editor Tex. Lawyers Weekly Letter, 1964. Home: 13176 Trail Hollow Houston TX 77024 Office: 510 Gulf Bldg Houston TX 77002

CALHOUN, MILBURN EUGENE, pub. co. exec., physician; b. West Monroe, La., Jan. 15, 1930; s. Darrell Lavelle and Mary (Crowell) C.; student N.E. La. State U., 1947-49; B.S., La. State U., 1951, M.D., 1955; m. Nancy Kathryn Harris, July 14, 1956; children—Kathleen Elizabeth, David Harris. Intern Charity Hosp. La., New Orleans, 1955-56; practice medicine, specializing in family practice, Buras, La., 1956-57, 59-65, Marrero, La., 1965—; mem. staff West Jefferson Gen. Hosp., Marrero; clin. instr. Med. Sch., La. State U., New Orleans, 1970—, Tulane U. Med. Sch., New Orleans, 1971—; founder, owner Bayou Books, Gretna, La., 1961—; pub., pres. Pelican Pub. Co., Inc., Gretna, 1970—; sec., dir. Nicholson Baehr Calhoun, M.D.'s, Ltd., Marrero, 1971—. Served with USAF, 1957-59. Diplomate Am. Bd. Family Practice. Mem. Assn. Am. Pubs., Am. Booksellers Assn., Am. Acad. Family Practice, A.M.A., La. Med. Soc. (com. on hwy. safety; hist. com.), La. Hist. Soc. Baptist. Pub., book rev. editor La. Hist. Quar., 1971—. Office: 829 Baratavia Blvd Marrero LA 70072 also 630 Burmaster St Gretna LA 70058

CALHOUN, NOAH ROBERT, dentist; b. Clarendon, Ark., Mar. 23, 1921; s. Son and Dwelley (Erving) C.; student Fisk U., 1940-41, Lincoln U., 1942-43, U. Pa., 1944-45; D.D.S., Howard U., 1946; M.Dental Surgery, Tufts U., 1955; m. Cecelia C. Christopher, Oct. 17, 1950; children—Stephen Marc, Cecelia Noel. Oral surgeon Tuskegee (Ala.) VA Hosp., 1950-53, chief dental service, 1955-57; oral surgeon, dir. oral surgery tng. VA Hosp., Washington, 1964—, asst. chief dental service, 1971—; oral surgeon Freedman Hosp., Washington, 1967—; prof. oral surgery Dental Sch., Howard U., 1968—; professorial lectr. Dental Sch., Georgetown U., 1970—; Naval Dental Sch., 1970—, Walter Reed Army Dental Sch., 1971-72. Asst. dir. Tuskegee chpt. A.R.C., 1961-62, dir. 1962-64. Served to capt. USAF, 1943-45, 1952-53. Recipient alumni award Howard U., 1969. Diplomate Am. Bd. Oral Surgeons (mem. adv. com. 1967-71). Fellow Am. Coll. Dentistry; mem. Am. Dental Assn., Am. Soc. Oral Surgeons, Nat. Dental Assn., Internat. Assn. Dental Research, Omicron Kappa Upsilon, Alpha Phi Alpha. Home: 1413 Leegate Rd NW Washington DC 20012 Office: 50 Irving St NW VA Hosp Washington DC 20012

CALHOUN, WANDA JUNE, librarian; b. Mayfield, Ky., Jan. 23, 1932; d. Thomas Lewis and Lucile (Hamlet) Calhoun; B.S., Murray State Coll., 1953; M.A. in L.S., U. Mich., 1955, postgrad., 1956-58; postgrad. U. Minn., 1960. Divisional librarian U. Mich., 1955-58; head librarian Heidelberg Coll., 1958-63, Fla. Presbyn. Coll., Eckerd Coll., St. Petersburg, 1963—. Vis. specialist in library services United Bd. for Christian Higher Edn. in Asia, 1965-66, 71; library cons. United Bd. Sch., Indonesia P.I., Hong Kong, Taiwan, Korea. Mem. Am. Assn. U. Women (chpt. v.p. 1962-63), Am., Fla. library assns., Am. Assn. U. Profs. Presbyn. Office: Eckerd Coll St Petersburg FL 33733

CALHOUN, WILLIAM MCCALL, physician; b. Arlington, Ga., Sept. 13, 1932; s. William Wright and Mary Maude (Taylor) C.; B.S., N.Ga. Coll., 1952; postgrad. U. Mich., 1953, U. Ga., 1953-54; M.D., Med. Coll. Ga., 1958; m. JoAnn LeSueur, Oct. 10, 1961; children—William McCall, Anne, Mary Clay, Virginia. Intern, U.S. Naval Hosp., Phila., 1958-59; gen. practice medicine and surgery, Buena Vista, Ga., 1961—; mem. staff, sec. med. staff, vice chief of staff Stewart-Webster Hosp., Richland, Ga. Served with USN, 1958-61. Hon. mem. Ala. Senate, 1971—; mem. gov's. staff Ala., 1971—. Mem. Am. Acad. Family Practice, A.M.A., Med. Assn. Ga., So. Med. Assn., Alpha Kappa Kappa, Sigma Alpha Epsilon. Mason (Shriner). Club: Tri County Country (Buena Vista). Home: Walton Woods Rd Buena Vista GA 31803 Office: E Court Square Buena Vista GA 31803

CALKIN, HOMER LEONARD, diplomatic historian; b. Clearfield, Ia., May 5, 1912; s. Henry Orlando and Ina Marie (Leonard) C.; student Simpson Coll., 1930-32; B.A., U. Ia., 1935, M.A., 1936, Ph.D., 1939; m. Mary K. Ferriss, June 12, 1971. Tchr., Lyons Twp. High Sch., La Grange, Ill., 1941-42; propaganda analyst Dept. Justice, Washington, 1942-43; intelligence officer War Dept. Gen. Staff, Washington, 1944-46; archivist Nat. Archives, Washington, 1946-50; mgmt. officer, historian Dept. State, Washington, 1950—; faculty Am. U., Washington, 1946-47. Mem. Commn. on Archives and History, United Methodist Ch., 1972—. Mem. Am. Hist. Assn., Orgn. Am. Historians, So. Hist. Soc. Club: Cosmos (Washington). Author: Castings From the Foundry Mold, 1968. Contbr. to Those Incredible Methodists, 1972. Co-editor: Documents on Germany, 1944-1970, 1971. Home: 3830 Columbia Pike Arlington VA 22204 Office: Hist Office Dept State Washington DC 20520

CALKINS, GARY NATHAN, lawyer; b. N.Y.C., Mar. 1, 1911; s. Gary Nathan and Helen R. (Williston) C.; student Ecole Internationale, Geneva, Switzerland, 1926-27, Storm King Sch., 1927-29; A.B., Columbia, 1933; LL.B., Harvard, 1936; m. Constantia Hommann, June 22, 1940 (div. Dec. 1948); m. 2d, Susannah Eby, Nov. 19, 1949; children—Helen, Margaret, Sarah, Abigail. Admitted to N.Y. bar, 1936, D.C. bar, 1955; asso. Beekman & Bogue, N.Y.C., 1936-41; staff Civil Aeros. Bd., 1941-56, chief internat. and rules div., 1947-56; partner Galland, Kharasch & Calkins, Washington, 1956-62; partner Galland, Kharasch, Calkins & Lippmann, 1962-69, Galland, Kharasch, Calkins, & Brown, Washington and N.Y.C., 1970—. Mem. U.S. del. legal com. Internat. Civil Aviation Orgn., 1947-55, delegation chmn. 1st, 3d, 5th, 9th and 10th meetings; chmn. U.S. delegation Internat. Diplomatic Conf. for Revision of Warsaw Conv., The Hague, 1955; chmn. legal div. U.S. Air Coordinating Com., 1955-56. Served as lt. USNR, 1943-45. Mem. Am., D.C. bar assns., Soc. Quiet Birdmen, Psi Upsilon. Clubs: Internat., Nat. Aviation, Internat. Aviation (Washington). Asso. editor United States and Canadian Aviation Reports, 1956; asso. editor Jour. Air Law and Commerce, 1956-58, editor-in-chief, 1958-63. Author profl. papers. Home: 6504 Dearborn Dr Falls Church VA 22044 Office: Canal Sq 1054 31st St Washington DC 20007 also 40 Wall St New York City NY 10022

CALKINS, JOHN THIERS, lawyer; b. Elmira, N.Y., May 14, 1925; s. John Thiers and Laura (Westervelt) C.; A.B., Syracuse U., 1949; postgrad. U. London, summer 1951; J.D., Georgetown U., 1957; m. Patricia Painton, Dec. 27, 1952; children—Sharon, Carolyn. Admitted to D.C. bar, 1958. Asst. to rep. J.C. Davies, Washington, 1949-51; account exec. Mellor Advt. Agy., Elmira, N.Y., 1952; asst. to Rep. Sterling Cole, Washington, 1953-58; exec. asst. to Rep. Howard W. Robison, Washington, 1958-70; exec. dir. Nat. Republican Congl. Com., Washington, 1970—; dir. Elmira Data Processing Co. Inc., 1964—. Chmn. Syracuse U. Alumni Giving Program, Washington, 1964. Chmn. com. spl. assts. Nat. Rep. Congl. Com., 1962-69. Trustee, Nat. Rowing Found., 1970—. Served with AUS, World War II. Congl. staff fellow Am. Polit. Sci. Assn., Inst. Internat. Studies, Geneva, Switzerland, 1965. Mem. D.C. Bar Assn., Psi Upsilon. Episcopalian. Clubs: Elmira City, Capitol Hill (Washington). Home: 2329 California St NW Washington DC 20008 Office: Congressional Annex Washington DC 20515

CALL, EVERETT RALPH, assn. exec.; b. Manchester, N.H., June 17, 1922; s. Ralph Harvey and Erna (Schricker) C.; B.S. in Exec. Bus. Adminstrn., Georgetown U., 1949; m. Rosalind Warner Kain, Mar. 23, 1945; children—M. Christine, Jocelyn G., Phyllis A. Asst. to sec. U.S. Ind. Telephone Assn., Washington, 1946-49; statistician Inst. Shortening and Edible Oils Inc., Washington, 1950-55; dir. mgmt. information Nat. Paint and Coatings Assn., Washington, 1955—; pres. Call Marketing Services, Washington, 1959—. Pres. Civic Assn., Fairfax, Va., 1953-54. Served with USMC, 1942-46. Mem. Washington Soc. Assn. Execs. (recipient Outstanding Contbrs. award 1966, v.p. 1969-70, pres. 1970-71), Color Marketing Group (dir. 1962—). Unitarian (trustee). Home: 2608 N Pocomoke St Arlington VA 22207 Office: 1500 Rhode Island Av NW Washington DC 20005

CALLAHAN, VINCENT FRANCIS, JR., publisher, state legislator; b. Washington, Oct. 30, 1931; s. Vincent Francis and Anita (Hawkins) C.; B.S. in Fgn. Service, Georgetown U., 1957; m. Dorothy Helen Budge, Aug. 27, 1960; children—Vincent Francis III, Elizabeth Lauren, Anita Marie, Cynthia Helen, Robert Bruce, Became partner Callahan Publs., 1957, now pres., editor numerous publs., 1957—; dir. McLean Savs. and Loan Assn.; past pres. Ind. Newsletters Assn., Washington; mem. Va. Ho. of Dels., 1968—. Candidate for lt. gov. Va., 1965; state finance chmn. Rep. Party of Va., 1966-68; dir. Washington Met. Council Govts. Served with USMC, 1950-53; as lt. USCGR, 1959-63. Mem. U.S. Naval Inst., Marine Tech. Soc., Am. Def. Preparedness Assn. Republican. Roman Catholic. Clubs: National Press; Kiwanis (past pres.) (McLean, Va.); Bull and Bear (Richmond, Va.). Author eight books including: Missile Contracts Guide, 1958; Space Guide, 1959; Underwater Defense Handbook, 1963; Military Research Handbook, 1963. Home: 6220 Nelway Dr McLean VA 22101 Office: 1427 Center St McLean VA 22101

CALLAWAY, HOWARD H., sec. Army, b. LaGrange, Ga., Apr. 2, 1927; s. Cason Jewell and Virginia (Hand) C.; student Ga. Inst. Tech., 1945; ed. U.S. Mil. Acad., 1945-49; m. Elizabeth Walton; children—Elizabeth Walton, Virginia Hand, Howard Hollis, Edward Cason, Ralph Walton. Pres. Callaway Gardens, Pine Mountain, Ga., 1953-72; pres. Interfinancial, Inc., Atlanta, 1972-73; sec. Army, Washington, 1973—. Mem. Adv. Commn. on Intergovtl. Relations, Washington, 1969-73; civilian aide to U.S. Sec. of Army. Mem. 89th congress from 3d Ga. dist.; Republican nominee gov. Ga., 1966; Ga. mem. Rep. Nat. Com., 1968-73. Mem. bd. regents univ. system Ga., 1953-64; trustee Freedoms Found, Valley Forge, Pa.; trustee Ida Cason Callaway Found. Served to 1st lt. AUS, 1949-52. Decorated Combat Infantryman badge, Korean Service medal with 3 bronze stars, Republic of Korea badge, UN Service medal. Episcopalian. Home: Pine Mountain GA 31822 Office: The Pentagon Washington DC 20301

CALLAWAY, RONALD FORREST, quality engr.; b. Mobile, Ala., Sept. 15, 1932; s. Raphael Leon and Forrest Estelle (Waldrop) C.; B.S., U. Ala., 1957; m. Margaret Louise Wooley, Aug. 18, 1950; children—Ronald Havard, Lynn Forrest, Jesse Leon. Nuclear engr. Lockheed Aircraft Corp., Ga. Nuclear Labs., 1957-63; electronics engr. missile guidance and control prodn. U.S. Army Missile Command, 1963-66, gen. engr. missile systems test, reliability and quality engring., 1966—. Served with AUS, 1950-52. Registered profl. engr., Ala. Mem. Assn. U.S. Army, Army Ordnance Assn., Nat. Rifle Assn., U. Ala. Alumni Assn. Clubs: Arab Country, Jaycees, Quarterback. Home: Route 4 Box 444B Arab AL 35016 Office: AMSMI-QEL Redstone Arsenal AL 35809

CALLAWAY, WILLIAM CHOTEAU, banker; b. Oakland, Miss.; May 4, 1914; s. Gilbert Evans and Bell (Duke) C.; student Miss. State U., 1931-33, George Washington U., 1934-36; m. Ann J. Monteith, May 18, 1947; 1 son, William Chouteau, 1 step-dau., Patricia Ann (Mrs. Jake Gibbs). With U.S. Dept. Interior, Washington, 1936-38, Dist. Govt. Washington, 1938-41; with Bank of Oakland (Miss.). 1951—, successively bookkeeper, cashier, exec. v.p., 1951-59, pres., 1959—. Mem. council Town of Oakland, 1957-61, mayor, 1965-69. Served with AUS, 1941-45; vet. adviser VA, 1946-51. Mem. Am. Legion, V.F.W. Presbyn. (elder). Rotarian. Office: Bank of Oakland Oakland MS 38948

CALLEN, IRWIN R., physician; b. Chgo., May 3, 1919; s. Harry and Esther (Levey) C.; student U. Chgo., 1936-39; B.S., U. Ill., 1941, M.D., 1943; M.S., 1949; m. Rose P. Cohen, Aug. 10, 1941; children—Jeffrey P., James Jay. Intern Ill. Research and Ednl. Hosps., U. Ill., 1943, fellowship dept. internal medicine, 1946-47, electrocardiographer, asso. attending physician, 1948-51; practice medicine specializing in internal medicine and cardiology, Chgo., 1947—; asso. attending physician Cook County Hosp., Chgo., 1951-57, attending physician dept. internal medicine, 1958—, prof. medicine and cardiology grad. sch., 1958—; instr. dept. medicine U. Health Scis., Chgo. 1951-56, asso. dept. internal medicine, 1956-66, asso. prof. medicine, 1966-72, prof. clin. medicine, 1972—; chmn. dept. internal medicine Edgewater Hosp., Chgo., 1964-68, v.p. med. staff, 1967, dir. cardiology, 1964—, pres. med. staff, 1968, 69, bd. dirs., 1968—; attending physician, Louis A. Weiss Meml. Hosp., Chgo., 1952—. Served as capt., M.C., AUS, 1944-45. Diplomate Am. Bd. Internal Medicine, Fellow Am. Coll. Cardiology (sec. Chgo. roundtable 1963. Am. Coll. Chest Physicians, Am. Assn. Bioanalysts; mem. Ill. Soc. for Med. Research, Am., Ill., Chgo., Greater Miami heart assns., Chgo. Diabetes Assn., Am., Ill., Chgo., Dade County med. assns., N.Y. Acad. Scis., Fla. Soc. Internal Medicine, A.A.A.S., Brain Research Found. Contbr. numerous articles in field to prof. jours. Address: 800 NE 195th St North Miami FL 33162

CALLENDER, MARTHA V. LINDER (MRS. RICHARD ERVIN CALLENDER), club woman, genealogist, artist; b. Prairie Dell, Tex.; d. Franklin Trimmier and Adeline (Hunter) Linder; student Baylor Coll., 1914-16; grad. Sam Houston State Tchrs. Coll., Huntsville, Tex., 1916; m. Richmond Ervin Callender, July 9, 1919; children—Catherine V. (Mrs. Merrill Smith), Richard Ervin (dec. 1963). Tchr. pub. schs., Rosenberg, Tex., 1917-18; sec. Gulf Oil Co., Houston 1918-19; exec. sec. Fed. Farm Loan Assn., Lockhart, Tex., 1925-30. Recipient various awards for artwork. Corr. sec. A. and M. Garden Club, 1968-69; mem. A. and M. Mother's Club, A. and M. Social Club, Extension Service Club, Fine Arts and Crafts Group. Mem. Tex. Hist. Soc., Tex. Fine Arts Assns., D.A.R. (chpt. corr. sec. 1952-54, librarian 1948-50; nat. vice chmn. scholarships com. 1960-63, Tex. chmn. geneal. records com. 1952-58, chpt. registrar 1950-52, 60-62, 71-74, chpt. regent 1965-67), Daus. Am. Colonists (Tex. chmn. colonial and geneal. records 1957-59, regent Louis Guion chpt. 1961-63, hon. regent, Tex. parliamentarian 1959-61, state registrar 1963-65, chmn. our colonial heritage com. 1965-67, 2d vice regent chpt. 1967-71), U.D.C. (pres. L.S. Ross chpt. 1961-63, chpt. registrar 1963-65 dist. chmn. 1964-66), Children Am. Colonists (nat. chaplain, sr. adv. council 1964-66, v.p. So. sect. 1971-73), Brazos County Bar Assn. Aux., United Daus. 1812 (state chmn. 1971-74), Tex. State Geneal. Soc., So. Linder Family Assn. (1st pres.), Tex. Folklore Soc., Brazos Valley Art Council, Art Gallery League, Operating and Performing Arts Soc. (charter), Tex. Hist. Assn. Club: Bryan College Station Art (charter). Home: 209 Lee Av College Station TX 77840

CALLIHAM, EDITH MADELIN ETHEREDGE (MRS. GEORGE NOLLON CALLIHAM, JR.), banker; b. Ridgeville, S.C., Jan. 4, 1928; d. John Beckwith and Exie (Singletary) Etheredge; grad. high sch.; m. George Nollon Calliham, Jr., Nov. 25, 1946; children—George Nollon III, Robert L. With S.C. Nat. Bank, Naval Base, S.C., 1944-49, supr. transit and bookkeeping dept. 1947-49; with 1st Nat. Bank of S.C., Charleston, 1952—, mgr. Air Base Facility, 1955-68, asst. cashier, 1961—, mgr. Air Base and Naval Base Facilities, 1961-68, asst. v.p., 1968-73, v.p., 1973—, operation and mgr. credit card dept., Charleston office, 1968-73, v.p. credit card dept., pub. relations, br. planning mgr., 1973—. Active P.T.A., Community Civic Club. Mem. Nat. Assn. Bank Women (past chmn. S.C. group, regional v.p. 1973-74), S.C. Bankers Assn. (exec. council women's div. 1971—, bank week coordinator 1972, 73), Altrusa Internat. (pres. Greater Charleston 1964-66), C. of C. Methodist (sec. jr. dept. ch. sch. 1962-64). Home: 1609 Holton Pl Charlestowne Estates Charleston SC 29407 Office: 1st National Bank of SC PO Box 959 Charleston SC 29402

CALLISON, CAROLINE HOLLINGSWORTH, physician; b. Charleston, S.C., Aug. 20, 1914; d. Henry Grady and Ethel (Jagar) Callison; B.S., Coker Coll., 1936; M.D., Med. Coll. S.C., 1939; M.P.H., Columbia, 1947. Intern, Crawford W. Long Meml. Hosp., 1939-41; health officer Washington Coosa, Clarke, St. Clair counties, Ala., 1941-45, McCormick and Greenwood counties, S.C., 1945-46; asst. health officer Charleston County, S.C., 1947-48; county health officer Marlboro, Chesterfield, Abbeville, McCormick counties, S.C., 1948-52; dept. state health officer Queen Anne's County, Md., 1952-61; health dir. Sampson and Bladen counties, N.C., 1961—. Mem. Am. Coll. Preventive Medicine, Am. Assn. Pub. Health Physicians, N.C. Med. Assn., A.M.A., Am., N.C. pub. health assns., Sampson County Med. Soc. Episcopalian. Home: 406 Parker Dr Clinton NC 28328 Office: County Health Dept Clinton NC 28328

CALLISON, GLENN BAYNE, broadcasting co. exec.; b. Paxton, Ill., Dec. 10, 1913; s. Cicero Edward and Georgella (Bayne) C.; student U. Ill., 1932-34, Coyne Elec. Sch., 1934-35; m. Helen Danner, Nov. 10, 1970; children—Charlene Callison, Beverly. Engr., WMBD radio, Peoria, 1940-47; v.p. engring. McLendon Corp., Dallas., 1947—, Liberty Broadcasting System, 1947-52; chief engr. KLIF, Dallas, 1947-71. Served with USNR, 1944-45. Mem. Assn. Fed. Communications Engrs. Mason. Club: Engineers. Home: 15745 Terrace Lawn Circle Dallas TX 75240 Office: 1917 Elm St Dallas TX 75201

CALMAN, EDWIN CHARLES, JR., editor, pub.; b. Bonne Terre, Mo., Aug. 21, 1928; s. Edwin C. and Ethel (Radle) C.; student U.S. Mil. Acad., 1946-47, U. N.C., 1948, U. Ky., 1949; B.S., Western State U., Bowling Green, Ky., 1951; m. Patsy J. McGaw, Aug. 20, 1950; children—Linda Kay, Keary, Karol, Kristy. With Sturgis (Ky.) News, 1953—, mng. editor, 1962-67, pub., 1968—. Served with AUS, 1945-49, to capt. USAF, 1951-53; now col. USAF Res. Decorated Bronze Star medal. Mem. Ky., Western Ky. (pres. 1967) press assns., Am. Legion (dist. comdr. 1956, state dir. publicity 1957). Kiwanian (pres. 1964). Home: 1124 Washington St Sturgis KY 42459 Office: Box 218 Sturgis KY 42459

CALVERLEY, JOHN ROBERT, physician, educator; b. Hot Springs, Ark., Jan 14, 1932; s. John A. and Della (O'Neill) C.; B.S., U. Ore., 1953, M.D., 1955; m. Alice Mae Feller, Dec. 27, 1953; children—Mark, David. Intern U. Ia., Iowa City, 1955-56, resident in neurology, 1956; resident internal medicine Mayo Found., Rochester, Minn., 1957, neurology resident, 1957-59; mem. faculty dept. neurology, med. br. U. Tex., Galveston, 1964—, asso. prof., 1966-70, prof., 1970—, chief div. neurology, 1967-73, chmn. dept. neurology, 1973—. Cons. neurology U.S. Air Force, 1965—. Served to capt. USAF, 1957-64. Diplomate neurology Am. Bd. Psychiatry and Neurology, 1962. Mem. A.M.A., Tex. Med. Assn., Am. Acad. Neurology, Am. Neurol. Assn., Am. Epilepsy Soc., Assn. Research Nervous and Mental Diseases, Sigma Xi. Home: 39 Colony Park Circle Galveston TX 77550 Office: 915 Strand St Galveston TX 77550

CALVERT, DAVID VICTOR, educator; b. Chaplin, Ky., Feb. 26, 1934; s. Stanford Byron and Willia (Neal) C.; B.S., U. Ky., 1956, M.S., 1958; Ph.D., Ia. State U., 1962; m. Joyce Faye LeMay, July 27, 1957; children—Victor Neal, Yvonne Carole. Grad. asst. U. Ky., 1956-58, Ia. State U., 1958-62; asst. prof. soil chemistry U. Fla., 1962-68, asso. prof., 1968—, ofcl. collaborator USDA-ARS So. Region, Fla. Area, 1969—. Scoutmaster, Boy Scouts Am., 1963-69. Served with AUS. CIBA-Geigy grantee; Environmental Protection Agy. grantee. Mem. Am. Soc. Agronomy, Soil Sci. Soc. Am., A.A.A.S., Fla. State Hort. Soc., Sigma Xi, FarmHouse Fraternity, Gamma Sigma Delta, Alpha Zeta. Baptist (deacon 1973). Kiwanian (dir. 1964-67, pres. 1968). Contbr. articles to sci. and tech. jours. Home: 1003 Tennessee Av Fort Pierce FL 33450 Office: Agrl Research Center PO Box 248 Fort Pierce FL 33450

CALVERT, DELBERT WILLIAM, corp. exec.; b. Bosworth, Mo., Jan. 29, 1927; s. William McKinley and Ruby (Berrier) C.; B.S. in Civil Engring., U. Mo., 1952; m. Mary Lee Brown, Feb. 10, 1947 (div. Mar. 1971); children—Gary D., Danial L.; m. 2d, Melva Allen Hurst, Sept. 4, 1971; stepchildren—Holly Hurst, Allen Hurst. With Phillips Petroleum Co., Bartlesville, Okla., 1952-63, supr. econ. devel., supply and transp. dept., 1956-60, asst. mgr. transp. div., 1960-61, mgr. automotive div.-supply and transp. dept., 1961-63; asst. to v.p. Tex. Eastern Transmission Corp., Houston, 1963-65; mgr. diversification dept. No. Natural Gas Co., Omaha, 1965-68; pres. Williams Bros. Pipe Line Co., Tulsa, 1968-71; exec. v.p. The Williams Cos., Tulsa, 1971—, also dir.; pres. Suburban Cos., Tulsa, 1972—, also dir.; dir. Edgcomb Steel Co., Phila., Williams Energy Co., Tulsa, Agrico Chem. Co., Tulsa, Sci. Pres., mem. exec. bd. Indian Nations council Boy Scouts Am., 1974—. Mem. adv. com. dean engring. U. Mo. Bd. dirs. Goodwill Industries Tulsa, Ark. Basin Devel. Assn., Inc., Devel. Fund U. Mo. Served with AUS, 1945-47. Mem. Okla. Petroleum Council (dir. 1968), Am. Petroluem Inst. (mem. gen. com. div. transp. 1971), Transp. Assn. Am. (mem. pipe line panel 1969), Tau Beta Pi, Chi Epsilon, Pi Mu Epsilon. Republican. Clubs: University, Southern Hills Country (Tulsa). Home: 7277 S Pittsburg St Tulsa OK 74105 Office: 825 Nat Bank Tulsa Bldg Tulsa OK 74103

CALVERT, FLOYD OLAN, educator; b. Mountain View, Okla., Aug. 23, 1925; s. Jesse Roy and Jewel (Bourns) C.; B.S., U. Okla., 1950, M.S., 1958, Engring. D., 1969; postgrad. U. Cal. at Berkeley, 1960-61, U. Ariz., 1963-64; m. Dorothy Jean Carnes, Nov. 25, 1947; children—Sherry Lynn, Hallie Ann, Paula Joyce, Cary Mark, Wendy Jean. Instr., asst. prof. mech. engring. U. Okla., Norman, 1956-60, asso. prof. Architecture and Mech. Engring., 1969—; asst. prof. Cal. State Poly. Coll., Pomona, 1961-62; asst. prof., asso. prof. mech. engring. U. N.M., 1962-67; mech. engr. Internat. Paper Co., Corp. Engrs., Bechtol Corp., 1950-56. Served to 2d lt. C.E., AUS, 1945-47. NSF Sci. Faculty fellow, 1960-61, 63-64. Registered profl. engr., Okla. Mem. Am. Soc. M.E., Am. Soc. Heating, Refrigeration and Air Conditioning Engrs., Am. Soc. Engring. Edn., Pi Tau Sigma, Tau Beta Pi. Baptist (deacon). Contbr. articles to profl. jours. Home: 731 Nancy Lynn St Norman OK 73069 Office: 180 W Brooks St Norman OK 73069

CALVERT, GASTON EVON, educator; b. Cullman, Ala., July 19, 1923; s. John Davis and Carrie (Fisher) C.; B.S., Jacksonville State U., 1949; M.A., U. Ala., 1952, Ph.D., 1970; m. Kenneith Carol Harbison, July 26, 1947; children—Rebecca, Bonnie. Teacher, coach, guidance dir., prin. Cullman County also Calhoun County, Ala. schs., 1949-62; critic tchr., supr. student tchrs. Jacksonville State U., 1962-68; student tchr. supr. U. Ala., 1968-70; prof., supr. student teaching Campbell Coll., 1970—, mem. President's Commn. on Curricular Reform, 1972—. Served with AUS, World War II. NDEA fellowship, 1965-66. Mem. Buies Creek, Nat. edn. assns., Assn. Supervision and Curriculum Devel., Outstanding Educators Am., Personalities of the South, Phi Delta Kappa, Kappa Phi Kappa. Baptist (deacon 1965, minister of music 1963—). Club: Civitan Internat. Home: PO Box 173 Buies Creek NC 27506 Office: Campbell Coll Buies Creek NC 27506

CALVERT, GORDON LEE, lawyer; b. Wardensville, W. Va., Sept. 2, 1921; s. Aaron Lee and Ada (Brill) C.; A.B. with distinction, George Washington U., 1943, J.D. with distinction, 1945; m. Margaret Frances James, June 9, 1945; children—Gordon Rodney, Roger Lee, Walter Randolph. Admitted to D.C. bar, 1946; asso. firm Covington and Burling, 1945-46; mem. staff Investment Bankers Assn. Am., Washington, 1946-71, municipal dir., asst. gen. counsel, 1955-66, exec. dir., gen. counsel, 1966-71; exec. v.p. gen. counsel Securities Industry Assn., Washington, 1972; v.p., gen. counsel N.Y. Stock Exchange, Washington, 1973—. Mem. adv. com. Harvard Law Sch. Study of State Securities Regulation, 1954-55. Active Boy Scouts Am. Mem. Am. Bar Assn., Order of the Coif, Pi Kappa Alpha, Phi Delta Phi, Omicron Delta Kappa, Pi Gamma Mu. Clubs: Metropolitan. Columbia (Washington). Author: Fundamentals of Municipal Bonds, 1959, 63, State Pension Funds-Digest of Authorized Investments and Actual Investments, 1960, 64. Home: 6712 Michaels Dr Bethesda MD 20034 Office: 1800 K St NW Washington DC 20006

CALVERT, ROBERT W(ILBURN), judge; b. nr. Pulaski, Tenn., Feb. 22, 1905; s. Porter and Maud (Richardson) C.; LL.B., U. Tex., 1931; m. Frances Freeland, June 6, 1933 (div. 1958); children—Carolyn, James Porter; m. 2d, Corinne Lundgren, Jan. 26, 1962. Admitted to Tex. bar, 1931, practiced in Hillsboro, 1931-50, with Morrow & Calvert, 1934-50; dist. atty. Hill County, 1943-47; asso. justice Supreme Ct. Tex., 1950-61, chief justice, 1961-72. Mem. Tex. Ho. of Reps., 1933-39, speaker, 1937-39. Chmn. Dem. State Exec. Com., 1946-48. Home: 1411 W 29th St Austin TX 78703 Office: Tex State Bank Bldg Austin TX 78701

CALVERT, STAUNTON KIRKBRIDE, statistician, author; b. Columbia, Mo., Aug. 22, 1912; s. Sidney and Elizabeth (Fyfer) C.; B.A., U. Mo., 1933, M.A., 1934. With Internal Revenue Service, Washington, 1940-67, chief wealth statistics staff Statis. div., 1963-67, ret., 1967; statistician U.S. Tax Project, Argentina, 1970. Author: The Difficult Estimate, 1947; Samizdat in the U.S.A., Vol. 1, 1973—. Mem. Soc. Internat. Devel. Home and office: 3528 S St NW Washington DC 20007

CALVIN, LARRY O., zoo adminstr. married; 1 son. Formerly curator Dallas Zoo, now dir. Mem. Am. Assn. Zool. Parks and Aquariums, Nat. Recreation and Park Assn. Kiwanian. Home: 1507 Oak Glen Trail Dallas TX 75232 Office: Clarendon Dr Dallas TX 75023*

CAMERON, AGNES PATRICIA, real estate broker; b. Bklyn., Nov. 1, 1917; d. Alexander and Agnes (Carberry) Cameron; student Germain Sch. Photography, 1949, Leo Lee Photographer, 1950; m. Samuel Brokenshire, May 28, 1934 (dec. 1973); children—Joan (Mrs. Carl Miller), Fredrick Brokenshire; m. 2d, Ford R. Carter, Sr. (dec.). Self-employed Patricia Cameron Comml. Photographer, N.Y.C., 1950-56, Mgmt. Personnel Employment Agy., 1953; owner, operator Patricia Cameron Realtor, Delray Beach, Fla., after 1957, now owner, operator Cameron's Corner Real Estate. Mem. Nat. Assn. Real Estate Bds., Nat. Inst. Real Estate Bds., Nat. Inst. Farm and Land Brokers, Boynton Beach-Ocean Ridge, Delray Beach bds. realtors, Women's Council Realtors, Internat. Realtors, League Women Voters, Boynton Beach C. of C. Address: 4659 N Ocean Blvd Delray Beach FL 33444

CAMERON, ALBERT MOSELEY, retail car agy. exec.; b. Hartford, Ky., Oct. 28, 1908; s. John Payton and Rena Jane (Moseley) C.; student Western Ky. Tchrs. Coll., 1929-32, U. Ky., 1946; m. Emma Lee Hinton, Aug. 14, 1928; children—Margaret Ann (Mrs. Thomas Y. Catron), Max Gordon, Gary Dale. Tchr. Whitesville (Ky.) High Sch., farmer, Whitesville, 1945-51; mgr. Farmers Coop. Store, Owensboro, Ky., 1951-53, salesman Short Bros., Owensboro, 1953-58; gen. mgr. Ohio Motor Co., Hawesville, Ky., 1958-69; pres. Cambron Chevrolet, Inc., Hawesville, 1969—. Mem. Hawesville C. of C. (pres. 1968), Owensboro chpt. Dale Carnegie Alumni Assn. (pres. 1966). Baptist. (chmn. bd. deacons 1971-72). Mason, Lion (pres. 1964). Contbr. articles to profl. pubs. Home: Box 295 Hawesville KY 42348 Office: Hwy 60 E Hawesville KY 42348

CAMERON, BENJAMIN FRANKLIN, JR., orgn. exec.; b. Meridian, Miss., Nov. 4, 1920; s. Benjamin Franklin and Polly (Paine) C.; B.S., U. South, 1942; M.S. in Engring., U. Cin., 1944, Sc.D., 1948; m. Ruth Anders, Dec. 21, 1942; children—Douglas Winston, Robert Boatner, Elizabeth Anne. Research asst. Cin. Milling Machine Co., 1942-44, 44-48; research chemist, 1948-49; asst. prof. chemistry U. South, Sewanee, Tenn., 1949-51, dir. admissions, 1951-59; trustee Coll. Entrance Exam. Bd., N.Y.C., 1958-59, So. regional dir., Sewanee, 1959-63, v.p., 1964-70; pres. Outdoor Enterprises, Inc., 1970—; bd. dirs. So. Edn. Reporting Service. Cons. in edn. Ford Found., 1964-65; research cons. Carlisle Chem. Co., Norwood, O., 1949-50. Chmn. Sewanee Community Chest, 1950-51, 63-64; pres. Sewanee Civic Assn., 1951-52, Sewanee P.T.A., 1959-60. Served to lt. (j.g.) USNR, 1944-46; PTO. Mem. Am. Chem. Soc., A.A.A.S., Am. Assn. Collegiate Registrars and Admissions Officers, Assn. Coll. Admissions Counselors (exec. bd. 1958-59), So. Coll. Scholarship Group (chmn. 1956-59), Blue Key, Sigma Xi, Alpha Chi Sigma, Omicron Delta Kappa, Kappa Alpha. Democrat. Episcopalian. Author: Family Circle Guide to Florida Campgrounds, 1972; N.Y. Times Guide to Outdoors U.S.A., Southeast, 1973, Northeast, 1973. Contbr. numerous articles on student financial aid to profl. publs. Home: Sewanee TN 37375 Office: Outdoor Enterprises Inc Sewanee TN 37375

CAMERON, C. ARNOLD, lawyer; b. Cookeville, Tenn., Apr. 5, 1916; s. Orren Edward and Bessie (Arnold) C.; B.S., Tenn. Technol. U., 1937; LL.B., Andrew Jackson U., 1940; M.A. in Econs. and Bus. Adminstrn., Vanderbilt U., 1953; m. Billie Scott, June 26, 1938; children—William A., Anne E. Admitted to Tenn. bar, 1946, since practiced in Cookeville; sr. partner Cameron, Oakley & Jared, attys.; city judge, Cookeville, 1947-50; county atty. Putnam County, 1948-49. Dir. Cookeville Fed. Savs. & Loan Assn. Vice pres., financial chmn. Middle Tenn. council Boy Scouts Am., 1963—. Served with USNR, 1943-45. Recipient Silver Beaver award Boy Scouts Am., 1963. Mem. Putnam County, Tenn., Am. bar assns. Democrat. Presbyn. Rotarian, Lion. Club: Golf and Country (Cookeville). Home and office: PO Box 654 Cookeville TN 38501

CAMERON, CURTIS ALFRED, rancher; b. Fredericksburg, Tex., Apr. 27, 1939; s. Alfred Louis and Helen Alma Mathilda (Dittmar) C.; B.B.A., S.W. Tex. State Coll., 1961; m. Mary Katharine Redman, Apr. 8, 1967; children—Catharine Helen, Cyrena Christine. Self employed rancher, Gillespie, Llano and Kimble counties, Tex., 1961—. Dir. Fredericksburg Nat. Bank. Pres. Gillespie County Fair Assn., 1964-65, now bd. dirs., futurity chmn. Served with USAF, 1961-67. Recipient Appreciation award Gillespie County Fair Assn., 1965. Mem. Tex. Sheep and Goat Raisers Assn., Fredericksburg Ex-Students Assn. (dir. 1971—), Am. Quarter Horse Assn., Farm Bur. Lutheran. Home: Route 1 Box 252 Fredericksburg TX 78624 Office: 155 E Main St Fredericksburg TX 78624

CAMERON, DAVID SHIELDS, JR., banker; b. Fayetteville, N.C., Oct. 23, 1928; s. D.D. Shields and Margaret Louise (Porter) C.; A.B., U. N.C., 1950, M.Ed., 1956; diploma Stonier Grad. Sch. Banking of Rutgers U., 1966; m. Edith L. Rogers, June 9, 1956; children—Edith Porter, Elizabeth O., Jane C., R. Neill. Mgr., 1st Nat. Bank of S.C., Charleston, 1957-60; asst. cashier N.C. Nat. Bank, Wilmington, 1960-63; v.p. 1st Union Nat. Bank, Fayetteville, 1963-70; pres. Bank of Va., Lynchburg, 1970-73, Liberty Bank of Bedford (Va.), 1973—. Served with USNR, 1950-53. Clubs: Lions, Bedford Country, Piedmont (Bedford). Home: 840 College Av Bedford VA 24523 Office: 130 W Main St Bedford VA 24523

CAMERON, DONALD FIELD, JR., retail trade exec.; b. Knoxville, Tenn., Feb. 11, 1916; s. Donald Field and Katherine Mae (Knight) C.; student U. Tenn., 1934-37; m. Elizabeth Rutelia McCampbell, Nov. 29, 1942; children—Virginia Susan (Mrs. Elbert Allen Springer, Jr.), Donald Field III. With Miller's Inc., retail trade, Knoxville, 1937, v.p., 1959—, merchandising mgr., 1961—; dir. Talcor, Inc., Jefferson City, Tenn. Pres. Cancer Soc., Knoxville, 1957-58; bd. dirs. United Fund, 1958-62. Served with Armed Forces, 1941-46, 50-52. Mem. Nat. Retail Mchts. Assn. (dir. 1958-64, 68-71. Mem. Christian Ch. (trustee 1969—, deacon 1953—, chmn. ch. bd. 1960-66). Clubs: Holston Hills

Country, Fort Loudoun Yacht. Home: 5110 E Sunset Rd Knoxville TN 37914 Office: 600 Henley St Knoxville TN 37902

CAMMENGA, JOHN ALDEN, furniture mfg. co. exec.; b. Rock Valley, Ia., Nov. 6, 1932; s. Andrew and Tillie (Visser) C.; student Davenport Inst. (Grand Rapids, Mich.), 1955-56; m. Esther Ellen Hoolsema, Mar. 18, 1955; children—Elizabeth M., Sarah L., John A., Anna K., Mary E. Vice pres., mgr. Drapery House Inc., Grand Rapids, 1955-60; adminstrv. head mfg. Furniture City Upholstery Co., Grand Rapids, 1960-66; v.p. mfg. La-Z-Boy Chair Co., Monroe, Mich., 1966-72, Dayton, Tenn., 1972—. Mem. budget com. Mich. chpt. United Fund, 1958-59; chmn. bd. Monroe County United Fund, 1971-72, campaign mgr., 1971; mem. adv. bd. Bryan Coll., 1974. Served with M.P., AUS, 1953-55; Korea. Mem. Dayton C. of C. (dir.). Mem. Christian Ref. Ch. (past elder). Kiwanian. Club: Dayton Golf and Country (dir.). Home: Rural Route 1 Dayton TN 37321 Office: Walnut Grove and Broadway Sts Dayton TN 37321

CAMP, CLIFTON DURRETT, JR., newspaper exec.; b. Trenton, Ky., Aug. 2, 1927; s. Clifton Durrett and Virginia (McElwain) C.; B.S., U. Ky., 1950; m. Jane Peters, June 9, 1950; children—Daniel Durrett, Thomas Clifton, Pamela Jane, Emily Ann. Accountant, Sheldon, Curry, Canning & Wells, St. Petersburg, Fla., 1950-54; asst. controller Times Pub. Co., St. Petersburg, 1954-57, controller, 1957-71, treas., 1960-73, v.p., 1967-73, sec., 1969-73, dir., 1962-73, bus. mgr., 1974—; pub. Sumter County Times, Wildwood Herald Express, Bushnell, Fla., 1973—; treas. Congl. Quar., Inc., 1962-73, sec., 1969-73. Treas., Poynter Fund, 1962-73, trustee, 1973—. Adv. bd. St. Petersburg Salvation Army, 1970-73; mem. Com. of 100 of Pinellas County. Served with USNR, 1945-46. Mem. Inst. Newspaper Controllers and Finance Officers, Am. Mgmt. Assn., Nat. Assn. Accountants, St. Petersburg C. of C. Methodist. Clubs: Yacht, Lakewood Country (St. Petersburg, Fla.). Home: 2411 Sunrise Dr SE St Petersburg FL 33705 Office: 490 1st Av South St Petersburg FL 33701

CAMP, JOHN CLAYTON, lawyer; b. Arab, Ala., Sept. 23, 1923; s. Roy H. and Alice (Cox) C.; student Birmingham So. Coll., 1940-42, U. Ala., 1943, Auburn U., 1944; LL.B., La. State U., 1948; m. Frances Spencer, Nov. 3, 1944; children—Elizabeth Ann, Martha Lynn, Charles Henry, John Clayton II. Admitted to La. bar, 1948, D.C. bar, 1973; asso. firm Thompson, Lawes & Cavanaugh, Lake Charles, 1948-55; partner firm Camp, Carmouche, Palmer, Carwile & Barsh, Lake Charles, 1955—. Dir., v.p. Land & Royalty Owners La.; dir. Marine Nat. Bank Lake Charles. Spl. counsel, legal adviser Gov. La., 1974. Chmn., Calcasieu Indsl. Devel. Bd., 1963-64; committeeman La. Bd. Edn.; adv. com. La. Law Inst.; mem. La. Pub. Affairs Research and Council for Better La. Assns.; adv. bd. La. div. Small Bus. Adminstrn., 1969-70. Served with USAAF, 1943-46. Fellow Internat. Acad. Law and Sci.; mem. Am., Fed., La., Fed. Power, D.C. bar assns., Fgn. Relations Assn. New Orleans, Houston Estate and Financial Forum, Am. Mgmt. Assn., La. Civil Service League (dir. 1970—), Miss. Valley World Trade Council, La.-Miss. Export Expansion Council, La. Intercoastal Seaway Assn. (dir. 1970—), U.S. (internat. com. 1972), La. (dir. 1971), Greater Lake Charles (pres. 1971, dir.) chambers commerce, Club: Propeller. Home: 224 W Spring St Lake Charles LA 70601 Office: PO Drawer 2001 Lake Charles LA 70601

CAMP, JOHN N. HAPPY, congressman; b. Enid, Okla., May 11, 1908; s. John Rowland and Minnie Catherine (Newbold) C.; ed. Phillips U., Enid; m. Vera Juanita Overman, Nov. 26, 1930; children—Patricia (Mrs. Roy G. Rainey), Kay (Mrs. Dan Dillingham), John N. III, Steven Richard. Pres. Waukomis State Bank; mem. Okla. Legislature, 20 years; chmn. Okla. Bd. Pub. Affairs; mem. 91st-93d congresses from 6th Dist. Okla., mem. Com. Interior and Insular Affairs, Com. Sci. and Astronautics, Com. Coms. Pres. Great Salt Plains council Boy Scouts Am.; legislative supt. Okla. Girls State; area dir. Okla. Northwest. Precinct chmn., then chmn. Garfield County Republican party, mem. Okla. state com. Bd. dirs. Miss Okla. Pageant; mem. grad. sem. council Phillips U.; mem. governing com. Christian Ch. Found. Recipient Silver Beaver award Boy Scouts Am.; Master Farmers certificate Future Farmers Am. Hon. mem. 4-H Clubs Okla.; mem. Okla. C. of C. (dir.), Hist. Soc. Mem. Disciples of Christ Ch. (charter). Mason (32 deg., Shriner, Jester). Office: House Office Bldg Washington DC 20515

CAMP, LAWRENCE H., business exec.; b. Brunswick, Va., 1915; ed. Ferrum Jr. Coll., Va. Mech. Inst. With Carter Bros., Inc., 1936-44; staff accountant Leach, Calkins & Scott, 1944-49, partner, 1949-61; with Chesapeake Corp. Va., 1961—, controller, 1961-63, treas., 1963-66, v.p. finance and treas., 1966-68, sr. v.p. and treas., 1968, exec. v.p., treas. and chief exec. officer, 1968-69, pres. and chief exec. officer, 1969—, also dir.; treas., dir. Balt. Box Co., Binghamton Container Co., Miller Container Corp., Scranton Corrugated Box Co., So. Corrugated Box Corp., David Weber Co.; dir. Greenlife Products Co. Address: Chesapeake Corp Va West Point VA 23181

CAMP, THOMAS EDWARD, librarian; b. Haynesville, La., July 12, 1929; s. Charles W. and Annie Laura (Brazzell) C.; B.A., Centenary Coll. La., 1950; postgrad. Div. Sch. Vanderbilt U., 1950-51; M.S., La. State U., 1953; m. Elizabeth Anne Sowar, Sept. 4, 1952; children—Anne Winifred, Thomas David. Asst. in binding dept. La. State U. Library, 1951-53; circulation librarian Bridwell Library, Perkins Sch. of Theology, So. Meth. U., Dallas, 1955-57; librarian Sch. Theology U. of South, Sewanee, Tenn., 1957—. Mem. credit com. Sewanee Credit Union. Served with AUS, 1953-55. Mem. Franklin County Assn. for Retarded Children and Adults (pres. 1971-72), Am. Guild Organists, Am. Theol. Library Assn. (exec. sec. 1965-67), Kappa Alpha, Omicron Delta Kappa, Phi Kappa Phi, Beta Phi Mu. Author: (with E.V. Aldrich) Using Theological Books and Libraries, 1963. Contbr. articles in field to profl. jours. Home: Carruthers Rd Sewanee TN 37375

CAMP, THOMAS LEE, judge; b. Fairburn, Ga., Mar. 9, 1905; s. Thomas Wiley and Lula (Duggan) C.; A.B., Oglethorpe U., 1925; LL.B., George Washington U., 1931; m. Gladys Palmer Hobgood, June 15, 1927; children—Gladys (Mrs. John Gordon Hiles), Sara Ann (Mrs. Julian Wilson Swann). Admitted Ga. bar, 1933; clk., Atlanta and Lowry Nat. Bank (now 1st Nat. Bank Atlanta), and high sch. tchr., 1925-27; sec. to congressman, clk., Civil Service Com. U.S. Ho. Reps., 1927-44; pvt. practice law, Atlanta; commr. Fulton County (Ga.), 1947-56; judge Civil Ct. Fulton County, 1957-66, chief judge, 1966—. Bd. trustees Oglethorpe U. Mem. Am., Ga. bar assns. Methodist (chmn. ofcl. bd. 1958-59). Mason (Shriner). Clubs: Lawyers, Kiwanis, Atlanta Athletic, Ansley Golf. Home: 169 Robin Hood Rd NE Atlanta GA 30309 Office: Civil Ct Bldg Atlanta GA 30303

CAMPBELL, AGNES KNIGHT (MRS. JOHN FRANKLIN CAMPBELL), social agy. exec.; b. Boom, Tenn.; d. George Allen and Nora (Clark) Knight; B.S., Tenn. Tech. U., 1934; postgrad. Vanderbilt U., 1935, U. Chgo. Sch. Social Service Adminstrn., 1942, 46; M.S., U. Tenn. Sch. Social Work, 1953; m. John Franklin Campbell, June 20, 1942. Regional dir. Tenn. Dept. Pub. Welfare, Nashville, 1942-55; social worker Youth Service, Child and Family Service, Knoxville, Tenn., 1955-58; exec. dir. Knoxville Travelers Aid Soc., 1958—. Bd. dirs. Knoxville Legal Aid Soc., planning council United Community Services Greater Knoxville. Mem. Nat. Assn. Social Workers (pres. 1951-53, sec. 1966-68), Tenn. Conf. of Social Work (state sec. 1955), Nat. Travelers Aid Assn., Profl. Execs. Knoxville (pres. 1967-68). Club: Social Service of Knoxville. Author script: Some of Those We Help, 1962; play: Trouble Away From Home, 1964. Home: 6515 Sherwood Dr Knoxville TN 37919 Office: 100 Magnolia Av Knoxville TN 37917

CAMPBELL, ARCHIBALD ALGERNON, lawyer, state legislator; b. Wytheville, Va., July 23, 1921; s. P. Fitzgerald and Mary (Austin) C.; B.S., Va. Mil. Inst., 1943; LL.B., U. Va., 1949; m. Eloise Richberg, Feb. 19, 1950; children—Donald Richberg, Marenda Ann, Florence Weed. Admitted to Va. bar, 1948; temporary foreign service officer Amfoge II, Greece, 1946; partner Campbell & Campbell, attys., Wytheville, Va., 1949—; mem. Va. Ho. Dels., 1966—; adv. bd. First Nat. Exchange Bank Va., Wytheville; dir., treas. Tourists, Inc., Wytheville, 1960—. Mem. exec. com. Va. State Tb. Assn., 1958-63; sec. Smyth-Wythe Joint Airport Commn., 1958-69; chmn. Wythe County Economy Commn., 1962-63. Served with USMCR, 1943-46. Decorated D.F.C. Mem. Am., Va. State (v.p. 1962-63) bar assns., Southwest Va. Horsemen's Assn. Democrat. Presbyn. Rotarian (local pres. 1958-59). Home: Pine Ridge Wytheville VA 24382 Office: 210 W Main St Wytheville VA 24382

CAMPBELL, CHARLES BOYLE, JR., city ofcl.; b. College Station, Tex., Nov. 13, 1922; s. Charles Boyle and Margaret (Boulware) C.; B.B.A., Tulane U., 1943; B.S., Tex. A. and M. U., 1948; m. Katherine Love Harrison, July 1, 1950; children—Ann Hamilton, Margaret Womack, Charles Brice. Asst. prof. naval sci. and tactics Tex. U., 1945-46; landscape architect Lambert Landscape Co., Dallas, 1948-49; mgr. R. Lacy Nursery Co., Longview, Tex., 1949-51; asst. mgr. Tex. Nursery Co., Sherman, 1951-54; dir. parks and recreation City of Midland, Tex., 1954-62, City of Ft. Worth, 1962—. Served with USNR, 1943-46; PTO. Mem. Am. Park and Recreation Soc. (dir.), Tex. Municipal Park and Recreation Assn. (pres. 1972), Tex. Turfgrass Assn. (past pres.), Phi Delta Theta. Developer 1st municipal zoo, Midland, 1954-62, Dennis the Menace playground, Midland, 1960. Home: 3600 Westcliff Rd N Fort Worth TX 76109 Office: 1000 Throckmorton St Fort Worth TX 76102

CAMPBELL, CHARLES CLINTON, ins. exec.; b. Bolivar, Tenn., Aug. 2, 1923; s. Charles Ray and Tommie (Clinton) C.; grad. high sch.; m. Johnsye Craft, Apr. 22, 1950; children—Theresa Lee, Charles Lamar, Philip Wayne, Pamela Louise. Clk., Comml. Nat. Bank, Little Rock, 1941; finance clk. U.S. Engrs., Little Rock, 1941-42; spl. agt. W.M. Apple & Co., Little Rock, 1946-56; exec. v.p. Rebsamen & Assos., Inc., Little Rock, 1956—. Vice pres. Optimist Internat., 1966-67, pres. elect, 1969-70, pres., 1970-71; bd. dirs. Optimist Internat. Found., pres., 1970-71. Bd. dirs. Presbyn. Village, pres., 1974-75; bd. dirs. Little Rock Boys Club. Served to comdr. USNR, 1942-46. Decorated Air medal with 2 oak leaf clusters. Mem. Ark. Assn. Ins. Agts. (mem. exec. com. 1964-68), So. Agts. Conf. (chmn. casualty com. 1967-69). Presbyn. (elder, deacon). Clubs: Pleasant Valley Country, Little Rock, Capital. Home: 7215 I St Little Rock AR 72207 Office: Tower Bldg Little Rock AR 72201

CAMPBELL, CLARENCE L., state ofcl.; b. Indpls., Sept. 24, 1921; s. Clarence L. and Louise (Altvater) C.; student Fla. So. Coll., 1939-41; D.V.M., Ohio State U., 1945; m. Dorothy Marguerite Watford, June 10, 1950. Pvt. practice vet. medicine, Kewanee, Ill., 1945; field veterinarian Fla. Livestock San. Bd., 1945-48; asst. state veterinarian of Fla., 1948-52, acting state veterinarian, 1952; sec. Fla. Livestock Bd., 1953; dir. div. animal industry Fla. Dept. Agr., 1961—; state veterinarian, dir. div. animal industry Fla. Dept. Agr. and Consumer Services, Tallahassee, 1961—. Recipient Man of Year award Progressive Farmer Mag., 1963; award for meritouious service, 1962. Mem. U.S., So. (pres. 1965-66) animal health assns., Am. (chmn. com. on council on pub. health and regulatory vet. medicine 1962, recipient Certificate of Service 1959-61), Fla. vet. med. assns., Nat. Assembly State Veterinarians, Am. Assn. Equine Practitioners, Arabian Horse Assn. Fla. (pres. 1969), Alpha Psi, Gamma Sigma Delta. Office: Div Animal Industry Fla Dept Agriculture and Consumer Services Room 328 Mayo Bldg Tallahassee FL 32304

CAMPBELL, CLYDE HENSON, project engr.; b. Tracy City, Tenn., June 22, 1924; s. Frank and Maude Adell (Sweeton) C.; student U. Miss., 1946-48; B.A., U.S. Naval Postgrad. Sch., 1952; m. Paula Inez Hammond, July 5, 1948; children—Clyde Henson, Paul, John, Ruth. Commd. ensign U.S. Navy, 1942, advanced through grades to lt. comdr., 1955; aviator, 1942-52; electronic specialist, 1952-62; ret., 1962; project engr. Reynolds Metals Co., 1963-71; gov. Rotary Internat. Dist. 686 of Ala., 1971-73; project engr. Martin Stove & Range Co., Florence, Ala., 1973—; audio design cons. Campbell Sound Engring. Dir. North Ala. Soc. Crippled Children and Adults. Decorated D.F.C., Air medal (3). Mem. I.E.E.E. Episcopalian. Mason, Rotarian (pres. 1965-66). Co-inventor device for making instantaneous measurements of alumina concentration percentage in aluminum reduction cells. Home: 1302 N Columbia Av Sheffield AL 35660 Office: Commerce St Florence AL 35630

CAMPBELL, EDWARD GROSS, govt. ofcl.; b. New Cumberland, Pa., May 20, 1912; s. John and Hannah Criswell (Gross) C.; A.B., Princeton, 1933; M.A., Columbia, 1934, Ph.D., 1938; m. Frances Watson James, Oct. 16, 1941; 1 son, John. With Nat. Archives, Gen. Services Adminstrn., Washington, 1938—, dir. Region 3, 1958-67, asst. archivist, 1967—. Served with AUS, 1943. Mem. Soc. Am. Archivists. Home: 1715 N Huntington St Arlington VA 22205 Office: Nat Archives Bldg 9th St and Pennsylvania Av NW Washington DC 20408

CAMPBELL, GEORGE SUMMERS, cons. engr.; b. Chattanooga, Tenn., Mar. 29, 1911; s. George Eugene and Winona Isabelle (Hinshaw) C.; B.S., U. Tenn., 1933; m. Irma Lee Carson; children—Nancy, George. Sales engr. Tenn. Elec. Power Co., 1935-37; sales engr. John Bouchard and Sons, contractors, 1938-40; owner George S. Campbell, cons. engr., 1940-41, 1946-50; pres. Campbell Industries, Inc., 1951-55; pres. George S. Campbell and Assos., Inc., cons. engrs., 1956—. Served to lt. USNR, 1942-46. Registered profl. engr., Ala., Ga., Tenn., Va. Mem. Am. Cons. Engrs. Council (pres. chpt. 1967—), Nat. Soc. Profl. Engrs., Am. Soc. Heating, Refrigeration and Air-Conditioning Engrs. (chpt. pres. 1973), Illuminating Engrs. Soc., Am. Soc. M.E., Am. Soc. Plumbing Engrs., Chattanooga C. of C. (com. chmn. 1967). Episcopalian. Rotarian. Club: Civitan (pres. 1951). Home: Cravens Terrace Route 4 Chattanooga TN 37409 Office: 701 E 4th St Chattanooga TN 37403

CAMPBELL, GLENN HARVEY, computer co. exec.; b. Lowesville, Va., July 7, 1932; s. Goede Danridge and Mary Louise (Harvey) C.; student Lynchburg Coll., 1949-52; B.S., Ind. Inst. Tech., 1959; elec. engr. Memps, Inc., Falls Church, Va., 1959-60; Am. Machine and Foundry Co., Alexandria, Va., 1960-61, Page Communications Engrs., Washington, 1961-63; v.p., dir. SAID, Inc., computers, Falls Church, 1963—; partner Nelson Lumber Co., Piney River, Va., 1967—, Cobweb Corner Antique & Upholstery, Glen Allen, Va., 1972—. Coach, Little League Baseball, 1968-73; mem. Commonwealth Council Girl Scouts, 1969-73; mem. pres.'s roundtable Va. Inst. Tech., 1971—. Served with USAF, 1952-56. Recipient grant NSF, 1959. Mem. Lynchburg C. of C., I.E.E.E., Data Processing Mgmt. Assn., Beta Sigma Tau. Clubs: Winton Country (Clifford, Va.); Sertoma (Vienna, Va.); Golden Hokie (Va. Inst. Tech.). Home: Piney River VA 22964 Office: 1243 W Broad St Falls Church VA 22046

CAMPBELL, GUY DOUGLAS, physician; b. Lauderdale, Miss., Oct. 15, 1915; s. Walter H. and Anna Adele (Nicholson) C.; B.S., U. Miss., 1946; M.D., Harvard, 1949; m. Margaret Mary Ford, May 20, 1950; 1 son, Guy Douglas. Intern, Charity Hosp., New Orleans, 1949-50; resident internal medicine Miss. State Sanatorium, 1950-51, VA Hosp., New Orleans, 1953-55; practice medicine, specializing in internal medicine, Jackson, Miss., 1955—; mem. staff VA Hosp., Univ. Hosp.; mem. faculty U. Miss. Sch. Medicine, Jackson, 1956—, asso. prof. medicine, 1967—; chief pulmonary disease sect. VA Hosp., Jackson, 1960—; coordinator Miss. Regional Med. Program, 1966-71. Pres. Miss. Lung Assn., 1966-68. Bd. dirs. Am. Lung Assn., 1972—. Diplomate Am. Bd. Internal Medicine, and subsplty. bd. pulmonary diseases. Fellow Am. Coll. Chest Physicians (gov. 1966-72), A.C.P. (gov.); mem. Am. Thoracic Soc. (dir.), Sigma Xi, Omicron Delta Kappa, Kappa Sigma. Methodist. Mailing Address: 2015 Cherokee Dr Jackson MS 39211 Office: VA Hosp Jackson MS 39216

CAMPBELL, HENRY ARVILLE, JR., coll. adminstr.; b. Cosmos, Wash., Aug. 27, 1925; s. Henry Arville and Viva Ethel (Blair) C.; A.B., U. Ky., 1949; M.A., N.M. State U., 1957, Ed.S., 1961; postgrad. Syracuse U.; Ph.D., U. Tex., 1963; m. Nancy Elizabeth Belew, Jan. 4, 1965; children—Micca Lauren, Jan Rebecca, Sheryl Robin. Tchr. high schs., Lancaster, Ky., 1949-51, Cumberland, Ky., 1951-54, Benham, Ky., 1954-55; tchr., chmn. math. dept. Alamogordo (N.M.) High Sch., 1955-63; pres. Crowder Coll., Neosho, Mo., 1963-64, dir.; Alamogordo Community Coll., 1957-63; dir. Prestonsburg (Ky.) Community Coll., 1963—; acting dir. Hazard Community Coll., 1967-68. Served with AUS, 1943-45. Mem. N.E.A., S.W. N.M. (chmn. math., sci. sect.), Ky., Eastern Ky. edn. assns., Am. Math. Assn., Nat. Council Math. Tchrs., N.M. Acad. Sci., Floyd County Hall of Fame, Order of Red, Red Rose. Democrat. Methodist. Lion, Kiwanian (dir.), Rotarian. Home: PO Box 589 Prestonsburg KY 41653 Office: PO Box 110 Prestonburg KY 41653

CAMPBELL, HOWARD WALLACE, ecologist; b. Balt., Oct. 23, 1935; s. Howard Wallace and Mary Catherine (Henkel) C.; B.A., U. Fla., 1958; M.A., U. Cal. at Los Angeles, 1963, Ph.D., 1967; m. Linda Kathleen French, Apr. 9, 1965; children—Sabra, Mariel Lee, Colin James. Postdoctoral fellow Center for Biology of Natural Systems, Washington U. of St. Louis, Panama, 1967-68; various positions U. Fla. Med. Sch., 1968-69, Fla. State Mus., 1969-70, U. Fla., 1970-72; dir. wildlife studies Jack McCormick & Assos., ecol. cons., Devon, Pa., 1972-73; staff scientist Office of Endangered Species, U.S. Dept. Interior, Washington, 1973—. Staff herpetologist Internat. Turtle and Tortoise Soc., 1966-73; mem. crocodile specialist group, survival service commn. Internat. Union for Conservation Nature and Natural Resources, Morgas, Switzerland, 1970—. Served with Med. Service Corps, AUS, 1958-60. Recipient research grants, fellowships. Mem. Am. Soc. Zoologists, Ecol. Soc. Am., Am. Soc. Ichthyologists and Herpetologists, Soc. for Study Amphibious Reptiles, Herpetologists League, Sigma Xi. Home: 9905 Renfrew Rd Silver Spring MD 20901 Office: Office Endangered Species US Dept Interior Washington DC 20240

CAMPBELL, HUGH BROWN, judge; b. Waynesville, N.C., Mar. 14, 1907; s. Wilburn Camrock and Stella (Brown) C.; A.B., Amherst Coll., 1929; J.D., U. N.C., 1932; m. Thelma Welles, Dec. 2, 1933; children—Hugh Brown, Thelma Elizabeth, Wilburn Welles. Admitted to N.C. bar, 1932, pvt. practice, Goldsboro, 1932-34, Charlotte, 1934-55; mem. Campbell, Craighill, Rendleman & Kennedy, 1952-55; judge N.C. Superior Ct., 1955-67, N.C. Ct. Appeals, 1967—; city atty., Charlotte, 1941-45. Mem. airport adv. com., 1945-61. Mem. St. Peters Hosp. Found. Mem. Am., N.C. bar assns. Democrat. Episcopalian. Kiwanian. Home: 1626 Queens Rd Charlotte NC 28207 Office: NC Ct Appeals Ruffin Bldg Box 888 Raleigh NC 27602

CAMPBELL, INEZ GIBSON, editor, publisher; b. Tyler, Tex., Feb. 24, 1914; d. Robert N. and Beatrice (Martin) Gibson; student E. Tex. State Tchrs. Coll., 1929-32; m. Jack W. Campbell, July 12, 1935; children—Melinda Lee, Melissa Ann. Supr. mail opening dept. Montgomery Ward, 1935-41; supr. recap dept. N.Am. Aviation, Inc., 1942-45; sec., aviation dept. mgr. Ft. Worth C. of C., 1946-47; sec. claims dept. Comml. Standard Ins. Co., Ft. Worth, 1947-49; owner Campbell Secretarial Service, Ft. Worth, 1952—; prodn., circulation mgr. Trade Jour., Bicycle Jour., 1954—; editor Ft. Worther Mag., 1956-64, editor and pub., 1964-67; editor, Pub. Key-Ft. Worth Mag., 1967—; editor Lawn Equipment Jour., 1959—; Yardware nat. trade publ. Dir. Nat. Visitor Mag. Group, Inc., Chgo., 1962-68. Publicity chmn. Ft. Worth chpt. Internat. Good Neighbor Council, 1963-64; rec. sec. Provarsu Study Club, Ft. Worth, 1963-64. Mem. Ft. Worth C. of C. (mem. conv. and tourist com.). Clubs: Press of Ft. Worth, The Ft. Worth, Woman's Club Ft. Worth, Ridglea Country, Casa Del Sol (dir.) (Ft. Worth). Home: 4020 White Settlement Rd Fort Worth TX 76107 Office: 3339 W Freeway PO Box 1570 Fort Worth TX 76107

CAMPBELL, JAMES WAYNE, educator; b. Highlandville, Mo., Mar. 2, 1932; s. Frank Pauline and Mable (Kentling) C.; B.S., S.W. Mo. State Coll., 1953; M.S., U. Ill., 1955; Ph.D. (USPHS fellow) U. Okla., 1958; m. Bonnalie Josephine Oetting, Sept. 4, 1960; children—Heather Anne, James Kentling. Nat. Acad. Sci-NRC fellow Johns Hopkins U., Balt., 1958-59; faculty dept. biology Rice U., Houston, 1959—, asso. prof., 1964-70, prof., 1970—, chmn. dept., 1974—. Vis. asso. prof. (USPHS fellow) U. Wis. Med. Sch., Madison, 1964-65; cons. govt. agys., 1969—; program dir. regulatory biology BMS, NSF, Washington, 1973-74. USPHS career devel. award grantee, 1966-70; NSF, USPHS grantee, 1960—. Fellow Am. Inst. Chemists, A.A.A.S.; mem. Am. Physiol. Soc., Am. Soc. Biol. Chemists, Biochem. Soc. Eng., Am. Soc. Zoologists, Sigma Xi, Phi Sigma, Phi Lambda Upsilon. Editor: Comparative Biochemistry of Nitrogen Metabolism, 2 vols., 1970; (with L. Goldstein) Nitrogen Metabolism and the Environment, 1972. Contbr. articles to profl. jours. Home: 2628 Fenwood Rd Houston TX 77005

CAMPBELL, JOHN ROBERT, ednl. adminstr.; b. Dalton, O., Aug. 6, 1927; s. Daniel Cavitt and Alice (Pinnock) C.; B.A., Sterling Coll., 1949; Ph.D., U. Kan., 1952; m. Margaret Eloise Treaster, June 8, 1948; children—Barry, Lynn, Brian, Daniel. Instr. Washington U., St. Louis, 1954-64; chmn. div. natural sci., prof. chemistry, asst. acad. dean Tarkio (Mo.) Coll., 1964-68; v.p. acad. affairs Midwestern U., Wichita Falls, Tex., 1968—. Research specialist Monsanto Co., St. Louis, 1952-64; chmn. commn. on ednl. relations, bd. dirs. Assn. Tex. Colls. and Univs., 1972—. Mem. exec. com., trustee United Way Commn. on Human Relations, Wichita Falls, 1969—; bd. dirs. Wichita Falls Symphony Orch. Mem. Am., So. confs. and acad. deans, Tex. Assn. Acad. Deans, Am. Chem. Soc., Sigma Xi, Phi Lambda Upsilon. Presbyn. Patentee in field. Home: 2401 Dartmouth St Wichita Falls TX 76308

CAMPBELL, JOSEPH EDWARD, dentist; b. Wilmington, N.C., Mar. 7, 1923; s. Cornell and Lulua (Harris) C.; B.S., N.C. Central U., 1950; D.D.S., Howard U., 1955; m. Dorothy Gwendolyn Wilson, Aug. 27, 1955;children—Joseph Edward, Kenneth B., Cynthia V.

With Del. Dept. Pub. Health, Dover, 1955; pvt. practice dentistry, Durham, N.C., 1955—; dentist Durham Pub. Health Dept., 1955-57; mem. cons. staff Lincoln Hosp. Mem. med. and dental adv. com. Durham County Hosp. Commn.; adv. com. on dental edn. N.C. Bd. Edn., N.C. Bd. Higher Edn., 1969—. Bd. dirs. Office Econ. Opportunity Antipoverty Program for Children, Mt. Gilead Bapt. Ch. Day Care Center, Delta Dental Plans Assn. N.C., Durham Community Health Center. Served with USNR, 1944-46. Fellow Royal Soc. Health; mem. Nat. (past state v.p.), Am., N.C., Old North (past pres.), Alexander Hunter (past program chmn.) dental socs., Durham Acad. Medicine (past pres.), Durham Mchts. Assn., Omega Psi Phi (sec.), Chi Delta Mu (sec.-treas.). Democrat. Baptist (trustee). Mailing Address: 905 Jerome Rd Durham NC 27707

CAMPBELL, JUNE COLLYER PETERS (MRS. LEROY M. CAMPBELL), social worker; b. Pitts., June 18, 1929; d. Nathaniel R. and Cleo (Minor) Peters; B.A., Howard U., 1951, M.S.W., 1964; M.A., Am. U., 1959; m. Leroy M. Campbell, Aug. 22, 1952; 1 dau., Sharon. With Prince George's County Dept. Social Services, Hyattsville, Md., 1957—, caseworker, 1957-64, supr., 1964-66, asst. dir., 1967-70, dir. Bur. Services to Families and Children, 1970—. Mem. task force treatment of emotionally disturbed youth Md. Gov.'s Conf. Crime and Delinquency, 1968—. Mem. Nat. Assn. Social Workers, Am. Pub. Welfare Assn., Nat. Conf. Social Welfare, Council Local Adminstrs. Social Services, Acad. Certified Social Workers, Alpha Kappa Alpha. Home: 8019 16th St NW Washington DC 20012 Office: Prince Georges County Dept Social Services 6525 Belcrest Rd Hyattsville MD 20782

CAMPBELL, LEROY MILLER, architect; b. N.Y.C., July 5, 1927; s. Allan and Roma Gwendolyn (Miller) C.; B.Arch., Howard U., 1951; m. June Collyer Peters, Aug. 22, 1952; 1 dau., Sharon June. Draftsman, Alexander Richter, Kensington, Md., 1952; draftsman, job capt. Hilyard R. Robinson, Washington, 1952-56; job capt. Mcleod Ferrara, Washington, 1956-59; job capt., designer John Hans Graham, Washington, 1959-63; job capt. Cohen Haft, Silver Spring, Md., 1963-66; partner Sulton Campbell Assos., Washington, 1966—. Bd. dirs. Neighbors, Inc., Washington Planning Workshop, 1970—, Met. Washington Planning and Housing Assos., 1970—. Served to cpl. USAAF, 1945-46. Mem. A.I.A., Nat. Orgn. Minority Architects, Nat. Tech. Assn., Alpha Phi Alpha. Democrat. Episcopalian. Home: 8019 16th St NW Washington DC 20012 Office: 7600 Georgia Av NW Washington DC 20012

CAMPBELL, MARY GRACE WILLIAMS (MRS. WALTER ROBERT CAMPBELL, JR.), business exec.; b. New Bern, N.C., Nov. 5, 1928; d. Leon Franklin and Sadie (Scurlock) Williams; student E. Carolina Coll., 1946-47; m. Walter Robert Campbell, Jr., July 8, 1949; children—Walter Robert III, Mary Lynn, Douglas Alan. With Barbour Boat Works, Inc., New Bern, 1947—, asst. sec.-treas., 1954-63, supr. office personnel, 1961—, sec.-treas., 1964—, also dir.; sec.-treas. Barbour Boats, Inc., 1962; sec.-treas., dir. Marine Trading Corp., New Bern, 1953—; sec., dir. Williams Oil Co., Inc., New Bern, 1955—. Pres., Brinson Meml. Sch. P.T.A., 1959-61; tchr. Sunday Sch. class Riverdale Meth. Ch., New Bern, 1960—, mem. ofcl. bd., 1952—; sub-dist. leader Woman's Soc. Christian Service Meth. Ch. 1964-68. Mem. Pi Omega Pi. Club: New Bern Golf and Country. Home: Route 6 Box 215 New Bern NC 28560 Office: PO Box 1069 New Bern NC 28561

CAMPBELL, MCCOY CLEMPSON, III, banker; b. Spring Hill, Tenn., Apr. 5, 1918; s. McCoy Clempson and Annie (Woodard) C.; B.A., Vanderbilt U., 1940; postgrad. Stonier Grad. Sch. Banking, Rutgers U. 1955-57; m. Josephine McHenry, Dec. 2, 1944; children—Lucinda (Mrs. John N. Peabody), Laura Ann. Mgr. personnel RFC custody depts. Fed. Res. Bank Atlanta, Nashville, 1940-50; v.p., dir. personnel First Nat. Bank Atlanta, 1950-68; v.p. personnel adminstrn. Am. Nat. Bank & Trust Co., Chattanooga, 1968-71, sr. v.p. personnel adminstrn., 1971—. Lectr. Stonier Grad. Sch. Banking, Rutgers U., 1959-62, 69—, Colo. Sch. Banking, U. Colo., Boulder, 1970, Sch. Bank Adminstrn., U. Wis., Madison, 1971—. Chmn. adv. com., bd. dirs. So. Coll. Placement Assn., 1965-68; bd. dirs. YMCA, Chattanooga. Served to 1st lt. F.A., AUS, 1942-46. Mem. Am. Inst. Banking, Am. Bankers Assn. (lectr. personnel adminstrn. 1964—), Ga. Personnel and Guidance Assn. (past pres.), Bank Adminstrn. Inst. (dir.), Greater Chattanooga C. of C. (gen. chmn. Career Opportunities Day 1970), Kappa Alpha Alumni Assn. Presbyn. Club: Lookout Moutain (Tenn.) Fairyland. Cons. editor: The Bankers Handbook, 1966. Home: 308 Henry Lane Lookout Mountain TN 37350 Office: PO Box 1638 Chattanooga TN 37401

CAMPBELL, NORMAN, ednl. adminstr.; b. Greenfield, Tenn., Jan. 4, 1911; s. Aron Green and Lochie Hale (Norman) C.; B.S., U. Tenn., 1937, M.S., 1938; Ph.D., U. Ill., 1961; m. Ruby Robinson, Dec. 30, 1934; children—Jane (Mrs. Jack Mitchell), Ruth (Mrs. Timothy White), Jo Ellen (Mrs. Charles Melvin Roe). Instr. chemistry Bethel Coll., McKenzie, Tenn., 1938-40; tchr., prin. Weakley County (Tenn.) Pub. Schs., 1940-43; instr. to prof. chemistry U. Tenn. at Martin, 1943-73, dean instrn., 1963-69, vice chancellor for acad. affairs, 1969—; vis. lectr. U. Ill., 1963. NSF Coll. Faculty fellow, 1959. Mem. Am. Chem. Soc., Am. Assn. Higher Edn., N.E.A., Tenn. Acad. Scis. Methodist. Rotarian. Home: 110 Willow Lane Martin TN 38237

CAMPBELL, ROBERT CLYDE, corp. rep.; b. Honea Path, S.C., May 18, 1903; s. John James and Leona (Elgin) C.; B.A., Furman U., 1926; M.A., George Peabody Coll., 1929; student U. N.C., 1930; m. Priscilla Augusta Dillard, May 2, 1931; 1 dau., Priscilla Ann. Tchr., prin. Norway (S.C.) High Sch., 1926-29; supt. pub. schs., Richburg, S.C., 1929-43, Bethune, S.C., 1943-45, Pageland, S.C., 1945-68; supt. Chesterfield County Sch. Dist., 1968-71; rep. Greater Carolinas Corp., Columbia, S.C., 1972—. Mem. N.E.A., Pageland C. of C., S.C. Ret. Educators Assn. Baptist. Mason, Lion. Home: PO Box 307 Pageland SC 29728

CAMPBELL, ROBERT KYLE, utility exec.; b. Chicota, Tex., July 6, 1926; s. Loy C. and Ruby (Carder) C.; Asso. Bus. Adminstrn., Paris Jr. Coll., 1948; B.A., East Tex. State U., 1949, M.Ed., 1951; m. Donna Jo Poole, Nov. 26, 1947; children—Ricky, Mark, Stacy. Sr. accountant firm Haskins & Sells, Dallas, 1951-59; with Tex. Power & Light Co., Dallas, 1959—, asst. sec., asst. treas., 1964-72, v.p., 1972—, v.p., asst. sec., asst. treas. Bi-Stone Fuel Co. div., 1973—, also dir. Served with AUS, 1945-46. C.P.A., Tex. Mem. Tex. Soc. C.P.A.'s, Am. Inst. C.P.A.'s. Home: 2620 Ripplewood St Dallas TX 75228 Office: 1511 Bryan St Dallas TX 75201

CAMPBELL, ROY TIMOTHY, JR., lawyer; b. Newport, Tenn., Aug. 8, 1927; s. Roy Timothy and Polly Vance (Brittain) C.; LL.B., J.D., U. Tenn., 1950. Admitted to Tenn. bar, 1951; practiced in Newport, 1951—; sr. partner Campbell and Hooper, Newport, 1965—; dir. Mchts. and Planters Bank, Newport, Tenn. City atty., Town of Newport, 1968—; vets.' service officer for Cocke County, Tenn., 1953-73. Sec. Rep. Exec. Com., Cocke County. Bd. dirs. Indsl. Devel. Bd., Cocke County, 1965—. Served with AUS, 1946-47. Mem. Newport C. of C. (pres. 1955-56), Tenn., Cocke County (pres. 1972—) bar assns., U. Tenn. Alumni Assn., Sigma Alpha Epsilon. Methodist (ofcl. bd. 1973—). Elk, Lion (pres. 1958-59). Home: 712 College St Newport TN 37821 Office: 406 E Main St Newport TN 37821

CAMPBELL, STEPHEN ROY, physician; b. New Orleans, Feb. 5, 1904; s. Stephen Frank and Mary Alice (Healy) C.; student Chenet's Inst., 1922-25; B.S., Tulane U., 1929, M.D., 1931; m. Marie McDowell Pilkington, Oct. 21, 1933; children—Marie (Mrs. Henry J. Legendre, Jr.), Judith (Mrs. Kennette C. Cranor), Stephenie (Mrs. William O. Jeansonne), Kathleen, Claire (Mrs. Joseph R. Gendron). Intern Charity Hosp., New Orleans, 1931-33; practice medicine Vacherie, La., 1933—. Active pub. health services, 1933-50; examining physician St. James Parish, SSS, 1942-50. Recipient Selective Service medal U.S. Congress, World War II. Mem. A.M.A., La., Tri-Parish med. socs. Address: Box 106 Route 2 Vacherie LA 70090

CAMPBELL, STUART BLAND, JR., lawyer; b. Wytheville, Va., July 30, 1916; s. Stuart Bland and Mary (Miles) C.; A.B., Presbyn. Coll., Clinton, S.C., 1937; LL.B., U. Va., 1941; m. Janet Reed Sutherland, Aug. 14, 1953; children—Stuart Bland III, Arthur Reed, Martha Miles. Admitted to Va. bar, 1940; partner firm Campbell & Campbell, 1941-42; sec. State Dept. Bd. Appeals on Visa Cases, 1942-44; div. dir. UNRRA Greece Mission, 1944-47; U.S. fgn. service officer, 1949-53; partner firm Campbell & Campbell, Wytheville, Va., 1953—. Mem. adv. bd., dir. Wytheville br. First Nat. Exchange Bank Va., 1971—. Del. Democratic Nat. Conv., 1960; chmn. Wytheville County Dem. Com., 1966-70. Mem. Wythe County Sch. Bd., 1964—. Bd. dirs. Wythe County Meml. Hosp.; trustee Union Theol. Sem., Richmond, Va. Fellow Am. Coll. Trial Lawyers, Am. Bar Found.; mem. Am. Law Inst., Am., Va. bar assns. Presbyn. (elder). Club: Commonwealth (Richmond). Home: Peppers Ferry Rd Wytheville VA 24382 Office: 210 W Main St Wytheville VA 24382

CAMPBELL, WALLACE GIBSON, JR., med. educator; b. Lockport, N.Y., July 25, 1930; s. Wallace Gibson and Grace Estelle (Morris) C.; A.B., Harvard, 1953; M.D., Cornell, 1957; m. Noreen Mary Keating, June 16, 1957; children—John, William, Julia, Donald. Intern pathology N.Y. Hosp.-Cornell Med. Center, N.Y.C., 1957-58, asst. resident pathology, 1958-59, USPHS trainee pathology, 1959-62, asst. in pathology, 1959-61, instr., 1961-62; asst. prof. pathology Emory U. Sch. Medicine, Atlanta, 1964-67, asso. prof. pathology, 1967-71, prof., 1971—. Served to capt. M.C., AUS, 1962-64. Mem. Am. Soc. Exptl. Pathology, Am. Soc. Pathologists and Bacteriologists, Internat. Acad. Pathology, A.M.A., N.Y. Acad. Sci., Ga. Heart Assn. Home: 643 Webster Dr Decatur VA 30033 Office: Woodruff Bldg Emory U Atlanta GA 30322

CAMPBELL, WILLIAM ROCKWELL, concrete co. exec.; b. Cleve., Dec. 3, 1926; s. Frank William and Ollie (Rockwell) C.; student Ohio U., 1946-48; B.S.I., Cleve. Coll., 1950; m. Doris Prestwood Holloway, May 5, 1950; 1 dau., Susan Nanette. Chief design engr. Cleve. Lathe & Machine Co., 1950-52; gen. mgr. mfg. div. Rinker Materials Corp., West Palm Beach, Fla., 1952—. Sec., West Palm Beach Camp Gideons, 1965. Served with USNR, 1944-45. Mem. Am. Inst. Indsl. Engrs. (chpt. v.p. 1965), Christian Bus. Mens Com. (sec.-treas. 1965; dir. South Am. mission), Nat. Concrete Masonry Assn. (tech. com., chmn. prodn. sub-com.), Fla. Engring. Soc., Am. Mgmt. Assn., Am. Concrete Inst., Fla. Concrete and Products Assn. (tech. com., jr. coll. com.), S.A.R. (sec. 1968, 1st v.p. 1969). Presbyn. (deacon 1966-69, elder 1969—). Home: 7387 Venetian Way West Palm Beach FL 33406 Office: 431 7th St West Palm Beach FL 33401

CANADAY, WILLIE VERNON, civil engr.; b. Lilington, N.C., Aug. 13, 1927; s. Hubert Rinso and Vivian (Draughon) C.; B.S. in Civil Engring., U. Miami, 1957; m. Barbara Lou Duncan, Nov. 25, 1955; children—Dennis D., Belle C. Civil engr., U.S. Army C.E., Jacksonville, Fla., 1957-60, 61-62, 64-66, area engr., Tampa, 1966—; civil engr. Dade County Dept. Pub. Works, Miami, 1960-61; mgmt. engr. NASA, Cape Kennedy, 1962-64. Served with USNR, 1945-46, 51-52. Registered profl. engr., Vt. Mem. Fla. Engring. Soc., V.F.W., Am. Legion, U. Miami Sch. Engring. and Environmental Design Alumni Assn., Alpha Tau Omega. Club: Propeller. Home: 1936 Arrowhead Dr NE St Petersburg FL 33703 Office: 3602 Hwy 301 N Tampa FL 33619

CANADY, GEORGE MASABEAU, JR., constrn. co. exec.; b. Charleston, S.C., Oct. 18, 1919; s. George Masabeau and Artha Marie (Stephens) C.; B.S., The Citadel, 1947; m. Evelyn Elizabeth Koenig, Nov. 24, 1940; children—Lynda Rae, George Masabeau III, Brian Lee. Trainee, Canady Constrn. Co., Charleston, 1940-41, v.p., 1947-61, pres., 1961-73, also chmn. bd.; dir. new sch. house planning Charleston County Sch. Dist., 1973—. Chmn. Gen. Contractors Licensing Bd. Charleston County, 1968—. Bd. dirs. Carolina Nursing Center. Served to capt. USAAF, 1941-45; lt. col. Res. ret. Mem. Asso. Gen. Contractors Am., Sigma Phi Sigma. Methodist (trustee). Mason (32 deg.). Club: Square and Level (pres.) (Charleston). Home: 706 Shamrock Lane Charleston SC 29407 Office: Box 932 Charleston SC 29412

CANAN, HOWARD VOORHEIS, cons. engr., author; b. Omaha, Aug. 6, 1894; s. Clarence John and E. Lizette (Voorheis) C.; B.S., U.S. Mil. Acad., 1918; postgrad. U.S. Army Engring. Sch., 1921, Command and Gen. Staff Coll., 1939, Naval War Coll., 1942. Commd. 2d lt. U.S. Army, 1918, advanced through grades to col.; with C.E., 1921-28; asst. prof. mil. sci. and tactics Colo. Sch. Mines, Golden, 1928-32; asst. dist. engr. Duluth, 1932-34; dist. engr. U.S. Lake Survey, 1934-36; gen. staff M.I. Div. War Dept., 1939-41; G-2 sec. GHQ, 1941-42; duty with Amphibious Corps and Force, Pacific Fleet, 1942-43; asst. to engr. ETO, 1943-46; dist. engr. Nashville, 1946-49; engr. 2d Army, Ft. Meade, Md., 1949-52; engring. insp. gen., 1952-53; asst. chief engrs. for real estate, 1953-54; ret., 1954; cons. practice, 1954-56; cons. civil engr. Melpar, Inc., Alexandria, 1956-60; cons. engr., 1960—. Trustee Patriotic Edn., Inc. Decorated Legion of Merit, Bronze Star medal (U.S.); Croix Guerre (France). Fellow Am. Soc. C.E., Am. Geog. Soc.; mem. Mil. Inst., Soc. Am. Mil. Engrs., S.A.R., Civil War Round Table. Clubs: Cosmos, Army and Navy. Contbr. articles to profl. and hist. jours. Home: Apt 522 1200 S Washington St Alexandria VA 22314

CANCIO, MIGUEL MANUEL, lawyer; b. San Sebastian, P.R., Sept. 17, 1923; s. Jose Luis and Narcisa Maria (Rodriguez) C.; student U. P.R., 1942, U. Md., 1943, Poly. Inst. P.R., 1944; B.Pharm. Scis., U. P.R., 1948, LL.B. magna cum laude, 1964; m. Sylvia B. Gonzalez, July 11, 1949; children—Sylvia E., Miguel Manuel, Jose R. Tchr., Aguadilla (P.R.) High Sch., 1945; owner, pharmacist Cancio Drug Store, Aguadilla, 1949—; admitted to P.R. bar, 1964, since practiced in Aguadilla; partner Cancio & Cancio, Aguadilla, 1967—. Mem. Jud. Conf., 1973—; legal counsel FEMI, Inc., 1973—; mem. P.R. Bd. Bar Examiners, 1973—. Mem. Ramey AFB Community Council, 1971-73. Mem. Colegio de Abogados de P.R., P.R. Bar Assn. (del. bd. dirs. 1971-72), Phi Sigma Alpha. Roman Catholic. Lion. Home: Villa Lydia Aguadilla PR 00603 Office: 19 Progreso St Box 65 Aguadilla PR 00603

CANCIO, PABLO R(AMÓN), lawyer; b. San Sebastian, P.R., Mar. 22, 1931; s. José Luis and Marcisa (Rodriguez) C.; A.B., U. P.R., 1952; J.D., U. Mich., 1955; m. Haydeé E. Reichard, July 17, 1960; children—Pablo G., Juan Carlos. Admitted to P.R. bar, 1956; asso. mem. firm Brownm Newsom & Cordova, San Juan, 1956-60; partner firm McConnell, Valdes & Kelly, San Juan, 1960-67, firm Cancio & Cancio, Aguadilla, P.R., 1967—. Mem. Bd. Bar Examiners P.R., 1965-66, Com. Rules Evidence Judicial Conf. P.R. Supreme Ct., 1973—. Mem. fellowship com. Colegio San Carlos, Aguadilla, 1972—, Aguadilla Indsl. Com., 1971—, Ramey AFB Community Council, Aguadilla, 1971-73; legal counsel FEMI, Inc., Mayaguez Med. Center, 1973—. Mem. Colegio de Abogados de P.R., P.R. Bar Assn. (dir.). Roman Catholic. Lion. Home: Villa Haydee Aguadilla PR 00603 Office: 19 Progreso St PO Box 65 Aguadilla PR 00603

CANDELA, FELIX, architect; b. Madrid, Spain, Jan. 27, 1910; s. Felix Candela Magro and Julia Outerino Echeverria; Architect, Escuela Superior de Aquitectura de Madrid, 1935; m. Eladia Martin, May 3, 1940 (dec. Sept. 5, 1963); children—Antonia, Manolita, Teresa and Pilar (twins). Practice architecture in Mexico City, also Acapulco; builder reinforced concrete shells, 1951—, important works include Church La Virgen Milagrosa, Mexico City; pres. Cubiertas Ala S.A., 1950—; prof. structures Escuela Nacional de Arquitectura, Universidad Nacional Autonoma de Mexico; Charles Eliot Norton prof. poetry Harvard, 1961-62. Served as capt., C.E., Republican Army, Spanish Civil War. Recipient Gold medal Instn. Structl. Engrs., London, 1961; Price Auguste Parret, Internat. Union Architects, 1961. Mem. Internat. Assn. Shell Structures (hon.), Sociedad Venezolana de Arquitectos (hon.), Sociedad de Arquitectos Colombianos, Sociedad de Arquitectos Mexicanos, Am. Concrete Inst., Internat. Assn. Bridge and Structural Engring., Institut Technique du Batiment of Des Travaus Publics, A.I.A. (hon.), Royal Inst. Brit. Architects (hon.). Home: Juarez 14 Tlacopac Mexico 20 DF Mexico Office: Ramon Guzman 123 Mexico 4 DF Mexico

CANDLER, BILLIE CHARLES, ednl. adminstr.; b. Greenville, Tex., Oct. 5, 1926; s. Charles Houston and Nettie (Graham) C.; B.S., N. Tex. State Coll., 1949, M.Health, Phys. Edn., Recreation, N. Tex. State U., 1952; m. Barbara Lynn Ezzell, Nov. 20, 1951. Dir. health, phys. edn., athletics, coach San Antonio Coll. 1949—. Safety chmn. Bexar County chpt. A.R.C., 1968-71. Served with inf. AUS, 1944-46. Mem. Tex. Jr. Coll. Tchrs. Assn. (pres. 1970), Tex., Am. assns. health, phys. edn. and recreation, Nat. Assn. Dirs. Colegiate Athletics, Phi Delta Kappa. Democrat. Mem. Ch. of Christ. Author: Physical Education Handbook, 1969. Home: 366 Maplewood St San Antonio TX 78216

CANDLER, JOHN SLAUGHTER, II, lawyer; b. Atlanta, Nov. 30, 1908; s. Asa Warren and Harriet Lee (West) C.; A.B. magna cum laude, U. Ga., 1929; J.D., Emory U., 1931; m. Dorothy Bruce Warthen, June 13, 1933; children—Dorothy Warthen (Mrs. Joseph W. Hamilton, Jr.), John Slaughter. Admitted Ga. bar, 1931, partner Candler, Cox, Andrews & Hansen and other law firms, 1931—; sec., dir. Leon Propane, Inc., Peachtree Realty & Ins. Co., Weatherly Corp., Propane Gas Service, Inc., D. M. Weatherly Co.; dir. P. D. Christian Co., Sungas, Inc., Equipment Sales Co., dep. asst. atty. gen. State of Ga., 1951-68. Mem. Greater Atlanta Council USO, 1969—. Trustee Ga. Student Ednl. Fund; trustee Kappa Alpha Scholarship Fund, pres., 1970-72. Served from capt. to col. AUS, 1941-46. Decorated Commendation Ribbon. Fellow Am. Coll. Probate Counsel (Ga. state chmn. 1965-68, regent 1968—), Internat. Acad. Law and Sci.; mem. Nat. Tax Assn., Tax Inst. Am. (adv. council 1969—), Newcomen Soc., Am. Judicature Soc., State Bar Ga. (chmn. sect. on fiduciary law 1964-65), Am., Atlanta bar assns., Internat. Platform Assn., Atlanta Estate Planning Council (pres. 1963-64), Lawyers Club Atlanta, Am. Legion (post comdr. 1949-50), Res. Officers Assn. (state pres. 1946, nat. exec. com. 1947), Mil Order World Wars, English-Speaking Union, Phi Beta Kappa, Phi Kappa Phi, Phi Delta Phi, Kappa Alpha, Sigma Delta Chi. Episcopalian (vestryman 1953-56, sr. warden, 1955, cathedral trustee 1957-67, Lay reader 1971—). Mason, Kiwanian (v.p. 1950, dir. 1948-50, 1958-59; trustee Northside Atlanta Found. 1959—, chmn. 1959—). Home: 413 Manor Ridge Dr NW Atlanta GA 30305 Office: 2400 Gas Light Tower Atlanta GA 30303

CANFIELD, CRAIG JENNINGS, physician; b. Pasadena, Cal., May 11, 1932; s. Ronald E. and Enid Clarice (Bellows) C.; B.S., U. Ore., 1955; M.D., 1957; m. Beatrice Kay Golding, Jan. 10, 1954; children—Joni Jean, Brian Craig, Kevin Brent, Todd Cameron. Intern, Good Samaritan Hosp., Portland, Ore., 1957-58; commd. 2d lt. AUS, 1958, advanced through grades to col., 1972; battle group surgeon 82d Div., Fort Bragg, N.C., 1958-60; resident internal medicine and research Walter Reed Hosp., Washington, 1960-64; chief med. service SEATO Med. Research Lab., Bangkok, Thailand, 1964-66; spl. asst. dir. div. medicine Walter Reed Inst. Research, Washington, 1966-68, fellow hematology, 1968-69, chief dept. metabolism, 1969-70, spl. asst. dir. inst., 1970—; prin. investigator U.S. Army antimalarial investigation new drugs, 1969—. Diplomate Am. Bd. Internal Medicine. Fellow A.C.P.; mem. A.M.A., Am. Soc. Tropical Medicine, Am. Fedn. Clin. Research, Am. Soc. Hematology. Home: 3508 Largo Rd Upper Marlboro MD 20870 Office: Walter Reed Army Inst Research Washington DC 20012

CANFIELD, EARL RODNEY, dentist; b. Toledo, O., Dec. 19, 1916; s. Howard Stowe and Alice (Wynn) C.; A.B., Emory U., 1938, D.D.S., 1942; m. Evelyn Louise Flowers, Dec. 26, 1940; children—Merilyn Canfield (Mrs. J. Arthur Mozley), Earl Rodney. Practice dentistry, Atlanta, 1942, 52, 70—, College Park, Ga., 1967, 69; partner College Park Supply Co., 1951-71, sec., treas., 1955-71; pres. Herff Jones Co., Indpls., 1968. Mem. Arts Festival, Atlanta, 1965—. Served to maj. Dental Corps, AUS, 1942-46, USAAF, 1951-54; Korea, CBI. Decorated Bronze Star medal. Fellow Am. Coll. Dentists, Internat. Coll. Dentists; mem. Am., Ga. dental assns., No. Dist., 5th Dist., Chgo. dental socs., Fedn. Dentaire Internationale (life), Am. Analgesia Soc., Atlanta Civil War Round Table, Am. Legion, Sigma Pi. Mason (32 degree, Shriner), Elk. Clubs: Cherokee Town and Country, (Atlanta). Home: 6 Montclair Dr Atlanta GA 30309 Office: 305 Buckhead Av Atlanta GA 30305

CANN, KENNETH THOMAS, educator; b. N.Y.C., Apr. 29, 1926; s. Kenneth Wilkins and Gladys (Harpell) C.; B.S., Georgetown U., 1950; M.A., Ind. U., 1960, Ph.D. (Midwest Universities Consortium grantee 1964-65), 1967; m. Maria Nilda de Carvelho Jordao, Jan. 21, 1962. Appraiser VA, Washington, 1950-56; real property officer FHA, Indpls., 1956-59; teaching asst. Ind. U., 1960-63, lectr., 1965-66, asst. prof., 1967-68; asso. prof. Western Ky. U., 1968-70, prof., head dept. econ., 1970—; instr. U. Wis., 1963-65. Served with AUS, 1944-46. Mem. Am., So., Midwest econ. assns., Soc. for Internat. Devel. Home: 1017 Ridgecrest Dr Bowling Green KY 42101 Office: Dept Economics Western KY U Bowling Green KY 42101

CANNIFF, JOSEPH HARRY, electronics engr.; b. South Houston, Tex., Nov. 29, 1931; s. Harry Bronson and Mary Jane (Brown) C.; B.Applied Sci. (Jesse H. Jones fellow), U. Houston, 1960; m. Pansy Ruth Dixon, June 3, 1955; children—Anita Gail, Sharon Lynn, Joseph Stephen. Engr. Heldenbrand Tubular Service Co., New Iberia, La., 1960-62; engr. Boeing Co., Seattle, 1962-64; sr. engr. Lockheed

Electronics Co., Houston, 1964—. Sectl. comdr. Royal Rangers, boys program Assemblies of God, Houston, 1969-70, nat. aide-de camp, South Tex. dist., 1970-71, dist. comdr., 1971-72. Served with USNR, 1950-54. Mem. Am. Radio Relay League, I.E.E.E., Instrument Soc. Am., Nat. Mgmt. Assn. (com. chmn. 1969; program div. com. chmn. 1970, dir. 1971), Am. Mgmt. Assn., Tau Alpha Pi. Mem. Assembly of God (trustee, supt. Sunday sch. 1966-71). Home: 103 Parliament St Houston TX 77034 Office: 16811 El Camino Real Houston TX 77058

CANNON, CARROLL CONWAY, lawyer; b. St. Louis, July 22, 1909; s. Thomas D. and Marguerite (Carroll) C.; student Washington U., 1926-28; LL.B., City Coll. Law, 1933; m. Helen Harrelson, Nov. 2, 1940; children—Carroll C., Cathlyn II., Helen M. Abstracter Title Ins. Corp., St. Louis, 1928-33; atty. Fed. Land Bank St. Louis, 1933-38; practice law, St. Louis, 1938-41; spl. agt. FBI, 1942-46; practice of law Forrest City, Ark., 1946—; pres. St. Francis County Abstract Co. Pres. St. Louis Jr. C. of C., 1942; dir., mem. exec. com. Forrest City C. of C., 1947-51. Mem. Am., Ark., St. Francis County (pres. 1963) bar assns., Ark. Land Title Assn. (pres. 1951-52). Lion (pres.). Home: 2917 E Broadway Forrest City AR 72335 Office: 112 S Izard Forrest City AR 72335

CANNON, HOWARD JOSEPH, marketing cons.; b. Beaumont, Tex., Oct. 10, 1930; s. Howard Joseph and Eunie (Grove) C.; B.A. in Speech, English, U. S.W. La., 1952; postgrad. U. Houston, 1956-58; m. Sandra Ann Boydston, Mar. 5, 1958; children—Blynn Claudina, Brian Joseph. Promotion mgr. KPRC Radio, audience promotion mgr. KPRC-TV, 1959-62; merchandiser, merchandising mgr. Tex. Instruments Inc., 1962-70; pres. Marketing Services Mgmt., Houston, 1970—. Cons. Small Bus. Assn., 1972-73. Bd. dirs. Cystic Fibrosis Research Found., Houston. Served with USMC, 1952-55. Mem. Pub. Relations Soc. Am., Houston Soc. Mgmt. Consultants. Home: 4822 McDermed St Houston TX 77035 Office: PO Box 35733 Houston TX 77035

CANNON, HUGH, lawyer; b. Albemarle, N.C., Oct. 11, 1931; s. Hubert Napoleon and Nettie (Harris) C.; A.B., Davidson Coll., 1953; B.A. (Rhodes scholar) Oxford U., 1955, M.A., 1960; LL.B., Harvard, 1958; m. Jessie Mercer, Jan. 26, 1956; children—John Stuart, Marshall, Martha Janet. Admitted to N.C. bar, 1958; mem. staff U. N.C. Inst. Govt., Chapel Hill, 1959; atty. Sanford, Phillips, McCoy & Weaver, Fayetteville, 1960; asst. to Gov. of N.C., Raleigh, 1961; dir. adminstrn. State of N.C., 1962-65, state budget officer, 1963; mem. firm Sanford, Cannon, Adams & McCullough, Raleigh, 1965—. Parliamentarian N.E.A., 1965—; lectr. N.S. State U., Raleigh, part-time, 1965, 66. State dir. N.C. Emergency Resources Planning Com., 1962-65; pres. Friends of Coll., Raleigh, 1963. Alternate del. Nat. Democratic Conv., 1964. Bd. govs. U. N.C.; trustee Davidson Coll. Mem. Phi Beta Kappa, Omicron Delta Kappa, Phi Gamma Delta. Democrat. Methodist. Home: 3333 Alleghany Dr Raleigh NC 27609 Office: Br Bank Bldg Box 389 Raleigh NC 27602

CANNON, LOUIS SIMEON, newspaper corr.; b. N.Y.C., June 3, 1933; s. Jack Ralph and Irene (Kohn) C.; student U. Nev., 1950-52, San Francisco State Coll., 1952-53; m. Virginia Oprian, Feb. 2, 1953; children—Carl, David, Judith, Jack. Editor, Contra Costa (Cal.) Times, 1960-61; asst. wire editor, state capitol bur. chief San Jose (Cal.) Mercury-News, 1961-69; Washington corr. Ridder Publs., 1969-71; nat. corr. Washington Post, 1971—; Washington corr. Cal. Jour., Sacramento, 1970—. Served with AUS, 1953-54. Recipient distinguished pub. affairs reporting award Am. Polit. Sci. Assn., 1968, edit. excellence award Cal. Taxpayers Assn., 1969. Mem. Nat. Press Club, Author's Guild, Am. Newspaper Guild, Sigma Delta Chi. Mem. Ch. Christ. Club: Capitol Hill (Washington). Author: Ronnie and Jesse: A Political Odyssey, 1969; The McCloskey Challenge, 1971. Home: 1934 Hull Rd Vienna VA 22180 Office: 1511 15th St NW Washington DC 20005

CANNON, MARK WILCOX, govt. jud. exec.; b. Salt Lake City, Aug. 29, 1928; s. Joseph Jenne and Ramona (Wilcox) C.; student Deep Springs Coll., 1944-46; B.A., U. Utah, 1949; M.A., Harvard, 1954, M.Pub. Adminstrn., 1955, Ph.D., 1961; m. Ruth Marian Dixon, Dec. 28, 1956; children—Lucile, Mark, Kristen. Missionary, Ch. of Jesus Christ of Latter-day Saints, Argentina, 1949-52; research analyst Utah Found., 1953; sec. Utah Sch. Merit Study Com., 1954; instr. Brigham Young U., 1955, chmn. dept. polit. sci., 1961-64, adminstrv. asst. to U.S. congressman, 1956-60; mem. staff Inst. Pub. Adminstrn., N.Y.C., 1964-72, dir. urban devel. program, Venezuela, 1964-65, dir. internat. programs, N.Y.C., 1965-68, dir., 1968-72; adminstrv. asst. to chief justice U.S. Supreme Ct., 1972—. Mem. inter Am. adv. Council Dept. State, 1972-74. Cons. unconventional war research studies project USN, 1962-63; mem. staff U.S. Senator W.F. Bennett, 1961, 62-63. Trustee Inst. Pub. Adminstrn., 1972—. Recipient Ann. award Western Polit. Sci. Assn., 1963. Mem. Internat. Studies Assn. (sec. 1962-63), Am. Polit. Sci. Assn., Am. Soc. Pub. Adminstrn., Nat. Acad. Pub. Adminstrn., Comparative Adminstrn. Group. Author: (with R. Joseph Monsen) The Makers of Public Policy: American Power Groups and Their Idealogies, 1965; (with Carlos Moran) The Challenge of Urban Development in Valencia, 1966; (with others) Partnership for Progress: Atlanta-Fulton County Consolidation, 1969. Home: 8404 Martingale Dr McLean VA 22101 Office: Supreme Ct of United States Washington DC 20543

CANNON, WILLIAM RAGSDALE, bishop; b. Dalton, Ga., Apr. 5, 1916; s. William Ragsdale and Emma (McAfee) C.; A.B., U. Ga., 1937; B.D., Yale U., 1940, Ph.D., 1942; D.D., Asbury Coll., 1950; LL.D., Temple U., 1955; L.H.D., Emory U., 1969. Dean, Candler Sch. Theology, Emory U., Atlanta, 1953-68; resident bishop Raleigh (N.C.) area United Methodist Ch., 1968—. Chmn. Am. sect. World Methodist Council; chmn. dept. ministry United Methodist Bd. Edn. Trustee, Emory U., Duke U., Asbury Coll. Author: A Faith for These Times, 1944; The Christian Church, 1945; The Theology of John Wesley, 1946; Our Protestant Faith, 1949; Our Faith in Love, 1949; The Redeemer, 1950; The History of Christianity in the Middle Ages, 1960; The Journeys after St. Paul, 1963. Home: 2301 Beechridge Rd Raleigh NC 27605 Office: Methodist Bldg 1307 Glenwood Av Raleigh NC 27605

CANTER, HALL GIBBONS, physician; b. Harrisonburg, Va., Feb. 26, 1929; s. Noland Mackenzie and Mary Virginia (Yancey) C.; B.S., Randolph Macon Coll., 1950; M.D., Med. Coll. Va., 1954; m. Martha Grizzelle Hardy, June 13, 1953; children—Hall Gibbons, Martha Jane, Jean, Grace. Intern, Med. Coll. Va., 1954-55; resident Georgetown Hosp., 1957-58, D.C. Gen. Hosp., 1958-59, VA Hosp., Washington, 1959-61; clin. investigator VA, Washington, 1961-64; asst. chief medicine VA Hosp., Washington, 1964-70; chief pulmonary disease section Georgetown U. Hosp., 1970—; asso. prof. medicine Georgetown U. Sch. Medicine, 1969—. Served with AUS, 1955-57. Fellow A.C.P., Am. Coll. Chest Physicians; mem. Am. Fedn. Clin. Research, Am. Thoracic Soc. Home: 505 Canterbury Lane Alexandria VA 22314 Office: 3800 Reservoir Rd NW Washington DC 20007

CANTEY, CRAIG COVINGTON, JR., lawyer; b. Fort Worth, July 15, 1929; s. Craig Covington and Maurine (Martin) C.; student Tex. Christian U., 1945, So. Methodist U., 1947; B.A., U. Tex., 1955, LL.B., 1957; m. Patricia Ann Hardin, 1957 (div. 1968); children—Craig Covington III, Frank Shelby, Cynthia Ann; m. 2d, Susan Thayer Wierum, Nov. 9, 1968. Admitted to Tex. bar, 1957; since practiced in Houston; partner firm Foreman, Dyess, Prewett, Henderson & Cantey, and predecessor firms, 1958-70; partner firm Cantey & Kendall, 1970—; mng. partner Barbour's Cut Co., 1971—, Atkinson Island Co., 1973—, South Loop Co., 1973—, other real estate investment cos., ranches; chmn. bd. Bowie Nat. Bank. Founding trustee SOS Houston, Inc. Served with USAF, 1951-54; Korea. Decorated Bronze Star. Mem. Houston Assn. Def. Attys. (pres. 1968-69), Am., Tex., Harris County bar assns., Bayshore, Houston chambers commerce. Mason (32 deg.). Clubs: Houston Yacht, Houston Athletic. Home: 2715 Crescent View St La Porte TX 77571 Office: 2148 Tenneco Bldg Houston TX 77002

CANTILLON, WILLIAM HOUCK, warehouse co. exec.; b. Cleve., Sept. 17, 1943; s. Daniel James and Genevieve (Houck) C.; B.S., Case Inst. Tech., 1965; M.B.A., Butler U., 1968; m. Barbara Lee Jackson, Feb. 19, 1966; children—Denice Renee, William Houck II. Co-ordinator planning, part div. Gen. Motors, Flint, Mich., 1969-72; nat. sales mgr. Nat. Distbn. Service, Inc., Atlanta, 1972—. Mem. Am. Marketing Assn., Nat. Council Phys. Distbn. Mgmt., Inst. Mgmt. Sci. Home: 4701 Flat Shoals Rd Union City GA 30291 Office: Suite 1100 1st Nat Bank Tower Atlanta GA 30303

CANTOR, BERNARD HAROLD, lawyer; b. Syracuse, N.Y., Apr. 13, 1920; s. Moses Ellis and Sarah (Livshin) C.; B.A., U. Tenn., 1941; J.D., Harvard, 1943; m. Evelyn Mach, Dec. 28, 1947; children—Judith, Susanna, Abigail. Admitted to D.C., Tenn. bars, 1944; law clk. U.S. Ct. Appeals, Washington, 1943-45; staff counsel OSRD, Washington, 1945-46; mem. firm Cantor & Kiener, 1972—. Pres., So. Home Bldg. Fund, Inc., Johnson City, Tenn., 1962—; dir. Tenn. Nuclear Spltys., Inc., Jonesboro, Tenn. Arbitrator labor relations, 1958—. Chmn. Washington County Democratic Orgn., 1971-72; del. Dem. Nat. Conv., 1972; Dem. candidate for U.S. Congress, 1st Congl. Dist., 1972. Mem. Harvard Law Sch. Assn. Tenn. Mem. B'nai B'rith. Home: 215 W Gilmer St Johnson City TN 37601 Office: 126 Spring St Johnson City TN 37601

CANTOR, ROBERT L., leasing co. exec.; b. N.Y.C., Apr. 30, 1928; s. Saul and Blanche (Bursutsky) C.; B.S., N.Y. U., 1952, M.A., 1953; m. Myra Werner, Dec. 8, 1966; children—Scott Howard, Nina Gail. In investment banking, 1955-60; exec. v.p., dir. C.F. Kirk Labs., N.Y.C., 1960-62; exec. v.p. Dragor Shipping Corp., N.Y.C., 1964-67; sr. v.p. Nat. Equipment Rental, Ltd., N.Y.C., 1965-68, pres., chmn. 1968-69; chmn. exec. com., dir. Detroit Steel Corp., N.Y.C., 1969-71; financial cons., 1971-72; pres., dir. Barnett Leasing Co. subsidiary Barnett Banks Fla. Inc., Ft. Lauderdale, Fla., 1973—. Vice pres. Am. Export Industries, N.Y.C., 1967-68. Served with USNR, 1946-48. Home: 3725 S Ocean Dr Hollywood FL 33020 Office: 1 Financial Plaza Ft Lauderdale FL 33394

CANTOW, EDWARD FRANCIS, physician; b. Balt., Jan. 17, 1936; s. Edward Henry and Cecilia (Hart) C.; B.S., Manhattan Coll., 1957; M.D., Georgetown U., 1961; m. Theresa Scala, July 11, 1959; children—Christine Marie, Loretta Ellen, Claire Denise, Diana Jacqueline, Edward Francis Jr. Commd. ensign, U.S. Navy, 1961, advanced through grades to comdr., 1971; intern U.S. Naval Hosp., Portsmouth, Va., 1961-62, resident, 1963-66, mem. staff internal medicine, 1967-68, asst. dir. hematology service, 1970-72; resigned, 1972; mem. staff internal medicine, hematologist Naval Hosp., Camp Pendleton, Cal., 1968-69; fellow in hematology Naval Hosp., Phila., 1969-71; pvt. practice medicine, specializing in hematology and oncology, Portsmouth, 1972—; cons. hematology USPHS Hosp., Norfolk, Va. Fellow A.C.P.; mem. Bur. Medicine and Surgery Grants for Clin. Investigation in Hematology, Am. Soc. Hematology, A.M.A., Am. Fedn. Clin. Research, Am. Bd. Med. Examiners, Phi Chi. Roman Catholic (dir. youth activities 1969-70, dir. tchrs. 1969-70). Home: 2904 Duke of York Dr Chesapeake VA 23321 Office: 4037 Taylor Rd Chesapeake VA 23321

CANTRELL, BERT MITCHELL, JR., utility exec.; b. Birmingham, Ala., Mar. 21, 1926; s. Bert Mitchell and Essie (Crow) C.; student Mercer U., 1943-44, U. N.C., 1944-45; B.E.E., Auburn U., 1948; m. Louise Anne Thomas, July 11, 1946; children—Lynn Carlisle, Kent Mitchell. With So. div. Miss. Power & Light Co., McComb, Miss., 1948—, div. engr., 1966-71, mgr. So. div., 1971—. Vice pres. McComb Planning Commn., 1971-73, pres., 1974; pres. McComb Aero. Assn. Inc., 1973—; mem. exec. bd. Andrew Jackson council Boy Scouts Am., 1973—, asst. scoutmaster, 1972—, recipient Dist. award merit Tall Pine Dist., 1973. Served with USNR, 1943-46; PTO. Registered profl. engr., Miss. Mem. I.E.E.E., Miss., Nat. socs. profl. engrs., McComb C. of C. (treas. 1973, v.p. 1974), Kappa Sigma, Tau Beta Pi, Eta Kappa Nu. Methodist (steward). Rotarian. Home: 325 Butler St McComb MS 29648 Office: 300 N Broadway St McComb MS 39648

CANTRELL, FRANK WILLIAM, business cons.; b. Poplar Bluff, Mo., Oct. 11, 1902; s. William Ambrose and Josephine (Catern) C.; student S.E. Mo. State Coll., 1918-21; m. Julia Peironnet Albert, Sept. 4, 1925; children—Frank Peironnet (dec.), Julie. With Western Electric Co., 1921-23; various editorial positions Ark. Gazette, Little Rock, 1924-44; exec. v.p. Ark. C. of C., Little Rock, 1945-68, Asso. Industries Ark., Inc., Little Rock, 1948-68. Industry mem. S.W. Regional Wage Stblzn. Bd., Dallas, 1950-52; chmn. Conf. So. Indsl. Assn., 1959-60, Nat. Indsl. Council, 1963; mem. adv. council Ark. Employment Security Div., 1962—. Mem. Ark. Constl. Conv., 1969-70. Mem. Beta Gamma Sigma. Presbyn. Clubs: Little Rock, Little Rock Country. Address: 15 Beverly Pl Little Rock AR 72207

CANTRELL, WILLIAM ALLEN, educator; b. Everton, Ark., Nov. 6, 1920; s. William E. and Vida (Vinson) C.; B.S., McMurry Coll., 1940; M.D., U. Tex., 1943; m. Joyce LaRee Hobbs, Jan. 17, 1945; children—Mary Elizabeth, William Robert. Rotating intern U.S. Naval Hosp., Corona, Cal., 1943-44; resident neuropsychiatry U. Tex. Med. Br. Hosps., 1947-49; asst. prof. neuropsychiatry U. Tex. Med. Br., 1949-54; practice medicine, specializing in psychiatry, Houston, 1951-63; prof. psychiatry Baylor Coll. Medicine, Houston, 1963—. Chief psychiatry service Meth. Hosp., Houston, 1966-73; mem. med. adv. com. Tex. Bd. Mental Health and Mental Retardation, 1965—, chmn., 1965-69, 72-73; bd. dirs. Tex. Assn. Mental Health, 1965-72. Served to lt. M.C., USNR, 1944-47. Fellow Am. Psychiat. Assn. (br. pres. 1958-59), Am. Coll. Psychiatrists; mem. A.M.A., Tex. Med. Assn., Tex. (v.p. 1958-59), Central neuropsychiat. assns., Houston Psychiat. Soc. (pres. 1956). Home: 5018 Loch Lomond St Houston TX 77035

CAPARROS, JENARO ALEXIS, lawyer; b. San Juan, P.R., May 5, 1943; s. Jenaro and Blanca Maria (Rivera) C.; B.A. magna cum laude, U. P.R., 1962, LL.B. magna cum laude, 1969; postgrad. Oxford (Eng.) U., 1964. Admitted to P.R. bar, 1969; mem. firm Trias & Francis, Hato Rey, P.R., 1969—. Mem. Forum for Contemporary History, 1970—. Mem. Am., P.R., Fed. bar assns. Club: Club Equestre de Puerto Rico. Home: 803 Condominium Torre Alta Hato Rey PR 00917 Office: Suite 1900 Popular Center Bldg Hato Rey PR 00918

CAPE, CHARLES ALBERT, physician, educator; b. Grand Forks, N.D., Apr. 27, 1933; s. Thomas Wilson and Julia (Porter) C.; B.S., U. N.D., 1955, B.A., 1956, B.S. in Medicine, 1957; M.D., Wake Forest Coll., 1959; m. Gloria Joyce Torgerson, Dec. 18, 1955; children—Cheryl Ann, Connie, Barbara Lee, Richard Charles, Catherine Joyce. Intern U. Ia., Iowa City, 1959-60, resident neurology, 1960-63, research neurologist, 1963-64, instr. dept. neurology, 1964-65; asst. prof. neurology U. Tenn., Memphis, 1965-69, asso. prof., 1969—; practice medicine specializing in neurology, Iowa City, 1963-65, Memphis, 1965—; mem. staffs City of Memphis, Baptist, Methodist hosps., Memphis. Mem. A.M.A., Am. Acad. Neurology. Contbr. articles to publs. Home: 724 Center Dr Memphis TN 38128 Office: Suite 101 B 20 S Dudley St Memphis TN 38103

CAPELOUTO, REUBEN, pest control co. exec.; b. Atlanta, Nov. 7, 1920; s. Gabriel and Sinoru (Galanti) C.; B.S. in Agr., U. Fla., 1947, M.S., 1949; m. Rachel Franco, May 28, 1953; children—Grant Alan, Raymond Aaron, Carl Creighton, Sue Linda. Mgr. Tallahassee (Fla.) office Orkin Exterminating Co., Inc., 1950-64; pres. Capelouto Termite & Pest Control, Inc., Tallahassee, 1964—. Adj. asso. prof. dept. entomology Fla. A. and M. U. Mem. Fla. Pest Control Commn., 1963-66. Bd. dirs. Tallahassee Municipal Hosp. Served with A.C., AUS, 1942-45. Republican. Jewish religion. Mem. B'nai B'rith; Mason (Shriner). Club: Capital City Country. Home: 1114 Lothian Dr Tallahassee FL 32303 Office: PO Box 3894 Tallahassee FL 32303

CAPERS, CHARLOTTE, state ofcl.; b. Columbia, Tenn.; d. Walter B. and Louise (Woldridge) Capers; student Millsaps Coll., 1930-32, U. Colo., 1932; B.A., U. Miss., 1934. With Miss. Dept. Archives and History, 1938—, successively sec., research and editorial assist., asst. dir., 1938-55, dir., 1955-69, dir. spl. projects, 1969-73, dir. edn. and information, 1973—; asst. editor Jour. Miss. History, 1942-43, asso. editor, 1943-55, editor-in-chief, 1956-69; columnist Jackson Daily News, 1944-55, State Times, 1955, Dixie Roto Mag., 1957; book revs. N.Y. Times Book Rev., various hist. jours. Bd. dirs. Miss. Arts Festival, Inc. Fellow Soc. Am Archivists; mem. Jr. League Jackson, Miss. State Hist. Soc. (pres.), Am. Assn. Museums. Episcopalian. Editor: (with William D. McCain) Papers of the Washington County Historical Society, 1954; Mississippi History Newsletter, 1974—; editorial dir. Mississippi in the Confederacy, 1961; mem. adv. editorial bd. Jefferson Davis Papers, Rice U.; publs. com. Mississippi as a Province, Territory and State (J.F.H. Claiborne), 1964; contbg. editor The Delta Review, 1966-70. Home: 4020 Berkley Dr Jackson MS 39211 Office: Box 571 Jackson MS 39205

CAPERTON, CHARLES LEE, lawyer; b. N.Y.C., Dec. 25, 1937; s. Albert Helvey and Loraine (Ellston) C.; B.B.A., So. Methodist U., 1961, J.D., 1964; m. Frances Ann McNatt, Dec. 23, 1963; children—Kelly Conder, Charles Lee II. Admitted to Tex. bar, 1964, U.S. Supreme Ct. bar, 1967; asst. dist. atty. Dallas County, 1964-68; partner Akin, Steinberg & Stanford, 1968-71; pvt. practice law, Dallas, 1971—. Mem. citizen's adv. com. Tex. Constl. Revision Commn., 1973—. Served with AUS, 1964. Mem. Tex. Criminal Def. Lawyers Assn. (charter), Am., Dallas (sec. treas. 1973, v.p., 1974), Tex. (state dir.) trial lawyers assns., Dallas (chmn. criminal law sect.), Am. bar assns., State Bar Tex. (speaker criminal law skills course 1973—), Kappa Alpha, Phi Alpha Delta, Alpha Kappa Psi. Democrat. Methodist (dir.). Mason (32 deg.), Lion. Club: Dallas Athletic. Home: 8133 Inwood Rd Dallas TX 75209 Office: Griffin Sq Bldg 900 Dallas TX 75202

CAPERTON, LUCIEN MARSHALL, bank exec.; b. Lawrenceburg, Tenn., Nov. 3, 1910; s. William Carrell and Sarah Leona (Dalton) C.; student Vanderbilt U., 1928-29; B.S. in Civil Engring., Va. Mil. Inst., 1929-33; m. Mary Elizabeth McMann, June 12, 1933; children—Beth (Mrs. Thomas Donald Rayfield), Jane (Mrs. Joe Gleaves), Melinda (Mrs. Donald Crews). Owner Caperton Ins. Agy., Lawrenceburg, 1933—, Caperton Chevrolet Co., Lawrenceburg, 1949-55; dir. Murray Ohio Mfg. Co., Nashville and Lawrenceburg, Tenn., 1958—; with 1st Nat. Bank, Lawrenceburg, 1954—, dir., 1954—, pres., 1954-69, chmn. bd., 1969—; v.p., dir. Bank Loretto (Tenn.), 1956—. Pres. Tenn. Fedn. Young Republicans, 1940-46. Served to maj. AUS, 1942-45. Mem. Lawrenceburg C. of C. (pres. 1952), Am. Legion (comdr. 1946-47), Phi Kappa Sigma. Republican. Mason (Shriner), Lion (pres. 1935). Home: 205 Caperton Av Lawrenceburg TN 38464 Office: 116 Pulaski St Lawrenceburg TN 38464

CAPO, BERNARDO GUILLERMO, agrl. cons.; b. Guayama, P.R., Dec. 28, 1908; s. Rafael E. and Dolores (Capo) C.; B.S., U.P.R., 1929; M.S., Cornell U., 1941, Ph.D., 1942; m. Juanita de Choudens, Jan. 4, 1930; children—Ada Teresa (Mrs. Jaime A. Colley), Carlota. Fertilizer chemist dept. agr., P.R., 1929-36; soil chemist agrl. expt. sta. U.P.R., 1936-42, acting head soils dept., 1942-43, biometrician, 1943-44, biometrician and head dept. agronomy and horticulture, 1944-48, asst. dir., 1948-50, asso. dir., 1951-64; project mgr. UN Spl. Fund agrl. research sta., Damascus, Syria, 1964-66; agrl. cons., P.R., 1966—; agrl. research cons. Land Authority P.R., 1967-73. Recipient Internat. award Gamma Sigma Delta, 1965. Mem. Coll. Chemists P.R., Internat. Soc. Sugarcane Technologists, Am. Statis. Assn., Inst. Math. Statistics, Soc. Agrl. Scis. P.R., Statis. Soc. P.R., Assn. Agrl. Cons. (pres. 1967-69). Contbr. articles profl. jours. Address: 1749 Santa Praxedes Rio Piedras PR 00926

CAPPS, CLIFTON ROWLAND, mfrs. rep.; b. nr. Middleburg, N.C., Dec. 17, 1893; s. Lewis Boyd and Mary Ida (Dowling) C.; student N.C. State U., 1942-43; m. Lida Jane Roberts, Nov. 12, 1930. Clk., bookkeeper Aberdeen Hardware Co. (N.C.), 1910-12; with Lee Hardware Co., Sanford, N.C., 1912-19; mgr. Capps Hardware Co., Sanford, 1919-26; with Shapleigh Hardware, St. Louis, 1927-28, Simmons Hardware Co., Atlanta, 1929-31; operator produce warehouse, Sanford, 1932-33; salesman, buyer Carolina Hardware, Raleigh, N.C., 1934-46; prin. Clifton R. Capps Co., mfrs. reps., Cary, N.C., 1946-70; dir. Council Tool Co., Wananish, N.C. Methodist (bd. stewards 1944-48). Mason. Address: 203 E Maynard Rd Cary NC 27511

CAPPS, GENE THOMAS, mus. ofcl.; b. Wilmington, N.C., Apr. 11, 1943; s. Lawrence Leonard and Anna Augusta (Turner) C.; A.B., U. N.C., 1965, M.A., 1967; m. Patricia Ann Ward, Apr. 2, 1972. Tchr., Charlotte-Mecklenburg Schs., Charlotte, N.C., 1965-71; dir. dept. edn. and interpretation Old Salem, Inc., Winston-Salem, N.C., 1971—. Mem. Winston-Salem Arts Council, 1973—; Southeastern Museums Conf., 1971—. Mem. Nat. Council for Social Studies, Am. Assn. for State and Local History, Am. Assn. Museums, N.C. Museums Council (dir.). Home: 440 S Main St Winston-Salem NC 27102 Office: Drawer F Salem Station Winston-Salem NC 27108

CAPPS, PAUL ROBERTS, lawyer; b. Nashville, Sept. 27, 1922; s. Paul and Sadie (Roberts) C.; LL.B., Cumberland U., 1948; m. Sarah Marie Ready, May 15, 1943; children—Diane (Mrs. H.N. Noe), Claudia (Mrs. Gordon Bonnyman), Paula (Mrs. Larry Duby), Chris. Admitted to Tenn. bar, 1947; since practiced at Morristown; partner Capps & Oakley; city atty. Morristown, 1960-62. Chmn. bd. Morristown Fed. Savs. & Loan Assn.; dir. Hamilton Bank, Morristown. Bd. dirs. Walters Found. Served with USAF, 1944-46, to 1st lt. AUS, 1950-51. Mem. Am., Hamblen County (past pres.), Tenn.

bar assns., Blue Key. Democrat. Methodist. Rotarian. Home: 848 Summit Ridge Dr Morristown TN 37814 Office: Hamilton Bank Bldg Morristown TN 37814

CAPPS, SHERRILL MAYNARD, accountant; b. Clayton, N.C., Feb. 8, 1941; s. Chester E. and Stella P. (Puckett) C.; B.S., U. N.C., 1963; m. Mary Ellis, Dec. 17, 1961; children—Mary Elizabeth, Kimberly Joyce. Staff accountant S.D. Leidesdorf & Co., Charlotte, N.C., 1963-69; controller Washburn Press, Inc., Charlotte, 1969—. Exec. dir. Miss N.C. Pageant, 1972-73, bus. mgr. Miss N.C., 1973-74. C.P.A., N.C. Mem. Am. Inst. C.P.A.'s, Nat. Assn. Accountants, N.C. Assn. C.P.A.'s, Charlotte Jr. C. of C. (chaplain 1966-67, internal v.p., 1969-70), Beta Gamma Sigma. Home: 6033 Sheppard Cove Charlotte NC 28211 Office: PO Box 10216 Charlotte NC 28201

CAPS, JAMES WILLIAM, civil engr.; b. Kansas City, Mo., Oct. 29, 1911; s. John C. and Florence Centennial (Fowler) C.; B.S. in Civil Engring., U. Kan., 1939; certificate in architecture U. London (Eng.) Sch. Arch., 1945; m. Grace Elizabeth Schroetter, May 29, 1941; children—Sharon Elizabeth, James William. Constrn. engr. C.E., 1941-55; with U.S. Air Force, 1955—, civil engr. constrn., design Arnold Air Force Sta., Tenn., 1964—. Served with AUS, 1942-46. Decorated Bronze Star. Registered profl. engr., Kan. Mem. Res. Officers Assn., Air Force Assn. (treas. Tullahoma br. 1973—), Nat., Tenn. socs. profl. engrs., Am. Soc. C.E. (pres. Colorado Springs br. 1953-55), Soc. Am. Mil. Engrs. (treas. Tullahoma post 1969-73), Am. Philatetic Soc., Am. Legion. Home: PO Box 509 107 Essex Ct Tullahoma TN 37388 Office: Arnold Air Force Sta TN 37389

CARABIA, ALEX GARCIA, physician; b. Guantanamo, Cuba, June 14, 1925; s. Alex Garcia and Rose (Carabia) Prieto; B.S., Inst. Secondary Edn., Santiago, Cuba, 1945; M.D., U. Havana, 1952; m. Bessie Florence Joines, Sept. 17, 1954; children—Mark Steven, Janet Leigh, Bruce Allen. Came to U.S., 1952, naturalized, 1958. Intern, St. Mary's Hosp., Huntington, W.Va., 1953-54, resident, 1954-58, asso. pathologist, 1958-61; dir. lab. Oak Ridge Hosp., 1961—; practice medicine specializing in pathology, Oak Ridge, Tenn., 1961—; med. examiner Anderson County, Tenn., 1967—; dist. pathologist Tenn. Med. Examiners System, 1971—; pathologist cons. Harriman, Rockwood, Athens Community hosps. Diplomate Am. Bd. Pathology. Fellow Am. Coll. Pathologists; mem. Am. Soc. Clin. Pathologists. Democrat. Baptist. Rotarian. Home: 1068 W Outer Dr Oak Ridge TN 37830 Office: 125 W Tennessee Av Oak Ridge TN 37830

CARAMEROS, GEORGE DEMITRIUS, JR., gas transmission co. exec.; b. El Paso, Mar. 1, 1924; s. George Demitrius and Esperanza (Purdy) C.; B.A., U. Tex. at El Paso, 1947; student U. Okla., 1944; m. Verna Narcissus Easterling, May 26, 1944; children—Cecille (Mrs. George Shannon), Cynthia (Mrs. John Blevins), Cathy, George Demitrius III, Carl. With El Paso Natural Gas Co., 1948—, mgr. new product devel. of subsidiary El Paso Products Co., 1957-60, mng. dir. El Paso Europe-Afrique, Paris, France, 1960-65, adminstrv. asst. to chmn. bd., N.Y.C., 1965-66, asst. v.p., 1966-70, v.p., 1970-73, exec. v.p., dir., El Paso, 1973—; dir. Tex. Commerce Med. Bank, Houston. Served to sgt., AUS, 1943-46. Decorated Bronze Star. Mem. Interstate Natural Gas Assn. Am. Methodist. Clubs: Houston, Lakeside Country, Houston Racquet (Houston). Home: 660 Shartle Circle Houston TX 77024 Office: 2727 Allen Pkwy Houston TX 77019

CARAS, THOMAS SAM, physician; b. Dayton, O., June 3, 1936; s. Sam L. and Helen (Macris) C.; B.A., U. Louisville, 1958, M.D., 1962; m. Carole A. Raque, July 31, 1960; children—David, Kathy, Margaret. Intern, Letterman Gen. Hosp., San Francisco, 1962-63; resident internal medicine Brooke Gen. Hosp., San Antonio, 1963-66; practice medicine, specializing in internal medicine, Marietta, Ga., 1969—; mem. staff Kennestone Hosp., Marietta. Mem. Met. Atlanta Council on Alcohol and Drugs. Served with AUS, 1968-69. Arthritis and Rheumatism Found. fellow, 1961. Diplomate Am. Bd. Internal Medicine. Mem. A.M.A., A.C.P., Ga. Heart Assn., Alpha Omega Alpha. Contbr. articles to profl. pubs. Home: 587 Heyward Circle Marietta GA 30060 Office: 641 Church St Marietta GA 30060

CARBAUGH, HARRY ALBERT, indsl. engr.; b. Tionesta, Pa., July 25, 1923; s. Curtis Custer and Eva May (Whitman) C.; student Gen. Electric Co. Night Sch., 1941-44, Pa. State Coll. Extension, 1951; m. Mary Helen Stanley, Dec. 12, 1948; children—Barbara (Mrs. Jimmy Downs), Lawrence, Ronald, Gary, David, Terry, Cindy. Apprentice tool maker Gen. Electric Co., Erie, Pa., 1941-44, tool maker, 1946-50, tool and process planner, foreman, quality control engr., advanced mfg. engr., Louisville, 1950-68, specialist methods and planning, supr., Greenville, S.C., 1968-73, quality control engr., 1973—. Mem. Pa. State Police, 1949-52. Served with AUS, 1944-46; ETO. Decorated Bronze Star medal with oak leaf cluster. Registered profl. engr., Ky. Republican. Lutheran (v.p. council). Mason, Elk. Home: 240 Greenbrier Dr Simpsonville SC 29681 Office: Box 648 Greenville SC 29602

CARDELLI, GIOVANNI GUIDO CARLO, architect, producer; b. London, Eng., Oct. 2, 1910; s. Count Giovanni and Ruth (Lamson) C.; M.A. Scis. Politiques, Lycee Jansen, Paris, France, 1928; m. Jacqueline Stewart, Nov. 22, 1931; children—Diane (Mrs. Lawrence O. Houghon), Giola (Mrs. Bourke Mason). Came to U.S., 1933. naturalized, 1941. Naval architect, designer, Chgo., N.Y.C., Southampton, N.Y., Westport, Conn., 1932-64; resident naval architect Rybovich & Sons Boat Works Inc., West Palm Beach, Fla., 1964-70; exec. v.p. John H. Witman Interiors, Palm Beach, 1970-72; dir. interior design Outcalt Environment, Stuart, Fla., 1972-73; pres. By Design, Inc., Jupiter, Fla., 1973—; asst. to pres. Chgo. Opera Co., 1938-40; gen. mgr. Opera Theater, Chgo., 1940-49; producer Rape of Lucretia, Chgo., N.Y.C., 1948-49; gen. mgrs. Dallas Symphony, 1949-52. Clubs: River, New York Yacht (N.Y.C.); Seawanhaka Yacht (Center Island, N.Y.), Arts Club (Chgo.); Westhampton Yacht, Delray Beach Yacht; Coral Harbor Yacht (Nassau); Sag Harbor Yacht (Long Island). Translator operas, 1939-54. Home: 166 Beacon Lane Jupiter FL 33458 Office: 1620 US Hwy No. 1 Jupiter FL 33458

CARDEN, WILLIAM RAYMOND, importer; b. Ft. Worth, Aug. 22, 1937; s. Willie Raymond and Minnie Catherine (Atkinson) C.; B.A., Baylor U., 1959, M.A., 1961; Ph.D. (Univ. fellow), Emory U., 1965; m. Merilyn Brown, Dec. 27, 1957; children—Michael Wayne, Amber Lynn. Asso. prof. history, dir. spl. projects Stetson U., Deland, Fla., 1965-67; contract research Bapt. Gen. Conv. of Tex., Dallas, 1967-68, mem. exec. com., 1971—; asso. prof. history, asst. to pres. for acad. affairs Baylor U., Waco, Tex., 1968-70; exec. v.p., Word, Inc., Waco, 1970-72, now cons.; pres., dir. Translinear, Inc., Dallas, 1972—; owner Intrada, 1973—; dir. Whittemore Assos., Boston. Cons. Dallas Bapt. Coll. Bd. dirs. Richardson Symphony Orch. Mem. Am. Mgmt. Assn., Ex-Students Assn. Baylor U. (dir., exec. com.). Democrat. Baptist. Club: Baylor Bear, Centre Tennis. Author: Financial and Curricular Efficiency of the Nine Baptist College and Universities in Texas, 1968. Mem. editorial bd. Faith at Work mag., 1970-72. Contbr. articles profl. jours. Home: 207 Shadywood Lane Richardson TX 75080 Office: First Nat Bank Bldg Dallas TX 75202

CARDENAS, EDUARDO, editor, publisher; b. Popayan, Colombia, S.Am., Aug. 10, 1901; s. Jeremias and Armida (Nannetti) C.; B.A., Universidad Naciornal, Bogota, Colombia, 1920; m. Esther Prentice, June 19, 1927; children—Esther (Mrs. Ramiro Hurtado), Teresa (Mrs. George F. Marshal, Jr.), Armida (Mrs. Ernesto Alcala), Marilu (Mrs. Gerald R. Donaty). Came to U.S., 1924, naturalized, 1952. Editor, pres. Editors Press Service, Inc., N.Y.C., 1933-40; editor Selecciones del Reader's Digest, N.Y.C., 1940-60; sr. editor internat. editions The Reader's Digest, 1945-60; pres. Editora Moderna, Inc., Enciclopedia Moderna, Inc., N.Y.C., 1960-71; mng. partner Eduardo Cardenas Assos., Ltd., Ft. Lauderdale, Fla., 1971—. Recipient Alberdi-Sarmiento prize La Prensa of Buenos Aires, 1955; Maria Moors Cabot prize Columbia U., 1958; Hammarskjoeld prize of journalism, 1969. Mem. Academia Colombiana de la Lengua, 1955. Author: Diccionario Moderno de la Lengua Espanola, 1950; Almanaque Mundial (Year Book of Facts), 1955—. Editor: Veintemil Biografias Breves, 1963; Gran Diccionario Enciclopedic. Ilustrado, 8 vols., 1971. Office: 4000 NE 29th Av Fort Lauderdale FL 33308

CARDER, KENDALL LYMAN, oceanographer, educator; b. Norfolk, Neb., Sept. 11, 1942; s. David Truman and Annabel (Ross) C.; B.S. (Arakelian Found. scholar), Fresno State Coll., 1964; M.S., Ore. State U., 1967, Ph.D., 1970; m. Sharon Franklin, June 20, 1971. Teaching asst. Ore. State U., 1964-65, research asst., 1965-69; asst. prof. Marine Sci. Inst., U. S.Fla., St. Petersburg, 1969—. Recipient research grants Fla. Power Corp., 1970—, NSF, 1970-71, Office Naval Research, 1972—. Mem. Optical Soc. Am., Am. Geophys. Union, Fla. Acad. Sci. Contbr. articles profl. jours. Office: 830 First St S St Petersburg FL 33701

CARDINAL, PAUL J(OSEPH), pharm. and mgmt. cons., writer; b. Paterson, N.J., Mar. 2, 1904; s. Alphonse A. and Mary M. (Froehlich) C.; student Stevens Prep. Sch., Hoboken; B.S. in Engring. and Bus. Adminstrn., Mass. Inst. Tech., 1924; m. Lorene F. Lapham, June 26, 1929; children—Lorene M. (Mrs. Walter Welsh), Joan R. (Mrs. Donald MacMurray), Paul Joseph, John, Richard, Anne (Mrs. Arthur O'Connell, Jr.), Carolyn (Mrs. C. Roy Walker, Jr.), Alan. Employed Hoffmann-LaRoche, Inc., Nutley, N.J., 1924-63, successively advt. asst., advt. mgr., office mgr., mgr. hosp. dept., co-dir. sales staff, mgr. bulk vitamin div., v.p. charge vitamin div., v.p. charge indsl. relations, 1958-63; cons. in relations Inst. Human Nutrition, Columbia, N.Y.C., 1963-71. Vice pres. Nat. Vitamin Found., 1958, treas., 1959-71; bd. dirs. N.Y. Bd. Trade, 1959-62; exec. com. Drug, Chem. and Allied Trades Assn., 1956-63, treas., 1961-62, v.p., 1962-63; vol. Internat. Exec. Service Corps. Recipient Coronat medal St. Edwards U., 1963. Mem. Naples Civic Assn., Pharm. Advt. Club (life), Phi Kappa Theta, Pi Delta Epsilon. Clubs: Mass. Inst. Tech. (Fla.). Home: 707 Port Side Dr Naples FL 33940

CARDONA, MARIA ELENA ARGUELLO (MRS. FRANCISCO J. CARDONA), librarian; b. Managua, Nicaragua, Jan. 18, 1925; d. Victorino and Rosa (Solorzano) Arguello; student Barnard Coll., 1945-46; B.A., magna cum laude, U. P.R., 1958; M.L.S., Pratt Inst., 1962; m. Francisco J. Cardona, Jan. 26, 1946; children—Francisco Victorino, Rosa Maria, Lidia Beatriz. Librarian, indsl. devel. lab. Indsl. Devel. Co., Hato Rey, P.R., 1955-57; with N.Y. Pub. Library, 1958-65, head Latin Am. bibliographic projects, 1962-64; Latin Am. cataloger U. Fla. at Gainesville, 1966-67; bibliographer, research asst. Inst. Caribbean Studies U. P.R., Rio Piedras, 1968-70; dir. Caribbean Regional Library, Hato Rey, 1970—. Cons. Latin Am. bibliography Bowker Co. N.Y.C., 1962-65; editor cataloging Fichero Bibliografico Hispanoamericano, 1962-64. Mem. A.L.A., Sociedad de Bibliotecarios de P.R., Assn. Caribbean U. and Research Libraries (exec. council, 1971-74, v.p., pres. elect), Seminars on Acquisition of Latin Am. Library Materials. Compiler, author index vols. 1-28 Handbook of Latin American Studies, 1968. Home: 2208 Park Blvd Santurce PR 00913 Office: 452 Ponce de Leon Av Hato Rey PR 00919

CARDONE, JOHN ELMO, investment co. exec.; b. Madisonville, La., Dec. 15, 1927; s. Joseph Salvador and Eunice Elizabeth (Stein) C.; B.S., La. State U., 1948, postgrad., 1951-52; m. Mary Magdalene Niel, Apr. 23, 1950; children—Gwendolyn Ann, John Elmo, Jay Anthony, Mary Ann. Chemist, Mathieson Chem. Co., Lake Charles, La., 1948-49, process engr., 1950-60, plant supt., 1961-62; co-founder Cesco, Inc., indsl. service and proprietary chem. co., Maplewood, La., 1962, v.p., 1962-71, operational mgr., 1967-69, mgr. engring and product line devel., 1967-71, mgr. fgn. operations, 1969-71, also dir.; self employed Cardone Enterprises, 1971—; dir. Cosmopolitan Life Ins. Co., Intraco, Lake Charles. Mem. Am. Chem. Soc., Maintenance Engr. Inst., Am. Inst. Chem. Engrs., Nat. Assn. Corrosion Engrs. Democrat. Roman Catholic. K.C. (grand knight 1960), Lion, Rotarian. Home: 1236 Bayouwood Dr Lake Charles LA 70601 Office: 107 Weber Bldg Lake Charles LA 70601

CARDOZO, JOSEPH ANTHONY, educator; b. New Orleans, May 18, 1918; s. Joseph S. and Mildred (Lewis) C.; B.A., Xavier U., 1949; M.A., Columbia, 1952; Ed.D., Ind. U., 1971; m. Ruby E. Dubuclet, Nov. 22, 1947; 1 dau., Eugenia M. Mem. faculty dept. fine arts So. U., Baton Rouge, 1950—, asso. prof., 1960-70, prof., 1970—. Mem. adv. bd. La. chpt. Youth Art Council Am., 1972. Served with AUS, 1942-45; PTO. So. U. Alumni Fedn. grantee, 1967. Mem. Phi Delta Kappa, Phi Beta Sigma. Democrat. Roman Catholic. Home: 1066 Mayhaw Dr Baton Rouge LA 70807

CARDUS, DAVID, physician, educator; b. Barcelona, Spain, Aug. 6, 1922; s. Jaume and Ferranda (Pascual) C.; B.A., B.S., U. Montpellier, France, 1942; M.D. magna cum laude, U. Barcelona, 1949, diploma in Cardiology, 1956; m. Francesca Ribas, July 19, 1951; children—Hellena (Mrs. Victor Guerra), Silvia, Bettina, David. Came to U.S., 1957, naturalized, 1969. Intern, Hosp. Clinico, U. Barcelona, 1950-53; resident Sanatorio del Puig de Olena, Barcelona, 1950-53; French Govt. fellow dept. cardiology Hosp. Boucicaut and Hosp. de la Pittie, Paris, 1953-54; research asso. dept. physiology U. Barcelona Med. Sch., 1954-55; Brit. Council fellow Manchester Royal Infirmary, U. Manchester, 1957; research asso. Lovelace Found., Albuquerque, 1957-60; instr. depts. physiology and rehab. Baylor Coll. Medicine, Houston, 1960-61, asst. prof., 1961-65, asso. prof., 1965—, dir. Biomath. Program, 1966-69, mem. adv. com. computer scis. to chief exec. officer, 1966-68, mem. grad. exec. com., 1968-69, chmn. biomath. com. Sch. Grad. Studies, 1968-69, prof. dept. rehab., 1969—, dept. physiology, 1973—; research asso. Tex. Inst. Rehab. and Research, Houston, 1960—, head exercise lab., 1960—, mem. active med. staff, 1960—, pres. staff, 1967-68, dir. research, 1962-66, chmn. library com., 1968—, head cardio-pulmonary lab., 1969—, dir. div. biomath., 1970; mem. sci. adv. council Common Research Computer Facility, Tex. Med. Center, 1965-66; NIH trainee Summer Inst. Math. for Life Scientists, U. Mich., 1966; adj. prof. math. scis. Rice U., 1970—. Cons. USPHS div. health facilities Planning and Constrn. Service, 1967—, Math. Assn. Am., VA Hosp. Houston. Chmn. bd. dirs. Inst. Hispanic Culture, Houston; vice chmn. Gordon Conf. on Biomaths., 1970. Recipient 1st prize for exhibit Am. Urol. Assn., 1967, August Pi i Sunyer prize Institut d'Estudis Catalans, 1968, 1st prize for sci. exhibit 5th Internat. Congress Phys. Medicine, 1968, Gold medal 6th Internat. Congress, 1972. Mem. A.A.A.S., Am. Assn. U. Profs., Am. Coll. Cardiology, Am. Coll. Chest Physicians, Am. Coll. Sports Medicine, Am. Congress Rehab. Medicine (Gold award for sci. exhibit 45th ann. session 1967), A.M.A., Tex. Med. Assn., Harris County, 9th Dist. med. socs., Am. Physiol. Soc., Am. Statis. Assn., Biomed. Engring. Soc., Fedn. Am. Socs. Exptl. Biology, Houston Acad. Medicine, N.Y. Acad. Scis., Postgrad. Med. Assembly South Houston, Soc. Math. Biology, Tex. Heart Assn., Tex. Med. Center Research Soc., Societat Catalana Biologia, Sigma Xi. Contbr. articles to profl. jours. Home: 14314 Cindywood St Houston TX 77024 Office: 1333 Moursund Av Houston TX 77025

CARDWELL, HORACE MILTON, hosp. adminstr.; b. Oklahoma City, Feb. 3, 1919; s. Horace M. and Lona (Bridges) C.; B.S. in Econs., Tex. A. and M. Coll., 1941; m. 2d, Billie Jo Cardwell; children (by previous marriage)—Barbara Ann, Beverly Kay, Horace Milton III. Asst. adminstr. Herman Hosp., Houston, 1946-48; adminstr. Meml. Hosp., Lufkin, Tex., 1948—. Chmn. Hosp.-Ins.-Physicians Joint Adv. Com. Tex., 1954—; mem. Tex. Commn. Patient Care, 1957-61; pres. State Bd. Vocational Nurse Examiners, 1962-68; dir. Med. Information, 1968—; bd. dirs. Blue Cross Tex., 1962—. Chmn. Lufkin United Fund, 1961; med. adv. com. State Dept. Pub. Welfare, 1968-70. Served AUS, 1941-46; ETO, PTO. Fellow Am. Coll. Hosp. Adminstrs.; mem. Am. (ho. dels. 1956-68, mem. council govt. relations 1966—, mem. council on adminstrv. practice 1957-61, trustee 1968-71, chmn. bd. trustees 1974—), Tex. (pres. 1956-57, chmn. council govt. relations 1958—, chmn. bldg. com. 1965—, Earl M. Collier award 1970) hosp. assns., Tex. Assn. Hosp. Accountants (pres. 1953-54), C. of C. Rotarian (local pres. 1969-70). Address: PO Box 1447 Lufkin TX 75902

CARDWELL, MILTON ALONZO, dentist; b. Lytton Springs, Tex., Dec. 24, 1911; s. Lawson Alonzo and Ann Vesta (Palmer) C.; D.D.S., Baylor U., 1935; m. Eloise Robertson, May 30, 1934; children—Milton Alonzo, Richard Kent. Pvt. practice dentistry, Lockhart, Tex., 1935-59; staff dentist Mexia (Tex.) State Sch., 1959—. Served to lt. USNR, 1944-46. Mem. Tex. Assn. Instnl. Dentists (pres. 1966), Tex. Public Employees Assn. (chpt. pres. 1966-67), Baylor Ex-Students Assn. (bd. dirs. 1951-54), Am. Legion (post-comdr. 1947). Methodist (ofcl. bd. 1935-50, 62-70). Clubs: Rotary (pres. 1965). Home: 814 Holly Lane Mexia TX 76667 Office: Box 1132 Mexia TX 76667

CARESS, EDWARD ALAN, educator; b. Columbus, Neb., Feb. 6, 1936; s. Arthur Edward and Helen Bernice (Williams) C.; A.B., Dartmouth, 1958; Ph.D., U. Rochester, 1963; m. Virginia Bayard Fonda, June 24, 1961; children—James Bayard, Rebecca Whiteley, Peter Newkirk. Research asso. Mass. Inst. Tech., 1963-65; asst. prof. chemistry George Washington U., 1965-70, asso. prof., 1970—, asst. dean Grad. Sch. Arts and Scis., 1971—. Mem. Am. Chem. Soc., The Chem. Soc. (London), Am. Assn. U. Profs., Sigma Xi. Contbr. articles profl. jours. Home: 3906 Cherrywood Lane Annandale VA 22003 Office: George Washington University Washington DC 20006

CAREY, ROLAND FRANKLIN, univ. computer center dir.; b. Lexington, Miss., Mar. 23, 1936; s. Samuel Gwin and Lillian Doris (Wadlington) C.; B.S., Tenn. A. and I. State U., 1956; M.S., U. Southwestern La., 1973; m. Alleen King, Aug. 26, 1961; children—Gina Rolanda, Ramon Gwinn, Greta Lynn, Randal Allan. Accountant, So. U., Baton Rouge, 1960-61, charge IBM sect., 1961-63, supr. data processing, 1963-68, asst. dir. computer center, 1968-73, dir., 1973—. Instr. computing and data processing; cons. devel. comml. data processing system applications and mgmt., tng. and devel. Active Boy Scouts Am. Served with USAF, 1956-59. Mem. Assn. Computing Machinery, Assn. Systems Mgmt., Coll. U. Machine Records Conf., Am. Mgmt. Assn., Alpha Phi Alpha. Baptist. Mason. Club: Conquistadors Social and Civic (Baton Rouge). Research on feasibility of computers in low-income coops. in South. Home: 1225 Bayberry Av Baton Rouge LA 70807

CARGILL, ROBERT LEE, JR., educator; b. Marshall, Tex., Sept. 11, 1934; s. Robert Lee and Pauline Elizabeth (Wood) C.; B.A., Rice U., 1955; Ph.D., Mass. Inst. Tech., 1960; postdoctoral fellow, U. Cal., 1960-62; m. Linda Ann Sanders, Aug. 29, 1965; children—William Robert, Thomas Oscar, Ann Hope. Asst. prof. chemistry U. S.C., 1962-67, asso. prof., 1967-73, prof., 1973—; cons. Columbia Organic Chems., Inc. Research grantee NSF, NIH, Petroleum Research Fund, Research Corp. Mem. Am. Chem. Soc., Chem. Soc. London, Sigma Xi. Research on photchemistry and organic synthesis. Home: 2408 Wilmot Av Columbia SC 29205

CARLAN, CHARLES HAMPTON, civil engr.; b. DeFuniak Springs, Fla., July 21, 1937; s. Loy and Eleanor (Flow) C.; B.C.E., Auburn (Ala.) U., 1960; m. Sandra Edwards, Apr. 12, 1958; children—David Loy, Larry Edward. Profl. baseball player Milw. Braves, 1959-60; trainee, project engr., maintenance engr. Fla. State Rd. Dept., 1960-65; supt. City of Pensacola, Fla., 1965-68, city engr., 1969-71; staff dir. transp. com. Fla. Senate, Tallahassee, 1971-72; dir. profl. devel. Barrett, Daffin & Figg, Engrs., Architects & Planners, 1972-73, v.p. Pensacola div., 1973—; pres. Carlan Constrn. Co., Inc. Chmn. employees exec. com. City of Pensacola, 1968-70. Mem. Fla. Engring. Soc. (past sec. N.W. Fla. chpt.), Pensacola Jr. C. of C. (dir.). Methodist. Lion. Home: 4650 Francisco Rd Pensacola FL 32504 Office: 880 N Reus St Pensacola FL 32573

CARLISLE, CHARLES HENRY, coll. adminstr.; b. Newberry, S.C., Sept. 15, 1924; s. Hubert Toland and Ora (Askins) C.; B.S., Newberry Coll., 1944, LL.D., 1972; M.A., U. S.C., 1947; postgrad. U. Omaha, 1959; m. Jean Kennedy Todd, June 1, 1950; children—Lucille Askins, Charles Todd, Catherine Kennedy. Prin. Williston-Elko High Sch., Williston, S.C., 1944-46; asst. prof. history Erskine Coll., Due West, S.C., 1947-54, bus. mgr., 1954-66, v.p. for bus. and finance, 1966—. Mem. Abbeville County Devel. Bd. Trustee, sec. bd. trustees Erskine Coll. Mem. S.C. Hist. Assn. (sec.-treas. 1949-54), So. Assn. Coll. and Univ. Bus. Officers. Presbyn. (elder, moderator 1972-73). Rotarian (pres. 1972). Home: Box 185 Due West SC 29639

CARLISLE, EDWARD JAMES, investment co. exec.; b. Madisonville, Ky., Feb. 13, 1912; s. Forest Elmo and Dollie Mae (Tomblinson) C.; student Dale Carnegie Sch., 1958; m. Lottie Mae Williams, Aug. 1, 1936; children—C. Ed, James F., Thomas L., Terry W. Owner, operator Edward J. Carlisle, Contractor, Madisonville, 1944-64, Carlisle Distributing Co. Inc., Madisonville, 1959—; exec. v.p., treas., dir. Am. Pyramid Cos., Inc., Louisville, 1966—; exec. v.p., dir., mem. exec. com. Independence Nat. Corp., Delaware, O., Am. Consol. Corp., Consol. Nat. Corp., Western Pioneer Life Ins. Co., Am. Holding Corp. (all Louisville). Mem. Civil Air Patrol, 1957-65, Air Bd., 1958-64, Game and Fish Conservation, 1951—. Mem. Perry Park Property Owner's Assn., Ky. C. of C. Baptist (deacon; finance com. 1972—), Mason (Shriner, K.T.). Clubs: Princeton (Ky.) Golf and Country; Glenwood Hall (Perry Park, Ky.). Home: 102 Chipping Way-5 Louisville KY 40222 Office: Am Pyramid Cos Inc 4211 Norbourne Blvd Louisville KY 40207

CARLO, ALPHONSE PHILIP, educator, violinist; b. New Haven, Aug. 14, 1913; s. Lawrence and Jennie (Petocchi) C.; student Yale Music Sch., 1927-29, Juilliard Music Sch., 1930-35, Nat. Orchestral Assn., 1936-40; m. Katherine Braun, Aug. 3, 1942. Mem. faculty So. Meth. U., 1942-44; mem. faculty Rollins Coll., Winter Park, Fla., 1944—, prof. violin, 1944—. Concertmaster Fla. Symphony Orch.,

1949—, Bach Festival of Winter Park (Fla.), 1944—; asso. condr. Fla. Youth Symphony, 1955—; mem. World Symphony Orch., 1971—; adjudicator Fla. State Music Tchrs. Convs., 1960—. Recipient William Freeman Blackman Medal of Honor for distinguished service Rollins Coll., 1972. Mem. Pi Kappa Lambda. Home: 2001 Dundee Dr Winter Park FL 32789

CARLOSS, HARRY WORTHINGTON, state cons.; b. Gracey, Christian County, Ky., Apr. 11, 1908; s. Harry Dabney and Anna Pearl (Tuggle) C.; B.S. in Mech. Engring., U. Ky., 1931; m. Rebecca Long, Dec. 21, 1935; children—Rebecca Anne (Mrs. Thomas Page), James D., Harry Worthington. With Ky. Utilities Co., Lexington, 1931—, comml. service adviser, 1935-40, indsl. engr., 1940-48, mgr. indsl. engring. and service, 1948-50, asst. dir. customer service, 1955-53, dir. customer service, 1953-56. dir. bus. devel., 1959-66, asst. v.p., 1966-67, v.p., 1967-73; cons. Ky. Dept. Commerce, 1973—. Pres., Ky. Council for Comml. and Area Devel., 1964-65; mem. Indsl. Devel. Com., 1949—; dir. Asso. Industries Ky., 1968—. Mem. Ky. Hist. Events Com., 1970—. Bd. dirs. Florence Crittendon Home, Lexington; pres. bd. Salvation Army. Registered profl. engr., Ky. Mem. Ky. Soc. Profl. Engrs., Edison Electric Inst. (chmn. area devel. com. 1961-62, mem. exec. com. marketing div.), U.S. (mem. constrn. and comml. devel. com. 1963-65, co-chmn. Ky. clean-up and beautification, 1965—), Ky. (regional v.p. 1963—), Lexington-Fayette County (dir. 1964-65) chambers commerce, Electric Heating Assn., Newcomen Soc. N. Am. Club: Optimist (pres. 1961-62) (Lexington). Home: 205 Albany Rd Lexington KY 40503 Office: Frankfort KY 40601

CARLOUGH, EDWARD F., labor union ofcl.; b. Bronx, N.Y., Aug. 31, 1903; ed. pub. schs.; m. Florence Sweeney. Journeyman sheet metal worker, N.Y.C., 1924-40; pres., bus. mgr. local 28, Sheet Metal Workers Internat. Assn., N.Y.C., 1940-51, gen. sec.-treas., Washington, 1951-59, gen. pres., 1959-70, gen. pres. emeritus, 1970—. Office: 1000 Connecticut Av NW Washington DC 20036

CARLSON, GORDON, state ofcl.; s.; Carl John and Laura Mathilda (Carlson) C.; student U. Tex., 1926-28; m. Mary Nell Fredrickson, Sept. 7, 1949; 1 son, John Gordon. Asst. dir. Tex. Motor Vehicle Div., Austin, 1926-53; owner, cons. Motor Vehicle Cons. Service, Austin, 1953-54; chief of staff services Tex. Water Devel. Bd.; owner, operator Carlson Trailer Village, Point Comfort, Tex., 1955-57, owner, 1957-63. Mem. City Council, Manor, Tex., 1965-67, 73—; mayor, Manor, Tex., 1967-71. Vice chmn. exec. com. Austin-Travis County Regional Planning Commn., 1967-70. Democrat. Baptist. Lion. Home: PO Drawer J Manor TX 78653 Office: PO Box 13087 Capitol Station Austin TX 78711

CARLSON, HOWARD LINN, dentist; b. Barnesville, Minn., July 15, 1919; s. Albert Amandus and Lillie Alfreda (Linn) C.; student Ia. State Coll., 1937-41; D.D.S., U. Minn., 1950; m. Sonia Etoile Carloss, Mar. 25, 1945; children—Paul Howard, Candace Linn. Pvt. practice dentistry, Red Wing, Minn., 1953-54, Spartanburg, S.C., 1954—. Bd. dirs., chmn. bd. Spartanburg Speech and Hearing Clinic, 1966-68; bd. dirs., chmn. bd. Charles Lea Rehab. Center. Served with F.A., AUS, 1941-46, Dental Corps, 1950-53. Mem. Am. (5th dist. del. 1971-72), S.C. (pres. 1971-72) dental assns., Am. Soc. Preventive Dentistry, S.E. Acad. Prosthodontics (pres. 1974), S.C. Acad. Practice Adminstrn., Piedmont Dist. Dental Soc. (pres. 1963-64). Rotarian. Home: 2094 E Main St Spartanburg SC 29302 Office: 2086 E Main St Spartanburg SC 29302

CARLSON, J(OHN) PHILIP, lawyer; b. Shickley, Neb., Apr. 16, 1915; s. Christopher Theodore and Klara (Blomquist) C.; student Luther Coll., Wahoo, Neb., 1931-33; A.B., Neb. State Tchrs. Coll. 1935; M.A., Columbia, 1967; J.D., Georgetown U., 1951; m. Maryjo Suverkrup, Oct. 14, 1950. Tchr., coach high sch., Bristow, Neb., Carroll, Neb., Ashland, Neb., 1935-42; vets. relations adviser OPA, Washington, 1946-47; tng. specialist Dept. Navy, Washington, 1947-56; minority counsel Com. on Govt. Operations, Ho. of Reps., Washington, 1956—; admitted to D.C. bar, 1952, U.S. Supreme Ct. bar, 1957, U.S. Ct. Mil. Appeals bar, 1970; Am. Polit. Sci. Assn. congl. staff fellow Columbia, 1964-65, 66-67. Served from aviation cadet to capt. USAAF, 1942-45; lt. col. USAF Res. ret. Decorated D.F.C., Air Medal with oak leaf cluster. Mem. Am. Econ. Assn., Am., Fed. bar assns., Am. Judicature Soc. Republican. Lutheran. Clubs: Nat. Lawyers, Capitol Hill, National Economists, George Town (Washington). Home: 2206 Belle Haven Rd Alexandria VA 22307 Office: House of Reps Washington DC 20515

CARLSON, JOHN SWINK, lawyer, petroleum co. exec.; b. Ft. Collins, Colo., June 16, 1911; s. George A. and Rosa (Alps) C.; A.B., U. Colo., 1932; LL.B., Harvard, 1936; m. Sara A. Mott, June 22, 1940 (div. 1973); children—John Swink, Lucie Pamela, Ann Brockenbrough, Virginia Charles, Thomas George (dec.); m. 2d Barbara Carlson, 1973. Admitted to Okla. bar, 1937; mem. legal staff Shell Oil Co., 1936-37, Turman Oil Co., 1937-38; legal asso. Yancey & Spillers, Tulsa, 1938-39; legal counselor Chapman, Barnard & McFarlin, oil, cattle and investments, Tulsa, 1939-42; gen. counsel Seismograph Service Corp., Tulsa, 1942-49; practice law, Tulsa, 1949-51; gen. counsel Okla. Natural Gas Co., 1951-61; sr. partner Carlson, Lupardus, Matthews, Holliman & Huffman, Tulsa, 1951-61; head legal firm John S. Carlson, Tulsa, 1961—. Sec., gen. counsel, dir. Century Geophys. Corp., 1951-71, sr. v.p., 1957-71; sec., dir., gen. counsel Hayward-Wolff Research Corp., 1951; v.p., sec., dir., gen. counsel Exploration Cons., Inc., 1951, Canadian Geophys. Measurements, Ltd., 1954, Venezuela Geophys. Measurements, S.A., 1957, 66; pres., dir., gen. counsel Petroleum Research Corp., 1957-66; chmn. bd., gen. counsel Community Merchandisers, Inc., 1959; pres., dir., gen. counsel Western Petroleum Co., Inc., 1960; v.p., sec., dir., gen. counsel Enterprises & Businesses, Inc., 1960-65; sec., dir. Western Hemisphere Trade & Credit Corp., 1960, v.p., 1961; sec., dir. Hemisphere Constrn. Co., 1960, v.p., 1961; v.p., sec., dir., gen. counsel Jameson Corp., 1961, Digital Resources Corp., 1972—; pres., chmn. bd. T'Oil, Inc., 1962-65; pres., dir. Oil Enterprises Inc., 1965—; dir. gen. counsel Applied Devices Corp., 1973—. Mem. Am., Okla., Okla. Jr. (pres. 1943-44), Tulsa County bar assns., Am. Soc. Internat. Law, Phi Beta Kappa, Delta Sigma Rho. Clubs: Tulsa, Harvard (pres. 1949-50) (Tulsa). Editor: Compendium of Laws Relating to Problems of Men in the Armed Forces, 1943. Contbr. sect. to report on 34th Nat. Fgn. Trade Council. Office: 15 W 6th St Tulsa OK 74119

CARLSON, MAURICE IRWIN, educator, editor; b. Fulton, Ky., July 26, 1914; s. Peter Arvid and Della Elizabeth (Irwin) C.; B.A. with honors, Southwestern Coll., Memphis, 1936; M.A., Vanderbilt U., 1937; postgrad., Brown U., La. State U., 1938-39; m. Martha Elizabeth Deniger, Jan. 13, 1939; children—Martha Ann, Martha Elizabeth (Mrs. Michael Wayne Crain). Agt., br. mgr. Acacia Mut. Life Ins. Co., Memphis, New Orleans, field supr., Washington, 1941-47; mgr. N.Tex. dept. Reliance Life Ins. Co. Pitts., Dallas, then supt. agys., Pitts., 1947-51; v.p. Universal Life and Accident Ins. Co., Dallas, 1951-59; with Life Ins. Co. N.Am., Tex., 1959; pres., dir. Reliance Life and Accident Ins. Co. Am., Dallas, 1959-65; mem. English and Greek faculties U. Tex., Arlington, 1966—, editor Arlington Quar., 1967—. Guest lectr. So. Meth. U., U. Tex., Arlington; a founder weekly newspaper Hudkins Jour. (now Dallas County Jour.), 1962. Gen. chmn. Dallas County Cancer Crusade, 1954, Dallas County chpt. Nat. Kidney Disease Found., 1960; organizer Greater Dallas Citizens Com. for Old-Time Celebration Am. Ind. Day, 1961, chmn. adv. bd., 1961-67; chmn. adv. bd. Operation LIFT, 1962-65; pres. Dads' Club So. Meth. U., 1963-64. Chmn., Dallas County Republican Exec. Com., 1958-60; co-founder Dallas Charter League, 1961, exec. com., 1961-65, pres., 1965. Bd. dirs. Dallas Council on World Affairs, Dallas UN Assn. U.S. C.L.U. Mem. Dallas Forum, Tex. Bur. Econ. Understanding (pres. 1971). Author: Aubrey Beardsley: A Study in Decadence, 1937; book reviewer Dallas Times-Herald, 1950—. Home: 3520 Centenary Dr Dallas TX 75225 Office: Box 366 Univ Station U Tex at Arlington Arlington TX 76010

CARLSON, MERLE THOMAS, phys. therapy co. exec.; b. Lodgepole, Neb., Nov. 28, 1932; s. Merle Dixon and Helen (Rubado) C.; B.B.A., U. Neb., 1957; M.A., George Washington U., 1963; M.A., Am. U., 1963; Cert. Phys. Therapy, Hermann Hosp. Sch. Plys. Therapy, 1964; m. Jacqueline Elizabeth Viau, Sept. 2, 1961; children—Thomas David, John Joseph, Deborah Anne, Nancy Catherine. Tchr. Lisco (Neb.) Pub. Schs., 1951-52; computer systems analyst Statis. div. Internal Revenue Service, Washington, 1957-58; internat. economist Office of Econ. Analysis Bur. Fgn. Commerce, Washington, 1958-62; partner pvt. phys. therapy practice, Houston, 1963-64; exec. v.p. Phys. Therapy Assos. Inc., Houston, 1964-69, pres., Wharton Tex., 1969—; chmn. bd. dirs., pres. Tocar Inc., Wharton, 1967—. Scoutmaster, Boy Scouts Am., 1968-71. Served with AUS, 1953-55. Mem. U.S. Jaycees, Am. Phys. Therapy Assn., Am. Registry of Phys. Therapists, Am. Econ. Assn., Am. Mgmt. Assn., Omicron Delta Epsilon. Republican. Roman Catholic. Lion, K.C. Patentee Swim-Trainer, 1967. Home: 1210 Oriole Lane Wharton TX 77488 Office: 1210 Oriole Lane Wharton TX 77488

CARLSON, ROBERT KENNETH, mfg. exec.; b. Chgo., July 7, 1928; s. Axel Frederick and Ester (Johnson) C.; Ph.B., Northwestern U., 1955; m. Marjorie Gwyne Norman, Dec. 3, 1954; children—Kevin Patrick, Kimberley Georgianne. Chemist, Great Lakes Carbon Research Center, Morton Grove, Ill., 1949-57; research chemist, project leader Borg Warner Research Center, Des Plaines, Ill., 1957-59; sr. materials engr., head materials scis. LTV Research Center, Dallas, 1959-64; v.p. Poco Graphite, Inc., Decatur, Tex., 1964—, also dir. Served with AUS, 1950-52. Fellow Am. Inst. Chemists; mem. Am. Chem. Soc., Research Soc. Am., Sigma Xi. Patentee in field. Home: Route 3 Box 32AA Decatur TX 76234 Office: PO Box 2121 Decatur TX 76234

CARLSON, WILLARD EMMETT, paper co. exec.; b. Ft. Dodge, Ia., May 11, 1923; s. Willard A. and Dorinda (Kehl) C.; B.S. in Chem. Engring., Ia. State U., 1947; M.S., Lawrence Coll., 1949; m. Evelyn DeCoster, June 17, 1950; children—Mary P., Ann D., Jane E., Joseph W. Tech. dir. Whiting-Plover Paper Co., Stevens Point, Wis., 1952-57; mgr. research St. Regis Paper Co., Carthage, N.Y., 1957-61, mgr. devel., West Nyack, N.Y., 1961-65, tech. dir. Kraft div., Jacksonville, Fla., 1965—. Pres., Jacksonville Port Com. for Spillage Control, Inc., 1970-71. Served with Signal Corps, AUS, 1943-46. Registered profl. engr., Fla. Mem. T.A.P.P.I. (chmn. S.E. 1970-72), Alpha Chi Sigma, Tau Beta Pi. Patentee in field. Home: 2751 E Holly Point Rd Orange Park FL 32073 Office: Gulf Life Tower Jacksonville FL 32207

CARLTON, ALWIN HORATIO, mech. engr.; b. Birmingham, Ala., Feb. 24, 1933; s. Basil Brown and Nannie Hope (Lee) C.; B.S., Auburn U., 1960; postgrad. U. Tenn., 1965-67; m. Dorothy Emma Bowles, Sept. 16, 1952; children—Patricia Ann, Linda Jane, James Alwin, Robert Duane. Mech. engr. Holston Def. Corp., Kingsport, Tenn., 1960-72, chief engr., 1972—. Mem. Eastman Adult Evening Sch. Adv. Com., 1972—, Mountain Empire Community Coll. Adv. Com. for Technologists. Registered profl. engr., Tenn. Mem. Am. Soc. M.E. (exec. com. Holston sect. 1971-72). Elk. Clubs: Bays Mountain Flying, Auburn. Home: 1417 Crescent Dr Kingsport TN 37664 Office: Holston Def Corp Kingsport TN 37660

CARLTON, CHARLES THADDEUS, judge; b. Ft. Pierce, Fla., Nov. 7, 1935; s. Thaddeus Hudson Carlton and June (Pinson) Carlton Vest; B.A., U. Fla., 1957; J.D., Stetson U., 1963; m. Ida May Peacock, Oct. 7, 1967; children—Charles Thaddeus II, Kelley, Marshall Hudson. Admitted to Fla. bar, 1963; asso. Carlton & McCain, Ft. Pierce, 1963-65; partner Carlton, McCain, Carlton & Brennan, Ft. Pierce, 1965-67; partner Carlton, Brennan & McAllen, Ft. Pierce, Fla., 1967-70; asst. city atty., Ft. Pierce, 1965-69; state atty. 19th Jud. Circuit, 1967-70; circuit judge 20th Jud. Circuit, Moore Haven, Fla., 1970—, dep. chief judge, 1971. Owner, operator citrus groves, cattle ranches, St. Lucie, Glades, Hendry counties, Fla.; pres. Legal Services, Inc., Ft. Pierce, 1966-67. First v.p. United Fund, 1966-67. Served to 1st. lt. USMCR, 1957-60. Mem. U. Fla. Alumni Assn. (pres. 1964), Stetsen Lawyers Assn., U.S. Dist. Atty.'s Assn., Fla. Pros. Atty.'s Assn., Fla. Circuit Judges Conf., U.S. Trial Judges Assn., Am., Fla. bar assns., Fla. Acad. Trial Lawyers, Am. Trial Lawyers Assn., Airplane Owners and Pilots Assn., Cattlemen's Assn. Elk. Club: Pelican Yacht (Ft. Pierce). Home: PO Box 235 Carlton Ranch Moore Haven FL 33471 Office: Circuit Judges Office Glades County Ct House Moore Haven FL 33471

CARLTON, DEAN, lawyer; b. Ft. Worth, Nov. 4, 1928; s. Robert Ardine and Marjorie (Box) C.; B.S., Tex. A. and M. Coll., 1949; LL.B., So. Meth. U., 1952; m. Mary Ellen Williams, Sept. 9, 1949; children—R. Mark, Scott Duane, Mary Ann. Admitted to Tex. bar, 1952, U.S. Supreme Ct., 1968; practiced in Dallas, 1952—; mem. firm Herbert Marshall, 1952-54, Marshall & Carlton, 1954-57, Speck, Johnson & Carlton, 1957-59, Turner, White, Atwood & McLane, 1959-67, Meer, Chandler & Carlton, 1967-70; atty. Dean Carlton, Inc., 1970—. Mem. City of Richardson Bd. Adjustment, 1966-67, Tex. Water Code Adv. Com., 1968-70. Co-founder, chmn. Dallas Martini Found. and Trust. Mem. Am., Tex., Dallas, Richardson (pres. 1967), Lawyers-Pilots bar assns., Aircraft Owners and Pilots Assn. Clubs: Aggie, Lancers, Kings. Home: 7038 Spring Valley Rd Dallas TX 75240 Office: 1055 One Main Pl Dallas TX 75250

CARLTON, EMORY LINWOOD, lawyer, state ofcl.; b. nr. Tappahannock, Va., July 15, 1906; s. Ellis Mortimer and Ruby Evans (Lumpkin) C.; B.B.A., U. Richmond, 1929, J.D., 1933; m. Nan Page Trent June 28, 1941; 1 dau., Betty Page (Mrs. Henry John Schroeder, Jr.). Admitted to Va. bar, 1933; practice law Tappahannock, 1933—; state's atty. bar Essex County, Va., 1936-42, 45-64; dir. Bank Essex, Tappahannock, 1954—. Served to lt. comdr. USN, 1942-45. Mem. Va. Bar Assn., Commonwealth Attys. Assn. (v.p. 1963), Nat. Dist. Attys. Assn. (v.p. 1962-63), Soc. Cincinnati, Jamestowne Soc. (gov. 1971-73), Kappa Sigma. Democrat. Baptist (former chmn. bd. deacons). Mason. Home: Box 605 Tappahannock VA 22560 Office: E 407 Prince St Tappahannock VA 22560

CARLTON, JACK KENNETH, ednl. adminstr.; b. Baileyville, Tex., Oct. 6, 1921; s. James M. and Gladys Eleanor (Askew) C.; B.S., Centenary Coll., 1942; M.S., La. State U., 1949, Ph.D., 1951; m. Mary Ellen Petree, June 1, 1948; children—Claudia, Anne (Mrs. Thomas J. Bryan), James, Jack Kenenth II. Research fellow La. State U., Baton Rouge, 1951-52; asst. prof. chemistry U. Ark. at Fayetteville, 1952-55; asso. prof. chemistry Ga. Inst. Tech., Atlanta, 1955-58; dean La. State U. Coll. Sci., 1958-66; dean U. West Fla. Coll. Arts and Scis., 1966-67; pres. Macon (Ga.) Jr. Coll., 1967-72; chancellor Western Carolina U., Cullowhee, N.C., 1972-73; asst. to pres. U. N.C. at Chapel Hill, 1973—. Dir. Wachovia Bank, Asheville, N.C. Sci. bldg. cons., 1958-68; cons. analytical chemistry, 1957-58. Vice pres. Middle Ga. Area Planning Commn., 1970-72; chmn. Macon Bi-Racial Com., 1970-72. Served to lt. (j.g.) USNR, 1943-46. Research grantee Research Corp., 1955-56, NIH, 1956-61, Petroleum Research Fund, 1961-62. Mem Am. Assn. for Higher Edn., Sigma Xi. Presbyn. (elder). Home: 1815 N Lakeshore Dr Chapel Hill NC 27514

CARLTON, LESSIE, educator; b. Etoile, Tex., Aug. 4, 1903; d. David H. and Mollie (Mayes) Carlton; B.S., North Tex. State U., 1932, M.S. 1939; Ed.D., U. Houston, 1963. Tchr., prin. various schs. Tex., 1921-55; mem. faculty Stephen F. Austin State Coll., Nacogdoches, 1947-55; prof. edn. Ill. State U., Normal, 1955-73, prof. emerita, 1972—; dir. Reading-Study Center, 1955-72; dir. Reading Study Center Cumberland Coll., Williamsburg, Ky., 1972—. Del., lectr. numerous seminars, confs. Mem. N.E.A., Internat. Reading Assn., Internat. Platform Assn., Delta Kappa Gamma, Kappa Delta Pi. Author: (with R.H. Moore) Reading, Self-Directive Dramatization, 1968. Contbr. numerous articles to profl. jours. Address: Melrose Acres Route 1 Sand Flat Rd Alto TX 75925

CARLTON, RICHARD JAMES, petroleum refining co. exec.; b. Mansfield, O., Apr. 3, 1924; s. Clinton Arbie and Carrie Pauline (Beach) C.; student North Tex. Agrl. Coll., 1946-47; B.S. in Chem. Engring., Tex. A. and M. U., 1949; m. Patricia Jones, Sept. 17, 1944; children—Caren (Mrs. Loyd M. Burns), Richard James. Asst. refinery foreman Shamrock Oil & Gas Corp., Sunray, Tex., 1949-53; project exec. Stearns-Roger Corp., Denver, 1953-64; mgr. Denver region Oil Shale Corp., 1964-68; mgr. processing U.P. R.R. Co., Los Angeles, 1968-70; refinery mgr. Champlin Petroleum Co. subsidiary U.P. R.R., Corpus Christi, 1970—. Dir. Corpus Christi Bd. of Trade, 1972—. Republican precinct committeeman, 1961-64, area chmn., 1964-68. Served to capt. AUS. Decorated Bronze Star medal, Purple Heart. Registered profl. engr., Colo. Mem. Am. Petroleum Inst., Ind. Petroleum Assn. Am., Nat. Petroleum Refiners Assn., Western Natural Gas and Oil Refiners Assn., Corpus Christi C. of C. Clubs: Corpus Christi Country, Corpus Christi Town, Corpus Christi Petroleum. Home: 6122 Pebble Beach Dr Corpus Christi TX 78413 Office: PO Box 9176 Corpus Christi TX 78408

CARLTON, ROBERT AUSTIN, educator; b. Brownsville, Tenn., Apr. 30, 1927; s. Albert M. and Lidie (Mann) C.; B.S., Lambuth Coll., 1950; M.A., Peabody Coll., 1951; Ph.D., Auburn U., 1958; m. Dorothy Jeane Lyles, Aug. 20, 1950; children—Robert Austin, David, Martha. Instr. N.E. Jr. Coll., Booneville, Miss., 1951-54; asso. prof. Delta State Coll., Cleveland, Miss., 1956-63; prof. biology Lambuth Coll., 1964—. Served with USNR, 1945-46. Recipient Nat. Sci. Found. Summer Inst. grants. Mem. Am. Inst. Biol. Scis., Assn. Southeastern Biologists, Am. Mus. Natural History. Methodist. Mason. Home: 15 Ridgeview St Jackson TN 38301

CARLTON, THOMAS CLARENCE, oral surgeon; b. Birmingham, Ala., Feb. 7, 1938; s. George Shelton and Rose (Park) C.; student Duke, 1956-60; D.M.D., U. Ala., 1964; m. Lois Elizabeth Bloodgood, June 10, 1967; children—Thomas C., Kathryn Howell, Richard Andrew. Intern oral surgery Jackson Meml. Hosp., Miami, Fla., 1967-68, resident, 1968-69; resident Georgetown U., 1970; practice oral surgery, Fort Lauderdale, Fla., 1970—; mem. staff Broward Gen. Hosp., Fort Lauderdale, Plantation (Fla.) Hosp., Holy Cross Hosp., Fort Lauderdale, Beach Hosp., Fort Lauderdale, Imperial Point Hosp. Served to lt. USNR, 1964-67. Diplomate Am. Bd. Oral Surgery. Mem. Am., Borward County dental assns., Fla., Atlantic Coast Dist. dental socs., Am., Fla. socs. oral surgeons, Psi Omega, Pi Kappa Alpha. Home: 2115 NE 67th St Fort Lauderdale FL 33308 Office: 906 NE 26th Av Fort Lauderdale FL 33304

CARLTON, THOMAS MABRY, county ofcl., agrl. co. exec.; b. Wauchula, Fla., July 2, 1901; s. Thomas Newton and Ada (Altman) Carlton; LL.B., Stetson U., 1929; m. Septa Virginia Savell, June 12, 1931; children—Thomas Mabry, Ben Savell, Winston Cambron. Admitted to Fla. bar, 1929; practiced in Wauchula, 1929-36; county tax assessor Hardee County, 1937-50; pres. Mabry Carlton & Sons Citrus Groves, Inc., Wauchula, 1959—, Mabry Carlton & Sons Ranch, Inc., Wauchula, 1959—. Chmn. Hardee County Park Bd., 1962—. Recipient award for service to the industry Fla. Cattleman's Assn., 1970. Mem. Am. Bar Assn., Fla. Farm Bur., Fla. Citrus Mut., Fla. Cattleman's Assn. (hon. life dir. 1968—), Peace River Valley Hist. Soc. (pres. 1970—), S.A.R., Sigma Nu Phi, Pi Gamma Mu, Delta Sigma Phi. Baptist (chmn. bd. deacons 1958-64, 67-73). Address: 708 E Main St Wauchula FL 33873

CARLTON, VASSAR BENJAMIN, judge; b. Island Grove, Fla., Nov. 13, 1912; s. Benjamin F. and Zeffie (Ergle) C.; student U. Fla., 1931; LL.D, Stetson U., 1937; m. Grace Ramer, Sept. 23, 1959 (dec.); children—Mary Carol (Mrs. Buddy Crisafulli), Martha (Mrs. Bryan Fulmer), Barbara, Pamela; m. 2d, Sue E. Collins, Feb. 16, 1974. Admitted to Fla. bar, 1937; county judge Brevard County, Titusville, Fla., 1941-54, circuit judge 9th jud. circut ct., 1954-69; justice Supreme Ct., Tallahassee, 1969—. Mem. Jr. C. of C. (pres. 1939). Baptist. Mason (32 deg., Shriner). Elk, Kiwanian. Home: 1103 Gardenia Dr Tallahassee FL 32303 Office: Supreme Ct Bldg Tallahassee FL 32304

CARMACK, NATHAN DYKES, rehab. agy. dir.; b. Columbus, Ga., Aug. 21, 1940; s. Comer Aston and Mary Kate (Mills) C.; student Emory U., 1956-60; A.B., U. Ga., 1967, M.Ed., 1971; m. Beth Heys, Aug. 20, 1967; 1 son, Nathan Dykes. Circuit probation officer Ga. State Bd. Probation, 1964-68; exec. dir. Kelley Workshop, Inc., Athens, Ga., 1968—. Chmn., Clarke County Bd. Health, 1971—, Athens Citizens for Better Govt., 1972. Named Outstanding Young Man of Am., Athens Jr. C. of C., 1970. Mem. Ga. Assn. Workshops and Rehab. Facilities (pres. 1972-73), Assn. Med. Rehab. Dirs. and Coordinators (dir.), Community Personnel Assn. (pres. 1972-73), Athens Area Indsl. Mgmt. Assn. (v.p. 1972-73), Athens Area C. of C., U.S. Jr. C. of C. (nat. dir. 1970-71). Methodist (adminstv. bd.). Club: Athens Sertoma (charter v.p.). Home: 120 Woodcrest Dr Athens GA 30601 Office: PO Box 967 Athens GA 30601

CARMAN, GEORGE HENRY, physician, educator; b. Albany, N.Y., Sept. 23, 1928; s. Simon Peter and Mary (Whish) C.; B.A., Cornell U., 1948, M.D., 1951. Intern, Barnes Hosp., St. Louis, 1951-52, asst. resident, 1952-53; asst. resident medicine Salt Lake County Gen. Hosp., Salt Lake City, 1955-56; chief resident VA Hosp., Salt Lake City, 1956-57; fellow cardio-vascular diseases U. Utah Coll. Medicine, 1957-60; pvt. practice Dallas, 1960—; clin. instr. internal medicine U. Tex. Southwestern Med. Sch., Dallas, 1960-66, clin. asst. prof. internal medicine, 1966-69, clin. asso. prof., 1969-72, clin. prof., 1972—; attending physician Baylor U. Med. Center, Gaston Episcopal Hosp., Dallas. Mem. med. adv. council Parkland Meml. Hosp. Served to 1st lt. M.C., AUS, 1953-55. Diplomate in cardiovascular disease Am. Bd. Internal Medicine. Fellow A.C.P. (asso.); mem. A.A.A.S., Am. Fedn. Clin. Research A.M.A., Tex. Acad. Internal Medicine, Am. (fellow council clin. cardiology), Tex. (dir.), Dallas (dir., past pres. heart assns., Dallas Acad. Internal Medicine, Confrerie de Chaine des Rotisseurs (chevalier), L'Alliance

Francaise, Phi Beta Kappa, Alpha Omega Alpha. Episcopalian. Clubs: Dallas Internist, Dallas Gun. Home: 6211 W Northwest Hwy Dallas TX 75225 Office: 3710 Swiss Av Dallas TX 75204

CARMICHAEL, JACK CHARLES, engr.; b. Dodd City, Tex., Oct. 11, 1918; s. Horace Henry and Edna (Gay) C.; B.S., U. Tex., 1942; M.S., Johns Hopkins, 1947; m. Doris Eloise Heuschkel, Mar. 14, 1942; children—Cynthia (Mrs. William H. Oliver III), Richard Charles, Lawrence Jack. Commd. 2d lt. USAF, 1942, advanced through grades to col., 1967; sr. san., indsl. hygiene engr. Hdqrs. USAF, Washington, 1950-54, chief med. facilities div., 1958-64; chief engring. br., chief enviromental health lab. br. hdqrs., Air Material Command, Dayton, O., 1954-58; chief of staff Aerospace Med. Div., San Antonio, 1964-65; asst. med. facilities planning Office Sec. Def., Washington, 1965-67; ret., 1967; asst. prof. dept. preventive medicine, asst. to dean Ohio State U. Coll. Medicine, Columbus, 1967-70; dir. Tex. Health Data Inst., Gov.'s Office, 1970-71; mgr. health and human resources div. Office of Gov., Austin, Tex., 1971—. Cons. environmental engring., med. facilities planning, 1967—. Decorated Legion of Merit with 2 oak leaf clusters. Registered profl. engr., Tex. Diplomate Am. Acad. Enviromental Engrs. Mem. Fed. Conf. Environmental Engrs. (pres. 1957-58), Aerospace Med. Assn., Am. Conf. Govtl. Indsl. Hygienists. Mason (Shriner). Home: 7214 W Rim Dr Austin TX 78731

CARMICHAEL, JOSEPH PLEDGER, editor, educator; b. Temple, Ga., July 27, 1917; s. Charles Rufus and Mae (Edmondson) C.; student W. Ga. Coll., 1935-37; A.B. in Journalism, U. Ga., 1940, M.S. in Agr., 1953; m. Stella Cornelia Daniel, Sept. 1, 1946 (dec. May 1972). Reporter Carroll Free Press, Carrollton, Ga., 1937-38, 40; news editor Carroll County Times, Carrollton, 1941; mng. editor Carroll Pub. Co., 1941-42; asst. extension editor U. Ga. Coll. Agr., Athens, 1942-43, acting editor, 1943-46, asso. editor, 1946-56, editor, 1956—, chmn. div. agrl. information, 1962—, prof. agrl. extension, 1963—; editorial columnist Athens (Ga.) Banner-Herald, 1967—. Mem. exec. com. Ga. Livestock Expn., 1965-68; hon. dir. Nat. Farm-City Com., 1969-70. Recipient Golden Anniversary medallion, Fed. Land Banks, 1967. Hon. mem. Master 4-H Club, Ga.; mem. Am. Assn. Agrl. Coll. Editors (pres. 1968-69, dir. 1969-70), Fanny Farmers (pres. 1966—), Atlanta C. of C. (Farmers club), Atlanta Metro Agribusiness Council, Nat. Assn. County Agrl. Agts., U. Ga. Alumni Assn., Sigma Delta Chi, Phi Kappa Phi, Epsilon Sigma Phi, Mu Zeta Alpha, Zeta Sigma Phi. Baptist (sec. bd. deacons 1963-68, 73—). Contbr. articles to mags., profl. publs. Home: 200 Plum Nelly Rd Athens GA 30601

CARMICHAEL, WILLIAM GREGORY, author; b. Birmingham, Ala., Mar. 27, 1922; s. Robert Edward and Annie (Noyes) C.; B.A., U. Ala., 1943; B.S., Princeton, 1945; masso-therapist, Johns-Hopkins, 1969. Graphics designer; pres. Three B's, Ltd., Great Falls, Va., 1964—; researcher, speech writer White House during adminstrns. Truman, Eisenhower, Johnson, Nixon. Dir. pub. relations and advt. Nat. Symphony Orch., 1949-53; dir. vol. radio, speech program A.R.C., 1959-61. Mem. Pub. Relations Soc. Am. Clubs: National Press, Arts (bd. govs.), 1925 F St. (all Washington). Author: Spaniel in the Lion's Den, 1947; Chatillion in Mexico, 1948; A Din of Antiquity, 1967; Alligators in the Bath Tub, 1969; Incredible Collectors, Weird Antiques and Odd Hobbies, 1971. Home: 8818 Jeffery Rd Great Falls VA 22066 Office: Box 1 Great Falls VA 22066

CARMODY, ARTHUR RODERICK, JR., lawyer; b. Shreveport, La., Feb. 19, 1928; s. Arthur R. and Caroline (Gaughan) C.; B.S., Fordham U., 1949; LL.B., La. State U., 1952; m. Renee Aubry, Jan. 26, 1952; children—Helen Bragg, Renee, Arthur Roderick III, Patrick, Timothy, Mary, Virginia, Joseph. Admitted to La. bar, 1952; mem. firm Wilkinson, Carmody & Peatross, Shreveport, 1952—. Dir. Kansas City So. Transport Co., Kansas City, Shreveport and Gulf Terminal Co., Shreveport Cable TV Co., Inc., Shreveport Braves Baseball Club. Chmn. Met. Shreveport Zoning Bd. Appeals, 1959-72; bd. dirs. Caddo Democratic Assn., Shreveport, 1966—. Trustee Jesuit High Sch., Shreveport, Schumpert Meml. Hosp., Shreveport; bd. dirs. La. State U. Found., Baton Rouge, Agnew Day Sch., Shreveport, Ridgewood Montessori Sch., Shreveport. Mem. Am., Fed., La., Shreveport bar assns., Am. Judicature Soc., Nat. Assn. R.R. Trial Counsel, Shreveport C. of C. (bd. dirs. 1967—), Soc. Hosp. Council, La. Civil Service League, Phi Delta Phi, Kappa Alpha. Roman Catholic. Clubs: Touchdown, Petroleum (Shreveport); Pierremont Oaks Tennis. Home: 255 Forest St Shreveport LA 71104 Office: Beck Bldg Shreveport LA 71102

CARMON, JAMES LAVERN, ednl. adminstr.; b. Mount Airy, Ga., May 7, 1926; s. Louie Whit and Anne (Mae (Funk) C.; B.S. in Agr., U. Ga., 1942; M.S., U. Md., 1950; Ph.D., N.C. State Coll., 1955; m. Betty Jo Lee, Feb. 15, 1946; 1 dau., Lee Ann. Mem. faculty, adminstrn. U. Ga., Athens, 1950—, dir. computing center, 1960—, also asst. vice chancellor computing systems Univ. System, 1968—. Trustee EDUCOM. Served with USNR, 1944-46. NSF fellow, 1960-61, NIH fellow, 1963-64. Elk. Home: 304 Greencrest Dr Athens GA 30601 Office: Computer Center U Ga Athens GA 30601

CARNAHAN, ROBERT GORDON, psychiatrist; b. Louisville, Nov. 18, 1913; s. Robert and Ida May (Holman) C.; student Vanderbilt U., 1931-33; M.D., U. Tenn., 1936; m. Sara Elisabeth Alexander, Sept. 8, 1938. Intern Yonkers (N.Y.) Gen., 1937; practice gen. medicine, San Antonio, Tex., 1938-44; resident psychiatry Colo. Psychiat. Hosp., Denver, 1944-48; ednl. dir. Ingleside Hosp., Hastings, Neb., 1949; mem. staff Ark. State Hosp., Little Rock, 1949—, sect. chief, 1966—; clin. prof. psychiatry U. Ark., 1966—. Bd. dirs. Pulaski County Assn. Crippled. Fellow Am. Psychiat. Assn.; mem. A.M.A., Mid-Continent, Ark. psychiat. assns. Home: 4313 W Markham St Little Rock AR 72201

CARNAHAN, ROBERT NARVELL, lawyer; b. Littlefield, Tex., Nov. 22, 1928; s. Clarence D. and Wilma L. (Hartness) C.; B.A., Tex. Technol. Coll., 1950; J.D., U. Tex., Austin, 1957; m. Betty L. Stewart, Mar. 25, 1952; children—Cynthia Lou, Michael S., Christopher Kelly. Admitted to Tex. bar, 1957; asst. county atty., Potter County, 1957; practice law, Amarillo, 1958—. Pres., Amarillo Little Theatre, Inc. Served from 2d lt. to 1st lt. USAF, Korean War. Named Outstanding Young Lawyer, Amarillo Jr. Bar Assn., 1964. Mem. Am. Judicature Soc., Tex. Assn. Def. Counsel, Tex., Amarillo bar assns., Phi Alpha Delta. Mem. Christian Ch. (dir.). Lion. Club: Tascosa Country (Amarillo). Home: 105 Palomino St Amarillo TX 79106 Office: Plaza One Amarillo TX 79101

CARNES, CECIL DWAIN, petroleum co. exec.; b. Hominy, Okla., Mar. 3, 1935; s. Carl S. and Jewell (Norwood) C.; B.S. in Bus., Okla. State U., 1958; m. Linda L. Pearce, June 23, 1962; children—Kimberli L., David D. Vice pres. Osage Oil & Transp., Inc., Cleveland, Okla., 1958-74, pres., 1974—. Served with USAF, 1958-62. Home: 411 North B St Cleveland OK 74020 Office: Box 29 Cleveland OK 74020

CARNES, JAMES OLIVER, gas co. exec.; b. Winnsboro, Tex., Apr. 11, 1927; s. Dolphus C. and Julia C. (Hanson) C.; ed. mgmt. courses U. N.M., 1958, Harvard, 1971; m. Joyce F. Smith, Dec. 26, 1947; children—Ned C., Kenneth E. Road and equipment accountant Tex. & Pacific Ry., Dallas, 1946-48, treas., gen. mgr. employee fed. credit union, 1948-50; office mgr. So. Union Gas Co., Galveston, Tex., 1952-55, office mgr., asst. dist. mgr., Albuquerque, dist. mgr., Farmington, N.M., 1955-63, v.p., dist. mgr., Flagstaff, Ariz., 1963-73, sr. v.p., Dallas, 1973—. Chmn. industry legislative com. utility taxation State of Ariz., 1967; mem. bd. adv. council State of Ariz. Tech. Services, 1963; mem. Coconino County Air Pollution Adv. Council, 1968-73; mem. personnel bd. City of Flagstaff, 1971-73; mem. exec. adv. com. to dean Coll. Bus. of No. Ariz. U., 1965-73. Bd. dirs. Ariz. Dept. Econ. Planning and Devel., 1969-73. Served with AUS, 1944-46, 50-52; PTO, CBI. Mem. Am., Pacific Coast, So. gas assns., Dallas Petroleum Club, Beta Gamma. Republican. Baptist. Mason. Club: Royal Oaks Country (Dallas). Home: 9522 Milltrail Dr Dallas TX 75238 Office: Fidelity Union Tower Dallas TX 75201

CARNES, JAMES ROBERT, trade assn. exec.; b. Acworth, Ga., Oct. 23, 1909; s. James Erwin and Fannie (McDowell) C.; B.S., Ga. Inst. Tech., 1930; J.D., Emory U., 1936; postgrad. George Washington U., 1962-63; m. Virginia Richmond, Aug. 20, 1940; 1 son, Thomas Peter. Operating mgr. B.F. Goodrich Co., Johnson City, Tenn., 1930-33; admitted to Ga. bar, 1935; practiced in Columbus, 1936-41, 46; commd. ensign USN, 1946, advanced through grades to capt., 1954; asst. judge adv. gen. Navy, 1959-61; ret., 1961; dir. govt. relations Mfg. Chemists Assn., Washington, 1962-67, sec.-treas., 1967—, v.p., 1972—. Decorated Bronze Star medal. Mem. Am. Soc. Assn. Execs., Alpha Tau Omega, Phi Delta Phi. Democrat. Conglist. Clubs: Army and Navy, Army Navy Country (Washington); Chemists (N.Y.C.). Home: 5702 Overlea Rd Washington DC 20016 Office: 1825 Connecticut Av NW Washington DC 20009

CARNETT, JOHN WILLIAM, librarian; b. Somerset, Ky., Dec. 13, 1913; s. James E. and Icy (McGahan) C.; B.A., East Tex. Bapt. Coll., 1952; M.S., East Tex. State U., 1967; m. Eunice Ashby, June 24, 1935; children—John Ashby, Judith Anne. Ordained to ministry Baptist Ch., 1947; pastor East End Bapt. Ch., Henderson, Tex., 1953-65; spl. edn. tchr., Longview, Tex., 1965-67; dir. library Kilgore Coll. (Tex.), 1967—. Mem. Am., Tex. library assns., Tex. State Tchrs. Assn., Tex. Jr. Coll. Assn. Home: 1308 Ash Lane Kilgore TX 75662

CARNEVALE, REYNOLDS ALFONSO, dentist; b. Newark, Dec. 18, 1923; s. Victor Nicholas and Margaret (Belfi) C.; B.S., U. N.C. at Raleigh, 1950; D.D.S., U. N.C. at Chapel Hill, 1961, M.S. in Periodontics, 1968; m. Myrtle Lee Debnam, Aug. 28, 1948; children—Victor Nicholas, Patricia Lee. Analytical chemist E.I. duPont de Nemours, Kinston, N.C., 1952-57; dentist, Goldsboro, N.C., 1961-66; practice dentistry, specializing in periodontics, Fayetteville, N.C., 1968—. Asst. prof. periodontics U. N.C., Chapel Hill, 1971—; lectr. periodontics in dental hygiene Fayetteville Tech. Inst. Pres., Cumberland County Cancer Soc., 1971-73. Served with AUS, 1942-45. Mem. Am. Dental Assn., N.C. Dental Soc., Cumberland County Dental Soc., Periodontal Study Club. Research in gingival healing after surgery, 1966-68. Home: Iron Gate Golf Club Fayetteville NC 28304 Office: 3419 B Melrose Rd Fayetteville NC 28304

CARNEY, FREEMAN HARDIN, assn. exec.; b. nr. Waco, Tex., June 27, 1910; s. Charles Hardin and Betty (Butler) C.; A.B., Baylor U., 1933; spl. courses Southwestern C. of C. Inst., Mich. State U.; m. Avis Lee McGinnis, June 19, 1938; 1 son, Jack F. Asst. mgr. Waco (Tex.) C. of C., 1938-42; mgr. Denison (Tex.) C. of C., 1946-57; exec. v.p. Tyler (Tex.) C. of C., 1957—. Served as capt. USAAF, 1942-46. Certified C. of C. exec. Mem. C. of C. Mgrs. Assn. E. Tex. (pres. 1956), Tex. C. of C. Mgrs. Assn. (pres. 1962), So. Assn. C. of C. Execs. (dir.) Am. C. of C. Execs., Tex. Indsl. Devel. Council (dir.), Tyler Petroleum Club. Methodist. Mason (Shriner), Rotarian. Club: Willowbrook Country (Tyler). Home: 1426 Westfield St Tyler TX 75701 Office: 301 N Broadway Tyler TX 75701

CARNLEY, SAMUEL FLEETWOOD, judge; b. Elba, Ala., Nov. 13, 1918; s. Jefferson A. and Mary (Ray) C.; B.A., U. Ala., 1939, LL.B., 1941; m. Mary Magdalene Talbot, Mar. 21, 1939; children—Nancy Hart (Mrs. Paul Clifford Morrow), Mary Oliver (Mrs. Donald Hubert Brown), Terry David, Samuel Fleetwood II, Melanie. Admitted to Ala. bar, 1941; practice law, Elba, 1941-44, 46, 53—; dir. indsl. relations State Ala., Montgomery, 1947-50; judge 12th Jud. Circuit Ala., Elba, Troy, 1950-52, Inferior Ct. Coffee County, Ala., 1969—. Mem. Interstate Conf. Employment Security Agys., 1947-50, mem. exec. com., dist. pres., 1948; mem. Elba Bd. Edn., 1953-58; pageant dir., master ceremonies Elba Centennial, 1953; mem. exec. com. Elba P.T.A., 1960-63, pres., 1966-68; chpt. chmn. A.R.C., 1966-68; program chmn. Elba Halloween Carnival, 1960-63; pres. Elba Little Theater, 1964-65; moderator Coffee County Bapt. Assn., 1967-68; mem. Ala. Bapt. Commn. on Higher Edn., 1967—. Trustee Judson Coll., 1960—, v.p. bd., 1964-67, pres. bd., 1967—, acting pres. coll., 1969-70. Served with AUS, 1944-45. Recipient Algernon Sidney Sullivan award Judson Coll., 1970. Mem. Am. Judicature Soc., Am., Coffee County (past pres.) bar assns., Ala. State Bar, Elba C. of C., Pi Kappa Phi (past pres.). Democrat. Baptist (chmn. bd. deacons, Sunday sch. tchr., trustee state pres. brotherhood). Club: Elba Country. Home: 416 W Collier St Elba AL 36323 Office: 463 Carnley Av Elba AL 36323

CARO, PAUL WILEY, research psychologist; b. Pensacola, Fla., Sept. 30, 1931; s. Paul W. and Doris (Hatton) C.; State U., 1955, M.A., 1956; Ph.D., U. Tenn., 1961; m. Mary Elizabeth Davis, Aug. 6, 1955; children—Philip Davis, Victoria Doris. Tng. psychologist Mead Corp., Chillicothe, O., 1961-62; with Human Resources Research Orgn., Fort Rucker, Ala., 1958-60, 63—, sr. staff scientist aviation div., 1969—. Sr. asso. Applied Psychology Assos., Dothan, Ala., 1965-70; pvt. practice psychology, 1970—; cons. sch. systems, mental health instns., industry, U.S. Air Force. Served with USAF, 1951-54. Fellow Am. Psychol. Assn.; mem. Southeastern, Ala. psychol. assns., Assn. Aviation Psychologists, Am. Helicopter Soc. (sect. v.p. 1967-71), Civil Air Patrol, Sigma Xi. Presbyn. (elder). Designer synthetic flight training systems and behavior control programs. Contbr. articles to profl. publs. Home: 1105 Evergreen Av Dothan AL 36301 Office: Human Resources Research Orgn Div No 6 PO Box 428 Fort Rucker AL 36360

CAROTHERS, DURELL MILLER, lawyer, parking co. exec.; b. Columbus, Tex., Aug. 25, 1909; s. Henry Walter and Mary (Towell) C.; B.A., Rice Inst., 1930; LL.B., South Tex. Sch. Law, 1934; m. Grace Drusilla Fewell, Dec. 16, 1933; children—Drusilla (Mrs. James M. Grisebaum), Mary K. (Mrs. Donald F. Evans), David D., John H., Anderson B. Admitted to Tex. bar, 1934, since practiced in Houston; chmn. bd. Allright Auto Parks, Inc., and predecessor firms, Houston, 1931—; pres., dir. B.A. Riesner & Son Co.; v.p., dir. Tex. Casualty Ins. Co., Austin, 1947-57, chmn. bd., 1955-62, dir., 1962—; dir. Lockwood Nat. Bank of Houston, Capital Devel. Corp. Bd. dirs. Big Bros. Am., Kiwanis Found. Houston. Presbyn. Kiwanian. Clubs: River Oaks Country, Houston, Houston Yacht. Home: 508 Hawthorne St Houston TX 77006 Office: Esperson Bldg Houston TX 77002

CAROW, RAYMOND EDWARD, TV exec.; b. Bklyn., Dec. 13, 1922; s. Edward and Jennie (Altenburg) C.; B.A., Hofstra U., 1950, postgrad., 1950-51; m. Elsie Frost Carow, Aug. 16, 1969; children—Kathleen J., Karen C. (Mrs. Thomas Ezell), Kurt, Cassandra, Jamie, Jayson. Prodn. mgr. WEAR-TV, Pensacola, Fla., 1953-55; mgr. WCTV, Tallahassee, 1955-57; gen. mgr. WALB-TV, Albany, Ga., 1957—; v.p. Gray Communications Systems, Inc., Albany, 1967—, also dir. Pres. Dougherty County Mental Health Assn., 1966. Asst. chmn. Ga. Democratic Com., 1966—. Served to lt. comdr. USNR, 1942-46, 50-53. Named Broadcaster of Year of Ga. Ga. Assn. Broadcasters, 1965. Mem. Ga. Assn. Broadcasters (pres. 1964-65), U.S. Navy League, Albany C. of C. Home: 2702 Doublegate Rd Albany GA 31705 Office: Gray Communications Systems Inc PO Box 3130 Albany GA 31706

CARPENTER, CARLTON LANIER, JR., dermatologist; b. Starville, Miss., Aug. 11, 1930; s. Carlton Lanier and Ruth (Deloach) C.; B.S., Miss. State U., 1951; M.D., Tulane U., 1955; m. Lynda Moss, Dec. 27, 1963; children—Carlton Lanier III, Will Moss, Michael Edward, Laura Elizabeth. Intern, Phila. Gen. Hosp., 1955-56; resident Charity Hosp., New Orleans, 1958-62; practice medicine specializing in dermatology, Baton Rouge, 1962—; mem. staff Our Lady of Lake Hosp.; asst. clin. prof. dermatology Tulane Sch. Medicine, 1962—, La. State U. Sch. Medicine, 1970—. Served to capt. USAF, 1956-58. Fellow A.C.P.; mem. Am. Acad. Dermatology, Baton Rouge C. of C., Baton Rouge Round Table, S.A.R. Rotarian. Home: 1151 S Cloverdale Baton Rouge LA 70808 Office: 1415 Main St Baton Rouge LA 70802

CARPENTER, CHARLES CONGDEN, educator, curator; b. Norman, Okla., June 2, 1921; s. Harry Alonzo and Myrtle Ruth (Barber) C.; B.A., No. Mich. Coll. Edn., Marquette, 1943; postgrad. Tarleton State Coll., Stephenville, Tex., 1943-44, Stanford, 1944, Wayne U., 1945; M.S., U. Mich., 1947, Ph.D., 1951; m. Mary F. Pitynski, Sept. 2, 1947; children—Janet Eleanor, Caryn Sue, Geoffrey Congden. Lab. asst. zoology No. Mich. Coll. Edn., 1941-43; teaching asst. zoology U. Mich., 1946, asst. herpetology and mammalogy Biol. Sta., summer 1948, teaching fellow zoology, 1947-51, instr. zoology, 1951-52; instr. U. Okla. Biol. Sta., Norman, summer 1952, instr. U. Okla., 1953, asst. prof. zoology, 53-59, asso. prof. zoology, curator reptiles U. Okla. and U. Okla. Biol. Sta., 1959-66, prof. zoology, curator reptiles, 1966—. Expdns. and field studies U. Mich. Paleontol. Expdn., Kan. and Colo., 1947, Jackson Hole Research Sta., Grand Teton Nat. Park, 1951, field trips throughout Mexico and S.W. U.S., 1956—, Galapagos Islands Expdn., 1962, expdns. to islands of Gulf of Cal., 1964; invited scientist mem. Galapagos Internat. Sci. Project to Galapagos Islands, Ecuador and Cocos Island, 1964; mem. sci. adv. com. Charles Darwin Found. for Galapagos Islands, 1966—; sec. Animal Research Council, Oklahoma City Zoo, 1972—. Served with AUS, 1943-46. Recipient Distinguished Alumni award No. Mich. U., 1972, numerous grants NSF, N.Y. Zool. Soc., U. Okla. Alumni Devel. Fund, U. Okla. Research Inst., 1951—. Fellow Animal Behavior Soc. (sec. 1966-68), Okla. Acad. Sci. (pres. 1970), Herpetologists League (v.p. 1972-73, pres. 1974-75); mem. Am. Ornithologists Union, Am. Soc. Zoologists, Am. Inst. Biol. Sci., Ecol. Soc. Am., Am. Soc. Ichthyologists and Herpetologists, Wilson Ornithol. Soc., Southwestern Assn. Naturalists (bd. govs. 1965-68, pres. 1968-69, permanent sec. 1971—), Am. Soc. Mammalogists, Brit. Ecol. Soc., Soc. Study Amphibians and Reptiles, Wilderness Soc., Nature Conservancy, Sigma Xi, Phi Kappa Phi, Phi Sigma. Contbr. articles profl. jours. Home: 1218 Cruce St Norman OK 73069 Office: Dept Zoology 730 Van Vlet Oval U Okla Norman OK 73069

CARPENTER, CHARLES DAVID, city ofcl.; b. Orlando, Fla., Aug. 30, 1938; s. John Kessler and Kate Eola (Willoughby) C.; student Orlando Jr. Coll., 1966-67, U. Ga., 1971; m. Dixie Lee Prater, Sept. 26, 1959; children—Sandra Lee, Susan Michelle, Charles Edward. With City of Orlando, 1965—, sanitation supt., 1972—. Cons. solid waste removal, Orlando, 1972—. Pres., Kingswood Civic Assn., Orlando. Mem. Am. Pub. Works Assn., Fla. Park Personnel Assn., Inst. for Solid Waste. Methodist. Home: 1603 Mosher Dr Orlando FL 32810 Office: 1046 W Gore St Orlando FL 32805

CARPENTER, CHARLES JEROULD, constrn. co. exec.; b. Norfolk, Va., Mar. 20, 1932; s. Charles Clinton and Phyllis (Stamp) C.; grad. Woodberry Forest Sch., 1950; B.S., Mass. Inst. Tech., 1954; m. Nancy Stephens Norfleet, Jan. 23, 1960; children—Margaret Courtney, Charles Clinton II. Jr. estimator, field engr. Carpenter Constrn. Co., Inc., Virginia Beach, Va., 1956-63, v.p., gen. exec., 1963-74, pres., 1974—. Jr. dir. Norfolk Central YMCA, 1962-65, pres., 1965, dir., 1966-68; capt. Va. Beach Rescue Squad, 1968, life mem., 1970; officer, dir. Cavalier Park-Bay Colony Community League, 1964-68, pres., 1967. Mem. ednl. council Mass. Inst. Tech., 1958-73; bd. dirs. Gen. Hosp. Virginia Beach, 1968—. Served from 2d lt. to 1st lt. C.E., AUS, 1954-56. Mem. Delta Kappa Epsilon. Episcopalian. Home: 1105 Brandon Rd Virginia Beach VA 23451 Office: PO Box 953 Virginia Beach VA 23451

CARPENTER, CLINTON RAY, JR., profl. assn. exec.; b. Monroe, N.C., Nov. 13, 1936; s. Clinton Ray and Rachel Frances (Greene) C.; student Pfeiffer Coll., 1955-58; student various courses U. Ga., 1963-69; m. Lucretia Leigh Hargette, Mar. 19, 1961; children—Angela Leigh, Clinton Ray III. Sales rep. Gen. Foods Corp., Hickory, N.C., 1960-63; exec. v.p. Monroe-Union County (N.C.) C. of C., 1963-66, Greater Rock Hill (S.C.) C. of C., 1966—. Bd. dirs. YMCA, Rock Hill, S.C., Girls Home; mem. Eagle rev. bd. Boy Scouts, 1969-73. Served with AUS, 1958-60. Named young man of the year Rock Hill Jr. C. of C., 1970. Mem. S.C. (pres. 1970-71, (dir. 1968-72), So. (dir. 1971—), Am. assns. chamber of commerce execs. Mason, Elk, Rotarian. Club: Rock Hill Country. Home: 637 University Dr Rock Hill SC 29730 Office: PO Box 590 Rock Hill SC 29730

CARPENTER, JAMES LINWOOD, JR., safety engr.; b. Fredericksburg, Va., Jan. 6, 1925; s. James Linwood and Edith Virginia (Bullock) C.; A.B., Coll. William and Mary, 1949, M.A., 1950; m. Margaret Rand Lomas, Sept. 2, 1947; children—Julia (Mrs. Dan Joseph Girouard), Blaine. Elec. engr. U.S. Navy Supr. Shipbldg., Newport News, Va., 1950-53, Newport News Shipbldg. and Dry Dock Co., Newport News, 1953-56; dir. plans and programs, def. products Chrysler Corp., Detroit, 1956-60; staff dir. logistics support Martin Marietta Corp., Balt., 1961-70, staff engr., Orlando, Fla., 1970—. Served with USNR, 1942-46. Recipient Edward Greer award for logistics mgmt. Nat. Security Indsl. Assn., 1970. Fellow Soc. Logistics Engrs. (pres. 1967-68), Am. Inst. Aeros. and Astronautics (asso.); mem. Aerospace and Electronics Soc., I.E.E.E., System Safety Soc. Home: 5214 Alleman Dr Orlando FL 32809 Office: Sand Lake Rd Orlando FL 32805

CARPENTER, KENNETH BENTSON, psychiatrist; b. Nashville, Feb. 18, 1932; s. Homer and Marie (Snell) C.; M.D., U. Tenn., 1960; m. Mary Elizabeth Smith, Jan. 7, 1954; children—David, Steven, Michael. Intern, John Gaston Hosp., Memphis, 1961-62; resident U. Tenn. Dept. Psychiatry, 1962-65; pvt. practice psychiatry, Knoxville, Tenn., 1965—; mem. staff U. Tenn. Meml., St. Mary's hosps., Knoxville; dir., clin. dir. Mental Health Center, Knoxville, 1965—. Served with USNR, 1951-54. Mem. A.M.A., Am. Psychiat. Assn. Home: 212 Seven Oaks St Concord TN 37720 Office: 1520 Cherokee Trail Knoxville TN 37920

CARPENTER, LONNIE CLOY, social welfare adminstr.; b. Panhandle, Tex., May 31, 1921; s. Lonnie Calvert and Lela (Toler) C.; B.A., McMurry Coll., 1941; B.D., So. Meth. U., 1944; M.S.,

Columbia, 1949; M.B.A., U. Louisville, 1972; m. Leonore Melnicoff, Aug. 18, 1946 (div.); children—Dean Kenneth, Sherry Linda. Adminstrv. asst. to med. dir. N.J. State Hosp., Trenton, 1945-48; cons. div. child care Fedn. Protestant Welfare Agys., N.Y.C., 1949-51; exec. dir. Children's Center, Greenville, S.C., 1951-55; asst. supt. Louisville and Jefferson County Children's Home, 1955-59, supt., 1959-67; dir. staff devel. and tng. Community Action Commn., Louisville, 1967-72, dep. dir., 1972—. Mem. Am. Soc. for Pub. Adminstrn., Nat. Assn. Social Workers, Acad. Certified Social Workers, Am. Soc. Tng. and Devel. Unitarian-Universalist. Home: 3621 A Brownsboro Rd Louisville KY 40207 Office: 1348 S 3d St St Louisville KY 40208

CARPENTER, LOUIS BENJAMIN, JR., mech. engr.; b. nr. Edgerton, Mo., Mar. 19, 1913; s. Louis Benjamin and Georgia (Winn) C.; B.S. in Mech. Engring., U. Kan., 1936; m. Mildred Dithe Stutzman, Apr. 8, 1946; children—Joyce Louise, Louis Benjamin III, Robert Daniel, Janice Lucile. Engr. trainee to sr. petroleum engr. Gulf Oil Corp., Tulsa, 1936-72; pvt. practice cons. engr. in oil and gas prodn., Oklahoma City, 1972—. Active Boy Scouts Am., 1960—. Served to lt. comdr. USNR, 1942-46. Registered profl. engr., Kan., Okla. Mem. Soc. Petroleum Engrs., Am. Inst. Mining, Metall. and Petroleum Engrs., Nat., Okla. socs. profl. engrs., Tau Beta Pi, Sigma Tau. Republican. Patentee in field. Home: 426 NW 44th St Oklahoma City OK 73118

CARPENTER, THOMAS GLENN, univ. pres.; b. Atlanta, Feb. 27, 1926; s. Walker Glenn and Loreta (Jackson) C.; student Ga. Inst. Tech., 1943-45; B.S., Memphis State U., 1949; M.A., Baylor U., 1950; Ph.D., U. Fla., 1963; m. Oneida Pruette, Oct. 30, 1948; children—Debra, Thomas Glenn. Gen. mgr, Laundry & Cleaning Co., Memphis, 1950-54; instr. econs. U. Fla., Gainesville, 1957-59, asst. dir. housing, 1959-64; dir. auxs. Fla. Atlantic U., Boca Raton, 1964; bus. mgr. U. West Fla., Pensacola, 1965, dean adminstrv. affairs, 1965-67, v.p. for adminstrv. affairs, 1967-69; pres. U. North Fla., Jacksonville, 1969—. Dir. Barnett Bank of Regency, Channel 7. Bd. dirs. Jacksonville Symphony Assn., Meml. Hosp. Jacksonville; adv. bd. Salvation Army. Served with USNR, 1944-46. Mem. Jacksonville C. of C. (gov.), Beta Gamma Sigma, Phi Delta Theta. Presbyn. (elder). Rotarian. Home: 806 Old Grove Manor Jacksonville FL 32207 Office: St Johns Bluff RD S PO Box 17074 Jacksonville FL 32216

CARPENTER, WILLIAM LEVY, marketing exec.; b. Columbia, S.C., May 26, 1926; s. Levy Leonidas and Lucille (O'Brien) C.; student N.C. State U., 1943-44; B.S., U.S. Naval Acad., 1947; m. Blanche Augusta Owen, Apr. 10, 1948; children—Becky (Mrs. Ralph Rothery Bouton), William Owen, Robert Meadors. Staff engr. Celanese Corp., Charlotte, N.C., 1954-56; v.p. bus. devel. J.E. Sirrine Co., Greenville, S.C., 1956—. Chmn. Non-Woven Industries, Inc., 1972—. Served to ensign, USNR, 1947-53. Registered profl. engr., S.C., La. Mem. S.C. Assn. Constrn. Engrs., Cons. Engrs. Council (nat. dir. 1966-69). Baptist (chmn. bd. deacons 1973—). Clubs: Sertoma, Greenville Country. Home: 227 Seven Oaks Dr Greenville SC 27605 Office: PO Box 5456 Greenville SC 29606

CARPENTER, WILLIAM M., diversified co. exec.; b. Burlington, Wis., Aug. 9, 1925; s. William and Olive (Eppers) C.; B.A., U. Wis., 1948; m. Elaine H. Jacobson, Aug. 17, 1945; children—William Scott, Deborah Elaine, Robert Todd. Asst. dir. pub. relations Kohler Co. (Wis.), 1949-56; pub. relations dir. Trane Co., LaCrosse, Wis., 1956-58; v.p., dir. Klau-Van Pietersom-Dunlap, Milw., Wis., 1959-62; dir. pub. relations Walker Mfg., Racine, Wis., 1962-67, dir. pub. relations, advt., sales promotion, 1967-69, v.p., 1969; v.p. Tenneco Inc., Houston, 1970—. Bd. dirs. Houston Kidney Found. Served with AUS, 1943-45. Mem. Pub. Relations Soc. Am., Pub. Relations Soc. Houston, Assn. Nat. Advertisers, Nat. Investor Relations Inst. Home: 11918 Churchill Ct Houston TX 77024 Office: PO Box 2511 Houston TX 77001

CARPENTER, WOODROW WILSON, ceramic engr.; b. West Union, Ill., Sept. 11, 1915; s. Marion E. and Margaretta (Fawver) C.; B.S. in Ceramic Engring. U. Ill., 1939; m. Fay D. Turner (div.); 1 dau., Gay M. (Mrs. Glenn E. Caldwell); m. 2d, Irmgard K. Toberg, Sept. 3, 1960. Research engr. Ingram Richardson Inc., Frankfort, Ind., 1939-42, sales engr., 1946-54; dir. research Barrows Corp., Cin., 1954-58; pres. Ceramic Coating Co., Newport, Ky., 1958—; pres. Florence Enameling Co. Inc. (Ala.), 1965—. Served to lt. col. AUS, 1942-46; PTO. Patentee in field. Home: 480 Winters Lane Cold Spring KY 41076 Office: PO Box 370 Banklick Rd Newport KY 41072

CARR, EARL VIVIAN, operations research analyst; b. Bowling Green, Ky., Aug. 5, 1926; s. Joe Wilson and Bonnie Marie (Morgan) C.; student Capitol Radio Engring. Inst., Washington, 1947-49; m. Mary Lee Lucas, July 10, 1948; children—Bonnie Lee (Mrs. James Carl Acton), Connie Marie (Mrs. Larry Daniel Chasteen). With Missile Test Project of Radio Corp. Am., Patrick Air Force Base, Fla., 1955-65; project engr. Philco-Ford Corp., Houston, 1965—. Served with USNR, World War II; ETO, PTO. Mem. I.E.E.E., Assn. Advancement Med. Instrumentation. Research and devel. of clin. technique to monitor electronically intra-uterine pressures, trans-vaginally, during labor. Home: 858 Seacliff Dr Houston TX 77058 Office: 1002 Gemini Av Houston TX 77058

CARR, FREDERICK LOUIS, lawyer, banker; b. Wilson, N.C., Sept. 6, 1909; s. Frederick Louis and Nancy (Branch) C.; student U. N.C., 1926-30, LL.B., 1932; m. Olivia Hart Chamberlain, June 4, 1932; 1 dau., Olivia (Mrs. John Ambrose Stuart). Admitted to N.C. bar, 1932, since practiced in Wilson; sr. partner firm Carr, Gibbons & Cozart, 1951—; with trust dept. Br. Banking & Trust Co., Wilson, 1932-33, gen. counsel, 1952—, chmn. bd. dirs., 1962—; dir. Atlantic Savs. & Loan Assn. Mem. Wilson County Bd. Edn., 1949-53; pres. Wilson County United Fund, 1960-61; pres. Wilson County chpt. A.R.C., 1950-51. Served with USNR, 1942-45. Mem. Am., N.C., Wilson County (pres. 1948-50) bar assns., Am. Hosp. Assn. Episcopalian. Club: Wilson Country (Raleigh, N.C.). Home: 402 S Kincaid Av Wilson NC 27893 Office: 302 Gold Profl Bldg Wilson NC 27893

CARR, GERALD PAUL, astronaut; b. Denver, Aug. 22, 1932; s. Thomas Ernest and Freda (Wright) C.; B. Mech. Engring., U. So. Cal., 1954; B.S. in Aero. Engring., U.S. Naval Postgrad. Sch., 1961; M.S. in Aero. Engring., Princeton, 1962; m. JoAnn Ruth Petrie, June 20, 1954; children—Jennifer, Jamee, Jeffrey, John, Jessica, Joshua. Commd. 2d lt. USMC, 1954, advanced through grades to lt. col., 1969; jet fighter pilot U.S., Mediterranean, Far East, 1956-65; astronaut NASA, Houston, 1966—, comdr. 3d Skylab Manned Mission. Mem. Marine Corps. Assn., Tau Kappa Epsilon. Presbyn. Office: Code CB NASA MSC Houston TX 77058

CARR, HAROLD N(OFLET), airlines exec.; b. Kansas City, Kan., Mar. 14, 1921; s. Noflet B. and Mildred (Addison) C.; B.S., Tex. A. and M. U., 1943; postgrad. Am. U., 1944-45; m. Mary Elizabeth Smith, Aug. 5, 1944; children—Steven Addison, Hal Douglas, James Taylor, Scott Noflet. Asst. dir. route devel. Trans World Airlines, Inc., 1943-47; exec. v.p. Wis. Central Airlines, Inc., 1947-52; mem. firm McKinsey & Co., 1952-54; dir. North Central Airlines, Inc., 1952—, pres., 1954-65, chmn. bd., pres., 1965-69, chmn. bd., chief exec. officer, 1969—; professorial lectr. mgmt. engring. Am. U., 1952-62; dir. Detection Scis., Inc., Temp Con, Inc., Stange Co. Councilor Tex. A. and M. Research Found. Bd. nominations Nat. Aviation Hall Fame. Bd. dirs. Minn. Safety Council, Airline Indsl. Relations Conf., Assn. Local Transp. Airlines. Served with AUS, 1942-43. Mem. World Bus. Council, Smithsonian Assos., Minn. Execs. Orgn., A.I.M. (pres.'s council), Tex. A. and M. Former Students Assn., Nat. Aero. Assn. (Washington), Am. Assn. Airport Execs., Nat. Def. Transp. Assn., Air Transp. Assn. (dir.), Am. Econ. Assn., Mpls., St. Paul chambers commerce, Stearman Alumnus Club, Pine Beach Peninsula Assn. Episcopalian. Clubs: Nat. Aviation, Aero (Washington); Wings (N.Y.C.); Nat. Aero (San Antonio); Briarcrest Country (Bryan); Racquet (Miami); Midway Civic (Mpls./St. Paul); Gull Lake Yacht (Brainerd, Minn.); Duluth Athletic; Minneapolis. Home: 3505 Parkway Terrace Bryan TX 77801 Office: 7500 Northliner Dr Minneapolis MN 55450

CARR, HOWARD ERNEST, ins. agy. exec.; b. Johnson City, Tenn., Oct. 4, 1908; s. William Alexander and Gertrude (Feathers) C.; B.S., E. Tenn. State U., 1929; M.Ed., Duke, 1935; postgrad. U. N.C., 1938-39; m. Thelma Northcutt, June 11, 1937; 1 son, Howard Ernest. Supt., Washington Coll. (Tenn.), 1929-35; ednl. advisor U.S. Office Edn., Ft. Oglethorpe, Ga., 1935-37; prin. Greensboro (N.C.) city schs., 1937-42; dir. activities First Presbyn. Ch., Greensboro, 1946-47; with Jefferson Standard Life Ins. Co., Greensboro, 1947—, spl. rep., 1947-54, supr. agy. Greensboro, 1964, mgr., 1964-67; pres. Everett's Lake Corp. Chmn. Guilford County Bd. Edn., 1950—; vice chmn. N.C. Gov's Com. Edn., 1956-60; N.C. rep. White House Conf. Edn., 1955. Mem. adv. com. Greensboro div. Guilford Coll., 1958—; head Guilford County Cancer Drive, 1956, bd. dirs. Cancer Soc., 1956—; v.p. N.C. State Sch. Bds. Assn., 1959-61; bd. dirs. Greensboro Jr. Mus., 1956-62, Sternberger Found. Served to lt. with USNR, 1942-46, asst. head motion picture dept., Washington; to capt., 1951-54, as head motion picture dept; ret. as capt., 1968. Recipient Nat. Quality award, Nat. Assn. Life Underwriters, 1948—; named Boss of the Year, Lou-Celin chpt. Am. Bus. Woman's Assn., 1967. Mem. Nat., N.C. (pres. 1964-65; Man of Year award 1969), Greensboro (pres. 1956-57) assns. life underwriters, N.C. Leaders Club, Greensboro C. of C. (chmn. edn. com. 1960-62). Presbyn. (elder). Mason (32 deg.), Kiwanian (pres. Greensboro 1951). Author: History of Higher Education in East Tennessee, 1935. Home: 3927 Madison Av Greensboro NC 27410 Office: 301 Battleground Av Greensboro NC 27401

CARR, JESSE CROWE, JR., author; b. Bland County, Va., July 27, 1930; s. Jesse Crowe and Flossie Elizabeth (Mitchell) C.; grad. Coyne Tech. Sch., 1949, Signal Sch., 1951; m. Lois Ainslie Domazet, June 18, 1955; children—Marsha, Susan, Catherine. With, Commonwealth Press Corp., Radford, Va., 1966-70, pres., gen. mgr., 1966-70; free lance author, Radford, 1970—. Speaker, lectr. various colls. Dir. Printing Industry of Virginias, 1965-68; v.p., dir. Radford Child Care Centers, 1968—. Bd. dirs. New River Valley Nat. Humanities Council, 1972—, pres., 1973-74. Served with USMC, 1951-52. Kiwanian (dir. 1966). Author: A Creature Was Stirring, 1970; The Second Oldest Profession, 1972; The Falls of Rabbor, 1973; The Saint of The Wilderness, 1974. Patentee childrens toy. Home and office: 1401 Madison St Radford VA 24141

CARR, JOSEPH A., JR., curator, planetarium exec.; b. Mpls., Sept. 26, 1920; s. Joseph A. and Vesta N. (Lindsey) C.; B.S., Gemol. Inst. Am., 1950; M.S., U. Minn., 1953; m. Anita R. Gibson, Mar. 12, 1943; 1 dau., Janine. Jeweler, Bemidji, Minn., 1947-53; curator, instr. dept. astronomy U. Minn., Mpls., 1953-60; curator, demonstrations lectr. dept. physics and phys. sci. U. S. Fla., Tampa, 1960-64, curator, dir. planetarium, 1964—, instr. dept. astronomy and phys. sci., 1964—; prof. astronomy Fla. Inst. for Continuing U. Studies, 1964, St. Leo Coll., 1965; cons. Tampa Mus. Sci. and Natural History; mem. solar eclipse expdn., El Cameron, Mexico, 1970. Served with Signal Corps, AUS, 1942-45. Fellow Royal Astron. Soc.; mem. Am. Assn. U. Profs., Am. Inst. Physics, Am. Assn. Physics Tchrs., Fla. Acad. Sci., Am. Astronomy League, Am. Astron. Soc., Sigma Pi Sigma. Mason (K.T.). Home: 3402 Riverview Dr E Tampa FL 33604 Office: 4202 Fowler Av Tampa FL 33620

CARR, LAWRENCE EDWARD, JR., lawyer; b. Colorado Springs, Colo., Aug. 10, 1923; s. Lawrence Edward and Lelah R. (Rubert) C.; B.S., U. Notre Dame, 1948, LL.B., 1949; LL.M., George Washington U., 1954; m. Agnes Isabel Dyer, Dec. 26, 1946; children—Mary Lee, James Patrick, Lawrence Edward III, Eileen Louise, Thomas Vincent. Admitted to Colo. bar, 1949, D.C. bar, 1952, Md. bar, 1961; with Travelers Ins. Co., 1949-51; practiced in Washington, 1952—; sr. partner firm Carr, Bonner, O'Connell, Kaplan, Thompson & Diuguid, 1960—. Pres., Capital Investment Co. of Washington, 1962—. Served with USMCR, 1943-46, 51-52; col. Res. Mem. Am. Bar Assn., Bar Assn. D.C. (dir. 1969-71, pres.-elect 1973). Home: 12001 Piney Glen Lane Potomac MD 20854 Office: 900 17th St NW Washington DC 20036

CARR, WESLEY ALLEN, dentist, oral surgeon; b. Truckee, Cal., June 2, 1913; s. Arthur and Ella (Podd) C.; A.A., Sacramento Jr. Coll., 1935; postgrad. U. Mo., 1936-37; B.S., U. Ga., 1938; D.D.S., Atlanta So. Dental Sch., 1942; m. Elizabeth Pauline Moss, July 1, 1938; children—Wesley Allen, Paula Karen. Practice dentistry, Royston, Ga., 1946-52, Augusta, Ga., 1952—; chief dental staff Univ. Hosp. Augusta, 1954—; mem. staff St. Joseph Hosp., Drs. Hosp.; asso. prof. Med. Coll., Ga. Sch. Dentistry, 1968—. Cons. U.S. Army, VA Hosp., Grace Wood State Hosp., Talmadge Meml. Hosp.; mem. adv. bd. Radiation Center, Augusta, 1971—. Mem. Ga. Bd. Health, 1964-72, regional Bd. Health, 1972—. Served with USNR, 1942-46; PTO. Fellow Royal Soc. Health, Am. Coll. Dentists, Internat. Coll. Dentists, Ga. Dental Assn. (hon.; pres. 1964); mem. Am., Ga. (pres. 1974) socs. oral surgeons, Eastern Dist. Dental Soc. (dentist of year 1965), Am. Dental Assn., Internat. Assn. Oral Surgeons, (pres. Eastern dist.), Ga. Acad. Dental Practice. Elk, Kiwanian. Clubs: West Lake Country (Augusta), Augusta Country. Home: 708 Aumond Rd Augusta GA 30904 Office: 1105 Druid Park Av Augusta GA 30904

CARR, WILEY NELSON, hosp. exec.; b. Dayton, O., Dec. 29, 1940; s. Russell Earl and Anna (Crane) C.; student Miami U. (Ohio), 1959-62; B.S. in Journalism, Ohio U., 1963, M.S., 1964; M.B.A., Xavier U., 1974; m. Grace Elizabeth Brown, June 4, 1960; children—Wiley Nelson, Alison, Elizabeth. Dir. pub. relations Western Coll., Oxford, O., 1964-68, dir. devel., pub. relations, 1968-70; dir. community relations, devel. St. Elizabeth Hosp., Covington, Ky., 1970-74, asst. adminstr., 1974—. Recipient certificate spl. merit Am. Coll. Pub. Relations, 1970; Ann. Giving Incentive award Women's Coll. div. Am. Alumni Council, 1970; MacEachern merit award Acad. Hosp. Pub. Relations, 1972. Mem. Am., Ky. hosp. assns., Nat., Ohio assns. hosp. devel., Pub. Relations Soc. Am., Am. Soc. Hosp. Pub. Relations, No. Ky. C. of C. Methodist (mem. adminstrv. bd.). Home: 355 Jerlou Circle Fort Mitchell KY 41017 Office: 20th and Eastern Sts Covington KY 41014

CARRABBA, MICHAEL PAUL, aircraft components mfg. co. exec.; b. Dayton, O., Jan. 31, 1945; s. Paul G. and Margie (Nichols) C.; student Miami Dade Jr. Coll., 1964—; m. Carol Frances Young, Nov. 1, 1968. Gen. mgr. D&C—Airparts Corp., Hialeah, Fla., 1969-70, pres., owner, 1970—, also chmn. bd.; pres. D.C. A/P Battery Co., 1974—. Served with USMCR, 1962-66. Mem. Nat. Pilots Assn., Profl. Aviation Maintenance Assn., Nat. Air Transp. Conf. Home: 5400 NW 159th St Miami FL 33014 Office: 483 W 27th St Hialeah FL 33010

CARRANZA, ALFRED S., cord. co. exec.; b. Havana, Cuba, Oct. 12, 1946; s. William L. and Adriana B. (Bernal) C.; came to U.S., 1960, naturalized, 1973; Asso. Degree of Bus., Miami Dade Jr. Coll., 1968; B.B.A., U. Miami, 1972. With Poncar Plastic Corp., Miami, Fla., 1965-71; v.p. Sunshine Cordage Corp., Miami, 1971—; v.p. Uxmal Corp. Ltd., Nassau, Bahamas. Mem. Hialeah-Miami Spring C. of C., Cordage Inst. Home: 9549 SW 20th Terrace Miami FL 33144 Office: 7250 NW 41st ST Miami FL 33144

CARRASQUER, GASPAR, physician, educator; b. Valencia, Spain, Dec. 21, 1925; s. Gaspar and Teresa (Paya) C.; B.S., U. Valencia, Spain, 1945, M.D., 1951; children—James Manuel, John Henry, Richard Gaspar. Came to U.S., 1952, naturalized, 1961. Intern, North Hudson Hosp., Weehawken, N.J., 1953; resident internal medicine City Hosp., Welfare Island, N.Y., 1954-55, Louisville Gen. Hosp., 1955-56; practice medicine specializing in internal medicine, 1959—; mem. staff Louisville Gen. Hosp.; fellow U. Louisville, 1956-59, instr., 1959-61, asst. prof., 1961-63, asso. prof., 1963-71, prof. exptl. medicine, 1971—. Vis. asso. prof. medicine Harvard Med. Sch., 1972; mem. asso. staff medicine Peter Bent Brigham Hosp., 1972. Bd. dirs. Kidney Found. Ky. Recipient Career Devel. award NIH, 1967-72; Am. Heart Assn. postdoctoral fellow, 1958-62. Mem. Am. Biophys. Soc., Am. Fedn. Clin. Research, Am. Physiol. Soc., Soc. Exptl. Biology and Medicine, Am. Heart Assn., A.A.A.S., Sigma Xi. Home: 1804 Bunker Hill Ct Louisville KY 40205 Office: U Louisville Health Scis Center Louisville KY 40201

CARRAWAY, HOWARD ERNEST, telephone exec.; b. Olanta, S.C., Oct. 22, 1917; s. Simeon Carlyle and Blanche (Ivy) C.; A.B., Furman U., 1940; m. Avis Cecelia Norman, Jan. 17, 1942 (dec. July 1970); children—Cathleen (Mrs. Duane T. Farmer), Nancy Ann (Mrs. John R. Leonard), John MacDonald; m. 2d, Barbara Begg Heilman, July 17, 1971; 1 stepson, Donald Keith Heilman. Mng. editor Florence (S.C.) Star, 1940-41; reporter Florence Morning News, 1946; owner, editor Pageland (S.C.) Jour., 1946-59; staff writer-columnist Ft. Pierce (Fla.) News-Tribune, 1959-63; pres. Pageland Printing Co., 1953-59, Times Pub. Co. Timmonsville, S.C., 1957-58; pres. Ft. Pierce Press., 1959-63; adminstrv. aide Fla. Pub. Service Commn., Tallahassee, 1963-67, adminstrv. sec., dir. adminstrv. services, 1967-70, asst. exec. dir., 1970-72; exec. dir. Fla. Telephone Assn., Tallahassee, 1972—. Mem. Chesterfield (S.C.) County Welfare Bd., 1957-59. Served with USNR, 1941-46, 51-53. Kiwanian (dir. 1968-70, v.p. 1970-71, pres. 1972-73, dist. chmn. 1973-74). Home: 2116 Spence Av Tallahassee FL 32303 Office: Suite 103 1030 East Lafayette St Tallahassee FL 32301

CARRELL, JOHN ROBERT, educator; b. Dallas, Aug. 15, 1921; s. William Beall and Beulah (Stewart) C.; student Duke U., 1939-41; B.B.A., So. Meth. U., 1943, J.D., 1947, LL.M., 1965; m. Norma Billingsley, June 9, 1956; children—Dianne, Brandon Lowry, Cindy, Bradley John. Admitted to Tex. bar, 1947; practiced in Dallas, 1947-59; faculty N. Tex. State U., Denton, 1959—, prof. bus. adminstrn., 1964—. Bd. dirs. Denton County Tchrs. Credit Union, 1969—, pres. 1971. Served with USAAF, 1942-45. Recipient Research grant N. Tex. State U., 1972. Mem. Am. Bus. Law Assn. (pres. 1968-69, mem. exec. com. 1969—), Am. Assn. U. Profs., Tex. Assn. Coll. Tchrs. (pres. 1973—), Southwestern Soc. Sci. Assn. (mem. membership com. 1966). Sect. editor: Venture, 1962-63; Am. Bus. Law Jour., 1962-64. Contbr. articles to profl. jours. Home: 601 E College St Denton TX 76201

CARRERA, ANA ESTRADA (MRS. GUILLERMO M. CARRERA), physician, pathologist; b. Rio Piedras, P.R., Apr. 16, 1921; d. Manuel and Josefina (Marquez) Estrada; student Stanford, 1945, Newcomb Coll., 1945-47; M.D., Tulane U., 1951; m. Guillermo M. Carrera, Sept. 5, 1945; children—Guillermo F., Carlos J. Am. Cancer Soc. research fellow Tulane U., New Orleans, 1951-53, research asso., instr. medicine, 1957-62, asso. prof. medicine, 1968-73, clin. prof., 1973—; clin. pathologist Ochsner Clinic, Ochsner Found. Hosp., New Orleans, 1958—, active staff clin. pathologist, 1961—. Mem. Am., Pan Am. med. assns., Am. Med. Women Assn., Coll. Am. Pathologists, Am. Soc. Clin. Pathologists, Am. Soc. Hematology, Alpha Omega Alpha, Sigma Xi. Contbr. articles to med. jours. Home: 3118 Jena St New Orleans LA 70125 Office: 1514 Jefferson Hwy New Orleans LA 70121

CARRERA, GUILLERMO MANUEL, pathologist; b. Vieques, P.R., Jan. 3, 1913; s. Guillermo and Carlota (Benitez) C.; B.S., U. P.R., 1933, M.D., Tulane U., 1937; m. Ana Luisa Estrada, Sept. 5, 1945; children—Guillermo Federico, Carlos Jose. Intern San Juan city hosps., 1937-39; resident surgery Univ. Hosp., San Juan, 1939-40, resident pathologist, 1940-45; instr. pathology and tropical medicine Tulane U. Sch. Medicine, New Orleans, 1945-48, asst. prof., 1948-52, asso. prof., 1952-54; head dept. pathology Ochsner Clinic and Ochsner Found. Hosp., New Orleans, 1954-73, sr. pathologist, 1973—. Mem. A.M.A., A.A.A.S., Soc. Exptl. Biology and Medicine, Am. Soc. Exptl. Pathology, Am. Soc. Clin. Pathology, Coll. Am. Pathologists, Am. Assn. Pathologists and Bacteriologists, So. Med. Assn., Sigma Xi. Home: 3118 Jena St New Orleans LA 70125 Office: 1516 Jefferson Hwy New Orleans LA 70121

CARRERE, CHARLES SCOTT, lawyer; b. Dublin, Ga., Sept. 26, 1937; B.A., U. Ga., 1959; LL.B., Stetson U., 1961. Admitted to Fla. bar, 1961, Ga. bar, 1960; law clk. to U.S. Dist. Judge, Orlando, 1962-63; asst. U.S. atty., Middle Dist. Fla., 1963-66, chief trial atty., 1965-66, spl. asst. to U.S. atty., 1966-67; partner firm Harrison, Greene, Mann, Davenport, Rowe, and Stanton, St. Petersburg, 1970—. Served with inf. AUS. Mem. Am., Fla., St. Petersburg bar assns., Stetson Lawyers Assn. (dir. 1968), Phi Beta Kappa, Phi Delta Phi. Office: First Federal Bldg St Petersburg FL 33701

CARRIER, GLASS BOWLING, JR., banker; b. Lexington, Ky., Sept. 2, 1931; s. Glass Bowling and Margaret (Sexton) C.; B.S., U. N.C., 1953; m. Dorothy Kay Olsen, June 15, 1957; children—Catherine Anne, David Bowling. Supr. Allstate Ins. Co., Charlotte, N.C., 1956-61, div. supr., St. Petersburg, Fla., 1961-62; sr. v.p., head investment div. First Union Nat. Bank, Charlotte, 1962—. Bd. dirs. N.C. Municipal Council. Served with USNR, 1953-56. Presbyn. (elder 1966—). Home: 3635 Severn Av Charlotte NC 28210 Office: 1 Jefferson First Union Plaza Charlotte NC 28201

CARRIER, OLIVER, coll. adminstr.; b. Detroit, Apr. 10, 1923; s. Oliver Joseph and Mary Ethel (Ryan) C.; B.S., Coll. Charleston, 1960; Ph.D. (NIH fellow), U. Miss., 1964; m. Mary Frances Malone, Jan. 15, 1944; children—Gerald Oliver, Robert Leroy, Deborah Star, Sharon Joy, Richard Wayne. Instr., U. Miss., 1964, asst. prof., 1964-67, asso. prof., 1967-68, instr. radiological defense U. Miss., Jackson, 1965-68; asso. prof. U. Tex. Med. Sch., San Antonio, 1968—, asso. prof. U. Tex. Dental Sch., 1972—, dir. grad. edn. pharmacology, 1968—. Instr. chemistry and physics Miss. State U., State College, 1960-65; instr. chemistry and pharmacology Miss. So. U., Jackson,

1961-68. Bd. dir. Nat. Cystic Fibrosis Research Found., 1962-68. Served with USNR, 1941-47, 50-51. Recipient NIH grant, 1965-68; NSF grant, 1967-69; S. Kieth Johnson Sci. medal, 1958. Fellow Am. Coll. Clin. Pharmacology; mem. A.A.A.S., Am. Soc. Pharmacology and Experimental Therapy, Am. Chem. Soc., Am. Physiol. Soc., Microcirculatory Soc., Soc. Crybiology, Soc. Biochem. Pharmacology, Tex. Acad. Sci., Western Pharmacology Soc., Sigma Xi. Author: The Pharmacology of the Peripheral Autonomic Nervous System, 1972. Editor: Am. Chem. Soc. Newsletter, 1967-68. Contbr. articles in field to profl. jours. Home: 15014 Heimer Rd San Antonio TX 78216

CARRINGTON, PAUL, lawyer; b. Mexico, Mo., Sept. 24, 1894; s. William Thomas and Mary (Holloway) C.; A.B., U. Mo., 1914; LL.B., Harvard, 1917; m. Frances DeWitt, Nov. 5, 1921; children—Frances (Lee), Paul DeWitt. Admitted to Tex. bar, 1919, since in practice civil law, Dallas; of counsel firm Carrington, Coleman, Sloman, Johnson and Blumenthal, attys.; adj. prof. So. Meth. U. Law Sch., 1974—. Chmn. North Tex. Com. Econ. Devel., 1943-46, Alien Enemy Hearing Bd. of N. Tex., 1942-45; pres. Greater Dallas Planning Council, 1948-53; chmn. bd. Dallas Council on World Affairs, 1953-54; trustee Southwestern Legal Found., 1947-74; v.p. Dallas Boy Scouts Am., nat. councilor, 1945-64; pres. Dallas YMCA, 1946-49. Served as 2d lt., instr. primary flying U.S. Army, 1918-19. Fellow Am. Bar Found. (chmn. 1965-66, 50 year award distinguished service 1973); mem. Am. Bar Endowment (dir. 1964-70), State Bar Tex. (chmn. revising corp. laws Tex. 1949-56, 1st chmn. sect. corp., banking and bus. law 1954, pres. 1960-61), Am. (mem. Ho. of Dels. 1958-70, chmn. sect. corp., banking and bus. law 1955-56, chmn. com. on lawyer referral service 1959-63), Dallas (pres. 1940) bar assns., U.S., Dallas (pres. 1940-42), East Tex. (pres. 1950-51) chambers commerce, Am. Soc. Internat. Law (exec. council 1961-67), Am. Arbitration Assn. (dir. 1935—), Am. Law Inst., Am. Judicature Soc. (dir. 1960-63), Harvard Law Sch. Assn. (pres. 1959-61, nat. council 1953—), S.A.R. Democrat. Mem. Christian Ch. (elder). Mason (32 deg.). Clubs: Dallas Country, Petroleum (Dallas); Harvard (N.Y.C.); Metropolitan (Washington). Home: 6315 Lupton Dallas TX 75225 Office: One Main Pl Dallas TX 75250

CARRION-SERNA, ASENSIO, ednl. adminstr.; b. Cartagena, Spain, Nov. 20, 1932; s. Asensio Carrion-Aviles and Pilar Serna-Gabaldon; student Nat. U. Mexico, 1950-52; C.P.A., Monterry Technol. Inst., 1956; M.B.A., Tex. Christian U., 1957; postgrad. Cornell U., 1959-62; m. Idalia Martinez, Apr. 17, 1969; children—Asensio, Alfonso José. Jr. accountant Despacho Freyssinier Morin, 1952, jr. auditor, 1955-56, sr. auditor, controller, 1956-57; prof. accounting Monterrey (Mexico) Technol. Inst., 1957-59, 62-64, head dept. accounting, 1964-68, asso. dean Sch. Bus., 1968-70, asso. dean div. adminstrn. and social scis., dir. grad. program in adminstrn., 1970—; cons. finance, accounting, mgmt.; guest prof. Mexican, Colombian Univs. Mem. Am. Finance Assn., Am. Econ. Assn., Am. Accounting Assn., Nat. Assn. Accountants, Financial Mgmt. Assn., Western Finance Assn., Inst. Mexicano de Contadores Publicos, Instituto de Contadores Publicos de N.L., Assn. de Ejecutives de Finanzes, Inst. Mgmt. Scis. Roman Catholic. Home: 132 A Ote Missouri Garza Garcia NL Mexico Office: ITESM Sucursal de Correos J Monterrey NL Mexico

CARRITHERS, PAUL NORMAN, realtor; b. Hindman, Ky., Apr. 16, 1923; s. Oliver Roy and Leah (Wiseman) C.; student, N.C. State Coll., Raleigh, 1940-41, Coll. William and Mary, 1949—; m. Marie Brown, July 20, 1944; children—Faye Jeanette, Kaye Louise, Gaye Elizabeth. Realtor Fidelity Real Estate Service, Newport News, Va., 1947—, mgr., 1950—; a founder 1st Peninsula Bank & Trust Co. of Hampton (Va.), 1970. Chmn. adv. bd. Salvation Army, 1965-68; bd. pres. Peninsula Family Counseling Agy., Newport News, 1956-60. Served with USAAF, 1944-46. Mem. Nat. Assn. Real Estate Bds., Nat. Inst. Real Estate Brokers, Va. Assn. Realtors, Newport News-Hampton Bd. Realtors, Peninsula C. of C. Mem. Unity Ch. (dir.). Mason. Clubs: Newport News Kiwanis. Home: 898 Cloverleaf Lane Newport News VA 23601 Office: 99 28th St Newport News VA 23607

CARROCCIO, CHARLES SALVATORE, dentist; b. N.Y.C., Nov. 25, 1920; s. Anthony and Josephine (Morello) C.; B.S. in Biology, Catholic U. Am., 1941; D.D.S., Georgetown U., 1944; m. Margaret Murray Brennan, Dec. 2, 1944; children—A. Thomas, Cristina (Mrs. Walter James Sears III), Charles, Maria, Margaret, Michelle, Andrea, Paul, Peter, John. Practice gen. dentistry, Washington, 1946—, Bethesda, Md., 1955—; mem. staff Providence Hosp., Washington, 1960—; instr. operative dentistry Sch. Dentistry, Georgetown U., 1946—. Cubmaster, Bethesda, 1954-56, pack chmn., 1956-57. Served with AUS, 1944-46. Mem. Am. Dental Assn., D.C. Dental Soc. (exec. com.), Acad. Gen. Dentistry, Pierre Fauchard Acad., Catholic U. Alumni Assn. (gov., past pres.), Xi Psi Phi. Roman Catholic (mem. parish council). K.C. Home: 5501 Albia Rd Bethesda MD 20014 Office: 2025 Eye St Washington DC 20016

CARROLL, CHARLES A., judge; b., 1898; B.A., U. Va., 1920; LL.B., Harvard, 1923. Judge, 3d Appellate Dist. Ct. Fla., Miami. Home: 4100 Malaga Miami FL 33133 Office: 1350 NW 12th Miami FL 33136

CARROLL, CHESTER COEN, univ. adminstr.; b. Boothton, Ala., Apr. 23, 1937; s. Earnest Elton and Eliza Antionette (Dunn) C.; student U. Va., 1956-57, Birmingham So. Coll., 1957-58; B.S. in E.E., U. Ala., 1961; M.S. in E.E., 1962, Ph.D., 1965; postgrad. U. Mich., 1963; m. Dezree Ann Cockrell, Sept. 7, 1958; children—Blake Michael, Andrea Lea, Burke Bradford. Student asst. in elec. engring. U. Ala., University, 1960-61, grad. asst., 1961-62, instr., 1962-65; asso. prof. elec. engring. Auburn (Ala.) U., 1965-68, prof., 1968-72, head dept., 1969-72, v.p. research, 1972—. Cons. New Generation Tech. Group, IBM, Hopewell Junction, N.Y., 1967, Nat. Acad. Sci., 1970-72; mem. adv. com. on data processing systems Anti-Ballistic Missile Def., 1970-72. Served witn Signal Corps, AUS, 1955-58. Registered profl. engr., Ala. Mem. I.E.E.E., Am. Soc. Engring. Edn., A.A.A.S., Nat. Soc. Profl. Engrs., Am. Assn. U. Adminstrs., Sigma Xi, Pi Mu Epsilon, Eta Kappa Nu. Methodist. Club: Saugahatchee Country (Auburn). Contbr. articles to profl. jours. Patentee in field. Home: 701 Wrights Mill Rd Auburn AL 36830

CARROLL, COLEMAN FRANCIS, archbishop; b. Pitts., Feb. 9, 1905; s. William J. and B. Margaret (Hogan) C.; B.A., Duquesne U., 1926; L.S.T., St. Vincent's Sem., Latrobe, Pa., 1930; J.C.D., Catholic U. Am., 1942. Ordained priest Roman Catholic Ch. 1930; asst. pastor Resurrection, St. Scholastica, St. Basil. Holy Cross, 1930-49; pastor St. Maurice Parish, Pitts., 1949-51, Sacred Heart Ch., East End, Pitts., 1951-58; became 1st Bishop, Miami, Fla., 1958; now archbishop Miami Beach, Fla.; domestic prelate, Rt. Rev. Msgr., 1952; aux. biship of Pitts., 1953-58. Address: 1633 Northview Dr Sunset Island No 1 Miami Beach FL 33140

CARROLL, DEWITT EDWARD, public relations co. exec.; b. Gastonia, N.C., Oct. 4, 1914; s. Wiley Tot and Constance (Hege) C.; student U. N.C., 1932-36; m. Marguerite Elizabeth Bishop, Apr. 8, 1943; 1 dau., Betsy Bishop (Mrs. Robert F. Alexander, Jr.). With U.P.I., 1936; with Raleigh (N.C.) Times, 1936-40, city editor, 1939-40; asst. city editor Greensboro Record, 1951-52; asst. city editor Greensboro Daily News, 1952-53; exec. sec. Piedmont Asso. Industries, 1953-60; v.p., sec. John Harden Assos., Greensboro, 1960-72; owner DeWitt Carroll/Pub. Relations, 1972—; exec. dir. Guilford County (N.C.) Bicentennial Commn., 1970-72. Cons. bus. letter and report writing, speech writing, pub. relations, co. publs., 1955—, lectr. in field. Exec. committeeman, pub. relations chmn. Carolinas United, 1966-67; mem. budget com., Greensboro United Fund, 1953-54; mem. adv. bd. Greensboro div. Guilford Coll., 1954-64, Guilford Tech. Inst., 1956-60. Served to capt. USAAF, 1942-45, USAF, 1950-52; Korea. Mem. Pub. Relations Soc. Am. (pres. Charlotte chpt. 1968, N.C. chpt. 1969, counselors sect.), Episcopalian (vestryman, lay reader 1969—). Home: 1503 Seminole Dr Greensboro NC 27408 Office: 1503 Seminole Dr Greensboro NC 27408

CARROLL, EDWARD JOSEPH, psychoanalyst; b. Pitts., Feb. 24, 1910; s. Edward Joseph and Stella (Bonner) C.; B.S., U. Pitts., 1933, M.D., 1934; m. Mildred Clark, Aug. 10, 1935; 1 son, Clark E. Intern St. Francis Hosp., Pitts., 1934-35, resident, 1935-37; individual practice pschoanalysis, Pitts., 1946-65, Miami, Fla., 1965—; dir. Craig House Children, Pitts., 1955-64; tng. analyst Phila. Psychoanalytic Inst., 1956-65, Psychoanalytic Inst., Pitts., 1962-65; clin. asso. prof. psychiatry U. Pitts., 1950-65; clin. asso. prof. psychiatry U. Miami, 1965-69, clin. prof., 1969—. Mem. Pa. Adv. Council Mental Health, 1960-65, chmn., 1963-65 mem. Pa. Bd. Pub. Welfare, 1963-65. Served with M.C., AUS, 1940-46. Mem. Am., Pitts., Fla. psychoanalytic socs. Address: 8201 Ponce de Leon Rd Miami FL 33143

CARROLL, FRANK ANDREW, JR., physician; b. Scranton, Pa., May 21, 1924; s. Frank Andrew and Evangeline (Farrell) C.; B.S., U. Scranton, 1947; M.D., Jefferson Med. Coll., 1951; m. Suzanne Teres Clarke, July 9, 1949; children—Suzanne, Drew, Ellen, Megan, David, Gail. Intern Scranton State Gen. Hosp., 1951-52; gen. practice medicine, Alexandria, Va., 1952—; dir. No. Va. Doctors Hosp. Corp., Circle Terrace Hosp. Corp., Alexandria; chief dept. family practice No. Va. Doctors Hosp., 1962—. Served with AUS, 1943-45. Decorated Purple Heart, Bronze Star. Diplomate Am. Bd. Family Practice. Fellow Am. Acad. Family Practice; mem. No. Va. Acad. Gen. Practice (pres. 1966-67), Va. Acad. Gen. Practice (dir. 1965-68), So., Va., Alexandria med. socs. Roman Catholic. Clubs: Belle Haven Country (Alexandria, Va.), Scranton Country (Scranton, Pa.). Home: 3505 Sterling Av Alexandria VA 22304 Office: 1707 Osage St Alexandria VA 22302

CARROLL, GALE GARTH, architect; b. Newman Grove, Neb., Jan. 14, 1936; s. Gale Orville and Marjorie Eleanor (Shain) C.; B.Arch., U. Tex., 1962; m. Katherine Elaine Carson, June 27, 1959; children—Christopher, Nicole, Ashley. With, Brooks & Barr, Austin, Tex., 1960-62; architect Caudill, Rowlett & Scott, Houston, 1963-67; owner Gale Garth Carroll, Architect, Corpus Christi, Tex., 1967—. Served with USAF, 1958-64. Mem. A.I.A., Kappa Sigma. Club: Beachcombers (Corpus Christi, Tex.). Home: 408 University St Corpus Christi TX 78412 Office: 1712 Santa Fe Corpus Christi TX 78404

CARROLL, GEORGE JOSEPH, physician; b. Gardner, Mass., Oct. 14, 1917; s. George J. and Kathryn (O'Hearn) C.; A.B., Clark U., 1939; M.D., George Washington U., 1944. Intern, Worcester (Mass.) City Hosp., 1944-45; resident Doctors Hosp., 1945-46, Sibley Hosp., 1948-49, VA Hosp., 1949-50, all Washington; asst. pathologist DC Gen. Hosp., 1950-51, pathologist, 1951-52; practice medicine, specializing in pathology, Suffolk and Franklin, Va., 1952—; pathologist Louise Obili Meml. Hosp., Suffolk, Southampton Meml. Hosp., Franklin, Greensville Meml. Hosp., Emporia, Va., all 1952—; instr. pathology Med. Sch., Georgetown U., Washington, 1950-52; instr. clin. micrology Am. U., Washington, 1950-51; asso. clin. prof. pathology Med. Coll. Va., Richmond, 1968—; clin. prof. pathology Health Sci. Center, Va. Commonwealth U., Richmond, 1970—. Mem. Va. Bd. Med. Examiners, 1967—, sec., treas., 1970—. Bd. dirs. Va. div. Am. Cancer Soc., 1955-62, Va. Med. Service Assn., 1960-71. Diplomate Am. Bd. Pathology. Fellow Am. Soc. Clin. Pathologists (dir. 1969—), Coll. Am. Pathologists, A.C.P.; mem. Am. Assn. Blood Banks (pres. 1973-74), Va. Soc. Pathology (sec., treas. 1954-68, mem. council), Va. Med. Soc. (mem. ho. of dels. 1960-73), Med. Soc. Va., So. Med. Assn. (councillor from Va. 1965-70, chmn. council 1969-70, 1st v.p. 1971-72, pres. 1973-74), 4th Dist. Med. Soc. Va. (pres. 1968), Internat. Acad. Pathology, A.M.A., George Washington, D.C. (asso.), Seaboard (past pres.) med. socs., Am. Soc. Clin. Pharmacy and Therapeutics, Soc. Nuclear Medicine. Rotarian. Home: 219 Northbrook Av Suffolk VA 23434 Office: Louise Obici Meml Hosp Suffolk VA 23434

CARROLL, JULIAN MORTON, lt. gov. Ky.; b. Paducah, Ky., Apr. 16, 1931; s. Elvie B. and Eva (Heady) C.; A.A., Paducah Jr. Coll., 1952; A.B., U. Ky., 1954, LL.B., 1956; m. Charlann Harting, July 22, 1951; children—Kenneth Morton, Iva Patrice, Bradley Harting. Admitted to Ky. bar, 1956; mem. Ky. Ho. of Reps., 1962-72, speaker of ho., 1968-72; lt. gov. of Ky., 1971—. Trustee Paducah (Ky.) Jr. Coll. Mem. Am., Ky., Paducah bar assns., Phi Delta. Optimist. Home: Old Mansion 420 High St Frankfort KY 40601 Office: State Capitol Frankfort KY 40601

CARROLL, RICHARD LYNN, govt. ofcl.; b. Laurel, Md., Oct. 1, 1932; s. Thomas Fenton and Hester Elizabeth (Doss) C.; B.A., George Washington U., 1960, M.A., 1962, Ph.D. (Gilbert H. Grosvenor teaching fellow 1962-64), 1966; m. Ruth Gail Hodges, Sept. 14, 1957; children—Alena Leticia, Park Kim. Cartographer supr. Army Map Service Dept. of Army, Washington, 1951-57; pub. health adviser D.C. Pub. Health Dept., 1966; spl. asst. Dept. Housing and Urban Devel., Washington, 1967-68; dir. policy and planning Am. Revolution Bicentennial Commn., Washington, 1969-70, exec. dir. dept., 1971-73; exec. assn. NSF, 1973—. Served with USNR, 1952-54. Ford Found. travel grantee, India, 1964-65. Home: 4720 20th Pl North Arlington VA 22207 Office: 1800 G St NW Washington DC 20550

CARROLL, ROBERT CLINTON, JR., elec. engr.; b. Florence, S.C., June 11, 1930; s. Robert Clinton and Harriet (Holland) C.; B.S., Clemson U., 1953; m. Helen White, Aug. 29, 1954; children—Robert F., Helen Haynsworth. Sr. elec. engr. Broad River Elec. Coop, Gaffney, S.C., 1956-57; extension engr. Clemson U., 1957-58; engr. Horry Elec. Coop, Conway, S.C., 1958-60; mgr. bd. pub. works Water Power & Sewer Utility, Gaffney, 1960-65; elec. engr. Harwood Beebe Co., Cons. Engrs., Spartanburg, S.C., 1965-73, dirs., 1971-73; mgr. Broad River Electric Coop., 1973—; pres. Dixie Ltd. Inc. Served with AUS, 1953-55. Mem. Spartanburg Soc. Profl. Engrs. (pres. 1968-69), S.C. Pollution Control Assn. (pres. 1965-66), Am. Water Works Assn., I.E.E.E. Rotarian. Home: 119 Hillside Dr Gaffney SC 29340 Office: PO Box 790 Gaffney SC 29340

CARROLL, ROBERT LEON, educator; b. Snohomish County, Wash., Jan. 15, 1910; s. Lillie May (Ritchie) C.; A.B., Fairmont State Coll., 1933; M.S., W. Va. U., 1940, Ph.D., 1944; m. Elsie Von Kautz, Dec. 10, 1970; children by previous marriage—Cynthia, Susette. Research staff mem. Mass. Inst. Tech., Field Expt. Sta., Bur. Standards, Washington, 1944-45, asso. project leader, proximity fuze research, ordnance devel. dir., 1945-46; head dept. physics Fairmont State Coll. (W.Va.), 1946-56; chief engr., dean of academics U.S. Naval Test Pilot Sch., Patuxent River, Md., 1956-58; propulsion unit head Bell Aircraft Corp., Buffalo, 1958-59; sr. scientist A.M.F. Co., Alexandria, Va., 1959-61; operations analyst Office of Chief of Naval Operations, Pentagon, 1961-62; mem. staff, office chief engr. Melpar, Inc., Falls Church, Va., 1962-65; faculty prof. physics, chmn. dept. physics Baptist Coll., Charleston, S.C., 1965—. Founder, pres. Carroll Research Inst., Hanahan, S.C., 1972—. Recipient Naval Ordnance Devel. award, 1945. Mem. Internat. Platform Assn., Math. Assn. Am., Sigma Xi, Sigma Pi Sigma, Sigma Zeta. Author: The Aerodynamics of Powered Flight, 1960; The New Physics, 1972; Number Theory, 1973. Patentee in field. Home: 115 Wisteria Rd Hanahan SC 29405 Office: Baptist College Charleston SC 29411

CARROLL, ROBROY CHARLES, constrn. co. exec.; b. Houston, Nov. 18, 1910; s. I.C. and Hattie (Rotten) C.; B.A. in Bus. Adminstrn., Rice U., 1934, B.S. in Architecture, 1935; m. Ilma Wilday, May 10, 1938. Sec.-treas. Tanglewood Corp., Houston, 1945-70, pres., 1970—, also pres. affiliated cos., 1970—. Served to maj. USAAF, 1942-45. Mem. Houston Builders Assn. (dir.), Nat. Assn. Home Builders (dir.). Kiwanian. Club: Briar (pres. Houston 1965). Home: 6239 Sugar Hill Houston TX 77027 Office: 1661 Tanglewood St Houston TX 77027

CARROLL, WILLIAM WENDALL, lawyer; b. Gainesville, Tex., Apr. 25, 1929; s. Clifton Haskell and Ruby Belle (Doty) C.; B.A., Tulane U., 1950; LL.B., U. Tex., 1952. Admitted to Tex. bar, 1952; practiced in Gainesville, 1952—; mem. firms Stark & Carroll, 1952-63, Carroll & Underwood, 1971—. City atty. City of Gainesville, 1958-62; county judge Cooke County Tex., 1963-70. Bd. dirs. Cooke County Devel. Found., City of Gainesville Indsl. Authority, 1968—; chmn. bd. dirs. Gainesville Housing Authority, 1968-73. Served with AUS, 1953-55. Mem. Am., North Tex., Cooke County bar assns., State Bar Tex. Home: 400 S Commerce St Gainesville TX 76240 Office: 106 W Main St Gainesville TX 76240

CARROON, LAMAR EVAN, engr.; b. University Park, N.M., Sept. 28, 1922; s. William Evan and Florence Ruth (Brownlee) C.; B.S., N.M. State U., 1943; m. Barbara Carter Paddock, Jan. 19, 1947; children—Robert Evan, Barbara Ann, Jean Carter. With U.S. Geol. Survey, 1946—, dist. engr., Montgomery, Ala., 1959-61, Tuscaloosa, Ala., 1961-64, regional staff engr., Denver, 1964-68, dist. chief water resources div., Jackson, Miss., 1968—. Guest lectr. Pan. Am. Health Orgn., Bridgetown, Barbados, 1967. Registered profl. engr., N.M., Ala., Colo., Miss. Fellow Am. Soc. C.E. (sec.-treas. sect. 1958-59, pres. Miss. sect. 1973-74), Miss. Soc. Profl. Engrs., Assn. Fed. Adminstrs. (sec.-treas. 1961), Fed. Exec. Assn., Am. Geophys. Union, Internat. Assn. Scientific Hydrology. Presbyn. (ruling elder 1954-68). Club: Jackson Yacht. Contbr. articles to profl. pubs. Home: 5818 N Dale St Jackson MS 39211 Office: 430 Bounds St Jackson MS 39206

CARRUTH, THOMAS PAIGE, ednl. adminstr.; b. Vernon, Tex., Mar. 17, 1931; s. Otho Thomas and Florine (Robinson) C.; student Tex. A. and M. U., 1948-49; B.S., West Tex. State U., 1952, M.Ed., 1955; Ed.D., Tex. Tech. U., 1958; m. Norma Lee Durrett, Aug. 15, 1952; children—Alan Wayne, Geraldine Louise, Joe Keith, Thomas Paige, Melissa. Social studies tchr. Kermit (Tex.) Ind. Sch. Dist., 1955-58; teaching fellow Tex. Tech. U., 1958-59; asst. dean men West Tex. State U., 1959-63, dean student life, 1963-70, v.p. student affairs, 1970—. Pres. Randall County chpt. Am. Cancer Soc., 1965-66, mem. pub. edn. com. Tex. div., 1971-74; mem. com. Llano Estacado council Boy Scouts Am., 1963-66. Served with AUS, 1952-54. Decorated many service medals. Mem. Tex. (pres. 1965-66), Southwestern (exec. com. 1964-65, 1967—) assns. student personnel adminstrs., Panhandle Sch. Leaders Assn. (pres. 1965-66), Canyon C. of C. (dir. 1962-65), Phi Delta Kappa (pres. Gamma Xi chpt. 1962-63). Methodist (lay leader 1965-67). Rotarian (pres. 1964-65, dist. gov. 1971-72). Home: Box 277 West Tex Sta Canyon TX 79015

CARRUTH, TOMMY TURNER, architect; b. Quanah, Tex., Feb. 17, 1928; s. Paul and Myra Katherine (Turner) G.; B.Arch., Tex. A. and M. U., 1958; m. Billie Gray Andrews, Nov. 24, 1951; children—Myra, Paul II (dec.), Tommy Turner, Alice. Draftsman, John G. York, Harlingen, Tex., 1948-49, 50; prin. Edward J. Romieniec & Assos., Harlingen, Tex., 1958-60; v.p. Uhlhorn Internat. Contractors, Balboa, Canal Zone, 1960-63; pres., owner Carruth Internat., Canal Zone, 1963-70; prin., owner Tommy T. Carruth Architect, Brownsville, Tex., 1971—. Served with USNR, 1952-56. Mem. A.I.A., Nat. Council Archtl. Registration Bds., Tex. Soc. Architects. Episcopalian (vestryman 1973—). Club: Valley Internat. Country (dir. 1973—) (Brownsville, Tex.). Home: 1114 Sycamore Dr Brownsville TX 78520 Office: 700 Paredes Av Brownsville TX 78520

CARRUTHERS, EWING, ins. agt.; b. Memphis, Mar. 14, 1917; s. Ewing and Willie Elmore (Vandegrift) C.; B.A. Southwestern Coll., Memphis, 1939; m. Mary Jane Ogden, Apr. 12, 1952; children—Jan, Ewing III, Cage, Tracy. Agt., Mass. Mut. Life Ins. Co., Memphis, 1939—. Speaker, cons. life ins. at various ednl. instn. seminars; guest lectr. U. Conn., U. Colo., U. Puget Sound. Mem. Shelby County Human Relations Commn., 1968-71, v.p., 1970-71; chmn. French Camp (Miss.) Project, 1951. Mem. Civil Service Bd., City of Memphis, 1969-71. Bd. dirs. Arts Appreciation, Memphis. Served to lt. (j.g.) USNR, 1942-46; now lt. Res. ret. C.L.U. Mem. Million Dollar Round Table (life mem.; mem. found ad hoc com. 1970-71), Nat. Assn. Life Underwriters (mem. fed. law and legislation com. 1959-71), Assn. for Advanced Life Underwriting (pres. 1966-67), chmn. long-range planning com. 1971-73), Memphis Life Underwriters Assn. (pres. 1955-56), Estate Planning Council Memphis. Republican. Episcopalian (v.p. Episcopalian Laymen of Tenn. 1964-65, mem. vestry 1966-69, 72-75, treas. 1974). Clubs: University, Tennessee, Country (Memphis). Author: A Way of Life, 1969. Contbr. articles to profl. jours. Home: 4134 Kriter Lane Memphis TN 38117 Office: 100 N Main St Memphis TN 38103

CARSON, DALE, city ofcl.; grad. Ohio State U., 1949; m. Doris N. Carson; children—Dale, Chris, Cynthia. Formerly with FBI; sheriff, Jacksonville, Fla., 1958-73, police chief, 1973—. Lectr. polit. sci. various colls. and univs. Mem. Fla. Police Standards Council; mem. Fla. Gov.'s Council on Criminal Justice. Mem. Nat., Fla. (past pres.), sheriffs assns., Internat. Assn. Chiefs of Police. Home: 3875 Rosalind Pl Jacksonville FL 32205 Office: Duval County Courthouse Jacksonville FL 32202*

CARSON, EDWARD FLOYD, ednl. adminstr.; b. Valley View, Tex., June 24, 1916; s. Thomas Augusta and Eva Lou (Fryer) C.; Asso. Sci., N. Tex. Agrl. Coll., 1937; B.S., Tex. A. and M. U., 1939; M.Ed., N. Tex. State U., 1966; m. Regina Jane Mitchell, June 28, 1959; children—Evalyn Dean, Mitchell Edward, Jane Grace. High sch. vocational agr. tchr. Southmayd (Tex.) High Sch., 1939-43; coordinator, Cooke County Vets. Vocational Sch., 1946-61; Cooke County sch. supt., Gainesville, Tex., 1963—. Treas. Nor-Tex. Fed. Credit Union, Gainesville, 1966—; fiscal officer Nor-Tex. Edn. Coop., 1968—. Served with USAAF, 1943-46; PTO. Decorated Bronze Star (3). Named Outstanding Conservation Farmer Upper Elm Red Soil Conservation Dist., 1956. Mem. Am., Tex. assns. sch. adminstrs., Tex. State Tchrs. Assn., Tex. County Supts. Assn., Manpower Adminstrv. Programs Assn. Tex., Tex. Farm Bur., V.F.W., Gainesville C. of C. (mem. edn. com. 1970—). Mason, Kiwanian. Club: Cooke County A.

and M. (pres. 1971—) (Gainesville). Home: Route 1 Box 87A Valley View TX 76272 Office: 100 California St Gainesville TX 76240

CARSON, GEORGE JOHN, lawyer; b. San Antonio, Nov. 12, 1936; s. John Chris and Sophia (Couloheras) C.; grad. Tex. Mil. Inst., 1954; B.S., Tex. A. and M. U., 1959; J.D., Tex. U., 1963; m. Georgia Williams, Nov. 26, 1971; 1 son, John George. Admitted to Tex. bar, 1963; partner Morrison, Dittmar, Dahlgren & Kaine, San Antonio, 1964—. Dir. State Jr. Bar of Tex., 1968-70; pres. San Antonio Jr. Bar, 1967. Mem. Am., Tex., San Antonio bar assns. Greek Orthodox (pres. ch. bd. trustees, mem. archdiocesan council). Home: 1045 Shook St San Antonio TX 78212 Office: Milam Bldg San Antonio TX 78205

CARSON, RICHARD LAFAYETTE, lawyer; b. nr. Knoxville, Tenn., Sept. 22, 1912; s. Thomas Callaway and Fannie (Cox) C.; J.D., U. Tenn., 1935; m. Ruth Elisabeth Brown, Oct. 31, 1942; 1 son, Bruce Alexander. Admitted to Tenn. bar, 1935; since practiced in Knoxville; mem. firm Hodges, Doughty & Carson, 1959—; trial atty. City of Knoxville, 1946-52. Chmn. bd. Royal Crown Bottling Co., Knoxville, Smoky Mountains Beverage Co.; dir. Tenn Mill and Mine Supply Co., Callaway Bldg. Products, Inc., Knoxville Parkrite, Inc., Knox Allright, Inc., Lenoir Co. Served as capt. AUS, 1942-45. Decorated Purple Heart. Fellow Am. Coll. Trial Lawyers; mem. Am., Tenn., Knoxville (pres. 1950-51) bar assns., S.R. (pres. 1950), Am. Judicature Soc., Phi Gamma Delta, Scarabbean. Presbyn. (deacon). Clubs: City, Cherokee Country. Home: Route 4 Westland Dr Concord TN 37720 Office: Hamilton Nat Bank Bldg Knoxville TN 37901

CARSON, RUBY LEACH, journalist; b. Joplin, Mo., June 9, 1894; d. John Milton and Minnie (Robinson) Leach; A.B., U. Miami; M.A., U. Fla.; m. James Milton Carson, Jan. 3, 1926 (dec.); children—Carol (Mrs. Thomas A. Stanford), Jackson C. Reporter, Miami (Fla.) Metropolis (now Miami News), 1916-22; v.p. South Dade Pub. Co., Homestead, Fla., 1923-27; instr. Fla. history U. Miami, 1939-41; co-founder Homestead Leader, 1923; free lance writer, 1924—. Mem. Hist. Assn. So. Fla. (dir.), Fla. Hist. Soc. (past dir.), Nat. League Am. Pen Women, Sigma Alpha Iota (patroness). Author: Fabulous Florida, 1942; Fla. story for Children of the U.S.A., 1946; (with others) The East Coast of Florida, 1961; (with C.W. Tebcau) Florida from Indian Trail to Space Age, 2 vols., 1965. Contbr. articles to hist. jours. Home: 3373 SW 7th St Miami FL 33135

CARSTEA, DUMITRU DUMITRU, research hydrologist, environmental scientist; b. Paduroiu, Rumania, Mar. 22, 1930; s. Dumitru Marin and Teodora (Soare) C.; B.S. in Agrl. Engring., Agrl. Inst. (Bucharest, Romania), 1954; M.S., Ore. State U., 1965, Ph.D., 1967; m. Eleanor Tolci, Nov. 14, 1956; children—Julius, Eugene, Virgil, Adina. Came to U.S., 1961, naturalized, 1965. Research scientist Rumanian Acad. Sci., Bucharest, 1954-60; research asst. dept. soils sci. Ore. State U., Corvallis, 1961-66; research scientist Canadian Dept. Agr., Vancouver, B.C., 1966-67; with U.S. Geol. Survey, Phila. and Arlington, Va., 1967—, hydrologist chemist, 1967-68, project chief hydrology, 1968—. Cons. environmental field; mem. B.C. Com. Soil Testing and Fertility, 1966-67; mem. Soil Conf. FAO, 1966, Internat. Soil Sci. Conf., Bucharest, 1958. Mem. Greenbriar Civic Assn., Fairfax, Va., 1969—. Mem. Internat., Am. soil sci. socs., Canadian, Western soil socs., Am. Geophys. Union, Internat. Assn. Study Clays, Am. Soc. Agronomy, Clay Minerals Soc. (mem. program quality com. 1971), Sigma Xi, Phi Kappa Phi. Contbr. articles to profl. jours. Home 12801 Point Pleasant Dr Fairfax VA 22030

CARSTENSEN, ROGER NORWOOD, coll. pres.; b. Tilden, Nev., Apr. 1, 1920; s. Lorenz Thomas and Birdie Alwilda (Norwood) C.; B.Th., N.W. Christina Coll., 1940; A.B., U. Ore., 1943, M.A. cum laude, 1946; B.D., Phillips U., 1952; Ph.D. (So. Fund fellow), Vanderbilt U., 1960; m. Maretta Marie Murphy, June 7, 1942; children—Karel (Mrs. James Eastman), Karren (Mrs. Robert Norris), Roger L., Connie, Phillip, Deborah. Ordained minister Christian Ch., 1939; part-time minister, Scotts Mills, Ore., 1938-40, Junction City, Ore., 1940-46, Sisters, Ore., 1946-49, Ceres, Okla., 1949-52; instr. N.W. Christian Coll., Eugene, Ore., 1941-49, prof., 1943-49; asst., then asso. prof. Phillips U., Enid, Okla., 1949-60, prof., 1960-65; pres. Christian Coll. Ga., Athens, 1966—. Dir., Disciples preaching seminars, 1963—; author, producer Professor's Story Hour, Oklahoma City, 1963-65. Dir. secretariat Nat. Interfaith Coalition on Aging, 1972. Mem. Soc. Bibl. Lit., Soc. Sci. Study Religion, Am. Inst. Oriental Research, Ga. Gerontology Soc. (pres. 1972). Author: Job, Defense of Honor, 1963; The Book of Jonah, 1971. Contbr. to Interpreters One Volume Commentary on the Bible, 1972. Home: 67 Gail Dr Athens GA 30601 Office: 220 S Hull St Athens GA 30601

CARSWELL, ELBA WILSON, journalist; b. nr. Bonifay, Fla., Jan. 4, 1916; s. John Robert and Victoria (Judah) C.; A.B., La. Poly. Inst., 1946; m. Mabel Bagley, Apr. 5, 1947 (dec. Jan. 1953); children—Carol, David Clements; m. 2d, Catherine Powell, Apr. 4, 1958; 1 dau., Catherine Melody. Exec. sec. Santa Rosa County C. of C., also asso. editor The Milton (Fla.) Gazette, 1946; asst. dir. publicity, asst. prof. journalism La. Poly. Inst., Ruston, 1947-49; editor The Milton Gazette, 1949-53, Graceville News, Graceville, Fla., Washington County News, Chipley, Fla., 1953-61; staff writer Pensacola News Jour.; editor, co-founder The Tri-County Gazette, Jay, Fla., 1951-53; staff writer Pensacola News-Jour., Chipley, 1961—; pres. Central Office Supply and Pub. Co., Bonifay, Fla., 1963-71. Mem. N.W. Fla. Regional Housing Authority, Citizens' Tax Council; chmn. Washington County Rural Area Devel. Council, 1961-66; chmn. Fla. adv. com. Farmers Home Adminstrn.; mem. regional adv. com. Fla. Dept. Recreation and Parks, 1972—; adv. com. on pub. relations Fla. State Welfare Bd., 1960-71; chmn. Fla. Bd. Parks and Historic Memls., 1966-69; chmn. Washington County Hist. Commn., 1965-66; bd. dirs. Children's Home Soc. Fla. Mayor, Chipley, Fla. 1963-67; chmn. Washington County Democratic Com., 1958-62. Adv. bd. Washington-Holmes Area Vocational-Tech. Sch., Chipley, Fla.; founder Carswell Found., pres. 1972. Recipient Florida Forestry editorial award, 1956, 57, 58, Fla. State U. editorial award, 1958, Fla. Gov.'s Festival of Fla. Products award, weekly newspaper div., 1958; Fla. Press Assn. editorial oscar, 1959; Fla. Outdoor Writers award, 1960; Fla. Outstanding Conservationist award Soil Conservation Soc. Am.; Fla. Man of Yr. for Agr., Fla. Assn. Agrl. Agts., 1966, Gov.'s appreciation award outstanding contbns. to State of Fla., 1969. Served with AUS, 1942-45. Mem. Fla. Municipal Judges Assn., Washington County C. of C. (pres. 1961-62), Fla. Hist. Soc., Washington County League Municipalities (pres. 1967), Carswell Assn. (pres. 1970), V.F.W., Am. Legion, Alpha Lambda Tau, Sigma Tau Delta. Tau Kappa Epsilon. Democrat. Methodist. Mason, Kiwanian (Chipley pres. 1960). Author: Among These Hills, 1968; Holmes Valley, 1969; Tempestuous Triangle; also numerous hist. articles. Home: Dekle St at Forest Av Chipley FL 32428 Office: PO Box 584 Chipley FL 32428

CARSWELL, T.N., loans, investments, income tax service, tax cons.; b. Homerville, Ga., Oct. 22, 1887; s. Andrew J. and Martha (Smith) C.; grad. Ga. Normal Coll. and Bus. Inst., 1908; A.B. magna cum laude, Simmons Coll., 1915; m. Byrdie P. Townley, Aug. 1921; 1 dau., Peggy A. (Mrs. William Peacock, Jr.). Tchr. bus. adminstrn. and comml. law; bus. mgr. and registrar, Simmons Coll.; treas. Western Produce Co.; mgr. Abilene C. of C. and W. Tex. Fair; organizer and pres. mgr. Merchants Paper Co.; owner Carswell Agy. and Carswell Travel Service. Adv. bd. Tex. Centennial. Served U.S.N.R.F., World War I; maj. Tex. Def. Guard, organized, commanded 10th Battalion. Chmn. Taylor Co. Vol. Parole Bd. Trustee Hardin-Simmons U.; trustee, co-founder Hendrick Meml. Hosp. Mem. Am. Legion (former dept. vice comdr.), Nat. Assn. Tax Cons., Tex. Cotton Coop. Assn. (state adv. bd.; organizer 7th dist.), Am. Cotton Coop. Assn. (nat. adv. bd.). Democrat (former mem., Taylor County exec. com.). Baptist (deacon). Mason (K.T., Shriner). Clubs: Abilene Country (charter), Lions (past dep. dist. gov.; instituted crippled children's work, local club, pres.). Speaker on moral, social and patriotic subjects. Home: 1501 Ambler Av Abilene TX 79601 Office: 1334 Pine St PO Box 2178 Abilene TX 79604

CARTER, ALLEN HUMPHREYS, lawyer; b. Athens, Tenn., June 26, 1938; s. L.A. and Nancy Sue (Humphreys) C.; student U. Ga., 1956-57; B.S., U. Tenn., 1960, J.D., 1962; m. Valerie Foster, July 9, 1967; 1 son, Allen Foster. Admitted to Tenn. bar, 1962; mem. firm Carter, Ayres & Reid, Athens, 1962—. Dir. Citizens Nat. Bank. East Tenn. campaign mgr. Senator Howard Baker, 1972. Mem. Am., McMinn County (pres. 1971-72) bar assns., Bar Assn. Tenn., Tenn. Def. Lawyers Assn., Assn. Ins. Attys., Sigma Chi, Phi Delta Phi. Kiwanian. Home: 405 Madison St Athens TN 37303 Office: 10 Madison St Athens TN 37303

CARTER, ARLEY WAYNE, elec. engr.; b. Kaufman, Tex., Jan. 16, 1932; s. Arthur George and Ethel Mae (Lake) C.; B.S., So. Meth. U., 1959, M.S. (Collins Radio grad. fellow), 1961; m. Carol Ann Strother, July 1, 1955; children—Susan, Catherine, Jennifer. Engr., Collins Radio, Dallas, 1954-60; with Gen. Electric Co., 1961—, mgr. in space div., Houston, 1965-73, dir. computer services, region 4 edn. service center, 1973—. Instr. electronics Alvin (Tex.) Jr. Coll., 1969-73, industry adviser to computing dept., 1971—. Adviser Jr. Achievement, 1964. Bd. dirs. Imperial Estates Civic Club, Friendswood, 1968. Served with USAF, 1950-54. Recipient Apollo Achievement award NASA, 1972. Registered profl. engr., Tex. Mem. I.E.E.E., Nat., Tex. socs. profl. engrs. Home: 8131 Birch Glen Lane Houston TX 77070 Office: PO Box 863 Houston TX 77001

CARTER, BETTY WERLEIN (MRS. HODDING CARTER), journalist; b. New Orleans; d. Philip and Elizebeth (Thomas) Werlein; B.A., Newcomb Coll., 1931; m. Hodding Carter, Oct. 14, 1931; children—Hodding III, Philip Dutartre Carter. Newspaper reporter Daily Courier, Hammond, La., 1932-36, Delta Star, Greenville, Miss., 1936-38; reporter Delta Democrat-Times, 1938-40, 45-72, pub., 1972—; researcher O.W.I., 1942-45; freelance writer. Mem. So. dist. Marshall Scholarship Com., 1961-69; mem. corp. U.S. Com. for UNICEF. Named Woman of the Year, Beta Sigma Phi, 1947. Episcopalian. Author: (with husband) So Great a Good, A History of the Episcopal Church in Louisiana, 1805-1955, 1955, Doomed Road of Empire, 1962. Home: Feliciana Greenville MS 38701 Office: Box 1618 Greenville MS 38701

CARTER, BRUCE GILBERT, coll. pres.; b. Elgin, Tex., July 29, 1904; s. Jefferson Lee and Emma (Condron) C.; B.A., Okla. Bapt U., 1928, LL.D. (hon.), 1951; M.A., U. Okla., 1932, Ed.D., 1950; m. Mary Nola Funderburk, July 4, 1929; children—Robert Bruce, Marilyn (Mrs. Jerry Owen), John Carroll. Tchr. Wewoka (Okla.) High Sch., 1929-38; postmaster, Wewoka, 1938-39; adminstr. Nat. Youth Adminstrn., Okla., 1940-43; pres. Northeastern Okla. A. and M. Coll., Miami, 1943-69; spl. adviser to Gov. of Okla., 1971-72; pres. Okla. Coll. Liberal Arts at Chickasha, 1972—. Okla. chmn. March of Dimes, 1952-60, Mental Health Assn., 1961-65; chmn. Okla. Ednl. TV Authority, 1968-69; exec. dir. Higher Edn. Alumni Council, Okla., 1969-71. Bd. dirs. Bapt. Found. Okla., Okla. Bapt. U. Mem. Miami C. of C. (pres. 1953), Council N. Central Jr. Colls. (pres. 1968—). Baptist (mem. exec. com. conv.). Home: Okla Coll Liberal Arts Chicasha OK 73019

CARTER, CHARLES HERSCHEL, physician; b. Castleberry, Ala., June 18, 1917; s. Joel and Fay (Menchien) C.; B.A., U. Ala., 1938; M.D., U. Tenn., 1940; m. Mary Dickson, Oct. 9, 1942; children—Nancy, David. Intern John Gaston Hosp., Memphis, 1941; resident U. Tenn. Teaching Hosp., 1941-43; practice medicine specializing in pediatrics, Memphis, 1943-51; med. dir. Sunland Tng. Center, Gainesville, 1951-60; med. and research dir. Sunland Hosp., Orlando, Fla., 1960—. Mem. Gov.'s Adv. Com. Mental Retardation, 1961—. Bd. dirs. Luther Rice Sem., Jacksonville, Fla., Edgewood Boys' Ranch, Orlando, Fla., Kradie-Kare, Maitland, Fla. Recipient various awards for outstanding service to mentally retarded. Fellow Am. Acad. Mental Retardation; mem. Am. Acad. Gen. Practice Am. Assn. Mental Deficiency, Am. Pediatric Asnn., A.M.A., So. Med., Christian Med. Soc. Baptist. Editor: Medical Aspects of Mental Retardation, 1965. Author: Handbook of Mental Retardation Syndromes, 2d edit., 1970. Contbr. articles to publs. Address: Box 3513 Sunland Hosp Orlando FL 32802

CARTER, CHARLES HILL, JR., county ofcl.; b. Charles City, Va., Aug. 16, 1919; s. Charles Hill and Emily (Harrison) C.; B.S. in Gen. Agr., Va. Polytech. Inst., 1943; m. Helle M. Klingemann, Aug. 4, 1960; children—Charles Hill, Robert Randolph, Harriet Emily. Owner Shirley Plantation, Charles City, 1957—; bd. suprs. Charles City County, 1953—, chmn., 1960-72. Mem. Charles City Planning Commn., 1955-72; chmn. County Democratic Com., 1961—. Served with AUS, 1943, Episcopalian (sr. warden 1966, 69). Home: Shirley Plantation Box 57 Route 2 Charles City VA 23030

CARTER, CHARLES LANDON III, elec. engr.; b. St. Augustine, Fla., Aug. 24, 1946; s. Charles Landon and Hortense (Shaw) C.; B.S., U. Fla., 1969; postgrad. Rollins Coll., 1970—. Asso. engr. dynatronics-electronics div. Gen. Dynamics, Orlando, Fla., 1970-71; electronic design engr. Martin Marietta Corp., Orlando, Fla., 1971—. Mem. I.E.E.E., Fla. Engring. Soc., Eta Kappa Nu. Republican. Presbyn. (deacon 1971—). Home: 212 W Winter Park St Orlando FL 32804 Office: E Sandlake Rd Orlando FL 32805

CARTER, CHARLES MITCHELL, civil engr.; b. Knoxville, Tenn., Dec. 16, 1924; s. Charles Benton and Cordie (Broyles) C.; B.S. in Civil Engring., U. Tenn., 1950; m. Margaret Barton Marsh, Dec. 23, 1944; children—Jeffrey Lynn, Victoria Barton. With nuclear div. Union Carbide Corp., Oak Ridge Nat. Lab., Oak Ridge, 1950—, engring. planning supr., 1960-73, supt. civil, archtl. engrin. dept., 1973—. Pvt. practice civil engring., Knoxville, also Oak Ridge, 1960—. Dist. commr. Great Smoky Mountains council Boy Scouts Am., 1967-70. Served with USAAF, 1943-46. Registered profl. engr., Tenn. Mem. Pi Kappa Alpha. Methodist (mem. adminstrv. bd.). Home: 920 Corning Rd Knoxville TN 37919 Office: PO Box X Oak Ridge TN 37830

CARTER, FRANK, real estate devel. and marketing co. exec.; b. Atlanta, July 21, 1925; s. Frank and Mary (Stewart) C.; B.S., Washington and Lee U., 1949; m. Jane Munnerlyn, June 25, 1949; children—Frank, Benjamin Munnerlyn, Wilson Munnerlyn, Jane Stewart. Salesman, Draper-Owens Co., Atlanta, 1952-59; pres. Pope & Carter Co., Atlanta, 1960-71, Crow, Carter & Assos., Atlanta, 1971—; dir. Alpha Fund, Inc. Trustee, treas. Lovett Sch.; trustee United Appeal; past mem. bd. visitors Emory U. Mem. Atlanta Real Estate Bd. (past officer, dir.; Realtor of Year 1966), Atlanta C. of C. (pres. 1969), Washington and Lee U. Alumni Assn. (past pres. Atlanta chpt.). Presbyn. (chmn. bd. deacons 1971). Clubs: Piedmont Driving (past dir.), Commerce, Capital, City (Atlanta). Home: 3800 Northside Dr NW Atlanta GA 30305 Office: 1100 Spring St NW Atlanta GA 30309

CARTER, FREDERICK JEROME, educator; b. Vernon, N.Y., Dec. 16, 1929; s. Howard Lyman and Mary Olive (Bartell) C.; B.S., LeMoyne Coll., 1956; M.A., U. Detroit, 1958; postgrad. U. Tex., 1965—; m. Dawn Marie Hoffman, Jan. 21, 1961; children—Frederick Jerome, Michael, Catherine, Susan, William. Teaching asst. U. Detroit, 1956-58; faculty LeMoyne Coll., Syracuse, N.Y., 1958-63, prof. math. St. Mary's U., San Antonio, 1963—, chmn. dept. math., 1970—. Cons. City Planning Com., San Antonio, 1973—. Served with AUS, 1950-53; ETO. Recipient, NSF Faculty fellowship, 1968-69. Mem. Am. Math. Soc., Math. Assn. Am. Democrat. Roman Catholic (mem. adv. bd. 1970—, parish youth orgn. pres. 1971—). Home: 1022 Morey Peak Dr San Antonio TX 78213 Office: Dept Math St Mary's University 2700 Cincinati San Antonio TX 78284

CARTER, HARRY NELSON, univ. adminstr.; b. Haileyville, Okla., Mar. 7, 1912; s. Ed and Cora (Baldwin) C.; B.S., Northeastern Okla. State Coll., 1940; M.S., U. Colo., 1950; grad. study U. Tulsa, U. Colo.; m. Bonnie Jackson, Oct. 27, 1939. Tchr. pub. schs., Ark. and Okla., 1936-41; instr. math. Spartan Sch. Aeros., 1941-45; instr. math. U. Tulsa, 1945-46, asst. prof., 1946-53, asso. prof., 1953-61, prof. 1961—, asst. dean of engring., 1958-59, acting dean, 1959-60, men's counselor, 1960-62, dean of students, 1962-70, coordinator student services, 1970—. Mem. Am. Soc. Engring. Edn., Am. Math. Soc., Okla. Acad. Sci., N.Y. Acad. Scis., Math. Assn. of Am., Am. Assn. U. Profs., A.A.A.S., Nat. Assn. Student Personnel Adminstrs., Omicron Delta Kappa, Kappa Mu Epsilon, Phi Eta Sigma, Alpha Phi Omega, Lambda Chi Alpha. Methodist. Club: University (Tulsa). Contbr. math. jours. Home: 3739 S Fulton Av Tulsa OK 74135

CARTER, HUGH (SEVIER), sociol. cons., writer; b. San Antonio, Apr. 5, 1895; s. David W. and Cornelia (Keith) C.; A.B., Southwestern U., 1916; M.A., U. Minn., 1922; Ph.D., Columbia, 1927; m. Isabel Gordon, June 22, 1925; children—Eleanor Jean (Mrs. Charles W. Brome), Janet C. (Mrs. Frank Hannigan). Prin. high sch., Hearne, Tex., 1916-17; instr. sociology U. Pa., 1924-29, asst. prof., 1929-45; chief gen. research Immigration and Naturalization Service, U.S. Dept. Justice, 1945-52; chief marriage and divorce statistics Nat. Center Statistics, U.S. Dept. Health, Edn., Welfare, 1952-65; vis. prof. sociology Purdue U., 1965; adj. prof. sociology Am. U., 1966; sociol. cons. and writer, Washington, 1966—. Statistician Com. Cost Med. Care, 1929-30; research analyst U.S. Housing Authority, 1939-40; mem. Del Internat. Union for Study of Popul, Vienna, Austria, 1959, London, Eng., 1969; mem. Nat. Council on Family Relations, Internat. Sci. Commn. on Family. Served to 2d lt. U.S. Army, 1917-18. Recipient Stuart A. Rice award, 1970. Mem. Am. Sociol. Assn. (council 1953-56, com. on govt. statistics), A.A.A.S. Am. Statis. Assn., Population Assn. Am. (sec.-treas. 1953-56, v.p. 1958), D.C. Sociol. Soc. (pres. 1953). Club: Cosmos (Washington). Author: Social Theories of L. T. Hobhouse, 1927, 2d edit., 1968; (with Paul C. Glick) Marriage and Divorce: A Social and Economic Study, 1970. Contbr. articles to profl. jours. Address: 2039 New Hampshire Av NW Washington DC 20009

CARTER, JAMES EARL, JR., govt. of Ga.; b. Plains, Ga., Oct. 1, 1924; s. James Earl and Lillian (Gordy) C.; student Ga. Southwestern U., 1941-42, Ga. Inst. Tech., 1942-43; B.S., U.S. Naval Acad., 1947; postgrad. Union Coll., 1952; m. Rosalynn Smith, July 7, 1946; children—John William, James Earl III, Donnel Jeffrey, Amy Lynn. Peanut farmer, warehouseman, 1953—; gov. State of Ga. (Atlanta), 1971—. Mem. Ga. Senate, 1962-66. Chmn. nat. campaign com. Dem. Nat. Com., 1974. Served with U.S. Navy, 1947-53. Home: 1 Woodland Dr Plains GA 31780 Office: Governors Office State Capitol Atlanta GA 30334

CARTER, JAMES EDWARD, JR., dentist, assn. ofcl.; b. Augusta, Ga., July 1, 1906; s. James Edward and Emma (Barnett) C.; D.D.S., Howard U., 1930; postgrad. Haines Normal and Indsl. Inst., 1920-24; m. Marjorie Butler, Jan. 7, 1928; 1 son, James Edward III. Pvt. practice dentistry, Augusta, 1930—. Mem. Nat. Council YMCA, 1958-64, 67-69; chmn. 9th St. YMCA, Augusta, 1950-57; active United Coll. Fund, Cancer Dr., United Chest Fund, Boy Scouts Am. Del. Republican Nat. Conv., 1960. Bd. dirs. Augusta-Richmond County Library. Recipient Achievement award in pub. service Upsilon Sigma chpt. Omega Psi Phi, 1949; award of merit Georgia Dental Soc., 1961; 55 Year award Thankful Bapt. Ch., 1973. Fellow Am. Coll. Dentists; mem. Nat. (life; past pres.; mem. exec. bd. 1940-52), Am., Ga., (pres. 1940-41, 35-year service plaque) dental assns., Stoney-Med. and Dental Soc. (pres. 1961-63), Acad. Gen. Dentistry, John A. Andrew Clin. Soc. (pres. dental sect. 1947), Omega Psi Phi (past basilius Psi Omega chpt. 1936-37, treas. 7th dist. 1943—; recipient achievement award human relations Psi Omega chpt. 1963), Sigma Pi Phi. Republican. Baptist (chmn. bd. trustees 1937; deacon 1961—). Club: Frontiers (Augusta, Ga.). Home: 2347 Fitten St Augusta GA 30904 Office: 1141 12th St Augusta GA 30901

CARTER, JAMES JOHNSTON, lawyer; b. Samson, Ala., Apr. 13, 1913; s. Castilla L. and Mary Ann (Smith) C.; LL.B., Jones Law Sch., 1934, grad. law study, U. Mich., 1940, U. Va., 1941; m. Eva Jane Edwards, Sept. 6, 1947; children—Harold M., David E. (stepsons), James M., Kathy Jane. Admitted to Ala. bar, 1934; atty. Montgomery County Probate Ct., 1935-38; law clk., sec. U.S. Circuit Judge Leon McCord, Montgomery, Ala. and New Orleans, 1938-47; mem. firm Hill, Hill, Carter, Franco, Cole & Black, Montgomery, 1947—; apptd. spl. judge 15th Jud. Circuit Ala., 1949, 51, 55, 60; pres. Jones Law Sch. 1963-72. Served from pvt. to 1st lt. AUS, 1943-46; spl. agt. criminal investigation div. S.W. Pacific, and pros. officer legal sect. H.Q. Supreme Comdr. for Allied Powers, Tokyo, Japan, 1945-46. Recipient Distinguished Service award U.S. Jr. C. of C. 1937. Mem. (hon.) Circuit Conf. U.S. Circuit and Dist. Judges, 5th Circuit. Fellow Am. Bar Found.; mem. Jud. Conf. Ala., Ala. State Bar (bd. bar examiners 1969—, pres. 1962-63), Am., Fed., Montgomery County (pres. 1957), Tenn. (hon.) bar assns., Ala. Law Inst. (mem. council 1970-72), Fedn. Ins. Counsel, Sigma Delta Kappa. Presbyn. (moderator E. Ala. Presbytery 1965). Clubs: Country, Beauvoir. Home: 2602 Wildwood Dr Montgomery AL 36111 Office: Hill Bldg PO Box 116 Montgomery AL 36101

CARTER, JOHN BOYD, JR., investment banker, oil operator; b. Ft. Worth, Oct. 19, 1924; s. John Boyd and Enlie (Corder) C.; student Kemper Mil. Sch., 1941-43, U. Tex., 1943-46, Babson Inst., 1946-47; m. Susie Ann Browne, Feb. 9, 1946 (div. Dec. 1968); children—Catherine Browne, John Mason; m. 2d, Winifred Trimble Runnells, Feb. 23, 1970. Mortgage loan supr. Am. General Investment Corp., 1947; ind. oil operator, 1948-49; sec., treas. Tex. Fund, Inc., 1949-52, mem. investment adv. bd., 1951—; pres. Tex. Fund Research and Mgmt. Assos., 1950-52; ind. oil operator and financial cons., 1952-58; southwestern rep. Lehman Bros., 1959-65, gen. partner, 1965—, mng. dir., 1970—; chmn. exec. com. Capital Nat. Bank; dir. Marine Service Corp.; dir. Am. Marine Corp., Hill and Hill Truck Lines, Inc., Austral Oil Co., Inc., Sea Drilling Corp. Trustee Houston Mus. Fine Arts, Baylor Coll. Medicine; bd. dirs. Houston

Symphony Soc. Mem. Ind. Petroleum Assn. Am., Tex. Ind. Producers and Royalty Owners Assn., Sigma Alpha Epsilon. Clubs: Bayou, Houston Country, St. Charles Hunting, Coronado; River (N.Y.C.). Home: 3682 Willowick Dr Houston TX 77019 Office: 1 Allen Center Houston TX 77002

CARTER, JOSEPH EMERSON, engring. firm exec.; b. Birmingham, Ala., Oct. 28, 1920; s. Joseph Emerson and Mildred (Rumph) C.; B.Engring. with honors, Johns Hopkins U., 1950; student U. Ala., 1945, postgrad., 1956, 57; m. Beth Miller, Nov. 24, 1945; children—Joseph Emerson, Beth Ann, Mary Ellen. Structural engr. Harbert Constrn. Corp., Birmingham, 1957-58; with Rust Engring. Co., Birmingham, 1954-57, 58—, v.p., chief engr., 1968-73, sr. v.p. environmental, 1973—. Served to capt. USAAF, 1941-45, USAF, 1951-53. Decorated Silver Star, Air medal with two oak leaf clusters. Registered profl. engr., Ala., Okla., Fla., Cal., Wash., Conn. Mem. Am. Soc. C.E., Nat. Soc. Profl. Engrs., Am. Inst. Chem. Engrs., T.A.P.P.I. Home: 3501 Westbury Pl Birmingham AL 35223 Office: PO Box 101 Birmingham AL 35202

CARTER, LAMORE JOSEPH, ednl. adminstr.; b. Carthage, Tex., Apr. 18, 1925; s. Peter and Nancy (Fite) C.; student Wiley Coll., 1946-47; A.B., Fisk U. 1950; M.S., U. Wis., 1952; Ph.D., State U. Ia., 1958; postgrad. U. Chgo., summer 1954, U. Tex., summer 1966, Columbia, summer 1967, Emory U. summer 1970; m. Lena Mae Jones, Aug. 18, 1957; children—Greta Lisa, Kris-Lana. Tchr. Union High Sch., Gallatin, Tenn., 1950-51; asso. prof. edn. and psychology, dir. spl. edn. center Grambling Coll. (La.), 1958-61, asso. dean of coll., 1971—, prof. edn. and psychology, dir. spl. edn. center, 1961-66, adminstr. Instl. Research, 1966-69; dean of faculties Tex. So. U., Houston, 1970-71; research asst. State U. Ia., 1956-58; licensed to practice psychology La. 1965—. Dir. Grambling Motel Internat. Cons. Social Security Adminstrn. Bd. Hearings and Appeals, 1965—, U.S. Office Edn., 1967—, Peace Corps, 1970-72, Commn. Colls., So. Assn. Colls. and Schs., 1970—. Served with AUS, 1943-46. Decorated Bronze Service Star medal; Distinguished prof. psychology Morehouse Coll., Atlanta, 1970; Nat. Edn. Research fellow U.S. Office Edn., 1969-70. Diplomate Am. Bd. Profl. Psychology. Mem. Am. Assn. U. Profs. (chpt. pres. 1960-63), Am., Southwestern, La. psychol. assns., Nat. Council Univ. Research Adminstrs., Assn. for Instl. Research, Am. Ednl. Research Assn., Assn. for Higher Edn., Nat. Soc. for Study Edn., Am. Assn. on Mental Deficiency, N.Y. Acad. Sci., La. Assn. Mental Health, N.E.A., Council Exceptional Children, Internat. Platform Assn., Phi Beta Sigma, Phi Delta Kappa. Democrat. Methodist. Mason (32 deg.). Contbr. articles to profl. jours., monographs, books. Home: 110 Richmond Dr Grambling LA 71245

CARTER, LEVONNE RAILEY, dentist; b. Tompkinsville, Ky., May 19, 1925; s. Earl Railey and Ovy Gladys (Pickerell) C.; B.S., Western Ky. State U., 1951; D.M.D., U. Louisville 1955; m. Hazel Idell Miller, Feb. 7, 1947; children—Vondell, Barry. Intern, Fla. State Hosp., 1955-56; gen. practice dentistry, Ft. Lauderdale, Fla., 1956—. Mem. exec. council Henry, Glades and Broward County Tb Assn., 1970—, trustee, 1971—. Served with USNR, 1943-46. Decorated Purple Heart. Mem. Ft. Lauderdale C. of C., Am., Fla., Atlantic Coast, Broward County (pres. 1973-74) dental assns. Baptist (deacon). Kiwanian. Club: Metropolitan Dinner (Ft. Lauderdale). Home: 181 Nurmi Dr Fort Lauderdale FL 33301 Office: 305 S Andrews Av Fort Lauderdale FL 33301

CARTER, NATHANIEL ONIS, judge; b. Vidalia, Ga., Feb. 15, 1926; s. Nathaniel Onis and Juel Judith (Darby) C.; student Princeton, 1945, Howard Coll., 1945, U. S.C., 1945-48; LL.B., Mercer U., 1949; m. Jeanne Marie Cone, Dec. 22, 1946; children—Gale (Mrs. Charles Goldenberg), Brenda J., Natalie Michelle. Admitted to Ga. bar, 1949, Middle Jud. bar, 1949; practice law, Vidalia, 1949-72; judge Recorder's Ct., City of Vidalia 1951-72. Dir. 1st Nat. Bank & Trust Co., Vidalia, United Communications, Inc., Vidalia; pres., owner Beverage Discount, Inc., Vidalia, 1970—. Served with USNR, 1943-46; PTO. Elk, Moose. Club: Vidalia Country. Died July 1, 1972. Home: 101 Darby Circle Vidalia GA 30474

CARTER, OTHA BURNETTE, supt. schs.; b. Gordo, Ala., Nov. 28, 1907; s. Earnest Atlas and Cora Bell (Free) C.; B.S., Auburn U., 1929; M.A., U. Ala., 1941; m. Sara Flewellen, Aug. 23, 1936; children—Sarah S. (Mrs. Carl Parrish), Otha Burnette, Louise F., Mary E. Coach, Louisville High Sch., 1929-34; tchr., Eufaula (Ala.) High Sch., 1934-41, prin., 1941-44, supt., 1944—. Mem. State Retirement Bd. Mem. Ala. Edn. Assn. (pres. 1965-66), Pi Kappa Phi. Baptist (chmn. bd. deacons 1935-71). Kiwanian. Club: Eufaula Country. Home: 343 N Randolph Av Eufaula AL 36027 Office: PO Box 270 Eufaula AL 36027

CARTER, ROBERT ALLEN, bakery exec.; b. Nashville, Feb. 9, 1931; s. William Franklin and Bessie (Spears) C.; student bus. mgmt. U. Tex., Austin, 1968; m. Juanita Joyce Smith, Nov. 26, 1952; children—Robert Allen, Ricky Alan. Mgr., Hill Grocery, Nashville, 1950-53; with Colonial Baking Co., various locations, 1953—, v.p., Memphis, 1968-69, pres., chmn. bd., Gulfport, Miss., 1969—; supr. Rainbo Baking Co., Beaumont, Tex., 1958; sales service Campbell Taggart Bakeries, Dallas, 1963-68; pres. R & G Devel. Corp., Ocean Springs, Miss., 1972—. Bd. dirs. Retarded Children Assn., Gulfport. Mem. exec. council to pres. Miss. Gov.'s Staff, 1973—. Served with AUS, 1952. Mem. So. Bakers Assn. (gov.), Gulfport C. of C. (dir.). Methodist. Rotarian. Club: Les Cavaliers (Gulfport). Home: 101 LaBranche St Ocean Springs MS 39564 Office: 1200 Pass Rd Gulfport MS 39530

CARTER, ROBERT LEON, physician; b. Meansville, Ga., Aug. 14, 1895; s. Robert Reid and Hattie Julia (Aldredge) C.; student U. Ga., 1912-13; M.D., Emory U., 1917; postgrad. U. Paris, 1919; m. Christine Lowe, Dec. 17, 1938; children—Evangeline (Mrs. Raymond C. Carter), Robert C. Intern, Riverside Hosp., N.Y.C., 1917; resident surgeon Ga. Bapt. Hosp., 1919-20; gen. practice medicine, Thomaston, Ga., 1920-67; mem. staff Upson County Hosp., Thomaston. Served with M.C., AUS, 1917-19. Mem. A.M.A., Ga. Med. Assn., Upson Med. Soc., Upson Hist. Soc. (pres. 1969-72), Thomaston C. of C. Democrat. Methodist. Kiwanian, Mason. Author weekly column Thomaston Times, 1968—. Home: 700 Andrews Dr Thomaston GA 30286

CARTER, ROBERT LEON, foundry exec.; b. Memphis, June 26, 1926; s. Harry Edward and Dollie Inez (Shearon) C.; B.S., Memphis State U., 1957; m. Dorothy Adrion, Feb. 16, 1966. Staff accountant Seidman & Seidman, C.P.A.'s, Memphis, 1957-62; controller Weis Butane Gas Cos., West Memphis, Ark., 1962-66; controller Kast Metals Corp., and Hica Corp., Shreveport, La., 1966-69, sec.-treas., 1969—, dir., 1969—. Active Jr. Achievement. Trustee, Mc Chesney, Miller, Dimond Trusts, Shreveport, La. Served with USAF, 1950-54. Mem. Am. Inst. C.P.A.'s, Tenn., Memphis socs. C.P.A.'s, Steel Founder Soc., Nat. Assn. Accountants, Shreveport C. of C., Delta Sigma Pi. Baptist. Mason. Clubs: East Ridge Country, Metropolitan Dinner, Little Theater (Shreveport). Home: 9523 Hollyoak St Shreveport LA 71108 Office: PO Box 6611M Shreveport LA 71106

CARTER, ROBERT PAGE, telephone co. engring. mgr.; b. Orange, N.J., June 12, 1932; s. Franklin Ives and Ellen Welles (Page) C.; B.S., Swarthmore Coll., 1954; postgrad. U. Colo., 1962-63; m. Virginia Perkins, Aug. 13, 1955; children—Robert Page, Michael Charles, Elizabeth Jane. With Am. Tel. & Tel. Co., 1954—, engring. mgr. long lines dept., Washington, 1969—. Pres. P.T.A., 1970-71; committeeman Boy Scouts Am., 1971-72, asst. scoutmaster, 1972-74. Served with Signal Corps, AUS, 1954-56. Mem. I.E.E.E. Home: 9703 Parkwood Dr Bethesda MD 20014 Office: 2000 L St NW Washington DC 20036

CARTER, ROLAND WHITE, mineral co. exec.; b. South Bend, Ind., Nov. 22, 1919; s. Roy Gee and Hazel (White) C.; student Purdue U. 1937-38; B.S. with distinction, U. Mich., 1941, postgrad., 1940-41; m. Helen Sue Smith, Feb. 20, 1954; 1 dau., Suzy Jean; children (by previous marriage)—Thomas M., William M., Stephen W. Party chief Seismograph Service Corp., Tulsa, 1941-48; geophysicist Union Producing Co., Shreveport, 1948-63, mgr. producing property acquisition, 1965-68; corporate planning asso. United Gas Corp., Shreveport, 1963-65; vice pres. exploration Freeport Oil Co. div. Freeport Minerals Co., New Orleans, 1968—. Mem. Soc. Exploration Geophysicists (Silver certificate 1969), Am. Assn. Petroleum Geologists, Soc. Petroleum Engrs., Phi Beta Kappa, Sigma Xi. Home: 6710 Canal Blvd New Orleans LA 70124 Office: PO Box 52349 New Orleans LA 70150

CARTER, ROY R., JR., banker; b. Fayetteville, Tenn., Nov. 13, 1915; s. Roy R. and Fannie Neil (Lamb) C.; student Marion County Bus. Sch., 1936; m. Marian Chase Woodfin, Nov. 24, 1937; children—Margaret (Mrs. C. Kenneth Adams), Katherine (Mrs. Rod P. Whittington). With First Nat. Bank, South Pittsburg, Tenn., 1936—, pres., 1963—; dir. B.C.W. Realty Co.; sr. partner Carter & Wilson Ins. Agy.; dir. Hamilton Bancshares, Inc., Chattanooga. Finance commr. South Pittsburg, 1956-57; chmn. South Pittsburg Planning Commn., 1964-68. Bd. dirs. Marion County Tb Assn.; trustee South Pittsburg Meml. Hosp., Wonder Cave. Mem. C. of C. (pres. 1966-67). Democrat. Methodist (trustee). Clubs: Sequatchie Valley Golf and Country. Lion. Editorial bd. Golfdom, 1968-69. Home: 701 Magnolia Ave South Pittsburg TN 37380 Office: 406 Cedar Av South Pittsburg TN 37380

CARTER, SELDEN BOOKER, SR., bank marketing exec.; b. Balt., Aug. 1, 1928; s. Minor Lee and Helen (Booker) C.; degree in liberal arts St. Albans Prep. Sch., 1949; B.A., Washington and Lee U., 1954; m. Shirley Abbott, Aug. 15, 1953; children—Melanie Sue, Selden Booker. Bus. trainee Gen. Electric Co., Pittsfield, Mass., 1954-56; advt. asst. The Nestle Co., Inc., White Plains, N.Y., 1956-59; account exec. Lambert & Feasley, Inc., N.Y.C., 1959-60; asst. account supr. Morse Internat., Inc., N.Y.C., 1960-63; new products dir. Vick Chem. Co., Inc., N.Y.C., 1963-65; v.p., mgmt. supr. Grey Advt., Inc., N.Y.C., 1965-70; dir. communications S.E. Banking Corp., Miami, Fla., 1970—. Coach football, baseball Hartsdale (N.Y.) Dad's Club, 1958-59. Served with USMC, 1946-48. Mem. Sigma Delta Chi, Pi Kappa Alpha. Republican. Episcopalian. Clubs: Jockey (Miami); Ponte Vedra (Fla.); Oakwood Country (Lynchburg, Va.). Home: 12820 SW 67th Av Miami FL 33156 Office: Southeast Banking Corp Miami FL 33131

CARTER, THOMAS D., sch. adminstr.; b. Oglesby, Tex., Sept. 7, 1931; s. O. Dan and Margrette (Baker) C.; student Tex. A. and I. Coll., 1948-49, Sam Houston State Coll., 1949-51, Tenn. Poly. Inst., 1951; B.A., Baylor U., 1956; M. Ed., U. Tex. at Austin, 1959, Ph.D., 1966; m. Jo Ann Respess, Aug. 31, 1952; children—Tommy Dan, Sheree. Tchr. English David Crockett High Sch., Conroe, Tex., 1956-58; intern prin. William B. Travis High Sch., Austin, 1959; tchr. English Brazosport High Sch., Freeport, Tex., 1959-60; supr., counselor pub. schs., Gonzales County, Tex., 1960-61; curriculum coordinator, Beeville, Tex., 1961-64; intern supt. schs., League City, Tex., 1965; teaching asst. U. Tex. at Austin, 1965-66; asst. supt. Alamo Heights Ind. Sch. Dist., San Antonio, 1966-71; dep. supt. research and devel. Goose Creek Consol. Sch. Dist., Baytown, Tex., 1971-72; supt. Eanes Ind. Sch. Dist., Austin, Tex., 1972—; designer ednl. research studies, individualized instrn. program for schs., other ednl. innovations. Dir. Bee County (Tex.) Assn. Retarded Children, 1961-63; v.p. Council Exceptional Children, Corpus Christi, 1962-63; mem. planning com. Bee County Jr. Coll., 1963. Served with USAF, 1951-54. Mem. N.E.A. (membership chmn. 1962-63), Tex. Elementary Prins. and Suprs. Assn. (membership chmn. 1961-63), Tex. Assn. Instructional Suprs., So. Assn. Colls. and Schs. (chmn. program studies 1962-71), Phi Delta Kappa. Methodist (mem. bd.). Kiwanian (sec. 1961-63), Rotarian (chmn. crippled children com. 1968-69). Contbr. articles to profl. jours. Home: 101-C Blue Ridge Terrace Austin TX 78746

CARTER, TIM LEE, physician, congressman; b. Tompkinsville, Ky., Sept. 2, 1910; s. James Clark and Idru (Tucker) C.; A.B., Western Ky. U., 1934; M.D., U. Tenn., 1937; m. Kathleen Bradshaw, Nov. 13, 1931; 1 son, Billy Starr. Gen. practice medicine, Tompkinsville, 1937—; mem. 89th to 93d Congress, 5th Ky. Dist., mem. interstate and fgn. commerce com. Dir. Deposit Bank of Monroe County, Tompkinsville. Mem. staff Monroe County War Meml. Hosp. Served to capt., inf. AUS, World War II. Decorated Combat Med. Badge, Bronze Star. Mem. Am., Ky. med. assns., Am., Ky. acads. gen. practice, Am. Legion, V.F.W., Alpha Omega Alpha. Republican. Mason (32 deg., Shriner). Home: 701 N Main St Tompkinsville KY 42167 Office: Rayburn Office Bldg Washington DC 20515

CARTER, WATT, state ofcl.; b. Sarepta, Miss., Jan. 25, 1911; s. John Wesley and Luna (Phillips) C.; B.S., Miss State U., 1938; m. Katie Will Edmondson, Aug. 13, 1939; children—Joe Jon, Phillip Conner. Tchr., Sarepta, 1934, prin., tchr., 1935-36; agr. tchr. Montpelier (Miss.) High Sch., 1938; tchr. agr. Vardaman (Miss.) High Sch., 1939-58, prin., 1959-63; dir. vocational tng. Miss. State Penitentiary, 1964-67; Miss. land commr., Jackson, 1968—. Mason. Home: 109 Old Canton Hill Dr Jackson MS 39211 Office: State Office Bldg Jackson MS 39205

CARTER, WILLIAM ALFRED, educator; b. Ada, Okla., Sept. 16, 1935; s. George F. and Flora E. (Summers) C.; B.S., E. Central State Coll., 1957; M.S., Okla. State U., 1960, Ph.D., 1965. Sci. tchr. Union High Sch., Broken Arrow, Okla., 1957-59; teaching asst. Dept. Zoology, Okla. State U., Stillwater, 1960-63; instr. biology Northwestern State Coll., Alva, Okla., 1963-64; asst. prof. East Central State Coll., Ada, Okla., 1964-66, asso. prof., 1966-71, prof. biology, 1971—. Research asso. ornithology U. Okla., Stovall Museum, Norman, 1971—. Mem. animal research council Oklahoma City Zoo, 1972. Fellow Okla. Acad. Sci. (pres. 1972); mem. Nat. Audubon Soc., Am. Ornithologists Union, Am. Soc. Ichtyologists and Herpetologists, Cornell Lab. Ornithology, Cooper, Wilson ornithol. socs., Ecol. Soc. Am., Herpetologists League, Inland, Northeastern bird banding assns., Okla. Ornithol. Soc. (pres. 1970-71), Southwestern Assn. Naturalists, Soc. for Study Amphibians and Reptiles, Phi Sigma. Home: Route 4 Box 468 Ada OK 74820

CARTER, WILLIAM EARL, coll. adminstr.; b. Dayton, O., Apr. 29, 1927; s. Homer Earl and Mabel (Martin) C.; B.A., Muskingum Coll., 1949; S.T.B., Boston U., 1954; M.A., Columbia, 1958, Ph.D., 1963; m. Bertha Garcia Roca, Dec. 26, 1954; children—Olivia D., Vivian L., Emily J. Nat. Inst. Mental Health research fellow, Bolivia, 1960-61; instr. Nat. Sch. Social Work, La Paz, Bolivia, 1961-62; research asso. Bur. Applied Social Research, Columbia, 1962-63; asso. prof. anthropology U. Wash., Seattle, 1966; asso. prof. anthropology U. Fla., Gainesville, 1966-67, prof., dir. Center for Latin Am. Studies, 1968—. Chief investigator Nat. Inst. Mental Health grant for study chronic cannabis use, Costa Rica, 1973—. Cons. U.S. Office Edn., 1969-70, Fgn. Area Fellowship Program, 1971. Pres., Southeastern Conf. on Latin Am. Studies, Gainesville, 1970; mem. steering com. Consortium on Latin Am. Studies Programs, 1973—; chmn. Southeastern Sr. Fulbright-Hays Scholars Conf., Gainesville, 1971. Recipient Fulbright-Hays Research award, 1965; NSF Research award, 1968. Fellow Am. Anthrop. Assn.; mem. Soc. for Applied Anthropology, So. Anthrop. Soc. Home: 1011 NW 21st Gainesville FL 32603

CARTER, WILLIAM HODDING, III, newspaper editor; b. New Orleans, Apr. 7, 1935; s. William Hodding and Betty Brunhilde (Werlein) C.; student Phillips Exeter Acad., 1949-51; B.A. summa cum laude, Princeton, 1957; postgrad. (Nieman fellow) Harvard U., 1965-66; m. Margaret Ainsworth Wolfe, June 21, 1957; children—Catherine Ainsworth, Elizebeth Fearn, William Hodding IV, Margaret Lorraine. Reporter, Delta Democrat-Times, Greenville, Miss., 1959-62, mng. editor, 1962-65, editor, asso. pub., 1965—; dir. Civic Communications Corp., Jackson, Miss. Juror, Pulitzer Prize Awards Com., 1971, 72, 74. Mem. exec. com. So. Regional Council. Mem. rules reform commn. Nat. Democratic Com., 1969-72; co-chmn. Young Dems. of Miss., 1965-68; co-chmn. Loyalist Dems. delegation Nat. Dem. Conv., 1968. Bd. dirs. Mary Holmes Coll., Miss. Action for Progress, 1966-72, Inst. of Politics, New Orleans, Robert F. Kennedy Meml., So. Poverty Law Center; trustee 20th Century Fund, N.Y.C. Served to 1st lt. USMCR, 1957-59. Recipient Urban Service award Office Econ. Opportunity, 1967, Appley Youth Leadership award Am. Mgmt. Assn., 1968, Silver Em award U. Miss., 1968. Mem. Miss. Press Assn., Miss. Council on Human Relations (R.F. Kennedy award), Am. Council Young Polit. Leaders (dir.), Atlantic Assn. Young Polit. Leaders (exec. com.), Atlantic Council (dir.), Am. Soc. Newspaper Editors, Com. for Pub. Justice. L.Q.C. Lamar Soc. (dir.), Sigma Delta Chi (award for editorial writing 1961). Episcopalian. Author: The South Strikes Back, 1959; contbr. to We Dissent, 1963, Race and the News Media, 1967. Home: 1203 Kirk Circle Greenville MS 38701 Office: Delta Democrat-Times North Broadway Extended Greenville MS 38701

CARTWRIGHT, CHARLES NELSON, lawyer; b. Ft. Worth, July 22, 1933; s. Charles L. and Mildred (Epperson) C.; student, U. Houston, 1952; B.A., U. Tex., 1956, J.D., 1960; m. Suzanne Oberwetter, Sept. 5, 1956; 1 son, Charles Rea. Admitted to Tex. bar, 1960; asst. city atty., City of Corpus Christi, Tex., 1960-63; asso. Utter & Chase, Corpus Christi, Tex., 1964-67, partner, 1967-73; mem. firm Howard, McDowell, Bennett & Cartwright, Corpus Christi, 1973—. Instr. real estate law Del Mar Coll., Corpus Christi, 1965-68, guest lectr., 1968-70. Mem. City Zoning and Planning Commn., Corpus Christi, Tex., 1970—, chmn., 1973—. Bd. dirs. Municipal Legal Studies Center, Southwestern Legal Found., Dallas, 1973—. Served to 2d lt. AUS, 1957. Mem. Am., Nueces County (v.p. 1973—) bar assns., State Bar Tex., Nueces County Trial Lawyers Assn. (dir. 1970-71). Mason. Home: 934 Barracuda Corpus Christi TX 78411 Office: United Savings Bldg Corpus Christi TX 78411

CARUBBI, ANGELO JOSEPH, JR., lawyer; b. Galveston, Tex., Jan. 1, 1932; s. Angelo Joseph and Madeline (La Barbera) C.; Ph.B. in Commerce, U. Notre Dame, 1952 LL.B., U. Tex., 1968 children—Kathy, Richard, Thomas, Kelly, Amy. Admitted to Tex. bar, 1957; asso. Gordon, Gordon & Buzzard, Pampa, 1958-60; sr. partner Carubbi, Warner & Jeter, Pampa, 1960-66; corp. ct. judge City of Pampa, 1960-62; exec. asst. to Atty. Gen. of Tex., 1966-68; asso. Dyche, Wheat, Thornton & Wright, Houston, 1969-70; partner Dyche, Wright, Sullivan, Bailey & King, 1971—. Bd. dirs. Gonzales Warm Springs Found., Gonzales, Tex., Tex. Jr. C. of C. Found., Grand Prairie Tex. Served with AUS, 1962-64. Recipient Distinguished Service award Pampa Jr. C. of C., 1966, named Outstanding Young Man in Community, 1966. Mem. Houston Bar Assn., State Bar of Tex., Tex. Jr. C. of C. (pres. 1965-66). U.S. Jr. C. of C. (legal counsel 1967-68), Phi Alpha Delta, Phi Kappa Theta. K.C. Home: 1310 Kipling St Houston TX 77006 Office: Mellie Esperson Bldg Houston TX 77002

CARUSO, VINCENT PASCAL, govt. ofcl.; b. New Orleans, Sept. 25, 1929; s. Pascal and Margaret (Caruso) C.; B.S. in Indsl. Engring., U. Ala., 1951; m. Johanna C. Castiglia, June 6, 1950; children—Michael, Margaret, Joseph, Lisa, Gerald. Plant indsl. engr. Standard Casket Mfg. Co., 1951-53, Gen. Steel Tank Co., 1953-55 (both Birmingham, Ala.); sr. indsl. engr Kaiser Aluminum Co., Baton Rouge and Ravenswood, W.Va., 1955-59; asst. chief indsl. engr. Reynolds Metal Co., Sheffield, Ala., 1959-60; sect. chief structural planning Marshall Space Flight Center, NASA, Huntsville, Ala., 1960-66, br. chief engring. planning br., 1966-69, dep. div. chief mfg. research and tech. div., 1969—; cons. indsl. engring. Baton Rouge Gen. Hosp., 1957—; cons. systems Ravenswood Sch. System, 1958. Vice pres. Diocese Birmingham Cath. Bd. Edn., 1971-73; pres. Grissom High Sch. P.T.A., 1972-73; mem. study commn. Huntsville Pub. Sch., 1970—; coach Huntsville Little League, 1968—, pres., 1972. Recipient several awards NASA. Registered profl. engr., Ala. Mem. Am. Assn. Indsl. Engrs. (award Baton Rouge chpt. 1957). Roman Catholic (parish council 1972-73). Lion, Toastmaster, K.C. Home: 6000 Chadwell Rd Huntsville AL 35802 Office: Marshall Space Flight Center Huntsville AL 35812

CARVER, JOHN GENE, cons. engr.; b. Gorman, Tex., Oct. 12, 1936; s. Arlie Madison and Billy (Hall) C.; B.S. in Civil Engring., So. Methodist U., 1960; m. Brenda Genell Dyer, Dec. 7, 1963; children—Renee Genell, John Madison. Asst. engr. M-K-T R.R., Denison, Tex., 1960-65; chief engr. firm Davis & Assos., Dallas, also Longview, Tex., 1965-69; operations mgr. Engring. Assos., Plano, Tex., 1969-70; owner, prin. engr. firm John G. Carver, Dallas, 1970—. Mem. bldg. fund com. Longview chpt. A.R.C., 1968. Registered profl. engr., Tex., Okla., La., Colo. Mem. Am. Inst. Steel Constrn., Tex. Soc. Profl. Engrs., Kappa Mu Epsilon, Kappa Sigma Alumni Assn. Baptist. Kiwanian, Elk. Home: 3012 Rockbrook St Plano TX 75074 Office: 10710 Shiloh Rd Dallas TX 75228

CARWILE, ATWOOD SMITH, banker; b. Gladys, Va., Sept. 27, 1925; s. Walter Ray and Mary Lucile (Smith) C.; grad. high sch.; m. Josephine Elaine Church, Apr. 5, 1947; children—Timothy C., William A. With Campbell County Bank, Rustburg, Va., 1946-63, asst. cashier, 1948-54, cashier, 1954-60, v.p., 1960-63; v.p. Fidelity Nat. Bank, Lynchburg, Va., 1963-70, sr. v.p., 1970-73; sr. v.p. Fidelity-Am. Bankshares, 1974—. Mem. Campbell County Redistricting Commn., 1967. Mem. Campbell County Sch. Bd., 1968-73. Served with USNR, 1944-46. Methodist (chmn. bd. 1967-69). Mason. Clubs: Exchange, Falling River Country (Appomattox, Va.). Home: Route 1 Box 61 Rustburg VA 24588 Office: 901 Main St Lynchburg VA 24505

CARY, WILLIAM EUGENE, civil engr.; b. Birmingham, Ala., Jan. 3, 1930; s. Walter E. and Lucille (Ozment) C.; B.S., La. State U., 1952; m. Gusta Ruth Vaughn, Aug. 3, 1955; children—William Vaughn,

Sally Kaye. Jr. engr. Am. Bridge div. U.S. Steel Co., 1952-56; sr. design engr. Rust Engring. Co., 1957-66; chief structural engr. Continental Engring. Ltd., 1966-67; sales engr. So. Prestressed Concrete Co., 1969-73; pres. William E. Cary, Inc., cons. engrs., 1973— (all Birmingham). Fellow Am. Soc. C.E.; mem. Tau Beta Pi, Phi Kappa Phi. Republican. Methodist. Home: 504 Lance Rd Birmingham AL 35206 Office: 2625 19th St S Birmingham AL 35209

CASA, VICTORIO, soccer player; b., 1944; married; 2 children. Profl. soccer player since age 16; mem. San Lorenzo (Argentina) soccer team in 1965 when lost right arm in freak shooting, returned to playing 22 days later; mem. Washington Whips club, 1968, Washington Darts, 1971—. Address: care Washington Darts 4832 MacArthur Blvd NW Washington DC 20007

CASADA, JAMES HUBERT, agrl. engr.; b. Pulaski, Ky., Sept. 24, 1931; s. Lewis Walter and Laura Gertrude (Vaught) C.; B.S., U. Ky., 1960, M.S., 1966; m. Emma Jean Simpson, Sept. 18, 1955; children—Rhonda Sue, Mark Edwin, Alan Thomas. Instr., U. Ky., Lexington, 1960-61, research specialist, 1967—; agrl. research engr. tobacco investigations Agrl. Research Service, Dept. Agr., Lexington, 1961-67. Served with USAF, 1953-57. Registered profl. engr., Ky. Mem. Am. Soc. Agrl. Engrs., Ky. Sect. Agrl. Engrs., Sigma Xi, Alpha Zeta. Baptist (deacon). Home: 3473 Dixiana Dr Lexington KY 40502

CASANOVA, RICHARD LOUIS, museum ofcl.; b. Buenos Aires, Argentina, Oct. 4, 1918; s. John and Martha Lillian (Franklin) C.; B.S., Columbia U., 1941; D.Sc., U. Paris, 1945; m. Mary Elizabeth Carson, Dec. 30, 1944; children—Patricia (Mrs. Robert Hinkle), Richard Louis, John F., Charles C. Came to U.S., 1927, naturalized, 1943. With Ward's Natural Sci. Establishment, Rochester, N.Y., 1947-49; dir. Paleontological Research Lab., Statesville, N.C., 1950-61; exec. scientist Nature Museum York County, Rock Hill, S.C., 1973—. Dir. world mollusca census project UNESCO, Charlotte, N.C., 1973; cons. Charlotte (N.C.) Nature Museum, 1957-59. Served with USAAF, 1941-45, 45-47. Decorated Bronze Star medal, Purple Heart, D.S.C. Mem. A.A.A.S., Oceanographic Inst. Author: The Silent Men, 1945; Fossil Collecting, 1957; Fossil Collecting in England, 1966. Contbr. articles in field to profl. jours. Home: 3616 Garden Club Lane Charlotte NC 28210 Office: Nature Museum York County Rock Hill SC 29730

CASARES-PONCE, ALBERTO, automotive exec.; b. Merida, Yucatan, Mexico, Jan. 10, 1921; s. Carlos Casares Perez and Maria Ponce; B.E.E., Catholic U. Am., 1943; m. Mercedes Urazandi, Aug. 16, 1947; children—Maria-Elisa (Mrs. Mario Rodriquez-Aguilar), Genoveva (Mrs. Mario Cervera-Ortiz), Patricia, Eulalia, Alberto, Anabelle. Engr. in charge installation, constrn. Cerveceria Yucateca, Merida, Mexico, 1947-50, maintenance supr., 1950-57, prodn. mgr., 1957-67; mgr. Automaya, S.A., Merida, 1967—; adminstr. Autos de Prestigio, S.A., Campeche, 1967—; mgr. Campeche & Diesel Sureste, S.A., Merida, 1969—. Pres., Centro Patronal de Merida, 1972; Consejero Confederacion Patronal de la Republica Mexicana, 1972—. Mem. I.E.E.E. Club: Serra de Merida. Home: 490 33rd St Merida Yucatan Mexico Office: 546 Av Juarez Merida Yucatan Mexico

CASCIO, JOSEPH ALFIERI, landscape architect; b. Hartford, Conn., Nov. 2, 1934; s. Peter Joseph and Helen Clara (Veselak) C.; B.Landscape Arch., Ohio State U., 1961; m. Yvonne Williams, Dec. 22, 1959; children—Peter, Gigi, Genevieve, Toni, Vice pres. Peter Cascio Nursery, Inc., West Hartford, Conn., 1963-65; asso. Allen W. Hixon & Assos., landscape architects, Simsbury, Conn., 1968-72; east coast div. mgr. Keith French Assos., landscape architects, Los Angeles, 1972-74; landscape cons. Environmental Systems Internat., Inc., Washington, 1972—. Judge, Ann. Mass. Horticulture Soc. Show, Boston, 1971-73. Served with inf. AUS, 1955-56. Registered architect, Conn., Mass., Md., Ga., Ohio, N.Y. Mem. Am. Soc. Landscape Architects, Sigma Phi Epsilon. Rotarian. Prin. works: Simsbury (Conn.) Farms Recreation Complex, 1971; Mainstreet Marketing and Recreation Complex, Atlanta, 1973; Greens, Branford, Conn., 1973; Churchill, Germantown, Md., 1974; Birchwood, Perkiomen, Pa., 1974; Hiddenbrook Marketing Complex, McLean, Va., 1972. Home: 10101 Capeway Ct Fairfax VA 22030 Office: 1048 Potomac St NW Washington DC 20007

CASE, GEORGE MILTON, state legislator; b. Canton, Miss., July 5, 1934; s. Willie and Mamie (Smith) C.; B.A., U. Miss., 1955, LL.B., 1956. Admitted to Miss. bar, 1956; partner Case & Montgomery, Canton, Miss., 1956—; mem. Miss. Ho. of Reps., 1960-64, 64-68, 68—; atty. towns Ridgeland, 1960, 65, Miss., Madison County sch. dist.,1959—. Trustee Madison County Library Commn., 1965-72; mem. Miss. Medicaid Commn. Served to 1st lt. with AUS, 1957-59. Mem. Omicron Delta Kappa, Phi Delta Phi. Mason (Shriner), Elk, K.P., Lion. Home: Green Acres Subdivision Canton MS 39046 Office: 360 N Liberty St Canton MS 39046

CASE, GEORGE PHILLIP, JR., naval officer; b. Parkersburg, W.Va., Oct. 3, 1929; s. George Phillip and Garnet Mae (Leary) C.; B.S., U.S. Naval Acad., 1952; B.S. in E.E., U.S. Naval Postgrad. Sch., 1962; M.S., George Washington U., 1972; m. Mary Louise Campbell, Oct. 15, 1955; children—Lisa Anne, G. Phillip. Commd. ensign U.S. Navy, 1952, advanced through grades to comdr., 1974; engring. duty officer Norfolk Naval Shipyard, Portsmouth, Va., 1962-66; repair officer U.S.S. Proteus, Guam, 1966-68; project mgr. and logistic mgr., aux. type ships Naval Ship Systems Command, Washington, 1968—. Decorated Navy Commendation medal (2). Registered profl. engr., Va. Mem. I.E.E.E. Lutheran (pres. ch. council 1973-74). Club: Woods of Ilda Swimming (Annandale, Va.). Home: 4913 Springbrook Dr Annandale VA 22003 Office: Navy Material Command (MATOOC) Navy Dept Washington DC 20360

CASE, KENNETH EUGENE, educator; b. Oak Ridge, Aug. 12, 1944; s. Richard T. and Vera L. (Peyton) C.; B.S., Okla. State U., 1966, M.S., 1967, Ph.D., 1969; m. Frances Lynn Curlee, Jan. 21, 1966; children—Kristin Lynn, David Rex. Prodn. engr. Humble Oil & Refining Co., Oklahoma City, 1965; design engr. Collins Radio Co., Cedar Rapids, Ia., 1966; grad. teaching asst. Okla. State U., Stillwater, 1967-68; asst. prof. indsl. engring. and operations research Va. Poly. Inst. and State U., Blacksburg, 1969-73, asso. prof., 1973—. Prin. investigator Navy Research grant to design optimal multifacility refuse disposal systems, 1973; cons. Cities Service Oil Co., 1968-69, TVA 1971-73, Williams Bros. Engring. Co., 1971-72. Registered profl. engr., Va., Okla. Mem. Nat. Soc. Profl. Engrs., Am. Inst. Indsl. Engrs. (editorial bd. Transactions 1973—, nat. dir. quality control and reliability engring. div. 1972-73), Am. Soc. Quality Control, Blue Key, Sigma Tau, Sigma Chi, Phi Kappa Phi, Alpha Pi Mu, Eta Kappa Nu, Pi Mu Epsilon. Contbr. articles to profl. jours. Home: 225 Craig Dr Blacksburg VA 24060

CASE, W(ARD) R(OLAND), JR., corp. exec.; b. Jamestown, Tenn., Oct. 31, 1918; s. Ward Roland and Mollie (Albertson) C.; LL.B., Cumberland U., Lebanon, Tenn., 1940; m. Sarah Helen Whitefield, July 26, 1940; children—Ward Roland III, John Howard. Title examiner TVA, Paris, Tenn., 1941-42; admitted to Tenn. bar, 1940, practice, Jamestown, Tenn., 1945-57; legal counsel Magnet Cove Barium Corp., Houston, 1957-65, sec., 1959-65; v.p. internat. dept., 1965-66; exec. v.p. Dresser Magcobar div. Dresser Industries, Inc., Houston, 1966-69, v.p. planning and adminstrn. Petroleum and Minerals Group, 1969-72, v.p., gen. counsel, 1972—. Chmn. bd. Union Bank, Jamestown, Tenn., 1949-59. Served with AUS, 1942-45. Mem. Bar Assn. Tenn., Am. Bar Assn. Republican. Mem. Ch. of Christ. Mason (Shriner). Home: 5014 Carew St Houston TX 77035 Office: 601 Jefferson St Houston TX 77002

CASEY, ALBERT E(UGENE), pathologist; b. N.Y.C., Mar. 13, 1903; s. Eugene Joseph and Anna Alma (Powell) C.; A.B., Spring Hill Coll., 1922; M.D., St. Louis U., 1927; m. Bourdon Eason Veazey, Apr. 19, 1928; children—Anna Elizabeth (Mrs. Clement Fisher Kent, Jr.), Bourdon Irene (Mrs. Charles Lee Payne), Albert Eugene; m. 2d, Joanne Gunn, Nov. 8, 1952; 1 son, Paul Travis. Intern St. Louis U. Hosp., 1926-27; asst. anatomy St. Louis U., 1924-27, asso. prof. pathology, 1936-38; asst. and asso. in pathology and bacteriology Rockefeller Inst., 1927-34; asso. prof. pathology U. Va., 1934-36; sr. asst. prof. pathology and bacteriology La. State U., 1938-42; sr. vis. pathologist Charity Hosp. of La., New Orleans, 1938-42; pathologist, dir. labs. Birmingham Bapt. Hosps., 1942-72, pres. staff 1956, chmn. exec. com., 1958; prof. pathology U. Ala., 1953—, dir. Meml. Inst. of Pathology, 1961—; pathologist Eye Found. Hosp., 1972—; cons. pathologist Childrens Hosp., pres. staff, 1947; pathologist Univ. Hosp., Hillcrest Hosp.; pathologist to coroner, 1942-67, Domestic Relations Ct., 1942-72. Field epidemiologist Nat. Found. Infantile Paralysis, 1941-42, 45-50. Bd. dirs. Blue Cross, Blue Shield of Ala., 1957-60. Diplomate Am. Bd. Pathology. Mem. Coll. Am. Pathologists (chmn. S.E. regional com. 1954-57), Ala. Assn. Pathologists (pres. 1947), Soc. Exptl. Biology and Medicine (council 1941-43), Am. Soc. Clin. Pathology, (counselor 1947-50), Am. Soc. Exptl. Pathology, Am. Inst. Chemists, Internat. Acad. Pathology, Internat. Cancer Congress, Am. Soc. Phys. Anthropology, Am. Assn. Anatomists, Am. Assn. Cancer Research, N.Y. Acad. Sci., A.A.A.S., Am. Assn. Blood Banks (Ala. rep. 1959-67), Am. Assn. Pathology and Bacteriology, Am. Pub. Health Assn., Am., So. (chmn. sect. pathology 1955-56) med. assns., Miss. Geneal. and Hist. Soc. (hon.), Am. Irish Hist. Soc. (v.p., life member), Sigma Xi, Phi Beta Pi, Alpha Omega Alpha. Democrat. Baptist. Mason (32 deg.). Clubs: Clinical, The Club, Exchange (Birmingham). Author: (with others) Amite County, Miss. History, 4 vols. 1948, 52, 57, 68; Slieve Lougher and Upper Blackwater in Ireland, 15 vols., 1954, 58, 59, 60, 62, 63, 64, 65, 66, 67, 68, 70, 72; Encyclopedia of Pathologists Southern U.S.A., 1963; Host Reaction and Cancer, 1962; Compilation of Common Physical Measurements on Adult Males of Various Races, 1969; articles on cancer, blood, virus diseases, med. edn., anthropology in profl. jours. Editor Jefferson County Med. Soc. Bull., 1956-59. Home: 2011 Southwood Rd Birmingham AL 35216 Office: 1025 18th St S Birmingham AL 35205

CASEY, BEVERLY ALLEN, JR., hotel exec.; b. N.Y.C., Jan. 5, 1934; s. Beverly Allen and Jennie Lynn (Toye) C.; student Auburn U., 1952-54, U. Chattanooga, 1954-55; m. Emma Berry Patten, Apr. 20, 1963; children—Lynn Patten, Elizabeth Patten. Partner, Caldwell-Casey Ins. Co., Chattanooga, 1958-70; pres. Town House Properties, Inc., Chattanooga, 1963—, also dir. Chmn. bd. dirs. Chattanooga Choo-Choo Co., 1973. Mem. allocations com. United Fund, 1971, Indsl. Com. of 100, 1971. Bd. dirs. Chattanooga YMCA, 1967-70. Named Jaycee of Year Chattanooga Jaycees, 1957. Mem. Tenn. Hotel and Motel Assn. (1st v.p. 1970-71), Jr. C. of C. (past state v.p.), Chattanooga Conv. and Visitors Bur. (dir. 1971), Chattanooga C. of C. (dir.). Episcopalian. Club: Lookout Mountain (Tenn.) Fairyland. Mailing Address: Terminal Sta Chattanooga TN 37402 Home: 113 W Fleetwood Dr Lookout Mountain TN 37350

CASEY, ELEANOR MURPHREY DANIELS (MRS. JEPHTHAH CASEY), librarian; b. nr. Goldsboro, N.C., Nov. 7, 1907; d. Jackson Isaac and Sallie Irene (Murphrey) Daniels; student Appalachian State Tchrs. Coll., 1948-50; m. Jephthah Casey, Feb. 5, 1925; children—Jephthah, Eleanor Joyce (Mrs. William Igoe). Head librarian Pender County Library, Burgaw, N.C., 1946—. Mem. Pender Welfare Bd., 1944-52; treas. Pender Red Cross, 1944-46, Crippled Children's Fund, 1950-52. Bd. dirs. Moore's Creek Battleground Assn. Mem. state exec. com. Democratic party, 1952-53. Recipient award for outstanding service Library Bd., 1966. Mem. Am., N.C. library assns., Burgaw Book Club. Methodist. Mem. Order Eastern Star. Home: Box 311 246 Bridgers St Burgaw NC 28425 Office: 103 Cowan St Burgaw NC 28425

CASEY, JAMES FRANCIS, physician; b. N.Y.C., May 2, 1930; s. James F. and Marcella A. (Reddy) C.; A.B., Holy Cross Coll., 1952; M.D., Columbia Coll., 1956; m. Lucille F. DeBevoise, Aug. 14, 1965; children—James Arthur, Arthur John. Intern, St. Vincent's Hosp., N.Y.C., 1956-57, resident, 1957-60; fellow cardiology Jackson Hosp., Miami, Fla., 1960-61; practice medicine specializing in internal medicine and cardiology, N.Y.C., 1963-67, Ft. Lauderdale, Fla., 1967—; mem. staff Holy Cross Hosp. Served to lt. comdr. USNR, 1961-63. Fellow A.C.P., Am. Coll. Cardiology; mem. Am., Fla., Broward County med. assns. Roman Catholic. Office: 4538 N Federal Hwy Fort Lauderdale FL 33308

CASEY, LIONEL JAMES, cons. co. exec.; b. Lowland, N.C., May 4, 1930; s. Lionel James and Emma (Brothers) C.; student Coll. William and Mary, 1951-52; B.S., Tulane U., 1954; M.A., Emory U., 1955; m. Garnett Eighme Seifert, Oct. 12, 1958; children—Amy Lynn, Judith Anne, Mary Catherine, Lionel James III. Pilot, Pan Am. World Airways, N.Y.C., 1955-57; pres. Colonial Chem. Co., Inc., Washington, N.C., 1958-62, dir., 1958—; pres., dir. Constrn. Consultants, Inc., Norfolk, Va., 1962—; chmn. bd. Timberlane Farms, Inc., Apollo Farms, Inc. Served with AUS, 1947-51. Mason. Home: 5404 Sherluck Rd Virginia Beach VA 23462 Office: 2408 Lafayette Blvd Norfolk VA 23509

CASEY, OFFA LUNSFORD, lawyer; b. Mobile, Ala., Apr. 22, 1912; s. Benjamin Dudley and Ethel Lou (Shivers) C.; student Jones County Jr. Coll., 1929-30; B.A., U. Miss., 1935, J.D., 1936; m. Muriel Elizabeth Terry, Nov. 21, 1936 (dec. Feb. 1973); children—Thomas Lunsford, Michael Reynolds. Admitted to Miss. bar, 1936; pvt. practice, Laurel, 1936-38, 46-48; atty. lands div. Dept. Justice, Washington, 1938-40; asst. to gen. counsel Adminstr. of Export Control, Washington, 1940-42; judge City Ct., Laurel, 1947-48; asst. U.S. Dist. Atty., So. Dist. Miss., 1949; judge county and youth cts., Laurel, 1951-55; circuit ct. judge 18th dist., Laurel, 1955-70; mem. firm Maxey, Clark & Casey, 1971—. Pres. Miss. Assn. Crime and Delinquency, 1953-55; chmn. Easter Seal Soc., Jones County, 1959-61. Served from 2d lt. to lt. col. AUS, 1942-46, PTO; now col. Res. ret. Mem. Am., Jones County (v.p. 1973-74) bar assns., Miss. State Bar (jud. adminstrn. com. chmn. 1969-70, commr. 1971-72), Miss. Circuit Judges Assn. (chmn. 1969-70), Jones County Bapt. Assn. (moderator 1957-58), Pi Kappa Phi, Phi Alpha Delta. Democrat. Baptist. Mason, K.P., Rotarian (pres. 1967-68). Home: 1006 Broadway Laurel MS 39440 Office: PO Box 185 Laurel MS 39440

CASEY, ROBERT RANDOLPH, congressman; b. Joplin, Mo., July 27, 1915; s. Samuel R. and Mabel (Caywood) C.; student U. Houston, also South Tex. Coll. Law, 1934-40; m. Hazel M. Brann, Aug. 13, 1935; children—Hazel Mary, Robert Randolph, Catherine, Bonnie, Michael, Shawn, Bridget, Eileen, Timothy, Kevin Casey. Admitted to Tex. bar, 1940, practice in Alvin, 1941-43, Houston, 1947-51; asst. dist. atty. Harris County, 1943-47; county judge, 1951-58; mem. 86th-93d Congresses from 22d Dist. Tex. Mem. Tex. Legislature, 1949-50. Club: Houston Yacht. Home: 2256 Dryden St Houston TX 77025 also 5406 Albia Rd Washington DC 20016 Office: Rayburn Office Bldg Washington DC 20515

CASEY, STEPHEN HUNTLEY, ins. agy. exec.; b. Anderson, S.C., Feb. 20, 1939; s. David Gordon and Lucy Marguerite (Leverett) C.; A.B., Duke, 1960; M.B.A., So. Meth. U., 1968; m. Terry Pearlstone, Jan. 31, 1961; children—Karen Elizabeth, Stephen Huntley. Partner, Pearlstone-Casey Agy., Inc., Dallas, 1964-70, pres., 1970—; dir. Main St. Nat. Bank, Dallas, Dallas-Ft. Worth Airport Bank. Pres. 500, Inc., 1971-72. Bd. dirs. Dallas Civic Opera Guild, 1968-69, Dallas Civic Opera, 1972-73, Dallas Arts Found., Inc., 1972-73, U.S.A. Film Festival, 1972-73. Served with USNR, 1960-64. Mem. Nat., Tex., Dallas assns. life underwriters, Chartered Life Underwriters (dir. Dallas chpt. 1971-72, sec.-treas. 1972-73, v.p. 1973-74), Assn. Advanced Life Underwriting, Dallas Assn. Ins. Agts., Dallas Estate Council, Million Dollar Roundtable, Tex. Leaders Roundtable, Dallas Jr. C. of C. (dir. 1967), Dallas Duke U. Alumni Assn. (pres. 1971-73). Club: City. Home: 4211 Arcady St Dallas TX 75205 Office: 1015 Elm St Dallas TX 75202

CASEY, THEOIDORE EVANS, apparel co. exec.; b. Harrogate, Tenn., July 28, 1920; s. Frazier B. and Hallie (Brooks) C.; student Bowling Green Coll. Commerce, 1939-41; B.S. cum laude Miss. State U., 1951; m. Ruth White, Feb. 12, 1945; 1 dau., Martha J. Auditor, M.M. Winkler Assos., C.P.A.'s, Tupelo, Miss., 1951-52; controller Meadow Sportswear, Okolona, 1952-72; partner Craig & Casey C.P.A.'s, 1972—; dir. First Citizens Nat. Bank. Mem. Mayor's adv. bd., Okolona, Miss., 1971. Bd. dirs. Miss. State U. Devel. Found., 1966-68; bd. dirs., treas. Shearer-Richardson Endowment Found., Okolona, Miss., 1965—. Served with USCGR, 1942-45. C.P.A., Miss. Mem. Okolona C. of C. (pres. 1957, Outstanding Community Service award 1972). Methodist (chmn. adminstrv. bd. 1971). Lion (pres. 1959). Home: Robertson St Okolona MS 38860 Office: PO Box 360 Okolona MS 38860

CASH, DEWEY BYRON, educator; b. Wadley, Ala., Dec. 22, 1930; s. Joe Jackson and Iola (McCormick) C.; Asso. Sci., So. Union Coll., 1950; B.S., Auburn U., 1955, M.Ed., 1957, M.S., 1964; m. Louise Hammock, Dec. 18, 1954; children—Paul, Sally. Tchr. pub. high sch., Fla., 1955-56, Ga., 1956-58; asso. prof. math. Columbus (Ga.) Coll., 1958—. Served with AUS, 1951-54. Mem. Math. Assn. Am. Home: 3317 Mustang Dr Columbus GA 31904

CASH, JOHNNY, singer, composer; b. Kingsland, Ark., Feb. 26, 1932; s. Ray and Carrie (Rivers) C.; grad. high sch.; D.Hum., Gardner-Webb Coll., Boiling Springs, N.C., 1971; m. June Carter, Mar. 1, 1968; 1 son, John Carter; children by previous marriage—Rosanne, Kathleen, Cindy, Tara. Rec. artist with Sun Records, 1955-58, Columbia Records, 1958—; researched and recorded documentary album, True West, for Columbia, 1965; pres. South Wind Music, N.Y.C.; motion pictures Five Minutes Live, A Gunfight, 1970; soundtracks for motion pictures I Walk the Line, Little Fuass and Big Halsy; star of Johnny Cash Show, ABC-TV, 1969—, star spl. Columbo; co-writer, narrator, singer in film The Gospel Road; owner House of Cash, Inc., pub. Song of Cash, Inc.; guest appearances numerous TV programs. Hon. com. mem. Israel's 25th Anniversary; co-host Muscular Dystrophy Telethon, 1972. Vice pres. Muscular Dystrophy Assn., 1973-74. Served with USAF 1950-54. Recipient Citation for USO shows in Far East, Def. Dept. Composer over 200 songs including: I Walk the Line, I Still Miss Someone, Don't Take Your Guns to Town. Address: PO Box 508 Hendersonville TN 37075

CASHEN, HENRY CHRISTOPHER, II, lawyer, b. Detroit, June 25, 1939; s. Raymond and Catherine C.; grad. Cheshire Acad., 1957; A.B. in Classics with honors, Brown U., 1961; postgrad. U. Mich., 1963; m. Leslie Renchard, June 28, 1967; 1 son, Raymond Cashen II. Admitted to Mich. bar; mem. firm Dickinson, Wright, McKean and Cudlip, Detroit, 1964-69; dep. asst. to Pres. Nixon, Washington, 1969-73; mem. firm Dickstein, Shapiro & Morin, Washington, 1973—. Mem. Barristers Soc., Psi Upsilon, Phi Delta Phi. Republican. Roman Catholic. Clubs: Country, University (Detroit). Home: 1231 33rd St NW Washington DC 20007 Office: 1735 New York Av NW Washington DC 20006

CASHION, ERNEST LOWERY, physician; b. Pine Bluff, Ark., Dec. 29, 1924; s. Ernest Lowery and Jessie (Mason) C.; M.D., U. Ark., 1951; m. Polly Funk, June 2, 1951; children—Brenda, Sidney, Charles. Intern, Univ. Hosp., Little Rock, 1951-52, asst. resident gen. surgery, 1952-53; resident neurol. surgery Kan. U. Med. Center, Kansas Ctiy, Kan., 1953-56, Murdock fellow surgery, 1954; practice medicine specializing in neurosurgery, Little Rock, 1956-59, Memphis, 1959-60, Great Falls, Mont., 1960-65, Salt Lake City, 1965-67, Memphis, 1967—; chief neurosurg. sect. VA Hosp., Memphis, 1967—; clin. instr. neurosurgery U. Ark. Sch. Medicine, Little Rock, 1956-59; isntr. surgery U. Utah Coll. Medicine, Salt Lake City, 1965-67; asst. prof. surgery U. Tenn. Coll. Medicine, Memphis, 1967—. Served with AUS, 1943-46; comdr. M.C., USN Res., 1959—. Diplomate Am. Bd. Neurol. Surgery. Mem. A.M.A., A.C.S., Am. Assn. Neurol. Surgeons, A.A.A.S., Congress Neurol. Surgeons, Rocky Mountain Neurosurg. Soc., Assn. VA Surgeons, So. Neurosurg. Soc., S.A.R. Presbyn. (ruling elder 1972—). Contbr. articles in field to profl. jours. Home: 3437 Clarke Rd Memphis TN 38118 Office: Veterans Administration Hospital 1030 Jefferson Av Memphis TN 38104

CASKIE, DABNEY HAMILTON, investment co. exec.; b. Proffit, Va., Mar. 11, 1925; s. Jaquelin Ambler and Margaret Lee (Minor) C.; student Mars Hill Coll., 1942-43, 46-47; B.S., U. Va., 1949; postgrad. U. Richmond, 1951-54, Va. Commonwealth U., 1964; m. Mary Jane Cannada, Sept. 6, 1947; children—Kathryn Ambler, Mark Hamilton. With Bank of Commerce & Trust, Richmond, Va., 1949-56, United Va. Bank, Richmond, 1956-72; v.p. Capitoline Investment Services, Inc., Richmond, 1973—. Active Community Fund, United Givers Fund, 1948-69; auditor Bon Air Community Center, Richmond, 1972. Served with USNR, 1943-45. Mem. Am. Inst. Banking, Richmond Soc. Financial Analysts, Inst. Chartered Financial Analysts, Beta Gamma Sigma. Baptist. Club: Bull and Bear (Richmond). Home: 8728 Trent Rd Richmond VA 23235 Office: PO Box 436 Richmond VA 23203

CASNER, STANLEY WAYNE, JR., physician; b. Marfa, Tex., Aug. 14, 1927; s. Stanley Wayne and Kathryn (Sheen) C.; student Tex. Tech U., 1948-50; M.D., U. Tex., 1958; m. Lucille Fay McGee, Apr. 18, 1957; children—John Wayne, Barbara Fay, Peggy Gayle. Intern Meth. Hosp., Houston, 1958-59; resident in surgery John Sealy Hosp., U. Tex. Med. br., Galveston, 1959-63; practice medicine specializing in family practice, Austin, Tex., 1968—; mem. staff Brackenridge Hosp., Holy Cross Hosp., St. Davids Hosp., Seton Hosp., Austin; team physician U. Tex. Student Health Center and Athletic, 1961-66; dir. Casner Research Labs., Austin, Tex., 1967—. Served with USAAF, 1944-46. Fellow Am. Coll. Family Practice; mem. A.M.A., Am. Diabetes Assn., Tex. Med. Assn., Travis County Med. Soc., Theta

Kappa Psi. Baptist. Kiwanian. Home: 4016 Rustling Oaks St Austin TX 78766 Office: 4019 Spicewood Springs Rd Austin TX 78766

CASON, CLEO STARGEL (MRS. CHARLES MONROE CASON, JR.), librarian; b. Dahlonega, Ga., June 24, 1910; d. John Jones and Georgia (Jones) Stargel; student North Ga. 1926-28; LL.B., Am. Sch. Law, 1949; postgrad. U. Ala., 1951-53, U. Chgo., 1954-55; m. Charles Monroe Cason, Jr., May 8, 1930; 1 son, Charles Monroe III. Adminstrv. asst. to comdr. Redstone Arsenal, Ala., 1944-47, chief office service br., 1947-49, tech. librarian, 1949—. Recipient Meritorious Civilian award Dept. Army, 1970, citation of Merit for outstanding service Madison County Ala., 1971. Mem. Spl. Libraries Assn. (pres. Ala. chpt. 1955-56), Southeastern, Ala. (pres. coll., univ. and spl. libraries div. 1959-60) library assns., Bus. and Profl. Women's Club (chpt. pres. 1950-51). Club: Aladdin (pres. 1958, 67) (Huntsville, Ala.). Home: 700 Watts Dr SE Huntsville AL 35801 Office: Redstone Sci Information Center Redstone Arsenal AL 35809

CASON, DICK KENDALL, physician; b. Beaumont, Tex., June 27, 1922; s. Dick Kendall and Maurine (Mills) C.; B.A., Rice U., 1945; M.D., U. Tex., 1945; m. Maxine Skocdopole, Apr. 4, 1946; children—Dick Mills, Alma Christine. Intern Kings County Hosp. Bklyn., 1945-46; med. resident Meth. Hosp., Dallas, 1948-49; gen. practice medicine, Hillsboro, Tex., 1949—; staff mem. Grant-Buie Hosp. Charter mem. Am. Bd. Family Practice. Pres. Hillsboro Indsl. Devel. Found., 1955-60; mem. regional adv. com. Dallas Civic Opera Co., 1960—. Served from 1st lt. to capt., AUS, 1946-48. Fellow Royal Soc. Health (Eng.); mem. Hill County Med. Soc. (pres. 1951), Tex. Med. Assn. (councilor 12th dist.), Am. Acad. Gen. Practice, N.Y. Acad. Sci., Am. Assn. Ry. Surgeons, Cotton Bowl Assn., C. of C., Hill County Soc. Crippled Children. Presbyn. (elder). Clubs: Hillsboro Country, Rotary (pres. Hillsboro 1955). Author articles profl. jours. Home: 1303 Park Dr Hillsboro TX 76645 Office: 150 Circle Dr Hillsboro TX 76645

CASON, M. LOUISE, physician; b. Lakeland, Fla., Mar. 26, 1923; d. L. Oscar and Mossie (Turner) Cason; B.S., Fla. State U., 1945; M.D., U. Chgo., 1950. Intern in pediatrics Duke U. Hosp., 1950-51; resident pediatrics Jewish Hosp. of Bklyn., 1951-53; practice medicine specializing in pediatrics, Miami, 1953—; clin. asso. prof. pediatrics U. Miami Sch. of Medicine, 1961—; chief dept. pediatrics Variety Children's Hosp., 1958-71, pres. med. bd., 1971—; attending pediatrician Jackson Meml. Hosp., Variety Children's Hosp.; cons. pediatrician to Children's Service Bur., Cath. Welfare Bur. Diplomate Am. Bd. Pediatrics. Fellow Am. Acad. Pediatrics. Mem. Am., So., Fla., Dade County med. assns., Miami Pediatric Soc., Fla. Pediatric Soc. Episcopalian. Office: 3041 Grand Av Miami FL 33133

CASON, THOMAS EDWARD, JR., sales co. exec.; b. Plain Dealing, La., June 22, 1921; s. Tom E. and Nettie (Bounds) C.; student So. State Coll., Magnolia, Ark., 1938-40; B.S., La. State U., 1942; m. Alma Dean Lester, Nov. 5, 1942; children—Cheryl Ann (Mrs. Doug Wallace), Gwendolyn (Mrs. Tommy Vaughan), Tommy, Randall. Tchr. high sch., Lutcher, La., 1942-43; tchr. Bradley (Ark.) High Sch., 1946-66; project instr. Ark. Dept. Edn., 1966-68; owner Cason Distbrs., Batesville, Ark., 1968—; v.p. Pennyrich Corp., Batesville, 1968—; pres. Pennyrich Distbrs. Assn., 1971—; gen. distbr. Holiday Magic Cosmetics, Batesville, 1965—; dir. Carolina Mfg. Corp. (P.R.). Civil def. dir., Bradley, 1958-66. Alderman, Bradley, 1948-50, 54-66. Served with AUS, 1943-46, ETO. Mem. Ark. Press Assn., N.E.A., Ark. Vocational Agr. Tchrs. Assn., Batesville C. of C., Little Rock Better Bus. Bur., Alpha Tau Alpha. Methodist (tchr., lay leader). Rotarian. Editor Bradley Pioneer, 1960-66. Home: 315 Craig St Batesville AR 72501 Office: 363 E Main St Batesville AR 72501

CASO Y ANDRADE, ALFONSO, scientist; b. Mexico City, Mexico, Feb. 1, 1896; s. Antonio and Maria (Andrade) C.; grad. U. Mexico, 1929; doctor honoris causa U. Nat. Mexico, U. Merida, U. Morelia, U. N.M., U. Cal. at Los Angeles; m. Maria Lombardo, Aug. 21, 1922; children—Beatriz (Mrs. Carlos Solorzano), Andres, Aleiandro Eugenia; m. 2d, Aida Lombardo. Prof. faculty philosophy and letters, 1918-40, Escuela de Layes, 1919-29; dir. Escuela Nacional Preparatoria, 1928; head dept. archeology Museo Nacional, 1930-33, dir., 1933-34; dir. explorations, Monte Alban, Oaxaca, 1931-44; dir. higher learning and sci. investigation, 1944; rector U. Nacional Mexico, 1944-45; sec. nat. properties and adminstrv. inspection, 1946-48; dir. Inst. Nacional Indigenista, Revista Estudios Antropologicos. Recipient First medal Viking Fund for Archaeology, 1952. Fellow Royal Anthrop. Inst. Great Britain and Ireland (hon.); mem. Nat. Acad. Scis. Antonio Alzate (pres.); Nat. Coll., Soc. Geography and Statistics, N.Y., Washington acads. sci., Archaeol. Inst. Am. (hon.), Am. Philos. Soc., Royal Anthrop. Inst. (hon.), Soc. Am. Paris (hon.), Brit. Acad. (hon.), Am. Anthrop. Assn., Soc. Geography and History Guatemala, Am. Assn. Tchrs. Spanish, Deutsche Gesellschaft fur Volkerkunde. Author numerous books including Urnas de Oaxaca, 1950; The People of the Sun, 1952; Codex Bodley, 1960; Codex Selden, 1964. Dir., founder Boletin Bibliog. de Antropologia Am. Home: Avenue Central 234 Tlacopac Sn Angel Mexico 20 DF Mexico Office: Instituto Nacional Indigenista Av Revolucion 1279 Mexico City 20 Mexico

CASSATA, JOHN T., clergyman. Ordained priest Roman Catholic Ch., 1932; apptd. bishop of Bida, aux. bishop of Dallas-Fort Worth, 1968; bishop of Fort Worth, 1969—. Address: 1206 Throckmorton St Fort Worth TX 76102*

CASSEDY, MARSHALL ROYAL, lawyer; b. Short Hills, N.J., July 28, 1928; s. Pierce A. and Callene (Thomas) C.; B.A., Hobart Coll., 1951; LL.B., Coll. Law Duke, 1956; m. Donna Louise Anderson, July 5, 1952; children—Marshall, Thomas A., Kristine C., Melissa H. Admitted to Fla. bar, 1956; asso. firm Turnbull & Senterfitt, Orlando, Fla., 1956-58; staff counsel Fla. Bar, Tallahassee, 1958-61, exec. dir., 1961—. Treas. Tallahassee YMCA, 1966-68. Served to lt. col. USMCR, 1951-53. Mem. Am. Bar Assn. (ho. of dels. 1971-72), Am. Judicature Soc., Fla. Am., Fla. (pres. 1966-67) socs. assn. execs., Nat. Assn. Bar Execs. (pres. 1967-68). Episcopalian. Home: 707 Live Oak Plantation Rd Tallahassee FL 32303 Office: The Florida Bar Tallahassee FL 32304

CASSEL, CHESTER, physician; b. N.Y.C., Feb. 23, 1918; s. Lionel and Florence (Dannenberg) C.; B.S. with high honors, U. Fla., 1939; M.D., Columbia, 1943; m. Carol Isaacson, Dec. 17, 1947; children—Karen, Laurie, Claudia, Juliet. Intern, Mt. Sinai Hosp., N.Y.C., 1943, resident, 1947-49; resident Bellevue Hosp., N.Y.C., 1946, Duke Hosp., Durham, N.C., 1949-51; practice medicine specializing in internal medicine and gastroenterology, Miami, Fla., 1951—; mem. staffs Cedars of Lebanon Hosp., Jackson Meml. Hosp., Miami; cons. VA Hosp., Victoria, Mercy hosps., Miami; clin. prof. medicine U. Miami Sch. Medicine, 1951—. Served to maj. AUS, 1944-46. Diplomate Am. Bd. Internal Medicine. Fellow A.C.P. (state gov. 1971-74); mem. Am. Gastroent. Assn., Fla. Gastroent. Soc. (pres. 1971), Phi Beta Kappa, Alpha Omega Alpha. Home: 1260 Shore Dr E Miami FL 33133 Office: 1150 NW 14th St Miami FL 33136

CASSEL, WILLIAM ALWEIN, educator; b. Phila., Mar. 25, 1924; s. William Andrew and Bessie Shriver (Alwein) C.; B.S., Phila. Coll. Pharmacy and Sci., 1946, M.S., 1947; Ph.D. (Phila. Lager Beer Brewers' Assn. fellow), U. Pa., 1952; m. Verne Madonna Finnell, June 18, 1949; children—William Stephen, Janet Lynn. Bacteriologist Phila. Gen. Hosp., 1947-48; asst. prof. Hahnemann Med. Coll., Phila., 1952-58; asso. prof. Emory U., Atlanta, 1958-69, prof. microbiology dept., 1969—. Recipient Lederle Med. Faculty award, 1955-58; USPHS Research Career Devel. award, 1960-65; Merit award Girard Coll. Alumni, 1966. Mem Am. Soc. Microbiologists, A.A.A.S., Am. Assn. Immunologists, Am. Assn. U. Profs., Tissue Culture Assn., N.Y. Acad. Sci., Soc. for Exptl. Biology and Medicine, Sigma Xi. Contbr. articles in field to profl. jours. Home: 2157 Willivee Pl Decatur GA 30033 Office: Dept Microbiology Woodruff Bldg Emory Univ Atlanta GA 30322

CASSELL, CHARLES IRVIN, architect, educator; b. Washington, Aug. 5, 1924; s. Albert Irvin and Martha Ann (Mason) C.; student Cornell U., 1942-44; grad. Rensselaer Poly Inst., 1951; divorced; children—Norma Elaine, Kathryn Annette. Asso. with Albert I. Cassell, architect, 1951-69; architect Bur. Yards and Docks, VA and GSA, 1951-68; pvt. practice as architect, part-time 1957—; dir. tech. services Reconstrn. and Devel. Corp., 1969-70; prof. Fed. City Coll., Washington, 1970—; architect-in-residence Urban Law Inst., 1971-72; founder, exec. dir. D.C. Council Black Architects, 1972—; lectr. colls. and univs.; cons. urban problems. Mem. D.C. Bd. Edn., 1970—; vice chmn. Emergency Com. Transp. Crisis; v.p. Nat. Caucus Black Sch. Bd. Mems., 1973—; chmn. Black United Front, 1967-68. Pres. D.C. Sch. Action Council, also editor, pub. newsletter; chmn. D.C. Statehood Party. Candidate U.S. Ho. Reps., 1972. Served with USAAF, 1942-44. Mem. A.I.A., Alpha Phi Alpha. Home: 1845 Summit Pl NW Washington DC 20009 Office: 1845 Summit Pl NW Washington DC 20009

CASSELL, RICHARD SAMUEL DAVID, real estate, oil investments; b. N.Y.C., June 30, 1938; s. Marvin and Junia (Schonwald) C.; B.A., Cornell U., 1960. Gen. mgr. Schonwald & Cassell, Oklahoma City, 1963-64; pres. Richard S. D. Cassell Co., Oklahoma City, 1964—. Chmn. Oklahoma City area Cornell U. Alumni Secondary Schs. Com.; treas. Class 1960 Cornell U., 1970—. Maj. AUS Res., 1974—. Mem. Oklahoma City Bd. Realtors, Nat. Inst. Real Estate Brokers, Internat. Real Estate Fedn., Okla. Zool. Soc., Oklahoma City C. of C., 89ers. Mason (Shriner). Clubs: City Athletic (N.Y.), Oklahoma City Press (dir.), Beacon, Young Men's Dinner. Home: 2753 Clermont Pl Oklahoma City OK 73116 Office: 415 N Broadway Oklahoma City OK 73102

CASSELL, ROBERT BERNARD, economist; b. Chattanooga, Feb. 16, 1918; s. Samuel and Katherine (Lesser) C.; B.A., U. Chattanooga, 1937; M.A., Vanderbilt U., 1938; m. Vylva Irene Holland, May 27, 1943; 1 son, Robert Holland. Supr. Hist. Records Survey, Nashville, 1938-42; indsl. economist Tenn. Planning Commn., Nashville, 1946-53; dir. research Tenn. Indsl. and Agrl. Devel. Commn., Nashville, 1953-60; prin. research scientist, editor Ga. Devel. News, Ga. Inst. Tech., 1960—. Served with AUS, 1942-46. Fellow Am. Indsl. Devel. Council (pres. 1971-72); mem. So. Indsl. Devel. Council (pres. 1968). Contbr. articles to profl. lit. Home: 2694 Briarcliff Rd NE Atlanta GA 30329 Office: Engring Expt Sta Ga Inst Tech Atlanta GA 30332

CASSELS, GORDON BERRY, state ofcl.; b. Pensacola, Fla., Sept. 1, 1942; s. Gordon Berry and Lois (Huff) C.; A.A., Pensacola Jr. Coll., 1964; B.S., Fla. State U., 1966; m. Bobbie Jo Wimberly, Dec. 11, 1973; children by previous marriage—Mark Jeffrey, Donna Sue, Christopher Lee. Semi-sr. accountant Peat, Marwick, Mitchell & Co., Houston, 1967; sr. accountant Saltmarsh, Cleaveland & Gund, Pensacola, 1967-69; dir. finance and accounting div. comml. devel. Dept. Commerce, State of Fla., Tallahassee, 1969-71, dir. finance and accounting div. vocational rehab. Dept. Health and Rehab., 1971-72, chief bur. auditing, beverage div. Dept. Bus. Regulation, 1972—. C.P.A., Tex., Fla. Mem. Nat. Tobacco Tax Assn. (chmn. com. on uniform action 1973), Am. Inst. C.P.A.'s, Am. Accounting Assn., Fla. State U. Alumni Assn., U.S. Jr. C. of C. Democrat. Baptist. Home: 2131 N Meridian St Tallahassee FL 32303 Office: Dept Business Regulation Division of Beverage Tallahassee FL 32304

CASSIDY, JUANITA NEWTON HARRIS (MRS. LEWIS C. CASSIDY), lawyer; b. Newtonville, S.C.; d. Giles Preston and Jessie Lee (Moore) Newton; student Wingate Coll., 1913-15, Ph.D. (hon.), 1960; student Duke, 1915-16; J.D., George Washington Nat. U., 1941; m. Everett Grant Harris, Apr. 14, 1918 (dec.); children—Everett G., Charles Giles, Newton Nolen (dec.); m. 2d, Lewis C. Cassidy, July 8, 1943 (dec. Feb. 1949). Admitted to Mont. bar, 1941, Fed. bar; atty. and counsellor Supreme Ct. of Mont., 1941-74, of U.S., 1973—. Gray Lady, A.R.C., 1952—. Recipient Certificate Alumni Achievement, Wingate Coll., 1960. Mem. Gold Star Wives Am. (nat. parliamentarian), U.D.C. (chpt. historian, state historian), D.A.R., Am. Legion Aux., Mont. Ia., state socs., Va., D.C. hist. socs., Nat. Soc. Magna Charta Dames, Eng. Speaking Union, U.S. Capitol Hist. Soc. (hon. life), George Washington U. Club (charter), Newton Reunion Assn., Daus. 1812 (asso.), Smithsonian Instn. (asso.), Sovereign Colonial Soc. Ams. Royal Descent, Colonial Order of Crown, Internat. Platform Assn., Daus. Brit. Empire U.S.A., Mont. Bar Assn., Sigma Chi Mothers Club, Gen. Fedn. Woman's Clubs, Villages Citizens Assn., Kappa Beta Pi (life). Mem. Order Eastern Star. Clubs: Woman's (bridge co-chmn., chaplain) (Lyon Village); Fort Meyer Officers (Arlington); Naval Officers (Bethesda, Md.). Home: 3137 Key Blvd North Arlington VA 22201

CASSIDY, PATRICK EDWARD, educator; b. East Moline, Ill., Nov. 8, 1937; s. Bert Garfield and Ilene Vertha (Anderson) C.; B.S., U. Ill., 1959; M.S., U. Ia., 1962, Ph.D., 1963; m. Judith Ann Grear, June 11, 1961; 1 son, Andrew Patrick. Fellow, U. Ariz., Tucson, 1963-64; staff mem. Sandia Corp., Albuquerque, 1964-66; sect. mgr. Tracor, Inc., Austin, Tex., 1966-71; asst. prof. chemistry S.W. Tex. State U., San Marcos, 1971—. Pres., Austin (Tex.) Skiers, Inc., 1972-73. DuPont fellow, 1962-63. Mem. Am. Chem. Soc. (chmn. 1969), Tex. Acad. Sci., Sigma Xi, Phi Lambda Upsilon. Presbyn. (elder 1973, chmn. bd. deacons 1972). Club: Town Lake Breakfast (pres. 1970) (Austin). Contbr. articles in field to profl. jours. Home: 6006 Shadow Valley Cove Austin TX 78731 Office: Dept Chemistry Southwest Texas State University San Marcos TX 78666

CASSIDY, ROBERT GORDON, elec. engr.; b. West Baden, Ind., Mar. 15, 1917; s. Elza and Alta (Wininger) C.; B.S. in Elec. Engring., Rose Poly. Inst., 1950; m. Lilah Beryl Pinnick, Jan. 31, 1946; children—Daniel G., Marcia G., Mary D., Christine M. Various positions including auto mechanic, store clk., 1934-42; elec. engr. Hill AFB, Utah, 1951-53; elec. engr. U.S.Army C.E., 1953—, chief, elec. sect. engring. div., Jacksonville Fla., 1967-73, elec. engr. constrn. div., 1973—. Served with AUS, 1942-45. Registered profl. engr., Fla., Ind. Methodist. Home: 5514 Norde Dr Jacksonville FL 32210 Office: 400 W Bay St Jacksonville FL 32201

CASSITY, LLOYD, dairy co. exec.; b. nr. Ashland, Ky., Aug. 10, 1918; s. Ted E. and Elizabeth (McGuire) C.; A.B., Morehead (Ky.) State U., 1941; m. Hazel Helmintoller, Oct. 14, 1939; 1 dau., Lynn Diane. Tchr., Boyd County High Sch., Ashland, Ky., 1941; accountant Stone & Webster Engring. Corp., Oak Ridge, 1942-43; gen. mgr. automobile agys., Morehead and Ashland, Ky., 1946-49; v.p. Johnson's Dairy, Ashland, 1949-68, pres., 1968—; dir. Birch Distbr., Home Fed. Savs. & Loan Assn., Am. Bus. Mens Life Ins. Co., Louisville, Ashland Indsl. Corp. Pres. Ky. Joint Alumni Council, Boyd County Community Chest. Former mem. Ashland Urban Renewal Authority. Vice pres. bd. regents Morehead State U. Served with AUS, 1943-46. Mem. Ky. Dairy Products Assn. (pres.), Assn. Dairy Food Mfrs. (dir.), Ashland area C. of C. (pres.), Morehead State U. Alumni Assn. (past pres.). Democrat. Mem. Christian Ch. Mason (Shriner), Kiwanian. Club: Bellefonte Country (Ashland). Home: 636 Amanda Dr Ashland KY 41101 Office: 2516 Carter Av Ashland KY 41101

CASSON, WALTER ANDREW, JR., civil engr.; b. Jacksonville, Fla., Nov. 11, 1933; s. Walter A. and Alice S. (Coney) C.; B.E., Vanderbilt U., 1956; m. Lauzanne D. Sims, Dec. 25, 1955; 1 son, Leonard Walter. Mgr. br. office C. Fred Deuel & Assos., 1956-62; pres. Casson Engring. Co., New Port Richey, Fla., 1963—; city engr. City of New Port Richey, 1963-71. Dir. First Nat. Bank of New Port Richey, Meadowlawn Meml. Gardens, Inc. Sec. Pithlachascotee water bd. S.W. Fla. Water Mgmt. Bd., 1962-66. Bd. dirs. Fla. Internat. Students. Served to 1st lt. AUS, 1956-57. Registered profl. engr., Fla. Mem. Am. Soc. C.E., Fla., Tampa Bay socs. profl. land surveyors, Fla. Sheriffs Assn., C. of C., Rotarian (pres. 1966-67, dir.). Home: 406 Carlton Rd New Port Richey FL 33552 Office: 106 N Boulevard St PO Box 1348 New Port Richey FL 33552

CASTEEL, WYNNE MARCUS, JR., lawyer; b. Binghamton, N.Y., Jan. 22, 1933; s. Wynne Marcus and Mona (Carnahan) C.; grad. U. Mo., 1950-54; LL.B., Stetson Coll. of Law. 1956-58; m. Sandra Lee Smith, July 31, 1954; children—Cathleen Lee, Mark Wynne, Russell Edmund. Admitted to Fla. bar. 1958; practiced in Ft. Lauderdale, Fla., 1958—; mem. firm Cabot, Scott, Wonkstern & Casteel; asso. municipal judge Fort Lauderdale, 1961, 68—, municipal judge, 1961-63. Served with AUS, 1954-56. Mem. Am., Broward County bar assns., Fla. Bar, Acad. Fla. Trial Lawyers, Phi Delta Theta. Republican. Baptist. Elk. Club: Touchdown. Home: 829 Ponce De Leon Dr Fort Lauderdale FL 33301 Office: 2190 SE 17th St Fort Lauderdale FL 37316

CASTILLO, EDMUND LUIS, govt. ofcl.; b. Toledo, O., Nov. 13, 1924; s. Carlos and Marian Ruth (Griffith) C.; B.S., Northwestern U., 1945; M.S., Boston U., 1954; postgrad. George Washington U., 1971—; m. Jane Catherine Taylor, Nov. 22, 1947; children—Edmund Christopher, James Carlos, Margaret Ann. Commd. ensign USN, 1945, advanced through grades to capt., 1966, press officer Dept. Navy, Washington, 1959-62; pub. affairs officer U.S. 6th Fleet, Mediterranean, 1963-65; asst. comdr. Def. Information Sch., Indpls., 1966; chief, press div. Dept. Def., Washington, 1967-68; ret., 1968; dir. pub. affairs Fairfax County (Va.) Govt., 1968—. Decorated Legion of Merit. Mem. Nat. Assn. County Information Officers (v.p. 1973-74), Pub. Relations Soc. Am. (dir. govt. sect. 1973—), U.S. Naval Inst., Nat. Press Club. Roman Catholic. Author: All About the U.S. Navy, 1961; The Seabees of World War II, 1963; Midway—Battle for the Pacific, 1967; Flat Tops—The Story of Aircraft Carriers, 1968. Home: 8404 Crossley Place Alexandria VA 22308 Office: Fairfax County Govt 4100 Chain Bridge Rd Fairfax VA 22030

CASTILLO, FELIX ARMANDO, civil engr.; b. N.Y.C., Sept. 23, 1933; s. Felix Edmundo and Rose Marie (Saldana) C.; B.C.E., Coll. City N.Y., 1961; m. Bernice Annie Tucker; children—Philip L., Lorie Anne, Lynn Marie. Structural engr. Kononoff & Smith, Coral Gables, Fla., 1962-64; structural engr. Met. Dade County, Fla. Pub. Works Dept., Miami, 1964-68, Bldg. and Zoning Dept., 1968-73; engr. Miami Testing Lab., Hialeah, Fla., 1973-74; structural design engr. Cont Conveyor & Equipment Co., Winfield, Ala., 1974—. Served to sgt. AUS, 1953-55. Registered profl. engr., Ala., Fla. Mem. Am. Soc. C.E., Am. Soc. Testing Materials. Baptist (deacon). Home: Rural Route #5 Box 210 Haleyville AL 35565 Office: PO Box 400 Winfield AL 35594

CASTLE, HENRY GRADY, JR., architect; b. Abilene, Tex. Oct. 4, 1923; s. Henry Grady and Mary (Gist) C.; B.Arch., U. Tex., 1951; children—Mina Johanna (Mrs. Dosier), Susan Reida (Mrs. von Rosenberg), Diane Castle. Asst. dir., regional architect properties and facilities Am. Airlines, Inc., N.Y., 1955, Dallas, 1955-57, Los Angeles, 1957-59; architect Page Southerland Page, A.I.A., 1960-64, Golemon & Rolfe, A.I.A., Houston, 1965-69, Lloyd, Morgan & Jones, architects, Houston, 1969-70; staff architect Walter W. Scarborough, Architect, Houston, 1970-74; individual practice architecture, Houston, 1974—. Served to 1st lt. USAAF, 1942-46, as lt. col. USAF, 1951-53, Korea; col. Res. Decorated Air medal with 3 oak leaf clusters, Air Force Commendation medal. Mem. A.I.A., Constrn. Specifications Inst., Tex. Soc. Fine Arts Assn., Tex. Soc. Architects, Soc. Am. Mil. Engrs., Air Force Assns., Sphinx Archtl. Soc., Res. Officers Assn., U. Tex. Ex-Student Assn. Home: 1300 Woodhollow Dr Houston TX 77027 Office: 1217 Woodhollow Dr Houston TX 77027

CASTRO, ALBERT, educator; b. San Salvador, El Salvador, Nov. 15, 1933; s. Alberto Lemus and Maria Emma (de la Cotera) C.; B.S., U. Houston, 1958; postgrad. Baylor U., 1958; Ph.D., U. El Salvador, 1962; m. Jeris Adelle Goldsmith, Oct. 19, 1956; children—Stewart, Sandra, Alberto, Juan, Richard. Came to U.S., 1952. Asst. prof. microbiology and biochemistry U. El Salvador, San Salvador, 1958-60, asso. prof. dental and med. sch., 1960-63, prof., head dept. basic sci., 1965-68, dir. research in basic sci. dental sch., 1964-68, co-dir. grad. research, 1965-66, bd. dirs. dental sch., 1961-66, mem. research and scholarship com., 1964-65; asst. prof. pediatrics, co-dir. pediatrics metalobic lab. U. Ore., Portland, 1969-73; dir. endocrinological dept. and research unit United Med. Lab., Portland, 1970-73; sr. scientist Papanicolaou Cancer Research Inst., Miami, Fla., 1973—; asso. prof. medicine U. Fla., Miami, 1973—. NIH postdoctoral fellow, 1966-70; U. Ore. Med. Sch. grantee, 1966-69; Northwest Pediatric Research fellow, 1971. Fellow Am. Inst. Chemists, Royal Soc. Tropical Med. and Hygiene; mem. N.Y. Acad. Scis., Am. Chem. Assn. Am. Assn. Microbiology, A.A.A.S., Tooth and Bone Research Soc., Acad. Sci. El Salvador. Roman Catholic. Contbr. articles to sci. publs. Basic research in diabetes and hypertension. Home: 14530 SW 64th Ct Miami FL 33158 Office: Papanicolaou Cancer Research Inst 1425 NW 10th Av Miami FL 33136

CASWELL, LYMAN RAY, educator; b. Omaha, Sept. 29, 1928; s. Omar and Emma E. (Richardson) C.; B.S., Ind. U., 1949, M.A., 1950; Ph.D., Mich. State U., 1956; m. Lynda L. Kinnard, July 17, 1964; children—Randy L., Timothy O., Amy. Asst. prof. chemistry Ohio No. U., Ada., 1955-56; head dept. chemistry Upper Ia. U., Fayette, 1956-61; mem. faculty Tex. Woman's U., Denton, 1961—, asso. prof., 1964-68, prof. chemistry, 1968—, acting chmn. chemistry dept., 1967-70. Fellow Am. Inst. Chemists, A.A.A.S.; mem. Am. Chem. Soc., Soc. for Applied Spectroscopy. Contbr. articles to profl. jours. Home: 2217 Burning Tree Lane Denton TX 76201 Office: Box 23973 Tex Women's U Denton TX 76204

CASWELL, PAUL EDWARD, judge; b. Savannah, Ga., June 28, 1907; s. Thomas E. and Florence Eva (Lee) C.; grad. Bradwell Inst., 1925; LL.B., U. Ga., 1930, J.D., 1969; m. Estelle Elizabeth Hendry,

Mar. 3, 1932; 1 son, Charles Thomas. Admitted to Ga. bar, 1930; mem. Ga. Ho. of Reps., 1935-37; judge City Ct., Hinesville, 1949-62; solicitor gen. Atlantic Circuit Ct., Hinesville, Ga., 1962-66, judge, 1966—. Dir. Hinesville (Ga.) Bank. Served to lt. col. AUS, 1941-46. Decorated Bronze Star medal, Presidential Unit Citation. Mem. Am. Judicature Soc., Am., Ga., Atlantic bar assns., C. of C. (pres. 1950-51), Circuit Bar Assn., Am. Legion, V.F.W. Democrat. Methodist. Lion (dist. gov. 1965-66), Mason. Home: 610 Oglethorpe Hwy Hinesville GA 31313 Office: 204 E Court St Hinesville GA 31313

CASWELL, RANDALL SMITH, physicist; b. Eugene, Ore., Feb. 7, 1924; s. Albert Edward and Mary (Edwards) C.; student U. Ore., 1940-42; S.B., Mass. Inst. Tech., 1947, Ph.D., 1951; m. Jean Marden Miller, June 14, 1945; children—William E., Virginia L., Anne (Mrs. Brian M. Flynn), Ellen S., Wendy J. (dec.), Julia C. With Nat. Bur. Standards, Washington, 1952—, chief neutron physics sect., 1957-67, dept. dir. Center Radiation Research, 1967—. Adj. prof. Am. U., Washington, 1957-70; mem. Nat. Council Radiation Protection, Measurement, 1967—, U.S. Nuclear Data Com., 1971—. Served to 1st lt. AUS, 1943-46. Fellow Am. Phys. Soc.; mem. Radiation Research Soc. (program com. 1968-69), Sigma Xi. Contbr. articles to profl. jours. Home: 2209 Salisbury Rd Silver Spring MD 20910 Office: Nat Bur Standards Washington DC 20234

CATALINO, ANTHONY, social worker; b. Reggio, Italy, July 13, 1916; s. Rocco and Angeline (Gallo) C.; B.S., U. Rochester, 1948; M.S.W., U. Buffalo, 1950; postgrad. U. Cal. at Berkeley, 1960; m. Isabell M. Small, Jan. 6, 1942; children—Suzanne, Raymond. Came to U.S., 1919, naturalized, 1935. Social worker youth parole Indsl. and Agrl. Sch., Industry, N.Y., 1950-58; dir. cottage program Highland Tng. Sch., 1958; dir. social services New Hampton Tng. Sch., 1959-60; asst. supt. Tng. Inst. Central Ohio, Columbus, 1960-62, supt., 1963-67; cons. child detention care N.Y. State, 1962-63; dir. Youth Devel. Center, Phila., 1967; dir. bur. children's instns. Pa. Dept. Pub. Welfare, Harrisburg, 1967-70; supt. Fla. Sch. for Girls, Ocala, 1970—. Field instr. St. Paul's Sch. Social Work, Ottawa, Ont., Can., 1958, Buffalo Sch. Social Work, 1958; vis. lectr. Franklin U., 1966, Ohio State U., 1966, Pa. State U., 1969. Served with F.A., AUS, 1941-45. Mem. Nat. Assn. Social Workers, Acad. Certified Social Workers, Nat. Assn. Tng. Schs. and Juvenile Agys. (gov.). Contbr. articles on social work to profl. publs. Address: Fla Sch for Girls Ocala FL 32670

CATANESE, ANTHONY JAMES, educator; b. New Brunswick, N.J., Oct. 18, 1942; s. Anthony James and Josephine Marlene (Barone) C.; B.A., Rutgers U., 1963; Ph.D., U. Wis., 1968; M.Urban Planning, N.Y. U., 1965; m. Sara Jean Phillips, Oct. 27, 1968; children—Mark Anthony, Michael Scott, Mark Alexander. Asst. prof. city planning Ga. Inst. Tech., Atlanta, 1967-68, asso. prof. city planning, 1968-73, chmn. doctoral studies com., 1970-73; mem. faculty U. Miami, Coral Gables, Fla., 1973—, James A. Ryder prof. transp. and planning, 1973—, dir. Ryder program in transp., 1973—. Sr. cons. State Wis., 1965-67; sr. planner State N.J., 1963-64; pres. A.J. Catanese & Assos., Inc., Cons. Planners, Atlanta, also Miami, 1967—; Sr. Fulbright prof. Colombia, 1971-72. Mem. Ga. Dunes Study Commn., 1972-73. Chmn. Middle DeKalb County Dem. Party, 1969-71; mem. 5th Congl. Dist. Dem. caucus, 1971; Aide-de-Camp Govs. Office, State Ga., 1971-72. Served with AUS, 1961-63. Recipient fellowships State N.J. Act, 1927, Werner Hegemann, 1964-65, Wis. Alumni Research Found., 1965-66, Richard King Mellon Trust, 1966-67, Ford Found., 1967. Mem. Am. Inst. Planners (bd. govs. 1971—; mem. exec. com. 1971—), Am. Soc. Planning Ofcls., Hwy. Research Bd., Regional Sci. Assn., Am. Acad. Polit. and Social Scis., Assn. Collegiate Schs. Planning, Jee Do Kwan Assn., Japanese Karate Assn. Author: Scientific Method of Urban Analysis, 1972; New Perspectives on Urban Transportation Research, 1972; Systemic Planning-Theory and Application, 1970; Planners and Local Politics; Impossible Dreams, 1973. Contbr. articles to profl. jours. Home: 15215 SW 77th Ct Miami FL 33157 Office: 1541 Brescia St Coral Gables FL 33124

CATER, KATHARINE C., educator; b. Macon, Ga., Sept. 1, 1914; d. Thomas J. and Maybelle (Moore) Cater; A.B. magna cum laude, Limestone Coll., 1935, Litt.D. (hon.), 1958; M.A., Mercer U., 1938; M.S., Syracuse U., 1942, postgrad., 1945-46. Tchr. Boiling Springs High Sch., Spartanburg, S.C., 1935-37; instr. English and French, Limestone Coll., Gaffney, S.C., 1937-40; dir. student personnel Furman U., Greenville, S.C., 1942-45; dean of women Auburn (Ala.) U., 1946—. Trustee Limestone Coll.; bd. dirs. Auburn Community Chest, 1955-57. Mem. Ala. Assn. Women Deans and Advisers (pres. 1947-49), Ala. Edn. Assn., Ala. Guidance Assn. (v.p. 1954-56, treas. 1957-58), Am. Coll. Personnel Assn., Am. Personnel and Guidance Assn., Am. Assn. U. Women (div. pres. 1954-56), Nat. Assn. Women Deans and Counselors, Assn. Coll. and Univ. Concert Mgrs. (life, mem. exec. bd. 1963-66), So. Coll. Personnel Assn. (adviser 1963-66), Garden Ala. (life), Kappa Delta Pi, Alpha Lambda Delta (nat. pres. 1970—), Assn. Coll. Honor Socs. (exec. com. 1972-74), Mortar Bd., League Women Voters (state dir. 1965-69), P.E.O., Delta Kappa Gamma (chpt. v.p. 1960-62), Phi Kappa Phi (chpt. pres. 1963-64). Democrat. Baptist. Clubs: Saugahatchee Country, Alabama Federation Womens, Auburn Campus, Auburn Faculty, Auburn Women's, Auburn Study. Home: Social Center Auburn U Auburn AL 36830

CATES, AUBREY MARION, JR., judge; b. Oklahoma City, Mar. 5, 1909; s. Aubrey Marion and Laura (Watkins) C.; B.A., U. Louisville, 1930; B.A. Jur. (Rhodes scholar), Oxford (Eng.) U., 1933, M.A., 1963; m. Dorothy May Bear, May 8, 1939; children—Dorothy Ellen (Mrs. Rex Dee Adams), Aubrey Marion III, Laura Compton (Mrs. Michael H. Luckett). Admitted to Ky. bar, 1933, Ala. bar, 1937; practiced in Louisville, 1932-33; counsel Pub. Works Adminstrn., Washington, Louisville, Montgomery, Ala., Austin, Tex., Lincoln, Neb., San Francisco, 1933-40, Maritime Commn., 1940-42; asst. gen. counsel War Shipping Adminstrn., Washington, 1942; practiced in Montgomery, 1942-56; mem. law firm Bear & Cates, 1942-43, Cates & Huddleston, 1950-56; judge Ala. Ct. Appeals, Montgomery, 1956-69; asso. judge Ala. Ct. Criminal Appeals, Montgomery, 1969-72, presiding judge, 1972—, chief judge Ala. Ct. Judiciary. Instr. econs. labor relations, real estate U. Ala. Montgomery Center, 1948-56. Pres. Montgomery Tb and Health Assn., 1952. Served from lt. (j.g.) to lt., USNR, 1943-46. Mem. Ala. State Bar, Am. Bar Assn., Am. Soc. for Legal History, Inst. Jud. Adminstrn., Selden Soc. (London). Democrat. Presbyn. Home: 1946 Ridge Av Montgomery AL 36106 Office: Jud Bldg Montgomery AL 36101

CATES, MICHAEL HAROLD, lawyer; b. Key West, Fla., July 23, 1937; s. Joseph Lovingston and Dorothy (Whitehead) C.; B.S. in Civil Engring., Valparaiso U., 1959; M.Engring., Tex. A. and M. U., 1960; J.D., U. Wash., Seattle, 1964; children—Keir Kayleen, Michelle Irene, Michael James. Engr. Boeing Co., Seattle, 1960-66; admitted to Fla. bar, 1967; contract mgr. EMR Corp., Sarasota, Fla., 1966-69; pvt. practice law, Key West, Fla., 1969—; atty. City Key West, 1971-74; atty. hosp. dist., 1970—. Dir. Fla. Keys Bldg. Supplies Inc., Spectrum Engring., Testing & Cons. Co. Inc., Big Fleet Inc. Registered profl. engr., Ala. Mem. Am., Fla., Monroe County, Fed. bar assns. Rotarian, Elk. Office: 505 Whitehead St Key West FL 33040

CATHEY, JAMES LEROY, city ofcl.; b. Arcadia, La., Apr. 30, 1919; s. John Leroy and Clotile (Brice) C.; student Centenary Coll., Shreveport, La., evenings 1939, 42; m. Dorothy Louise Williams, July 7, 1941; children—Sharon (Mrs. Robert Durwood Thorn), Karen (Mrs. Frederick Lee Green), Kathe (Mrs. Donald Lee Townsend). Safety insp. Camp Polk (La.) Fire Dept., 1940; fireman, Camp Livingstone, La., 1941, La. Ordnance Plant, 1942; mcht. dept., furniture and grocery stores, Bossier City, La., 1946-49; policeman Bossier City Police Dept., 1949-53, chief of police, 1953-70; asst. to mayor Bossier City, 1965-70, adminstr., coordinating agt., 1970-72, mayor, 1973—. Instr., La. Law Enforcement Inst., Bossier City, 1966; dep. sheriff Bossier Parish, 1963-73; 1st juvenile officer Bossier City and Parish, 1950-53. Chmn., Bossier City March of Dimes, 1951-52, chmn. northwest La. dist. Muscular Dystrophy Assn. Am., 1968—; chmn. Bossier Parish chpt. A.R.C., 1967—; chmn. Bossier Parish Heart Fund, 1970-73, bd. dirs. state com., 1971; co-chmn. Barksdale AFB Domes-Action Com., 1970-71; Bossier City chmn. United Fund, 1973; co-chmn. Council on Local Govts. for Shreveport and Bossier City, 1973. Mem. Bossier City Central Democratic Com., 1948-52. Bd. dirs. N.W. La. Fed. Law Enforcement Adv. Com., chmn., 1973; bd. dirs. Family Counseling and Children's Service of Bossier and Caddo Parish, Home Health Services Bossier Parish. Served with USAAF, 1943-46; lt. col. USAF ret. Named Most Courteous Policeman, Optimist Club, 1950; recipient Young Man of Year award Bossier Jr. C. of C., 1953; James Cathey Appreciation Day city of Bossier, 1968. Mem. Am. Legion (comdr. 1952-53), C. of C. (charter mem., dir. 1951-54, 70-71), V.F.W., La. Peace Officers Assn. (dir., past pres.), La. Municipal Police Assn. (dir. 1953—), La. Chiefs of Police (dir. 1953). Methodist (ofcl. bd. 1947-73, trustee 1967—, chmn. bd. trustees 1973). Lion (pres. Bossier City 1953-54), Mason (Shriner). Home: 317 Yarbrough St Bossier City LA 71010 Office: 630 Barksdale Blvd Bossier City LA 71010

CATHEY, MAURICE, lawyer; b. Paragould, Ark., June 23, 1910; J.D., Washington U., 1931. Admitted to Mo. bar, 1931, Ark. bar, 1933; mem. firm Cathey, Brown, Goodwin & Hamilton, Paragould; dep. pros. atty. Greene County, Ark., 1935-36. Mem. Am., Greene County, Northeast Ark., Ark. (chmn. jurisprudence and law reform com.; chmn. probate law com. 1950-51, mem. exec. com. 1962-67, pres. 1966-67), Delta Theta Phi. Office: 206 W Emerson St Paragould AR 72450*

CATHEY, RODNEY DEAN, ednl. adminstr.; b. Childress, Tex., Jan. 30, 1924; s. James E. and Gertrude (Land) C.; B.A., Hardin-Simmons U., 1948, M.A., 1950; Ed.D., U. Tex., 1962; m. Martha Carolyn Brown, Aug. 24, 1948; children—Blake, Christine, Deana, Ross. Prin. Sudan (Tex.) Elementary Sch., 1949; prin. Sanderson (Tex.) High Sch., 1949-51; prin. Winters (Tex.) High Sch., 1952-60; asst. supt. schs., Pharr, Tex., 1961; supt. schs., Bay City, Tex., 1963-69; supt. schs., McAllen, Tex., 1969—. Pres. Pan Am. U. Coop. Tchr. Edn. Center Bd., 1973—. Bd. dirs. Gladys Porter Zoo, Brownsville, Tex., 1973—. Served with AUS, 1943-46. Mem. Tex. Assn. Sch. Adminstrs. (mem. exec. com. 1967-69), Brazos-Colo. Adminstrs. Assn. (pres. 1967-69), Nat. Assn. Sch. Adminstrs., N.E.A., Tex. State Tchrs. Assn., Phi Delta Kappa (pres. Rio Grande Valley chpt. 1970-71). Lion. Home: 800 Jonquil St McAllen TX 78501 Office: 110 S 10th St McAllen TX 78501

CATLIN, AVERY, univ. adminstr.; b. N.Y.C., Jan. 29, 1924; s. Randolph and Hannah (White) C.; B.E.E., U. Va., 1947, M.A., 1949, Ph.D., 1960; m. Edith J. Reed, Sept. 7, 1946; children—Avery W., Edith (Mrs. Francis Lawrence), Beverly L., Frederic F. Faculty, U. Va., Charlottesville, 1948—, asso. prof., 1962-67, chmn. dept. math. sci., 1962-63, prof. materials sci., asso. dean engring., 1967-74, exec. v.p., 1974—. Cons. Westinghouse, Pitts., 1959-60, Hewlett-Packard, Cupertino, Cal., 1969-73, NSF, Washington, 1967, NASA, Washington, 1965-73, NIH, Bethesda, Md., 1965-72. Mem. Albemarle County Planning Commn., Charlottesville, 1966-74, chmn., 1968-74. Served with USNR, 1941-46. Home: Thimble Farm Route 5 Charlottesville VA 22901

CATO, ROBERT LOUIS, museum curator; b. Winters, Tex., Nov. 26, 1915; s. Joseph Henry and Babe (Murrell) C.; grad. high sch. Dept. county clk. Jefferson County, Beaumont, Tex., 1946; with Mil. Air Transport Service, Tripoli, Libya, 1948-50; with state Dept. in Tehran, 1950-52, Rome, 1953-55; now curator D.A.R. Mus., Washington. Served with AUS, 1943-46. Mem. S.A.R., S.C.V. Roman Catholic. Home: 216 Maryland Av NE Washington DC 20002 Office: 1776 D St NW Washington DC 20006

CATON, IRMA JEANNE, educator; b. Newport, Tenn.; d. Benjamin Dickerson and Bernice (Easterly) Caton; B.S., East Tenn. State U., 1946; M.S., U. Tenn., 1949, Ed.D., 1962. Tchr. pub. schs. Marion, Va., 1946-47, Newport, Tenn., 1947-48, Parrottsville, Tenn., 1949-50; asso. prof. phys. edn. Concord Coll., Athens, W.Va., 1950-60; instr. U. Tenn., Knoxville, 1961-62; asso. prof. phys. edn. North Tex. State U., Denton, 1962-65, prof., chmn. women's div. dept. health, phys. edn. and recreation, 1965—. Mem. Gov.'s Phys. Fitness Commn., 1971—. Mem. Am., Tex. assns. health, phys. edn. and recreation, N.E.A., Am. Assn. U. Women, Am. Assn. U. Profs., Tex. Assn. Coll. Tchrs., Pi Lambda Theta, Beta Sigma Phi, Kappa Delta Alumni Assn., Delta Psi Kappa. Mem. Christian Ch. Contbr. articles to profl. jours. Home: 1003 Eagle Dr Denton TX 76201

CATUCCI, HENRY GABRIEL, telecommunication co. exec.; b. Washington, Jan. 29, 1916; s. Ernesto and Francesca (Trozini) C.; LL.B., Cath. U., 1940; m. Margaret J. Halden, Apr. 6, 1947. Regional mgr. Western Union Cables, Washington, 1947-58; exec. dir. Western Union Telegraph Co., N.Y.C., 1959-64; v.p. Western Union Internat., Inc., Washington, 1964—; dir. several corps. Bd. dirs. Villa Rosa Home for Aged, Mitchelville, Md. Recipient Order of Merit, St. Penford (Spain), 1960. Mem. Armed Forces Communications and Electronic Assn. K.C. Clubs: Nat. Press, University, Columbia Country. Home: 3001 Veazey Terrace NW Washington DC 20008 Office: 2100 M St NW Washington DC 20037

CAUDILL, ESTILL LEFTRAGE, JR., surgeon, utility exec.; b. Narrows, Va., Aug. 21, 1916; s. Estill Leftrage and Flora (Weatherly) C.; student U. Tenn., East Tenn. State U., Va. Poly. Inst., 1934-37; M.D., Med. Coll. Va., 1941; m. Lucy Denny Bolton, Nov. 25, 1939; children—Estill L. III, Anne (Mrs. Clifton Reginald Lewis, Jr.), Lucy (Mrs. John Newby Austin, Jr.). Intern Baroness Erlanger Hosp., Chattanooga, 1941-42; individual practice gen. surgery, Elizabethton, Tenn., 1946-66; med. dir. Beaunit Corp. div. El Paso Natural Gas, Elizabethton, 1966—. Dir., Elizabethton Security Fed. Savs. and Loan Assn., Citizens Bank; med. examiner Carter County, 1961—. Mem. Tenn. Bd. Med. Examiners, 1964-71; mem. Carter County Bd. Health, 1946—. A founder Appalachian Regional Center for Healing Arts, 1968, bd. dirs.; sec.-treas. Elizabethton Airport Commn., 1972-73, chmn., 1973—. Served with M.C., AUS, 1942-46, USPHS Res., 1960—. Decorated Bronze Star medal, Combat Med. badge. Past Pres. Tenn. Acad. Gen. Practice, 1960. Mem. Tenn. Med. Assn. (trustee 1963-66), Am. Soc. Abdominal Surgeons, A.M.A., Phi Gamma Delta, Theta Kappa Psi. Rotarian (pres. 1950), Mason (32 deg.). Home: PO Box 551 Elizabethton TN 37643 Office: Beaunit Fibers Elizabethton TN 37643

CAUDILL, JOHN, agriculturist; b. Blackey, Ky., May 28, 1927; s. George Matt and Dora Alice (Fields) C.; B.S. in Agr., U. Ky., 1953, M.S., 1962, postgrad., 1968, 72; m. Alma Florence Lane, June 11, 1949; children—Aaron Mark, John Maurice. Asst. county agrl. extension agt. U.S. Dept. Agr., Whitley and Perry Counties, Ky., 1953, county agrl. extension agt., Owsley and Wolfe Counties, Ky., 1954-66, area extension resource devel. specialist, Quicksand Area, 1967-68, county extension agt. for agr., Wolfe County, Ky., 1969—. Bd. dirs. vol. fire depts., Hazel Green and Campton, Ky., 1968—. Served with AUS, 1945-47. Recipient award Ky. Div. Natural Resources, 1968, Ky. Service to Agr. citation, 1971, Distinguished Service award Nat. Assn. County Agrl. Agts., 1971. Mem. Nat. Assn. County Agrl. Agts., Community Devel. Soc., Epsilon Sigma Phi. Kiwanian (pres. Wolfe County 1965, dir. 1965—). Instrumental in mobilizing and organizing local leaders to bring improvements to area, including new electronics plant, pub. library, city water and sewer systems, 2 vol. fire depts., other. Home: PO Box 163 Hazel Green KY 41332 Office: PO Box 146 Campton KY 41301

CAUGHMAN, MARGUERITE WHITE (MRS. FRANCIS WILFRED CAUGHMAN), food products co. exec.; b. Columbia, S.C., Sept. 1, 1933; d. Chester Arthur and Mary Ella (Bone) White; grad. high sch.; m. Francis Wilfred Caughman, Aug. 25, 1951; children—Francis Wilfred, Ronald Alan, Alacia Lynn. Co-owner, bookkeeper Caughman's Meat Plant, Inc., Lexington, S.C., 1954-67; sec., dir. Lexington Frozen Foods, 1957—, gen. mgr., 1967—; bookkeeper C-Bar-D Farms, Inc., Abbeville, S.C., 1971—; bookkeeper, co-owner Bilmar Farms, Lexington, 1964—. Mem. Nat. Inst. Locker and Freezer Provisioners, S.C. Frozen Food Lockers Assn. (v.p. 1970-71, dir. 1968-71), Nat. Frozen Food Handling Com. (S.C. rep., 1971—). Democrat. Lutheran. Home: Route 5 Box 17 Lexington SC 29072 Office: 147 Columbia Av Lexington SC 29072

CAUGHRAN, BENNETT WILEY, orthopedic surgeon; b. Fayetteville, Tenn., May 21, 1927; s. Clarence Sloan and Ira Rebecca (Jackson) C.; B.A., Vanderbilt U., 1950, M.D., 1953; m. Phyllis Anne Wyrick, June 14, 1953; children—Frederick Daniel, Philip Bennett, Rebecca Elizabeth. Intern U. Va. Hosp., Charlottesville, 1953-54, resident, 1954-56; resident Vanderbilt U. Hosp., Nashville, 1956-58; practice medicine specializing in orthopedic surgery, Chattanooga, 1958—; mem. staffs Baroness Erlanger, Parkridge, Meml. hosps. Diplomate Am. Bd. Orthopedic Surgery. Fellow Am. Acad. Orthopedic Surgeons, A.C.S. Home: 100 Hilldale Dr Chattanooga TN 37411 Office: 1000 E 3d St Chattanooga TN 37403

CAULEY, JOHN ROWAN, newspaper corr.; b. Rushville, Ind., Apr. 25, 1908; s. Thomas S. and Mary Ann (Kelly) C.; student Rockhurst Coll., Kansas City, Mo., 1926-28, L.H.D., 1968; B.J., U. Mo., 1932. Pub. weekly newspaper The Summit News, Kansas City, Mo., 1933-36; mem. staff Kansas City (Mo.) Star, 1936—, news editor, 1954, fgn. affairs editor Washington bur., 1957-64, chief bur., 1964—. Recipient Pro-Meritis award Rockhurst Coll., 1960. Mem. A.P. Mng. Editors Assn. (dir. 1952-54). White House Corr. Assn., John Carroll Soc., Mo. Acad. Squires, Sigma Delta Chi. Roman Catholic (usher). Clubs: Kansas City Press (pres. 1950); Nat. Press (bd. govs.), Gridiron (Washington). Home: 1727 Massachusetts Av NW Washington DC 20036 Office: 1750 Pennsylvania Av NW Washington DC 20006

CAULEY, WILLIAM HARVEY, ins. co. exec.; b. Miami, Oct. 16, 1917; s. William Harvey and Onie (Hill) C.; student U. Fla., 1934, 36, U. Miami (Fla.), 1935; m. Naomi Padgett, Nov. 16, 1937; children—Vicki (Mrs. Richard Alexander Dennis), Susan (Mrs. Robert Andrew Barth). Prin., pres. Cauley & Martin Cos., Miami Springs, 1946-64, Americas Aviation & Marine Ins. Co., Miami Springs, Fla., 1963—; ins. cons. Dade County, Dade County Port Authority, 1961—; dir. Holsum Bakery, South Miami, South Miami Fed. Savs. & Loan Assn. Mem. diplomatic adv. bd. City of Coral Gables (Fla.), 1965-67; mem. Braniff Internat. Council, 1961-74, Dade County Grand Jury, 1964; mem. council Sch. Medicine, U. Miami, 1958-59; mem. interview bd. Air Force Acad., 1962. Co-chmn. Fla. Democratic Finance Com., 1964. Served to lt. USAAF, 1942-46. Mem. Greater Miami Ins. Bd. Methodist. Rotarian. Clubs: Coral Gables Country, Riviera Country; Carriage (Miami Springs). Home: 2715 DeSoto Blvd Coral Gables FL 33134 Office: 5353 NW 36th St Miami Springs FL 33166

CAUSEY, JACK QUIN, physician; b. Liberty, Miss., Sept. 29, 1932; s. Jack and Marguerite Eva (Quin) C.; B.S., Miss. Coll., 1953; M.D., Tulane U., 1957; m. Mary Elizabeth Cook, July 3, 1958; children—Jack Quin II, Edward Bruce, William David. Intern, Confederate Meml. Med. Center, Shreveport, La., 1957-58; resident medicine Charity Hosp., New Orleans, 1960-61, 63-65; clin. dir. medicine Lallie Kemp Hosp., Independence, La., 1965-66; practice medicine, specializing in internal medicine, Baton Rouge and Centreville, Miss., 1966—; chief of staff Field Meml. Hosp., Centreville, Miss., 1969-70, chief of medicine, 1969—; mem. staff Baton Rouge Gen. Hosp.; Instr., Tulane U. Sch. Medicine, 1960-66; clin. instr. La. State U. Sch. Medicine, 1968—. Adv. bd. Farmers Exchange Bank. Served with AUS, 1961-63. Diplomate Am. Bd. Internal Medicine. Fellow A.C.P.; mem. Am. Soc. Internal Medicine, A.M.A., So., Miss. med. assns., Amite Wilkinson Med. Soc. (pres. 1969-70), Centreville C. of C. (pres. 1970), Alpha Omega Alpha. Home: Centreville MS 39631 Office: Field Clinic Centreville MS 39631

CAUSEY, JAMES DAVID, lawyer; b. Tolerville, Miss., Jan. 31, 1926; s. R.C. and Ena (Gray) C.; ed. Delta State Tchrs. Coll., 1948; LL.B., U. Fla., 1950; m. Evelyn Lumbley, June 6, 1948; children—James Anderson, Catherine. Admitted to Fla. bar, 1950, Tenn. bar, 1951; individual practice law, Memphis. Served with USAF, 1943-46. Home: 4495 Park Av Memphis TN 38117 Office: 208 Adams St Memphis TN 38103

CAUSEY, NELL B. (MRS. DAVID CAUSEY), zoologist; b. Trenton, Tenn., Dec. 8, 1910; d. Harvey M. and Nettie (Hester) Bevel; B.S., Coll. of Ozarks, 1931; M.A., U. Ark., 1937; Ph.D., Duke, 1940; m. David Causey, Aug. 2, 1938. Tchr. high sch., Alma, Van Buren, Ark., 1931-36; biologist Marine Lab., Duke, 1944; instr. zoology U. Ark., 1943, 45-48; ind. investigator, 1948-64; asst. prof. zoology La. State U., 1964-66, asso. prof. zoology, 1966-71, prof., 1971—. Contbr. numerous articles to profl. jours. Research in taxonomy of the Diplopoda. Home: 1110 Magnolia Woods Dr Baton Rouge LA 70808

CAUTHEN, IRBY BRUCE, JR., univ. dean; b. Rock Hill, S.C., Aug. 24, 1919; s. Irby Bruce and Ruth (Kimbrell) C.; B.A., Furman U., 1940; M.A., U. Va., 1942, Ph.D., 1951; m. Elizabeth Bagby Greear, Aug. 28, 1954; children—Irby Bruce III, James Noah Greear. Asst. prof. English, Hollins Coll., 1951-54; mem. faculty U. Va., 1954—, prof. English, 1964—, asso. dean, 1958-62, dean coll., 1962—, chmn. Peters Rushton Seminars, 1958-61, 68—, asso. dir. summer sessions, 1958-72. Chmn. regional selection com. Woodrow Wilson Fellowship Found., 1961-72; exec. com. United Givers Fund, 1966-72. Trustee Belfield Sch., 1963-70. Served to lst lt. AUS, 1942-46; N. Africa, Italy. Decorated Bronze Star. Mem. Bibliog. Soc. U. Va. (v.p. 1961—), Modern Lang. Assn., Shakespeare Assn., Am. Assn. U. Profs., Va. Assn. Summer Sch. Deans (chmn. 1967-68), Phi Beta Kappa (U. Va.

pres. 1969-71), Omicron Delta Kappa. Democrat. Presbyn. Clubs: Colonnade, Farmington, Greencroft (Charlottesville). Editor: Norton and Sackville's Gorboduc; Two Mementoes from the Poe-Ingram Collection; (with J.L. Dameron) E.A. Poe: A Bibliography of Criticism. Contbg. editor Beaumont and Fletcher Canon. Contbr. articles to profl. jours. Home: 1824 Winston Rd Charlottesville VA 22903

CAUTHEN, WILEY MITCHELL, pipe line co. engr.; b. Montgomery, Ala., Aug. 27, 1935; s. George Ernest and Lois Ilean (Mitchell) C.; Asso. Sci. (Nat. LP Gas Assn. scholar), So. Tech. Inst., 1955; B.S., Auburn U., 1962; M.B.A., Rollins Coll., 1965; m. Jo Ann Watkins, Mar. 23, 1957; children—Wade Nelson, LoisAnn, Carol Rene. Asso. engr. Martin Marietta Corp., Orlando, Fla., 1962; staff engr., v.p. sales Fla. Gas Transmission Co., Winter Park, 1962-63, distbn. sales engr., 1963-64, mgr. indsl. sales, 1964-73, project engr., 1973—. Bd. mgmt. Central Fla. YMCA, Orlando. Served to lt. (j.g.) USNR, 1957-59. Registered profl. engr., Fla. Mem. Am. Soc. Heating, Refrigerating and Air-Conditioning Engrs. (chpt. pres. 1972-73), Nat. Soc. Profl. Engrs., Fla. Engring. Soc., Am. Soc. M.E., Asso. Industries Fla., Fla. Natural Gas Assn. Baptist. Home: 832 Orwell St Orlando FL 32809 Office: PO Box 44 Winter Park FL 32789

CAVALLO, PETER JOSEPH, dentist; b. Utica, N.Y., Feb. 14, 1904; s. Joseph and Theresa (Motto) C.; A.B., Colgate U., 1927; postgrad. City Coll. N.Y., 1927; D.D.S., U. Tenn., 1932; m. Irene Cullings Carr, Nov. 27, 1944; children—Joseph P., Peter J., Christopher C. Gen. practice dentistry, Memphis, 1932-48; staff dentist VA Hosp., Memphis, 1948—, chief VA Tb Dental Clinic, 1954-65, chief endodontia, 1965—. Asst. prof. operative dentistry U. Tenn. Dental Coll., 1955—. Diplomate Am. Bd. Endodontics. Mem. Am. Acad. Gold Foil Operators (gold key mem.), Am., Tenn. dental assns., Memphis Dental Soc., Am. Assn. Endodontists, Omicron Kappa Upsilon, Alpha Chi Sigma, Delta Sigma Delta. Republican. Roman Catholic. Clubs: Colgate Alumni, Forest Hill Civic (bd. dirs. 1963). Home: 3595 Forest Hill Rd Forest Hill TN 38031 Office: 1030 Jefferson Av Memphis TN 38104

CAVANAUGH, CHARLES JOHNSON, educator; b. Vernon Parish, La., Jan. 23, 1911; s. Patrick Henry and Fannie Jane (Smart) C.; B.A., La. Coll., 1932; M.S. (Teaching fellow 1932-34), U. Tenn., 1934; postgrad. (Teaching fellow 1935-37), N.Y. U., 1935-38; m. Eloise Wise Gill, Aug. 24, 1938; children—Charles Johnson, Jr., John Robert, Richard Lynn, William Denzell, David Albert. Head sci. Blytheville (Ark.) High Sch., 1935-36; asst. prof. biology Hofstra Coll., Hempstead, N.Y., 1937-41; prof. biology Union U., Jackson, Tenn., 1942-44; prof. biology La. Coll., Pineville, 1945—. Mem. undergrad. research com. La. Heart Assn., New Orleans, 1952—, chmn. bd. dirs., 1967-69; mem. So. regional heart com. Am. Heart Assn., Atlanta, 1968-73, mem. central com. for med. and community programs, 1970-73. Mem. La. Acad. Sci. (pres. 1964), Alpha Chi, Alpha Epsilon Delta, Omicron Delta Kappa. Democrat. Baptist. Author: Effects of Pituitary Substances on Adrenalectomized Rats, 1937; Life and Living, 1943; Clubfoot and Congenital Hand Anomalies, 1953; Situs Inversus Viserum Perfectus in the Rat, 1962. Home: 210 Stilley Rd Pineville LA 71360

CAVE, JERRY FRANK, architect; b. Forney, Tex., Jan. 25, 1924; s. Homer Samuel and Frank Ben (Yates) C.; student East Tex. State Tchrs. Coll., 1946-47, U. Tex., 1947-50; m. Myra Lynn Riley, Feb. 14, 1951; children—Ben Riley, Batina Lynn, Dorcas Lou. With archtl. firms Christensen & Christensen, 1951-53, Hidell & Decker, 1953-56, Broad & Nelson, 1956, Braden & Jones, 1956-64 (all Dallas); design architect Louis B. Gohmert, Architect—Planner, Mt. Pleasant, Tex., 1964—. Active Boy Scouts Am. Served with AUS, 1943-46. Mem. A.I.A., Tex. Soc. Architects, Nat. Rifle Assn. Mem. Christian Ch. (deacon 1964—). Club: Optimist (bd. dirs. 1965-66) (Mt. Pleasant). Home: PO Box 248 Mount Pleasant TX 75455 Office: PO Box 10 Mt Pleasant TX 57455

CAVENDER, JACK EDMOND, architect; b. Atlanta, Oct. 12, 1929; s. Jewel Edmond and Dallie Lou (McGiboney) C.; B.S. in Architecture, Ga. Inst. Tech., 1957; m. Bobbie Garrett, July 27, 1951 (dec. Dec. 1969); children—Jackie, Jenny, David; m. 2d, Celeta Estes, Feb. 12, 1971; 1 son, Jack Edmond. Architect, East Point, Ga., 1960-61; asso. Shugart & Cavender, Atlanta, 1961-63; architect, Decatur, Ga., 1963-71; prin. Cavender Assos. (name now Cavender/Kordys/Assos. Inc.), East Point, 1971—. Vice pres. Summit Investment Co., Inc., East Point, 1966—. Mem. A.I.A. Kiwanian. Prin. archtl. works include 1st Alliance Ch., S.W. Christian Ch., Emmanuel Luth. Ch., W.D. Luckie Masonic Lodge, Bottle Hill Masonic Lodge (all Atlanta), Gulf Disney Facility, Walt Disney World, Fla., Clayton-Rabun Community Center, Clayton, Ga., Wells Med. Pavilion, Hapeville, Ga. Home: 3830 Old Fairburn Rd SW Atlanta GA 30331 Office: 1677 Dorsey Av East Point GA 30044

CAVINESS, VERNE STRUDWICK, physician; b. Hillsborough, N.C., Feb. 9, 1895; s. Newby and Nora (Cummings) C.; A.B., Trinity Coll., 1915; student U. N.C., 1916-19; M.D., Jefferson Med. Coll., 1921; postgrad. McGill U., 1936; m. Alice Webb, Oct. 14, 1933; children—Verne Strudwick Jr., Elizabeth (Mrs. George E. Levings III), Alice (Mrs. Richard Hardy). Intern Jefferson Med. Coll., 1921-22, resident, 1922-23; pvt. practice medicine, specializing in internal medicine and cardiology, Raleigh, N.C., 1923—; chief cardiovascular medicine Rex Hosp., Raleigh, 1937-65; med. dir. Occidental Life Ins. Co., Raleigh, 1926-52; asso. prof. clin. medicine U. N.C., 1952-65, prof. emeritus, 1965—; cons. physician Methodist Home for Children, Raleigh, 1923—. Pres. Travelers Aid, 1928-29; pres. Raleigh Salvation Army, 1938-39; pres. Broughton High Sch. P.T.A., 1951-52; pres. Daniels Jr. High Sch. P.T.A., 1960-61. Served with U.S. Army, 1918. Fellow A.C.P.; mem. Am., Raleigh (past pres., dir.) heart assns., Am., N.C., Wake County (past pres.) med. assns., Raleigh Acad. Medicine (past pres.), Raleigh Med. Writers Soc. (past pres.), Am. Diabetes Assn. Democrat. Methodist. Mason (Shriner). Home: 913 Vance St Raleigh NC 27608 Office: 109 N Boylan Av Raleigh NC 27603

CAVNESS, PAT EDWARD, lawyer; b. Lampasas, Tex., Oct. 25, 1942; s. Damon Edward and Bernice (Parisher) C.; B.A., U. Tex., 1964, LL.B., 1966; m. Venona Goodwin, Aug. 17, 1962; children—Lorri Lynn, David Edward, Joel Patrick, Lindy Leigh. Admitted to Tex. bar, 1966; county atty. Lampasas County, 1966-70; individual practice, Lampasas, 1968-70; mem. firm Hammett, Hammett, & Cavness, Lampasas, 1970-72, Hammett, Hammett, Cavness & Builta, 1972—. Mem. Ch. of Christ (deacon 1970-73). Kiwanian. Home: Old Izoro Rd Lampasas TX 76550 Office: First Nat Bank Bldg PO Box 409 Lampasas TX 76550

CAWTHON, ELENORA ALBRECHT (MRS. JOHN ARDIS CAWTHON), coll. administr.; b. nr. Victoria, Tex., Dec. 6, 1917; d. Otto H. and Lillie (Lassmann) Albrecht; A.A., Victoria Jr. Coll., 1936; B.S.; U. Tex., 1938, M.S., 1939, Ed.D., 1948; m. John Ardis Cawthon, May 30, 1948; 1 dau., Elisabeth Albrecht. Tchr. pub. schs., Bandera, Tex., 1938-40, Woodsboro, Tex., 1940-46; asst. depts. govt., elementary edn., curriculum and instrn. U. Tex., Austin, 1936-38, summers 1943-46, 46-48; dir. tchr. edn. Ark. Polytech. Coll., Russellville, 1948-54; dir. dept. placement and service La. Polytech. Inst., Ruston, 1955-73, dean student services, 1973—, sec. faculty senate, 1966-67, senate mem., 1967-68. Trustee Coll. Placement Council Found., 1967-68; chmn. visitation teams Coll. Placement Services, Inc., 1967-68; bd. dirs. Bus. and Profl. Womens Found., 1956-57; scholarship com. Delta Kappa Gamma Soc., Epsilon State Orgn., 1961—. Mem. Bus. and Profl. Womens Club (pres. Ark. fedn. 1954-55), La. Fedn. Womens Clubs, Coll. Placement Council, (v.p. editorial 1967-68, pres. 1972-73), S.W. Placement Assn. (pres. 1959-61), La. Council Coll. Placement Officers (pres. 1967-68), La. Tchrs. Assn., Am. Personnel and Guidance Assn., Am. Coll. Personnel Assn., Am. Assn. U. Women, Delta Kappa Gamma, Pi Sigma Alpha, Pi Lambda Theta, Alpha Tau Delta, Phi Kappa Phi. Club: Pierian. Contbr., articles to profl. jours. Home: 815 Wilaford St Ruston LA 71270

CAWTHON, JOHN ARDIS, educator; b. Koran, La., Mar. 16, 1907; s. James Alexander and Maggie Mae (Dance) C.; B.A., La. Poly. Inst., 1934; M.A., La. State U., 1937; Ed.D., U. Tex., 1948; m. Elenora Albrecht, May 30, 1948; 1 dau., Elisabeth Albrecht. Tchr., Sarepta High Sch., 1934-39; supr. Demonstration Sch., La. Poly. Inst. at Ruston, 1940-41, vis. prof., 1948, head secondary edn. dept., 1954—; supr. Demonstration Sch., La. State Normal Coll., 1941-42, 46; grad. teaching asst. U. Tex., 1946-48; chmn. edn. dept. Ark. Poly. Inst., 1948-54. Served to capt. AUS, 1942-45. Mem. N.E.A., Assn. Supervision and Curriculum Devel., Assn. Student Teaching, La. Tchrs. Assn., La., North La., Darlington (S.C.) hist. assns. Phi Kappa Phi, Phi Delta Kappa, Sigma Tau Delta, Omicron Delta Kappa. Author: The Inevitable Guest-Life and Letters of Jemima Darby, 1965. Contbr. articles to profl. jours. Home: 815 Wilaford St Ruston LA 71270 Office: PO Box 6245 Tech Sta Ruston LA 71270

CAWTHON, PETER WILLIS, JR., banker; b. Mexia, Tex., Aug. 26, 1921; s. Peter Willis and Virginia (Smith) C.; B.S. in Petroleum Engr., U. Okla., 1947, M.Petroleum Engring. (Amoco Prodn. Co. fellow), 1949; grad. Columbia Exec. Program in Bus. Adminstrn., 1970; m. Charlsie Elaine McLaughlin, Jan. 23, 1947; children—Peter Willis III, Mark McLaughlin, David Kelly. Petroleum prodn. employee Exxon, U.S.A., Wink, Tex., 1947; petroleum engr. Phillips Petroleum Co., Eureka Kan., 1948-49, Midland, Tex., 1949-50; with First City Nat. Bank of Houston, 1950—, sr. v.p., mgr. petroleum and minerals dept., 1973—; dir. Highland Village State Bank, Houston. Served to 1st lt. Ordnance Corps, AUS, 1943-46; ETO. Registered profl. engr., Tex. Mem. Soc. Petroleum Engrs. of Am. Inst. Mining and Mineral. Engrs. (chmn. Gulf Coast sect. 1960, nat. dir. 1965-67), Tau Beta Pi, Sigma Tau, Sigma Gamma Epsilon, Phi Delta Theta. Methodist. Club: Petroleum (dir. Houston). Home: 11719 Wood Lane Houston TX 77024 Office: 1001 Main St Houston TX 77002

CAWTHON, WOODSON ARTHUR, health assn. exec.; b. Roxton, Tex., Oct. 5, 1918; s. William Arthur and Lura (Denton) C.; A.A., Paris Jr. Coll., 1937; B.S., Tex. A. and M. U., 1940; m. Merle Nance, July 4, 1942; children—Ann, Wesley Arthur. Mgr. W.A. Cawthon Wholesale Petroleum Co., Paris, Tex., 1946-54; owner, mgr. Cawthon's, Paris, 1955-67; mgr. Silsbee (Tex.) C. of C., 1967-73; asst. exec. dir. Tex. Home Health, Inc., Silsbee, 1973—. Mem. Paris (Tex.) City Council, 1959-61; mayor, Paris, 1961-63. Served to maj. AUS, 1942-46. Mem. Ch. of Christ (deacon 1948-60, elder 1960-67). Lion (pres. 1971—). Home: Route 1 Box 406 Silsbee TX 77656 Office: 1180 Railroad St Silsbee TX 77656

CAYCE, EDGAR EVANS, elec. engr.; b. Selma, Ala., Feb. 9, 1918; s. Edgar and Gertrude Salter (Evans) C.; B.S. in E.E., Duke, 1939; m. Kathryn Anderson Bane, June 13, 1942; children—Edgar Evans, Janet Gail. With Va. Electric & Power Co., Norfolk, 1940—, engr. dist. planning dept., 1955—. Vice pres. Edgar Cayce Found., 1960—. Trustee Atlantic U. Served to capt. AUS, 1941-45. Registered profl. engr., Va. Mem. Assn. for Research and Enlightenment (trustee 1960—). Presbyn. Author: Edgar Cayce on Atlantis, 1968; (with Hugh Lynn Cayce) The Outer Limits of Edgar Cayce's Power, 1971. Home: 1565 Michigan Av Virginia Beach VA 23453 Office: 2700 Cromwell Rd Norfolk VA 23510

CAYCE, LEE FARRAR, physician; b. Nashville, Jan. 12, 1915; s. John Smith and Martha (Farrar) C.; B.A., Vanderbilt U., 1936; M.D., Washington U., St. Louis, 1940; m. Mary Baker Gregory, Dec. 30, 1937; children—Mary Farrar (Mrs. Alfred George Nicols), Patricia Lee (Mrs. Lucien Caldwell Simpson). Intern Nashville Gen. Hosp., 1940-41, resident 1941-43; practice medicine specializing in otolaryngology and ophthalmology, Nashville, 1945—; chmn. dept. ophthalmology Mid-State Bapt. Hosp., Nashville, 1965—, mem. med. adv. com., 1965—; mem. staffs St. Thomas, Park View hosps. Bd. and hon. mem. Bill Wilkerson Hearing and Speech Center, Nashville. Served to capt. AUS, 1943-46. Mem. Tenn. State, Nashville med. socs., Nashville Acad. Ophthalmology and Otolaryngology, Contact Lens Assn. of Ophthalmology, Am. Assn. Ophthalmology, Pan Am. Assn. Ophthalmology, Royal Soc. Health. Mem. Ch. of Christ. Clubs: Nashville, Civitan. Home: 915 Robertson Academy Rd Nashville TN 37220 Office: Mid-State Med Bldg Nashville TN 37203

CAZAN, MATTHEW JOHN, educator; b. Beclean, Romania, Mar. 10, 1912; s. John and Marie (Sipos) C; student U. Bucharest Law Sch., Youngstown Coll., Georgetown U. Sch. Fgn. Service; m. Sylvia Marie Buday, July 14, 1935; 1 son, Matthew John George. Lectr. Georgetown U., 1942-44; spl. lectr. Indsl. Coll. of the Armed Forces, 1947; asso. in Romanian Georgetown U. Inst. Langs. and Linguistics, 1949—, lectr. polit. sci. and econs. Sch. Fgn. Service, 1943-57; lectr. The Inst. Fgn. Service Officer Preparation, 1953—; lectr. polit. sci. George Washington U., 1963—; spl. employee U.S. Dept. of Justice, 1947-60, 63—; internat. claims analyst fgn. claims settlement commn., 1960-63. Chmn. Lobarca youth guidance com. Va. Gov.'s Conf. Youth. Mem. Am. Assn. U. Profs., Am. Polit. Sci. Assn., Am. Soc. Internat. Law, Conf. Democratic Theory, Pi Gamma Mu. Home: 6369 Lakeview Dr Lake Barcroft Estates Falls Church VA 22041 Office: George Washington U Washington DC also Dept Justice Washington DC

CAZAN, SYLVIA MARIE BUDAY (MRS. MATTHEW JOHN CAZAN), realtor; b. Youngstown, O., Nov. 17, 1915; d. John J. and Sylvia (Grama) Buday; student U. Bucharest (Rumania), 1933-35, Youngstown Coll., 1936-38, Georgetown U. Inst. Langs. and Linguistics, 1950; m. Matthew John Cazan, July 14, 1935; 1 son, Matthew John G. Adminstrv. asst. statistics U.S. Dept. Def., 1941-52; spl. employee Dept. Justice, 1956-58; mgr. James L. Dixon & Co. Realtors, Falls Church, Va., 1959-70; Va. sub div. mgr. Lewis & Silverman, Inc., 1970—. Mem. Bd. Examiners Georgetown U., 1950. Bd. dirs. Magnolia Internat. Debutante Ball. Recipient Commendation and Meritorious award Dept. Justice, 1958. Mem. Gen. Fedn. Women's Clubs (pres. 1955-56), Interscholastic Debating Soc., Washington, No. Va. real estate bds. Mem. Rumanian Orthodox Ch. Home: 6369 Lakeview Dr Lake Barcroft Estates Falls Church VA 22041 Office: 8401 Connecticut Av Chevy Chase MD 20015

CEBOLLERO, CARLOS, lawyer; b. San Juan, P.R., Dec. 6, 1927; s. Tomas and Margarita (March) C.; A.B., Harvard Coll., 1948; J.D., Harvard Law Sch., 1951; m. Maybeth Lema, June 14, 1952; children—Carlos Jose, Maria Mercedes. Admitted to P.R. bar, 1951; asso. law firm Cordova & Gonzalez, San Juan, 1954-59; partner firm Cordova & Cebollero (firm name changed at time of merger to Brown, Newsom & Cordova), San Juan, P.R., 1959—; dir. P.R.-Am. Ins. Co., San Juan, 1961—, vice-chmn. bd., 1963—. Chmn. bd. dirs. San Juan Legal Services Inc.; mem. P.R. Bd. Bar Examiners, 1969-72. Mem. P.R., Am., Fed. (treas. P.R. chpt. 1973—) bar assns. Roman Catholic. Home: 64 Santiago Iglesias Santurce PR 00907 Office: PO Box S-2152 San Juan PR 00903

CECIL, DAVID ROLF, educator; b. Tulsa, July 12, 1935; s. Neil McKinley and Ola Ethel (Turner) C.; student Carnegie Inst. Tech., 1954-55, Okla. A. and M. U., 1955-56; B.A., Tulsa U., 1958; postgrad. Tulane U., 1958-59; M.S., Okla. State U., 1960, Ph.D., 1962; m. Betty Lou Poe, June 14, 1958; 1 son, Eric Alan. Asst. prof. mathematics N. Tex. State U., 1962-67, asso. prof., 1967-69; prof. mathematics Butler U., 1969-70; asso. prof. mathematics Tex. A. and I. U., 1970-73, prof., 1973—. Cons. magnetic div. Vero, Inc., Region I Edn. Service Center (Edinburg, Tex.); lectr. Mem. supervisory com. Denton County Tchrs. Credit Union, 1968-69. Research fellow Tulane U., 1958-59; Nat. Sci. Found. summer fellow, 1960, 61; recipient grant, North Tex. State U., 1968-69, Tex. A. and I. U., 1971, 72, 73. Fellow Tex. Acad. Sci.; mem. Am. Math. Soc., N.Y. Acad. Scis., Tex. Assn. Children Learning Disabilities, Sigma Xi. Methodist. Contbr. articles to profl. jours. Home: PO Box 1484 1921 S Park Dr Kingsville TX 78363

CECIL, SAM KENNETT, distillery exec.; b. Bardstown, Ky., Oct. 26, 1918; s. Francis Lavielle and Mary Elizabeth (Thompson) C.; student U. Louisville, 1939-40, 46-48, Bellarmine Coll., 1960-64; m. Mary Bernadine Greenwell, Oct. 30, 1940; children—Bernardine (Mrs. Joe Robert Strange), Beverly (Mrs. William K. Roberts), Francis Lavielle, Anthony Gerst, Sam Kennett III. Chemist, T.W. Samuels Distillery, Deatsville, Ky., 1937-41, Heaven Hill Distilleries, Bardstown, 1945-52; quality control supr. Dant Distillery, Gethsemane, Ky., 1952-54; prodn. mgr., v.p. Star Hill Distillery, Loretto, Ky., 1954—, also dir. Vice pres. P.T.A., Bardstown, 1963-64, pres., 1964-65, 70-71. Served with AUS, 1941-46; PTO. Decorated Bronze Star medal. Mem. Nat. Assn. Power Engrs. (sec. local chpt. 1963-64, pres. 1964-65), Newcomen Soc. N.Am. Democrat. Roman Catholic. Club: Old Kentucky Home Country (Bardstown). Home: Route 3 Box 98A Bardstown KY 40004 Office: Star Hill Farm Loretto KY 40037

CEDERVALL, ANTON ARNOLD, architect; b. Peking, China, Mar. 29, 1923; s. Anton Adolf and Sara Margareta (Elmgren) C.; student North Park Jr. Coll., 1941-42, Harvard, 1943-44; B.A., U. Mich., 1949, postgrad., 1949-50; m. Georgiana Gale Clark, Jan. 6, 1945; children—John, Edward, Jari, Sharon, Lisa, Sara; m. 2d, Brenda O. Burns, Feb. 5, 1972. Architect, various archtl. firms, 1960-68; partner, Eugene Lawrence, Assos., Architects, Palm Beach, Fla., 1968-69; pvt. practice as architect, Riviera Beach, Tequesta, Fla., 1969—; dir., cons. architect Modular Industries, Inc., Indiantown, Fla. Mem. planning and zoning bd., Longboat Key, Fla., 1958-59, Palm Beach Shores, Fla., 1969-70; bldg. ofcl., Juno Beach, Fla., 1966-68. Served with AUS, 1943-48, 51-56. Mem. A.I.A., Fla. Assn. Architects, Jupiter-Tequesta C. of C. (chmn. com. 1970—). Episcopalian. Kiwanian, Rotarian (pres. 1972). Prin. archtl. works include Overseas Service Corp. Bldg., West Palm Beach, Fla., St. Maurice Cath. Ch., Hollywood, Fla. Home: 1492 Carolina Dr Tryon NC 28782 Office: 113 S Trade St PO Box 1346 Tryon NC 28782

CELITANS, GERARD JOHN, educator; b. Riga, Latvia, Feb. 1, 1937; s. John and Anna (Stivrins) C.; B.Sc. (Commonwealth scholar), U. New South Wales (Sydney, Australia), 1959, Ph.D., 1963; m. Barbara Anne Valeska, Dec. 16, 1966. Came to U.S., 1964, naturalized, 1971. Vis. prof., research asso. New Eng. Inst., Ridgefield, Conn., 1966—, research scientist, 1964-66; asso. prof. chemistry Fla. Atlantic U., 1966-68; vis. prof. physics U. Toronto, summer 1968; asso. prof. bioengring. U. Tex. Med. Sch., San Antonio, 1968—. Recipient Commonwealth Postgrad. award, 1959-62. Mem. N.Y. Acad. Scis., A.A.A.S., Am. Phys. Soc., Am. Assn. Physics Tchrs. Author: Calculus, 1973; Basic Electronics, 1973; Ionizing Radiation, 1973. Contbr. articles to sci. jours. Home: 2818 Whisper Hill San Antonio TX 78230 Office: U Tex Med Sch San Antonio TX 78284

CENTER, DANIEL HAYDN, JR., computer processing co. exec.; b. Campton, Ky., Aug. 5, 1930; s. Daniel Haydn and Ruth (Tutt) C.; B.S., Ohio State U., 1961, M.S., 1961; student Berea Coll., 1947-48, 50-51, Am. U., 1953, George Washington U., 1953-55; m. Barbara Ann Willis, Feb. 10, 1973; children—Timothy Joseph, Brendan Dale. Supr. Communications Center CIA, Washington, 1951-56; research asst. Ohio State U., 1960-61; maj. projects mgr. Gen. Tel. of Fla., Tampa, 1961-66; statis. dir. Gen. Tel. of Cal., Santa Monica, 1967-69; dir. mgmt. services dept. GTE Data Services, Tampa, 1969—. Served with AUS, 1948-49. Named Ky. Col. Registered profl. engr., Ohio, Fla., Cal. Mem. Am. Inst. Indsl. Engrs., Nat. Soc. Profl. Engrs., Fla. Soc. Profl. Engrs., Am. Statist. Assn., Am. Inst. Indsl. Engrs. (sec. 1973, pres. elect 1974), Am. Statis. Assn., Tampa C. of C. (chmn. research com. 1962-63), Am. Marketing Assn. (v.p. 1962, 64, pres. 1965), Tau Beta Pi, Alpha Pi Mu. Home: 620 Riviera Dr Tampa FL 33606 Office: Box 1548 First Financial Tower Tampa FL 33606

CENTIFANTO, YSOLINA MEJIA, microbiologist, educator; b. Panama City, Panama, Sept. 12, 1928; d. J. and Benelda (Paneda) Mejia; B.S., U. Panama, 1951; M.S., Western Res. U., 1954; Ph.D., U. Fla., 1964; div.; children—Loraine, James, Anthony, Matthew. Came to U.S., 1951, naturalized, 1960. Asst. prof. U. Panama, 1955-56, physiology asst. Sch. Medicine, 1955-56; instr. E.Carolina Coll., 1958; research technologist Kodak Tropical Research Lab., Panama City, 1956-58, Eastman Kodak Research Lab., Rochester, N.Y., 1958-61; abstractor Chem. Abstracts, Rochester, 1960-61; research asst. dept. ophthalmology Coll. Medicine, U. Fla., Gainesville, 1964-65, instr., 1965-66, asst. prof., 1966-72, asso. prof. ophthalmology, immunology and med. microbiology, 1972—. Mem. Am. Chem. Soc., Am. Soc. Microbiology, A.A.A.S., Assn. for Research in Ophthalmology, N.Y. Acad. Scis., Sigma Xi. Contbr. articles to profl. jours. Home: 2809 NE 11th Terrace Gainesville FL 32601

CERNAN, EUGENE A., astronaut; b. Chgo., Mar. 14, 1934; s. Andrew C. Cernan; B.S. in Elec. Engring., Purdue U., 1956; postgrad. student U.S. Naval Postgrad. Sch., Monterey, Cal.; m. Barbara Jean Atchley; 1 dau., Teresa Dawn. Joined U.S. Navy, 1956, advanced through grades to lt.; former mem. attack squadrons 126, 113, Miramar (Cal.) Naval Air Sta.; now astronaut with Manned Spacecraft Center, NASA. Mem. Tau Beta Pi. Address: care Manned Spacecraft Center NASA Houston TX 77001*

CERNY, SAM J., petroleum co. exec.; b. Enid, Okla., June 21, 1932; s. Lafayette Hugh and Ila (Dague) Bingham; student Phillips U., 1950-51, No. Okla. Jr. Coll., 1951-52; B.S. in Geol. Engring., Okla. U., 1955; m. Virginia Lou Greene, Nov. 14, 1964; 1 dau., Jennifer Diane. With Shell Oil Co., various locations, 1955-62; sole practice petroleum cons., Oklahoma City, 1962-65; v.p. prodn. Cleary Petroleum Corp., Oklahoma City, 1965-71, exec. v.p., 1971-74, pres., 1974—, also dir.; pres. Petrodyne Ltd. (Canadian) subsidiary, 1971—. Mem. Oklahoma City Petroleum Club, Oklahoma U. Club Oklahoma City (pres. 1969), U. Okla. Alumni Assn., Oklahoma City C. of C. Methodist. Club: Oklahoma City Golf and Country. Home: 2005 NW

56th Terrace Oklahoma City OK 73118 Office: Prentice Bldg 63d and N Broadway Oklahoma City OK 73116

CERUTTI, PETER ADRIAN, educator, biochemist; b. Zurich, Switzerland, Oct. 8, 1931; M.D., U. Zurich, 1956, Ph.D., 1963, postdoctoral fellow, 1963; m. Patricia Ann Rogers, 1972. Came to U.S., 1964, naturalized, 1970. Asst. prof. George Washington U., 1965, Princeton, 1966-71; prof., chmn. dept. biochemistry U. Fla., Gainesville, 1971—. Served to 1st lt. Swiss Army, 1951-63. Mem. Am. Chem. Soc., Am. Soc. Biol. Chemists, Am. Soc. Photobiology, N.Y. Acad. Scis., Biophys. Soc. Home: 1111 NW 22d St Gainesville FL 32601

CERVERA, NICHOLAS JOSEPH, lawyer; b. N.Y.C., Sept. 25, 1940; s. Joseph J. and Rose (Romano) C.; B.S., Troy State U., 1963; J.D., Cumberland Sch. Law, Samford U., 1966; m. Patricia Ann Summer, June 2, 1967; children—Richard David, Michael James, Lisa Marie. Econ. researcher Eastern Air Lines, Inc., N.Y.C., 1964-65; prof. law Troy State U., Ala., 1966—; admitted to Ala. bar, 1966; practiced in Troy, 1966— mem. firm Cervera and Folmar, 1966—. Pres., Fonceco, Inc., 1967—; treas. Lakewood, Inc., 1968—. Mem. Am. Bus. Law Assn., Pike County Bar Assn. (pres. 1967—), Am. Assn. U. Profs., Phi Alpha Delta, Tau Kappa Epsilon. Mason (Shriner). Club: Lions. Home: 106 Lakeview Circle Troy AL 36081 Office: Box 325 Troy AL 36081

CHABLE, E(UGENE) ROBERT, clergyman; b. Cleve., June 7, 1920; s. Eugene Ray and Marion Margaret (Skym) C.; B.B.A., Cleve. State U., 1944; M.Div., Colgate Rochester Div. Sch., 1946; M.A., U. Rochester, 1948; Ph.D., Columbia, 1955; postgrad. Union Theol. Sem., 1951-54, Princeton, 1952; m. Marion Hayes Boynton, Oct. 26, 1946. With Elizabeth Jones Studios, Cleve., summer 1938, Gage Gallery, part-time 1939-40, Fed. Res. Bank, 1940-41, Crane Co., 1941-44; ordained to ministry Bapt. Ch., 1946; asso. minister Brighton Presbyn. Ch., Rochester, N.Y., 1944-45; minister 1st Bapt. Ch., Palmyra, N.Y., 1945-51; interim minister Wyckoff (N.J.) Reformed Ch., 1951-53; asso. minister Park Av. Meth. Ch., N.Y.C., 1954; dir. student personnel, dean of men, asso. prof. history Hillsdale Coll., 1954-57; dean of student personnel, acting registrar, prof. philosophy and religion Rio Grande Coll., 1957-59; incorporator, mem. exec. com. New Coll., Inc., Sarasota, Fla., 1959-62; v.p., bus. rep. Venice-Nokomis Bank, Venice, Fla., 1959-63; minister Venice United Ch. of Christ, 1963—. First v.p. Fla. Migrant Ministry, 1967-68. Asso. mem. Fla. Soc. for Prevention of Blindness, 1964—; mem. Am. Mus. Natural History; v.p. Sarasota County Community Health and Welfare Council. Bd. dirs. S. Sarasota County Retarded Children's Assn., 1961-63, Venice-Nokomis Art Assn., 1961-63; bd. dirs. Venice Little Theatre, 1962-65, treas., 1963-64, 64-66; bd. dirs. Family Service Assn., Sarasota County, 1963-65; trustee New Coll., Sarasota, Fla.; mem. S. Sarasota County Meml. Hosp. Assn., chmn. nominating com. 1962, chmn. major gifts, 1973—. Mem. Venice Area Ministerial Assn. (pres. 1967-69), Soc. Bibl. Lit. and Exegesis Am. Council of Learned Socs., Fla. Conf. United Ch. of Christ (moderator 1972-73), Wilderness Soc., Audubon Soc., Nat. Geog. Soc., Delta Sigma Phi. Rotarian, Mason (33 deg., K.T., Shriner); mem. Order DeMolay. Club: Venice (Fla.) Yacht. Contbr. articles to profl. jours. Home: 104 Alba St W Venice FL 33595 Office: PO Drawer 998 Venice FL 33595

CHABON, STEVE, ret. army officer, elec. co. exec.; b. Gilberton, Pa., Mar. 4, 1931; s. Onufer and Anna (Bobiak) C.; B.A. in Govt. and Politics, U. Md., 1968; m. Roberta Jean McGuire, Oct. 30, 1954; children—Stephen J., Gregory M. With Johns-Manville Corp., 1950; served with USNR, 1949-50; joined USAF, 1950, resigned as master sgt., 1962; commd. lt. U.S. Army, 1962, advanced through grades to maj., 1968; stationed in Korea, 1962-63, Vietnam, 1968-69; mil. asst. to spl. asst. Office Sec. of Def., Washington, 1965-67; exec. asst. to asst. sec. Office Asst. Sec. of Army, 1969-71; dir. adminstrn. Def. Systems Mgmt. Sch., 1971-72; mem. profl. staff Gen. Electric Co. Center for Advanced Studies, Washington, 1972-73; office adminstr. law firm Williams, Connolly & Califano Washington, 1973—. Decorated Legion of Merit, Meritorious Service medal, Joint Service Commendation medal. Club: Army-Navy Country (Arlington, Va.). Composer: Rhapsody in Notes, 1953; also ballads. Home: 6026 Haverhill Ct West Springfield VA 22152 Office: 1000 Hill Bldg Washington DC 20006

CHACKO, GEORGE KUTTICKAL, operations researcher; b. Trivandrum, India, July 1, 1930; s. Geevarghese Kuttickal and Thankamma (Mathew) C.; certificate advanced tng. Indian Statis. Inst., Calcutta, India, 1951; B. Commerce, Calcutta U., 1952; M.A., Madras U., Tambaram, India, 1950; Ph.D., New Sch. Social Research, 1959; m. Yo Yee, Aug. 10, 1957; children—Rajah Yee, Ashia Yo. Came to U.S., 1953. Asst. editor Indian Finance, Calcutta, 1951-53; comml. corr. Times of India, Calcutta, 1953; asso. test devel. math. Ednl. Testing Service, Princeton, N.J., 1955-57; dir. marketing mgmt. research Royal Metal Mfg. Co., N.Y.C., 1958-60; operations research cons. RAND Corp., Santa Monica, Cal., 1961-62; mgr. operations research dept. Hughes Semicondr. div. Newport Beach, Cal., 1960-61; operations research cons. Union Carbide Corp., N.Y.C., 1962-63; staff mem. Research Analysis Corp., McLean, Va., 1963-65; staff mem. MITRE Corp., Arlington, 1965-67; sr. staff scientist TRW Systems Group, Washington, 1967-70; asst. prof. U. Cal. at Los Angeles, 1960-61; lectr. U.S. Dept. Agr. Grad. Sch., 1965-67, asst. professorial lectr. George Washington U., Washington, 1965-68; professorial lectr. Am. U., Washington, 1967-70, adj. prof., 1970—; vis. prof. systems mgmt. U. So. Cal., 1970-71, prof., 1971—. Cons. UN Pub. Adminstrn. Div., N.Y., Milcom Systems Corp., Rockville, Md., Aries Corp., McLean, Va., Macro Systems Inc., N.Y.C. and Silver Spring, Md., Fujitsu Ltd., Tokyo, Japan, Inst. Creative Studies, Washington, York U. Kenya Project, Dept. Def. Ind. Coll. Armed Forces, So. Ry. System, others. Sec.-treas. Am. Com. Friends of Serampore, N.Y.C., 1959-63, treas., 1963-65; youth cons. World Council Chs. Trustee Washington Operations Research Council, 1967-69. Fellow A.A.A.S., Am. Astron. Soc. (nat. v.p. publs. 1969-71, dir. 1972—, rep. to A.A.A.S. 1968-71); mem. Operations Research Soc. Am. (nat. vice-chmn. health applications sect. 1966-68, mem. sect. council 1971-73, mem. nat. com. meetings 1966-67, mem. nominations com. 1972—, chmn. arrangements nat. meeting 1970, nat. council 1968-73, rep. to A.A.A.S. 1972—, rep. to Internat. Inst. Applied Systems Analysis 1974), World Future Soc., Washington Operations Research Council, World Future Soc., Policy Scis. Assn. Presbyn. (mem. nat. council 1969-71). Kiwanian (chmn. support chs. com. 1965-66, chmn. internat. relations com., 1966-77, chmn. boys and girls com. 1967, 68, 1st v.p. 1961; dist. chmn. agr. and conservation com. 1967, dist. chmn. spl. communications 1969-70, div. chmn. newsletter 1968-70, div. chmn. internat. relations 1971—, pres. chpt. 1972-73, div. chmn. adminstrn. 1972). Author: India-Toward an Understanding, 1959; International Trade Aspects of Indian Burlap-An Econometric Study, 1961; Today's Information for Tomorrow's Products, an Operations Research Approach, 1966; Studies for Public Men, 1969; Applied Statistics in Decision-Making, 1971; Computer-Aided Decision-Making, 1972; Technological Forecontrol—Prospects, Problems, Policy, 1974; Systems Approach to Public and Private Sector Problems, 1974; Operations Research Approach to Problem Formulation and Solution, 1974. Translator: Mar Thoma Syrian Liturgy, 1956; Mar Thoma Syrian Church—Order of Holy Matrimony, 1957. Editor: Reducing the Cost of Space Transportation, 1969; The Recognition of Systems in Health Services, 1969; Systems Approach to Environmental Pollution, 1971; Alternative Approaches to the National Delivery of Health Care, 1972; co-editor: Planning Challenges of the 70's in the Public Domain, 1971. Editor: Washington Operations Research Council Newsletter, 1967-68; Operations Research Soc. Am. Health Applications Sect. Newsletter, 1966—; acting mng. editor Jour. Astronautical Scis., 1969-70, mng. editor, 1971—; editor Kiwanis Newsletter, Capitol dist., div. 1, 1968-70, Am. Astron. Soc. jour., 1968-70. Contbr. articles to profl. jours. Home: 6809 Barr Rd Washington DC 20016 Office: U So Cal Systems Mgmt Center 4301 Columbia Pike Arlington VA 22204

CHADICK, T. C., civil ct. judge; b. Winnsboro, Tex., Sept. 21, 1910; s. Walter Martin and Carrie (Mars) C.; LL.B., Cumberland U., 1933;; m. Doris Adlyne Scruggs, Apr. 14, 1941; children—Mary Susan, Nancy Doris. Admitted to Tex. bar, 1933; pvt. law practice, 1934-40; county atty., Wood County, Tex., 1939-40; state senator, 1941-49; dist. judge, Quitman, Tex., 1949-56; chief justice Ct. of Civil Appeals, Texarkana, Tex., 1956—. Mem. Tex. Constl. Revision Commn. Pres. Tex. Civil Jud. Council, 1961-64. Democrat. Methodist. Mason (Shriner). Home: 4017 Potomac St Texarkana TX 75501 Office: Texas City Hall Texarkana TX 75501

CHADWICK, CHARLES WILLIAM, veterinarian; b. Jackson, Miss., Mar. 8, 1912; s. Hudson and Anne Louise (Eley) C.; student Hinds Jr. Coll., 1933; D.V.M., Tex. A. and M. Coll., 1938; m. Evelyn Elizabeth Clark, June 14, 1938; children—Charles Eley, Martha Ann, Evelyn Elizabeth, William Lyon, Hudson Barnett, Clara Gene. With U.S. Bur. Animal Industry, Jacksonville, Fla., 1938-42; practice vet. medicine, Jackson, Miss., 1946—. Cons., veterinarian Union Stock Yards, Jackson, 1946—. Vice pres. S.W. Jackson Improvement Assn.; mem. Jackson Pub. Schs. Survey Com., 1961; parent council Wilkins Sch., 1963—. Trustee Forest Hill Sch., 1955; bd. dirs. YMCA. Served as officer Vet. Corps, AUS, World War II. Col. Gov.s Staff, State of Miss., 1960—. Mem. Am., Miss. Vet. Medicine assns., Miss., Cattlemen's Assn., Farm Bur., Tex. A. and M. Former Student's Assn., Sons Confederate Vets. Methodist. Mason (Shriner). Contbr. cartoons, articles vet. publs. Home: 1426 Raymond Rd Jackson MS 39204

CHADWICK, GEORGE GILBERT, electronics exec.; b. Lawrence, Mass., Mar. 20, 1933; s. Gilbert Roy and Rita Blanche (Simmers) C.; B.S., U. N.H., 1955; m. Mary Ann Newman, Feb. 14, 1959; children—George A., Caroline A. Sr. engr. Melpar, Inc., Falls Church, Va., 1956-58; electronics dir. antenna lab. Aero Geo Astro Corp., Alexandria, Va., 1958-60; electronics sr. v.p. engring. Radiation Systems, Inc., McLean, Va., 1960—. Mem. electronics tech. adv. bd. No. Va. Community Coll., 1967—, chmn., 1969-70. Mem. Profl. Group Antennas and Propagation (nat. chmn. 1968-69), I.E.E.E. Patentee in field. Home: 1505 Mintwood Dr McLean VA 22101 Office: 1755 Old Meadow Rd McLean VA 22101

CHADWICK, ROBERT WILLIAM, toxicologist; b. Buffalo, Mar. 16, 1930; s. Elihu Clair and Helen (Murray) C.; B.A., Western Res. U., 1957, M.S., 1962; Ph.D., Utah State U., 1967; m. Claire Jeannette Crisp, Aug. 20, 1966. Electrician apprentice Doan Electric Co., Cleve., 1950-51; chemist Republic Steel Research Center, Cleve., 1957-62; toxicologist Environmental Protection Agy. Primate and Pesticide Effects Lab., Perrine, Fla., 1966-73, Research Triangle Park, N.C., 1973—. Served with AUS, 1951-53. Recipient certificate for outstanding vol. service in field recreation Coral Gables (Fla.) Recreation Dept., 1973. Mem. A.A.A.S., Am. Chem. Soc., N.Y. Acad. Scis., Fla. Chess Assn. (pres.), U.S. Chess Fedn., Miami Chess Internat. (v.p.), Sigma Xi, Pi Delta Epsilon. Democrat. Club: Coral Gables Chess (pres. 1969-73). Contbr. articles to profl. jours. Home: PO Box 977 Apex NC 27502 Office: US Environmental Protection Agy Nat Environmental Research Center Research Triangle Park NC 27711

CHAET, ALFRED BERNARD, marine physiologist, coll. adminstr.; b. Boston, June 7, 1927; s. Joseph and Viola (Ellis) C.; B.S., U. Mass., 1949, M.S., 1951; Ph.D., U. Pa., 1953; postgrad. Oak Ridge Inst. Nuclear Studies, 1961; m. Shirley Rice, Sept. 2, 1950; children—Douglas Lee, Mark Steven, Judi Elise. Sci. investigator Marine Biol. Lab., Woods Hole, Mass., 1949, 51-53, 55-63; instr. zoology U. Me., Orono, 1953-56; asst. prof. physiology Boston U., 1956-58; prof. biology Am. U., Washington, 1958-66; NIH fellow Scripps Inst. of Oceanography, U. Cal. at San Diego, LaJolla, 1964-66; provost Gamma Coll., prof. biology U. W. Fla., Pensacola, 1966—. Active sci. workshops, panels. Served with AUS, 1944-46. Recipient numerous research grants. Mem. Am. Zoology Soc., Am. Soc. Oceanography, Am. Physiol. Soc., Marine Biol. Lab. Soc., Soc. Cell Biology, Soc. Gen. Physiology, Biophysics Soc., A.A.A.S., Am. Inst. Biol. Sci., Sigma Xi, Beta Beta Beta, Phi Kappa Phi. Contbr. articles to profl. jours. Office: U W Fla Pensacola FL 32505

CHAFFE, LEWIS KENNETH, tobacco co. exec.; b. Buckfastleigh, Devon, Eng., Oct. 20, 1913; s. William James and Ada (Bowerman) C.; grad H. Ffoulks Lynch Accounting Corr. Coll. (Eng.), 1934; m. Violet Catherine Moseley, Aug. 26, 1939; 1 son, Roger Lewis. Came to U.S., 1951. Auditor, Tax asso. Binder Hamlyn & Co., London, Eng., 1935-46; tax accountant Brit.-Am. Tobacco Co. Ltd., London, 1946-50; finance cons. Brown & Williamson Tobacco Corp., Louisville, 1951-59; with Export Leaf Tobacco Co., Richmond, Va., 1959—, treas., 1967-74, dir., 1967—, v.p. finance, adminstrn., 1969-72, sr. v.p., 1973—; asst. sec. Brit.-Am. Tobacco Co., 1962—. Air raid warden, London, 1939-45. Fellow Inst. Chartered Accountants (Eng.). Episcopalian. Club: Salisbury Country (Richmond). Home: 2214 McRae St Richmond VA 23235 Office: 1601 W Leigh St Richmond VA 23261

CHAFFIN, CHARLES HUBERT, JR., ins. agt.; b. Macon, Ga., Aug. 18, 1933; s. Charles Hubert and Jesse (Wasdin) C.; student Mercer U., 1955-56; m. Bonny Gayle Register, Mar. 15, 1956; 1 dau., Melinda Lori. Spl. agt. Ins. Co. of N. Am., 1957-65; v.p. broker The Wightman Agy., Inc., 1965-69; ins. agt. Murphy, Taylor & Ellis, Inc., Macon, 1969; ins. agt., asst. v.p. Fickling & Walker Agy., Inc., Macon, 1969—. Served with AUS, 1952-55. Mem. Soc. Chartered Property and Casualty Underwriters, Soc. Chartered Life Underwriters. Presbyn. Home: 3065 Stuart Dr Macon GA 31204 Office: 577 Mulberry St PO Box 779 Macon GA 31202

CHAFIN, JAMES L., mining co. exec.; b. Port Arthur, Tex., Apr. 25, 1922; s. James L. and Mary Josephine (Oney) C.; B.S., Southwestern U., 1948; m. Emma Dell Matherne, Apr. 17, 1952; children—Mary Susan, Debra Ann, James L., III, Peggy Lynn. Vice-pres. sales L.A. Mud Co., Inc., Houma, La., 1963—. Served with USMCR, 1942-46. Mem. Am. Petroleum Inst. (pres. 1964-65). Presbyn. (deacon 1970-71, elder 1971—). Elk. Club: Ellendale Country (Houma). Home: 409 Mire St Houma LA 70360 Office: Box 1187 Foot of Palm Av Houma LA 70360

CHAFIN, WILLIAM VERNON, JR., assn. exec.; b. Waycross, Ga., Dec. 4, 1936; s. William Vernon and Sara (Whitaker) C.; A.B., U. Ga., 1958; m. Kaye Beth Cleveland, June 21, 1958; children—Sally, Mary Kaye, Will. Bus. office supr. So. Bell Tel. Co., Atlanta, Savannah and Albany, Ga., 1961-63; agt. Aetna Life Ins. Co., Albany, Ga., 1963-64; asst. mgr. Albany (Ga.) C. of C., 1964-68; exec. dir. Maury County C. of C., Columbia, Tenn., 1968—. Served with AUS, 1959-61. Mem. Am. C. of C. Execs., So. Assn. C. of C. Execs., Tenn. C. of C. Execs. (pres. 1973-74), So., Tenn. indsl. devel. councils. Methodist (sec. adminstrv. bd. 1970-71, tchr. ch. sch. 1969—, work area chmn. 1973-74). Kiwanian. (sec. club). Home: 1110 Sunnyside Dr Columbia TN 38401 Office: 308 W 7th St Columbia TN 38401

CHAIKIN, GERALD, indsl. engr.; b. N.Y.C., Apr. 5, 1934; s. Jack and Leah (Schultz) C.; student Hunter Coll., 1951-53; B.S., Purdue U., 1956; m. Clarice Mary Barrett, June 27, 1957; children—Jamine Jean, Stewart Phillip. Product engr. Sperry Gyroscope Co., Great Neck, N.Y., 1956-57; gen. engr. human factors U.S. Army Human Engring. Labs., Aberdeen Proving Ground, Md., 1959-60; gen. engr. human factors U.S. Army Missile Command, Redstone Arsenal, Ala., 1960—. Served with AUS, 1957-59. Registered profl. engr., Ala. Mem. Human Factors Soc. (chpt. pres. 1968), Assn. U.S. Army, Air Force Assn., Am. Def. Preparedness Assn. Home: 906 Four Mile Post Rd Huntsville AL 35802 Office: AMSMI-RLH US Army Missile Command Redstone Arsenal AL 35809

CHAKALES, HAROLD HARRY, physician; b. Bklyn., June 11, 1934; s. Harry John and Venus (Trakas) C.; B.S., Wake Forest Coll., 1955, M.D., Bowman Gray Sch., 1958; m. Linda Carol Haskett, Sept. 25, 1965; children—Harry John II, Carrie Glenn. Rotating intern Jefferson Davis Hosp., Houston, 1958-59; resident Baylor U. Coll., Houston, 1959-61, U. Ark. Med. Center, Little Rock, 1961-63; practice medicine, specializing in orthopedic surgery, Little Rock, 1963—; staff orthopedist VA Hosp., Little Rock; instr. orthopedic surgery U. Ark. Med. Center, 1963-65, asst. prof., 1965-69, clin. asst. prof. orthopedics, 1969—. Diplomate Am. Bd. Orthopedic Surgery. Fellow A.C.S.; mem. A.M.A., Pulaski County, So. med. assns., Ark. Orthopedic Assn., Am. Acad. Orthopedic Surgery. Home: 11119 Eden Lane Little Rock AR 72207 Office: 405 N University St Little Rock AR 72209

CHALFANT, RAY KING, JR., civil engr.; b. Barnesville, O., Aug. 27, 1920; s. Ray King and Margaret Elizabeth (Shaw) C.; B.S., Rose Poly. Inst., 1942; M.Eng., Yale, 1947; m. Allene Virginia Westbrook, Mar. 29, 1945; children—Karen (Mrs. Jack Wray), Ray King III, Melanie J., Todd W. Instr. civil engring. Yale, 1947-48; asst. prof. civil engring. Ga. Inst. Tech., 1947-55; part time positions as structural engr. S. Atlantic div. U.S. Engr. Dept.; design cons. W.H. Armstrong Structural Engr., 1947-55; structural engr. Atlanta dist. Am. Marietta Co., 1955-60; pvt. practice cons. engr., Atlanta, 1960—. Pres., Clairmont Civic Assn., 1951-52. Served to capt. C.E., AUS, 1942-46. Registered profl. engr., Ga., Fla., Ala., Miss., Tenn., N.C., N.J. Fellow Am. Soc. C.E.; mem. Tau Beta Pi, Chi Epsilon, Tau Nu Tau. Home: 1278 Valley View Rd Dunwoody GA 30338 Office: 4246 Peachtree Rd NE Atlanta GA 30319

CHALKER, ROY FLETCHER, editor, pub.; b. Swainsboro, Ga., Sept. 12, 1915; s. Gozie Fletcher and Isla (Brown) C.; student John Marshall Law Sch., 1955-56; m. Mae Evelyn Gisson, July 21, 1944; children—Roy Fletcher, Philip C. Founder, editor The Ga. Guide, Gibson, 1936-42; owner, editor The True Citizen, Waynesboro, Ga., 1945—; co-owner, radio sta. WBRO, Waynesboro, 1954-55. Mayor, Gibson, 1936; mayor, Waynesboro, 1954-55; state dir. parks, 1955-56; chmn. State Hwy. Dept., 1957-58; chmn. Rural Rds. Authority, 1957-58; chmn. State Bridge Bldg. Authority, 1957-58. Served with SUNR, 1941-44. Mem. Ga. Press Assn. (pres. 1953-54, dir. 1951-52), Sigma Delta Chi. Democrat. Baptist. Mason, Rotarian. Home: 514 Forest Dr Waynesboro GA 30830 Office: 202 E 6th St Waynesboro GA 30830

CHALLINOR, DAVID, museum ofcl.; b. N.Y.C., July 11, 1920; s. David and Merecedes (Crimmins) C.; B.A., Harvard, 1943; M.F., Yale, 1959, Ph.D., 1966; m. Joan Ridder, Nov. 22, 1952; children—Julia M., Mary E., Sarah L., D. Thompson. With Offerman-Anderson, Clayton & Co., Houston, 1947-51; cotton farmer, Culberson County (Tex.), 1951-53; asst. sec. First Mortgage Co. Houston, 1953-57; research asst. Conn. Agr. Expt. Sta., New Haven, 1959-60; dep. dir. Yale Peabody Mus., New Haven, 1960-65, acting dir., 1965-66; spl. asst. in tropical biology Smithsonian Instn., Washington, 1966-67, dep. dir. Office Internat. Activities, 1967-68, dir., 1968-70, asst. sec. (sci.) Smithsonian Instn., 1971—. Am. adminstrv. sec. Charles Darwin Found., 1971—; mem. biol.-agr. com. Nat. Acad. Scis., 1971—. Trustee Manhattanville Coll. Served with USNR, 1943-46. Fellow A.A.A.S.; mem. Sigma Xi. Contbr. articles to sci. jours. Home: 3117 Hawthorne St NW Washington DC 20008 Office: 114 Smithsonian Institution Washington DC 20560

CHAMBERLAIN, NUGENT FRANCIS, chem. researcher; b. Henderson, Tex., Mar. 10, 1916; s. Hubbard Bailey and Emmie (Chamberlin) C.; student N. Tex. Agrl. Coll., 1933-35; B.S., Tex. A. and M. U., 1938; m. Barbara Wilsdon Hall, Oct. 2, 1943; children—John Harold, Scott Nugent, David Alan. Trainee Humble Oil & Refining Co., 1938, jr. chemist, 1939-41, research chemist, 1941-50, sr. research chemist, 1950-61, research specialist, 1961-63; research asso. Esso Research & Engring. Co., Baytown, Tex., 1963-69, sr. research asso., 1969—. Mem. bd. reviewers Thermodynamics Research Center of Tex. A. and M. U.; mem. NMR subcom. and adv. com. Nat. Bur. Standards; mem. extramural adv. com. chemistry dept. U. Houston; vis. scientist Tex. Acad. Sci., 1959-67; seminar leader; speaker. Served to maj. C.W.S., AUS, 1942-46. Decorated Legion of Merit; recipient profl. progress award, Soc. Profl. Chemists and Engrs., 1961, Southeastern Tex. sect. award, S.W. regional award, Am. Chem. Soc., 1969. Mem. Am. Chem. Soc. (councillor 1972, dir. 1973), Am. Inst. Chemists, Tex. Inst. Chemists, Am. Soc. Testing and Materials, Am. Def. Preparedness Assn. Republican. Presbyn. (elder). Author: A Catalog of the Nuclear Magnetic Resonance Spectra of Hydrogen in Hydrocarbons and Their Derivatives, 1958; Chemical Shift and Spin Coupling Data, 1963; Nuclear Magnetic Resonance Data for Hydrogen, 1965, Nuclear Magnetic Resonance Data for Sulphur Compounds, 1971; The Practice of NMR Spectroscopy, in press. Contbr. articles profl. jours. Patentee in field. Home: 209 Edgewood St Baytown TX 77520 Office: PO Box 4255 Baytown TX 77520

CHAMBERLAIN, VON DEL, univ. adminstr.; b. Kanab, Utah, Feb. 24, 1934; s. Edward Leo and Cora (Esplin) C.; B.A., U. Utah, 1958; M.S., U. Mich., 1960; m. Marre Hollingsworth, Aug. 9, 1957; children—Marsh Edward, Blake Von, Drew Fen, Ven Cameron, Brent Avery. Observing asst. McMath-Hulbert Obs., 1959; instr. Flint Community Coll., 1960-64; staff astronomer Robert T. Longway Planetarium, instr. U. Mich. Extension, 1960-64; staff astronomer Abrams Planetarium, Mich. State U., East Lansing, 1964-68, dir., 1968-73; chief presentations and edn. div. Nat. Air and Space Museum Smithsonian Instn., Washington, 1973—. Chmn. Armand N. Spitz Meml. Fund, 1971—. Fellow Meteoritical Soc.; mem. Internat. Soc. Planetarium Educators (council 1970—), Am. Astron. Soc. (task group on edn. in astronomy 1972—), Great Lakes Planetarium Assn. (pres. 1965-67). Home: 1519 Bal Harbor Ct Herndon VA 22070 Office: Nat Air and Space Mus Smithsonian Instn Washington DC 20560

CHAMBERLIN, GARWOOD, printing exec.; b. Evanston, Ill., May 29, 1920; s. Richard and Elizabeth (Garwood) C.; B.S., U. Md., 1942; m. Sarah Ann Bemis, Dec. 22, 1959; children—Garwood Bemis, Sarah Hepworth. Vice pres. Merkle Press, Inc., Washington, 1946-67, Publishers Co., Inc., Washington, 1967-71; pres. Kaufmann/Graphics, Inc., 1971—. Served with AUS, 1942-45. Mem. Printing Industry of Washington (pres. 1955-56), Beta Alpha Psi. Home: 5404 Burling Rd Bethesda MD 20014 Office: 1110 Okie St NE Washington DC 20002

CHAMBERLIN, HOPE, journalist; b. Portland, Ore., Dec. 2, 1919; d. Willard Joseph and Frieda (Jones) Chamberlin; B.A., Ore. State U., 1938; M.S., Northwestern U., 1939. Reporter-photographer Portland Oregonian, 1939-41; regional pub. relations dir. USO, Chgo., 1942-45; information and editorial specialist U.S. Mil. Govt. for Bavaria, Munich, Germany, 1945-47; information specialist U.S. Army Hdqrs., Zone Command Austria, Salzburg, 1947-50; dir. pub. relations, asst. prof. English, Montclair (N.J.), State Coll., 1951-58; dir. pub. relations NBC-TV Continental Classroom, N.Y.C., 1958-61, Land-Grant Coll. and U. Centennial Washington, 1961; editor The Nat. Pub. Accountant, Washington, 1964-65; writer-editor pub. information division Internal Revenue Service, Washington, 1965-67; free-lance writer, editor, researcher, 1968—. Cons. journalism Prince George's Community Coll., 1962-65. Mem. Am. Assn. UN, Am. Assn. U. Women, Am. Women in Radio and Television, League Women Voters, Women in Communications, Gamma Phi Beta. Club: Overseas Press (N.Y.C.). Author: A Minority of Members: Women in the U.S. Congress, 1973. Home: 1884 Columbia Rd NW Washington DC 20009

CHAMBERLIN, JAMES ALLEN, surgeon; b. Houston Nov. 19, 1911; s. Willis West and Eva (Allen) C.; B.A. Rice U., 1936; M.D., Tulane U., 1942; m. Caryl Jean Wirth, Mar. 21, 1942; 1 dau., Caryl Jayne. Fellow obstetrics and gynecology Ochsner Clinic, New Orleans, 1942-43; asst. surg. resident Meml. Cancer Center, N.Y.C., 1943-44, surg. fellow, 1946-48, sr. surg. resident, 1948-49; surg. intern Jersey City Med. Center, 1944-45, house surgeon, 1945-46; chief surg. resident, chief of residents Roper Hosp., Charleston, S.C., 1945-46; asso. surgeon, acting chief clinics, head div. head and neck surgery M.D. Anderson Hosp., Houston, 1949-50; practice medicine specializing in surgery of head and neck, Houston, 1950— teaching asst. obstetrics and gynecology Tulane U., 1942-43; teaching fellow surgery Med. Coll. S.C., 1945-46; asso. prof. surgery U. Tex. Postgrad. Sch. Medicine 1949-50; clin. asso. prof. Baylor U. Coll. Medicine, Houston 1950—; attending surgeon Hermann, St. Joseph's Med. Arts, Heights, Twelve Oaks, Sharpstown, VA, Ben Taub Gen. hosps., Houston; cons. head and neck surgery St. Luke's Episcopal Tex. Children's hosps., Houston; courtesy staff Meml. Hosp. Houston; asso. surgeon Meth. Hosp., Houston. Dir. Med. Center Nat. Bank, Buffalo Savs. & Loan Assn. Fellow A.C.S; mem. Harris County Med. Soc. Am. Tex. (mem. com. on atomic energy and nuclear medicine 1955-67), med. assns., Am. Radium Soc., James Ewing Soc., Tex. Surg. Soc., Am. Thyroid Assn., Soc. Nuclear Medicine (pres. Southwestern chpt. 1963-64). Club: Doctors (bd. govs.) (Houston). Author: Lectures on Gynecological Pathology, 1943. Contbr. articles to med. jours. Home: 2722 Country Club Blvd Sugarland TX 77478 Office: Hermann Profl Bldg Houston TX 77025

CHAMBERS, BARBARA MAE FROMM (MRS. CHARLES MCKAY CHAMBERS), educator; b. Syracuse, N.Y., Nov. 23, 1940; d. George Edward and Wanda Roselia (Wollos) Fromm; B.S., U. Ala., 1962, M.A., 1964, Ph.D., 1969; m. Charles McKay Chambers, June 9, 1962; children—Charles, Catherine, Christina. Grad. asst. U. Ala., 1962-69; pvt. cons., Washington, 1969-70; lectr. math. U. Va., 1970-71; asst. prof. math. George Mason U., Fairfax, Va., 1971—. Adviser No. Va. Sci. Fair, 1972. Grad. fellow NASA, 1963-65. Mem. Math. Assn. Am., Pi Mu Epsilon. Home: 4220 Dandridge Terrace Alexandria VA 22309 Office: Dept Math George Mason U Fairfax VA 22030

CHAMBERS, CHARLES MCKAY, educator; b. Hampton, Va., June 22, 1941; s. Charles MacKay and Ruth Ellanora (Wallach) C.; B.S. (Gorgas fellow), U. Ala., 1962, M.S. (Nat. Def. Edn. Act fellow), 1963, Ph.D. in Physics, 1964; postgrad. math. (NSF fellow), Harvard, 1964-65; m. Barbara Mae Fromm, June 9, 1962; children—Charles Catherine, Christina. Aerospace engr. NASA, 1962-63; research asso. U. Ala. Research Inst., 1963-64, asso. prof. math. univ., 1965-69; research fellow Harvard, 1964-65; asso. dean George Washington U., 1972—; partner Univ. Assos., Inc., Washington, 1969-72, also dir.; dist. mgr. Life Ins. Co. Am.; cons. U.S. Congress, NSF, U.S. Office Edn., Salk Inst., Office Equal Opportunity, H & R Block, Health Facilities Resources, Inc.; lectr. in field. Recipient Tau Beta Pi award, Am. Legion citizenship award. NSF research grantee, NASA grantee. Mem. N.Y. Acad. Sci., Am. Math. Assn., A.A.A.S., Am. Assn. Physics Tchrs., Am. Assn. U. Adminstrs., Internat. Platform Assn., Phi Beta Kappa, Sigma Xi (chpt. pres. 1974), Pi Mu Epsilon, Sigma Pi Sigma. Contbr. articles to profl. jours. Home: 4220 Dandridge Terrace Alexandria VA 22309 Office: Coll Gen Studies George Washington U Washington DC 20006

CHAMBERS, EARL LAWRENCE, r.r. engr.; b. Birmingham, Ala., June 9, 1923; s. Earl Lawrence and Effie Mae (Burks) C.; student Howard Coll., 1945-46; m. Mary Emma Richards, Dec. 14, 1946; children—Gale (Mrs. Frank Cusamino), Pat (Mrs. Don Hiltbruner), Mary Lisa, Mary C. With Ala. Hwy. Dept., 1946-48, Tenn. Coal & Iron Co., 1948; with So. Ry. Co., Birmingham, 1948—, asst. engr. indsl. devel., 1963—. Pres. St. Barnabas Credit Union, 1973—. Served with USMCR, 1942-45. Home: 732 S 81st St Birmingham AL 35206 Office: 2201 1st Av N Birmingham AL 35203

CHAMBERS, FRANKLIN DELANO, bus. exec.; b. Lawrenceburg, Tenn., Nov. 8, 1932; s. Carl C. and Leona Mae (Morgan) C.; student Middle Tenn. State U., 1951-53; B.S. in Indsl. Engring., U. Tenn., 1963; M.B.A., U. Louisville, 1966; m. Helen L. Stewart, Dec. 31, 1955; children-Sandra, Jeffrey W. Indsl. engr. Am. Air Filter, Louisville, 1963-66; with Trane Co., Clarksville, Tenn., 1966-68; v.p., gen. mgr. Universal Wire Container Corp., Clarksville, 1968-69; v.p., gen. mgr. mfg. div. Convenient Industries Am., Louisville, 1969-71; pres. Munday Modular Homes Mfg. Co., Inc., Madisonville, Ky., 1971—; developer, pres. Marion Modular Homes (Ky.), 1972—; broker Frank Chambers Real Estate. Served with USAF, 1955-60. Mem. Nat. Home Builders Assn., Alpha Pi Mu. Republican. Mem. Ch. of Christ. Home: 227 Mitchell Dr Madisonville KY 42431 Office: Madisonville KY 42431

CHAMBERS, JOHN ED, banker; b. Danville, Ark., Mar. 17, 1917; s. John E. and Lydia (Littlejohn) C.; A.B. U. Ark. 1939, LL.B., 1940; postgrad. Grad. Sch. Banking of the South, summers 1953-56; m. Patricia Sloan, Feb., 1941; children—Eugenia Carol (Mrs. Jerral W. Jones), John Ed III, Patricia Dian (Mrs. William R. Meeks), Catherine Sloan. Admitted to Ark. bar 1940; practiced in Danville, 1940-43; ct. reporter, Danville, 1940-43; pres. Danville State Bank, 1946—; mayor of Danville, 1940-43, 56-60. Chmn. Yell County Soil Conservation Dist. 1940—; chmn. conservation and devel. project Ark. River Valley Resources, 1966—; exec. council ARVAC, Inc. area v.p. Ark. Assn. Soil Conservation Dist., 1952-57, pres. 1957-59, state treas., 1967—; Chmn. Yell County Devel. Council, 1962—; mem. Yell County Hosp. Bd. Trustee Ark. Polytechnic Coll. Served from ensign to lt. USNR, World War II 1943-46. Recipient Boss of Yr. award Ark. Jaycees, 1971. Mem. Am. (exec. council 1967-69), Ark. (mem. exec. council, mem. advt. and promotion com.) bankers assns., Ark. Library Assn., U. Ark. Alumni Assn. (alumni bd. 1964—, pres. 1969-70). Democrat. Methodist. Lion (past pres.). Address: Danville AR 72833

CHAMBERS, TORRENCE HARRISON, radar signal processing systems cons.; b. Ardmore, Pa., June 11, 1919; s. William Wilkie and Minnie (Harrison) C.; B.S., Haverford Coll., 1941; M.S., U. Md., 1950; m. Marion Joan Warman, June 2, 1945; children—William Wilkie, Frank Warman. Mem. TV tech. staff CBS, N.Y.C., 1941; cons. radar signal processing Radar div. search radar br. Naval Research Lab., Washington, 1941-71; ind. cons. signal processing systems, Washington, 1971—. Recipient Dept. Def. Meritorious Civilian Service award, 1945. Home: 3729 S St Washington DC 20020 Office: 3729 S St Washington DC 20020

CHAN, CHIA-HWA, educator; b. Shanghai, China, Apr. 28, 1936; s. Pei-Ling and Shun-Chun (Chang) C.; B.Sc., Imperial Coll. London U., 1958, Ph.D., 1962; m. Kathy Lu, June 28, 1961; children—David A., Debora, Gregory. Came to U.S., 1964. Vis. asst. prof. Middle East Tech. U., Ankara, Turkey, 1962-64; asst. research physicist U. Cal. at San Diego, 1964-66; asst. prof. Purdue U., 1966-70; asso. prof. physics U. Ala., 1970—, chmn. physics dept., 1972—. Mem. Am. Phys. Soc., Am. Assn. Physics Tchrs. Home: 3015 Barcody Rd Huntsville AL 35802

CHANCE, DONALD PAUL, surgeon; b. Hagan, Va., Feb. 28, 1916; s. David Preston and Berneice (Parkey) C.; student Tenn. Wesleyan Coll., 1932-34; B.S., U. Tenn., M.S., 1938; M.D., U. Va., 1943; m. Marie Elizabeth Garley, Sept. 10, 1952; children—Elizabeth Anne, Margaret Rose, Donald Paul II. Teaching fellow zoology in comparative anatomy U. Tenn., 1936-68; prof. zoology Tenn. Wesleyan Coll., 1938-39; intern dept. surgery U. Va. Hosp., 1943, asst. resident surgery, 1946-47; fellow in surgery, first asst. in surgery, asst. surgeon Mayo Found. and Mayo Clinic, 1948-54; head sect. thoracic surgery, asso. dept. surgery Foss Clinic, Geisinger Hosp., Danville, Pa., 1954-58; attending surgeon Holston Valley Community Hosp., Kingsport, Tenn., 1958—. Served with USNR, 1944-46. Diplomate Am. Bd. Surgery. Fellow A.C.S., Southeastern Surg. Assn.; mem. Raven Soc., Pi Kappa Alpha, Alpha Omega Alpha, Omicron Delta Kappa. Republican. Presbyn. Moose, Eagle. Home: 3709 Hemlock Park Kingsport TN 37663 Office: 613 Watauga St Kingsport TN 37660

CHANCE, FRANKLIN SOWELL, JR., writer; b. Springfield, Tenn., Sept. 3, 1915; s. Franklin Sowell and Walter Gertrude (Randolph) C.; B.S., U. Tenn., 1939, Ph.D., 1951; m. Melba Leona Greer, Nov. 12, 1939; children—Franklin Sowell III, John Randolph, Ethel Allison (Mrs. Richard Paul Britell). Chemist, Tenn. Eastman, Kingsport, Tenn., 1933-37; chem. engr. E.I. duPont de Nemours & Co., Inc., Wilmington, Del., 1939-48; chem. mgr. Chas. Pfizer & Co., Bklyn., 1951-58; fellow Oak Ridge Inst. for Nuclear Studies, 1950-51; tech. and corporate dir. Pfizer Internat., N.Y.C., 1958-62; head sci. dept., acad. dean Mackinac Coll., Mackinac Island, Mich., 1966-70. Bd. dirs. Am. Emergency Com. Tibetan Refugees. Mem. Am. Inst. Chem. Engrs., A.A.A.S., Alpha Chi Sigma, Tau Beta Pi. Rotarian. Patentee chem. and pharm. compounds, processes. Address: 633 Retta Esplanade W Punta Gorda FL 33950

CHANDLER, ARTHUR CECIL, JR., ophthalmologist; b. Hinton, W.Va., Feb. 14, 1933; s. Arthur Cecil and Laura Davis (Smith) C.; student Washington and Lee U., 1949-51; A.B., Fla. So. Coll., 1953; M.S., U. Tenn., 1955; M.D., Duke, 1959; m. Deborah Wren Sparkes, June 20, 1957; children—Arthur Cecil III, Laura Ashley, Matthew Davis, John Benjamin. Intern, Duke Hosp., 1959-60; resident ophthalmology Columbia-Presbyn. Hosp., N.Y.C., 1960-63; practice medicine, specializing in ophthalmology, Palo Alto, Cal., 1963-65, Durham, N.C., 1965—; lectr. Stanford, 1963-65; asso., asst. prof., asso. prof. ophthalmology Duke, 1965—, dir. residency program, dept. ophthalmology, 1965—, asso. dept. anatomy, 1966—; chief ophthalmology Durham VA Hosp., 1966—. Diplomate Am. Bd. Ophthalmology. Fellow A.C.S.; mem. Am., So. med. assns., Pan Am., Am. assns. ophthalmology, Soc. Eye Surgeons, Am. Acad. Ophthalmology and Otolaryngology, Durham C. of C., Sigma Xi, Alpha Omega Alpha. Presbyn. Home: 3508 Cambridge Rd Durham NC 27707 Office: Box 3802 Duke U Eye Center Durham NC 27710

CHANDLER, CLARENCE CLATEN, elec. engr.; b. Garrison, Tex., Oct. 10, 1915; s. Lonnie Clarence and Clara May (Hamrick) C.; B.E.E., Stephen F. Austin State Tchrs. Coll., 1934; m. Elizabeth Bogdanovich, Nov. 22, 1958; 1 dau., Lisa. With Southwestern Bell Telephone Co., Houston, 1934-50, Gustav Hirsch Orgn., cons., Columbus, O., 1950-60, Gen. Electric Co., Syracuse, N.Y., 1960-64; engr. Def. Communications Agy., Washington, 1964—. Cons., Am. Nat. Standards Inst. Served with Signal Corps AUS, 1942-46. Mem. I.E.E.E., Nat. Soc. Profl. Engrs., Telephone Pioneers, Am. Legion. Episcopalian. Elk. Club: Military District Washington Officers. Home: 3115 Savoy Dr Fairfax VA 22030 Office: 1860 Wiehle Av Reston VA 22090

CHANDLER, ISAAC, JR., county agt.; b. Havana, Fla., Oct. 9, 1922; s. Isaac and Lillie (McGriff) C.; B.S., Fla. A. and M. Coll., 1952; m. Gene Elizabeth Hopkins, Aug. 12, 1961; children—Marcia Elizabeth, Isaac Eugene. Farmer, Havana, Fla., 1946-48; county agrl. agt. Hamilton County, Fla., 1952-63, asst. county agt., 1963-69, county extension agr. agt., 1969—. Served with AUS, 1942-45. Mem. Am. Legion. Methodist (sec.-treas. 1970-71). Mason. Home: PO Box 101 Jasper FL 32052 Office: PO Drawer K Jasper FL 32052

CHANDLER, JOHN H., govt. ofcl.; b. Bklyn., Nov. 22, 1921; s. John R. and Ethel C. (Woodward) C.; A.B., Antioch Coll., 1943; postgrad. Am. U., 1950-53; m. Barbara Mann, Oct. 30, 1943; children—Richard, Janet, Kenneth, Martha. With UNRRA, Washington, 1946-49; with wage and hour div. U.S. Dept. Labor, Washington, 1950-60, chief div. fgn. labor statistics and trade Bur. Labor Statistics, 1960—. Served to lt. (j.g.) USNR, 1943-46. Mem. Am. Statis. Assn., Indsl. Relations Research Assn. Home: 6718 Persimmon Tree Rd Bethesda MD 20034 Office: US Dept Labor Bur Labor Statistics Washington DC 20212

CHANDLER, THOMAS WALTER, JR., librarian; b. Carrollton, Ga., Nov 12, 1924; s. Thomas Walter and Florence (Pope) C.; student West Ga. Coll., 1942-43, 46-47; B.A., Emory U., 1949, M.Library Sci., 1951. With Ga. State Coll., 1951-61, beginning as book order librarian, 1951-57, head acquisitions dept., 1957-61; head librarian Oglethorpe U., Atlanta, 1961—. Served AUS, 1943-45. Decorated Purple Heart. Mem. Ga. Library Assn. Democrat. Address: 2873 Hermance Dr NE Atlanta GA 30319

CHANDLER, WAYNE A., sports publicity exec.; b. Richmond, Ind.; A.B., Ind.; U., 1950; m. Viola Eschliman; children—Justin, Abigail, Amy Beth. Formerly newspaperman, Ohio, Fla.; joined Houston Sports Assn., 1963, asst. publicity dir. Houston Astrodome, 3 years, publicity dir. Astroworld, 2 years, now pub. relations dir. Astrodomain Corp. which includes Astros baseball team, Astrodome, Astrohall, Astroworld Hotels. Office: Houston Astros Houston TX 77001*

CHANDLER, WINSTON GRIGGS, transp. corp. exec.; b. Clinton, Ark., Oct. 9, 1919; s. Lester W. and Mattie (Griggs) C.; student Coll. Ozarks, 1940; LL.B., Ark. Law Sch., 1951; m. Ouida G. Hunnicutt, Sept. 16, 1942; children—Winston Griggs, Michael Lee, Jeffrey Scott. Owner Chandler 5 and 10, Clinton, Ark., 1946-48; safety insp. Ark. Pub. Service Commn., Little Rock, 1949-53; chmn. bd. Chandler Trailer Convoy, Inc., Little Rock, 1953—, dir., 1963-67; v.p. Razorback Realty; dir. Safety Boom, Inc. Mem. Ark. Athletic Commn., 1954-56; formerly chmn. Sch. Bd., Pulaski County; mem., chmn. Ark. State History Commn., Little Rock, 1957-67; mem. pres. devel. council Harding Coll., Searcy, Ark. Mem. finance com. Democratic Nat. Com., 1974. Served to maj. USAAF, 1941-45. Mem. Am. Legion, Ark. Pioneers, Air Force Assn. (charter), Ark. Truck and Bus. Assn., Tenn. Walking Horse Assn., Internat. Platform Assn. Democrat. Mem. Ch. of Christ (deacon). Lion. Home: 545 Valley Club Circle Little Rock AR 72207 Office: 8828 N Benton Hwy Little Rock AR 72204

CHANDLER, WYETH, city ofcl. Former mem. Memphis City Council, 4 years; mayor Memphis, 1972—. Office: City Hall Memphis TN 38103*

CHANDRA, KAILASH SRIVASTAVA, educator; b. Kanpur, India, Aug. 20, 1938; s. Sheosagar Lal and Prem Pyari Srivastava; B.S., Dayanand Anglo Vedic Coll., Kanpur, 1956, M.S., 1958; Ph.D., Gorakhpur U. (India), 1967; m. Sushma Srivastava, June 29, 1961; children—Sangeeta, Parul, Ravi. Came to U.S., 1968. Lectr. Kanya Kubja Degree Coll., Lucknow, India, 1958-60; research fellow Gorakhpur U., India, 1960-62, lectr. physics, 1962-68; research asso. dept. physics U. Ga., 1968-69; asso. prof. Savannah State Coll., 1969-73, prof. physics, 1973—. Chmn. bd. govs. Student Loan Fund, 1972-73; chmn. supervisory com. Savastate Tchrs. Fed. Credit Union, 1973—; coll. rep. acad. adv. com. on physics Univ. System Ga., 1970—. Council Sci. and Indsl. Research fellow, 1960-62. Mem. Southeastern sect. Am. Phys. Soc., Am. Assn. Physics Tchrs., Am. Math. Soc., Calcutta Math. Soc. (referee). Contbr. articles to sci. jours. Home: 110 Paradise Dr Savannah GA 31406

CHANEY, BOBBY LEE, supt. schs.; b. Graham, Ky., Sept. 5, 1934; s. Volla T. and Hazel D. (Matheney) C.; B.S., Murray State U., 1961, M.A., 1963; postgrad. Eastern Ky. State U., 1969; m. Drue Malone, Nov. 22, 1956; children—Leesa Drue, Terrea Jean, Robert Eric. Tchr., coach Christian County Schs., 1954, Calloway County Schs., 1956-60, Muhl County Schs., 1955; tchr., prin. Webster County Schs., 1961-66, supt., 1969—; high sch. prin., Harrodsburg, Ky., 1966-69. Mem. Am., Ky. assns. sch. adminstrs., Kappa Delta Pi. Methodist. Lion. Home: Clay KY 42404

CHANEY, CHARLES BUREN, JR. (DICK), ins. agt.; b. Birmingham, Ala., June 6, 1937; s. Charles Buren and Mildred Myra (Herrin) C.; student Ga. So. Coll., 1955-57, U. Ala., 1960-61, Jones Law Sch., 1969-71; m. Carole Wilson, Feb. 11, 1967; children—William Scott, Christen Lane. Scout exec. Boy Scouts Am., Montgomery, Ala., 1963-67; ins. adjuster Ala. Farm Bur., Montgomery, 1967-72; owner ins. agy., Monroeville, Ala., 1972—; real estate appraiser. County chmn. A.R.C., 1971—; chmn. United Fund campaign, 1972, pres., 1973; chmn. Vanity Fair Golf Com., 1971—. Co-chmn. Monroe County Republican party, 1972—. Served with USMCR, 1957-60. Mem. Monroeville Jr. C. of C. (pres. 1969). Methodist. Kiwanian. Home: Longleaf Circle Monroeville AL 36460 Office: 721 S Alabama Av Monroeville AL 36460

CHANEY, WILL WILSON, oil co. exec.; b. Ameagle, W.Va., Feb. 9, 1922; s. John F. and Parlee (Farley) C.; student Draughon's Bus. Sch., Tulsa, 1946; m. Anna Mae Trout, July 8, 1945; children—James, William, Michael, Richard. Purchasing agt. Western Supply Co., Tulsa, 1946-63; v.p., mgr. Mylon C. Jacobs Supply Co., Tulsa, 1963—. Served with AUS, 1942-45. Decorated Purple Heart with 2 oak leaf clusters, Bronze Star with 2 oak leaf clusters. Mem. Purchasing Mgmt. Assn. (dir. Tulsa 1968), Transp. Club. Elk. Home: 3816 E 55th St Tulsa OK 74135 Office: PO Box 2366 Tulsa OK 74101

CHANG, JEFFREY P., research scientist, educator; b. Changteh, Hunan, China; came to U.S., naturalized; grad. Nat. Central U. China; M.S., U. Ill., 1946, also Ph.D. Acting chief, sect. exptl. pathology U. Tex. M.D. Anderson Hosp., Houston, until 1964, prof. biology, also mem. faculty Grad. Sch. Biomed. Scis., 1964-71; prof. cellular biology U. Tex. Med. Br., Galveston, 1971—. Formerly cons. NIH, USAF Sch. Aerospace Medicine, Brooks AFB, Tex.; chmn. Symposium Preparative Histochemistry, 1st Internat. Congress Histochemistry and Cyto Chemistry, Paris, session chmn. 4th congress, Japan, 1972; vis. prof., lectr. Vanderbilt U., U. Kan. Sch. Medicine, U. Taiwan, Chin Hwa U., Med. Coll. of Dept. Defense, Republic of China, others. Contbr. articles to profl. publs. Developer open-top cryostat sect. freeze substitution; research tumors, electron microscopy, histochemistry, reproductive biology. Office: Div Cell Biology U Tex Med Branch Galveston TX 77550*

CHANG, PAUL KEUK, educator; b. Korea, Apr. 8, 1913; s. Leo Kibin and Lucia (Huang) C.; Dipl. Ing., Technische Hochschule, Berlin, 1940; student Fed. Inst. Tech., Zurich, 1944-45; M.A.E., N.Y. U., 1948; M.S., Harvard, 1949; Sc.D., U. Notre Dame, 1951; Dr. Ing., Technische Universität, Berlin, 1963; m. Frances Wha Shik Min, Nov. 26, 1955; children—Sophia Wha Sun, Teresa Wha Soo. Aero. engr. Siebel-Flugzeugwerke, Halle, Germany, 1940-41; mech. engr. Brown Boveri Co., Baden, Switzerland, 1946-47; instr. U. Notre Dame, 1949-51; with Airesearch Mfg. Co., Los Angeles, 1952-54; research specialist Lockheed Aircraft Corp., Cal., 1954-58; prof. mech. engring. Cath. U. Am., 1958—; cons. U.S. Naval Ship Research and Devel. Center (Carderock, Md.), U.S. Naval Research Lab. (Washington), Naval Ordnance Lab. (White Oak, Md.), Naval Ordnance Sta. (Indian Head, Md.); adviser to Seoul Nat. U. (Korea); mem. univs. adv. com. Korea Advanced Inst. Sci. (Seoul). Chmn. bd. Korean Sch. (Washington). Recipient Fulbright-Hays grants, Spain, 1964-65, Seoul, 1972, Orgn. Am. States and NSF grants, Peru, 1973. Asso. fellow Am. Inst. Aeros. and Astronautics; mem. Assn. Korean Scientists and Engrs. in Am. (hon.), Sigma Xi, Tau Beta Pi. Author: Separation of Flow, 1970; Control of Flow Separation, in press. Contbr. articles sci. jours. Home: 8005 Falstaff Rd McLean VA 22101 Office: Catholic University of America Washington DC 20017

CHANTRY, WILLIAM AMDOR, chem. engr.; b. Corning. Ia., Sept. 21, 1924; s. William Kline and Jessie May (McKee) C.; B.S., State U. Ia., 1949, M.S., 1951; Ph.D. (duPont fellow), Cornell U., 1953; m. Patricia Claire Lorenz, Dec. 17, 1949; children—Patricia (Mrs. William Forrest Martin), William Amdor, Elizabeth Ann. Paint technologist Sherwin Williams Co., Chgo., 1949-50; technologist Shell Chem. Corp., Martinez, Cal., 1953-56, sr. technologist, Houston, 1956-59; with E.I. duPont de Nemours & Co., Inc., Kinston, N.C., 1959—, research engr., 1959-63, sr. research engr., 1963-67, research and devel. asso. Dacron Research Lab., 1967—. Instr. Lenoir Community Coll., Kinston, 1969—. Precinct chmn. Dem. Party, 1968—. Served with AUS, 1943-46. Decorated Bronze Star. Mem. Am. Inst. Chem. Engrs. (charter), U.S. Power Squadron, Sigma Xi,

Tau Beta Pi, Phi Kappa Phi, Phi Lambda Upsilon, Alpha Chi Sigma. Home: 1708 St George Pl Kinston NC 28501 Office: Dacron Research Lab EI du Pont de Nemours & Co Inc Kinston NC 28501

CHAO, JING, thermodynamicist; b. Chia-hsing, Chekiang, China, Nov. 7, 1924; s. Li Chi and Pei Tsun (Hsia) C.; B.S., Nat. Central U., 1947; Ph.D., Carnegie-Mellon U., 1961; m. Chao Mei Chen, Dec. 21, 1952; 1 son, William Chih Hsin. Came to U.S., 1957, naturalized, 1971. Asst. chem. engr. Hsinchu Research Inst., Taiwan, 1947-54; asso. chem. engr. Union Indsl. Research Inst., Hsinchu, 1954-57; phys. chemist Dow Chem. Co., Midland, Mich., 1961-69; sr. thermodynamicist Thermodynamics Research Center, Tex. A. and M. U., 1969-73, asst. dir. molecular thermodynamics, 1973—. Mem. Am. Chem. Soc., A.A.A.S., Bryan-College Station C. of C., Sigma Xi. Methodist. Author: (with others) JANAF Thermochemical Tables, 1971. Home: 3415 Spring Lane Bryan TX 77801 Office: Thermodynamics Research Center Tex A and M U College Station TX 77843

CHAO, RAUL EDUARD, educator; b. Havana, Cuba, Dec. 21, 1939; s. Thomas and Engracia (Galdo) C.; student Villanova U., 1957-59; B.S.Ch.E. magna cum laude, U. P.R., 1961; Ph.D., Johns Hopkins, 1965; m. Olga Isabel Nodarse, Dec. 26, 1964; 1 son, Raul Octavio. Engr., research engr., group leader Esso Research & Engring. Co., Florham Park, N.J., 1965-68; asso. prof. chem. engring. U. P.R., 1968—, chmn. dept., 1970—. NASA-ASEE fellow, 1973. Registered profl. engr., N.J., Ill. Mem. Am. Inst. Chem. Engrs., Am. Chem. Soc., Inst. Chem. Engrs. P.R., Sigma Xi, Phi Kappa Phi, Tau Beta Pi. Lion. Contbr. articles profl. jours. Home: NF 16 Magnolia St Mayaguez PR 00708

CHAO, TYNG TSAIR, educator; b. Ching Yuan Hsien, China, Oct. 14, 1927; s. Tien-shi and Shan-hua (Wang) C.; B.S., Nat. Taiwan U., 1952, M.S., 1957; Ph.D., Va. Poly. Inst. and U., 1961; m. Anna Lee, Mar. 9, 1962; children—Teresa Linchih, Albert Chungkwang, Richard Chungming. Came to U.S., 1957, naturalized, 1968. Teaching asst. Nat. Taiwan U., 1954-57; research asst. Va. Poly. Inst., 1957-60; research fellow N.C. State U., 1961; prof. phys. sci., prof. chemistry Fayetteville (N.C.) State U., 1961—. Mem. Am. Chem. Soc., Agrl. Chem. Soc. China, Soil Sci. Soc. Am., N.C. Acad. Sci., N.C. Tchrs. Assn., Sigma Xi, Phi Sigma. Contbr. articles profl. jours. Home: 1510 Cardiff Dr Fayetteville NC 28304

CHAPIN, CATHERINE MAYFIELD WISWELL (MRS. TROY ALBERTUS CHAPIN, JR.), civic worker; b. Jacksonville, Ill., Sept. 10, 1916; d. Earl Burr and Clara (Mayfield) Wiswell; A.B., MacMurray Coll., 1937; M.S., U. Colo., 1945; m. Troy Albertus Chapin, Jr., May 15, 1950; children—Catherine Virginia, Louise Tunison. Tchr., Mt. Pulaski (Ill.) High Sch., 1937-38, Lincoln (Ill.) High Sch., 1938-43, U. Colo., Boulder, 1943-44; office mgr., comptroller Conf. Am. Small Bus. Orgns., Chgo., 1945-46; exec. sec. Northwestern U., Chgo. and Evanston, Ill., 1946-50. Pres. Evanston Aux. Cradle Soc., 1961-62; mem. bd. Citizens Alert Youth Program, Tampa, Fla., 1968-70; mem. Nat. Com. for Support Pub. Sch., Washington, 1968—; mem. bd. Hillsborough County Council Parent-Tchrs. Assn., Tampa, 1965—; pres. P.T.A., Tampa, 1967-68, pres. Fla. council, 1974—, mem. bd. Community Concert Assn., 1966-69. Mem. Evanston Bd. Edn., 1964-65; mem. Fla. Courses Study Council; mem. Fla. Career Services Commn., 1973—. Bd. dirs. Mental Health Assn. Hillsborough County. Recipient Alumna of Year award MacMurray Coll., 1965. Mem. Bus. Profl. Women Chgo. (pres. 1951-52), D.A.R. (first vice regent 1963-64), Mayflower Soc., Nat. Soc. Daus. Founders and Patriots Am., Nat. Soc. New Eng. Women, Am. Assn. U. Women (dir. 1970—), P.E.O. (chpt. pres. 1961-63), Krewe of Venus. Presbyn. Clubs: Tampa Woman's, Palma Ceia Golf and Country (Tampa); Tides Bath and Tennis (Redington Beach, Fla.). Address: 4524 Brookwood Dr Tampa FL 33609

CHAPIN, DOUGLAS SCOTT, govt. adminstr.; b. Muskegon, Mich., July 14, 1922; s. Ernest Knight and Lillian Augusta (Yuill) C.; B.S., Kan. State U., 1944; M.S., Ill. Inst. Tech., 1948; Ph.D., Ohio State U., 1954; m. Margaret Jane Gordon, Jan. 29, 1944; children—Jane (Mrs. Robin H. Grieves), Ruth (Mrs. Peter R. Chambers), Julia Jean, Ernestine Lillian. Fellow, Inst. Gas Tech., Ill. Inst. Tech., 1946-48; research asst. cryogenic lab Ohio State U., 1948-52, 53-54; sr. cryogenic operator Operation Ivy, Eniwetok Atoll, S.Pacific, 1952; cryogenic engr. Herrick L. Johnston, Inc., Columbus, O., 1954; asst. prof. dept. chemistry U. Ariz., 1954-59, asso. prof., 1959-66; staff mem. Lincoln Lab., Mass. Inst. Tech., 1963-64; sr. research scientist Jet Propulsion Lab., Cal. Inst. Tech., summer 1965; asso. program dir. grad. fellowships and traineeships NSF, Washington, 1966-68, program dir., 1968-73, head fellowships and traineeships sect., 1973—. Served with AUS, 1944-46. Research grantee AEC, 1955-62, NSF, 1959-61, Petroleum Research Fund, Am. Chem. Soc., 1959-66, Research Corp., 1959-60. Mem. Am. Chem. Soc. (sect. chmn. 1958), A.A.A.S., Am. Assn. U. Adminstrs. (dir.), Sigma Xi, Phi Kappa Phi, Phi Lambda Upsilon, Sigma Pi Sigma. Contbr. articles to profl. jours. Home: 9303 Fernwood Rd Bethesda MD 20034 Office: 1800 G St NW Washington DC 20550

CHAPIN, FRANCIS STUART, JR., educator; b. Northampton, Mass., Apr. 1, 1916; s. Francis Stuart and Nellie Estelle (Peck) C.; A.B., U. Minn., 1937; B.Arch., Mass. Inst. Tech., 1939, M. City Planning, 1940; m. Mildred Louise Canfield, Oct. 10, 1941; children—F. Stuart III, Alison L. (Mrs. Frederick A. Skidmore), Steven W. Regional planner TVA, Knoxville, Tenn., 1940-42, community planner, 1946-47; intelligence analyst War Dept., Washington, 1942-43; dir. planning City of Greensboro, N.C., 1947-49; asso. prof. planning U. N.C., 1949-54, prof., 1954-69, alumni distinguished prof., 1969—. Dir. urban studies program Inst. Research in Social Sci., 1957-62; research dir. Center Urban and Regional Studies of U. N.C., 1962-74; adviser div. slum clearance HHFA, 1951-52; chmn. com. land use evaluation Hwy. Research Bd., Nat. Acad. Sci., 1964-67; mem. Pres.'s Task Force on Cities, 1966-67. Served to lt. USNR, 1943-46. Recipient distinguished service award Am. Inst. Planners, 1969; Guggenheim fellow, 1972-73. Mem. Am. Inst. Planners (v.p. 1957, gov. 1951-53, 54-56, 58-61), Regional Sci. Assn. (v.p. 1961), Assn. Collegiate Schs. Planning (pres. 1964-65), Am. Soc. Planning Ofcls. Author: Communities for Living, 1941; Urban Land Use Planning, 2d ed., 1965. Editor, contbr.: (with S.F. Weiss) Urban Growth Dynamics, 1962. Contbr. to Urban Life and Form, 1963, Urban Development Models, 1968, The Quality of the Urban Environment, 1969, Ency. Urban Planning, 1973. Home: 206 Burlage Circle Chapel Hill NC 27514

CHAPLIN, ROBERT ROGERS, JR., physician; b. Emporia, Va., Jan. 4, 1936; s. Robert Rogers and Gertrude Mae (Michael) C.; B.S., Hampden Sydney Coll., 1958; M.D., Med. Coll. Va., 1962; m. Judith Falconer Preddy, Mar. 7, 1969; children—Robert Rogers III, James Michael. Intern, Stuart Circle Hosp., Richmond, Va., 1962-63, house physician, 1965-68, now mem. staff; gen. practice medicine, Richmond, 1968—; mem. staff Johnston-Willis, Chippenham, Grace, St. Luke's, St. Elizabeth hosps., all Richmond. Served as capt. USAF, 1963-65. Mem. Richmond Acad. Medicine, Med. Soc. Va. Episcopalian. Mason. Home: 2720 Kenbury Rd Richmond VA 23225 Office: 7111 Jahnke Rd Richmond VA 23225

CHAPMAN, CECIL CAREY, cons. hydraulic and san. engr.; b. White Pond, S.C., July 18, 1908; s. Carl McNeil and Myra (Scott) C.; B.S. in Civil Engring., U.S.C., 1931; m. Gertrude Rowe, Sept. 30, 1933. Insp., S.C. Hwy. Dept., 1931-32; chief draftsman U.S. Forest Service, 1933-34; engr. S.C. Geod. Survey, 1934-35; engr. U.S. Soil Conservation Service, 1935-41, drainage and irrigation engr., 1946-48, hydraulic engr. flood control, 1948-51; design engr. U.S.C.E., 1941-42; asso. Walter E. Rowe, municipal engring., 1935-41; partner Rowe & Chapman, designing and cons. engrs., Williston, S.C., 1951-53; co-partner Chapman Engring. Co., design and cons. engrs., Williston, 1953—. Served with USNR, 1943-45; PTO. Registered profl. engr., S.C., Ga., N.C., Fla. Diplomate Am. San. Engrs. Intersoc. Bd. Mem. Am. Soc. C.E., Nat. Soc. Profl. Engrs., Am. Concrete Inst., Am. Water Works Assn., Am. Soc. for Testing and Materials, Water Pollution Control Fedn., S.C. Water and Pollution Control Assn., S.C. Soc. Cons. Engrs., Cons. Engrs. Council, Am. Iris Soc., Am. Legion. Home: 312 W Main St Williston SC 29853 Office: PO Box 218 Williston SC 29853

CHAPMAN, JERRY WAYNE, govt. ofcl.; b. McKinney, Tex., Jan. 14, 1941; s. Grady and Marie (Blasingame) C.; B.A., Austin Coll., 1963; M.A., U. Okla., 1964; m. Martha Jackson, Aug. 19, 1961; children—Shain, Ashley. Asst. area coordinator HUD, Ft. Worth, 1965-68; exec. dir. Texoma Regional Planning Commn., Denison, Tex., 1969—. Commr., Texoma Valley council Boy Scouts Am. Mem. Internat., Tex. city mgmt. assns., Am. Soc. Planning Ofcls. Rotarian. Home: 2715 Shoreline St Sherman TX 75090 Office: 1000 Arnold St Denison TX 75020

CHAPMAN, JOEL ALVIN, supt. schs.; b. Anderson, S.C., Apr. 14, 1918; s. Joseph Wilhite and Eliza Eugenia (Hall) C.; B.A., Presbyn. Coll., 1939; M.A., Columbia, 1949; m. Carolyn Woods Embry, Jan. 26, 1942; 1 dau., Diana (Mrs. Richard John Monsour). Prin., Chambliss Jr. High Sch., Americus, Ga., 1939-40, Taylors (S.C.) Elementary Sch., 1940-41, Leland (Miss.) High Sch., 1946-51; Supt. Port Gibson (Miss.) Pub. Schs., 1953-65, Bolivar County Sch. Dist., Shelby, Miss., 1965—. Bd. dirs. Little Theatre Groups. Served to col. AUS, 1941-45, 51-53. Mem. Am. Assn. Sch. Adminstrs., Miss. Assn. Sch. Supts., Miss. State Guidance Council, Miss. Lang. Tchrs. (pres. 1950-51). Presbyn. (elder). Mason, Rotarian, Lion. Home: 119 Lauderdale St Shelby MS 38774 Office: Box 28 Shelby MS 38774

CHAPMAN, MARY LUCILE, educator; b. Louisa, Ky.; d. Napoleon Bonaparte and Ida Belle (Porter) Chapman; A.B., U. Ky., 1929; A.M., 1937; Ph.D., 1945. Tchr. pub. schs. Ashland, Ky., 1922-40, supr., 1940-56; asst. prof., history Marshall Coll., Huntington, W.Va., 1946-48; asso. prof. history E. Tenn. State Coll., Johnson City. 1948-55; prof. social studies Jr. Coll., 1955-57; prof. history Ashland Center U. Ky., 1957-59; head dept. history Piedmont Coll., Demorest, Ga., 1959-62; asso. prof. history Jacksonville (Ala.) State U., 1962-65, prof., 1965—, chmn. div. social studies, 1959-62. Mem. Nat. Council Social Studies, Am., So., Ala. hist. assns., Nat., Ga. hist. socs., Am. Assn. U. Women (pres. Anniston br. 1967-69, mem. Ala. div. bd.), Internat. Fedn. U. Women, Am. Assn. U. Profs., Calhoun County Hist. Assn., Orgn. of Am. Historians, Atlantic Council of U.S., Nat., Ala. edn. assns., Acad. Polit. Sci., So. Polit. Sci. Assn., Coalition for Better Schs. in Ala., Ala. Woman's Civil Def. Orgn., Polit. Sci. Soc., Council So. Life and Work, Internat. Platform Assn., Am. Acad. Polit. and Social Sci., U.D.C., Intercontinental Biog. Assn., D.A.R., Marquis Library Soc., Alpha Phi Theta, Kappa Delta Pi. Democrat. Methodist. Club: Jacksonville State College Faculty. Home: 703 12th Av Jacksonville AL 36265

CHAPMAN, RICHARD LEROY, polit. scientist; b. Yankton, S.D., Feb. 4, 1932; s. Raymond Young and Vera (Trimble) C.; B.S., S.D. State U., 1954; postgrad. Cambridge U., 1954-55; M.P.A., Syracuse U., 1958, Ph.D., 1967; m. Marilyn Jean Nicholson, Aug. 14, 1955; children—Catherine Ruth, Richard Matthew, Michael David, Stephen Raymond, Amy Jean. Mgmt. asst. Office Sec. Def., 1958-59; asst. dir. research S.D. Legislative Research Council, Pierre, 1959-60; budget examiner U.S. Bur. Budget, Washington, 1960-61; adminstrv. officer, project mgr. Adv. Research Projects Agy., Dept. Def., Washington, 1961-63; staff asst. Office Dir., NIH, Washington, 1965-66, exec. sec. Grants Assos. Program 1967-68; mem. profl. staff Govt. Operations Com., U.S. Ho. of Reps., Washington, 1966-67; sr. research asso Nat. Acad. Pub. Adminstrn., Washington, 1968—; staff dir., then cons. Rep. Frank Denholm, 1973—. Served with inf., AUS, 1955-57. Rotary Found. fellow, 1954-55, Syracuse U. fellow, 1957, 63, Brookings Instn. fellow, 1964. Mem. Royal Inst. Pub. Adminstrn., Am. Soc. Pub. Adminstrn., So. Polit. Sci. Assn., A.A.A.S., Phi Kappa Phi, Pi Kappa Delta. Republican. Methodist. Mason. Home: 8204 Chivalry Rd Annandale VA 22003 Office: 1225 Connecticut Av NW Washington DC 20036

CHAPMAN, SAMUEL GREELEY, educator; b. Atlanta, Sept. 29, 1929; s. Calvin C. and Jane (Greeley) C.; A.B., U. Cal. at Berkeley, 1951, M.A., 1959; m. Patricia Hepfer, June 19, 1949; children—Lynn Randall, Deborah Jane. Officer, Police Dept., Berkeley, Cal., 1950-56; police cons. Pub. Adminstrn. Service, Chgo., 1956-63; police chief Multnomah County, Portland, Ore., 1963-66; asst. dir. Nat. Crime Commn., Washington, 1966-67; prof. dept. polit. sci. U. Okla., Norman, 1967—, chmn. athletic council, 1971-72. Mem. Norman City Council, 1972—. Author: The Police Heritage in England and America, 1962; Police Patrol Readings, 1964, rev. edit., 1970. Home: 2421 Hollywood St Norman OK 73069

CHAPMAN, STEVEN FRANKLIN, lawyer; b. Waxahachie, Tex., May 8, 1940; s. Richard Franklin and Hazel (Stevens) C.; B.B.A., So. Meth. U., 1962, LL.B., 1965; m. Hilda Harbin, June 12, 1964; children—Jim, Jill. Admitted to Tex. bar, 1965; since practiced in Waxahachie, Tex., 1965—; mem. firm Chapman and Chapman, 1967—; city atty., Waxahachie, 1969—, Midlothian, Tex., 1970—. Judge, City Corp. Ct., Waxahachie, Tex., 1967-69. Bd. dirs. Ellis County Hist. Mus. and Art Gallery, pres., 1972-73; bd. dirs. Community Chest and United Fund, 1967-69, pres., 1968-69. Mem. Am., Ellis County (pres. 1970-71) bar assns., State Bar of Tex. Presbyn. (pres. bd. trustees 1972, 73). Rotarian (pres. 1969-70). Home: 419 Bird Lane Waxahachie TX 75165 Office: Citizens Nat Bank Bldg Waxahachie TX 75165

CHAPMAN, THEODORE EVERETT, trucking co. exec.; b. Waltham, Mass., Feb. 3, 1939; s. Theodore W. and Beatrice (Strong) C.; B.B.A., Central Mo. State Coll., Warrensburg, Mo., 1963; M.S. in Finance, U. Kan., 1966; m. Virginia Lee Martin, Mar. 4, 1960; children—Theodore Everett, Gillian K. With Arthur Andersen & Co., C.P.A.'s, Kansas City, Mo., 1963-65; dir. corporate accounting Yellow Freight System, Kansas City, Mo., 1966-71; exec. v.p., treas. Superior Trucking Co., Atlanta, 1971—, also dir. Chmn. econ. rate com. Rocky Mountain Tariff Bur. Mem. Kansas City (Mo.) Sports Commn., 1969-71; mem. fund raising com. Greater Atlanta Christian Schs. Served with AUS, 1957-60. Grad. teaching scholar, 1965-66. Mem. Ga. Motor Trucking Assn. (dir.). Mem. Ch. of Christ (deacon 1973—). Clubs: Atlanta Athletic; Indian Hills Country (Atlanta). Home: 742 Indian Hills Pky Marietta GA 30062 Office: PO Box 916 Atlanta GA 30301

CHAPMAN, WILLIAM FRED, JR., coll. dean; b. Belton, S.C., Apr. 13, 1931; s. William Fred and Iver (Cooper) C.; B.S., Clemson U., 1957, M.S., 1958; Ph.D., U. Fla., 1963; m. Nancy Jean Bryant, June 10, 1955; children—William Anthony, Nancy Jean. Asst. prof. Clemson U., 1957-59, prof., 1965-66; marketing economist Econ. Research Service, U.S. Dept. Agr., U. Fla., Gainesville, 1959-64; prof., head dept. econs. and bus. adminstrn. Presbyn. Coll., Clinton, S.C., 1964-65, 66-69, acad. dean, prof., 1969—. Cons., Clemson U., 1964-65, 66-67, U.S. Dept. Interior, 1966-67, U.S. Dept. Agr., 1964-65, 65-66. Served from pvt. to 1st lt. AUS, 1951-53. Decorated Combat Infantry badge, Purple Heart, Silver Star. Mem. Am., So. econs. assns., Am. Farm Econs. Assn., Am. Assn. U. Profs., Am. Statis. Assn., Alpha Zeta, Gamma Sigma Delta. Contbr. monographs, bulls. to profl. jours. Home: Huntingdon Rd Clinton SC 29325

CHAPMAN, WILLIE LASCO, JR., educator, veterinarian; b. Chattanooga, Dec. 17, 1928; s. Willie Lasco and Pearl (Spitzer) C.; B.S., U. Tenn., 1950; D.V.M., Auburn U., 1957; M.S., Colo. State U., 1963; Ph.D., U. Wis., 1968; m. Betty Ann Smith, May 10, 1958; children—Susan Ann, Karen Leigh. Pvt. practice veterinary medicine, Chattanooga, 1957-62; resident Colo. State U., 1962-63; asst. prof. dept. medicine and surgery U. Ga. Coll. Vet. Medicine, 1963-64; spl. fellow U. Wis., 1964-67; asst. prof. pathology U. Ga., Athens, 1967-71, asso. prof., head dept. medicine and surgery, 1971—. Cons. primate medicine. Served with AUS, 1950-52. Nat. Cancer Inst. Spl. fellow, 1965-67. Mem. Sigma Xi, Gamma Sigma Delta, Omega Tau Sigma, Phi Zeta. Methodist. Home: 565 Brookwood Dr Athens GA 30601

CHAPPELEAR, JOHN WILLIS, JR., architect; b. High Point, N.C., Feb. 3, 1929; s. John Willis and Floyce Lee (Goodson) C.; student N.C. State Coll., 1945-48; m. Betty Jean Hooker, Aug. 24, 1948; children—John III, Donald Eugene, Karen Lynn, Jean Marie. Designer, Eric G. Flannagan, Henderson, N.C., 1949-52, Frantz & Addkison, Roanoke, Va., 1953-59; designer, asso. Randolph Frantz & Assos., Roanoke, 1959-64; partner Frantz & Chappelear, Roanoke, 1965—. Apptd. by gov. to Va. Art Commn., 1970; pres. Downtown Roanoke, Inc., 1965; chmn. Roanoke Bd. Zoning Appeals, 1964—; pres. Central Roanoke Devel. Found., 1968—. Registered profl. architect, N.C., Va. Mem. A.I.A. (pres. Va. chpt. 1972). Prin. archtl. works include Roanoke Civic Center, Hollins Coll. (Va.) Sci. Bldg., Va. Western Community Coll., Madison Jr. High Sch., Roanoke, Melrose Towers Apts., Roanoke. Home: 2535 Robin Hood Rd Roanoke VA 24014 Office: 606 State and City Bldg Roanoke VA 24011

CHAPPELL, BUFORD SOUTER, physician; b. Bookman, S.C., July 28, 1914; s. Oscar and Belva (Lever) C.; M.D., Med. Coll. S.C., 1938; m. Mary Marjorie Cooper, Nov. 8, 1940; children—Buford Souter, Mary (Mrs. Charles F. Mills), Richard F., Pamela A. Intern, St. Francis Infirmary, Charleston, S.C., 1937-38, U. Kan. Hosp., Kansas City, 1938-39; asst. resident urology U. Va., 1945-46, resident urology, 1947; sr. resident urology VA Hosp., Columbia, 1948-49, cons. urology, 1949—; practice medicine, specializing in urology Columbia, 1949—; chief urology service Columbia (S.C.) Hosp., 1950-60; active urology staff Providence Hosp., Columbia, Bapt. Hosp. Served from capt. to lt. col. M.C., AUS, 1942-46. Fellow Internat. Coll. Surgeons; mem. A.M.A., So. Med. Assn., Am. Urol. Assn. Home: 1373 Kathwood Rd Columbia SC 29206 Office: 2011 Hampton St Columbia SC 29204

CHAPPELL, FRED, author; b. Canton, N.C., May 28, 1936; s. James Taylor and Anne (Davis) C.; B.A., Duke, 1961; m. Susan Nichols, Aug. 2, 1959; 1 son, Heath. Gen. mgr. Brown Supply Co., Candler, N.C., 1957-59; credit mgr. Candler Furniture Co., 1959-60; proofreader Duke U. Press, Durham, N.C., 1961. Woodrow Wilson fellow, Nat. Def. Edn. Act fellow. Mem. Southeastern Renaissance Assn. Author: It Is Time, Lord, 1963; The Inkling and Dagon, The World Between The Eyes, 1971; The Gaudy Place, 1973. Former editor The Archive; former contbg. editor Skyhook. Contbr. to Holiday, little mags. Adv. editor Greensboro Review. Address: care English Dept U of NC at Greensboro Greensboro NC 27412*

CHAPPELL, THOMAS WARREN, agrl. engr.; b. Newport News, Va., July 18, 1943; s. Richard Jennings and Edith (Brown) C.; B.S., Va. Poly. Inst. and State U., 1965, M.S., 1967; m. Margaret Louise White, Oct. 14, 1967; children—David, Michael, Wallace. Research agrl. engr. Forest Service, U.S. Dept. Agr., Auburn, Ala., 1967—. Mem. Am. Soc. Agrl. Engrs., Forest Products Research Soc., Alpha Epsilon, Gamma Sigma Delta. Home: 1212 Old Mill Rd Auburn AL 36830 Office: USDA Forest Service Agrl Engring Bldg Auburn U Auburn AL 36830

CHARDON, FERNANDO, adj. gen. P.R.; b. Ponce, P.R., Sept. 5, 1907; s. Carlos Felix and Isabel (Palacios-Pelletier) C.; B.S.A., Cornell U.; LL.D., Interam. U. P.R.; m. Carmin Guyar Gatell, Aug. 1931; children—Diana Maria (Mrs. Rengel), Carmen Isabel (Mrs. Ortiz), Fernando Luis, Marissa. Asst. agronomist for research in sugar cane and tobacco U. P.R., 1928-39; chief sect. agrl. rehab. div. P.R. Reconstrn. Adminstrn., 1937; field mgr. Constancia Sugar Mill, Toa Baja, P.R., 1939-41; dir. appraisal div. P.R. Land Authority, 1946-47; v.p. in charge operations and colonies Eastern Sugar Assn., Fajardo Eastern Sugar Assn., 1947-61; sec.-treas. P.R. Sugar Producers Assn., 1962—; sec. of state, P.R., then lt. gov., now adj. gen. Served to lt. col. AUS, 1941-46; PTO. Mem. Internat. Soc. Sugar Cane Technologists (sec. gen.), P.R. Technologists Assn. Mem. New Progressive Party. Roman Catholic. Address: Hdqrs PR NG Box 3786 San Juan PR 00904

CHARLES, GEORGE JAMES, lawyer; b. Toronto, Ont., Can.; s. James E. and Despina C.; came to U.S., 1934, naturalized 1940; B.A. with honors, U. Pa., 1950; J.D. with honors, George Washington U., 1952; m. Helen Clara Chigges, June 20, 1947; children—James George, Deborah, Mary Elizabeth, Constance. Admitted to D.C. bar, 1953, Md. bar, 1958, U.S. Supreme Ct. bar, 1960; press and information officer Royal Greek Embassy, 1950-57; pvt. practice law, Washington, 1953—. Press aide to King and Queen of Greece on royal tour of U.S., 1953. Pres. bd. trustees St. Sophia Cathedral, Washington, 1963-68; mem. exec. com. Archdiocesan Council Greek Orthodox Archidocese N. and S. Am.; chmn. Met. Washington Council Greek Orthodox Chs., 1963-73; mem. Order St. Andrew, Eucemenical Patriarchate Eastern Orthodox Ch.; mem. gen. bd. Nat. Council Chs. of Christ, U.S.A., 1969—. Served as maj. USAAF, World War II, Africa, Italy, Germany; lt. col. USAF Res. ret. Decorated Bronze Star, medal, Greek Gold Cross of George I. Mem. Am. Bar Assn., Bar Assn. D.C., Phi Delta Phi. Clubs: Nat. Lawyers; Bethesda Country. Home: 7604 Carter Ct Bethesda MD 20034 Office 1250 Connecticut Av NW Washington DC 20036

CHARLESWORTH, ARTHUR RIGGS, clergyman, educator; b. South Fork, Pa., Sept. 23, 1911; s. Thomas and Cora Orina (Riggs) C.; B.A. with honors, U. Pitts., 1933; B.D., M.Div., Theol. Sch., Drew U., Ph.D., 1946; m. Martha Jean Hamilton, July 11, 1935; children—Lois Jean, James Hamilton, Arthur Thomas. Ordained to ministry United Methodist Ch., 1938; minister, then sr. minister Bryan Meml. United Meth. Ch., Miami, Fla., 1959-63; head religion and philosophy Bethune-Cookman Coll., Daytona Beach, Fla., 1963—, also pres.

faculty assn. Participant seminar Near Eastern Civilizations, Holy Land and Greece, summer 1968, seminar The Living God, Oxford U., Eng., summer 1969, seminar Profs. to Africa, summer 1970; mem. summer inst. Inst. on Theology, Princeton Theol. Sem., 1971. Mem. Am. Assn. U. Profs. (pres. 1967), N.E.A., Drew U. Alumni Assn. (pres. Fla. chpt. 1967-70), Am. Acad. Religion, Soc. Bibl. Lit., Am. Sch. Oriental Research. Rotarian. Author: Paradise Found, 1973. Home: 1231 Florence Ct Holly Hill FL 32017 Office: Box 303 Bethune-Cookman Coll Daytona Beach FL 32015

CHASE, FRANK REYNOLDS, librarian; b. Chgo., June 9, 1915; s. Frank Maxwell and Ethel R. (Drummond) C.; B.A., U. Ill., 1942; B.L.S., Columbia, 1947; m. Anne Margaret Cameron, Aug. 18, 1962. Head reference librarian Bradley U., Peoria, Ill., 1947-52; asst. reference librarian Peoria Pub. Library, 1952-59; asst. sci. librarian Morris Library, So. Ill. U., Carbondale, 1959-65; head reference and law sects. John Grant Crabbe Library, Eastern Ky. U., Richmond, 1965—. Served with AUS, 1942-43. Mem. A.L.A., Ky. Library Assn., Alpha Phi Omega (adviser 1949-65). Home: Box 30-A Route 2 Richmond KY 40475

CHASE, LORING DUBOIS, clergyman; b. Greenfield, Mass., July 13, 1916; s. Loring Bertie and Edith (MacLaury) C.; A.B., Middlebury Coll., 1937; B.D., Yale, 1941; m. Helene Giannina Cosenza, Aug. 17, 1939; children—Christopher L., David M. Ordained to ministry Congl. Ch., 1941; minister Ledyard (Conn.) Congl. Ch., 1939-44; minister-at-large Conn. Conf. Congl. Chs., 1944-47; minister New Canaan (Conn.) Congl. Ch., 1947-64, Westmoreland Congl. Ch., Washington, 1964—. Dir. office of communication United Ch. Christ, 1965—; pres. United Ch. Bd. for World Ministries, 1969-73; sec. Commn. to Prepare a Statement of Faith United Ch. Christ, 1957-59. Author: Words of Faith, 1968; The Church, Community of Response and Mission, 1969. Home: 5107 Dalecarlia Dr Washington DC 20016 Office: 1 Westmoreland Circle Washington DC 20016

CHASTAIN, BENJAMIN BURTON, educator; b. Tuscaloosa, Ala., Dec. 21, 1936; s. Benjamin McCullough and Martha Louise (Burton) C.; B.S., Birmingham-So. Coll., 1956; M.A., Columbia, 1957, Ph.D., 1967; m. Doris Audra Dyer, Dec. 29, 1962; children—Edward Benjamin, Jonathan Dyer. Asso. chemist So. Research Inst., Birmingham, Ala., 1957-58; tchr. Birmingham Pub. Schs., 1958-59; instr. chemistry Samford U., Birmingham, 1959-63, asst. prof., 1963-67, asso. prof., 1967-70, prof., 1970—. Mem. Sec.'s Adv. Com. on Coal Mine Safety Research of U.S. Dept. Interior, 1971—; coordinator Central Ala. Regional Sci. Fair, 1968—. NSF predoctoral fellow, 1956-57; NSF sci. faculty fellow, 1965-66; NIH spl. fellow, 1966-67. Mem. Ala. Acad. Sci., Am. Chem. Soc., Am. Assn. U. Profs., Phi Beta Kappa, Sigma Xi, Phi Kappa Phi, Omicron Delta Kappa, Pi Kappa Alpha. Episcopalian. Contbr. articles profl. jours. Home: 3651 Haven View Circle Birmingham AL 35216

CHASTAIN, WALTER RALPH, JR., banker; b. Columbia, S.C., Mar. 26, 1939; s. Walter Ralph and Maitland Pearl (Mitchell) C.; B.A., U. South, 1961; M.B.A., U. S.C., 1963; m. Nell Williams Stevenson, Dec. 6, 1969. Asst. cashier Citizens and So. Nat. Bank, Charleston, S.C., 1965-66, bond officer, 1966-68, asst. v.p., mgr. bond dept., 1968-69, v.p., mgr. bond dept., 1969—. Instr. U. S.C., 1963, Fla. State U., 1966-72, Bapt. Coll. Charleston, 1967-72, Am. Inst. Banking, 1963-71, Bank Adminstrn. Inst., U. Wis., 1971—. Treas. Charleston County Heart Assn., 1965-72; mem. investment com. S.C. Heart Assn., 1971—. Served with S.C. N.G., 1963-69. Recipient Service award S.C. Heart Assn., 1969. Mem. Nat. Assn. Accountants, Bank Adminstrn. Inst., Huguenot Soc. Va., S.A.R., S.C. Bankers Assn. (mem. investment com. 1971—), Sewanee Alumni Assn. of Charleston (pres. 1969), Sewanee Alumni Assn. of Columbia (v.p. 1973), S.C. Municipal Council. Episcopalian. Clubs: Carolina Yacht (Charleston); Spring Valley Country (Columbia). Home: 2802 Forest Dr Columbia SC 29204 Office: Jefferson Sq Plaza Columbia SC 29201

CHASTEEN, JOSEPH WILEY, JR., property devel. co. exec.; b. Huntsville, Ala., Dec. 9, 1921; s. Joseph Wiley and Ola Lee (Brown) C.; A.B., William Jewell Coll., 1950; postgrad. U. Pa., 1952-55; Drexel Inst. Tech., 1956; M.B.A., Rollins Coll., 1962; m. Mae Lyndal Miller, Oct. 31, 1941; children—Joseph Wiley III, David A. Tchr., Central Tech. Inst., Kansas City, Mo., 1946-50; engr. RCA, Camden, N.J., 1951-56; group engr. Martin Co., Balt., 1956-57; asst. mng. engring. Martin Marietta Corp., Orlando, Fla., 1957-63, engring. mgr., 1963-67, tech. mgr., 1967-69; advance projects mgr. Emerson Electric Co., St. Louis, 1969-70; pres. PWC Assos., Inc., Orlando, 1970—; mgr. project office staff space shuttle Honeywell, Inc., St. Petersburg, Fla., 1973—. Chmn., Pine Hills Area Round Table, 1963-64; pres. Robinswood Civic Assn. 1963-65; commr. Pine Hills Fire Dist., 1964-65, Orange County (Fla.) Local Study Group. Bd. dirs. Robinswood Recreation Park, Orlando. Served with USNR, 1944-46, 50-51. Asso. fellow Am. Inst. Aero. and Astronautics; mem. I.E.E.E. (sr.), Sigma Pi Sigma, Kappa Mu Epsilon. Contbr. articles to profl. jours. Home: 1824 Hasting Terrace Orlando FL 32808 Office: PO Box 15606 Orlando FL 32808

CHATHAM, GEORGE NORTON, govtl. cons.; b. Cleburne, Tex., Aug. 20, 1923; s. Norton Sweeny and Mabel Amanda (Fisher) C.; B.A., U. Tex., 1949; m. Lois Rommel, Mar. 14, 1959; 1 son, Bruce. Exec. v.p. Chatleff Controls, Inc., Austin, Tex., 1953-63; program mgr. NASA, 1963-69; sci. policy transp. specialist Library of Congress, Washington, 1969—. Sci. writer, cons. aerospace forecasting. Served with USAAF, 1943-46; PTO. Mem. Am. Inst. Aeros. and Astronautics, A.A.A.S., Am. Aviation History Soc., Nat. Aero. Assn., Nat. Space Club. Author: The Supersonic Transport, 1971. Contbr. articles to profl. jours. Patentee in field. Home: 657 E St SE Washington DC 20003 Office: Library of Congress CRS/SPRD Washington DC 20540

CHATTIN, CHESTER COLES, judge; b. Winchester, Tenn., Nov. 2, 1907; s. Edward Walter, and Ellen (Shadow) C.; B.S., U. South, 1929; LL.B., Cumberland U., 1930; m. Mary Kiningham, May 15, 1935; 1 dau., Mary Kay. Admitted to Tenn. bar, 1930; practiced law, Winchester, 1930-47; asst. dist. atty. Gen. 18th Jud. Circuit, Winchester, Tenn., 1935-37, 39-47; dist. atty. Gen. 18th Jud. Circuit, Winchester, Tenn., 1947-58; circuit judge, 1958-62; judge Ct. Appeals Tenn., Winchester, 1962-64, Supreme Ct. Tenn., Winchester, 1964—; dir. rep. Franklin County, Tenn., 1941-43; dir. Farmers Nat. Bank, Winchester. Served with USNR, 1945. Mem. Tenn. Bar Assn., Tenn. Jud. Conf., Franklin County C. of C., Franklin County Hist. Soc., Am. Legion, Phi Gamma Delta. Episcopalian. Mason (Shriner). Club: Franklin County Country. Home: 801 S Jefferson St Winchester TN 37398 Office: 35 S Porter St Winchester TN 37398

CHAUVIN, ROBERT SILAS, coll. dean; b. West Beekmantown, N.Y., Nov. 20, 1920; s. Silas Nelson and Marie (Woodley) C.; B.S., State U. Coll. N.Y., 1943; M.Ed., U. Houston, 1947; M.A., Columbia, Ed.D., 1950; m. Della Faye Freeman, May 16, 1947; children—Robert Silas, Randall Freeman. Prof. geography, geology Stetson U., DeLand, Fla. 1960, dean sciences, 1968-69, dean Coll. Liberal Arts, 1969—; vis. asst. prof. geography Columbia U., 1954; vis. prof. geography-geology Neb. State Coll., Kearney, 1957. Mem. Govs. Bd. on Resource-Use, State of Fla., 1958—. Served with AUS, 1943-46. Mem. Assn. Am. Georgraphers, U.S. Naval Inst., Lambda Chi Alpha, Gamma Theta Upsilon. Democrat. Baptist. Home: 851 E Minnesota Av DeLand FL 32720

CHAVES-GARCIA, CARLOS FRANCISCO, dentist; b. Isabela, P.R., Nov. 2, 1937; s. Francisco Chaves and Martina Garcia; B.S., U. P.R., 1959, D.M.D., 1963; m. Celida Nieves Maldonado, Dec. 27, 1962; children—Aixa Odette, Elga Enid, Carlos Omar. Practice dentistry, Barbosa Isabela, P.R., 1963—, P.R. Health Dept., Isabela, 1965—. Pres. Gallitos de Isabela, Inc., 1967-68, Coop. Credito Isabela, 1968-69; v.p. Cooperativa Consumo Isabela, 1970-71. Mem. P.R. Dental Assn., Omicron Kappa Upsilon, Xi, Psi Phi. Mem. Popular Party. Roman Catholic. Lion. Home: Rural Route 2Bo Coto Isabela PR 00662 Office: Barbosa 8 Isabela PR 00662

CHAVEZ, CARLOS, condr., composer; b. Mexico, June 13, 1899. Former head Dept. of Fine Arts of Mexico, past dir. Nat. Conservatory, Mexico; founder Symphony Orch. of Mexico City, 1928, and since condr.; has been guest condr. of many major orchs. U. S.; Charles Eliot Norton prof. poetry Harvard, 1958-59. Decorated many fgn. govts. Hon. mem. Am. Acad. Arts and Scis., Nat. Inst. Arts and Letters. Composer Sinfonia Antigona, Sinfonia India, music for ballet symphony, H.P. (the initials standing for Horse Power), 4th Symphony, Romantica, 1959, Soil Number 1 for Wind Quartet, and many other leading works. Author: Toward a New Music, 1937; Musical Thought, 1960. Address: Av Pirineos 775 Lomas de Chapulltepec Mexico City 10 Mexico

CHAVEZ, GILBERTO JESUS, govt. ofcl.; b. Cottonwood, Ariz., June 12, 1931; s. Enrique and Henrietta (Brest) C.; A.A., Phoenix Coll., 1956; B.A., Ariz. State U., 1958, M.A., 1964; m. Yolanda Maria Vasquez, Dec. 26, 1968; children—Stuart Jess, Cristal Yolanda. Asst. boys dir. City of Phoenix, 1955-60; elementary sch. tchr. Maricopa County, Ariz., 1960-67; dir. Headstart, 1966-67; migrant dir. State of Wash., 1967-69; program planning and devel. officer U.S. Office of Edn., Washington, 1969-70, dep. to equal employment officer, 1970-71, dir. office for Spanish-speaking Am. affairs, 1971—. Served with USAF, 1951-55. Mem. Phi Delta Kappa. Home: 1306 E Holly Av Sterling VA 22170 Office: 400 Maryland Av SW Washington DC 20202

CHAVEZ, IGNACIO, physician; b., 1897; ed. Nat. U. of Mexico; hon. degrees univs. Paris, Montpellier, Lyon, Mexico, Sao Paulo, Oxford, Bologna, Praga, others. Clin. prof. Nat. U. of Mexico, 1923-50, dir. Faculty Medicine, 1933-34, prof. cardiology Sch. Grads., 1946-61, rector Nat. U., 1961-66. Founder, dir. Nat. Inst. Cardiology of Mexico; founder, mem. Colegio Nacional. Hon. rector U. Michoacan; hon. prof. univs. Guadalajara, Guatemala, San Salvador, Rio de Janeiro, others. Recipient Palmes Academiques. Decorated Legion of Honor, Order Pub. Health (France); comdr. Order Finlay (Cuba); Order Quetzal (Guatemala); Order Cruzeiro do Sul (Brazil); Medal of Civil Merit, (Mexico); Order Nassau (Holland); Merito (Italy); Polonia Restituta; Roi Leopoid (Belgium); recipient Scientific prize of Mexico. Mem. Inter-Am. Soc. Cardiology (hon. pres.), Acads. Medicine of Mexico, N.Y., Buenos Aires, France, Rome, others. Author books. Address: Paseo de la Reforma 1310 Lomas City 10 Mexico Office: Avenida Nuevo Leon 78 Mexico City 11 Mexico

CHEATHAM, FRANK SELLARS, JR., judge; b. Savannah, Ga., Jan. 11, 1924; s. Frank S. and Margaret (Caldwell) C.; student Armstrong Coll., 1942-44; A.B., U. Ga., 1946, LL.B., 1948. Admitted to Ga. bar, 1948; gen. practice, Savannah, 1948-72; judge Superior Ct., Eastern Jud. Dist. Ga., 1972—. Dir. First Bank of Savannah, 1968-72. Mem. Ga. Ho. of Reps., 1953-60, chmn. appropriations com., 1959-60; mem. Gov's Commn. on Jud. Selection, 1963-67. Pres. YMCA Bd., 1964-68. Trustee Candler Gen. Hosp. Named Outstanding Young Man in Ga., Ga. Jr. C. of C., 1951. Mem. Savannah Bar Assn. (pres. 1966), Blue Key, Sigma Alpha Epsilon, Phi Delta Phi, Omicron Delta Kappa. Kiwanian (pres. Savannah 1969). Home: 4622 Cumberland Savannah GA 31405 Office: 214 County Court House Savannah GA 31401

CHEATHAM, JOHN BANE, JR., educator; b. Houston, June 29, 1924; s. John Bane and Winnie (Carr) C.; B.S. in Mech. Engring., So. Meth. U., 1948, M.S., 1953; M.E., Mass. Inst. Tech., 1954; Ph.D., Rice U., 1960; m. Juanita Faye Burns, July 19, 1947; children—Preston, Curtis. Design engr. Linkbelt Co., Dallas, Houston, 1949-50; research engr. Atlantic Refining Co., Dallas, 1950-53; research asso., head drilling research Shell Devel. Co., Houston, 1954-63; prof. dept. mech., aerospace engring. Rice U., Houston, 1963—. Cons. in field. Served to 2d lt. USAAF, 1943-45. Registered profl. engr., Tex. Mem. Am. Soc. M.E., Am. Inst. Mining and Petroleum Engrs., Am. Soc. Engring. Educators, Sigma Xi. Contbr. articles to profl. jours. Home: 4402 Briarbend St Houston TX 77035

CHEATHAM, ROBERT CARL, city mgr.; b. Frostproof, Fla., Feb. 14, 1935; s. Milton Rufus and Mabel (Morris) C.; A.S. in Civil Engring. Tech. with honors, Polk Community Coll., 1969; m. Barbara Ann Lamb, Aug. 23, 1953; 1 son, Robert Carl. With City Lake Wales, Fla., 1959—, dir. utilities, 1967-69, city mgr., 1969—. Mem. adv. bd. adult edn. Polk Community Coll., 1971-72, Fla. Pollution Control Assn., 1959—. Bd. dirs. Ampitheater Assn., YMCA, both Lake Wales. Mem. Ridge (pres.), Fla. (mem. resolution com.) leagues municipalities, Internat., Polk County (chmn. 1972) city mgr. assns. Baptist (deacon). Kiwanian. Home: 823 E Ocesola St Lake Wales FL 33853 Office: PO Box 1320 Lake Wales FL 33853

CHEATHAM, WILLIAM JOSEPH, educator, physician; b. Jackson, Tenn., June 18, 1925; s. William G. and Rosalie (Pacaud) C.; student Gen. Motors Inst. Tech., 1943-44; B.A., Vanderbilt U., 1947, M.D., 1950; m. Jean Brandon, July 10, 1948; children—William J. Jr., David B. Intern, Vanderbilt U. Hosp., Nashville, 1950-51, resident, 1951-53; Nat. Found. Infantile Paralysis fellow div. infectious disease research Children's Med. Center, Boston, 1953-54, asst. pathologist, 1954-55; faculty dept. pathology Vanderbilt U. Sch. Medicine, Nashville, 1957—, prof., 1970—. Mem. staff VA Hosp., Nashville, 1966—. Served to capt. AUS, 1955-57. Diplomate Am. Bd. Pathology. Mem. Internat. Acad. Pathology, Tenn. Med. Assn., Tenn. Soc. Pathology, Am. Soc. Pathologists and Bacteriologists, Am. Soc. Exptl. Pathology, N.Y. Acad. Scis. Mem. Ch. of Christ. Editorial bd. Archives of Pathology, 1974. Contbr. articles to profl. jours. Home: 2472 Abbott Martin Rd Nashville TN 37215

CHEEK, CHARLES WALL, investment co. exec.; b. Lexington, N.C., Mar. 20, 1921; s. John Merritt and Maud (Wall) C.; B.S., Wake Forest U., 1941; m. Betty Green Johnson, Dec. 28, 1944; children—Mary Charles (Mrs. Charles Torrence Armstrong), Catherine, Alexander. Prodn. mgr. Cheek-Holton Co., Durham, N.C., 1946-50; trust officer Fidelity Bank, Durham, 1952-56; vice-pres. Wachovia Bank, Durham, 1956-60; v.p. First Nat. Bank of S.C., Charleston, 1960-63; vice-chmn. Piedmont Financial Co., Greensboro, N.C., 1963—, also dir.; chmn. bd. Templeton Dobrow and Vance; pres., dir. Richardson Corp.; dir. Piedmont Adv. Corp., Piedmont Mgmt. Co.; dir. Reinsurance Corp. of N.Y., Lexington Growth Fund, Lexington Research Fund. Pres. Charleston Civic Ballet, 1962; pres. Greensboro Civic Ballet, 1965. Pres., bd. dirs. United Arts Council, 1968; mem. exec. bd. Gen. Greene council Boy Scouts Am., 1970; trustee Wake Forest U., Smith Richardson Found., Weatherspoon Art Gallery, Baptist Med. Center. Served to capt. USNR, 1950-52. Mem. Greensboro C. of C. (dir.). Clubs: Greensboro Country, Greensboro City, Carolina Yacht. Home: 804 Sunset Dr Greensboro NC 27408 Office: PO Box W-1 Greensboro NC 27402

CHEEK, GEORGE CURTIN, trade assn. exec.; b. Seattle, Jan. 23, 1931; s. George C. and Evelyn (Kinvig) A.; B.S., Gonzaga U., 1954; postgrad. Harvard, 1957; m. Nancy May Powers, June 13, 1953; children—Allison, David, Jennifer, Sarah. Reporter, editor The Spokesman Rev., Spokane, 1951-59; writer, pub. relations mgr. information services Am. Plywood Assn., Tacoma, 1959-68; account supr. Cole & Weber, Seattle, 1968-69; dir. plans and programs Nat. Forest Products Assn., Washington, 1969-70; exec. v.p. Am. Forest Inst., Washington, 1970—. Pres. Tacoma Municipal League, 1968-69. Chmn. bd. advisers St. Patrick's and Aquinas Acad., Tacoma, 1967-68. Mem. Arctic Inst., Wilderness Soc., Pub. Relations Soc. Am., Am. Soc. Assn. Execs. Home: 2522 Lakevale Dr Vienna VA 22180 Office: 1619 Massachusetts Av NW Washington DC 20036

CHEETHAM, ALAN HERBERT, museum curator; b. El Paso, Tex., Jan. 30, 1928; s. Herbert and Marguerite (Moreton) C.; B.S., N.M. Inst. Mining and Tech., 1950; M.S., La. State U., 1952; Ph.D. (NSF fellow), Columbia, 1959; m. Marjorie Rogers, Apr. 20, 1951; children—Alan Christopher, Jan, Susan, Hilary. Instr. geology La. State U., Baton Rouge, 1954-60, asst. prof., 1960-64, asso. prof., 1964-66; asso. curator invertebrate paleontology Nat. Mus. Natural History, Smithsonian Instn., Washington, 1966-69, curator invertebrate paleontology, 1969—. Vis. prof. paleontology U. Stockholm (Sweden), 1964-65; cons. prof. geology La. State U., Baton Rouge, 1966—. NSF fellow, 1961-62. Mem. A.A.A.S., Paleontol. Soc., Palaeontol. Assn., Internat. Palaeontol. Assn., Paleontol. Soc. Washington, Internat. Bryozoology Assn., Soc. Econ. Paleontologists and Mineralogists, Sigma Xi. Editor: (with Richard S. Boardman, William A. Oliver, Jr.) Animal Colonies: Development and Function Through Time, 1973. Contbr. articles to profl. jours. Home: 6215 Winnebago Rd Washington DC 20016 Office: Smithsonian Instn Washington DC 20560

CHEGIN, LEE JOSEPH, civil engr.; b. Donora, Pa., Mar. 4, 1929; s. George Julius and Irene Helen (Szabo) C.; B.S., Va. Mil. Inst., 1950; M.S., Ohio State U., 1962; m. Betty Lee Lodek, Dec. 18, 1954; children—Catherine, John, Thomas. Commd. 2d lt. U.S. Army, 1950, advanced through grades to lt. col., 1970; combat engr., Korea; constrn. engr., France; mem. faculty U.S. Army Engr. Sch., Ft. Belvoir, Va.; chief constrn. and inspection, Taiwan; bn. comdr., Ft. Devens, Mass.; chief mapping, charting and geodesy, Vietnam; personnel exec. office Chief Engrs., Washington; ret., 1970; supr. plans and specifications City Water Bd., San Antonio, 1971—. Decorated Bronze Star medal with oak leaf cluster. Registered profl. engr., Ala., Tex. Mem. Am. Soc. C.E., Soc. Am. Mil. Engrs., Am. Water Works Assn. Home: 4006 Oakhaven San Antonio TX 78217 Office: 1001 E Market San Antonio TX 78298

CHEITLIN, MELVIN DONALD, physician; b. Wilmington, Del., Mar. 25, 1929; s. James and Mollie (Budman) C.; B.A., Temple U., 1950, M.D., 1954; m. Hella Hochschild, July 4, 1952; children—Roger, Kenneth, Julie. Commd. 1st lt. U.S. Army, 1954, advanced through grades to col., 1970; intern Walter Reed Army Hosp., Washington, 1954-55, resident, 1956-58, chief cardiovascular service, 1971-74; chief cardiovascular service Letterman Gen. Hosp., San Francisco, 1968-71, clin. prof. medicine, 1974—; asst. clin. prof. U. Cal. Med. Center, San Francisco, 1968-71, asso. clin. prof. Georgetown U., Washington, 1971-74; ret., 1974; now with cardiology service San Francisco Gen. Hosp. Fellow Am. Coll. Cardiology, A.C.P., Council Clin. Cardiology Am. Heart Assn.; mem. Am. Fedn. Clin. Research, Assn. Mil. Surgeons U.S., Alpha Omega Alpha. Contbr. articles to med. jours. Home: 224 Castenada Av San Francisco CA 94116 Office: Cardiology Service San Francisco Gen Hosp San Francisco CA 94110

CHELPON, THEODORE HARRY, clergyman; b. Huron, S.D., Mar. 4, 1932; s. Harry Theodore and Antonia (Szourou) C.; B.A., Holy Cross Orthodox Theol. Sch., Brookline, Mass., 1957; S.T.B., Gen. Theol. Sem., N.Y.C., 1961; S.T.M., Va. Episcopal Sem., Alexandria, 1967; postgrad. Catholic U., Washington, 1967-73; m. Theodora Gouvas, Sept. 29, 1957; children—Charalambes, George, Constantine, Antonia. Ordained deacon Greek Orthodox Ch., 1957, priest, 1957; asst. to pastor St. Demetrios Greek Orthodox Ch., Astoria, N.Y., 1957-62; pastor St. Katherine's, Falls Church, Va., 1962—; adj. prof. patristics Va. Episcopal Sem., Alexandria, 1971—. Recipient Legion of Honor award Order DeMolay, 1964. Mem. Order AHEPA. Kiwanian. Home: 3916 Gallows Rd Annandale VA 22003 Office: 3149 Glen Carlyn Rd Falls Church VA 22041

CHEN, PI-FUAY, elec. engr.; b. Taipei, Taiwan, Aug. 17, 1930; s. Tsa-Mo and Che (Wu) C.; student Taipei Inst. Tech., 1953-56; M.S. in Elec. Engring., Va. Poly. Inst., 1962; D.Sc., U. Va., 1969; m. Bertha Lin Chen, Sept. 26, 1964; children—Theodore Carl, Eugene Samuel. Came to U.S., 1960, naturalized, 1971. Asst. engr. Taipei Telecommunication Office, 1956-60; engr. Internat. Tel. & Tel. Corp., Raleigh, 1963-65, sr. engr., 1966; asst. prof. George Washington U., Washington, 1968-69; research engr. Army Engr. Topographic Labs., Alexandria, Va., 1969—. Recipient six awards Dept. Army, including research and devel. achievement award, 1970, outstanding performance award, 1970. Mem. I.E.E.E., Pattern Recognition Soc., Sigma Xi, Eta Kappa Nu. Home: 1805 Cool Spring Dr Alexandria VA 22308 Office: 701 Prince St Alexandria VA 22314

CHENAULT, B(ERTIE) J(EAN), pub. accountant; b. Mart, Tex., Apr. 21, 1927; s. Davis Oscar and Bertie (Mills) C.; B.B.A., Baylor U., 1950; m. Helen Louise Hancock, Mar. 8, 1947; children—Robert Louis, Catherine Ann. Jr. staff accountant Burns B. DuBois, Waco, Tex., 1947-49, Harry Wrench, 1949; semi-sr. staff accountant F. G. Masquelette & Co., Houston, 1949-51, Henslee & Hopson, 1951-52, John E. Doyle, San Antonio, 1952-53; sr. staff accountant Peat, Marwick, Mitchell & Co., Dallas, 1953-54, Payne Harrison & Co., 1954-55, F.W. LaFrentz & Co., 1955-56; internal auditor, controller Bush Enterprises, 1956-57; staff accountant supr. Lybrand, Ross Bros. & Montgomery, 1957-63; v.p., treas. Annuity Bd., So. Bapt. Conv., Dallas, 1963—. Crusader, Am. Cancer Soc. Served with USNR, 1945-46. C.P.A., Tex. Mem. Am. Inst. C.P.A.'s, Tex. Soc. C.P.A.'s, Internat. Platform Assn. Baptist (deacon). Club: Dallas Civitan. Home: 10456 Coleridge St Dallas TX 75218 Office: N Akard Bldg Dallas TX 75201

CHENERY, PETER JASPERSEN, govt. ofcl.; b. Chgo., May 26, 1919; s. William Ludlow and Dai (Smith) C.; B.S., Harvard, 1940; m. Faeth Rider-Hall, Nov. 22, 1941; children—Peter Taylor, Gilbert Rider, Mary Faeth. Research asst. Mass. Inst. Tech., Cambridge, 1940-42; asst. product engr., engr. sect. head Sperry Gyroscope Co., Great Neck, N.Y., 1942-44, 46-54; dir. research and devel. Wright Machinery Co., Div. Sperry-Rand Corp., Durham, N.C., 1954-63; dir. N.C. Bd. of Sci. & Tech., Research Triangle Park, N.C., 1963—; chmn. bd. Faeth Co., Kansas City, Mo., 1967—. Chmn. So. Interstate Nuclear Bd., 1974—; pres. Assn. Scientific Information

Dissemination Centers, 1972-74. Served with USNR, 1944-46. Mem. I.E.E.E., A.A.A.S., Am. Soc. Information Scis. Clubs: Harvard (pres. 1960-61, 65-66, 67-69) (Eastern N.C.). Home: 50 Beverly Dr Durham NC 27707 Office: Box 12235 Research Triangle Park NC 27709

CHENEY, REYNOLDS SMITH, lawyer; b. Jackson, Miss., Oct. 17, 1910; s. William Newton and Emma Laura (Wilson) C.; A.B., Millsaps Coll., Jackson, Miss., 1931; LL.B., Jackson Sch. of Law, 1932; m. Winifred Tunstall Green, Oct. 25, 1934; children—Reynolds Smith, William Garner, Winifred Calhoon. Admitted to Miss. bar, 1931, since practiced Jackson, mem. firm Green, Cheney, Jones & Hughes. Dir., Miss. Cottonseed Products Co., Mchts. Co., Engle Acoustic and Tile, Inc. Organizer, trustee St. Andrews Episcopal Sch., 1947-56, 60-70. Fellow Am. Coll. of Probate Counsel; mem. Am. Newcomen Soc., Jackson Symphony Orch. Assn., Family Service Assn. (dir., pres. 1958), Am., Miss., Hinds County bar assns., Estate Planning Council Miss., Am. Judicature Soc., Omicron Delta Kappa, Kappa Alpha (knight comdr., nat. pres. Episcopalian (dep. to gen. conv. 1958, 61, 64, 67, 69, 70, 73, vice chancellor 1947-66, chancellor 1966—, standing com. Diocese Miss. 1948-66). Club: Capitol City Petroleum (Jackson). Home: 1407 Riverside Dr Jackson MS 39202 Office: Electric Bldg Jackson MS 39201

CHENEY, STEPHEN EDWARD, land devel. co. exec.; b. Waterloo, Ia., Apr. 30, 1941; s. Frank Edward and Ethelee (Rochelle) C.; B.S., U. Ark., 1967; m. Judy Lynn Cash, Dec. 21, 1963; children—Kelly Joelle, Kyle Andrew. Dir. computer services Powers-Willis & Assos., Iowa City, 1970; asso. Bell-Burrough-Uerling Cons. Engrs., Ft. Smith, Ark., 1971-72; v.p. engring. Genesis Concern, Inc., Round Mountain, Ark., 1973—. Trustee Round Mountain Improvement Dist., 1973. Registered profl. engr., Ark., Ia., Tenn. Mem. Nat., Ark. socs. profl. engrs., Am. Soc. C.E. Baptist. Club: Fort Smith Engineers. Asst. editor Ark. Engr., 1972-73. Home: 178 Charjean Dr Jackson TN 38301 Office: 1805 Hwy 45 By-Pass Jackson TN 38301

CHENEY, WILLIAM ROBERT, utilities engr.; b. Boulder, Colo., July 23, 1921; s. Johnathan Plowman and Sadie (Jamison) C.; student U. Colo., 1940, 46-48, U. Cal., 1952, U. Denver, 1963, No. Va. Jr. Coll., 1971; m. Corinne K. Maness, Oct. 26, 1962; children—Linda K. (Mrs. Gary Grehber), Margaret E. (Mrs. Eric Singer). Asst. mgr. Fox Boulder Theatres, 1948-50; quality control engr. Poultry Producers Central Cal., 1951-55; engr. Coberly & Leffel, Denver, 1955-59; parks planner Colo. Game, Fish and Parks Dept., 1959-68; utilities engr. Arlington County (Va.) Dept. Transp., 1969—; free-lance artist, 1965—. Served with AUS, 1940-45, 49-51. Registered profl. engr., Colo. Mem. Nat. Soc. Profl. Engrs., Assn. Conservation Engrs., Nat. Conf. State Parks. Illustrator: Justice in Jeopardy, 1973. Home: 4627 31st Rd S Arlington VA 22206 Office: 1400 Courthouse Rd Arlington VA 22201

CHENG, TSUNG O., educator; b. Shanghai, China, Mar. 30, 1925; s. Keith S. and Fanny (Wang) C.; B.S., St. John's U. (China), 1945; M.D., U. Pa., 1950, M.S., 1956; m. Marie Ellen Roe, June 18, 1955; children—Mark Dudley, Yvonne Joyce. Came to U.S., 1950, naturalized, 1960. Intern, St. Barnabas Hosp., Newark, 1950-51; resident Cook County Hosp., Chgo., 1952-55; fellow in cardiovascular disease George Washington U. Sch. Medicine, Dist. of Columbia Gen. Hosp., Washington, 1955-56; instr. cardiology Mass. Gen. Hosp., Boston, 1956-57; fellow cardiorespiratory physiology Johns Hopkins U. Sch. Medicine and Hosp., Balt., 1957-59; acad. medicine, specializing in cardiology, Washington, 1970—; asst. prof. medicine U. State N.Y., 1959-70; asso. prof. medicine George Washington U. Sch. Medicine, 1970-72, prof. medicine, 1972—; chief cardiology D.C. Gen. Hosp., Washington, 1971-72; asso. dir. div. cardiology, dir. cardiac catheterization lab. George Washington U. Med. Center, Washington, 1972—; asst. physician Cardiac Clinic, Johns Hopkins Hosp., Balt., 1957-59, mem. staff cardiac catheterization lab., 1957-59; dir. cardiopulmonary lab. Bklyn. Hosp., 1959-66, co-chief Pediatric Cardiac Clinic, 1959-66, chief Adolescent Cardiac Clinic, 1961-66, attending physician Adult Cardiac Clinic, 1959-66; chief pediatric cardiac clinic Cumberland Hosp., Bklyn., 1963-66; asst. chief cardiology VA Hosp., Bklyn., 1966-69, chief Cardiovascular Lab., 1966-70; asst. vis. physician Kings County Hosp. Med. Center, Bklyn., 1964-70; attending physician Univ. Hosp., State U. N.Y., 1967-70; chief cardiology VA Hosp., Bklyn., 1969-70; co-chief cardiology George Washington U. Med. div. D.C. Gen. Hosp., 1970-71. Diplomate Nat. Bd. Med. Examiners. Fellow A.C.P., Am. Coll. Chest Physicians, Am. Coll. Cardiology, Am. Heart Assn. Council Clin. Cardiology, Internat. Coll. Angiology; mem. Am. Fedn. Clin. Research, Am. Heart Assn., Washington Heart Assn., A.A.A.S., D.C. Med. Soc., A.M.A. Contbr. numerous articles to sci., med. jours. Home: 7508 Cayuga Av Bethesda MD 20034 Office: George Washington Univ Med Center 2150 Pennsylvania Av NW Washington DC 20037

CHENNAULT, ANNA CHAN (MRS. CLAIRE LEE CHENNAULT), journalist, author, lectr.; b. Peiping, China, June 23, 1925; d. Sam Y.W. and Bessie (Jeong) Chan; B.A. in Journalism, Ling Nan U., Hong Kong, 1944; Litt. D., Chungang U., Seoul, Korea, 1967; LL.D., Lincoln U., 1970; H.H.D., Manahath Ednl. Center, 1970; m. Claire Lee Chennault, Dec. 21, 1947 (dec.); children—Claire Anna, Cynthia Louise. Came to U.S. 1948, naturalized, 1950. War corr. Central News Agy., 1944-48; feature writer Hsing Ming Daily News, Shanghai, China, 1946-49; pub. relations officer Civil Air Transport, Taipei, 1947-57, editor Civil Air Transport Bull., Taiwan, 1946-57; U.S. corr. Hsin Sheng Daily News, Washington, 1958—. Lectr., 1950—; fashion designer, 1952—; Chinese sect. chief machine translation research Georgetown U., Washington, 1958-63; with Voice of Am., Washington, 1963-66; spl. corr. to Washington Central News Agy., 1965—; v.p. internat. affairs The Flying Tiger Line, Inc.; dir. D.C. Nat. Bank. Pres. Gen. Claire L. Chennault Found., Chinese Refugee Relief; Mem. U.S. nat. commn. UNESCO; membership adviser Nation's Capital chpt. Air Force Assn.; adviser Radio Free Asia, Nat. League Families Am. Prisoners and Missing in S.E. Asia. Mem. finance com. D.C. Republican Com.; chmn. nat. women's finance com. Republican Campaign, 1967-68; chmn. nat. adv. com. Women for Nixon, 1967-68; del. platform com. Rep. Nat. Conv., 1972; co-chmn. Finance Com. to Re-Elect the Pres., 1972; co-chmn. Republican Heritage Groups Council, 1972; mem. spl. com. Transpo '72, also chmn. sec.'s com. for spl. activities; chmn. U.S. Citizens in Asia for Nixon, 1972; spl. asst. to chmn. Asian-Pacific Council of Amchams. Mem. Pres.'s adv. com. on arts John F. Kennedy Center for Performing Arts; mem. Women's Adv. Com. on Aviation Dept. of Transp.; trustee Center for Study of Presidency; mem. exec. com. Am. Acad. Achievement, Dallas; bd. visitors Civil Air Patrol. Decorated Order of Lafayette; recipient Freedom award Free China Relief Assn., 1966; Golden Plate award Am. Acad. of Achievement, 1967. Mem. Free China Writers Assn., Nat. League Am. Pen Women, Flying Tigers Assn., 14th Air Force Assn. (chmn. awards). Republican. Clubs: U.S. Air Force Wives, Capitol Hill, Internat., F Street, Am. Newcapper Women's (Washington). Author 15 books in Chinese, 1948—; Thousand Springs, 1962; Dictionary of New Simplified Chinese Characters, Telegraphic Code Chinese-English Dictionary, 1963; Chennault and the Flying Tigers, 1963. Translator: Way of a Fighter, 1955. Home: 2510 Virginia Av NW Washington DC 20037 Office: Investment Bldg Washington DC 20005

CHERRY, CHARLES LOUIS, stockbroker; b. Jacksonville, Fla., Mar. 8, 1936; s. Sam and Gussie (Rabinowich) C.; B.S. in Bus., U. Fla., 1959; postgrad. Sch. of Banking of South, 1963-65, Am. Inst. Banking, 1966; m. Carole Safer, Dec. 29, 1957; children—Brian Howard, Amy Frances. Asst. cashier First Nat. Bank of Orlando (Fla.), 1960-63, trust investment officer, 1963-67; registered rep., stockbroker Smith, Barney & Co., Tampa, Fla., 1967—. Mem. sales council Jewish Community Center, Tampa, 1967—. Served with USNR, 1955-57. Recipient Wall St. Jour., Mrs. Charles Ulrick Bay awards in finance, 1959. Mem. Inst. Chartered Financial Analysts, Am., So. finance assns., U. Fla. Alumni Assn., Central Fla. Analysts Soc. (bd. dirs. 1973-74), Financial Analyst Soc. Jacksonville, Financial Analyst Soc. Miami. Jewish religion. Lion (pres. Orlando 1967). Clubs: University (Tampa); River (Jacksonville). Home: 4402 Brookwood Dr Tampa FL 33609 Office: Smith Barney & Co 610 Florida Av Tampa FL 33602

CHERRY, DAVID EARL, lawyer; b. Fort Worth, Sept. 10, 1944; s. Leonard Earl and Dorothy (Brown) C.; B.B.A., Tex. Christian U., 1967, J.D., Baylor U., 1968; m. Katherine Ann Yarbrough, Dec. 23, 1967; 1 dau., Lisa Michelle. Admitted to Tex. bar, 1968; asso. firm Pakis & Cherry and predecessor firms, Waco, 1969-71, partner, 1971—. Mem. Planning, Zoning Commn. Woodway, Tex., 1972—, mem. City Charter Commn., 1973—. Voter's rights chmn. Com. to Re-elect Pres., Tex. Region V, 1972. Bd. dirs. Waco Lighthouse for Blind, Waco-McLennan County Legal Aid Soc. Served with Tex. Army Nat. Guard, 1968. Mem. Waco-McLennan County Jr. (pres.-elect), Am., Waco-McLennan County bar assns., State, State Jr. bars Tex., Am. Judicature Soc., Delta Sigma Pi. Methodist. Republican. Lion. Office: 504 1st Nat Bldg Waco TX 76701

CHERRY, JIM DAVID, cons., ret. supt. schs.; b. Edison, Ga., Jan. 1, 1911; s. Drew Fred and Nannie Iver (McKinnon) C.; B.S., Ga. So. Coll., 1936; M.A., U. N.C., 1939; postgrad. U. Ga., 1947-49, Emory U., 1949; Ph.D. (hon.), Oglethorpe U., 1972; m. Virginia Brown, June 4, 1939; children—Lynn (Mrs. George Rose), Jim David, Vicki (Mrs. Robert Fowler), Sally (Mrs. Jack Ferguson). Tchr., sci. coach Douglas (Ga.) High Sch., 1937-39; dir. guidance Waycross (Ga.) High Sch., 1939-42; dir. guidance and curriculum Albany (Ga.) High Sch., 1942-43; state sch. supr. Ga. Dept. Edn., 1946-47; supt. schs., DeKalb County (Ga.), 1949-73, ret.; organizer Counseling Services, Inc., Atlanta, 1973—. Mem. DeKalb Bd. Health, 1949—. Bd. dirs. Fulton-Rockdale-DeKalb chpt. Nat. Found., 1949-73, sec., 1954; bd. dirs. Ga. unit Am. Cancer Soc., past pres. DeKalb unit; bd. dirs. YMCA, Ga. So. Found. Served with USNR, 1943-46; PTO. Recipient award for patriotic service U.S. Treasury, 1957, Award of Merit, and Minute Man award, 1966, Freedom Found. award, 1958. Mem. N.E.A., Am. Assn. Sch. Adminstrs., Am. Legion, Ga. Ednl. Assn. (pres. 1951), Ga. Assn. Educators, DeKalb C. of C., Baptist. Elk, Rotarian. Home: 1052 N Jamestown Rd Decatur GA 30033 Office: 1784 Piedmont Av Atlanta GA 30307

CHERRY, LLOYD BENJAMIN, univ. dean; b. Weatherford, Tex., Mar. 1, 1915; s. Benjamin Franklin and Posie Ann (Heifrin) C.; B.A., U. Tex., 1936, M.A., 1937; B.S., Okla. State U., 1951, E.E., 1951; m. Kathryn Ruth Parrott, Nov. 24, 1938; children—Margaret Ann (Mrs. Osborne P. Wiggins, Jr.), Franklin Robinson. Head dept. math. Edinburg Coll., 1941-42; research engr. Brown Instrument Co., 1942-45; asso. prof. physics Hardin-Simmons U., 1945-46; head physics dept. Lamar U., Beaumont, Tex., 1946-51, head elec. engring., 1951-67, dir. research, 1961-67, dean Coll. Engring., 1967—. Chmn., Jefferson County Welfare Bd., 1963. Recipient award for teaching excellence Piper Found., 1967; named Engr. of Year, Tex. Soc. Profl. Engrs., 1972. Fellow I.E.E.E. (regional dir. 1972-73); mem. Am. Soc. Engring. Edn. (award Western Electric 1964, pres. Houston chpt. 1972-73), Eta Kappa Nu (nat. pres. 1971-72). Methodist (mem. higher edn. com. 1969—). Rotarian. Patentee in field. Home: 1418 Central Dr Beaumont TX 77706

CHESELDINE, ANNE MILLIGAN (MRS. RICHARD J. CHESELDINE), realtor; b. Cin., Aug. 16, 1914; d. William John and Anna (Brand) Milligan; grad. high sch., Cin.; m. Richard J. Cheseldine, Oct. 16, 1937; 1 son, Richard J. Saleswoman, broker Lind Davis Real Estate Co., Montgomery, Ala., 1962-64, owner, 1964—, sec.-treas., 1972—, also mng. broker. Recipient Million Dollar award, 1967. Mem. Montgomery Real Estate Bd. (dir. 1968-71), Ala., Nat. assns. real estate bds. Roman Catholic. Club: Woodley Country. Home: 2859 McGehee Rd Montgomery AL 36111 Office: Lind Davis Real Estate Co Inc 404 E South Blvd PO Box 2627 Montgomery AL 36105

CHESNUT, DONALD BLAIR, educator; b. Richmond, Ind., Dec. 27, 1932; s. James Lyons and Naomi Irene (Wright) C.; B.S., Duke, 1954; Ph.D., Cal. Inst. Tech., 1958; m. Deborah Berry, Dec. 21, 1954; children—Lauren, Blair, Lynn. Postdoctoral fellow, instr. physics, Duke U., Durham, N.C., 1957-58, asso. prof. chemistry, 1965-71, prof. chemistry, 1971—; research chemist E.I. duPont de Nemours, Inc., Wilmington, Del., 1958-65. Mem. Am. Chem. Soc., Am. Phys. Soc., Sigma Xi. Home: 4404 Malvern Rd Durham NC 27707 Office: Dept Chemistry Duke U Durham NC 27706

CHESNUT, LAWRENCE JAMES, clergyman, educator, author, broadcaster; b. Westplains, Mo., Dec. 6, 1908; s. Jim Jackson and Ida Louisa (Luna) C.; student Sherwin Cody Sch. English, Wyo., 1931-33, Central State Tchrs. Coll., Edmond, Okla., 1935-36; B.Th., Berean Bible Coll., Elk City, 1946; D.D., Universal Bible Inst., 1973; m. Jessie Mae Hill, Dec. 10, 1927; children—Daniel Lawrence, Samuel Joseph. With Ohio Oil Co. of Okla., 1927-36; ordained to ministry Ch. of God, 1931; pastor Capitol Hill Ch. of God, Oklahoma City, 1938—. Radio broadcaster, 1945—; TV broadcaster, 1955—; extension tchr. Anderson (Ind.) Coll. and Theol. Sem., 1938—; speaker to ministerial convs., camp meetings, youth convs.; leader religious dept. Nat. Radio Conv. Am., Norman, Okla., 1954; various nat., state positions in Ch. of God, including nat. Day-man rep., mem. nat. steering com., pres. 15 years, sec.-treas. 6 years of Bd. Ch. Extension of Ch. of God of Okla., pres. Campgrounds Assn., 12 years, pres. State Youth conv., 12 years, now ofcl. mem. Campgrounds Assn., mem. state program com. Ch. of God Okla. Past mem. Oklahoma City Police Reform Com.; spl. asst. to dist. judge working with problem children. Bd. dirs. Central Okla. Camp Meeting Assn. Decorated for outstanding ability in radio broadcasting. Author: True Bible Tongues, Their Proper Place and Use in the Church, 1948; The Battle of Armageddon-What, Where and When, 1949; Divine Physical Healing for You, 1949; Twentieth Chapter of Revelation Explained, 1954; The Sabbath, Mosaic and Christian, 1959; Will There Be a Millennium?, 1973; The Kingdom of God, Time, Nature, and Place, 1973. Contbr. numerous articles to profl. jours. Home: 3121 S Harvey Av Oklahoma City OK 73109 Office: 3120 S Harvey Av Oklahoma City OK 73109

CHESNUT, RALPH CARL, ret. petroleum refining co. owner; b. West Planes, Mo., Dec. 28, 1909; s. James Jackson and Ida (Luna) C.; grad. pub. schs.; m. Ruby May Taylor, Oct. 11, 1930. Gang pusher Marathon Oil Co., Bristow, Okla., 1929-32, Deep Rock Oil Co., Bristow, 1932-36; prodn. foreman Barnsdall Oil Co., Odessa, Tex., 1936-39; prodn. mgr. Brodrick & Calvert, Odessa, 1939; prodn. foreman Phillips Petroleum Co., Odessa, 1940-55; owner Chesnut Well Service, Odessa, 1955-73; pres. Posture Magic Cushion Co., Rosenberg, Tex., 1967—. Foreman, Ector County Petty Jury, 1958-62; mem. Ector County Sheriff's Posse, 1961—; life mem. Odessa Meteorite Mus.; mem. Permian Playhouse, Odessa, Tex., 1967—. Bd. dirs. Otto's Boys Club of Odessa, 1957-63. Mem. Am. Petroleum Inst. Moose. Clubs: Odessa Basin Lions, Odessa Country. Home: 3008 N Century Av Odessa TX 79760 Office: PO Box 1491 Odessa TX 79760

CHESNUTT, NELSON PHELPS, natural gas utility exec.; b. Henrietta, Tex., May 15, 1911; s. Robert Cleveland and Cora (Gragg) C.; B.S. in Mech. Engring., U. Okla., 1935; grad. Advanced Mgmt. Program, Harvard, 1964; m. Mary Gertrude Schreck, Nov. 26, 1936; children—Robert P., Mary Patricia (Mrs. Richard A. Strother). With So. Union Gas Co., Dallas, 1935—, chief engr., 1948-60, v.p., operating mgr., 1960-72, pres., 1972—. Served from 1st lt. to lt. col., AUS, 1941-46. Decorated Bronze Star. Registered profl. engr., Colo., N.M., Ariz., Tex. Mem. Am. (service award), So. (service award) gas assns., Dallas Club, Dallas Petroleum Club. Mason (32 1/2 deg.). Home: 6653 Gaston Av Dallas TX 75214 Office: Fidelity Union Tower Dallas TX 75201

CHESS, RICHARD BENJAMIN, JR., lawyer; b. Canonsburg, Pa., Mar. 3, 1935; s. Richard B. and Teresa (Marchio) C.; B.A. in Govt., Tufts U., 1957; LL.B., George Washington U., 1962; m. Cynthia A. Hooper, June 10, 1957; children—Dana R., Susan H., Taylor O. Admitted to Va. bar, 1962; atty. civil rights div. Dept. Justice, Washington, 1962-64; partner Kelly, Louk, Lawson & Chess, 1964-72, Chess & Roeder, Fairfax, Va., 1972—; substitute judge Fairfax City Dist. Ct., 1972—. Served to 1st lt. USMCR, 1957-59. Mem. Sigma Alpha Epsilon. Democrat. Roman Catholic. Club: Country (Fairfax). Home: 5111 Brookridge Pl Fairfax VA 22030 Office: 4085 Chain Bridge Rd Fairfax VA 22030

CHESSER, VICTOR LEON, dentist; b. Bessemer, Ala., Jan. 21, 1931; s. Ophus Charles and Mabel (Griffith) C.; student Livingston State Coll., 1949-51; A.B., Birmingham So. Coll., 1954; D.M.D., U. Ala., 1958; student N.Y.U., 1962; m. Jacqueline Ruth Cogbill, May 11, 1956; children—Karl Eric, Mark Victor. Lab. asst. Birmingham So. Coll., 1952-53; first aid man, ambulance driver Lloyd Noland Hosp., Fairfield, Ala., 1952-54, part-time, 1954-58; dentist USPHS, N.Y. State Dept. Health, 1962-63; profl. edn. radiol. health dental X-ray program Central Radiation Health Lab., Rockville, Md., 1963-69; ret., 1969. Served with USNR, 1958-62. Fellow Royal Soc.; mem. Phi Eta Sigma. Presbyn. Prin. author: Physical Survey Manual, 1964, rev. edn., 1967. Home: 5036 Pleasant Hill Rd SE Bessemer AL 35020

CHEVES, HARRY LANGDON, JR., physician; b. Birmingham, Ala., Oct. 17, 1924; s. Harry Langdon and Myrtle (Churchill) C.; A.B., Mercer U., 1949; M.D., Med. Coll. Ga., 1953; m. Lois Rebecca Corry, Dec. 25, 1949; children—Rebecca Churchill, Harry Langdon III; m. 2d, Mary Agnes Moon. Intern Univ. Hosp., Augusta, Ga., 1953-54; practice medicine, East Point, Ga.; mem. staff S. Fulton Hosp. Served with USAAF, 1942-46. Fellow Internat., Am. colls. angiology; mem. A.M.A., So. Med. Assn., Am. Acad. Gen. Practice, Atlanta Med. Soc., Am. Geriatric Soc., Med. Assn. Ga., Ga. Heart Assn., Phi Delta Theta. Clubs: Am. Antique Automobile, Classic Car Club Am., Packard Automobile Classics. Home: 333 Plantation Circle Riverdale GA 30274 Office: 2726 Felton Dr East Point GA 30344

CHIANG, CHI YU, educator; b. Chungking, China, Dec. 12, 1942; s. Chien Lo and Lien (Mao) C.; B.S., Tunghai U., 1964; M.S., U. Fla., 1967, Ph.D., 1970; m. Wei Tan, July 12, 1965; 1 son, Henry. Came to U.S., 1965, naturalized, 1971. Mem. faculty Hazard Community Coll. of U. Ky., Hazard, 1969—, chmn. phys. sci. div., 1971—, asst. prof. chemistry 1969—. NSF summer faculty research fellow, 1970-71; Summer Faculty Improvement grantee, 1973. Mem. Alpha Chi Sigma. Home: PO Box 992 Hazard KY 41701

CHICHESTER, JOHN D., real estate cons.; b. Birmingham, Ala.; s. John D. and Minnie Mae (Jolly) C.; student Gulf Coast Mil. Acad., 1913-14, U. Ala. Law Sch., 1915-16; m. Mattie Eugenia Ormond, Nov. 20, 1916; 1 son. Real estate cons., appraiser, Birmingham, 1925—; lectr. real estate. Mem. Ala. Ho. of Reps. 2 terms; real estate commr. State Ala. Mem. Ala. Real Estate Assn. (past pres.), Birmingham Real Estate Bd. (past pres.), Am. Inst. Real Estate Appraisers (pres. Ala. chpt., dir.), Nat. Assn. Real Estate Bds. (past v.p.), Omicron Delta Kappa, Phi Kappa Sigma. Club: Relay House. Home: 2057 S 20th Av Birmingham AL 35205 Office: Jefferson Fed Bldg Birmingham AL 35203

CHICK, JOHN BRADLEY, real estate appraiser, broker; b. Titusville, Pa., Feb. 8, 1900; s. Maxwell Benedict and Rose (Bradley) C.; A.B., Princeton, 1922; m. Alice Irene Sutton, Apr. 17, 1928 (dec. Oct. 1965); children—John Bradley, William Maxwell, Cynthia Ann (Mrs. Nolan Bruce Pitsinger); m. 2d, Helen Hine Benson, Mar. 4, 1967 (dec. Oct. 1972). Real estate sales Clark T. Chambers, Inc., N.Y.C., 1922-23; pres. Maxwell B. Chick Co., Titusville, Pa., 1923-38, owner, 1938-41; self-employed, 1941-43, 46-51; served as lt. col. U.S. Air Force, 1951-60, chief installations div., Paris (France) office 1958-60; real estate appraisals and sales, Ft. Lauderdale, Fla., 1960-63, 66—; exec. dir. Redevel. Authority, Titusville, Pa., 1963-65. Served from lt. to comdr. USNR, 1943-46. Mem. Am. Inst. Real Estate Appraisers, Navy League, Air Force Assn., Ret. Officers Assn. Presbyn. Mason, Rotarian. Club: Princeton (N.Y. and Ft. Lauderdale, Fla.); Nassau (Princeton, N.J.) Home: 2840 N Ocean Blvd Fort Lauderdale FL 33308 Office: care Wm H West & Co 2425 E Commercial Blvd Fort Lauderdale FL 33308

CHIERI, PERICLE ADRIANO C., ret. educator, mech. and aero. engr., naval architect; b. Mokanshan, Chekiang, China, Sept. 6, 1905; s. Virginio and Luisa (Fabbri) C.; Dr. Engring., U. Genoa, Italy, 1927; M.E., U. Naples, Italy, 1927; Dr. Aero. Engring., U. Rome, 1928; m. Helen Etheredge, Aug. 1, 1938. Came to U.S., 1938, naturalized, 1952. Naval architect. mech. engr. research and exptl. divs., submarines and internal combustion engines, Italian Navy, Spezia, 1929-31; naval architect, marine supt. Navigazione Libera Triestina Shipping Corp., Libera Lines, Trieste, Italy, 1931-32, Genoa, 1933-35; aero. engr., tech. adviser Chinese Govt. commn. aero. affairs, Nat. Govt. Republic of China, Nanchang and Loyang, 1935-37; engring. exec., dir. aircraft materials test lab., supt. factory's tech. vocational instrn., SINAW Nat. Aircraft Works, Nanchang, Kiangsl, China, 1937-39; aero. engr. FIAT aircraft factory, Turin, Italy, 1939; aero. engr. and tech. sec. Office: Air Attache, Italian Embassy, Washington, 1939-41; prof. aero. engring. Tri-State Coll., Angola, Ind., 1942; aero. engr., helicopter design Aero. Products, Inc., Detroit, 1943-44; sr. aero. engr. ERCO Engring. & Research Corp., Riverdale, Md., 1944-46; asso. prof. mech. engring. U. Toledo, 1946-47; asso. prof. mech. engring., faculty grad. div. Newark (N.J.) Coll. Engring., 1947-52; prof., head dept. mech. engring. U. Southwestern La., Lafayette, La., 1952-72; cons. engr., Lafayette, 1973—; research engr., adv. devel. sect., aviation gas turbine div., Westinghouse Electric Corp., South Philadelphia, Pa., 1953. Instr. Water Safety A.R.C. Nat. Aquatic Schs., summers 1958-67. Bd. dirs. Lafayette Parish chpt. A.R.C. Registered profl. engr., Italy, N.J., La., S.C.; chartered engr., U.K. Fellow Royal Instn. Naval Architects London (life); asso. fellow Am. Inst. Aeronautics and Astronautics; mem. Soc. Naval Architects and Marine Engrs., A.A.A.S., Am. Assn. U. Profs.

(emeritus), Am. Soc. Engring. Edn. (life), Am. Soc. M.E., Soc. Automotive Engrs., Instrument Soc. Am., Soc. Exptl. Stress Analysis, Nat. Soc. Profl. Engrs., N.Y. Acad. Scis., La. Engring. Soc., La. Tchrs. Assn., A.A.H.P.E.R., La. Acad. Scis., Commodore Longfellow Soc., Phi Kappa Phi. Pi Tau Sigma (hon.). Home: 142 Oak Crest Dr Lafayette LA 70501 Office: PO Box 52923 Lafayette LA 70501

CHIESA, CARMEN (DE PEREZ), author; b. Yabuoca, P.R., June 1, 1914; d. Pedro Chiesa and Damiana (Nieves) C.; B.S., Pa. State Coll., 1939; M.A., Columbia U., 1946, postgrad., 1946-47; postgrad., U. P.R., 1950-60; m. Juan Perez Cruz, June 25, 1939; children—Dra. Ivette, Marta, Janet. Tchr. pub. schs., P.R., 1936-56; instr. U. P.R., 1958-59; faculty Ursuline Coll., New Orleans, 1947-48; prin. schs. P.R., 1940-43; 1948-49; vocational guidance counsellor Central High Sch., Santruce, P.R., 1948-49. Mem. Damas Auxiliares de Rio Piedras, Agrupacion de Maestros Retiradosde de R.P., Asociacion de Maestros, Pa. State Alumni Assn., Soc. de. Autores Puertorriquenos, Union de Mujeres Americanas, Graduadas de la U. P.R. Author: Enjoy Puerto Rico, 1961: (short story) Principe, 1963; (essay) Proyecciones del Modernismo, 1964: (novel) La Telarana, 1971. Address: Flamboyanes 208 Hyde Park Rio Piedras PR 00927

CHILD, LEILA AVERELL (TONI), editor; b. Milw., Mar. 24, 1926; d. Frank Moore and Leonora Averell (Cowdrey) Child; student U. Ga., 1943-44; A.B., U. S.C., 1947. Editor, U.S. Army Intelligence, Manila, Philippines, 1947-48; editor lit. and cultural events, news reporter Columbia (S.C.) Record, 1949-55; pub. information dir., dir. personnel City of Columbia, 1955-61, dir. pub. information, 1961-65; editor, designer, pub. all books, booklets, tchrs. guides and publs. S.C. Dept. Edn., Columbia, 1965—. Mem. pub. relations com. United Fund, 1971-72; chmn. pub. relations Tb Assn., 1955; mem. League Women Voters, 1950-55; chmn. publicity Town Theatre, 1950-57; v.p. Drama Club, 1971, pres., 1972; v.p. Players Club, 1968. Bd. dirs. U.S.O., 1953-55, Family Services bd., 1972-74. Recipient awards for excellence of publs. design, Nat. Sch. Pub. Relations Assn., Sch. Mgmt. Mag., 1968-72. Mem. Alpha Delta Pi, Alpha Kappa Gamma (life). Roman Catholic. Home: 3000 Wilmot Av Columbia SC 29205 Office: 1429 Senate St Columbia SC 29201

CHILD, ROBERT DANVERS, rancher; b. El Dorado, Ark., Sept. 21, 1927; s. Thomas Harold and Sarah (Wallace) C.; B.S., U. Ark., 1950, M.S., 1966; m. Wanda Gay Daniel, May 3, 1951; children—Lisa Gay, Robert Danvers, Jr. Research and teaching asst. U. Ark., 1962-65; div. mgr. Carlisle div. Winrock Farms, Carlisle, Ark., 1965-67, operations mgr., Morrilton, Ark., 1967-69, gen. mgr., 1969—; dir. Riceland Foods, Inc. Served with USNR, 1944-46. Mem. Nat. Livestock and Meat Bd. (dir.), Am. Nat. Cattlemen's Assn. (regional v.p.), Santa Gertrudis Breeders Internat. (mem. exec. com.), Ark. Cattlemen's Assn. (past pres.), Alpha Zeta, Gama Sigma Delta. Contbr. articles to farm jours. Address: Route 3 Morrilton AR 72110

CHILDERS, FRANK MCDOWELL, aerospace engr.; b. Canton, N.C., Dec. 10, 1921; s. Joseph E. and Connie E. (Penland) C.; B.S., Ind. Inst. Tech., 1949; m. Hilda Pauline Conley, Aug. 16, 1945; children—Erika Gwynette, Jeffery Conley. Electronic engr. Dept. of Commerce, CAA, Atlanta, 1949-52, Dept. of Army, Huntsville, Ala., 1952-60; aerospace technologist, instrumentation systems NASA, John F. Kennedy Space Center, Fla., 1960-69, aerospace engr., 1969—. Pres. Asbury Arms, Inc., Cocoa, Fla., 1970—. Scoutmaster, Boy Scouts Am., Cocoa, Fla., 1956-64; mem. exec. bd. Central Fla. Council, 1968—. Served with USAAF, 1941-45. Recipient Silver Beaver award Boy Scouts Am., 1963. Mem. Am. Soc. Quality Control. Republican. Methodist. Home: 33 Little John Lane Rockledge FL 32955 Office: John F Kennedy Space Center FL 32899

CHILDERS, WYON DALE, state legislator; b. Fla., Nov. 25, 1933; s. Neil R. and Myrtle R. (Smith) C.; B.S., Fla. State U., 1955; m. Ruth A. Johnson, Dec. 21, 1953; children—Gail, Jeanna, Karen, Marvel. Tchr., Santa Rosa County Schs., 1956; pres., gen. mgr. A & E Stores, Pensacola, Fla., 1957; mem. Fla. Senate. Mem. Fla. Council on Crime and Delinquency. Mem. Farm Bur., Am. Pharm. Assn. Baptist. Lion. Home: 5901 Memphis Av Pensacola FL 32506 Office: Box 3327 Pensacola FL 32506*

CHILDS, H(ENRY) PRENTISS, broadcasting co. exec.; b. Iowa City, June 9, 1927; s. Marquis W. and Lue (Prentiss) C.; student Mass. Inst. Tech., 1944-45; B.A., Yale, 1949; postgrad. Columbia, 1962-63; m. Nancy Jane Craze, Jan. 24, 1960; children—Catherine Clenn, Christina Prentiss, Marquis Bradley. Asst. producer CBS News, 1956-60, producer, 1960—; produced Lamp Unto My Feet, 1960-62, Face The Nation, 1963—. Served with USNR, 1945-46. Home: 5045 Reno Rd NW Washington DC 20008 Office: 2020 M St NW Washington DC 20036

CHILDS, JAMES BENNETT, librarian; b. Van Buren, Mo., June 2, 1896; s. Trall Bennett and Mary (Michener) C.; A.B., U. Ill., 1918, B.L.S., 1921; m. Eleanor Atala Pirkner, Nov. 20, 1927; children—James Bennett Jr., Herbert A., Robert F., Daniel B., Rudolph W., Philip D., Richard P. Cataloger John Crerar Library, Chgo., 1921-25; chief Documents div. Library of Congress, Washington, 1925-29, 34-43, chief catalog div., 1929-34, chief documents officer, 1943-54, specialist govt. document bibliography, 1954-67, hon. cons. govt. document bibliography, 1967—. Mem. A.L.A., Library Assn. U.K., Bibl. Soc. Am., Am. Polit. Sci. Assn., Am. Econ. Assn., Phi Beta Kappa. Clubs: Cliff Dwellers, Cosmos. Author: Entry for Government Publications, 1941; German Democratic Republic Official Publications, 1960-61; German Federal Republic Official Publications, 1958; Government Document Bibliography in the U.S. and Elsewhere; Guide to the Official Publications of Other American Republics, 1945-48; Memorias of the Republics of Central America and of the Antilles, 1932; Spanish Government Publications after July 17, 1936, 1965-69. Home: 1221 Newton St NE Washington DC 20017 Office: Library of Congress Washington DC 20540

CHILDS, MARQUIS WILLIAM, journalist; b. Clinton, Ia., Mar. 17, 1903; s. William Henry and Lilian Malissa (Marquis) C.; A.B., U. Wis., 1923; A.M., U. Ia., 1925; LL.D., Upsala Coll., 1943; Litt. D., U. Wis., 1966, U. Ia., 1968; m. Lue Prentiss, Aug. 26, 1926 (dec.); children—Prentiss, Malissa (Mrs. Elliott); m. 2d, Jane Neylan McBaine. With United Press, 1923, 25-26, St. Louis Post-Dispatch, 1926-44, spl. corr., 1954-62, chief Washington corr., 1962-69, contbg. editor, 1969—. Columnist, United Feature Syndicate, 1944-54; made 3 mos. tour battlefronts, 1945; lectr. Columbia U. Sch. Mexico 1950. Decorated Order of North Star (Sweden); recipient Sigma Delta Chi award for best Washington corr., 1944; award for journalism U. Mo.; Pulitzer prize for commentary, 1970. Mem. Kappa Sigma, Sigma Delta Chi. Clubs: Overseas Writers (pres. 1943-45); Century (N.Y.C.); Washington Press, Gridiron (pres. 1957), Metropolitan, Cosmos (Washington). Author: Sweden—The Middle Way, 1936; They Hate Roosevelt, 1936; Washington Calling, 1937; This Is Democracy, 1938; This Is Your War, 1942; I Write From Washington, 1942; The Cabin, 1944. Edited and wrote Evaluation for New Edition of Brooks Adams' America's Economic Supremacy, 1947; The Farmer Takes a Hand, 1952; Ethics in Business Society with Douglass Cater), 1954; The Ragged Edge, 1955; Eisenhower. Captive Hero, 1958; The Peacemakers, 1961; A Taint of Innocence, 1967. Co-editor: Walter Lippmann and His Times, 1959. Home: 3554 Edmunds St NW Washington DC 20007 Office: 1028 Connecticut Av Washington DC 20036

CHILES, LAWTON, U.S. senator; b. Lakeland, Fla., Apr. 3, 1930; B.S., U. Fla., 1952, LL.B., 1955; m. Rhea Grafton; children—Tandy, Lawton III, Edward G., Rhea Gay. Admitted to Fla. bar, practiced in Lakeland; mem. Fla. Ho. of Reps., 1958-66; mem. Fla. Senate, 1966-70; U.S. Senator from Fla., 1971—. Served with AUS; Korea. Democrat. Home: Lakeland FL 33801 also 3807 N Woodstock St Arlington VA 22207

CHILTON, ALICE PLEASANCE HUNTER (MRS. ST. JOHN POINDEXTER CHILTON), state ofcl., vocational counselor; b. Boyce, La., Apr. 16, 1911; d. Albert Eugene and Maggie (Texada) Hunter; B.A., La. Coll., 1931; M.S., La. State U., 1934, Guidance Counselor certificate, 1954; m. St. John Poindexter Chilton, Mar. 2, 1935. Tchr. secondary sch., Glenmora, La., 1931-35; with La. Div. Employment Security and USES, Baton Rouge, 1937-74, employment interviewer and supr., 1937-43, personnel officer, 1943-46, operations analyst, 1946-55, supr. counseling and tech. services, 1955-74. Vice pres., dir. LaPlace Enterprises, Inc., Belle Pointe Enterprises, Inc. Mem. curriculum study com. East Baton Rouge, Parish Sch. Bd., 1968—; rec. sec. Quota Internat., 1961-62, 2d v.p., 1963-64. Bd. dirs. YWCA. Recipient certificate merit La. Acad. Sci., 1960; certificate 30 years meritorious service La. Div. Employment Security, 1967. Mem. Am. Personnel and Guidance Assn., Nat. Vocational Guidance Assn., Am. Sch. Counselor Assn., Assn. Counselor Edn. and Supervision, Nat. Employment Counselors Assn., La. Guidance Assn., Internat. Assn. Personnel in Employment Security, Menninger Found., La. Geneal. and Hist. Soc. (pres. 1957), La. Landmarks Soc., Found. for Hist. La. Club: Campus Louisiana State University (Faculty Wives); Methodist. Home: 3617 Hyacinth Av Baton Rouge LA 70808 Office: 802 Life Sciences Bldg La State U Baton Rouge LA 70803

CHIOU, CHUNG YIH, educator; b. Hsinchu, Taiwan, July 11, 1934; s. Chang and Mei (Wei) C.; B.S. in Pharmacy, Nat. Taiwan U., 1957, M.S. in Pharmacology, 1960; Ph.D. in Pharmacology (Research fellow Mead Johnson & Co. 1964-67), Vanderbilt U., 1967; m. Tricia T.S. Tsen, Sept. 23, 1961; children—Linda, Faye. Came to U.S., 1964, naturalized, 1973. Pharmacist William Pharm. Works, Hsinchu, Taiwan, 1960-61; instr. China Med. Coll., Taichung, Taiwan, 1962-64; research asst. pharmacology Vanderbilt U., Nashville, 1964-67, research asso. pharmacology, 1967-68; postdoctoral fellow pharmacology U. Ia., Iowa City, 1968-69; asst. prof. pharmacology U. Fla., Gainesville, 1969-73, asso. prof. pharmacology, 1973—. Served to 2d. lt. Chinese Air Force, 1961-62. Recipient Health Scis. Advanced award NIH, 1967-68; Research grants from NIH Gen. Research Support Grant, 1969-71, Nat. Inst. Neurol. Diseases and Stroke, 1971—. Mem. N.Y. Acad. Scis., Am. Soc. Pharmacology and Exptl. Therapeutics, Sigma Xi. Contbr. articles to profl. jours. Home: 3451 NW 35th Pl Gainesville FL 32605

CHIOVAROU, ROY EDWARD, archtl.-engring. firm exec.; b. Summit, N.J., Jan. 21, 1944; s. Edward and Ruth (Woodside) C.; B.S., N.Y. U., 1965; m. Maud Ann Cauley, June 4, 1966. With Edward Chiovarou & Son, Inc./Chiovarou Painting Co., Inc., Summit, 1964-69, treas., 1966-69; adminstrv. and financial exec. Ins. Services Office, 1969-71; adminstr., financial exec. Francisco & Jacobus, N.Y.C., after 1971; now financial exec. Greenleaf & Telesca, Inc., Miami, Fla. Mem. Areopagus, Aircraft Owners and Pilots Assn. Office: 1451 Brickell Av Miami FL 33131

CHIPLEY, ALFRED SANGSTER, govt. ofcl.; b. Uniontown, Pa., Oct. 24, 1912; s. Edmund Lee and Grace (Noble) C.; B.S. in M.E., U. Fla., 1936; m. Willie Josephine Page, July 7, 1937; children—Jo Ann (Mrs. William P. Blair, Jr.), Richard Lee, Carol Grace (Mrs. David M. Mastro), Robert Page. Research engr. Burgess Battery Co., Madison, Wis., Chgo., 1936-42; chief research engr. Burgess-Menning Co., Libertyville, Ill., 1945-51; poultry farmer, Bokeelia, Fla., 1951-62; vector control specialist USPHS, Fla., 1963-68, also state project officer, Ala.; dir. div. solid waste and vector control Ala. Dept. Pub. Health, Montgomery, 1968—. Served from 2d lt. to maj. Ordnance Corps, AUS, 1942-46; ETO. Registered profl. engr., Ill., Ala. Mem. Am. Mosquito Control Assn., Ala. Sanitarians Assn., Am. Pub. Health Assn., Sigma Tau. Patentee in air velocity, air distbn., air cleaning, radiant heating and cooling, and engine exhaust and intake silencing devices. Home: 3728 Princeton Rd Montgomery AL 36111 Office: Dept Health State Office Bldg Montgomery AL 36104

CHIPMAN, DENNIS CLARENCE, psychiatrist; b. Seattle, Jan. 7, 1934; s. Dennis Clarence and Esther Ronghild (Lund) C.; student U. Wash., 1952-55, M.D., 1959; m. Karen Ekern, Mar. 17, 1968; children—Kimberly Maria, Jason. Intern U. Neb. Hosp., Omaha, 1959-60; resident U. Wash. Hosp. System, 1960-63; pvt. practice, Seattle, 1963-66; dir. Kingsport (Tenn.) Mental Health Center, 1969-73; pvt. practice, Kingsport, 1973—; mem. staff Holston Valley Community Hosp., Indian Path Hosp.; dir. Kingsport Mental Health Center, Kingsport Center Opportunity; clin. instr. psychiatry U. Wash. Sch. Medicine, 1963-69. Served wiht M.C., AUS, 1966-68. Diplomate Am. Bd. Psychiatry and Neurology. Mem. Am. Psychiat. Assn., A.M.A., Kappa Sigma. Republican. Episcopalian. Clubs: Kingsport Dinner, Ridgefields Country (Kingsport). Home: 516 Forestdale Rd Kingsport TN 37660 Office: 1920 Brookside Dr Kingsport TN 38664

CHIPPS, HENRY DAVIS, physician, educator; b. Smithland, Ky., Aug. 30, 1909; s. Henry Duley and Gene (Davis) C.; student U. Va., 1926-28; B.S., U. Ala., 1930; M.D., U. Louisville, 1934; m. Frances Sydnor deButts, Nov. 7, 1937; children—Mary Elizabeth (Mrs. Mark Dent-Broklehurst), Genie Davis. Intern Lloyd Nolan Hosp., Birmingham, Ala., 1934-35; resident Meth. Hosp., Indpls., 1937-39, Royal Victoria Hosp., Montreal, Que., Can., 1939-41; practice medicine specializing in pathology, Lexington, Ky., 1954—; mem. staff Bapt. Hosp., Lexington; instr. pathology McGill U. Med. Sch., Montreal, 1939-41; asso. prof. pathology U. Wash. Sch. Medicine, Seattle, 1947-52; dir. pathology Ochsner Found. Hosp., New Orleans, 1952-54; prof. clin. pathology U. Ky. Sch. Medicine, Lexington, 1960—. Bd. dirs. Ky. div. Am. Cancer Soc., 1960—, pres. Ky. div., 1970; bd. dirs. Order Lafayette, 1962—. Served to col. M.C., AUS, 1942-46. Fellow Coll. Am. Pathologists (founding mem.); mem. Am. Assn. Pathologists and Bacteriologists, Ky. Hist. Soc., Civil War Round Table, The Lexington Club, Sigma Xi, Phi Chi, Phi Delta Theta. Home: 101 S Hanover St Lexington KY 40502 Office: 1740 S Limestone St Lexington KY 40503

CHISHOLM, ARTHUR GORDON, med. book distbg. co. exec.; b. New Orleans, July 22, 1911; s. Arthur Caspar and Annie (Thomas) C.; student Loyola U., New Orleans, 1943-44; m. Andrea Francis, Oct. 8, 1931; children—Arthur Gordon, Carol Ann, Andrea (Mrs. John J. Kuglar). With J.A. Majors Co., New Orleans, 1926—, chief clk., 1943-47, mgr. Atlanta office, 1948-56, v.p., 1956—. Mem. Atlanta C. of C., Atlanta Hist. Soc., Clan Chisholm Soc. Home: 1905 Sandgate Circle College Park GA 30349 Office: 3770 Zip Industrial Blvd NE Atlanta GA 30354

CHISHOLM, DAVID HUGH, librarian; b. Philadelphia, Miss., Mar. 23, 1922; s. Robert Benjamin and Fanny Ellen (Randoll) C.; A.A., East Central Jr. Coll., 1946; B.B.A., U. Miss., 1948, B.A., 1948; B.S. in L.S., La. State U., 1952; postgrad. U. Tex., 1952-62. Field asst. CCC, Wash. and Ore., 1941; clk. Civil Service, Washington, 1942, 48-49; tchr. English and comml. subjects La. State U., 1952, sec. to Grad. Sch. Library Sci., summer 1952; reference librarian U. Tex., 1952-54, acquisitions librarian, 1954—. Served with USNR, 1942-45. Decorated D.S.M. Mem. A.L.A. Home: 407 W 18th St Apt 300 Austin TX 78701 Office: 1802 Main Bldg Library U Tex Austin TX 78712

CHISHOLM, LESLIE LEE, JR., physician, surgeon; b. Cairo, Ill., Feb. 6, 1931; s. Leslie Lee and Lila (Cates) C.; B.S., U. Neb., 1953, M.D., 1960; m. Phyllis June Segar, Aug. 13, 1953; children—Leslie Lee III, Douglas Scott, Philip Kent. Intern, Tampa Gen. Hosp., 1961; eye resident U. Louisville Gen. Hosp., 1961-64; civil service med. project officer Wright Patterson AFB, Dayton, O., 1967; practice medicine specializing in ophthalmology, Tampa, Fla., 1964—; teaching staff Tampa Gen. Hosp., vice chief sect. on ophthalmology, 1967, chief sect. ophthalmology, 1968-70; mem. sr. attending staff St. Joseph, U. Community, Centro Astruiano hosps.; cons. staff Tampa Vets. Hosp., Tampa Meml., Centro Espanol, Lykes Meml. hosps.; asst. clin. prof. dept. ophthalmology U. S. Fla., 1972—. Pres., Doctor's Optical Co., Inc. Bd. dirs. Fla. Council for Blind. Served with USAF, 1954-56. Diplomate Am. Bd. Ophthalmology. Mem. A.M.A., Am. Assn. Ophthalmologists, Contact Lens Assn. Ophthalmologists, Assn. Am. Physicians and Surgeons, So., Fla., Hillsborough County med. assns., Soc. Eye Surgeons, Am. Acad. Ophthalmology and Otolaryngology, Pan Am. Soc. Ophthalmology. Republican. Home: 10913 Carrollwood Dr Tampa FL 33618 Office: 5206 N Armenia Av Tampa FL 33603

CHISHOLM, TOMMY, utilities exec.; b. Baldwyn, Miss., Apr. 14, 1941; s. Thomas Vaniver and Ruby (Duncan) C.; B.S. in Civil Engring., Tenn. Tech. U., 1963; J.D., Samford U., 1969; m. Janice McClanahan, June 20, 1964; children—Mark Alan (dec.), Andrea, Stephen Thomas. Civil engr. TVA, Knoxville, Tenn., 1963-64; with So. Services, Inc., 1963-73, coordinator spl. projects, Atlanta, 1971-73; admitted to Ala. bar, 1969; asst. to pres. So. Co., Atlanta, 1973—. Active local United Appeal fund drives, 1967, 68, 72. Registered profl. engr., Ala., Fla., Ga., Miss. Mem. Am. Bar Assn., Ala. State Bar, Am. Soc. C.E., Phi Alpha Delta. Home: 2918 Deerview Trail Marietta GA 30062 Office: PO Box 720071 Atlanta GA 30346

CHISMAN, JAMES ALLEN, educator; b. Ravenna, O., Mar. 4, 1935; s. Wallace Forbray and Marthalee (Wood) C.; B.S. in E.E., Akron U., 1958; M.S. in Indsl. Engring., Ia. U., 1960, Ph.D. in Mgmt. Engring., 1963; m. Lois Ann Lessig, May 11, 1957. Devel. engr. Def. Research Div. Firestone, Akron, O., 1958-59; mem. faculty Clemson U., Clemson, S.C., 1963—, asso. prof. systems engring., 1965—, dir. engring. tech. program, 1974—, mem. faculty senate, 1974—. Pres. Clemson Investment & Devel. Co., 1963—; mgmt. cons. Consumers Power Co., Jackson, Mich., 1963—. Chmn. troop com. Boy Scouts Am., Clemson, 1968-70; pres. Clemson Arts Council, 1972—; dir. Clemson Youth Theater, 1972—. Mem. Am. Inst. Indsl. Engrs. (sr.), Am. Soc. Engring. Edn., Operations Research Soc. Am., Inst. Mgmt. Scis., Tau Beta Pi, Sigma Xi. Mem. editorial bd. Am. Inst. Indsl. Engrs. Transactions, 1969—. Home: PO Box 1111 Clemson SC 29631

CHISOLM, CHARLES SMITH, foundry exec.; b. Selma, Ala., Sept. 10, 1916; s. James Satterfield and Ernestine (Smith) C.; B.S. in Chem. Engring., Auburn (Ala.) U., 1938, M.S., 1939; postgrad. student Birmingham So. Coll., 1940; m. Martha Elizabeth Gilbert, Nov. 6, 1942; children—Betsy (Mrs. Tony Silberman), John Grier, Catherine. Instr. chemistry Auburn U., 1939; with metall. dept. U.S. Steel Corp., 1939-41; supt. metallurgy and quality control Wheland Foundry div. N.Am. Royalties, Chattanooga, 1946-56, plant mgr., 1956—; pres. Valley Farms, Selma, 1950—, Chisolm Corp., Selma, 1969—, Satterfield Co., Selma, 1970—, Peter Pan Industries, Lookout Mountain, Tenn., 1954—. Vice chmn. Lookout Mountain Planning Bd., 1968—. Served to lt. col. AUS, 1941-45. Registered profl. engr., Tenn. Mem. Am. Soc. Metals, Am. Foundrymen's Soc. (nat. dir. 1973—), Am. Soc. Testing Materials, Omicrom Delta Kappa, Spades, Kappa Alpha. Presbyn. (ruling elder). Clubs: Mountain City (Chattanooga); Fairyland (Lookout Mountain). Home: 1213 Peter Pan Rd Lookout Mountain TN 37350 Office: 1800 S Broad St Chattanooga TN 37401

CHITTY, ARTHUR BENJAMIN, JR., assn. exec.; b. Jacksonville, Fla., June 15, 1914; s. Arthur Benjamin and Hazel Talitha (Brown) C.; student U. Fla., summer 1934; A.B., U. of South, 1935; M.A., Tulane U., 1952; L.H.D., Canaan Coll., 1970; m. Mary Elizabeth Nickinson, June 16, 1946; children—Arthur Benjamin III, John Abercrombie Merritt, Em Turner, Nathan Harsh Brown. Vice pres. Chitty & Co., Jacksonville, Fla., 1937-41, chmn. bd. dirs., 1963-67, dir. pub. relations U. of South, 1946-65, 70-73, historiographer, 1955—, exec. dir. Asso. Alumni 1946-65; pres. Assn. of Episcopal Colls., N.Y.C., 1965-70, 74—, sec., dir., 1971—. Pres. Sewanee Civic Assn., 1948-49; mem. Tenn. Bishop and Council, 1956-65; nat. convenor Episcopal historiographers, 1961-66, 71—; nat. council Brotherhood St. Andrew, mem. exec. com., 1966—, v.p., 1968; Am. coordinator Oxford Scholar Program, Keble Coll., Eng. 1970—. Bd. dirs. Living Ch. Found., Ch. Hist. Soc.; trustee St. Augustine's Coll.; trustee, sec. bd. St. Andrew's Sch. Served with USNR, 1942-45. Mem. N.Y. Acad. Scis., St. George's Soc., English-Speaking Union (nat. bd. 1973; pres. local chpt. 1972-73), Phi Beta Kappa (pres. 1963-64), Pi Gamma Mu, Phi Alpha Theta, Sigma Upsilon, Sigma Nu, (pres. Ednl. Found. 1969—). Episcopalian. Clubs: Century Assn., Church (N.Y.C.). Author: Reconstruction at Sewanee, 1954. Contbr. articles to profl. jours. Editor: Sewanee News, 1946-65; Historiographical Newsletter, 1962-67; Franklin County (Tenn.) Historian, 1965-69. Editor: (with Elizabeth N. Chitty) Ely: Too Black, Too White, 1970. Home: Sewanee TN 37375 Office: 815 2d Av New York City NY 10017

CHIU, KUN-YOUNG, cons. engr.; b. Taipei, Taiwan, Formosa, June 23, 1937; s. Jiun and Luan-Yin (Lin) C.; B.S., Nat. Taiwan U., 1960; M.S., U. Fla., 1964; 1 dau., Michelle Karen. Came to U.S., 1963. Asst. mgr. Yun-long Engring. Co. Inc., Taipei, Taiwan, 1956-60; research and teaching asst. Nat. Taiwan U., Taipei, 1961-63; research asst. U. Fla., Gainesville, 1963-64; structural engr. Wm. T. Mathis & Assos., Jacksonville, Fla., 1964-67, resident engr., Valdosta, Ga., 1967-70; prin. Kun-young Chiu & Assos., cons. engrs., Valdosta, 1970—, Jacksonville, 1972—. Registered profl. engr., Fla., Ga., Ky., S.C. Mem. Am. Soc. C.E., Am. Concrete Inst., Chinese Inst. Civil Engring., Nat. Soc. Profl. Engrs., Cons. Engrs. Council. Contbr. articles in field to profl. jours. Address: 109 E Adair St Valdosta GA 31601

CHIU, WEN JUNG, physician; b. Taiwan, Formosa, May 6, 1924; s. Yi Pau and Chuan Hau (Chen) C.; M.D., Nat. Taiwan U., 1947; m. So-Khim Tan, Dec. 14, 1953; children—Mark, Peter, James. Came to U.S., 1952, naturalized, 1969. Intern, 1st Mil. Forces Gen. Hosp., Taipei, Taiwan, 1947-48; resident in anesthesiology Peter Bent Brigham Hosp., Boston, 1953, Boston Children's Hosp., 1954, Boston Lying-in Hosp., 1954; resident U. Tex., M.D. Anderson Hosp. and

Tumor Inst., Houston, 1954-57, asso. anesthesiologist, asst. prof., 1965—; anesthesiologist E. Tex. Tb Hosp., Tyler, 1957-61; asst. prof. U. Tex. Med. Sch., Houston, 1971—. Fellow Am. Coll. Anesthesiologists; mem. Internat. Anesthesia Research Soc., Am. Soc. Anesthesiologists, A.M.A., Tex. Med. Assn., Harris County Med. Soc., Doctors' Club Houston. Presbyn. Home: 5034 Glenmeadow St Houston TX 77035 Office: 6723 Bertner Dr Houston TX 77025

CHO, YOUNG WON, med. educator; b. Seoul, Korea, Mar. 3, 1931; s. Dae Hyun and Chung-Tai (Kim) C.; M.D., Seoul Nat. U., 1956; M.S., Emory U., 1962; Ph.D., Nihon U., Tokyo, 1972; m. Mia Myungja Hur, June 30, 1971; children—Ann Marie, Clifford Oscar. Came to U.S., 1956, naturalized, 1969. Intern, Vanderbilt U. Affiliated Hosp., Nashville, 1956-57, resident internal medicine, 1957-60; fellow cardiovascular Emory U. Sch. Medicine, Atlanta, 1960-63; chief cardiovascular research lab., physician Phila. Gen. Hosp., 1964-67; instr. pharmacology U. Pa., Phila., 1964-70; asso. prof. medicine and pharmacology La. State U. Med. Center, New Orleans, 1970-73; asso. prof. pharmacology U. N.C. Sch. Medicine, Chapel Hill, 1973—. Cons. in research Castle Point (N.Y.) VA Hosp., 1969-72, Merrell-Nat. Lab., Cin., 1971-72, Cooper Lab., Cedar Knoll, N.J., 1972—; prin. investigator NIH project Emory U., 1963-64, Phila. Gen. Hosp., 1964-67. Fellow Am. Coll. Chest Physicians, Am. Coll. Clin. Pharmacology, Royal Soc. Health, Am. Coll. Angiology; mem. Am. Pharm. Assn. (chmn. antihyperlipidemic agts., sci. rev. panel, drug interaction project 1972—), Am. Soc. Pharmacology and Exptl. Therapeutics, Soc. Exptl. Biology and Medicine, Am. Heart Assn., Internat. Soc. Nephrology. Home: 102 Lilac Dr Chapel Hill NC 27514 Office: Room 227 Swing Bldg U NC Sch Medicine Chapel Hill NC 27514

CHOATE, JIM KEITH, mfg. co. exec.; b. Snyder, Okla., May 27, 1931; s. Walter D. and Dorothy M. (Farr) C.; B.B.A., Tex. Tech U., 1952; J.D., U. Tex., 1958; m. Carolyn Hannah, Feb. 10, 1952; children—Shannon, Bryan C. Admitted to Tex. bar, 1957; mem. firm Geary, Brice, Barron, & Stahl, Dallas, 1958-64, Choate & Kelly, Dallas, 1964-68; pres. Internat. Merchandising Systems, Dallas, 1964-68; with Am. Hydroponic Systems, Inc., Dallas, 1965—, pres., 1966—; dir. Equidynne Investments, 1973—, Data Automation Co., 1973—, N.Y. Asset Mgmt., Inc., 1972—. Pres. North Dallas Democrats, 1964-66; mem. steering com. Kennedy-Johnson campaign, 1960, Johnson-Humphrey campaign, 1964. Served to capt. USAF, 1952-55. Mem. Am. Bar Assn., Phi Alpha Delta. Mason. Home: 4330 Allencrest Dallas TX 75234 Office: 1137 Frito Lay Tower Dallas TX 75235

CHOATE, WILLIAM WESLEY, civil engr., lawyer; b. Oklahoma City, July 25, 1939; s. Irvan Wesley and Fleeta Stapleton (Moritzky) C.; B.S. in Geol. Engring., U. Okla., 1960; J.D., Oklahoma City U., 1973; m. Edna Beth Petersen, Feb. 8, 1964; children—LaNae, William, James, Steven, Carol, Linda. Missionary, Ch. of Jesus Christ of Latter-day Saints, Brazil, 1960-63; civil engr. Bur. Reclamation, 1963-64; planning engr. Okla. Water Resources Bd., 1969-71; civil engr. U.S. Army Corps Engrs., Oklahoma City, 1971—; cons. ground water geologist, 1971—; cons. to pvt. schs. Western Area Bd. Information. Mem. Nat. Eagle Scout Assn., Boy Scouts Am. County conv. del. Democratic Party, 1972. Served to capt. USAF, 1964-69. Registered profl. engr., Okla., Neb. Mem. Okla. Soc. Profl. Engrs. (ethics com.), Soc. Mil. Engrs., Okla. Bar Assn., Okla. Trial Lawyers Assn. (legislative com.), Okla. Cattlemen's Assn. Mem. Ch. of Jesus Christ of Latter-day Saints (Sunday sch. pres. Okla. stake, 1971-73). Home: 1605 Classen Blvd Oklahoma City OK 73106 Office: Okla Resident Office Army Corps Engrs Tinker AFB OK 73145

CHODKOWSKI, HENRY, JR., educator, painter; b. Hartford, Conn., Mar. 20, 1937; s. Henry and Bronislawa (Rzasa) C.; B.F.A., U. Hartford, 1961; M.F.A., Yale U., 1963; m. Elizabeth Cowell Goss, Oct. 16, 1964; children—Ivor Alexander, Ariadne Mayo. Draughtsman, New Haven Redevel. Project, 1962-63; faculty U. Louisville, 1963—, asso. prof. advanced and grad. painting, 1973—; one-man shows U. Louisville, 1964, Va. Poly. Inst., Blacksburg, 1968, Speed Mus., Louisville, 1968, 72, Duke U. Mus., Durham, N.C., 1972; exhibited in numerous group shows; represented in permanent collections Speed Mus., Montgomery (Ala.) Mus. Fine Arts, Jewish Community Center, New Haven, others. Cons. Ky. Arts Commn., 1973—, Philip Morris Co., Louisville, 1973—. Polaroid Corp. research grantee, 1968; recipient numerous prizes and awards. Home: 2015 Baringer Av Louisville KY 40204

CHOPRA, KULDIP PRAKASH, educator; b. Srinagar, India, Mar. 25, 1932; s. Madan Gopal and Shanti Devi (Handa) C.; B.S. with honors, U. Delhi, 1951, M.S., 1953, Ph.D., 1960; m. Phyllis Shirley McGrath, July 15, 1968. Came to U.S., 1957, naturalized, 1968. Research asso. physics U. Md., 1957-58; vis. asst. prof. physics, research scientist U. So. Cal., Los Angeles, 1958-60; research asst. prof. astronautics Poly. Inst. Bklyn., 1960-63; head and sr. scientist, space sci. lab. Melpar, Inc., Falls Church, Va., 1963-65, cons., 1965-66; dir. summer sch. of environmental and planetary scis., asso. prof. atmospheric and space scis. U. Miami, Coral Gables, Fla., 1965-67; prof. applied physics Nova U., Ft. Lauderdale, Fla., 1967-69; prof. physics Old Dominion U., Norfolk, Va., 1969—; vis. prof. Va. Inst. Marine Scis., Gloucester Point, Va., 1972—. Mem. adv. bd. Sci. Spectrum, 1970. Fellow Am. Phys. Soc.; mem. Am. Geophys. Union (life), A.A.A.S., Am. Inst. Aeros. and Astronautics, Am. Assn. U. Profs., Am. Meteorol. Soc. Contbr. articles to profl. jours. Home: 1372 W Little Neck Rd Virginia Beach VA 23452 Office: Old Dominion U Norfolk VA 23508

CHOPRA, NAITER MOHAN, educator; b. Amritsar, India, Nov. 23, 1923; s. Harbans Lal and Tara Wati (Kohli) C.; B.S. Honors, Punjab U., Lahore, India, 1944, M.S. Honors, 1945; Ph.D., U. Dublin, 1955; m. Santosh Bala Dhanda, Feb. 11, 1953; children—Kiran, Ashok, Hersh, Siddharth. Came to U.S., 1965, naturalized, 1971. Demonstrator chemistry F.C. Coll., Lahore, 1946-47; asst. lectr. Agrl. Inst., Allahabad, India, 1946-49; Research fellow U. Toronto, 1955-57; research officer Can. Dept. Agr., Winnipeg, Man., 1957-65; mem. faculty N.C. Agrl. and Tech. State U., Greensboro, 1965—, prof. chemistry, 1967—, dir. tobacco and pesticide research project, 1967—. Sec. India League Toronto, 1956-57; pres. India Assn., Greensboro, N.C., 1971-72. Govt. of Eire Research grantee, 1954-55; Post-doctoral fellow U. Toronto, 1955-57; research grantee Council for Tobacco Research—U.S.A., 1967-71; research grantee U.S. Dept. Agr., 1972—. Mem. Am. Chem. Soc. (sect. dir. 1970-72), N.C. Acad. Sci. Home: 1803 Red Forest Rd Greensboro NC 27410

CHOUDHURY, ABDUL LATIF, educator; b. Dacca, Bangladesh, Jan. 1, 1933; s. Abdur Rub and Umme Arefa (Khatun) C.; B.S. with honors in Physics, Dacca U., 1953, M.S. in Physics, 1954; Dr.rer.nat. in Theoretical Physics, Freie Universitaet, Berlin, West Germany, 1960; m. Jutta Kausch, Nov. 4, 1960; children—Kadjol, Marcel. Came to U.S., 1966, naturalized, 1969. Asst. to prof. Dacca U., 1955, sr. lectr. physics, 1961-66, reader, 1968-69; asst. to prof. Freie Universitaet, 1959-60; asso. prof. State U., Elizabeth City, N.C., 1966-68, 69-73, prof. physics, math., 1973—. Gen. sec. Dacca U. Tchrs. Assn., 1969. W. German Exchange scholar Deutscher Akademischer Austauschdienst, 1955-59; Research fellow Fritz-Haber-Institut of Berlin, 1960; Research fellowship dept. Theoretical Physics Imperial Coll., London, U.K., 1960-61. Mem. Am. Phys. Soc., Assn. Am. U. Profs. Contbr. articles to profl. jours. Home: 218 E Broad St Elizabeth City NC 27909

CHOW, SIDNEY HSINHUAI, chem. engr.; b. China, Nov. 3, 1936; s. Chow Kwan and Sui Fei (Yee) C.; M.S., Kan. State U., 1962; Ph.D., Vanderbilt U., 1967; m. E-Yen Foo, Mar. 16, 1963; children—George, Wade, Howard. Came to U.S., 1959, naturalized, 1973. Research engr. I.E. duPont de Nemours & Co., Niagara Falls, N.Y., 1966-70, sr. engr., La Porte, Tex., 1970—. Named Hon. Citizen of State Tenn., 1964. Mem. Pi Mu Epsilon, Phi Lambda Upsilon, Sigma Xi. Home: 4118 Bayou Grove Dr Seabrook TX 77586 Office: PO Box 347 La Porte TX 77571

CHOW, YUNG-TEH, educator, author; b. Wu-Yi, Chekiang, China, Oct. 28, 1916; s. Fang-Ping and Hsiu-Ning (Li) C.; B.A., Nat. Tsing Hua U., 1937; M.A., U. Chgo., 1951, Ph.D., 1958; m. Tsun-Hsun Li, Aug. 21, 1968. Editor, Nat. Assn. for Advancement of Mass Edn., Changsha, Hunan, China, 1937-39; research asst. Socio-econ. Inst., Nat. Yunnan U., Kunming, 1939-41; research instr. Inst. for Census Research, Nat. Tsing Hua U., Chengkung and Kunyang, Yunnan, 1941-46; instr. sociology Nat. Tsing Hua U. at Peiping (now Peking), China, 1946-48; asst. prof. sociology Eastern Mich. U., Ypsilanti, 1958-61; research on Chinese population in Chgo. 1961-62; asso. prof. sociology Moorhead (Minn.) State Coll., 1962-65, prof., 1965-67; prof. sociology No. Mich. U., Marquette, 1967-72; vis. prof. sociology U. Ala., 1973—. Mem. Am. Sociol. Assn., Am. Assn. U. Profs., Assn. Asian Studies, Population Assn. Am. Author: (with Hsiao-tung Fei) China's Gentry, 1953; Social Mobility in China, 1966. Home: U Ala PO Box 5694 University AL 35486

CHRIS, HARRY JOSEPH, architect; b. Beaumont, Tex., Sept. 13, 1938; s. Harry Adam and Lucille Helen (Junca); B.Arch., Tulane U., 1961; M.B.A., Memphis State U., 1969; m. Jimmie Lea Bowen, Sept. 21, 1966; children—Mary Elizabeth, James, William, Mark, Lisa. Architect, Tex. Bldg. Commn., 1966-68, Holiday Inn Am., 1968-69; pres. Archtl. Designers Inc., Dallas, 1969—. Served to lt. comdr. USNR, 1961-66. U.S. Navy scholar, 1956-61. Mem. A.I.A., Dallas Jr. C. of C., Beta Theta Pi. Roman Catholic. K.C. Clubs: Toastmasters, Lancer's (Dallas). Prin. works include Met. Club, Chgo., 1973, Cascade Club, Akron, O., 1972, Dayton (O.) Racquet Club, 1972, Plaza Club, Houston, 1972, Univ. Club, Houston, 1972; Citrus Club, Orlando, Fla., 1971. Home: 3654 Ridgebriar St Dallas TX 75234 Office: 4448 Sigma St Dallas TX 75240

CHRISTENSEN, DAVID LEE, tech. and bus. cons.; b. Birmingham, Ala., Apr. 7, 1932; s. Arne Scove and Susie (Harvey) C.; student U. Ala., 1955-57; m. Doris Margaret Baker, Mar. 19, 1949; children—David Lee, Erik Lane. Design engr. Hayes Internat., Birmingham, Ala., 1955; cons. engr. Cons. & Designers, Inc., Redstone Arsenal, Ala., 1956-60; aerospace cons., 1960—; to Arthur D. Little, Inc., 1969—; pres. TEC Prodns., Inc., Huntsville, Ala., 1960-63; Served with AUS, 1953-55. Mem. Am. Inst. Aeros. and Astronautics, Soc. Tech. Writers and Pubs., Rocket City Astron. Soc., Aviation Space Writers Assn., Huntsville C. of C. (pub. relations com.). Co-author: Twenty Centuries of Space Travel, Dividends from Space, Stations in Space. Asst. editor Space Jour., 1957-60. Chmn. lit. com. Ala. Space and Rocket Center; research asso. U. Ala. Center for Environmental Studies, Huntsville. Home: 11015 Vivian Dr Huntsville AL 35810 Office: PO Box 3180 Huntsville AL 35810

CHRISTENSEN, JOHN LAWRENCE, air force officer; b. St. Anthony, Fremont, Ida., July 10, 1939; s. John Rulon and Veda Caroline (Taylor) C.; B.S., Brigham Young U., 1961; M.Computer Sci., Tex. A. and M. U., 1968; m. Nina Marie Rex, Dec. 18, 1959; children—John Lawrence, David R., Debora M., Rebecca A., Lisa C., Lara L., Susan E. Commd. 2d lt. USAF, 1962, advanced through grades to maj., 1973; automatic data processing mgmt. officer, Robins AFB, Ga., 1962-66; chief data automation br. Takhli Royal Thai AFB, Thailand, 1968-69; computer systems analyst comdr. in chief Pacific, Camp Smith, Hawaii, 1969-73; assigned Data Services Center, Pentagon, Washington, 1973—. Tchr. bus. mgmt. Far East div. U. Md., 1968-69. Decorated Air Force commendation medal, Joint Services commendation medal. Mem. Upsilon Pi Epsilon. Mem. Ch. of Jesus Christ of Latter-day Saints (bishop Halawa ward 1971-73). Home: 3905 Desoto Ct Woodbridge VA 22191 Office: Data Services Center Pentagon Washington DC 20301

CHRISTENSON, VICTOR JUNIOR, univ. adminstr.; b. Jackson, Minn., May 12, 1924; s. Victor Edwin and Mina Maurine (Thornburg) C.; B.A., Buena Vista Coll., 1949; M.Ed., Mont. State U., 1956; Ed.D., U. Neb., 1967; m. Inez Mildred Johnson, Oct. 28, 1924; children—Bruce Martin, Brett Junior. High sch. tchr., Cleghorn, Ia., 1949-52; high sch. prin., Sutherland, Ia., 1954-58; supt. schs., Royal, Ia., 1958-63; exec. sec., dir. Neb. Council Ednl. TV, Inc., Lincoln, Neb., 1963-67; supt. schs., Oskaloosa, Ia., 1967-69; head dept. sch. adminstrn. Western Ky. U., Bowling Green, Ky., 1969—; owner Sporting Goods Store, 1960-65. Cons. Ednl. TV, 1963-65; Served with AUS, 1943-46, 52-54. Decorated Bronze Star medal. Mem. N.E.A., Nat. Council Profs. Ednl. Adminstrn., Am., Ky. assns. sch. adminstrs., Ky. Edn. Assn., Ky. Assn. Sch. Bus. Ofcls., Assn. Supervision Curriculum Devel., Nat. Elementary Schs. Prins., Ky. Assn. Pupil Personnel Workers, Sch. Facilities Council, Council Ednl. Facility Planners, Assn. Sch. Bus. Ofcls., Phi Delta Kappa. Elk. Home: 1316 Willow Lane Bowling Green KY 42101

CHRISTERSON, ROBERT KELLY, coll. adminstr.; b. nr. Springfield, Ky., May 10, 1924; s. Garnett Phillip and Mattie (Goode) C.; m. Alberta Jones, Mar. 22, 1947; children—Garnett Kelly, Marcus Allen, Sandra Gail. Bookkeeper, First Nat. Bank, Springfield, Ky., 1946-58; asst. cashier First and Peoples Bank, Springfield, 1959-63, asst. v.p., 1964-66; controller Campbellsville (Ky.) Coll., 1967-69, bus. mgr., 1970-72; cashier Springfield (Ky.) State Bank, 1972—. Treas., Taylor County Park Bd. Served with AUS, 1944-47. Baptist. Mason. Home: Route 1 Springfield KY 40069 Office: Springfield State Bank Springfield KY 40069

CHRISTIAN, GEORGE LLOYD, JR., newspaper editor; b. Houston, May 29, 1927; s. George Lloyd and Hazel Margaret (Singleton) C.; B.S. in Journalism, U. Houston; m. Mary Frances Blount, Sept. 22, 1956; children—Stephen Scott, Karen Elizabeth, Devin Alan. With Houston Post, 1949—, successively reporter, film critic, drama critic, mag. editor, now asst. mng. editor. Free-lance writer. Served with AUS, 1945-46. Home: 1108 Danbury Rd Houston TX 77055 Office: 4747 Southwest Freeway Houston TX 77001

CHRISTIAN, JOHN KENTON, publisher; b. Pana, Ill., Nov. 6, 1927; s. Ben Ross and Ruth (Stevenson) C.; student Westminster Coll., 1945, Colo. Coll., 1948, Emerson Coll., 1949; B.S., Boston U., 1951; student Am. U., 1954-55; m. Marjorie Adair Pollock, Nov. 28, 1958; children—Jefrey, Dwane, Kevin. Relief editor, rep., columnist St. Louis Daily Record, 1950-51; reporter Commerce Clearing House, Washington, 1952; with U.S. News and World Report, 1953-68, regional sales mgr., Los Angeles, 1960-63, marketing mgr., Washington, 1964-68; pub. Nation's Cities Mag., Washington, 1968—; dir. marketing services Nat. League of Cities and U.S. Conf. Mayors, Washington, 1971—. Served with USAAF, 1945-48. Mem. Nat. Press. Club, Am. Marketing Assn., Delta Tau Delta. Presbyn. Home: 5217 Wapakoneta Rd Washington DC 20016 Office: 1620 Eye St NW Washington DC 20006

CHRISTIAN, JOSEPH ROY, banker; b. Tenaha, Tex., June 20, 1927; s. Joe Richard and Irene Elizabeth (Brown) C.; student Tex. Technol. Coll., 1944, N.M. A. and M. Coll., 1944-45; B.S. in Petroleum Engring., La. State U., 1949; m. Mary Delores Dooley, Nov. 16, 1951; children—Randall Allen, Marc Richard. Petroleum engr., div. prodn. geologist Shell Oil Co., Hobbs, N.M. and Odessa, Tex., 1949-57; petroleum engr. DeGolyer & MacNaughton, Dallas, 1957-59; area engr., chief engr. Stekoll Petroleum Corp., Dallas, 1959-61; sr. engr. Colo. Interstate Gas Co., Colorado Springs, 1961-62; petroleum engr. R.F. Kravis Assos., Tulsa, 1962-63; v.p. Oliver & West, Inc., Dallas, 1963-65; sr. v.p., trust officer First Nat. Bank in Dallas, 1965—. Group chmn. Dallas County United Fund, 1970, 71. Served with AUS, 1945-47. Mem. Am. Inst. M.E., Soc. Petroleum Engrs., Ind. Petroleum Assn. Am., Mid-Continent Oil and Gas Assn., Tex. Mid-Continent Oil and Gas Assn., Am. Assn. Petroleum Landmen, West Tex. Geol. Soc., Am. Petroleum Inst., Petroleum Engrs. Toastmaster (pres. White Rock Club 1971-72). Club of Dallas (program com. 1971-72), Engrs. Club of Dallas. Home: 9480 Timberleaf Dr Dallas TX 75231 Office: PO Box 6031 Dallas TX 75222

CHRISTIAN, WAYNE GILLESPIE, geophysicist; b. King City, Mo., Oct. 28, 1918; s. Elza Orval and Maude Amelia (Gillespie) C.; B.S., West Tex. State U., 1939; M.S., U. Denver, 1948, D.Sc. in Edn., 1951; m. Kara Lorraine Groom, Oct. 29, 1943; children—Kara Lo, Karl Wayne. Mus. technician West Tex. State U., 1936-37, hist. geology lab. supr., 1936-39; supr. ground water surveys and mineral survey U.S. Dept. Interior and State Tex., 1937-39; field and lab. supr. paleontol., archaeol. work Plains Hist. Mus., Canyon, Tex., 1939-40; chief computer Western Geophys. Co., Los Angeles, 1940-44; supt. schs. Darlington, Mo., 1943-44; tchr. sci. and social studies, Pickering, Mo., 1944-45; prin. jr.-sr. high sch., Tarkio, Mo., 1945-46; supt. schs., Pickering, 1946-48; grad. teaching fellow, part-time instr. gen. biology U. Denver, 1948-56; dep. dir. Colo. Home Children, Denver, 1951-52; sr. geophysicist Sun Oil Co., Dallas, 1952—. Mem. Met. Council Denver, 1967-69; mem. bd. Denver's War on Poverty, 1967-69; chmn. city-wide Head Start Program, 1968-69. Bd. Home Assn. Colo., 1964-70; pres. Rocky Mountain Bapt. Assn., 1963-70. Chmn. bd. dirs. Curtis Park Community Center, Denver, 1965-70. Mem. Soc. Exploration Geophysicists, Soc. Vertebrate Paleontologists, Dallas Geophys. Soc., Dallas Geol. Soc. Contbr. articles to profl. jours. Home: 3636 Shenandoah St Dallas TX 75205 Office: Sun Oil Co 12850 Hillcrest St Dallas TX 75230

CHRISTIE, DUDLEY BENJAMIN, supt. schs.; b. Parrott, Ga., Jan. 13, 1918; s. Dudley Whaley and Mary (Kirksey) C.; B.S., U. Ga., 1942, M.S., 1943, 6 yr. certificate U. Ga., 1963; m. Hazel Mixon, Aug. 21, 1943; children—Dudley Benjamin, Hugh Allen. Tchr., coach high sch., Ludowici, Ga., 1937-40; prin., coach Washington (Ga.) High Sch., 1943-44; prin. Fitzgerald (Ga.) High Sch., 1944-48; supt. city schs., Eastman, Ga., 1948-51; prin. Griffin (Ga.) High Sch., 1951—; supt. Griffin-Spalding County Schs., 1967—. Mem. Ga. Improvement Council; merit counsellor Flint River council Boy Scouts of Am., 1951-64; v.p. Boys Club, Griffin; treas. Flint River Regional Library, 1967—; mem. Spalding County Bd. Health, 1967. Bd. dirs. State YMCA, 1965, Central West Dist. YMCA, 1966-68; mem. bd. Southeastern Regional Lab. Served with USMC, 1936-37. John Hay fellow U. Ore., 1964. Mem. N.E.A., Ga., Dodge County (past pres.) edn. assns., Am., Ga. assns. sch. adminstrs., Ga. Congress Parents and Tchrs., Nat., Ga. (past pres.) prins. assns., So. Assn. Colls. and Schs. (mem. Ga. com.), Ga. Assn. Sch. Supts. (pres. 1972-73), Ga. Tchr. Edn. Council, Middle Ga. Coll., Ga. Tchrs. Coll. alumni assns., Sigma Nu. Baptist (deacon). Kiwanian (v.p. 1959), Elk. Club: Griffin Country. Home: 621 Forest Av Griffin GA 30223 Office: PO Box 622 Griffin GA 30223

CHRISTMAN, JON DAVID, land devel. exec.; b. Dayton, O., Aug. 15, 1936; s. James E. and Minnie S. (Humphrey) C.; B.A., Wittenberg Coll., 1958; m. Carol Ann Weaver, July 6, 1956; children—Scott, Jennifer, Jeffrey, Tamera, Teresa, Jill. Personnel mgr. McCall Printing Co., 1959-61, dir. customer service, 1961-69; pres. Foote & Davies, Doraville, Ga., 1969-73, Shenandoah Devel., Inc., 1973—; v.p., dir. McCall Printing Co. Chmn. indsl. com. United Appeal, Dayton, O., 1968. Mem. DeKalb C. of C. (dir. 1970-71, v.p. 1972), Pi Kappa Alpha. Republican. Lutheran. Mason. Clubs: Commerce, Athletic (Atlanta). Home: 5384 Pheasant Run Stone Mountain GA 30083 Office: 3240 Whipple St Atlanta GA 30354

CHRISTMAS, JOSEPH THEODORE, physician; b. Vienna, Ga., Jan. 9, 1923; s. George B. and Edye Mae (Sangster) C.; student Ga. Southwestern Coll., 1939-41; B.S. in Agr., U. Ga., 1943, postgrad., 1949-50; M.D., Med. Coll. Ga., 1954; m. Lucy Farris Smith, Apr. 7, 1944; children—Karen Sue, Timothy Lane. Tchr. vocational agr. Americus (Ga.) High Sch., 1943-44; county agrl. extension agt., Lanier County, Ga., 1946-49; intern Macon Hosp., 1954-55; gen. practice medicine, Vienna, Ga., 1955—; mem. staff Dooly Med. Center, Vienna, Crisp County Hosp., Cordele, Ga. Chmn., Dooly County Bd. Edn., 1959-69. Bd. dirs. Ga. Med. Care Found. Served with USNR, 1944-45; PTO. Mem. Ga. Acad. Gen. Practice (dir. 1969—), Med. Assn. Ga. (dist. councilor 1968—), Flint Med. Soc., Am., Ga. Holstein-Fresian assns., Alpha Omega Alpha. Baptist (deacon 1966-69). Lion. Address: PO Box 247 Vienna GA 31092

CHRISTOPHER, WILFORD SCOTT, assn. exec.; b. Enid, Okla., Feb. 8, 1916; s. W. Scott and Mary Elizabeth (Heaton) C.; B.A., Phillips U., 1938; M.A., U. Ia., 1941; m. Marjorie Lois Lester, Dec. 30, 1941; 1 son, Scott Douglas. Asst. prof. speech Phillips U., 1939, asso. prof. sociology, 1940-42; pub. relations dir. Miami (Fla.) C. of C., 1946-51; gen. mgr. Greater Tampa C. of C., 1951-64, exec. v.p. 1964—. Chmn. Nat. Adv. Council Urban Devel., 1959-60; mem. adv. council U. Tampa, 1966-69; mem. tech.-occupation adv. com. Hillsborough Jr. Coll., 1969—, chmn. advanced mgmt. curriculum com., 1958-59; mem. Adv. Group on Continuing Edn. for Urban Leadership, 1967-68. Bd. dirs. Tampa Philharmonic Orch. Assn., Tampa Oral Sch. for Deaf. Trustee U. South Fla. Found., 1959-65; trustee Berkeley Prep. Sch., 1963, v.p., 1965—. Named Tampa Citizen of the Year, 1972, Reid Humanitarian of Year award, 1973. Mem. Fla. C. of C. Execs. Assn. (pres. 1954), Southeastern Inst. C. of C. Execs. (pres. 1956), So. Assn. C. of C. Execs. (pres. 1972), Inst. Orgn. Mgmt. (bd. regents), Am. C. of C. Execs. (sec.-treas., v.p. 1960, pres. 1961-62, chmn. nat. panel on exec. certification 1966). Clubs: Tampa Exchange (pres. 1955), Executive (past pres.), University (dir.), Tampa Yacht and Country; Ye Mystic Kreme of Gasparilla. Contbr. to Chamber of Commerce Administration. Home: 10701 Carrollwood Dr Tampa FL 33618 Office: 801 E John F Kennedy Blvd Tampa FL 33601

CHRISTOPHERSON, MERRETH EUGENE, sales co. exec.; b. Canton, S.D., Apr. 5, 1926; s. Ole C. and Annie Sabina (Swanson) C.; B.S., S.D. State U., 1947; M.S., Kan. State U., 1951; m. Marian Kathryn Schaeffer, Nov. 23, 1946; children—Mary Pamela, Paige Ann, Janet Kay. Athletic dir., coach, tchr. South Sioux City, Neb.

1947-55; ins. rep., mgr. N.Y. Life Ins. Co., Mankato, Minn., 1955-63; v.p., marketing mgr. Kayot, Inc., Mankato, 1963-69; pres. C & S Sales Co., Inc., Easley, S.C., 1969—. Councilman, Mankato, 1962-64; mem. exec. com. Blue Earth County, Minn., 1964-69. Served with USNR, 1943-45. Mem. Boating Industry Assn. (mem. govt. relations com. 1965—), Am. Legion, Am. Marketing Assn., Phi Kappa Phi, Phi Epsilon Kappa. Republican. Presbyn. (elder, trustee, deacon). Mason, Rotarian (dir. Easley 1970, 73). Club: Pickens (S.C.) County Country. Home: Old Stagecoach Rd Easley SC 29640 Office: 149 Cumberland Av Easley SC 29640

CHUBB, GEORGE HENRY, steel co. exec.; b. Prides Crossing, Mass., Aug. 15, 1912; s. George Henry and Sigrid (Malgren) C.; B.S., U. Miami, 1937; m. Marion Leachman, Feb. 22, 1965; children—Barbara Louise, Heather Merrill. With Carnegie-Ill. Steel Co., Pitts., 1939; with Republic Steel Corp., Cleve., 1947-58; with Jessop Steel and Green River Steel Corp., Owensboro, Ky., 1958—, v.p. sales 1969—. Dir. Harbor Mfg. Co. Served with RCAF, 1940-42, USMC, 1942-46. Mem. Am. Iron and Steel Inst., Am. Ordnance Assn., Nat. Sales and Marketing Execs. Club, Am. Inst. Aeros. and Astronautics, Nat. Steeplechase and Hunt Assn., Am. Horse Shows Assn. (sr. judge 1947), Midwest Hunt Racing Assn. (dir. 1962), Ky. Hunter and Jumper Assn., Pa. Thoroughbred Breeder Assn., Forging Industry Assn., Open Die Forging Inst., Gamma Delta Psi, Sigma Chi. Episcopalian. Clubs: University (Cleve.); Cornell (N.Y.C.); Muncie (Ind.); Thoroughbred Club of Am. (Lexington, Ky.); Campbell Owensboro Country (Owensboro); Creve Coeur (Peoria, Ill.). Home: 1411 Marycrest Dr Owensboro KY 42301 Office: Hwy E 60 Owensboro KY 42301

CHUCULATE, RICHARD WOODROW, social worker; b. Sallisaw, Okla., Apr. 16, 1913; s. Isaac and Nellie (Christie) C.; B.A., U. Chgo., 1942; M.S.W., U. Okla., 1957; m. Ada Maxine Breuninger, Nov. 18, 1938; children—Richard William, Max James. Asst. community worker Bur. Indian Affairs, Rosebud, S.D., 1936-42, ednl. field agt., Harlem, Mont., 1942-43; timekeeper Engring. Labs., Inc., Tulsa, 1943-44; caseworker Dept. Pub. Welfare, Sallisaw, 1944-52, dist. child welfare supr., 1957-72, social service rep., 1967-72; project dir. Cherokee social work Sch. Social Work, U. Okla., Norman, 1972—; community worker Cherokee Indian Found., Bartlesville, Okla., 1952-55. Mem. exec. com. Cherokee Nation of Okla., 1958—; Indian adv. com. mem. Bd. Nat. Missions of U.P. Ch. Am., 1962—; chmn. Sequoyah County March of Dimes; mem. Sequoyah County Selective Service Bd.; trustee Sequoyah County Devel. Found. Mem. Nat. Assn. Social Workers Presbyn. (elder). Mason; mem. Order Eastern Star. Home: 419 Poplar Pl Sallisaw OK 74955

CHURCH, ARCHER EDWARD, JR., naval officer; b. Bradford, Pa., Apr. 23, 1929; s. Archer Edward and Berta Marie (Unger) C.; B.S., U.S. Naval Acad., 1951; B.Civil Engring., Rensselaer Poly. Inst., 1955; M.S., Princeton, 1962; m. Marie Lucy Ciampitti, June 27, 1970. Commd. ensign U.S. Navy, Civil Engr. Corps, 1951, advanced through grades to comdr., 1965; asst. dir. engring. Navy facilities, Southeastern U.S., 1962-63; asst. pub. works officer Pensacola Naval Air Sta., 1963-65; constrn. program mgr. mil. assistance, Vietnam, 1965-66; asst. dist. civil engr., 4th Naval Dist., 1966-67; chief civil engr. U.S. facilities, Antarctica, 1967-70; spl. asst. for contracts Naval Ship Systems Command Hdqrs., Washington, 1970—. Decorated Bronze Star medal, Air medal. Registered profl. engr., Ala. Mem. Am. Soc. C.E., Soc. Am. Mil. Engrs., Tau Beta Pi, Chi Epsilon. Episcopalian. Author: (with G. Breese et al) The Impact of Large Installations on Nearby Areas, 1965. Home: 332 M St S W Washington DC 20024 Office: NAVSHIPSYSCOM HQ Code 70C Washington DC 20360

CHURCH, GORDON EDWARD, savs. and loan exec.; b. Kansas City, Mo., Oct. 24, 1928; s. Ernest Edward and Mabel Price (Majors) C.; student Kansas City Jr. Coll., 1946-47, 49-50, U. Mo., 1957-60; m. Carolyn Joyce Manning, Dec. 21, 1956; 1 dau., Susan Elaine. Accountant Safety Fed. Savs., Kansas City, Mo., 1947-50, Forum Cafeterias, Kansas City, 1951-52; accountant Safety Fed. Savs., Kansas City, 1952-55, br. mgr., 1958-59; savs. and loan commr. State Mo., Jefferson City, 1960-63; v.p. Fed. Home Loan Bank, Little Rock, 1964-68; pres. Meridian (Miss.) Fed. Savs. & Loan, 1969—. Mem. Fed. Savs. & Loan Adv. Council, Washington, 1963. Bd. dirs. Salvation Army, Meridian, 1970-73, chmn., 1973; dir. United Fund, Meridian, 1970-73, campaign chmn., 1972, budget chmn., 1973. Served with AUS, 1955-57. Mem. Nat. Assn. State Savs. and Loan Commrs. (sec., treas. 1962-63), Miss. Savs. and Loan League (v.p. 1973, mem. exec. com. 1972-73), Meridian C. of C. Rotarian. Clubs: Downtown, Northwood Country (Meridian). Home: 5313 17th Av Meridian MS 39301 Office: 905 23d Av Meridian MS 39301

CHURCH, ROBERTA, govt. ofcl.; d. Robert R. and Sara (Johnson) Church; A.B., Northwestern U., 1935, M.A., 1937. Social worker Family and Child Welfare div. Chgo. Welfare Adminstrn., 1940-43, adoption div. Ill. Children's Home and Aid Soc., Chgo., 1943-53; cons. for minority groups U.S. Dept. Labor, 1953-61; cons. Rehab. Services Adminstrn., U.S. Dept. Health, Edn. and Welfare, 1961—. Mem. Pres.'s Nat. Adv. Council on Adult Edn., 1970—; mem. Rep. State Exec. Com. Tenn., 1952-53. Recipient Certificate of Merit, Alpha Phi Alpha, 1956. Mem. Nat. Assn. Social Workers, Delta Sigma Theta. Republican. Episcopalian. Home: 1629 Columbia Rd NW Washington DC 20009 Office: US Dept Health Edn and Welfare Washington DC 20201

CHURCHILL, DARRELL OLIVER, oil co. exec.; b. Pipestone, Minn., Jan. 6, 1917; s. Ernest L.M. and Parthenia (Patterson) C.; LL.B. cum laude, U. Omaha, 1938; J.D. cum laude, U. Neb. at Omaha, 1969; m. Velma Caroline Bell, Nov. 6, 1949; children—John O., James E. Admitted to Neb. bar, 1938, Cal. bar, 1950; stenographer legal and claims dept. Woodmen of World Life Ins. Soc., 1934-37, Interstate Transit Lines, Omaha, 1937-38; sec. to gen. claim agt. Union Pacific R.R. Co., Omaha, 1938-39, sec. to gen. atty., 1939-40, sec. to Western gen. counsel, 1940-41, sec. to pres., 1941-42, 46-49, asst. spl. counsel, devel. 1949-56, gen. atty., Los Angeles, 1956-58, asst. to v.p. oil dept., 1958-61, asst. to chief exec. officer natural resources div., 1961-66, asst. sec., 1965-72, gen. mgr. mineral lands and contracts natural resources div., 1966-71; v.p. land and leasing Champlin Petroleum Co., Ft. Worth, 1971-73, v.p. domestic land, 1973—; dir. Uinta Devel. Co.; sec. Calnev Pipe Line Co., 1967-70, 71—, Union Pacific Resources Ltd., Calgary, Alta., Can., 1968—; asst. sec. Union Pacific Resources Corp., 1969—. Exec. asst. to rubber dir. WPB, Washington, 1942-43. Served with AUS, 1943-46; PTO. Mem. Rocky Moutain Oil and Gas Assn. (dir., mem. exec. com. 1971—, vice chmn. pub. lands com. 1969-71, chmn. pub. lands com. 1971-73), Western Oil and Gas Assn. (mem. pub. lands com., 1968-70), Am., Ft. Worth, Denver assns. petroleum landmen, Cal., Neb. bar assns. Clubs: Ridglea Country Petroleum (Ft. Worth). Home: 6929 Serrano Dr Fort Worth TX 76126 Office: 5301 Camp Bowie Blvd Fort Worth TX 76107

CHYTIL, FRANK, educator; b. Prague, Czechoslovakia, Aug. 28, 1924; s. Frantisek and Ruzena (Vitouskova) C.; M.S., Sch. Chem. Tech., Prague, 1949, Ph.D., 1952; C.Sc., Czechoslovak Acad. Sci., Prague, 1956; m. Lucie Scheinost, Nov. 26, 1949; children—Frank, Anna, Helena. Came to U.S., 1965, naturalized, 1971. Research biochemist Charles U., Prague, Czechslovakia, 1949-51; research fellow Inst. Human Research, Prague, 1952-63; sr. scientist Czechoslovakia Acad. Sci., Prague, 1956-64; sr. research fellow Brandeis U., Waltham, Mass., 1964—, sr. research asso., 1965-66; head sect. enzymology S.W. Found. Research and Edn., San Antonio, 1966-69; mem. faculty Vanderbilt U., Nashville, 1969—, asso. prof. biochemistry, 1972—. Adj. asso. prof. U. Tex., San Antonio, 1968-69. Served with Czechoslovakian Army, 1952-56. USPHS grantee, 1967—. Mem. Am. Chem. Soc., Am. Soc. Biol. Chemists, Am. Inst. Nutrition, Endocrine Soc., Am. Assn. U. Profs., Sigma Xi. Contbr. to profl. jours., books. Home: 914 Lynnwood Blvd Nashville TN 37205

CICIO, ANTHONY LEE, lawyer; b. Birmingham, Ala., July 8, 1926; s. Joseph and Rosa Tom (Burello) C.; B.S., Samford U., 1951; student U. Ala., 1952; LL.B., Birmingham Sch. Law, 1955; m. Yvonne Antonio, Nov. 4, 1959; children—Valerie, Anthony Lee, Mark. Admitted to Ala. bar, 1956; individual practice law, Birmingham, 1959—; partner firm Cicio & Winston. Mem. Democratic Com., Birmingham, 1960—. Served with USAAF, 1944-46. Mem. Birmingham, Ala., Am. bar assns., Am. Trial Lawyers Assn., Pi Kappa Alpha, Sigma Delta Kappa. Roman Catholic. Clubs: Roma Country, The Club (Birmingham); Mountain Brook Swim and Tennis. Home: 3128 N Woodridge Rd Birmingham AL 35223 Office: 1316 2121 Bldg Birmingham AL 35203

CIMIJOTTI, LEW F., architect; b. Mason City, Ia., May 18, 1931; s. Leo M. and Mary E. (Pedelty) C.; A.A., Mason City Jr. Coll., 1951; B.S., Ia. State U., 1958; m. Patricia J. Kennedy, Sept. 17, 1956; children—Mark Trenton, Bruce Trenton, Laura Denise (dec.). Practice architecture, Chgo., 1960-65, Fairborn, O., 1965-68; with Dept. Housing and Urban Devel., 1968—. Prodn. mgr. Space Jour. mag., Huntsville, Ala., 1958. Served with AUS, 1956-58. Recipient Lincoln Arc Welding Found. award, 1958. Mem. Ill. Soc. Architects, Am. Registered Architects, A.I.A., Toastmasters Internat. Home: 963 Parkridge Circle W Jacksonville FL 32211

CIRIACKS, KENNETH W., geologist; b. West Bend, Wis., May 7, 1938; s. Edwin Fred and Diana Melida (Oelke) C.; B.S., U. Wis., 1958; Ph.D., Columbia, 1962; m. Betty Joyce Bryant, July 17, 1965; children—Nicole Rene, Jennifer Diane. Geologist, Pan Am. Petroleum Corp (co. name change to Amoco Prodn. Co. 1971), Calgary, Alta., Can., 1962-63, research scientist, Tulsa, 1963-72, project geologist, Houston, 1972-73, dist. geologist, 1973—. NSF fellow, 1960, 62. Mem. Geol. Soc. Am., Paleontol. Soc., Houston Geol. Soc., Soc. Econ. Paleontologists and Mineralogists, Paleontol. Assn., Alpha Tau Omega. Home: 406 Riverforest Ct Houston TX 77024 Office: PO Box 3092 Houston TX 77001

CITTY, JIM CHARLES, physician; b. Idabel, Okla., May 24, 1939; s. Lester and Odell Mattie (Green) C.; B.S., Harding Coll., 1961; M.D., U. Tenn., 1965; m. Maralyn Bailey, June 9, 1961; children—Kelee, Kent, Kris, Kyle. Intern William Beaumont Gen. Hosp., El Paso, Tex., 1965-66; resident Brooke Army Med. Center, San Antonio, 1966-68; pvt. practice medicine specializing in family practice, De Queen, Ark., 1968—; mem. staff DeQueen Gen. Hosp. Instr. Med. Field Service Sch., San Antonio, 1966-68. Mem. bd. Sevier County Airport Commn., 1970—; bd. dirs. City De Queen, Ark., 1972—; mem. president's devel. council Harding Coll., Searcy, Ark., 1972—. Served with M.C., AUS, 1965-68. Mem. A.M.A., Am. Acad. Family Practice, Ark. Med. Soc., Phi Rho Sigma. Mem. Ch. of Christ (lay minister 1961—). Lion. Home: 707 N 12th St De Queen AR 71832 Office: Hwy 70 By-Pass De Queen AR 71832

CLAGETT, BRICE MCADOO, lawyer; b. Washington, July 6, 1933; s. Brice and Sarah Fleming (McAdoo) C.; A.B. summa cum laude, Princeton, 1954; postgrad. (Rotary Internat. fellow), U. Allahabad, India, 1954-55; J.D. magna cum laude, Harvard, 1958; m. Virginia Lawrence Parker, Sept. 18, 1965; children—John Fitzhugh de Treville, Ann Calvert Brooke. Research asst. in history Princeton, 1952-53; tutor in history St. Albans Sch., 1956, 57, mem. bd. freshmen advisers and teaching fellow, 1957-58; admitted to D.C. bar, 1958; asso. firm Covington & Burling, Washington, 1958-67, partner, 1967—. Juridical counsellor Cambodian delegation to Internat. Ct. of Justice, 1960-62. Trustee Md. Hist. Trust, chmn., 1972—, Md. State House Trust, Clagett Sch., Inc. Decorated comdr. Royal Order of Cambodia; recipient Bishop Satterlee medal, 1950, Lawrence Hutton prize in history, 1954. Mem. Internat. Law Assn., Washington Inst. Fgn. Affairs, Am. Soc. Internat. Law, Sons Confederate Vets., Soc. Cincinnati Md., Am. Bar Assn., Phi Beta Kappa. Episcopalian. Clubs: Princeton, Metropolitan (Washington); Harvard (N.Y.). Bd. editors Harvard Law Rev., 1956-58. Contbr. articles to legal and hist. jours. Home: Holly Hill Friendship MD 20758 Office: 888 16th St NW Washington DC 20006

CLAIN-STEFANELLI, VLADIMIR, museum curator; b. Czernowitz, Austria, Jan. 2, 1914; s. Wilhelm Klein and Theodora Stefanelli; M.A., U. Carol II, 1936, Ph.D., 1938; m. Elvira Eliza Olinescu, Dec. 29, 1938; 1 son, Alexander. Came to U.S., 1951, naturalized, 1956. Librarian, Seminar for South-East European History, 1932-37; asst. Seminar Greek and Roman Epigraphy, in charge coin collections Carol II U., Cernauti-Czernowitz, 1936-38; asst. in temporary charge excavations at Mangalia, 1936-37; museum asst. Museul Regele Carol II, 1937-38; charge Greek Coin Corpus, Prussian Acad. Scis., 1939; cons. coins and medals, firms in Rome and N.Y.C., 1949-56; curator div. numismatics U.S. Nat. Mus., Smithsonian Instn., 1956—. Adviser on status gold coins Dept. Treasury. Recipient Prix de Rome, 1939-40, Exceptional Service Gold medal Smithsonian Inst., 1973. Fellow Am. Numis. Soc., Royal Numis. Soc. (London); mem. Am. Numis. Assn. (hon. life mem., curator), Internat. Bank Note Soc., Washington, Md., N.Y., Ga. numis. socs., Archeol. Inst. Am. (gov., past pres. Washington), Internat. Inst. Conservation Historic and Artistic Works, Bavarian, Austrian, French numis. socs. Author: History of the National Numismatic Collections, 1968. Contbr. papers on numismatics to tech. lit. Home: 2608 N Nelson St Arlington VA 22207 Office: Smithsonian Institution Washington DC 20560

CLAIRE, WILLIAM FRANCIS, editor; b. Northampton, Mass., Oct. 4, 1935; s. William Cahill and Vena Marie (Lasonde) C.; B.A., Columbia, 1958. Legislative asst. U.S. Rep. Silvio O. Conte, 1961-63; dir. govt. relations Am. Paper Inst., 1963-68; exec. dir. World Federalists U.S.A., 1968-71; dir. Washington office State U. N.Y., 1971—; editor, pub. Voyages, 1967—. Trustee, Internat. Devel. Corp., 1968-69; exec. bd. Coalition on Nat. Priorities, 1968-69. Chmn. Columbia Students for Stevenson, 1956; state coordinator Humphrey-Muskie U.S. presdl. campaign, 1968. Served with AUS, 1958-59. Recipient Ernie Pyle award Pacific Stars and Stripes, 1959; Editors award Nat. Found. Arts and Humanities, 1970. Mem. Friends of Kennedy Center, Friends of Folger Library. Clubs: National Press, International (Washington). Contbr. articles, poems, essays and revs. tech. lit. Home: 2101 Connecticut Av NW Washington DC 20008 Office: State Univ New York Island Av NW Washington DC 20036

CLAPP, ALLEN LINVILLE, cons. engr.; b. Raleigh, N.C., Oct. 8, 1943; s. Byron Siler and Alene (Linville) C.; B.S., N.C. State U., 1967, M. Econs., 1973; m. Anne Stuart Calvert, Dec. 18, 1966. Asst. engr. Booth-Jones & Assos. Inc., Raleigh, N.C., 1964-67; elec. engr., asst. research U.S. Army, Picatinny Arsenal, Dover, N.J., 1967-69; cons. engr. Booth-Jones & Assos., Raleigh, 1969-71; utilities engr. N.C. Utilities Commn., Raleigh, 1971—, now chief econ. analysis sect. engring. div.; pvt. cons. practice, Raleigh, 1971—. Served with AUS, 1967-69. Registered profl. engr., N.J., N.C. Mem. Nat. Soc. Profl. Engrs., Profl. Engrs. N.C., Am., So. econs. assns., Am. Statis. Assn., Am. Finance Assn., Soc. Govt. Economists, Ecometric Soc. Home: 3206 Queens Rd Raleigh NC 27612 Office: Box 991 Raleigh NC 27602

CLAPP, NEAL KEITH, exptl. pathologist, clergyman; b. Waldron, Ind., Oct. 14, 1928; s. Worrill Groven and Dora M. (Hurst) C.; B.S., Purdue U., 1950; D.V.M., Ohio State U., 1960; M.S., Colo. State U., 1962, Ph.D., 1964; m. Dorothy Louise Stockwell, Dec. 19, 1953; children—Cheryl Lynne, Mark Allen, Stephen Neal. Faculty, Colo. State U. Coll. Vet. Medicine, 1961, NIH postdoctoral fellow radiation biology, 1961-64; exptl. pathologist biology div. Oak Ridge Nat. Lab., 1964—, cons. biology div. Union Carbide Corp. at lab., 1968—; tchr. comparative pathology U. Tenn., 1967—. Ordained to ministry Christian Ch., 1966; pastor Clinton (Tenn.) Christian Ch., 1972—. Coach local Little League Baseball. Served with USAF, 1951-55. Mem. Am. Vet. Med. Assn., Am. Assn. Cancer Research, Radiation Research Soc., N.Y. Acad. Scis., Sigma Xi, Phi Zeta, Omega Tau Sigma. Republican. Author: An Atlas of RF Mouse Pathology: Disease Descriptions and Incidences, 1973. Contbr. articles to profl. jours. Home: 404 Hicks Circle Clinton TN 37716 Office: Biology Div PO Box Y Oak Ridge TN 37830

CLAPPER, THOMAS WAYNE, chem. co. exec.; b. Middleboro, Pa., Oct. 15, 1915; s. Thomas H. and Magdalene Ann (Sterrett) C.; student Gannon Coll., 1933-35; B.S., St. Vincent Coll., 1937; M.S., Pa. State U., 1940, Ph.D., 1942; m. Anne M. Anderson, Aug. 2, 1941; children—Thomas H., Robert A., Andrea M. Research chemist Calco Chem. div. Am. Cyanamid Corp., Bound Brook, N.J., 1940-44, asst. chief chemist pharm. div., 1944-45, chief chemist, 1945-48, prodn. mgr., 1948-50, prodn. mgr., 1950-51, tech. dir. Atomic Energy div., Idaho Falls, Ida., 1951-52, gen. supt., 1952-53, asst. gen. mgr., 1953-54; plant mgr. Calera Mining Co., Chem. Constrn. Corp., cobalt refinery, Garfield, Utah, 1954-56; mgr. research Am. Potash and Chem. Corp., Henderson, Neb., 1956-63, dir. research, Whittier, Cal., 1963-68; dir. research Kerr-McGee Corp., Oklahoma City, 1968—. Mem. Am. Chem. Soc., Indsl. Research Inst., Electrochem. Soc., Sigma Xi, Alpha Chi Sigma. Elk. Patentee in field. Contbr. articles to profl. pubs. Home: 12104 Camelot Place Oklahoma City OK 73120 Office: Kerr McGee Technical Center PO Box 25861 Oklahoma City OK 73125

CLARE, MICHAEL JAMES, lawyer; b. Louisville, Dec. 22, 1920; s. James John and Hannah (Guider) C.; student Morehead State Coll., 1946; LL.B., U. Ky., 1950; m. Mary Helen French, June 13, 1953 (dec. Jan. 1968); children—Michael, Mary Helen, Teresa Lynn, James Gregory, Cynthia Anne, Brian Edward, Stephen Thomas. Admitted to Ky. bar, 1950; trial atty., office chief counsel Internal Revenue Service, U.S. Treasury Dept., Cin., Cleve., 1951-54; practiced in Louisville, 1954—; instr. bus. law Bellarmine Coll., 1955-59. Mem. Jefferson County (Ky.) Registration and Purgation Bd., 1956-60, chmn., 1961-69. Served with AUS, 1943-46. Decorated Bronze Star medal with oak leaf cluster. Mem. Am., Fed. (pres. Louisville 1961-62), Ky., Louisville bar assns., Am. Legion, Phi Alpha Delta. Roman Catholic. Lion, K.C. Home: 33 Hill Rd Louisville KY 40204 Office: Ky Home Life Bldg Louisville KY 40202

CLARK, ARTHUR BARNETT, JR., judge; b. Indianola, Miss., Oct. 19, 1920; s. Arthur B. and Ada (Neill) C.; B.A., U. Miss., 1942; postgrad. U. Ala., 1945; LL.B., Harvard, 1948; m. Dollie Hughes, June 16, 1943; 1 son, Arthur Barnett III. Admitted to Miss. bar, 1948; mem. firm Neill, Clark & Townsend, Indianola, 1948-58; judge 4th Circuit Ct. Dist. of Miss., Indianola, 1959—. Bd. dirs. Delta area council Boy Scouts Am. Served to 1st lt., inf., AUS, 1942-45; ETO. Decorated Purple Heart with 2 oak leaf clusters. Mem. Am., Miss., Sunflower County (past pres.) bar assns., Am. Legion, Vets. Fgn. Wars. Democrat. Episcopalian. Rotarian (past pres. Indianola). Home: W Augusta St Indianola MS 38751 Office: Courthouse Indianola MS 38751

CLARK, ARTHUR WATTS, life ins. co. exec.; b. Seattle, Nov. 28, 1922; s. Irving Marshall and Nell Snowden (Watts) C.; A.B., U. N.C., 1943; M.A., U. Cal. at Berkeley, 1948; postgrad. U. N.C., 1960; m. Mary Dick Cannon, Nov. 21, 1942; children—Arthur Watts, Claiborne Marshall, Johnston Jewell. With Home Security Life Ins. Co., Durham, N.C., 1948—, dir. planning, 1952-59, v.p., 1959-64, exec. v.p., 1964-67, pres., 1967—, chmn. finance com., 1967—, also dir.; dir., chmn. bd. Home Security Broadcasting Co.; mem. exec. com., finance com., dir. Capital Holding Corp. Treas., mem. exec. com. Research Triangle Regional Planning Commn., 1959-67; mem. N.C. Health Ins. Adv. Bd., 1966-70. Served with USAF, 1942-46, 50-52; maj. gen. Res. Mem. Nat. Assn. Flight Instrs., Pres.'s Assn., Am. Mgmt. Assn., Life Office Mgmt. Assn. (dir. life insurers' conf.), Am. Life Ins. Assn. (dir.), Phi Beta Kappa, Sigma Xi. Presbyn. (elder 1964-69, 72—). Home: 3540 Rugby Rd Durham NC 27707 Office: Box 61 Durham NC 27702

CLARK, BILLY PAT, physicist; b. Bartlesville, Okla., May 15, 1939; s. Lloyd A. and Ruby Laura (Holcomb) C.; B.S., Okla. State U., 1961, M.S., 1964; Ph.D., 1968. Postdoctoral research fellow dept. theoretical physics U. Warwick, Coventry, Eng., 1968-69; sr. mem. tech. staff Booz-Allen Applied Research, 1969-70; sr. mem. tech. staff field services div. Computer Scis. Corp., Leavenworth, Kan., 1970—. Grad. asst. dept. physics Okla. State U., 1961-68. Recipient undergrad. scholarships Phillips Petroleum Co., 1957-61, Am. Legion, 1957-58, Okla. State U., 1957-58. Mem. Am. Phys. Soc., A.A.A.S., N.Y. Acad. Scis., Pi Mu Epsilon, Sigma Pi Sigma. Clubs: Victory Hills Golf and Country (Kansas City, Kan.). Home: 502 S Hamilton St Dewey OK 74029

CLARK, CECIL WILLIAM, physician; b. Natchitoches, La., June 7, 1924; s. Cecil William and Elizabeth Virginia (Jones) C.; B.S., Northwestern State Coll., 1948; M.D., La. State U., 1951; m. Sybil Ruth Baccigaloni, Nov. 1, 1947; children—John David, Cecil Joseph, Elizabeth Dianne, Celia Marie, Jack Benjamin, Cecil William III, Jennings Patrick, Mary Elise, Paul Benjamin. Intern Touro Infirmary, 1951-52; gen. practice medicine, Cameron, La., 1952—; mem. La. State Hosp. Bd.; sec.-treas. bd. South Cameron Hosp., 1959-61; pub. health officer Cameron Parish, 1960-62; chief of staff South Cameron Meml. Hosp., 1964-73; coroner Cameron Parish, 1964-72; USPHS physician, 1969-72. Mem. council nursing Edn. McNeese State Coll., 1954-56. Served to sgt., AUS, 1946-47. Recipient humanitarian award B'nai B'rith, 1958; named gen. practitioner of the year A.M.A., 1957, outstanding gen. practitioner La. Med. Soc., 1957, Lion of the year, 1962; recipient award for distinguished achievement Jour. Modern Medicine, 1958, distinguished service award U.S. Jr. C. of C., 1957, distinguished intern-resident alumni award Touro Infirmary, 1958, certificate of merit V.F.W., 1958. Mem. A.M.A., La., Calcasieu med. socs., So., Indsl. med. assns., Am. Acad. Gen. Practice, Am. Legion, V.F.W., Alpha Kappa Kappa, Phi Kappa Nu. Democrat. Home: PO Box 411 Cameron LA 70631 Office: PO Box 400 Cameron LA 70631

CLARK, CHARLES ALPHA, accountant, rancher; b. Thurber, Tex., Dec. 4, 1914; s. Alpha V. and Sue Isobelle (Brumley) C.; B.B.A., Tex. Technol. U., 1938; m. Rose B. Hart, Jan. 21, 1949; children—Jeannette (Mrs. Robert Gorman), Charles Alpha, Diana. Accountant, Reynolds Mfg. Co., Cisco, Tex., 1938-40; v.p. Reynolds Oil Co., Cisco, 1940-51; rancher, Eastland County, 1952—; C.P.A., Cisco, 1957—. Dir. Sawyers Oil Co., Cisco, Low Drilling Co., Cisco; sec., treas., dir. Desert Water Supply Corp., Eastland, 1973—. C.P.A., Tex. Mem. Cisco C. of C. (pres. 1972-73), Tex. Soc. C.P.A.'s. Mason (master 1945-46), Lion. Club: Country (Cisco dir., sec., treas. 1971—). Home: Hwy 80 E 7 Miles Cisco TX 76437 Office: 700 Av DD PO Box 752 Cisco TX 76437

CLARK, CHARLES FRANKLIN, supt. schs.; b. Van Lear, Ky., Jan. 1, 1913; s. John Brown and Campbell (Chadwick) C.; B.A., U. Ky., 1938, M.A., 1952; m. Annis Conley, Dec. 29, 1938; children—Jon Darrol, Michael Chadwick. Tchr. English and social studies, 1938-42; prin. Garrett (Ky.) High Sch., 1946-60; supt. Floyd County (Ky.) Schs., 1960—. Chmn. region II Regional Orgn. Promotion Ednl. Services; mem. Floyd County Library Bd., Big Sandy Area Devel. Bd. Mem. Nat., Ky. assns. schs. adminstrs. Home: Garrett KY 41630 Office: care Supt of Schs Prestonsburg KY 41653

CLARK, CHARLES M(ARVIN), psychologist; b. Johnstown, O., Nov. 25, 1927; s. Floyd Monroe and Josephine (Willard) C.; B.A., U. Akron, 1951, M.A., 1956; Ph.D., Ohio State U., 1960; m. Mary Jane Koury, Nov. 22, 1951; children—Cheryl L., Mark C., Christopher S. Coordinator child study and guidance Pub. Schs., Marion, O., 1955-58; instr., counseling psychologist Ohio State U., Columbus, 1958-60; asst. prof. U. Tex., 1960-65; asso. prof. Cal. State Coll. at Hayward, Cal., 1965-67; dir. psychology and assessment Corpus Christi (Tex.) Ind. Sch. Dist., 1967-72; pvt. practice psychology, 1972—. Cons. prof. U. Corpus Christi, 1970; dir. Inst. Child Devel., 1970. Served with AUS, 1951-52. Diplomate in sch. pscyhology Am. Bd. Profl. Psychology. Mem. Am. Psychol. Assn., Am. Personnel and Guidance Assn., Am. Group Psychotherapy Assn., Am. Ednl. Research Assn., A.A.A.S., Tex. Psychol. Assn. (pres. div. sch. psychology 1970), Phi Delta Theta, Phi Delta Kappa. Episcopalian. Mason. Home: 710 Burkshire Corpus Christi TX 78412 Office: 1202 Third St Corpus Christi TX 78404

CLARK, CLINTON COX, educator, clergyman; b. Oxford, N.C., May 2, 1924; s. Samuel Marsh and Bessie (Moore) C.; A.A., Pfeiffer Coll., 1945; A.B., Catawba Coll., 1947; B.D., Ref. Episcopal Sem., 1951; M.A., Western Carolina U., 1963; D. Christian Edn. (hon.) Geneva Theol. Coll., 1968; m. Lois Louise Hamrick, July 16, 1949; children—Stephen Goodwin, Anelia Beth, Samuel Arboth, Priscilla Lois, Timothy Clinton. Ordained to ministry Presbyn. Ch., 1948; pastor various chs., 1953, 57-58, 67-68; tchr. various schs., 1953-66; prin. Galilean Christian Sch., Yalaha, Fla., 1955-57, Christian Sch. of Germantown, Phila., 1963-65, Broad River Christian Sch., Mooresboro, N.C., 1966-68, Christian High Sch., Charlotte 1968-69, Gibbon-Sherrill Christian Acad., Charlotte, 1969-70; pastor Bible Presbyn. ch., Edmonton, Alta., Can., 1970-72; mem. faculty Edmonton Christian schs., 1970-72; adminstrv. asst. to pres. East Coast U., Dade City, Fla., 1972-73. Sec. bd. Am. Assn. Christian Schs., 1958—; v.p. Voice of the Unborn, 1972—. Fellow Am. Geog. Soc.; mem. Philos Soc. Eng. (asso.), Eastern (sec. 1962-63), Mid-Atlantic (dir. 1964-65), Southeastern Christian tchrs. assns., Assn. Christian Educators, Nat. Union Christian Schs., N.C. Christian Educators Assn. (treas. 1969-70), Am. Accrediting Assn. Coll. and Secondary Schs. (steering com. 1969-70), Sons of Temperance. Home: PO Box 146 Mooresboro NC 28114 also 3646 110th Av Edmonton AB Canada

CLARK, DENNIS ALLEN, mining engr.; b. Chgo., June 5, 1940; s. Joseph Patrick and Theresa Cathryn (Prester) C.; B.S., U. Mo., 1963. Mine engr. ASARCO, Tucson, 1965-67; cons. engr. Rock Mechanics, Louisville, 1967-70; asst. to v.p. operations USNR Mining & Minerals, Inc., Louisville, 1970—; cons. drilling and blast design. Served to 1st lt. C.E., AUS. Registered profl. engr., Ky. Mem. Am. Soc. Mining Engrs. Home: 1040 Cherokee St Louisville KY 40204 Office: 3825 Bardstown Rd Louisville KY 40218

CLARK, DONALD KARL; broadcasting co. exec.; b. Irvine, Ky., Jan. 2, 1924; s. Arch Matthew and Harriet (Beaty) C.; A.B., U. Ky., 1949; m. Anne von Thurn, Aug. 20, 1949; children—James Richmond, Barbara Anne. News mgr., Paintsville (Ky.) Herald, 1949-50; advt. mgr. Bill Auto Stores, Louisville, 1950-56; exec. v.p. Bluegrass Advt. Agy., Louisville, 1956-59; gen. mgr. Rounsaville Radio Stas., Inc., Tampa, Fla., 1959—. Founder, Gasparilla Sidewalk Art Show, Tampa, 1969. Served with USAAF, 1943-45. Decorated Air medal. Mem. Greater Tampa Mchts. Assn. (pres.), Sales and Marketing Execs. Tampa (past pres.), Tampa Advt. Fedn. (Ad Man of Year award 1971), Sigma Delta Chi, Lambda Chi Alpha. Presbyn. (past elder). Clubs: Tampa Sailing Squadron, Carrollwood Golf and Country, Tower (Tampa). Home: 3024 Samara Dr Tampa FL 33618 Office: 101 N Tampa St Tampa FL 33602

CLARK, DOROTHY TWITCHELL, psychiatrist; b. Owatonna, Minn., Dec. 22, 1926; d. Caryl Emory and Dorothy (Buxton) Twitchell; student Cornell Coll., Mt. Vernon, Ia., 1944-46; B.A., U. Cal. at Berkeley, 1948; M.D., Harvard, 1952; m. Clarence Benson Clark, Apr. 2, 1952 (div. Feb. 1969); children—Elizabeth Dorothy, Susan Elizabeth. Intern Orange Meml. Hosp., Orlando, Fla., 1952-53; gen. practice medicine, Winter Park, Fla., 1953-60; resident psychiatry VA Hosp., Augusta, Ga., 1961-63, Med. Coll. Ga., Augusta, 1963-64; practice medicine specializing in psychiatry, Cocoa Beach, Fla. 1967—; mem. staff Cape Canaveral Hosp., Cocoa Beach, Wuesthoff Hosp., Rockledge, Fla. Cons. Brevard County Mental Health Center, Rockledge, 1968—. Mem. Brevard County Med. Soc., Fla. Med. Assn., A.M.A., Am., Fla. Central Fla. psychiat. assns., Cape Kennedy C. of C., Boylston Soc. Harvard Med. Sch., Am. Assn. U. Women. Republican. Episcopalian. Club: Womans. Office: 1325 N Atlantic Av Cocoa Beach FL 32931

CLARK, EMORY EUGENE, ins. agy. exec.; b. Opelika, Ala., Jan. 24, 1931; s. Bunk Henry and Dorothy (Bolt) C.; grad. pub. schs.; m. Jean F. Reed, Sept. 30, 1951; children—Steven E., Michael E. With Mgrs. Life Ins. Co., 1956—, agt., supr., Los Angeles, 1956-60, mgr. Hawaii br., 1960-65, Pitts. br., 1965-68, Houston br., 1968—. Served with AUS, 1950-56. Mem. Houston Life Underwriters Assn., Am. Soc. Life Underwriters, Houston Gen. Agts. and Mgrs. Assn., Houston C. of C. Home: 11719 Flintwood Dr Houston TX 77024 Office: 2100 Travis St Houston TX 77002

CLARK, EUGENIE, zoologist; b. N.Y.C., May 4, 1922; B.A., Hunter Coll., 1942; M.S., N.Y. U., 1946, Ph.D. (Pacific Sci. Bd. fellow 1949), 1950; m. Roy Umaki, 1942; m. 2d, Ilias Konstantinu, 1949; 4 children; m. 3d, Chandler Brossard, 1967; m. 4th, Igor Klatzo, 1969. Research asst. ichthyology Scripps Instn. Oceanography, 1946-47; with N.Y. Zool. Soc., 1947-48; research animal behavior Am. Mus. Nat. History, N.Y.C., 1948-49, research asso., 1950-54; instr. Hunter Coll., 1954; exec. dir. Cape Haze Marine Lab., Sarasota, Fla., 1955-67; asso. prof. biology College City N.Y., 1966-67; now asso. prof. zoology U. Md.; spl. research reproductive behavior fishes, morphology and taxonomy plectognath fishes, isolating mechanisms poecillid fishes. Fellow AEC, 1950; Fulbright scholar, Egypt, 1951; Saxton fellow, 1952; Breadloaf Writer's fellow; recipient Alumnae award Hunter Coll. Mem. Am. Soc. Icthyology and Herpetology, Soc. Women Geographers. Author: Lady with a Spear, 1953; Lady and the Sharks, 1969. Home: Bethesda MD 20034 also Cape Haze Marine Lab Sarasota FL 33578

CLARK, FLOYD EVERETT, coll. adminstr., clergyman; b. McTaggart, Sask., Can., Apr. 23, 1916; s. Edward Everett and Bonnie (Cave) C., came to U.S., 1937, naturalized, 1953; A.B., Johnson Bible Coll., 1941, D.D., 1968; B.D., Butler Sch. Religion, 1944; m. Lillian A. Frazier, July 2, 1941; 1 dau., Betty Ann. Prof., Greek and New Testament, Johnson Bible Coll., Kimberlin Heights, Tenn., 1944—, dean of men, 1945—, acad. dean, 1962-67, 68—, acting exec. v.p., 1967-68, mem. council of 70, 1972—; ordained to ministry Christian Ch., 1938; student minister Christian chs., Gap Creek, 1938-39, Bernard St., Knoxville, 1940-41 (all Tenn.), Buck Creek Chapel, Indpls., 41-44; minister 1st Christian Ch., Maryville, Tenn., 1944-59, Thorn Grove Christian Ch., Strawberry Plains, Tenn., 1960-63, Meadowbrook Christian Ch., Maryville, 1963-66, Forest Av. Christian Ch., Knoxville, 1966—. Mem. council advisers Internat. Christian U., 1972—. Chmn. French Christian Mission, 1956—; bd. dirs. Christian Mission to S. Korea, 1965—, Sunny Hills Children's Home, Kimberlin Heights, 1962—. Address: Johnson Bible Coll Kimberlin Heights TN 37920

CLARK, FRANKLIN JACOB, JR., architect; b. Anderson, S.C., Dec. 7, 1937; s. Franklin Jacob and Corrie Elizabeth (Watson) C.; B.Arch., Clemson U., 1962; m. Beverly Thornton Bowie, Nov. 19, 1960; 1 son, Franklin Jacob III. Designer A.G. Odell, Jr., & Assos., 1966, Ledbetter & Earle Architects, 1966-67; dir., asso. architect, v.p. Odell Assos., Inc., Charlotte, N.C., 1967—; pres., treas. Clark Godwin Harris & Li, Architects, Charlotte, 1973—; partner CGHL Planning, CGHL Engring. Served to lt., USAF, 1962-66. Registered architect, S.C., N.C., Tenn.; certified Nat. Council Archtl. Registration Bds. Mem. A.I.A., N.C. Soc. Preservation of Antiquities, Charlotte C. of C. Presbyn. (elder). Club: Charlotte City. Works include Cedar Forest Rackett Club, Charlotte, N.C. State Govt. Office Bldg., Raleigh. Mem. Mint. Mus. Art. Home: 3600 Wheaton Pl North Charlotte NC 28211 Office: 230 S Tryon Charlotte NC 28202

CLARK, GEORGE TAYLOR, JR., propr. art gallery; b. Baton Rouge, Jan. 9, 1936; s. George Taylor and Pearl (DeLaune) C.; B.S. in Commerce, La. State U., 1958; m. Jane Powers, June 5, 1961; children—George Taylor III, Amy Jane, Delia Lynne. Propr., Taylor Clark's Inc. paintings, prints and rare books, Baton Rouge, 1958—. Bd. mem. La. Arts and Sci. Center, Baton Rouge Gallery. Mem. Appraisers Assn. Am., Sigma Chi. Methodist (mem. bd.). Club: Baton Rouge Country. Home: 2125 Richland St Baton Rouge LA 70808 Office: 2623 Government St Baton Rouge LA 70806

CLARK, HARRY MCDONOUGH, ednl. adminstr.; b. Mobile, Ala., Dec. 18, 1937; s. Harry Patrick and Margaret Ellen (McDonough) C.; student Tulane U., 1955-58; B.S., Auburn U., 1960; M.A., U. Ala., 1962; Ed.D., Columbia, 1967; m. Clara Mildred Ball, July 21, 1962; children—Connolly Lightfoot, Erin McDonough. Teaching fellow U. Ala., 1961; instr. art U. So. Miss., 1962-64; asso. fellow ednl. adminstrn. Columbia Tchrs. Coll., 1964-67; asst. prof. ednl. adminstrn. U. So. Ala., 1968-69; asso. prof. ednl. adminstrn. U. S.C., 1969-70; asso. prof. ednl. adminstr. U. So. Miss., Biloxi, 1970—; adminstrv. dir. Coastal Med. Center, Biloxi, 1971—; pres. Mgmt. Approach Planning; sec.-treas. R.W. Bell Cos., Inc. Acting headmaster Gulf Day Sch., Ocean Springs, Miss., 1971-72; compliance insp. VA, 1971—. Bd. dirs. Gulf Day Sch., Ocean Springs. Mem. Council Ednl. Facilities Planners, Am. Assn. U. Profs., Am. Assn. Sch. Adminstrs., Southeastern Sch. Bus. Ofcls., Med. Group Mgmt. Assn., Phi Delta Kappa, Kappa Pi. Republican. Club: St. Andrews Country (Ocean Springs); Broadwater Country (Biloxi). Author: Methods for Computing School Building Capacity, 1967. Home: 306 Lovers Lane Ocean Springs MS 39564 Office: Box 4080 Biloxi MS 39531

CLARK, ISAAC EDGAR, publisher; b. Schulenburg, Tex., Dec. 9, 1919; s. Harvey Robert and Annie Ruby (Miekow) C.; B.A., U. Tex. at Austin, 1941, M.A., 1945; m. Lila Rhea Norwood, Sept. 1, 1945; children—Candace Ann, Robin Rhea. Rancher, 1945—; tchr., theatre dir., publs. dir., lang. arts coordinator Schulenburg Pub. Schs., 1945—; founder, owner I.E. Clark, Pub., Band Magic Halftime Shows and Stage Magic Plays, 1959—; tchr. Newspaper Fund seminars U. Tex. at Austin, summers 1961-66; regional observer for Nat. Observer, 1961; mem. Tex. Edn. Agy. Commn. for Lang. Arts Curriculum Revision, 1958-59. Mem. Fayette County His. Survey Com., 1969—; founder, artistic dir., bd. dirs., officer Backstage, Inc., Fine Arts Council for South Central Tex., 1969—; adv. dir. 1st Nat. Bank of Schulenburg, 1974—. Democratic precinct chmn., Fayette County Dem. Exec. Com., 1955—; county campaign chmn. Lyndon B. Johnson, 1949, 55; area campaign chmn. Tex. Lt. Gov. Bill Hobby, 1972. Bd. dirs. Schulenburg Hist. Soc. Recipient Finest Journalism Tchr. in Tex. award U. Tex. Interscholastic League, 1967; named Hon. State Farmer, Future Farmers Am., 1956. Newspaper Fund fellow, 1959. Mem. Am. Theatre Assn., Am. Community Theatre Assn., Childrens Theatre Assn., Tex. Secondary Theatre Conf. (dir., Newsletter editor, 1966-69, mem. Interscholastic League adv. com.), Tex. Ednl. Theatre Assn., Tex. Tchrs. Assn., Modern Music Masters (hon. life), English Speaking Union, Farm Bur., Phi Beta Kappa, Delta Tau Delta, Sigma Delta Chi, Phi Eta Sigma. Methodist. Mason (Shriner). Author: (plays) Twelve Dancing Princesses, 1969; Hansel and Gretel, 1970; It's A Dungaree World, 1974; also several one-act plays including The Christmas Dream, transl. into Spanish, produced TV, Ecuador, 1973. Home: Bermuda Valley Farm Schulenburg TX 78956 Office: PO Box 246 Schulenburg TX 78956

CLARK, JACK CROWLEY, physician; b. Whitleyville, Tenn., Feb. 24, 1936; s. Cordell Hull and Clio Elizabeth (Cassetty) C.; student Vanderbilt U., 1954-57; M.D., U. Tenn., 1961; m. Janet Sue Chailland, June 21, 1959; children—Jack Crowley, Christopher David, Julie Elizabeth. Intern, Nashville Gen. Hosp., 1961-62; gen. practice medicine, Lafayette, Tenn., 1962-71; resident in radiology U. Tenn., 1972—, chief resident, 1974—; mem. staff Smith-Chitwood Hosp., Lafayette, 1962-71. Med. dir. Cordell Hull Econ. Opportunity Corp., Lafayette, 1967-71; former dir. Citizens Bank, Lafayette, Tenn. Mem. Gov's. Adv. Bd. on Mental Retardation, 1969—. Mem. City Council, Lafayette, 1964-68; mem. Macon County Election Commn., 1968-70. Bd. dirs. Macon County Cancer Soc.; trustee Tenn. Dept. Mental Health; chmn. bd. advisers Arlington Devel. Center, 1972—. Mental Health Dept. Mem. Am. Acad. Gen. practice, So., Tenn. med. assns., Memphis, Shelby County roentgen socs., Phi Chi, Pi Kappa Alpha. Democrat. Methodist. Rotarian. Home: 1349 Hickory Ridge Cove Memphis TN 38116 Office: U Tenn Dept Radiology 865 Jefferson St Memphis TN 38103

CLARK, JAMES ANDREW, JR., pediatrician; b. Ruleville, Miss., Dec. 18, 1911; s. James Andrew and Virginia (Miller) C.; student Sunflower Jr. Coll., 1933; B.S., U. Miss., 1936; M.D., U. Tenn., 1938; m. Margaret Ellen Smith, June 5, 1946 (dec. Feb. 1971); children—James Andrew III, Mary Charlotte, John Arthur, Margaret Ellen. Intern, John Gaston Hosp., Memphis, 1938-40; house physician Good Samaritan Hosp., West Palm Beach, Fla., 1940-41; resident pediatrics U. Tenn., 1953-54; gen. practice medicine, Ruleville, Miss., 1946-52; practice medicine specializing in pediatrics, Memphis, 1955—; mem. staffs LeBonheur Children's, Bapt. Meml., Meth., St. Joseph hosps. Served from 1st lt. to maj. M.C., AUS, 1941-46. Mem. Am., Tenn. med. assns., Memphis, Shelby County med. socs., Tenn., Memphis pediatric socs., Am. Legion, V.F.W., D.A.V., Disabled Officers Assn., Ret. Officers Assn., Mil. Order World Wars. Presbyn. Home: 4149 Poplar Av Memphis TN 38117 Office: 4515 Poplar Av Memphis TN 38117

CLARK, JAMES ANTHONY, author, journalist, petroleum historian and biographer; b. Abita Springs, La., Sept. 7, 1907; s. Edward Arlie and Laura (Page) C.; student Lamar Tech. Coll., 1928; m. Estelle Walton, Apr. 8, 1934. Partner James A. Clark Co., 1953-73, pres., 1963—; pres. Clark Book Co. Trustee Houston Mus. Natural Sci.; founding mem., pres., dir. Energy Research and Edn. Found.; columnist Energy News. Served with AUS, 1941-46; PTO. Decorated Bronze Star Medal; recipient first annual journalistic award Am. Assn. Petroleum Geologists, 1972. Mem. Authors Guild. Roman Catholic. Clubs: Nat. Press, Headliners. Author: (with Michel T. Halbouty) Spindletop, 1952; (with Weldon Hart) The Tactful Texan, 1958; Three Stars for the Colonel, 1954; The Chronological History of the Petroleum and Natural Gas Industries, 1963; (with Nathan Broch) A Biography of Robert Alonzo Welch, 1963; Founders of Oil Industry, 1967; A Geography of Oil, 1959; Marrs McLean, A Biography, 1969; (with Michel T. Halbouty) The Last Boom, 1972; An Oilman's Oilman, 1974. Home: 2171 University Blvd Houston TX 77025 Office: Houston Club Bldg Houston TX 77002

CLARK, JAMES EDWIN, educator; b. Winnsboro, S.C., Mar. 3, 1933; s. James Edward and Annie Mae (Cooper) C.; B.S. in C.E., U. S.C., 1957, M.E., 1964; Ph.D., N.C. State U., 1967; m. Becky Jo Davis, Sept. 8, 1956; children—Teresa Jo, Davis Edward, Melissa Becky. Civil engr., Union Bag Camp Paper Corp., Franklin, Va., 1957-60; sr. bridge designer Smith, Pollitte & Assos., Columbia, S.C., 1960-64; instr., N.C. State U., Raleigh, 1964-65; asst. prof. Miss. State U., State College, 1967-70; asso. prof. civil engring. Clemson (S.C.) U., 1970—. Vice chmn. Clemson Planning Commn., 1971—. Served with USAF, 1951-53. Lyles Bissett Carlisle & Wolfe fellow, 1963, Nat. Defense Edn. Act fellow, 1965-67. Mem. Inst. Traffic Engrs. (pres. S.C. div. 1972-73), Am. Soc. Engring. Edn., Hwy. Research Bd. (com. mem. 1969—). Home: 114 E Brookwood Dr Clemson SC 29631

CLARK, JOE RICHARD, oil co. exec.; b. Burleson, Tex., Feb. 26, 1927; s. Hugh Milton and Mary (Baker) C.; B.M.E., Tex. A. and M. U., 1948; m. Betty Nan White, Aug. 21, 1948; children—James Rod, Carolyn Louise, Joseph Breen. Dist. reservoir engr. Stanolind Oil & Gas Co., Lubbock, Tex., 1948-55; div. reservoir engr. TXL Oil Corp., Midland, Tex., 1955-62; div. sec. reservoir engr. Texaco Inc., Midland, 1962-63; ind. cons. engr. Midland, 1963-64; v.p. prodn. Tex. Pacific Oil Co., Dallas, 1964—. Served to 1st lt. AUS, 1951-53. Mem. Am. Petroleum Inst., Am. Inst. Mining and Metal. Engrs., Tex.-Mid Continent Oil and Gas Assn., N.M. Oil and Gas Assn., Nat., Tex. socs. profl. engrs. Mason. Club: Dallas Petroleum. Home: 3605 Colgate St Dallas TX 75225 Office: 1700 One Main Pl Dallas TX 75250

CLARK, JOHN MARTIN, JR., research engr.; b. San Antonio, Oct. 5, 1916; s. John Martin and Dorothy (Hilgers) C.; B.S. in Mech. Engring., Rice Inst.; Tech., 1940, M.S., Mass. Inst. Tech., 1941; m. Mary Frances Dittmar, Aug. 23, 1941; children—Anne (Mrs. Jack Johnson), Marsha (Mrs. Ed Page), John Martin III. Powerplant designer, test engr. Douglas Aircraft, Santa Monica, Cal., 1941-47; pres. John Clark Industries, San Marcos, Tex., 1947-55; sr. research engr. Southwest Research Inst., San Antonio, 1955-58, dir. dept. automotive research, 1958—, tech. v.p., 1972-74, v.p., 1974—. Mem. Soc. Automotive Engrs., Sci. Research Soc. Am. Republican. Episcopalian. Contbr. articles to profl. jours. Patentee in field. Home: 707 Lake Placid Dr Seguin TX 78155 Office: 8500 Culebra Rd San Antonio TX 78206

CLARK, JOHN RAY, state legislator; b. Hancock, Md., June 9, 1924; s. John N. and Della M. (Alderton) C.; A.B., Transylvania Coll., 1947; M.A., U. Ky., 1949; m. Geneva Rolfe, Nov., 18, 1962; children—John (dec.), Douglas, Robert, James, Sandra, Edward, Randall. Formerly tchr., prin. elementary schs.; mem. Fla. Ho. of Reps. 1966—. Bd. dirs. Polk County (Fla.) Juvenile Home. Served with AUS, 1940-45. Mem. Am. Legion, Pi Kappa Alpha. Democrat. Elk, Moose. Home: 515 Queens Loop Lakeland FL 33803 Office: 417 Arcade Bldg Lakeland FL 33801

CLARK, JOHN WILLARD, JR., lawyer; b. Dallas, Nov. 7, 1938; s. John Willard and Grace Lillian (Hobgood) C.; student Washington & Lee U., 1956-57; B.A., So. Meth. U., 1960; J.D., So. Meth. U. Sch. Law, 1963; m. Ann Louise Burnett, Feb. 16, 1962; children—Catherine Gibson, Sue Frost. Admitted to Tex. bar, 1963; asso. Douglas E. Bergman, Dallas, 1963-68; partner Turner Hitchins McInerney Webb & Hartnett, Dallas, 1968—. Dir. Global Graphics, Inc., Global Tech. Services, Inc. Del. Dem. County Conv., 1964-65. Bd. dirs. So. Meth. U. Law Sch., Dallas, 1970—, vice chmn., 1973. Mem. Am. (bd. govs. 1972—; ho. of dels. 1972—), Dallas bar assns., State Bar Tex., Am. Bar Found., Am. Bar Endowment, Phi Alpha Delta, Kappa Alpha. Democrat. Methodist. Club: Royal Oaks Country (Dallas). Home: 3637 Rosedale St Dallas TX 75205 Office: 1700 Mercantile Bank Bldg Dallas TX 75201

CLARK, LAMAR SHAFFER, clergyman; b. Durant, Okla., Dec. 19, 1911; s. Alexander Marion and Donna Marie (Hilton) C.; student Lon Morris Jr. Coll., 1931-32, B.A., U. Southwestern La., 1934; student Perkins Sch. Theology, So. Meth. U., 1935-37, B.D., 1944; D.D. (hon.) Southwestern U., 1966; m. Lenora Fay Newbern, Apr. 26, 1936; children—Donna Dean (Mrs. Gerge H. Hutcherson), Jan Carolyn (Mrs. George M. Atkinson). Ordained to ministry Methodist Ch., as deacon, 1939, elder, 1941; pastor Meth. chs., Bellville, 1937-41, Pleasant Retreat, Tyler, 1941-42, Frankston, 1945-47, Glenwood Ch., 1947-50, St. John's Ch., Richmond, 1950-56, 1st Ch., Jasper, 1956-61, 1st Ch., Texarkana, 1961-64 (all Tex.); exec. sec. Tex. Annual Conf. United Meth. Ch., 1964-70; pastor Grace United Meth. Ch., Baytown, 1970-72, First United Meth. Ch., La Marque, 1972—. Chmn. United Meth. Communications Council of Tex., 1968-70; del. World Meth. Conf., London, 1966, Denver, 1971; mem. World Meth. Council, 1971—; trustee, sec. bd. trustees Mt. Sequoyah United Meth. Assembly, Fayetteville, Ark.; chmn. bd. trustees Tex. Ann. Conf. United Meth. Ch., 6 years, vice chmn. bd. edn., 8 years. Trustee Lydia Patterson Inst., El Paso, Tex., San Jacinto Meth. Hosp., Baytown, Tex., Happy Harbor Home for Older People, La Porte, Tex. Served as chaplain AUS, 1942-46. Decorated Bronze Star, Purple Heart. Mason (32 deg.), Rotarian (pres. Jasper 1958). Home: 10 Perthius Dr La Marque TX 77568 Office: First United Meth Ch Scott and Howell Sts La Marque TX 77568

CLARK, LAWRENCE BEARDEN, civil engr.; b. Birmingham, Ala., Dec. 15, 1935; s. Cortex Brown and Myrtle Willadean (Bearden) C.; grad. Phillips Exeter Acad., 1953; B.C.E., Ala. Poly. Inst., 1959; postgrad. Tex. Christian U., 1956-58, Nashville Law Sch., 1964-67; M.S. (Chow fellow) Auburn (Ala.) U., 1960; m. Nancy Kate Woolley, July 18, 1964; children—Shirley Elizabeth, John Lawrence. With engring. dept. So. Ry. Co., 1953-55; jr. engr. Frisco Ry. Co., Ft. Worth, 1956-58; tchr. civil engring. Auburn U., 1950-60; san. engr. C.&O. Ry., 1960-62; constrn. engr. E.I. du Pont de Nemours & Co., Inc., 1963-68; design engr. Courtaulds N.Am., Inc., Mobile, Ala., 1968—. Sec., Mobile Civic Roundtable, 1970-71, v.p., 1971-72. Del. Democratic Nat. Conv., 1960. Bd. dirs. Mobile Area Safety Council. Recipient numerous C. of C. awards. Registered profl. engr., Va., Ala. Mem. Am. Soc. C.E., Mobile (v.p. 1970-71), Ala. (v.p. 1970-71) jr. chambers commerce, Delta Sigma Phi, Chi Epsilon. Presbyn. Editor: Forum mag., 1970. Home: 405 Pine Ct Mobile AL 36608 Office: PO Box 2648 Mobile AL 36601

CLARK, MORTON HUTCHINSON, lawyer; b. Norfolk, Va., Apr. 21, 1933; s. David Henderson and Catharine Angelica (Hutchinson) C.; B.A., U. Va., 1954, LL.B., 1956; m. Lynn Harrison Adams, Aug. 12, 1961; children—Allison Adams, David Henderson, Susan West, Julia Dixon. Admitted to Va. bar, 1960; practiced in Norfolk, Va., 1960—; asso. firm Vandeventer, Black, Meredith & Martin, 1960-65, partner, 1965—; dir. Allied Marine Industries, Norfolk. Chmn. Va. Commn. Children and Youth, 1968-72; pres. Friends Norfolk Juvenile Ct., Inc., 1971-72; pres. Norfolk Forum, 1973. Bd. dirs. United Cancer Soc. Served to comdr. USNR, 1956-59. Mem. Maritime Law Assn. U.S., Am. Bar Assn., Va. State Bar. Clubs: Yacht and Country Harbor (Norfolk, Va.). Home: 1428 Daniel Av Norfolk VA 23505 Office: 2050 Virginia Nat Bank Bldg Norfolk VA 23510

CLARK, ROBERT EARL, JR., assn. exec.; b. Louisville, Miss., Mar. 1, 1934; s. Robert Earl and Charlie Mae (Garriques) C.; student Miss. State U., 1952-54; B.S., U.S. Mil. Acad., 1958; student Rensselear Poly. Inst., 1964; m. Sylvia Duck, July 19, 1958; children—George Robert, Camille. Commd. 2d lt. U.S. Army, advanced through grades to maj., 1970; resigned, 1970; mgr. Clark Ranch, Louisville, 1970—, Louisville-Winston County C. of C., 1970—. Decorated Commendation medal, Bronze Star medal. Mem. Am. Legion (post comdr.), Louisville Businessmen's Club. Methodist (sec. adminstrv. bd., mem. council ministries). Rotarian (dir. Louisville). Home: Box 373 Louisville MS 39339 Office: Box 551 Louisville MS 39339

CLARK, ROSCOE CONKLING, petroleum engr.; b. Kansas City, Mo., Dec. 21, 1917; s. Roscoe C. and Mary A. (Anderson) C.; M.S. in Petroleum Engring., U. Tulsa, 1952; m. Ruby O. Plemons, Nov. 7, 1941; 1 son, Mike S. Service engr. Dowell, Inc., Great Bend, Kan., 1946-47; engr. Amoco Research, Tulsa, 1947-52; research engr. Conoco, Ponca City, Okla., 1952-54; v.p. operations The Western Co., Ft. Worth, 1954-65; pres. Scott Corp., Houston, 1965-67; chief drilling engr. Conoco, Houston, 1967—. Youth tennis commr. Houston Tennis Assn., 1972-73. Served to lt. col. AUS, 1940-46. Mem. Am. Inst. Mining and Metall. Engrs., Am. Petroleum Inst., Soc. Petroleum Engrs., Internat. Assn. Drilling Contractors. Patentee in field. Home: 201 Vanderpool St Houston TX 77024 Office: Box 2197 Houston TX 77001

CLARK, ROY THOMAS, JR., educator; b. Lockhart, Tex., Feb. 22, 1922; s. Roy Thomas and Ada Louise (Masur) C.; B.S. in Chemistry, S.W. Tex. State Coll., 1947, M.A. in Chemistry, 1950; m. Lavanie Anne Busby, Jan. 3, 1948; 1 son, Thomas David. Commd. 2d lt. USAAF, 1943; advanced through grades to lt. col. USAF, 1966; various assignments U.S., 1943-59; project officer propulsion br. Agena div. Directorate Space Systems, Air Force Ballistic Missile Div., Los Angeles, 1959-60; chief propulsion sect., astrovehicle br. Agena div. Office Dep. Comdr. Satellite Systems, Space Systems Div., Los Angeles, 1960-61; asst. prof. chemistry USAF Acad., Colo., 1961-63, asso. prof., 1963-64; student Air Force Inst. Tech., Edn.-with-Industry Program, Aerojet Gen. Corp., Sacramento, 1964-65; project officer 6595th Aerospace Test Wing, Vandenberg AFB, Cal., 1965-66; chief Titan Launched Satellite Systems Office, 1966-69; ret., 1969; adminstrv. officer dept. chemistry U. Tex. at Austin, 1969—. Decorated Air medal, Air Force Commendation medal, Meritorious Service medal. Mem. Am. Chem. Soc. Episcopalian. Home: 7711 Shadyrock Dr Austin TX 78731

CLARK, THOMAS ALEXANDER, librarian; b. Iuka, Miss., Mar. 12, 1936; s. Ezekiel Candler and Arvis (Fancher) C.; student N.E. Miss. Jr. Coll., 1954-56; B.S., U. So. Miss., 1958; M.L.S., U. Miss., 1966. Librarian Belmont (Miss.) High Sch., 1958-66, Valdosta (Ga.) State Coll., 1966—. Active Valdosta Lowndes YMCA. Mem. Valdosta Lowndes Mental Health Assn., Ga., Southeastern library assns. Methodist. Mason. Club: Civitan (pres. 1960-61) (Belmont, Miss.). Home: 1709 N Ashley St Valdosta GA 31601

CLARK, VERNON RAY, petroleum engr.; b. McPherson, Kan., May 5, 1932; s. Martin Joel and Laura (Wann) C.; student McPherson Coll., 1955-56; B.S., Kan. State U., 1959; m. Donna Marlene Alexander, May 5, 1955; children—Kyanna Kay, Kevin Ray, Keith Warren, Kayla Ann. Asso. engr. Nortronics Inc., Hawthorne, Cal., 1959-61; design engr. Gen. Dynamics Astronautics, Salina, Kan., 1961-62; sr. engr. Chrysler Space Div., Huntsville, Ala., 1962-65; project engr. Applied Automation, Bartlesville, Okla., 1965—. Served with AUS, 1953-55. Registered profl. engr., Ala. Mem. Bartlesville Bible Ch. (deacon 1970—). Research, devel. latest state-of-the art computerized process control systems. Patentee in field. Home: 3308 Nowata Rd Bartlesville OK 74003 Office: 215 RB2 PRC Pawhuska Rd Bartlesville OK 74003

CLARK, VICTOR C., former govt. ofcl.; b. Falmouth, Mass., Aug. 24, 1917; s. E. Frank H. and Maude (Kelley) C.; B.S. in Bus. Adminstrn., George Washington U., 1971; m. Hester C. Rice, Nov. 24, 1941; children—Kenneth, Andrew, Beth, Miriam, Roger, Jennifer. Chief nav. aids sect. CAA, Washington, 1953-55; chief instrument landing system br. FAA, Washington, 1955-58, chief plans and programs br., internat. aviation service 1958-62; dir. electronics engring. lab. USCG, Alexandria, Va., 1963—. Mem. I.E.E.E. (sr.), Am. Radio Relay League (charter life, 1st v.p. 1974—), No. Va. Amateur Radio Council (dir. 1972—), Quarter Century Wireless Assn., Potomac Valley Radio Club (charter, pres. 1948, 51, 53). Home: 12927 Popes Head Rd Clifton VA 22024

CLARK, WARREN JAMES, clin. psychologist; b. Syracuse, N.Y., Oct. 20, 1920; s. Robert Warren and Mae Louise (Corcoran) C.; A.B., Syracuse U., 1943; M.A., U. Denver, 1947, Ph.D., 1953; m. Faye Louise Manning, Aug. 8, 1969; children—Kay Natalie, Roy, Robert, David. Dir. speech clinic Children's Hosp., Columbus, O., 1943; Fulbright lectr. phonetics for fgn. students U. Denver, 1950, dir. Hearing and Adult Speech Center, 1953-55; vis. asst. prof. linguistics State U. Ia., 1955-56; psychologist Fulton County (Ga.) Child Guidance Center, 1956-60; individual practice clin. psychology, Atlanta, 1960—. Cons. Ga. Dept. Vocational Rehab., Fulton County Adult Probation Dept., Ethel Harpst Home Children, Cedartown, Ga., 1960—. Bd. dirs. Arbor Acad., Atlanta. Mem. Am., Ga. psychol. assns., Psychologists in Pvt. Practice (pres. elect 1974). Presbyn. Clubs: Atlanta Artists; Lake Lanier (Ga.) Sailing. Office: 3384 Peachtree Rd NE Atlanta GA 30326

CLARK, WESLEY GLEASON, educator; b. Wadsworth, O., July 1, 1933; s. Alfred William and Mary June (Starn) C.; B.A., U. Colo., 1955, M.S., 1958; Ph.D. (USPHS Predoctoral Research fellow 1958-61, USPHS trainee 1961-62), U. Utah. 1962; m. Yvonne Lee Stanfield, Apr. 16, 1965; children—David Lee, Rebecca Lynne, Roger Dale. Instr. U. Tex. Southwestern Med. Sch., Dallas, 1962-63, asst. prof., 1963-72, asso. prof. pharmacology, 1972—. NIH research grantee USPHS, 1964-66, 70—. Mem. A.A.A.S., Am. Soc. Pharmacology and Exptl. Therapeutics, Soc. Exptl. Biology and Medicine, Phi Lambda Upsilon. Home: 1334 Carriage Dr Irving TX 75062 Office: 5323 Harry Hines Blvd Dallas TX 75235

CLARK, WILLIAM DONALDSON, banker; b. Haltwhistle, Northumberland, Eng., July 28, 1916; s. John McClare and Marion (Jackson) C.; M.A., Oriel Coll.; postgrad. (Commonwealth fellow) U. Chgo., 1938-40. With Ministry of Information and Brit. Information Services, Chgo., 1941-44; press attache, Washington, 1945-46; London (Eng.) editor Ency. Brit., 1946-49; diplomatic corr. Observer, London, 1950-55; pub. relations adviser to prime minister, London, 1955-56; editor Week, London, 1958-60; dir. Overseas Devel. Inst., London, 1960-68; dir. information and pub. affairs World Bank, Washington, 1968-73, dir. external relations, 1973—. Various appearances on TV shows including Right to Reply. Clubs: Athenaeum, Sevile (London); Athletic (Washington). Author: Less than Kin: A Study of Anglo-American Relations, 1957; What is the Commonwealth?, 1958; (with Ronald Millar) Number 10, 1966; Special Relationship, 1968. Home: 3407 Rodman St NW Washington DC 20008 Office: 1818 H St NW Washington DC 20433

CLARK, WILLIAM FREDERICK, county ofcl.; b. Washington, July 10, 1936; s. Abner Stephenson and Elsie Agusta (Feusahrens) C.; B.S., U. Md., 1959; Master Pub. Works, U. Pitts., 1970; m. Eleanor Janet Munsey, July 10, 1959; children—Richard William, Sandra Ann, Sara Elizabeth. Civil engr. City of Downey, Cal., 1960-62; asst. to dir. pub. works City of Rockville, Md., 1962-64; city engr. City of Roanoke, Va., 1965-70, dir. pub. works, 1970-72, asst. city mgr., 1972-73; county adminstr. Roanoke County, Va., 1973—. Trustee United Fund of Roanoke Valley, 1971-73, Am. Pub. Works Assn. Edn. Found., 1971-73. Mem. Am. Pub. Works Assn. (chpt. pres. 1967-68), Soc. for Preservation and Encouragement Barber Shop Quartet Singing in Am. (chpt. pres. 1974—), Sigma Alpha Epsilon. Methodist (mem. bd. 1973—). Kiwanian. Home: 3514 Kenwick Trail Roanoke VA 24018 Office: PO Box 168 Salem VA 24153

CLARK, WILLIAM KEMP, physician, educator; b. Dallas, Sept. 2, 1925; s. James and Florine (Kemp) C.; B.A., U. Tex., 1945, M.D., 1948; m. Fern Blair, Mar. 30, 1952; children—Elizabeth, Sarah, Florine, Blair, Peter, Jonathan. Intern, Ind. U., 1948-49; resident Neurol. Inst. N.Y., 1953-56; practice medicine specializing in neurosurgery, Dallas, 1956—; prof. div. neurosurgery Southwestern Med. Sch., Dallas, 1956—; dir. neurosurg. service Parkland Meml., Children's Meml. hosps., 1956—, St. Paul Hosp., 1960—; cons. VA Hosp., 1956—. Chmn., Nat. Manpower Com. for Neurosurgery, 1971—; mem. Linz Award Com., 1972. Mem. lay adv. bd. St. Michael's Sch., Dallas, 1973—. Bd. dirs. Tex. div. Am. Cancer Soc. Served to capt. USAF, 1950-52. Mem. Am. Bd. Neurol. Surgery (sec. 1972—), Soc. Neurol. Surgeons, Am. Assn. Neurol. Surgery. Clubs: Brookhollow Golf, City (Dallas). Home: 3909 Euclid St Dallas TX 75205 Office: 5323 Harry Hines Dallas TX 75235

CLARK, WILLIS KENLEY, oil co. exec.; b. Crockett, Tex., Sept. 21, 1911; s. John Thomas and Jonie (Kenley) C.; B.S., U. Tex., 1936; m. Marybelle Henning, Feb. 25, 1939; 1 dau., Mary Kay. Jr. geologist Shell Oil Co., Houston, 1934-37; geologist Transwestern Oil Co., San Antonio, 1937-39; geologist Superior Oil Co., Houston, 1939-44, dist. geologist, Shreveport, La. 1944-49, chief geologist, Houston, 1949-62, v.p. geology, Houston, 1962—, also dir. Mem. Am. Assn. Petroleum Geologists, Sigma Gamma Epsilon. Home: 5644 Lynbrook Dr Houston TX 77027 Office: 1st City Nat Bank Bldg Houston TX 77001

CLARKE, CLIFFORD MONTREVILLE, civic assn. exec.; b. Ludowici, Ga., July 20, 1925; s. Clifford Montreville and Lella Bertrue (Hightower) C.; A.B. in Polit. Sci., Emory U. 1951. Radio engr. and announcer WSAV, Savannah, 1941-43; pub. relations dir. Dept. Ga., Am. Legion, 1945-47; instr. Armstrong Coll., Savannah, 1947-48; asst. supt. Savannah Park and Tree Commn., 1951; instr., then supr. tng. dept. Lockheed Aircraft Corp., Marietta, Ga., 1951-52, mgr. employee services dept., 1952-53; exec. v.p. Asso. Industries Ga., 1953-68; pres. Ga. Bus. and Industry Assn., 1968-73; exec. dir. Bicentennial Council 13 Original States, 1973—; mem. Am. Soc. Execs., 1955—, bd. dirs., 1958-67, mem. exec. com., 1960-67, treas., 1962-64, sr. v.p., 1964-65, pres., 1965-66; pres. Ga. Soc. Assn. Execs., 1958-60; chmn. state group Nat. Indsl. Council, 1970-72. Mem. Ga. Urban and Tech. Assistance Adv. Council, 1965-70, Ga. Intergovtl. Relations Commn., 1966; mem. Ga. Ednl. Improvement Council, 1964-69, chmn., 1967-69, vice chmn., 1970-71; mem. Forward Ga. Commn., 1969-72; vice chmn. Ga. Commn. for Nat. Bicentennial Celebration, 1969-73, chmn., 1973—; chmn. Chartered Assn. Exec. Chartering Bd.; 1969-71; bd. dirs. Atlanta Conv. Bur., 1968-71; exec. com. Conf. State Mfrs. Assns., 1969-72; Ga. del. to Bicentennial Council 13 Original States, 1971-73, chmn., 1972-73; chmn. Gov.'s Commn. Student Financial Aid, 1972—. Mem. policy com. Grad. Sch. Bus., U. Ga., 1966-71; adv. bd. Ga. Vocational Rehab., 1964-70; dirs. Arthritis Found. Ga., 1965-71; Atlanta Community Services to Blind, Coop. Services for Blind, 1964-71, Atlanta Sch. Art. Served with inf. AUS, World War II. Decorated Purple Heart with 2 oak leaf clusters; hon. consul Mexico, 1970-72. Mem. Am. Soc. Assn. Execs. (trustee Found. 1968-71), Chartered Assn. Execs. (trustee 1967-73). Home: 1115 Beechhaven Rd NE Atlanta GA 30324 Office: Suite 2001 400 Colony Sq Atlanta GA 30361

CLARKE, DAVID SCOTT, architect, assn. exec.; b. Kenosha, Wis., Jan. 2, 1942; s. Donald Edwin and Martha Jean (Chatterton) C.; B.S. in Philosophy, U. Wis., 1965; B.Arch., U. Ore., 1969; m. Karin Anne Wanner, Apr. 24, 1965. Designer, Skidmore, Owings & Merrill, N.Y.C., 1969-70; pvt. practice architecture, Vancouver, B.C., Can., 1970-71; exec. dir. Assn. Collegiate Schs. Architecture, Inc., Washington, 1971—; dir. edn. programs A.I.A. Guest lectr. Carnegie-Mellon U., 1971, Am. U., 1972; cons. Pres.'s Com. on Barrier-Free Architecture, Health, Edn. and Welfare Office Environmental Edn., 1972, Nat. Park Service, 1972. Mem. planning com. Washington Urban League, 1972—; mem. adv. bd. Group for Environmental Edn., Phila. Mem. Am. Inst. Planners, N.E.A., Inst. Humanistic Psychology. Edn. editor A.I.A. Jour., 1972—. Home: 407 A St NE Washington DC 20002 Office: 1735 New York Av NW Washington DC 20006

CLARKE, EUGENE SINGLETON, accountant; b. Hollandale, Miss., June 15, 1933; s. Eugene Singleton and Georgia (Wicks) C.; B.S. in Accounting, Miss. State U., 1955; m. Grace Ellen Oakes, June 19, 1955; children—Eugene Singleton, David Estill. Staff accountant Dick D. Quin & Co., Jackson, Miss., 1957-60; staff accountant Peat, Marwick, Mitchell & Co., Jackson, 1960-62; partner firm Moody & Clarke, C.P.A.'s, Hollandale, Greenville and Leland, Miss., 1962-67; individual practice as C.P.A., Hollandale, 1968-70; partner Clarke & Wicks, Hollandale, 1970—. Dir. Hollandale Indsl. Found., 1964—; sec.-treas. Washington County Devel. Commn.; treas. Hollandale Minority Devel. Corp. Scoutmaster, Boy Scouts Am., Hollandale, 1962—. Trustee, Hollandale Consol. Sch. Dist. Served to 1st lt. USAF, 1955-57, Mem. Am. Inst. C.P.A.'s (treas.), Miss. Soc. C.P.A.'s (past pres. Miss. Delta chpt.), Hollandale C. of C. (past pres.), Sigma Alpha Epsilon. Methodist. Rotarian (past pres. Hollandale). Clubs: Sharkey Country, Highland. Home: Treadway Circle Hollandale MS 38748 Office: Bank of Hollandale Bldg Hollandale MS 38748

CLARKE, HARVEY EDEN, electronic engr.; b. Birmingham, Ala., July 26, 1924; s. Fredrick William and Helen (Scott) C.; B.E.E., Ala. Poly. Inst., 1952; m. Iva M. Williams, Feb. 9, 1947; children—Linda Eden (Mrs. John Martin Willcox), James Harvey. Electronic technician Civil Service Commn., U.S. Air Force, Brookley AFB, 1946-49, electronic engr., 1954-62; instr., field engr. Westinghouse Elec. Corp., Balt. and Jacksonville, Fla., 1952-54; electronic engr. U.S. Corps Engrs., Mobile, Ala., 1962—. Served with USNR, 1943-46. Registered profl. engr. Ala. Baptist (deacon 1964—, Sunday sch. tchr. 1955-67, dir. adult dept. 1969—). Mason. Home: 507 Newport Dr W Mobile AL 36609 Office: Corps Engrs Mobile Dist Office Box 2288 Mobile AL 36628

CLARKE, JAY, newspaper editor; b. Jacksonville, Fla., Oct. 6, 1927; s. Charles Williamson and Gabrielle (Creusot) C.; A.B., U. Miami, Coral Gables, Fla., 1950; m. Patricia Hughes, Nov. 2, 1963; children—Anne Patrice, Dougan, Paul. Mng. editor Trilane Publs., N.Y.C., 1951-52; copy editor Fairchild Publs., N.Y.C., 1952-55; Sunday editor The Miami (Fla.) Herald, 1955—. Served with AUS, 1946-48. Mem. Soc. Am. Travel Writers (dir.), Sigma Delta Chi, Omicron Delta Kappa, Sigma Alpha Epsilon. Episcopalian. Contbr. to mags. and newspapers. Home: 1001 Sunset Dr Coral Gables FL 33143 Office: 1 Herald Plaza Miami FL 33101

CLARKE, JESSE EDWARD, engr. corp. exec.; b. Louisville, Aug. 3, 1914; s. Edward Hokar and Jesse (Miles) C.; student U. Louisville, 1936; m. Marie Dorothy Kornacki, Jan. 1, 1946; children—Richard S., Virginia L. (Mrs. Francis Greeley), Betty J. (Mrs. Leslie Konicki), David E., Philip J., Rose M. (Mrs. Frederic Harbour), Bonnie M. (Mrs. Michael Donaldson), Deborah (Mrs. Terrence Illes). Supr. elec. power wiring Jeffersonville Boat Works, 1941-43; tech. sales and service Rotating Parts Co., 1945-46, v.p., 1946-47; pres. Autoquip Corp., 1948—, chmn. bd., 1970—. Mem. Nat. Right to Work Com. Served as pvt. USMC, 1943-45. Mem. Am. Inst. Mgmt. (mem. pres.'s council), Ill. C. of C., U.S. C. of C., Nat. Mfrs. Assn., Chgo. Commerce Assn. Patentee in field. Home: 1276 Laurel Ct Marco Island FL 33937 Office: 1140 S Washtenaw St Chicago IL 60612

CLARKE, LEE BEN, II, hosp. adminstr.; b. Atlanta, Dec. 18, 1931; s. Maurice Lee Ben and Frances Myrinie (Scruggs) C.; student U. Ga., 1950-53; B.B.A., Ga. State U., 1957, certificate in hosp. adminstrn., 1958; m. India Katherine Harvey, Dec. 12, 1953; children—Lee Ben III, Frances Lynn, Harrell Harvey. Adminstrv. resident Macon Hosp., 1957-58, bus. office mgr., 1958; asst. adminstr. City-County Hosp., LaGrange, Ga., 1958-60; adminstr. Humphreys Meml. Hosp., Fernandina Beach, Fla., 1960-66, Glades Gen. Hosp., Belle Glade, Fla., 1966—. Mem. Palm Beach County Health Planning Council, Glades Pub. Health Adv. Bd.; adv. com. West Area Palm Beach County Sch. System. Bd. dirs. Palm Beach County Mental Health Center, 1967-71. Served with AUS, 1953-55. Mem. Am. Coll. Hosp. Adminstrs., Am., Fla. (trustee 1964-65) hosp. assns., East Central Fla. Hosp. Council, Palm Beach County Soc. Hosp. Adminstrs., Am. Mgmt. Assn. N.E. Fla. Hosp. Council (pres. 1964-65), Belle Glade C. of C. (pres. 1973-74), Pi Epsilon Rho. Presbyn. (deacon, elder 1963-66). Elk, Lion. Home: 1125 1/2 S Main St Belle Glade FL 33430 Office: 1201 S Main St Belle Glade FL 33430

CLARKE, LEWIS JAMES, landscape architect; b. Carlton Notts., Eng., Mar. 10, 1927; s. Roland and May (Pringle) C.; Dip. Arch. Sch. Architecture, 1950; Dip. L.D., Kings Coll., U. Durham, 1951; M.W.A., Harvard, 1952; m. Abbie Pearl Swinson, Nov. 24, 1954; children—Lewis Nigel, Jennifer Kay, Rachel May, Liza Elaine. Came to U.S., 1951. Prin. Lewis Clarke Assos., landscape architecture and site planning, Raleigh, 1952—; prof. Sch. Design N.C. State U., Raleigh, 1952-68, acting head dept. landscape architecture, 1967-68. Mem. Planning Commn. Raleigh, 1967-69. Recipient Fulbright grant, Smith Mundt award; Distinguished Tchr. award, 1961, 67. Mem. Am. Soc. Landscape Architects; Royal Inst. British Architects, British Inst. Landscape Architects. Home: 3215 Darien Dr Raleigh NC 27607 Office: Kroger Exec Center Raleigh NC 27612

CLARKE, L(ULA) BEATRICE FLEMING (MRS. ALLEN CLARENCE CLARKE), educator; b. Jacksonville, Fla., Oct. 1, 1910; d. Lucius Samuel and Eva (Jackson) Fleming; B.S., Fla. A. and M. Coll., 1931; M.A., U. Mich., 1933, postgrad. summer, 1951; postgrad. summers U. Chgo., 1938, (fellow) Brown U., 1945, (NSF fellow) U. Kan., 1958, 59, Tufts U., 1968; m. Allen Clarence Clarke, Nov. 21, 1942; 1 dau., Karen Eileen. Tchr. sci. Howard Acad., Ocala, Fla., 1931-32; tchr. high sch. math. Edward Waters Coll., Jacksonville, 1933-34; instr. English and math. Fla. and A. and M. Coll., 1934-40, asst. prof., 1940-45; asst. prof. math., 1947-49, asso. prof., 1949—, dir. 13 coll. curriculum program, 1969—, acting chmn. dept., 1949-62; substitute tchr. pub. schs., Bridgeport, Conn., 1946. Vice pres. Leon Interfaith Child Care, Inc., 1969-73; active Jack and Jill Club Am., 1952-65. Bd. dirs. Leon Interfaith Child Care, Inc., 1969-73. Named Tchr. of Year, Fla. A. and M. Coll., 1954. Mem. Math. Assn. Am., Delta Sigma Theta, Alpha Kappa Mu, Beta Kappa Chi. Presbyn (elder). Author: (with others) College Algebra, 1956; College Algebra and Basic Set Theory, 1962. Home: 1442 Coleman St Tallahassee FL 32304

CLARKE, LYNN BENJAMIN, univ. adminstr.; b. N.Y.C., Aug. 2, 1926; s. Lynn Banks and Mary Louise (Farrell) C.; B.A., Princeton, 1947; m. Mildred Kate Stine, Dec. 18, 1950; children—Lynn Bernard, Stephen Dawson, Edward Joseph. Mem. editorial, promotion and advt. sales staffs Time Inc., N.Y.C., 1947-53, Chgo., 1953-57; pres. Russell Clarke, Inc., St. Petersburg, Fla., 1957-65; dir. pub. relations U. Miami, Coral Gables, Fla., 1966-73, dir. legislative relations, 1973—. Exec. dir. Ind. Colls. and Univs. Fla., 1962-65. Served to lt. USNR, 1944-46, 49-51. Mem. Pub. Relations Soc. Am. (pres. S. Fla. chpt. 1969-71, nat. vice chmn. Southeast dist. 1972), Am. Coll. Pub. Relations Assn., Children Am. Revolution, Coral Gables C. of C. (dir. 1969-71), Fla. Presbyn. Coll. Charter Alumni Assn., Alpha Kappa Psi. Democrat. Roman Catholic. Club: Charter (Princeton, N.J.). Home: 9450 Palmetto Club Lane E Miami FL 33157 Office: PO Box 8073 U Miami Coral Gables FL 33124

CLARKSON, ALLEN B., clergyman; b. Columbia, S.C.; B.A., U. S.C.; B.D., U. of South, also D.D. Rector, Ch. of Good Shepherd, Augusta, Ga. Founder, rector Episcopal Day Sch., Augusta, Ga. Dep. to 6 gen. convs. Episcopal Ch.; pres. standing com. Diocese Ga.; mem. council Province Sewanee; mem. council Assn. Episcopal Schs.; chmn. Day Sch. Province, Sewanee, Tenn. Home: 2347 Walton Way Augusta GA 30904

CLARKSON, LAWRENCE WILLIAM, aircraft co. exec.; b. Grove City, Pa., Apr. 29, 1938; s. Harold William and Jean Henrietta (Jaxtheimer) C.; A.B., DePauw U., 1960; J.D., U. Fla., 1962; m. Barbara Louise Stevenson, Aug. 20, 1960; children—Michael, Elizabeth, Jennifer. Admitted to Fla. bar, 1963; mem. firm, Caldwell, Pacetti, Barrow, Palm Beach, Fla., 1965-67; dept. counsel Pratt & Whitney, Fla. Research and Devel. Center, West Palm Beach, 1967-69, mgr. contract adminstrn., 1969-72, program mgr.

F-100/F401 Engine Program, 1972—; asst. sec. United Aircraft, 1971—. Musical dir. North County Choral Soc., 1968—; mem. nat. council Met. Opera. Mgr., Leroy Collins campaign U.S. Senate, Palm Beach County, 1968; mem. Palm Beach County Democratic Exec. Com., 1967-68; town counsel, Town of Haverhill, Fla., 1968-72, pres. town counsel, 1971-72, judge, 1970-72. Bd. dirs. Palm Beach County Goodwill Industries, 1966-68, Palm Beach County chpt. Am. Cancer Soc.; chmn. Palm Beach County Cancer Crusade, 1973-74. Served to capt. USAF, 1962-66. Mem. Am. Bar Assn., Fla. Bar, Am. Judicature Soc., Phi Delta Phi, Delta Chi, Phi Mu Alpha. Episcopalian (vestryman). Club: LaCoquille (Palm Beach, Fla.). Home: 2255 S Flagler Dr West Palm Beach FL 33405 Office: Box 2691 Beeline Hwy West Palm Beach FL 33402

CLARSON, JOHN PATRICK, lawyer; b. Bklyn., June 7, 1946; s. Thomas A. and Ann (Kelly) C.; B.A., John Carroll U., 1967; J.D., So. Meth. U. Law Sch., 1970; m. Laura Banks, June 20, 1969. Admitted to Tex. bar, 1970; mem. firm Spafford, Gay & Whitham, Dallas, 1970—. Mem. State Bar Tex., Am. Bar Assn. Home: 4706 Jason St Dallas TX 75206 Office: Adolphus Tower Dallas TX 75202

CLATOR, IRVIN GARRETT, educator; b. Huntington, W.Va., Nov. 2, 1941; s. Charles Eugene and Wanda Roberta (Garrett) C.; B.S., W.Va. U., 1963, M.S., 1965, Ph.D., 1969. Sr. scientist U.S. Naval Weapons Lab., Dahlgren, Va., 1969-70; asst. prof. physics U. N.C., Wilmington, 1970-74, asso. prof., 1974—, chmn. dept. physics, 1970—. Mem. A.A.A.S., N.Y. Acad. Scis., N.C. Acad. Sci. Contbr. articles to profl. jours. Patentee in field. Home: Wrightsville Village Wilmington NC 28401

CLAUDEL, CALVIN ANDRÉ, educator; b. Goudeau, La., July 7, 1909; s. André Émile and Leota Anna (Edwards) C.; B.A., Tulane U., 1931, M.A., 1932; Ph.D., U. N.C., 1947; diploma Sorbonne, Paris, 1962; m. Alice Mcleod Moser, Feb. 23, 1943; 1 stepson, William Mcleod Rivera. Tchr., chmn. langs. New Orleans Pub. High Schs., 1932-43, 53-65; instr. French, U. N.C., 1943-47; prof., chmn. Romance langs. W.Va. Wesleyan Coll., Buckhannon, 1966-69; prof. French and Spanish, Salisbury (Md.) State Coll., 1969-72; asst. prof. French and Spanish, Eastern Shore Community Coll., Wallops Island, Va., 1972—. Cons., NASA. Scoutmaster, Wallops Island, 1972-73. Served with USMCR, 1942-43. Decorated Acad. Palms (France); recipient prize Athenee Louisianais. Mem. Modern Lang. Assn., Inst. for Internat. Sociol. Research (life fellow), Am. Assn. Tchrs. French (v.p. Md. 1969-72), Md. Fgn. Lang. Assn. (2d v.p.), Fgn. Lang. Tchrs. Assn. La. (dist. chmn. 1956-60), Nat. Fedn. State Poetry Socs. (chancellor 1969-72), La. Poetry Soc. (pres. 1963-64), N.E.A. (life), Am. Assn. Tchrs. French, Am. Assn. Tchrs. Spanish and Portuguese, Am. Folklore Soc., Am. Assn. U. Profs., Am. Legion (post historian 1957-60), Athenee Louisianais (v.p. 1960-65), Md. Poetry Soc., Paul Claudel Soc. (hon. founder pres. 1968-69). Contbr. to various publs. Home: Box 1083 Chalmette LA 70043 Office: Eastern Shore Community Coll Wallops Island VA 23337

CLAUTICE, WILLIAM EDWARD, aerospace engr.; b. Balt., Jan. 12, 1918; s. Edward P. and Edith (Adams) C.; B.S. in Mech. Engring., Johns Hopkins, 1943, postgrad. metallurgy, 1948-51; m. Lois Orma Russell, Aug. 2, 1958; children—Paula E., William Edward, John R., Laurie E., Russell L., Richard B., Ronald B. Metall. engr. Westinghouse Electric Corp., Pitts., 1946-47; mech. engr. C.E., U.S. Army, Balt. dist., 1947-48; metall. engr. Bur. Ships, Navy Dept., Washington, 1948-62; aerospace engr., structural materials tech. staff, design engring. NASA, Kennedy Space Center, Fla., 1962—. Bd. dirs. Community Assn., Severna Park, Md., 1961-62. Served to lt. with USNR, 1943-46. Registered profl. engr., Ala. Mem. Canaveral Council Tech. Socs., Am. Inst. Aero. and Astronautical Engrs., Am. Soc. Metals, Am. Welding Soc. (chmn. Central Fla. sect. 1966-67), Am. Soc. M.E.s. Home: 68 Westview Lane Cocoa Beach FL 32931 Office: Design Engineering DD-MDD-1 Kennedy Space Center FL 32899

CLAY, HARRIS AUBREY, chem. engr.; b. Hartley, Tex., Dec. 28, 1911; s. John David and Alberta (Harris) C.; B.S., U. Tulsa, 1933; Ch.E., Columbia, 1939; m. Violette Frances Mills, June 19, 1948 (dec. June 1972); m. 2d, Garvice Stuart Shotwell, Apr. 28, 1973. Pilot plant operator Phillips Petroleum Co., Burbank, Okla., 1939-42, resident supr. Burbank pilot plants, 1942-44, process design engr., Bartlesville, Okla., 1944-45, process engring. supr. Philtex Plant, Phillips, Tex., 1946-56, tech. adviser to pilot plant mgr., Bartlesville, 1957-61, chem. engring. asso., 1961-74; cons. engr., 1974—; chmn. tech. com. Fractionation Research, Inc., 1966-71, mem. tech. com., 1972-73. Mem. Am. Inst. Chem. Engrs., Am. Chem. Soc., Electrochem. Soc. Presbyn. Elk. Contbr. articles to profl. jours. Patentee in field. Home: 1723 Church Ct Bartlesville OK 74003

CLAY, JAMES HORACE BEVERLEY, forestry exec.; b. Crewe, Va., Feb. 13, 1924; s. Charles Richard and Augusta (Redford) C.; student U. Richmond, 1946-47, U. Rochester, 1943; m. Phyllis Laughlin, Oct. 26, 1963; children—Vivian, Adrian. Press sec. to congressman, Washington, 1958-60; staff mem. Senate Republican Policy Com., Washington, 1960-61; legislative asst. Senator John Tower, Washington, 1961-63; free lance polit. writer, 1963-66; founder, pres. Washington Nat. Press, Inc., 1967-70; pres. Pub. Affairs Book Club, Inc., 1968-70; co-founder with Orville L. Freeman, pres. U.S. Tree Farms System, Inc., Houston, 1970—. Served with USAAF, 1943-45, with USAF, 1952-53. Mem. Am. Polit. Sci. Assn. Republican. Episcopalian. Clubs: Capitol Hill, Forest Cove Country. Author: Hoffa, 1965. Home: 8986 Chatsworth Dr Houston TX 77024 Office: 8989 Westheimer Rd Houston TX 77042

CLAY, PAUL EUGENE, mech. engr.; b. Texarkana, Tex., Dec. 16, 1933; s. Paul Eugene and Ruth (Elmer) C.; B.S. in Mech. Engring., U. Ark., 1960; M.S. in Mech. Engring., La. Poly. Inst., 1965; M.B.A., La. State U., 1973; m. Mary Elizabeth Brown, June 11, 1955; children—Paul Eugene III, Charlotte Elizabeth, Mitchell Brown. Engr., AMF Beaird Inc., Shreveport, La., 1960-62, sr. engr., 1963-66, product engr., 1967-69, asst. mgr. engring. Maxim Silencer div., 1969-70, mgr. engring., 1970-72, dir. engring., 1972-73; gen. mgr. Pulsco div. Am. Air Filter Inc., 1973—. Served with USMCR, 1955-58. Registered profl. engr., Ark. Mem. Am. Soc. M.E. Republican. Methodist. Contbr. articles to profl. jours. Patentee in field. Home: 6253 Kearny Ventura CA 93003 Office: 126 W Santa Barbara St Santa Paula CA 93060

CLAY, ROSS COLLINS, educator; b. Conehatta, Miss., Dec. 15, 1908; s. George Walker and Ida (Hambrick) C.; B.S., Jackson State Coll., 1934; M.A., Fisk U., 1940; Mus. M., Northwestern U., 1953; postgrad. Ind. U., 1961-62; m. Lillie James, 1940 (dec.); 1 son, Ross Collins; m. 2d, Ollie D. Billingslea, Aug. 7, 1955. Dir. music Easom High Sch., Corinth, Miss., 1934-36, Ark. Bapt. Coll., Little Rock, 1936-38, Geeter High Sch., Whiteheaven, Tenn., 1940-43, Friendship Jr. Coll., Rock Hill, S.C., 1945-46, Philander Smith Coll., Little Rock, 1946-48, Lane Coll., Jackson, Tenn., 1948-53; def. worker, Detroit, 1943-45; dir. music edn. Jackson (Miss.) State Coll., 1953—; church pianist, organist. Mem. Miss. Tchrs. Assn., Nat. Assn. Negro Musicians, N.E.A., Am. Assn. U. Profs., Music Educators Nat. Conf. Baptist. Mason. Club: Harmonia (Jackson). Home: 1750 Topp St Jackson MS 39204

CLAY, WILLIAM CALDWELL, JR., lawyer, corp. exec.; b. Mt. Sterling, Ky., Dec. 28, 1915; s. William Caldwell and Kathryn (Greene) C.; A.B., Dartmouth, 1937; J.D., Yale, 1940; LL.D., Transylvania Coll., 1973; m. Esther Briggs, Apr. 13, 1946; children—Jeanette Dobbs, Sally Sue, Kathryn Caldwell. Admitted to Ky. bar, 1939, since practiced in Mt. Sterling; with Anti-trust div. Dept. Justice 1938-40; counsel pub. relations Burley Auction Warehouse Assn., 1946-56; chmn. bd. Exchange Bank of Ky., Soundiana, Inc., Clay Tobacco Co.; pres. The Cola Corp.; sec., dir. Cowden Mfg. Co., Montgomery Nat. Bank, Hwy. Concrete Pipe, Inc. Mem. bd. curators, mem. exec. com. Transylvania Coll. Mem. Am., Ky. bar assns., C. of C., Sigma Alpha Epsilon. Mem. Christian Church. Odd Fellow, Mason, Rotarian. Author: Farmers Tax Manual, 1943; How to Read and Understand the Bible, 1974. Contbr. to trade publs. Office: 50 Broadway Mount Sterling KY 40353

CLAYBORNE, RICHARD BOOKER II, clergyman; b. Wheeler, Tex., Sept. 12, 1915; s. Mason Webster and Abbie Dorenda (LaRue) C.; student Baylor U. Law Sch., 1933-38; B.A., Tex. Christian U., 1940, M.Div., 1943, D.D., 1963; m. Lula Jean Johnson, Sept. 30, 1943; children—Richard David, Dixie Jean (Mrs. E.L. McIntyre), Terry Mason. Ordained to ministry Christian Ch., 1943; minister Main St. Christian Ch., Waxahachie, Tex., 1946-48, First Christian Ch., Borger, Tex., 1948-54, Woodlawn Christian Ch., San Antonio, 1954-57, First Christian Ch., Midland, Tex., 1957-68, Meml. Dr. Christian Ch., Houston, 1968—. Mem. exec. com. Christian Ch. in Tex., 1971—; v.p. Coastal Plains Area Christian Ch., 1971—. Served with USNR, 1943-46; PTO. Recipient Community Builder award Midland C. of C., 1967. Mem. Tex. Assn. Christian Chs. (pres. 1961-63). Mason (32 deg.). Club: Optimist International (life, lt. gov. 1951-52, pres. Midland 1961-62, Community Service award Midland 1968). Author: The Doctrine of Freedom in the New Testament, 1943; (booklet) A Christian Approach to Race Relations, 1958. Home: 14126 Cindywood St Houston TX 77024 Office: 11750 Memorial Dr Houston TX 77024

CLAYTON, BYRL WASHINGTON, educator; b. Linglevile, Tex., Sept. 7, 1920; s. Byrl Washington and Dollie Mae (Whitefield) C.; B.S., S.W. Tex. State U., 1948; M.Ed., U. Houston, 1953; m. Audie Mae Wheeler, Dec. 24, 1941; children—Janie Ilene (Mrs. Richard Wolters), Danny Byrl, Honee Wynona, Randy Jack. Tchr. indsl. arts, head coach Santa Fe High Sch., Alta Loma, Tex., 1948-50, Van Vleck (Tex.) High Sch., 1950-53; tchr., coach Burnet (Tex.) High Sch., 1953-54, Eldorado (Tex.) High Sch., 1954-59, LaMarque (Tex.) High Sch., 1959-67; dir. health, phys. edn., recreation and athletics, tennis coach Central Tex. Coll., Killeen, 1967—. Served with USCG, 1942-45. Mem. Tennis Coaches Assn., Nat. Jr. Coll. Athletic Assn. (Tennis Coach of Year 1973), Tex. High Sch. Tchrs. Assn., Tex. Indsl. Arts Club, Tex. Assn. Health, Phys. Edn. and Recreation, Tex. Jr. Coll. Tchrs. Assn. Home: 1104 Arkansas St Killeen TX 76541

CLAYTON, CHARLES PRENTICE, city planner; b. Savannah, Mo., Apr. 30, 1911; s. William Prentice and Blanche (Vail) C.; B.S. in Landscape Architecture, Ia. State Coll., 1938; m. Elinor Hale, Sept. 3, 1935; children—Charles Harrison, Elinor Ann (Mrs. Joe L. Clark), Thomas Hale. Landscape foreman Nat. Park Service, Devil's Den State Park, Fayetteville, Ark., 1933-36; landscape architect regional office Resettlement Adminstrn., Little Rock, 1936-37; landscape designer; field supt. Maurice Shamburger, landscape contractor, Tyler, Tex., 1938-39; asso. with Ruth London, Houston, 1939-41; landscape architect U. Ark.; pvt. practice in Mpls., summers 1941-43; site planner Skidmore, Owings & Merrill, Oak Ridge, 1943-44; prin. planning technician Ala. Planning Bd., Birmingham, 1944-47; town planner FHA, land planning sect., Southeastern states, 1947-50, chief land planning cons., 1950-51; mgr. Southeastern office Harland Bartholomew & Assos., 1951—, partner, 1961—. Fellow Am. Soc. Landscape Architects; mem. Am. Inst. Planners, Am. Soc. Planning Ofcls., Am. Planning and Civic Assn., Ga. Engring. Soc., Tau Sigma Delta, Alpha Zeta. Presbyn. (elder). Home: 479 S Woodland Dr Marietta GA 30060 Office: 1401 W Paces Ferry Rd NW Suite D-216 Atlanta GA 30327

CLAYTON, CURTIS ABBITT, hosp. adminstr.; b. Portsmouth, Va., July 25, 1927; s. Graham W. and Charlotte (Williamson) C.; B.S., Va. Inst. Tech., 1952; M.H.A., Med. Coll. Va., 1954; m. Betty Cook, June 17, 1952; children—Debra Rea, Mark W., David A. Asst. supt. Md. Gen. Hosp., Balt., 1954-55; hosp. specialist Kendall Co., Chgo., 1955-59; asst. dir. U. Va. Hosp., Charlottesville, 1959-64; adminstr. Circle Terrace Hosp., Alexandria, Va., 1964-74; exec. dir. West Fla. Hosp., Pensacola, 1974—; chmn., mgr. engring. for hosps. State of Va., 1969; pres. Blue Ridge Hosp. Council, 1970—. Served with AUS, 1945-47. Fellow Am. Coll. Hosp. Adminstrs.; mem. Va. Hosp. Assn. (dir. 1972—), Alumni Assn. Med. Coll. Va. Sch. Hosp. Adminstrn. (past pres.). Methodist (lay leader 1968-72, chmn. bd. 1972—). Rotarian. Home: 4560 Francisco Dr Pensacola FL 32503 Office: 200 E Burgess Rd Pensacola FL 32504

CLAYTON, LAURA BLAND (MRS. CHARLES LINDSAY CLAYTON), educator; b. Winston-Salem, N.C.; d. Joseph Franklin and Mozella (Dugan) Bland; A.B., Salem Coll., 1938; M.A., U. N.C., 1939, Ph.D., 1950; diploma Am. Acad. Rome, 1950; m. Charles Lindsay Clayton, May 25, 1958; Piano, organ instr. Bland Piano Co., Winston-Salem, 1938-50, cons., partner, 1940-58; instr. Latin, Salem Acad., Winston-Salem, 1948-50; asso. prof. English, journalism, dramatics, speech Lees-McRae Coll., Banner Elk, N.C., 1950-53; asst. prof. English, Latin, Lenoir Rhyne Coll., Hickory, N.C., 1963-65, asso. prof., 1966-67, prof., 1969—, also chmn. humanities div. Mem. S. Atlantic Modern Lang. Assn., N.C. Edn. Assn., N.E.A., Am. Classical League, Classical Assn. Middle West and South, Vergilian Soc., Am. Assn. U. Women, Am. Assn. U. Profs., Modern Lang. Assn., N.C. Classical Assn. (pres. 1971-73), Am. Translators Soc., Internat. Platform Assn., Mu Sigma Epsilon. Clubs: Lake Hickory Country; Lenoir (N.C.) Country, Cedar Rock Country (Lenoir), Blowing Rock Country (N.C.) Home: 327 2d St NE Hickory NC 28601

CLAYTON, WILLIAM HOWARD, univ. ofcl.; b. Dallas, Aug. 16, 1921; s. William Howard and Blanche (Phillips) C.; B.S., Bucknell U., 1949; Ph.D., Tex. A. and M. U., 1956; m. Diane Dougherty, June 8, 1963; children—Jill, Gregory. Instr., Bucknell U., 1948; grad. asst. Ohio State U., 1949, U. N.M., 1949-50; research asst. oceanography and meteorology Tex. A. and M. U., College Station, 1950-51, asst. oceanography, 1951-54, asso. oceanography, instr. math., 1954-56, micrometeorologist U. Research Found., instr. math., 1956-58, faculty oceanography, meteorology, 1958—, prof. oceanography, 1965—, prin. investigator Research Found., 1956-65, asso. dean Coll. Geoscis., 1970-71, dean Moody Coll. Marine Scis. and Maritime Resources, Galveston, 1971-74, provost, 1974—. Vis. prof. U. Hawaii, 1963-64; tech. dir. Project Themis, U.S. Army Electronics Command, 1967-74; chmn. field observing facility adv. panel Nat. Center for Atmospheric Research, 1973-74. Trustee Gulf Univs. Research Consortium, 1971—. Served with RCAF, 1940-44, USAAF, 1944-45. Mem. Am. Geophys. Union, Am. Meteorol. Soc., Galveston C. of C., Sigma Xi, Pi Mu Epsilon, Sigma Pi Sigma, Phi Kappa Phi, Sigma Phi Epsilon. Elk. Contbr. articles to profl. lit., chpts. to books. Home: 54 Adler Circle Galveston TX 77550 Office: Tex A and M U Moody Coll Marine Scis and Maritime Resources PO Box 1675 Galveston TX 77550

CLEAR, JAMES ARTHUR, JR., city ofcl.; b. Petersburg, Va., June 1, 1916; s. James Arthur and Catherine B. (Hammond) C.; student in surveying Internat. Corr. Schs., 1940; student Engring. Sch., Ft. Belvoir, Va., 1943; student in municipal pub. works U. Tenn., 1956; m. Hazel Marsh, Apr. 21, 1935; 1 dau., Catherine Jane. Instrument man survey party Tenn. Hwy. Dept., Knoxville, 1938-40; surveyor Am. Bemberg Corp., Elizabethton, Tenn., 1940-41; cartographer U.S. Coast and Geodetic Survey, Washington, 1941-43; asst. city mgr., dir. pub. works City of Elizabethton, 1946—. Pres., United Fund, 1963-64, campaign dir., 1964-65; pres. Boys Club, 1964-65; chmn. Carter County, Nat. Found. March of Dimes, 1966-67. Served with AUS, 1943-46; PTO. Named Outstanding Citizen of Carter County, V.F.W., 1968; recipient Honor award Carter County C. of C., 1963; Outstanding Community Service award Elizabethton Jr. C. of C., 1964; Outstanding Citizenship award United Fund, 1964, 65. Mem. Elizabethton C. of C. (pres. 1963-64), Am. (nat. dir. 1969—), Tenn. (pres. 1969-70) pub. works assns., Tenn. Municipal League, Tenn. Water and Waste-Water Assn., Am. Legion, V.F.W., Y's Men. Methodist (chmn. bd. stewards 1966-67). Club: Civitan (Elizabethton). Home: 505 Carter Blvd Elizabethton TN 37643 Office: Municipal Bldg Elizabethton TN 37643

CLEARY, ROBERT EDWARD, univ. provost; b. East Orange, N.J., Feb. 27, 1932; s. Charles A. and Mary J. (Solomon) C.; B.A. in Social Sci., Montclair (N.J.) State Coll., 1953; M.A. in Polit. Sci., Rutgers U., 1959, Ph.D., 1962; m. Marilyn F. Jacoby, Apr. 21, 1956; children—Barbara, Kevin, Charles. Asst. dir. secondary sch. project Eagleton Inst. Politics, Rutgers U., 1959-61; asst. prof. polit. sci. George Peabody Coll. for Tchrs., 1961-64; asst. dir. Am. Polit. Sci. Assn., 1966-67; asso. prof., asso. dean Sch. Govt. and Pub. Adminstrn., Am. U., Washington, 1965-70, prof. govt., 1970—, dean acad. devel., 1970-72, provost, 1972—. Mem. Am. Polit. Sci. Assn. (Congl. fellow 1964-65), Nat. Council Social Studies. Contbr. articles to profl. jours. Home: 7503 Elmore Lane Bethesda MD 20034 Office: American University Washington DC 20016

CLECKLEY, JAMES JENNINGS, psychiatrist; b. Bamberg, S.C., Feb. 17, 1914; s. John Jennings and Mary Cliffton (Cope) C.; B.S., The Citadel, 1935; M.D., Med. Coll. S.C., 1939; m. Martha Carter, May 23, 1942; children—Jenny Jaudon, James Jennings, Jr., Marther Carter. Intern Charity Hosp., New Orleans, 1939-40, Tri County Hosp., Orangeburg, N.C., 1940-41; resident U.S. Naval Hosp., Phila., 1944-46, VA Hosp., Columbia, S.C., 1946-47, Med. Coll. S.C., Charleston, 1947-49; practice medicine specializing in psychiatry, Charleston, 1947—; dir. Charleston County Mental Health Clinic, 1952-56; mem. staffs Roper, St. Francis hosps., Charleston; mem. faculty Med. U. S.C., Charleston, 1947—, prof. psychiatry, 1968—, chmn. dept. psychiatry, 1956-68; cons. U.S. Naval Hosp., Charleston, 1950—, Charleston VA Hosp., 1966—. Served with USNR, 1942-46. Fellow Am., So. psychiat. assns.; mem. A.M.A., Charleston County Med. Soc., Alpha Omega Alpha. Home: 14 Country Club Dr Charleston SC 29412 Office: 80 Barre St Charleston SC 29401

CLEGG, GILES CONNELL, JR., lawyer; b. San Angelo, Tex., Apr. 1, 1929; s. Giles Connell and Eula (Griggs) C.; B.S., Tex. A. and M. U., 1951; LL.B., So. Meth. U., 1960; M. Nancy Moore, July 25, 1953; children—Stephen, Karen, Richard; m. Lynaveta Bates, Dec. 30, 1967. With Tex. Eastern Transmission Corp., 1953-55, Tex. Instruments, Inc., 1955-61; admitted to Tex. bar, 1960, since practiced in Dallas. Served to lt. USAF, 1951-53. Mem. I.E.E.E., Am. Patent Law Assn., Am. Bar Assn., State Bar Tex., Dallas-Ft. Worth Patent Assn. Home: Route 3 Roanoke TX 76262 Office: 1950 One Main Pl Dallas TX 75250

CLEGG, LEONARD BRUCE, food co. exec.; b. Milw., July 31, 1928; s. Gilbert and Nina (Oatman) C.; B.B.A., U. Wis., 1950, M.B.A., 1951; m. Gretchen Joy Zentner, Dec. 10, 1955; children—David Bruce, Julie Ann, Laura Lynn. With Red Dot Foods, Inc., Madison, Wis., 1951-61, dir. tng., 1957-58, dir. personnel, 1958-61; with Frito-Lay, Inc., Detroit and Dallas, 1961—, mgr. labor relations, Dallas, 1964-69, v.p. labor relations, 1969—. Lectr. supervisory tng. extension div. U. Wis., Madison, 1969. Troop chmn. Circle Ten council Boy Scouts Am., 1969—. Served with AUS, 1951-53. Mem. Am. (workshop chmn.), Tex. (mem. Tex. labor relations com.) mfrs. assns. Methodist. (chmn. council on ministries). Kiwanian. Club: Brookhaven Country (Dallas). Home: 4927 Forest Bend Rd Dallas TX 75234 Office: Box 35034 Dallas TX 75235

CLEM, JAMES WILLIAM, JR., aircraft instrument co. exec.; b. Dallas, Sept. 12, 1923; s. James William and Frances Byrde (Kendrick) C.; student So. Meth. U., 1959; m. Frances Anne Voss, Dec. 18, 1959; children—James William III, Michael Frank. Owner, Hobby Nook, Dallas, 1947-49; shop supr. Carruth Lab. Inc., Dallas, 1949-61; with Executive Instruments Inc., Addison, Tex., 1961—, pres., 1964—; cons. Tex. Instruments Inc., Dallas, 1966—, Azimuth Indsl. Design, Addison, 1965—. Trustee Exec. Instruments Employee Pension Trust. Mem. Acad. Model Aeronautics (v.p. 1957-59), Sports Car Club Am. Home: 8240 Greenhollow Dallas TX 75240 Office: 771 Wiley Post Rd Addison TX 75001

CLEMENS, DONALD FAULL, educator; b. Dover, O., Aug. 14, 1929; s. John William and Ruth Adelaide (Faull) G.; B.S., Fla. So. Coll., 1961; M.S., U. Fla., 1963, Ph.D., 1965; m. Martha Katharine Lemmon, July 2, 1950; children—Richard, Nancy (Mrs. Hyman Spruill Legett), Barbara, Rebecca, Margaret. Machinist Greer Steel Co., Dover, O., 1947-57; instr. U. Fla., Gainesville, 1963-65; asso. prof. East Carolina U., Greenville, 1965-69, prof. chemistry, 1969—. Petroleum Research Fund grantee Am. Chem. Soc., 1966-68. Mem. Am. Chem. Soc. (sect. chmn. 1969-70; sec. treas. 1967-68), Sigma Xi (pres. 1970-71). Methodist (chmn. council ministries 1969-71; chmn. adminstrv. bd. 1971-72; chmn. finance com. 1972-73). Mason, Kiwanian. Author: (with W.A. McAllister) Fundamental Laboratory Operations, 1968, 70, 72. Home: 1701 Sulgrave Rd Greenville NC 27834

CLEMENS, GERALD O'NEAL, lawyer; b. Christiansburg, Va., Mar. 20, 1936; s. Maury Hampton and Clairmont Estelle (Snider) C.; B.S., Va. Poly. Inst., 1956; LL.B., Washington and Lee U., 1960; LL.M. (Ford Found. fellow 1960-61), Northwestern U., Evanston, Ill., 1961; m. Patricia Jean Lugar, Sept. 3, 1960; children—Cynthia Neal, John Christopher, Charles Thomas. Admitted to Va. bar, 1960; law clk. U.S. Dist. Ct., Western Dist. Va., Roanoke, 1960-62; partner Kime, Jolly, Clemens & Canterbury, Attys., Salem, Va., 1962—. Part-time instr. Roanoke Coll., Salem, Va., 1964-69; pres. Holiday Estates, Inc., Salem, 1972—; sec., treas. Hundley Painting Co., Roanoke, 1971—; commr. in chancery Circuit Ct., Salem, Va., 1968—, County Roanoke, Va., 1962—. Pres. Luth. Children's Home of South, Salem, 1972—, bd. trustees, 1971—; bd. dirs. Legal Aid Soc., Roanoke Valley, 1968—. Mem. Am., Va., Salem (past pres.) bar assns., Salem Jr. C. of C., Alpha Kappa Psi, Alpha Phi Omega, Phi Kappa Phi, Phi Alpha Delta. Lutheran. Clubs: Town, Racquet (Salem, Va.). Home: 135 Lewis Av Salem VA 24153 Office: 430 E Clay St Salem VA 24153

CLEMENT, BESSE ALBERTA, educator; b. Norman, Okla., Nov. 10, 1902; d. Thomas Egbert and Daisy Alberta (Armstrong) Clement; student Nat. Park Coll., 1920-21; Franco-Am. exchange scholar Lycee de Jeunes Filles, St.-Germain-en-Laye, France, 1922-23; B.A., U. Okla., 1925, M.A., 1928; postgrad. Columbia, 1934; Ph.D. (Univ. Grad. scholar 1938-39), Stanford, 1947. Asst. modern langs. Ouachita Coll., Arkadelphia, Ark., 1925-26; mem. faculty U. Okla., 1926—, prof. Romance langs., 1958-63, David Ross Boyd prof. Romance langs., 1963—. Recipient Teaching award U. Okla., 1955. Mem. Modern Lang. Assn., Am. Assn. Tchrs. French, South Central Modern Lang. Assn., Phi Beta Kappa (past pres. U. Okla. chpt.), Delta Delta Delta. Translator: (Roger Le Tourneau) Fez in the Age of the Marinides, 1961. Home: 1108 Chautauqua St Norman OK 73069

CLEMENT, G. FRANK, ins. co. exec.; b. Roanoke, Va., Aug. 22, 1907; s. George Abner and Susan (Pollard) C.; ed. at Radford, Va. Agt., Jefferson Standard Ins. Co., 1930-34, mgr. Roanoke br. office, 1934-48; mgr. home office agy. Shenandoah Life Ins. Co., Roanoke, 1949-52, v.p. charge agys., 1952-60, exec. v.p., 1960, pres., dir. 1960-71, chmn. bd., pres., 1971, chmn. bd., 1972—; dir. Colonial-Am. Nat. Bank of Roanoke, Roanoke Electric Steel Corp., Roy H. Park Broadcasting Co., Roanoke. Bd. dirs. Community Hosp. of Roanoke Valley. C.L.U. Home: 2237 Brambleton Av SW Roanoke VA 24015 Office: 2301 Brambleotn Av SW Roanoke VA

CLEMENT, ROBERT LEBBY, JR., lawyer; b. Charleston, S.C., Dec. 14, 1928; s. Robert Lebby and Julia Axson (Thayer) C.; A.B., The Citadel, 1948; J.D., Duke, 1951; m. Helen Mathilda Lewis, Nov. 26, 1954; children—Jeanne Marie, Robert Lebby III, Thomas L.T. Admitted to N.C. bar, 1951, S.C. bar, 1954; practiced in Charlotte, N.C., 1951-53, Charleston, 1955—; partner Cornish, Clement & Horlbeck, 1955-60, Hagood, Rivers & Young, 1960-65, Young, Clement & Rivers, 1965—; judge Municipal Ct. City of Charleston, 1961-64. Pres., Charleston Automotive Parts, 1969—; dir. Am. Mut. Fire, Carolina Am. Life Ins. Co.; mem. Charleston adv. bd. dirs. Citizens and So. Nat. Bank. Chmn., Gov.'s Higher Edn. Study Com. for Charleston County, 1967-68; mem. Planning and Zoning Commn. City of Charleston, 1968—; asst. corp. counsel City of Charleston, 1960; chmn. Broad St. Beautification Com., 1968-71, Am. St. Com. Bi-Centennial Program, 1973—, Downtown Council, 1971-72; mem. Trident Devel. Council, 1973—. Trustee Charleston Mus. Served to capt. USAF, 1953-55. Mem. Am., S.C. (v.p. 1965-66), N.C., Charleston County bar assns., Soc. Colonial Wars State S.C. (gov. 1972—), Soc. Cin., S.C. Hist. Soc. (curator 1965-66), Charleston Trident C. of C. Democrat. Presbyn. (deacon 1959-60). Rotarian. Clubs: Charleston Lawyers (pres. 1959-60), St. Andrews Society (v.p. Charleston 1971—), Sertoma (pres. Charleston 1963-64, gov. 1965-66). Home: 7 Legare St Charleston SC 29401 Office: 28 Broad St Charleston SC 29401

CLEMENT, WALTER STONE, railroad exec.; b. Roanoke, Va., Sept. 12, 1912; s. Allen W. and Berta L. (Bousman) C.; ed. Washington and Lee U., Boston Coll.; m. Jane Henderson, Nov. 15, 1940; children—Zack, Tiffany. With N. & W. Ry., 1935—, asst. roadmaster, 1947-50, roadmaster, 1950-54, asst. trainmaster, 1954-55, trainmaster, 1955-57, supt., 1957, asst. gen. supt., 1957-59, gen. supt., Roanoke, Va., 1959-60, resident v.p., Norfolk, Va., 1960-64, v.p. lake region, Cleve., 1964-66, v.p. Western region, St. Louis, 1966-69, v.p. Washington, 1969-71, v.p. pub. affairs, Roanoke, 1971—. Served to capt. C.E., AUS, 1942-46. Mem. Ohio C. of C. (dir.). Democrat. Baptist Clubs: Burning Tree (Washington); Roanoke Country. Office: 8 N Jefferson St Roanoke VA 24011

CLEMENT, WILLIAM JOHN, bank exec.; b. Rover, Ark., Feb. 14, 1906; s. Charles A. and Ada Belle (Fry) C.; student pub. schs.; m. Thelma Jessica Webb, June 25, 1948; 1 son, William John. Farmer nr. Yell County (Ark.), 1925-42; cattle rancher, Dardanelle, Ark., 1948-52, 59-64; owner, ins. agt. Clement-Cox Agy., Dardanelle, 1942-48; owner Clement Feed Co., Russellville, Ark. and Dardanelle, 1952-59; with First State Bank, Plainview, Ark., 1961—, pres., 1965—; pres. Clement Ins. Agy., Ola, Ark., 1966—; dir. Dardanelle Industries, Inc., 1952—, chmn. bd. 1968—; dir. Lake Dardanelle, Inc., 1971—, chmn. bd., 1971-73. Circuit clk. Yell County, 1936-45. Named Boss of Year, Plainview Jr. C. of C., 1973. Mem. Ark. Bankers Assn., Bank Adminstrn. Inst. (pres. Central Ark. chpt. 1971-72). Democrat. Methodist. Mason, Lion, Rotarian. Club: Bay Ridge Boat and Golf (Dardanelle). Home: 419 S 2d St Dardanelle AR 72834 Office: Box 277 Plainview AR 72857

CLEMENTS, ABRAHAM WALLER, state ofcl.; b. nr. Morganfield, Ky., Dec. 9, 1916; s. Baldwin Johnson and Margaret Elizabeth (Kagey) C.; grad. high sch.; m. Lena Ray Sosh, Nov. 25, 1939; 1 dau., Bonnie Lou (Mrs. DeMotte Little); m. 2d, Mildred T. Corum Woodruff, Feb. 11, 1972; stepchildren—James Woodruff, Larry Woodruff. With Ky. Dept. Hwys., 1934—, chief constrn. engr., 1963-66, dist. engr., Madisonville, 1966—. Served with USNR, 1942-45. Registered profl. engr., Ky. Mason (Shriner), Kiwanian. Home: 24 Valley Dr Madisonville KY 42431 Office: P O Drawer D Madisonville KY 42431

CLEMENTS, OMER RANDOLPH, petrochem. mfg. co. exec.; b. Ida, La., Aug. 14, 1925; s. Quilla Zedoic and LaVada (Slay) C.; B.S., La. Poly. Inst., 1950; m. Lovenia Holder, Dec. 22, 1950; 1 son, Terence Christopher. Plant engr. Southwest Gas Producing Co., 1950-51; with Western Co., Midland, Tex., 1951-52, Henderson Engring. Co., Shreveport, La., 1952-53, El Paso Natural Gas Co., 1953-61, operations mgr., 1963-65; with El Paso Products Co., Odessa, 1961—, v.p., gen. mgr., mfg. operations, 1968—. Bd. regents Odessa Coll., now pres. bd. Served with AUS, 1943-45. Registered profl. engr., Tex. Mem. Am. Inst. Chem. Engrs., Nat., Tex. socs. profl. engrs., Tex. Mfrs. Assn. (dir., regional chmn.), West Tex. (dir., dist. v.p.), Odessa (dir.) chambers commerce. Home: 2927 Kirkwood St Odessa TX 79760 Office: PO Box 3986 Odessa TX 79760

CLEMENTS, REXFORD SCOTT, banker; b. Hartford, Conn., Aug. 30, 1936; s. Rolf Victor and Eleanor Benedict (Baldwin) C.; B.A. in Econs., Dickinson Coll., 1959; M.A. in Econs., Trinity Coll., 1968; grad. Stonier Grad. Sch. Banking, Rutgers U., 1972; m. Arline Florence Bishop, Aug. 17, 1962; children—Kate Baldwin, Amy Elizabeth, Rebecca Lee, Sarah Lynn. Asst. cashier Hartford Nat. Bank and Trust Co. (Conn.), 1963-68; v.p. Atlantic Nat. Bank of Jacksonville (Fla.), 1968-73, v.p., sr. bond officer, 1973—; v.p. Atlantic Bancorp., 1972—; v.p. finance, dir. Atlantic Financial Services, 1973—. Instr., Am. Inst. Banking, 1968—. Treas., United Negro Coll. Fund, 1971—; mem. budget com. United Fund, 1970—. Served with USNR, 1959-62. Mem. Greater Jacksonville C. of C. (mem. state and local govt. com. 1970—), Financial Analysts of Jacksonville, Municipal Forum of Washington, Am. Inst. Banking, Nat. Assn. Bus. Economists. Unitarian. Clubs: San Jose Country, University (Jacksonville). Home: Route 6 Box 332 Jacksonville FL 32223 Office: West Bay Sta Jacksonville FL 32203

CLEMENTS, ZEKE, musician; b. Dora, Ala., Sept. 6, 1911; s. Andrew Jackson and Vjola (Peters) C.; student pub. schs.; m. Helen E. Dalton, May 21, 1944; 1 dau., Sally R. Star of Grand Ole Opry, Nashville; writer numerous songs including Just a Little Lovin, Smoke on the Water, Why Should I Cry, Live and Learn, Somebody's Been Beatin' My Time, Me and My Big Mouth, I Love the Name of Jesus. Mem. Song Writers Hall Fame. Address: PO Box 35 Nashville TN 37202

CLEMMONS, ROBERT STARR, minister, educator, author; b. New London, O., Oct. 21, 1910; s. William E. and Tella (Tissot) C.; B.A., Ohio Wesleyan U., 1933; M.Div., Union Theol. Sem., 1936; S.T.M., Oberlin Coll., 1951; postgrad. Vanderbilt U., George Peabody Coll., U. Pitts., Columbia; m. Beatrice Marian Winter, Aug. 27, 1936; children—Lynne Marie (Mrs. Judson Henry Morris, Jr.), David Robert. Ordained to ministry Methodist Ch., 1934; mem. staff Ch. of All Nations, N.Y.C., 1934-36; minister, Brecksville, O., 1936; dir. Wesley Found., State U., Kent, O., 1940-45; mem. staff young adult work Gen. Bd. Edn. United Meth. Ch., Nashville, 1945-57, dir. Council of Adult Work, 1957-67, asst. to gen. sec. program design and coordination task force ethnic minorities, 1967—. Lectr. Emory U., Iliff Sch. Theology, Scarritt Coll.; field work cons. Vanderbilt U. Divinity Sch.; mem. nat. family life com. United Meth. Ch., 1956-68, mem. nat. curriculum com., 1945-68, mem. interagy. staff planning task force, 1968—. Mem. Am. Acad. Religion, Adult Edn. Assn., Am. Acad. Arts and Scis., World Futurist Soc. Methodist. Author: Dynamics of Christian Adult Education, 1957; Young Adults in the Church, 1959; Adult Education in the Methodist Church, 1961; Education for Churchmanship, 1966. Home: 2019 Overhill Dr Nashville TN 37215 Office: PO Box 871 1001 19th Av S Nashville TN 37203

CLEMMONS, SLATON, lawyer; b. Rome, Ga., July 19, 1909; s. Thomas Edmondson and Annie Ross (Slaton) C.; student Davidson Coll., 1926-27; LL.B., U. Ga., 1929; postgrad. U. Pa., 1929-30; m. Starr Reynolds Quigg, 1939 (div. 1957); children—Diana Edmondson, Byard Quigg, Thomas Slaton; m. 2d, Frances Mansell Crowder, Nov. 1965. Admitted to Ga. bar, 1929; practiced in Rome, 1930-35, 46-54; spl. atty. U.S. Dept. Justice, 1935-37, 42-46; spl. atty. gen. Ga., 1938-39; spl. asst. to atty. gen. U.S., 1940-41; asst. U.S. atty. No. dist. Ga., 1954-62; 1st asst. U.S. atty., 1962-70, ret., 1970. Served as lt. (j.g.) USNR, 1942. Fellow Internat. Acad. Law and Sci.; mem. Am., Ga., Rome (past pres.) bar assns., Am. Judicature Soc., Am. Acad. Polit. and Social Sci., Am. Legion, Mil. Order World Wars, Phi Delta Phi, Sigma Alpha Epsilon. Democrat. Presbyn. Mason. Clubs: Coosa Country, Nine O'clock Cotillion (Rome, Ga.). Home: 412 E 3d Av Rome GA 30161

CLENDENING, JOHN ALBERT, palynologist; b. Martinsburg, W.Va., Mar. 6, 1932; s. Charles Brady and F.D. Myrtle (Remsburg) C.; student Shepherd Coll., 1954-56; B.S., W.Va. U., 1958, M.S., 1960, Ph.D., 1970; m. Cleo Dorothy Bond, Sept. 26, 1954; children—Kyra Lynn, Rebecca Lea, Shawna Ruth. Coal geologist-palynologist W.Va. Geol. Survey, Morgantown, 1960-68; palynologist Pan Am. Petroleum Corp., Ft. Worth, 1968-71, Amoco Prodn. Co., Houston, 1971—. Served with inf., U.S. Army, 1951-54. Decorated Purple Heart. Fellow Geol. Soc. Am.; mem. Bot. Soc. Am., W.Va. Acad. Sci. Methodist. Mason (K.T.). Author: (with W.H. Gillespie) West Virginia Geology, Archeology and Pedology, 1964; (with Gillespie & Latimer) Plant Fossils of West Virginia, 1966; Sporological Evidence on the Geological Age of the Dunkard Strata in the Appalachian Basin, 1970. Contbr. articles to profl. jours. Home: 1018 Tulip Tree Lane Houston TX 77090 Office: Box 3092 Houston TX 77001

CLERICO, LOUIS RICHARD, interior designer; b. Yonkers, N.Y., Mar. 30, 1918; s. Ludovico Michael and Mary Lucia (Esposito) C.; grad. Newark Fine and Indsl. Arts Sch., 1935; student Art Students League, 1945-46, N.Y.U., 1946-49; m. Antoinette Francis Oliveri, June 6, 1952; children—Louis, Candace, Melodi, Valerie. Owner, Louis R. Clerico Assos., N.Y.C., 1948-62; pres., chief designer Louis R. Clerico, Miami, 1962-69; sr. partner I.D. Assos., Miami, 1969-70; v.p. charge design Louis R. Clerico Assos., Inc., Miami, 1970—. Cons. for design and color Jo Gresite Ceramic Tile Corp., Milan, Italy, 1961-63. Mem. Fla. Gov's. Council, 1967-70. Served to 1st lt. AUS, 1940-45. Recipient 1st prize for package design Art Dirs. Club Greater Miami, 1953, award for outstanding design achievements Euster Merchandise Mart, 1970, Interior Design award Miami Mdse. Mart, 1969; decorated comdr. Mil. Order St. Brigite (Sweden); created knight (Italy). Mem. Am. Inst. Interior Designers, Indsl. Designers Soc. Am. (chmn. S.W. chpt. 1965). Designers and Decorators Guild (pres. 1962-63), Miami Design Assn. (v.p. design 1967-68), Nat. Home Builders Assn., Ret. Officers Assn. Clubs: Country (Coral Gables, Fla.); Jockey (Miami); Delray Beach (Fla.), Sky Lake (North Miami, Fla.); Inverrary Racquet (Ft. Lauderdale, Fla.). Co-author, illustrator Never Unarmed, 1944. Home: 235 NE 122d St Miami FL 33161 Office: 54 NE 54th St Miami FL 33137

CLEVELAND, CONRAD PIERCE, JR., banker; b. Spartanburg, S.C., Sept. 6, 1914; s. Conrad P. and Louise (Williams) C.; B.S., The Citadel, 1935. Realtor, 1946-48; organizing dir. Piedmont Nat. Bank, 1947-63, v.p., mgr. Main St. br., 1953-63; v.p. Main St. office S.C. Nat. Bank, Spartanburg, 1963-65, v.p. charge Montgomery bldg. office, 1965—; owner Clevedale Farms. Past pres. Spartanburg Music Found.; active Boy Scouts Am., formerly dist. commr. Spartanburg; adv. com. Third Army. Served from 1st lt. to lt. col. AUS, 1940-46; col. Res. Recipient Silver Beaver, Distinguished Eagle Scout awards Boy Scouts Am. Mem. Assn. Citadel Men (past pres., life mem.). Assn. U.S. Army, Res. Officers Assn. Episcopalian (sr. warden, layreader, vestryman; sec. Upper S.C. Diocese Found.). Clubs: Country, Piedmont (Spartanburg). Home: Clevedale Farms Spartanburg SC 29301 Office: South Carolina National Bank Spartanburg SC 29301

CLEVELAND, COURTS KENDALL, JR., rancher; b. Acton, Tex., Oct. 29, 1922; s. Courts Kendall and Olga (Collins) C.; A.S., Tarleton State Coll., 1942; B.S., Tex. A. and M. Coll., 1946. Owner, C & C Candy Co., Ft. Worth, 1946-72; partner Met. Parking Co., Ft. Worth, 1957; owner Cleveland Sales Co., Ft. Worth, 1959-71; owner Clear Fork Ranches, Parker and Hood County, 1949—; dir. Texarado Corp., Internat. Ventures, Inc., Midland Minerals, Inc. Vice pres. Big Brothers Assn., 1957, Jr. C. of C., 1958; pres. Ft. Worth Rehab. Center, 1962. Served with AUS, 1943-45. Decorated Purple Heart. Methodist. Mason (K.T., Shriner). Home: PO Box 215 Granbury TX 76048 Office: 18 Island Village Estates Granbury TX 76048

CLEVEN, CATHERINE LOUISE SEWARD (MRS. EDMUND H. CLEVEN), author; b. Dayton, O.; d. Edmund Garfield and Elizabeth (Smith) Seward; B.A., U. Ill., 1927; m. Edmund H. Cleven, Oct. 18, 1930. Mem. Nat. League Am. Penwomen (v.p. Ft. Lauderdale, Fla. br. 1968-70), Women's Nat. Book Assn., Mystery Writers Am., Inc., Soc. Midland Authors, Chgo. Children's Reading Round Table. Author: Secret of the King's Field, 1952; Flight Angel, 1961; Pirate Dog, 1962; John Hancock, 1963; Black Hawk, Young Sauk Warrior, 1966; Eddie Rickenbacker: Young Racer, Ace Pilot, 1974. Home: 1545 SE 14th St Deerfield Beach FL 33441

CLEVEN, GALE WINSTON, govt. ofcl.; b. Perkins County, S.D., Dec. 27, 1918; s. James and Bertha V. (Mahoney) C.; B.A., U. Wyo., 1946, M.A., 1956; M.B.A., Harvard, 1949; postgrad. Air War Coll., 1956-57, Georgetown U., 1957-60, Indsl. Coll. Armed Forces, 1962; Ph.D., Georgetown U., 1962; m. Esther Lee Athey, June 11, 1954. Joined USAAF, 1940, advanced through grades to col., 1951; dir. atomic energy research and devel. programs, USAF, 1957-58, mgr. data processing and computational center, 1958-60, dir. research, devel., 1960-62; programs mgr. Office Dir. Behavioral Scis. and Information Processing Research, Advanced Research Projects Agy./Office Sec. Def., Washington, 1963-64; dir. operations Hughes Aircraft Co., Aerospace Group, Culver City, Cal., 1964-67; sci. adviser Fed. Hwy. Adminstrn., Washington, 1967-70, asso. adminstr. research and devel., 1970—. Lectr. astronomy Georgetown U., Washington, 1964-68. Decorated D.F.C., Air medal with three oak leaf clusters, D.S.C. Recipient Adminstrs. award for superior service Fed. Hwy. Admins., 1969, 72. Mem. Washington, N.Y. acads. scis., Gold Key Soc., Sigma Xi, Alpha Sigma Nu. Mason (Shriner). Club: Capitol Hill (Washington). Home: Normandy House 1701 N Kent St Arlington VA 22209 Office: 2100 2d St SW Washington DC 20590

CLEVENGER, ERNEST ALLEN, mfg. co. exec.; b. Chattanooga, Oct. 22, 1908; s. Charles Robert and Myrtle Minerva (Hinds) C.; student McKenzie Coll., 1925-26, Cooke Sch. Engring., 1926-27, Internat. Corr. Sch., 1929-36, Cadek Conservatory of Music, 1946-50; m. Mary Ellen Fridell, Dec. 23, 1928; children—Ernest Allen, Jr., Robert Graham, Michael Dale, Alice (Mrs. Larry Wayne Cooper). With Corley Mfg. Co., Chattanooga, 1929—, asst. sales mgr., 1934-39, sales mgr., 1939-47, v.p., 1947-69, pres., 1969—. Instr. Dale Carnegie course McKenzie Coll., Chattanooga, 1948-60. Pres. Chattanooga Opera Assn., 1943-44; exec. com. Citizen's Com. for Better Schs., Chattanooga, 1970—; mem. Chattanooga Vocational Edn. Adv. Council, 1973-74; mem. allocations com. United Fund, 1969—. Bd. dirs. Boyd-Buchanan Sch., 1962—, Heart Fund Assn., 1973-74; bd. dirs., v.p. TB and Respiratory Diseases Assn., 1973-74. Recipient Patriot's medal S.A.R., named Tenn. Outstanding Man of Year in Forestry, 1957. Mem. C. of C. (chmn. edn. com. 1970-71), Forest Products Research Soc., Am. Wood Preservers Assn., Tenn. Forestry Assn. (pres. 1956-57), S.A.R. (state pres. 1957-58, nat. trustee 1972-73). Republican. Mem. Ch. of Christ. Rotarian. Club: Signal Mountain (Tenn.) Golf and Country. Contbr. articles to nat. mags. Home: 602 Georgia Av Signal Mountain TN 37377 Office: PO Box 471 Chattanooga TN 37401

CLEVERLY, WILLIAM STEPHEN, elec. engr.; b. Fitchburg, Mass., Feb. 19, 1941; s. Clayton G., Jr. and Marguerite A. (Rienstra) C.; B.E.E., Clarkson Coll. Tech., 1963; m. Anne Marie Hood, May 6, 1967; 1 son, Clayton Gibson. Asst. engr. N.Y. Telephone Co., Buffalo, 1963-64; project engr., asst. dir. transmission engring., asso. dir. planning, program mgr., dir. Sudan programs Page Communications Engrs., Vienna, Va., 1967—. Bd. dirs. Tysons Manor Homeowners Assn., 1969—. treas., 1971-72, pres., 1973—; v.p. Tysons-Wheystone Civic Assn. Served from 2d lt. to capt. Signal Corps, U.S. Army, 1964-67. Decorated Bronze Star medal, Army Commendation medal. Mem. I.E.E.E., Am. Mgmt. Assn., Armed Forces Communications Electronics Assn., Pi Delta Epsilon. Home: 8146 Larkin Lane Vienna VA 22180 Office: Page Communications Engrs Inc Northrop Page Tech Park Vienna VA 22180

CLIBURN, CECIL DEBERRY, computer programmer; b. Hazlehurst, Miss., Jan. 13, 1927; s. Charles Inge and Addie Ruth (Bufkin) C.; B.S., U. So. Miss., 1950; postgrad. New Orleans Baptist Theol. Sem., 1955-57; B.D., Emory U., 1964; M.Combined Scis., U. Miss., 1968; m. Dorothy Nell Stovall, Aug. 23, 1949; children—Charles William, Robert Rynearson, Cecilia Nell. Asst. computer programmer Continental Oil Co., 1953-55; tchr. math. and sci., Stonewall, Miss., 1957-59; ordained elder Methodist Ch., 1964; minister Meth. Chs. in So. Miss., 1959-68; computer programmer, Eglin AFB, Fla., 1968—. Served with USNR, 1945-46, to lt. AUS, 1949-50, 51-53. NSF grantee, 1967-68. Mem. Kappa Mu Epsilon. Mason. Author article. Home: 219 Staff Dr Fort Walton Beach FL 32548 Office: TSXCS-2 Eglin AFB FL 32542

CLIBURN, JOSEPH WILLIAM, educator; b. Hazlehurst, Miss., Jan. 20, 1926; s. Grady W. and Catherine (Raggio) C.; B.S., Millsaps Coll., 1947; M.A., U. So. Miss., 1953; Ph.D., U. Ala., 1960; m. Lonette Bryant, Apr. 4, 1950; children—Joseph William, Jr., Gregory Bryant. Tchr. pub. schs. Miss., 1947-53, Copiah-Lincoln Jr. Coll., Wesson, Miss., 1953-55; mem. faculty U. So. Miss., Hattiesburg, 1955—, prof. zoology, 1963—. Environmental cons. to pvt. industry, 1972—. Scoutmaster Boy Scouts Am., Hattiesburg, 1965—. Mem. Sigma Xi, Beta Beta Beta, Omicron Delta Kappa. Methodist. Home: 2606 Sutton Pl Hattiesburg MS 39401

CLIFFORD, PAUL INGRAHAM, psychologist, assn. exec.; b. Martinsburg, W.Va., Jan. 22, 1914; s. J. Paul and Mabel (Douglass) C.; B.S., State Tchrs. Coll., Shippensburg, Pa., 1938; A.M., Atlanta U., 1948; Ph.D., U. Chgo., 1953; m. Elizabeth Edith Sterrs, Jan. 21, 1950. Civilian administrv. asst. USAAF, 1941-46; prof. chemistry Paine Coll., Augusta, Ga., 1947-48; instr. in edn. Atlanta U., 1948-51, asst. prof., 1952-54, asso. prof., 1954-57, prof., 1957-68, registrar, 1954-66, dir. admissions, 1954-66, dir. summer sch., 1957-68; staff psychologist Am. Mgmt. Psychologists, Inc., 1966—, v.p., dir., 1969—, nat. dir. profl. services, 1971—; prof., chmn. dept. psychology S.C. State Coll., 1971—. Cons. U.S. Office Edn., 1961—; vis. prof. edn. U. Cal. at Berkeley, 1968-69; cons. psychologist various indsl. orgns. Bd. dirs. So. Fellowships Fund, Nat. Fellowships Fund; trustee Zale Found., Dallas. Licensed psychologist, Ga., Ill. Fellow A.A.A.S., Ga., Pa. psychol. assns.; mem. Am., Southeastern, S.C., Ill. psychol. assns., Soc. for Psychol. Study Social Issues, Nat. Soc. Study Edn., Am. Assn. U. Profs., Assn. for Higher Edn., N.E.A., Am. Ednl. Research Assn., Am. Personnel and Guidance Assn., Nat. Vocational Guidance Assn., Nat. Assn. Guidance Suprs., Assn. Counselor Edn. and Supervision, Assn. Measurement Edn. and Guidance, Nat. Council on Measurement in Edn., Am. Acad. Polit. and Social Scis., N.Y. Acad. Scis., Internat. Platform Assn., Phi Delta Kappa, Omega Psi Phi. Episcopalian. Author monograph, articles for ednl. and psychol. jours. Home: 859 Woodmere Dr NW Atlanta GA 30318 Office: SC State Coll Orangeburg SC 29115

CLIFTON, DREW SPENCER, judge; b. Meridian, Miss., Nov. 26, 1909; s. Sid Spencer and Frances (Whitlock) C.; student Tex. Christian U., 1929-31, Columbia, 1931, Cumberland U., 1935-36; LL.B., Jefferson U., 1938; m. Mildren Inez Jones, July 3, 1938. Asst. mng. dir., mng. dir., Panther Boys Club, Ft. Worth, 1929-32; agt. N.M. Rural Rehab. Corp., 1934-35; admitted to Tex. bar, 1936; practicing lawyer, Dallas, 1936-38, Ft. Worth, 1938-42, 45; asst. dist. atty., Tarrant Co., 1944; judge County Ct. 1946—; judge adv., dir. Vets. Meml., Inc.; lectr. Rep. Mid.-Century White House Conf. Children and Youth, Tex., 1950. Trustee Greenwood Cemetery Perpetual Fund; bd. dirs. Tarrant County Mental Health Assn. Fort Worth Rehab. Farm, Ft. Worth-Tarrant County Employment Handicapped. Served from pvt. to warrant officer (j.g.), U.S. Army, 1942-44. Mem. State Bar Tex. (exec. com. jud. sect.), Ft. Worth, Am. bar assns., Am. Judicature Soc., Am. Authors and Composers Assn., Council Social Agencies (mem. bd. and exec. com.), Ft. Worth C. of C., Am. Vets. World War II, Disabled Veterans Am., Tex. Judiciary Conf., Am. Legion (nat. child welfare com.; Tex. child welfare com.), V.F.W., Forty and Eight. Democrat. Baptist. Mason (K.T., Shriner). Clubs: Tex. Gridiron, Kiwanis (v.p.). Home: 5208 Byers Av Fort Worth TX 76107 Office: Tarrant County Courthouse Fort Worth TX 76101

CLIFTON, NOEL SAMUEL, state bar ofcl.; b. Danville, Va., Dec. 11, 1929; s. Noel Samuel and Lessie Adele (Megginson) C.; B.S. in Commerce with honors, U. Va., 1952; LL.B., George Washington U., 1959; m. Barbara Hyams, June 1, 1969. Admitted to Va. bar, 1960, practiced in Alexandria until 1962; dir. econs. dept. Am. Bar Assn., Chgo., 1963-66; asst. dir. Va. State Bar, Richmond, 1967-69, exec. dir., 1969—. Served as lt. USNR, 1952-56; Korea. Mem. Delta Theta Phi, Phi Eta Sigma. Home: 4903 Sulky Dr Richmond VA 23228 Office: Virginia State Bar Imperial Bldg Richmond VA 23219

CLIFTON, ROBERT WENDELL, metal finishing co. exec.; b. Middletown, O., Aug. 19, 1921; s. Everett and Mary (Armitage) C.; grad. Middletown High Sch., 1941; m. Agnes Marie Robinette, June 7, 1942; children—Robert James, Susalee, Cathy Jo. Pres., Valley Plating Co., Richmond, Va., 1958—; pres. Richmond Galvanizing Co., Richmond, 1962—. Served with USAAF, 1942-46. Home: Ingleside Farm Box 296 Mechanicsville VA 23111 Office: 920 E Laburnum Av Richmond VA 23222

CLINE, FRANCIS XAVIER, JR., orthopedic surgeon; b. Monroe, La., Mar. 16, 1927; s. Francis X. and Josephine (La Baume) C.; student N.E. State Coll., 1944-46; diploma La. Tech. Inst., 1947; M.D., La. State U., 1951; postgrad. Tulane U., 1957-58; m. Ann Merriman; children—Colleen, Francis Xavier III, Catherine, Pamela M.J. Intern, Touro Infirmary, New Orleans, 1951-52; resident orthopedic surgery Confederate Meml. Med. Center, Shreveport, La., 1957-60; gen. practice medicine, Delhi, La., 1955-57; practice orthopedic surgery, Monroe, La., 1960—; vis. staff St. Francis Hosp.; vice chief staff Glenwood Hosp., 1968; cons. E.A. Conway Meml. Hosp.; cons. handicapped children's service La. Bd. Health; med. adviser Social Security Adminstrn.; vice pres. Doctors Bldg., Monroe. Bd. dirs. Carolyn Strauss Rehab. Center, Ouachita chpt. A.R.C. Served to capt. with USAF, 1953-55. Fellow A.C.S. (mem. La. com. on trauma 1966—), Am. Acad. Orthopedic Surgeons; mem. A.M.A., So. Med. Assn., La. Orthopedic Assn., Ouachita Parish Med. Soc. (v.p. 1968-69), U.S. Power Squadron (comdr.), La. Farm Bur., Monroe C. of C. Episcopalian (vestryman 1969-71). Clubs: Bayou De Siard Country, D'Arbonne Yacht (commodore 1968-70). Home: 503 Speed Av Monroe LA 71201 Office: 313 Wood St Monroe LA 71201

CLINE, FRANK RAY, investment exec.; b. Greenville, S.C.; s. Hunley and Lila (Ballew) Cline; m. Betty Virginia Smith; 1 dau., Deborah Anne. Asst. mgr. J.C. Penney Co., 1951-56; now v.p. Cisco of Am., Inc. Dir. Cumberland County United Fund, 1958-59; gen. campaign chmn. United Services Fund for Fayetteville, Ft. Bragg, Pope Field, 1965-66. Mem. 3d Army Adv. Bd., 1957-58. Served as staff sgt. AUS, 1942-46. Mem. Internat. Platform Assn., Assn. U.S. Army. Methodist (steward). Clubs: Lions (past pres.), Executives (dir., past pres.) (Fayetteville). Home: 2518 Dartmouth Dr Fayetteville NC 28304 Office: Bordeaux Shopping Center Mall Fayetteville NC 28304

CLINE, RANDALL EUGENE, educator; b. Marietta, O., Oct. 4, 1931; s. William Wesley and Lorama Pearl (Fordham) C.; B.A. magna cum laude, Marietta Coll., 1953; M.S., Purdue U., 1955, Ph.D., 1963; m. Marilyn Elizabeth Krebs, Jan. 7, 1956; children—Deborah E., Dennis E., Sherri A. Instr., research asst. Purdue U., Lafayette, Ind., 1955-59; research asso. U. Mich., Ann Arbor, 1959-63, research mathematician, 1965-68; vis. asst. prof. Math. Research Center, U. Wis., Madison, 1964-65; asso. prof. math., computer sci. U. Tenn., Knoxville, 1968-72, prof. math., computer sci., 1972—. NSF grantee, 1970-73. Mem. A.A.A.S., Assn. Computing Machinery, Soc. Indsl. and Applied Math., Phi Beta Kappa, Sigma Xi, Alpha Tau Omega. Home: 5312 Yosemite Trail Knoxville TN 37919

CLINGAN, FRANK HARRINGTON, elec. engr.; b. El Cajon, Cal., Sept. 6, 1902; s. Robert Lee and Elva Jane (Richey) C.; grad. Westminster Jr. Coll., 1924; B.S. in Elec. Engring., U. Mich., 1929, postgrad., 1929, 32; m. Elnora S. Clingan, June 4, 1938. With Utah Power & Light Co., Salt Lake City, 1924, Chevrolet Gear & Axle Div., Detroit, 1925; maintenance supr. Chevrolet and Chrysler Corp., 1926-29; apprentice electrician Detroit Bd. Edn., 1929-35, elec. journeyman, 1935-37, asst. foreman, 1937-38, foreman, 1938-42, gen. foreman, 1942-44, asso. elec. engr., 1944-52, sr. asso. elec. engr., 1952-62; asst. elec. engr. Kaisrlik, Snell & Whitehead, Sarasota, Fla., 1962-63; asso., Kaisrlik, Snell & Assos., 1963-66; owner Clingan & Assos., Inc., Bradenton, Fla., 1966-67; sr. elec. engr. Watson & Co., architects, engrs., planners, Tampa, Fla., 1967-69, asst. dept. head elec. engring. dept., 1969-71; chief elec. engr. Rowe-Paras & Assos., Tampa, Fla., 1971-72, Lanbanque Engring., Holiday, Fla., 1972-73; elec. engr. Edward Dean Wyke, architect, Bradenton, 1974—. Registered profl. engr., Mich., Fla. Mem. Nat. Soc. Profl. Engrs., Fla. Engring. Soc., Illuminating Engring. Soc., Aircraft Owners and Pilots Assn. Presbyn. Club: Schoolmen's (Detroit). Patentee in field. Home: 500 S Park Blvd Apt V15 PO Box 357 Venice FL 33595 Office: 2530 Manatee Av W Bradenton FL 33505

CLINGERMAN, EDGAR ALLEN, business exec.; b. Wolf Lake, Ind., Dec. 27, 1934; s. Virgil Wilson and Jessie Pauline (Miller) C.; B.S. in Bus. Adminstrn., Ball State U., 1960; student Ball State U., Purdue U.; m. Betty Gean White, Dec. 9, 1966; children—Tammera, Sarah, Johnny, Edgar Allen. Sr. accountant Lybrand, Ross Bros., Montgomery, Ft. Wayne, Ind., 1960-63; controller Monteith Bros. Co., Elkhart, Ind., 1963-66; plant controller Joy Mfg. Co., Michigan City, Ind., 1966-68; treas., controller Milton Roy Co., St. Petersburg, Fla., 1968—; dir. E-C Apparatus Corp. Active local Boy Scouts Am. Served with USNR, 1952-55. Mem. Nat. Assn. Accountants, Am. Mgmt. Assn., Corporate Controllers Assn., Sci. Apparatus Mfg. Assn. (chmn. financial execs. group 1973-74). Mem. Christian Ch. (deacon, dir.). Mason, Rotarian (pres. local group 1963). Home: 11144 Hammock Dr Largo FL 33540 Office: 5000 Park St St Petersburg FL 33733

CLINGMAN, WILLIAM HERBERT, JR., mgmt. cons.; b. Grand Rapids, Mich., May 5, 1929; s. William Herbert and Elizabeth (Davis) Clingman; B.S. with distinction and honors, in Chemistry, U. Mich., 1951; M.A., Princeton, 1954, Ph.D., 1954; m. Mary Jane Wheeler, Feb. 6, 1951; children—Mary Constance, James Wheeler. Chemist, Am. Oil Co., Texas City, Tex., 1954-57, group leader, 1957-59; head thermoelectric sect. Tex. Instruments, Inc., Dallas, 1959-61, dir. energy research lab., 1961-62, mgr. corporate research and devel. marketing dept., 1962-67; pres. W.J. Clingman Co., Inc., Dallas, 1967—. Speaker, cons. Small Bus. Adminstrn., 1967-70. Mem. adv. com. on sci., tech. and economy Nat. Planning Assn., 1966-69. Mem. Am. Chem. Soc., I.E.E.E., Assn. for Computing Machinery, Sigma Xi. Club: Brook Hollow Golf (Dallas). Mem. editorial adv. bd. Jour. Advanced Energy Conversion, 1961-66. Home: 4416 McFarlin St Dallas TX 75205 Office: 2001 Bryan St Dallas TX 75201

CLIZER, HERALD KENNETH, food co. exec.; b. Savannah, Mo., Oct. 31, 1932; s. Kenneth Herman and Iva May (Sheppard) C.; B.S. in Agr., U. Mo., 1954; m. Martha Francis, Jan. 11, 1963. With Wilson & Co., Inc., 1954—, v.p. subsidiary Wilson Certified Foods, Oklahoma City, 1969-72, corp. v.p., 1972—. Bd. dirs. Am. Royal, Kansas City, 1966—; vice chmn. Kansas City United Appeal, 1967. Served to capt. AUS, 1954-56. Mem. Alpha Gamma Rho, Alpha Zeta, Mystical Seven. Clubs: Oklahoma City Golf and Country, Petroleum. Home: 2604 60th St Oklahoma City OK 73112 Office: 4545 Lincoln Av Oklahoma City OK 73105

CLODY, HARRY WILLIAM, ins. cons.; b. S.I., N.Y., Mar. 28, 1917; s. Harry William and Marie J. (Allen) C.; student N.Y.U., 1934-35; grad. exec. program U. N.C., 1960; m. Marcia Hope Fisher, Aug. 11, 1941; 1 son, William F.M. With group ins. dept. Equitable Life Assurance Soc., N.Y.C., 1934-46; group service mgr. Pilot Life Ins. Co., Greensboro, N.C., 1946-48; mgr. group div. State Capital Life Ins. Co., Raleigh, N.C., 1948, v.p., 1949-70; v.p. Durham Life Ins. Co., 1970; exec. v.p. Mid-South Ins. Co., 1970-71; owner, cons. Carolina Ins. Advisors, 1971—; chmn. bd. So. Roofing & Metal Co., Raleigh; v.p., dir. Soramco Corp. Bd. dirs. N.C. Assn. for Blind, Raleigh Lions Clinic for Blind. Served from pvt. to staff sgt. USAAF, 1942-46. Mem. Acad. Polit. Sci., Internat. Platform Assn., Assn. U.S. Army, Am. Legion, Newcomen Soc., N.C. Fraternal Congress (past pres., dir.), Am. Acad. Consultants, Life Office Mgmt. Assn. (group ins. adminstrn. com.), Ins. Accounting and Statis. Assn. (research com., group ins. com.). Lion (pres., dir., zone chmn., dist. gov.), K.C. (past state dep.). Clubs: Raleigh Sales and Marketing Executives (dir.), Raleigh Country. Home: 2805 Churchill Rd Raleigh NC 27607 Office: Box 2416 Raleigh NC 27602

CLOER, CARROLL MARTIN, textile engr.; b. Patterson, N.C., Jan. 29, 1926; s. Carl Elisha and Nannie (Holder) C.; B.S., N.C. State Coll., 1950; grad. Air War Coll., 1970, Indsl. Coll. Armed Forces, 1971; m. Rachel Tuttle, Oct. 2, 1954. Overseer, Hudson (N.C.) Mfg. Co., 1950-52; head quality control Rhodhiss (N.C.) Mills, Burlington Industries, 1952-61; supt. quality control polyester plant Beaunit Fibers, Elizabethton, Tenn., 1961-68; asst. prof., head textile dept. Danville Community Coll., 1968-69; mfg. supt. Arista Mills, Winston-Salem, N.C., 1969-70, Virginia Mills, Swepsonville, N.C., 1970-71; quality control mgr. Firestone Textiles, Gastonia, N.C., 1971—; treas. Burkwell Investors, Rhodhiss, 1960—. Staff officer Tenn. Dept. Civil Def., 1967—. Served with USAAF, 1944-45; now maj. USAF Res. Decorated Air medal with three oak leaf clusters. Mem. Am. Soc. for Testing and Materials, Am. Soc. Quality Control, Soc. Aerospace and Material Engrs., Am. Assn. Textile Technologists, Am. Mgmt. Assn., V.F.W., Air Force Assn., Res. Officers Assn., Sigma Tau Sigma. Kiwanian. Home: 2005 Monticello Dr Gastonia NC 28052 Office: Firestone Textiles Gastonia NC 28052

CLONTZ, LUTHER HALL, physician; b. Morganton, N.C., Mar. 19, 1932; s. Vester Herman and Annie Ophelia (Butler) C.; M.D., U. N.C., 1957; m. Fannie Ruth Cagle, Sept. 9, 1954; children—Geoffrey, Deborah, Dana. Intern, U.S. Navy Hosp., Charleston, S.C., 1957-58; pvt. practice medicine, Morganton, N.C., 1960-63; dir. Alcoholism and Drug Program, Broughton Hosp., 1963-66; asst. supt. med. services Western Carolina Center, Morganton, 1966—. Fund-raising chmn. Cerebral Palsy Burke County, 1960-61. Served with USNR, 1957-60. Mem. Phi Beta Kappa. Democrat. Baptist. Home: 408 W Union St Morganton NC 28655 Office: Western Carolina Center Morganton NC 28655

CLOUD, FITZ-HUGH WELBORN, banker; b. Vicksburg, Miss., Mar. 13, 1919; s. William Buchanan and Georgia Belle (Maxwell) C.; B.S., Miss. Coll., 1946; M.B.A., Tulane U., 1947; m. Margaret Katherin Causey, June 17, 1945; 1 dau., Margaret (Mrs. John Christopher Kolstad). Accounting and statis. clerk, Texaco Inc., N.Y.C., 1950-51, New Orleans, 1952-53; sec.-treas. Norton Drilling Co. & predecessor, 1954-62; exec. v.p. Washington Bank & Trust Co., Franklinton, La., 1963—, dir. since 1974—. Served with AUS, 1941-44, served to staff sgt., USAAF, 1944-45. C.P.A., La., Chartered Bank Auditor. Mem. Soc. C.P.A.'s La., Am. Inst. C.P.A.'s. Democrat. Baptist. Rotarian. Home: PO Box 1183 Bogalusa LA 70427 Office: PO Drawer L Franklinton LA 70438

CLOUD, RUSSELL WALKER, textile co. exec.; b. Albemarle, N.C., May 24, 1932; s. Jesse Walker and Etta Ramelle (Russell) C.; student Davidson Coll., 1950, Elon Coll., 1951; student U. N.C., 1951-53; m. Isabel N. Blackburn, Mar. 21, 1953; children—Judy, Kathryn, Jeanne, Ruth, Carol. With Jackson & Jackson, Inc., Tryon, N.C., 1960—, sec., asst. treas., 1961-68, v.p., 1968-70, pres., treas., 1970—; dir. Northwestern Bank, Tryon, 1971—. Served with AUS, 1953-55. Club: Tryon Country. Home: Wilderness Rd Tryon NC 28782 Office: 240 Pacolet St Tryon NC 28782

CLOUTIER, ROGER JOSEPH, health-physicist; b. North Attleboro, Mass., July 25, 1930; s. Joseph Donat and Ludovique M. (Precourt) C.; B.S., U. Mass., 1956; M.S., U. Rochester, 1957; m. Linda S. McAuslan, June 12, 1954; children—Richard, Michelle, Katherine, Rita, Raymond. Engr., Westinghouse Atomic Power Dept., Pitts., 1957-59; scientist Oak Ridge Asso. Univs., 1959—. Dir. Radiopharm. Internal Dose Information Center, Oak Ridge, 1969—. Bd. dirs. Tenn. Council Human Relations, Nashville, 1964-73; pres. Youth Haven, Oak Ridge, 1971-73. Served with USNR, 1948-52. Diplomate Am. Bd. Health Physics; mem. Health Physics Soc. (treas. 1971-73), Tenn. Acad. Sci., Soc. Nuclear Medicine. Home: 168 Cumberland View Dr Oak Ridge TN 37830 Office: Med Div Oak Ridge Asso Univ Oak Ridge TN 37830

CLOWDIS, CHARLES WILBURN, JR., mgmt. cons.; b. Lafayette, Ga., Sept. 5, 1944; s. Charles Wilburn and Margaret Mae (Robinson) C.; A.A., Young Harris Coll., 1964; B.B.A., U. Ga., 1966; M.B.A., Hamilton State U., 1971. Exec. trainee Gulf & Western Industries, Houston, 1966-67; exec. asst. Provident Life & Accident Ins. Co., Chattanooga, 1967-68, with PLA Securities subsidiary, 1968, asst. sec., 1968-69, sec.-treas., 1970-71; sr. partner Charles W. Clowdis Jr. & Assos., Lafayette, 1972—; pres., treas. Mich.-Ga. Auto Ventures, Inc., Lafayette, 1972—; chmn. bd. Lafayette Automotive Supply Co., 1972—; propr. Clowdis Ins. Agy., Lafayette, 1973—; sec., dir. Actuarial Services of Mich., Inc., Grand Rapids, Mich., 1970—; sr. partner Aviation Assos., Lafayette, Ga., 1970—. Mem. Lafayette C. of C. (charter), Young Harris Alumni Assn. (dir. 1969—), Nat. Assn. Pub. Accountants, Internat. Assn. Financial Counsellors, Am. Marketing Assn. Democrat. Elk, Rotarian. Home: PO Box 592 301 Sequoia Lane Lafayette GA 30728 Office: 200 Oak St Lafayette GA 30728

CLOWES, ROYSTON COURTENAY, educator; b. Swansea, Wales, Sept. 11, 1921; s. William John and Prudence Alice (King) C.; B.S., U. Birmingham, U.K., 1942, Ph.D., 1951, D.Sc., 1965; m. Janet Shopland, Apr. 5, 1952; children—Martin Anthony, Christopher Tobias, David Malcolm. Came to U.S., 1965. Research asso. St. Marys Hosp. Med. Sch., London, Eng., 1951-57; mem. staff Med. Research Councils Microbial Genetics Research Unit, Hammersmith Hosp., London, Eng., 1958-65; prof. biology Southwest Center for Advanced Studies, Dallas, 1965-69; prof., head div. biology U. Tex., Dallas, 1969—. Vis. prof. dept. microbiology U. Cal., Berkeley, 1961-62; mem. microbial chemistry study sect. Dept. Health, Edn. and Welfare—NIH, 1971-73, chmn., 1973—. Served to capt. Brit. Army, 1943-47. Recipient Damon Runyon Cancer Research fellowship, 1955-56; numerous grants. Author: The Structure of Life, 1964. Editor: Experiments in Microbial Genetics, 1968. Mem. editorial bd. Jour. Gen. Microbiology (U.K.), 1960-65; Jour. Bacteriology, 1970-72; Antimicrobial Agents and Chemotherapy, 1973—. Home: 7148 Meadowcreek Dr Dallas TX 75230

CLUM, DENNIS PATRICK, city ofcl.; b. Poughkeepsie, N.Y., May 1, 1925; s. Frederick J. and Margaret M. (Murphy) C.; B.A., Union Coll., Schenectady, 1947; LL.B., Fordham U., 1951; m. Dorothy M. Diederichs, Oct. 14, 1953; children—Dennis Patrick, Robert, Laura. Sr. v.p., trust officer, dir. Miami Beach, First Nat. Bank (Fla.), 1954-71; sr. v.p., dir. United Bancshares of Fla., Inc., 1965-71; exec. v.p., trust officer First State Bank of Miami (Fla.), 1972, also dir.; now dir. Crime Commn., Miami. Past pres. Estate Planning Council Dade County; bd. dirs. Miami Heart Inst., Variety Childrens Hosp., Dade Found., Com. of 100 Miami Beach; mem. adminstrv. bd. Biscayne Coll.; mem. devel. fund bd. Barry Coll.; co-chmn. endowment fund com. U. Miami. Served to lt. USNR, 1943-46, 51-54. Mem. Miami Shores C. of C., Corporate Fiduciaries Assn. Kiwanian. Clubs: Surf, La Gorce, Miami Shores Country, Rod and Reel, Miami, Palm Bay, Racquet, Standard, Jockey, Army and Navy. Home: 898 NE 95th St Miami Shores FL 33138 Office: 8017 NE 2d Av Miami FL 33138

CLUTTERHAM, DAVID ROBERT, educator; b. Chgo., Feb. 10, 1922; s. Fred Wilford and Margaret (Thomas) C.; B.A., Cornell Coll., 1945; M.S., U. Ariz., 1948; Ph.D., U. Ill., 1953; m. Jean Mildred Ballou, Oct. 20, 1945; children—Lars Thomas, Beth Marie (Mrs. Victor Alan Ramey), Ann Hali (Mrs. William Gilford Crouch), Jack Wesley. Design specialist Convair Aircraft, Ft. Worth, 1953-58; mgr. computer and information scis. dept. Martin Co., Orlando, Fla., 1959-64; staff scientist Bunker Ramo, Canoga Park, Cal., 1964-65; sr. scientist Radiation Inc., Melbourne, Fla., 1965-68; prof., head math. scis. dept. Fla. Inst. Tech., 1968—. Mayor, Lakeside, Tex., 1958. Served to lt. (j.g.) USNR, 1943-46. Decorated Silver Star medal. Mem. Assn. for Computing Machinery (chmn. Central Fla. chpt. 1962-64), I.E.E.E., Math. Soc. Am., Sigma Xi, Pi Mu Epsilon. Home: 200 Miami Av Indialantic FL 32903 Office: Fla Inst Tech Math Scis Dept Melbourne FL 32901

CLYBURN, THOMAS MILBURN, scientist; b. Lancaster, S.C., Mar. 15, 1906; s. Lewis Marcellus and Elizabeth (Belk) C.; B.S., Clemson Coll., 1929; postgrad. Ia. State U., 1937-38; m. Bess Edith Plyler, June 3, 1933; 1 son, Thomas Milburn. Coop. agt. agrl. research Clemson Coast Sta., U.S. Dept. Agr., S.C., 1930-37, asst. county agt., Greenwood, S.C., 1938-46; asso. animal husbandry Clemson Coast Sta., Summerville, 1946-51; asst. prof. animal sci. U. Ga., Ga. State Prison Farm, Reidsville, 1951-73. Instr. Clemson Coll., 1938. Served to maj. USAAF, 1942-46. Mem. Am. Soc. Animal Sci., Alpha Zeta. Methodist (supt. Sunday Sch. 1949-50). Mason, Lion, Rotarian. Club: Exchange (Greenwood). Home: Route 6 Box 339 Lancaster SC 29720

COAD, PETER, oil co. exec.; b. San Francisco, Oct. 17, 1926; s. John Francis and Mary (David) C.; B.S., U. Cal. at Berkeley, 1948, M.S., 1949; Ph.D., Ore. State U., 1953; m. Raylene Elizabeth Adams, June 25, 1950; children—Anne (Mrs. Jerry Cornelius), Peter, Mike, Patrick, Molly. Instr. chemistry U. San Francisco, 1952-54, Coll. San Mateo, 1954-56; prof. chemistry, head div. natural sci. Chapman Coll., Orange, Cal., 1956-63; chemist Dept. Army, Walter Reed Army Research Inst., Washington, 1963-65; project chemist Kerr-McGee Corp., Oklahoma City, 1965-66, sect. head, 1966-69, mgr. chem. research, 1969-72, sr. bus. analyst, 1973—. Served with AUS, 1947. NSF fellow, 1958; DuPont fellow, 1951-52. Mem. Am. Chem. Soc. (pres.-elect local sect. 1962-63), Sigma Xi, Phi Kappa Phi. Mem. Christian Ch. (elder). Contbr. articles to profl. jours. Home: 3603 Woodvale Dr Midwest City OK 73110 Office: Kerr-McGee Center Robert Kerr St Oklahoma City OK 73102

COAD, RAYLENE ELIZABETH ADAMS (MRS. PETER COAD), educator; b. South Pasadena, Cal., Apr. 11, 1926; d. Charles Donald and Dorothy (Morgan) Adams; B.S., M.S., U. Cal. at Berkeley, M.S., 1947; M.A. (Thomas Dana fellow), Radcliffe Coll., 1949; Ph.D., U. Cal. at Berkeley, 1950; m. Peter Coad, June 25, 1950; children—Anne (Mrs. Jerry Cornelius), Peter, Mike, Patrick, Molly. Research asst. Ore. State U., Corvallis, 1950-52; instr. chemistry San Jose State Coll., 1954-55; asst. prof. chemistry Chapman Coll., Orange, Cal., 1957-63; instr. phys. sci. Trona (Cal.) Unified Sch. Dist., 1968; instr. chemistry Oscar Rose Jr. Coll., Midwest City, Okla., 1970—. Chemist, U.S. Dept. Agr., Beltsville, Md., 1964-65; abstractor Chem. Abstracts Service, 1967—. Mem. Am. Chem. Soc., Sigma Xi, Phi Beta Kappa, Iota Sigma Pi. Mem. Christian Ch. Home: 3603 Woodvale Dr Midwest City OK 73110

COALSON, ROBERT ELLIS, educator; b. Hobart, Okla., Dec. 7, 1928; s. Ellis Ernest and Lucy Belle (Foster) C.; B.S., U. Okla., 19—, M.S., 1951, Ph.D., 1955; m. Jacqueline Lynne Jones, Dec. 27, 1962; children—Danon Lynne, Robert Lowell, Diane Laverne. Instr. anatomy Vanderbilt U., Nashville, 1957-60; asst. prof. anatomy U. Okla. Med. Center, Oklahoma City, 1960-64, asso. prof. anatomy, 1964-70, prof. anatomy, 1970—. Served with AUS, 1955-57. Mem. Am. Assn. Anatomists, Tissue Culture Assn., Am. Soc. Zoologists, Sigma Xi, Phi Sigma. Home: 10900 Maple Grove Oklahoma City OK 73120 Office: 801 NE 13th St Oklahoma City OK 73104

COATES, JESSE, educator; b. Baton Rouge, Mar. 12, 1908; s. Charles Edward and Ollie (Maurin) C.; B.S., La. State U., 1928; student Mass. Inst. Tech., 1930-31; M.S., U. Mich., 1932, Ph.D., 1936; m. Judith Mills Williams, Apr. 16, 1938; children—Judith Mills, Jesse, Victor Maurin (dec.). Chemist, treating engr. Nat. Lumber and Creosoting Co., 1928; chemist Internat. Paper Co., 1928-29, Meeker Sugar Refinery, 1930-31, Punta Alegre Sugar Co., 1931; chem. engr. Tex. Pacific Coal & Oil Co., 1932-33, United Gas Pub. Service, 1933-36; asst. prof. chem. engring., La. State U., 1936-42, asso. prof., 1942-47, prof., 1947-69, Alumni prof. chem. engring., 1969—, chmn. dept., 1955-67; cons. chem. engr.; mem. La. Bd. Registration Profl. Engrs. Active Boy Scouts Am. Recipient Technol. Accomplishment medal La. Engring. Soc., 1958, Charles E. Coates meml. award Am. Chem. Soc.-Am. Inst. Chem. Engrs., 1958; named Man of Month, Chem. Engring. Mag., 1958, distinguished service certificate Nat. Council Engring. Examiners, 1969. Fellow Am. Inst. Chemists; mem. Am. Chem. Soc., La. Acad. Sci., Am. Inst. Chem. Engrs., Am. Soc. Engring. Edn., Sigma Xi, Phi Kappa Phi, Alpha Chi Sigma, Phi Lambda Upsilon, Kappa Alpha, Omicron Delta Kappa. Episcopalian (past vestryman). Contbr. numerous articles to La. State U. Engring. Expt. News, Chem. Eng. mag., other publs. Home: 2320 Terrace Av Baton Rouge LA 70806

COATS, WILLIAM EDWARD, supt. schs.; b. Coal Hill, Ark., Nov. 25, 1933; s. Earl and Xenya (Meyers) C.; A.A., Ft. Smith Jr. Coll., 1953; B.S., Coll. Ozarks, 1957; M.Ed., U. Ark., 1961, postgrad., 1966; m. Jimmy Lue Coffee, Sept. 3, 1955; children—Thomas, Karen. Tchr., Ft. Smith (Ark.) Pub. Schs., 1959-61; supt., Hartman (Ark.) Pub. Schs., 1961-63, Smackover (Ark.) Pub. Schs., 1963-66, Batesville (Ark.) Pub. Schs., 1966—. Served with USAF, 1954-59. Mem. N.E.A., Am. Assn. Sch. Adminstrs., Ark. Sch. Adminstrs. Assn., Ark. Edn. Assn., Phi Delta Kappa. Democrat. Presbyn. (deacon 1968-69). Mason, Lion, Rotarian. Club: Optimist (Batesville). Home: 385 17th St Batesville AR 72501 Office: 507 7th St Batesville AR 72501

COBB, DAN, newspaper editor; m. Stella Morris; 1 son, David Childs. Formerly city editor Birmingham News, also Houston Chronicle; now news editor Houston Chronicle. Home: 1322 Palm Av Houston TX 77004 Office: 801 Texas Av Houston TX 77002

COBB, JERRIE M., aviation/aerospace cons.; b. Norman, Okla., Mar. 5, 1931; d. William Harvey and Helena Butler (Stone) Cobb. Profl. pilot, 1949—; chief pilot South American Fleetway, Inc.; mem. adv. com. FAA, 1964-69; now aviation/aerospace cons. in pvt. practice, also missionary jungle pilot in South Am. Founder, Jerrie Cobb Found. Named 1 of 9 women selected in the 100 most important in U.S., 1962; first woman to pass astronaut tests, 1960; recipient Gold Wings, Fedn. Aeronautique Internationale; named Woman of Yr. in Aviation, Women's Nat. Aero. Assn.; hon. pilot Colombian Air Force, 1964; recipient Harmon Internat. Trophy, 1973. Mem. Am. Inst. Aeronautics and Astronautics, Am. Astronautical Soc., Aerospace Medicine Assn., Nat. Aero. Assn., 99's (Amelia Earhart Gold medal), Profl. Pilots Assn. (Pilot of Year 1959), Women's Nat. Aero. Assn. Club: Whirlygirls. Author: (with Jane Rieker) Woman Into Space: The Jerrie Cobb Story, 1963. Home: 4057 Malaga St Miami FL 33133

COBB, JOE HACKLER, civil engr.; b. nr. Brownsville, Tenn., Mar. 6, 1927; s. Paul Hackler and Zina Maie (Proctor) C.; B.S., U. Tenn., 1965; m. Myrtle Louise Wilson, Sept. 20, 1969. Rodman, instrument man Tenn. Hwy. Dept., Covington, 1958-62; jr. engr. Brown Engring. Co., aerospace, Huntsville, Ala., 1965-67; structural engr. Brighton Engring. Co., cons. engrs., Nashville, Tenn. and Frankfort, Ky., 1967-69; prin. civil engr. Met. Dept. Pub. Works, Nashville, 1969—. Registered profl. engr., Tenn., Ky. Mem. Am. Soc. C. E., Nat. Soc. Profl. Engrs., Am. Pub. Works Assn., Tau Beta Pi. Baptist. Home: 2929 Berry Hill Dr Nashville TN 37204 Office: 720 S 5th St Nashville TN 37206

COBB, JOHN BYNUM, II, lawyer; b. Memphis, Oct. 24, 1932; s. John Bynum and Edna Geneva (Sennett) C.; B.S., Memphis State U., 1955; LL.B., Vanderbilt U., 1960, J.D., 1964; m. Mary Lee Billingsley, Mar. 3, 1964; children—Lynn Ann, John Bynum, III. Admitted to Tenn. bar, 1960; trial atty., Memphis, 1960—; mem. firms Burch, Porter & Johnson, 1960-62, J.B. Cobb, 1962-73. Mem. exec. com. Shelby County Democratic party, 1960-72, chmn., 1968-72. Served to capt. USAF, 1955-58. Recipient Paul H. Sanders award Vanderbilt U. Sch. Law, 1960. Mem. Tenn. Bar Assn., Tenn. (bd. govs. 1971-73), Memphis (pres. 1964) trial lawyer's assns., Kappa Sigma, Phi Delta Phi. Home: 83 W Walnut Grove Circle Memphis TN 38117 Office: 99 N 3d St Memphis TN 38103

COBB, LAWRENCE DEAN, lawyer; b. Marlin, Tex., Mar. 16, 1936; s. Lawrence Morgan and Ruth (Day) C.; B.A., U. Tex., 1958; J.D., Baylor U. Sch. Law, 1962; m. Patricia Grace Threadgill, July 1, 1961; children—Kendall McKay, Courtney Read, Susanna Ruth. Admitted to Tex. bar, 1962; pvt. practice law, Dumas, Tex., 1962—; partner Lovell, Lyle, Cobb & Renfer, Dumas, Tex., 1965—. County atty. Moore County, 1964-68; mem. Tex. Ho. of Reps., 1968—. Chmn. advance gifts div. Community Chest, Dumas, 1963-64; pres. Moore unit Am. Cancer Soc., Dumas, 1963-64. Served to 1st lt. AUS, 1958-59. Mem. C. of C. (bd. dirs. 1966-68). Mason, Rotarian (pres. 1966-67). Home: 109 Amherst St Dumas TX 79029 Office: 113 Bliss Av Dumas TX 79029

COBB, THOMAS TRACY, lawyer; b. Washington, Nov. 13, 1916; s. William M. and Bessie (Coghill) C.; LL.B., John B. Stetson U., 1939; m. Jane Carter Campbell, Mar. 15, 1941; children—Jane Tracy (Mrs. Jerry M. Trammell), Thomas Carter, Charlotte Susan (Mrs. Thomas Clayton), Jennifer Jerome. Admitted to Fla. bar, 1939; trustee Lawyer's Title Guaranty Fund, Orlando, Fla., 1949-51; city atty., Daytona Beach, Fla., 1953-55; gen. counsel Fla. State Road Bd., 1961-65; mem. Fla. Bd. Bar Examiners, 1969-73, chmn., 1971-73; gen. counsel, dir., sec. News-Jour. Corp., Daytona Beach, 1961—; gen. counsel. dir. 1st Atlantic Nat. Bank, Daytona Beach. Mem. Fla. Legislature, 1946-56. Served with USNR, 1944-45. Mem. Volusia County, Am. bar assns., Fla. Bar, Am. Judicature Soc. Presbyn. (elder). Kiwanian. Home: 58 S Beach St Ormond Beach FL 32074 Office: 444 Seabreeze Blvd Daytona Beach FL 32015

COBBS, JAMES HAROLD, petroleum engr.; b. Bristow, Okla., Aug. 25, 1928; s. Harold M. and Ella (Rouintree) C.; B.S., U. Okla., 1949, postgrad., 1949-51; postgrad. U. Tulsa, 1955-67; m. Charlotte Marie Fisher, Aug. 16, 1953; children—James Harold, David C., Gregory L., Matthew L. Grad. asst. U. Okla., 1949-51; asso. engr. Tidewater Oil Co., Midland, Tex., 1951-52, reservoir engr., Houston, 1952-55, div. reservoir engr., Tulsa, 1955-59; pvt. practice engring., Tulsa, 1959-63, 69—; sr. engr. Fenix & Scisson, Inc., Tulsa, 1963-69. Committeeman, asst. scoutmaster Indian Nations council Boy Scouts Am., 1962—; instr. first aid A.R.C., 1969—. Precinct chmn. Republican party, 1961-62. Fellow A.A.A.S.; mem. Soc. Petroleum Engrs., Nat., Okla. socs. profl. engrs., Sigma Phi Epsilon. Mem. Christian Ch. (elder, chmn. bd. 1971-72). Patentee in field. Home: 5144 S New Haven St Tulsa OK 74135 Office: 5200 S Yale St Tulsa OK 74135

COCHRAN, CLAY LEE, govt. ofcl., economist; b. Endee, N.M., Oct. 7, 1914; s. Charles Leon and Mary Dona (Gray) C.; B.A., M.A., U. Tex., 1938; Ph.D., U. N.C., 1950; m. Anne Weidner, Sept. 27, 1957; children—Carole Jean, Mary Anne. Admitted to Tex. bar, 1939; social worker Tex. Welfare Dept., 1938-39; migratory labor and labor specialist Farm Security Adminstrn., 1939-43; instr. econs. U. La., 1946, U. N.C., 1947-49; asst. prof. econs. U. Okla., 1949-50, asso. prof., 1951-52; dir. dept. legislation, research and mgmt. Nat. Rural Electric Coop. Assn., 1952-58; legislative cons. resources and agr., indsl. union dept. AFL-CIO, 1958-66; exec. dir. Rural Housing Alliance, Washington, 1967—. Mem. Sec. Agr. Adv. Com. on Coops., 1953-54, Adv. Com. on Feed Grains, 1961-62, Citizen's Adv. Com. on Civil Rights, 1963-68; sec.-treas. Group Research, 1961—; dir. Nat. Housing Conf., 1970-72; mem. community relations com. Am. Friends Service Com., 1968—; mem. rural adv. com. Nat. Assn. Housing and Urban Devel. Orgn., 1971-72; dir., sec. Housing Assistance Council, 1971—; dir. Nat. Council Agrl. Life and Labor, 1960—; chmn., chmn. legislative com. Nat. Rural Housing Coalition, 1969—; dir. Western States Water and Power Consumers Conf., 1954—. Served with AUS, 1943-46. Democrat. Home: 1920 Martha's Rd Alexandria VA 22307 Office: 1346 Connecticut Av NW Washington DC 20036

COCHRAN, JAMES ALAN, educator; b. San Francisco, May 12, 1936; s. Commodore Shelton and Gwendolyn Audrey (Rosenau) C.; B.S. in Physics, Stanford, 1956, M.S. in Physics, 1957, Ph.D. in Math., 1962; m. Katherine Koehler Kern, Sept. 6, 1958; children—Cynthia, Sarah. Mem. tech. staff, supr. applied math. Bell Telephone Labs., Whippany, N.J., 1962-72; prof. dept. math. Va. Poly. Inst. and State U., Blacksburg, 1972—; vis. prof. math. Stanford, 1968-69. Young man pres. Nat. Eagle Scout Assn., Boy Scouts Am., 1957-58, adviser, 1958-71, mem. nat. com., 1972—. Chmn. bd. commrs. Morris County (N.J.) Area Library System, 1971-72. Mem. Am. Math. Soc., Soc. Indsl. and Applied Math., Phi Beta Kappa, Sigma Xi, Alpha Phi Omega. Republican. Presbyn. (deacon). Author: Analysis of Linear Integral Equations, 1972; also numerous tech. reports and articles. Home: 836 Hutcheson Dr Blacksburg VA 24060

COCHRAN, MCKENDREE THOMAS, JR., dairy co. exec.; b. Altus, Okla., May 24, 1918; s. McKendree Thomas and Ray (Wheeler) C.; Asso. B.A., Kemper Mil. Sch., 1937; B.A., U. Okla., 1939; m. Mary Delores Coleman, June 22, 1940; children—Mary Chris (Mrs. Alexander Pryor Murray), McKendree Thomas, III, William Chesley, James Coleman. Asst. to pres. Eskimo Pie Corp., Bloomfield, N.J., 1940-52; gen. mgr. ice cream div. DCA Food Industries, N.Y.C., 1952-57; v.p., gen. mgr. dairies div. Southland Corp., Dallas, 1957—. Served to lt. USNR, 1943-46. Mem. Nat. Dairy Council (dir.), Dairy Products Inst. Tex. (pres. 1966-67), Internat. Assn. Ice Cream Mfrs. (dir. 1968—), So. Assn. Dairy Food Mfrs. (pres. 1971-72), Dallas Sales Exec. Club, Kappa Alpha. Presbyn. Club: Northwood Country (Dallas). Home: 6440 Northport Dr Dallas TX 75230 Office: 2828 N Haskell St Dallas TX 75230

COCHRAN, OLIVE LEIGH MYATT (MRS. RAYMOND NEVITT COCHRAN), ednl. adminstr.; b. Monroe, La., Sept. 8, 1907; d. Webster Andrew and Martha Fidelia (Morton) Myatt; student La. State Normal Coll., 1923-25; Kindergarten certificate Harris Tchrs. Coll., 1926; B.S. cum laude, La. State U., 1942; M.Ed., Northeast La. U., 1962; m. Raymond Nevitt Cochran, June 4, 1940; children—Kathleen (Mrs. Knowless), Susan (Mrs. Eric Mingledorff). Tchr. rural schs., Ouachita Parish, La., 1925-27, Georgia Tucker Elementary Sch., Monroe, 1927-43, 55-62; tchr., owner Cochran Nursery Sch., 1949-51; supr. elementary edn. Monroe Sch. System, 1962-67, dir. elementary curriculum, 1967-73, supr. spl. edn., 1964-73. Organizer first spl. edn. classes Monroe schs., 1964; supr. spl. edn. Monroe City schs., 1964-73; ret., 1973. Active Civil Def. during World War II. Mem. Internat. Reading Assn. (dir. local unit 1970-73), Am. Legion Aux. Assn. Childhood Edn. Internat. (br. pres. 1967-71, treas. 1971—), Assn. Supervision and Curriculum Devel., La. Assn. Supervision and Curriculum Devel., La. Sch. Suprs. Assn., La. Tchrs. Assn., Assn. Elementary, Kindergarten, Nursery Edn., Am. Assn. U. Women, Delta Kappa Gamma, Sigma Tau Delta. Democrat. Baptist. Home: 1105 N 7th St Monroe LA 71201

COCHRAN, THAD, congressman; b. Pontotoc, Miss., Dec. 7, 1937; s. William Holmes and Emma Grace (Berry) C.; B.A., U. Miss., 1959, J.D. cum laude, 1965; postgrad. (Rotary Found. fellow), U. Dublin (Ireland), 1963-64; m. Rose Clayton, June 6, 1964; children—Thaddeus Clayton, Katherine Holmes. Admitted to Miss. bar, 1965, practiced in Jackson, 1965-72; asso. firm Watkins & Eager, 1965-72; mem. 93d Congress from Miss. Mem. exec. bd. Andrew Jackson council Boy Scouts Am., 1973—. Served to lt. USNR, 1959-61. Named Outstanding Young Man of Jackson, 1971, One of Three Outstanding Young Men of Miss., 1971. Mem. Am., Miss. (pres. young lawyers sect.) bar assns., Omicron Delta Kappa, Phi Kappa Phi, Pi Kappa Alpha. Republican. Baptist. Rotarian. Home: Route 5 Jackson MS 39212 Office: 1609 Longworth House Office Bldg Washington DC 20515

COCKE, WILLIAM MARVIN, JR., physician, educator; b. Balt., Aug. 2, 1934; s. William Marvin and Clara Emma (Bosley) C.; B.S., Tex. A. & M. Coll., 1956; M.D., Baylor U., 1960; m. Janice Ann McBride, Aug. 20, 1955; children—William Marvin, III, Catherine Lynn, Deborah Kay, Brian Thomas. Intern Vanderbilt Univ. Hosp., Nashville, 1960-61; fellow gen. surgery Ochsner Clinic and Found. Hosp., New Orleans, 1961-64; clin. research fellow surgery Am. Cancer Soc. Grant, Ochsner Clinic, 1962-63; chief resident surgery, clin. dir. Monroe (La.) Charity Hosp., 1963-64; resident surgeon plastic surgery Cornell U. Med. Center, N.Y., 1964-66; resident head and neck surgery Roswell Park Inst., Buffalo, 1965; clin. instr. plastic surgery U. Tex. Med. Sch., San Antonio, 1968; asst. prof. surgery Vanderbilt U. Sch. Medicine, Nashville, 1968-69, developer div. plastic surgery, 1969, asst. clin. prof. plastic surgery, 1969—; mem. staffs Vanderbilt Univ. Hosp., Nashville Gen. Hosp., Nashville Meml. Hosp., St. Thomas Hosp., Parkview Hosp., Bapt. Hosp., West Side Hosp. (all Nashville), Donelson (Tenn.) Hosp. Served with USAF, 1966-68. Diplomate Am. Bd. Plastic Surgery. Fellow A.C.S.; mem. Am. Soc. Plastic and Reconstructive Surgeons, Am. Cleft Palate Assn., Am. Burn Assn., Southeastern Soc. Plastic Surgeons, Tenn. Soc. Plastic and Reconstructive Surgeons (pres. 1971-73), Pan Am. Med. Soc., Soc. Head and Neck Surgeons, Assn. Academic Surgery, A.M.A., Herbert Conway Soc., Alton Oshsner Surg. Soc., Soc. Mil. Plastic Surgeons, Soc. Air Force Clin. Surgeons, Nashville Acad. Medicine, Nashville Surg. Soc., Tenn. Med. Assn., Nashville Whippets (founder 1972), Am. Pentathlon and Biatholon Assn., U.S. Track Coaches Assn. Contbr. articles to various publs. Home: New Dunkeld Farm Route 3 Franklin TN 37064 Office: 1916 Patterson St Nashville TN 37203

COCKERHAM, COLUMBUS CLARK, educator; b. Mountain Park, N.C., Dec. 12, 1921; s. Corbett C. and Nellie Bruce (McCann) C.; B.S., N.C. State Coll., 1943, M.S., 1949; Ph.D., Ia. State Coll., 1952; m. Joyce Evelyn Allen, Feb. 26, 1944; children—Columbus Clark, Jr., Jean Allen, Bruce Allen. Asst. prof. biostatistics U. N.C., Chapel Hill, 1952-53; asso. prof. exptl. statistics N.C. State Coll., Raleigh, 1953-59, prof. statistics, 1959-72, William Neal Reynolds prof. statistics and genetics, 1972—. Mem. genetics study sect. NIH, 1965-69; cons. FDA, 1967-69. Served with USMCR, 1943-46. Fellow Am. Soc. Agronomy; mem. A.A.A.S., Am. Soc. Agronomy, Am. Soc. Animal Sci., Am. Soc. Naturalists, Nat. Acad. Scis., Biometric Soc., Genetics Soc. Am., Sigma Xi, Phi Kappa Phi, Gamma Sigma Delta. Mem. editorial bd. Genetics, 1969-72. Home: 2110 Dixie Trail Raleigh NC 27607

COCKRELL, ANGUS HARDEE, JR., ret. accountant; b. Floresville, Tex., Jan. 17, 1911; s. Angus Hardee and Vera (Cocke) C.; student Tex. A. and M. Coll.; m. Vivian Smith, Dec. 25, 1933; children—Barbara Ann, Joan. C.P.A., San Antonio, 1933—; mem. firm George, Thrift & Cockrell, 1941-64; partner Ernst & Ernst, 1964—. Mem. pub. safety com. U.S. Jr. C. of C., 1944-46. Mem. Tex. State Bd. Pub. Accountancy, Nat. Assn. State Bds. Pub. Accountancy. Bd. mgrs. San Antonio City-County Hosp.; vice chmn. bd. commrs. San Antonio Urban Renewal Agy. Mem. Tex. (chmn. pub. safety com., recipient distinguished service award), San Antonio (past pres.) jr. chambers commerce, C. of C. (v.p. 1966). Mem. Christian Ch. Clubs: San Antonio (past pres.), Oak Hills Country, St. Anthony. Home: 2300 Nacogdoches Rd San Antonio TX 78209 Office: Frost Tower San Antonio TX 78205

COCKRELL, CLAUDE O'FLYNN, JR., container co. exec.; b. Memphis, May 10, 1937; s. Claude O'Flynn and Audrey (Roberts) C.; student Memphis State U., 1955, U. Miami, 1955-57; div.; children—Cana Lynn, Claude O'Flynn III. Pres., Shelby Paper Box Co., Memphis, 1952-56; pres.-owner Memphis Corrugated Container Co., 1956-61; adminstr., owner Cockrell Container Co., Memphis, 1961—; owner West Corp., Memphis, 1971—, Diamond Bar Ranch, Memphis, 1972—. State marshall Freedom Trail Found. Tenn., 1973—. Head campaign George Wallace for Pres., Memphis and Tri-state area, 1968. Mem. Pi Kappa Alpha. Presbyn. Moose. Home: 6700 Cabot Dr Nashville TN 37209 Office: PO Box 90387 Nashville TN 37209

COCKRILL, EDITH HERRING, lawyer, judge; b. Covington, Tenn., Mar. 11, 1914; d. Lucian and Martha (McLennan) Cockrill; student So. Meth. U., 1936-37; A.B., U. Tenn., 1936, LL.B., 1940. Admitted to Tenn. bar, 1940; govt. atty. 1943-44; pvt. practice law Washington, 1944-49; juvenile ct. judge, Washington, 1949-57. Trustee United Community Services D.C.; dir. Soc. for Prevention of Blindness D.C., D.C. Rehab. Service White House Conf., 1950; hearing examiner ICC, 1960-72, adminstrv. law judge, 1972—. Mem. Nat. Council Juvenile Court Judges (treas. 1952-54, exec. com. 1953-55), Profl. Panhellenic Assn. D.C., Fed. Women's Bar Assns., Fed. Trial Examiners Conf., Mortar Board, Washington Heart Assn., D.C. Crippled Children's Soc., YWCA, Kappa Delta, Phi Kappa Phi, Phi Delta Delta. Presbyn. Clubs: Altrusa, Am. Newspaper; Farmington Country. Home: 3016 Tilden St Washington DC 20008 Office: ICC Washington DC 20423

CODDING, FREDERICK HAYDEN, lawyer; b. Hopewell, Va., Dec. 13, 1938; s. Francis Chadwick and Ruthcille Sharon (Craven) C.; A.B., Coll. William and Mary, 1962; J.D., Georgetown U., 1966; m. Judith Willis Hawkins, Apr. 30, 1966; children—Forrest Hayden, Judith Chadwick, Cally Willis. Legal asst. VA, Washington, 1963-65; Capitol Hill reporter, editor Congl. Monitor, Washington, 1966; admitted to Va. bar, 1966, D.C. bar, 1968; law clk. to chief judge D.C. Ct. Appeals, 1966-68; atty. firm Swayze, Parris, Cowles & Tydings, Fairfax, Va. and Washington, 1968-70; v.p., counsel Nat. Assn. Miscellaneous, Ornamental and Archtl. Products Contractors, Fairfax, 1970—; counsel, dir. Nat. Assn. Reinforcing Steel Contractors, Fairfax, 1970—. Mem. federally established rev. bds. for constrn. industry, N.Y.C. Bldg. Standards Com. Mem. Am., D.C., Va., Fairfax bar assns., Nat. Council Erectors, Fabricators and Riggers, Sigma Nu. Editor, pub. legislative, adminstrv., bldg. and constrn. industry newsletters, reports. Office: 10533 Main St Fairfax VA 22030

CODY, MARTHA JANE BALLARD (MRS. WILLIAM JOSEPH CODY), ret. educator; b. Washington, June 25, 1897; d. Thomas Victor and Ada E. (Janney) Ballard; student Ala. Coll., 1914-16; B.S., U. Ala., 1918; M.S., U. Chgo., 1935; postgrad. U. Fla.,; Ph.D. (hon.), Colo. State Christian Coll., 1973; m. William Joseph Cody, Dec. 16, 1954. Tchr. English, art in pub. schs., Ala., Fla., 1918-30; dept. head fine arts and home arts State Tchrs Coll., Troy, Ala., 1931-51; arts and crafts supr. Southeastern Area A.R.C., Keesler Field, Ft. Jackson, 1944-46; asst. prof. U. Fla. Coll. Edn., Gainesville, 1951-57. Dir. Boys' Clubs Am., Gainesville, 1956—, sec. bd., 1965—, chmn. arts and crafts, library, 1962— mem. Safety Council, 1958—. Bd. dirs. Sante Fe Library, Gainesville. Mem. Ala. Tchrs. Art (pres. 1941), Nat. League Am. Pen Women (pres. Gainesville chpt. 1961-63, rec. sec. 1963-65, sec. 1965-67), Internat. Platform Assn., Zeta Tau Alpha, Delta Kappa Gamma (v.p. Ala. 1941, sec. Delta chpt. 1965-67), Kappa Delta Pi, Pi Lambda Theta (charter). Episcopalian (mem. St. Patrick's woman's club 1957—, St. Margaret's Circle, Holy Trinity Ch. 1951, Women of Ch. 1951—). Research on family life of Ala. tenant farmer, devel. of curriculum for Korean schs. Home: 1831 NE 7th Terrace Gainsville FL 32601

CODY, WALTER JAMES MICHAEL, lawyer; b. Memphis, Mar. 13, 1936; s. Walter James and Bessie Lou (Hill) C.; B.A. with distinction, Southwestern U., Memphis, 1958; J.D., U. Va., 1961; m. Alice Jones, June 9, 1962 (div.); children—Jane Barton, Michael Walter James. Admitted to Tenn. bar, 1961; mem. firm Burch, Porter & Johnson, Memphis, 1961, partner, 1966—; prof. polit. sci. Southwestern U., Memphis, 1970-73. Spl. city judge, Memphis, 1971. Pres. Lamar Soc., Memphis, 1969-70. Chmn. Memphis and Shelby County Dem. Party, 1972-74. Mem. Am., Tenn. bar assns., Phi Delta Phi, Sigma Alpha Epsilon, Omicron Delta Kappa. Episcopalian (mem. vestry 1967-71). Home: 2232 Washington St Memphis TN 38104 Office: 130 N Ct Av PO Box 3115 Memphis TN 38103

COE, MIRIAM, writer, librarian; b. Liverpool, Eng., July 1, 1902; d. David Avrom and Shaynah Froma (Lippsman) Cohen; honors diploma, Oulton Coll.; diploma, Skerry's Coll.; student Liverpool U., Liverpool City Sch. Art, U. Rochester (N.Y.), Columbia U., N.Y. Sch. Theatre, Carnegie Hall Studios, Sch. Chinese Brushwork, L.I. U., George Peabody Coll. for Tchrs., Utah, Fla., La. State univs. Sec., J. Ogden Co., Shipbrokers, Eng., 1916-19; tchr. violin, 1924-29; article writer Liverpool Express, 1928; lectr. on psychology of music Sta. WHAM, Stromberg Carlson Telephone Co., Hotel Sagamore, Rochester, 1929-30; comml. artist, N.Y.C.; coach in English lang.; librarian, Baton Rouge; one-woman shows, Baton Rouge; exhibitor paintings, N.Y., La. Recipient various awards and prizes. Mem. A.L.A. (coll. and research div., Roundtable for the Blind), La., Southwestern library assns., Am. Assn. Sch. Librarians, Am. Assn. State Librarians, Am. Assn. Polit. and Social Scis., Am. Hist. Soc., Am. Sociol. Assn., Am. Assn. for Natural History, Am. Judicature Soc., Am. Pub. Health Assn., Am. Soc. Photogrammetry, Smithsonian Assos., Liverpool Psychol. Assn. (asso.), Alumni Palmer Grad. Sch. L.S., Am. Assn. Museums, La. Water-color Soc., La. Art and Artists Guild, Am. Dickens League (hon.), Southwestern Poetry Soc., Mystery Club N.Y., Alpha Beta Alpha. Author: Librarians Manual; Librarianship as a Career Field; Development of Education in England; Careers in Art, Poems, Juveniles; Dictionary of Terms Related to Photogrammetry. Editor: Anthology of World Literature, A Sociological Cyclopedia; Pitirim Sorokin: Anthology, Haiku, Old and New. Developed original color system for teaching typewriting; inventor spectrum color system for teaching music theory; inventor type-face, adjuncts for mechanism in constructing typewriters. Home: Apt 29 839 Azalea Baton Rouge LA 70802 Office: Box 18184 La State U Baton Rouge LA 70803

COE, WILLIAM CLITUS, JR., accountant; b. Swifton, Ark., Sept. 18, 1941; s. William Clitus and Mary Inez (McCall) C.; B.S. in Bus. Adminstrn., U. Ark., 1963; M.B.A., Wharton Grad. Sch. Finance, 1965; m. Yvonne Marie Ross, Nov. 16, 1969; children—Mary, Rebeecka. Office mgr. Frank Whitbeck for Gov., Little Rock, 1968; supr. Ernst & Ernst, New Orleans, C.P.A.'s, 1968—. Adviser Jr. Achievement, New Orleans, 1971-72. Bd. dirs. Jefferson Place Civic Assn., New Orleans, 1971—, pres., 1972-73, v.p., 1973—; bd. dirs. New Orleans Floral Trail, 1973—. Served to 1st lt. Finance Corp, AUS, 1966-68. C.P.A., La., Ark. Mem. Goals to Grow Found., Am. Inst. C.P.A.'s, New Orleans, La. Socs. C.P.A.'s, Financial Analyst Soc., New Orleans Jr. C. of C. (dir. 1972-73, state dir. 1972-73), Phi Eta Sigma, Alpha Kappa Psi, Phi Delta Theta, Omicron Delta Kappa. Democrat. Methodist. Clubs: Variety dir. 1973-75), Young Men's Business (dir. 1971-73, treas.) (New Orleans). Editor: Action, 1972-73. Home: 211 Bienville Dr Gretna LA 70052 Office: 1824 International Trade Mart New Orleans LA 70130

COERPER, MILO GEORGE, lawyer; b. Milw., May 8, 1925; s. Milo Wilson and Rose (Schubert) C.; B.S., U.S. Naval Acad., 1946; LL.B., U. Mich., 1954; M.A., Georgetown U., 1957; Ph.D., 1960; m. Lois Hicks Coerper, Apr. 11, 1953; children—Milo Wilson, Allison Lee, Lois Paddock. Admitted to D.C. bar, 1954; asso. firm Wilmer & Broun, Washington, 1954-60, firm Coudert Brothers, 1961-63, partner, 1964—. Trustee Sheridan Sch., vice chmn., 1972—; trustee House of Mercy, pres., 1970—. Served to ensign USN, 1946-49, to lt., 1951-53. Mem. Bar Assn. D.C., Assn. Bar City N.Y., Am. Bar Assn., Am. Soc. Internat. Law. Internat. Law Assn., Am. Law Inst. Contbr. articles to profl. jours. Home: 7315 Brookville Rd Chevy Chase MD 20015 Office: 1 Farragut Square S Washington DC 20006

COFER, MALCOLM THOMAS, accountant; b. Petersburg, Va., May 29, 1943; s. Thomas Linwood and Pauline (Johnson) C.; student Va. Poly. Inst., 1961-64, Old Dominion U., 1967-69, Christopher Newport Coll., 1970-73; m. Edna Watson Powell, Aug. 27, 1966.

Processing foreman Smithfield (Va.) Packing Co., 1963-69, time study clk., 1967-69, dir. cost accounting, 1971—; accounting clk. Stone & Webster Engring. Corp., 1970. Mem. Smithfield Little Theatre, 1970—. Recipient Keyman award Jaycees, 1972; named Jaycee of year, 1968, 69, Most Outstanding Regional chmn., 1969. Mem. Smithfield Jaycees (chmn. bd. 1973—), Va. Jaycees (region v.p. 1971—), Nat. Assn. Accountants. Methodist. Home: 923 Magruder Rd Smithfield VA 23430 Office: Route 1 Smithfield VA 23430

COFER, VERNON LONSDALE, JR., physician; b. Norfolk, Va., Apr. 9, 1924; s. Vernon Lonsdale and Nancy Carola (Ross) C.; student Coll. William and Mary, 1942-44; M.D. with honors, Med. Coll. Va., 1948; m. Judith Ball Wysong, July 1, 1950; children—Thomas L., James S. Intern, Wis. Gen. Hosp., Madison 1948-49; resident internal medicine Kansas City Gen. Hosp., 1950-51; fellow, 1st asst. in internal medicine Mayo Clinic, 1951-53; practice medicine, specializing in internal medicine and hematology, Norfolk, 1954—; dir. dept. medicine DePaul Hosp., 1964-69, dir. hematology clinic, 1955-69; pres. med. staff, 1970-71; attending staff, teaching faculty Norfolk Gen. Hosp., 1954—. Served to capt. M.C., AUS, 1948-50. Mem. Am., So. med. assns., Va. Med. Soc., Norfolk County Med. Soc. (exec. com.), Am. Soc. Internal Medicine, A.C.P. (life mem.). Clubs: Norfolk Yacht and Country, Izaak Walton, Tidewater Anglers' (Norfolk); Cape Hatteras (N.C.) Billfish; Ocean Reef (Key Largo, Fla.). Home: 5326 Edgewater Dr Norfolk VA 23508 Office: 530 Wainwright Bldg Norfolk VA 23510

COFFEE, CHARLES WENDELL, lawyer; b. Loraine, Tex., Mar. 10, 1925; s. Charlie Childress and Edith Wilson (Hurd) C.; B.S. in Mech. Engring. with honors, Tex. Technol. Coll., 1947; J.D. with honors, U. Tex., 1954; m. Dorothy Jean Nesmith, Aug. 30, 1947; children—Camille Lane (Mrs. Fred Flournoy), Celia Jean (Mrs. Mike Davis), Mark Wayne, Charles Creed. Admitted to Tex. bar, 1953; engr. Humble Oil & Refining Co., Baytown, Tex., 1947-48; partner Coffee & Coffee, 1948-51; tchr. Tex. Technol. Coll., 1949; examiner U.S. Patent Office, 1954-55; patent adviser U.S. Army, Washington, 1955-56; practice law, Lubbock, Tex. 1956—. Served with USNR, 1944-46. Mem. State Bar Tex. (chmn. patent, trademark and copyright sect. 1972-73), Am. Patent Law Assn., Am. Bar Assn., Tau Beta Pi, Phi Delta Phi. United Methodist (chmn. commn. Christian social concerns N.W. Tex. conf. 1967-71). Mason, Rotarian. Club: White River Yacht (commodore 1971-72). Home: 3210 55th St Lubbock TX 79413 Office: 1507 13th St Lubbock TX 79401

COFFEE, JAMES MADISON, JR., educator; b. Douglas, Ga., Nov. 18, 1918; s. James Madison and Bessie (Hatfield) C.; B.A. in History, Duke, 1949; M.A. in History, Cornell U., 1950; Ed.D. in Guidance and Counselling, Harvard, 1957. Mem. faculty Clark U., Worcester, Mass., 1954-68, asso. prof. edn., 1962-68, acting chmn. dept., 1967-68, dir. guidance and placement, 1954-67; prof. edn. Jacksonville (Fla.) U., 1968—, dir. tchr. edn., 1970—, dir. M.A. in Teaching program, 1972—, chmn. div. edn., 1968—. Co-chmn. edn. com. Jacksonville Sesquicentennial Com., 1971-72. Served to 2d lt. USAAF, World War II. Named Man of Year, Clark U. chpt. Lambda Chi Alpha, 1957. Mem. Am. Personnel and Guidance Assn., Am. Psychol. Assn., Am. Ednl. Research Assn., Fla. Council Deans and Dirs. Tchrs. Edn., Fla. Assn. Tchr. Edn., Phi Beta Kappa, Phi Delta Kappa, Kappa Delta Phi. Baptist. Home: 5903 Woodside Dr Jacksonville FL 32210

COFFEY, JOHN WALTER, dentist; b. Shawnee, Okla., May 9, 1939; s. Thomas Ray and Edna May (Poindexter) C.; student U. Okla., 1957-61; D.D.S., Baylor U., 1965; m. Joy Diane Arrington, Aug. 6, 1960; children—Dana Catherine, Jennifer Diane, Anne Elizabeth, Emilie Lyn. Practice dentistry, Stillwater, Okla., 1968—; mem. staff, cons. Stillwater Municipal Hosp. Active YMCA memberships drs.; mem. budget com. United Fund, 1969-72; regional chmn. Children's Dental Health Week, 1973-74. Served to capt., USAF, 1965-68. Mem. Am. Soc. Preventive Dentistry, Am. Soc. Dentistry for Children (sec.-treas. Okla. unit 1971-72, pres. 1974—), Acad. Gen. Dentistry (charter mem. Okla.), Am., Okla. (del.) dental assns., Stillwater, Ponca City dental study clubs, Sigma Nu. Republican. Presbyn. Home: 220 Ridge Rd Stillwater OK 74074 Office: 823 S Pine Stillwater OK 74074

COFFIELD, CONRAD EUGENE, lawyer; b. Hot Springs, S.D., Nov. 26, 1930; s. Eugene M. and Alice (Hotvet) C.; student S.D. Sch. Mines and Tech., 1948-49; B.B.A., Washington U., St. Louis, 1952; LL.B., U. Tex., 1959; m. Maggie Lee Murphey, Aug. 1, 1953; children—Conrad Eugene, Michael, Megan, Edward, Philip. Admitted to Tex., N.M. bars, 1959; practiced in Roswell, N.M., 1959-66, Midland, Tex., 1966—; mem. firm Hervey, Dow & Hinkel, 1959-64; gen. partner Hinkle, Bondurant, Cox & Eaton, Roswell, 1964-66, resident partner, Midland, 1966—; dir., counsel Grammer-Murphey, Inc., Midland. Mem. N.M. Republican party orgn., 1959-66, Midland County Rep. party orgn., 1966—; 1st v.p. Midland County Rep. Men's Club, 1971—. Served with USCGR, 1952-56. Mem. Am., Tex., N.M., Midland County bar assns., N.M. Oil and Gas Assn. Episcopalian (vestryman). Kiwanian (Man of Year 1969). Clubs: Midland Petroleum, Midland Country, Torero, Cotillion. Home: 2813 W Dengar St Midland TX 79701 Office: Midland Tower Midland TX 79701

COFFIN, DAVID LUKENS, pathologist; b. Neshameny, Pa., Feb. 24, 1913; s. Samuel Malcolm and Katherine Fraley (Glacken) C.; V.M.D., U. Pa., 1938; m. Viola DiFranceschi, Dec. 10, 1964; 1 son, Robert David. Asst. veterinarian, diagnostic lab. Pa. Bur. Animal Husbandry, Summerdale, 1938-39; asst. vet. practice, Peekskill, N.Y., 1939; mem. faculty U. Pa., 1939-46, 1956-61; Herbert Fox Meml. fellow in comparative pathology Phila. Zool. Soc., 1943-45; head dept. pathology Angell Meml. Hosp., Boston, 1946-56; research asso. pathology Children's Med. Center, Boston, 1947-56; instr. pathology Harvard Med. Sch., Boston, 1946-56; dir. research, pathologist Animal Med. Center, N.Y.C., 1956-61; spl. cons. div. air pollution Bur. State Services— Pub. Health Service, Cin., 1961-62, acting chief exptl. pathology sect., 1962-67; asso. prof. pathology U. Cin. Sch. Medicine, 1961, adj. asso. prof. environmental health, 1968-71; chief exptl. pathology sect. Nat. Air Pollution Control Adminstrn., Cin., 1968-71; chief pathobiology research br. Exptl. Biology Lab., Nat. Environmental Research Center; sr. research advisor Environmental Protection Agy., Research Triangle Park, N.C., 1971—. Adj. prof. pharmacology Duke U. Med. Sch., Durham, N.C. Fellow N.Y. Acad. Sci.; mem. Am. Coll. Vet. Pathologists, Internat. Acad. Pathology, Research Workers Animal Diseases, A.A.A.S., Soc. Toxicology, Am. Littoral Soc., WHO, Am. Pub. Health Assn., Inc., Conf. Pub. Health Vets., Nat. Wildlife Fedn., Am. Assn. Pathologists and Bacteriologists, Air Pollution Control Assn. Author: Laboratorio Clinico en Medicine Veterinaria, 1952; Manual of Veterinary Clinical Pathology, 1953. Contbr. numerous articles to various publs. Home: 1023 Sycamore St Durham NC 27711 Office: Pathobiology Research Br EBL Tech Center Research Triangle Park NC 27711

COFFLAND, ARTHUR WESLEY, utility exec.; b. Mpls., Apr. 6, 1918; s. Carl Melville and Alma Elma (Wissman) C.; B.B.A., U. Minn., 1954; m. Martha Jane Burlingame, May 19, 1944; children—Carol Lynn (Mrs. Carol L. Slack), Brooks Carleton, Laura Leigh (Mrs. Stephen E. Lewis), Leslie Ellen. Portfolio mgr. Investors Diversified Services, Inc., Mpls., 1954-60; dir. research No. Natural Gas, Omaha, 1960-62; sr. analyst Duff & Phelps, Inc., Chgo., 1962-66; dir. financial research, economist Tex. Gas Transmission Corp., Owensboro, Ky., 1966—. Asst. prof. mil. sci. Yale, 1948-53; instr. finance U. Minn., Mpls., 1953-58. Mem. Owensboro Symphony Orchestra. Served with USAF, 1940-48. Mem. Am. Gas Assn., Ind. Natural Gas Assn. Am., Financial Analysts Fedn. Rotarian. Contbr. articles to various publs. Home: 1515 Brentwood Dr Owensboro KY 42301 Office: 3800 Frederica St Owensboro KY 42301

COFFMAN, BEN F., ednl. adminstr.; b. Slaughters, Ky., Nov. 17, 1905; s. John Frank and Virginia (Cox) C.; A.B., U. Ky., 1929, M.A., 1940; postgrad. Columbia, Harbridge House, Brookings Instn., Center for Continuing Edn., U. Okla.; m. Jean Ruhlman, May 18, 1935; children—Virginia Ann (Mrs. William Case), Linda Lee (Mrs. Thomas Scott), Nancy Jean (Mrs. Lawrence Goodwin), Donald F. Tchr., coach, prin., supt. South Portsmouth (Ky.) Schs., 1930-40; supt. schs., Russell, Ky., 1940-50, Bourbon County, Paris, Ky., 1952-56; asst. supt. pub. instrn. for rehab. Ky. Dept. Edn., Frankfort, 1956—. Vice pres. Slaughters Merc. Co.; owner Sarahlawn Farms, Hopkins County (Ky.). Active fund drives A.R.C., United Fund; v.p. Area council Boy Scouts Am. Bd. dirs. Ky. YMCA. Mem. Nat. Rehab. Assn. (pres. region III). Home: 1019 Chicksaw St Frankfort KY 40601 Office: Capital Plaza Office Tower Frankfort KY 40601

COFFMAN, CHARLIE QUINN, educator; b. Lula, Miss., Feb. 20, 1923; s. Tulus Jackson and Addie (Mick) C.; B.S., Delta State Coll., Cleveland, Miss., 1948; M.A. (scholar), U. So. Miss., Hattiesburg, 1951; D.Ed. (scholar), U. Miss., 1964; m. J'Nell Posey, Aug. 23, 1947; children—Deborah (Mrs. Gerald Juzwiak), Marilyn Mick. Athletic dir. Tunica (Miss.) High Sch., 1948-50; prin. Shelby (Miss.) High Sch., 1951-53; supt. schs., Arcola, Miss., 1953-56; asst. supt. schs., Cleveland, 1957-60, Hinds County (Miss.) schs., 1961-67; dir. lay renewal United Methodist Ch., 1967-69; asso. dir. for planning in higher edn. State of Miss., 1969—; tchr. grad. studies ednl. adminstrn. U. Miss., 1964—; coordinator Title I Higher Edn. Act for Miss., 1969—. Asso. lay leader, chmn. conf. program council, conf. leadership devel. United Meth. Ch.; dir., charter mem. Jackson (Miss.) Contact Telephone Ministry; tng. officer Explorer Scout leaders. Bd. dirs. local A.R.C., Delta State Coll. Found. Served with USMC, 1941-45. Decorated Purple Heart. Mem. Am. Assn. Sch. Adminstrs., Assn. Instl. Research, Phi Delta Kappa. Mason, Lion. Club: Brookwood Country (Jackson). Author: Ministry of the Laity Training Program, 1968; Growing Together in Small Groups, 1968. Home: Route 9 Box 110 Jackson MS 39212 Office: PO Box 2336 Jackson MS 39205

COFFMAN, FRANK LEE, JR., savs. and loan exec.; b. Harrison, Ark., June 24, 1922; s. Frank Lee and Fannie Lou (Maggard) C.; student Hendrix Coll., 1939, U. Ark., 1940; m. Wanda L. Magness, Feb. 4, 1947; children—Cathy (Mrs. Larry J. Brandt), Cynthia. Owner, mgr. Coffman Motor & Implement Co., Harrison, Ark., 1946-53; with Motels, Inc., Harrison, 1953-61; with Harrison Fed. Savs. & Loan Assn., 1961—, pres., 1968—; dir. First Nat. Bank of Harrison. Chmn. Ark. Savs. and Loan Commn., 1967-72. First v.p. W. Ark. council Boy Scouts Am., 1968-73. Chmn. City Planning Commn., Harrison, 1964-72; mem. Boone County Airport Commn., 1970—. Served with USAF, 1942-45. Decorated Air medal, D.F.C.; recipient Silver Beaver award Boy Scouts Am., 1967. Mem. Nat. League Insured Savs. Assn. (exec. com. 1968—), Southwestern Savs. & Loan Conf. (1st v.p. 1973-74), Ark. Savs. and Loan League (pres. 1967, Distinguished Service award 1973), Ark. C. of C. (dir. 1973—). Elk, Rotarian (pres. 1969-70). Home: 100 S Highland St Harrison AR 72601 Office: 200 W Stephenson St Box 550 Harrison AR 72601

COFFMAN, PENELOPE DALTON (MRS. ALDINE J. COFFMAN, JR.), lawyer; b. Pulaski, Va., Apr. 16, 1938; d. Gomez and Hazel (Davis) Dalton; A.B., Randolph-Macon Womans Coll., 1958; J.D., Coll. William and Mary, 1966; m. Aldine J. Coffman, Jr., Mar. 27, 1965; 1 dau., D'Maris Dalton. Research chemist, research biologist Arthur D. Little, Inc., Cambridge, Mass., 1958-63; admitted to Va. bar, 1966; law clk. Asso. Justice C. Vernon Spratley, Va. Supreme Ct. Appeals, Hampton, Va., 1966-67; practiced in Norfolk, Va., 1967-68, Virginia Beach, Va., 1968—; mem. firm Coffman & Coffman; asst. commonwealth atty. for City Virginia Beach, 1971-73. Mem. Va. Adv. Council on Ednl. TV, 1971—. Mem. Va. State, Virginia Beach bar assns., Nat. Assn. Women Lawyers, William and Mary Alumni Assn., William and Mary Soc., Randolph-Macon Womans Coll. Alumni Assn., Zeta Tau Alpha. Home: 2861 River Rd Virginia Beach VA 23454 Office: 4999 Cleveland St Virginia Beach VA 23462

COGGESHALL, KENNETH MORRISON, pub. relations exec.; b. St. Louis, June 27, 1920; s. Kenneth McCandless and Eva Louise (Morrison) C.; B.A. in Journalism, B.A. in English, U. Mo., 1948; certificate in pub. relations Washington U., 1951; m. Corinne Beard, May 23, 1942; children—Diane (Mrs. Ralph Conlin), David Knight. Asst. pub. relations dir. McDonnell Aircraft Corp., 1949-53; dir. pub. relations Bank Bldg. Corp., St. Louis, 1953-58; cons. pub. affairs, Washington, 1958—. Dir. 1st Internat. Trauma Symposium, 1970; mem. Pub. Relations Soc. Task Force on Environment, 1970—. Served with USAAC, 1942-46. Recipient Silver Anvil award Pub. Relations Soc. Am., 1961; Pub. Service citation Am. Pub. Relations Assn. Mem. Pub. Relations Soc. Am. (chmn. eligibility com. Nat. Capital chpt. 1967). Am. Helicopter Soc., Helicopter Assn. Am. Home: 8212 Carrleigh Pkwy Springfield VA 22152 Office: 400 Maryland Av SW Washington DC 20202

COGGESHALL, ROBERT WALDEN, ret. cons.; b. Darlington, S.C., Sept. 11, 1912; s. Robert Werner and Beulah (Walden) C.; B.S., U. S.C., 1932; M.A., George Washington U., 1964; postgrad. Am. U., 1964-69; m. Ellie Mason Thomas, Sept. 3, 1934; children—Peter Collin V., John Pennington. Adminstrv. analyst Home Owners Loan Corp., Washington, 1934-41; budget analyst Fed. Works Agy., 1941-43; asst. dep. adminstr. for rent control OPA, 1943-46; chief systems and procedures Bur. Reclamation, 1946-53; editor Postal Manual, Office Postmaster Gen., 1954; chief mgmt. analysis Bur. Indian Affairs, 1954-57; chief div. mgmt. sci. Office of Sec., Dept. Interior, Washington, 1957-68; research fellow Brookings Instn., 1968-69; mem. faculty U.S. Dept. Agr. Grad. Sch., 1959-65. Mem. Am. Soc. Pub. Adminstrn., A.A.A.S., Common Cause, Alpha Tau Omega. Episcopalian. Author: Administrative Functions of the Fish and Wildlife Service, 1958; Coordination of Federal Oceanography, 1963. Home: Shaggy Acres Ballentine SC 29002

COGGINS, WADE THOMAS, assn. exec.; b. New Market, N.C., Dec. 12, 1924; s. Charles Lee and Laura Jean (Hinshaw) C.; B.S., Nyack Missionary Coll., 1955, LL.D., 1973; M.A., U. Md., 1965; m. Jane Marguerite Wells, Aug. 18, 1945; 1 son, Robert Charles. Ordained to ministry Christian and Missionary Alliance Ch., 1947; minister, Norwoodville Ch., Des Moines, 1945-47; missionary, tchr. Christian and Missionary Alliance, Columbia, 1948-55; minister Alliance Ch., Knoxville, Tenn., 1956-58; asso. exec. sec. Evang. Fgn. Missions Assn., Washington, 1958—. Mem. Alumni Assn. Nyack Missionary Coll. (v.p. 1966-67). Mem. Christian and Missionary Alliance Ch. (elder 1959—). Editor: (with Clyde W. Taylor) Protestant Missions in Latin America, 1961; (with Clyde W. Taylor) Mobilizing for Saturation Evangelism, 1970. Editor, Missionary News Service, 1958—. Home: 4913 Bangor Dr Kensington MD 20795 Office: 1405 G St NW Washington DC 20005

COGSWELL, GEORGE WALLACE, chem. co. exec.; b. N.Y.C., Feb. 8, 1923; s. Charles Wallace and Anna Cecelia (Rean) C.; B.S., Coll. City N.Y., 1953; postgrad. Bklyn. Poly. Inst., 1954-55; M.S., Fordham U., 1955, Ph.D., 1960; m. Helen Elizabeth Conrad, Nov. 26, 1949; children—Ann Elizabeth, Steven Charles, Janet Louise, Linda Helen. Asst. chemist Colgate Palmolive Co., Jersey City, 1951-53; grad. teaching asst. Fordham U., N.Y.C., 1953-57; research asso. Cornell U. Med. Coll., N.Y.C., 1957-58; sr. devel. chemist Staley Mfg. Co., Decatur, Ill., 1958-63; sec. mgr. research Armour & Co., Beverly, Mass., 1964-66; mgr. market devel. Hooker Chem. Corp., Niagara Falls, N.Y., 1966-68; v.p. Vanguard Industries, Anderson, S.C., 1968-72; pres. Arlington Services Corp., Anderson, 1972—; treas. Higher Coating & Finishing, Inc., Anderson, 1973—; dir. Woodburn Analytical Lab., Anderson. Cons. polymer and electrochemicals, 1965—. Chmn. bd. dirs. Anderson Civic Chorale, 1970-72; bd. dirs. Anderson Community Theater, 1969-72. Served with AUS, 1942-46. Decorated Bronze Star. Mem. Am. Chem. Soc., N.Y. Acad. Sci., T.A.P.P.I. (chmn. coating com. 1973-74), Am. Pharm. Assn., V.F.W., Sigma Xi, Phi Lambda Upsilon. Methodist (dist. trustee 1973—). Elk, Rotarian. Club: Toastmasters (gov. Ill. area 1961-62). Home: 411 Ravenal Rd Anderson SC 29621 Office: 118 N Fant St Box 1048 Anderson SC 29621

COHEN, EUGENE ERWIN, univ. adminstr.; b. Johnstown, Pa., Nov. 1, 1917; s. LeRoy S. and Ann (Aronson) C.; B.B.A., U. Miami, 1941, M.B.A., 1951; postgrad. Wayne State U., 1944-45, U. N.C., 1951-52; m. Lee Woodard Edmundson, Dec. 31, 1944; children—William Palmer, Margaret Gene, Ann Woodard. Mem. faculty U. Miami, 1945—, asso. prof. accounting, 1954-67, prof., 1967—, treas., 1957—, v.p., treas., 1958-72, v.p. financial affairs, 1972—, also treas. Univ. Research Found.; v.p., dir. Dormitory Housing Assn., Inc.; chmn. pres. Laurel Corp., 1971-73; dir. Am. Laser Corp., Garrett & Co., Consortium Investors Corp., Corad Corp., Univ. Fed. Savs. and Loan Assn.; mem. adv. bd. Am. Bankers Ins. Co. Fla. Cons., NSF, NIH, U.S. Office Edn., So. Assn. Colls. and Schs., Greyhound Corp., Plastetics, Inc., Reynolds & Co.; mem. com. taxation Am. Council Edn.; rep. Univ. Corp. Atmospheric Research, 1969-73. Vice pres. Nat. Childrens Cardiac Hosp.; mem. Health Planning Council South Fla.; asso. mem. Orange Bowl Com.; dir. Greater Miami Indsl. Commn.; mem. Miami Mayor's Spl. Adv. Com. on Interama.; chmn. Dade County Higher Edn. Facilities Authority, 1969—. Bd. dirs. Goodwill Industries, Miami, Dade County Citizens Safety Council, Jackson Found.; trustee United Fund Dade County. Served with AUS, 1941-45. Mem. So. Assn. Coll. and Univ. Bus. Officers (pres. 1963), Financial Execs. Inst. (pres. Fla. chpt. 1963). Nat. Assn. Coll. and Univ. Bus. Officers, Am. Mgmt. Assn., Coll. and Univ. Personnel Assn., Coll. and Univ. Housing Officers Assn., Nat. Assn. Cost Accountants, Newcomen Soc., Dade County C. of C., Econ. Soc. South Fla., Financial Analysts Soc. Miami, Nat. Accounting Assn., Beta Gamma Sigma, Omicron Delta Kappa, Phi Mu Alpha, Alpha Phi Omega, Alpha Kappa Psi. Methodist. Mason. Clubs: Ocean Reef Yacht, Miami University Yacht. Cons. editor Coll. and Univ. Bus. Mag., 1963-68. Home: 6700 SW 117th St Miami FL 33156 Office: Ashe Adminstrn Bldg U Miami Coral Gables FL 33124

COHEN, H(ERMANN) E(DMOND), ret. textile co. exec., civic worker; b. Ukraine, Oct. 10, 1889; s. Edell and Sarah (Rosenstein) C.; Came to U.S., 1892, naturalized citizen; extension student Mechanics Inst. Va., 1909-10, U. Va., 1912; m. Claire Rosenberg, Apr. 6, 1921 (dec. Apr. 1960). Formerly textile selling agt.; pres. Priestly Knitting Co., 1948; owner Chester Knit Goods Co., Charlotte, N.C., 1948-72. Mem. adv. com. So. Sch. for Workers, 1940-55; mem. adv. com. League for Mut. Aid, 1959—; charter mem. Am. Civil Liberties Union, Charlotte-Mecklenburg Council on Human Relations, Charlotte-Mecklenberg Symposium on World Affairs; mem. Central Com. for Conscientious Objectors; mem. internat. com. Thomas Paine Found., 1958—, organizer Charlotte chpt. Thomas Paine Soc., 1963. Recipient awards Nat. Conf. Christians and Jews, 1958, 63. Mem. Internat. Platform Assn., C. of C. Jewish religion (mem. temple adult edn. com., pres. Men's Club): Unitarian; mem. Community Ch. Mason (Shriner). Elk (chaplain). Clubs: Executives, Toastmasters (Charlotte). Former mem., editorial bd., cofounder The Carolina Israelite. Home: 301 W 10th St Charlotte NC 28202

COHEN, HYMAN JACOB, lawyer; b. Boston, July 27, 1905; s. Benjamin L. and Kate (Bazol) C.; B.S., Tufts U., 1928; LL.B., Harvard, 1931; m. Ann Rosen, Nov. 1940; children—Amy Rose (Mrs. Mark P. Scher), Judith F. (Mrs. David C. Wilson), Kate B. (Mrs. Cohen Schachter). Admitted to D.C. bar, 1947, Va. bar, 1948; pvt. practice law, 1931-42; field worker U.S.O., 1942-43; atty. U.S. Govt., 1943-47; pvt. practice law, Washington, Va., 1947—; print collector, exhibiting D.C., Md. and Va. Mem. adv. bd. Independence Fed. Savs. & Loan Assn. Mem. min. standards housing bd. Arlington County Youth Commn., 1960—; mem. nat. council U.S.O. 1959—; mem. dist. adv. council Small Bus. Adminstrn.; mem. region 3 archives adv. council Gen. Services Adminstrn.; mem. Arlington County Hist. Commn., World Peace Through Law Center, Arlington County Bicentennial Commn., Arlington History Commn.; mem. adv. com. N.E. region Nat. Park Service. Trustee United Jewish Appeal, Greater Washington Jewish Community Found.; bd. regents James Monroe Law Office-Mus. and Meml. Library; bd. dirs. Touro Synagogue-Nat. Historic Shrine. Mem. Am., Va. bar assns., Bar Assn. D.C., Am. Trial Lawyers Assn. (asso. editor), Am. Forestry Assn., Nat. Trust for Historic Preservation, Nature Conservancy (life), UN Assn. U.S.A., Wilderness Soc., Jewish Hist. Assn. Greater Washington (pres.), Am. Jewish (exec. council), U.S. Capitol hist. socs., Pi Lambda Phi. Mem. Washington Hebrew Congregation (dir.). Mason; mem. B'nai B'rith (Jewish hist. com.). Clubs: Torch, Nat. Press. Home: 5300 36th St N Arlington VA 22207 Office: 910 17th St NW Washington DC 20006

COHEN, LAWRENCE LOUIS, otolaryngologist, allergist; b. Memphis, Jan. 1, 1924; s. Jacob William and Anna (Friedman) C.; student Vanderbilt U., 1941-42, Southwestern U., 1942-43, Memphis State U., summers 1941-42; M.D., U. Tenn., 1947; m. Kay Allenberg, Apr. 9, 1955; children—Kathryn Ann, Lawrence Louise. Interne John Gaston Hosp., Memphis, 1947; resident U. Ill., 1948-49; practice medicine specializing in otolarynology and allergy, Memphis, 1950—; mem. staffs Baptist, Methodist, St. Joseph, LeBonheur hosps. Served with USAF, 1953-55. Mem. Am. Acad. Otolaryngology. Kiwanian. Home: 261 Wakefield Dr Memphis TN 38117 Office: 4515 Poplar Av No 510 Memphis TN 38117

COHEN, ROY JAY, lawyer; b. N.Y.C., Oct. 17, 1926; s. Isidore and Florence B. (Bluh) C.; B.A., Yale, 1946, J.D., 1949; m. Yolanda Shoreman, Aug. 21, 1960 (div. 1972); children—Mark R., Brian J., Alan I. Admitted to N.Y. bar, 1950, P.R. bar, 1953; asso. Hirsh, Newman & Rosenson, N.Y.C., 1949-50; atty. Nat. Labor Relations Bd., P.R., 1951-52; asso. McConnell, Valdes, Kelley & Sifre, P.R., 1953-57; partner Roy J. Cohen, Hato Rey, P.R., 1957—. Mem. president's adv. council InterAm. U., P.R., 1967-72. Mem. Assn. Labor Practitioners (pres. 1970-71), Fed. (chpt. treas. 1972-73), Am., P.R. bar assns. Rotarian (pres. 1955-56, 1959-60; dist. gov. 1966-67). Clubs: Caparra Country, Dorado Beach Hotel and Country (P.R.);

Bankers of Puerto Rico (San Juan); Caribe Hilton Hotel Swimming and Tennis (P.R.). Home: 31 A St Villa Caparra Bayamon PR 00619 Office: PO Box 1718 Hato Rey PR 00919

COHEN, TED ELLIS, pub. relations exec., state legislator; b. N.Y.C., Aug. 13, 1922; s. Irving and Gertrude (Cantor) C.; student U.S. Naval Acad., 1942-45; m. Carolyn Bloom, June 1944 (div. Sept. 1960); children—Constance Diane, James David, Ellen Jane. Partner, DiLido Hotel, Miami Beach, Fla., 1950-53; real estate salesman J.A. Cantor Assos., Miami, 1952-53; real estate broker Ted Cohen, Realtor, Miami Beach, 1953-56; pres. Ted Cohen Assos., Pub. Relations, Miami Beach, 1956—. Exec. dir. Fla. Fashion Council, 1965-68. Mem. Mayor's Safety Com., Miami Beach, 1955-70, chmn. 1959-61; pres. Pres.'s Council, 1964-65; chmn. S. Fla. council Boy Scouts Am., 1960. Democratic committeeman, 1962-70, state Dem. committeeman, 1971-74; pres. Young Dems., 1959-61; chmn. Dade County Dem. Exec. Com., 1971-72; mem. Fla. Ho. of Reps., 1972-74. Served with USN, 1942-45. Named Outstanding Young Man Miami Beach 1959, Outstanding Citizen Fla., 1961 (both Jaycees). Elk (exalted ruler 1971-72). Clubs: Civic League (pres. 1967-68), Civitan (pres. 1959-60). Home: 5 Island Av Miami Beach FL 33139 Office: 1 Lincoln Rd Miami Beach FL 33139

COHN, ERNST MAX, govt. ofcl.; b. Mainz, Germany, Mar. 31, 1920; s. Martin and Lorle Flora (Wertheimer) C.; B.S., U. Pitts., 1942, M.S., 1952; m. Margaret M. Miller, July 8, 1949. Phys. chemist U.S. Bur. Mines, Pitts., Washington, 1942-60, Army Research Office, 1960-62; with NASA, Washington, 1962—, mgr. solar and chem. power, 1971—. Mem. Electrochem. Soc., Am. Chem. Soc., A.A.A.S. (reviewer 1965—), Postal History Soc. (v.p. 1972—), Pi Tau Phi, Phi Eta Sigma, Sigma Pi Sigma, Phi Lambda Upsilon. Contbr. articles to various publs. Patentee in field. Home: 103 G St SW Washington DC 20024 Office: NASA Code RPP Washington DC 20546

COHN, ISIDORE, JR., surgeon, educator; b. New Orleans, Sept. 25, 1921; s. Isidore and Elsie (Waldhorn) C.; M.D., U. Pa., 1945, M.Med.Sci. in Surgery, 1952, D.M.S. in Surgery, 1955; m. Jacqueline Heymann, July 4, 1944 (div. Aug. 27, 1971); children—Ian Jeffrey, Lauren Kerry. Intern, Grad. Hosp. U. Pa., 1945-46, resident in surgery, 1949-52; fellow dept. surg. research U. Pa., 1947-48; vis. surgeon Charity Hosp., New Orleans, 1952-62, sr. vis. surgeon, 1962—; surgeon-in-chief La State U. Service, Charity Hosp., 1962—; cons. surgeon VA Hosp, Touro Infirmary (both New Orleans); instr. surgery La. State U. Sch. Medicine, New Orleans, 1952-53, asst. prof., 1953-56, asso. prof. 1956-59, prof., 1959—, chmn. dept. surgery, 1962—. Mem. surg. research rev. com. VA, Washington; mem. Am. Bd. Surgery, 1969—. Served to capt. M.C., AUS, 1946-47. Diplomate Am. Bd. Surgery. Fellow A.C.S.; mem. A.M.A., Soc. Exptl. Biology and Medicine, Am., So., La. (2d v.p. 1966, 1st v.p. 1967, pres. 1968) surg. assns., So. Med. Assn., La., Orleans Parish med. socs., Internat., New Orleans (v.p. 1966, pres. 1967) surg. socs., Soc. Univ. Surgeons, Southeastern Surg. Congress (chmn. forum on progress in surgery 1967-69, councillor for La. 1967-73, 2d v.p. 1965, 1st v.p. 1969, pres. 1972), Surg. Biology Club II, Assn. Acad. Surgery, Allen O. Whipple, James D. Rives surg. socs., Am. Gastroenterol. Assn., Bockus Soc. Gastroenterology, So. Soc. Clin. Research, Soc. Surgery Alimentary Tract (trustee 1969—, recorder 1973—), Am. Soc. Microbiologists, N.Y. Acad. Scis., Soc. Surg. Chmn., Am. Assn. Cancer Research, Collegium Internationale Chirurgiae Digestivae, Am. Cancer Soc. (vice chmn. clin. investigation adv. com. 1969, chmn. clin. investigation adv. com. 1969-73), Sigma Xi. Mem. editorial bd. Am. Surgeon, Review of Surgery, Am. Jour. Surgery, Surgery Digest. Home: 510 Iona St Metairie LA 70005 Office: Louisiana State Univ School of Medicine New Orleans LA 70112

COHN, JACK, educator; b. Rock Island, Ill., May 6, 1932; Howard and Sarah (Abrams) C.; B.S., State U. Ia., 1953, M.S., 1956, Ph.D., 1963; m. Rebecca R. Whitice, Sept. 5, 1953 (div. 1972); children—David William, Eve Mari, Michael Jerome, Roddey Lynn. Mem. staff U. Okla., Norman, 1960—, prof. physics, 1969—. Office: Dept Physics U Okla Norman OK 73069

COHN, JAY NORMAN, cardiologist; b. Schenectady, July 6, 1930; s. Morris Mandel and Rose (Gold) C.; B.S., Union Coll., Schenectady, 1952; M.D., Cornell U., 1956; m. Syma Cheris, June 14, 1953; children—Cynthia, Lauren, Joshua. Intern, then asst. resident medicine Beth Israel Hosp., Boston, 1956-58; clin. investigator VA Hosp., Washington, 1962-65, chief hypertension and clin. hemodynamics, 1965—; fellow cardiovascular research Georgetown U. Med. Sch., 1960-61, faculty, 1962—, prof. medicine, 1971—, co-dir. cardiovascular research div., 1970—; cons. Provident Hosp., Washington Hosp. Center. Served with USPHS, 1958-60. Recipient Arthur S. Femming award Downtown Washington Jr. C. of C., 1969. Mem. Am. Heart Assn., Am. Fedn. Clin. Research, Am. Soc. Clin. Investigation, Am. Coll. Cardiology, Am. Physiol. Soc., Am. Soc. Pharmacology and Exptl. Therapeutics, Am. Soc. Clin. Pharmacology, So. Soc. Clin. Investigation, Am. Soc. Nephrology, Alpha Omega Alpha. Contbr. to books, articles to profl. jours. Home: 10503 Streamview Ct Potomac MD 20854 Office: 50 Irving St NW Washington DC 20422

COHN, SIDNEY ARTHUR, educator; b. Toronto, Ont., Can., May 8, 1918; s. Benjamin and Mollie (Haymond) C.; B.S., U. Conn., 1940, M.S., 1947; Ph.D., Brown U., 1951; m. Dorothy Jane Sampson, Aug. 14, 1946; children—Nancy Jane (Mrs. Stephen Ziskind), Richard Aaron. Mem. faculty U. Tenn., Memphis, 1951—, prof. anatomy, 1966—. Served with AUS, 1940-43; served to capt. USAF, 1943-46. Decorated Air medal. USPHS grantee Nat. Inst. Dental Research, 1971-74. Mem. Nat. Bd. Dental Examiners, Internat. Assn. Dental Research, Am. Assn. Anatomists, Sigma Xi. Contbr. articles to sci. jours. Home: 5350 Denwood Av Memphis TN 38117

COINER, RICHARD TIDE, JR., aviation cons., ret. air force officer; b. Washington, Sept. 2, 1910; s. Richard T. and Emily (Hall) C.; B.S., U.S. Mil. Acad., 1932; m. Helen Lanier Nix, Feb. 22, 1936; children—Richard Tide III, Beverly Nix, William Lanier. Commd. 2d lt. U.S. Army, 1932, advanced through grades to maj. gen. USAF, 1952; exec. to asst. sec. of war for air, 1941-43; comd. 397th Bomber Group, ETO, 1943-45; RAF Staff Coll., 1946; Hdqrs. U.S. Air Force Europe, 1946-49; div. mil. application AEC, 1949-51; dep. comdr., field command Armed Forces Spl. Weapons Project, 1951-54; asst. dep. chief of staff Operations for Atomic Energy, Hdqrs. USAF, 1954-58, asst. chief staff, Air and Spl. Operations, SHAPE, 1958-61; comdr. Headquarters Ninth Air Force, 1961-63; dir. transp. Hdqrs. USAF, 1963-66; ret., 1966; pres. Nix Profl. Bldg. Corp., San Antonio. Mem. Nat. Rifle Assn. (life), Nat. Def. Transp. Assn. Episcopalian. Clubs: Argyle, San Antonio Country (San Antonio); Army and Navy (Washington). Home: 140 Patterson Av #403 San Antonio TX 78209

COIT, ROBERT DANIEL, lawyer; b. Enterprise, Miss., Mar. 31, 1930; s. Robert Edwin and Faye (Armstrong) C.; student Meridian Jr. Coll., 1947-49; B.S., Miss. State Coll., 1952; LL.B., U. Miss., 1956; m. Elna Faye Haden, Aug. 2, 1959; children—Lauren Faye, Linda Ann, Nancy Margaret, Edwin Daniel. Admitted Miss. bar. 1956; since practiced in Meridian; mem. firm Huff & Williams, 1956-62; gen. practice, Meridian, 1962—. Mem. Selective Service Bd. Incorporator, pres. Lamar Sch. Found., 1964-72. Served to lt. AUS, 1952-54. Col. on Gov.'s Staff, 1972—. Mem. Am., Miss. State, Lauderdale County bar assns., Miss. Forestry Assn., Phi Alpha Delta, S.C.V., Miss. Pvt. Sch. Assn. (dir.), Am. Legion, Am. Right of Way Assn., Miss. Claims Assn. Presbyn. Mason. Home: 2305 36th Av Meridian MS 39301 Office: Lamar Bldg Meridian MS 39301

COKE, CRAWFORD CALVIN, accountant; b. Marshall, Tex., Sept. 2, 1917; s. Rogers and Norma Crawford (Nickell) C.; B.B.A., U. Tex., 1948; m. Annette Coleman, June 7, 1945; children—Cerry (Mrs. Ralph Garrett Jr.), Crawford Calvin. With United Gas Pipeline Co., Shreveport, La., 1948-51, Internal Revenue Service, Tyler, Tex., 1951-58; C.P.A., Crawford C. Coke, Longview, Tex., 1958—. Served with USAAF, 1940-44. Decorated D.F.C., Air medal with 2 oak leaf clusters. C.P.A., Tex. Mem. Am. Inst. C.P.A.'s, Tex. Soc. C.P.A.'s. Clubs: Pinecrest Country (Longview); Koon Kreek (Athens, Tex.). Home: 900 LeDuke St Longview TX 75601 Office: Longview Nat Bank Bldg Longview TX 75601

COLBENSON, PAUL DAHLE, trade assn. exec.; b. Rushford, Minn., Mar. 20, 1920; s. Henry Carl and Clara (Dahle) C.; student Winona State Tchrs. Coll., 1938-40; U. Fla., 1947; B.S., U. Tenn., 1950; m. Thelma Peters, Apr. 16, 1943; children—Peter D., Peggy Jane (Mrs. James B. Brown). Instr., U. Tenn., 1947-50; appraiser engr. U.S. Dept. Agr., Knoxville, Tenn., 1950-54; engr. Douglas Fir and Am. Plywood Assn., Tacoma, Wash., 1954-56, field rep., Birmingham, Ala., 1956-57, Clearwater, Fla., 1957-63, regional mgr., Atlanta, 1963—. Served to lt. comdr. USNR, 1941-46. Decorated Air medal with one star. Mem. Am. Soc. Agrl. Engrs., Phi Kappa Phi, Alpha Zeta. Home: 1710 Timothy Dr SW Atlanta GA 30311 Office: PO Box 90550 Atlanta GA 30344

COLBERT, JOE, lawyer; b. Columbia, Miss., Apr. 1, 1935; s. David Womack and Nell (Rankin) C.; B.S., U. Ala., 1958; LL.B., U. Tex. Law Sch., 1964; m. Linda Moore, Apr. 1, 1973; children—Mark, David, Becca, Alexandra. Accountant USAF, Weisbaden, Germany, 1958-60; v.p. Rankin Co., Columbia, Miss., 1960; mgr. bookkeeping dept. Citizens Bank, Columbia, 1961-62; admitted to Tex. bar, 1964; practiced in Austin, 1964—; former mem. firm Garey, Colbert & Kidd, Austin. Served with USMC, 1954-56. Mem. Am., Travis Country (dir. 1969-70) bar assns., Am. Trial Lawyers Assn., State Bar Tex., Tex. Trial Lawyers (dir. 1971—), Austin Jr. Bar (dir. 1966-68). Clubs: Headliners (Austin), Austin Skiers (pres. 1970). Asso. editor: Tex. Law Review, 1964. Home: 2201 McCullough St Austin TX 78703 Office: 115 E 5th St Austin TX 78701

COLE, FRANK W., petroleum cons.; b. Connerville, Okla., Aug. 14, 1925; s. Fred W. and Velma (Ingram) C.; B.S., U. Okla., 1948, M.S., 1949; m. Martha Barton, Feb. 7, 1968; 1 son, Frank Warren. Petroleum engr. Humble Oil & Refining Co., Houston, 1949-51, 53-55; asso. prof. petroleum engring. U. Okla., 1955-63; pres. Frank W. Cole Engring. Co., Dallas, 1963-73, Continental Energy Corp., Dallas; vice chmn. Lamco Energy Corp. Served with USNR, 1943-46, 51-53. Author: (with A.W. McCray) Oil Well Drilling Technology, 1959; Reservoir Engineering Manual, 1961; Well Spacing in the Areth Reservoir, 1962; Basic Principles of Reservoir Engineering, 1963; (with P.L. Moore) Drilling Operations Manual, 1964. Contbr. papers to tech. lit. Home: 5710 Forest Lane Dallas TX 75230 Office: Meadows Bldg Dallas TX 75206

COLE, GEORGE DAVID, educator; b. Minden, La., June 23, 1925; s. Stephen Peru and Willie Lee (White) C.; B.S., Northwestern State Coll., 1950; M.A., Peabody Coll., 1954; Ph.D., U. Ala., 1963; m. Ruth Alvera Moore, Mar. 1, 1947; children—Lindy Barry, Karen (Mrs. Steven Leeds), George Marcus. Tchr. Morgan City (La.) High Sch., 1950-54; asso. prof. Nicholls State Coll. La., Thibodaux, 1954; mem. faculty U. Ala., University, 1963—, asst. prof., 1964-67, asso. prof., 1967-68, head dept. physics and astronomy, 1968—, prof., 1972—. Cons. physics Stillman Coll., Tuscaloosa, Ala., 1968-69. Served with USAF, 1943-46. NSF Sci. Faculty fellow, 1961-62. Mem. Am. Phys. Soc., Am. Assn. Physics Tchrs., Pi Mu Epsilon, Sigma Pi Sigma, Sigma Xi (chpt. pres. 1968-69). Contbr. numerous articles to profl. jours. Home: 13 Hickory Hill Tuscaloosa AL 35401 Office: Box 1921 University AL 35486

COLE, HARPER LEROY, JR., educator; b. Pasadena, Cal., Dec. 5, 1921; s. Harper Leroy and Maidie Belle (McBride) C.; A.B., Bethany Nazarene Coll., 1965; M.A., U. Okla. 1970, now postgrad.; m. Pearl Mae Cook, Aug. 2, 1942; children—Stephen Leroy, Myrla Dawn (Mrs. Carl Ray Cook). Ordained to ministry Nazarene Ch., 1945; minister Christian edn. Ch. of Nazarene, Bethany, Okla., 1945-48, Kansas City, Mo., 1949-51, Oklahoma City, 1953-56; asst. to gen. treas. Ch. of Nazarene, Kansas City, Mo., 1951-53, 56-66; administrv. asst., asst. prof. bus. Bethany Nazarene Coll., 1966-72, dir. data processing, 1966-73, asso. prof., 1973—. Mem. Soc. for Advancement Mgmt., Nat. Assn. Accountants, Acad. of Mgmt., Am. Mgmt. Assn., Okla. Edn. Assn., Beta Gamma Sigma, Delta Pi Epsilon. Kiwanian. Home: 3117 N Mueller St Bethany OK 73008

COLE, HERSCHEL EUGENE, lawyer; b. Dallas, Ga., May 23, 1905; s. Jesse T. and Pearl (Cole) C.; LL.B., Atlanta Law Sch., 1925; LL.D., Cleveland-Marshall Law Sch., 1954; m. Rose B. Dumas, Jan. 15, 1930; 1 dau., Barbara Ann. Admitted to Ga. bar, 1925; practice law, Atlanta, 1925—; instr. Atlanta Law Sch., 1934-55, sec., 1937-53, dean, 1958—; judge traffic div. City Ct., Atlanta, 1959—. Vice pres., dir. Kings Mountain Mica Co. (N.C.); dir. English Mica Co., Kings Mountain, N.C. Mem. Ga., Atlanta bar assns., Sigma Delta Kappa. Baptist. Mason. Home: 831 Crestridge Dr NE Atlanta GA 30306 Office: Rhodes Haverty Bldg Atlanta GA 30303

COLE, LUTHER FRANCIS, judge; b. Alexandria, La., Oct. 25, 1925; s. Clem and Catherine (Wiley) C. ; student La. Poly. Inst., 1943-44; J.D., La. State U., 1950; grad. Nat. Coll. State Trial Judges; m. Juanita Barton, Mar. 9, 1945; children—Frances Jeannette, Jeffrey Martin, Christopher Warren. Admitted to La. bar, 1950; mem. firm Cole & Mengis, Baton Rouge, 1950-66; dist. judge 19th Jud. Dist., 1966—. Mem. La. Ho. of Reps., 1964-66. Served to lt. (j.g.) USNR, 1943-46. Mem. La. Law Inst., Jud. Council La. Supreme Ct., Judiciary Commn. La., Am., La., Baton Rouge (pres. 1966) bar assns., Am. Judicature Soc., La. Dist. Judges Assn. (pres. 1972). Baptist. Club: Exchange (past pres.). Home: 9525 Donna Dr Baton Rouge LA 70815 Office: Court House Bldg Baton Rouge LA 70801

COLE, NOMAN MONROE, JR., nuclear engr.; b. Parris Island, S.C., Mar. 10, 1933; s. Noman Monroe and Bessie (Owens) C.; B.M.E., U. Fla., 1955; grad. AEC Nuclear Engring. and Physics Grad. Sch., Bettis Lab., 1957; m. Janet Audrey Nelson, Mar. 1, 1958; children—Keith Noman, Nelson Owens. Project mgr. AEC Natural Circulation Reactor Devel. Project, U.S. Navy, 1960-66; asst. dept. dir. Howard Research div. Control Data Corp., Washington, 1966-67; sr. engr. MPR Assos., Inc., Washington, 1967—. Treas. Gunston Hall Sch., 1966-67; pres. Mason Neckand and Hallowing Point Civic Assn., 1963-70. Chmn. Va. State Water Control Bd., 1970—; mem. Va. Gov.'s Environmental Council, 1972—. Served to lt. USNR, 1956-60. Named one of ten Ten Washingtonians of Year Washingtonian mag., 1971. Mem. Phi Delta Theta. Methodist. Home: 5917 River Dr Lorton VA 22079 Office: 1140 Connecticut Av NW Washington DC 20036

COLE, ROBERT JOBE, dentist; b. Galesburg, Ill., Feb. 21, 1924; s. Glen R. and Marian Vinnie (Robinson) C.; B.S., U. Ia., 1945, D.D.S., 1946; m. Kathryn Ann O'Brien, June 17, 1944; children—Brian Robert, Jo Anne. Pvt. practice dentistry, St. Petersburg Beach, Fla., 1948—. Mem. adv. com. Dental Hygiene Sch., St. Petersburg Jr. Coll., 1964-69, lectr., 1966—; mem. adv. com. Dental Sch., U. Fla., Gainesville, 1966—. Chmn. fluoridation com. City of St. Petersburg, 1952-58; coach Little League, 1958-62; active Boy Scouts Am. Served to lt. (j.g.) USNR, 1946-48. Recipient Distinguished Service award Jr. C. of C., 1959. Fellow Internat., Am. colls. dentists; mem. Am. (del.), Fla. (v.p.) dental assns., West Coast (pres. 1968), Pinellas County (pres. 1959) dental socs., Beta Theta Pi, Delta Sigma Delta. Methodist (dir. 1958-71). Kiwanian. Club: Lakewood Country (St. Petersburg). Home: 960 Boca Ciega Isle St Petersburg Beach FL 33706 Office: 511 76 Av St Petersburg Beach FL 33706

COLE, SAMUEL JENNINGS, sch. supt.; b. Elizabethtown, N.C., Mar. 21, 1930; s. Roland Jennings and Eva (Quale) C.; diploma, Louisburg (N.C.) Jr. Coll., 1950; A.B., High Point (N.C.) Coll., 1952; postgrad. U. N.C., 1954-55; M.A., East Carolina U., 1957; m. Martha Ann Lewis, Aug. 3, 1952; children—Sharon, Nancy, Tracy, Samuel II. Supt., Fremont (N.C.) City Schs., 1958-62; asst. supt. Gov. Morehead Sch., Raleigh, N.C., 1962-67, supt., 1968—. Served with M.C. AUS, 1952-54. Rotarian. Home and Office: 301 Ashe Av Raleigh NC 27606

COLE, THOMAS EARLE, phys. and nuclear engr.; b. Winter Park, Fla., Dec. 13, 1922; s. Henry Earle and Lizzie Bell (Perrine) C.; student U. Miami, 1943, Columbia, 1944, U. Tenn., 1946-47; B.S., Rollins Coll., 1946; m. Jean Holden, Feb. 24, 1944; children—Henry Earle, Edmund Platt, Peter Bartlett. With Oak Ridge Nat. Lab., 1946—, project dir. nuclear research reactors, 1954—. Cons. to various orgns., 1955—; lectr. Oak Ridge Sch. Reactor Tech., 1952-53. Bd. dirs. Oak Ridge Tech. Enterprises Corp. Served to lt. (j.g.) USNR, 1943-46; PTO. Mem. Am. Phys. Soc., Am. Nuclear Soc., Research Soc. U.S., Kappa Alpha. Episcopalian. Patentee in field. Home: 103 Disston Rd Oak Ridge TN 37830 Office: PO Box X Oak Ridge TN 37830

COLE, THOMAS EDWARD, lawyer, judge; b. Knoxville, Tenn., May 14, 1920; s. Vernon Edward and Katherine (Ellis) C.; B.S., U. Tenn., 1946, J.D., 1948; m. Mary Jean Bell, May 26, 1943; children—Thomas Marshall, Robert Armistead, William Edward. Admitted to Tenn. bar, 1947; practiced in Knoxville, 1948-51, 53-61; judge 2d Circuit Ct., Knox County, Tenn., 1961—. Commr. of elections, Knox County, 1958-61; pres. Tenn. Jud. Conf., 1971-72. Served with AUS, 1942-45; as 1st lt. Judge Adv. Gen.'s Corps, AUS, 1951-53. Mem. Order of Coif, Phi Delta Phi, Delta Tau Delta. Democrat. Lutheran. Home: 201 Geneva Rd Knoxville TN 37919 Office: Knox County Court House Knoxville TN 37902

COLE, WILFRED QUALLS, JR., physician; b. Jackson, Miss., Nov. 28, 1924; s. Wilfred Q. and Laurie (Shotwell) C.; student U. Miss., 1943, 46-49; M.D., U. Va., 1951; m. Gwen Walker, Aug. 5, 1949; children—Wilfred Q. III, Craig Addison, Ashley. Intern U. Ala. Hosp., Birmingham, 1951-52, resident pediatrics, 1952-54; fellow pediatric allergy Duke Med. Center, 1961; practice medicine specializing in pediatric allergy, dir. pediatric allergy clinic U. Miss., Jackson, 1961—, clin. asso. prof. pediatrics, 1970—, co-dir. Cystic Fibrosis Research Center, 1962—; mem. staffs Univ., Miss. Bapt., St. Dominic hosps., Jackson. Mem. Miss. State Bd. Health, Jackson, 1972—. Served with AUS, 1943-46; ETO. Decorated Bronze Star. Diplomate Am. Bd. Pediatrics, Am. Bd. Allergy and Immunology. Fellow Am. Acad. Pediatrics, Am. Acad. Allergy, Am. Coll. Allergy; mem. Alpha Omega Alpha, Omicron Delta Kappa, Sigma Alpha Epsilon. Episcopalian. Home: 4036 Boxwood Circle Jackson MS 39211 Office: 940 N State St Jackson MS 39201

COLEMAN, CARL DUBOIS, lawyer; b. Danville, Va., June 19, 1910; s. Charles Cornelious and Vetie (Brown) C.; A.B., Howard U., 1931, LL.B., 1935; m. Pearl Elfreda Goodlow, June 8, 1943. Admitted to D.C. bar, 1936; practice law, Washington, 1936-50; asst. corp. counsel, 1950-62; spl. asst. Bd. Commrs., 1962-67; spl. asst. to Mayor, 1967-68 (all Washington); chmn. D.C. Bd. Parole, 1968—. Mem. Montgomery County (Md.) Human Relations Comm., 1961-65; chmn. non-discrimination com. Health and Welfare Council, 1969. Served with AUS, 1943-45. Mem. Nat., Fed., Washington, D.C. bar assns., Kappa Alpha Psi. Conglist. Home: 2 Elwyn Ct Silver Spring MD 20910 Office: 614 H St NW Washington DC 20001

COLEMAN, FRANK CARTER, physician, med. lab. adminstr.; b. Jackson, Miss., May 14, 1915; s. Francis Marion and Emma (Carter) C.; B.A., Miss. Coll., 1935; M.D., Tulane U., 1941; m. Ruth Yvonne Ellzey, Sept. 2, 1937; children—Nancy Ruth (Mrs. James Lujan), Stephen Carter, John Timothy, Jeanne Laurie. Intern Touro Infirmary, New Orleans, 1941-42, resident in pathology, 1942-45, asst. dir. pathology, 1945; practice medicine specializing in pathology, Des Moines, 1946-64, Tampa, Fla., 1964—; dir. labs. Mercy Hosp., Des Moines, 1945-64, Patterson Coleman Labs., Tampa, 1964—; dir. dept. pathology Centro Asturiano Hosp., Tampa, 1964—, Citrus Meml. Hosp., Inverness, Fla., 1964—, Hillsborough County Hosp., Tampa, 1964—, Jackson Meml. Hosp., Dade City, 1965—, Hardee Meml. Hosp., Wauchula, Fla., 1970—, Centro Espanol Hosp., Tampa, 1967—, DeSoto Meml. Hosp., Arcadia, Fla., 1969—, Community Hosp., New Port Richey, 1971—, Tarpon Springs (Fla.) Gen. Hosp., 1967—, West Pasco Hosp., New Port Richey, 1966—, G. Pierce Wood Meml. Hosp., Arcadia, 1971—; resident asst. in pathology Sch. Medicine Tulane U., 1942-44, instr. pathology, 1944-45; asst. clin. prof. dept. pathology Coll. Medicine U. Neb., 1951-64; clin. prof. pathology U. South Fla., Tampa, 1973—; cons. Tampa Gen. Hosp., 1964—, dept. pathology residency program St. Joseph's Hosp., Tampa, 1967—; med. dir. S.W. Fla. Blood Bank, 1971—. Mem. Pres.'s Com. Health Services Industry, 1971-72, Gov.'s Community Hosp. Edn. Council, 1971-73; mem. subcom. profl., sci. and tech. manpower Nat. Manpower Adv. Com. Dept. Labor, 1973—. Vice pres. Gulf Coast Symphony, 1970-72. Bd. dirs. Blue Shield of Fla., 1967-70; bd. dirs. Am. Med. Polit. Action Com., 1960-69, chmn., 1965-67. Recipient award of merit Ia. Med. Soc., 1957; Sci. Products Found. award for outstanding service to pathology and medicine, 1965. Diplomate Am. Bd. Pathology (trustee 1964—, sec.-treas. 1973—). Fellow Am. Soc. Clin. Pathologists, Coll. Am. Pathologists (bd. govs. 1953-58, pres. 1960-61, mem. nat. legislative com. 1966—, chmn. legislative com. 1971—), A.C.P., Am. Coll. Chest Physicians; mem. A.M.A. (chmn. council legislative activities 1963-64, chmn. council health manpower 1972-73, profl. standards rev. orgns. adv. com. 1973—), Fla. Med. Assn. (chmn. com. on blood 1969—), Hillsborough County Med. Soc. (chmn. membership com. 1966-67, 69, mem. exec. council 1967—, chmn. pub. service com. 1970—, del. to Fla. Med. Assn.), Am. Assn. Pathologists and Bacteriologists, Am. Assn. Blood Banks (pres. 1968-69, dir.), N.Y. Acad. Scis., Fla. Soc. Pathologists (chmn. ins. com. 1966—, chmn. com. contractual and profl. ethics 1968—), Soc. Nuclear Medicine, Am. Therapeutic Soc., A.A.A.S., Am. Soc. Cytology, Fla. Assn. Blood Banks (pres. 1969-70), Internat. Acad. Pathologists, Am. Pub. Health Assn., Tampa C. of C. (chmn. air pollution task force 1971—, chmn. med. sch. com. 1966-67, chmn. health care com. 1969—), Theta Kappa Psi, Alpha Omega Alpha. Presbyn. (elder). Rotarian. Clubs: Krewe of Venus, University,

Carrollwood Golf and Country. Contbr. articles to profl. jours. Contbg. editor Recent Advances in Clinical Pathology, 1971. Home: 4111 Carrollwood Village Dr Tampa FL 33624 Office: 4807 N Armenia Av Tampa FL 33603

COLEMAN, JAMES JULIAN, lawyer, banker, business exec.; b. New Orleans, May 5, 1915; s. William Ballin and Millie (Davis) C.; B.A., Tulane U., 1934, LL.B., 1937; m. Dorothy Louise Jurisich, July 30, 1940; children—James Julian, Thomas Blaise, Peter Dee, Dian Judith. Admitted to La. bar, 1937; sr. partner Clay, Coleman, Dutrey & Thomson; chmn. bd. Internat. Tank Terminals, Ltd.; Internat. Tank Terminals, Ltd., Karachi, West Pakistan, Chittagong, Bangladesh, and Ulsan, South Korea, Daisy Oil Co.; formerly chmn. bd. Internat. City Bank & Trust Co., Loving Enterprises, Civic Center Site Devel. Co., Inc.; former dir. New Orleans & Lower Coast R.R. Co.; v.p., gen. counsel Internat. Trade Mart. Treas. Cordell Hull Found. Former pres. Adult Edn. Center, Inc.; past mem. exec. com. Internat. Relations Com., Mississippi Valley World Trade Council; past pres. Jr. Achievement New Orleans. Trustee Loving Found., Bradley Family Found. Principia Coll.; bd. dirs. Tulane U. Bus. Sch. Hon Counsulgen. Republic Korea. Mem. Internat., Am., La., New Orleans bar assns., Greater New Orleans area (past pres.), U.S. (bd. 1964-68) chambers commerce, Beta Gamma Sigma (hon.). Christian Scientist. Home: 10 Audubon Pl New Orleans LA 70118 Office: 321 Charles Av New Orleans LA 70130

COLEMAN, JOHN DEE, veterinarian; b. Dozier, Tex., Oct. 2, 1932; s. Jay Dee and Paralee (Brock) C.; D.V.M., Tex. A. and M. U., 1956; M.S., Auburn U., 1964; m. Sandra Burden, Aug. 26, 1954; children—Carol, Susan, Scott. Vet. ednl. cons. Tex. A. and M. U., 1956-60; post veterinarian, Ft. Rucker, Ala., 1960-62; NIH fellow Auburn U., 1962-64; sr. research scientist Abbott Labs., North Chicago, Ill., 1964-68; pvt. practice veterinary medicine, McLean, Tex., 1968-70; asso. prof. feedlot cattle disease research Tex. A. and M. U., Bushland, 1970—. Served with AUS., 1960-62. Mem. Am., Tex. vet. med. assns., Am. Assn. Vet. Nutritionists, Am. Soc. Animal Sci., Plains Nutrition Council. Club: Rotary of Mymensingh (East Pakistan). Home: 705 15th St Canyon TX 79015 Office: TAES-USDA Research Center Bushland TX 79012

COLEMAN, JOHN SHERRARD, orgn. exec.; b. Oahu, Hawaii, Jan. 15, 1914; s. Sharrard and Mary Comstock (Griswold) C.; B.S., Coll. William and Mary, 1935; M.S., Mass. Inst. Tech., 1940; m. Beverly Reynolds Bridge, Dec. 24, 1944; children—Sherrard, Deborah Reynolds. Residential constrn. and design, 1936-38; mem. Nat. Def. Research Com., 1940-43; research asso. Harvard, 1943-44; London rep. OSRD, 1944; div. war research Columbia U., 1945-46; com. underseas warfare NRC, 1947-53; prof. engring. research Pa. State U., 1953; exec. sec. div. phys. scis. Nat. Acad. Scis.-NRC, 1953-65; exec. officer Nat. Acad. Scis., Washington, 1965—. Chmn. acoustics panel Research and Devel. Bd., 1952-53; cons. Air Research and Devel. Command, 1952-53, Office Sec. Def., 1953-55; chmn. Pres.'s Com. for Local Action in Sci. and Engring. Recipient Meritorious Pub. Service award, 1958. Clubs: Fairfax Country, Cosmos. Home: 3010 N Florida St Arlington VA 22207 Office: 2101 Constitution Av NW Washington DC 20418

COLEMAN, MARION LESLIE, ins. co. exec.; b. Mobile, Ala., Mar. 20, 1925; s. Luther Woodward and Carrie (Lockler) Coleman; student pub. schs.; m. Joyce Kelley, Aug. 29, 1944; children—Connie, Woodward L. and Franklin M. (twins). Agt., Life Ins. Co. of Ga., Mobile, 1946-53, staff mgr., Texarkana, Ark., 1953-55, dist. mgr., El Dorado, Ark., 1955-56, Hattlesburg, Miss., 1957-60, Meridian, Miss., 1957-60, Meridian, Miss., 1960-64; v.p., agy. dir. Nat. Preferred Life Ins. Co., Atlanta, 1964-65; v.p. tng. Found. Life Ins. Co., Atlanta, 1965-67; v.p., dir. agys. Tenn. Nat. Life Ins. Co., Nashville, 1967—, also dir.; v.p. Kelley Blakeley Land Co., Inc., Mobile, Ala.; owner Meridian Sportarama, Inc. Yamaha Sports World, Mel co Ltd., Fashion Tailors (all Meridian). Served with USNR, 1943-46. Mem. Life Underwriters Assn., Sales and Marketing Execs. Club, Civitan Club (pres. Meridian). Home: 2100 23d Av Meridian MS 39301 Office: Citizen National Bank Bldg Meridian MS 39301

COLEMAN, MARY JANE (MRS. NATHANIEL R. COLEMAN, JR.), assn. ofcl.; student Coll. William and Mary. Formerly in advt. Active Youth Builders Club Greeneville; founder, pres. Greeneville Arts Guild; Tenn. co-partner Partnership for the Arts; active Tenn. Arts Commn. 1968—, sec., 1972—, mem. exec. com., long range planning com., purchase com., adv. to Film Panel, now chmn. Film Panel. Bd. dirs. Friends Carroll Reece Mus.; founder, dir. Sinking Creek Film Celebration, 1970—. Address: Creekside Farm Route 8 Greeneville TN 37743

COLEMAN, NATHANIEL RAGSDALE, JR., lawyer; b. Hamburg, Germany, Nov. 9, 1922; s. Nathaniel Ragsdale and Frances (Esders) C.; B.A., Coll. William and Mary, 1943; LL.B., U. Va., 1948; m. Mary Jane Riddick, Apr. 15, 1944; children—Caroline (Mrs. William Gourly), Jane. Admitted to Tenn. bar, 1948; partner Millegar, Coleman, Fletcher & Gaby, Greeneville, Tenn., 1958—. Sec., dir., gen. counsel Hauni Richmond, Inc., 1953—; sec. to bd., dir. First Nat. Bank, Greeneville, 1958—. Served with USNR, 1943-46. Mem. Am., Tenn., Va. Green County (pres. 1958—) bar assns. Episcopalian (mem. vestry 1949—). Home: Creekside Farm Route 8 Greeneville TN 37743 Office: 1st Nat Bank Bldg Greeneville TN 37743

COLEMAN, ROBERT BOISSEAU, JR., lawyer; b. Birmingham, Ala., Mar. 15, 1916; s. Robert Boisseau and Jessie (Wheeler) C.; B.S., N.C. State U., 1939; postgrad. Mass. Inst. Tech., 1940; LL.B., Birmingham Sch. Law, 1952; m. Ann Alderson, Mar. 16, 1956; children—Clayton L. Campbell, Claire Campbell Lindberg, Mary Virginia, Robert Boisseau III, Barbara Anne, Caroline. Metall. engr. Am. Cast Iron Pipe Co., Birmingham, 1940-41; acid plant supr. E.I. duPont de Nemours & Co., Inc., Kankakee Ordnance Plant, 1941-42, metall. engr. Kings Mills Ordnance Plant, 1942-43, chem. engr. ammonia dept., Charleston, W.Va., 1943-44; tech. asst. to plant mgr. Indsl. Rayon Co., Covington, 1944-48; research engr. So. Research Co., Birmingham, 1948-50, So. Cement Co., Birmingham, 1948-53; admitted to Ala. bar, 1952; Okla. bar, 1953; patent atty. Phillips Petroleum Co., Bartlesville Okla., 1953-59; real estate, ins. broker Alderson Coleman Agy., Ada, Okla., 1959-64; supr. patents and trademarks Continental Oil Co., Ponca City, Okla., 1964—; partner Coleman Bros. Investments; dir. Investors Security. Past pres. Ada Boys Club. Registered profl. engr., Ala., Okla. Mem. Am. Inst. Chem. Engrs., Am. Chem. Soc., Nat. Soc. Profl. Engrs., Am. Patent Layers Assn. (past com. chmn.), Am., Okla., Pontotoc County (past sec.-treas.) bar assns. Episcopalian. Mason, Rotarian. Home: 2513 Mockingbird Lane Ponca City OK 74601 Office: 1000 S Pine St Ponca City OK 74601

COLEMAN, ROBERT EMERSON, clergyman, educator; b. Dallas, Apr. 28, 1928; s. James Henry and Helen (Hood) C.; A.B., Southwestern U., 1948; B.D., Asbury Theol. Sem., 1951; M.Th., Princeton, 1952; Ph.D., U. Ia., 1954; m. Marietta Louise Emmons, June 3, 1951; children—Alathea Dawn, Angela Denise, James Russell. Evangelist, 1947—; pastor chs. in Ind., N.J., Ia., 1949-55; prof. Evangelism, Asbury Theol. Sem., 1955—. Pres. Christian Outreach, 1962—; conf. speaker nat. convs., S. Africa; v.p. Acad. for Evangelism in Theol. Edn., 1973—; mem. Bd. for Good News, 1968-72; del. World Congress Evangelism, Berlin, Germany, 1966, Internat. Congress Evangelism, Switzerland, 1974. Author: The Master Plan of Evangelism, 1964; Dry Bones Can Live Again, 1969; Written in Blood, 1972. Contbr. articles to profl. jours. Editor: One Divine Moment, 1971. Home: 200 Asbury Dr Wilmore KY 40390

COLEMAN, RUSSELL, assn. exec.; b. Montpelier, Miss., Dec. 23, 1913; s. Oscar Willis and Alice (Marshall) C.; B.S., Miss. State Coll., 1936; M.S., 1937; Ph.D., U. Wis., 1941; m. Laura Elizabeth Burrous, Aug. 18, 1937; children—Peggy (Mrs. Robert H. Best, Jr.), Susan (Mrs. Garry Blunt), Russell Clayton. Grad. asst. Miss. Agr. Expt. Sta., 1936-37, asst. agronomist, 1937-39, asst. dir., 1946, dir., 1947-48; grad. asst. U. Wis., 1939-40; asso. prof. soils Miss. State Coll., 1940-45; pres. Nat. Fertilizer Assn., 1948-55, exec. v.p. Nat. Plant Food Inst., 1955-60; pres. Sulphur Inst., Washington, 1960—. Mem. fertilizer industry adv. panel FAO, 1963—. Fellow Am. Soc. Agronomy; mem. Soil Sci. Soc. Am., Alpha Zeta. Presbyn. Clubs: Cosmos, University (Washington); Columbia Country (Chevy Chase, Md.). Contbr. numerous articles to tech. jours. Home: 3806 Woodbine St Chevy Chase MD 20015 Office: Sulphur Inst 1725 K St NW Washington DC 20006

COLEMAN, THOMAS STOKELEY, JR., lawyer; b. Spotsylvania, Va., Oct. 24, 1910; s. Thomas Stokeley and Alice Teasdale (Graves) C.; B.A., Va. Mil. Inst., 1931; B.A., U. Va. Law Sch., 1936; m. Evelyn Cosby Massey, Oct. 15, 1938; children—Anne L. (Mrs. James E. Jarrell, Jr.), Carol L. (Mrs. John Parker), Thomas Stokeley, James Richlieu. Admitted to Va. bar, 1936; pvt. practice law, Spotsylvania, 1936-58, Fredericksburg, Va., 1962; commonwealth atty. Spotsylvania (Va.) County, 1942-62, commr. of accounts, 1956-73; sr. partner Coleman & Scaife, Fredericksburg, Va., 1958-60; sr. partner Coleman & Jarrell (name changed to Coleman, Jarrell & Hicks 1973), Spotsylvania, also Fredericksburg, 1968—. Chmn. bd. Rappahannock Savs. & Loan Assn., Fredericksburg, 1973—; pres. Fredericksburg Data Services, 1973—. Served with AUS, 1944-45. Mem. Am. Judicature Soc., Am., Va., Fredericksburg, 15th Jud. Circuit bar assns., Am., Va. trial lawyers assns. Home: PO Box 885 Fredericksburg VA 22401 Office: 315 William St Fredericksburg VA 22401

COLEMAN, WILLIAM BALLIN III, textile co. exec.; b. New Orleans, Oct. 8, 1943; s. William Ballin, Jr. and Stella (Scheyer) C.; B.S., Trinity U., San Antonio, 1967, M.S. in Econs. and Bus. Adminstrn., 1969; m. Cynthia Anita Groos, May 12, 1973. With William B. Coleman Co., Inc., New Orleans, 1969—, v.p., 1971-73, pres., 1973—; pres. Joint Enterprises, Inc., New Orleans, 1971—. Pres., trustee CCC Found.; bd. dirs. Trinity U. Alumni Bd. Named Triniteer of Yr., Trinity U., 1967, recipient Triniteer Outstanding Service award, 1967. Mem. Nat. Branded Distbrs. Assn. (bd. dirs.), New Orleans C. of C. Mem. Christian Sci. Ch. Home: 217 Friedrichs Av Metairie LA 70005 Office: 4001 Earhart St New Orleans LA 70125

COLES, ELBERT HOUSTON, lawyer; b. Goodlettsville, Tenn., Sept. 9, 1938; s. Jesse Eugene and Teddie Wilson (Ricketts) C.; B.A., U. Tenn., 1960; LL.B., Vanderbilt U., 1962; m. Donna Rhea Goodman, Apr, 1, 1966. Admitted to Tenn. bar, 1962; trial atty. NLRB, Memphis, 1962-64; asso. firm Seligman & Seligman, N.Y.C., 1964-70; partner firm McKnight, Hudson & Coles, Memphis, 1970-73; pvt. practice, Memphis, 1973; sr. asso. firm Coles & Swain, 1974—. Mem. Am., Tenn., Memphis and Shelby County bar assns., Memphis Jaycees, Delta Phi. Republican. Mem. Ch. of Christ. Home: 5641 Gaywinds Av Memphis TN 38118 Office: 531 Sterick Bldg Memphis TN 38103

COLES, WILLIAM SWANEY, banker; b. Nashville, July 12, 1936; s. John William and Margaret Jackson (Swaney) C.; B.S., Bowling Green Coll., 1958; postgrad. U. Ala., 1971-72; m. Trula Faye Dailey, Aug. 5, 1962; 1 son, John William II. Asst. cashier, br. mgr. Commerce Union Bank, Nashville, 1958-62; asst. v.p. First Peoples Bank, Johnson City, Tenn., 1962-63; v.p., personnel dir. Central Bank Ala. N.A. (formerly State Nat. Bank), Decatur, 1963-73, v.p., mgr. nine brs., 1973—. Pres., Ala. United Cerebral Palsy Assn., 1969-70, Southeastern regional v.p., 1971-72. Served with Tenn. Air Nat. Guard, 1954-62. Mem. Am. Inst. Banking (chmn. Southeastern regional sch. relations com. 1964, pres. Decatur chpt. 1970, Ala. Bankers Assn. (group chmn. jr. sect. 1967, named outstanding chmn. in state 1967). Clubs: Decatur Country, Decatur Toastmasters (pres. 1972). Home: 3307 Hastings Rd Huntsville AL 35801 Office: 200 W Court Sq Huntsville AL 35804

COLEY, DEE DEE OREN, diamond coring engr.; b. Lexington, Okla., Feb. 6, 1910; s. John Lewis and Orah Estell (Nesbitt) C.; student Oklahoma City U., 1932-36; m. Helen Evanoff, Jan. 25, 1936; children—Gary, Dorla (Mrs. Don Fudge), Karen (Mrs. Michael Gregory), Lynna (Mrs. Jim Hannah). With oilfield drilling crew, 1937, Okla. Hwy. Patrol, 1937-46; sargeant-at-arms Okla. Senate, 1947; investigator LuPer Freight Lines, 1947; with oilfield drilling crew, 1947-48; diamond coring, engr., sales, service, 1949—; Diamond Bits Oilfield, 1956—; pres. Diacore Inc., Oklahoma City, 1956—. Mem. Nat. Football Found. Mem. Am. Petroleum Inst. Methodist. Mason (Shriner). Clubs: Petroleum (Oklahoma City); Touchdown (Okla. U.). Home: 1210 Camden Way Norman OK 73069 Office: 9201 S Shields St Oklahoma City OK 73109

COLEY, FRANCIS HAMILTON, govt. ofcl.; b. Fieldale, Va., Oct. 16, 1923; s. Lee Andrew and Nannie Mae (Long) C.; B.S., Va. Poly. Inst., 1943; M.Gas Tech., Ill. Inst. Tech., 1949; Ph.D., Pa. State U., 1955; m. Marie Carolyn McMillan, Oct. 11, 1949; children—Carolyn (Mrs. Jeffrey Converse Young), Marilyn (Mrs. John Harvey Shafer, Jr.), Beth Hamilton. Engr., Tenn. Eastman Corp., Kingsport, 1944-47, East Ohio Gas Co., Cleve., 1949-50; research asso. Pa. State U., University Park, 1950-55; research engr. E.I. du Pont de Nemours & Co., Inc., Aiken, S.C., 1955-65; engr. Office Saline Water, U.S. Dept. Interior, Washington, 1965-66, chief materials div. Office Saline Water, 1966—. Instr., Augusta (Ga.) Coll., part-time 1957-65; lectr. desalination. Served with C.E., AUS, 1944-46. Recipient Meritorious Service award U.S. Dept. Interior, 1973. Mem. Am. Inst. Chem. Engrs., Nat. Assn. Corrosion Engrs., Sigma Xi, Phi Lambda Upsilon. Club: Evergreen Country. Home: 9717 Laurel St Fairfax VA 22030 Office: 1951 Constitution Av Washington DC 20240

COLIANNI, VINCENT ALPHONSE, lawyer; b. Greensburg, Pa., Nov. 20, 1938; s. Vincent A. and Mary L. (Grant) C.; A.B., U. Pa., 1960; J.D., U. Pitts., 1963; m. Eileen Reutzel, Nov. 30, 1963; children—Elena, Vincent. Admitted to Pa. bar, 1963; practiced in Pitts., 1963-68, St. Croix, V.I., 1968—; asst. U.S. atty., Western Dist., Pa., 1966-68, V.I., 1968; U.S. atty., V.I., 1969; mng. partner Isherwood & Colianni, Christiansted, St. Croix, 1970—. Teaching instr. Coll. V.I., 1969. Founder, pres. Civic Searchlight, 1971-73; mem. Selective Service Appeals Bd., 1972-73. Trustee, chmn. bd. Tamarind Sch., 1972-73. Mem. Am., V.I., D.C., Allegheny County bar assns., C. of C. (pres. 1972-73). Home: 46 King St Christiansted St Croix VI 00820

COLINS, CHRISTOPHER, social worker; b. Lynn, Mass., Sept. 3, 1925; s. James and Pota (Scipitari) Kolinites; B.A., U. Mass.; M.S.W., U. Pa., 1950, postgrad., 1955-56; m. Christine Maynard, Aug. 3, 1953. Social worker VA Regional Office, Roanoke, Va., 1952-56; dir. social services Embreeville (Pa.) State Hosp., 1956-60; program adminstr. Piedmont Mental Health Complex, Concord, N.C., 1960-70; clin. social worker Lenoir County Mental Health Clinic, Kinston, N.C., 1970—. Mental health cons. various community resources. Served with USAAF, 1943-46. Recipient certificate for dedicated service Pa. Mental Health Assn., 1960. Methodist (chmn. social concerns com.). Home: 310 Sherwood Pl Kinston NC 28501 Office: 111 S McElwean St Kinston NC 28501

COLLETT, HENRY AUGUSTUS, dentist, lawyer; b. Phila., May 19, 1914; s. Henry A. and Nettie Jean (Morris) C.; D.D.S., Temple U., 1939; J.D., U. Miami, 1962; m. Virginia Houston, Sept. 11, 1959. Commd. lt. (j.g.) USN, 1940, advanced through grades to capt. Dental Corps, 1955, ret., 1960; pvt. practice dentistry, Phila., 1939-40, Jacksonville, Fla., 1962—; prof. restorative dentistry N.J. Coll. Medicine and Dentistry, 1968-69; admitted to Fla. bar, 1962; individual practice law, Jacksonville, 1962—. Diplomate Am. Bd. Prosthodontics. Fellow Acad. Denture Prosthetics; mem. Am., Fla. dental assns., Jacksonville Dental Soc., Fla. Prosthodontic Assn. (pres. 1972), Fla. Bar, Nat. Sojourners (pres. 1972-73). Democrat. Episcopalian. Mason (Shriner). Contbr. articles to dental jours. Address: 2231 Post St Jacksonville FL 32204

COLLETTE, BRUCE BADEN, zoologist; b. N.Y.C., Mar. 14, 1934; s. Raymond Hill and Agnes Hellen (Anderson) C.; B.S., Cornell U., 1956, Ph.D., 1960; m. Sara Elizabeth Foster, June 14, 1956; children—Karen, Sheila, Claire. With Nat. Marine Fisheries Service, Washington, 1960—, asst. lab. dir. systematics lab., 1963—. Research asso. Smithsonian Instn. Mem. exec. bd. Little Hunting Creek Civic Assn., Mt. Vernon, Va., 1971—; vice chmn., environmental affairs and recreations com. Mt. Vernon Council Citizen's Assns., 1973—; mem. adv. council natural and environmental resources No. Va. Planning Dist. Commn., 1973—; mem. Fairfax County Environmental Quality adv. council, 1974—. Served to capt. Med. Service Corps, AUS, 1960. Fellow A.A.A.S., Herpetologists League; mem. Am. Soc. Ichthyologists and Herpetologists (exec. com. 1964-68), Am. Fisheries Soc., Ecol. Soc. Am. Contbr. articles to profl. jours. Home: 2629 Stirrup Lane Alexandria VA 22308 Office: Nat Marine Fisheries Service Systematics Lab US Nat Mus Natural History Washington DC 20560

COLLIE, KELSEY EUGENE, educator; b. Miami, Fla., Feb. 21, 1935; s. James George and Malinda Elizabeth (Moxey) C.; student Hampton Inst., 1953-57; A.B., George Washington U., 1967, M.F.A., 1970; m. Doris Jean Sims, June 13, 1959; 1 dau., Kim Denyse. Documents librarian Library of Congress, Washington, 1965-70; asso. prof. drama Howard U., Washington, 1970—. Bd. dirs. St. Stephen's Enterprises, Inc., 1970—, Washington Home for Foundlings, 1973—. Mem. exec. com. Council on Adoptable Children, 1971—. Served with AUS, 1958-60. Mem. Am. Theatre Assn. Episcopalian. Major plays produced include Good Friday, 1962, Maybe Someday, 1968, Fiesta, 1969, Celebration, 1973; Author: The Gift (play), 1973; Youth Ministry Notebook, 1973. Home: 7519 12th St NW Washington DC 20012

COLLIER, BOYD DEAN, educator, mgmt. cons.; b. Waco, Tex., Jan. 16, 1938; s. Denis Lee and Annie Alice (Berry) C.; B.B.A., Baylor U., 1963, M.S. (Earhart Found. fellow), 1965; Ph.D. (Earhart Found. fellow, NSF fellow), U. Tex., 1970; m. Barbara Nell Joseph, June 20, 1966; 1 dau., Deirdre Michelle. Asst. prof. econs. U. N.C., Greensboro, 1969-71; mem. com. acad. policies, 1970-72; asso. prof. behavioral mgmt. sci. U. Houston, 1972; v.p. tax planning Consilium, Inc., Austin, Tex., 1973; chief internal auditor Glastron Boat Co., Austin, 1973-74; asso. prof. St. Edward's U., Austin, 1974—. Mgmt. cons., 1974—. Precinct chmn. Austin Democratic Com., 1968. Served with USNR, 1955-59. Mem. Am. Assn. U. Profs. (chpt. v.p. 1971), Am. Inst. C.P.A.'s, Am. Econs. Assn., Phi Kappa Phi, Beta Gamma Sigma. Home: 9602 Newfoundland Circle Austin TX 78758

COLLIER, CALVIN JEFFERSON, JR., tool co. exec.; b. Cedar Valley, Tex., Aug. 20, 1923; s. Calvin Jefferson and Bathsheba Mary (Milam) C.; B.B.A., U. Tex., 1949; m. Doris Elaine Fritts, Oct. 20, 1945; 1 dau., Tracy Diane. Staff accountant Haskins & Sells, C.P.A.'s, Houston, 1949-54; adminstrv. asst. to v.p. and treas. Hughes Tool Co., Houston, 1954-60, asst. sec., 1960-72, sec., 1972—, asst. treas., 1960-63, v.p., treas., 1963—, also dir.; dir. Hughes Tool Co. Ltd., Hughes Tool Co. Australia Ltd., Hughes de Mexico, S.Am. de C. V., Hughes Tool Co. de Mexico, S.Am. de C.V. Served with USAAF, 1943-46. Decorated D.F.C., Air medal with two oak leaf clusters. C.P.A., Tex. Mem. Am. Inst. C.P.A.'s, Tex. Soc. C.P.A.'s, Am. Soc. Corporate Secs., Beta Alpha Psi. Home: 8119 DeLeon Dr Houston TX 77017 Office: 5425 Polk Av Houston TX 77023

COLLIER, COURTLAND ALDEN, civil engr.; b. Buffalo, July 29, 1925; s. Leo Robert and Marcheniel Overton (Bass) C.; B.E. in Civil Engring., Yale, 1949; grad. Canadian Summer Inst. Linguistics, Carenport, Sask., 1955; M.E., U. Fla., 1963; m. Albertine Elizabeth Taylor, Aug. 8, 1946 (div. Feb. 1963); children—Deborah Elizabeth, Nathan Stafford, Dennis Brainerd; m. 2d, Marian Fryer Legate, Feb. 22, 1971; stepchildren—Alexis Arthur, Amy Alice, Michael Fryer, Becky Marie. Jr. civil engr. Cal. Div. Hwys., 1950-51; office engr. Western Contracting Corp., 1951; asst. city engr. Dodge City, Kan., 1951-52; asso. resident engr. Tex. Hwy. Dept., Pharr, 1952-55; instr. mechanics div. Coll. Engring., Lehigh U., 1955-56; field engr. Raymond Conc. Pile Co., Havana, Cuba, 1956-57; design engr. Lummus Co., Edmonton, Alta. and Maracaibo, Venezuela, 1957-59; design engr. D.E. Britt & Assos., Ft. Lauderdale, Fla., 1960-61; cons. engr., asst. prof. Coll. Engring., U. Fla., 1961—; v.p. C.A.V. Inversiones Zulianas, Maracaibo. Mem. Gainesville (Fla.) City Commn., 1967-73; chmn. Pub. Works Commn. Gainesville, 1967-73, chmn. pub. safety commn., 1971-73. Mem. Am. Soc. C.E. (pres. Gainesville br. 1966-67), Fla. Engring. Soc., Am. Assn. Cost Engrs., Am. Arbitration Assn. Club: 300 (Gainesville). Home: 2809 SW 1 Way Gainesville FL 32601

COLLIER, DURWARD REED, dentist; b. Weir, Miss., Jan 6, 1932; s. George Hester and Eva Mae (Braswell) Collier; B.S., Miss. State U., 1955; D.D.S., U. Tenn., 1957; M.P.H., U. Mich., 1958; m. Doris Jeanette Morrow, June 8, 1950; children—Lisa Kay, Cheryl Lynn, Gina Laura, Paul Reed. Dir. div. dental Health, Ark. State Bd. Health, 1958-59; practice dentistry, Brandon, Miss., 1959-60; regional dental officer Tenn. Dept. Pub. Health, 1960-67; asst. chief, div. dental health, Ill. Dept. Pub. Health, chief Bur. Spl. Projects and Research Dental Div., 1967-68; dir. div. dental health services Tenn. Dept. Pub. Health, Nashville, 1968—. Clin. asso. prof. Coll. Dentistry, U. Tenn. Diplomate Am. Bd. Dental Pub. Health. Fellow Am. Pub. Health Assn. (mem. governing council 1969-71); mem. Am. Dental Assn. (cons. council on edn. 1973—), Am. Assn. Pub. Health Dentists (sec.-treas. 1970-73, pres.-elect 1973-74), Tenn. Pub. Health Assn. (sec.-treas. 1971—; chmn. dental sect. 1971—), Pierre Fauchard Acad. Mason (32 deg., Shriner). Baptist (deacon). Contbr. articles to profl. jours. Home: 2442 Rychen Dr Nashville TN 37217 Office: 310 Capitol Towers Nashville TN 37219

COLLIER, GAYLAN JANE, educator; b. Fluvanna, Tex., July 23, 1924; d. Ben Vivian and Narcis (Smith) Collier; B.A., Abilene Christian Coll., 1946; M.A., U. Ia., 1949; Ph.D., U. Denver, 1957. Instr. speech and drama Woman's Coll. U., N.C., 1947-48; asst. prof. Greensboro (N.C.) Coll., 1949-50; asst. prof., then asso. prof., dir. theatre Abilene Christian Coll., 1950-60; asso. prof. Ida. State U., 1960-63, summers 1958, 59; asso. prof. speech and drama Sam Houston State Coll., Huntsville, Tex., 1963-65, prof. drama, 1965-67; prof. theatre arts Tex. Christian U., Ft. Worth, 1967—; dir. Pkwy. Playhouse, Burnsville, N.C., summer 1951; guest dir. U. Denver, summer 1962; dir. Scott Theatre Actors' Repertory Co., summers 1968, 69; dir. Tex. Christian U. Prodn. The Imaginary Invalid, Eng., summer 1970. Mem. Am. Ednl. Theatre Assn., Southwestern Theatre Conf. (past v.p. Rocky Mountain Theatre conf. 1962-63), Children's Theatre Conf. (past dir., editor region 4, adminstrv. asst. to dir. 1965-67). Center for Research in Frontier Theatre, Zeta Phi Eta. Author: Assignments in Acting, 1966. Contbr. articles to profl. jours. Home: 2725 Lubbock Av Fort Worth TX 76109

COLLIER, HENRY MORGAN, JR., physician, surgeon; b. Savannah, Ga., Aug. 7, 1916; s. Henry M. and Annie B. (Gilliard) C.; A.B. cum laude, Savannah State Coll., 1935; M.D. Meharry Med. Coll., Nashville, 1942; m. Mozella B. Gaither, June 22, 1943; children—Vincent Louis, Roberle E., Henry M. III. Resident Kate Bitting Reynolds Meml. Hosp., Winston-Salem, N.C., 1942-43; practice medicine, Savannah, 1943-52, 55—; treas., chief staff Charity Hosp., 1959-64; asso. staff St. Josephs Hosp., Warren A. Candler Hosp.; pres. bd. dirs. William A. Harris Hosp. and Nursing Home; active staff Meml. Hosp. of Chatham County, Ga., Ga. Infirmary, Savannah. Treas. Seaside Devel. Corp., Hilton Head, S.C.; owner, operator Collier Meml. Beach, Hilton Head. Mem. Savannah Port Authority, 1970-73, Savannah Devel. Authority, 1971-73. Vice pres. Coastal Empire council Boy Scouts Am., 1972-73; chmn. Savannah State Coll. Found., 1973—. Trustee W. Broad St. YMCA; past pres. Savannah chpt. Nat. Guardsmens, Inc. Served to capt. USAF, Force, 1952-55. Recipient Silver Beaver award Boy Scouts Am., 1970. Fellow Am. Soc. Abdominal Surgeons; mem. A.M.A., Ga. Med. Soc., Med. Assn. Ga., Nat., Ga. (pres. 1961-62) med. assns., South Atlantic Med. Soc. (past pres.), Mid Town C. of C. of Savannah (pres. 1956-69), N.A.A.C.P., Alpha Phi Alpha. Democrat. Episcopalian. Club: Hub Business and Professional Men's (pres. 1961-62). Home: 1827 Mills B Lane Blvd Savannah GA 31405 Office: Collier Profl Bldg 900 W Broad St Savannah GA 31401

COLLIER, LOLA GAMBLE (MRS. JOHN WAYNE COLLIER), owner clothing store; b. Stonegia, Va., Oct. 9, 1911; d. Waymond Walter and Mary Elizabeth (Maggard) Gamble; grad. high sch.; student U. Va. Extension, 1958; m. John Wayne Collier, June 11, 1937; children—Gale Annette (Mrs. Charles Lawrence Wright), Kenneth Wayne, John Chadriek. Dress maker, designer, Appalachia, Va., 1935; owner, propr. The Grill, Appalachia, 1936-47; owner, buyer, mgr. Collier's Style Shop, Appalachia, 1947—, St. Paul, Va., 1949—, Lexington, Ky., 1952—, Kingsport, Tenn., 1966-71. Asst. in town politics regarding better civic conditions; coordinator Ky. div. Am. Cancer Soc.; vol. Road for Recovery program. Mem. Women's Soc. (leader 1937-47), Baptist. Clubs: Woman's (pres. 1954-58), Bridge. Home: 1001 Castleton Way Lexington KY 40502 Office: 201 Eastland Shopping Center Lexington KY 40505

COLLIER, ROBERT ARTHUR, lawyer, oil co. exec.; b. Wichita Falls, Tex., Apr. 3, 1917; s. Robert Heber and Lulu (Cross) C.; LL.B., U. Tex., 1940; m. Jeanne Claybrook, Sept. 19, 1942; children—Claybrook, Deborah Leigh. Admitted to Tex. bar 1940, D.C. bar, 1954; partner Collier, Shannon, Rill & Edwards, and predecessor firm Washington, 1956—. Chmn. bd. Macmillan Ring-Free Oil Co., N.Y.C., 1963—. Mem. Pres.'s Com. on Mental Retardation; mem. nat. adv. com. Jobs for Vets. Home: 6202 Fort Hunt Rd Alexandria VA 22307 Office: 1666 K St NW Washington DC 20006

COLLIER, ROBERT HOYAL, JR., surgeon; b. Cherokee County, N.C., Aug. 15, 1939; s. Robert Hoyal and Barbara Phyllis (Ries) C.; B.S., U. Tenn., 1961, M.D., 1963; m. Louise Thompson, Dec. 29, 1960; children—Robert Hoyal, Ries, Lara. Intern, Grady Hosp., 1963-64; surg. resident Emory, Grady, VA hosps., Atlanta, 1964-68; pvt. practice gen. and vascular surgery, Knoxville, Tenn., 1970—; mem. staff St. Mary Meml., Ft. Sanders Presbyn., E. Tenn. Bapt. hosps., U. Tenn. Research Center and Hosp. Bd. dirs. Knoxville chpt. Am. Cancer Soc. Served with USAF, 1968-70. Diplomate Am. Bd. Surgery. Fellow A.C.S.; mem. Am., Tenn. med. assns., Knoxville Acad. Medicine, Knoxville Surg. Soc., Alpha Omega Alpha. Presbyn. Home: 1325 Fieldwood Dr Knoxville TN 37918 Office: 939 Emerald Av Knoxville TN 37917

COLLIER, SHELLEY HALE, JR., banker; b. Mercedes, Tex., July 1, 1928; s. Shelley Hale and Marguerite (Feike) C.; B.B.A., U. Tex., 1950; postgrad. La. State U., 1960-63; m. Caryl Ann Hunt, Nov. 24, 1958; children—Michael Melinda, Shelley Hale III, Susan Gail, Kay Caryl. Asst. cashier First Nat. Bank, Mercedes, 1951-54, cashier, 1954-57, v.p., 1957-60, pres., 1960-71, also dir.; pres., dir. Valley Nat. Bank, McAllen, Tex., 1971—; dir. First Nat. Bank, LaFeria, Tex., J & C Royalty Corp., B & P Bridge Co., Mid-Valley Community Motor Hotel Devel. Co. Bd. regents Pan Am. Coll., Edinburg, Tex., 1961-65; bd. dirs., sec. Rio Grande Valley Pollution Control Authority, until 1973. Mem. Tex. (mem. exec. council 1969-71), Rio Grande Valley (pres.) bankers assns. Rotarian. Home: 1520 Ulex St McAllen TX 78501 Office: 2400 N 10th St McAllen TX 78501

COLLIER, VIRGINIA ROLLWAGE, music patroness, assn. exec.; b. Forrest City, Ark., July 5; d. Otto Benjamin and Virginia (Anderson) Rollwage; student Lenox Hall, St. Louis, Nat. Coll. Edn., Evanston, Ill., Columbia, George Washington U.; m. John Francis Collier (div.). Tchr. math. Comstock Sch. for Girls, N.Y.C., 2 years; econ. analyst and internat. economist U.S. Dept Commerce, Washington, 1943-53. Pres. Motion Picture and TV Council D.C., 1952—. Chmn. Embassy of Iran Benefit Ball for Blind, 1965; judge U.S. Navy Band Ann., 1970. Mem. Dept. State com. Partner in Alliance. Mem. Nat. Assn. Am. Composers and Condrs. (award for outstanding service to Am. music 1953, founder D.C. chpt. 1950, pres.), Nat. League Am. Pen Women (gen. chmn. nat. biennial conv. 1960, nat. membership chmn. 1974-76), U.D.C. (chmn. Confederate meml. com. 1963, 64; bd. trustees Confederate Meml. Hall; pres. Stonewall Jackson chpt. 1967-68), Nat. Soc. Arts and Letters (nat. 1st v.p. 1964-66; gen. chmn. nat. 20th anniversary; gen. chmn. ann. chpt. benefit 1967-68, chpt. program chmn. 1974—), Nat. Fedn. Women's Clubs (chmn. dept. pub. affairs 1970-72, chmn. dept. performing arts 1972—), D.C. Soc. Dames Ct. Honor (state treas. 1971-73), Pan Am. Liaison Com. Women's Orgn.; Internat. Platform Assn., Friends Kennedy Center. Club: Washington. Author govtl. publs.; columnist Box Office, weekly mag., 1961—. Home: 5112 Connecticut Av NW Washington DC 20008

COLLIER, WILLIAM MARION, state ofcl.; b. Colorado City, Tex., Dec. 11, 1908; s. William M. and Rebecca (Gore) C.; B.S., Tex. A. and M. U., 1931; m. Mable Leona Bowlin, June 12, 1943; children—William M. III, Caroline Jane (Mrs. John M. Pinson). Archtl. practice, Abilene, Tex., 1941-60; chief, health facilities constrn. sect. Tex. State Dept. of Health, Austin, 1960—. Mem. adv. council Mental Health Dept., 1968—. Mem. Tex. Soc. Architects, A.I.A. Home: 2803 Greenlawn Pkwy Austin TX 78757 Office: 1100 W 49th St Austin TX 78756

COLLIGNON, ARTHUR P., safety cons.; b. Cin., Dec. 9, 1889; s. John F. and Elizabeth (Bidner) C.; C.E., U. Cin., 1915; Aero. Engr., Mass. Inst. Tech., 1918; B.S., N.Y.U., 1923; m. Marion Tourison, July 10, 1924 (dec.); m. 2d, Charlotte Field, Jan. 16, 1954. Eastern mgr. Brunhoff Mfg. Co., merchandising mgr. nat. advt. N.Y. Eve. Jour.; asst. agt. N.Y. dist. Standard Brands, Inc.; pres. mgr. Putnam County Reporter; asst. state safety cons. N.Y. State F. W.A.; former dist. engring mgr. Am. Mut. Liability Ins. Co., ret. 1955; now engaged as safety cons. Chmn. com. vehicle sect., mem. operating com. Greater N.Y. Safety Council; vice chmn. marine ins. safety com. N.Y. Shipping Assn. Mem. Safety Execs. Club N.Y., Am. Soc. Safety Engrs., Am. Legion, Army Athletic Assn., Vets. of Safety, Naples Moorings Assn., Nat. Audobon Soc., Canopus Civic Assn., Inc. (pres.), Naples Civic Assn., Delta Tau Delta. Presbyn. Mason (32 deg.). Clubs: Country (Naples, Fla.); Square (Putnam Valley). Author engring. articles for co. mag. Address: 3400 Gulf Shore Blvd Naples FL 33940

COLLINS, ANN ELIZABETH AVERITT (MRS. GALEN FRANKLIN COLLINS), civic leader; b. Peru, Ind., July 28, 1934; d. Robert Chancellor and Cleo (Hite) Averitt; student Ind. U., 1952-55; Goshen Coll., 1958, East Tenn. State U., 1967-68; m. Galen Franklin Collins, Sept. 30, 1956; children—Galen Robert, Amelia Lynn, Scott Franklin, Daniel Chancellor. Co-soc. editor Elkhart (Ind.) Truth, 1955-56; mem. Elkhart Civic Theatre, 1957-60; mem. Chenango County Community Players, N.Y., 1960-63; co-founder Dogwood Playhouse, Bristol Va.-Tenn., 1964, bd. dirs., 1964-69; co-founder Collero Puppets, Bristol, 1967; writer, performer puppet shows, Miami, Fla., 1972—; free lance writer, 1972—. Mem. Editor Threshold, publ. Dade County Assn. Retarded Citizens. Musical compositions include Why Am I Old, 1969; Little Boy, My Dear Son, 1969; Color, 1969; Willows, 1969; Soldier Boy, 1969; Is That Your Voice I Hear, 1969. Home: 10800 SW 69th Av Miami FL 33156

COLLINS, ARLEE GENE, chemist; b. Forest City, Ia., Dec. 20, 1927; s. Paul Wilbur and Esther E. (Matson) C.; B.A., Kletzing Coll., 1951; M.S. in Chemistry, Kan. State Coll., 1955; M.S. in Earth Scis., Tulsa U., 1972; postgrad. Drake, 1951-52, George Washington U., 1969-70; m. Barbara Joan Howard, Sept. 1, 1961; children—Michael Gene, Sandra Diane. Chemist Howard Moffit, Cons. Chemist, Des Moines, 1951-52, Spencer Chem. Co., Pittsburg, Kan., 1952-55; asst. chief chemist Co-op. Refinery Assn., Phillipsburg, Kan., 1955-56; chemist, project leader Bur. Mines, U.S. Dept. Interior, Bartlesville, Okla., 1956—. Served with AUS, 1946-47. Mem. Am. Soc. Testing and Materials (vice chmn. subcom.), Am. Chem. Soc., Geochem. Soc. Am., Internat. Assn. Geochemistry and Cosmochemistry, N.Y. Acad. Scis., Soc. Applied Spectroscopy. Elk. Clubs: Engineers, Sportsmen's, Adams Golf (Bartlesville, Okla.); Horseshoe Bend (Ark.). Home: 1428 Valley Rd Bartlesville OK 74003 Office: Virginia and Cudahy Sts Bartlesville OK 74003

COLLINS, ARTHUR ANDREWS, inventor, mfr.; b. Kingfisher, Okla., Sept. 9, 1909; s. M.H. and Faith (Andrews) C.; student Coe Coll., 1926-27, D.Sc. (hon.), 1954; student Amherst Coll., 1927-28; spl. study U. Ia.; D.Sc. (hon.), Mount Mercy Coll., 1974; D. Engring. (hon.), Poly. Inst. Bklyn., 1968, So. Methodist U., 1970; m. Margaret Van Dyke, Jan. 4, 1930 (dec. Dec. 1955); children—Susan, Michael; m. 2d, Mary Margaret Meis, June 10, 1957; children—Alan, David. Pioneer in devel. of high frequency radio communication; founder Collins Radio Co., Cedar Rapids, Ia., 1931, propr., 1931-33, pres., chmn., 1933-71; pres. Arthur A. Collins, Inc., 1972—; inventor electronic equipment, including automatic tuned multi-channel radio equipment. Trustee Coe Coll., 1945-51, Grad. Research Center of S.W., 1962-69, Herbert Hoover Found., 1965—. Fellow I.E.E.E. Author: Telecommunications-A Time for Innovation. Amateur radio operator; patentee radio electronic inventions. Home: 13731 Danvers Dr Dallas TX 75240 Office: 13601 Preston Rd Suite 509W Dallas TX 75240

COLLINS, CLARENCE TILLMAN, educator; b. Greenup, Ky., May 20, 1933; s. John Tillman and Marie (Stevens) C.; B.S., Eastern Ky. State U., 1957; Materials Handling Engr., Detroit Indsl. Tech., 1959; postgrad. U. Mich., 1959, Mich. State U., 1960-63; M. Engring., U. Ky., 1967, postgrad., 1969-71; m. Ruby Dean Holbrook, July 3, 1954;children—Toni Dee, John Tillman II. Tchr., Ottawa Hills High Sch., Grand Rapids, Mich., 1957; asst. to mgr. Rapids Standard Co., Inc., 1958, field engr., 1959, asst. mgr. engring. dept., 1960; tchr. indsl. engring. Mich. State U., 1959-60; tchr. tech. writing Grand Rapids Jr. Coll., 1961-62; mgr. Westdale Co., Inc., 1961-62; tchr. Kenowa Hills High Sch., 1962-63; chmn. dept. English Wolfe County High Sch., 1967-68; instr. English and philosophy Lees Jr. Coll., Jackson, Ky., 1968-69, chmn. dept. humanities, asso. prof. English and philosophy, 1969—, dir. devel., 1970-71. Corp. mgr. Rapistan Carolinas, Charlotte, 1963. Mem. adv. staff Govt. Housing, 1969-71; ednl. cons. So. Consortium of 14 Colls. on Ednl. Media and Philosophy of Edn., 1969-71. Bd. dirs. Career Opportunities Program. Served with USNR, 1950-53. Mem. Nat. Reading Assn., N.E.A., Nat. Assn. Material Handling Engrs., Am. Assn. U. and Coll. Profs., Am. Assn. Jr. Colls., Nat. Assn. Tchrs. English, Ky. Edn. Assn. Methodist. Lion. Club: Wolfe County Fish and Game (pres. 1970-71) (Campton, Ky.). Author: First Aid to Composition, 1968; Easy Street, 1969; To Each His Own, 1971; Strange Lady, 1972. Home: Collinswood Pine Ridge KY 41360 Office: 601 Jefferson St Jackson KY 41339

COLLINS, DAVID ARTHUR, univ. ofcl.; b. Greenville, S.C., July 4, 1927; s. Ernest Fleming and Lula (Weeks) C.; student Am. U., 1947-48; B.A., Presbyn. Coll., 1954; M.A., Memphis State U., 1962; postgrad. U. Tenn., 1964-66; m. Anna Kay Maples, July 31, 1957; children—Debra Ann, David Arthur. Field sec., adminstrv. asst., asst. exec. sec. Pi Kappa Alpha, Memphis, 1954-61; asst. dean student affairs Auburn (Ala.) U., 1962-64; asst. dean students Memphis State U., 1964-69, dean student activities, 1969-71, asst. v.p. for student affairs, 1971—. Exec. sec. So. Univ. Student Gov't. Assn., 1967-70. Served with USNR, 1945-46. Mem. Tenn. Edn. Assn., So. Coll. Personnel Assn., So. Deans Assn., Assn. for Coordination Univ. Religious Affairs, Blue Key, Pi Kappa Alpha, Omicron Delta Kappa, Phi Delta Kappa. Presbyn. (elder). Home: 1591 Page Cove Memphis TN 38117

COLLINS, DAVID BROWNING, clergyman; b. Hot Springs, Ark., Dec. 18, 1922; s. Charles Frederick and Agnes Elizabeth (George) C.; B.A., U. of South, 1943, B.D., 1948, S.T.M., 1962, D.D., 1974; diploma St. Augustine's Coll., Canterbury, Eng., 1961; m. Maryon Virginia Moise, Oct. 14, 1945; children—Melissa (Mrs. Mark Sterling), Christopher B., Matthew B., Geoffrey C. Ordained to ministry Episcopal Ch.; rector St. Andrew's Ch., Marianna, Ark., 1948-53; chaplain, asso. prof. religion U. of South, Sewanee, Tenn., 1953-66; dean Cathedral of St. Philip, Atlanta, 1966—. Vice pres. Christian Council Met. Atlanta, 1968-70; dep. Episcopal Gen. Conv., 1967, 69, 70, 73. Bd. dirs. Nat. Conf. Christians and Jews, Nat. Clergy Devel. Bd. Served as lt. (j.g.) USNR, 1943-46. Mem. Blue Key, Phi Beta Kappa, Omicron Delta Kappa, Kappa Sigma. Contbr. articles to religious publs. Home: 2799 Andrews Dr NW Atlanta GA 30305 Office: 2744 Peachtree Rd NW Atlanta GA 30305

COLLINS, FRED TILLMAN, JR., mfg. co. exec.; b. Ahoskie, N.C., Nov. 2, 1920; s. Fred Tillman and Genevieve (Kimbrough) C.; B.S., Wake Forest Coll., 1942; B.E.E. with honors, N.C. State U., 1948; m. Mildred Frances Roberson, May 1, 1943; children—Fred, Hobart. Design engr., motors and control Gen. Electric Co., Schenectady, 1948-50, applications engr., mining industry, 1950-52, mgmt. trainee GE Apparatus Shop, Pitts., 1952-53, mgr. GE Apparatus Shop, Richmond, Va., 1953-56, mgr. GE Apparatus Shop, Houston, 1956-73, regional mgr. Southwestern operations, apparatus service div., 1973—. Served to 1st lt. USAAF, 1942-46. Mem. I.E.E.E. Republican. Baptist (deacon 1950—, trustee 1972—). Club: Houston Engineers. Office: 3115 West Loop South Suite 27 Houston TX 77027

COLLINS, GALEN FRANKLIN, pharm. chemist; b. Winona Lake, Ind., Dec 29, 1927; s. Harry Franklin and Elsie (Bahney) C.; B.S., Purdue U., 1949, M.S., 1952, Ph.D., 1954; m. Ann Elizabeth Averitt, Sept. 30, 1956; children—Galen Robert, Amelia Lynn, Scott Franklin, Daniel Chancelor. Grad. asst. Purdue U., 1949-52, research fellow, 1952-53; pharm. chemist Miles Labs., Inc., Elkart, Ind., 1953-58, asst. to dir. Miles-Ames pharm. research lab., 1958-59, sr. research scientist, sect. head Ames Products, 1959-60; sect. chief Norwich Products Devel., Norwich Pharmacal Co. (N.Y.), 1960-63; mgr. research div. S.E. Massengill Co., Bristol, Tenn., 1963-67, dir. research, 1967-71; v.p. research and devel. Dade div. Am. Hosp. Supply Corp., Miami, Fla., 1971—. Bd. dirs. Bristol unit Am. Heart Assn., 1967-71, pres., 1969-71. Fellow A.A.A.S., Am. Inst. Chemists; mem. A.I.M., Am. Chem. Soc., Am. Pharm. Assn., Acad. of Pharm. Scis., Multiple Sclerosis Soc., Sigma Xi, Rho Chi, Phi Lambda Upsilon. Presbyn. Elk. Patentee in field. Home: 10800 SW 69th Av Miami FL 33156 Office: PO Box 672 Miami FL 33152

COLLINS, GENEVIEVE (MRS. FRANK COLLINS, JR.), organist, choir dir.; b. Meeker, La., July 12, 1912; d. Claude E. and Bessie (Hamberlin) Cox; Mus. B., La. State U., 1933; Mus.M., 1934; pvt. study with Louis Vierne, Paris, 1935 ; m. Frank Collins, Jr., June 7, 1933; 1 son, James F. C. Organist, choirmaster Temple B'nai Israel, Baton Rouge, 1935-67, 68—; organist First Meth. Ch., 1943-45; organist, choirmaster Trinity Episcopal Ch., 1949—; recitalist; mem. faculty Hardtner Choir Camp, 1956-62; tchr. piano, 1944-58. Mem. music commn. Episcopal Diocese La. Mem. Am. Guild Organists (dean La. chpt. 1945-47; 50-51, 59-61, state chmn. 1966—, sub-dean, program chmn. Baton Rouge chpt. 1972), Past Presidents Assn. Baton Rouge (pres. 1952), Baton Rouge Piano Tchrs. Assn. (pres. 1951), Pan-Hellenic Assn. Baton Rouge (pres. 1939), Alpha Chi Omega (pres. alumnae club 1938), Sigma Alpha Iota. Episcopalian. Home: 406 Delgado Dr Baton Rouge LA 70808 Office: 3552 Morning Glory Av Baton Rouge LA 70808

COLLINS, HAROLD RAY, supt. schs.; b. Hartford, Ala., Mar. 14, 1919; s. Francis Alex and Vestie (Kinsaul) C.; B.S., Troy State Coll., 1946; M.A., U. Ala., 1953, Ed.D., 1966; m. Ruth Bassett, Mar. 1, 1941; children—Harold Ray, Gene Bassett. Prin. Zion Chapel Sch., Jack, Ala., 1944-48, Goshen (Ala.) High Sch., 1948-66; supt. Pike County Schs., 1966-70, Mobile County (Ala.) Pub. Schs., 1970—. Mem. Ala. State Textbook Commn.; mem. Ala. Jr. Coll. Selection Com. Mem. Nat., Ala. assns. secondary sch. prins., Am., Ala. assns. sch. adminstrs., N.E.A., Ala. Edn. Assn., Nat. Assn. Sch. Bds., Ala. Assn. Elementary Sch. Prins, Kappa Phi Kappa, Kappa Phi Delta. Baptist. Rotarian. Club: Civitan (Mobile). Home: 3251 Rivere du Chien Dr Mobile AL 36606 Office: PO Box 1327 Mobile AL 36601

COLLINS, JAMES ALTON, editor; b. Pecos, Tex., Nov. 24, 1934; s. Harlin Alton and Ada Belle (Hayes) C.; B.A., Tex. A. and M. U., 1956; candidate M.A., U. Tex., 1964; m. Jerry LaVerne Ratliff, Apr. 29, 1963; 1 dau., Christina Carmen. Reporter, Pecos (Tex.) Enterprise, 1956; tchr., coach Barstow (Tex.) Ind. Schs., 1956-59; reporter Wichita Falls (Tex.) Times, 1959-60, Roswell (N.M.) Daily Record, 1960-61, Pecos Daily News, 1961; reporter U.P.I., Albuquerque, 1962; reporter, photographer New Mexican, Santa Fe, 1962-63, sports editor, 1964; editor N.M. Farm and Ranch Mag., 1964-65; staff writer The Pipeliner, El Paso Natural Gas Co., 1965-68, editor, 1968-73, staff rep., 1973—. Served with AUS, 1957. Mem. Internat. Assn. Bus. Communicators. Democrat. Home: 9925 Bourbon St El Paso TX 79924 Office: Box 1492 El Paso TX 79978

COLLINS, JAMES SPENCER, petroleum co. exec.; b. Dallas, Jan. 10, 1922; s. Robert Oron and Hallie Rhea (Jowell) C.; B.S., Tex. Coll. Mines, 1947; postgrad. Harvard Bus. Sch., 1964; m. Mary White, Apr. 15, 1944; children—Gregory Newton, Kelly Anne. Geologist, Union Oil Co., Corpus Christi, Tex., 1947-50; geologist York & Harper, Midland, Tex., 1950-52; div. geologist Tenneco Oil Co., Houston, 1952-57, exploration mgr., 1957-59, v.p., 1959-73; v.p., dir. oil and gas J.M. Huber Corp., 1973—. Chmn. oil industry sect. United Fund, 1969. Served with USMCR, 1942-46. Mem. Am. Assn. Petroleum Geologists, Soc. Exploration Geophysicists, Am. Assn. Petroleum Landmen. Club: Houston. Home: 3815 Olympia St Houston TX 77019 Office: JM Huber Corp 2000 West Loop S Houston TX 77027

COLLINS, JASON HAYDEL, physician; b. New Orleans, Aug. 13, 1918; s. Charles and Amelie (Haydel) C.; B.S., Tulane U., 1938, M.D., 1941; m. Marie Elaine White, June 30, 1949; children—Denise Adele, Marie Elaine, Janine Ann, Jason Haydel, Lynette Joan, Charles Louis. Intern, Wis. Gen. Hosp., 1941-42; resident Ochsner Clinic, New Orleans, 1946-48; practice medicine, specializing in obstetrics and gynecology, New Orleans, 1946—; prof. clin. obstetrics and gynecology, Tulane U., 1959-71, prof., acting chmn. dept. obstetrics and gynecology Sch. Medicine, 1971-72, C. Jeff Miller prof., chmn., 1972—; dir. med. edn. So. Bapt. Hosp., New Orleans; sr. cons. obstetrics and gynecology USPHS Hosp., New Orleans; cons. Mercy Hosp., Touro Infirmary. Served with AUS, 1942-45; PTO. Mem. Am. Gynecol. Soc., A.C.S., Am. Coll. Obstetrics and Gynecology, Am. Assn. Obstetrics and Gynocology, Am. Gynecol. Club, Delta Kappa Epsilon. Club: Boston (New Orleans). Home: 7801 St Charles Av New Orleans LA 70118 Office: 1430 Tulane Av New Orleans LA 70112

COLLINS, JOHN P., football exec. Exec. v.p. Houston Oilers. Office: 6910 Fannin Houston TX 77025*

COLLINS, LESTER ALBERTSON, landscape architect; b. Moorestown, N.J., Apr. 19, 1914; s. Lester and Anne (Albertson) C.; grad. Choate Sch., Wallingford, Conn., 1933; A.B., Harvard, 1938, M.L.A., 1942; m. Petronella le Roux, July 8, 1947; children—Abigail Anne, Lester Adrian, Oliver Michael. Chmn. dept. landscape architecture, Harvard, 1950-53; prin. Collins, Simonds and Simonds, landscape architects and planners, Washington, Pitts., 1955-70, Lester Collins Assos., 1971—. Mem. Am. the Beautiful Fund of Natural Area Council, Washington; mem. Hubbard Ednl. Trust, Boston; pres. Innisfree Found., Millbrook, N.Y., 1960—. Fullbright scholar, 1953-54. Fellow Am. Soc. Landscape Architects. Mem. Soc. of Friends (with Am. Field Service 1942-45). Clubs: Harvard (Boston); Cosmos (Washington); Century Assn. Address: 1619 33d St NW Washington DC 20007

COLLINS, MARVIN BOBBY, retail grocery exec.; b. Tarpon Springs, Fla., Mar. 17, 1929; s. Marvin Bartow and Elsie Idella (Hughes) C.; student pub. schs.; m. Mary Marie Mock, June 20, 1948; children—Mark Ryan, Marcia Ann. Mgr. meat dept. Winn Dixie Food Stores, Inc., Tallahassee, 1947-55, Melbourne, Fla., 1955-58; owner pres. Minit Saver Food Stores, Inc., Melbourne, 1958-66; v.p. Certified Grocers of Fla., Ocala, 1963-64, dir., 1963-66; v.p., dir. Minit Ranch, Inc., Melbourne, 1965-68; pres. Quik Way Food Stores, Inc., Anderson, S.C., 1966—; pres. Quik Way of Carolina, Inc., 1967—; dir., pres. Asso. Grocers Inc. of S.C., 1968—; chmn. Travelers Petroleum, Inc., Self Way Stores, Inc., 1974—; partner Lease Way Enterprises; dir., chmn. Sports Way Stores, Inc.; dir. So. Bank & Trust Co., Anderson, S.C., A.G. Investment Co. Chmn. bd. dirs. Salvation Army Adv. Bd., Anderson; bd. dirs. Boys Club, Anderson. Served with AUS, 1952-54. Mem. Retail Grocers Assn. of Fla. (dir. until 1966), Food Retailers Assn. S.C. (dir. 1973—), Nat. Assn. Convenience Stores (dir.), C. of C. (sec., dir. 1962-66). Baptist. Mason (32 deg., Shriner), Elk, Rotarian. Home: 221 Timberlake Rd Anderson SC 29621 Office: 1007 N Fant St Anderson SC 29621

COLLINS, MICHAEL, museum dir.; b. Rome, Italy, Oct. 31, 1930 (parents Am. citizens); s. James L. Collins; B.S., U.S. Mil. Acad., 1952; m. Patricia Mary Finnegan, 1957; children—Kathleen, Ann Stewart, Michael Lawton. Commd. 2d lt. USAF, advanced through grades to col.; formerly exptl. test pilot Air Force Flight Test Center, Edwards AFB, Cal.; formerly astronaut with Manned Spacecraft Center, NASA, pilot Gemini X, nation's 3d space walker, command module pilot Apollo 11, mem. 1st lunar landing crew, 1969; asst. sec. state for pub. affairs, Washington, 1970-71; dir. Nat. Air and Space Mus., Smithsonian Instn., Washington, 1971—. Mem. Soc. Exptl. Test Pilots. Office: National Air and Space Museum Smithsonian Instn Washington DC 20560

COLLINS, MIKE GOURLEY, chem. co. exec.; b. Charleston, W.Va., Mar. 4, 1929; s. Otha Benjamin and Laura Valera (Gourley) C.; student Morris Harvey Coll., 1946-48; B.S. in Chem. Engring., W. Va., State U., 1950, M.S. in Chem. Engring., 1966; m. Eva Mae Canterbury, Oct. 27, 1956. Engr. Union Carbide, South Charleston, W.Va., 1950-54, dept. head, 1957-65, plant mgr. Frederick, Md., 1954-56, chem. prodn. supt., Ponce, P.R., 1966-67, chem. asst. plant mgr., Port Lavaca, Tex., 1967—. Dir. Jr. Achievement, Victoria, Tex., 1969—, pres., 1973—. Served with AUS, 1954-56. Registered profl. engr., W.Va. Mem. Victoria C. of C., Am. Chem. Soc., Am. Inst. Chem. Engrs., Tau Beta Pi, Sigma Gamma Epsilon, Phi Lambda Upsilon, Chi Beta Phi. Methodist. Club: Country (Victoria, Tex.). Home: 111 Dover Dell Victoria TX 77901 Office: PO Box 186 Port Lavaca TX 77979

COLLINS, MORRIS LAVERNE, lawyer; b. Pleasanton, Tex., Dec. 16, 1923; s. Benjamin Franklin and Luke (Brite) C.; B.A., St. Mary's U., 1957, LL.B., 1958; m. Mary Louise Garza, Apr. 13, 1947; children—Michael Joseph and Martin James (twins). Admitted to Tex. bar, 1957, since practiced in San Antonio; mem. firm Waltz, Bretz & Collins, San Antonio, 1957—. Charter mem. laity, adv. bd. Assumption Sem., The Major Sem. Archdiocese San Antonio, 1968-70; commr., Urban Renewal Agy., 1962-71; active United Fund, Heart Fund. Bd. dirs. Good Govt. League. Served with USNR, 1950-52. Mem. Am. Legion, Res. Officers Assn., Naval Res. Officers Assn., Navy League, Phi Delta Phi. K.C., Lion. Home: 134 Shannon Lee San Antonio TX 78216 Office: 600 Nat Bank Commerce Bldg San Antonio TX 78205

COLLINS, MURIEL MORSE (MRS. DENIS AUGUSTUS COLLINS), ret. journalist; b. Bklyn., Apr. 15, 1912; d. Frederick and Henrietta (Grasser) Morse; grad. high sch; m. Denis Augustus Collins, Nov. 15, 1952. Dept. head Uniform Printing & Supply Co., Bklyn, 1935-45; sec., bookkeeper Borough Press, Inc., N.Y.C., 1945-52; pvt. sec. to service mgr. Atlantic Service Co., 1952-57; asst. sec., asst treas., confidential sec. to pres. Shaker Mus. Found., Inc., Old Chatham, N.Y., 1957-68; sec. Port Charlotte (Fla) C. of C., 1969-70; reporter Sarasota Jour., 1970-72. Mem. Old Chatham Improvement Assn., 1952-69; chaplain Old Chatham Grange, 1962-69; charter mem. v.p. Tri-Village Fire Aux., 1963-64, pres., 1965-68; sec. Charlotte County Pageant Assn., Inc. Mem. Nat Fedn. Bus. and Profl. Women's Clubs (charter pres. Chatham club 1968), Port Charlotte Bus. and Profl. Women's Club (2d v.p. 1971), Am. Assn. Ret. Persons, Animal Welfare League Charlotte County, Port Charlotte Civic Assn., Fla. Sheriffs Assn. (hon.), St. Joseph Hosp. Aux. Clubs: Empire State (Charlotte County, Fla.); Alan Devoe Bird. Home: 3159 Windmill Village Punta Gorda FL 33950

COLLINS, REED, physician; b. Big Spring, Tex., Nov. 16, 1929; s. Alfred Reed and Bess Francis (Adams) C.; student Abilene Christian Coll., 1947-48; B.S., U. Tex., 1951; M.D., 1956; m. Geraldine Katherine Koenig, Sept. 4, 1954; children—Roxanne, Robin, Alan. Intern, Tripler Army Hosp., Honolulu, 1956-57; practice medicine specializing in family practice, Midland, Tex., 1959—; mem. staff Midland Meml. Hosp. Vice-pres. Midland chpt. Am. Cancer Soc., 1969-70. Served with USAF, 1956-59. Mem. Am. Assn. Gen. Practice, Am., Tex. med. assns., Am. Assn. Physicians and Surgeons, Alpha Omega Alpha. Home: 1704 Mayberry St Midland TX 79701 Office: 503 N Garfield St Midland TX 79701

COLLINS, ROYAL EUGENE, educator, physicist; b. Corsicana, Tex., Feb. 25, 1925; s. Royal and Jewell Anna (Truhitte) C.; B.S. in Physics, U. Houston, 1947-49; M.S., Tex. A. and M. U., 1950, Ph.D., 1954; m. Brunella T. Boneaux, Sept. 3, 1962; children—Royal Eugene, Cindy Ann. With Magnolia Petroleum Co., Dallas, 1951-52, Stanolind Oil & Gas Co., Tulsa, 1954-55, Humble Oil & Refining Co., Houston, 1955-59; faculty U. Houston, 1959—, prof. physics, 1967—; staff cons. med. biophysics Baylor Coll. Medicine, 1962—. Cons. to govt., industry, 1959—. Served with USNR, 1942-45. Research grantee Tex. Heart Assn., 1960-62, NSF, 1962, Research Corp. Am., 1969-70, U. Houston, 1970. Mem. Am. Phys. Soc., Am. Assn. Physics Tchrs., Sigma Xi, Sigma Pi Sigma. Author: Flow of Fluids Through Porous Materials, 1961, Russian edit., 1965; Mathematical Methods for Physicists and Engineers, 1968. Home: Route 1 Box 662 Manvel TX 77578 Office: Physics Dept U Houston Houston TX 77004

COLLINS, STANLEY NEWCOMB, JR., airline pilot, state legislator; b. Alexandria, Va., Jan. 30, 1937; s. Stanley Newcomb and Mary Elsie (Bloxom) C.; B.S., U. Md., 1962; M.Ed., Coll. William and Mary, 1965; m. Joyce Diane Pratt, July 18, 1958; children—Kendra Ann, Andrew, Daniel, Katie Louise. Tchr. Richmond (Va.) Pub. Schs., 1962-64; pilot Delta Air Lines, Atlanta, 1965—; dir. Fly-In Concept Inc. Mem. Ga. Ho. of Reps., 1969-70, 71-72. Served with USMC, 1956-60; maj. Res. Mem. Airline Pilots Assn., Res. Officers Assn., Marine Corps Res. Officers Assn. (sec., treas. Atlanta chpt. 1970-71), Iota Lambda Sigma. Address: 1727 W Nancy Creek Dr Atlanta GA 30319

COLLINS, WILLIAM COLDWELL, lawyer; b. El Paso, Tex., June 19, 1921; s. William Ruben and Julia (Coldwell) C.; B.A., U. Tex., 1943, LL.B., 1949; m. Marian Bainbridge, May 2, 1944; children—Nancy, Cynthia, Marian. Admitted to Tex. bar, 1949; asst. county atty., El Paso County, 1950-54; pvt. practice law, El Paso, 1954-59; partner Collins, Langford & Pine, El Paso, 1959—. Pres. alumnae U. Tex., El Paso, 1958. Served to capt. A.C., AUS, 1943-46. Mem. Am., El Paso bar assns., El Paso Hist. Soc., Am. Philatelic Soc. Episcopalian. Club: Country (El Paso, Tex.). Home: 4040 N Stanton St El Paso TX 79902 Office: 1100 Bassett Tower El Paso TX 79901

COLLINS, WILLIAM EDWARD, research psychologist; b. Bklyn., May 16, 1932; s. William Edward and Loretta Agnes (Brasier) C.; B.S., St. Peter's Coll., 1954; M.A., Fordham U., 1956, Ph.D. in Exptl. Psychology, 1959; m. Corliss Jean Barnes, June 20, 1970; 1 dau., Corliss Adora. Psychol. research asst. Fordham U., 1954-56, teaching fellow, 1958, psychol. research asst. Office Naval Research contract, 1958-59, grad. instr., 1958-59; research psychologist U.S. Army Med. Research Lab., Ft. Knox, Ky., 1959-61; research psychologist Civil Aeromed. Inst. FAA, Oklahoma City, 1961-63, chief sensory integration sect., 1963-65, chief psychology lab., 1965—; adj. asso. prof. psychology U. Okla., 1963-70, adj. prof., 1970—; adj. asso. prof. research psychology U. Okla. Med. Sch., 1965-71, adj. prof., 1971—. Mem. Nat. Acad. Sci.-NRS Com. Vision, 1963—; mem. Nat. Acad. Sci.-NRC Com. Hearing, Bioacoustics, and Biomechanics, 1963—, exec. council, 1973—; founding mem. Internat. Research Group on Colour Vision Deficiences, 1970—; lectr. in field. Judge, Okla. Sci. Fair, 1964. Recipient award FAA, 1964, 66, 67, 68, 69, 70, 71. Fellow Am. Psychol. Assn., A.A.A.S. (life), N.Y. Acad. Sci. (life), Aerospace Med. Assn. (Raymond F. Longacre award 1971); mem. Psychonomic Soc., Eastern Psychol. Assn., Assn. Aviation Psychologists, Bárány Soc., Sigma Xi (life). Editorial bd. Aerospace Medicine, 1974—. Contbr. numerous articles to profl. jours. Patentee in field. Home: 8900 Sheringham Dr Oklahoma City OK 73132 Office: FAA Civil Aeromed Inst AAC-118 PO Box 25082 Oklahoma City OK 73125

COLLISTER, EARL HAROLD, geneticist; b. Galva, Ill., Mar. 25, 1923; s. Harold Harrison and Judith Matilda (Ericson) C.; B.S., Purdue U., 1947, M.S., 1948, Ph.D. in Plant Genetics, 1950; m. Mary Vashti McCormack, May 19, 1945; children—Gregory Earl, Gary Alan, Guy Duane. With Tex. Research Found., 1950-59, prin. agronomist, chmn. plant sci. dept., 1956-59; with High Plains Research Found., 1959-67, dir., chief agronomist, 1962-67; exec. v.p. World Seeds, Inc., Salinas, Cal., 1967-68; pres. Internat. Grain, Inc., Dallas, 1968-71, Transera Research, Inc., Richardson, Tex., 1971—; cons. Francisco Sugar, Inc., Cuba, 1956-58. Hon. trustee Internat. Sesamum Found. Served to 1st lt. USMCR, 1943-45. Research fellow Am. Seed Trade Assn., 1947; research grantee Purdue U., 1947; named Distinguished Student, Purdue U., 1947. Mem. A.A.A.S., N.Y. Acad. Scis., Am. Soc. Agronomy, Am. Legion, Ceres, Sigma Xi, Alpha Zeta. Methodist (steward). Author: Culture of Sesame, 1954; also articles, bulls. Address: 530 Park Lane Richardson TX 75080

COLMERY, BENJAMIN HERRING, govt. ofcl.; b. Mobile, Mar. 10, 1921; s. Benjamin Herring and Bess Birdsong (White) C.; B.S. with distinction, U.S. Naval Acad., 1943; M.S., Ohio State U., 1951; M.E., U. Cal. at Los Angeles, 1959; children—Benjamin Herring III, Aimee P., Wesley B.; m. Frances Barber Sullivan, Aug. 16, 1970. Commd. ensign USN, 1943, advanced through grades to lt. comdr., 1954; destroyer navigator, naval aviator, nuclear weapons specialist; resigned, 1955; proposal coordinator, research supr., program mgr. N.Am. Aviation, 1955-59; mgr. nuclear dept. Bendix Systems div., Ann Arbor, Mich., 1959-63; dir. research Indsl. Nucleonics, Columbus, O., 1963-64; br. head nuclear rocket systems Lewis Research Center, NASA, Cleve., 1964-66; marketing mgr. Brown Engring. Co., Huntsville, Ala., 1966-68; br. head, asst. div. dir. logistics mgmt. Naval Air Systems Command, Washington, 1969—. Recipient Outstanding Performance award Naval Air Systems Command, 1972. Mem. Soc. Logistics Engrs. Club: Army-Navy Country (Arlington, Va.). Author, patentee in field. Introduced use radioactive gold seeds for cancer therapy; mgr. 1st organic moderated nuclear reactor program. Home: 6640 Midhill Pl Falls Church VA 22043 Office: Code 401A Naval Air Systems Command Navy Dept Washington DC

COLON, ANGEL ALBERTO, educator; b. Rio Piedras, P.R., Nov. 5, 1915; s. Isidoro A. and Josefina (Olivieri) C.; B.S., La. State U., 1937, M.S., 1939; D.Sc., Carnegie Inst. Tech., 1943; M.D., U. Madrid (Spain), 1962; m. Madeline Terry, Sept. 15, 1938; children—Madeline L., David A. Instr. chemistry U. Rio Pedras, 1937-39, asst. prof., 1939-43, asso. prof., 1943-46, prof. chemistry, 1946; asst. prof. medicine in charge biochem. research Med. Sch., Hato Rey, P.R., 1963-67, asst. clin. prof. medicine, 1967-71, prof. medicine, 1971—; research chemist Merck & Co., Rahway, N.J., 1946-50; supr. research Econ. Devel. Adminstrn., Hato Rey, 1950-56, asst. dir. research, 1951-58; dir Inst. Health Labs., Dept. Health P.R., Hato Rey, 1967—; asst. sec. for environmental health and consumer protection Dept. Health P.R., 1969-71; dean student affairs U. P.R. Med. Scis. Campus, 1971—; clin. pathologist P.R. Cancer Hosp., Rio Piedras, 1967—. Exec. sec. Gov.'s Com. on Pollution; mem. Adv. Council on Air Pollution Control; mem. P.R. Environmental Quality Bd., 1972—. Fellow Am. Heart Assn., Am. Inst. Chemists, A.A.A.S.; mem. Colegio Quimicos de P.R. (pres. 1953-65), Am. Chem. Soc. (local chpt. pres. 1954), P.R. Med. Assn., Am. Pub. Health Assn., Asociacion de Salud Publica de P.R., Academia Puertorriquena de Artes y Ciencias, Assn. Food and Drug Ofcls. U.S., Sigma Xi, Alpha Chi Sigma, Phi Lambda Upsilon, Phi Kappa Phi. Rotarian (pres. 1945). Roman Catholic. Home: 1817 Miosotis St Rio Piedras PR 00927 Office: GPO Box 5067 San Juan PR 00936

COLON, RAMERY LUIS E., lawyer; b. Ponce, P.R., Aug. 5, 1943; s. Gustavo Colon Aluztiza and Araceli Colon Ramery; B.A., Cath. U., 1965, LL.B., 1968; m. Teresita Guillemard, Dec. 22, 1967; children—Teresita Maria Colon, Anna Maria Colon. Admitted to P.R. bar; legal cons. P.R. Urban Renewal and Housing Adminstrn., San Juan, 1968-69; legal counsel in charge fed. housing programs P.R. Urban Renewal and Housing Corp., San Juan, 1969-71; asso. counsel law firm Blanco Lugo, Martinez Munoz, Moran and Lavastida, Santurce, P.R., 1971—; sec. Noloc, Inc., Ponce, 1973. Vice pres. student council Cath. U. P.R. Mem. P.R., Am. bar assns., Phi Eta Mu (sec. 1961-63, v.p. 1964-65). Lion (sec. 1974). Home: 108 Akron Collegeville Devel San Juan PR 00916 Office: 1252 Ponce de Leon Av Santurce PR 00910

COLONEY, WAYNE HERNDON, civil engr.; b. Bradenton, Fla., Mar. 15, 1925; s. Herndon Percival and Mary Adore (Cramer) C.; B.C.E. summa cum laude, Ga. Inst. Tech., 1950; m. Anne Elizabeth Benedict, June 21, 1950; 1 dau., Mary Adore. Project engr. Fla. Rd. Dept., Tallahassee, 1950-55; hwy. engr. Gibbs & Hill, Inc., Guatemala, 1955-57, project engr., Tampa, Fla., 1957-59; prject engr. J.E. Greiner Co., Tampa, 1959-62, asso., 1962-63; partner Barrett, Daffin & Coloney, Tallahassee, 1963-70; pres. Wayne H. Coloney Co., Inc., Tallahassee, 1970—. Dir. Internat. Enterprises, Inc. Pres. United Fund of Leon County, 1971-72; chmn. adv. com. Area Vocational Tech. Sch., 1965—. Bd. dirs. Springtime Tallahassee, 1970-72, Heritage Found., 1967. Served with AUS, 1943-46. Registered profl. engr. and land surveyor, Fla., Ga., N.C., Nat. Council Engring. Examiners. Fellow Am. Soc. C.E.; mem. Nat. Soc. Profl. Engrs., Fla. Engring. Soc. (sr.), Am. Water Works Assn., Fla. Inst. Cons. Engrs., Fla. Soc. Profl. Land Surveyors, C. of C., Anak, Koseme Soc., Phi Kappa Phi, Omicron Delta Kappa, Sigma Alha Epsilon, Tau Beta Pi. Episcopalian. Club: Metropolitan Dinner (dir.). Contbr. articles to profl. jours. Patentee in field. Home: Argyle House 2540 Marston Rd Tallahassee FL 32303 Office: PO Drawer 3966 Tallahassee FL 32303

COLQUITT, JOHN ORVILLE, JR., beverage co. exec.; b. Macon, Ga., June 11, 1923; s. John Orville and Isabel Harris (Denham) C.; A.A., Wentworth Mil. Acad., 1941; student W. Tex. State Coll., 1941, U. Tex., 1941-42; m. Margaret Jane Jones, Oct. 18, 1944; children—R. Jeff, John Orville 3d, James M. With Dalhart Coca-Cola Bottling Co. (Tex.), 1947—, pres., 1969—; dir. First Nat. Bank, Dalhart. Mem. Dalhart Ind. Sch. Dist., 1963-69, pres., 1967-69; mem. Dalhart City Council, 1971—; mayor pro-tem of Dalhart, 1972, mayor, 1973; chmn. Panhandle Regional Planning Commn., 1973. Trustee Coon Meml. Hosp., Dalhart. Served to 1st lt. USAAF, 1942-45. Recipient Most Outstanding Citizen award Dallam-Hartley County C. of C., 1958, Man With A Heart award Community Services Bur., 1958, Silver Beaver award Llano Estacado council Boy Scouts Am., 1964. Mem. Tex. Municipal League (dist. pres. 1973). Methodist (chmn. ofcl. bd. 1972). Mason (32 deg., Shriner). Home: 1717 Denrock St Dalhart TX 79022 Office: 819 Chicago St Dalhart TX 79022

COLQUITT, WALTER TERRY, ins. agy. exec.; b. Atlanta, July 11, 1915; s. Walter Terry (dec.) and Julia Elizabeth (Dunning) C.; student Ga. Inst. Tech., 1934-35, Va. Mil. Inst., 1936-37; m. Jean L. Cissel, Feb. 19, 1966; children—Gilbert Fuller, Susan Lynne (Mrs. Glenn Hogeland). Pres. Colquitt & Martin Ins., Miami, Fla., 1945-49, B & C Recording, Inc., N.Y.C., 1953-62, Time & Tide, Inc., Boca Raton, Fla., 1963-68, Gen. Ins. Agy., Boca Raton, Inc., Boca Raton, 1968—. Bd. dirs. YMCA, Atlanta, 1950. Served to lt. USCG, 1942-45. Clubs: Cruising of America (commodore 1966-67); Bankers (Boca Raton, Fla.). Home: 300 E Royal Palm Rd Boca Raton FL 33432 Office: 855 S Federal Hwy Boca Raton FL 33432

COLSKY, JACOB, physician; b. Memphis, Dec. 5, 1921; s. Abraham Samuel and Jennie (Shefsky) C.; student Memphis State Coll., 1938-40; M.D., U. Tenn., 1944; m. Irene Vivian Belen, July 26, 1953; children—Liane Caryl, Arthur Spencer, Andrew Evan. Intern, Jackson Meml. Hosp., Miami, Fla., 1944-45; fellow dept. preventive medicine Johns Hopkins Med. Sch., 1947-50, instr. dept. preventive medicine, 1950-51; asst. chief clin. research unit Nat. Cancer Inst., Balt., 1951-52; asst. physician, out-patients Johns Hopkins Hosp., 1947-52; asso. dir. medicine Maimonides Hosp., Bklyn., 1952-57; asso. attending physician Kings County Hosp. Med. Center, 1955-57; instr. medicine State U. N.Y. Coll. Medicine, N.Y.C., 1952-54, asst. prof. medicine, 1954-55, asso. prof. 1955-57; pvt. practice medicine, specializing in internal medicine and med. oncology, Miami, Fla., 1957—; mem. staffs Cedars of Lebanon, Jackson Meml. hosps., Miami; cons. Bapt., Mount Sinai, VA hosps., Miami; asso. prof. medicine U. Miami Sch. Medicine, 1957—; dir. med. oncology sect. dept. medicine U. Miami and Jackson Meml. Hosp., 1960-70; chief med. oncology sect. Cedars Lebanon Hosp., 1972—; sr. investigator Eastern Coop. Oncology Group, 1960—, mem. exec. com. 1971—; pres. Med. Oncology and Chemotherapy Found. Miami, Inc., 1970-73. Bd. dirs. Papanicolaou Cancer Research Inst., 1969—. Served to capt. M.C., AUS, 1945-47. Diplomate Am. Bd. Internal Medicine with subsplty. in med. oncology. Fellow Bklyn. Soc. Internal Medicine, N.Y. Acad. Medicine, A.C.P.; mem. N.Y. Acad. Sci., A.A.A.S., Am. Fedn. Clin. Research, Am. Assn. Cancer Research, Am. Geriatrics Soc., Leukemia Soc. (state bd. dirs. 1970—), Am. Cancer Soc. (county bd. dirs. 1968-71), Fla. Med. Soc. (vol. health agy. com. 1971—), Am. Soc. Clin. Oncology (founding mem.). Contbr. numerous articles to profl. jours. Home: 8220 S W 52d Av Miami FL 33143 Office: 1150 NW 14th St Miami FL 33136

COLSON, BILLY EDMON, civil engr.; b. Tennille, Ga., May 19, 1938; s. Thomas Jefferson and Lona Oceile (Stewart) C.; A.A., Young Harris Coll., 1958; B.S. in C.E., Ga. Inst. Tech., 1963; m. Linda Patricia Smith, Apr. 27, 1963; children—Cynthia Ellen, Jennifer Anne. Hydrological engr. U.S. Geol. Survey, Atlanta, 1962-64, Charleston, W.Va., 1968-71, hydrologist, Jackson, Miss., 1971—; tech. adviser U.S. AID, Kano, Nigeria, 1964-68. Registered profl. engr., W.Va., Miss. Mem. Am. Soc. C.E., Miss. Engring. Soc. Author: Water Resources of the Yobe River Basin, 1969; Efficiency of Earthen Spur Dikes, 1973; Excavations Beneath Bridges, 1973. Home: 101 Old Canton Hill Dr Jackson MS 39211 Office: 430 Bounds St Jackson MS 39206

COLTHARP, LELAND HOMER, JR., lawyer; b. Maringouin, La., Mar. 8, 1926; s. Leland Homer and Una Mae (Lefeaux) C.; student McNeese State Coll., 1946-47; LL.B., La. State U., 1950; m. Barbara Anne Bennett, Aug. 16, 1947; children—Karen L., Debra J., Pamela A. Admitted to La. bar, 1950; practice law, La., 1950-51; asst. U.S. atty. Western Dist. La., 1951-53; partner LeCompte, Hall & Coltharp, DeRidder, La., 1953-60, Hall & Coltharp, DeRidder, 1960—; asst. dist. atty. 30th Dist. of La., 1955-64; city atty. City of DeRidder, 1960-70; gen. counsel So. Casualty Ins. Co. Mem. Beauregard Parish Pub. Library, 1964—, pres., 1968—; mem. Library Devel. Com. La., 1968—, chmn., 1970-73; mem. La. State Adv. Council on Libraries, 1971—. Trustee Beauregard Meml. Bapt. Hosp., 1954-66, chmn. bd., 1958-59. Served with USNR, 1944-46. Recipient Modisette award, 1972. Mem. Am., La. bar assns., S.W. La. Def. Counsel Assn. (pres. 1967-68), Am. (intellectual freedom com.), La. library assns. Methodist (trustee). Club: Lions (DeRidder). Home: 605 S Division St DeRidder LA 70634 Office: 205 W 2d St DeRidder LA 70634

COLTMAN, CHARLES ARTHUR, JR., physician; b. Pitts., Nov. 7, 1930; s. Charles Arthur and Sara Margaret (Carman) C.; student Bethany Coll., 1948-51; B.S., U. Pitts., 1952, M.D., 1956; M.S., Ohio State U., 1963. Intern, Del. Hosp., Wilmington, 1956-57, resident pathology, 1957; jr. asst. resident, asst. in medicine Ohio State U. Hosp., 1959-60; sr. asst. resident hematology, asst. instr. medicine, 1961-62, chief med. resident, demonstrator in medicine, 1962-63, attending physician, instr. medicine, 1963; clin. asso. prof. medicine U. Tex., Tex. Health Sci. Center, San Antonio, 1970—; commd. capt. USAF, 1957, advanced through grades to col., 1971; flight surgeon Walker AFB, N.M., 1957-59; staff hematologist Wilford Hall USAF Med. Center, 1963-66; mil. cons. Surgeon Gen., USAF, 1964—; chief hematology-oncology service Wilford Hall USAF Med. Center, 1966—. Bd. dirs. Am. Cancer Soc. Bexar County, Tex. div. Am. Cancer Soc. Recipient Moseby Book Co. Pub. Scholarship award, 1955, 56. Meml. prize U. Pitts. Sch. Medicine, 1956; Heard Sr. prize U. Pitts. Sch. Medicine, 1956; Mederi award Aerospace Med. Div., 1969; Harold Brown award USAF, 1971. Diplomate Am. Bd. Internal Medicine, Subsplty. Bds. Hematology, Oncology. Fellow A.C.P.; mem. Am. Fedn. Clin. Research, Am. Soc. Hematology, Am. Assn. Cancer Research, Am. Soc. Clin. Oncology, Soc. Air Force Physicians, Assn. Mil. Surgeons (Stitt award 1970), A.M.A., A.A.A.S., Central Soc. Clin. Research, San Antonio Research Club (pres. 1966). Home: 10411 Moonglow St San Antonio TX 78236 Office: Hematology-Oncology Service Wilford Hall USAF Med Center Lackland AFB TX 78236

COLVIN, (OTIS) HERBERT, JR., educator; b. El Dorado, Ark., Mar. 18, 1923; s. Otis Herbert and Irene (Hammons) C.; B.A., Baylor U., 1944, M.B., 1948; Mus.M., U. Colo., 1950; Ph.D., U. Rochester (N.Y.), 1957; m. Mary Ila Ullom, June 18, 1948; children—Carol Kay (Mrs. James Lee Smith), Mary Edith, Susan Elizabeth. Instr. music

Tex. Technol. Coll., 1950-55; chmn. piano dept. Baylor U., Waco, Tex., 1957-62, chmn. dept. theory and composition, 1962—; teaching asst. Eastman Sch. Music, Rochester, 1955-57. Served USNR, 1944-46; PTO. Mem. Music Tchrs. Nat. Assn., Am. Guild Organists (dean Waco chpt. 1958-60), Phi Mu Alpha. Baptist. Mason (32 deg.). Editor choral compositions. Composer: Organ Voluntaries Based on Early American Hymn Tunes, Short Pieces Organ, For Sunday (6 organ pieces based on modal melodies). Editor choral compositions. Contbr. to profl. publs. Home: 9121 Pin Oak Dr Waco TX 76710

COLWELL, GENE THOMAS, educator; b. Chattanooga, Aug. 3, 1937; s. William Clarence and Mary Virginia (Smith) C.; B.S., U. Tenn., 1959, M.S., 1962, Ph.D., 1966; m. Peggy Ann Fletcher, June 1, 1973. Research engr. Oak Ridge Nat. Lab., 1959-62, design specialist, 1965-66; instr. U. Tenn., Knoxville, 1962-65; asst. prof. Sch. Mech. Engring. Ga. Inst. Tech., Atlanta, 1966-71, asso. prof., 1971—. Postgrad. prof. U. Carabobo, Valencia, Venezuela, 1971; cons. various indsl., govt. orgns. Registered profl. engr., Ga. Mem. Am. Soc. M.E., Sigma Xi, Pi Tau Sigma. Contbr. articles to profl. jours. Patentee gas turbine engine, 1973. Home: 1420-A Post Oak Dr Clarkston GA 30021 Office: Sch Mech Engring Ga Inst Tech Atlanta GA 30332

COMBS, AUSTIN OLIN, real estate and ins. broker; b. Harr, Tenn., Aug. 5, 1917; s. Clyde Harmon and Bess (Widner) C.; student Stetson Bus. Coll.; m. Marjorie Thayer Mason, Dec. 28, 1947; 1 dau. by previous marriage, Hope; 1 dau., Carolyn; adopted children—Dianne, Marjorie, Dunnan Dowling III. Vice pres. Kipp & Combs, Inc., 1952-54; partner Combs-Sibley, 1954; pres. Austin O. Combs, Inc., Daytona Beach, Fla., 1954—; airplane pilot. Mem. Air Def. Command, Air Res. Adv. Bd., 1946-47. Trustee Volusia County Heart Assn., 1955-56, pres., 1965; trustee, chmn. bd. visitors Embry-Riddle Aero. U.; bd. dirs. YMCA; bd. dirs., pres. Fla. Internat. Festival Com. Served with USAAF, 1944-46. Mem. Flying Realtors, Fla. Aero Club, Aircraft Owners and Pilots Assn., Daytona Beach C. of C., Tomoka Gems and Minerals Soc. (past pres.), Internat. Platform Assn., Quiet Birdmen. Mason (Shriner, Jester). Elk, Moose. Clubs: Elinor Village Country (past pres., dir.), Daytona Beach Yacht, (Daytona Beach); Miami Springs Executive, Oceanside Country. Home: 3756 Cardinal Blvd Daytona Beach FL 32019 Office: 2008 S Atlantic Av Daytona Beach FL 32018

COMBS, BENNETT ALBERT, advt. exec., bus. film producer; b. Oklahoma City, Apr. 1, 1941; s. William Grady and Ina (Shultz) C.; B.A., U. Ark., 1964; postgrad. Columbia, 1964-65, sch. Marketing U. Colo. Nat. field rep. Am. Cancer Soc., N.Y.C., 1964-66; promotion dir. KTHV, Little Rock, 1966-67; pub. affairs dir. KATV, Little Rock, 1967-69; pub. relations dir., editor Briggs Assos., Little Rock, 1969; v.p., creative dir. Carroll & Assos., Little Rock, 1970-72; v.p. McCarty-Phelps, Inc., 1972—. Pub. relations bd. Am. Cancer Soc., 1967-68. Mem. Ark. Advt. Fedn., Sales and Marketing Execs., Pub. Relations Soc. Am. Home: 47 Scenic Blvd Little Rock AR 72207 Office: Commerical Bank Bldg Little Rock AR 72201

COMBS, CLARENCE H., dentist; b. Beattyville, Ky., Mar. 10, 1919; s. Joseph Oscar and Maude M. (Congleton) C.; tchrs. certificate, Eastern Ky. State Coll., 1941; B.S., U. Ky., 1947; D.M.D., U. Louisville, 1951; m. Maxine Land, Feb. 29, 1964; children—Clarence H., Gene Alan, Brian Keith. Gen. practice dentistry, Beattyville, Ky., 1951—; pub. health dentist Lee County Pub. Healty Dept., part-time 1951—. Mem. Lee County Bd. Health, 19——. Scoutmaster Eastern Tng. Sch. br. Richmond (Ky.) council Boy Scouts Am., 1941-42. Served with USNR, 1943-45. Decorated Purple Heart. Mem. Blue Grass Dental Soc. (pres. 1970-71), Am. Legion, Psi Omega. Democrat. Mem. Christian Ch. Kiwanian. Address: Box 387 Beattyville KY 41311

COMBS, JOSEPH FRANKLIN, author, columnist; b. Center, Tex., Nov. 23, 1892; s. Frank and Annie Mae (Beck) C.; student Tex. A. and M. Coll., 1917; m. Addie Laura Brittain, Sept. 8, 1912; children—Talmage Franklin, Doris Addie Mae (Mrs. Aubrey Bedford), Thomas Buchanan, Jo Ruth (Mrs. Travis Price). Rural sch. tchr. Shelby County, Tex., 1910-17; agrl. agt. Tex. A. and M. Coll. Extension Service, Montgomery County, Tex., 1917-27; county agrl. agt., Beaumont, Tex., 1927-55; farm editor Beaumont Enterprise, 1955-58; farm columnist Beaumont Enterprise, 1958—. Adminstr., New Deal Agrl. Acts, Jefferson County, Tex., 1933-38; operator German Prisoner of War Farm Labor Camp, Jefferson County, 1944-45; pres. Montgomery County Fair, 1923-27. Bd. dirs. Houston Fair and Exposition, 1923. Bd. dirs. Camp Fire Girls. Served with Tex. State Guard, 1941-47; mem. Res. Mem. Am. Mus. Natural History, Smithsonian Assos., Tex. Guard Assn., Coastal Cattleman's Assn. (sec. Jefferson County 1934-54), Tex. and Southwestern Cattle Raisers Assn. (dir. Ft. Worth 1948-55), C. of C. Baptist. Mason. Author: Growing Pastures In The South, 1936; Farm Corner, Nature Stories, 1963; Legends of the Pineys, 1965; Gunsmoke in the Redlands, 1968; Kudjo Quatterman, 1972. Discoverer grass species. Home: 5635 Duff Av Beaumont TX 77706

COMBS, PAUL NAPIER, charitable soc. exec.; b. Hazard, Ky., Jan. 5, 1919; s. Emanuel and Mollie (Napier) C.; student Hazard Jr. C. Coll., 1936-37, Georgetown Coll., 1939-40; A.B., U. Ky., 1947; m. Lottie Louise Herald, Apr. 8, 1951; children—Nancy, Rebecca. Writer, Ky. Hwy. Dept., Frankfort, 1947; promotion mgr., news dir. Radio Station WKIC, Hazard, 1948-49; news editor Hazard Herald, 1949; dep. commr. Dept. Indsl. Relations, Commonwealth of Ky., 1950-53, acting commr., 1953-55, dep. commr., 1955-56; field rep. Ky. Soc. for Crippled Children, Louisville, 1956-57, pub. relations dir., 1957—. Mem. Ky. Ho. of Reps., 1950. Served with Armed Forces, 1942-45. Mem. Pub. Relations Soc. Am., Ky. Press Assn., Nat. Easter Seal Exec. Assn., Combs Family Assn. (dir. 1963—), U. Ky. Alumni Assn., Advt. Club of Louisville. Democrat. Presbyn. Mason. Home: 9510 Aylesbury Dr Louisville KY 40222 Office: 233 E Broadway Louisville KY 40202

COMBS, ROBERT HEARIN, utilities exec.; b. El Dorado, Ark., Feb. 11, 1923; s. John Hearin and Estelle (Hammons) C.; student U. Ark., 1940-43, 47, U. Okla., 1958, Okla. State U., 1959, U. Tex., 1961; m. Toni Louise Rogers, June 12, 1945; children—Gary L., William Bryce. Sales mgr. Ark.-La. Gas Co., 1947-56; dist. sales mgr. Okla. Natural Gas Co., Tulsa, 1956-63; dir. sales, promotion Am. Gas Assn., N.Y.C., 1963-65; v.p. marketing Western Ky. Gas Co., Owensboro, 1965—. Pres. Audubon council Boy Scouts Am., 1969-71, mem. Region II exec. bd. Bd. dirs., trustee Ky. Ind. Coll. Found.; bd. dirs. Owensboro United Fund. Served to maj. USAF, 1943-47, 51-52. Recipient Gas Industries Hall of Flame award, 1959, Silver Beaver award Boy Scouts Am., 1971; named Boss of Year, Am. Bus. Womens Assn., 1968. Mem. Tulsa Exec. Assn. (past pres.), Am., So. (sect. chmn.), Ky. (past pres.) gas assns., Sales and Marketing Exec. Internat., Tulsa (life), Ky. (dir., pres. elect), Owensboro chambers commerce. Baptist. Mason (32 deg., Shriner), Rotarian, Kiwanian (past pres.). Home: 2169 N Stratford Dr Owensboro KY 42301 Office: 311 W 7th St Owensboro KY 42301

COMER, DONALD, JR., textile mill exec.; b. Birmingham, Ala., May 18, 1913; s. Donald and Gertrude (Miller) C.; grad. U. N.C.; m. Isabel Anderson, Oct. 29, 1936; children—Donald, Isabel Anderson. With Avondale Textile Mills, Sylacauga, Ala., 1932—, exec. v.p. textiles, 1954-70, pres., treas., 1970—, also mem. exec. com., dir.; with Cowikee Mills, Eufaula, Ala., 1943—, pres., treas., 1956-67, chmn. bd., 1967—; dir. First Nat. Bank Birmingham, First Fed. Savs. and Loan Assn., Sylacauga, Home Fed. Savs. & Loan, Birmingham, Am. Mut. Liability Ins. Co., Boston; mem. exec. com. Chem. Bank N.Y. Trust Co. Bd. dirs. Ala. Aero. Bd.; trustee So. Research Inst., Birmingham, Birmingham Symphony Assn.; pres. bd. trustees Choccolocco council Boy Scouts Am.; bd. govs. Ala. Assn. Ind. Colls. and Univs.; trustee Cowikee Edn. and Charitable Found., Avondale Ednl. and Charitable Found. Mem. Am. Textile Mfrs. Inst. (dir., pres. 1973-74), Nat. Assn. Mfrs. (dir.), So. Indsl. Relations Conf. (dir.), Asso. Industries Ala. (dir.), Ala. Textile Mfrs. Assn., Newcomen Soc., Phi Psi. Methodist. Clubs: Birmingham Country, Downtown, Mountain Brook Country Relay, The Club (Birmingham); Coose Valley Country (Sylacauqa, Ala.); Union League, Weavers (N.Y.C.); Boca Grande Yacht (Fla.). Home: Comer Hill Sylacauga AL 35150 Office: Avondale Av Sylacauga AL 35150

COMER, DONALD, III, textile products co. exec.; b. N.Y.C., June 23, 1938; s. Donald and Isabel (Anderson) C.; B.S., U. Ala., 1962; m. Jane Stephens Comer, May 4, 1962; children—Jason Legare, Luke MacDonald, Carrie St. George. With Cowikee Mills, Eufaula, Ala., 1962—, plant mgr., 1965-66, v.p., 1966-68, pres., treas., dir. 1968—. Dir. 1st Nat. Bank, Eufaula, Allied Sports Co., Eufaula; adv. dir. Southeast div. Am. Mut. Ins. Cos., Boston. Dir. Ala. Safety Council, Eufaula Heritage Assn., Ala. Ethics Commn. Dir. Ala./Fla. Council Boy Scouts Am., 1972-73. Bd. dirs. Cowikee Trust, Eufaula, trustee; bd. dirs. E.T. Comer Trust, Catherine Corner Sch. Trust. Served with USAF, 1961-64. Named Boss of Year Jr. C. of C., 1972; Citizen of Year Kiwanis, 1966. Mem. Ala. Textile Mfrs. Assn. (pres., dir. 1967-73). Clubs: Country (Eufaula, Ala.); Mountain Brook Country (Birmingham). Home: St Francis Point Eufaula AL 36027 Office: 117 Front St Eufaula AL 36027

COMM, EDWARD DANIEL, mgmt. and civil engring. cons.; b. Fargo, N.D., Jan. 10, 1912; s. Otto Ben and Emily (Riebhoff) C.; B.S., N.D. State U., 1933; grad. U.S. Army War Coll., 1953. Practice civil engring., N.D., 1933-40; commd. 1st lt. C.E., U.S. Army, 1940, advanced through grades to col., 1944, ret., 1967; served N. Africa, Italy, France, Germany, 1942-45; exec. asst. to Q.M. Gen. and dir. logistics, Washington, 1946-52; asst. chief of staff logistics, France, 1953-56; engr. U.S. Army Engr. Dist., Louisville, 1956-58; mem. Joint Chiefs Staff, Washington, 1958-60; comdg. officer Advanced Individual Tng. Regiment, Ft. Leonard Wood, Mo., 1960-62; spl. asst. to dep. chief staff for logistics Dept. Army, Washington, 1962-67; dir. Washington operations Howard Needles Tammen & Bergendoff, cons. Engrs., 1968—; cons. to Dept. Def., Washington, 1967-69. Mem. directorate Presdl. Task Force on Structure SSS, 1967. Decorated D.S.M., Legion of Merit with two oak leaf clusters, Bronze Star, Army Commendation medal, officer Order Brit. Empire; Legion of Honor, Croix de Guerre (France) comdr. Crown of Italy Medahla de Guerra (Brazil). Fellow Am. Soc. C.E.; mem. Soc. Am. Mil Engrs., Amateur Trapshooting Assn., Phi Kappa Phi, Tau Beta Pi. Clubs: Army and Navy (Washington); Army-Navy Country (Arlington, Va.). Address: 1111 Army Navy Dr Arlington VA 22202

COMOLA, JAMES PAUL, govt. ofcl.; b. Leland, Miss., Nov. 16, 1931; s. Wilson and Freda (Saba) C.; student Hinds Jr. Coll., 1950; B.A., Millsaps Coll., 1957; profl. social worker Fla. State U., 1958; postgrad. U. Miss., 1959-62; m. Mary Jacqueline Petermann, May 27, 1956; children—James Paul, Jon Ronald. Asst. buyer Kennington's, 1954-57; dir. Miss. Dept. Pub. Welfare, Yazoo County, 1957-59; tech. liasion Commn. Small Watersheds, U.S. Ho. of Reps., 1959-60; exec. v.p. Miss. Rivers and Harbors Assn., 1960-62; asst. gen. mgr. Trinity Improvement Assn., Arlington, Tex., 1962-66, gen. mgr., 1967-70; now asst. regional adminstr. Environmental Protection Agy., Dallas; cons., 1970—. Mem. Bedford City Council, Tex., 1963-65, chmn. mid-cities adv. council, 1963-66. Served with USNR, 1950-54. Recipient award Rivers and Harbors Assn. Miss., 1962; Appreciation award Bedford Council Good Govt., Bedford, 1966. Mem. Miss. Valley Assn. (dir.), Tex. Water Conservation Assn., Nat. Rivers and Harbors Congress (dir.), Nat. Waterways Conf., Water Resources Asso., Internat. Navigational Congress, Gulf Intracoastal Canal Assn. Lion (dir. Bedford), Editor Trinity Valley Progress, 1963-67. Contbr. articles to profl. jours. Home: 1301 Cliffwood Rd Euless TX 76039 Office: 1600 Patterson St Dallas TX 75201

COMPTON, DEWEY PRESTON, television host; b. New Salem, Tex., Nov. 12, 1926; s. Fred Ray and Elizabeth Victoria (Hodges) C.; B.S., Tex. A. and M. U., 1949; m. Curtis Lee Perry, July 19, 1947; children—Ronnie, Kerry, Cathy Ann. Asst. county agt., Carthage, Tex., 1949-51; county agt. Tex. Extension Service, Cuero, 1951-53; agrl. bus. dir. radio sta. KTRH, Houston, 1953—, host farm show KTRK-TV, 1956—. Bd. dirs. Houston Livestock Show. Served with AUS, 1944-47. Recipient Tex. 4-H Alumni award, 1958, Am. Farm Bur. award, 1958, Tex. Forestry award, 1959, Vocational Agr. Tchr.'s Distinguished award, 1972, Houston Hadassah award, 1973. State Farmer award, 1959, Shrine Circus award, 1972, Billy Goldberg award, 1973. Mem. Nat. Assn. Farm Burs., Nat. Agrl. and Marketing Assn., Houston Farm and Ranch Club. Mem. Ch. of Christ (deacon). Pub. Gulf Coast Gardener, 1961, Southwest Gardener, 1967, Early Morning Dew Drops, Vols. I and II, 1967-68. Editor: Dewey Compton's Gardening Newsletter, 1971—, Old Dew's Gardening Almanac, 1972—. Home: 2222 Brooktree St Houston TX 77008 Office: 510 Lovett Blvd Houston TX 77005

COMPTON, HENRY TAYLOE, JR., savs. and loan assn. exec.; b. Savannah, Ga., June 5, 1925; s. Henry Tayloe and Sarah Millward (Walthour) C.; B.S. in Commerce, U. N.C., 1948; divorced; children—Randall Adams, Cameron Walthour, Tayloe Bond. Staff accountant D.F. Stewart, C.P.A., Savannah, 1948-51; partner William Lattimore, realtor, Savannah, 1951-66; with First Fed. Savs. & Loan Assn., Savannah, 1966—, mgr. data processing, 1967—, v.p., 1972—. Served with USNR, 1943-46. Mem. Data Processing Mgmt. Assn., Controllers Soc. Savs. Instns. (chmn. off-line computer com. 1972, chmn. regional conf. 1974), Soc. Colonial Wars (registrar Ga. 1972—). Clubs: Oglethorpe, Cotillion, Century, Exchange (dir. 1972-73) (Savannah). Home: Star Route Box 50R Bluffton SC 29910 Office: PO Box 8206 Savannah GA 31402

COMPTON, JOSEPH OTTO, city ofcl.; b. Bowling Green, Ky., Dec. 3, 1921; s. Joseph Otto and Marjory Cora (Pierce) C.; student U. Fla., 1940-43, Ga. Inst. Tech., 1943; m. Eleanor Opal Henderson, May 22, 1943; children—Joseph Otto III, Michael, Harold, Marjory (Mrs. Conan R. Martin), Victoria (Mrs. Dennis Fountain). Joined USMC, 1942, advanced to maj., 1954, ret., 1964; with City of Winter Park, Fla., 1964—, dir. pub. works, 1973—. Mem. Am. Soc. C.E., Am. Pub. Works Assn., Inst. for Transp., Inst. for Solid Wastes. Home: 6615 Beamer Way Orlando FL 32807 Office: 401 Park Av S Winter Park FL 32789

COMPTON, ROBERT CURRAN, lawyer; b. El Dorado, Ark., Mar. 27, 1929; s. Thomas J. and Virginia (Knox) C.; B.A., Hendrix Coll., Conway, Ark., 1949; LL.B., U. Ark., 1952; m. Margaret Tyler Villee, Apr. 7, 1951; children—Robert Curran, Cathleen Villee, Walter Knox. Served with FBI, Washington and Pitts., 1952-54; admitted to Ark. bar, 1952; practiced in El Dorado, 1954—; partner Brown, Compton & Prewett and predecessors, 1957—. Chmn., Cancer Drive, 1956. Candidate for Gov. Ark., 1970. Bd. dirs. Salvation Army. Mem. Am., Ark. (mem. exec. com.), Union County (past pres.) bar assns., El Dorado C. of C., Am. Coll. Trial Lawyers, Blue Key, Kappa Sigma. Democrat. Presbyn. (trustee). Mason (Shriner), Rotarian. Club: El Dorado Golf and Country (past pres.). Home: 2504 Forestlawn Dr El Dorado AR 71730 Office: 423 N Washington St El Dorado AR 71730

COMPTON, SUSAN LANELL, librarian; b. Batesville, Ark., Aug. 20, 1917; d. Thomas Smith and Susan (Whitlow) Compton; B.S. in Edn., Ark. State Tchrs. Coll., 1939; B.S. in L.S., Peabody Coll. Tchrs., 1948. Asst. cataloger U. Ark. Gen. Library, Fayetteville, 1948-49; head catalog dept. Ark. Library Commn., Little Rock, 1949—. Free lance writer. Mem. Nat. League Am. Pen Women v.p., program chmn. Ark. Pioneer br. 1972-73, pres. 1974-75), UN Assn. (rec. sec. Ark. chpt.), Ark. Choral Soc., Am. Assn. U. Women, Ark. Hist. Assn., Ark. Fedn. Women's Clubs. Christadelphian. Author: Beauty Transient & Other Poems, 1969. Contbr. to Collier's Ency., 1971. Home: 4911 Lee Av Little Rock AR 72205 Office: 506 1/2 Center St Little Rock AR 72201

CONAWAY, PAUL MAGNUS, lawyer; b. Sylacauga, Ala., Oct. 16, 1903; s. Magnus Eli and Kitty (Jackson) C.; student U. Ala., 1919-20; B.S., Cumberland U., 1924; LL.B., Maynard Law Sch., 1931; postgrad. Mercer U., 1934, also Ohio State U.; m. Faye Overton, Dec. 24, 1928; children—Paula Faye, Lessie Elizabeth. Admitted to Ga. bar; practiced in Macon, 1932—; dir. pub. relations Ga. Dental Assn., 1938-54, after gen. counsel, 1954, then exec. dir., to 1972, exec. dir. emeritus, 1972—. Mem. Am., Ga., Macon bar assns., Omicron Kappa Upsilon. Presbyn. Author: Pipeline to the Clouds, 1954. Contbr. articles to profl. jours. Home: 231 Beverly Pl Macon GA 31204 Office: Suite 310 So United Bldg Macon GA 31201

CONCEPCION, CARLOS VICTOR, dentist; b. Santa Clara, Cuba, July 28, 1933; s. Jose M. De La and Maria Zoila (Garcia) C.; B.S., Instituto de Santa Clara, 1951; D.D.S., U. Havana, 1956; D.M.D., U. Pitts., 1967; postgrad. U. Miami, 1965; m. Teresita Machado Concepcion, Sept. 8, 1956; children—Carlos Francisco, Jorge Luis, Eduardo Gerardo. Came to U.S., 1962, naturalized, 1968. Dental student Municipal Pub. Health, Cuba, 1955-56; oral surgeon Santa Clara Clinic, 1956-62; dentist, oral surgeon Marta Abreu Central Clinic, 1956-62; individual practice dentistry, 1956-62; dental officer Avon Park Correctional Instn., Fla. Div. of Correction, 1967-68; individual practice dentistry, Miami, Fla., 1968—. Tech. instr. crown and bridge U. Havana, 1955-56. Mem. Cuban, Santa Clara, Am., Fla. dental assns., Cuban Soc. Dentistry for Children, Pan Am. Council Dentistry for Children, Pa. Acad. Gen. Dentistry, Cuban Dental Assn. in Exile, East Coast Dist. Dental Soc., Miami Dental Soc. Cuban Soc. Orthodontics, Cuban Soc. Oral Surgeons, Delta Sigma Delta. Episcopalian (sr. warden 1969—). Rotarian. Clubs: American (Miami), Miami Tennis. Home: 14401 Cedar Ct Miami Lakes FL 33014 Office: 705 Huntington Bldg 168 S E 1st St Miami FL 33131

CONCON, ARCHIMEDES ABAD, physician; b. San Fernando, La Union, Philippines, Jan. 30, 1929; s. Juan Sumabong and Rosario (Aquino Abad) C.; A.A., Silliman U., Dumaguete City, Philippines, 1948; M.D., U. Santo Tomas, Manila, 1953; m. Janis Marie Kothe, Dec. 20, 1967; children—Roswell Timothy, Darwin Finlay, Peter Anthony, Larissa Hayley, Paul Jonathan, Pamela Dawn, Sarah Susan. Intern Baptist Meml. Hosp., Memphis, 1954, resident, 1955-58; head sect. electrocardiography Philippine Nat. Rwys. Hosp., Caloocan City, 1960-68; asso. staff dept. internal Medicine Bapt. Meml. Hosp., Memphis, 1974—; jr. staff Doctors Hosp., Memphis, 1973—, Meth. Hosp., Memphis, 1973—; practice medicine specializing in internal medicine, Caloocan City, Philippines, 1960-68, Memphis, 1968—; mem. staffs Philippines Nat. Rwys. Hosp., Caloocan City, Baptist Meml., Meth., Doctors Hosps. (all Memphis). Recipient Physician's Recognition award A.M.A., 1972. Diplomate Faculty Hemeopathy (London, Eng.). Mem. Memphis, Shelby County med. socs., Tenn., Mid-South med. assns., A.M.A., Memphis Acad. Internal Medicine, Brit. Amateur Sci. Research Assn., Internat. Soc. for study L'Altra Medicina. Presbyn. Contbr. articles to profl. jours. Home: 5450 Flowering Peach Dr Memphis TN 38118 Office: 910 Madison Av Suite 828 Memphis TN 38103

CONDIE, JAMES MCMURRIN, statistician, data processor; b. Hailey, Ida., Aug. 20, 1930; s. Marion Asher and Lillie Alice (Ivie) C.; B.S., Utah State U., 1956, M.S., 1957; postgrad. Ia. State U., 1963-64; m. Marilyn Margaret Lincoln, May 27, 1954 (dec.); children—Elden James, Emily Lenore, John Matthew, Margaret (dec.); m. 2d, Geraldine Faye Olson, Oct. 19, 1962; children—Colleen Faye, Karyn Gay, Eric Andrew, Jamie Michelle, Julie Marie, Jeri Lynn. Agrl. statistician U.S. Dept. Agr., Boise, Ida., 1960-63, math. statistician, Washington, 1964-68; statistician, bd. govs. Fed. Reserve System, Washington, 1968—. Mem. faculty U.S. Dept. Agr. Grad. Sch., Washington, part time, 1967—. Missionary Ch. of Jesus Christ of Latter-day Saints, Berlin, Germany, 1950-53. Served with AUS, 1953-55. Home: 2216 Emporia St Woodbridge VA 22191 Office: Div Data Processing Bd Gov Fed Reserve System Washington DC 20551

CONDOM, JAIME ERNESTO, hosp. adminstr., physician; b. Mariel, Cuba, Feb. 27, 1932; s. Jaime Simeon and Maria Matilde (Valera) C.; B.S., U. Havana, 1957; M.D., U. Madrid, 1962; 1 dau., Marie Elizabeth. Came to U.S., 1960, naturalized, 1966. Intern, Mobile Gen. Hosp., 1962-63; staff physician Searcy State Hosp., Mt. Vernon, Ala., 1963-68, acting clin. dir., 1968-69, clin. dir., 1969-70, acting supt., clin. dir., 1970, supt., 1970—. Mem. Am. Assn. Med. Supts. Mental Hosps., Med. Assn. State Ala., Mobile County Med. Soc., Gulf Coast Soc. Neurology, Psychiatry, Neurosurgery and Psychology. Address: Searcy Hosp PO Box 23 Mount Vernon AL 36560

CONDON, CHARLES FRANCIS M(ICHAEL), psychologist; b. Quincy, Mass., Dec. 20, 1940; s. Charles Francis and Helen Anna (Wassell) C.; A.B., Boston Coll., 1962; M.S., Purdue U., 1964. Staff psychologist, electric boat div. Gen. Dynamics, Groton, Conn., 1965-67, head human factors sect., Quincy (Mass.) div., 1967-69; with Systems Operations Support, Inc., San Diego, 1969-72; sr. research scientist URS Matrix Co., Alexandria, Va., 1969-73, dir. 1973-74; sr. systems analyst Bradford Computer & Systems Co., Rockville, Md., 1974—. Mem. Nat. Mgmt. Assn., Nat. Speleological Soc., Am. Civil Liberties Union, Am. Psychol. Assn., Internat. Platform Assn., Am. Nat. Standards Inst., Human Factors Soc. (dir. New England chpt. 1968), Mensa (pres. D.C. chpt. 1972—). Home: 6100 Duke St Apt 205 Alexandria VA 22304 Office: 6001 Executive Blvd Rockville MD 20852

CONDRAY, BEN ROGERS, educator; b. Waco, Tex., July 4, 1925; s. Benjamin Sadler and Elise (Rogers) C.; student U. Chattanooga, 1942-44; B.S., Baylor U., 1948; M.S., Purdue U., 1950; Ph.D. (Bapt. Faculty fellow 1955-58; NSF Faculty fellow 1958), Baylor U., 1965; postgrad. Tex. A. & M., 1968; m. Mickey Ida Grady, Aug. 23, 1951; children—Suzanne E., Mary Catherine, Benjamin G. Mem. faculty East Tex. Bapt. Coll., Marshall, 1950—, asst. prof., 1950-55, asso. prof., 1958-65, prof. chemistry, chmn. dept., 1965—; instr. Baylor U., Waco, Tex., 1955-58. Active Boy Scouts Am., 1962—. Bd. dirs. Marshall (Tex.) Assn. Retarded Children, 1970—. Served with AUS,

1944-46. Mem. Am. Chem. Soc. (alternate councelor 1969-73), A.A.A.S., Sigma Xi, Alpha Chi. Baptist (deacon 1954—). Rotarian. Home: 2201 George Gregg St Marshall TX 75670

CONDRON, STEWART LEWIS, accountant; b. Elgin, Tex., Oct. 17, 1919; s. Harvey Elmo and Ruth (Carter) C.; B.S., Bowling Green Coll. Commerce, 1942; M.B.A., Harvard Bus. Sch., 1947; m. Helen Johnson, Sept. 24, 1943; 1 dau., Helen Ruth (Mrs. John M. Balentine, Jr.). With S.D. Leidesdorf & Co., C.P.A.'s, Greenville, S.C., 1947—, partner, 1958—. Adj. prof. bus. adminstrn. U. S.C., Columbia, 1972-73. Pres. United Fund Greenville County, 1961, Little Theatre, Greenville, S.C., 1962, 64. Chmn. Greenville County Found., 1967, Greenville Hosp. System, 1971. Served with USNR, 1942-46. Recipient Diamond Merit award Adminstrv. Mgmt. Soc., 1960; named Outstanding Boss Greenville Jr. C. of C., 1961. C.P.A., S.C., Tex., N.C., La. Mem. Greater Greenville C. of C. (dir. 1963-66), S.C. Assn. C.P.A.'s (pres. 1964), Am. Inst. C.P.A.'s (mem. council 1964). Kiwanian (pres. 1964). Clubs: Poinsett, Green Valley Country, Country (all Greenville, S.C.); Biltmore Forest Country (Asheville, N.C.). Home: 11 Indian Spring Greenville SC 29607 Office: 1814 Daniel Bldg Greenville SC 29602

CONDRY, CARSON EMMITT, mech. engr.; b. Liberal, Kan., July 12, 1923; s. Sterling H. and Gladys B. (Carson) C.; B.S., Kan. State U., 1948; m. Martha Elizabeth Baker, July 9, 1944. Prodn. draftsman, design engr., asst. chief engr. The J.B. Ehrsam & Son Mfg. Co., Enterprise, Kan., 1948-50; chief engr. Hamilton Constrn. Co., Salina, Kan., 1950-51; with A.J. Boynton & Co., of Texas, Dallas, 1951-66, successively draftsman, design engr., project engr., asst. chief engr., 1951-61, chief engr., 1961-66; v.p., dir. Zetterlund-Boynton-Condry & Assos., engrs. and tech. counselors, 1966-67; pres. Condry, Cayton, Burford & Assocs., cons. engrs., indsl. specialists, Dallas, 1967—. Served from pvt. 1st class to 1st lt. A.C., AUS, 1941-45; ETO. Decorated Air medal. Registered profl. engr., Tex., Okla., Kan. Mem. Am. Soc. M.E., Tex., Nat., Tex. socs. profl. engrs., Engrs., Alumni Assn. Kan. State U., Nat. Geog. Soc., Profl. Engrs. Soc., Cons. Engrs. in Pvt. Practice, Joint Engrs. Council, Greater Dallas Planning Council, Nat Wildlife Fedn. Home: 2216 Longwood Lane Dallas TX 75228 Office: 10901 Garland Rd Dallas TX 75218

CONE, A. CLYDE, JR., real estate broker; b. Mexia, Tex., July 24, 1923; s. A. Clyde and Ruby Maurine (Nettles) C.; student Tarleton Coll., 1941-42; m. Virginia Elizabeth Baker, Jan. 19, 1946; children—Adrian Christine (Mrs. Everett M. Crainer), Stephen Clyde, John Stanley, Matthew Robert. Mem. Carr-Stamps Quartet, 1937-40; with Dow Chem. Co., Freeport, Tex., 1946-66, purchasing buyer, 1960-66; owner, real estate broker Clyde Cone Co. Realtors, Clute, Tex., 1966—. Instr. real estate Brazosport Coll., Lake Jackson, Tex., 1973—. Served with USMC, 1943-46. Mem. Brazoria County Bd. Realtors (pres. 1969, 73), Brazosport C. of C. (dir. 1968-70), Soc. Preservation and Encouragement Barber Shop Quartet Singing Am. (pres. 1950). Mason. Home: 124 Red Bud St Lake Jackson TX 77566 Office: 1227 Hwy 332 Clute TX 77531

CONE, WICE EARL, state ofcl.; b. Montgomery, Ala., Feb. 8, 1925; s. Wice C. and Florence Inez (Farmer) C.; C.E., Internat. Corr. Schs., 1966; m. Hazel Padgett, Jan. 17, 1948; children—Carolyn Hazel, Nancy Ann. With Ala. Conservation Dept., 1946-48; with Ala. Hwy. Dept., 1948—, asst. secondary road engr., Montgomery, 1963—. Served with USNR, 1943-46. Mem. Nat. Soc. Profl. Engrs., Ala. Soc. Profl. Land Surveyors (charter). Home: Route 1 Box 264 A Montgomery AL 36105 Office: Ala Hwy Dept 11 Union St Montgomery AL 36104

CONGER, NORMAN LEE, electronics engr.; b. Tulsa, July 5, 1930; s. Norman Robert and Edith Juanita (Drake) C.; B.S. in Physics, Tulsa U., 1952; M.S. in Electronics Engring., Air Force Inst. Tech., 1954; postgrad. Northeastern U., 1955-57, Mass. Inst. Tech., 1955-56, Okla. State U., 1957-67; m. Bonnie Lucille Sanders, Nov, 3, 1950; children—Alan Lee, Norman Lester, Debra Ellen. With Continental Oil Co., Ponca City, Okla., 1957—, now supervising instrument engr. process control, engring. center. Served to 1st lt. USAF, 1952-57. Registered profl. engr., Okla. Mem. Instrument Soc. Am. (dir. standards and practices bd. 1972—). Mem. Christian Ch. (elder 1969—). Patentee in field. Home: 939 N 4th St Ponca City OK 74601 Office: PO Box 1267 Ponca City OK 74601

CONGER, STEPHEN HALSEY, lumber co. exec.; b. Asheville, N.C., July 14, 1927; s. Allen Ford and Margery (Evans) C.; B.S., U. Ga., 1949; m. Marian Lansdell Meiere, June 29, 1951; children—Susan deCamp, Stephen Halsey, Robert Cody Lansdell, Marian Lansdell Meiere. Forester, Coastal Lumber Co., Lake City, S.C., 1950-51; asst. sales mgr. Commonwealth Lumber Co., Murphy, N.C., 1951-52; sales Ga. Pacific Corp., Augusta, 1952-54; pres. Coastal Sales Co., Weldon, N.C., 1954-68, Pioneer Lumber Corp., Dailey, W.Va., 1961-70; exec. v.p. Coastal Lumber Co., Weldon N.C., 1969—, also dir.; pres. Coast Lumber Internat., Inc., 1972—, also dir. Chmn. Halifax County Republican party, 1960-65; mem. exec. com. N.C. Rep. party, 1963-65; treas. Am. party, N.C., 1969-71, mem. exec. com. of central com., 1969-71, mem. nat. com., 1969-71. Served with C.E., AUS, 1945-46. Mem. Soc. Am. Foresters, Nat Forest Products Assn., (dir.), So. Cypress Mfrs. Assn. (pres.), N.C. Pvt. Sch. Assn. (treas.), S.A.R., Holland Soc. N.Y., Sigma Alpha Epsilon. Baptist. Club: Chockoyotte Country. Office: Box 829 Weldon NC 27890

CONGER, THOMAS DECKMAN, architect; b. Dallas, Aug. 7, 1927; s. Thomas Doris and Margaret Bell (Deckman) C.; B.Arch., U. Tex., 1953; m. Pauline Djerf, July 29, 1950; children—Natalie, Norman, Nathan. With archtl. firm Bennett & Crittenden, Dallas, 1953-55, Tatum & Quade, Dallas, 1955-58; with 8th Naval Dist., New Orleans, 1958-59; with Bur. Yards & Docks, Washington, 1959-61; with NASA, Langley Field, and Houston, Tex., 1961—. Mem. A.I.A., Tex. Soc. Architects, Constrn. Specifications Inst., U. Tex. Alumni Assn., Phi Kappa Tau. Club: Officers (Ellington AFB). Home: 322 Ravenhead St Houston TX 77034 Office: Engineering Division Johnson Space Center Nat Aeros and Space Adminstrn Houston TX 77034

CONGLETON, JAMES CLEVELAND, JR., ednl. adminstr.; b. Parkersburg, W.Va., Jan. 24, 1921; s. James Cleveland and Bessie (Sprout) C.; student Carson-Newman Coll., 1938-40; B.S. in Advt., U. Fla., 1970; m. Dorothy Louise Satterfield, Apr. 29, 1942; children—Bruce Arthur, James Patrick. Engaged in retail music bus., W. Va., Fla., 1947-69; mem. faculty Seminole Jr. Coll., Sanford, Fla., 1971—, spl. projects dir. Served with USAF, 1941-45. Decorated Air medal, Group Citation with two clusters. Mem. Fla. Assn. Community Colls. (mem. com. 1971-73). Presbyn. Home: 801 W 18th St Sanford FL 32771 Office: Seminole Jr Coll Sanford FL 32771

CONKLIN, JAMES BYRON, JR., ednl. adminstr.; b. Charlotte, N.C., July 29, 1937; s. James Byron and Gerta (Reithmuller) C.; B.S., Mass. Inst. Tech., 1959, M.S., 1962, Sc.D., 1964; m. Elizabeth Bradford Calef, July 7, 1962; children—David Bradford, Anne Elizabeth. Asst. prof. physics U. Fla., Gainesville, 1964-71, asso. prof. physics, 1971—, asso. dir. for instrn. and research N.E. Regional Data Center, State U. System Fla., 1973—. Bd. dirs. N.W. Neighborhood Daycare Center, Gainesville, 1966-74, v.p., 1968, pres., 1969-70, 73; bd. dirs. Alachua County Coordinated Child Care, 1971—, v.p., 1973, pres., 1974. Mem. A.A.A.S., Assn. Computing Machinery, Am. Phys. Soc., Am. Assn. Physics Tchrs., Sigma Xi, Tau Beta Pi, Eta Kappa Nu, Sigma Pi Sigma. Home: 600 NW 36th St Gainesville FL 32607

CONLEY, CECIL, coll. dean; b. Tomahawk, Ky., June 1, 1922; s. Leander David and Carrie (Swain) C.; B.S., U. Ky., 1948, M.S., 1950; Ph.D., N.C. State U., 1954; m. Naomi Lee, Sept. 5, 1964. Researcher dairy sci. Clemson U., 1956-63; chmn. div. sci. and math. Pembroke (N.C.) State U., 1963-67, Livingston (Ala.) U., 1967-70; prof. chemistry Palm Beach Jr. Coll., Lake Worth, Fla., 1970-72, exec. dean, Belle Glade, Fla., 1972—. Vice pres. Carolina Inst. Aeros., 1961-68; chmn. Adv. Com. on Edn. Adult Offenders, 1973—. Pres., Loxahatchee Landowners Assn., 1972—. Served with AUS, 1943-45. Mem. Sigma Xi, Alpha Zeta. Democrat. Mem. Community Ch. (chmn. trustees 1971-74). Mason (32 deg.), Lion. Home: PO Box 26 Loxahatchee FL 33470 Office: 1185 S Main St Belle Glade FL 33370

CONLEY, NAOMI LEE (MRS. CECIL CONLEY), educator; b. Lumberton, N.C., Sept. 27, 1928; d. Richard Henry and Emma (Carter) Lee; B.S., Pembroke State Coll., 1961; M.Ed., U. N.C., 1962; Ed.D., U. Tenn., 1965; m. Cecil Conley, Sept. 5, 1964. Sec. for dist. mgr. Buckeye Cotton Oil Co., Charlotte, N.C., 1948-49; sec. personnel dept. Navy Dept., Washington, 1949; sec. to supt. Lumberton City Schs., 1950-61; tchr. Massey Hill High Sch., Fayetteville, N.C., 1961-62; prof. edn. Pembroke (N.C.) State Coll., 1962-63, 64-67, dean of Women 1962-63; asst. tchr. U. Tenn. 1963-64, counselor for freshman dormitory, 1963-64; asso. prof. edn. Livingston (Ala.) U., 1967-70; counselor Indian River Community Coll., also prof. Palm Beach Atlantic Coll., 1970-71; area leader dept. marketing mgmt. Broward Community Coll., Ft. Lauderdale, Fla., 1971-73; psychologist Palm Beach Community Mental Health Center, Belle Glade, Fla., 1973—. Sec., Loxahatchee Land Owners Assn., 1970-72. Mem. Am. Assn. U. Women, Sales and Marketing Execs. Internat., Delta Kappa Gamma, Phi Epsilon Chi, Delta Pi Epsilon, Pi Lambda Theta. Presbyn. Club: Primrose. Home: 1222 E Rd Loxahatchee FL 33470 Office: Palm Beach Community Mental Health Center 300 W Canal St South Belle Glade FL 33430

CONLEY, RONALD WILLIAM, govt. ofcl.; b. Ft. Worth, Aug. 25, 1935; s. William Earnest and Sammy Cathryn (Courtney) C.; B.A., U. Wash., 1958; Ph.D., Johns Hopkins, 1963; m. Josephine Villerreal, Dec. 4, 1955 (div. Feb. 1972); children—Annette, Debbie, Tami, Kathy, Edward, Patricia; m. 2d, Carol G. Bellotti, 1973. Economist, Nat. Inst. Mental Health, Rockville, Md., 1963-67. Pres.'s Com. on Mental Retardation, Washington, 1967-70; sr. program analyst Rehab. Services Adminstrn., Washington, 1971—. Instr. evening div. U. Md., College Park, 1962—. Served with AUS, 1954-56. Nat. Def. fellow. 1959-61, Vocational Rehab. Tng. grantee, 1961-62. Mem. Am. Econ. Assn., Phi Beta Kappa. Author: The Economics of Vocational Rehabilitation, 1965; The Economics of Mental Retardation, 1973. Home: 2702 Players Mill Rd Silver Spring MD 20902 Office: 330 C St Washington DC 20201

CONN, FREDERICK JAMES, JR., pub. co. exec.; b. Lynchburg, Va., Feb. 20, 1908; s. Charles Richard and Bessie E. (Stemple) C.; B.A., U. Ky., 1929; m. Blanche Montgomery, Jan. 31, 1936; children—Frederick James III, Cathy. Advt. salesman Sherman (Tex.) Democrat, 1926-36; advt. mgr. Marshall (Tex.) News Messenger, 1936-40; v.p. Denison (Tex.) Herald, 1940-44, publisher, 1944-64; publisher San Angelo (Tex.) Standard Times, 1964—. Mem. Presdl. Adv. Bd. Water Pollution Control, 1972—. Head restoration com. Eisenhower Birthplace, Denison, 1952-62; pres. Denison Camp Fire Girls, 1957; chmn. indsl. devel. coms., Denison, 1946-60, San Angelo, 1965, 68; pres. Denison C. of C., 1956; v.p. Denison Library, 1945-64; chmn. Miss. Wool of Am. Pageant, San Angelo, 1965; chmn. Denison Meml. Hosp. 1960-64; chmn. Houston Harte Found., Angelo State U., 1971; mem. Upper Colorado River Authority Bd., 1966-72; pres. San Angelo Entertainment Assn., 1969. Named Most Valuable Citizen, San Angelo C. of C., 1970. Mem. Sigma Delta Chi, Alpha Delta Sigma, Delta Chi. Rotarian (pres. 1955). Clubs: San Angelo Tex Country, River. Home: 1525 Paseo de Vaco San Angelo TX 76901 Office: 28 W Harris St San Angelo TX 76901

CONNALLY, HERSCHEL JOSEPH, lawyer; b. San Angelo, Tex., July 15, 1935; s. Herschel Christian and Hazel Corinne (Faris) C.; student Southwestern U., 1953-54, 1957, San Angelo Coll., 1955-56, U. Tex., 1960-61; J.D., U. Tex. Law Sch., 1964; m. Vella Cloe Redwine, Sept. 21, 1957; children—Vella Katherine, Jennifer Robin. Admitted to Tex. bar, 1964; practiced in Abilene, Tex., 1964, Odessa, 1964—; mem. firms Jackson & Jackson, Abilene, 1964; mem. firm Turpin, Smith, Dyer, Harman & Dawson, Odessa, Tex., 1964—, partner, 1967—. Chmn. zoning bd. adjustment City Odessa, Tex., 1972—; mem. Tex. Bd. Pvt. Investigators and Pvt. Security Agys., 1973—; v.p. Presidential Mus. Odessa, Tex., 1971—, bd. trustees, 1969—. Mem. Tex. Dem. Exec. Com., 1972—; campaign mgr. U.S. Senator Lloyd Bentsen, 1970, Gov. Dolph Briscoe, 1972. Served with AUS, 1958-60. Mem. State Bar Tex., Ector County Bar Assn. (chmn. grievance com. 1972), Kappa Sigma, Phi Alpha Delta. Democrat. Methodist. Club: Exchange (Odessa, Tex.). Home: 6217 Glenhaven St Odessa TX 79760 Office: 1010 American Bank Bldg Odessa TX 79761

CONNALLY, JOHN BOWDEN, lawyer; b. Floresville, Tex., Feb. 27, 1917; s. John Bowden and Lela (Wright) C.; LL.B., U. Tex., 1941; m. Idanell Brill, Dec. 21, 1940; children—John Bowden III, Sharon (Mrs. Robert Ammann), Mark. Admitted to Tex. bar, 1938; pres., gen. mgr. radio sta. KVET, Austin, Tex., 1946-49; adminstrv. asst. to Senator Lyndon B. Johnson, 1949; mem. firm Powell, Wirtz & Rauhut, Austin, 1949-52; atty. for Sid. W. Richardson & Perry R. Bass, ind. oil operators, Ft. Worth, 1952-61; sec. of the navy, 1961; gov. of Tex., 1963-69; partner Vinson, Elkins, Searls, Connally & Smith, Houston, 1969-71, 72—; sec. treasury, 1970-72; spl. adviser to Pres. Nixon, 1973. Mem. U.S. Adv. Council Exec. Orgn., 1969-70; mem. Pres.'s Fgn. Intelligence Adv. Bd., Adv. Com. Reform Iternat. Monetary System. Recipient Distinguished Alumnus award U. Tex. Ex-Students Assn., 1961. Republican. Office: First City Nat Bank Bldg Houston TX 77002

CONNAR, RICHARD GRIGSBY, surgeon; b. Zanesville, O., Jan. 11, 1920; s. Virgil Norwood and Anna Margaret (Grigsby) C.; B.A., Duke, 1941, M.D., 1944; m. Elizabeth Dickens, May 18, 1946; children—Cathleen, Elizabeth Ann, Richard Grigsby. Intern, Duke Hosp., Durham, 1944-45, resident in internal medicine, 1945-46, resident in gen. and thoracic surgery Duke U. Sch. Medicine, 1948-53, asst. prof. surgery, 1953-55; practice medicine specializing in thoracic and cardiovascular surgery, Tampa, 1955—; clin. prof. surgery, chief sect. thoracic and cardiovascular surgery U. South Fla.; cons. throacic and cardiovascular surgery Fla. Crippled Children's Commn., MacDill AFB Hosp., S.W. Fla. Tb Sanitarium; chmn. med. adv. bd. Hillsborough County Hosp. and Welfare Bd., 1962-64; mem. Fla. Tb Bd., 1964—. Bd. dirs. Fla. (award 1967), Hillsborough County (award 1960) heart assns., U.S. Fla. Found.; chmn. Duke U. Nat. Council, 1970-71. Served as capt. with USAAF, 1946-48. Fellow A.C.S. (bd. govs. 1970—, pres. Fla. chpt. 1967—); mem. A.M.A. ho. of dels. 1971—), Fla., Hillsborough County (pres. 1970-71) med. assns., So. Surg. Assn., Am. Assn. Thoracic Surgery, So. Thoracic Surg. Assn., Fla. Thoracic Soc. (pres. 1971-72), Soc. Thoracic Surgeons, Duke U. Alumni Assn. (v.p. 1971-72, pres. 1973-74), Phi Beta Kappa, Alpha Omega Alpha. Clubs: University, Tampa Yacht and Country; Ye Mystic Krewe of Gosparilla; Palma Ceia Golf and Country. Contbr. articles in field to profl. jours. Home: 3305 Jean Circle Tampa FL 33609 Office: 1 Davis Blvd Tampa FL 33606

CONNELL, EDWARD PEACOCK, lawyer; b. Memphis, Apr. 8, 1936; s. Charles Willis and Georgia (Peacock) C.; student Tulane U., 1954-55; B.B.A., U. Miss. 1958; LL.B., 1961; postgrad. N.Y.U., 1962; m. Eva B., Nov. 23, 1968. Admitted to Miss. bar, 1961; since practiced in Clarksdale; mem. Holcomb, Dunbar, Connell, Merkel & Tollison, and predecessor firms, 1961—; municipal judge, Clarksdale, 1961-68; adj. prof. law U. Miss., 1963—. Mem. Miss. Jr. Bar (pres. 1966-67), Am., Miss (2d v.p. 1967-68) bar assns., Young Lawyers Conf. (exec. council 1966-68). Rotarian (pres. 1967-68). Home: 111 Cypress Av Clarksdale MS 38614 Office: 152 Delta Av Clarksdale MS 38614

CONNELL, JAMES FREDERICK LOUIS, educator; b. Balt., June 25, 1920; s. James Edward and Elizabeth Johanna Maria (Henning) C.; B.S. in Geology, La. State U., 1949; M.S. in Geology, U. Okla., 1951, Ph.D. in Geology, 1955; m. Martha Carol Matthews, Feb. 7, 1943; 1 son, James Jeffery Charles. Asst. prof. geology La. Poly. Inst., Ruston, 1953-56; asso. prof. geology U. So. Miss., Hattiesburg, 1956-57, State U. N.Y., New Paltz, 1957-58, U. S.W. La., Lafayette, 1958-62; prof. geology, U. Montevallo (Ala.), 1962—. Ind. cons. geologist, Montevallo, 1962—. Served with USN, 1936-40, Royal Canadian Army, 1940-41, AUS, 1941-43. Decorated Canadian Star, Canadian Vol. Service medal, Canadian Def. medal, U.S. Pearl Harbor medal. Mem. Yorkshire Geol. Soc. (Brit.), Am. Inst. Profl. Geologists, Paleontol. Soc., Soc. Vertebrate Paleontology, Am. Geol. Inst., Ala. Geol. Soc., Ala. Acad. Sci., Ga. Geol. Soc., Ga. Acad. Sci., Royal Regiment Can. Assn. Mason. Home: Box 144 Montevallo AL 35115

CONNELL, MARY WEBB (MRS. BILL MITCHELL), pub. relations exec.; b. Cherry Ridge, La.; d. W.C. and Ora (Henderson) Webb; student Draughn Bus. Coll.; m. W.W. Connell, Jr.; m. 2d, Bill Mitchell, May 15, 1966. Librarian, radio sta. KLRA, Little Rock; sec. radio sta. KTHS, Little Rock; programming radio sta. WNOE, New Orleans; artist, producer, co-host TV show Eye on Arkansas, KTHV-TV, Little Rock, to 1973; nat. mdsg. dir. Holland's Assos., Little Rock, 1973, now pub. relations dir.; also pub. relations dir. Jimmy Dean Meat Co. Dir. television, pub. relations com. Pulaski County United Fund; active Kiddie Bag Program, Salvation Army. Recipient awards Am. Cancer Soc., Salvation Army, Am. Heart Fund, United Fund, USAF, 2 awards for show Eye on Arkansas TV Radio Mirror Mag.; citation merit Muscular Dystrophy Am., Inc.; certificate Better Bus. Bur. Ark. Home: 2100 Rebsamen Park Rd Little Rock AR 72202 Office: 1600 Union Nat Plaza Little Rock AR 72201

CONNELL, RICHARD GRANT, JR., metall. engr.; b. Richmond, Va., Jan. 3, 1938; s. Richard Grant and Alice Caroline (Richardson) C.; B.S., Va. Poly. Inst., 1960; M.S., Va. Poly. Inst., 1965; Ph.D., U. Fla., 1973; m. Linda Dare Lane, Aug. 13, 1960; children—Deborah Lane, Richard Grant III. Metall. engr. Reynolds Metals Co., Richmond, Va., 1960-62; instr. Va. Poly. Inst., Blacksburg, 1962-65; grad. asst. U. Fla., Gainesville, 1965-73, asst. engr., dept. materials sci. and engring., 1973—. Registered profl. engr., Fla. Mem. Metall. Soc., Am. Inst. Mining, Metall. and Petroleum Engrs., Am. Welding Soc., Am. Soc. Metals, Internat. Soc. Stereology, Nat. Assn. Corrosion Engrs., Sigma Xi, Alpha Sigma Mu, Sigma Gamma Epsilon.

CONNER, EUGENE HAYWARD, anesthesiologist; b. Balt., Dec. 2, 1921; s. James Moses and Mary (Fader) C.; M.D., U. Md., 1945; m. Mary Lou Brown, Sept. 7, 1946; children—Janice, Jeffrey, Marcia, Melissa. Intern, Univ. Hosp., Balt., 1945-46; resident Univ. Hosp., Balt., 1947-49, Hosp. Univ. Pa., Phila., 1949-50; practice medicine specializing in anesthesiology, Phila., 1950-57, Louisville, 1957—; mem. staffs Louisville Gen., Meth.-Evang. hosps.; asst. prof. anesthesiology U. Pa. Sch. Medicine, 1951-57; mem. faculty U. Louisville, 1957-71, prof. anesthesiology, chmn. dept., 1957-71. Served with USAAF, 1946-47. Mem. Am. Soc. Anesthesiologists, Assn. U. Anesthetists, Assn. for History Medicine, Alpha Omega Alpha. Home: 5704 Apache Rd Louisville KY 40207

CONNER, NED FELL, ret. air force officer, hosp. adminstr.; b. Bethlehem, Pa., June 6, 1915; s. Max Bowman and Mayda (Schmidt) C.; student Pa. Sch. Phys. Therapy, 1937, Moravian Coll., 1940, Miss. So. U., 1951; m. Desiree Pamela Palmer, Oct. 7, 1944; children—Cheryl, Peter, Christopher, Daniel, David. Commd. 2d lt. USAAF, 1942, advanced through grades to col. USAF, 1966—; mem. med. adminstrn. office U.S. Army, India and Burma, 1941-45; hosp. adminstr. Keesler AFB, Miss., 1946-51, Parks AFB, Cal., 1951-53, Burderop, Eng., 1953-56, Barksdale AFB, La., 1956-61; chief med. financial programming 2d Air Force, Shreveport, La., 1961-63; dir. med. adminstrv. service 3d Air Force, Eng., 1963-66; chief med. constrn. programming USAF, Washington, 1966-67; hosp. adminstr. Homestead AFB, Fla., 1967-71; ret., 1971. Mem. Am. Coll. Hosp. Adminstrs., Am. Acad. Med. Adminstrn., Royal Soc. Health (Eng.) Northwest La. Hosp. Council (pres. 1961), Fla., South Fla. hosp. assns. Home: 8480 SW 143d St Miami FL 33158

CONNER, WARREN WESLEY, lawyer; b. Cat Spring, Tex., Aug. 14, 1932; s. George William and Frieda Johanna (Kollatschny) C.; B.B.A., So. Meth. U., 1959, J.D., 1963; m. SuZanne Rosser, Oct. 29, 1955; children—Connie SuZanne, Cathy Lorraine. With M., K. & T. R.R., 1951-53, 55-57, So. Union Gas Co., 1959-63; admitted to Tex. bar, 1963, since practiced in Sealy; sr. partner firm Conner & Odom, 1968—. Chmn. bd. Austin County Abstract and Title Co. Pres. Austin County unit Am. Cancer Soc., 1974. Bd. dirs. Sealy Indsl. Found., 1972-73, Sealy Pub. Library, 1972-73. Served with AUS, 1953-55. Mem. Austin County Bar Assn. (past pres.), Am. Legion, Phi Delta Phi. Mason (Shriner), Rotarian (past pres. Sealy). Home: RFD 1 Box 41 Cat Spring TX 78933 Office: 311 Fowlkes St Sealy TX 77474

CONNER, WILLIAM FRED, accountant; b. Crandall, Tex., Dec. 8, 1933; s. Cecil Theodore and Ola Virginia (Yandell) C.; B.B.A., U. Houston, 1955; J.D., S. Tex. Coll. Law, 1969; m. Wanda Lue Shoemaker, Nov. 18, 1954; children—Gail Ann, Mark Allen. Accounting supr., econ. analyst Tenneco Inc., Houston, 1955-69; admitted to Tex. bar, 1969; financial analyst, asst. to v.p. finance foods div. Coca-Cola Co., Houston, 1969-71; pvt. accounting practice, Houston, 1971—; dir. Brittain's Fine Furniture, Inc., Bob's Men's Wear, Brame Constrn. Co., Solar Rec. Corp. Bd. dirs. Variety Boys' Club, Houston, 1970—, sec., 1971—; bd. dirs. Boys's Country, 1964—, sec.-treas., 1969—. C.P.A., Tex. Mem. Am. Inst. C.P.A.'s, Tex., Houston (chmn. speaker's bur.) socs. C.P.A.'s, Am., Houston bar assns., State Bar Tex. Baptist (deacon). Home: 7726 Pagewood St Houston TX 77042 Office: 3115 W Loop S Suite 22 Houston TX 77027

CONNOR, SEYMOUR VAUGHAN, educator; historian; b. Paris, Tex., Mar. 4, 1923; s. Aikin Beard and Gladys (Vaughan) C.; B.A., U. Tex., 1948, M.A., 1949, Ph.D., 1952; 1 son, Charles Seymour. Archivist, W. Tex. State U., 1952-53, Tex. State Library, 1953-55;

prof. history, dir. S.W. collection Tex. Tech. U., Lubbock, 1955-63, prof. history, editor, 1965—. Served with AUS, 1943-45; ETO. Fellow Tex. Hist. Assn. (mem. exec. council 1957-71, pres. 1967-68); mem. Panhandle-Plains Hist. Soc. (editor Rev. 1954-59; life mem.), W. Tex. Hist. Assn. (exec. council 1960-63), W. Tex. Mus. Assn. (exec. council 1956-62), Western Hist. Assn., Am. Assn. State and Local History, Orgn. Am. Historians, Phi Kappa Tau, Phi Kappa Psi, Phi Alpha Theta. Author: Preliminary Guide to Texas Archives, 1956: Peters Colony of Texas, 1959; A Biggers Chronicle, 1961; Adventure in Glory, 1965; Texas: A History, 1971; (with Odie Faulk) North America Divided, 1971; (with W.C. Pool) Texas, the 28th state, 1971. Editor: Texas Treasury Papers (3 vols.), 1955; The West Is for Us, 1957; Builders of the Southwest, 1959; Saga of Texas (6 vols.), 1965; Dear America, 1971. Contbr. articles to profl. jours. Home: 3503 45th St Lubbock TX 79413

CONOMOS, WILLIAM G., newspaper pub.; b. Blairsville, Pa., Apr. 29, 1931; s. Van H. and Grace (Hoover) C.; student Orlando (Fla.) Jr. Coll., Rollins Coll., Winter Park, Fla.; m. Dorothy Bradford McGuffin, Mar. 17, 1956; children—Andrew, Christopher; stepchildren—Bradford, Amelia, Joanna Silliman. Pres., pub., editor Orlando Sentinel & Star. Home: 1223 Ensenada St Orlando FL 32801 Office: 633 N Orange Av Orlando FL 32801

CONOVER, CLYDE STUART, govt. ofcl.; b. Springfield, Ill., June 25, 1916; s. Carey Stuart and Mildred Primrose (Andreas) C.; B.S. in C.E., U. N.M., 1938; postgrad. Mass. Inst. Tech., 1942-43; m. Marguerite Agnes Nolan, Oct. 22, 1943; children—Carol (Mrs. Ernest L. Quinn), Catherine (Mrs. Ernest M. Duvall). Hydraulic engr. Ground Water Br., Water Resources Div., U.S. Geol. Survey, Albuquerque, 1938-41, hydraulic and supervising engr., 1946-57, asst. chief, 1957-62, dist. engr., dist. chief, Tallahassee, 1962—. Served to capt. USAAF, 1941-46. Registered profl. engr., N.M. Mem. Am. Geophys. Union, Am. Soc. C.E., Am. Water Resources Assn. (sect. pres. 1973—), Am., Nat. (div. dir., chmn. div. 1964-65) water works assns., Am. Geol. Inst., S.E. Geol. Soc., Sigma Xi. Lion. Contbr. articles to various publs. Office: Bldg F John Knox Rd Tallahassee FL 32303

CONOVER, FRED JOE, city ofcl.; b. Ft. Cobb, Okla., Dec. 15, 1930; s. Joseph Boone and Elva Alberta (Churchill) C.; ed. pub. and police schs.; m. Nancy Carolyn Lowe, Apr. 28, 1951; children—Steve, Ronnie, Patricia. With LTV, 1949-50, 52-54; with Grand Prairie (Tex.) Police Dept., 1954—, chief of police, 1961-72, dir. pub. safety, 1972—. Dir. Dallas Area Organized Crime Task Force, 1970—; mem. N. Central Tex. Crime Information Center Policy Bd., Dallas County Criminal Justice Council, 1971-72; dir. N. Central Tex. Regional Police Acad.; dep. dir. Grand Prairie Civil Def., 1961—. Mem. adv. com. to police sci. program El Centro Coll., 1969-70; bd. dirs. YMCA. Served with USMC, 1948-52. Named Outstanding Young Man of Year, Grand Prairie Jr. C. of C., 1961. Mem. Internat. Assn. Chiefs Police, Tex. Police Assn., Tex., N. Tex. (pres. 1965-66) chiefs of police assns., Nat. Police Officers of Am., Sheriff's Assn. Tex., Internat. Fire Chiefs Assn., N. Tex. Teletype Assn., Grand Prairie C. of C. (dir., life mem.). Mem. Christian Ch. Rotarian (dir. Grand Prairie club 1964). Home: Route 2 Box 323K Grand Prairie TX 75050 Office: 702 S Carrier Pkwy Grand Prairie TX 75050

CONRAD, C. CARSON, govt. ofcl.; b. New Albany, Ind., Apr. 28, 1911; s. Claude H. and Mary B. (Carson) C.; student Butler U., 1929-32; A.B. in Phys. Edn., U. Cal. at Santa Barbara, 1940; postgrad. U. So. Cal., 1946-47; M.A., Sacramento State U., 1953; m. Margret Claire Padrick, May 19, 1946; children—William R. and Robert W. (twins). Cons. Dept. Edn., State of Cal., Sacramento, 1947-54, chief Bur. Health Edn., Phys. Edn., Athletics and Recreation, 1954-70; exec. dir. Pres.'s Council Phys. Fitness and Sports, Washington, 1970—; past mem. staff San Francisco State Coll., U. So. Cal.; past dir. municipal and sch. recreation, cons. in phys. edn. Alhambra (Cal.) Schs.; past sports dir., Santa Barbara, Cal. Served with USAAF, 1942-46, USAF, 1951-53; col. Res. ret. Recipient Verne S. Landreth Meml. award Cal. chpt. A.A.H.P.E.R.; Service award Athletic Inst.; Distinguished Service award Cal. Coaches Assn.; Certificate of Appreciation, Cal. Interscholastic Fedn.; William S. Rockwell Meml. award, 1973; named Alumnus of Year U. Cal. at Santa Barbara, 1965. Clubs: Hoffman Golf, Andrews Golf, Del Norte Swim and Tennis. Contbr. articles to profl. jours. Home: 901 6th St SW Apt 415 Washington DC 20024 Office: Room 3030 400 6th St SW Washington DC 20201

CONRAD, CHARLES, JR., astronaut; b. Phila., June 2, 1930; s. Charles and Frances V. (Sargent) C.; B.S. in Aero. Engring., Princeton, 1953, M.A. (hon.), 1966; LL.D., Lincoln-Wesleyan U., 1970; D.Sc. (hon.), Kings Coll., 1971; m. Jane DuBose, June 17, 1953; children—Peter, Thomas, Andrew, Christopher. Commd. U.S. Navy, 1953, advanced through grades to lt. comdr., 1964; project test pilot, armaments test div. Dept. Navy, 1959-60; flight instr., performance engr. U.S. Naval Test Pilot Sch., 1960-61; flight instr. for F4H, Naval Air Sta., Miramar, Cal., 1961-62; safety flight officer Fighter Squadron, 96, 1963; astronaut Manned Spacecraft Center, NASA, Houston, 1964—, now chief Skylab operations; pilot Gemini V, 1965; comdg. pilot Gemini XI, 1966; spacecraft comdr. Apollo XII, 1969. Recipient Distinguished Service medal NASA, 2 Exceptional Service medals (NASA); D.S.M., D.F.C. with oak leaf cluster (Navy); various other awards. Asso. fellow Am. Inst. Aero. and Astronautics; mem. Soc. Exptl. Test Pilots. Home: 102 Whispering Oaks Seabrook TX 77586 Office: Manned Spacecraft Center NASA Houston TX 77058

CONRAD, HAROLD THEODORE, physician; b. Milw., 1934; M.D., U. Chgo., 1958; m. Elaine Conrad; 5 children. Intern USPHS Hosp., San Francisco, 1958-59; resident USPHS Hosp., Lexington, Ky., 1959-61; chief psychiatry USPHS Hosp., New Orleans, 1962-67, clin. dir., 1968; chief clin. research center Nat. Inst. Mental Health, Lexington, 1969—. Diplomate in psychiatry Am. Bd. Psychiatry and Neurology. Mem. A.M.A., Am. Psychiat. Assn., Alpha Omega Alpha. Office: Nat Inst Mental Health Clin Research Center Leestown Pike Lexington KY 40507

CONRAD, MARCEL EDWARD, JR., hematologist; b. N.Y.C., Aug. 15, 1928; s. Marcel Edward and Lulu Marie (Geraghty) C.; B.S., Georgetown U., 1949, M.D., 1953; m. Patricia Jane Hutchon, Jan. 16, 1948; children—Marcel Edward, III, Mark E., Carol J. Commd. 1st lt. U.S. Army, 1953, advanced through grades to col., 1968; intern Walter Reed Gen. Hosp., Washington, 1953-54, resident internal medicine, 1955-58, chief resident dept. medicine, 1958-60, chief hematology service, 1965-74; chief dept. gastroenterology Walter Reed Army Inst. Research, Washington, 1961-62, asst. chief dept. hematology, 1963-65, chief dept. hematology. 1965-74, dep. dir. div. medicine, 1966-69, dir. div. medicine, 1969-71; chief clin. investigation service Walter Reed Army Med. Center, Washington, 1971-74; clin. asst. prof. medicine Georgetown U. Sch. Medicine, Washington, 1964-68, clin. asso. prof. medicine, 1968-74; dir. div. hematology and oncology, prof. medicine U. Ala. at Birmingham, 1974—; cons. in hematology to Surgeon Gen., 1965—; mem. staff Walter Reed Gen. Hosp. Mem. sickle cell adv. com. Health Edn. and Welfare, 1971—; mem. med. adv. com. Am. Nat. Red Cross, 1969—, mem. ad hoc com. for evaluation of in-house research, 1968—; mem. adv. panel on hematologic and neoplastic diseases therapy U.S. Pharmacopeia, 1970—; mem. research adv. com. Washington Heart Assn., 1968-73; mem. hepatitis adv. com. Nat. Heart and Lung Inst., 1970—. Decorated Legion of Merit. Fellow Internat. Soc. Hematology, A.C.P.; mem. Am. Fedn. Clin. Research, Am. Soc. Hematology, A.A.A.S., Soc. Exptl. Biology and Medicine, Internat. Soc. Blood Transfusion (councillor 1970—), Am. Assn. Blood Banks, A.M.A., Am. Soc. Clin. Investigation, Assn. Am. Physicians, Am. Physiol. Soc. Contbr. articles to various publs. Office: Div Hematology and Oncology U Ala Birmingham AL 35294

CONRAD, THEODORE CHARLES, accountant, lawyer; b. Anderson, Ind., July 29, 1903; s. Charles William and Lydia (Lukens) C.; A.B., DePauw U., 1925; J.D., Harvard, 1933; postgrad. bus. adminstrn. Northwestern U., 1936-39; m. Mary Emma Gilby, Mar. 30, 1935; children—Mary Jo (Mrs. James L. Cresimore), Theodore Charles, Carolyn Jane (Mrs. Vann O. Trapp), Jeanne Minette (Mrs. Louis A. Trosch), Virginia Dianne (Mrs. Gene Draper), Doris Ellen. Admitted to Ill. bar, 1934, N.C. bar, 1953; pvt. practice law, Chgo., 1934-40; mgr. tax dept. Baumann Finney & Co., Chgo., 1940-44; supr. tax dept firm Ernst & Ernst, Boston, 1944-49; mgr. tax dept. George G. Scott & Co., Charlotte, N.C., 1950-52; sr. partner Conrad, Hoey, East & Co., Charlotte and Spartanburg, S.C., 1952—. Republican candidate for state auditor, 1968, for state treas., 1972. C.P.A., Ill., Mass., Ky., N.C., S.C. Mem. N.C. Assn. C.P.A.'s (pres. Charlotte chpt. 1956-57), Am. Inst. C.P.A.'s, Nat. Assn. Accountants (nat. dir., v.p. 1963-64), N.C. Bar, 26th Jud. Bar Assns., Baptist. Mason (Shriner); Kiwanian. Clubs: Charlotte Execs., Charlotte City, Harvard Charlotte. Home: 4615 Walker Rd Charlotte NC 28211 Office: 301 N Caswell Rd Charlotte NC 28204 also 447 Kennedy St Spartanburg SC 29302

CONRAD, TROY LAVERNE, petroleum co. exec.; b. Frederick, Okla., Jan. 8, 1932; s. Harold Raymond and Mary Ruth (Harwood) C.; B.S., U. Okla., 1958; m. Gloria Darlene Knox, June 20, 1954; children—Mark R., Kirk W., Beth Ann. Petroleum engr. Felmont Oil Corp., Owensboro, Ky., 1958-60; dist. petroleum engr. Ashland Oil & Refining Co., Monroe, La., 1960-65; prodn. supt. Grigsby Oil & Gas Co., Shreveport, 1965—. Served with USAF, 1951-53. Mem. Am. Inst. Mech. Engring. (chpt. dir. 1971—). Elk. Club: Petroleum (Shreveport). Home: 340 Carroll St Shreveport LA 71105 Office: 1108 Commercial National Bank Bldg Shreveport LA 71101

CONREY, KENNETH KERWIN, city ofcl.; b. Cheyenne, Wyo., Aug. 25, 1924; s. John Wesley and Mable (Kerwin) C.; B.A., U. Denver, 1950; postgrad., mgmt. seminar, U. Chgo., 1963; m. Donna Jean Sapp, Sept. 18, 1944; children—Megganey Sue, James Todd, Calvin Frank. IBM operator and various other positions, Union Pacific R.R., N. Platte, Neb., 1942-59, treas. Union Pacific employee credit union, 1953-57; sec.-treas. Local 609, Am. Fedn. Musicians, N. Platte, Neb., 1950-59; city clk., N. Platte, 1957-59; adminstrv. asst. to city mgr., Borger, Tex., 1959-60; city mgr., Spearman, Tex., 1960-65, Weatherford, Tex., 1965-68; city clk., Pensacola, Fla., 1968-72; dir. finance, Pensacola, 1972—. Served with USAF, 1943-45; ETO. Decorated Air medal with three clusters. Mem. Fla. City Mgrs. Assn. (asso.), Internat. City Mgrs. Assn., Fla. Municipal Finance Officers Assn. Presbyn. (elder). Lion (pres. 1962-63). Home: 3790 Tom Lane Dr Pensacola FL 32504 Office: City Hall PO Box 12910 Pensacola FL 32521

CONROY, DAVID JEROME, lawyer; b. New Orleans, Dec. 27, 1929; s. George E. and Lilyon (Bowling) C.; B.A., Tulane U., 1950, J.D., 1952; m. Ann Kathryn Gunderson, May 15, 1954; children—Kathryn Ann, David Michael, Elizabeth Helen, Mary Daire, Peter George Edward, Patrick Frank. Admitted to La. bar, 1952; partner firm Milling, Benson, Woodward, Hillyer & Pierson, New Orleans, 1956—; sec. Jahncke Service Inc., New Orleans, 1961-69, Pub. Grain Elevator New Orleans, 1964—; sec., dir. C.B. Fox Co., New Orleans, 1965—. Del., La. Constl. Conv., 1973. Bd. dirs. New Orleans Speech and Hearing Center, 1968-74, pres., 1970-72; bd. dirs. Family Service Soc., 1972—, Beverly Knoll Civic Assn., 1972—, Greater New Orleans Tourist and Conv. Commn., 1971—; bd. dirs. Louise S. McGehee Sch., 1970—, 1st v.p., 1973—; trustee United Way Greater New Orleans, 1974—, Pub. Affairs Research Council La., Inc., 1974—. Served with AUS, 1952-54. Mem. Am., La. (chmn. sect. corp. law 1968-69, mem. ho. of dels. 1970-71), New Orleans bar assns., Internat. House, St. Thomas More Cath. Lawyers Assn. (bd. govs. 1969-73, 1st v.p. 1972-73), La. Hist. Soc. (exec. council 1971-73). Roman Catholic. Clubs: Pickwick, New Orleans Country, Plimsoll, Essex. Home: 437 Dorrington Dr Metairie LA 70005 Office: Whitney Bldg New Orleans LA 70130

CONROY, JOHN ALBERT, psychiatrist; b. Bound Brook, N.J., Jan. 31, 1906; s. Dennis Martin and Mary Ellen (Cusick) C.; student Middlesex U., Waltham, Mass., 1927-29; M.D., Kan. City U., 1933; m. Rita Margaret Ginty, Oct. 25, 1934. Intern Broad St. Hosp., N.Y.C., 1933-34; resident St. Mary's Meml. Hosp., Knoxville, Tenn., 1934-35; gen. practice, Gatlinburg, Tenn., 1935-40, Newton Centre, Mass., 1940-57; staff psychiatrist VA Hosp., Murfreesboro, Tenn., 1958-71, acting chief psychiatry, 1971—. Served with USPHS-USCGR, 1942-45. Mem. Mass. Med. Soc., Assn. Mil. Surgeons, Assn. Res. Officers USPHS, V.F.W., Am. Legion, Am. Radio Relay League. Republican. Roman Catholic. Elk. Home: 1003 Elliott Dr Murfreesboro TN 37130 Office: VA Hosp Murfreesboro TN 37130

CONSTANT, CLINTON, chem. engr.; b. Nelson, B.C., Can., Mar. 20, 1912; s. Vasile and Annie (Hunt) C.; B.Sc. with honors, U. Atla., 1935, postgrad., 1935-36; Ph.D., Western Res. U., 1939; m. Mary E. Dunlap, Apr. 21, 1950. Came to U.S., 1936, naturalized, 1942. Devel. engr. Harshaw Chem. Co., Cleve., 1936-38, mfg. foreman, 1938-43, sr. engr. semi-works dept., 1948-50; supt. hydrofluoric acid dept. Nyotex Chems., Inc., Houston, 1943-47, chief devel. engr., 1947-48; mgr. engring. Ferro Chem. Co., Bedford, O., 1950-52; tech. asst. mfg. dept. Armour Agrl. Chem. Co. (formerly Armour Fertilizer Works), Bartow, Fla., 1952-61, mgr. research and devel. div., 1961-63, mgr. spl. projects, research div. (co. name changed to USS Agri-Chems, 1968), 1963-65, project mgr., 1965-70; chem. adviser Robert & Co. Assos., Atlanta, 1970—. Fellow A.A.A.S., Am. Inst. Chemists; mem. Am. Inst. Chem. Engrs., Am. Chem. Soc., Am. Inst. Aeros. and Astronautics, Am. Astron. Soc., Astron. Soc. Pacific, Royal Astron. Soc. Can., N.Y. Acad. Scis., Am. Water Works Assn., Ga. Water and Pollution Control Assn. Author tech. reports, sci. fiction. Patentee in field. Home: PO Box 1221 Atlanta GA 30301 Office: Robert and Co Assos 96 Poplar St Atlanta GA 30303

CONSTANTIN, JAMES ALFORD, educator; b. Tulsa, June 15, 1922; s. Jules Joseph and Nelle (Alford) C.; B.B.A., U. Tex., 1943, M.B.A., 1944, Ph.D., 1950; m. Wanda Anita Moyer, May 18, 1941; children—Nina Katherine (Mrs. Robert Dean Beaird), James Alford, Jr., Jules Joseph II, Anne Louise (Mrs. Michael Gordon Keown). Instr., U. Tex., 1946-47; asst. prof., asso. prof., asst. dir. Bur. Bus. Research, U. Ala., Tuscaloosa, 1947-52; asso. prof. U. Wash., 1952-53; prof. marketing and transp. U. Okla., Norman, 1953-69, David Ross Boyd prof. marketing and transp., 1969—; chmn. bd. The Constantin Distbn. Corp. Served with USAAF, 1942-43. Mem. Am. Econ. Assn., Transp. Research Forum, Am. Soc. Traffic and Transp., S.W. Social Sci. Assn. Author: (with W.J. Hudson) Motor Transportation, 1958, Principle of Logistics Management, 1966; (with W.N. Peach) World Resources and Industries, 1972; (with R.E. Evans and M.L. Morris) Planning and Managing the Marketing Function, 1974. Home: 929 W Lindsey St Norman OK 73069

CONSTANTINE, OLEINICK PAVLOVITCH, neuropsychiatrist; b. Ostrog, Ukraine, Oct. 22, 1908; s. Pavel Ivanovich and Thekla (Doschuk) Oleinik; student Polish Tchrs. Sch., 1924-26; B.S., Eastern U., 1931; B.A., Columbia Bible Coll., 1932; M.A., U.S.C., 1932; M.D., Baylor Coll., 1937; m. Ethelwyn G. Brown, Dec. 23, 1935; children—Paula Joy (Mrs. Ted L. Edwards, Jr.), Paul D. Came to U.S., 1926, naturalized, 1937. Intern Baylor U. Hosp., Dallas, 1937-38; asst. physician Tex. San Antonio State Hosp., 1938-39; resident Kings Park State Hosp., N.Y., 1941-43; psychiatrist VA Hosp., Canandaigua, N.Y., 1943-49, chief continued treatment service, 1946-49; psychiatrist VA Hosp., Waco, Tex., 1949-70, chief combined treatment service, 1949-56; neurologist Columbia Presbyn. Med. Center, N.Y.C., 1942-44. Served to maj. M.C., AUS, 1944-46. Diplomate Am. Bd. Psychiatry and Neurology. Fellow Am. Psychiat. Assn., A.M.A., Royal Soc. Health; mem. Tex. Med. Assn. Mason. Home: 3825 Austin Av Waco TX 76710

CONSTANTINIDES, CONSTANTINE (DINOS) DEMETRIOS, composer, violinist, educator; b. Ioannina, Greece, May 10, 1929; s. Demetrios Constantine and Magdaleni (Papastergiou) C.; diploma in violin Greek Conservatory, 1950, in theory, 1957; diploma in violin (Found. of Greece scholar) Juilliard Sch. Music, 1960; M.Music, Ind. U., 1965; Ph.D. in Composition, Mich. State U., 1968; m. Judith Rose Hursh, July 1, 1962; children—Lenna Rose, John Demetrios. Came to U.S., 1957, naturalized, 1967. First violin Athens (Greece) State Orch., 1952-57, 61-63, also 1st violin Radio Symphony Orch.; 1st violin Indpls. Symphony Orch., 1963-65; asso. prof. violin, composition and theory La. State U., Baton Rouge, 1966—, dir. prep. dept. for strings, 1971—, Grad. Research grantee, 1973. Concertmaster Baton Rouge Symphony, 1966—, Baton Rouge Civic Ballet, 1967—, Beaumont (Tex.) Civic Opera, 1967—; mem. Festival Arts Trio, La. State U., 1966—; tchr., coach La. State U. Extension Div., 1966. Co-founder, co-chmn. New Times, orgn. promoting performance contemporary music, Baton Rouge, 1971—. Grad. Research grantee La. State U., 1970; Distinguished Faculty fellow La. State U. Found., 1971-72. Mem. Am. Assn. U. Profs., Am. Musicological Soc., Coll. Music Soc., Music Educators Nat. Conf., Music Tchrs. Nat Assn. (teaching award So. div. 1970), Am. String Tchrs. Assn., Am. Fedn. Musicians, Webern Soc., Phi Kappa Phi, Phi Mu Alpha, Pi Kappa Lambda. Mem. Greek Orthodox Ch. Composer: Symphony No. 1, 1966; Woodwind Quartet, 1966; Trio, 1967; String Quartet, 1966; Triple Concerto, 1967; Composition for String Orch., 1968; Twentieth Century Studies for Two Violins, 1970; Study for Brass, 1970; Sonata for Viola and Piano, 1971; Designs for Strings, 1971; Kaleidoscope for Voice, Violin, Cello, Piano and 2Slide Projectors, 1972; Exploding Parallels for Instrumental Ensemble, Reader and Audience, 1972; Antigone, music drama, 1973. Home: 947 Daventry Dr Baton Rouge LA 70808

CONTACOS, PETER GEORGE, physician; b. Springfield, Mass., Mar. 19, 1926; s. George Demetrios and Aphrodite (Klonis) C.; A.B., Harvard, 1947; M.A., Boston U., 1949; Ph.D. in Med. Parasitology, Tulane U., 1954, M.D., 1957. Instr. parasitology Tulane U., 1951-53; intern Methodist Hosp., Bklyn., 1957-58, commd. surgeon USPHS, 1958; USPHS physician Tech. Cooperation Mission to India, 1958-60; med. officer in charge NIH Malaria project U.S. Penitentiary, Atlanta, 1960-65; head sect. cytology Lab. Parasite Chemotherapy Nat. Inst. Allergy and Infectious Diseases NIH, Chamblee, Ga., 1965-66, head sect. primate malaria, Chamblee-Atlanta, 1966-70; head sect. primate malaria Lab. Parasitic Diseases NIH, Atlanta-Chamblee, 1970-72; asst. to dir. research malaria program Center Disease Control, Atlanta, 1972-73, asst. to dir. research tropical disease program, 1973-74, chief host parasite studies br. Vector Biology and Control Div., Bur. Tropical Diseases, 1974—. Mem. WHO Expert Adv. Panel Malaria, 1966—; asso. mem. Commn. Malaria Armed Forces Epidemiolofical Bd., 1967-72; mem. sci. group immunology malaria, Geneva, Switzerland, 1967; hon. chmn. session immunology malaria, Geneva, Switzerland, 1967; hon. chmn. session immunology of malaria 9th Internat. Congress Tropical Medicine, Athens, Greece, 1973; cons., lectr. in field. Recipient Walter Reed Meml. medal La. State Med. Soc., 1957; Commendation medal USPHS, 1968. Fellow Royal Soc. Tropical Medicine and Hygiene (life); mem. Am. Soc. Tropical Medicine and Hygiene, A.M.A., Am. Acad. Microbiology, Sci. Research Soc. Am. Author: (with Coatney, Collins and Warren) The Primate Malarias, 1971. Contbr. numerous articles to profl. jours. Home: 2946 Greenbrook Way NE Atlanta GA 30345 Office: Center Disease Control Atlanta GA 30333

CONTE, NICHOLAS FERDINAND, physician; b. Scranton, Pa., Dec. 6, 1918; s. Matthew Arthur and Mary Ann (Jordan) C.; B.S., U. Scranton, 1941; M.D., U. Pa., 1944; m. Virginia Mae Bertolett, Sept. 22, 1944;children—Norman Richard, Claude V. (dec.), Frederic Arthur. Intern, Phila. Gen. Hosp., 1944-45; resident VA Hosp., Aspinwall, Pa., 1948-50; commd. capt. U.S. Army, 1950, advanced through grades to col., 1968; asst. chief Med. Service, U.S. Army Hosp., Ft. Carson, Colo., 1956-61; chief med. service 121 Evacuation Hosp., Korea, 1961-62; fellow basic scis. Walter Reed Inst. Research, 1960-61; fellow endocrinology U. Cal. Sch. Medicine, San Francisco, 1962-63; asst. chief, then chief dept. medicine, Valley Forge Gen. Hosp., Phoenixville, Pa., 1963-67; med. cons. to surgeon gen. U.S. Army, Vietnam, 1967-68; co-dir. U.S. Army Med. Research Lab., Ft. Knox, Ky., 1969-72; chief med. cons. Office Surgeon Gen., Washington, 1972—. Asst. clin. prof. medicine Woman's Med. Coll., Phila., 1964-67; Dept. Def. rep. Nat. Program for Dermatology, 1972—. Served to capt. M.C., AUS, 1945-47. Decorated Legion of Merit. Diplomate Am. Bd. Internal Medicine. Fellow A.C.P. (gov. 1972—); mem. A.M.A., N.Y. Acad. Scis., Am. Assn. Blood Banks, Assn. Mil. Surgeons U.S. Republican. Contbr. articles to profl. pubs. Home: 4100 Tidewater Ct Alexandria VA 22309

CONTNEY, JOHN JOSEPH, assn. exec.; b. Milw., Oct. 15, 1932; s. Francis Anthony and Rose (Nowicki) C.; B.S., Marquette U., 1956, M.B.A., 1965; m. Dawn Georgette Wintz, Sept. 7, 1963; children—Wade Anthony, Ross Joseph. Asst. to v.p. Boston Store, Milw., 1950-56; v.p., sales mgr. Records Unltd., Inc., Milw., 1956-60; v.p., sales mgr. Columbia S.E., Miami, Fla., 1960-63; asst. to pres. Color Corp., Tampa, Fla., 1964-65; mgr. marketing Linen Supply Assn. Am., Miami Beach, Fla., 1965—; lectr. in field. Served with AUS, 1954-56. Mem. Am. Marketing Assn., Am. Pub. Health Assn. (mem. environmental control com.), Alpha Delta Sigma. Contbr. articles to profl. jours. Home: 705 NE 94th St Miami Shores FL 33138 Office: 975 Arthur Godfrey Rd Miami Beach FL 33140

CONTRERAS, FERMIN M., banker; b. Santurce, P.R., Jan. 20, 1944; s. Benigno and Argelia (Bordallo) C.; B.B.A. cum laude, U. P.R., 1965; M.B.A., Inter-Am. U., 1971; m. Gisela Gómez, Sept. 3, 1965; children—Fermin, Omar, Gisela, Mariana. Trainee, Chase Manhattan Bank, San Juan, 1965-66, credit analyst, credit officer, 1966-67; asst. mgr. Banco Economias, San German, P.R., 1967-68, asst. v.p. in charge of operations and personnel, 1968-69, v.p. in charge of S.W. credit operations, 1969-72, sr. v.p., 1972—. Mem. Am. Banking Assn.

Club: Mayaguez (P.R.) Hilton Tennis and Swimming. Home: Rd 108 K3-5 Mayaguez PR 00708 Office: Box 146 San German PR 00753

CONVERSE, J. GERARD, physician; b. Boston, Sept. 21, 1918; s. Frederick F.B. and Rosita (McVey) C.; B.A. cum laude, Boston Coll., 1940; M.D. cum laude, Tufts Med. Sch., 1943; m. Gwendolyn Stone Connor, Sept. 26, 1964; children by previous marriage—Sharon Ann, Geoffrey Michael. Intern, U.S. Naval Hosp., Chelsea, Mass., 1944; resident Boston City Hosp., 1947-48, VA Hosp., W. Roxbury, 1948-49, Children's Med. Center, Boston, 1949; instr. anesthesiology Albany (N.Y.) Med. Coll., 1949-50, asst. prof., 1950-52, prof., chmn. dept., 1952-56; prof., chmn. dept. anesthesiology U. Miami (Fla.) Sch. Medicine, 1956-62, clin. prof., 1963—; dir. dept. anesthesiology Albany Hosp., 1952-56, Jackson Meml. Hosp., Miami, 1956-62; attending anesthesiologist Winter Haven (Fla.) Hosp., 1962—. Cons. VA Hosp., Albany, 1950-56, Coral Gables, Fla., 1956-62; asso. examiner Am. Bd. Anesthesiologists, 1955—. Hon. mem. Fla. Sheriff's Assn., 1963—. Served to lt. with M.C., USN, 1944-47. Decorated Bronze Star medal. Fellow Boston Med. Library. Mem. Am., Fla., So. med. assns., Am. (dir. 8th dist.), Fla. (pres. 1966, dir. 1961—) socs. anesthesiologists, Am. Heart Assn., Assn. U. Anesthetists, Internat. Anesthesiologists Research Soc., A.A.A.S., Am. Conservative Union, Alpha Omega Alpha. Clubs: Faculty (U. Miami); Capitol Hill (Washington); Lake Region Yacht and Country. Contbr. articles to profl. jours. Home: W Lake Hamilton Drive Winter Haven FL 33880 Office: Med Arcade Bldg 1st St N Winter Haven FL 33880

CONWAY, CHARLES MILTON, JR., steel co. exec.; b. Jacksonville, Fla., June 30, 1940; s. Charles Milton and Lucille (Dunn) C.; A.B., Washington & Lee U., 1962, LL.B., 1964, J.D., 1965; m. Minna Ann Corbin, Oct. 13, 1962; children—Charles M., III, Minna Corbin. Trainee Aetna Steel Co., Jacksonville, Fla., 1964-65, mgr., 1965-67, v.p., 1967-71, dir., 1967—, pres., 1971—. Mem. Regional Export Expansion Council, 1971-72; v.p. Big Brothers Greater Jacksonville, Inc., 1972-73; bd. mgmt. Jacksonville (Fla.) YMCA, 1972-73. Bd. trustees Riverside Presbyn. Day Sch., Jacksonville, Fla., 1968-74. Served with USMC, 1959-65. Mem. Jacksonville C. of C. (pres. 1970), Fla. Bar Assn. Clubs: Florida Yacht, Seminole (both Jacksonville). Home: 4341 Venetia Blvd Jacksonville FL 32210 Office: 5007 New Kings Rd Jacksonville FL 32203

CONWAY, DWIGHT COLBUR, educator; b. Long Beach, Cal., Nov. 14, 1930; s. Dee Allyson and Ruth Ermia (Mills) C.; B.S., U. Cal. at Berkeley, 1952; M.S., U. Chgo., 1953, Ph.D. (Teaching fellow 1954-55; U.S. Rubber Co. fellow 1953-54), 1956; m. Diane Faye Coulter, Aug. 25, 1962; children—Kathleen, Karyn, Michael, Patrick. Asst. prof. chemistry Purdue U., 1957-63; asso. prof. Tex. A. & M. U., College Station, 1963-67, prof. chemistry, 1967—. Recipient Outstanding Teaching award Standard Oil Co. of Ind., 1969. Mem. Am. Chem. Soc. (sect. chmn. 1971), Am. Phys. Soc., Am. Soc. Mass Spectrometry, Phi Beta Kappa, Sigma Xi, Alpha Chi Sigma. Home: 1104 Sul Ross Bryan TX 77801 Office: Dept Chemistry Tex A & M U College Station TX 77843

CONWAY, FRENCH HOGE, lawyer; b. Danville, Va., June 11, 1918; s. Lysander Broadus and Mildred (Hoge) C.; B.S., U. Va., 1942, LL.B., 1946; m. Louise Throckmorton, Feb. 3, 1961; children—French Hoge, William Chenery, Helen (Mrs. W.C. Brann), Donna (Mrs. W.B. Salmon). Admitted to Va. bar, 1942, since practiced in Danville; mem. firm Clement, Conway & Winston, 1950-60. Dir., Danville Industries (Va.). Sec. Danville Election Bd., 1969—, v.p. Va. Election Bd. Assn., 1974. Served with USNR, 1942-46. Mem. Am., Va., Danville bar assns., Ret. Officers Assn., Boat Owners Assn. U.S. Kiwanian, Mason. Home: 912 Main St Danville VA 24541 Office: 105 S Union St Danville VA 24541

CONWAY, MACK HOWARD, JR., profl. assn. exec.; b. Jacksonville, Fla., Aug. 20, 1926; s. Mack Howard and Roberta (Arnold) C.; student Va. Comml. Coll., 1946-48; m. Agnes Mae Powell, Sept. 17, 1948; children—Mack Howard III, Richard, Patricia, Christine. Accounting mgr. Gen. Motors Acceptance Corp., Roanoke, Va., 1948-54; bus. mgr. Paul H. Pusey, Inc., Richmond, Va., 1954-56; treas., gen. mgr. Nick Allen Motors, Inc., Newport News, Va., 1956-60; pres. Conway Ford Sales, Inc., Blackstone, Va., 1960-65; exec. v.p. Housing and Builders Assn., Hampton, Va., 1965—. Pres., Newport News Homeownership Assn., 1970—; mem. citizens adv. com. to City Council, Newport News; pub. Guide to Peninsula Living, Newport News, 1969—. Served with USNR and USMCR, 1943-46. Recipient awards Nat. Assn. Home Builders, 1965, 69, 70, 71. Mem. Am. Legion (post comdr. 1969-70). Mason. Moose. Home: 8 Meadow Dr Newport VA 23606 Office: 2607 W Mercury Blvd Hampton VA 23366

CONWAY, MARTHA BELL, ednl. adminstr.; b. Raleigh, N.C., July 24, 1917; d. Elijah James and Cora (Henderson) Conway; student William and Mary Coll., 1932-35; LL.B., U. Richmond, 1939. Admitted to Va. bar, 1940, since practiced in Richmond; commr. chancery Hanover Co. Circuit Court, 1943-51; real estate broker, 1951-55; sec. of Commonwealth of Va., 1952-70; adminstr. grants and contracts Va. Commonwealth U., Richmond, 1970—. Dist. counsel OPS, 1951-52; dir. Richmond Nat. Bank, 1972—. Registered patent atty., Va. Mem. Am. Assn. U. Women. Democrat. Methodist. Author: Compacts of Virginia, 1963; also profl. publs. Home: 2500 Grove Av Richmond VA 23220 Office: Va Commonwealth U Richmond VA 23220

CONWAY, ROBERT NELSON, cons.; b. Rochester, N.Y., Nov. 15, 1917; s. Reginald J. and Anne (Nelson) C.; B.Aero. Engring., Rensselaer Polytech. Inst., 1939; m. Janet Grant Alling, May 25, 1940; children—Bruce A., Michael A., David L. Aero. engr. NASA Langley Research Center, Hampton, Va., 1939-47, asst. budget officer, 1947-61, budget officer, 1961-68, dep. asst. dir. resources, 1968-71, asst. dir. adminstrn., 1971-73; cons., 1973—. Committeeman, Boy Scouts Am., Hampton, Va., 1951-61; dir. Peninsula Community Services Planning Council, Newport News, Va., 1965-67. Mem. Pennisula Engrs. Club. Episcopalian. Club: Hampton Yacht (commodore 1967). Home: 39 Hampton Roads Av Hampton VA 23661

CONWAY, WALTER PHILIP, real estate developer; b. Honolulu, Jan. 16, 1940; s. Walter Clem and Dorris (Garrett) C.; B.B.A., U. Tex., 1967; m. Sandra Matassa, July 4, 1968; 1 son, Michael Garrett. Audit sr. Arthur Andersen & Co., C.P.A.'s, Houston, 1967-70; sr. v.p. Kickerillo Co., Houston, 1971—, also dir. C.P.A., Tex. Mem. Am., Tex. socs. C.P.A.'s. Home: 5403 Pebble Springs Dr Houston TX 77066 Office: 1300 Texas Av Houston TX 77002

CONWAY, WILLIAM RAYFORD, state legislator; b. Green Cove Springs, Gla., July 25, 1911; s. James Franklin and Idella Jane (Minton) C.; B.S. in Bus. Adminstrn., U. Fla., 1936; m. Dianne Anger, Feb. 4, 1950; children—William Rayford, Robert Fisher, James Marvin, Julia Ann, John Charles. Pres., Fla. Liquified Gas Assn., 1950; mem. Fla. Ho. of Reps., 1966—. Chmn., Cancer Crusade, 1965. Served from lt. (j.g.) to lt. comdr. USNR, 1942-45; PTO. Decorated Bronze Star. Mem. U. Fla. Nat. Alumni Assn. (pres. 1963), Pi Kappa Phi. Episcopalian. Mason (Shriner), Kiwanian (local pres. 1953). Club: University. Address: 213 Riverside Dr Ormond Beach FL 32074

CONWELL, JOSEPH THOMAS, lawyer; b. Oakman, Ala., Nov. 9, 1914; s. Joe D. and Elma Pettus (Wells) C.; student Transylvania Coll., 1934-35; B.A., U. Ala., 1937, LL.B., 1940; m. Winifred Maxwell, June 25, 1946; 1 son, Joseph Thomas. Admitted to Ala. bar, 1940; pvt. practice law, Jasper, Ala., 1940-42, Birmingham, Ala., 1946-48, Huntsville, Ala., 1955—; atty. ICC, Atlanta, 1948-49; claim and ins. investigator, San Francisco, 1949-54. Pres., Madison County Citizens Council, 1965-66; mem. Huntsville Indsl. Expansion Com. Served with AUS, World War II, lt. col. Ala. State Militia. Mem. Am., Ala., Huntsville-Madison County bar assns., Ala. Trial Lawyers Assn., Am. Judicature Soc., Farrah Law Soc., Civitan Club, Am. Legion. Democrat. Episcopalian. Mem. Woodmen of World. Home: 7118 Chadwell Rd SW Huntsville AL 35802 Office: Conwell Legal Bldg 607 Madison St Huntsville AL 35801

COODY, RICHARD HOWARD, gen. contractor; b. Dodge County, Ga., Jan. 27, 1931; s. Robert W. and Audrey (Shepherd) C.; grad. high sch.; m. Joyce Moore, June 15, 1951; children—Richard Howard, Robin. Engaged in home constrn., Eastman, Ga., 1948-55; job. supt. A.C. Samford, Inc., also A.C. Samford Overseas, Inc., 1954-62; owner R.H. Coody & Assos., Inc., Albany, Ga., 1972—; dir. First Nat. Bank Albany. Bd. dirs. Sowega Youth Home, Albany. Mem. Assn. Gen. Contractors (dir. Ga. Br.). Mason (Shriner), Elk. Clubs: Doublegate Country, Sportsmens (Albany). Home: 5002 Holly Hill Rd Albany GA 31707 Office: PO Box 3349 Westover Rd Albany GA 31706

COOK, ALLYN AUSTIN, educator; b. Grandview, Ill., Feb. 14, 1927; s. Floyd Lester and Kathryn (Kime) C.; B.S. in Edn., Eastern Ill. State Tchrs. Coll., 1948; M.S., U. Wis., 1950, Ph.D. in Plant Pathology, 1951; m. Carolyn Jean Shores, May 30, 1948; children—Jacalyn, Cheryl (Mrs. Robert Patrick Kriegner). Asst. prof. S.D. State Coll., Brookings, 1952-54; agt. plant pathologist U.S. Dept. Agr., Gainesville, Fla., 1954-56; mem. faculty U. Fla., Gainesville, 1956—, prof. plant pathology, 1968—. Served with USNR, 1945-46. Mem. Am. Phytopath. Soc., Fla. Hort. Soc. Home: 1311 NW 107th Terrace Gainesville FL 32601

COOK, AUGUST JOSEPH, pub. accountant; b. Devine, Tex., Sept. 25, 1926; s. August E. and Mary H. (Schmidt) C.; B.S., Trinity U., 1949; B.B.A., U. Tex., 1954; LL.B., St. Mary's U., San Antonio, 1960; m. Matie M. Brangan, July 12, 1952; children—Lisa Ann, Mary Beth, John Joseph. Staff accountant Ernst & Ernst, C.P.A.'s, San Antonio, 1949-50; bus. mgr., sec., dir. Life Enterprises, Inc., Beverly Studios, Inc., Castle Land Co., Inc., Randolph Studios, Inc., San Antonio, 1950-58; admitted to Tex. bar, 1960; with Ernst & Ernst, 1960—, mgr., Memphis, 1969-70, partner, Memphis, 1970—. Vice pres. Tex. Municipal League, 1968-69. Alderman, Castle Hills, Tex., 1961-63, mayor, 1963-69; chmn. Bexar County Council Mayors, 1967-69. Bd. dirs. Met. YMCA San Antonio. Served with AUS, 1945-46. C.P.A., Tex. Mem. Am. Inst. C.P.A.'s., Tex. Soc. C.P.A.'s, Tex. Bar Assn., Estates Planners Council San Antonio (pres. 1967), Delta Theta Phi, Kappa Pi Sigma. Clubs: Optimist (dir.), Toastmasters (pres. San Antonio 1963). Home: 6785 Slash Pine Ct Memphis TN 38138 Office: Sterick Bldg Memphis TN 38103

COOK, BUREN EUGENE, agriculturist; b. Colquitt, Ga., Mar. 10, 1917; s. Booley C. and Ethel D. (Donley) C.; grad. high sch.; m. Vera E. Grogan, Sept. 24, 1938; 1 son, Buren E. With B.C. Cook & Sons, Inc., Haines City, Fla., 1931—, sec., sales mgr., 1970—. Bd. dirs. Brotherhood of Ridge Bapt. Assn. Mem. Polk County Farm Bur. (past pres., v.p., dir. 1971), Fla. Aberdeen-Angus Assn. (past dir.), C. of C., Fla. Citrus Commn. (mem. citrus juice extractor com.), Future Farmers Am. (life hon.), Farm Bur. (chmn. citrus com., mem. farm labor relations com. Fla. chpt.). Baptist (chmn. bd. deacons 1965-66). Kiwanian (pres. 1969, chmn. agr. and conservation com. 1970-72). Home: Lake Elsie Dr Haines City FL 33844 Office: 413 N 12th St Haines City FL 33844

COOK, CHARLES DEVERE, JR., accountant; b. Waco, Tex., Mar. 5, 1943; s. Charles DeVere and Wanda Elizabeth (Maedgen) C.; B.B.A., U. Tex., 1964; M.B.A., Baylor U., 1970; m. Ann Elizabeth Stephani, Mar. 9, 1968. C.P.A. Wilcox, Pattillo, Brown & Hill, Waco, Tex., 1970-72, Main Lafrentz & Co., Waco, 1972—. Bd. dirs. Friends of Waco-McLennan County Pub. Library, Waco, 1972-73. Served with USNR, 1964-69. Decorated Army Commendation medal, Navy Commendation medal with Combat V. C.P.A., Tex. Mem. Naval Reserve Assn. (chpt. sec., treas. 1971-73), Navy Supply Corps Alumnai Assn. (life) (area adminstr. 1971-73), Tex. Soc. C.P.A.'s, Am. Inst. C.P.A.'s, Beta Gamma Sigma. Kiwanian (bd. dirs. 1971-72), K.P. Home: 2111 Wooded Acres Waco TX 76710 Office: 219 N 8th St Waco TX 76703

COOK, CHARLES WILLIAM, govt. ofcl.; b. Yankton, S.D., Sept. 27, 1927; s. William O. and Kathryn S. (Eymer) C.; A.B. summa cum laude, U. S.D., 1951; M.S., Cal. Inst. Tech., 1954, Ph.D., 1957; m. Virginia M. Fosness, May 30, 1950; children—Jennifer L., William O. II, Amy E. Head nuclear physics Convair, San Diego, 1957-60; chief ballistic missile def. br. Inst. for Def. Analysis, Washington, 1960-61, Advanced Research Projects Agy., Washington, 1961; corporate dir. N.Am. Aviation, El Segundo, Cal., 1961-67; dep. div. chief CIA, Washington, 1967-71; asst. dir. Office Sec. Def., Dir. Def. Research and Engring., Washington, 1971—. Served with USAAF, 1944-47. Dean Akeley fellow, 1951-52; Dobbins scholar, 1954-55; Inst. scholar, 1955-57. Asso. fellow Am. Inst. Aeros. and Astronautics; mem. I.E.E.E. (sr.), Am. Phys. Soc., N.Y. Acad. Scis., Am. Inst. Physics, Sigma Xi, Phi Beta Kappa, Sigma Pi Sigma. Contbr. articles to tech. jours. Home: 1180 Daleview Dr McLean VA 22101 Office: OSD ODDR&E Room 3D136 Pentagon Washington DC 20301

COOK, CLARENCE RICHARD, city ofcl.; b. Houston, Oct. 11, 1927; s. John Thomas and Mary Jane (Mills) C.; grad. Aldine High Sch.; m. Mary Belle Bennett, Oct. 11, 1944; 1 son, Richard Carlton. Engaged in bus., Houston, 1945-50; chauffeur Houston Fire Dept., 1950-53, jr. capt., 1953-56, sr. capt., 1956-58, dist. chief, 1958-64, dep. dist. chief, 1964-67, asst. fire chief, 1967-68, fire chief, 1968—. Office: 410 Bagby Houston TX 77002

COOK, CLAYTON HENRY, rancher; b. Moundridge, Kan., Apr. 21, 1912; s. Herbert and Bertha (Wilkening) C.; student pub. schs., Moundridge; m. Margery Maxine Manning, Apr. 13, 1941; children—Larry Clayton, Ronald Leigh, Michael Craig, Melanie Beth. Engaged in ranching. Vega, Tex. Mem. Tex. Econ. Commn., 1950-57-59, 62—; mem. Gov.'s Com. on Aging; mem. Tex. Constn. Revision Com. Past mem. governing bd. Amarillo Little Theatre; mem. governing bd. High Plains Center of Performing Arts. Chmn. Oldham County Democratic Exec. Com. Mem. Internat. Platform Assn. Methodist. Mason, Kiwanian (lt. gov. Tex.-Okla. dist. 1959, chmn. new club bldg. 1960, chmn. past lt. govs. 1967). Club: Amarillo Knife and Fork. Home: Box 57 Vega TX 79092

COOK, CLORVAL ALLEN, accountant; b. Tulsa, Oct. 31, 1919; s. John and Nellie M. (Latham) C.; B.B.A., U. Tulsa, 1949, M.B.A., 1950; m. Edna Earle Hanson, Jan. 25, 1951; children—Cheryl Earle, Robert Alan. Auditor Sohio Petroleum Co., Oklahoma City, 1953-60; joint interest supr. Richfield Oil Corp., Los Angeles, 1960-65; budget/performance analyst Atlantic Richfield Co., Phila., 1966-68; dir. joint operations accounting Atlantic Richfield Co., Dallas, 1969—. Instr. accounting, finance econs. Okla. Mil. Acad., Claremore, Okla., 1950. Acting baseball commr. Spring Valley Athletic Assn., Richardson, Tex., 1972. Served to capt. USAF, 1941-45, 1951-53. C.P.A., Okla., Cal., Tex. Mem. Petroleum Acct. Soc. Dallas (chmn. com. 1970-71), Council Petroleum Accountants Socs. N.Am. Republican. Baptist. Mason. Home: 7861 La Sobrina Dr Dallas TX 75240 Office: PO Box 2819 Dallas TX 75221

COOK, DAMON GRANT, lawyer; b. Fort Worth, Tex., Mar. 27, 1937; s. W.E. and Edith Lorene (Grant) C.; student Tulane U., 1955-58; J.D., Baylor U. Sch. Law, 1961; m. Evelyn Erickson Crady, Mar. 8, 1959; children—Kyle Crady, Kelly Colleen. Admitted to Tex. bar, 1961; asso. atty. Bracewell, Reynolds & Patterson, Houston, 1961-66; partner Reynolds, White, Allen & Cook, Houston, 1966—. Spl. prosecutor grievance com. State Bar Tex., 1970-71; tchr. South Tex. Sch. Law, Houston, 1961-62; corporate dir. Granada Land & Cattle Co., Inc., Houston, Service Brokerage Co., Inc., Houston. Mem. Council Sch. Attys. Nat. Sch. Bds. Assn. Recipient Am. Jurisprudence award Baylor U. Sch. Law, 1959, Law Review scholarship, 1960, Tex. Assn. Plaintiffs' Attys. award 1961. Mem. Am., Houston, bar assns., Nat. Orgn. Legal Problems of Edn., Sigma Chi, Phi Alpha Delta. Presbyn. Clubs: Houston, Brae-Burn Country (Houston). Editor: Baylor Law Review, 1960-61. Contbr. articles to various publs. Home: 12522 Mossycup St Houston TX 77024 Office: Milam Bldg Houston TX 77002

COOK, DAVID RAY, mech. engr.; b. Tulsa, June 19, 1936; s. Artie Wrothal and Nellie Mae (Miller) C.; B.S. in M.E., Okla. State U., 1959; M.S. in Systems Mgmt., Fla. Inst. Tech., 1969, M.S. in Contract, 1970; student Internat. Corr. Schs., 1963, 70; m. Benetta Borne, May 26, 1959; children—Kathryn, Karlene, Kristine. Design engr. Douglas Aircraft Co., Santa Monica, Cal., 1959-60; sr. design engr. Convair, Omaha, 1960-62; design engr. Boeing Co., Huntsville, Ala., 1962-65; sect. supr. Launch Support div. Bendix Corp., Kennedy Space Center, Fla., 1965-69, dept. mgr., 1969—; v.p. Profl. Cons., 1972—; instr. mgmt. Bay State Coll., Titusville, Fla., 1971, Rollins Coll., 1971—, Brevard Community Coll., 1972—. Vol. counselor Brevard County (Fla.) Econ. Devel. Commn., 1971; mem. Nat. Council Small Bus. Mgmt. Mem., pres. bd. Brevard Symphony Orch. Recipient Citizenship award Am. Legion, Broken Arrow, Okla., 1954. Registered profl. engr., Ala. Mem. Am. Mgmt. Assn., Am. Soc. M.E. (chmn. small bus. com., vice chmn. Cannaveral sect. 1972), Fla. Engring. Soc., Soc. Automotive Engrs. (mem. space transp. com. 1972—), Nat. Soc. Profl. Engrs. Methodist (vice chmn. ch. finance com., pres. Meth. Men's Fellowship). Mason (32 deg.). Contbr. articles and tech. papers to profl. jours. Home: 2932 E Carriage Dr Titusville FL 32780 Office: Bendix Corp BEN 4300 PO Box 21086 Kennedy Space Center FL 32815

COOK, EDWARD WILLINGHAM, bldg. products mfr., commodity mcht.; b. Memphis, June 19, 1922; s. Everett Richard and Phoebe (Willingham) C.; grad. Hotchkiss Sch., 1940; A.B., Yale, 1944; m. Patricia L. Weaver, Mar. 17, 1973; children from previous marriage—Edward Willingham, Everett Richard II, Barbara Moore. Pres., Cook Industries, Inc., Memphis, N.Y.C., Chgo., Fresno, Cal., Los Angeles, Kansas City, Osaka, Tokyo, Japan, Hong Kong, Singapore, Rotterdam, Paris, Melbourne, Sao Paulo, Guatemala City, London, Rome, Geneva, 1952—, Cook Y Cia, de Mexico, S.A., 1952—; dir. S.L.-S.F. Ry., First Tenn. Nat. Corp. Mem. Cotton Adv. Commn., 1964-68; mem. exec. com. Nat. Council U.S.-China Trade, 1973—, Pres.'s Export Council, 1973—; dir. Chgo. Bd. Trade, 1974—. Chmn. Memphis-Shelby County Airport Authority, 1968—. Served to maj. USAAF, 1943-45; MTO. Decorated D.F.C., Bronze Star, Air medal with six oak leaf clusters. Mem. Am. Cotton Shippers Assn. (pres. 1966-67). Democrat. Episcopalian. Clubs: Memphis Country, Memphis Hunt and Polo; Links (N.Y.C.); Boston (New Orleans); Everglades (Palm Beach, Fla.). Office: 2185 Democrat Rd Memphis TN 38116

COOK, ERNEST EWART, oil exploration co. exec.; b. Wiltshire, Eng., Mar. 23, 1926; s. Edgar John and Dorothy May (Wiltshire) C.; B.A. in Natural Scis., Cambridge (Eng.) U., 1946, M.A., 1950; m. Nina Cairo, Sept. 23, 1953; 1 dau., Julia Ann. Came to U.S., 1946. Geophysicist, Cia Shell de Venezuela, Maracaibo, 1947-56; chief geophysicist Pakistan Shell Oil Co., Karachi, 1956-57; with Signal Oil & Gas Co., 1957-67, internat. exploration mgr., Los Angeles, 1966-67; v.p. Seismic Computing Corp., Houston, 1968-70; pres. Invent Inc., Houston, 1971—; dir. Holland Sea Search N.V., The Hague, Netherlands. Fellow Geol. Soc. London; mem. Soc. Exploration Geophysicist, Seismological Soc. Am., Marine Tech. Soc., Am. Geophys. Union, Am. Assn. Petroleum Geologists. Home: 624 Hedwig Rd Houston TX 77024 Office: Suite 430 9235 Katy Freeway Houston TX 77024

COOK, EVERETT LUNDIN, financial co. exec.; b. Alton, Ill., Oct. 17, 1927; s. James Everett and Alice R (Lundin) C.; student U. Colo., 1947-48; B.Indsl. Engring., Ga. Inst. Tech., 1950; m. Patricia Margaret Doherty, Dec. 26, 1949; children—James Dennis, John Patrick, Betsy Ann. Appraiser, Prudential Ins. Co., Denver, 1950-54; dist. mgr. Pacific Mut. Ins. Co., Salt Lake City, 1954-55; mortgage officer Tchrs. Ins. & Annuity Assn., N.Y.C., 1955-61; v.p. T.J. Bettes Co., Houston, 1961-65; real estate investor, 1965-70; v.p. Lincoln Financial, Inc., Houston, 1970—; pres., dir. Lincoln Liberty Investment Corp., 1970—; v.p., dir. Lincoln Liberty Life Ins. Co., 1970—; dir. Benjamin Franklin Savs. Assn. Mem. real estate adv. bd. Ill. Central Industries, Inc., 1972—. Served with USNR, 1945-46. Mem. Mortgage Bankers Assn., Internat. Council Shopping Centers, Greater Houston Ga. Tech. Alumni Assn., (dir., past pres.), Chi Psi. Clubs: Houston, Lakeside Country (treas., dir.). Home: 12115 Old Oaks St Houston TX 77024 Office: 711 Polk St Houston TX 77002

COOK, GEORGE GLENN, landscape architect; b. Port Arthur, Tex., June 20, 1940; s. James Dykes and Clairbell (Creswell) C.; student McNeese State Coll., 1961; B.S. in Landscape Architecture, La. State U., 1964; m. Wanda Guidry, June 3, 1961; children—Stephen Keith, Gary Paul. Landscape architect Stewart E. King & Asso., San Antonio, 1966-70; owner Glenn Cook, Landscape Architect, San Antonio, 1970—. Mem. Old Spanish Missions Restoration Com., San Antonio, 1970—; mem. San Antonio Bd. Rev. Hist. Dists., 1974—. Served to 1st lt. C.E., AUS, 1964-66; capt. Res. ret. Mem. Am. Soc. Landscape Architects (v.p. S.W. chpt. 1974—). Club: Toastmaster Internat. (San Antonio). Home: 5507 Gleason St San Antonio TX 78240 Office: 528 King William St San Antonio TX 78204

COOK, GLORIA HOUSTON (MRS. JAMES THOMAS COOK, JR.), civic worker; b. Portland, Me., Aug. 22, 1933; d. Ellwyn Kenelm May Elvera (Delay) Houston; student U. Fla., 1950-51; m. James Thomas Cook, Jr., Jan. 28, 1952; children—Victoria Ann, Sheryl Ann. Del., White House Conf. on Food, Nutrition and Health, 1969, Fla. Conf. on Food, Nutrition and Health, 1970; mem. President's Com. on Employment Handicapped, 1963—; Gray lady A.R.C., 1964-70; mem. Welsh Area planning com. State Div. Vocational Rehab., 1971—; chmn. Christmas Cotillion, 1971—; active campaign worker for various local civic orgns. Bd. dirs. Nat. Easter Seal Soc. (ho. of dels.

1965—), Fla. Easter Seal Soc. (sec. 1964-66, 1st v.p. 1970—), Volusia County Easter Seal Soc. (sec. 1962-64, pres. 1965-67), Jr. Service League Daytona Beach, 1956— (pres. 1967-68, chmn. future policies com. 1968—); bd. mem. Jr. Service League Orthopedic Center, 1957-66, v.p., 1967, parliamentarian, 1972—; bd. mem. Volusia County Cancer Soc., sec., 1963-66, v.p., 1969-71; bd. dirs. Fla. Internat. Festivals, Inc., sec. trustee bd. 1967—. Named Woman of Year, Halifax Area Selection Com., 1965, Woman of Year, Palmetto Jr. Woman's Club, 1957. Mem. United Ch. (trustee, pub. relations dir. 1974—). Clubs: Hibiscus Garden (bd. mem., v.p., sec. 1958-62), Oceanside Country. Home: 825 John Anderson Dr Ormond Beach FL 32074

COOK, H. K., banker; b. Mooreland, Okla., Jan. 22, 1933; s. William C. and Mary B. (Egbert) C.; student Cameron Jr. Coll., Lawton, Okla., 1952; student Trinity U., San Antonio, 1953-55; grad. Southwestern Grad. Sch. Banking, So. Meth. U., 1969; m. June B. Toepperwein, July 31, 1954; children—Darrell and Cheryl (twins), Pamela, Bradley. Profl. football player, Can., 1956-57; with SIC Finance Loan, San Antonio, 1957-63, br. mgr., Ponca City, Okla., 1963-65; v.p. loans and pub. relations, dir. Bank of Commerce, Tonkawa, Okla., 1965-68; v.p. Community Nat. Bank, Oklahoma City, 1968—. Pres., Tonkawa Safety Council, 1968; mem. Community Council No. Okla. Coll. and city of Tonkawa, 1968. Bd. dirs. United Fund, Tonkawa, 1966-68, pres., 1966; bd. dirs., treas. Tonkawa Youth Recreation, 1966-68. Mem. City Council, Tonkawa, 1967, mayor, 1968. Mem. Okla. Bankers Assn. (vice chmn. pub. relations and marketing com. 1971—; mem. econ. edn. com. 1973), Oklahoma City Installment Bankers Assn. (sec. 1973, v.p. 1974), C. of C. (pres. 1974). Lutheran. Elk. Home: 4202 N Barr Oklahoma City OK 73122 Office: 5800 N W 39th St Oklahoma City OK 73122

COOK, HENRY MORGAN, JR., physician; b. Belton, Tex., June 23, 1922; s. Henry Morgan and Maude Hazel (Gaeckler) C.; B.S., U. Neb., 1945, M.D., 1945; m. Nancy Leontine Gill, July 7, 1947; children—Carol Ann (Mrs. Truman Harris), Henry Morgan III, William, James. Commd. 2d lt. U.S. Army, 1942, advanced through grades to col., 1968; ret., 1972; intern Kings Daus. Hosp., Temple, Tex., 1945-46; resident internal medicine Brooke Gen. Hosp., San Antonio, Tex., 1949-52; resident pulmonary diseases Fitzsimons Gen. Hosp., Denver, 1952-53; chief med. service U.S. Army Hosp., Okinawa, 1953-56; resident allergy U. Va. Hosp., 1957-58; chief outpatient service Letterman Gen. Hosp., San Francisco, 1958-62; chief med. service U.S. Army Hosp., Ft. Carson, Colo., 1962-63; chief med. adv. div. MAAG, Taiwan, 1963-67; med. rep. U.S. Army Standardization Group, Ottawa, Ont., Can., 1967-70; chief profl. services, chief dept. medicine Womack Army Hosp., Ft. Bragg, N.C., 1970-72; dir. med. service, clin. dir. San Antonio Chest Hosp., 1972—. Diplomate Am. Bd. Internal Medicine. Mem. A.M.A., A.C.P., Assn. Mil. Surgeons. Home and office: PO Box 23340 Highland Hills Station San Antonio TX 78223

COOK, JAMES JOSEPH, city ofcl.; b. El Dorado, Kan., Aug. 22, 1934; s. Roy Andrew and Ada Josephine (Jones) C.; B.A. (honors scholar), Yale, 1956; postgrad. (grad. fellow) Kan. U., 1956-58, (Housing and Urban Devel. Scholar) Okla. U., 1971-73; m. Martha Ann Saunders, Dec. 7, 1960; children—David Johnston, James Lloyd. Asst. city mgr., El Dorado, Kan., 1957-58; budget analyst, Cin., 1959-61; budget dir., asst. city mgr., Winston-Salem, N.C., 1961-64; village mgr., Northfield, Ill., 1964-69; city mgr., Ada, Okla., 1969—. Cons. finance Okla. State U., 1973—. Trustee, treas. Okla. Municipal Retirement Fund, 1970—. Mem. Am. Soc. Pub. Adminstrn., Internat., Oklahoma (dir. 1973—) cities mgmt. assns. Lion (first v.p. 1973). Club: Yale (Tulsa). Home: 2207 Foster Dr Ada OK 74820 Office: 13th and Townsend Sts Office City Mgr Ada OK 74820

COOK, KENNETH GRAHAM, research psychologist; b. Phila., Aug. 21, 1931; s. Joseph and Anna (Graham) C.; B.S., Pa. State U., 1954, M.S., 1955; Ph.D., Am. U., 1967; m. Jane Davis, Dec. 17, 1955; children—Kenneth Graham, Sara Ann. Residence hall counselor Pa. State U., University Park, Pa., 1954-55; personnel asst. Chrysler Corp., Detroit, 1955; survey asst., personnel mgmt. br. The Adjutant General's Office, U.S. Army, Washington, 1956-57, statistical research asso., personnel research br. 1957-59; research asso. Century Research Corp., Arlington, 1959—, v.p., 1961—, dir., 1962—. Served with AUS, 1955-57. Mem. Am., Eastern, D.C. psychol. assns., Human Factors Soc., A.A.A.S., Phi Beta Kappa, Kappa Phi Kappa, Phi Kappa Phi, Phi Eta Sigma, Psi Chi. Contbr. articles in field to profl. jours. Home: 6542 35th Rd N Arlington VA 22213 Office: 4113 Lee Hwy Arlington VA 22207

COOK, LELAND BLANCHARD, civil engr.; b. Tupelo, Miss., June 7, 1920; s. Thomas Blanchard and Verlie Rebecca (Christian) C.; B.S., Miss. State U., 1942; m. Mary Agnes Livingston, Sept. 30, 1942; children—Mary Lee (wife of Dr. John Paul Bryson), Rebecca Caye, Stephen Roy. With Ingalls Shipbldg. Corp., Pascagoula, Miss., 1942-44; cons. engr., Tupelo, 1946-60; partner Cook Coggin Engrs., Inc., Tupelo, 1960—; pres. Found. Services, Inc.; v.p. Planning Consultants, Inc. Past mem. Miss. Bd. Registration for Profl. Engrs.; mem. engring. adv. com. Miss. State U. Served as lt. USNR, 1944-46. Mem. Cons. Engrs. Council Miss. (past pres.), Miss. Soc. Profl. Engrs., Am. Soc. C.E. (dir. Miss. sect.), Miss. Profl. Engrs. Pvt. Practice (past pres.), Miss. State U. Engring. Alumni Assn. (pres.). Baptist. Home: 1006 Jackson St Tupelo MS 38801 Office: 703 Crossover St Tupelo MS 38801

COOK, MARLOW WEBSTER, U.S. senator; b. Akron, N.Y., July 27, 1926; s. Floyd Truman and Mary Lee (Webster) C; LL.B. U. Louisville, 1950; m. Nancy Elizabeth Remmers, Nov. 22, 1947; children—Christine, Caroline, Nancy, Mary Louise, Marlow Webster. Admitted to Ky. bar, 1950; mem. firm Hotell and Stephenson, Louisville, 1952-61; judge Jefferson County, 1961-65, 66-68; mem. U.S. Senate from Ky., 1969—. Mem. Ky. Ho. of Reps., 1958-61. Served with USN, 1944-46. Home: 4000 River St North Arlington VA 22207 Office: Old Senate Office Bldg Washington DC 20510

COOK, MAURICE GAYLE, educator; b. Frankfort, Ky., Dec. 26, 1932; s. Price Cash (dec.) and Evelyn (Moore) (dec.) C.; B.S. (NSF fellow 1957), U. Ky., 1957, M.S., 1959; Ph.D., Va. Poly. Inst., 1961; m. Eva Nancy Blalock, Aug. 27, 1966; 1 son, Stephen Price. Mem. faculty N.C. State U., Raleigh, 1961—, prof. soil sci., 1968—. Bd. dirs. Nat. Alpha Zeta Found., Lafayette, Ind., 1972—. Served with AUS, 1957-58. Named Outstanding Prof. N.C. State U., 1970. Mem. Soil Sci. Soc. Am., Clay Minerals Soc., U.S. Army Reserve, Alpha Zeta, Gamma Sigma Delta, FarmHouse, Sigma Xi, Phi Delta Kappa, Phi Kappa Phi. Democrat. Baptist. Contbr. articles to profl. jours. Home: 3458 Leonard St Raleigh NC 27607

COOK, RALDO WOLFORD, evangelist; b. Milford, Ill., Dec. 2, 1927; s. Franklin G. Harlan and Ella Corrine (Robb) C.; A.B., Johnson Bible Coll., 1950; M.Ed., U. Pitts., 1956; m. Beverly Lynn Price, Oct. 15, 1950; children—Terrie Lynn, David Franklin, Timothy Wayne, Stephen Mark. Ordained to ministry Christian Ch., Ch. of Christ, 1950; minister Midway Christian Ch., Bluefield, W.Va., 1949-53, First Christian Ch., Greensburg, Pa., 1953-58, Ch. of Christ, Greensburg, 1958-70; owner Cook's Religious Supplies and Gift Shop, Greensburg, 1958—; dir., evangelist Total Evangelism, Altamonte Springs, Fla., 1971—; regional sales mgr. World-Wide Group Tours, N.Y.C., 1971—; owner Inspirational Recs., Altamonte Springs; rec. artist, music dir. various religious gatherings, including N.Am. Christian Conv. Lectr. various colls., univs.; adviser Pension Plan Christian Chs., 1969—. Mem. Council of 70, Johnson Bible Coll., Knoxville, Tenn., 1970—. Mem. Christian Booksellers Am., United Comml. Travellers Am. (chaplain). Author: Your First Year As A Christian, 1973; The Work of the Holy Spirit-Today, 1973; Is Your Congregation in the Dark About the Holy Spirit, 1973. Address: 120 Peacock Dr Altamonte Springs FL 32701

COOK, WILLIE EDWARD, accountant; b. Roosevelt, Okla., Apr. 1, 1919; s. Ira and Clara Ann (Wallis) C.; B.B.A., U. Tex., 1943, B.A., 1948; C.P.A., 1951; grad. Draugh's Bus. Coll., Wichita Falls, Tex., 1940, Internat. Accountants Soc., 1941; m. Alice Delorne Wilson, June 9, 1967; children—Dwayne J., Delorne Gay. Accountant, City of Wichita Falls, 1940-41; chief accountant Consol. Vultee Aircraft Co., Wichita Falls, 1941-42; partner Rodney B. Horton & Co., C.P.A.'s, Ft. Worth, 1942-48, resident partner, Del Rio, Tex., 1948-50; resident partner Horton, Leatherwood & Ward, C.P.A.'s, Del Rio, 1950-54; propr. W.E. Cook, C.P.A., Del Rio, 1954—; pres. Vista De Amistad, Inc., Rio Grande Realty Co., Inc., Aimstad Realty and Investment Co., Inc. (all Del Rio). Past chmn. Del Rio Park Devel. Bd.; dir. Big Bend Nat. Park Devel. Commn.; vice chmn. Amistad Reservoir Commn., 1950-72; fund chmn., exec. chmn. Boy Scouts Am.; active Nat. Flood Disaster Relief; mem. exec. council U. Tex., 1973—; mem. White House Youth Conf., Tex. Youth Conf.; hon. mem. Del Rio Fire Dept.; active local drives March of Dimes; co-chmn. Val Verde Hosp. Found. Commn. Bd. dirs. Five States, Tex. and Mexico Good Neighbor Com., Old Spanish Trails, Del Rio Indsl. Found., Columbus Internat. Celebration. Mem. Am. Inst. C.P.A.'s, Tex. Soc. C.P.A.'s, Tex. Soc. Pub. Accountants, Dep. Sherrif's Assn., W. Tex., Del Rio (past pres.), chambers commerce, U.S. 90 Assn., Old Spanish Trails Assn., U. Tex. Execs. (past pres. Del Rio). Baptist. Rotarian (past pres. Del Rio; numerous internat. offices). Club: Knife and Fork. Home: Gilchrist Lane Box Y Del Rio TX 78840 Office: Cook Bldg 114 W Martin St Box 1347 Del Rio TX 78840

COOKE, HERMAN GLENN, educator; b. Petersburg, Va., Nov. 28, 1918; s. Joseph P. and Vinia (Goode) C.; B.S., Va. State Coll., 1936; M.S., U. Pa., 1939; Ph.D., U. Wis., 1962. Histologist, Children's Hosp. of Phila., 1942-44; taxonomist, entomologist U.S. Research Center, Washington, 1944-45; asst. prof. biology Hampton Inst., 1946-53; prof. biology Elizabeth City (N.C.) State Coll., 1961—. Post-doctoral research Max-Planck-Institut fur Limnologie, West Germany, 1967; lectr. in field. Recipient citation for research work, Elizabeth City State Coll., 1966. Mem. Am. Entomol. Soc., A.A.A.S., Acad. Sci. Phila., Acad. Sci. N.C., Elisha Mitchell Sci. Soc., Sigma Xi, Psi Sigma, Omega Psi Phi, Beta Beta Beta. Contbr. articles to profl. jours. Home: 4 Ross Ct Petersburg VA 23803 Office: Elizabeth City State Coll Elizabeth City NC 27909

COOKE, JAMES L., educator; b. Canyon, Tex., Sept. 20, 1929; s. Elzie B. and R. Vita (Heasley) C.; B.S. in Elec. Engring., Tex. Tech U., 1951; M.S. in Elec. Engring., U. Tex., 1952; Ph.D., Northwestern U., 1960; m. Ina Lee Crowell, Nov. 10, 1950; children—Diane, Linda. With Southwestern Pub. Service Co., Amarillo, Tex., 1952-53; mem. faculty Lamar U., Beaumont, Tex., 1956-58, 60—, now Regents prof. elec. engring.; cons. engr. Gulf States Utilities Co., 1956-58, 60-65, 72—, Texaco, 1966-71. Served with AUS, 1953-55. Registered profl. engr., Tex. Mem. I.E.E.E. (sr.), Sigma Xi, Tau Beta Pi. Methodist. Home: 6235 Westgate Dr Beaumont TX 77706

COOKSEY, WAYNE EARL, food co. exec.; b. Centralia, Ill., Jan. 4, 1943; s. Earl Heber and Avadel (Bundy) C.; student Centralia Jr. Coll., 1961-62; B.S., Murray State Coll., 1965; M.S., St. Louis U., 1969; m. LaDonna Baker, Apr. 4, 1965; children—Jason Wade, Mason Wayne. Counselor, Murray State U., 1963-65; sales analyst Ralston Purina Co., St. Louis, 1965-67, market anaylst, 1967-69, mgr. sales analysis, 1969-70, marketing mgr., 1972-73; dir. new product devel. Farmbest, Inc., Jacksonville, Fla., 1973—. Tchr., Belleville Area Coll., 1970-72. Active United Fund of St. Louis. Mem. Am. Marketing Assn., Alpha Tau Omega. Club: Toastmasters (pres. 1969-70). Home: 3309 Cypresswood Dr S Jacksonville FL 32217 Office: PO Drawer R Jacksonville FL 32203

COOKSEY, WILLIAM TRAVIS, bus. exec.; b. Phenix City, Ala., Mar. 20, 1915; s. Samuel Hill and Verna (Brodnax) C.; student pub. schs.; m. Mildred Alice Jenkins, May 16, 1936. Accounting dept. Tom Huston Peanut Co., Columbus, Ga., 1931-39; salesman Liley Ames Corp., Columbus, O., 1939-40; chief clk. supply Q.M.C., Ft. Benning, Ga., 1940-44; gen. mgr. Blue Springs Farms-Cason J. Callaway, Hamilton, Ga., 1944-60; sec. Ida Cason Callaway Found., Pine Mountain, Ga., 1951—, treas., 1960—, exec. sec., 1964—. Instl. rep. Boy Scouts. Chmn. Harris County (Ga.) Planning Commn. Bd. dirs. Harris County Mental Health Assn.; bd. dirs. Harris County chpt. A.R.C., chmn. finance com., 1963—; life bd. dirs., past pres. Ga. Lions Lighthouse Found.; sec.-treas., trustee Pine Mountain Clinic; bd. dirs., v.p. Peach Bowl, Inc. Mem. U.S. Hwy. 27 of Ga. (dir., past pres.). Methodist. (steward, chmn. ofcl. bd., lay speaker). Mason (K.T.), Lion (past pres., zone chmn., dep. dist. gov.). Home: Blue Springs Rd Hamilton GA 31811 Office: Pine Mountain GA 31822

COOLEY, CALEB BERNARD, accountant; b. Prestonsburg, Ky., Sept. 10, 1944; s. Otis and Viola (May) C.; B.S., Morehead State U., 1966; m. Sandra Kay Annett, Aug. 15, 1970; children—Tambra Lynn, James Christian, Matthew Todd. Auditor U.S. Gen. Accounting Office, Los Angeles, 1966-68; c.p.a., Linton & Co., Pikeville, Ky., 1968—. C.P.A., Ky. Mem. Ky. Soc. C.P.A.'s, Am. Inst. C.P.A.'s, Blue Key. Kiwanian. Home: Wells St Pikeville KY 41501 Office: PO Box 111 Pikeville KY 41501

COOLEY, DAVID WILLIAM, assn. exec.; b. Hendersonville, N.C., Feb. 6, 1929; s. Arthur Gullford and Reina (McNee) C.; student pub. schs.; m. Diane Clair Miller, Oct. 24, 1953; children—Ann, David William, John, Philip, Matthew. Chief exec. officer Greer (S.C.) C. of C., 1951-52, Hendersonville C. of C., 1952-58, Greenville (S.C.) C. of C., 1958-64, Jacksonville (Fla.) C. of C., 1964-68, Memphis C. of C., 1968-73; pres. Dallas C. of C., 1973—. Served with USMCR, 1948-50. Mem. Am. C. of C. Execs. (pres. 1973-74). Episcopalian. Mason (Shriner). Home: 4909 Ridgeside Dr Dallas TX 75234 Office: Dallas Chamber of Commerce 1507 Pacific Av Dallas TX 75201

COOLEY, DENTON, surgeon, educator; b. Houston, Aug. 22, 1920; s. Ralph C. and Mary (Fraley) C.; B.A., U. Tex., 1941; M.D., Johns Hopkins, 1944; m. Louise Goldsborough Thomas, Jan. 15, 1949; children—Mary, Susan, Louise, Florence, Helen. Asso. prof. surgery Baylor U. Coll. Medicine, Houston, 1954-62, prof. surgery, 1962—; chief cardiovascular service St. Luke's Hosp., Tex. Children's Hosp. Dir. Southwestern Savs. Assn., Bank of Tex. Trustee St. Stephens Episcopal Sch., Austin, Tex. Served as capt. M.C., AUS, 1946-48. Named one of Ten outstanding Young Men in U.S., by U.S. Jr. C. of C., 1955; decorated Condecoracion Al Merito (Republic Ecuador); recipient Grande Medaille, U. Ghent, Belgium, 1963, Humanitarian award Variety Clubs Internat., 1963, Coronet medal St. Edwards U., 1963; Kappa Sigma Man of Year, 1964; Distinguished Citizen award Rotary Club Houston, 1965. Diplomate Am. Bd. Surgery, Am. Bd. Thoracic Surgery (mem. bd. 1965—). Fellow A.C.S. (gov. 1965-68); mem. Soc. Thoracic Surgeons, Thoracic Soc., So. Med. Assn., Am. Assn. Thoracic Surgery, Soc. U. Surgeons, Am. Coll. Cardiology, Am. Coll. Chest Physicians, Am., Pan-Pacific, Western surg. assns., Tex. Acad. Sci., Soc. for Clin. Surgery, Internat. Cardiovascular Soc., Soc. for Vascular Surgery, Western So. surg. assns., Halsted Soc., Tex. Surg. Soc., Internat. Soc. Surgery. Home: 3014 Del Monte Dr Houston TX 77019

COOLEY, JAMES FRANKLIN, clergyman, educator; b. Rowland, N.C., Jan. 11, 1926; s. James Franklin and Martha (Buie) C.; A.B., Johnson C. Smith U., 1953, B.D., 1956; D.D., Shorter Coll., 1971; D.D., Life Sci. Coll., 1972; M.A. in Sociology, East Neb. Christian Coll., 1972; M.Div., Interdenominational Theology Sem., 1973; m. Louvenia McCallum, Oct. 20, 1946; children—Virginia M., James Francis, Glady M. (Mrs. Edward Taylor), Franklin Donell. Ordained to ministry Presbyn. Ch., 1956; pastor Grant Chapel Presbyn. Ch., Darien, Ga., 1956-57, St. Andrews Presbyn. Ch., Forrest City, Ark., 1957-69, New Elbenzer A.M.E. Ch., Little Rock, 1969—; tchr. social sci. Lincoln Jr. High Sch., Forrest City, 1957-69; acad. dean Shorter Jr. Coll., 1969—. Juvenile probation officer, protector for young offenders, 1959—; chaplain Tucker Prison; dep. sheriff St. Francis County, hon. dep. sheriff, Pulaski County, 1969; established basic adult edn. class St. Andrews Ch., 1965, St. Andrews Day Care Center, 1966, Com. for Peaceful Co-existence, 1969; Justice of Peace, Big Rock Twp.; dep. pros. atty., 1973; staff mem. Atty. Gen.'s Office, 1973. Recipient citation Ark. Dept. Edn., 1964. Served with AUS, 1944-46. Mem. Ark. Tchrs. Assn. (certificate award, recognition), Forrest City Profl. Tchrs. Assn., Forrest City Council on Human Relations (pres.), Interdenominational Ministerial Alliance (sec.), N.A.A.C.P., Johnson C. Smith U. Alumni Assn., Vegetable Growers Assn., Omega Psi Phi (Citizen of Year award 1972). Mason (32 deg.). Writer weekly column So. Mediator Newspaper, 1970-73. Address: 2415 W 13th St Little Rock AR 72202

COOLEY, JOSEPH BERNARD, physician; b. Atlanta, July 1, 1920; s. Lewis Robert and Pallie Clementine (Hudgins) C.; A.B., Emory U., 1942; M.D., Med. Coll. Ga., 1945; m. Mary Elizabeth Longley, Oct. 11, 1946; children—William Robert, Joseph Howell, John Cline, Stephen Lewis. Intern, Crawford W. Long Meml. Hosp., Atlanta, 1945-46, now mem. staff; gen. practice medicine, Lithonia, Ga., 1949-52, Atlanta, 1952—; mem. staff DeKalb Gen. Hosp., Decatur, Ga. Served with M.C., AUS, 1942-48. Mem. John Birch Soc. (chpt. leader 1968—), Theta Kappa Psi. Baptist. Home: 5127 Stratmor Ct Stone Mountain GA 30083 Office: 572 Fayetteville Rd SE Atlanta GA 30316

COOLIDGE, EDWIN CHANNING, educator; b. Mt. Vernon, O., Jan. 30, 1925; s. Walter Hatheral and Sarah Helen (Fay) C.; B.A., Kenyon Coll., 1944; Ph.D., Johns Hopkins, 1949; m. Bonita Mae Warner, May 1, 1953; 1 son, Edwin Channing IV. Research chemist Procter & Gamble Co., Cin., 1949-54; asst. prof. Hamilton Coll., Clinton, N.Y., 1954-58; asst. prof. N.M. Inst. Mining and Tech., Socorro, 1959-61; asso. prof. Stetson U., Deland, Fla., 1961-64, prof. chemistry, 1964—. Dir. Asso. Mid-Fla. Colls. Year Abroad Program, 1968-69, resident dir., Freiburg, Germany, 1969-70. Served with AUS, 1951-53. Mem. Am. Chem. Soc. (sect. chmn. 1973), Chem. Soc. London, A.A.A.S., N.Y. Acad. Scis., Am. Assn. U. Profs., Phi Beta Kappa, Sigma Xi, Gamma Sigma Upsilon. Contbr. articles to profl. jours. Home: 2446 E New York Av Deland FL 32720

COOLIDGE, JOEL BOOTH, lawyer; b. Ft. Worth, Dec. 25, 1922; s. Clarence Earle and Marian (Booth) C.; B.S., Tex. A. & M. U., 1947; LL.B., U. Tex. at Austin, 1949; m. Dorothy Sue Roemer, Aug. 18, 1950; children—Jennifer Sue, Roberta Gayle. Admitted to Tex. bar, 1949; partner Coolidge & Coolidge, Houston, 1949-60; practiced in Houston, 1960-63; partner Urban, Coolidge, Pennington & Scott, Houston, 1963—. Trustee Continental Bank Employees Profit Sharing Plan, Houston; dir. Jetty-Fagg, Inc., Houston. Chmn. Harris County Democratic Exec. Com., 1962-63. Chmn. bd. Tex. Bill of Rights Found., Houston, 1968-70, mem., 1965—; pres. interim bd. Westheimer Ind. Sch. Dist., Houston, 1971—; trustee Houston Legal Found. 1973—. Served with AUS, 1942-45; ETO. Mem. Am., Houston (dir. 1965-66, v.p. 1967-68, sec. 1974) bar assns., Galveston Bay Cruising Assn. (dir. 1968—, commodore 1971), Kappa Sigma. Methodist (sec. 1960; mem. ofcl. bd. 1955-62). Clubs: Yacht (mem. bd. 1970—), Inns of Court (sec. bd. dirs. 1971—). Racquet (Houston). Home: 6231 Terwilliger St Houston TX 77027 Office: 777 S Post Oak Bldg Suite 808 Houston TX 77027

COOLIDGE, WARREN H., lawyer; b. Plattsburg, N.Y., July 30, 1930; s. Victor A. and Laura (Cook) C.; A.A., Campbell Coll., 1957; A.B., U. N.C., 1958, J.D., 1961; m. Nancy Harnish, Mar. 19, 1951. Admitted to N.C. bar, 1961; practiced in Fayetteville, N.C.; instr. N.C. State U., 1962; city solicitor, Fayetteville, 1965-69; U.S. atty. Eastern Dist. N.C., 1969-72; now atty. firm Coolidge, Anderson & Clarke, Fayetteville. Exec. sec. N.C. Republican Party, 1960; Cumberland County Rep. chmn., 1961, 7th dist. chmn., 1962-63. Served with AUS, 1947-55. Mem. Am., N.C., 7th Dist., Cumberland County bar assns., Campbell Coll. Alumni Assn. (county pres. 1965-66), Nat. Dist. Attys. Assn. Mason (32 deg., Shriner, K.T.), Home: 224 Woodcrest Rd Fayetteville NC 28305 Office: 1008 Hay St Fayetteville NC 28302

COOMBS, VIRGINIA RUTH HILL, home economist; b. Punta Gorda, Fla., Feb. 1, 1931; d. David Sylvester and Lillian Violet (Peile) Hill; B.S. in Home Econs. Edn., Fla. State U., 1952; m. Richard John Coombs, July 22, 1961 (dec. Apr. 1964). Vocational home econs. tchr., Highlands County, Fla., 1952-54; extension home econs. agt. Fla. Coop. Extension Service, Hillsborough County, Fla., 1954—. Sec., Hillsborough County Nutrition Com., 1963, chmn., 1964. Mem. West Coast Dist. Home Econs. Assn. (sec.-treas. 1957-58, vice chmn. 1958-59), Nat., Fla. (sec. 1964) assns. extension home economists, Am., Fla. home econs. assn., Nat. Assn. Extension 4-H Agts. Home: 220 6th Av SW Ruskin FL 33570 Office: 101 14th Av SE Ruskin FL 33500

COONEY, JOSEPH CHARLES, entomologist; b. Harrisburg, Pa., Aug. 13, 1940; s. Cloyd Howard and Mary Emma (Katzaman) C.; B.S. with honors, Florence State U., 1962; Ph.D., Auburn U., 1967; m. Mary Settle Wright, Aug. 18, 1962; children—Joseph Charles, Robert Howard. Chief entomology sect. Environmental Biol. Br., TVA, Sheffield, Ala., 1969—. Bd. dirs. Colbert County United Fund. Mem. Sheffield Bd. Edn., 1973—. Served with USPHS, 1966-68. Mem. Entomol. Soc. Am., Am. Mosquito Control Assn., Am. Registry Certified Entomologists, Phi Kappa Phi, Gamma Sigma Delta, Beta Beta Beta. Methodist (mem. adminstrv. bd. 1970—), Kiwanian. Club: Tennessee Valley Country (v.p. Sheffield 1973, bd. mem. 1974). Contbr. articles to sci. jours. Home: 117 Highland Pl Sheffield AL 35660 Office: E & D Bldg TVA Sheffield AL 35660

COONEY, LEO JOSEPH, librarian; b. Jacksonville, Ill., Mar. 30, 1935; s. Riley Joseph and Mary Ellen (Chumley) C.; B.S. in Bus. Adminstrn., U. Fla., 1959; postgrad. Ga. Inst. Tech., 1965-66; M.L.S., Peabody Coll., 1969; m. Virginia Ann McCaskill, July 1, 1961; children—Patricia Marie, Leo Joseph, Michael Joseph. Systems analyst RCA, Palm Beach Gardens, Fla., 1961-62; systems analyst Gen. Electric Co., Huntsville, Ala., 1962-63; computer specialist Redstone Sci. Information Center, Huntsville, 1963-71; chief cataloging div. Copyright Office, Library Congress, Washington, 1971—. Served with AUS, 1960-61. Mem. Nat. Microfilm Assn., Am. Soc. Information Sci., Beta Phi Mu. Home: 400 O St SW Washington DC 20024 Office: Copyright Office Library Congress Washington DC 20559

COONS, THOMAS ELMER, milling co. exec.; b. Mt. Sterling, Ky., Dec. 7, 1903; s. John Thomas and Lucy (Duff) C.; B.S. in Commerce, U. Ky., 1926; m. Louise Atkins, July 12, 1929. Farmer, Mt. Sterling, 1926—; field supr. FCA, St. Louis, 1934-42; assn. supr. farm credit Prodn. Credit Corp., Louisville, 1942-45; owner, operator Monarch Milling Co., Mt. Sterling, Ky., 1945—; pres., chmn. bd. dirs. Central Ky. Prodn. Credit Assn., Lexington, 1960—, past pres. Ky. fedn.; dir. Exchange Bank Ky., Mt. Sterling. Mem. Montgomery County Agrl. Council, 1968—. Mem. Phi Kappa Tau. Democrat. Mem. Christian Ch. (deacon 1944—; trustee 1950—). Home: 195 Antwerp Av Mount Sterling KY 40353 Office: 101 S Maysville St Mount Sterling KY 40353

COOPER, AGNES PEARSON (MRS. DAVID ACRON COOPER), educator; b. Bonner Springs, Kan., Oct. 18, 1910; d. James P. and May B. (Luther) Pearson; B.S., Kan. State Tchrs. Coll., 1932; M.S., U. Denver, 1938; postgrad. Harvard, 1939, 40; m. David Acron Cooper, Oct. 15, 1941; 1 son, David Acron. Tchr. high schs., Kan., Mo., 1929-37; tchr. Wyandotte High Sch., Kansas City, Kan., 1937-39; instr. secretarial sci. Alfred U., 1939-41; instr. U. Tenn., 1941-42; dir. edn. and placement Knoxville (Tenn.) Bus. Coll., 1942-48; dir. edn., treas. Cooper Inst., Inc., Knoxville, 1948—. Mem. Knox County adv. com. Tenn. Welfare Dept., Knoxville, 1955—, chmn. 1959; mem. East Tenn. Community Improvement Central Com., 1952—, pres., 1968; hostess spl. luncheons Tenn. Valley Agrl. and Indsl. Fair, 1956—. Mem. nat. bd. Woman's Med. Coll. of Pa. Mem. East Tenn. Edn. Assn. (chmn. bus. sect. 1958, sec. 1957), Nat. Office Mgrs. Assn., Am. Assn. U. Women, Am. Bus. Women's Assn., Better Bus. Bur. Baptist. Club: Quota (gov. 23d dist. 1956-57, gov. 8th dist. 1949-51, trustee ednl. revolving fund Knoxville 1962-63, internat. pres. 1965-66). Home: 720 N 5th Av NE Knoxville TN 37917

COOPER, ALAN BRUCE, psychoanalyst, psychiatrist; b. N.Y.C., Aug. 19, 1928; s. Harold and Florence (Zeisler) C.; B.A., Conn. Wesleyan U., 1949, M.A., 1951; M.D., N.Y. Med. Coll., 1955; children—Nanette Michele, Robin Angele. Intern Lenox Hill Hosp., N.Y.C., 1955-56; chief resident pathology Boston Lying-In Hosp., 1958, Free Hosp. for Women, Brookline, Mass., 1959; instr. pathology, clin. pathology N.Y. Med. Coll., N.Y.C., 1956-58; teaching fellow pathology Harvard Med. Sch., Boston, 1958-59; chief resident pathology Mass. Meml. Hosp., Boston, 1959-60; exptl. pathologist toxic hazards sect. aerospace med. research lab., Wright Patterson AFB, Dayton, O., 1960-62, cons. pathologist, 1962-65; chief research and tng. Am. Registry Pathology, Armed Forces Inst. Pathology, Washington, 1962-63; chief Biomed. Materials Exchange Center, Washington, 1963-65; asst. curator Med. Mus., 1963-65, acting curator, 1964; candidate, fellow New Orleans Psychoanalytic Inst., 1966—; cons. psychiatry Rice U., Houston, 1967-68, Kelsey Seybold Clinic, Houston, 1968-69; clin. asst. prof. psychiatry Baylor Coll. Medicine, 1973—; practice medicine specializing in psychoanalysis, Houston, 1968—. Mem. visitor com. on toxicology Nat. Scis., NRC, 1963-65. Bd. dirs. F.A.H. Cooper Found. Served to maj., USAF. Diplomate Nat. Bd. Med. Examiners. Mem. A.M.A., Assn. Mil. Surgeons U.S., A.A.A.S., Am. Chem. Soc., Air Force Assn., Soc. Cryobiology (chmn. publs. com. 1963-65, mem. nominating com. 1963-65), Aerospace Med. Assn., Am. Psychiat. Assn., Am. Psychoanalytic Assn., N.Y. Acad. Scis., Montgomery County, Harris County (mem. com. mental health 1971—) med. socs., Lenox Hill Hosp. Alumni Assn., Stamford-Darien-New Calman Heart Assn., Mass. Meml. Hosp. Med. and Surg. Soc., Washington Pathology Soc., Houston Psychiat. Assn., Cor et Manus, Phi Delta Epsilon. Club: John Wesley (Middletown, Conn.). Editor USAF Toxicol. Newsletter, 1961-63. Office: 1400 Hermann Dr Houston TX 77004

COOPER, ALFRED JOSEPH, civil engr.; b. New Orleans, Feb. 2, 1913; s. Alfred Joseph and Eloise Mary (Douglas) C.; B.S. in C.E., Tulane U., 1934; M.S. in C.E., U. Tenn., 1951; postgrad. Colo. State U., 1941; m. Helen Irene Powell, Oct. 25, 1936; children—Helen Anne (Mrs. Henry Ernest DeSaix), Betty Gail (Mrs. Dennis Howard Peters). With TVA, 1934—, head hydrology sect., Knoxville, Tenn., 1954-57, head river and reservoir forecasting sect., 1957-58, asst. chief river control br., 1958-60, chief river control engr., 1960—. Tchr. Knoxville Adult Evening High Sch., 1946-47; lectr. fluid mechanics, U. Tenn. at Knoxville, 1948-50. Pres. Teen Center, Inc., Knoxville, Tenn., 1962; chmn. water task group Tenn. Emergency Resource Mgmt., 1965-66; mem. Tenn. Water Agy., 1966—. Bd. dirs. Knoxville Children's Found., 1970—, pres., 1972-74. Recipient Clifford B. Scott medal, 1931, 33. Fellow Am. Soc. C.E. (br. pres. 1960; sect. pres. 1963); mem. Knoxville Tech. Soc., Phi Kappa Phi, Tau Beta Pi, Chi Epsilon, Sigma Phi Epsilon. Club: Deane Hill Country (Knoxville). Home: 3843 Kenilworth Dr SW Knoxville TN 37919 Office: TVA Evans Bldg Knoxville TN 37902

COOPER, ARTHUR WIGGINS, govt. ofcl.; b. Fairfield, Ala., Mar. 3, 1918; s. Obie Boland and Corrie (Wiggins) C.; B.S., Auburn U., 1939, M.S., 1941; Ph.D., Mich. State U., 1956; m. Dorothy Summers, July 20, 1949; children—Robert Wayne, Donald Summers, Arthur Wiggins, Mary Corinne (Mrs. Edward A. Askins). Instr., Auburn (Ala.) U., 1939-41, asst. prof., 1941-45, asso. prof., 1946; mem. grad. faculty, 1958-70; in charge farm elect research Purdue U., Lafayette, Ind., 1946-49; project supr. U.S. Dept. Agr. Soil Conservation Service, 1949-53, asst. dir. Nat. Tillage Machinery Lab., Auburn, 1953-58, dir., 1958-70, dep. adminstr. Agr. Research Service, Washington, 1971-72, So. region, New Orleans, 1972—. Served with USNR, 1945-46. Recipient Outstanding Performance award Agr. Research Service, 1961. Fellow Am. Soc. Agrl. Engrs. (John Deere Gold medal 1969, Outstanding Paper award 1956), A.A.A.S.; mem. N.Y. Acad. Scis., Sigma Xi, Tau Beta Pi, Sigma Pi Sigma, Gamma Sigma Delta. Kiwanian. Contbr. articles to profl. jours. Home: 7151 Benson Ct New Orleans LA 70127 Office: 701 Loyola Av Box 53326 New Orleans LA 70153

COOPER, BERNARD LABE, owner retail clothing store; b. Hampton, Va., Sept. 27, 1922; s. Morris Samuel and Rose Mary (Harris) C.; student U. Va., 1939-41; m. Pearl Strauss, Nov. 23, 1947; children—Sharman Fae (Mrs. Joseph Jeffrey Leinwand), Wayne, Marla Sue. With Coopers Dept. Store, Hampton, Va., 1937-39, 1946—, partner, 1948-64, owner, 1964—. Treas. Phoebus Civic Assn., Hampton, 1959-63, pres., 1964. Pres. B'nai Israel Cong. and Synagogue, Hampton, Va., 1968-69. Served with A.C. AUS, 1943-46. Mem. Hampton Retail Mchts. Assn. (dir. 1949-50), Peninsula Retail Mchts. Assn. (dir. 1973—). Elk, Mason (Shriner). Home: 104 Eggleston Av Hampton VA 23669 Office: 14-16 E Mellen St Hampton VA 23663

COOPER, BILLY KAY, civil engr.; b. Melbourne, Ark., July 23, 1933; s. Robert Troy and Nona (Campbell) C.; A.S., Ark. Poly. Coll., 1953; B.S., U. Ark., 1955; M.S. (Automotive Safety Found. fellow), Purdue U., 1957; m. Madeline Baker, June 6, 1970; children—Lonnie, Phyllis. Traffic engr. Ark. State Hwy. Dept., Little Rock, 1957-65, design engr., 1965-67, asst. chief engr., 1967-70, chief engr., 1970-73, dep. dir., chief engr., 1973—. Pres., Lake Nixon Christian Recreation Area, Little Rock, Ark., 1969. Recipient Distinguished Alumnus award Purdue U., 1973. Mem. Nat. Soc. Profl. Engrs., Am. Assn. of State Hwy. and Transp. Ofcls., Hwy. Research Bd., Chi Epsilon. Baptist (mem. bd. deacons 1968-70). Kiwanian. Club: Toastmasters (pres. 1966) (Little Rock, Ark.). Home: 618 N Mellon Little Rock AR 72205 Office: PO Box 2261 Little Rock AR 72203

COOPER, CHARLES DEWEY, educator; b. Whittier, N.C., Jan. 11, 1924; B.S., Berry Coll., 1940; M.A., Duke, 1948, Ph.D., 1950; m. Corrie Willie Johnson, Dec. 21, 1946; children—Norma Louise, Virginia Claire, Edward Howell. Asst. prof. physics U. Ga. at Athens, 1950-55, asso. prof., 1955-61, prof., 1961—; research fellow Harvard, 1954-55. Cons. Oak Ridge Nat. Lab., 1968—. Served to lt USNR, 1944-46. Fellow A.A.A.S.; mem. Am. Inst. Physics (regional counselor 1967-70), Am. Phys. Soc., Am. Assn. U. Profs., Sigma Xi. Home: Route 3 Athens GA 30601

COOPER, CHARLES ELLIS, communications co. exec.; b. Everglades, Fla., Dec. 25, 1928; s. Charles Burnett and Lettie Anora (French) C.; student Rochester Inst. Tech., 1946-48; B.S. in Elec. Engring., U. Fla., 1951. Electronic technician Stromberg-Carlson Co., Rochester, N.Y., 1946-48, service engr., 1952-53; equipment engr. Peninsular Telephone Co., Tampa, Fla., 1954-55; cons. engr., Central and S.Am., 1955-60; pres., gen. mgr. Servicios Technicos S.A., San Jose; Costa Rica, 1961-67; founder, chief exec. Continental Communications Constrn. Corp., Tampa, 1968-70; pres. Arcata Installation Inc., Tampa, 1970—; dir. Telephone Plant Corp., Continental Finance Corp., Miami, Fla., Arcata Installation Can. Ltd., Montreal, Que.; mem. operating com. Arcata Nat., Menlo Park, Cal. Industry rep. Tampa Concentrated Employment Program, 1970—; asst. dir. Appalachian Council Manpower Devel. Program, 1970—. Mem. U.S. Telephone Pioneers Assn., U.S. Ind. Telephone Assn. (charter). Republican. Roman Catholic. Home: Pleasure Island Everglades FL 33929 Office: 5440 Mariner St Suite 221 Tampa FL 33609

COOPER, CLAUDE GEORGE, county ofcl.; b. Buffalo, June 16, 1940; s. Paul Andrew and Elsbeth Julia (Schuler) C.; B.C.E., Clarkson Coll. Tech., 1963; m. Elma May Triebel, Aug. 18, 1962; children—Timothy Alan, Kyryn Linda. With Va. Dept. Hwys., Richmond, 1963-72; dir. inspection service County of Fairfax, Fairfax, Va., 1972—. Chmn. region 3 tech. com. Va. Bd. Housing, 1973. Mem. edn. adv. bd. on bldg. No. Va. Community Coll., 1974—. Registered profl. engr., Va. Mem. Nat. Soc. Profl. Engrs., Am. Concrete Inst., Am. Soc. C.E. (asso.), Met. Washington Council Govts. (chmn. codes and regulations com. 1973-74), Am. Nat. Standards Inst. (mem. com. on concrete formwork 1974—). Mason. Club: Fairfax (Va.) Rod and Gun. Home: 13519 Pennsboro Dr Chantilly VA 22021 Office: 4100 Chain Bridge Rd Fairfax VA 22030

COOPER, CLEMENT THEODORE, lawyer; b. Miami, Fla., Oct. 26, 1930; s. Benjamin Leon and Louise (Bethel) C.; A.B., Lincoln U. of Mo., 1952; postgrad. Boston U., 1954-55; J.D., Howard U., 1958; postgrad. Hastings Coll. Law at San Francisco, 1971; m. Nannie Coles; children—Stephanie L., Bridgette L., Patricia E., Karen G., Stacie L. Admitted to Mich., D.C. bars, 1960, Supreme Ct. bar, 1963; gen. practice Washington, 1960—; pres., gen. counsel Bayshore Resources Co., Inc. Mem. D.C. Pub. Welfare Adv. Council, 1966-68. Bd. dirs. Rocky Mountain Meml. Law Found. Served with AUS, 1952-54. Mem. U.S., D.C. chambers commerce, Bar Assn. D.C., Am., Nat., Washington bar assns., Am. Civil Liberties Union, Am. Judicature Soc., Am. Trial Lawyers Assn., Alpha Phi Alpha. Author: The Sealed Verdict, 1964. Home: 728 Dahlia St NW Washington DC 20012 Office: 918 F St NW Washington DC 20004

COOPER, DAVID ACRON, coll. pres., public accountant, tax cons.; b. Charlotte, N.C., October 16, 1910; s. David P. and Roberta (Lewis) C.; B.S., U. Tenn., 1931, M.S., 1934; A.M., Columbia, 1938; postgrad. Harvard, 1939, Washington & Jefferson Coll., 1943, Am. U., Biarritz, France, 1945; m. Agnes Pearson, Oct. 15, 1941; 1 son, David A. Tchr. Knoxville (Tenn.). High Sch., 1931-34; spl. cons. bus. edn. Southwestern Pub. Co., Cin., 1935-39; personnel dir. S. H. George & Sons, Knoxville, 1941-48; owner, mgr. Dapco Sales & Services, 1949—; pres. Cooper Inst., Inc., 1948—; instr. Am. U., Biarritz, France, 1945; asso. prof. bus. Knoxville Coll., 1967—. Treas. Mental Health Clinic; mem. Com. on Teaching Bible in Pub. Schs. Sec. Bd. Edn. Served as tech. sgt. U.S. Army, ETO, 1943-45. Mem. Am. Mgmt. Assn., Nat. Assn. Accountants, Internat. Platforms Assn., C. of C., Baptist. Clubs: Kiwanis, North Knoxville Business Men's. Home: 720 N 5th Av Knoxville TN 37917

COOPER, DONALD CHARLES, hat co. exec.; b. Cleve., Feb. 6, 1917; s. Charles Edward and Elsie Helen (Hausler) C.; B.S., Western Res. U., 1938-41; postgrad. Cleve. Coll., Baldwin Wallace Coll., Fenn Coll., Case Western Res. U.; m. Blanca Julieta Delano, Apr. 19, 1942; children—Donna (Mrs. Robert Osterthaler), Karen (Mrs. Albert Warfield), Leslie (Mrs. Robert Stewart), Gayle, Charles. With Undustrias Unidas de Nuevo Laredo (Mexico), 1946-47; with Tex. Hat Co., Laredo, 1947—, pres., 1969—. Vice pres. Laredo (Tex.) Internat. Fair and Expn., 1969-74. Served to maj. USAAF, 1941-46. Decorated Air medal, D.F.C. Elk. Home: 2301 Clark St Laredo TX 78040 Office: PO Drawer 619 Laredo TX 78040

COOPER, EARL DANA, govt. engr.; b. Washington, Apr. 16, 1926; s. Dana Cockrill and Mildred (Schultz) C.; student Hampden Sydney Coll., 1944; B.E.E., George Washington U., 1948; postgrad. U. Md., 1949-51; m. Elaine LaDona Tibben, Apr. 16, 1949; children—Denise Kay, Karl Dennis. Elec. engr. Bur. Ships, Washington, 1948-55; guided missile design engr. and ordance engr. Navy Bur. of Ordnance, 1955-59; aerospace engr. Bur. Naval Weapons, 1959-62, tech. dir. air launched weapon systems 1962-66, tech. dir. advanced systems Naval Air Systems Command, Washington, 1966—; cons. to exec. com. Aircraft Armament div. Am. Def. Preparedness Assn. Served with USNR, 1944-45. Mem. U.S. Naval Inst., Assn. Naval Engrs. and Scis. (past sec.), Am. Def. Preparedness Assn., I.E.E.E., Am. Inst. Aeros. and Astronautics. Lutheran. Home: 8265 The Midway Annandale VA 22003 Office: Code AIR-03P1 Washington DC 20361

COOPER, EUGENE BRUCE, speech pathologist, educator; b. Utica, N.Y., Dec. 20, 1933; s. Clements E. and Beulah (Wetzel) C.; B.S., State U. N.Y. at Geneseo, 1955; M.Ed., Pa. State U., 1957, Ed.D., 1962; m. Crystal Silverman, Sept. 12, 1965; children—Philip Adam, Ivan Bruce. Asst. prof. Ohio U., 1962-64, Pa. State U., 1964-66; program specialist Bur. Edn. Handicapped, U.S. Office Edn., 1966; exec. sec. sensory study sect., research and demonstrations div. Rehab. Services Adminstrn., Dept. Health, Edn. and Welfare, 1966-67; prof., chmn. communicative disorders, dir. Speech and Hearing Center, U. Ala., 1967—; cons. in field. Mem. Gov. Ala. Adv. Council Devel. Disabilities Services Act, 1972—. Bd. dirs. Tuscaloosa County Crippled and Adults Assn., chmn., 1974; bd. dirs. United Cerebral Palsy W. Ala. Fellow Am. Speech and Hearing Assn. (legislative councilor 1971-73; asso. editor jour.); mem. Assn. Advancement Behavior Therapies, Council Exceptional Children (pres.-elect. div. for children with communicative disorders), Nat. Assn. Speech and Hearing Agencies, Nat. Rehab. Assn., Speech and Hearing Assn. Ala., Sigma Xi, Kappa Delta Pi. Contbr. profl. jours. Authority on stuttering. Home: 88 Woodridge St Tuscaloosa AL 35401 Office: PO Box 1965 University AL 35486

COOPER, HARRY EZEKIEL, educator; b. Kansas City, Mo., Dec. 10, 1897; s. Ezekiel and Helen (Moore) C.; Mus.B., Horner Inst. Fine Arts, 1920; Mus.D., Bush Conservatory, 1923; A.B., Ottawa U., 1937; m. Agnes Bickford, Nov. 18, 1926; children—Robert Ezekiel, Alice Caroline (Mrs. Theo Robert Potter). Supt. music Liberty (Mo.) Schs., 1917-19; prof. music, chmn. dept. William Jewell Coll., 1919-28; dean music Ottawa U., 1928-37; chmn. dept. music, prof. music Meredith Coll., 1937—. Organist, choirmaster Kansas City (Mo.) Chs., 1911-37, Christ Ch., Raleigh, N.C., 1937-47, 1st Bapt. Ch., 1948—; organist N.C. Symphony Orch., 1949. Condr., Raleigh Oratorio Soc., 1940-48. Fellow Am. Guild Organists; mem. N.C. Music Tchrs. Assn. (pres. 1943-44), Raleigh Chamber Music Guild (pres. 1942-43). Writer musical articles, various songs, others. Home: 3 Henderson St Raleigh NC 27607

COOPER, JEROME MAURICE, architect; b. Memphis, Jan. 24, 1930; s. Samuel and Bessie (Phillips) C.; B.S., Ga. Inst. Tech., 1952, B. Arch., 1955; postgrad. Universita di Roma, Rome, Italy, 1956-57; m. Jean Kanter Cooper, Dec. 29, 1957; children—David Franklin, Samuel Randolph, Beth Lauren. Draftsman Willner & Millkey, Atlanta, 1955-56; Fulbright fellow Rome, Italy, 1956-57; designer Abreu & Robeson, Atlanta, 1957-59, Heery & Heery, Atlanta 1959-60; pres. Cooper, Salzman & Carry, 1960—. Chmn. citizens adv. bd. for urban devel. City of Atlanta. Served to lt. (j.g.) USNR, 1952-54. Mem. A.I.A. (pres. Atlanta chpt.). Prin. archtl. works include: Classroom-Arts bldg. W. Ga. Coll., Briarcliff Village Shopping Center, Atlanta, Chateau-Fleur-di-Lis Restaurant, Atlanta, Sheraton Emory Inn, Riverbend Apts., Macon Youth Devel. Center, Landmark Office Bldg., Westlake Mall Shopping Center, also elementary schs. Home: 1070 Judith Way NE Atlanta GA 30324 Office: 836 W Peachtree St NW Atlanta GA 30308

COOPER, OWEN, ret. chem. co. exec., religious orgn. exec.; b. Warren County, Miss., Apr. 19, 1908; s. William S. and Malena (Head) C.; student Culkin Acad., 1925; B.S. in Agr., Miss. State Coll., 1929; M.A., U. Miss., 1936; grad. Jackson (Miss.) Sch. Law, 1938; postgrad. U. So. Cal., 1934; LL.D., Miss. Coll., 1960; m. Elizabeth Thompson, Sept. 2, 1938; children—Nancy (Mrs. Spencer Gilbert), Carolyn (Mrs. Ben Ladner), Owen, Elizabeth (Mrs. Joe Johnson II), Frances (Mrs. Charles Niles). Tchr. vocational agr., 1930-35; asst. dir. Miss. Planning Commn., 1936-40; exec. dir. Miss. Farm Bur. Fedn., Jackson, 1940-48; exec. v.p. Miss. Chem. Corp., Yazoo City, 1948-60, pres., 1960-72; exec. v.p. Coastal Chem. Corp., 1956-60, pres., 1960-72; dir. Fed. Res. Bd. Atlanta. Pres. So. Baptist Conv.; v.p. Bapt. World Alliance, also deacon ch. Home: 1826 Grand Av Yazoo City MS 39194

COOPER, RICHARD HOLCOMB, judge; b. Birmingham, Ala., Aug. 30, 1920; s. William Gerald and Ethel (Cobb) C.; A.B., Fla. So. Coll., 1940, LL.D., 1965; J.D., Stetson U., 1948; m. Bess Constantine Blanton, June 15, 1941 (dec. 1972); children—Bess Ann (Mrs. Robert L. Castlen), Sharon Lorraine (Mrs. J. Roger Efird), Thomas Richard. Admitted to Fla. bar. 1949; practiced in Orlando, 1949-67; prosecutor Orange County Criminal Ct. Record, 1953-59, judge, 1959-66; circuit judge 9th Jud. Circuit, Orlando, 1966—; moderator Moral Issues of Our Times, weekly panel program WFTV, 1962-71. Served to col. AUS, 1942; brig. gen. Res. Recipient First prize for Law Day address Am. Bar Assn., 1968. Mem. Fla. So. Coll. Nat. Alumni Assn. (past pres.), V.F.W. (state chmn. N.C. and res. activities), Res. Officers Assn. (pres. dept. 1973-74), Am. Legion. Methodist. Lion, Elk. Home: 80 Loudon Ct Maitland FL 32751 Office: Orange County Court House Orlando FL 32802

COOPER, ROBERT GILBERT, librarian; b. St. Louis, Feb. 24, 1930; s. Robert Kehr and Irma Emilie (Wagner) C.; B.S. in Edn., Union Coll., 1952; M.S. in L.S., U. So. Cal., 1966; m. Vivian Bernice Rabun, Aug. 9, 1953; children—Teresa Lynette, Stanley Wayne. Tchr., Tex. Conf. Seventh-day Adventists, Ft. Worth, 1952-62; librarian Loma Linda U., 1962-67, Findley Meml. Library, Southwestern Union Coll., Keene, Tex., 1967—. Mem. A.L.A., Tex. Library Assn. Home: 408 N College Dr Keene TX 76059 Office: Findley Meml Library Southwestern Union Coll Keene TX 76059

COOPER, SELDON AMZI, civil engr.; b. Dixon, Miss., Sept. 26, 1913; s. John Jessie and Carry Lucinda (Thomas) C.; B.C.E., Miss. State Coll., 1935; m. Monta Glee Allman, Sept. 11, 1940. Asst. engr. Gulf, Mobile & No. R.R. (name later changed to Gulf, Mobile & Ohio R.R. Co.), 1935-37, asst. supr., 1937-38, asst. engr., 1938-41, resident engr., 1941-57, chief engr., 1957-72; chief engr. So. lines Ill. Central Gulf R.R. Co. (consol. Gulf, Mobile and Ohio R.R. with Ill. Central R.R.), 1972—. Mem. Am. Ry. Engring. Assn. (dir. 1968-71). Democrat. Methodist. Office: 104 St Francis St Mobile AL 36624

COOPER, WALTER GERALD, lawyer; b. Atlanta, Mar. 22, 1904; s. Walter G. and Belle (Bacon) C.; A.B., U. Ga., 1924; student Harvard Law Sch., 1925-27; LL.B., Emory U., 1929. Admitted to Ga. bar, 1929; regional atty. NLRB, 10th Region, 1936, litigation atty., 1937; chief enforcement atty. Southeastern states for OPA, Altanta, 1942; mem. firm Tye, Cooper & Bill, 1952-55, McFarland & Cooper, Atlanta, 1955-64; mem. law firm Poole, Pearce, Cooper & Smith, and predecessor firm, Atlanta, 1964—; mem. law faculty Emory U., 1932-64. Served as lt. USNR, World War II. Mem. Am., Ga., Atlanta bar assns., Res. Officers Assn., Atlanta Lawyers Club (past. v.p. and sec.), Phi Beta Kappa, Phi Delta Phi. Democrat. Baptist. Mason, Optimist. Club: Ansley Golf. Contbr. articles to Ga. Bar Assn. Jour. Home: 200 Montgomery Ferry Dr NE Atlanta GA 30309 Office: 1642 Nat Bank of GA Bldg Atlanta GA 30303

COOPER, WILLIAM ANDERSON, JR., educator; b. Archer City, Tex., Feb. 4, 1927; s. William Anderson and Vera Bess (Herron) C.; B.S. in Biology, North Tex. State U., 1948, M.S., 1950; Ph.D., Tex. A. & M. U., College-Station, 1957; m. Scottie Charlene Snodgrass, July 14, 1952; children—Viki, Andy, Ken, Judy. Instr. natural scis. Paris Jr. Coll., Paris, Tex., 1953; instr. biology North Tex. State U., Denton, 1953; grad. instr. biology Tex. A. & M. U., College Station, 1954-57; mem. faculty West Tex. State U., Canyon, 1957—, prof. biology, 1966—. Seismograph operator Continental Oil Co., Ponca City, Okla., 1952-53; ecol. cons. Ecology Audits, Inc., Dallas, 1973—, Tex. Water Quality Bd., Amarillo, 1965—, Nat. Parks Service, 1965—, Tex. Parks and Wildlife Dept., 1957—, Killgore Researcher Water Quality, 1966—. Vice pres. Little League Baseball, Randall County, Tex., 1966-69; pres. Babe Ruth League Baseball, Randall County, Tex., 1970-73; v-p. Canyon High Sch. Booster Club, 1973-74. Served with USNR, 1945-46, 50-52. NIH research grantee for nutritional-heart devel. research, 1959-64; Water Quality Tex. Lakes Faculty Research grantee, 1965-73. Recipient ex-student assn. Faculty Excellence award West Tex. State U., 1965. Fellow Tex. Acad. Sci.; mem. Am. Micros. Soc., Am. Soc. Zoologists, Nat. Geog.

Soc., Tex. Assn. Coll. Tchrs., Sigma Xi, Beta Beta Beta. Author: (with L.S. Dillon) A Laboratory Survey of Biology, 1962, 2d edit., 1969. Home: 3205 Conner Dr Canyon TX 79015

COOVER, HARRY WESLEY, JR., chem. co. exec.; b. Newark, Dela., Mar. 6, 1918; s. Harry Wesley and Anna (Rohm) C.; B.S., Hobart Coll., 1941; M.S., Cornell U., 1943; Ph.D., 1944; m. Muriel Zumbach, Sept. 17, 1941; children—Harry Wesley III, Stephen R., Melinda R. Research chemist Eastman Kodak Co., Rochester, N.Y., 1944-49; sr. research chemist Tenn. Eastman Co., mfr. plastics, chemicals, fibers, Kingsport, 1949-54, research asso., 1954-63, div. head, 1963-65, dir. research, 1965-70, v.p., 1970-73, exec. v.p., 1973—. Recipient So. Chemist award Memphis sect. Am. Chem. Soc., 1960. Mem. A.A.A.S., Am. Chem. Soc., Am. Ordnance Assn., Am. Assn. Textile Tech., N.Y. Acad. Sci., Sigma Xi, Epsilon Pi Sigma, Phi Kappa Phi. Patentee in field. Contbr. articles to profl. pubs. Home: 1335 Linville St Kingsport TN 37660 Office: Tennessee Eastman Company PO Box 511 Kingsport TN 37662

COPE, LAWRENCE LYNDON, editor; b. N.Y.C., Oct. 5, 1918; s. Oliver Franklin and Gladys Edith (Willes) C.; B.A., Fla. So. Coll., 1940; postgrad. Northwestern U., 1941-42, Loyola U., New Orleans, 1953, U. Ill. at Urbana, 1957, U. Chgo., 1964; m. Dorothea Anne Herrick, June 25, 1944; children—Patricia (Mrs. Theodore T. Tackett), Laurence B. Asst. advt. mgr. Greenwich (Conn.) Times, 1945-47; mgr. sales promotion Nat. Circulation Co., N.Y.C., 1947-52; field editor H.L. Peace Publs., New Orleans, 1952-53; mgr. promotion Simmons-Boardman Pub. Co., N.Y.C., 1953-56; mgr. devel. Am. Chem. Soc., Washington, 1956-65; editor Jour. Opticianry, Opticians of Am., Washington, 1966—; cons. publs., Washington, 1965—. Coordinator Community Chest, New Orleans, 1952. Served to lt. comdr., USNR, 1941-45. Recipient Lloyd F. Wood Meml. award Mail Advt. Club, Washington, 1970. Mem. Am. Med. Writers Assn., Direct Mail Advt. Assn. (chmn. com. 1963-66). Roman Catholic. Clubs: National Press, Advertising, Mail Advertising (dir. 1959-62) (Washington). Editor, The Eye Physician, 1967-69; asso. editor Volta Rev., 1968-70. Home: 5407 Newington Rd Washington DC 20016 Office: Cope Assos 1629 K St NW Washington DC 20006

COPELAND, EMILY AMERICA, educator, librarian; b. Tifton, Ga.; d. Jerry and America (Vaughn) Copeland; A.B., Spelman Coll., 1937; B.S. in L.S. (Carnegie grantee) Atlanta U., 1942; M.S., Columbia, 1948, postgrad., 1959-60; postgrad. N.Y. U., 1949-50, U. S.C., 1969. Tchr., Tift County Indsl. High Sch., Tifton, 1937-38; librarian Finley High Sch., Chester, S.C., 1938-41; library asst. Atlanta U. Library, summers 1938-40, 42; head librarian Gammon Theol. Sem., Atlanta, 1942-44; acquisitions librarian Atlanta U., 1944-46; reference, sch. work sst. N.Y. Pub. Library, N.Y.C., 1945-46; head dept. library sci. S.C. State Coll., 1946-51; prof., chmn. dept. library service Fla. A. and M. U., Tallahassee, 1951—; pres., founder Black Research Information Coordinating Service, Inc., 1972—. Recipient certificate of merit Spelman Coll., 1968. Mem. S.C. Library Devel. Com., 1947-51, S.C. Library Edn. Planning Com., 1948-51; mem. Fla. com. Columbia Campaign Fund, 1967-69. Mem. Am. (mem. nat. planning com. 1956-62, E.P. Dutton McRae award com. 1971, mem. right to read com. pub. library div. 1972—, minority recruitment cons. 1972), Southeastern, Fla. (pres. 1953-56) library assns., Smithsonian Instn. (asso.), Information Industry Assn., Marquis Biog. Library Soc. Author: A Handbook for the Guidance of Students in School Library Intership, 1964; A Guide to Minority Resources, 1973. Contbr. articles to profl. jours., World Book Ency., Black Librarian in Am. Home: 614 Howard Av Tallahassee FL 32304 also 1212 Peachtree St Tifton GA Office: 540 W Brevard St Tallahassee FL 32301

COPELAND, HARRY ELBERT, JR., pub. relations and advt. counselor; b. Houston, June 16, 1931; s. Harry Elbert and Laura Elizabeth (Robertson) C.; B.J., U. Tex., 1952; m. Ann Bryan, Sept. 15, 1955; children—Elaine Suzette, Douglas Carter. Pub. relations and advt. counsel Hal Copeland Co., Dallas, 1957—. Mem. Pub. Relations Soc. Am. (pres. North Tex. chpt. 1965), Dallas C. of C. (communications com. 1971—), Phi Delta Theta, Alpha Delta Sigma. Presbyn. Rotarian (pub. relations chmn. 1971-72). Club: Press (Dallas). Home: 2800 McFarlin Blvd Dallas TX 75205 Office: 6517 Hillcrest Suite 302 Dallas TX 75205

COPELAND, JAMES WILLIAM, superior ct. judge; b. Woodland, N.C., June 16, 1914; s. Luther Clifton and Nora (Benthall) C.; A.B. Guilford Coll., 1934; J.D., U. N.C., 1937; m. Nancy Hall Sawyer, Oct. 11, 1941; children—Emily, James William, Buxton. Admitted to N.C. bar, 1936; pvt. practice law, Woodland, 1937-42, Murfreesboro, 1946-61. Mayor, Woodland, 1938-42, Murfreesboro, 1947-50; mem. N.C. Senate, 1951, 53, 57, 59, chmn. judiciary com., 1957, mem. adv. budget commn., 1957-61, chmn. appropriations com., 1959, legislative counsel to gov. 1961 session; spl. judge Superior Ct., 1961—. Delegate Dem. National Conv., 1956. Served as lt. USNR, 1942-45. Mem. Am. Legion, Am. (del. trial judges conf. 1969—), N.C. bar assns., V.F.W. Mason (Shriner). Home: 407 E High St Murfreesboro NC 27855

COPELAND, PAUL WILLIAM, journalist; b. Columbus, O., Aug. 12, 1917; s. Paul Walter and Helen Marie (Kanmacher) C.; student Ohio State U., 1933-34, Franklin U., 1934-35; m. Annita Auteri, Jan. 28, 1949; children—Robert, Judith, Mary, Constance. Radio, TV dir. Byer & Bowman Advt. Agy., Columbus, O., 1936-45, 49-50; pub. relations dir. Hallmark Motion Pictures, Hollywood, Cal., 1950-51; columnist Sarasota (Fla.) Jour., 1951—; columnist McCall's, mag., 1969-70. Served with AUS, 1945-49; PTO. Author: The File on Charlie, 1968. Home: 5720 Antilles Dr Sarasota FL 33581 Office: Sarasota Journal Box 1719 Sarasota FL 33578

COPELAND, ROGER PRENTICE, sch. supt.; b. Philadelphia, Miss., Sept. 22, 1926; s. Linard Gaston and Effie Aurilla (Cumberland) C.; B.S., U. So. Miss., 1951, M.A., 1954; postgrad., 1970; m. Dorothy Ree Irons, Oct. 21, 1945; children—Roger Lynn, Rex Byron. Coach Neshoba County Schs., Philadelphia, 1951-61; prin. Neshoba County High Sch., Philadelphia, 1961-65, supt., 1965—. Bd. edn. East Central Jr. Coll., 1965. Served with AUS, 1945-46, 1950-51. Mem. Miss. Tchrs. Assn., Miss. Assn. Sch. Adminstrn., Miss. Sch. Supts. Assn., Nat. Assn. Sch. Adminstrs. Rotarian (dir. 1971), Mason. Home: Route 2 Philadelphia MS 39350 Office: Ct House Philadelphia MS 39350

COPELAND, THOMPSON PRESTON, educator; b. Snyder, Ark., Mar. 11, 1921; s. Hosea Preston and Pearl M. (Thompson) C.; B.S., Ouachita Baptist Coll., Arkadelphia, Ark., 1947; M.A., George Peabody Coll., 1950; Ph.D., U. Tenn., 1962; m. Iva Jean Scott, Aug. 21, 1950; children—Rebecca Jean, David Scott. Instr. biology Ouachita Bapt. Coll., 1947-49; guest prof. Union U., Jackson, Miss., summers 1952, 53; instr. biology East Tenn. State U., 1950, asst. prof. to asso. prof., 1954-62, prof. biology, 1962—, chmn. dept., 1963—. Served with USNR, 1942-46. NSF fellow, 1961-62. Fellow Tenn. Acad. Sci.; mem. A.A.A.S., Am. Inst. Biol. Sci., Assn. Southeastern Biologists, Tenn. Edn. Assn., Biol. Soc. Washington, Soc. Systematic Zoologists, Sigma Xi. Mason, Kiwanian (dir. Johnson City 1970-73). Democrat. Contbr. articles to profl. jours. Home: 1 Tallapoosa Rd Johnson City TN 37601

COPLEY, WAVERLY EMMETT, supt. schs.; b. Lynchburg, Va., Apr. 23, 1931; s. Horace Otis and Nell Hardy (Hurt) C.; B.A., Randolph-Macon Coll., 1953, M.A., Longwood Coll., 1963 (both Coll. William and Mary); m. Mary Anne Hammer, Apr. 16, 1960; 1 dau., Anne Simmons. Athletic dir., coach Amelia County (Va.) Pub. Schs., 1955-62, supt., 1967—; prin. Amelia High Sch., 1962-67. Scoutmaster Piedmont council Boy Scouts Am., 1955-57. Served with AUS, 1953-55. Mem. Am. Assn. Sch. Adminstrs., P.T.A., Va. Edn. Assn. Methodist (tchr. men's Bible class). Home: PO Box 65 Amelia VA 23002 Office: PO Box 276 Amelia VA 23002

COPPAGE, WILLIAM THOMAS, state ofcl.; b. nr. Front Royal, Va., May 1, 1929; s. Alvin T. and Emma (Eastham) C.; B.A., U. Richmond, 1951; M.A., U. Va., 1962; M.S. in Rehab. Counseling, Richmond Profl. Inst., 1968; m. Beverly Manning, May 30, 1959; children—Linda Beth, William Thomas, John Robert. Area supr. Bus. Enterprises For Blind, 1951-55, asst. workshop supt., 1955-61; asst. dir. State Agy. for Blind, Richmond, Va., 1961-64, dir., 1964—. Instr., Va. Commonwealth U. Mem. adv. council Sch. Community Services, Dept. Rehab. Counseling; mem. Gov.'s Overall Adv. Com. on Needs Handicapped Children, 1964-72, chmn., 1967-71; service adv. com. Am. Found. for Blind, 1969-73; mem. Gov.'s Manpower Planning Council, 1973—; mem. health execs. roundtable Richmond Area Community Council, vice chmn., 1972-73; mem. Gov.'s Com. Employment of Handicapped, 1965—; mem. Developmental Disabilities Adv. Council, 1972—. Bd. dirs. Nat. Council Workshops for Blind, 1968-71, Nat. Accreditation Council Agys. Serving Blind and Visually Handicapped, 1973—. Recipient certificate of award for service as mem. Va. Mental Health Study Commn., Gov. Va., 1965; certificate of recognition Va. Rehab. Assn., 1969, R.N. Anderson award, 1971. Mem. Am. Soc. Quality Control, Nat. Rehab. Assn., Am., Va. (dir., 1966-72) assns. workers for Blind, Nat. Council State Agys. for Blind (pres. 1968-69), Council State Adminstrs. Vocational Rehab., Internat. Platform Assn., Va. Soc. Prevention of Blindness (dir., treas. 1971-72), Lambda Chi Alpha. Lion. Home: 8000 Moorfield Rd Richmond VA 23229 Office: 3003 Parkwood Av Richmond VA 23221

COPPEDGE, DONALD LEROY, newspaper pub.; b. Hollywood, Cal., May 29, 1931; s. Charles M. and Loraine (Fultz) C.; B.A., N. Tex. State U., 1956; m. Bettye Suzanne Crawford, Jan. 12, 1952; children—Dana (dec.), D'on, Denise, Derek. Wire editor Denton (Tex.) Record-Chronicle, 1956; state editor San Angelo (Tex.) Standard-Times, 1956-58; editor Brownwood (Tex.) Bull., 1958-62; press aide Gov. John Connally, Fort Worth and Austin, 1962, dist. coordinator, 1962—; v.p., co-pub., exec. editor Waxahachie (Tex.) Daily Light, 1962—; v.p., dir. Craco, Inc.; v.p., part owner Stephenville (Tex.) Daily Empire. Mem. Waxahachie Park Bd., 1966—, chmn., 1971-72; mem. Waxahachie Charter Commn., 1969; founding dir. Ellis County Hist. Mus. and Art Gallery, 1967—; bd. dirs. Community Chest, 1962-65, Brazos River Authority, 1967—; mng. dir. Waxahachie Family Welfare Fund.; dir. Blue Bonnet Trails Dist. council Boy Scouts of Am., 1966—, dist. chmn. Bluebownet dist., 1969-71; bd. dirs. Waxahachie YMCA, Camp Grady Spruce, Dallas, 1970—; bd. dirs. Emergency Sch. Assistance Program, Waxahachie Ind. Sch. Dist., 1971-72, Emergency Sch. Assistance Act, 1973—. Served with AUS, 1953-55. Named Outstanding Young Man, Waxahachie, 1964. Mem. Tex. Press Assn. (dir. 1963—, pres. 1972-73, chmn. bd. 1973-74), N. and E. Tex. Press Assn. (dir. 1964—, pres. 1969), C. of C. (dir. 1964-67, pres. 1968). Episcopalian (vestryman 1963-68). Home: 307 Monticello St Waxahachie TX 75165 Office: PO Box 354 Waxahachie TX 75165

COPPICK, GLENDON CLEON, clergyman; b. Stigler, Okla., Mar. 18, 1926; s. Cleo Clarence and Gerty (Speer) C.; B.A., Tex. Christian U., 1952; M.Div., Ch. Div. Sch. of Pacific, Berkeley, Cal., 1955; postgrad. San Francisco Theol. Sem., 1967—; m. Shirley Jane Pederson, Nov. 21, 1954; children—Stephen Cleon, John Christen, Mary Katherine. Ordained to ministry Episcopal Ch., 1955; rector Episcopal Ch. of Good Shepherd, Dallas, 1955-59, Trinity Episcopal Ch., Owensboro, Ky., 1959—. Mem. exec. council Diocese of Ky., 1962-65, 70-73, convocation dean, 1970—; dep. Gen. Conv., 1970; faculty Brescia Coll., Owensboro, 1971—. Mem. Mayor's Commn. on Human Rights, 1965-69. Bd. dirs. Welfare League; trustee U. of South, Sewanee, Tenn. Served with USNR, 1944-46. Nat. Bd. Theol. Edn. grantee, 1972. Mem. Acad. Parish Clergy. Lion. Home: 1517 Dean Av Owensboro KY 42301 Office: 720 Ford Av Owensboro KY 42301

COPPIN, JOHN STEPHENS, artist, portrait painter; b. Mitchell, Ont., Can., Sept. 13, 1904; s. Thomas Pascoe and Maude (Levette) C.; stu., Stratford Collegiate Inst., 1918-21, Wicker Art Sch., 1923-27, study trip, Europe, 1938; m. Sidni Lovelace, Feb. 7, 1948; 1 son, Torry John. Art dir. Mich. Motor News, 1930-60; art instruction, 1928; free lance artist and illustrator, 1928—; portrait painter. Recipient Scarab gold medals, 1941, 1944, 1946; Detroit Inst. Arts popular prize, 1933, 1939, 1946, 1950. Carl F. Clark award, 1953. Murals in Mich. Bar Assn. Bldg., Lansing, Detroit Central High Sch., Detroit Gas Co., Adam Strohm Hall, Detroit Pub. Library; works in Detroit Inst. Arts, Nat. Historic Mus., Frederiksborg, Denmark, others. Portraits include Edgar A. Guest, Alvan McCauley, Mrs. Alfred Glancey, George Romney, Dr. Henry Vaughan, George W. Stark; ex-governors Wagoner, Kelly and Sigler; Henry Ford, Paul Paray, Alec Guinness, Mennen G. Williams, Wm. S. Knudsen, James M. Roche and others; numerous commissioned portraits of prominent persons; hist. paintings Mich. State U. Fellow Internat. Inst. Arts and Letters; mem. Am. Fedn. Artists, Mich. Acad. Sci., Arts and Letters, Sarasota, Longboat Key art assns., Ringling Mus. Assn. Clubs: Prismatic (hon. pres.), Scarab (past pres.), Detroit Press, Acanthus (Detroit); St. Dunstan's Guild, Cranbrook (past pres.) (Bloomfield Hills, Mich.); Sarasota Yacht. Selected works of John S. Coppin, 1948. Home: 226 Golden Gate Point Sarasota FL 33577 Studio: Key Towers 1750 Benjamin Franklin Dr Sarasota FL 33577

COPSON, DAVID ARTHUR, educator; b. Boston, June 16, 1918; s. David H. and Alvina M. (Webb) C.; B.S., U. Mass., 1940; Ph.D., Mass. Inst. Tech., 1953; m. Valeda Mary Michaud, Sept. 4, 1960; children—Anna (Mrs. David Alan Lindsley), Janice (Mrs. Donald M. Cannistraro), Wendy Elena, Laurie Carolyn, David Arthur, Jr., Tilin Rose Marie. With Am. Mut. Ins. Co., Boston, 1941, Birdseye div. Gen. Foods, 1942-48; mgr. microwave applications research group Raytheon Co., Waltham, Mass., 1953-58; prof. Quincy (Mass.) Jr. Coll., 1959; prof. biophysics and radiation biology U. P.R., Mayaguez, 1960—. Pres. Camp Dorchester Assn., Boston YMCA, 1950-53. Served to capt. USNR, 1944-46. Registered profl. engr., Mass. Fellow A.A.A.S.; mem. I.E.E.E., Biophys. Soc., Naval Res. Assn. (chpt. pres. 1948-49), Sigma Xi. Author: Microwave Heating, 1963, rev., 1973. Contbr. articles to various publs. Patentee in field. Home: PO Box 3661 Mayaguez PR 00708

CORBETT, LESLIE WILLIAM, banker; b. Britton, Okla., Aug. 6, 1915; s. Leland M. and Laura M. (Leslie) C.; student Central State U., 1933-34, Am. Inst. Banking, 1936-38; m. Opal Jane McWilliams, Apr. 6, 1957. With First Nat. Bank, Edmond, Okla., 1935-41; asst. nat. bank examiner, 1946-51; with Okla. Nat. Bank, Duncan, 1951—, pres., 1968—. Pres., Duncan Community Chest, 1957. Served with USNR, 1941-46. Mem. C. of C. (dir. 1961-65, v.p., 1964-65). Elk, Rotarian (pres. 1962-63). Home: 1001 Oakview Dr Duncan OK 73533 Office: Box 1508 Duncan OK 73533

CORBOY, MICHAEL ROBERT, communications equipment co. exec.; b. Chgo., Aug. 1, 1930; s. William J. and Eileen (Dunne) C.; B.S. in Elec. Engring., U.S. Naval Acad., 1953. With Tex. Instruments, Inc., Dallas, 1957-68, successively sales engr., dist. mgr., midwest and central region mgr. U.S., field sales mgr., European marketing mgr. Semicondr.-Component div., Geneva, Switzerland, corporate mgr. investor relations, Dallas, 1966-68; gen. partner New Bus. Resources—Venture Capital Partnership, Dallas, 1968-71; pres. Tocom, Inc., Dallas, 1973—; chmn. bd. Southwest Bus. Devel. Corp., 1973—. Chmn. bd. advisers Jesuit Coll. Prep. Sch., Dallas. Served with USN, 1953-57. Mem. U.S. Naval Acad. Athletic Assn. Clubs: Las Colinas Country; N.Y. Athletic. Home: 3883 Turtle Creek Blvd Dallas TX 75219 Office: 3301 Royalty Row Irving TX 75247

CORCORAN, VINCENT JOHN, elec. engr.; b. Chgo., Oct. 7, 1934; s. Vincent Anthony and Mae (DeNardo) C.; student Fournier Inst. Tech., 1952-55; B.S., U. Notre Dame, 1957; M.S., U. Ill., 1958; postgrad. Ill. Inst. Tech., 1958-63; Ph.D., U. Fla., 1968; m. Anne Marie Fitzgerald, June 29, 1957; children—Kevin V., Margaret M., Kathleen M., Karen M., Brian J. Mem. staff U. Chgo. Lab. Applied Scis., 1958-62; v.p. Astromarine Products Corp., Melrose Park, Ill., 1962-63; sr. research scientist, aerospace div. Martin Marietta corp., Orlando, Fla., 1963-73; research staff mem. Inst. for Def. Analyses, Arlington, Va., 1973—. Adj. prof. Rollins Coll., Winter Park, Fla., 1972-73; cons. radiation Stanford Co., 1962, Motorola, Inc., 1963, Martin Marietta Corp., 1967-68. Dir. Q.E.D. Corp., 1968-73, Ecoterra, Inc., 1971—. A.J. Schmidt Found. scholar, 1952-57; recipient Achievement award Martin Marietta Co., 1965. Mem. I.E.E.E. Clubs: Notre Dame Alumni; Fournier Alumni (v.p. 1961-63) (Chgo.). Contbr. articles in field to profl. jours. Home: 1638 Dempsey St McLean VA 22101 Office: 400 Army-Navy Dr Arlington VA 22202

CORDELL, DEWITT BYNUM CROMER (MRS. ALFRED ROBERT CORDELL), civic worker; b. Winston-Salem, N.C., Feb. 27, 1930; d. Clarence Franklin and Grace (Bynum) Cromer; A.B., Duke, 1950; postgrad. U. Buffalo, 1956-57; m. Alfred Robert Cordell, June 4, 1955; children—Alfred Robert, Franklin Cromer, Carl DeWitt, Mark Bynum. Pres., Winston-Salem Jr. League, 1963-64; dir. region XIII Assn. Jr. Leagues Am., 1965-67, 2d v.p., 1967-68; treas., 1st v.p., pres., bd. dirs. YWCA, 1962-68; pres., v.p., bd. dirs. Forsyth-Stokes County Med. Aux., 1967-69; asst. sec., pres., bd. dirs. Nature-Sci. Center, 1965-72; v.p. Civic Music Assn., 1964-68; pres. Amos Cottage Guild, 1969-70; mem. bd. United Fund, 1968-73; bd. dirs. Experiment in Self Reliance, 1969-70, v.p., 1970-73; mem. exec. com. N.C. Council on Crime and Delinquency, 1969-70, 1st v.p., 1970—; v.p. Regional Health Planning Council, 1971-73, pres., 1974—; sec. Forsyth Health Planning Council, 1970-71, v.p., 1971-73; mem. Mayor's Com. on Historic Preservation Winston, 1971—, Mayor's Com. on Status of Women, 1973—. Bd. dirs. Forsyth County Heart Assn. (pres. 1969-70), Amos Cottage. Mem. Winston-Salem Symphony Guild, Bowman Gray Guild, Alpha Delta Pi. Home: 349 Arbor Rd Winston-Salem NC 27104

COREY, ORLIN RUSSELL, theatrical producer; b. Nowata, Okla., May 4, 1926; s. Lue Amosa and Nada Gladys (Patton) C.; B.A., Baylor U., 1950, M.A., 1952; certificate Central Sch. Speech and Drama, London, 1956; m. Irene Lockridge, Aug. 25, 1949. Asst. prof. speech and drama, theatre dir. Georgetown (Ky.) Coll., 1952-59; asso. prof. drama, chmn. theatre dept., dir. theatre Centenary Coll. of La., Shreveport, 1960-68; founder, producer Everyman Players, Inc., 1959—; producer, dir. Romans by St. Paul, 1964; Pilgrim's Progress, 1970 (nat. tour U.S. 1973). Guest artist U. N.H., 1968, U. South Fla., 1971, Blue Mountain (Miss.) Coll., 1974, Fla. State U., 1974; guest lectr. theatre U. Cape Town, Grahamstown U., U. Natal (South Africa), Bristol (Eng.) U., Southampton (Eng.) U., Ohio State U., U. Ill., U. Mass., others. Served with USNR, 1944-46. Recipient award for religious drama Nat. Cath. Theatre Conf., 1968. Mem. Am. Assn. U. Profs., Am. Theatre Assn. (Jennie Heiden award for profl. theatre for children 1969), Children's Theatre Assn. Am. (pres. 1971-73), Internat. Assn. Theatre for Children and Youth (chmn. U.S. center 1972—), Brit. Drama League, Religious Drama Soc. Gt. Britain. Republican. Baptist. Rotarian. Author: Theatre for Children: Kid-Stuff or Theatre?, 1974. Adapted to stage The Book of Job, 1957, book pub., 1960. Home: 810 Kimbrough St Shreveport LA 71104 Office: Box 4154 Shreveport LA 71104

CORK, ROBERT LANDER, lawyer; b. Central, S.C., Oct. 27, 1927; s. James Walter and Emma Lila (McNeill) C.; A.B. in Law, U. Ga., 1951, LL.B., 1953; m. Anne McNeill Ward, Oct. 11, 1952; children—Mary Leah, Robert Lander, Travis Walter, Patrick Carlyle. Admitted to Ga. bar, 1951, Fla. bar, 1958; partner Cork & Gaines, Athens, Ga., 1951-53; gen. practice, Valdosta, Va., 1953—; gen. counsel Warrior Land & Cattle Co. S. Ga., 1961—; local counsel, agt. Louisville Title Ins. Co., 1962—. Atty., City of Dasher (Ga.), 1967—, Sch. Bd. of Ga. Christian Sch., 1967—; pros. atty. for Ga., So. Jud. Circuit, 1970-71. Council adviser Boy Scouts Am. Vice chmn. Valdosta and Lowndes County sect. Ga. Goldwater for Pres. drive, 1964; mem. exec. com. American Party of Ga. Served with 101st Airborne Inf. Div., AUS, 1945-46, Q.M.C., 1955. Mem. Am. So. Circuit, Valdosta bar assns., State Bar Ga., The Fla. Bar, Am. Judicature Soc., Citizens Councils Am. (mem. nat. bd. 1969), S.A.R., Am. Legion (mem. nat. law and order com. 1968-69, judge adv. 8th Congl. dist.). Methodist (trustee, chmn. bd. stewards). Mason (Shriner, K.T.), Lion (pres. 1971-72, mem. Lighthouse for Blind 1964). Home: Sunnyside Frances Lake RFD Lake Park GA 31636 Office: 505 N Patterson St Valdosta GA 31601

CORLEY, JOHN BRYSON, physician; b. Calgary, Alta., Can., Aug. 29, 1913; s. Robert Bryson and Anna May (Amos) C.; B.A. with honors in Psychology, U. Alta., 1936, M.D., 1942; m. Lidje Corley de Jong, May 23, 1947; children—Nolly Elisabeth, James Bryson. Intern Univ. Hosp., Edmonton, Ala., 1942; resident Col. Belcher Hosp., Calgary, 1946-47; family physician Chinook Med. Clinic, Calgary, 1946-73; chief examiner Coll. Family Physicians Can., 1969-73; asst. prof. dept. ednl. planning and assessment Faculty Medicine, U. Calgary (Alta., Can.), 1969-73; asso. prof. dept. family practice Med. U. S.C., Charleston, 1973—, also chief div. evaluation; dir. Canadian Project for Devel. Post-grad. Tng. in Family Medicine, 1967-70. Served to maj. Canadian Army, 1942-45; ETO. Mem. Canadian Med. Assn. (chmn. sect. gen. practice 1962-64), Coll. Family Physicians Can. (hon. treas. 1969-71), Am. Soc. Clin. Hypnosis (1st v.p. 1971-72). Asso. editor Self Assessment, Jour. Continuing Edn. Home: 377 Grove St Charleston SC 29401

CORLISS, JACK ARTHUR, librarian; b. Brookings, S.D., May 6, 1933; s. Fred Arthur and Annie (Boulton) C.; M.A., Baylor U., 1961; m. Barbara Ann Mann, Aug. 29, 1961. Grad. library asst. Baylor U. 1960-61; young adult librarian Waco Pub. Library, 1961-65; dir. libraries Arlington (Tex.) Pub. Library, 1965—. Served to capt. USAF, 1953-60. Mem. Am., Tex. (mem. council 1970), Tarrant Regional (pres. 1966, 67, 71) library assns. Rotarian (dir. 1973—). Club: Civitan (pres. 1969) (Arlington, Tex.). Home: PO Box 1165 Arlington TX 76010 Office: 101 E Abram St Arlington TX 76010

CORMAN, WILLIAM FRANKLIN, telephone co. exec.; b. Louisville, Mar. 26, 1916; s. Minor and Willye (Bright Pierce) C.; B.B.A., U. Ore., 1937; M.B.A., Harvard, 1939; m. Gladys Juliette Temple, June 19, 1952; children—Jim, Myna, Julie, Page. Bookkeeper Collierville Telephone Co. (Tenn.), 1939-41; mgr. Southland Telephone Co., Atmore, Ala., 1945—. Pres., Atmore United Fund, 1958; chmn. Atmore Indsl. Devel. Bd., 1965—. Mem. Escambia County Republican Exec. Com., 1967. Served to lt. col. USAAF, 1941-46. Decorated Bronze Star. Named Man of Year, Ala.-Miss. Ind. Telephone Assn., 1966, Nat. Tel. Coop. Assn., 1968. Mem. Ala.-Miss. Ind. Telephone Assn. (pres. 1954), Orgn. Protection and Advancement Small Telephone Cos. (pres. 1963-65), Nat. R.E.A. Telephone Assn. (dir.), U.S. Ind. Telephone Assn. (dir.), Atmore C. of C. (pres. 1947, 61), Ala. Safety Council (dir.), I.E.E.E. Presbyn. (elder). Club: Atmore Lions (pres. 1955). Author: Cost Studies, a Tool for Management, 1963; The Misunderstood Half Billion Dollars, Independent Toll Revenue, 1967; The Pricing of Telephone Service, 1971. Contbg. editor Telephone Engr. and Magmt., 1949—. Home: 800 1st Av Atmore AL 36502 Office: 201 S Pensacola Av Atmore AL 36502

CORMIER, RICHARD, orch. condr.; b. Orange, Mass., May 10, 1929; s. Ernest A. and Doris Hunt (Deane) C.; B.Mus., New Eng. Conservatory Music, 1951; M.A., Columbia Tchrs. Coll., 1955, Ed.D., 1964. Mem. Birmingham (Ala.) Symphony Orch., 1951, Kansas City (Mo.) Philharmonic Orch., 1955-62, Santa Fe Opera Orch., summers 1957, 58; music dir., condr. Charlotte (N.C.) Symphony Orch., also Charlotte Symphony Youth Orch., 1963-67; dir. instrumental music Park Coll., Parkville, Mo., 1956-63, asso. prof., chmn. music dept., 1961-63; music dir., condr. Chattanooga Symphony and Youth Orch., 1967—; music dir. Oak Ridge Civic Music Assn. Symphony and Chorus, 1968-71; instr. conducting and brass instruments Tchrs. Coll., Columbia, summers 1964-67. Condr. Cormier Chamber Orch., Kansas City, Mo., 1956-63; Youth Symphony Orch., Kansas City, 1959-61, St. Joseph (Mo.) Symphony Orch., 1959-63; guest condr. U.S. and Europe. Served with USMC, 1952-53, Res., 1953-58. Recipient Distinguished Citizen award, Chattanooga, 1973. Mem. Pi Kappa Lambda, Phi Mu Alpha Sinfonia. Home: 1209 Peter Pan Lookout Mountain TN 37350 Office: 730 Cherry St Chattanooga TN 37402

CORNELL, CORWIN DAVID, ednl. adminstr.; b. Des Moines, Feb. 5, 1924; s. Corwin S. and Margaret (Hardie) C.; student U. Kan., 1943-44; B.A., U. Ia., 1947, M.A., 1949, postgrad., 1949-50, 55; postgrad. U. Cal. at Los Angeles, 1959-60; m. Ruth Marian Reininga, Sept. 7, 1946 (div. 1965); children—Barbara Jean, Corwin Bruce, Philip Craig, Stewart David; m. 2d, Jean S. Harkness, Nov. 4, 1966. Civilian chief, instr. tng. br. Plans and Operations Office, Adj. Gen.'s Sch., Ft. Harrison, Ind., 1952-54; instr. speech Pomona Coll., Claremont, Cal., 1954-56; staff asst. to mgr. indsl. relations Gen. Dynamics/Pomona, (Cal.), 1956-57, asst. to pres., 1957-64; asst. v.p. Newhall Land & Farming Co., Valencia, Cal., 1964-65; dir. pub. affairs Cal. Land Co., Valencia 1964-65; dir. devel. and planning Scripps Coll., Claremont, Cal., 1965-69; dir. office agy. liaison, office v.p. for ednl. devel. and research U. Ia., Iowa City, 1969-71; v.p. finance and devel. Davidson (N.C.) Coll., 1971—. Dir. Davidson Community Properties, Inc., 1971—; mem. Davidson bd. Piedmont Bank and Trust Co., 1971—, chmn., 1973—. Cons. communication field, 1955—; lectr. indsl. communication Cal. Inst. Tech., Pasadena, 1958, 59, 61, 67; lectr. organizational communication Claremont Men's Coll., 1956-57, 59-69; lectr. exec. communication U. Ida., Moscow, 1960-71. Nat. council Old Gold Devel. Fund, State U. Ia. Found., 1962-69; community leader 4-H Club, LaVerne, Cal., 1962-64; pres. Pomona C. of C., 1964; chmn. Archtl. Commn., Claremont, 1962-64. Bd. dirs. Pomona Valley United Fund, 1958-61, Claremont chpt. A.R.C., 1960-63; trustee Pomona Valley Community Hosp., 1964-65, Mercy Hosp., Iowa City, 1970-71. Served with AUS, 1942-46; ETO; 1950-52; lt. col. Res. ret. Recipient George Washington Honor medal, 1968. Mem. State Hist. Soc. Ia. (life), Pub. Relations Soc. Am., U. Ia. Alumni Assn. (pres. Los Angeles chpt. 1968-69, life), Am. Bus. Com. Assn., Am. Coll. Pub. Relations Assn., U. Cal. at Los Angeles Alumni Assn. (life), Am. Alumni Council, Am. Acad. Polit. and Social Sci., Am. Assn. Higher Edn., Nat. Assn. Coll. and U. Bus. Affairs, Nat. Council U. Research Adminstrs. Phi Beta Kappa, Omicron Delta Kappa, Delta Sigma Rho. Episcopalian. Club: Charlotte (N.C.) Athletic. Home: 544 Concord Rd Davidson NC 28036

CORNISH, EDWARD SEYMOUR, editor; b. N.Y.C., Aug. 31, 1927; s. George Anthony and Elizabeth Furniss (McLeod) C.; diplome d'etudes U. Paris (France), 1948; A.B., Harvard, 1950; m. Sally Woodhull, Oct. 12, 1957; children—George Anthony, Jefferson Richard Woodhull, Blake McLeod. Copy boy, cub reporter Evening Star, Washington, 1950-51; staff corr. U.P. Assn., Richmond, Va., 1951-52, Raleigh, N.C., 1952-53, London, Eng., 1953-54, Paris, 1954-55, Rome, Italy, 1956; staff writer Nat. Geog. Soc., 1957-69; founder, pres., World Future Soc., Washington, 1966—, creator, editor The Futurist jour., 1966—, editor World Future Soc. Bull., 1968—. Cons. to other govt., bus., ednl. orgns. Mem. A.A.A.S., Soc. Internat. Devel. Editorial cons. Nat. Goals Research Staff, 1970, White House report Toward Balanced Growth, 1970; mem. editorial bd. Assn. Vol. Action Scholars. Home: 5501 Lincoln St Bethesda MD 20034 Office: World Future Soc 4916 St Elmo Av Washington DC 20014

CORRADA, BALTASAR, lawyer; b. Morovis, P.R., Apr. 10, 1935; s. Romulo and Ana Maria (Del Rio) C.; B.A., U. P.R., 1956, LL.B., 1959; m. Beatriz Betances, Dec. 24, 1959; children—Ana Isabel, Francisco Javier, Juan Carlos, Jose Baltasar. Tchr. P.R. High Sch. of Commerce, San Juan, 1958; admitted to P.R. bar, 1959, Supreme Ct. P.R. bar, 1959, U.S. Dist. Ct. P.R. bar, 1960, U.S. Ct. Appeals, 1961; asso. mem. firm Sifre & Ruiz Suria Law Offices, San Juan, 1959-67; partner firm McConnell, Valdes, Kelley, Sifre, Griggs & Ruiz-Suria, San Juan, 1969—. Dir. Clinica Dr. M. Julia, Inc., 1970—. Mem. Commonwealth of P.R. Civil Rights Commn., 1969, pres., 1970-72; mem. P.R. Bar Exam. Bd., 1970. Mem. adv. commn. on drug abuse to Archbishop of San Juan, 1970; mem. com. for study legislative system Commonwealth of P.R. Council for the Reform of Justice, 1973-74. Mem. platform com. New Progressive party, 1972, chmn. status com., 1973. Mem. Am., P.R. (mem. com. on constl. law 1970—) bar assns., P.R. C. of C., Phi Eta Mu. Roman Catholic. Clubs: Bankers, Caparra Country (San Juan). Chmn. editorial bd. P.R. Human Rights Review, 1970-72. Home: 154 Tulipan Rio Piedras PR 00927 Office: GPO Box 4225 San Juan PR 00936

CORRADO, BENJAMIN WILLIAM, marketing cons.; b. Bklyn., July 16, 1911; s. Anthony and Genevieve (La Guardia) C.; student Sch. Commerce, N.Y. U., 1930-32; m. Virginia M. McCormick, June 23, 1939. Chief statisician, investment counsellor Standard Statistics Co.; news editor, Washington editor Am. Machinist; Cleve. editor Iron Age mag.; metals and beverage specialist Poor's Pub. Co.; asst. pub. relations dir. Am. Iron and Steel Inst., 1946-48; coordinator advt., spl. asst. to pres. Market Research Dir., Publicker Industires, Inc., 1948-50; research cons., beverage Specialist, 1950-55; v.p. charge market research and industry relations Nat. Distillers Products Co., 1955-66; v.p. industry relations Nat. Distillers & Chem. Corp., 1966-72; marketing cons., broker Benjamin W. Corrado Assos., 1972—. Jr. economist, munitions br. WPB, 1943; v.p. dir. Bourbon Inst.; v.p., dir. Ky. Distillers Assn.; v.p. Md. Distillers Assn.; author nat. liquor consumption estimate by states and by types, 1950-54; per diem cons. NPA, 1951-52. Recipient indsl. marketing award of merit for best pub. research Am. Machinist, 1945. Mem. Am. Legion, Am. Mgmt. Assn., Nat. Assn. Bus. Economists, Am. Marketing Assn. Asso. Cooperage Ind. Am. Club: Nat. Press (Washington). Author: Distilled Spirits Industry-Public Revenues, 1943; Newsweek Liquor Advt. Exp. Mags., 1951, 52, 53, 54; Trne's Beer Consumption Report, 1952, 53; Am. Mag. Wine Consumption Report, 1952, 53; Liquor Marketing Handbook, 1954, 55. Contbr. articles to nat. mags. Home: 401 Briny Av Pompano Beach FL 33062

CORRELL, WARD FORREST, shopping center exec.; b. Delta, Ky., Jan. 7, 1928; s. Charlie and Clora Alice (Hammonds) C.; grad. high sch.; m. Regina Tarter, Mar. 27, 1953; children—Rebekah, Kirk, Jesse, Vincent, Susan, Christa, Melinda. Transmission tester Chrysler Corp., Detroit, 1948; farmer, Somerset, Ky., 1949-50, 52-54; partner Sci. Hill Stockyards, Science Hill, Ky., 1955-60; partner Correll Auto Sales, Somerset, 1956—; pres. Tradewinds Shopping Center, Somerset, 1966—; sec. Trademart Shopping Center, Corbin, Ky., 1973—. Fund raising chmn. for Pulaski County, Lake Cumberland 4-H Center, 1967; pres. Cumberland Lake Shell, Somerset, 1972—. Served with AUS, 1950-52. Baptist (Sunday sch. tchr. 1953-71). Home: Box 44 Route 2 Somerset KY 42501 Office: Tradewinds Shopping Center Somerset KY 42501

CORWIN, WILLIAM, physician; b. Boston, Oct. 28, 1908; M.D., Tufts Coll., 1932; m. Frances M. Wetherell (dec.) m. 2d, Joyce S. Newman, 1965. Intern Wesson Meml. Hosp., Springfield, Mass., 1932-33; physician Met. State Hosp., Waltham, Mass., 1933-37, asst. supt., 1937-42; research fellow Harvard, 1937-46; practice medicine, specializing in psychiatry, Springfield, Mass., 1946-54, Miami, Fla., 1954—; mem. staff Jackson Meml. Hosp., Miami; instr. psychiatry Boston U., 1937-46, Tufts Coll., 1941-46; clin. asso. prof. psychiatry U. Miami, 1955-70, clin. prof., 1970—. Dir. Pan Am. Bank, Coral Gables. Past mem. State Fla. Adv. Com. on Mental Health; agy. operations com. United Fund. Bd. dirs. Family and Childrens Services Miami. Served to lt. col. M.C., USAAF, 1942-46. Diplomate Am. Bd. Psychiatry and Neurology. Fellow Am. Psychiat. Assn. (life); mem. A.M.A., Fla. Psychiat. Soc. (councillor). Contbr. articles on physiology of schizophrenia to profl. publs. Home: 3929 Granada Blvd Coral Gables FL 33134 Office: Dupont Plaza Center Miami FL 33131

CORWIN, WILLIAM MOORE, farm coop. exec.; b. Port Huron, Mich., July 13, 1912; s. William Henry and Columbia Camdelia (Moore) C.; A.B., W.Va. U., 1932; m. Mary Rose Kimmell, Nov. 20, 1940; 1 dau., Cathryn Ann (Mrs. William Anthony Meyer). Reporter, Clarksburg (W.Va.) Exponent, 1933-34; asst. in pub. relations dept., editor co. mag. Monongahela Power Co., Fairmont, W. Va., 1934-44; dir. publs. So. States Coop., 1944-48, dir. information publs. service, 1947—. Active Richmond area Tb Assn. Mem. Nat. Council Farmer Coops. (chmn. pub. relations com. 1957-58, 69-70), Nat. Coop. Editorial Assn. (pres. 1963), Nat. Coop. Advt. Council (pres. 1964-65), Advt. Relations Council (dir. 1962-64), Richmond Pub. Relations Assn. (pres. 1951-52), Richmond Advt. Club (dir. 1964-67), Richmond (chmn. agrl. com. 1963-65), Va. chambers commerce, Phi Kappa Tau, Kappa Tau Alpha. Democrat. Methodist. Home: 5106 Riverside Dr Richmond VA 23225 Office: 7th and Main Sts Richmond VA 23219

COSBY, HARRY, JR., physician; b. Memphis, Apr. 6, 1923; s. Harry and Mary (Johnson) C.; student Memphis State U., 1940-42; M.D., U. Tenn., 1945; m. Mary Elizabeth Richardson, Dec. 16, 1944; children—Walter Nathan, Harry Thomas. Intern, John Gaston Hosp., Memphis, 1945-46; practice gen. medicine, Iuka, Miss., 1947—; mem. staff Tishomingo County Hosp., Iuka, Miss.; Project dir. N.E. Miss. Multiphasic Testing Unit, 1970—. Mem. planning com. Memphis Regional Med. Program, 1971-72, county adv. bd. Head Start, 1968—, Miss. Comprehensive Planning Med. Agy., 1970—; cons. preventive medicine dept. U. Tenn., 1971—. Served with AUS, 1946-47. Mem. Am., N.E. Miss., Miss. med. assns., So. Med. Soc., Soc. for Advanced Med. Systems. Established first rural, doctor-oriented preventive med. testing unit, 1970. Home: Hwy 25 N Iuka MS 38852 Office: 309 N Main St Iuka MS 38852

COSSAR, GEORGE PAYNE, lawyer, state legislator; b. Webb, Miss., Aug. 26, 1907; m. children—John, Bill, George Payne. Lawyer, mem. Miss. Ho. of Reps., 1944-48, 52—. Mem. exec. com. Council of State Govts.; exec. com. Nat. Conf. State Legislative Leaders. Mem. Omicron Delta Kappa, Phi Alpha Delta, Sigma Nu. Methodist. Mason (Shriner), Rotarian. Home: Box 50 Charleston MS 38921 Office: Mississippi House of Reps Jackson MS 39201

COSTELLO, JOSEPH MARK, III, broadcaster; b. New Orleans, Nov. 8, 1940; s. Joseph Mark and Josephine (Cortese) C.; student Loyola U. of South, 1959-61. Program dir. Dixie Stas. of La. and Tex., 1960-63; pres., dir. Broadcasting Inst. Am., 1963—; owner, pres., gen. mgr. WRNO Radio, New Orleans, 1966—; owner KSMI, Donaldsonville, La., KXOR, Thibodaux, La. Cons. radio sta. mgmt. and engring. Mem. Algiers Centennial Com. Recipient Pub. Service Broadcaster award U.P.I., 1965; Abe Lincoln award, 1973. Mem. Nat., La. (dir.), Greater New Orleans (officer) assns. broadcasters, Soc. Broadcast Engrs., Radio Advt. Bur., Nat. Assn. FM Broadcasters, Soc. for Preservation and Encouragement Barbershop Quartet Singing in Am. K.C. Home: 4042 S Pin Oak St New Orleans LA 70114 Office: 3400 N Causeway Blvd New Orleans LA 70114

COSTON, HAROLD PRESTWOOD, hosp. adminstr.; b. Winston-Salem, N.C., Aug. 30, 1926; s. Fred E. and Lula Gertrude (Prestwood) C.; B.S., Wake Forest Coll., 1946; M.P.H., Johns Hopkins, 1952; m. Vivian Landis Johnson, Oct. 18, 1949; children—Carolyn (Mrs. Terry Leap), Deborah, Pamela. Adminstr. Levering Hosp., Hannibal, Mo., 1960-66; asso. prof. hosp. adminstrn. U. N.C. Sch. Medicine at Chapel Hill, 1966-68; adminstrv. dir. N.C. Meml. Hosp., U. N.C. at Chapel Hill, 1968-72; exec. dir. Lubbock (Tex.) County Hosp. Dist., 1972—; dir. Tex. Tech U. Med. Sch. Hosp., Lubbock, 1972—. vis. lectr. Washington U. Sch. Hosp. Adminstrn., St. Louis. Pres. P.T.A., Rawls County, Mo.; chmn. bldg. fund YMCA, Hannibal; mem. St. Louis Commn. Hosps. and Homes, Meth. Ch., NIH Gen. Clin. Research Center grantee Bethesda, Md.; Bur. Health Services, Dept. Health, Edn. and Welfare grantee, Washington. Mem. Am. Coll. Hosp. Adminstrn. (fellowship award 1965), Am. Hosp. Assn., Am. Pub. Health Assn., Assn. Am. Med. Colls., N.C. Hosp. Assn. Methodist. Rotarian. Club: Men's Garden. Author pamphlets, booklets in field. Home: 4509 8th St Rushland Park Lubbock TX 79416 Office: Drane Hall Tex Tech U Lubbock TX 79409

COTEY, HADDON EUGENE, clergyman; b. Alexandria, La., Apr. 30, 1927; s. Haddon Spurgeon and Eloise (Cordill) C.; B.A., Union U., 1949; B.D., So. Bapt. Theol. Sem., 1952, Th.D., 1957; m. Jean Lipsey, June 6, 1952; children—Sara Elizabeth, David Eugene, Stephen Ray, James Cavin. Ordained to ministry Bapt. Ch., 1948; pastor 1st Bapt. Ch., Oxford, Ala., 1957-60, 1st Bapt. Ch., Murfreesboro, Tenn., 1961—. Pres. exec. bd. Tenn. Bapt. Conv., 1969; mem. hist. commn. So. Bapt. Conv.; mem. arrangements com. Tenn. Bapt. Conv. Mem. Rutherford County Job Opportunity Com.; chmn. Murfreesboro chpt. A.R.C., 1965-67; chmn. profl. div. United Givers Fund, Murfreesboro, 1965-66. Trustee Nashville Bapt. Hosp., 1965-73, Belmont Coll., Nashville, 1971-74. Served with USNR, 1945-46. Mem. Soc. Bibl. Lit. Democrat. Rotarian. Contbr. to Teaching Adult Life and Work Lessons, 1970—. Home: 723 N Rutherford Blvd Murfreesboro TN 37130 Office: 200 E Main St Murfreesboro TN 37130

COTHRAN, SAMUEL ALEXANDER, newspaper editor; b. Laurens, S.C., Dec. 13, 1915; s. Frank Harrison and Blanche (Clardy) C.; student Davidson Coll., 1938; B.A. cum laude, U. S.C., 1939; m. Nona Owens Crane, Apr. 8, 1942; children—Samuel Alexander, Thomas Crane, Frank Chiles. Reporter, Index-Jour., Greenwood, S.C., 1939; reporter News and Courier, Charleston, S.C., 1939-41, asst. city editor 1947-51, city editor, 1951-58, mng. editor, 1958-68; pres., editor Aiken (S.C.) Standard, 1968—; pres. Aiken Communications, Inc., S.C. A.P., 1964; v.p. Aiken Cablevision, Inc. Served from 2d lt. to lt. col. Inf., AUS, 1942-45; ETO. Mem. Phi Delta Theta. Presbyn. (elder). Rotarian. Clubs: Carolina Yacht, Country of Charleston; Palmetto Golf. Home: 553 Sumter St SE Aiken SC 29801 Office: PO Box 456 124 Rutland Dr Aiken SC 29801

COTNER, NORMAN ANDREW, physician; b. Booneville, Ark., Mar. 28, 1927; s. Harrison H. and Myrtle E. (Rothwell) C.; B.S., Okla. A. and M. U., 1950, postgrad., 1951-54; M.D., U. Okla., 1958; m. Ruth Anna Giem, Dec. 22, 1949; children—Mark, Paul, Jeffrey, Sarah, Martha. Intern, Mercy Hosp., Oklahoma City, 1958-59; gen. practice medicine, Grove, Okla., 1959—; pres. Grove Med. Center, Inc., 1963—; chief staff Grove Gen. Hosp. Dir. State Bank Grove, Glassmaster Plastics. Chmn. Airport Authority, 1964-68; chmn. Grove Airport Bd., 1969—; chmn. Grove Indsl. Devel. Authority, 1968—. Chmn. town bd. trustees, 1962. Served with USN, 1944-48; PTO. Recipient Seabees Nat. Meml. Scholarship Fund award, 1971. Mem. Am. Acad. Gen. Practice, A.M.A., Okla., Delaware County med. assns., Tri-County Med. Soc. (pres. 1961-62), Okla. Rural Med. Assn. (mem. scholarship bd. 1970-71), Okla. Med. Alumni Assn., Phi Chi. Democrat. Elk. Home: PO Box 370 Grove OK 74344 Office: 1200 S Main St Grove OK 74344

COTNOIR, RAYMOND EUGENE, ins. co. exec.; b. Lowell, Vt., Oct. 12, 1934; s. Antoine Hercules and Rose Elda (Girouard) C.; student Tex. A. and M. U., 1953; B.A., So. Meth. U., 1965; m. Sybil Ann Fain, Sept. 13, 1957; children—Caryn Renee, Charon Nicole, Julie Michelle. With U.S. Fidelity & Guaranty Co., Dallas, 1956—, underwriter, 1958-68, asst. supt., 1968-70, supt., 1970—. Gen. chmn. Cotton Bowl Invitational Intercollegiate Basketball Tournament, 1970, adv. com. mem., 1971. Served with Tex. Air N.G., 1957-69. Mem. Surety Underwriters Assn. Dallas (pres. 1970), St. Augustine Home and Sch. Assn. (pres. 1969-71), Pi Kappa Alpha. K.C. Club: Mustang. Home: 1524 Brockham Circle Dallas TX 75217 Office: Mercantile Bank Bldg Dallas TX 75201

COTTER, VINCENT P., meat and food products co. exec.; b., 1927; B.S. in Bus. Adminstrn., Northeastern U., 1952, M.B.A., 1965. Office mgr. Wilson Sporting Goods Co., Chgo., 1953-65; adminstrv. asst. to treas., asst. treas., Wilson & Co., Inc., Chgo., 1965-68, treas., 1968-69, v.p., treas., 1969—. Home: 8016 Lakehurst Dr Oklahoma City OK 73120 Office: 4545 N Lincoln Blvd Oklahoma City OK 73105

COTTON, RICHARD GENE, baking co. exec.; b. Alexandria, La., Jan. 18, 1935; s. William F. and Genevieve Winifred (Hathorn) C.; B.S., La. State U., 1957; m. Nancy Wilson, Aug. 9, 1958; children—Richard, William, Tracy. With Cotton Bros. Baking Co., Inc., Alexandria, La., 1957—, gen. mgr., 1963-66, v.p., 1966-67, pres., 1967—; chmn. bd. Data Route, Inc., Dallas; dir. W. E. Long Co., Chgo. Pres., Alexandria Country Day Sch.; mem. Pub. Affairs Research Council, Civil Service Council, La. State U. Found. Bd. dirs. Rapides United Givers, Alexandria. Served with U.S.N.G., 1951-65. Mem. Young Pres. Orgn., C. of C. (bd. dirs. 1964-65, 67-68), La. Mfg. Assn., Kappa Sigma. Mason (Shriner), Kiwanian. Home: 4511 Willowick Blvd Alexandria LA 71301 Office: PO Box 5405 Alexandria LA 71301

COTTON, WILLIAM FREDERICK, bakery exec; b. Corley, Ark., Oct. 23, 1897; s. John Thomas and Emily (Peters) C.; student U. Ark., 1921-22; m. May Compton, De. 9, 1969; children—William Frederick, Richard Gene. Chmn., Cotton Bros. Baking Co., Cotton Baking Co., Cotton's, Inc., Cotton's Holsum Bakers, Cotton's Ouchita Bakery, Alexandria, La., 1965—; dir. Guaranty Bank & Trust Co. Finance adviser, Alexandria, 1946—. Dir., mem. exec. com. Rapides Parish Sch. Bd., 1963—. Served with USN, World War I. Democrat. Baptist. Mason (Shriner), Lion. Clubs: Baton Rouge Country; Alexandria Country; Shreveport (La.). Home: 1516 City Park Blvd Alexandria LA 71301 Office: 3400 McArthur St Alexandria LA 71301

COTTRELL, SAMUEL, engring. cons.; b. Washington, Oct. 4, 1898; s. Samuel and Ella (Kaufman) C.; Chem. E., Lehigh U., 1922; m. Elise Mardorf, Apr. 22, 1936 (dec. Aug. 1969); children—Susan Elise, Samuel IV: m. 2d, Lucille L. Summers, June 26, 1971. With Trojan Powder Co., Allentown, Pa., 1922-29, where advanced from foreman to supt. acid plants and supt. of a power plant; with Monsanto Chem. Co., 1929-46, advancing from asst. supr. to asst. plant mgr., Monsanto, Ill., plant; with Am. Potash & Chem. Corp., Los Angeles, 1946-49, sucessively tech. asst. to exec. v.p., v.p. in charge tech. operations; asst. to dir. operations Mathieson Chem. Corp., Balt., 1949-52, v.p., dir. operations, agrl. chems. div., Little Rock, 1952-54; dir. operations, agrl. chems. div. Olin Mathieson Chem. Corp., Little Rock, 1954-61, mgr. prodn. chems. div.-agrl., 1961-63; v.p., gen. mgr. Universal Moulded Fiber Glass Corp., Bristol, Va., 1963-65; adviser engring. World Bank, Washington, 1965-74; cons., 1974—. Pres. Little Rock Chamber Music Soc., 1956-57. Served as 2d lt. inf. U.S. Army, World War I. Mem. C. of C., Nat. Safety Council, Am. Chem. Soc., Electrochem. Soc., Am. Inst. Chem. Engrs. (chmn. St. Louis sect.). Unitarian (pres., trustee). Rotarian. Home: 5101 River Rd Washington DC 20016

COUCH, DONALD PETER, diversified bus. exec.; b. New Orleans, Mar. 20, 1940; s. Harvey Crowley, Jr. and Beatrice (Kearney) C.; B.A., Notre Dame U., 1962; m. Susan Kay Watkins, June 6, 1962; children—Laura Kay, Cynthia Marie, Donald Peter. Trainee, First Nat. Bank, Magnolia, Ark., 1963-64, also dir.; trainee Union Nat. Bank, Little Rock, 1964-68, v.p., dir., 1968, pres., co-chmn. bd., 1968-70; pres. Internat. Properties, Inc., Circle Realty Co., Railroad Lodging, Inc., Little Rock, 1970—. Mem. exec. bd. Quapaw Area council Boy Scouts Am. Mem. Little Rock C. of C. Clubs: Little Rock Country, Little Rock. Home: 2321 N Rodney Parham Little Rock AR 72207 Office: Cantrell Pl Office Bldg 2311 Biscayne St Little Rock AR 72207

COUCH, JAMES HOUSTON, educator; b. Easley, S.C., June 5, 1919; s. A. Waverly and Gertrude (Foster) C.; B.S., Clemson U., 1941, M.S., 1952; grad. Inst. for Materials Handling Tchrs., Northwestern U., 1969; grad. Materials Handling Inst., Purdue U., 1972; m. Sarah Crenshaw, Jan. 11, 1942; children—James F., Dorothy C. (Mrs. Stafford). Asst. prof. indsl. engring. Clemson (S.C.) U., 1941-56, asso. prof. indsl. engring., 1956-74, asso. prof. systems engring., 1974—. Research engr. Lockheed Aircraft Corp., part time, Lockheed-Ga.

Co., part-time 1955-69. Bd. dirs. Foundry Edn. Found., Cleve. Mem. Am. Welding Soc. (Meritorious award 1964, Adams Meml. membership award 1965), Am. Soc. for Metals, Am. Foundrymen's Soc. Author: Manufacturing Processes and Materials, 1967; Engineering Manufacturing Processes, 1960. Home: 408 College Av Clemson SC 29631

COUCH, WILSON PAUL, physician; b. Louisville, Feb. 17, 1929; s. Joseph M. and Flora Freda (Thom) C.; A.B., Snead Jr. Coll., 1948; B.S., Tulane U., 1953, M.D., 1956; m. Merle Louise Kepler, Jan. 26, 1952; children—David K., Stephen W., Wilson Paul II. Intern, William Beaumont Army Hosp., El Paso, Tex., 1956-57; post-grad. tng. LaLee Kemp Charity Hosp., 1957; gen. practice medicine, Paradis, La., 1957—; mem. med. staff St. Anne's Hosp., Raceland, La., St. Charles Hosp., Luling, La. Mem. St. Charles Parish Bd. Health, 1962—; mem. Council Med. Staffs, 1971; asst. coroner St. Charles Parish, 1967—. Mem. St. Charles Parish Bd. Drainage, 1965-71. Served with USMC, 1946-48, 50-51, as capt. M.C., AUS, 1956-57. Diplomate Am. Bd. Family Practice. Fellow Am. Geriatric Soc., Am. Acad. Family Physicians (charter); mem. Am. Acad. Gen. Practice (pres. 2d dist. 1968-70), La., Tri-Parish med. socs., La. Acad. Family Physicians, Tulane Alumni Assn., Am., La. heart assns., Assn. Mil. Surgeons, Phi Kappa Sigma, Theta Kappa Psi. Home: Route 1 Luling LA 70070 Office: Box 3498 Paradis Medical Clinic Paradis LA 70080

COULTER, BORDEN MCKEE, JR., indsl. engr.; b. Casper, Wyo., Feb. 9, 1917; s. Borden McKee and Josephine Helen (Grother) C.; B.S., U. Cal. at Los Angeles, 1939, M.B.A., 1947; m. Emily Sawtelle, Aug. 23, 1950; children—Borden, Terry Lynn, Leigh, Richard. Research analyst Australian Nat. R.R., 1939-40; indsl. engr. Lockheed Aircraft, 1940-47, staff indsl. engr., 1948-50; with div. indsl. engring. U.S. Steel Corp., 1947; mgr. prodn. control Bakewell Products, 1947; supr. orgn. and procedures Norris Thermador Corp., 1950-53; gen. mgr. Roed Engring. Assos., 1943—; prin., v.p., dir. The Emerson Cons., Inc., mgmt. cons., N.Y.C., 1954—. Mem. Am. Inst. Indsl. Engrs. (pres. Los Angeles), Am. Mgmt. Assn., Am. Inst. Plant Engrs., Nat. Assn. Accountants Am., Newcomen Soc., U.S. Naval Inst., Navy League U.S., Am. Forestry Assn., Inst. Mgmt. Consultants, Nat. Petroleum Refiners Assn., Am. Arbitration Assn., Nat., Tex. socs. profl. engrs., Houston Soc. Cons. Engrs., Blue Key, Kappa Kappa Psi, Alpha Kappa Psi, Tau Kappa Alpha, Phi Gamma Delta. Club: Petroleum (Houston). Home: 2112 Amberly Ct Houston TX 77042

COULTER, DOUGLAS WILSON, wholesale grocery co. exec.; b. Knoxville, Tenn., Sept. 3, 1925; s. John Wilson and Minnie Lucille (Matlock) C.; student U. of South, 1943-44, U. N.C., 1945; B.S., U. Tenn., 1953; m. Parthena Faye Sterchi, Mar. 28, 1958; children—Lynn (Mrs. Max Wayne McTeer), Douglas Wilson, Melissa Jane. Warehouseman, Pay Cash Grocery Co., Inc., Knoxville, 1947-48, foreman, 1948-49, salesman, 1950-54, buyer, 1954-62, gen. mgr., 1963-67, chmn. bd., 1971—; exec. v.p. U.S. Wholesale Grocers Assn., Washington, 1967-69; v.p. Nat. Am. Wholesale Grocery Assn., N.Y.C., 1969-71; dir. Scriverner-Boogaart Co., Oklahoma City. Cons. on food distbn. to city govt., Sao Paula, Brazi, 1970-71. Served with USNR, 1943-45. Mem. Full Gospel Bus. Men's Fellowship Internat. (Knoxville pres. 1972-73), Tenn. Wholesale Grocers Assn. (dir. 1971-74, v.p. 1972-73), Sigma Chi. Kiwanian. Presbyn. (elder). Home: Box 272 Route 5 Lenoir City TN 37771 Office: 2121 Stephenson Dr Knoxville TN 37901

COULTER, WILLIAM WALLACE, JR., physician; b. Hensley, Ark., Jan. 16, 1916; s. William Wallace and Sue Virginia (Tilton) C.; B.S., Agrl. and Mech. Coll. Tex., 1936; M.D., La. State U., 1940; m. Martha Lilly Harper, Feb. 18, 1944; children—Martha Lee, Carol (Mrs. Joseph L. Pritchett III), Augusta (Mrs. Robert G. Szabo). Intern, Jefferson Davis Hosp., Houston, 1940-41; practice medicine, Kerrville, Tex., 1941-44; instr. medicine Baylor U. Coll. Medicine, 1944-45; resident Tex. State Sanatorium, 1945-46; practice medicine, McAllen, Tex., 1946-49; clin. asso. prof. medicine La. State U. Coll. Medicine, 1967-72, instr., 1949-50; resident pathology Jefferson Davis Hosp., Houston, 1949; practice medicine, specializing in internal medicine, Lafayette, La., 1960—; mem. staffs Lafayette Charity Hosp., Our Lady of Lourdes Hosp., Lafayette Gen. Hosp.; med. dir. Lafayette Charity Hosp. Tb Annex, 1957-60. Diplomate Am. Bd. Internal Medicine, Am. Bd. Pulmonary Diseases. Fellow Am. Coll. Chest Physicians, A.C.P.; mem. Am. Assn. Tb Physicians, La. Thoracic Soc. (pres. 1959-60), A.M.A., La., Lafayette Parish (sec.-treas. 1960-61) med. assns., La. Tb Assn. (pres. 1960-62), S.A.R., Alpha Kappa Kappa. Roman Catholic. Clubs: Oakbourne Country, Town House (Lafayette). Home: 1000 W Bayou Pkwy Lafayette LA 70501 Office: 1229 Coolidge Lafayette LA 70501

COUNTS, GURDON WRIGHT, JR., physician; b. Prosperity, S.C., Nov. 12, 1933; s. Gurdon Wright and Violet Marjorie (Epting) C.; B.S., Newberry Coll., 1955; M.D., Med. Coll. S.C., 1959; m. Elizabeth Mae Rickenbacker, Dec. 20, 1959; children—Gurdon Wright III, Karl F., Walter E., Philip J., Anthony J. Intern, Greenville (S.C.) Gen. Hosp., 1960, resident, 1961-62; practice medicine, specializing in family practice, Prosperity, S.C., 1961, Batesburg-Leesville, S.C., 1964—; mem. staff Lexington County Hosp. Served with USAF, 1962-64. Named Batesburg-Leesville Young Man of the Year, Jr. C. of C., 1967. Mem. A.M.A., S.C., Ridge med. socs., Batesburg-Leesville C. of C. (dir. 1965-69), Batesburg-Leesville Jaycees (pres. 1967-68, state dir. 1968-71, (hon. life mem.). Lutheran (mem. ch. council 1965-68, 70-73). Home: 501 E Church St Leesville SC 29070 Office: E Columbia Av Batesburg SC 29006

COURSEN, RICHARD DENNISON, assn. exec., govt. cons.; b. Newark, Dec. 2, 1917; s. H. Preston and Ruth (Dennison) C.; grad. Phillips Andover Acad., 1936; B.A., Yale, 1940; m. Helen Wilson Stevens, July 18, 1942; children—Timothy S., Christopher D.; m. 2d, Carolyn Hinman Yeaw, May 22, 1971. Advt. product mgr. Pillsbury Mills, Inc., 1945-48; account exec. Campbell-Mithun, 1948-49; dir. marketing Northrup, King & Co., 1949-54; dir. edn., editor Council Agrl. and Chemurgic Research, 1954-57; v.p., dir. Cornwell, Inc., 1954-57; dir. Malayan Tin Bur., Washington, 1957—; pres. Coursen & Co., govt. consultants, Washington, 1970—. Served from pvt. to capt. cav. AUS, 1940-45. Decorated Bronze Star. Republican. Episcopalian. Clubs: Burning Tree, Chevy Chase, 1925 F Street, Capitol Hill, Yale (past pres.). Home: 5053 Loughboro Rd NW Washington DC 20016 Office: 2000 K St NW Washington DC 20006

COURTNEY, ALBERT KENNETH, physician; b. Wills Point, Tex., Feb. 5, 1929; s. Albert and Lottie Ethel (Miracle) C.; B.A., U. Tex., 1953, M.D., 1963; m. Eleanor Kay Dunks, July 1, 1961; children—Steven Paul, Deborah Kay, David Allen, Philip Edward. Intern, U. N.M. Hosp., 1963-64; gen. practice resident Monterrey County Hosp., Salinas, Cal., 1964-66; gen. practice medicine, Midland, Tex., 1967—; mem. med. staff Midland Meml., Parkview hosps., Midland; chief staff Parkview Hosp., 1973—. Served to lt. (j.g.) USNR, 1954-57. Mem. Am. Acad. Family Physicians, Assn. Am. Physicians and Surgeons, So. Tex. (mem. com. on pvt. practice 1970-71), Midland County med. assns., Phi Beta Pi. Republican. Baptist (deacon 1966—). Mason. Clubs: Antique Automobile, Permian Basin Rifle and Pistol (Midland). Office: 210 N C St Midland TX 79701

COURTNEY, EDWIN RALEIGH, hardware co. exec.; b. Dunbrooke, Va., Mar. 14, 1904; s. Peachie Clarence and Ida (Powers) C.; grad. high sch.; m. Irene Trible, Jan. 14, 1926; children—Dorothy Mae (Mrs. William Gilmer), Jene Francis. With Watkins Cottrell Co., Richmond, Va., 1925—, v.p., 1953-56, pres., dir., 1956-70, pres., chmn. bd., dir., 1970—. Mem. So. Hardware Golf Assn., Va. Wildlife Fedn. Baptist (trustee). Kiwanian. Home: 3103 Moss Side Av Richmond VA 23222 Office: 109-125 S 14th St Richmond VA 23219

COURTNEY, J(OHN) CAL(HOUN), investment and found. exec., rancher; b. Aiken, S.C., Apr. 12, 1916; S. James Edwin and Alice (Guy) C.; B.S. in Civil Engring., George Washington U., 1939, M.S. in Mgmt. Engring., 1948; m. Zoleta Meachum, Jan. 19, 1947; children—John Calhoun IV, Winfree Meachum, Zoleta Guy. Staff asst. White House, Washington, 1948-52; indsl. cons. Tex. Power & Light Co., Dallas, 1952-57; pres. Tex. Investment & Mgmt. Co., Dallas, 1959—, Sam Rayburn Found., Dallas, 1962—; pres. Greater Laredo Devel. Found., Laredo, Tex., 1968-72; dir. Ga.-Fla. Oil & Refining Co., Jacksonville, Internat. Projects & Devel. Co., Dallas, Continental Sulphur & Phosphate Co., Dallas, Graham Land & Devel. Co., Dallas, Bank Tex., Hounston; exec. v.p. Nat. Conv. Corp., Dallas, 1956. Chmn., Vets. Com. for Eisenhower-Nixon, 1956; ind. candidate for U.S. Senate from Tex., 1957. Trustee, Hosp. of S.W.; bd. dirs. Tex. Found. for Higher Edn. Served to col. USAAF, 1946. Named Outstanding Citizen Mil. Order Equalizers, 1957; recipient Distinguished Service award V.F.W., 1962. Mem. Am. Polit. Sci. Assn., V.F.W., Am. Mgmt. Assn., Am.-Mexican Assn. (pres.). Methodist Clubs: Brookhaven Country (Dallas); Willowbrook Country (Tyler, Tex.); Army-Navy. Contbg. editor Commodity Year Book, 1948. Home: 7210 S Jan Mar Dr Dallas TX 75230 Office: Dallas Fed Savs and Loan Bldg 1505 Elm St Dallas TX 75201

COUSINS, THOMAS G., diversified bus. exec.; ed. U. Ga.; m. Ann Draughon; children—Jane Caroline, Lillian, Thomas G. Chmn. bd., chief exec. officer Cousins Properties Inc., Atlanta, subsidiaries including 1st Am. Investment Corp., Investment Mortgage Co., Retail Planning Corp., Southeastern Land Fund, Inc., Investment Adv. Co.; prin. owner Atlanta Hawks, 1968-70; mem. Atlanta bd. Citizens and So. Nat. Bank. Mem. exec. com. Central Atlanta Progress, Inc. Trustee Atlanta Arts Alliance, Rockefeller U. Presbyn. (chmn. bd. deacons). Club: Commerce of Atlanta (dir.). Office: Cousins Properties Inc 300 Interstate N Atlanta GA 30339

COVINGTON, CECIL LYONS, electronics co. exec.; b. Dallas, Nov. 21, 1911; s. William Roper and Mary Eliza (Lyons) C.; A.B. cum laude, Baylor U., 1933; LL.B., Nat. U., 1939, M.P.L., S.J.D., 1940; m. Phyllis Ruth McIntyre, Feb. 17, 1943; 1 son, Mark Roper. Adminstrv. asst. PWA Washington, 1933-40; clk. to Senator Tom Connally of Tex., 1940-41; spl. asst. on contracts OSRD, 1941-43; spl. asst. to dir. tng., facilities service VA, in charge review contracts negotiated with all schs. and colls. Ark., La., Okla., Miss., Kan., Tex., Mo., 1946-53; contract adminstr. Texas Instruments, Inc., 1953-56, controller apparatus div., 1956-58, mgr. govt. contracts adminstrn., 1958-61, mgr. govt. contracts and banking relations, 1962-63, mgr. govt. relations, 1964-66, adminstrv. asst. to chmn. bd., 1967, contracts mgr. govt. products div., 1968, mgr. govt. relations equipment group, 1969—. Served as lt. USNR, 1944-46. Mem. Financial Execs. Inst. (govt. bus. com.), Nat. Security Indsl. Assn. (chmn. procurement adv. com.), N.A.M. (nat. def. com.), Sigma Tau Delta, Beta Pi Theta, Sigma Nu Phi. Presbyn. Club: Twin Points (Hot Springs, Ark.). Home 9531 Windy Hill Rd Dallas TX 75238 Office: 13500 North Central Expressway Dallas TX 75222

COVINGTON, ROBERT NEWMAN, educator; b. Evansville, Ind., Sept. 9, 1936; s. George M. and Roberta (Newman) C.; B.A., Yale U. 1958; J.D., Vanderbilt U., 1961; m. Paula Anne Hattox, July 29, 1972. Admitted to Tenn. bar, 1961; asst. prof. Vanderbilt U. Sch. Law, Nashville, 1961-64, asso. prof., 1964-69, prof., 1969—, asso. dean, 1972—; cons. Tenn. State Law Library Commn., 1965—; chmn. Southern Law Review Conf., 1963-64; mem. Labor Law Group Trust, 1969—. Pres. Henry County (Tenn.) Young Democrats Club, 1959. Mem. Am., Tenn. bar assns., Am. Judicature Soc., Order of Coif, Phi Beta Kappa, Phi Delta Phi. Democrat. Episcopalian. Club: University (pres. 1968-70) (Nashville). Author: Problems in Professional Responsibility: Insurance, 1966; co-editor: (with Thomas G. Roady Jr.) Essays in Procedure and Evidence, 1961 (with others) Cases and Materials on Legal Methods, 1969; (with A. Caghan) Social Legislation, 1971; (with J. Jones and A. Cagham) Discrimination in Employment, 1971. Contbr. articles in field to legal jours. Home: 907 Estes Rd Nashville TN 37215

COWAN, CHARITY ALLENE, educator; b. Lancaster, Ky., Oct. 1, 1924; d. John Theo and Julia Mae (Stevens) Cowan; B.S., Eastern Ky. U., 1946; M.A., U. Ky., 1952; postgrad. U. Ky., 1959-60. Tchr. Locust Street Sch., Erlanger, Ky., 1946-58; gen. supr. Erlanger-Elsmere Bd. Edn., 1958—. Mem. Assn. Childhood Edn. (state sec. 1956-58, chpt. pres. 1968—), N.E.A. (life mem., br. pres. 1967—), Eastern State U. Alumni Assn. (life), U. Ky. Alumni Assn. (life), Ky. Edn. Assn., Assn. for Childhood Edn. (life), Ky. Assn. for Ednl. Suprs., Assn. for Supervision and Curriculum, Am. Assn. U. Women (v.p. 1964-66; program chmn. 1964-66), Ky. P.T.A. (life), Ind. Order Foresters, Kappa Delta Pi, Delta Kappa Gamma. Baptist (sec. chmn. kindergarten 1964—). Home: 440 B Graves Av Erlanger KY 41018 Office: 39 Erlanger Rd Erlanger KY 41018

COWAN, JOEL HARVEY, real estate exec.; b. Marietta, Ga., June 23, 1936; s. Charles A. and Bernice (Kemp) C.; B.S., Ga. Inst. Tech., 1958; m. R. Geraldine Matthews, Dec. 21, 1957; children—Joel H., Mark Kemp, Jennifer Matthews. Pres. Phipps Land Co., Atlanta, 1968—; chmn. Phipps-Harrington Corp., Atlanta, Fayette State Bank, Peachtree City, Ga.; dir. Interstate Gen. Corp., San Juan, P.R., Nat. Bank Ga., Atlanta. Chmn. Gov.'s Commn. on Planned Growth. Trustee, Rabun Gap-Nacoochee Sch., Rabun Gap, Ga.; bd. dirs. Central Atlanta Progress. Kiwanian. Home: Pebble Point Peachtree City GA 30269 Office: One Northside 75 Atlanta GA 30318

COWAN, RICHARD SUMMER, systematic botanist; b. Crawfordsville, Ind., Jan. 23, 1921; s. Walter Harrison and Eura B. (Walker) C.; A.B., Wabash Coll. 1942; M.S., U. Hawaii, 1948; Ph.D., Columbia, 1952; m. Mary Frances Minnich, June 28, 1941; children—Richard A., Diedra Anne, Charles Ian. Teaching asst. U. Hawaii, 1946-48; tech. asst. N.Y. Bot. Garden, N.Y.C., 1948-52, asst. curator, 1952-57; asso. curator Smithsonian Instn., Washington, 1957-62, asst. dir. Mus. Natural History, 1962-65, dir., 1965-73, sr. botanist, 1973—; sec. nat. com. XI Internat. Bot. Congress; mem. nat. com. Internat. Biol. Program. Served with USNR, 1943-45. NSF fellow, 1952-53. Mem. Am. Inst. Biol. Scis., A.A.A.S., Am. Soc. Plant Taxonomists, Internat. Assn. Plant Taxonomy. Methodist. Contbr. articles profl. jours. Home: 4409 Tonquil Pl Beltsville MD 20705 Office: Smithsonian Instn Washington DC 20560

COWAN, SWAFFIELD, cons. elec. engr.; b. Moss Point, Miss., Dec. 1, 1907; s. Oliver Bingham and Mary (Swaffield) C.; B.S. in Elec. Engring., U. S.C., 1929; E.E., 1931; m. Anne Bryan Lawton, July 2, 1935; children—Anne Lawton (Mrs. Wade H. Barber), William Swaffield. With N.Y.C. R.R., 1929-30; teaching fellow U. S.C., Columbia, 1930-31; with S.C. Power Rate Investigating Com., Columbia, 1931, Underwriters Labs., Inc., Chgo., 1935-46; with Factory Ins. Assn., Charlotte, N.C., 1946-72, sr. elec. engr., 1960-72; cons. elec. engr., Georgetown, S.C., 1972—. Mem. Elec. Council Underwriters Labs., Chgo., 1956-72. Bd. dirs. Joint Indsl. Council, 1967-72. Registered profl. elec. engr., Ill., N.C. Mem. Am. Inst. E.E. (chmn. textile com. 1952-54, mem. gen. industry applications com. 1952-65, safety com., 1961-65, industry div. com., 1961-65), I.E.E.E. (life, mem. industry applications soc. 1965—, chmn. group safety com. 1966-69, mem. group tech. operations dept. 1966-69, mem. textile industry com. 1966—), Nat. Fire Protection Assn. (mem. nat. elec. code correlating com. 1966-72, chmn. machine tool elec. standards com. 1956-72, chmn. elec. equipment maintenance com. 1968-72), Internat. Assn. Elec. Insps., N.C., S.C. socs. engrs. Contbr. articles to profl. jours. Address: 29 Palmetto St Georgetown SC 29440

COWART, DAVID GEORGE, ednl. adminstr.; b. Ludowici, Ga., Jan. 18, 1940; s. William Madison and Alta Mae (Bacon) C.; B.S., Ga. So. Coll., 1961, M.Ed., 1966; postgrad. U. Ga., summer 1962, Valdosta State Coll., 1971; m. Carole Biddy, Dec. 17, 1960; children—Leisha, Michael. Tchr. math., sci. Swainsboro (Ga.) High Sch., 1961-62; prin. Brookfield (Ga.) Jr. High Sch., 1962-63, Monroe County Elementary Sch., Forsyth, Ga., 1963-68, Carver Elementary Sch., Milledgeville, Ga., 1968-71; dir. Elementary Secondary Edn. Act project PRIDE, Waycross, Ga., 1971-73; coordinator acad. programs Fla. State Hosp., Chattahoochee, 1973—. Named Outstanding Young Educator, Monroe County Jaycees, 1968, by Milledgeville Jaycees, 1969; recipient Humanitarian Service in Edn. award Baha'i Faith, 1970. Mem. N.E.A., Council Exceptional Children, Phi Delta Kappa. Home: PO Box 548 Chattahoochee FL 32324 Office: PO Box 109 Fla State Hosp Chattahoochee FL 32324

COWART, GRIGGSBY THOMAS, physician; b. Atlanta, Aug. 19, 1919; s. Griggsby Thomas and Gilley Pearl (Johnson) C.; A.B., Emory U., 1941, M.D., 1944; m. Anne Henderson, Mar. 4, 1944; children—Dorothy Anne, Griggsby Thomas. Intern, Emory U. Hosp., Atlanta, 1944-45, asst. resident surgery, 1945-46; resident urology Lawson VA Hosp., Chamblee, Ga., 1948-51; chief of urology Atlanta VA Hosp., 1951-54, cons., 1954—; individual practice medicine, specializing in urology, Atlanta, 1954—; clin. asst. prof. surgery Emory U. Sch. Medicine, 1964—. Dir. So. Fed. Savs. and Loan Assn., Atlanta. Served to capt. M.C., AUS, 1946-48. Diplomate Am. Bd. Urology. Fellow A.C.S.; mem. A.M.A., So. Med. Assn., Am., Southeastern, Ga. Urol. assns., Phi Beta Kappa, Sigma Nu. Contbr. articles to profl. jours. Home: 18 Blackland Rd NW Atlanta GA 30342 Office: 384 Peachtree St Atlanta GA 30308

COWLES, MILLY, educator; b. Ramer, Ala., May 29, 1932; d. Russell Fail and Sara (Mills) Cowles; B.S., Troy State U., 1952; M.A., U. Ala., 1958; Ph.D. (grad. fellow), 1962. Tchr. pub. schs., Montgomery, 1952-59; asst. then asso. prof. Grad. Sch. Edn., Rutgers U., 1962-66; asso. prof. U. Ga., 1966-67; prof. early childhood devel. and edn. Sch. Edn., U. S.C., Columbia, 1967-73; prof. Sch. Edn., U. Ala. at Birmingham, 1973—, asso. dean, 1974—. Cons. So. Edn. Found., Atlanta, Ga. Inst. Higher Edn. U. Ga., also numerous sch. systems throughout Northeast and South; chief cons. Williamsburg County (S.C.) Pub. Schs., 1968—. Pres. bd. dirs. 2d Reformed Ch. Nursery Sch., New Brunswick, N.J., 1963-66. Mem. Am. Ednl. Research Assn., Soc. for Research Child Devel., A.A.A.S., Am. Assn. U. Profs., Nat. Council Tchrs. English, Internat. Reading Assn., Nat. Assn. for Edn. Young Children, N.E.A. (mem. parent involvement com. elementary, kindergarten and nursery educators dept. 1972—), Assn. for Supervision and Curriculum Devel. (mem. council on early childhood edn. 1969-71), Am. Psychol. Assn., N.Y. Acad. Sci., Kappa Delta Pi (chpt. treas. 1964-66), Delta Kappa Gamma. Editor, contbg. author: Perspectives in the Education of Disadvantaged Children, 1967. Contbr. articles to profl. jours. Home: 1022 Essex Rd Birmingham AL 35222

COWLEY, LEONARD MERWYN, real estate appraiser, cons.; b. Bladen, Neb., Mar. 16, 1899; s. Charles Wesley and Flora (Cramer) C.; A.B., U. Neb., 1922; postgrad. So. Meth. U., 1947-49, B.F.A., 1972; U. So. Cal., 1939; m. Irene Leona Holston, Aug. 13, 1922; 1 dau., Barbara Lou (Mrs. C. Russell Smith, Jr.). Vice pres. Cowley, Higgins & Delph Investment Co., Phoenix, 1927-37; owner Cowley & Co., 1937-40; mgr. Appraisal Assos., Dallas, 1952-55; mng. partner Leonard M. Cowley & Assos., Dallas, 1955—; pres. Appraisal Library, Inc., 1959—. Adj. gen. Ariz., 1929. Sec. Ariz. Republican Central Com.; chmn. Maricopa County Rep. Com., 1932. Served to col. C.E., AUS, 1940-47. Decorated Legion of Merit. Mem. Am. Inst. Real Estate Appraisers (charter pres. N. Tex. chpt.), Am. Soc. Appraisers (past chpt. pres., regional gov.), Farm and Ranch Mgrs. and Appraisers, Retreads (past comdr. Tex. dept., past nat. vice comdr.), Sigma Delta Chi, Phi Sigma Kappa. Mason (Shriner). Clubs: Dallas Press. Contbr. articles profl. jours. Home: 6305 Lange Circle Dallas TX 75214 Office: 6162 E Mockingbird Lane Dallas TX 75214

COWLING, HERFORD TYNES, photographic engr., movie producer, explorer, ret. air force officer; b. Nansemond County, Va., Aug. 20, 1890; s. John Phillips and Caroline Weaver (Tynes) C.; student George Washington U., 1912-13; m. Virginia Hardin, Jan. 14, 1927. Chief photographer U.S. Reclamation Service, 1909-16; traveled extensively in U.S., Canada and Mexico, 1913-16; headed cinematographic expdn., 1917, to Formosa. Philippines, Indo-China, Siam, Malay States, Indonesia, Australia, Tasmania, China, Japan, New Zealand and South Sea Islands, producing Paramount—Burton Holmes Travel Films; produced motion pictures of Europe, 1919, including France, Belgium, Germany, Austria, Switzerland, Czechoslovakia, Italy, also Algeria, Tunisia, Tangier, Morocco, Sicily, Spain, Egypt, Palestine, Turkey, Cuba and Mexico, 1921-23; expdns. to Brit. East Africa, Uganda, Belgian Congo and The Sudan, filming big game hunting, 1922; India, Kashmir, Tibet, Burma, Sumatra, Malaysia, 1924; China war corr. Fox News Movietone Films, produced motion picture of coronation of Maharaja of Kashmir, 1926; tech. dir. teaching films dept. Eastman Kodak Co., 1927-32; ofcl. photographer Century of Progress, Chgo., 1933; supr. motion picture prodn. Emergency Conservation Works in Nat. Parks, 1934; tech. dir. div. motion pictures and sound rec. U.S. Nat. Archives, Washington, 1935-37; tech. asst. to adminstr. Nat. Unemployment Census, Washington, 1937; sr. adminstrv. asst. Dept. Commerce, 1938-40, then chief photog. services U.S. Dept. Labor. Served with USAAF, 1941-46, USAF, 1946-50; col. USAF ret. Fellow Royal Photog. Soc. (Gt. Britain); mem. U.S. Photog. Soc. (pres. 1915-16, hon. mem.), Biol. Photographic Assn., Am. Soc. Cinematographers, Soc. Motion Pictures Engrs., S.A.R. Mason (Shriner). Clubs: Explorers (fellow) (N.Y.C.); Army-Navy Country, Army and Navy (Washington). Home: 808 S Ode St Arlington VA 22204

COWPER, ALBERT WALLACE, superior ct. judge; b. Kinston, N.C., July 14, 1911; s. George Vernon and Rosabel (Rountree) C.; LL.B., U. N.C., 1935; m. Virginia Bland Lee, Apr. 10, 1943; children—Richard Green, Lee Fitzgerald. Admitted to N.C. bar, 1934; individual practice law, Kinston, 1935-41, 60—; spl. agt. FBI, 1941-45; Judge Recorder's Ct., Kinston, 1946-56, Superior Ct., 1960—. Pres., N.C. Conf. Superior Ct. Judges, 1970. Served with AUS, 1945-46. Home: 604 Edwards Av Kinston NC 28501 Office: Lenoir County Superior Courthouse Kinston NC 28501

COX, ALBERT EDWARD, ins. exec.; b. Chatham, Va., Aug. 21, 1910; s. Albert Henry and Anna (Jackson) C.; student William and Mary Coll., 1927-29, U. Va., 1929-30; m. Glenn Jones; children—Albert Jones, Anna Glenn, Sally Ruth. Pres. Cox & Goodridge, Inc., Danville, Va., 1940—; ins. agt., Danville, 1934-40; owner South Side Gen. Agy., Danville, 1951—; mem. Danville bd. Va. Nat. Bank. Chmn. ins. adv. com. City of Danville. Chmn. bd. trustees Anderson Student Aid Fund. Co-chmn. War Fund of Pittsylvania County, Va., 1944-45, citation for service. Mem. Va. Gov.'s Redistricting Commn., 1961. Del. Dem. Nat. Conv., 1960. Mem. Va. Assn. Ins. Agts. (pres. 1954-55). Va., Danville chambers commerce, Nat. Assn. Ins. Agts. (state bd. dirs.), Kappa Alpha. Baptist. Mason, Rotarian (pres. 1956-57). Clubs: Danville Golf (pres. 1963); Commonwealth (Richmond, Va.). Fire Insurance Field (award Agent of Year 1951). Home: 491 Hawthorne Dr Danville VA 24541 Office: 128 S Market St Danville VA 24541

COX, BERTHA MAE HILL (MRS. WILLIS L. COX), educator; b. Kosse, Tex., Mar. 10, 1901; d. Marshall Victor and Ollie Evelyn (Phifer) Hill; student Southwest Tex. U., 1922, Baylor U., 1923, So. Meth U.; B.S., North Tex. State U., 1935, M.S., 1950; m. Willis L. Cox, June 8, 1924. Prin. rural sch., Harmony, Tex., 1918; acting postmaster, Kosse, Tex., 1919-21; tchr. pub. schs., Kosse, 1922-24; Dallas County, 1925-29; prin. Dallas City Schs., 1930-33, tchr., 1934-64; tchr. Dallas Ind. Sch. Dist., after 1964, now ret.; founder, now dir. emeritus Kessler Park United Meth. Ch. Day Sch., Dallas. Named tchr. of the year Dallas Times Herald, 1950. Mem. Dallas Assn. Childhood Edn. (pres. 1938, state sec.-treas., 1940), Speech Arts Tchrs., (pres. 1954), N.E.A., (life), Tex. Tchrs. Assn. (life), Tex. Parents and Tchrs. Assn. (hon. life), Wesleyan Service Guild (hon. life), Kappa Delta Pi, Delta Kappa Gamma. Democrat. Methodist. Author: True Tales of Texas, 1949; Susan's Happy Year, 1957; Let's Read about Texas, 1963; Our Texas, 1964; also ch. sch. materials for Meth. Ch. Editor: Tell Us about Texas, 1947; The Texans Texas to Today, 1972. Editorial adviser Ideas readers series, 1973. Contbr. articles to profl. jours. Home: 1130 N Winnetka St Dallas TX 75208

COX, CARL THOMAS, ednl. adminstr.; b. Bridgeton, N.C., Jan. 12, 1925; s. Henry Albert and Emily Alice (Miller) C.; B.S., East Carolina Coll., 1949; postgrad. Atlantic Christian Coll., 1960-63; M.A., East Carolina U., 1967; m. Scottie Winstead, Nov. 23, 1950; children—Scott Lee, Carla Sue. Office mgr. utility dept. T.A. Loving & Co., constrn., Goldsboro, N.C., 1949-58; office mgr. Carolina Plywood Dist. and Patelos Door Corp., Wilson, N.C., 1959-63; instr. Wayne Community Coll., Goldsboro, 1963-65; bus. mgr., 1965—. Mem. N.C. accreditation com. Dept. Community Colls., 1967-72. Served with USNR, 1943-46. Mem. Nat., N.C. edn. assns., Community Coll. Bus. Ofcls. Mem. Christian Ch. (chmn. bd. 1965-67). Mason (Shriner), Elk. Club: Goldsboro Country. Home: 709 Pittman St Goldsboro NC 27530 Office: PO Box 1878 Goldsboro NC 27530

COX, EDITH GLORIA (MRS. HOWARD REEVES COX JR.), banker; b. Angleton, Tex., Dec. 15, 1923; d. Henry Fred and Eva Eleanor (Bozarth) Raiford; student U. Houston, 1948-49; prestandard certificate Am. Inst. Banking, 1963, standard certificate, 1966, gen. certificate, 1972; m. Howard Reeves Cox., Jr., Nov. 25, 1947. With plant protection dept. Dow Chem. Co., Freeport, Tex., 1943; bookkeeper Velasco (Tex.) State Bank, 1950-55; with East End State Bank, Houston, 1956—, asst. cashier, 1967—. Mem. Corrigan Civic Club, 1969—. Served with WAC, 1944-45. Named Outstanding Woman of Year, Am. Inst. Banking, 1969. Mem. Nat. Assn. Bank Women, Am. Inst. Banking (mem. bd. govs. 1967-69, co-chmn. nat. conv. publicity 1971). Home: 5302 Carmona Lane Pearland TX 77581 Office: 4200 Leeland St Houston TX 77023

COX, GAYLORD HAINES, design engr.; b. Jacksonville, Ore., Mar. 26, 1906; s. Alva Carl and Emma Mildred (Haines) C.; B.A., U. Ore., 1931; m. 2d, Edith Rogers, 1968; children (by previous marriage)—Dennis, Phillip, Rosemary Louise. Pvt. engring. practice, Portland, Ore., 1931-35; gen. engr. Crosby Chem. Co., DeRidder, La., 1945-49; design engr. Cit-Con Oil Corp., Lake Charles, La., 1949-65; mem. W.H. Woodward & G.H. Cox, Architects and Cons. Engrs., 1951—, prin., 1965—; dir. Mid-South Financial Corporation. Adviser Boy Scouts. Capt., U.S. Army, 1935-45. Mem. Nat. Assn. Corrosion Engrs., I.E.E.E., La. Engring. Soc., Am. Legion (chmn., mem. commn. Americanism, mem. nat. com. constitution and bylaws), Nat. Rifle Assn., Nat. Soc. Profl. Engrs., Air Craft Owners and Pilots Assn. Methodist. Home: 1362 W Jefferson St Lake Charles LA 70601 Office: 714 Hodges St Lake Charles LA 70601

COX, JACK FRANK WELLS, oil producer, real estate resort exec.; b. Kingwood, W.Va., May 20, 1914; s. Frank Wells and Helen (Berry) C.; B.S. in Petroleum Engring., Stanford, 1932-36; m. Marilyn Edna Hawbaker, Oct. 18, 1952; children—Lynne, John, Berry. Pres., Cox Drilling Co., Owensboro, Ky., 1938—, Bahama Reef Devel. Co., Freeport, Grand Bahama, 1962-67, Royal Oak Country Club Resort, Royal Oak Devel. Co., Titusville, Fla., 1962—. Served to lt. comdr. USNR, 1941-46. Mem. Delta Kappa Epsilon. Episcopalian. Elk. Home: 1114 SE 12th Terrace Deerfield Beach FL 33441 Office: Country Club Dr Titusville FL 32780

COX, JACKSON BARCUS, utilities exec.; b. Mexico, D.F., Mexico, Sept. 10, 1910 (parents Am. citizens); s. Jackson Berry and Julia (Barcus) C.; A.B., U. Tex., 1933; m. Beatrice Deborah Von Zuben, Nov. 24, 1941; children—Julia (Mrs. Stuart Howard Lee), Deborah (Mrs. John Andrew Styrsky). Editor U. Tex. Student Publs., 1932-33; reporter, sports editor Austin (Tex.) Daily Dispatch, 1934-35; asst. to welfare officer Civilian Conservation Corps, Ft. Worth, 1935-37; clk. accounting Community Pub. Service Co., Ft. Worth, 1937-42, asst. sales mgr., 1946-66, mgr. advt., 1956-66, dir. advt. and pub. relations, 1966—, editor Communicator, 1966—. Served from pvt. to capt. AUS, 1942-46. Mem. Pub. Utilities Advt. Assn., W. Tex. Press Assn., Pub. Relations Soc. Am. Methodist. Clubs: Fort Worth Press, Advertising (Ft. Worth). Home: 3608 Wedgway Dr Fort Worth TX 76133 Office: Community Pub Service Co 501 W 6th St Fort Worth TX 76102

COX, JAMES M(IDDLETON), JR., publisher; b. Dayton, O., June 27, 1903; s. James Middleton and Mary Simpson (Harding) C.; student Culver Mil. Acad., 1917-20, Cheshire (Conn.) Acad., 1922-24; Ph.B., Yale, 1928; m. Helen Rumsey, Nov. 21, 1930. Joined Dayton Daily News, 1929, gen. mgr., 1931-38, asst. pub., 1938-39, asst. pub. and v.p., 1939-49, dir., pres., 1949-56; pres. dir. Dayton Journal-Herald, 1948-56; vice chmn., pres. Dayton Newspapers, Inc., 1957-58, chmn., pres., 1958—; established Radio Sta. WHIO, Dayton, 1934; pres., dir. Miami Valley Broadcasting Corp., Dayton, 1949-58, chmn. bd., pres., 1958—; chmn. bd. Atlanta Newspapers, Inc., 1957—; v.p. Springfield (O.) Daily News and Sun, 1938-54; pres., dir. Springfield Newspapers Inc., 1954-58, chmn. bd., pres., 1958—; chmn. bd. Carolina Broadcasting Co., 1959—; pres. Miami (Fla.) Daily News, 1957—; v.p., dir. radio sta. WIOD, Miami, 1947-56; v.p. Biscayne TV Corp., Miami, 1956—; pub. Miami News, Miami. Active Community Chest, A.R.C., Salvation Army. Mem. asso. bd. lay trustees U. Dayton. Served as lt. comdr. Naval A.S., USNR, 1942-45. Episcopalian. Home: 4358 N Bay Rd Miami Beach FL 33139 Office: care The Miami News Miami FL 33132

COX, LOEL DENE, agrl. exec.; b. Sidney, Tex., Apr. 12, 1926; s. Ottie Scott and Gladys (McCarty) C.; A.S., John Tarleton Agrl. Coll., 1946; B.S., Tex. A. and M. U., 1948; m. Sara Lou McCarrol, Feb. 26, 1949; 1 son, Lowell Dean. Instr. agr. San Angelo Coll., 1948-50; instr. Comanche County Vocational Sch., 1951-52; salesman Moorman Mfg. Co., Comanche, Tex., 1952, dist. mgr., San Antonio, Tex., 1952-53, state sales mgr., Comanche, 1953—, profl. feed counsellor, 1971—; dir. Comanche Nat. Bank, 1965—. Served with USNR, 1944-46. Decorated Purple Heart; recipient Lone Star Farmer degree Tex. Future Farmers Am. Mem. S.A.R. Mem. Ch. of Christ. Home: 203 Williams Dr Comanche TX 76442 Office: 203 Williams Dr Comanche TX 76442

COX, PAUL JEFFERSON, textile mill exec.; b. Wilcoe, W. Va., Aug. 9, 1934; s. Andrew Jackson and Emma (Presley) C.; B.S., Ohio State U., 1960, M.A. (William Green Meml. fellow), 1961; m. Pearl Louise Cheek, Aug. 9, 1952; children—Pamela Gwyn, Paula Jeanine. Mgr. labor relations Whirlpool Corp., St. Joseph, Mich., 1961-64; mgr. flight contracts Eastern Airlines, Miami, 1964-65; mfg. mgr. Collins & Aikman Corp., Albemarle, N.C., 1965—. Trustee Marion (N.C.) Gen. Hosp., 1970-71. Served with USNR, 1952-56. Mem. Albemarle Jr. C. of C. (pres. 1967-68), Am. Bus. Club (v.p. 1968-69), Am. Econ. Assn., McDowell County C. of C. (bd. dirs.). Methodist. Lion. Home: 900 Honeysuckle Lane Albemarle NC 28001 Office: Box 580 Albemarle NC 28001

COXE, EMILY BADHAM (MRS. THOMAS CHATTERTON COXE), civic worker; b. Edenton, N.C., May 3, 1910; d. Richard Paxton and Emily Wood (Fagan) Badham; grad. St. Mary's Jr. Coll., 1929; m. Thomas Chatterton Coxe, Jr., Nov. 6, 1929; children—Thomas Chatterton III, Emily Wood (Mrs. William Alfred Winburn III), Patricia Barringer (Mrs. Marshall Taylor Ware), Charlotte Victoria (Mrs. Charles E. Commander, III), Richard Badham. Mem. state bd. dirs. S.C. div. Am. Cancer Soc.; mem. area bd. dirs. Tb Assn.; mem. S.C. Ednl. TV Commn., 1973—. Mem. bd. visitors St. Mary's Jr. Coll. Mem. Nat. Soc. Colonial Dames Am., Internat. Platform Assn., Darlington County Hist. Soc. Episcopalian. Clubs: Garden Am., Palmetto Garden S.C. Author: (with Frances Warfield) Mother of the Maid, 1960. Home: Skufful Farm Darlington SC 29532

COXWELL, ALVIN BARTLEY, JR., dentist; b. Monroeville, Ala., May 14, 1913; s. Alvin Bartley and Margaret (Mims) C.; B.S., U. Ala., 1934; D.M.D., U. Louisville, 1942; m. Frances Louise Mize; children—Margaret (Mrs. Wright), Madolyn (Mrs. Campbell). Practice dentistry, Louisville, 1942—; instr. dept. prosthetics U. Louisville, 1943-60, now guest lectr., also mem. cancer control com. Med. Center; courtesy staff Bapt. Hosp., St. Anthony's Hosp., Gen. Hosp. (all Louisville); guest lectr. U. Ky., mem. adv. com. Med. Center; acting dir. Ky. Dental Services Corp., 1965. Mem. adv. com. Ky. Dept. Health, 1951-60; surgeon Bklyn. Health Moblzn., 1960; sr. dental surgeon USPHS, 1960. Trustee Nat. Assn. Dental Service Plans. Mem. Louisville Dental Soc. (sec.-treas. 1946), Ky. (sec.-treas. 1947), Am. (del. 1948-68, spl. com. trustee dists. 1965-66) dental assns., Am., Internat. colls. dentists, Am. Dental Assn. Officers (sec. 1959, v.p. 1961, pres. 1962), Am. Soc. Oral Surgeons (hon., chmn. council on allied med. services 1952, exec. sec. 1952-56, Louisville Philol. Soc., Omicron Kappa Upsilon. Office: Ky Dental Assn 1940 Princeton Dr Louisville KY 40205

COY, CHARLES R., lawyer; b. Madison County, Ky., Jan. 12, 1926; grad. Eastern Ky. U.; LL.B., U. Ky., 1951; m. Gay Alley; children—Russell Gay, Reba Jane. Admitted to Ky. bar, 1951, U.S. Supreme Ct. bar, 1960; mem. firm Coy and Coy, Richmond, Ky.; commonwealth's atty. 25th Jud. Dist., 1969. Mem. Republican Nat. Com., 1973—; chmn. Ky. Rep. Com., 1973—. Mem. Madison County, Ky. State (bd. govs. 1964-66, pres. 1967-68), Am. (ho. of dels. 1967-69) bar assns., Internat. Assn. Ins. Counsel, Am. Judicature Soc. (dir. 1968—). Office: 212 N 2d St Richmond KY 40475

COZBY, JOE BLANTON, profl. assn. exec.; b. Robert Lee, Tex., Apr. 30, 1918; s. Leonard Drew and Cossie Lee (Turner) C.; student John Tarleton Coll., 1937-38, Tex. U., 1938-40; grad. Southwestern Inst., 1950; m. Nona Denney, May 15, 1959; children—Rosalind (Mrs. Gary Ray Huckabey), Donna (Mrs. James Edwards), Karen (Mrs. Albert Linker), Judi (Mrs. Clayton Pulley), Linda (Mrs. Ricky Ray). Mgr., Odessa C. of C. (Tex.), 1947; bus. mgr. Odessa Chuck Wagon Gang, 1947-56; owner Alamo Directory Co., pub. city directory, Alamagordo, N.M., 1957-65, Uptown Cleaners and Laundry, 1959-64; mgr. Monahans (Tex.) C. of C., 1969—. Sec., Monahans Indsl. Found. Served with AUS, 1940-44. Decorated Purple Heart. Home: 1203 E 9th St Monahans TX 79756 Office: 4th and Dwight Sts Monahans TX 79756

CRABB, TOMMY BERT, savs. and loan exec.; b. Killeen, Tex., Jan. 12, 1939; s. Willie Bert and Lola Beatrice (Truelove) C.; B.B.A., Tex. Christian U., 1964; postgrad. U. Ind., 1972; m. Claire Jane Knapp, Aug. 26, 1959; children—Debora Claire, Julie Carroll. Clk., teller, asst. controller, asst. sec., loan officer Ft. Worth Savs. & Loan Assn., 1960-64; v.p., controller Ellis County Savs. Assn., Waxahachie, Tex., 1964-68, sr. v.p., 1969—; v.p., mgr., dir. Henderson County Savs. & Loan Assn., Athens, Tex., 1968-69. Drive chmn. Community Chest of Henderson County, 1968, Athens Indsl. Found., 1969; v.p., bd. dirs. United Fund, Waxahachie, 1969-72; mem. Waxahachie Planning and Zoning Commn., 1970—. Bd. dirs. United Presbyn. Home, Waxahachie. Mem. Nat. Assn. Savs. and Loan Controllers, N.Tex. Savs. and Loan Mgrs., Waxahachie C. of C. (v.p. 1971-72). Presbyn. (elder). Mason, Lion. Club: Waxahachie Country. Home: 1615 Little Creek Dr Waxahachie TX 75165 Office: 400 Ferris Av Waxahachie TX 75165

CRADDOCK, GEORGE BARKSDALE, physician; b. Lynchburg, Va., Oct. 24, 1908; s. Abram Poindexter and Ella Elizabeth (Goodwin) C.; A.B., Washington and Lee U., 1930; M.D., Jefferson Med. Coll., 1935; m. Mary Spencer Jack, Feb. 1, 1941; children—George Barksdale, Theodore Jack, Alice Ashley. Rotating intern Phila. Gen. Hosp., 1935-37, resident pathology, 1937-38; asst. resident medicine Med. Coll. Va., 1938-39, resident, 1939-40; practice medicine specializing in internal medicine, Lynchburg, 1940-42, 46—. Mem. alumni bd. dirs. Washington and Lee U. Served to maj. M.C., AUS, 1942-46. Diplomate Am. Bd. Internal Medicine. Fellow A.C.P.; mem. Lynchburg Acad. Medicine (past pres.), Va. Soc. Internal Medicine (past pres.), Va. Bd. Med. Examiners (pres.), Sigma Alpha Epsilon, Omicron Delta Kappa. Episcopalian. Club: Boonsboro Country. Home: 1500 Langhorne Rd Lynchburg VA 24503 Office: 2011 Tate Springs Rd Lynchburg VA 24503

CRADDOCK, THOMAS ELMORE, utility exec.; b. Seymour, Tex. Dec. 13, 1893; s. E. L. and Susan (Birdsell) C.; student high sch.; engring. dept. U. Tex., 1911-13; m. Marie Knoerr, Apr. 12, 1919. Engaged in business for self; city mgr., 1929-47; pres. Nat. Rural Electric Coops. Assn., 1947-48, now sec.-treas., mgr. rural electrification project; sec.-treas. Brazos River Power Coop.; dir. Farmers Nat. Bank, Vice pres. N.W. Tex. council Boy Scouts Am., Bd. regents Mid-Western U. Vice chmn. Region IX Tex. Edn. Service Center. Served as sgt., 1st class, Q.M.C. Finance Div., 13 mos. during World War I. Named Man of Year in Tex. Agr., 1972. Mem. C. of C., Am. Legion. Democrat. Mem. Christian Ch. Clubs: Lions, Golf and Country. Address: Box 672 Seymour TX 76380

CRAFT, OTHO E., JR., civil engr.; b. Covington, Va., Aug. 17, 1938; s. Otho Estel and Roxie (Entsminger) C.; B.S. in Civil Engring., Va. Poly. Inst., 1960; m. Margaret Sue Hollyfield, July 4, 1964; children—Laura Ruth, Connie Jo, Eric Michael. Civil engr. firm Hayes, Seay, Mattern & Mattern, Roanoke, Va., 1962-69; head dept. civil engring. firm Wiley & Wilson Inc., Lynchburg, Va., 1969—, also asso. mem. firm, 1973—. Served with AUS, 1961-67. Recipient All Stars award Va. chpt. 4-H, 1955. Registered profl. engr., Va., W.Va. Mem. Am. Soc. C.E., Nat. Soc. Profl. Engrs., Richmond Engrs. Club. Presbyn. (elder). Club: Bear Loop Hunt (Clifton Forge, Va.): Home: 203 Windingway Rd Lynchburg VA 24502 Office: 2310 Langhorne Rd Lynchburg VA 24501

CRAFT, RANDAL ROBERT, realtor; b. Ellisville, Miss., July 13, 1918; s. Tilden Bayard and Annie Laurie (Vining) C.; student Miss. State U., 1935-37; m. Elisabeth Ann Nelson, Feb. 3, 1940; children—Randal Robert, Ann Elizabeth. With Belzoni Provision Co. (Miss.), 1937-42; partner, sales mgr. Craft Co., Jackson, Miss., 1946-49; real estate salesman Reid-McGee & Co., Jackson, Miss., 1949-51; owner Craft Hosiery Co., Dallas, 1952-54; v.p. in charge sales Craft Co., Dallas, Jackson, 1954-64; owner Randal Craft, Realtor, Jackson, 1964—; pres. Craft Builders, Inc., Jackson, 1969—; dir. Multiple Listing Service, Inc., Jackson, pres., 1967; dir. All Points Relocation Service, Atlanta, 1966-70. Pres., Hinds County Heart Assn., 1968-69. Served with USAAF, 1942-45, served to capt. USAF, 1951-52. Mem. Nat. Inst. Real Estate Brokers (mem. governing council 1972—, mem. edn. com. 1969—), Jackson Bd. Realtors (dir., sec.-treas. 1966-68), Miss. Assn. Realtor Bds. (sec.-treas. 1968), Nat. Inst. Farm and Land Brokers, C. of C., Rho Epsilon (dist. dir. 1969—). Baptist (deacon). Clubs: Knife and Fork (pres. 1970-71), Civitan (pres. 1969-70). Home: 2310 Twin Lakes Circle Jackson MS 39211 Office: 4554 Office Park Dr Jackson MS 39216

CRAGO, H. CARMAN, II, glass co. exec.; b. Wheeling, W.Va., Aug. 23, 1921; s. Homer C. and Ethel (Kittle) C.; A.B., W.Va. U., 1943; postgrad. U. Pitts., 1950-51; m. Sarah Kathleen Carter, Aug. 4, 1945; children—David Hughes, John Carman. Adminstrv. asst. Hazel-Atlas Glass Co., Wheeling, W.Va., 1944-49, product mgr. beverage containers, 1950-55; dist. sales mgr. Glass div. Continental Can Co., Cleve., 1955-56, Clin. 1957-60. Midwest area mgr., Chgo., 1961-64; regional mgr. Knox Glass, Inc., Palestine, Tex., 1964-69; mgr. S.W. region Glass Containers Corp., Dallas, 1969-70; nat. sales mgr. Obear-Nester Glass, 1971-74; gen. sales mgr. Windor Industries, Inc., Dallas, 1974—. Served to lt. (j.g.) USNR. 1943-44. Mem. Nat. Assn. Bus. Econs., Ret. Officers Assn. Washington, Phi Delta Theta Alumni Assn. Presbyn. (elder). Mason. Club: Cincinnati (O.). Home: 7606 Chattington Dr Dallas TX 75240 Office: Windor Industries Inc Dallas TX

CRAIG, GERALD NICHOLS, lawyer; b. Los Angeles, Apr. 4, 1938; s. Neal Adams and Virginia Adele (Abel) C.; B.S. magna cum laude, Abilene Christian Coll., 1962; J.D., Tulane U., 1965; M.B.A., Tex. Christian U., 1971; m. Shirley Ann Hebert, Aug. 3, 1957; children—Gerald Nichols II, Darly N., Kendall P., Anne Elizabeth. Exec. trainee Bank of Commerce, Abilene, Tex., 1959-61; investigator Willmark Service System, New Orleans, 1963-65; landman Chevron Oil Co., Denver, 1965-66; trust officer Ft. Worth Nat. Bank, 1966-69; admitted to Tex. bar, 1967; mem. firm Wilson, McGee, Craig & Owen, Ft. Worth, 1969—; faculty Evening Coll., Tex. Christian U., 1968—. Adv. dir., asst. sec. Equities Internat. Life Ins. Co.; dir. Lee's Country Candies, Inc. Sponsor, Jr. Achievement, 1967-68. Bd. dirs. Ft. Worth Ballet Assn. Served with USCG, 1955-59. Mem. Am., Colo., Tex., Ft. Worth bar assns., Ft. Worth Bus. and Estate Council, Met. Opera Guild, Phi Alpha Delta, Alpha Chi. Rotarian. Clubs: Petroleum, Shady Oaks Country (Ft. Worth). Home: 8909 Mahan Dr Fort Worth TX 76116 Office: Ft Worth Nat Bank Bldg Fort Worth TX 76102

CRAIG, H. CURTIS, utilities exec.; b. Ky., May 4, 1913; s. James T. and Mollie Catherine (Wilkins) C.; student Western Ky. U., 1932-35; LL.B., U. Louisville, 1939; m. Evelyn Taylor Robinson, Nov. 26, 1947; 1 dau., Penryn Lee. With Louisville Gas & Electric Co., 1936—, advt. mgr., 1946-62, asst. v.p. sales and pub. relations, 1962-63, v.p. sales and pub. relations, 1963—. Bd. dirs. Asso. Industries Ky., Better Bus. Bur. Louisville, Ky. Shorthorn Cattlemens Assn., Louisville chpt. A.R.C., Old Ky. Home council Boy Scouts Am., Cherokee sect. City of Indian Hills, Sts. Mary and Elizabeth Hosp., Nat. Found. Infantile Paralysis; trustee James Graham Brown Found., U. Louisville Law Alumni Found. (treas.). Served with USNR, World War II. Mem. Ky., Louisville (award for outstanding contbn. to orgn.) bar assns., Louisville Med. Found., U. Louisville Sch. Medicine, Ky. C. of C. Rotarian (v.p. Louisville club). Clubs: Advertising of Louisville, Louisville Boat. Home: 125 Travois Rd Louisville KY 40207 Office: 311 W Chestnut St Louisville KY 40202

CRAIG, JAMES CONOVER, life ins. exec.; b.Jacksonville, Fla., Dec. 2, 1908; s. Marion Bookman and Elizabeth (Stork) C.; student U. Fla., 1926-29; m. Julia Bryan, Dec. 28, 1932; children—Julia Olive (Mrs. Richard Brooke, Jr.), Cynthia Bryan (Mrs. John McKey, Jr.). Mem. editorial staff Fla. Times-Union, Jacksonville, 1929-57; dir. pub. relations Ind. Life & Accident Ins. Co., Jacksonville, 1957—, v.p., 1958—; v.p. Herald Life Ins. Co. Pres., Duval County chpt. Mental Health Assn., 1962. Mem. Pub. Relations Soc. Am., Fla. Pub. Relations Assn., Life Advertisers Assn., S.A.R. (chpt. pres. 1950), Fla. (pres. 1970-72), Jacksonville (pres. 1958-59) hist. socs., English Speaking Union (br. pres. 1965), Jacksonville C. of C., So. Hist. Assn., Com. of 100, Ye Mystic Revellers. Episcopalian. Clubs: Timuquana Country; University; Ponte Vedra; Fla. Yacht; River. Contbr. numerous articles profl. jours. Home: 4201 Yacht Club Rd Jacksonville FL 32210 Office: 233 W Duval St Jacksonville FL 32201

CRAIG, JAMES WILLIAM, forestry supply co. exec.; b. Pope, Miss., Sept. 30, 1912; s. John William and Annie Laurie (Craig) C.; B.S. in Forestry, Purdue U., 1936; M.S., N.Y. State Coll. Forestry, 1938; m. Dorabel Moore, Dec. 14, 1941; children—Mary Elizabeth, Annie Laurie, John Moore. Watershed forester, Rochester, N.Y., 1938-41; asst. chief forest fire control, Miss., 1946-47, chief, 1947-48; cons. forester, merchandiser forestry supplies, 1948-52; Miss. State forester, 1952-56; mgr. cons. div. Forestry Suppliers, Inc., Jackson, Miss., 1956, gen. mgr., 1956-69, pres., 1956—. Served from 1st lt. to lt. col. AUS, 1941-45; ETO. Mem. Soc. Am. Foresters (vice chmn. Gulf States sect. 1949, chmn. 1958), Forest Products Research Soc. (chmn. 1954), Miss. Forestry Assn. (pres. 1963, dir. 1952—), Forest Farmer's Assn. (dir. 1973). Methodist (treas.) Rotarian. Home: 5420 Red Fox Rd Jackson MS 39211 Office: 205 W Rankin St Jackson MS 39204

CRAIG, LOUIS ELWOOD, chem. co. exec.; b. Clifton Hill, Mo., Dec. 10, 1921; s. Clyde Allen and Elsie (Metcalf) C.; A.B., Central Coll., 1943; Ph.D. in Organic Chemistry, U. Rochester, 1948; m. Lorene Virginia Higgins, July 17, 1943; children—James Allen, David Andrew, Margaret Louise, Barbara Jean. Chemist Am. Cyanamid Co., Stamford, Conn., 1943-46; research fellow U. Rochester, 1946-48; research chemist Gen. Aniline Film Corp., Easton, Pa., 1948-54; dir. research John Deere Chem. Co., Tulsa, 1954-59, dir. research and tech. service, 1959-61, dir. marketing services, 1961-65; mgr. market research and devel. Kerr-McGee Chem. Corp., Oklahoma City, 1965-67, Western area marketing mgr., 1967-68, v.p. mfg., 1968-70, v.p. chem. mfg. div., 1972—; v.p. information services Kerr-McGee Corp., Oklahoma City, 1970-72. Mem. Am. Chem. Soc. (past chmn. Tulsa sect.), A.A.A.S., Am. Mgmt. Assn. Contbr. articles profl. jours. Patentee. Home: 4921 NW 32d St Oklahoma City OK 73122 Office: Kerr McGee Center Oklahoma City OK 73125

CRAIG, NANCY RYAN (MRS. WILLIAM JOSEPH CRAIG), physician; b. Norman, Okla., June 24, 1924; d. Henry Grady and Anna (Butler) Ryan; B.S., U. Okla., 1946; M.D., U. Okla., 1949; m. William Joseph Craig, Apr. 25, 1946; children—John Joseph, Christopher Patrick, Mary Elizabeth, Kathleen Frances. Intern, U. Okla. Hosps., 1949-50; resident anesthesiology, 1955-57, dir. health service, 1951-53; mil. dependent in Alaska, 1953-54; practice medicine specializing in anesthesiology, 1957—; mem. staffs St. Anthony, Presbyn., Baptist Meml., Mercy, Oklahoma City Gen., U. Okla. hosps.; asst. attending anesthesiologist Mt. Sinai Hosp., N.Y.C., 1968; asso. clin. prof. U. Okla. Hosp. Mem. Okla. Art Center, Oklahoma City Symphony Soc., Oklahoma City Ballet Soc. Diplomate Am. Bd. Anesthesiology. Mem. Am., So., Okla., Oklahoma County med. assns., Am., Okla. (pres. 1974-75) socs. anesthesiologists, Internat. Anesthesia Research Soc., Oklahoma City Clin. Soc., N.Y. Acad. Scis., Phi Beta Kappa, Alpha Lambda Delta, Alpha Epsilon Delta, Phi Sigma, Alpha Epsilon Iota. Republican. Roman Catholic. Club: Oklahoma Medical Faculty. Home: 525 NW 39th St Oklahoma City OK 73118 Office: 525 NW 11th St Oklahoma City OK 73103

CRAIG, PETER STEBBINS, lawyer; b. Bklyn., Sept. 30, 1928; s. Clarence Tucker and Rena (Stebbins) C.; B.A. Oberlin Coll., 1950; LL.B., Yale, 1953; m. Lois Achor, June 9, 1950 (div. Oct. 1969); children—Stephen, Carolyn, Jennifer; m. 2d, Sally Love Banks, Feb. 14, 1970; 1 dau., Katherine. Spl. asst. Ho. of Reps. Judiciary Com., Washington, 1951-52; admitted to D.C. bar, 1953; practiced in Washington, 1953-63; commerce counsel So. Ry. Co., Washington, 1964-67; asst. gen. counsel, litigation Dept. of Transportation, Washington, 1967-69; gen. atty. So. Ry. Co., Washington, 1969—. Urban transp. planning cons., 1960-67, 69—. Trustee, Com. of 100 on the Fed. City, 1965—. Named Washingtonian of Yr., Washingtonian mag., 1973. Mem. Am., D.C. bar assns. Quaker. Home: 3406 Macomb St NW Washington DC 20016 Office: So Ry Bldg McPherson Sq Washington DC 20013

CRAIG, ROBERT E. LEE, physician; b. Toledo, Oct. 7, 1936; s. Robert L. and Virginia Mae (Trautman) C.; A.B., Harvard, 1958, M.P.H. (NASA fellow), 1967, S.M. in Hygiene (NASA fellow), 1968; M.D., C.M., McGill U., 1962; m. Elisabeth M. Welter, June 24, 1961; 1 son, Graham Robert. Intern Royal Victoria Hosp., Montreal, Que., Can., 1962-63; resident in occupational medicine Harvard Sch. Pub. Health, 1966-68, TVA, 1968-69; gen. practice medicine, Wilmington, Vt., 1965-66, specializing in occupational medicine, Chattanooga, 1968—; asst. med. dir. TVA, 1971-74, med. dir., 1974—. Sec., bd. dirs., mem. exec. com. Hillandale Center, Signal Mountain, Tenn. Served as capt. M.C., USAF, 1963-65. Diplomate Am. Bd. Preventive Medicine. Fellow Indsl. Med. Assn., Am. Coll. Preventive Medicine; mem. A.M.A., Mass., Chattanooga-Hamilton County med. socs., Am. Acad. Occupational Medicine, Tenn. Indsl. Med. Assn. (sec.-treas. 1971-73, pres. 1973—). Home: 7112 Saratoga Lane Chattanooga TN 37421 Office: Edney Bldg Chattanooga TN 37401

CRAIG, THOMAS E., accountant; b. Moulton, Ala., Sept. 25, 1915; s. R. Clyde and Lassie (Fretwell) C.; student pub. schs. of Leon County, Tallahassee. Partner Partner Pentland & Cowles, C.P.A.'s, Tampa, Fla., 1952-63. Cowles, Craig, Silverman & Wooten, C.P.A.'s, Tampa, 1963—. Served with USAAF, World War II. C.P.A., Fla. Mem. Am. Inst. C.P.A.'s, Fla. Inst. C.P.A.'s. Clubs: Propellor, University (Tampa). Home: 212 S Church Tampa FL 33609 Office: 1st Financial Tower Tampa FL 33602

CRAIGE, BRANCH, JR., physician; b. El Paso, Tex., Feb. 6, 1915; s. Branch and Else (Kohlberg) C.; student Tex. Coll. Mines and Arts, U. Tex., 1931-32; A.B., U. N.C., 1935; M.D., Harvard, 1939; m. Jean Mohler McCracken, Aug. 18, 1945; children—Betty Jean, Mary Josephine (Mrs. Bruce B. Johnson), Branch Criage III. Intern, New Haven Hosp., 1940-41, resident, 1941-43; practice medicine specializing in internal medicine, El Paso, 1946—; mem. staffs Hotel Dieu, El Paso, Providence Meml. Hosp., El Paso, Southwestern Gen. Hosp., El Paso, Sun Tower Hosp., El Paso, St. Joseph's Hosp., El Paso; dir., pres., Med. Center Corp., 1956-58, 61-63, 68-71, pres., 1963; cons. William Beaumont Gen. Hosp., 1947-71; pres. Kohlberg Corp., 1951—; pres. El Paso County Bd. Health, 1950-51. Served with AUS, 1943-46. Diplomate Am. Bd. Internal Medicine. Fellow A.C.P.; mem. Am., So., Tex. med. assns., El Paso County Med. Soc., Tex. Soc. Internal Medicine, Alpha Omega Alpha, Sigma Nu. Club: Coronado Country. Contbr. articles to profl. pubs. Home: 2432 Savannah Av El Paso TX 79930 Office: 5B 1501 Arizona Av El Paso TX 79902

CRAIGHEAD, GORDON FULTON, JR., hotel exec.; b. Pitts., Apr. 2, 1925; s. Gordon Fulton and Gladys (McKinnon) C.; student Carnegie Inst. Tech., 1943, U. Rochester, 1943-44; B.S., B.Mgmt. Engring., Rensselaer Poly. Inst., 1947; B.S. in Hotel Adminstrn., Cornell U., 1949; m. Eugenia Anne Garard, Sept. 10, 1951; children—Eugenia Anne, Barbara Evans, Cameron Garard. Steward, Madison Hotel, Atlantic City, N.J., 1949-50; asst. mgr. Hidden Valley Inn, Somerset, Pa., 1950; mgr. Langwell Hotel, Elmira, N.Y.., 1951; resident mgr. The Inn, Ponte Vedra Beach, Fla., 1952; asst. mgr. Cloister Hotel, Sea Island, Ga., 1952-57; restaurant mgr. Marshall Field & Co., Chgo., 1957-60; asst. dir. Presbyn.-St. Lukes Hosp., Chgo., 1960-66; v.p. Sea Pines Co., Hilton Head Island, S.C., 1966-72; pres. Atlantis Devel. Co., Hilton Head Island, 1972—. Mem. Council on Hotel, Restaurant and Instl. Edn., 1969—. Pres. bd. dirs. Beaufort County United Way, 1974. Served to lt. (j.g.) USNR, 1943-46. Mem. Hilton Head Island (dir., pres. 1969-70), Beaufort County (dir.) chambers commerce, S.C. Innkeepers Assn., So. Innkeepers, Am. Hotel and Motel Assn., Nat. Restaurant Assn., Hotel Sales Mgrs. Assn., Cornell Soc. Hotelmen (regional v.p. 1970). Republican. Clubs: Oglethorp, Chatham (Savannah, Ga.); Plantation, Hilton Head Golf (Hilton Head Island). Home: Beach Lagoon Rd Hilton Head Island SC 29928 Office: Atlantis Devel Co Hilton Head Island SC 29928

CRAIN, DARRELL CLAYTON, JR., physician; b. Washington, Mar. 29, 1910; s. Darrell Clayton and Annie (Rau) C.; M.D., George Washington U., 1932; m. Louise Moore, July 12, 1934; children—Barbara (Mrs. Mark Rollinson), Anne (Mrs. Richard Fitzgerald), Darrell Clayton III. Intern, Central Dispensary and Emergency Hosp., Washington, 1932-33, resident, 1933-34; med. officer Walter Reed Gen. Hosp., Washington, 1934-37; practice medicine, specializing in Reumatic diseases, Washington, 1937-42, 45—; mem. staff Georgetown U. Hosp., Drs. Hosp.; cons. Surgeon Gen. U.S. Army, Surgeon Gen. USPHS; clin. prof. medicine Georgetown U., 1969—. Mem. med. adv. bd. Vis. Nurses Soc., Washington, 1960—. Bd. dirs. Westminster Found., Annapolis, Md., Arthritis Rehab. Center. Served to maj. M.C., AUS, 1942-45. Diplomate Am. Bd. Internal Medicine. Fellow A.C.P.; mem. Med. Soc. D.C. (pres. 1972, chmn. exec. bd. 1973), A.M.A., Am. Soc. Internal Medicine, Am. Rheumatism Assn., Rheumatism Soc. D.C. (pres. 1946-48; sec.-treas. 1948-52), Am. Therapeutic Soc., Am. Congress Phys. Medicine and Rehab., So. Med. Assn., A.A.A.S., N.Y. Acad. Sci., Pan-Am., Internat. med. socs., Washington Acad. Medicine, Am. Med. Authors, Arthritis and Rheumatism Assn. Met. Washington (pres. 1948-52, dir., adv. bd. 1948-72), Assn. Oldest Inhabitants D.C. Contbr. numerous articles to Crain, Darrell Clayton, Jr., profl. jours. Home: 6422 Garnett Dr Kenwood Chevy Chase MD 20015 Office: 1234 19th St NW Washington DC 20036

CRAIN, HAROLD STARK, civil engr.; b. Elkhart, Ind., Nov. 7, 1899; s. George M. and Harriett (Stark) C.; B.S., Purdue U., 1922; m. Nelle R. Snyder, Sept. 1926 (dec. May 1955); children—Mary Helen (Mrs. Laurence D. Savadove), Harold Stark, Elizabeth T. (dec.); m. 2d, Virginia Ruth Floyd, May 26, 1956. Estimator, supt. Am. Crain & Co., Chgo., 1922-26; v.p., mgr. Frost Constrn. Co., Tampa, Fla., 1927-29; estimator, supt. McMillan & Shelton, Enid, Okla., 1929-31; v.p., gen. mgr. William Muirhead Constrn. Co., Durham, N.C., 1932-41, 42-46; project mgr. Triangle Constrn. Corp., Army Cantonment, Camp Butner, N.C., 1941-42; pres. Crain & Denbo Inc., Piedmont Housing & Constrn. Co., Thrift Investment Co. (all Durham), 1946—; v.p. Durham Excavating Co., 1946—. Project mgr. Def. Housing, Portsmouth, Va., 1939-40; chmn. N.C. Licensing Bd. for Contractors, 1950-51. Pres., Constrn. Edn. Found. N.C., 1959—; pres. Watts Hosp., Durham, 1962-68. Served with S.A.T.C., 1918. Recipient Spl. Recognition award Friends of Watts Hosp., 1969. Mem. Durham Contractors Assn. (pres. 1962), N.C. Soc. Engrs. (pres. 1955-56), Assn. Gen Contractors Am. (br. pres. 1951), S.A.R., U.S. Power Squadron (comdr. Durham 1970; Outstanding Comdr.'s award dist. 27, 1971, sec. dist. 27, 1973-74), Purdue Alumni Assn., Sigma Phi Epsilon. Mason. Lion (past pres. Durham). Home: 10th St W and Yacht Dr Long Beach NC 28461 Office: Highland and Britania Sts Durham NC 27702

CRAIN, JOSEPH, chief of police; b. N.Y.C., Aug. 19, 1915; s. Ike and Rose Marie (Strikoff) C.; grad. high sch.; m. Helen Louise Smith, Sept. 7, 1951; 1 son, Thomas Michael. With oil heat co., N.Y.C., 1935-37; self-employed Ace Trucking Co., N.Y.C., 1937-42; with police dept. City of Hot Springs, Ark., 1947—, chief of police, 1969—. Served with AUS, 1942-47. Mem. Internat., Ark. chiefs police assns., Ark. Municipal Assn. Baptist. Mason, Elk. Home: 133 Mount View St Hot Springs AR 71901 Office: Police Dept Box 700 Hot Springs AR 71901

CRAIN, SOLON PATRICK, orthodontist; b. nr. McMinnville, Tenn., Mar. 1, 1895; s. Isaac Denton and Elizabeth Emmaline (Johnson) C.; D.D.S., Baylor U., 1927; M.Dental Surgery, Northwestern U., 1944; m. Ethal Good, Apr. 15, 1921; children—Valois (Mrs. Wayne Holder), Marvin Good. Practice gen. dentistry, Wichita Falls, Tex., 1927-31, Gladewater, 1931-38, Dallas, 1938-42; practice dentistry limited to orthodontics, Midland, 1950—. Asst. instr. dental lab. Baylor Dental Coll., 1948. Served with AEF, 1918-19. Mem. Am. Dental Assn., Charles H. Tweed Found. for Dental Research (pres. 1956), Edward H. Angle Orthodontic Assn., Am. Assn. Orthodontists, Permian Basin Dental Soc. (pres. 1955), Tex. Dental Soc., Am. Bd. Orthodontia, S.A.R. (chpt. pres. 1972), Am. Legion (post comdr. 1936). Baptist. Mason (32 deg. Shriner), Rotarian (pres. 1935). Home: 1203 W Cuthbert St Midland TX 79701 Office: 503 N N St Midland TX 79701

CRAIN, WILLIAM HENRY, curator; b. Victoria, Tex., July 19, 1917; s. William Henry and Margaret James (McFaddin) C.; student Tex. Mil. Inst., 1933-36; B.A., U. Tex., 1940, M.A., 1943, B.F.A., 1947, M.F.A., 1949, Ph.D., 1965. Resident playwright Artillery Lane Theatre, San Augustine, Fla., 1950-51; dir. David G. Benjamin Inc., Austin, Tex., 1957-59 Austin Mfg. Corp., 1957-59; publicity asst. drama dept. U. Tex., Austin, 1959-60; humanities research asso. II, 1965-70; curator Hoblitzelle Theatre Arts Library, Austin, 1971—; dir. Waterloo Press, 1971—. Bd. dirs. Austin Civic Theatre, 1961-64. Served with AUS, 1941-45. Recipient Cross of Mil. Service, U. D.C., 1961. Mem. Am. Theatre Assn., Sons Republic Tex., Phi Eta Sigma, Phi Kappa Phi, Delta Kappa Epsilon. Roman Catholic. Writer numerous plays produced including Brains and Eggs, 1948, Sweet Old Thing, 1961. Home: 2511 San Gabriel Austin TX 78705 Office: 7204 B Humanities Research Center PO Box 7219 Austin TX 78712

CRAM, JACK RANDOLPH, bus. exec., govt. cons.; b. Berkeley, Cal., Feb. 25, 1906; s. Frank A. and Etta D. (Story) C.; B.S. cum laude, U. Wash., 1929; m. Emma Jane Hahn, June 6, 1952. Pilot, Gov. of Wash., Olympia, 1934-38; mgr. Olympia Airport, 1935-38; owner Cram Flying Service, Olympia, Port Angeles, Wash., 1935-38; insp. CAA, Washington, 1938-39, chief devel. div. Civil Pilot Tng. Program, 1939-40; commd. 2d lt. USMC, 1932, advanced through grades to brig. gen., 1959; ret., 1959; naval aviator, 1932; squadron group comdr., World War II; test pilot, 1946-47; MCEB, 1948-51; Korea, 1952; Naval War Coll., 1954-55; comdg. officer MCAS, Kaneohe, 1956-58; cons. pres. Air Transport Assn., 1959-60; pres. Nat. Aircraft Noise Abatement Council, Inc., Washington, 1960-65; pres., dir. Cram Mining & Devel. Corp., 1960—; pres. Barbequed Spare Ribs, Inc., 1967-69; pres. The Bar-B-Que Corp., Rosslyn, Va., 1970—, dir. Airdiv. Transp. Cons., Inc., 1965-67. Decorated Navy Cross, Legion of Merit, D.F.C. with 3 bronze oak leaf clusters, Air medal with 2 silver, 1 bronze oak leaf cluster, Presdl. Unit Citation. Mem. Master Mechanics and Foremans Assn., Am. Inst. Aeros. and Astronautics, Acoustical Soc. Am., Nat. Aviation Club, Am. Assn. Airport Execs., Am. Helicopter Soc., Phi Beta Kappa, Alpha Delta Phi, Pi Sigma Alpha. Clubs: Internat. of Washington, Wings. Home: 3802 Densmore Ct Alexandria VA 22309 Office: 10750 Columbia Pike Silver Spring MD 20901

CRAMER, ARDIS LAHANN (MRS. HOWARD ROSS CRAMER), parasitologist, educator; b. Chgo., Jan. 22, 1927; d. Paul Harold and Helen Etheline (Lowry) Lahann; B.S. in Edn., Northwestern U., 1948; M.S. in Biology, Emory U., 1963, Ph.D. (NSF Coop. fellow), 1967; m. Howard Ross Cramer, Dec. 16, 1950. Tchr. elementary and high sch. Chgo. Pub. Schs., 1948-53; practice teaching supr., dept. edn. Emory U., 1963; vis. instr. biology Agnes Scott Coll., Decatur, Ga., 1968-69, vis. asst. prof., 1969-70, asst. prof., 1970-72; vis. asst. prof. biology Ga. Inst. Tech., Atlanta, 1973—; sci. coordinator Westminster Sch., 1973—. Mem. Am. Soc. Parasitologists, Assn. Southeastern Biologists, Ga. Acad. Sci., League Women Voters, Phi Sigma, Phi Theta Kappa. Contbr. articles to profl. jours. Home: 1431 Cornell Rd Atlanta GA 30306

CRAMER, GEORGE HALLOCK, electronics co. exec.; b. St. Louis, Apr. 9, 1927; s. George Hallock and Pearl (Patterson) C.; B.S. in Elec. Engring. with honors (physics scholar), So. Meth. U., 1949; M.S. in Elec. Engring., Stevens Inst. Tech., 1952; m. Patsy Rhea Thrasher, Oct. 10, 1949; children—Georgia Sue, Scott Patrick, George Hallock. Research microwave engr. RCA, 1949-52; sr. microphysics engr. Convair, 1952-54; corporate dir. electronics Ling Temco Vought, Dallas, 1954-69; founded Resalab, Inc., Dallas, 1969, pres., 1969—; dir. 1st State Bank of Dennison (Tex.), Metrocom, Dallas, Town North Plaza, Dallas. Cons. to various cos.; industry rep. for U.S. govt. to Internat. Standardization Com., 1970. Asst. scoutmaster Boy Scouts Am., Dallas, 1968. Served with USNR, 1945-46. Registered profl. engr., Tex. Mem. I.E.E.E., Old Crows (pres. Dallas 1970), Alpha Tau Omega, Eta Kappa Nu, Kappa Mu Epsilon, Delta Phi Alpha, Sigma Tau. Research in magnetron tuning and electronic reconnaissance systems. Home: 4248 Armstrong Parkway Dallas TX 75205 Office: Town North Plaza Dallas TX 75234

CRAMER, JOHN OLIVER, oral surgeon; b. Albuquerque, Oct. 30, 1942; s. Oliver Steward and Rhoda Bliss (Crouch) C.; student U. N.M., 1960-64, Eastern N.M. U., 1964-65; D.D.S., U. Mo. at Kansas City, 1969, grad. oral surgery, 1972; m. Martha Louise Donner, Aug. 20, 1965. Resident oral surgery Kansas City (Mo.) Gen. Hosp., 1969-72; practice oral surgery, Ada, Okla., 1972—; chief dental staff Valley View Hosp., Ada, 1972—. Mem. Am., Okla. dental assns., Psi Omega (sec. treas. 1967, pres. 1968, achievement award 1969, Kappa Alpha Order. Home: 1904 E 15th St Ada OK 74820 Office: 314 S Broadway Ada OK 74820

CRAMER, JOHN SCOTT, banker; b. Charlotte, N.C., Dec. 10, 1930; s. Stuart Warren, Jr. and Julia (Scott) C.; A.B., U.N.C., 1953; m. Nancy Arnott, Aug. 9, 1952; children—Julia Baxter, Alice Arnott. With Wachovia Bank & Trust Co., 1955—, asst. v.p., Charlotte, 1958-61, v.p., 1961-64, sr. v.p., bd. mgrs. Charlotte office, 1964-71, exec. v.p., head banking div., Winston-Salem, N.C., 1971-74, vice chmn. bd., head fiduciary div., 1974—; v.p., dir. John M. Scott & Co.; dir. Am. Credit Corp., Shadowline, Inc., Linville Resorts, Inc.; sec., treas., dir. Cramer Realty Co. Mem. adv. bd. Salvation Army; bd. dirs. YMCA; mem. exec. com. Arts Council; mem. central selection com. Morehead Found. Served to 1st lt. USAF, 1953-55. Named one of Charlotte's Ten Outstanding Young Men, Jr. C. of C., 1964. Clubs: Charlotte Country; Linville Golf; Old Town Club (Winston-Salem). Home: 2700 Reynolds Dr Winston-Salem NC 27104 Office: PO Box 3099 Winston-Salem NC 27102

CRAMER, WILLIAM MONROE, microfilm electronics mfg. co. exec.; b. St. Louis, Oct. 12, 1928; s. George Hallock and Pearl (Patterson) C.; B.S. in Elec. Engring., U. Tex., 1955; m. Judith Sue Hitchcock, May 25, 1970; children—Wayne William, Gary Lewis. With Rockwell Internat. Co., Anaheim, Cal., 1955-70, supr. Minuteman and Navy ground support equipment, 1963-66, Minuteman flight control equipment, 1966-70; pres. Research Tech. Inc., Dallas, 1971-72; pres. chief exec. officer Seaco Computer Display, Garland, Tex., 1972—. Served with USNR, 1947-50. Mem. Am. Mgmt. Assn. Elk. Home: 3311 Chaparral St Dallas TX 75234 Office: 2800 W Kingsley Rd Garland TX 75040

CRANCE, JOHNIE HAMPTON, fisheries mgmt. adminstr.; b. Pell City, Ala., Apr. 4, 1929; s. Alabama Dixon and Maudie Florence (Savage) C.; B.S., Auburn U., 1956, M.S., 1958; postgrad. Tex. A. and M. U., 1970-71; m. Mary Ann Rook, Apr. 18, 1952; children—Gregory Hampton, Wade Eddamond. Fisheries biologist Ala. Dept. Conservation, Montgomery, 1958-66, dir. Ala. Marine Resources Lab., Dauphin Island, 1966-71; marine fisheries specialist Tex. A. and M. U., Galveston, 1971-72; fisheries adminstr. Nat. Marine Fisheries Service, St. Petersburg, Fla., 1972—. Served with USAF, 1946-49, 50-51. Decorated Air medal; recipient Sports Fisheries Inst. stipen for Pa. State U. Mgmt. Program for Resource Mgrs., 1966. Mem. Am. Fisheries Soc., Nat. Shell Fisheries Assn., World Mariculture Soc., Gulf and Caribbean Fisheries Inst. Baptist. Club: Civitan (chpt. sec. 1968-69). Editor: Ala. Marine Resources Bull., 1966-72. Home: 7798 16th Av N St Petersburg FL 33710 Office: 9450 Gandy Blvd St Petersburg FL 33702

CRANE, KENT B., govt. ofcl.; grad. with honors, Dartmouth, 1957; married; two children. Assigned Am. embassy, Djakarta, Indonesia, 1960-62; with U.S. Dept. State, Washington, 1963-64; served in Zanzibar, 1964-65, Accra, Ghana, 1965-67; sr. research asso. fgn. affairs and sec. task force on conduct of fgn. relations Rep. Nat. Com., 1967-68; spl. asst. to U.S. Senator George Murphy, 1968-69; asst. for nat. security affairs Office of Vice Pres., Washington, 1969-71; asst. dir. for East Asia and Pacific, USIA, Washington, 1972-74; adminstrv. asst. to Rep. Peter H.B. Frelinghuysen of N.J., Washington, 1974—. Office: 2110 Rayburn House Office Bldg Washington DC 20515

CRANE, LAWRENCE LOUIS, JR., trading stamp co. exec.; b. Phila., Sept. 25, 1938; s. Lawrence Louis and Camila A. (Hoffman) C.; B.S., Fairfield (Conn.) U., 1960; grad. Mgmt. Devel. Program, Harvard, 1968; m. Kathe Ann McConville, Aug. 10, 1963; children—Deirdre, Christine. Sales rep. Addressograph-Multigraph Corp., 1960-62; with Quality Stamp Co. Inc., Memphis, 1962—, pres., 1967—, also dir. Chmn. bd. Trading Stamp Inst. Am., 1974. Kiawanian. Clubs: Harvard, University (Memphis). Home: 5652 Barfield Rd Memphis TN 38117 Office: 4681 Burbank Rd Memphis TN 38118

CRANE, MARILYN JOYCE, paleontologist; b. Grand Rapids, Mich., May 10, 1931; d. H.D. and Dorris (Northrup) Crane; B.S., Mich. State U., 1953, M.S., 1955. Geologist, Ind. Geol. Survey, Bloomington, 1955-56; paleontologist Humble Oil & Refining Co. (now Exxon), 1956—. Mem. Nat. Audubon Soc. (charter Houston, sec. 1971), Am. Assn. Petroleum Geologists, Soc. Econ. Mineralogists, and Paleontologists, Houston Geol. Soc., Gulf Coast Soc. Econ. Mineralogists and Paleontologists, Conservation Arts of Houston, Houston Outdoor Club, Corpus Christie Outdoor Club (sec. 1965, chmn. Christmas bd. count 1967); Ornithology Group (chmn. 1972, 73). Contbr. articles to profl. jours. Home: 3601 Alley Pky Houston TX 77019 Office: PO Box 2180 Houston TX 77001

CRANE, PAUL SHIELDS, surgeon; b. Oxford, Miss., May 2, 1919; s. John Curtis and Florence (Hedleston) C.; B.S., Davidson Coll., 1941, D.Sc., 1969; M.D., Johns Hopkins, 1944; m. Sophie Earle Montgomery, June 2, 1942; children—Virginia (Mrs. Robert Gleser), John Curtis, Letitia, Janet, James. Intern, resident surgery Union Meml. Hosp., Balt., 1944-46, 51-52; fellow surgery Johns Hopkins Hosp., Balt., 1960-62; med. missionary to Korea, Bd. World Missions, Presbyn. Ch. U.S., 1947-69, dir., chief surgeon Presbyn. Med. Center, Chonju, Korea, 1948-69; asst. chief surgery VA Hosp., Atlanta, 1969-70; asso. Miller Clinic, Nashville, 1970—; clin. prof. surgery Yonsei U., Seoul, Korea, 1964-69; asst. clin. prof. surgery Emory U., Atlanta, 1969, Vanderbilt U., 1971—. Chmn. Korean Presbyn. Mission, 1956; dir. Program for Intestinal Parasite Eradication in Korea through Korean Assn. Vol. Agys.; chmn. Philatelic Soc. Korea; council mem. Korea br. Royal Asiatic Soc. Bd. dirs. Med. Benevolent Found., Yonsei U., Wilson Leprosy Colony, Korea. Served as 1st lt. M.C., AUS, 1946-47; to maj. Res., 1956-58, 60, 65, 68. Decorated Commendation medal, Order Cultural Merit (Korea); recipient UN World Day of Health medal Korea, 1963. Mem. A.C.S., Tenn. Acad. Medicine, Nashville Surg. Soc. Presbyn. (elder). Author: Korean Patterns, 1967. Writer monthly column Korea Times Newspaper, Seoul, 1964. Contbr. articles to profl. jours. Home: 1203 Riverside Rd Old Hickory TN 37138 Office: 602 Gallatin Rd Nashville TN 37206

CRANE, WILLIAM HARRY, public accountant; b. Montgomery, Ala., Mar. 21, 1925; s. Harold Curtis and Alvira (Landon) C.; student Clemson Coll., 1943, Duke, 1946-47; B.S., M.S., U. Ala., 1950; m. Joanna Breedlove, Sept. 1970; children—(by previous marriage) Dorothy Jean (Mrs. Alan Adams), Lucy Anne (Mrs. Duane Newby), Mary Elizabeth (Mrs. Clifford Hornady), Suzanne Victoria. Partner, Crane, Jackson & Thornton, C.P.A.'s, Montgomery, 1953-64 Crane

& Crane, C.P.A.'s, Montgomery, 1964-67; pres. William H. Crane & Co., C.P.A.'s, Montgomery, 1967—. Budget dir., exec. com. United Appeal, Montgomery, 1962-64. Bd. dirs. Montgomery chpt. A.R.C. Served with AUS, 1943-45. Decorated Bronze Star medal, Silver Star medal; named Ky. col. C.P.A., Ala. Mem. Ala. Soc. C.P.A.'s (chmn. council 1964-65), Am. Inst. C.P.A.'s, Montgomery Assn. C.P.A.'s (pres. 1961-62), Delta Sigma Pi. Rotarian (dist. gov. 1969-70). Home: 3300 Drexel Rd Montgomery AL 36106 Office: 200 S Hull St Montgomery AL 36104

CRANFILL, HENRY LEE, JR., supt. schs.; b. Clairette, Tex., Nov. 25, 1917; s. Henry Lee and Mary Frances (Sowell) C.; B.A., Baylor U., 1946, M.S., 1950; m. Irma Geraldine King, Apr. 4, 1938; children—Carol, John, Charles. Supt. schs., Alexander, Tex., 1948-50, China Spring, Tex., 1950-52, Oglesby, Tex., 1952-56, La Vega, Waco, Tex., 1964—. Served with USAAF, 1943-46. Mem. Am., Tex. assns. sch. adminstrs. Mason. Home: 2141 Charboneau Waco TX 76705 Office: 3100 Bellmead Dr Waco TX 76705

CRANFILL, WILBURN FRANKLIN, food broker; b. Winston-Salem, N.C., June 1, 1920; s. David Calvin and Mattie Elizabeth (Chandler) C.; student Mars Hill Coll., 1941-42, Piedmont Bible Coll., 1946-47, Food Service Inst., 1971; m. Ella Louise Threatt, Oct. 21, 1948; children—David Hoyt, Donald Eugene. With Am. Home Foods, 1947-48, Pilot Brokerage Co., 1948-54, 55-58, Cates Pickle Co., 1954-55, Cranfill Merchandising Service, 1958-59; with Southgate Brokerage Co. of Raleigh, Inc., 1959—, dir., pres., treas., 1971—. Cons. in field personology, 1969—. Served with AUS, 1943-46; PTO. Named Optimist of Year, 1966. Mem. Raleigh Food Brokers Assn. (pres. 1961, 74), Asso. Brokers Am. (chmn. bd., past pres., v.p.). Baptist (chmn. bd. deacons 1964). Clubs: Optimist of Raleigh (pres. 1964-65), Optimist International, Pinehurst Country. Home: 3325 Buffaloe Rd Raleigh NC 27604 Office: 1525 S Blount St Raleigh NC 27603

CRANFORD, HENRY CLAY, JR., health service plan exec.; b. Monroe County, Ala., Sept. 20, 1920; s. Henry Clay and Minnie Idelia (Barton) C.; student U. N.C., 1940-45; m. Lois Adele Ribelin, Nov. 8, 1943; children—Susan Carole, Kathryn Gail. Reporter, Durham (N.C.) Sun, 1940-41; exec. dir. N.C. Good Health Assn., 1946-49; dir. pub. relations Hosp. Care Assn., Durham, 1949-68; v.p. N.C. Blue Cross and Blue Shield, Durham, 1968—. Campaign chmn. Durham (N.C.) United Fund, 1968, pres., 1969; chmn. N.C. Com. Patient Care, 1963-64; pres. Family Counseling Service and Better Health Found., Durham, 1965-66. Served with USMCR, 1942-45. Mem. Pub. Relations Soc. Am., N.C. Health Council (pres. 1973-74), Greater Durham C. of C. (pres. 1972). Baptist. Rotarian. Home: 8 Chantilly Pl Durham NC 27707 Office: Hwy 15-501 Durham NC 27702

CRANFORD, WAYNE, advt. exec.; b. Bald Knob, Ark., Jan. 1, 1933; s. Benjamin Franklin and Rachel (Jacobs) C.; B.S.E., State Coll. Ark., 1953; m. Frances Jane Anderson, Sept. 15, 1962; children—Jay Wayne, Anderson Ross, Christopher Benjamin. Instr. Bald Knob High Sch., 1953-55; reporter Ark. Democrat, Little Rock, 1955-56; dir. pub. relations Little Rock C. of C., 1956-57; account exec. The Hockersmith Agy., Little Rock, 1957-61; pres. Cranford/Johnson/Hunt & Assos., Inc., Little Rock, 1961—. Dir. River Devel. Corp.; adviser Jr. League Little Rock, 1973. Bd. dirs. A.R.C., state fund chmn., 1966-67; bd. dirs. Ark. State Festival of Arts, Pulaski County chpt. Nat. Found., Presbyn. Found Synod Ark.-Okla., 1969-72, Capital City 150th Anniversary, 1971, Ark. Orch. Soc.; trustee Ark. Arts Center, 1970-73. Named one of Ark.'s Outstanding Young Men, Ark. Jr. C. of C., 1969. Mem. Am. Assn. Advt. Agys. (bd. govs. S.W. council 1967-71, chmn. 1970-71), Ark., Little Rock (dir.) chambers commerce, Pub. Utilities Adv. Assn., Ark. Press Assn. Bank Marketing Assn., Ark. Hall Fame, Pub. Relations Soc. Am. (mem. counselor's sect.), Fifty for the Future, Phi Sigma Epsilon. Presbyn. Clubs: Capital (dir. 1971-73), Country of Little Rock. Home: 1917 N Spruce Little Rock AR 72207 Office: First National Bank Bldg Little Rock AR 72201

CRANK, JAMES ELDON, hosp. adminstr.; b. Puxico, Mo., Aug. 22, 1925; s. John C. and Luda (Harty) C.; B.S. in Edn., S.E. Mo. State Coll., 1950; M.P.H., U. N.C., 1952; m. Vera Emma Rau, May 18, 1949; children—Kyla Rau, Kimberly Ann, James Floyd. Field rep. Ga. Tb Assn., Atlanta, 1949-51; asst. to dir. local health services Ga. Dept. Health, Atlanta, 1952-54; with U. Ala. Hosp., Birmingham, 1954-65, asso. gen. dir., 1963-65; adminstr. Meth. Hosp., Inc., Birmingham, 1965-69; hosp. dir., prof. health care adminstrn. U. Ark. Med. Center, Little Rock, 1969—. Clin. asso. prof. Med. Coll. Ala., Birmingham, 1965-69; hosp. cons. Ariz. Med. Sch. Study, 1961—; adj. asso. prof., preceptor U. Ala. Sch. Community and Allied Health Resources, 1970—; mem. Ark. Commn. Renal Disease, 1971—. Founder, Health Careers Council Ala., 1964, pres., 1964-69; chmn. Joint Am. Hosp. Assn.-Nat. Health Council Com. on Health Careers Councils, 1968-70. Fellow Am. Coll. Hosp. Adminstrs., Am. Pub. Health Assn.; mem. Am. Assn. Med. Colls. (mem. council teaching hosps. 1969—). Presbyn. (trustee). Home: 50 Nob View Circle Little Rock AR 72205 Office: U Ark Med Center Little Rock AR 72201

CRASILNECK, HAROLD BERNARD, clin. psychologist; b. San Antonio, Apr. 4, 1921; s. John N. and Kate (Wolfson) C.; B.A., Trinity U., 1947; M.A., U. Tex., 1949; Ph.D., U. Houston, 1954; m. Sherry Gold Knopf, Jan. 18, 1959; children—Robert Ingram, Susan Carol, Candace Elizabeth (Mrs. Philip Eugene Rosen), Jonathan, John, Robert. Asst. prof. psychology Trinity U., 1948-51; instr. psychology U. Houston, 1951-52; lectr. psychology So. Meth. U., 1952-53; asst. prof. psychiatry Southwestern Med. Sch., U. Tex., 1954-60; clin. psychologist Dallas Neurol. Clinic, 1960-61; pvt. practice clin. psychology, Dallas, 1961—; clin. asso. prof. psychology and anesthesiology Southwestern Med. Sch., 1970—. Served with USMCR, 1942-45. Diplomate Am. Bd. Examiners Psychol. Hypnosis (sec., treas. 1959-62). Fellow Am. Soc. for Clin. Hypnosis (Merit award for outstanding dissertation 1958, Ben Raginsky award, 1965, Morton Prince award 1968, certificate merit best clin. paper 1969, 71, 72, Roy M. Dorcus award 1971), Soc. for Clin. and Exptl. Hypnosis (pres. 1963-65); mem. Am., Tex., Dallas (pres. 1959-60) psychol. assns., Ecuatoriana de Medicina (hon. pres. 1972), Pan-Am. Congresso (hon. v.p. 1973), Sigma Xi, Phi Kappa Phi. Contbr. articles to various publs. Home: 5635 Yolanda Circle Dallas TX 75229 Office: 712 N Washington St Dallas TX 75246

CRAVEN, FRANKLIN DUVAL, heavy equipment distbn. co. exec.; b. Greensboro, N.C., May 30, 1906; s. Eli Franklin and Minnie (Phipps) C.; ed. pub. and pvt. schs.; m. Ora Hankal, Mar. 26, 1935; 1 son, Franklin Duval. Pres., E.F. Craven Co., Asheville, N.C., 1927-32, Greensboro, 1932—. Bd. dirs. Jr. Achievement, Greensboro, Masonic and Eastern Star Home, Greensboro. Mem. Soc. Friends (treas.). Mason (Shriner); mem. Woodmen World. Club: Greensboro Country. Home: 2202 Lafayette Av Greensboro NC 27408 Office: 315 Swing Rd PO Box 20807 Greensboro NC 27420

CRAVEN, WILLIAM HERBERT, JR., educator; b. Bamberg, S.C., Nov. 1, 1929; s. William Herbert and Marion (Easterling) C.; B.S., Clemson U., 1950; postgrad. U. Wis., 1956; m. Lois Anita Kearse, July 21, 1951; children—William Herbert III, Pamela Ann. Agronomist, Epting Distbn. Co., Leesville, S.C., 1950-52; asst. county agt. Clemson U. Extension service, Edgefield, S.C., 1953-56, county agt., Saluda, S.C., 1956-71; county agt. Ga. Extension Service, Waynesboro, Ga., 1971—. Weekly newspaper columnist 5 area newspapers, 1956—. Sec. Ridge Farmers Mut., Ridge Spring, S.C., 1965-71, Ridge Mut. Ginnery, 1961-71. Dist. chmn. Central S.C. council Boy Scouts Am., 1964. Sec., Saluda County Aeros. Commn., 1967-71. Served to 1st lt., AUS, 1952-53. Recipient Silver Beaver award Boy Scouts Am., 1969; named Coop. Man of Year S.C., 1967; 1st nat. award as farm columnist Nat. Assn. County Agrl. Agts., 1973. Methodist. Lion (dist. gov. 1969-70). Home: PO Box 112 Waynesboro GA 30830

CRAVER, WILLIAM EVERETT, JR., finance, mfg., real estate, shipping exec.; b. Columbus, Ga., Aug. 14, 1922; s. William Everett and Myrtle (Ivey) C.; student George Washington U., 1940-43; B.S., U.S. Mcht. Marine Acad., 1945; m. Jane Honour McDonald, Oct. 19, 1946; children—Virginia St. Clair (Mrs. Joseph C. Good, Jr.), Ellen Lloyd, Jane Honour, William Everett III. Administrv. asst. OPM, WPB, Washington, 1940-43; founder, partner Bradham-Craver Co., 1946-49; founder, owner, partner Craver and Co., pub. accountants, Charleston, S.C., 1948-58; founder, pres. So. Gen. Corp. (formerly Craver Industries, Inc.), Charleston, 1949—, also dir.; founder, pres. Carolina Gen. Corp., Charleston, 1952—; founder, pres. Coastal Investors, Inc., 1955-56, Beautyguard Mfg. Corp., 1962-67, Craver Indsl. Park, Inc., 1963-67, Leasemasters, 1968—; founder, pres. Universal Financial Corp., 1962—, also dir.; founder, pres. Financial Resources Corp., 1973—. Vice chmn. Charleston Cancer Crusade, 1965; mem. Charleston County Aviation Authority, 1970—, chmn., 1971—; chmn. parents adv. council Converse Coll., 1972—, trustee, 1972—. Served to lt. USNR, 1945-46; PTO, ETO. Recipient Outstanding Bus. Achievement award U.S. Mcht. Marine Acad. Alumni, 1960, Meritorious Alumni award, 1970. Mem. Am. Soc. Metals, Hibernian Soc., Navy League (pres. Charleston council 1971-73, mem. nat. exec. com.), Greater Charleston C. of C., U.S. Mcht. Marine Acad. Alumni Assn. (chpt. charter pres. 1964-65, S. Atlantic regional gov. 1965-71, life mem.), S.C. Hist. Soc., Preservation Soc. Charleston, Pi Kappa Alpha. Democrat. Presbyn. (deacon). Clubs: Metropolitan (N.Y.C.); Piedmont (Spartanburg, S.C.); Charleston Country, Albemarle (pres. 1965-66), Sertoma (past dir., life mem.), Propeller (Charleston). Patentee metal forming equipment and device field. Home: 82 Tradd St Charleston SC 29401 also Sullivan's Island SC Office: PO Box 1014 Charleston SC 29402

CRAWFORD, ANDY WILLIAM, veterinarian; b. Ashland, Miss., Feb. 23, 1904; s. J.A. and Ella (Elliott) C.; student U. Tex., 1923-24, Millsaps Coll., 1924-25; D.V.M., Kan. State Coll., 1930; m. Muriel Hallock, July 29, 1931; children—Jo Anne, Pat. Gen. practice vet. medicine, Rolling Fork, Miss., 1933-40, 45—; also cons. animal health and nutrition. Mem. sec. agr.'s hog cholera eradication com. Sheriff Sharkey County, Miss., 1946-51, 56-59. Served with AUS, 1940-45; col. Res. Mem. Am. Vet. Med. Assn. (v.p., 1961-62, house dels., ednl. council), Am. Bovine Practitioners Assn. (past pres.), Am. Soc. Agrl. Cons. Mason, Rotarian. Home: 400 Race St Rolling Fork MS 39159 Office: 305 Race St Rolling Fork MS 39159

CRAWFORD, CARL LEROY, physician; b. Grinnell, Ia., Oct. 26, 1928; s. William Lester and Eva Wilma (Flanigan) C.; B.S., U. N.M., 1953; M.D. (fellow), Med. Coll. Ga., 1965; m. Joe Ann Simmons, Nov. 22, 1959; 1 dau., Constance S. Tchr. sci. high sch., Ia., 1953-56; profl. service rep. Geigy Pharm., Macon, Ga., 1957-61; intern Macon (Ga.) Hosp., 1965-66; gen. practice medicine, Americus, Ga., 1966-68, Warner Robins, Ga., 1968—; mem. med. staff Americus and Sumter County Hosp., 1966-68, Houston County Hosp., Warner Robins, 1968—; med. dir. Plains (Ga.) Convalescent Home, 1966-67; coll. physician Ga. Southwestern Coll., 1967; med. dir. Hallmark Nursing Home, Warner Robins, 1968—. Profl. v.p. Houston County chpt. Am. Cancer Soc., 1969—; pres. Houston County Assn. Exceptional Children, 1971—. Bd. dirs. A.R.C., chmn. Houston County Bloodmobile program, 1971—; bd. dirs. Atlanta Regional Blood Program, Warner Robins chpt. Houston County United Givers Fund; chmn. adv. bd. Salvation Army. Served with AUS, 1946-49. Recipient Citizen of Yr. award Warner Robins Jaycees, 1971; Community Service award Warner Robins C. of C., 1973. Mem. A.M.A., Am., Ga. acads. gen. practice, Am. Heart Assn., So. Med. Assn., Med. Assn. Ga., 3d Dist. Med. Soc. (sec.-treas. 1967-69), Air Force Assn. (life), Franklin Mint Collectors Soc., Med. Coll. Ga. Alumni Assn., Alpha Kappa Kappa. Republican. Episcopalian. Rotarian. Club: Houston Lake Country (Perry, Ga.). Home: 105 Granada Terrace Warner Robins GA 31093 Office: 124 Hospital Dr Warner Robins GA 31093

CRAWFORD, EDWIN MCNEILL, ednl. adminstr.; b. Montgomery, Ala., May 14, 1929; s. William H. and Mary (Thomas) C.; B.S., Auburn U., 1951; m. Mary Jean Barrett, Mar. 5, 1955; children—Ellen McNeill, Edwin Barrett, Graham Thomas. Reporter, Decatur (Ala.) Daily, 1951; editor Auburn (Ala.) U. Alumnews, 1952, Montgomery Examiner, 1953-54; account exec. Sparrow Advt. Agy., Birmingham, 1954-58; exec. asso. So. Regional Edn. Bd., Atlanta, 1958-62; dir. univ. relations Auburn U., 1962-66; asso. dir., dir. Office Instl. Research, Nat. Assn. State Univs. and Land-Grant Colls., Washington, 1966-70; v.p. for pub. affairs U. Va., Charlottesville, 1970—. Asso. dir. NSF Regional Sci. Seminar, U. Fla., 1961. Mem. Ala. Civil War Centennial Commn., 1962-64. Del., Democratic Nat. Conv. from 9th Dist. Ala., 1956; mem. Jefferson County Dem. Exec. Com., 1958. Recipient Silver Anvil awards Pub. Relations Soc. Am., 1962, 64. Mem. Am. Coll. Pub. Relations Assn. (certificate of exceptional achievement 1963, trustee 1971—, chmn. elect 1974-75), Edn. Writers Assn., Mid-South St. Andrews Soc., Omicron Delta Kappa, Sigma Nu. Presbyn. Home: 68 Tanglewood Rd Charlottesville VA 22901

CRAWFORD, FELIX CONKLING, dentist; b. Midland, Tex. Jan. 11, 1938; s. Marshall Holloway and Lela Mary (Heard) C.; student Tex. Technol. Coll. 1956-59; D.D.S., U. Tex., 1963; m. Roberta Jeanne Craze, July 22, 1961; children—Christin Kay, Boyd William. Pvt. practice dentistry, Plainview, Tex., 1965—. Chmn. Hale County Health Bd., 1972. Served with Dental Corps, AUS, 1963-65. Mem. Am., Tex. dental assns., S. Plains Dist. Dental Soc. (v.p., 1972), Psi Omega, Sigma Alpha Epsilon. Rotarian (pres. 1970). Clubs: Knife and Fork (pres. 1967), Plainview Country (bd. dirs. 1969-72, pres. 1973-74), Toastmasters (pres. 1968) (Plainview). Home: 1409 Canyon St Plainview TX 79072 Office: 2615 W 24th St Plainview TX 79072

CRAWFORD, GRADY LELAND, judge; b. Palatka, Fla., Mar 22, 1915; s. Grady Leland and Emma (Creekman) C.; LL.B., John B. Stetson U., 1939; m. Alleyne Carolyn Foster, May 8, 1942; 1 dau., Lee Carolyn. Admitted to Fla. bar, 1939; asso. Shutts, Bowen, Simmons, Prevatt and Julian, 1939-42, partner, 1949-51; circuit judge 11th Judicial Circuit Fla. 1951—. Chmn. Fla. State Conf. Circuit Judges, 1971—. Chmn. Gov.'s Com. on Seminole Indian Affairs, 1959-60. Served from ensign to lt. comdr. USN, 1942-46. Mem Am., Fla., Dade County bar assns., Navy League, Am. Legion. Democrat. Episcopalian. Mason (33 deg.), Kiwanian (pres. 1959). Home: 7911 SW 58th St Miami FL 33143 Office: Court House Miami FL 33130

CRAWFORD, HEWLETTE SPENCER, JR., ecologist; b. Syracuse, N.Y., June 4, 1931; s. Hewlette Spencer and Gladys Amy (Cole) C.; B.S., U. Mich., 1954, M.S. in Wildlife Mgmt., 1957; Ph.D., U. Mo., 1967; m. Joyce Marie Henley, Aug. 8, 1952; children—June Marie, Nancy Louise, Bruce Evin, Patricia Ann. Research forester So. Forest Expt. Sta., Harrison, Ark., 1957-63; research ecologist, project leader N. Central Forest Expt. Sta., Columbia, Mo., 1964-68; prin. ecologist, project leader Southeastern Forest Expt. Sta., U.S. Forest Service, Blacksburg, Va., 1968—; adj. prof., mem. adv. com., div. forestry and wildlife Va. Poly. Inst. and State U. Mem. Environmental Controls Com., Town of Blacksburg, 1970-71. Served with Signal Corps, AUS, 1954-56. Recipient certificate of appreciation Southeastern Forest Expt. Sta., 1973. Mem. Ecol. Soc. Am., Wildlife Soc. (treas., sec., v.p. Mo. chpt. 1965-68), Sigma Xi, Phi Sigma. Author: Ozark Range and Wildlife Plants, 1971. Contbr. articles profl. jours. Home: Dogwood Lane Radford VA 24141 Office: 104 Hubbard St Blacksburg VA 24060

CRAWFORD, HORACE RANDOLPH, diversified industry exec.; b. Stamford, Tex., Mar. 4, 1928; s. John Milton and Annie Maud (Williams) C.; B.Ch.E., Tex. Tech. U., 1949; M.S., U. Tex., 1954, Ph.D. (Humble Oil fellow), 1958; m. Mary Louise Holcombe, July 10, 1955; children—Michael Earl, Donald Kevin, Nancy Esther, Barbara Ann. Engine opr. Sun Oil Co., Rio Grande, Tex., 1949, plant chemist, 1950, gas engr., Silver, Tex., 1954-55; instr. math U. Tex. at Austin, 1956-57; research asso. Western Co., Dallas, 1957-59, research group supr., 1959-61, asst. div. mgr., 1961-63, mgr. chem. engring. dept., 1963-67, mgr. contract research and devel. dept., Richardson, Tex., 1967-68; mgr. chem. engring. Lone Star Gas Co., Dallas, 1969-72, dir. fuels sect. corp. devel. and research, 1972—. Vice-chmn. finance North Trail Dist. Boy Scouts Am., 1971, chmn. finance, 1972, chmn. dist., 1973—. Served with AUS, 1950-52. Mem. Engring. Soc. Tex. Tech. (pres. 1948-49), Am. Inst. Chem. Engrs. (chmn. Dallas 1968), Am. Soc. Gas Engrs. (pres. Southwest chpt. 1972-73, nat. dir. 1972-74), Nat. Solid Waste Mgmt. Assn., Sigma Xi, Alpha Chi, Kappa Mu Epsilon, Tau Beta Pi, Omega Chi Epsilon (pres. Tex. chpt. 1954). Contbr. articles to profl. jours. Patentee in field. Home: 7227 Oakbluff St Dallas TX 75240 Office: 301 S Harwood St Dallas TX 75201

CRAWFORD, J. M., hosp. adminstr.; b. Waynesville, N.C., Feb. 7, 1931; s. Jerry Morris and Pearl (Davis) C.; B.S., Western Carolina U., 1953; postgrad. Duke U., 1968-69; m. Susie J. Stamey, June 9, 1952; children—Susan Leigh, Gregory Morris. Bus. mgr., asst. adminstr. Haywood County Hosp., Waynesville, 1953-67; adminstr. Angel Community Hosp., Franklin, N.C., 1967—. Bd. dirs., mem. exec. com. State of Franklin Health Council. Mem. Am. Coll. Hosp. Adminstrs., N.C. Hosp. Assn. (chmn. Dist. I 1971-72). Democrat. Baptist. Home: Childress Rd Franklin NC 28734 Office: Riverview St Franklin NC 28734

CRAWFORD, JIMMIE G., banker; b. O'Donnell, Tex., Jan. 10, 1926; s. Jefferson Davis and Ethel Imogene (Flack) C.; B.B.A., West Tex. State Coll., 1950; m. Pauletta Fannon, June 10, 1950; children—Mary Diane, James Douglas. Bookkeeper, Berryhill Equipment Co., Lubbock, Tex., 1950-51; bookkeeper, cashier, gin mgr. Western Cottonoil Co., Lubbock, Aiken, Muleshoe and Loop, Tex., 1951-53; bookkeeper Tex. Sesame Growers, Inc., Muleshoe, 1963; asst. v.p. Muleshoe State Bank, 1964-66, cashier, 1966-71, v.p., 1971—, trust officer, 1969—. Asst. coach Muleshoe Little League, 1955, coach, 1956-58; sec.-treas. Muleshoe Athletic Boosters, 1957-59; rep. Easter Seal Appeal for Crippled Children and Adults of Bailey County, 1967—; sec. com. Muleshoe Stegall Opportunity Plan, 1969-71. Served with USNR, 1944-46. Recipient Jr. Citizenship award Muleshoe C. of C., 1957. Mem. Muleshoe C. of C. (dir. 1956-58, 64-66, 70-72, 2d v.p. 1970, sec.-treas. elect 1972), V.F.W. (trustee 1969-71). Baptist. Mason, Lion (3d v.p. 1955-59, 63-71). Home: 1725 West Av E Muleshoe TX 79347 Office: Drawer K Muleshoe TX 79347

CRAWFORD, JOE EARL, railroad exec.; b. nr. Bertram, Tex., May 14, 1933; s. Ralph Albert and Rena Vesta (Rowney) C.; student Dunham Sch. of Accounting, 1955; m. Geneva Henry, July 27, 1956; children—Joel Scott, Victor Dale, James Barton. With Georgetown R.R. Co. (Tex.), 1962—, v.p. operations, 1965—; v.p. Eureka Terminal Co., Houston, 1965—. Campaign chmn. Heart Fund, 1971; pres. Indsl. Corp. Georgetown, 1970-71. Mem. Georgetown City Council, 1970—; mayor, Georgetown, 1972—. Served with USN, 1951-55. Mem. Georgetown C. of C. (pres. 1968). Mem. Ch. of Christ. Mason (32 deg.), Rotarian. Club: Georgetown Country. Home: 1804 Louise St Georgetown TX 78626 Office: 310 Austin Av Georgetown TX 78626

CRAWFORD, JOHN MILTON, JR., assn. exec.; b. Tyler, Tex., Jan. 7, 1939; s. John Milton and Winifred (Robinson) C.; B.B.A., U. Tex, 1961; m. Carolyn Tyson DeVault, Aug. 29, 1963. Field rep. U. Tex. Ex-Students Assn., 1961-62; asst. promotional dir. S.W. Republic Corp. 1965; exec. dir. Tex. Nursing Home Assn., 1965-69 (all Austin, Tex.); exec. v.p. Screen Printing Assn. Internat., Falls Church, Va., 1969—; guest lectr. univs., 1966-67. Loan exec. United Fund, 1965; mem. exec. com. printing and pub. sect. Nat. Safety Council; mem. McLean Hamlet Citizens Assn. Mem. governing bd. McLean Community Center. Served with Intelligence Corps, AUS, 1962-65. Recipient SPOKE Jaycee award, 1961; Sparkplug Jaycee award, 1970, 71. Mem. McLean Jr. C. of C. (pres. 1971), Tex. Soc. Washington, Am., Washington socs. assn. execs., Internat. Platform Assn., Soc. Assn. Mgrs. (charter mem.), Meeting Planners Internat. (charter mem.), Postal Commerative Soc., Graphic Arts Assn. Execs., Nat. Assn. Exec. Club, Nat. Hist. Soc., Cowboy Hall of Fame, U. Tex. Ex-students Assn., Delta Sigma Pi. Baptist. Editor: Caring, 1965-69, Spotlights, 1961-62, 65-66, Highlights, 1965. Contbr. articles newspapers, mags. in U.S. Home: 1318 Macbeth St McLean VA 22101 Office: 150 S Washington St Falls Church VA 22046

CRAWFORD, LESTER MILLS, JR., ednl. adminstr.; b. Demopolis, Ala., Mar. 13, 1938; s. Lester Mills and Susan Doris (Mitchell) C.; D.V.M., Auburn U., 1963; Ph.D., U. Ga., 1969; m. Catherine Walker, July 27, 1963; children—Catherine Leigh, Mary Stuart. Intern, Dr. J. P. Carney, Meridian, Miss., 1963; asso. veterinarian in group practice, Birmingham, Ala., 1963-64; regional tech. dir. S.E. region Am. Cyanamid Co., Atlanta, Ga., 1964-66; instr. pharmacology Coll. Vet. Medicine, U. Ga., Athens, 1966-68, asst. dean, 1968-70, asso. dean, 1970—. Lectr. Council on Gerontology, U. System of Ga., 1968—. Pres. Cedar Creek Civic Assn., Athens, Ga., 1971-72; chmn. Ga.-S.C. Vet. Conv., 1969. Bd. dirs. Wesley Found.; regional bd. dirs. Am. Cancer Soc. Mem. Am., Ga. vet. med. assns., History of Sci. Soc., Am. Soc. Animal Sci., Ga. Acad. Sci., A.A.A.S., Phi Kappa Phi, Sigma Xi, Phi Zeta, Omicron Delta Kappa, Jr. C. of C. Methodist (chmn. council on ministries 1971-73). Club: University of Georgia Faculty (bd. dirs. 1971-72). Contbr. articles to profl. pubs. Home: 260 Cedar Creek Dr Athens GA 30601

CRAWFORD, OLIVER RAY, paper co. exec.; b. Amarillo, Tex., July 19, 1925; s. George Gordon and Bell Elizabeth (Allston) C.; student Wash. State Coll., 1943-44, S. Tex. Sch. Law, 1953-55; m. Margaret Ann Barker, Jan. 1, 1946; children—Lynda Ann, Carolyn Rae, Richard Alan. Div. mgr. Phillips Petroleum Co., Midland, Tex., 1947-52; mgr. tax and tile dept. Houston Oil Co. Tex., 1952-56; asst.

to gen. mgr. Southwestern Settlement and Devel. Co., Jasper, Tex., 1956-59; gen. mgr. Southwestern Timber Co., 1959-73; v.p. Eastex, Inc., 1956-73; v.p., treas. Jasper Timber Co., Newton Timber Co., Bleakwood Timber Co., San Augustine Timber Co., 1960-72; pres. Eastern Tex. Cable TV Services, Inc., 1967-71; asst. to pres. Temple Industries, 1973-74; partner firm real estate investment and counseling, Austin, Tex., 1974—; dir. First State Bank, Jasper. Mem. Tex. Liquor Control Bd., 1965-69. Pres. So. Forest Research Inst., 1963—; adv. com. Tex. Forest Service, 1957-74; dir. Tex. forest industries com. Am. Forest Products Industries. Pres. Jasper Youth Baseball Assn., 1958-74. Bd. dirs. A.R.C., Operation Orphans, Inc., Tex. Law Enforcement Found.; mem. century council Tex. A. and M. U.; trustee Southwest Research Inst., Tex. and M.U. Research Found.; v.p., bd. dirs. Tex. chpts. Leukemia Soc. Am.; mem. regent's devel. council Lamar U. Served as fighter pilot USAAF, 1943-45; brevet maj. gen. U.S. Air N.G. Named Man of Month, East Tex. C. of C., 1961; recipient hon. Lone Star Farmer degree Tex. Assn. Future Farmers; Forest Mgmt. award Nat. Lumber Mfrs. Assn.; Mr. East Texas award, operating dirs. of Tyler County Dogwood Festival, 1967; Sportsman Conservationist of Yr. award Tex. Outdoor Writers Assn.; decorated comdr.'s cross order of merit (Fed. Republic of Germany). Hon. life mem. Jasper Youth Baseball, Nat. Congress P.T.A., Future Farmers Am.; mem. Am. Pulpwood Assn. (dir.), Tex. Forestry Assn. (dir., pres. 1970-71), Sportsman's Clubs Tex. (v.p., mem. exec. com., dir. 1960—), Jasper C. of C. (pres. 1964), Def. Orientation Conf. Assn. Presbyn. Home: 1106 Crooked Creek Dr Lufkin TX 75901 Office: 2210 Hancock Dr Austin TX 78756

CRAWFORD, PAUL BERLOWITZ, research adminstr.; b. Stamford, Tex., July 28, 1921; s. John Milton and Annie Maud (Williams) C.; B.S., Tex. Tech. Coll., 1943; M.S., U. Tex., 1946, Ph.D., 1949; m. Bernice Lydia Murray, June 12, 1948; children—Rebecca Joan (Mrs. B.D. Russell, Jr.), Janice Anne, Patricia Grace. With Am. Cyanamid & Chem. Co., 1943-44, Magnolia Petroleum Co., 1947-52; asst. dir. Tex. Petroleum Research Com., prof. Tex. A. and M. U., College Station, 1952—; vis. lectr. Tex. Acad. Sci. Chmn. long range planning com. Sul Ross, 1960-64, Interstate Oil Compact Long Range Research Planning, 1964—; vice chmn. College Station Community Chest, 1962-63; mem. gov.'s com. A.L.A., 1963-66; v.p. Jr. Mus., 1970-71; pres. Band Boosters, 1969-72. Served with C.E., AUS, 1941-43. Recipient Community Leader award, 1970, Best Paper award Boston, 1971; named Tex. Library Trustee of Year, 1973. Mason, Rotarian. Contbr. articles profl. jours. Home: 1100 Edgewood St Bryan TX 77801 Office: TPRC-Tex A and M U College Station TX 77843

CRAWFORD, RICHARD GEORGE, newspaper publisher; b. Sequim, Wash., Aug. 15, 1911; s. George E. and Julia T. (Fritz) C.; student Western Inst. Accounting, 1931-32, Adj. Gen.'s Sch., 1942; m. Olive O. Ericksen, Aug. 5, 1933; children—James Richard, Lawrence Robert. Joined U.S. Army, 1931; advanced through grades to lt. col., 1953; with 3d Inf. Div., II Corps, 5th Army, 1942-45; adj. gen. officer, 1945-49; adj. gen. Engring. Center, Ft. Belvoir, Va., 1949-52; sec. joint staff Alaskan Command, 1952-54; exec. officer; adj. gen. sect. Ft. Jackson, 1954-57; ret., 1957; founder Cape Coral (Fla.) Breeze Newspaper, 1961, mng. pub., 1966—. Treas., dir. Citizens Mut. of Cape Coral, Inc., 1965—; dir. Cape Coral Bank. Bd. dirs. Lee County Assn. Retarded Children, 1962-67, Lee County Cancer Soc., 1961-68. Decorated Bronze Star medal. Mem. Cape Coral C. of C. (pres. 1968). Home: 5363 Nautilus Dr Cape Coral FL 33904 Office: 1620 SE 47th Terrace Cape Coral FL 33904

CRAWFORD, ROBERT SIMMONS, JR., lawyer; b. Batesville, Tex., May 29, 1920; s. Robert Simmons and Clio (Childress) C.; B.A., Tex. A. and M. U., 1942; J.D., U. Tex., 1949; m. Betty E. Zimmerman, Aug. 8, 1945; children—Betty Ann (Mrs. Stacy Mathis), Larry D., Terry D. Admitted to Tex. bar, 1949; practice law, Crystal City, Tex., 1949-61, Uvalde, Tex., 1961—; partner Crawford & Crawford, 1949—, dist. atty. 38th Jud. Dist., Tex., 1957-71. Served to maj. AUS, 1942-46. Mem. Phi Alpha Delta. Mason (Shriner). Home: 920 Laurel St Uvalde TX 78801 Office: 223 N Getty St Uvalde TX 78801

CRAWFORD, WILLIAM FRANKLIN, banker; b. Brookhaven, Miss., July 31, 1929; s. William F. and Lena (Moreton) C.; B.S., U. So. Miss., 1951, M.A., 1952, postgrad., 1953; m. Anne S. Jordan, Oct. 15, 1955; 1 son, Robert Michael. Asst. cashier, dir. State Bank & Trust Co., Brookhaven, 1954-58, asst. v.p., 1958-60, v.p., 1960-65, vice chmn. bd., 1965, chmn. bd., 1966—. Treas., Brookhaven Beautiful; mem. adv. bd. Copiah-Lincoln Vocational Tech. Sch. Treas., bd. dirs. Brookhaven Music Assn.; bd. dirs. S.W. Miss. Devel. Dist. Chmn. bd. dirs. Miss. Sch. Banking, 1971. Mem. Am., Miss. bankers assns., Newcomen Soc. N.Am., Lincoln County C. of C. (pres.), Phi Delta Kappa, Kappa Delta Pi. Presbyn. Kiwanian. Club: Brookhaven Country. Home: 613 S Jackson St Brookhaven MS 39601 Office: PO Drawer 319 Brookhaven MS 39601

CREECH, FULTON HUNTER, shipbldg. co. exec.; b. Washington, July 8, 1929; s. Fulton Hunter and Pauline MacKay (Bryan) C.; B.A., U. Va., 1951, LL.B., 1957; postgrad. Harvard, 1971; m. Betty Frost; children—Kathryn, Nancy, Leslie, Kenneth, Carol, Maxwell, Hunter. Admitted to Va. bar, 1957; atty. Navy Dept., Washington, 1957-61; contract adminstr. Kaman Aircraft Co., Bloomfield, Conn., 1961-62; atty. Ingalls Shipbldg. div. Litton Industries, Pascagoula, Miss., 1962-64; asst. to gen. counsel Newport News Shipbldg. & Dry Dock Co. (Va.), 1964-66, asst. personnel mgr., 1966, asst. gen. counsel, 1966-67, asst. sec., asst. gen. counsel, 1967-70, sec., gen. counsel, 1970-74, v.p., 1974—; dir. United Va. Bank/Citizens & Marine. Bd. dirs. Peninsula Symphony Orch.; trustee Hampton Rds. Acad. Served to lt. (j.g.) USN, 1951-54. Mem. Fed., Va. bar assns., Va. C. of C. (v.p. Tidewater chpt.), Sigma Nu. Presbyn. (elder). Mason. Clubs: Propeller, James River Country (Newport News). Home: 117 Yorkville Rd Yorktown VA 23490 Office: 4101 Washington Av Newport News VA 23607

CREEDEN, JOHN JAMES, JR., drug store chain exec.; b. Phila., Apr. 6, 1916; s. John James and Rosella Cecilia (Haley) C.; B.S., St. Joseph's Coll., Phila., 1939; student Georgetown U. Law Sch., 1939-41; m. Betty DeVere Hodgin, June 19, 1948; children—Kathy (Mrs. Kermit Treibs), Cecilia, Carol. Investigator, adminstr. FBI, 1939-67; v.p. Sommers Drug Stores Co., San Antonio, 1967—; security cons. Nat. Assn. Chain Drug Stores, 1972—; pres. Jack Creeden Assos., security consultants; conductor seminars on security, 1971—; dir. Southwest Seminars, San Antonio, 1971—; dep. sheriff, Bexar County, Tex. Mem. Internat. Assn. Chiefs Police, Am. Soc. Indsl. Security, Soc. Former Agts. FBI, Forgery Investigators Assn. Tex. Home: 109 Tuttle Rd San Antonio TX 78209 Office: 3130 E Houston St San Antonio TX 78298

CREEKMORE, DAVID DICKASON, judge; b. Knoxville, Tenn., Aug. 8, 1942; s. Frank Benson and Betsey Olivia (Beeler) C.; B.S., U. Tenn., 1964, LL.B., 1965, J.D., 1965. Clk., Gen. Sessions Ct., Knoxville, 1963-64, judge Div. 2, 1972—; admitted to Tenn. bar, 1965; partner Creekmore & Thompson, Knoxville, 1965-72; asst. county atty. Knox County, 1965-70. Col. gov.'s staff Tenn., 1972—; sgt. at arms Tenn. Ho. of Reps., 88th Gen. Assembly, 1972-73. Mem. Tenn. Judiciary Conf. Mem. Am., Tenn. bar assns., Am. Judicature Soc., S.A.R., Sigma Alpha Epsilon. Republican. Mason (32 deg., Shriner), Kiwanian, Eagle. Clubs: Exchange, City, Cherokee Country, Deone Hills Golf and Country. Home: 4734 Sylvan Lane Knoxville TN 37919 Office: 14 S Gay St Knoxville TN 37901

CREIGHTON, WILLIAM FORMAN, bishop; b. Phila., July 23, 1909; s. Frank Whittington and Maud R. (Hawk) C.; B.A., U. Pa., 1931, S.T.B., Phila. Div. Sch., 1934, D.D., 1957; D.D., Va. Theol. Sem., 1959; L.H.D., Rikkyo U. (Tokyo, Japan), 1964; m. Marie-Louise Forrest, June 2, 1934; children—William Wendel, Michael Whittington, Maxwell Forrest. Ordained deacon Episcopal Ch., priest, 1934; vicar, St. Mark's, Oakes, N.D., 1937-37; rector St. Clements Ch., St. Paul, 1937-43, St. Johns Ch., Bethesda, Md., 1946-59; bishop co-adjutor Diocese of Washington, 1959-62, bishop of Washington, 1962—. Mem. overseas rev. com. and overseas program group Episcopal Ch., 1970—. Trustee Va. Theol. Sem., 1962—; chmn. bd. trustees Ch. Pension Fund. Served as chaplain USNR, 1943-46. Home: Mount St Alban Washington DC 20016 Office: Episcopal Ch House Mt Saint Alban Washington DC 20016

CRELLIN, DAVID ALEXANDER, pub. relations exec.; b. St. Clair Shores, Mich., Apr. 1, 1926; s. Charles G. and Kathleen M. (Carroll) C.; student Mich. State U., 1946-47, Wayne State U., 1947-50; m. Patricia J. Guzinski, May 18, 1964; children—Timothy M., Charles E., Wendy P., Michelle L., David Alexander, Heather K. Gen. reporter Detroit Times, 1947-51; sect. supr. sales operation Ford Motor Co., Dearborn, Mich., 1951-56, staff rep. pub. relations office, 1956-64, southwest pub. relations mgr., 1964-67; exec. v.p., partner Thomas J. Tierney & Assos., Inc., Dallas, 1967-70; pres. Glenn Pub. Relations, Dallas, 1970—. Served with AUS, 1944-46. Mem. Press Club (bd. dirs. 1968), Pub. Relations Soc. Am. (bd. dirs. N. Tex. chpt. 1967-70). Home: 7261 Ashington St Dallas TX 75225 Office: Republic Bank Tower Dallas TX 75201

CREMINS, WILLIAM DANIEL, lawyer; b. Boston, Feb. 21, 1939; s. Eugene Joseph and Dorothy (Forbes) C.; B.A., St. Bonaventure U., 1960; J.D., George Washington U., 1967; m. Susan P. Shenkman, June 25, 1960; children—Kathryn, Michael, Jennifer. Admitted to Va. bar, 1967; partner, prin. Mackall, Mackall & Cremins, Fairfax, 1967—; lectr. No. Va. Community Coll., Annandale. Bd. dirs. Brookfield P.T.A., 1970-71, Brookfield Swim Club, Inc. Served to 1st lt. AUS, 1961-63. Mem. Am., Va. bar assns., Am. Judicature Soc., Am., Va. trial lawyers assns., Delta Theta Phi. Home: 1513 Millikens Bend Rd Herndon VA 22070 Office: 4031 Chain Bridge Rd Fairfax VA 22030

CRENSHAW, GORDON LEE, tobacco co. exec.; b. Richmond, Va., Jan. 19, 1922; s. Walter and Hattie (Ready) C.; B.A. in Econs., U. Va., 1943; m. Deubre Anne Roper, May 12, 1945; children—Clarke Hutchins, Gordon Lee. With Universal Leaf Tobacco Co., 1946—, v.p., 1958-65, pres., 1965—, chief exec. officer, 1966—, also dir.; dir. Life Ins. Co. Va., Va. Indsl. Devel. Corp., State Planters Bank of Commerce and Trusts. Bd. dirs. Richmond Boys Club Am., Nat. Tobacco Festival; bd. govs. Richmond Home for Boys. Served to lt. USNR, 1943-46. Mem. Tobacco Assn. U.S. (bd. govs., past pres.). Episcopalian. Home: 111 Windsor Way Richmond VA 23221 Office: 201 S 3d St Richmond VA 23219

CRENSHAW, JOHN THOMAS, physician; b. Maysville, Ga., Sept. 2, 1933; s. Howard and Annie Elizabeth (Morris) C.; B.S., U. Ga., 1960; M.D., Med. Coll. Ga., 1964; m. Frances Hallie Goodyear, June 15, 1964; children—Hallie Alisa, Elizabeth Ann. Intern, Spartanburg (S.C.) Gen. Hosp., 1964-65; gen. practice medicine, St. Marys, Ga., 1965-66, Clayton, 1967-72; Jefferson, Ga., 1973—; mem. staff Du Pont Corp., Jefferson, Ga., 1972-73; mem. staff Banks-Jackson-Commerce (Ga.) Hosp. Served with USNR, 1952-56. Mem. A.M.A., Ga., Rabun County (sec. 1971) med. socs. Home: 155 Hill St Jefferson GA 30549 Office: PO Box 219 Jefferson GA 30549

CRENSHAW, JOSEPH WILLIAM, state ofcl.; b. Millington, Tenn., Nov. 7, 1914; s. Ura and Helen (Anderson) C.; B.S., Memphis State U., 1935; M.A., Columbia, 1947, Ed.D., 1953; m. Mary E. Carmignani, Dec. 29, 1951; children—William Donald, Helen Camille. Asst. prin. Bolton High Sch., Arlington, Tenn., 1935-42; dean students, prof. edn. Pratt Inst., 1946-57; dean students, prof. edn. Jersey City State Coll., 1957-61; asst. dir. instructional services Fla. Dept. Edn., 1961-65, asst. commr. edn., 1965—; dir. Southeastern Ednl. Lab., Atlanta, 1969-71. Vis. prof. Western Carolina U., summers 1963-70; cons. in field. Vice pres. Tallahassee Little Theater, 1966-67. Served with AUS, 1942-45; ETO. Mem. Am. (dir. 1965—), Fla. (pres. 1970-71, v.p. 1971-72) assns. supervisions curriculum devel., Am. Psychol. Assn., Future Farmers Am. (hon.), Phi Delta Kappa (pres. 1973-74), Kappa Delta Pi, Alpha Phi Omega. Democrat. Author: Student Administration of Activity Funds, 1954. Contbr. articles to profl. jours. Home: 1008 Shadowlawn Dr Tallahassee FL 32303 Office: Knott Bldg Tallahassee FL 32304

CRENTZ, WILLIAM LUTHER, govt. ofcl.; b. Balt., May 1, 1910; s. William and Nettie Mae (Rice) C.; B.S., U. Md., 1932, M.S., 1933; m. Regina McKeever, Jan. 3, 1957. Researcher, Dept. Treasury, Washington, 1935-37; econ. analyst Nat. Bituminous Coal Commn., 1937-43; chem. engr. U.S. Bur. Mines, Washington, 1943-68, dir. coal research, 1968-70, asst. dir. energy, 1970—. U.S. rep. on various internat. coms. Recipient Distinguished Service award U.S. Dept. Interior, 1968; decorated Chevalier Order of Crown (Belgium), 1960. Club: Cosmos (Washington). Home: 3850 Tunlaw Rd NW Washington DC 20007 Office: US Bureau of Mines 18th and C St NW Washington DC 20240

CRESIMORE, JAMES LEONARD, food broker; b. Statesville, N.C., Jan. 24, 1928; s. Fred Clayton and Cleo (Edison) C.; B.S. in Bus. Adminstrn., High Point Coll., 1949; m. Mary Josephine Conrad, June 3, 1956; children—James Conrad, Jennifer Cheryl, Joel Clayton. Gen. mgr. Home Service Stores, Inc., High Point, N.C., 1948-50; co-founder, sec. Red Dot Food Stores, Inc., 1952-56; sec. Consol. Wholesale Corp., 1952-56; owner Village Super Market, High Point, 1953—; co-owner Bunker Hill Packing Corp., Bedford, Va., 1964—, chmn. bd. Asso. Brokers, Inc., Raleigh, N.C., 1956—; founding dir. State Bank Raleigh. Chmn. Mayor's Manpower Com., Raleigh. Chmn. Wake County Republican Party, 1963—, del. nat. conv. San Francisco, 1964; 4th Congl. dist.; mem. platform com. Rep. Nat. Convention, Miami, Fla., 1968. Mem. adv. bd. Salvation Army. Served with AUS, 1950-52. Mem. Internat. Sales and Marketing Execs. Club (mem. bd., pres. Raleigh), Raleigh (past pres.), Nat. (lt. regional dir.) food brokers assns., Raleigh C. of C. (dir. 1973-74). Rotarian. Home: 3720 Williamsborough Ct Raleigh NC 27609 Office: 3309 Drake Circle Raleigh NC 27609

CRESSE, JOSEPH PARKER, state ofcl.; b. Cutler, Ind., Oct. 7, 1928; s. Bruce Dudley and Lela Mariam (Fisher) C.; B.A., U. Fla., 1950; m. Susie Marlene Heflin, June 11, 1955; children—Elaine, Kay. Jr. auditor Price Waterhouse & Co., N.Y.C., 1953-54; auditor State of Fla., Tallahassee, 1954-55; internal auditor, controller State Tb Bd., Tallahassee, 1955-60; budget examiner Budget Commn., State of Fla., Tallahassee, 1960-64, asst. budget dir., 1964-69, chief Bur. Budgeting, Dept. Adminstrn., 1969-71, asst. dir. planning and budgeting Dept. Adminstrn., 1971—. Served with Adj. Gen. Corps, AUS, 1950-52. Mem. Nat. Assn. State Budget Officers, Beta Alpha Psi. Presbyn. Toastmaster (pres. 1964). Club: Killearn Golf and Country (Tallahassee). Home: 419 Vinnedge Ride Tallahassee FL 32303 Office: Dept Adminstrn The Capitol Tallahassee FL 32304

CRESSEY, ROGER FRANK, JR., parasitologist; b. Stoughton, Mass., June 9, 1930; s. Roger Frank and Florence (English) C.; A.B., Boston U., 1956, A.M., 1958, Ph.D., 1965; m. Nancy Marie Foster, Sept. 13, 1969; children—Brenda, Linda, Michael. Instr. Boston U., 1964-65; curator Smithsonian Instn., Washington, 1965—; research asso. Mote Marine Lab., Sarasota, Fla., 1972—; mem. expert adv. panel UNESCO, 1973—. Served with AUS, 1947-50. Recipient Smithsonian Research awards, 1968, 1970, 1971—; Office Naval Research grantee, 1966. Mem. Biol. Soc. Washington (pres. 1972-73, editor 1969-71), Am. Soc. Parasitologists. Contbr. articles to profl. jours. Home: 10935 Wickshire Way Rockville MD 20852 Office: Nat Museum Natural History Smithsonian Instn Washington DC 20560

CREWS, MALCOLM KNIGHT, city ofcl.; b. Arcadia, Fla., Apr. 2, 1923; s. Chester Arthur and Florence Hortenze (Meliza) C.; student S.Fla. Jr. Coll., 1968-69; m. Betty G. Lanier, Apr. 16, 1955; children—Dennis Mark, Keith Knight. Asst. operations clk. Lodwick Aviation Mil. Acad., 1941-44; asst. sec.-treas. Avon Park Citrus Growers Assn. (Fla.), 1944-51; city clk., treas., tax collector city of Avon Park, 1951-55, city clk., treas., 1967—; gen. mgr. Wells Better Homes Co., Avon Park, 1955-60; sec.-treas. Wells Motor Co., Avon Park, 1960-67; appraiser, dir. 1st Fed. Savs. and Loan Assn. Hardee County, Wauchula, Fla., 1960—. Mem. Chrysler Corp. Accountants Inst. (life), Fla. Assn. Realtors, Fla. Municipal Finance Officers Assn., Fla. Assn. Assessing Officers, Fla. Pollution Control Assn., Avon Park C. of C. (past pres.), Internat. Inst. Municipal Clks., Avon Park Area Bd. Realtors (sec.-treas.). Baptist (treas., deacon, Sunday sch. tchr.). Lion. Home: 421 E State St Avon Park FL 33825 Office: City Hall Avon Park FL 33825

CREWS, WILLIAM DARYL, cons. engr.; b. Chickasha, Okla., Mar. 31, 1927; s. Ralph William and Beryl (Callahan) C.; student Rice U., 1945-48; B.S., U. Colo., 1949; postgrad. U. So. Cal., 1949-50, U. Tulsa, 1953-56; m. Dortha Louise Parsons, Oct. 14, 1950; children—Darryl Lee, Gary Wayne, Peggie Lynn, Rebecca Louise. Research chemist, engr. Cities Service Research and Devel. Co., Tulsa, 1950-59; ind. cons. engr., Tulsa, 1959—; prin. Exploration Unltd., Inc., Bentley Royalties, Beeline Ranch Ltd., Beeline Devel. Corp., Nat. Mfg. & Supply Corp.; propr. mgr. farm and ranching operations. Served with USNR, 1944-46, AUS, 1950-52. Registered profl. engr., Okla. Mem. Soc. Petroleum Engrs., Kappa Sigma. Patentee well stimulation techniques. Home: 2625 E 67th St Tulsa OK 74136 Office: 420 Philtower Bldg Tulsa OK 74103

CRIDLIN, JOSEPH NELSON, judge; b. Jonesville, Va., Apr. 13, 1913; s. George P. and Sallie (Smith) C.; A.B., B.C.L., Coll. of William and Mary, 1935; m. Fay Fuller, June 12, 1946; children—George F., Josephine. Admitted to Virginia bar; practiced law in Jonesville, 1935-60; judge 24th Jud. Circuit of Va., 1961—. Served as 2d lt. AUS, 1942-46. Mem. Am. Legion, 40 and 8. Methodist (bd. stewards). Mason, Lion. Home: Jonesville VA 24263

CRIM, STERLING CROMWELL, mathematician, educator; b. Corsicana, Tex., Jan. 5, 1927; s. Churchill Wilbur and Francis Willard (Cromwell) C.; A.A., Kilgore Jr. Coll., 1948; B.S., Baylor U., 1950; M.Ed., N.Tex. U., 1953; M.A., Peabody Coll., 1958; Ph.D., U. Tex., Austin, 1968; m. Mary Louise Mayes, June 26, 1954; children—Kathryn, Randall. Tchr., N.W. High Sch., Justin, Tex., 1951-53; tchr. math. Hobbs (N.M.) Jr. High Sch., 1953-57; asst. prof. W. Ga. Coll., Carrollton, 1958-59; spl. instr. U. Tex., Austin, 1959-64; asso. prof. math. Lamar U., Beaumont, Tex., 1964-68, prof. math., 1968—, summer research grantee, 1973, 74. Served with AUS, 1946-47. Mem. Am. Assn. U. Profs., Nat. Council Tchrs. Math., Math. Assn. Am., Tex. Assn. Coll. Tchrs. (pres. Lamar chpt., state exec. com.), Tex., Sabine Area (pres.) councils tchrs. math. Methodist. Author: Directed Practice in Algebra, 1958. Home: 525 Peyton Dr Beaumont TX 77706

CRINER, JAMES ELLIS, naval officer; b. Ripley, Tenn., Feb. 12, 1918; s. James Alfred and Rosa Agnes (New) C.; student Lake Forest Coll., 1950-51, U. Ill., 1948-49; B.S., U.S. Naval Postgrad. Sch., 1958; m. Ruth Elizabeth Hall, Dec. 15, 1945; children—James Ellis, David Hall, George Keith, Nancy Suzanne. Enlisted as apprentice seaman USN, 1938, advanced through grades to capt., 1972; tchr. USN Warrant Officer Electronic Engrs. Sch., Washington, 1947-48; tchr. elec. sci. U.S. Naval Acad., Annapolis, Md., 1963-66; comdg. officer Naval Electronic Systems Engring. Center, Charleston, S.C., 1973—. Served with U.S. Army, 1935-38. Decorated Bronze Star medal, Navy Commendation medal. Mem. I.E.E.E., U.S. Naval Inst., Armed Forces Communications and Electronics Assn. Mason (Shriner). Home: Quarters AA US Naval Sta Charleston SC 29408 Office: 334 Meeting St Charleston SC 29403

CRINKLEY, RICHMOND DILLARD, theatrical producer; b. Richmond, Va., Jan. 20, 1940; s. James Epes and Sarah Elizabeth (Beck) C.; B.A., U. Va., 1961, M.A., 1962, Ph.D. (Seven Soc. fellow), 1966. Asst. prof. English, U. N.C., 1967-69; dir. programs Folger Shakespeare Library, Washington, 1969-73; founder, producer Folger Theatre Group, 1970-73; producer Kennedy Center Prodns., Inc., spl. asst. to chmn. Kennedy Center, Washington, 1973—. Bd. dirs. Stage II, Hampstead Theatre Club, London; mem. exec. com. bd. trustees Greater Washington Ednl. Telecommunications Authority. Fulbright fellow Oxford U., 1965-67, Nat. Def. Edn. Act fellow, 1961-64, Bennet Wood Green Traveling fellow, 1965. Mem. Nat. Assn. Arts and Letters (adv. bd.), Raven Soc., Phi Beta Kappa, Pi Delta Epsilon (Journalism award 1964). Author: Walter Pater, Humanist, 1970. Mem. editorial bd. Shakespeare Quarterly, 1972. Contbr. articles to profl. jours. Home: 10 3d St SE Washington DC 20003 Office: John F Kennedy Center for the Performing Arts Washington DC 20566

CRIPPEN, ROBERT LAUREL, astronaut; b. Beaumont, Tex., Sept. 11, 1937; s. Herbert W. and Ruth (Andress) C.; B.S. in Aerospace Engring., U. Tex., 1960; m. Virginia E. Hill, Sept, 8, 1959; children—Ellen M., Susan L., Linda R. Commd. ensign USN, 1960, advanced through grades to lt. comdr., 1969; completed naval aviation tng., 1962; attack pilot in U.S.S. Independence, 1962-65; student USAF Test Pilot Sch., Edwards AFB, Cal., 1965; mem. flight crew USAF Manned Orbiting Lab., 1966-69; astronaut NASA Manned Spacecraft Center, Houston, 1969—. Office: Astronaut Office NASA Manned Spacecraft Center Houston TX 77058

CRISMAN, ORVIL WAYNE, oil prodn. co. exec.; b. Mansfield, La., Nov. 15, 1916; s. Guy S. and Minnie Lee (Dagnell) C.; B.S., Tex. A. and M. U., 1938; m. Ruby Pearl Keeling, Oct. 20, 1939; children—Waynell (Mrs. Sterling Joseph Kuhlman), Brenda (Mrs. Michael George Liverman). W. Tex. mgr. Fred M. Allison Products Co., Corsicana, 1938-41; mgr. S. La. offshore operations Gulf Oil Co., Morgan City, 1945-59; v.p. prodn. Delhi Taylor Oil Corp., Dallas, 1959-64; pres. Oleum, Inc., Longview, Tex., 1964—, also dir.; v.p. Falcon Seaboard, Inc., Houston, 1970-73, pres., 1973—, also dir. Served with AUS, 1941-45. Decorated Bronze Star medal with oak leaf cluster. Mem. Am. Petroleum Inst. (Meritorious Service award 1958), Ind. Petroleum Assn. Am., Tex. Mid-Continent Oil and Gas

Assn., Longview C. of C., Smithsonian Assn. Methodist (steward 1968-72, mem. finance com. 1966-72). Kiwanian. Clubs: Dallas Petroleum; Tyler (Tex.) Petroleum; Houston Petroleum, Houston; Pinecrest Country, Cherokee (Longview, Tex.). Contbr. articles to profl. jours. Patentee in field. Home: 32 Brownwood Pl Longview TX 75601 Office: Drawer 2232 Longview TX 75601

CRISSMAN, WALTER EDGAR, superior ct. judge; b. nr. Siloam, N.C., Dec. 11, 1902; s. Charles Edgar and Ollie (Huff) C.; A.B., U. N.C., 1926, grad. law sch., 1928; m. Wilma Planzer, Apr. 6, 1935; children—Walter Edgar Jr., Kathryn Jane. Admitted to N.C. bar, 1929; individual practice law, High Point, N.C., 1929-55; asst. atty., High Point, 1938-44, pros. atty. municipal ct., High Point, 1945-46; judge superior ct. 18th Jud. Dist. N.C., 1955—; dir. Carson's Inc., Crestwood Furniture Co., Davidson Electric Wholesale Supply Inc., Piedmont Electric Repair Co., Central Stone Works Inc. Chmn. High Point Democratic Exec. Com., 1933-43; mem. N.C. Ho. of Reps., 1945, 47, 49, 51, 53. Trustee Children's Home, Lexington, N.C., Wake Forest U., 1959-67. Mem. N.C. Bar Assn. (v.p. 1968-69), Conf. Superior Ct. Judges (pres. 1968-69), Chi Psi. Baptist (trustee, deacon, past state pres. brotherhood). Kiwanian, Mason. Home: 1310 Longcreek Dr High Point NC 27260 Office: City-County Bldg S Hamilton St High Point NC 27260

CRIST, ALLAN GILBERT, ret. editor; b. Harrisburg, Pa., Dec. 14, 1908; s. Charles West and Mabel (Weand) C.; grad. high sch.; m. Violet Mary Stuart, June 1, 1931 (dec. Apr. 24, 1945); children—Larry Stuart, Diane (Mrs. James Prichard); m. 2d, Margaret Jean Zimmerman, Nov. 26, 1953; children—Lucinda, Ann, Laura. Reporter The Patriot, Harrisburg, 1926-29, U.P., Harrisburg, Buffalo, 1929-30, N.Y.C., Harrisburg, 1931, Brit. United Press, Ltd., Toronto, Ont., Can., 1930-31, A.P., Phila., Harrisburg, 1931-36, Harrisburg, 1937-40, 45-46, Phila. Inquirer, 1937, Pa. Dept. Mil. Affairs, 1946; editor Nat. Guardsman, Nat. Guard Assn. U.S., Washington, 1947-74. Served with AUS, 1940-45. Home: 705 Woodside Pkwy Silver Spring MD 20910 Office: Nat Guardsman Nat Guard Assn U S 1 Massachusetts Av NW Washington DC 20001

CRITES, SHERMAN EDWIN, communications co. exec.; b. Chadron, Neb., Jan. 12, 1918; s. Frederick A. and Marion (Hart) C.; student Neb. State Coll., 1934-37; B.S., Mass. Inst. Tech., 1941; M.S., N.Y. U., 1947; m. Florence Virginia Stiles, Dec. 22, 1940; children—Sherman Edwin, Patricia L., James F. Various engring. positions Pan Am. World Airways, N.Y.C., 1941-47, asst. prof. A. and M. Coll. of Tex., 1947-49, asso. prof. 1949-50; product planning engr. aircraft gas turbine div. Gen. Electric Co., Lynn, Mass., 1950-52, mgr. new product planning, Evendale, O., 1952-55, from mgr. product planning to mgr. marketing, small aircraft engine dept., Lynn, 1955-60; v.p., gen. mgr. transmission products dept. ITT Kellogg, Raleigh, N.C., 1960-62; pres., chief exec. officer Aero Electronics, Inc. (now Aerotron, Inc.), Raleigh, 1962-65, pres., chmn. bd., 1965-71; pres., chmn. bd. C.H. Electronics, Inc., Raleigh, 1971—, also dir. Mem. Gov.'s Tech. Utilization Adv. Bd. for State of N.C., 1967-68; active various community drives. Bd. dirs. United Fund Wake County, 1965-70; adv. bd. N.C. Vet. Research Found. Mem. Am. Horse Show Assn. Clubs: Carolina Country, Sphinx; United Hunt Racing. Home: Pine Hall Farm 5300 Castlebrook Dr Raleigh NC 27604 Office: PO Box 14042 Raleigh NC 27610

CROCKER, RICHARD R., editor; b. Wichita, Kan., June 6, 1938; s. Cecil R. and Hazel (Cheatham) C.; B.S. in Journalism, U. Kan., 1960; m. Elvira J. Valenzuela, May 21, 1966; 1 son, Christopher M. Reporter, Salina (Kan.) Jour., 1960-62, Sunday editor, 1962-63; with Wichita (Kan.) Eagle, 1963-72, Sunday editor, 1964-65, night city editor, 1965-66, city editor, 1966-70, asst. mng. editor, 1970-72; asst. editor news Washington Post, 1972—. Mem. Sigma Delta Chi (charter Kan. chpt.; pres. Kan. profl. chpt. 1971). Home: 4408 Elm St Chevy Chase MD 20015 Office: 1150 15th St NW Washington DC

CROCKER, ROBERT MERROW, labor union exec.; b. Auburn, Me., Sept. 24, 1917; s. Ralph Erwin and Eva Eudora (Merrow) C.; B.A., Bates Coll., 1938; m. Dorothy Evelyn Mawdsley, June 19, 1943; children—Steven A., Janet E. (Ms. Curtis). Reporter Lewiston (Me.) Eve. Jour., 1939-41, Worcester (Mass.) Eve. Gazette, 1941-47; newsman A.P., Portland, Me., 1947, corr., Augusta, Me., 1947-69; sec., treas. The Newspaper Guild, Washington, 1969—. Baptist (moderator 1965-69). Mason. Club: Bates College (Lewiston, Me.). Office: 1125 15th St NW Room 835 Washington DC 20005

CROCKER, ROWELL THOMAS, lawyer; b. Bruce, Miss., Feb. 20, 1898; s. George Campbell and Catherine (Chrestman) C.; M.A., Baylor U., 1949. Admitted to Miss. bar, 1920, D.C. bar, 1950, Supreme Ct. U.S., 1944; mem. law firm Evans & Crocker, Calhoun City, Miss., 1920-28; head dept. history Clarke Meml. Coll., Newton, Miss., 1930-34; mem. law firm Horne & Crocker, Jackson, Miss., 1936-37; pvt. law practice and legal and hist. research Tex. and S.W. U.S., 1937—. Mem. Miss. Ho. of Reps., 1920-24. Mem. Am. Bar Assn., Am. Judicature Soc. Home: Box 1163 Jackson MS 39205

CROCKETT, GIBSON MILTON, editorial cartoonist, artist; b. Washington, Sept. 18, 1912; s. Hal Gibson and Gertrude (Lentz) C.; student pub. schs.; m. Florence Elizabeth Crockett, July 4, 1937; children—David (dec.), Gary Abbott (dec.), Sandra Lea. Apprentice, Washington Evening Star, 1933-34, successively artist, gen. cartoonist, ct. sketching, 1942-47, sport cartoonist, editorial cartoonist, 1948—; art dir. Am. Pub. Co., Washington, 1944—; portrait painter; exhibited one man shows, George Washington U. Library, Evening Star; group shows Smithsonian Inst., Arts Club (all Washington), Rockville (Md.) Civic Center, Silver Spring (Md.) Gallery, Am. Watercolor Soc., N.Y. Bd. trustees Am. Art League. Mem. Washington Landscape Club (pres. 1961-62). Club: Manor Country (Norbeck, Md.). Home: 4713 Great Oak Rd Rockville MD 20853 Office: 225 Virginia Av SE Washington DC 20003

CROCKETT, HENRY BOWEN, lawyer; b. Pulaski, Va., Feb. 24, 1922; s. Henry Bowen and Willie Marie (Flanagan) C.; B.A., Washington and Lee U., 1943, LL.B., 1948, J.D., 1969; m. Ruth Ann Phillips, Nov. 12, 1949; children—Ann Bowen, William Henry. Admitted to Va. bar, 1948; practiced in Alexandria, 1948—. Served with A.C. AUS, 1943-46. Mem. Am., Va., Alexandria bar assns., Va. State Bar, Va. Trial Lawyers Assn., Phi Delta Phi, Pi Kappa Alpha. Club: Businessmens (Alexandria, Va.). Home: 2618 Stirrup Lane Alexandria VA 22308 Office: 108 North St Asaph St Alexandria VA 22314

CROFT, CHARLES BENJAMIN, architect; b. Enid, Okla., Nov. 10, 1927; s. Glenn W. and Esther (Lewis) C.; Design and Planning, Technologico y de Estudios Superiores de Monterrey (Mexico), 1952; B.Arch., U. Tex., 1953; m. A. Carolyn McWilliams, Dec. 20, 1948; children—David, Cathy, Janet, Charles B., Carol. Draftsman-designer John Linn Scott & Asso., Austin, Tex., 1953-54; architect, designer Fehr & Granger Architects, Austin, 1954-59; asso. partner John G. York & Asso., Harlingen, Tex., 1959-60; partner Taniguchi & Croft, Harlingen, 1960-62; asso. partner Jessen Assos., Austin, 1966-72; owner Charles B. Croft, Harlingen, 1962-66, Charles B. Croft, Architect, Austin, 1972—. Cons. architect Valley Regional Airport, Cameron County, 1963-65; mem. Elec. Examining Bd., Harlingen, 1963-66. Commr. Capital council Boy Scouts Am., 1955-58. Precinct presiding judge Cameron County Democratic Com., 1960-66, precinct chmn., 1964-66; del. Tex. Dem. Conv., 1960, 64. Bd. dirs. YMCA, Harlingen, 1960-63. Served with USMC, 1946-48; PTO. Recipient Honor award Tex. Soc. Architects, 1962, Merit award, 1962. Mem. A.I.A. (chpt. pres. elect 1966, chpt. sec. 1974), Tex. Soc. Architects, Harlingen C. of C. (chmn. pub. relations com. 1964-66). Presbyn. (deacon 1964-66). Home: 6001 Bullard Dr Austin TX 78731 Office: 3810 Medical Pkwy Austin TX 78756

CROFTS, DAN WILLIAM, elec. engr.; b. Port Arthur, Tex., Dec. 24, 1933; s. Albert A. and Mary Edith (Pankey) C.; B.S. in Elec. Engring., U. Tex., 1958; m. Helen Claire Berkman, Feb. 22, 1958. With Tex. Elec. Service Co., 1958, 60; with Tex. Power & Light Co., 1961—, transmission and substa. engr., Dallas, 1968—. Mem. elec. systems and equipment com. Edison Electric Inst.; mem. program and arrangement com. Ann. Transmission and Substa. Design and Operating Symposium, U. Tex. at Arlington, 1972-75. Pres., chmn. bd. Dallas Horseless Carriage Club Am., 1969, dir., 1970-71, 74—; sec., dir. South Central Swap Meet Assn., 1972-74. Bd. dirs., 1st v.p. Irving (Tex.) Humane Soc., 1971-73. Served to capt. USAF, 1958-60. Registered profl. engr., Tex. Mem. I.E.E.E., Dallas Power Engring. Soc. (past sec., financial officer), Dallas Electric Club, Antique Automobile Club Am., Phi Kappa Sigma. Home: 1411 Moss Rose Circle Irving TX 75061 Office: PO Box 6331 Dallas TX 75222

CROGGON, JEREMY COLDSTREAM, mining co. exec.; b. Cornwall, Eng., Oct. 13, 1938; s. John Rawson and Nancy Beatrice (Thompson) C.; B.Comm., McGill U., 1960; m. Christiane Francoise Cogne, Sept. 8, 1962; children—Ian, Marc. Came to U.S., 1967, naturalized, 1973. Trainee, English China Clays Ltd., Cornwall, Eng., 1961-62; sales service Anglo-Am. Clays Corp., Montreal, Que., Can., 1962-67, pres., N.Y.C., 1967-70, Atlanta, 1970—; dir. English China Clays Sales Co., Ltd., Cornwall, Eng. Mem. Am. Ceramic Soc., N.C., Syracuse pulp and paper founds., Atlanta C. of C. Clubs: Canadian (N.Y.C.); Country (Dunwoody, Ga.). Home: 5334 Vernon Lake Dr Dunwoody GA 30338 Office: 52 Executive Park South Atlanta GA 30329

CROLEY, JAMES EVERETT, JR., dentist; b. Corbin, Ky., May 14, 1924; s. James Everett and Huldah (Schormann) C.; student Cumberland Coll., 1941-43, Berea Coll., 1943-45; D.D.S., U. Mo., 1947; m. Anna Lou House, June 8, 1947; children—James Everett III, Jennifer Lou. Pvt. practice dentistry, Middlesboro, Ky., 1947-50, Pineville, Ky., 1953-73, Harlan, Ky., 1973—. Mayor, City of Pineville, 1958-62. Mem. adv. com. Ky. Tourist and Travel Commn., 1960-64, Union Coll. Environmental Ednl. Center, 1970—, Ky. Med. Assistance Program, 1972—. Trustee Cumberland Coll.; bd. dirs. outdoor drama Book of Job. Served with USNR, 1943-45, 51-53. Named Outstanding Young Man, Ky., 1957. Mem. Am., Ky. State dental assns., Southeastern Dist. Dental Soc. (pres. 1954-55, 1968-69). Republican. Baptist. Home: Intermont Apts Harlan KY 40831 Office: Gunn Bldg Harlan KY 40831

CROMARTIE, JOHN LLOYD, poultry exec.; b. Gainesville, Ga., June 10, 1905; s. Jefferson and Mary Magadline (Richardson); ed. pub. schs.; m. Frances Williard Hubbs, Dec. 22, 1935; children—Margaret Lee (Mrs. Robert L. Walls), John Lloyd, Sarah Huske. With Ga. Hwy. Dept., 1923-29; bookkeeper, salesman, sales mgr., gen. mgr., v.p. wholesale feed, grocery and bldg. material co., Gainesville, 1929-50; founder, head John L. Cromartie Co., Gainesville, 1950—; founder Twin Oaks Hatchery, Inc., Gainesville, 1950, pres., dir., 1954—; pres., dir. Helen Feed Store, Inc. (Ga.), 1954—, C.W.T. Farms, Inc., 1958—; v.p., dir. Lanier Feed Mills, Inc., 1954—; sec., dir. Lanier Sales Co., Inc., 1962—, Orbit Egg Co., Inc., 1964—; dir. Mar-Jac Poultry Co., Inc. Commr., City Gainesville, 1960-65, mayor pro tem, 1963-64, mayor, 1965-70. Scoutmaster, N.E. Ga. council Boy Scouts Am., 1935-40, troop committeeman, treas. exec. com., 1935-72; mem. Upper Chattahoochee Devel. Commn., 1965—; mem. community devel. com. Nat. League Cities, 1964—; mem. Ga. Mountains Planning-Devel. Commn., 1964—, Gainesville-Hall County Econ. Opportunity Orgn., 1965—; mem. Hall County Library Bd., 1964—. Trustee Joint Municipal Employees Retirement System. Recipient Silver Beaver award Boy Scouts Am., 1961. Mem. United Comml. Travelers, Ga. Poultry Producers' (pres. 1965), Ga. Poultry Fedn. (dir.), Ga. Municipal Assn. (pres. 1966-67, exec. bd., dir.), Gainesville-Hall County C. of C., Ga. Feed Dealers Assn. (sec.-treas. 1960-61). Methodist (ofcl. bd. 1963-65). Lion, Elk. Club: Chattahoochee Country. Home: 1171 Dixon Circle NW Gainesville GA 30501 Office: PO Box 1396 Gainesville GA 30501

CROMER, DAVID ANDREWS, supt. schs.; b. Tryon, N.C., Nov. 24, 1922; s. John S. and Ruth (Farr) C.; A.B., Wofford Coll., 1944; M.A., Columbia, 1954. Instr., Carlisle Mil. Sch., Bamberg, S.C., 1944-49; tchr. Tryon High Sch., 1950; prin. Stearns Sch., Columbus, N.C., 1951-55, Alamance Sch., Greensboro, N.C., 1956-59; supt. Polk County Schs., Columbus, 1959—. Treas. N.C. State Theatre; pres. Western N.C. Lung Assn., Tryon Fine Arts Center; trustee Patterson Sch.; v.p. Tryon Little Theatre; bd. dirs. Vagabond Sch. Drama; mem. bd. visitors Brevard Music Center. Served with AUS, 1943. Mem. Am. Assn. Sch. Adminstrs., N.E.A., Am. Guild Organists, Tryon Concert Assn. (pres.), N.C., Polk County edn. assns., Lambda Chi Alpha. Episcopalian. Clubs: Men's (past pres.), Kiwanis. Home: Box 428 Tryon NC 28782 Office: Box 697 Columbus NC 28722

CROMER, JERRY HALTIWANGER, educator; b. Anderson, S.C., Apr. 4, 1935; s. Phillip and Ethel Irene (Tribble) Cromer; B.S., Wofford Coll., 1957; postgrad. Med. U. S.C., 1957-58; M.S., U. S.C., 1965; Ph.D., Vanderbilt U., 1968; m. Anne Olevia Palmer, June 9, 1962; 1 son, Jeffrey Philip. Instr. biology Vanderbilt U., Nashville, 1965, teaching fellow, 1966-67; asst. prof. biology Converse Coll., Spartanburg, S.C., 1968-73, asso. prof., 1973—, organizer, dir. pre-profl. med. and paramed. programs, 1971—. Served as ensign USNR, 1959-61. USPHS tng. grantee, 1963-64; faculty research grantee Converse Coll., 1968, 73. Mem. A.A.A.S., Assn. Southeastern Biologists, S.C. Acad. Scis., Sigma Xi. Presbyn. Home: 202 Shelton Dr Spartanburg SC 29302

CRONIN, DONALD JOSEPH, lawyer; b. Huntsville, Ala., July 1, 1925; s. Raymond Francis and Jean Marie (Snow) C.; B.S., U. Ala., 1951, J.D., 1953; m. Mary Edna Andress, Apr. 10, 1957; 1 dau., Mary Anne. Field rep. Dun & Bradstreet, Tuscaloosa, Ala., 1950-52; research asst. Bur. Bus. Research, U. Ala., Tuscaloosa, 1950-53, asst. prof. Sch. Commerce, 1951-52; adminstrv. asst. to U.S. Senator Lister Hill, 1953-68; admitted to Ala. bar, 1953, D.C. bar, 1969, U.S. Supreme Ct. bar, 1963; mem. firm Corcoran, Foley, Youngman & Rowe, Washington, 1968—. Active Democratic Presdl. campaign coms., 1960, 64, 68; campaign mgr. U.S. Senator Lister Hill, 1962. Recipient Distinguished Service award U.S. Senate, 1968, Distinguished Citizens award, 1969, Distinguished Alumni award U. Ala., 1969. Mem. Interam., Am., Ala. bar assns., Bar Assn. D.C., U. Ala. Alumni Assn. (pres. 1960). Episcopalian. Club: University, Touchdown (Washington); Columbia Country (Bethesda, Md.). Home: 5406 Blackstone Rd Bethesda MD 20016 Office: 1511 K St Washington DC 20005

CRONIN, THOMAS RAYMOND, devel. co. exec.; b. Hartford City, Ind., Feb. 23, 1939; s. Thomas Edmond and Pauline Ray (Pruden) C.; grad. high sch.; m. Sandra Constance Hamilton, Aug. 14, 1966; children—Thomas, Martine. Pres. Flordeco, Inc., Ft. Myers, Fla., 1973—; pres. Cronin Distbrs.; v.p. King Symonds Realty, Inc. Pres. Colonial Ranchettes and Colonial Farms Subdivs. Bldg. and capital fund chmn. Million Dollar YMCA, 1969-70, also dir., v.p., pres.; chmn. Lee County United Way Drive, 1972; mem. Mayor's Urban Transp. Study Com., 1972—, Planning Bd. City Ft. Myers, 1974-76. Pres., Ft. Myers Community Hosp.; bd. dirs. Alcoholism Council, United Way. Served with U.S. Army, 1957-60. Recipient Outstanding Jaycee of Year award, 1964, Red Triangle award YMCA, 1969, certificate of award Alcoholism Council, 1971, Outstanding Young Man of Am. award, 1971, Distinguished Service award, 1970, Hadassah Service award, 1973, Service to Youth award, 1973. Mem. Beer Industry Fla. (past dir.), Wine Industry Fla. (founder), Nat. Beer Wholesalers Am. (adv. bd.). Home: 3402 W Riverside Dr Fort Myers FL 33901 Office: 3916 Cleveland Av Fort Myers FL 33901

CRONK, ALFRED EDWARD, educator; b. Hudson, Wis., July 1, 1915; s. Walter Eli and Alma Serena (Simonson) C.; B.S., Coll. St. Thomas, 1937; M.S., U. Minn., 1946; m. Nora Viola Pepin, Sept. 7, 1940; children—Andrew, Alfred, Susan, Nancy. Math. and physics instr. Cretin High Sch., 1940-43; instr. U. Minn., 1943-46, asst. prof., 1946-53, asso. prof., 1953-56; prof., head dept. aerospace engring. Tex. A. and M. U., College Station, 1956—. Cons. Mpls.-Honeywell, Gen. Mills Co., 3 M Co., Fluidyne Engring. Corp., 1950-56. Fellow Tex. Acad. Scis., Am. Inst. Aeros. and Astronautics; mem. Am. Soc. Engring. Edn. (chmn. aero. div. 1951-52), Sigma Xi, Tau Beta Pi, Sigma Gamma Tau, Theta Tau. Club: Briarcrest Country (Bryan, Tex.). Home: 727 N Rosemary St Bryan TX 77801 Office: Tex A and M U College Station TX 77843

CROOK, ANGUS MCDONALD GREEN, physician; b. Jackson, Tenn., Oct. 10, 1927; s. Jere Lawrence and Millian Cooke (Green) C.; B.A., U. South, 1949; M.D., U. Va., 1953; m. Nancy Nadine Ferrier, May 29, 1965; children—William Grant, Anne Ferrier, Millian McDonald. Intern, Henry Ford Hosp., Detroit, 1953-54; resident, N.Y. Hosp., Cornell Med. Center, N.Y.C., 1957-59; practice medicine specializing in obstetrics and gynecology, Wichita, Kan., 1960-68, Nashville, 1968—; asst. prof. obstetrics and gynecology Vanderbilt U. Sch. Medicine, Nashville, 1968—. Med. dir. Planned Parenthood Reproductive Health Center, Nashville, 1973—. Served with USNR, 1945-47, 54-57. Diplomate Am. Bd. Obstetrics and Gynecology. Fellow A.C.S., Am. Coll. Obstetricians and Gynecologists; mem. Phi Delta Theta, Nu Sigma Nu. Episcopalian. Club: Belle Meade Country (Nashville). Home: 407 Leake Av Nashville TN 37205 Office: Vanderbilt U Hosp Nashville TN 37232

CROOK, ROBERT LACEY, state senator, lawyer; b. Bolton, Miss., Apr. 22, 1929; s. Walter Barber and Louise (Lacey) C.; student U. Miss., 1952-53; LL.B., Jackson Sch. Law, 1965; m. Brigita Vija Nerings, Sept. 20, 1953; children—Robert Lacey II, Hubert William. Operator, Ruleville (Miss.) Dry Cleaners, 1953-60; Miss. dir. Civil Def., Jackson, 1960-64; admitted to Miss. bar, 1965, since practiced firm R.L. Crook, Ruleville; mem. Miss. Senate, 1964—. Mem. adv. bd. St. Dominic Hosp., Jackson, Miss. Served with USMC, 1949-51. Mem. State Civil Def. Dirs. Assn. (nat. v.p. 1962-63), Miss. Bar Assn., Am. Legion, S.C.V., Order Stars and Bars. Democrat. Home: 3615 Crane Jackson MS 39216 also 125 N Oak Av Ruleville MS 38771 Office: 118 N Ruby Av Ruleville MS 38771

CROOK, TROY NORMAN, petroleum co. exec.; b. Wall, Tex., May 24, 1928; s. Otis Allen and Viola (Aylor) C.; B.S., Tex. A. and M. U., 1949; B.S., U. Houston, 1961; m. Ruby Mae Keel, June 5, 1949; children—David, Larry. Jr. geophysicist, seismic operator Humble Oil & Refining Co., La., Miss., Ala., Fla., 1949-54; asst. div. geophysicist, Houston, 1968-69, div. geophysicist, 1969-71; research geophysicist Humble Oil & Refining Co., Houston, 1955-64; research supr. Esso Prodn. Research Co., Houston, 1965-67, mgr. basic geophysics, 1967-68, mgr. exploration systems div., 1971—. Trustee Soc. Exploration Geophysicists Found., 1973—. Registered profl. engr., Tex. Mem. Am. Assn. Petroleum Geologists, I.E.E.E., Soc. Exploration Geophysicists, Geophys. Soc. Houston, Tau Beta Pi, Sigma Gamma Epsilon, Phi Kappa Phi. Patentee in field. Home: 5527 Sylmar Houston TX 77036 Office: PO Box 2189 Houston TX 77001

CROOM, WILLIAM STERLING, physician; b. Morrilton, Ark., July 3, 1925; s. Adlai Stevenson and Margaret Price (Harris) C.; student Phillips U., 1943, Harding Coll., 1943, Abilene Christian Coll., 1943-44; M.D., U. Okla., 1948; m. Karen Ausburn, June 3, 1968; children—William Sterling, Brad Franklin, Christian. Intern, U. Ind. Med. Center, Indpls., 1948-49; resident internal medicine U. Okla. Hosp., 1949-52; pvt. practice internal medicine, Oklahoma City, 1952-53, Lubbock, Tex., 1953—; mem. staff Methodist, St. Mary's hosps., (both Lubbock); courtesy staff W. Tex. Hosp., Lubbock; clinical asst. internal medicine U. Okla. Hosps., 1952-53; asso. clin. prof. medicine Tex. Technol. U., 1972—. Served to lt. USNR, 1954-56. Diplomate Am. Bd. Internal Medicine. Fellow. Am. Coll. Chest Physicians; mem. A.C.P., Tex. Acad. Internal Medicine, Am. Heart Assn., Tex. Med. Assn., Phi Chi. Republican. Mem. Ch. of Christ. Club: Lubbock Country. Home: 6219 Kenosha Dr Lubbock TX 79413 Office: 3801 19th St Lubbock TX 79410

CROSBY, DAVID S., educator; b. St. George, Utah, June 4, 1938; s. Samuel Wallace and Mae (Dodds) C.; A.B. magna cum laude, Am. U., 1962; M.S., U. Ariz., 1964, Ph.D., 1966; m. Anna Jo Hovermale, Apr. 15, 1962; children—Anna Danisha, Mae Melinda. Asso. prof. math. and statistics Am. U., Washington, 1966—. Statis. cons. Nat. Oceanographic and Atmospheric Adminstrn., 1969—. Mem. Math. Assn. Am., Inst. Math. Statistics, Am. Statis. Assn., Phi Beta Kappa, Phi Kappa Phi. Home: 206 Independence St Berkeley Springs WV 25411 Office: Dept Math and Statistics Am U Washington DC 20016

CROSBY, HAROLD BRYAN, univ. pres.; b. Jacksonville, Fla., Sept. 21, 1918; s. Arthur Francis and Marie (Long) C.; student Northwestern U., 1934-35, 36-37; LL.B., U. Fla., 1948; m. Margaret Frances Dutton, Apr. 18, 1939; children—Susan Frances, Anne Bryan. With Atlantic Coast R.R. Co., 1937-41; resident prof. law U. Fla. Coll. Law, 1948; admitted to Fla. bar, 1948; pvt. practice, Kissimmee and Pensacola, 1948-55; circuit judge 1st Jud. Circuit Fla., 1955-60; prof. law U. Fla., 1960-64, asst. dean Coll. Law, 1961-62, dean univ. relations and devel., 1962-64; pres. U. West Fla., Pensacola, 1964—. Dir. Fla. Trial Judges Seminar, 1960-61, 64; Southeastern dir. Joint Com. Effective Adminstrn. Justice, 1961-62; dir. S.E. Seminar State Trial Judges, 1962; mem. Nat. Conf. Commrs. Uniform State Laws, 1962-64; cons. Fla. Constl. Adv. Commn., 1956-57; Fla. commr. to promote uniformity legislation, 1962-64; mem. com. standard jury instructions Supreme Ct. Fla., 1962-64; mem. commn. on colls. So. Assn. Colls. and Schs., 1970—; pres. Assn. Upper Level Colls. and Univs., 1970—; mem. exec. com. Fla. Assn. Colls. and Univs., 1970—; mem. exec. council Commn. Colls., 1973-74. Chmn. Fla. Citizens Com. Humanities, 1974. Trustee U. Fla. Law Rev., 1961, U. Fla. Law Center Assn., 1961; bd. dirs. U. Fla. Center, 1962-64. Served to maj. USAAF, 1942-45, USAF, 1951-53. Mem. Fla. Bar (bd. govs. 1950-52, pres. jr. bar sect. 1951-52), Am. Bar Assn. (Fla. chmn. jr. bar sect. 1951), Order of Coif, Theta Xi, Blue

Key, Phi Alpha Delta, Phi Kappa Phi. Methodist (trustee, past ofcl. bd.). Contbr. articles to legal jours. Home: 30 Rockwood Rd River Gardens Pensacola FL 32504

CROSBY, WARREN MELVILLE, educator; b. Topeka, Mar. 19, 1931; s. Warren Melville and Sarah Elizabeth (Frost) C.; B.S., Washburn U., 1953; M.D., Kan. U., 1957; m. Joanne D. Banaka, June 13, 1954; 1 dau., Sarah. Intern, St. Luke's Hosp., Kansas City, Mo.; resident U. Cal., 1957-62; practice medicine specializing in obstetrics and gynecology Oklahoma City, 1962—; mem. staff U. Okla. Hosp.; instr. obstetrics and gynecology U. Okla., 1962—, prof., vice chmn. obstetrics and gynecology, 1969—. Diplomate Am. Bd. Obstetrics and Gynecology. Mem. A.M.A., Soc. Gynecologic Investigation, Assn. Profs. Gynecology and Obstetrics, Central Assn. Obstetricians and Gynecologists, Alpha Omega Alpha. Home: 1713 Guilford Lane Oklahoma City OK 73120

CROSS, BILLY BENSON, supr. schs.; b. Lebanon, Va., Dec. 25, 1935; s. Floyd Gilmer and Bessie Lee (Price) C.; B.S., Va. Poly. Inst., 1958; M.S., E. Tenn. State U., 1966; m. Clara Ruth Caudill, Oct. 10, 1957; children—Billy G., Diane Rebecca, Vicki Sue. Tchr. chemistry Lebanon High Sch., 1958-65, asst. prin., 1965-68; gen. supr. Russell County Schs., Lebanon, 1968—, chmn. sci. dept., 1966—; farmer raising dairy-cattle, Lebanon 1959—; operator, owner West and East Lebanon Laudromatts, 1962—, retail gasoline sta., Lebanon, 1965—, beauty salons, 1968—, bldg. contracting and real estate, 1970—. Bd. dirs. Boy Scouts Am., Lebanon. Named Russell County Bus. Man of Year, Lebanon Jaycees, 1966. Mem. Nat., Va., Russell County (treas. 1967) edn. assns., Russell County Tchr. Assn. (treas. 1968—), Lebanon Jr. C. of C. (sec. 1966), Phi Delta Kappa, Methodist (supr. Sunday sch. 1969-71). Woodsman. Home: Box 576 Lebanon VA 24266

CROSS, CHARLES BRINSON, JR., lawyer; b. Portsmouth, Va., Mar. 10, 1914; s. Charles Brinson and Ethel Maywood (Bland) C.; student William and Mary Coll., 1930-32; J.D., Washington and Lee U., 1936; m. Eleanor Royce Phillips, Apr. 19, 1944; children—Martha Eleanor, Charlotte Marie. Admitted to Va. bar, 1936; law practice in Portsmouth, Norfolk, South Norfolk and Norfolk County, 1936-61; comr. in chancery Circuit Ct., Chesapeake, Va., 1949, Portsmouth, 1950-53, Norfolk, 1956-61, Corp. Ct., South Norfolk, 1953-56; clk. Circuit Ct., County of Norfolk, 1961-63, City of Chesapeake, Va., 1963—. Dir. First & Merchants Nat. Bank, Chesapeake Region. Mem. Va. Ho. of Dels., 1956-61; mem. Va. Commn. Constnl. Govt., 1959-63. Mem. Democratic State Central Com., 1964-66. Chpt. chmn. Portsmouth A.R.C., 1950-51; chmn. Eastern Va. Bi-Centennial Com., 1971—; bd. visitors Old Dominion U., 1962-68. Bd. dirs. Va. State Library, Tidewater Community Coll. Served to lt. comdr. USNR, 1941-45. Recipient Outstanding Civic Achievement award Chesapeake C. of C., 1966; First Citizen award Jr. C. of C., 1970; Certificate of Commendation Am. Assn. State and Local History. Mem. Va., Norfolk-Portsmouth, Chesapeake bar assns., So., Va. hist. socs., Norfolk County Hist. Soc. of Chesapeake, (charter), Co. of Mil. Historians, Chesapeake Friends Music (charter), Friends Chesapeake Pub. Library (charter), Chesapeake C. of C. (v.p.), U.S.C.G. Aux. (v.p.), Kappa Alpha, Phi Delta Phi. Democrat. Methodist. Mason (32 deg., Shriner), Kiwanian (pres. Portsmouth 1942, Chesapeake 1966). Club: Churchland Ruritan (pres. 1962). Author: The County Court 1637-1904, Norfolk County, Virginia; The Chesapeake-A Biography of a Ship (Am. Assn. State and Local History certificate of commendation 1969); Memoirs of Helen Calvert Maxwell Read, 1970. Co-author: Glencoe Diary: It Happened Here: From the Archives, 1968. Editor: Historical Sketch of Norfolk County: An Historical Review. Home: 320 Kemp Lane Chesapeake VA 23325 Office: Civic Center PO Box 15205 Chesapeake VA 23322

CROSS, EARLE ALBRIGHT, JR., educator; b. Memphis, Nov. 23, 1925; s. Earle Albright and Florence Irene (Hale) C.; B.S., Utah State U., 1951; M.A., U. Kan., 1955, Ph.D., 1962; m. Dorthy Jean Showalter, Aug. 15, 1948; children—John Broughton, Stephen Earle, Robert Randall, Scott Lewis. Instr. entomology Purdue U., 1956-57, U. Kan., 1957-58; NIH research asso., 1958-59; asst. prof. biology Northwestern State U. La., 1960-63, asso. prof., 1964-66, prof., 1967-70; asso. prof. biology U. Ala., Tuscaloosa, 1970-73, prof., 1973—. Dist. commr. Boy Scouts Am., 1966-69. Served with USNR, 1943-46. NIH research grantee, 1965-67, NSF teaching grantee, 1962, 66, U.S. Forest Service research grantee, 1965-66; NSF Undergrad. Research Participation grantee, 1971; NSF coll. tchrs. grantee, 1972; NSF research grantee, 1972—. Mem. Entomol. Soc. Am., Ecol. Soc. Am., Soc. Systematic Zoology, Central States Entomol. Soc., Assn. Southwestern Naturalists, Sigma Xi, Phi Kappa Phi. Home: 5 Berkeley Hills Tuscaloosa AL 35401

CROSS, GERTRUDE SARA ERHARD (MRS. ROBERT BLACK CROSS), physician; b. Pa., June 2, 1916; d. Elmer Sylvester and Lydia Mae (Park) Erhard; student Beaver Coll. Women, 1933-34; B.M., Grove City Coll., 1937; student Mansfield State Tchrs. Coll., 1938; D.O., Kirksville (Mo.) Coll. Osteopathy and Surgery, 1945; grad. student Kirksville Coll. Osteopathy, 1946, 62. Phila. Coll. Osteopathy, 1950-66; m. Dr. Robert Black Cross, Nov. 29, 1938. Intern, resident Kirksville Osteo. Hosp.; gen. practice osteo. medicine, Columbus, O., 1946-70, ret.; vis. intern lectr. Doctors Hosp., Columbus, with dept. manipulation, physio-therapy and rehab., cons. manipulative therapy, 1966-68. Mem. sustaining bd. Boys Ranch. Diplomate Am. Bd. Osteo., Gen. Practice. Fellow Am. Coll. Gen. Practice in Osteo. Medicine and Surgery (sec., treas. Ohio chpt.; mem. Columbus Dist. Acad. Osteo. Medicine and Surgery, Ohio (sec.-treas. 1962-66), Nat. (component socs. com. 1965-68) acads. applied osteopathy, Nat. Coll. Gen. Practitioners (nominating com.), Kirksville Alumni Assn. (past pres. Ohio chpt.), Am. Ohio osteo. assns., Am. Assn. U. Women, D.A.R., Am. Osteo. Coll. Phys. Medicine and Rehab., Theta Alpha Phi, Theta Kappa (past pres.), Delta Omega (past pres., past nat. chpt. treas., nat. pres. 1964-66). Clubs: Zonta Internat. (past pres., past bd. dirs., past program chmn. Columbus Chpt.), Masquers. 750 (Kirksville Coll. Osteopathy and Surgery). Home: 5961 Emerald Harbor Dr Longboat Key Sarasota FL 33577

CROSS, HANSELL FLYNN, educator; b. Wilson, La., Oct. 30, 1913; s. Hansell Pinkney and Mary Virginia (Dawson) C.; B.S., La. State U., 1936, M.S., 1941; Ph.D., U. Md., 1955; m. Mary Lucille McDonald, Mar. 17, 1943; children—James Flynn, Pamela J. (Mrs. Daniel Dimsdale). High sch. tchr., Clinton, La., 1936-39; high sch. prin., Bluff Creek, La., 1939-42; asst. entomologist La. Expt. Sta., 1942-43; asst. entomologist U.S. Dept. Agr., Orlando, Fla., 1946-49; asst. prof. Ga. State U., Atlanta, 1949-53, prof. biology, entomology, 1962—; research asst. U. Md., 1953-55; asso. prof. N.E. La. State Coll., 1955-60; prof., head dept. biology Huntingdon Coll., 1960-62. Served with AUS, 1943-45. NIH grantee, 1957-62. Mem. Soc. Med. entomology, Entomol. Soc. Am., Entomol. Soc. Washington, Entomol. Soc. Ga., Helminthological Soc. Washington, N.Y., Miss. acad. scis., Sigma Xi, Phi Sigma. Contbr. articles to profl. jours. Home: PO Box 66 Covington GA 30209 Office: 34 Gilmer St Atlanta GA 30303

CROSS, JAMES EDWARD, educator; b. Hampton, Va., May 29, 1937; s. Hampton and Julia (Cross) Morgan; B.Engring. Sci. (scholar), Johns Hopkins, 1960; M.S., La. State U., 1967, postgrad., 1972-73; postgrad. (grantee) U. Fla., 1971-72; m. Velta Rose Jones, Dec. 1, 1965; children—Michael, Andre, Michelle. Mem. faculty So. U., Baton Rouge, La., 1962—, chmn. dept., 1964—, asso. prof. elec. engring. dept., 1965—, mem. senate, 1973—. Teaching asst. U. Fla., Gainesville, 1971-72. Mem. Baton Rouge Council on Human Relations, 1969—; adviser Explorer Scouts, 1968-71. Served with C.E., AUS, 1960-62; capt. Res. Mem. Am. Soc. Engring. Edn., I.E.E.E., Am. Assn. U. Profs. (chpt. pres. 1969-71). Democrat. Baptist. Mason. Club: Quarterback (So. U.). Home: 381 Mills Av Baton Rouge LA 70807

CROSS, JAMES STANTON, JR., lawyer; b. Valdosta, Ga., Feb. 17, 1942; s. James Stanton and Lilliam (Riley) C.; B.S., Clemson U., 1964; J.D., U. S.C., 1967; m. Mary Virginia Allen, Aug. 7, 1965; children—Mary Catherine, James Stanton III. Admitted to S.C. bar, 1967; asso. mem. firm Singleton & Singleton, Conway, S.C., 1967-70, partner, 1970-73; partner, Myrtle Beach, S.C., 1973—; partner firm Cross & Singleton, Conway, 1973—. Recorder, City of Conway, 1970—. Bd. dirs. Horry County Mental Health Assn. Mem. Am., Horry County, S.C. bar assns. Methodist (trustee). Home: Route #5 Conway SC 29526 Office: PO Box 121 Conway SC 29526

CROSS, JOSEPH RUSSELL, ednl. adminstr.; b. Cross, S.C., Feb. 24, 1914; s. Joseph Pressley and Addie Lea (Russell) C.; A.B., Wofford Coll., 1935; M.Ed., U.S.C., 1950; m. Julia Harrington Rogers, Aug. 23, 1941; children—Gertrude Celeste (Mrs. Wiggins Ellison Singletary), Julia Harrington (Mrs. Warren Shuler Lambert), Elizabeth Rogers (Mrs. William Spencer Hutto), Joseph Russell. Supt. Cross (S.C.) area schs., 1946-71; asst. supt. for pupil affairs Berkely County Sch. Dist., Moncks Corner, S.C., 1971—. Extension instr. U. S.C., 1969—. Chmn., Berkeley County Hist. Commn., 1968—. Pres., Cross Democratic Club, 1960-70; del. Dem. County Conv., 1946—, Dem. State Conv., 1966. Trustee Berkeley County Library. Served with AUS, 1941-46. Named Hon. State Farmer, Future Farmers of Am. Mem. Berkeley County Edn. Assn. (pres.), Huguenot Soc. S.C. (v.p.), N.E.A. (life), Am. Assn. Sch. Adminstrs., Berkeley County Hist. Soc. (pres. 1973—), S.C. Hist. Soc., Am. Legion, 40 and 8, Blue Key. Methodist (lay del. S.C. ann. conf.). Rotarian. Contbr. articles on early Berkeley County history to hist. jours. Home: Cherokee Path Cross SC 29436 Office: Court House Moncks Corner SC 29461

CROSS, LOUISE PORTLOCK, mfg. co. exec.; b. Norfolk, Va., Jan. 20, 1907; d. William Seth and Mary Louise (Fanshaw) Portlock; grad. high sch.; m. James Byron Cross, July 17, 1929; children—Blanche (Mrs. Charles Louis Kerzanet). With J.B. Cross, Inc., Norfolk, 1952—, exec. pres., 1959-60, pres., chief exec. officer, 1960—. Mem. Phi Sigma Alpha. Episcopalian. Mem. Order Eastern Star, Altrusa Internat. Home: 1605 Mayflower Apts Virginia Beach VA 23451 Office: 3797 Progress Rd Norfolk VA 23502

CROSS, MATTHEW PHILIPS, civil engr.; b. Jacksonville, Fla., Nov. 22, 1932; s. Fred Edgar and Margerite (Philips) C.; B.C.E., U. Fla., 1956; m. Dorothy Faye Getford, Dec. 5, 1960; children—Mary, Lillian. Partner, East Lake Co., Eustis, Fla., 1958-62; engr. Fla. Road Dept., Bartow, 1962-64; county engr., Suwannee County, Fla., 1964-67; city engr., Orlando, Fla., 1968-72; owner Burchfield, Cross & Assos., cons. engrs., Orlando, 1972—. Mem. Orange County Pollution Control Bd., 1969—. Served with AUS, 1956-58. Mem. Orlando Area C. of C. (mem. environmental resources com.). Elk, Kiwanian. Home: 2002 Chippewa Trail Maitland FL 32751 Office: 1516 E Hillcrest St Orlando FL 32803

CROSSLAND, EDWARD JOHN, seismograph co. exec.; b. Okmulgee, Okla., Jan. 17, 1927; s. Samuel Hess and Iva (Jones) C.; B.S., U. Tulsa, 1954; m. Joyce Gardner, Dec. 28, 1963; children—Joy Lorraine, Iva Lynn, Lisa Pauline. Engr., Philco Corp., Phila., 1950-51; research engr. Seismograph Service Corp., Tulsa, 1951-56, mgr. new product devel., 1957-59, engring. mgr. voting machine div., 1959-65, nat. marketing mgr. voting products, 1966-68, exec. engring. cons. P.E.D./Seiscor Div., 1969—. Mem. Okla. State Bd. Registration for Profl. Engrs., 1962-67, chmn., 1966-67. Trustee Tulsa State Fair Bd., 1956-57. Served with USAAF, 1945-49. Registered profl. engr., Okla. Mem. Nat., Okla. socs. profl. engrs. Patentee in field. Home: 7022 E 64th Pl Tulsa OK 74133 Office: 6200 E 41st St PO Box 1590 Tulsa OK 74102

CROSSWHITE, WILLIAM EUGENE, lawyer; b. Bristol, Va., Apr. 26, 1933; s. Lawrence F. and Juanita (Thomas) C.; A.B., Catawba Coll., 1956; J.D., Wake Forest U., 1961; m. Jessie Neil Sowers, June 2, 1956; children—Joseph Neil, Robert Neil, Rebecca Neil. Admitted to N.C. bar, 1961; mem. law firm Sowers, Avery & Crosswhite, Statesville, N.C., 1961—; solicitor Statesville Records Ct., 1962-70. Served with AUS, 1956-58. Mem. N.C., 22d Jud. Dist. (v.p. 1971-72), Iredell County (pres. 1970-71) bar assns., Am. Assn. Trial Lawyers, N.C. Acad. Trial Lawyers, Phi Alpha Delta, Sigma Pi Alpha. Presbyn. Elk, Lion. Home: 564 Stoneybrook Rd Statesville NC 28677 Office: First Savs and Loan Bldg Statesville NC 28677

CROTTS, MARCUS BOWMAN, mech. engr.; b. Winston-Salem, N.C., Aug. 6, 1931; s. Marcus James and Daphne (Bowman) C.; B.Mech.Engring., N.C. State U., 1953; postgrad. Wake Forest U., 1954; M.S. in Mech.Engring., U. Ill., 1956; m. Margo Jackson, May 12, 1955; children—Van, Laura. Asso. engr. Duke Power Co., Winston-Salem, 1947-49; Mech. engr. Babcock & Wilcox Co., Canton, O., 1950-51, Western-Electric Co., Winston-Salem, 1954-55; partner Crotts & Saunders Engring., Inc., Winston-Salem, 1956—. Dir. Electronic Data Control. Pres. alumni assn. N.C. State U.; dist. commr. Boy Scouts Am. Served to lt. USAF, 1954-56. Registered profl. engr., N.C., S.C., Va. Mem. Am. Soc. M.E. (past nat. v.p., mem. council), Soc. Mfg. Engrs. (past chmn. Winston-Salem chpt., Piedmont chpt., nat. dir., past regional chmn., Nat. Soc. Profl. Engrs., Numerical Control Soc., Profl. Engrs. N.C. (dir.), N.C. Soc. Engrs. (dir.), Instn. Prodn. Engrs. (Eng.), Winston-Salem C. of C., Alumni Assn. N.C. State U. (dir., past pres.), Phi Kappa Phi, Tau Beta Pi, Theta Tau, Pi Tau Sigma. Mem. United Ch. Christ (deacon, elder, trustee). Rotarian (dir., pres. Stratford club). Club: Engineers (past pres.) (Winston-Salem). Contbr. numerous articles to tech. jours. Home: 10 Gomar Lane Winston-Salem NC 27106 Office: PO Box 5058 4000 Silas Creek Pkwy Winston-Salem NC 27103

CROUCH, JAMES HAMPTON, ins. agt. exec.; b. Hartsville, S.C., Jan. 8, 1923; s. Manning C. and Tincie (Yarborough) C.; m. Harriette Cato, Aug. 16, 1952; 1 son, James Banjamin. Vice pres. W.D. Arthur & Co., ins. and real estate, Hartsville, S.C., 1952—; dir. First Peoples Nat. Bank, vice chmn. bd., 1970—. Chmn. fund dr. Hartsville chpt. A.R.C., 1953, Boy Scouts Am., 1955; pres. Friends Hartsville Library, 1965-66; co-chmn. bus. dist. fund dr. United Fund, 1968. Pres., Alumni Fund Wofford Coll., 1963; trustee James Byrnes Acad., 1970-73. Named Young Man of Year, Hartsville Jr. C. of C., 1957, Hartsville Citizen of Year, 1972; recipient alumni citation Wofford Coll., 1957. Mem. Darlington County Assn. Ins. Agts. (pres. 1956), Am. Legion, Hartsville C. of C. (pres. 1966), Civitan (dist. gov. 1962-63, dist. lt. gov. 1961, Civitan of Year award 1960, 68, 69). Methodist. (treas. 1961-62). Mason (Shriner). Club: Wofford Coll. Eleven (dir. 1960-73). Home: Box 75 Hartsville SC 29550 Office: Box 248 Hartsville SC 29550

CROUCH, (NORA) JOSEPHINE, librarian; b. Hereford, Tex.; d. Joseph Evvy and Nora (Betts) Crouch; B.S., Ga. Coll., 1942; M.L.S., George Peabody Coll., 1950 Librarian, Boy's High Sch., Rome, Ga., 1942-44, Parker High Sch., Greenville, S.C., 1944-46; library supr. Bartow (Fla.) Sch. System, 1946-47; librarian high sch. Aiken, S.C., 1950-53; chief librarian Aiken County Pub. Library, 1954-58; dir. Aiken-Bamberg-Barnwell-Edgefield Regional Library, Aiken, 1958—. Appointed dir. to establish 1st S.C. Regional Demonstration Library, 1958—; library rep. 2d to 9th S.C. Governor's Conf. Bus., Industry, Edn. and Agr., 1960-68; mem. S.C. Gov.'s Conf. Pub. Libraries, 1965; mem. S.C. Gov's Conf. State-wide Traffic Safety, 1961-63; mem. spl. com. S.C. Progress, 1962. Sec. Dibble Meml. Library Bd., 1963—, S.C. Council Common Good, 1968-69, 69-70. Mem. A.L.A., Southeastern, S.C. (chmn. pub. library sect. 1956-58, mem. exec. bd. 1956-58, 64-70, mem. state exec. com. 1965-69, pres. 1966, 67; A.L.A. fed. relations coordinator 1963-65), Central Savannah River Area library assns., Am. Assn. U. Women (mem. state bd. 1957-58, br. bd. 1958—; state div. parliamentarian 1965-67; exec. bd. 1964-67; br. pres. 1966-67), Council for Common Good (sec. 1968-70). Aiken County Hist. Soc. Club: Pilot. Contbr. to profl. publs. Home: 823 Fermata Pl SW Aiken SC 29801 Office: 504 Richland Av W Aiken SC 29801

CROVITZ, HERBERT FLOYD, educator; b. Providence, R.I., May 21, 1932; s. Jacob and Natalie (Turick) C.; B.A., Clark U., 1953, M.A., 1954; Ph.D., Duke U., 1960; m. Elaine Sandra Kobrin, Dec. 19, 1957 (div. Aug. 1973); children—Gordon, Deborah, Sara. Research psychologist VA Hosp., Durham, N.C., 1961—; mem. faculty Duke U., Durham, 1961—, prof. med. psychology dept. psychiatry, 1973—, lectr. dept. psychology, 1961—. Mem. A.A.A.S., Am. Psychol. Assn., Optical Soc. Am., Psychonomic Soc. Author: Galton's Walk: Methods for the Analysis of Thinking, Intelligence and Creativity, 1970. Home: 3600 Tremont Dr Durham NC 27705

CROW, ALONZO BIGLER, educator; b. Warren, Pa., Aug. 27, 1910; s. Charles Rohrer and Mary Donaldson (Wilson) C.; student Pa. State Forest Sch., 1928-29, U. Mont., 1929-30, U. Pitts., 1930; B.S., N.C. State Coll., 1934; M.Forestry, Yale, 1941; m. Margaret Isabel Rinaman, June 22, 1935; children—Nancy (Mrs. Joseph Hamlin Barham, Jr.). Jr. forester, research forester U.S. Forest Service, Mo., Pa., Md., 1934-40; farm forester U.S. Soil Conservation Service, Md., 1941-44; regional cons. Am. Forestry Assn., Md., Del., Ill., W.Va., 1945-46; asst. prof. Sch. Forestry and Wildlife Mgmt., La. State U., Baton Rouge, 1946-52, asso. prof., 1952-64, prof., 1964—. Recipient Sci. Faculty Fellowship, NSF, 1958, 60, Teaching award Gamma Sigma Delta, 1964. Mem. Soc. Am. Foresters, Am. Forestry Assn., Forest Farm Assn., La. Forestry Assn., Sigma Xi, Phi Kappa Phi, Gamma Sigma Delta, Alpha Zeta, Xi Sigma Pi. Home: 1957 Cherrydale Av Baton Rouge LA 70808

CROW, BOBBY JOE, banker; b. Alvarado, Tex., Dec. 13, 1929; s. Oliver S. and Oma (Smith) C.; student N. Tex. State U., 1947-48, Tex. Christian U., 1954-56; m. Betty Louise Bryant, Apr. 1, 1956; children—James Gregory, Carol Annette, Lisa Gayle. With First Nat. Bank, Ft. Worth, 1948—, v.p., sr. trust officer, 1960-73, sr. v.p., trust officer, 1973—. Bd. dirs. Wesley Found., Tex. Christian U., All-Church Home for Children, Tarrant County chpt. Easter Seal Soc. Served with USAF, 1951-54. Mem. Am. Inst. Banking. Methodist. Clubs: Optimist (dir.), Colonial Country. Home: 229 Hallbrook Dr Fort Worth TX 76134 Office: 1 Burnet Plaza Fort Worth TX 76102

CROW, (FRED) TRAMMELL, real estate co. exec.; b. Dallas, June 10, 1914; s. Jeff B. and Mary (Simonton) C.; student So. Meth. U., 1933-40; m. Margaret Doggett, Aug. 15, 1952; children—Robert, Howard, Harlan, Trammell, Lucy, Stuart. Founder, partner Trammell Crow Co., Dallas, 1948—; owner Dallas Market Center. Home: 4500 Preston Rd Dallas TX 75205 Office: 32d Floor 2001 Bryan St Dallas TX 75201

CROW, GORDON ALLEN, banker; b. Newark, O., Nov. 29, 1923; s. Allen G. and Avanelle D. (Frenier) C.; B.A., Otterbein Coll., 1947; B.S., Ohio State U., 1949; grad. Sch. Financial Pub. Relations, 1959; m. Evelyn McFeeley, Aug. 31, 1946; children—Deborah, Rebecca, Gordon Allen. Salesman, WLEC Radio, Sandusky, O., 1949-50; dept. mgr. Neiman-Marcus Co., Dallas, 1952-55; with First Nat. Bank, Ft. Worth, 1955-67, 70—, v.p. 1970—; account exec. Tracy-Locke Co., Dallas, 1968-69, Witherspoon & Assos., Ft. Worth, 1969-70. Mem. service to mil. families com. A.R.C., Ft. Worth, 1971—. Bd. dir. Casa Manana Musicals, 1972—. Served with AUS, 1950-52. Mem. Bank Marketing Assn. (chpt. pres. 1966), Advt. Fedn. Am. (dir. 1963-65). Clubs: Advt. (pres. 1964); Press (treas. 1965); Colonial Country. Home: 3808 Trailwood Lane Fort Worth TX 76109 Office: One Burnett Plaza Fort Worth TX 76102

CROW, HELEN CAROL, social worker; b. Little Rock, Mar. 30, 1935; d. Johnnie S. and Helen Frances (Rice) Crow; student Tex. Womens U., 1953-55; B.A., U. Tex., Austin, 1957; M.S.W., La. State U., 1960. Social worker mental health div. Tex. Dept. Health, 1961-63; sr. psychiat. social worker Dallas Child Guidance Clinic, 1963-69; social work cons. Childrens Med. Center, 1969-71; dir. profl. services Family Guidance Center, Dallas, 1971—; clin. instr. pediatrics Southwestern Med. Sch., 1969-71; field instr. Worden Sch. Social Work, Our Lady of Lake Coll., 1965-71, Sch. Social Welfare, La. State U., 1966-69, U. Tex., Austin and Arlington Schs. Social Work, 1968-71. Social work cons. Palo Pinto Community Action Council Mental Health Services, 1966; trainer vols. Suicide Prevention Center, Dallas, 1969. Mem. Nat. Assn. Social Workers (v.p. Dallas chpt.), Tex. Soc. Clin. Social Workers, Am. Orthopsychiat. Assn., Delta Zeta. Home: 7136 Pasadena Av Dallas TX 75214 Office: 2200 Main St Dallas TX 75201

CROW, JAMES SYLVESTER, banker; b. Mobile, Ala., June 23, 1915; s. James S. and Elizabeth (Jackson) C.; student U. Ala., 1946-48; grad. Rutgers Sch. Banking, 1959; m. Helen De Blanc, Apr. 20, 1945; children—Michele Marie (Mrs. John Z. Higg, III), Denise Anne (Mrs. Walter C. Andrews, Jr.), Marcia Lynn, Deborah Jane. Clk. First Nat. Bank Mobile, 1932-41, 45-48, mgr. bond dept., 1949-50, asst. cashier, 1951, asst. v.p., 1952; sales mgr. Hendrix & Mayes Investment Bankers, Birmingham, Ala., 1952-53; asst. cashier First Nat. Bank Birmingham, 1954-55, asst. v.p., 1955-56, v.p., 1957-60, sr. v.p., 1961-66, exec. v.p., 1966-67; v.p. finance So. Ry. Co., Washington, 1967-70; exec. v.p. First Nat. Bank Mobile, 1970-71, pres., 1971-74, chmn. bd., 1974—; pres., chmn. bd. First Bancgroup Ala., 1973—; dir. First Nat. Bank, Mobile, First Bancgroup Ala., Ala. Gt. So. R.R., Ala. Dry Dock & Shipbldg. Co., Lerio Corp. Trustee So. Research Assn. Mem. Ala. Banker Assn. (v.p. 1966-67), Newcomen Soc. N.Am. Episcopalian. Clubs: Birmingham Country, Downtown (Birmingham); Athelstan, Country, Lakewood, Internat., Isle Dauphine (Mobile); Metropolitan (Washington). Home: 217 Berwyn Dr Mobile AL 36608 Office: PO Box 1467 Mobile AL 36601

CROW, LESTER DONALD, educator, author; b. Dundee, O., Mar. 31, 1897; s. William Caldwell and Mary (Olmstead) C.; A.B., Ohio U., 1923, Litt.D. (hon.), 1972; M.A., N.Y. U., 1924, Ph.D., 1927; m. Alice von Bauer, June 11, 1927 (dec. Jan. 1966); m. 2d, Rosamond M. Hardy, July 9, 1969. Tchr. high schs., Ohio, 1919-22, Pelham, N.Y., 1924-26; prof. edn. Mary Washington U., Fredericksburg, Va., 1926-27; asst. prof. edn. Leigh U., Bethlehem, Pa., 1927-28; prof. edn. N.Y. U., 1929-30; dir. edn. Pelham Inst., N.Y.C., 1930-32; faculty Bklyn. Coll., 1932-67, emeritus prof. edn., 1967—. Mem. com. to evaluate secondary schs. Middle Atlantic States Colls. and Secondary Schs., 1947-49; pres. Midwood Park Property Assn., Bklyn., 1955-65; mem. U.S. govt. commn. to set up Tchr. Edn. Program, Japan, 1950-51. Recipient Certificate of Merit, Ohio U. Alumni Assn., 1970; Alumni award Mt. Union Coll., 1974. Mem. Am. Personnel and Guidance Assn. (life), N.Y. Acad. Sci. (life), Kappa Delta Pi (hon. life), Phi Delta Kappa (life). Club: N.Y. Schoolmaster's (pres. 1965-66). Author numerous books including An Introduction to Education, 1947, 3d edit., 1974; Educational Psychology, 1948, rev. edit., 1963; Introduction to Guidance, 1951, 2d edit. 1961; High School Education, 1951; Readings in General Psychology, 1954; Sex Education in a Growing Family, 1959; How to Study, 1963; Psychology and Human Adjustment, 1967; Human Development and Adjustment, 1973. Contbr. articles to profl. jours. Home: 5300 Washington St Apt 301D Hollywood FL 33021

CROW, MICHAEL RAY, financial analyst; b. Oklahoma City, Mar. 15, 1947; s. Melvin B. and Helen L. (Rand) C.; A.A., South Plains Coll., 1967; B.B.A., Tex. Tech U., 1969, M.B.A., 1970; m. Leta Mae Campbell, Jan. 25, 1969; 1 dau., Rhonda Lynne. Research asst. Tex. Tech U., Lubbock, 1969-70; staff auditor Arthur Andersen & Co., Ft. Worth, 1970-71; sr. acquisitions analyst First City Bancorp. Houston, 1971-73, financial controls officer, 1973—. C.P.A., Tex. Mem. Am. Inst. C.P.A.'s, Tex. Soc. C.P.A.'s, Phi Beta Lamba, Beta Gamma Sigma. Home: 7352 Crownwest Dr Houston TX 77072 Office: PO Box 2557 Houston TX 77001

CROW, NEIL EDWARD, physician; b. Belton, Tex., July 12, 1926; s. Floyd Charles and Mary (Martin) C.; student Henderson Coll., 1943-44, Tex. Christian U., 1944-45; B.S., U. Tex., 1946; M.D., U. Ark., 1951; m. Mary Katherine Claxton, Sept. 11, 1948; children—Neil E., Katherine Lee. Intern U. Ark. Med. Center, 1951-52, splty. tng. in radiology, 1953-56, asso. clin. prof. radiology, 1960—; gen. practice medicine, Hope, Ark., 1952-53; radiologist Holt-Krock Clinic and Sparks Med. Center, Fort Smith, Ark., 1960—; cons. USPHS, USAF Surgeon Gen. Pres., Ft. Smith Sch. Bd., 1971-72. Trustee Ark. Poly. Coll., 1972—, Sparks Regional Med. Center, 1974—. Served to lt. (j.g.) USNR, 1944-47; to lt. col. USAF, 1953-60; now col. M.C. Res. Diplomate Am. Bd. Radiology. Mem. Am. Coll. Radiology, A.M.A., Ark. Med. Soc., Air Force Assn., Am. Fedn. Clin. Research, U. Ark. Sch. Medicine Alumni Assn. (pres. 1972-74), Alpha Omega Alpha, Phi Chi. Democrat. Presbyn. Contbr. articles to profl. jours. Home: 19 Berry Hill Rd Fort Smith AR 72901 Office: 1500 Dodson Av Fort Smith AR 72901

CROW, WILLIAM CECIL, govt. ofcl.; b. Oneonta, Ala., Oct. 4, 1904; s. Mandeville McAlpin and Flora Jane (Brice) C.; A.B., Maryville Coll., 1924; A.M., U. Chgo., 1929; LL.D., Maryville College, 1969; m. Mary Lucille Johnson, July 5, 1935; 1 son, William Cecil. Asst. prof. econs., Ala. Poly. Inst., 1930-35; with U.S. Dept. Agr., 1935—, successively with Bur. Agrl. Econs., 1935-42, War Food Adminstrn. and Prodn. and Marketing Adminstrn., 1942-53, dir. transp. and facilities research div., and liaison with state dept. agr. Agrl. Marketing Service, 1953-63, dir. transp. and facilities research div. Agrl. Research Service, 1963—. Mem. Arlington (Va.) Com. of 100; chmn. Arlington County Pub. Utilities Commn. Trustee Presbytery of Washington. Decorated Chevalier de l'Ordre du Merite Agricole (France); Order of Long Leaf Pine (N.C.); recipient Achievement award Nat. Assn. Produce Market Mgrs., also plaque for exceptional service; Superior Service award U.S. Dept. Agr.; citation Greater Phila. Movement; named Ky. Col. Hon. life mem. Nat. Assn. Refrigerated Warehouses; mem. Am. Farm Econs. Assn., A.A.A.S. Presbyn. Club: Springfield Golf and Country. Author many publs. Home: 1258 N Buchanan St Arlington VA 22205 Office: US Dept Agr Washington DC 20025

CROWDER, CHARLIE CLEMONS, JR., municipal ofcl.; b. Danville, Va., July 26, 1940; s. Charlie Clemons and Avis Louise (Griffith) C.; B.S., Va. Mil. Inst., 1962; m. Carolyn Marie Willis, June 16, 1962; children—Coni, Christin, Catherine. Commd. 2d lt., U.S. Army, 1962, advanced through grades to capt., 1965; combat engr. unit comdr., Ft. Meade, Md., 1962-64; post engr., Aschaffenburg, Germany, 1964-66; comdr. Port Constrn. Co., Ft. Belvoir, Va. and Qui Nhou, Vietnam, 1966-67; post engr., Tobyhanna (Pa.) Army Depot, 1968; ret., 1968; dir. pub. works City of Danville, 1969-72; mgr. store engring. Asso. Service Corp., Danville, Va., 1972-73; adminstrv. engr., asst. to dir. pub. utilities, City of Pensacola, Fla., 1973, water supt. dept. pub. utilities, 1973—. Decorated Bronze Star (U.S.); Order of Merit 2d Class (Vietnam). Mem. Am. Pub. Works Assn., Internat. City Mgmt. Assn. (cooperating mem.). Baptist. Mason. Home: 6000 Sarah Dr Pensacola FL 32503 Office: Dept Pub Utilities Pensacola FL 32576

CROWDER, GENE AUTRY, educator; b. Wichita Falls, Tex., Oct. 25, 1936; s. Raymond Melvin and Jewel Marie (Saylors) G.; B.S., Central State U., 1958; M.S., U. Fla., 1961; Ph.D. (Petroleum Research Fund fellow), Okla. State U., 1964; m. Marita Faye Barnes, Nov. 25, 1965; children—Kevin Scott, Kathryn Lyn. Asst. prof. W. Tex. State U., Canyon, 1964-65, asso. prof., 1965-68, prof. chemistry, 1968—, head chemistry dept., 1970—, coordinator phys. scis. research Killgore Research Center, 1971—. Recipient Petroleum Research Fund fellowship, 1966. Mem. Am. Chem. Soc. (sect. chmn. 1968), Chem. Soc. London, Coblentz Soc., Soc. for Applied Spectroscopy, Sigma Xi, Alpha Chi Sigma, Phi Lambda Upsilon. Contbr. articles in field to profl. jours. Home: Box 188 West Texas State University Canyon TX 79016

CROWDER, JACK ANDREW, trade assn. exec.; b. Charleston, W.Va., Jan. 2, 1927; s. John Amos and Helen (Gallagher) C.; B.A. magna cum laude, Washington and Lee U., 1948, LL.B. cum laude, 1950 ; m. Barbara Grace Ochtman, Nov. 4, 1950; children—Mary C., Jack Andrew, Marjorie H., Barbara E., Patricia F., James T. Admitted to District of Columbia Bar, 1950; gen. practice law, Washington, 1950-65; exec. v.p., counsel Nat. Assn. Wool Mfrs., Washington, 1965-67, pres., 1967-71; gen. counsel Am. Textile Mfrs. Inst., Washington, 1971—. Mem. Pres.'s Labor-Mgmt. Textile Adv. Com.; mem. U.S. delegation Internat. Wool Textile Orgn. Cons. Nat. Council Catholic Men. Served with AUS, 1945-46. Mem. Am. Bar Assn., Phi Beta Kappa, Omicron Delta Kappa, Sigma Alpha Epsilon. Roman Catholic. Home: 3607 Bent Branch Ct Falls Church VA 22041 Office: 1150 17th St NW Washington DC 20036

CROWDER, JOSEPH LOUIS, JR., cement co. exec.; b. Apex, N.C., June 22, 1921; s. Joseph Louis and Cathryne Pearl (Lowry) C.; grad. high sch.; m. Mary Lou Stubblefield, June 27, 1947; children—Linda Ruth (Mrs. Thomas Arthur Brennison), Joseph Louis III, Virginia Glenn. Customers engr. IBM, Charlotte, N.C., 1945-47; salesman Robert E. Mason Co., mfrs. rep., Charlotte, 1947-51; salesman Giant Portland Cement Co., Columbia, S.C., 1951-53, sales mgr. So. div., 1953-69, v.p. sales, 1969-70, exec. v.p., 1970-71, pres., 1971—, also dir., mem. exec. com.; dir. Columbia adv. bd. Citizens and So. Nat. Bank of S.C. Served with USAAF, 1940-44; PTO. Mem. S.C., Columbia chambers commerce, Com. One Hundred. Presbyn. Clubs: Palmetto, Summitt, Columbia Country, Spring Valley Country (Columbia); Santee Cooper Country (Santee, S.C.). Home: 4816 Shadow Lawn Rd Columbia SC 29206 Office: 3006 Devine St Columbia SC 29206

CROWDER, ROBERT SCOTT, assn. exec.; b. Durand, Ga., Sept. 23, 1910; s. Robert Scott and Willie (Scaife) C.; B.S. in Chem. Engring., Ga. Inst. Tech., 1932; m. Julia Johnston, Mar. 31, 1937; children—Robert Scott Jr., Henry Johnston, William Scaife. Pres., Johnston-Crowder Mfg. Co. Inc., Birmingham, Ala., 1946-56; asst. dir. Birmingham's Com. 100, 1956-62; mgr. research dept. Birmingham Area C. of C., 1962—. Sec. Birmingham Regional Planning Commn., 1963-70; mem. Birmingham Nat. Alliance Businessmen, 1968-70; mem. adv. com. vocational edn. Jefferson County Bd. Edn., 1970—; mem. vocational edn. funding com. Ala. Bd. Edn., 1972-73; mem. Re-Apportionment Task Force, Ala. Legislature, 1973; dist. chmn. Birmingham Area council Boy Scouts Am., 1944—; pres. Ala. Council Epilepsy, Inc., 1973. Served to lt. col. Ordnance Corps, AUS, 1940-46. Mem. Am. C. of C. Research Assn. (nat. sec.), Am. Marketing Assn. (dir. Birmingham Chpt.), Am. Mgmt. Assn., Am. Statis. Assn., Regional Sci. Assn., Am. Soc. Metals (pres. chpt. 1944), Am. Inst. Mining, Metall. Engrs., Am. Ordnance Assn. Republican. Baptist (deacon). Clubs: Executive, The Club (Birmingham). Home: 1308 S 17th St Birmingham AL 35205 Office: 1914 6th Av N Birmingham AL 35203

CROWE, CHRISTOPHER, geophysicist; b. London, Eng., Dec. 4, 1928; s. George Kenneth and Dorothy Mowat (Duff) C.; B.S., U. Western Ont., 1952, Ph.D., 1956; postgrad. (Royal Commn. Exhbn. 1851 research scholar), U. Cambridge (Eng.), 1956-58; m. Janet Marilyn Adsett, July 12, 1952; children—Brian Charles, Rodger Thomas, Sheila Florence. Came to U.S., 1958; Canadian citizen. Tchr. rural schs., Kenilworth, Ont., Can., 1946-47; asst. prof. geophysics Pa. State U., State College, 1958-63; staff geophysicist Geoscis. Operations and Sci. Services div. Tex Instruments, Inc., Dallas, 1964-69; sr. geophysicist, exploration and prodn. research lab. Sun Oil Co., Dallas, 1969-70, research scientist, 1970—. Cons. earth sci. curriculum project Am. Geol. Inst., 1963-65. Mem. Inst. Physics, Canadian Assn. Physicists, Am. Geophys. Union, Soc. Exploration Geophysicists, A.A.A.S. Methodist. Rotarian. Home: 6225 Alpha Rd Dallas TX 75240 Office: 503 N Central Expressway Richardson TX 75080

CROWE, ELLENIA AUGUSTA BATES, artist, author; b. Dardanelle, Ark. ; d. James Fillmore and Alice (Putnam) Bates; student Columbia, 1946; m. Theopholis Waldon Crowe; children—Blonnie Dell (Mrs. Eugene Lambert), Adrian Bates, Rodney Page Thomas, Doris Ellenia (Mrs. Shannon Townley). Sales, Macy's, N.Y.C., 1946; one-man shows Little Rock Fine Arts Bldg., Old South Restaurant; exhibited in group shows at Philbrook, Tulsa, U. Ark., Ark. Arts Center, Verdigris Valley, Independence, Kan., Fort Smith Arts Center. Mem. Ark. Art Center, D.A.R. (treas.), Friends of Library, League Women Voters, Fort Smith Asso. Artists, Ark. Letos, Phi Sigma Alpha. Methodist. Author: volume of poetry, 1954; (novel) Hilda's Miracle, 1955; Days of Passion, Nights of Love, 1964. Home: 718 N 16th St Fort Smith AR 72903

CROWELL, HENRY HARLAND, JR., real estate broker; b. Kansas City, Mo., May 23, 1917; s. Henry H. and Frances (Menchan) C.; student Georgetown U., 1935-37; LL.B., Columbus U., 1940; m. Patricia McKinney, Nov. 19, 1965; children—Henry Harland III, Michael W., Samuel F. Pres. Crowell & Co., Inc., Arlington, Va., 1955—, Crowell Ins. Agy., Inc., Arlington, 1959—, Relocation Consultants, Inc., 1969—. Dean Realtors' Inst., U. Va., 1961—; v.p., dir. Commonwealth Nat. Bank, Arlington. Recipient awards No. Va. Bd. Realtors, Va. Real Estate Assn., Chattanooga, San Antonio, Montgomery County (Md.), Prince Georges County (Md.) bds. realtors; named Realtor Year. Mem. Nat. Assn. Real Estate Bds., Va. Real Estate Assn. (pres. 1966), Nat. Inst. Real Estate Brokers (regional v.p. 1969, gov. 1969), Rho Epsilon (pres. 1969-70). Clubs: Washington Golf and Country (Arlington). Contbr. articles to profl. jours. Home: 6010 Oakdale Rd McLean VA 22101 Office: 2160 N Glebe Rd Arlington VA 22207

CROWELL, WAYNE ALLEN, veterinarian; b. Sterling, Colo., Nov. 25, 1940; s. Carl L. and Lorraine E. (Rambow) C.; B.S., Colo. State U., 1963, D.V.M., 1964; postgrad. U. Neb., 1962, Ind. State U., 1969; Ph.D., U. Ga., 1973; m. Mary Linn Scott, Apr. 27, 1962; children—Cheryl Linn, George Scott. Pvt. practice vet. medicine, Glasgow, Ky. and Colorado Springs, Colo., 1964-66; research veterinarian Comml. Solvents Corp., Terre Haute, Ind., 1968-70; research asso. Coll. Vet. Medicine, U. Ga., Athens, 1970-73, asst. prof., 1973—. Served with AUS, 1966-68. Decorated Army Commendation medal. NSF Student Research grantee, 1962, Colo. State U. Alumni award of Merit, 1963. Diplomate Am Coll Vet. Pathologists. Mem. Am. Vet. Med. Assn., Internat. Acad. Pathology, Soc. Vet. Urologists, Assn. Am. Vet. Med. Colls., A.A.A.S., Am. Legion, Alpha Gamma Rho (pres.), Phi Zeta, Beta Beta Beta. Republican. Presbyn. Mason. Home: 120 Richard Way Athens GA 30601

CROWLEY, BILLIE BLALACK (MRS. H.W. CROWLEY), newspaper editor; b. Mt. Vernon, Ill., Mar. 25, 1930; d. William James and Mildred Alice (Barefield) Elliott; student Kilgore Coll., 1967-69; North Tex. U., 1949-50, So. Meth. U., 1958-59; m. Joe Blalack, Aug. 30, 1950 (dec. Feb. 1966); children—John, Jack, James, Jay, Jill; m. 2d, H.W. Crowley, May 26, 1970. Owner, operator Blalack Oil Co., Longview, Tex., 1966—; founder, owner Am. Real Estate Co., Longview, 1968—; co-pub., editor Woman's World Weekly, newspaper, Longview 1969—; syndicated columnist, 1972—; editor, v.p., co-pub. Greater Longview Post, 1974—; co-owner Tri-W Pub. Co.; news commentator radio sta. KOCA, 1974—. Mem. Tex. Press Women (rec. sec. 1971-73, pres. dist. 1974-75, 9 awards ann. Writers contest 1972, sweepstakes writing award 1973), Nat. Fedn. Press Women (journalism award 1970), C. of C. (ambassador). Presbyn. Home: 1803 Hughey Dr Longview TX 75601 Office: Box 3206 Longview TX 75601

CROWSON, WILLIAM NATHAN, physician; b. Calhoun City, Miss., Dec. 21, 1922; s. Quinton T. and Estelle Priscilla (Lamar) C.; B.S., B.A., U. Miss., 1943; M.D., Harvard, 1946; m. Jewel Evelyn Snipes, July 5, 1952; children—Cynthia Lynn, William Nathan, Chris Lamar, Elizabeth Amy. Intern, Nashville Gen. Hosp., 1946-47, resident, 1949; practice medicine specializing in surgery, Clarksdale, Miss., 1954-70; mem. staff Coahoma County Hosp., Clarksdale; prof. surgery U. Tenn., Memphis, 1970—; asst. chief surgery VA Hosp., Memphis, 1970—. Pres., Greenbough, Inc., Clarksdale, 1965—; dir. CFG Realty Co., Clarksdale, 1969—, Coahoma Opportunities, Clarksdale, 1966-69. Served to lt. USNR, 1947-49. Diplomate Am. Bd. Surgery. Fellow A.C.S., Southeastern Surg. Congress; mem. A.M.A. Methodist (chmn. ofcl. bd. 1966-67, trustee 1968-70). Home: 561 Claycreek Rd Memphis TN 38138 Office: 1030 Jefferson Av Memphis TN 38138

CROZIER, GEORGE FREDRICK, marine biologist; b. New Orleans, Oct. 8, 1941; s. George Frederick and Dorsey (Long) C.; B.S. in Biology, Loyola U., New Orleans, 1963; Ph.D. in Marine Biology, U. Cal. at San Diego, 1966; m. Deanna Kay Kennedy, Aug. 28, 1965; children—George Frederick, Holly Lorraine, William Matthew. Asst. prof. dept. biology U. So. Miss., Hattiesburg, 1966-68; asst. dir. Marine Scis. Inst., U. Ala., Bayou La Batre, 1968-73; asso. dir. Marine Environmental Scis. Consortium/Miss.-Ala. Sea Grant, Dauphin Island (Ala.) Sea Lab., 1973—. Vice pres. Environmental Cons. Internat., Gulf Shores, Ala., 1973—. Adviser Explorer Post 365, Boy Scouts Am. Miss. Heart Assn. grantee, 1967, Alpha Helix Expdn., Bering Sea grantee, 1968. Mem. Am. Soc. Zoology, Am. Littoral Soc., Marine Tech. Soc., N.Y. Acad. Scis., Sigma Xi, Beta Beta Beta. Home: Route 1 Box 256 Irvington AL 36544 Office: PO Box 386 Dauphin Island AL 36528

CRUM, WALLACE ELLIOTT, banking exec.; b. Orangeburg, S.C., Nov. 26, 1910; s. William Wallace and Rebecca Collier (Elliott) C.; B.S., in Elec. Engring., U. S.C., 1932, B.S. in Civil Engring., 1937; m. Mary Lou Funderburk, Sept. 16, 1939; children—Mary Lou (Mrs. John Asbil Cloyd), Collier (Mrs. John Robert Turnbull), Wallis Elliott. Bridge design engr. S.C. Hwy. Dept., 1933-42, mgr. bridge design group, 1946-56, chief bridge engr. design, 1956—; pres., chmn. bd. E.C. Bldg. & Investment Corp., Columbia, S.C., 1963—. Hon. mem. spl. choir Westminster Abbey, London, Eng., 1968—. Served as lt. comdr. USNR, 1942-46. Mem. Am., Southeastern (chmn. bridge com. 1958—) assns. state hwy. ofcls., Am. Soc. C.E., S.C. Soc. Engrs., Internat. Assn. Bridge and Structural Engrs. (chmn. bridge com. design 1968—), English Speaking Union (br. pres. 1971—, dir. 1968-71). Episcopalian. Clubs: Columbia Ball Debutant, Kiwanis (chmn. tennis com. 1959—), Corsair, Arrow, Forest Lake Country. Address: 2710 Canterbury Rd Columbia SC 29204

CRUM, WILLIAM BARTON, physician; b. Ft. Deposit, Ala., May 8, 1922; s. William Salley and Willa Frances (Holston) C.; B.A., U. Ala., 1943; M.D., U. Pa., 1946; m. Gertrude LaBotz, Nov. 26, 1953; children—Margurite Joan, William Barton, Laura Lynn, Richard Eric. Intern, Phila. Gen. Hosp., 1946-47, resident, 1951-55; practice medicine specializing in internal medicine, Montgomery, Ala., 1955—; mem. staff Montgomery Baptist Hosp. Served with USNR, 1947-49. Fellow A.C.P., Am. Coll. Cardiology, Montgomery C. of C., Med. Soc. Montgomery County (pres. 1970). Club: Montgomery Country. Home: 3355 Allendale Pl Montgomery AL 36111 Office: 1301 E South Blvd Montgomery AL 36111

CRUMB, GLENN HOWARD, educator; b. Harveyville, Kan., Dec. 21, 1927; s. Clifford Myers and Katie (Turner) C.; B.S., Kan. State Tchrs. Coll., 1951, M.S., 1956; Ph.D., U. Neb., 1965; m. Neva Joyce Graber, Nov. 24, 1950; children—Judith Kay, James Dan, Nancy June, Steven Ray. Tchr. sci. pub. schs., Darby, Kan., 1951-54, Wichita, Kan., 1954-56; instr. phys. sci. U. Neb., 1959-63; prof. phys. sci. Kan. State Tchrs. Coll., 1963-72, dir. research grants, 1968-72; dir. grant and contract services, prof. physics and elementary sci. Western Ky. U., Bowling Green, 1972—. Pres. Emporia State Coll. Coop. Fed. Credit Union, 1967-68; cons. program devel. and evaluation State of Kan. Title III Elementary and Secondary Edn. Act, 1971-73. Bd. dirs. Jayhawk Area council Boy Scouts Am., 1969-71; bd. dirs. United Fund, Lyon County, Kan., 1969-71. Mem. project adv. bd. CFK, Ltd. Found. Served with USNR, 1945-47. Sci. faculty fellow Stanford U., 1969; DuPont fellow Harvard, 1956; Danforth Found. asso., 1965. Mem. Nat. Assn. Research in Sci. Teaching (editorial bd. 1969-72), Nat. Sci. Tchrs. Assn., Am. Assn. Physics Tchrs., Assn. Edn. Tchrs. Sci. (pres. S.W. sect. 1970-71), Alpha Kappa Lambda, Phi Delta Kappa, Sigma Pi Sigma. Mason. Contbr. articles to profl. jours. Home: 2251 Smallhouse Rd Bowling Green KY 42101

CRUMBLEY, GEORGE PIERCE, JR., advt. exec.; b. Atlanta, June 15, 1923; s. George Pierce and Mary (Hicks) C.; A.B., Emory U., 1949; m. Sarah Carolyn Hardy, July 4, 1944; children—Thomas McMahan, Cheryl Marie. Sales mgr. WSB-TV, Atlanta, 1948-57; southeastern mgr. Headley-Reed Radio-TV Reps., 1957-59, CBS Radio, 1959-62; pres. Crumbley, Robertson, Riley Advt., Inc., 1962—. Chmn. DeKalb County Cancer Crusade, 1965-67; chmn. spl. study com. Ga. Industries for Blind. Bd. dirs. Met. Atlanta Better Bus. Bur., Met. Atlanta Assn. for Blind; trustee Found. Visually Handicapped Children; exec. dir. Peach Bowl, Inc. Served with USAAF, 1942-46; lt. col. Res. ret. Mem. Atlanta Advt. Club (dir.), Alpha Delta Sigma, Sigma Delta Chi. Methodist. Mason, Lion (life dir. Lighthouse for Blind; past dist. gov.). Club: Druid Hills Country. Home: 873 Castle Falls Dr NE Atlanta GA 30329 Office: 20 Marietta St NW Atlanta GA 30303

CRUME, RONALD GLENN, dentist; b. Covington, Ky., Sept. 19, 1935; s. Thomas Clinton and Helen Madiline (Craddock) C.; U. Ky., 1954-57, Austin Peay Coll., 1959-60, Thomas Moore Coll., 1961; D.M.D., U. Louisville, 1966; m. Barbara Ann Denham, June 12, 1954; children—Lou Ann, Ronald Glenn. Practice dentistry, Florence, Ky., 1966—. Cons. Boone County (Ky.) Bd. Health, 1969—, Woodspoint Extended Care Home, 1970—. Magistrate, Boone County, 1970—. Trustee Ohio, Ky., Ind. Regional Planning Authority. Served with AUS, 1959-61. Named Ky. col., 1971, Tenn. Squire, 1970. Mem. Boone County Jr. C. of C. (Outstanding Young Man of Year 1969), Boone County Businessmen's Assn., Phi Delta, Psi Omega. Democrat. Baptist. Home: 7544 Dogwood St Florence KY 41042 Office: 8315 US 42 Florence KY 41042

CRUMMER, ROGER NELSON, communications co. exec.; b. Essexville, Mich., Dec. 21, 1931; s. John Ernest and Ethel Linea (Nelson) C.; B.S., Mich. State U., 1957; m. Jacqueline Sue Meade, Oct. 7, 1960; children—Laura Ann, James Einar, Margaret Leigh. Sr. engr. Creole Petroleum Corp., Maracaibo, Venezuela, 1957-64; supervisory engr. Page Communications Engrs., Inc., Washington, 1964-67; v.p. Telcom, Inc., McLean, Va., 1967—. Communications systems cons. Republic of Venezuela, Fed. Mil. Govt. Nigeria, Republic of Bolivia. Served with USN, 1949-53. Mem. I.E.E.E. Republican. Home: 4127 Lenox Dr Fairfax VA 22030 Office: 8027 Leesburg Pike McLean VA 22101

CRUMP, HAROLD CRAFT, broadcasting exec.; b. Amory, Miss., Sept. 28, 1931; s. Harold Williams and Eva (Craft) C.; B.B.A., U. Miss., 1953; m. Lannese M. Thompson, Apr. 30, 1952; children—Harold T., William L., Laurie M. Asst. advt. mgr. Blytheville (Ark.) Courier Jour., 1955-56; account exec. WLAC-TV, Nashville, 1956-59, local sales mgr., 1959-62, gen. sales mgr., 1962-66, v.p., dir. sales, 1966-69, v.p., str. mgr., 1969—; dir. Omega Ranches, Inc., Nashville. TV cons. athletic dept. U. Miss., 1970—. Bd. dirs. Better Bus. Bur., 1967-73, vice chmn. bd., 1973-74; mem. corp., bd. dirs. Muscular Dystrophy Assns. Am., 1971-74; bd. dirs. Jr. Achievement, 1966-73, Jr. Pro Football League, 1966-69. Served to 1st lt. USAF, 1953-55. Named Man of Yr. in Advt., Nashville, 1971; recipient Silver medal Advt. Fedn. Am., 1971. Mem. Nat., Tenn. (dir. 1970-74) assns. broadcasters, Nashville Advt. Fedn. (pres. 1965-66), Sales and Marketing Execs. (dir. 1968-71), U. Miss. Alumni Assn. (chpt. pres. 1962-68, dir. 1962-74), Nashville Area C. of C., Delta

Kappa Epsilon, Alpha Delta Sigma. Presbyn. (deacon). Club: Nashville City. Home: 3505 Hampton Av Nashville TN 37215 Office: WLAC-TV 474 James Robertson Pkwy Nashville TN 37219

CRUMP, KENNY SHERMAN, educator; b. Haynesville, La., Oct. 13, 1939; s. Sherman and Travis Elsie (Hardaway) C.; B.S., La. Tech. U., 1961; M.A., U. Denver, 1963; Ph.D., Mont. State U., 1968; m. Shirley Rae Edmondson, June 2, 1961; children—Frankie Faith, Tanya Travis, Kenny Sherman. Instr. math. Mont. State U., Bozeman, 1963-66; prof. math. La. Tech. U., Ruston, 1966—; research asso. State U. N.Y., Buffalo, 1967-68. Cons. Nat. Inst. Environmental Health Scis., 1972, Nat. Heart and Lung Inst., 1972. Mem. Biometric Soc., Inst. Math. Statistics. Democrat. Baptist (deacon 1963—). Kiwanian. Home: Route 1 Box 38 Ruston LA 71270

CRUMPLER, HARRY ABNER, judge; b. Magnolia, Ark., Oct. 4, 1914; s. Samuel Abner and Kathleen (Warnock) C.; student So. State Coll., Magnolia, 1933-34; LL.B., U. Ark., 1939; m. Laura Hays, July 22, 1950; children—Kathleen W., Harry A., Laura Ann. Admitted to Ark. bar, 1939; city atty., Magnolia, 1940-42; dep. pros. atty. Columbia County, Ark., 1946-48; pros. atty. 13th Jud. Circuit, 1949-52; pvt. practice law, Magnolia, 1953-64; circuit judge 13th Jud. Circuit, 1st Div., Magnolia, 1965—. Mem. Constl. Revision Study Commn. of Ark., 1967-68. Served with AUS, 1942-45. Named Ky. col. Mem. Ark., 13th Dist. (v.p. 1950-52), Columbia County (pres. 1956-58) bar assns., Kappa Sigma. Home: RFD 1 Box 67E Magnolia AR 71753 Office: 114 E Calhoun St Magnolia AR 71753

CRUSE, DONALD MARION, govt. ofcl.; b. Smackover, Ark., Nov. 16, 1927; s. John Thomas and Louella (Davis) C.; B.A., La. Tech., 1953; M.A., La. State U., 1955; m. Jeanne Marie Thibodeaux, Mar. 11, 1957; stepchildren—Charlene, Cynthia; 1 dau., Gail. Instr. La. State U., Baton Rouge, 1954-55; field economist Bur. Labor Statistics, Atlanta, 1955-57, economist, 1957-59, br. chief, 1959-63, asst. regional dir., 1964—. Bd. dirs. Peachtree Fed. Credit Union, Atlanta, 1973—. Served with AUS, 1946-49. Mem. Am. Statis. Assn. (chpt. pres. 1970-71), Indsl. Relations Research Assn. Baptist. Club: Atlanta Economics. Home: 1568 Rainier Falls Dr NE Atlanta GA 30329 Office: Room 540 1371 Peachtree St NE Atlanta GA 30309

CRUSE, JULIUS MAJOR, JR., physician, educator; b. New Albany, Miss., Feb. 15, 1937; s. Julius Major and Effie (Davis) C.; B.A., U. Miss., 1958, B.S. with honors, 1958; D.Microbiology with honors (Fulbright fellow), U. Graz, Austria, 1960; M.D., U. Tenn., 1964, Ph.D. in Pathology (USPHS fellow), 1966. USPHS postdoctoral fellow in pathology U. Tenn., 1964-66; faculty U. Miss., University, 1967—, research prof. immunology, prof. biology, Grad. Sch., 1967—, asst. prof. pathology, Sch. Medicine, 1973-74, prof., 1974—, asst. prof. microbiology, 1968—. Lectr. pathology U. Tenn. Coll. Medicine, Memphis, 1967—. Fellow A.A.A.S., Royal Soc. for the Promotion of Health, Am. Acad. Microbiology, Intercontinental Biographical Assn.; mem. Am. Assn. Pathologists and Bacteriologists, Am. Soc. for Experimental Pathology, Am. Chem. Soc., British, Canadian socs. for immunology, Am. Soc. Microbiology, Internat. Acad. Pathology, Am. Assn. Immunologists, Am. Inst. Biol. Scis., Am. Soc. Clin. Pathologists, Canadian Soc. Microbiologists, N.Y. Acad. Scis., Soc. for Experimental Biology and Medicine, Societe Francaise d'Immunologie, Reticuloendothelial Soc., Transplantation Soc., Electron Microscopy Soc. Am., Internat. Platform Assn., Sigma Xi, Phi Kappa Phi, Phi Eta Sigma, Alpha Epsilon Delta, Gamma Sigma Epsilon, Beta, Beta, Beta. Episcopalian. Author: Immunology Examination Review Book, 1971, rev. edit., 1974; Introduction to Immunology, 1974. Contbr. articles to profl. jours. Home: Jackson MS Office: Dept of Pathology University of Miss Medical Center 2500 N State St Jackson MS 29213

CRUTCHER, WILLIAM EDWARD, newspaper pub.; b. Louisa, Ky., Oct. 8, 1912; s. Clarence Buck and Emma (Raines) Crutcher; A.B., Morehead State U., 1934; m. Darlyn Miller, Jan. 21, 1934 (dec. Oct. 1962); children—Mrs. Clayton Z. Skaggs, Mrs. Jerry Franklin. Owner, pub. Morehead (Ky.) News, Greenup News, Grayson Jour.-Enquirer, Olive Hill Times; pres. Morehead Pub. Co. Birthdate Calendar Co.; partner, sec. Hobac Co. Chmn. Cave Run Reservoir Assn.; chmn. Housing Authority Morehead, 1960—; chmn. exec. com., sec. N.E. Ky. Hosp. Found., 1960—. Named Morehead's Outstanding Citizen of 20th Century, City Council, 1965; recipient gold medallion Morehead State U. Bd. Regents, 1969; Outstanding Pub. Service award Alumni Assn. Morehead State U., 1972. Mem. Ky. Press Assn. (pres. 1974), Morehead C. of C. (past pres.). Mem. Ch. of Christ (bus. bd.). Clubs: Lafayette, Keeneland. Office: 722 W 1st St Morehead KY 40351

CRUTCHFIELD, ALBIN PILKINGTON, citrus groves exec.; b. Sewickley, Pa., Dec. 24, 1908; s. James Stapleton and Alice (Pilkington) C.; student Princeton, 1927-29, Duff's Iron City Coll., 1930, U. Pitts., 1930-31; m. Mary Elizabeth Fiske, Apr. 4, 1935; children—James S. II, Albin P. Jr., Sheldon F., Mary (Mrs. Jimmy R. McDowell). With AFG, Inc., various locations, 1938-46, dist. sales mgr., Atlanta, 1940-41, Fort Worth, Tex., 1942-43, asst. mgr., Weslaco, Tex., 1944-46; partner Crutchfield Bros., Weslaco, 1947-51; sales mgr., exec. v.p. Vaughn Griffin Packing Co., Howey-in-the-Hills, Fla., 1952-68; pres. Deerfield Groves Co., Wabasso, Fla., 1969-74; chmn. bd. dirs. Union Fruit Auction Co., Pitts.; pres. Central Fla. Truck Brokers, Inc., Orlando, 1959-73, Central Fla. Produce, Inc., Sanford, 1972—, Wabasso Fruit Co. Inc., 1970-74, Deerfield of St. Lucie, Fort Pierce, Fla., 1970-74. Advancement chmn. troop 567, Treasure Coast council Boy Scouts Am., 1972—; mem. Fla. Citrus Commn., 1972—. Mem. city council, Howey-in-the-Hills, 1956-58. Bd. dirs. Indian River County Farm Bur., Vero Beach, Fla., YMCA, Vero Beach; trustee Howey Acad., 1955-58. Mem. Vero Beach C. of C. (dir.), Indian River Citrus League (v.p.), Fla. Fresh Citrus Shippers Assn. (v.p.), Growers and Shippers League (v.p.), United Growers and Shippers Assn. (pres.). Presbyn. (elder). Club: Riomar Bay Yacht (Vero Beach). Home: 3040 Par Dr Vero Beach FL 32960 Office: Wabasso FL 32970

CRUTCHFIELD, SAM SHAW, JR., lawyer, assn. exec.; b. Nashville, July 15, 1934; s. Sam Shaw and Alfreda (Whitworth) C.; B.A., George Washington U., 1960, J.D., 1963; m. Sylvia Ann Dinneen, May 14, 1958; children—Catherine Anne, Firmadge Whitworth, Elizabeth Victoria. Admitted to D.C. bar, 1963; jud. law clk. Hon. Frank H. Myers, D.C. Ct. of Appeals, 1963-64; exec. dir. Va. Commn. Constl. Govt., 1964-67; asso. counsel Am. Enterprise Inst. Pub. Policy Research, Washington, 1967-70, asst. to pres., 1970-73, dir. legal studies, 1973; gen. counsel U.S. Postal Rate Commn., 1973-74; exec. dir. Phi Delta Phi, internat. legal frat., Washington, 1974—. Mem. Jud. Conf. for D.C. Circuit, 1969. Vice pres. Young Republican Club, Arlington, Va., 1968-69; mem. Arlington County Rep. Com., 1968-70; exec. dir. Young Rep. Fedn. Va., 1968-69. Trustee Del. Law Sch. Served with AUS, 1953-56. Mem. Am., D.C. (asst. editor jour. 1971-73, editor D.C. Bar Report 1973—), Fed. bar assns., Am. Judicature Assn., Phi Delta Phi. Contbr. articles to profl. jours. Editor: D.C. Young Lawyer, 1968-69. Home: 1804 N Quinn St Arlington VA 22209 Office: 1750 N St NW Washington DC 20036

CRUZAN, CHARLES GRANT, physicist; b. Cushing, Okla., Feb. 23, 1912; s. Ulysses Grant and Mamie Amanda (Montgomery) C.; B.S., Okla. State U., 1934, M.S., 1938; m. Leonore Scott, May 25, 1937; children—Carlyn G., Marletta (Mrs. Raymond Howard Walker), Jo Ann (Mrs. James Charles Smith), Donald C. Asst. mathematician Okla. State U., Stillwater, 1937-38; instr. math. and physics Woodward (Okla.) Jr. Coll., 1938-41; instr. Tech. Schs. USAF, Chanute Field, Ill., 1941-43; with Phillips Petroleum Co., Bartlesville, Okla., 1946—, chief physicist Patent div., 1947—. Pres. McKinley Sch. P.T.A., Bartlesville, 1948-49; mem. adv. com. Washington County, Bartlesville, 1973-74; asst. dist. commr. Boy Scouts Am., Bartlesville, Okla., 1967-69. Del. State Rep. Conv., 1971-72. Served to comdr. USNR, 1943-46. Mem. Am. Phys. Soc., Am. Legion (pres. 1955-56, dir. 1950-58), Pi Mu Epsilon, Kappa Delta Pi. Baptist (pres. mens brotherhood 1963-64). Mason (32 deg.), Lion (pres. 1969-70). Clubs: Hillcrest Country; Frank Phillips Mens (Bartlesville, Okla.). Home: 1950 Dewey Bartlesville OK 74003 Office: 308 A FPB Bartlesville OK 74004

CRYMBLE, ALFRED CARTER, elec. engr.; b. Bristol, Va., Jan. 15, 1897; s. Ellis Kennon and Maud (Carter) C.; student Washington and Lee U., 1914-16, Carnegie Inst. Tech., 1916-17; B.S. in Elec. Engring., Ga. Inst. Tech., 1919; m. Lucy May Boswell, Mar. 14, 1936; children—Lucy Boswell (Mrs. Thomas Emerson Morse), Alfred Carter. With Tenn. Eastman Co., Kingsport, Tenn., 1933-62, spl. projects engr., 1945-47, asst. supt. engring. div., 1947-60; engring. cons., 1960-62; sole practice cons. elec. engring., Kingsport, 1962—. Mem. Tri-City Airport Commn., Kingsport, 1948-67, chmn., 1955-63; chmn. camp com. Girl Scouts U.S., Tri-Cities, 1950-52. Registered profl. engr., Va., N.J., Tenn., Tex. Fellow I.E.E.E.; mem. Am. Soc. M.E. (Pub. Service award Region IV, 1972), Nat., Tenn. (Outstanding Service award 1967) socs. profl. engrs., Nat. Council Engring. Examiners, Tau Beta Pi, Phi Gamma Delta. Presbyn. (elder). Mason, Rotarian. Club: Ridgefield Country (Kingsport). Home: 1348 Linville St Kingsport TN 37660 Office: 135 E New St Kingsport TN 37660

CSAKY, T(IHAMER) Z(OLTAN), med. educator; b. Maramarossziget, Hungary, Aug. 12, 1915; s. Tihamer L.G. and Olga (Rudolf) C.; M.D., U. Budapest, 1939; spl. degree in pub. health and hygiene State Hygienic Inst., Budapest, 1942; m. Susan Dischka, June 18, 1953; children—Catharina M., Karl G. Came to U.S., 1949, naturalized, 1954. Instr. physiology U. Budapest (Hungary), 1938-40, asst. prof. physiology, 1940-46; research adj. Hungarian Biol. Research Inst., 1946-47; research fellow biochemistry Inst., Helsinki, Finland, 1947-48; research fellow Microbiology Inst., Uppsala-Ultuna, Sweden, 1948-49; research asso. Duke U. Med. Sch., Durham, N.C., 1949-51; asst. prof. pharmacology U. N.C. Sch. Medicine, Chapel Hill, 1951-55, asso. prof. pharmacology, 1955-61; prof. pharmacology U. Ky. Coll. Medicine, Lexington, 1961—, chmn. dept. pharmacology, 1961—. Vis. prof., USPHS spl. fellow U. Milan (Italy), 1968-69. Guggenheim fellow, 1958-59. Mem. Am. Chem. Soc., Am. Soc. Pharmacology and Exptl. Therapeutics, Soc. Exptl. Biology and Medicine, Am. Physiol. Soc., Soc. Gen. Physiologists, Am. Coll. Clin. Pharmacology and Chemotherapy, Sigma Xi. Home: 1032 The Land Lexington KY 40504

CUBA, BENJAMIN JAMES, lawyer; b. San Antonio, Dec. 12, 1936; s. Ben and Patricia (Machalek) C.; A.A., Temple Jr. Coll., 1957; B.B.A., U. Tex., 1959; J.D., Baylor U., 1963; m. Bernadette Theresa Haney, Sept. 4, 1964; children—Benjamin Courtney, Tristan Konrad. Admitted to Tex. bar, 1964; partner firm Cuba, Johnson & Lagow and predecessor firms, Temple, Tex., 1964—. Dir. Temple Savs. Assn. Mem. Bell, Lampasas and Mills Counties (pres.), Am. Bar assns., State Bar Tex., Tex. Assn. Def. Counsel, Am. Judicature Soc., Temple C. of C., Phi Delta Phi. Home: 3700 Gila St Temple TX 76501 Office: First Nat Bldg Temple TX 76501

CUBA, PATRICK DAVID, savs. assn. exec.; b. Temple, Tex., Mar. 23, 1939; s. Ben and Patricia (Machalek) C.; A.A., Temple Jr. Coll., 1959; B.B.A., U. Tex. at Austin, 1961; postgrad. Baylor U., 1967; m. June Ada McCabe, Sept. 20, 1958; children—Nancy, Sallie, Windy. Asst. v.p. First Fed. Savs. & Loan Assn., Temple, 1961-67; with Temple Savs. Assn., 1968—, pres., 1970—, also dir.; pres., dir. Differential, Inc., Temple, 1973—; dir. So. Republic Corp., Temple. Mem. City Temple Charter Commn., 1972. Home: 3609 Gila St Temple TX 76501 Office: 402 N Main St Temple TX 76501

CUDAHY, WILLIAM BREWER, banker; b. Chgo., Jan. 23, 1912; s. Edward Ignatius and Leonore (Brewer) C.; grad. Middlesex Sch., 1930; B.A. magna cum laude, Harvard, 1934; J.D., Northwestern U., 1937; m. Evelyn Wilkinson, Apr. 5, 1951; children—Joseph Michael, Victoria Fenton. Sec., dir. Callaghan & Co., Chgo., 1937-41; asst. sec. No. Trust Co., Chgo., 1945-51; v.p. Am. Nat. Bank & Trust Co., Chgo., 1951-60; sr. v.p., dir. 1st Nat. Bank in Palm Beach (Fla.), 1960—; dir. Sterling Precision Corp., West Palm Beach. Served as lt. USCG, 1941-45; ETO, PTO. Mem. Nat. Fedn. Financial Analysts. Republican. Episcopalian. Clubs: Everglades (dir., sec., treas.), Bath and Tennis (dir.) (Palm Beach). Home: 742 Slope Trail Palm Beach FL 33480

CUDDINGTON, RUTH A., sch. adminstr.; b. Hickory, N.C., May 27, 1910; d. Donald E. and Elizabeth (Clark) Abee; A.B., U. S.C., 1943, M.A., 1945; postgrad. Lenoir Rhyne Coll., Radford Coll.; m. William Franklin Cuddington, Jr., Aug. 29, 1932; children—William Franklin III, Betty (Mrs. Richard O. Newman), David Abee. Tchr., Wagner (S.C.) Centralized High Sch., 1943-45, Hickory High Sch., 1944-45; prin. Cloverdale Elementary Sch., Botetourt County, Va., 1946-54; tchr. Lee Jr. High Sch., Roanoke, 1954-55; prin. Belmont Elementary Sch., Roanoke, 1955-69, Monterey Elementary Sch., Roanoke, 1969-72. Active YWCA, 1955-70. Bd. dirs. Crippled Children's Soc., Mental Hygiene Assn., Cerebral Palsy Assn., Roanoke Council Christians and Jews. Named Woman of Year, Roanoke, 1959. Mem. Nat. (state pres., nat. bd. mem., nat. rec. sec.), Va., councils adminstrv. women in edn., Va., Roanoke City, Botetourt County (v.p.) edn. assns. Nat., Va., Roanoke depts. elementary sch. prins, N.E.A., Am. Assn. U. Women, Internat. Platform Assn., Smithsonian Assos. Home: 233 Christian Av NE Roanoke VA 24102

CUDDY, DAVID BRUCE, poultry co. exec.; b. London, Ont., Can., Dec. 17, 1946; s. Alfred MacInroy and Dilys (Scott) C.; B.S. in Agrl. Econs., U. Guelph (Can.), 1970; m. Sally Ann Peever, July 17, 1970. Came to U.S., 1970. Vice pres. Cuddy Farms Inc., Marshville, N.C., 1970—, also dir.; dir. Cuddy Farms Ltd., Strathroy, Ont. Mem. N.C. Poultry Fedn. (dir.), Nat., N.C. (pres.) turkey fedns. Office: PO Box 247 Marshville NC 28103

CUEVAS, JOSE LUIS, artist; b. Mexico City, Mexico, Feb. 26, 1933; student Nat. Sch. Painting and Sculpture, Mexico City. One man shows Mexico City, 1947, Pan-Am. Union, Washington, 1954, Galerie Edouard Loeb, Paris, France, 1955, Havana, Cuba, 1956, N.Y.C., 1957, 60, Caracas, Venezuela, 1958, Buenos Aires, Argentina, 1959, Sao Paulo, Brazil, 1959; represented in permanent collection Museum Modern Art, others; prof. art Universidad Iberoamericana, Mexico City, 1956—; vis. prof. Phila. Museum Art Sch., 1957. Illustrator The Worlds of Kafka and Cuevas, 1959; Poems (W. McLeod Rivera), 1960. Contbr. to newspapers, mags. Address: 1766 Lanier Pl NW Washington DC also 1028 Calle del Valle Providencia Mexico DF Mexico

CULBERTSON, GEORGE EDWARD, ednl. adminstr.; b. Cranes Nest, Va., Oct. 23, 1937; s. Fred and Anna (Johnson) C.; student Emory and Henry Coll., 1955-56, Clinch Valley Coll., 1956-57; B.S., Va. Poly. Inst., 1959, M.S., 1962, Ph.D. (NDEA fellow), 1970; m. Nancy Gayle Bise, June 7, 1959; children—Jeffrey Brian, Deidre Ann, James Edward. Asst. prof. U.S. Naval Acad., Annapolis, Md., 1964-70; asso. prof. dept. math. Clinch Valley Coll. of U. Va., Wise, 1970—, asso. dean coll., 1972—. Dir. Systech Corp., Severna Park, Md.; cons. IIT Research Inst., Annapolis, 1966-69. Mem. Norton (Va.) Planning Commn., 1971—. Naval Acad. Research Council grantee, 1970—. Mem. Alumni Assn. Clinch Valley Coll. U. Va. (dir.), Sigma Xi, Pi Mu Epsilon, Sigma Zeta. Home: 825 Ridge Av Norton VA 24273 Office: Clinch Valley Coll Wise VA 24293

CULBRETH, RAYWARD BILL, clergyman; b. Columbia, Ala., Dec. 17, 1921; s. Jesse A. and Ettie (Webb) C.; A.B., Howard Coll., 1944; B.D., So. Bapt. Theol. Sem., 1947, Th.M., 1948, Th.D., 1951; m. Ella Florine Eaton, June 3, 1943; children—Karen F., Randall E. Ordained to ministry Baptist Ch., 1942; pastor, Choccolocco, Ala., 1942-44, New Haven, Ky., 1945-47, Clermont, Ky., 1947-49, First Bapt. Ch., Miami, Fla., 1949-58, Miami Springs (Fla.) Bapt. Ch., 1958-61, Met. Bapt. Ch., Washington, 1961-66, Huffman Bapt. Ch., Birmingham, 1966-72, First Bapt. Ch., South Miami, 1972—. Moderator Miami (Fla.) Bapt. Assn., 1957; mem. Christian life commn. So. Bapt. Conv., 1958-61, mem. Sunday Sch. Bd., 1962-66; pres. D.C. Pastor's Conf., 1966; mem. Ala. Bd. Missions, 1967-72; mem. exec. bd., chmn. evangelism com. Birmingham Bapt. Assn., 1968; chmn. Evangelism com. Miami Bapt. Assn., 1973-74. Chmn. bd. Cook Springs Home for Sr. Citizens 1968-72. Recipient Freedoms Found. Valley Forge Freedom award, 1962. Address: 6767 Sunset Dr Miami FL 33143

CULLINAN, GERALD, assn. exec.; b. San Francisco, Jan. 6, 1916; s. Eustace and Katherine (Lawler) C.; B.A., Oxford U. (Eng.), 1937, M.A., 1957; m. Barbara Lynch, Jan. 2, 1943; children—Mary Patricia, Thomas. Reporter, editor San Francisco Call-Bull., 1938-43; partner Mooney & Cullinan, Dallas, 1946-53; asst. to postmaster gen., Washington, 1953-58; asst. to pres. Nat. Assn. Letter Carriers, Washington, 1959—. Mem. Inst. on Fgn. Relations (chmn. Friends Service com. 1950). Roman Catholic. Clubs: Serra Internat., National Press (Washington); Kenwood Country (Chevy Chase, Md.). Author: 4000 Years in San Antonio, 1949; A Financial Policy for the U.S. Post Office, 1955; The Post Office Department, 1967; The U.S. Postal Service, 1973. Home: 6205 Nebraska Av Washington DC 20015 Office: 100 Indiana Av Washington DC 20001

CULLINS, JOHN GRAYDON, physician; b. Junction City, Ark., Dec. 11, 1893; s. John Robert and Mary Elizabeth (Gardner) C.; Ph.B., Little Rock Coll., 1930; M.D., U. Ark., 1917; m. Alma B. Conrad, Aug. 9, 1918. Asst. attending surgeon USPHS, Little Rock, San Antonio, Ft. Worth, 1918-19, U.S. Pellagra Hosp., Spartanburg, S.C., 1919-20; neuropsychiatrist VA Hosp., Lake City, Fla., 1920-21, North Little Rock, Ark., 1921; neuropsychiatrist, roentgenologist VA Hosp., Bronx, N.Y., 1922-28, Northport, N.Y., 1928-31; clin. dir. VA Hosp., North Chicago, Ill., 1931-37, Marion, Ind., 1937-39; mgr. VA Hosp., Am. Lake, Washington, 1939-45, Knoxville, Ia., 1945-47 chief neuropsychiat. service VA Hosp., Wadsworth, Kan., 1947-61; with Benton unit State Hosp., Ark., 1961-63. Served as col. M.C., AUS, 1942-47. Diplomate Am. Bd. Psychiatry and Neurology. Fellow A.M.A., Am. Psychiat. Assn.; mem. Union County Med. Soc., Ark. Med. Soc., Radiol. Soc N.A., Assn. Mil. Surgeons of U.S., Heroes of '76, Nat. Sojourners, Chi Zeta Chi, Phi Rho Sigma. Mason. Contbr. articles med. jours. Address: 1412 S Taylor St Little Rock AR 72204

CULP, DELOS POE, univ. pres.; b. Clanton, Ala. July 26, 1911; s. Joseph Daniel and Lela (Popwell) C.; student Jacksonville State Coll., 1932-34; B.S., Auburn U., 1937, M.S., 1940; Ed.D., Columbia, 1949; m. Martha Edwardine Street, Dec. 23, 1934; children—Martha Jean, James David, John Stephen. Tchr., prin. Chilton, Butler counties, Ala., 1935-42; supt. Chilton County Schs., Ala., 1942-46; supr. pub. sch. trans., asst. dir. div. adminstrn. and finance State Dept. Edn., Montgomery, Ala., 1946-51; prof. edn. Ala. Polytech. Inst., 1951-54; pres. Livingston State Coll., 1954-63; pres. Ala. Coll., Montevallo, 1963-67; pres. E. Tenn. State U., Johnson City, 1967—. Dir. First Peoples Bank. Mem. com. on studies Am. Assn. State Colls. and Univs., 1970—. Chmn. Nat. Commn. on Safety Edn., 1965—; mem. survey team for Philippine Sch. Bur. Survey, 1959-60; mem. bd. advisers Meth. Children's Home, Selma, Ala.; mem. nat. com. on exploring Boy Scouts Am., 1971—. Mem. Ala. Edn. Commn. (exec. dir. 1957-59), Ala. Edn. Assn. (chmn. policies commn. 1965—), Am. Assn. U. Profs., Ala. Acad. Sci., Am. Assn. Sch. Adminstrs., Ala. Hist. Assn., Kappa Delta Pi, Kappa Phi Kappa, Phi Delta Kappa, Phi Kappa Phi. Democrat. Methodist. Rotarian. Home: Pres's Home East Tenn State University Johnson City TN 37601

CULP, MARTHA EDWARDINE STREET (MRS. DELOS POE CULP), educator, civic worker; b. Gadsden, Ala., Nov. 4, 1915; d. Alonzo Cranford and Mattie (Miller) Street; student Jacksonville State Coll., 1932-34; B.S., Auburn U., 1940; postgrad. Columbia, 1948, Birmingham Mus.; m. Delos Poe Culp, Dec. 23, 1934; children—Martha Jean (Mrs. William McIver Flanigan), James David, John Stephen. Tchr, elementary grades, Ala. Schs., 1934-42; sec. to sch. supt. Chilton County, Ala., 1942-45; tchr. pub. kindergarten Tappan, N.Y., 1948-49; tchr. Marbury, Ala., 1950-51, Auburn, Ala., 1952-53; coll. registrar Livingston State Coll., 1957-63. Chmn., Easter Seal Soc. for Crippled Children and Adults. Pres.'s rep. to bd. Carroll Reece Mus. Soc.; mem. bd. United Fund, Johnson City Symphony Orch., Vol. chpt. Easter Seal E. Tenn. Area. Mem. D.A.R. (vice regent), U.D.C. (v.p.), Nat. League Am. Pen Women, Am. Hemerocallis Soc., Tenn. Women's Press and Authors, Johnson City Area C. of C. (v.p. Women's div., Outstanding Mem. award 1973), Watauga Valley Art League (charter), Delta Kappa Gamma, Kappa Delta Pi. Clubs: Johnson City Garden; Faculty Women's (past pres.); Monday; Music. Contbr. articles newspapers, mags. Home: Shelbridge East Tenn State University Johnson City TN 37601

CULP, WILLIAM WALLACE, JR., clergyman; b. Union, S.C., Jan. 16, 1935; s. William Wallace and Frances Walton (Greer) C.; A.B., Wofford Coll., 1957; B.D., Emory U., 1960; m. Mildred Hembree, Aug. 20, 1960; children—William Wallace III, David Edward, Timothy Eugene, Stephen Hembree. Ordained to ministry Methodist Ch., 1959; minister Liberty Ch., Spartanburg, S.C., 1956-57; asso. minister Avondale (Ga.) Meth. Ch., 1958, Cherokee Place Methodist Ch., Charleston, S.C., summer 1958; minister Chicopee Ch., Walhalla, S.C., 1959-63, Calhoun Falls (S.C.) Meth. Ch., 1963-67, Mathews Ch., Greenwood, S.C., 1967-71, First Meth. Ch., Clover, S.C., 1971—. Dean area tng. schs. Meth. Ch., 1966-71. Pres. Asheville County Mental Health Assn., 1966-68. State bd. dirs. S.C. Mental Health Assn., 1966-70. Named Minister of Yr. in Anderson Dist., S.C. Meth. Ch., 1965. Mem. Blue Key, Pi Kappa Alpha. Lion (dir. 1965-67), Optimist (Clover). Address: Box 225 Clover SC 29710

CULPEPPER, FRED CARROLL, JR., engring. and constrn. co. exec.; b. Monroe, La., Nov. 16, 1918; s. Fred Carroll and Elizabeth (Schulze) C.; B.C.E., Va. Mil. Inst., 1940; m. Mary Frances Moore, June 3, 1941; children—Fred Carroll III, Carol (Mrs. J. Wayne Smith), Dorothy (Mrs. John Schween), Patricia. Project mgr. Ford, Bacon & Davis, 1941-63, mgr. bus. devel., 1963-69, exec. v.p., resident mgr., Monroe, La., 1970—, dir., 1963—; pres. Sealants Internat. Inc.; dir. Ouachita Nat. Bank, Monroe, La. Mem. council Small Bus. Adminstrn. for La., 1969-70; mem. La.-Miss. Regional Export Council Dept. Commerce, 1969-70; mem. exec. com. Jr. Achievement of Monroe, La., 1970—. Served with AUS, 1941-45. Decorated Bronze Star medal with one oak leaf cluster; Purple Heart medal with one oak leaf cluster. Mem. Nat. Soc. Profl. Engrs., La. Engring. Soc. (dir. 1970), Am. Soc. C.E. (mem. exec. com. 1970-71), Nat. Constructors Assn. Clubs: N.Y. Athletic, Harbor View, Bayou de Siard Country. Home: 3506 Loop Rd Monroe LA 71201 Office: PO Box 1762 Monroe LA 71201

CUMBIE, CALVIN ARTIMUS, univ. adminstr.; b. Athens, Tex., July 19, 1922; s. Artimus and Rubie (Richardson) C.; B.A., North Tex. State U., 1943, M.A., 1948; B.S., Tex. Christian U., 1953, M.Ed., 1951. Tchr., San Marcos Mil. Acad., 1946-47; instr. Tex. Mil. Coll., 1947-49; asst. registrar Tex. Christian U., 1949-54, registrar, 1954—. Served to col. AUS, 1942; now active Res. Mem. Assn. U.S. Army, Res. Officers Assn., Am. (pres. 1972-73), Tex. pres. 1962-63), So. (pres. 1968-69) assns. collegiate registrars and admissions officers. North Tex. State U., Tex. Christian U. (sec. 1962-63) ex-student assns., Phi Delta Kappa, Alpha Phi Omega, Pi Omega Pi, Alpha Sigma Lambda. Baptist. Rotarian. Home: 3141 Cockrell Av Fort Worth TX 76109 Office: Sadler Hall Tex Christian U Fort Worth TX 76129

CUMBO, HAROLD WALLACE, govt. ofcl.; b. Philomath, Ore., Apr. 1, 1920; s. George Wallace and Jennie T. (Hockema) C.; B.A., Walla Walla Coll., 1944; postgrad. Andrews U., 1944-45; m. Dorothy Catherine Blasko, June 17, 1951; children—Sharon Lael, Cathy Uel. With Library of Congress, Washington, 1945—, reference asst., 1945-51, head spl. study facilities, 1951-62, librarian spl. collections, 1962-67, editor Nat. Register Microform Masters, 1967—; stock broker Financial Planning Co., Hyattsville, Md., 1961-66. Mem. Nat. Microfilm Assn., D.C. library Assn. Home: 8402 11th Av Silver Spring MD 20903 Office: Library of Congress Washington DC 20540

CUMFER, DONALD ALONZO, JR., paper co. exec.; b. Oak Park, Ill., Jan. 31, 1924; s. Donald Alonzo and Ruth (Shannon) C.; B.E., Vanderbilt U., 1949; m. Winifred Eugenia Johnson, Oct. 2, 1925; children—Cynthia Dee, Neil Shannon, Shawn Johnson, Eric Michael. Mgr. Dura-Containers, Inc., Clarksville, Tenn., 1961-65; product planning and devel. mgr. Mead Packaging Co., Atlanta, 1965-68; v.p. Hamilton Mfg. Co., Richmond, Va., 1968—. Chmn., Ashland Christian Emergency Service, 1969—; chmn. Hanover County FISH, 1971—; chmn. Ashland Planning Commn., 1973. Served with USAAF, 1942-46. Decorated D.F.C., Air medal with 1 oak leaf cluster. Mem. T.A.P.P.I., Am. Soc. for Testing and Materials. Presbyn. (elder). Mason. Home: 301 College Av Ashland VA 23005 Office: 7400 Ranco Rd Richmond VA 23228

CUMMING, HUGH SMITH, JR., former govt. ofcl.; b. Richmond, Va., Mar. 10, 1900; s. Hugh Smith and Lucy A. (Booth) C.; student Va. Mil. Inst., Lexington, Va., 1917-20, U. Va., 1920-24; m. Winifred Burney West, Sept. 21, 1935. Mem. Va. bar; banker, London, Bombay, Singapore, Peking, 1924-27; tech. advisor U.S. State Dept., 1928; asst. to U.S. delegation Internat. Econ. Conf., London, and 7th Pan-Am. Conf., Montevideo, 1933; exec. asst. to Sec. of State, 1934, detailed to U.S. Consulate, Geneva, in connection Italo-Ethiopian affairs, 1935-36; spl. mission to Scandinavia and Netherlands, 1939; mem. exec. com. U.S Antartic Service, 1939-41; spl. mission Greenland, 1941; mem. Econ. Warfare Mission, also U.S. del. Internat. Whaling Conf., London, 1943; spl. mission to Sweden, 1943; rep. State Dept. on Anglo-Swedish-Am. Commn., and chief div. No. European Affairs, 1944; polit. liaison officer U.S. delegation UN Conf. on Internat. Orgn., San Francisco, 1945; spl. mission Iceland, 1946; counselor of Embassy, Stockholm, 1947-50; counselor of Embassy with personal rank of minister, Moscow, 1950-52; dep. sec. gen. for polit. affairs NATO, Paris, 1952-53; ambassador to Indonesia, 1953-57; spl. asst. to sec. of state, ir. Intelligence, Dept. of State, 1957-61, cons., 1961-64; mem. bd. examiners Am. Fgn. Service, 1957-62; adv. bd. Fgn. Service Inst., 1957-62; v.p. West-Wilholt Co., Stockton, Cal., 1961-63. Former mem. bd. govs. Columbia Hosp. for Women, Washington. Trustee Washington Inst. Fgn. Affairs, Meridian House Found., Washington, Family and Child Services of Washington; v.p. Overseas Mission Soc., 1963—. Chmn. adv. com. John Foster Dulles Library, Princeton; mem. adv. council Sch. Internat. Service, Am. U.; trustee Washington Cathedral; bd. dirs. Historic Georgetown, Inc.; adv. bd. Woodrow Wilson House Nat. Trust; pres., mem. bd. mgrs. Bath County Community Hosp., Hot Springs, Va. Served as 2d lt. U.S. Army, 1918. Mem. U. Va. Law Sch. Assn., Mil. Order World Wars, S.A.R., Nat. Cathedral Assn. (trustee, pres. 1962-65, 73—). Diplomatic and Consular Officers Ret. (pres.), Com. 100 for Fed. Capital, Raven Soc., Zeta Psi. Episcopalian (vestryman). Clubs: Metropolitan (past pres.), Cosmos, Alibi (Washington); Chevy Chase (Md.); Royal Swedish Yacht, Sallskopet (Stockholm). Home: 2811 O St NW Washington DC 20007 also Overlook Hot Springs VA 24445 Office: 2811 O St NW Washington DC 20007

CUMMINGS, DONALD LAWRENCE, engr.; b. Boston, Sept. 13, 1922; s. Dennis L. and Hazel (Beaton) C.; student Tufts Coll., 1941-42, Boston Architecture Center, 1946-47; Engrs. degree with honors, Northeastern U., 1951; postgrad. Mass. Inst. Tech., 1952-53; m. Irene B. Budrick, Mar. 11, 1945; children—Pamela Gail, Cynthia, Valerie. Draftsman, John P. Heffernan, architect, 1939-40, Stone & Webster, 1940-41; architect, project engr., dir. constrn., dir. estimating dept. Metcalf & Eddy, Boston, 1946-63; asst. project engr., mgr. engring. Reston Va., Inc., 1963-66; v.p. planning, engr. Gulf Reston, Inc., 1966-72; v.p. planning, engr. Gulf Oil Real Estate Devel. Co., 1972—. Mem. bd. elevator appeals Commonwealth of Mass., 1961-71; mem. com. reviewing and revising zoning ordinance County of Fairfax, Va., 1970-74. Served as naval aviator USNR, 1942-46. Registered profl. engr., Mass., Conn., N.Y., Va. Mem. Boston Soc. Civil Engrs., Am. Soc. C.E., Nat. Soc. Profl. Engrs. Contbr. numerous papers on land devel., erosion and sedimentation control, New Town devel., related fields. Home: 3700 Whispering Lane Falls Church VA 22041 Office: Reston VA

CUMMINGS, HATCH WHITFIELD, JR., physician; b. Hearne, Tex., Dec. 6, 1903; s. Hatch Whitfield and Pauline (Eckerle) C.; student U. Tex., 1921-24; M.D., Tulane U., 1928; m. Olivette Wise Nunn, June 22, 1935; stepchildren—Huberta Read Nunn (Mrs. Vernon Gerald Wright), Robert Read Nunn. Intern Grad. Hosps., U. Pa., 1928-29; preceptorship Dr. Marvin L. Graves, emeritus prof. U. Tex., Houston, 1929-33; practice medicine, specializing in internal medicine, Houston, 1933—; chief medical service Meth. Hosp., 1946-70; prof. clin. medicine Baylor U. Coll. Medicine, 1946—. Served to capt. M.C., USNR, 1942-46. Fellow A.C.P. (gov. Tex. 1963-69); mem. Tex. Acad. Medicine (past pres.), Tex. Club Internal Medicine (past pres.), Alpha Omega Alpha, Phi Gamma Delta, Nu Sigma Nu. Home: 2137 Chilton Rd Houston TX 77019 Office: 6516 Bertner Av Houston TX 77025

CUMMINGS, JILL, lawyer; b. N.Y.C., Dec. 1, 1936; A.B., Vassar Coll., 1958; student Am. U., Columbia; J.D., George Washington U., 1970. Admitted to D.C. bar, 1970; now resident asso. firm Cadwalader, Wickersham & Taft, Washington. Mem. Bar Assn. D.C. Address: Cadwalader Wickersham & Taft 1000 Connecticut Av NW Washington DC 20036

CUMMINGS, JOHN MATHEWS, utility co. exec.; b. Waseca, Minn., July 17, 1928; s. Raymond Henry and Isabelle (Mathews) C.; B.S., Tex. A. and M. U., 1950; m. Linda Leiper, May 27, 1950; children—Carol (Mrs. James E. Hunt), Bruce, Paul. Engr., Lone Star Gas Co., Dallas, 1950-61, div. indsl. engr., 1961-67, dir. data processing dept., 1967-73, dir. bldg. mgmt. dept., 1973—. Registered profl. engr., Tex. Mem. Am. Soc. C.E., Tex. Soc. Profl. Engrs. Home: 4232 Hallmark St Dallas TX 75229 Office: 301 S Harwood St Dallas TX 75201

CUMMINGS, WILLIAM BRUCE, lawyer; b. Bronxville, N.Y., Apr. 26, 1939; s. Frederick Otis and Ethel (Malm) C.; B.A. in Econs., Randolph-Macon Coll., 1961; LL.B., U. Va., 1964; m. Dianne Abbott, Jan. 29, 1964; children—Kimberly, Colette. Admitted to Va. bar, 1964; since practiced in Fairfax; mem. firm Tolbert, Lewis & Fitzgerald, Ltd., Arlington and Fairfax, Va., 1964-74; partner Lewis, Wilson, Cowles, Cummings & Lewis, Ltd., Arlington and Fairfax, Mem. exec. com. alumni bd. Randolph-Macon Coll., Ashland, Va., 1970—; vice chmn. bd. mgmt. Arlington YMCA, 1972-74. Mem. Am., Arlington County (sec.), Fairfax County, Va. bar assns., Am., Va. trial lawyers assns., Alexandria Jr. C. of C. Home: 211 Courthouse Circle Vienna VA 22180 Office: 4085 Chain Bridge Rd PO Box 321 Fairfax VA 22030

CUMMINS, LIGHT TOWNSEND, dentist; b. San Antonio, Feb. 15, 1916; s. Light Townsend and Alta Amanda (Crook) C.; B.B.A., U. Tex., 1937; D.D.S., Baylor U., 1944; m. Agnes Roberta Kelley, June 24, 1945; children—Light Townsend III, Bobbe K., Mannti C. Pvt. dental practice, San Antonio, 1947—; chmn. bd. dirs. L.T. Cummins, D.D.S., Inc.; bd. dirs. E.H. Ramsey D.D.S., Inc. Mem. exec. council Alamo council Boy Scouts Am., 1948-49, 55-56; chmn. U.S. Selective Service Bd. 146, 1966—. Served to capt. AUS, 1944-47. Mem. Am., Tex. (exhibit chmn. 1952, 55, 59) dental assns., San Antonio Dental Soc. (pres. 1957-58, dir. 1953-60), Southwest Soc. Dental Medicine (dir. 1956-61), Order of Good Fellow Tex. Dental Assn., Southwestern and Tex. Cattle Raisers Assn., Alumni Assn. Tex. Mil. Inst. (pres. 1962-63), Psi Omega, Alpha Tau Omega. Episcopalian (vestryman). Home: 120 Tuxedo St San Antonio TX 78209 Office: 3830 McCullough San Antonio TX 78209

CUMMISKEY, CHARLES JOSEPH, educator; b. St. Louis, Feb. 12, 1924; s. Charles Joseph and Sarah (Hickey) C.; B.S. in Edn., U. Dayton, 1943; M.S. in Secondary Sci., Northwestern U., 1952; Ph.D. in Inorganic Chemistry, U. Notre Dame, 1956. Tchr. pvt. schs., Detroit, 1942-44, St. Louis, 1944-52, St. Boniface, Man., Can., 1946-47; mem. faculty dept. chemistry St. Mary's U., San Antonio, 1955—, asso. prof., 1960-65, prof., 1965—, chmn. dept., 1957-66, v.p., dean faculties, 1966—. Vis. scientist for secondary schs. Am. Chem. Soc., 1962-65. Robert A. Welch Found. grantee, 1962—. Mem. Am. Chem. Soc. (past pres. San Antonio sect.), Albertus Magnus Guild, Tex. acad. Sci., Sigma Xi. Home and office: 2700 Cincinnati Av San Antonio TX 78284

CUNNINGHAM, CALVIN, JR., govt. ofcl.; b. Memphis, Dec. 19, 1940; s. Calvin and Lovie Pearl (Henderson) C.; B.A. in Social Sci. and Sociology, LeMoyne Coll., 1966; M.A. in Edn., Memphis State U., 1971; m. Lillie Mae Redmond, June 30, 1962; children—Roderic, Calvetta, Utica, Craig. Mgmt. trainee Phillips Petroleum Co., 1966-67; probation counselor Tenn. Dept. Corrections, 1967-68; attendance tchr. Memphis Bd. Edn., 1968-72, acting adminstrv. aid, 1972; probation officer U.S. Cts., Memphis, 1972—. Pres. Longview Heights Civic Club, 1972-73; sponsor local Boy Scouts Am.; swimming instr. Memphis chpt. A.R.C., 1969—. Mem. Memphis Edn. Assn., Fed. Probation Assn., Phi Delta Kappa. Home: 853 E Dempster Av Memphis TN 38106 Office: 167 N Main St Memphis TN 38103

CUNNINGHAM, E. BRICE, lawyer; b. Buffalo, Tex., Feb. 17, 1931; s. Hattie and Tessie (Roblow) C.; B.A., Howard U., 1960, LL.B., 1960; m. Rosie Nell Portis, Mar. 6, 1964; children—Ledner Vernard, Michele Denise, Elana Brice. Admitted to Tex. bar, 1960, U.S. Dist. Ct., 1962, U.S. Ct. Appeals, 1966, U.S. Supreme Ct. bar, 1972; asso. counsel W.J. Durham, Dallas, 1960-64; mem. firm Finch, Lockridge & Cunningham, Dallas, 1964-68; individual practice, Dallas, 1968—. Municipal judge City of Dallas, 1971-72; mem. Dallas City Plan Commn., 1973—; vice chmn. Park South br. YMCA, Dallas, 1969—, chmn., 1970—. Bd. dirs. Children's Aid Soc. Served with AUS, 1948-54. Mem. State Bar Tex., Dallas Bar Assn. Mason. Club: Idlewild (Dallas). Home: 2210 Van Cleave Dallas TX 75216 Office: 2606 Forest Av Suite 202 Dallas TX 75215

CUNNINGHAM, EMORY O., publisher; b. Kansas, Ala., Mar. 17, 1921; s. Emory O. and Belle (Kelly) C.; B.S. in Agrl. Sci., Auburn U., 1948; m. Jeanne Loftis, Dec. 21, 1951; children—James Emory, David Lee, Sara Jeanne, Mary Lou. Advt. dir. Progressive Farmer and Southern Living, 1966-67, pub., 1967—; pres. Progressive Farmer Co., 1968—; dir. Birmingham Trust Nat. Bank. Bd. dirs. Audit Bur. Circulation, Ala. Heart Assn., Salvation Army; exec. bd. Birmingham Area council Boy Scouts Am. Bd. govs. Internat. Ins. Seminar, Inc. Named Man of Year, Birmingham Advt. Club, 1971, Hall of Fame award Miss. Gulf Coast Jr. Coll., 1973. Mem. Agrl. Pubs. Assn. (pres., dir.), Mag. Pubs. Assn. (dir.), Birmingham Area C. of C. (dir.). Home: 1605 Gentilly Dr Birmingham AL 35226 Office: 820 Shades Creek Pkwy Birmingham AL 35209

CUNNINGHAM, FAYE GABBERT, religious assn. ofcl.; b. Oakland, Miss., May 29, 1928; d. Elmer and Ruby (Cobb) Gabbert; student Bus. Coll. Jackson, Miss., 1946, Am. Inst. Banking Los Angeles, 1953-56; m. Fred Harold Cunningham, Apr. 11, 1970. With Koppers Co., Inc., Grenada, Miss., 1946-48, atty. Leon Provine, Grenda, 1948; sec., bookkeeper, licensed saleslady Life Ins. Co. Ga., Grenada, 1948-50; accounting clk. Anderson Tully Co., Memphis, 1950-51; in bank operations Bank Am., Hawthorn, Cal., 1952-57; teller Union Planters Bank, Memphis, 1958; accounting clk. Allens Chevrolet Co., Grenada, 1958-60; treas. No. Miss. United Meth. Conf. (merger Black Upper Miss. Conf.), Grenada, 1960—. Mem. Southeastern Jurisdictional Conf. Secs., Treasurers, Statisticians and World Service Chmn. (sec.-treas. 1967-72, sec. treas.'s sect. 1972—). Home: 260 Katherine Dr Grenada MS 38901 Office: 111 3d St Grenada MS 38901

CUNNINGHAM, FLOYD WADE, lawyer; b. Marietta, Miss., Feb. 23, 1905; s. James Andy and Carolyn Nancy (Floyd) C.; student Millsaps Coll., 1921-24; LL.B., U. Miss., 1928; m. Ouida Marie. Admitted to Miss. bar, 1928; pros. atty. Prentiss County, Miss., 1932-36; dist. atty. First Jud. Dist. Miss., 1936-44; mem. firm Cunningham & Smith, Booneville, Miss., 1945—; prosecutor Internat. Prosecution sect. in trial of Tojo, et al, before Internat. Mil. Tribunal for the Far East, Tokyo, Japan, 1947-48. Served as capt. USAAF, 1942-45. Mem. Internat. Soc. Barristers, Am., Miss., 1st Circuit Ct. Dist. (pres. 1965-66) bar assns., Am. Judicature Soc., V.F.W. (past State dept. adviser, past dist. comdr.) Am. Legion (past comdr. local post, past dist. comdr.), 40 and 8 (past grande advocate, Miss.), Miss. Assn. Hosp. Governing Bds., Kappa Sigma, Sigma Upsilon. Methodist. Mason (32 deg., Shriner), Elk, Rotarian. Home: PO Box 168 Booneville MS 38829

CUNNINGHAM, JACQUELYN MARIE, librarian; b. Glouster, O., Aug. 16, 1926; d. Raymond Linscott and Wilhelmine (Grothaus) Cunningham; B.A., Westhampton Coll., U. Richmond, 1949; M.A., George Peabody Coll. Tchrs., 1958. Tchr., Garden High Sch., Oakwood, Va., 1949-51; librarian, Powhatan (Va.) High Sch., 1951-55, Waterloo (Md.) Jr. High Sch., 1955-56; asst. librarian Norview Jr. High Sch., Norfolk, Va., 1956-58; children's librarian Belmont br. Richmond (Va.) Pub. Library, 1958-60; asst. librarian Tuckahoe Jr. High Sch., Richmond, 1960-62; librarian Henrico High Sch., Richmond, 1962—; mem. adj. faculty Va. Commonwealth U., 1969-73. Mem. N.E.A., Va., Henrico edn. assns., A.L.A., Va. Library Assn. (chmn. sch. libraries sect. 1964-65), Am. Assn. U. Women, Children's Book Council Richmond, Wesleyan Service Guild (local pres. 1963-65, Richmond dist. sec. 1965-68, chmn. Ashland dist. 1972-73), Bus. and Profl. Women's Clubs (1st v.p. 1972-74, pres. 1974—). Methodist (v.p. dist. women's group 1974—). Home: 4902 Laurie Lane Richmond VA 23223 Office: 302 Azalea Av Richmond VA 23227

CUNNINGHAM, JAMES ALLEN, supt. schs.; b. Shamrock, Tex., July 1, 1927; s. Thomas Riley and Cordelia Lillian (Glazner) C.; B.S., Tex. Technol. U., 1950, M.Ed., 1959, postgrad., 1963—; m. Ethyl Faye Neeley, June 2, 1951; children—Allen Ray (dec.), Mark Thomas. Tchr., Whiteface (Tex.) Ind. Sch. Dist., 1951-62, coach, 1951-62, adminstr., 1962-68; supt. Spearman (Tex.) Ind. Sch. Dist., 1968—. Chmn. Hansford County unit A.R.C., 1969—; mem. Hansford County Library Bd. Served with AUS, 1945-47. Mem. Tex. Assn. Sch. Adminstrs. (chmn. adminstrs. sect. dist. 16 1970-71), Nat. Assn. Sch. Adminstrs., Tex. State Tchrs. Assn., N.E.A. Home: 1107 Bernice St Spearman TX 79081

CUNNINGHAM, JOHN ROOD, JR., sch. adminstr.; b. Gainesville, Fla., Jan. 4, 1925; s. John Rood and Rubie (Ray) C.; student Northwestern U., 1944; B.S., Hampden-Sydney Coll., 1948, Davidson Coll., 1948; M.Ed., U. N.C., 1954; postgrad. Wake Forest U., 1964, Shorter Coll., 1962; m. Gladys Potts, July 23, 1948; children—Margaret Orlyn, John Rood III. Tchr. physics and chemistry Darlington Sch., Rome, Ga., 1948—, chmn. sci. dept., 1960—, dir. admissions, 1967—. Dir. Fla. Salt Springs Corp., 1968—. Served to lt. (j.g.) USNR, 1943-46. NSF grantee, 1964; recipient Distinguished Service award Ga. Assn. Ind. Schs., 1973. Mem. Nat., Ga. assns. sci. tchrs., S.A.R. (pres. Rome chpt. 1969-72), Order of Founders and Patriots of Am., Sons of Confederate Vets., Order of Stars and Bars, Cum Laude Soc., Mil. Order World Wars, St. David's Soc., St. Andrew's Soc., Huguenot Soc., Nat. Soc. Sons and Daus. Pilgrims, Theta Chi, Chi Beta Phi. Presbyn. (elder 1958—, clk. of session 1972—). Club: Coosa Country (Rome). Home: Darlington School Rome GA 30161

CUNNINGHAM, JOSEPH CONRAD, librarian; b. Asheville, N.C., Jan. 10, 1925; s. Cornelius Carman and Bernice Anna (Fry) C.; B.A., U. Ore., 1949; B.S. in L.S., U. Cal. at Berkeley, 1950; m. Nella Mae Steussy, Oct. 20, 1970. Catalogue librarian Fresno (Cal.) State Coll. Library, 1950-51; catalogue librarian Los Angeles State Coll. Library, 1951-54; catalogue librarian U. Tex. Library, Austin, 1954—. Served with AUS, 1943-46; ETO. Mem. Am. Assn. U. Profs. Democrat. Unitarian. Home: 1904 Miles St Austin TX 78745

CUNNINGHAM, RONNIE WALTER, devel. co. exec., former astronaut; b. Creston, Ia., Mar. 16, 1932; s. Walter Wilfred and Gladys Thelma (Backen) C.; B.A., U. Cal. at Los Angeles, 1960, M.A., 1961; m. Lo Ella Irby, July 8, 1956; children—Brian Keith, Kimberly Anne. Research asst. Planning Research Corp., Westwood, Cal., 1959-60; physicist Rand Corp., Santa Monica, Cal., 1960-63; astronaut NASA, Manned Spacecraft Center, Houston, 1963-71, crew mem. Apollo 7, 1968; sr. v.p. operations Century Devel. Corp., Houston, 1971—. Founding dir. Earth Awareness Found. Served with USMC, 1952-56. Recipient Exceptional Service medal NASA, Astronaut Wings, USN; Alumni Profl. Achievement award U. Cal. at Los Angeles, 1969; Spl. Trustees award Nat. Acad. Television Arts and Scis., 1969; co-recipient Haley Astronautics award Am. Inst. Aeros. and Astronautics, 1969. Asso. fellow Am. Inst. Aeros. and Astronautics; mem. Soc. Exptl. Test Pilots, Marine Air Res., Am. Geophys. Union, Sigma Xi, Sigma Pi Sigma. Club: Explorers. Office: 5 Greenway Plaza East Suite 1700 Houston TX 77046

CUPP, HORACE BALLARD, JR., physician; b. Bristol, Va., Nov. 30, 1930; s. Horace B. and Laura (Reece) C.; B.A., U. Tenn., 1951; M.D., Duke, 1955; m. Ann Miller, Dec. 3, 1958; children—Robert Ballard, Laura Ann. Intern Duke Hosp., 1955-56; resident Duke Med. Center, 1958-64; practice medicine specializing in neurosurgery, Johnson City, Tenn., 1964—; mem. staff Johnson City Meml., Carter County Meml., Unicoi County, Johnson County Meml. hosps.; cons. VA Center, Mountain Home, Tenn., 1964—. Served to lt. comdr. USNR, 1956-58. Diplomate Am. Bd. Neurol. Surgery. Mem. A.M.A., Tenn. Med. Assn., Congress Neurol. Surgeons, Assn. Neurol. Surgeons, A.C.S., U.S. Power Squadron (past comdr.), U.S. Coast Guard Aux. Mason, Rotarian. Home: 604 E Holston Av Johnson City TN 37601 Office: 407 Profl Bldg Johnson City TN 37601

CURL, SAMUEL EVERETT, univ. adminstr.; b. Fort Worth, Tex., Dec. 26, 1937; s. Henry Clay and Mary Elva (Watson) C.; student Tarleton State Coll., 1955-57; B.S., Sam Houston State U., 1959; M.S., U. Mo., 1961; Ph.D., Tex. A. and M. U., 1963; m. Betty Doris Savage, June 6, 1957; children—Jane Ellen, Julia Kathleen, Karen Elizabeth. Mem. faculty Tex. Tech. U., Lubbock, 1961—, prof. animal physiology and genetics, asst. dean, asso. dean, interim dean, dir. research Coll. Agrl. Scis., 1968-72, asso. v.p. acad. affairs, 1973—. Cons. beef cattle breeding field. Served as 2d lt. AUS, 1959. Am. Council Edn. fellow, 1972-73. Mem. Am. Soc. Animal Sci., So. Assn. Agrl. Scientists, Profl. Agr. Workers Tex., Sigma Xi, Gamma Sigma Delta, Alpha Zeta. Mem. Christian Ch. (mem. ofcl. bd.). Rotarian. Club: Lubbock Agriculture. Author: (with others) Progress and Change in the Agricultural Industry, 1973. Contbr. profl. jours. Home: 3512 78th Dr Lubbock TX 79423 Office: 104 Adminstrn Bldg Tex Tech U Lubbock TX 79409

CURLESS, LESTER DEVERE, JR., elec. engr.; b. Peoria, Ill., Nov. 9, 1947; s. Lester Devere and Alba (Abreu) C.; A.A., St. Johns River Jr. Coll., 1967; B.S. in Elec. Engring., U. Fla., 1970; m. Carolyn Ann Wilson, July 1, 1972. Elec. engr. avionics equipment design br. Nav. Air Rework Facility, Jacksonville, Fla., 1970—. Mem. I.E.E.E., Profl. Assn. Diving Instrs. Democrat. Baptist. Club: Jacksonville Ping-Pong. Home: Route 2 Box 213-C Green Cove Springs FL 32043 Office: Code 613 NARF/NASJAX Jacksonville FL 32212

CURLIN, JAMES WILLIAM, lawyer; b. Pine Bluff, Ark., Oct. 4, 1932; s. James Alexander and Virginia (Barth) C.; B.S. in Forestry, U. Ark. at Monticello, 1954; M.S. in Forest Soils, La. State U., 1959, Ph.D. in Environmental Sci., 1964; J.D., U. Tenn., 1972; m. Patricia

Ann Stevens, May 15, 1954; children—Kimberly, James. Research scientist TVA, Norris, Tenn., 1959-63; environmental scientist Oak Ridge Nat. Lab., 1964-72; environmental policy specialist Congl. Research Service, Library Congress, Washington, 1972—; admitted to Tenn. bar, 1972, D.C. bar, 1973; since practiced in Washington. Vice mayor City Norris (Tenn.), 1963-64. Served with C.E., AUS, 1955-56; Korea. Mem. Audubon Soc., Ecol. Soc. Am., A.A.A.S., Fed., Am. bar assns., Nat. Lawyers Club, Sigma Xi, Alpha Zeta, Xi Sigma Pi, Phi Alpha Delta. Club: National Lawyers (Washington). Contbr. articles to profl. jours. Home: 2928 28th St NW Washington DC 20008 Office: 1st and Independence Av SE Washington DC 20540

CURRAN, CHARLES EDWARD, educator, clergyman; b. Rochester, N.Y., Mar. 30, 1934; s. John Francis and Gertrude Louise (Beisner) C.; B.A., St. Bernard's Sem. and Coll., 1955; S.T.D., Pontifical Gregorian U., Rome, Italy, 1961; S.T.D., Pontifical Lateran U., Rome, Italy, 1961. Ordained priest Roman Cath. Ch., 1958; prof. moral theology St. Bernard's Sem., Rochester, N.Y., 1961-65; prof. theology Cath. U. Am., Washington, 1965—. Fellow Kennedy Center Bio-ethics, 1972; faculty fellow grantee Am. Assn. Theol. Schs., 1971-72. Mem. Cath. Theol. Soc. Am. (pres. 1969-70), Am. Soc. Christian Ethics (pres. 1971-72), Coll. Theology Soc., Am. Assn. U. Profs. Author: Christian Morality Today, 1966; A New Look at Christian Morality, 1968; Contemporary Problems in Moral Theology, 1970; Catholic Moral Theology in Dialogue, 1972; Crisis in Priestly Ministry, 1972; Politics, Medicine, and Christian Ethics, 1973; (with others) Dissent in and for the Church, 1969, The Responsbility of Dissent: The Church and Academic Freedom, 1969. Editor: Absolutes in Moral Theology, 1968; Contraception: Authority and Dissent, 1969, Shared Responsibility in the Local Church, 1970. Contbr. articles to profl. jours. Address: Caldwell Hall Catholic University Washington DC 20017

CURRAN, HELEN, educator; b. Chgo., Aug. 6, 1916; d. Samuel Audley and Edna (Sandiford) Curran; student Lewis Inst. Tech., 1935-37; B.S., Ill. Inst. Tech., 1946; M.E. in Guidance and Counseling, U. Ill., 1952; postgrad. Internat. Inst. Edn., 1957, U. Me., 1962, U. London, 1963, No. Ill. U., 1964; Advanced certificate in ednl. adminstrn., U. Ill., 1966; m. William Zorn, 1937 (div.); 1 dau., April; m. 2d, J.W. Fenner, May 10, 1972. Tchr. pub. schs., Maywood, Ill., 1946-47, tchr., Fox Lake, Ill., 1947-49, guidance dir., dean girls, 1949-57; dean girls, Peoria Heights, Ill., 1957-59, dir. guidance, 1959-63, adminstrv. asst., dir. curriculum, McHenry (Ill.) Pub. Schs., 1963-66, asst. supt., 1966-71; asst. supt. instrn. Tech. Information Center, Charleston, S.C., 1972—; tchrs. summer sessions The Citadel. Bd. dirs. Orphans of the Storm, Mem. Ill. Assn. Sch. Adminstrs., Ill., Nat. edn. assns., Ill., Nat. assns. women deans and counselors, Nat. Ill. assns. supervision and curriculum, Ill. Sch. Pub. Relations Assn., Am. Legion Aux., Delta Kappa Gamma. Office: Tech Information Center 64 Society St Charleston SC 29401

CURRIE, F.A., judge; b. Vancouver, B.C., Oct. 17, 1907; s. George Graham and Lulu Marion (Angevine) C. (parents Am. citizens); LL.B., U. Fla., 1932, J.D. (hon.), 1967; m. Reese Tumlin Vermilya, Aug. 15, 1958. Admitted to Fla. bar, 1932; practiced in West Palm Beach, Fla., 1932-51; judge Small Claims-Magistrate Ct., Palm Beach County, Fla., 1951-73; judge Palm Beach County Ct., 1973—. Municipal judge, West Palm Beach, Fla., 1943-46; mem. Fla. Childrens Commn., 1949-52. Served with AUS, 1942-43. Mem. Fla., Palm Beach County bar assns., Sigma Chi. Democrat. Episcopalian. Mason, Elk, Kiwanian. Home: 200 Rugby Rd West Palm Beach FL 33405 Office: Palm Beach County Ct House West Palm Beach FL 33401

CURRIE, JOHN STUART, psychologist; b. McBee, S.C., Oct. 6, 1938; s. William Margret and Lona (Cruse) C.; student Mercer U., 1957-59; B.A. Fla. State U., 1961; M.A., U. Fla., 1962, Ph.D., 1965; m. Beverly Jo Unick, Sept. 2, 1962; children—William Kennedy, Donya Lynn. Clin. psychologist Macon-Bibb County Health Dept., 1965-68; pvt. practice psychology, Atlanta, 1968—. Mem. staff Atlanta Psychiat. Clinic; cons. Ga. Depts. Family and Children Services; asst. prof., Mercer U., Macon, Ga., 1966-67, Ga. Inst. Tech., Atlanta, 1968; mem. Collegium Musicum, Emory U., 1968—. Fellow Ga. Psychol. Assn., (treas. 1969-71, gov.'s adv. council psychologists 1972); mem. Am. Acad. Psychotherapists, Assn. Aviation Psychologists (charter), Am. Psychol. Assn., Aeros. Med. Assn., Aircraft Owners and Pilots Assn. (charter), Am. Psychology-Law Soc. Home: 6422 Cherry Tree Lane NE Atlanta GA 30328 Office: 6363 Roswell Rd Atlanta GA 30328

CURRIE, ROYCE ALEXANDER, engr.; b. Anniston, Ala., July 14, 1929; s. Royce Alexander and Cora Lee (Morrison) C.; B.M.E., Auburn U., 1953; m. Martha Ann Hughes, Aug. 22, 1952. Supervisory engr. U.S. Steel Corp., Birmingham, Ala., 1953-65; engring. mgr. Steel City div. Midland-Ross Corp., Athens, Tenn., 1965-68; chief mfg. engr., mfg. engring. mgr. Gabriel div. Maremont Corp., Pulaski, Tenn., 1968—. Served as sgt. U.S. Army, 1946-49. Registered profl. engr., Tenn., Ala. Mem. Am. Soc. M.E., Nat., Tenn. socs. profl. engrs., Soc. Mfg. Engrs. (sr.), Exptl. Aircraft Assn., Giles County C. of C., Pi Tau Sigma, Tau Beta Pi. Methodist. Club: Pulaski Exchange (dir.). Home: Route 6 Pulaski TN 38478 Office: Maremont Corp PO Box 617 Pulaski TN 38478

CURRIER, ROBERT DAVID, physician, educator; b. Grand Rapids, Mich., Feb. 19, 1925; s. Frederick Plummer and Margaret (Hoedemaker) C.; student Carleton Coll., 1942-43; A.B., U. Mich., 1948, M.D., 1952, M.S. in Neurology, 1956; postgrad. Nat. Hosp., U. London (Eng.), 1955, Medico-Social Research Bd. (Dublin, Ireland), 1972; m. Marilyn Jane Johnson, Sept. 1, 1951; children—Mary Margaret, Angela Maria. Intern Univ. Hosp., Ann Arbor, Mich., 1952-53; resident U. Mich. at Ann Arbor, 1953-56, instr., 1956-57, asst. prof., 1957-60, asso. prof., 1960-61; asso. prof. neurology Med. Center, U. Miss., Jackson, 1961-71, prof., 1971—, chief div. neurology, 1961—. Cons. VA Hosp., Ann Arbor, 1957-61, Jackson, Biloxi and Gulfport, all Miss., 1961—. Mem. nat. adv. bd. Epilepsy Found. Am., 1970—; dir. med. adv. bd. Miss. chpt. Multiple Sclerosis Found., 1967—, med. adv. bd. Miss. Council Epilepsy, 1966—. Bd. dirs. Miss. Heart Assn., 1966-68. Served with USAAF, 1943-45; ETO. Decorated Air medal with 2 oak leaf clusters. NIH grantee, 1961-74, others. Fellow Am. Acad. Neurology; mem. Am. Neurol. Assn., Central Soc. Neurol. Research (pres. 1971), Sigma Xi. Author: (with A.F. Haerer) Neurology Notes, 1966. Contbr. articles to profl. jours. Home: 828 Adkins Blvd Jackson MS 39211 Office: 2500 N State St Jackson MS 39216

CURRY, A.F., III, lawyer; b. Tulia, Tex., Apr. 5, 1933; s. Alfred Foy and Rae (Potter) C.; B.A., U. Tex. at Austin, 1955; J.D., Baylor U., 1960; m. Virginia Gayle Glass, Apr. 5, 1958 (div. Jan. 1972); children—Alfred Foy IV, Alison Claire. Admitted to Tex. bar, 1960; since practiced in Fort Worth; partner firm Curry & Curry, Fort Worth, 1963—. Dir. Equities Internat. Life Ins. Co., Fort Worth, Evergreen Salvages & Constrn. Co., Fort Worth. Bd. dirs. Safety Council Fort Worth-Tarrant County, Westside YMCA, Fort Worth; trustee Presbyn. Childrens Home, Itasca, Tex., Fort Worth Cancer Soc. Named Outstanding Young Lawyer Fort Worth-Tarrant County, Fort Worth Jr. Bar Assn., 1969. Mem. State Bar Tex., Fort Worth Jr. (pres.), Fort Worth-Tarrant County (dir.) bar assns., State Jr. Bar Tex. (dir., sec.-treas.), Lambda Chi Alpha, Phi Alpha Delta. Democrat. Presbyn. (chmn. bd. deacons). Mason (Shriner). Clubs: Fort Worth, River Crest Country, Petroleum (Fort Worth). Home: 1333 Roaring Springs Rd Fort Worth TX 76114 Office: 300 Union Bank Bldg Fort Worth TX 76102

CURRY, CHARLES EFFRIDGE, lawyer; b. Mullins, S.C., Apr. 18, 1940; s. Hagood and Laura (Lee) C.; B.S., U. S.C., 1962, LL.B., 1965; m. Virginia Williams, Oct. 16, 1969; children—Susan Lee, Martha Lynn. Admitted to S.C. bar, 1965; asso. mem. firm Marion Kinon, Dillon, S.C., 1966-68, partner firm Kinon & Curry, 1968—; magistrate Dillon County, 1972-73. Dir. Fed. Savs. & Loan Assn., Dillon. City chmn. Dillon chpt. Am. Heart Assn., 1969-70; bus. chmn. Dillon chpt. United Fund drive, 1969-71. Vice chmn. Dillon Democratic Com., 1971. Served with AUS, 1966-67. Recipient Distinguished Service award Dillon Jaycees, 1971. Mem. Dillon County (sec. treas. 1970-71), S.C. bar assns., S.C. State Bar. Baptist. Home: 200 N Roberts St Dillon SC 29536 Office: 105 S 3d Av Box 191 Dillon SC 29536

CURRY, JOHN WILLIAN, food wholesale co. exec.; b. Tampa, Fla., Oct. 18, 1921; s. Allen Benjamin and Vashti (Hewett) C.; B.Bus.Sci., Tampa Coll., 1950; m. Mildred Luella Spindler, May 8, 1942—; children—John Allen, David Christian, Donald William. Instr. accounting Tampa Coll., 1950-51; accountant Winn-Dixie Supermarkets, Tampa, 1951-53, div. controller, Louisville, 1953-61; v.p. Gafford Brokerage Co., Louisville, 1962-63; dir. systems and procedures Stevens Supermarkets, Miami, 1963-64; with Hill Bros., Inc., Miami, 1964—, operations mgr., 1968-70, v.p., sec., 1968—, also dir. Served with USN, 1941-47; PTO. Mem. Phi Theta Pi. Rotarian. Home: 6245 W 10th Av Hialeah FL 33012 Office: 3501 NW 60th St Miami FL 33152

CURRY, LEONARD PRESTON, educator; b. Cave City, Ky., Mar. 23, 1929; s. Daniel Preston and Ruby (Downey) C.; student Campbellsville Coll., 1947-49; B.A., Western Ky. State Coll., 1951; M.A. (Haggin fellow, Colonial Dames Am. scholar), U. Ky., 1956, Ph.D. (So. Fellowships Fund fellow), 1961; m. Mary Campbell Prichard, June 25, 1959; children—Fletcher Preston, Justin Campbell. Instr. history Memphis State U., 1958-60, asst. prof., 1960-62; asst. prof. history U. Louisville, 1962-66, asso. prof., 1966-69, prof., 1969—; vis. asst. prof. history U. Me., Orono, 1964-65; vis. asso. prof. history U. Md., College Park, 1968-69; vis. research asso. Smithsonian Instn., Washington, 1970-71. Mem. adv. com. Ky. Archives and Records Commn., 1972—. Served to 2d lt. USAF, 1951-53. Am. Philos. Soc. research grantee 1962, 72; faculty research grant U. Louisville, 1963, 66, 67, 73. Mem. Am. Hist. Assn., Orgn. Am. Historians, So. Hist. Assn., Phi Alpha Theta, Lambda Chi Alpha. Democrat. Presbyn. Author: Blueprint for Modern America: Nonmilitary Legislation of the First Civil War Congress, 1968; Rail Routes South: Louisville's Fight For the Southern Market, 1865-1872, 1969. Contbr. articles to profl. jours. Home: 1801 Spring Dr Apt N Louisville KY 40205

CURTIN, THOMAS EDWARD, physician; b. Washington, Oct. 27, 1920; s. Edward Gregory and Mary (Deenahan) C.; B.S., U. Scranton, 1942; M.D., Georgetown U., 1945; m. Helen Marie Fitzsimmons, June 23, 1945; children—Thomas E., Gregory P., Mary Elizabeth, Michael W., Kathleen Mary. Intern, Providence Hosp., Washington, 1945-46, resident internal medicine, 1948-50; practice medicine specializing in internal medicine, Washington, 1950-68; med. dir. Providence Hosp., Washington, 1968—; mem. clin. faculty Georgetown U. Med. Sch., 1950—, asso. clin. prof. medicine, 1970—; cons. continuing edn., met. area Regional Med. Program, 1969-72. Served to capt. AUS, 1948-50. Diplomate Am. Bd. Internal Medicine. Fellow A.C.P.; mem. Am., D.C. (pres. 1966-67) socs. internal medicine, D.C. Med. Soc., A.M.A., Assn. Hosp. Med. Edn. (exec. com. 1972—). Club: Kenwood Country (Bethesda, Md.). Home: 7206 Exfair Rd Bethesda MD 20014 Office: Providence Hospital 1150 Varnum St NE Washington DC 20017

CURTIN, WILLIAM JOSEPH, lawyer; b. Auburn, N.Y., Mar. 9, 1931; s. W. Joseph and Edith (Murray) C.; B.S., Georgetown U., 1953, J.D., 1956, LL.M., 1957; m. Helen Bragg White, Aug. 3, 1956; children—Helen Bragg, Caroline Goddard, William Joseph III, Christopher Newport. Admitted to D.C. bar, 1956; asso. firm Morgan, Lewis & Bockius, Washington, 1960-64, partner, 1965—. Pub. mem. Adminstrv. Conf. U.S., 1968-72. Recipient Outstanding Service award Am. Arbitration Assn., 1966; John Carroll Soc. award Georgetown U., 1973. Mem. Am. Bar Assn. (chmn. spl. com. to study nat. strikes in transp. industries), Bar Assn. D.C. (mem. labor law com. 1960—, chmn. 1969-70). Editor-in-chief Legal Legislative Reporter of Internat. Found. Employee Benefit Plans. Contbr. articles to law jours. Home: 5206 Dorset Av Chevy Chase MD 20016 Office: 1140 Connecticut Av NW Washington DC 20036

CURTIS, CHARLES WILLIAM, JR., mortgage banker; b. Daytona Beach, Fla., Sept. 24, 1938; s. Charles William and Ila Maria (Hernandez) C.; B.A., Jacksonville (Fla.) U., 1961, M.A. in Teaching, 1968; m. Nancy Ethel Mulligan, Aug. 22, 1959; children—Nancy Lynne, Ula Michele, Barbara Ann, Charles William III. Tchr., coach Duval County schs., Jacksonville, 1961-66, Jacksonville U., 1966-69; marketing officer Jacksonville Nat. Bank, 1969-73; v.p. marketing Charter Mortgage Co., Jacksonville, 1973—. Co-chmn. spl. gifts. Jacksonville chpt. Am. Cancer Soc., 1972-73. Bd. dirs. Duval Assn. Retarded Children. Served with USMCR, 1957-63. Mem. Bank Marketing Assn., Com. 100, Jacksonville C. of C., Phi Delta Theta. Democrat. Roman Catholic. Clubs: University (gov.), Racquet (gov.) (Jacksonville). Home: 11455 Beacon Dr Jacksonville FL 32225 Office: 815 S Main St Jacksonville FL 32207

CURTIS, DON TEEL, oral surgeon; b. Amarillo, Tex., Aug. 29, 1937; s. Stephen Teel and Zallee (Williams) C.; student U. Colo., 1955-56, U. Tex., 1956-58; grad. Baylor U. Coll. Dentistry, 1962; m. Suzanne Stokes, June 16, 1961; children—Margaret Anne, Stephen Teel, II, Sara Catharine. Resident, Parkland Meml. Hosp. Dallas, 1962-65; exchange resident Queen Victoria Hosp., East Grinstead, Eng., 1965; pvt. practice oral surgery, Amarillo, Tex., 1965—. Clin. instr. Baylor U. Coll. Dentistry, 1962-65; chief dental sect. N.W. Tex. Hosp., Amarillo, 1969-72; instr. Amarillo Coll. Sch. Biomed. Arts and Scis.; mem. task force on cancer Regional Med. Program Tex., 1970-72. Bd. dirs. Potter County Unit Am. Cancer Soc., Amarillo, 1966—, pres., 1971, dir. at large Tex. div., 1969—; bd. dirs. Amarillo Area Acad. Health Center Corp., 1973—, pres., 1973, 74; mem. Amarillo Mental Health Coordinating Com., 1972, 73; bd. dirs. Amarillo Health Sci. Mus.; bd. dirs. Amarillo Little Theater, 1969—, pres., 1972; bd. dirs. Kilgore Childrens Psychiat. Hosp. and Center, 1969—, pres., 1972, 73. Diplomate Am. Bd. Oral Surgery. Mem. Potter-Randall (pres. 1973), Panhandle Dist. dental socs., Am., Tex. dental assns., S.W. Soc. Oral Surgery, Am. Soc. Oral Surgeons, Amarillo C. of C. (dir. 1973—). Presbyn. (deacon 1971-73, elder 1974—). Office: 1901 Medi-Park Amarillo TX 79106

CURTIS, JAMES ROBERT, lawyer; b. Ft. Worth, Oct. 4, 1905; s. Charles Robert and Betty (Lacy) C.; B.A., Tex. Christian U., 1927, B.E., 1928; M.A., So. Meth. U., 1929; LL.B., Cumberland U., 1930; diploma Grad. Sch. of Banking, Rutgers U., 1945; J.D., Samford U., 1969; m. Sarah DeRue Armstrong, June 30, 1935; children—Elizabeth DeRue, James Robert. Admitted to Tex. bar, 1930; practice of law 1930—; city judge Longview, Tex., 1933-35; sec., mgr. First Fed. Savs. and Loan Assn., 1934, dir., 1935—, v.p., 1955-72, pres., 1972—; pres. Voice of Longview Radio Sta. KFRO (established 1935, 1000 watts,) 1934—, Workmen's Oil Co., 1933—, Nat. Security Ins. Co., 1947-63, Courtesy Life Ins. Co., 1955-57, Trans. Security Investment Co., 1955-60; owner Etex Sales Co., 1940-42; v.p., dir. Rogers Nat. Bank, Jefferson, Tex., 1942-50; pres. First Internat. Co., 1966-67; dir. Gillespie Paint Co., Longview. Pres., Jr. C. of C., 1935, E. Tex. Girl Scouts, 1950-52; dist. dir. Am. Cancer Soc., 1957-58; dir. Longview Salvation Army, 1957—, chmn. bd., 1958; bd. dirs. E. Tex. area council Boy Scouts Am., 1956—, dist. chmn., 1959-63, council v.p., 1965-73, recipient Silver Beaver, 1966; mem. Tex. Blind Commn., 1959-65, chmn., 1963-65; bd. devel. So. Meth. U., 1966—; trustee Tex. Christian U., 1973—; (dir. 1964-66), pres. Curtis Found., 1945—. Hon. col. Tex. N.G. Diploma Life Ins. Mgmt. Assn., 1951. Mem. Am. Inst. Mgmt. (charter mem. pres. council), Tex. Broadcasters Assn., Nat. Assn. Broadcasters (bd. dirs. 1964-66), Am., Tex. bar assns., Fed. Communications Bar, Colonial Order Crown, C. of C. (v.p. 1955-56), Radio Pioneers, Sovereign Colonial Soc., Am. Royal Descent, Am. Radio Relay League, Oil Belt Assn. Life Underwriters (v.p. 1954-56), S.R., Tex. Ind. Producers and Royalty Owners Assn. (exec. com. 1957-58), S.A.R., Magna Charta Barons, Sigma Alpha Epsilon, Mem. Christian Ch. Mason. Clubs: Knife and Fork (pres. 1948, 59-60). Lions (pres. 1952, dist. gov. 1954-55; v.p. Tex. Lions Crippled Children Camp 1957-66), Pinecrest Country. Home: 2118 E Marshall Av Longview TX 75601 Office: Curtis Bldg Box 792 Longview TX 75601

CURTIS, JAMES WYLIE, psychologist; b. Madison, Ind., July 3, 1913; s. Wylie Ralph and Gertrude (Allison) C.; A.B., U. Ky., 1937, M.S., 1938; postgrad. Princeton, 1942-43, Universidad de Panama, 1946-47; m. Mildred Louise Fisher, Apr. 29, 1942; children—James W.A., Carol Ann. Cons. psychologist Ill. Div. Vocational Rehab., Springfield, 1947—; staff psychologist Meml. Hosp.; personnel cons. Capitol Bank of Springfield, Town and Country Bank, 1962—; prof. Lincoln Land Community Coll., also chmn. Behavioral Sci. Div. Cons. psychologist Sangamo Electric Co., Hosp. Order St. Francis. Served from 1st lt. to lt. col., USAAF, 1941-47. Recipient medal of Merit Am. Numismatic Assn., 1955, medal of Merit. Central States Numismatic Soc., 1950, Heath Lit. award, Am. Numismatic Assn., 1957, Lit. award, Chgo. Coin Club, 1955. Fellow Royal Numismatic Soc., A.A.A.S.; mem. Sociedad Numismatica de Mexico, Am. Numis. Assn. (gov.), Ill., Midwestern psychol. assns., Springfield Personnel Assn. (dir. 1960-72), Am. Research Center Egypt. Egypt Exploration Soc., Pi Kappa Alpha. Club: Windcrest Golf. Author: (tests) Curtis Completion Form, 1953; Curtis Classification Form, 1951; Curtis Checking Test, 1954; Curtis Interest-Aptitude Index, 1952; Curtis Interest Scale, 1959; Curtis Capacity Test, Curtis Cross Reference Test, Curtis Computation Test, 1965; (books) Media of Exchange in Ancient Egypt, 1951; The Tetradrachms of Roman Egypt, 1957; The Coinage of Roman Egypt, 1956; United States Pattern Coin Handbook, 1949; (monographs) Coinage of Pharaonic Egypt, 1956, Domitius Domitianus and His Coinage, 1957; Pictorial Coin Types at the Roman Mint at Alexandria, 1955; A Study of the Relationship Between Hypnotic Susceptibility and Intelligence, 1943; Administration of the Purdue Pegboard Test to Blind Individuals, 1950. Home: 634 Weatherly Dr San Antonio TX 78239

CURTIS, JOHN CARLOS, lawyer; b. nr. Dowelltown, Tenn., Nov. 4, 1926; s. Amon Carlos and Willie (Norton) C.; B.S. in Bus. Adminstrn., Tenn. Tech. U., 1950; LL.B., McKenzie Coll. Law, 1956; m. Linnie Rhea Davis, June 8, 1950; children—Peggy Lynn, John C. Jr. Admitted to Tenn. bar, 1956; practiced in Chattanooga, 1956-58, 69—; asst. dist. atty., Chattanooga, 1958-69. Served with AUS, 1945-46. Mem. Chattanooga (past pres.), Tenn. (v.p.), Am. (state committeeman) trial lawyers assns. Club: Valleybrook Golf and Country (Hixson, Tenn.). Home: 1602 S Rugby Pl SE Chattanooga TN 37402 Office: 308 Profl Bldg Chattanooga TN 37402

CURTIS, JOHN RUSSELL, psychiatrist, univ. adminstr.; b. Bessemer City, N.C., Nov. 7, 1934; s. John Richard and Nelle C. (Williams) C.; A.B. in History, U. N.C., 1956, M.D., 1960; m. Elizabeth Hunter Dent, Aug. 23, 1958 (div.); children—Russell, Elizabeth, Mary. Intern, Med. Coll. Ga., Augusta, 1960-61; resident N.C. Meml. Hosp., Chapel Hill, 1961-64; chief mens addiction service Nat. Inst. Mental Health Clin. Research Center, Lexington, Ky., 1965-66; dir. psychiat. sect. Student Health Service, U. Ky., Lexington, 1966-68; dir. Univ. Health Service, U. Ga., Athens, 1968—; cons. psychiatry Stephens County Pub. Health Dept., Toccoa, Ga., 1969—. Fellow Am., Ga. psychiat. assns.; mem. A.M.A., Am., So. coll. health assns., Ga. Mental Health Assn., Gridiron Secret Soc. Rotarian. Home: 115 Hanover Pl Athens GA 30601 Office: Director's Office University Health Service University of Georgia Athens GA 30602

CURTIS, JOSIAH MONTGOMERY, publishing co. exec.; b. Elm Grove, W.Va., Nov. 11, 1905; s. Allen and Zelda (Epstein) C.; A.B., W.Va. U., 1928, L.H.D., 1966; postgrad. U. Buffalo, 1931-32; m. Alma Heidee, Oct. 13, 1945. Reporter, sub-editor Wheeling (W.Va.) News-Register, 1928-29; city editor Morgantown (W.Va.) Dominion-News, 1930-31; reporter Buffalo Evening News, 1931-34, asst. city editor, 1934-37, city editor, 1937-42; asso. dir. Am. Press Inst., 1947-51, dir., 1951-65, exec. dir., 1965-67; v.p. devel. Knight Newspapers, Miami, Fla., 1967—; trustee Trenton Times Newspapers. Prof. Columbia Grad. Sch. Journalism, 1947-67; lectr. in field. Mem. journalism com. DePauw U., 1968—; mem. adv. bd. Am. Press Inst., 1968—. Served to maj. AUS, 1942-45. Recipient citation Philippine Govt., 1958. Nat. fellow Sigma Delta Chi, 1958. Mem. Phi Delta Theta, Sigma Delta Chi. Home: 6601 Roxbury Lane Miami Beach FL 33141 Office: 1 Herald Plaza Miami FL 33101

CURTIS, MARILYN S. (MRS. JON E. CURTIS), pharmacist, flight instr.; b. Astoria, L.I., N.Y., Aug. 25, 1934; d. Bernard P. and DeRetta (Williamson) Smith; B.S., U. Tex., 1955; m. Charles Stoneberg, June 28, 1958 (dec. Apr. 1968); m. 2d, Jon E. Curtis, Mar. 28, 1969. Pharmacist, Med. Arts Pharmacy, San Antonio, 1955-56, Northside Drug, San Antonio, 1956-58, Jones Apothecary, Houston, 1958-68, 73—, Madings Drugs, 1968-69, Phillips Pharmacy, 1968-70, Gloyer's Pharmacy, 1969-73, Fed-Mart Pharmacy, Pasadena, Tex., 1970-72. Flight instr. Barstow Aviation, Houston, 1962, free lance, 1962-64, Consol. Aero, Houston, 1967-68; participant Powder Puff Derby, 1960, Internat. Air Race, 1962, All Women's Internat. Air Race, 1964, other races; mem. 1st Women's Nat. Pylon Racing Team, 1967-71. Mem. Tex. State Aviation Assn. (sec.-treas. 1962-64), Petticoat Pilots (pres. 1964-65), 99's (pres. Houston 1966-68), Aircraft Owners and Pilots Assn., Nat. Assn. Flight Instrs., Animal Behavior Soc. Home: 25414 Friar Lake Lane Spring TX 77373 Office: 5322 W Bellfort St Houston TX 77035

CURTIS, MARY GERVASE BARNETT (MRS. BUFORD C. CURTIS), publisher, genealogist, author; b. Little Rock, June 8, 1924; d. Edgar Wheeler and Nellie (O'Neal) Barnett; grad. high sch.; m. Buford C. Curtis, Sept. 19, 1943; children—Mary Michele (Mrs. William Boyd Hill), Buford C., Robert Thornton Higgins, Eura Melisa, Sidney Watson, Katherine Victoria. Editor, South Fort

Worthian, weekly, 1954-56, Strickland & Allied Families Query & Answer Exchange, quar., 1958—; owner Arrow Printing Co., Ft. Worth, 1953—; founder, pres. Am. Reference Publishers, Inc., 1967-72; owner In Print Books, 1972—; publisher, owner Mag. of Bibliographie's, 1972—; dir. Ft. Belknap Archives, Inc., 1971— Chmn. ramp com. Tarrant County of Tex. Hist. Survey Com., 1959-66; judge genealogy and heraldry Okla. State Fair, 1972-73. Mem. Tex. (charter mem., rec. sec. 1960—), Ft. Worth (charter mem., chmn. publicity 1959-60) geneal. socs., Tex., Cath. (pres. Ft. Worth 1959—), Tarrant County (dir. 1962—, rec. sec. 1962-63) hist. socs., Cath. Daus. Am., S.W. Council Geneal. and Hist. Socs. (sec. 1973), S.W. Archivists (charter). Author: Early East Tennessee Tax Lists. Editor: Stirpes, Quar. Tenn. Geneal. Soc., 1973. Home: 3812 Lafayette Fort Worth TX 76107 Office: 2921 Morton St Fort Worth TX 76107

CURTIS, RALPH FRANKLIN, JR., life ins. co. exec.; b. Carmichaels, Pa., Feb. 5, 1929; s. Daniel Ralph and Retha (Dugan) C.; B.S., Waynesburg Coll., 1951; m. Margaret Rizer, July 3, 1954; children—Linda Joyce, Thomas David, Steven Douglas. Agt., Fidelity Union Life Ins. Co., Houston, 1955-56, gen. agt., Pasadena, Tex., 1956-59, div. mgr., Dallas, 1959-60, regional v.p., Dallas, 1960-64; v.p., agy. dir. Western Security Life Ins. Co., Oklahoma City, 1965-69, also Gulf Atlantic Life Ins. Co. (both cos. merged with Gulf Atlantic Surviving Co. 1971); v.p. marketing Gulf Atlantic Surviving Co., Dallas, 1971—. Bd. dirs. Cub Scouts of Am., 1965-67, North Side All Sports Program, 1965-67. Served with USAF, 1951-56. Mem. Sales and Exec. Club. Presbyn. Club: Prestonwood Golf and Country. Home: 6562 Briarmeade Dr Dallas TX 75240 Office: 8435 N Stemmons St Dallas TX 75247

CURTIS, WILLIAM DWIGHT, orthodontist; b. Columbia, Mo., June 14, 1905; s. Winterton Conway and Marion (Hitchcock) C.; A.B., U. Mo., 1930; D.D.S., Washington U., 1935; m. Elizabeth Ilda Poulter, July 3, 1931; children—Marion, Elizabeth Anne, Caroline, Constance. Intern Forsyth Dental Infirmary for Children, Boston, 1935-36, New Haven Hosp., 1936-38; mem. staff Childrens Hosp., Washington, 1942—. Diplomate Am. Bd. Orthodontics. Fellow Am. Coll. Dentists; mem. Am. Dental Assn., Am. Assn. Orthodontists, D.C. Dental Soc. (v.p. 1947-48), So. Soc. Orthodontists (v.p. 1954-55), Washington Dental Club (pres. 1960). Lion (pres. 1945-46). Home: 5408 Moorland Lane Bethesda MD 20014 Office: 1726 Eye St NW Washington DC 20006

CUSACK, CLARENCE FRANK, lawyer; b. Dallas, Sept. 27, 1905; s. Clarence Eugene and Carrie (Watson) C.; ed. pub. schs.; m. Gilberte Bourdel, Nov. 27, 1945; children—Jack, Frankie (Mrs. Alan Hirschberg), Pat. Admitted to Tex. bar, 1930; practiced in Dallas, 1930-43, 46—, founder, pres., gen. counsel Security Savs. Assn., Dallas, 1965-71, now dir.; dir. Hampton State Bank, Dallas. Served to capt. Transp. Corps, AUS, 1943-46. Decorated Bronze Star. Mem. Tex., Dallas bar assns., Tex Savs. and Loan League. Mem. Christian Ch. Mason. Club: Oak Cliff Country (Dallas). Home: 1305 Briarbrook St DeSoto TX 75115

CUSH, JOSEPH WILBUR, dentist; b. Natchitoches, La., Aug. 22, 1929; s. Samuel and Angeline Marie (Catanese) C.; student Centenary Coll., 1946-48; D.D.S., Loyola U. of So., 1953; m. Beverly Jean Burch, Aug. 21, 1954; children—Joseph Wilbur, Derrie Anne, Gregory Samuel, Bryan Stephan, Angela Marie. Intern oral surgery Charity Hosp., New Orleans, 1953-54; resident oral surgery Confederate Meml. Med. Center, Shreveport, La., 1956-58; pvt. practice oral surgery, Shreveport, 1958—; mem. staffs La. State Sch. Medicine Post Grad. Dept. Pres. N.W. La. Cancer Soc., 1970. Served with USAF, 1954-56. Fellow Acad. Internat. Dentistry; mem. Am. Dental Soc. of Anesthesiology, Am., La., 4th Dist. (pres. 1965) dental assns., Pierre Fauchard Acad., C. of C., Delta Sigma Delta, Am. Legion. Roman Catholic. K.C., Rotarian. Clubs: Serra, Pierremont Oaks Tennis, East Ridge Country. Home: 307 Deborah St Shreveport LA 71106 Office: 915 Shreveport Barksdale Hwy Shreveport LA 71105

CUSHING, BARRY EDWIN, educator; b. Lansing, Mich., July 6, 1945; s. William Eldon and Abigail (Stevens) C.; B.A. with high honors, Mich. State U., 1966; Ph.D. (Ernst & Ernst Found. fellow 1968), 1969; m. Cherry Lee Barker, June 25, 1966; 1 son, Dennis Earl. Asst. prof. dept. accounting U. Tex. at Austin, 1969-71, asso. prof., 1971—; vis. asst. prof. U. Ill. at Urbana, 1972-73. Recipient Elijah Watts Sells hon. mention award for high score C.P.A. exam., 1970. C.P.A., Tex. Mem. Am. Accounting Assn., Am. Inst. C.P.A.'s, Nat. Assn. Accountants, Phi Kappa Phi, Beta Alpha Psi. Author: Accounting Information Systems and Business Organizations, 1974. Home: 9201 Quail Meadow Dr Austin TX 78758 Office: BEB 316 U Tex Austin TX 78712

CUSTER, DOROTHY ELIZABETH MASSIE (MRS. LYLE EDGAR CUSTER), educator; b. Amherst, Va., Apr. 15, 1922; d. William Joseph and Winnie (Coleman) Massie; A.B., Lynchburg Coll., 1948; M.Ed., U. Va., 1953, Ed.D., 1971; m. Edward Perkins Faulconer, Apr. 9, 1942 (dec. July 1967); m. 2d, Lyle Edgar Custer, May 1, 1971. Tchr., Amherst County (Va.) Schs., 1943-45, elementary supr., 1953-55; prin. Clifford (Va.) Elementary Sch., 1945-47; tchr. Amherst High Sch., 1948-52, Garland Rodes Sch., Lynchburg, 1952-53; gen. and high sch. supr. Buckingham County Schs., Buckingham, Va., 1955-60; dir. Sweet Briar Coll. Nursery Sch., instr. edn. Sweet Briar Coll., 1960-65, dir. reading improvement program, 1962-65; instr. U. Va. Sch. Gen. Studies, 1963-65; asst. supr. elementary edn. Va. Dept. Edn., Richmond, 1965-72; asso. prof. edn., div. chmn. J. Sargeant Reynolds Community Coll., Richmond, 1972—. Mem. Am. Assn. U. Profs., Am. Assn. U. Women (br. chmn. 1964-65), N.E.A., Va. Edn. Assn., Assn. Supervision and Curriculum Devel. (area chmn. 1958-59), Coll. Reading Assn., Va. Assn. Ednl. Communications and Tech., Va. Assn. Ednl. Research, Nat. Council Tchrs. English, D.A.R. (chmn. chpt. edn. com. 1964-65), Kappa Delta Pi, Delta Kappa Gamma (chmn. chpt. profl. affairs com. 1966-68). Mem. Order Eastern Star (past worthy matron). Home: 3117 Windsorview Dr Richmond VA 23225 Office: 108 E Grace St Richmond VA 23219

CUSUMANO, CHARLES LOUIS, physician, educator; b. Bklyn., Jan. 16, 1936; s. Charles Louis and Catherine Maniscako C.; B.S. in Chemistry cum laude, U. Notre Dame, 1957; M.D., Georgetown U., 1961; m. Joann Elaine DeSimone, Aug. 16, 1958; children—David, Barbara, Jeanne, Mark. Intern, Georgetown Hosp., Washington, 1961-62; resident Mt. Alto VA Hosp., Washington, 1962-63, Georgetown Hosp., 1965-66; surgeon USPHS, Bethesda, Md., 1963-65, spl. fellow lab. chem. biology, 1966-68; asst. prof. immunology, medicine, Med. Sch., U. Fla., Gainesville, 1968-74, asso. prof., 1974—; attending physician Shands Teaching Hosp., Gainesville 1968—, head sect. med. oncology, 1973—; clin. investigator VA Hosp., Gainesville, 1969-72, attending physician, 1968—. Served with USPHS, 1963-65. Am. Cancer Soc. grantee, 1969, 70, 72, Nat. Cancer Inst. grantee, 1970—. Diplomate Am. Bd. Internal Medicine. Fellow A.C.P.; mem. Am. Fedn. Clin. Research, N.Y. Acad. Sci., Fla., Alachua County med. assns. Contbr. profl. jours. Office: Box 727 Coll Medicine Univ Fla Gainesville FL 32610

CUTRIGHT, EUGENE ALBERT, chem. co. exec.; b. Seminole, Okla., Jan. 26, 1934; s. Albert Henry and Emule Lourine (Conner) C.; B.Chem.Engrng., Ga. Inst. Tech., 1957; m. Jeanne Lippy, May 20, 1960; children—Eugene Albert, H. Gilmore. Prodn. supr. Monsanto Co., Texas City, Tex., 1957-58, engr., Nitro, W.Va., 1960-62, prodn. supr., 1962-66, prodn. supt., 1966-69, prodn. supr., Luling, La., 1969-70; plant mgr. Betz Labs., Inc., Macon, Ga., 1970—. Vice pres. McKibben-Lane P.T.A., 1972-73. Served with C.E., AUS, 1958-60. Registered profl. engr., W.Va. Mem. Macon Mfrs. Bur., Macon Lawn Tennis Assn., Lambda Chi Alpha. Moose. Home: 1474 Maplewood Dr Macon GA 31204 Office: PO Box 406 Wilson Experiment Station Macon GA 31204

CUTTING, RICHARD HAWLEY, architect; b. Woodsfield, O., July 4, 1901; s. Orville Blanchard and Nora Ella (Dempsey) C.; B.S. in Architecture, Carnegie Inst. Tech., 1926; M.Arch. (scholar), Harvard, 1934; m. Jean Smith McKenzie, Oct. 23, 1925; children—Malcolm M., Nancy (Mrs. John C. Young). Architect, Walker & Weeks, 1926-29; pvt. archtl. practice, 1929-30, 32-33, 39-44; architect Abraham Garfield, 1930-31, Garfield, Stanley-Brown, Harris & Robinson, 1931-32, Garfield, Harris, Robinson & Schafer, 1934-39; partner Cutting, Ciresi & Assos., 1945-49; owner Richard H. Cutting & Assos., Architects-Engrs., West Palm Beach, Fla., 1949—. Cons. USAF, 1951-58; profl. cons. West Palm Beach Downtown Devel. Authority, 1973—. Active Boy Scouts Am., 1913—. Mem. A.I.A. (chmn. com. on relationship architects to bldg industry 1964), Architects Soc. Fla., Fla. Engrs. Soc., Nat. Soc. Profl. Engrs., Am. Soc. C.E., Am. Soc. Heating and Ventilating Engrs., S.A.R., Delta Upsilon. Clubs: Old Port Yacht (West Palm Beach, Fla.), Hermit (Cleve.), Ambassadors. Contbr. articles to profl. jours. Inventor: aluminum tee sqs., rolling fire screen for fireplaces, paper cornerbead, others. Home: 3405 S Flagler Dr West Palm Beach FL 33405 Office: 2806 S Dixie Hwy West Palm Beach FL 33405

CUTTS, ERNEST A(LLEN), newspaperman; b. Augusta, Ga., Nov. 27,, 1912; s. Allen Sherrod and Mary (Moorman) C.; student Acad. Richmond County, Jr. Coll. of Augusta, U. S.C., 1933-35; m. Susan Maner Dotterer, May 2, 1942; children—Susan Dotterer, Mary Allen (Mrs. James A. Gardner), Anna Maner (Mrs. Harold J. Burns). Reporter Augusta Herald, 1937-40; reporter News and Courier, Charleston, 1940-42, sports editor 1943; reporter Charleston Evening Post, 1944, city editor, 1945—, news editor, 1953, mng. editor, 1954—. Pulitzer Prize juror, 1972-73. Hon. asso. curator zoology Charleston Mus., 1956—, trustee, 1959-68. Past pres. S.C. Asso. Press News Council, S.C. U.P.I. Mem. A.P. Mng. Editors Assn. (dir. 1964-69, exec. com., treas. 1971, charter mem. regents), S.C. Press Assn. (exec. com.), Am. Soc. Newspaper Editors, Charleston Natural History Soc. (pres. 1967-68), Wilson Ornithol. Soc., Carolina Bird Club, Sigma Delta Chi (S.C. chpt. v.p. 1967-70). Club: Country of Charleston (dir. 1970-73). Asso. editor Chat mag., 1954-70. Home: 1466 S Edgewater Dr Charleston SC 29407 Office: 134 Columbus St Charleston SC 29402

CUTTS, VIRGINIA ALLEN PAIRO (MRS. HARVEY CLARK CUTTS), former advt. exec.; b. Atlanta, Jan. 12, 1903; d. Louis Prescott and Lucy Walthall (Jones) Pairo; A.B., Oglethorpe U., 1924; m. Harvey Clark Cutts, Apr. 12, 1962; 1 stepdau., Caroline Cutts (Mrs. Randall Edmund Jones). Sales promotion Allyn & Bacon Pub. Co., 1924-25; advt. mgr. Philbosian, home furnishings, 1925-27, J.M. High Dept Store, 1928, Loeb Advt. Agy., 1929-35, Loeb & Pairo, 1935-47; owner Pairo Advt. Agy., Atlanta, 1947-66. Mem. housing com. YWCA, 1934-35; active A.R.C., Am. Heart Assn., Jr. Achievement. Mem. Fashion Group, Inc. (sec. 1953-54), Advt. Fedn. Am., Atlanta Advt. Club (dir. 1953-58), Am. Women in Radio and TV, Atlanta Hist. Soc., Atlanta Art Assn., Atlanta Symphony Guild (policy bd. 1959-62, v.p. 1961-63), D.A.R., English-Speaking Union, Atlanta Opera Guild. Episcopalian. Pub.: Maum Nancy (Susan Merrick Haywood). Home: Greenville GA 30222 also 3701 Scenic Hwy Pensacola FL 32504

CWIKLA, JOSEPH ROBERT, dentist; b. Hartford, Conn., June 7, 1940; s. Joseph Michael and Julia (Orzech) C.; B.S., St. Bonaventure U., 1964; D.M.D., Tufts U., 1966; certificate in Endontics, State U. N.Y. at Buffalo, 1971; m. Priscilla Ann Bouvier, Sept. 14, 1968; 1 dau., Deborah Ann. Instr., teaching fellow Sch. Dentistry, State U. N.Y. at Buffalo, 1969-71; faculty Sch. Dental Medicine, Harvard, 1971; practice dentistry, specializing in endodontics, Hartford, 1961-72, Melbourne, Fla., 1972—. Served with USNR, 1966-68. Mem. Am., Conn. dental assns., Am. Assn. Endodontists. Home: 924 Jamestown Av Indian Harbor Beach FL 32935 Office: 1341 S Hickory St Suite 111 Doctors Bldg Melbourne FL 32901

CYLKE, FRANK KURT, librarian; b. New Haven, Feb. 13, 1932; s. Frank Anton and Helen Mary (Callahan) C.; B.A., U. Conn., 1954; M.L.S., Pratt Inst., 1957; postgrad. Fairfield U., 1959, Am. U., 1968-69; m. Mary Elizabeth Zembroski, Dec. 28, 1962; children—Frank Kurt, Mary Amanda. Librarian Graham-Eckes Sch., Palm Beach, Fla., 1957-58; reference librarian Bridgeport (Conn.) Pub. Library, 1958-62; head pub. services New Haven Pub. Library, 1962-65; asst. librarian Providence Pub. Library, 1965-68; chief library and information scis. research program U.S. Office Edn., 1968-69; exec. sec. Fed. Library Com., Library Congress, Washington, 1970-73, chief div. blind and physically handicapped, 1973—. Instr. U. R.I. Grad. Library Sch., 1967-68. Exec. sec. panel on edn. and tng. Com. on Sci. and Tech. Information; chmn. librarians tech. com. Met. Washington Council Govts., 1970-71; sec. U.S. Book Exchange, 1972—; sec.-treas. Joint Venture Pub. Activity, 1970—. Mem. East Greenwich (R.I.) Free Library Corp., 1967—; adv. bd. Ednl. Resources Information Center/Clearinghouse on Library and Information Sci., 1970-72. U.S. Office Edn. grantee to develop a survey fed. libraries, 1972. Mem. A.A.A.S., Am., D.C., Mass., New Eng. library assns., Am. Soc. for Information Sci., Internat. Fedn. for Documentation, Pvt. Libraries Assn., Spl. Libraries Assn., Lewes Hist. Soc. Roman Catholic. Clubs: Branford Yacht; Dinghy Cruising Assn. Editor: Captains Shelf, 1964-66, FLC Newsletter, 1970-73. Home: 1032 Harriman St Great Falls VA 22066 Office: Library of Congress Washington DC 20540

CYR, LOUIE MCGOWEN, lawyer; b. Jeanerette, La., May 12, 1913; s. Paul N. and Mary (McGowen) C.; b.a., southwestern La. Inst., 1936; LL.B., La. State U., 1940; m. Mary Elizabeth Junot, Aug. 19, 1942; children—Patricia Jean, Paul N. Admitted to La. bar, 1940; practiced in New Iberia, 1940—. pres. Iberia Savings & Loan Assn., New Iberia, 1967—, dir., 1952—; dir. La. Land and Royalty Owners Assn., 1964—. Chmn. Iberia Crippled Children's Assn., 1942-62; v.p. La. Sugar Cane Festival and Fair Assn., 1946; pres. Iberia Municipal Concert Assn., 1947; pres. Community Chest, 1954; mem. Park and Recreation Commn., 1951—, chmn., 1964—; city judge, 1943-46 (all New Iberia). Recipient Distinguished Service award, New Iberia Jr. C. of C., 1947; citation La. Recreation and Parks Assn., 1963. Mem. Am., La. State, Iberia Parish (pres. 1950-51) bar assns., Am. Judicature Soc., New Iberia Jr. C. of C. (pres. 1946), C. of C. (bd. dirs. 1947-49, 51-55), Iberia Parish Rod and Gun Club (pres. 1954-56). Kiwanian (pres. New Iberia 1947, lt. gov. Div. 1957). Home: 409 Loreauville Rd New Iberia LA 70560 Office: 301 Julia St New Iberia LA 70560

CYRUS, JOHN HOLMAN, state ofcl.; b. Louisburg, N.C., Aug. 14, 1920; s. John Henry and Bettie (Hicks) C.; B.S. in Agrl. Edn., N.C. State U., 1948; m. Billie Marie Watkins, Feb. 11, 1950; children—John Michael and Gary Holman (twins). Tchr. vocational agr. Moncure (N.C.) High Sch., instr. Vets. Farm Tng. Program, 1946-49; specialist tobacco marketing N.C. Dept. Agr., Raleigh, 1949-65, dir. tobacco marketing sect., 1966-72, chief field crops sect., 1973—, pub. anh. N.C. Tobacco Report, 1949—. Adv., cons. Industry-Wide Flue-Cured Marketing Com., 1967—; bd. dirs. Nat. Tobacco Growers Information Com., 1966—; bd. dirs., exec. com., treas. Nat. Tobacco Tax Council, since 1966—. Mem. Democratic Precinct Election Com., 1969—. Bd. dirs. Nat. Tobacco and Cotton Mus. Served with USAAF, 1942-45; ETO. Decorated Air medal with three oak leaf clusters; named Tarheel of Week, Raleigh (N.C.) News and Observer, 1968; recipient commendation N.C. Grange, 1971. Mem. Kappa Phi Kappa, Alpha Gamma Rho. Baptist (deacon, chmn. bd., tchr. Sunday sch.). Clubs: Farm Hands, North Carolina State University Alumni (Raleigh). Editor: The Tobacco Story, 1966. Contbr. articles newspapers and profl. jours. Home: 113 Clarendon Crescent Raleigh NC 27610 Office: N C Dept Agr PO Box 27647 Raleigh NC 27611

DABBS, CHESTER NORWOOD, food processing co. exec.; b. nr. Quitman, Miss., Sept. 25, 1904; s. Willis Sanders and Margaret Ruth (Fortner) D.; B.S., Miss. State U., 1930, postgrad., 1932; m. Miriam Adair, Dec. 24, 1933; 1 son, Willis Norwood. Vocational agrl. tchr., athletic coach Shady Grove High Sch., Jones County, Miss., 1930-33; agronomist Dept. Agr. Soil Conservation Service, North Miss., 1935-47; asst. mgr. Planters Mfg. Co., Clarksdale, Miss., 1947—. Baptist (deacon). Lion. Club: Ward Lake Hunting. Home: 321 Maple St Clarksdale MS 38614 Office: Planters Mfg Co Clarksdale MS 38614

DABBS, CLYDE HARWELL, physician; b. Tupelo, Miss., Nov. 5, 1921; s. Clyde Harwell and Lucille (Feemster) D.; B.S., Millsaps Coll., 1942; M.D., Washington U., 1945; m. Beth Barron, Aug. 1, 1942; children—Beth (Mrs. Boyd Spellman), Ruth Ann, Diana (Mrs. David Taylor), Barron Harwell, Deborah. Intern, Barnes Hosp., St. Louis, 1945-46; resident in surgery USPHS Hosp., Balt., 1947-50; practice medicine specializing in gen. and thoracic surgery, Knoxville, Tenn., 1952-73, Rockwood, Tenn., 1973—; surgeon Rockwood Med. Group; med. dir. Cumberland Valley Med. Group, 1952-54, Acuff Clinic, 1954-60. Med. adviser So. div. Nat. Ski Patrol. Served to lt. col. AUS, 1946. Diplomate Am. Bd. Surgery. Fellow A.C.S.; mem. Knoxville Surg. Soc. (past pres.). Clubs: Deane Hill Country, Rockwood Country, Knoxville Ski, Beach Mountain Ski. Contbr. articles to profl. jours. Inventor of Dabbs disc. Home: Route 1 Dabbs Dr Spring City TN 37381 Office: 450 S Chamberlain Av Rockwood TN 37859

DABBS, JOHN WILSON THOMAS, physicist; b. Nashville, Dec. 11, 1921; s. John Wilson Thomas and Ruth (Fuqua) D.; B.S., U. Tenn., 1944, Ph.D., 1955; m. Elizabeth Jane Hicks, Sept. 16, 1945; children—Carol Jane, John Richard, David Frederick. Research asst. metall. lab. U. Chgo., 1944-45; jr. engr. applied physics lab. Johns Hopkins U., Balt., 1945; physicist Oak Ridge Nat. Lab., 1946—, sr. staff physicist, 1968—; pres. Oak Ridge Devel. Corp., 1973; v.p. Pic-Air, Inc., Oak Ridge, 1971—; dir. Elographics, Inc., Oak Ridge. Fulbright lectr. Instituto de Fisica, San Carlos de Bariloche, Argentina, 1961; vis. scientist Centre d'Etudes Nucleaires, Saclay, France, 1967-68. Pres., Karns (Tenn.) Community Club, 1956. Served with ordnance AUS, 1945-46. Fellow Am. Phys. Soc.; mem. Am. Mgmt. Assn., Oak Ridge C. of C. (chmn. local industry com. 1972), Mobile Steam Soc. (pres. 1973), Delta Tau Delta. Republican. Home: 106 Osage Rd Oak Ridge TN 37830 Office: PO Box X Oak Ridge TN 37830

DABBS, MIRIAM ADAIR (MRS. CHESTER NORWOOD DABBS), journalist, artist; b. Rialto, Cal., May 6, 1908; d. Watts McIntosh and Betty (Pearson) Adair; B.A., Miss. State Coll. for Women, 1930; m. Chester Norwood Dabbs, Dec. 24, 1933; 1 son, Willis Norwood. English instr., Jones County Jr. Coll., Ellisville, Miss., 1933-34; instr. Am. history Northwest Jr. Coll., Senatobia, Miss., 1935-36; soc. editor Clarksdale (Miss.) Daily Register, 1942-47; feature writer, corr. Clarion-Ledger, Jackson, Miss., 1964—; corr. Jackson Daily News, 1968—, Press-Scimitar, Memphis, 1969-74, Here's Clarksdale mag., 1973—. Exhibited one-man shows Galeries Raymond Duncan, Paris, France, 1970, 71, Ligoa Duncan Gallery, N.Y.C., 1971, also regional exhbns.; works represented in pvt. and museum collections; lectr. in field, 1972. Chmn., Missionary Soc. Bapt. Ch., 1952-53; mem. Clarksdale Beautification Commn., chmn., 1952-54, 56-63, sec., 1955, 68. Recipient Beautification Merit award, Miss. C. of C. community program at Clarksdale, 1961; Prix de Paris for painting Bridge to Sunrise, 1970, for The Rising Flood, 1974. Mem. Nat. League Am. Pen Women (award; editor Pen Drifts, 1957), Ulster-Scot Hist. Soc. (Belfast, Ireland), D.A.R. Clubs: Clarksdale Woman's (past pres.), Town and Country Garden (Clarksdale, Miss.). Author: Idyls of the Delta: Coahoma, 1948; The Passing Storm; Sepaled Horns; Sonnets From India, 1962. Contbr. articles on founding families of Miss. to tech. lit. Research in genealogy. Home: 321 Maple St Clarksdale MS 38614 Office: Clarion Ledger Jackson MS 39205

DACUS, PERCY MELVIN, lumber co. exec.; b. Kilmichael, Miss., July 4, 1910; s. Aubrey P: and Eulalee (Watson) D.; grad. Miss. Heights Acad., 1928; B.S., U. Tenn., 1932; m. Chloe Weaver, July 18, 1937; children—Robert A., Marvin W., Clara, Chloe (Mrs. Raymond Charette). Partner, Dacus Lumber Co., West Memphis, Ark., 1933-50, inc., 1950, sec., 1950-59, pres., 1959—; sec.-treas. Dacbra, Inc. Mayor City of West Memphis, 1946. Mem. bd. Crittenden Meml. Hosp. Named man of year in West Memphis, Crittenden County Rep. Com., 1946; recipient industry award, Ark. Wood Products Assn., 1962. Mem. So. Hardwood Lumber Mfg. Assn. (pres. 1962), West Memphis C. of C. (pres. 1948), Lumbermen's Club, Sigma Nu. Methodist (trustee). Clubs: Summit, Meadowbrook County (West Memphis). Home: 607 Graham St West Memphis AR 72301 Office: 1105 N Missouri St West Memphis AR 72301

DAEHLER, MARK, physicist; b. Cedar Rapids, Ia., Mar. 21, 1934; s. Max and Mary (Bingham) D.; B.A., Coe Coll., 1955; student U. Ia., 1955; M.A., U. Wis., 1957, Ph.D., 1966. Staff mem. Los Alamos Sci. Lab., 1966-68; guest scientist Inst. for Plasma Physik, Garching, West Germany, 1968-71; physicist U.S. Naval Research Lab., Washington, 1971—. Mem. Am. Phys. Soc., Optical Soc. Am., Sigma Xi. Home: 900 Massachusetts Av NE Washington DC 20002 Office: US Naval Research Lab Washington DC 20375

DAGGS, RAY GILBERT, ret. assn. exec.; b. McKees Rocks, Pa., June 26, 1904; s. Myrvyn Dorsa and Clara Etta (Wolstoncroft) D.; B.S., Bucknell U., 1926, D.Sc., 1954; Ph.D., U. Rochester, 1930; m. Mary Agnes Dwyer, June 14, 1929; children—Vertie (Mrs. Donald Kunkle), William D. Instr. U. Rochester (N.Y.) Sch. Medicine, after 1930, asst. prof. physiology, to 1936; asso. prof., head dept. physiology U. Vt. Coll. Medicine, 1936-41; dir. research U.S. Army Med. Research Lab., Ft. Knox, Ky., 1946-56; exec. sec.-treas. Am. Physiol. Soc., Bethesda, Md., 1956-73. Served with AUS, 1941-46. Mem. Phi Beta Kappa, Sigma Xi. Editor Physiologist; asso. editor Physiol. Revs.

Editorial bd. Am. Jour. Physiology, Jour. Applied Physiology. Contbr. articles to profl. jours. Home: 5013 Alta Vista Ct Bethesda MD 20014

DAGLEY, FRANK ALLEN, cons. engr.; b. Charlotte, N.C., Mar. 12, 1940; s. Ray Harrison and Elizabeth Alice (Graham) D.; B.C.E., Auburn U., 1964; m. Catherine Marquis Slaughter, Dec. 21, 1963; 1 dau., Valerie Annette. Asst. engr. Atlantic Coast Line R.R., Florence, S.C., 1964-65, cons. engr., Hensley-Schmidt, Inc., Marietta, Ga., 1965-67, Palmer & Baker Engrs., Inc., Mobile, Ala., 1967-73, David Volker & Assos., Inc., Mobile, 1973—. Registered profl. engr., Ala., S.C. Presbyn. Home: 5538 Nassau Dr Mobile AL 36608 Office: 3809 Moffat Rd Mobile AL 36605

DAHIYA, RAGHUNATH SINGH, microbiologist; b. India, Oct. 4, 1931; s. Jage Ram and Chander Kaur (Khatri) D.; came to U.S., 1958, naturalized, 1971; B.Sc., M.Sc., Punjab, India; Ph.D., N.C. State U., 1962; m. Swarn Kanta, Nov. 5, 1955; children—Surinder, Narinder. Asst. prof. N.C. State U., 1965-71; chief microbiologist N.C. Dept. Agr., Raleigh, 1971—. Mem. Am. Soc. Microbiology, Inst. Food Technologists. Contbr. articles to sci. jours. Home: 621 Brooks Av Raleigh NC 27607 Office: NC Dept Agr Raleigh NC 27611

DAHL, EDWARD, economist; b. Buffalo, Mar. 15, 1900; s. Edward George and Augusta (Sommer) D. ; B.A., Yale, 1923; m. Clemence Eirene Liesching, Oct. 11, 1932; children—Georgia Hermione (Mrs. Clare A. Schmutz), Edward Carle. Asst. mgr. Socony Vacuum Corp., Calcutta, India, also Colombo, Ceylon, 1927-33; mgr. Dodge & Seymour, Ltd., Rangoon, Burma, 1933-36, asst. to v.p., N.Y.C., 1936-40; mgr. export office Reynolds Metals Corp., Richmond, Va., 1940-41; supr. Va. Dept. Edn., Richmond, 1941-42; internat. economist Dept. State, Washington, 1947-50, 52-70, pub-affairs officer, 1952-62, chief fgn. reporting staff, 1962-70; cons. South Asia, 1970—; comml. attache Am. embassy, Karachi, Pakistan, 1950-52. Served with U.S. Army, World War I, 1918; to lt. comdr. USNR, 1942-46. Mem. Internat. Council for Christian Leadership (chmn. exec. com. Internat. Luncheon Group 1954—), Ret. Officers Assn., Nat., Md. ret. officers assns., English-Speaking Union, Am. Fgn. Service Assn., Am. Legion, Lambda Chi Alpha. Clubs: Dacor, Yale, Army and Navy (Washington). Author: Christ, the Man. Home: The Spruces 7800 Old Chester Rd Bethesda MD 20034

DAHL, ELMER VERNON, physician, educator; b. Colby, Kan., Apr. 17, 1921; s. Henry S. and Marie A. (Berg) D. ; B.S., U. So. Cal., 1943, M.D., 1952; m. Josephine M. Townzen, June 14, 1944; children—Linette, Jonathan, Hans, Elizabeth, Andrew. Intern Walter Reed Hosp., Washington, 1952-53; instr. and fellow in pathology Duke, Durham, N.C., 1953-54, Mayo Found., Rochester, Minn., 1954-59; commd. 1st lt., USAF, 1952; advanced through grades to col., 1966; chief pathology br. Sch. Aerospace Medicine, San Antonio, 1959-61, cons., 1961-68; comdr. Epidemiological Lab., San Antonio, 1961-68; comdr. Epidemiological Flight, Manila, P.I., 1968-69; research asso. prof. pathology U. Tex. Med. Br., Galveston, 1969—; cons. lab. medicine to Surgeon Gen. U.S. Air Force, 1961-65; spl. cons. pathology to 6571st Aeromed. Research Lab., Holloman AFB, N.M., 1964-68. Recipient Research award Mayo Alumni Assn., 1958. Diplomate Am. Bd. Pathology. Fellow Coll. Am. Pathologists; mem. Am. Soc. Exptl. Pathology, Am. Soc. Tropical Medicine and Hygiene, A.M.A., Sigma Xi. Home: 124 Tuna Galveston TX 77550

DAHL, ORVILLE JEROME, tire co. exec.; b. Chgo., Jan. 10, 1917; s. Harold P. and Rachel A. (Ibsen) D.; B.S., U. Wis., 1941; m. Roma W. Wenger, Feb. 21, 1942; children—Barbara (Mrs. Charles F. Struck), Mary (Mrs. Thomas W. Winton). Chemist, Pitts. Plate Glass Co., Milw., 1941-42; chemist B.F. Goodrich Co., Akron, Los Angeles, The Netherlands, 1942-53, tech. mgr., Miami, Okla., 1953—. Home: 1223 N Elm St Miami OK 74354 Office: 1000 Goodrich Blvd Miami OK 74354

DAHLBERG, WALTER GUNNARD, landscape architect; b. Bryan, Tex., June 14, 1940; s. Frank Iver and Jewell (Thomas) D.; B.S., Tex. A. and M. U., 1962; m. Genelle Mary Hoffman, Oct. 11, 1968; 1 son, Scott Iver. Landscape architect U.S. Forest Service, Sitgraves Nat. Forest, Phoenix, 1965-66, Caudill Rowlett Scott, Houston, 1966-69, Myrick-Newman-Dahlberg, Ind., Dallas, 1969—. Mem. Town Lake Environmental Awareness Com., 1972; chmn. environmental com. Operation Get Involved of Dallas, 1971-72; mem. Sign Ordinance Adv. Com. Dallas, 1972-73. Served to 1st lt. USAF, 1962-65. Mem. Am. Soc. Landscape Architects (Nat. Merit award 1972, Merit award S.W. chpt. 1973), Tex. design landscape architect, landscape master plan Dallas-Fort Worth Regional Airport, 1973. Home: 8207 San Benito Way Dallas TX 75208 Office: 5207 McKinney Av Dallas TX 75205

DAHLGREN, JOHN ONSGARD, lawyer; b. Missoula, Mont., Sept. 7, 1913; s. John and Geneva (Newhouse) D.; B.A., George Washington U., 1936; J.D., Georgetown U., 1939; children—John Robert, Robin Reed. Admitted to D.C. bar, 1939, Md. bar, 1956; chief counsel requisition div. Bd. Econ. Warfare, Washington, 1941-42; partner law firm Dahlgren, Darragh and Close, 1946—; Pres. Internat. Humanities, Inc. Served from ensign to lt. comdr. USNR, 1941-46; comdr. Res. ret. Mem. Am., Inter-Am. (sec. gen. 1967—), Fed. bar assns., Am. Soc. Internat. Law, Am. Judicature Soc., Bar Assn. D.C. Lutheran. Clubs: University, Internat. Home: 4952 Sentinel Dr Bethesda MD 20016 Office: 1000 Connecticut Av NW Washington DC 20036

DAILEY, GEORGE CURTIS, dentist; b. Newcastle, Pa., Oct. 29, 1941; s. George William and Ann Stuart (Miller) D.; D.D.S., Ohio State U., 1966; certificate in Orthodontics, U. Ala., 1971; m. Marianne L. Barker, June 27, 1964; children—Suzanne Renee, Curtis William. Dental intern Brooke Army Med. Center, San Antonio, 1966-67; resident in orthodontics U. Ala., 1969-71; practice dentistry, specializing in orthodontics, Hampton, Va., 1971—. Served to capt. AUS, 1966-69. Mem. Am., Va. dental assns., Am. Assn. Orthodontists, So. Soc., Orthodontists, Va. Peninsula Dental Soc., Tidewater Orthodontic Soc., Omicron Kappa Upsilon, Delta Sigma Delta. Home: 216 Shifting Log Hampton VA 23369 Office: 1610 B Aberdeen Rd Hampton VA 23366

DAILEY, MARTEL JENNINGS, physician; b. Powellsville, N.C., Oct. 6, 1925; s. Louis Ellsworth and Mary Elizabeth (Owens) D.; B.A., U. Va., 1947; M.D., Med. Coll. Va., 1951; m. Olive Thomas Trader, June 10, 1950 (div. Aug. 1970); children—Charles, Jean, Olivia, John. Intern Norfolk (Va.) Gen. Hosp., 1951-52; practice gen. medicine, Reedville, Va., 1952-63, Williamston, N.C., 1963—; mem. staff Bertie County Hosp., Windsor, N.C., 1963-71; Martin Gen. Hosp., Williamston, 1963-71 officer in charge USPHS, Reedville, 1955-63; med. dir. Martin County Health Dept., Williamston, 1970-71; clinician Planned Parenthood Clinic, Martin County, 1966-71. Co-founder Am. Hepatic Found., Inc., now sec.-treas. Chmn. Martin County A.R.C., 1963-69. Mem. Bertie County Med. Soc. (sec., 1965—), Alpha Omega Alpha, Alpha Chi Sigma. Baptist. Club: Roanoke Country. Research in fetal and neonatal hepatitis. Home: Williamston By Pass Williamston NC 27892 Office: Smithwick St Williamston NC 27892

DAILEY, THOMAS MILLS, JR., gas co. exec.; b. Austin, Tex., Oct. 16, 1913; s. Thomas Mills and Renee E. (Tinney) D.; B.B.A., U. Tex., 1934, postgrad., 1935-36; postgrad. Houston Law Sch., 1937-38; m. Inez Fleming, Sept. 30, 1944; children—Thomas Mills, William Anson. Petroleum economist, Humble Oil, Houston, Tex., 1946-55; mgr. coporate planning and research Tidewater Oil Co., Los Angeles, 1955-64; v.p. West Fla. Natural Gas Co., Panama City, 1964—; also dir. Served to lt. USNR, 1944-46. Mem. Am. Petroleum Inst., Fla. Natural Gas Assn. Episcopalian. Clubs: Bay West Country, Signal Hill Country, St. Andrews Bay Yacht. Home: 405 Bayshore Dr Panama City FL 32401 Office: PO Box 1460 Panama City FL 32401

DALE, BILLY GENE, clergyman; b. Harrisburg, Ill., Aug. 27, 1930; s. James Arthur and Louise Elizabeth (Batey) D.; B.S., Eastern Ill. U., 1961; m. Doris Jean Aldridge, May 18, 1952; children—Pamela Beth, Lisa Ann, William Leighton, Bruce Gregory. Mem. staff chief clk.'s office FBI, Washington, 1956; ordained to ministry Ch. of God, 1957; pastor First Chs. of God, Sullivan, Ill., 1956-61, Sarasota, Fla., 1961-65, Louisville, 1965—. Gen. Assembly chmn. Ch. of God in Ky., 1973—. Served with USAF, 1951-55. Hon. chief of police, Louisville. Ky. Col. Address: 4408 Taylorsville Rd Louisville KY 40220

DALE, GEORGE WILLIAM, sales cons., real estate broker; b. Coldwater, Kan., July 15, 1912; s. George William and Nellie (Haynes) Dale; B.A. in Bus., Fairmount Coll., 1936; postgrad. U. Kan., 1945-50; m. Bernita Bates, Nov. 22, 1933; 1 son, Roger Dean. Tng. course planner N.Am. Aviation, Kansas City, Kan., 1941-44; operations mgr. Consumers Co-op. Assn., Kansas City, Mo., 1944-54; pres. Pallister Mfg. Co., Wichita, Kan., 1954-57; pres. Hollidays Blueprint & Supply, Inc., Wichita, Kan., 1957-65; realtor, cons., Eureka Springs, Ark., 1966—. Mem. Eureka Springs Real Estate Bd. (pres. 1968-70). Mem. Christian Ch. (chmn. bd. elders 1946-50). Mason (Shriner). Address: Rural Route 2 Eureka Springs AR 72632

DALE, GLENN HILBURN, chem. engr.; b. Mountain Park, Okla., Aug. 25, 1923; s. Otis Elbridge and Eula (Hoover) D.; B.S., U. Okla., 1944; m. Vivian B. Jewitt, Aug. 30, 1947; children—Denise Ann, Marsha Jane, Laura Ellen. With Phillips Petroleum Co., Bartlesville, Okla., 1944—, beginning as asso. chemist, successively process design engr., pilot plant supr., br. mgr. separation, staff engr. refining process, 1944-72, staff engr. refining and separation, 1973—. Mem. Vol. Tech. Assistance Program. Mem. Am. Chem. Soc., Am. Inst. Chem. Engrs. Methodist (lay del.). Patentee in field. Home: 2900 Staats Dr Bartlesville OK 74003 Office: 128 RB 3 Phillips Petroleum Co Bartlesville OK 74004

DALE, GROVER CLEVELAND, physician; b. nr. Seven Springs, N.C., Apr. 7, 1897; s. Curtis James and Julia (Thompson) D. ; A.B., U. N.C., 1920; M.D., U. Pa., 1925; m. Sarah Maud Eason, May 18, 1929. Intern St. Joseph's Hosp., Lancaster, Pa., 1925-26; practice medicine, specializing in proctology, Goldsboro, N.C., 1926—; electrocardiologist Wayne Meml. Hosp., Goldsboro, 1936—; med. dir. Wayne County Sanitorium, 1940-53. Served as seaman 2d class USN, 1918-19. Fellow A.C.P.; mem. N.C., Fourth Dist., Wayne County (pres. 1939) med. socs., A.M.A. Democrat. Presbyn. Mason (32 deg.). Contbr. articles med. jours. Home: 307 S Pine View Av Goldsboro NC 27530 Office: Wachovia Bldg Goldsboro NC 27530

DALE, JAMES C., JR., lawyer; b. Dec. 14, 1906; M.A., Vanderbilt U., 1929. Admitted to Tenn. bar, 1931; clk., master Chancery Ct., 1939-46; now mem. firm Dale, Thompson & Miles, Nashville. Mem. Nashville, Tenn., Am. bar assns., Phi Beta Kappa. Office: Nashville City Bank & Trust Bldg Nashville TN 37201

DALE, JOHN IRVIN, III, chemist; b. Knoxville, Tenn., May 14, 1935; s. John Irvin, Jr., and Cecile Lurline (Chandler) D.; B.S., Carson-Newman Coll., 1956; M.A., U. N.C., 1959; Ph.D., U. Va., 1963; m. Emily Louise Fornes, Sept. 1, 1962; 1 dau., Susan Marie. Grad. teaching asst. U. N.C., 1956-58; asso. chemist Oak Ridge Nat. Labs., 1957-58; with Tenn. Eastman Co., research labs., Kingsport, Tenn., 1962-67, organic chems. div., 1967—, sr. chemist devel. and control dept., 1967-69, sr. chemist dyes dept., 1969-73, sr. chemist hydroquinone dept., 1973, sr. chemist intermediate dept., 1973—. Mem. Kingsport Citizens Adv. Com., 1965-67; dir. Kingsport Girls Club, 1965-68. Justice of peace Sullivan County, Tenn., 1969-72. Shell Found. fellow, 1961-62; recipient Pres.'s and Bd. Visitors prize, Soc. of Sigma Xi, U. Va., 1964. Mem. Am. Chem. Soc., Am. Assn. Textile Chemists and Colorists, Carson-Newman Coll. Alumni Assn., Sigma Xi, Alpha Chi Sigma, Blue Key. Republican. Presbyn. (elder). Moose. Club: Orebank Ruritan (Kingsport). Contbr. articles profl. jours. Patentee in field. Home: 5300 Orebank Rd Kingsport TN 37664 Office: Tennessee Eastman Co Kingsport TN 37662

D'ALESSANDRO, EDWARD ANTHONY, library adminstr.; b. Cleve., Mar. 11, 1913; s. Rocco M. and Isabella (Romanelli) D'A.; B.A. magna cum laude, John Carroll U., 1937; B.S. in L.S. (William Howard Brett scholar), Western Res. U., 1938; m. Grace Martha Musche, Nov. 29, 1947; children—Edward R., Paul A. With Cleve. Pub. Library, 1927-70, jr. asst. librarian sociology div. main library, 1938-41, asst. br. librarian Euclid-100 br., 1941-42, br. librarian Woodland br., 1942-43, Fleet br., 1946-49, Eastman br., 1949-51, head book repair dept. 1951-54, asst. head main library, 1954-56, bus. mgr., 1956-59, asst. dir., 1959-66, dep. dir., 1966-69, dir., 1969-70; spl. asst. for planning mgmt. reference dept. Library of Congress, Washington, 1970—. Mem. personnel com., trustee Cleve. U. Settlement, 1948-51; mem. Citizen's League Cleve., 1963-70; mem. Fairfax Police Youth Club, 1970—. Served with USAAF, 1943-45, AUS, 1945-46. Mem. A.L.A. (past mem. library equipment com.), John Carroll U., Western Res. alumni assns., D.C. Library Assn., Library of Congress Profl. Assn., Library of Congress Welfare and Recreation Assn. Lutheran. Home: Apt 19 9930 Fairfax Sq Fairfax VA 22030 Office: Library of Congress Washington DC 20540

DALEY, ROGER A., newspaper exec. Pres. Knoxville News-Sentinel Co. Office: 294 W Church St Knoxville TN 37901*

DALL, CURTIS BEAN, patriotic orgn. exec.; b. N.Y.C., Oct. 24, 1896; s. Charles Austin and Mary (Bean) D.; grad. Mercersburg Acad., 1916; degree Princeton, 1920; m. Anna Roosevelt, June 5, 1926 (div. 1933); children—Anna Eleanor, Curtis Roosevelt; m. 2d, Katharine Miller Leas, Dec. 15, 1938; children—Katharine G. (Mrs. Earle Boulton III), Stephen A., James H., Mary B. (Mrs. C. Dary Dunham Jr.). Mem. N.Y. Stock Exchange, gov. Assn. Stock Exchanges Firms, 1933-40; organizer Tenn. Gas & Transmission Co., 1940; natural gas and oil exploration, San Antonio, 1945-51, Phila., 1951; with Liberty Lobby, Washington, 1960—, chmn. bd., 1963—; speaker. Nat. chmn. Constn. party, 1960-64. Served as ensign, USN, 1918-19, with N.Y. N.G., 1920-23, to col. USAAF, 1942-45. Recipient Patrick Henry award Va. Conservative party, 1969; citation Polish Freedom Fighters in U.S., 1971, Order of Lafayette, 1971. Mem. Mil. Order World Wars, S.R., S.C.V., V.F.W. Clubs: Nassau, Cap and Gown (Princeton); Army-Navy (Washington). Author: F.D.R., My Exploited Father-in-Law, 1964; The War Lords of Washington, 1972. Home: 5375 Duke St Alexandria VA 22304 Office: 300 Independence Av SE Washington DC 20003

DALLDORF, FREDERIC GILBERT, educator; b. N.Y.C., Mar. 12, 1932; s. Gilbert J. and Frances E. (Barnhart) D.; A.B., Bowdoin Coll., 1954; M.D., Cornell U., 1958; m. Joanna S. Stein, June 26, 1956; children—Peter, Sharon, Carolyn. Intern, N.Y. Hosp., N.Y.C., 1958-59, resident, 1959-60; resident N.C. Meml. Hosp., Chapel Hill, 1960-63; faculty U. N.C. Sch. Medicine, Chapel Hill, 1965—, prof., 1973—. Med. examiner Orange County, 1965—. Served to capt. AUS, 1963-65. Diplomate Bds. Anatomic and Clin. Pathology. Mem. A.M.A., N.C. Med. Soc., Am. Soc. for Exptl. Pathology, Am. Assn. Pathologists and Bacteriologists. Research with heart disease, capillary permeability, effects of bacterial toxins. Home: 11 Woodhaven St Chapel Hill NC 17514

DALLMAN, GLENN ROBERT, library dir.; b. Oconomowoc, Wis., July 31, 1927; s. Henry William and Alma (Baehler) D.; B.A. magna cum laude, Northland Coll., 1950; M.Ed., U. Wis. at Milw., 1954; M.S. in Library Sci., Western Res. U., 1962; m. Charlotte Marie Frank, June 26, 1954; children—Jeffry Paul, Jaclyn Marie. Tchr. Trinity High Sch., Fort Lauderdale, Fla., 1950-51; tchr., prin. Lutheran Tchrs. Tng. Coll., Ibakachi, Nigeria, 1951-57; tchr., librarian Concordia Coll., Portland, Ore., 1957-58; tchr. Luth. High Sch., Cleve., 1959-61; librarian Cleveland Heights (O.) Pub. Library, 1961-62; dir. library Indian River Community Coll., Fort Pierce, Fla., 1962-66, St. Petersburg Jr. Coll., Clearwater, Fla., 1966—. Served with USNR, 1945-46. Mem. A.L.A., Southeastern, Fla., St. Lucie County (dir., pres., 1965-66) library assns., Fla. Assn. Community Colls. Home: 1740 Harmony Dr Clearwater FL 33516 Office: 2465 Drew St Clearwater FL 33515

DALRYMPLE, DAVID EDWARD, physician; b. Elkhart, Ind., Nov. 10, 1936; s. Thurlow Edward and Irene Guinevere (Northrop) D.; A.B., DePauw U., 1958; M.S., Purdue U., 1960; postgrad. Ind. U., 1960-61; M.D., U. Chgo., 1965; m. Carol Mae Anderson, Aug. 2, 1959; children—David Northrop, Brian Anderson. Intern State U. Ia., 1965-66, resident, 1966-68; NIH fellow Washington U. Sch. Medicine, St. Louis, 1968-69; practice medicine specializing in internal medicine, Atlanta, 1971—; chmn. patient care and dictary com., exec. com., sec. dept. medicine Northside Hosp., Atlanta. Vis. clin. instr. Med. Coll. Ga., Augusta, 1969-70. Chmn. med. com. drug abuse Sandy Springs (Atlanta), Ga.; mem. N. Fulton County Medically Indigent Program; med. adviser Kalarooso Puppet Drug Abuse Show. Served with AUS, 1969-71; med. officer Specialized Treatment Center, Ft. Gordon. Recipient Resident award U. Ia., Iowa City, 1965. Diplomate Am. Bd. Internal Medicine, Am. Bd. Med. Examiners. Mem. Am. Fedn. for Clin. Research, Fulton County Med. Soc., A.C.P., Am., Ga. socs. internal medicine, A.M.A., U.S. Handball Assn., Atlanta (jr. trustee), Ga. med. assns., Diabetes Assn. Atlanta (v.p.), Ga. Thoracic Soc., Ga. Wildlife Fedn., Sigma Xi, Alpha Tau Omega. Episcopalian. Club: Flying. Publisher, Atlanta Medicine. Contbr. articles to profl. jours. Home: 5515 Whitewood Ct Dunwoody GA 30338 Office: 6500 Vernon Woods Dr Atlanta GA 30328

DALTON, ALVIN RAY, banker; b. Plainview, Tex., Nov. 28, 1932; s. Bernice A. and Clarice (Harlin) D.; student Tenn. Poly. Inst., 1951; courses Am. Inst. Banking; grad. Southwestern Grad. Sch. Banking, So. Meth. U., 1972; m. Barbara Ann Bowers, Nov. 27, 1953; children—Terry Ray, Kathryne Sheree. With 1st Nat. Bank of Fort Worth, 1955—, v.p. data processing, 1968—. Active Boy Scouts Am., Civil Air Patrol. Served with USAF, 1951-55. Mem. Data Processing Mgrs. Assn. (past chpt. pres., individual performance award), Am. Inst. Banking, Nat. Rifle Assn. Baptist. Home: 6328 Friar Ct Fort Worth TX 76119 Office: 1 Burnett Plaza Fort Worth TX 76101

DALTON, DAVID LANDRESS, urologist; b. Chattanooga, Feb. 17, 1944; s. Sethur White and Mary Elizabeth (Landress) D.; B.A., Vanderbilt U., 1966; M.D., U. Tenn., 1969; m. Jeanne Maria Hervio, May 11, 1968; 1 dau., Nathalie Jeanne. Mixed med. intern City of Memphis Hosps., 1970; resident surgery Bapt. Meml. Hosp., Memphis, 1971; sr. asst. resident gen. and thoracic surgery Duke Med. Center, Durham, N.C., 1972, resident urology, 1973—; mem. univ. staff 1974—. Mem. Alpha Omega Alpha, Phi Delta Theta, Phi Chi. Episcopalian. Home: 1011 Anderson St Durham NC 27705 Office: Box 3225 Duke Med Center Durham NC 27710

DALTON, DONALD H., lawyer; b. Stitzer, Wis.; s. Charles Christian and Alvina D.; student U.S. Naval Acad., 1925-29, Columbia U., 1930; B.S., U. Chgo., 1931; postgrad. Yale, 1934-35; J.D., Georgetown U., 1947; m. Virginia Brady, Sept. 20, 1931; 1 dau., Sylvia (Mrs. Howard R. Searight); m. 2d, Irene Martin, Sept. 16, 1939; children—Doris J. (Mrs. John R. Harper), Donald H., Diane I. Reporter Washington Post, 1945; admitted D.C. bar, 1946, Ill. bar, 1947, Md. bar, 1952; pvt. practice law, Washington, Ill., Md.; prof. pub. bar, relations Southeastern U., 1949-58. Trustee Legal Aid Soc. D.C. Served with USNR, World War II. Recipient certificate of pub. relations achievement Am. Pub. Relations Assn., 1957; Distinguished Alumni award Columbia U. Club, Washington, 1968. Mem. Am. (chmn. pub. relations com. gen. practice sect.), Fed., D.C. (1st v.p., dir.), Md. (mem. pub. relations com.), Chgo. bar assns., Am. Arbitration Assn. (adv. com. to pub. relations com.), English-Speaking Union, Am. Legion, Res. Officers Naval Service (pres.), Judge Advocates Gen. Assn. (dir.), The Counsellors, U.S. Capitol, Montgomery County hist. socs., U. Chgo. Alumni Assn., U.S. Naval Acad. Alumni Assn., Lincoln Group D.C. (pres. 1971—), Newcomen Soc., S.A.R., Mil. Order Fgn. Wars, Civil War Round Table, Nat. Sojourners (pres. Washington chpt.), Delta Theta Phi. Mason (Shriner). Clubs: Columbia U. (pres. Washington 1960-71); Army and Navy Country, Yale, Army and Navy, Nat. Lawyers, Nat. Press. Home: 8603 Springdell Pl Chevy Chase MD 20015 Office: Dalton Matthews & Sheehy Fed Bar Bldg W 1819 H St NW Washington DC 20006

DALTON, JESS NEWMAN, lawyer; b. Independence, Kan., Feb. 3, 1912; s. Edward Andrew and Floss Ellen (Newman) D.; A.B., Washburn U., Topeka, 1934, J.D., 1937; Mexican Legal Title, Universidad Nacional de Mexico, 1939; grad. Advanced Mgmt. Program, Harvard, 1952; m. Elaine Virginia Courtney, Dec. 7, 1957; children—Nancy McNeese, Laurie Bernat, Jess Newman, Corneilia Virginia, Molly Adrienne. Admitted to Mexican bar, 1939; since practiced in Mexico City; partner firm Basham, Ringe & Correa, Mexico City, 1937-45, Goodrich, Dalton, Little & Riquelme, 1945—. Chmn. bd. Mexico City Valley Coca Cola Bottling Co.; dir. Mexican subsidiaries Procter & Gamble, Scott Paper Co., Owens-Corning Fiberglas, Burlington Industries, Pan Am. Ins., Aluminum Co. Am., others; dir. Am. Standard, N.Y.C., Sistemas Banco de Comercio Mexico City. Past chmn. fund drive Mexico City Community Chest; past pres. Am. Soc. Past chmn. bd. dirs. Am. Brit. Cowdray Hosp., Mexico City; bd. dirs., mem. exec. com. U. Ams., Puebla, Mexico, 1965—. Mem. S.A.R., Sons Am. Colonists. Clubs: University, River (N.Y.C.). Home: 2570 Paseo de la Reforma Pvt 115 Mexico City 10 Mexico Office: 355 Paseo de la Reforma PO Box 93 Bis Mexico City 5 Mexico

DALTON, JOHN NICHOLS, lawyer, lt. gov. Va.; b. Emporia, Va., July 11, 1931; s. Ted R. and Mary (Turner) D.; A.B., William and Mary Coll., 1953; LL.B., U. Va., 1957; m. Edwina Jeanette Panzer, Feb. 18, 1956; children—Katherine Scott, Ted Ernest, John Nichols, Mary Helen. Admitted to Va. bar, 1957; partner Dalton, Stone &

Clay, Radford, Va., 1957—; lt. gov. Va., 1974—. Vice pres., dir. Meredith & Tate, Pulaski, Va., 1961—; dir. Sutton Devel. Corp., Radford, 1st & Mchts. Nat. Bank, Radford. Pres., Young Republican Fedn. Va., 1960; treas. Va. Rep. Com., 1960, gen. counsel, 1961-72. Mem. Va. Ho. of Dels., 1966-72, Va. Senate, 1973. Served to 1st lt. AUS, 1954-56. Mem. Am. Legion, Sigma Alpha Epsilon. Mason (Shriner, 32 deg.), Moose, Odd Fellow. Home: 411 4th St Radford VA 24141 Office: Norwood St Radford VA 24141

DALVIT, LEWIS, symphony condr.; b. Denver; B.A., Beloit Coll.; M.A., Vandercook Coll. Mus.; studied with Pierre Monteux, William Steinberg, Richard Lert, Boris Goldovsky, Thor Johnson, Lillian Poenisch; m. Patricia Dougan, 1949; children—Jacqueline, Stephanie. Founder, condr. Beloit (Wis.) Symphony Orch., 1953-65; asst. condr. Honolulu Symphony, 1963-64; artist in residence Beloit Coll., 1964-65, chmn. dept. music, 1965; condr. Jackson (Miss.) Symphony Orch., 1965—; mem. music faculty Belhaven Coll., 1965—; guest condr. symphony orchs. Germany, Mexico, U.S., including Carnegie Hall Symphony of Air, Pitts. Symphony, Atlanta Symphony; guest condr. Pierre Monteux Meml. Concerts, Sewanee Summer Music Center; condr. ballet Atlanta Ballet, 1969, 70, 72, Jackson Ballet Guild, 1965—, Rockford (Ill.) Youth Ballet, 1958-64, Honolulu Ballet Orch.; guest condr. Wolf Trap Center for Performing Arts, 1973. Served with AC, AUS, 1943-46. Mem. Phi Mu Alpha Sinfonia (1st Ann. Achievement award). Address: Box 4584 Jackson MS 39216

DALY, JOHN J., lawyer; b. Scranton, Pa., June 7, 1927; s. Stanley W. and Clare L. (Hagan) D.; B.A., George Washington U., 1949, J.D., 1953; div.; children—Dean R., Christopher J. Admitted to Va. bar, 1954; U.S. Supreme Ct. bar; asst. commonwealth atty. Commonwealth of Va., 1954-58; partner Siciliano, Daly, Ellis, Sheridan & Dyer, Arlington, Va. and predecessor firms, 1958-73, pvt. practice, 1973—. Mem. Am., Va., Arlington bar assns., Bar Assn. D.C., No. Va. Trial Lawyers Assn., Counsellors, Am. Arbitration Assn., Va. Assn. Def. Attys. Home: 1200 N Nash St Arlington VA 22209 Office: 1911 Ft Myer Dr Arlington VA 22209

DALY, VICTOR REGINALD, former govt. ofcl.; b. N.Y.C., Nov. 22, 1895; s. Thomas Henry and Marie (Maynard) D.; B.A., Cornell, 1919; m. Adelaide Cook, Feb. 5, 1918 (dec. 1954); children—Peggy Adelaide (Mrs. John L. Waters), Millicent Cook; m. 2d, Lenore Brown, Aug. 18, 1958. With U.S. Dept. Labor, Washington, 1932-67, dep. dir. U.S. Employment Service, 1959-67. Served to 1st lt. 367th Inf., U.S. Army, 1917-19. Decorated Croix de Guerre (France). Mem. Am. Bridge Assn. (a founder, charter mem. 1932, pres. 1949-64, pres. emeritus 1964—), Alpha Phi. Club: Cavendish Bridge (N.Y.C.). Home: 1612 Manchester Lane NW Washington DC 20011

DAMBRAUSKAS, VINCENT, army officer; b. Utena, Lithuania, June 17, 1933; s. Thomas and Sophie (Dumbrava) D. (parents Am. citizens); B.S., U. Mich., 1955, B.S. in Engring. Math., 1963, M.S., 1963; postgrad. U.S. Army Command and Gen. Staff Coll., 1965, U.S. Army War Coll., 1972-73; m. Milda Fricas, Apr. 7, 1956; children—Peter T., Donna M., Sofia A. Commd. 2d lt. U.S. Army, 1955, advanced through grades to lt. col., 1968; operations officer 53d Signal Bn., Ft. Hood, Tex., 1955-57; operations officer 97th Signal Bn., Germany, 1958-61; instrumentation planning officer Combat Devels. Command Experimentation Command, Ft. Ord, Cal., 1963-68; with Def. Communications Agy., Vietnam, 1967; mem. Army Gen. Staff, Washington, 1968-70; comdr. 143d Signal Bn., Germany, 1970-71; communications and electronics rep. to Nat. Mil. Command System Office Joint Chiefs of Staff, Washington, 1973—. Decorated Legion of Merit, Bronze Star medal, Meritorious Service medal with oak leaf cluster, Army Commendation medal. Mem. I.E.E.E. Office: Office Joint Chiefs of Staff J-6 Pentagon Washington DC 20315

DAMERON, THOMAS BARKER, JR., orthopaedic surgeon; b. Rocky Mount, N.C., June 1, 1924; s. Thomas Barker and Isa (Sills) D.; student The Citadel, 1941-42, U. N.C., 1942-44, Duke, 1947; M.D., U. Cal., 1945; m. Nancy Jane Henry, Aug. 26, 1949; children—Thomas Barker III, David Henry, Christopher Buxton Williams, Nancy Van Vleet, Rebecca Jane. Intern, Baylor U. Hosp., 1947-48; surg. house staff Grady Meml. Hosp., 1948-49; resident orthopaedic surgery Johns Hopkins Hosp., Balt., 1949-54; practice medicine, specializing in orthopaedic surgery, Raleigh, N.C., 1954—; mem. staff Rex Hosp., Wake Meml. Hosp.; clin. asso. prof. surgery (orthopedics) U. N.C. Sch. Medicine; adj. prof. poultry sci. N.C. State U. Mem. regional com. Morehead scholarships U. N.C.; bd. dirs. Raleigh United Fund; accreditation com. N.C. Crippled Children's Services. Served with USNR, 1943-45, 59-61. Diplomate Am. Bd. Orthopaedic Surgery. Mem. Am. Acad. Orthopaedic Surgery, Assn. Bone and Joint Surgeons, N.C. (past pres.), Am. (exec. com.), Piedmont orthopaedic assns., Am., So. councilor, mem. exec. com.), N.C., Wake County (pres.) med. socs., N.Y. Acad. Sci. Methodist (ofcl. bd.). Asso. editor Clin. Orthopaedics and Related Research. Contbr. articles profl. jours. Home: 414 Scotland St Raleigh NC 27609 Office: 600 Wade Av Raleigh NC 27605

DAMIAN, RAYMOND TRAIAN, parasitologist, educator; b. Phila., Aug. 11, 1934; s. Romulus and Christina (Pepici) D.; B.S., U. Akron, 1956; M.S., Fla. State U., 1958, Ph.D., 1962; m. Anna Jean Clifton, Aug. 31, 1957; children—Jane Camille, David Clifton, Leah Dawn. Research asso. Fla. State U., Tallahassee, 1962-63; asst. prof. biology Emory U., Atlanta, 1963-67; immunologist Southwest Found. for Research and Edn., San Antonio, 1967-69, asso. found. scientist, 1969-73; adj. asso. prof. microbiology U. Tex. Med. Sch., San Antonio, 1972-73; asso. prof. Zoology U. Ga., Athens, 1973—. Mem. Royal Soc. Tropical Medicine and Hygiene, Am. Assn. Immunologists, N.Y. Acad. Scis., Am. Soc. Parasitologists, A.A.A.S., Am. Soc. Tropical Medicine and Hygiene, Southwest Assn. Parasitologists, Am. Assn. U. Profs., Sigma Xi. Contbr. sci. articles to books and profl. jours. Home: Route 2 180 Northwoods Rd Watkinsville GA 30677 Office: Dept Zoology U Ga Athens GA 30602

DAMON, GLENN HERBERT, phys. chemist; b. Winnebago, Minn., Nov. 3, 1901; s. Albert Charles and Grace (Rundall) D.; B.Ch.E., U. Wis., 1927, Ph.D., 1932; m. Laura Eleanore Gillingham, June 22, 1932; children—Paul, Carolyn, Keith. Instr., Mich. Coll. Mining and Tech., 1927-30, asst. prof., 1932-40, asso. prof., 1940-43; group leader Manhattan Project, N.Y.C., 1943-46; asst. chief research lab. U.S. Bur. Mines, Pitts., 1946-60, staff coordinator, Washington, 1960-73, cons., 1973—; cons. explosives, fires and explosions, accident investigations. Recipient U.S. Dept. Interior Distinguished Service award, 1970. Fellow Am. Inst. Chemists, Am. Inst. Aeronautics and Astronautics (asso.); mem. Combusion Inst., Am. Chem. Soc., Am. Inst. Chem. Engrs., N.Y. Acad. Sci., Sigma Xi, Phi Lambda Upsilon. Club: Internat. Town and Country. Author: (with Maki) Qualitative Analysis, 1939, rev. edit., 1941. Contbr. numerous research articles to sci. jours. Patentee missile fuels; atomic energy. Home: 2445 N Sycamore St Arlington VA 22207 Office: US Bur Mines Washington DC

DAMRON, RALPH FORD, savs. and loan assn. exec.; b. Weeksbury, Ky., Oct. 12, 1921; s. Fred and Myrtle (Atkins) D.; B.B.A., Bowling Green Bus. U., 1948; m. Elizabeth Jeanette Goodall, Mar. 1, 1944; 1 son, Gregory Ford. Airport controller FAA, Birmingham, Ala., 1945-46; salesman Burroughs Corp., various locations, 1948-58; v.p., br. mgr. El Paso Fed. Savs. & Loan Assn., 1958—; financial counselor, 1958—; tchr., cons. Nat. Inst. Savs. and Loans, El Paso, 1960—; real estate broker, ins. recorder, 1967—. Served with USAF, 1942-45. Mem. Am. Inst. Savs. and Loans. Methodist (mem. bd. finance 1968-73). Rotarian, Optimist (v.p. El Paso br. 1960-65, Kiwanian. Home: 8717 Parkland Dr El Paso TX 79925 Office: 1401 McRae Blvd El Paso TX 79925

DANBY, JOHN MICHAEL ANTHONY, educator; b. London, Eng., Aug. 5, 1929; s. Herbert and Hilda (Waddy) D.; B.A., Christ Church Oxford U., 1950; Ph.D., U. Manchester (Eng.), 1953; m. Phyllis Creighton, Sept. 6, 1958; children—Colin, Arthur, Michael, Dinah, Winifred. Came to U.S., 1957, naturalized, 1965. Prin. oboist London Philharmonic Orch., 1956-57; asst. prof. astronomy U. Minn., Mpls., 1957-61; asso. prof. Yale, 1961-67; prof. math., physics N.C. State U., Raleigh, 1967—. Pres., Wake County chpt. N.C. Symphony Soc., 1973—. Mem. exec. com. Wake County Democratic party, 1968-72. Mem. Royal, Am. astronom. socs., Internat. Astronom. Union. Editorial com. Celestial Mechanics, 1970—. Home: 707 Lakestone Dr Raleigh NC 27609

DANDRIDGE, WILLIAM SHELTON, orthopedic surgeon; b. Atoka, Okla., May 21, 1914; s. Theodore Oscar and Estelle (Shelton) D.; B.A., U. Okla., 1935; M.D., U. Ark., 1939; M.S., Baylor U., 1950; m. Pearl Sessions, Feb. 3, 1941; 1 dau., Diana Dawn. Intern St. Paul's Hosp., Dallas, 1939-40; surgical residence Med. Arts Hosp., Dallas, 1940; commd. 1st lt. USAF, advanced through grades to lt. col., 1950; chief reconditioning service and reconstructive surgery Ashburn Gen. Hosp., McKinney, Tex., 1945-46; neurosurg. resident Brooke Army Med. Center, San Antonio, 1946-47; orthopedic surg. resident, 1947-50; chief orthopedic service and gen. surgery Francis E. Warren AFB, Cheyenne, Wyo., Travis AFB, Susan, Cal., 1950-51; chief orthopedic service and gen. surgery Shepherd AFB, 1951-52; comdg. officer, chief orthopedic service, chief gen. surgery Craig AFB Hosp., Selma, Ala., 1952-53; practice medicine specializing in orthopedic surgery Muskogee, Okla., 1954-69, 72—; active staff Muskegon Gen. Hosp.; orthopedic econs. McAlester (Okla.) Gen. Hosp., VA Hosp., Muskogee. Exec. mem. Eastern Okla. council Boy Scouts Am. Fellow A.C.S., Internat. Coll. Surgeons; mem. Am. Fracture Assn., Nat. Found. (adviser 1958-61), N.Y. Acad. Sci., Okla. State, Pan-Am., So., Aerospace med. assns., A.M.A., Eastern Okla. Counties med. socs., S.W. Surg. Congress, Am. Rheumatology Soc., Democrat. Methodist. Mason (32 deg., K.T. Shriner, Jester), Lion. Club: Muskogee Country. Contbr. articles to profl. jours. Home: 3504 University Blvd Muskogee OK 74401 Office: 1601 W Okmulgee St Muskogee OK 74401

DANIEL, ARTHUR RATCLIFFE, JR., engring. co. exec.; b. Blackstone, Va., Aug. 19, 1932; s. Arthur Ratcliffe and Susie (Waller) D.; B.S.C.E., Va. Poly. Inst., 1954; m. Eva Delorous Foster, May 18, 1952; children—Sherri Delorous, Arthur Ratcliffe III. Div. traffic engr. Ohio Dept. Hwys., Marietta, 1955-59 area traffic engr. N.C. Hwy. Commn., Raleigh, 1959-64; dir. Louisville-Jefferson County (Ky.) Dept. Traffic Engring., 1964-69; pres. Sherridan Engring. Inc., Louisville, Ky., 1966—. Chmn. engring. com. Citizens Traffic Commn., Marietta, 1956-59; mem. Ky. Gov.'s Efficiency Task Force, 1967. Registered profl. engr., Ind., Ky., N.C., Ohio, Tenn., W.Va., Fla. Mem. Inst. Traffic Engrs. (gen. chmn. 1967 ann. meeting So. sect.), Ohio Soc. Profl. Engrs. (sec.-treas. Muskingum Valley chpt. 1958-59), Ky., Nat. socs. profl. engrs. Elk. Clubs: Plantation Country, Jeffersonville-Elks Country. Author: Urban Transportation in Louisville, Kentucky, 1966. Home: 3511 Forest Brook Dr Louisville KY 40207 Office: 120 Village Louisville KY 40243

DANIEL, AUBREY MARSHALL, III, lawyer; b. Monks Corner, S.C., May 16, 1941; s. Aubrey Marshall, Jr. and Laura Frances (Morris) D.; grad. Woodberry Forest Sch., 1959; B.A., U. Va., 1963; LL.B., U. Richmond, 1966; m. Shirley Virginia Hanbury, June 19, 1965; children—Laura Elizabeth, Ann Meade. Admitted to Va. bar, 1966, D.C. bar, 1971; mem. firms Minor, Thompson, Savage, Richmond, Va., 1966-67, Williams, Connolly & Califano, Washington, 1971—. Served to capt. AUS, 1967-71. Decorated Army Commendation medal; recipient Outstanding Service award Nat. Dist. Attys. Assn., 1971; Elliott-Black award Am. Ethical Union, 1972. Mem. Am., Va., D.C. bar assns., Am., Va. trial lawyers assns., Phi Delta Phi, Delta Phi. Home: 3010 1/2 R St NW Washington DC 20005 Office: Williams Connolly & Califano 839 17th NW Washington DC 20006

DANIEL, CLAUDE PIPPO, dentist; b. Franklinton, La., Feb. 27, 1916; s. Chester Pippo and Elizabeth Van Dora (Simmons) D.; student La. State U., 1935-36; D.D.S., Loyola U., 1940; postgrad. Northwestern U., 1949, Washington U., 1951, U. Ala., 1954; m. Erephile Margaret Gremillion, June 22, 1940; children—Claudia (Mrs. John Atkins Melton), Janis (Mrs. Joseph Albert Roman), Anne (Mrs. Greg Herman Briese), Claude Pippo. Pvt. practice dentistry, Bogalusa, La., 1950—, Slidell, La., 1952—; mem. staff Charity Hosp. chief orthodontics Bogalusa Community Med. Center, 1955—. Pres. Crippled Children Bogalusa, 1960-72; active United Fund. Served to 1st lt. USAAF, 1941-45. Decorated Bronze Star medal. Mem. Acad. Internat. Dentistry, Am. Dental Soc., Kells Hon. Orthological Soc., Am., So. socs. orthodontics, La., New Orleans orthodontic assns., Am. Legion, V.F.W., D.A.V., Bogalusa C. of C., Psi Omega. Democrat. K.C., Rotarian. Home: 1532 Founders Dr Bogalusa LA 70427 Office: 315 Memphis St Bogalusa LA 70427

DANIEL, HAROLD TURNER, sch. supt.; b. Locust Grove, Ga., May 26, 1916; s. Emmett Benjamin and Willie (Mae) D.; A.B., U. Ga., 1937, M.Ed., 1948, postgrad., 1963, Specialist in Edn., 1971; m. Mary Rowan, Mar. 3, 1940; children—Harold Turner, Evelyn Claire, Randolph. Tchr., Spalding County Bd. Edn., 1938-39; prin. Butts County Bd. Edn., 1941-42; prin. Pike County Bd. Edn., 1942-44; supt. Pike County Schs., Zebulon, Ga., 1945-72; adminstrv. cons. Coop. Ednl. Service Agy., Griffin, Ga., 1972—. Bd. dirs. Flint River Regional Library. Mem. N.E.A., Ga. Edn. Assn., Ga. Assn. County Sch. Supts. (pres.). Methodist. Mason, Lion. Address: Route 2 McDonough GA 30253

DANIEL, JOSEPH CARL, JR., educator; b. Murphysboro, Ill., Aug. 21, 1927; s. Joseph Carl and Alice (G'Sell) D.; B.S., St. Louis U., 1949; M.S., U. Mich., 1950; Ph.D., U. Colo., 1956; m. Mary Patricia Hurley, June 30, 1951; children—Catherine (Mrs. David Johnson), Joseph, Mark, Judith, Edward, Alice. Instr. Adams State Coll., 1952-55, asst. prof., 1955-59, asso. prof., 1959-60; sr. research fellow in biophysics U. Colo. Med. Center, 1960-62, asst. prof., 1962-65, asso. prof., 1965-71; vis. scientist Cambridge (Eng.) U., 1968-69; prof., head dept. zoology U. Tenn., Knoxville, 1971—. Asso. dir. Population Research Inst., Oak Ridge, Tenn., 1972—; cons. biology div. Oak Ridge Nat. Lab., 1973. Served with USNR, 1945-47. Fellow Am. Soc. Zoologists; mem. A.A.A.S., Am. Genetics Assn., Am. Soc. Cell Biology, Soc. Developmental Biology, Soc. Study of Reprodn., Internat. Soc. Developmental Biologists, Perinatal Research Soc., Sigma Xi, Phi Sigma. Author: Methods in Mammalian Embryology, 1971. Mem. editorial bd. Jour. of Experimental Zoology. Contbr. numerous articles to sci. jours. Home: 5505 Crestwood Dr Knoxville TN 37914

DANIEL, KATHRYN BARCHARD, educator; b. Foley, Ala., Jan. 9, 1931; d. Frank Vernon and Myrtle (Morris) Barchard; B.S., U. Ala., 1952, M.A., 1961, Ph.D., 1963; m. James L. Daniel, 1954 (div. 1958); 1 dau., Pamela Kathryn. Tchr. pub. schs. Baldwin County, Foley, Ala., 1952-60; asst. prof. ednl. psychology Monmouth Coll., West Long Branch, N.J., 1963-64; asso. prof. ednl. psychology Newark State Coll., Union, N.J., 1964-66; asso. prof. U. S.C., Columbia, 1966-69, prof., chmn. com. ednl. psychology, 1969-73; prof., coordinator research and devel. Sch. Nursing, U. Ala., Birmingham, 1973—. Cons., Regional Ednl. Lab., pub. schs. N.C., S.C., Va., N.J., 1963-68; evaluation cons. pilot kindergarten program S.C. Dept. Edn., 1969-72, early childhood edn. program Williamsburg County (S.C.) Sch. Dist., 1968—. Nat. Def. Edn. Act fellow, 1960-63. Mem. Am. Psychol. Assn., Am. Personnel and Guidance Assn., Am. Ednl. Research Assn., Assn. Supervision and Curriculum Devel., Soc. Research Child Devel., Am. Assn. U. Profs., Assn. Student Tchrs., A.A.A.S. Contbr. articles to profl. jours. Home: 1022 Essex Rd Birmingham AL 35222

DANIEL, LARKIN TAYLOR, religious assn. exec.; b. Hampton, Ark., Mar. 8, 1909; s. Joseph Thomas and Gena (McDonald) D.; student Ark. A. and M. Coll., 1928; B.A., Ouachita Baptist U., 1940; B.D., So. Bapt. Theol. Sem., 1950; D.D., East Tex. Bapt. Coll., 1953; m. Emma Jean Hargrove, Mar. 30, 1929; children—Joan (Mrs. Frank Neal Pennington), Gene Paul. Ordained to ministry, Baptist Ch., 1938; tchr., prin. Tinsman High Sch., Calhoun County, Ark., 1929-33; ins. salesman Met. Life Ins. Co., Hot Springs, Ark., also Gen. Underwriters, Pine Bluff, Ark., 1933-38; pastor Plum Bayou Bapt. Ch., Wright, Ark., also 1st Bapt. Ch., Hagler, Ark., 1938-40, 1st Bapt. Ch., Almyra, Ark., 1940-42, Elm Grove Bapt. Ch., Murray, Ky., 1942-45, 1st Bapt. Ch., Simpsonville, Ky., 1945-47, 1st Bapt. Ch., Woodville, Tex., 1947-51, 1st Bapt. Ch., Palestine, Tex., 1951-53; endowment exec. Tex. Bapt. Conv., 1953-55; pension bd. exec., sr. v.p. mktg. Annuity Bd. of So. Bapt. Conv., Dallas, 1955—; mem. exec. bd. Bapt. Gen. Conv. of Tex. Trustee Southeast Tex. Bapt. Hosp., Beaumont; trustee East Tex. Bapt. Coll. Home: 3948 Wentwood Dr Dallas TX 75225 Office: 511 Bldg 511 N Akard St Dallas TX 75201

DANIEL, RALPH WINFIELD, electronics engr., fraternal exec.; b. Greensboro, N.C., Sept. 27, 1940; s. Ray Edward and Hattie Rema (Jones) D.; B.S., N.C. State U., 1964. Mem. Mu Beta Psi, 1960—, nat. v.p., 1961-63, nat. editor, 1962-63, nat. pres., chpt. v.p., 1963-64, exec. sec., 1965—; sr. electronics engr. Lockheed Ga. Co., Marietta, 1966—. Lutheran. Address: 3401 Hickory Crest Dr Marietta GA 30060

DANIEL, ROBERT WILLIAMS, JR., congressman; b. Richmond, Va., Mar. 17, 1936; s. Robert Williams and Charlotte (Bemiss) D.; B.A., U. Va., 1954-58; M.B.A., Columbia, 1961; m. Sally Lewis Chase, May 2, 1964; children—Robert, Charlotte, Nell. Financial analyst J.C. Wheat Co., Richmond, 1961-62; instr. econs. U. Richmond Sch. Bus., 1963; instr. CIA, Washington, 1964-68; owner, operator Brandon Plantation, Prince George County, Va., 1968—; mem. 93d Congress from Va. Mem. Commonwealth of Va. Bd. Conservation and Econ. Devel., 1972; mem., sec. Prince George County Planning Commn., 1972; mem. Va. Farm Bur. Marketing Com., 1971-72. Trustee Atlantic Rural Expn., Sheltering Arms Hosp., Richmond. Served with AUS, 1959. Mem. Phi Beta Kappa, Phi Kappa Psi. Republican. Episcopalian (vestryman 1968-72). Moose. Clubs: N.Y. Yacht, Knickerbocker (N.Y.C.); Metropolitan (Washington); Commonwealth (Richmond). Home: Brandon Plantation Spring Grove VA 23881 Office: 1331 Longworth Bldg Washington DC 20515

DANIEL, WILBUR CLARENCE (DAN), U.S. congressman; b. Chatham, Va., May 12, 1914; m. Ruby McGregor. Formerly asst. to chmn. bd. Dan River Mills, Inc.; mem. Va. Ho. of Dels., 1960-68; mem. 91st-93d congresses from 5th Va. Dist. Dir. Bank Va., Danville. Mem. Va. Commn. on Constl. Govt., Govt. Com. on Employment; permanent mem. People to People Com.; mem. Va. Independence Bicentennial Com. Bd. dirs. Dulles Internat. Airport Devel. Com.; trustee Averett Coll., Danville. Served with USNR. Decorated Star Italian Solidarity, Croix de Merit. Mem. Am. Legion (past. nat. comdr.), Va. State C. of C., Omicron Delta Kappa (hon.). Baptist. Mason, Elk, Kiwanian. Club: Danville Golf. Address: Post Office Bldg Danville VA 24541 also 520 N St SW Washington DC 20024

DANIELL, HERMAN BURCH, educator, pharmacologist; b. Cadwell, Ga., May 25, 1929; s. Walter and Ruby Florence (Burch) D.; B.S., U. Ga., 1951, M.S., 1963; Ph.D., Med. Coll. S.C., 1966; m. Ottie Lorraine Smith, June 30, 1957; children—Kimberley, Anthony, Walter. Owner-pharmacist retail pharmacies, Savannah, Ga., 1953-62; instr. U. Ga. Sch. Pharmacy, Athens, 1962-63; NIH research fellow Med. Coll. S.C., Charleston, 1964-66, instr. pharmacology, 1966-67, asso. in pharmacology, 1967-68, asst. prof., 1968-70, asso. prof. pharmacology, 1970—. Served to capt. Med. Service Corps, AUS, 1951-53. USPHS research grantee, 1968-71, S.C. Heart Assn. research grantee, 1966-73. Mem. Am. Soc. Pharmacology and Exptl. Therapeutics, Sigma Xi, Kappa Sigma, Rho Chi. Episcopalian. Lion. Contbr. articles to profl. jours. Home: 1549 Burningtree Rd Charleston SC 29412 Office: Dept Pharmacology Med U SC Charleston SC 29401

DANIELS, FRANK A(RTHUR), newspaper exec.; b. Raleigh, N.C., June 8, 1904; s. Josephus and Addie Worth (Bagley) D. A.B., U. N.C., 1927; m. Ruth Aunspaugh, Nov. 20, 1929; children—Frank Arthur, Patricia Woronoff. With mech., circulation and advt. depts. News and Observer, Raleigh, N.C., 1927-32, treas., 1932-56, gen. mgr., 1942-68, pres., 1956-70, chmn. bd., 1970—, editor, pub. News & Observer, Raleigh Times, 1966-70; dir. A.P., 1964-67; mem. Raleigh bd. N.C. Nat. Bank. Chmn. N.C. Bd. Pub. Welfare, 1948-56; mem. N.C. Tax Study Commn., 1956-57. Trustee Rex Hosp., 1950-68; bd. dirs. Research Triangle Inst., 1960—. Mem. Am. (treas., dir.), So. (pres. 1951-52, newsprint mills com.) newspaper pubs. assns., N.C. Press Assn. (pres. 1948-49), Raleigh C. of C. (past pres.), Delta Kappa Epsilon. Presbyn. Clubs: Carolina Country, Sphinx (Raleigh). Home: 1515 Glenwood Av Raleigh NC 27608 Office: News and Observer Raleigh Times 215 S McDowell St Raleigh NC 27601

DANIELS, JACK B., sch. supt.; b. Hallettsville, Tex., Dec. 14, 1930; s. Ernest S. and Roxie (Moore) D.; B.S., N. Tex. State U., 1952, M.Ed., 1958; postgrad. Coll. So. Utah, fall 1969; m. Betty Endres, Jan. 3, 1955; children—Jack Bobbie, Lyndon S., Debra Ann. Tchr., prin. elementary sch. McMullen County Sch. System, 1955-61; mem. adminstrv. staff N. Tex. State U., Denton, 1961-63; asst. bus. mgr. Victoria (Tex.) Ind. Sch. Dist., 1963-66; bus. mgr. Bay City (Tex.) Ind. Sch. Dist., 1966-67; asst. adminstr. fed. programs Yoakum (Tex.) Ind. Sch. Dist., 1967-68; supt. schs. Normangee (Tex.) Ind. Sch. Dist., 1968-69, Warren (Tex.) Ind. Sch. Dist., 1969-73, Mirando City (Tex.) Ind. Sch. Dist., 1973—. Cons. wage and hour law Tex. Tech. U., Lubbock, 1967, local taxation and sch. desegregation Tex. A. and M. U., 1969. Served with AUS, 1952-54. Named Hon. Senator Tex., 1967, Outstanding Educator Am., 1970, 73. Mem. Am. Assn. Sch. Adminstrs., N.E.A., Assn. Sch. Bus. Ofcls. U.S. and Can., Tex. Tchrs. Assn., Tex. Assn. Sch. Bd. Ofcls., C. of C., Nat. Sch. Pub. Relations Assn. (pres.-elect 1974-75), Phi Delta Kappa. Presbyn. (deacon). Lion. Author: (with J.A. Anderson) Bond Issue, Techniques Used in Promoting School Bond Elections, 1966. Mem. editorial bd. Tex. Sch.

Bus. Mag., 1967-68, 71-73. Home: PO Box 307 Mirando City TX 78369 Office: PO Box 471 Mirando City TX 78369

DANN, ALEXANDER WILLIAM, JR., lawyer; b. Sewickely, Pa., Mar. 20, 1923; s. Alexander William and Ella (Berry) D.; B.A., Cornell U., 1948, LL.B., 1951, L.D., 1969; m. Mimi Elise Semmes, July 5, 1947; children—Alexander William III, Thomas Semmes, Elise Selden, Katherine Montgomery. Admitted to Tenn. bar, 1951; asso. mem. firm Canada, Russell & Turner, Memphis, 1951-55; partner Tual, Younger & Dann, 1955-58, Younger & Dann, 1958-61, Dann & Hills, 1961-68, Dann, Hills & Blackburn, 1968-71, Dann, Blackburn & Smith, Memphis, 1971—. Cons. Gov. Tenn., 1970—. Chmn., Republican party Shelby County, 1970-71. Vice chmn. trustees Brooks Meml. Art Gallery 1968-72, chmn., 1972—; mem. exec. com. bd. dirs. Memphis Acad. Arts, 1966—. Served to lt. (j.g.) USNR, 1943-46. Mem. Am. Judicature Soc., Am., Tenn., Shelby County bar assns., Alpha Delta Phi. Episcopalian. Clubs: Memphis Hunt and Polo, Memphis Country; Chevaliers de Tastevin, Tred Avon Yacht (Oxford, Md.). Home: 6246 Greenmeadows Cove Memphis TN 38138 Office: 100 N Main Bldg Memphis TN 38103

DANNAHOWER, WILLIAM ROY, dentist; b. Ft. Pierce, Fla., July 10, 1927; s. Franklin Roy and Ruth Merry (Landis) D.; A.B., U. Mo., Kansas City, 1950, D.D.S., 1953; m. Lucia Ann Sevier, June 23, 1950; children—William D., James L., Stephen B., Linda A. Asst. prof. diagnosis and roentgenology U. Mo., Kansas City, 1953-56; individual practice dentistry, Ft. Pierce, Fla., 1956—. Chmn., Govt. Study Commn., 1970-72; mem. Fla. Bd. Dentistry, 1971—. Mem. Ft. Pierce City Commn., 1962-64, mayor, 1964-66. Served with AUS, 1945-46. Recipient Distinguished Service award Ft. Pierce Jr. C. of C., 1960, Good Govt. award, 1966; Recognition plaque USPHS, 1966; Silver Beaver award Boy Scouts Am., 1971. Mem. Fla. Dental Assn. (chmn. state fluoridation com. 1962—), Am. Dental Assn., Delta Sigma Delta. Democrat. Presbyn. Elk, Kiwanian. Home: 809 S Indian River Dr Fort Pierce FL 33450 Office: 1205 Delaware Av Fort Pierce FL 33450

DANNE, HERBERT JOHN, mfg. co. exec.; b. Kingfisher, Okla., Mar. 11, 1926; s. John L. and Helen Irene (Thompson) D.; B.S., Okla. State U., 1950; m. Helen Marie Baird, Aug. 21, 1948; children—John G., William A., Susan M., Carol J., Karen L., James R., Lynn A. Sales engr. Standard Magnesium Corp., Tulsa, 1950-51; sales and design engr. Western Supply Co., Tulsa, 1951-58; v.p. sales and engring. Indsl. Fabricating Co. div. Bendix-Fram, Tulsa, 1958-63, exec. v.p., 1963-70; chmn. bd., pres. Thermic, Inc., 1971—; exec. v.p., operations mgr. Indsl. Fabricating Co., 1973—. Pres., Bishop Kelly Found., 1971-72. Served with USNR, 1944-46. Mem. Am. Inst. Chem. Engrs., Tubular Exchanger Mfrs. Assn. (past pres.), Phi Kappa Theta. Republican. Roman Catholic. K.C. Clubs: University, Harvard. Mailing Address: 5823 E 57th St Tulsa OK 74135

DANNENBAUM, JAMES DENNY, cons. engr.; b. Houston, July 22, 1939; s. Joseph B. and Janice (Denny) D.; B.S., U. Tex., 1962; m. Shirley Kay McKinley, Dec. 21, 1963; 1 dau., Kay Elizabeth. Pres., Dannenbaum Engring. Corp. Houston, 1962—; adv. dir. Transport Life Ins. Co.; dir. Bank Harris County N.A.; co-chmn. Southwestern Bank; mem. exec. com., dir. Surety Savs. Assn. Mem. Harris County Hist. Survey Com.; mem. Houston Adv. Com. Rapid Transit; mem. Tex. Adv. Com. Intergovtl. Relations; vice-chmn. Gulf Coast Water Resources Council Tex.; mem. exec. com. Houston chpt. March of Dimes, Tex. Urban Devel. Commn., The Houston Com. Trustee, Tex. Air and Water Resources Found.; exec. bd. Sam Houston area council Boy Scouts Am.; mem. exec. com. Soc. for Performing Arts, Houston; bd. dirs. Tex. Bill of Rights Found.; devel. council Houston Museum Natural Sci.; bd. dirs. Tex. Beta Student Aid Fund, Coastal Indsl. Water Authority, Arts and Scis. Found. U. Tex., Tanglewood Homes Assn. Named Outstanding Young Engr., Sam Houston chpt. Tex. Soc. Profl. Engrs., 1967; Outstanding Young Man, Jr. C. of C., Houston, 1969; One of 5 Outstanding Young Texans, Texas Jaycees, 1970. Mem. Houston C. of C., Ex-Students Assn. U. Tex. (exec. council), Friar Soc., Nat., Tex. (chmn. engrs. council state affairs) socs. profl. engrs., Am. Soc. C.E. (chmn. pub. affairs com.), Am. Indsl. Hygienists Assn., Constrn. Industry Council, Engrs. Council Houston, Newcomen Soc., Beta Theta Pi, Tau Beta Pi, Chi Epsilon, Phi Eta Sigma. Episcopalian. Clubs: Lakeside Country, Plaza. Home: 5324 Holly Springs Houston TX 77027 Office: PO Box 22292 Houston TX 77027

DANNENBAUM, JOSEPH BOWMAN, cons. engr.; b. Houston, Sept. 15, 1898; s. Henry Joseph and Sadie (Bowman) D.; student Tex. A. and M. Coll., 1920; m. Janice Denny, Apr. 10, 1929; 1 son, James D. Asst. engr. Humble Oil & Refining Co., Goose Creek, Tex., 1919; party chief Humble Pipe Line Co., Houston, 1919; asst. engr. Crown Oil & Refining Co., Pasadena, Tex., 1919-20; engr. James Stewart & Co., Houston, 1920, Tellepsen Constrn. Co., 1922; constrn. engr. Am. Constrn. Co., Houston, 1923-24; owner J. B. Dannenbaum, Inc., Houston, 1924-33; city chief water works engr., Houston, 1933-35; mgr., pres. San Jacinto Constrn. Co., 1935-38; plant and prodn. engr. Water Dept., Houston, 1938-40; asst. chief engr. Helland & Drought, Camp Wallace, Tex., 1940-41; office engr. Hubbard, Knutson-Mitchell, San Jacinto Ordnance Depot, Houston, 1941; chief civil engr. Monsanto Chem. Co., Texas City, 1941, Arthur G. McKee & Co., Sheffield Steel Co., Houston, 1942; chief purchasing engr. J. F. Pritchard Co., Sweeney and Houston, 1942, USN sponsored addition to Todd-Galveston Dry Docks, Galveston, 1943; office engr. San Jacinto River Water Div., City Houston, 1943-45; pvt. practice cons. engr., Houston, 1945—; chmn. bd. Dannenbaum Engring. Corp. Registered profl. engr., Tex., La. Fellow Am. Soc. C.E.; mem. Tex. (pres. 1956), Nat. socs. profl. engrs., Am. Pub. Works Assn., Water Pollution Control Fedn., Am. Water Works Assn., Newcomen Soc., C. of C., Chi Epsilon. Episcopalian. Club: Briar. Home: 5622 Lynbrook Dr Houston TX 77027 Office: 4543 Post Oak Pl Dr Houston TX 77027

DANNENBURG, WARREN NATHANIEL, biochem. pharmacologist; b. Tulsa, Jan. 9, 1926; s. Grady Winfield and Thelma Mary (Setley) D.; B.S., Va. Poly. Inst., 1948; M.S. (research fellow), Tex. A. and M. U., 1955, Ph.D., 1957; m. Mary Nelle Lindsay, July 16, 1949; children—Warren Nathaniel, Mary, Sara. Teaching fellow Va. Poly. Inst., 1947-48; bacteriologist S.E. Massengill Co., Bristol, Tenn., 1948-53; biochemist R.J. Reynolds Tobacco Co., Winston-Salem, N.C., 1957-60; research asst., prof. biochemistry Bowman Gray Sch. Medicine, 1960-65; group mgr. biochem. pharmacology A.H. Robins Co., Inc., Richmond, Va., 1965—. Recipient career devel. award NIH, 1964-65. Mem. Soc. Exptl. Biology and Medicine, Am. Chem. Soc., Am. Inst. Nutrition, Sigma Xi (award 1957). Democrat. Presbyn. Home: 7730 Brentford Dr Richmond VA 23225 Office: 1211 Sherwood Av Richmond VA 23220

DANSBY, HUDDIE, land surveyor; b. Uniontown, Ala., June 11, 1941; s. Joseph Afenious and Sarah Ann (Brooks) Dansby; student Internat. Corr. Schs., 1966-69; m. Dorothy Jean Watkins, June 28, 1958; children—Joseph, Huddie, Belinda, William, Jessie, John. Rodman, Coulter Engring. Co., Homewood, Ala., 1959, J.M. Keel, Birmingham, 1960; rodman, head chainman W.M. Douglas, land surveyor, Birmingham, 1960-66; instrument man R.E. Clement, land surveyor, Fairfield, Ala., 1966, part chief, 1966-67, partner, 1968-69; with Jim Walter Homes, Inc., Birmingham, 1970-73; self-employed as Huddie Dansby & Asso., land surveyors and mappers, Bessemer, 1973—. Mem. Nat. Fedn. Engrs. and Land Surveyors, Nat. Fedn. Ind. Bus. Home: 2808 Dowell Ct SW Birmingham AL 35211 Office: 1822 3d Av N Bessemer AL 35020

DANTZLER, ERNEST RAYMOND, JR., broadcasting exec.; b. Orangeburg, S.C., Nov. 27, 1924; s. Ernest Raymond and Olive Lurline (Bozard) D.; B.A. in Speech, U. Fla., 1950; m. Nancy Raye Frey, Oct. 23, 1963; children—Ernest Raymond III, Samuel Raymond. Asst. mgr., producer WRUF, Gainesville, Fla., 1950-57; TV news reporter, editor, anchorman sta. WFGA-TV, Jacksonville, Fla., 1957-62; with sta. WTVT, Tampa, Fla., 1962—, TV dir. programs, news, pub. affairs, 1968—. Pres., TV Programmers Conf., 1973-74. Served with USNR, 1942-46, 50-52. Mem. Nat. Assn. TV Program Execs. Mason (32 deg.), Rotarian. Home: Route 2 Box 989 Odessa FL 33556 Office: 3213 Kennedy Blvd Tampa FL 33609

DAPPRICH, JOHN WILLIAM, interior designer; b. Dearborn, Mich., Mar. 6, 1937; s. Elton and Ellen (Ketchum) D.; student Easter U., 1956-57; diploma Kendall Sch. Design, 1962. Interior designer Burdines Dept. Stores, Miami, Fla., 1963-64, Jordan Marsh Dept. Store, Miami, 1964-66; interior designer Waldo Perez Interiors, Coconut Grove, Fla., 1967-68; owner Dapprich Interiors, Coconut Grove, 1968-70; dir. interior design Deltona Corp., Miami, 1970—. Served with AUS, 1957-59. Mem. Am. Inst. Designers. Interior designer pent-house Joe Garagiola, Marco Island, 1970, also interior designer for Jack Paar, Key Biscayne, 1972, Henry Kissinger, Key Biscayne, 1972, Gene Sarazen, Marco Island, 1972, also Adm. Rickenbacker, Senator George Smathers, Ara Parseghian. Home: 3927 Douglas Rd Coconut Grove FL 33133 Office: 3250 SW 3d Av Miami FL 33133

DARABARIS, ALEX, welfare orgn. adminstr.; b. Birmingham, Ala., May 25, 1927; s. John and Mary (Contorupis) D.; student Birmingham So. Coll., 1946-49; B.S., U. Ala., 1951; M.S.W., U. Tenn., 1958; postgrad. Tulane U., 1954; m. Dorothy Lee Williams, Aug. 17, 1951; children—Bruce Steven, Gus Alexander, Thomas Andrew. Caseworker, Dept. Pub. Welfare, Birmingham, 1951-53, supr., 1955-57; coordinator Aftercare for Mental Patients, Birmingham, 1958-59; social worker VA, 1959-60; dir. social services Ala. Boys Indsl. Sch., Birmingham, 1960-68; dir. Youth Devel. Center, Milledgeville, Ga., 1968—; dir. Aftercare Project for Delinquents, 1961-65; mem. adv. council Central State Hosp., 1974-75. Cons., Fla. Child Care Assn., 1965. Nat. Inst. Mental Health grantee, 1958. Mem. Nat. Inst. on Crime and Delinquency, Nat. Assn. Social Workers, Ala. Conf. Child Caring Agys. and Instns. (pres. 1962-63), Ala. Probation and Parole Assn., Jefferson County Social Workers Club (pres. 1965-66), So. Assn. Tng. Schs. (pres. 1973-74). Baptist (deacon). Rotarian. Club: All Nations (pres. 1965-67). Home: PO Box 617 Milledgeville GA 31061 Office: PO Box 788 Milledgeville GA 31061

DARBY, JOHN FEASTER, univ. adminstr.; b. Chester, S.C., Oct. 22, 1916; s. John Feaster and Kathryn (Gregory) D.; B.S.A., U. Fla., 1948, M.S.A., 1949; Ph.D., U. Wis., 1951; m. Marjorie Bellah, Sept. 20, 1941; children—Lizbeth Claire, John Feaster. Asst. plant pathologist U. Fla. Indian Field Lab., Ft. Pierce, 1951-54; asso. plant pathologist U. Fla. Central Fla. Expt. Sta., 1954-64, plant pathologist, 1964-66, plant pathologist, head exptl. sta., 1966-70; plant pathologist, center dir. Agrl. Research and Edn. Center, U. Fla., Sanford, 1970—. Sec., local Civil Service Bd.; active P.T.A. Served to 1st lt. Q.M.C., AUS, 1942-46. Mem. Am. Phytopath. Soc., Fla. Hort. Soc., Sigma Xi, Phi Sigma, Gamma Sigma Delta, Phi Kappa Phi. Kiwanian. Club: Men's Garden. Home: 1324 E 24th St Sanford FL 32771

DARBY, LLOYD HUBERT, III, dentist; b. Metter, Ga., June 18, 1937; s. Lloyd Hubert, Jr. and Carolyn Adamson (Hale) D.; student Medill Sch. Journalism, Northwestern U., 1956-57; B.A., Emory U., 1959, D.D.S., 1964; postgrad. U. Ga., 1959-60; m. Loretta Wilkes, Aug. 16, 1958; children—Carolyn Leslie, Jennifer Wilkes, Pamela Elaine. Individual practice dentistry, Vidalia, Ga., 1966—. Chmn., Toombs County Republican party, 1969—; vice chmn. 1st Congl. Dist. Ga. Rep. Com., 1970—; alt. del. Rep. Nat. Conv., 1972. Served to lt., Dental Corps USNR, 1964-66. Recipient Am. Coll. Dentists Essay award, Emory U., 1964, Block Drug Co. Essay award Emory U. Mem. Am., Ga. dental assns., Central Dist. Dental Soc., Acad. Gen. Dentistry, Phi Delta Theta, Psi Omega. Home: 202 W 9th St Vidalia GA 30474 Office: 308 Jackson St Vidalia GA 30474

DARBY, LUTHER ODELL, utility exec.; b. Columbia, S.C., Sept. 23, 1926; s. John Clarence and Agnes (Gibbons) D.; B.S. in Civil Engring., The Citadel, 1951; m. Lelia Oates, July 3, 1949; 1 son, John Jackson. With So. Carolina Electric & Gas Co., Charleston, 1949—, dist. engr., 1953-58, comml. mgr., 1962—. Chmn. Charleston dist. Boy Scouts Am., 1971-72, exec. bd. Coastal Carolina council. Chmn. Charleston County Park, Recreation and Tourist Commn., 1968-70; mem. Charleston County Sch. Bd., 1970-74. Bd. dirs. S.C. Tb and Respiratory Disease Assn.; exec. bd. dirs. Met. Charleston YMCA. Served with USNR, 1945-46. Mem. I.E.E.E., S.C., Charleston Trident chambers commerce, Exec. Assn. Greater Charleston (past dir., v.p.), E. Charleston Sertoma Club (life; past v.p., dir.), Navy League. Methodist (past lay leader, tchr., chmn. bldg. com., steward). Mason. Home: 20 Bayview Dr Mount Pleasant SC 29464 Office: PO Box 760 Charleston SC 29402

DARBY, MICHAEL RUCKER, furnace mfg. co. exec.; b. Dallas, Nov. 24, 1945; s. Joseph Jasper, Jr. and Frances Adah (Rucker) D.; A.B., Dartmouth, 1967; M.A., U. Chgo., 1968, Ph.D., 1970; m. Emily Ann Loutrel, June 19, 1965; 1 dau., Margaret Loutrel. Vice pres., economist Paragon Industries, Inc., Dallas, 1961—, dir., 1964—; asst. prof. econs. Ohio State U., 1970-73; asso. prof. econs. U. Cal. at Los Angeles, 1973—. Woodrow Wilson fellow, 1967-68, NSF Grad. fellow, 1967-69, Fed. Deposit Ins. Corp. Grad. fellow, 1969-70. Mem. Am. Econ. Assn., Econometric Soc., Am. Statis. Assn., Phi Beta Kappa, Omicron Delta Epsilon. Episcopalian. Club: Hyannis Port Yacht (Hyannis Port, Mass.). Contbr. articles to profl. jours. Home: 3937 Purdue St Dallas TX 75225 also 1442 Yale St Santa Monica CA 90404 Office: PO Box 10133 Dallas TX 75207 also Dept Econs U Cal Los Angeles CA 90024

DARBY, WILLIAM JEFFERSON, med. educator, found. exec.; b. Galloway, Ark., Nov. 6, 1913; s. William Jefferson and Ruth (Douglass) D.; B.S., U. Ark., 1936, M.D., 1937; M.S., U. Mich., 1940, Ph.D., 1942, D.Sc., 1966; D.Sc., Utah State U., 1973; m. Elva Louise Mayo, June 12, 1935; children—William Jefferson III, James Richard, Thomas Douglass. Asst. prof. biochemistry and medicine Vanderbilt U. Med. Sch., Nashville, 1944-46, asso. prof. biochemistry and medicine, 1946-48, dir. div. nutrition, 1949-71, prof. biochemistry, chmn. dept., 1949-71, prof. medicine in nutrition, 1965—; pres. Nutrition Found., N.Y.C., 1972—. Vis. prof. U. Cal. at Davis, 1967; ofcl. U.S. del. 7th Internat. Congress Nutrition, 1966; mem. expert adv. panel on nutrition WHO, 1950—; mem. Tenn. Gov.'s Pesticide Council, 1965—; co-chmn. hazardous materials adv. com. Environmental Protection Agy., 1971—; mem. expert adv. panel food safety and nutrition Nat. Acad. Scis., 1971-72; mem. Tenn. Com. on Aging, 1972—; pres. Citizens' Comm. on Sci., Law and Food Supply, 1973—. Decorated Order of Cedars of Lebanon (Lebanon); Star of Jordan (Jordan), Order of Rodolfo Robles (Guatemala); recipient Osborne-Mendel award Am. Inst. Nutrition, 1962, Conrad A. Elvhjem award for pub. service in nutrition, 1972, Joseph F. Goldberger award in clin. nutrition A.M.A., 1964, Distinguished Service award Nutrition Council Met. N.Y., 1969, Thomas Jefferson award Vanderbilt U., Nashville, 1969, Spencer award for outstanding achievement in agrl. chemistry Kansas City sect. Am. Chem. Soc., 1972. Fellow A.A.A.S., A.C.P.; mem. Am. Chem. Soc., Am. Coll. Nutrition (dir. 1972), Am. Fedn. for Clin. Research, Am. Inst. Nutrition (pres. 1958), A.M.A. (chmn. council on foods and nutrition 1960-62, 67-70), Am. Pub. Health Assn. (mem. governing council 1957), Am. Soc. Clin. Investigation (mem. council 1953-55), Am. Soc. Biol. Chemists, Assn. Am. Physicians, Inst. Food Technologists, Nutrition Soc. (Britain), Soc. Exptl. Biology and Medicine, Soc. Toxicology, So. Soc. Clin. Research (v.p. 1948), Sigma Xi, Phi Lambda Upsilon, Alpha Omega Alpha; hon. mem. Austrian Pub. Health Assn., Nat. Med. Soc. Panama, El Colegio de Guatemala, Serbian Acad. Sci., Philippine Dietetic Assn. Corr. editor Jour. Nutrition and Dietetics, India, 1966—. Clubs: Cosmos (Washington); Union League (N.Y.C.). Home: Route 2 Box 165 Thompson Station TN 37179 Office: Nutrition Foundation Inc 489 Fifth Av New York City NY 10017

DARBY, WILLIAM THOMAS, lawyer; b. nr. Vidalia, Ga., May 12, 1914; s. Lloyd H. and Embelle (Dickens) D.; student Mercer U., 1930-31; grad. Brewton-Parker Jr. Coll., 1932; LL.B., Atlanta Law Sch., 1935; grad. So. Bus. U., 1935; m. Gladys Wood, Dec. 8, 1940; children—William T., Robert Wood. Admitted to Ga. bar, 1935; city atty. Vidalia, 1947-48, county atty., 1951-52; solicitor county, 1953-57; county judge, 1961—; county juvenile judge, Vidalia, 1963-70; dir., sec., gen. counsel Rosebud Mfg. Co. div. Athlone Industries, Vidalia; pres., gen. counsel Aimwell Enterprises, Inc.; dir., gen. counsel Darby Banking Co., Inc., Darco, Inc., Piggly Wiggly So., Inc., Shuman Saveway; div. counsel Belle Interiors, Inc.; pres. land devel. corps.; part owner cattle ranches; trust officer, financial cons. Gen. counsel Vidalia Devel. Authority. Active Boy Scouts. Served with USNR, 1944-45. Mem. Am. Judiciary Soc., Am. Trial Lawyers Assn., Am., Ga. bar assns., State Bar of Ga., Vidalia C. of C. Rotarian (pres. club), Mason (Shriner), Lions. Elk. Home: 1007 Center Dr Vidalia GA 30474 Office: PO Box 648 Vidalia GA 30474

DARDEN, CONRAD LYNN, lawyer; b. Tyler, Tex., June 6, 1934; s. Robert Webster and Willie Oleta (Jones) D.; B.A., Baylor U., 1956; J.D., U. Tex., 1959; m. Margaret Alice Furr, June 16, 1956; children—Kimberly, Victoria, Sally. Admitted to Tex. bar, 1959; with Kouri, Banner & Darden, Wichita Falls Tex., 1959-61; adminstrv. asst. to U.S. Congressman Graham B. Purcell, Jr., Washington, 1961-62; partner Humphrey, Gibson & Darden, Wichita Falls, 1962-69, Gibson, Darden & Hotchkiss, Wichita Falls, 1969—. Mem. Civil Def. Adv. Commn., 1960; chmn. Wichita Falls Planning Bd., 1960-65; dir. Wichita Falls Citizens Adv. Com., 1965—; chmn. bd. N. Tex. Mental Health Clinic, Inc., 1965-68; bd. dirs. Tex. Mental Health and Mental Retardation Found.; dir. Vol. Services Council State Hosp. and Spl. Schs. for Tex., 1965-66; chmn. bd. Wichita County Mental Health and Mental Retardation Center, 1969-73; dir. Children's Aid Soc. of W. Tex., 1965—. Del. Dem. Nat. Conv., 1972. Recipient awards, U. Tex. Bar Assn., 1958, U. Tex. Counsel, 1959, Wichita Falls Mental Health Assn., 1973. Mem. Am., Tex. bar assns., Delta Sigma Pi, Delta Theta Phi. Democrat. Presbyn. Mason (32 deg., Shriner), Rotarian. Home: 2100 Berkley St Wichita Falls TX 76308 Office: City National Bank Bldg Wichita Falls TX 76301

DARDEN, PAUL ALBERT, educator; b. Gadsden, Ala., Apr. 11, 1929; s. Edward LaFayette and Hazel Christian (Estes) D.; B.Arch., Auburn U., 1952; m. Juanita Faulkner, Nov. 22, 1971; children—Janet Sue, Paul Albert, Steven Mark, Nancy Anne. Head structural dept. Van Keuren, Davis & Co., Birmingham, Ala., 1953-58; asso. prof. bldg. tech. Auburn U., 1958—; cons. structural engr.; works include Am. Family Life Bldg., Columbus, Ga., Bill Heard Chevrolet, Columbus. Trustee Lee Acad., 1970. Hon. lt. col., aide-de-camp Ala. State Militia, 1973. Mem. Scarab, Sigma Lambda Chi. Methodist. Elk. Home: 349 Brookside Dr Auburn AL 36830 Office: Box 1309 Auburn AL 36830

DARDEN, WILLIAM ALLEN, engr., govt. ofcl.; b. Nashville, Mar. 29, 1910; s. William Allen and Kathryn Belle (Edwards) D.; student Vanderbilt U., 1930-31; B.S., Ga. Inst. Tech., 1935; grad. Army Command and Staff Coll., 1952, Strategic Intelligence Sch., 1956; M.S., George Washington U., 1970; m. Mary Elizabeth Ransom, Jan. 7, 1939; children—Kathryn, Michael, Cynthia, Richard. Civil engr. C.E., Nashville, 1935-42; commd. lt. U.S. Army, 1942, advanced through grades to col., 1959, ret., 1965; area engr., Nashville, Atlanta, Wright Field engring. dists., 1942-43; planning officer Ohio River div., 1944; engr. brigade engring. officer, New Guinea, Philippines, Okinawa, 1944-45; corps staff officer, Korea, 1946; post engr., squadron comdr., March Field, 1947-48; mil. adviser, air engr. Mil. Mission to Greece, 1948-51; asst. dist. engr., Tullahoma, 1952-55; attache Am. embassy, New Delhi, 1956-59; bn. comdr., Ft. Dix, N.J., 1959-60; mem. staff Dept. Army, Washington, 1960-62; comdr. Army sect. Joint Mil. Mission to India, 1962-63; chief operations inspections Dept. Army Insp. Gen., 1963-65; spl. asst. to U.S. Army Dist. Engr., Nashville, 1966-71, exec. asst., 1971—. Dist. chmn. camping and activities Boy Scouts Am., 1953-55, chmn. pack com., 1964-65, chmn. explorer post com., 1972—. Decorated Legion of Merit, Bronze Star with oak leaf cluster; Royal Order of George I (Greece); Philippine Liberation medal. Registered profl. engr., Tenn. Fellow Am. Soc. C.E. (past officer); mem. Nat., Tenn. socs. profl. engrs., Soc. Am. Mil. Engrs. (post pres. 1954-55, sec. 1972-73), Engrs. Assn. Nashville (dir. 1970-72), Soc. Am. Value Engrs. (Tenn. chpt. pres. 1974—), Middle Tenn. Fed. Exec. Assn., Internat. Assn. Nav. Congresses, Am. Mgmt. Assn., Assn. U.S. Army, Tenn. Hist. Soc., Phi Kappa Sigma. Republican. Episcopalian. Club: Brentwood Country, Propeller (Nashville). Home: 1300 Old Hickory Blvd Brentwood TN 37027 Office: Federal Office Bldg Nashville TN 37203

DARDEN, WILLIAM HOWARD, JR., educator; b. Tuscaloosa, Ala., Apr. 25, 1937; s. William Howard and Jannie Belle (Herring) D.; B.S., U. Ala., 1959, M.S., 1962; Ph.D. (NIH fellow, Microbiology Tng. grant fellow) Ind. U., 1965; m. Caroline Jackson Sullivan, July 15, 1959; children—Leanne Carol Darden, Michael Howard. Faculty, U. Ala., Tuscaloosa, 1965—, prof. biology, 1973—, chmn. dept., 1974—. Mem. Am. Soc. Cell Biology, Sigma Xi, Beta Beta Beta, Omicron Delta Kappa. Contbr. articles to profl. jours. Home: 11B Springhill St Tuscaloosa AL 35401 Office: Box 1927 Dept Biology U Ala University AL 35486

DARLAND, DWIGHT DAVID, edn. assn. exec.; b. Coleridge, Neb., Aug. 11, 1917; s. Floyd Lambert and Hazel Maude (Roland) D.; B.S., Neb. State Tchrs. Coll., 1939; M.A., U. Wyo., 1942; Ed.D., Columbia, 1947; m. Elinore M. Fritz, Dec. 28, 1940; children—David Floyd and Dallas Leland (twins). Tchr. sci., prin. high sch., Newcastle, Wyo., 1939-42; supt. schs. Teton County, Jackson, Wyo., 1942-45; instr. psychology Newark State Tchrs. Coll., 1945; tchr. sci. Birch-Wathen Sch., N.Y.C., 1946-47; asst. dir. community services U. Wyo.,

Laramie, 1947-48; dean students, prof. edn., chmn. grad. com. Pacific U., Forest Grove, Ore., 1948-53; ednl. cons. Am. Osteo. Assn., Chgo., 1953-56; dir. profl. services Ore. Edn. Assn., Portland, 1956-59; exec. sec. div. instructional and profl. devel. (formerly Nat. Commn. on Tchr. Edn. and Profl. Standards) N.E.A., Washington, 1959—, editor Jour. Tchr. Edn., 1962—. Professorial lectr., tchr. edn. George Washington U., 1959—; program specialist Ford Found., Colombia, Venezuela, 1963-64; cons. on tchr. edn. AID Mission to East Africa, 1966; cons. to bd. trustees State Colls. Md., 1966-68; coordinator Antioch-Putney Grad. Sch. Edn., Washington, 1967-68. Mem. governing bd. Futures for Children, Washington. Mem. N.E.A. (life), Am. Assn. Sch. Adminstrs., Am. Assn. U. Profs., Higher Edn. Assn. Washington, Wilderness Soc., Assn. for Student Teaching, Assn. for Supervision and Curriculum Devel., Phi Delta Kappa, Lambda Delta Lambda, Kappa Delta Pi. Club: City (Portland). Contbr. articles to profl. publs., also chpts. to books. Home: 341 O St SW Washington DC 20024 Office: 1201 16th St NW Washington DC 20036

DARLING, JOSEPH WARREN, army officer, govt. ofcl.; b. Chestnut Hill, Phila., May 5, 1908; s. Joseph Robinson and Charlotte (Kelsey) D.; student U. Madrid, Spain, 1926; S.B., Harvard, 1931; M.B.A., U. Pa., 1934; student Temple Law Sch., Phila., 1935-37, student George Washington U., 1941-43, LL.B., 1954, LL.M., 1959; m. Helene Manley, May 29, 1943; children—Mary Beal, Albert Beal, Venie Helene McNab. Bank examiner Commonwealth Pa., 1935-37; financial coordinator Socony Vacuum Oil Co., Hamburg, The Hague, N.Y.C., Caracas, Venezuela, 1937-42; served as officer U.S. Army, 1942—, now col. Ordance Corps and Res.; administrv. exec. officer Office Chief Ordnance, Washington, 1942-44; with econs. div. Office Mil. Govt., Eng., France, Germany, also acting chief control and inspection sect. Western zones Germany, 1944-48, dep. chief, acting chief econs. br., Berlin, assisting in policy and procedures Berlin airlift, policy advisor concerning Berlin Trade Assn., C. of C., industry and handicraft, 1948-50; U.S. land observer Dept. State, providing information to H.I.C.O.G. on devels. Land Nordrhein-Westfalen, Brit. Zone, Germany, rep. U.S. in zone, assisting Brit. by advice, cons. reports to obtain uniformity in adminstrn. Germany, responsible to U.S. High Commr., 1950-51; chief European br. Fgn. div. NPA, Washington, 1951-55; cons. Office Sec. Def. for Internat. Security Affairs, 1955-56; dep. dir. investment devel. div. Bur. Fgn. Commerce, Dept. Commerce, 1956-57; fgn. investment adviser Econ. and Financial Mission to Govt. Chile, Santiago, 1957-58; with investment div. Small Bus. Adminstrn., 1959-62; dir. Office Fgn. Econ. Affairs, Office Sec. Def., Washington, 1962—; pres., chmn. D & D Ventures Corp., Washington; pres., dir. Chestnut Hill Investment Corp., Phila.; dir. Darling Investment Corp.; financial adviser A. W. Kelsey and C. C. Washburn estates. Mem. Washington Bd. Trade. Chmn. disaster com. Wissahickon area E. Pa. chpt. A.R.C.; mem. zoning com. Springfield Twp. Civic Assn. Bd. dirs. Thomas A. Roberts Sch., Montgomery County (Pa.) Citizens Council; trustee Israel Washburn Home, Livermore Falls, Me. Mem. Am., Fed., Inter-Am. (mem. mil. justice com.) bar assns., Bar Assn. D.C. (com. relationships with internat. bar assns., del.), Washington Soc. Investment Analysts, C. of C., Res. Officers Assn. (past pres. chpt.), Soc. Internat. Devel. (com. law devel.), Washington Fgn. Law Soc. (dir.), Greater Phila. and South Jersey Council, Phila. Assn. Profl. Consultants, S.A.R. Episcopalian (treas. 1965—). Mason. Clubs: Chevy Chase (Md.); Harvard, Cricket, Penn (Phila.); Harvard (Boston); American (London); Sporting Club de France (Paris); Am. Yacht, American (Berlin); University, Harvard, International, University, National Lawyers, National Sojourners (Washington). Home: 423 New Jersey Av SE Washington DC 20003 Office: Office Sec of Def Pentagon Washington DC 20025

DARNELL, ROBERT DAVID, real estate devel. co. exec.; b. Abilene, Tex., Nov. 13, 1922; s. Edward Phillip and Lena Elizabeth (Adkisson) D.; student U. N.M., 1941-44, U. Tex., 1947; B.S., Hardin Simmons U., 1949; m. Jerre Jean Hynds, Oct. 18, 1947; children—David, Sylvia, Patrick, Rebecca. With Computer Geophys. Service, Inc., Dallas, 1949-51; purchasing, office mgr., sales rep. Stauffer Chem. Co., Ft. Worth, Houston, 1951-67; v.p., pres., dir. Tex. Gulf Industries, Inc., Houston, 1968—; chmn. bd. Bowie First Fed. Savs. & Loan Assn. (Tex.), 1970-72; dir. South Central Savs. & Loan Assn., Brenham, Tex., 1969. Vice pres., dir. Ashford Lake Civic Assn.; mem. bd. Houston-Galveston Area Conv. and Vistors Council. Trustee Robert C. Lanier Found., Robert C. Lanier Operating Found. Served from ensign to lt. (j.g.) USNR, 1943-46. Mem. Kappa Alpha. Presbyn. Club: Braeburn Country. Home: 1205 Shannon Valley St Houston TX 77077 Office: 2525 N Loop W Houston TX 77008

DARROW, SUSAN HORNSTEIN, ednl. adminstr.; b. Orlando, Fla., Dec. 25, 1941; d. Louis Albert and Mildred (Bruce) Hornstein; A.B., Wheaton Coll., 1963; postgrad. Fla. State U., 1963; M.S. in Edn., No. Ill. U., 1967. Tchr. English, Apopka, Fla., 1964; with WMFE-TV, Orlando, 1965; residence hall dir. Wheaton (Ill.) Coll., 1965-67, asst. dean students, 1967-68; asso. dean students Gordon Coll., Wenham, Mass., 1968-71; counselor Valencia Community Coll., Orlando, Fla., 1971-73; dir. Thee Door Residential Center, drug rehab., Orlando, 1973—. Mem. Nat. Assn. Student Personnel Adminstrs., Nat. Assn. Women Deans and Counselors, Am. Personnel and Guidance Assn., Christian Women Deans. Address: 551 E Semoran St Fern Park FL 32730

DARSEY, JOSEPH FREDERICK, clothing mfg. exec.; b. Amsterdam, Ga., Apr. 11, 1926; s. Charles H. and Mettie (Connell) D.; B.Indsl. Engring., Ga. Inst. Tech., 1949; m. Parkerlyn Florence, Dec. 27, 1952; children—Laurie, Joseph, Steven, Jonathan. Mgmt. trainee Stockham Valves & Fittings Co., Birmingham, Ala., 1948-49; engr. Jaco Pants, Inc., Ashburn, Ga., 1950, plant mgr., 1951-53; v.p., gen. mgr. Anniston (Ala.) Sportswear Corp., 1954-59; founder, pres., gen. mgr. Darsey Mfg. Co., Tallapoosa, Ga., 1960—; pres. Darsey Clothing Co., Inc., East Point, Ga. Dir. W. Ga. Bank of Tallapoosa. Mem. exec. bd. Ga. div. Am. Cancer Soc. Mem. adv. bd. Shorter Coll., Rome, Ga. Named Man of Yr., City of Tallapoosa, 1969. Served with AUS, 1944-46. Mem. Ga. Inst. Tech. Alumni Assn. (trustee), Tau Beta Pi, Alpha Tau Omega. Presbyn. (elder). Home: 3325 Old Fairburn Rd SW Atlanta GA 30331 Office: Darsey Mfg Co Box 187 Stoffel Dr Tallapoosa GA 30176

DART, STEPHEN PLAUCHE, lawyer; b. New Orleans, Sept. 21, 1924; s. Benjamin Wall and Clarabel (Cromwell) D.; B.B.A., Tulane U., 1946; B.S. in Elec. Engring., La. State U., 1951, LL.B., 1951, J.D., 1970; m. Elisabeth Ann Kilbourne, Feb. 3, 1951; children—James K., Ann Holcombe. Admitted to La. bar, 1951; practice law, New Orleans, 1952-53, St. Francisville, La., 1951-52, 1953—; sr. v.p. Bank of Commerce & Trust Co., St. Francisville, La., also dir., 1964—. Mem. adv. com. La. Law Inst. Com. of Continuous Revision of Code Civil Procedure, 1962—; lectr. probate, immovable property, trust estates, 1962-63. Mem. Democratic State Central Com., 1958—; chmn. West Feliciana Parish Dem. Exec. Com., 1968—. Served as lt. (j.g.) USNR, 1941-46. Mem. Am., La. bar assns., Am. Judicature Soc., Delta Kappa Epsilon, Phi Delta Phi. Clubs: Boston, Pickwick, New Orleans City; Baton Rouge. Address: Box 489 St Francisville LA 70775

DARTER, VERNON WEBSTER, univ. adminstr.; b. Hiltons, Va., Feb. 6, 1904; s. Ernest D. and Margaret Pearl (Howard) D.; A.B., King Coll., 1926; B.S., U. Tenn., 1930; M.P.A., Harvard, 1952, D.P.A., 1955; m. Ida Sue Taylor, Oct. 6, 1930. Prin., Sullivan County (Tenn.) Elementary Sch., 1926-27; tchr. Church Hill High Sch., Hawkins County, Tenn., 1927-28; dir. milk sanitation Bur. Health, Knoxville, Tenn., 1930-35; asst. county agt. U. Tenn., Johnson County, 1935-42, county agt., 1942-43; dep. dir. food and agr. Office Mil. Govt., Bavaria, 1946-49; chief agrl. prodn. and distbn. br. Office High Commr., Frankfort, Germany, 1949-51; Eastern rep. Fund for Adult Edn., 1953-54; prof., leader extension tng. and studies Coll. Agr., U. Tenn., Knoxville, 1954-57, dir. Agrl. Extension Service, 1957-68, dean, 1968-72, emeritus, 1972—. Served to capt. AUS, 1943-46. Named Man of Yr. in Service to Tenn. Agr., Progressive Farmer mag., 1971. Mem. Am. Agrl. Econs. Assn., Phi Kappa Phi, Alpha Zeta, Gamma Sigma Delta. Presbyn. (elder). Kiwanian. Home: 2300 Lakemoor Dr Knoxville TN 37920

DAS, NIRMAL KANTI, educator; b. Chittagong, India, Mar. 1, 1928; s. Surya and Swarmalata (Das) D.; B.Sc. with honors U. Calcutta (India), 1948, M.Sc., 1950; Ph.D., U. Wis. at Madison, 1957; m. Faye Ann Paske, June 28, 1958; children—Robin, Anita. Came to U.S., 1952, naturalized, 1964. Asso. research zoologist U. Cal. at Berkeley, 1958-73; asso. prof. dept. cell biology Med. Center, U. Ky., Lexington, 1973—. Mem. Am. Bot. Soc., A.A.A.S., Am. Soc. Cell Biology, Internat. Soc. Cell Biology. Contbr. profl. jours. Home: 112 Edgemoor Av Lexington KY 40503 Office: Dept Cell Biology Univ Ky Med Sch Lexington KY 40506

DASCOMB, HARRY EMERSON, physician; b. Bath, N.Y., Aug. 12, 1916; s. William Everett and Mildred Bell (Emerson) D.; A.B. cum laude, Colgate U., 1938, M.D., 1943; m. Helen Lucille Bowyer, Aug. 29, 1939; children—Alan William, Sharon Lee, Wendy Jane (Mrs. Walker A. Long). Intern, Iola Sanitarium, Rochester, N.Y., 1944-45; resident Strong Meml. Hosp., Rochester, 1945-46; Buswell fellow in medicine U. Rochester, 1946-47; practice medicine, New Orleans, 1947—; instr., asst. prof., asso. prof., prof. medicine and preventive medicine La. State U., 1947—; asst. vis. physician Charity Hosp., 1947-56, sr. vis. physician, 1956—; adj. prof. dept. epidemiology and biostatistics Tulane U. Sch. Pub. Health and Tropical Medicine, 1972—. Cons. Pike Meml. Hosp., Kentwood, La., 1951—, Beacham Meml. Hosp., Magnolia, Miss., 1951—, VA Hosp., Biloxi, Miss., 1955—, USPHS Hosp., New Orleans, 1969—; dir. Office Hosp. Infectious Control, 1968—. Served as capt. M.C., AUS, 1953-55. USPHS fellow, Latin Am., 1960. Fellow A.C.P.; mem. A.M.A., La., Orleans Parish med. socs., Am. Fedn. Clin. Research, So. Soc. Clin. Investigation, La. Heart Assn., La. Thoracic Soc., N.Y. Acad. Scis., Infectious Diseases Soc. Am., Phi Beta Kappa, Sigma Xi, Alpha Omega Alpha, Omicron Delta Kappa. Home: 129 Brockenbraugh Ct Metairie LA 70005 Office: 1542 Tulane Av New Orleans LA 70112

DASH, SAMUEL, lawyer, educator; b. Camden, N.J., Feb. 27, 1925; s. Joseph and Ida (Weinberg) D.; B.S., Temple U., 1947; J.D. cum laude, Harvard, 1950; m. Sara Goldhirsh, July 14, 1946; children—Judy, Rachel. Teaching asso. Northwestern U. Law Sch., 1950-51; admitted to Ill. bar, 1950, Pa. bar, 1952; trial atty. criminal div. Dept. Justice, 1951-52; asst. dist. atty., chief appeals div., Phila., 1952-54, 1st asst. dist. atty., 1954-55, dist. atty., 1955-56; dir. nationwide investigation of wiretapping Pa. Bar Assn., 1956-59; dir. Phila. Com. for Community Advancement, 1963-65, D.C. Jud. Conf. on Mental Disorders, 1965-70; prof. law Georgetown U. Law Sch., 1965—; chief counsel Senate Com. on Presdl. Campaign Activities, 1973. Cons. Ford Found., 1958-63, Nat. Assn. Attys. Gen., 1971—; chmn. bd. trustees Pub. Defenders Service D.C., 1967—. Mem. Human Relations Commn. Phila., 1957-65; mem. exec. com. Jewish Relations Council Phila., 1960-65, Jewish Community Council Met. Washington, 1973—. Bd. dirs. Internat. League for Rights of Man. Served to 2d lt. USAAF, 1943-46; ETO. Recipient Civic award for service as dist. atty., 1956; Ann. award Nat. Assn. Criminal Lawyers, 1959. Mem. Am. Law Inst., Am. Bar Assn. (certificate of commendation as chmn. criminal law sect. 1971, del. 1972), Nat. Assn. Criminal Def. Lawyers (pres. 1958). Mem. B'nai B'rith (Phila. regional chmn., nat. commn. Anti-Defamation League 1960-63). Author: The Eavesdroppers, 1959. Contbr. articles to profl. jours. Home: 110 Newlands St Chevy Chase MD 20015 Office: New Senate Office Bldg Washington DC 20510

DASHIELL, THOMAS RONALD, chem. engr.; b. Salisbury, Md., Sept. 9, 1927; s. Elmer Thomas and Dortha Lee (English) D.; B.S. in Biology, Western Md. Coll., 1950; B.S. in Chem. Engring., Johns Hopkins, 1962; m. Mabel Virginia Trout, Apr. 13, 1949; children—Thomas M., Tina Louise. Bacteriologist Dept. Army, Ft. Detrick, Frederick, Md., 1951-53, lab. supr., 1953-59, supervisory chem. engr., 1959-69, asst. sci. dir., 1969-70; staff specialist for chem. tech. Office Sec. Def., Washington, 1970—. Vice pres. West Frederick (Md.) Jr. High Sch. P.T.A., 1966-67, pres., 1967-68. Served with USAAF, 1946-47. Recipient Spl. Service award Dept. Army, 1970, Meritorious Civilian Service award, 1971. Mem. Am. Inst. Chem. Engrs., Am. Soc. Microbiology, Am. Chem. Soc., Sci. Research Soc. Am. (A.J. Rawson Meml. Engring. award 1965), N.Y. Acad. Scis., A.A.A.S., Am. Ordnance Assn., Nat. Acad. Scis. (Dept. Def. liaison mem.), V.F.W. Democrat. Methodist. Home: 504 Thomas Av Frederick MD 21701 Office: Office Dir Def Research and Engring Environmental and Life Sciences The Pentagon Washington DC 20301

DASLER, ADOLPH FREDERICK, psychiatrist; b. St. James, Minn., Sept. 9, 1906; s. Adolf and Melanie (Agather) D.; B.A., U. Wis., 1929; M.D., U. Kan., 1931; Ph.D., Naval Nat. Med. Center; m. Anita D. Buck, Sept. 29, 1931; children—Barbara Anne (Mrs. Liev M. Rydland), Adolph R. Intern, Hackley Hosp., Muskegon, Mich., 1931-32; practice medicine, Conklin, Mich., 1932-34, Muskegon Heights, Mich., 1931-42; practice medicine specializing in psychiatry, Muskegon, 1946-50, 53-71. Cons. to Plainwell Sanitarium. Served with USNR, 1942-46; served to comdr. M.C., USNR, 1950-53. Fellow Am. Geriatrics Soc.; mem. N.Y. Acad. Sci., Acad. Religion and Mental Health, Am. Psychiat. Assn., Mich. Assn. Neurologists and Psychiatrists, Mich. Skeet Assn. (pres. 1962-64), Mich. Assn. Professions (charter), Assn. Med. Psychiatrists, Disabled Am. War Vets (life), Nat. Rifle Assn. (life), Nat. Muzzle Loading Assn. (life). Home: 2208 Glendale Rd Augusta GA 30904

DASTUGUE, FERNAND JOSEPH, JR., physician; b. New Orleans, Apr. 26, 1922; s. Fernand Joseph and Frances Eliza (Brownson) D.; B.S., Tulane U., 1941, M.D., 1944; m. Shirley Louise Labbe, Dec. 10, 1955; children—Patrice L., Suzanne M., Michele C. Intern Charity Hosp., New Orleans, 1944-45; asst. dept. anatomy Tulane U., 1946-47; resident internal medicine Charity Hosp., 1947-50; staff physician VA Center, Biloxi, Miss., 1950-60, Ochsner Clinic, New Orleans, 1960—; sec. staff Ochsner Found. Hosp., 1966-69. Served to comdr., USNR, 1945-46, 52-54. Diplomate Am. Bd. Internal Medicine. Mem. A.C.P. (asso.), A.M.A., So. Med. Assn., Orleans Parish Med. Soc., New Orleans Acad. Internal Medicine, Cath. Physicians Guild, Pub. Affairs Research Council La., Phi Beta Kappa, Omicron Delta Kappa, Alpha Omega Alpha. Democrat. Roman Catholic. Clubs: Timberlane Country, Empire, New Orleans Opera (New Orleans). Home: 35 Colony Rd Gretna LA 70053 Office: 1514 Jefferson Hwy New Orleans LA 70121

DAUBEN, DWIGHT LEWIS, petroleum engr.; b. Ft. Smith, Ark., Feb. 28, 1938; s. Harry and Flossie Amy (Hindman) D.; B.S., Tex. Technol. U., 1961; M.S. (Amoco Prodn. fellow), Tulsa U., 1963; Ph.D. (Conoco fellow), Okla. U., 1966; m. Melonnie Long, July 25, 1963; children—Paul, David. Engr., Chevron Oil Co., Denver, 1962; staff research engr. Amoco Prodn. Co., Tulsa, 1966—. Mem. Soc. Petroleum Engrs., Pi Epsilon Tau, Tau Beta Pi. Club: Toastmasters (local pres. Tulsa 1971-72, area gov. 1972-73). Patentee in field. Home: 5641 S 83d E Av Tulsa OK 74145 Office: PO Box 591 Tulsa OK 74102

DAUBENSPECK, WAYNE MARTEL, clergyman; b. Selinsgrove, Pa., Nov. 25, 1904; s. Lloyd Mosheim and Della Almeda (Burns) D.; A.B., Susquehanna U., 1927; grad. Susquehanna Theol. Sem., 1930; m. Ethel Mason, July 15, 1931; children—Richard Edward, Ruth Elizabeth (Mrs. G. Keith Kistler), Henry Mason. Ordained to ministry Luth. Ch., 1930; minister ch., Oshkosh, Neb., 1930-35; chaplain Neb. Dist. CCC, 1936-38, U.S. Penal System (Northeastern and Ft. Leavenworth), 1938-40; Luth. service pastor Japan and Korea, 1954-63; pastor St. David's Ch., Kannapolis, N.C. 1964-70; ret., 1970. Served as chaplain AUS, 1940-54, commd. 1st. lt., 1935; col. Res. ret. Decorated Bronze Star medal. Mem. V.F.W. (chaplain N.C. dept. 1973). Mason (32 deg.). Home: 208 W 22d St Kannapolis NC 28081

DAUBIN, SCOTT CRITTENDEN, engr., educator; b. New London, Conn., Sept. 20, 1922; s. Freeland Allyn and Elizabeth Virginia (Scott) D.; B.S., U.S. Naval Acad., 1944; postgrad. U.S. Naval Postgrad. Sch., 1950-51; Ph.D., Princeton, 1954; m. Jacqueline Williams, Jan. 17, 1970; children by previous marriage—Larry E. Porter, Pamela (Mrs. Carl F. Brady, Jr.), Scott Crittenden, Jean (Mrs. Lonnie Arnold), Susan (Mrs. Leonard Garber). Commd. ensign U.S. Navy, 1944, advanced through grades to comdr., 1960; served in destroyers and submarines; with Office of Naval Research, Portsmouth Naval Shipyard, until 1961; head marine scis. AC Electronics Def. Research Labs., Gen. Motors Corp., Santa Barbara, Cal., 1961-67; chmn. dept. ocean engring. Woods Hole Oceanographic Inst., 1967-71; prof., chmn. dept. ocean engring. U. Miami (Fla.), 1971—. Mem. Deep Submergence Systems Review Group, 1963; mem. com. submersible vehicles, Am. Bur. Shipping Tech., 1966—; mem. panel buoy tech. marine bd. Nat. Acad. Engring., Fla. Commn. Marine Scis. and Tech.; mem. Sci. and Engring. Council Santa Barbara, 1962-67, vice chmn., 1966. Registered profl. engr., N.H. Mem. Acoustical Soc. Am., Am. Assn. Physics Tchrs., Marine Tech. Soc., Am. Soc. M.E. (chmn. underwater tech. div. 1965-66), Soc. Naval Architects and Marine Engrs., Sigma Xi. Home: 115 Sunrise Dr Key Biscayne FL 33149 Office: 10 Rickenbacker Causeway Miami FL 33149

DAUGHERTY, BILLY JOE, banker; b. Timpson, Tex., Jan. 31, 1923; s. David Albert and Kate (Smith) D.; grad. Tyler Comml. Coll., 1942; postgrad. So. State Coll., 1945-47; grad. Southwestern Grad. Sch. Banking So. Meth. U., 1969; student Nat. Credit Lending Sch. U. Okla., 1969; m. Martha Carroum, May 14, 1942; children—Stephen Michael, Tony Fares, Kathryn Love. Asst. v.p., asst. trust officer First Nat. Bank Magnolia, Ark., 1947-52; plant accountant Republic Steel Corp., Magnolia, 1953-54; with Union Nat. Bank Little Rock, 1954-70, v.p., cashier, 1965-70; exec. v.p., dir., sec. to bd. dirs. First State Bank & Trust Co., Conway, Ark., 1970-73, pres., dir., sec. to bd. dirs., 1973—. Dir. Ark. Banking Sch. Mem. adv. bd. Salvation Army, 1967—; bd. dirs. Met. YMCA, Little Rock, 1966-70; chmn., Columbia chpt. A.R.C., Magnolia, 1952; mem. budget com. United Fund Pulaski County, Ark., 1962-65; treas., City Beautiful Com., Little Rock, 1965-67; treas. Ark. br. Am. Assn. UN, 1965-67; pres. Heart of Ark. Travel Assn., 1971—; pres., dir. United Fund of Faulkner County, 1972; state treas. Radio Free Europe, 1960—; chmn. Faulkner County Heart Fund Campaign, 1971. Sec. to bd. dirs., trustee Union Nat. Found.; bd. dirs. Ark. Heart Assn., 1971—; trustee Ark. Baptist Med. Center, sec.-treas., 1965-69. Served with USAAF, 1943-46. Mem. Little Rock Clearing House Assn. (v.p. 1969, pres. 1965-66, sec.-treas. 1967-68), Ark. Bankers Assn. (pres. jr. bankers sect. 1950; bank dirs. adv. com. 1971—), Conway C. of C. (1st v.p.). Baptist (supt. Sunday sch.; chmn. bldg. com. 1964-66; chmn. bd. deacons 1962-63; mem. finance com. 1960-68, chmn. stewardship com. 1968). Clubs: Top of Rock (dir. 1969—); Little Rock; Conway Country; Pleasant Valley Country; Western Hills Country (dir., sec. 1968-69). Home: 4 Oakdale Dr Conway AR 72032 Office: First State Bank & Trust Co Oak & Front Sts Conway AR 72032

DAUGHERTY, CHAUNCEY O'HARA, physician; b. Dublin, Miss., Dec. 8, 1933; s. Julius E. and Cleopatra (Reese) D.; A.A., Coahoma Jr. Coll., 1952; M.D., Meharry Med. Coll., 1958; m. Bernia Louise Williams, June 28, 1958; children—Chauncey, Vincent, Patricia, Valerie. Intern, Detroit Receiving Hosp.; resident VA hosps., Tuskegee, Ala., Des Moines and Oteen, N.C.; practice medicine, specializing in gen. thoracic and cardiovascular surgery, Memphis, 1967—; chmn. bd. dirs., pres. Asso. Surgeons and Physicians, Inc., Memphis, 1970—; med. dir. Memphis Health Center Med. Group; chmn. Memphis Health Center; dir. Mid-South Med. Center Council, 1969-70. Served to lt. comdr. USN, 1959-67. Diplomate Am. Bd. Surgery, Am. Bd. Thoracic Surgery. Fellow A.C.S., Royal Soc. Health. Mason. Home: 837 Lucille St Memphis TN 38106 Office: 256 E McLemore St Memphis TN 38106

DAUGHERTY, FREDERICK ALVIN, judge; b. Oklahoma City, Aug. 18, 1914; s. Charles L. and Felicia A. (Mitchell) D.; LL.B., Cumberland U., 1934; postgrad. Oklahoma City U., 1934-35, U. Okla., 1936-37; m. Marjorie E. Green, Mar. 15, 1947 (dec. Feb. 1964); m. 2d, Betsy F. Amis, Dec. 15, 1965. Admitted to Okla. bar, 1937; practiced in Oklahoma City, 1937-40; mem. firm Ames, Ames & Daugherty, Oklahoma City, 1946-50, Ames, Daugherty, Bynum & Black, Oklahoma City, 1952-55; judge dist. ct. 7th Jud. Dist. Okla., 1955-61; U.S. dist. judge Western, Eastern, No. dists. Okla., Oklahoma City, 1961-72; chief judge Western Dist. Okla., 1972—. Mem. profl. adv. com. Okla. County Assn. Mental Health, 1964-70; mem. exec. com. Oklahoma City Council on Alcholism, 1964—, Okla. Med. Research Found., 1966-69. Nat. bd. govs. A.R.C., 1963-69, 3d vice chmn., 1968-69, nat. fund vice chmn. Okla., 1956-58; trustee United Fund Greater Oklahoma City, v.p., 1960, pres., 1961; bd. dirs. Community Council Oklahoma City and County, pres., 1967-69. Served with AUS, 1940-45; PTO; 1951-52; Korea; served to maj. gen. Okla. N.G., 1934-64. Decorated Legion of Merit with two oak leaf clusters, Bronze Star with oak leaf cluster, UN Distinguished Service medal; recipient Okla. Distinguished Service medal, recipient award to mankind Oklahoma City Sertoma Club, 1962, Outstanding Citizen award Oklahoma City Jr. C. of C., 1965, U. Okla. Distinguished Service citation, 1973, named to Okla. Hall of Fame, 1969. Mem. Jud. Conf. U.S., Okla., Am., Fed. bar assns., Am. Bar Found., Oklahoma City C. of C. (dir. 1960-61, 66-70, 72—), N.G. Assn. U.S. (Distinguished Service medal 1965), 45th Inf. Div. Assn., Amvets, Am. Legion, Assn. U.S. Army (Okla. pres. 1962-65, dir. 1964-70), Okla. N.G. Assn. (pres. 1947), V.F.W., Mil. Order World Wars (chpt comdr. 1968-69), Sigma Alpha Epsilon, Phi Delta Phi. Episcopalian Kiwanian (pres. Oklahoma City 1957), Mason (32 deg., Shriner, Jester). Club: Oklahoma City Men's Dinner (exec. com. 1963-65, pres. 1966-69). Home: 1800 Coventry Lane Oklahoma City OK 73120 Office: US Courthouse Oklahoma City OK 73102

DAUGHTREY, ZOEL WAYNE, soil scientist, educator; b. Sulphur Springs, Tex., June 30, 1940; s. Jewel D. and Hazel (Kostris) D.; B.S., Tex. Tech. U., 1963; M.S., Okla. State U., 1966; Ph.D., N.C. State U., 1970; m. Jackie E. Burch, Dec. 18, 1965; 1 dau., Heather Lynn. Materials analyst Tex. Hwy. Dept., Paris, 1963-64; expediter UARCO, Paris, 1964; instr. Okla. State U., 1964-66; agronomist soil testing div. N.C. Dept. Agr., Raleigh, 1966-70; asso. prof., head dept. earth scis. Northwestern State U., 1970—. Mem. agrl. adv. com. La. Bankers Assn.; cons. agrl. enterprises Natchitoches Area Action Assn. Mem. Citizens for Better Schs., 1973—; v.p., program chmn. agrl. sect. Conf. La. Colls. and Univs., 1972-73, pres., 1973-74. Named hon. State Farmer of La., Future Farmers Am. 1973. Mem. Am. Soc. Agronomy, Soil Sci. Soc. Am., Crop Sci. Soc. Am., La. Assn. Agronomists, La. Hort. Soc., So. Beef Conf., Sigma Xi, Phi Kappa Phi, Phi Theta Kappa. Home: 1006 Oma St Natchitoches LA 71457

DAUSSMAN, GROVER FREDERICK, cons. engr.; b. Newburgh, Ind., May 6, 1919; s. Grover Cleveland and Madeline (Springer) D.; student U. Cin., 1936-38, Carnegie Inst. Tech., 1944-45, George Washington U., 1948-56; B.S. in Elec. Engring., U. Ala., 1963, postgrad., 1963-64; postgrad. Indsl. Coll. Armed Forces, 1955, 63; Ph.D. (hon.), Hamilton State U., 1973; m. Elli Margrite Kilian, Dec. 27, 1941; children—Cynthia Louise (Mrs. Kenneth E. Quinn), Judith Ann, Margaret Elizabeth (Mrs. Robert T. Davidson). Coop. engr. Sunbeam Elec. Mfg. Co., Evansville, Ind., 1936-38; engr. draftsman Phila. Navy Yard, 1941-42; resident engr. supr. shipbldg. USN, Neville Island, Pa., 1942-45; engr. Pearl Harbor Navy Yard, 1945-48; with Bur. Ships, USN, Washington, 1948-56; with Guidance and Control Tech. Liaison, Army Ballistic Missile Agy., Huntsville, Ala., 1956-58, chief program coordination Guidance and Control Lab., 1958-60; chief program coordination Astrionics Lab., Marshall Space Flight Center, Huntsville, 1960-62, staff asst. for advanced research and tech. Astrionics Lab., 1962-70; engring. cons., 1970—; project dir. fallout shelter surveys Mil. Dept. Tenn., 1971-73. Recipient certificate Hon. Service, USN, 1945; Performance Award certificate U.S. Army, 1960; NASA Apollo Achievement award, 1969. Registered profl. engr., Ala., Va., D.C. Mem. U. Ala. Alumni Assn., Ala. (Engr. of Yr. award 1968, pres. chpt. 1966-67, state dir. 1962-65, 68-71), Nat. socs. profl. engrs., I.E.E.E. (sr. mem., sect. chmn. N.Ala. sect. 1961-62, engring. mgmt. chpt. chmn. 1964-65, mem. adminstrv. com. engring. mgmt. soc. 1966—, sec. soc. 1969-73, Engr. of Yr. award 1969, research com. 1965-67, dir. S.E. region, mem. inst. bd. dirs. 1972-73), A.A.A.S., Am. Def. Preparedness Assn. (post dir. Tenn. Valley), Am. Inst. Aeros. and Astronautics, Am. Soc. Naval Engrs., Missile, Space and Range Pioneers, U.S. Naval Inst., Assn. U.S. Army, Internat. Platform Assn., Huntsville Assn. Tech. Socs. (sec. 1969-71, v.p., dir.), Marshall Space Flight Center Retirement Assn. (v.p. 1973-74). Democrat. Mem. United Ch. of Christ (sec. ch. council 1965-66, vice moderator Ala-Tenn. Assn. 1965-68, bd. dirs. S.E. conv. 1965-66). Home: 1910 Colice Rd SE Huntsville AL 35801

DAVENPORT, FOUNTAIN ST. CLAIR, electronic engr.; b. Harmony, N.C., Jan. 16, 1914; s. Dennis F. and Margaret E. (Winfield) D.; B.S., U. Miami, 1950; postgrad. U. Miami, U. Balt., Johns Hopkins, U. Fla., Rollins Coll., Brevard Engring. Coll., 1952-64; M.S., Fla. Inst. Tech., 1970; m. Jane Helena Hermann, June 11, 1948 (dec. Sept. 1973); 1 dau., Sylvia Jane; m. 2d, Joyce Allen Huff, Mar. 16, 1974. Engr., Bendix Aviation Corp., Towson, Md., 1951-53; project engr. Vitro Labs., Eglin AFB, Fla., 1953-55; engr. A, RCA Missile Test Project, Patrick AFB, Fla., 1955-60; spur. radar engring., guided missiles range div., Pan Am. World Airways, Inc., Patrick AFB, Fla. 1960-65, sr. systems engr. Aerospace Services Div., 1965—. Cons. N.R.C., Churchill Research Range, Man., Can., 1966-67; faculty Fla. Inst. Tech., 1958-60, 62-63, mem. edn. com., 64. Served with USN, 1934-37; with USNR, 1942-45. Life mem. Friends Melbourne Library; patron Indian River Players. Mem. Fla. Engring. Soc. (sr.), Nat. Soc. Profl. Engrs., Am. Ordnance Assn. (life), Missile and Space Pioneers (life). Mason (32 deg.). Home: 2110 Shannon Av Indialantic FL 32901 Office: Mail Unit 6090 Pan Am World Airways Inc Patrick AFB FL 32925

DAVENPORT, O. MALCOLM, educator; b. Pittston, Pa., Feb. 13, 1908; s. Frank Garfield and Cora May (Rader) D.; B.S. in Forestry, Pa. State U., 1933; M.S., Purdue U., 1940; m. Sara Elkins, Aug. 31, 1935; children—Sue (Mrs. Ray M. Ware), Peter, Martha. Forestry formen ECW, Summer, N.J., 1933; instr. forestry Pa. State U., 1933-35; asst. prof. forestry Purdue U., 1935-42; shop specialist U.S. War Dept., 1943-47; prof. forestry U. Ky., Lexington, 1947-74. Cons. on wood utilization. Mem. Soc. Am. Foresters, Ky. Conservation Council, Ky. Forestry Council, Am. Assn. U. Profs., Alpha Zeta, Gamma Sigma Delta. Home: 4425 13th St Vero Beach FL 32960

DAVENPORT, WILLIAM HAROLD, mathematician; b. Jackson, Tenn., Dec. 21, 1935; s. John Heron and Mary (Troutt) D.; B.S. in Engring. Physics, U. Tenn., 1962; M.S. in Math., Tex. A. & M. U., 1966; Ph.D. in Math., U. Ala., 1971; m. Mary Janice Johnson, Mar. 18, 1960; children—Mark Edson, Amber Yvette; m. 2d, Sandra Elaine Holloway, June 30, 1973. Aerospace tech. NASA Manned Spacecraft Center, Houston, 1962-64; research mathematician Brown Engring. Co., Huntsville, Ala., 1966-67; teaching fellow, instr. math. U. Ala., 1967-71; mathematician U.S. Army Missile Command, Huntsville, 1971-72; asst. prof. Coll. Petroleums and Minerals, 1972—. Served with USN, 1954-58. Mem. Am. Math. Soc., Sigma Pi Sigma, Phi Kappa Phi, Pi Mu Epsilon. Home: 307C Cedar Crest Tuscaloosa AL 35401 Office: Box 26 CPM Dhahran Saudi Arabia

DAVEY, KENNETH ROGER, lawyer; b. nr. Chippewa Falls, Wis., Dec. 25, 1929; s. Wilbur T. and Nell (Paynter) D.; B.A., U. Wis., 1950, postgrad. Law Center, 1951; LL.B., So. Methodist U., 1956; m. Susan Putman, May 16, 1953; children—Alice L., Elizabeth Ann. Admitted to Tex. bar, 1955; partner firm Baker, Jordan, Davey & Shaw, 1955-62, Stark & Davey, 1962-67, Shaw, Davis & Davey, 1967-70; chmn. Davey-Davis, Inc., 1970-72; partner firm Davey, Conrad, Enderby & FitzGerald, Dallas, 1972—. Finance chmn. Cooke County Democratic Com., 1964. Served to 1st lt. AUS, 1951-54. Mem. Tex. Bar Found., Tex., Dallas, Cooke County (pres. 1966) bar assns., Comml. Law League, Tex. Trial Lawyers Assn., Phi Delta Phi. Home: 4404 Fairfax St Dallas TX 75205 Office: 1212 Main Tower Dallas TX 75202

DAVEY, WALTER FLETCHER, physician; b. Bayonne, N.J., June 25, 1911; s. Thomas Nelson and Evelyn (Peterson) D.; B.S., Rutgers U., 1933; M.D., Temple U., 1937; m. Mildred Berkey, Aug. 30, 1969; children—(by previous marriage) Walter Fletcher, Sandra Edwards. Intern, Temple U. Hosp., Phila., 1937-39; gen. practice medicine, Stuart, Fla., 1939—. Served with USAAF, 1942-45. Mem. A.M.A. Elk. Clubs: Stuart Golf and Country, Yacht and Country, Martin Golf and Country (dir. 1945-60) (Stuart). Home: St Lucie Blvd Stuart FL 33494 Office: Box 258 401 Ocean Blvd Stuart FL 33494

DAVIDOW, HOWARD BRUCE, aerospace co. exec.; b. Lakeland, Fla., Mar. 16, 1933; s. Samuel and Rose (Lefkowitz) D.; B.A., U. Miami, 1959; m. Vasaliki Jacqueline Voyantzis, July 5, 1959; Gen. sales mgr. E. Farnell & Co., Inc., West Palm Beach, Fla., 1958-62; pres., dir. H. M. Melard Corp., Miami, 1959—; pres. Maru Avionics, Inc., 1963-67; exec. v.p. Aero Sytems, Inc., Miami, 1967-72, also dir.; pres., dir. Aero Systems Avionic Sales Div. subsidiary, Miami, 1967-72; sec., dir. Microtenna Corp., Miami, 1969. Mem., pres. Living Inst. for Edn., Miami. Served to 1st lt. SAC, USAF, 1954-57. Home: 6705 SW 117th St Miami FL 33156 Office: Virginia Plaza Bldg 6501 NW 36th St Miami FL 33166

DAVIDSON, MRS. CHARLES (KATE S. DAVIDSON), educator; b. Emporia, Va., May 13, 1910; d. John William and Ida Florence (Hill) Saunders; student Chowan Coll., 1926-27; A.A., Louisburg Coll., 1927-28; summer student Forest Coll., 1928, 29. Longwood Coll., 1932; m. Charles Reuber Davidson, July 1, 1933; 1 dau., Katharine Saunders (Mrs. John Byers Horner). Tchr. Emporia High Sch., 1930-33, 1946-50, substitute tchr., 1950—. Gen. chmn., dir. Greenville Tb Assn.; 2d v.p. Southside area council Girl Scouts U.S.A.; dir. Southside Area Planning Bd., A.R.C.; sec. Emporia Band Boosters Club; mem. state nursing scholarship com. Tb and Respiratory Disease Assn.; pres. Greenville Meml. Hosp. Aux.; rep. dir. Va. Tb Assn.; bd. dirs. Commonwealth council (Va.) Girl Scouts, Richmond council Girl Scouts, Southside Tb and Health Assn., Va. Lung Assn.; rec. sec. pub. affairs Ch. Hosp. Aux. Mem. P.T.A. (asst. dist. dir. Southside area, dir. Emporia, Va.), U.D.C. (ures local chpt.; registar), Va. Hist. Soc., Butts Tavern Assn. (dir., trustee), Woman's Soc. Christian Service (promotion sec. corr.; edn. ch. pres., Dora Armstrong zone leader, pres., mem. bd. Petersburg dist.), United Meth. Women (pres. Petersburg dist., chmn. community improvement projects). Methodist (supt. CradleRoll, mem. bd. edn., mem. ch. adminstrv. bd., dir.). Clubs: Emporia Ladies Golf Assn. (pres.), Riparian Federated Woman's (v.p.), Woman's (past pres., parliamentarian, edn. chmn., mental health chmn.), Emporia Federated Garden, Wednesday. Home: 506 Ingleside Av Emporia VA 23847

DAVIDSON, CHARLES NELSON, chemist; b. Kankakee, Ill., Oct. 19, 1937; s. Arthur Nelson and Maxine Elizabeth (Garrett) D.; B.S., The Citadel, Charleston, S.C., 1959; Ph.D. (NSF fellow), Fla. State U., 1962; m. Juanita Louise Davey, Aug. 1, 1959; children—Charles Nelson, Kevin Arthur, Timothy Michael. Nuclear effects officer U.S. Army Combat Devels. Command CBR Agy., Ft. McClellan, Ala., 1962-66, physicist Combat Devels. Command Inst. Nuclear Studies, Ft. Bliss, Tex., 1966-68, sci. adviser to comdr. U.S. Army Nuclear Agy., Ft. Bliss, 1968—; asso. prof. dept. chemistry Jacksonville (Ala.) State Coll., 1965-66. Tng. chmn. Yucca council Boy Scouts Am., El Paso, Tex., 1968-70, cubmaster, 1969-72, 73—, dist. chmn., 1970-72, cubmaster Keystone Area council, 1972-73; coach Little League Baseball, 1969, 73. Served as capt. U.S. Army, 1962-64. Decorated Army Commendation medal. NSF postdoctoral fellow, 1962. Mem. Am. Chem. Soc., Am. Nuclear Soc. Roman Catholic. Rotarian. Home: 10116 Monaco Dr El Paso TX 79925 Office: US Army Nuclear Agy Fort Bliss TX 79916

DAVIDSON, DONALD ROBERT, numerical control engr.; b. Charleston, W.Va., July 16, 1937; s. Robert H. and Ava (Ratcliff) D.; B.S., U. Tenn., 1965, M.S., 1974; m. Gwendolyn Sue Parker, Sept. 26, 1959; children—Robert Wesley, Benjamin Parker. Clk., Union Carbide, Oak Ridge, 1958-61, part programmer, 1961-65, engr., supr. numerical control, 1967—; engr. E.I. DuPont de Nemours & Co., Inc., Chattanooga, 1965-67. Math. instr. Chattanooga State Tech. Inst., 1966-67; cons. Modular Home Industry, Rockwood, Tenn., 1971-72. Mem. Gulf Park Civic Assn., 1967—. Registered profl. engr., Tenn. Mem. Am. Inst. Indsl. Engrs., Nat., Tenn. socs. profl. engrs. Club: Gulf Park Recreation Assn. Home: 829 Naples Rd Knoxville TN 37919 Office: PO Box Y Bldg 9201-4/2 Oak Ridge TN 37830

DAVIDSON, GORDON BYRON, lawyer; b. Louisville, June 24, 1926; s. Paul Byron and Elizabeth (Franz) D.; A.B., Centre Coll., 1949; J.D., U. Louisville, 1951; LL.M., Yale, 1952; m. Geraldine B. Geiger, Dec. 21, 1948; children—Sally Burgess, Stuart Gordon. Asst. Army staff judge advocate of First Army, Govs. Island, N.Y., 1952-54; law clk. Mr. Justice Stanley Reed, Supreme Ct. of U.S., Washington, 1954; partner Wyatt. Grafton and Sloss, 1955—; lectr. U. Louisville Law Sch., 1958—. Dir. Courier-Jour. & Louisville Times Co., WHAS, Inc., Standard Gavure Co. Pres. Louisville Central Area, Inc., 1971-73; chmn. River City Mall Com., 1973-74; mem. Ky. Derby Festival Com.; mem. Louisville Commn. Fgn. Relations. Bd. dirs., chmn. Norton-Children's Hosps., Inc., Louisville Fund for Arts; trustee St. Francis Sch., Centre Coll., Louisville Theatrical Assn. Served as cadet midshipman U.S. Mcht. Marine Acad., 1944-45; 1st lt. AUS, 1952-54; Korea. Mem. Am., Ky., Louisville, Fed. bar assns., Louisville Area C. of C. (dir.), Phi Delta Theta, Omicron Delta Kappa, Phi Kappa Phi. Democrat. Presbyn. Clubs: Harmony Landing Country; Jefferson (bd. govs.), Louisville Country (bd. govs.); Tavern; Lawyer's; Pendennis; Delray Beach. Home: 435 Lightfoot Rd Louisville KY 40207 Office: 28th Floor Citizens Plaza Louisville KY 40202

DAVIDSON, IVAN WILLIAM FREDERICK, pharmacologist, educator; b. Winnipeg, Man., Can., July 31, 1926; s. Adam Grieve and Ella Lea (Crowell) D.; B.Sc., U. Man., 1954; M.A. (Banting and Best fellow), U. Toronto, 1956, Ph.D. (Banting and Best fellow), 1959; m. Audrey Kathleen Murray, Sept. 16, 1950; children—Linda Lea, Craig Murray, Brian Stuart, Beth Susan. Came to U.S., 1959, naturalized, 1969. Research asso. Banting and Best Dept. Med. Research, U. Toronto, 1958-59; research biochemist Union Carbide Chems. Co., S.Charleston, W.Va., 1959-61; asst. prof. physiology and pharmacology Bowman Gray Sch. Medicine, Winston Salem, N.C., 1961-63, asst. prof. pharmacology, 1963-66, asso. prof., 1966-70, asso. in physiology, 1963—, prof. pharmacology, 1970—. Recipient Lederle Med. Faculty award, 1964-67, Bowman Gray Sch. Medicine Preclin. Teaching award, 1964, 66. Med. Life Ins. fellow, 1956-59. Mem. Am. Physiol. Soc., Am. Soc. Pharmacology and Exptl. Therapeutics, Am. Soc. Exptl. Medicine and Biology, A.A.A.S., N.Y. Acad. Scis., Am. Inst. Biol. Scis., Sigma Xi. Mem. editorial bd. Drug Metabolism Revs., 1972—. Home: 4934 Stonington Rd Winston-Salem NC 27103

DAVIDSON, JAMES BLAINE, educator; b. Oklahoma City, Nov. 10, 1923; s. Richard Blaine and Bessie Lowrance (Greene) D.; student U. Okla., 1941-43; B.S., U.S. Naval Acad., 1946; B.S. in Elec. Engring., U.S. Naval Postgrad. Sch., 1952; M.S., U. Cal., Los Angeles, 1953; m. Anna Ruth Cox, Dec. 18, 1948; children—Annette Jan (Mrs. George Board, Jr.), Jeannette Ann (Mrs. Alex McCallum), James Blaine. Commd. ensign USN, 1946, advanced through grades to comdr., 1962; dir. undersea programs Office Naval Research, 1965-67; ret., 1967; prof. ocean engring. Fla. Atlantic U., Boca Raton, Fla., 1967—. Research cons. City of Deerfield Beach, Fla., Metallgesellschaft AG. Recipient Advanced Sci. Study grant USN, U. Cal., Los Angeles, 1952. Mem. Am. Soc. Engring. Edn., Acoustical Soc. Am., Marine Tech. Soc., Fla. Shore and Beach Preservation Assn. Republican. Presbyn. Club: Sandalfoot Cove Golf and Country. Home: 1190 SW 11th St Boca Raton FL 33432

DAVIDSON, JOHN KENNETH, sociologist, educator; b. Augusta, Ga., Oct. 25, 1939; s. Larcie Charles and Betty (Corley) D.; student Augusta Coll., 1956-58; B.S. Ed., U. Ga., 1961; M.A., 1963; postgrad. U. Fla., 1971—; m. Josephine Frazier, Apr. 11, 1964; children—John Kenneth, Stephen Wood. Asst. prof. dept. psychology and sociology Armstrong State Coll., Savannah, 1963-67; asst. prof. dept. sociology Augusta Coll., Augusta, Ga., 1967-74; asst. prof. dept. sociology Ind. U., South Bend, 1974—; research cons. dept. obstetrics and gynecology Med. Coll. Ga., Augusta, 1969-74, pediatrics, 1972-73, also asso. dir. health care project, 1971-73, research instr., summer 1971, research asso., summer 1972-73. Program coordinator Community Devel. in Process Phase II and III, Title I Higher Edn. Act of 1965, 1970; mem. sociology and anthropology Univ. System Ga., 1970-74, chmn. curriculum sub-com., 1970-72; mem. Nat., Ga., Southeastern councils on family relations. Bd. advisers Augusta Area Planned Parenthood Assn. Mem. Ga. Acad. Sci., Am. Sociol. Assn., So., Ga. sociol socs., Am. Assn. U. Profs., Augusta Coll. Alumni Soc., Law and Soc. Assn., U. Ga. Alumni Soc., Ga. Sociol. and Anthropol. Assn. (sec.-treas. 1969-71), Kappa Delta Pi, Phi Kappa Phi, Phi Theta Kappa, Alpha Kappa Delta (pres. Beta chpt. 1971-72, nat. exec. com. 1972—). Episcopalian. Home: 1908 Valley Spring Rd Augusta GA 30904

DAVIES, DAVID CHRISTOPHER, oil co. exec.; b. Casper, Wyo., Aug. 11, 1927; s. Edward Earl and Anna Katherine (Christopher) D.; B.S., U. Tulsa, 1953; m. Opal Christine Hobbs, July 19, 1953; children—David Christopher, John L., Charles H. Petroleum engr. Tidewater Oil Co., Garnett, Kan., 1954-55, Salmon Oil Corp., Tulsa, 1955-57, Home-Stake Prodn. Co., Tulsa, 1957-71; co-owner, petroleum engr. Davies & Fitzgerald oil prodn., Tulsa, 1971—. Bd. dirs. Gilcrease Mus. Assn., Tulsa. Served with AUS, 1946-47. Registered profl. engr., Okla. Mem. Soc. Profl. Evaluation Engrs., Am. Inst. Metall. and Mining Engrs., Am. Petroleum Inst. Episcopalian. Home: 2653 S Birmingham Pl Tulsa OK 74114 Office: Philtower Bldg Tulsa OK 74103

DAVIES, ROBERT STOCKWELL, mfg. co. exec.; b. Syracuse, N.Y., Apr. 25, 1925; s. Harry William and Ruth (Heath) D.; student Dartmouth, 1943-45; B.Arch., Syracuse U., 1951; m. Janice Hudson, Feb. 20, 1954; children—Gail Brewer, Robert Stockwell, James Hudson. Project architect Carl W. Clark, Syracuse, 1954-59; adminstr. Lockwood Green Engrs., Inc., Spartanburg, S.C., 1962-65; asst. to pres. Blackman Uhler Industries, Spartanburg, 1965-68; sec.-treas., Synalloy Corp. (formerly Blackman Uhler Industries), Spartanburg, 1968-69, v.p. adminstrn., sec., 1970—, dir., 1971—; dir. Whiting Engring. Co., Camden, S.C., Multifab, Inc., Spartanburg, Balco Realty Co., Spartanburg, Delmar Equipment Co., Spartanburg. Mem. Spartanburg Safety Council, 1968-69. Served to lt. USNR, 1943-46, 51-53. Mem. Spartanburg Council Architects, Gargoyle Soc., Phi Delta Theta. Republican. Presbyn. Home: Quailhurst Route 2 Campobello SC 29322 Office: PO Box 5627 Spartanburg SC 29301

DAVIS, ABRAHAM ERIC, clergyman; b. New Orleans, Nov. 16, 1934; s. Herbert L. and Christina (Jase) D.; B.A., So. U., B.D., M.Div.; m. Muriel Jean McCall, June 17, 1957; children—Gretenal Marie, Carol Ann, Iris Ann, Anita Coleen. Ordained to ministry Methodist Ch.; asst. pastor Bowen United Meth. Ch., Atlanta, 1957-60; pastor Trinity and Mason United Meth. Chs., 1960-63; instr., chaplain Sager Brown Elementary Sch., 1960-63; pastor St. Paul United Meth. Ch., Shreveport, La., 1963—. Mem., elder, full connection La. Annual Conf. United Meth. Ch., Acad. of Parish Clergy. Pres. Interdenominational Ministerial Alliance, Shreveport-Bossier City, La. Bd. dirs. Confederate Meml. Med. Center, Open Ear, Vols. of Am. Recipient Crusade scholarship, 1960; Community Service award Mt. Canaan Baptist Ch., 1970. Mem. N.A.A.C.P. (mem. exec. com.). Mason. Home: 1852 Abbie Shreveport LA 71103 Office: 1001 Pierre Av Shreveport LA 71103

DAVIS, ALVIE LEE, chemist, educator; b. Richardson, Tex., Jan. 22, 1931; s. John Caleb and Jewell Estelle (Hawk) D.; B.S., Abilene Christian Coll., 1955; Ph.D., U. Tex., 1960; m. Jana Showalter, Apr. 18, 1941; children—Jeffrey Scott, Lisa Carol. Asst. prof. chemistry Abilene (Tex.) Christian Coll., 1959-62, asso. prof., 1962-68, prof., 1968—. Robert A. Welch Found. research grantee, 1962—. Mem. Am. Chem. Soc., N.Y. Acad. Scis., Sigma Xi, Alpha Chi, Phi Lambda Upsilon, Gamma Sigma Epsilon. Contbr. articles to profl. jours. Home: 2549 Campus Ct Abilene TX 79601

DAVIS, ARCHIBALD KIMBROUGH, banker; b. Winston-Salem, N.C.; Jan. 22, 1911; s. Thomas W. and Frances (Conrad) D.; A.B. U. N.C., 1932; student Grad. Sch. Banking Rutgers U., 1940; m. Mary L. Haywood, May 12, 1938; children—Archibald Hilliard, Louise, Haywood, Thomas W., III. With Wachovia Bank & Trust Co., 1932-46, sr. v.p. charge Winston-Salem, office, 1946-56, chmn., 1956—, also dir.; dir. Charlotte br. Fed. Res. Bank of Richmond, 1959-61; dir. Am. Tel. & Tel. Co., Chatham Mfg. Co., Jordan Spinning Co., Sellers Mfg. Co., Sellers Dyeing Co., Royal Cotton Mills, So. Ry. Co., Media Gen., Inc. Founder, 1st pres. Northwest N.C. Indsl. Devel. Assn.; mem. Nat. Commn. Productivity, Commodity Credit Corp. Pres. Research Triangle Found. N.C., 1959—. Chmn. bd. trustees N.C. Found. Ch.-Related Colls., pres., 1971-72, chmn. bd., 1972-73; vice chmn. Duke Endowment. Mem. U.S. C. of C. (v.p. 1958-61, dir. 1973—), Soc. of Cincinnati, Am. Bankers Assn. (pres. state bank div. 1956-57, nat. pres. 1965-66), Joint Council Econ. Edn., Com. Econ. Devel. (trustee), Phi Beta Kappa. Rotarian (pres. 1958-59). Home: 2828 Forest Dr Winston-Salem NC 27104 Office: 612 S Main St Winston-Salem NC 27108

DAVIS, AUDREY B., govt. ofcl.; b. Hicksville, N.Y., Nov. 9, 1934; B.S., Adelphi Coll., 1956; Ph.D. (NIH fellow), Johns Hopkins, 1969. Tchr. biology, chemistry and physics Sewanhaka High Sch., Floral Park, N.Y., 1956-59, Saugus (Mass.) High Sch., 1960-61, Windsor Sch., Boston, 1961-62; cons. Sci. Service, 1964-66; asst. curator div. med. scis. Smithsonian Instn., Washington, 1967-70, asso. curator, 1970—, supr., 1972—. NSF research grantee, 1958, 59, 59-60; Commonwealth Found. grantee, 1972-74, Smithsonian Research Found. grantee, 1971-72. Mem. Assn. Curators Nat. Mus. History and Tech. (chmn. 1972-73), History Sci. Soc., Am. Assn. History of Medicine, History Tech. Soc., Am. Hist. Assn., Brit. Soc. Social History of Medicine, Am. Acad. Polit. and Social Sci., Am. Inst. History of Pharmacy. Author: Handbook for Secondary School Science Projects, 1966; Circulation Physiology and Medical Chemistry, 1650-1680, 1973; Bibliography on Women: With Special Emphasis on Their Role in Science and Society, 1974; contbr. chpts. to books. Contbr. articles to profl. jours. Address: Smithsonian Instn Washington DC 20560

DAVIS, BEN ARTHUR, JR., assn. exec., mgmt. cons.; b. Meridian, Miss., Oct. 27, 1930; s. Ben Arthur and Sarah (Combs) D.; student Meridian Jr. Coll., 1948-49, Miss. State U., 1949-50; B.S. in Forestry, Auburn U., 1955; m. Georgia Ann Coleman, Aug. 20, 1954; children—Anne Miller, Ben Arthur III. Fire prevention specialist Miss. Forestry Commn., 1955; asst. exec. sec. Miss. Forestry Assn., Jackson, 1956-57, exec. sec., 1957-58, exec. v.p., 1958-73; founder Ben Davis Assos., Jackson, 1974—. Served with USAF, 1951-52. Certified assn. exec. Mem. Pub. Relations Assn. Miss. (pres. 1961), Am., Miss. (pres. 1961) socs. assn. execs., Nat. Council Forestry Assn. Execs. (pres. 1964-65), Miss. Hwy. Users Conf. (dir.). Address: 5420 Charter Oak Pl Jackson MS 39211

DAVIS, BEN REEVES, newspaper editor; b. Huntington, Ark., Apr. 1, 1927; s. Lester Belton and Jessie (Reeves) D.; B.A. in Journalism, U. Ala., 1949; m. Margaret Lee Rogers, Nov. 26, 1950 (div.); 1 son, Ben Reeves. Reporter, Selma (Ala.) Times-Jour., 1949-50; mng. editor Jasper (Ala.) Mountain Eagle, 1950-52; sports writer, copy editor Birmingham (Ala.) News, 1952-56; mng. editor Tuscaloosa (Ala.) News, 1956-64; exec. mng. editor Montgomery Advertiser and Ala. Jour., 1964—. Bd. dirs. Montgomery United Appeal. Served with USNR, 1945-46. Mem. A.P. Mng. Editors Assn., Ala. A.P. Assn. (pres. 1964-65), Sigma Delta Chi, Pi Kappa Phi. Methodist. Office: 200 Washington Ave Montgomery AL 36102

DAVIS, BERNARD BYRD, lawyer; b. nr. Shelbyville, Ky., Feb. 17, 1912; s. John Fulton and Annie (Bailey) D.; LL.B., Washington and Lee U., 1933; m. Sarah Ware, Aug. 12, 1933. Admitted to Ky. bar, 1932, gen. practice, Shelbyville, 1933-63, Louisville, 1971—; spl. agt. FBI, 1942-45; commr. Ky. Ct. of Appeals, Frankfort, 1963-71. Chmn. Shelby County Democratic Exec. Com., 1936-40. Home: 1315 Walnut St Shelbyville KY 40065 Office: Citizens Plaza Louisville KY 40202

DAVIS, BERTRAM HYLTON, educator, assn. exec.; b. Ozone Park, N.Y., Nov. 30, 1918; s. Hubert Edwin and Gladys (Greenidge) D.; grad. Phillips Acad., Andover, Mass., 1933-37; student Hamilton Coll., Clinton, N.Y., 1937-39; A.B., Columbia, 1941, M.A., 1948, Ph.D., 1956; m. Ruth Austin Benedict, Jan. 11, 1946; children—Ralph Paul, Kathryn Austin (Mrs. Person), Richard Austin. Lectr. English, Hunter Coll., 1947-48; instr., then asst. prof. English, Dickinson Coll., 1948-57; staff asso. Am. Assn. U. Profs., 1957-63, dep. gen. sec., 1963-67, gen. sec., 1967-74. Served to capt. AUS, 1941-46. Mem. Modern Lang. Assn., Johnsonians, Am. Soc. 18th-Century Studies. Author: Johnson Before Boswell, 1960; A Proof of Eminence, 1973. Editor: (Sir John Hawkins) Life of Samuel Johnson LL.D., 1961. Editor bull. Am. Assn. U. Profs., 1960-65. Home: 3009 Daniel Lane NW Washington DC 20015 Office: Suite 500 1 DuPont Circle Washington DC 20036

DAVIS, BEVERLY ANDREW, III, judge; b. Chgo., Mar. 25, 1925; s. Beverly Andrew, Jr., and Julia Elizabeth (Waters) D.; LL.B., J.D., Washington and Lee U., 1951; m. Elizabeth Ann Davis, Dec. 21, 1946; children—Sarah Elizabeth, Richard Andrew, Jane Reid. Admitted to Va. bar, 1951; asst. U.S. atty., 1953-55; gen. practice law, 1955-73; circuit ct. judge, Rocky Mount, Va., 1973—; spl. prosecutor Commonwealth of Va., 1967-68. Mem. Va. Adv. Hosp. Council. Trustee Franklin Meml. Hosp. Served with USAAF, 1943-46. Mem. Am., Va. bar assns., Va. Jaycees (v.p. 1954). Home: Ferrum Rd Rocky Mount VA 24151 Office: Court House Rocky Mount VA 24151

DAVIS, BILLY JOE, educator; b. Hobart, Okla., Oct. 27, 1932; s. Stafford Madison and Vera May (Bryan) D.; B.S., Southwestern State Coll. at Weatherford, Okla., 1954, M.T., 1957; Ph.D., Okla. State U., 1966; m. Oletta Faye Sharry, July 2, 1953; children—Joe Bill, Tommy Kent, Karen Marie, Sheila Kaye. Tchr. pub. schs., El Reno, Okla., 1954-63; faculty La. Tech. U., Ruston, 1966—, asso. prof. zoology, 1969-73, prof., 1974—. Cons. water pollution Continental Can Co., 1968—. Mem. Am. Soc. Ichtyologists and Herpetologists, Herpetologists League, Soc. for Study Amphibian and Reptiles, Assn. Southwestern Naturalists, Assn. Southeastern Biologists, Sigma Xi, Phi Kappa Phi, Beta Beta Beta. Home: Route 5 Box 141 Ruston LA 71270

DAVIS, BRIAN, paneling co. exec.; b. N.Y.C., May 20, 1934; s. Putnam and Louise Taylor (Schwab) D.; grad. Phillips Exeter Acad., 1952; B.A., Yale, 1956; m. Martha Mathers, Feb. 21, 1959 (div. Feb. 1974); children—Peter, Katherine, Emily. Salesman, Inmont Corp., Cin., 1957-63; div. sales mgr. Reliance Universal, Inc., Louisville, 1963-70, gen. sales mgr., 1970, gen. mgr., 1970-71; pres., dir. Tech-Panel Corp., Springfield, Ky., 1971—; treas., dir. Environment Plus, Inc., Louisville, 1974—; treas., dir. Wehmeyer Piano Co., Louisville, 1974—. Vice pres. Anchorage Childrens Theatre, 1967, 71, 73—, pres., 1968, 72; mem. Anchorage Trails, Inc., 1969-71; mem. Anchorage Bd. Edn., 1969—, chmn., 1973; pres. Mummers and Minstrels, 1973. Served with F.A., AUS, 1959. Clubs: Yale (N.Y.C.); Owl Creek Country (dir. 1970-72, sec. 1970, treas. 1972) (Anchorage). Home: Apt 513 3201 Leith Lane Louisville KY 40218 Office: PO Box 429 Springfield KY 40069

DAVIS, CLIFFORD YOUNG, JR., banker; b. Memphis, Sept. 21, 1932; s. Clifford Young and W.E. (Wells) D.; B.S., U. of South, 1954; postgrad. Sch. Bank Marketing, Northwestern U., 1964; m. E. June Hargis, Aug. 7, 1955; children—Melissa Dawn, Clifford Young III. Editor So. Motor Cargo mag., Memphis, 1957-59; pub. relations rep. Fla., Inc., Miami, 1959-61; mgmt. trainee 1st Nat. Bank Memphis, 1961-62, sr. v.p., dir. marketing, 1970—. Bd. dirs. Memphis and Shelby County Health and Welfare Planning Council, 1971—. Served with USAF, 1955-56. Mem. Bank Marketing Assn. (dir. 1970), Pub. Relations Soc. Am., Memphis Advt. Fedn., Alpha Delta Sigma. Club: Colonial Country. Home: 6218 Malloch Dr Memphis TN 38117 Office: 165 Madison Av Memphis TN 38103

DAVIS, COURTLAND HARWELL, JR., neurol. surgeon; b. Alexandria, Va., Feb. 14, 1921; s. Courtland Harwell and Mary Helen (Fox) D.; A.B., George Washington U., 1941, M.D., U.Va., 1944; m. Marilyn Bauer, Sept. 14, 1942; children—Courtland Harwell III, Randon, Richard, Jean Campbell, Cameron, Marilyn. Rotating intern U.S. Marine Hosp., New Orleans, 1944-45; asst. resident neurosurgery U. Va., 1945-46; postdoctoral research fellow neuropathology NIH, Duke Med. Center, 1948-49; asst. resident neurosurgery Duke Hosp., 1950-51, resident, 1951-52; practice medicine, specializing in neurosurgery, Winston-Salem, N.C., 1952—; instr. medicine Duke Hosp., 1949-50; instr. neurosurgery Bowman Gray Sch. Medicine, 1952-55, asst. prof., 1955-59, asso. prof., 1959-67, prof., 1967—; mem. staff N.C. Bapt. Hosp., 1952—, Kate Bitting Reynolds Meml. Hosp., 1953-58, City Meml. Hosp., 1953-58; cons. VA Hosp., Salisbury, N.C., 1954—, Regional Office VA, Winston-Salem, 1954; vis. prof. neurosurgery CARE-MEDICO, Malaysia, 1966; vis. prof. neurosurgery Christian Med. Coll., Vellore, India, 1966; vis. neurosurgeon HOPE, Cartagena, Colombia, S.Am., 1967, Kingston, Jamaica, 1971. Vice chmn. Gov.'s Commn. on Mental Retardation, 1962-64, N.C. Legislative Council on Mental Retardation, 1964-71. Pres. Bowman Gray Med. Found., Goodwill Industries, Assn. for Handicapped Childrens Center; bd. dirs. Forsyth County Rehab. House, Forsyth County Sheltered Workshop. Served to capt. M.C., AUS, 1946-48. Diplomate Am. Bd. Neurol. Surgery. Fellow A.C.S.; mem. A.M.A., So., Med. Assn., Med. Soc. N.C. (past del.), Forsyth County Med. Soc., Am. Assn. Mental Deficiency, Congress Neurol. Surgeons, So. Neurol. Soc., Am. Assn. Neurol. Surgeons, Neurol. Soc. Am. (pres.), Nat. Assn. for Retarded Children, Assn. for Research in Nervous and Mental Disease, Am. Acad. Neurol. Surgeons, So. Neurol. Surgeons, Soc. Brit. Neurol. Surgeons (hon.), Alpha Omega Alpha. Presbyn. (elder). Rotarian. Home: 921 Goodwood Rd Winston-Salem NC 27106 Office: 300 Hawthorne Rd Winston-Salem NC 27103

DAVIS, DAVID KEITHLEY, petroleum co. exec.; b. Sayre, Okla., July 19, 1926; s. Orville Keithley and Ruth (Johnson) Wilson; student Oklahoma City U., 1943-44, 46-47; student Cameron State Coll., 1955; m. Wanda Jean Martin, July 20, 1944; children—David Michael, Derek Hamilton, D'Et Suzanne. Bombsight technician Air Service Com., Oklahoma City, 1943; computer, party chief seismograph crew Century Geophys. Corp., Tulsa, 1947-50; party chief, supr. seismograph Midwestern Geophys. Lab., Tulsa, 1950-55; supr. Exploration Surveys Inc., Dallas, 1955-58; chief geophysicist Frankfort Oil Co., Dallas, 1958-62; exec. v.p. Longhorn Prodn. Co., Dallas, 1962-64; exec. v.p. Exploration Surveys Inc., Dallas, 1964-71; pres. Computer Systems Corp., Dallas, 1967-71; ind. geophys. cons., exec. v.p. Natural Gas Finders Inc., Dallas, 1971—; pres. Exploration Service Co., 1967-71; owner D.K. Davis: Geosci., Dallas, 1972—; partner Landmark Geosci. Assos., Dallas, 1972—, dir. Norandco Mining Co., Calgary, Alta., Can.; dir. Mustang Computing Co., Dallas. Served with USAAF, 1944-45. Mem. Soc. Exploration Geophysicists, Dallas Geol. Soc., Dallas Geophys. Soc., Houston Geophys. Soc., Petroleum Engrs. Club, Internat. Oceanographic Found., Mensa. Republican. Baptist. Mason (32 degree, Shriner). Toastmaster, Kiwanian. Home: 10850 Ridge Spring Dr Dallas TX 75218 Office: 532 Meadows Bldg Dallas TX 75206

DAVIS, D'EARCY PAUL, JR., architect; b. Zuni, Va., Sept. 12, 1917; s. D'Earcy Paul and Laura Mae (Joyner) D.; B.S. Archtl. Engring., Va. Poly. Inst.; postgrad. naval architecture U. Va., 1941-42; m. Frances Marye Brooks, Apr. 11, 1942; children—D'Earcy Paul III, Wayne Howard. Mem. prodn. staff Newport News Shipbuilding & Drydock Co. (Va.), 1940-46; draftsman Clarence Wenger architect, Harrisonburg, Va., 1947; chief engr., treas. Nielsen Constrn. Co., Harrisonburg, 1947-54; pvt. practice architecture and civil engring., Harrisonburg, 1955—. Dir. Va. Nat. Bank, Harrisonburg; pres. Rockingham Devel. Co., Harrisonburg, 1959—, Fran-El Corp., Harrisonburg, 1964—. Chmn., Harrisonburg Electric Commn., 1956-61, Planning Commn., 1954-62. Bd. dirs. Friendship Industries. Named Outstanding Man Rockingham County and City Harrisonburg C. of C., 1964. Mem. A.I.A., Nat. Soc. Profl. Engrs. Presbyn. (elder). Elk, Rotarian. Home: 539 S Dogwood Av Harrisonburg VA 22801 Office: 110 Newman Av Harrisonburg VA 22801

DAVIS, DON ERWIN, coll. pres.; b. Aulne, Kan. Nov. 7, 1906; s. Charles William and Ida Belle (Pratt) D.; A.B., Southwestern Coll., 1930; B.S., Kan. State Tchrs. Coll., 1935, M.S., 1943; Ed.D., Wayne State U., 1951; m. Eva Marcille Bard, Aug. 14, 1939; 1 dau., Jacqueline Jo. Tchr. pub. schs., Protection, Kan., 1935-39; prin. pub. sch., Clements, Kan., 1939-43, Emporia, Kan., 1946-47; supt. lab. schs., dir. supervised teaching Kan. State Tchrs. Coll., 1947-49, chmn. div. tchr. edn., 1951-58; instr. Wayne State U., 1949-51, asst. prof., 1958-59, asso. prof., 1959-61, prof., chmn. dept. elementary edn., 1961-62; pres. Coll. Ozarks, 1962—. Dir. Western Ark. Devel. Assn.; mem., v.p. W. Central Ark. Econ. Devel. Dist.; mem. adv. council South Central Region Ednl. Lab; mem. Gov's Adv. Council; del. to State Constl. Conv., 1969, Ark. Health Planning Commn. Served with USNR, 1943-45. Mem. Nat., Ark. edn. assns., Internat. Platform Assn., Newcomen Soc., Johnson County C. of C. (past pres.), Kappa Delta Pi, Phi Epsilon. Democrat. Presbyn. Mason, Rotarian (dist. gov. 1973-74). Contr. profl. articles publs. Home: 603 Buchanan St Clarksville AR 72830

DAVIS, DONALD DEAN, civil engr.; b. Decatur, Ill., May 28, 1928; s. Chauncey Depew and Gertie (Owen) D.; Asso. Sci. in Indsl. Elec. Engring., Arlington State Coll., 1949, student 1951-52; B.S. in Civil Engring., Tex. A. and M. U., 1954. Jr. elec. engr. Tex. Electric Service Co., Ft. Worth, 1949-51; sr. engring. asst. Tex. Hwy. Dept., 1954-57; civil engr. S.W. region FAA, Ft. Worth, 1957-61, chief radar plant unit, 1961-62, chief plant engring. sect. for design and constrn. air navigational and facilities So. region, Atlanta, 1962-65, chief terminal sect., 1965-66, chief plant engring. br., 1966-69, asst. chief airway facilities div. So. region, Atlanta, 1969—. Lt. col. C.E., U.S. Army Res. Registered profl. civil engr., Tex., Ga., Miss., Ala., Tenn. Mem. Am. Soc. C.E., Am. Mgmt. Assn., Soc. Am. Mil. Engrs., Res. Officers Assn., Am. Concrete Inst., Ga. Engring. Soc., Assn. U.S. Army. Home: 2567 Headland Dr East Point GA 30344 Office: FAA PO Box 20636 Atlanta GA 30302

DAVIS, DONALD ECHARD, educator; b. Charleston, Ill., Jan. 12, 1916; s. Leonard Ernest and Jessie Alice (Echard) D.; B.Ed., Eastern Ill. State U., 1938; M.S., Ohio State U., 1940, Ph.D., 1947; Ped.D. (hon.), Eastern Ill. U., 1956; m. Dorothy Dale Richey, June 5, 1940; children—Leonard Richey, Dorothy Ann (Mrs. Miles McKenzie Majure). Research fellow U. Tenn.-AEC, 1951; asso. prof. plant physiology and ecology Auburn (Ala.) U., 1952-55, prof., 1955-68, alumni prof., 1968—. Mem. adv. panel weed research U.S. Dept. Agr.; mem. com. persistent pesticides residues Nat. Acad. Sci.-NRC; mem. adv. panel Environmental Protection Agy. Served with AUS, 1942-45. USPHS, U.S. Dept. Agr., Water Resources Research Inst. research grantee. Mem. So. Weed Sci. Soc. (past pres.), Am. Soc. Plant Physiologists, Weed Sci. Soc. Am., Ala. Acad. Sci., Am. Inst. Biol. Sci., A.A.A.S., Sigma Xi, Phi Kappa Phi, Kappa Delta Pi, Gamma Sigma Delta, Phi Epsilon Phi, Gamma Alpha. Lion (past pres. Auburn). Author: Alabama Trees, 1963; Guide and Key to Alabama Trees, 1965, 72. Contbr. articles to sci. jours. Home: 512 Auburn Dr Auburn AL 36830

DAVIS, DONALD GOODWIN, JR., chemist, educator; b. Stoneham, Mass., Aug. 23, 1932; s. Donald Goodwin and Elizabeth (Fowler) D.; B.A., Wesleyan U., 1954; Ph.D. (Shell fellow), Harvard, 1957; m. Janet Mary Alford, June 26, 1954; children—Donna Lee (Mrs. Benjamin Beeson), Barbara Elizabeth, Scott Jeffries. Asst. prof. Ga. Inst. Tech., 1957-59; asso. prof. La. State U., New Orleans, 1959-63, chmn. dept. chemistry, 1960-64, prof., 1963—, dean Grad. Sch., 1965-69. Sci. adviser FDA, 1965-72; v.p. New Orleans Sci. Fair, 1966-73. NSF, NIH, New Orleans Cancer Soc., Reserach Corp. research grantee. Mem. Am. Chem. Soc., N.Y. Acad. Scis., A.A.A.S., Phi Beta Kappa, Sigma Xi. Democrat. Episcopalian. Contbr. articles to profl. jours., chpts. in books. Home: 6802 Willow Lane New Orleans LA 70127

DAVIS, DONNELL PRESTON, lawyer; b. Shop Springs, Tenn., Sept. 27, 1924; s. Elmer H. and Julia G. (Donnell) D.; A.B., U. S.C., 1945; LL.B., George Washington U., 1949; m. Helen Warrene Welch, Aug. 20, 1949; children—Julia Lynn, Randall Preston. Dist. claims mgr. Govt. Employees Ins. Co., Washington, 1948-52; v.p. claims Carolina Casualty Ins. Co., Jacksonville, Fla., 1952-64; admitted to Va. bar, 1951; practiced in Norvolk, Va., 1964—. Vice moderator Norfolk Baptist Assn. Bd. dirs. Martus, Inc. Virginia Beach, Va., 1971—. Mem. Virginia Beach Electoral Bd., 1969—. Served with USNR, 1943-46. Republican. Baptist (chmn. bd. deacons). Lion (pres. Virginia Beach 1970-71). Home: 3216 Queensbury Dr Norfolk VA 23452 Office: Plaza One Bldg Norfolk VA 23510

DAVIS, DREXEL CARTER, dentist; b. Kilsyth, Tenn., Feb. 7, 1914; s. John Calvin and Ida Bell (Drake) D.; B.S., U. Tenn., 1939, D.D.S., 1949; m. Bertha Irene McNew, June 1, 1938; children—Drexel Carter II, Stanley Paul; m. 2d, Nora Jane Townsend Hawk, Feb. 5, 1972; 1 stepdau., Kathryn Elaine Hawk. Tchr., prin. Westbourne (Tenn.) Elementary Sch., 1936-38; prin. Midway Sch., Knox County (Tenn.), 1938-39; tchr. sci. Halls High Sch., Knox County (Tenn.), 1940-43; tchr. adult edn., supr. practice tchrs. U. Tenn., 1945-46; indsl. engr. Fulton Sylphon Co., Knoxville, 1942-46; pvt. practice dentistry, Knoxville, 1950—. Active Boy Scouts Am.; mem. Knox County Clean Air League. Bd. dirs. Knox County Cancer Soc. Recipient Distinguished Service award Kiwanis Club, 1970; named Outstanding Kiwanian, 1971. Mem. Acad. Hypnosis, Am. Dental Assn., 2d Dist. Dental Soc., Knox County Hist. Soc., Appalachian Zool. Soc., Delta Sigma Delta. Republican. Mason (32 degree), Kiwanian. Home: Route 18 Oak Ridge Hwy Knoxville TN 37921 Office: 5317 Clinton Hwy Knoxville TN 37912

DAVIS, EARL VALENTINE, banker; b. Russellville, Ky., Feb. 13, 1916; s. Young and Tina (Valentine) D.; grad. high sch.; m. Mary Williston Riley, Dec. 24, 1937; children—Richard E., Raymond R. With Citizens Nat. Bank, Russellville, 1936—, pres., 1969—, chmn. bd., 1972—, also dir. Pres., Russellville-Logan County Civic Devel. Corp., 1955—; mem. Barren River Area Devel. Health Planning Council, 1966-71. Served from 2d lt. to lt. col. AUS, 1941-46. Decorated Bronze Star medal. Mem. Russellville-Logan County C. of C. (pres. 1950-55, dir.). Kiwanian. Home: Route 6 Russellville KY 42276 Office: 138 N Main St Russellville KY 42276

DAVIS, ERNST MICHAEL, educator; b. Victoria, Tex., Oct. 12, 1933; s. Robert and Helen (Lamprecht) D.; B.A., N. Tex. State U., 1956, M.A., 1962; Ph.D., U. Okla., 1966; m. Claudia Dixon, July 21, 1973. Research asso. U. Tex. at Austin, 1966-68, asst. prof., 1968-70; asst. prof. U. Tex. at Houston, 1970-73, asso. prof. san engring., 1973—; cons. water pollution abatement, waste treatment, ecological effects of discharges. Served with Chem. Corps, AUS, 1956-58. USPHS scholar, 1964-66. Registered profl. engr., Tex. Mem. A.A.A.S., Water Pollution Control Fedn., Am. Water Works Assn., Internat. Assn. Water Pollution Research, Assn. Environmental Engring. Profs., Tex. Soc. Profl. Engrs., Tex. Water Pollution Assn., Sigma Xi, Beta Beta Beta, Kappa Sigma. Contbr. articles profl. jours. Home: 6900 Bissonnet St Houston TX 77036 Office: U Tex Sch Pub Health PO Box 20186 Houston TX 77025

DAVIS, FRANCES IRENE, ct. reporter; b. Lathrop, Ala., Mar. 2, 1924; d. John Everette and Samantha Texanna (O'Bryant) Davis; student pub. schs. Timekeeper, DeBardeleben Coal Corp., Holt, Ala., 1943-46; town clk., Reform, Ala., 1946-47; chief probate clk. to probate judge of Pickens County, Carrollton, 1953-59; bookkeeper D. T. Hannah Lumber Co., Gordo, 1959-61; sec. Ala. Farm Bur. Ins. Co., Carrollton, 1962; ct. reporter 24th Jud. Circuit Ala., Carrollton, 1963—. Sec. Civic Improvement Council, Reform, 1963-66. Sec. Pickens County Democratic Exec. Com., 1963—. Mem. Bus. and Profl. Women's Club, Ala. Shorthand Reporters Assn., Wesleyan Service Guild (pres. 1958-59, v.p. 1965-66). Methodist. Mem. Order Eastern Star (sec. 1965-66, worthy matron 1955-56, 63-64). Club. Reform Homemakers (sec. 1963-66). Home: PO Box 566 Reform AL 35481 Office: PO Box 299 Carrollton AL 35447

DAVIS, FRANK WILBUR, aero. engr.; b. Charleston, W.Va., Dec. 6, 1914; s. Madison T., Jr., and Julia (Staunton) D.; B.S. in Mech. Engring., Cal. Inst. Tech., 1936; D.Sc., W.Va. U. 1960; m. Frances Washington, Mar. 15, 1941; children—Caroline (Mrs. O. D. Calvert, Jr.), Frank Wilbur, William Brewster. With Convair div. Gen. Dynamics Corp., 1940—, successively engring. test pilot, chief aerodynamics and flight test, chief design engr., asst. chief engr., asst. to v.p. engring., chief engr., 1940-54, pres., mgr., chief engr. Ft. Worth div., 1954-70, corporate sr. v.p., 1959—, also pres. Convair Aerospace div., 1970-74; dir. Canadair, Ltd. Bd. dirs. Ft. Worth YMCA, Internat. Sci. Fair. Served with USMC, 1937-40. Recipient Silver Anniversary All Am. award Sports Illustrated mag. Registered profl. engr., Cal., Tex. Fellow Am. Inst. Aero. and Astronautics, Soc. Exptl. Test Pilots (hon.); mem. Tex. (Engr. of Year award Ft. Worth sect. 1957), Nat. socs. profl. engrs., Soc. Automotive Engrs., Nat. Alliance Businessmen (met. chmn. 1968-71), Nat. Acad. Engring., S.W. Center Advanced Studies, Air Force Assn., Navy League U.S., Assn. U.S. Army, Nat. Aeros. Assn., Airpower Council. Patentee spring tab for aircraft control, ejection seat for escape from aircraft. Pioneer design of intercontinental ballistic missile. Home: 6328 Curzon St Fort Worth TX 76116 Office: Fort Worth Div Gen Dynamics Box 748 Fort Worth TX 76101

DAVIS, GARNETT STANT, accountat; b. Mt. Vernon, Tex., Oct. 24, 1916; s. James Stant and Ivey (Hightower) D.; student E. Tex. State Tchrs. Coll., 1938-39; B.B.A., Tex. Tech. Coll., 1942; M.S., Tex. A. and M. U., 1943; LL.B., So. Meth. U., 1947; m. Emogene Campbell, Oct. 3, 1943; children—Patricia Jean (Mrs. Peter E. Medine), Cynthia Ann, Mary Helen. Grad. asst. Tex. A. and M. Coll., 1942-43; instr. Tex. Tech. Coll., 1943-44; mem. staff Haskins & Sells, Dallas, 1944-46; asst. prof. Tex. Christian U., 1946-48; asso. prof. Tex. Coll. Arts and Industries, 1948-51; partner Hart, Veale, Davis & Co., 1951-53, Veale, Davis & Kendall, 1953-55; pvt. accounting practice, 1955-65; partner Davis & Olson, Kingsville, Tex., 1965—. Named Kingsville Lion of the year, 1966. C.P.A., Tex. Baptist (deacon). Club: Lions (Kingsville). Home: 720 Santa Clara St Kingsville TX 78363 Office: 701 E King Kingsville TX 78363

DAVIS, GERALD LYNN, physician; b. Chgo., Oct. 22, 1934; s. Langdon Giles and Madelon (Raven) D.; student U. Mich., 1955, M.D., 1959; m. Diane Helene Slates, June 15, 1957; children—Jeffrey, Peter, Efren, Minerva, Jennifer, Kathryn, Christopher. Intern U.S. Naval Hosp., Boston, 1960; resident U.S. Naval Hosp., Portsmouth, Va., 1961-65, staff orthopedist, 1967-69; commd. ensign U.S. Navy 1957, advanced through grades to comdr., 1968; staff orthopedist in U.S.S. Repose, 1966; chief profl. services U.S. Naval Hosp., Subic Bay, Philippines, 1969-71; practice medicine, specializing in orthopedic surgery and scoliosis surgery, New Orleans, 1971—; mem. staff Ochsner Clin., New Orleans, Crippled Childrens Hosp., New Orleans; clin. instr. Sch. Medicine, Tulane U., New Orleans, 1971—. Decorated Vietnam Medal Gallantry. Diplomate Am. Bd. Orthopedic Surgery. Fellow A.C.S., Am. Acad. Orthopedic Surgery; mem. Scoliosis Research Soc., Philippine Orthopedic Assn. Contbr. articles to profl. jours. Home: 28 Swallow St New Orleans LA 70124 Office: Ochsner CLinic 1514 Jefferson Hwy New Orleans LA 70124

DAVIS, GORDON WILLIAM, educator; b. Galva, Ill., Oct. 7, 1910; s. William George and Beatrice (Gordon) D.; A.B., Knox Coll., 1934; M.S., Washington U., 1938. Asst. plant physiology Washington U., 1935-39; head sci. dept. Leadwood (Mo.) High Sch., 1937-39; tch. sales dir. Printograph Co., Kansas City, Mo., 1939-41; instr. sci., English, math. Morgan Park Mil. Acad., Chgo., 1941; head sci. dept. Elkader (Ia.) Jr. Coll., 1941-42; asst. prof., sci. supr. Winthrop Coll., Rock Hill, S.C., 1957-58; prof. biology and chem., chmn. sci. dept., Frederick Coll., Portsmouth, Va., 1958-59; asst. prof. chem. and math. Ferris State Coll., Big Rapids, Mich., 1959-63; asso. prof. phys. scis. Miami-Dade Jr. Coll., Miami, 1963—. Commd. capt. AUS, 1942, advanced through grades to lt. col., Res., 1953; chem. br. advisory S.C. Mil. Dist., also chem. U.S. Army Res. adviser for chem. units, Charleston, S.C., 1953•57. Mem. Mo. Acad. Sci., Res. Officers Assn., Armed Forces Chem. Soc., Nat. Honor Soc., Nat. Sci. Tchrs. Assn. (life), Am. Assn. U. Profs. (pres., founder Miami-Dade Jr. Coll. chpt. 1966—), Am. Chem. Soc., Dade County Classroom Tchrs. Assn., Am. Assn. Physics Tchrs., Am. Ordnance Assn. (life), N.E.A., Fla. Edn. Assn., Assn. for Higher Edn., Internat. Platform Assn., Fla. Acad.

Sci., Sigma Xi, Phi Sigma. Club: Chemist. Home: 10545 NW 28th Av Miami FL 33147

DAVIS, HAL D., banker; b. Toccoa, Ga., Oct. 7, 1905; s. Jefferson and Myrtle (Yow) D.; student U. Miami, 1945-47; m. Margaret Brown Wilson, Oct. 3, 1934; children—Jefferson II (dec.), Margaret Moseley, Myra Anne. With 1st Fed. Savs. & Loan Assn. Miami, 1938—, v.p., sec., 1950-69, sr. v.p., sec., 1969—, sr. v.p., sec.-treas., 1971, dir., sr. v.p., sec.-treas., 1972—. Bd. dirs. Grand Jury Assn., Inc., 1968—. Mem. S.A.R., Hist. Assn. So. Fla., Fla. Hist. Assn. Presbyn. (elder). Club: Riviera Country of Coral Gables. Kiwanian. Home: 1420 Sopera Av Coral Gables FL 33134 Office: 100 NE 1st Av Miami FL 33132

DAVIS, HARRY GORDON, pub. co. exec.; b. Houston, June 26, 1912; s. Harold Richard and Elsie Claire (Barrett) D.; student Houston Jr. Coll. and Houston Law Sch., 1937-38; m. Bernice Shannon Davis, Sept. 2, 1950. With circulation dept. Houston Post, 1930-34, police reporter, 1934-37; criminal investigator Harris County, 1937-39; dist. circulation mgr. Houston Post, 1939-42, 46-47; sec.-mgr. Gulf Coast Express, Inc., Houston, 1947-51; v.p., gen. mgr. Bluebonnet Express, Houston, 1950-52; part owner G.A. White Express, Houston and Dallas, 1953-57; with Houston Post, 1958—, purchasing mgr., 1962-71, dir. distbn., 1971—. Pres., Houston Post Employees Credit Union, 1973. Served with AUS, 1942-46. Mem. Newspaper Purchasing Mgrs. Assn., Ret. Officers Assn., Tex. Circulation Mgrs. Assn., Am. Legion, Am. Auto Assn., Internat. Circulation Mgrs. Assn. Democrat. Methodist. Mason (32 deg.); mem. Eastern Star. Club: Indian Shores Golf. Home: 2040 Westcreek Lane Apt 29C Houston TX 77027 Office: 4747 Southwest Freeway Houston TX 77001

DAVIS, HARTWELL, lawyer; b. Auburn, Ala., Dec. 18, 1906; s. Christopher Hartwell and Elizabeth Myrick (Dowdell) D.; student U. Fla., 1923-24; B.S., Auburn U., 1928; Woodrow Wilson Meml. scholar U. Va. Law Sch., 1929-30; LL.B., Emory U., 1931; LL.D., 1970; m. Elizabeth Mardre, Feb. 24, 1933; children—Hartwell, Letitia Dowdell (Mrs. R. Wilkins Hamill, III). Clk. Bradenton Bank & Trust Co. (Fla.), 1924-25; admitted to Ga., Ala. and Fla. bars, 1931, and since practiced at Opelika and Montgomery, Ala.; asst. U.S. atty. Middle Dist. Ala., 1932-51, U.S. atty., 1953-62; atty. City of Montgomery, 1951-53; spl. asst. atty. gen. Ala., 1964-71. Del. S. E. jurisdictional confs. Meth. Ch., 1948, 52, 56; mem. Meth. Gen. Bd. Evangelism, 1952-56; sec.-treas. Meth. Ala. Conf. Bd. Lay Activities, 1945-60. Pres. Montgomery YMCA, 1938-40, bd. dirs., 1935-57; chmn. Ct. Honor, Tuckabatchie area Boy Scouts Am., 1951-52, chmn. merit badge com., 1953; bd. dirs. Ala. Meth. Children's Home, 1953—, 1st v.p., 1973—; trustee George Wheeler Meml. Scholarship Fund, 1941-71. Mem. Fed., Am., Ala., Montgomery bar assns., C. of C., Am. Judicature Soc., Am., Ala. trial lawyers assns., Sigma Nu, Phi Alpha Delta, Theta Alpha Phi. Republican. Kiwanian (pres. 1938). Clubs: Montgomery Gun, Montgomery Fresh Air Domino. Home: 2216 Allendale Pl Montgomery AL 36111 Office: 1st Nat Bank Bldg Montgomery AL 36104

DAVIS, MRS. HARTWELL (ELIZABETH MARDRE), educator, civic worker; b. Lumpkin, Ga.; d. Wilson Little and Sarah (Bivins) Mardre; student U. Cal. at Berkeley, 1927; B.S., Auburn U., 1929; m. Hartwell Davis, Feb. 24, 1933; children—Hartwell, Letitia Dowdell. Tchr. English, Clift High Sch., Opelika, Ala., 1929-33, Lanier High Sch., Montgomery, Ala., 1934-36, 39, Robert E. Lee High Sch., Montgomery, 1962-68, Jefferson Davis High Sch., Montgomery, 1968-69. Mem. Ala. Citizens Adv. Ednl. Council, Ala. Com. for Better Schs., Inc.; pres. Montgomery Know-Your-Schs. Com., 1951-52. Trustee Carnegie Library Assn. Mem. Montgomery County Republican Exec. Com., 1956-66, 70-72; vice chmn. Rep. State Exec. Com., 1961-62; mem. Congl. Dist. and State Republican exec. coms., 1960-66; pres. Montgomery County Rep. Women, 1970-72. Mem. United Church Women (pres. Montgomery 1951-53, pres. Ala. 1955-57, mem. adminstrv. and exec. coms. gen. dept. 1957-58), D.A.R., League Women Voters (exec. bd. Montgomery 1952-54), Auburn U. Alumni Assn. (v.p. 1946-48), Kappa Delta, Phi Kappa Phi, Kappa Delta Pi. Methodist. (exec. com., sec. promotion Ala.-W. Fla. Woman's soc. 1952-58, mem. Ala.-W. Fla. Conf. Bd. Missions 1960-62). Clubs: 20th Century Literary (pres. 1944-45, 72-73), Hypatia Literary (pres. 1944-45). Panjandrum Literary (pres. 1948-49). Home: 2216 Allendale Pl Montgomery AL 36111

DAVIS, HENRY GORDON, JR., physician; b. Sylvester, Ga., Feb. 21, 1919; s. Henry Gordon and Lillie (Wingate) D.; B.S., U. Ga., 1941; student Young Harris Coll., 1939, U. Okla., 1943, Med. Coll. Ga., 1941-45; M.D., Cook County Grad. Sch. Medicine, 1955; m. Francis Marion Salisbury, Dec. 7, 1941; children—Henry Gordon III, Francis Marion, Margaret Davis, Barbara Jeanne. Intern, resident Coker Hosp., Cantonga, 1945-46, U.S. Army Hosp., 1946-48; pvt. practice medicine, Sylvester, 1948—; staff Worth County Hosp., chief staff, 1955; chmn. bd. Worth Loans, Inc.; dir. Sylvester-Worth County Tobacco Co., Sylvester Banking Co., Security Bank & Trust Co., Albany, Ga. Pres. Ga. Care, Inc., S.W. Ga. Nursing Home Council; bd. dirs. Ga. Nursing Home Assn. Served from 1st lt. to capt. AUS, 1946-48. Diplomate Am. Bd. Abdominal Surgeons. Fellow Am. Geriatrics Soc.; mem. Am., So., Ga. med. assns., Am., Ga. (dir.) acads. family practice, Worth County (pres. 1953, 57, 61), 2d Dist. (pres. 1964-65) med. socs., Am. Heart Assn. Democrat. Baptist. Kiwanian (pres. 1963). Home: 305 King St Sylvester GA 31791 Office: 108 Liberty Av Sylvester GA 31791

DAVIS, HILLIS DWIGHT, librarian; b. Selma, Ala., Jan. 24, 1932; s. Jordan and Mary Emma (Wright) D.; B.S., Johnson C. Smith U., 1954; M.S., Atlanta U., 1958; m. Marian Louise Anderson, Dec. 23, 1958; children—Hillis D., Marian P. Asst. librarian, head cataloger W.Va. State Coll., Institute, 1957-65; dir. libraries Hampton (Va.) Inst., 1965-69; dir. Coop. Coll. Library Center, Atlanta, 1969—. Cons. So. Assn. Colls. and Schs., 1970-71. Served with AUS, 1955-57. Mem. Am., Ga. library assns., Omega Psi Phi. Home: 3855 Village Dr SW Atlanta GA 30331 Office: 159 Forest Av NE Atlanta GA 30303

DAVIS, HORANCE GIBBS, JR., educator, journalist; b. Manchester, Ga., 1924; B.A. with high honors, U. Fla., also M.A. in Journalism; m. Marjorie Lucile Davis, 1948; children—Gregory, Jennifer. Formerly columnist Bradford County (Fla.) Telegraph, state capitol corr. Jacksonville (Fla.) Times-Union, Tallahassee; mem. faculty Coll. Journalism, U. Fla., 1954—, now prof.; editorial writer Gainesville (Fla.) Sun. Recipient Sigma Delta Chi Distinguished Service award, 1963, Sidney Hillman award, 1963, Pulitzer prize editorial writing, 1971; named Distinguished Alumnus, U. Fla., 1972. Mem. Sigma Delta Chi (nat. v.p. acad. affairs 1969-72), Omicron Delta Kappa. Address: Sch Journalism U Florida Gainesville FL 32605 also Gainesville Sun Box 14425 Gainesville FL 32601

DAVIS, HOWARD HALL, newspaper editor; b. Crandall, Fla., Sept. 4, 1915; s. Howard Hall and Beulah (Mizell) D.; student U. Ga., 1935-36; m. Kathleen Knight, June 30, 1946; 1 son, Howard Hall. Owner, editor Fernandina (Fla.) Beach News, 1937-42; owner Davis Motors, 1947-54; mgr., editor Southeast Georgian, Kingsland, 1954—. Pres., dir. Citizens State Bank, Kingsland; profl. photographer, 1950—. Past exec. sec. Camden Community Chest. Mem. Kingsland City Council; mem., chmn., clk. Camden County SSS Bd., 1948—; mem. Camden Hist. Commn. Served with AUS, 1942-45. Mem. Kingsland C. of C. (pres. 1967-68). Methodist (steward 1938—, chmn. ofcl. bd. 1961-62, treas.). Mason, Lion (past sec.-treas., pres. 1962-63). Home: 112 E William St Kingsland GA 31548 Office: 112 S Lee St Kingsland GA 31548

DAVIS, HUGH EDWARD, hosp. adminstr.; b. Pulaski, Tenn., Mar. 30, 1925; s. Ray and Rosa (Cole) D.; LL.B., Andrew Jackson U., 1949; m. Bettye Van Landingham, Oct. 4, 1953; children—Stephen, Linda. Fiscal officer various VA hosps., 1950-61; asst. hosp. dir. trainee VA Hosp., Biloxi, Miss., 1961-63; asst. hosp. dir. VA hosps., Fayetteville, Ark., 1963-65, Johnson City, Tenn., 1965-67; asso. dir. hosp. constrn. services VA, Washington, 1967-68, dir. hosp., Hot Springs, S.D., 1968-72, Salem, Va., 1972—. Mem. Gov.'s Com. on Employment Handicapped, 1968-72. Served with AUS, World War II. Fellow Am. Coll. Hosp. Adminstrs.; mem. Hot Springs C. of C. Kiwanian. Clubs: Country (Roanoke, Va.). Home: Quarters 18 VA Hosp Salem VA 24153 Office: VA Hosp Salem VA 24153

DAVIS, HUMPHREY DENNY, journalist; b. Fayette, Mo., May 8, 1927; s. Lionel Winchester and Sarah Elizabeth (Denn) D.; B.J., U. Mo., 1949; m. Barbara Ellen Hartsgrove, June 6, 1954; 1 son, Thomas Shackelford. With Fayette Democrat-Leader, 1944-47, Cape Girardeau Southeast Missourian, 1949-54; with U.P.I., 1954—, assigned Oklahoma City, 1954-55, Tulsa, 1955, Denver, 1955, Albuquerque, 1955-56, Lima, Peru, 1956-58, Rio de Janeiro, Brazil, 1958-68, mgr. for Mexico and Central Am., 1968—. Cape Girardeau (Mo.) community ambassador to Yugoslavia, Expt. in Internat. Living, 1953. Served with USNR, 1946-47, 50-51, Clubs: Club de Golf la Hacienda (Mexico City); Overseas Press (N.Y.C.). Home: Calle San Diego de los Padres 56 Mexico City Mexico Office: Av Morelos 110 Suite 1107 Mexico City 1 Mexico

DAVIS, JACQUELINE MARIE VINCENT (MRS. LOUIS REID DAVIS), educator; b. Birmingham, Ala.; d. Jud Fred and Marie (Yates) Vincent; A.B. cum laude, Birmingham-So. Coll., 1943; M.A., Columbia, 1950; M.S., U. Ala., 1958, Ed.D., 1961; postgrad. U. Va., George Washington U.; m. Louie Reid Davis, July 17, 1943. Tchr., Fork Union (Va.) Mil. Acad., 1943-46, Ft. Belvoir, Va., 1946-48; tchr., adminstrv. asst., supr. Quantico (Va.) Post schs., 1950-52; instr., prof. dept. child devel. and family life U. Ala. Sch. Home Econs., 1952-57, asso. prof., 1957-67, prof. child devel., dir. Child Devel. Center, 1967—, mem. grad. council, adminstr. head start tng. program. Dir. Ala. Presch. Inst., 1964—; mem. NASA scholarship selection bd. U. Ala., 1966; mem. Gov.'s Adv. Com. on Day Care, 1963-66; mem. State Adv. Com. on Children and Youth, 1960—; coordinator Head Start supplementary tng. programs State of Ala. Adviser, mem. selection com. Tombigbee council Girl Scouts U.S.A., 1961-66; cons. Tuscaloosa Community Action Program, 1965-66. Mem. Nat. Assn. for Edn. of Young Children (mem. planning bd. 1963-64), U.S. Nat. Com. for Early Childhood Edn., World Orgn. for Early Childhood Edn., Southeastern Council Family Relations, So. (pres. 1961, mem. exec. bd. 1961—, chmn. 19th ann. conf.), Ala. (pres. 1963-64) assns. children under six, Ala. Home Econs. Assn. (chmn. profl. sect. family life and child devel. 1963—, v.p., mem. governing bd. 1969-70), Comparative Edn. Soc., N.E.A., Am. Home Econs. Assn., Phi Beta Kappa, Kappa Delta Pi, Kappa Delta Epsilon. Methodist. Contbr. articles to profl. jours. Home: 47 Guilds Wood Tuscaloosa AL 35401 Office: PO Box 1211 University AL 35486

DAVIS, JAMES BUFORD, JR., educator; b. Stratford, Okla., Apr. 5, 1933; s. James Buford and Annie G. (Cole) D.; B.B.S., Okla. State U., 1956, M.S., 1958, Ed.D. (NSF fellow, Haskins and Sells scholar), 1966; m. Donna Jean Sims, Sept. 9, 1967; children—Gaye Lynn, Louise, LaMoyne, Terry, Dustin. Prof. Central State U., Edmond, Okla., 1958-67; prof., head dept. accounting West Tex. State U., Canyon, 1967—. Ednl. cons. State of Okla.; indsl. cons. Lear Siegler Co.; cons. Amarillo Bd. City Devel. Active Boy Scouts Am. Bd. dirs. Ednl. Endowments, Inc., Mich. Sch. Bus. C.P.A., Tex., Okla. Mem. Canyon C. of C., Beta Alpha Psi, Alpha Kappa Psi, Delta Pi Epsilon. Methodist. Kiwanian. Club: Canyon Country. Conducted feasibility study of mobile home industry, 1972. Home: 1000 4th Av Canyon TX 79015

DAVIS, JAMES EVANS, surgeon; b. Goldsboro, N.C., Mar. 2, 1918; s. Daniel Wilborn and Maude (Evans) D.; A.B., U. N.C., 1940; M.D., U. Pa., 1943; m. Margaret Royall, June 14, 1943; children—James Evans, Kenneth Royall, George Harrison. Intern and resident surgery New York Hosp.-Cornell U. Med. Center, N.Y.C., 1944-45, 46-51; practice of surgery in Durham, N.C., 1951-53, 54—; chief surg. service Watts Hosp.; attending staff Lincoln Hosp., Durham, Dorothea Dix Hosp., Raleigh, N.C.; asso. prof. surgery U. N.C. Med. Sch., Duke U. Med. Sch. Served as lt. comdr. USNR, 1945-46, 53-54. Diplomat Am. Bd. Surgery. Fellow A.C.S. (past pres. N.C. chpt.); mem. So. Surg. Assn., So. Soc. Clin. Surgeons, Southeastern Surg. Congress, A.M.A., So. Med. Assn., N.C. Med. Soc. (speaker ho. dels.), N.C. Surg. Assn., Alpha Tau Omega, Phi Chi. Episcopalian. Kiwanian. Home: 7 Beverly Dr Durham NC 27707 Office: 1200 Broad St Durham NC 27705

DAVIS, JAMES FRANKLIN, atty.; b. Ft. Wayne, Ind., Aug. 11, 1934; s. John Forrest and Lucrece (Shoemaker) D.; B.S. in Chem. Engring. with honors, U. Ill., 1957; J.D., Georgetown U., 1963; m. Mary Karen Biddle, Dec. 29, 1957; children—John Montgomery, Mary Melinda, Jennifer Susan. Admitted to Ill. and D.C. bars, 1964; examiner U.S. Patent Office, 1961-62; patent atty. firm Wenderoth, Lind & Ponack, Washington, 1962-63; law clk. to Judge Rich, U.S. Ct. Customs and Patent Appeals, 1963-64; patent atty. firm Bair, Freeman & Molinare, Chgo., 1964-66; trial judge U.S. Ct. of Claims, 1966-72; mem. firm Howrey, Simon, Baker & Murchison, Washington, 1972—; instr. chemistry U.S. Naval Acad., 1959-61; adj. prof. law Georgetown U. Law Sch., 1966-68. Served with USNR, 1957-59; lt. comdr. Res. Mem. Am. Bar Assn., Am. Patent Law Assn., Phi Lambda Upsilon, Theta Chi. Home: 8000 Hampden Lane Bethesda MD 20014 Office: 1730 Pennsylvania Av Washington DC 20006

DAVIS, JAMES VERLIN, univ. dean; b. De Kalb, Ill., Dec. 14, 1935; s. Verl James and Esther Jane (Thomas) D.; B.A., Wabash Coll., 1957; M.A., Vanderbilt U., 1963; Ph.D. (Research scholar), Cornell U., 1967; m. Bessie Anita Taylor, June 10, 1961; children—Elizabeth Lee, Jonathan James, Amy Lynn. Systems analyst Prudential Ins. Co., Chgo., 1957-58, 60-61; financial analyst Ford Motor Co., Dearborn, Mich., 1963-64; asso. dean Grad. Sch. Mgmt., Vanderbilt U., 1970-73, acting dean, 1973—, prof., 1967—. Trustee, treas. Nashville Child Center, Inc. Served with AUS, 1958-60. Recipient Madison Saratt Prize for excellence in undergrad. teaching Vanderbilt U., 1969. Ford Found. fellow, 1964-66. Mem. Am. Econ. Assn., Am., Western, So. finance assns., Financial Mgmt. Assn., Financial Execs. Inst. Club: University (dir. 1970-72) (Nashville). Home: 519 Colice Jeanne Rd Nashville TN 37221

DAVIS, JAMES WILFRED, editor, publisher, advt. agy. exec.; b. Knoxville, Ia., June 15, 1934; s. Wilfred W. and Ethel (Shutter) D.; student Gen. Motors Inst., Flint, Mich., 1951-52; m. Georgia Elizabeth Baggett, June 17, 1955 (div. Jan. 1968); children—Linda Diane, Robin Teresa, John Douglas; m. 2d, Sue Jenkins, Aug. 9, 1968. Mech. designer United Design Service, Arlington, Va., 1954-64; partner Eastern Pub. Co., 1964-69; owner Jim Davis Prodns., Inc., Alexandria, Va., 1969—; owner Art Studio, Alexandria. Clubs: Nat. Potomac Yacht (gov.); Tantallon Yacht (charter mem.). Home: 1600 S Eads St Arlington VA 22202 Office: 3112 Mt Vernon Av Alexandria VA 22305

DAVIS, JEFFERSON CLARK, JR., chemist, educator; b. Jacksonville, Fla., Mar. 20, 1931; s. Jefferson Clark and Margaret Olivia (Pippin) D.; B.S., U. Ariz., 1953, M.S., 1954; Ph.D., U. Cal. at Berkeley, 1959; m. Sylvia Belle Conelly, June 4, 1954; children—Nancy, Susan, Gretchen. DuPont teaching fellow U. Cal. at Berkeley, 1956-59; instr. to asst. prof. U. Tex., Austin, 1959-65; asso. prof. to prof. chemistry U. South Fla., Tampa, 1965—. Dir. Willard Grant Press. Cons. Wadsworth Pub. Co., McGraw-Hill, Holt-Rinehart-Winston, Marcel Dekker, Edn. Devel. Center. Mem. adv. council coll. chemistry NSF. Served to lt., AUS, 1954-56. Fellow Am. Inst. Chemists; mem. Am. Chem. Soc., A.A.A.S., Am. Assn. U. Profs., Fla. Acad. Sci., Phi Beta Kappa, Sigma Xi, Phi Kappa Phi, Lambda Phi Alpha, Sigma Pi Sigma. Unitarian. Author: Advanced Physical Chemistry, 1965; A Laboratory Manual for General Chemistry, 1968, 72; Spectroscopy Film Series, 1970. Mem. bd. Chemistry Mag., 1969-72. Contbr. articles to profl. jours. Home: 19615 Carrollwood Dr Tampa FL 33618

DAVIS, JEFFERSON LEE, judge; b. Cartersville, Ga., Aug. 28, 1912; s. William Robert and Deborrah (Hobgood) D.; student Ga. Inst. Tech., 1930-31; LL.B., Atlanta Law Sch., 1943; postgrad. Nat. Coll. State Trial Judges, U. Nev., 1969; m. Eloine Greene, Apr. 1, 1942; children—Ronald L., Jefferson Lee, Sarah Grace. Admitted to Ga. bar, 1943; practiced in Cartersville, 1943-58; judge Superior Cts. Cherokee Jud. Circuit, Cartersville, 1958—. Pres., First Ga. Financial Corp., Johnson-Davis Co.; sec. Gurvis Corp.; vice chmn., dir. Bartow County Savs. & Loan Assn.; dir. Fulton Fed. Savs. & Loan Assn., Atlanta. Chmn., Cartersville Bd. Edn., 1954-57. Mem. Ga. Ho. of Reps., 1947-51; Senate, 1955-56. Mem. Ga. Bar Assn. (past bd. govs.), Demosthenian Lit. Soc., Gridiron Secret Soc. Episcopalian. Mason (Shriner), Lion. Home: Old Alabama Rd Cartersville GA 30120 Office: Savs & Loan Bldg Cartersville GA 30120

DAVIS, JESSE DUNBAR, lawyer; b. Burden, Kan., June 19, 1908; s. Jesse Bowman and Hazel (Dunbar) D.; student U. Okla., 1926-28; LL.B., U. Tulsa, 1944; m. Frances Lou Vinson, June 19, 1929; children—Sydney (Mrs. William Albert Russell, Jr.), Brett Vinson. Asst. mgr. Long-Bell Lumber Co., Muskogee, Okla., 1928-32, gen. mgr., Tulsa, 1933-48, div. mgr., Kansas City, Mo., 1949-57; admitted to Okla. bar, 1944, U.S. Supreme Ct. bar, 1950, Mo. bar, 1959, Fed. bar, 1963; v.p., dir. Tamko Asphalt Products, Inc., Joplin, Mo., 1958-59; gen. counsel Southwestern Lumberman's Assn., Kansas City, Mo., 1960-65, corporate sec., 1962-65; gen. practice law, Kansas City, Mo., Tulsa, 1960—; mgmt. cons., Tulsa, 1965—; realtor, Tulsa, Columnist, Retail Lumberman Mag., 1962-65; cons. industry Sch. Forestry, U. Mo., 1962-65; tchr. bus. law U. Mo., 1946-65; tchr. real estate law U. Tulsa, 1969—; v.p., dir., asso. editor Retail Lumberman Pub. Co., Kansas City, 1962-65. Served to lt. USNR, 1944-46. Recipient Civic award Tulsa YMCA, 1946-47. Mem. Am. Judicature Soc., Lawyers Assn. Kansas City, Tulsa Bd. Realtors (dir. 1970-72, treas. 1971, corporate sec. 1972), Tulsa C. of C. (Civic award 1939), Res. Officers Assn. U.S., Claremore C. of C. (dir. 1972—, v.p. 1973), Am., Tulsa County, Rogers County, Kansas City bar assns., S.A.R., U.S. Navy League, Phi Delta Theta, Phi Beta Gamma. Republican. Presbyn. Clubs: University (charter mem.), Kiwanis (pres. Tulsa 1941, sec.-treas. Tex.-Okla. dist. 1942). Home: 3231 S Utica Av Tulsa OK 74105 Office: 3233 S Utica Av Tulsa OK 74105

DAVIS, JESSE EDWIN, JR., wood products exec.; b. Atlanta, Feb. 4, 1910; s. Jesse Edwin and Eufa (Swilling) D.; B.S., Ga. Sch. Tech., 1933; LL.B., Woodrow Wilson Coll., 1937; m. Sarah Etta Fitzpatrick, Apr. 7, 1938; children—Carolyn W. (Mrs. Edward W. Riser), Sarah K. (Mrs. M. Rick Taylor), Jesse Edwin III, Marion H. Admitted to Ga. bar, 1937; sales rep. Atlantic Steel Co., 1937-43, Tidewater Supply Co., 1943-49; v.p., treas. Thackston-Davis Supply, 1949-59; with Marwin Co., Columbia, S.C., 1959—, pres., treas., 1959— (all Columbia). Chmn. religious work com. Columbia YMCA, 1956—, also bd. dirs. Trustee, United Community Services. Mem. Columbia Com. of 100, Sigma Chi, Alpha Kappa Psi, Pi Delta Epsilon. Baptist (deacon). Mason (Shriner), Lion. Home: 4829 Carter Hill Rd Columbia SC 29206 Office: PO Box 9126 Atlas Rd Columbia SC 29209

DAVIS, JOE WALTER, ch. ofcl.; b. Hobart, Okla., Aug. 11, 1913; s. Lee and Willie (Stewart) D.; B.S., Southwestern U., 1935; B.C.S., Benjamin Franklin U., Washington, 1942; m. Ethel Lois Wiemers, Apr. 24, 1937; children—Edith Marie (Mrs. Alan W. Loveland), Eugene Stewart, George Edward, Mary Ellen (Mrs. Phillip H. Arnold), Elizabeth Ann. Identification officer FBI, Washington, 1937-42, spl. agt., 1942-44; auditor Southwestern U., 1944-54; treas., bus. mgr. television, radio and film communication United Meth. Ch., 1954—, asst. gen. treas. Council Finance and Adminstrn., 1973. Past mem. bd. mgrs., bus. finance com. of broadcasting and film commn. Nat. Council Chs. Sch., bd. sec., Georgetown, Tex., 1951-54. Home: 210 Emery Dr Nashville TN 37214 Office: 1525 McGavock St Nashville TN 37203

DAVIS, JOHN EDWARD, JR., coll. adminstr.; b. Welch, W.Va., Nov. 18, 1922; s. John Edward and Bessie Irene (Cline) D.; student Randolph-Macon Coll., 1939-41; B.A., U. Va., 1947, M.A., 1949, Ph.D., 1955; m. Katherine Vivian Smith, Aug. 27, 1949; 1 son, John Edward III. Instr. biology Washington and Lee U., 1949-51, 54-56; asst. prof. biology Wake Forest U., 1956-62, asso. prof., 1962-67, prof., 1967-68; chmn. dept. biology Madison Coll., Harrisonburg, Va., 1968-71, acting provost, 1971-72, provost div. arts and scis., 1972—; cons. N.C. State Dept. Edn.; mem. study commn. allied health scis. State Council Higher Edn. Va. Ednl. coordinator Madison Coll. United Fund, 1973. Mem. adv. com. Rockingham Meml. Hosp. Sch. Nursing. Served with M.C., AUS, 1942-46. Phipps and Bird research fellow, 1948; research asso. N.C. Heart Assn., 1962; Am. Cancer Soc. research fellow, 1963. Mem. A.A.A.S., Assn. Southeastern Biologists, Va. Acad. Sci., N.Y. Acad. Scis., Sigma Xi, Kappa Alpha. Republican. Methodist. Elk. Clubs: Spotswood Country, Harrisonburg Kiwanis. Contbr. articles profl. jours. Research in biology, effects of radiation on coronary blood vessels, avian embryology. Home: Forest Hills Harrisonburg VA 22801

DAVIS, JOHN EMERSON, educator; b. Detroit, Jan. 1, 1907; s. Emerson and Marion (Biegler) D.; A.B., Oberlin Coll., 1930; M.S., U. Mich., 1931; Ph.D., U. Chgo., 1936; m. Unni Dorothea Haerem, Sept. 2, 1935; 1 dau., Barbara Jean. Instr. physiology Med. Coll. Va., 1935-37; instr. U. Ala., 1937-38; asst. prof. pharmacology U. Vt., 1938-42; asso. prof., prof. U. Ark., 1942-51; prof. U. Tex., Austin, 1952-73, prof. emeritus, 1973—. Sec. staff U. Ark. Med. Sch. Hosp., 1951. Mem. Pharmacology and Endocrinology Fellowships Rev. Panel, NIH, 1960-64. Fellow Am. Coll. Angiology, A.A.A.S., Am. Coll. Cardiology; mem. Am. Heart Assn. (council on basic scis.), Am. Physiol. Soc., Am. Soc. Pharmacology and Exptl. Therapeutics, Soc. Exptl. Biology and Medicine, N.Y. Acad. Scis., Western Pharmacology Soc. Contbr. articles to med. jours. Home: 1413 Larkwood Dr Austin TX 78723

DAVIS, JOHN GRIFFITH, assn. exec.; b. Frostburg, Md., Sept. 13, 1933; s. John Gerard and Virginia (Griffith) D.; student Frostburg State Coll., 1951-53; B.A., George Washington U., 1956; m. Mildred Eliose Ward, Apr. 8, 1956; children—Stephen Robert, Scott Richard, John William. Sports reporter Washington Post, 1954-61; pub. relations asst. Nat. Assn. Real Estate Bds., Washington, 1961-62; asst. exec. v.p. Soc. Indsl. Realtors, Washington, 1962-73; v.p., asst. gen. mgr. Nat. Assn. Bus. and Ednl. Radio, 1973—. Served with AUS, 1957-59. Mem. Pub. Relations Soc. Am. Republican. Mem. United Ch. Christ (elder). Club: Nat. Press. Home: 7306 Statecrest Dr Annandale VA 22003 Office: 1330 New Hampshire Av NW Washington DC 20036

DAVIS, JOHN OLDHRAM, lawyer; b. Nacogdoches, Tex., Feb. 10, 1942; s. William J. and Vera L. (Myers) D.; B.B.A., U. Tex. at Austin, 1964, J.D., 1967; m. Sharon Ann Myers, Feb. 1, 1964; 1 dau., Dana Myers. Admitted to Tex. bar, 1967; staff accountant Peat, Marwick, Mitchell & Co., Dallas, 1967-68; asso. Tate McCain, Palestine, Tex., 1968-70; pvt. practice law, Palestine, 1970-71, 73—; partner Price & Davis, 1971-72. Dir. 1st Nat. Bank of Palestine. Mem. Palestine City Council, 1971-72. Dir. Palestine Indsl. Found. Mem. Anderson County Bar Assn. (pres. 1970-71), Beta Theta Pi. Home: 501 S Magnolia St Palestine TX 76801 Office: 505 N Church St Palestine TX 75801

DAVIS, JOHN WILLIAM, congressman; b. Rome, Ga., Sept. 12, 1916; s. John Camp and Era (DeLay) D.; A.B., U. Ga., 1937, LL.B., 1939; m. Vivian Hawkins, Feb. 6, 1944 (dec.); children—Katherine DeLay (Mrs. Lloyd Mewbourne), John William, Mary Ellen; m. 2d, Bridget O'Sullivan Chrisman, June 26, 1971; stepchildren—Norman Chrisman, Paul Chrisman. Admitted to Ga. bar, 1939; practice in Rome, 1939-42, Summerville, 1946-55; solicitor gen. Rome Circuit, 1950-53; judge Lookout Mountain Jud. Circuit, 1950-53; judge Lookout Mountain Jud. Circuit, 1955-60; mem. 87th-93d congresses from 7th Dist. Ga. Served with AUS, World War II. Democrat. Mason, Lion. Home: 100 Espy St Summerville GA 30747 Office: House Office Bldg Washington DC 10025

DAVIS, JOSEPH SOLOMON, coll. adminstr.; b. Macon, Ga., Apr. 8, 1938; s. Oscar Lee and Alice Mae (Lucas) D.; B.S., Tuskegee Inst., 1960, M.Ed., 1968; m. Sarah Frances Striggles, July 28, 1962; children—Joan Yvette, Oscar Wendall. Tchr., counselor Boggs Acad., Keysville, Ga., 1961-67; dir. financial aid Stillman Coll., Tuscaloosa, Ala., 1967—. Fellow Assn. Colls. and Secondary Schs., 1967. Home: 8 Oak Ridge Tuscaloosa AL 35401 Office: Stillman College Tuscaloosa AL 35401

DAVIS, JUNIUS AYERS, research psychologist; b. Raleigh, N.C., Feb. 4, 1925; s. Roy and Vivian (Johnson) D.; A.B., U. N.C., 1946; A.M. Columbia, 1950; Ph.D., 1956; m. Pegge Jill Morris, Nov. 9, 1946; children—Michael Ayers, Christopher Morris, Cynthia Jill. Control buyer Sears Roebuck, Greensboro, N.C., 1946-48; asst. dir. counseling service Princeton, 1952-54; asst. prof. psychology Emory U., 1954-57; dir. testing and guidance bd. regents Univ. Systems, Ga., 1957-58; grad. dean U. N.C., Greensboro, 1958-61; research psychologist Ednl. Testing Service, Princeton, N.J., 1961-67; dir. southeastern office Ednl. Testing Service, Durham, N.C., 1967-73; dir. Center for Ednl. Research and Evaluation, Research Triangle Inst., Research Triangle Park, N.C., 1973—. Adj. prof. edn., lectr. psychology Duke, 1968—; lectr. edn. U. N.C. at Chapel Hill, 1970—. Served from ensign to lt. (j.g.), USNR, 1942-46, 48-49. Mem. Am. Psychol. Assn., Am. Personnel and Guidance Assn., Am. Ednl. Research Assn., Assn. for Instl. Research, Sigma Xi, Phi Delta Kappa, Kappa Delta Pi. Presbyn. (ruling elder 1964-67). Home: 405 Holly Lane Chapel Hill NC 27514 Office: PO Box 12194 Research Triangle Park NC 27709

DAVIS, LEW ARTER, clergyman; b. Marietta, Okla., Jan. 3, 1930; s. Louis Albert and Marie Mamie (Petree) Davis; B.A., Phillips U., 1951; postgrad. Okla. State U., 1952-53, Hartford Sem. Found., 1954; B.D., Tex. Christian U., 1954, M.Th., 1968; m. Dorothy Elsie Armstrong, July 12, 1950; children—John, Bruce, Carolyn, Glenn. Missionary to India, United Christian Missionary Soc., 1954-71, field adminstr., 1965-66, 68-71; minister First Christian Ch., Blackwell, Okla., 1971—. Mem. negotiating com. Ch. in N. India, 1968-70; mem. council ring of camps farthest out No. Okla. camp Internat. Camps Farthest Out, 1971—; pres. Blackwell Assn. for Growth, 1972—; chmn. Mayor's Adv. Com., Blackwell, 1972, Blackwell Overall Econ. Devel. Plan Com., 1973; mem. task force for new acad. units, pres.'s adv. council Phillips U., 1972-73. Bd. dirs. Kay County Guidance Assn. Mem. Okla. Conf. Chs. (dir. 1972—), United Christian Missionary Soc. (mem. investment adv. com. 1971-73), Blackwell Ministerial Alliance (pres. 1972-74), Blue Key, Theta Phi. Author: The Layman Views World Missions, 1964. Home: 1806 S 1st St Blackwell OK 74631 Office: 306 E Coolidge St Blackwell OK 74631

DAVIS, MACLIN PASCHALL, JR., lawyer; b. Nashville, July 13, 1926; s. Maclin Paschall and Edith Chamberlin (Uhler) D.; student Va. Mil. Inst., 1943-44, U. N.C., 1944-45; B.A., Vanderbilt U., 1947, LL.B., 1950; m. Dorothy Jane Savage, June 24, 1953; children—Maclin Paschall III, Joseph N., Dorothy S. Admitted to Tenn. bar, 1950; practice law with Waller Lansden, Dortch & Davis (and predecessor firms), Nashville, 1950—. Dir. Am. Health Profiles, Inc., Nashville, Met. Mgmt. Co., Nashville; v.p., dir. Tenn. Foundry & Machine Co., Nashville. Mem. Tenn. Ho. of Reps., 1954-56. Bd. dirs. Day Care Center and Sch. for Retarded Children. Served with USNR, 1944-46. Mem. Nashville (dir., 2d v.p. 1963-66), Tenn., Am. bar assns., Omicron Delta Kappa, Delta Kappa Epsilon, Phi Alpha Delta. Episcopalian. Clubs: Belle Meade, Sequoia, Seven Hills, Capitol. Home: 411 Lynwood Blvd Nashville TN 37205 Office: American Trust Bldg Nashville TN 37201

DAVIS, MARION JOHNSON, lawyer, corp. exec.; b. Winston-Salem, N.C., May 5, 1929; s. John Neal and Elva Martha (Wall) D.; B.S., Wake Forest U., 1951, J.D., 1953; m. Carrie Chamberlain, Dec. 28, 1950; children—Martha Ann Joslin, Marion Johnson. Admitted to N.C. bar, 1953; pvt. practice law, 1953-54; atty., asst. sec. Security Life & Trust Co., 1954-56, atty., asst. v.p., 1959-63, v.p., gen. counsel, 1963-69; v.p., sec., gen. counsel Integon Corp., Winston-Salem, 1969—. Bd. dirs. Goodwill Industries, 1962-73, Forsyth County chpt. A.R.C., 1953-73; pres., bd. dirs. Forsyth County Heart Assn., 1961-65. Mem. Assn. Life Ins. Counsel, Am., N.C., Forsyth County bar assns. Baptist (past deacon, trustee). Clubs: Twin City, Old Town (Winston-Salem). Home: 2525 Warwick Rd Winston-Salem NC 27104 Office: 420 N Spruce St Winston-Salem NC 27102

DAVIS, MARK VINCENT, mfg. co. exec.; b. Wabash, Ind., Aug. 26, 1913; s. Joseph A. and Edna (Firth) D.; student U. Toledo, 1931-32; m. Josephine DeVaux Hissong, Dec. 29, 1934; children—Judy Jo (Mrs. John David Rainey), Mark Vincent Jr. Mem. staff stores dept. Libbey-Owens-Ford Glass Co., Toledo, O., 1935-43; mgr. Charles R. Baum Constrn. Co., Houston, 1946-50; operations mgr., div. mgr. Ada Oil Co., Houston, 1950-59; pres. Marand Sales Co. Inc., Houston, 1959-70, dir., 1959—; pres. Jet Mfg. Co. Inc., Houston, 1964—, also dir. Served with AUS, 1943-45; ETO. Mem. Petroleum Equipment Inst., Houston C. of C., Houston Power Squadron. Roman Catholic. K.C. Home: 12343 Rip Van Winkle Dr Houston TX 77024 Office: 5611 Clinton Dr Houston TX 77001

DAVIS, MENDEL JACKSON, congressman; b. North Charleston, S.C., Oct. 23, 1942; s. Felix Charles and Elizabeth (Jackson) D.; B.S., Coll. Charleston, 1966; J.D., U. S.C., 1970; m. Suzanna Henley, Nov. 25, 1965; 1 dau., Lila Salisbury. Admitted to S.C. bar, 1970; mem. staff Rep. L. Mendel Rivers, 1970-71; mem. 92d-93d Congresses from S.C. Keynote speaker Charleston County Democratic Conv., 1972. Named One of Outstanding Young Men of Am., 1972. Mem. S.C. State, Am. bar assns., Air Force Assn., Navy League. Democrat. Methodist. Mason, Elk. Home: 4342 Patricia St Charleston Heights SC 29405 Office: 1726 Longworth Bldg Washington DC 20515

DAVIS, MERTON LOUIS, research chemist; b. Detroit, Nov. 27, 1918; s. Alfred and Etta (Sellings) D.; B.A., DePauw U., 1942; Ph.D., U. Mich., 1951; m. Eliza White, June 18, 1962; children—Eliza, Sarah, Albert, Miriam. Analytical chemist Bohn Aluminum & Brass, 1942; x-ray technician Los Alamos Sci. Labs., 1943-46; research chemist E.I. duPont de Nemours & Co., Camden, S.C., 1951—. Served with AUS, 1943-45. Mem. Am. Chem. Soc. Home: 3A Palmetto Arms Camden SC 29020 Office: PO Drawer A Camden SC 29020

DAVIS, MILTON WICKERS, JR., chem. engr., educator; b. Frederick, Md., Apr. 5, 1923; s. Milton Wickers and Elizabeth H. Griffith (Wood) D.; B.E., Johns Hopkins, 1943; M.S., U. Cal. at Berkeley, 1949, Ph.D., 1951; m. Jane Crayton, May 21, 1955 (div.); children—Gaither Griffith, Richard Render. Research asst. U. Cal. Radiation Lab., 1947-50; research engr. atomic energy div. E.I. duPont de Nemours & Co., Wilmington, Del., 1950-54, research supr. Savannah River plant, Aiken, S.C., 1954-62; prof. engring. U. S.C., Columbia, 1962—. Mem. Aiken County Water Pollution Control Commn. Served from ensign to lt., USNR, 1943-46. Mem. Am. Inst. Chem. Engrs., Am. Chem. Soc., Md. Soc. War of 1812, Sigma Xi, Delta Phi. Episcopalian. Club: Plantation (Hilton Head Island, S.C.). Contbr. to Chemical Processing of Nuclear Fuels, 1960. Home: PO Box 242 Columbia SC 29202

DAVIS, N. KNOWLES, public utility cons.; b. Atlanta, Feb. 20, 1904; s. Archibald H. and Susan (Topliff) D.; B.S., Ga. Inst. Tech., 1925; E.E., Cornell U., 1926; m. Jean Nutting, June 21, 1932; 1 dau., Jean (Mrs. Daniel Fort Flowers). Transmission engr. Ga. Power Co., Atlanta, 1926-32; chief engr. Ga. Pub. Service Commn., 1933-41, dir. utilities div., 1945-55; chief power allocation WPB, Washington, 1942-44; dir. rates Tenn. Gas Transmission Co., Houston, 1956-58, v.p., 1959-67, sr. v.p., asst. to pres., 1967-69; pub. utility cons., Houston, 1969—. Guest lectr. Ia. State U., 1963, 72, Am. Law Inst., 1954, 67. Bd. dirs. Epilepsy Fodn. Am. Mem. Nat., Tex. socs. profl. engrs., Am., Fed. Power, Ga. bar assns., Am., So. gas assns., Am. Judicature Soc., Chi Psi. Presbyn. Rotarian. Home: 3420 Overbrook Lane Houston TX 77027 Office: 1932 Chamber of Commerce Bldg Houston TX 77002

DAVIS, NANCY BRAWLEY HOWARD (MRS. BENJAMIN CUMMINGS DAVIS), librarian; b. Mooresville, N.C., Dec. 9, 1910; d. Henry North and Jessie Anna (Brawley) Howard; A.B. in L.S., Woman's Coll., U. N.C., 1931; m. Benjamin Cummings Davis, Mar. 29, 1936; children—Nancy Elizabeth (Mrs. Francis Michael Fennegan), John Allen. Library asst. Woman's coll. U. N.C., Greensboro, 1927-31; librarian, also tchr. Taylorsville (N.C.) City Schs., 1933-35; librarian Hugh Morson High Sch., Raleigh, N.C., 1935-36; supr. WPA Library Project, Mecklenburg and Stanley counties, N.C., 1937-38; librarian Harding High Sch., Charlotte, N.C., 1938-40, 49-55; librarian Southern Pines (N.C.) Sch., 1942-43; children's librarian Greensboro Pub. Library, 1943-44; librarian Mooresville (N.C.) High Sch., 1944-46; librarian elementary schs., Charlotte, 1947-49; tchr. Mooresville Jr. High Sch., 1955-57; librarian Iredell County Pub. Library, Statesville, N.C., 1957-59; reference, circulation librarian Davidson (N.C.) Coll. Library, 1959-60; librarian Kenly Sch., Tampa, Fla., 1960-61, John McKnitt Alexander Jr. High Sch., Huntersville, N.C., 1961—. Ednl. chmn. Iredell County Cancer Soc., Statesville, 1958-60; chmn. Mooresville Community Achievement Program, 1961-62. Bd. dirs. Mooresville Community Fund, 1958-60. Mem. Am., N.C., Charlotte-Mecklenberg library assns., N.E.A., N.C., Charlotte-Mecklenburg edn. assns., Iredell County Friends of the Library (chmn. membership com.). Democrat. Presbyn. (ch. librarian). Club: Mooresville Woman's (pres. 1958-60). Specializes in organizing and reorganizing sch. and community libraries. Home: 313 W McLelland Av Mooresville NC 28115 Office: Route 1 Huntersville NC 28078

DAVIS, NOAH RICHARD, univ. adminstr.; b. Dallas, Oct. 30, 1926; s. Noah Schley and Gussie Merle (Dielman) D.; B.B.A., So. Meth. U., 1950; m. Sandra Lee Burt, May 22, 1965; children—Linda, Richard, Susan, Scott, Leslie. With Merrill, Lynch, Pierce, Fenner & Smith, Dallas, 1950-74, v.p., resident mgr., 1966-74; athletic dir. So. Meth. U., Dallas, 1974—. Dir. Circle 10 council Boy Scouts Am., 1970—; vice chmn. So. Meth. U. Sustenation, 1971; div. dir. United Fund, 1969. Served with USAAF, World War II. Mem. Dallas C. of C., Mustang Club (dir. 1959-66), Sigma Alpha Epsilon. Home: 3945 Amherst St Dallas TX 75225

DAVIS, RAYMOND GILBERT, assn. exec.; b. Fitzgerald, Ga., Jan. 13, 1915; s. Raymond Roy and Zelma Miranda (Tribby) D.; B.S. with honors in Chem. Engring., Ga. Inst. Tech., 1938; grad. Nat. War Coll., 1960; m. Willa Knox Heafner, Apr. 25, 1942; children—Raymond Gilbert, Gordon Miles, Willa Kay. Commd. 2d lt. U.S. Marine Corp., 1938, advanced through grades to gen.; asst. comdt. USMC, 1971-72; ret., 1972; exec. v.p. Ga. C. of C., Atlanta, 1972—. Bd. dirs. U.S. Marine Youth Found.; trustee Marine Mil. Acad.; bd. visitors Berry Coll., Rome, Ga. Decorated Medal of Honor, D.S.M. (2), Silver medal (2), Legion of Merit (2), Bronze Star, Purple Heart, also fgn. decorations. Mem. Marine Crops League, First Marine Div. Assn. (pres. 1966-68), Ret. Officers Assn. (dir.), V.F.W., D.A.V., Congl. Medal of Honor Soc. Methodist. Club: Commerce (Atlanta). Contbr. articles to mil. jours. Home: Route 2 32 Dogwood Lane McDonough GA 30253 Office: Ga C of C 1200 Commerce Bldg Atlanta GA 30303

DAVIS, ROBERT EARL, publishing co. exec.; b. Waco, Tex., Apr. 26, 1933; s. Earl R. and Grace Truman (Abernathy) D.; student Baylor U., 1951-52, 55-56; m. Mary Ann Boehne, Dec. 15, 1957; children—Earl Ray, Pamela Ann. Partner, co-owner Texian Press, Book Pubs., Waco, 1960—; editor Texana, hist. jour., 1962—; pres. Davis Bros. Pub. Co., Waco, 1972—. Chmn., Waco Library Commn., 1966-70; pres. Waco Hist. Found., 1967-71; mem. Tex. Library and Hist. Commn., 1968-73; chmn. adv. bd. Confederate Research Center, Hill Jr. Coll. Served with USMCR, 1952-53. Mem. Order Red Men, (nat. sec.). Pub.: William Barrett Travis Dairy, 1966. Home: 1020 Sleepy Hollow St Waco TX 76710 Office: 1301 Jefferson St Waco TX 76708

DAVIS, RON WILLSON, ednl. adminstr.; b. Spokane, Wash., Dec. 5, 1918; s. Roncisco Harold and Beatrice Antonette (Willson) D.; B.A., Reed Coll., Portland, Ore., 1947; M.A., Columbia, 1948, Ed.D., 1952, postgrad., 1966; postgrad. U. Pa., 1955-56; m. Lucy Elizabeth Tolbert, Aug. 28, 1948; children—Ronald Redd, Margaret Willson, Elisabeth Southard. Tchr., Wilmette (Ill.) Schs., 1948-50; research asso. Columbia, 1952-54; sch. prin., Bristol Twp. and Cheltenham Twp., Pa., 1954-64; asst. supt. pub. schs., Euclid, O., 1964-67; asso. prof. U. N.C., Chapel Hill, 1967-70; dir. continuing edn. N.C. Regional Med. Program, Durham, 1970—; faculty dept. community health scis. Duke, 1970—. Ednl. cons. N.C. Med. Soc.; writer monthly column N.C. Med. Jour. Dist. orgn. and extension chmn. Greater Cleve. council Boy Scouts Am., 1965-67. Bd. dirs. YMCA, Euclid, 1965-66. Served with AUS, USAAF, 1942-45. Mem. Am. Soc. for Health Manpower Edn. and Tng., Am. Assn. Sch. Adminstrs. (life), Nat. Soc. for Study Edn., Phi Delta Kappa, Kappa Delta Pi. Rotarian. Club: Chapel Hill Country. Editor: Committee Guidelines Handbook, N.C. Med. Soc., 1974. Home: 705 Gimghoul Rd Chapel Hill NC 27514 Office: PO Box 8248 Durham NC 27704

DAVIS, RUSSELL LEWIS, lawyer, state ofcl.; b. Rocky Mount, Va., Mar. 8, 1903; s. Beverly A. and Mary (Gravely) D.; student Augusta Mil. Acad., 1919-20; student Roanoke Coll., 1920-23, U. Va., 1926; m. Winifred Skinnell, Oct. 8, 1933; children—Emily (Mrs. C. Dean Londos), Russell L., William G., Julia W., Katherine. Admitted to Va. bar, 1926; practiced in Rocky Mount, 1926—; mem. firms Davis, Davis, Davis & Raine; mem. Va. Ho. of Dels., 1966—. Dir. Peoples Nat. Bank, Rocky Mount. Mem. Va. State Bar Assn., Pi Kappa Phi, Phi Alpha Delta. Republican. Mason, Lion. Home: 116 Taliaferro St Rocky Mount VA 24151 Office: 113 E Court St Rocky Mount VA 24151

DAVIS, RUSSELL REID, clergyman; b. Lexington, N.C., May 5, 1928; s. Russell Martin and Helen Pearl (Clodfelter) D.; B.A., U. N.C., Chapel Hill., 1950; M.Div., Union Theol. Sem., Richmond, Va., 1957; M.A. in Edn., E. Carolina U., Greenville, N.C., 1970; m. Eleanor Jane Doubles, Sept. 1, 1965; children—Catherine, Elizabeth, Anne. With Davis Linen Service, Danville, Va., 1950-54; ordained to ministry Presbyn. Ch., 1957; pastor, Plymouth, N.C., 1957-60, Buena Vista, Va., 1960-64, Boyd Meml. Presbyn. Ch., Greenville, 1965-74; adminstrv. minister Amelia County (Va.) Presbyn. Chs. Cluster, 1974—; chaplain Buena Vista Fire Dept., 1960-65, Stonewall Jackson Dist. council Boy Scouts Am., 1963-64, Pitt County Boy's Club, 1968-72. Chmn. homes. Gen. Council Lexington Presbytery, 1961-64, chmn. Christianity and health, 1960-65, ch. extension, 1961; chmn. ch. and soc. gen. council Albermarle Presbytery, 1966—. Mem. Am. Assn. Pastoral Counselors, Pitt County Ministerial Assn. (chmn. health ministeries 1966-68), Kappa Delta Phi, Delta Phi Alpha, Sigma Chi. Club: Candlewick Swim and Tennis (Greenville). Author papers. Home: Deekens St Amelia VA 23002

DAVIS, SAM WARREN, cons. engring. firm exec.; b. Doniphan, Mo., Apr. 20, 1902; s. Daniel H. and Emily Belle (Warren) D.; B.S. in Elec. Engring., Okla. State U., 1928; m. Marion Elizabeth White, Sept. 14, 1930; children—Warren Eugene, Stanley Kent, Jerry Marshall, Rebecca Ann. With Tex. Power & Light Co., Dallas, 1928-29, Cosden Oil Co., Big Spring, Tex., 1929-30; with Southwestern Pub. Service Co., Amarillo, 1930-48, div. engr., 1940-48; self employed elec. engr., contractor Panhandle Engrs. & Contractors (inc. 1971), Amarillo, 1948-66, partner, 1965-71, chmn. bd., treas., 1971—; chmn. bd. Deltex Systems, Inc., 1973—; sec.-treas., dir. Audio-Video Corp., Amarillo, 1959—, now also chmn. bd. Mem. adv. bd. Salvation Army, 1968-73, pres. adv. bd.. 1973—; bd. dirs. Amarillo Little Theater, 1970-73; mem. Tex. N.G., 1941-45. Named Outstanding Young Man of Year Amarillo Jr. C. of C., 1941. Registered profl. engr., Tex., N.M., Okla. mem. I.E.E.E. (life mem.), Tex. Soc. Profl. Engrs. (chpt. pres. 1945-46), Kappa Alpha. Presbyn. (elder). Lion (Lion of Yr. award Downtown Amarillo Club 1971, bd. dirs. 1971-72). Club: Amarillo. Contbr. articles to publs. Home: 2611 Henning St Amarillo TX 79106 Office: 216 Lipscomb St Amarillo TX 79105

DAVIS, STAFFORD GRISE, pub. relations exec.; b. Bremen, Ind., May 21, 1924; s. Stafford Wine and Violet Lucille (Grise) D.; B.S., Northwestern U., 1947; postgrad. Fgn. Service Inst., 1956-57; m. 2d, Suzanne Marie Wilkinson, Feb. 25, 1967; children—Stafford Bruce, Laura, Scott B. Editor, asst. gen. mgr. Nat. Editorial Assn., Chgo., 1946-49; asst. dir. publicity Northwestern U., 1949-52; dir. information services, 1960-64; supr. state area information Ill. Bell Telephone Co., Chgo., 1953-56; press attache U.S. Embassy, Saigon, Vietnam, 1957-60; v.p. devel. Shimer Coll., 1964-67; pres., owner The Idea Fund, Chgo., 1967-69; v.p., dir. Pub. Relations Internat. Ltd., Tulsa, 1969-71, exec. v.p., dir., 1971—; v.p., dir. Dean Pub. Relations Ltd., London, Eng.; cons. Stone-Brandel Center, Chgo., 1967. Pres. Epis. Churchmen Chgo., 1967-68. Bd. dirs. Okla. Lung Assn., 1970—, Okla. Lung Research, 1971—; trustee Found. African Communications Tng., N.Y.C., Am. Friends Vietnam, N.Y.C. Served to lt. USNR, World War II. Mem. Pub. Relations Soc. Am. (dir. Tulsa chpt. 1969—), Internat. Platform Assn., Newcomen Soc., Sigma Delta Chi, Phi Kappa Psi. Club U. Tulsa. Contbr. articles to profl. jours. Home: 2144 N Elwood Av Tulsa OK 74106 Office: 522 S Boston St Tulsa OK 74103

DAVIS, STAFFORD WINE, ret. coll. adminstr.; b. Buffalo, Dec. 3, 1902; s. Vernon John and Arvilla W. (Stafford) D.; student Northwestern U., Chgo., 1932-36; m. Violet Lucille Grise, June 3, 1923; 1 son, Stafford Grise. Accountant, South Bend, Ind. and Chgo., 1922-47; partner Raymond S. Blunt & Co., C.P.A.'s, Chgo., 1947-65; controller Para-Tone, Inc., LaGrange, Ill., 1965-68; finance officer Fla. Keys Community Coll., Key West, 1968-72. C.P.A., Ill. Mem. Am. Inst. C.P.A.'s. Home: 509B Key West Towers Key West FL 33040

DAVIS, SUSAN SCOTT (MRS. GAYLORD DAVIS), civic worker; b. Kearney, Neb.; d. Thomas Jefferson and Mary Estelle (Grant) Scott; A.B., U. Neb., 1918, Neb. State Tchrs. Coll., 1919; M.A., Columbia, 1935; m. Gaylord Davis, July 4, 1925; 1 dau., Susanne (Mrs. Daniel Oliver Newberry). Dir. tng. sch., dept. kindergarten Neb. State Tchrs. Coll., 1914-16; mem. casts plays in N.Y. theatres, 1921-23. Mem. Council Juvenile Planning Group, Asheville and Buncombe County, N.C., 1956-59; sec. exec. com. Buncombe County Com. White House Conf. Children and Youth, 1960; dir. Children's Welfare League, Asheville, N.C., 1949, 52, 60, pres., 1955-57; bd. dirs. Family and Children's Service Agy., Asheville, N.C., 1948-55, Asheville Community Concerts Assn., 1973—; mem. Family and Children's Services Buncombe County Planning Council, 1967—. Bd. dirs. United Social Services, 1955-60, Candelight Concerts, Inc., 1960-63, Civic Arts, Inc., 1960-68; bd. dirs. Asheville Day Nursery, 1960-62, 68—, v.p., 1963-64, pres., 1964-66. Mem. Buncombe County Republican Women's Club, 1963—; mem. Women's Nat. Rep. Club, N.Y.C., 1963—, mem. nat. council, 1963—, mem. membership com., 1969—; mem. exec. com. permanent conf. Buncombe County Planning Council, 1965-70. Mem. English-Speaking Union, Ikebana Internat., Pi Beta Phi. Republican. Christian Scientist. Clubs: Biltmore Forest Country, The Duetters (founder 1947). Home: 12 Fairway Pl Biltmore Forest Asheville NC 28803

DAVIS, TERRY HUNTER, JR., lawyer; b. Charlottesville, Va., Mar. 19, 1931; s. Terry Hunter and Mattie (Parsons) D.; B.A., Va. Mil. Inst., 1953; LL.B., U. Va., 1958; m. Mary Jane Davis, Sept. 3, 1960; 1 son, Terry Hunter III. Admitted to Va. bar, 1958; atty. law firm Thacher, Proffitt, Prizer, Crawley & Wood, N.Y.C., 1958-60; law clk.

to Hon. Walter E. Hoffman, Chief U.S. Dist. Judge, Norfolk, Va., 1960-61; partner law firm Taylor, Gustin, Harris, Fears & Davis, Norfolk, Va., 1961—. Republican candidate for Va. House of Dels., 1967, 1969. Served with AUS, 1953-55. Named to State Electoral Bd. City Norfolk, 1970-73, chmn., 1972. Mem. Norfolk-Portsmouth, Va. State, Am. bar assns., Am. Judicature Soc., S.A.R., Norfolk C. of C. Clubs: Norfolk Yacht, Virginia, Kiwanis. Contbg. author to: The Virginia Lawyer's Basic Practice Handbook, 2d edn., 1964. Home: 7451 North Shore Rd Norfolk VA 23505 Office: 1440 Virginia Nat Bank Bldg Norfolk VA 23510

DAVIS, THAD WESLEY, lawyer; b. Galveston, Tex., Sept. 13, 1924; s. Thad and Lottie Annie (Wolverton) D.; LL.B., U. Tex., 1950; m. Margaret Nan Strickland, July 12, 1944; children—Nancy Sue, Michael Thad, Diane, Mark Robert. Admitted to Tex. bar, 1949; mem. firm Davis, Stovall & Newton, Freeport, Tex., 1950—, sr. partner, 1968—; municipal judge City Freeport, 1966—. Dir. 1st Freeport Nat. Bank, Freeport Unltd., Inc., Brazosport Abstract Co., Mr. Chip, Inc. Precinct chmn. Democratic party, 1956—. Trustee Community Hosp. Brazosport. Served as pilot USAAF, 1943-46; PTO. Decorated Air medal (5). Mem. Brazoria County Bar Assn. (pres. 1956-57), Phi Alpha Delta. Methodist. Rotarian, Mason. Home: 1611 W 9th St Freeport TX 77541 Office: 415 W 2d St Freeport TX 77541

DAVIS, THOMAS HENRY, airline exec.; b. Winston-Salem, N.C., Mar. 15, 1918; s. Egbert L. and Annie (Shore) D.; student U. Ariz., 1935-39; m. Nancy Caroline Teague, Oct. 28, 1944; children—Thomas Henry, Winifred (Mrs. Alfredo Torres Bond), George Franklin, Nancy Caroline, Juliana. Aircraft salesman Piedmont Aviaton, Inc., Winston-Salem, 1940, v.p., treas., 1941-43, pres., treas., 1943—; dir., mem. exec. com. Wachovia Corp. Mem. Urban Redevel. Commn., 1955—. Trustee Wake Forest U. Recipient Winston-Salem and N.C. Jr. C. of C. Distinguished Service award, 1954, Frank Davison trophy for outstanding service to aviation in N.C., 1949. Mem. Air Transport Assn. (dir.), Nat. Aviation Club, Soaring Soc. Am., Newcomen Soc., Winston-Salem C. of C. (past pres.), Pi Kappa Alpha. Democrat. Baptist. Rotarian. Clubs: Forsyth Country, Old Town (Winston-Salem); Wings (N.Y.C.). Home: 1190 Arbor Rd Winston-Salem NC 27104 Office: Smith Reynolds Airport Winston-Salem NC 27102

DAVIS, TRUE, banker; b. St. Joseph, Mo., Dec. 23, 1919; s. William True and Helen (Marstella) D.; student Cornell U., 1937-40; L.H.D., Tarkio Coll., 1963; m. Virginia Bruce Motter, Jan. 24, 1948 (dec. Sept. 1969); children—William True, Bruce Motter, Lance Barrow. Salesman Anchor Serum Co., So. St. Joseph, 1940-42, v.p., sales mgr., 1945-50, pres., 1950-60; pres., dir. Research Labs., Inc., 1952-60, Pet's Best Co., 1954-60; v.p., dir. Phillips Electronics & Pharm. Industries Corp., N.Y.C., 1959-63; pres., dir. Philips-Roxane, Inc., N.Y.C., 1959-63, Med. Industries, Inc., 1956-63, True Davis Founds., Inc., 1955—, Carolina Vet Supply, Inc., Charlotte, N.C., 1956-60, Wilke Labs, Inc., West Plains, Mo., Wilke Labs of Tenn., Inc., Memphis, 1956-60, Peters Serum Co., Kansas City, 1956-60, Gothic Advt., Inc., St. Joseph, Mo., 1956-60, World Health Inst., Ltd., 1958-60, Peerless Serum Co., 1956-60, Certified Labs., Inc., 1958-60, Davis Estate, Inc., Anchor Serum Co. of N.J., 1959-60, Anchor Serum Co. of Ind., 1959-60, Anchor Serum Co. of Minn., 1960-63; chmn. Thompson-Hayward Chem. Co., Kansas City, Mo., 1961-63; chmn., dir. Chemico Labs., Inc., Miami, Fla., 1960-63; U.S. ambassador to Switzerland, 1963-65; asst. sec. U.S. Treasury, 1965-68; U.S. exec. dir. Inter-Am. Devel. Bank, 1966-68; chmn. bd., dir. Nat. Bank Washington, 1968-73, pres., 1970-73. Dir. Laurel (Md.) Race Course, 1970—; mem. adv. bd. Washington Mut. Investors Fund, 1971—. Bd. dirs. Animal Health Inst., 1946-59, pres., 1954-56; mem. Nat. Serum Control Agy., 1947-58, chmn. 1954-55; chmn. U.S. Port Security Com., 1966-68, N.Y. Pier Com., 1966-68, Pub. Adv. Com. on Customs Adminstrn., 1966-68; mem. exec. com. United Fund, 1960; mem. Adv. Council on Naval Affairs, 1958-60; pres. Met. Washington Urban Coalition, 1971-72; chmn. Met. Washington Invest-in-Am. Council, 1970-71; mem. steering, nat. coms. Corcoran Gallery Art, 1970-72, spl. commn. on urban renewal D.C. City Council, 1971-73, D.C. Bicentennial Commn., 1971-73. Police commr., St. Joseph, 1949; mem. Democratic Nat. Finance Council, 1970-72. Bd. dirs. Little League, Nat. Assn. Boys Club Am., Children's Hosp. Washington, Washington div. Am. Health Found., Agrl. Hall Fame; trustee Missouri Valley Coll., 1969-71, Coll. Mt. St. Vincent's, 1969-71, Fleming Coll. and Inst. Fgn. Affairs, Switzerland, 1968—; bd. dirs. Close-Up, D.C. chpt. A.R.C., World Information Found., Nat. Capital Area council Boy Scouts Am., Research Found. Washington Hosp. Center, Meridian House Found., Washington; trustee Fed. City Council, Washington Center for Met. Studies, D.C. chpt. Am. Cancer Soc., Downtown Progress Assn. D.C., Washington Bd. Trade; adv. bd. Md. Commn. on Dope Addiction. Served to lt. USNR, 1942-45. chief test pilot Naval Air Sta., Pearl Harbor; lt. col. staff Mo. Gov., 1949-54, 60-72, Ky. Gov., 1953-54. Recipient Boss of Year award St. Joseph Jr. C. of C., 1960; Exceptional Service award U.S. Treasury, 1968. Hon. fellow Consular Law Soc.; mem. N.A.M. (nuclear energy com.), N.Y. Acad. of Scis., Washington Drama Soc. (dir.), Ballet Soc. (dir.), Performing Arts Soc. (dir.), Am. Royal Assn. (gov. 1960), Mo. C. of C. (dir. 1963-64), UN Assn. (dir. capital area div.), Newcomen Soc., Mo. Soc. of N.Y., Nat. Thoroughbred Breeders Assn., Am. Legion, V.F.W. (mem. nat. Americanism com., Mo. chmn. Americanism com., outstanding citizen award St. Joseph 1960, Nat. Gold Medal for Americanism 1967), Council on Fgn. Relations, Res. Officers Assn. (hon. life), Am. Soc. for Friendship with Switzerland (hon. life), Mil. Order World Wars, 40 and 8, Phi Gamma Delta Elk. Clubs: Benton (pres. 1949-50) (St. Joseph); Keeneland, Thoroughbred of Am. (Lexington, Ky.); Cornell (N.Y.C.); Minnesouri Angling; Metropolitan, City Tavern, F Street (Washington); Brook (N.Y.C.). Author: Americanism vs. Communism, 1962; The Partnership Between the Federal Government and American Universities in Financing Scientific Enquiry, 1967. Contbr. articles to various trade and farm publs. Home: 2860 Woodland Dr NW Washington DC 20008 also 3000 Ashland Av St Joseph MO 64506

DAVIS, VINCENT, educator; b. Chattanooga, May 3, 1930; B.A., Vanderbilt U., 1952; M.P.A., Woodrow Wilson Sch. Pub. and Internat. Affairs Princeton, 1959, M.A., 1960, Ph.D., 1961; m.; 3 children. Mem. faculty dept. politics, research asst. Center Internat. Studies Princeton, 1959-61, vis. research prof., 1969-70; mem. faculty Dartmouth, 1961-62; mem. faculty Grad. Sch. Internat. Studies, research asso. Social Sci. Found. U. Denver, 1962-71; Patterson Chair prof. internat. studies, dir. Patterson Sch. Diplomacy and Internat. Commerce U. Ky., Lexington, 1971—; Nimitz prof. polit. Sci. U.S. Naval War Coll., 1970-71; mem. exec. council Inter-Univ. Seminar on Armed Forces and Soc. U. Chgo., 1972—; cons., lectr. in field. Served with Armed Forces, 1952-56. Mem. Internat. Studies Assn. (exec. dir. 1964-71; chmn. intensive panels 1972-74), Am. Polit. Sci. Assn., Am. Assn. U. Profs., A.A.A.S., Internat. Inst. Strategic Studies (London). Author: Postwar Defense Policy and the U.S. Navy, 1943-46, 1966; The Admirals Lobby, 1967; The Politics of Innovation, 1967; The Analysis of International Politics, 1971, also monographs, spl. reports. Editor Sage Profl. Papers in Internat. Studies. Contbr. articles to profl. jours. Address: Patterson Sch Diplomacy and Internat Commerce U Ky Lexington KY 40506

DAVIS, VIRGIL LEON, elec. engr.; b. Nashville, Mar. 30, 1945; s. Jesse Norman and Eleanor Lee (Buck) D.; B.S., David Lipscomb Coll., 1966; B.S. in Elec. Engring., Tenn. Technol. U., 1969; m. Reatha Juelene Savely, Aug. 26, 1967; children—Darla Michelle, Jennifer Dawn. Engr., measurement and instrumentation systems NASA, Kennedy Space Center, Fla., 1969-70, engr., control systems, 1970-73, lead engr., spl. projects staff, 1973—. Mem. Eta Kappa Nu. Home: 240 Cherry Av Merritt Island FL 32952 Office: DE-DEO-1 Kennedy Space Center FL 32899

DAVIS, WALLACE, JR., nuclear chem. engr.; b. Pawtucket, R.I., Dec. 17, 1918; s. Wallace and Alice (Hardman) D.; Sc.B., Brown U., 1941; Ph.D., U. Rochester, 1947; m. Ruth Ellen Butler, Nov. 29, 1942; children—Wallace III, Adrienne (Mrs. Ronald R. Harris), Sharon Lynn. Univ. fellow U. Rochester, 1947; group leader phys. chemistry Oak Ridge Gaseous Diffusion Plant, 1947-58; group leader, chem. engr. nuclear fuels reprocessing Oak Ridge Nat. Lab., 1958-65, nuclear engr. environmental impact analysis, 1966—; guest scientist U.K. Atomic Energy Research Establishment, Harwell, Eng., 1965-66. Tchr. phys. chemistry Oak Ridge Nat. Lab., 1963-65. Fellow A.A.A.S., Am. Inst. Chemists; mem. Am. Chem. Soc. (chmn. E. Tenn. sect. 1970), Sigma Xi. Kiwanian. Contbr. articles to tech. jours., chpts. in books. Home: 601 Florida Av Oak Ridge TN 37830 Office: Oak Ridge Nat Lab Oak Ridge TN 37830

DAVIS, WILBUR MCLAURIN, JR., oral surgeon; b. Orlando, Fla., Sept. 5, 1939; s. Wilbur McLaurin and Emilie May (Haneaur) D.; D.D.S., Emory U., 1964, M.S., 1967; postgrad. U. Pa., 1964-65; m. Roselyn Marie David, Aug. 1, 1964; 1 dau., Mary McLaurin. Resident oral surgery Grady Meml. Hosp., Atlanta, 1965-67; individual practice oral surgery, Orlando, Fla., 1969—. Pres. Orange County Dental Research Dental Clinic, 1971-72. Bd. dirs. Orange County br. Am. Cancer Soc. Served to lt. USNR, 1967-69. Diplomate Am. Bd. Oral Surgeons. Mem. Am., Fla. dental assns., Am., Southeastern socs. oral surgeons, Orange County Dental Soc., Sigma Chi, Psi Omega. Home: 1007 Greentree Dr Winter Park FL 32789 Office: 508 N Mills Av Orlando FL 32803

DAVIS, WILLIAM DUNCAN, JR., physician; b. Brookhaven, Miss., Apr. 4, 1918; s. William Duncan and Jessie (Mounger) D.; B.S., Tulane U., 1939, M.D., 1943; m. Sylvia Saunders, Dec. 3, 1949; children—Cary McLaurin, William Duncan III, Eugene Saunders. Intern, Cleve. City Hosp., 1943-44, resident, 1944-45; joined Ochsner Clinic, New Orleans, 1945, head sect. gastroenterology, 1953—, head dept. internal medicine, 1968—, mem. bd. mgmt., 1963—; v.p., trustee Alton Ochsner Med. Found., 1970—; prof. clinic medicine Tulane U. Mem. subcom. on gastroenterology Surgeon Gen.'s Adv. Com. on Gen. Medicine, 1963-69. Served to comdr. M.C., USNR, 1954-56. Diplomate Am. Bd. Internal Medicine. Fellow A.C.P.; mem. A.M.A., Am. Fedn. Clin. Research, Central Soc. Clin. Research, Am. Assn. Study of Liver Disease, Am. Gastroent. Assn., So. Soc. Clin. Investigation, Am. Soc. Internal Medicine, Phi Beta Kappa, Sigma Xi, Phi Kappa Sigma, Theta Kappa Psi, Alpha Omega Alpha, Omicron Delta Kappa, Kappa Delta Phi. Home: 2129 Palmer Av New Orleans LA 70118 Office: 1514 Jefferson Hwy New Orleans LA 70121

DAVIS, WILLIAM GLENN, JR., orthodontist; b. High Point, N.C., June 28, 1938; s. William Glenn and Hazel (Hicks) D.; B.S., U. N.C., 1956, D.D.S., 1963, M.S., 1967; m. Ann Sherrill, July 29, 1961; children—William Glenn III, Katherine Ann, Ashlyn Lee, Carolyn Kelly. Individual practice orthodontics, Chapel Hill, N.C., 1967—. Lectr., U. N.C., 1967—. Served with USNR, 1963-65. Mem. Am., N.C. dental assns., Am. Assn. Orthodontists, So. Soc. Orthodontists, N.C. State Orthodontic Assn. (v.p. 1969), Phi Beta Kappa, Omicron Kappa Upsilon. Rotarian. Home: 2014 N Lakeshore Dr Chapel Hill NC 27514 Office: Conner Dr Profl Bldg W Willow Dr Chapel Hill NC 27514

DAVIS, WILLIAM PRATHER, designer; b. Waco, Tex., July 30, 1914; s. James Lee and Frances Kirkpatric (Prather) D.; grad. Hill Sch., 1933; ed. U. Tex., 1933-37; m. Rosalie Jenkins, Oct. 15, 1949; 1 son, Donald Benjamin. Farmer, rancher, Waco, 1938-66; pres., Brazos Valley Cotton Oil Co., Waco, 1942-48; pres., owner Braswell-Davis & Assos., Waco, 1946—. Pres. St. Paul's Day Sch. Bd., 1972-73. Trustee J.T. Davis Estate. Fellow Am. Inst. Interior Designers (nat. v.p. 1962-63), C. of C. (chmn. cultural relations com. 1971-72). Episcopalian (sr. warden). Rotarian. Home: Lake Air Tower Waco TX 76710 Office: 701 New Rd Waco TX 76710

DAVIS, WILLIAM ROBERT, physicist, educator; b. Oklahoma City, Aug. 22, 1929; s. Cecil Samuel and Virgie Vanolia (Fowler) D.; B.S., U. Okla., 1953, M.S., 1954; postgrad. U. Gottingen, Germany, 1955-56; Doktor der Naturwissenschaften-Technol. U. Hannover, Germany, 1956; m. Robin Nell Reed, May 21, 1970; 1 son, Eric Reed. Physicist, Trisophia Enterprises, Oklahoma City, 1956-57; asst. prof. physics N.C. State U., Raleigh, 1957-62, asso. prof., 1963-66, prof., 1966—. Cons., Bahnson Co., Inc., Winston Salem, N.C., 1961-66, Lab. for Electronics, Inc. (Tracerlab), Richmond, Cal., 1962-64, NASA Langley Research Center, Hampton, Va., 1969-70, Research Triangle Inst., Durham, N.C., 1966—; pres. Regulus Corp. of Okla., 1957-59. John Simon Guggenheim Meml. Found. fellow, 1970. Fellow Am. Phys. Soc.; mem. Am. Assn. Physics Tchrs., A.A.A.S., Sigma Xi, Sigma Pi Sigma, Pi Mu Epsilon, Tau Beta Pi, Sigma Tau. Author: Classical Fields, Particles and the Theory of Relativity, 1970. Contbr. chpt. to Lanczos Festschrift, 1973. Contbr. articles profl. jours. Home: PO Box 5383 Raleigh NC 27607

DAVIS, WINBORN ELTON, med. facilities cons.; b. Heflin, La., Aug. 26, 1917; s. John Henry and Joanna (McKinney) D.; student La. Poly. Inst., 1935-37; B.A., La. State U., 1940; M.S.W., Tulane U., 1948; m. Edith Claire Causey, Aug. 5, 1940; 1 son, David Michael. Family service supr. U.S. Dept. Agr., Thibodaux, La., 1941-42; social worker VA, Shreveport, La., 1946-47; chief div. mental health La. Dept. of Hosps., Baton Rouge, 1949-51, dir. tng. and research, 1958-61, asst. dir., 1962-63, dir., 1964; asso. prof. mental health Southeastern La. Coll., Hammond, 1952-55; dir. La. Evaluation Center for Exceptional Children, New Orleans, 1956-57; adminstr. Student Health Service, asso. prof. mgmt. La. State U., 1965-70, adminstr. dept. psychiatry Sch. Medicine, 1970-71, asst. dean for adminstrn. Sch. Medicine, 1971-73; lectr. dept. psychiatry Tulane U., 1950—, adj. asso. prof. Sch. Pub. Health, 1970—; mgmt. cons. health facilities, 1957—; spl. cons. U.S. Surgeon Gen., 1964-68. Mem. adv. council La. Commn. on Aging, 1963-66; mem. adv. com. Baton Rouge Family Ct., 1957-61; sec. Gov.'s Com. on Mentally Retarded, 1959-60; sec. State Adv. Com. on Edn. Handicapped, 1950-55. Chmn. adv. council Protestant Childrens Home, 1964-65; dir. Baton Rouge Guidance Center, 1952-54. Trustee La. State Employees Retirement System, 1962-66, chmn., 1964-66; bd. dirs. La. Dept. Hosps. Credit Union. Served to lt. (j.g.) USNR, 1942-45. Mem. Nat. Assn. Social Workers (charter mem., mem. cabinet div. of profl. standards), La. Conf. on Social Welfare (pres. 1961-63), La. Psychiat. Assn., New Orleans Soc. Neurology and Psychiatry (asso.), Nat. Assn. State Mental Health Program Dirs., La. Assn. Mental Health, Am. Coll. Health Assn., La. Hosp. Assn. Democrat. Baptist. Author: (with James A. Knight) Manual for Comprehensive Mental Health Clinics, 1964. Contbr. articles to profl. jours. Home: 5057 Whitehaven St Baton Rouge LA 70808

DAVISON, DENVER N., justice Okla. Supreme Ct.; b. Rich Hill, Mo., Oct. 9, 1891; s. Benjamin P. and Lottie (Jones) D.; LL.B., U. Okla., 1915, J.D., 1973; m. Barbara Wilhelm, July 29, 1917; 1 son, Denver B. (dec.). Practiced law, Coalgate, Okla., 1915-1927, Ada, Okla., 1927-37; mem. Supreme Ct. of Okla., Oklahoma City, 1937—, chief justice on 3 occasions. Mem. original Will Rogers Commn. Served with U.S. Army, World War I. Mem. Alpha Tau Omega, Phi Delta Phi. Elk, Mason, K.P. Home: 1806 Huntington St Oklahoma City OK 73116 Office: State Capital Bldg Oklahoma City OK 73105

DAVISON, FREDERICK CORBET, univ. pres.; b. Atlanta, Sept. 3, 1929; s. Fred C. and Gladys (Carsley) D.; D.V.M., U. Ga., 1952; Ph.D., Ia. State U., 1963; m. Dianne Castle, Sept. 3, 1952; children—Frederick, William C., Anne. Pvt. practice vet. medicine, Marietta, Ga., 1952-58; research asso. Ia. State U., Ames, 1958-59, asst. prof., 1960, asso. inst. for atomic research, 1960; asst. dir. sci. activities Am. Vet. Med. Assn., Chgo., 1963-64; dean sch. vet. medicine U. Ga., Athens, 1964-66; vice chancellor Univ. System Ga., Atlanta, 1966-67; pres. U. Ga. at Athens, 1967—; dir. Clarke Fed. Savs. & Loan Assn. Mem. rural devel. com., exec. com. 6th region Boy Scouts Am.; mem. Council of Synod of Ga. Trustee Rabun Gap-Nacoochee Sch. Mem. Am. (council on biol. and therapeutic agts.), Ga. vet. med. assns., Inst. Lab. Animal Research of Nat. Acad. Scis., Nat. Com. on Pharmacy and Vet. Medicine, Sigma Xi, Phi Kappa Phi, Sigma Alpha Epsilon, Omega Tau Sigma, Alpha Zeta, Phi Zeta, Gamma Sigma Delta. Contbr. articles to profl. jours. Home: 570 Prince Av Athens GA 30601 Office: U Ga Athens GA 30601

DAVISON, JOSEPH WADE, petroleum co. exec.; b. Kansas City, Kan., Nov. 14, 1921; s. Elmer Joseph and Lucile (Ranney) Davison; B.S., U. Kan., 1943; m. Leatha Belle Sanford, Feb. 3, 1951; children—Teresa Ann, Diane Leslie. With Phillips Petroleum Co., Bartlesville, Okla., 1943—, mgr. process evaluation, research and devel. dept., 1957-64, dir. process devel., research and devel. dept., 1965-69, dir. rubber, carbon black and polyolefine, research and devel. dept., 1969-71, vice chmn. operating com., 1971-73, chmn. operating com., 1973—. Served with USNR, 1946-48. Mem. Am. Inst. Chem. Engrs. Home: 1205 Oakdale Dr Bartlesville OK 74003 Office: Phillips Bldg Phillips Petroleum Co Bartlesville OK 74004

DAVISON, THOMAS III, lawyer; b. Scranton, Pa., Mar. 16, 1923; s. Thomas and Ann (Kellaway) D.; A.A., Keystone Jr. Coll., 1943; A.B., Bucknell U., 1945; J.D., U. Miami, 1949; m. Virginia M. Seymour, May 23, 1952; 1 son, Thomas IV. Admitted to Fla. bar, 1949; title officer Land Title Co., Coral Gables, 1949-52; practiced law, Miami, 1952-55, Coral Gables, 1955—; mem. firm Padgett, Teasley, Niles & Davison, and predecessor firm, 1955—. Dir. Coll. Law, U. Miami Alumni. Mem. Am., Dade County, Coral Gables (pres. 1961-62) bar assns., Fla. Bar, U. Miami Alumni Assn. (dir., pres.), U. Miami Law Sch. Alumni Assn. (pres.), Lambda Chi Alpha. Republican. Mem. Christian Ch. (elder, chmn. bd.). Mason, Kiwanian (pres. Coral Gables club). Club: Riviera Country. Home: 1436 Ancona Av Coral Gables FL 33146 Office: 2505 Ponce de Leon Blvd Coral Gables FL 33134

DAVISSON, NELSON MARC, dentist, army officer; b. Winchester, Ind., Sept. 16, 1938; s. Ray Marcus and Garnet Rebecca (Addington) D.; A.B., DePauw U., 1960; D.D.S., Ind. U., 1964; m. Patricia Ann Crossen, Aug. 24, 1963; children—George William Tennis, Lani Catherine. Commd. capt. U.S. Army, 1964, advanced through grades to lt. col., 1973; practice dentistry, Ft. Gordon, Ga., 1964-68, Viet-Nam, 1968-69, Fort Sam Houston, Tex., 1969-70; asst. chief crown and bridge service Walter Reed Hosp., Washington, 1971-72; chief crown and bridge dental detachment, Ft. Leavenworth, Kan., 1972—. Decorated Bronze Star. Mem. Am. Dental Assn., V.F.W., Psi Omega. Mem. Ch. of Jesus Christ of Latter-day Saints (elder 1971—). Home: 717 Virginia St Dunedin FL 33528 Office: Dental Activities MEDDAC Fort Leavenworth KS 66027

DAWES, CHARLES EDWARD, mfg. co. exec.; b. Peoria, Okla., Feb. 7, 1923; s. Charles Gates and Lottie (Nonkesis) D.; A.A., Joplin (Mo.) Jr. Coll., 1950; B.S., U. Ark., 1953; m. Lorraine Mercer, Apr. 16, 1948; children—Charla Rene, Kevin Lawrence. Mgr. mfg. Vickers, Inc., Joplin, 1953-57; sales engr. Sebastian Diesel Co., Joplin, 1957-59; gen. mgr. Duplex Mfg. Co., Ft. Smith, Ark., 1959—. Chief, Ottawa Indians of Okla. Pres., bd. dirs. Abilities Unlimited, Inc.; bd. dirs., mem. exec. com. Ft. Smith United Fund; mem. adv. bd. Seneca Indian Sch. Served with USAAF, 1943-46. Mem. Am. Soc. Tool and Mech. Engrs., Ft. Smith C. of C. (dir.), Personnel Assn. N.W. Ark., Western Ark. Purchasing Assn., Nat. Congress Am. Indians, Okla. Inter-Tribal Council. Republican. Presbyn. Mason. Home: 2010 Wolfe Lane Fort Smith AR 72901 Office: 1415 N 32d St Fort Smith AR 72901

DAWN, FREDERIC SHINYUAN, aerospace engr., govt. ofcl.; b. Wusih, Kiangsu, China, Nov. 24, 1914; s. Yung Tsien and Yufu (Yufu) D.; B.S., Kwang Hwa U., 1934; B.S. in Textile Engring., Inst. Tech., 1936, D.Sc. 1949; postgrad. Lowell Technol. Inst., 1938; M.S. in Textile Engring., U. N.C., 1939; postgrad. in plastic tech. U. Wis., 1956; D.Sc., Nat. Acad. Scis. Republic China, 1967; m. Marie Dunn, Oct. 1, 1934; children—Robert C., William S., Victoria W. Came to U.S., 1951, naturalized, 1961. Chmn. dept. textile engring. Nantung U., 1939-42, China Inst. Agr. and Textiles, 1942-43, Shanghai Inst. Tech., 1943-45, Shanghai Municipal Inst. Tech., 1946-49; v.p. China Inst. Tech., 1946-48, pres., 1948-50; v.p., dir. Standard Plastics Corp., 1940-50, China Chem. and Pharm. Co., 1941-50, China Gen. Import & Export Co., 1941-50, Kai Yuan Textile Mfg. Co., 1946-50, China Indsl. Devel. Corp., 1946-50; gen. mgr. Yih Hsing Textile Mfg. Corp., 1939-45; tech. dir. China Textile Industries, Inc., 1946-49; cons. textile and allied industries for S.E. Asian and S.Am. countries, 1951-54; lab. dir. Decar Plastic Corp., Middleton, Wis., 1956-60; sr. research engr. Aero. Systems div. U.S. Air Force, Wright-Patterson AFB, O., 1960-62; aerospace engr. Manned Spacecraft Center, NASA, Houston, 1962-64, chief materials lab., 1964-69, dir. materials research, 1969—. Mem. adv. com. Ministry Econ. Affairs, Ministry Agr. and Forestry, Ministry Edn., Ministry Industry, 1946-49; mem. Bd. Profl. Certification Exam., Yuan, 1946-49. Bd. dirs. Dawn Found., St. Luke's Hosp. Recipient various citations and award from Chinese govt. agys., NASA, also indsl. and ednl. orgns. on indsl. and ednl. devel. programs. Registered profl. engr., Tex. Fellow Am. Inst. Chemists, Am. Ordnance Assn.; mem. Am. Chem. Soc., N.Y. Acad. Scis., Am. Inst. Aeros and Astronautics, Internat. Platform Assn., A.A.A.S., Soc. Plastics Engrs., Am. Soc. M.E., Nat. Soc. Profl. Engrs., Soc. Aerospace Materials and Processes Engrs., Phi Lambda. Methodist. Mason (32 deg., Shriner). Club: Optimist (Madison, Wis.). Contbr. numerous articles profl. jours. Patentee textiles, plastics and machinery fields. Home: 1615 Richvale Lane Houston TX 77058 Office: Manned Spacedreft Center NASA Houston TX 77058

DAWSON, AMOS COUNCIL, ednl. adminstr.; b. Jacksonville, N.C., Sept. 9, 1915; s. Amos Council and Emma (Raynor) D.; A.B., Atlantic Christian Coll., 1937; M.A., U. N.C., 1954; LL.D., Atlantic Christian Coll., 1955; m. Margaret Virginia Hilburn, July 19, 1941; children—Donna (Mrs. James Van Ness IV), Amos Council III, Linda, Pamela. Tchr. Southern Pines (N.C.) High Sch., 1937-39, prin., 1939-51; supt. schs., Southern Pines, 1951-59; exec. sec. N.C. Edn. Assn., 1959-70; exec. sec. N.C. Assn. Educators, 1970—. Dir. Horace

Mann Ins. Cos.; chmn. bd. Horace Mann Mut. Ins. Co. Trustee Nat. Edn. Assn. Ins. Trust Mem. Am. Assn. Sch. Adminstrs., Horace Mann League, Nat. Assn. State Pres. and Exec. Secs., N.C. Edn. Assn. (acting pres. 1947-48, pres. 1948-49, state chmn. legislative com. 1949, 1951, 1955, 57), Nat. Council State Edn. Assns. (pres. 1968-69). Home: 2104 Barfield Ct Raleigh NC 27602 Office: NC Assn Educators Raleigh NC 27602

DAWSON, DAVID FLEMING, mathematician, educator; b. Denton, Tex., Sept. 16, 1926; s. William Augustus and Carrie Lurlein (Fleming) D.; B.S., North Tex. State U., 1947, M.S., 1948; Ph.D., U. Tex., Austin, 1957; m. Mildred Catherine McCarty, June 5, 1948; children—Dan, David, Sharon, Donald, John, Catherine. Asst. prof. U. Mo., 1957-59; mem. faculty North Tex. State U., Denton, 1959—, prof. math., 1964—. Mem. Civic Fund Com., 1970—. Served with USNR, 1951-53. Mem. Am., London math. socs., Tex. Acad. Sci. Contbr. articles to profl. jours. Home: 1015 Ector St Denton TX 76201

DAWSON, EARL BLISS, educator; b. Perry, Fla., Feb. 1, 1930; s. Bliss and Linnie (Callaham) D.; B.A., U. Kan., 1955; student Bowman Gray Sch. Medicine, 1955-57; M.A., U. Mo., 1960; Ph.D., Tex. A. & M. U., 1964; m. Winnie Ruth Isbell, Apr. 10, 1951; children—Barbara Gail, Patricia Ann, Robert Earl, Diana Lynn. Research instr. dept. obstetrics and gynecology U. Tex. Med. br., Galveston, 1963-67, asst. prof., 1967-70, asso. prof., 1970—; cons. Interdeptl. com. on Nutrition for Nat. Defense, 1965-68; cons. Nat. Nutrition Survey, 1968-69. Served with USNR, 1951-52. Nutrition Research fellow, 1960-61; NSF scholar, 1961-62; Nat. Insts. Health Research fellow, 1962-63. Mem. Am. Chem. Soc., Tex., N.Y. acad. scis., A.A.A.S., Am. Inst. Physicists, Am. Inst. Nutrition, Am. Soc. Clin. Nutrition, Soc. Environmental Geochemistry and Health, Sigma Xi, Phi Rho Sigma. Baptist. Mason. Club: Mic-O-Say (Kansas City, Mo.). Contbr. numerous articles to profl. jours. Home: 15 Chimney Corners LaMarque TX 77568 Office: Dept Obstetrics and Gynecology U Tex Med Br Galveston TX 77550

DAWSON, FRANCES TRIGG (MRS. CARL H. DAWSON), author, lectr.; b. Chesterfield County, S.C., Oct. 31, 1901; d. John Wilson and Frances (Harris) Warr; B.A., Western Res. U., 1947; M.S., N.C. U., 1957; Ed.D., N.C. State U., 1969; m. Harry E. Trigg, June 18, 1918 (dec. Nov. 1929); children—Margaret Alice (Mrs. Margaret Sanderson), Harry Edward, Virginia Mae (Mrs. J.P. Ellington); m. 2d, Carl Horn Dawson, Apr. 6, 1946. Social worker Colo. Emergency Relief Adminstrn., Denver, 1929-30, asst. state supr., 1930-32; asst. dir. edn. Dept. Vocational Edn., Denver, 1932-37; supr. Vocational and Adult Edn., Wilmington, N.C., 1937-43; spl. rep. U.S. Office Edn., Washington, 1943-45; chief personnel counselor Office Indsl. Relations Dept. Navy, Washington, 1945-47; dir., supr. Vocational and Adult Edn., Burlington, N.C., 1947-67. State treas. League Women Voters N.C., 1967-69, state pres., 1969-73; mem. Gov.'s Com. on State Govt. Reorgn., 1970-72; mem. curriculum study com. State Dept. Pub. Instrn. N.C., 1969-73; mem. N.C. Adv. Com. on Pub. Edn., 1970—, also mem. exec. com. Named Mother-of-Yr., 1958. Mem. Am. Assn. U. Women (br. pres. 1952-54, 63-64), N.C. Vocational Assn. (sec. 1938-40), N.C. Ednl. Assn. (pres. Burlington unit 1948-49), Am. Acad. Polit. and Social Sci., Bus. and Profl. Womens Club (pres. Burlington 1952-54), Altrusa Internat. (dist. gov., mem. internat. bd. dirs. 1958-62). Methodist (supt. young peoples div. Sunday sch. 1949-53). Author: (with Earl M. Bowler) Counseling Employees, 1945; More Efficient Use of Women In Industry, 1943; The Job Of The Counselor, 1943; Training Counselors, 1944; The Relationship of Satisfaction of Service Club Members to Perception of Club Management Systems; also pamphlets, brochures. Home: PO Box 505 Elon Coll NC 27244

DAWSON, JACK, asso. supt. schs.; b. Bloomfield, Ky., July 11, 1906; s. Charles B. and Agnes (Allen) D.; A.B., Georgetown Coll., 1930; M.A., U. Louisville, 1948; m. Allice Scott, June 21, 1933. With Jefferson County Sch. System, Louisville, 1931—, adminstr., 1954-60, asso. supt., 1960—. Mem. adv. com. Croft Sch. Bus. Service, New London, Conn., 1966—. Bd. dirs. YMCA, 1962-70. Served with USNR, 1942-45. Mem. High Sch. Prins. Assn. (past pres.), Ky. High Sch. Adminstrs. Assn. (bd. control 1952-61), Pi Kappa Alpha. Mason, Rotarian (pres. St. Matthews 1972-73). Clubs: Middletown, St. Matthews. Home: 100 Bellemeade Rd Louisville KY 40222 Office: 3332 Newburg Rd Louisville KY 40218

DAWSON, JAMES PAUL, real estate co. exec.; b. Cloud Chief, Okla., Jan. 19, 1903; s. William David and Mary (Martin) D.; teaching certificate Central State Coll., 1924; m. Martha Vandivere, June 13, 1942. Tchr. Cool Br. sch., Carter County, Okla., 1921, prin. Washington High Sch., 1923-24; P.O. clk., San Diego and Atlanta, 1930-47; salesman Southwest Text Book div. Prentice Hall Inc., Dallas, 1947-51, salesman Addressograph Corp., Atlanta, 1952-54; real estate and securities sales, 1955-68; pres. Southern Planning Co., Atlanta, 1969-71; exec. v.p. Camelot of Ga., Inc., 1972—; instr. Clemson U., 1962—. Dist. Sec. Democratic Party, 1971-72. Served with USMCR, 1927, AUS, 1942-43. Mem. Christian Ch. (life elder emeritus, lay minister 1964-69). Mason. Home: 310 Westchester Dr Decatur GA 30030 Office: 1670 NE Expressway NE Atlanta GA 30329

DAWSON, JERRY FLOYD, coll. dean; b. Borger, Tex., Dec. 28, 1933; s. Frank Alden and Nellena (Gibson) D.; student Wayland Bapt. Coll., 1952-54; B.A., Miss. Coll., 1956; M.A., U. Tex., 1958, Ph.D., 1964; m. Margie Jo Clements, June 21, 1952; children—Kim Alden, Carey Austin, Jamie Lynn. Head history dept. Wayland Bapt. Coll., Plainview, Tex., 1960-68; asso. prof. history Tex. A. and M. U., College Station, 1968-71; dean Grad. Sch., prof. history S.W. Tex. State U., San Marcos, 1971—. Chmn. drive United Fund Hays County, 1973. Bd. dirs. A.R.C., Hays County, Tex. Alcohol-Narcotics Edn.; trustee San Marcos Acad. Mem. Conf. Borderlands (gen. dir. 1972—), Southwestern Social Sci. Assn., Conf. Faith and History, Am. Studies Assn. Tex., So. Conf. Grad. Deans, Tex. Assn. Grad. Deans. Author: Friedrich Schleiermacher: The Evolution of a Nationalist, 1966; Folktales and Footprints: Stories from the Old World, 1973. Asst. editor Rocky Mountain Social Sci. Jour., 1967-72; editor Rocky Mountain Social Sci. Newsletter, 1967-72. Home: 220 N Johnson St San Marcos TX 78666

DAWSON, JOHN LEO, JR., hardwood lumber co. exec.; b. Louisville, May 3, 1922; s. John Leo and Omega (Fitzhugh) D.; S.B. in Naval Architecture and Marine Engring., Mass. Inst. Tech., 1944; postgrad. U. Louisville, 1966-72; m. Mary Jane Rehm, June 23, 1945; children—John Leo III, Enid Rehm. With Dawson Lumber Co., Louisville, 1946-50, 53—, chmn. bd., pres., 1953—; sales and gen. mgr. Christian Lumber Co., Monticello, Ky., 1950-52. Mem. Louisville and Jefferson County Planning and Zoning Bd. Adjustment and Appeals, 1962-65, chmn., 1965. Mem. M.I.T. Ednl. Council, 1963-73. Served to lt., USNR, 1942-46. Registered profl. engr., Ky. Mem. Nat. Wholesale Lumber Distbg. Yard Assn. (pres. 1971-72), So. Hardwood Traffic Assn. (pres. 1972-73), Nat. Hardwood Lumber Assn. (dir. 1973—), Louisville Area C. of C., Ky. Soc. Profl. Engrs., Soc. Naval Architects and Marine Engrs., Delta Kappa Epsilon. Episcopalian. Mason (Shriner). Clubs: M.I.T. of Kentucky (pres. 1967), Louisville Boat, Glendale Flying. Home: 7913 Westover Dr Prospect KY 40059 Office: Box 8305 Station E Louisville KY 40208

DAWSON, THOMAS HENRY, educator; b. Fredericksburg, Va., Oct. 13, 1940; s. Bryant Kitching and Pauline Mabel (Lewis) D.; B.S., Va. Poly. Inst. and State U., 1963; M.S., Johns Hopkins, 1965, Ph.D., 1968; m. Lois Stevens, Sept. 16, 1969; 1 dau., Tamalyn. Physicist U.S. Naval Weapons Lab., Dahlgren, Va., 1963-68; asst. prof. civil engring. U. Va., 1968—; cons. U.S. Army Fgn. Sci. and Tech. Center; dir. U.S. Navy research contracts. Whitehead fellow, 1964, 68; NASA fellow, 1965-68; recipient Nat. Sci. Found. research grant, 1970-72. Mem. A.A.A.S., Va. Acad. Sci., Sigma Xi. Contbr. articles prof. jours. Home: 505 Nottingham Rd Charlottesville VA 22901

DAWSON, WILLIAM JOHN, cons. engr.; b. Batesville, Ark., Feb. 12, 1925; s. Allie Raphael and Mary (Smith) D.; B.S., La. State U., 1952; m. Madge Kenny, Sept. 2, 1950; children—Donna Louise, William John, Mary Ann, David Charles. Cons. engr., pres. Dawson Engrs., Inc., Baton Rouge, 1954—. Served with USMCR, 1942-46. Mem. Am. Soc. C.E. Home: 7623 Bocage Blvd Baton Rouge LA 70809 Office: 5700 Florida Blvd Baton Rouge LA 70806

DAWSON, WILLIAM SIDNEY, JR., physician; b. West Logan, W.Va., July 2, 1932; s. William Sidney and Mary Elizabeth (Bratton) D.; B.A., Berea Coll., 1954; M.D., W.Va. U. and Med. Coll. Va., 1961; m. Sylvia Copley, Jan. 13, 1961; children—William Sidney III, John Stuart, Mary Elizabeth. Intern, Mound Park Hosp., St. Petersburg, Fla., 1961-62; gen. practice medicine, Fremont, N.C., 1962-66; partner with E.B. Aycock, Greenville, N.C., 1966—; mem. staff Pitt County Meml. Hosp., Greenville, N.C. Charter mem. E. Carolina U. Found., Greenville, 1968-69. Served with AUS, 1954-56. Mem. A.M.A., Med. Soc. N.C., Pitt County Med. Soc. Methodist. Home: 203 King George Rd Greenville NC 27834 Office: 210 W 4th St Greenville NC 27834

DAWSON, WINTER WOOD, dentist; b. Cary, Miss., Oct. 1, 1908; s. Walter Putnam and Carrie (Byerly) D.; student Miss. State U., 1926-28; D.D.S., U. Tenn., 1932; m. Helen Virginia Moore, Aug. 3, 1935; children—Thomas Winter, Helen Virginia. Gen. practice dentistry, Brooksville, Miss., 1932-38, Meridian, Miss., 1938—. Served with USNR, 1942-46. Fellow Internat. Coll. Dentists; mem. Pierre Fauchard Acad., Miss., Am. dental assns., Psi Omega, Omicron Kappa Upsilon. Methodist. Rotarian. Home: 2214 39th St Meridian MS 39301 Office: 601 22d Av Meridian MS 39301

DAY, CHARLES RICHARD, architect; b. Johnson City, Tenn., Oct. 1, 1933; s. John Harvey and Nannie (Byrd) D.; B.S. in Architecture, U. Cin., 1957; m. Rebecca Louise Wyatt, Dec. 28, 1968; children—Charles Franklin, Richard Wyatt. Draftsman, Beeson & Beeson, architects, Johnson City, 1960-63; architect, partner, Abingdon, Va., 1963—. Washington County chmn. March of Dimes, 1962, Heart Fund, 1965-69; mem. citizens adv. com. Va. Highlands Community Coll., 1969-72. Served to lt. USAF, 1958-60. Mem. Jr. C. of C. (v.p. 1961-63). Presbyn. Rotarian (past pres.). Clubs: Washington County Sportsman's Abingdon. Prin. archtl. works include: Mchts. and Farmers Bank, Galax, Va.; addition to Johnston Meml. Hosp., Abingdon; YMCA Bldg., Bristol, Tenn.-Va.; Service Bldg. Appalachian Power Co., Abingdon; E.B. Stanley Elementary Sch., Abingdon. Home: 179 Hillside Dr Abingdon VA 24210 Office: Lee Hwy PO Box 650 Abingdon VA 24210

DAY, DON, broadcasting co. exec.; b. Sherman, Tex., May 15, 1939; s. Robert Eugene and Georgia Pauline (Sheridan) D.; grad. high sch.; m. Nancie Marie Baldwin, Apr. 27, 1973; children by previous marriage—Lisa, Charles, Sissy, Walt, Sheri, Steven, Holly. With KTXO Radio, Sherman, Tex., 1959, KDSX Radio, Sherman, 1959, 66-68, KXOL Radio, Ft. Worth, 1960, 62-66, WMPS Radio, Memphis, 1961, KFJZ Radio, Ft. Worth, 1968-70; with WBAP Radio, Ft. Worth, 1970—, operations mgr., 1971—. Named Country Music Program Dir., Billboard Mag., 1971. Home: 3529 Westfield Fort Worth TX 76133 Office: 3900 Barnett Fort Worth TX 76101

DAY, MELVIN SHERMAN, govt. exec.; b. Lewiston, Me., Jan. 22, 1923; s. Israel and Frances (Goldberg) D.; B.S., Bates Coll., 1943; postgrad. U. Tenn., 1953-54; m. Annette Barbara Berman, Feb. 8, 1948; children—Cynthia, Wendy, Robert. Chemist, Metal Hydrides, Inc., 1943-44, Tenn. Eastman Corp., 1944-46; sci. analyst AEC, 1946-49, asst. chief tech. information service extension, 1950-56, chief, 1956-58, dir. office of tech. information, 1958-60; dep. dir. Office of Tech. Information and ednl. program NASA, 1960-61, dir. Office Sci. and Tech. Information, 1961-67, dep. asst. adminstr. for tech. utilization, 1967-70, chmn., 1967-69; head Office Sci. Information NSF, Washington, 1970-72; dep. dir. Nat. Library Medicine, Dept. Health, Edn. and Welfare, 1972—. Cons. IAEA, 1959-60, OECD, 1970, Ford Found., 1973-74; mem. documentation com. AGARDNATO, 1960-70; chmn. adv. bd. Sci. Information Exchange, 1963-68; chmn. com. on sci. and tech. information Fed. Council, 1970-72; mem. adv. bd. CAS, 1965-67; mem. Com. on Intergovtl. Sci. Relations; chmn. Environmental Quality Information Panel OECD, 1970—; mem. com. libraries, documentation and archives UNESCO, 1971—, del. intergovtl. conf., 1971, conf. human environment, 1972; mem. panel tech. information for developing countries Nat. Acad. Scis., 1971-72, mem. panel transp. research, 1972; mem. Fed. Library Com., 1969-72, chmn. exec. adv. com., 1973—. Bd. dirs. Smithsonian Sci. Information Exchange, 1972; trustee Found. Center, 1972—. Served with AUS, 1944-46. Recipient Sustained Superior Performance award AEC, 1960; Exceptional Service medal NASA, 1970. Mem. Am. Chem. Soc., Am. Soc. Information Service, A.A.A.S., N.Y. Acad. Scis., Med. Library Assn., D.C. Library Assn., Am. Soc. Information Sci., Spl. Libraries Assn., Nat. Microfilm Assn. Clubs: Nat. Space, Nat. Aviation, Internat. (Washington). Home: 7805 Beech Tree Rd Bethesda MD 20034 Office: 8600 Rockville Pike Bethesda MD 20014

DAY, ROBERT EMMETT, optometrist; b. Van Alsteyne, Tex., May 19, 1924; s. Emmett Vester and Louise (Maphis) D.; B.S., N.Tex. State U., 1947; Dr. Optometry, So. Coll. Optometry, 1949; postgrad. U. Houston, 1971-73; m. Sarah Elizabeth Kelsey, Aug. 1, 1947; children—Robert Emmett, Cynthia Beth. Pvt. practice optometry, Garland, Tex., 1950—. Pres., Garland Jr. C. of C., 1954, Garland Band and Choral Booster, 1966; v.p. Garland Tennis Assn., 1967; mem. State Commn. for Blind, 1972-73, chmn. optometric adv. com., 1974—. chmn. A.R.C. drive, 1952, March of Dimes, 1953. Vice pres., mem. Garland Sch. Bd., 1951-58, Dallas County Sch. Bd., 1968—; chmn. Park Bd., City of Garland, 1954-56; State chmn. for optometrists Preston Smith for Gov., 1968; Garland chmn. Senator Lloyd Bentson of U.S. Senate, 1970. Bd. dirs. Found. for Edn. and Research in Vision. Served with USAAF, 1943-46. Fellow Am. Acad. Optometry; mem. Am. (pres., past v.p., dir. depts., com. chmn., trustee), Tex. (dir., pres., chmn. bd., com. chmn., Distinguished Service award 1970) optometric assns., Tex. Optometric Found. (dir.), N.Tex. Optometric Soc. (past pres., com. chmn.), Garland C. of C. (past pres., dir.), Am. Contract Bridge League, Alpha Phi Omega, Beta Sigma Kappa. Methodist (ofcl. bd.). Mason (32 deg.), Lion. Club: Pleasant Valley (pres. 1950). Contbr. articles profl. jours. Home: 706 Carroll Dr Garland TX 75041 Office: 3034 Broadway Garland TX 75041

DAY, STEPHEN MARTIN, physicist, educator; b. N.Y.C., Dec. 17, 1931; s. James V., Jr., and Mildred Elinor (Forbes) D.; B.S., La. State U., 1957; M.A., Rice U., 1959, Ph.D., 1961; m. Sara Shinault, Jan. 24, 1953; children—Linda Carol (Mrs. Larry Garriot), Sandra Karen, Jeffrey Shinault, Marcus Forbes, Stephen Martin, Mary Kathleen. Asst. prof. physics U. Ark., Fayetteville, 1961-66, asso. prof., 1966-70, prof., 1970—, chmn. dept., 1968—. Teaching fellow U. Nottingham, Eng., 1967-68. Vice chmn. Washington County Republican Com., 1963-65; mem. Ark. Rep. Platform Com., 1964. Mem. pres.'s council Subiaco Acad., 1966-69. Served with USAF, 1950-54. Mem. Ark. Acad. Sci. (chmn. physics sect.), Am. Phys. Soc., Am. Assn. Physics Tchrs., Phi Kappa Phi, Sigma Pi Sigma. Club: Fayetteville Country. Home: 112 W Sycamore St Fayetteville AR 72701

DEABLER, HERDIS LEROY, clin. psychologist, educator; b. Howell, Mich., Jan. 27, 1910; s. John S. and Mary (Dunkelberger) D.; A.B., N. Central Coll., 1931; Ph.D. Lucinda Bidwell Beebe fellow, Boston U., 1936; m. Oleva Gingrich, Sept. 12, 1933; children—Donna Jean (Mrs. Donna J. DuRant), JoAnn (Mrs. Frank E. Crawford), Herdis LeRoy, Mary Elizabeth (Mrs. Fredric William Corwin Jr.). Personnel dir. N. Central Coll., 1936-45, asst. prof., 1937-40, asso. prof., 1940-43, prof. psychology, 1943-45, prof., head dept., 1946-49; sr. counselor, asst. prof. psychology U. Minn., 1945-46; chief clin. psychologist VA Hosp., Gulfport, Miss., 1949-60; asst. prof. psychology, coordinator Gulf Coast Extension Center, U. Miss., Gulfport, 1951-60; area chief psychologist VA Area Med. Office, Boston, 1960-64; asso. prof. psychology State Coll. Boston, 1963-67; chief clin. psychologist VA Outpatient Clinic, Boston, 1964-67; extension asst. prof. psychology Boston U., 1966-67; chief psychology service VA Hosp., New Orleans, 1967—; clin. asso. prof. dept. neurology and psychiatry Tulane U. Sch. Medicine, New Orleans, 1967—; clin. prof. psychology La. State U., New Orleans, 1970—. Vis. lectr. psychology La. State U. Sch. Medicine, New Orleans, 1957-60; vis. prof. psychology Tulane U., 1968—. Pres., Citizens Scholarship Found., Hingham, Mass., 1965-67. Diplomate Am. Bd. Examiners in Profl. Psychology. Mem. La. Psychol. Assn. (chmn. bd. profl. affairs 1968—). Home: 6509 Center St New Orleans LA 70124 Office: 1601 Perdido St New Orleans LA 70140

DEAL, CARL HOSEA, JR., chemist, petroleum refining co. exec.; b. Spartanburg, S.C., Dec. 26, 1919; s. Carl Hosea and Caroline Jane (Rhodes) D.; B.S., Duke, 1942, Ph.D. in Chemistry, 1944; m. Virginia Betty Zerfass, Apr. 15, 1944; children—Julia Z., Carl H., Milton Z., Nicolaas R. Chemist, Shell Devel. Co., Emeryville, Cal., 1944-55, supr., 1956-62, supr., 1963-72, sr. staff research chemist, Houston, 1972—, also supr. separation processes; exchange scientist Royal Dutch Shell Labs., Amsterdam, The Netherlands, 1962-63. Mem. Am. Chem. Soc., Phi Beta Kappa, Sigma Xi. Contbr. articles to sci. publs. Patentee in field. Home: 5 Lazee Trail Houston TX 77024 Office: PO Box 481 Houston TX 77001

DEAN, ALINE HONEYCUTT (MRS. JOHN FOSTER DEAN), trucking co. exec.; b. Corinth, Miss., Aug. 1, 1906; d. William Lee and Maude (Ellington) Honeycutt; grad. high sch.; m. John Foster Dean, Sept. 7, 1924; 1 son, John Foster. Bookkeeper, McRae Hosp., Corinth, Miss., 1923-24; pvt. sec. Corinth (Miss.) Machinery, 1924-25; co-founder Dean Truck Line, Corinth, Miss., 1935—; pres. Dean Truck Line, Inc., 1956-66, chmn. bd., 1966—; pres. Miss. Warehouse Corp., Corinth, 1964—; chmn. bd. Debbin Co., Corinth. Bd. dirs. Boys Club, Corinth, 1970—. Methodist (mem. finance com. 1970—, mem. ofcl. bd. 1971—). Mem. D.A.R. Mem. Order Eastern Star. Home: Shiloh Rd Corinth MS 38834 Office: Fulton Dr Corinth MS 38834

DEAN, BOB WESLEY, mech. engr.; b. Birmingham, Ala., Aug. 6, 1924; s. Robert Leon and Gertrude (Griffith) D.; B.Mech. Engring., Auburn U., 1945; M.S. in Engring., U. Ala., 1948; m. Martha Stone Grace, July 15, 1944; children—Robert Allbritton, Elizabeth Cary, Thomas Wesley, DeForest DeSha, David Bryant. Various positions, 1948-52; mfrs. rep. F. J. Evans Engring. Co., Atlanta, 1952-57; design engr. Robert & Co., Atlanta, 1957-62; with Mallory & Evans, Inc., Scottdale, Ga., 1962—, v.p., project engr., 1965—; asso. Mech. Engring., Inc., Scottdale, Ga., 1965-70. Mem. State Ga. Bd. Examiners Warm Air Heating Contractors, 1970—. Registered profl. engr., Ind., Pa., Cal., Miss., Ala., Ga., Fla., Tenn., S.C., N.C., Neb., N.Y., Va., Ky., Del., Minn., Ark. Mem. Am. Soc. Heating, Refrigeration and Air Conditioning Engrs. (chpt. pres. 1963-64). Home: 760 Old New York Rd NE Atlanta GA 30342 Office: 646 Kentucky St Scottdale GA 30079

DEAN, CHARLES ALBERT, JR., elec. engr.; b. Stockton, Cal., Sept. 9, 1921; s. Charles Albert and Vera Lenore (Benefiel) D.; A.A., Sacramento City Coll., 1942; B.S., U. Cal. at Berkeley, 1947; m. Ida Sue Gilliam, June 14, 1958; children—Julia Ann, Jennifer Kay. With Pacific Gas & Electric Co., Sacramento, 1947-64, domestic sales field supr., 1963-64; sr. power sales engr. Pub. Service Co. Okla., Tulsa, 1964—. Lectr. seminars. Chmn. speakers bur. United Crusade, Sacramento, 1955. Served to lt. USNR, 1943-46. Recipient Recognition award I.E.E.E., 1958; Key award Sacramento Jr. C. of C., 1953. Registered profl. engr., Okla., Tex., Cal. Mem. Illuminating Engring. Soc. (chmn. oil capital sect. 1971-72), I.E.E.E., Engrs. Soc. Tulsa (pres. 1972-73). Presbyn. (elder 1957—). Mason (worshipful master 1955). Contbr. articles in field to profl. jours. Home: 5386 S 74th E Av Tulsa OK 74145

DEAN, CHARLES EARLE, translation editor; b. nr. Central, S.C., May 23, 1898; s. Charles Lewis and Eloise (Earle) D.; A.B., Harvard, 1921; M.A., Columbia U., 1923; Ph.D., Johns Hopkins U., 1927; m. Mildred Caroline Waters, Sept. 10, 1927; children—Robert Waters, Margaret Lewis (Mrs. Robert Morris Vogel). Tech. asst. Bell Tel. Labs., N.Y.C., 1921-24; various positions including cons. engr. Hazeltine Corp., Little Neck, N.Y., 1929-63; translation editor Scripta Pub. Corp., Washington, 1964—. Mem. Am. Civil Liberties Union, Americans for Democratic Action. Fellow I.E.E.E., Radio Club of Am.; mem. Wash. Ethical Soc. Co-editor book Principles of Color Television, 1956. Home: 115 Sherman Av Takoma Park MD 20012 Office: 1511 K St NW Washington DC 20005

DEAN, CLAY HUTCHINSON, state ofcl.; b. Moultrie, Ga., July 23, 1917; s. Clay Lehman and Chloe Fay (Hutchinson) D.; B.S. in Civil Engring., Auburn U., 1938; M.S., Harvard, 1948; postgrad. Oxford (Eng.) U., 1943, U. Ala., 1965; m. Vickie Wilkerson, July 30, 1938; children—Vickie Fay (Mrs. E. C. Missildine), Joseph Clay. Draftsman Ala. Hwy. Dept., Montgomery, 1938; sanitation officer Clay County Health Dept., Ashland, Ala., 1938-41; with Ala. Dept. Health, Montgomery, 1941—, distr. engr. sanitation bur., 1941-42, asst. san. engr. bur. sanitation, 1945-47, dir. hosp. planning div., 1948-65, dir. bur. health facilities constrn., 1966—. Mem. Ala. Adv. Council Rehab. Facilities, 1968-72, Ala. Adv. Council Sheltered Workshops, 1968-72, Gov.'s Ad Hoc Com. Comprehensive Cancer Control, 1969-72, planning com. U. Ala. Med. Center, 1968-73, Ala. Planning and Adv. Council of Developmental Disabilities Act, 1971-73, nat. com. health services data collection USPHS, 1970-72, nat. states plans adv. council, 1971-72. Active Boy Scouts Am., Montgomery. Served to 1st lt., AUS, 1942-45; ETO, maj. Res. ret. Registered profl. engr., land surveyor, Ala. Mem. Am., Ala. pub. health assns., Am. Assn. Hosp. Planning, Am. Assn. Pub. Adminstrn., Forest Farmers Assn., Res. Officers Assn., Ala. Hist. Assn., Am. Heritage Soc., Nat. Geog. Soc.,

Chi Epsilon, Sigma Phi Epsilon. Methodist. Club: Dixie Sailing. Home: 3143 Gilmer Av Montgomery AL 36105 Office: Ala Dept Health 501 Dexter Av Montgomery AL 36104

DEAN, DAVID PARKS, oil co. exec.; b. Detroit, Tex., July 23, 1898; s. William Alexander and Minnie (Lee) D.; student Austin Coll., 1915-16, U. Tulsa, 1916-17; B.A., Okla. U., 1920; m. Ruby Macy Boren, Mar. 12, 1953. Geologist, Waite Phillips Co., later Barnsdall Oil Co., 1921-30; partner Dean Bros., 1931-48; pres., Great Expectations Oil Corp., Fort Worth, 1948—. Trustee Reformed Theol. Sem., Jackson, Miss., 1968-71. Served as pvt. U.S. Army, World War I, to capt. AUS, World War II. Recipient 50 yr. award Am. Assn. Petroleum Geologists, 1969, Austin Coll., Sherman, Tex., 1966. Presbyn. Author: Smackover Rose, 1967, adaptation for play, 1971. Home: 2125 Park Pl Av Fort Worth TX 76110 Office: First Nat Bank Bldg Fort Worth TX 76102

DEAN, DONALD LEE, educator; b. Litchfield, Ill., Nov. 25, 1926; s. George Walter and Leola (Henry) D.; B.S., U. Mo., 1949, M.S., 1951; Ph.D., U. Mich., 1955; m. Jewel Lynn Knigge, Aug. 28, 1949; children—Philip Douglas, Cynthia Ann. Asst. prof. U. Mo., Rolla, 1949-55; asso. prof. U. Kan., Lawrence, 1955-60; prof. civil engring. U. Del., Newark, 1960-65, chmn. civil engring. dept., 1960-65; prof. N.C. State U., Raleigh, 1965—, head dept. civil engring. 1965—. Cons. on design and analysis of complex structural systems, I awrence, Newark, 1955-65. Mem. Del. Commn. on Air Pollution, 1961-65. Served with USNR, 1945-46. Mem. Internat. Assn. for Shell and Spatial Structures, Internat. Assn. for Bridge and Structural Engring., Am. Soc. C.E. (Walter L. Huber civil engring. research prize 1967), Am. Soc. Engring. Edn. Contbr. articles to profl. jours. Home: 3005 Sandia Dr Raleigh NC 27607

DEAN, HARDY ROBINSON, city ofcl.; b. Jacksonville, Fla., Sept. 13, 1913; s. William Henry and Callie (Easterlin) D.; student pub. schs.; m. Gladys Estell Cooper, Apr. 25, 1952; children—Hardy R., Patricia Ann, Verley E., Steven C., Susan C. Agt. Liberty Nat. Life Ins. Co., Chiefland, Fla., 1939-41, staff mgr., 1941-43; agt. Life Ins. Co. of Ga., Chiefland, 1946-59; city mgr. Chiefland, 1959—; owner Suwannee Valley Cleaners, Chiefland, 1964-69. Mem. Chiefland City Commn., 1957-59, Chiefland Planning Commn., 1963-71. Bd. dirs. Chiefland Activities Inc., 1965—. Served with USNR, 1943-46. Mem. Fla. City Mgrs. Assn., Internat. City Mgmt. Assn. Club: Lions (sec. 1967-71). Home: 903 W Boundary St Chiefland FL 32626 Office: 25 N Main St Chiefland FL 32626

DEAN, JACK FREDERICK, dentist; b. Ponca City, Okla., Nov. 16, 1923; s. Herman Hilbert and Lula May (Adair) D.; student No. Okla. Jr. Coll., 1941-43; D.D.S., St. Louis U., 1946; B.S. with honors, Baylor U., 1958. Private practice gen. dentistry, Ponca City, 1949-57; pvt. practice oral surgery, Dallas, 1961—. Asst. prof. physiology Baylor Dental Sch., 1966-72; mem. sr. attending staff Dept. Oral Surgery, U. Tex. Southwestern Med. Sch., 1966—. Served with USPHS, 1946-49. Diplomate Am. Bd. Oral Surgery. Fellow Am. Coll. Dentists; mem. Am. Dental Assn., Am., S.W. socs. oral surgery. Mason (Shriner). Home: 1631 Windchime Dallas TX 75224 Office: 223 W 10th St Dallas TX 75208

DEAN, JAMES, state legislator, univ. ofcl.; b. Atlanta, Mar. 14, 1944; s. Steve and Dorothy (Cox) D.; student San Francisco City Coll., summer 1962; B.A., Clark Coll., 1966; certificate Fisk U., summer 1967, U. Ga., 1967; M.S.W., Atlanta U., 1968; m. Vyvyan Ardena Coleman, June 12, 1966; 1 dau., Sonya Velika. Clk., Magic Carpet, Atlanta, 1957-58; rep. Atlanta Daily World, 1957-62; mgr. edn. bd. Atlanta Inquirer Inc., 1962-65; clk. BMC Realty Co., BMC Ins. Co., 1965-66; counselor, asst. manpower dir. Office Econ. Opportunity, Atlanta, 1965-66; community relations specialist, 1968; tchr. Atlanta Bd. Edn., 1966; recreation project dir., field rep. Atlanta Urban League, 1967, dir. Lynwood Park Neighborhood Center; mem. Ga. Ho. of Reps., 1968—; now dir. alumni affairs Clark Coll., Atlanta. Mem. Nat. Com. in Support of Pub. Schs., Eastlake Civic League, Eastside Community Council; chmn. spl. interest groups and edn. com. Dekalb unit Am. Cancer Soc.; mem. Met. Mental Health Assn. Recipient Achievement award Atlanta Inquirer; named Outstanding Young Man, Atlanta Jaycees, 1973. Mem. Am. Acad. Social Sci., Am. Acad. Polit. Sci., Nat. Assn. Social Workers, Acad. Certified Social Workers, Internat. Platform Assn., Am. Acad. Social and Polit. Sci., Soc. Fund Raisers, Am. Alumni Council, Soc. State Legislators, Nat. Assn. Black Elected Ofcls., Alpha Kappa Delta, Alpha Phi Alpha. Home: 17 Eastlake Dr NE Atlanta GA 20217 Office: 240 Chestnut St NW Atlanta GA 30319

DEAN, JANET E. VAUGHN, ednl. adminstr.; b. Baldwin City, Kan., Jan. 5, 1934; d. Earl William and Waneta (Sowers) Vaughn; B.A., Baker U., 1955; M.S., Barry Coll., 1963; H.H.D. (hon.), London Inst. for Applied Research, 1974; m. Wendell Hungtington Dean, May 21, 1957 (div. Sept. 1961). Tchr. speech, counselor Carol City Jr. High Sch., Miami, Fla., 1958-66; pres. Dade County Classroom Tchrs. Assn. Inc., Miami, 1966-70; asst. prin. for curriculum Miami Northwestern Sr. High Sch., 1970—. Mem. exec. com. Miami Emergency Planning Commn. on Human Relations, 1968—. Bd. dirs. P.T.A. Dade County. Mem. Democratic Exec. Com., Dist. 7, Dade County, 1966-68. Recipient award N.E.A., 1967. Mem. Fla. Edn. Assn. (chmn. urban com. 1967-68), Nat. Com. Educators for Human Rights, Nat. (pres. 1968-69), Fla. (pres. 1967-68) council urban edn. assns., Am. Assn. Univ. Women, Nat. Assn. Supervision and Curriculum Devel., League Women Voters, Alpha Chi Omega. Home: 367 NW 153 St Miami FL 33169 Office: 7007 NW 12th Av Miami FL 33150

DEAN, JOHN EDWARD, lawyer, accountant; b. Carrie, Va., Feb. 16, 1914; s. George Paris and Mary (Breeding) D.; A.B., Emory and Henry Coll., 1934; M.B.A., U. Ga., 1948, J.D., 1950; m. Priscilla Ross, Nov. 25, 1944; children—Nancy Karen, John Edward, George Ross, Robert David. Tchr., Jenkins (Ky.) Consol. Schs., 1934-35; head social sci. dept. Beckley (W.Va.) Coll., 1936-38; pres. Logan (W.Va.) Coll., 1938-39; pub. accountant, Louisville, 1939-41; head bus. adminstrn. dept. N.M. Mil. Inst., Roswell, 1941-42, asst. prof. U. Ga., 1946-51; admitted to Ga. bar, 1951; atty. Internal Revenue Service, Washington, 1951-52, So. Garment Mfrs. Assn., Washington, 1952-53, FCC, Washington, 1954; sr. auditor, staff mgr. Army Audit Agy., Atlanta, 1954-59; asst. atty. gen. Ga., Atlanta, 1959-66; pvt. practice law, Atlanta, 1966—. Bd. dirs. Atlanta Met. Area A.R.C. Served from apprentice seaman to lt. USCGR, 1942-46. C.P.A., Tenn., Ga. Mem. Ga., Clayton County bar assns., Am. Arbitration Assn. (nat. panel arbitrators), Internat. Platform Assn., Am. Acad. Polit. and Social Sci., Am. Judicature Soc., Clayton County C. of C. (pres. 1962-65), Delta Theta Phi, Alpha Kappa Psi, Lambda Chi Alpha, Artus Club, Phi Kappa Phi. Home: Route 2 Lovejoy Hampton GA 30228

DEAN, LYDIA MARGARET CARTER (MRS. HALSEY ALBERT DEAN), food and nutrition cons.; b. Bedford, Va., July 11, 1919; d. Christopher C. and Hettie (Gross) Carter; grad. Averett Coll.; B.S., Madison Coll., 1941; M.S., Va. Poly. Inst. and State U., 1951; postgrad. U. Va.; m. Halsey Albert Dean, Dec. 24, 1941; children—Halsey Albert, John Carter, Lydia Margaret. Dietetic Intern, therapeutic dietitian St. Vincent de Paul Hosp., Norfolk, Va., 1942; physicist U.S. Naval Operating Base, Norfolk, 1943-45; clin. dietitician, instr. Va. Poly. Inst. and State U., 1946-51, asso. prof. nutrition, 1951-53; community nutritionist and supr. sch. lunch program Roanoke (Va.) Pub. Schs., 1953-60; dir. nutrition and dietetics dept. Southwestern Va. Med. Center, Roanoke, 1960-67; food and nutrition cons. Nat. Hdqrs. A.R.C., Washington, 1967-73; nutrition scientist, cons. Dept. Army, Washington, 1973—, also Dept. Agr., A.R.C. Cons. Am. Dietetic Assn., 1969—; mem. task force White House Conf. Food and Nutrition, 1969—; chmn. fed. com. Interagy. Com. on Nutrition Edn., 1970-71; now tech. rep. to AID; chmn. Crusade for Nutrition Edn., Washington, 1970—; participant, cons. Nat. Nutrition Policy Conf., 1974. Fellow Am. Pub. Health Assn.; mem. Am. Dietetic Assn., Bus. and Profl. Women's Clubs (cons. 1970—), Am. Home Econs. Assn. (rep. and treas. Joint Congl. Com.), Am. Assn. U. Women, Food Service Execs. Assn. Author: (with Virginia McMasters) Community Emergency Feeding, 1972; Help! My Child Won't Eat Right, 1973. Contbr. articles to profl. jours. Home: 7816 Birnam Wood Dr McLean VA 22101 Office: Dept Army Washington DC

DEAN, PAUL CLEMENT, geologist, oil co. exec.; b. Detroit, July 23, 1898; s. William Alexander and Minnie Lee (Dean) D.; student Austin Coll., 1915-16, U. Tulsa, 1917-18; B.A., Okla. U., 1920; m. Lola Mae Guyer, Mar. 20, 1935; children—Jane (Mrs. Robert S. Travis), Nancy (Mrs. John S. McClane); m. 2d, Irene Morgan Poppewell, July 31, 1966; 1 stepdau., Kay (Mrs. G. Warren Holly). Planetable geol. mapper, various areas Kan., Okla., Tex., 1918-23; ind. geologist, Tex., 1923-47; v.p., treas. Gt. Expectations Oil Corp., Ft. Worth, 1948—. Served with inf. U.S. Army, 1918. Recipient certificate of award Austin Coll., Sherman, 1964. Mem. Ind. Petroleum Assn. Am., Am. Assn. Petroleum Geologists, Soc. Petroleum Engrs. (sr.), Ft. Worth Geol. Soc. (pres. 1934), Sigma Gamma Epsilon. Clubs: Shady Oaks, Colonial Country (Ft. Worth), Fort Worth Petroleum; Chaparral (Dallas). Home: 2309 Pembroke Dr Fort Worth TX 76110 Office: 1215 First Nat Bank Bldg Fort Worth TX 76102

DEAN, ROMEO BARNES, JR., bank exec.; b. Greenville, S.C., May 19, 1928; s. Romeo Barnes and Pearle (Griffin) D.; grad. Palmetto Inst. Accountancy, 1950, Sch. Consumer Banking, U. Va., 1959, Stonier Grad. Sch. Banking, Rutgers, 1966; m. Eileen Knutson, Sept. 11, 1946; children—Claudia (Mrs. Thomas E. Chandler), Julie (Mrs. John W. Flowers), Carol (Mrs. Paul A. Thompson). With S.C. Nat. Bank, Greenville, 1947—, v.p., city exec. officer, Florence, S.C., 1972—. Campaign chmn. United Fund, Sumter, 1969, pres., 1971; pres. United Way S.C., 1972. Served with USAAF, 1945-47. Recipient Boss of Yr. award Sumter Jaycees, 1970; named S.C.'s United Way Man of Yr., Gov. S.C., 1970. Mem. C. of C. (pres. 1972), Am. Legion (vice comdr. 1957-58). Episcopalian. Home: 1427 Dorchester Rd Florence SC 29501 Office: PO Box 551 Florence SC 29501

DEAN, STANLEY ROCHELLE, physician; b. Stamford, Conn., Feb. 13, 1908; s. Jacob and Gerta (Rochelle) D.; B.S., U. Mich., 1930, M.D. cum laude, 1934; children—Lori (Mrs. Joel Schonfeld), Michael Louis; m. 2d, Marion Jamieson, Nov. 8, 1967. Intern, Hurley (Mass.) Hosp., 1934-35; resident psychiatry Taunton (Mass.) State Hosp., Boston Psycopathic Hosp., 1935-37; sr. physician Fairfield State Hosp., Newtown, Conn., 1937-40; practice medicine, specializing in psychiatry, Stamford, 1940-64, Miami, Fla., 1964—; clin. prof. psychiatry U. Fla. Coll. Medicine, Gainesville, also U. Miami Med. Sch.; chief Stamford Hosp., Psychiat. Clinic, 1934-43. Founder, v.p. Research in Schizophrenia Endowment, 1958-62. Served to lt. AUS, 1943-45. Recipient New Eng. Psychiat. Assn. prize for research, 1942; namesake Stanley R. Dean award for research in psychiatry. Diplomate Am. Bd. Psychiatry. Fellow Am. Psychiat. Assn., Am. Coll. Psychiatrists, A.A.A.S., Royal Soc. Medicine (Gt. Britain); mem. Internat. Assn. Social Psychiatry (trustee), Am. Assn. Social Psychiatry (mem. exec. council), Internat. Fedn. Hygiene, Preventive Medicine and Social Medicine (mem. exec. council). Adv. bd. Transcultural Psychiat. Review. Contbr. articles to profl. jours. Address: 2121 N Bayshore Dr Miami FL 33137

DEAN, THOMAS SCOTT, educator; b. Sherman, Tex., July 6, 1924; s. Lura Cecil and Lucille (Scott) D.; B.S., N. Tex. State U., 1947; M.S., Mass. Inst. Tech., 1949; postgrad. So. Meth. U., 1955-59; Ph.D., U. Tex., 1963; m. Jan Marie Dixon Irvine, June 1, 1945; children—Tamarie, Dixon Lee, Thomas Scott. Individual practice as architect and engr., Dallas, 1950-60; lectr., cons. So. Meth. U., Dallas, 1955-59; lectr. archtl. engring. U. Tex. at Austin, 1960-64; prof. architecture Okla. State U., Stillwater, 1964—; vis. prin. lectr., cons. North East London Poly., 1973. Cons. Tex. Industries, Inc., Dallas, 1955-59. Served with C.E., AUS, 1943-44. Research fellow Latin Am. Studies Inst., 1963. Registered profl. engr., Tex., Okla.; registered architect, Tex., Okla. Mem. A.I.A., Nat. Soc. Profl. Engrs., Am. Soc. Engring. Edn., Am. Soc. C.E., Am. Soc. Heating, Refrigeration and Air conditioning Engrs. Contbr. articles to profl. jours. Home: 2002 Cresent Dr Stillwater OK 74074

DEAN, TROY WENDELL, data processor; b. Electra, Tex., Sept. 5, 1936; s. Jodie Frank and Zelma Ellen (Walker) D.; student U. Houston, 1954-65; m. Faith Ann Rowe, July 28, 1961; children—Theresa Ann, Tina Louise. With Transcontinental Gas Pipe Line, Houston, 1954-57; tab operator Union Carbide Internat., Houston, 1957-62; jr. engr. So. Nat. Bank, Houston, 1962-66; with Tex. Data Center, Inc., Bryan, 1966—, now exec. v.p. Instr. data processing Alvin (Tex.) Jr. Coll., 1963-64, San Jacinto Jr. Coll., Pasadena, Tex., 1963. Mem. Data Processing Mgmt. Assn., C. of C. (chmn. pub. affairs, congl. action coms. 1973-74). Mason (Shriner), Rotarian. Home: 3009 Tennessee St Bryan TX 77801 Office: 114 S Bryan St Bryan TX 77801

DEAN, WILLIAM CORNER, elec. engr.; b. Pitts., Nov. 21, 1926; s. William Edward and Doris Lucy (Brown) D.; B.S., Carnegie Inst. Tech., 1949, M.S., 1950, Ph.D., 1952; m. Sara Jane Prichard, Apr. 1, 1950; children—Amy Susan, Martha Ellen. Geophysicist, Gulf Research & Devel. Co., Pitts., 1952-60; project mgr. United Electrodynamics div. Teledyne, Alexandria, Va., 1961—, tech. dir. geophysics, research and devel., 1968—. Cons. coal mine safety Arthur D. Little Inc., Cambridge, Mass., 1972. Treas., Burgundy Farm Sch., Alexandria, 1966-69, pres., 1970; pres. Tauxemont Community Assn., Alexandria, 1965. Served with USNR, 1945-46. Registered profl. engr., Pa. Mem. I.E.E.E., Soc. Exploration Geophysicists, Am. Geophys. Union, Sigma Xi, Eta Kappa Nu. Home: 1301 Namassin Rd Alexandria VA 22308 Office: PO Box 334 Alexandria VA 22313

DEANS, PARKER DUDLEY, atomic energy engr.; b. Coshocton, O., Jan. 27, 1916; s. Alvah Wilkins and Bessie (Joynes) D.; B.S. in Chem. Engring., Ga. Inst. Tech., 1938; m. Marie Edgeworth Killen, June 27, 1941; children—Margaret Virginia, Catherine Edgeworth. Research chemist So. Cotton Oil Co., Savannah, Ga., 1938-41; engr. E. I. duPont de Nemours & Co., Old Hickory, Tenn., 1941-42, research engr., sr. engr., Bridgeport, Conn., 1942-45, quality control supr., Old Hickory, 1945-49, research engr., statis. cons., Richmond, Va., 1949-51, quality control supt., area supt. Savannah River Plant, Aiken, S.C., 1951—. Pres., Crosland Park Civic Assn., 1952-53; commr. Aiken (S.C.) Recreation Commn., 1953-54; pres. Aiken Community Playhouse, 1962-64, 65. Sr. mem. Am. Soc. Quality Control (chmn. Tenn. sect. 1946-47, nat. dir. 1946-48); mem. Am. Statis. Assn., Internat. Platform Assn. Episcopalian (pres. Men's Club 1954, jr. warden 1960-62, sr. warden 1973). Home: 539 Highland Park Av SW Aiken SC 29801 Office: Savannah River Plant Aiken SC 29801

DEAR, HOWARD MARSHALL, banker; b. Houston, Apr. 5, 1939; s. Johnnie Maxwell and Evelyn Nell (Berry) D.; student Henderson County Jr. Coll., 1958-59, Grad. Sch. Banking Lon Morris Jr. Coll., 1959-60; B.B.A., Stephen F. Austin State Coll., 1962; m. Phyllis June Vaughan, May 26, 1961 (div. Jan. 1971); m. 2d, Peggy Kay Emmons, July 8, 1972; children—Angela, Holly, Darla. Vice pres. First State Bank, Rusk, Tex., 1961-68; exec. v.p. First Nat. Bank, New Boston, Tex., 1968—; pres. Dear & Co., Inc., New Boston, 1970—; owner New Boston Real Estate Agy., New Boston, 1968—, New Boston Ins. Agy., 1968—. Dist. vice chmn. Caddo Area council Boy Scouts Am., 1969-71; pres. Athletic Booster Club, 1969-70. Mem. New Boston C. of C. (dir.). Baptist. Lion (v.p. 1969-70). Home: 520 Anderson St New Boston TX 75570 Office: Box 608 New Boston TX 75570

DEARMAN, WILBUR ELISHA, judge; b. Cuba, Ala., Oct. 9, 1908; s. John Albert and Annie (Shaw) D.; B.S., Auburn U., 1931; LL.B., Cumberland U., 1933; J.D., Samford U., 1969; m. Mary Emma Turner, Aug. 15, 1942; children—Marianne (Mrs. George D. Rainer), Jean Shaw (Mrs. Walter Mark Anderson III), Juanita (Mrs. Eladio Rubira II). Admitted to Ark. bar, 1934, Ala. bar, 1935; mem. firm Patton & Patton, Livingston, Ala., 1935—. Pres., Livingston P.T.A. Mem. Ala. Ho. of Reps., 1939-46; chmn. Sumter County Democratic Exec. Com., 1944-46; probate judge Sumter County, Ala., 1953—. Mem. Sumter County Hist. Soc. (pres.), Am., Ala. bar assns., Ala. Hist. Soc., Ala. Law Inst., Continuing Legal Edn. Ala. (exec. com.), Barristers, Blue Key, Tau Kappa Epsilon. Baptist (deacon, supt. Sunday sch.). Lion. Club: Commercial (Livingston). Home: Main and Spring Sts Livingston AL 35470 Office: Courthouse Livingston AL 35470

DEASEY, LUCILLE VALLO (MRS. DANIEL WALTER), educator; b. Chgo., Nov. 11, 1912; Dominic and Jennie (Corve) Vallo; student Chgo. Tchrs. Coll., 1930-33; B.S. in Edn., DePaul U., 1939; M.Ed., Our Lady of Lake Coll., 1957; m. Daniel Walter, Oct. 7, 1939. Tchr., Chgo. Pub. Schs., 1932-45, Harlandale Ind. Sch. Dist., San Antonio, 1950-55, occupational orientation coordinator, 1970-71, dir. career edn., 1971-73, psychologist, 1973—; counselor Terrell Wells Jr. High Sch., San Antonio, 1955-61; dean girls McCollum High Sch., San Antonio, 1961-70, Lectr. Our Lady of Lake Coll., San Antonio; mem. S.W. regional bd. Am. Coll. Testing Program, 1968-70. Mem. sch. adv. bd. Minnie Stevens Piper Found., 1971—. Mem. Tex. Assn. Women Deans, Counselors (2d v.p. 1960-62, pres. 1962-65), South Tex. Personnel and Guidance Assn. (pres. 1959, treas. 1967-68), San Antonio Women Deans and Counselors (treas. 1956, pres. 1970-71), Tex. Tchrs. Assn. (br. pres. 1962-63), Nat. Assn. Women Deans and Counselors (membership chmn.), P.T.A. (life), Delta Kappa Gamma. Home: 118 E Ackard St San Antonio TX 78221 Office: 102 Genevieve St San Antonio TX 78285

DEATHERAGE, JAMES W., lawyer; b. Cainsville, Mo., Aug. 8, 1933; s. Virgil P. and Fern L. (Woodward) D.; B.S., Austin Coll., 1956; LL.B., So. Meth. U., 1964; m. Mary Jo Wyatt, June 8, 1956; children—Todd W., James H. Admitted to Tex. bar, 1964; agt. N.Y. Life Ins. Co., Sherman, Tex., 1958-59; claim examiner Allstate Ins. Co., Dallas, 1959-64; mem. firm Brewer & Deatherage, Irving, Tex., 1964-67, Tabor & Deatherage, Irving, 1967-70; partner firm English, Deatherage & Boyle, Irving, 1970—; dir. McCrary Powell Advt. Inc., Dallas, Draperies Unlimited, Lewisville, Tex. Bd. dirs. Dallas County Mental Health Assn. Served with AUS, 1956-58. Mem. Austin Coll. Hall of Fame, 1970—. Mem. Austin Coll. Alumni Assn. (v.p. 1974), Tex. (dir.), Irving (pres. 1968-69), Dallas, Am. bar assns., Am. Judicature Soc., Nat. Council Sch. Attys., Irving C. of C., Delta Theta Phi. Presbyn. (elder). Rotarian. Club: Las Colinas Country. Home: 1204 N Irving Heights Irving TX 75060 Office: SW Bank Bldg Irving TX 75060

DEATHERAGE, WILLIAM GEIER, banker; b. Carrollton, Ky., Aug. 26, 1912; s. George William and Florence (Geier) D.; A.B., Centre Coll., 1933; m. Helen Frances Early, June 5, 1943; children—William G., Sara Jane, Julie Ann. Asst. cashier First Nat. Bank, Carrollton, Ky., 1934-37; cashier Deposit Bank, Shelbyville, 1937-40; bank examiner State of Ky., Frankfort, 1940-42; cashier Bank of Oldham County, LaGrange, 1947-50; v.p. Planters Bank & Trust Co., Hopkinsville, 1950-61, pres., 1961—; dir. Louisville br. Fed. Res. Bank St. Louis, Pennyrile Rural Electric Coop. Corp., Lincoln Income Life Ins. Co. Past bd. dirs. Hopkinsville Givers Fund; mem. Mayor's Adv. Com., 1963. Bd. dirs. Hopkinsville Servicemen's Center; bd. dirs., sec.-treas. Hopkinsville Indsl. Found.; mem. adv. bd. U.Ky., Hopkinsville Community Coll. Served to capt. AUS, 1942-46. Mem. Assn. Mil. Banks (past pres., dir.), Am. Bankers Assn. (regional v.p.), Ky. (dir.), Hopkinsville (dir.) chambers commerce, Sigma Alpha Epsilon. Democrat. Mem. Disciples of Christ Ch. Rotarian. Home: Route 1 Hopkinsville KY 42240 Office: 712 S Main St Hopkinsville KY 42240

DE AVILA, ALEJANDRO, physician; b. Oaxaca, Mexico, Aug. 16, 1922; s. Alejandrino and Refugio (Cervantes) de Avila; student Universidad Autonoma de San Luis Potosi, 1937-41; M.D., Universidad Nacional Automona de Mexico, 1949; m. Alice Blomberg, Mar. 24, 1956; children—Alejandro, Mark Edward, David Michael, Elizabeth. Physician, Social Service, El Fuerte, Sinaloa, 1948-49; intern, King County Hosp. System, Seattle, 1951-52; anesthesia resident King County Hosp. System, Children's Orthopedic Hosp., Seattle, 1952-54; anesthesiologist Am. Brit. Cowdray Hosp., Mexico, 1959—, dir. inhalation therapy service, 1966—. Mem. Am. Soc. Anesthesiologists, Sociedad Mexicana de Anesthesiologia, World Fedn. Neurology, Pan Am. Med. Assn., Asociacion Mexicana de Hospitales, Nacional Fire Protection Assn., Phi Chi. Rotarian. Author (with Everado Ortiz) Temas Medico Quirurgicas; (with Juan Cardenas) Neurologia, 1960. Editor: Revista Mexicana de Anesthesiologia, 1959-61. Address: 810 Crater St Mexico DF Mexico

DEBAKEY, MICHAEL E(LLIS), surgeon; b. Lake Charles, La., Sept. 7, 1908; s. Shaker Morris and Raheega (Zerba) DeB.; B.S., Tulane U., 1930, M.D., 1932, M.S., 1935, LL.D., 1965; Dr. honoris causa, U. Lyon (France), 1961, U. Brussels (Belgium), 1962, U. Ghent (Belgium), 1964, U. Athens (Greece), 1964, U. Turin (Italy), 1965, U. Belgrade (Yugoslavia), L.L.D., 1967; Lafayette Coll., 1965, U. Cin., McNeese U., 1972; D.Sc., D'Youville Coll., 1967, U. Mich., 1967, Fla. State U., 1968, MacMurray Coll., 1971, Hahnemann Med. Coll. and Hosp., 1973; Dr. Med. Scis. (hon.), Aristotelean U. of Thessaloniki (Greece), 1971; D.Sc. honoris causa, Assumption Coll., 1971, L.I. U., 1971; Hon. Dr., Ljubljana U., 1971; M.D. honoris causa, U. Louvain; m. Diana Cooper, Oct. 15, 1936; children—Michael Maurice, Ernest Ochsner, Barry Edward, Denis Alton. Intern Charity Hosp., New Orleans, 1932-33, asst. in surgery, 1933-35; asst. in surgery U. Strasbourg (France), 1935-36; asst. surgery U. Heidelberg (Germany), 1936; instr. surgery Tulane U., 1937-40, asst. prof., 1940-46, asso. prof., 1946-48; prof. surgery, chmn. dept. Baylor U.,

Houston, 1948—, v.p. med. affairs, 1968—, chief exec. officer Baylor Coll. Medicine, 1968-69, pres., 1969—, Distinguished Service prof., 1968—; surgeon in chief Ben Taub Gen. Hosp., Houston, 1963—; practice medicine Ochsner Clinic, New Orleans, 1946-48; sr. attending surgeon, dir. Cardiovascular Research Center, Methodist Hosp., Houston, 1967—; hon. faculty medicine U. Chile, Santiago, 1964; cons. staff, mem. exec. com. St. Luke's Episcopal Hosp., Houston; cons. surgery M.D. Anderson Hosp. and Tumor Inst., Tex. Children's Hosp., Houston; clin. prof. surg. U. Tex. Dental Br., Houston, 1971-72; distinguished prof. surgery Tex. A. and M. U., 1972—; cons. Tex. Inst. Rehab. and Research, Brooke Gen. Hosp., Ft. Sam Houston; area cons. thoracic surgery to VA, 1946—. Mem. med. adv. com. sec. of def., 1948-50; chmn. com. on surgery NRC, 1953, mem. exec. com., 1953; mem. task force Commn. for Reorgn. Exec. Br. Govt.; mem. Nat. Adv. Health Council, 1961-65, Nat. Adv. Council Region Med. Programs, 1965—, Civilian Health and Med. Adv. Council Office Asst. Sec. Def.; mem. med. adv. bd. Am. Hosp. of Paris, 1971—; cons. cardiovascular surgery to surgeon gen. U.S. Air Force; mem. adv. council Nat. Heart Inst.; chmn. Albert Lasker Clin. Med. Research Jury awards, 1973, Citizens for Treatment High Blood Pressure, 1974, numerous other adv. positions. Bd. visitors Tulane U., 1970—; trustee S.W. Research Inst., 1972—. Served as col., Office of Surgeon Gen., AUS, 1942-46, surg. cons. to surgeon gen., 1946—. Decorated Legion of Merit, knight comdr. Order of Merit Italian Republic, Grand Cross Order Leopold (Belgium); recipient Rudolph Matas award, 1954; Hektoen Gold Medal A.M.A.; Internat. Soc. Surgery Distinguished Service award, 1958, 59; Distinguished Service award A.M.A., 1959; Albert Lasker award for clin. research, 1963; St. Vincent prize med. scis. U. Turin, 1965; Orden del Libertador Gen. San Martin, Argentina, 1965; Hunterian medal St. George's Hosp. Med. Sch., London, Eng., 1966; Centennial medal Albert Einstein Med. Center, 1966; Eleanor Roosevelt Humanities award, 1969; P.A. Gertzin medal Internat. Med. Sci. Orgn. of Surgeons, Moscow, 1971, medallion Tex. Med. Center, 1972, Spl. Recognition award Merck Sharp & Dohme, 1971, Distinguished Citizens award Rotary Club, 1972, USSR Acad. Sci. 50th Anniversary Jubilee medal, 1973, numerous others; named Dr. of Year Med. World News, 1965, Med. Man of Year, 1966. Diplomate Am. Bd. Surgery, Am. Bd. Thoracic Surgery, Nat. Bd. Med. Examiners. Fellow A.C.S. (ann. award extraordinary performance 1973), Am. Coll. Cardiology (hon.), Royal Coll. Surgeons (Eng.) (hon.); mem. Internat Cardiovascular Soc. (pres. N.Am. chpt. 1964), Southwestern Surg. Congress (pres. 1952), Soc. Vascular Surgery (pres. 1953), A.M.A., Tex. Med. Assn. Council on med. edn. and hosps. 1971—), Am., So., Western surg. assns., Am. Assn. Thoracic Surgery (pres. 1959), Soc. Clin. Surgery, Soc. U. Surgeons, Internat. Soc. Surgery, Soc. Exptl. Biology and Medicine, Sociedad Nacional de Cirugia, Am. Acad. Achievement (gov.), A.A.A.S., Am. Assn. Cancer Research, Am. Soc. Contemporary Medicine and Surgery (pres. 1971—; achievement award 1973), Am. Trauma Soc. (founding), N.Y. Acad. Scis., World Med. Assn., Philos. Soc. Tex., Mexican Acad. Surgery, Cuban Med. Assn. in Exile (hon.), Udruzenje Kirurga Jugoslavia (hon.), Acad. Medicine of Turin (fgn. hon. asso.), Am. Geriatric Soc., Am. Heart Assn. (founding mem. council cerebrovascular disease, mem. council on thrombosis), C. of C., Sigma Xi, Alpha Omega Alpha. Democrat. Episcopalian. Rotarian (hon. Houston). Clubs: Cosmos, University (Washington); Press (Houston). Author: (with Robert Kilduffe) Blood Transfusion, 1942; (with Gilbert W. Beebe) Battle Casualties, 1952; (with Alton Ochsner) Textbook of Minor Surgery, 1955; (with T. Whayne) Cold Injury, Ground Type, 1958. Editor surg. vols. AUS Medical History of World War II; Year Book of General Surgery, 1958—. Editorial bd. surg. jours.; mem. editorial adv. bd. Biomed. Materials and Artificial Organs, 1971—. Home: 5323 Cherokee St Houston TX 77005 Office: 1200 Moursund Av Houston TX 77025

DEBARDELEBEN, LEWIS TYUS, civil engr.; b. Burnsville, Ala., Mar. 18, 1902; s. Joseph Gindrat and Maude Graham (Tyus) D.; B.S., Auburn U., 1926; m. Mary Logue, Mar. 31, 1929; children—William L., Joseph L. Draftsman, Ala. Hwy. Dept., Montgomery, 1926-27, transitman, 1927-29, resident engr., 1934-36, project engr., 1939-41; with Mo. Hwy Dept., Macon, 1929-34; jr. engr. Resettlement Adminstrn., Scottsboro, Ala., 1936-37; office engr. Tenn. Coal, Iron & R.R. Co., Fairfield, Ala., 1937-39; civil engr. U.S. Corps Engrs., Mobile, Ala., 1941-45; county engr. Talladega County (Ala.) Commn., 1945—. Registered profl. engr., Ala. Mem. Nat. Assn. County Engrs. (sec., treas. 1957-67, Rural County Engr. award 1970), Am. Soc. C.E., Assn. County Engrs. Ala. (pres. 1956-57). Methodist (chmn. ofcl. bd. 1965-66). Home: 721 S Spring St Talladega AL 36150 Office: 106 W South St Talladega AL 36150

DE BAUERNFEIND, JOSEPH BUFFINGTON, chem. co. exec.; b. Nelson, Neb., Nov. 7, 1916; s. Frank E. and Nell M. (Buffington) de B.; B.A., Ohio Wesleyan U., 1938; m. Marjorie Anne Skelton, Jan. 17, 1942; 1 dau., Deborah Lee. Vice-pres. S. S. Skelton Co., Cleve., 1947-52; product mgr. Glidden Co., Jacksonville, Fla., 1953-62; mgr. sales and marketing, terpene and aromatics div. Union Camp Corp., Jacksonville, 1962—. Asso. trustee Ohio Wesleyan U. Served with USNR, 1941-45. Mem. Essential Oil Assn., Phi Gamma Delta. Presbyn. (elder 1949—). Club: Timuquana Country (Jacksonville). Home: 4242 Ortega Blvd Apt 4 Jacksonville FL 32210 Office: PO Box 6170 Jacksonville FL 32205

DE BEAUBRIEN, PHILIP FRANCIS, banker; b. Conneaut, O., Feb. 9, 1913; s. Jay William and Eileen Anne (Schubert) deB.; student pub. schs.; m. June Elizabeth Hesse, June 18, 1937; children—Philip Francis, Suzette Marie (Mrs. George L. Brown III), Hugo Hesse. Detroit mgr. Good Housekeeping mag., 1945-50; central zone mgr. Look Mag., 1950-56; pub. Detroit Times, 1956-61; v.p. Comml. Bank, Daytona Beach, Fla., 1963-71; dir. news bur. First at Orlando Corp., 1972—. Writer nat. syndicated news column under pseudymon Homer Holiday. Pres., Halifax Cultural Found., 1965-67. Mem. Fla. Bankers Assn. (chmn. pub. edn. com. 1966-67, chmn. advt. com. 1967-69). Home: 855 Ocean Shore Blvd Ormond Beach FL 32074 Office: Ormond Ocean Club Ormond Beach FL 32074

DEBENPORT, JERALD RANDOLPH, JR., indsl. engr., mayor; b. Tyler, Tex., Jan. 10, 1928; s. Jerald Randolph and Maurinne (Teller) D.; B.S., E. Tex. State U., 1953; m. Martha Sue Allsopp, Aug. 12, 1950; children—Cliff Edmund, Don Albert. Asso. customer engr., customer engr. IBM Corp., Tyler, 1953-60, sr. customer engr., 1960-70; area dir. Combined Ins. Co., Tyler, 1970-72; formed own toy mfg. co. Tiny Tent Co., 1972—; mayor, Tyler, 1970—. Chmn. Smith County Youth Adv. Bd., 1963-65; scoutmaster Rose City council Boy Scouts Am., 1953-59. Mem. Tyler City Commn., 1969-70. Served with USNR, 1945-46. Republican. Baptist (deacon). Kiwanian. Patentee in field. Home: 1220 Parkdale St Tyler TX 75701 Office: 1224 Winona St Box 4386 Tyler TX 75701

DE BLIEUX, JOSEPH DAVIS, state senator; lawyer; b. Columbia, La., Sept. 12, 1912; s. Honore Louis and Ozet (Perot) BeB.; student Ouachita Parish Jr. Coll., 1932-34; LL.B., La. State U., 1938; m. Dorothy Lepine, Apr. 22, 1946; 1 son, Paul Louis. Admitted to La. bar, 1938, U.S. Supreme Ct. bar, 1958; practiced in Baton Rouge, 1938—; mem. firm DeBlieux Guidry & Lowe, Baton Rouge, 1959—; mem. La. Senate, 1956-60, 64—. Mem. Pub. Affairs Research Council, Baton Rouge, 1952—; chmn. La. Adv. Com., U.S. Commn. on Civil Rights, 1960—. Bd. dirs. Community Advancement, Inc., Greater Baton Rouge Mental Health Assn. Del. Democratic Nat. Conv., 1956, 64, 68; mem. La. Central Com., 1960—. Served with AUS, 1942-45. Decorated knight St. Gregory the Great, Pope Pius XII, 1958. Mem. Am., La. Baton Rouge bar assns., Baton Rouge C. of C., Am. Legion, Amvets. Roman Catholic. Moose, K.C., Lion. Club: Serra (Baton Rouge). Home: 3755 Churchill Av Baton Rouge LA 70808 Office: PO Box 3574 Baton Rouge LA 70821

DEBNATH, LOKENATH, educator; b. Hamsadi, India, Sept. 30, 1935; s. Jogesh Chandra and Surabala (Nath) D.; B.S. (scholar), U. Calcutta, India, 1954, M.S. (scholar), 1956, Ph.D. (scholar), 1964; D.I.C., U. London, 1967, Ph.D., 1967; m. Sadhana Bhowmik, Aug. 1, 1969; 1 son, Jayanta. Came to U.S., 1968. Lectr. U. Calcutta, India, 1957-60, asst. prof. math. 1960-64; research fellow Imperial Coll. Sci. and Tech., London U., 1965-67, teaching fellow, 1965-67; sr. research fellow Cambridge (Eng.) U., 1967-68; asso. prof. East Carolina U., Greenville, 1968-69, prof. math., 1969—, research grantee, 1970-73. Vis. prof. Centre Advanced Study in Applied Math., U. Calcutta, 1972. Served to 2d. lt. Nat. Cadet Corps, 1961-62. Recipient certificate of spl. merit for excellence in teaching East Carolina U. Fellow Inst. Math. and its Applications (Eng.); mem. Am., Calcutta (bull. editor 1973—) math. socs., Tensor Soc. Japan, Indian Sci. Congress Assn., Jnan O Bigyan Calcutta, Sigma Xi, Pi Mu Epsilon, Sigma Pi Sigma. Author: Elements of General Topology, 1964; Elements of Elliptic and Associated Functions with Applications, 1965. Contbr. numerous articles on pure and applied math., math. physics to profl. jours. Home: 204 N Elm St Apt 8 Greenville NC 27834

DEBORD, ROBERT EDWARD, physician; b. Marion, Va., Sept. 28, 1922; s. John Thompson and Emma (McCready) DeB.; B.S., Emory and Henry Coll., 1949; M.D., Med. Coll. Va., 1953; m. Martha Jane Porter, Feb. 6, 1954; children—Martha, Nancy, Emily, Robert, David. Intern Med. Coll. Va., 1953-54; practice medicine specializing in family practice, Williamsburg, Va., 1954—; coll. physician Coll. William & Mary, Williamsburg, 1954—; mem. staff Community Hosp., pres., 1969-70. Vice pres. Mill Creek Corp., Williamsburg, 1970-71; med. examiner James City County and Williamsburg, 1956—. Bd. dirs. Jamestown Acad., Williamsburg, 1966—. Served with AUS, 1942-46. Mem. James City County Med. Soc. (pres. 1961-62), Ruritan. Home: 202 Matoaka Ct Williamsburg VA 23185 Office: 224 Monticello Av Williamsburg VA 23185

DEBRUCQUE, WILLIAM ROBERT, dentist; b. Tulsa, Apr. 23, 1929; s. Phillip Baldwin and Ruby (Ragan) DeB.; B.S., U. Tulsa, 1958; D.D.S., Baylor U., 1957; m. Linda Sue Thompson, Sept. 23, 1955; children—Valerie Kay, Natalie Rae. Practice gen. dentistry, Dallas, 1957—. Bd. dirs. Tex. Found. for Dental Health. Served with AUS, 1946-48, 50-52. Mem. Dallas County (bd. dirs.), Tex., Am. dental assns., Internat. Assn. Orthodontics, Psi Omega, Kappa Sigma. Republican (del. to state conv. 1970—). Editor Dallas Dental Soc. News, 1969-70. Contbr. to profl. jours. Home: 522 Brook Valley Lane Dallas TX 75232 Office: 4323 Lemmon Av Dallas TX 75219

DEBUS, KURT HEINRICH, govt. ofcl.; b. Frankfurt-am-Main, Germany, Nov. 29, 1908; s. Heinrich P.J. and Melly (Graulich) D.; M.S. in Elec. Engring., Darmstadt Tech. U., 1936, Ph.D. in Elec. Engring., 1939; LL.D. (hon.), Rollins Coll., 1967; D.Eng., Fla. Technol. U., 1969; D.Sc., Fla. Inst. Tech., 1970; m. Irmgard Helene Brueckmann, June 30, 1937; children—Ute Irmgard, Sigrid Monika (Mrs. William R. Northcutt). Came to U.S., 1945, naturalized, 1959. Asst. prof. Darmstadt Tech. U., 1939-42; test engr., flight test dir. Peenemuende Rocket Center, 1942-45; dep. dir. guidance and control div., staff asst. to Wernher von Braun, Army Ballistic Missile Agy., U.S. Army, Huntsville, Ala., 1945-52, dir. missile firing lab., Cape Canaveral, Fla., 1952-60; dir. launch operations directorate G.C. Marshall Space Flight Center, NASA, Cape Canaveral, 1960-62, dir. Launch Operations Center, 1962-63, dir. John F. Kennedy Space Center, Fla., 1963—. Mem. sr. mgmt. council Office Manned Space Flight, NASA. Chmn. Brevard County U.S. Savs. Bond Drives, 1962—; chmn. Brevard-Indian River campaign Muscular Dystrophy Assn. Am., 1969-70. Recipient Exceptional Civilian Service award U.S. Army, 1959; Frank A. Scott gold medal Am. Ordnance Assn., 1964; NASA Outstanding Leadership award, 1964; Pioneer of Windrose award Order of the Diamond, 1965; AAS Space Flight award, 1968; Outstanding Achievement award U.S. Treasury Dept., 1968; Nat. Civil Service League Career award, 1969; Distinguished Service medal for Apollo 8, NASA, 1969, for Apollo 11, 1969, Apollo Achievement award, 1969; named to Nat. Space Hall of Fame, 1969; recipient Americanism medal D.A.R., 1969; decorated comdr.'s cross Order of Merit Fed. Republic of Germany, 1971. others. Fellow Am. Inst. Aeros. Astronautics (Louis W. Hill Space Transp. award 1973); mem. Hermann Oberth Geselischaft (hon., recipient Honor Ring 1971), Brit. Interplanetary Soc. (adv. bd. 1968), Am. Ordnance Assn. (life), German Soc. Rocket Tech. and Space Flight (hon.), Instrument Soc. Am. (hon.). Club: Nat. Space (gov. 1963). Home: 280 Bahama Blvd Cocoa Beach FL 32931 Office: John F Kennedy Space Center NASA Kennedy Space Center FL 32899

DEBUSK, ARON GIB, biochem. geneticist, educator; b. Lubbock, Tex., Jan. 15, 1927; s. Elias Clint and Ollie Myrtle (Lewis) D.; B.S., U. Wash., 1950; M.S., U. Tex., 1952, Ph.D., 1954; children—Michele, Barrett, Brook, Melissa, Clint, Cara. Instr., Northwestern U., Evanston, Ill., 1955-57; faculty Fla. State U., Tallahassee, 1957—, prof. dept. biol. scis. 1969—, dir., genetics group, 1962—. Research scholar Inst. Advanced Studies, Australian Nat. U., 1968. Vice pres. DeBusk Enterprises, Inc., Dallas, Tallahassee, 1969—; pres. Wayah Lodges, Inc., Aquon, N.C., 1971—; dir. Unidev Corp. Mem. Fla. Park Adv. Bd., Tallahassee, 1970-71. Served with AUS, 1945-46. Mem. Am. Chem. Soc., Genetics Soc. Am., Biophys. Soc., Soc. Am. Microbiologists, Sigma Xi. Author: Molecular Genetics, 1968. Home: 3583 Doris Dr Tallahassee FL 32303

DECAMP, RICHARD SURRIDGE, hist. assn. exec.; b. St. Louis, Dec. 5, 1931; s. Frank Baker and Nancy (Surridge) DeC.; B.A., Brown U., 1955; m. Patricia Storey, Dec. 5, 1966; 1 stepson, A.G. Patterson Boyce. Exec. dir. Blue Grass Trust for Historic Preservation, Lexington, Ky., 1970-73, Lexington-Fayette County Historic Commn., 1973—. Mem. adv. bd. Nat. Trust Historic Preservation. Trustee Lexington Pub. Library. Served with AUS, 1956-58. Home: 644 Montclair Dr Lexington KY 40502 Office: 187 Market St Lexington KY 40507

DE CARDONA, JORGE HIRAM, dentist; b. Aguadilla, P.R., Nov. 13, 1915; s. Francisco and Maria (Quinones) de C.; student U. P.R., 1933-34; D.D.S., Temple U., 1938; postgrad. in surgery U. P.R., 1971, in oral cancer, 1971-72;; m. Alicia Martinez Bianchi, Mar. 16, 1942; children—Alicia (Mrs. Nelson Fernandez), Hiram Arsenio, Olga Maria. Dentist, Am. Jr. Red Cross, 1938-40, Aguadilla (P.R.) Health Dept., 1940-42; pvt. practice dentistry, Aguadilla, 1938—. Served from 1st lt. to maj., AUS, World War II. Mem. Am. Dental Assn., Colegio Cirujanos Dentistas (pres. Aguadilla dist. 1963-64), Cirujanes Dentistas de P.R., Order San Juan Bautista, Phi Eta Mu. Roman Catholic. Home: 62 Betances St Aquadilla PR 00603 Office: 62 Altos Betances St Aguadilla PR 00603

DECHOUDENS-LABOY, JOSE MIGUEL, social worker; councelor; b. Guayama, P.R., Feb. 14, 1934; s. Rafael and Felicita (Laboy) DeC.; B.S., John Carroll U., Cleve., 1957; M.S.W., Fordham U., 1959; postgrad. U. P.R., 1965-69, Carribean Center for Postgrad. Studies, 1970-73; m. Dimna Marrero-Aulet, July 25, 1959; children—Yvonne, Lourdes. Psychiat. social worker Childrens Village, N.Y.C., 1959-61, Northside Center for Child Devel., N.Y.C., 1961-65, Family Inst. P.R., 1965—; U.S. probation officer U.S. Dist. Ct., San Juan, 1972; research interviewing Community Council Greater N.Y. Bd. dirs. Puerto Rican Family Inst.-N.Y.C., 1960-64, Legal Service P.R. Mem. Nat., P.R. (sec.) assns. social workers, Acad. Certified Social Workers. Home: JJ-13 Fiqueras Villa Andalucia Rio Piedras PR 00926 Office: 154 Los Myrtis St Hyde Park Rio Piedras PR 00928

DECK, MARVIN EDWARD, JR., surgeon; b. Nashville, Oct. 28, 1933; s. Marvin Edward and Volanda (Chronister) D.; A.B. cum laude, Vanderbilt U., 1955, M.D., 1963; m. Rose Deck, Sept. 9, 1956 (div.); children—Kathy, Karen, Phillip; m. 2d, Pamela Paulette Eakin, Oct. 30, 1972. Intern, Butterworth Hosp., Grand Rapids, Mich., 1963-64; resident, 1964-68; practice surgery, Rutherford County, Tenn., 1968-72, South Pittsburg, Tenn., 1973—; mem. staff South Pittsburg Municipal Hosp. Served with USNR, 1955-58. Diplomate Am. Bd. Surgery. Mem. Alpha Omega Alpha, Phi Kappa Alpha. Moose, Rotarian. Home: PO Box 404 South Pittsburgh TN 37380 Office: South Pittsburg Municipal Hosp South Pittsburg TN 37380

DECKARD, CHARLES, financial exec.; b. nr. Bloomington, Ind., June 1, 1927; s. James Andrew and Nora (Sipes) D.; B.S., Ind. U., 1951; m. Emily Jane Dwyer, Dec. 25, 1948; children—Norita Charlene, Charles Kevin, Mark Alison. Instr. Ind. U., 1951-52; with Bendix Corp., South Bend, Ind., 1951-61, asst. to mgr. internal audit staff, 1956-61, controller Sheffield Corp., Dayton, O., 1961-66, div. controller Automation and Measurement div. Bendix Corp., Dayton, 1966-69, Automotive Electronics div., Balt., 1969-70, Newport News, Va., 1971—. Served with AUS, 1945-46. Methodist. Club: Four Seasons Towne (founding trustee, treas.) (Dayton). Home: 1 Digges Dr Newport News VA 23602 Office: 615 Bland Blvd Newport News VA 23602

DECKER, ALLAN FRANCIS, banker; b. Fairbury, Neb., Sept. 17, 1929; s. Oscar C. and June L. (Brunner) D.; B.S., U. Neb., 1951, LL.B., 1955; m. Teckla Ellen Stelling, Aug. 22, 1953; children—Kathy A., Robert E., William J. Spl. agt. FBI, 1956-59; trust officer S.C. Nat. Bank, Charleston, 1959-64; sr. v.p., trust investment officer, also dir. First Nat. Bank, Fort Myers, Fla., 1964—. Pres. Estate Planning Council, Lee County, Fla. Mem. Lee County exec. com. Republican party, 1966-69. Served to 1st lt. AUS, 1951-53. Mem. Financial Analysts Soc. Central Fla., Neb. State Bar Assn., Soc. Former Spl. Agts FBI (pres. S.W. Fla. chpt. 1969-70), C. of C. Home: 1096 N Town and River Dr Fort Myers FL 33901 Office: PO Box 130 Fort Myers FL 33902

DECKER, GEORGE PHARES, educator; b. Holton, Kan., Aug. 1, 1909; s. George W. and Anne Elizabeth (Longenecker) D.; B.S., Kan. State U., 1934; M.S. (Tex. Gulf Sulfur Co. fellow), Tex. A. and M. U., 1935; Ph.D., Cornell U., 1941; m. Velma Fern Thompson, June 6, 1937; children—Glenn Allen, David George, Pharlee Fern (Mrs. James Shellenberger). Research asst. U. Minn., St. Paul, 1935-37; teaching asst. Cornell U., Ithaca, N.Y., 1937-38, research asst., 1938-40, research instr., 1940-42; asso. prof. dept. plant pathology U. Fla., Gainesville, 1942-47, prof., 1947-67, research prof., 1967—, head dept. plant pathology, 1955-67. Adv. chmn. N. Fla. council Boy Scouts Am., 1954—, troop chmn., 1954—. Chmn. bd. dirs. Georgia Seagle Trust, 1962—. Mem. A.A.A.S., Am. Potato Soc. (pres. So. div. 1950-51), Fla. Hort. Soc., Fla. Soil Crops Soc., Gamma Sigma Delta, Sigma Phi. Club: Atheneaum (Gainesville). Home: 903 SW 13th St Gainesville FL 32601

DECKER, ROLAN VAN, chemist, educator; b. Bartlesville, Okla., Nov. 4, 1936; s. Willis Ivan and Marjorie Evelyn (Bashaw) D.; B.S. (NSF fellow 1959-60), Okla. State U., 1958; Ph.D., Purdue U., 1965; m. Priscilla Ruth Smith, Jan. 24, 1961; children—Brian Patrick, Joel Kent. Jr. research chemist Shell Oil Co., Houston, 1957; tech. salesman Charles Pfizer & Co., Oklahoma City, 1958; faculty Southwestern State Coll., Weatherford, Okla., 1965—, prof. chemistry, 1973—. Research asso. Okla. State U., Stillwater, 1973. Precinct chmn. Weatherford Democratic Com., 1971—. Mem. Am. Chem. Soc., Am. Assn. U. Profs. (pres. Okla. conf. 1969-70, 71-72, co-chmn. Okla. conf. com. R 1972—), Phi Lambda Upsilon, Omicron Delta Kappa, Phi Kappa Phi, Kappa Kappa Psi. Home: Rural Route 1 Weatherford OK 73096

DE COLLAZO, FLOR DE MARIA QUINONES, realtor; b. Guanica, P.R., Jan. 6, 1909; d. Eduardo Quinones Martorell and Ma Domilita Rivera de Quinones; student Colegio Puertorriqueno de Ninas, 1928, U. P.R., 1931, N.Y. U., 1929; m. Jorge R. Collazo, June 25, 1938; children—Jorge R., Flor de Mar (dec.). Comml. tchr., P.R., 1930-39; dist. coordinator Govt. P.R., 1939-45; plant supr. Nuzone Cleaners, 1945-59; divisional mgr. Waddell & Reed, Inc., 1960-63; office mgr. Collazo Mortgage & Investment Co., Ponce, 1964—; charge Adventures Overseas Program, Colgate U., 1954—. Pres. Ponce Heart Assn., 1953; mem. bd. Juvenile Red Cross P.R., 1954; mem. Adv. Com. Ch. Properties P.R., 1966. Pres. Fundacion Dr. Pila Hosp., 1971-73. Mem. Ponce Bd. Realtors (past pres.), Altrusa Club (pres. Ponce 1946, coordinator P.R. 1950). Clubs: Deportivo, Yacht and Fishing (Ponce). Author: El Arte de Vender, 1943. Home: 12 Alcazar Alhambra Ponce PR 00731 Office: 12 Alcazar Alhambra Ponce PR 00731

DEDRICK, JOHN HENRY, metals co. exec.; b. Milw., July 10, 1913; s. John Henry and Mathilde Ernestine (Phlamer) D.; B.S. in Chem. Engring., U. Wis., 1935; postgrad. metallurgy Pa. State U., 1936-37; D.Sc., Mass. Inst. Tech., 1948; m. Irene McWhorter, Apr. 1959. With Reynolds Metals Co., 1950—, dir. basic research, 1966-70, exec. asst. v.p. research and devel., 1970-72, gen. dir. metall. research div., Richmond, Va., 1972—. Fellow Am. Chem. Soc.; mem. Am. Soc. Metals, Am. Inst. Metall. Engrs., Brit. Inst. Metals, Va. Acad. Sci., Sigma Xi, Alpha Chi Sigma. Clubs: Sertoma (Richmond), Mass. Inst. Tech. of Va. (v.p.). Contbr. chpts. to books, numerous articles to profl. jours. Patentee field phys. metallurgy. Home: 7618 Cornwall Rd Richmond VA 23229 Office: 4th and Canal Sts Richmond VA 23218

DEEB, RICHARD JAMES, state senator; b. Tallahassee, Sept. 8, 1924; s. George and Mary (Shaheen) D.; B.S. in Civil Engring., U. Notre Dame, 1947; m. Catalina Panayotti, Jan. 7, 1950; children—Alex, Richard, Teresa, Thomas. Operator Dick Deeb Realtor, St. Petersburg, Fla., 1952—; pres. Deeb Constrn. Co., Inc., St. Petersburg, 1952—; mem. Fla. Ho. of Reps., 1963-66; mem. Fla. Senate, 1966—, Republican floor leader, 1971-72, senate minority floor leader, 1972; chmn. 15 state sub-com. on Local Govt. Fiscal Affairs, 1967-68. Dir. Bank of Holiday. Rep. Fla. Legislature to Nat. Legislative Council, 1963-64, 67-68, 73-74. Chmn. St. Petersburg Minimum Housing Standards Bd., 1963-64; vice chmn. nat. com. Constnl. Amendment to Prohibit Forced Busing; nat. v.p. Aiding Leukemia Stricken Am. Children, St. Jude Children's Hosp., 1962-63;

mem. Fla. Select Com. on Aging, Central Pinellas Transit Authority. Served with AUS, 1945-46. Recipient award for outstanding service to all Fla. Vets. AMVETS, 1967; award for outstanding service on behalf all civic orgns. Lions Internat., 1967; Distinguished Pub. Service award Fla. Assn. Realtors, 1967; Distinguished Service award Contractors and Builders Assn., 1969; award for assistance to Fla. citrus industry Fla. Citrus Mut., 1969; Distinguished Service award K.C., 1968. Mem. St. Petersburg Bd. Realtors, Contractors And Builders Assn. Pinellas County, St. Petersburg Audubon Soc., Amvets., Am. Legion. K.C. Clubs: Exchange, Rod and Gun (St. Petersburg). Home: 5750 7th Av N St Petersburg FL 33710 Office: 5675 5th Av N St Petersburg FL 33710

DEEN, BRASWELL DRUE, JR., judge; b. McRae, Ga., Aug. 16, 1925; s. Braswell Drue and Emma Corinne (Smith) D.; LL.B., Ga. Law Sch., 1950; m. Jean Strickland Buie, June 9, 1953; children—Braswell Drue III, Sanders Buie. Admitted to Ga. bar, 1949; practiced in Alma, 1950—; sr. mem. firm Deen & Powell, 1950-52, Deen, 1963—; county atty. Bacon County, 1958-64; judge Ga. State Ct. Appeals, 1965—. Mem. Ga. Ho. of Reps., 1950-58. County chmn. fund drive A.R.C., 1953-54; past pres. Alma Devel. Council; pres. Alma Credit-Trade Bur.; chmn. bd. County Library Bd.; asst. scoutmaster Boy Scouts Am., 1951-52; third vice chmn. Ga. Dem. Exec. Com. Served with USMC, 1943-45. Decorated Purple Heart. Mem. Ga. Chess Assn. (state pres.), Am. Legion, V.F.W. (comdr.; dist. judge adv.), Pi Kappa Alpha, Delta Theta Phi. Methodist (bd. stewards). Lion (dep. dist. gov.). Clubs: Atlanta Athletic, Piedmont Driving, Capitol City, Atlanta County (Atlanta). Home: 4715 Kitty Hawk Pl NW Atlanta GA 30305 Office: State Jud Bldg Atlanta GA 30334

DEERE, CHARLES JOSEPH, physician; b. Lexington, Tenn., June 28, 1909; s. Joe Allen and Annie Louise (Hesse) D.; B.S., Union U., 1929, M.S., 1932, Ph.D., 1937; M.D., U. Tenn., 1939; m. Ella Ingram, Sept. 19, 1933. Teaching fellow, instr. chemistry U. Tenn., Memphis, 1929-37; intern John Gaston Hosp., Memphis, 1939-40; practice medicine, specializing in internal medicine, Memphis, 1945—; mem. staff Bapt. Meml. Hosp., John Gaston Hosp., Meth. Hosp., St. Joseph Hosp.; instr., then asst. and asoo. prof. U. Tenn., 1946-66, clin. prof. medicine, 1966—. Served to maj. AUS, 1941-45. Diplomate Am. Bd. Internal Medicine. Fellow A.C.P.; mem. A.M.A., Tenn. State, Memphis, Shelby County med. assns., Alpha Omega Alpha. Home: 5381 Pecan Grove Lane Memphis TN 38117 Office: 910 Madison St Memphis TN 38103

DEERIN, JAMES BENEDICT, assn. exec.; b. Orange, N.J., Sept. 4, 1915; s. James Benedict and Beatrice (Connolly) D.; student Seton Hall Prep. Sch., 1930-34. Army Command and Gen. Staff Coll., 1951; m. Lucy Lewis, Jan. 17, 1942; children—James Benedict, Margaret Lesesne, Beatrice C., Virginia W., John E. Reporter, Newark News, 1938-41, 46-52; mag. editor, pub., N.J., 1952-54; news corr., Vietnam, 1965; exec. dir. N.G. Assn. of U.S., Washington 1958—. Served with AUS, 1941-46; to col. U.S. Army, 1954-58. Decorated Bronze Star medal, Army Commendation medal. Mem. Nat. Pres Club. Author: Guide for Army National Guardsman, 1959. Home: Oxford MD Office: 1 Massachusetts Av NW Washington DC 20015

DEERING, RONALD FRANKLIN, librarian; b. Paxton, Ill., Oct. 6, 1929; s. Minor Franklin and Grace Gilmore (Perkins) D.; B.A. summa cum laude, Georgetown Coll., 1951; B.D., So. Bapt. Theol. Sem., 1955, Th.D., 1961; M.S. in Library Sci., Columbia, 1967; m. Edith Ann Proctor, June 12, 1966; children—Mark David, Daniel Timothy. Ordained to ministry Bapt. Ch., 1950; instr. religion Georgetown (Ky.) Coll., 1951; pastor Blue River Bapt. Ch., Salem, Ind., 1955-58; instr. Greek, So. Bapt. Theol. Sem., Louisville, 1958-61, research librarian, 1962-67, asso. librarian, 1967-71, librarian, 1971—. Recipient Lilly Fund grant, 1967. Mem. Am. Assn. U. Profs., Am. Acad. Religion, Soc. Bibl. Lit., Phi Alpha Theta, Sigma Tau Delta, Beta Phi Mu. Home: 3803 Layside Dr Louisville KY 40220

DEES, JAMES PARKER, clergyman; b. Greenville, N.C., Dec. 30, 1915; s. James Earl and Margaret Burgwin (Parker) D.; A.B., U. N.C., 1938, postgrad., 1938-39; B.D., Va. Theol. Sem., 1949; D.D. honoris causa, Bob Jones U., 1965; m. Margaret Lucinda Brown, Aug. 10, 1940; children—Margaret Lucinda, Eugenia Johnston. Ordained priest Protestant Episcopal Ch., 1949; priest Aurora, N.C., 1949-52, Beaufort, N.C., 1952-55, Statesville, N.C., 1955-63; resigned, 1963; founder Anglican Orthodox Ch., Statesville, 1963, consecrated bishop, 1964, metropolitan Anglican Orthodox Communion, 1969. Baritone soloist, N.Y.C. Opera Co., 1945. Pres. P.T.A., 1964-66; founder, pres. N.C. Defenders of States' Rights, Inc., 1956; mem. editorial bd. Citizen's Councils Publ., Jackson, Miss., 1959; mem. policy bd. Liberty Lobby, Washington. Bd. dirs. Fedn. Constl. Govt., New Orleans, 1957-60, Independence Found., Portland, Ind., Nat. Conservative Council, Richmond, Va. Served with inf. AUS, 1943-45: Italy. Recipient Liberty award Congress of Freedom, 1969, 70. Mem. Mayflower Soc. Home: 618 Walnut St Statesville NC 28677 Office: 323 Walnut St Statesville NC 28677

DEES, THOMAS HAROLD, real estate exec.; b. Keiser, Ark., May 7, 1940; s. William Thomas and Lucinda Evelyn (Scott) D.; B.S., Ark. State Coll., 1962; M.S., Ark. State U., 1968; m. Nellie Katherine Bowman, Mar. 26, 1963; children—Leslie DeAngela, Lucinda Michelle. Prin. schs., dir. fed. programs Keiser (Ark.) High Sch., 1963-67; prin. schs. Osceola (Ark.) Pub. Schs., 1967-68; bus. mgr., v.p. bus. affairs Ark. Coll., Batesville, 1968-70; treas. Hot Springs (Ark.) Village Property Owners Assn., 1970-71; asst. to financial v.p. Cooper Communities, Inc., Bentonville, Ark., 1971-73; controller Shangri-La, Afton, Okla., 1973—. Chmn. Mississippi County Heart Fund, 1968. Mem. Nat. Assn. Accountants, Mississippi County Edn. Assn. (pres. 1966-67), Phi Delta Kappa, Alpha Kappa Psi. Baptist. Address: Shangri-La Route 3 Afton OK 74331

DEFALCO, LAWRENCE MICHAEL, bishop; b. McKeesport, Pa., Aug. 25, 1915; s. Rosario and Margret (Desmone) DeF.; student St. Vincent's Coll., Latrobe, Pa., 1933-35, St. John's Mission Sem., Little Rock, 1935-42; J.C.L., Gregorian U., Rome, Italy, 1955. Ordained priest Roman Catholic Ch., 1942; asst. pastor St. Patrick's, Ft. Worth, 1942-52, pastor, 1962; asst. pastor Sacred Heart Cathedral, Dallas, 1952; vice chancellor Dallas-Fort Worth Diocese, 1952-55, sec. Marriage Tribunal, 1955-62; pastor Our Lade Perpetual Help Ch., Dallas, 1956-62; bishop of Amarillo, Tex., 1963—. Address: 1800 N Spring St Amarillo TX 79107

DE FELICE, FRANK, economist; b. Boston, Dec. 20, 1932; s. Frank and Karoline (Reis) De F.; B.A. magna cum laude, Mich. State U., 1961; M.B.A., U. N.C. (Nat. Def. Edn. Act fellow 1961-64), 1963, Ph.D., 1967; m. Eleanor Elizabeth Sullivan, June 20, 1950; children—Frank, Kathleen Ann, William. Asst. prof. div. econs. and bus. adminstrn. U. N.C., Charlotte, 1966-69; asso. prof. econs. East Carolina Coll., 1965-66; asso. prof. econs., dir. Computer Center, Queens Coll., 1969-71; prof. econs. Belmont Abbey Coll., Belmont, N.C., 1971; dir., pres., gen. mgr. Frank DeFelise & Assos., Inc. Vis. asso. prof. Davidson Coll., 1970. Chmn. adv. bd. West Charlotte High Sch., 1972—. Ford postdoctoral fellow, 1968-69. Mem. Am., So. econ. assns., Beta Gamma Sigma, Phi Kappa Phi, Alpha Kappa Psi, Tau Sigma. Author: A Primer on Business Finance, 1974. Contbr. articles to profl. jours. Home: 5032 Allen Rd E Charlotte NC 28213 Office: Box 26576 Charlotte NC 28213

DEFEO, RICHARD JOSEPH, chem. co. exec.; b. Kansas City, Mo., June 10, 1932; s. John Michael and Barbara (Weitzel) DeF.; B.S., U. Mo., 1953, Ph.D., 1958; m. Phyllis Ballow, June 3, 1953; children—Debra Ann, John Michael. Chemist, Esso Research Labs., Baton Rouge, 1958-69; process supr. Exxon Chem. Co., Baton Rouge, 1969—. Pres., Baton Rouge Little Theater, 1971—. Served with AUS, 1953-55. Mem. Am. Chem. Soc., Sigma Xi, Phi Beta Kappa, Pi Mu Epsilon, Tau Kappa Epsilon. Patentee in field. Home: 1142 Ashbourne Dr Baton Rouge LA 70815 Office: Exxon Chemical Co Baton Rouge LA 70815

DEFFEYES, ROBERT JOSEPH, powder metals and magnets co. exec.; b. Oklahoma City, Aug. 16, 1935; s. Joseph Alfred and Hazel (Stover) D.; B.S., Cal. Inst. Tech., 1957; postgrad. U. Cal. at Berkeley, 1958-69, Stanford, 1964-66, San Jose State U., 1967; m. Ethel Bell Black, Aug. 2, 1958; children—Joan E., Suzanne C. Engr., Dow Chem. Co., Pittsburg, Cal., 1957-61, devel. engr., Kalama, Wash., 1961-63; mgr. mfg. tech. service Memorex, Inc., Santa Clara, Cal., 1963-69; v.p. Graham Magnetics, Inc., also pres. Cobaloy div., Arlington, Tex., 1969—. Served with U.S. Army, 1958. Fellow Am. Inst. Chemists; mem. Am. Inst. Chem. Engrs., Am. Assn. Contamination Control. Home: 804 Red Oak St Arlington TX 76012 Office: 626 Great SW Pkwy Arlington TX 76011

DEFOREST, ELBERT MURRAY, petroleum engr.; b. Natoma, Kan., July 17, 1917; B.S., Tulsa U., 1940; m. Lois Ellen Wimmer, Sept. 25, 1942; children—Elbert Lee, Kenneth. Jr. petroleum engr. Gulf Oil Corp., 1940-41; chemist, E. I. duPont de Nemours & Co., 1941-42, devel. process engr., 1942-46; sr. process engr. Spencer Chem. Co., 1946-47, mgr. process engring., 1947-49; sr. project engr. Pan Am. Petroleum Corp., Standard Oil Co., 1949-50, supt. chem. mfg., 1950-52; mgr. new projects Frontier Chem. Co. div., Vulcan Materials Co., Birmingham, Ala., 1952-59, mgr. research and devel., 1959-67, v.p. research and devel. Vulcan Materials Chems. and Metals, 1967-73, dir. tech., 1973—. Mem. Am. Inst. Chem. Engrs., Am. Chem. Soc., A.A.A.S., Am. Inst. Mining, Metall. and Petroleum Engrs., Licensing Execs. Soc. Home: 412 S Maize Rd Wichita KS 67209 Office: PO Box 7497 Birmingham AL 35223 also PO Box 545 Wichita KS 67201

DEFOREST, JOHN DUANE, economist; b. Peabody, Kan., Jan. 13, 1930; s. John Daniel and Cleo (Marsh) D.; B.S., Kan. State U., 1955, M.S., 1957; postgrad. (Cordell Hull fellow), Vanderbilt U., 1956-57; Ph.D., U. Ia., 1961; post-doctoral fellow U. Mich., 1964-65; m. Peggy Glee Stratman, June 15, 1952; children—Debra Dru, Denise Sue, Deanne. Asst. prof. econs. Denison U., Granville, O., 1959-62; program economist U.S. Aid Mission to Colombia, 1962-64; prof. econs. Parsons Coll., Fairfield, Ia., 1965-67; economist Econ. Devel. Adminstrn., U.S. Dept. Commerce. Washington, 1967-71, sr. economist Office of Environmental Affairs, 1971-74. Professorial lectr. bus. adminstrn. George Washington U., Washington, 1968—. Served with USMC, 1948-51. Mem. Am. Men Sci., Am. Econ. Assn., A.A.A.S., Phi Kappa Phi, Alpha Kappa Psi, Beta Theta Pi. Home: 3204 Wessynton Way Alexandria VA 22309

DE FRANK, VINCENT, condr.; ed. Juilliard Sch. Music; hon. D.Music, Ind. U., Southwestern at Memphis. Debut as condr. radio sta. WNYC Radio Orch.; formerly mem. Detroit Symphony, St. Louis Symphony; founder, condr. Memphis Sinfonietta (became Memphis Symphony 1960), 1952; condr. Memphis Youth Symphony; guest condr. numerous musical groups, summer music camps, clinics. Address: 1503 Monroe Memphis TN 38104

DEGEER, MYRON WINTERSTEIN, civil engr.; b. Deerhead, Kan., June 2, 1912; s. Vaughn Eugene and Hazel (Race) D.; B.S., Kan. State U., 1938; m. Ethelyn Nichols, Nov. 11, 1933 (dec.); 1 dau., Mary (Mrs. DeJarnette Herring). With div. water resources Kan. Bd. Agr., Topeka, 1938-39; with U.S. Army Corps of Engrs., Tulsa, 1939—, chief engring. div., 1963—. Recipient Meritorious Civilian Service award U.S. Army, 1971. Fellow Am. Soc. C.E.; mem. Nat. Soc. Profl. Engrs., Soc. Am. Mil. Engrs. Home: 4060 S 54th St Apt 106 Tulsa OK 74135 Office: PO Box 61 Tulsa OK 74102

DEGGES, IRA DONALD, civil engr.; b. Gulledge, Ark., Apr. 17, 1929; s. Ira Dwight and Annie (Gibbs) D.; B.S. in Civil Engring., La. Poly. Inst., 1958; m. Vonnie Faye Mayo, Apr. 15, 1960; children—James Ira, Paul Donald, Karen Elizabeth, Bruce Neal. Self-employed pulpwood producer, Hamburg, Ark., 1947-51, 53-54; project engr. La. Dept. Hwys., Monroe, Tallulah, 1958-62; with Fed. Hwy. Adminstrn., 1962—, asst. area engr., Austin, Tex., 1962-63, area engr., Oklahoma City, 1963-66, dist. engr., Little Rock, 1966-69, asst. div. engr., engring. coordinator, Nashville, 1969—. Served with AUS, 1951-53. Mem. Am. Soc. C.E., Nat. Soc. Profl. Engrs. Baptist. Home: 2662 Forest View Dr Antioch TN 37013 Office: Fed Hwy Adminstrn 4004 Hillsboro Rd Nashville TN 37215

DEHAAN, HENRY J., psychologist; b. East St. Louis, Ill., Nov. 23, 1920; s. Henry J. and Fanny (Haislip) deH.; A.B., Washington U., St. Louis, 1942, M.A., 1949; Ph.D. U. Pitts., 1960; m. Mary J. Farrell, Oct. 22, 1943. Research psychologist VA Hosp., Coatesville, Pa., 1960-62; research scientist Human Resources Research Office, George Washington U., 1962-64; research psychologist Armed Forces Radiobiology Research Inst., Naval Med. Center, Bethesda, Md., 1965-69, U.S. Army Research Inst., Arlington, Va., 1969—. Faculty, U.S. Dept. Agr. Grad. Sch., 1967—. Served with USNR, 1944-46. Mem. A.A.A.S., Am. Psychol. Assn., Internat. Primatological Soc., Soc. for Neurosci., Sigma Xi. Contbr. articles to profl. lit. Home: 5403 Yorkshire St Springfield VA 22151 Office: US Army Research Inst Arlington VA 22209

DEHART, ROBERT CHARLES, research co. exec.; b. Laramie, Wyo., Aug. 16, 1917; s. Charles Edward and Harriet Irene (Tapling) DeH.; B.S., U. Wyo., 1938; M.S., Ill. Inst. Tech., 1940, Ph.D., 1953; m. Ethel M. Thompson, Sept. 20, 1941 (dec. Apr. 1970); children—Michael R., Dayle Ann; m. 2d, Marion W. McDonald, Aug. 21, 1970. Design engr., Standard Oil Co., Wood River, Ill., 1940-46; asso. prof. Mont. State U., Bozeman, 1946-53; analyst Armed Forces Spl. Weapons Project, Washington, 1953-58; mgr. structural mechanics S.W. Research Inst., San Antonio, 1958-59, dir. structural research, 1959-72, tech. v.p., 1972—. Lectr., George Washington U., Washington, 1955-58. Mem. Am. Soc. C.E., Am. Soc. M.E., N.Y. Acad. Scis., Sigma Xi, Phi Kappa Phi, Tau Beta Pi, Sigma Tau. Home: 403 LaJara St San Antonio TX 78209 Office: 8500 Culebra Rd San Antonio TX 78284

DEHAVEN, ERNEST THOMAS, hosp. adminstr.; b. Hiram Twp., O., Aug. 7, 1928; s. Ernest Roy and Bertha Catherine (Thomas) DeH.; A.B., Hiram Coll., 1949; M.H.A., Med. Coll. Va., 1957; m. Barbara Ann Hoskin, Aug. 21, 1955; children—Matthew, Stephen, Catherine. Adminstr. Albert Schweitzer Meml. Hosp., Haiti, 1958-59, Jackman Meml. Hosp., Bilaspur, India, 1959-64; asst. adminstr. Lake County Meml. Hosp., Painesville, O., 1965-67; adminstr. Carroll County Meml. Hosp., Carrollton, Ky., 1967—. Trustee No. Ky. Health and Social Planning Council. Served with AUS, 1953-54. Mem. Ky. Hosp. Assn. (v.p. 1969-70, trustee 1970—), Am. Coll. Hosp. Adminstrs. Mem. Christian Ch. Rotarian. Home: 119 Comanche Trail Carrollton KY 41008 Office: 309 11th St Carrollton KY 41008

DEHOFF, ROBERT THOMAS, educator; b. Sharon, Pa., Jan. 15, 1934; s. George Leo and Zita Marie (Kelley) D.; B.E., Youngstown State U., 1955; M.S. (Alcoa fellow 1957-59), Carnegie Mellon U., 1958, Ph.D., 1959; m. Marjorie Linnea Davis, June 8, 1957; children—Robert Thomas II, Susan Linnea. Asst. prof. U. Fla., Gainesville, 1959-62, asso. prof., 1962-70, prof. dept. materials sci. and engring., 1970—. Cons. Hanford Atomic Power, 1962, Argonne Nat. Labs., 1972, Inst. for Gas Tech., 1973. Mem. Internat. Soc. for Stereology, Am. Soc. for Metals, Am. Inst. Mining, Metall. and Petroleum Engrs., Am. Metal Powders Inst., Sigma Xi, (Outstanding Tchr. award 1964), Alpha Sigma Mu, Tau Beta Pi. Author: Quantitative Microscopy, 1968. Editor: Stereologia, 1963-67. Home: 1500 NW 30th St Gainesville FL 32605

DEHUECK, GEORGE THEODORE M., finanical holding co. cons.; b. Toronto, Ont., Can., July 17, 1921; s. Baron Boris and Baroness Catherine (deKolychkine) deH.; B.A., Queen's U., 1946; postgrad. U. Chgo., 1946-48; m. Elena Tcherbatchev; children—Sharon Diane Castelin, Paul, Mary Catherine, Pete, Ian. Agt., Lincoln Nat. Life Ins. Co., Chgo., 1948-50; sales research asst. Conn. Gen. Life Ins. Co., Hartford, 1950-52; agy. v.p. Am. Bankers Life Assurance Co., Miami, Fla., 1952-54; cons. Life Ins. Industry, 1954-56; pres. Am. Insurors Devel. Co., 1956-61; owner George T. deHueck & Assos., Mobile, Ala. Served from rifleman to lt., Canadian Army, 1940-45. C.L.U. Mem. Am. Soc. C.L.U.'s, Am. Numis. Soc. Club: Bienville (Mobile); Lotos (N.Y.C.); Adventurers. Office: 413 One Office Park Bldg Mobile AL 36609

DEICHMANN, WILLIAM BERNHARD, coll. adminstr.; b. Kiel, Germany, Sept. 7, 1902; s. Johann Wilhelm and Mathilde Gesine (Bollenhagen) D.; came to U.S., 1924, naturalized, 1930; A.B., Western Res. U., 1932, M.S., 1934; Ph.D., U. Cin., 1939; M.D. (hon.) Christian Albrechts U., Kiel, Germany, 1972; m. Hedy Gruebler, Aug. 4, 1928; children—Herbert, Herta (Mrs. John Hayse Holly). Asst. biochemistry Western Res. U., Cleve., 1928-34; jr. pharmacologist DuPont Haskell Lab. Indsl. Toxicology, Wilmington, Del., 1934-37; asst. Kettering Lab., instr. pharmacology U. Cin., 1947; asso. prof. Union U., Albany Med. Coll., Schenectady, 1947-50, prof. pharmacology, 1950-53; prof., chmn. dept. pharmacology U. Miami Sch. Medicine, Carol Gables, Fla., 1953-69, prof. pharmacology, dir. Research and Teaching Center Toxicology, 1969—. Mem. Nat. Bd. Med. Examiners, 1948-53; cons. pharmacology and toxicology Sterling Winthrop Research Inst., Rensselaer, N.Y., 1947—, Esso Research & Engring. Co., Linden, N.J., 1950—, Lehn & Fink Products Co., Montvale, N.J., 1971—. Fellow A.A.A.S., Am. Coll. Clin. Pharmacology and Chemotherapy, Ohio, N.Y. acads. sci., Royal Soc. Medicine (Eng.); mem. Am., Pan Am. (pres. sect. toxicology 1963—) med. assns., Am. Indsl. Hygiene Assn. (sect. pres. 1949), Am. Therapeutic Soc., Am. Soc. for Pharmacology and Exptl. Therapeutics (emeritus), Soc. Toxicology (founder, treas. 1961-64), Deutsche Pharmakologische Gesellschaft), N.Y. State Soc. for Med. Research, Permanent Commn. and Internat. Assn. on Occupational Health, U.S. Naval Inst. (asso.), Oceanographic Soc., U.S. Power Squadrons, Sigma Xi. Clubs: Navigators of So. Fla. (pres. 1959-60); U. Miami (Fla.) Yacht (founder, commodore 1955-59, dir.); U. Miami Faculty (pres. 1965-68). Author: (with H.W. Gerarde) Toxicology of Drugs and Chemicals, 4th edit., 1969; others. Asso. editor: Industrial Medicine and Surgery, 1970—; mem. hon. adv. bd. Food and Cosmetics Toxicology, 1970—; bd. editors Archives of Toxicology, 1970—. Contbr. numerous articles to profl. jours. Home: 1931 S Bayshore Dr Miami FL 33133 Office: Research and Teaching Center of Toxicology U Miami Sch Medicine PO Box 8216 Coral Gables FL 33124

DEIDESHEIMER, HAROLD JACOB, advt. exec.; b. N.Y.C., Feb. 1, 1917; s. Charles Phillip and Adeline (Erdenbrecher) D.; student pub. schs.; m. Mary Ann Moroni, Jan. 26, 1958; 1 dau., Annamaria E. Dir. printing Hazard Advt. Co., N.Y.C., 1948-53; salesman, printing cons. Reiman Conway Assos., N.Y.C., 1953-55; prodn. mgr., dir. printing and purchasing Harris & Whitebrook & Co., Miami Beach, Fla., 1955-57; prodn. mgr. C.J. LaRoche & Co., N.Y.C., 1957-58; asso. mgr. advt. prodn. controls Gen. Food Corp., White Plains, N.Y., 1959-64; adminstrv. mgr., account exec. firm Bishopric Green Fielden Advt., Miami, Fla., 1966-71; pres. Financial Plaza Advt. Co., Ft. Lauderdale, Fla., 1971—. Recipient Cronite awards Art Dirs. Club N.Y., 1952. Miami, 1956, Detroit, 1958. Address: 2100 NW 12th Av Fort Lauderdale FL 33311

DEININGER, ROBERT WADE, educator; b. Monroe, Wis., Aug. 15, 1927; s. Ernest Michael and Lena (Wenger) D.; B.S., U. Wis., 1950, M.S., 1957; Ph.D., Rice U., 1964; m. Margaret Atkinson Donaldson, Sept. 4, 1960; children—Mary, Elizabeth. Geologist, U.S. Army Engrs., Jacksonville, Fla., 1951-53; field geologist Tidewater Oil Co., Casper, Wyo., 1957-58; instr. geology U. Conn., 1960-62; instr. U. Ala., 1962-64, asst. prof. geology, 1964-66; asst. prof. geology Memphis State U., 1966-68, asso. prof., 1968—. Served with USNR, 1945-46. Fellow Geol. Soc. Am.; mem. Geochem. Soc., Internat. Assn. Geochemistry and Cosmochemistry, Sigma Xi. Home: 4707 Sequoia Rd Memphis TN 38117

DEITENBECK, WILLIAM, editor; b. LaGrange, Ill., Oct. 30, 1919; s. Max and Sarah Claire (Collins) D.; B.A., Birmingham So. Coll., 1942; m. Madelyn Ruth Downs, Mar. 9, 1948; 1 son, William. Mgr. Paramount Theatres, So. cities, 1945-56; dir. pub. relations, editor Cinderella Internat. Corp., 1957-59, Viviane Woodard Corp., 1960-62; mgr. advt. Fla. Field Report, Orlando, 1963-64, editor, 1965—, owner, 1968—. Treas. United Cerebral Palsy of Miss., 1954-56. Served with USAAF, 1942-45; PTO. Recipient Distinguished Service award Fla. Dairy Products Assn., 1971. Mem. Agribus. Inst. Fla. (bd. dirs.), Fla. Mag. Assn. (award 1970; bd. dirs., pres.), Fla. Press Assn. Democrat. Presbyn. Home: 3000 Delaney Av Orlando FL 32806 Office: Fla Field Report 17 S Lake Av Orlando FL 32801

DEITZ, ROBERT EUGENE, journalist; b. Winona, W.Va., May 8, 1940; s. Merritt Singleton and Irene Elizabeth (Wilder) D.; student U. Ky., 1959-62; m. Marsha Ann Kingsley, Aug. 1, 1964; children—Marcus Wilder, Robert Addison, Adam Kingsley. Reporter, Lexington (Ky.) Herald, 1962-63; polit. reporter Louisville Courier-Jour., 1963-67, asso. editor, 1970-72, dir. pub. relations, 1973—; staff writer Nat. Observer, Silver Spring, Md., 1967-68; mgr. systems planning Louisville Courier-Jour. and Louisville Times, 1968-70; Nieman fellow, Harvard, 1971-72. Served with USMCR, 1957-61. Home: 2366 Valley Vista Rd Louisville KY 40205 Office: Louisville Courier-Journal 525 W Broadway Louisville KY 40202

DEJARNETTE, JAMES TERRY, state ofcl.; b. Bessemer, Ala., Jan. 30, 1909; s. James Terry and Daisy Laura (Marbut) deJ.; A.B., U. Ala., 1931; postgrad. Ala. Poly. Inst., 1940. Ga. State Coll., 1961-63; m. Dorothy Leona Davis, June 27, 1946; 1 dau., Ethel Terry (Mrs. Earl Lamar Robertson). Chief engr. Ala. Dept Conservation, 1941-42; bus. mgr. Ga. Youth Devel. Center, Milledgeville, 1969—. Served to col C.E., AUS, 1958-62. Decorated Legion of Merit. Registered profl. engr., Ga. Mem. Delta Chi. Clubs: Milledgeville Country,

Milledgeville Rotary; Old Guard (Atlanta). Home: Pine Valley Rd Milledgeville GA 31061 Office: PO Box 1092 Milledgeville GA 31061

DEJEAN, CHARLES ELWOOD, constrn. co. exec.; b. Biloxi, Miss., July 15, 1912; s. Charles and Ethel (George) DeJ.; B.A., Baylor U., 1935, postgrad., 1936-37; m. Doris Gamble, Sept. 20, 1944; children—Sandra (Mrs. Thomas L. Patterson), Jon Cherrie. Insp. Blue Bonnet Ordnance Plant, McGregor, Tex., 1942-43; asst. chief chemist Premier Oil Co., Cotton Valley, La., 1943-45; owner Eze Orange Bottling Co., Prichard, Ala., 1945-47; soils dir. A.W. Williams Inspection Co., Mobile, Ala., 1947-53; co-owner, pres., sr. engring. technician, dir. soils chemistry and asphalt depts. Dixie Labs., Inc., Mobile and Dothan, Ala. and Columbus, Ga., 1953—. Pres. Exchange Club, Prichard, 1963. Mem. Am. Chem. Soc., Am. Soc. Testing Materials, C. of C., Better Bus. Bur. Baptist (bd. deacons 1958-71). Club: Lake Forrest Country (Spanish Fort, Ala.). Home: 113 Baratara Dr Mobile AL 36611 Office: 604 Loeffler St Mobile AL 36607

DE JESUS TORO, ROBERTO, banker; b. San Juan, P.R., July 27, 1918; s. Francisco and Graciela (Toro) de Jesus; B.S. in Econs., Wharton Sch. Finance and Commerce, U. Pa., 1940; M.B.A., 1943; m. Sylvia Pou, Aug. 17, 1947; children—Roberto, Sylvia, Nestor, Ana Maria. Dir. Bur. of Budget, Govt. of P.R., 1945-51; v.p. Govt. Devel. Bank of P.R., San Juan, 1951-54; exec. v.p. Banco de Ponce (P.R.), 1954-59, pres., 1959—, also dir.; dir. Puerto Rican Cement Co. Inc., Puerto Rican and Am. Ins. Co., Ponce Hotel Corp., Union Carbide Caribe Inc., Union Carbide Corp. Served to sgt. AUS, 1943-45. Home: Condominio Palma Real 15 G Calle Madrid Santurce PR 00731 Office: Banco de Ponce PO Box 4228 Ponce PR 00731

DELAAT, BART, petroleum cons.; b. Montpelier, Ind., Dec. 15, 1904; s. William Penn and Beth (Pearson) DeL.; Petroleum Engr., Colo. Sch. Mines, 1930; m. Helen Margaret Ryan, June 6, 1971. Engr., asst. supt. Gulf Oil Corp., 1930-38; asst. chief engr., dist. mgr. Pure Oil Co., 1939-46; gen. mgr., exec. cons. Dow-Brazos, 1947-53; petroleum cons. in mgmt. engring. and geology, Houston, 1954—; exec. v.p., dir. Pano Tech Exploration Corps., now chmn. bd. Vice-chmn. bd. dirs. Served as lt. Hdqrs. Bn., Engrs. Res. Corps, 1930-34. Mem. Am. Petroleum Inst., Am. Inst. Mining, Metall. and Petroleum Engrs., Houston Petroleum Club, Tex. Mid-Continent Oil and Gas Assn. Clubs: Houston; Cercle de l'nion (San Francisco); South Shore Country (Chgo.). Home: 3822 Piping Rock Lane Houston TX 77027 Office: C & I Bldg Houston TX 77027

DE LA HOUSSAYE, EDWARD ANTHONY, III, judge; b. Franklin, La., May 4, 1930; s. Edward Anthony and Heloise (Fay) de la H.; B.S., La. State U., 1951; LL.B., Tulane U., 1956, J.D., 1956; grad. Nat. Coll. State Trial Judges, Reno, 1969; m. Mary Kay Oakley, Dec. 21, 1957; children—Mary Downs, Jeanne Marie, Heloise Marie, Lisette Anne, Adrienne Claire. Admitted to La. bar, 1956; practiced in Franklin, 1957-66; 1st asst. dist. atty. 16th Jud. Dist. La., 1964-66; judge 16th Jud. Dist. Ct. La., 1966—. Dist. chmn. Teche dist. Evangeline Area council Boy Scouts Am., 1963, 64, chmn. finance drive, 1965-66; chmn. finance drives A.R.C., 1959-60, March of Dimes, 1960-61. Chmn. Municipal Democratic Exec. Com., Franklin, 1961-64. Served to 1st USAF, 1951-53. Mem. Moot Ct. Bd. Tulane U. Law Sch. Mem. La. Juvenile Judges Assn. (pres. 1970-71, dir.), La. Dist. Judges Assn. (v.p., dir.), La. Soc., S.A.R., Beta Theta Pi, Phi Delta Phi. K.C. (4 deg.). Club: Belleview Golf and Country (past pres.) (Franklin). Home: 112 Oakwood Dr Franklin LA 70538 Office: St Mary Parish Court House Franklin LA 70538

DELAITSCH, DALE M., educator; b. Colfax, Wis., Dec. 18, 1922; B.S., U. Chgo., 1944; A.B., St. Olaf Coll., 1946; Ph.D. in Chemistry, U. Minn., 1950; m. 1945; 2 children. Asst. prof. chemistry U. Southwestern La., Lafayette, 1950-52, asso. prof., 1952-63, prof., 1963—. Served to 1st lt. USAAF, 1943-46. Mem. Am. Chem. Soc. Address: Dept Chemistry U Southwestern La Lafayette LA 70501*

DELAMERENS, SERGIO ANDRES, hematologist; b. Havana, Cuba, Feb. 4, 1928; s. Arturo A. and Dolores (deZayas) DeL.; B.S., PreUniv. Inst., Matanzas, Cuba, 1946; M.D., Havana U., 1953; M.S., U. Tenn., 1967; m. Maria Teresa Ortiz, June 22, 1957; children—Sergio, Maria Teresa, Goar. Intern, U. Hosp., Havana, 1953-54; resident in pediatrics Univ. Hosp., Havana, 1954-56, Frank Tobey Hosp., Memphis, 1961-63; practice medicine, specializing in pediatrics, Havana, 1956-60, Milw., 1965-67, Memphis, 1967-73; instr. pediatrics U. Havana Med. Sch. 1956-60 asst. prof. pediatrics Marquette U., 1965-67; asst. prof. pediatrics, chief pediatric hematology U. Tenn. Med. Sch., 1967-73, asso. prof. pediatrics, chief pediatric hematology, 1972-73; dir. div. hematology and oncology Variety Children's Hosp., Miami, 1973—; hematology cons. Milw. Childrens Hosp., Meth. Hosp., Bapt. Hosp., St. Joseph Hosp., LeBonheur Hosp., Memphis. Chmn. med. adv. council chpt. Memphis Hemophilia Found., 1967-69. Recipient Cabrera Saavedra award, 1956, Aballi award, 1956 Havana. Mem. So. Soc. Pediatric Research, Am. Hematology Soc., Am. Acad. Pediatrics, A.M.A., Pediatric Soc. Medellin, Bogota and Cali, Sigma Xi. Contbr. articles profl. jours. Home: 120 Sunrise Av Coral Gables FL 33133 Office: Variety Children's Hosp Miami FL 33155

DELANEY, THOMAS CALDWELL, JR., museum exec.; b. Danville, Va., Jan. 1, 1918; s. Thomas C. and Ethel (Loving) D.; B.S., Spring Hill Coll., 1941; M.A., U. Ala., 1952; m. Lois Jean Fitzsimmons, July 20, 1960. Dean U. Mil. Sch., Mobile, Ala., 1941-56; founder, supt. Julius T. Wright Sch. for Girls, Mobile, 1956-65; mus. dir. City of Mobile, 1965—. Mem. adv. bd. Providence Sch. Nursing, 1956-59, U.S. Civil War Centennial Commn., 1958-65; rep. Mobile County Ala. First Capital Commn., 1961-65. Historian Mobile 250th Anniversary Celebration, 1961, Mobile Civil War Centennial Comm., 1961-65, Mobile Sesquicentennial Comm., 1969. Bd. dirs. Mobile Civic Music Assn., Mobile Symphony, Historic Mobile Preservation Soc. Recipient Ala. Penwomen award, 1962. Mem. Ala. Hist. Assn. (pres. 1962-63), Mobile Art Assn. Rotarian, Author: Deep South, 1942; Remember Mobile, 1948, 69; The Story of Mobile, 1953, 61; Madame Octavia Walton LeVert, 1961; Mary McNeil Fenollosa, 1963; The Phoenix Volunteer Fire Company of Mobile 1838-1888, 1967; The First Hundred Years, 1968; Craighead's Mobile, 1968; Confederate Mobile, 1971. Home: 8 S Ann St Mobile AL 36604 Office: 203 S Claiborne St Mobile AL 36602

DELAP, JAMES HARVE, educator; b. Carbondale, Ill., Feb. 6, 1930; s. Harve Eugene and Adena Rosetta (Harriss) DeL.; B.A., So. Ill. U., 1952; postgrad. U. Cal. at Berkeley, 1954-55; M.A., Duke U., 1959, Ph.D., 1960; m. Prudence Todd, Mar. 29, 1959; children—Carolyn, Mary, Margaret, Todd. Chemist, Chemstrand Research Center, Durham, N.C., 1960-62; faculty Stetson U., DeLand, Fla., 1962—, asso. prof. chemistry, 1966-71, prof., 1971—. Served with AUS, 1952-54. James B. Duke fellow, 1957-60; Fulbright lectr., Nepal, 1970-71. Mem. Am. Chem. Soc., Am. Phys. Soc., Am. Assn. U. Profs., Sigma Xi, Gamma Sigma Epsilon (grand visor). Presbyn. Home: 1103 N Boston St DeLand FL 32720 Office: Dept Chemistry Stetson U DeLand FL 32720

DE LA PARTE, LOUIS ANTHONY, state senator; b. Tampa, Fla., July 27, 1929; s. Louis and Dulce (Santa Cruz) de la P.; B.A., Emory U.; LL.B., U. Fla.; m. Helen C. White, Nov. 23, 1957; children—Louis David, Martha Ann. Admitted to Fla. bar; practice law, Tampa; spl. asst. atty. gen. State of Fla., 1953; asst. county solicitor, Hillsborough County, Fla., 1957-60; asst. state atty. 13th Jud. Circuit, 1960-61; mem. Fla. Senate, 1966—, senate pres. pro tempore, 1973-74, pres., 1974—. Mem. Fla. Ho. of Reps., 1962-66; del. Democratic nat. conv., 1968. Served to capt. USAF, 1953-56. Recipient Allen Morris award, 1967, 71, 73, Outstanding Senator award Tax Assessors Assn. Fla., 1972, award for service Cuban Vet. Med. Assn. in Exile, 1972, Outstanding State Legislator award Fla. Young Dems., 1972, award for leadership Hillsborough County Classroom Tchrs. Assn., 1972-74, award for service Cuban Drs. in Exile, 1973, award for service Cuban Lawyers in Exile, 1973; named Most Valuable Senator St. Petersburg (Fla.) Times, 1969, 70, 74, Legislator of Year Fla. Assn. Retarded Children, 1969-74, Legislator of Year Fla. Vol. Health Assns., 1970, Legislator of Year, Pros. Attys. Assn., 1972, Mem. Am., Fla. bar assns., Am., Fla. trial lawyers assns., Fla. Blue Key (hon.), Phi Delta Phi, Eta Sigma Phi, Sigma Alpha Epsilon. Roman Catholic. Home: 8003 N Rome St Tampa FL 33604 Office: 725 E Kennedy Blvd Tampa FL 33602*

DE LA SIERRA, ANGELL ORTIZ, coll. adminstr.; b. Santurce, P.R., Feb. 28, 1936; s. Juan Ortiz and Barbara de la S.; B.S., U. P.R., 1954; M.S., Coll. City N.Y., 1958; Ph.D., St. John's U., 1963; m. Judith Sheffer-Lavalle, Dec. 31, 1960; children—Angell Ortiz II, John Arthur, Daniel Gerard, Barbara Grace, Denise Roxanne. Research analyst Smithsonian Instn., Washington, 1963-64; research chemist Defense Atomic Support Agy., Washington, 1964-65; NIH fellow Georgetown U., Washington, 1965-67; vis. prof. Faculty of Medicine, U. P.R., 1967-68, dir. Faculty of Natural Scis., 1968—. Lectr. on univ. and community interactions at various academic and civic orgns. Served with USAF, 1963-70. Mem. Am. Phys. Soc., Am. Chem. Soc., N.Y. Acad. Scis., Biophys. Soc., Sigma Xi. Contbr. articles in field to profl. jours. Home: 1-7 Faculty Residence University of Puerto Rico Cayey PR 00633

DELAUGHTER, GEORGE W., automobile agy. exec.; b. Sparkman, Ark., Oct. 11, 1916; s. George W. and Mary Pearl (Cookston) DeL.; student Ouachita Bapt. Coll., 1935-38; m. Martha Jean Taylor, Apr. 28, 1946; children—Abigail (Mrs. Larry F. Pennington), Susan (Mrs. Jerry Young). Mgr., Sparkman Motor Co., 1940—; pres. DeLaughter Butane Co., Sparkman, 1946, Zero Gas Co., Inc., Arkadelphia, Ark., 1950—; sec. Quality L.P. Gas Co., Inc., Nashville, Ark., 1964-68; pres. DeLaughter Transport Co., Inc., Sparkman, 1962—; v.p., dir. Mchts. & Planters Bank, Sparkman. Mem. Ark. Liquefied Petroleum Gas Control Bd. Chmn., Sparkman Housing Authority, 1964—; mayor, Sparkman, 1952-64. Past pres. Dallas County Fair Assn. Trustee Ouchita Bapt. U. Served to maj., inf. AUS, 1942-46. Decorated Bronze Star. Mem. Res. Officers Assn., Am. Legion. Democrat. Baptist. Lion. Address: PO Box 97 Sparkman AR 71763

DELAUGHTER, JERRY WILLFRED, journalist; b. nr. Brookhaven, Miss., Jan. 1, 1935; s. H. M. and Grace E. (Rials) DeL.; B.A., Miss. Coll., 1958; M.A., U. Miss., 1959; m. Mary Norman Van Zandt, Oct. 28, 1960. Sports editor The Natchez (Miss.) Democrat, 1957; sports writer The Clarion-Ledger, Jackson, Miss., 1957-58, editorial staff, 1959-63; writer, travel dept. Miss. Agrl. and Indsl. Bd., Jackson, 1964-66; chief Miss. bur. Memphis Comml. Appeal, Jackson, 1966-70; dir. Inst. of Politics in Miss., Millsaps Coll., Jackson, 1970-73. Recipient Sullivan Writing Award, 1958; A.P. Newswriting award, 1963. Mem. Sigma Delta Chi, Sigma Tau Delta.

DE LAURÉAL, WILLIAM DAVID, cons. engr.; b. Broussard, La., Jan. 8, 1914; s. George Rene and Marie Olymphe (Ducrest) d.; student Southwestern La. Inst., 1930-32; B.S., La. State U., 1934; m. Eva Wilkinson Allen, Dec. 27, 1941; children—William David, Carolyn (Mrs. John Roxburgh Jr.), Martin Rene, Eva Marie. Founder, W. David de Lauréal, cons. engr., New Orleans, 1946— (inc. 1965 under name of de Lauréal Engrs., Inc.), pres., 1965—. Served to capt. C.E. AUS. Mem. Am. Soc. Mil. Engrs., Cons. Engrs. Council. Home: 1912 State St New Orleans LA 70118 Office: 2 Canal St New Orleans LA 70130

DELAY, CLARENCE NORTON WARREN, petroleum co. exec.; b. Salina, Kan., Feb. 3, 1920; s. Nathan Henry and Mary (Peterson) D.; student Houston U., 1951-54, Dale Carnegie Course, 1967; m. Lillian Pearl Wedel, Feb. 20, 1940; children—Galen Arnie, Gary Lee, Dale Gene. Service sta. attendant, clk. George R. Hess, 1937-38; roustabout Hamner McLean Drilling Co., Galva, Kan., 1938-40, Warren Petroleum Corp., Galva, 1940-41; supt. Warren Petroleum Co. div. Gulf Oil Corp., Breckenridge, Tex., 1965—. Active Boy Scouts Am.; Fairbanks, (Tex.) pres. United Fund Drive, Breckenridge, 1967-68. Mem. Planning and Zoning Commn., Breckenridge, 1968-71; city commr. with mayor pro-tem, 1972, city commr., 1973. Bd. dirs. YMCA, Breckenridge. Served with USMCR, 1945-46; PTO. Recipient award plaque for planning and zoning service, 1968-71. Mem. Nat. Gas Petroleum Assn., Breckenridge C. of C. (dir. 1971) Methodist. Mason, Odd Fellow, Rotarian (pres. local chpt. 1968-69). Club: Breckenridge Country (dir. 1966). Home: 1313 Cypress St Breckenridge TX 76024 Office: PO Box 991 Breckenridge TX 76024

DELCO, EXALTON ALFONSO, JR., coll. dean; b. Houston, Sept. 4, 1929; s. Exalton Alfonso and Pauline (Broussard) D.; B.A., Fisk U., 1949; M.S., U. Mich., 1950; Ph.D., U. Tex., 1962; m. Wilhelmina Ruth Fitzgerald, Aug. 23, 1952; children—Deborah Diane, Exalton Alfonso III, Loretta Elmirle, Cheryl Pauline. Instr. biology Tex. So. U., Houston, 1950-54, asst. prof., 1957-60; research asst. vertebrate speciation lab. U. Tex., Austin, 1958-62; asso. prof. biology Huston-Tillotson Coll., Austin, 1960-63, prof., 1963—, Piper prof., 1967—, acad. dean coll., 1967—, dir. Upward Bound project, 1965-67. Cons. NSF, 1959—. Eagle dist. commr. Boy Scouts Am., Austin, 1965-68; bd. dirs. Central Tex. Comprehensive Health Planning Comm., 1966-68, Natural Sci. Center, Austin, 1967-68. Served with AUS, 1955-56; Germany. Fellow A.A.A.S., Tex. Acad. Sci. (vis. sci. tchr. 1960-66); mem. Travis County Grand Jury Assn., Am. Inst. Biol. Scis., Assn. Coll. Honor Socs. (council 1963-68), Am. Fisheries Soc., Am. Soc. Ichthyologists and Herpetologists (Stoye prize 1960), Am. Soc. Limnology and Oceanography, N.Y. Acad. Sci., Sigma Xi, Beta Kappa Chi (exec. sec. 1964-68, v.p. S.W. region 1964-67). Contbr. articles profl. jours. Home: 1805 Astor Pl Austin TX 78721

DELEEUW, SAMUEL LEONARD, civil engr., educator; b. Grand Rapids, Mich., Aug. 2, 1934; s. Samuel Bastion and Gertrude (Vanderploeg) D.; B.S., Mich. State U., 1956, M.S., 1958, Ph.D., 1961; m. Nancy Kay Newton, Sept. 8, 1956; children—David, Daniel, Deborah. Asst. prof. civil engring. Yale, New Haven, 1960-65; prof. U. Miss., University, 1965—, chmn. dept. civil engring. 1965—. Mem. Am. Soc. C.E. (pres.-elect. Miss. sect. 1973-74), Am. Soc. M.E., Am. Soc. for Engring. Edn., Soc. for Natural Philosophy., Miss. Engring. Soc., Tau Beta Pi, Chi Epsilon, Phi Lambda Tau. Author: (with Ray Southworth) Digital Computations and Numerical Methods, 1965. Contbr. articles to profl. jours. Home: Box 1355 University MS 38677

DELEON, EDWIN LAZARO, oral surgeon; b. Aguadilla, P.R., Jan. 20, 1937; s. Candido E. and BeLen (Sein) DeL.; B.A., Fla. State U., 1961; D.M.D., U. Louisville, 1965; m. Helen Amelia Sheppard, Sept. 9, 1960; children—Melinda Amelia, Jon Deni. Intern, Hillsborough County Dental Research Clinic, 1965-66; oral surgery resident U. Tenn. Meml. Research Center and Hosp., 1966-69; pvt. practice oral surgery, Madison, Tenn., 1969—. Served with USAF, 1954-58. Fellow Royal Soc. Health; mem. Am., Southeastern socs. oral surgeons, Am., Nashville dental assns., Psi Omega. Episcopalian. Author numerous articles in field. Office: 500 Lentz Dr Madison TN 37115

DELEONIBUS, PASQUALE SALVITORE, govt. ofcl.; b. Chester, Pa., Jan. 13, 1926; s. Joseph and Carmela (Ubaldi) D.; B.S., N.Y. U., 1952; M.S., Am. U., 1963; m. Nancy Louise Smothers, July 7, 1963; 1 dau., Adria. With U.S. Naval Oceanographic Office, Washington, 1954—, dir. phys. oceanography div., 1973—. U.S. rep. on wave forecasting and wave instrumentation Commn. on Maritime Meteorology, 1971-73. Served with AUS, 1944-46. Decorated Purple Heart. Mem. Am. Geophys. Union, Am. Meteorol. Soc., Research Soc. Am. Home: 1111 Wimbledon Dr McLean VA 22101 Office: Code 8050 c/o Naval Research Lab Washington DC 20375

DELGADO, HUMBERTO, broadcasting exec.; b. Havana, Cuba, Mar. 24, 1940; s. Emilio and Gloria (Martinez) D.; student Centro Sperimentale di Cinematografia, Rome, Italy, 1962; Italian Govt. scholar for study TV producing and directing Italian TV Network, Rome, 1960; m. Aurora Muniz, Jan. 12, 1963; children—Humberto, George. Came to U.S., 1962, naturalized, 1967. Mgr. operations sta. WNEW-TV, N.Y.C., 1967-69; exec. producer spls. sta. WNJU-TV, Newark, 1969-70; program controller for news spl. events ABC, N.Y.C., 1970; program dir., pub. service dir. sta. WCIX-TV, Miami, Fla., 1970—. Tchr. cinematography Miami Dade Coll., 1972—. Recipient award for best producer, best show WNJU-TV, 1969; award merit WCIX-TV, 1970; key to City Miami, certificates appreciation, 1971. Home: 310 SW 64th Way Pembroke Pines FL 33023 Office: 111 Bricknell Av Miami FL 33131

DELGADO, MARIA ELENA, sculptress; b. Monclova, Coahuila, Mexico, Nov. 5, 1921; student Technol. Inst. High Studies, Monterrey, Mexico, 1946-55, U. Nuevo Leon, 1955; pupil Adolpho Laubner. One-man shows include Arts A.C., Monterrey, 1956, Soc. Architects, Mexico City, 1957, Regional Inst. Fine Arts, Acapulco, Mexico, 1958, Mexican Plastics, 1968, Welna Gallery, Chgo., 1968, Museum Ciudad Juarez, 1969, Escudero Gallery, 1970, Visual Arts Orgn. Am. States, Washington, 1972, also Mexico Cultural Inst., Ft. Worth Mus. Sci. and History, Ft. Worth Art Center, Misrachi Gallery, Mexico City; works included in group exhbns., Mexica, U.S., Can., Europe; represented in permanent collections U. Nuevo Leon, Teatro Juarez, Monterrey, La Ciudadela, Monterrey; bust John F. Kennedy in brass exhibited Mexico Pavilion World's Fair, N.Y.C., 1964. Address: Nube 724 Lomas Quebradas Mexico 20 DF Mexico

DELGADO, PRIMITIVO, coll. dean; b. Caibarien, Cuba, Dec. 9, 1912; s. Victor Mariano and Andrea (Perez) D.; came to U.S., 1935; A.B., Carson-Newman Coll., 1941; Th.M., So. Bapt. Theol. Sem., 1944, Th.D., 1948; M.S., Radford Coll., 1971; m. Hazel Frances Martin, Oct. 20, 1944; children—Lofton Primo, Andrea Maria. Ordained to ministry Baptist Ch., 1939; minister Marion (Va.) Bapt. Ch., 1947-57; prof. religion Bluefield (Va.) Coll., 1957-58, acad. dean, prof. religion and philosophy, 1958—. Bd. dirs. Bluefield chpt. A.R.C., Mercer County Mental Health Assn. Mem. Assn. Bapt. Profs. Religion, Am. Acad. Religion, W.Va. Psychol. Assn., Assn. Deans So. Colls. Rotarian. Address: Bluefield Coll Campus Bluefield VA 24605

DELIUS, JACK CORAM, city ofcl.; b. Smyrna, Ga., Mar. 18, 1933; s. Charles Harold and Emma (Coram) D.; B.B.A., Ga. State U., 1965; certificate N.C. State U., 1967; postgrad. U. Ga., 1968; m. Lillian Rozella Bullard, Oct. 22, 1966; 1 son, John Charles. Traffic engr. asst. City of Atlanta 1953-56, 57-61, office mgr., sec. parks com., 1961-64, gen. mgr. parks and recreation, 1964—. Cons. Vice Pres.'s Council on Summer Youth Sports and Recreation, 1968—, del. White House Conf. on Natural Beauty, 1965. Bd. dirs. Arts Festival of Atlanta, Dogwood Festival of Atlanta, Community Council of Atlanta, Model Cities, Econ. Opportunity Atlanta; trustee Leisure Careers Found., Atlanta Zool. Soc. Recipient Civic Design Commn. Bernice Raiford award, 1973, award merit outstanding achievement creative urban landscape planning Ga. Land Devel. Assn. Served with AUS, 1955-56. Fellow Nat. Recreation and Park Assn.; mem. Assn. Adminstrn. Dept. Heads (pres. 1971—), Am. Assn. Zool. Parks and Aquariums (asso.), DeKalb Hist. Soc. Episcopalian. Lion, Elk. Home: 4313 Riverwood Circle Decatur GA 30032 Office: 260 Central Av SW Atlanta GA 30303

DELLERT, CHARLES EDWARD, elec. engr.; b. Jersey City, Aug. 7, 1941; s. Charles Frederick and Gladys Constance (Domm) D.; B.S., U. N.M., 1965; M.S., U. Tex. at El Paso, 1969; m. Ina Marie Work, May 27, 1960; children—Charles Edward, Michael Allen. Div. engr. El Paso Natural Gas Co., 1965-67, area engr., 1967-69, sr. elec. and instrument engr., 1969-70, div. plant engr., 1970—. Leader Polaris dist. Yucca council Boy Scouts Am., 1969-74. Registered profl. engr., Tex. Mem. Gas Turbine Users Assn. (chmn.), Tex. Soc. Profl. Engrs., Train Collectors Assn. Methodist. Mason. Home: 4747 Emory Way El Paso TX 79922 Office: PO Box 1492 El Paso TX 79978

DELLINGER, HUBERT LOGAN, physician; b. Memphis, Feb. 16, 1933; s. Hubert Logan and Clara Ellen (Deal) D.; B.S., Memphis State U., 1954; M.D., U. Tenn., 1957; m. Lauran Waldran, Oct. 23, 1966; children—James Preston, Laura Clare. Intern, Meth. Hosp., Memphis, 1958-59, resident pediatrics, 1959-61; practice medicine specializing in pediatrics, Memphis, 1961—; mem. staffs Meth. Hosp., chmn. pediatric dept. 1968-71, Bapt., St. Joseph, LeBonheur hosps. Diplomate Am. Bd. Pediatrics. Fellow Am. Acad. Pediatrics; mem. Am., Tenn. med. assns., Memphis Mid-South Pediatric Soc. (pres. 1972-73), Phi Rho Sigma, Pi Kappa Alpha. Lutheran. Club: Century (Memphis). Home: 245 W Cherry St Memphis TN 38117 Office: 5270 Knight Arnold Rd Memphis TN 38118

DELOACH, MARVA LAVERNE, librarian; b. Ludowici, Ga., Oct. 24, 1946; d. Tom and Maggie (Boyd) DeLoach; B.S. in Math., Savannah State Coll. (Regents scholar 1965-66), 1967; M.S. in L.S. (Title II grantee), Atlanta U., 1968; postgrad. Hampton Inst., 1970—. Head catalog librarian Voorhees Coll., Denmark, S.C., 1968-70; instr. head catalog librarian Hampton Inst. (Va.), 1970—. Library cons. Hampton Inst. Drug Edn., 1971—. Sec. N.A.A.C.P., Savannah State Coll., 1965-66, pres., 1966-67; vol. worker A.R.C., 1965—. Recipient outstanding community service award Savannah State Coll., 1965, Math. award, 1966.Mem. Am. Assn. U. Profs. (sec. 1969, 71), Am., Ga., Va., Southeastern library assns., Am. Assn. U. Women, Alpha Kappa Mu, Beta Kappa Chi. Home: PO Box 6599 Hampton VA 23368 Office: CP Huntington Library Hampton VA 23368

DE LORENZI, JOHN, assn. exec.; b. Perth Amboy, N.J., Nov. 21, 1921; s. Otto and Honora (Martin) deL.; B.J., U. Mo., 1947. Reporter-editor Baytown (Tex.) Sun, 1947-48; night editor, cable editor Internat. News Service, Dallas and N.Y.C., 1948-51; account exec. Carl Byoir & Assos., N.Y.C., 1951-57; asst. pub. relations dir., asso. editor King Features Syndicate, N.Y.C., 1957-62; pub. relations dir. Am. Automobile Assn., Washington, 1963-65, mng. dir. pub. and govt. relations, 1966-73, mng. dir. pub. policy div., 1974—. Vice-pres. Martin Estates Inc., Edison, N.J., 1969—. Mem. adminstrv. com. Nat. Hwy. Users Conf., Washington, 1966-69; chmn. pub. relations adv. com. Pres.'s Com. on Traffic Safety, 1964-66; mem. policy adv. com. Hwy. Users Fedn. for Safety and Mobility, 1970—. Served with USAAF, 1942-45. Decorated Air medal with 2 oak leaf clusters. Mem. Internat. Platform Assn., Pub. Relations Soc. Am., Discover Am. Travel Orgns., Ark. Traveler, Kappa Tau Alpha, Sigma Delta Chi. Clubs: Nat. Press (Washington); Overseas Press (gov. 1961-65) (N.Y.C.). Home: 1500 Massachusetts Av NW Washington DC 20005 Office: 8111 Gatehouse Rd Falls Church VA 22042

DEL TORO TORRES, PEDRO ENRIQUE, church adminstr.; b. Sabana Grande, P.R., Dec. 8, 1920; s. Thomas and Generosa (Torres) del Toro; B.B.A. cum laude, U. P.R., 1954, postgrad., 1961-63; m. Panchita Garcia, Mar. 9, 1945; 1 son, Pedro Enrique. Chief accountant Sharp & Dohme, Inter-Am. Corp., Santurce, P.R., 1948-53; pub. accountant, mem. auditing staff Deloitte, Plender, Haskins & Sells, San Juan, P.R., 1954-55; asst. comptroller Commonwealth Oil Refining Co., Inc., Ponce, P.R., 1955-58, asst. treas., 1958-61; comptroller Passalacqua & Cia, Inc., Santurce, 1961-64; mem. auditing staff Haskins & Sells, C.P.A.'s, 1964-67; controller Ochoa Investment Corp., Hato Rey, P.R., 1967-72, Gonzalez Padin Co., San Juan, 1972-73; archbishopric of San Juan, 1973—. Pres., Credit Union of Employees Commonwealth Oil Refining Co., 1957-58; lectr. Cath. U. P.R., 1958-59. Served with AUS, 1946. C.P.A., P.R. Mem. Nat. Assn. Accountants, Am., P.R. (treas. Ponce chpt. 1959-60) insts. C.P.A.'s. Lion. Home: Apt 7-C El Dorado Condominium Ponce de Leon Av and Trigo Miramar Santurce PR 00907 Office: 3d floor Gonzalez Padin Bldg Plaza de Armas San Juan PR 00901

DELYANNIS, LEONIDAS THEODORE, cons. engr.; b. Athens, Greece, Nov. 8, 1926; s. Theodore L. and Xanthi (Mamouri-Goura) D.; B.S., Greek Mil. Acad., 1947; B.S., Greek Tech. Mil. Coll., 1954; M.S., U. Ill., 1958; m. Georgia H. Alexander, Feb. 21, 1957; children—Theodore, Harry-Michael. Came to U.S., 1957, naturalized, 1963. Chief structural engr. Ben Dyer & Assos., Hyattsville, Md., 1958-60; chief bridge engr. David Volkert & Assos., Washington, 1960-70; prin. L.T. Delyannis & Assos., Arlington, Va., 1970—. Program chmn. Internat. Symposium on Concrete Bridge Design, Toronto, Ont., Can., 1967, Chgo., 1969. Mem. Nixon-Agnew Inaugural Com., 1968, 72; 2d vice chmn. Nat. Republican Heritage Groups Council; chmn. Va. Rep. Nationalities Council; alternate del. at large Rep. Nat. Conv., 1972. Bd. dirs. Arlington Dance Theater. Registered profl. engr., Ala., Md., Va., D.C. Mem. Am. Soc. C.E., Nat. Soc. Profl. Engrs., Am. Concrete Inst. (com. on concrete bridge design), Soc. Am. Mil. Engrs., Prestressed Concrete Inst., Arlington C. of C., Pan-Arcadian Fedn. Am., Internat. Assn. for Bridge and Structural Engring., AHEPA. Mem. Greek Orthodox Ch. (dir.). Club: Republican Capitol Hill (life); Washington Golf and Country. Contbr. articles to tech. publs. Home: 2350 N Taylor St Arlington VA 22207 Office: 4620 Lee Hwy Arlington VA 22207

DEMAYA, CHARLES BERTRAND, lab. exec.; b. Belem, Para, Brazil, Sept. 12, 1909; s. Charles and Lucilla M. (Pinho) D.; came to U.S., 1919, naturalized, 1929; A.B., Columbia, 1931, B.S., 1933, Chem. E., 1935; m. Janet Moore Ewart, Oct. 10, 1931 (dec. 1971); children—Kathryn E. (Mrs. William C. Armstrong), Charles C. M. Foreman hydrogenation dept. Durkee Famous Foods, Inc., 1935-36; night supt. Wecoline Products Co., Boonton, N.J., 1936; devel. engr. essential oils dept. Trubek Labs., Inc., Rutherford, N.J., 1936-37; supt. cosmetics Spl. Toiletries Corp., N.Y.C., 1937; from devel. engr. to research mgr. Gen. Foods Corp., N.Y.C. and Hoboken, N.J., 1937-54; owner, dir. Sun Tests Unltd., Sarasota, Fla., 1954—; pres. Food Products Corp., Sarasota, 1967—. Mem. A.A.A.S., Am. Assn. Textile Colorists and Chemists, Am. Chem. Soc., Inst. Food Technologists, Am. Oil Chemists Soc., Am. Assn. Candy Technologists, Am. Ordnance Assn.; Electro-chem. Soc. (sec. 1933). Episcopalian. Contbr. articles to food publs.; patentee in field. Address: Box 3707 Sarasota FL 33578

DEMECS, DESIDERIO DEZSO, educator; b. Bolyk, Hungary, Nov. 8, 1923; s. Dezso and Erzsebet (Szulak) D.; Ph.D. in Econs., Universita degli Studi, Bologna, Italy, 1955, D.C.S., 1955; Ph.D. in Philosophy, State U. N.Y. at Buffalo, 1965. Came to U.S., 1956, naturalized, 1961. Asso. prof., head dept. philosophy U. Dubuque (Ia.), 1965-66; asso. prof. humanities and philosophy U. Ark. at Pine Bluff, 1967—. Mem. Am. Philos. Assn., Am. Assn. U. Profs., Internat. Phenomenological Soc., Internat. Platform Assn., U. Profs. for Acad. Order (dir.), Lecomte Du Nouy Assn., Alumni Assn. State U. N.Y. at Buffalo (club leader for Central Ark.). Home: PO Box 4066 Pine Bluff AR 71601

DEMELLO, WALMOR CARLOS, educator; b. Florianopolis, Brazil, Sept. 11, 1931; s. John Carlos and Alba (Baptiste) DeM.; B.S., Colegio Catarinese, 1949; M.D., U. Brazil, 1955, D.M., 1964; m. Celina Storino, Sept. 15, 1956; children—Alexandre, Andriana, Claudia, Patricia. Prof. dept. pharmacology Sch. Medicine, U. P.R., Rio Piedras, 1970-71, prof., dir. dept. pharmacology, 1972—. Cons. Am. Heart Assn., 1973. Nat. Heart and Lung Inst. grantee, 1966—, P.R. Heart Assn. grantee, 1968-71. Mem. Sociedade Brasilera de Biologia, Am. Physiol. Soc., Biophys. Soc., N.Y. Acad. Scis. Author: The Specialized Tissues of the Heart, 1961; Electrical Phenomena in the Heart, 1973. Home: 0-12 C St Extension Alto Apolo-Guaynabo PR Office: Dept Pharmacology Med Scis Campus PO Box 5067 San Juan PR 00936

DE MENT, IRA, U.S. atty.; b. Birmingham, Ala., Dec. 21, 1931; s. Ira and Helen Virginia (Sparks) De M.; Asso. in Sci., Marion Inst., 1951; A.B., U. Ala., 1953, J.D., 1958; m. Ruth Lester Posey, Sept. 22, 1959; 1 son, Charles Posey. Admitted to Ala. bar, 1958, U.S. Ct. Appeals for 5th Circuit, 1958, U.S. Dist. Ct. for Middle Dist. Ala., 1958, U.S. Supreme Ct. bar, 1965, U.S. Dist. Ct. for So. Dist., 1967, U.S. Tax Ct., 1972, U.S. Ct. Claims, 1972, other fed. cts.; law clk. to asso. justice Supreme Ct. Ala., 1958-59; asst. U.S. atty. for middle dist. of Ala., Montgomery, 1959-61, U.S. atty., 1969—; practiced in Montgomery, 1961-69; asst. atty. City of Montgomery, 1965-69; spl. asst. atty. gen. State of Ala., 1966-69. Instr. agy., criminal and constl. law Jones Law Sch., 1961-63, Montgomery Police Acad., 1964—, U. Ala. extension, 1967. Served to 1st lt., inf. AUS, 1953-55; lt. col. Res. Mem. Am., Fed., Montgomery, D.C. bar assns., Ala. State Bar, Am. Judicature Soc., Nat. Dist. Attys. Assn., Ala. Trial Lawyers Assn., Assn. Trial Lawyers Am., Am. Arbitration Assn. (nat. panel arbitrators), Res. Officers Assn. Fraternal Order Police, Ala. Peace Officers Assn., Phi Alpha Delta, Sigma Chi. Republican. Methodist. Mason (32 deg., Shriner). Club: Montgomery Country. Editorial adv. bd. Ala. Lawyer, 1966-72. Contbr. articles to legal jours. Home: 3437 Warrenton Rd Montgomery AL 36111 Office: Lock Drawer 197 Montgomery AL 36101

DEMING, FRANK CAMMACK, civil engr.; b. Suggsville, Ala., Aug. 14, 1922; s. Lon Albert and Gertrude (Cammack) D.; B.S., U. Ala., 1948; m. Gloria A. Herndon, Apr. 15, 1950; 1 son, Herndon Cammack. With C.E., U.S. Army, Mobile, 1948—, asst. chief engring. div., 1967-68, chief design br., engring. div., 1968-73, chief engring. div., 1973—. Instr. U. Ala. Extension at Mobile, 1949. Served with AUS, 1943-45; ETO. Decorated Purple Heart. Recipient Outstanding Performance ratings Army Dept. Fellow Am. Soc. C.E. (dir. Ala., 1970-71), Soc. Am. Mil. Engrs. (recipient Merit award, 1970, v.p., 1971), Internat. Commn. Large Dams, Nat. Assn. Govt. Engrs., Capstone Engr. Soc., S.A.R., 95th Inf. Div. Assn., 320th Engring. Bn. Assn., Chi Epsilon, Tau Beta Pi. Mason. Clubs: Skyline Country, Skyline Swim. Mailing Address: 4155 Belvedere St Mobile AL 36609

DEMING, LOUISE MACPHERSON (MRS. OLCOTT HAWTHORNE DEMING), civic worker; b. Evanston, Ill., July 8, 1916; d. C. Rust and Helen (Bennett) Macpherson; B.A., Rollins Coll., 1937; postgrad. Am. U., 1955-57, George Washington U., 1960-62; m. Olcott Hawthorne Deming, June 2, 1937; children—Rust Macpherson, John Hawthorne, Rosamond Bennett. Tchr., Fairfield Country Day Sch., 1937-40; mgmt. planning OWI, 1940-41; vis. prof. history Am. lit. Chulalongkom U., Bangkok, Thailand, 1949-51. Fgn. policy chmn. Montgomery County (Md.) League Women Voters, 1946; grey lady A.R.C.-Tokyo Army Hosp., 1951-53, Bethesda Naval Hosp., 1955-57; founding mem., bd. dirs. Fgn. Service Council, 1957-72; pres. Okinawa Internat. Women's Club, 1957; founder Okinawa chpt. Ikebana Internat. Club, 1958; organizer Folkcraft exhibit Smithsonian Inst., 1959; curator William Meads Prince Collection, Ackland Mus., Chapel Hill, N.C., 1967. Mem. Am. Assn. Fgn. Service Women (pres. 1962). Kappa Alpha Theta. Club: Cosmopolitan (N.Y.C.). Episcopalian. Author: The History of Uganda Museum, 1964. Editor: Letters of Sophia Peabody Hawthorne, 1964. Home: 1510 Dumbarton Rock Ct Washington DC 20007

DEMING, OLCOTT HAWTHORNE, assn. exec., former ambassador; b. N.Y.C., Feb. 28, 1909; s. William Champion and Imogen (Hawthorne) D.; grad. Loomis Sch., 1929; B.A., Rollins Coll., 1935; postgrad. U. Tenn., 1935-36; m. Louise Macpherson, June 2, 1937; children—Rust, John, Rosamond (Mrs. Luis de Larrega). Tchr. pvt. schs. New Eng., 1937-42; asst. indsl. placement TVA, Knoxville, 1935-37; ednl. asst. Coordinator Inter-Am. Affairs, Washington, 1942-44; exec. sec. interdepartmental com. State Dept., Washington, 1944-48; with U.S. Fng. Service, 1948-69, ambassador to Uganda, 1963-66; diplomat in residence U. N.C., 1966-67; coordinator nat. indepartmental seminar, 1967-69; dir. Fgn. Student Service Council, Washington, 1969—. Leader, Expt. in Internat. Living, Putney, Vt., 1938-41; 1st v.p. Georgetown Citizens Assn., Washington, 1973-74; mem. Nat. Trust for Historic Preservation, 1971—. Trustee Rollins Coll., Winter Park, Fla., 1964-70; bd. dirs. Exptl. in Internat. Living, Brattleboro, Vt. Mem. Diplomatic and Consular Officers Ret. (bd. govs. 1973—), Fgn. Service Assn., Siam Soc. (editor Jours. 1948-51). Clubs: Metropolitan, City Tavern (Washington); Chevy Chase (Md.). Home: 1510 Dumbarton Rock Ct Washington DC 20007 Office: 1860 19th St NW Washington DC 20009

DE MONTFORT, HAROLD, educator; b. Birmingham, Ala., Oct. 5, 1912; s. Harold R.E. and Marie (Greene) de M.; A.A., Tex. Mil. Coll., 1932; B.A., U. Chgo., 1937; M.A., U. Ala., 1958; postgrad. Harvard, Tulane U., Fla. State U., Auburn U.; M.S., U. So. Miss., 1970, Ph.D., 1973. Unemployment claims examiner, administrv. office supr., dept. mgr. employment service office, labor market analyst La. Div. Employment Security, 1945-47; tng. officer regional office VA, New Orleans, 1947-51; orgn., methods examiner Cal. Mil. Dist., U.S. Army, 1951; adminstrv. asst. Baton Rouge Engr. Depot, U.S. Army, 1951-52; administrv. asst. New Orleans Civil Def., 1952; individual practice, personal vocational counseling, 1953-56; grad. asst. guidance Fla. State U., 1957-58; sch. psychologist Brevard Guidance Center, Cocoa, Fla., 1958-59; grad. asst. psychology Auburn U., 1959; instr. Lyman Ward Mil. Acad., Camp Hill, Ala., 1960; asst. comdt., prof. mil. sci. Chamberlain-Hunt Acad., Port Gibson, Miss., 1961-62; dean of students, sch. psychologist Jr. U. New Orleans, 1962-63; became dean Monticello Acad., Jefferson Parish, La., 1964; col. govs. staff La. Militia, a.d.c. to gov., 1964; headmaster The Sanctuary Sch., New Orleans, 1964-65; ednl. counseling, 1966-72; headmaster Kenner (La.) Acad., 1972—. Mem. exec. com. New Orleans Meml. Day Assn., 1960, 63. Served with Royal Canadian Army, 1939-43, AUS, 1943-45. Decorated knight grand cross Sovereign Greek Order of St. Dennis of Zante; comdr. Nat. Order of Honor and Merit (Haiti); Cross Order St. Justinian; Royal Yugoslav Commemorative War Cross (1941-45); recipient medal for essay, Internat. Colonial and Overseas Expedition, Paris, 1931; Cross of Merit, Nat. Legion of Greek-Am. War Veterans in Am., 1966; gold medal City of Mesolongi (Greece), 1966; medal Japanese Red Cross Soc., 1967. Mem. La. State Rifle and Pistol Assn. (past pres., mem. exec. council), Am. Legion, V.F.W., Internat. Platform Assn., Mensa, Am. Personnel and Guidance Assn., Nat. Vocational Guidance Assn., Intertel., So. Polit. Sci. Assn., Pi Gamma Mu, Kappa Delta Pi. Club: New Orleans Shooting (pres., dir.). Home: 241 Chartres St New Orleans LA 70130

DEMPSEY, BRUCE HARVEY, mus. curator; b. Camden, N.J., July 4, 1941; s. Lawrence Aloysius and Audrey Ruth (Harvey) D.; B.A., Fla. State U., 1964, M.F.A., 1966; m. Gabriele Katarina Heerling, July 12, 1970. Faculty, Fla. State U., Tallahassee, 1966—, gallery dir., 1973—, instr. Fla. State U. Study Center, Florence, Italy, 1967-68. Bd. dirs. Tallahassee Arts Council, 1973—. Mem. Fla. Art Mus. Dirs. Assn., Fla. League Arts. Home: 1405 Broome St Tallahassee FL 32301

DEMPSEY, WILLIAM HENRY, JR., lawyer; b. New Ulm, Minn., Dec. 1, 1930; s. William H. and Myra (Seifert) D.; A.B., U. Notre Dame, 1952; LL.B., Yale, 1955; m. Mary Studer, Aug. 25, 1954; children—William Henry III, Robert J., Timothy M., Elizabeth, Thomas, Mary. Admitted to D.C. bar, 1955; law clk. to Judge Charles Fahy, U.S. Ct. Appeals, 1955-56; chief law clk. Chief Justice of U.S., Washington, 1959-60; mem. firm Shea & Gardner, Washington, 1960-72; chmn. Nat. Ry. Labor Conf., Washington, 1972—. Served as 1st lt. with Judge Adv. Gen.'s Corps. AUS, 1956-59. Mem. Yale Law Sch. Assn. Washington (pres. 1966; mem. exec. com.), Phi Alpha Delta. Roman Catholic. Home: 3311 N Glebe Rd Arlington VA 22207 Office: 1225 Connecticut Av NW Washington DC 20036

DENABURG, CHARLES ROBERT, metall. engr.; b. Birmingham, Ala., Apr. 23, 1935; s. Simon and Mary (Rosenblum) D.; B.S. in Metall. Engring., U. Ala., 1959; m. Sara Rose Lepp, Aug. 12, 1956, children—Elisa Jan, Cheryl Lyn, Danial. Mem. staff aerospace tech. and materials NASA, Marshall Space Flight Center, Ala. 1963-67, mem. staff aerospace tech. and materials failure analysis, Kennedy Space Center, Fla., 1967—. Past vice chmn., mem. Indian Harbour Beach (Fla.) Planning and Zoning Bd. Served with AUS, 1961-62. Recipient Snoopy award Astronaut Office NASA, 1969. Registered profl. engr., Ala. Mem. Am. Soc. Metals, Nat. Assn. Corrosion Engrs. Mem. B'nai B'rith (past chmn.). Home: 325 Eutau Court Indian Harbour Beach FL 32937 Office: Kennedy Space Center FL 32899

DENBO, BRUCE FREDERICK, editor; b. Port Arthur, Tex., May 20, 1913; s. Bruce Emerson and Ursula (Hamilton) D.; B.A., La. State U., 1936; M.A., La. State U., 1940; Litt.D., Berea Coll., 1970; m. Helen Lenora Hunt, Dec. 18, 1939; 1 dau., Geri Lynn (Mrs. John L. Greenway). Editor La. State U. Press, 1938-46, mgr., 1946-50; dir. U. Ky. Press, Lexington, 1950-69, U. Press of Ky., 1969—. Served to capt. USAAF, 1943-46. Mem. Assn. Am. U. Presses (v.p. 1965), Orgn. Am. Historians, So. Hist. Assn., S.O.R., Ky. Heritage Found., Lexington Civil War Round Table (program chmn., 1955—). Episcopalian. Rotarian (pres. 1972-73). Author: Notice by Publication in Louisiana, 1942. Home: 525 Ridge Rd Lexington KY 40503 Office: University Press Ky Lexington KY 40506

DENHAM, GLENN WILDER, lawyer; b. Pulaski, Tenn., Sept. 6, 1918; s. Ernest Myers and Dove (Browning) D.; student Cumberland Coll., 1935-37; LL.B., U. Ky., 1946; m. Lyda Belle Culver, Dec. 1, 1949; children—Suzanne, Steven Culver, Rebecca D., David Wilder. Admitted to Ky. bar, 1941; law clk. Ky. Ct. Appeals, 1946-47; practices law, Williamsburg, Ky., 1947-51, Middlesboro, Ky., 1951—. Dir. Comml. Bank, Middlesboro. Pres. Middlesboro Indsl. Found.; trustee Appalachian Regional Hosps. Inc. Served with USNR, 1942-45. Decorated Navy Cross, Air medal. Mem. Middlesboro C. of C. (pres. 1963—), Ky. C. of C. (dir. 1969—), Ky. Bar Assn. (v.p. 1971-72, pres. 1973-74). Home: 207 Arthur Heights Middlesboro KY 40965 Office: 2121 1/2 Cumberland Av Middlesboro KY 40965

DENISON, MRS. FRANKLIN AUGUSTUS, shipyard exec.; b. Chgo., Feb. 25, 1915; d. Clarence Morton and Geraldine (Strickland) Winslow; student Lyons Twp. Jr. Coll., 1935; m. Franklin Augustus Denison, Dec. 27, 1947; children—Christopher Winslow, Franklin Augustus, Keneim Winslow. Sec.-treas. Broward Marine, Inc., Ft. Lauderdale, Fla., 1948—, interior decorator, designer of yacht interiors G. Winslow Denison, 1960. Mem. D.A.R. Home: 1801 SW 20th St Fort Lauderdale FL 33302 Office: 1601 SW 20th St Fort Lauderdale FL 33302

DENISON, HENRY CLARK, elec. engr.; b. Norman, Okla., Sept. 17, 1900; s. Jesse Irvin and Ada Irene (Naylor) D.; B.S., U. Okla., 1924; m. Mary Ella McBride, Apr. 23, 1927; children—Gilbert Walter, Harvey Clark. Student engr. Dallas Power & Light Co., 1924-25; test engr. Gen. Electric Co., Schenectady, N.Y., 1925-26; statistical engr. Kan. City (Mo.) Power & Light Co., 1926-29; with Okla. Gas & Electric Co., Oklahoma City, 1929-65; elec. design engr. Benham-Blair & Affiliates, Oklahoma City, 1965-67; elec. study and design engr. C.H. Guernsey & Co., Oklahoma City, 1967-69, 73—; ind. elec. cons. Oklahoma City, 1972—. Precinct chmn. Rep. party, 1964. Registered profl. engr., Okla. Mem. Nat. Soc. Profl. Engrs., Okla. Soc. Profl. Engrs. (mem. municipal affairs com. 1972—), I.E.E.E., Sigma Tau, Eta Kappa Nu. Club: Engring. (Oklahoma City). Contbr. articles in field to profl. jours. Home: 2816 NW 25th St Oklahoma City OK 73107 Office: 2701 N Oklahoma Av Oklahoma City OK 73105

DENLINGER, WILLIAM WATSON, pub. co. exec.; b. Bethesda, Md., May 30, 1924; s. Milo Grange and Dorothy (Watson) D.; Spl. student Radcliffe Coll., 1954; m. Shirley Lou Spehn, Feb. 8, 1969; children—Kathleen L., Diane C., Tamara R., Carrie. Engaged in pub., 1953—; with Denlingers Pubs., Fairfax, Va., 1963—; pres. Man, Inc., 1963—, Baronat Men's Shop, Inc., 1970—; asso. Atwell Assos., Inc., 1969—; dir. Red Fox Inn. Served with AUS, 1943-46. Mem. Am. Legion (dist. comdr. 1965-66). Lion, Mason, Elk. Author: The Complete Boston, 1956; The Complete Beagle, 1957. Editorial cons. Howell Book House, 1961-64, Hawthorne Books, 1964-68. Home: 12515 Chronicle Dr Fairfax VA 22030 Office: Box 76 Fairfax VA 22030

DENMAN, ANDREW JACKSON, optometrist; b. Atlanta, Aug. 8, 1915; s. Julius L. and Minnie Irene (Murphy) D.; D.Optometry, So. Coll. of Optometry, 1949, Dr. Ocular Sci., 1963; m. Ruth H. Schillinger, Sept. 28, 1940; children—Andrew Jackson, Steven W., Sylvia L. Pvt. practice optometry Athens, Ga., 1949—. Trustee So. Coll. of Optometry, 1960-68. Served with AUS, 1943-45. Recipient Man of Year award Ga. Optometric Assn., 1957. Mem. Am., Ga. (pres. 1957) optometric assns., Am. Acad. Optometry, S.E. Ednl. Congress Optometry (pres. 1956), Omega Delta. Presbyn. (elder 1956). Kiwanian (pres. 1956, lt. gov. 7th div. 1958). Home: 230 Beechwood Dr Athens GA 30601 Office: 489 N Milledge Av Athens GA 30601

DENMAN, BEN P., ins. co. exec.; b. Brownwood, Tex.; student Howard Payne Coll.; B.B.A. with high honors, U. Tex. at Austin, 1942; m. Nell Denman; children—W. Edwin, Marajen. Formerly sec.-treas. wholesale grocery firm, Brownwood; with Southwestern Life Ins. Co., Dallas, 1951—, successively salesman, regional mgr., v.p., agy. dir., exec. v.p., 1969-73, chief operating officer, 1972-73, pres., 1973—; v.p., dir. Southwestern Life Corp.; chmn. exec. com. Southwestern Gen. Life Ins. Co.; dir. Southwestern Mgmt. & Research Corp., Southwestern Investors, Inc., Southwestern Investors Growth Fund, Inc., Fund Southwest, Inc., MESBIC Financial Corp., Dallas. Bd. dirs. Dallas Alliance Minority Enterprise, Tex. Bur. Econ. Understanding. Served with USNR, World War II. C.L.U. Mem. Am. Coll. Life Underwriters (mem. devel. bd.). Presbyn. (elder). Club: Bent Tree Country. Address: Southwestern Life Ins Co Dallas TX 75201

DENMAN, EUGENE DALE, elec. engr., educator; b. Farmington, Mo., Mar. 15, 1928; s. Charles Mathias and Flora B. (Ward) D.; B.S., Washington U., St. Louis, 1951; M.S., Vanderbilt U., 1955; D.Sc., U. Va., 1963; m. Lorene Norma J. Hodge, June 28, 1952; children—Stephen D., Laura K. Engr., Magnavox Co., Ft. Wayne, Ind., 1951-52, Sperry Gyroscope Co., Great Neck, N.Y., 1954-56, Midwest Research Inst., Kansas City, Mo., 1956-60; research scientist U. Va., Charlottesville, 1960-63; asso. prof. elec. engring., asst. prof. medicine Vanderbilt U., Nashville, 1963-69; prof. elec. and systems engring. U. Houston, 1969—. Cons. Boeing Co., Huntsville, Ala., 1965-67, Oak Ridge Nat. Labs., 1966. Committee chmn. Cub Scouts Am., Brentwood, Cal., 1967. Served with Signal Corps, AUS, 1946-48. Mem. I.E.E.E., Eta Kappa Nu, Tau Beta Pi. Methodist. Author: (with Roy N. Adams) Wave Propagation and Turbulent Media, 1966; Coupled Modes in Plasmas, Elastic Media and Parametric Amplifiers, 1970. Home: 13402 Taylorcrest Houston TX 77024

DENNARD, LILLIAN MAURINE WHEELER (MRS. MACK WILLIAM DENNARD, SR.), secretarial service exec.; b. Dodd City, Tex., Feb. 25, 1929; d. Mitchell Gail and Florence Lillian (Glover) Wheeler; grad. high sch.; m. Mack William Dennard, Sr., Sept. 22, 1973; children by previous marriage—Danny Gail Campbell, Dorita Jean Campbell (Mrs. Ronnie Henderson), Mark Weldon Campbell. Owner, mgr. Sherman Telephone Answering & Secretarial Service (Tex.) 1962—; bldg. mgr. Sherman Exchange Office Bldg., 1968—; mgr. Woodland Terrace Apts., Sherman, 1972-73. Named Boss of Year, 1968-69. Methodist. Club: Soroptimist. Home: Route 1 Box A482 Pottsboro TX 75076 Office: 2007 Hwy 75 N Sherman TX 75090

DENNEN, WILLIAM HENRY, geologist, educator; b. Gloucester, Mass., Apr. 8, 1920; s. William Llewellyn and Ruth Louise (Lufkin) D.; S.B., Mass. Inst. Tech., 1942, Ph.D., 1949; m. Charlotte Davidson, Dec. 20, 1942; children—William S., Peter D., Susan O. Faculty, Mass. Inst. Tech., Cambridge, 1949-67; prof., chmn. dept. geology U. Ky., Lexington, 1967—, dir. Cabot Spectrographic Lab., 1954-67, acting grad. dean, 1970-72. Sr. Fulbright lectr. Ecuador, 1971; geologist U.S. Geol. Survey, 1957—; vis. prof. U. Central Venezuela,

1967. Dir. Rigolets Corp. Served with USMCR, 1942-46. NSF grantee, 1960-72, U. Ky. Research Found. grantee, 1967-72. Fellow Geol. Soc. Am.; mem. Geochem. Soc., Soc. Applied Spectroscopy, Ky. Acad. Sci., Geol. Soc. Ky., Sigma Xi. Author: Principles of Mineralogy, 1959. Contbr. articles to profl. jours. Home: 809 Hildeen Rd Lexington KY 40502

DENNERY, PHYLLIS S. (MRS. MOISE W. DENNERY), civic worker; b. N.Y.C.; d. Harry and Frieda (Seydel) Sugarman; grad. Collegiate Inst., N.Y.C., 1937; m. Moise W. Dennery, June 7, 1941; children—Harry, Richard. Exec. com. Adult Edn. Assn. La.; nat. conv. chmn. Nat. Council Jewish Women, 1959, pres. New Orleans, 1952-54; pres. Friends New Orleans Pub. Library, 1955-59; chmn. com. ways and means, teen age adviser Madison (Settlement) House, N.Y.C., 1938-40; active ARC, 1941-42; chmn. vols. United Seamen's Service, New Orleans, 1944-45; v.p. League Jewish Women, New Orleans, 1953-55; women's adv. com. Crusade for Freedom, New Orleans, 1958—; co-chmn. New Orleans Am. Jewish Com., 1958-60, bd. dirs. 1958—; chmn. budget com. Jewish Welfare Fund, 1959, chmn. women's div., 1958; exec. com. Cultural Attractions Fund, Nat. Friends Pub. Broadcasting; mem. La. Co-ordinating Council Higher Edn.; mem. La. Bd. Regents. Bd. dirs. Jewish Community Center, New Orleans, Anti-Defamation League, New Orleans Pub. Library, Urban League, Newman P.T.A., Jewish Fedn., Charity Hosp.; pres. Greater New Orleans Ednl. TV Found., 1966-69; trustee Nat. Citizens for Pub. TV. Mem. Touro Sisterhood, League Women Voters, Am., La. library assns. Home: 2303 Broadway New Orleans LA 70125

DENNETT, EDWARD MOORE, mfg. co. exec.; b. Central Falls, R.I., Mar. 10, 1935; s. Edward Moore and Gertrude May (Pelote) D.; B.S., Worcester Poly. Inst., 1957; m. Katherine L. Kapesis, June 15, 1957; 1 son, Mark E. Sales engr. Sangamo Electric Co., Birmingham, Ala., 1960-62, dist. mgr., 1963-68, sales mgr. automotive and indsl. div., Springfield, Ill., 1969, asst. regional mgr., Atlanta, 1970-71, mgr. marketing and sales Oliver div., Atlanta, 1972—. Served to 1st lt. AUS, 1958-60. Registered profl. engr., Fla., Miss. Mem. I.E.E.E., Alpha Tau Omega. Republican. Roman Catholic. K.C. Contbr. articles to profl. jours. Office: 22 Perimeter Park Atlanta GA 30341

DENNEY, JEAN STONE, state ofcl.; b. Milan, Tenn., May 27, 1918; s. John Dunlap and Mina (Stone) D.; B.A., Cumberland U., 1942; LL.B., Memphis State U., 1967; m. Wanda Hundley, Sept. 29, 1946; children—Hundley Stone, Janet Lynn, Lisa Luanne. Foreman, Wolf Creek Ordnance Plant, Proctor & Gamble Def. Corp., Milan, 1942-44; reemployment rep. U.S. Dept. Labor, 1944-45, Gibson County service officer, 1945-49; field rep. Div. Vets. Affairs, State of Tenn., 1949-60; v.p. Milan Banking Co., 1961-63; fiscal mgmt. officer Tenn. Dept. Conservation, Nashville, 1963—. Dir. Milan Banking Co. Chmn. Gibson County Adv. Citizen's Com., 1963-64. Founding dir. 4H Club Am., 1962—. Served with AUS, World War II. Named Man of Year Milan C. of C., 1963; recipient G.W. Stegall trophy Am. Legion, 1960, 61, 63. Mem. Tenn. (group pres. 1963), Gibson County (pres. 1963) bankers assns., Nat. Outdoor Recreation Fiscal Officers Assn. (v.p.), Am. Records Mgmt. Assn. (chpt. charter mem., pres. 1973—), Am. Legion (mem. nat. rehab. commn. 1956-61, nat. com. for post activities 1960-70, service officer 1943-69), Milan C. of C. (pres. 1962-64), Sigma Alpha Epsilon. Presbyn. (Sunday sch. supt. 1960—, ruling elder). Clubs: Rotary (pres. 1962), Am. Legion Century (recipient Diamond pin). Home: 6825 Pennywell St Nashville TN 37205 Office: 2611 West End Av Nashville TN 37203

DENNIS, CHARLES EDWIN, JR., bldgs. engr.; b. Balt., Oct. 26, 1894; s. Charles Edwin and Annie (Wetzel) D.; student Balt. Poly. Inst., 1908-12; B.S. in Civil Engring., U. Wis., 1918; m. Emma Brown Griswold, Nov. 27, 1929; children—Charles Edwin III, Roy Oliver. Instr., Balt. Poly. Inst., 1912-14, 15-16; research work U.S. Forest Products Lab., Madison Wis., 1918-19; draftsman constrn. work Union Shipbldg. Co., Balt., 1919-21; asst. engr. charge telephone bldg. planning Chesapeake and Potomac Telephone Cos., Washington, 1921-29; engr. bldgs. Chesapeake and Potomac Telephone Co. Va., Richmond 1929-59; pres. Project Services, Inc., Richmond, 1959-60; chief architect's insp. for municipal housing project, Richmond, 1961-62. Mem. Telephone Pioneers Am., Triangle. Republican. Episcopalian. Home: 1737 Braeburn Dr Apt C-11 Salem VA 24153

DENNIS, DANNY PAUL, sch. ofcl.; b. DeRidder, La., Nov. 17, 1923; s. Ledger Paul and Elsie Aline (Bailey) D.; B.B.A., Lamar U., 1957; m. Mary Margaret Mullen, June 14, 1944; children—Dan Michael (dec.), William Richard. Yield clk. Neches Butane Products Co., Port Neches, Tex., 1946-56; accountant Western Natural Gas Co., Houston, 1957-59, supr. prodn. accounting, 1959-60; budget supr. Jefferson Chem. Co., Houston, 1960-67; bus. mgr. Richmond (Tex.) State Sch., 1967—. Del., Republican County Com., 1972. Served with USAAF, 1943-45, USAF, 1951-52. Decorated D.F.C., Air medal with 4 oak leaf clusters. C.P.A., Tex. Mem. Richmond C. of C. (govtl. affairs com. 1973). Mem. Ch. of Christ (deacon 1967-69, elder 1969-71). Home: 1227 Frances St Rosenberg TX 77471 Office: 2100 Preston St Richmond TX 77469

DENNIS, EDWARD FRANCIS, plant utility engr.; b. Fernwood, Miss., Sept. 17, 1921; s. Oscar Newton and Josie (Case) D.; student Internat. Corr. Schs., 1941-42; B.S. in Elec. Engring., U. Ala., 1950; m. Mary Beatrice Kilpatrick, Oct. 11, 1941. Head plant engring. Rohm & Haas Co., Redstone Arsenal, Ala., 1950-59; chief engr., gen. mgr. Bagwell Co., 1959-65; chief operating engr. Stewart Co., Merril Co., 1965-67; chief appliance engr. Bendix-Westinghouse Refrigerator Div. (name later changed to Americold Compressor Corp.), Cullman, Ala., 1967—; partner Asso. Engrs., Montgomery, Ala., 1960-65. Served with USNR, 1943-45; PTO. Mem. I.E.E.E. (nat. com. automatic control; pres. Huntsville, Ala., sect.), Nat. Soc. Profl. Engrs., S.A.R. Methodist (tchr. sunday sch.). Lion. Principal work design of spl. equipment for rocket motor. Home: 125 Stovall Dr Florence AL 35630 Office: Diamond Shamrock Chem Corp Sheffield AL 35660

DENNIS, ROGER MITCHELL, ins. co. exec.; b. Hattiesburg, Miss., Mar. 10, 1939; s. Mitchell Michael and Annie Laurie (Bryant) D.; student Western Ky. State U., 1957-58; B.S., U. So. Miss., 1960; m. Merrill Flowers, Aug. 31, 1960; children—Michael Roger, Annie Laurie, Theresa Merrill. Agt., N. Am. Co. for Life, Health and Accident Ins., Tallahassee, 1960-61, Franklin Life Ins. Co., Jackson, Miss., 1962; with Coastal States Life Ins. Co., Maryville, Tenn., 1962—, v.p. sales, 1967—. Pres., Crest Enterprises, Inc., Maryville, 1969—; sales v.p. Aquila Life Ins. Co. subsidiary Vico Corp., Indpl., 1970—; chief exec. officer Exec. Equity Corp. Served with AUS, 1962. Recipient Gold Plaque award Nat. Assn. Life Cos., 1966-70. Mem. Omicron Delta Kappa, Pi Sigma Epsilon. Republican. Methodist. Home: 1018 Oak Park Av Maryville TN 37801 Office: Blount Nat Bank Bldg Maryville TN 37801

DENNISON, HAROLD CLAY, JR., surgeon; b. Nashville, June 6, 1932; s. Harold Clay and Bessie Marie (Stroud) D.; B.A., Vanderbilt U., 1954; M.D., U. Tenn., 1957; m. Laura Sue Yeager, June 18, 1957; children—Susan Denise, Harold Clay III. Intern, Baptist Hosp., Nashville, 1958, now mem. staff; resident Thayer VA Hosp., Nashville, 1959, Nashville Gen. Hosp., 1959-63; practice medicine specializing in surgery, Nashville, 1963—; mem. staffs Vanderbilt, St. Thomas, Park View, West Side hosps.; asst. clin. prof. surgery Vanderbilt U., Nashville, 1963—. Chmn. bd. dirs. Franklin Road Acad., 1973-74. Diplomate Am. Bd. Surgery. Fellow A.C.S.; mem. A.M.A., Tenn. Med. Assn., Nashville Surg. Soc., Nashville Acad. Medicine. Club: Hillwood Country (Nashville). Home: 1611 Tyne Blvd Nashville TN 37215 Office: 1916 Patterson St Suite 203 Nashville TN 37203

DENNISON, JOHN MANLEY, geologist, educator; b. Keyser, W.Va., Apr. 13, 1934; s. Raymond Lewis and Edna (Sturm) D.; B.S., W.Va. U., 1954, M.S., 1955; Ph.D., U. Wis., 1960; m. Sondra Wise, Dec. 22, 1972; 1 son, John Robert. Asst. prof. U. Ill., Urbana, 1960-64, asso. prof., 1964-65; asso. prof. U. Tenn., Knoxville, 1965-67; prof. geology U. N.C., Chapel Hill, 1967—, chmn. dept. geology, 1969—. Served with AUS, 1955-57. Fellow Geol. Soc. Am.; mem. Am. Assn. Petroleum Geologists, Am. Statis. Assn., Paleontol. Soc. Author: Concepts in Physical Science, 1965; Analysis of Geologic Structures, 1968; Geology, 1974. Contbr. articles to profl. jours. Home: D Chalet Green St Chapel Hill NC 27514

DENNY, CHARLOTTE CURTI (MRS. ERNEST O. DENNY), educator; b. Boston; d. Harry and Olive (Drewett) Curti; diploma Central Islip State Hosp. Sch. Nursing, B.S. magna cum laude, N.Y. U., 1955; M.A., U. Ky., 1959; postgrad. Coll. City N.Y.; m. Ernest O. Denny, Feb. 16, 1941 (div. 1972); children—Warren, Linda. Pub. health nurse Nassau County (N.Y.), 1949-52; sch. nurse, tchr. Harborfields Sch. Dist., Greenlawn, N.Y., 1954-57; coordinator practical nurses edn. Huntington (N.Y.) High Sch., 1957-58; asst. prof. Coll. Nursing, U. Ky., Lexington, 1959-66; asso. prof., chmn. dept. nursing Eastern Ky. U., Richmond, 1967—. Vice pres. Northport-Ocean Av. P.T.A., 1953; chmn. health, nutrition, mental health, exec. council 7th Congl. dist. P.T.A., Ky., 1960-63. Recipient Founder's Day certificate N.Y. U., 1956. Fellow Am. Sch. Health Assn., Am. Pub. Health Assn.; mem. Am., Ky. (dist. pres. 1970-72, bd. dirs. 1972-76) nurses assns., Royal Soc. Health, Nat. League Nursing (chmn. health and career com. Ky. 1960-62, v.p. 1968-70), Am. Personnel and Guidance Assn., Assn. Higher Edn., Zonta Internat. Home: 3569 Olympia Rd Lexington KY 40502 Office: Eastern Ky U Richmond KY 40475

DENNY, J(AMES) WILLIAM, music pub.; b. Nashville, Aug. 25, 1935; s. James R. and Margaret (Osment) D.; student Vanderbilt U., 1953-57; m. June Ralls Denny, Aug. 31, 1957; children—Kevin, Steven, Jennifer. Rd. mgr. Philip Morris Country Music Show, 1957-58; pres. So. Star Investors Assos., 1960; account exec. McDonald & Alsup Advt. Agy., 1958-59; mgmt. trainee Third Nat. Bank, 1959-61; mgr. Columbia Records Rec. Studio & Columbia Records Custom Prodns., 1961-63; exec. v.p. radio stas. WJAT, Inc., Swainsboro, Ga., WRBO, Waynesboro, Ga., WSNT, Sandersville, Ga., 1963—; pres. Cedarwood Pub. Co., Inc., 1963—, pres., dir. Country Music Assn., 1965—; partner Hatch Show Print, 1964—. Bd. dirs. Nashville Cancer Soc., 1967-69, Brentwood Acad.; chmn. bd. Country Music Found., 1967; trustee, chmn. Wilkerson Speech and Hearing Center. Recipient Spl. Achievement award Record World mag., 1967; named Country Music Pub. of Yr., Music Bus. mag., 1964. Mem. Nat. Acad. Rec. Arts and Scis. (bd. govs., sec. Nashville chpt. 1964—), Nashville Jr. C. of C. (bd. govs.; man of yr. award 1967), Sigma Alpha Epsilon, Alpha Phi Omega. Methodist (dir. 1967—). Home: 800 Caldwell Lane Nashville TN 37204 Office: 815 16th Av Nashville TN 37203

DENT, BEN, dentist; b. Nashville, Nov. 11, 1908; s. David and Rebecca (Ballon) D.; student West Tenn. State Tchrs. Coll., 1926-28; D.D.S., U. Tenn., 1932; m. Regina Rose Brandt, Oct. 24, 1933; 1 son, Amiel Joseph. Practice dentistry, Hayti, Mo., 1932-34, Memphis, 1934—; mem. cons. staff St. Joseph Hosp., LeBonheur Childrens Hosp.; lectr. operative dentistry U. Tenn., 1951-56; vis. lectr. So. Coll. Optometry, 1947-66, instr., 1966-69, adj. instr., 1969—. Bd. dirs. West Tenn. chpt. Nat. Found. Neuromuscular Diseases, 1961-65. Fellow Am. Soc. for Advancement Gen. Anesthesia (citation for outstanding achievement as lectr. 1971), Acad. Gen. Dentistry (dir. 1959-73, Outstanding Service Citation), Royal Soc. Health (Eng.); mem. Am., Tenn. dental assns., Memphis Dental Soc., Am. Acad. Dental Medicine, Tenn. Soc. Dentistry for children, dir. 1949, Am. Acad. for Plastics Research in Dentistry (v.p. 1961-62, pres. 1963-64, Meritorious Service award 1964), Tenn. Acad. Gen. Dentistry (pres. 1964), Pierre Fauchard Acad., Southeastern Acad. Prosthodontics, Chgo. Dental Soc. (asso.), Canadian Dental Assn. (asso.), Acacia (hon.), Alpha Omega, Theta Nu Epsilon. Mason (32 deg.); mem. Order of Eastern Star. Contbr. articles to profl. jours. Home: 5442 Laurie Lane Memphis TN 38117 Office: Suite 310 1st Nat Bank Bldg 4990 Poplar Av Memphis TN 38117

DENT, FREDERICK BAILY, govt. ofcl.; b. Cape May, N.J., Aug. 17, 1922; s. Magruder and Edith (Baily) D.; grad. St. Paul's Sch., 1940; B.A., Yale, 1943; m. Mildred C. Harrison, Mar. 11, 1944; children—Frederick Baily, Mildred Hutcheson, Pauline Harrison, Diana Gwynn, Magruder Harrison. Dir., Joshua L. Baily & Co., Inc., N.Y.C., 1946-47; pres. Mayfair Mills, Arcadia, S.C., 1947-73, also dir.; former dir. Gen. Electric Co., S.C. Nat. Bank, Crompton Co., Scott Paper Co., Mut. Life Ins. Co. N.Y.; sec. of commerce, Washington, 1973—. Chmn. Spartanburg County Planning and Devel. Commn.; mem. Bus. Council, 1960-72. Former trustee Inst. Textile Tech., Spartanburg Day Sch. Served with USNR, 1943-46. Recipient Man of Year award N.Y. Bd. of Trade, 1971, Soc. for Advancement of Mgmt., 1973. Mem. S.C. Textile Mfrs. Assn. (dir.), Am. Textile Mfrs. Inst. (dir.). Episcopalian. Home: 2964 University Terrace NW Washington DC 20016 Office: US Dept Commerce Commerce Bldg Washington DC 20230

DENT, HARDY LEE, JR., profl. assn. exec.; b. Hale Center, Tex., Dec. 3, 1920; s. Hardy Lee and Clara (Allen) D.; student C. of C. Inst., 1957, U. Colo., 1958-59; m. Juanita Carmickle, Apr. 17, 1946; 1 child, Hardy Lee. Mgr. Ponca Wholesale Co., Austin, 1947-50; owner Dent Service Sta., Hale Center, 1951-56; gen. mgr. Hale Center C. of C., 1956—. Exec. dir. Fed. Housing Authority, Hale Center, 1966—. Chief Hale Center Vol. Fire Dept., 1953—; sec. Community Fund Bd., Hale Center, 1968—; coordinator Disaster and Clean-up orgn. tornado disaster, 1965. Bd. dirs. Salvation Army, Hale Center; mem. Hale Center Indsl. Found., 1971—. Served with AUS, 1941-46, 50-51. Recipient Service to Youth award Am. Legion, 1962, Service to Youth award 4-H Club, 1965, Lion of Year award, 1964-65. Mem. C. of C. Execs. Assn. West Tex., Tex. C. of C. Mgrs. Assn., Panhandle Fireman's Assn. (pres. 1967, sec.-treas. 1969-74), Internat. Assn. Fire Chiefs. Lion (sec.-treas. 1970—). Baptist. Home: 407 Main St Hale Center TX 79041 Office: City Hall Main St Hale Center TX 79041

DENT, JAMES NORMAN, biologist, educator; b. Martin, Tenn., May 10, 1916; s. James Rolandus and Alta Anne (Norman) D.; A.B., U. Tenn., 1938; Ph.D., Johns Hopkins U., 1941; m. Valgerda Nielsen, Dec. 27, 1945 (div.); children—Julie Anne (Mrs. Michael L. Carlyle), Martha Elizabeth. Asst. prof. biology Marquette U., Milw., 1945-46; asst. prof. biol. sci. U. Pitts., 1946-49; faculty U. Va., Charlottesville, 1949—, prof. biology, 1957—. Guggenheim fellow St. Andrews (Scotland) U., 1959-60; USPHS fellow Harvard, Cambridge, Mass., 1968-69. Served with USAAF, 1942-46; lt. col. Res. ret. Mem. Am. Soc. Zoologists, Am. Assn. Anatomists, Assn. Southeastern Biologists (pres. 1974—), Sigma Xi. Club: Farmington Country (Charlottesville). Contbr. numerous articles to profl. jours. Home: 1940 Thomson Rd Charlottesville VA 22903

DENT, JOHN ROBERT, elec. engr.; b. Rainelle, W.Va., Oct. 26, 1932; s. George Livingston and Reba Ammi (Reid) D.; B.S., Va. Poly. Inst., 1957, postgrad., 1969; postgrad. Rensselaer Poly. Inst., 1967; m. Bonnie Heather Plahte, Aug. 15, 1953; 1 son, John Robert II. Sr. engr. Melpar, Falls Church, Va., 1957-63; project engr. Tri-State Electronics, Falls Church, 1963-64; with Harry Diamond Labs., Washington, 1964—, chief research and devel. br., 1973—. Instr. Va. Poly. Inst., Blacksburg, 1956; cons. to Gen. Abram's sci. adviser, Republic of Vietnam, 1969. Judge regional sci. fair judge Fairfax and West Prince William Counties (Va.), 1965-73; dir. regional contest Acad. Model Aeronautics, Washington, 1971-73. Served with AUS, 1953-57. Recipient Hinman award for annual outstanding tech. leader Harry Diamond Labs., 1971; Research and Devel. Tech. Achievement award Dep. Sec. Army, 1972. Mem. I.E.E.E., A.A.A.S., Fairfax Model Assn. (pres. 1970-71). Patentee in field. Home: 9932 Clearfield Av Vienna VA 22180 Office: Harry Diamond Labs Connecticut Av and Van Ness Sts Washington DC 20438

DENT, MAGRUDER, lawyer; b. Augusta, Ga., May 8, 1919; s. Magruder and Edith Houston (Baily) D.; A.B., Yale, 1940; J.D., U. Va., 1954; m. Rosemary Romeyn, Dec. 7, 1946; children—Peter, Susan, Magruder III. With Joshua L. Baily & Co., Inc., N.Y.C., 1946-51, now dir.; dir. Mayfair Mills, Inc.; admitted to Va. bar, 1953; pvt. practice law, Charlottesville, Va., 1954-58; mem. firms Michael & Dent, 1958-72, Michael, Dent & Brooks, Ltd., 1972—. Served with USNR, 1940-46. Mem. Am., Va., Charlottesville-Albermarle bar assns., U. Va. Rowing Assn. (pres. 1966—). Clubs: Farmington Hunt (sec. 1962—), Farmington Country (Charlottesville). Home: Polaris Farm Rural Route 5 Charlottesville VA 22901 Office: PO Box 895 Charlottesville VA 22902

DENTON, EMMA MANEY, banker; b. Hiawassee, Ga., Oct. 25, 1905; d. Milton M. and Missouri (Eller) Maney; student pvt. schs., Hiawassee, Ga.; m. James Young Denton, May 20, 1920; children—J.C., Evelyn Isabel (Mrs. William T. Groves), Ruth Elois (Mrs. Robert L. Anderson), J. William, Emma Jean (Mrs. Ray W. Anderson). Cashier, Bank of Hiawassee, Ga., 1936—, dir., 1950—. Chmn. county dr. Am. Cancer Soc., 1944-60. Mem. D.A.R., Friendship Community Club, Hiawassee Garden Club (charter mem., pres. 1960—). Baptist. Address: Hiawassee GA 30546

DEODATI, JOSEPH BENJAMIN, aero. engr.; b. San Antonio, Dec. 17, 1916; s. Michael N. and Lydia (Rotondi) D.; B.S., Tex. A. and M. U., 1939 M.S., Cal. Inst. Tech., 1946, Aero. Engr., 1947; m. Mildred Perkins, Mar. 2, 1944; children—Debora (Mrs. Michel Breger), Joseph Benjamin. Commd. ensign USN, 1941, advanced through grades to comdr., 1953; naval aviator, World War II; aero. engr., Pacific and Atlantic fleets, U.S.; ret., 1961; dir. research, engrng. systems engring. div. Pnuemo Dynamics Corp., Bethesda, Md., 1961-63; aero. engr. advanced programs Gen. Dynamics Co., Ft. Worth, 1963—. Decorated Air medal with two gold stars. Mem. Operations Research Soc. Am., Nat. Mgmt. Assn., Navy League U.S. (dir.), Air Force Assn., Am. Security Council, Cal. Inst. Tech. Alumni Assn., Sigma Xi. Club: De Cordova Bend Country. Home: 2512 Ridgmar Fort Worth TX 76116 Office: PO Box 748 Fort Worth TX 76101

DEPALMA, NICHOLAS, clin. psychologist; b. Naples, Italy, Aug. 30, 1913; s. Joseph and Caroline (Musto) DeP.; A.B., Harvard, 1939; M.A., Boston U., 1942; Ed.D., Calvin Coolidge U., 1955; m. Ruth A. Warren, Apr. 24, 1944; children—W. Brett, Nicholas B., Niki A. Came to U.S., 1921, naturalized, 1921. Psychologist, VA, Murfreesboro, Tenn., 1959-62; chief psychologist Met. Bordeaux Hosp., Nashville, 1957—; pvt. practice psychology, Nashville, 1957—. Tchr. U. Tenn., 1960—. Served with USAAF, 1942-45. Mem. Nat. Assn. Vocational Rehab., Am., Tenn. psychol. assns. Author: Professional Ethics: A Survey, 1955; Psychotherapy with Low Grade Morons, 1956; Rorschack Combined Location and Record Form, 1957; The 16 PF Test and Alcoholics, 1960. Home: 811 Caldwell Lane Nashville TN 37204 Office: 1619 17th Av S Nashville TN 37212

DEPASQUALE, NICHOLAS DOMINIC, aerospace exec.; b. Balt., June 5, 1927; s. George C. and Carmella M. (Tuminella) DeP.; B.E., Johns Hopkins, 1951; M.S. (Sloan fellow), Mass. Inst. Tech., 1971; m. Mary Carol Cooper, Apr. 21, 1951; children—Michael N., Deborah. With Martin Marietta Corp., 1951—, asst. project engr., Orlando, Fla., 1958-61, program mgr., 1968-67, program dir., 1967-73, dir. tactical weapons systems program, 1973—. Served with USNR, 1945-46. Mem. I.E.E.E., Am. Ordnance Assn., Am. Inst. Aeros. and Astronautics, Laser Inst. Am., Armed Forces Communications and Electronics Assn., Assn. U.S. Army. Home: 1881 Shiloh Lane Winter Park FL 32789 Office: PO Box 5837 MP-292 Orlando FL 32805

DEPREIST, JAMES ANDERSON, condr.; b. Phila., Nov. 21, 1936; s. James Henry and Ethel (Anderson) DeP.; B.S., U. Pa., 1958, M.A., 1961; student Phila. Conservatory Music, 1959-61; m. Betty Louise Childress, Aug. 10, 1963. Music dir. Contemporary Music Guild, Phila., 1959-62; v.p. charge music Allen's Lane Art Center, Phila., Am. specialist music for Dept. State, 1962-63; condr.-in-residence, Bangkok, Thailand, 1963-64; asst. condr. to Leonard Bernstein and N.Y. Philharmoic Orch., 1965-66; music dir., condr. sta. WCAU-TV, Phila., Music-Spls. series, 1965, 66; music dir., summer music program Westchester County, N.Y., 1965, 66; asso. condr. Nat. Symphony, Washington, 1971—. Recipient 1st prize gold medal Dimitri Metropoulos Internat. Music Competition for Condrs., 1964. Mem. Sigma Pi Phi. Composer: (ballet scores) Vision of America, 1960, Tendrils, 1961, A Sprig of Lilac, 1964; (theme music) Eye on N.Y., series WCBS-TV, 1965; (concert) Requim, 1965. Address: care Nat Symphony Orch 2480 16th St Washington DC 20009

DE PUY, MARY BONNAR (MRS. HENRY C. DE PUY), librarian; b. New Bedford, Mass., Aug. 19, 1917; d. James Miller and Jane (Forsyth) Bonnar; A.B., Colby Coll., 1940; B.A. in L.S., Simmons Coll., 1941; m. Henry C. DePuy, Sept. 29, 1967. Reference librarian N.Y. Pub. Library, N.Y.C., 1941-45; lit. searcher Am. Chem. Soc., N.Y.C., 1945-46; librarian Burroughs Wellcome & Co., Inc., Tuckahoe, N.Y., 1947—. Cons. H.W. Wilson Co., 1965-70; mem. adv. bd. N.C. Central U. Sch. Library Sci., 1973. Mem. Am. Soc. Information Sci., Spl. Libraries Assn. (chmn. pharm. div. 1957-58). Home: 5918 Winthrop Pl Raleigh NC 27612 Office: Burroughs Wellcome & Co Inc 3030 Cornwallis Rd Research Triangle Park NC 27709

DERAMUS, JUDSON DAVIE, ednl. adminstr.; b. Speigner, Ala., June 22, 1896; s. William Neal and Josephine (Flinn) DeR.; B.S., U. Ala., 1917; student Pell Law Sch., Raleigh, N.C., 1923-24; m. Nina D. Jerome, Nov. 26, 1940; 1 son, Judson Davie. Admitted to N.C. bar, 1926; with VA, Raleigh, Charlotte, Fayetteville, N.C., 1923-42, mgr. N.C. regional office, Winston-Salem, 1946-66; cons. asso. Mgmt. Inst. Wake Forest U., 1966-70, dir., 1970—. Dir. Winston-Salem United Fund, 1959-65; chmn. adv. bd. Winston-Salem, Forsyth County Civil Def., 1967-69; chmn. Winston-Salem Army Adv. Com. Dir. of

Winston-Salem Goodwill Industries, 1962-68, Winston-Salem Industries for Blind, 1962-68, Expt. in Self Reliance, 1967-69. Served with U.S. Army, World War I; AEF in France; served to col. AUS, World War II. Decorated Purple Heart; recipient Humanitarian Service award Winston-Salem Hadassah, 1957, V.A.s Exceptional Service award, 1958, VA'S Distinguished Career award, 1965; selected by Nat. Civil Service League as one of top ten career employees in fed. govt., 1960. Mem. Am. Legion (citation N.C. 1964), V.F.W. (citation 1965), D.A.V. (citation N.C. 1960), Res. Officers Assn. U.S., N.C. Fed. Personnel Mgmt. Council (life), Mil. Order World Wars, Beta Gamma Sigma (hon.). Methodist. Rotarian. Home: 2201 Buena Vista Rd Winston-Salem NC 27104

DERBY, ROGER MALCOLM, elec. engr.; b. Chgo., Oct. 13, 1933; s. Malcolm Richard and Sylvia Nevada (Damon) D.; B.S., U. Ill., 1960; m. Joyce Elaine Roach, May 25, 1958; children—Kevin, Bryan, Sharon. With Gen. Electric Co., 1960—, project engr., Daytona Beach, Fla., 1968—. Served with AUS, 1955-58. Mem. I.E.E.E., Halifax Sailing Assn. (sec. 1973—, commodore 1974—). Home: 407 Jessamine Blvd Daytona Beach FL 32018 Office: Box 2500 Daytona Beach FL 32015

DERHAM, JOHN PICKENS, JR., banker; b. Green Sea, S.C., Apr. 27, 1896; s. John Pickens and Loula Jackson (McGougan) D.; B.S., Clemson U., 1917; m. Sarah Louella Ivy, Apr. 19, 1968; children by previous marriage—Mary L. (Mrs. Junius P. Roberts), Anne A. (Mrs. Gilbert Coleman). With Seaboard R.R., 1920-66, beginning as devel. agt., successively contracting freight agt., comml. agt., dist. freight agt., asst. freight traffic mgr., all Jacksonville, Fla., freight traffic mgr., asst. v.p., both Norfolk, Va., 1920-54, v.p., Richmond, Va., 1954-66; sr. v.p., dir. Barnett Bank of Winter Haven (Fla.), 1966—; sr. v.p. Barnett Bank of Cypress Gardens; v.p. Auburndale Barnett Bank. Served to 1st lt. inf., U.S. Army, 1917-19. Mem. Nat. Freight Traffic Assn. (life), Nat. Def. Transp. Assn. (life), Jacksonville Traffic Club (life, past pres.), Fla. Traffic Assn., Future Farmers Am. (hon.), Future Farmers Fla. (hon.), Newcomen Soc. N.Am. Mason (Shriner). Clubs: Deerwood (Jacksonville, Fla.); Lake Region Yacht and Country (Winter Haven). Home: 700 Mirror Terrace Winter Haven FL 33880 Office: 11 5th St Winter Haven FL 33880

DERIAN, PATRICIA MURPHY (MRS. PAUL S. DERIAN), Democratic nat. committeewoman; b. N.Y.C.; d. Ronald and Ruby (Hardiman) Murphy; ed. Palos Verdes Coll., Millsaps Coll.; grad. U. Va. Sch. Nursing; m. Paul S. Derian, Mar. 7, 1953; children—Michael Tabore, Thomas Craig, Renee Brooke. Chmn. Women in Miss. for Humphrey-Muskie, 1968, Miss. McGovern campaign, 1972; mem. Dem. Nat. Com., 1968—; del. Dem. Nat. Conv., 1968, 72, vice chmn. rules com., 1972; mem. exec. com. So. Regional Council, Dem. Policy Council, 1969-72; co-chmn. Policy Council Com. on Women's Polit. Power; mem. Dem. Charter Commn.; mem. Nat. Women's Polit. Caucus; v.p. So. Regional Council. Bd. dirs. Miss. Council Human Relations, Operation Shoestring, Mississippians for Pub. Edn., Delta Ministry, Miss. office Children's Television Workshop, Center for Correctional Justice; chmn. bd. dirs. Civic Communications Corp. Am. Civil Liberties Union (nat. dir.), Gallery Guild, League of Women Voters. Address: 2349 Twin Lakes Circle Jackson MS 39211

DERIAN, PAUL SAHAK, educator; b. L.I., N.Y., July 25, 1922; s. Sahak B. and Renee (Tabore) D.; student N.Y. U., 1940-41; B.A., U. Va., 1946, M.D., 1947; m. Patricia S. Murphy, Mar. 7, 1953; children—Michael, T. Craig, Renee Brooke. Intern St. Vincent's Hosp., N.Y.C., 1951-52; resident orthopedic surgery U. Va., Charlottesville, 1952-53; sr. resident, 1956-57; resident Alfred I. Dupont Inst., Wilmington, Del., 1954-55, Children's Hosp., Cerebral Palsy, Reisterstown, Md., 1955, Rehab. Center, Fisherville, Va., 1955; practice medicine specializing in orthopedic surgery, Pineville, W.Va., 1953-54, Marion, O., 1959; instr. orthopedic surgery Ohio State U., 1958-60, also chief orthopedic surgery F.C. Smith Clinic; asso. prof., chief orthopedic surgery U. Miss. Med. Center, Jackson, 1960-66, prof., chief orthopedic surgery, 1966—, also adj. prof. law; vis. lectr. Sch. Law, Oxford; cons. Jackson VA Hosp., 1960—, Keesler AFB, Biloxi, Miss.; adj. prof. U. Miss. Sch. Law, Oxford, dir. Medicolegal program Univ. Med. Center. Served with USNR, 1942-45. Fellow Nat. Polio Found., 1956-57. Diplomate Am. Bd. Orthopedic Surgery, also examiner; fellow Am. Acad. Orthopedic Surg., A.C.S.; mem. Am., Miss. State, So., Va., Ohio, W.Va. med. assns., Soc. Nuclear Medicine, Am. Med. Colls., Am. Assn. U. Profs., Miss. Assn. Medicine (bd. advisers), Southeastern Surg. Congress, Tri-County, Central, Hinds County med. socs., Am. Assn. Surgery of Trauma, Miss. Orthopedic Soc. (pres. 1968-69), Research Soc. Am., Nat. Rehab. Soc., Am. Arthritic and Rheumatology Soc., Am. Civil Liberties Union, Sigma Xi, Raven Soc. (U. Va.). Author: Outline Orthopedic Surgery, 1968. Contbr. articles in field profl. jours. Home: 2349 Twin Lakes Circle Jackson MS 39211

DERRICK, GEORGE LYNN, physician; b. Columbia, S.C., Feb. 13, 1932; s. Curtis Eugene and Pearle (Derrick) D.; student U. S.C., 1954; M.D., Med. Coll. S.C., 1958; postgrad. Colby Coll., 1964, U. Miami, 1965, U. Chgo., 1966; m. Sylvia Anne Turner, June 1, 1956; children—George Lynn, Katherine Laine. Intern, Med. Center Hosp., Charleston, S.C., 1958-59; resident internal medicine Columbia Hosp., 1959-60; pvt. practice medicine, Columbia, 1960-63; resident ophthalmology Med. Coll. Hosp., Charleston, 1963-66; teaching fellow Med. Coll. S.C., 1965-66; clin. fellow Johns Hopkins, 1966; instr. ophthalmology Med. Coll. S.C., Columbia, 1966—; instr. spl. studies U. S.C., 1968—. Cons. Eye Bank, 1966—, S.C. Blind Commn., 1966-71; mem. rotating surg. staff Project Hope, Ceylon, 1968-69. Participant 2d Congress Internat. Group Medicine, Rio de Janeiro, Brazil, 1973; mem. med. adv. staff Social Security Adminstrn. Bur. Hearings and Appeals, 1973—. Bd. dirs. S.C. Eye Bank, 1972—. Served with AUS, 1950-52. Diplomate Am. Bd. Ophthalmology. Fellow Am. Acad. Ophthalmology and Otolaryngology; mem. Am. Assn. Ophthalmology. Club: Sertoma (Richland). Home: 4859 Forest Ridge Lane Columbia SC 29206 Office: 1520 Laurel St Columbia SC 29201

DERRICK, HOMER, banker, ins. exec.; b. Lexington, S.C., Dec. 10, 1906; s. Edwin Paris and Mayme Eva (Hughes) D.; student U. S.C., 1923-24; grad. Am. Inst. Banking, 1932; m. Mabel Ellison Beckham, Sept. 1, 1924; children—Jeanne (Mrs. James E. Morris), Betsy (Mrs. Philip S. Calvo), Homer E. Vice pres. S.C. Nat. Bank, Columbia and Greenville, 1926-50; pres. Carolina Nat. Bank, Easley and Pendleton, S.C., 1951-54; pres., chmn. bd. First Nat. Bank, Lexington, Va., 1955—; organized and 1st pres. Great Eastern Life Ins. Co., Greenville, 1954— Eastern Fire & Casualty Ins. Co., Greenville, Atlantic & Gulf States Ins. Co., Easley, S.C., partner The Sherwood Co., 1951-73; pres. First Eastern Financial Corp.; chmn. bd. First Eastern Securities Corp., Lexington, Virginia; past pres. Financial Internat. Corp., Washington; past chmn. adv. council Financial Gen. Corp., Washington; dir. Appalachian Fruit Growers Coop. Assn., Raphine, Va. Episcopalian. Club: Lexington Country (1st pres.). Home: Windswept Lexington VA 24450 Office: First Nat Bank Bldg 22 S Main St Lexington VA 24450

DERRICK, JOHNNY B., ednl. adminstr.; b. Gilmer, Tex., Feb. 27, 1930; s. Avery and Fessie (Jeffrey) D.; B.A., Tex. Coll., 1957; M.B.A., Tex. So. U., 1967; m. Pearlia Mae Wallace, July 18, 1953; children—Frederick D., LeNard D. Cashier, Fla. Meml. Coll., St. Augustine, 1957-65, business mgr., 1963-65; fed. loans officer Tuskegee Inst., Ala., 1965-68; dir. student financial aid Tex. Coll., Tyler, 1968—. Active Boy Scouts Am. Mem. Bi-racial com. Tyler div. Eastern Dist. of Tex., 1971—; mem. Bd. of Adjustment, Tyler, Pk. Bd., Tyler. Served with AUS, 1951-53. Mem. Am. Assn. Colls. and U Bus. Adminstrn., So. Assn. Student Financial Aid Adminstrs., Tex. Assn. Student Financial Aid Adminstrs., Nat. Assn. Student Financial Aid Adminstrs., Tyler Orgn. Men (treas. 1968—), Tex. Coll. Alumni Assn. (chpt. treas. 1970—), Alpha Phi Alpha. Baptist (trustee). Home: 1602 Northridge Dr Tyler TX 75701 Office: 2404 N Grand Av Tyler TX 75701

DERRYBERRY, EVERETT, univ. pres.; b. Columbia, Tenn., Oct. 11, 1906; s. Felix Oscar and Bonnie Everett (McDonald) D.; B.A., U. Tenn., 1928; B.A. (Rhodes scholar), U. Oxford (Eng.), 1932, M.A., 1939; O.Litt., U. Chattanooga, 1965; LL.D. (hon.), Pepperdine Coll., 1967; m. Joan Pitt-Rew, Aug. 5, 1933; children—Walter Everett, June Elisabeth. Prof. English, Burritt Coll., Spencer, Tenn., 1932-33; head dept. English, U. Tenn. Jr. Coll., 1933-38; head dept. langs. and lit. Murray (Ky.) State Coll., 1938-40; pres. Tenn. Technol. U., Cookeville, 1940—. Regional dir. U.S.O. and Nat. War Fund, 1943-46. Chmn. Tenn. Edn. Legislative Com., 1943, 44, 45; adv. bd. Tenn. Congress P.T.A.; sec. Conf. on Public Instns. in So. States, 1949; mem. Tenn. Jud. Council; pres. Tenn. Water Safety Congress, 1951. Recipient Outstanding Civilian service medal Dept. Army, 1968. Mem. Am. Assn. U. Profs., Nat. Council English Tchrs., U. Tenn. Alumni Assn. (pres. 1946), Tenn. Coll. Assn. (pres. 1945), So. Assn. Colls. (commn. on higher edn.), Phi Delta Kappa, Sigma Chi, Phi Kappa Phi, Pi Kappa Delta, Omicron Delta Kappa, Kappa Delta Pi. Rotarian. Lion. Address: Tenn Technol U Cookeville TN 38501

DERRYBERRY, WALTER EVERETT, obstetrician, gynecologist; b. Martin, Tenn., May 9, 1935; s. William Everett and Gertrude Joan (Pitt-Rew) D.; B.S., Tenn. Tech. U., 1957; M.D., U. Tenn., 1959; m. Alice Hamilton Sprunt, May 14, 1966; children—Douglas Everett, William Pitt-Rew. Intern, Cook County Hosp., Chgo., 1960; resident Vanderbilt U. Hosp., Nashville, Tenn., 1963-66; practice medicine specializing in obstetrics and gynecology Cookeville, Tenn., 1966—; mem. staffs Lady Ann Meml. Hosp., Livingston, Tenn., Cookeville (Tenn.) Gen. Hosp. Bd. dir. Cookeville Symphony Orchestra, 1967-73, Cookeville Summer Theater, Inc., 1973-74, Louise Mercer Found., 1968. Served with USPHS, 1961-63. Fellow Am. Coll. Obstetrics and Gynecology; mem. Am. Fertility Soc., Royal Soc. Medicine, Sigma Chi, Phi Chi. Democrat. Episcopalian (warden 1966-67, mem. vestry 1966-70). Rotarian. Home: 717 E 6th St Cookeville TN 38501 Office: 137 W 2nd St Cookeville TN 38501

DESANDERS, (ALICE) JANET, journalist; b. Dallas, Dec. 30, 1943; d. William Dwayne and Alice Madeline (Jones) DeSanders; student Whittier Coll., 1961-62; B.S., So. Meth. U., 1965. Asst. to dir. customer relations Neiman-Marcus, Dallas, 1967-68; soc. editor Dallas Times Herald, 1970—, editor, pub. Soc. Sect.; pres. Soc. Publs. Inc. Mem. Chi Omega. Office: 3511 N Hall St #110 Dallas TX 75219

DE SAUSSURE, RICHARD LAURENS, JR., surgeon; b. Macon, Ga., Dec. 29, 1917; s. Richard Laurens and Margaret (Hamilton) DeS.; A.B., U. Va., 1939, M.D., 1942; m. Phyllis Helen Falk, June 12, 1948; children—Alexis, Richard Laurens III, Denise. Intern, U. Va. Hosp., Charlottesville, 1942-43, resident neurosurgery, 1946-47; vol. fellow neurosurgery Cin. Gen. Hosp., 1947-48; asst. chief neurosurgery Kennedy VA Hosp., Memphis, 1949-50, chief neurosurgery, 1950; practice medicine specializing in neurosurgery, Memphis, 1950—; clin. prof. neurosurgery U. Tenn. Coll. Medicine; chief staff Bapt. Meml. Hosp., Memphis, pres., 1966; mem. courtesy staff Meth., St. Joseph, William F. Bowld, John Gaston hosps. (all Memphis). Served from 1st lt. to maj. with M.C., AUS, 1943-46; ETO. Decorated Bronze Star medal; recipient Superior Leadership award Memphis area C. of C., 1966. Diplomate Am. Bd. Neurol. Surgery (mem. bd. 1966-72, sec. 1970-73). Mem. Tenn. Med. Assn. (speaker ho. of dels. 1969-71), Am. Assn. Neurol. Surgery (v.p. 1966), Congress Neurol. Surgeons (past pres.), A.C.S. (chmn. adv. council neurol. surgery 1964-69), Am. Acad. Neurol. Surgeons (v.p.), Memphis and Shelby County Med. Soc. (v.p.). Home: 4290 Heatherwood Lane Memphis TN 38117 Office: 20 S Dudley St Memphis TN 38103

DES CHAMPS, JOHN LEFEBER, mech. engr.; b. Muskogee, Okla., Apr. 23, 1913; s. John William and Mary B. (Cordray) D.; B.S., Okla. State U., 1936; m. Ludie B. Sullivan, July 18, 1933; children—Michael, Mary Lee (Mrs. Guy L. Butler). Chief engr. Allied Steel Products Corp., Tulsa, 1939-47; Star Mfg. Co., Oklahoma City, 1947-59; self-employed cons. structural engr., Oklahoma City, 1959-69; chief engr. Harter Concrete Products Corp., Oklahoma City, 1969—. Instr. structural steel design U. Tulsa, Engring. Defense Program, 1941-43. Scoutmaster, Boy Scouts Am., Oklahoma City, 1956-57, merit badge counciler, 1956—; little league baseball coach, Oklahoma City, 1953-54. Registered profl. engr., Okla., Tex., Ind., Tenn. Baptist (deacon 1954—). Rotarian (charter pres. 1949-50). Home: 3716 NW 25th St Oklahoma City OK 73107 Office: Harter Concrete Products 1628 W Main Oklahoma City OK 73103

DESELM, HENRY RAWIE, biologist, educator; b. Columbus, O., Nov. 1, 1924; s. Ralph Emerson and Helen (Rawie) D.; student Miami U., Oxford, O., 1943-44; B.S., Ohio State U., 1948, B.S. Edn., 1949, M.Sc., 1950, Ph.D., 1953; m. Mary Hersee, 1948; children—Diane (Mrs. Jerry Overcast), Richard Lowell. Asst. instr. botany dept. Ohio State U., Columbus, 1952-54; instr. biology Middle Tenn. State U., Murfreesboro, 1954-56; faculty U. Tenn., Knoxville, 1956—, now prof. botany. Served with USMCR, 1943-46. Fellow A.A.A.S., Tenn. Acad. Sci.; mem. Assn. Southeastern Biologists, Bot. Soc. Am., Brit. Ecol. Soc., Ecol. Soc. Am. (membership com.), Assn. Tropical Biology, Internat. Soc. Tropical Biology, Am. Assn. Stratigraphic Palynologists, Am. Soc. Photogrammetry, Internat. Assn. for Ecology, Soc. Am. Foresters, Soil Sci. Soc. Am., U. Tenn. Arboretum Soc., Tenn. Citizens for Wilderness Planning, Tenn. Trails Assn., Tenn. Scenic Rivers Assn., Smoky Mountain Hiking Club, So. Appalachian Bot. Club, Sigma Xi, Gamma Sigma Delta, Phi Epsilon Phi. Asso. editor Am. Midland Naturalist, 1964-70. Contbr. articles to profl. jours. Home: 424 W Hillvale Turn Knoxville TN 37919

DESIDERIO, DOMINIC MORSE, JR., educator; b. McKees Rocks, Pa., Jan. 11, 1941; s. Dominic Morse and Jewell Aline (Hull) D.; B.A., U. Pitts., 1961; S.M., Mass. Inst. Tech., 1964, Ph.D., 1965; m. Julia Marie Thomas, Oct. 9, 1965; children—Annette Marie, Dominic Michael. Research asst. Mass. Inst. Tech., Cambridge, 1962-65; research chemist Am. Cyanamid Co., Stamford, Conn., 1966-67; asst. prof. chemistry Baylor Med. Sch., Houston, 1967-71, asso. prof., 1971—. Cons. Recipient fellowships Internat. Assn. for Exchange of Students, 1962, Intra-sci. Research Found., 1971—. Mem. Am. Chem. Soc. (mem. awards com. 1972—), Am. Inst. Chemists, A.A.A.S., Am. Soc. Mass Spectrometry, Am. Assn. U. Profs. (sec. 1972-73), N.Y. Acad. Sci., Sigma Xi. Home: 3514 Dumbarton St Houston TX 77025

DESLOGE, EDWARD AUGUSTINE, physicist, educator; b. St. Louis, Aug. 31, 1926; s. Louis Francis and Angela (Burdeau) D.; B.S., U. Notre Dame, 1947; M.S., St. Louis U., 1955, Ph.D., 1957; m. Helen Moira Dunne, Dec. 15, 1968; children—Bryan, Matthew, Rosemary, Angela, Bruce. Engr., Watlow Electric Mfg. Co., 1947-48, dir. 1971—; instr. Yale, New Haven, 1958-59; asst. prof. physics Fla. State U., Tallahassee, 1959-65, asso. prof., 1965-69, prof., 1969—. Served to ensign USNR, 1945-47. Mem. Am. Phys. Soc. Roman Catholic. Elk. Author: Statistical Physics, 1966; Thermal Physics, 1968. Home: 2213 Demeron Rd Tallahassee FL 32303

DESMOND, MURDINA M. MACFARQUHAR (MRS. JAMES L. DESMOND), physician; b. Isle of Lewis, Scotland, Nov. 14, 1916; d. Alexander and Margaret Muir (Graham) MacFarquhar; B.A., Smith Coll., 1938; M.D., Temple U., 1942; m. James L. Desmond, July 10, 1948; children—Margaret Graham, James Alexander. Intern, Lincoln Hosp., N.Y.C., N.Y. Hosp., N.Y.C., 1942-44; resident D.C. Gen. Hosp., Washington, 1946-47; fellow pediatrics George Washington U., 1947-48; practice medicine, specializing in pediatrics, Houston, 1948—; mem. staff Methodist Hosp., Tex. Children's Hosp., St. Luke's Hosp.; instr. Baylor U., Houston, 1948-53, asst. prof., 1953-57, asso. prof., 1957-65, prof. pediatrics, head newborn sect., 1965-72, prof. pediatrics and community medicine 1970—, head sect. developmental pediatrics, 1972—, dir. Center for Developmental Pediatrics, 1972—. Diplomate Am. Bd. Pediatrics. Fellow Am. Assn. Mental Deficiency, Acad. Cerebral Palsy; mem. Am. Soc. Pediatric Research, Am. Pediatric Soc. Research into newborn disease and care. Home: 2210 Bellefontaine St Houston TX 77025 Office: Baylor Coll Medicine 1200 MD Anderson Blvd Houston TX 77025

DESNOYERS, THOMAS HOLLISTER, transp. exec.; b. Chgo., Mar. 27, 1928; s. Harry B. and Browning (Hollister) D.; Ph.B., Ill. Wesleyan U., 1951; M.B.A., Northwestern U., 1953; m. Margery N. Foster, Mar. 22, 1952; 1 dau., Aimee Louise. Clk., C. & N.-W. Ry. Co., Chgo., 1950-52, Pa. R.R., Chgo., 1955; asso. editor Ry. Age, Chgo., 1955-58; dir. traffic research C.M., St. P. & P. R.R., Chgo., 1958-66, dir. marketing and research, 1966-67; dir. marketing N. & W. Ry., Roanoke, Va., 1967-69; dir. codes and standards Transp. Data Coordinating Com., Washington, 1969—. Served with AUS, 1953-55. Mem. Am. Econ. Assn., Transp. Research Forum, Am. Marketing Assn., Phi Kappa Phi, Pi Gamma Mu, Research in field. Home: 8124 Birnam Wood Dr McLean VA 22101 Office: 1101 17th St NW Washington DC 20036

DE SOMBRE, ROBERT MAGNUS, publisher; b. Washington, Oct. 7, 1915; s. John William and Helena (Magnus) de S.; student pub. schs.; m. Patricia Ann Sullivan, Apr. 17, 1948; children—Diane, Patricia Ann, Joanne. With Kiplinger Washington Letters, 1942-50; with Gulf Pub. Co., Houston, 1950—, v.p., dir., 1956-68, sr. v.p., dir., 1968—. Mem. Am. Petroleum Inst., Houston C. of C., Direct Mail Advt. Assn. (past gov.). Club: Houston. Home: 4410 Ingersoll St Houston TX 77027 Office: 3301 Allen Pkwy Houston TX 77019

DESPAIN, DAYSIE SPENCER (MRS. CHARLES RICHARDSON DESPAIN), pub.; b. Ft. Spring, Ky., Dec. 11, 1894; d. Joseph and Julia (Vaughan) Spencer; student Ky. Western State Tchrs. Coll., 1920; m. Charles Richardson DeSpain, May 15, 1922 (dec. Feb. 1949); 1 son, Charles Richardson. Pub., Anchorage (Ky.) Press. Mem. Nat. League Women's Service, World War I; vol. worker A.R.C., World War II. Mem. Nat. Soc. D.A.R. (registrar 1951-56), Ky. Soc. Mayflower Descs. (corr. sec. 1953—), U. Ky. Library Assos., English-Speaking Union, Historic Homes Found., Nat. Soc. Magna Charta Dames, Colonial Order of the Crown, Order of Washington, Alden Kindred Am., Wilderness Soc., Anchorage Home Makers No. One, Nat. Trust for Hist. Ky. Hist. Soc., Nat. Soc. Magna Charta Dames, Plantagenet Soc., Sovereign Colonial Soc. Ams. Royal Descent, UN Assn., Smithsonian Inst., English Speaking Union, Knights Most Noble Order Garter. Presbyn. Clubs: Anchorage Civic; Filson. Pub.: Anchorage (Leone Hallenberg), 1959. Home: 11402 Ridge Rd Anchorage KY 40223

DESPALJ, PAVLE, condr.; b. Yugoslavia; grad. Zagreb (Yugoslavia) Music Acad., 1960; m. Majda Radic; children—Nadja, Simon. Condr. Zagreb opera, 1959-66; founder Zadar Music Festival, 1961; music dir. Zagreb Radio TV Chamber Orch. and Symphony, 1962-67; founder Belgrade Chamber Orch., 1966; asso. condr. Fla. Symphony Orch., Orlando, 1968-70, music dir., condr., 1970—; condr. Grant Park Symphony Orch., Chgo., 1972—; composer works for string quartet, piano and strings, orch., chamber orch., sonatas. Address: Florida Symphony Orchestra PO Box 782 Orlando FL 32802

DESPORTE, JOHN STANLEY, physician; b. New Orleans, Jan. 10, 1911; s. Charles Alexander and Marie Olivia (Meyer) D.; B.S., Tulane U., 1931, M.D., 1935; m. Janet Elizabeth Voorhies, Sept. 14, 1936; children—Elizabeth Ann (Mrs. James Oliphant Lilly), Janet (Mrs. John Edwin Boelte II). Intern, Touro Infirmary, New Orleans, 1935-36; gen. practice medicine and surgery, Bogalusa, La., 1936-66; co. physician Great So. Lumber Co., Gaylord Container Corp., Bogalusa, La., 1936-43; founder Desporte Clinic-Hosp., Bogalusa, La., 1943-66; mem. staff Bogalusa Community Med. Center, 1936-66. Examining physician, med. adviser Selective Service System, Washington Parish, La., 1942-66. Head Civic Music Assn., Washington Parish, La., 1950-60. Bd. dirs. Community Concerts, New Orleans, 1967-68. Mem. Am. Acad. Family Practice, A.M.A., So. Med. Assn., La. State Med. Soc., Alpha Omega Alpha, Nu Sigma Nu, Sigma Chi. Democrat. Episcopalian. Club: Country (New Orleans). Address: 1550 2d St New Orleans LA 70130

DES PORTES, BERNARD BARUCH, corp. exec.; b. Winnsboro, S.C., Mar. 28, 1922; s. Fay Allen and Elise (Lyles) D.; A.B. in Econs., Tulane U., 1951; m. Elise Harleston Ham, Nov. 25, 1953; children—Sally, Faye, Ann. Susan. Personnel mgr. Owen Roofing Co., Columbia, S.C., 1951-52; employee relations mgr. Kendall Co., Charlotte, N.C., 1952-58; labor relations mgr. combustion Engr. Co., Chattanooga, 1958-60; group dir. personnel Deering Milliken, Inc., Spartanburg, S.C., 1960-68; corporate dir. personnel Sonoco Products Co., Hartsville, S.C., 1968-70, v.p. indsl. relations, 1970-71, v.p. adminstrn., 1972—. Trustee, Byerly Hosp., Hartsville, 1971—. Served with AUS, 1944-46. Mem. Florence C. of C. (adv. council 1971—). Episcopalian. Rotarian. Home: Churchill Rd Hartsville SC 29550 Office: 2d St Hartsville SC 29550

DESROSIERS, NORMAN ALFRED, psychiatrist, clergyman; b. East Providence, R.I., Aug. 6, 1924; s. Frederick Israel and Desneiges (Charette) D.; A.B., Duke, 1949, B.D., 1953; M.D., U. N.C., 1959; m. Frances Lorraine Lueders, Sept. 11, 1943; children—Bruce, Paul, David, Mark. Chaplain, John Umstead Hosp., Butner, N.C., 1951-55, staff physician, 1960-62, resident, 1967-69; intern Watts Hosp., Durham, N.C., 1959-60; resident in psychiatry U. N.C., 1961-62; dir. N.C. Alcoholic Rehab. Center, 1962-65; staff psychiatrist, tng. regional dir., 1969—; med. dir. W.Va. Dept. Mental Health, 1965-66. Served with USNR, 1942-46. Home: 1919 W B St Butner NC 27509 Office: NC Alcoholic Rehabilitation Center E St Butner NC 27509

DESSAUER, HERBERT CLAY, biochemist, educator; b. New Orleans, Dec. 30, 1921; s. Herbert Andrew and Shirley Ross (Patin) D.; student U. N.M., 1943, Cal. Inst. Tech., 1943-44; B.S., La. State

U., 1949, Ph.D., 1952; m. Frances Jane Moffatt, Dec. 10, 1949; children—Dan Winston, Rebecca Lynn, Bryan Clay. Faculty, La. State U., New Orleans, 1951—, prof. dept. biochemistry, 1963—. Mem. Alpha Helix Expdn. to New Guinea, 1969; cons. VA Hosp., New Orleans, 1962—; mem. panel in advanced sci. edn. NSF, 1965-67, mem. panel in systematic biology, 1972—; mem. task force on fluoridation New Orleans Health Planning Council, 1971-72. Served to 1st lt. USAAF, 1943-46. NSF research grantee, 1961—, Am. Philos. Soc. grantee, 1964. Fellow A.A.A.S.; mem. Am. Physiol. Soc., Soc. for Exptl. Biology and Medicine (sect. sec. 1959-61), Am. Soc. Icthyology and Herpetology, Herpetologists League, Soc. Systematic Zoology, Sigma Xi, Phi Kappa Phi. Mem. editorial bd. Herpetologica, 1967—. Contbr. articles to profl. jours. Home: 7100 Dorian St New Orleans LA 70126

DESSOUKY, DESSOUKY AHMAD, med. educator; b. Mit-Ghamr, Egypt, Jan. 18, 1932; s. Ahmad A. and Aleia M. (Ahmad) D.; M.D., Ain-Shams U., Cairo, Egypt, 1956; Ph.D., Tulane U., 1964; m. Caroline Justice, Aug. 2, 1969; 1 son, Dean Ahmad. Came to U.S., 1961, naturalized, 1972. Intern, Ain-Shams U. Hosps., 1956-57, resident, 1957-59; practice medicine specializing in obstetrics and gynecology, Cairo, 1959-61; research asso. Georgetown U., Washington, 1961-64, asst. prof. anatomy, 1966-67, asst. prof. obstetrics and gynecology, dir. Electron Microscope Lab., 1967—, resident univ. hosp., 1967-70. Rockfeller Family Planning grantee, 1970—. Mem. Am. Assn. Anatomists, Am. Fertility Soc., Am. Coll. Obstetricians and Gynecologists, D.C. Med. Soc. Home: 1116 Dominion Court McLean VA 22101 Office: Dept Obstetrics and Gynecology Georgetown U 3800 Reservoir Rd NW Washington DC 20007

DETAR, DELOS FLETCHER, chemist, educator; b. Kansas City, Mo., Jan. 18, 1920; s. DeLos and Laura Serena (Fletcher) D.; B.S., U. Ill., 1941; M.S., U. Pa., 1943, Ph.D., 1944; m. Frances Patty Livesay, Sept. 4, 1943; children—Carleton E., Caroline J. (Mrs. Robert K. Mautz), Marvin B., Martha G. With E.I. DuPont de Nemours & Co., Buffalo, 1945-46; instr. Cornell U., Ithaca, N.Y., 1946-50, asst. prof., 1950-53; asso. prof. U. S.C., Columbia, 1953-56, prof. chemistry, 1956-60; prof. chemistry Fla. State U., Tallahassee, 1960—. Mem. Am. Chem. Soc., Chem. Soc. Gt. Britain, Sigma Xi, Acacia. Editor: Computer Programs for Chemistry, 1968, Computers and Chemistry, 1973. Contbr. articles to profl. jours. Home: 1912 Sharon Rd Tallahassee FL 32303

DETJEN, DON WHEELER, oil co. exec.; b. St. Louis, Oct. 31, 1925; s. C. Wheeler and Irma H. (Grounds) D.; student Ia. State Coll., 1943-44, Ill. State Normal U., 1944; B.S., Mo. Sch. Mines and Metallurgy, 1948; exec. tng. program Ind. U., 1965-66; m. Shirley Anne Pence, Mar. 1, 1947; children—David, Anne, Michael, John, Allison. With Ashland Oil Co., Inc. (Ky.), 1948-58; exec. asst. Valvoline Oil Co., Ashland, 1959-68, v.p. operations, 1968—. Mem. Ashland Zoning Adjustment Bd., 1961-65. Served with USNR, 1943-46. Home: 2931 Lucille St Ashland KY 41101 Office: Ashland Oil Inc Ashland KY 41101

DETLEFS, DALE RALPH, air filter mfg. co. exec.; b. Stickney, S.D., Jan. 12, 1927; s. William Frederick and Anna (Peterson) D.; student Purdue U., 1945-46; A.B., U. Neb., 1947; J.D., U. Ia., 1950; B.S. in Commerce, U. Louisville, 1961, M.B.A., 1968; m. Claire McIntosh, Aug. 29, 1953; children—Paul Steven, Ann, William Frederick. Admitted to Ia. bar, 1950, Ky. bar, 1957; editor Bur. of Analysis, Davenport, Ia., 1950-51; sales rep. regulatory and legal div. Prentice Hall, Inc., Davenport, 1951-55; indsl. relations asst. Bendix Aviation Corp., Davenport, 1955-56; mgr. Corporate personnel services Am. Air Filter Co., Louisville, 1956—. Asst. prof. Grad. Sch. Bus., U. Louisville. Bd. dirs. Louisville Urban League, 1962-70, Louisville chpt. A.R.C. Served with USNR, 1945-46. Mem. Ia., Ky. bar assns., Louisville Personnel Assn. (pres. 1966-67), Am. Mgmt. Assn., Am. Compensation Assn., Am. Soc. Personnel Adminstrn. Presbyn. (deacon). Club: Hurstbourne Country (Louisville). Home: 9001 Peterborough Ct Louisville KY 40222 Office: 215 Central Av Louisville KY 40208

DE TONNANCOUR, PAUL ROGER GODEFROY, library adminstr.; b. Fall River, Mass., May 22, 1926; s. R. Godefroy and Emilie (St. Germain) de T.; A.B. cum laude, Providence Coll., 1952; M.S., Simmons Coll., 1953; m. Mary E. Fenno, Apr. 9, 1955; children—Paul Godefroy, Camille Marie. Asst. librarian Enoch Pratt Library, Balt., 1953-54; chief librarian, tech. analyst Armco Steel Corp., Balt., 1954-56; mgr. Information Services-Gen. Dynamics, Ft. Worth div., 1957-69, mgr. information programs, 1969—; cons. Modern Lang. Assn. Am.; cons. on sci. information personnel U.S. Office Edn. John Cotton Dana lectr., 1966. Singer Ft. Worth Opera Assn., Chorus. Active United Fund; mem. exec. com. Big Bros. Tarrant County. Trustee Cosmopolitan Internat., 1961-63. Served with USNR, 1943-46. Named Boss of Year, Am. Bus. Women's Assn., 1965. Mem. Am. Library Assn., Fort Worth Art Assn., Spl. Libraries Assn., (adv. council, chmn. aerospace div.), Am. Soc. Information Sci., Delta Epsilon Sigma. Episcopalian, (vestryman). Mason. Club: Fort Worth Boat. Author: The Exploitation of Technical Information, 1966. Co-author: Science Information Personnel, 1963. Contbr. articles to profl. jours. Home: 6332 Genoa Rd Fort Worth TX 76116 Office: PO Box 748 Fort Worth TX 76101

DETRO, RANDALL AUGUSTUS, librarian; b. Grand Bayou, La., July 6, 1931; s. Clarence Augustus and Clarice Vivian (Lay) D.; B.A., Northwestern La. State Coll., 1952; M.S., La. State U., 1954; Ph.D., 1970; m. Ruby Charlene Lyles, Aug. 23, 1957; children—Barron Randall, Frederick Charles. Library dir. Northeast La. State Coll., Monroe, 1954-55, Mars Hill (N.C.) Coll., 1955-57; serials librarian Northwestern La. State Coll., Natchitoches, 1957-59; prof. geography, library dir. Nicholls State U., Thibodaux, 1959—. Mem. La. State U. Library Sch. Alumni Assn. (pres. 1962-63), Am., La. library assns., Am. Geog. Soc., Assn. Am. Geographers, Am. Name Soc., La. Hist. Assn., Pioneer Am. Soc., Am. Littoral Soc., Delta Sigma Phi, Alpha Beta Alpha. Home: 1014 Peoples St Thibodaux LA 70301

DETYENS, WILLIAM JAMES, ship repair co. exec.; b. Georgetown, S.C., Mar. 21, 1917; s. Hasford Walker and Sally Maria (Cox) D.; student pub. schs., Charleston, S.C.; m. Marjorie Alice Greene, June 10, 1954; children—William Ronald, Judy Ann (Mrs. David Loy Stewart), Margaret Ann, Mary Alice, Hasse Harold, James William. Founder, chmn. bd. Detyens Shipyards, Inc., Mt. Pleasant, S.C., 1956—, Berkeley Industries, Inc., Mt. Pleasant, 1962—, Wando Enterprises, Inc., Mt. Pleasant, 1970—; dir., mem. adv. bd. Citizens and So. Nat. Bank. Mem. U.S. Draft Bd., 1962-71. Bd. dirs. Trident Ungraded Acad., Easter Seal Soc. Crippled Children and Adults; bd. dirs., chmn. bd. Mt. Pleasant Meml. Gardens. Served with U.S. Mcht. Marines, 1932. Mem. Southeastern Shipyard Assn., Inc. (v.p. 1972-73), Hibernian Soc. Baptist (mem. bd. 1970-73). Elk. Home: 123 Hobcaw Dr Mount Pleasant SC 29464 Office: Route 2 Box 180 Hwy 41 Mount Pleasant SC 29464

DEUPREE, CHARLES LAMAR, assn. exec., cons.; b. New Orleans, Feb. 2, 1917; s. Elijah Julius and Della (Morgan) DeuP.; B.B.A., U. Tex., 1940; m. Grace Fisher, Mar. 26, 1946; children—Della Grace (Mrs. Lawrence Mitchell Ryan), Anne Colista (Mrs. John Allen Richardson), Cecilia Valerie, Elisabeth Frances. Ind. oil operator and owner; exec. v.p. Assn. Oilwell Servicing Contractors, Dallas, 1961—. Mem. exec. com. Nat. Safety Council, 1966—. Bd. dirs. Tex. Safety Council. Served from pvt. to capt. AUS, 1942-46; ETO. Decorated Purple Heart, Bronze Star medal. Mem. Am. Soc. Assn. Execs. (dir. 1964—), Tex. Soc. Assn. Execs. (v.p. 1966, pres. 1967—), U.S. C. of C., Patriotic Soc. Colonial Wars (founder Tex. gentleman council 1966—, gov. 1974), Am. Petroleum Council (adv. com. 1966—), Am. Petroleum Inst., Huguenot Soc., Ret. Officers Assn. (mem. nominating com. 1974), Assn. Petroleum Writers, Sigma Nu. Episcopalian. Mason (32 deg., Shriner), Rotarian. Address: 4414 Alta Vista Lane Dallas TX 75229

DEUTSCH, EBERHARD PAUL, lawyer; b. Cin., Oct. 31, 1897; s. Gotthard and Hermine (Bacher) D.; student Tulane U., 1924-25; LL.D. (hon.), U. Messina (Sicily), 1943, Loyola U., New Orleans, 1972; m. Rhea Loeb, Aug. 1, 1929 (dec. Mar. 1961); 1 son, Brunswick G. Admitted to La. bar, 1925, since practiced in New Orleans; spl. asst. to atty. gen. U.S. on Texas City Disaster litigation, 1950-53; prin. legal adviser to Gen. Mark W. Clark in Mil. Adminstrn. of Austria, 1945-46, also chmn. Allied Legal Directorate. Civilian aide for La. to sec. of army; hon. consul gen. of Austria for La. and Miss.; mem. Met. Crime Commn. Chmn. bd. visitors Judge Adv. Gen.'s Sch. of Army; adv. council Sch. Law, Loyola U. Served as lt. with F.A., U.S. Army, 1917-19, col., Gen. Staff Corps, 1942-46. Decorated Silver Star, Bronze Star, Legion of Merit, Purple Heart, Army Commendation; Gold Cross of Merit (Austria); Croix de Guerre with Palm and Fourragere, Order of Lafayette (France). Mem. Internat., Fed., Inter-Am., Am. (chmn. admiralty and maritime law com. 1961-62, com. peace and law through UN 1962-63, 65-68, mem. council sect. internat. and comparative law 1967—, mem. com. on marine resources 1968—), La. (chmn. com. law reform; chmn. commn. on revision of La. corp. law 1962—, chmn. supreme ct. com. on jury instrns. 1968—), New Orleans bar assns., Assn. Bar City N.Y., Am. Judicature Soc. (dir. 1935-56), Maritime Law Assn., Am. Fgn. Relations Assn. (dir.), Assn. ICC Practitioners, C. of C., Alumni Assn. Tulane U., Scribes, Athene Louisianais, Audubon Soc., Confrerie des Chevaliers du Tastevin, English Speaking Union, Fellowship U.S.-Brit. Comrades, Heroes of '76, Internat. Order of Blue Goose, Order of Lafayette, Le Petit Theatre du Vieux Carre, Met. New Orleans Safety Council, Mil. Govt. Assn., Mil. Order World Wars, Nat. Aero. Assn., Nat. Geog. Soc., Res. Officers Assn., Seldon Soc., 33d Div. War Vets. Assn., Tulane Alumni Fund, Assn. Am. Indian Affairs, Inc., Am. Soc. Legal History, Am. Civil Liberties Union, Internat. Law Assn., Internat. Legal Aid Assn., Assn. of Average Adjusters, Assn. U.S. Army, Information Council of Americas, Nat. Trust Historic Preservation (nat. devel. com.), Am. Arbitration Soc., Research Fellows Southwestern Legal Found., also numerous local assns. and socs. Mason (Shriner); mem. B'nai B'rith. Clubs: Army and Navy, Insurance, International House (dir., mem. exec. com.), Press, University, Petroleum, Round Table, Southern Yacht (New Orleans); Lotos, Downtown Athletic (N.Y.C.); Petroleum (Houston); Propeller U.S., Skyriders; Nat. Lawyers, Cosmos (Washington); Nat. Sojourners; City (Baton Rouge); Escoffiers, New Orleans Athletic, New Orleans Yacht, Plimsoll, Lamplighter (New Orleans); Tulane Side Lines Mariners. Editor-in-chief Internat. Lawyer, 1968—. Home: Pontchartrain Hotel New Orleans LA 70140 Office: One Shell Sq New Orleans LA 70139

DEUTSCH, STANLEY, govt. ofcl.; b. Yonkers, N.Y., Oct. 28, 1921; s. Benjamin and Helene Pepi (Klein) D.; basic engring. certificate R.I. State Coll., 1944; B.A., Bklyn. Coll., 1948; M.S., Purdue U., 1951, Ph.D., 1957; m. Thelma Ruth Fogel, June 8, 1948; children—Ellen Sue, Robert Jay, Paula Jean. Research psychologist USN Electronics Lab., San Diego, 1948-57; head human factors support group Martin Co., Denver, 1957-58; supervisory psychologist USAF Ballistic Missiles Div., Inglewood, Cal., Vandenberg AFB, Cal., 1958; supr., head human factors space systems Douglas Aircraft Co., Santa Monica, Cal., 1958-62; v.p., dir. Consad Corp., 1962-63; chief systems research and man-systems integration NASA, 1962-70, dir. bioengring. div., 1970—. Exec. sec. Research Adv. Com. on Biotech. and Human Research, 1962-65; chmn. NASA Com. on Teleoperators and Extravehicular Activities, 1972—. Served with AUS, 1942-46; ETO. Recipient Scholarship award USN, 1953. Fellow A.A.A.S., Human Factors Soc. (pres. 1972-73, exec. council 1960—); mem. N.Y. Acad. Scis., Sigma Xi. Home: 7109 Lava Rock Lane Bethesda MD 20034 Office: Hdqrs NASA Washington DC 20546

DEVALL, CHARLES KLINGMAN, newspaper exec.; b. Mount Vernon, Tex., Nov. 7, 1908; s. Charles Robert and Leila (Milam) D.; student John Tarleton State Coll., 1925-26; B.J., U. Tex., 1931; m. Lyde Gwynne Williford, July 15, 1939. Owner-pub. Kilgore (Tex.) Herald, 1935-40, Kilgore Daily News Herald, 1940—; dir. Kilgore Ceramics Corp., Kilgore Nat. Bank, Kilgore Indsl. Found., Inc. Pres., Tex. Good Rds. Assn., 1956-58. Mem. Tex. Democratic party Exec. Com., 1934-38, presdl. elector, 1940. Chancellor's council U. Tex. at Austin. Served to lt. comdr. USNR, 1942-45. Recipient George Washington awards Freedoms Found. Valley Forge, Pa., 1956, 63; Appreciation award East Tex. Freedom Forum, 1968. Mem. Tex. Daily Newspaper Assn., So. Newspaper Assn., Tex. (past pres., N.E. Tex. (past pres., award 1964) press assn., Kilgore C. of C. (past pres.), Sigma Delta Chi. Presbyn. (elder). Lion (past pres. Kilgore). Clubs: Laird Country (Kilgore); Cherokee (Longview, Tex.); Headliners (Austin) Home: 820 Crimwood Lane Kilgore TX 75662 Office: 610 E Main St Kilgore TX 75662

DEVANEY, AMOGENE FOWLER, educator; b. Canyon, Tex., May 2, 1913; d. William Haywood and Odie (Brooks) Fowler; B.A., West Tex. State Tchrs. Coll., 1934, M.A., 1948; Ph.D., N.Y. U., 1965; m. Walter William DeVaney, Dec. 19, 1936; children—Will Earl, David Brooks. Tchr. pub. schs., Vega, Tex., 1934-35, Fritch, Tex., 1935-36; draftsman Dept. Engring. Amarillo (Tex.), 1945-46; tchr. engring. graphics West Tex. State U., Canyon, 1946-47; prof. engring. graphics and math. Amarillo Coll., 1947—, dir. teach aide inst., 1968. Chmn. workshop on testing in engring. graphics A. and M. U. Tex., 1960. Recipient Founders Day award N.Y. U., 1965. Mem. Am. Soc. Engring. Edn. (exec. com. Gulf-S.W. sect. 1950—), Soc. Women Engrs. (chmn. profl. guidance and edn. 1967-69), Tex. Tchrs. Assn. (unit pres. 1964-65), N.E.A., Math. Assn. Am., Tex. Jr. Coll. Tchrs. Assn. (chmn. engring. graphics sect. 1957-59), Am. Assn. U. Women (br. treas. 1955-59), A.A.A.S. Home: 2410 Parker St Amarillo TX 79109

DEVANEY, JAMES PHILLIPS, civil engr.; b. Birmingham, Ala., Mar. 27, 1926; s. Claude and Mona P. (Peaman) D.; B.S., U. Ala., 1951; m. Peggy White DeVaney, Dec. 26, 1948; 1 dau., Sharon Lee. With S. Central Bell Telephone, Birmingham, 1951—, dist. engr., 1967—. Active United Appeal, Birmingham, 1960-72. Served with USNR, 1944-46. Mem. I.E.E.E. Mason, Elk. Home: 3629 Dabney Dr Birmingham AL 35243 Office: Box 2662 Birmingham AL 35202

DEVAUGHN, JAMES EVERETTE, educator; b. Deatsville, Ala., Apr. 30, 1913; s. Stanly and Medie (Lewis) DeV.; B.S., Auburn U., 1936; M.Ed., Emory U., 1955; Ed.D. (Proctor and Gamble fellow), Columbia, 1964; m. Lillie Hazel Wood, Oct. 26, 1947 (dec. Mar. 1968); children—Kay (Mrs. Joseph Edwards), Emilie Michelle, Wanda Hazel; m. 2d, Jane Gray Rushin, June 14, 1970. Tchr. pub. schs., Atlanta, 1936-52, prin., 1952-61, asst. supt., 1961-68; prof. edn. Ga. State U., Atlanta, 1968—. Cons. various schs. Served with AUS, 1941-45. Mem. P.T.A. (life), Nat. Assn. Sch. Personnel Adminstrs., N.E.A., Am. Assn. Sch. Adminstrs., So. Assn. Colls. and Schs. (exec. sec. Ga. Com., 1969—), Nat. Orgn. Legal Problems in Edn., Phi Kappa Phi. Author; Adminstrative Error in Separation or Reassignment of Professional Personnel in Education, 1964; Teacher Employment, Legal Aspects: Separation and Demotion, 1971; Policies and Procedures for Teacher and Administrator Evaluation, 1971. Contbr. articles to profl. jours. Home: 60 Burdette Rd NW Atlanta GA 30327

DEVAUGHN, WALTER CALVIN, govt. ofcl.; b. Tampa, Fla., Nov. 3, 1926; s. Ellsworth Calvin and Alice (Pumphrey) DeV.; B.C.S., Benjamin Franklin U., 1948; B.S. in Bus. Adminstrn., Am. U., 1961, J.D., 1963; m. Catherine Virginia Griffith, June 21, 1952; children—David Griffith. Douglas Walter, Lynn Allison. Auditor, Theodore Bollt & Co., C.P.A.'s Silver Spring, Md., 1948-49, Potomac Electric Power Co., Washington, 1949-54; accountant Gen. Accounting Office, Washington, 1954-67; comptroller, gen. counsel U.S. Govt. Printing Office, Washington, 1967-70, acting asst. pub. printer for mgmt. and adminstrn., 1970-71, asst. pub. printer, 1973—, gen. counsel, 1971-73. Prof. accounting Benjamin Franklin U., Washington, 1965—; prof. law Am. Inst. Washington, 1966-67; admitted to D.C. bar, 1964, Supreme Ct. bar, 1967. Pres. Huntington Citizens Assn., Colesville, Md., 1964-66; bd. dirs. Wheaton (Md.) Rescue Squad; treas. Allied Civic Group, Silver Spring, Md., 1966-71. Served with USNR, 1945-46. C.P.A., Md. Mem. Am., D.C., Fed. bar assns., Am. Inst. C.P.A.'s Fed. Govt. Accountants Assn., Am. Assn. Atty.-C.P.A.'s, Washington Club of Printing House Craftsmen, Fed. Exec. Inst. Alumni Assn. Club: Argyle Country, Silver Spring, Md., Nat. Lawyers (Washington). Home: 200 Eldrid Dr Silver Spring MD 20904 Office: US Govt Printing Office N Capitol & H Sts NS Washington DC 20401

DE VAULT, ELMER EMMERT, engr.; b. Bristol, Tenn., Apr. 10, 1916; s. Elmer Emmert and Myrtle (Senter) DeV.; student High Point Coll., 1946-48, U. Tenn., 1948-50; m. Ida Blanche Cunningham, June 4, 1937; one dau., Myrtle Nell (Mrs. Hubert Leroy Brant). Engr. aide U.S. Bur. Pub. Roads, Roanoke, Va., 1938-43, 50-53; supt. constrn. Troitiono Constrn. Co., Asheville, N.C., 1953-56; engr. N.C. State Hwy. Commn., Graham, 1956-66, resident engr., Reidsville, 1966—. Served with AUS, 1943-46; ETO. Registered profl. engr., N.C. Mem. Nat. Soc. Profl. Engrs., N.C. Assn. Professions, D.A.V. Democrat. Home: PO Box 732 Wentworth Rd Reidsville NC 27320 Office: Box 1318 Reidsville NC 27320

DEVAULT, JOHN LEE, geophysicist; b. Kansas City, Mo., Aug. 4, 1937; s. Isaac Henderson and Evelyn (Rowell) DeV.; B. Chem. Engring., Case Inst. Tech., 1959; B.S. in Math., MacMurray Coll., 1960; m. Audrey McBlaine, Feb. 10, 1966. Geophysicist, Companie Generle de Geophyque, Paris, France, N. Algeria, Libya, Persia, 1960-62; geophysicist United Geophys. Corp., Australia and Alaska, 1962-65, Digital Playback Center, Houston, 1965-69; mgr. Siesmic Explosives div. Austin Powder Co., 1969-71; mgr. S.Am.-Digicon Inc., 1971-73; v.p. Sercel Inc., 1973—. Mem. Soc. Exploration Geophysicists, European Soc. Exploration Geophysicists, Am. Siesmol. Soc., Am. Math. Soc., Soc. Indsl. and Applied Math., Houston, Dallas, S.E. La., S.W. La., Ark.-La.-Tex., Ft. Worth, Alaska, Denver geophys. socs., Houston Geol. Soc., Canadian Soc. Exploration Geophysicists, Am. Geophys. Union. Mason (K.T., 32deg., Shriner), Elk. Home: 1319 M'Ardi St Houston TX 77055

DE VEER, WILLIAM KIPP, banker; b. Hoboken, N.J., Nov. 18, 1914; s. William H. and Henrietta (Kipp) deV.; A.B., N.Y. U., 1937; LL.B., 1940, J.D., 1968; m. Frances Hutchison, June 9, 1945; children—William H., Nancy K. (Mrs. William M. Edwards III). Admitted to N.Y. State bar, 1941; with Bank of Manhattan Co., N.Y.C., 1935-37, Empire Trust Co., N.Y.C., 1938-42, Chase Nat. Bank, N.Y.C., 1946; pres., dir. Financial Consultants, Inc., Miami, Fla., 1946-65; v.p. First Nat. Bank, Palm Beach, Fla., 1955-57, pres., dir., 1965—; chmn. bd., dir. Palm Beach Mall Bank, 1969—; pres., dir. Arthur V. Davis Co., 1959-65; dir. Am. Bankers Life Assurance Co., Miami. Mem. Palm Beach Civic Assn., 1955—; bd. dirs., pres. Civic Opera Palm Beaches, Inc., 1972—. Served to lt. comdr. USNR, 1942-46. Mem. Phi Delta Phi. Episcopalian. Clubs: Everglades, Palm Beach Sailfish (pres. 1973—), Beach (Palm Beach); Miami. Home: 200 Orange Grove Rd Palm Beach FL 33480 Office: 255 S County Rd Palm Beach FL 33480

DEVENS, WILLIAM GEORGE, coll. adminstr.; b. Ft. Eustis, Va., Mar. 2, 1926; s. William George and Mary Margaret (Hammond) D.; B.S., U.S. Mil. Acad., 1946; M.S., U. Ill., 1953; C.E., Command and Gen. Staff Coll., 1961; m. Mary Katharine Tansey, Dec. 1, 1948; children—William, Patrick, Mary, Robert, Diane, Timothy, Thomas, James. Commd. 2d lt. U.S. Army, 1946, advanced through grades to lt. col., 1963, ret. 1966; dept. comdt. cadets Norwich U., Northfield, Vt., 1966-67; prof. Coll. Engring., dir. div. engring. fundamentals Va. Poly. Inst. and State U., Blacksburg, 1967—. Pres., Blacksburg High Sch. Athletic Found., 1971-72. Decorated Bronze Star medal. Registered profl. engr., N.Y., Vt. Recipient George C. Marshall Gold medal U.S. Army, 1961. Mem. Am. Soc. for Engring. Edn. (S.E. sect. chmn. engring. design graphics 1971-72), Ret. Officers Assn., Nat. Geog. Soc., Soc. Am. Mil. Engrs. Club: Blacksburg Country. Home: 1306 Highland Circle Blacksburg VA 24060

DEVERE, DAVID ERSKINE, optometrist; b. Marion, N.C., Jan. 15, 1939; s. Princhas Neilds and Harriet (Arneson) DeV.; student U. N.C., 1957-62; B.S., Ill. Coll. Optometry, 1966, Dr. Optometry, 1966; m. Martha E. Pierce, June 1, 1962; children—David Grainger, John Sloan. Pvt. practice optometry, Roanoke Rapids, N.C., 1966—; co-founder Optometric Mgmt. Cons., Inc., Raleigh, N.C., 1969. N.C. chmn. Am. Optometric Found., 1972-73. Mem. Am., N.C. optometric assns., Roanoke Rapids C. of C., Ducks Unlimited (area chmn. 1969—, mem. N.C. com. 1970—), Tomb and Key, Beta Sigma Kappa, Zeta Psi. Episcopalian. Kiwanian (pres. 1970-71). Club: Chockoyotte Country (Weldon, N.C.). Home: 622 Cedar St Roanoke Rapids NC 27870 Office: Drawer 1125 Roanoke Rapids NC 27870

DEVEREAUX, WILLIAM JOSEPH, govt. ofcl.; b. Balt., May 21, 1922; s. Paul and Pauline (Cornwell) D.; B. Mech. Engring., Johns Hopkins U., 1950; M. Engring. Adminstrn., George Washington U., 1960; M.A., U. Pa., 1966; m. Mary Louise Moltz, Sept. 2, 1944; children—William Joseph, Peter Wheaton. Engr., Norden Labs., White Plains, N.Y., 1952-56; sr. engr. Melpar Electronics, Falls Church, Va., 1956-61; chief engr. program mgmt. staff RCA, Moorestown, N.J., 1961-66; instr. econs. Pa. State U., 1966-67; asst. prof. mgmt. Temple U., 1967; mgr. market analysis and planning Atlantic Research Corp., Alexandria, Va., 1967-69; mem. staff Office of Sec., U.S. Dept. Transp., Washington, 1969-70; mem. staff Nat. Aeronautics and Space Council, Exec. Office of Pres., Washington, 1970-73; mem. staff office of sec. U.S. Dept. Transp., Washington, 1973—; instr. mgmt. Drexel Inst. Tech., 1962-65; asst. prof. lectr. George Washington U., 1968—. Served with USNR, 1942-45. Mem. Am. Econ. Assn., Am. Inst. Aeros. and Astronautics. Home: 8824

Southwick St Fairfax VA 22030 Office: US Dept Transp Washington DC 20590

DEVERO, KENNETH RAY, city ofcl.; b. Morris, Okla., May 21, 1938; s. Roy W. and Alta (Harrell) D.; B.S., Okla. State U., 1961; M.A., U. Okla., 1969; m. Miriam Locke Jordan, Sept. 1, 1963; children—Kenneth Ray II, Richard Reynolds, Christopher Edward. City adminstr. City of Newbern (Tenn.), 1965-66; city mgr., exec. dir. housing authority City of Elizabethton (Tenn.), 1966-69, City of Maryville (Tenn.), 1969-73; city mgr., Beaumont, Tex., 1973—. Mem. solid waste adv. com. State of Tenn., 1971. Past bd. dirs. United Fund, Sr. Citizens Orgn., local unit Am. Cancer Soc., Elizabethton. Served with USMCR, 1961-64; now capt. Res. Mem. Nat. League Cities, Acad. Polit. Sci., Nat., Tenn. (dir.), Tex. municipal leagues, Am. Soc. for Pub. Adminstrn., Internat. City Mgmt. Assn., Tenn. City Mgrs. Assn. (pres. 1969-70), Am. Soc. Planning Ofcls. Methodist (adminstrv. bd. 1968-70). Moose, Kiwanian (dir. 1969). Home: 6120 Pinkstaff Lane Beaumont TX 77706 Office: PO Box Beaumont TX 77704

DEVOE, DONALD E., basketball coach; b. Greene County, O., Dec. 31, 1941; s. Fred Neal and Vivian Annette (Atkinson) DeV.; B.S. in Edn., Ohio State U., 1964, M.S. in Higher Edn., 1970; m. Marianne Woodside, June 9, 1971; 1 dau., Donna Lee. Asst. basketball coach U.S. Mil. Acad., West Point, N.Y., 1965-69, Ohio State U., 1970; head varsity basketball coach Va. Poly. Inst. and State U., Blacksburg, 1971—. Served with AUS, 1965-67. Mem. Nat. Assn. Basketball Coaches (mem. selection com. 1971-73). Home: 614 Alleghany St Blacksburg VA 24060

DEVOLL, CHARLES WESLEY, radio co. exec.; b. Madelia, Minn., Nov. 23, 1926; s. Otis and Clara Bernice (Riggle) DeV.; B.S. in Elec. Engring., Ia. State U., 1950; student Franklin and Marshall Coll., 1951; m. Marcella Maxine Viersen, Aug. 3, 1946; children—Robert Allen. Engr., RCA, Lancaster, Pa., 1950-51, Bendix Aviation Co., Kansas City, Mo., 1951-53; with Collins Radio Co., 1955—, mgr. microwave sales, Dallas, 1959—. Recipient Silver Beaver award Boy Scouts Am. Served with USNR, 1944-46. Registered profl. engr., Tex. Mem. I.E.E.E., Eta Kappa Nu, Tau Beta Pi, Phi Kappa Phi. Club: Richardson (Tex.) Quarterback (pres.). Home: 500 St Lukes Dr Richardson TX 75080 Office: 1200 N Alma Rd Richardson TX 75080

DEVOY, CHARLES STEPHEN, port authority exec.; b. N.Y.C., May 12, 1923; s. Harold Edwin and Loretta Veronica (McNamee) D.; B.S., Georgetown U., 1947; postgrad. Northwestern U., 1963; m. Dee Bryan, Nov. 21, 1946; children—Deeanne, Stephen Douglas, Charles Bryan. With Lykes Bros. Steamship Co., Inc., 1947-57, deep sea traffic mgr., Galveston, Tex., 1948-57; dir. Port N.Y. Authority, London, Eng., 1957-62; chief exec. Galveston Wharves, 1963—; dir. Galveston Cotton Exchange, Bd. Trade, Am. Bank. Pres. Am. Assn. Port Authorities, Inc. Served to capt., USAAF, 1943-46. Mem. Am. Indsl. Devel. Assn., Galveston County Research Assn., Inc. (past dir., mem. exec. com.), Tex. Ports Assn., Inc. (pres. 1965), Gulf Ports Assn., Inc. (pres. 1967-68). Clubs: Propellor, Warwick. Home: 2 Port aux Princes Galveston TX 77550 Office: PO Box 328 Galveston TX 77550

DEW, JESS EDWARD, chem. engr.; b. Okemah, Okla., July 18, 1920; s. Jess Edward and Colleen (Norman) D.; student Okla. Mil. Acad., 1939-41; B.S. in Chem. Engring., U. Okla., 1943; M.S., Mass. Inst. Tech., 1948; m. Mary Ann Burns, Jan. 3, 1944; children—Anne, Stephen Dodson, David Burns. Asst. chem. engr. Standard Oil N.J., Baytown, Tex., 1943-47; chem. engr. Standard Oil Ind., Tulsa, 1948-52; v.p., John Deere Chem. Co., Pryor, Okla., 1952-63; gen. supt. John Deere Planter Works, Moline, Ill., 1963-65; v.p. Arkia Chem. Corp., Helena, Ark., 1965-69; project mgr. Chem. Constrn. Co., N.Y.C. hdqrs. 1969—, posts include Eng., Argentina, Arabia, Algeria. Pres., dir. Pryor Indsl. Conservation Co., 1961-63. Mem. Pryor Municipal Utility Bd., 1955-60, Pryor City Council, 1962-63; Rivers and Harbor Commn., Helena, 1966-70. Mem. Am. Inst. Chem. Engrs., Am. Soc. M.E., Sigma Xi, Beta Theta Pi, Alpha Chi Sigma, Tau Beta Pi. Republican. Roman Catholic. Elk. Clubs: Tulsa, Okmulgee Country. Home: 1402 E 7th St Okmulgee OK 74447 Office: c/oChemico One Penn Plaza New York City NY 10022

DEW, JOHN KENNETH, radio sta. exec.; b. Detroit, Nov. 5, 1939; s. Albert Nelson and Irene (Morris) D.; student U. Mich. (Nat. Merit scholar), 1958-60; B.A., Wayne State U., 1963, postgrad., 1963-66; m. Beverly Ann Lisiecki, Apr. 14, 1967; children—Mary Elizabeth, Kimberly Ann and Julie Lynn (twins). Producer, dir. pub. relations WXYZ radio and TV, Detroit, 1958-66; dir. advt., sales Orange Blossom Diamond Rings div. Traub Co., Detroit, 1966-68, San Francisco, 1968-70; account exec. KABL radio, San Francisco, 1970-71; gen. mgr. WWWW radio, Detroit, 1971-73; mgr. WFAA-AM and KZEW-FM radio, Dallas, 1973—. Tchr., St. Leo High Sch., Detroit, 1963, Howard Sch. Broadcasting, Detroit, 1972-73; columnist, Observer newspaper, Detroit, 1963-66. Mem. Avon Players, Rochester, Mich., 1971-73; vice pres. Stoneridge (Cal.) Homeowners Assn., 1969-70; mem. Common Cause. Mem. Oakland County Campaign Com. McGovern for Pres., 1972. Bd. dirs. Ridgedale Theatre, Ferndale, Mich., 1965-66. Democrat. Roman Catholic. Clubs: Milline (San Francisco); Variety, Adcraft (Detroit); Baypoint Country (Waterford, Mich.); Lancers (Dallas); Rochester (Mich.) Racquet. Home: 7416 Winterwood St Dallas TX 75240 Office: Communications Center Dallas TX 75202

DEWAR, MILDRED (JO) ELLER (MRS. DONALD NORMAN DEWAR), librarian; b. Wilkesboro, N.C., Nov. 9, 1925; d. Charles Franklin and Golda(Velt) Eller; student Brevard Coll., 1942-44; diploma Jr. Coll., 1944; A.B., Berea Coll., 1946; B.S. in L.S., U. N.C., 1948; postgrad. Barry Coll., U. Fla.; m. Donald Norman Dewar, Mar. 6, 1954; 1 dau., Heather. Tchr., librarian Mountain View High Sch., Hays, N.C., 1946-47; chief librarian Tenn. Wesleyan Coll., Athens, 1948-50; dept. head U. Tex. Library, Austin, 1951; librarian U.S. Army Spl. Services, Ft. Jackson, S.C., 1951-52; chief post library system, Ft. Stewart, Ga., 1952-54; librarian Olsen Jr. High Sch., Dania, Fla., 1955-56; librarian Lauderdale Manors Sch., Ft. Lauderdale, Fla., 1956-63; head readers services Miami-Dade Jr. Coll. Library, Miami, Fla., 1963-70; library dir. Miami-Dade Jr. Coll., South, 1970—. Vis. instr. library edn. U. Ga., summer 1967. Co-exec. dir. Nat. Library Week Fla., 1966. Mem. Am. Assn. U. Women (past br. v.p.), Am., Fla. library assns., Nat., Fla. edn. assns., Am., Fla. (past pres.) assns. sch. librarians, Fla. Audio-Visual Assn., Delta Kappa Gamma. Author articles in field. Home: 3520 Crystal View Ct Coconut Grove FL 33133 Office: 11011 SW 104 St Miami FL 33156

DEWETTE, FREDERIK WILLEM, educator; b. Bussum, Netherlands, June 29, 1924; s. Willem Hendrik and Cornelia (Boogerd) D.; B.S., U. Utrecht, Netherlands, 1947, doctoral degree cum laude, 1950, Ph.D., 1959; m. Theodora deGaay Fortman, July 21, 1952; children—Julia Regina, Hetty Helene, Nicolaas Willem. Came to U.S., 1960. Research asso. U. Utrecht, Netherlands, 1950-52, asst. prof. physics, 1955-60; vis. lectr. Brown U., Providence, R.I., 1952-53; research asso. U. Md., College Park, 1953-55; research asst. prof. U. Ill., Urbana, 1960-62; research physicist Netherlands Reactor Center, 1962-63; resident research asso. Argonne (Ill.) Nat. Lab., 1963-65; faculty U. Tex., Austin, 1965—, prof. physics 1965—, chmn. physics dept., 1969-74. Cons. Argonne Nat. Lab., 1965-72. Mem. bd. trustees Argonne Universities Assn., 1972—. Recipient Research grants Air Force Office Scientific Research, 1967—, Robert A. Welch Found., 1971—. Fellow Am. Phys. Soc.; mem. A.A.A.S., Am. Assn. U. Profs., European Phys. Soc. Contbr. articles in field to profl. jours. Home: 5912 Carleen Dr Austin TX 78731

DEWITT, ROSCOE PLIMPTON, architect; b. Dallas, Feb. 18, 1894; s. Edgar A. and Imogene (Walker) DeW.; A.B., Dartmouth, 1914, M.A. (hon.), 1937; Harvard, 1917, M.Arch.; m. Elizabeth Boyd Newcomb, 1943; children by previous marriage—Sylvia Louise (Mrs. Tom Ferguson), Elizabeth Frances (Mrs. Julian Acker). Engaged in archtl. practice, Dallas, 1919—. Mem. Tex. Fine Arts Commn., 1967-69. Bd. dirs. Dallas Civic Opera, 1960—. Served from 2d lt. to capt., U.S. Army, World War I; capt. to lt. col. AUS, World War II. Fellow A.I.A., Soc. Am. Registered Architects; mem. Internat. Hosp. Fedn., Soc. Am. Mil. Engrs., Am. Hosp. Assn., Assn. for Hosp. Planning, Royal Soc. Arts, Tex. Soc. Architects (dir. 1956-58), Phi Delta Theta. Clubs: Dallas Athletic, Dallas Country, Brookhollow Golf, City (Dallas); Harvard (N.Y.C.); Cosmos (Washington). Prin. works include: Methodist, Parkland Meml., Presbyn., St. Paul, Tex. Childrens hosps. (all Dallas), Hotel Dieu (New Orleans), Sheppard AFB, Carswell AFB hosps., Bay Front Med. Center, St. Petersburg, Fla., St. Vincents Med. Center, Jacksonville, Fla.; office bldgs. for Republic Financial Services, N.Y.C., Dallas, Los Angeles, stores and service bldg. for Neiman-Marcus, sch. and coll. bldgs. in Dallas and numerous other Tex. cities, Sam Rayburn Library, Bonham, Tex.; remodeled Cannon House Office Bldg., Washington; (with others) Tex. State Bldg., Dallas Mus. Fine Arts, extension of East Front of Nat. Capitol, James Madison Meml. Bldg. of Library of Congress; housing projects in Dallas and elsewhere. Home: 4657 Mockingbird Lane Dallas TX 75209 Office: No 2 Turtle Creek Village Dallas TX 75219 also 425 13th St NW Washington DC 20004

DEWITT, WINSON LEE, tobacco co. exec.; b. Hart County, Ky., June 14, 1931; s. Herbert Stenson and Ethel Myrtle (Caswell) D.; B.S., U. Louisville, 1957; m. Margaret June Grisham, June 11, 1955; children—Kevin Lee, Kimberly Ann, Michael Kent. With Brown & Williamson Tobacco Co., Louisville, 1957—, corporate exec., dir., 1970—; dir. Kohl Corp., Milw., Vita Food Products, N.Y.C., Gimbel Bros., N.Y.C. Chmn. bd. trustees City of Bancroft, Ky., 1970-71, mem., 1972-73. Served with USAF, 1951-54. Mem. Assn. for Systems Mgmt. (internat. dir. 1968-69), Pi Kappa Phi, Omicron Delta Kappa. Club: Hunting Creek Country (Louisville). Office: 1600 W Hill St Louisville KY 40210

DEWTON, JOHANNES LEOPOLD, librarian; b. Vienna, Austria, Sept. 27, 1905; s. Eduard and Elsbeth (Brauchbar) Deutsch; Jur.D., U. Vienna, 1927; B.S. in Library Scis., U. Ill., 1941, M.S., 1944; m. Hedwig Marianne Strauss, Apr. 7, 1935; children—Elizabeth Ann (Mrs. John B. Cordaro), Doris Jean. Came to U.S., 1939, naturalized, 1944. Court sec., lawyer's asst., Vienna, 1928-34; lawyer, Vienna, 1935-38; cataloger Library U. Ill., Urbana, 1941-45, research asst. English dept., 1944-45; tech. adviser USSTAF, Europe, 1945; with Library Congress, Washington, 1945—, chief shared cataloging div., 1966-67, head Nat. Union Catalog Publ. Project, 1967—. Bd. dirs. Council on Research and Bibliography, N.Y.C., 1962-73. Mem. A.L.A., D.C. Library Assn., Beta Phi Mu. Jewish religion. Contbr. articles to profl. jours. Home: 4201 7th Rd S Arlington VA 22204 Office: Library Congress 10 1st St SE Washington DC 20540

DEZENBERG, GEORGE JOHN, elec. engr.; b. Tientsin, China, Jan. 12, 1935; s. John and Fanny (Philipsova) D.; came to U.S., 1943, naturalized, 1943; B.E.E., Auburn U., 1960; M.S., U. Ark., 1962; Ph.D. (Ford fellow), Ga. Inst. Tech., 1966; m. Theresa Marie Kenny, Sept. 10, 1960; children—George John, Paul Joseph, Carl Vincent, Gary Francis. Instr., U. Ark., Fayetteville, 1960-61; with Army Missile Command, Redstone Arsenal, Ala., 1965—, research electronic engr., 1967—. Served to capt., Ordnance Corps, AUS, 1965-67. Mem. Sigma Pi Sigma, Eta Kappa Nu, Pi Mu Epsilon, Tau Beta Pi, Pi Tau Pi Sigma. Roman Catholic. Contbr. articles to profl. jours. Home: 910 San Ramon Av Huntsville AL 35802 Office: Army Missile Command Redstone Arsenal AL 35809

DEZOORT, EDITH JUNE, physician; b. Paterson, N.J., June 26, 1934; d. Wilem and Lavina Mae (Judge) DeZoort; B.S. cum laude, U. Ga., 1956; M.S., Med. Coll. Ga., 1960. Intern Meml. Hosp. Chatham County, Savannah, Ga., 1960-61; resident pediatrics Sinai Hosp. Balt., 1961-62, Talmadge Meml. Hosp., Augusta, Ga., 1962-63; pvt. practice pediatrics, Decatur, Ga., 1963—; chief pediatrics DeKalb Gen. Hosp., Decatur, 1969-71; mem. staff DeKalb Gen., Henrietta Egleston hosps., Decatur. Recipient Bausch Lome award, 1952, Phi Sigma award, 1954. Mem. DeKalb County Med. Soc., Med. Assn. Ga., A.M.A., Phi Beta Kappa, Phi Kappa Phi, Alpha Epsilon Delta, Tau Epsilon Delta, Phi Sigma. Office: 6 Lavista Perimeter Office Park Tucker GA 30084

DIAL, ALLARD HEYWARD, broadcasting exec.; b. Charleston, S.C., Feb. 13, 1944; s. Warlwell Robertson and Nina (Heyward) D.; student St. Andrews Coll., 1965-67. With S.C. Ednl. TV, Columbia, 1967-68; dir. WNOK-TV, Columbia, 1968-69, prodn. mgr., 1969—. Served with USN, 1962-65. Mem. U.S. Polo Assn. Clubs: Tarentella, Spring Valley Country, Columbia Bachelors. Home: 312 Country Club Dr Columbia SC 29206 Office: WNOK-TV PO Box 5307 Columbia SC 29205 also RFD 1 Montgomery Rd Columbia SC 29203

DIAMOND, HINDI ALTMAN (MRS. WALTER DIAMOND), editor; b. N.Y.C., Sept. 11, 1924; d. Saul and Esther (Kijewski) Altman; student Canal Zone Jr. Coll., Republic of Panama, 1947-49, U. Miami (Fla.), 1966-69; m. Walter Diamond, Nov. 25, 1943; children—Linda, Stephen, Mark. Reporter, photographer The Panama Am. daily English newspaper, 1951-58; Panama corr. McGraw-Hill and Vision mag., 1951-61; pub., editor Panama/This Month, 1958-65; editor Industria Turistica mag. Diamond Pub. Co., South Miami, Fla., 1957—; editor Caribbean Travel Report, 1972—. Bd. dirs. Am. Jewish Com., editor Newsletter, 1969—. Mem. Am. Soc. Mag. Photographers (chmn. Fla. chpt. 1960—), Theta Sigma Phi. Home: 7250 SW 126th St Miami FL 33156 Office: Industria Turistica Box 52 South Miami FL 33143

DIAMOND, JACOB JOSEPH, govt. ofcl.; b. N.Y.C., July 25, 1917; s. Isaac and Anna (Elfant) D.; A.B. cum laude, Bklyn. Coll., 1937; m. Pauline Elizabeth Taube, July 2, 1944; children—Ellen (Mrs. Robert Meeropol), Carol (Mrs. Craig Johnson). Analytical chemist Nat. Bur. Standards, Washington, 1940-55, high temperature chemist, 1955-70, program mgr. protective equipment standards, 1970-72, chief law enforcement standards lab., 1972—. Recipient medal Am. Inst. Chemists, 1937. Fellow A.A.A.S., Washington Acad. Scis.; mem. Am. Chem. Soc., Am. Ceramic Soc., Am. Soc. Testing Materials, Internat. Assn. Chiefs of Police. Editor: Bibliography of the High Temperature Chemistry and Physics of Materials, 1957-70. Contbr. articles to profl. jours. Home: 6436 Bannockburn Dr Bethesda MD 20034 Office: Nat Bur Standards Physics B-150 Washington DC 20234

DIAMOND, THOMAS MULFORD, JR., lawyer; b. Long Beach, Cal., Mar. 28, 1923; s. Thomas Mulford and Violet Eleanor (Williams) D.; B.S., Stanford, 1949; J.D., Baylor U., 1957; m. Carolyn Reed Culbertson, Jan. 1, 1949; 1 son, John Culbertson. Appraiser, Prudential Ins. Co., Los Angeles, 1949-50; scout, landman Sunray Oil Co., Tulsa, 1953-55; engr. Tex. Hwy. Dept., Waco and El Paso, 1957-59; admitted to Tex. bar, 1957; atty. Diamond, Rash, Leslie & Schwartz, Inc., El Paso, 1960—. Cattle ranching interests in Catron and Sierra counties, N.M. Chmn., El Paso Open Space Com., 1971-72; mem. Mayor's Hist. Preservation Com., 1973—. Chmn., El Paso County Democratic Com., 1962-67. Bd. dirs. El Paso Heritage Found. Served to capt. AUS, World War II and Korean Conflict. Recipient Conquistador award City of El Paso, 1963, award of exceptional merit El Paso C. of C., 1966, award of merit El Paso County, 1968. Registered profl. engr., Tex. Mem. El Paso Bar Assn. (past sec.), El Paso C. of C. (dir.), Am. Right-of-Way Assn., Phi Delta Phi, Theta Chi. Methodist. Mason (Shriner). Club: El Paso Country. Home: 5022 Columbine St El Paso TX 79922 Office: 1208 Southwest Center El Paso TX 79901

DIAZ, HECTOR JOSEPH, civil engr.; b. Tampa, Fla., Dec. 21, 1930; s. Manuel Vega and Corina (Trujillo) D.; B.C.E., Ga. Inst. Tech., 1954; m. Ingeborg M. Ratajczak, June 30, 1956; children—Catherine, Felicia, Caroline. Engr., Fla. Prestressed Concrete Co., Tampa, 1956-61; chmn. bd., chief exec. Diaz, Seckinger & Assos., Tampa, 1962—. Served as 1st lt. U.S. Army, 1954-56. Home: 2419 Sunset Dr Tampa FL 33609 Office: 800 W Buffalo Av Tampa FL 33603

DIAZ, JOSE ARMANDO ANTONSANTI, sch. personnel dir.; b. Yauco, P.R., Nov. 10, 1935; s. Armando Antonsanti and Rosario (Diaz) Rodgriguez; B.A., Interamerican U., 1958; student Salamanca Med. Sch., 1958-64; student Catholic U. Ponce, 1965-66; m. Maria Enriqueta Gonzalez, Dec. 31, 1962; children—Jose, Carlos. Prof. Yauco (P.R.) High Sch., 1958-65; adminstr. Lincoln Hosp., N.Y., 1965-67; supr. indsl. Gen. Electric Co., Juana Diaz, P.R., 1968-69; supr. indsl. mgmt. Nat. Packing div. Ralston Purina Co., Ponce, P.R., 1971-73; personnel dir. P.R. Trade and Tech. Schs., Santurce, 1973—. Roman Catholic. Club: N.Y. Shell. Home: 21 Vivaldi Pachero Yauco PR 00768 Office: 1225 Ponce de Leon Av 18 Stop Santurce PR 00908

DIAZ, RICK, hotel exec.; b. Havana, Cuba, Nov. 6, 1940; s. Juan Enrique and Maria Celida (Castillo) D.; student Sharron-William Comml. Coll., Miami, 1954-56, Walsh Sch. Bus. Sci., Miami, 1956-58, Lindsey-Hopkins Hotel Sch., Miami, 1958-59, Cornell U., summers 1967, 68; m. Georgette Catherine Schufa, Feb. 8, 1964; children—Tashia Marya, Tiara Elleny. Came to U.S., 1960, naturalized, 1965. Page boy, bellman Varadero Internat. Hotel, Cuba, 1951; various positions Robert Clay Hotel, Miami, Fla., 1954-59; various positions to mgr., dir. sales. Taft Hotel, New Haven, Conn., 1961-62; shop mgr., asst. maitre Allison Hotel, Miami Beach, Fla., 1962; asst. reservations mgr., gen. mgr. Antlers Resort Hotel, Lake George, N.Y., summers 1960, 61, 63; resident mgr., exec. asst. mgr. El Convento Hotel, San Juan, P.R., 1962-63; with Causeway Inn Beach Resort, Tampa, Fla., 1964—, gen. mgr., 1964-70, pres., mgr. dir., 1970—. Mem. Fla. Restaurant Assn., Greater Tampa C. of C., Fla. Retail Liquor Dealers Assn. Inc., Fla. Hotel and Motel Assn., Hotel Sales Mgmt. Assn., Pan Am. Commn., Bon Vivants. Address: Causeway Inn Beach Resort Courtney Campbell Causeway Tampa FL 33607

DIAZ-COLLER, CARLOS, physician; b. Villahermosa, Tabasco, Mexico, Sept. 2, 1916; s. Jose Diaz-Coller and Maria Gonzalez; M.D., Army Med. Sch., Mexico, 1945; M.P.H., Harvard, 1948; m. Ana Maria de la Garza, Dec. 17, 1945; children—Carlos, Jose Alberto, Mario, Juan Antonio and Anna Maria Elisa (twins). Del. from Mexico, WHO, 1956, 57, 58; exec. bd. alternate WHO, 1956-57, v.p. exec. bd., 1958-59; del. from Mexico to directing council Pan-Am. San. Orgn., 1956-57, exec. com., 1957-58, pres. exec. com., 1958-59; del. from Mexico, XV Pan Am. San. Conf., 1958; dir. div. exptl. studies in pub. health Ministry Pub. Health and Welfare, Mexico, 1957, 58; former chief dept. profl. edn., chief editorial services Pan Am. Health Orgn. of WHO; now dep. sec. gen. Nat. Health Plan, Ministry of Health and Welfare, Mexico. Pub. health supr. Mexican Army, 1948-56; dir. Sch. Pub. Health, Mexico, 1953. Mem. Mexican Pub. Health Soc. (pres. 1957-58), Am. Pub. Health Assn., Nat. Geog. Soc. Editor: Jour Mexican Pub. Health Soc., 1955-58. Home: California 180 Churubusco Mexico 21 DF Mexico Office: Medellin 43 Quinto Piso Mexico 7 DF Mexico

DIAZ-NORIEGA, JOSÉ MIGUEL, electronics component co. exec.; b. México, D.F., Mexico, May 1, 1929; s. José and Emilia deDiaz (Noriega) Diaz de la Fuente; B.A., Universidad de Oviedo (Spain), 1948; B.S., Stanford, 1951, M.S., 1952; m. María del Carmen Sotres, Aug. 22, 1953; children— María José, José Miguel, María del Carmen, Francisco Javier, Juan Ignacio, Teresa de Jesús, Ignacio. Gen. Elec. fgn. student scholar, 1952-53, electronics and elec. small appliance mgr. Gen. Electric de México, S.A., 1954-56; mgr. engring. Sylvamex Electrónica, S.A., 1956-58; mfrs. rep., 1958-62; pres., gen. mgr. Electrey, S.A., Monterrey, Mexico, 1962—. Asst. prof. Instituto Tecnológico y de Estudios Superiores de Monterrey. Dir. Christian Family Movement, 1964-69. Mem. I.E.E.E. (sr.). Roman Catholic. Club: Casino del Valle Athletic (Monterrey). Patentee in field; designer test and mfg. machines for fuses and breakers. Home: 425 Río Colorado Colonia del Valle NL México Office: Apartado 1393 Monterrey NL México

DIBRELL, GEORGE EDWARD, city mgr.; b. Dallas, Sept. 22, 1928; s. Waymen Eugene and Maude (Helton) D.; B.B.A., So. Meth. U., Dallas, 1951; LL.B., U. Tex. at Austin, 1957; m. Georgene Valas, May 30, 1953; 1 dau., Deborah Jeanne. Admitted to Tex. bar, 1956; pvt. practice law, Austin, 1956-57; asst. city atty., Port Arthur, Tex., 1958-62, city mgr., 1962—. Adj. prof. Lamar U. Mem. State Bar Tex., Jefferson County, Am. Port Arthur bar assns., C. of C., Internat., Tex. (pres. region 6, dir. 1973) city mgmt. assns., Municipal Finance Officers Assn., Phi Alpha Delta, Sigma Nu. Mason, Rotarian. Home: 3919 Platt Port Arthur TX 77640 Office: City Hall 444 4th St Port Arthur TX 77640

DICARA, C(OSTANTE) JOHN, economist; b. Winsted, Conn., Dec. 31, 1927; s. Salvo P. and Rosalia (Colombi) DiC.; B.A., Yale, 1950; M.A., U. Conn., 1952; postgrad. London Sch. Econs., 1965, Am. U., 1969; m. Lolita Mae Lanpher, Sept. 12, 1953; children—Laurie Anna, Andrea Lynn. Economist, Conn. Labor Dept., Hartford, 1952, Conf. Bd., N.Y.C., 1953, N.Y. Stock Exchange, 1954-58; officer, economist AID, Kabul, Afghanistan and Washington, 1959-64, coordination attaché Embassies London and Bonn., 1965-68; sr. area economist CIA, Washington, 1969—. Participant, U.S. German Aid Confs., Berlin and Bochum, Germany, 1968. Active Great Falls (Va.) Citizens Assn. Mem. Soc. Internat. Devel., Am. Econ. Assn. Democrat. Lion (pres. 1970-72, mem. state adv. com. 1970-72). Contbr. articles to profl. pubs. Home: 10605 Good Spring Av Herndon VA 22070 Office: Headquarters Central Intelligence Agency McLean VA 22101

DICE, HENRY KIMMELL, chem. engr.; b. Somerset, Pa., May 31, 1908; s. John E. and Edna (Kimmell) D.; student Antioch Coll., 1926-28, Ohio No. U., 1929-30; B.S., U. Pitts., 1932; m. Janet K. Womer, Sept. 1, 1934; children—Janet (Mrs. Thomas A. Maierhofer, Henry Kimmell. Chem. engr. Celanese Corp., Cumberland, Md., 1934-40, supt. research and devel., 1940-44, prodn. supt., Bishop, Tex., 1944-47, mgr. research and devel., Clarkwood, Tex., 1947-59, v.p. tech. dir., Corpus Christi, Tex., 1959-61, cons., 1963—; sub-dir. gen. Quimica Gen., S.A., Mexico, 1961-63; sr. resident engr. Tex. Hwy. Dept., Houston, 1966-73; sr. chem. engr. E.N. Wolcott Corp., Houston, 1973—. Mem. Am. Inst. Chem. Engrs., Am. Chem. Soc., Nat. Soc. Profl. Engrs., Alpha Chi Sigma, Sigma Tau. Patentee in field. Home: 10215 Briar Dr Houston TX 77042 Office: 9099 Westheimer Houston TX 77042

DICK, GEORGE WALTER, state ofcl.; b. Berea, Ky., Aug. 24, 1934; s. George Arthur and Alice (Muth) D.; A.B. in Math., Berea Coll., 1956; postgrad. bus. adminstrn., U. Ky., 1962; m. Jane Lee Kavanaugh, Dec. 12, 1958; children—David Arthur, Dana Anne. Trainee, Westinghouse Electric Corp., Pitts., 1956-58; adminstrn. analyst Hwy. Dept., State of Ky., Frankfort, 1960-62, fiscal and personnel officer Dept. Pub. Information, 1962-69, budget dir. Dept. Edn., 1969-71, 72—, systems analyst Dept. Finance, 1971-72. Developer tourist promotion matching funds program, charge account procedure for state toll facilities and indirect cost negotiations. Bd. dirs. Commonwealth Credit Union. Served with AUS, 1958-60. Mem. Pub. Personnel Assn. Home: 524 Timothy Dr Frankfort KY 40601 Office: Capitol Plaza Tower Frankfort KY 40601

DICK, LEW, cons.; b. N.Y.C., June 9, 1906; s. Jacob and Taube (Eigen) D.; B.S., Columbia, 1928, M.A., 1929; Ph.D., London Coll. Applied Sci., 1970; m. Georgette Augusta Goldman, Sept. 19, 1934 (dec. Feb. 1962). With N.Y.C. Dept. Parks, 1932-71, playground dir., 1932-38, asst. supr., 1938-45, supr. recreation, Manhattan, 1945-71; now marriage and family counselor, Fort Lauderdale, Fla., 1973—; asso. Sam Ross Theatrical Agy.; owner Lew Dick Enterprises; profl. magician, hypnotist, mentalist, ventriloquist, juggler; co-owner Gladys Olin Art Gallery, N.Y.C.; lect. hypnotism and recreation. Dist. capt. Democratic Club, Rockaway Beach, 1940—. Bd. dirs. Peninsula Gen. Hosp. Served with U.S.O., 1940-43. Mem. Soc. Illustrators, Ind. Order Foresters (high chief ranger 1937-39), Knights of Magic, Internat. Guild Presdigitators (pres.), Soc. Am. Magicians (dir. pub. relations parent assembly), N.Y. State Police Chiefs (asso.), Internat. Brotherhood Magicians, Magic Circle London, All-India Magic Club. K.P., Mason. Author: What is Hypnotism? World Tour, 1964. Address: 201 NE 2d St Fort Lauderdale FL 33301

DICK, LOIS A. (MRS. CARL E. DICK), ret. coll. adminstr.; b. Decatur, Ind., June 19, 1907; d. J.F. and Mabel (Schlegel) Hildinger; student Internat. Bus. Coll., Ft. Wayne, Ind., 1926, Mrs. Davis Secretarial Sch., Ft. Wayne, 1929; m. Carl E. Dick, Dec. 31, 1939. Sec., Koerbers Jewelers, Inc., Ft. Wayne, 1932-50; sec. Fruehauf Trailer Co., Ft. Wayne, 1952-53; sec. to registrar Fla. So. Coll., Lakeland, 1956-60; exec. sec. to dean coll. basic studies U. South Fla., Tampa, 1960-62, exec. sec. to dean acad. affairs, 1962-65, adminstrv. asst. to dean, 1965-67, staff asst. to v.p. acad. affairs, 1967-70; part time cons., asso. med. sec. X-Ray dept. Sun Coast Osteo. Hosp., Largo, Fla. Mem. fund raising com. Greater Largo Recreational Complex. Named 1 of 100 outstanding women to attend Conf. Fla., 1964. Mem. Nat. Secs. Assn. (parliamentarian Tampa 1960-61), Lakeland Bus. and Profl. Women's Club (v.p. 1958-59, pres. 1959-60), North Tampa (pres. 1963-64), North Largo bus. and profl. women's clubs, Temple Terrace Bus. and Profl. Women's Club (co-organizer, 2d v.p. 1966), Retired Group of Nat. Assn. Ednl. Secs. Lutheran. Mem. Order Eastern Star, White Shrine Jerusalem, Beauceant, Order Amaranth. Clubs: Pilot (parliamentarian Lakeland 1959-60, charter mem. Bay Area); Woman's (U. South Fla.). Home: 79 Rainbow Ct 1159 Clearwater Rd Largo FL 33540

DICK, WILLIAM ARTHUR, banker; b. Hornell, N.Y., Sept. 4, 1941; s. William Prentice and Erma (Almy) D.; B.S. in Econs., W.Va. U., 1963; LL.B., Atlanta Law Sch., 1966; m. Carol Louise Truax, Nov. 13, 1964; children—William Arthur, Robert Peyton. With First Nat. Bank Atlanta, 1963-69, mgr. credit investigations, 1966-67, mgr. corporate lending, 1967-69; pres. First Bank Savannah, 1969—, also dir. Mem. Ga. Com. for Care, 1973—, Regional Export Expansion Council, 1972—, Savannah Port Authority, 1971—; pres. Savannah Symphony Soc., 1972-73. Bd. dirs. Salvation Army, United Community Services, A.R.C., Hist. Savannah Found.; trustee St. Joseph's Hosp. Lion. Clubs: Oglethorpe, Chatham (Savannah). Home: 27 E 56th St Savannah GA 31405 Office: 136 Bull St Savannah GA 31402

DICKASON, ORVILLE O., accountant; b. Lampasas, Tex., Dec. 28, 1908; s. Henry Frank and Fay (Mitchell) D.; student Tex. A. and M. U., 1928-29, Okla. U., 1930-31; LL.B., Blackstone Sch. Law, 1953; m. Barbara Ford, July 8, 1964; children—Jeanette (Mrs. Brian A. Hilsabeck). With Arthur Young & Co., C.P.A.'s, 1935-36; auditor Fed. Land Bank, Houston, 1936-40; with Lybrand, Ross Bros. & Montgomery, C.P.A.'s, Houston, 1940-42, Peat, Marwick & Mitchell, C.P.A.'s, Houston, 1947-51; pvt. practice pub. accounting, Dallas, 1955—; pres. Dickason & Co., Inc. Served with AUS, 1942-46; to maj. USAF, 1951-55. Mem. Am. Legion, V.F.W., Am. Inst. C.P.A.'s, Tex. Soc. C.P.A.'s. Mason. Club: Brookhaven Country. Home: 5451 Glenwick Lane Dallas TX 75209 Office: 11111 N Central Expressway Suite E Dallas TX 75231

DICKENS, ALBERT EDWARD, economist; b. Mt. Vernon, Ill., May 19, 1904; s. Robert Lee and Laura (Polk) D.; A.B., Ind. U., 1930, M.S., 1939, postgrad. Law Sch., 1932-33; m. Rose Mary Salinardi, Mar. 25, 1954. State statistician Ind., Indpls., 1931-39; dir. research Chgo. Plan Commn., 1941-45; chief surplus property div. Allied Commn., Rome, Italy, 1945-47, chief control br. Joint Export-Import Agy., Frankfurt, Germany, 1947-49; spl. cons. Nat. Acad. Scis., Washington, 1950; owner, prin. Albert E. Dickens & Co., Washington, 1951—. Cons. Internat. Devel. Services, Inc.; expert cons. AID; cons. Washington Bd. Trade. Mem. Am. Econ. Assn., Am. Statis. Assn., Inst. Urban and Regional Affairs, Soc. Internat. Devel., Phi Beta Kappa, Beta Gamma Sigma, Lambda Alpha. Club: Economists (Washington). Author: Growth and Structure of Real Property Uses in Indianapolis, Indiana, 1939. Home: 1500 Massachusetts Av NW Washington DC 20005 Office: 1627 K St NW Washington DC 20006

DICKENS, H. DERRELL, lawyer; b. Little Rock, Apr. 24, 1918; A.B., Washington and Lee U., 1940, LL.B., 1947; M.B.A., Harvard, 1943. Admitted to Ark. bar, 1947, Tex. bar, 1957, Mo. bar, 1961; atty. legal dept. Lion Oil Co., 1947-55, v.p., gen. counsel, 1973—; dir. legal dept., dep. sec. Monsanto Chems. Ltd., London, Eng., 1965; sr. atty., asst. sec. Monsanto Co., 1966-68; now practice law, El Dorado, Ark. Mem. Union County, Ark., Am. bar assns., State Bar Tex., Order Coif, Phi Beta Kappa, Phi Delta Phi. Address: 814 Lion Oil Bldg El Dorado AR 71730

DICKERSON, ARTHUR JAMES, petrolem refining co. exec.; b. Ft. Worth, Aug. 25, 1929; s. Walter R. and Beatrice B. (McKinney) D.; B.A., Arlington State Coll., 1950; M.B.A., Pepperdine U., 1962; m. Patricia E. Gross, Apr. 14, 1951. With sales dept. Southwestern Petroleum Corp., Ft. Worth, 1950-58, dir., gen. mgr., 1958-60, exec. v.p., 1960-64, pres., chief exec. officer, 1964—, also pres., dir. Southwestern Petroleum Corp. in Europe, Can., Venezuela; dir., v.p. Data Computer Center, Ft. Worth, 1968—. Treas., bd. dirs. Ft. Worth Met. YMCA. Bd. dirs. Opera Assn. Mem. Young Presidents Orgn. (chmn. W. Tex. chpt.), Ft. Worth Area C. of C. (v.p. planning, dir., mem. exec. com.), Newcomen Soc. Rotarian. Clubs: Ft. Worth, Colonial Country. Home: 4132 Hildring Dr E Fort Worth TX 76109 Office: Box 789 534 N Main Fort Worth TX 76101

DICKERSON, HAROLD OSCAR, dentist; b. nr. Elco, Ill., May 8, 1924; s. Grover Alexander and Sophia Stella (Shelton) D.; A.A., Lamar Coll., 1948; B.S., U. Houston, 1950; D.D.S., U. Tex., 1960; m. Doris Naomia Sheffield, June 17, 1945; children—Melanie Verline (Mrs. Mack Neal Hooker), Harold Oscar. Pvt. practice dentistry, Groves, Tex., 1960—. Served with USNR, 1942-45. Fellow Royal Soc. Health; mem. Am., Tex. dental assns., Nat. Analgesia Soc., South Jefferson County Acad. Dental Sci., Sabine Dist. Dental Soc., Nat. Rifle Assn., Xi Psi Phi. Baptist. Optimist (sec.-treas. 1961-62). Home: 4048 Willowoak Dr Groves TX 77619 Office: 4114 Main Av Groves TX 77619

DICKERSON, HERMAN EDWARD, city mgr.; b. Greensboro, N.C., Nov. 1, 1915; s. Raymond Rufus and Blanche Eve (Welker) D.; B.S. in Bus. Administrn., Va. Poly. Inst., 1937; m. Nell Taylor, Dec. 25, 1943; children—Herman E., Robert Taylor, William Lawrence, Dennett Haywood, Thomas Welker, James Marshall, Diane. With Security Nat. Bank, Greensboro, N.C., 1937-40, city of Charlotte (N.C.), 1950-51; adminstrv. asst. to city mgr., city Laurinburg (N.C.), 1951-55; city mgr., Statesville, N.C., 1955—. Served to maj. AUS, 1940-46. Mem. N.C. League Municipalities (George C. Franklin award 1956, dir. 1961-63), Am. Legion, N.C. Soc. Engrs., Internat. City Mgmt. Assn. (dir. 1971-73), N.C. City and County Mhrs. Assn. (pres. 1960-61). Presbyn. (deacon 1948—, elder 1973). Rotarian. Home: 335 Holland Dr Statesville NC 28677 Office: City Hall 227 S Center St Statesville NC 28677

DICKERSON, MERLE LEROY, banker; b. Cairo, Neb., Feb. 9, 1921; s. Arthur Sinclair and Florence Mabel (Elliot) D.; student Grand Island (Neb.) Bus. Coll., 1938-40; m. Bettie Florence Cothran, June 27, 1943; children—Bettie Ann (Mrs. George Johnson, Jr.), Merle Leroy. Asst. cashier Little River Bank, Lepanto, Ark., 1946-56; pres. Mchts. & Planters Bank, Clarendon, Ark., 1956-64; pres. Tunica County Bank (Miss.), 1964-67; sr. v.p. Peoples Bank & Trust Co., Russellville, Ark., 1967—. Served with USNR, 1941-46. Mem. Am. Legion, V.F.W. Democrat. Mem. Ch. of Christ (elder). Rotarian, Lion. Home: 205 Candlewick Dr Russellville AR 72801 Office: People's Bank & Trust Co Russellville AR 72801

DICKERSON, MILDRED GORTNEY (MRS. Z.S. DICKERSON, JR.), educator; b. Harrodsburg, Ky., Sept. 18, 1920; d. Oscar E. and Bessie (Marshall) Gortney; B.S., Eastern Ky. State U., 1942; M.S. U. Ky., 1951; m. Z.S. Dickerson, Jr., June 26, 1943; children—Richard Evans, Margaret Ann. Tchr. pub. schs., Shelby, O., 1942-43, Bradstown, Ky., 1944-45; instr. Ala. State Coll., Florence, 1950, 55-58; asst. prof. edn. Madison Coll., Harrisonburg, Va., 1958—, coordinator early childhood edn. program, 1967—. Instr., U. Ky., Lexington, summer 1951. Cons. pub. schs., 1965—. Chmn. parent edn. Va. Congress Parents and Tchrs., 1962-64, chmn. presch. services, 1964—, also bd. mgrs. Mem. N.E.A., Va. Edn. Assn., Nat. Assn. for Edn. Young Children, Assn. Childhood Edn., Va. Assn. for Early Childhood Edn. (pres., 1971-73), So. Assn. on Children Under Six (sec.), Delta Kappa Gamma. Democrat. Methodist. Home: Route 1 Harrisonburg VA 22801

DICKEY, JAMES, poet, critic; b. Atlanta, Feb. 2, 1923; s. Eugene and Maibelle (Swift) D.; student Clemson Coll., 1942; B.A., Vanderbilt U., 1949, M.A., 1950; m. Maxine Syerson, Nov. 4, 1948; children—Christopher Swift, Kevin Webster. Poet in residence Reed Coll., Portland, Ore., 1963-64, San Fernando (Cal.) Valley State Coll., 1964-65, U. Wis., 1966; cons. in poetry Library of Congress, 1966-68; now writer in residence U. S.C. Served with USAAF and USAF, World War II, Korea. Decorated Air medal. Recipient Union League prize, 1958; Vachel Lindsay award, 1959; Longview award, 1959; Melville Cane award, 1965-66. Sewanee Rev. fellow, 1954-55; Guggenheim fellow, 1962-63; Nat. Inst. grant of, 500, 1966. Fellow Am. Acad. Arts and Scis.; mem. Nat. Inst. Arts and Letters. Author: (poems) Into the Stone, 1960; Drowning With Others, 1962; Helmets, 1964; Two Poems of the Air, 1964; Buckdancer's Choice, 1965 (Nat. Book Award for poetry 1966); Poems, 1957-67; (criticism) The Suspect in Poetry, 1964; Babel to Byzantium, 1968; The Eyebeaters, 1970; Self Interviews, 1970; Sorties, 1971; (novel) Deliverance, 1970. Address: 4620 Lelia's Ct Lake Katherine Columbia SC 29206

DICKEY, LEE DOWLING, aerospace co. engring. exec.; b. Lubbock, Tex., Jan. 2, 1928; s. Emory Dowling and Lucy Golden (Hooten) D.; student E. Tex. State U., 1944-45; B.S., Tex. Technol. U., 1951; m. Lena Mae Payne, Apr. 12, 1949; children—Jerry Lee, Richard Allan, Sharon Kay. Jr. engr. J.B. Payne & Assos., Enid, Okla., 1951; with Vought Systems div. LTV Aerospace Corp., Dallas, 1951—, supr. elec. electronic design, 1963-71, chief systems design, 1971-72, supr. armament, crew systems and elec./electronic design, 1972—. Instr. aerospace design So. Meth. U., 1969, Naval Air Sta., Dallas, 1970. Coach, Little League Baseball, 1961-63. Bd. dirs. Arlington Christian Youth Center. Served with USAAF, 1946. Mem. I.E.E.E., Aerospace and Electronics Systems Soc. (dir.). Mem. Ch. of Christ (deacon). Contbr. to Power Semiconductor Applications, vol. II, 1972. Research on application of solid state switching to aircraft elec. systems. Home: 1615 White Way Dr Arlington TX 76013 Office: PO Box 5907 Dallas TX 75222

DICKINSON, ELIZABETH ANN KANOZIK (MRS. EDGAR RANDOLPH DICKINSON), city ofcl.; b. Greenwich, Conn.; d. Frank and Rose (Matlak) Kanozik; tchrs. certificate State of Fla., 1965; m. Edgar Randolph Dickinson, Dec. 6, 1935. Mgr., buyer book dept. Cranston Co., Norwich, Conn., 1942-50; radio dispatcher Orlando (Fla.) Police Dept., 1953-54, supr. adminstrv. bur., 1956-69, police statistician, 1970—; sec. to dir. communications City of Orlando, 1954-55. Mem. credit com. City of Orlando, 1954-55. Mem. credit com. City of Orlando Employees Credit Union, 1964-65; mem. Citizens Adv. Council on Aging, Orange County, Fla., 1967-69; mem. membership com. Central Fla. Heart Assn. Bd. dirs. Orange County Citizens Safety Council, 1958-61, sec., 1959-60. Recipient Carol Lane award Nat. Safety Council and Shell Oil Co., 1959; Dale Carnegie scholar, 1960. Episcopalian. Club: Altrusa (1st v.p. Orlando 1959-60, corr. sec. 1963-64, editor 1963-64, pres. 1967-69, chmn. coms). Home: 1021 Fleck Av Orlando FL 32804 Office: Municipal Justice Bldg 100 S Hughey St Orlando FL 32801

DICKINSON, WILLIAM ANDREW, lawyer; b. Roanoke, Va., Sept. 15, 1916; s. George Nelson and Shirley Carter (Hart) D.; B.S., U. Va., 1939, LL.B., 1941; m. Nancy McQuown Ring, Jan. 10, 1942; children—William Andrew, Michael W., Nancy Adele. Admitted to Va. bar, 1940; law clk. Judge Herbert Gregory Va. Supreme Ct. Appeals, 1941-42; asso. firm Hazlegrove, Carr & Shackelford, Roanoke, 1946-49; partner firm Hazlegrove, Carr, Dickinson, Smith & Rea, Roanoke, 1949—. Bd. dirs. Roanoke United Fund, 1956-58, Roanoke Symphony, 1964-67, YMCA, 1961-64. Trustee, v.p. Roanoke Hosp. Assn., 1956—. Served to lt. USNR, 1942-46. Mem. Roanoke C. of C. (dir. 1957-58), Roanoke Bar Assn. (dir., pres. 1958-59). Episcopalian. Clubs: Roanoke Country; Shenandoah. Home: 2616 Stanley Av Roanoke VA 24014 Office: 202 S Jefferson St Roanoke VA 24011

DICKINSON, WILLIAM LOUIS, congressman; b. Opelika, Ala., June 5, 1925; s. Henry K. and Bernice (Lowe) D.; LL.B., U. Ala., 1950; m. Mary Patterson Stanfield, 1948; children—Chris, Mike, Tara, William Louis. Admitted to Ala. bar, 1950, practiced in Opelika, 1950-63; judge Opelika City Ct., 1951-53; judge Ct. Common Pleas, 1953-59; judge Juvenile Ct. Lee County, 1953-59; judge 5th Jud. Ct. Ala., 1959-63; asst. v.p. So. Ry. System, Montgomery, Ala., 1963-64; mem. 89th-93d congresses from 2d Ala. Dist.; mem. com. on govt. operations, com. on house adminstrn. Chmn. Opelika Bd. Edn., 1960-61; mem. Gov.'s Indsl. Com. of 100, 1963-64; dir. Lee County Civil Def., 1961-62. Past pres. Ala. Mental Health Assn. Chmn. Ala. Republican Congl. Delegation. Pres., bd. dirs. Lee County Mental Health Clinic; bd. dirs. Lee County Rehab. Center. Served with USNR, World War II; now capt. USAF Res. Named Man of Year Opelika Jr. C. of C., 1961, One of Four Outstanding Young Men in Ala., 1961. Mem. Ala. Bar Assn., U. Ala. Alumni Assn., Sigma Alpha Epsilon. Mason, Kiwanian, Elk. Home: 6236 Edgewater Dr Falls Church VA 24041 Office: Cannon House Office Bldg Washington DC 20515

DICKS, JOSEPH LEWIS, JR., dentist; b. Augusta, Ga., Oct. 9, 1935; s. Joseph Lewis and Wesley Townsend (O'Neall) D.; student Acad. Richmond County, 1949-53, Emory-at Oxford Coll., 1953-55; D.D.S., Emory U. Sch. Dentistry, 1959; M.S., Tufts U. Sch. Dentistry, 1969; M.P.H., U. Minn., 1973; m. Dorothy Ann Lowery, July 1, 1970. Individual practice dentistry, Columbus, Ga., 1961-63; staff dentist Gracewood (Ga.) Hosp., 1963-64; instr. Arhus (Denmark) Sch. Dentistry, 1964-65; instr. Royal Coll. Dentistry, Copehagen, Denmark, 1965-67; dir. dental program Ga. Retardation Center, Atlanta, 1969—. Guest lectr. U. Minn., 1973. Cons. Atlanta Cerebral Palsy Assn., 1969-70; instr. Emory U. Sch. Dentistry, U. Ga., 1969—. Served to capt. USAF, 1959-61. Recipient Outstanding Unit award 837th Tactical Hosp., 1961. Fellow Royal Soc. Health; mem. Am., Ga. dental assns., Am. Assn. Mental Deficiency, Ga., Atlanta assns. retarded children, Ga. Pub. Health Assn., So. Assn. Institutional Dentists (vice chmn.), Acad. Dentistry for Handicapped, Xi Psi Phi. Home: 2670 Ridgemore Rd NW Atlanta GA 30318 Office: 4770 N Peachtree Rd Atlanta GA 30341

DICKS, ROBERT STANLEY, environmental engr.; b. Barnwell, S.C., Dec. 23, 1917; s. Robert S. and Wilhelmina (Antley) D.; B.S., U. N.C., 1938, M.S., Va. Poly. Inst., 1939; Ph.D., U. Pa., 1944; m. Frances G. Findley, Oct. 25, 1945; children—Stan, Greg, Carol. Group leader research and devel. Shell Oil Co., Houston and N.Y.C., 1944-53; dir. mfg. devel. Celanese Fibers Co., Charlotte, N.C., 1953-63; plant mgr. Celanese Chem. Co., Bay City, Tex., 1963-72; engr. Tex. Water Quality Bd., Austin, 1972—; dir. 1st Nat. Bank Bay City. Vice pres. Matagorda County United Fund, 1969-71. Recipient Silver Beaver award Boy Scouts Am., 1958. Registered profl. engr., Tex. Mem. Am. Inst. Chem. Engrs., C. of C., Tex. Mfrs. Assn., Tex. Chem. Council, Sigma Xi, Tau Beta Pi, Alpha Chi Sigma. Home: 7602 Long Point Dr Austin TX 78731 Office: Tex Water Quality Bd 314 W 11th St Austin TX 78711

DICKSON, ALFRED GRANBERY, ret. newspaper exec.; b. Liberty, S.C., Oct. 28, 1908; s. John G. and Cora (Mauldin) D.; student N.C. State U., 1925-26, Wofford Coll., 1926-29; m. Cornelia E. Weaver, Oct. 18, 1932 (dec. Sept. 1958); 1 son, John Hines; m. 2d, Maggie Lee Madry, June 27, 1959; 1 stepson, Robert W. Madry, Jr. Reporter, Wilmington (N.C.) News, 1929, 30-36; sports editor Durham (N.C.) Morning Herald, 1929-30; mng. editor Wilmington Star, 1936-41; mng. editor Wilmington News, 1941-47; editor Wilmington News and Wilmington Star, 1947-55, exec. editor Star-News Newspapers, Wilmington, 1955-70, asst. to pub., 1970-72. Bd. dirs. Cornelia Nixon Davis Nursing Home. Former pres. N.C. Assn. Asso. Dailies; pres. UPI Editors Assn. N.C., 1963-64, Asso. Daily Newspapers N.C., 1966-67. Recipient Forrestal citation, 1947; 6 awards ann. editorial competition N.C. Press Assn., 1954-63; award in new plant competition Am. Press mag., 1969. Mem. Sigma Delta Chi (Distinguished Service award for journalism in editorial writing 1965), Alpha Phi Gamma, Lambda Chi Alpha. Democrat. Methodist. Clubs: Cape Fear, Rotary. Author: Histories of N.C. Shipbuilding Co. Home: Route 1 Box 603 Wilmington NC 28401

DICKSON, FRANK ALEXANDER, journalist, author; b. Townville, S.C., Oct. 29, 1911; s. Frank Alexander and Laura (Holland) D.; grad. high sch.; m. Renthy Pruitt, Feb. 10, 1938; children—Larry Pruitt (dec.), Milton Alexander, Horace Ansel. Feature writer, columnist Anderson (S.C.) Ind. Anderson Daily Mail, 1929—; columnist Writer's Digest, Cin., 1939—, asso. editor, 1967—; editorial staff Quote Mag., Anderson, 1965—. Democrat. Methodist. Author: 2000 Articles You Can Write and Sell, 1955; Freelancer's Treasury of Article Ideas 1961; Editor: Writers Digest Handbook of Article Writing, 1968. Co-editor: Writer's Digest Handbook of Short Story Writing, 1969. Contbr. articles to newspapers, mags. syndicated publs. Home: 1006 Elizabeth St Anderson SC 29621 Office: The Anderson Independent Hwy 29 N Anderson SC 29621

DICKSON, KENNETH PEARL, hosp. adminstr.; b. New Summerfield, Tex., June 29, 1935; s. Coy and Esther (Richey) D.; B.A., North Tex. State Coll., 1957, M.A., 1962; m. Lucy Ellen Baker, Oct. 26, 1963; children—Kenneth Lowell, Kevin Neal. Lab., X-ray technician, Med. Surg. Clinic, Lewisville, Tex., 1953-63; adminstr. Newton County (Tex.) Hosp., 1963-64, Hardeman County Hosp., Quanah, Tex., 1964-68; adminstr. Simmons Meml. Hosp., Sweetwater, Tex., 1968—. Vice pres. Am. Cancer Soc., Nolan unit, Sweetwater, Tex., 1970-71. Served with AUS, 1958-60. Recipient Pub. Service award Am. Radio Relay League, 1966. Mem. Tex. Hosp. Assn. (pres. midwestern hosp. div. 1967-68; pres. S.W. hosp. div. 1970-71; del. 1968-72), N.W. Tex. Hosp. Assn. (trustee, v.p. 1973-74). Presbyn. (deacon). Mason, Lion. Home: 1411 Sunnyvale St Sweetwater TX 79556 Office: 1301 Hailey St Sweetwater TX 79556

DICKSON, LILLIAN DURHAM, author, editor, artist, art gallery exec.; b. Atlanta; d. Joseph Idelbert and Annie Rosbell (Meeks) Durham; student Sch. Fine Arts, Washington U., St. Louis, 1910-12, Ft. Worth Conservatory Music, 1928, Tex. Christian U., 1930-31; m. Henry McHaney Dickson, Sept. 16, 1917 (dec. July 1956); 1 son, Henry McHaney; m. 2d, B. Houston Cogdell, Sept. 5, 1966 (div.). Propr. real estate firm, Ft. Worth, 1914-59; mgr., supr. Lloyd Surveying and Engring. Co., Houston, 1958-60; mgr. Tarrant County Surveyor's Office, Ft. Worth, 1961-63; dir., mgr. Westbrook Hotel Art Gallery, Ft. Worth, 1963-64, 69-72; art tchr., propr. Four-Arts Studio, Ft. Worth, 1964—; dir. Westbrook Art Gallery; founder, pub., editor mag. Composers, Authors, Artists Am., 1940—, chief editor, 1940-43, 48-49, contbg. editor, 1943—; contbr. poetry, articles mags., newspapers, 1920—; exhibited paintings in ann. group shows Tex. Fine Arts Soc., Ft. Worth, 1920—, also other regional shows; one-man shows, 1969-71; chmn. Tex. Council Promotion Poetry, Austin, 1949-59, co-chmn., 1960-66; nat. cultural coordinator Avalon Poetry Shrine, San Antonio, 1941-44; Tex. chmn. Nat. Poetry Day Com., Austin, 1960-65; nat. pres. Composers, Authors, Artists Am., 1940-43, historian, 1948-50, 60-67, hon. life pres., 1944—, organizer Ft. Worth br., pres., 1938, v.p., 1951-52; organizer Ft. Worth Water Color Soc., 1952, bd. dirs., 1952-67, recipient art awards, 1952, 53, 54, 63, 68-70; pres. Ft. Worth Poetry Soc., 1960-61. Recipient award of merit, Gold medal Tex. Press Woman's Assn., Houston, 1948, also awards in poetry and music, art exhibits. Mem. Nat. League Am. Pen Women (v.p. Ft. Worth br., 1951-52), Poetry Soc. Tex., A.S.C.A.P., Tex. Fine Arts Assn., Ft. Worth Poetry Soc., Marquis Biog. Library Soc. (adv. mem.). Clubs: Euterpean, Music Study, O'Henryettes (Ft. Worth). Author: The Enchanted Mesa, 1937; Amber In The Sun, 1947. Composer: Sentimental Over Texas, 1946. Home: 200 Burnet St Fort Worth TX 76102

DICKSON, ROY SHELTON, petroleum co. exec.; b. Lewiston, Ida., Aug. 29, 1933; s. Roy S. and Ethel (Means) D.; B.S., U. Tulsa, 1958; m. Cassandra G. Bennett; children—Laura Ann, Julia Kay. Sci. computer programmer research and devel. Phillips Petroleum Co., Bartlesville, Okla., 1957, systems analyst computing dept., 1958-61, supt. computing systems computing dept., 1961-62, supr. tech. programming systems, 1962-65, dir. computing systems and evaluations, 1965-67, asst. mgr. operations div., 1967-69, mgr. operations div., 1969—. Vice pres. SHARE, Internat., 1964-65, pres., 1965-66. Served with USMCR, 1952. Mem. Assn. Computing Machinery. Home: 2065 S Osage Bartlesville OK 74003 Office: Computing Dept Phillips Petroleum Co Bartlesville OK 74003

DICUS, R. EARL, bishop; b. Jerome, Ariz., Sept. 1, 1910; s. Harry Everett and Matilda Elizabeth (Lawrence) D.; B.A., U. of South, 1936, B.D., 1937, D.D., 1956; m. Mildred Dawson, Sept. 10, 1938; 1 child. Ordained deacon Episcopal Ch., 1938, priest, 1938; vicar Good Samaritan Ch., Phoenix, 1938-41; priest-in-charge St. Andrew's Ch., Tucson, 1941-42; rector St. Paul's Ch., Batesville, Ariz., 1942-46; vicar Trinity Ch., Searcy, Ark., 1944-46; Locum Tenens St. Thomas Ch., Los Angeles, 1946; rector Redeemer Ch., Eagle Pass, Tex., 1946-55; priest-in-charge Holy Trinity Ch., Carrizo Springs, Tex., 1946-53; consecrated suffragen bishop West Tex., 1955. Dep. Gen. Conv. Epis. Ch., 1949. Address: PO Box 6885 San Antonio TX 78209*

DIDEA, ARTHUR ANTHONY, dentist; b. N.Y.C., Jan. 4, 1925; s. Charles and Rebecca (Schmeltzer) DiD.; B.S. with honors, U. City N.Y., 1945; postgrad. Washington U., St. Louis, 1945-47; D.D.S., U. Ill., 1952; m. Viola Mae Rodenmayer, Feb. 8, 1947; children—Barbara (Mrs. David Haines Phillips), Mark Brian, Linda Katherine, Gregory Scott, Karen Lee. Tchr. gen., qualitative and quantitative chemistry Harris Tchrs. Coll., St. Louis, 1947; research bacterial chemist St. Louis Health Dept. Endemic Typhus Fever Study, 1948; asst. prof. oral histology, pathology and operative dentistry U. Ill., 1952-53; practice dentistry, Orlando, Fla., 1955—; dental staff Winter Park (Fla.) Hosp., also Fla. Hosp., Orlando, 1956-62. Chief Hawkeye tribe Indian Guides of YMCA, Orlando, 1963-64, nation chief, 1965; pres. P.T.A., 1970; active Little League, Cub Scouts Am. Bd. dirs. Civic Theater, 1963-66. Served as 1st lt. AUS, 1953-55. Mem. Fla. (ins. chmn. 1965), Orange County (program chmn. 1970) dental socs., Kappa Alpha, Phi Beta Pi, Omicron Kappa Upsilon, Psi Omega. Episcopalian (mem. vestry 1970-74, jr. warden 1971-73). Mason (Shriner); mem. Order Eastern Star. Clubs: Executive (pres. 1966-68); Sertoma (chmn. bd. 1963, 65, pres. 1964); University (Winter Park). Contbr. articles to profl. jours. Home: 1921 N Forest Av Orlando FL 32803

DIDIER, LYDIA MARCHIVE, guidance counselor; b. Baton Rouge, Dec. 23, 1922; d. Marcel M. and Jewel (Furlow) Marchive; B.S., La. State U., 1951, M.Ed., 1953; m. Fabius Odell Didier, Sept. 3, 1940 (dec. 1949); 1 son, Marcel Furlow. Librarian, Gonzales (La.) High Sch., 1951-55, Pride High Sch., Baton Rouge, 1955-59; guidance counselor Westdale Jr. High Sch., Baton Rouge, 1959-73, Sherwood Jr. High Sch., Baton Rouge, 1973—. Tutor retarded children, 1958—; vocational counselor Presbyn. Ch., 1960—. Active A.R.C., East Baton Rouge Mental Health Assn., Broadmoor Assn. Greater Baton Rouge, Baton Rouge Little Theater, Broadmoor P.T.A., Westdale Jr. High Sch. P.T.A., La. Assn. Mental Health. Mem. Am. La., personnel and guidance assns., Am. Sch. Counselor Assn., East Baton Rouge Parish Guidance Assn. (pres. 1966, 67), La. Tchrs. Assn., Assn. Classroom Tchrs. East Baton Rouge Parish, Royal Order Daffy, Daffy Daffodil, Phi Lambda Phi (certificate of Merit 1953), Theta Xi (Mothers' Club), Beta Sigma Phi. Democrat. Presbyn. Clubs: Womans', Readers' (Baton Rouge). Home: 2545 Woodland Ridge Blvd Baton Rouge LA 70815 Office: 1020 Maribrook Dr Baton Rouge LA 70815

DIEDERICH, JOHN WILLIAM, pub. co. exec.; b. Ladysmith, Wis., Aug. 30, 1929; s. Joseph Charles and Alice Florence (Yost) D.; Ph.B., Marquette U., 1951; M.B.A. with high distinction (Baker scholar), Harvard, 1955; m. Mary Theresa Klein, Nov. 25, 1950; children—Mary Theresa (Mrs. Flint Baxter Evans), Robert Douglas, Charles Stuart, Michael Mark, Patricia Anne, Donna Maureen (dec.), Denise Brendan, Carol Lynn, Barbara Gail, Brian Donald, Tracy Maureen, Theodora Bernadette, Tamara Alice, Lorraine Angela. Research dir. Landmark Communications, Inc., Norfolk, Va., 1955-61, controller, 1961-64, sec.-treas., 1964-65, v.p., treas., dir., 1965-73, exec. v.p. finance, dir., 1973—; instr. Boston U., 1954, Old Dominion U., 1955-59. Bd. dirs. De Paul Hosp., Landmark Charitable Found., Virginian-Pilot and Ledger-Star Joy Fund Found., Norfolk. Served to lt. col. USMC, 1951-53; Res. ret. Mem. Nat. Assn. Accountants, Inst. Newspaper Controllers and Finance Officers, Inst. Broadcasting Financial Mgmt., Am. Numismatic Assn., Nat., Wis. geneal. socs., Geneal. Soc. Pa., Soc. Profl. Journalists, Sigma Delta Chi. Roman Catholic. Club: Harbor (Norfolk). Home: 3751 Oyster Point Quay Virginia Beach VA 23452 Office: 150 W Brambleton Av Norfolk VA 23501

DIEHM, FLOYD LEE, clergyman; b. Perry, Okla., May 1, 1925; s. John William and Hortence (Russell) D.; B.Th., N.W. Christian Coll., Eugene, Ore., 1951; M.Div., Phillips Sem., Enid, Okla., 1954; D.Religion, Claremont Sch. Theology, 1970; m. Emily Louise Helseth, Dec. 21, 1951; children—Kenneth John, Janet Kay. Ordained to ministry Christian Ch., 1950; nat. evangelist, 1955-58; pastor Belmont Christian Ch., Roanoke, Va., 1958-62, 1st Ch., Modesto, Cal., 1964-66, Midwest Blvd. Ch., Midwest City, Okla., 1970—. Bd. dirs. Bicentennial Celebration Com.; trustee Phillips U. Mem. Phillips Alumni Assn. (pres.). Rotarian. Author: Fully Alive!, 1974. Home: 3617 Oak Grove St Midwest City OK 73110 Office: 320 N Midwest Blvd Midwest City OK 73110

DIENHART, CHARLOTTE MARIE, educator; b. Sioux Falls, S.D., Aug. 14, 1923; d. Arthur Peter and Mae (Donahue) Dienhart; B.S., Coll. St. Catherine, 1945; M.S., State U. Ia., 1947; postgrad. U. Minn., 1956-58, Emory U. Sch. Medicine, 1962-64; Ph.D., Mich. State U., 1960. Research asst. U. Minn., 1947-48, grad. teaching asst. physiology, 1957-58; instr. dept. biology Coll. St. Catherine, 1948-57; grad. teaching asst. anatomy Mich. State U., 1958-60; mem. faculty Emory U., Atlanta, 1960—, asst. prof. anatomy, 1966—. Served to lt. comdr. M.C., USNR. Mem. A.A.A.S., N.Y. Acad. Scis., So. Soc. Anatomists, Ga. Acad. Sci., Sigma Xi, Sigma Delta Epsilon, Omicron Nu. Beta Beta Beta. Author: Basic Human Anatomy and Physiology, 1967, 2d edit., 1973. Home: 1943 N Decatur Rd NE Atlanta GA 30307

DIERCKS, FRED HERMAN, microbiologist, educator; b. Greenville, Tex., Aug. 1, 1920; s. Fred Amanuel and Louise Elmo (Johnson) D.; B.A., East Tex. State Tchrs. Coll., 1941; M.S., U. Md., 1951; M.P.H., U. Pitts., 1957, D.Sc., 1959; m. Viviene A. Davis, Dec. 24, 1942; children—Susan (Mrs. Charles F. Lindner), Margaret Ann, Mary E., William F. Served as hosp. apprentice 1st class USNR, 1942-45; commd. 2d lt. U.S. Army, 1948, advanced through grades to lt. col., 1963; assigned Inst. Med. Research, Kuala Lumpur, Malaysia, 1948-56, Walton Reed Army Inst. Research, Washington, 1956-61, U.S. Army Med. Research Unit, Panama, 1961-64, Hdqrs. Research and Devel. Command, Office Surgeon Gen., Washington, 1964-67; ret., 1967; asso. prof. biology Mars Hill (N.C.) Coll., 1967—. Sec. bd. dirs. Mountain Ramparts Health Planning, Inc. Diplomate Am. Bd. Microbiology. Mem. Am. Pub. Health Assn., Am. Soc. Microbiology, A.A.A.S., N.Y. Acad. Sci., Bot. Soc. Am., Am. Soc. Tropical Medicine and Hygiene. Democrat. Baptist (deacon). Mason (Shriner). Club: Civitan (pres. 1971). Contbr. articles to profl. jours. Home: 122 Mt View Rd Mars Hill NC 28754

DIERCKS, FREDERICK OTTO, govt. ofcl.; b. Rainy River, Ont., Can., Sept. 8, 1912 (parents Am. citizens); s. Otto Herman and Lucy (Plunkett) D.; B.S., U.S. Mil. Acad., 1937; M.S. in Civil Engring., Mass. Inst. Tech., 1939; M.S. in Photogrammetry, Syracuse U., 1950; m. Kathryn Frances Transue, Sept. 1, 1937; children—Frederick William, Lucy Helena. Commd. 2d lt. U.S. Army, 1937, advanced through grades to col., 1952; comdg. officer U.S. Army Map Service, Washington, 1957-61; dir. U.S. Army Coastal Engring. Research Center, Washington, 1964-67; ret., 1967; asso. dir. U.S. Coast and Geodetic Survey (now Nat. Ocean Survey), Rockville, Md., 1967—. U.S. mem. commn. cartography Pan. Am. Inst. Geography and History, OAS, 1961-67, alt. U.S. mem. directing council, 1970—. Decorated Legion of Merit (U.S.); Grand Cross of Order of King George II (Greece); Most Exalted Order of White Elephant (Thailand). Registered profl. engr., D.C. Fellow Am. Soc. C.E.; mem. Am. Soc. Photogrammetry (pres. 1970-71), Sigma Xi. Republican. Presbyn. Mason. Clubs: Army-Navy, Cosmos (Washington). Home: 9313 Christopher St Fairfax VA 22030 Office: 6001 Executive Blvd Rockville MD 20852

DIES, DOUGLAS HILTON, assn. exec.; b. St. Paul, Sept. 9, 1913; s. Edward Jerome and Maresta (Cole) D.; A.B., Harvard, 1934; postgrad. Oxford U., 1934-35; m. Mary Frances Doreen Harding, Nov. 25, 1939; children—Harding Mogridge, Andrea Frances. Editorial staff Grand Forks (N.D.) Herald, summer 1933, Mpls. Star, summer 1934, London Sunday Chronicle, summer 1935; staff London bur. U.P., 1935-38, Knoxville (Tenn.) Jour., 1938-40; pub. relations dept. Westinghouse Electric Co., 1940-41; staff A.P., Cleve., 1941-42; pub. relations staff U.S. Bd. Econ. Warfare, Washington, 1942-43; pub. relations, Washington, 1946—; asso. world trading corps, 1947—; asst. to pres. Nat. Inst. Oilseed Products, 1947—; Washington rep. Pillsbury Co., 1956-64, East Asiatic Co., 1956—, Woodward & Dickerson, Inc., 1958—; asst. sec., bur. raw materials Am. Vegetable Oils and Fats Industries, 1961-62, sec., 1962—; exec. sec. Am. Council Ind. Labs., 1963—; guest lectr. fgn. trade Georgetown U., 1966—. Mem. Republican City Com., Alexandria, 1953-61. Served from ensign to lt. comdr., USNR, 1943-46. Mem. S.R. (gov. D.C. 1956-62), Mil. Order World Wars, Sigma Alpha Epsilon. Episcopalian (vestryman). Clubs: Harvard (N.Y.C., Washington); University, Oxford-Cambridge (Washington). Editor: Chemurgic Digest, 1950-53. Home: 505 Robinson Ct Alexandria VA 22302 Office: 1725 K St NW Washington DC 20006

DIES, FEDERICO, educator; b. Paris, France, Mar. 17, 1936; s. Haroldo and Pilar (Angulo) D.; M.D., Universidad Autónoma de México, 1959; Ph.D., U. Rochester, 1966; m. Rosa María Cobos, Aug. 11, 1962; children—Juan Antonio, Gonzalo. Asst. chmn. dept. clin. physiology Instituto Nacional de la Nutrición México, 1965-70; med. dir. Eli Lilly Co., Mexico, 1970-72; chmn., prof. physiology and pharmacology dept. Sch. Medicine, Universidad Autónoma de San Luis Potosí (Mexico), 1973—. Nat. Acad. Medicine (Mexico). Fellow A.C.P.; mem. Academia de Investigación Científica, Sociedad Mexicana de Ciencias Fisiológicas (pres.), Sociedad Mexicana de Nutrición y Endocrinología (Alfonso Rivera award 1967, pres.-elect 1972), Internat., Am. socs. nephrology, N.Y. Acad. Scis., Am. Physiol. Soc., Academia Nacional de Medicina (Dr. Eduardo Liceaga award 1972), Asociación Latinoamericana de Ciencias Fisiológicas (sec.). Contbr. articles to profl. jours. Home: 1030 Fray Diego de la Magdalena San Luis Potosí SLP Mexico Office: 2405 Venustiano Carranza San Luis Potosí SLP Mexico

DIETRICH, EDWIN JERRY, cons. engr., lawyer; b. Shreveport, La., July 14, 1926; s. Merwyn and Vera (Eaves) D.; student Centenary Coll., Shreveport, 1944, Miss. Coll., Clinton, 1944, Tulane, 1945; B.S., U. Tex. at Austin, 1949; LL.B., So. Tex. Coll., 1958; m. Adele Marie Odom, June 5, 1946; children—Shelle (Mrs. Michael Dean Wright), Melanie Gae. Field engr. Farnsworth & Chambers, Houston, 1949; head reports and specifications Lockwood Andrews & Newman, Houston, 1950-56; sr. v.p. Bernard Johnson, Inc. engrs., architects, planners, Houston, 1956—; admitted to Tex. bar, 1958, U.S. Supreme Ct. bar, 1966. Bd. dirs. Greater Houston Council Camp Fire Girls, Inc., 1965-68. Served to capt. USMCR, 1944-47, 51. Fellow Am. Soc. C.E.; mem. Houston Bar Assn., Cons. Engrs. Council, Houston C. of C., Tex. Soc. Profl. Engrs., Houston Engring. and Sci. Soc. (dir.). Clubs: Houston, University. Home: 23 Hickory Ridge Houston TX 77024 Office: 5050 Westheimer St Houston TX 77027

DIETRICH, HELEN RUSSELL, court reporter, conv. service co. exec.; b. Birmingham, Ala., May 4, 1912; d. William Crawford and Lucy Adelaide (Powell) Russell; B.A., Newcomb Coll., 1933; m. Norman Edward Dietrich, July 31, 1935 (div. Oct., 1949); 1 dau., Emilie (Mrs. Henry William Griffin). Sec., ct. reporter 8th Dist. U.S. Navy, 1941-42; founder, pres. Dietrich & Pickett, Inc., court reporting, New Orleans, 1942—; founder, pres. Helen R. Dietrich, Inc., conv. service, New Orleans, 1966—, Habersham Corp., pub., supplier ct. reporting machines, New Orleans, 1966—. Rec. sec. Le Petit Theatre du Vieux Carre, 1964-66. Mem. Nat. Shorthand Reporters Assn., La. Hist. Soc. (corr. sec. 1962-71), D.A.R., Colonial Dames XVII Century, Dames Magna Charta, Newcomb Alumnae Assn. (2d v.p. 1947-49, treas. 1949-51), Internat. House, Southampton Colonial Soc. Democrat. Episcopalian. Editor, pub.; Of Time and Chase (Edison B. Allen), 1969. Home: 2033 Jefferson Av New Orleans LA 70115 Office: 333 St Charles Av New Orleans LA 70130

DIETZ, ROBERT SINCLAIR, marine geologist; b. Westfield, N.J., Sept. 14, 1914; B.S., U. Ill., 1937, M.S., 1939, Ph.D. in Geology, 1941; m. 1955; 2 children. Asst. Ill. State Geol. Survey, 1935-37; with Scripps Instn., Cal., 1937-39; oceanographer U.S. Naval Electronics Lab., 1946-52, 54-58; with U.S. Coast and Geod. Survey, Rockville, Md., 1958-67; marine geologist Nat. Oceanic and Atmospheric Adminstrn. Atlantic Oceanographic and Meteor. Lab., Miami, 1967—; lectr. in field. Served to lt. col. USAAF, 1941-46. Fulbright scholar, Tokyo, Japan, 1952-53. Fellow London Geol. Soc., Geol. Soc. Am.; mem. Am. Geophys. Union, Soc. Limnology and Oceanography, Am. Mineral Soc., Am. Meteoritical Soc., Marine Tech. Soc. Address: 365 Heather Lane Key Biscayne FL 33149*

DIETZE, CHARLES EDGAR, clergyman; b. Savannah, Ga., Jan. 21, 1919; s. Ernest and Mary (Fetzer) D.; A.B., Transylvania Coll., 1940; B.D., Lexington Theol. Sem., 1944; D.D., Atlantic Christian Coll., 1965; m. Mary Nettie Peavyhouse, Dec. 28, 1940; children—Mary Katherine (Mrs. Jimmie G. Lamm), Charles William. Ordained to ministry Christian Ch. (Disciples of Christ), 1943; pastor, Ky., 1940-55; v.p. Lexington Theol. Sem. (Ky.), 1955-65; exec. minister Christian Ch. in N.C., Wilson, 1965—. Vice pres., bd. higher edn. Christian Ch., 1966-68, pres.-elect, conf. regional ministers, 1974—. Trustee Atlantic Christian Coll., Wilson. Recipient Distinguished Service award Henderson (Ky.) Jr. C. of C., 1951. Spl. Centennial citation Lexington Theol. Sem., 1965; named outstanding young man Ky., Jr. C. of C., 1951. Mem. N.C. Council Chs. (pres. 1972-73). Editor N.C. Christian, 1965—. Contbr. articles to profl. jours. Home: 805 Trinity Dr Wilson NC 27893 Office: Box 521 Wilson NC 27893

DIEZ, FLORENCIO, coll. dean; b. Salamanca, Spain, Apr. 28, 1933; s. Jose Antonio and Natalia (Pacho) D.; B.A., La Santa Coll., 1952; S.T.B., St. John's Coll., 1958; M.A., U.Salamanca, 1959. Ph.D., 1962; came to U.S., 1963. Tchr. philosophy La Santa Coll., 1959-62; gen. sec. Nat. Inst. Spirituality, Madrid, 1962-63; asso. prof. philosophy Cath. U. Puerto Rico, Ponce, 1963-71, prof., 1971—, dean Coll. Arts and Humanities, 1968—. Mem. Am. Cath. Philos. Assn. Roman Catholic. Author: Los Complutenses, 1962. Home: San Antonio Devel Ponce PR 00731

DIEZ-RIVAS, FEDERICO MANUEL, physician; b. Caguas, P.R., June 17, 1920; s. Carlos and Elvira (Rivas-Soto) Diez-Ramos; B.S., U. P.R;, 1941; M.D., Med. Coll. Va., 1944; m. Elsie Cardona, July 28, 1963; children—Elsie Marie, Federico, Juan Carlos. Intern Med. Coll. Va. Hosp., Richmond, 1944-45; resident U. Mich. Hosp., Ann Arbor, 1945-49; practice medicine, specializing in internal medicine and cardiology, San Juan and Caguas, P.R., 1950—; mem. staff San Juan City, San Rafael hosps., Rio Piedras Med. Center; chief cardiology clinic Caguas Subregional Hosp., 1972—; asst. prof. medicine U. P.R. Sch. Medicine 1950-58. Served to 2d lt. with AUS, 1942-44. Diplomate Am. Bd. Internal Medicine. Fellow A.C.P.; mem. A.M.A., P.R., Am. heart assns., P.R. (past pres.), Pan-Am. med. assns. Contbr. articles in field to profl. jours. Address: 572 Munoz Rivera Av Hato Rey PR 00918

DI FILIPPI, ARTURO, operatic mgr.; b. Lucera, Italy, Aug. 15, 1894; s. Henry and Frieda di F.; came to U.S., 1913; student Highland Park Coll., 1914-15; student Kan. Wesleyan U., 1915-19, hon. doctorate, 1946; student Juilliard Sch. Music, 1919-22; m. Dec. 5, 1933. Studied and sang in Germany and Italy, 1922-28; debut as operatic tenor Cin. Summer Opera, 1928; mem. Roxy Gang, Radio City Music Hall, N.Y.C., also tenor with numerous symphony and opera orgns. throughout U.S., 1929-39; founder Opera Guild Greater Miami, 1939, artistic dir., gen. mgr., 1939-72; chmn. singing dept. U. Miami (Fla.), 1939-63, also prof. Mem. Fla. Arts Council. Recipient awards for outstanding operatic activities Italian Govt., gov. of Salzburg (Austria), French Govt., Presdl. citation Nat. Fedn. Music Clubs, 1965. Mem. Am. Assn. U. Profs., Nat. Assn. Tchrs. Singing (past pres. Miami chpt., regent South Fla.). Mason (32 deg., Shriner), Rotarian. Club: Flamingo Dinner. Home: 625 SW 29th Rd Miami FL 33129 Died June 27, 1972.

DIGGS, MELVIN M., lawyer; b. Trenton, Tex., Apr. 11, 1914; s. Harvey Washington and Juanita (Moore) D.; A.B., Tex. Christian U., 1936; LL.B., Georgetown U., 1941; m. Virginia Haley, May 3, 1948; children—Susan, Nancy, Ann. Admitted to Tex. bar; lawyer U.S. Govt., Ft. Worth, 1945—; U.S. atty. No. Dist. Tex., Ft. Worth, 1965-68. Served with AUS, 1941-45. Mem. State Bar. Tex., Fed., Tarrant County bar assns., Mil. Intelligence Assn., Texas Christian U. Ex-Lettermen's Assn. Club: Colonial Country (golf com.) (Ft. Worth). Home: 4316 Briar Haven Rd Fort Worth TX 76109

DILIBERTO, BERNARD (BUDDY) SAVERIO, JR., TV sta. exec.; b. New Orleans, Aug. 18, 1931; s. Bernard Savert and Mar (Carr) D.; B.S. in Journalism, Loyola U. (New Orleans), 1955; m. Jeanne Chester, July 23, 1971; children by previous marriage—Christopher, Michael, Kathleen, Debra Ann. With Times-Picayune Pub. Co., New Orleans, 1950-66, sports columnist, 1955-66, asst. sport editor, 1962-66; sports dir. WVUE-TV, New Orleans, 1966—; columnist Gridweek mag., 1967—, Clarion-Herald, New Orleans, 1967—. Served with AUS, 1951-53; Korea. Decorated Purple Heart, Bronze Star; named Sportswriter Year La., Nat. Sportswriters and Sportscasters Assn., 1963, Sportscaster of Year, 1968, 69, 71, 72. Mem. Delta Sigma Pi. Roman Catholic. Clubs: New Orleans Athletic; Touchdown (New Orleans). Home: 3225 Ridgelake St Apt A Metarie LA 70003 Office: 1025 S Jefferson Davis Pkwy New Orleans LA 70012

DILL, BILLY CLIFF, elec. engr.; b. Sulligent, Ala., Aug. 28, 1935; s. Ernest Albert and Flora Mae (Burnett) D.; B.S. in E.E., U. Ala., 1963; m. Emma Kathryn Lankford, Dec. 11, 1965; 1 dau., Susan Kathryn. Design engr. Brown Engring. Co., Huntsville, Ala., 1963-64, Chrysler Corp., Huntsville, Cape Canaveral, Fla., 1964-66, Rust Engring. Co., Birmingham, Ala., 1966—; instr. U. Ala. Sch. Engring. at Birmingham, 1966-67. Served with USMCR, 1954-57. Registered profl. engr., Ala., Ga. Mem. I.E.E.E., Instrument Soc. Am. Home: 5401 10th Ct Birmingham AL 35222 Office: Rust Engring Co 1130 S 22d St Birmingham AL 35201

DILL, GEORGE CURTIS, airways exec.; b. Tampa, Fla., Nov. 20, 1937; s. George Erin and Edith Carmen (Gonzalez) D.; student U. Tampa, 1955-56; B.S., Fla. So. Coll., 1959; Advt. asst. Fla. div. FMC Corp., Lakeland, 1961-63; supr. pub. relations aerospace services div. Pan Am. World Airways, Cape Kennedy, Fla., 1963—. Served with USNR, 1959-61. Mem. Cape Kennedy Pub. Relations Assn. (chmn. 1969), Delta Sigma Pi. Republican. Episcopalian. Home: PO Box 1370 Cocoa Beach FL 32931 Office: Pan Am World Airways Box 4187 Patrick AFB FL 32929

DILLABER, PHILIP ARTHUR, govt. budget analyst; b. Springfield, Mass., Aug. 24, 1922; s. Ralph E. and Grace (Holman) D.; B.A., Am. Internat. Coll., 1949; M.B.A., Ind. U., 1950; postgrad. U. Mich., Ind. U., 1950-54; m. Jacqueline M. Bertin, July 16, 1946; children—Anne Erline (Mrs. Donald Youngblood), Katherine Marie, John Philip, Patricia Elizabeth. Clk. research and devel. div. Springfield Armory, 1946-47; research asst. dept. econs. Ind. U., 1951, lectr. econs., 1955-57; orgn. and methods examiner U.S. Air Force, Gulfport, Miss., 1952-53; mgmt. analyst 5th U.S. Army, Chgo., 1954-61; program progress and resources mgmt. analyst Continental Army Command, Ft. Monroe, Va., 1962-66; adminstrv. officer U.S. Army NIKE-X System Office, Alexandria, Va., 1967; program analyst Office Asst. Chief Staff Force Devel., Dept. Army, Washington, 1967-71; budget analyst Office Dep. Chief Staff Logistics Dept. Army, Washington, 1971-74; budget analyst Office Dep. Chief Staff Research, Devel. and Acquisition, 1974—; guest lectr. econs. Purdue U., 1959-61. Served with AUS, 1943-46. Mem. Am. Econ. Assn., Am. Soc. Pub. Adminstrn., Beta Gamma Sigma. Home: 3003 N Arkendale St Woodbridge VA 22191 Office: Dept Army Office Dep Chief Staff Research Devel and Acquisition Pentagon Washington DC 20301

DILLAHUNTY, WILBUR HARRIS, U.S. atty.; b. Memphis, June 30, 1928; s. Joseph Silas and Octavia (Jones) D.; J.D., U. Ark., 1954; m. Emma Cox, Nov. 25, 1948; 1 dau., Sharon Kaye. Admitted to Ark. bar; practiced, West Memphis, Ark., 1954-58; U.S. dist. atty., Eastern Ark., Little Rock, 1968—. West Memphis city atty., 1958-68. Served with AUS, 1945-48. Named Young Man of Year, Crittenden County, Ark., 1961. Mem. Crittenden County Bar Assn. (past pres.), Omicron Delta Kappa, Delta Theta Phi. Club: Meadowbrook Country (West Memphis). Home: 9710 Catskill Rd Little Rock AR 72207 Office: Courthouse Bldg 5th and Gaines Sts Little Rock AR 72203

DILLARD, ALEXANDER FLEET, JR., lawyer; b. Richmond, Va., May 18, 1938; s. Alexander Fleet and Elizabeth Burwell (Ware) D.; B.A., Hampden-Sydney Coll., 1959; LL.B., U. Richmond, 1962; m. Rebecca Lucretia Keesee, Feb. 22, 1964; children—Ella Grey, Sarah Browne, Alexander Fleet III. Admitted to Va. bar, 1962; practiced in Tappahannock, 1966—; substitute county judge, Essex, Richmond, Northumberland, Lancaster and Westmoreland counties, 1967-68. Trustee Aylett County Day Sch., Millers Taverns, Va. Served to lt. comdr. USNR, 1963-66. Mem. Theta Chi, Delta Theta Phi. Rotarian. Club: Essex County Ruritan (pres. 1972). Home: RFD Dunnsville VA 22554 Office: 221 Queen St Tappahannock VA 22560

DILLARD, JACK HAMNER, research adminstr.; b. Charlottesville, Va., Aug. 4, 1924; s. Charles Leo and Addie (Fairfax) D.; B.C.E., U. Va., 1950, M.C.E., 1954; m. Mildred Amelia Newton, Jan. 1, 1948; children—Lisa Marie, Charles Fairfax, Robert Newton. Head bituminous research activities U. Va., 1952-68, lectr. dept. humanities Sch. Continuing Edn., 1955-68; head Va. Hwy. Research Council, Charlottesville, 1968—. Served with USNR, 1943-46. Mem. Assn. Asphalt Paving Technologists, Hwy. Research Bd. (bituminous sect.), Am. Soc. Testing Materials. Contbr. articles to profl. jours. Home: Route 1 Box 3N Keswick VA 22947 Office: Box 3817 Univ Sta Charlottesville VA 22903

DILLARD, JAMES WILLIAM, coll. pres.; b. Lubbock, Tex., June 28, 1910; s. Robert Jefferson and Mary (Gearing) D.; student Clarendon Jr. Coll., 1929-31; B.S. and M.A., West Tex. State Coll., 1939; m. Edna Gerlach, Aug. 22, 1932; children—Barbara Elaine, Edna Carolyn. Supt. Alanreed (Tex.) pub. sch., 1931-37; prin. Spring Creek pub. sch., Borger, Tex., 1937-46; supt. Hutchinson County Schs., Borger, 1946-48; dean Frank Phillips Coll., Borger, 1948-55, pres., 1955—. Dist. chmn., area exec. com. Adobe Walls council Boy Scouts Am. Served as lt. USNR, 1943-46. Decorated Am. Theatre, Phillippine Asiatic-Pacific, Victory medals. Mem. N.E.A., Am. Assn. Sch. Adminstrs., Tex. Tchrs. Assn., Tex. Jr. Coll. Tchrs. Assn., Panhandle Plains Supts. Assn. (past pres.), Tex. Jr. Coll. Athletic Conf. (past pres.), Alpha Chi. Methodist. Mason, Rotarian (past pres.). Home: 1105 College Av Borger TX 79007

DILLARD, MAX MURRAY, oil drilling co. exec.; b. Lueders, Tex., Nov. 21, 1935; s. Alva Clemens and Effie Carroll (Murray) D.; B.S., U. Tex. at Austin, 1959; student Ranger Jr. Coll., 1953-55; m. Carol Gayle Jenkins, Dec. 27, 1957; children—Denise Gayle, Pamela Deann, Julie Ann. Drilling engr. Offshore Co., Houston, 1959-61, Great Western Drilling Co., Midland, Tex., 1961-63; operations mgr. Arrow Drilling Co., Tulsa, 1963-64; Western states sales mgr. Reed Drilling Tools, Inc., Los Angeles, 1964-67; operations mgr. Peter Bawden Drilling, Inc., Long Beach, Cal., 1967-69; chmn. bd., pres. Bandera, Inc., 1969—; pres. Bandera Drilling Co., Dallas, 1969—, also dir.; exec. v.p. Drillers, Inc., Wichita. Mem. Los Angeles Petroleum Club, Am. Petroleum Inst., Nat. Soc. Profl. Engrs., Internat. Assn. Drilling Contractors. Republican. Club: Los Angeles Athletic. Contbr. articles to profl. jours. Home: 7949 LaCosa St Dallas TX 75240 Office: Bandera Inc 160 Meadows Bldg Dallas TX 75206

DILLARD, RODNEY JEFFERSON, real estate broker; b. Short Hills, N.J., Jan. 1, 1939; s. Albert Jefferson and Anne E. (Willingham) D.; student Morristown Sch. (N.J.), 1953-55, Salisbury Sch. (Conn.), 1955-57; B.A., Rollins Coll., 1961; m. Anne Palfrey Lanston, June 10, 1961; children—Courtney Lanston, Carter Jefferson. With A.M. Kidder Co., N.Y.C., 1961-62; with Previews Inc., N.Y.C., 1962-63, Palm Beach, Fla., 1963—, regional v.p. 1967-70, v.p., 1970—. Mem. Internat. Real Estate Fedn. Clubs: Everglades, Bath and Tennis (Palm Beach). Home: 1555 N Lake Way Palm Beach FL 33480 Office: 309 Royal Poinciana Plaza Palm Beach FL 33480

DILLINGHAM, PAUL L., JR., soft drink co. exec.; b. Madisonville, Ky., Nov. 16, 1927; s. Paul L. and Mary Elizabeth (Braun) D.; B.S., U. Ky., 1950; postgrad. Harvard, 1966; m. Barbara Ruth Rosson, Apr. 21, 1951; children—Deborah Ruth (Mrs. William L. Durham, Jr.), Doris Elizabeth, Karen Sue. Supr. income taxes Ky. Dept. Revenue, 1950-55; pvt. practice pub. accounting, Frankfort, Ky., 1955-57; controller So. Transport Inc., Atlanta, 1957-58; prin. tax accountant, asst. dir. taxes, asst. treas., dir. taxes, v.p. Coca Cola Co., Atlanta, 1958—. Co-chmn. Greater Atlanta Heart Fund Campaign, 1970-72; pres. Consumer Credit Counseling Greater Atlanta, 1972-73. Mem. pres.'s council Oglethorpe U., Atlanta; mem. exec. com. agy. relations and allocations div. United Way of Atlanta. Served with AUS, 1946-47. Mem. Ga. Soc. C.P.A.'s, U.S. C. of C., Financial Execs. Inst., Tax Execs. Inst. (internat. pres. 1972—), Sigma Nu. Presbyn. Kiwanian. Home: 975 River Overlook Ct NW Atlanta GA 30328 Office: PO Drawer 1734 Atlanta GA 30301

DILLINGHAM, WILLIAM PYRLE, economist, educator; b. Dorset, Vt., Mar. 4, 1909; s. Stephen R. and Mary Luisa (Chapman) D.; A.B., U. Fla., 1934; M.S., U. Tenn., 1942; Ph.D., Duke U., 1950; m. Mary Marjorie Carter, Dec. 25, 1943; children—William Pyrle (dec.), Robert Carter, Sharon Elizabeth. Tchr. high sch., Ft. Lauderdale, Fla., 1934-38, Durham, N.C., 1938-42; mem. faculty South Ga. Coll., Douglas, 1942-43, Madison Coll., Harrisonburg, Va., 1943-44; instr. Duke, 1944-47; asst. prof. econs. U. Ga., Athens, 1947-49; asst. prof. econs. Fla. State U., Tallahassee, 1949-52, asso. prof., 1952-56, prof., 1956—, dir. grad. studies, 1963-70, dir. Center for Econ. Edn., 1971—. Fulbright prof. U. Madrid, U. Barcelona, 1961-62; Fulbright prof. Nat. U. del Rosario (Argentina), 1970. Sr. cons. President's Commn. on Vets. Pensions, 1955. Asso. mem. Fla. Citizens Tax Council, 1955-56. Mem. Am., Soc. econ. assns., Nat. Tax Assn., Tax Inst., Kappa Phi Kappa, Kappa Delta Pi, Phi Delta Kappa, Omicron Delta Epsilon, Alpha Kappa Psi, Pi Omega Pi, Phi Kappa Phi, Sigma Delta Pi. Home: 2109 Trescott Dr Tallahassee FL 32303

DILLMAN, GEORGE FRANKLIN, operating co. exec.; b. Coronado, Cal., Sept. 5, 1934; s. Wilbur Mitchell and Meadie (Ables) D.; student Abilene Christian Coll., 1952; B.S., B.B. A., U. Tex., 1958; m. Virginia Gayle Yeary, Sept. 1, 1961; children—Leesa Gayle, Mitchell Lynn, Virginia Louise, Laura Lynn. Asso. Bus. Research Corp. Tex., Austin, 1957-61; dir. econ. research Pacific Western Properties, Inc., Los Angeles, 1961; dir. corporate relations, econ. research Diversa, Inc., Dallas, 1961-62, Corporate Sec., 1962-65, v.p., corp. sec., dir., 1965-67; chmn. bd., pres. Bonanza Internat., 1965-67; chmn. Dillman-Berry & Assos., Dallas, 1968—; chmn., dir. Richardson Savs. & Loan Assn., 1965—. Mem. univ. bd. Pepperdine Coll., Los Angeles. Mem. bd., past pres. Dallas Assembly; chmn. Tex. Tourist Devel. Agy., Urban Rehab. Standards Bd. City of Dallas. Served with USNR, 1952-55. Democrat. Mem. Ch. of Christ. Clubs: Royal Oaks Country, Dallas Press (Dallas); Headliners (Austin). Contbr. articles to profl. and ch. jours. Home: 13361 Peyton Dr Dallas TX 75214 Office: Richardson Savs and Loan Bldg Richardson TX 75080

DILLON, CLARENCE EDWARD, clergyman; b. South Charleston, W.Va., Jan. 30, 1933; s. James Wesley, Sr., and Hurtle Gladys (King) D.; student W.Va. State Coll., 1955-64, Morris Harvey Coll., 1963-64; m. Shirley Ann Hill, Apr. 3, 1953; children—Karen Lynn (Mrs. Johnnie Hayes Milstead), Sharon Kay (Mrs. Anthony Eugene Pompelia), Angela Carol, Judith Ann. Laborer, lab. asst. chemist Union Carbide Chems. Co., 1951-64; ordained to ministry Ch. of God-Anderson, Ind., 1965; pastor 1st Ch. of God, Point Pleasant, W.Va., 1964-67, Rock Creek Ch. of God, Bessemer, Ala., 1967-72, Parkview Ch. of God, Meridian, Miss., 1972—. Chmn. Ala. Ministers Fellowship Ch. of God, 1970-71; active numerous regional ch. bds. and coms. Served with AUS, 1953-55; ETO. Mason. Home: 1739 46th Av Meridian MS 39301 Office: 1625 45th Av Meridian MS 39301

DILLON, ROBERT CHESTER, lawyer; b. Birmingham, Ala., May 17, 1931; s. Chester C. and Martha R. (Keith) D.; A.B., U. Ala., 1953, LL.B., 1957; m. Helen C. Frizzle, Sept. 20, 1957; children—Robert C., Susan B., Helen Leigh. Admitted to Ala. bar, 1957; law clk. Supreme Ct. Ala., 1957-58; asst. atty. gen. Ala., 1958-59; individual practice law, Anniston, Ala., 1959—; mem. firm Knox Jones Woolf & Merrill. Chmn. Calhoun County A.R.C., 1970-71. Served to 1st lt. AUS, 1953-55. Mem. Am., Ala., Calhoun County (pres. 1972) bar assns. Rotarian. Club: Anniston Country. Home: 421 Wildwood Rd Anniston AL 36201 Office: PO Box 580 Anniston AL 36201

DILLON, ROBERT MORTON, research exec.; b. Seattle, Oct. 27, 1923; s. James Richard and Lucille (Morton) D.; student U. Ill., 1946-47; B.Arch., U. Wash., 1949; M.Arch., U. Fla., 1954; m. Mary Charlotte Beeson, Jan. 6, 1943; children—Robert Thomas, Colleen Marie, Patrick Morton, Draftsman, Williams and Longstreet, Architects, Greenville, S.C., 1949-50; designer G. Lyles, Bissett, Carlisle & Wolf, Architects, Columbia, S.C., 1950, Robert M. Dillon and Wm. B. Eaton, Architects, Gainesville, Fla., 1952-55; staff architect, proj. dir. Bldg. Research Adv. Bd., Nat. Acad. Scis.-NRC, Washington, 1955-58, exec. dir., 1958—, exec. sec. U.S. nat. com. for Conseil Internat. du Batiment, 1962—. Sec. U.S. Planning Com. 2d Internat. Conf. on Permafrost, U.S.S.R., 1973. Asst. prof. architecture Clemson Coll., 1949-50; instr., asst. prof. architecture U. Fla., 1950-55; lectr. civil engring. Catholic U. Am., 1957-63; distinguished faculty Acad. Code Adminstrn. and Enforcement, U. Ill., 1972—; Professorial lectr. engring. George Washington U., 1973—. Cons. Ednl. Facilities Labs., N.Y.C., 1958-71. Mem. adv. com., low-income housing demonstration program Dept. Housing and Urban Devel., Washington, 1964-67; mem. sub-panel on housing White House Panel on Civilian Tech., Washington, 1961-62; mem. adv. council Basic Homes Program OEO and HUD, 1972—. Served with USNR, 1942-45. Mem. A.I.A. (mem. com. on research for architecture 1962-67, chmn. 1969; chmn. com. archtl. barriers 1967-68, mem. housing com. 1970-72), N.Y. Acad. Sci., A.A.A.S., Nat. Acad. Code Adminstrn., Am. Real Estate and Urban Econs. Assn., Sigma Lambda Chi. Author: (with S.W. Crawley) Steel Buildings: Analysis and Design, 1970. Home: 811 Arrington Dr Silver Spring MD 20901 Office: 2101 Constitution Av Washington DC 20418

DILS, ROBERT JAMES, educator; b. Dayton, O., Oct. 2, 1919; d. Lawrence Elsworth and Maudie Marguerette (Koogler) D.; B.S., Eastern Ky. U., 1939-43; M.A., Marshall U., 1960; postgrad. Ohio State U., 1962-64; m. Juanita B. Graber, Aug. 9, 1947; children—Susan (Mrs. Leroy Mayne), Robert James II, Norma, Jo. Tchr. Ashland (Ky.) High Sch., 1948-51, Jr. Coll., Ashland, 1951-57; chmn. sci. dept. Paul G. Blazer High Sch., Ashland, 1958-62; asso. prof. sci. Marshall U., Huntington, W.Va., 1964—. Mem. exec. com. Tri-State council Boy Scouts Am., 1970—; radiol. def. officer Cabel County Civil Def., 1968—. Served with USAAF, 1943-45. Decorated Air medal. NSF grantee. Mem. A.A.A.S., Phi Delta Kappa, Kappa Delta Pi. Republican. Baptist (deacon 1964—). Home: 2514 Elm St Ashland KY 41101 Office: 3d Av and 16th Huntington WV 25701

DILWORTH, BILLY D., newspaperman; b. Martin, Ga., Oct. 4; 1934; s. B.Q. and Pearl (Davis) D.; student journalism U. Ga. Ga. editor Anderson (S.C.) Ind., 1953-63; state editor Atlanta Times, 1964-65, Athens (Ga.) Daily News, 1967-72, The Anderson Independent, 1972—; host programs radio sta. WLET, Toccoa, Ga., 1960—, sta. WSPA-TV, Spartanburg, S.C., 1968—. Mem. Ga. Scholarship Commn., 1971—. Recipient A.P. award reporting and news photo, 1963. Address: Box 117 Carnesville GA 30521

DILWORTH, JAMES WELDON, lawyer; b. San Antonio, Jan. 1, 1928; s. William H. and Bertie (Lawrence) D.; student U. Houston, 1949-51; LL.B. cum laude, Baylor U., 1953; m. Marie Miller, Mar. 10, 1945; children—Patricia Ann, Pamela Sue, James Weldon. Admitted to Tex. bar, 1953; asso. Andrews, Kurth, Campell & Jones, Houston, 1953-64, partner, 1964—. Spl. counsel for trustee in charge investigation Westec Corp., Houston, Dallas, Chgo., N.Y.C., 1966—. Bd. dirs. Houston Grand Opera Assn. Mem. Houston Heritage Soc., Mus Fine Arts. Served with AUS, 1946-47. Mem. Tex. Bar. Am. (mem. anti-trust, family law sects.), Houston bar assns. Methodist. Clubs: Houston Country, Petroleum (Houston). Home: 1 Hedwig Ct Houston TX 77024 Office: Exxon Bldg Houston TX 77002

DIMITROFF, EDWARD, chemist; b. Nancy, France, Feb. 27, 1917; s. Stantcho Stantcheff and Marguerite Louise (Virrion) D.; student U. Medicine, Nancy, 1946-48; B.S., U. Denver, 1956; M.S., St. Marys U., San Antonio, 1965; m. Dorothy Mae Queen, Nov. 24, 1951; children—John, Monique. Came to U.S., 1950, naturalized, 1955. Aero. research chemist Naval Ordnance Test Sta., China Lake, Cal., 1956-59; mgr., staff scientist petroleum chemistry research Southwest Research Inst., San Antonio, 1959—. Fellow Am. Inst. Chemists; mem. Am. Chem. Soc., Am. Soc. Testing Materials, N.Y. Acad. Scis., Soc. Automotive Engrs. Contbr. articles to profl. jours. Home: 4838 Rollingfield Dr San Antonio TX 78228 Office: 8500 Culebra Rd San Antonio TX 78228

DIMLING, JOHN ARTHUR, JR., assn. exec.; b. Pitts., Apr. 9, 1938; s. John A. and Elizabeth (Powell) D.; A.B., Dartmouth, 1960; M.S., Carnegie Inst. Tech., 1962; m. Anne Stewart Hogg, Sept. 10, 1960. Trainee U.S. Steel Corp., Pitts., 1960-62, cost analyst, 1962-63; sr. scientist Spindletop Research, Lexington, Ky., 1965-67, mgr. communications and systems, 1967-69; v.p. Nat. Assn. Broadcasters, Washington, 1969—. Sec.-treas. Broadcast Rating Council, N.Y.C., 1971—; adviser Ky. Ednl. TV Authority, 1968-69. Served to 1st lt. AUS, 1963-65. Mem. Operations Research Soc. Am., Inst. Mgmt. Scis., Am. Econ. Assn., Am. Assn. for Pub. Opinion research. Spindletop Hall, Phi Beta Kappa. Club: Dartmouth (N.Y.C.). Home: 7923 Inverness Ridge Potomac MD 20854 Office: 1771 N St NW Washington DC 20036

DIMMITT, KATHRYNE ELDER COOKSEY (MRS. JAMES E. COREY), artist; b. Washington, May 8, 1910; d. Claude Bonifant and Bessie (Suite) Cooksey; A.B., Conn. Coll., 1932; m. E. Hewitt Dimmitt, July 11, 1939 (dec. Aug. 1957); m. 2d, James E. Corey, Jan. 19, 1971. Illustrator, mus. preparator artist Nat. Park Service, Dept. Interior, Washington, and Yorktown, Va., 1934-35, illustrator Bur. Reclamation, Washington, 1935-38, 40-45, 60-65; diorama artist Office of Exhibits, N.Y. World's Fair, 1938-40. Exhibited in groups shows at Smithsonian Instn., 1946-52, Corcoran Gallery of Art, 1944-46, Arts Club Washington, 1962-74. Recipient 1st prize Mid-Atlantic Regional Art Exhibit, 1955; 1st prize landscape Nat. League Am. Pen Women, 1948, 55, 63, best oil in show, 1963; Superior Performance award Dept. Interior, 1961. Mem. Nat. League Am. Pen Women (nat. art bd. 1956-66), Miniature Painters, Sculptors and Gravers Soc. Washington (pres. 1970-72), Arts Club Washington (exhibits chmn. 1968-70), Conn. Coll. Alumnae Assn. (chpt. pres. 1943-44), P.E.O. (chpt. pres. 1953-55). Home: 5801 Massachusetts Av Washington DC 20016

DI PIETRO, ROBERT JOSEPH, sci. linguist; b. Endicott, N.Y., July 18, 1932; s. Americo and Mary Di P.; B.A., Harpur Coll., State U. N.Y. at Binghamton, 1950-54; M.A., Harvard 1955; Ph.D., Cornell U., 1960; m. Vincenzina Angela Giallo, Sept. 5, 1953; children—Angela Maria, Mark Andrew. Instr. English, Boston Sch. Modern Lang., 1955-56; instr., grad. fellow Cornell U., 1957-60; jr. lectr. linguistics U. Rome (Italy), 1960; asst. prof. linguistics Georgetown U., Washington 1961-64, asso. prof., 1964-69, prof., 1969—, head div. Italian, 1966-68, sr. lectr. linguistics U. Madrid (Spain), 1963-64; Spanish lang. proficiency tester Peace Corps Vols., Venezuela, 1965; cons. editor Ginn-Blaisdell Pub. Co., Waltham, Mass., 1964-72. Fulbright grantee, 1960, 63. Mem. Am. Assn. Tchrs. Italian (chpt. pres. 1968-69), Linguistic Soc. Am., A.A.A.S., Am. Anthrop. Assn., Washington Linguistics Club (pres. 1967-68). Author: (with F.B. Agard) Sounds of English and Italian (Vol. I), 1965; Grammatical Structures of English and Italian (vol. II), 1965, 2d edit., 1969; Language Structures in Contrast, 1971. Book rev. editor Modern Lang. Jour., 1972—. Contbr. articles in field to profl. jours. Home: 1706 Woodman Dr McLean VA 22101 Office: Georgetown U Washington DC 20007

DIPLACIDO, FRANCIS PAUL, JR., dentist; b. Phila., Dec. 25, 1934; s. Francis Paul and Elizabeth Marie (deMaria) DiP.; B.S. in Biology, St. Josephs Coll., 1956; D.D.S., U. Pa. Sch. Dentistry, 1962; postgrad. U. Pa. Grad. Sch. Medicine, 1965; m. Noreen M. Bamford, June 14, 1969; children—Francis Paul, III, Damon Samuel. Resident oral surgery U. Pa., 1965-68; pvt. practice oral surgery, Fort Myers, Fla., 1968—. Sec., S.W. Fla. Flyers; pres. Southwest Amusements, Inc., 1970-71; v.p. Palace Constrn. Co., Inc., 1971—; treas., dir. Flordeco, Inc. Bd. dirs. Boys Clubs of Lee County. Served with AUS, 1962-65. Diplomate Am. Bd. Oral Surgery. Mem. Am., Fla. dental assns., Southwest Fla. Dental Soc. (pres. 1974), Am. Soc. Oral Surgeons, Internat. Assn. Oral Surgeons, Internat. Soc. Maxillofacial Surgeons, Am. Dental Soc. Anesthesiology. Republican. Roman Catholic. Clubs: Cypress Lake Country, Royal Palm Yacht, Sandpiper (dir.) (Fort Myers). Home: 6696 Overlook Dr Fort Myers FL 33901 Office: 3900 S Broadway Fort Myers FL 33901

DIRECTOR, HERMAN, furniture co. exec.; b. Bremen, Germany, May 15, 1915; s. Simon and Bertha (Yeserski) D.; m. Lillian Rosenzweig; children—Steven, Dennis, Toby. Came to U.S., 1934, naturalized 1939. Pres. Dir. Enterprises, Inc., Savannah, Ga., 1970—. Pres., Savannah Jewish Council, 1959-61; chmn. Israeli Bond drive, 1960-61; mem. Park and Tree Commn., 1961-66; mem. Bd. Edn., 1963-69, pres., 1969. Bd. dirs. A.R.C., 1960-62. Served with USAAF, 1942-46. Mem. Savannah Retail Furniture Assn. (pres. 1959-61), Greater Downtown Bus. Assn. (pres. 1971). Home: 4710 Fairfax Dr Savannah GA 31405 Office: 401 W Broughton St Savannah GA 31402

DI SANT'AGNESE, PAUL EMILIO ARTOM, physician; b. Rome, Italy, Apr. 23, 1914; s. Valerie Artom and Rosita (Sinigaglia) di Sant'A.; M.D., U. Rome, 1938; D.M.S., Columbia, 1948; Dr. Med. (hon.), Justus Liebig U., Giessen, West Germany, 1962; m. Elizabeth Boryzewski, Feb. 14, 1943; children—Paul Anthony, Valerie Anne. Came to U.S., 1939, naturalized, 1945. Rotating intern, Rome, 1938-39; intern N.Y. Postgrad. Hosp., 1940-41, asst. resident, 1942-43, chief resident, 1943-44; intern Willard Park Hosp., N.Y.C., 1941-42; Koplik fellow pediatrics Babies Hosp., N.Y.C., 1944; asst. in pediatrics Presbyn. Hosp., N.Y.C., 1944-46, asst. attending pediatrician, 1948-59, chief cystic fibrosis and celiac clinic, head cystic fibrosis program, 1951-59; instr. pediatrics Columbia Coll. Phys. and Surg., 1944-46, asso. in pediatrics, 1946-51, asst. prof. pediatrics, 1951-59; chief pediatric div. Vanderbilt Clinic, 1944-53; chief pediatric metabolism br. Nat. Inst. Arthritis and Metabolic Diseases, NIH, 1960—; clin. prof. pediatrics Georgetown U. Med. Sch., 1960—; dir. cystic fibrosis care Research and Teaching Center, Children's Hosp., Washington, 1960-67, cons., 1960—. Vice chmn., chmn. gen. med. and sci. adv. council, trustee Nat. Cystic Fibrosis Research Found., 1962-67, founder-mem. exec. com., chmn. research com., 1967—; chmn. med. sci. adv. council Internat. Cystic Fibrosis Assn., 1965-69, founder-trustee, mem. exec. com., 1965—. Diplomate Am. Bd. Pediatrics. Mem. Am. Pediatric Soc., Soc. Pediatric Research, Am. Acad. Pediatrics, N.Y. Acad. Medicine, N.Y. Acad. Scis., Harvey Soc., A.M.A., Babies Hosp. Alumni Assn., Med. Soc. D.C., Am. Inst. Nutrition, N.Y. County Med. Soc., Am. Pub. Health Assn., Am. Thoracic Assn. Research cystic fibrosis, pancreas, pediatric gastroenterology, glycogen storage disease, immunology in children. Home: 4928 Sentinel Dr Washington DC 20016 Office: NIH Bethesda MD 20014

DISANTO, FRANK MICHAEL, industrialist; b. N.Y.C., July 12, 1924; s. Rocco and Filomena (DiBiase) DiS.; B.S., Phila. Textile Inst., 1949; m. Grace Johanna DeMarco, Aug. 30, 1946; children—Frank Richard, Bernadette Mary, Roxanne Judith. Plant mgr. Housatonic Dyeing & Printing Co., Derby, Conn., 1951-54; pres. Bay State Dyeing & Finishing Corp., Bondsville, Mass., 1954-61; pres. Morganton Dyeing & Finishing Corp. (N.C.), 1961—; sec. Grace Sales Corp., N.Y.C.; pres. Mimosa Specialty Co., Morganton, Rank Realty Co., Morganton; v.p. Joel Finishing, Inc., Wilmington, Del.; sec. Astro Chem. Corp., Morganton; dir. Wachovia Bank & Trust Co., Western Carolina Industries; mem. exec. com. Attacoa, Inc. Bd. dirs. United Fund, Western Piedmont Community Coll. Found. Served with USNR, 1943-46. Mem. Am. Assn. Textile Colorists and Chemists, Community Mgmt. Soc. (pres.), Newcomen Soc. N.Am., C. of C., Phi Psi. Roman Catholic. Clubs: Catawba Valley Executives, Mimosa Golf, Lenoir Country; Asheville City, Grandfather Golf and Country. Home: 218 Riverside Dr Morganton NC 28655 Office: Morganton Dyeing and Finishing Corp Morganton NC 28655

DI SANTO, GRACE JOHANNE DEMARCO (MRS. FRANK MICHAEL DI SANTO), civic worker; b. Derby, Conn., July 12, 1924; d. Richard and Frances (DeMarco) De Marco; student N.Y. U. Sch. Journalism, 1941-43; m. Frank Michael Di Santo, Aug. 30, 1946; children—Frank Richard, Bernadette Mary, Roxanne Judith. Newswriter, Australian Asso. Press, N.Y.C., 1942-43; staff reporter Ansonia Sentinel, Derby, 1943-45; feature writer, drama critic Bridgeport Herald, New Haven, 1945-46; editor monthly bull. Pa. State Coll. Optometry, Phila., 1947-48; free-lance writer, 1949-54; founder, pres. bd. Investors Ltd., Morganton, N.C., 1966-67. Pres., Catholic Ladies' Guild, Morganton, 1965-66, Morganton Garden Club, 1966-67, Burke County chpt. N.C. Symphony Soc., 1968-70; mem. exec. bd. Community Concerts Assn., 1962-73; mem. Am. Field Service program Burke County, 1969-70; active Burke County Heart Fund, Burke County Council Garden Clubs; mem. exec. bd., chmn. room reps. Forest Hill P.T.A., 1968-70; Burke County chmn. nat. humanities series Woodrow Wilson Fellowship Found. Bd. dirs. Burke county chpt. March of Dimes, 1966—; trustee N.C. Symphony Soc., 1965-73. Republican. Roman Catholic (pres. St. Charles Borromeo Ladies Guild 1965-66. Clubs: Schubert Music; Morganton Friday Afternoon Bridge, Lenoir Country (N.C.); Grandfather Golf and Country (Linville, N.C.); Mimosa Hills Golf. Address: 218 Riverside Dr Morganton NC 28655

DISTELHORST, CARL FREDERICK, financial cons.; b. Burlington, Ia., May 16, 1906; s. Charles H. and Augusta (Loose) D.; B.S. in Commerce, U. Ia., 1928; M.Litt., U. Pitts., 1936; m. Josephine Harris Smith, July 9, 1932; children—Craig T., Lynn H. Instr. accounting and Finance U. Tenn., 1928-30; instr. accounting U. Pitts., 1930-38, Am. Inst. Banking, 1930-42, Am. Savs. and Loan Inst., 1931-42; asst. to pres. Fed. Home Loan Bank Pitts., 1938-42; staff v.p. U.S. Savs and Loan League, also sec. Am. Savs. and Loan Inst., 1942-43; pres. Council Insured Savs. Assns. N.Y. State, 1943-46; exec. v.p. Am. Savs. and Loan Inst., exec. dir. Grad. Sch. Savs. and Loan, 1946-55; exec. v.p. Fla. Savs. and Loan League, 1955-62; financial cons., Winter Park, Fla., 1962—; dir. Winter Park Fed. Savs. & Loan Assn., Farm & Home Savs. Assn., Nevada, Mo., Comml. Loan Ins. Corp., N.Y. Guaranty Ins. Corp., MGIC Investment Corp.; dir. Mortgage Guaranty Ins. Corp. Wis., 1960—, mem. exec. com., 1965—; dir., mem. exec. com. MGIC Financial Corp., Financial Data Scis., Inc.; dir. Am. Municipal Bond Assurance Corp., Fla. Informanagement Services, Inc., MGIC Credit Ins. Corp., Caltrop Corp., Caltex Corp., Fiscanex, Ltd. (Can.). Mem. Savs. and Loan Adv. Com. to Sec. Treasury, 1956-71; mem. adv. council on naval affairs 6th Naval Dist., 1957-63. Mem. Highland Park (Ill.) Dist. Sch. Bd., 1950-53. Bd. dirs., sec. Savs. and Loan Found., Washington. Mem. Am. Savs. and Loan Inst. (hon. life trustee dir.); Nat. Planning Assn. (nat. council), Royal Soc. Arts (London, Eng., Benjamin Franklin fellow), Navy League U.S., Am. Finance Assn., Lambda Alpha, Beta Gamma Sigma, Omicron Delta Kappa, Alpha Sigma Phi, Delta Sigma Pi. Republican. Presbyn. Rotarian. Club: Citrus (Orlando, Fla.). Contbr. to books, encys., profl. jours. Address: 141 Alexander Pl Winter Park FL 32789

DIVERS, ALAN GERALD, banker; b. Detroit, Sept. 17, 1935; s. Earle Leland and Dorotha Evelyn (Unger) D.; B.S. in Bus. Adminstrn. U. Fla., 1957; m. Jean Bacon, Apr. 18, 1964; children—Alan Blaec, Brett Devereux. With Exchange Nat. Bank of Tampa, Fla., 1961—, v.p., 1967-73, sr. v.p., 1973—, also dir.; v.p. Exchange Bancorp; dir. Exchange Bank & Trust Co., Clearwater, Exchange Bank of West Shore, Tampa. Pres., Southwest Fla. Blood Bank, Inc., 1970—; treas., Fla. West Coast Ednl. TV, 1967—. Bd. dirs. Community Coordinating Council, Fla. State Fair and Gasparilla Assn., The Childrens Home, Old Peoples Home Assn.; treas., trustee Berkeley Preparatory Sch. Served to lt. comdr. USNR, 1957-61. Mem. Robert Morris Assos., Am. Inst. Banking, Phi Delta Theta. Republican. Episcopalian. Rotarian. Clubs: Merrymakers, University (dir.), Ye Mystic Krewe of Gasparilla, Tampa Yacht and Country (Tampa). Home: 812 Bayside Dr Tampa FL 33609 Office: PO Box 1809 Tampa FL 33601

DIXON, ALVIN TERRELL, mgmt. cons.; b. Okmulgee, Okla., July 4, 1909; s. Alvin Ernest and Minnie (Ramsey) D.; student U. Mo., 1926-27; B.A., U. Okla., 1962; m. Virginia Lee Francis, Sept. 17, 1938; 1 son, Terrell Francis. Prodn. mgr. Denver Producing & Refining Co., Oklahoma City, 1930-37; chief accountant Seaboard Oil Co. Del., Dallas, 1937-43; dir. controls Nat. Geophys. Co., Dallas, 1943-45; propr. Dixon-Dallas, Bus. Consultants, 1945-48; comptroller Okla. State Tech. Coll., 1949-55; cost accountant Ball Bros. Glass Co., Okmulgee, Okla., 1955-57; mgmt. cons. USAF, Oklahoma City, 1958—. Bd. dirs. Creek Nation council, Boy Scouts Am., Okmulgee, 1955-57, Ark. River Devel. Com., 1956-57. Mem. Am. Inst. C.P.A.'s, Am. Accountants Assn., Tex., Okla. State socs. C.P.A.'s, Fed. Govt. Accountants Assn., Tinker AFB Mgmt. Club, Delta Sigma Pi. Republican. Mem. Christian Ch. Clubs: Rotary, Toastmasters (pres. 1954-55). Home: 1215 Caddell Lane Norman OK 73069 Office: Tinker AFB USAF Logistics Command Oklahoma City OK 73145

DIXON, CLARENCE CURTIS, ednl. adminstr.; b. Richlands, Va., Dec. 12, 1935; s. Clarence Miller and Carrie May (Elam) D.; B.S., E. Tenn. State Coll., 1958, Ma.A., 1963; Ed.D., U. Ga., 1972; m. Rosemary Ferguson, June 7, 1958; children—Curtis Shelburne, Christopher Charles. With Atlanta Pub. Schs., 1959—, prin. Roosevelt High Sch., 1969-73, Northside High Sch., 1973—. Mem. vis. faculty Bank St. Coll. Edn., summer 1967; cons. to sch. systems in Ala. Bd. dirs. Central Community Br. YMCA. Mem. Nat., Ga., Atlanta (v.p. 1967-68) edn. assns., N.G. Assn. U.S. and Ga., Assn. Supervision and Curriculum Devel., Kappa Phi Kappa. Club: Civitan (pres. 1969-70). Home: 2745 Old Spanish Trail College Park GA 30349 Office: 2875 Northside Dr NW Atlanta GA 30305

DIXON, EVA CRAWFORD JOHNSON, librarian; b. Evinston, Fla., Aug. 28, 1909; d. William Alpheus and Willie (Crawford) Johnson; A.B. in Edn. with honors, U. Fla., 1937, M.A., 1948; postgrad. Fla. State U., 1950, Appalachian State Tchrs. Coll., 1955; Ph.D. (hon.), Colo. State Christian Coll., 1973; m. Thomas Gordon Dixon, Dec. 14, 1935 (div. 1944). Tchr., English, librarian Jefferson High Sch., Monticello Fla., 1945-47; audio-visual dir. Jefferson County Schs., 1948-50; tchr. English, librarian Meigs (Ga.) High Sch., 1954-55; librarian Chipola Jr. Coll., Marianna, Fla., 1955-57, dir. library services, 1958—, chmn. student aid and scholarship com., 1961-65. Mem. Jefferson County Edn. Assn. (pres. 1948-50), Fla. Edn. Assn. Honor Socs. (chmn. 1950-51), Bus. and Profl. Women's Club (pres. 1958-59, 62-63), Fla. Fedn. Bus. Profl. and Women's Clubs (dist. dir. 1962-63), Women of 1st Presbyn. Ch. (pres. 1962-65), Kappa Delta Pi. Contbr. articles to profl. jours. Home: 506 Kelson Av Marianna FL 32446 Office: Chipola Jr Coll Marianna FL 32446

DIXON, FRED WHITE, meat packing co. exec.; b. Salisbury, N.C., Jan. 2, 1929; s. Willis N. and Louise (White) D.; student Wake Forest Coll., 1946-47; B.B.A., Tulane U., 1950; m. Mildred Joyce Myers, Sept. 15, 1951; children—Fred White, Mark, Brian. With White Packing Co., Salisbury, N.C., 1951—, sales mgr., 1965-70, prodn. mgr., v.p., 1971—. Committeeman, Central Carolina council Boy Scouts Am., 1965—. Trustee Hargrave Mil. Acad., Chatham, Va.; bd. dirs. Sch. Nursing, Rowan Tech. Inst. Served with AUS, 1950-51. Recipient Outstanding Alumnus award Hargrave Mil. Acad., 1972. Mem. N.C. Meat Packers Assn. Soc. for Advancement Mgmt. Baptist (chmn. bd. deacons 1969-70). Kiwanian. Home: 1624 Wiltshire Rd Salisbury NC 28144 Office: White Packing Co Kerr St Salisbury NC 28144

DIXON, HAL BERNARD, ch. exec.; b. Wake Forest, N.C., Mar. 6, 1928; s. Dudley Burgwin and Cynthia Lou (Crowder) D.; grad. Wake Forest Coll., 1951; student N.C. State Coll., 1951, U. Chattanooga, 1962-63; m. Starr Faye Stone, Sept. 29, 1951; children—Hal Bernard, Valerie Starr, Candace Starr, Vanessa Starr. Successively credit and sales mgr., sales mgr., gen. sales mgr., dir. marketing Ch. of God Pub. House, Cleveland, Tenn., 1955—; pres. M.I.T., Inc., Wilson, N.C.; v.p., dir. Dixon Food Service, Inc., Wilson, N.C.; dir., sec. First Citizens Bank of Cleveland. Former chmn. Bradley County Bd. Edn. Pres. North Cleveland Towers. Mem. Pres.'s Council Lee Coll. Served with AUS, 1946-47. Mem. Christian Booksellers Assn. (dir. Colorado Springs 1960-69, sec. 1967-69). Rotarian. Club: Cleveland Optimist (pres. 1966-67). Home: 3550 Edgewood Circle NW Cleveland TN 37311 Office: 1080 Montgomery Av Cleveland TN 37311

DIXON, JACK OWENS, fabricated metal co. exec.; b. Portsmouth, O., Dec. 3, 1929; s. Norman T. and Minnie (Clare) D.; C.E., U. Ala., 1952; m. Cora Lee Barnard, Aug. 31, 1952; children—James Lee, Judy Lynn, Jack Owens, Jr. Jr. engr. Brunswick Corp., Marion, Va., 1952-56; with Panelfab, Inc. (name changed to Panelfab Internat. 1969), Miami, Fla., 1956—, v.p. sales, 1969—. Served with USMC, 1950-51. Mem. Ednl. Industries Assn. (dir. 1969-71), Metal Builders Assn., Alpha Sigma Phi. Republican. Moose. Club: Quarter Back (Hollywood, Fla.). Home: 6960 SW 28th St Miramar FL 33121 Office: 1600 NW LeJeune Rd Miami FL 33126

DIXON, JAMES THEODORE, III, electronics co. exec.; b. Fairfield, Ala., Aug. 28, 1940; s. James Theodore, Jr. and Mildred Rosamond (Ireland) D.; B.S. (Alcoa fellow), U. Ala., 1963, M.S., 1969, M.B.A., 1971; m. Janice Gail Wilson, Feb. 5, 1966; children—Lara Anne, Suzanne Marie. Electronic engr. Space Craft, Inc., Huntsville, Ala., 1963-65; test engr. Motorola, Inc., Scottsdale, Ariz., 1965-66; project engr. Sci. Electronics, Inc., Huntsville, 1966-69; marketing mgr., asst. to pres., program mgr. SCI Systems, Inc., Huntsville, 1970—. Pres. Coll. Engring., U. Ala., 1962-63. Named Outstanding Engring. Sr., U. Ala., 1962-63. Registered profl. engr., Ala. Mem. I.E.E.E., Nat. Assn. Profl. Engrs., Am. Mgmt. Assn. Nat. Mgmt. Assn. (chpt. pres.), Phi Eta Sigma, Pi Mu Epsilon, Chi Alpha Phi, Eta Kappa Nu, Tau Beta Pi, Theta Tau, Omicron Delta Kappa, Delta Nu Alpha. Author: Network Analysis By Means of Digital Computer, 1962; Using A Digital Computer in the Undergraduate Instructional Program, 1963; An Analysis of Nonlinearity In Voltage Controlled Astable Multivibrators, 1968; Complementary Transistor Buffer for IC Interfaces, 1970. Home: 9017 Craigmont Rd Huntsville AL 35802 Office: PO Box 4208 Huntsville AL 35802

DIXON, JOHN ALLEN, JR., judge; b. Orange Tex., Apr. 8, 1920; s. John A. and Louella (Stark) D.; B.A., Centenary Coll., 1940; LL.B., Tulane U., 1947;; m. Imogene K. Shipley, Oct. 20, 1945; children—Stella, Diana (Mrs. L. C. Morehead, Jr.), Jeannette. Tchr., coach Tallulah High Sch., 1940-42; admitted to La. bar, 1947; pvt. practice law, Shreveport, La., 1947-57; asst. dist atty., Shreveport, 1954-57; judge First Dist. Ct., 1957-68, La. Ct. Appeal, Shreveport, 1968-70; asso. justice La. Supreme Ct., 1971—. Bd. dirs. Woolworth Found., 1968—. Served with AUS, 1942-45. Democrat. Methodist. Mason. Home: 3718 Bobbitt St Shreveport LA 71107 Office: 301 Loyola Av New Orleans LA 70112

DIXON, RICHARD REMY, city ofcl.; b. New Orleans, Oct. 13, 1911; s. Richard Andrew and Marie (Charles) D.; student Loyola U., New Orleans, 1932-36, Tulane U., 1931-32; m. Mimi Eddy, Sept. 12, 1936; children—Richard Lawrence, Marie F. (Mrs. Frank Perez), Jeanne E. Pub. relations dir. City of New Orleans, 1961-65, exec. sec. to mayor, 1955-61, asst. dir. pub. recreation, 1950-54; mng. dir. New Orleans Municipal Auditorium, 1965—; editor, pub. Westside News, 1932-36. Sec., pub. relations dir., exec. asst. dir. New Orleans Recreation Dept., 1947-54; chmn. Algiers unit A.R.C., 1967-70. Mem. Democratic exec. com., 1952-69. Trustee Our Lady of Holy Cross Coll., Sunshine Club. Mem. New Orleans C. of C., Young Mens Bus. Club, La. Hist. Soc. and Assn., Internat. House. Author: History of Algiers, 1954; This is Algiers, 1718-1970, the Centennial History of Algiers, 1971; The Battle on the West Side, 1965; The Heart of New Orleans—Algiers, 1973. Contbr. articles to profl. jours., newspapers. Home: 1236 Shirley Dr New Orleans LA 70114 Office: 1201 St Peter St New Orleans LA 70116

DIXON, ROBERT BEATTIE, securities dealer; b. Hoboken, N.J., Oct. 9, 1908; s. James Monroe and Anna Louise (Sawyer) D.; Ph.B., Emory U., 1931; postgrad. Atlanta Law Sch., 1931-32; m. Mary Florence Gillmore, May 20, 1935; children—Robert Beattie, Marion M. With Hooper-Holmes Bur., Inc., credit bur., Atlanta, 1931-32, Charlotte, N.C., 1931-33, state mgr., Columbia, S.C., 1933-36, state mgr., Greensboro, N.C., 1936-45; mng. partner McDaniel Lewis & Co., broker-dealer, Greensboro, 1945-55; pres. United Securities Co., Greensboro, 1955-66; sr. v.p., dir. Interstate Securities Corp., Greensboro, 1966—; dir. Beaman Corp., Greensboro, Wyson & Miles Co., Greensboro. Mem. Phila.-Balt.-Washington Stock Exchange, 1963-66; allied mem. N.Y. Stock Exchange, 1966—, Am. Stock Exchange, 1966—. Mem. Securities Dealers of Carolinas (pres. 1959-60), Greensboro C. of C. (dir. 1960), S.A.R., Sigma Pi. Democrat. Methodist (chmn. trustees 1972-74). Odd Fellow, Woodmen of World (state pres. 1961-63). Clubs: Civitan (pres. 1953), Greensboro Country, Merchants and Manufacturers (dir. 1973—), Greensboro City (Greensboro). Home: 202 Homewood Av Greensboro NC 27403 Office: 500 First Union Bank Bldg Greensboro NC 27401

DIXON, SAMUEL MCCLURE, constrn. co. exec.; b. Parrall, W.Va., July 19, 1906; s. Fred Fenwick and Anna (McClure) D.; B.S. in Civil Engring., Tri-State Coll., 1926; m. Sara Courtney, Oct. 12, 1930. Pres., dir. S.M. Dixon Constrn. Co., Warren, Ark., 1947—, Michey's Inc., Warren 1946—; dir., mem. exec. com. Mo. Pacific R.R. Co., First Nat. Bank Little Rock; dir. First Sav. & Loan, Warren. Chmn., Ark. Contractors Licensing Bd., 1945-70. Pres., YMCA, Warren, 1946-49, bd. dirs., 1945—. Chmn. Oaklawn Jockey Club, Hot Springs, Ark., 1970—. Recipient R.L. Newton award YMCA, 1966. Mem. Asso. Gen. Contractors Am. (pres. Ark. chpt. 1950-51). Methodist. Clubs: Warren Country, Little Rock Country. Office: 307 Chestnut St Warren AR 71671

DOAN, PATRICIA NAN, librarian; b. Fayetteville, Ark., Oct. 27, 1930; d. William Rader and Olga (White) Rogers; B.A., U. Ark., 1951; m. John Cannon Doan, Apr. 2, 1950; children—William Curtis, Sarah Cannon, Mary Virginia. Librarian, Okmulgee (Okla.) Pub. Library, 1967—. Treas. Okmulgee Art Guild, 1969-71; sec. Okmulgee County Devel. Council, 1971—. Mem. Okmulgee Meml. Hosp. Found. Mem. Am., Okla. (sec. pub. library div. 1970) library assns., Okmulgee County Genealogical Soc. (v.p. 1970), Sigma Alpha Iota, Zeta Tau Alpha. Democrat. Episcopalian. Author: Index of the 1907 Census of Okmulgee, Oklahoma, 1971. Home: 540 N Morton St Okmulgee OK 74447 Office: 218 S Okmulgee St Okmulgee OK 74447

DOANE, HAROLD EVERETT, record co. exec.; b. N.Y.C., Oct. 17, 1904; s. Thomas J. and Mary S. (Blaisdell) D.; student Edison Sch. Arts, 1919-23, Columbia, 1924; m. Mary G. Gardner, Dec. 20, 1936 (div. 1941) ; m. 2d, Faith S. Tracy, Oct. 17, 1943 (div. 1966); children—Priscilla Clare, Richard Henry Tracy; m. 3d Vivian Dillon Dunn, May 3, 1966. Asst. cameraman D.W. Griffith Orienta Point Studios, Mamaroneck, N.Y., 1921-22; radio announcer sta. WGBU, Fulford, Fla., 1925-26, WBNY, N.Y.C., 1926-27, WMCA, 1927 WKBQ, 1927-28; owner radio sta. WCOH, Mt. Vernon, N.Y., 1928-29; research engr., N.Y.C., 1929-35; dir. Gramercy Pictures Corp., N.Y.C., 1935-37; producer Spotlight Prodns., Inc., 1940-41; tech. operations dir. War Finance Com., N.Y. State div. U.S. Treasury Dept., N.Y.C., 1941-44; gen. mgr. Art Records, Miami, Fla., 1945-59, pres., 1959—; dir. Mizmor Internat., Inc., Hollywood, Fla. Mem. Nat. Acad. Rec. Arts and Scis., N.Y. Advt. Club. Republican. Home: 5800 Marlin Dr Plantation Isles FL 33314 Office: 991 SW 40th Av Plantation FL 33314

DOAR, WILLIAM WALTER, JR., lawyer, state senator; b. Rock Hill, S.C., Mar. 9, 1935; s. William Walter and Julia (Poag) D.; B.S., U. S.C., 1957, LL.B., 1959; m. Louise Terrell Davis, Aug. 24, 1957; children—Elizabeth Beckham, Julia, Terrell. Admitted to S.C. bar, 1959; mem. firm McKay, McKay, Black & Walker, Columbia, 1962-64, Moore, Flowers & Doar, Georgetown, 1964—; mem. S.C. Ho. of Reps., 1966-72, S.C. Senate, 1972—. Served as judge adv. USAF, 1959-62. Rotarian. Home: 232 Queen St Georgetown SC 29440 Office: Smith Bldg Screven St Georgetown SC 29440

DOBBIE, ROBERT PAUL, JR., surgeon; b. Buffalo, June 2, 1924; s. Robert Paul and Adeline (Pfleghaar) D.; B.S., U. Mich., 1944, M.D. cum laude, 1946; m. Barbara Louise Smith, July 2, 1949; children—David Scott, Sarah Leigh. Commd. ensign, U.S. Navy, 1943, advanced through grades to capt., 1963; intern Univ. Hosp., Ann Arbor, Mich., 1947-48, resident in gen. surg. 1948-50, 1951-53; resident in cardiothoracic surgery Glover Clinic, Presbyn. Hosp., Phila., 1958-60; mem. surg. staff U.S. Naval Hosp., Phila., 1953-54; sr. med. officer U.S. Naval Sta. Hosp., Athens, Greece, 1954-56; mem. surg. staff, Bethesda, Md., 1956-58, asst. chief surgery, 1960-62, cardio-thoracic surgeon, 1962-64, sr. med. officer, 1960-64; chief surgery U.S. Naval Hosp., Memphis, 1964-65, chief surgery, exec. officer, 1965-66; chief surgery U.S. Naval Hosp., Oakland, Cal., 1966-69, exec. officer, 1968-69; ret., 1969; asso. prof. surgery U. Tenn. Coll. Medicine, 1969—; mem. surg. staff City of Memphis Hosp.; cons. thoracic and gen. surgery Methodist Hosp., VA Hosp., Memphis, 1969—, St. Joseph Hosp., 1969—, U.S. Naval Hosp., Millington, Tenn., 1969—; mem. jr. staff gen. and thoracic surgery Baptist Hosp., Memphis, 1969; mem. courtesy staff LeBonheur Children's Hosp., Memphis, 1969—; dir. Cancer Center Program, U. Tenn. Med. Units, 1972—; mem. attending staff West Tenn. Chest Disease Hosp., Memphis, 1973—. Mem. A.M.A., Frederick A. Coller, Memphis surg. socs., Am. Thoracic Soc., Am. Cancer Soc., Memphis Med. Seminar, So. Thoracic Surg. Assn., San Francisco Surg. Assn., Memphis and Shelby County Med. Soc., Soc. Med. Cons. to Armed Forces, Assn. Mil. Surgeons, Phi Kappa Phi, Alpha Omega Alpha. Mem. editorial bd. Tenn. Med. Alumnus, 1972—. Home: 1399 Pecan Trees Dr Germantown TN 38138 Office: 951 Court Av Memphis TN 38163

DOBBS, GLENN, JR., pub. relations mgr.; b. McKinney, Tex., July 12, 1920; s. Glenn and Mary Tennie (McGraw) D.; B.A., U. Tulsa, 1943, postgrad., 1962-63; m. June Marie Manchester, Jan. 16, 1942; children—Glenn III, John Saxon. Owner stock ranch, Tulsa, 1946-53; profl. football player Bklyn. Dodgers, 1946-47, Los Angeles Dons, 1947-49; profl. football player, backfield coach Sask. Roughriders, 1951-53; football coach U. Tulsa, 1961-68, dir. athletics, 1955-70; pub. relations mgr. Jim Harrell Pontiac, Tampa, Fla., 1971—. Football coach U. Tulsa at Bluebonnet Bowl, 1964, 65; coach teams in Miami North-South Shrine Game, 1964, Blue-Gray games, 1965, 66; dir. Ann. Celebrity Golf Tournament, Tampa. Mem. Tampa chpt. Nat. Football Found. and Hall of Fame, 1971—; charter mem. bd. dirs. Okla. Sports Hall of Fame; mem. sports adv. com. Hillsboro Jr. Coll., Tampa, 1971—; fund-raiser Colt Baseball World Series, 1972. Served as 1st lt. USAF, 1943-46. Named to Consensus All— Am. football team, 1942, All-Pro team, 1946, Canadian All-Pro team, 1951, Helms Hall of Fame, 1952; elected to Okla. Sports Hall of Fame, 1970; named Rookie of Year, 1946, Most Valuable Player, All-Am. Conf., 1946, Most Valuable Player, Canadian Football League, 1951, Most Valuable Player, Chgo. Tribune All-Star Game, 1944. Mem. Tampa C. of C., Pi Kappa Alpha. Mem. Christian Ch. Rotarian (pres. N.W. Tampa 1972-74). Club: Carrollwood Village Golf and Tennis (dir. 1974-75). Home: 3712 Carrollbrook Rd Tampa FL 33618 Office: 3800 W Hillsborough St Tampa FL 33614

DOBBS, HENRI TALMAGE, JR., ins. exec.; b. Atlanta, Oct. 14, 1915; s. Henri Talmage and Maggie Stanton (Austin) D.; student Emory U., 1932-34; B.C.S., Ga. State U., 1939; m. Ruth Reynolds, Mar. 21, 1941; children—Henri Talmage III, Joan, Nancy, Ruth. With Life Ins. Co. of Ga., Atlanta, 1933—, v.p., treas., 1953-63, exec. v.p. finance, 1963-72, sr. v.p., 1972—, dir., 1948-72. Trustee Trinity Presdl. Trust Fund, Ga. State U. Found. Served with USNR, 1944-45. Chartered financial analyst. Mem. Alpha Kappa Psi, Delta Tau Delta. Presbyn. Rotarian. Club: Capital City (Atlanta). Home: 439 Blackland Rd NW Atlanta GA 30342 Office: 600 W Peachtree St Atlanta GA 30308

DOBBS, SOLON CARTER, dentist; b. Akron, O., Sept. 13, 1919; s. Solon Levelle and May Plen (Carter) D.; student U. Miss., 1937-39; D.D.S., U. Tenn., 1943; m. Kathleen Hathorn, Apr. 25, 1943 (dec. 1963); children—Solon Carter, Jimmy Gage, Frances Maybelle; m. 2d, Marjorie House, Jan. 3, 1964. Individual practice dentistry, Calhoun City, Miss., 1948—; mem. staff Hillcrest Hosp.; missionary dentist, San Blas Islands, Panama, 1967, 69-72, 74. Chmn. various fund drives. Chmn. A.R.C., Calhoun County, 1960—; v.p. scoutmaster Pushmataha council Boy Scouts Am., 1950-64. Recipient Silver Beaver award Boy Scouts Am., 1964. Alderman, Calhoun City, 1965-69, mayor pro-tem, 1965-69. Served to lt. Dental Corps USNR, 1943-48; PTO. Mem. North Miss. (past pres.), Miss. (v.p. 1959-60) dental assns. Baptist (deacon). Rotarian, Mason. Editor San Blas Newsletter, 1969-71. Home: Monroe at Wells St Calhoun City MS 38916 Office: Calhoun City MS 38916

DOBBS, WALTER EDWARD, pub. accountant; b. Haskell, Ark., Nov. 18, 1922; s. Dewell Gann (Caple) and Hester D.; B.S., B.A., U. Ark., 1947; m. Marilyn R. Middleton, Dec. 22, 1946; children—Scott, Jeffrey, Douglas. With R.A. Lile & Co., C.P.A.'s, 1949-56; pub. accountant Hennigen, Croft & Cotham, C.P.A.'s, Little Rock, 1958-60; controller A. Tenenbaum Co., Inc., Little Rock, 1960-63; practice of accounting, Little Rock, 1963-68; partner Dobbs, Albright & Co.; C.P.A.'s, Little Rock, 1968—. Served as 1st lt. USMC, 1943-46. Decorated Purple Heart. Mem. Am. Inst. C.P.A.'s, Ark. Soc. C.P.A.'s (sec. 1971—). Lion (sec. 1959-63). Home: 64 White Oak Lane Little Rock AR 72207 Office: Tower Bldg Little Rock AR 72201

DOBBS, WAYNE, basketball coach; b. Smyrna, Ga., June 12, 1939; s. L.F. and Floy (Herren) D.; B.A., Oglethorpe U., 1961; M.A., Peabody Coll., 1964. Head basketball coach S.W. Dekalb High Sch.; Decatur, Ga., 1961-63, head basketball coach, athletic dir. Bronton Parker Jr. Coll., Mt. Vernon, Ga., 1963-64; Belmont Coll., Nashville, 1964-66; head basketball coach George Washington U., Washington, 1966-70; asst. basketball coach Vanderbilt U., Nashville, 1970—. Author: Basketball's Stunting Defenses, 1964. Home: 1199 Murfreesboro Rd Nashville TN 37217

DOBES, WILLIAM LAMAR, JR., dermatologist; b. Atlanta, Apr. 16, 1943; s. William Lamar and Sara (Wilson) D.; B.A., Emory U., 1965, M.D., 1969; m. Martha Husmann, June 16, 1966; children—Margaret Alison, William Shane. Intern Grady Meml. Hosp., Atlanta, 1969-70; fellow dermatology Mayo Clinic, 1970-71; fellow U. Miami, 1971-73; clin. instr. Emory U., Atlanta, 1973—; mem. staff Crawford Long, West Paces Ferry, Bolton Rd. hosps. (all Atlanta). Diplomate Am. Bd. Dermatology. Mem. Soc. Investigative Dermatology, Am. Acad. Dermatology, So., Ga. med. assns., A.M.A.,

A.C.P., Ga. Conservancy, Sierra Club, Ga. Wildlife Fedn., Am. Civil Liberties Union, Phi Delta Theta, Phi Chi. Clubs: Key Biscayne (Fla.) Yacht; Little Cumberland, Cherokee Town & Country (Atlanta). Contbr. articles to profl. jours. Home: 232 Pineland Rd Atlanta GA 30342 Office: 478 Peachtree St Atlanta GA 30308 also Dept Dermatology Emory U School Medicine Atlanta GA 30308

DOBRIANSKY, LEV EUGENE, educator, economist; b. N.Y.C., Nov. 9, 1918; s. John and Eugenia (Greshchuk) D.; B.S. (Charles Hayden Meml. scholar), N.Y.U., 1941, Hirshland Polit. sci. fellow, 1943-44, tchg. fellow econ., 1942-43, M.A., 1943, Ph.D., 1951; LL.D., Munich, Germany, 1952; m. Julia Kusy, June 29, 1946; children—Larisa Eugenia, Paula Jon. Faculty mem. N.Y.U., 1942-48; asso. editor Ukrainian Quar., 1946-58, chmn. editorial bd. 1958—; econs. editor Washington Report, Am. Security Council, 1963—; asst. prof. econ. Georgetown U., 1948-52, became asso. prof. econs. 1952, acting chmn. dept. econs., 1953-54; mem. faculty Nat. War Coll., 1957-58; prof. econs. Georgetown U., 1960—; lectr. on Soviet Union; econ. research and cons.; cons. USIA, also State Dept., 1971—; splty. Thorstein Veblen, Ukraine. Mem. Economists' Nat. Com. on Monetary Policy exec. com., Free World Forum; chmn. National Captive Nations Com., 1959—. Asst. sec. Republican Nat. Conv., 1952; Rep. Nat. Com. 1956; Rep. Com. Program and Progress, 1959. Col. Res. 352d Civil Affairs Mem. Acad. Polit. Sci., Nat. Acad. Econs. and Polit. Sci., Am. Assn. U. Profs., Am. Acad. Polit. and Social Sci., Am., Cath. econ. assns., Am. Finance Assn., Nat. Soc. Study Edn., Shevchenko Sci. Soc., Common Cause, Inc. Ukrainian Cong. Com. Am. (chmn.), Fedn. Am. Central and E. European Descent (exec. v.p.), N.Y.U. Alumni Assn., Gold Key Soc. Beta Gamma Sigma, Delta Sigma Pi. Author: A Philosophico-Economic Critique of Thorstein Veblen. 1943; The Social Philosophical System of Thorstein Veblen, 1950; Free Trade Ideal, 1954; Veblenism, A New Critique, 1957; The Great Pretense, 1956; The Crimes of Khrushchev, 1959; Decisions for a Better America, 1960; Nations, Peoples, and Countries in the USSR, 1964; (with others) Peace and Freedom Through Cold War Victory, 1964; The Vulnerable Russians, 1967; U.S.A. and the Soviet Myth, 1971. Contbr. articles field. Radio and TV appearances. Home: 4520 Kling Dr Alexandria VA 22312 Office: Georgetown U Washington DC 20001

DOBSON, CHARLES WILLIAM, dentist; b. Morganton, N.C., Aug. 11, 1925; s. Cecil Burgin and Mary Virginia (Sparks) D.; B.S., Wake Forest Coll., 1951; D.D.S., Emory U., 1953; m. Stella Flora Smith, Mar. 17, 1956; 1 son, Carl Wilhelm. Commd. 2d lt. Dental Corps U.S. Army, 1952, advanced through grades to lt. col., 1966; chief prosthetics, Nurnberg, Germany, 1956-59; chief hosp. dental service, Ft. Gordon, Ga., 1963-65; chief preventive dentistry, Ft. Gordon, 1967-69; ret., 1969; pvt. practice dentistry, Flat Rock, N.C., 1969—. Pres. parents panel Cerebral Palsy Assn., Columbus, Ga., 1961. Served to lt. (j.g.) Air Corps, USNR, 1943-47. Mem. Am., N.C., Buncombe, Henderson County (pres.) dental assns., Am. Legion, V.F.W., Ret. Officers Assn., Assn. U.S. Army. Presbyn. (deacon). Club: Henderson Country. Author, producer, star TV movie preventive dentistry, U.S. Army, 1968. Home: Route 7 Box 120 Hendersonville NC 28739 Office: Box 458 Flat Rock NC 28731

DOBSON, GERARD RAMSDEN, educator; b. East Rockaway, N.Y., May 4, 1933; s. Edward Ramsden and Harriet (Bowman) D.; B.S., Fla. So. Coll., 1955; Ph.D., Fla. State U., 1964; m. Kay Ann Tauscher, June 16, 1962; children—Charles, Thomas, Edward. Asst. prof. chemistry U. Ga., 1963-67; asso. prof. chemistry U. S.D., 1967-69; asso. prof. chemistry North Tex. State U., 1969-72, prof. chemistry, 1972—. Mem. Clarke County (Ga.) Republican Exec. Com., 1964-67, Denton County (Tex.) Rep. Exec. Com., 1974—. NSF grant, 1969-72; Petroleum Research Fund grant, 1963-72; Robert A. Welch Found. grant, 1971—. Mem. Am. Chem. Soc., Chem. Soc. (London), Soc. Sigma Xi, Beta Beta Beta, Pi Kappa Phi, Alpha Chi Sigma (dist. counselor 1974—). Mason. Contbr. numerous articles to sci. jours. Home: Box 273 Justin TX 76247 Office: Dept Chemistry North Tex State U Denton TX 76203

DOBSON, HAROLD LAWRENCE, physician; educator; b. nr. Hightower, Tex., May 10, 1921; s. Starrett Washington and Polly (Cole) D.; student Lee Jr. Coll., 1937; B.S., Baylor U., 1943, M.D., 1946, M.S., 1956; m. Yvonne Annette Fudge, July 15, 1945; children—Harold Lawrence, Laura Yvonne, Robin Leah, Steven Craig. Intern, Salt Lake County Hosp., 1946-47; instr. biochemistry Baylor Coll. Medicine, Waco, Tex., 1947-48, USPHS fellow depts. internal medicine, biochemistry, 1948-50; resident internal medicine VA Hosp., Houston, 1950-51; practice medicine specializing in diabetes mellitus endocrinology, Houston, 1953—; mem. staff Hermann, Meth. hosps., Houston. Faculty, Baylor Coll. Medicine, 1953—, asso. prof., 1962—; clin. prof. U. Tex. Sch. Medicine, Houston, 1973—; cons. staff Tex. Inst. Rehab. and Research, Houston, 1968—; mem. med. adv. com. Vis. Nurses Assn., 1969—. Served with USNR, 1943-45, USAF, 1951-53. Diplomate Am. Bd. Internal Medicine. Fellow Council Atherosclerosis; mem. Am. (com. pub. edn. and detection), Tex., S. Tex. diabetes assns., Am. Fedn. Clin. Research, Am. Heart Assn., Am. Coll. Nephrology. Contbr. articles to profl. jours. Home: 5414 Maple St Bellaire TX 77401 Office: Med Sch U Tex Houston TX 77025

DOBSON, JOHN HARRISON, librarian; b. Greeneville, Tenn., June 1, 1924; s. Benjamin H. and Leta S. (McAmis) D.; student Tusculum Coll., 1942-43; B.A., U. Tenn., 1948; M.S., Columbia, 1951. Librarian, Greeneville (Tenn.) High Sch., 1951-54, Tusculum Coll., 1952-54; sr. cataloger U. Tenn. Library, Knoxville, 1954-59, spl. collections librarian, 1959—, curator Estes Kefauver Collection, 1966—, archivist, 1971—. Bd. dirs. Greene County Library, 1954-56. Served with AUS, 1943-46. Mem. Am., Southeastern, Tenn. library assns. Editor U. Tenn. Library Lectures, 1955-57, Tenn. Librarian, 1962-67, U. Tenn. Libraries Occasional Publ., 1970—. Home: 1111 Kenesaw Av Knoxville TN 37919

DOBYNS, NORMAN LESTER, can co. exec.; b. Lynchburg, Va., Jan. 13, 1933; s. Lloyd Allen and Helen (Stokes) D.; B.A., Washington and Lee U., 1954; postgrad. Wharton Sch. Bus. U. Pa., 1957-58; masters certificate communication Am. U., 1971; m. Yvonne Elizabeth Fox, Nov. 28, 1958; children—Cynthia Lynn, Barbara Diane. Adminstrv. asst. Rep. T. Downing, Newport News, Va., 1960-67; with Am. Can Co., Washington, 1967—, dir. govt. relations, 1969-71, v.p. govt. relations, 1971—. Pres. West Springfield (Va.) Civic Assn., 1964-67; mem. Fairfax (Va.) Council Cultural Com., 1965-66; pres. Springfield Community Council, 1965-66. Served with AUS, 1954-56. Recipient Savs. Bond Sales award Treasury Dept., 1956. Mem. Washington and Lee Alumni Assn., Phi Beta Kappa, Kappa Sigma. Clubs: University, George Town (Washington). Home: 8501 Brook Rd McLean VA 22101 Office: 1660 L St NW Washington DC 20036

DOBYNS, ROY ARMSTEAD, educator; b. Bristol, Va., Jan. 31, 1931; s. Roy Armstead and Francis (Williams) D.; A.B., Carson-Newman Coll., 1953; M.A., Vanderbilt U., 1954; Ph.D., George Peabody Coll., 1963; m. Kathryn Louise Williams, June 19, 1955; children—Roy, John, Joe. Asst. prof. math. Lee Coll., 1956-58; prof. math. McNeese State U., 1958-68; chmn. dept. math Georgetown Coll., 1968-73; prof., chmn. div. sci. and math Clayton Jr. Coll., 1973—. Served with AUS, 1954-56. Recipient Ford grant, 1961-62; NSF fellowship, 1963. Mem. Math. Assn. Am. (chmn. Ky. sect. 1971-73), Nat. Council Tchrs. Math. Baptist (deacon 1964—). Author: Programmed Guide to Trigonometry, 1968; Programmed Guide to Algebra, 1969; Programmed Guide to Algebra & Trigonometry, 1970; Programmed Guide to Elementary Functions, 1971. Home: 2223 Carmen Ct Morrow GA 30260 Office: Clayton Jr Coll Morrow GA 30260

DOCKRAY, GEORGE HENRY, editor; b. Phila., May 4, 1920; s. George L. and Mary (Finan) D.; B.S., Phila. Coll. Textiles and Sci., 1948; m. Louise Stedman, Nov. 9, 1942 (dec. May 1970); children—Karen E., George Henry, Andrea; m. 2d, Audrey Laney Cochran, June 2, 1973. Textile research asso. Research Inst. Temple U., Phila., 1948-49; textile engr. Nat. Cotton Council Am., Washington, 1949-53; asso. editor Textile Industries, Atlanta, 1953-56, exec. editor, 1956-57, editor, 1957-68, editor-in-chief 1968—; v.p., dir. W.R.C. Smith Pub. Co., Atlanta. Served with AUS, 1941-45. Mem. Fiber Soc., Textile Inst. (Eng.), Am. Assn. Textile Chemists and Colorists, Sigma Delta Chi, Delta Kappa Phi. Home: 4064 Navajo Trail NE Atlanta GA 30319 Office: 1760 Peachtree Rd NW Atlanta GA 30309

DOCKSTADER, WILMER BELDON, govt. ofcl.; b. St. Ansgar, Ia., Sept. 23, 1918; s. Wilmer Lot and Caroline (Hansen) D.; B.S., Ia. State U., 1941; M.S. (Hormel fellow), U. Minn., 1949; Ph.D., Wash. State U., 1952; m. Geraline Ferrell, July 18, 1941; children—Carolyn (Mrs. K.C. Stewart), Steven Walter, Sue. Research asso. Bauer & Black div. Kendall Co., Chgo., 1952-55; devel. chemist Froedtert Malt Corp., Milw., 1955-56; fermentologist Clinton Corn Processing div. Standard Brands, Inc. (Ia.), 1956-62; supervisory microbiologist NIH, Bethesda, Md., 1962-68; with FDA, Washington, 1968—, consumer safety officer, 1971—. Mem. Judges' Panel for Ford Future Scientists of Am., 1963-68, Judges' Panel for Finals of NASA Sci. Talent Search, 1963-65; treas. Hawthorne Sch. PTA, Clinton, 1957-58; co-chmn. membership com. West Fernwood Citizens Assn., 1963-65; sci. adviser Nat. Capitol Area council Boy Scouts Am., 1967—. Served with AUS, 1941-46. Fellow Am. Inst. Chemists; mem. Am. Soc. Microbiology, Am. Inst. Biol. Sci., Sci. Research Soc. Am. (mem. admissions com. 1972—), Alpha Sigma Phi. Methodist (Sunday sch. tchr. 1963-65, mem. ch. governing bd. 1953-55, mem. edn. bd. 1963-65). Mason. Patentee unitary non-adherent dressings (Telfa); preparation antioxidant from rootlets; devel. presumptive test medium for salmonella. Home: 6804 Buttermere Lane Bethesda MD 20034 Office: 200 C St SW Washington DC 20204

DOCTERMAN, GERT N., mfg. co. exec.; b. Stuttgart, Germany, July 9, 1933; s. Alfred N. and Else (Bornstein) D.; came to U.S., 1955, naturalized, 1961; student LaSalle U. Extension, 1961; B.B.A., Ga. State U., 1967; m. Edna Richards, Feb. 7, 1959; children—Michael, Anna, Mark. Accountant Union Camp Corp., Atlanta, 1956-63; exec. v.p., dir. Vintage Enterprises, Atlanta, 1963—. Mem. Nat. Assn. Accountants, Am. Mgmt. Assn., Ga. Mobile Home Assn. (dir., 1971-72). Home: 5875 Musket Lane Stone Mountain GA 30083 Office: 3825 NE Expressway Atlanta GA 30340

DOCTOR, VASANT MANILAL, educator; b. Surat, India, Mar. 19, 1926; s. Manilal Ramlal and Kusum (Bhambhani) D.; M.S., U. Wis., 1951; Ph.D., Tex. A & M. U., 1953; m. Pushpa Broker, Nov. 17, 1953; children—Shreenath, Uday, Ravi. Came to U.S., 1949, naturalized, 1973. Asst. prof. biochemistry U. Tex. M.D. Anderson Hosp., Houston, 1953-59, asso. prof. dental br., 1959-62; chief biochemist H.A. Ltd., Pimpri, India, 1962-65; asso. prof. biochemistry U. Houston, 1965-67; prof. biochemistry Prairie View (Tex.) A. & M. U., 1967—. Cons. U. Houston Biochemistry and Biophysics dept., Houston Research Inst. Committeeman Sam Houston Area council Boy Scouts Am., 1957-62. NIH grantee 1961-62; Am. Cancer Soc. grantee, Welch Found. grantee, 1968, Research Career Devel. award NIH, 1959-64. Mem. Am. Soc. Biol. Chemists, Soc. Exptl. Biology and Medicine, A.A.A.S., Sigma Xi. Contbg. author: Nucleic Acids, 1965. Contbr. numerous articles to sci. jours. Home: 2115 10th St Hempstead TX 77445 Office: Chemistry Dept Prairie View A & M U Prairie View TX 77445

DODD, DANIEL PHILLIPS, veterinarian; b. St. Louis, July 8, 1919; s. George Deming and Nellie (Phillips) D.; D.V.M., Ia. State U., 1942; m. LaVern Shattuck, June 15, 1946; children—Barbara Ann, Carol Jean. Research asso. Ia. State Coll., 1946-47; pvt. practice vet. medicine, Washington, 1947—. Served from pvt. to maj., AUS, 1942-46 lt. col. Res., ret. Mem. Am., D.C. vet. med. assns., D.C. Acad. Vet. Medicine, Ia. State U. Vet. Assn., Assn. Mil. Surgeons U.S., Ia. State U. Alumni Assn., Sigma Nu. Republican, Methodist. Lion (local pres., zone chmn., dep. dist. gov.). Home: 9806 Ashby Rd Fairfax VA 22030 Office: 317 Massachusetts Av NE Washington DC 20002

DODD, FADRA REBECCA DEAN, govt. ofcl.; b. Corinth, Miss., Dec. 23, 1924; d. Sam Richard and Ruby Pearl (Meeks) Dean; student Miss. State U., 1942-43; m. James R. Dodd, Feb. 25, 1945 (div. Dec. 1951); children—James Andre, Myra Kathryn. Dept. circuit clk., part-time 1952-57; legal sec. county atty., 1952-57; solicitor, sec. Mut. Ins. Agy., 1957-60; circuit ct. clk., county registrar Alcorn County, 1960— (all Corinth). Chmn., Alcorn County Polio Assn., Corinth, 1960. Mem. Circuit Clks. Assn. Miss. (legislative com. 1960-62, 67-73, pres. 1965, exec. com. 1966-73, sec.-treas. 1967-73), Internat. Platform Assn., Bus. and Profl. Women's Club Corinth (corr. sec. 1968-69, chmn. legislative com. 1967—), Miss.-Tenn. Peace Officers Assn., C. of C. Baptist. Co-author: Handbook for Circuit Clerks in Mississippi. Home: 2010 E 6th St Corinth MS 38834 Office: Alcorn County Courthouse Waldron St Corinth MS 38834

DODD, LAMAR, artist, educator; b. Fairburn, Ga., Sept. 22, 1909; s. Francis Jefferson and Etta Irene (Cleaveland) D.; student Ga. Sch. Tech., 1926-27, Art Students League of N.Y., 1929-33; L.H.D., LaGrange Coll., 1949; A.F.D., U. Chattanooga, 1959; m. Mary Lehmann, Sept. 25, 1930; 1 dau., Mary Irene. Art tchr., Five Points, Ala., 1927-28; asst. mgr. Spivy-Johnson Co., Birmingham, Ala., 1933-37; asso. prof. art U. Ga., Athens, 1937-40, prof. art, 1940—, head dept. art, 1940—, Regents prof., 1948—, chmn. dept. fine arts, 1960—. Chmn. Ga. Art Commn.; mem. com. on arts U.S. Dept. State. Numerous awards and prizes 1936-57; 2d award, Painting of Year, Pepsi-Cola Art Exhbn., 1947; Va. Biennial Purchase award, 1948; 1st purchase prize Southeastern Art Exhbn., 1949; Nat. Inst. Arts and Letters grantee, 1950; Grumbacher Oil award Fla. Internat. Exhibit, 1952; Edwin Palmer Meml. prize N.A.D., 1953; 1st transparent watercolor prize, Southeastern Art Assn. Exhbn., 1953. Exhbn. Am. Art (N.Y. World's Fair), 1940. Exhibited throughout U.S. 1930-57; Whitney Mus. Ann. Exhbn. (1937-57), Neb. Ann. Exhbn. (1940), Carnegie Internat. (Pittsburgh, 1936), N.Y. World's Fair (1939, 1940), San Francisco Fair (1939); work represented in Met. Mus., N.Y.C., by "Sand, Sea and Sky," also in collections of Telfair Acad., Savannah, High Mus., Atlanta, Pa. Acad. Fine Arts, Whitney Mus. Am. Art, many pvt. collections. One man shows: various mus. and galleries, such as Corcoran Museum, Washington, 1942; Grand Central Art Gallery, N.Y., Rochester Meml. Art Gallery, 1949; Witte Meml. Mus., San Antonio, 1951; and many others. Nat. Academician. Mem. Sphinx, Phi Kappa Phi. Contbr. articles to art mags., jours. Home: 590 Springdale St Athens GA 30601

DODD, PARKS ALLEN, JR., state ofcl.; b. Rome, Ga., Mar. 23, 1943; s. Parks Allen and Frances Anne (Booker) D.; B.S., Ga. Inst. Tech., 1965; M.B.A., Ga. State U., 1967, Ph.D., 1974; m. Barbara Elaine Minor, June 19, 1965; children—Parks Allen III, Andrew Hunter. Adminstrv. trainee Trust Co. of Ga., Atlanta, 1965-67; asso. dir. Ga. Higher Edn. Facilities Commn., 1967—. Mem. Am., So. econ. assns., Omicron Delta Epsilon, Chi Phi. Home: 6770 Wright Rd Atlanta GA 30328 Office: Suite 614 Equitable Bldg 100 Peachtree St NW Atlanta GA 30303

DODD, RICHARD WINNE, physician; b. Syracuse, N.Y., Mar. 18, 1934; s. Donald Cameron and Irene (Winne) D.; B.S., St. Lawrence U., 1956; M.D., State U. N.Y., 1960; m. Jean Susan Petrock, Nov. 12, 1961; children—Richard Paul, Helen Jeanine. Intern U. Va. Hosp., 1960-61; resident J. Hillis Miller Health Center, Gainesville, Fla., 1961-62; practice family medicine, Daytona Beach, Fla., 1962-73; mem. active hosp. staff Halifax Dist. Hosp., 1962—, vice-chmn. family practice resident teaching program, 1970—, mem. credential com. and exec. com., 1969-71; dir. family practice residency program Halifax Hosp. Med. Center, 1973—. Pres. Mental Health Bd. Volusia County, 1971. Bd. dirs. Daytona Beach Symphony Soc., 1967-70, Fla. Internat. Music Festivals, Inc., 1969. Named Doctor of the Day Fla. Legislature, 1970. Diplomate Am. Acad. Family Physicians. Mem. A.M.A., Fla. Med. Assn., Am., Fla. (ed. com. chmn. 1969-71, dir. 1973—) acads. gen. practice, Volusia County Med. Soc. (pres. 1971-72), C. of C. (med. facilities com. chmn. 1969). Republican. Editor Volusia County Med. Soc. Bull., 1967-68. Home: 513 Riverview Blvd Daytona Beach FL 32018 Office: 157 S Halifax Av Daytona Beach FL 32018

DODDS, ALVIN FRANKLIN, pharmacist, educator; b. Starkville, Miss., Jan. 20, 1919; s. Charles Richey and Cora (Floyd) D.; B.S., Miss. State U., 1940; M.S., Northwestern U., 1942, Ph.D., 1943; postgrad. Loyola U. of South, 1945-47; B.S. in Pharmacy Med. U. S.C., 1949; m. Annie Ruth Arnold, Sept. 7, 1943; children—Kenneth Arnold, Carolyn Ruth, William Russell. Chemist, Pan Am. Refining Corp., Texas City, Tex., 1943-45; asst. prof. Loyola U. of South, 1945-47; asso. prof. pharmacy Med. U. S.C., Charleston, 1947-53, prof., 1953—. Mem. Am. Pharm. Assn., Sigma Xi, Rho Chi, Phi Lambda Upsilon, Kappa Mu Epsilon, Beta Beta Beta. Presbyn. Home: 425 Geddes Av Charleston SC 29407

DODDS, JOSEPH J., surgeon; b. Farrell, Pa., Feb. 9, 1929; s. Joseph Burns and Julia (Scott) D.; B.S., Univ. Pitts., 1951, M.D., 1955; m. Vina Mae Elder, June 19, 1954; children—Lynn Eider, Sandra Allison. Intern, Shadyside Hosp., Pitts., 1955-56; resident Mayo Clinic, Rochester, Minn., 1958-62; practice medicine specializing in surgery, Chattanooga, 1962—; pres. Patterns, Inc.; dir. S.E. Tenn. Area Health Edn. Center, Inc., Profl. Systems Inc., Chattanooga. Mem. Tenn. Manpower Commn. Bd. dirs. Ga.-Tech. Regional Health Commn. Served with USAF, 1956-58. Diplomate Am. Bd. Surgery. Fellow A.C.S., Southeastern Surg. Congress, Am. Soc. Abdominal Surgeons, Royal Soc. Health, Pan. Pacific Surg. Assn., Pan. Am. Med. Assn.; mem. A.M.A., So. Med. Assn., Fedn. Am. Hosps. (pres. 1971-72, dir.), Tenn., Chattanooga and Hamilton County med. socs., Royal Coll. Medicine. Republican. Presbyn. (deacon). Lion. Club: Capital. Home: 1105 E Brow Rd Signal Mountain TN 37377 Office: 525 McCallie Av Chattanooga TN 37402

DODEK, SAMUEL MAYER, physician; b. Chgo., June 14, 1902; s. Mayer B. and Lena (Ettinger) D.; A.B., George Washington U., 1923; M.D., Jefferson Med. Coll., 1927; M.A. in Obstetrics, Western Res. U., 1932; m. Miriam Joyce Selker, Apr. 13, 1936; children—Marianne (Mrs. Benjamin Brauzer), Samayla (Mrs. John M. Deutch). Intern, Albert Einstein Med. Center, Phila., 1927-29; asst. house surgeon N.Y. Lying-in Hosp., N.Y.C., 1929; resident, fellow, teaching fellow dept. obstetrics and gynecology Western Res. U., Cleve., 1929-32; practice medicine specializing in obstetrics and gynecology, Washington, 1932—; sr. attending staff George Washington Hosp.; chmn. dept. obstetrics and gynecology Washington Hosp. Center, 1959-64, now sr. adv. staff; faculty George Washington U. Sch. Medicine, 1932—, clin. prof. obstetrics and gynecology, 1960-72, prof. emeritus, 1972—. Chmn. med. adv. com. Planned Parenthood, Inc., 1962-67. Bd. dirs. Research Found. Washington Hosp. Center. Chmn., Obstet. Bd. D.C., 1965—; chmn. allied professions group United Jewish Appeal, 1950-53; mem. profl. com. United Givers Fund, 1952. Diplomate Am. Bd. Obstetrics and Gynecology. Fellow A.C.S., Am. Coll. Obstetrics and Gynecology; mem. Am. Fertility Soc., A.M.A., Med. Soc. D.C. (1st v.p. 1954, chmn. profl. conduct and ethics com. 1970-72), Washington Gynecol. Soc. (pres. 1953), So. Med. Assn., Royal Soc. Medicine, Sigma Xi. Clubs: Woodmont Country, Internat. Med., Bass Rocks Beach, Nat. Press, George Washington University, Cosmos. Author: Shakespeare's Knowledge of Medicine. Cons. editor Gynecology; Am. Jour. Proctology; editorial staff Obstetric-Gynecology News. Contbr. numerous articles in field to profl. jours. Invented instrument for study human uterine physiology and monitoring of labor in humans, 1932; co-developer isotope localization of human placenta, 1963. Home: 2930 Woodland Dr Washington DC 20008 Office: 5480 Wisconsin Av Washington DC 20015

DODGE, CHARLES FREMONT III, geologist, educator; b. Dallas, May 28, 1924; s. Hale Barbour and H.C. (Clark) D.; B.S., So. Methodist U., 1949, M.S., 1952; Ph.D., U. N.M., 1966; m. Kathryn Charlyne Pond, Aug. 4, 1950; children—Deborah Kathryn, Rebecca Lee. Jr. geologist T.Y. Pickette Valuation Engring. Co., Dallas, 1947-48; instr. Arlington State Coll., 1948-50; field geologist Bur. Econ. Geology, Big Bend Area, Tex., summer 1949; instr. So. Methodist U., summer 1950; petroleum geologist Concho Petroleum Co., N.M., Colo., Utah, Tex., 1950-51; petroleum geologist Intex Oil Co., South Tex., Okla., 1951-52; dist. geologist Am. Trading and Prodn. Corp., West Tex., S.E. N.M., 1952-57; lectr. Odessa Jr. Coll., spring 1956; asso. prof. geology U. Tex., Arlington, 1957-67, prof., 1967—, acting chmn. dept., 1971-74, chmn., 1974—. Cons. Core Labs. Citronelle Field, Ala., 1958, McCord & Assos., Sumatra, Indonesia, 1958-59, Algeria, Venezuela, 1962-63, Atlantic Refining Research and Devel. Lab., 1959-61, James A. Lewis Engring., Cal., Mont., Wyo., N.M., La., Tex., 1959-63, Sun Oil Co. Research and Devel. Lab., 1966-67, Gt. Am. Industries, 1967; Tex. Steel Inc., 1969, Sonatrach-Alcore, Sahara, Algeria, 1969-70; vis. scientist Tex. Acad. Sci., 1963-64. Served with USAAF, 1943-47; with AUS, 1951-53. NSF Sci. Faculty fellow, 1965-66. Mem. Am. Assn. Petroleum Geologists, Assn. Am. Geographers, West Tex., Ft. Worth geol. socs., Dallas-Tarrant County Council Sci. Socs., Soc. Econ. Paleontologists and Mineralogists, Nat. Assn. Geology Teachers, Am. Inst. Profl. Geologists, Sigma Xi, Sigma Gamma Epsilon, Sigma Gamma Xi. Contbr. numerous articles to sci. jours. Home: 1301 Briarwood Arlington TX 76013

DODGE, DONALD W., artist; b. New Albany, Ind., Apr. 21, 1934; B.S., Ind. U., 1956, also postgrad.; M.A., U. Louisville, 1957. One man shows Art Center Assn. U. Louisville, 1958, Moorehead State Coll., 1960, Downtown Gallery, New Orleans, Ohio U., Cin. Art Museum, So. Ind. Studio Gallery, 1961, Bellarmine Coll., 1962, U. Ala., 1963, Ligoa Duncan Gallery, 1964, others; represented in pvt. collections; now head art dept., prof. art Georgetown Coll. Recipient Nat. Soc.

Arts and Letters award, 1962; Prix de Paris, 1963, 64. Address: 315 Warrendale Ct Georgetown KY 40324*

DODGE, JOSEPH JEFFERS, artist, art mus. adminstr.; b. Detroit, Aug. 9, 1917; s. Joseph Morrell and Julia (Jeffers) D.; grad. with honors Choate Sch., 1936; B.S. in Fine Arts with honors, Harvard, 1940; postgrad. Wayne U., 1941; m. Jane Halliday Pike, 1938 (div. 1947); m. 2d, Dorothy MacArthur, 1949 (div. 1973); children—Joseph Morrell II, Dorothy, Julia, Jeffers, Lisa. Curator, Hyde Collection, Glen Falls, N.Y., also tchr. drawing and painting, 1942-62; dir. Cummer Gallery Art, Jacksonville, Fla., 1962-72. Tchr. art history Hamilton Coll., 1947, Adirondack Community Coll., 1961-62; tchr. drawing and painting Ft. Edward Art Center, 1952-62; exhibited one-man shows at Wildenstein Galleries, N.Y.C., Hirschl and Adler Galleries, N.Y.C., Cummer Gallery Art, Jacksonville, Fla., Tampa (Fla.) Art Inst., Group Gallery, Jacksonville, Fla., Columbus (Ga.) Mus. Arts and Crafts, George Thomas Hunter Gallery Art, Chattanooga, Ga. Mus. Art, U. Ga., Athens, Columbia (S.C.) Mus. Art, Jacksonville (Fla.) U., Mint Mus., Charlotte, N.C., U. Fla., Gainesville, Gibbes Gallery, Charleston, S.C., The Hyde Coll., Glen Falls, N.Y., Art Celebration, Jacksonville, Fla. Mem. Jacksonville C. of C. (fine arts com.). Clubs: Harvard, (N.Y.); River (Jacksonville). Home: 843 Alderman Rd Jacksonville FL 32211

DODGE, NELSON LOWELL, lawyer; b. New Haven, Sept. 11, 1940; s. Nelson Hovey and Elizabeth (Adams) D.; B.A., Yale U., 1963; J.D., Harvard, 1969; m. Elizabeth Bickley Smith, Oct. 5, 1963, (div. Jan. 1973); 1 dau., Shannon Elizabeth. Admitted to D.C. bar, 1969; dir. Avalon Community Tutorial, Los Angeles, 1964; dir. tutoring N.C. Advancement Sch., Winston-Salem, 1964-65; co-dir. Youth Ednl. Services, Durham, N.C., 1965-66; intern Legal Defense Fund of NAACP, Bolivar County, Miss., 1967; dir. Center for Auto Safety, Washington, 1969—. Bd. dirs. Action for Child Transp. Safety. English-Speaking Union Exchange fellow, 1958-59; Ralph Nader Auto Safety fellow of Consumers Union, 1970-73; Coro Found. fellow in Urban Affairs, 1963-64. Mem. Bar of D.C. Author: (with Ralph Nader) What To Do with Your Bad Car: An Action Manual for Lemon Owners, 1971; (with others) Small on Safety: The Designed-In Dangers of the Volkswagen, 1972. Home: 1612 Riggs Pl NW Washington DC 20009 Office: Dupont Circle Bldg Washington DC 20036

DODGE, WARREN FRANCIS, physician, educator; b. Scottdale, Pa., May 5, 1928; s. Charles Hulbert and Mary Ann (Shubert) D.; B.S., U. Tenn., 1953, M.D., 1955; postgrad. U. Minn., 1968; m. Elizabeth Ann Walton, Jan. 29, 1949; children—Lisa, Kent. Intern Baylor U., 1955-56; fellow Baylor Affiliated Hosp., 1958-60; practice medicine specializing in pediatrics, Galveston, Tex., 1960—; mem. staff U. Tex. Med. Br. Hosp., Galveston, asst. prof. pediatrics, dir. pediatric nephrology U. Tex. Med. Br., 1960-66, asso. prof., 1966-68, asso. prof. pediatrics and preventive medicine and community health, 1968-72, chmn. dept. health care scis., 1972—, asso. dir. pediatric nurse practitioner program, 1972—, prof. pediatrics and preventive medicine and community health, 1972—, chmn. adv. com. on ednl. support services 1973-74. Dir. Kidney Disease Detection Program, 1967-73; prin. investigator Ayerst Lab. Grant, 1969-73, Sch. Health and Nutrition Demonstration Project, 1971-74; dir. sch. health Galveston Ind. Sch. Dist., 1969-73; cons. Nat. Bd. Med. Examiners, 1972—. Served with USAAF, 1945-48. Jessie Jones fellow Baylor Coll. Medicine, 1968. Mem. A.M.A., Am. Fedn. Clin. Research, Am. Soc. Nephrology, Am. Acad. Pediatrics, Ambulatory Pediatric Assn., Am. Pediatric Soc., So. Soc. Clin. Investigation, Tex. Pediatric Soc., So. Soc. Pediatric Research (pres. 1974-75), Am. Soc. Pediatric Nephrology. Contbr. articles to profl. jours. Home: 2 Maple Lane Galveston TX 77550 Office: 1202 Market St Galveston TX 77550

DODSON, BC, educator; b. Magnolia, Ark., Dec. 6, 1924; s. Sam and Linnie Belle (Camp) D.; B.S., State Coll. Ark., 1948; M.S., U. Ark., 1958; Ed.S., Kan. State Teachers Coll., 1961; student Okla. State U., 1960-61; Ed.D., U. Okla., 1969; m. Norma Dene Norwood, Aug. 10, 1946; children—Tekla Regina (Mrs. Harold R. Barr), Barton Clifford, Debbie Diane. Tchr. Ark. High Schs., 1948-54; tchr. Tex. High Sch., 1954-55; tchr., sci. coordinator Crossett (Ark.) High Sch., 1955-60; prof. chemistry., sci. edn. So. State Coll., head chemistry dept., 1966-68, prof., chmn. div. scis. and math., 1968-72, prof., 1970—. Served with USAAF, 1943. NSF Summer Inst. grants, 1956-59, HEW Small Coll. Research grant, 1967-68; Nat. Sci. Found. Cooperative Coll. Sch. grants, 1968-69, 1971-72. Mem. Am. Legion, Ark. Edn. Assn. (pres. 1964-65, pres. So. State Coll. chpt. 1970), Assn. Edn. Teachers of Sci. (regional treas. 1969-70), Ark. Sr. Acad. Sci., Ark. Sci. Tchrs. Assn., Nat. Sci. Tchrs. Assn., Assn. for Edn. of Teachers of Sci. (regional treas. 1969-70). Presbyn. Home: PO Box 1397 Southern State Coll Magnolia AR 71753 Office: PO Box 1397 So State Coll Magnolia AR 71753

DODSON, BERTRAM FELIX, exterminating co. exec.; b. Lynchburg, Va., June 9, 1927; s. Albert Sydnor and Hallie Turpin (Holland) D.; student pub. schs.; m. Dorothy Lee Hayes, Mar. 8, 1952; children—Bertram Felix, Karen Lee, Bonny Lynn. Founder, chief exec. officer Dodson Bros. Exterminating Co., Inc., Lynchburg, 1944—, pres., chmn. bd. 41 branches; owner, officer Dodson Florist, Lynchburg, 1961—, Dodson Real Estate, Lynchburg, 1962—, Dodson Farms and Aireactor Chem., Lynchburg, 1966—, Hapiday Motor Lodge, Pearisburg, Va., 1963—. Pres. Va. Counties Assn., 1960-61, Campbell County Rescue Squad, 1969-70; mem. P.T.A., 1960-71. Pres. Campbell County Bd. Suprs., 1958-61. Bd. dirs. Lynchburg United Fund, 1964-65, A.R.C., 1963-64, Lynchburg Gen. Hosp., 1957-64, U. Va. Extension Coll. at Lynchburg, 1960-63. Mem. C. of C., Pest Control Assn. Va. (pres. 1954-55), Nat. Pest Control Assn., Ruritan. Presbyn. Mason (Shriner), Lion, Elk. Club: Lynchburg Track. Home: 1022 Oakmont Circle Lynchburg VA 24502 Office: 3712 Campbell Av Lynchburg VA 24505

DODSON, DURWOOD RANDOLPH, supt. schs.; b. Picton, Tex., Sept. 3, 1915; s. Joel Marshall and Della Lou (Randolph) D.; B.S., East Tex. State U., 1937, M.S., 1947; m. Joe Louise Amos, June 2, 1938; children—Keith, Mark. Supt. schs. Rural High Sch., Tahoka, Tex., 1941-43, Merit, Tex., 1946-51, Roxton, Tex., 1951-57, Honey Grove, Tex., 1958-65, Cameron, Tex., 1965—. Mem. faculty So. Meth. U., 1946. Active Community Chest, 1966-71. Served with AUS, 1943-45. Mem. Am., Tex. assns. sch. adminstrs., Tex. State Tchrs. Assn., Phi Delta Kappa. Mason, Lion, Rotarian. Home: 702 E 7th St Cameron TX 76520 Office: PO Box 712 Cameron TX 76520

DODSON, EUGENE BENEDICT, TV exec.; b. Woodward, Okla., Nov. 25, 1912; s. William Benedict and Minnie (Richards) D.; B.A., U. Okla., 1933; m. Grace Beaulieu, Apr. 4, 1941; children—Jean Ann (Mrs. Jean D. Hibbs), George. Reporter, Okla. News, Oklahoma City, 1933-34, Daily Oklahoman, Oklahoma City, 1934-42; reporter, deskman Asso. Press, Washington, 1945-47; news editor Daily Transcript, Norman, Okla., 1947-49; promotion mgr. WKY Television System, Oklahoma City, 1949-51, adminstrv. asst. 1951-54, dir. radio operations, 1954-55, asst. mgr., 1955-56, acting mgr., 1956-57; mgr. WSFA-TV, Montgomery, Ala., 1957-58, WTVT, Tampa, Fla., 1958—; exec. v.p. WKY Television System, Inc., 1970—; dir. Okla. Pub. Co., 1974—. Past mem. CBS-TV affiliates adv. bd. for Dist. No. 3. Campaign chmn. Tampa United Fund, 1965, pres., 1968-69; pres. Tampa Horse Show Assn., 1966—, Tampa Citizens Safety Council, 1965, Tampa Philharmonic Assn., 1962-66; fellow U. Tampa. Served with AUS, 1942-45. Decorated Legion of Merit (U.S.); Order of Vasco Nunez de Balboa (Republic of Panama); recipient Silver Medallion of Brotherhood award Fla. Region Nat. Conf. Christians and Jews, 1974; named Citizen of Yr., Civitan Club, Tampa, 1967. Mem. Nat. (television bd. dirs. 1974—), Fla. (dir., past pres.) assns. broadcasters, Broadcast Pioneers, Nat. Press Club, Greater Tampa C. of C. (pres. 1969-70), Sigma Delta Chi. Episcopalian. Rotarian (pres. Tampa club 1966-67). Clubs: University, Tampa Yacht and Country, Palma Ceia Golf and Country. Home: 10703 Carrollwood Dr Tampa FL 33618 Office: PO Box 22013 Tampa FL 33622

DODSON, JAMES MARVIN, ednl. adminstr.; b. Bonnieville, Ky., Mar. 29, 1910; s. Clive and Cola (Riggs) D.; A.B., Western Ky. U., 1936, M.A., 1942; Ph.D., Ind. U., 1960; m. Narvilla Burns, Dec. 28, 1931; 1 dau., Barbara Ann (Mrs. Joseph Macaluso). Classroom tchr., Bonnieville, Ky., 1931-38; prin. Meml. High Sch., Hardyville, Ky., 1938-42; supt. Hart County Schs., 1942-43, Horsecave Schs., 1943-48; dir. pupil transp. Dept. Edn., 1948-50; dir. pub. relations Ky. Edn. Assn., Louisville, 1950-54, exec. sec., 1954—. Mem. N.E.A., Nat. Council State Edn. Assns., Horace Mann League, Am. Assn. Sch. Adminstrs., Sigma Phi Sigma, Phi Delta Kappa. Methodist. Mason (Shriner). Author: Desirable Practices in Promoting State Legislation, 1960. Home: 925 Packard Av Louisville KY 40217 Office: 101 W Walnut St Louisville KY 40202

DODSON, MAYHEW WILSON (PAT) III, advt. firm exec.; b. Pensacola, Fla., Oct. 7, 1929; s. Mayhew Wilson and Marcelle (Statham) D.; B.A., Vanderbilt U., 1951; M.A., U. Fla., 1955; LL.D. (hon.), U. W.Fla., 1974; m. Peggy Bond, June 11, 1951; children—Deborah Ann, David Bond. Chmn. bd. Dodson, Craddock & Born Advt., Inc., Pensacola, 1958—; pres., dir. Gaberonne, Inc., 1962—, Lavallet, Inc., 1968; pres. Pensacola Hist. Properties, Inc., Climax Corp.; dir. First Nat. Bank Pensacola, 1972, chmn. bd., 1972-74. Past pres. Pensacola Preservation Soc., United Cerebral Palsy Pensacola; exec. chmn. Fla. Bicentennial Steering Com.; chmn. Bicentennial Commn. Am. Revolution for Fla., 1970-72, vice chmn., 1972-74, City Pensacola, Jackson Day Sesquicentennial, 1971, City-Country Inner-City Task Force; mem. W. Fla. Resources Council; dir. adminstrn. Fla. Dept. Transp., 1970; past chmn. Pensacola Hist. Restoration and Preservation Commn., Gov.'s Conf. Devel. Fla.'s Hist. Resources, 1968; past v.p., bd. dirs., chmn. bldg. com. Ninety and Nine Boys Ranch; past vice chmn. Pensacola Hist. Adv. Com.; past mem. Pensacola Archtl. Rev. Bd.; mem. Fla. Bd. Regents, also chmn. instructional tech. com., 1969-70; pres. Pensacola Hist. Properties, Inc.; charter mem. Citizens Com. for establishment four year coll. Pensacola, Miracle Strip Council; mem. Pres.' Adv. Council on Hist. Preservation, 1974—. Active numerous Republican campaigns, including organizer Escambia County Nixon-for-Pres. campaign, 1968; organizing dir. Pensacola Rep. Club: organizer Pensacola Young Rep. Club; coordinator Gov.'s adv. com. for N.W. Fla. Past bd. dirs. Pensacola Hist. Soc., Pensacola Sports Assn., Fiesta Five Flags, Dorothy Walton Found.; bd. dirs. Action '76 Steering Com., Pensacola, Fla. Hist. Soc. (also recording sec.), Hist. Pensacola, Inc. Served with USNR, 1947-51, with USMCR, 1951-53. Recipient A.C. Blount award Pensacola Action '76 Program, 1974; named Businessman of Year, Pensacola News-Jour., 1974. Mem. Pensacola C. of C. (past chmn. annexation com.), Pensacola Sales and Marketing execs. Club (past v.p.), Advt. Fedn. Am. (Ink Silver medal and Advt. Man of Year award, both 1962), Sigma Nu. Episcopalian. Editor: Journey Through the Old Everglades, 1973. Contbr. to profl. jours. Home: 4845 Andrade St Pensacola FL 32504 Office: 4711 Scenic Hwy PO Drawer A Pensacola FL 32502

DODSON, RONALD FRANKLIN, neurocytologist; b. Paris, Tex., Feb. 14, 1942; s. Benjamin Franklin and Vera (Eubank) D.; A.A., Paris Jr. Coll., 1962; B.A., East Tex. State Coll., 1964, M.A., 1965; Ph.D., Tex. A. & M. U., 1969; m. Sandra Jim Roberson, Nov. 13, 1965; 1 dau., Diana Lynn. Teaching asst. East Tex. State U., 1964-65; grad. coll. fellowship in electron microscopy Tex. A. & M. U., 1965-69; research asso. dept. anatomy U. Tex. Med. Sch., 1969-70; instr. depts. neurology and pathology Baylor Coll. Medicine, 1970, asst. prof. neurology and pathology, 1971—, ultrastructural research in cerebrovascular disease. Mem. Am. Heart Assn. (fellowship in stroke council 1971—), British Brain Research Assn., Tex., N.Y. acad. scis., A.A.A.S., Am. Men and Women of Sci., Am. Chem. Soc., Am. Inst. Biol. Sci., Tex. Soc. Electron Microscopy, Electron Microscopy Soc. Am., Soc. Neurosci. Home: 9440 Tooley St Houston TX 77071 Office: Dept Neurology Baylor Coll Medicine Tex Med Center Houston TX 77025

DOENGES, RUDOLPH CONRAD, educator; b. Tonkawa, Okla., Dec. 7, 1930; s. Rudolph Soland and Helen (Lower) D.; A.B. magna cum laude, Harvard, 1952, M.B.A., 1954; D.Bus. Adminstrn., U. Colo., 1965; m. Ellen Ione Gummere, Oct. 5, 1963; children—Rudolph Conrad, John Soland, William Gummere. Marketing analyst Ford Motor Co., Dearborn, Mich., 1954; gen. mgr. Doenges-Long Motors Inc., Colorado Springs, Colo., 1958-61; asst. prof. U. Tex. Grad. Sch. Bus., Austin, 1964-67, asso. prof., 1967—, asso. dean, 1972—. Dir. Doenges-Glass, Inc., Aurora, Colo. Served to lt. (j.g.) Supply Corps, USNR, 1954-58. Harvard Nat. scholar, 1948-54; Ford Found. Dissertation fellow, 1963-64. Mem. Am. Econ. Assn., Am., Southwestern (pres.) finance assns., Financial Mgmt. Assn., Phi Beta Kappa, Beta Gamma Sigma, Delta Sigma Pi. Republican. Methodist. Rotarian. Author: (with others) Case Problems in Financial Management, 1968; (with G.A. Jentz) Consumer Credit in Texas, 1969. Editor: (with H.A. Wolf) Readings in Money and Banking, 1968; asso. editor finance Social Sci. Quar., 1966—. Home: 3500 Hillbrook Circle Austin TX 78731

DOGGETT, LOWELL, judge; b. Council Grove, Kan., Jan. 6, 1917; s. Walter Martin and May (Jasper) D.; A.B., U. Okla., 1938, LL.B., 1940; m. Shirley Ruth Jackson, June 6, 1947; children—Bruce Jackson, Robert Lowell. Admitted to Okla. State bar, 1940; pvt. practice law, Ponca City, Okla., 1940-48 county atty. Kay County Okla., 1948-52; county judge Kay County, Okla., 1959-69; asso. dist. judge 8th Judicial Dist. Okla., 1969-71, dist. judge, 1971—. Pres., No. Okla. Coll. Found., 1966; pres. Ponca City YMCA, 1957-58; pres. Kay County Tb. Assn., 1950-51. Served with AUS, World War II. Mem. Okla. Assn. County Judges (pres. 1966-67), Okla. Assn. County Bar Pres. (pres. 1963), Kay County (pres. 1962), Am., Okla. bar assns., Am. Judicature Soc., Nat., Okla. councils juvenile ct. judges, Ponca City C. of C., Kay Council Community Services, Kay County Assn. Child Guidance, Am. Legion (comdr. 1953). Methodist (lay leader). Club: Exchange (dist. gov. 1956). Home: 2509 Robin Rd Ponca City OK 74601 Office: Kay County Courthouse PO Box 424 Newkirk OK 74647

DOHERTY, JAMES EDWARD III, physician; b. Newport, Ark., Nov. 22, 1923; s. James Edward and Ida Josephine (Parish) D.; B.S., U. Ark., 1944, M.D., 1946; m. Margaret Walton Croskeys, June 5, 1948; children—Richard Edward, Margaret Elise. Intern, Columbus (Ga.) City Hosp., 1946-47; resident in internal medicine U. Ark. Sch. Medicine, Little Rock, 1949-52, instr., 1952-53, asst. prof. medicine, 1953-61, asso. prof., 1962-68, prof., 1968—, dir. cardiology div., 1969—; chief cardiology section VA Hosp., Little Rock, 1956-68, dir. cardiology div. 1969—. Served with AUS, 1943-46, 47-49. Diplomate Am. Bd. Internal Medicine. Mem. A.C.P., Am. Coll. Cardiology (state gov. 1962-65, 68-71), Soc. Nuclear Medicine, N.Y. Acad. Scis., A.M.A., So. Soc. Clin. Investigation, Am. (chmn. So. regional research com. 1969-71), Ark. (dir. 1955, pres. 1959-60) heart assns., Ark. Arts Center, Ark. Orch. Soc., Med. Center Camera Club, Sigma Xi, Sigma Chi, Phi Chi, Alpha Omega Alpha, Alpha Epsilon Delta. Mason. Club: Little Rock Racquet. Contbr. articles to profl. pubs. Home: 48 Wingate Dr Little Rock AR 72205 Office: 4301 W Markham St Little Rock AR 72201 also 300 E Roosevelt Rd Little Rock AR 72206

DOHERTY, JAMES PAUL, banker; b. Central Falls, R.I., Dec. 20, 1914; s. James and Mary (Brady) D.; Ph.B., Providence Coll., 1935; m. Miriam Louise Barnett, Mar. 3, 1943; children—James Paul, Mary (Mrs. John F. Lally III), Miriam (Mrs. Robert Baldwin, Jr.), Patrick, John. Tchr. high sch., Central Falls, 1935-41; v.p., mgr. Cotton Products Co., Inc., 1945-58; v.p., trust officer Am. Bank and Trust Co., Opelousas, La., 1958-73, exec. v.p., 1973—. Vice pres. Evangeline Area council Boy Scouts Am., 1948—; sec. Krotz Springs Port Commn., 1966—; pres. Acad. Immaculate Conception Parent Tchr. Club, 1960-61. Bd. dirs. Regional Export Expansion Commn. Served to capt. AUS, 1941-45. Recipient Sertoma Service to Mankind award, 1965; Silver Beaver award Boy Scouts Am., 1969; named Citizen of Year, C. of C., 1966, Man of Year, Acad. Immaculate Conception, 1962. K.C. (3 deg, 4 deg). Roman Catholic (mem. ch. council 1968—). Home: Route 1 Box 30 Opelousas LA 70570 Office: PO Box 271 Opelousas LA 70570

DOHERTY, MICHAEL FOWLER, university adminstr.; b. San Antonio, Feb. 23, 1945; s. John Gerard and Elizabeth (Fowler) D.; A.S., San Antonio Coll., 1966; B.S., St. Mary's U., 1969; m. Shirley Jean Keller, Sept. 29, 1944; 1 dau., Michelle Jean. Research asst. Southwest Research Inst., San Antonio, Tex., 1966-69; computer programmer Trinity U. Computer Center, San Antonio, 1969-70, mktg. mgr., 1970-72, asst. dir., systems programming mgr., 1972—; cons. Tektronix, Inc., 1973. Mem. Assn. for Computing Machinery, Share. Roman Catholic. Author: Trinity APL Users Manual, 1973. Development of an APL Shared Variables System which allows for easy use of computers by non-computer personnel, 1973. Home: 12614 Prima Vista Dr San Antonio TX 78233 Office: 715 Stadium Dr San Antonio TX 78284

DOHERTY, THOMAS ROSS, dentist, oral implantologist; b. Pine Bluff, Ark., Aug. 13, 1938; s. Neumie Ray and Pocahontas (Guthrie) D.; student U. Ark. at Monticello, 1956-59; D.M.D., Washington U., 1964; m. Ruth Esther Willoughby, Dec. 31, 1963; children—Christopher Michael, Johnathan Maxwell. Asso. of Drs., Pine Bluff, Dumas, Ark., 1966-67; pvt. practice dentistry, Pine Bluff, 1967—; mem. dental staff Jefferson, Davis hosps., sec. dental staff, 1968. Chmn., Nat. Children's Dental Health Week, 1968-69; dental dir. Office Econ. Opportunity, 1967-69. Served to capt. Dental Corps, AUS, 1964-66. Diplomate Am. Bd. Oral Implantology. Fellow Acad. Gen. Dentistry; mem. Am. Dental Assn., Ark., Jefferson County (pres. 1974), Armed Forces dental socs., Acad. Gen. Dentistry, Am. Acad. Implant Dentistry, Exptl. Aircraft Assn., Aircraft Owners and Pilots Assn., C. of C., Flying Dentists, Quiet Birdmen, Exptl. Aircraft Assn., Xi Psi Phi. Mason (Shriner). Club: Little Rock Hangar. Home: 904 Wisconsin St Pine Bluff AR 71601 Office: 1700 Doctors Dr Pine Bluff AR 71601

DOKE, MARSHALL J., JR., lawyer; b. Wichita Falls, Tex., June 9, 1934; s. Marshall J. and Mary Jane (Johnson) D.; B.A. magna cum laude, Hardin-Simmons U., 1956; LL.B. magna cum laude, So. Meth. U., 1959; m. Betty Orsini, June 2, 1956; children—Gregory J., Michael J., Laetitia Marie. Admitted to Tex. bar, 1959; practiced in Dallas, 1959, 62—; partner Rain, Harrell, Emery, Young & Doke, 1965—. Lectr. govt. contract law So. Meth. U., 1965—. Mem. bd. visitors So. Meth. U. Law Sch., Dallas, 1966-69; mem. bd. young assos. Hardin-Simmons U., Abilene, Tex., 1964-69; bd. dirs. Hope Cottage-Children's Bur., Dallas, 1964-71, pres., 1969-70. Served with Judge Adv. Gen.'s Corps, AUS, 1959-62. Mem. Am. (chmn. sect. pub. contract law 1969-70, mem. ho. of dels. 1970-72), Fed., Dallas bar assns., State Bar Tex. Methodist (chmn. com. edn. 1967-68). Home: 6910 Dartbrook Dallas TX 75240 Office: Republic Bank Tower Dallas TX 75201

DOLBEARE, ROBERT LORING, lawyer; b. Richmond, Va., Oct. 26, 1936; s. Walter Irving and Jeanne (Biggs) D.; B.Mgmt. Engring., Rensselaer Poly. Inst., 1958; LL.B., U. Va., 1965; m. Anne Cottrell Daffron, Feb. 5, 1966; children—Kenneth W., Mary Anne. Admitted to Va. bar, 1965; law clk. to Judge John Butzner, U.S. Eastern Dist. Va., 1965-66; asso. firm Hunton, Williams, Gay, Powell & Gibson, Richmond, 1966-70; partner firm Obenshain, Hinnant & Dolbeare, Richmond, 1970—; asst. county atty. County of Henrico (Va.), 1970-74. Bd. mgmt. South Richmond-Chesterfield YMCA, 1973—; bd. dirs. Southampton Citizens Assn., Richmond, 1972—. Served to comdr. USNR, 1958-65; mem. Res. Mem. Res. Officers Assn., Naval Reserve Assn., Am., Va., Richmond bar assns., Assn. Am. Trial Lawyers, Va. Trial Lawyers Assn., Tau Beta Pi. Roman Catholic. Home: 7625 Granite Hall Av Richmond VA 23225 Office: 7th & Franklin Bldg Suite 912 Richmond VA 23219

DOLCE, CARL JOHN, coll. dean; b. New Orleans, June 3, 1928; s. John and Nina (Puglia) D.; B.A., Tulane U., 1947; M.Ed., Loyola U. of South, 1955; Ed.D., Harvard, 1963; m. Nancy Lockwood, July 27, 1955; children—Carla, John. Elementary sch. tchr. 1948-54; secondary sch. tchr., 1954-55; acting supr. textbooks, 1955; prin. jr. high sch., 1955-63; faculty Harvard, 1963-65; supt. pub. schs. City of New Orleans, 1965-69; dean Sch. Edn., N.C. State U., 1969—. Mem. vis. com. Harvard Grad. Sch. Edn., 1967-73; mem. adv. com. for new ednl. media U.S. Office Edn, 1966-68; mem. Nat. Citizens Com. for Pub. TV, 1967-68, Inst. for Services to Edn., Inc., Washington, 1967—. Served with AUS, 1951-53. Home: 801 Macon Pl Raleigh NC 27609

DOLCE, PETER SEBASTIAN, dentist; b. Chgo., Sept. 9, 1923; s. Sebastian Anthony and Rosaria Elizabeth (Dolce) D.; D.D.S., Loyola U., Chgo., 1947; m. Joan Haberkorn, Apr. 16, 1952; children—Kathryn Ann, Peter Joseph. Practice oral reconstrn., Oak Park, Ill., 1947-52, 54-57, Delray Beach, Fla., 1957—. Prof. prosthetics U. Seoul, Korea, 1952-53. Served with AUS, 1943-45; with USNR, 1952-55; Korea. Mem. Am., Dental Assn., East Coast, Palm Beach dental socs., Am. Acad. Dental Practice Adminstrn., Pierre Fauchard Acad. (Fauchard medal 1953), Acad. of 100. Roman Catholic. Kiwanian. Club: Delray Beach; Loyola University (Chgo.). Inventor mouth irrigation device, de-burring mechanism. Mailing Address: 1045 E Atlantic Av Delray Beach FL 33444 Home: 1227 Harbor Dr Delray Beach FL 33444

DOLEZAL, HENRY, judge; b. Perry, Okla., Jan. 11, 1905; s. James H. and Ella (Kasl) D.; A.B., U. Okla., 1926, LL.B., 1933; student U. Chgo., 1930-31. Admitted to Okla. bar, 1933, pvt. practice, Perry, 1933-35, 37-38, 46-68; asso. dist. judge, Noble County, Okla., 1969—; county atty. Noble County, 1935-37, county judge, 1938-41; city atty., Perry, 1937-38. County adviser to registrants under Selective

Service Law, 1940-41, 46—; mayor City of Perry, 1947-49, 51-57; mem. Okla. Ho. Reps., 1957-64. Chmn. finance com. Noble County Rep. Central Com., 1948-52, chmn. central com. 1954-58. Served to maj. AUS, 1941-46. Mem. Am., Okla., Noble County (pres. 1953-55) bar assns., Am. Judicature Soc., V.F.W. (comdr. post 1948-49), Am. Legion (chaplain Okla. dept. 1960), 40 and 8, Phi Delta Phi. Presbyn. (elder, clk. session 1966-69). Mason (32 deg., K.T.), Rotarian (pres. Perry 1946-47), Odd Fellow, Knight of Pythias; mem. Order of Eastern Star, White Shrine of Jerusalem. Home: 1102 Delaware St Perry OK 73077 Office: County Courthouse Perry OK 73077

DOLL, MAX, paper co. exec.; b. Soldiers Grove, Wis., Feb. 21, 1932; s. Leo E. and Genevieve (Martin) D.; student Loras Coll., 1950-51, Wis. State Coll., 1951-52; m. Karen Mary Bender, Dec. 28, 1955; children—Peter, Mark, Christopher, Mary Kathryn, John. With Cellu Products Co., Patterson, N.C., 1955—, v.p., 1958—, sec., 1968—. Trustee Caldwell Community Coll. and Tech. Inst. Served with AUS, 1953-55. Rotarian (pres. 1969-70). Home: Pine Hill Patterson NC 28661 Office: Cellu Products Co River and Roby Martin Rd Patterson NC 28661

DOLLAHITE, JAMES WALTON, educator, veterinarian; b. Center Point, Tex., May 1, 1911; s. William Walter and Lucy (Thomason) D.; D.V.M., Tex. A. and M. U., 1933, M.S., 1961; m. Willie Mae Bishop, Dec. 22, 1933; children—Alice Jane (Mrs. Arthur James Hustins, Jr.), Jamie Sue (Mrs. Gregory Peter Wene). Veterinarian pvt. practice, Marfa, Tex., 1933-52; researcher USDA, Beltsville, Md., 1934-39; head Animal Disease Lab. Tex. Agrl. Expt. Sta., Marfa, 1952-61; asso. prof. vet. medicine Tex. A. and M. U., 1962-65, prof., researcher, 1965—. Cons. to physicians, veterinarians, industry on toxicology, pollution. Served with AUS, 1942-46. Fellow A.A.A.S., Am. Bd. Vet. Toxicology; mem. Am. Coll. Vet. Toxicologists (pres. 1970-71), Soc. Toxicology, Am. Acad. Clin. Toxicology, N.Y. Acad. Sci., Am., Tex. vet. med. assns., Sigma Xi, Phi Zeta. Contbr. numerous articles to sci. jours. Home: 4200 Milam St Bryan TX 77801 Office: Vet Sci Bldg College Station TX 77843

DOLLISON, ROBERT BENSON, govt. ofcl.; b. N.Y.C., June 2, 1930; s. Dwight Israel and Laura Blair (Maxwell) D.; B.S., Columbia Coll., 1951; postgrad. George Washington U., 1962 65; m. Sally Chamberlin Scott, Dec. 25, 1969; children—Robert Maxwell, Elizabeth Anne. Engr., Westinghouse Electric Corp., Pitts., 1951-53; fgn. service officer Dept. State Washington, El Salvador and Thailand, 1958-63; internat. economist Dept. Commerce, Washington, 1963—. Served to lt. USNR, 1953-56. Episcopalian. Home: 2229 Bancroft Pl NW Washington DC 20008 Office: Dept of Commerce 14th and Constitution Av Washington DC 20230

DOMAN, LEWIS ALBERT, JR., banker; b. Alton, Ill., Mar. 21, 1930; s. Lewis Albert and Clara Rosalie (Johnson) D.; student Shurtleff Coll., 1948-49, Washington U., St. Louis, 1950, U. Md., 1960-61; m. Alice Louise Reese, May 3, 1957; children—David, Patrick, James, Anne, Amy, Michael. Commd. 2d lt. USMC, 1950, advanced through grades to capt., 1958; U.S. Naval aviator Korean campaign, 1953-54; ret., 1962; sr. v.p., dir. Citizens & Peoples Nat. Bank, Pensacola, Fla., 1962—. Pres., Community Mental Health Center Escambia County; 1st v.p. Fiesta of Five Flags, 1973, pres. elect; active YMCA; treas. United Way of Escambia County, Gulf Coast council Boy Scouts Am., 1968-70. Bd. dirs. Blue Shield of Fla.; pres., bd. dirs. Mental Health Dist. 1 State of Fla. Mem. Am. Inst. Banking (past pres. Pensacola chpt.), Fla. Bankers Assn., Pensacola Sports Assn., Pensacola C. of C. (dir.). Roman Catholic. Rotarian. Clubs: Pensacola Country; Order of Tristan; Rebellaires. Home: 604 Fairpoint Dr Gulf Breeze FL 32561 Office: PO Box 1072 Pensacola FL 32595

DOMBALIS, CONSTANTINE NICHOLAS, clergyman; b. Norfolk, Va., July 30, 1925; s. Nicholas John and Helen Florence (Matinos) D.; B.A., Greek Orthodox Theol. Sem., 1947, B.Th., 1949; postgrad. (Gregory Taylor scholar), Harvard, 1949-50; S.T.B., Gen. Episcopal Theol. Sem., 1951; postgrad. Columbia, 1952; m. Mary Chris Fourgis, June 6, 1954; children—Nicholas, Christopher. Ordained to ministry Greek Orthodox Ch., 1954; pastor Sts. Constantine and Helen Greek Orthodox Ch., Richmond, Va., 1954—. Lectr. dept. humanities Va. Union U., Richmond. Mem. Nat. Presbyters Bd. of Greek Archdiocese; vicar Greek Archdiocese of Va.; rep. Nat. Council Chs., 1970—; v.p. Mediterranean Inst., U. Richmond, 1970-71; founder, Pre-Naturalization Classes (cited by Freedom Found.), 1958; mem. Richmond Human Relations Commn., 1970-72; pres. UN Assn. Central Va., 1972—, Boys Club, 1971. Bd. dirs. James Branch Cabell Library, Va. Commonwealth U.; bd. govs. United Givers Fund, 1966-69. Recipient citation award D.A.R., 1968. Mem. Richmond Area Ministers Assn. (pres. 1964). Club: James River Catfish. Contbr. articles to profl. jours., mags. and newspapers, sermons to numerous books. Home: 304 Sandalwood Dr Richmond VA 23229 Office: 30 Malvern Av Richmond VA 23221

DOMEIER, DOUGLAS DRATH, journalist; b. Berwyn, Ill., June 30, 1939; s. Erwin Jesse and Julia Katharine (Drath) D.; B.J., U. Mo., 1961. Reporter, Dallas Morning News, 1965—, religion editor, 1965-66, editor for aviation, sci. and space, 1966—. Served with AUS, 1962-65. Recipient 3 Dallas News Dealey awards for outstanding reporting; winner Best Spot News Story, Dallas Press Club, 1968; co-recipient S.W. Journalism Forum award, 1969. Mem. Sigma Phi Epsilon, Sigma Delta Chi. Home: 3900 W Northwest Hwy Dallas TX 75220 Office: Young & Houston Sts Dallas TX 75222

DOMENGEAUX, JEROME ERASTE, judge; b. Lafayette, La., Mar. 3, 1919; s. Joseph Rodolph and Marthe (Mouton) D.; B.A., U. Southwestern La., 1940; postgrad. Georgetown U. Sch. Law, 1941; LL.B., Tulane U., 1948, J.D., 1968; m. Julia Marie Harvey, Oct. 5, 1945; children—Jane Ann (Mrs. William J. Bayard), Julia Martha (Mrs. Anthony D. Moroux), Joan Marie, Jerome E. Jr., James H. Admitted to La. bar, 1948; gen. practice law, Lafayette, 1948-62; mayor, Lafayette, 1956-60; judge 15th Jud. Dist. Ct. La., Lafayette, 1962-70, 4th La. Ct. of Appeal, New Orleans, 1969-70, 3d Circuit Ct. Appeal, 1970—. Served to capt., AUS, 1942-46. Decorated Bronze Star; recipient Mayor of Distinction award La. Municipal Assn. 1959. Home: 1217 Myrtle Blvd Lafayette LA 70501 Office: Jourdan Bldg Lafayette LA 70501

DOMINGUEZ, DANIEL, C.P.A.; b. Buenos Aires, Argentina, Oct. 20, 1945; s. Vicente and Josefa (Santangelo) D.; brought to U.S., 1964, naturalized, 1970; B.A., U. Houston, 1968, M.S., 1970; m. C. Naomi Liendo, Dec. 15, 1966; children—Andrea, Daniel. Staff accountant Seidman & Seidman, C.P.A.'s, Houston, 1968, sr. accountant 1970-71, mgr. taxes, 1971-72, mgr. in charge profl. devel., scheduling, 1972-73, prin., 1974—. Recipient Standard Oil of Tex. scholarship, 1967-68, Heine fellowship, 1968-69. C.P.A., Tex. Mem. Tex. Soc. C.P.A.'s, Am. Inst. C.P.A.'s. Mem. Spanish Bible Chapel (trustee, elder 1971—). Home: 8215 Twin Hills Houston TX 77074 Office: 1525 Americana Bldg Houston TX 77002

DOMINGUEZ, ERNESTO, educator; b. Veracruz, Mexico, Oct. 6, 1927; s. Ernesto and Ernestine (Quiroga) D.; Chem. Engr., Escuela Nacional de Ciencias Químicas, Universidad Nacional Autónoma de México, 1950, Ph.D., 1963. Tchr. gen. chemistry Universidad Iberoamerica, Mexico City, 1960-61, prof. chemistry, 1960—, dir. Sch. Chem. Scis., 1962-63, dir. chemistry dept., 1968-69; tchr. Universidad Nacional Autónoma de México, 1961-62. Mem. Mexican Inst. Chem. Engrs. (dir. 1972), Mexican Chem. Soc., Am. Chem. Soc., Instituto Mexicano de Ingenieros Químicas (dir. jour. 1972-73). Home: 1 Rio Hondo Mexico DF 20 Mexico

DOMINGUEZ, GERALD HENRY, physician; b. Tampa, Fla., Apr. 12, 1933; s. Jose Antonio and Dolores A. (Amoedo) D.; B.S., Tulane U., 1955, M.D., 1959; m. Maralyn G. Childress, June 27, 1964; children—Erin Lynn, Nancy Lauren. Intern, Charity Hosp., New Orleans, 1959-60; resident internal medicine, 1960-63, clin. instr., 1962-64; gastroenterology fellow, mem. faculty dept. medicine Tulane Med. Sch., 1963-64; practice medicine, specializing in internal medicine, Tampa, Fla., 1965—; mem. staff Tampa Gen. Hosp., St. Joseph's Hosp., Tampa; asst. clin. prof. medicine U. South Fla., 1972—. Recipient physician's recognition award A.M.A., 1970-73. Diplomate Am. Bd. Internal Medicine. Fellow A.C.P.; mem. Am. Soc. Internal Medicine, Fla. Soc. Gastroenterology, Am., Fla., Hillsborough med. assns., West Coast Soc. Internal Medicine. Clubs: Palma Ceia Golf and Country. Contbr. articles to profl. publs. Home: 1504 Sheridan Forest Dr Tampa FL 33609 Office: 1921 W Buffalo Av Tampa FL 33607

DOMINGUEZ, JAMES FRANCIS, dentist; b. New Orleans, June 13, 1920; s. James Louis and Frances Beatrice (Buchert) D.; B.S., Tulane, 1943; D.D.S., Loyola U., New Orleans, 1945; m. Estelle Viola Haase, Jan. 24, 1945; 1 dau., Carlos Ann (Mrs. Gary Jude Danos). Individual practice dentistry, New Orleans, 1945—. Dir. Assn. Upper State St. Inc., 1966—. Served with USNR, 1943-45, 52-54. Mem. C. Victor Vignes Hon. Dental Fraternity, Am., La., New Orleans dental assns., Xi Psi Phi. Roman Catholic. Home: 2323 State St New Orleans LA 70118 Office: 2233 Jefferson Hwy New Orleans LA 70121

DOMINGUEZ, JOSE RAMON, physician; b. Perico, Matanzas, Cuba, Oct. 28, 1924; s. Jose Ramon and Margarita (Daniel) D.; B.S. in Letters and Sci., La Progresiva Presbyn. Coll., 1942; M.D., Havana U., 1952; m. Elise Whetsell, Dec. 3, 1967; 1 dau., Elyse Joley. Intern Christian Hosp., St. Louis, 1953-55; surg. resident St. Francis Hosp., Miami Beach, Fla., 1955-56; gen. practice resident Halifax Dist. Hosp., Daytona Beach, Fla., 1956-58; practice medicine, specializing in geriatrics, West Palm Beach, Fla., 1959-68, Daytona-Ormond Beach, Fla., 1968—; chief of medicine Ormond Beach Meml. Hosp., 1972-74. Fellow Am. Geriatrics Soc.; mem. A.M.A., Fla. Med. Assn., Volusia County Med. Soc. Mason (32 deg.). Home: 4 Bayberry Dr Ormond Beach FL 32074 Office: 1184 Ocean Shore Blvd Ormond Beach FL 32074

DONALD, JAMES ROBERT, agrl. economist; b. Omega, Ga., Dec. 31, 1933; s. Clinton Ernest and Lorena (Branan) D.; B.S., U. Ga., 1954; M.S., N.C. State U., 1957; m. Nancy Ripple, Sept. 16, 1961; children—Gordon, Mary. Agrl. economist U.S. Dept. Agr., Washington, 1957—. Served with AUS, 1957. Mem. Am. Agrl. Econ. Assn., Alpha Zeta. Editor: Cotton Situation, 1962-72. Author: The Demand for Textile Fibers in the United States, 1963. Home: 1046 Carper St McLean VA 22101 Office: 500 12th St SW Washington DC 20250

DONALD, WILLIAM DAVID, physician; b. Donalds, S.C., Apr. 27, 1924; s. Emmett Clifton and Ruth (Kennedy) D.; B.A., Erskine Coll., 1943; M.D., Vanderbilt U., 1947; m. Lola Jane Callaway, Sept. 11, 1948; children—William Kennedy, Janice Marie, James Herbert, David Clifton. Intern, Vanderbilt Hosp., Nashville, 1947, now staff mem.; resident U. Va., Charlottesville, 1948-50; asst. prof. dept. pediatrics U. Ala. Med. Sch., 1952-54, asso. prof., 1954-59; asso. prof. pediatrics Med. Coll. Ga., 1959-60; asso. prof. pediatrics Vanderbilt U. Med. Sch., 1960—; practice medicine specializing in pediatrics, Nashville, 1960—; mem. staff Nashville Gen. Hosp. Served with USAF, 1950-52. Diplomate Am. Bd. Pediatrics. Mem. Am. Acad. Pediatrics, So. Soc. Pediatric Research, Am. Fed. Clin. Research, Ambulatory Pediatric Assn., Sigma Xi, Alpha Omega Alpha. Home: 2311 Warfield Ln Nashville TN 37215 Office: Vanderbilt U Hosp Nashville TN 37232

DONALDSON, DAVID, san. engr.; b. Boulder City, Nev., June 17, 1932; s. Arthur and Myrtle (Dallenty) D.; B.S. in Civil Engring., Mont. State Coll., 1955; M.S., U. N.C., 1960; m. Alfrieda Elizabeth Chambers, Dec. 18, 1954; children—Bruce Arthur, Brian David, Blair Whitney. Profl. engr., Hazen & Sawyer, cons. engrs., N.Y.C., 1960-63, project mgr., Managua, Nicaragua, 1963-66; adviser to Peruvian Govt., Pan Am. Health Orgn., Lima, 1966-68, regional adviser in rural water supply, Washington, 1968-71, regional adviser in instl. devel. pub. services, 1971—. Cons. World Bank Group, Washington, 1972; v.p., Health Services Adminstrn., Washington, 1972-73. Served to lt. USNR, 1956-59. Trainee grantee Pub. Health Service, 1959-60. Registered profl. engr., N.Y. Mem. Assn. Nicaragua Soc. Engrs. and Architects, Am. Assn. C.E. (sec. local chpt. 1956), Am. Water Works Assn. (mem. internat. com. 1967—), Interam. Soc. San. Engrs. (sec. treas. 1968—). Home: 2526 Trophy Lane Reston VA 22091 Office: 525 23d St Washington DC 20037

DONALDSON, MERLE RICHARD, elec. engr., educator; b. Silverdale, Kan., Apr. 7, 1920; s. Harry Richard and Alma (Bowman) D.; B.E.E., Ga. Inst. Tech., 1946, M.E.E., 1947, Ph.D., 1959; m. Maideth Erlaine Bennett, Oct. 23, 1943; children—Donna Sharon (Mrs. David A. Jones), Merle Richard. Instr., asst. prof. elec. engring. dept. Ga. Inst. Tech., 1946-50; engr. Oak Ridge Nat. Lab., 1950-57; elec. engr.; lab. dir. Electronic Communications, Inc., St. Petersburg, Fla., 1957-63; asso. prof. U. Fla., 1963-64; prof., chmn. elec. engring. dept. U. South Fla., Tampa, 1964—. Cons. Sperry Microwave Co., Trak Microwave Co. Served with USNR, 1940-46. Fellow I.E.E.E.; mem. A.A.A.S., Am. Soc. Engring. Edn., Sigma Xi, Tau Beta Pi, Eta Kappa Nu, Phi Kappa Phi. Editor: I.E.E.E. Transactions on Communications Systems, 1959-60. Home: 1833 Almeria Way S St Petersburg FL 33712 Office: Dept Elec Engring Coll Engring U South Fla Tampa FL 33620

DONALDSON, WILLIAM EMMERT, nutrionist, educator; b. Balt., Dec. 19, 1931; s. Clarence Emmert and Lillian (Creekmore) D.; B.S., U. Md., 1953, M.S., 1955, Ph.D., 1957; m. Josephine Doran Blair, Aug. 2, 1955; children—Katherine, Anne, William, Rita, Jennifer, Robert. Asst. prof. U. R.I., 1957-62; asst. prof. dept. poultry sci. N.C. State U., Raleigh, 1962-64, asso. prof., 1964-68, prof., 1968—. Mem. Am. Inst. Nutrition, Poultry Sci. Assn. Am., A.A.A.S., Sigma Xi (research award N.C. state chpt.), Phi Kappa Phi. Contbr. numerous articles to sci. jours. Home: 4401 Laurel Hill Rd Raleigh NC 27612

DONAN, WILLIAM PAGE, lawyer; b. Morganfield, Ky., May 17, 1914; s. David C. and Adeline (Callaway) D.; LL.B., Cumberland U., 1939; m. Helen Pauline Hinch, Oct. 19, 1940; 1 son, Thomas Arthur. Asst. warehouse mgr. Pitts. Steel Co., Evansville, Ind., 1935-36, St. Louis, 1936-38; clk. land dept. Phillips Petroleum Co., Bartlesville, Okla., 1940; asso. Newton Belcher, attys., Greenville, Ky., 1940-42; partner Belcher & Donan, 1945-51; pvt. practice, 1951-56; partner Donan & Vick, 1956—; atty. Greenville, 1946-48, judge, 1954-70. Pres. Greenville Indsl. Devel. Corp., 1960-67. Mem. Gov.'s Judicial Adv. Council, 1972—. Mem. Muhlenberg County Library Bd., 1969-70. Trustee Greenville Boy Scouts; fund campaign chmn. A.R.C., 1956. Trustee Med. Research Found., Greenville, Muhlenberg County Law Library, Lon Rogers Ednl. Trust, Jessie Rogers Ednl. Trust. Served to 1st lt. AUS, 1942-45. Decorated Bronze Star medal, Silver Star. Fellow Am. Coll. Probate Counsel; mem. Greenville C. of C. (pres. 1960-62), Sports Philatelists Internat., Am., Ky. (ho. dels.; chmn. ho. dels. 1968-69, v.p. 1970-71, inquiry tribunal 1971—), Muhlenberg County bar assns., Am. Judicature Soc., Law-Sci. Acad. of Am., Am. Philatelic Soc., Am. Topical Assn., Ky. Hist. Soc., Am. Legion, V.F.W., S.A.R., Blue Key. Presbyn. Democrat. Mason. Clubs: Kiwanis (past pres., lt. gov. dist. 2 Ky.-Tenn. dist.), Greenville Country (past pres.). Home: 306 E Main Cross St Greenville KY 42345 Office: 110 E Court Sq Greenville KY 42345

DONATELLI, FELIX FRANCIS, pharmacist; b. Newport, Ky., Aug. 29, 1929; s. Mario and Angela Sophie (Ferrara) D.; B.S.P., U. Fla., 1951; m. Barbara Ann Donatelli; children by previous marriage—Nick, Felicia, Steve, Petey. Pharmacist, mgr. Liggett-Rexall Stores, 1951-58; founder Donatelli's Pharmacies, Lakeland, Fla., 1959; pres. Donnaco, Inc., D & F Goaves; dir. Holiday Nursing Homes, Inc. Mem. utilization rev. com. Presbyn. Extended Care Facility, 1954; dir. Pharmashield, 1967-70. Founder Gator Youth Athletic Assn.; dir. Polk County Heart Assn., 1968-70; chmn. Citizens Adv. Com. City of Lakeland, Lakeland Planning and Zoning Bd., 1969. Named vol. of year Fla. Heart Assn., 1969, outstanding young man Lakeland Jr. C. of C., 1965, Fla. pharmacist of the year, 1964, 65. Served with USNR, 1951. Mem. Am., Fla. (pres. 1965), Polk County (pres. 1960) pharm. assns., Nat. Assn. Retail Druggists, U. Fla. Coll. Pharm. Alumni Assn. (pres. 1966). Rotarian (dir.). Home: 2256 Collins Lane Lakeland FL 33803 Office: 1400 Lakeland Hills Blvd Lakeland FL 33801

DONAUBAUER, ELTON HENRY, univ. administr; b. Marion, Tex., Nov. 9, 1921; s. Edwin O. and Melanie (Schultze) D.; B.A., Sul Ross State Coll., 1949, M.A., 1950; M.Ed., George Peabody Coll. for Tchrs., 1951; m. Dorothy Mauryne Lindley, Oct. 17, 1947; children—Melanie, Allyn, Craig. Asst. mgr. J. C. Penney Co., New Braunfels, Tex., 1939-42, 1946; prof. edn., polit. sci. S.W. Tex. Jr. Coll., Uvalde, 1949-50; dir. pub. relations Community Chest, Nashville, 1951-54, Allegheny County, Pitts., 1954-55; regional dir., dir. information services Pa. United Fund, 1955-57; instr. Watkins Inst. High Sch., Nashville, 1952-54; mem. pub. relations adv. com. United Community Funds and Councils of Am., Inc., 1955-57, mem. United Fund adv. com., 1957-60; exec. dir. United Fund of Shenango Valley Area, Sharon, Pa., 1957-60; exec. dir. Community Chest, United Fund, Health and Welfare Council, Pulaski County, Little Rock, 1960-64; dir. devel. and planning George Peabody Coll. for Tchrs., also lectr. Sociology and Social scis. Watkins Inst., Nashville, 1964-68; dir. devel. U. Ark., Fayetteville, 1968—; pres. S.W. Regional Conf. United Community Funds and Councils Am., 1963—; part-time instr. social scis. Little Rock U. Chmn. United Fund Campaign, 1970; div. chmn. Washington Regional Hosp. Devel. Campaign; co-chmn. Ridgehouse campaign, Fayetteville; chmn. Washington County United Way; pres. United Community Services of Northwest Ark., 1974—. Vice chmn. Fayetteville Planning Commn. Bd. dirs. Westark Boy Scout Council; bd. dirs., pres. United Fund Fayetteville, United Community Services, Fayetteville. Served with USAAF, 1942-46. Mem. Pub. Relations Soc. Am., Ark., Springdale, Fayetteville chambers commerce, Nat. Soc. Fund Raisers, Internat. Platform Assn., Phi Delta Kappa, Kappa Delta Pi. Methodist (bd., pres. Meth. men). Rotarian (dir.). Home: 1101 Woolsey Fayetteville AR 72701

DONAVAN, GEORGE EDGAR, JR., banker; b. Jackson, Miss., Feb. 23, 1916; s. George Edgar and Annie Mivian (Nelson) D.; student Miss. State U., 1933-34; B.S., U. Miss., 1937; postgrad. La. State U., 1964; m. Katie Bell Holmes, Dec. 3, 1938; children—George Edgar III, Carl Howard. With Lamar Life Ins. Co., Jackson, 1937-43; state mgr. Scharff & Jones, Inc., investment bankers, New Orleans, 1946-60; sr. v.p. First Nat. Bank, Jackson, 1960—. Pres. Magnolia Speech Sch.; state fund dir. A.R.C., Am. Cancer Soc. Served with USNR, 1943-46. Mem. Pi Kappa Alpha, Omicron Delta Kappa. Episcopalian. Rotarian. Clubs: Jackson (past pres.), Capital City Petroleum, Country (Jackson). Home: 3949 Eastwood Dr Jackson MS 39211 Office: First Nat Bank Jackson MS 39205

DONEGAN, CHARLES KENDALL, cardiologist; b. St. Petersburg, Fla., Oct. 21, 1920; s. Charles Edward and Cecel (Shaw) D.; A.A., St. Petersburg Jr. Coll., 1939; M.D., Duke, 1943; m. Barbara McGuire Bowman, Nov. 20, 1962; children—Anna, Martha, Charles Thomas. Intern, Duke Hosp., Durham, N.C., 1944-45, resident in medicine, 1945-46, fellow in cardiovascular disease, 1946-48; practice medicine specializing in internal medicine, St. Petersburg, 1948—; cons. Bayfront Med. Center; cardiologist St. Petersburg Med. Clinic, 1952—; vice-chief staff St. Anthony's Hosp., 1964-65, mem. exec. com. 1964-66, now sr. staff; clin. prof. medicine U. South Fla. Bd. dirs. Fla. Blue Shield, 1970—. Mem. Fla. Tb. Bd., 1957-64; Bd. dirs. Pinellas County Tb. Health Assn., 1957-64, Fla. Tb. and Respiratory Disease Assn., 1964-65, Youth City, 1974—; trustee Mus. Fine Arts. Served to lt. comdr. USNR, 1946, 53-54. Diplomate Am. Bd. Internal Medicine. Fellow A.C.P., Am. Coll. Cardiology, Am. Coll. Chest Physicians; mem. Am. (fellow council clin. cardiology 1963—), Fla. (dir. 1958-61), Suncoast (dir. 1950—, pres. 1972-73, chmn. bd. 1973-74) heart assns., New Orleans Acad. Internal Medicine, Am. (trustee 1959-64, pres. 1962-63), Fla. (sec.-treas. 1956-62) socs. internal medicine, A.M.A. (alt. del.), Pinellas County Med. Soc., Fla. Thoracic Soc., Fla. (bd. govs. 1969-71, adv. mem. 1971-72, relative value study com. 1966—), So. (chmn. section on medicine 1969-70) med. assns., Confrerie de la Chaine des Rotisseurs. Episcopalian (vestry). Clubs: St. Petersburg Yacht, Quarterback, Xanadu. Asst. editor Jour. Fla. Med. Assn., 1960-64. Home: 5401 Leilani Dr St Petersburg Beach FL 33706 Office: 501 11th St N St Petersburg FL 33705

DONEHUE, JOHN DOUGLAS, newspaper exec.; b. Cramerton, N.C., July 5, 1928; s. John Sidney and Annie (Shepherd) D.; student Am. Press Inst., Columbia, 1964, 71, 73; m. Mary Phelps (dec. 1964); children—Teresa Jean, Marilyn Phelps; m. Sylvia Louise McKenzie, Feb. 11, 1966 (dec. 1971); children—Hayden Shepherd, John Douglas. Sports writer Charleston, S.C. News and Courier, 1947, telegraph editor, 1956, state editor, 1959-62, city editor, 1962-68, mng. editor, 1968-71, dir. promotion and pub. service, 1971—, compiler News and Courier Style Book, 1969; sports editor Orangeburg (S.C.) Times and Democrat, 1948-50; polit. reporter Montgomery (Ala.) Advertiser, 1954-55; faculty advisor Bapt. Coll. at Charleston Student Newspaper. Spl. adviser comdt. 7th USCG dist. for establishment dist.-wide pub. information program, 1960-61; journalism lectr. Baptist Coll., Charleston, sec. 1st bd. founders, 1969. Mem. bd. S.C. Commn. for Blind, 1969—, S.C. Tricentennial Parade Com., 1969—. Mem. exec. com. Low Country Council Boy Scouts Am.; mem. adv. bd. Salvation Army. Served with USAF, 1950-54. Recipient Freedoms Found. award, 1971. Mem. John Ancrum Soc. of Soc. Prevention Cruelty to Animals, Carolina Art Assn., Internat. Newspaper Promotion Assn., YMCA, Toastmasters Internat. (charter mem. Okinawa club), Okinawa Soc. Baptist (deacon, Sunday sch. supt.). Clubs: Country, Rotary (Charleston). Home: 66 Bull St Charleston SC 29401 Office: 134 Columbus St Charleston SC 29401

DONGES, GEORGE NIKOLAS, clergyman; b. Ashland, O., Apr. 19, 1943; s. George H. and Cathleen (Vanosdall) D.; B.A., Ashland Coll., 1965; M.Div., Lexington Theol. Sem., 1970; m. Eunice Cecelia Racey, Aug. 22, 1965; 1 son, Kent Braden. Psychiat. social worker Apple Creek (O.) State Hosp., 1965-66; ordained to ministry Christian Ch., 1970; minister Salem Fork Christian Ch., Dobson, N.C., 1970-72, Wendell (N.C.) Christian Ch., 1972—. Sec. treas. N.C. Disciple Ministers, 1973—, Wake Meml. Chaplain Assos., 1973—; oboist Wooster (O.) Symphony Orch., 1960-63, Ashland Chamber Orch., 1960-65. Mem. Wendell Council Chs. (vice chmn. 1973-74), Ky. Assn. Christian Chs. (dist. rep. to council 1969-70), Nat. Honor Soc., Order Demolay (pres. 1960—). Lion. Club: Union Cross Ruritan. Address: PO Box 874 409 Mattox St Wendell NC 27591

DONLEY, MARSHALL OWEN, JR., edn. editor and writer; b. Christiana, Pa., Mar. 20, 1932; s. Marshall O. and Edna (Detwiler) D.; B.A., Pa. State U., 1954; postgrad. U. So. Cal., 1954-55; M.A., Am. U., 1966, Ph.D., 1971; m. Margaret T. Reagan, Sept. 18, 1971; 1 son, Owen. Newspaper reporter Lancaster (Pa.) Intelligencer Jour., 1950-52; radio-tv writer WGAL and WGAL-TV, Lancaster, 1953; linguist U.S. Army Security Agy., Ft. Meade, Md., 1955-58; edn. writer, exec. editor N.E.A., Washington, 1958—. Instr. spl. sessions U. N.Y. at Buffalo, summers 1964-65. Served with AUS, 1955-58. Mem. Ednl. Press Assn. (chpt. past pres.), N.E.A. (dept. editorial cons. 1960-67; pres. staff orgn. 1967-68), Phi Kappa Phi, Phi Delta Kappa, Phi Sigma Kappa, Sigma Delta Chi. Contbr. articles to profl. jours. Home: 5213 Andover Rd Chevy Chase MD 20015 Office: 1201 16th St NW Washington DC 20036

DONNELL, BEN ADDISON, lawyer; b. Wichita Falls, Tex., Nov. 18, 1936; s. Ralph Shirley and Mary Anita (Crocker) D.; B.B.A., U. Tex., 1959, LL.B., 1961; m. Elinor Drake, Aug. 16, 1958; children—Elinor Allison, Amy Lauren. Admitted to Tex. bar, 1961; briefing atty. Supreme Ct. of Tex., 1961-62; mem. firm Keys Russell, Watson & Seaman, Corpus Christi, Tex., 1962-73; partner firm Meredith and Donnell, Corpus Christi, 1973—. Campaign chmn. United Way, 1973; chmn. leadership Corpus Christi Selection Com., 1972. Chmn. Lloyd Bentsen campaign for U.S. Senate, 1970. Trustee Cliff Maus Village; bd. dirs. Bethune Day Nursery. Served to capt. AUS, 1967. Rotarian. Clubs: Beachcombers (pres. 1968), Corpus Christi Country. Home: 4902 Olympia Dr Corpus Christi TX 78413 Office: PO Box 2624 Corpus Christi TX 78403

DONNELLAN, THOMAS A., bishop; b. N.Y.C., Jan 24, 1914; s. Andrew and Margaret (Egan) D.; A.B., St. Joseph's Sem., 1939; J.C.D., Catholic U. Am., 1942. Ordained priest Roman Catholic Ch., 1939; chancellor Archdiocese of N.Y., 1958-62; synodal judge Marriage Tribunal, 1950-58; rector St. Joseph's Sem., 1962-64; bishop of Ogdenburg, N.Y., 1964-68, archbishop of Atlanta, 1968—. Treas. Nat. Conf. Cath. Bishops/U.S. Cath. Conf., 1972—; trustee Catholic U. Decorated knight grand cross Knights Holy Sepulchre. Mem. Nat. Conf. Catholic Bishops (adminstrv. bd.), Sacred Congregation Religious and Secular Insts. Address: 136 W Wesley Rd NW Atlanta GA 30305

DONNELLY, DONALD TRACY, editor; b. Chester, Mass., Mar. 29, 1915; s. Samuel J. and Lucy (Mahan) D.; B.S., U. Mass., 1936; m. Dorothy M. Joyce, May 28, 1938; 1 son, John Samuel. Editor, Mass. Agrl. Extension Service, Springfield, 1936-46; editor Conn. State Farm Bur., New Haven, also Conn. Milk Producers Assn., Hartford, 1946-51; editor Am. Farm Bur. Fedn., Washington, 1951—. Asso. editor Am. Farmer, 1954—; editor Farm Bur. News, 1951—; farm broadcaster, 1936—. Republican. Roman Catholic. Home: 6760 Baron Rd McLean VA 22101 Office: 425 13th St NW Washington DC 20004

DONNELLY, HAROLD IRVIN, JR., sch. adminstr.; b. Phila., Jan. 21, 1923; s. Harold Irvin and Beatrice Irene (Wetherbee) D.; A.B., Princeton, 1947; postgrad. Harvard, summer 1950; M.Ed., U. Va., 1954; m. Ellen Lovell Taylor, Mar. 17, 1951; children—Charlotte Radcliffe, Harold Irvin III, Margaret Wetherbee. Tchr., Deerfield (Mass.) Acad., 1947-48; guidance counselor, tchr., Woodbury Forest (Va.) Sch., 1948-64; headmaster Spartanburg (S.C.) Day Sch., 1964—. Mem. ednl. com. Spartanburg Found., 1968—; mem. Wofford Coll. Bd. Assos. Served with Combat Engrs., AUS, 1943-45. Mem. So. Assn. Colls. and Schs. (sec. S.C. secondary com. 1969—, mem. central reviewing com. 1969—), Nat. Assn. Secondary Sch. Prins., Nat. Assn. Coll. Admission Counselors, Am. Alumni Council, S.C. Assn. Sch. Adminstrn., S.C. Princeton U. Alumni Assn. (pres. 1967-69), Carolinas Ind. Schs. (pres. 1969-70). Episcopalian. Club: Spartanburg Country. Home: 300 Beechwood Dr Spartanburg SC 29302

DONOGHUE, GERALD THOMAS, horse breeder; b. Beaumont, Tex., Sept. 17, 1906; s. Thomas Joseph and Mary Evangelist (Sullivan) D.; grad. Canterbury Sch. (New Milford, Conn.), 1925; B.A., Holy Cross Coll., 1929; m. Louise Huggins, Jan. 27, 1932; children—William T., Clare (Mrs. T. T. Beck, Jr.), Timothy H. Reporter, asst. city editor Houston Chronicle, 1929-43; founder Donoghue Arabian Farm, Goliad, Tex., 1943—. Pres. Arabian Horse Owners Found., 1970-71. Served with AUS, 1944-45, Mem. Am. Horse Shows Assn., Internat. Arabian Assn. (v.p.), Arabian Horse Club Tex. (past pres.). Author: For Peace Comes Dropping Slow, 1946. Contbr. articles to popular mags. including The Atlantic, Esquire. Address: Donoghue Arabian Farm Goliad TX 77963

DONOHOO, HORRIE VAN WALDO, mining co. exec.; b. Tucumcari, N.M., June 7, 1914; s. Horrie Van Waldo and Pearl (Wilson) D.; student Drake U., 1931-34; student Colo. Sch. Mines, 1936-39, 1945-46, Columbia, 1947; m. Norma Stegmann, Dec. 1, 1933; children—Michael O., Van Brian. Seismic computer Stanolind Oil & Gas Co., 1939-40, Phillips Petroleum Co., Gulf Coast, Tex., La., 1940-41; instr. mechanics Cornell U. Buffalo campus, 1941-43; instr. geophysics Colo. Sch. Mines, 1945-46, Columbia, 1947; asst. prof. geophysics U. Utah, 1947-51; exploration geophysicist Columbia-Geneva div. U.S. Steel Corp., San Francisco, 1953-57; chief geophysicist, asst. mgr. exploration Tex. Gulf Sulphur Co., N.Y.C., 1957-61, Houston, 1961-66, gen. mgr. potash div., Moab, Utah, 1966-67, v.p., gen. mgr. potash div., 1967-70, v.p. agrl. div., Raleigh, N.C., 1970-71, sr. v.p., 1972-73, exec. v.p., 1973—. Served to lt. comdr. USNR, 1943-45, 51-53. Recipient medal Colo. Sch. Mines, 1968. Mem. Am. Assn. Petroleum Geophysics, Soc. Exploration Geophysicists, European Assn. Exploration Geophysicists, Soc. Econ. Geologists, Am. Inst. Mining and Metall. Engrs., Mining and Metall. Soc. Am., Newcomen Soc. N.Am., Raleigh C. of C., Canadian Geophys. Soc. Home: 5309 Parkwood Dr Raleigh NC 27612 Office: Tex Gulf Sulphur Co 410 Oberlin Rd Box 30321 Raleigh NC 27605

DOODY, LOUIS CLARENCE, JR., C.P.A.; b. New Orleans, Feb. 5, 1940; s. Louis Clarence and Elsie Clair (Connors) D.; B.C.S., Tulane U., 1963; m. Mary Evelyn Barba, Nov. 13, 1965; children—Dana Lori, Mary Lyn, Kathleen Louise. Accountant, Louis C. Doody, C.P.A., 1963-68, partner Doody and Doody, C.P.A.'s, 1969—. C.P.A., La., Tex., Miss. Mem. Am. Inst. C.P.A.'s, La. Soc. C.P.A.'s. Home: 231 Atherton Dr Metairie LA 70005 Office: 1160 Commerce Bldg 821 Gravier St New Orleans LA 70112

DOOLEY, MARIE LOUISE BOYETT, ednl. adminstr.; b. Bryan, Tex.; d. Oran H. and Mary (Mitchell) Boyett; B.S., Tex. Woman's U., 1954, M.S. in Home Econs. Edn., 1956; M.Ed., East Tex. State U., 1961; Ed.D., 1972; m. James C. Dooley, May 5, 1942 (div. Nov. 1966); children—Bobby Curtis, Marilu. Tchr. home econs. Garland Ind. Sch. Dist., 1954-55; tchr. home econs. Richardson Ind. Sch. Dist., 1955-60, counselor, 1958-66; dir. spl. project drug and crime prevention edn. Tex. Edn. Agy., Austin, 1967—. Mem. Am., Tex. (pub. relations com. 1966) personnel and guidance assns., Am. (membership chmn. 1966, 67), Tex. (pres. 1966-67, exec. bd. 1967) sch. counselors assns., Richardson Edn., Assn. (pres. 1957-58), Tex. Tchrs. Assn., Am. Vocational Assn., North Central Tex. Vocational Guidance Assn. (sec. 1963), Am., Tex. home econs. assns., Phi Sigma Alpha (chpt. charter mem.). Methodist. Club: Altrusa Internat. (chpt. charter mem.). Home: 3 Sugar Shack St Austin TX 78761 Office: Tex Edn Agy 201 E 11th St Austin TX 78701

DOOLEY, WALLACE TROY, physician; b. Conway, Ark., June 15, 1917; s. Thomas Pierce and Dalice (Hawkins) D.; A.B., Kan. U., 1939, M.A., 1941; M.D., Meharry Med. Coll., 1947; m. Orealia Clara Robinson, Dec. 10, 1939; children—Wallace Troy, Orealia Leola. Intern Hubbard Hosp., Nashville, 1947-48, resident, 1948-51; practice medicine specializing in orthopedic surgery, Nashville, 1955; mem. staff George W. Hubbard Hosp., Riverside Hosp., Nashville; resident orthopedic surgeon Mercy Hosp., Iowa City, 1951-53; orthopedic resident Children's Hosp., State U. Ia., Iowa City, 1953-55; with Meharry Med. Hosp., Nashville, 1955—, head dept. orthopedic surgery, 1955—, asso. prof. surgery, 1955-68, prof. orthopaedic surgery, 1968—. Mem. Frontiers Am., med. adv. bd. Nat. Found., 1959-60; co-chmn. March of Dimes, 1957-58; bd. dirs. N.A.A.C.P., 1958-61; pres. Community Conf. Employment, 1960-64. Bd. dirs. Nat. Found. Fellow Royal Soc. Health; mem. R.F. Boyd Med. Soc. (sec.), Vol. State Med. Assn., Nat. Med. Assn., Am. Congress Preventive Medicine and Rehab., Assn. Med. Rehab. Dirs. and Coordinators, Nashville C. of C., N.Y. Acad. Sci., A.A.A.S., Kappa Pi. Kappa Alpha Psi. Republican. Baptist. Elk. Home: 3404 Geneva Circle Nashville TN 37209 Office: 1005 18th Av N Nashville TN 37208

DOOLEY, WILLIAM GERALD, football coach; b. Mobile, Ala., May 19, 1934; s. William Vincent and Nellie Agnes (Stauter) D.; student Miss. State U., 1956; m. Mary Christine Paolucci, July 14, 1962; children—Jim Bill. Asst. coach Miss. State U., 1956-57, head freshman coach, 1958-60, offensive line coach, 1963; head line coach George Washington U., 1961-62; head offensive coach U. Ga., 1964-66; head coach U.N.C., 1967—. Rotarian. Home: 110 Fern Lane Chapel Hill NC 27514

DOOLITTLE, JESSE WILLIAM, JR., lawyer; b. Wheaton, Ill., May 19, 1929; s. Jesse William and Selma (Schacht) D.; A.B., DePauw U., 1951; LL.B., Harvard, 1954; m. Annette Danforth Bush, May 5, 1962; children—Danforth Bush, Alice Walters. Admitted to D.C. bar, 1954; law clerk U.S. Supreme Ct. Justice, Felix Frankfurter, Washington, 1957-58; associated with the firm Covington & Burling, Washington, 1958-61; asst. to solicitor gen. of U.S., U.S. Dept. of Justice, Washington, 1961-63, 1st asst., civil div., 1963-66; gen. counsel U.S. Dept. Air Force, 1966-68, asst. Sec. Air Force, 1968-69; partner firm Prather, Levenberg, Seeger, Doolittle, Farmer & Ewing, Washington, 1969—. Mem. council Harvard Law Sch. Assn., 1964-68; mem. Harvard Coll. overseers' com. to visit ROTC programs, 1967-69, com. to visit Law Sch., 1969—, overseer Harvard Law Rev., 1967-72; pres., bd. trustees Nat. Child Research Center, 1972-74. Served to 1st lt., AUS, 1954-57. Recipient Career Service award Nat. Civil Service League, 1968, Air Force Exceptional Civilian Service award, 1969. Mem. Am. Law Inst., Bar Assn. D.C., Delta Chi, Phi Beta Kappa. Clubs: Metropolitan, Internat. (Washington). Episcopalian (former vestryman, sr. warden 1973—). Home: 4238 50th St NW Washington DC 20016 Office: 1101 16th St NW Washington DC 20036

DORATI, ANTAL, composer-condr.; b. Budapest, Hungary, Apr. 9, 1906; s. Alexander and Margit (Kunwald) D.; student composition and piano, Acad. of Music, Budapest, diploma, 1924; student U. Vienna, 1923-25; Mus.D., Macalester Coll., 1957. Condr. Budapest Royal Opera House, 1924-28, Dresden State Opera, 1928-29, Munster State Opera, 1929-32, Ballet Russe de Monte Carlo, 1933-37; mus. dir. original Ballet Russe, 1938-40, Ballet Theatre, 1940-44; mus. dir. Dallas Symphony Orch., 1945-49; mus. dir. Mpls. Symphony Orch., 1949-60; chief condr. BBC Symphony Orch., London, 1962-66; chief condr. Stockholm Philharmonic, 1966—; music dir. Washington Nat. Symphony, 1969—; guest condr. all maj. orchs., U.S., Europe, Latin America, Australia. Compositions include string quartet, quintet for oboe and strings, divertimento for small orchestra, two Am. serenades for string orch., cello concerto; 2 Hungarian Peasant Tunes for violin and piano, 1945; La Vie Parisienne by Offenbach, 1941; The Way (Cantata); The Two Enchantments of Li Tai Pe (lyric scene for baritone and small orchestra); Symphony (for large orchestra); Missa brevis (for mixed choir and percussion instruments); Magdalena (ballet); 7 Pictures for Orchestra; Octet for Strings; Madrigal Suite (chorus and orch.); Largo Concertato for String Orchestra; Chamber Music for Soprano and String Orchestra; Night Music for flute and small orch.; arrangements include: Graduation Ball, Bluebeard, Helen of Troy, Pavillon, Fair at Sorochinsk, Harvest Time. Recs. for Mercury Recording Co. EMI, Philips, RCA-Victor, Decca, London. Office: care Nat Symphony Orch Kennedy Center Washington DC 20566

DORENKAMP, HENRY JOSEPH, JR., accountant, lawyer; b. Louisville, May 25, 1925; s. Henry Joseph and Mary J. (O'Hern) D.; B.S., Xavier U. 1949; LL.B., U. Louisville, 1952, J.D., 1952; m. Mary Virginia Rassinier, May 31, 1952; children—Stephen Henry, Jill Ann, Kent Robert, Dayle Ann. Admitted to Ky. bar, 1953; individual practice, Louisville; owner Glendale Office Center; treas. Seignior, Inc. Served USAAF, 1943-46. Decorated Air medal with oak leaf cluster. C.P.A., Ky. Mem. Am. Inst. C.P.A.'s Ky. Soc. C.P.A.'s, Am. Assn. Atty.-C.P.A.'s, Ky., Louisville bar assns., Am. Legion. Home: 2340 Gladstone Av Louisville KY 40205 Office: Glendale Office Center 2305 Taylorsville Rd Louisville KY 40205

DORMAN, DONALD WILBUR, accountant; b. Los Angeles, Dec. 9, 1928; s. Wilbur Alanson and Helen (Baxter) D.; student Texas A. and M. U., 1945-46, Tyler Jr. Coll., 1946; B.B.A., Tex. Technol. U., 1950; m. Mildred Nelson, May 2, 1952; children—Donna, David, Dean, Daniel. Staff accountant Condray, Pratas & Smith, C.P.A.'s, Lubbock, Tex., 1951-55; propr. Donald W. Dorman, C.P.A., Lubbock, 1955-57; partner Dorman & Newsom, C.P.A.'s, Dorman Newsom & Caraway, Dorman & Caraway, Dorman, Caraway & Howard, 1957-66; mng. partner Lubbock office Main Lafrentz & Co., C.P.A.'s 1966—; pres., dir. Donall, Inc.; v.p., dir. Dorman & Co. Past pres. S. Plains Trust and Estate Council. Bd. dirs. Lubbock United Fund, chmn. budget div., 1969, 70, v.p., 1971; bd. dirs. Tex. Technol. U. Found.; past pres., trustee Ednl. Found. Tex. Soc. C.P.A.'s. Recipient award for meritorious service to pub. accounting profession in Tex., Tex. Soc. C.P.A.'s, 1968. Mem. Am. Inst. C.P.A.'s, Tex. Soc. C.P.A.'s (past v.p.), Lubbock Chpt. C.P.A.'s (past pres.), Beta Alpha Psi (hon.). Home: 3202 57th St Lubbock TX 79413 Office: 1st Nat Pioneer Bldg Lubbock TX 79401

DORMAN, JOHN FREDERICK, genealogist; b. Louisville, July 25, 1928; s. John Frederick and Sue Carpenter (Miller) D.; B.A., U. Louisville, 1950; M.A., Emory U., 1955. Asst. archivist Coll. of William and Mary, 1953-55; genealogist, Washington, 1955—; lectr. Am. U. Inst. Geneal. Research, 1963—. Fellow Am. Soc. Genealogists (treas. 1959-66); mem. Soc. of Cincinnati, Soc. Colonial Wars (dep. registrar gen. 1969—), Soc. War of 1812, S.R., S.A.R. (D.C. pres. 1967-68), Newcomen Soc., Nat. Geneal. Soc. (v.p. 1958-59, 68-70, librarian, 1959-60), Children Am. Revolution (sr. nat. registrar 1960-62, sr. nat. treas. 1962-64, 66-68, sr. nat. 2d. v.p. 1968-70), Descs. Colonial Govs. (gov. gen. 1973—), Deses. Lords Md. Manors (registrar 1971—). Republican. Episcopalian. Club: Cosmos (Washington). Editor: The Va. Genealogist, 1957—. Home: 2022 Columbia Rd NW Washington DC 20009

DORMOIS, JOHN CARL, physician; b. Kansas City, Kan., May 3, 1945; s. John F. and Mary (Reeder) D.; B.A., Kan. State Coll., 1965; M.D., U. Kan., 1969; m. Carllyn Lee Mathis, Aug. 14, 1965; children—Andrew John, Amy Brooke, Matthew David. Intern U. Kan. Hosp., 1969-70; resident Vanderbilt U. Hosp., Nashville, 1970-71, fellowship in clin. pharmacology, 1973—. Served with USNR, 1971-73. Home: 6825 Cloudland Dr Nashville TN 37205 Office: Vanderbilt Hosp Nashville TN 37203

DORN, RICHARD DONALD, oil and gas lease broker; b. Tulsa, Oct. 8, 1923; s. Kenneth C. and Laura Mae (Crooks) D.; B.S., U. Tulsa, 1950; m. Ann Adelle Miller, Sept. 11, 1950; children—Patricia Ann, Tracy. Dist. landman Cities Service Oil Co., Oklahoma City, 1950-65; ind. oil and gas operator and producer, 1965-68; ind. oil and gas lease broker, Oklahoma City, 1968—; cattle rancher; pres. Creo Oil Co., Inc. Served with USAAF, World War II. Mem. Am., Oklahoma City assns. petroleum landmen, Sigma Chi. Republican. Presbyn. Mason (K.T.). Home: 7208 Shoreline Dr Oklahoma City OK 73132 Office: Cravens Bldgs Oklahoma City OK 73102

DORNAN, JAMES EDWARD, JR., educator; b. Bklyn., Jan. 3, 1938; s. James Edward and Florence (Gouch) D.; A.B. magna cum laude, LeMoyne Coll., 1959; Ph.D., Johns Hopkins, 1968; m. Patricia Ann Capezzuti, Jan. 19, 1959 (separated 1972); children—James Edward III, Patrick Francis, Erin Maureen, Kieran Christopher, Mieghan. Asst. instr. polit. sci. Johns Hopkins, 1960-61; research asst. Gov.'s Ednl. Commn., Balt., 1961-62; asst. prof. polit. sci. Purdue U., Lafayette, Ind., 1963-67; asst. prof. Inst. Internat. Law and Relations Cath. U., Washington, 1967-68, asst. prof. politics, 1968—, chmn. dept. politics, 1973—; asst. prof. polit. sci. Johns Hopkins, evenings and summer session 1969—; research and writing Hon. John J. Rhodes, 1970—. Lectr., Utah State U., U.S. Naval Acad., Rockford (Ill.) Coll., numerous others. Republican precinct committeeman Tippecanoe County (Ind.), 1966-68, campaign chmn., 1966, v.p. Critical Issues Council, 1965-67; v.p. Tippecanoe County Republican Club, 1966, pres., 1967. Recipient Best Instr. award Sch. Humanities Purdue U., 1965, Univ. Tchr. of Year, 1966. Earhart and NATO Research fellow, 1973-74. Mem. Am. Polit. Sci. Assn., Am. Assn. U. Profs. (pres. chpt. 1970-73), Acad. Polit. Sci., Phila. Soc., U.S. Strategic Inst., U.S. Naval Inst., Royal United Services Inst., Pi Sigma Alpha, Omicron Delta Kappa. Contbg. editor Report mag., N.Y.C., 1964-66, Intercollegiate Rev., 1970—. Contbr. articles to profl. jours. Office: Dept of Politics Catholic University Washington DC 20017

DORNAUS, WALTER PERRY, lawyer; b. Bloomington, Ill., Apr. 27, 1915; s. Walter J. and Minnie E. (Perry) D.; A.B., Ill. Wesleyan U., 1937; LL.B., U. Okla., 1939; m. Aragene Lane, Sept. 15, 1938; children—Elizabeth Ann, Sara Jeanne, Margaret Lane, Vera Carolyn. Admitted to Okla. bar, 1940, Tex. bar, 1945; asso. firm Crouch, Rhodes & Crowe, Tulsa, 1940-42, Milsten & Milsten, Tulsa, 1942; with legal dept. Shell Oil Co., Tulsa, 1942-44, Stanolind Oil & Gas Co., Ft. Worth, also Tulsa, 1944-52; chief counsel, head legal dept. Kewanee Oil Co., Tulsa, 1952-71; practice law, Tulsa, 1971—; past bd. suprs. Nat. Oil Co. of Libya; dir., sec. Sound Refining, Inc., Tacoma; pres., dir. Bromandor Corp., Tulsa. Mem. legal com. Interstate Oil Compact Commn., 1963-71; lectr. legal insts. Southwestern Legal Found., Dallas, 1952-53. Mem. Tulsa Mayor's Com. for Charter Revision, 1959-60. Mem. City-County Republican Exec. Com., 1949-60, chmn. state speakers bur., 1950. Mem. State Bar Tex., Okla., Tulsa County, Am. (chmn. oil com. of mineral sect. 1964-65, chmn. spl. ad hoc com. congl. pub. and law rev. commn. 1966) bar assns., Mid-Continent (exec. com.), N.M., Ill. oil and gas assns., Oil Industry Information Council, Independent Petroleum Assn., Petroleum Club Tulsa, S.A.R. (Tulsa pres. 1966—, state pres. 1969-71), Tau Kappa Epsilon, Pi Kappa Delta, Phi Alpha Delta. Methodist. Mason (Shriner). Author: The Fountain and Other Poems. Contbr. articles to law revs. Home: 1344 E 26th Pl Tulsa OK 74114

DOROUGH, VIRGINIA ANN, banker; b. Birmingham, Ala., Dec. 26, 1930; d. Joseph Southern and Gladyce Mildred (Wilson) Dorough; B.S., U. Ala., 1952, postgrad., 1964-65; postgrad. Ga. State Coll., 1964; certificates Am. Inst. Banking, 1967, 69, 71; grad. Sch. Banking South, 1973. Tchr. sci. Munford (Ala.) High Sch., 1952, Cahaba Heights Jr. High Sch., Birmingham, 1952-53; loan clk. First Nat. Bank of Birmingham, 1953-55; reservations agt. Eastern Airlines, Birmingham and Atlanta, 1955-64; programmer Exchange Security Bank, Birmingham, 1965-67, systems analyst, 1967—, asst. cashier, 1969—; mem. planning com. U. Ala. Ann. Data Processing Conf., 1968-72. Recipient Bausch & Lomb Hon. Sci. award, 1948. Mem. Am. Inst. Banking, Nat. Assn. Bank Women, Am. Soc. Women Accountants (pres. 1972-73), Mountain Brook Bus. and Profl. Women's Club (v.p. 1972-73, pres. 1974-75), Am. Assn. U. Women, Assn. for Computing Machinery. Methodist. Soroptimist; mem. Order Eastern Star (worthy matron 1957-58). Home: 2140 Shadybrook Lane Birmingham AL 35226 Office: Exchange Security Bank PO Box 10247 Birmingham AL 35202

DORR, ANNIE MAUDE DEAN (MRS. WILLIAM HENRY DORR), educator; b. Ashland, Ala.; d. William Thomas and Dora (Griffin) Dean; A.B. cum laude, diplomas in piano and speech, Judson Coll., 1928; M.A., George Peabody Coll., 1945; m. William Henry Dorr, June 22, 1954. Tchr. English, Tallapoosa County High Sch., Dadeville, Ala. 1928-32, Clay County High Sch., Ashland, 1932-43; dir. YWCA-USO, Carolina Beach, N.C., 1943-44, Durham, N.C., 1944, Montgomery, Ala., 1945-47; asst. prof. edn. and psychology Huntingdon Coll., 1947-48; tchr. English, St. Petersburg (Fla.) High Sch., 1948—, chmn. dept., 1958-65, 68—; tchr. English, St. Petersburg Jr. Coll., evening div., 1956-62. Chmn. constitution and by-laws com. Pinellas County Tchrs. English Council, 1965-66. Fla. sponsor Nat. Honor Soc., 1962-63. Mem. Pinellas (2d v.p. 1953-54, pres. 1954-55, 62-63, 1st v.p. 1963-64), Fla. (treas. 1955-57, chmn. textbook evaluation com. 1962-64, chmn. state conv. 1960), Nat. (membership com. 1962, del. 1954, 62), councils tchrs. English, Pinellas County Classroom Tchrs. Assn., St. Petersburg Community Concert Assn., St. Petersburg Little Theater, Alph Delta Kappa (chpt. corr. sec., chpt. pres. 1972-74). Baptist (organist 1938-43). Mem. Order Eastern Star. Home: 1300 6th Av N St Petersburg FL 33705 Office: St Petersburg High Sch 2501 5th Av N St Petersburg FL 33713

DORROH, JAMES ROBERT, mathematician, educator; b. Marion, Ala., Apr. 20, 1937; s. Joe Lee and Jaime (Benson) D.; student Tex. Arts and Industries U., 1955-56; B.A., U. Tex., 1958, M.A., 1961, Ph.D., 1962; m. Elizabeth Jones Brett, June 20, 1959; 1 dau., Rebecca Ruth. Instr. math. dept. Laredo Jr. Coll., 1959-60; asst. prof. math. dept. La. State U., Baton Rouge, 1962-67, asso. prof., 1967-71, prof., 1971—. Home: 723 Seyburn Ct Baton Rouge LA 70808

DORSET, VIRGIL JACKSON, physician; b. Washington, Feb. 1, 1909; s. Marion and Emily Kerfoot (Jackson) D.; A.B. George Washington U., 1931, M.D., 1934; m. Laurie Harris, Nov. 10, 1937; children—Emily, Sally, Richard. Intern, Emergency Hosp., Washington, 1934-35; resident USPHS Hosp., Balt., 1946-48; officer USPHS, 1935-62, med. dir. ret., 1962—; plant physician E.I. du Pont de Nemours & Co., Inc., Belle, W.Va., 1962-69; staff physician U.S. VA Hosp., Bay Pines, Fla., 1969—. Served with AUS, 1941-45; PTO. Decorated Bronze Star. Diplomate Nat. Bd. Med. Examiners, Am. Bd. Internal Medicine. Fellow A.C.P. Home: 122 Live Oak Lane Largo FL 33540 Office: US VA Bay Pines FL 33504

DORSEY, HAROLD WINSTON, clergyman; b. Shelbyville, Ky., Dec. 31, 1916; s. Earl Vanhorn and Angie Marie (Hancock) D.; A.B. Ky. Wesleyan Coll., 1938, D.D., 1959; B.D., Emory U., 1941; m. Irene Cochran, Aug. 31, 1941; 1 son, Edwin Cochran (dec.). Ordained to ministry Meth. Ch., 1940; minister various congregations, 1942—, Pikeville (Ky.) United Ch., 1960-63; dist. supt. Danville dist. United Meth. Ch., 1963-69; minister Epworth United Ch., Lexington, Ky., 1969—. Del. Southeastern Jurisdictional Conf., 1968, 72; alternate del. Gen. Conf. United Meth. Ch., 1968, 72; mem. Southeastern Jurisdictional Council, 1968—; chmn. various bds. and agencies Ky. ann. conf. United Meth. Ch. Trustee Ky. Wesleyan Coll. Ky. col.; named to Floyd County Hall of Fame, 1959. Mem. Bluegrass Exec. Club, Civil War Roundtable. Mason (K.T., Shriner), Kiwanian. Club: Mountain (Lexington). Home: 1774 Bryan Station Rd Lexington KY 40505 Office: 1015 N Limestone St Lexington KY 40505

DORSEY, JASPER NEWTON, communications co. exec.; b. Marietta, Ga., Jan. 19, 1913; s. John Tucker and Annie (Coryell) D.; A.B., U. Ga., 1936, postgrad. Lumpkin Law Sch., U. Ga., 1935-36; m. Callender Weltner, Oct. 16, 1937; children—Sally (Mrs. William E. Danner), John Tucker (dec.). With So. Bell Tel. & Tel. Co., Inc., 1937-61, 68—, v.p., Atlanta, 1968—; mgr. govt. relations Am. Tel. & Tel., Washington, 1962-68; dir. Fulton Nat. Corp., Fulton Nat. Bank, Atlanta, Ga. Motor Club, Inc., Atlanta. Vis. distinguished lectr. Coll. Bus. Adminstrn. U. Ga. Mem. adv. bd. Salvation Army, Atlanta, 1970—; Ga. fund chmn. A.R.C.; chmn. exec. bd. Ga. World Congress Center. Bd. dirs. Ga. Safety Council, Atlanta Boys Club, Easter Seal Soc., Kidney Found. Ga. vice chmn., mem. exec. com. U. Ga. Found., Atlanta; trustee Ga. Student Ednl. Fund, Athens; pres. adv. bd. U. Ga. Henry Grady Sch. Journalism; bd. visitors Emory U., Atlanta, mem. exec. com.; treas., mem. exec. com. Richard B. Russell Found., Atlanta. Served to lt. col. Inf. AUS, 1941-46. Recipient Blue Key award U. Ga., 1967; Outstanding Contbn. to U. Ga. award, 1969; Alumni Merit award U. Ga., 1970; Georgian of Year award Ga. Assn. Broadcasters, 1971; named Citizen of Year for Cobb County, Ga., Atlanta Daily Jour., C. of C., 1974. Mem. Ga. (pres., dir.), Atlanta (former dir.) chambers commerce, Newcomen Soc. N.Am., U. Ga. Alumni Assn. (nat. pres., 1967-69, chmn. bd., 1969-73), Blue Key, Sphinx, Gridiron, Greek Horsemen, Omicron Delta Kappa, Sigma Delta Chi, Sigma Iota Epsilon, Phi Delta Theta. Presbyn. (elder). Kiwanian. Clubs: Capital City, Commerce, Peachtree Golf, Piedmont Driving (Atlanta); Nat. Press, Army-Navy, Kenwood (Washington). Office: So Bell Telephone & Telegraph Co 805 Peachtree St Atlanta GA 30308

DORSEY, LEONA FEHLER, educator; club woman; b. Balt.; d. Henry J. and Fredericka (Dolch) Fehler; student U. Heidelberg (Germany), summer 1929; A.B., Goucher Coll., 1931; M.A., Johns Hopkins, 1933; m. Ridgely Corbin Dorsey, Jan. 12, 1935 (div. July 1965); 1 dau. Deborah Worthington (Mrs. William Anthony Trebilcock). Tchr. history Kenwood High Sch., Balt., 1932-36; asso. in secretarial studies George Washington U., 1952-60; tchr. history Burdick High Sch., Washington, 1963-74. Pres., Salvation Army Aux. Alexandria, 1964-65; mem. Alexandria Hosp. Aux. Bd., 1938—, sec., 1943-44. Mem. Nat. League Am. Pen Women (nat. corr. sec. 1954-56), Internat. Platform Assn., English-Speaking Union, Nat. Trust for Historic Preservation, Friends of the Y, Phi Delta Gamma (nat. pres. 1932-34). Clubs: Belle Haven Country, Carlyle Womans (pres. Alexandria, Va. 1939-41); Washington Arts, Friday Morning Music (Washington). Home: 506 Crown View Dr Alexandria VA 22314

DORTCH, LAWRENCE, lawyer; b. Columbia, Tenn., Jan. 21, 1914; B.A., Duke, 1936; LL.B., U. Va., 1940. Admitted to Tenn. bar, 1939; mem. firm Waller Lansden Dortch & Davis, Nashville. Mem. Nashville, Tenn., Am. bar assns., Phi Delta Phi. Address: Waller Lansden Dortch & Davis 12th Floor Am Trust Bldg Nashville TN 37201

DOSCHER, JÜRGEN HENRY, lawyer; b. Houston, Jan. 5, 1921; s. J. Henry and Maynette (Shearn) D.; B.A., Amherst Coll., 1942; M.A., Hardin-Simmons U., 1973; J.D., U. Tex., 1948. Law clk. Supreme Ct. Tex., 1949-50; admitted to Tex. bar, 1948; partner, Wagstaff, Alvis, Pope, Doscher & Charlton, 1950-66; practiced in Abilene, Tex., 1966—; adj. prof. law McMurry Coll., Abilene, 1969—. Mem. Dodge-Jones Found., 1973—. Bd. dirs. Abilene Fine Arts Mus., 1971-72, W. Tex. Rehab. Center, Abilene. Served to capt. USNR, 1942-46. Mem. Am., Abilene (pres. 1971-72) bar assns., State Bar Tex., Sons Rep. Tex., Phi Gamma Delta, Phi Delta Phi. Club: Country (Abilene). Home: 2301 Sayles Blvd Abilene TX 79605 Office: Citizens Nat Bank Bldg Abilene TX 79601

DOSKOCIL, SISTER MARY RAYMOND, librarian; b. Cyclone, Tex., July 11, 1930; d. Joseph and Matilda (Manak) Doskocil; B.A., U. St. Thomas, 1960; M.L.S., U. Tex., 1966. Tchr. parochial schs., Houston, 1952-64; librarian Our Lady of Perpetual Help Jr. Coll., Bellaire, Tex., 1965-66; librarian Marian High Sch., Bellaire, 1966-68, 68-71, dir. learning resource center, 1971—; librarian Incarnate Word Acad., Houston, 1968-71. Mem. A.L.A., Cath. Library Assn., Assn. Ednl. Communications and Tech., Tex. Library Assn. Home: 4600 Bissonnet St Bellaire TX 77401 Office: 4621 Gulfton Dr Bellaire TX 77401

DOSS, JAMES HOUSTON, bank dir.; b. Weatherford, Tex., Mar. 15, 1915; s. James Houston and Annie Lee (Goodman) D.; grad. Weatherford Jr. Coll., 1934; B.B.A., U. Tex., 1936; postgrad. Sch. Bus. Adminstrn. Harvard, 1937-38; m. Dorothy Jane Smith, Aug. 17, 1940; children—Nancy (Mrs. Billy Francis Knight), James Houston III, John Edgar. With Weatherford Mchts. and Farmers State Bank, 1937—, pres., 1945-55, dir., 1940—; dir. Continental State Bank, Boyd, Tex. Tchr. accounting Weatherford Jr. Coll., 1938-39; owner, devel. Shepherd Mall, Oklahoma City, 1964—; builder S.W. area James Doss Enterprises, 1952-63. Vice pres. Weatherford Pub. Schs., 1958; mem. adv. bd. Southwest Med. Center, Dallas, 1958-61. Trustee Weatherford Jr. Coll., 1938-45; mem. bd. control Weatherford Mcpl. Water and Electric, 1945-48; trustee Trinity U., San Antonio, 1955—, mem. finance com., 1960—. Recipient Outstanding Civic Service

citation Weatherford, 1958; named Outstanding Layman of Tex., Tex. Council Chs., 1961. Mem. Weatherford C. of C. (bd. dirs. 1942-48). Lion. Presbyn. (pres. Synod Tex. Found., 1954—, mem. United Presbyn. Found. 1972—. Home: 616 Baylor St Weatherford TX 76086 Office: James Doss Enterprises 536 Braniff Tower Dallas TX 75235

DOSS, SHANNON LOWELL, govt. ofcl.; b. Wilmar, Ark., Aug. 24, 1923; s. Elvin Payton and Jewell (Ault) D.; B.S., Ark. A. & M. U., 1949; M.S., U. Ark., 1952; student U. Tex., 1968-71; m. Robbye Lee Thompson, July 1, 1948; children—Debra Jo, David Shannon, Dayna Lee. Tchr. pub. schs., Monticello, Ark., 1949-51; prin., Springdale, Ark., 1952-55; asst. prin., counselor Wilson and Matthews jr. high schs., Lubbock, Tex., 1955-61; supt. schs., Claude, Tex., 1961-64; supt. schs., Memphis, Tex., 1964-66; supt. schs., San Marcos, Tex., 1966-70; chief govtl. relations div. Office of Economic Opportunity, Dallas, 1970—; mem. adv. bd. ednl. TV sta. KLRN, Austin, Tex. Bd. dirs. San Marcos Community Action Agy. Served with USMCR, 1942-45. Decorated Air medal. Mem. Dallas Fed. Bus. Assn. (dir. 1970—), Tex. Assn. Sch. Adminstrs., Tex. State Tchrs. Assn. (dist. pres. 1968-69), N.E.A., Am. Assn. Sch. Adminstrs., Tex. Congress Parents and Tchrs., San Marcos C. of C. (dir. 1968-70). Methodist (steward 1948—). Mason. Rotarian, Lion (dir. 1954-66). Home: 3205 Greenbriar Plano TX 75074 Office: Office of Economic Opportunity 1100 Commerce St Dallas TX 75202

DOSSETT, JAMES KEARNEY, lawyer; b. Sanford, Miss., Feb. 10, 1914; s. Jesse Christopher and Mary Elizabeth (Lott) D.; B.S., U. So. Miss., 1939; LL.B., Jackson Sch. Law, 1954; m. Ina Fewell, May 31, 1941; children—James Kearney, Anita Kathryn (Mrs. James Harrold Jones), William Edward. Tchr. Miss. pub. schs., 1939-41; office mgr. Farm Security Adminstrn., Prentiss, Miss., 1941-42; agt. Internal Revenue Service, Jackson, Miss., 1952-54, chief rev. staff, 1954-58; admitted to Miss. bar, 1954; practice law, Jackson, 1958—. Mem. Estate Planning Council Miss.; mem., chmn. delegation S.E. Region Tax Liaison Com., 1967-72; chmn. taxation com. Miss. Econ. Council, 1973. Trustee Clarke Meml. Coll., Newton, Miss., U. So. Miss. Found. Served with USNR, 1942-45. Mem. Hinds County, Miss. (chmn. taxation com. 1965-70), Am. (mem. taxation sect.) bar assns., Miss. Bar Found. (trustee 1962-65), Phi Kappa Phi, Sigma Delta Kappa. Baptist (deacon; adult sch. supt.). Kiwanian. Clubs: Country, Knife and Fork (Jackson). Home: 353 Northside Circle Jackson MS 39206 Office: 1801 Deposit Guaranty Bank Bldg Jackson MS 39201

DOSSETT, WALTER BROWN, JR., furniture co. exec.; b. Waco, Tex., Aug. 20, 1927; s. Walter Brown and Alethea Halbert (Sleeper) D.; B.B.A., U. Tex. at Austin, 1950; m. Mary Martha Dickie, Aug. 4, 1951; children—Walter Dickie, Markham Brown, Susan Sleeper, Martha Beckham, Pauline Reeder. Asst. sec., treas. Exporters & Traders Compress & Warehouse Co., Waco, Tex., 1952-65, sec., treas.; 1965-70; chmn., chief exec. officer Royal Seating Corp., Cameron, Tex., 1970—; dir. 1st Nat. Bank Waco, Tex. Life Ins. Co., Waco, Rogers Delinted Cotton Seed Co., Waco; pres., Central Tex. Compress Co., Waco, 1965—. Chmn. Waco Library Commn., 1961-62; pres. United Fund Waco, 1969-70. Mem. Waco City Council, 1970-74, mayor pro tem, Waco, 1973-74. Served with AUS, 1950-52. Mem. Kappa Sigma. Episcopalian (exec. bd. Tex. 1967-69). Rotarian. Club: Ridgewood Yacht. Home: 1609 College Dr Waco TX 76708 Office: PO Drawer 1339 Waco TX 76703

DOSTER, JAMES FLETCHER, educator; b. Tuscaloosa, Ala., Dec. 8, 1912; s. James Jarvis and Mabel (Cowart) D.; A.B., U. Ala., 1932; M.A., U. Chgo., 1936, Ph.D., 1948; postgrad. Harvard (research fellow), 1953-54; m. Nina Hall, Dec. 22, 1936; children—James Hall, Nina Katherine (Mrs. Michael S. Stoddard). Instr. U. Ala., 1936-39, 40-44, asst. prof., 1948-55, asso. prof., 1955-62, prof. history, 1962—; instr. Samford U., Birmingham, 1944-45; asso. Danforth Found., 1950-53; vis. prof. U. Houston (Tex.), 1956, U. Western Ont. (Can.), 1965. Cons. Creek Nation, 1957-65, 68-73; lectr. U. Chattanooga (Tenn.), 1961, 63. Vice pres. Tuscaloosa Sesqui-Centennial Com., 1963-64. Mem. S.A.R. (chpt. pres. 1965-66), Tuscaloosa C. of C., Ala. Acad. Sci. (v.p. 1961-62), Ala. (exec. com. 1959-70), Am., So. (exec. com. 1958-61) hist. assns., Am., So. econ. assns., Am. Statis. Assn., Tuscaloosa Hist. Soc. (trustee, 1960-73, pres. 1960-62), Orgn. of Am. Historians, Econ. Hist. Assn., Forest Hist. Soc., Phi Beta Kappa, Delta Chi (Ala. trustee), Phi Delta Kappa, Kappa Delta Pi. Democrat. Methodist. Researcher in history of Am. railroads. Author: Alabama's First Railroad Commission, 1881-1885, 1949; Railroads in Alabama Politics, 1875-1914, 1957. Contbr. articles on railroad history to profl. jours. Home: 10 Guilds Woods Tuscaloosa AL 35401 Office: PO Box 1955 University of Alabama University AL 35486

DOSWELL, JAMES MARSHALL, JR., textile mills exec.; b. Richmond, Va., Aug. 13, 1921; s. James Marshall and Margaret Lewis (Miller) D.; B.S., Hampden-Sydney Coll., 1942; postgrad. Drake U., 1947-48, U. N.C., 1967-68; m. Gloria Virginia Stacy, Dec. 22, 1947; children—Julia, Margaret, Laura. News editor Chgo. Bur., A.P., 1948-55; editor Covington (Va.) Virginian, 1956; asso. editor, mng. editor Evening Herald, Rock Hill, S.C., 1957-62; dir., v.p. pub. relations Springs Mills, Inc., Ft. Mill, S.C., 1962—. Bd. dirs. S.C. State Library, Rock Hill Speech and Hearing Center, Rock Hill Sheltered Workshop. Served with AUS, 1942-46. Internat. Press Inst. grantee, 1958; recipient Distinguished Reporting award Atlanta chpt. Sigma Delta Chi, 1960. Mem. Rock Hill C. of C. (pres. 1961), Pub. Relations Soc. Am. (pres. S.C. chpt. 1971), Charlotte Pub. Relations Soc. (pres. 1972), S.C. Textile Mfrs. Assn. (chmn. pub. relations div. 1965), Presbyn. Men of Ch. Bethel Presbytery (pres. 1970, moderator 1973), Sigma Delta Chi. Home: 937 Meadow Lakes Rd Rock Hill SC 29730 Office: Springs Mills Inc Exec Office Bldg Fort Mill SC 29615

DOTY, DONALD D., banker; b. Independence, Kan., June 30, 1928; s. Laton L. and Dorothy (Russell) D.; B.S., Okla. State U., 1950; grad. Grad. Sch. Banking, U. Wis., 1963; m. Cheri F. Montgomery, June 14, 1952; children—John Scott, Susan Dorothy, Mark Montgomery. Cattle rancher, nr. Bartlesville, Okla., 1950-53; with First Nat. Bank Bartlesville, 1955—, asst. cashier, 1956-60, asst. v.p., 1960-62, v.p., 1962-69, exec. v.p., 1969—, also dir.; pres. First Bancshares, Inc., First Okla. Ventures Corp., Oklahoma City; v.p., dir. Rocking D Land & Cattle Co., Bartlesville, 1969—; dir. New Camp Minerals, Inc. Bd. dirs. Bluestem Cattlemens Assn., 1966; pres. Bartlesville Credit Bur., 1971; pres. Bartlesville Area Indsl. Devel. Co., 1971; chmn. bd. trustees Jane Phillips Episcopal Meml. Med. Center, 1971. Served to capt. USAF, 1953-55. Recipient Distinguished Service award Bartlesville, 1957; named Outstanding Local Jaycee Pres., 1958, Outstanding Young Man in Okla., 1958. Mem. Bartlesville C. of C. (dir. 1966—), Wis. Sch. Banking Alumni Assn. (pres . Okla. 1966). Republican. Presbyn. (pres. bd. trustees 1970). Mason (32 deg., Shriner, Jester). Club: Hillcrest Country (Bartlesville). Home: 1447 Valley Rd Bartlesville OK 74003 Office: Box 999 Bartlesville OK 74003

DOTY, LOCKWOOD RICHARD II, pub. relations and advt. exec.; b. Lockport, N.Y., Mar. 24, 1921; s. Lockwood West and Flora (Weaver) D.; student Trinity Coll.; D.Bus. Adminstrn. (hon.), Ind. No. U., 1971; H.L.D., Ft. Lauderdale U., 1974; m. Mary Alice Brayer, Oct. 6, 1945; children—Mary Louise Brayer, Jennifer West (dec.),

Sara Cady. News editor WCOP, Boston, 1945-47, WCON, Atlanta Constn., 1947-49; commentator NBC, N.Y.C., 1949-52; asso. news dir. WOR-TV, N.Y.C., 1953; program dir. WHAM, Rochester, 1953-57; pres. Blue Skies Broadcasting Corp., 1957-60; exec. v.p., gen. mgr. Fla. Air Power, Inc., 1960-61; v.p. WINZ, Miami, 1961-62; newscaster WTVJ, Miami, 1962-67; pres. Group One, Inc., 1967; sr. v.p. Campbell-Dickey Advt., 1967; pres. Dick Doty & Assos. Inc., pub. relations, advt. and marketing, Ft. Lauderdale, 1968—; exec. v.p., sec.-treas. PRAMtee, Inc., 1972—. Chmn. bd. trustees Ft. Lauderdale U.; bd. dirs. Am. Revolution Bicentennial Commn. Mem. Pub. Relations Soc. Am., Greater Ft. Lauderdale Advt. Fedn. (pres. 1970-71), Fla. Pub. Relations Assn. (dir., pres. Gold Coast chpt. 1971-72), Sigma Delta Chi (pres. Fla. East Coast chpt. 1965-67). Republican. Episcopalian. Rotarian. Home: 2749 NE 19th St Fort Lauderdale FL 33305 Office: Suite 310 2701 E Sunrise Blvd Fort Lauderdale FL 33304

DOUBLES, MALCOLM CARROLL, clergyman, educator; b. Richmond, Va., Aug. 14, 1932; s. Malcolm Ray and Catherine Clifford (Carroll) D.; B.A., Davidson Coll., 1953; B.D., Union Theol. Sem., 1957; postgrad. Faculty of Theology, Montpellier, France, 1955-56; Ph.D., St. Andrews U., Scotland, 1960; postgrad. Oxford (Eng.) U., 1970-71; m. Jacqueline Elisabeth McLeod, Dec. 21, 1956; children—Malcolm McLeod, John Carroll, Mary Blake. Ordained to ministry Presbyn. Ch., 1957; minister Presbyn. churches, Lebanon, Va., and Castlewood, Va., 1960-65; faculty St. Andrews Presbyn. Coll., Laurinburg, N.C., 1965—, asso. prof. religion, 1969—, dean students, 1974—. Commr. to gen. assembly Presbyn. Ch. U.S., 1967. Mem. Va. Legislative Mental Health Study Commn., 1963-65. Del. N.C. Dem. Conv., 1970. Chmn. bd. dirs. Russell Area Devel. Corp., 1963-65; exec. bd. Lonesome Pine council Boy Scouts Am., 1962-65. Recipient Younger Humanist fellowship Nat. Endowment for Humanities, 1971-72. Mem. Nat. Council Soc. Bibl. Lit., 1967—. Mem. Soc. Bibl. Lit. (sec. So. sect. 1967-75), Assn. for Targumic Studies (chmn. 1972—), Phi Gamma Delta. Mng. editor St. Andrews Rev., 1972—; contbg. editor History of Jews in the Time of Christ, 1973. Contbr. to publs. in field. Home: Route 1 Box 197-A Laurinburg NC 28352

DOUD, DAVID LAWRENCE, computer co. exec.; b. Ferguson, Ia., Feb. 11, 1943; s. Walter William and Cheryl Jean (Finders) D.; B.S., Drake U., 1969; m. Diane Marie Cathcart, July 3, 1964; children—Deborah Jean, Kristine Michelle. Audit sr. Arthur Young & Co., C.P.A.'s, Dallas, 1969-73; mgr. financial reporting Univ. Computing Co., Dallas, 1973—. C.P.A., Tex. Mem. Am. Inst. C.P.A.'s, Tex. Soc. C.P.A.'s. Home: 1614 Villanova Dr Richardson TX 75080 Office: PO Box 47911 Dallas TX 75247

DOUGHERTY, EDDIE LEE, cons. engr.; b. Kansas City, Kan., Dec. 1, 1925; s. Henry Leslie and Sylvia (Garrett) D.; B.S., U. Mo., 1949; m. Mary Lucille Campbell, June 9, 1948; children—Sylvia Louise, Mary Lorrice, Vicky Lee (Mrs. Frank Monczewski), Patricia Lorraine (Mrs. John Marin), Michael Leslie, Terry Lynn, Dennis Leroy. Constrn. engr. Mo. Dept. Hwys., 1949-50; field engr. Howard, Needles, Tammen & Bergendoff, 1950-54, resident engr., Wheeling, W.Va., 1954-55, Emporia, Kan., 1955-56, Sault Ste. Marie, Mich., 1956-58, Rock Island, Ill., 1958-61, project engr., Orlando, Fla., 1961-64, New Castle, Del., 1964-66, engr. in charge, Richmond, Va., 1966-70, project mgr. Greater Buffalo Airport, 1970-71; asso. W.K. Dougherty, Cons. Engrs., Miami, Fla., 1971-74; organizer, v.p. P.E. Cons., Inc., Miami, 1973—. Com. chmn. Boy Scouts Am., 1967-69. Served with AUS, 1943-45. Decorated Air medal with 6 oak leaf clusters. Registered profl. engr., Mo., Fla., N.Y., Del., N.J., N.C., Va. Mem. Am. Soc. C.E., Nat. Soc. Profl. Engrs., Fla. Engring. Soc., N.J. Soc. Profl. Planners, Aero Club of Buffalo, Engrs. Club, Theta Tau. Home: 7565 SW 135th St Miami FL 33156 Office: PO Box 1162 Kendall Branch Miami FL 33156

DOUGHERTY, FRANK MARION, judge; b. Diboll, Tex., July 26, 1912; s. Frank E. and Della M. (Fitts) D.; LL.B., Baylor U., 1949; LL.B., Loyola U., New Orleans, 1950; m. Paulyn Gill, Feb. 17, 1946; children—Glenda Ruth, John Michael. Admitted to La. bar, 1950; pvt. practice law, Homer, 1952-57; judge 2d Jud. Dist. Ct., Homor, La., 1958—. Served with USMC and USNR, 1942-45. Mem. Am., La. bar assns., Am. Judicature Soc., La. Law Inst., N. La. Hist. Soc. Mason (32 deg., Shriner). Baptist. Home: 722 S Main St Homer LA 71040 Office: 1 Public Sq Homer LA 71040

DOUGHERTY, HUGH LARRABEE, JR., savs. & loan assn. exec.; b. Norfolk, Va., Apr. 15, 1932; s. Hugh Larrabee and Effie (Griffin) D.; B.S. in Civil Engring., Va. Mil. Inst., 1954; grad. Am. Savs. & Loan Inst., 1966; m. Barbara Woodside, Sept. 11, 1971; children—Deborah Lynn, Carey Ann, Katherine Griffen, Scarlett C., Donald, Guy. With Atlantic Permanent Savs. & Loan Assn., Norfolk, Va., 1963—, teller, 1965-69, personnel dir., 1965-69, asst. v.p., asst. sec., 1969-72, exec. v.p., 1972-73, pres., 1973—, dir., 1971—; chmn. bd. dirs. Data Systems Corp. Computer & Mortgage Broker Co. Bd. dirs. Tidewater Heart Assn. Served with USMCR, 1954-63; now lt. col. Res. Mem. Norfolk C. of C. (treas. 1973-74), Downtown Norfolk Assn., Hampton Rds. council Navy League, Va. Mil. Inst. Alumni Assn., Homebldrs. Assn., Soc. Real Estate Appraisers, Am. Savs. & Loan Inst. (pres. Tidewater chpt. 1969-70), Tidewater Group Savs. & Loan Assn. (pres. 1970-71), Va. Savs. & Loan League (bd. govs. 1973-75), U.S. Savs. & Loan League (mem. legislative com. 1969—). Mason. Home: 3884 Thalia Dr Virginia Beach VA 23452 Office: 740 Boush St Norfolk VA 23510

DOUGHERTY, J(OHN) CHRYS(OSTOM), lawyer; b. Beeville, Tex., May 3, 1915; s. John Chrysostom and Mary V. (Henderson) D.; B.A., U. Tex., 1937; LL.B., Harvard, 1940; diploma, Inter-Am. Acad. Internat. and Comparative Law, Havana, Cuba, 1948; m. Mary Ireland Graves, Apr. 18, 1942; children—Mary Ireland, John Chrysostom IV. Admitted to Tex. bar, 1940; atty. Hewit & Dougherty, 1940-41; partner Graves & Dougherty, 1946-50, Graves, Dougherty & Greenhill, Austin, Tex., 1950-57, Graves, Dougherty & Gee, 1957-60, Graves, Dougherty, Gee & Hearon, 1961-66, Graves, Dougherty, Gee, Hearon, Moody & Garwood, 1966-73, Graves, Dougherty, Hearon, Moody & Garwood, 1973—; spl. asst. atty. gen., 1949-50. Dir. Austin Nat. Bank. Hon. French consul for Tex., Austin, 1971—. Mem. Tex. Submerged Lands Adv. Com., 1963-72, Tex. Bus. and Commerce Code Adv. Com., 1964-66, Gov.'s Com. Marine Resources, 1970, Colo. River Basin Water Quality Mgmt. Study Com., 1972-73, Legislative Property Tax Com., 1973—. Bd. dirs. Advanced Religious Study Found.; trustee Nat. Pollution Control Found., 1966—, St. Stephen's Episcopal Sch., 1966—, U. Tex. Law Sch. Found., 1971—. Served as capt. C.I.C., U.S. Army, 1941-44, Judge Adv. Gen. Corps. 1944-46, maj., 1953—. Fellow Tex. Bar Found., Am. Bar Found.; mem. Am. Arbitration Assn. (mem. nat. panel arbitrators 1958—), S.W. adv. council 1965—) Am., Travis County bar assns., State Bar Tex. (chmn. sect. taxation 1965-66), Internat., Am. fgn. law assns., Am. Law Inst., Am. Soc. Internat. Law (exec. council 1959-62), Inter-Am. Bar Assn., Cum Laude Soc. (hon.), Phi Beta Kappa, Phi Eta Sigma, Beta Theta Pi (dir. Tex. Beta Students Aid Fund). Presbyn. Rotarian. Co-editor: Texas Appellate Practice, 1964. Contbr. Bowe, Estate Planning and Taxation; Texas Lawyers Practice Guide, 1967, 71, How to Live and Die with Texas Probate, 1968; Texas Estate Administration, 1973. Home: 6 Green Lanes

Austin TX 78703 Office: Austin Nat Bank Bldg PO Box 98 Austin TX 78767

DOUGLAS, BARTON THRASHER, lawyer; b. Gainesville, Fla., Mar. 23, 1908; s. James Byers and Rebecca (Hicklin) D.; J.D., U. Fla., 1932; m. Monica Karlene Darling, May 30, 1958; children—Barton A. J. Zachariah Hicklin II, Alexander Scott II, Monica Karlene. Admitted to Fla. bar, 1932, Tex. bar, 1935; practiced in Gainesville, 1932—. Served to lt. comdr. USNR, 1942-45, judge advocate U.S. Naval Forces Western Australia. Mem. Am., Fla. State, Tex. State, Fed. bar assns., Academia Internationali Lex Et Scientia, Eighth Jud. Bar Assn. (past pres.), Delta Chi. Democrat. Presbyn. (elder). Elk, K.P. Home: 612 NE 4th Av Gainesville FL 32601 Office: 103 N Main St Gainesville FL 32601

DOUGLAS, CHARLES HERBERT, univ. research adminstr.; b. Loughman, Fla., Dec. 2, 1926; s. Herbert and Delia (Sutton) D.; student La. State U., 1943-44, 46-47; Mus.B., Converse Coll., 1949, Mus.M., 1958; Ph.D., Fla. State U., 1965; m. Jane Caroline Long, Aug. 25, 1949; children—Daron Maudel, Carolyn Grove. Tchr. pvt. schs., New Orleans, 1950-57; asst. prof. Converse Coll., Spartanburg, S.C., 1957-60; asst. prof. U. Ga., Athens, 1961-65, asso. prof., 1965-67, asst. dean arts and scis., 1967-68, asst. v.p., 1968-71, dir. gen. research, 1971—. Guest lectr. Agnes Scott Coll., 1966; clinician, adjudicator Ga. Music Educators Assn., 1961-66; dir. Spartanburg Civic Band, 1959-61. Served with USNR, 1943-45, 51-53. Spartanburg Found. teaching fellow, 1957-58. Mem. Nat. Council U. Research Adminstrs., Ga. Composers (pres. 1966-67), Phi Mu Alpha, Pi Kappa Lambda. Presbyn. Author: Harmony, 1954; Rhythmic Excerpts, 1954; Piano Class Teaching Method, 1955; Basic Music Theory, 1965; Playing Social Instruments, 1972. Mus. composer: Symphonic Suite for Band, 1958; Rhapsody for String Orchestra, 1962; String Quartet, 1963. Home: 460 Forest Rd Athens GA 30601

DOUGLAS, CHARLIE (DOUGLAS CHINA), radio personality; b. Miami, Fla., Mar. 11, 1933; s. Douglas Elwood and Susan Kyle (Beggs) C.; student Wofford Coll., 1950-51; m. Martha Claire McGee, July 8, 1954; children—Helen Claire, George Douglas, Cynthia Anne. Disc jockey radio stas. KLIC, Monroe, La., 1953-57, KTSA, San Antonio, 1957-61, WKBW, Buffalo, 1961-64, WINZ, Miami, 1964-67, KPRC Houston, 1967-70, WWL, New Orleans, 1970—; v.p. Rand Broadcasting, 1965-67. Cons. in field; lectr., guest speaker. Named Disc Jockey of Year, Billboard mag., 1973, Disc Jockey of Year, Overdrive mag., 1972. Mem. Country Music Assn. (dir., Disc Jockey of Year award 1973). Office: 1024 N Rampart St New Orleans LA 70176

DOUGLAS, HUBERT PRENTISS, engring. exec.; b. Richton, Miss., Dec. 4, 1918; s. Washington Scott and Stacy Elizabeth (Myrick) D.; student E. Miss. Jr. Coll., 1937-38, Miss. State Coll., 1938-39, Bklyn. Coll., 1940-46; B.E.E., Bklyn. Poly. Inst., 1949; postgrad. Brown U., 1949-50; m. Anne Corinne Picke, Jan. 20, 1945; children—Gregory, Therese (Mrs. Michael Dana Murphy), Janet (Mrs. James Daniel Anslow), Jeffery. Instr. elec. engring. U.S. Naval Sch., Newport, R.I., 1949-51; with Lockheed Electronics Co., Inc., 1951—, mgr. field engring., 1958-64, dir. Houston operations, 1964-65, dir. program control, 1965-69, mgr. information systems, 1969-71, mgr. gen. engring., 1971—. Pres., Lake Land Civic League, Norfolk, Va., 1956-57; chmn. Clear Lake Little League Fund-Raising Activity, Seabrook, Tex., 1967-71. Served with USNR, 1941-45. Mem. I.E.E.E., Am. Inst. Aeros. and Astronautics, Soc. Logistics Engrs. (chpt. chmn. 1967-68). Democrat. Roman Catholic (chmn. bldg. fund 1967). K.C., Elk (chmn. trustees 1969-73). Home: 418 Terrace Dr Seabrook TX 77586 Office: 16811 El Camino Real Houston TX 77058

DOUGLAS, JAMES NATHANIEL, radio astronomer, educator; b. Dallas, Aug. 14, 1935; s. Loyd and Nell (Curtis) D.; B.S., Yale, 1956, M.S., 1958, Ph.D., 1961; m. Charlotte Cummings, Aug. 30, 1956; children—Neva, James, Alan. Instr. Yale, 1960-61, asst. prof., 1961-65; asso. prof. astronomy U. Tex., Austin, 1965-71, prof., 1971—, dir. Radio Astronomy Obs., 1965—. Mem. astronomy adv. panel NSF, 1971-74. Mem. A.A.A.S., Am. Astronom. Soc., Am. Geophys. Union, Internat. Astronom. Union, Union Radio Scientifique Internationale, Phi Beta Kappa, Sigma Xi. Contbr. numerous articles to sci. jours. Home: 2300 Leon Av Austin TX 78705

DOUGLAS, JOHN F., JR., indsl. engr.; b. Lake City, Fla., Nov. 18, 1929; s. John F. and Elsie B. Douglas; B.S. in Indsl. Engring., U. Fla., 1951. With Tenn. Eastman Co., Kingsport, Tenn., 1953—, formerly indsl. engr., now dir. distbn. Served to 1st lt. USAF, 1951-53. Registered profl. engr., Tenn. Mem. Nat. (dir. Ednl. Found.), Tenn. (chmn. policy rev. com., presdl. award 1971), Upper East Tenn. (past pres., dir.) socs. profl. engrs., Am. Inst. Indsl. Engrs. Baptist (charter mem., deacon, Sunday sch. supt.). Club: Kiwanis (pres., dir.) (Kingsport). Address: Route 6 Edens View Kingsport TN 37664

DOUGLAS, MELVYN LEE, lawyer; b. Seattle, May 28, 1945; s. Arden Ray and Avie (Squier) D.; B.B.A., So. Methodist U., 1967, J.D., 1970. Admitted to Tex. bar, 1970; C.P.A. firm Touche Ross & Co., Dallas, 1970-72; pvt. practice law Neary & Ives, Inc., Attys., Dallas, 1972—. Mem. Am., Tex., Dallas bar assns., Am. Inst. C.P.A.'s, Tex. Soc. C.P.A.'s, Phi Delta Phi, Kappa Sigma. Club: The 500 Inc. Home: 3851 Windsor Lane Dallas TX 75205 Office: 1100 Fidelity Union Tower Dallas TX 75201

DOUGLAS, OMER RAY, ednl. adminstr.; b. Hamilton, Tex., May 4, 1919; s. Eli Erwin and Nettie Laura (Johnson) D.; B.S., Howard Payne Coll., 1942; M.A., North Tex. State U., 1949; Ed.D., Tex. Tech U., 1965; m. V. Pauline Fergusson, Aug. 14, 1940; children—Donna Kay (Mrs. Darrell Franks), Randal Ray, Phyllis Jo, Bruce Wayne. Prin. Hess-Averitt Sch., San Angelo, Tex., 1939-42; prin. Winters (Tex.) High Sch., 1942-44, 46-49; prin. Brownfield (Tex.) High Sch., 1949-51; supt. Brownfield pub. schs., 1951-67; exec. dir. Edn. Service Center-Region XVII, Lubbock, Tex., 1967—. Gen. fund chmn. Brownfield Community Chest, 1959. Served with AUS, 1944-46. Mem. Am., Tex. (past pres. Dist. IV and XIII) assns. sch. adminstrs., Tex. Tchrs. Assn. (past pres. Dist. IV). Lion (pres. 1952-53). Home: 6221 Lynnhaven Dr Lubbock TX 79413 Office: 700 Tex Commerce Tower Lubbock TX 79401

DOUGLAS, WILLIAM ORVILLE, asso. justice U.S. Supreme Ct.; b. Maine, Minn., Oct. 16, 1898; s. William and Julia Bickford (Fisk) D.; B.A., Whitman Coll., 1920, LL.D., 1938; LL.B., Columbia, 1925; hon. M.A., Yale, 1932; LL.D., Wesleyan U., 1940, Washington and Jefferson Coll., 1942, Coll. William and Mary, 1943, Rollins Coll., 1947, Nat. U., 1949, New Sch. Social Research, 1952, U. Toledo, 1956, Bucknell U., 1958, Colgate U., 1973; m. Mildred Riddle, Aug. 16, 1923; children—Mildred Riddle (Mrs. Norman T. Read), William Orville; m. 2d, Mercedes Hester, Dec. 14, 1954; m. 3d, Joan Martin, Aug. 5, 1963; m. 4th, Cathleen Heffernan, July 15, 1966. High school tchr., Yakima, Wash., 1920-22; admitted to N.Y. bar 1926; practiced N.Y.C., 1925-27; law faculty Columbia 1925-28, Yale, 1928-34; bankruptcy studies Yale Inst. Human Relations and U.S. Dept. Commerce, 1929-32; sec. Com. Bus. Fed. Courts, Nat. Commn. on Law Observance and Enforcement, 1930-32; dir. protective com. study SEC, Washington, 1934-36, commr. and chmn., 1936-39; nominated asso. justice U.S. Supreme Ct. by Pres. Roosevelt Mar. 20, 1939, confirmed by Senate Apr. 4, 1939, and took seat on bench Apr. 17, 1939. Served as pvt. U.S. Army, 1918. Mem. Royal Geog. Soc. (London), Phi Beta Kappa, Beta Theta Pi, Phi Alpha Delta, Delta Sigma Rho. Democrat. Presbyn. Mason. Clubs: Yale; Himalayan (Delhi, India); University (Washington); Overseas Press. Author various law case books, also books: Of Men and Mountains, 1950; Strange Lands and Friendly People, 1951; Beyond the High Himalayas, 1952; North from Malaya, 1953; An Almanac of Liberty, 1954; We The Judges, 1955; Russian Journey, 1956; The Right of the People, 1958; Exploring the Himalaya, 1958; West of the Indus, 1958; My Wilderness, The Pacific West, 1960; My Wilderness: East to Katahdin, 1961; A Living Bill of Rights, 1961; Muir of the Mountains, 1961; Democracy's Manifesto, 1962; Mr. Lincoln and the Negros, 1963; The Anatomy of Liberty, 1963; A Wilderness Bill of Rights, 1966; Farewell to Texas, 1967; Towards a Global Federalism, 1969; Points of Rebellion, 1970; International Dissent, 1971; Holocaust or Hemispheric Co-op, 1971; The Three Hundred Year War, 1972; Go East Young Man, Vol. I, 1974. Contbr. articles to law jours. Home: Goose Prairie WA 98929 Office: US Supreme Ct Washington DC 20543

DOUGLASS, CURTIS LINDSEY, elec. co. engr.; b. Gilmer, Tex., Dec. 20, 1929; s. Robert George and Christell (Lindsey) D.; B.S., So. Meth. U., 1952; m. Owenda Lee Hardy, Oct. 27, 1956; children—Caren Lynn, Cathy Ann. Elec. design engr. Tex. Power & Light Co., Dallas and Waco, Tex., 1948-57, Phillips Petroleum Co., McGregor, Tex., 1957; engring. mgr. Fed. Pacific Elec. Co., Dallas, 1958—; investor rental properties. Registered profl. engr., Tex. Mem. I.E.E.E., Constrn. Specifications Inst., Delta Chi. Methodist. Home: 1417 Boca Chica Dr Dallas TX 75232 Office: 901 Regal Row Dallas TX 75247

DOUGLASS, FRANK EUGENE, judge; b. Houston, June 29, 1925; s. Young Eugene and Ethel (Haag) D.; B.B.A., Tex. Technol. Coll., 1951; m. Virginia Dale Lankford, Mar. 1, 1951; children—Stephen Frank, Cary Dale. Sales rep. Procter & Gamble, Ft. Worth, 1951-54; sales mgr. Blue Bonnet Drug Sales, Arlington, Tex., 1954-57; non-foods purchasing agt. Affiliated Foods, Dallas, 1957-66; mayor pro-tem City of Euless (Tex.) 1968-72, asso. municipal judge, 1973—. Sec., Euless (Tex.) Planning and Zoning Bd., 1962-63, chmn., 1963-64; councilman, Euless 1964-68; sec., treas., mem. adv. council Northeast Cities, 1964-72; mem. Euless Civil Service Commn., 1973—. Served with USNR, 1942-45. Lion (pres. 1962-63). Home: 502 Martin Lane Euless TX 76039 Office: 298 N Main St Euless TX 76039

DOUGLASS, JESSE BURTON, food co. exec.; b. Johnson City, Tenn., Apr. 12, 1914; s. Sidney B. and Mary (Edwards) D.; student Washington and Lee U., 1936, U. Ky., 1937; m. Joan Colgan, July 3, 1941; children—Sidney Barns, Jesse Burton, Daniel O. Mgr. Jellico Grocery Co., Harlan, 1946—; pres. Tri-State Wholesale Co., Middlesboro, Ky., Jellico Grocery Co. (Tenn.). Former dir. Harlan County Planning and Devel. Assn.; commr. Harlan Municipal Water Works; former mem. Blue Grass council Boy Scouts Am., Lexington, voted scouter of the year Harlan dist., 1950. Served to master sgt. USAAF, 1941-45. Mem. Nat. Am. Wholesale Grocers Assn., Ky. Wholesale Grocers (pres. 1964, dir.), Pi Kappa Alpha. Presbyn. (chmn. 1958-59, trustee). Kiwanian (dir., pres. 1963, lt. gov. div. 10 Ky-Tenn. dist. 1964, chmn. pub. and bus. affairs com. Ky-Tenn. dist.). Club: Harlan Country (pres.). Home: Good Neighborhood Rd Loyal KY 40854 Office: 102 E Rail Rd Harlan KY 40831

DOUGLASS, ROBERT JOSEPH, forest products co. exec.; b. Moline, Ill., Sept. 8, 1913; s. Ralph Allison and Fannie Josephine (Moore) D.; student Augustana Coll., 1933-34; B.S., U. Miss., 1937; m. Hattie Jane Holmes, Feb. 2, 1947; children—Jane (Mrs. John E. Rhodes, Jr.), Robert Joseph. Area mgr. Weyerhaeuser Corp., Tacoma 1954-61; v.p. marketing Gen. Plywood Corp., Louisville, 1961-63; pres., chmn. bd. Gamble Brothers, Inc., Louisville, 1963—; dir. Ernest Homes, Co., Chattanooga, Reliance Universal, Inc., Plastic Parts, Inc., Shelbyville, Ky., Martin Sweets Co., Louisville. Trustee Old Ky. Home council Boy Scouts Am., 1968. Served to lt. comdr. USNR, 1941-46. Mem. Ky. Forestry Council, Nat. Forest Products Assn. (dir. 1966), Internat. Woodworking Machinery and Furniture Supply Fair (dir. 1969—), Ky. Wood Industry Assn. (dir. 1967—), Sigma Chi. Rotarian. Clubs: Flight, Louisville Country, Pendennis, Rock Creek Riding (Louisville). Home: 6213 Glen Hill Rd Louisville KY Office: 4601 Allmond Av Louisville KY 40221

DOUMA, JACOB HENDRICK, civil engr.; b. Hanford, Cal., May 30, 1912; s. Hendrik Jackob and Gertje (Kok) D.; B.S., U. Cal. at Berkeley, 1935; m. Allene Vartia, Apr. 4, 1939; children—Mark Hendrick, Allen Jacob. With C.E. U.S. Army, various locations, 1935—, chief hydraulic engr., Washington, 1961—. TAMS, N.Y.C., 1961-70, CASECO, Vancouver, B.C., Can., 1964-71, Quinones Assos., P.R., 1965-71. Mem. Am. Soc. C.E., Nat. Acad. Engring., Internat. Commn. Irrigation, Drainage and Flood Control, Internat. Commn. Large Dams, Internat. Assn. Hydraulic Research, Permanent Internat. Assn. Nav. Congresses, Tau Beta Pi, Chi Epsilon. Contbr. articles to profl. jours. Home: 1001 Manning St Great Falls VA 22066 Office: 1000 Independence Av Washington DC 20314

DOUMAR, ROBERT GEORGE, lawyer; b. Norfolk, Va., Feb. 17, 1930; s. George Joseph and Margot (Meshaka) D.; B.A., U. Va., 1951, LL.B., 1953, J.D., 1972; m. Dorothy Mundy, Apr. 28, 1962; children—Robert George, Charles C. Admitted to Va. bar, 1952; asso. firm Venable, Parson, Kyle & Hylton, Norfolk, 1955-58; sr. partner firm Doumar, Pincus, Knight & Harlan, Norfolk, 1958—. Pres., Tidewater Legal Aid Soc., 1966-68. Mem. Va. Republican Central Com., 1972—, chmn., Norfolk, 1965—; del. Rep. Nat. Conv., 1968, 72. Served with AUS, 1953-55. Mem. Norfolk, Portsmouth, Va., Am. bar assns., Raven Soc., Am. Legion, Order of Coif. Roman Catholic. Elk. Clubs: Norfolk Yacht and Country, Harbour, Mallary Country. Mem. editorial bd. Va. Law Rev., 1952-53. Home: 1400 Armistead Bridge Rd Norfolk VA 23507 Office: 1350 Virginia Nat Bank Bldg Norfolk VA 23510

DOVE, LLOYD ALVIN, civil engr.; b. Washington, May 8, 1928; s. Charles Elmer and Thelma Estelle (Trewalla) D.; B.S., Ia. State U., 1952; postgrad. Northwestern, 1960-61, U.S. Fla., 1972—; m. Sylvia Gladys Thompson, Aug. 14, 1949; children—JoAnn, Stephen, Gary. Cons. engr., Black & Veatch, Kansas City, Mo., 1952-54; city mgr. Nevada, Ia., 1954-56; dir. pub. works Ames, Ia., 1956-59; asst. exec. dir., author pub. works manuals Am. Pub. Works Assn., Chgo., 1960-62, 68-70; land mgmt. adviser to Ministers Finance and Interior, Royal Govt. Afghanistan, 1963-68; dir. pub. works St. Petersburg, Fla., 1971-73; regional mgr. West Fla., Black, Crow & Eidsness, Inc., Engrs., Clearwater, 1973—. Mem. utilities com. Hwy. Research Bd., 1970—. Served with AUS, 1946-48. Mem. Fla. Engring. Soc., Am. Water Works Assn., Am. Soc. C.E., Am. Pub. Works Assn., Nat. Soc. Profl. Engrs., Am. Pollution Control Assn., Am. Soc. Pub. Adminstrn., Pi Sigma Alpha. Kiwanian. Author: Land Surveying and Registration Manual of Afghanistan, 6 edits., 1963-68; also articles. Home: 1978 Massachusetts Av NE St Petersburg FL 33703 Office: PO Box 5066 Clearwater FL 33518

DOWD, EDWARD JOSEPH, JR., assn. exec.; b. Holyoke, Mass., May 24, 1921; s. Edward Joseph and Nora M. (Kennedy) D.; A.B., Am. Internat. Coll., 1947; M.Ed., Springfield Coll., 1952; m. Henrietta Laura Moran, Dec. 21, 1943; children—John Edward, Nancy Beth, Christopher John. Restaurant owner, Springfield, Mass., 1947-50, mgmt. trainee Libby-Owens-Ford Glass Co., Toledo, 1952-53; employment supr., tng. dir. Toledo Edison Co., 1953-55; exec. sec. Employers' Assn. Toledo, 1955-58; v.p., pres. Central Piedmont Industries, Charlotte, N.C., 1958—; vocational cons. Dept. Health, Edn. and Welfare, Washington, 1962—. Exec. com. N.C. Manpower Devel. Com. Bd. dirs. Belmont Abbey Coll., Belmont, N.C. Served with USNR, 1943-46. Mem. Am., Southeastern, N.C. psychol. assns., Nat. Indsl. Council (exec. com. 1960-63, chmn. indsl. relations group), Am. Soc. Assn. Execs., Knights Malta. Rotarian. Clubs: University (N.Y.C.); Charlotte City, Carmel Country; Capital Hill (Washington). Home: 5200 Rounding Run Rd Matthews NC 28105 Office: 420 Hawthorne Lane Charlotte NC 28204

DOWDEN, THOMAS CLARK, cable television exec.; b. Nashville, Tenn., May 6, 1935; s. James Robert and Anna (Hunter) D.; A.B., U. Ga., 1962, M.A., 1963; m. Wendy Vereen, Jan. 27, 1962; children—Anna V., Constance H., John T. TV dir., newswriter WMAR-TV, Balt., 1960-62; TV acct. exec. Corinthian Broadcasting Corp., Houston, 1963-65; v.p., sec. Cox Cable Communications, Inc., Atlanta, Ga., 1965—; instr. U. Ga., 1962-63. Served with AUS, 1955-58. Mem. U. Ga. Alumni Assn. (mem. President's adv. com. 1970-71), Di Gamma Kappa, Sigma Delta Chi, Pi Sigma Alpha. Democrat. Episcopalian. Club: Cherokee Country. Home: 6311 Mountain Brook Way NW Atlanta GA 30328 Office: 53 Perimeter Center Atlanta GA 30346

DOWDY, JOE HOLLAND, dentist; b. High Springs, Fla., Mar. 29, 1930; s. Terrell Joe and Azilene (Holland) D.; B.Mech. Engring. with high honors, U. Fla., 1951; D.D.S. with highest honor, Baylor U., 1960; m. Billye Clarice Arledge, Oct. 26, 1952; children—Kaye Ann, David William. Engr., Westinghouse Electric Corp., Pitts., 1951; practice dentistry, High Springs, Fla., 1960—. Served to 1st lt. USAF, 1951-55. Mem. Alachua County Dental Soc. (pres. 1971-72), Fla. Dental Assn. (dist. del. 1970-71), High Springs, (dir.), Greater Gainesville (com. of 100) chambers commerce, Phi Kappa Phi, Omicron Kappa Upsilon, Delta Sigma Delta. Democrat. Baptist (deacon, trustee, supt. young people dept. 1964—). Home: 230 NE 7th Av High Springs FL 32643 Office: 60 S Main St High Springs FL 32643

DOWELL, JAMES DALE, lawyer; b. Goose Creek, Tex., July 17, 1932; s. James Dale and Margaret (King) D.; B.A., Tex. A. & M. U., 1954; LL.B., U. Tex., 1957; m. Patricia Jo Skaggs, Feb. 2, 1957; children—Terry, James Dale III. Admitted to Tex. bar, 1957; asso. firm King, Sharfstein & Rienstra, Beaumont, Tex., 1957-63, partner, 1963-68; partner firm Rienstra, Rienstra & Dowell, Beaumont, 1968—. Mem. Tex. Democratic Exec. Com., 1966-68. Mem. State Bar of Tex., Am. Bar Assn. Democrat. Rotarian. Home: 6275 Wilchester Ln Beaumont TX 77706 Office: 707 Beaumont Savs Bldg Beaumont TX 77701

DOWIS, WILLIAM SHAFER, JR., architect; b. Sumter, S.C., Dec. 23, 1923; s. William Shafer and Patricia (Bunn) D.; student Wofford Coll., 1941-43; B.S. in Architecture with honors, Clemson Coll., 1950; m. Joyce Norfleet Dickinson, Apr. 3, 1947; children—William Shafer III, George Dickinson, Mary Norfleet. Architect, specifications writer J.E. Sirrine Co., Greenville, S.C., 1950-54; partner firm Lewis & Dowis, Florence, 1954-71; prin. firm William S. Dowis, Jr., Florence, 1972—. Mem. S.C. Arts Commn., 1967-73; chmn. S.C. Art Collection Com., 1970-73. Trustee Florence (S.C.) Mus., pres. 1960-70, 73. Served with inf. AUS, 1943-46. Decorated Bronze Star; recipient Distinguished Service award Jr. C. of C., Florence, 1969. Mem. A.I.A. (pres. S.C. 1961), Constrn. Specifications Inst., Guild S.C. Artists (pres. 1970). Methodist. Lion. One-man shows paintings Florence Mus., Banks Haley Gallery, Albany Ga., Sandlapper Gallery, Columbia, S.C., The Art Center, Spartanburg, S.C., 1971. Home: 322 W Pine St Florence SC 29501 Office: PO Box 368 Florence SC 29501

DOWLING, FRED BENNY, environmental cons.; b. Jackson, Miss., Jan. 3, 1937; s. Harry E. and Lozelle (Beasley) D.; B.S., Millsaps Coll., 1959; B.S. in Chemistry, La. State U., 1961; m. Betty Jean Burgdorff, May 23, 1959; children—James Hampton, Charles Edward, Nicole Elizabeth. With Kem-Tech Labs., Inc., Baton Rouge, 1961—, chemist, 1961-62, air pollution chemist, 1962-65, air pollution chemist, sec.-treas., dir., sec. bd., 1965—, v.p., 1972—. Mem. Am. Chem. Soc., Air Pollution Control Assn., Aircraft Owners and Pilots Assn. Methodist. Club: Fairwood Country. Contbr. articles to profl. jours. Patentee in field. Home: 12270 E Milburn St Baton Rouge LA 70815 Office: 16550 Highland Rd Baton Rouge LA 70808

DOWLING, JOAB MAULDIN, lawyer; b. Greenwood, S.C., Nov. 26, 1917; s. Grafton Geddes and Leonora Connors (Mauldin) D.; B.S., U. S.C., 1939, J.D., 1941; m. Katharine Elizabeth Douglas, Mar. 23, 1943; children—Jane (Mrs. Sherwood N. Fender), Joab Mauldin, John D., Katharine Louisa, May D. Admitted to S.C. bar, 1941, U.S. Supreme Ct. and all state and fed. cts.; partner firm Dowling, Dowling, Sanders & Dukes, P.A. and predecessors, Beaufort, S.C., 1941—; civilian aide to Sec. of Army, 1971—. Chmn. bd. Palmetto State Savs. & Loan Assn.; dir., officer Sea Island Investment Co., 1st Beaufort Corp., Coastal Securities Corp.; dir. Blue Channel Corp. Trustee Dowling Found., Bapt. Found. S.C., Beaufort Acad. Served with USNR, 1943-45. Mem. Am., S.C., Beaufort County bar assns., Am. Judicature Soc., Am. Legion, Beaufort County C. of C. (past v.p.). Elk, Rotarian (past pres. Beaufort Club). Home: 1 Spinnaker Ct Hilton Head Island SC 29928 Office: 1105 Bay St Beaufort SC 29902 also Pope Av Hilton Head Island SC 29928

DOWNEY, ELEANOR PAULINE LONG, med. researcher; b. Birmingham, Ala., Nov. 27, 1942; d. Roger Winston and Ruby Pauline (King) Long; A.B., Birmingham So. Coll., 1964; postgrad. U. Ala., 1965-67, 68—; m. Stanford H. Downey, Jr., July 4, 1964 (div.); 1 son, Stanford Harmon III. Lab. asst. Seale Harris Clinic, 1959-60; cancer research technologist Meml. Inst. Pathology, Birmingham, Ala., 1960-64, anthropology and clin. research asso., 1963—, now coordinator research activities. Med. sec. to dr., 1960-62; high sch. tchr., Trussville, Ala., 1963-64. Mem. A.A.A.S. (award 1960), Internat. Cancer Congress, Internat. Acad. Pathology, Ala. Acad. Sci., Am. Assn. Phys. Anthropologists, Am. Statis. Assn., Caucus for Women in Statistics, Alpha Chi Omega (adv. bd. 1964—). Kappa Delta Epsilon. Unitarian (Sunday sch. tchr., summer program coordinator). Contbr. numerous articles to profl. jours. Home: 5323 Tenth Av S Birmingham AL 35222 Office: 1025 S 18th St PO Box 3406-A Birmingham AL 35205

DOWNEY, THOMAS ALBERT, JR., structural engr.; b. Alexandria, Va., Jan. 1, 1936; s. Thomas Albert and Thelma Marguerite (Miles) D.; B.S. in Archtl. Engring., Va. Poly. Inst., 1958; M. C.E., Cath. U. Am., 1968; m. Doris Ann Cool, Sept. 8, 1956; children—Karen Lynn, Jane Lee. Draftsman, Fortune Engring. Asso., Alexandria, Va., 1958-60, chief design engr., 1960-68; partner Fortune, Downey, Elliott, cons. engring., Alexandria, 1968—. Served to 2d lt. C.E., AUS, 1958. Registered profl. engr., Md., Va., D.C.

Mem. Cons. Engrs. Council, N. Va. Builders Assn. (dir.), Alexandria C. of C. Kiwanian. Home: 8505 Cyrus Pl Alexandria VA 22308 Office: 4660 Kenmore Av Alexandria VA 22304

DOWNEY, WILLIAM GERALD, JR., lawyer, banker, ret. army officer; b. Bklyn., June 20, 1914; s. William Gerald and Mary Veronica (Ryder) D.; B.S.S., Coll. City N.Y., 1937; M.A., Catholic U., 1938; J.D., Georgetown U., 1951; certificate internat. law, U. Mich., 1937, Latin Am. area tng., 1946; student U. Iceland, 1941-42; grad. Command and Gen. Staff College, 1962; m. Ellen Wagle, Apr. 17, 1942 (dec.); 1 son, William G. III (dec.); m. 2d, Laufey Arnadottir, June 5, 1947; children—Richard, Elizabeth, Mary, Catherine, William Gerald IV, Karen. Commd. 2d lt. inf. res., 1936, advanced through the grades to col. Judge Adv. Gen.'s Corps, 1964, ret., 1969; chief internat. law br., 1946-50, Group Judge Adv., Formosa, 1952-54; sr. partner Downey & Lennhoff, Springfield, Va.; practice law, Va. and Washington; founder, past chmn. bd. No. Va. Bank; pres. Springfield Corp.; fellow internat. law Cath. U., 1936-37; fellow internat. law, Georgetown U., 1937-40, instr. govt., 1937-40; prof. internat. law Soochow U. Law Sch., 1952-54. Mem. Fairfax County Democratic Com.; del. Va. Dem. Conv., 1960, 64, 68; candidate Va. State Senate, 1963. Mem. Springfield C. of C. (pres. 1961-62, dir.), Washington, Va. bar assns. Kiwanian (pres. Springfield 1961-62; lt. gov. select Capital dist. 1973-74). Clubs: Army-Navy, Army-Navy Country; Morgan Horse. Author articles on mil. and internat. law. Contbr. to Ency. Britannica. Home: Roscrea 5611 Guinea Rd Fairfax VA 22030 Office: Springfield Tower Bldg PO Box 6 Springfield VA 22150

DOWNING, HUDSON URQUHART, stock broker; b. Columbus, Ga., Feb. 26, 1923; s. Lemuel Tyler and Frances Ruth (Hudson) D.; grad. Truman and Smith Inst., 1942, N.Y. Inst. Finance, 1960; m. Barbara Ann Parker, Oct. 11, 1953. Tchr. pub. schs. Va., Phenix City. Ala., 1946-50; mgr. Ala., Ga. Cigarette Service, Columbus, Ga., 1950-56; asst. mgr. Western Auto Supply Store, Columbus, 1956-59; v.p., partner First Southeastern Co., brokerage firm, Columbus, 1963—; organizer, bd. dirs. Phenix Nat. Bank, Phenix City. Served with USAAF, 1942-46. Presbyn. Club: Stock Investment (Phenix City). Home: Route 1 Box 870 Phenix City AL 36867 Office: 103 12th St Columbus GA 31901

DOWNING, THOMAS NELMS, U.S. congressman; b. Newport News, Va., Feb. 1, 1919; s. Samuel and Lucille (Nelms) D.; B.S., Va. Mil. Inst., 1940; LL.B., U. Va., 1947; m. Virginia Dickerson Martin, Feb. 17, 1947; children—Susan Nelms, Samuel Dickerson Martin. Admitted to Va. bar, 1947; with Downing, Andrews & Durden, Hampton, Va., 1955-58; substitute judge Municipal Ct., City of Warwick (now Newport News), 1953-58; mem. 86th-93d congresses from 1st Va. Dist.; mem. Mcht. Marine and Fisheries Com., Sci. and Astronautics Com. Bd. visitors Mcht. Marine Acad., Kings Point, N.Y. Coll. Served from 2d lt. to maj. Cav., AUS, World War II. Decorated Silver Star. Mem. Am. Legion, Am., Va. State, Hampton, Newport News-Warwick (past pres.) bar assns., Assn. U.S. Army, V.F.W. Democrat. Episcopalian (trustee). Lion, Jr. Order United Am. Mechanics. Club: Propeller. Home: 27 Indigo Dam Rd Washington DC 20007 Office: Rayburn House Office Bldg Washington DC 20515

DOWNS, ELDON WILSON, air force officer; b. Buffalo, Okla., Feb. 7, 1918; s. Hawley Wilson and Pearl (Clark) D.; A.B., Okla. State U., 1940, M.A., 1941; Ph.D., U. Wis., 1959; m. Elyn Dorothy Howell, Feb. 14, 1947; children—DeAnne, Denise, Danielle, DeLys. Served to maj. AUS, 1941-46, recalled as lt col. U.S. Air Force, 1951; prof. mil. history Air U., 1951-54, chief hist. office, 1951-54; historian Allied Air Forces, Central Europe, NATO, 1954-58; asst. prof. history U.S. Air Force Acad. (Colo.), 1960-61, asso. prof., dir. instrn., 1961-62, asso. prof., dep., 1962-63, asso. prof., spl. asst., 1963-64; plans and programs officer Aerospace Studies Inst., Air U., Maxwell AFB, Ala., 1964—, editor Air Univ. Rev., 1965—; instr. polit. sci. Okla. State U., 1946, grad. asst. history U. Wis., 1946-49, instr. history, 1949; instr. history, counselor Stephens Coll., 1949-51. Cons. curriculum Officer Tng. Sch., San Antonio, 1962. Recipient mil. commendation for U. Press Study, 1964. Mem. Am., Western hist. assns., Orgn. Am. Historians, Air Force Hist. Found., Am. Mil. Inst., Am. Aviation Hist. Soc., Phi Kappa Phi, Phi Alpha Theta. Baptist (former mem. bd.). Author: Histories of Headquarters AIRCENT, 1955-58; Army and the Airmail-1934, 1962. Editor: Golden Arrow, 6 vols., 1965; The U.S. Air Force in Space, 1966. Co-author: Out of the Darkness, 1969. Office: Editor Air U Rev Maxwell AFB AL 36112

DOWNS, JON FRANKLIN, educator; b. Bartow, Fla., Sept. 15, 1938; s. Clarence Curtis and Frankie Mae (Morgan) D.; student Ga. State Coll., 1956-58; B.F.A., U. Ga., 1960, M.F.A., 1969. Dir. The Beastly Purple Forest (marionettes) U. Ga., 1968, Dracula: A Horrible Musical, DeKalb Coll., 1971, Streetcar Named Desire, DeKalb, 1974, others; actor Wedding in Japan, N.Y.C., 1960, Dark at the Top of the Stairs, N.Y.C. and tour, 1961, Night Must Fall, DeKalb Coll., 1970, others; designer Sweeney Todd, DeKalb Coll., 1970, Romulus, 1971, Grass Harp, 1972, others; author, dir. Gold, tour, summer 1974; drama dir. Dekalb Coll., Clarkston, Ga., 1969—. Writer, dir. play Tokalitta, on tour of Ga., summers 1973, 74. Ga. Dept. Planning and Budget arts sect. grantee, 1973. Mem. Southeastern (state rep. 1971-73), Ga. (area rep. 1970-73) theatre confs. Home: 116 Springdale St Decatur GA 30030 Office: Dekalb Coll 555 N Indian Creek Dr Clarkson GA 30021

DOWTIN, MAUDE CHILES, librarian; b. Troy, S.C., Oct. 27, 1912; d. Robert Lee and Clifford Gallagher (Chiles) Dowtin; student Winthrop Coll., 1930-32; A.B., U. S.C., 1934; A.B in L.S., Emory U., 1939. Tchr. pub. schs., S.C., 1934-38; library supr. state-wide library project WPA, Columbia, S.C., 1939-43; librarian Post Library No. 4, Fort Jackson, S.C., 1943-45, No. 5, 1945-46, chief librarian, Post Library System, 1946—. Mem. Am., Southeastern, S.C. library assns. Home: 3012 Manchester Rd Columbia SC 29204 Office: Post Library Fort Jackson SC 29207

DOXEY, WALL, JR., lawyer; b. Memphis, Jan. 11, 1926; s. Wall and Myrtle (Johnson) D.; B.B.A., J.D., U. Miss., 1950; m. Sarah Mozelle Smith, Apr. 19, 1945; children—Ralph Hindman, Helene. Admitted to Miss. bar, 1950; practiced in Holly Springs, Miss., 1950-73; county atty. Marshall County, Miss., 1952-56; now atty. Marshall County Bd. Suprs. Served with USAAF, 1943-46. Mem. Am., Miss. bar assns., Phi Delta Theta, Delta Sigma Pi. Home: 510 Randolph St Holly Springs MS 38635 Office: Doxey Bldg Memphis St Holly Springs MS 38635 Died Dec. 17, 1973.

DOYLE, CHARLES THOMAS, investment banker; b. Mangum, Okla., Aug. 3, 1934; s. Roy Leo and Mattie (Carter) D.; A.A., Kemper Mil. Acad., 1954; B.B.A., U. Okla., 1956; M.B.A., U. Houston, 1961; m. Mary Ellen Hipp, Aug. 25, 1956; children—Matthew, David, Denise, Patrick, Christopher. With Mangum Brick & Tile Co., 1952-56; indsl. relations Union Carbide Corp., Texas City, Tex., 1956-69; investments and real estate broker, Houston, 1969—; impartial arbitrator labor mgmt. arbitration, 1964—; dir. Buffalo Savs. & Loan Assn., Houston, Copperstone Constructors Inc., Houston, O'Neill, Anderson & Assos. Inc. Houston); pres., 1st dir. State Bank, Hitchcock, Tex.; chmn. bd. U.S. Mgmt. Corp., Houston. Adult adviser Catholic Youth Orgn., 1964-68. Mayor pro tem, Texas City, 1964—; pres. Galveston County Mayors and Councilmens Assn., 1968-69. Bd. dirs. Galveston County Community Action Council, 1964-68. Served to capt. Armored Div., AUS, 1956-58. Recipient Texas City Distinguished Service award, 1963; named One of Five Outstanding Young Texans, 1965. Mem. Texas City Jr. (life), Texas City (dir.) chambers commerce, Beta Gamma Sigma, Sigma Iota Epsilon, Omicron Chi Epsilon, Phi Gamma Delta. Contbr. articles to profl. jours. Home: 1526 19th Av N Texas City TX 77590 Office: First State Bank PO Box 104 Hitchcock TX 77563

DOYLE, JOHN F., judge; b. Kansas City, Mo.; grad. Rockhurst (Mo.) Coll., Georgetown U. Law Sch. Formerly asst. corporation counsel D.C.; asst. U.S. atty.; mem. staff Ho. of Reps. appropriations com., 1952; then asst. gen. counsel U.S. Cath. Conf., Washington; judge U.S. Dist. Ct., Washington, now superior Ct. judge. Address: 5th and E Sts NW Washington DC 20001

DOYLE, TERRY, lawyer, state legislator; b. Port Arthur, Tex., Jan. 14, 1939; s. Patrick John and Frances Louise (Owsley) D.; B.S., Lamar U., 1960; LL.B., Tex. U., 1963; m. Barbara Palermo, Aug. 23, 1959; children—Kelly Ann, Paddy. Admitted to Tex. bar, 1963; asst. dist. atty., Jefferson County, Tex., 1963-66; practiced in Port Arthur, 1966—; partner firm Provost, Umphrey, Doyle & Mehaffy, 1971—; mem. Tex. Ho. of Reps., 1971—. Mem. Port Arthur Bar Assn. (pres. 1965). Home: 2801 Glacier Port Arthur TX 77640 Office: 3747 Doctors Dr Port Arthur TX 77640

DOYLE, WALTER ARNETT, dentist; b. Los Angeles, Aug. 9, 1933; s. Walter James and Ruth (Journey) D.; student Glendale Coll., 1951-52, U. Hawaii, 1952-53, Joliet Jr. Coll., 1953-54, U. Ill., 1954-55; D.D.S., Emory U., 1959; M.S. in Pedodontics, Ind. U., 1961; m. Betty Ann Parrott, Dec. 28, 1957; children—Shannon, Elizabeth, Sally, Walter Arnett. Practice dentistry, specializing in pedodontics, Lexington, Ky., 1962—; pres. Bluegrass Orthodontic-Pedodontic Labs., Inc., Lexington, 1971—; instr. pedodontics U. Ky., Lexington, 1964-65, guest lectr., 1965—; mem. staff St. Joseph's Hosp., Central Baptist, Good Samaritan hosps., Lexington. Partner Coca Cola Bottling Co., Campbellsville, Ky., 1971—. Mem. Com. Am. Dental Assn. Task Force Nat. Dental Care Program, Chgo., 1970-71; mem. Blue Grass Trust for Historic Preservation, 1970—. Recipient Travel South photography award, 1968. S.S. White teaching fellow. Fellow Internat. Coll. Dentists; mem. Am. Bd. Pedodontics (examining mem.), Am. (pres. 1964), Ky. socs. dentistry for children, Internat. Assn. Dental Research (pres. 1969), Southeastern Soc. Pedodontics, Ky. Dental Service Corp. (past dir.), Lexington C. of C. Rotarian. Clubs: Polo, Keeneland, Athletic (Lexington). Contbr. to profl. jours. and textbooks. Home: 3800 Nicholasville Rd Lexington KY 40503 Office: 1628 Nicholasville Rd Lexington KY 40503

DOZIER, MABRY FRAZIER, lumber sales co. exec.; b. Mobile, Ala., Apr. 4, 1927; s. Mabry F. and Frances (Gray) D.; student Spring Hill Coll., 1946-47; m. Frances Gay, Dec. 24, 1955; children—Mabry Frazier III, Frances. Gen. mgr. Jim Walter Doors, Century, Fla., 1963—; v.p. sales, dir. Alger-Sullivan Co., Century, 1965—; dir. Clancy Lumber Co., Grayson, Ala. Trustee Escambia County Hosp. Served with AUS, 1945-46. Mem. So. Pine Assn., Tri-City C. of C. (pres. 1965-66), Hoo-Hoo Internat. Methodist. Lion (pres. Century 1967-68), Toastmaster (pres. Tri-City 1964-65). Home: 100 N Jefferson Av Century FL 32535 Office: Century FL 32535

DOZIER, MAURICE FRANCIS, corp. exec.; b. Richmond, Va., Aug. 20, 1920; s. Curtis M. and Rosa (Conaty) D.; B.S.S., Georgetown U., 1941; m. Ann T. O'Connor, May 7, 1949; children—Curtis M. and Ann O'Connor (twins), Thomas C. Sales rep. Hamilton Paper Corp., Richmond, 1949-51; pres. Colonial Paper Co., Inc., Richmond, 1951-54; sales mgr. Richmond Container Corp., 1954-64; pres. Commonwealth Corp., Richmond, 1964—; v.p., treas. Fibre Tube Corp., 1969—. Republican dist. chmn. 3d Congl. Dist. Va., 1952-56. Served with AUS, 1941-46. Decorated Purple Heart (3), Bronze Star. Roman Catholic. Home: 5900 S Crestwood Av Richmond VA 23226 Office: 1003 Commerce Rd Richmond VA 23224

DOZIER, WILLIAM ALBERT, elec. engr.; b. Winfield, Ga., Mar. 11, 1932; s. Thomas Albert and Josie Hall (Large) D.; B.E.E., Ga. Inst. Tech., 1956; m. Martha Virginia Morris, May 24, 1958; children—William Albert, Steven Daniel. With Ga. Power Co., Columbus, 1955—, dist. engr., 1969-71, div. planning engr., 1971—. Registered profl. engr., Ga. Mem. I.E.E.E., Ga. Soc. Profl. Engrs. Originator 3 stake method of locating faults on underground cables using radar; inventor dead cable certifier. Home: 5921 Leonard's Ct Columbus GA 31904 Office: PO Box 1220 Columbus GA 31902

DRAEGER, ARTHUR ANDREW, JR., petroleum co. exec.; b. Seguin, Tex., Mar. 23, 1911; s. Arthur Andrew and Cora (Schaper) D.; B.S., M.S., U. Tex., 1932, Ph.D., 1935; m. Billy Bob White, July 24, 1937; children—Carolyn (Mrs. David J. Rhoads), Madeleine (Mrs. R.T. McCulley). Jr. engr. Humble Oil & Refining Co. (co. name changed to Exxon Co. U.S.A. 1973), Baytown, Tex., 1935-38, new project engr., 1938-47, div. head research and devel., 1947-58, mgr. gen. sales, 1958-61, mgr. marketing research, 1961-64, mgr. corporate planning, 1964-74, exec. asst. to pres., 1974—. Budget chmn. Community Chest, Baytown, 1956-59. Mem. Am. Inst. Chem. Engrs., Am. Chem. Soc., Am. Petroleum Inst., Sigma Xi. Home: 5406 Tilbury St Houston TX 77027 Office: Exxon Co USA PO Box 2180 Houston TX 77001

DRAKE, AVERY ALA, JR., geologist; b. Kansas City, Mo., Jan. 17, 1927; s. Avery Ala and Mary Genevieve (Wilson) Drake; B.S., Mo. Sch. Mines, 1950, M.S., 1952; m. Colette J.J.E. Buino, Aug. 10, 1963; children—Avery Ala III, Isabelle G.P. Research geologist Colo. front range U.S. Geol. Survey, 1952-55, Central Appalachians, 1957—, Antarctica, 1960-61, Nat. Center, Reston, Va., 1971—. Teaching asst. mining geology Mo. Sch. Mines, Rolla, 1950-52; prof. advanced structural geology U. Goiania, Brazil, 1973. Served with inf. AUS, 1945-47. Fellow Geol. Soc. Am.; mem. Soc. Econ. Geologists, Geochem. Soc., Geol. Soc. Washington (sec. 1963-64), Pa. Acad. Sci., Pi Kappa Alpha, Sigma Gamma Epsilon. Club: Cosmos (Washington). Contbr. articles to profl. jours. Home: 1575 44th St NW Washington DC 20007 Office: US Geol Survey Nat Center Reston VA 22092

DRAKE, ROBERT WILLIAM, agrl. co. exec.; b. Attica, Ind., Jan. 10, 1933; s. George William and Clara Marian (Winks) D.; B.S., Ind. U., 1954. With Cargill, Inc., 1957—, mgr. soybean processing operation, Chesapeake, Va., 1971—. Bd. dirs. Va. Soybean Commn. Served with USAF, 1955-57. Mem. Va. Feed Assn. (pres. 1965), Va. Soybean Assn. (dir.), C. of C., Delta Tau Delta. Home: 1124 Michaelwood Dr Virginia Beach VA 23452 Office: PO Box 7502 Chesapeake VA 23324

DRAKE, VAUGHN PARIS, JR., telphone co. exec.; b. Winchester, Ky., Nov. 6, 1918; s. Vaughn Paris and Margaret Turney (Willis) D.; student U. Ky., 1936-41; m. Lina Louise Wilson, May 5, 1946; 1 son, Samuel Willis. With Gen. Telephone Co. Ky., Lexington, 1945—, asst. engr., 1945-50, field engr., 1950-54, dist. engr., 1954-56, div. engr., 1956-57, depreciation engr., 1957-62, valuation and cost engr., 1962—. Mem. profl. adv. bd. Zoning Commn., Lexington and Fayette County (Ky.), 1955-57. Served with AUS, 1941-45. Registered profl. engr., Ky. Mem. Ky. Soc. Profl. Engrs. (chmn. engrs. in industry sect. 1967-68), I.E.E.E. (sr.), Ky. Hist. Soc. Author: (manual) Conduit Engineering for Telephone Engineers, 1958. Home: 633 Portland Dr Lexington KY 40503 Office: 2001 Harrodsburg Rd Lexington KY 40507

DRAPER, CLARE HILL, III, bldg. material co. exec.; b. Anderson, S.C., June 17, 1928; s. Clare Hill and Helen (Watkins) D.; student bus. adminstrn. U. Va., 1946-48; B.S. in Textile Mfg., Clemson Coll., 1952; m. Eulalie Thomas Jenkins, Dec. 8, 1956; children—Clare Hill IV, Eulalie Crommelin, Raleigh Jenkins. Salesman Pacific Mills, Inc., Atlanta, 1954-55; exec. asst. to v.p. Pacific Mills, N.Y.C., 1955-56, asst. mdse. mgr., 1956-57, sales and merchandising mgr., 1957-58; exec. v.p. Jenkins Mfg. Co., Anniston, Ala., 1958—; dir. Nat. Sash & Door Jobbers Assn., Chgo., 1971-73. Bd. dirs. United Fund, Calhoun County, 1970-73. Served to 1st lt. inf. AUS, 1952-54. Mem. Anniston C. of C. (dir. 1972-74), Chi Phi. Episcopalian. Rotarian. Club: Anniston Country. Home: 940 Montvue Rd Anniston AL 36201 Office: 315 W 17th St Anniston AL 36201

DRAPER, DANIEL D., supt. schs.; b. Elk Point, S.D., June 26, 1911; s. Jesse Sylvester and Bertha (Sawtelle) D.; elementary certificate Northeastern State Coll., 1933, B.A., 1937; M.A., Okla. State U., 1949; postgrad. U. Ark., 1957-59; m. Elva Anderson, July 3, 1937; children—Shirley Ann (Mrs. Don Allen Gard), Daniel D., Marjorie Kay (Mrs. William E. Miller). Prin., Stone Chapel Sch., Cherokee County, Okla., 1931-40; supt. Pierce (Okla.) Pub. Schs., 1945-54, Colcord (Okla.) Pub. Schs., 1954—. Mem. Okla. Ho. Reps., 1938-42; chmn. Dem. Central Com., Delaware County; mayor Colcord, Okla. Mem. Anti-Thief Assn. (nat. pres.), Cherokee County (pres. 1940-41), McIntosh County (pres. 1951-52), Delaware County (pres. 1958-59) tchrs. assns., N.E. Dist. Sch. Adminstrs. Assn. (pres.), Colcord C. of C. (pres.). Mason. Address: 102 W Blocker St Colcord OK 74338

DRAPER, ERNEST LINN, JR., educator; b. Houston, Feb. 6, 1942; s. Ernest Linn and Marcia Lee (Saylor) D.; student Williams Coll., 1960-62; B.A., Rice U., 1964, B.S., 1965; Ph.D., Cornell U., 1970; m. Deborah Doyle, June 9, 1962; children—Susan Elizabeth, Robert Linn, Barbara Ann, David Doyle. Asst. prof. nuclear engring. U. Tex., Austin, 1969-73, asso. prof., 1973—, dir. Nuclear Reactor Lab., 1971—. Dir. NuTex Corp. Recipient U. Tex. at Austin Engring. Found. Faculty award, 1972. AEC fellow, 1967-69; NSF trainee, 1965-67; Ford Found. fellow, 1968. Mem. Am. Nuclear Soc., Am. Phys. Soc., Am. Inst. Chem. Engrs., Sigma Tau, Pi Tau Sigma. Editor: Implications of Nuclear Power in Texas, 1973; Texas Symposium on the Technology of Controlled Thermonuclear Fusion Experiments and the Engineering Aspects of Fusion Reactors, 1973. Contbr. articles to profl. jours. Home: 8007 Hillrise Austin TX 78759

DRAPER, JAMES F., assn. exec.; b. Auburn, N.Y., Feb. 27, 1931; s. John Reed and Cora (Fallon) D.; A.B., Harvard, 1951, postgrad. Bus. Sch., 1954-55. With J.P. Morgan & Co., N.Y.C., 1955-56, McDonnell & Co., N.Y.C. and Boston, 1956-68; v.p., mgr. Butcher & Sherrerd, N.Y.C., 1968-70; pres. James F. Draper Corp., Boston, 1970-72; stockbroker F.S. Smithers & Co., N.Y.C., 1972-73; spl. asst. to pres. Govt. Nat. Mortgage Assn., Washington, 1973—. Trustee Draper Charitable Found. Club: Harvard. Home: 2800 Woodley Rd NW Washington DC 20008

DRAPER, ROBERT BRUCE, architect; b. Gainesboro, Tenn., July 28, 1927; s. Herbert Ridley and Hallie (Reeves) D.; student U. Chgo., 1947-48, Frank Lloyd Wright Found., 1948-50; m. Jane Helen Caplinger, Dec. 11, 1953; children—Cynthia, Christopher Louis, Elizabeth. Draftsman, designer Chgo. firms William F. Deknatel, and Barancik & Conte, 1951-52; draftsman, designer Marr & Holman, Nashville, 1952-53; gen. practice architecture, Nashville, 1953—. Served with USNR, 1945-46. Mem. Soc. Am. Registered Architects. Unitarian. Home: 613 Estes Rd Nashville TN 37215 Office: 2535 Franklin Rd Nashville TN 37204

DRAWDY, JOHN WESLEY, lawyer; b. Orangeburg, S.C., Nov. 11, 1925; s. Lonnie Wesley and Agnes (Wilson) D.; B.A. magna cum laude, Furman U., 1952; postgrad. Wash. U. Sch. Law, 1952-53; LL.B., U. S.C., 1955, J.D., 1970; m. Brenda Jones, Dec. 24, 1960; children—Wesley, Doireann Lynn, Peter Warren, Dawn Aleta. Admitted to S.C. bar, 1955; asso. atty. firm Haynsworth, Perry, Bryant, Marion & Johnston, Greenville, S.C., 1955-57; atty. Allstate Ins. Co., Charlotte, N.C., 1957; adjuster John Rattery & Co., Grier, S.C., 1957-58; partner firm McCants & Drawdy, Columbia, S.C., 1958-60, Smith & Drawdy, Columbia, 1961-63; pvt. practice law, Columbia, 1963-70; partner firm Drawdy, Faucette & Rothwell, Columbia, 1971-72; prin. firm J. Wesley Drawdy, Columbia, 1972—. Served with U.S. Mcht. Marine, 1944-47. Nat. Law scholar, 1952. Fellow Comml. Law Found.; mem. Fed., Am., S.C., Richland County bar assns., Am. Judicature Soc., Comml. Law League Am. Republican. Unitarian. Elk (exalted ruler 1969-70). Home: 4901 Carter Hill Dr Columbia SC 29206 Office: 2014 Sumter St Columbia SC 29201

DRAWDY, VANCE BRABHAM, lawyer; b. Orangeburg, S.C., Jan. 29, 1928; s. Lonnie Wesley and Agnes Jane (Wilson) D.; B.A. cum laude, Furman U., 1952; J.D. (Root Tildeon scholar), U. S.C., 1955; m. Mary Earle, Aug. 4, 1962; children—Vance Earle. Admitted to S.C. bar, 1955; asso. Rainey, Fant & Horton, Greenville, S.C., 1955-62, partner, 1963-70; v.p. Horton, Drawdy, Dillard, Marchbanks, Chapman & Brown, Greenville, 1970—; sec., dir. Patewood Corp., Greenville; dir. Byrd Furniture Co., Inc., Greenville, Pleasantburg Warehouse Co., Greenville. Gen. counsel S.C. Republican party, 1972—. Served as 1st lt. Signal Corps, AUS, 1947-49. Mem. S.C.V. Elk. Clubs: Poinsett, Exchange (pres. 1974—) (Greenville). Home: Route 4 Box 256 Piedmont SC 29673 Office: 307 Pettigru St Greenville SC 29603

DRECHSLER, WILLIAM GLENN, elec. products mfg. co. exec.; b. Alburg, Vt., Dec. 27, 1928; s. Francis Arthur and Alice (Perry) D.; B.S. in Elec. Engring., Purdue U., 1957; postgrad. Syracuse U., 1957-59; m. Elizabeth Glynn Niblett, Feb. 13, 1953; children—Linda, Sandra, Dianne, Karen, Nancy. Staff engr. IBM Corp., Endicott, N.Y., 1957-61; with Dynatronics, Inc., Orlando, Fla., project mgr., 1961-65, v.p. engring., Gen. Dynamics Electronics div. 1965-74; program mgr. TRW Financial Data Scis., Winter Park, Fla., 1974—. Mem. adv. com. computer sci. program Seminole Jr. Coll., Sanford, Fla., 1970-72. Trustee Central Fla. Mus., Orlando, 1st v.p., 1970-72. Served with USNR, 1951-55. Recipient pub. service award NASA, 1969. Mem. I.E.E.E. (sr.), Am. Mgmt. Assn., Gen. Dynamics/Orlando Mgmt. Assn. (past chmn. dirs.), Kappa Sigma. Republican. Home: 2814 Rapidan Trail Maitland FL 32751 Office: PO Box 1300 Winter Park FL 32789

DRELL, ANNIE DEE FLINN (MRS. THEODORE LOUIS DRELL), realtor; b. Fulton, Ky., June 11, 1916; d. Dillingham Dodson and Alma (Bradley) Flinn; student real estate appraising Tulane U., 1966-67; m. Theodore Louis Drell, Aug. 31, 1935; children—Barbara Anne (Mrs. Austin Allen), Robert Louis (dec.), Theodore Louis III, Dee Dodson. Sec.-treas. Ted Drell, advt. art and design, 1939—; real estate agt. Carriere & Harper, New Orleans, 1959-66; broker, 1966-67; v.p. Waguespack, Pratt, Inc., 1967; staff broker Stan Weber & Assos., New Orleans, 1968—. Organizing mem.

Lake Terrace Woman's Club, New Orleans, 1957, rec. sec. 1969-70, v.p., 1970-71, 72-73, pres., 1973-74; mem. Methodist Hosp. Woman's Aux., 1968—. Mem. D.A.R. (charter Bayou St. John chpt. regent chpt. 1958-59, 62-63, treas. 1970-72), Jefferson Bd. Realtors, Nat. Assn. Real Estate Bds. (treas. women's council New Orleans chpt. 1972), Real Estate Bd. New Orleans. Baptist. Home: 1336 New York St New Orleans LA 70122 Office: 6244 Argonne Blvd New Orleans LA 70124

DRESSER, KENNETH BULLARD, JR., theatrical designer; b. N.Y.C., Aug. 21, 1938; s. Kenneth Bullard and Gertrude (McMahon) D.; B.F.A. in Interior Archtl. Design, R.I. Sch. Design, 1961. Free lance designer Interior Space & Graphic Design, Washington, 1961—. Served with AUS, 1961-64. Recipient Designer's Drama Theatre Key award R.I. Sch. Design, 1961, various govt. scenic design awards, 1963, 66, 68. Mem. U.S. Inst. Theatre Tech., Theatre Hist. Soc., Am. Theatre Assn. (pres. Mid-Atlantic 1972-73). Author, designer: Production Guide I: The Thematic Production, 1964; Production Guide II: Scenic Adaptations for Musicals, 1966. Cons. numerous orgns., including, Smithsonian Instn., Kennedy Center for Performing Arts, Disney World (Fla.), Disneyland (Cal.), White House, also numerous theatre, stage and TV prodns. Home and office: 320 2d SE Washington DC 20003

DRESSLER, ROBERT, elec. engr.; b. N.Y.C., May 5, 1925; s. Sam and Bertha (Bernblut) D.; B.S. in Elec. Engring., Columbia, 1946, M.S. in Elec. Engring., 1948; postgrad. Bklyn. Poly. Tech., 1948, 57, Northeastern U., 1962-67; m. Fay Goodkin, June 8, 1946; children—Sherl, Lori, Carrie. Mgr. research and devel. Paramount Pictures, N.Y.C., 1946-51; v.p. Chromatic TV Labs, Ins., N.Y.C., 1951-57; exec. v.p. Autometric Corp., N.Y.C., 1957-61; dir. advanced systems research and engring. Raytheon Corp., 1961-68; pres., chief exec. officer Riker-Maxson Corp., 1968-73; exec. v.p. Crown Industries, Tampa, Fla. Served with USNR, 1943-46. Recipient Nat. TV Systems Com. Award for color TV standards. Mem. I.R.E. (sr.), Am. Inst. E.E., Am. Soc. Photogrammetry, N.Y. Acad. Sci., Am. Phys. Soc., Am. Optical Soc., Am. Mgmt. Assn., Air Force Assn., Am. Rocket Soc. (sr.), Am. Geophys. Union, Soc. Motion Picture and TV Engrs. Patentee electric analogue circuit and method, others in field. Home: 2626 NE 37th Dr Ft Lauderdale FL 33308 Office: 3825 Henderson Blvd Tampa FL 33609

DREVO, JOSEPH CHARLES, refrigeration equipment designer; b. Balt., Feb. 18, 1908; s. Joseph and Johanna (Lukova) D.; diploma architecture Md. Inst., 1926; certificate City Coll. Balt., 1937; m. Dorothy Jacobs, Dec. 23, 1949; children—Robert J., Norman C. Mfg. shop foreman Ottenheimer Bros., Balt., 1927-37; research designer Innovative Frozen Foods, Stanguard Dickerson Co., N.Y.C., 1937-39; then designer, supr. Moss Mfg., Bklyn.; now prodn. supr. Revere Group Quality Inns Internat., Washington, 1939—. Research asso. in natural resource food systems investigative studies. Leader Boy Scouts Am., 1952-57. Recipient Pub. service award D.C., 1944. Mem. Soc. Am. Mil. Engrs., World Assn. Nat. Wildlife Fedn. Roman Catholic. Home: 6004 Jamestown Rd Hyattsville MD 20782 Office: 10750 Columbia Pike Silver Spring MD 20901 20011

DREVO, WILLIAM LUK, SR., architect; b. Pacov, Czechoslovakia, May 27, 1905; s. Joseph and Johanna (Lukova) D.; brought to U.S., 1905, naturalized, 1939; Diploma Architecture, Md. Inst., Balt., 1925; student George Washington U., 1929-31; research studies Richard J. Neutra Inst., 1966-70, George Washington U., 1970—; m. Olga Nenadel, Mar. 25, 1931; children—William L., Richard N. Asso. architect Fed. Constrn. Agys., 1927-43; sr. engr. applied physics lab. Johns Hopkins, Silver Spring, Md., 1943-46; asso. architect firm F. Grad & Sons, Washington, 1946-51; archtl. planning cons. William L. Drevo, Sr., Washington, 1951—. Cons. Graphics Ednl. Communications Assn., 1949-56. Active campaigns various Congl. ofcls., 1952—. Recipient Civilian award Navy Dept., 1945. Mem. A.I.A., George Washington U. Alumni Assn., Soc. Am. Mil. Engrs. Republican. Presbyn. Nat. Accelerator Lab. site studies, 1964, now environmental, natural resource investigative studies, Atlantic Ocean Coastal estuary flood plain regional analyses, satellite potentials NASA. Performing pianist, 1930—. Home: 6125 29th St NW Washington DC 20015 Office: 6125 29th St NW Washington DC 20015

DREW, ELIZABETH BRENNER, writer, television commentator. Washington editor Atlantic mag., 1967-73; moderator program Thirty Minutes With..... Pub. Broadcasting Service, 1971-73; commentator Washington Post-Newsweek stas., 1973—. Recipient award for excellence Soc. Mag. Writers, 1970; DuPont-Columbia award for broadcast journalism, 1973. Contbr. articles to mags., including New Yorker, N.Y. Times Mag., Atlantic. Address: 3112 Woodley Rd NW Washington DC 20008

DREW, HORACE RAINSFORD, JR., lawyer; b. Jacksonville, Fla., Jan. 1, 1918; s. Horace Rainsford and Margaret Louise (Phillips) D.; B.S. in Bus. Adminstrn., U. Fla., 1940, LL.B., 1941, J.D., 1967; m. Rae Berger, Oct. 28, 1944; children—Shelley Louise, Robert Fairbanks, Horace Rainsford III. Admitted to Fla. bar, 1941; estate tax examiner Office Internal Revenue Agt. in Charge, Jacksonville, 1946-50; practice law, Jacksonville, 1951—; partner Buck, Drew & Glocker. Bd. dirs. Childrens Home Soc. Fla., Family Consultation Service, Duval County unit Am. Cancer Soc., 1962-71; founder, trustee Episcopal High Sch., Jacksonville; trustee Frank Lubbock Miller, Jr. Ednl. Found.; founding mem. So. Acad. Letters, Arts and Scis. Served to maj. F.A., AUS, 1941-45; ETO; lt. col. Res. (ret.). Mem. Am., Fla. (chmn. estate and gift tax com. 1956-58, chmn. tax sect. 1959-60), Jacksonville (chmn. spl. liaison tax com. Southeastern region 1962-63, chmn. com. on taxation 1955-56, 64-65) bar assns., Am. Judicature Soc., Jacksonville C. of C., Am. Security Council, Newcomen Soc. N.Am., Phi Delta Phi, Sigma Alpha Epsilon. Episcopalian. Clubs: River; San Jose Country, San Jose Yacht; Officers U.S. Naval Air Sta. (Jacksonville). Home: 861 Waterman Rd N Jacksonville FL 32207 Office: Fla Title Bldg Jacksonville FL 32202

DREW, JAMES MULCRO, composer; b. St. Paul, Feb. 9, 1929; s. James Joseph and Gladys Jeanette (Drew) Mulcro; student N.Y. Sch. Music, 1954-56; pupil with Wallingford Riegger, 1956-59, Edgard Varese, 1956; M.A., Tulane U., 1964; m. Gloria Kelly, Apr. 26, 1960; children—Drummond, Kelly Anne. Composer, 1968—; instr. composition and theory Northwestern U., Chgo., 1965-67; vis. prof. Washington U., St. Louis, 1967; asst. prof. composition Yale, 1967-73; composer-in-residence La. State U., Baton Rouge, 1974—. Served with USNR, 1945-46. Northwestern research grantee for electronic music, 1965; Morse fellow, 1967-69; Calhoun fellow, Yale, 1968-73; Guggenheim fellow, 1972-73; commns. Fromm Music Found., 1973, Berkshire Music Center, 1973. Mem. Am. Soc. Composers and Condrs., Am. Soc. Composer, Authors and Pubs. (award 1974). Composer: The Lute in the Attic, 1963; October Lights, 1969; Primero Libro de Referencia Laberinto, 1970; Metal Concert, 1971; Symphony No. 2, 1971; Chamber Symphony, 1972; Lux Incognitus, 1973; West Indian Lights, 1973; Mysterium, 1974. Home: 1078 Rodney St Baton Rouge LA 70808

DREW, JOHN, chem. engr.; b. Tampa, Fla., Jan. 24, 1915; s. Anon John and Addie (Sumner) D.; B.Ch.E., Ga. Inst. Tech., 1940; M.E., U. Fla., 1968; m. Frances McKay, Sept. 6, 1941; 1 son, John Drew IV. Research chemist Hercules Inc. Naval Stores, Hattiesburg, Miss., 1940-50; asst. to v.p. Crosby Chems. Inc. Naval Stores, Deridder, La., 1950-56; div. engr. SCM-Glidden-Durkee div. Organic Chem. group, Jacksonville, Fla., 1956-59, mgr. mfg., 1960-66, dir. devel., 1966-72, mgr. tech. services, 1972—. Chmn., Fores Gen. Hosp. Com., 1948-50; Gulf County chmn. fund raising Red Cross, 1959. Bd. dirs. Air Improvement Authority. Registered profl. engr., Fla., La. Mem. Am. Chem. Soc., Am. Inst. Chem. Engrs., Pulp Chems. Assn., T.A.P.P.I., United Inventors and Scientists of Am., Am. Oil Chemists Soc. Methodist (chmn. bd. stewards 1955-56). Lion, Elk, Kiwanian. Clubs: Deerwood, Ponte Vedra, San Blas (pres. 1961), Toastmasters (pres. 1964-65). Patentee organic chemistry and engring., ednl. toys. Chief editor: Sulfate Turpentine Recovery, Library of Congress Catalogue 1971. Home: 3759 Jose Terrace Jacksonville FL 32217 Office: PO Box 389 Jacksonville FL 32201

DREW, ROBERT TAYLOR, toxicologist; b. Red Bank, N.J., Apr. 22, 1936; s. Jerome Bradley and Jesse (Taylor) D.; B.S., Rensselaer Poly. Inst., 1958; M.S., N.Y. U., 1962, Ph.D., 1968; m. Cornelia Hoyt, May 26, 1962; children—Judith Bradley, Stephanie, Christiana. Chemist, N.Y. Dept. Health, Albany, 1958-60, N.J. Dept. Health, West Orange, 1960; instr. N.Y. U., Inst. Environmental Medicine, Sterling Forest, 1961-70; toxicologist Nat. Inst. Environmental Health Sci., Research Triangle Park, N.C., 1970—. Cons. inhalation toxicology, indsl. hygiene. Mem. Soc. Toxicology, Am. Indsl. Hygiene Soc. Contbr. articles to profl. jours. Home: 4513 Lindsay Dr Raleigh NC 27612 Office: Box 12233 Research Triangle Park NC 27709

DREWRY, GUY CARLETON, author; b. Stevensburg, Va., May 21, 1901; s. Rev. Samuel Richard and Julia Harriet (Pinckard) D.; student pub. schs. Va.; m. Margaret Elizabeth McDonald, Apr. 2, 1942; children—Barbara Louise, Guy Carleton. Asso. editor The Lyric, 1929-49; vis. lectr. English, Am. poetry Hollins Coll., 1952-53; instr. creative writing U. Va. Extension Div. Counselor Blue Ridge Writers Colony, 1965-66. Contbr. poetry to The Dial, later The Nation, The New Republic, Poetry: A Magazine of Verse also Voices. Work appears in N.Y. Times, N.Y. Herald Tribune, The Ga. Rev., Prairie Schooner, Sat. Rev., Queen's Quar., Va. Quar. Rev. and Yale Rev.; included in following anthologies: American Writing, Lyric Virginia Today, Moult's Best Poems, Virginia Reader, Poetry Awards (1949, 51). Proud Horns, 1933: The Sounding Summer, 1948; A Time of Turning, 1951; The Writhen Wood, 1953. Winner The Voices Award, 1940; Lyric Virginia Today, No. 2, The Best Poems of 1956; Cloud Above Clocktime, 1957 also The Golden Years, The Diamond Anthology, N.Y. Times Anthology of Verse, Modern Religious Poetry. Recipient Poetry Awards prize for best book of poetry pub. in 1951; poet laureate Va. Mem. Poetry Soc. Va. (pres. 1952-55, mem. adv. bd.), Poetry Soc. Am. (regional v.p.), Authors Guild of Authors League Am. Club: Virginia Writers (hon.). Editor of Southern Issue of Voices, 1952. Home: 2305 Maiden Lane SW Roanoke VA 24015

DREWYER, ROLAND PAUL, civil engr.; b. Waco, Tex., Feb. 17, 1935; s. Cecil Arnold and Sarah Edna (Arnold) D.; student Baylor U., 1953-54, 57-59; B.S. in C.E., U. Tex., 1961; m. Madelyn Elizabeth Coppin, Aug. 22, 1958; children—Roland, Patricia. Div. engr., City Waco, 1961-64; bridge design engr. Tex. Hwy. Dept., Waco, 1964-66; mgr. civil structural design group Dow Chem. Co., Houston, 1966-70; chief civil structural engr. J.F. Pritchard & Co., Houston, 1970-73; mgr. civil structural engring. Lummus Co., Houston, 1973—. Served with C.E., AUS, 1954-57. Registered profl. engr., Tex., Ark., La. Baptist (deacon). Home: 13307 Butterfly Lane Houston TX 77024 Office: 2000 West Loop Houston TX 77027

DREXLER, DAVID, savs. and loan exec.; b. Wynne, Ark., Jan. 8, 1903; s. Meyer Mike and Dora (Glass) D.; student Wynne Bus. Coll., 1921-22; m. Christine Elizabeth West, May 12, 1943. With Drexlers' Dry Goods Store, Wynne, 1920-30; owner David's cafe and soda fountain, Wynne, 1930-42; owner Wynne Ins. and Loan Co., 1943-70; dir. Wynne Fed. Savs. and Loan Assn., 1934, pres., 1964—; dir. Cross County Bank. Mem. Wynne Planning Commn., 1952—, chmn., 1956-69. Served with AUS, 1942-43. Mem. Jewish religion. Rotarian; mem. B'nai B'rith. Club: Razorback (Wynne). Home: 909 Hamilton Av Wynne AR 72396 Office: 363 E Union Av Wynne AR 72396

DREYFUS, DANIEL AUGUSTUS, engineer, govt. ofcl.; b. Bklyn., Mar. 5, 1931; s. James and Edna (Hogan) D.; student Northwestern U., 1950-52; B.C.E., George Washington U., 1957, M.E.A., 1965; postgrad. Am. U., 1966—; m. Josephine Catherine Sime, Sept. 21, 1957; children—Barbara, Patrick, Teresa, Karin, Lisa. Civil engr. Tex. Co., Lockport, Ill., 1957-59; civil engr. U.S. Corps Engrs., Anchorage, Alaska, 1959-61; planning engr. U.S. Bur. Reclamation, Washington, 1961-68; profl. staff mem. U.S. Senate, Washington, 1968—. Served with AUS, 1952-54. Mem. Am. Soc. C.E., Nat. Soc. Profl. Engrs., Soc. Am. Mil. Engrs., Theta Tau. Roman Catholic. Home: 1536 Forest Lane McLean VA 22101 Office: New Senate Office Bldg Washington DC 22101

DRIGGERS, J(AMES) CLYDE, coll. pres.; b. Ft. Green, Fla., Jan. 10, 1917; s. Uria Alonzo and Mary (Stephens) D.; B.S.A., U. Fla., 1938, Ph.D., 1949; m. Doris Esther McCullough, Aug. 25, 1940; children—David, Billie Kay (Mrs. John Pehler), Stephen, James McCullough. Instr. poultry husbandry U. Fla., 1939-40, asst. prof., 1946-49, asso. prof., 1949-55, prof., 1955-57; chmn. poultry div. U. Ga., 1957-64; pres. Abraham Baldwin Coll., Tifton 1964—. Pres. Ga. Assn. Jr. Colls. Bd. dirs. Internat. Inst. Edn. Served with AUS, 1941-46; col. Res. Mem. Poultry Sci. Assn. (past pres.), World's Poultry Sci., Assn. So. Agrl. Workers (past chmn. poultry sect.), Ga. Poultry Fedn., Sabres, Fla. Blue Key, Sigma Xi, Gamma Sigma Delta (past chpt. pres.), Alpha Tau Alpha, Alpha Gamma Rho (past grand pres.), Alpha Zeta (past high censor), Kappa Kappa Psi, Gamma Sigma Epsilon, Sigma Delta Psi. Democrat. Methodist. Rotarian (past pres., zone chmn. Rotaract) (Tifton, Ga.). Club: F (U. Fla.). Home: Abraham Baldwin Coll Tifton GA 31794

DRISKELL, CARL ROWLAND, elec. engr.; b. Forsyth, Ga., June 5, 1939; s. Cecil Searcy and Mary Susan (Bullard) D.; B.E.E., Ga. Inst. Tech., 1962, M.S., 1964; m. Nancy Lee Mastin, Aug. 20, 1966; 1 son, Robert Scott. Systems engr. Western Electric Co., Atlanta, 1962-63; asst. research engr. Ga. Tech. Engring. Expt. Sta., Atlanta, 1964-68, lectr. dept. elec. engring., 1967-68; electronics engr. Naval Tng. Equipment Center, Orlando, Fla., 1968—. Mem. I.E.E.E., Soc. Information Display, Sci. Research Soc. Am., Eta Kappa Nu, Tau Beta Pi. Home: 412 Cornwall Rd Winter Park FL 32789 Office: Naval Tng Equipment Center Code N212 Orlando FL 32813

DRISKELL, MELVILLE MORGAN, physician; b. Sparta, Ga., Jan. 16, 1909; s. William Walter and Lulu (Houser) D.; B.S., Emory U., 1932, M.D., 1935; m. Alice Center, Feb. 19, 1933; children—William Clark, Margaret Josephine. Intern, Macon (Ga.) Hosp., 1936-37, resident, 1937-38; commd. lt. (j.g.), M.C., U.S. Navy, 1938, advanced through grades to capt., 1957, ret., 1958; practice medicine specializing in internal medicine and cardiology, St. Petersburg, Fla., 1958—. Decorated Bronze Star. Diplomate Am. Bd. Internal Medicine. Fellow A.C.P., Am. Coll. Cardiology; mem. A.M.A., Fla. Med. Assn., Am., Fla., Suncoast heart assns., Phi Delta Theta, Phi Chi. Home: 747 Brightwaters Blvd St Petersburg FL 33704 Office: 404 12th Av N St Petersburg FL 33701

DRISKELL, ORVAL LEWIS, pub. co. exec.; b. Kalmath Falls, Ore., Mar. 19, 1927; s. Sylvester Clyde and Olive (Stanyer) D.; B.A., Walla Walla Coll., 1948; m. Arlene LaVerne Babbitt, Nov. 14, 1948; children—Karen (Mrs. C. Russell Edwards), Kathleen (Mrs. William L. Matthews), Barbara (Mrs. Ricardo F. Burks). With Pitney-Bowes, Seattle, 1948-50; with Pacific Press Pub. Assn., Mountain View, Cal., 1950-64; with So. Pub. Assn., Nashville, 1964—, mgr. book dept., dir., 1971—. Served with AUS, 1944-45. Mem. Seventh-day Adventist Ch. (ordained minister 1970). Home: 3223 Healy Ct Nashville TN 37207 Office: 1900 Elm Hill Pike Nashville TN 37210

DRISKOLL, BAYNE EVANS, religious orgn. exec.; b. Bedford, Tex., Apr. 18, 1905; s. George Douglas and Martha (Evans) D.; A.B., Phillips U., 1932, M.A., 1933, LL.D., 1955; B.D., Tex. Christian U., 1946; D.D., N.W. Christian Coll., 1953; m. Edna Agnes Horton, Dec. 23, 1927; children—John Ray, Robert Bayne. Ordained to ministry Christian Ch., 1932; dir. pub. relations Phillips U., Enid, Okla., 1935-38; pastor Central Christian Ch., Galveston, Tex., 1938-43; dir. pub. relations Tex. Christian U., Ft. Worth, 1943-45; pastor Magnolia Av. Christian Ch., Fort Worth, 1945-48; dir. pub. relations Yale Sch. Alcohol Studies, Ft. Worth, 1948-49; exec. dir. All-Ch. Evangelism, Inc., Edmond, Okla., 1950—; pastor First Christian Ch., Grand Prairie, Tex., 1964-69. Office: 404 E 14th St Edmond OK 73034

DROEGE, ROBERT WALTER, mfg. co. exec.; b. Detroit, Sept. 23, 1943; s. Henry and Gertrude (Brenicka) D.; B.S., Wayne State U., 1966. With General Electric Co., Lynchburg, Va., 1968-72, Florence, S.C., 1972—, specialist mfg. systems, 1969-72, mgr. product control, 1973—. Mem. Central Va. Sports Car Club (pres. 1971). Home: 1519 S Wood Dr Florence SC 29501 Office: 1 Radio Av Florence SC 29501

DROOZ, ARNOLD THOMAS, entomologist; b. Albany, N.Y., Nov. 17, 1921; s. Albert Samuel and Della (Davis) D.; B.S., N.Y. State Coll. Forestry, 1948, M.S., 1949; m. Dorothy Golden Thornton, July 25, 1955; children—David Thornton, Alain Thomas. With Bur. Entomology Plant Quarantine, U.S. Dept. Agr., Beltsville, Md., 1949-50, New Haven, 1950-52, Milw., 1952-54; with Forest Service Lake States Forest Expt. Sta., St. Paul, 1954-56, East Lansing, Mich., 1956-57; with Pa. Dept. Forest and Waters, Harrisburg, 1957-60; with Southeastern Forest Expt. Sta., Forest Service, U.S. Dept. Agr., Asheville and Research Triangle Park, N.C., 1960—, prin. entomologist, 1968—. Served with USAAF, 1943-46. Mem. Soc. Am. Foresters, Entomol. Soc. Am. (sec. sect. ecology, behavior and bionomics 1972-73, vice chmn. sect. 1973-74), Entomol. Soc. Can., Internat. Orgn. for Biol. Control. Home: 705 Jefferson Dr Cary NC 27511 Office: Forestry Scis Lab Box 12254 Research Triangle Park NC 27709

DRUCE, HERMAN L., milling co. exec.; b. Cordell, Okla., May 12, 1910; s. Arthur Jack and Ursula Ann (Perkins) D.; student Draughans Bus. Coll., West Falls, Tex., 1930; m. Myrtle Claire Hassman, Sept. 10, 1938; children—Linda Ann (Mrs. Gabriel Zablatnik), Teddy Katherine (Mrs. Herman Moore Jr.), Martha Jean (Mrs. Jerry Derby). Traffic clk. Gen. Mills, Inc., Wichita Falls, Tex., 1931, Oklahoma City, 1931, El Reno, Okla., 1932-35, traffic mgr., Oklahoma City, 1935-38, Wichita Falls, 1938-45, asst. div. traffic mgr., Oklahoma City, 1945-53; traffic mgr., grain buyer Morrison Milling Co., Denton, Tex., 1953-60, v.p. purchasing and traffic, 1960—. Mason, Lion. Home: 2619 Robinwood St Denton TX 76201 Office: Morrison Milling Co 319 E Prairie St Denton TX 76201

DRUCKER, MELVIN BRUCE, psychologist; b. Phila., May 27, 1927; s. Maxwell Lionel and Sylvia (Layton) D.; B.S., Western Res. U., 1950; M.A., Ohio U., 1951; Ph.D., George Peabody Coll. for Tchrs., 1956; m. Miriam Elizabeth Koontz, Aug. 22, 1957. Intern clin. psychology S.C. Mental Health Commn., 1955-56; psychologist Fulton County Child Guidance Clinic, Atlanta, 1956-58; chief psychologist community mental health service Ga. Dept. Pub. Health, Atlanta, 1958-65; clin. and research psychologist Georgian Clinic div. Ga. Mental Health Inst., Atlanta, 1965-70; chmn., asso. prof. dept. Mental Health Assts., Sch. Allied Health Scis., also asso. prof. psychology and urban life Ga. State U., 1970—. Diplomate in clin. psychology Am. Bd. Examiners in Psychology, Mem. Ga. Psychol. Assn. (sec. 1965-68, pres. 1970). Author: (with Fox, Dominick, Crow) Pilot Project for the Clinical Training of Clergymen in the Field of Alcoholism, 1967. Home: 424 Glenndale Av Decatur GA 30030 Office: Dept Mental Health Assts Ga State U Atlanta GA 30303

DRUCKER, STANLEY WOLFFE, lawyer; b. Newport News, Va., Feb. 22, 1931; s. A. Louis and Loraine B. (Blechman) D.; B.S. in Commerce, U. Va., 1951, LL.B., 1953; m. Margo Mound, June 13, 1954; children—Karen, Laurie, Ann. Admitted to Va. bar, 1952; mem. firm Diamonstein & Drucker, Newport News, 1959—. Served with AUS, 1954-57. Home: 8 Booth Circle Newport News VA 23606 Office: 103 28th St Newport News VA 23607

DRUDGE, J. HAROLD, educator; b. Bremen, Ind., Feb. 7, 1922; s. Alfred M. and Respa Elizabeth (Bowser) D.; D.V.M. (Gunson scholar), Mich. State U., 1943; D.Sc. (Am. Vet. Med. Assn. research fellow), Johns Hopkins, 1950; m. Ethelyn Laura Thomas, July 19, 1946; 1 dau., Karin Lynn. Parasitologist vet. parasitology research Miss. State U., Starkville, 1950-51; prof. vet. parasitology research U. Ky., Lexington, 1951-63, prof. dept. vet. sci., 1951—, chmn. dept. vet. scis., 1963-73. Served with Vet. Corps, AUS, 1943-46. Mem. Am., Ky. (Distinguished Service award 1970), vet. med. assns., Am. Assn. Vet. Parasitology, Am. Soc. Parasitology, World Assn. for Advancement Vet. Parasitology, Helminthol. Soc. Washington, Conf. Research Workers N.Am., Research Workers So. State, Sigma Xi, Alpha Psi, Gamma Sigma Delta. Club: Optimists (Lexington). Home: 3220 Breckenwood Dr Lexington KY 40502

DRUMMOND, ALFRED ALEXANDER, cattle rancher, oil producer; b. Pawhuska, Okla., Dec. 2, 1896; s. Fred and Addie (Gentner) D.; B.S., Okla. A. and M. Coll., 1915; postgrad. U. Ill., 1916; m. Madelaine Russell, June 2, 1920; children—Madelaine II (Mrs. Oliver F. Bush); m. 2d, Ferne Boles, Jan. 22, 1943; 1 adopted son, James Alexander. Cattle rancher, Madill, 1920—; First Nat. Bank, Hominy, 1924-30; organizer, mgr. Okla. Live Stock Marketing Assn.; organizer Nat. Livestock Credit Corp., Oklahoma City, 1932; dir. Fed. Land Bank Assn. of Durant, 1956—; adv. com. Okla. to Fed. Land Bank Wichita, 1961-64; nat. adv. com. Washington Fed. Land Bank System representing 9th dist. Okla., Kan., Colo., N.M., 1962-64. Served from 2d lt. to capt., U.S. Army, 1917-19; served from maj. to lt. col., AUS, 1942-46. Mem. Okla. Fedn. of Fed. Land Bank Assns. (pres. 1960, dir. 1958-64), Am. Nat. Cattlemen's Assn., Tex. State and Southwestern Cattle Raisers Assn., Okla. Cattlemen's Assn., Scabbard and Blade, Phi Gamma Delta. Presbyn. Rotarian. Address: 510 W Tishomingo St Madill OK 73446

DRUMMOND, CHARLES EDGERTON, JR., civil engr.; b. Cedar Rapids, Ia., Mar. 5, 1898; s. Charles E. and Lula (Pollans) D.; B.A., Cornell Coll., Ia., 1920; m. Beulah Mae Tull, Aug. 12, 1924; 1 dau., Nancy Lee (Mrs. Howard H. McCall III). Draftsman, Caldwell

Engring. Co., Jacksonville, Ill., 1920-24; engr. Clinchfield Portland Cement Co., Kingsport, Tenn., 1924-25, Mees & Mees, Charlotte, N.C., 1925-26; head bridge dept. Piedmont & No. Ry., Charlotte, 1926-29; engr. Robert & Co., Atlanta, 1929-30; self-employed as cons. engr., Atlanta, 1930-34; with Wiedeman & Singleton, Atlanta, 1934-72, partner, 1959-71, cons., 1972-73; now ret. Mem. Ga. Environmental Health Task Force, 1969—. Served with S.A.T.C., 1918. Recipient Bedell award Ga. Water and Pollution Control Assn., 1956, Wyckoff award, 1968. Registered profl. engr., Ala., Fla., Ga., N.C., S.C., Tenn., Va. Mem. Am. Inst. Cons. Engrs., Am. Soc. C.E. (Ga. pres. 1954), Nat. Soc. Profl. Engrs., Ga. Engring. Soc. (charter, pres. 1952), Am. Acad. Environmental Engrs. (charter), Water Pollution Control Fedn. (dir. Ga. 1953-56; chmn. Atlanta conv. 1972). Episcopalian. Kiwanian. Clubs: Atlanta Athletic, Commerce. Address: 4700 Dudley Lane NW Atlanta GA 30327

DRUMMOND, KENNETH HERBERT, diversified co. exec.; b. Riverside, Cal., Jan. 19, 1922; s. Finlay Mackay and Eve Mery (Holland) D.; student Bates Coll., 1941-43; B.S., U. Ariz., 1949; postgrad. Tex. A. and M. U., 1950-57; m. Marion Emily Deane, May 14, 1955; children—Laurie, Finley, Carter. Asso. in oceanography Tex. A. and M. U., College Station, 1950-57; asst. dir. Smithsonian Astrophys. Obs., Cambridge, Mass., 1957-60; asst. to chancellor U. Cal. at San Diego, 1960-62; Washington rep. Tex. Instruments, 1960-67; exec. sec. panel industry and investment Commn. on Marine Sci., Exec. Office Pres., Washington, 1967-68; dir. program devel. Teledyne, Inc., Washington, 1969-72; asst. to pres. Ensco, Inc., Springfield, Va., 1972—. Mem. adv. council La. State U., 1969—. Served with USNR, 1943-46; PTO. Fellow A.A.A.S., Tex. Acad. Sci., Explorers Club; mem. Nat. Space Club, Marine Tech. Soc., Nat. Ocean Industries Assn. (dir. 1966—). Mason (32 deg.). Club: Washington Hilton Racquet. Author: (with Eloise Engle) Sky Rangers, 1965. Editor: (with C.A. Whitten) Contemporary Geodesy, 1959. Home: 9104 Santayana Dr Fairfax VA 22030 Office: 5408 A Port Royal Rd Springfield VA 22151

DRUMWRIGHT, GEORGE WELLS, dentist; b. Washington, Sept. 2, 1924; s. Leo O. and Emma (Wells) D.; student Western Md. Coll., 1942-43; D.D.S., Georgetown U., 1947; m. Mary Ann Spicer, Nov. 12, 1948; children—Marie (Mrs. William Joseph Pepper Jr.), George Wells, Janet Lee. Individual practice dentistry, Washington, 1947—. Served with USAF, 1953-55. Mem. Am. Dental Assn., D.C. Dental Soc., Dental Progress Study Club, Columbia Dental Study Club, D.C. Acad. Gen. Dentistry (pres. 1974-75). Club: Civitan of Washington. Home: 3 Whitingham Terrace Silver Spring MD 20904 Office: 1722 Eye St NW Washington DC 20006

DRURY, THOMAS JOSEPH, bishop; b. County Sligo, Ireland, Jan 4, 1908; s. Michael and Margaret (Lannon) D.; student St. Benedict's Coll., Atchison, Kan., 1926-29; A.B., Kenrick Sem., 1931-35. Ordained priest Roman Catholic Ch., 1935; asst. and pastor Sacred Heart Cathedral, Amarillo, Tex., 1935-45; pastor St. Elizabeth's Ch., Christ the King Ch., Lubbock, Tex., 1956-61; bishop Diocese of San Angelo, 1961-65; consecrated, 1962; bishop Diocese of Corpus Christi, 1965—. Sec. Matrimonial Ct., 1935, promotor of justice, 1938—, defender of the bond, 1939—; diocesan dir. Confraternity of Christian Doctrine, 1936, Soc. Propagation of the Faith, 1936—, Cath. Action, Holy Name Soc.; mem. bd. Diocesan Adminstrn., 1938—. Chmn. Amarillo council Boy Scouts Am.; v.p. Amarillo Cath. Welfare Bur. Served to maj. Chaplains Corps, USAAF, 1945-47, USAF, 1949-55. Editor, bus. mgr. Texas Panhandle Register, 1936-38. Home: 4109 Ocean Dr Corpus Christi TX 78411 Office: 620 Lipan St Corpus Christi TX 78401

DRY, HAL SMITH, metal products co. exec.; b. Winters, Tex., Nov. 19, 1924; s. John Ray and Dora Elizabeth (Williamson) D.; grad. high sch.; m. Eleanor Jearldine Bryan, Jan. 14, 1946; children—Rickey A., Gary Lynn. Plant mgr. to exec. v.p. Dry Mfg. Co., Inc., Winters, 1947-69; exec. v.p. to v.p., gen. mgr. Dry Mfg. Co., Inc. div. Wallace Murray Corp., Winters, 1969—; dir., cons. John's Internat. Mem. City Council, Winters, 1969—. Served with USNR, 1942-45. Mason, Lion. Home: 201 S Frisco St Winters TX 79567 Office: 205 N Melwood St Winters TX 79567

DRY, WILLIAM ARTHUR, interior designer; b. Apollo, Pa., Nov. 16, 1928; s. Victor George and Daisy (Hugar) D.; grad. N.Y. Sch. Interior Design, 1955. Interior designer Ruth Miller Interiors, Winston Salem, N.C., 1957-61, Modern Day Furniture, Knoxville, Tenn., 1961-62, Bromberg & Co., Birmingham, Ala., 1962—. Served with AUS, 1951-53. Mem. Am. Inst. Interior Designers (pres. Ala., 1971-72; nat. dir. 1973-75). Home: 2930 Clairmont Av Birmingham AL 35205 Office: 123 N 20th St Birmingham AL 35203

DRYDEN, WILLIAM BERNARD, JR., dentist; b. Quincy, Ill., July 5, 1943; s. William Bernard and Dorothy Jean (Long) D.; student Murray State Coll., 1961-62; postgrad. U. Louisville, 1962-64, D.M.D., 1968; m. Sandra Lee Saxton, June 18, 1965; children—Debra Lee, Wendy Ann. Practice dentistry Louisville, 1970—. Instr. dept oral diagnosis U. Louisville Sch. Dentistry, 1971—. Active Ky. Dept. Child Welfare, Louisville, 1971—. Served with USAF, 1968-70. Mem. Am. Endontic Soc., Am., Ky. socs. for preventive dentistry, Louisville Dental Soc., Am., Ky. dental assns., Tau Kappa Epsilon (sec. 1963-64), Delta Sigma Delta. Republican. Methodist. Club: Midland Trail (Ky.) Golf. Home: 1902 Crossgate Lane Louisville KY 40222 Office: 1005 Dupont Sq Louisville KY 40207

DRYE, RICHARD LEVEN, lawyer; b. Bradfordsville, Ky., Sept. 16, 1912; s. Don Victor and Edna Baker (Thornton) D.; A.B., U. Ky., 1937; LL.B., U. Louisville, 1940; B.Fgn.Trade, Am. inst. Fgn. Trade, Phoenix, 1948; acad. postgrad., diploma in law, London Sch. Econs. and Polit. Sci., U. London, 1953-54; postgrad. Queens' Coll., Cambridge U., 1954. Admitted to Ky. bar, 1940; asst. atty. gen., Commonwealth of Ky., 1946-48; practice law, Louisville, 1948—; asst. Jefferson County atty., 1964-70; treas. Don. V. Drye, Inc., Lebanon, Ky., 1973. Bd. dirs. Neighborhood Devel. Corp. Republican candidate for rep. of Ky., 1957. Served as spl. agt., CIC, AUS, 1942-45; 2d lt. Ky. N.G., 1946-48. Mem. Am., Ky., Louisville bar assns., St. James Ct. Assn., V.F.W., Ky. Hist. Soc., Kappa Alpha. Mem. Christian Ch. Mason. Club: Lincoln of Kentucky (sec. 1958-59). Home: 1453 St James Ct Louisville KY 40208 Office: 546 Starks Bldg Louisville KY 40202

DRYER, DOROTHEA MERRILL (MRS. EDWIN JASON DRYER), lawyer; b. Salt Lake City; d. George Edmund and Lillian (Chapman) Merrill; A.B., Stanford, 1936; LL.B., Yale, 1940; m. Edwin Jason Dryer, Feb. 28, 1942; children—Diana Claire, Faith Ellen. Admitted to Utah bar, 1941; clk. for Chief Justice Wolfe of Utah Supreme Ct. 1941; atty. Bur. Immigration, Dept. Justice, Washington, 1941-42; practice in Salt Lake City, 1943-47, Washington, 1948—; dep. county atty., Salt Lake County, 1947-48; admitted to bar U.S. Supreme Ct., U.S. Ct. Mil. Appeals. Fellow Am. Assn. Criminology; mem. Am., Fed., Utah bar assns., Internat. Platform Assn., Oral History Assn., Jr. League Washington, Nat. Assn. Women Lawyers, Nat. Assn. for Gifted Children, Assn. for Gifted, Kappa Kappa Gamma. Unitarian. Clubs: Nat. Lawyers, Potomac Business and Professional Women's. Home: 5126 Palisade Lane NW Washington DC 20016 Farm: Running Brook Farm Browntown VA 22610

DUANE, FRANK, author; b. Chgo., Aug. 8, 1926; s. Frank and Florence (Kednay) Rosengren; B.A., U. Chgo., 1951; fellow Yale, 1955-56; m. Emily Camille Sweeney, Jan. 13, 1951; 1 dau., Emily Duane Ferry. Vice pres. Rosengrens Bookshop, San Antonio, program cons. sta. KENS-TV, San Antonio, 1963—; staff writer Omnibus, 1956-57; workshop coordinator Elinor Morgenthau New Dramatists Workshop, N.Y.C., 1954-55; producer On The Spot, KENS-TV, 1961—; editor El Abrazo, 1967—; chief spl. features HemisFair, 1968; exec. producer KLRN-TV, San Antonio-Austin, 1968—; exec. dir. Presentation Assos. Bd. dirs. Music Theatre, Inc.; chmn. adv. bd. Coll.-Community Creative Arts Center, Our Lady of Lake Coll.; dir. concept devel. Telesis, 1972—. Served with USAAF, 1944-46. Mem. Dramatists Guild, Writers Guild of Am., New Dramatists Com., Acad. TV Arts and Scis., Nat. Assn. Ednl. Broadcasters, San Antonio Theatre Council, U. Chgo. Alumni Assn. Writer various plays, motion picture, TV shows including: Jimmy and the River, 1958; Prophets of Light, 1966; Pilgrims to the West, 1971; After Cortez, 1973. Home: 801 Garraty Rd San Antonio TX 78209

DUBACH, HAROLD WILLIAM, oceanographer, sci. cons.; b. St. Joseph, Mo., Nov. 25, 1920; s. Henry William and Susan (Cornelius) D.; A.B., Baker U., 1942; postgrad. U. Chgo., 1942-43, Johns Hopkins, 1949-51; m. Roberta Pauline Rose, Sept. 26, 1946; children—Linda Joy, Deborah Ann, Nancy Lee, David Wesley. Research meteorologist Thunderstorm Project, U.S. Weather Bur., Chgo., 1946-48; research oceanographer U.S. Naval Hydrographic Office, Washington, 1948-60; oceanographer, dep. dir. Nat. Oceanographic Data Center, Washington, 1960-69; oceanographer, asst. dir. Center for Marine Devel., Coastal Plains Regional Commn., 1969-73; head marine industries dept. Beaufort (S.C.) Tech. Inst., 1973—. Panel examiner in meteorology U.S. Civil Service Commn., 1957-60, in oceanography, 1954-63; mem. Fed. Adv. Com. Water Pollution, 1966-69; chmn. U.S. delegation Working Group on Marine Data Systems, Internat. Council Exploration of Seas, 1968. Pres. Bellemead (Md.) Citizens Assn., 1955-56; lay del. Balt. Conf. Meth. Ch., 1956-71. Bd. dirs. Youth Services Inc., Landover Hills, Md., 1956-57. Served to capt. USAAF, 1942-46. Recipient CIA-U.S. Navy Commendation, 1959; Superior Accomplishment award U.S. Navy, 1962, commendation award for invention, 1967, Distinguished Alumni award Baker U., 1970. Mem. Am. Meteorol. Soc., Am. Shore and Beach Preservation Assn., Internat. Oceanographic Found., Marine Tech. Soc. (coastal zone mgmt. com. 1969—), Oceanographical Soc. Japan, Marine Tech. Soc., Australian Marine Scis. Assn. Methodist (trustee 1956-57; ofcl. bd. 1956—, mem. social concerns com. 1967; steward). Author tech. reports, book reviews and papers profl. jours. Mem. editorial bd. Geoscience Documentation (London, Eng.). Patentee in field. Home: 4609 Dean Dr Wilmington NC 28401 Office: Beaufort Tech Inst Ribaut Rd Beaufort SC 29902

DUBAR, JULES RAMON, geologist, educator; b. Canton, O., June 30, 1923; s. Joseph Adolphe and Inez Ismay (Simlar) D.; B.S., Kent State U., 1949; M.S., Ore. State U., 1950; Ph.D., U. Kan., 1957; m. Susan Stokes Davidson, July 31, 1964; children—Nicole Mae, Scott Johnson. Instr. geology So. Ill. U., Carbondale, 1951-57; asso. prof. U. Houston, 1957-62, Duke, Durham, N.C., 1962-64; with Esso Prodn. Research Co., Houston, 1964-67; prof. geology Morehead (Ky.) State U., 1967—, head dept. geosci., 1967—. Vis. prof. U. N.C., Chapel Hill, 1963. Served with USCGR, 1942-46. NSF grantee, 1959-70. Fellow A.A.A.S., Geol. Soc. Am.; mem. Am. Assn. Petroleum Geologists, Soc. Econ. Mineralogists and Paleontologists, Internat. Paleontol. Union. Contbr. articles to profl. jours. Home: 148 Flemingsburg Rd Morehead KY 40351

DUBERG, HELMUTH PRINCE JOHN, banker; b. Des Moines, Feb. 21, 1907; s. Helmuth Frederick Christian and Kathryn Prince (Needham) D.; A.B., Yale, 1930; postgrad. N.Y. U., 1931, U.S. Naval War Coll., 1953; m. Dorys Hall McConnell, June 24, 1964. With Otis & Co., N.Y.C., 1930; with City Trust Co., Bridgeport, Conn., 1931—, trust officer, 1935—. Mem. adv. com. YMCA, Palm Beach, Fla., 1967—; mem. exec. com., finance com., bd. govs. Nature Conservancy, Washington, 1968—. Bd. dirs., v.p. Pestalozzi Found. of Am., N.Y.C., N.Y., 1955—. Comdr., Conn. Naval Militia, 1952—. Served to capt. USNR. Episcopalian. Home: Gomez Rd Jupiter Island Hobe Sound FL 33455 Office: City Nat Bank Conn Bridgeport CT 06602

DUBERG, JOHN EDWARD, research scientist; b. N.Y.C., Nov. 30, 1917; s. Charles Augustus and Mary (Blake) D.; B.S., Manhattan Coll., 1938; M.S., Va. Polytech. Inst., 1940; Ph.D., U. Ill., 1948; m. Mary Louise Andrews, June 11, 1943; children—Mary Jane, John Andrews. Field engr. Caulowell Wingate Builders, N.Y.C., 1938-39; research fellow Va. Polytech. Inst., 1939-40; research asst. U. Ill., 1940-43; aero. research scientist Langley Labs., NACA, Langley Field, Va., 1943-46; research engr. Standard Oil Co. (Ind.), Chgo., 1946-48; chief structures research Langley Lab. NACA, 1951-56; mgr. aero. mechanics Aeronutronics, Glendale, Cal., 1956-57; prof. structures U. Ill., 1957-59; asst. to chief theoretical mechanics div. Langley Research Center, NASA, Langley AFB, Va., 1959-61, tech. asst. to asso. dir., 1951-64, asst. dir., 1954-68, asso. dir., 1968—; instr. U. Va. Extension, 1944-45; adj. prof. George Washington U.; dir. Joint Inst. Acoustics and Flight Scis., 1971. Dir. Newport News Savs. & Loan Assn. Mem. NACA adv. com. on materials, 1950, adv. com. on structures, 1951-56, NASA, 60-63; mem. materials adv. bd. Nat. Acad. Scis., 1950; mem. subcom. profl., sci. and tech. manpower Nat. Manpower Adv. Com., Dept. Labor, 1971; participant Fed. Exec. Inst., Charlottesville, Va., 1971. Trustee Peninsula United Fund, 1963—, campaign chmn., 1965-66; exec. bd. Peninsula council Boy Scouts Am., 1968—; sci. adv. bd. Va. Assn. Research Center; bd. dirs. Peninsula Jr. Nature Mus.; mem. Pres.'s Adv. Council Christopher Newport Coll., 1973. Fellow Am. Inst. Aeros. and Astronautics (asso.), Research Soc. Am. (pres. Hampton chpt. 1963), Soc. Indsl. and Applied Math., Engrs. Club Va. Peninsula (pres. 1955), Sigma Xi, Gamma Alpha, Phi Kappa Phi, Sigma Tau, Tau Beta Pi. Episcopalian (mem. vestry). Rotarian (pres. 1967-68), Huntington (founding mem., dir., pres. 1972-73; chmn. bd. 1973-74) (Newport News, Va.), Club: James River Country. Contbr. numerous articles to profl. jours. Home: 4 Museum Dr Newport News VA 23601 Office: Langley Station Hampton VA 23365

DUBOIS, EUGENE ELI, assn. exec.; b. Rochester, N.Y., Mar. 2, 1937; s. Eugene E.R. and Ursula R. (Johnson) DuB.; A.B., Hillsdale (Mich.) Coll., 1960; M.S., Boston U., 1962; Ed.D., Wayne State U., 1966. Asst. to v.p. Jr. Coll. Dist. St. Louis, 1963; adminstrv. asst. to pres. Monroe Community Coll., Rochester, 1963-67; mem. faculty Boston U., 1967-73, asso. prof. edn., 1970-73, coordinator spl. services, 1972-73; exec. sec. spl. interest groups Am. Assn. Community and Jr. Colls., Washington, 1973—; cons. in field. Trustee Garland Jr. Coll., Boston; bd. dirs. Montgomery Neighborhood Center, Rochester, 1965-66. Kellogg fellow, 1962-64; recipient Alumni Achievement award Hillsdale Coll., 1973. Mem. Adult Assn. U.S., Am. Assn. U. Profs., Am. Assn. Higher Edn., Tau Mu Epsilon, Phi Delta Kappa. Baptist. Clubs: Boston University; George Washington University. Contbr. articles to profl. jours. Home: 925 25th St NW Washington DC 20037 Office: 1 DuPont Circle NW Washington DC 20036

DUBOSE, DOROTHY GAMBLE (MRS. WILLIAM SHELTON DUBOSE), civic worker; b. St. Louis, Dec. 23, 1925; d. Andrew Suter and Dorothy (Collier) Gamble; student Swarthmore Coll., 1942, 43, Tex. Christian U., 1964, 67; m. William Shelton DuBose, Jan. 14, 1944; children—Dorothy, Frances, Julie, William Shelton, Suter Gamble. Vice pres. W. S. DuBose, Inc., Ft. Worth, 1956—. Bd. mem. Family Service Assn. Tarrant County (Tex.), 1964-66; v.p. Fort Worth (Tex.) Art Center Guild, 1963; mem. Charitable Solicitations Commn., Fort Worth, 1965—; asso. mem. Mayor's Com. on Status of Women, 1971. Bd. dirs. North Tex. chpt. Arthritis Found., Tarrant County YWCA. Mem. Soc. for Study Democratic Instns., Am. Civil Liberties Union (bd. mem., pres. Greater Ft. Worth chpt. 1971), Nat. Orgn. Women (pres. Ft. Worth chpt. 1970-72, legislative coordinator Tex.). Democrat. Episcopalian. Home: 2928 Owenwood St Fort Worth TX 76109 Office: Suite 234 2630 West Freeway Fort Worth TX 76109

DUBOSE, JAMES DAULTON, dentist; b. Turbeville, S.C., July 14, 1938; s. Robert Alvin and Olive (Dennis) DuB.; B.S., U. S.C., 1961; D.M.D., U. Louisville, 1965. Practice dentistry, Bishopville, S.C., 1965-70, Aiken, S.C., 1970-72, Manning, S.C., 1972—. Chmn. Heart Fund, Lee County, S.C., 1966. Mem. Am. Dental Assn., Am. Soc. Dentistry for Children, Augusta Dental Soc., Pee-Dee Dist. Dental Soc., Delta Sigma Delta. Baptist. Mason. Clubs: Century (Columbia, S.C.); Sertoma (Aiken, S.C.). Home: Church St Summerton SC 29148 Office: Mill and Hospital Sts Manning SC 29102

DUBOSE, ROBERT N(EWSOM), clergyman; b. Hartsville, S.C., Sept. 4, 1914; s. John Boyd and Belle (Newsome) DuB.; A.B., Wofford Coll., 1936; B.D., M.Div., Duke, 1942; D.D., Salem Coll., 1946; m. Marie King, Sept. 10, 1937; children—Mary Virginia (Mrs. Jean Derrick), Barbara Anne (Mrs. J.M. Terry). Ordained to ministry Meth. Ch., 1939; pastor, Jamestown, 1937-39, Lake View, 1939-40; asso. pastor Asbury Ch., Durham, N.C., 1940-41; dir. religious activities Duke U., 1945-48; exec. sec. Commn. Christian Higher Edn., Assn. Am. Colls., 1948-51; pastor First Meth. Ch., Whitmire, S.C. 1951-54, Shandon Meth. Ch., Columbia, S.C., 1954-60; dist. supt. Spartanburg Dist., S.C. Conf., 1960-65; pastor Buncombe St. Meth. Ch., Greenville, S.C., 1965-71, 1st United Meth. Ch., Myrtle Beach, S.C., 1971—. Mem. bd. edn. S.C. Conf., Meth. Ch., 1968-72. Pres. Myrtle Beach Camp Ground Ministry Commn. Past pres., dir. Columbia chpt. A.R.C., S.C. fund chmn., 1963-65; pres. S.C. Crippled Children's Soc.; chmn. Caroling Program, 1969-70; mem. S.C. Tricentennial Com., 1969-70, Mayor's Adv. Com., 1969-70; adv. bd. Mental Health Clinic; dir. Jr. League Speech and Hearing Clinic. Vice chmn. bd. trustees Wofford Coll; chmn. bd. trustees Spartanburg Jr. Coll., 1967-68, exec. com., 1969-72. Vice Chmn. bd. dirs. U.S.C. Wesley Found.; trustee Meth. Home Aging; chmn. S.C. Meth. Credit Union. Served as chaplain AUS, 1943-45; PTO. Mem. S.C. Conf. Meth. Ch. (chmn. conf. com. Christian vocation, chmn. credit com., chmn. interboard com.), Lambda Chi Alpha. Rotarian, Kiwanian (conf. bd. edn.). Author articles on Christian edn, Editor: College and Church (ofcl. publ. Assn. Am. Colls.), 1948-51. Home: 5408 Hampton Circle Myrtle Beach SC 29577 Office: 1st United Methodist Church Myrtle Beach SC 29577

DUCHARME, JEAN MARC, engring. exec.; b. Boston, Nov. 16, 1910; s. Armand A. and Adelaide J. (Desnoyers) D.; C.E., Rensselaer Poly. Inst., 1931; m. Irene Tarala, 1938; children—Jeanne L. (Mrs. Joshua Taylor), Jean Marc II, Denise (Mrs. Thomas Constantino); m. 2d, Thelma L. Phipps, Mary 26, 1967. Land and mine surveyor, miner, structural designer, 1931-39; pres., chief engr. Crandall Dry Dock Engrs., Cambridge, Mass., 1939-53; cons. engr., Boston, N.Y.C. and Amsterdam, Netherlands, 1953-57; chief engr. Wilputte Coke Oven div. Allied Chem. Corp., 1957-66; project mgr. Olin Mathieson Chem. Corp., N.Y.C. and Ky., 1966-68; v.p. engring. Finfrock Industries, Inc., Orlando, Fla., 1968—. Mem. Am. Soc. C.E. (life), Tau Beta Pi. Patentee roller system improvements for endhaul ry. dry docks, method of cooling byproduct coke oven batteries. Home: 2807 Cady Way Winter Park FL 32789 Office: PO Box 7006 Orlando FL 32804

DUCK, BOBBY NEAL, educator; b. Reagan, Tenn., Sept. 6, 1939; s. George Franklyn and Frankie (Austin) D.; B.S., U. Tenn., Martin, 1961; M.S. (Nat. Def. Edn. Act. fellow 1961-64), Auburn U., 1963, Ph.D., 1964; m. Barbara Ann White, Sept. 2, 1962; 1 dau., Leigh Anne. Grad. asst. Auburn U., 1961-64; research asst. Coker's Seed Co., Hartsville, S.C., 1962; asst. prof. U. Fla., Gainesville, 1964-66; asst. prof. U. Tenn., Martin, 1966-70, asso. prof., 1970-73, prof., 1973—, asst. dean, 1970—. Mem. Am. Soc. Agronomy, Crop Sci. Soc. Am., Am. Farm Bur. Fedn., Assn. So. Agrl. Scientists, Soil Conservation Soc. Am. (sec.-treas. So. sect.), Alpha Gamma Rho, Phi Kappa Phi. Kiwanian (sec. 1968-70). Contbr. articles to sci. jours. Home: Route 1 Martin TN 38237

DUCKER, JOHN LACKNER, state senator; b. Ft. Thomas, Ky., Sept. 3, 1922; s. Stuart Reilly and Margaret (Lackner) D.; student U. Ia., 1943, U. Neb., 1944; B.A., Yale, 1944, LL.B., 1950. Admitted to Fla. bar; mem. Fla. Senate, 1968—. Mem. Fla. Ho. of Reps., 1960-68; mem. Orange County (Fla.) Republican exec. com. Served with USAAF, 1943-46. Mem. Fla., Orange County bar assns., Am. Legion, Nat. Rifle Assn., Fla. Edn. Assn., Orange County Sportsmen's Assn. Episcopalian. Elk, Optimist. Club: University (Winter Park, Fla.). Home: 2810 W Fairbanks Av Winter Park FL 32789 Office: 205 E Jackson St Orlando FL 32801*

DUCKETT, CHARLES HOWARD, physician; b. Asheville, N.C., Nov. 11, 1932; s. Virgil Howard and Maude (Johnson) D.; B.S., Wake Forest Coll., 1954; M.D., Bowman Gray Sch. Medicine, 1957; m. Evelyn Carolyn Garrison, Apr. 1, 1956; children—Deborah Lynn, Ralph Howard, Charles Garrison, Sarah Carolyn. Intern U. Va. Hosp., Charlottesville, 1957-58; practice medicine specializing in family practice, Canton, N.C., 1958—; asso. Midway Clinic, 1959—; mem. staff Haywood County Hosp., chief staff, 1967—. Pres. Midway Inc., Canton, 1968—; dir. Canton Savs. and Loan Assn. Alderman, City of Canton, 1967-73; mem. exec. com. Haywood County Council of Govt., 1971-73. Served to capt. USAF, 1961-63. Diplomate Am. Bd. Family Practice. Fellow Am. Acad. Family Practice; mem. A.M.A., N.C. Acad. Family Practice (dir. 1973-75), N.C., Haywood County (pres. 1965—) med. socs., Omicron Delta Kappa. Democrat. Home: 11 Forest Hill Dr Canton NC 28716 Office: Midway Clinic Canton NC 28716

DUCKWORTH, WILLIAM CLIFFORD, endocrinologist; b. Athens, Tenn., Oct. 21, 1941; s. James Clifford and Vesta (Walker) Duckworth; B.S. with highest honors, U. Tenn., 1963, M.D., 1966; m. Nancy Caroline Hannah, Aug. 19, 1962. Intern, City of Memphis Hosp., 1966-67, resident internal medicine, 1967-69; fellow endocrinology U. Tenn., Memphis, 1969-71; research and edn. asso. VA, Memphis, 1971-73; clin. investigator, 1973—; asst. prof. medicine U. Tenn., Memphis, 1972—. USPHS fellow, 1969-71. Diplomate Am. Bd. Internal Medicine, Bd. Endocrinology and Metabolism. Mem. Am. Diabetes Assn., Endocrine Soc., Am. Fedn. Clin. Research, Sigma Xi, Alpha Omega Alpha, Phi Kappa Phi. Home:

3924 Mickey St Memphis TN 38116 Office: 1030 Jefferson St Memphis TN 38104

DUCKWORTH, WILLIAM THOMAS, JR., real estate appraiser; b. Asheville, N.C., Mar. 7, 1920; s. William Thomas and Margaret (Ball) D.; A.A., Mars Hill Coll., 1940; B.S., Wake Forest Coll., 1942; postgrad. Duke Div. Sch., summer 1953; m. Mary Watson Corpening, June 16, 1942; 1 dau., Lynne Revell. Partner, W. T. Duckworth Co., Asheville, 1946-60, owner, 1960—; dir. Asheville Fed. Savs. & Loan Assn. Mem. bd. adjustment Asheville Zoning and Planning Commn., 1950—; mem. Asheville Housing Authority, 1952-55; mem. chmn. bd. Buncombe County Welfare Bd., 1952-58. Sec., Young Democrats Club, 1951-52. Trustee Revell Meml. Mission, 1960—. Mars Hill Coll., 1955-58, Realtors Inst., 1958-61; past dir. YMCA; mem. Greater Asheville Council. Served with AUS, 1942-46. Mem. Am. Inst. Real Estate Appraisers, Soc. Real Estate Appraisers (sr.), Central Asheville Assn. (pres. 1965), Asheville Jr. C. of C. (life, pres. 1954), C. of C. (past dir.), Asheville Mchts. Assn. (dir. 1969-71), Kappa Sigma. Baptist. Rotarian. Clubs: Rhododendron Royal Brigade Guards (chief of staff 1972), Asheville Country (gov.), Asheville City. Home: 32 Maywood Rd Asheville NC 28804 Office: Northwestern Bank Bldg Asheville NC 28801

DUCY, CLEMENT AMBROSE, economist, govt. ofcl.; b. Pueblo, Colo., Dec. 7, 1911; s. Cornelius Leo and Emma Ann (Boylan) D.; A.B. (J.K. Mullen scholar), Cath. U. Am., 1933; m. Ellen Catherine O'Brien, Aug. 5, 1939; children—Ellen Catherine (Mrs. Hernan Perez-Montas), Mary Elizabeth, Patricia Cornelia. Staff asst. Sen Alva B. Adams of Colo., Washington, 1933-35; adminstrv. officer Fed. Pub Works Adminstrn., Colorado Springs and Denver, 1935-40; mgmt. and econ. cons. Clement A. Ducy, Pueblo, 1940-42, Washington and N.Y.C., 1945-68; auditor Cheyenne (Wyo.) Modification Center, USAAF, 1942-44; economist Office of Small Bus., Nat. Prodn. Authority, Washington, 1950-51; dir. materials div. Small Def. Plants Adminstrn., Washington, 1951-53; staff economist Bd. Govs. Fed. Res. System, 1968—. Mem. Nat. Prodn. Policy Com., Requirements and Allocations Bd., Rev. and Appeals Bd., Strategic Stockpile Com., 1951-53. Co-founder Nat. Young Democratic Clubs Am., Washington, 1930; mem. Nat. Young Dem. Com. for Colo., 1931-33; asst. exec. dir. Nat. Bus and Profl. Com for Stevenson, 1956. Chmn. bd., founder Cath. Youth Orgn. Trust Found., 1964. Recipient Civilian Meritorious Service award War Dept., 1944. Mem. Am. Econ. Assn., A.A.A.S., Am. Petroleum Inst., Am. Assn. Applied Solar Energy, Washington Bd. Trade, Pi Gamma Mu. Democrat. Roman Catholic (bd. dirs. Cath. Youth Orgn., Archdiocese Washington, 1954—, pres. 1962-63; mem. Cardinal's Com. Laity 1967—). Home: 4313 Chesapeake St NW Washington DC 20016 Office: Board of Governors Federal Reserve System Washington DC 20551

DUDA, EDWIN, educator; b. Donora, Pa., Oct. 15, 1928; s. John and Julia (Widuch) D.; B.A., Washington and Jefferson Coll., 1951; M.S., W.Va. U., 1953; Ph.D., U. Va., 1961; m. Emma Lou Cheney, Sept. 6, 1955; children—Mark, Kent, Wendy, Amy, Heather. Instr. math. U. W.Va., Morgantown, 1955-57, U. Va., Charlottesville, 1961; faculty U. Miami, Coral Gables, Fla., 1961—, prof. dept. math., 1972—. Served with AUS, 1953-55. Research grantee NSF, 1965-71. Mem. Am. Math. Soc., Math. Assn. Am. Contbr. articles to profl. jours. Home: 5771 94th St Kendall FL 33156 Office: U Miami Coral Gables FL 33124

DUDLEY, JAMES TIM, JR., elec. engr.; b. Ft. Benning, Ga., July 3, 1942; s. James Tim and Daphne (Bouseman) D.; B.S., Va. Poly. Inst., 1965; m. Dianne Constance Smoot, Apr. 16, 1966; children—Shannon Leigh, Christine Susanne, Michael Tim. Asst. gen. mgr., systems engr. Dixie Electric Power Assn., Laurel, Miss., 1968—. Served with C.E., AUS, 1966-68. Mem. I.E.E.E., Electric Power Assns. Miss. (sect. pres.), Laurel C. of C. Kiwanian (sec. membership com., chmn. pub. and bus. affairs com., agr. com). Home: 1223 2d Av Laurel MS 39440 Office: PO Box 88 Laurel MS 39440

DUDLEY, KENNETH HARRISON, educator; b. Hagerstown, Md., Nov. 12, 1937; s. Kenneth Earle and Fredericka (Angle) D.; B.S., Elon Coll., 1959; Ph.D., U. N.C., 1963; postgrad. (NSF fellow), U. Basel, Switzerland, 1963-64; m. Betty Jean Kirchdorfer, July 16, 1966; children—Christopher, Angela. With Research Triangle Inst., N.C., 1964-67; faculty U. N.C., Chapel Hill, 1967—, asso. prof. pharmacology, 1973—. Mem. Am. Chem. Soc., Am. Soc. Pharmacology and Exptl. Theraputics. Home: 5311 Pelham Rd Durham NC 27707 Office: Sch Medicine U NC Chapel Hill NC 27514

DUDLEY, VIRGINIA (EVELYN), artist; b. Spring City, Tenn.; d. Charles Newton and Laura (Thompson) Dudley; student U. Chattanooga, 1937-40, Art Students League, N.Y.C., 1940-45, New Sch. Social Research, 1942-43, 45, Atelier 17, N.Y.C., 1945-46, N.M. Coll., 1947-48, Coll. William and Mary, 1958-59, U. Md., Seoul, Korea, 1959-60; M.F.A. Claremont (Cal.) Grad. Sch., 1950; m. Joseph Spenser Moran, Apr. 20, 1946. Works exhibited Met. Mus. Art, San Francisco Mus. Art, Library of Congress, also London, Eng., San Francisco, Buffalo, Los Angeles, Phila., Vancouver, Washington, other; one man shows U. Chattanooga, 1943, Hunter Gallery Art, Chattanooga, 1952; Ga. Mus., Athens, 1954, Newport News, Va., 1959, Rome, Ga., 1964, 69, 71, Columbus (Ga.) Mus. Art, 1970, Reinhart Coll., Walleska, Ga., 1971, Next Door Gallery, Chattanooga, 1972, Macon (Ga.) Mus. Arts and Scis., 1973; represented in permanet collections including Met. Mus. Art, N.Y.C., Library of Congress, Scripps Coll., Ga. Mus. Art, U. Miami, Art Students League, Everson Mus. Art, Pa. State Mus., Albright Mus. Art, U. Tenn., Columbus (Ga.) Mus., Macon Mus. Arts and Scis. Asso. prof. art Shorter Coll., Rome, 1963-71; pres. Next Door Gallery, 1972; dir. Am. Craftsmen, Rising Fawn, Ga., Virginia Dudley Studios lectr. at large on Southeast Asia and the Orient. Regional bd. dirs. Am. Crafts Council, also Ga. rep.; regional rep. Ga. Designer Craftsmen, 1974-75. Recipient Rosenwald fellowship painting and lithography, 1943, 1st award So. Highland Handicraft Guild, 1953, Sarasota Found. Craft and Sculpture Show, 1953, Internat. Crafts Show, Canadian Pacific Expn., Vancouver, 1945, Nat. Ceramic Exhbns., Everson Mus. Fine Arts, 1956, others. Art dir. Coronado Playmakers, N.M. State Coll., 1947-48 art editor Rio Grande Writer, lit., mag., 1947-48; staff arts and crafts dir. 8th U.S. Army, Korea, 1959-61; staff arts and crafts dir. Hdqrs. Eighth Air Force, Westover, Mass., 1961-63. Fellow Internat. Art Guild, World Crafts Council (life), mem. Am. Crafts Council, Ga. Designer Craftsmen, So. Highland Handicraft Guild, Soc. Am. Graphic Arts, Chattanooga Art Assn., Royal Asiatic Soc., So. Assn. Sculptors, Internat. Inst. Arts and Letters. Home and studio: Lookout Mountain Route 2 Rising Fawn GA 30738

DUDNEY, DORIS ANN, lawyer; b. Sebring, Fla., June 9, 1934; d. Fred Stanton and Opal (Laine) Dudney; B.A., Vanderbilt U., 1954, LL.B., 1956. Admitted to Fla. bar, 1956, since practiced in Tampa; asso. firm Fowler, White, Gillen, Humkey & Trenam, 1956-61; mem. firm Fowler, White, Gillen, Humkey, Kinney & Boggs, P.A., and predecessor firms, 1961-74; individual practice, 1974—. Vice chmn., sec. Law Inc. Hillsborough County (Fla.), 1967-70, pres., chmn. bd., 1970—, also dir. Bd. dirs., vice chmn. YWCA Tampa, 1964-69, 71—; bd. dirs. Big Sisters, Tampa, 1966-69; bd. dirs. Girls Clubs Tampa 1966—, pres., 1971-74; nat. bd. dirs. Girls Clubs Am., 1972—; bd. dirs. Hillsborough Assn. Retarded Children, 1st v.p., 1973-74; bd. dirs. Mental Health Assn. Hillsborough County, pres., 1973-74; vice-chmn. local SSS bd., Tampa; trustee, mem. exec. com. Tampa-Hillsborough County Drug Abuse Comprehensive Coordinating office. Named Outstanding Young Woman Am., Vanderbilt U. and Tampa chpt. Am. Assn. U. Women, 1966. Mem. Am., Tampa, Hillsborough County bar assns., Fla. Bar (chmn. standing com. on econs. of law practice 1970-72; chmn. com. prepaid legal ins. 1972-73, chmn. steering com. delivery legal service, 1973-74), Am. Assn. U. Women, Am. Judicature Soc., Nat. Legal Aid and Defenders Assn., Greater Tampa C. of C., Am. Dog Owners Assn. (dir.), Order of Coif, Kappa Delta. Republican. Contbg. author: How to Live-and Die-with Florida Probate, Handbook for Newsmen. Clubs: Zonta (local pres., dist. gov. 1974—), Palma Ceia Golf and Country, Tower (Tampa); Boston Terrier (Miami); Tampa Bay Kennel; Tampa Woman's (courtesy mem.). Home: 2407 Ardson Pl Tampa FL 33609 Office: Suite 2001 First Financial Tower Tampa FL 33602

DUERKSEN, DEAN FARISS, dentist; b. Chickasha, Okla., Feb. 14, 1931; s. Cornelius Arthur and Flossie (Fariss) D.; B.A., Oklahoma City U., 1952; postgrad. So. Methodist U., 1953-57, 59-60; D.D.S., Baylor U., 1964; m. Alice Leigh Tilton, Dec. 28, 1970; children by previous marriage—Michael D., Paul D., Joseph D. Ordained to ministry Methodist Ch., 1953; minister Meth. Ch., Wheatland, Okla., 1952; television dir. WFAA-TV, Dallas, 1953-60; pvt. practice dentistry, Ft. Stockton, Tex., 1964—. Mem. Midland-Odessa Symphony and Chorale, 1965-73. City councilman, Crane, Tex., 1964-67. Bd. dirs. Crane Meml. Hosp. Named Outstanding Young Man of Am. Nat. Jr. C. of C., 1967. Mem. Am., Tex. dental assns., Am., Tex. acads. gen. dentistry, Crane C. of C. (dir.), Blue Key. Lion, Rotarian. Home: Sands Apts Fort Stockton TX 79735 Office: 905 W Dickinson Blvd Fort Stockton TX 79735

DUERKSEN, LELAND EMERSON, hotel co. exec.; b. Reedley, Cal., Jan. 10, 1927; s. Daniel Emerson and Lelah (Shelton) D.; student Mont. State U., 1944-48, Jefferson City Jr. Coll., 1947-48; m. Lois Lucile Calavan, Feb. 2, 1952; children—Debrah Lee, Daniel Charles. With Holiday Inns, Inc., Memphis, 1963—, dir. indsl. relations, 1967—, v.p., 1969—. Served with USAF, 1950-56. Elk. Home: 5295 Dargen Av Memphis TN 38118 Office: 3742 Lamar Av Memphis TN 38118

DUFF, WILLARD EARL, social worker; b. Miami, Okla., Jan. 22, 1939; s. Earl and Edith (Woodard) D.; B.A., Northeastern State Coll., Tahlequah, Okla., 1962; M.S.W., U. Okla., 1965; m. Lola Jean Tosh, June 23, 1962; 1 dau., Pamela Jean. Chief social worker Childrens Center, Central State Hosp., Norman, Okla., 1966—; pvt. practice social work, 1969—. Adj. asst. prof. U. Okla., 1970—, traveling prof. advanced studies sect., 1971—; spl. instr. Okla. State U., 1972—; group and family therapist Coyne Campbell Hosp., Oklahoma City. Elk, Mason (32 deg.); mem. Order Eastern Star. Club: Norman Civitan (pres.). Home: 400 Rosewood St Norman OK 73069 Office: Box 151 Norman OK 73069

DUFF, WILLIAM GRIERSON, elec. engr.; b. Alexandria, Va., Dec. 16, 1936; s. Johnnie Douglas and Annetta Osceola (Rind) D.; B.E.E., George Washington U., 1959, postgrad., 1959-72; M.S., Syracuse U., 1969; m. Joan Lilla King, June 27, 1964; children—Warren David, Valerie Lynn, Dawn Elizabeth. Program mgr. Atlantic Research Corp., Alexandria, 1959—; asst. prof. Capitol Inst. Tech., Kensington, Md., 1972—; instr. Inst. for Electromagnetic Compatibility, Don White Cons., Inc., Germantown, Md. Counselor, Meth. Sr. High Youth Group, 1965-73. Recipient D.A.R. Good Citizenship award, 1955; Math. award George Washington High Sch., Alexandria, 1955. Mem. I.E.E.E. (asso. editor EMC Group Newsletter 1970—), Am. Inst. E.E. (Best Paper award 1961), George Washington U. Engring. Alumni Assn. (pres. 1963-64), Sigma Tau, Theta Tau. Clubs: Springfield Golf and Country; Occoquan (Va.) Water Ski. Author: EMI Handbook, vol. 5, EMI Prediction and Analysis Techniques, 1972. Contbr. articles to profl. jours. Home: 8601 Greeley Blvd Springfield VA 22152 Office: 5390 Cherokee Av Alexandria VA 22314

DUFFEY, DONALD CREAGH, educator; b. Winchester, Va., Feb. 9, 1931; s. Hugh Sisson and Vera (Lynch) D.; B.S., Va. Poly. Inst., 1953; M.A., Rice U., 1955; Ph.D., Ga. Inst. Tech., 1959; m. Elizabeth Mallard, Aug. 25, 1965. Asst. prof. dept. chemistry Miss. State U., State College, 1960-62, asso. prof., 1962-67, prof., 1967—; fellow Pa. State U., 1959-60, U. Pa., 1964-65; vis. prof. U. Cin., 1967-68, Max-Planck-Institut, Gottingen, 1968. Fellow Am. Inst. Chemists; mem. Am. Chem. Soc., Sigma Xi, Phi Kappa Phi. Contbr. articles to profl. jours. Home: PO Box 35 State College MS 39762

DUFFIELD, PAULINE, librarian; b. Sutton, W.Va., June. 30, 1910; d. John Byrn and Mary (Marlow) Duffield; B.S., George Peabody Coll., Nashville, 1936, B.S. in L.S., 1940; student Chgo. Normal Sch. Phys. Edn., Chgo., 1929. Tchr., librarian Richwood (W. Va.) High Sch., 1930-41; librarian Parker Dist. High Sch., Greenville, S.C., 1941-43; asst. librarian Vanderbilt U. Sch. Med., Nashville, 1944-45; librarian Med. and Chirurg. Faculty of Md., Balt., 1945-52, Tex. Med. Assn., 1952—. Mem. Med. Library Assn. (treas. 1954-58, chmn. recruitment com. 1961-63, chmn. nominating com. 1968-69), Tex. Med. Assn. Assts. (hon.), Spl. Library Assn., Tex. Council Health Sci. Libraries (sec.-treas. 1968-72), Austin Library Club (v.p. 1961-62). Club: Zonta. Home: 1219 Castle Hill Austin TX 78703 Office: 1801 N Lamar Blvd Austin TX 78701

DUFFY, BERNARD READ, chem. engr.; b. Oklahoma City, Dec. 7, 1926; s. William and Bessie (Bayless) D.; B.S., Oklahoma City U., 1949; m. Mary Louise Bezner, May 31, 1963; children—William J., Julia Dyan. Chemist, pres., div. engr. North Tex. div. Oil Well Mud Co., Inc., Gainesville, Tex., 1952—. Served to ensign, USNR, 1944-47. Mem. Am. Petroleum Inst., Am. Chem. Soc., Am. Legion, Petroleum Club, Beta Beta Beta, Phi Chi Phi. Democrat. Roman Catholic. Home: 1925 Tulane St Gainesville TX 76240 Office: 1618 N Dixon St Gainesville TX 76240

DUFFY, JOHN JOSEPH, ednl. adminstr., educator; b. Charleston, S.C., Apr. 25, 1931; s. John Joseph and Mary (McMahon) D.; student Fordham U., 1948-49; B.S., Coll. Charleston, 1952; M.A., U. S.C., 1955, Ph.D., 1963; m. Marcia Fletcher Tinkham, Aug. 15, 1959; children—Katharine, John Joseph, Eleanor. Dir. U. S.C. at Beaufort, 1959-66, acad. coordinator Coll. Gen. Studies at Columbia, 1966-67, asst. provost for regional campuses, 1967-68, asso. provost for regional campuses, 1968—, asso. prof. history 1964—. Dist. chmn. Midlands council Boy Scouts Am., 1969—. Served with AUS, 1954-56. Named Young Man of Year Beaufort County Jaycees, 1964; recipient Garnet and Black award for distinguished service U. S.C., 1969. Mem. So., S.C. hist. assns., Phi Beta Kappa. Democrat. Roman Catholic. Elk. Home: 315 Harden St Columbia SC 29204

DUFLOT, LEO SCOTT MELLOO, med. educator; b. Mayfield, Ky., June 24, 1919; s. Joseph Leo and Elizabeth Shanklin (Melloo) D.; B.A., U. Tex., 1939; M.D., U. Tex., 1943; m. Rosemary Collins, Mar. 24, 1951; children—Rene, Jeanne, Carol, Merrie, Joseph. Intern, Parkland Hosp., Dallas, 1943-44; gen. practice medicine, Canyon, Tex., 1946-48; resident anesthesiology U. Tex. Med. Br., Galveston, 1949-52, faculty, 1952—, prof. anesthesiology, 1972—. Served with M.C., USNR, 1944-46. Diplomate Am. Bd. Anethesiology. Fellow Am. Coll. Anesthesiologists; mem. Internat. Anethesia Research Soc., Am. Soc. Anesthesiologists, A.M.A., A.A.A.S. Home: 176 San Marino St Galveston TX 71550

DUGAN, CHARLES CLARK, physician; b. Penn Yan, N.Y., Jan. 24, 1921; s. Charles Emmanuel and Wilhelmina May (Clark) D.; A.A., Wentworth Mil. Jr. Coll., 1940; A.B., Cornell U., 1942; M.D., Jefferson Med. Coll., 1946; m. Ruth Louise Fugh, Dec. 2, 1966; children—Charles Clark II, Douglas Craig, Timothy Gene, C. Dain Walters, C. Jay Walters. Jr. resident in psychiatry Pa. Psychiat. Hosp., Phila., 1946; rotating intern Harrisburg (Pa.). Gen Hosp., 1946-47; resident in dermotology and syphilogy U. Colo. Med. Center, Denver, 1956-57; resident in dermotology and syphilogy Henry Ford Hosp., Detroit, 1957-59, tng. in allergy, 1957-59; tng. in allergy Ohio State U., Columbus, 1961, Montefiore VA Hosp., Pitts., 1962; practice medicine specializing in dermotology and allergy, West Palm Beach, Fla., 1959—; staff Good Samaritan Hosp., West Palm Beach, Bethesda Meml. Hosp., Boynton Beach, Fla., Palm Beach Gardens Community Hosp., Banyan Psychiat. Inst., Lake Worth. Past med. adviser aviation medicine USAFE, SHAPE, other mil. groups. Served to lt. col. M.C., USAAF, USAF, 1943-56. Recipient Meritorious Service award Am. Cancer Soc., 1960. Diplomate Am. Bd. Dermotology, Am. Bd. Preventive Medicine, Am. Bd. Allergy and Immunology. Fellow Am. Coll. Preventive Medicine, Am. Acad. Dermatology, Am. Assn. Clin. Allergy and Immunology, Aerospace Med. Assn. (asso.); mem. A.M.A. (Continuous Edn. award), Pan Am. (med. council pediatric allergy), Fla. med. assns., Am. Acad. Allergy, Am. Coll. Allergy, Noah Worcester Dermatol. Assn., Soc. Investigative Dermatologists, Am. Soc. Dermatologic Surgeons, Fla. Dermatol. Soc. (pres.) S.E., South Central dermatol. assns., Internat. Corr. Soc. Allergists, Internat. Congress Dermatology, Internat. Congress Allergology, Internat. Soc. Tropical Medicine and Dermotology, N.Y. Acad. Scis., Assn. Modern and Contemporary Medicine and Surgery. Republican. Mason. Club: Catillian. Research in short-time accelerations and cerebral concussion. Home: 2600 Broadway West Palm Beach FL 33407 Office: MD Center 2600 Broadway West Palm Beach FL 33407

DUGDALE, MARION (MRS. JAMES G. MCCLURE), physician, educator; b. Bellavista, Callao, Peru, Oct. 7, 1928; d. Herbert and Sarah Emily (Read) Dugdale; came to U.S., 1946, naturalized, 1959; B.A., Bryn Mawr Coll., 1950; M.D., Harvard, 1954; m. James G. McClure, Dec. 17, 1955; children—Emily Marie, John Michael. Intern, U. N.C., Chapel Hill, 1954-55, resident, 1955-57; fellow in hematology Duke Hosp., Durham, N.C., 1957-58; fellow and research fellow in hematology U. Tenn., Memphis, 1958-60; faculty, 1960—, prof. medicine, prof. pathology, 1973—. Mem. Am. Soc. Hematology, Am. Heart Assn., N.Y. Acad. Scis., Internat. Soc. on Thrombosis and Haemostosis, Am., Tenn., Shelby County med. assns., Sigma Xi. Home: 2957 Iroquois Rd Memphis TN 38111 Office: 800 Madison Av Memphis TN 38163

DUGGAN, MINOR, med. editor, writer; b. Cork, Ireland, Apr. 9, 1924; s. Cornelius and Eugenia (Sposchum) D.; M.B., B.Ch., B.A.O., Univ. Coll., Cork, Nat. U. Ireland 1952; m. Doloria Arlene Zelasko, July 10, 1959. Came to U.S., 1958, naturalized, 1963. Asst. editor Merck Manual, Merck Sharp and Dohme, 1961-64; dir. med. services White Labs., Inc., div. Schering Corp., Kenilworth, N.J., 1967-72; dir. med. illustration and publs. dept. Miami (Fla.) Heart Inst., 1972—. Mem. Assn. Med. Dirs., Am. Med. Writers Assn., Am. Assn. for History Medicine, Drug Information Assn., Brit. Med. Assn. Home: 251 Winston Blvd Apt 1820 Miami Beach FL 33160 Office: Miami Heart Inst 4701 N Meridian Av Miami Beach FL 33140

DUGGER, GORDON SHELTON, educator, neurosurgeon; b. Vilas, N.C., July 17, 1921; s. John Gray and Ruth (Combs) D.; A.B., U. N.C., 1941; M.D., Johns Hopkins, 1945; m. Josephine Conrath, June 14, 1958. Intern, Bowman Gray, 1941-46; resident neurosurgery Montreal Neurol. Inst., 1949-53; asso. div. neurosurgery U. N.C. Sch. Medicine, Chapel Hill, 1954—, now prof. surgery, chief div. neurosurgery. Mem. exec. bd. N.C. Hist. Commn. Served with M.C., AUS. Diplomate Am. Bd. Neurol. Surgery. Mem. Congress Neurol. Surgeons, Am. Assn. Neurol. Surgeons, A.C.S., So. Neurol. Soc. (v.p. 1970), Phi Beta Kappa. Contbr. chpt. to Pediatric Neurology, 1964

DUKE, CHARLES MOSS, JR., astronaut; b. Charlotte, N.C., Oct. 3, 1935; s. Charles Moss and Willie (Waters) D.; B.S., U.S. Naval Acad., 1957; M.S., Mass. Inst. Tech., 1964; grad. USAF Aerospace Research Pilot Sch., 1965; m. Dorothy Meade Claiborne, June 1, 1963; children—Charles Moss III, Thomas Claiborne. With 526th Fighter Interceptor Squadron, Germany, 1958-62; instr. USAF Aerospace Research Pilot Sch., 1965-66; astronaut NASA, Houston, 1966—. Mem. Air Force Assn., S.A.R. Episcopalian. Landed on moon abroad Apollo 16, Apr. 1972. Home: 410 Lakeshore Dr Seabrook TX 77586 Office: Code CB NASA-MSC Houston TX 77058

DUKE, CHARLES WAYNE, lawyer; b. Belton, Tex., Dec. 7, 1905; s. Charles and Elsie (Wheeler) D.; B.B.A., Baylor U., 1928; LL.B., U. Tex., 1931; m. Lorena Dodson, Feb. 2, 1935; children—Charles Wayne, Lorena (Mrs. John E. Furrh). Admitted to Tex. bar, 1931; practiced in San Antonio, 1932—; mem. firm Dodson and Ezell, 1932-53, Dodson, Duke, Branch, 1953—. Dir., gen. counsel Handy-Andy, Inc., San Antonio; v.p., dir., gen. counsel Main Savs. Assn., 1964—; dir. Noranda Oil Co., Midland, Tex. Mem. Tex. Turnpike Authority, 1972—. Bd. dirs. San Antonio Live Stock Expn., HemisFair 68; pres., dir. St. Anthony Hotel, San Antonio; bd. govs., exec. com. S.W. Found. for Research and Edn. Bd. regents North Tex. U., Denton, 1950-57; trustee U. Tex. Law Sch. Found. Served to maj. USAAF, 1942-45. Recipient Outstanding Alumnus award U. Tex. Law Sch., 1968. Mem. San Antonio Zool. Soc. (dir. 1967—), San Antonio Bar Assn. (past pres.), State Bar Tex. (dir. 1948-50). Home: 724 College Blvd San Antonio TX 78209 Office: Travis Park West 711 Navarro San Antonio TX 78205

DUKE, DOUGLAS EARLE, elec. engr.; b. Nashville, Apr. 11, 1924; s. Andrew Earle and Gertrude Christina (Schlerp) D.; B.S. in Elec. Engring., Vanderbilt U., 1950, postgrad., 1969-73; m. Anna Lou Brown, July 28, 1950; children—Robert, Timothy, Charlotte, Alan, Dianna. Elec. engr. TVA, 1950-54; elec. engr. Electric Power Bd., Nashville, 1954—; tchr. co. course electric power distbn. Served with USAAF, 1942-46. Sr. mem. I.E.E.E. Presbyn. (elder). Author: Electric Power Distribution, 1970. Home: 2026 Rosecliff St Nashville TN 37206 Office: 1214 Church St Nashville TN 37246

DUKE, MICHAEL BENTON, lunar sample curator; b. Los Angeles, Dec. 1, 1935; s. Leon and Eva (Siegel) D.; B.S., Cal. Inst. Tech., 1957, M.S., 1961, Ph.D., 1963; m. Mary Carolyn Creamer, July 17, 1967; children—Lisa, Stuart, Kenneth, Donna. Geologist, U.S. Geol. Survey, Washington, 1963-70, lunar sample prin. investigator, 1968-70; lunar sample curator NASA, Houston, 1970—. Recipient NASA Superior Achievement award, 1971; NASA Exceptional Sci. Achievement medal, 1973. Mem. Am., Geophys. Union, A.A.A.S., Sigma Xi. Contbr. articles to profl. jours. Home: 1015 Woodland Dr

Seabrook TX 77586 Office: NASA Johnson Space Center/TL Houston TX 77058

DUKES, PHILIP DUSKIN, plant pathologist, educator; b. Reevesville, S.C., Jan. 16, 1931; s. Henry L. and Roberta E. (Reeves) D.; B.S., Clemson U., 1953; M.S., N.C. State U., 1960, Ph.D., 1963; student Colo. State U., 1957; m. Marlene Hart, July 28, 1956; children—Marla Hart, Philip Duskin. Plant chief clk. Davison Chem. Corp., Savannah, Ga., 1953-54; asst. county agt. S.C. Extension Service, Saluda, 1956-58; research asst. N.C. State U., Raleigh, 1958-62; asst. prof. U. Ga., Tifton, 1962-67, asso. prof. plant pathology, 1967-70, research plant pathologist U.S. Vegetable Lab., Agrl. Research Service, U.S. Dept. Agr., Charleston, S.C., 1970—. Mem. Tobacco Variety Adv. Com., 1967-70; chmn. Tobacco Disease Evaluation Com., 1969-70, Sweetpotato Disease Com., 1970. Mem. local bd. SSS. Served with Signal Corps, AUS, 1954-56. Mem. Am. Phytopath. Soc., Mycol. Soc. Am., Bot. Soc. Am., Internat. Soc. Tropical Root Crops, So. Agrl. Workers, Nat. Sweetpotato Cooperator Group, Sigma Xi, Phi Kappa Phi, Alpha Zeta. Methodist. Research on physiology of phytopathogenic fungi, physiology of parasitism of root and stem pathogens, breeding disease resistant vegetables. Home: US Vegetable Lab PO Box 3348 Charleston SC 29407

DULANEY, GENE LANDIS, lawyer; b. Murray, Ky., Nov. 27, 1919; s. James A. and Edith (Bourland) D.; B.A. magna cum laude, Vanderbilt U., 1942; LL.B., St. Mary's U., San Antonio, 1949; m. Mary Arthur Bloomer, Sept. 2, 1948; children—Mary Jean, John Landis. Admitted to Tex. bar, 1949; practice law, San Antonio, 1949-50, Snyder, 1950—; city judge, Snyder, 1964—. Mem. Snyder Sch. Bd., 1960-63. Mem. Republican State Exec. Com., 1964-66; del. Rep. Nat. Conv., 1964. Bd. dirs. Colorado River Municipal Water Dist., Scurry County Boys Club. Served to 1st lt. USAAF, World War II; ETO. Decorated Air medal, D.F.C., Purple Heart. Mem. Am., Tex. bar assns., Snyder C. of C. (past pres., dir.). Episcopalian. Rotarian. Home: 3112 Av X Snyder TX 79549 Office: W Tex State Bank Bldg Snyder TX 79549

DULANEY, LUTHER THOMAS, JR., distbg. co. exec.; b. Oklahoma City, Feb. 23, 1939; s. Luther T. and Virginia (Piersol) D.; student U. Okla., 1957-61; m. Barbara Holmes, Feb. 16, 1963 (div.); children—Luther Thomas III, Lisa, Geoffrey P. Partner L. T. Dulaney Co., Oklahoma City; pres. Dulaneys, Inc.; dir. First Nat. Bank & Trust Co. Bd. dirs. Salvation Army Oklahoma City, 1967—, Oklahoma City Symphony, 1967—, A.R.C., 1968—, Okla. Sci. and Arts Found., 1968—, Oklahoma City Better Bus. Bur., 1969—, Oklahoma City Beautiful, 1970—, Southwestern Coll. of Oklahoma City, St. Anthony Hosp., State Fair Okla.; exec. com. Frontiers of Sci. Found. of Okla., 1971—, Water Devel. Found. Okla., 1966—. Mem. Young Pres.'s Orgn., Oklahoma City C. of C. (dir. 1967-71, 73—), Phi Gamma Delta. Episcopalian (vestryman). Rotarian (pres. 1972-73). Clubs: Oklahoma City Golf and Country, Young Mens Dinner. Office: PO Box 1292 100 NW 44th St Oklahoma City OK 73101

DULIN, WILLIAM EASTERDAY, electronic engr.; b. Washington, June 28, 1911; s. Charles Thomas and Mary (Easterday) D.; student George Washington U., 1944, 60-62, 65, Am. U., 1946-51; B.S., Phoenix U., 1959; grad. Capitol Radio Engring. Inst., 1943; Ph.D., Taylor U., 1970; Ph.I.D., World U., 1973; m. Mary Barker Wintringham, Mar. 28, 1952; 1 son, Charles Thomas II. With Dulin Radio Service, Dulin Audio Lab., Washington, 1930-36; in charge radio dept. Warfield Motor Co., 1937-38; buyer, estimator Lighthouse Electric Co., 1939; radio technician Md. State Forestry Radio Network, Laurel, 1940; contract radio engr. Naval Research Lab., Washington, 1941; chief engring. aide Office of Chief Signal Officer, War Dept., 1942; electronic engr. FCC, 1945-48, electronic engr. chief tech. br. Marine Div., 1948-51; industry analyst, chief radio communication equipment sect. Electronics div. Nat. Prodn. Authority, 1951-53; indsl. specialist, asst. to dir. for moblzn. planning Electronics div. Bus. and Def. Services Administrn., 1953-55; sci. staff asst., research and devel. Nat. Security Agy., 1955-56, gen. engr., 1956-57; electronic engr., chief radio propagation unit Frequency div. USIA, 1957-60, supervisory electronic engr., dep. chief, 1960—. Grad. instr. Concept Therapy Inst., 1971. Founder, mem. World U., also trustee World U. Roundtable. Served to lt. USNR, 1942-45. Registered profl. engr., D.C., Va. Mem. Va. Soc. Profl. Engrs., I.E.E.E., Internat. Writer's Assn., Assn. Advancement Med. Instrumentation, Soc. Advancement Free Energy, Audio Engring. Soc., Mensa, S.A.R. Mem. Unity Ch. Home: 3522 Washington Ct Alexandria VA 22302 Office: Frequency Div US Information Agy Washington DC 20547

DULLEA, JOHN JOSEPH, city ofcl.; b. Manchester, N.H., Dec. 19, 1926; s. Denis J. and Mildred A. (Brady) D.; B.A., St. Bonaventure U., 1950; M.A., Syracuse U., 1951; m. Elizabeth Cooper Elder, Feb. 28, 1960; children—Stephanie, Mark, Kara. Personnel technician County of Westchester (N.Y.), 1951-54; asst. to city mgr. City of Winston-Salem (N.C.), 1954-59, budget dir., 1959-61; twp. mgr. Levittown, N.J., 1961-63; city mgr. City of Sidney (O.), 1963-67, City of Burlington (Ia.), 1967-71, City of Greenville (S.C.), 1971—. Bd. dirs. Goodwill Industries, Greenville. Served with USNR, 1944-46. Mem. Internat., S.C. city mgmt. assns. Roman Catholic. Rotarian. Home: Riverbend Greenville SC 29601 Office: City Hall Greenville SC 29601

DULLER, NELSON MARK, JR., physicist, educator; b. Houston, Mar. 6, 1923; s. Nelson Mark and Sue (Hardcastle) D.; B.S., Tex. A. and M. U., 1948; M.A., Rice U., 1951, Ph.D., 1953; m. Joe Ann Chappell, June 18, 1955; 1 son, David Chappell. Mem. faculty physics dept. Tex. A. and M. U., College Station, 1953-54, 62—; mem. faculty U. Mo., Columbia, 1954-62. Served with AUS, 1943-45. Alfred P. Sloan Fellow, 1956-58. Mem. Am., Italian phys. socs., Am. Geophys. Union, Am. Assn. Physics Tchrs. Contbr. articles to profl. jours. Home: 818 N Rosemary St Bryan TX 77801 Office: Tex A and M University College Station TX 77843

DULOCK, VICTOR AUGUST, JR., physicist; b. Waco, Tex., Feb. 26, 1939; s. Victor August and Libbie (Zalman) D.; B.A., U. St. Thomas, 1960; Ph.D., U. Fla., 1964; m. Maryann Welhoelter, Dec. 26, 1959; children—Victoria, Richard, Sharon, Kathryn, Michael. Research asso. U. Fla., Gainesville, 1964-65; asst. prof. La. State U., New Orleans, 1965-67; research engring. specialist, cons. Chrysler Corp. Space div., New Orleans, 1966-67; mem. tech. staff TRW Inc., 1967-69, sect. head, Houston, 1969, staff engr., 1969-72, project mgr., Cape Canaveral, Fla., 1972—. Lectr., U. Houston, 1968-70. Mem. Am. Phys. Soc., Am. Assn. Physics Tchrs. Sigma Xi. Democrat. Roman Catholic. Home: 341 W Osceola Ln Cocoa Beach FL 32931 Office: 7001 N Atlantic Av Cape Canaveral FL 32920

DUMA, RICHARD JOSEPH, physician, educator; b. Bethlehem, Pa., Apr. 2, 1933; s. Joseph Anthony and Helen Veronica (Bartek) D.; B.S., Va. Poly. Inst., 1955; M.D., U. Va., 1959; m. Mary Alyce Fridley, Apr. 18, 1957; 1 son, Scott. Intern, U. Ala. Med. Center, Birmingham, 1959-60; resident, 1962-65; research fellow Harvard Med. Sch. and Mass. Gen. Hosp., 1965-67; instr. medicine Med. Coll. Va., Richmond, 1967-68, asst. prof., 1968-70, asso. prof., 1970—, acting chmn. div. immunology and infectious diseases. Chmn., U.S. Pharmacopeia Adv. Panel on Hosp. Practices, 1971—; chmn. subcom. on microbial contamination Nat. Coordination Com. on Large Volume Parenterals. Vice pres. bd. dirs. Nat. Found. for Infectious Diseases, 1973—. Served with USN, 1960-62. Diplomate Am. Bd. Internal Medicine. Mem. Am. Fedn. Clin. Research, Am. Va. socs. microbiology, A.C.P., Am., Va., Richmond socs. internal medicine, Infectious Diseases Soc. Am., A.A.A.S., So. Soc. Clin. Investigation, Am. Thoracic Soc., Royal Soc. Medicine, Med. Soc. Va., Richmond Acad. Medicine, Sigma Xi. Home: 2410 Castlebridge Rd Midlotian VA 23113 Office: Med Coll Va PO Box 92 Richmond VA 23219

DUMAN, BARRY LANCE, educator; b. N.Y.C., Jan. 6, 1943; s. James B. and Zelda M. (Steinberg) D.; A.A., George Washington U., 1962, B.A. (Emma K. Carr scholar), 1964; M.A. (University fellow), U. Del., 1966; Ph.D. (Cal. State Grad. fellow), U. So. Cal., 1971; m. Sofia L. Baruch, Dec. 26, 1965; 1 dau., Laura Suzanne Gabrielle. Teaching asst. U. So. Cal., Los Angeles, 1966-69; asst. prof. Northrop Inst. Tech., Inglewood, Cal., 1968; faculty West Tex. State U., Canyon, 1969—, asso. prof., head dept. econs., 1973—, univ. research grantee. Mem. Am. Econs. Assn., Assn. for Comparative Econ. Studies, Rocky Mt. Social Sci. Assn., Am. Assn. U. Profs. Rotarian (participant in Internat. group study program to Chile 1970). Home: 1501 26th St Canyon TX 79015

DUNAGAN, JOHN CONRAD, bottling co. exec.; b. Midland, Tex., Dec. 31, 1914; s. John C. and Ada L. (Hicks) D.; student U. Tex., 1937; m. Kathlyn Cosper, Aug. 21, 1933; children—Deanna, John C., Carol, Kathleen, William C. Mgr. Midland Bottling Co., 1931-33; mgr. Coca-Cola Bottling Co., Monahans, Tex., 1933-35, 41-46, pres., 1946-71, chmn. bd., 1971—; asst. cashier 1st State Bank, Monahans, 1937-39, dir., v.p., 1942—, chmn. bd., 1968—; asst. bank examiner Fed. Res. Bank, Dallas, 1940-41; chmn. bd. Tex. Savs. & Loan Assn., Monahans, 1965—; dir. Kermit State Bank (Tex.) 1943—; pres. Monahans Enterprises, Inc., 1953—, Midessa TV, Inc., Midland, 1954—, S.W. Canners Inc., 1973—. Mem. Tex. Finance Adv. Commn., 1960, U. Tex. Bus. Adminstrn. Adv. Council, 1960-61; mem. standardization com. Bottlers of Coca-Cola (U.S.), 1960—, chmn., 1968-72; mem. Tex. Good Neighbor Commn., 1955-62; pres. Monahans Sandhills Park Assn., 1958-61. Bd. dirs. Tex. Hist. Found., 1971—. Mem. Tex. Bottlers Assn. (pres. 1958), Tex. Hist. Assn., Tex. Folklore Soc. (councilor 1968—), Tex. Permian Hist. Soc. (pres. 1962-63), Nat. Soft Drink Assn. (exec. bd. 1961-73). Rotarian (pres. Monahans 1952-53). Home: 1107 S Dwight Av Monahans TX 79756 Office: 500 S Main Av Monahans TX 79756

DUNAWAY, DONNA ELIZABETH KASTLE, computer scientist, co. exec.; b. Ft. Worth, Mar. 16, 1935; d. Joseph A. and Susie (Garrett) Kastle; B.A., Tex. Christian U., 1956; M.S., So. Meth. U., 1969, Ph.D., 1972; children—Diane Elizabeth, Thomas Kastle. Mathematician Gen. Dynamics, Ft. Worth, 1956-57, Humble Oil and Refining Co., Houston, 1957-58; operations research analyst Atlantic Richfield, 1972-73; owner, pres. Ditrec Corp., Dallas, 1971—; cons. Tex. Instruments, Inc.; mem. faculty U. Tex. at Dallas. Mem. Math. Assn. Am., Assn. Computing Machinery, Kappa Kappa Gamma. Republican. Presbyn. Home: 3706 Dartmouth St Dallas TX 75205

DUNAWAY, JAMES LEE, JR., educator; b. Molino, Fla., Nov. 4, 1922; s. James Lee and Jahaza (Rooks) D.; B.S., U. Fla., 1948, M.Agr., 1952, Rank I Advanced Post grad. Teaching Certificate, 1955; m. Frances DuBose, Aug. 10, 1950; children—Michael Lee, Frances Ann, Rosemary, Marcia Lynn (dec.). Tchr. vocational agr. Columbia High Sch., Lake City, Fla., 1948-56; owner farm supply bus. Mobile Feed Mill Service, Jasper, Fla., 1955-69; tchr. sci. and vocational edn. Columbia High Sch., 1948-55, Lake City Jr. High Sch., 1961-62; tchr. vocational agr. Jasper High Sch. and Hamilton High Sch., 1962-69; supt. Hamilton County Schs., Jasper, 1969-73; tchr. career edn. Daytona Beach (Fla.) high schs.; instr. Daytona Beach Community Coll.; also salesman ins. and real estate. Active North Fla. council Boy Scouts Am., 1963-72; registered donor North Fla. Eye Bank for Restoring Sight, Inc., U. Fla. Med. Center, 1969—. Councilman, Jasper, 1959-69; mayor pro-tem. Jasper, 1966-68. Served with arty. AUS, 1942-45; ETO. Decorated Purple Heart with oak leaf cluster; recipient complete mobile feed mill as 1st prize Nat. Feed Dealers' Essay Contest, 1956. Am. Assn. Sch. Adminstrs. travel grantee, Europe, 1971. Mem. Jasper P.T.A. (past pres.), Hamilton County Farm Bur., Fla., Nat. vocational tchrs. assns., Hamilton County, Fla. tchrs. assns., Columbia, Hamilton County, Volusia County, White Springs chambers commerce, V.F.W., Alpha Gamma Rho, Alpha Tau Alpha. United Methodist (dir.). Lion. Club: Antique Auto (Daytona Beach). Home: 265 Center St Ormaond Beach FL 32074

DUNBAR, JAMES CURTIS, physician; b. Mountain Home, Ark., Nov. 21, 1921; s. Felton F. and Eilleen (Love) D.; M.D., U. Ark., 1946. Intern Luth. Hosp., Cleve., 1946-47; practice medicine, Mountain Home, 1949—. Served from lt. (j.g.) to lt. comdr. M.C., USNR, 1943-49; PTO. Fellow Am. Coll. Angiology, Am. Geriatrics Soc.; mem. N.Y. Acad. Scis., A.M.A., Ark., Baxter County med. socs., U. Ark. Alumni Assn. Mem. Christian Ch. Home: 806 E 9th St Mountain Home AR 72653 Office: 617 S Baker St Mountain Home AR 72653

DUNCAN, DAVID ALLEN, mech. engr.; b. Tulsa, Mar. 1, 1941; s. Lawrence Jackson and Virginia Caroline (Decker) D.; B.S., Kan. State U., 1964; m. Lenora M. Bartone, Sept. 17, 1966; children—Scott Allen, Ashley Shay. With Burns & McDonnell Engring. Co., Kansas City, Mo., 1966-70; project mgr. Limbach Co., Washington, 1970—. Vice pres. Lake Ridge Communities Civic Assn., Woodbridge, Va., 1972—. Served to 1st lt. AUS, 1964-66. Registered profl. engr., Kan., Va., D.C. Mem. Nat. Environmental Balancing Bur., Am. Soc. Heating, Refrigeration and Air Conditioning Engrs. Home: 2552 Paxton St Woodbridge VA 22191 Office: PO Box 39 Springfield VA 22151

DUNCAN, DAVID TURNER, lawyer; b. Bowie, Tex., Feb. 4, 1929; s. John Thomas and Lee (Turner) D.B.B.A., U. Tex. A. and M. U., 1951; J.D., U. Tex., 1956; m. Betty Virginia Watson, Aug. 25, 1956; children—David Turner, Marshall Thomas, Brian Randolph, John William. With FBI, Houston, 1951; admitted to Tex. bar, 1956; practiced in Baytown, Houston, 1956-61, Brownsville, Tex., 1961—; mem. firms Cunningham, Yznaga & Duncan, 1961-65, Cox, Wilson, Duncan & Clendenin, 1965-69, Cox, Wilson, Duncan & Black, 1969—. Dir. Pan Am. Bank, Brownsville. Devel. fund chmn. Tex. A. and M. U., 1965. Trustee Brownsville Pub. Schs., 1964-67; dir., co-chmn. Brownsville Music Festival, 1962-63; dir., trustee Rio Grande Valley council Boy Scouts Am. Served to 1st lt. USAF, 1951-53. Fellow Tex. Bar Found.; mem. State Bar Tex., Am., Cameron County bar assns., Am. Judicature Soc., Tex. Assn. Def. Counsel, Def. Research Inst., C. of C., Delta Theta Phi. Episcopalian. Rotarian (pres. 1965-66), Aggie (dir. 1963—). Club: Valley International Country. Home: 1404 Mulberry Lane Brownsville TX 78520 Office: 422 E Elizabeth St Brownsville TX 78520

DUNCAN, JAMES LOUGHLIN, bishop; b. Greensboro, N.C., Sept. 11, 1913; s. Robert and Mary (Loughlin) D.; B.A., Emory U., 1935, M.A., 1936; B.D., U. of South, 1939, D.D., 1962; m. Evelyn Burgess, July 25, 1943 (dec. Jan. 1967); children—Mary Anna (Mrs. Edward B. Waters), John Robert, James Loughlin; m. 2d, Mrs. Elaine B. Gaither, Oct. 7, 1967. Ordained to ministry Episcopal Ch., 1938; asst. rector in Atlanta, 1939-40; rector in Rome, Ga., 1940-45, Winter Park, Fla., 1945-50, St. Petersburg, Fla., 1950-61; suffragan bishop Episcopal Diocese So. Fla., 1961-69; bishop S.E. Fla., 1969—. Exchangee, U.S.-S. African Program, 1961. Chmn. Dade County Community Relations Bd., 1965. Mem. Kappa Alpha (knight comdr. 1957-58). Home: 3800 Alhambra Ct Coral Gables FL 33134 Office: 525 NE 15th St Miami FL 33132

DUNCAN, JOHN ALEX, govt. appraiser; b. Marianna, Fla., Aug. 22, 1944; s. Finley J. and Vivian Marie (Johns) D.; A.A., Chipola Jr. Coll., 1964; B.S., Troy State Coll., 1966. Trainee Fla. Pub. Welfare Dept., Marianna, 1966-67; cashier Fla. Bank at Chipley, 1967-71; mgr. service center Agrico Chem. Co., Chipley, 1971-72; state R/W appraiser, Dept. Transp., 1972—. Bd. dirs. Chipley Housing Authority, 1970-74, Holmes Valley Authority, 1971-75. Meml. chmn. Am. Cancer Dr. Washington County, 1971. Mem. Bank Adminstrn. Inst. (v.p. 1970-71). Democrat. Baptist. Lion. Club: Quarterback (treas.). Home: 801 S 8th St Chipley FL 32428 Office: Dept Transp Chipley FL 32428

DUNCAN, JOHN JAMES, congressman; b. Scott County, Tenn., Mar. 24, 1919; married, four children. Asst. atty. gen., 1947-56; dir. law, Knoxville, Tenn., 1956-59, mayor, 1959-64; mem. 89th-93d congresses from 2d dist. Tenn. Served with AUS, 1942-45. Mem. Am., Tenn., Knoxville bar assns., Am. Legion (comdr. Tenn. 1954), V.F.W. Presbyn. Republican. Home: 5403 E Sunset Rd Knoxville TN 37914 also 3803 Cameron Mills Rd Alexandria VA 22305 Office: Cannon House Office Bldg Washington DC 20515

DUNCAN, JOSEPH, environmental engr.; b. Decatur, Ala., Feb. 5, 1943; s. Robert Paul and Nettie Belle (Coker) D.; B.S. in C.E., U. Ala., 1965; M.S., W.Va. U., 1969; M.S. in Environmental Engring., U. Tenn., 1975; m. Patsy Ann Martin, May 29, 1964; children—Latisha Ann, Leslie Ann. Dir. air pollution control sect. Met. Health Dept. Nashville, 1966-67; environmental engr. TVA, Muscle Shoals, Ala., 1967-70; asst. dir. Knox County (Tenn.) Air Pollution Control Dept., Knoxville, 1970-72; v.p. Harmon Engring., Opelika, Ala., 1972—. Adj. instr. chem. engring. Auburn (Ala.) U., 1973. NASA summer fellow, 1970. Registered profl. engr., Ala., Tenn. Mem. Am. Soc. C.E. (atmospheric pollution commn.), Air Pollution Control Assn. (sec.-treas. So. sect. 1970-71, treas. 1972-74), Sigma Xi, Chi Epsilon. Editor: (with others) Industrial Air Pollution Control, 1973; Industrial Air Pollution Control II, 1974; Industrial Odor Control, 1974. Contbr. articles to profl. jours. Home: 1550 Pumphrey Av PO Box 2249 Auburn AL 36830 Office: 413 Etowah Av Opelika AL 36801

DUNCAN, POPE ALEXANDER, coll. pres.; b. Glasgow, Ky., Sept. 8, 1920; s. Pope Alexander and Mabel (Roberts) D.; B.S., U. Ga., 1940, M.S., 1941; Th.M., So. Bapt. Theol. Sem., 1944, Th.D., 1947; postgrad. U. Zurich (Switzerland), 1960-61; m. Margaret Flexer, June 30, 1943; children—Mary Margaret, Annie Laurie, Katherine Maxwell. Instr. physics U. Ga., 1940-41; fellow So. Bapt. Theol. Sem., 1944-45; dir. religious activities Mercer U., 1945-46, Roberts prof. church history, 1948-49; prof. religion Stetson U., 1946-48, 49-53; prof. ch. history Southeastern Bapt. Theol. Sem., 1953-63; dean Brunswick Coll., 1964; pres. S. Ga. Coll., Douglas, 1964-68; v.p. Ga. So. Coll., Statesboro, 1968-71, pres., 1971—. Pres. Wake Forest Civic Club, 1959-60, Ga. Assn. Colls., 1968-69; pres. Coastal Empire Council Boy Scouts Am., 1973-74. Mem. Am. Hist. Assn., Am. Soc. Ch. History, Douglas-Coffee County C. of C. (dir. 1966-68), Statesboro-Bulloch County C. of C. (dir. 1971—), Phi Beta Kappa, Omicron Delta Kappa, Phi Kappa Phi, Phi Delta Kappa, Kappa Delta Pi, Pi Mu Epsilon, Phi Eta Sigma, Sigma Phi Sigma. Democrat. Baptist. Rotarian (dir. 1965-66, 1970-72, pres. 1967-68). Author: Our Baptist Story, 1958; The Pilgrimage of Christianity, 1965 Hanserd Knollys, 1965. Home: 16 Golf Club Circle Statesboro GA 30458

DUNCAN, ROBERT SMITH, JR., savs. and loan exec.; b. Montgomery, Ala., June 24, 1936; s. Robert Smith and Mildred (Hamm) D.; B.S., Auburn U., 1957; m. Judy White, July 19, 1959; children—Richard, Michaele. With Peat, Marwick, Mitchell & Co., Birmingham, Ala., 1959-64, Jackson, Miss., 1964-68; with First Fed. Savs. & Loan Assn. of Hattiesburg (Miss.), 1968—, exec. v.p., 1971—. Bd. dirs., sec.-treas. United Givers Fund Forrest County, 1969—. Served to capt. AUS, 1965. C.P.A., Ala., Miss. Mem. Nat. Soc. Controllers and Financial Officers of Savs. Instns. (Miss. pres. 1973-74), Am. Inst. C.P.A.'s, Miss. (gov. 1973-74), Ala. socs. C.P.A.'s, Forrest County C. of C. Kiwanian. Home: 1209 Carter Dr Hattiesburg MS 39401 Office: 130 W Front St Hattiesburg MS 39401

DUNCAN, THOMAS RAY, radiologist; b. Linden, Tenn., Jan. 18, 1934; s. Bernard Ray and Bonnie Laura (DePriest) D.; B.A., cum laude, Vanderbilt U., 1955; M.D., U. Tenn., 1958; m. Judith Gayle Buchanan, Feb. 1, 1964; children—Jeffrey, Darrell. Intern, Kings County Hosp., Bklyn., 1958-59; resident Vanderbilt U. Hosp., Nashville, 1961-64, asst. prof. radiology, 1966-73, asst. clin. prof. radiology, 1973—, lectr. skeletal roentgenology, 1970—; chmn. radiology dept. Met. Gen. Hosp., Nashville, 1966-73; practice medicine specializing in diagnostic radiology, Brentwood, Tenn., 1973—; mem. staffs Vanderbilt U., Lewisburg (Tenn.) Community, Williamson County hosps., Nashville Gen. Hosp., 1965—, sec. exec. com., 1970—. Chmn., Brentwood Park Bd., 1973—; vice chmn. River Oaks Civic Assn., Brentwood, 1971. Bd. dirs. devel. found. David Lipscomb Coll. Mem. Am. Contract Bridge League (treas. 1963). Republican. Mem. Ch. of Christ. Club: Delta Duplicate Bridge (Brentwood, Tenn.). Address: River Oaks Rd Brentwood TN 37027

DUNCAN, WAYNE JOHNSON, realtor; b. Alexandria, Va., Sept. 22, 1940; s. Samuel Guy, Sr. and Sally Ann (Vohun) D.; student U. Ga., 1963; B.A., Piedmont Coll., 1965; m. Mary Betty Burger, Dec. 18, 1965. Purchasing agt. Old Dominion Mfg. Co., 1965; advt. salesman, reporter Culpeper (Va.) Star Exponent, 1965-66; salesman Met. Life Ins. Co., 1967-69; salesman Otis Burke Realty, Culpeper, 1966-67, 69—. Pres. Mental Health Assn. of Culpeper, 1968-70, bd. dirs., 1966-70; pres. Culpeper United Givers Fund, 1971. Pres. Young Democratic Club of Culpeper, 1967-69; mem. Culpeper Dem. Com., 1968—, chmn., 1973—. Bd. dirs. Culpeper Mental Health Clinic, Inc., 1969—, Culpeper Sr. Center, 1972—, Culpeper Library, 1972—. Recipient Mental Health Service award, 1970, Outstanding Young Man award, Jaycees, 1973, Appreciation award United Givers Fund, 1972, Service award A.R.C., 1973. Mem. Piedmont Bd. Realtors (sec.-treas.). Episcopalian (lay reader). Lion, Toastmaster. Home: 605 S West St Culpeper VA 22701 Office: 420 Sunset Lane Culpeper VA 22701

DUNGAN, THOMAS MILLER, clergyman; b. Paris, Tenn., Mar. 19, 1920; s. Robert Hall and Nina Beatrice (Holman) D.; A.B., Transylvania U., 1943; B.D., Lexington Theol. Sem., 1955, M.Div., 1972; m. Gradie Irene Scarborough, Oct. 26, 1943; children—Diana (Mrs. Donald L. Parker), Karen (Mrs. Charles Edward Maddux). Ordained to ministry Christian Ch. (Disciples of Christ), 1942; minister Parkland Christian Ch., Louisville, 1947-51, First Christian Ch., Morehead, Ky., 1951-55, North Middletown Christian Ch., 1955-60, First Christian Ch., Clarksville, Tenn., 1960-62, First Christian Ch., Houston, 1966-73, Hillside Meml. Christian Ch., Ft. Worth, 1973—. Tchr., prin. elementary sch.; tchr. history high sch.

Pres., La. Bd. Christian Chs., 1964, Gulf Coast Area of Christian Ch., 1970, 71; mem. recommendations com. Tex. State Conv., 1971, Internat. Conv., 1963-64. Mem. Hermann Hosp. Nurses Scholarship Com., 1970-71. Mem. Disciples of Christ Hist. Soc. (life), Religious Instns. Planning (sec.-treas.). Contbr. articles to newspapers and mags. Home: 3517 Madrid Dr Fort Worth TX 76133 Office: 6410 South Freeway Fort Worth TX 76134

DUNHAM, DONALD HARRISON, ins. exec.; b. Davies County, Mo., Sept. 15, 1913; s. Emory H. and Zula (Crain) D.; A.A., Pomona Coll., 1935; LL.B., Nat. U. Washington 1941, LL.M. 1942; J.D., George Washington U., 1968; m. Lillian Mae Ingram, Aug. 21, 1941; 1 dau., Carol-Lynn Shirley. Instr. ins., office mgmt. Nat. Inst. Tech., Washington, 1946-47; dist. mgr. group dept. Mass. Mut. Life Ins. Co., 1947-48; regional mgr. group dept. U.S. life, N.Y.C., 1948-50; group dept. dir. Eastern Seaboard, Minn. Mut. Life Ins. Co., 1950-51; dir. retirement, safety and ins. dept., also contbg. editor of Rural Electrification mag. Nat. Rural Electric Coop. Assn., 1951-58; asst. v.p. Church Life Ins. Corp., 1958-59; adminstrv. v.p., 1959-64; v.p., mgr., mem. exec. com., dir., 1964-72; sec. Ch. Agy. Corp., 1966-72, Ch. Finance Corp. 1966-72; asst. v.p. Ch. Pension Fund P.E. Ch., 1959-72; ins. cons., 1950—; ins. cons. Nat. Telephone Coop. Assn.; dep. asst. adminstr. Tex. Bd. Ins., Austin, 1972—. Mem. Planning Bd., Borough of New Providence, 1964-72. Asst. v.p. govt. relations Ch. Pension Fund, 1959-72; bishop's com. St. Andrews Epls. Ch., 1961-72; Epis. ch. rep. to coms. Nat. Assn. Ins. Commrs., 1959-72. Mem. Gov.'s Com. Traffic Safety; mem. Pres.'s Conf. Traffic, Indsl. and Farm Safety; nat. safety counsel, ins. conference Cooperative League, U.S. Group Health Federation Am. Served with USNR, 1944-46. Mem. A.I.M. (fellow pres.' council), Am. Legion (past post comdr., legislative rep. to N.J. and Fed. govt. depts.), Acad. of Polit. Sci., Borough Council of New Providence (chmn. adv. com.), N.J. Problems of Aging Com., Minn. State Soc. (past pres.), V.F.W., D.A.V., Sigma Delta Kappa, Delta Psi Omega. Mason (master New Jersey 1967, 32 deg.). Clubs: Craftsman, Kerwood Golf and Country (Chevy Chase, Md.). Home: 4213 Endcliffe Dr Northwest Hills Austin TX 78731 also 10008 Edwards Av Bethesda MD Office: State Bd Ins 1110 San Jacinto St Austin TX 78786

DUNKIN, MILLARD LEE, dentist; b. Ala., Mar. 20, 1931; s. Robert Lee and Sarah Ruth (Drake) D.; B.S., U. Ala., 1958, D.M.D., 1961; m. Mary Lou Boerschel, Dec. 27, 1953; children—Jeffery, Bethany, Gregory, Malcolm. Practice dentistry, Columbia, S.C., 1961—. Served with USAF, 1951-55. Mem. Central Dist. Dental Soc. (sec.-treas. 1968-70), Am., S.C. (sec., 1970—) dental assns., Greater Columbia Dental Soc., S.C. Acad. Practice Adminstrn., Am. Acad. Dental Electrosurgery, Am. Soc. Dentistry for Children, So. Acad. Clin. Nutrition, Omicron Delta Kappa, Delta Sigma Delta. Optimist (lt. gov., 1967-68). Home: 6909 Longbrook Rd Columbia SC 29206 Office: 2800 Rosewood Dr Columbia SC 29205

DUNLAP, ESTELLE CECILIA DIGGS (MRS. LEE A. DUNLAP), educator; b. Washington, Sept. 26, 1912; d. John F. and Mary F. (Chasley) Diggs; B.S., D.C. Tchrs. Coll., 1937; M.S., Howard U., 1940; m. Lee A. Dunlap, May 16, 1941; children—Gladys C. (Mrs. Kimbrough), Dolly A. (Mrs. Sparkman). Tchr. math. Garnet-Patterson Jr. High Sch., Washington, 1941-56, head dept. math., 1950-56; tchr. math., sci. MacFarland Jr. High Sch., Washington, 1956-72. Vis. instr. math. D.C. Tchrs. Coll., 1963—. Mem. N.W. Boundary Civic Assn., Washington, 1954—, rec. sec., 1964-66. NSF fellow, 1959. Fellow Intercontinental Biog. Assn.; mem. A.A.A.S., Nat. Edn. Council, Nat. Council Tchrs. Math. Nat. Aviation Edn. Council, Internat. Platform Assn., Washington Performing Arts Soc., Soc. Indsl. and Applied Math., Am. Ordnance Assn., Am. Math. Soc., Math. Assn. Am., Washington Urban League, Washington Opera Soc., UN Assn., Met. Opera Guild, Smithsonian Assos., Fgn. Policy Research Inst., Assos. Nat. Archives. Republican. Club: Stardusters' V.I.P. (Waldorf, Md.). Home: 719 Shepherd St NW Washington DC 20011

DUNLAP, JAMES ALBERT, broadcasting co. exec.; b. Wheeling, W.Va., July 18, 1939; s. Clifford Leslie and Irma (Heinlein) D.; B.A., W.Va. U., 1959; m. Sandra Elaine Puronen, Oct. 14, 1961; children—Shawn, Shannon. With WKWK, Wheeling, 1960-61, WIRK, West Palm Beach, Fla., 1961-62; with WQAM, Miami Beach, Fla., 1963—, program dir., 1968—. Served with AUS, 1956-59. Home: 220 NE 175th Terrace North Miami Beach FL 33162 Office: 767 41st St Miami Beach FL 33140

DUNLAP, JERRY J., lawyer; b. Chelsea, Okla., Feb. 12, 1925; B.S. in Mech. Engring., U. Okla., 1948; J.D., U. Tulsa, 1952. Admitted to Okla. bar, 1952, U.S. Supreme Ct. bar, 1969; practiced in Oklahoma City, 1952—; mem. firm Dunlap, Laney, Hessin & Dougherty. Asst. prof. patent trademark and copyright law Oklahoma City U., 1962-67. Served to lt. (j.g.) USNR, 1943-46, 52-53. Registered profl. engr., Okla. Mem. Nat. Soc. Profl. Engrs., Am., Oklahoma County, Okla. bar assns., Am. Patent Law Assn. Office: 200 Lawyers Bldg 219 Couch Dr Oklahoma City OK 73102*

DUNLAP, JOE EVERETT, dentist; b. Delaware, O., May 11, 1930; s. Arthur Calvin and Mary Irene (Jones) D.; student Ohio Wesleyan U., 1949-50, 54; D.D.S., Ohio State U., 1959; m. Mary Susan King, June 17, 1959; children—Marlene, Todd, David, Sherrie, Dru. With Fla. Instl. Dental Service, Gainesville, Ft. Myers, 1959-60; individual practice dentistry, Clearwater, Fla., 1961—; sr. mem. dental group Dunlap, Vance, Reinhold, Yeager & Montreuil. Sec.-treas. Cedardale Properties, Inc. Served to 2d lt. Med. Service Corps, AUS, 1950-53. Mem. Am., Fla., West Coast Dist. dental assns. Home: 1816 Lombardy Dr Clearwater FL 33515 Office: 1455 Sunset Point Rd Clearwater FL 33515

DUNLAP, ROY L., civil engr.; b. Canyon, Tex., Aug. 15, 1927; s. Richard and Leona Blanche (Easter) D.; B.S. in Civil Engring., Tex. Technol. Coll., 1949; m. Riley Fae Butler, Jan. 29, 1950; 1 son, Roy Joe. Asst. design engr. City of Lubbock (Tex.), 1950-53; engr. City of Snyder (Tex.), 1953-54, mgr., 1955-62; mgr., City of Killeen, Texas, 1962-68; coordinator City of Hamlin (Tex.), 1954-55; asst. to sr. v.p., head project mgmt. div. Turner, Collie & Braden, Inc., cons. engrs., Houston, 1969-71; chief engr. Wilkinson Welding, Killeen, Tex., 1971-72; pres., owner Dunlap & Assos., 1972—. Bd. dirs., sec. Scurry County Indsl. Found., Snyder, Tex. Served with USMCR, 1945-46; now capt. CEC, USNR; recalled to active duty comdg. officer U.S. Naval Constrn. Bn. 22, South Vietnam, 1968-69. Decorated Legion of Merit; named Outstanding Young Man, Snyder Jr. C. of C., 1957. Registered prof. civil engr., Tex. Mem. Am. Soc. C.E., Internat., Tex. city mgrs. assn., Am. Legion (sch. award Crosbyton, Tex. 1944), V.F.W., Navy League, Killeen C. of C. Methodist. Mason. Rotarian (pres. Snyder 1957-58). Home: 1512 Alta Mira Killeen TX 76541 Office: 5902 E Hwy 190 Killeen TX 76541 also 211 N 2d St Temple TX 76540

DUNLOP, JAMES NATHANIEL, JR., missile co. exec.; b. Yonkers, N.Y., Apr. 19, 1921; s. James Nathaniel and Katharine W. (Lyon) D.; B.S. in Engring., Princeton, 1942; E.E., 1943; m. Rosemary Royce, Jan. 12, 1948; children—James, William, Rosemary, Paul Dunlop. Engr., Kelex Corp., Silver Spring, Md., 1946-47; with Martin Co., Balt., 1947-55, dir. quality, Orlando, Fla., 1959-61; dir. electronic programs Martin Marietta Corp., Orlando, 1961-69, operations dir. communications and electronics, 1969-71, mgr. contracts services and configuration, data mgmt., 1971—. Past bd. dirs. Orange County chpt. A.R.C. Served as lt. USNR, 1942-46. Mem. Armed Forces Communications and Electronics Assn. (regional v.p.), Am. Ordance Assn., I.E.E.E., U.S. Naval Inst., Winter Park C. of C. (past dir.). Republican. Episcopalian. Home: 1807 Via Amalfi Winter Park FL 32784 Office: Martin Marietta Corp Orlando FL 32805

DUNN, ADOLPHUS WILLIAM, physician; b. Eden, N.C., Nov. 23, 1922; s. Adolphus William and Sally (Gray Ivie) D.; B.S., Wake Forest Coll., 1942; M.D., Duke, 1945; children—John Bullard Ray, Adolphus William III. Intern New Haven Hosp., 1945-46; commd. lt. (j.g.) 1945, med. officer, 1946-65, ret. as capt. M.C.; head dept. orthopaedic surgery Ochsner Clinic and Ochsner Found. Hosp., New Orleans, 1967—; clin. asso. prof. orthopaedic surgery Tulane U. Sch. Medicine, New Orleans. Diplomate Am. Bd. Orthopaedic Surgery. Fellow A.C.S., Am. Acad. Orthopaedic Surgeons; mem. Am. Orthopaedic Assn., Phi Beta Kappa. Republican. Home: 110 Mark Twain Dr Apt 15 Harahan LA 70123 Office: 1514 Jefferson Hwy New Orleans LA 70121

DUNN, CHARLES EDWARD LEE, JR., ordnance co. exec.; b. New Orleans, Sept. 25, 1921; s. Charles Edward Lee and Eugenia Cecelia (Quinn) D.; B.S., Loyola U. of the South, New Orleans, 1941; m. Billie Louise Odom, Apr. 16, 1943; children—Charles E.L. III, Robert T., Kenneth B. Inspection supr. U.S. Govt., La. Ordnance Plant, Shreveport, 1941-48; asst. chief chemist Silas Mason Co., Ia. Ordnance Plant, Burlington, 1948-51; chief chemist Day and Zimmermann, Inc., Lone Star Ordnance Plant, Texarkana, Tex., 1951-54; chief chemist Thiokol Chem. Corp., Longhorn div., Marshall, Tex., 1954-57, process engr. supr., 1957-60, quality control mgr. Elkton div., Bristol, Pa., 1965-70, prodn. supr. Elkton (Md.) div., 1970-74; mgr. dept. Ga. div. Thiokol Corp., Woodbine, 1974—. Served to sgt. U.S. Army, 1944-46. Mem. Am. Chem. Soc., Am. Inst. Chem. Engrs. Home: 845 Beachview Dr Jekyll Island GA 31520 Office: Thiokol Corp Ga div Woodbine GA 31569

DUNN, CHARLES JEROME, state ofcl.; b. Phila., June 29, 1934; s. Charles Rome and Lelia Mae (Whitley) D.; A.B., U. N.C. at Chapel Hill, 1956, postgrad., 1956-60; m. Martha Ellen Sherrill, Dec. 29, 1963; children—Sherrill, Jay, Lelia. With Chapel Hill Weekly, 1951-52, Durham (N.C.) Morning Herald, 1956-63; legislative asst. to Congressman Horace Kornegay, 1963-64; spl. asst. to Gov. Dan Moore, N.C., 1965-68; dir. State Bur. Investigation, Raleigh, 1969—. Served with AUS, 1957-59. Democrat. Methodist. Home: 6512 Raceview Terrace Raleigh NC 27609 Office: 421 N Blount St Raleigh NC 27601

DUNN, CHARLES THOMAS, clergyman, psychologist; b. Brookhaven, Miss., Apr. 4, 1920; s. John W. and Josephene (Norman) D.; B.A., Abilene Christian Coll., 1949; M.A., U. Houston, 1952; m. Celeste Mae Cate, Mar. 14, 1946; children—James Nelson, Deanne Lee, Dianna Lynn. Ordained to ministry Church of Christ, 1947; minister in Abilene, Tex., 1948-49, Corpus Christi, 1950, Turkey, 1951, Baytown, 1952, Rodeo Cal., 1954; minister, bishop Hardy and Hopper St. Ch. of Christ, Houston, 1954—; guidance dir. psychologist Channelview Sch. Dist., 1954-71; prin. Marathon (Tex.) High Sch., 1971-72; supt. schs., Waelder, Tex., 1972—. Served with AUS World War II. Mem. Am., Tex. personnel and guidance assns., Nat. Vocational Guidance Assn., Tex. Edn. Assn., Am. Sch. Counselors Assn. Republican. Contbr. numerous articles to Gospel Tidings. Address: PO Box 564 Waalder TX 78959

DUNN, FLOYD WARREN, coll. dean; b. Huntington, Ark., Dec. 15, 1920; s. Fred H. and Mattie (Waters) D.; B.S., Abilene Christian Coll., 1944; M.S., U. Colo., 1946, Ph.D., 1950; m. Ila Pauline Witt, Oct. 21, 1944; children—Shirley (Mrs. Philip E. Woods), James Floyd, Nina Jene. With Abilene Christian Coll., 1946-60, prof. chemistry, 1954-60, 68-72; asso. dir. research, 1970-72, dean Grad. Sch., 1972—; asso. prof., prof. biochemistry U. Tenn. Med. Units, 1960-65; prof. biochemistry U. Ill.-Chiengmai U. (Thailand), 1965-68. Vis. prof. Chulalong Koriv U., Bangkok, Thailand, 1958-59. NIH predoctoral fellow, 1948-50; Robert A. Welch Found. research grantee, 1969—. Mem. Am. Soc. Biol. Chemists, Am. Chem. Soc., Sigma Xi. Contbr. articles to profl. jours. Home: 933 Washington Blvd Abilene TX 79601

DUNN, HARRISON A., constrn. co. exec.; b. Tellico Plains, Tenn., Sept. 22, 1920; s. Charles Edmund and Ella (Ware) D.; ed. pub. schs.; m. Tennie Arlene Cochran, Jan. 10, 1943; children—Harrison David, Pamela (Mrs. David Brockwell Kidd). Employed with various constrn. firms, 1940—; with Brock & Blevins Co., Ins., Rossville, Ga., 1950—, mgr. power constrn., 1958—, v.p., 1969—, dir., 1969—. Baptist. Mason (Shriner). Home: 7109 Saratoga Lane Chattanooga TN 37421 Office: 411 W Gordon Av Rossville GA 40741

DUNN, HENRY HAMPTON, editor; b. Floral City, Fla., Dec. 14, 1916; s. William Harvey and Nannie L. (Hemrick) D.; student Mercer U., Macon, Ga., U. Tampa (Fla.); m. Charlotte Rawls, Aug. 16, 1941; children—Janice Kay, Henry Hampton, Dennis Harvey. Mem. staff Tampa (Fla.) Times, 1936-58, city editor, 1946-51, mng. editor, 1951-58; polit. analyst and newscaster WCKT-TV, Miami, 1958-59; pub. relations dir. Peninsula Motor Club, 1959—, also v.p.; editor Fla. Explorer. Adv. council Gordon Keller Sch. Nursing, 1955—, chmn. 1956-59, adv. bd. Salvation Army, 1953—, chmn., 1955-56; dir. United Cerebral Palsy of Tampa, state pres.; dir., treas. Tampa A.R.C.; selections com. Girl Scouts; dir., v.p. Vis. Nurses Assn. Greater Tampa 1956, pres., 1973-74; mem. Nat. AAA Traffic and Safety Com., Nat. AAA Pub. Relations Com., Nat. AAA Hwy. Com.; mem. West Central Fla. Com. Mil. Assistance to Safety and Traffic, Citizen's Adv. com. Tampa Urban Area Transp. Study. Charter trustee Historic Pensacola Preservation Bd.; trustee Historic Tallahassee Preservation Bd.; pres. DWI Counterattack Tampa-Hillsborough County; mem. Carrollwood Civic Assn.; dir. Girl's Club of Tampa, Hillsborough County unit Am. Cancer Soc.; adv. com. Hillsborough Community Coll.; bd. dirs. Hillsborough Community Mental Health Center, Inc. Served to maj. USAF, World War II; MTO. Decorated Bronze Star, 5 Battle Stars. Recipient award for best news story A.P., 1946; Award of Merit, Fla. Hist. Soc.; Torch award Citrus County C. of C., 1969; Jefferson Davis medal United Daus. Confederacy; Fla. History award Peace River Valley Hist. Soc., 1974. Mem. Am. Legion, Tampa C. of C. (tourist com., mem. hwy. com.), Fla. Hist. Soc., Hist. Assn. So. Fla., U. Tampa Alumni Assn. (past pres.), Asso. Press Assn. Fla. (pres. 1955-56), Internat. Platform Assn., Tampa Hist. Soc. (pres. 1973-74), Old Timers Assn. Hillsborough County (dir.), Sigma Delta Chi (pres. Fla. West Coast chpt. 1954-55). Baptist. Mason, Rotarian (pub. relations chmn., bd. dirs., pres. Tampa, dist. gov.); mem. Order Eastern Star. Author: Re-Discover Florida; WDAE, Florida's Pioneer Radio Station; Yesterday's Tampa; Yesterday's St. Petersburg; Yesterday's Clearwater; Yesterday's Tallahassee; Re-explore Florida. Hist. writer Fla. Trend mag., Tampa Tribune, Tampa Times; writer syndicated hist. column. Home: 10610 Carrollwood Dr Tampa FL 33618 Office: 1515 N Westshore Blvd Tampa FL 33607

DUNN, J. D., educator, labor arbitrator; b. Freeport, Tex., Jan. 18, 1928; s. James Arlee and Martha (Gipson) D.; student Tex. A. and M. U., 1945-46; B.F.A., U. Tex., 1951, M.B.A., 1955; Ph.D., U. Ala., 1961; m. Paula Ann Huston, June 17, 1950; 1 son, Gary Paul. Asst. prof. bus. adminstrn. U. Tex., Arlington, 1955-58; chmn. bus. adminstrn. dept. Ala. Coll., Montevallo, 1960-63; prof. bus. adminstrn. N. Tex. State U., Denton, 1963—, dir. Tech. Information and Mgmt. Services Center, 1963—; labor arbitrator, Denton, 1965—. Cons. Victor Equipment Mfg. Co., Denton, 1966. Served with AUS, 1946-47, 1st lt., 1951-53. Mem. Am. Arbitration Assn., Indsl. Relations Research Assn. (chpt. pres. 1965-66). Author: (with Frank M. Rachel) Wage and Salary Administration), 1971; (with Elvis C. Stephens) Management of Personnel: Manpower Management and Organizational Behavior, 1972; (with E.C. Stephens and J.R. Kelley) Management Essentials: Resource, 1973, Management Essentials: Practicum, 1973. Contbr. articles to profl. jours. Home: 1311 Greenwood St Denton TX 76203

DUNN, JOHN THORNTON, physician, educator; b. Washington, Oct. 27, 1932; s. William LeRoy and Thelma (Brumfield) D.; A.B., Princeton U., 1954; M.D., Duke, 1958; m. Margaret Ann Davis, June 30, 1962; children—Catherine Thornton, Margaret Scudder, Robert Davis. Intern N.Y. Hosp., N.Y.C., 1958-59; resident U. Utah Hosp., 1959-61; research fellow in medicine Mass. Gen. Hosp., Harvard, Boston, 1961-62, 63-64, Columbia Presbyn. Hosp., 1962-63; research fellow in biochemistry Harvard, 1964-66; asst. prof. medicine U. Va., Charlottesville, 1966-70, asso. prof., 1970—; mem. staff U. Va. Hosp. Cons. endemic goiter Pan Am. Health Orgn. Nat. Inst. Health Career Devel. award, 1971. Mem. Am. Thyroid Assn. (Van Meter prize 1968), Endocrine Soc., Am. Fedn. Clin. Research, So. Soc. Clin. Investigation. Contbr. articles to sci. and med. jours. Address: Dept Medicine School Medicine University of Virginia Charlottesville VA 22901

DUNN, LEON ALGERNON, JR., diversified pub. corp. exec.; b. Greenville, N.C., Oct. 6, 1938; s. Leon Algernon and Mary Magdalene (Tripp) D.; B.S., U. N.C., 1960, grad. Exec. Program, Grad. Sch. Bus., 1974; m. Pattie Gene McCay, Apr. 27, 1963; children—Mary Eugenie, Jane McCay. Tchr. pub. schs., Chesapeake, Va., 1960-61; trust adminstr. Wachovia Bank & Trust Co., Winston-Salem, N.C., 1965-66; exec. v.p., dir. Guardian Corp., Rocky Mount, N.C., 1966-72, pres., 1972—, chief adminstrv. officer, 1972—, also dir. 19 subsidiaries; dir. Planters Nat. Bank & Trust Co., Rocky Mount. Bd. dirs. Rocky Mount area Wesleyan Coll. Found., 1971—, pres., 1973-74; bd. dirs. United Fund, 1971-73. Served to capt. USMCR, 1961-64. Mem. N.C. Health Care Facilities Assn. (pres. East dist. 1967-68, treas. 1968-69, sec. 1969-70, dir. 1967-70), Sigma Phi Epsilon. Republican. Episcopalian. Kiwanian. Club: Benvenue Country (dir.). Home: 165 Candlewood Rd Rocky Mount NC 27801 Office: 3801 Sunset Av W Rocky Mount NC 27801

DUNN, MICHAEL KIELLY, steel tower mfg. co. exec.; b. Sentinel, Okla., Apr. 22, 1943; s. Robert Patrick and Marion Mildred (Morris) D.; B.S. (real estate fellow), U. Okla., 1965; m. Mary Ballow Hammer, July 16, 1966; 1 dau., Amy Michelle. Accountant, auditor Peat Marwick, Mitchell & Co., C.P.A.'s, Houston, 1968-71; sec.-treas. Tenn-Tex Alloy Corp. of Houston, 1971-72; partner firm Laurel, Dunn & Co., C.P.A.'s, Houston, 1972—; financial v.p. Allied Tower Co. Inc., Houston, 1972—, dir., 1973—; financial cons. Tenn-Tex Alloy Corp., Rig A Lite Inc., both Houston. Trustee, bd. dirs. Calvary Mission. Served with AUS, 1965-68. C.P.A., Tex. Mem. Am. Inst. C.P.A.'s, Tex. Soc. C.P.A.'s. Home: 11407 Sandstone St Houston TX 77072 Office: 11105 Bellaire Blvd Houston TX 77072

DUNN, NEAL JOSEPH, lawyer; b. Steubenville, O., Oct. 26, 1919; s. Neal Joseph and Anna (Behne) D.; student Ohio State U., 1937-46; LL.B., U. Miami, 1951; m. Rose Camp; children—Felisa Ayn, Ayn, Alan Reid. Admitted to Fla. bar, 1951; gen. practice Miami, 1951—. Served with AUS, 1942-46. Club: Clewiston (Fla.) Country. Home: 3300 Spanish Moss Terrace Apt 404 Lauderhille FL 33313 Office: 23 NW Le Jeune Rd Miami FL 33126

DUNN, THOMAS T(INSLEY), lawyer; b. Petersburg, Va., Aug. 27, 1901; s. George W. and Emma (Tinsley) D.; B.S., U. Va., 1925, LL.B., 1926; m. Elizabeth Campbell, Dec. 31, 1927; children—Janet E., Thomas C. Asst. trust officer First Nat. Bank, St. Petersburg, Fla., 1926-30; v.p., trust officer United Savs. Bank, Detroit, 1930-35; asst. v.p. Pub. Nat. Bank & Trust Co., N.Y., 1935-36; dir. trust new bus. Citizens and So. Nat. Bank, Atlanta, 1938-41; v.p., trust officer First Nat. Bank, St. Petersburg, 1941-54; practice law, 1954—. Co-founder Goodwill Industries-Suncoast, Inc. Republican primary candidate U.S. Congress, 1954. Mem. Am. Judicature Soc., Fla., Va. bars, Am. Bar Assn., S.A.R., Soc. Mayflower Descs., Huguenot Soc., Newcomen Soc. N.Am., Alpha Chi Rho, Phi Alpha Delta. Clubs: St. Petersburg Yacht, Bath. Co-author: Trust Accounting Act, 1951. Contbr. articles to profl. jours. Home: 7400 Sun Island Dr S St Petersburg FL 33707 Office: 3023 Central Av St Petersburg FL 33713

DUNN, WILLIAM EDWARD, trade assn. exec.; b. Ohio, Ill., July 30, 1909; s. James Patrick and Anna (Manning) D.; LL.B., DePaul U., 1937; m. Margaret Lyons, Apr. 19, 1937; children—James Albert, Mary Virginia (Mrs. Robert T. Metz), William Frederick, Roger, Mary Suzanne. Admitted to Ill. bar, 1937, U.S. Supreme Ct., 1947; practice in Chgo., 1937-44; regional atty. WLB, Chgo., 1945-46; mem. staff Asso. Gen. Contractors Am., Washington, 1946—, exec. dir., 1961-72, exec. v.p., 1972—. Mem. Pres.'s Missile Sites Labor Commn., 1962—; mem. nat. coms. apprenticeship and tng. Labor Dept., 1961—; dir. Programs Safety in Constrn., 1960—; mem. Citizen's Adv. Com. on Transp. Quality. Clubs: Nat. Lawyers, Georgetown (Washington); Moles (N.Y.C.). Home: 4828 Fort Sumner Dr Washington DC 20016 Office: 1957 E St NW Washington DC 20006

DUNN, (WILLIAM) EDWIN, communications exec.; b. Cleveland, Miss., Aug. 21, 1938; s. Sam Edwin and Rachel (Reed) D.; B.A., Memphis State U., 1959. Copywriter radio sta. WCLD, Cleveland, Miss., 1959-60; mgr. radio sta. WOLT, Indianola, Miss., 1960-61; writer Delta-Democrat Times, Greenville, Miss., 1961-63; edn. editor Memphis Press-Scimitar, 1963-69, bus. editor, 1969-73; dir. communications Bell, Norfleet Enterprises, Memphis, 1973—. Recipient Superior Writing award Tenn. Edn. Assn., 1965; Sch. Bell award Memphis Edn. Assn., 1966. Mem. Edn. Writers Assn., Maywood Civic Club. Home: 1746 Peach St Memphis TN 38112 Office: 3003 Airways Memphis TN 38130

DUNN, WILLIAM HARP, constrn. co. exec.; b. nr. Salisbury, N.C., Nov. 17, 1935; s. Robert Ernest and Frances Eltra (Harp) D.; B.S. in Civil Engring. with honors, N.C. State U., 1957; m. Molly Ann Elledge, Sept. 9, 1956; children—Leo Elledge, Jennifer Ann, Sally Mae. Draftsman, J.N. Pease Co., architects and engrs., Charlotte, N.C., 1957-58; estimator C.D. Spangler Co., Charlotte, 1958-61; v.p. estimating and engring. Foster-Sturdivant Co., Inc., North Wilkesboro, N.C., 1961-72, pres., 1972—, also dir.; dir. Sturdivant Devel. Co. Mem. bd. commrs. Redevel. Commn., North Wilkesboro, 1967—, sec., 1968-71; active Boy Scouts Am., 1948—, committeeman Old Hickory council Boy Scouts Am., 1969—. Mem. Profl. Constrn. Estimators Assn., Wikes C. of C. (v.p. 1973), Home Builders Assn. (sec. 1968-70; pres. 1971). Republican. Methodist. Mason. Home: 76 Townsend St North Wilkesboro NC 28659 Office: Box 1009 North Wilkesboro NC 28659

DUNN, WILLIAM LEROY, ret. physician; b. Gordonsville, Va., Aug. 30, 1899; s. William Melville and Vira Ellis (Hunter) D.; student Randolph-Macon Coll., 1915-18; B.A., U. Va., 1919, M.A., 1922, M.D., 1926; m. Thelma Flournoy Brumfield, Dec. 26, 1929; children—William Hunter, John Thornton, Mary Flournoy (Mrs. Thomas R. Degges). Intern Blue Ridge Sanatorium, Charlottesville, Va., 1926, St. Luke's Hosp., N.Y.C., 1927-29; resident Tb div. Bellevue Hosp., N.Y.C., 1929-30; practice medicine specializing in internal medicine, Washington, 1930-71; clin. instr. medicine George Washington U., Washington, 1930-36; attending physician Chest Clinic, Washington, 1936-57; attending physician Garfield Hosp., Washington, 1938-58; sr. attending physician Washington Hosp. Center, 1958-71, Doctor's Hosp., Washington, 1965—; cons. chest diseases S.S.S., Washington, 1940-50. Served with U.S. Army, 1918. Diplomate Am. Bd. Internal Medicine. Fellow A.C.P., Am. Coll. Chest Physicians; mem. A.M.A., Med. Soc. D.C. (pres. 1959), So. Med. Assn., Am. Thoracic Soc., Am. Soc. Internal Medicine, Phi Beta Kappa, Alpha Omega Alpha. Contbr. articles to prof. jours. Home: 1604 Jamestown Dr Charlottesville VA 22901

DUNN, WILLIAM ROBERT, supt. edn.; b. Shoals Junction, S.C., Mar. 21, 1911; s. Larkin Barmore and Sara E. (Barmore) D.; B.S., U. S.C., 1933, LL.B., 1935; m. Ruth E. Polatty, June 23, 1943; children—Jane Barmore, William Robert. Admitted to S.C. bar, 1935; practice law, Greenwood, 1935-41; county supt. edn. Greenwood County, 1943-71; asst. supt. for bus. Greenwood Sch. Dist. 50, 1971—. Chmn. Greenwood County Bd. Edn., 1943-65. Served with AUS, 1941-43. Mem. N.E.A., S.C., Greenwood County edn. assns., Am. Legion (past adj.), S.C. Assn. County Supts. (pres. 1960), Am. Assn. Sch. Adminstrs., S.C. Bar. Baptist. Club: Greenwood Kiwanis (sec.-treas. 1952—). Home: 223 Gracemont Dr Greenwood SC 29646 Office: Adminstrv Bldg Magnolia St Greenwood SC 29646

DUNN, WILLIAM RUFUS, broadcasting exec.; b. El Paso, Tex., Mar. 23, 1938; s. Rufus Monroe and Hazel Kathrine (Bolton) D.; grad. high sch.; m. Virginia Fabela, Dec. 30, 1966; children—Diedra Jilene, Marissa Kai. Dir., KROD-TV, Trigg Vaughn Broadcasting Co., El Paso, 1960-67; operations mgr., programming mgr. Doubleday Broadcasting Co., Dallas, 1967-73; account exec. KPLX-FM, Susquehanna Broadcasting Co., Ft. Worth, 1974—. Mem. TV Cluster adv. com. Skyline High Sch. Career Devel. Center, Dallas, 1970—. Vice pres., bd. dirs. Dallas Ballet Theatre, 1973-74. Served with USNR, 1956-58. Home: 12228 High Meadow St Dallas TX 75234 Office: 6465 Spur 303 Fort Worth TX 76112

DUNN, WINFIELD, gov. Tenn.; b. Meridian, Miss., July 1, 1927; s. Aubert C. and Dorothy (Crum) D.; B.B.A., U. Miss.; postgrad. Memphis State U.; D.D.S., U. Tenn.; m. Betty Jane Prichard, Dec. 30, 1950; children—Charles W., Donna Gayle, Julie Claire. Field rep. Aetna Casualty & Surety Co., New Orleans, 1950-51; practice gen. dentistry Memphis, 1956-70; gov. Tenn., 1970—. Chmn. Tenn.-Tombigbee Waterway Devel. Authority; chmn. Edn. Commn. States. Chmn. Shelby County (Tenn.) Republican Com., 1964-68, mem. exec. com., 1962-70; chmn. Rep. Govs. Assn. Trustee Memphis-Shelby County Hosp., 1968-70. Served with USNR, 1945-47. Mem. Am., Tenn. dental assns., Memphis Dental Soc., Kappa Alpha, Omicron Kappa Upsilon, Omicron Delta Kappa, Delta Sigma Delta, Delta Sigma Pi. Home: Governor's Mansion Curtiswood Lane Nashville TN 37204 Office: State Capitol Nashville TN 37219

DUNNING, WILHELMINA FRANCES, cancer researcher, pathologist; b. Topsham, Me., Sept. 12, 1904; d. Fred J. and Evelyn (Williams) Dunning; A.B., U. Me., 1926, D.Sc., 1960; M.A., Columbia, 1928, Ph.D., 1932. Asso. cancer research Columbia, 1930-41; instr. pathology Wayne State U., 1941-48, asst. prof. oncology, 1948-50; asso. cancer research Detroit Inst. Cancer Research, 1944-50; prof. zoology U. Miami, 1950-52, research prof. exptl. pathology 1952—, dir. cancer research lab., 1950-71, sr. scientist Papanicolaou Cancer Research Inst., 1971—. Mem. bd. dirs. Coconut Grove Civic Club, Coconut Grove Residents Club. Mem. A.A.A.S., Am. Assn. for Cancer Research (dir.), Am. Soc. Zoologists, Genetics Soc. Am., Soc. for Exptl. Biology and Medicine, N.Y. Acad. Scis. Club: Pilot (Miami). Home: 2850 Coconut Av Miami FL 33133 Office: Papanicolaou Cancer Research Inst 1155 NW 14th St Miami FL 33136

DUNSTAN, EDGAR MULLINS, med. cons.; b. Rio de Janeiro, Brazil, Mar. 7, 1902 (parents Am. citizens); s. Albert Lafayette and Sarah (Silvey) D.; B.S., U. Ga., 1923; M.A., Mercer U., 1924; M.D., Emory U., 1928; m. Florene Anita Johnson, Aug. 26, 1926; 1 dau., Dorothy Florence (Mrs. Walter E. Brown). Intern, Ga. Bapt. Hosp., Atlanta, 1928-29; resident Elkins (W.Va.) City Hosp., 1929-31; chief resident Baylor U. Hosp., Dallas, 1930-31; practice medicine specializing in internal medicine, Atlanta, 1946-70; cons. VA Hosp., Atlanta, 1970—; instr. internal medicine med. sch. Emory U., Atlanta, 1946-70. Active Civil Def., Atlanta. Served with M.C., AUS, 1941-46. Recipient Aven Citizenship Cup, Fulton County Med. Soc., 1955. Diplomate Am. Bd. Internal Medicine. Fellow A.C.P.; mem. A.M.A., Am. Heart Assn. Democrat. Baptist (deacon). Contbr. articles to prof. jours. Home: 710 Pinetree Dr Decatur GA 30030 Office: VA Hosp 1670 Clairmont Rd Decatur GA 30033

DUNSTAN, FLORENE JOHNSON, educator; b. Baxley, Ga., Mar. 21, 1904; d. Joseph James and Emma Frances (Nash) Johnson; A.B., Tift Coll., 1924; M.A., So. Meth. U., 1932; Ph.D., U. Tex., 1936; postgrad. U. Madrid, 1951, Nat. U. Mexico, 1932-44, U. Paris, 1938; m. Edgar Edgar Mullins Dunstan, Aug. 26, 1926; 1 dau., Dorothy Florene (Mrs. Walter E. Brown). Instr. romance langs. So. Meth. U., 1936-41; instr. Spanish, Agnes Scott Coll., Decatur, Ga., 1941-43, asst. prof., 1943-51, prof., chmn. dept. Spanish, 1966—. Mem. budget com. Met. Atlanta Community Service, 1956-57; exec. com. Atlanta Com. for Internat. Visitors. Trustee Tift Coll., 1948-54, 71—. Recipient Carnegie research grant, Brazil, 1949, Spain, 1951; named Atlanta Woman of Yr. in Edn., 1963. Mem. Am. Assn. Tchrs. Spanish and Portuguese (Ga. pres. 1965-67), South Atlantic Modern Lang. Assn., UN Assn. U.S.A., Am. Assn. U. Women (past pres. Atlanta br., exec. bd.; area chmn. Ga. div.), English-Speaking Union, Cirulo Hispano-Americano, D.A.R. Am. Assn. U. Profs. (pres. local chpt. 1968-69), U.D.C. Baptist. Clubs: Woman's, Pan American (chmn. internat. affairs dept.; past pres.) (Atlanta). Home: 710 Pinetree Dr Decatur GA 30030

DUNTON, JAMES GERALD, assn. exec.; b. Circleville, O., Nov. 10, 1899; s. Oscar Howard and Florence (Nightengale) D.; A.B., Harvard, 1923, M.Ed., 1928; m. Dorothy Winfough, Oct. 10, 1944. Free lance author, 1925-34; Fed. Projects dir., Ohio, 1935-37; spl. rep. Fed. N.W. Terr. Sesquicentennial Commn., 1938; editor Ohio Democracy, 1939-40; Ohio field rep. Office Govt. Reports, Exec. Office of Pres., 1940-41; dir. spl. activities Office Sec. Def., 1950-61; exec. dir. Va. Nursing Home Assn., 1965—; Washington rep. Am. Chess Found., 1962—; adv. council Oliver Wendell Holmes Assn., 1966—. Mem. vets. com. Presdl. Inaugurations, 1965, 69; pres. Nat. Capital U.S.O., Washington, 1966-67; mem. Nat. Council of U.S.O., 1966—; Va. State Adv. Com. Adult Services, 1972; distinguished sponsor 100th Anniversary 1st Battle of Bull Run, 1961. Served with Ambulance Corps, A.E.F., U.S. Army, 1918-19, to maj. AUS, World War II. Recipient certificate of appreciation Nat. Press Club, 1955, Commendation award Pres.'s Com. on Employment of Handicapped, 1963; decorated Army Commendation medal. Mem. Nat. Assn. Execs. Club, Am. Legion, Vets. World War I (dir. pub. relations 1969), V.F.W., Res. Officers Assn., Va. Soc. Assn. Execs., Mil. Order World Wars, Ohio Soc. Washington, Soc. of Va. Presbyn. (elder). Club: Harvard (Washington). Author: Wild Asses, 1925; Murders in Lovers Lane, 1927; Maid and a Million Men, 1928; Counterfeit Wife, 1930; Honey's Money, 1933; Queen's Harem, 1933; (anthology) C'est La Guerre, 1927. Contbr. articles to mags., newspapers. Address: 2820 Bisvey Dr Falls Church VA 22042

DUNWODY, EUGENE COX, architect; b. Macon, Ga., July 19, 1933; s. W. Elliott and Mary Bennet (Cox) D.; B.S., Ga. Inst. Tech., 1955, B.Arch., 1956; m. Susan Howe Foxworth, June 15, 1957; children—Susan Howe, Eugene Cox, George Foxworth, Mary Bennet Cox. With archtl. firm W. Elliott Dunwody, Jr. Architect Inc., and successor Dunwody Dunwody & Assos. Architects, Inc., Macon, Ga., 1959-69, 1st v.p., treas., 1966; pres. Dunwody & Co., Architects, 1969—. Chmn. Macon Bibb County Planning and Zoning Commn. Trustee United Givers Fund; pres. Macon Nursery Schs., Inc. Served with C.E.C., USNR, 1956-59. Mem. A.I.A., Constrn. Specifications Inst. (past pres. Macon chpt.), Kappa Alpha. Presbyn. Rotarian (pres. 1973-74). Home: 330 Wesleyan Dr Macon GA 31204 Office: 205 Broadway Macon GA 31201

DUNWODY, KENNETH WEBSTER, brick and tile mfg. co. exec.; b. Macon, Ga., Apr. 12, 1897; s. William Elliott and Elizabeth Lowe (Webster) D.; B.M.E., Ga. Sch. Tech., 1918; student U. Ill., 1926, Ohio State U., 1927, U. Wis., 1923; m. Pauline Coleman Hinkle, June 24, 1920; children—Elizabeth (Mrs. Thomas Alfred Sams), Kenneth Webster. With Cherokee Brick & Tile Co., Macon, Ga., 1918—, various positions, 1918-44, v.p., 1944-48, pres., 1948-58, chmn. bd. dirs., 1958—; v.p., dir. West Coast Land Co., Tampa, Fla., 1957—; v.p., dir. East Side Water Co., Tampa, Fla., 1957—; v.p., dir. Coleman, Meadows, Pate Drug Co., Macon, Ga., 1950—; dir. Ga., So. & Fla. Ry. Co., Macon, Ga., 1962—, Mid-Atlanta Investment Co., Atlanta, 1966—, Interstate Motor Hotels, 1965—. Mem. council Ga. Found. for Ind. Colls., 1959-60; bd. dirs. Exec. Equities, Atlanta, Ga.; bd. mgrs. Assn. County Commnrs. Ga., Atlanta, 1950—; mem. rds. and hwys. com. Nat. Assn. County Ofcls., 1958-60; chmn. Ga. State Toll Bridge Com., 1952-62. Mem. So. Brick & Tile Mfrs. Assn. (pres. 1948-49, 1952-53, v.p. 1950-51, dir. 1950—), Structural Clay Products Inst. (pres. 1957-59, v.p. 1956-57, dir. 1953), Nat. Assn. Mfrs. (mem. indsl. relations com. 1955—), Am. Ceramic Soc., Am. Soc. Testing Materials (1st vice-chmn. 1972—), Am. Legion, Kappa Alpha. Democrat. Presbyn. (elder 1965—, trustee 1953—). Rotarian. Home: 4727 Rivoli Dr Macon GA 31204 Office: PO Box 4567 Macon GA 31208

DUPEPE, F(RANK) CLANCY, lawyer, real estate exec.; b. New Orleans, Mar. 6, 1934; s. Vernon Wilfred and Eunice (Clancy) D.; B.A., Tulane U., 1955; LL.B., Loyola U., 1962; m. Susan Fautt; children—Michele Tanguis, Mignon Wattigny, Andree Nicole. Tchr., Jefferson Parish (La.) Sch. System, 1958-60; admitted to La. bar, 1962; practiced in New Orleans, 1962—; pres. Dupepe and Assos., Ltd., New Orleans, 1971—; chmn. bd. Provincial Motor Hotels, Inc., 1962—; pres. La. Boucherie, Inc., Duman Investments, Inc.; pres., dir. Mchts. Trust & Savs. Bank; treas., dir. French Market Corp. Chmn. La. State Museum Bd.; treas., bd. dirs. Greater New Orleans Tourist and Conv. Commn. Served to 1st lt. USMCR, 1955-58. Mem. S.A.R., Order Stars and Bars, Sons Confederate Vets., La. Bar Assn., Tulane, Loyola alumni assns., C. of C. Clubs: Le Moyne de Bienville, Iris, Bacchus. Home: 5420 Camp St New Orleans LA 70115 Office: 337 Chartres St New Orleans LA 70130

DUPONT, MARTHA ANNE CAROLINE VERGE (MRS. HENRY ELEUTHÈRE IRÉNEE DUPONT), civic worker; b. Long Beach, Cal.; d. William E. and Martha Anne Caroline (Bready) Verge; student Notre Dame Acad., 1949-53; children—Catherine Foree, Christopher Hans, William Garey, Martha Anne Caroline, Henri Verge; m. 2d, Henry Eleuthére Irénee duPont, Sept. 25, 1967; children—Sophie Madeleine, Henry Eluethere Irenee. Founder Del. Pony Club, Wilmington, 1959; pres. Council of Agys. on Children and Youth, 1970-74; mem. Mental Health Assn. Del., 1964-74. Trustee Nat. Council on Crime and Delinquency, mem. exec. com., 1964-74; trustee; pres., chmn. Child Found., 1963-74; founder, pres. Del. Council Agys. Children and Youth, 1970-74. Mem. Del. Hist. Soc. Clubs: Wilmington Country; Annapolis (Md.) Yacht; Talbot Country (Easton, Md.). Address: Box 4000 "Montmorency" Greenville DE 19807 (summer) Gemini Manalapan FL

DUPRÉ, GRACE ANNETTE, portrait painter; b. Spartanburg, S.C.; d. Daniel Allston and Helen Capers (Stevens) DuPre; student Converse Coll. and Converse Coll. Sch. Music. Grand Central Sch. Art, 1931-32; pvt. studies various tchrs., including Wayman Adams and Frank V. DuMond. Solo violinist, tchr. violin, painter, 1932—. Several one man shows; exhibited Fine Arts League of Carolinas, Gibbs Art Gallery, Mint Museum, Charlotte, Blue Ridge, N.C., Allied Artists Am., Nat. Arts Club, Audubon Artists, Am. Artists Profl. League, Ogunquit (Me.) Nat. Exhbn. Paintings; portraits include judges of U.S. Ct. Appeals, 7th Circuit, Chgo., chief justice S.C. Supreme Ct., pres. of Wofford Coll., gov. of S.C., others; portraits in permanent collections Columbia, Main P.O., N.Y.C., U. Ind. Law Bldg., White House, U.S. Supreme Ct., U.S. 7th Circuit Ct. of Appeals, Chgo., Charleston (S.C.) City Hall Collection of Portraits, S.C. State House, numerous pub. and ednl. instns., pvt. collections. Recipient various awards including award 31st Ann. Exhbn. Am. Paintings, Ogonquit, Me., 1951, portrait prize Catherine Lorillard Wolfe Art Club ann. show N.Y.C., 1955. Mem. M.B.L.S. Mem. Grand Central Art Galleries, Inc., Pen and Brush, Nat. Arts Club N.Y.C., Am. Artists Profl. League (nat. exec. bd.), Allied Artists Am., Carolina Art Assn., Gramercy Park Assn., Huguenot Soc. S.C., Portraits, Inc. Clubs: Woman's Music (Spartanburg, S.C.); Catherine Lorillard Wolfe Art (N.Y.C.). Studio: 361 Mills Av Spartanburg SC 29302 also 302 S Pine St Spartanburg SC 29302

DUPREE, JAMES HENRY, retail trade exec.; b. N.C., June 28, 1929; s. Paul Earnest and Dixie Pauline (Lamm) D.; grad. high sch.; m. Frances Deloris Mayo, Nov. 12, 1950; children—Kimberly Ann, Connie Frances. Asst. office mgr. Nat. Biscuit Co., Greenville, N.C., 1947-52; bookkeeper M.O. Blount & Sons, Bethel, N.C., 1954-60; gen. mdse. gen. mgr., sec. L.J. Whitehurst & Sons, Inc., Bethel, 1960-64; gen. mdse. sec., mgmt. exec. M.O. Blount & Sons, Inc., Bethel, 1964—, Blount Fertilizer Co., Inc., Greenville, N.C., 1964—, Allied Petroleum Corp., Greenville, N.C., 1965—, Ayden Tractors, Inc. (N.C.), 1965—; v.p. Superior Wholesale Distbg., Inc., Bethel, 1968—. Dir. Mut. Tobacco Barn Fire Ins. Assn., Robersonville, N.C. Sec., treas. Bethel Little League, 1958-60; commr. Town of Bethel, 1969—, mayor, 1971—. Bd. dirs. Greenville Christian Acad., Bethel Better Bus. Bur. Served with AUS, 1952-54. Baptist (treas. 1958-69). Rotarian, Lion (sec. Bethel 1957-58). Home: McWhorter St Bethel NC 27812 Office: 225 W Railroad St Bethel NC 27812

DUPRIEST, BETTE RUTH HORTON (MRS. DENNIS BLACK DUPRIEST, JR.), club woman; b. Dallas, June 8, 1922; d. Frederick Reece and Frances Mellersh (Martyn) Horton; student Tex. State Coll. Women, 1941; B.A. in Spanish, B.S. in Journalism, So. Meth. U., 1944; m. Dennis Black DuPriest, Jr., Nov. 28, 1958. Mem. staff Internat. News Service, Dallas, 1944-45, Dallas Morning News, 1945-49; with Petroleum Engr. Pub. Co., Dallas, 1955-57; translator Spanish and French letters Trinity Portland Cement div. Gen. Portland Cement Co., Dallas, 1950-58. Recipient Sigma Delta Chi scholastic award, 1944. Chpt. pres. Delta Zeta, 1942-44, mem. chpt. alumnae adv. bd., 1950-53, 67-68, Dallas chpt. pres., 1955-56; corr. sec., pub. relations chmn. Maj. James McGregor chpt. Colonial Dames of XVII Century, 1967-69, curator, 1969-73. Mem. Magna Charta Dames (registrar 1970-72, historian 1974-76), Local History and Geneal. Soc., Colonial Order of Crown, Order of Washington, Sovereign Colonial Soc., Ams. Royal Descent, Tenn. Geneal. Soc., Maury County Hist. Soc., Script and Score, Mortar Bd., Nat. Trust Historic Preservation, Sigma Delta Pi, Pi Sigma Alpha, Theta Sigma Phi. Presbyn. Home: 5621 McCommas Av Dallas TX 75206

DUPUIS, ROBERT THOMSEN, constrn. co. exec.; b. Chgo., Aug. 25, 1937; s. Robert Newell and Eleanor (Thomsen) DuP.; B.S., Davidson Coll., 1959; M.B.A., Columbia, 1963; m. Patty Willis Pendleton, June 24, 1961; children—Robert Thomsen, Arthur P., Andrew W. Sales engr. E.I. duPont de Nemours & Co., Wilmington, Del., 1963-68; v.p., sec., dir. Pendleton Constrn. Corp., Wytheville, Va., 1968—; pres. Southwestern Devel. Corp., 1971—. Commr., Wythe County Planning Bd., 1970—. Treas., bd. dirs. Pendleton Constrn. Corp. Found.; bd. dirs. Wythe County Community Hosp. Served with C.E., AUS, 1959-61. Mem. Am., Va. rd. builders assns., Va. Asphalt Assn., Gt. Lakes to Fla. Hwy. Assn., Wythe County C. of C., Eumanean Soc., Alpha Tau Omega, Gamma Sigma Upsilon, Delta Phi Alpha, Alpha Epsilon Delta. Rotarian. Club: Wytheville Country. Author: (with others) Linen Supply News, 1966-68. Home: 360 Withers Rd Wytheville VA 24382 Office: Box 549 Wytheville VA 24382

DUPUY, BURTON PAUL, JR., optometrist; b. Bunkie, La., Sept. 27, 1919; s. Burton Paul and Mary Elizabeth (Helm) D.; student Southwestern La. Inst., 1937-39, 48-49; B.S., So. Coll. Optometry, 1953, Dr. Optometry, 1953; m. Yvonne Walther, July 24, 1947; children—Burton Paul III, Mary Lynn, Lillian Alice, Yvonne Patrice, Marc Walther. Practice optometry with Dr. Carlyle Bordelon, Lake Charles, La., 1954; pvt. practice optometry, Natchitoches, La., 1954—. Pres., La. Bd. Examiners in Optometry, 1970-72, sec.-treas., 1973-74. Pres., Natchitoches Parish Assn. for Retarded Children, 1959. Served to lt. col. USAAF, 1940-46. Named La. Optometrist of Year, 1962. Mem. La. Assn. Optometrists (pres. 1960, exec. sec. 1961-64). Episcopalian. Club: Natchitoches Civitan (pres. 1962). Address, PO Box 2656 Natchitoches LA 71457

DUQUE, HOMER ADOLPH, city ofcl.; b. Belcher, La., Mar. 27, 1918; s. Adolph and Ann (Bullard) D.; student La. Poly., 1939-40; B.A., Centenary Coll., La., 1947; m. Melba Juanita Sisemore, Feb. 15, 1940; 1 dau., Melba Kathryn. Dist. mgr. Shreveport Times, 1946-50; mgr. B.H. Rainwater Ins. Agy., Ruston, La., 1950-55; exec. dir. Ruston Housing Authority, 1956—. Sec., v.p., pres. Housing Council La., 1967—. Served with USNR, 1943-45; PTO. Mem. Nat. Assn. Housing and Redevel. Ofcls., Am. Legion, V.F.W. Democrat. Baptist. Home: 1805 Huey Dr Ruston LA 71270 Office: 615 N Farmerville St Ruston LA 71270

DURAN, OTIS S(AMUEL), ins. and real estate broker; b. nr. Haywood, Okla., Dec. 17, 1911; s. Montgomery Samuel and Fannie (Plunkett) D.; student Hershey Bus. Coll., 1930-32, Walton Sch. Commerce, 1932-34; m. Alberta Mary Sites, June 21, 1932; children—Sim, Annette; m. 2d. Evelyn Sewell, Oct. 7, 1946; children—Robert, Christine; 1 stepdau., Mrs. Mary Minyard, Mgr. Duran & Duran, ins. and real estate brokers, 1930—; owner, also mgr. Duran Investment Co., McAlester, Okla.; pres. Duran Mortgage Co., Inc., McAlester; partner McAlester Devel. Co.; sec.-treas. Profl. Bldg. of McAlester, Inc.; dir. First Nat. Bank of McAlester. Councilman, McAlester, 1948-53. Pres. Berry Manor Nursing Home, McAlester; active Boy Scouts Am.; bd. dirs. McAlester United Fund, pres., 1962; v.p. McAlester Ambulance Authority; Bd. dirs. McAlester Boys Club, pres., 1968; bd. dirs. Bapt. Found. Okla., 1971—; trustee McAlester Hosp. Found., McAlester Gen. Hosp. (pres. 1957—); adv. bd. Kiamichi Vo-Tech Schs. Served in USAF, 1943-45. Dir., officer Jr. C. of C., 1933-42. Mem. Okla. Assn. for Crippled Children (life mem.), Okla. Assn. Real Estate Bds. (dir. 1953-62), McAlester Bd. Realtors (pres. 1954-55, 68-69), Eastern Okla. Frontiers Sci. (charter), C. of C. (pres. 1959, dir.), McAlester Ins. Assn. (pres. 1962), Am. Legion, V.F.W. (trustee 1946—), Navy League. Baptist (deacon, trustee, pres. Brotherhood 1967, 68). Mason (32 deg., Shriner), Rotarian (pres. 1955-56). Club: Knife and Fork (pres. 1958). Home: Red Bud at Hickory Bend McAlester OK 74501 Office: Profl Bldg 10 E Washington McAlester OK 74501

DURAND, GERALD CLIFFORD, r.r. exec.; b. Atlanta, Apr. 25, 1937; s. Howard Taft and Lois Lucille (Paden) D.; B.S., Ga. Inst. Tech., 1961; m. Sandra Barbara Slate, May 25, 1957; children—Deborah Elaine, Michael Jeffrey, Deanna Leigh. Engring. technician Lockheed Ga. Co., Marietta, 1959-61; with So. Ry. Co., Atlanta, 1961—, asst. v.p., 1969—. Tchr. computer programming Atlanta Area Tech. Sch., 1972. Mem. Assn. for Computing Machinery, Data Processing Mgmt. Assn., Atlanta Rail Exec. Club (pres. 1973). Home: 450 Safari Circle Stone Mountain GA 30083 Office: 125 Spring St Atlanta GA 30303

DURANT, JOHN RIDGWAY, physician; b. Ann Arbor, Mich., July 29, 1930; s. Thomas Morton and Jean (deVries) D.; B.A., Swarthmore Coll., 1952; M.D., Temple U., 1956; m. Ruth Wolfe, Dec. 28, 1954 (div. July 1973); children—Christine Joy, Thomas Arthur, Michele Grace. Intern Hartford (Conn.) Hosp., 1956-57, jr. asst. resident in medicine, 1957-58; resident in medicine Temple U. Med. Center, Phila., 1960-62; spl. fellow in med. neoplasia Meml. Hosp., N.Y.C., 1962-63; Am. Cancer Soc. advanced clin. fellow Temple U. Health Scis. Center, Phila., 1964-67, instr. medicine, 1963-65, asst. prof. medicine, 1965-67; clin. asso. chemotherapy Moss Rehab. Hosp., Phila., 1964-67; instr. medicine, 1963-65, asst. prof. medicine, 1965-67; clin. asso. chemotherapy Moss Rehab. Hosp., Phila., 1964-67; research asso. Fels Research Inst., Phila., 1965-67; asso. prof. medicine U. Ala. Med. Center, Birmingham, 1968-70, head sec. oncology, div. hematology, dept. medicine, 1968-69, dir. div. hematology-oncology, 1969-71, dir. cancer tng. grant, 1968-70, prof. medicine, 1970—, asso. dir. for cancer, 1968—, dir. cancer research and tng. program, 1970—; mem. staff Univ. Hosp., Birmingham, 1968—; cons. VA Hosp., Tuskegee, Ala., 1970—. Mem. external rev. com. cancer program, Howard U., Washington, 1972—; mem. external rev. com. U. Tenn., 1972—, Wilmington (Del.) Med. Center, 1972—, U. Louisville, 1973—; mem. extramural adv. com. Boston U., 1972—; chmn. extramural adv. com. Med. Coll. S.C., 1973—; chmn. extramural advisors Med. Coll. Va., 1973—. Served with USNR, 1958-60. Bd. dirs. Ala. div., Am. Cancer Soc., pres., 1973, also mem. advanced clin. fellowship com.; mem. exec. com. Southeastern Cancer Chemotherapy Study Group. Diplomate Am. Bd. Internal Medicine. Fellow A.C.P.; mem. Am. Fedn. Clin. Research, Am. Assn. Cancer Research, Am. Assn. Cancer Edn., James Ewing Soc., Soc. Clin. Investigation, A.A.A.S., Am. Soc. Clin. Oncology, Am. Soc. Hematology, Alpha Omega Alpha. Author: (With R.V. Smalley): The Chronic Leukemias—Chemistry, Pathophysiology and Treatment,

1972. Contbr. numerous articles to med., sci. and profl. jours. Home: 1105 Altadena Rise Birmingham AL 35243

DURANT, PAUL DILLINGHAM, II, ins. co. exec.; b. Ann Arbor, Mich., Feb. 20, 1931; s. Wentworth Tenney and Katherine (Henning) D.; B.B.A., North Tex. State U., 1958; m. Carolyn Peterson, June 2, 1967; 1 son, Jon Paul. Staff accountant Peat, Marwick, Mitchell & Co., Dallas, 1958-59; comptroller Steere Tank Lines, Inc., Dallas, 1959-64; accountant Paul D. Durant, C.P.A., Dallas, 1964-65; v.p., controller, asst. treas. Gt. Commonwealth Life Ins. Co., Dallas, 1965-68; pres., dir. Investers Found. Life Ins. Co., Dallas, 1969; cons. Finance and Acquisitions, Dallas, 1968-69; exec. v.p., treas., dir., co-founder Am. Bus. & Comml. Life Ins. Co., Dallas, 1969-73; Controller, asst. v.p. Southland Life Ins. Co., 1973—. Served with Signal Corps, AUS, 1951-53. Mem. Am. Inst. C.P.A.'s, Am. Accounting Assn., Tex. Soc. C.P.A.'s. Methodist. Club: Lancers. Home: 6905 Kingsbury Dr Dallas TX 75231 Office: Southland Center Dallas TX 75201

DURANT, WENTWORTH T(ENNEY), lawyer; b. Milw., Sept. 27, 1907; s. Paul Dillingham and Frances Josephine (Linck) D.; A.B., U. Mich., 1930, LL.B., 1932; postgrad. So. Meth. U., 1950-51; m. Katherine Louise Henning, Feb. 8, 1926 (dec. 1971); children—Paul II, Patricia, Wentworth, Frederick; m. 2d, Lucille D. Lang, Aug. 4, 1972. Admitted to Mich., Wis. bars, 1933, D.C. bar, 1944, Tex. bar, 1949; practiced in Milw., 1933-43; with law office Robert Ash, Washington, 1944-48; partner Durant, Mankoff, Davis & Wolens, and predecessor firms, practice restricted to tax law field, Dallas; lectr. fed. taxation N.Y. Inst., 1948, Am. U., 1948, Southwestern Legal Found., First Ann. Inst. Fed. Taxation, 1949, So. Meth. U. Law Sch., 1952, Tex. Technol. Tax Inst., 1962. Mem. Am. (mem. tax ct. procedure sect. taxation 1948-70), Dallas bar assns., State Bar Tex. Mason. Contbg. author Handbook of Tax Techniques, 1951. Contbr. articles to legal mags. Home: 10740 Pagewood St Dallas TX 75230 Office: 1st Nat Bank Bldg Dallas TX 75202

DURANT, WILLIAM STINSON, chem. engr.; b. Mobile, Ala., Sept. 5, 1932; s. Dolive and Winnie (Stinson) D.; B.Ch.E., Auburn U., 1953, M.Ch.E., 1955; m. Beulah Mae Williams, Dec. 26, 1959; children—Clark, Renee. Engr., E.I. duPont de Nemours & Co., Inc. Savannah River Lab., Aiken, S.C., 1955-67, sr. engr., 1967-70, sr. research engr., 1970—, cons., adv. com. for reactor safeguards, 1970. Served to capt. AUS, 1955-57. Contbr. articles to sci. jours. Home: 1828 Bolin Rd North Augusta SC 29841 Office: Savannah River Lab EI duPont Aiken SC 29841

DUREK, THOMAS ANDREW, computer exec.; b. Sharpsville, Pa., July 1, 1929; s. Joseph A. and Helen B. (Ondish) D.; B.A., Pa. State U., 1953; M.A., Baylor U., 1957; M.S., Stanford, 1959. Commd. officer USAF, 1953-65; assigned as mathematician, mgmt. sci. analyst at Hdqrs. USAF, 1959-65; head data processing and analysis space and information systems div., Project Cloud Gap, N.Am. Aviation, 1965-68; sr. staff engr. software and information systems div. TRW, Inc., Washington, 1968—; asst. prof., lectr. statistics George Washington U., 1961-66. Mem. Am. Statis. Assn., Assn. Computing Machinery, Inst. Mgmt. Scis. (treas. D.C. chpt. 1969-70, treas. internat. meeting 1971), Washington Operations Research Council. Home: 2510 Virginia Av NW Washington DC 20037 Office: Westgate Research Park McLean VA 22101

DURELL, JACK, physician; b. N.Y.C., July 5, 1928; s. Sam and Helen (Schwartzman) D.; A.B. summa cum laude, Harvard, 1949; M.D. cum laude, Yale, 1953; m. Viviane M. diGioja, May 19, 1955. Intern, USPHS Hosp., Balt., 1953-54; resident Yale Dept. Psychiatry, 1957-59; practice medicine specializing in psychiatry, Bethesda, Md., 1961-72, Washington, 1961—; mem. staff Psychiat. Inst. Washington, George Washington U. Hosp.; biochemist Nat. Inst. Mental Health, Bethesda, 1954-57, research psychiatrist, 1960-63, chief sect. on psychiatry, 1963-67; clin. dir. Psychiat. Inst., research dir. Psychiat. Inst. Found., Washington, 1967-72; med. dir. Psychiat. Inst., 1972—, pres., 1973; v.p., dir. Psychiat. Insts. Am., 1969—. Asso. clin. prof. dept. psychiatry George Washington U., Washington, 1967—. Served with USPHS, 1953-67. Recipient Anna Monica Commemorative award, 1967. Fellow Am. Psychiat. Assn.; mem. Am. Coll. Psychiatrists. Assn. Research in Nervous and Mental Diseases, Psychiat. Research Soc., N.Y. Acad. Scis., Am. Civil Liberties Union. Home: 706 Belgrove Rd McLean VA 22101 Office: 4460 MacArthur Blvd Washington DC 20007

DUREN, JOSEPH PERCY, JR., utilities co. exec.; b. Helena, Ark., Feb. 28, 1922; s. Joseph Percy and Crynn Viola (Poteete) D.; student Ark. Poly. Coll., 1940-42; m. Dorothy Helen Spears, Aug. 23, 1947; children—Deborah Jean, Joseph Percy III, Cheryl Denise, Donna Lynn. Mgr. power accounting and records Ark. Power & Light Co., Pine Bluff, 1947-71, Middle South Services, Inc., Pine Bluff, 1971—. Served with USAAF, 1942-45, USAF, 1951-52. Decorated Air medal with 2 oak leaf clusters. Mason (32 deg., Shriner). Club: Pine Bluff Arsenal Officers. Home: 311 Steve Dr Pine Bluff AR 71601 Office: PO Box 6100 Pine Bluff AR 71601

DURHAM, FRANK EDINGTON, physicist, educator; b. Jonesboro, La., July 12, 1935; s. Joseph Byron and Marylou (Edington) D.; B.S., La. Tech. U., 1956; M.A., Rice U., 1958, Ph.D. (M.D. Anderson fellow), 1960; m. Mona Henry, Aug. 5, 1956; children—Frank, Joseph, Caroline. Postdoctoral research asso. Rice U., summer, 1960; asst. prof. physics Tulane U., New Orleans, 1960-64, asso. prof., 1964-67, prof., 1967—, head arts and scis. physics, 1972—. NSF grantee in nuclear physics, 1967-72. Mem. Am. Phys. Soc., Sigma Xi. Democrat. So. Baptist. Research on nuclear structure, 1966—. Home: 1315 Broadway New Orleans LA 70118

DURHAM, HARVEY RALPH, univ. adminstr.; b. Perry, Fla., Feb. 25, 1938; s. William Ralph and Clara Elizabeth (Swift) D.; B.S., Wake Forest U., 1959; M.A., U. Ga., 1962, Ph.D., 1965; m. Susan Brooks Stephens, Aug. 31, 1963; children—William Harvey, Stephen Bryan, David Logan. Asst. prof. math. Appalachian State U., Boone, N.C., 1965-67, asso. prof. math., 1967-71, chmn. dept. math., 1967-71, asso. vice chancellor for acad. affairs, 1971—. Intern, Am. Council on Edn. acad. adminstrn. internship program Ohio U., 1969-70. Named An Outstanding Educator Am., 1973. Mem. Math. Assn. Am., Am. Assn. Advancement Sci., N.C. Assn. Acad. Deans. Home: 204 Hillcrest Circle Boone NC 28607

DURHAM, HUGH NELSON, univ. basketball coach; b. Louisville, Oct. 26, 1937; s. Samuel Hayes and Mary S. (Sparrow) D.; B.S. in Bus. Adminstrn., Fla. State U., 1959, M.S., 1961; m. Malinda Jane Dixon, Apr. 22, 1959; children—David, Douglas, James. Asst. basketball coach Fla. State U., Tallahassee, 1960-66, head basketball coach, 1966—. Home: 914 Ivanhoe St Tallahassee FL 32303

DURHAM, JOSEPH THOMAS, ednl. adminstr.; b. Raleigh, N.C., Nov. 26, 1923; A.B., Morgan State Coll., 1948; Ed.M., Temple U., 1949; Ed.D., Columbia, 1962. Instr. edn., dean Coll. Edn., Va. Sem. and Coll., 1949-51; acting dir. student teaching Morgan State Coll., 1951-56; core tchr. English and social studies New Lincoln Sch., N.Y.C., 1956-58; asso. prof. edn. So. U., 1958-60; prof. Coppin State Coll., 1960-63, prof. edn. and dean, 1965-68; prof. Albany State Coll., 1963-65; prof. edn., asso. dean Coll. Edn., Ill. State U., 1968-71; dean Sch. Edn., Howard U., Washington, 1971—; sr. cons. Research Corp. Am., 1968—. Mem. Am. Assn. Supervision and Curriculum Devel., Alpha Phi Alpha, Phi Delta Kappa. Co-author chpt. in Readings on the Culturally Disadvantaged, 1969; author: Sense and Non-Sense about Busing, 1973. Office: Howard Univ 2401 6th St NW Washington DC 20001

DURHAM, LEE GATLIFF, JR., physician; b. Williamsburg, Ky., Oct. 4, 1944; s. Lee Gatliff and Dixie (Holt) D.; B.A., Cumberland Coll., 1965; M.D., U. Louisville, 1969; m. Janis Curwood, Dec. 13, 1968; children—Lara Lee, Lee Gatliff III. Intern Louisville Gen. Hosp., 1969-70; practice medicine, Jellico, Tenn., 1970-73; emergency room physician S.E. Ky. Bapt. Hosp., Corbin, 1973—. Served with AUS, 1970. Mem. Am., Tenn., Ky. med. assns., Am. Coll. Emergency Physicians. Home: 502 Wright St Jellico TN 37762 Office: 201 S Main St Jellico TN 37762

DURHAM, LUCY ELIZABETH (MRS. DOUGLAS F. DURHAM), banker; b. Atlanta, Nov. 18, 1929; d. George Washington and Elizabeth Ganahl (Black) Sciple; student U. Ga., 1948; grad. Fla. Sch. Banking, U. Fla., 1971; m. Douglas Franklin Durham, Jan. 20, 1951; 1 dau., Sandra Elizabeth. File clk. First Nat. Bank, Atlanta, 1946-48, mgr. installment loan files, 1948-49, loan teller, 1949-51, comml. teller, drive-in teller, savs. teller, relief head teller, 1956-60; comml. teller First Nat. Bank Tampa (Fla.) (name changed to First Financial Nat. Bank Tampa 1973), 1964-66, head teller, 1967-70, asst. mgr. mil. facility, 1968-70, new accounts officer, 1968-73, asst. v.p., 1973-74, v.p., 1974—. Vice pres. elementary sch., Atlanta, 1961; troop leader Girl Scouts Am., 1958-62; charter mem. Piedmont Hosp.'s Women's Aux.; mem. Women's Aux. Tampa Gen. Hosp., bd. dirs., 1963. Mem. Am. Bus. Women's Assn. (treas. 1970-71, pres. 1971-72), Nat. Assn. Bank Women (2d vice-chmn., membership chmn. 1973-74), Am. Bus. Women's Assn. (Woman of Year 1973-74), Credit Mgrs. Assn., Am. Inst. Banking (dir. 1972—). Episcopalian. Clubs: West Coast Orchid Soc., Palma Ceia Golf and Country. Co-author Teller's Manual First Nat. Bank Tampa. Home: 512 Channel Dr Tampa FL 33606 Office: PO Box 17656 Tampa FL 33612

DURICK, JOSEPH ALOYSIUS, bishop; b. Dayton, Tenn., Oct. 13, 1914; s. Stephen and Bridget (Gallagher) D.; student St. Bernard Coll., Cullman, Ala., 1930-33; B.A., St. Mary's Sem., Balt., 1936; B.Th., Urban Coll. Propagation of Faith, Rome, Italy, 1940. Ordained priest Roman Catholic Ch., 1940, domestic prelate, 1952—, aux. bishop, 1955—; chaplain St. Mary's Summer Camp for Children, Batties Wharf, Ala., 1940; asst. to Rev. Frank Giri, Birmingham, later priest St. John's Ch., Birmingham; dir. North Ala. Missions, 1940-57; pastor St. Margaret's Ch., Birmingham, 1949-57, St. Francis Xavier Ch., Mountain Brook, Birmingham, 1957-64; aux. bishop Mobile-Birmingham, 1955-62, became vicar gen. Mobile-Birmingham, 1962; coadjutor bishop Diocese of Nashville, 1964-65, vicar gen., 1965-66, apostolic adminstr., 1966—, now bishop of Nashville. Founder, dir. Catholic Information Center, Birmingham; dir. Nocturnal Adoration Movement, Birmingham Holy Name Soc.; asst. diocesan dir. Confraternity of Christian Doctrine; diocesan dir. Priests Eucharistic League, 1954—. Mem. Holy Name Union, Toy Bowl Assn. K.C. (4 deg.). Club: Catholic Men's (past chaplain, trustee). Home: 4000 Brookhaven Dr Nashville TN 37204 Office: 421 Charlotte Av Nashville TN 37219

DURISCH, LAWRENCE LOGAN, JR., otolaryngologist; b. Knoxville, Tenn., Jan. 18, 1936; s. Lawrence Logan and Gladys Winefred (Johnson) Durisch; B.S., U. Tenn., 1958, M.D., 1963; m. Joanne Ferrell, June 23, 1961; children—Lawrence Logan, Anne Bailey. Intern, City Memphis and U. Tenn. hosps., 1963-64; resident U. Louisville, 1966-68, Med. Coll. Va., Richmond, 1968-70; practice medicine specializing in otolaryngology, Gainesville, Ga., 1970—; mem. staff Hall County Hosp., Gainesville. Served to capt. AUS, 1964-66. Fellow A.C.S., Am. Acad. Ophthalmology and Otolaryngology. Elk, Kiwanian. Home: 2256 Riverside Dr Gainesville GA 30501 Office: 304 S Enota St Gainesville GA 30501

DURKIN, MARY LUCILE, librarian; b. Battle Creek, Mich.; d. James Henry and Ella M. (McQuillen) Durkin; B.S., Simmons Coll., 1936; B.A., U. Tenn., 1944; M.A., Columbia, 1955; Advanced Master in L.S., U. Mich., 1972; postgrad. U. Okla., 1973—. Librarian, Chattanooga Sch. System, 1936-41; dist. supr. U.S. Govt. Program, Chattanooga, 1941-42; supr. city sch. library and Negro brs., Chattanooga, 1942-44; dir. field clubs A.R.C., Eng., Scotland, Germany, 1944-45; dir. USIS Libraries, Egypt, Morocco, Greece, 1948-58; librarian U.S. Army Aviation Sch., Ft. Rucker, Ala., 1959—. Home: 207 Westview Dr Enterprise AL 36330 Office: Bldg 5907 Fort Rucker AL 36360

DURRETT, JACK WESLEY, auto air conditioner mfr.; b. Jacksonville, Tex., Feb. 1, 1906; s. Thomas Lloyd and Mollie (Embry) D.; student pub. schs.; children—Jack, Sherry (Mrs. Howard Dudley); m. Billie Raye Bickerdike Dudley, Mar. 9, 1971; 1 stepdau., Shirley Anne (Mrs. Robert Hillier). Master mechanic, owner Tyler Service Parts Co. (Tex.), 1938—; owner Auto Indsl. Warehouse, Dallas, 1957—; pres. 'Climatic Air, Inc., Dallas, 1957—. Mason. Dallas. Home: Hutchins TX 75141 Office: 615 N Good Latimer PO Box 805 Dallas TX 75221

DURYEA, LYMAN CHANDLER, physician; b. Boston, Jan. 10, 1898; s. Lyman C. and Alice E. (Adelstein) D.; M.D., U. Vt., 1931; M.P.H., Johns Hopkins, 1939; m. Myrtle Holland Ryder, Sept. 6, 1924; children—Arthur Warren (dec.), Lyman Chandler. Intern DeGresbriand Hosp., Burlington, Vt., 1933-34; resident Bklyn. State Hosp.; practice gen. medicine, Ewa Plantation, Oahu, Hawaii, 1931, Sheldon Springs, Vt., 1935, Lyndonville, Vt., 1939; asso. dir. div. med. care N.Y. State Temporary Emergency Relief Adminstrn., 1935-38; dir. div. physically handicapped Dept. Health, N.Y.C., 1938-41; mem. com. for study care and edn. physically handicapped children pub. schs., N.Y.C., 1938-41; Commd. officer M.C. U.S. Army, 1941, advanced through grades to col.; ret., 1958; dist. health officer N.M. State Dept. Health, 1958-63; dep. dir. N.M. Dept. Pub. Health, 1963—; mem. staff Sunland Hosp., Orlando, Fla., 1964-70. Lectr. part-time Columbia, Fordham U. Bd. dirs. Cerebral Palsy Assn., Inc. Decorated Army Commendation Ribbon, Legion of Merit. Rockefeller Found. fellow, 1939. Fellow Am. Pub. Health Assn., Am. Sch. Health Assn.; mem. Ret. Officers Assn., Assn. U. S. Army, N.Y. State, N.M., West End med. socs., Fed. Hosp. Inst. Alumni Assn., Advt. Execs. Club. Contbr. articles to profl. jours. Home: 2727 Amsden Rd Winter Park FL 32789

DUSENBURY, JOSEPH HOOKER, phys. chemist; b. Troy, N.Y., Nov. 18, 1923; s. Fred Morgan and Eola Loretta (Benack) D.; B.S., Union Coll. 1947; Ph.D., U. Cal. at Berkeley, 1950; m. Bernice Katherine Iwinski, Aug. 23, 1947. Chemist, Am. Cyanamid Co., Bound Brook, N.J., 1947, research chemist, 1950-53; sect. leader Textile Research Inst., Princeton, N.J., 1953-58, asso. research dir., 1958-61; sect. leader Deering Milliken Research Corp., Spartanburg, S.C., 1961-66, research dept. mgr., 1966—. Teaching asst. U. Cal. at Berkeley, 1947-49; guest lectr. textile dept. Clemson U., 1972. Served with AUS, 1942-45. Recipient Fuller prize in Chemistry, Union Coll., 1947. Fellow A.A.A.S., Textile Inst. (Great Britain), Am. Inst. Chemists; mem. Am. Chem. Soc. (chmn. div. cellulose wood and fiber chemistry 1971), Fiber Soc. Inc., Soc. Rheology, Am. Inst. Physics. Clubs: Nassau (Princeton); Piedmont (Spartanburg). Contbr. articles to tech. jours. Contbr. chpt. on wool chemistry to Wool Handbook, 3d edn., vol. I, 1963. Patentee modification wool and nylon fibers, manufacture elastic yarns and fabrics. Home: 413 Overland Dr Spartanburg SC 29302 Office: Deering Milliken Research Corp PO Box 1927 Spartanburg SC 29301

DUSI, JULIAN LUIGI, educator; b. Columbus, O., Nov. 10, 1920; s. Marion Luigi and Fay Marguerite (Beard) D.; student Capital U., 1938-39; B.S., Ohio State U., 1943, M.S., 1946, Ph.D., 1949; postgrad. Albion Coll., 1943; m. Rosemary Twyla Dearth, Nov. 22, 1947. With W.Va. Conservation Commn., 1948; faculty Auburn U., Auburn, Ala., 1949—, prof. dept. zoology-entomology, 1963—. Cons. environmental research Anderson Devel. Co., Dauphin Island, Ala., Ala. and Ga. power cos. Served to 2d lt. USAAF, 1943-45. Mem. Am. Inst. Biol. Scis., Am. Ornithologists Union, Am. Soc. Mammalogists, Wilson Ornithol. Soc., Sigma Xi, Gamma Sigma Delta. Republican. Episcopalian. Home: 560 Sherwood Dr Auburn AL 36830

DUSINA, LOUIS, elec. design engr.; b. Lynch, Ky., Dec. 1, 1921; s. John and Agnes (Silvini) D.; B.E.E., U. Ky., 1946, M.E.E., 1949, B.S. in Commerce, 1949; m. Ruby Leora Warwick, Sept. 9, 1951; children—Sharon Leora, Mary Lynn, Daniel Louis, John Leslie. Elec. control engr. U.S. Steel Corp., Gary, W.Va., 1947-48; instr. engring. U. Ky., 1948-49; project engr. Union Carbide Nuclear div. Tenn. Atomic Energy Program, Oak Ridge, Tenn., 1950-61, elec. splst., 1961-66; sr. facilities engr. Dow Chem. Co. Aerospace div., Kennedy Space Center, Fla., 1966-69; sr. facilities engr. North Am. Rockwell Aerospace div., Kennedy Space Center, Fla., 1967-69; elec. design, project engr. NASA, Kennedy Space Center, Fla., 1969—. Pres. Cripple Children PTA, Knoxville, Tenn., 1959-60. Served with AUS, 1943-46. Registered Profl. Engr., W.Va. Democrat. Baptist. Mason. Home: 2656 Baywood Dr Titusville FL 32780 Office: NASA Kennedy Space Center FL 32899

DUSON, WALTER WEBB III, architect; b. Bay City, Tex., Oct. 8, 1935; s. Donald McNaughton and Savanna Pearl (Hawkins) D.; B.Arch., U. Tex., 1959; M.Arch., U. Cal. at Berkeley, 1969; m. Lisabeth Kerr, Apr. 4, 1970. With Mackie & Kamrath, architects, Houston, 1961-68; owner W.W. Duson Assos., Houston, 1969—. Vis. lectr. Tex. A. and M. U., 1970—; vis. critic U. Houston, 1971-72, lectr., 1971. Served with C.E. Corps, USNR, 1959-61. Mem. A.I.A. (award for design excellence), Tex. Soc. Architects, Houston C. of C., Sphinx, Pi Kappa Alpha. Club: Houston Racquet. Home: 8501 Burkhart St Houston TX 77055 Office: 4904 Travis St Houston TX 77002

DUTT, RAY HORN, animal scientist, educator; b. Bangor, Pa., Aug. 26, 1913; s. Elmer James and Viola (Horn) D.; B.S., Pa. State U., 1941; M.S., U. Wis., 1942, Ph.D., 1948; m. Louise Elizabeth Gettys, June 22, 1946; children—Philip, Kathleen. Asst. prof. animal sci. U. Ky., Lexington, 1948-51, asso. prof., 1951-58, prof., 1958—; asso. editor Jour. Animal Sci., 1961-63, editor, 1964-66. Served to maj. USMCR, 1942-46. Recipient Sang award for outstanding contbn. to grad. edn. U. Ky., 1970-71, Distinguished Alumnus award Pa. State U. Coll. Agr., 1967. Fulbright research grantee, New Zealand, 1957. Mem. Am. Soc. Animal Sci. (pres. 1968, Distinguished Service award 1971), Soc. Study Reprodn., A.A.A.S., Biometrics Soc., Genetics Soc. Am., Sigma Xi, Gamma Sigma Delta. Research on control of mammalian estrous cycle. Home: 437 Bristol Rd Lexington KY 40502

DUTTON, ARTHUR MORLAN, statistician, educator; b. Des Moines, July 28, 1923; s. Arthur W. and Letta (Morlan) D.; B.S. in Elec. Engring., Ia. State U., 1945, Ph.D., 1951; m. Joanne McHenry, Sept. 3, 1945; children—David, Margaret. Teaching fellow, research asso. Ia. State U., 1946-51; instr. U. Rochester, 1951-54, asst. prof., 1954-61, asso. prof., 1961-68; prof., chmn. math. sci. dept. Fla. Technol. U., Orlando, 1968—. Cons. Xerox Corp., 1956-58. Served with USNR, 1942-46. USPHS Postdoctoral fellow, 1965-66. Fellow Am. Statist. Assn.; mem. Biometric Soc., A.A.A.S., Am. Math. Soc., Sigma Xi, Tau Beta Pi, Eta Kappa Nu, Phi Kappa Phi, Pi Mu Epsilon, Phi Delta Theta. Contbr. articles to statis. jours. Home: 9953 Lake Georgia Dr Maitland FL 32751 Office: Box 25000 Orlando FL 32816

DUTTON, BENSON LEROY, civil engr.; b. Phila., Jan. 7, 1910; s. Bert Leroy and Beatrice (Thomas) D.; B.S., Pa. State U., 1933, C.E., 1949; postgrad. Lehigh U., summer 1955, U. Pa., 1956-57; m. Josephine Olivia Brown, June 24, 1939; children—Marie Elizabeth (Mrs. Kenneth Brown), Benson Leroy, Michael Eric. Chief-of-party Bur. Engring., 1933-34; constrn. engr. F. Massiah, contractor, Phila., 1935-36; project engr. Nat. Park Service, U.S. Dept. Interior, 1937-40; asst. prof., cons. engr. Hampton Inst., Va., 1940-47; dean engring. Tenn. State U., Nashville, 1947-56; chief design engr. bridges City of Phila., 1956-65; mgmt. engr. Office Edn., U.S. Dept. Health, Edn. and Welfare, Washington, 1965-67, chief constrn. service operations, 1967-70, dir. Office Federally Assisted Constrn., 1970—. Asst. dir. radiol. def. Civil Def., Nashville, 1953-56. Pres., bd. dirs. Mt. Airy/Rittenhouse YMCA; bd. dirs. North Phila. Area Health and Welfare Council, W.Mt. Airy Neighbors; trustee Germantown YMCA, Phila.; chmn. bd. mgrs. Mt. Airy YMCA, Phila.; bd. dirs. YMCA Met. Washington. Recipient prize for welded structures Lincoln Found., 1966; Distinguished Alumnus award Pa. State U., 1971. Registered profl. engr., D.C., Pa., Tenn., Va. Fellow Am. Soc. C.E.; mem. Am. Pub. Works Assn., Assn. Sch. Bus. Ofcls., Omega Psi Phi. Episcopalian. Planner sch. engring. Tenn. State U., 1949; designer Spring Garden St. bridges over Schuylkill River, Phila.; improvements Art Mus. Complex, 1963-65. Home: Town Sq Towers 700 7th St SW Washington DC 20024 Office: 330 Independence Av SW Washington DC 20201

DUVAL, CLAUDE BERWICK, lawyer, state senator; b. Houma, La., Oct. 24, 1914; s. Stanwood and Mamie (Richardson) D.; student La. State U., 1931-32; LL.B., Tulane U., 1937; m. Betty Bowman, Apr. 6, 1938; 1 dau., Dorothy. Admitted to La. bar, 1937; practiced in Houma, La., 1937—; mem. law firm Duval, Arceneaux & Lewis. Chmn. bd. First Nat. Bank Houma; dir. Pelican Lake Oyster & Packing Co., Ltd., Duval-Whitney-Stevenson, Inc. Mem. La. Senate, 1967—. Mem. com. A.R.C., 1947-48; chmn. 3d Congl. dist. Area Cancer Drive, 1949-50; mem. devel. council Tulane U., 1958; trustee Pub. Affairs Research Council; bd. dirs. Council for Better La.; state chmn. Radio Free Europe, 1968. Campaign mgr. deLesseps S. Morrison, Democratic candidate for gov. La., 1959; candidate for lt. gov. La., 1963. Served from 2d lt. to capt. USMCR, 1941-46; PTO. Decorated Bronze Star, Purple Heart. Letter of Commendation, Presdl. Unit Citation; recipient award as Outstanding Young Man of Year, Houma Jr. C. of C., 1947. Mem. Am., La. (mem. house of dels. 1957-60, mem. law reform com.) bar assns., Am. Legion (La. comdr. 1950; mem. nat. exec. com. 1952-54), La. State (pres. 1961-62), Houma (pres. 1959) chambers commerce, Young Mens' Bus. Clubs of La. (state pres. 1948). Democrat. Episcopalian. Mason (Shriner), Elk, Rotarian (pres. 1958), Houma Exchange (pres. 1940). Home: 18 Country Club Dr Houma LA 70360 Office: 504 Belanger St Houma LA 70360

DUVAL, MILES P., JR., ret. naval officer; b. Portsmouth, Va., Apr. 19, 1896; s. Miles P. and Minnie Lee (Chalkley) DuV.; B.S., U.S. Naval Acad., 1918, student U.S. Naval War Coll., 1925-26; U.S. Naval Post Grad. Sch., 1930-31; M.F.S., Fgn. Service Sch., Georgetown U., 1937. Commd. ensign USN, 1918, and advanced through grades to capt., 1945; served as comdg. officer, U.S.S. Dupont, 1933-35, participated in naval demonstration off Cuban ports, 1933-34; sec. Shore Sta. Devel. Bd., Navy Dept., Washington, 1936-38; comdg. officer U.S.S. Antares, 1939-40; capt. of port, Balboa, C.Z., in charge marine operations of Pacific subdiv. of Panama Canal, 1941-44; planned and coordinated enlargement of Balboa Harbor, 1942-43; developed high level terminal lake plan for improvement of Panama Canal, 1943; comdg. officer U.S.S. Dade, 1944-46, participated in Okinawa campaign, 1945; designated as Navy Dept. liaison officer and coordinator for modernization studies of Panama Canal by Sec. of Navy, 1946; ret. active service, 1949. Vice pres., gen. cons. John F. Stevens Hall of Fame com. Bd. dirs. Gorgas Meml. Inst. Tropical and Preventive Medicine. Decorated Legion of Merit (Army), 1945, World War I Victory medal with Atlantic and Grand Fleet clasps, 1918, Am. Defense with Fleet and Base clasps, 1939-41, Am. campaign, 1941-44, Asiatic-Pacific campaign with bronze star, 1945. Fellow A.A.A.S.; mem. Va. Hist. Soc., Naval Hist. Found., Soc. of Va. in Washington (past v.p.), Permanent Internat. Assn. Nav. Congresses (life), U.S. Naval Inst., U.S. Strategic Inst., Soc. Am. Mil. Engrs., Panama Hist. Soc. (corr. mem.), Panama Canal Soc. of Washington (pres.), Panama Canal Natural History Soc. (past v.p.), Phi Alpha Theta. Clubs: Explorers; Propeller of U.S., Cosmos, Army and Navy (Washington); Yacht (N.Y.C.). Author: Series on Panama Canal: Cadiz to Cathay, 1940; And the Mountains Will Move, 1947; Matthew Fontaine Maury: Benefactor of Man Kind, 1964; Sam Houston: The Washington of the Vast Southwest, 1966; George Rogers Clark: Conqueror of the Old Northwest, 1970; The Future Canal; also papers on interoceanic canal problems. Home: 5120 King William Rd Richmond VA 23225

DUVALL, HARRY MAREAN, chemist, educator; b. Lanham, Md., Oct. 27, 1910; s. Harry Gilbert and Margaret (Rogers) D.; B.S., U. Md., 1932, Ph.D., 1936; m. Honora Holmes, Oct. 24, 1955. Research fellow U. Va., 1936-38; research chemist E.I. du Pont de Nemours & Co. Inc., Deepwater, N.J., 1938-50; research chemist Thiokol Chem. Corp., Trenton, N.J., 1950-53; research chemist Masonite Corp., Laurel, Miss., 1954-58; prof. chemistry, head dept. Valdosta (Ga.) State Coll., 1958—. Mem. Am. Chem. Soc., Sigma Xi, Phi Kappa Phi. Home: Box 52C Route 6 Valdosta GA 31601

DUVALL, RICHARD MAREEN, JR., mfg. co. exec.; b. Richmond, Va., Oct. 1, 1930; s. Richard Mareen and Azele Pogue (Mehl) D.; student Randolph-Macon Coll., 1949-50; B.S., Va. Poly. Inst., 1958; m. Shirley Christine Jones, Sept. 22, 1951; children—Edward Mehl, Julie Lynne, Richard Mareen III. With Albemarle Paper Mfg. Co., Richmond, 1959-67, maintenance supt., 1964-66, asst. paper mill supt., 1966-67; chief engr., asst. to pres. Georgia Bonded Fibers, Inc., Buena Vista, Va., 1967-71, v.p. operations, 1971—; dir. Bontex S.A., Stembert, Belgium. Pres. Va. Heights Civic Assn., Henrico County, 1960. Served with USAF, 1951-54. Mem. Paper Industry Mgmt. Assn., Blue Ridge Safety Assn. (dir. 1970—). Methodist. Kiwanian. Home: 605 Ross Rd Lexington VA 24450 Office: PO Box 751 Buena Vista VA 24416

DUVALL, WILLIAM CLYDE, JR., ednl. adminstr.; b. Farmville, Va., Feb. 4, 1917; s. William Clyde and Harriet King (Bugg) D.; student Hampden-Sydney Coll., 1934-36, Washington Mus. Inst., 1936-38, Old Dominion U., 1946, U. Va., 1951, Coll. William and Mary, 1962-63; m. Ruth Elizabeth Jones, Sept. 30, 1939; children—William Clyde III, George Drummond, Charles Montgomery, Elizabeth Leigh, Thomas King. Tchr. band pub. schs. Charlotte County (Va.), 1939-43, Norfolk County (Va.), 1945-51; dir. music Norfolk County Schs., 1951-55, dir. music and teaching materials, 1955-63; dir. music and teaching materials Chesapeake (Va.) Pub. Schs., 1963—. Band clinician, music festival adjudicator. Pres., Chesapeake Friends of Music, 1967-68. Bd. dirs. Young Audiences, Inc., Norfolk, 1970—. Served with USNR, 1943-45. Mem. Va. Band and Orch. Assn. (pres. 1953-54), Pi Kappa Alpha. Democrat. Episcopalian. Author: High School Band Director's Handbook, 1960. Home: 4714 River Shore Rd Portsmouth VA 23703 Office: 300 Cedar Rd Chesapeake VA 23320

DVORETZKY, ISAAC, petroleum co. exec.; b. Houston, Jan. 24, 1928; s. Max and Anna (Greenfield) D.; B.A., Rice U., 1948, M.A., 1950, Ph.D. in Chemistry, 1952; m. Zelda Benowitz, June 29, 1958; children—Rachel Leah, Aaron Benjamin, Rebecca Esther. With Shell Oil Co., various locations, 1952—, mgr. unconventional raw materials dept., Emeryville, Cal., 1969-72, mgr. profl. recruitment, univ. relations Shell Devel. Co. div., Houston, 1972—. Mem. Sigma Xi, Phi Beta Kappa, Phi Lambda Upsilon. Jewish religion (synagogue officer, trustee). Contbr. to profl. jours. Patentee hydrocarbon chemistry and catalysis. Home: 9714 KIT Houston TX 77035 Office: PO Box 481 Houston TX 77001

DWIGGINS, BAILEY LEE, broadcasting co. exec.; b. Statesville, N.C., July 5, 1938; s. J. Lee and Jane (Woodruff) D.; B.F.A., Va. Commonwealth U., 1962; m. Elizabeth Cornwell, Aug. 30, 1958; children—Allison Hollin, Bailey Tolson. With Meml. Guidance Clinic, Richmond, Va., 1960-63; graphic artist Cox Broadcasting Co., WSOC-TV, Charlotte, N.C., 1963-64; with Alderman Studios, High Point, N.C., 1964-66; art dir. Gen. Electric Co., Winston-Salem, N.C., 1966-68; creative services promotion mgr. Jefferson-Pilot Broadcasting, Richmond, 1968—. Served with AUS, 1956-57. Bd. dirs. Grace House, 1973—. Mem. Richmond Soc. of Communicating Arts (dir. 1973—). Home: 2521 Hanover Av Richmond VA 23220 Office: PO Box 12 5710 Midlothian Turnpike Richmond VA 23220

DWIGGINS, CLAUDIUS WILLIAM, JR., chemist; b. Amity, Ark., May 11, 1933; s. Claudius William and Lillian (Scott) D.; B.S., U. Ark., 1954, M.S., 1956, Ph.D. (Am. Oil Co. fellow, Coulter-Jones scholar), 1958. With U.S. Dept. Interior Bur. Mines, Bartlesville (Okla.) Research Center, 1958—, chemist, 1958-60, project leader surface physics project, 1960-65, project leader petroleum composition research project, 1965—. Mem. Am. Chem. Soc., N.Y. Acad. Scis., A.A.A.S., Am. Crystallographic Assn., Am. Inst. Physics, Sigma Xi (sec. 1966-67), Alpha Chi Sigma, Delta Sigma Phi (treas. 1952). Contbr. articles to profl. jours. Home: 1211 S Keeler St Bartlesville OK 74003 Office: US Bur Mines Petroleum Research Center Bartlesville OK 74003

DWORNIK, JULIAN JONATHAN, univ. dean; b. Colonsay, Sask., Can., Mar. 11, 1938; s. John Martin and Marie Jay (Babuik) D.; B.A., Andrew's U., 1961; M.S., U. Man., 1964, Ph.D., 1969; m. Diane Joan St. Goddard, June 7, 1963; children—Pamela, Marie, Joan. Research fellow U. Man., 1965-67; instr. U. Louisville Med. Coll., 1967-69, asst. prof., 1969-70; asst. prof. dept. anatomy U. South Fla. Coll. Medicine, Tampa, 1970-73, asso. prof., 1973—, asst. dean admissions, 1972—. Pres., Univ. Sq. Homeowners Assn., 1972-73. Mem. Canadian, Pan Am., So. assns. anatomists. Home: 10019 N 52d St Temple Terrace FL 33617 Office: U South Fla Coll Medicine Tampa FL 33620

DWYER, JEAN AGNES FERGUSON, U.S. magistrate; b. Atlanta, Feb. 14, 1927; d. Frederick Kilby and Rose (Norris) Ferguson; A.B., George Washington U., 1948, LL.B., 1951; 1 dau., Maureen M. Admitted to D.C. bar, 1951, Va. bar, 1965; mem. firm John J. and Jean F. Dwyer, Washington, 1952-72; U.S. magistrate U.S. Dist. Ct., Washington, 1972—. Del. Jud. Conf., 1972; mem. criminal rules adv. com. Superior Ct., 1971-72; bd. dirs. Nat. Council U.S. Magistrates, 1974-75. Mem. Rappahannock League for Environmental Protection. Mem. Women's Bar Assn., D.C., Va. bar assns., Nat. Capitol Great Pyrenees Club. Home: 7214 Davis Ct McLean VA 22101 Office: US District Courthouse 3d and Constitution Av NW Washington DC 20001

DYAL, WILLIAM M., JR., found. exec.; b. Austin, Tex., May 13, 1928; s. William M. and Mildred Eleanor (Taylor) D.; A.B., Baylor U., 1949; M.Th., So. Theol. Sem., Louisville, 1953; certificate Sch. Langs., San Jose, Costa Rica, 1954; m. Edith Colvin, May 6, 1950; children—Kathy Lynn, Deborah Irene, Maria Lisa. Field rep. Baptist Fgn. Mission Bd., Central Am., 1954-59, S.Am., 1959-62; dir. Christian Life Commn., Nashville, 1963-66; dir. Peace Corps, Colombia, 1967-69, regional dir., North Africa, Near East, South Asia, 1969-71; pres. Inter-Am. Found., 1971—. Bd. govs. Dag Hammarsjkold Coll., Columbia, Md. Recipient Best Book on Youth and Current Issues award A.P., 1966; Gold medal of Santander, Pres. Colombia, 1968. Mem. Latin Am. Studies Assn. Author: It's Worth Your Life, 1966; Un Desafio al Discipulado, 1971; contbr. chpts. to Word Books, 1967, 69. Home: 4018 Fort Worth Av Alexandria VA 22304 Office: 1515 Wilson Blvd Rosslyn VA 22209

DYCK, WALTER PETER, physician; b. Winkler, Man., Can., Dec. 7, 1935; s. Isaac P. and Maria (Penner) D.; B.A., Bethel Coll., 1957; M.D., U. Kan., 1961; m. Lana Lee Kushnir, June 12, 1965; children—Christa Anne, Lauren Maria, Jon Andrew, Paul Bradley. Intern, Henry Ford Hosp., Detroit, 1961-62, resident internal medicine, 1962-63, 65-66; research fellow U. Zurich (Switzerland), 1963-64, U. Toronto (Ont., Can.), 1964-65; research and clin. fellow Mt. Sinai Sch. Medicine, N.Y.C., 1966-68; cons., dir. gastrointestinal physiology and research labs. Scott and White Clinic, Temple, Tex., 1968—, chief sect. gastroenterology, 1974—; clin. instr. internal medicine Southwestern Med. Sch., Dallas, 1969—. Cons. NIH, 1973—. Pres., Central Tex. Orchestral Soc., 1972—. Fellow ACP; mem. Am. Gastroent. Assn. (com. on research 1971—), Am. Physiol. Soc., So. Soc. Clin. Investigation, Am. Fedn. Clin. Research, A.M.A. Home: 2614 Marland Wood Circle Temple TX 76501 Office: Scott and White Clinic Temple TX 76501

DYER, ALVAH FRANCIS, petroleum co. exec.; b. Longton, Kan., May 18, 1929; s. Frank and Lorena Opal (Jones) D.; B.S., Kan. State U., 1950; m. Joan A. Endicott, Aug. 11, 1950; children—Lynn Ann, Jane Carol. Design engr. Phillips Petroleum Co., Bartlesville, Okla., 1951-54, tech. rep., 1954-63, mgr. codes, regulations and standards br. engring. dept., 1963—; pres., Caney (Kan.) Airpark, Inc., 1970—. Mem. City Council Caney, 1969-70, Bd. Edn. Caney, 1970—. Recipient Certificate of Appreciation, Am. Petroleum Inst., 1968, 73; Tech. Com. award Nat. Fire Protection Assn., 1971. Methodist (mem. adminstrv. bd. 1960—, chmn. finance commn. 1971—). Mason, Elk. Contbr. articles to profl. jours. Patentee in field. Home: 208 S Fawn St Caney KS 67333 Office: Phillips Bldg Bartlesville OK 74004

DYER, ELBA LORRAINE, ret. social worker; b. Wardensville, W.Va., Apr. 19, 1906; d. Thomas A. and Mary Alice (Orndorff) Dyer; B.A., Shepherd Coll., 1933; diploma social work Columbia, 1939; M.Ed. in Sociology, Temple U., 1941. Med. social worker Lankenau Hosp., Phila., 1939-41; psychiat. social worker, student supr. Norristown (Pa.) State Hosp., 1941-47; med. social work cons. Ariz. Dept. Pub. Welfare, 1947-49; chief psychiat. social worker Child Guidance Clinic, Des Moines, 1949-51, Tulsa, 1951-55; chief psychiat. social worker, acting dir. Cumberland County Guidance Center, Fayetteville, N.C., 1955-61; chief psychiat. social worker, supr. students Psychiat. Clinic, Portsmouth, Va., 1961-66; psychiat. social worker aftercare program Dept. Hosps. and Mental Hygiene, Roanoke (Va.) Guidance Center, 1966-73. Fellow Am. Orthopsychiat. Assn.; mem. Nat. Assn. Social Workers (pres. Montgomery County Welfare Conf. 1945-46), Mental Health Assn. Roanoke, Nat. Conf. Social Welfare, Internat. Council Social Welfare, Phi Delta Gamma. Democrat. Lutheran (deaconess 1933-41). Club: Pilot. Home: PO Box 4361 Roanoke VA 24015 Office: 1125 2st St SW Roanoke VA 24016

DYER, FREDERICK CHARLES, author, cons.; b. St. Louis, Feb. 17, 1918; s. George Leo and Katherine Mary (Dobson) D.; B.A., Holy Cross Coll., 1938; M.B.A., Dartmouth, 1948. Ednl. writer, editor tng. pubs. Bur. Naval Personnel, 1948-58, asst. for spl. projects, leadership staff, 1958-64; spl. asst. to Undersec. Navy, 1964-66; asst. for spl. projects Office Civilian Manpower Mgmt., Navy Dept., 1966-68; dir. program analysis div. Navy Publs. and Printing Service, Washington, 1968-74, ret., 1974. Chmn., U.S. Civil Service Task Force on Mgmt. Edn. for Computers, 1965-66; profl. lectr. George Washington U., 1956-60; adj. prof. Drexel Inst. Tech., 1962-67; professorial lectr. Am. U., 1967-73. Councilman, Town of Somerset, Md., 1962-64. Served with USNR, 1943-46, 48-52. Recipient Writing award Navy League, 1959; Superior Civilian Service award Navy Dept., 1961. Mem. Authors Guild, Authors League Am., Internat. Communications Assn., Fed. Profl. Assn., Nat. Assn. Profl. Bureaucrats (Order of Bird award 1971). Clubs: Army Navy Country (Arlington, Va.); Columbia Country (Chevy Chase, Md.); University, Cosmos, National Press (Washington); Sycamore Island (Montgomery County, Md.). Author or co-author: Blueprint for Executive Success, 1964; Bureaucracy Vs Creativity, 1965, rev. edit., 1969; Executive's Guide to Effective Speaking and Writing, 1962; Executive's Guide to Handling People, 1958; Export Financing, 1964; How to Make Decisions About People, 1966; The Petty Officer's Guide, 1966; Putting Yourself Over in Business, 1957; The Enjoyment of Management, 1971. Home: 4509 Cumberland Av Chevy Chase MD 20015

DYER, LLOYD EDWARD, communications exec.; b. Carthage, Ind., June 2, 1921; s. Larry Everett and Estella (Dayhoff) D.; A.B., DePauw U., 1942; grad. mgmt. programs Harvard, 1959, Dartmouth, 1961; m. Dorothy Harriett Levien, Dec. 26, 1942 (dec.); children—Lloyd Edward, Nancy H., Mark F., Wendy A. With Ill. Bell Telephone Co., Chgo., 1945-51, 53-62, asst. v.p., 1961-62; exec. dir. pub. relations and publ. Bell Telephone Labs., Murray Hill, N.J., 1962-64; asst. v.p. pub. relations Am. Tel. & Tel. Co., N.Y.C., 1964-65; v.p. personnel Chesapeake & Potomac Telephone Cos., Washington, 1965—. Dir. at large Met. Washington Bd. Trade, 1972-73, chmn. employment and edn. bur., 1971-73. Dir. Opportunities Industrialization Center, Washington, 1969—. Served with USNR, 1942-45. Mem. Telephone Pioneers Am., Sigma Delta Chi. Club: Harvard Business School (Washington). Home: 3 Savannah Ct Bethesda MD 20034 Office: 1710 H St NW Washington DC 20006

DYER, ROBERT THEODORE, elec. engr.; b. Jacksonville, Fla., Nov. 15, 1945; s. Theodore Mains and Mildred Inez (Fuqua) D.; A.A., Fla. Jr. Coll., 1969; B.S., U. Fla., 1971; m. Robin Jean Dizor, Sept. 1, 1973. Engr. in tng. system planning div. Jacksonville Electric Authority, 1971-73, instr. engring. technician tng. program, 1973; elec. engr. Buena Vista Engring. Co. (Fla.), 1973—. Served with USAF, 1963-67. Recipient service key Benton Engring. Council, 1971. Mem. I.E.E.E., U.S. Parachute Assn., Phi Theta Kappa. Home: 5308 Glasgow Av Orlando FL 32805 Office: PO Box 40 Lake Buena Vista FL 32830

DYER, ROSS WATKINS, state justice; b. Halls, Tenn., Mar. 10, 1911; s. Clarence W. and Zona (Smith) D.; student U. Tenn., 1929-30, Cumberland U., 1930-31; LL.B., YMCA Law Sch., Nashville, 1937; m. Agnes Rebecca Moss, Nov. 1, 1936; 1 son, Thomas Ross. Insp. Tax Dept. Tenn., 1933-39; admitted to Tenn. bar, 1939; adjustor various ins. cos., 1939-41; practice, Halls, Tenn., 1941-61; asso. justice Supreme Ct. Tenn., 1961—. Mayor of Halls, 1947-49; mem. Tenn. Constl. Conv., 1953; mem. Tenn. Senate, 1957-59. Trustee Lauderdale County Hosp. Served from pvt. to 1st lt. AUS, 1943-46. Methodist. Mason. Home: Halls TN 38040 Office: Supreme Ct Tenn Nashville TN 37203

DYER, SALLIE (MRS. ROBERT FRANCIS DYER), genealogist, club woman; b. Washington, Oct. 16, 1891; d. Nathaniel Talmadge and Emma (Hutchins) Worley; student Cazenovia Jr. Coll., 1908-12, George Washington U., 1912-13, Strayer's Bus. Coll., 1914; m. Robert Francis Dyer, Jan. 2, 1926; children—Robert F., Nancie (Mrs. Edward C. Santelmann), Richard Hutchins, David Marcus. Sec. Brit. Embassy, Washington, 1914-15, Adj. Gen.'s Office, War Dept., 1915-16; owner Dyer's Geneol. Office, Washington, 1914-26. Pres. Washington alumnae club Pi Beta Phi, 1946-47; mem. war work com. D.A.R., 1943-45, vice-regent Dorothy Hancock chpt., 1945—, del. Eastern Shore Va. chpt. to nat. congresses, 1952-73. Mem. spl. com. U.S.O., 1941-45, mem. Belasco Theater, 1942-45; nurse's aid A.R.C., 1943-45; woman's bd. George Washington U. Hosp., Hosp., 1946-56; mem. George Washington U. Alumni Assn. Recipient service award A.R.C., 1945; Golden Arrow award Pi Beta Phi. Mem. So. Dames Am. (charter mem., state v.p. 1963-66), Tex. Geneal. Soc., Md. Hist. Soc. Clubs: Washington, Chevy Chase Woman's, Arts, Army-Navy, Annapolis Yacht. Home: 3813 Garrison St NW Washington DC 20016

DYESS, BOBBY DALE, lawyer; b. Waxahachie, Tex., Jan. 27, 1935; s. Robert Olin and Rubie Lee (Odom) D.; B.A., North Tex. State U., 1956; J.D., So. Methodist U., 1959; m. Janet Lee Hassell, Jan. 30, 1960, (dec. Mar. 1973); children—Robert Dale, Jonathan David, Juliana Georgette. Admitted to Tex. bar, 1959; asso. law firm Brundidge, Fountain, Elliott & Churchill, Attys., Dallas, Tex., 1963—, partner, 1965—; dir. Combined Am. Ins. Co.; dir. Rainbow Sound, Inc. Voting mem. East Dallas Y.M.C.A., 1970—, chief Y.M.C.A. Indian Guides, 1971; chmn. Cub Scout pack com. Boy Scouts Am., 1970. Served with USAF, 1960-63. Mem. Am., Tex., Dallas bar assns., Scribes. Methodist (trustee 1971-72). Club: North Tex. Weimaranaer. Editor: The Legal Spotlight - Best's Review, Life Health Ins. edn., 1968—. Home: 6869 CarolynCrest Dallas TX 75214 Office: 2020 Live Oak St Dallas TX 75201

DYESS, WILLIAM ALFRED, lawyer; b. Stratford, Tex., Apr. 1, 1940; s. Ernest Roscoe and Doris Hettie (Pronger) D.; student Panhandle Agrl. and Mech. Coll., 1958; B.S., W. Tex. State U., 1962; LL.B., Baylor U., 1964; postgrad. George Washington U., 1968; m. Glenda Agnes Allison, May 12, 1962; children—William Shane, Allison Dianne, Alisha Dawn. Admitted to Tex. bar, 1964; practiced in Stratford, 1964-65; partner Sheehan, Dubuque & Dyess, Stratford, 1970—; atty., Sherman County, Tex., 1973—. Instr. bus. law N.M. State U., 1969-70. Chmn., Sherman County chpt. Internat. Red Cross, 1970—, Sherman County Fair Com., 1971; mem. Sherman County Hist. Com., 1971—; v.p., Stratford Community Center, 1972—. Served to capt. Judge Adv. Gen. Corps, AUS, 1966-70. Decorated Army Commendation medal with oak leaf cluster. Mem. Am., Tex., 69th Jud. Dist. bar assns., Tex. Dist. and County Attys. Assn., Am. Legion (comdr. 1972—), Delta Theta Phi, Kappa Alpha. Lion. Home: 1207 N Chestnut St Stratford TX 79084 Office: 401 N 3d St Stratford TX 79083

DYKEMAN, WILMA (MRS. JAMES ROREX STOKELY, JR.), writer; b. Asheville, N.C., May 20, 1920; d. Willard Jerome and Bonnie Cushman (Cole) Dykeman; B.S. in Speech, Northwestern U., 1940; m. James Rorex Stokely, Jr., Oct. 12, 1940; children—Dykeman Cole, James R. III. Lectr. various orgns., 1955—; tchr. numerous writers' confs. Mem. def. adv. com. on Women in the Services, 1967-70; exec. com. Tenn. Com. Humanities, 1973—; mem. adv. com. Tenn. Arts Commn., 1973—. Trustee Berea (Ky.) Coll., 1968—. Recipient Thomas Wolfe Meml. award Western N.C. Hist. Soc., 1955, Hillman award, 1957, Chgo. Friends Am. Writers Waukegan Club award, 1962, Mary Mildred Sullivan medallion, 1971; named Tenn. Conservation Writer Year, 1973. Guggenheim fellow, 1956. Mem. Am. PEN, Lit. Guild, Tenn. Hist. Commn. (mem. exec. com. 1966-71). Author: The French Broad River, 1955; (with husband) Neither Black Nor White, 1957; (with husband) Seeds of Southern Change, 1962; The Tall Woman, 1962; The Far Family, 1966; Prophet of Plenty, 1966; Look to This Day, 1968; (with husband) The Border States, 1968; Return the Innocent Earth, 1973; Too Many People, Too Little Love, 1974. Author numerous short stories and articles, Editorial columnist Look to This Day For News Sentinel, Knoxville, Tenn., 1962—; editorial adviser Appalachian Jour., So. Voices. Address: 405 Clifton Heights Newport TN 37821

DYKES, NORMAN WAYNE, city ofcl.; b. Dallas, May 18, 1942; s. Welton Wayne and Cora Jane (Walker) D.; B.S., Tex. Tech. U., 1964; postgrad. E. Tex. State U., 1973—; m. Brenda Lee Jackson, Aug. 31, 1963; children—Sherry Lee, Billy Norman. Asso. engr., Gen. Dynamics Corp., Fort Worth, 1964-66; systems engr. LTV Electrosystems, Greenville, Tex., 1968; dir. pub. works City Sulphur Springs, Tex., 1969—. Officer, Young Farmers, 1970-72. Mem. Tex. Soc. Profl. Engrs. (dir., v.p. 1974-75). Baptist. Rotarian (dir. 1972-74, sec. 1974-75). Home: Route 1 Brashear TX 75420 Office: Municipal Bldg Sulphur Springs TX 75482

DYKSTRA, RONALD WILLIAM, ins. co. exec.; b. Holbrook, N.Y., Feb. 25, 1939; s. Kenneth Charles and Viola Miriam (Schmidt) D.; grad. high sch.; m. Kristina Elizabeth Jelstrom, Feb. 11, 1968; children—Craig Taylor, Christiaan Kal. With So. Bell Tel. & Tel. Co., Fla., 1956-67, Phone Cons., Inc., Miami, Fla., 1967-69; owner Profl. Communications Cons., Ft. Lauderdale, Fla., 1969-70; br. mgr. Arcata Communications, Inc., Ft. Lauderdale, 1970, regional mgr., Atlanta, 1970-71; pres. Ft. Lauderdale Telephone Co., subsidiary Telephone Cos., Inc., also pres., chmn. bd. Telephone Cos., Inc., 1973; br. mgr. Litton Bus. Telephone Systems, Sunnyvale, Cal., 1973-74; now with Pa. Life Ins. Co., Birmingham, Ala. Served with AUS, 1958-61. Mem. Sales and Marketing Execs., Ft. Lauderdale Bus. Assn. Presbyn. Club: Gulfstream Sailing (Ft. Lauderdale). Home: 1030 41st St S Birmingham AL 35222

DYLLA, EDWARD VINCENT, lawyer; b. San Antonio, May 29, 1937; s. Frank Tofiel and Victoria (Korus) D.; B.A., St. Mary's U., 1957, J.D., 1960; m. Margaret Ann Quinn, Apr. 4, 1964; children—David Edward, Andrew Gerald, Barrett Ross. Admitted to Tex. bar, 1960; practiced in San Antonio, 1960—. Served to maj. AUS, 1970. Mem. San Antonio Bar Assn., Delta Theta Phi. Club: Toastmasters (dist. gov. 1973-74). Home: 10919 Janet Lee San Antonio TX 78230 Office: 615 NBC Bldg San Antonio TX 78225

DYSON, SAMUEL ARCHER, librarian; b. Shreveport, La., Sept. 3, 1928; s. Leslie Paul and Bessie (Archer) D.; student Tulane U., 1945-46; B.S., Northwestern State Coll., Natchitoches, La., 1950; postgrad. North Tex. State U., 1951-52, La. Coll., 1957, La. Tech. U., 1967-69; M.S., La. State U., 1953; LL.D., Bapt. Christian Coll., 1974; m. June Katherine Wallace, May 6, 1950; children—Stuart Alan, Karen Ernestine. Head librarian La. Coll., Pinesville, 1953-60; asso. librarian La. Tech. U., Ruston, 1960-66, dir. libraries, 1966—, asso. prof. library sci. Coll. Edn., 1966—. Sec. treas. adv. bd. Recreation Program for Blind, YWCA, 1960; mem. exec. bd. Quachita Valley council Boy Scouts Am., 1966—; range and information officer Ruston Civil Air Patrol, 1964. Served with USNR, 1948. Mem. La. (1st v.p. 1972-73, pres. 1973-74), S.W. (mem. exec. bd.) library assns., La. Coll. Conf. (chmn. library sect. 1957, 63), Conf. La. Acad. Librarians (chmn. 1958), Alpha Tau Omega, Alpha Beta Alpha. Lion. Author: Library Automation, 1971. Editor: Planning and Implementing Academic Library Automation Programs, 1970. Editor abstracts of theses, 1968—. Home: 2 Westwood Hills Ruston LA 71270 Office: Prescott Library La Tech Univ Ruston LA 71270

DZIADEK, FRED, govt. ofcl.; b. Vienna, Austria, June 4, 1934; s. Morris and Ray (Horowitz) D.; came to U.S., 1940, naturalized, 1946; A.B., Columbia, 1955; postgrad. (White fellow econs.), Cornell, 1955-56; Ph.D. (Univ. fellow), Johns Hopkins, 1960; m. Ilana H. Zuckerman, July 31, 1955; children—Tamara, Margaret, Mark. Economist IMF, Washington, 1959-65; asso. chief socio-econs. div. Battelle Meml. Inst., Columbus, O., 1965-66; asst. chief office program and policy coordination AID, Washington, 1966-68; asst. dir. internat. div. U.S. Gen. Accounting Office, Washington, 1968—. Instr. polit. economy Johns Hopkins, part-time 1960-65; lectr. econs. part time Georgetown U., Washington, 1960-65. Mem. Am. Econ. Assn. Contbr. articles to profl. jours. Home: 909 Annmore Dr Silver Spring MD 20902 Office: 441 G St NW Washington DC 20548

EADS, EDWIN MOUZON, architect, civil engr.; b. Ben Wheeler, Tex., Oct. 4, 1914; s. William Daniel and Lola Roselle (Sides) E.; B.Arch., Tex. A. and M. Coll., 1937; m. Billie Frances Curran, Oct. 29, 1937; children—Lynn (Mrs. John William Black III), Sara (Mrs. John Eugene Walsh). Commd. 2d lt., USAF, 1940, advanced through grades to col., 1952, ret., 1967; dir. planning and new constrn. Jefferson County Sch. Dist., Colo., 1967-70; Alaska dist. engr. Facilities Engring. and Constrn. Agy., U.S. Dept. Health, Edn. and Welfare, Anchorage, 1970-73, project mgr. Research Triangle Park, N.C., 1973—. Decorated Legion of Merit; recipient Newman award Soc. Am. Mil. Engrs., 1956. Registered profl. engr., Colo., D.C.; registered profl. architect, D.C. Mem. Nat. Soc. Profl. Engrs., Soc. Am. Mil. Engrs. (pres. post 1953, 62, 65, 73), Tex. A. and M. Alumni. Mason. Contbr. articles to tech. mags. Home: Raleigh NC Office: Box 12233 Research Triangle Park NC 27707

EAGLETON, E. JOHN, lawyer; b. Tulsa, Jan. 22; s. W.L. and Pauline F. (Dellinger) E.; B.A., then J.D., U. Okla., 1950-56; m. Norma Haddad, Oct. 6, 1956; children—Courtney Jean, Richard John. Admitted to Okla. bar, 1956; jr. accountant Peat, Marwick Mitchell & Co., Dallas, 1956-57; regional counsel Internal Revenue Service, Dallas and New Orleans, 1957-62; mem. firm Houston, Klein & Davidson, Tulsa, 1962-65, Kothe & Eagleton, Tulsa, 1965—. Lectr. on tax, bus. planning and estate planning. Mem. Fed., Okla. bar assns., Okla., Tex. socs. C.P.A.'s, Tulsa Tax Forum, Tulsa Estate Tax Forum. Rotarian. Home: 3210 E 65th St Tulsa OK 74105 Office: 124 E 4th St Tulsa OK 74103

EAGLETON, JAMES RICHARDSON, lawyer; b. Pawnee, Okla., June 17, 1903; s. William L. and Mattie (Saunders) E.; B.A., U. Okla., 1924, J.D., 1925; m. Ruby M. Moffett, Nov. 30, 1923 (dec. Apr. 1971); children—Suzanne (Mrs. Don R. Nicholson II), Robert M. (dec.); m. 2d, Rosemary E. Callahan, June 24, 1972. Admitted to Okla. bar, 1925; lease buyer and requirements, land dept. Foster Oil Co., Tulsa, 1926-30; gen. practice, Oklahoma City, 1931-40, 1945—; legal asst. Okla. Supreme Ct., Oklahoma City, 1941-44; pres., dir. Royalties, Inc., Oklahoma City, 1970—. Mem. Am., Okla., Oklahoma County bar assns., Phi Alpha Delta, Sigma Chi. Democrat. Presbyn (elder). Home: Apt 1 6305 N Villa St Oklahoma City OK 73112 Office: 217 N Harvey St Investors Capital Bldg Oklahoma City OK 73102

EAGON, ROBERT GARFIELD, educator; b. Salesville, O., Oct. 29, 1927; B.Sc., Ohio State U., 1951, M.Sc., 1952; Ph.D., 1954; m. Margretta Buchanan, Aug. 30, 1952; 1 dau., Victoria. Asst. prof. microbiology U. Ga., Athens, 1955-59, asso. prof., 1959-66, prof., 1966—. Served with M.C., AUS, 1946-49; now lt. col. Res. Fulbright fellow, 1954-55. Fellow Am. Acad. Microbiology; mem. Am. Soc. for Microbiology, Am. Soc. for Biol. Chemists. Editorial bd. Jour. of Bacteriology, 1972—. Contbr. articles in field to profl. jours. Home: 455 Riverview Rd Athens GA 30601

EAKER, NICK, elec. engr.; b. Amarillo, Tex., Sept. 4, 1933; s. Autha Dale and Viola Junita (Speck) E.; B.S. in Elec. Engring., 1958; M.Applied Sci., So. Methodist U., 1970; m. Delores Ann Moore, Feb. 18, 1956; children—Randall Nick, Lori Charisse, Pamela Dawn. Research, devel. engr. Collins Radio Co., Richardson, Tex., 1958-61; research engr. Hallmark Instruments, Inc., Dallas, 1961-62, chief engr., 1962-63, v.p. engring., 1963-64; research scientist U. Tex., Dallas, 1964—, program mgr., 1966—. Cons. analog and digital control systems, telemetry systems. Served with USN, 1952-56. Mem. I.E.E.E., Richardson Jr. C. of C. (dir. 1963-64). Contbr. articles on atmospheric measurements to sci. jours. Home: 312 Canyon Ridge Dr Richardson TX 75080 Office: U Texas-Dallas Box 30365 Dallas TX 75230

EAMES, WILLIAM JAMES, electric co. exec.; b. Lakeview, Pa., Aug. 29, 1927; s. James Timothy and Marguerite (Christ) E.; B.S., Carnegie Inst. Tech., Pitts., 1949; M.B.A., Xavier U., Cin., 1960. Mgr., Eames Butter-Krust Bakery, Tamaqua, Pa., 1952-56; mgmt. analyst aircraft nuclear propulsion Gen. Electric Co., Cin., 1956-61, operations analyst air weapons system, Syracuse, N.Y., 1961-63, mgr. long range mfg. planning, refrigerator div., Louisville, 1964—; lectr. operations research U. Louisville, 1965-66. Served with AUS, 1950-52. Registered profl. engr., Ohio. Mem. Inst. Mgmt. Scis., Am. Soc. Quality Control, Appliance Engrs. Soc. Club: Catholic Alumni. Home: 3501 Illinois Av Louisville KY 40213 Office: Gen Electric Co Appliance Park Louisville KY 40225

EANES, EDWIN COLEY, real estate exec.; b. Sapulpa, Okla., Dec. 18, 1921; s. Arthur Musgrove and Floy Glenn (Coley) E.; B.S., U. Tulsa, 1949; M.S. in Indsl. Adminstrn., USAF Inst. Tech., 1955; m. Betty Jo Winton, May 27, 1945; children—Donna Jo, Edwin Coley. Commd. 2d lt. U.S. Army, 1945, advanced through grades to lt. col. USAF, 1965; resident rep. of auditor gen., San Antonio, Tex., 1955-59; supervisory mgr. Auditor Gen.'s Office, 1959-61, exec. officer, 1961-67; chief research and plans div. USAF, 1965-67; chief mgmt. review, 1967; ret., 1967; gen. mgr. Ray Conard Constrn. Co., Tulsa, 1967-71; mgr. properties Tri State Devel., Tulsa, 1971-73; regional property mgr. Clark-Frates Corp., Dallas, 1973—. Decorated D.F.C., Air medal with clusters. Formed and headed 1st research orgn. in internal audit in U.S., 1965. Home: Apt 2 4908 573d E Av Tulsa OK 74145 Office 7605 E 49th St Tulsa OK 74145

EANES, GORDON LEA, financial exec.; b. Danville, Va., June 24, 1937; s. Douglas R. and Grace (Dehart) E.; B.S., U. Richmond, 1962; student Va. Poly. Inst., 1958-60; m. Nancy Carolyn Hodnett, Aug. 21, 1960; children—Gordon Lea, Leila Carolyn. With Price Waterhouse & Co., Charlotte, N.C., 1962-65, Atlanta, 1965-70, mgr., 1967-70; v.p. finance Air Treads, Inc., Forest Park, Ga., 1970—. Served with USAF, 1954-58. C.P.A., Ga., N.C. Mem. Am. Inst. C.P.A.'s, Ga., N.C. Socs. C.P.A.'s, Alpha Kappa Psi. Republican. Home: 2338 Kings Point Dr Atlanta GA 30341 Office: 5075 Pine Tree St Forest Park GA 30050

EARLEY, HUBERT RANDOLPH, dentist; b. Epworth, Ga., July 20, 1936; s. Homer Cleve and Frankie Iowa (Queen) E.; student U. Fla., 1954-57; D.D.S., Emory U., 1961; m. Lynn Elizabeth Williams, June 8, 1957; children—Jeffrey Thorpe, Clay Randolph. Individual practice dentistry, Orlando, Fla., 1963—. Dir. Barnett S. Orlando Bank; pres. Earlco Inc., land devel. corp. Served to capt. USAF, 1961-63. Mem. Am., Fla., Orange County dental assns., Phi Delta Theta. Republican. Presbyn. Club: Country, University (Orlando). Home: 2112 Santa Antilles Rd Orlando FL 32806 Office: 1319 S Orange Av Orlando FL 32806

EARLEY, JOSEPH EMMETT, educator; b. Providence, Apr. 6, 1932; s. Daniel McGlynn and Margaret Teresa (Doran) E.; B.S. cum laude, Providence Coll., 1954; Ph.D., Brown U., 1957; m. Shirley Ann Titus, June 23, 1956; children—Thomas Daniel, David Gilbert, Joseph Emmett. Research asso. U. Chgo., 1958; asst. prof. Georgetown U., Washington, 1958-63, asso. prof., 1963-69, prof. chemistry, 1969—; vis. asso. Cal. Inst. Tech., 1967-68. Cons., coordinator Chemistry Research Evaluation Service for USAF Office Sci. Research, 1963—. Served to 1st lt. Chem. Corps, U.S. Army, 1957. Recipient Potter prize Brown U., 1957; grantee Smith, Kline & French Found., 1959, NSF, 1960—, AEC, 1961-69, Air Force Office Sci. Research, 1964—. Mem. Am. Chem. Soc., Philosophy of Sci. Assn., A.A.A.S. (life). Democrat. Roman Catholic. K.C. Club: Albertus Magnus Guild. Contbr. articles to profl. jours. Home: 2348 N Greenwich St Falls Church VA 22046 Office: Dept Chemistry Georgetown U Washington DC 20007

EARLS, JAMES ROE, mech. engr.; b. Summerfield, Okla., Apr. 18, 1943; s. James Henry and Fannie Bell (Wooten) E.; student Eastern Okla. A. and M. Coll., 1962-64; B.S., Okla. State U., 1967; M.B.A. Program, Oklahoma City U., 1972, Central State U., 1973—; m. Linda Kay Bradley, Dec. 5, 1970. Aerospace engr. McDonnell-Douglas Corp., St. Louis, 1967-68; mech. engr. USAF, Tinker AFB, Oklahoma City, 1968—. Registered profl. engr. Okla. Mem. Am. Soc. M.E. Democrat. Home: 4724 Crest Pl Oklahoma City OK 73117 Office: Tinker Air Force Base Oklahoma City OK 73145

EARLY, JACK JONES, coll. pres.; b. Corbin, Ky., Apr. 12, 1925; s. Joseph M. and Lela (Jones) E.; A.B., Union Coll., Barbourville, Ky., 1948; M.A., U. Ky., 1953, Ed.D. (So. scholar 1955-56), 1956; B.D., Coll. of Bible, Lexington, Ky., 1956; D.D., Wesley Coll., Grand Forks, N.D., 1961; LL.D., Parsons Coll., 1962; Litt.D., Dakota Wesleyan U., 1969; LL.D., Ia. Wesleyan Coll., 1972; m. Nancye Bruce Whaley, June 1, 1952; children—Lela Katherine, Judith Ann, Laura Hattie. Ordained to ministry Methodist Ch., 1954; pastor Rockhold Circuit (Ky.), 1943-44, Craig's Chapel and Laurel Circuit, London, Ky., 1944-47, Trinity Ch., Oak Ridge, summer 1945, Hindman Ch. (Ky.), 1947-52; dean of men Hindman Settlement Sch., 1948-51; asso. pastor Park Ch., Lexington, Ky., 1952-54; asst. to pres., dean Athens (Ala.) Coll., 1954-55; v.p., dean of coll. Ia. Wesleyan Coll., Mt. Pleasant, 1956-58; pres. Dakota Wesleyan U., 1958-69, Pfeiffer Coll., Misenheimer, N.C., 1969-71; exec. dir. edn. The Am. Bankers Assn., Washington, 1971-73; pres. Limestone Coll., Gaffney, S.C., 1973—. Active Boy Scouts Am. Mem. Ky. Ho. of Reps., 1952-54; v.p. Young Republican Clubs of Ky., 1949-50. Dir. S.D. Found. Pvt. Colls., S.D. Meth. Found., YMCA. Recipient Spoke award Mitchell Jr. C. of C., 1959, Distinguished Service award, 1960; Distinguished Service award S.D. Jr. C. of C., 1960; named Outstanding Former Kentuckian, 1963. Hon. fellow Wroxton Coll., Oxfordshire, Eng. Mem. Jr. C. of C. (dir. 1959), C. of C., Blue Key, Kappa Delta Pi, Phi Delta Kappa, Kappa Phi Kappa, Alpha Psi Omega, Theta Phi, Pi Tau Chi. Home: Limestone Coll Box 39 Gaffney SC 29340

EARLY, JOHN LEVERING, lawyer; b. Staunton, Va., Dec. 19, 1896; s. Charles E. and Ida (Clark) E.; A.B., Washington and Lee U.; LL.B., U. Va., 1923; m. Maebelle C. Brooks, June 2, 1924; 1 son, Charles Edward. Admitted to Va. bar, 1923, W.Va. bar, 1924, Fla. bar 1924; practice law Welch, W.Va., 1923-24, Sarasota, Fla., 1924—; cattleman, breeder thoroughbred Shorthorns. Mem. Sarasota-Bradenton (Fla.) Airport Authority, 1951-53. Mem. Ho. Reps., 1933-39; municipal judge, 1944-46; mayor City Sarasota, 1951-53. Served as pvt., inf., 1918-19. Ky. col. Mem. Sarasota County Bar Assn. (pres.), Am. Legion, D.A.V., Helping Hands (pres.), Rodeheavers Boy's Ranch Assn., Founders Club, Fla. Sheriffs Boys Ranch, Order of Coif. Methodist. Mason, Odd Fellow. Home: 1841 Oak St Sarasota FL 33577 Office: 920 1st Fed Bldg Sarasota FL 33577

EARLY, JULIAN QUAYLE, physician; b. Riner, Va., Mar. 31, 1918; s. James Lawrence and Lottie E. (Lucas) E.; B.A., Bridgewater Coll., 1940, M.D., U. Va., 1943; m. Marion Juanita Shaver, Mar. 21, 1942; children—Susan (Mrs. Rees Russell Jr.), Julian Quayle, Jane Lucas, Stephen Vest. Intern, Phila. Gen. Hosp., 1944-45, asst. chief resident, 1945-46; resident and fellow in cariology U. Va., Charlottesville, 1947-49; practice medicine specializing in internal medicine, Bristol, Tenn., 1950—; mem. staff Bristol Meml. Hosp., 1950-69, chief staff, 1955, 68—; chief cardiology VA Hosp., Columbia, S.C., 1966-68. Served to lt. J.G., USNR, 1945-46. Mem. A.M.A., Tenn.-Va., Sullivan-Johnson County Med. socs., So. Med. Assn., Am. Soc. Internal Medicine, A.C.P., U. Va. Alumni Assn. Home: 301 Robin Rd Bristol TN 37620 Office: 104 Memorial Dr Bristol TN 37620

EARNEST, CHARLES MANSFIELD, chemist, educator; b. Goodsprings, Ala., June 7, 1941; s. Woodrow Wilson and Helen Lee (Hawkins) E.; B.S., U. Ala., 1964, Ph.D. (NSF fellow), 1970. Grad. asst. dept. chemistry U. Ala., Tuscaloosa, 1964-67; prof. chemistry Stillman Coll., Tuscaloosa, 1969—. Mem. Consensus 21. NIH research grantee, 1973. Mem. Am. Chem. Soc. (treas. Ala. sect.), Sigma Xi, Gamma Sigma Epsilon. Presbyn. Contbr. articles to profl. jours. Home: Stillman Faculty Apts Tuscaloosa AL 35401

EARP, JAMES FRANCY, civil engr.; b. Spencer, W.Va., Feb. 11, 1935; s. Fogle Francy and Hettie Catherine (Langford) E.; B.S. in Civil Engring., W.Va. U., 1958; divorced; children—James Kevin, Gregory Allen, Shannetta Sue, Jennifer Lynn. Sec., mgr. F.F. Earp & Son, Inc., Fairmont, W.Va., 1958-60; pres. Laurel Materials & Engring., Inc., Fairmont, 1960-65; engr. Anderson's Black Rock, Inc., Charleston, W.Va., 1965-68, Polk County Engring. Dept., Bartow, Fla., 1969-70; owner J.F. Earp Assos., cons. engrs., Lakeland, Fla., 1970—; cons. transactional analysis, 1973—. Mem. Am. Soc. C.E. (past pres. Ridge chpt.), Fla. Engrs., Soc., Nat. Soc. Profl. Engrs. Methodist (tchr., mem. choir). Home: PO Box 620 Lakeland FL 33802 Office: PO Box 1095 Lakeland FL 33802

EARP, ROBERT DEAN, lawyer; b. El Paso, Tex., July 21, 1941; s. Marion Dean and Pina Mae (Hays) E.; B.B.A., U. Tex., 1962, J.D., 1964; m. Mary Helen McGrath, Dec. 20, 1963; 2 children—Robert Dean, Dean Alan. Admitted to Tex. bar, 1964, U.S. Supreme Ct. bar, Fed. Ct. Western Dist. Tex. bar; practiced in El Paso, 1964—; asst. dist. atty., City of El Paso, 1964-68; mem. firm Diamond, Rash, Leslie & Schwartz, 1968—. Mem. Tex., El Paso County (chmn. Law Day com.) bar assns., Am., Tex. trial lawyers assns. Home: 6308 Fiesta St El Paso TX 79912 Office: Suite 1208 1208 SW Center El Paso TX 79901

EASLEY, CHARLES TAYLOR, ins. co. exec.; b. Hillsboro, Tex., Oct. 24, 1930; s. Knight Homan and Ruth Crow (Lambert) E.; B.A., Tex A. and M. U., 1951; m. Janelle Hicks, Aug. 1, 1953; children—Paul Alan, Janelle. Asso. actuary, chief underwriter Amicable Life Ins. Co., Waco, Tex., 1953-60; owner Hicks, Easley & Co. ins. agy., Waco, 1960—; v.p. Lake Waco Golf Course, Inc., 1965—; dir. Westview Nat. Bank Waco. Lectr. Am. art history Baylor U., 1971—. Bd. dirs. Historic Waco Found., Better Bus. Bur. Waco, Waco Pub. Library. Served with AUS, 1951-53. Mem. Nat., Tex. assns. ins. agts. Clubs: City, Waco, Lake Waco Country, Ridgewood Country. Two-man show with son, photography, Klaras Art Gallery, 1973; exhbns. at Baylor U., 1973, Waco Pub. Library, 1974. Home: 5108 Lake Jackson Dr Waco TX 76710 Office: 516 Golden Triangle Waco TX 76710

EASON, HELGA RUTH HALVORSEN (MRS. MORRIS JACKSON EASON), librarian; b. Nebraska City, Neb.; d. Lee Roy and Luella (Strong) Halvorsen; student Evansville (Ind.) Coll., 1924-25; A.B., Ohio Wesleyan U., 1927; B.S., Simmons Coll., 1929; m. Morris Jackson Eason, Nov. 23, 1947. Circulation asst. N.Y. Pub. Library, 1930-39; br. librarian Evansville Pub. Library, 1941-45; head reference dept. Miami (Fla.) Pub. Library, (name Miami-Dade Pub. Library System 1971—), 1947-52, head community relations dept., 1952—. Mem. program com. WTHS-TV Community TV Found. South Fla., 1955-70. Bd. dirs. Miami Finance Welfare Employees Fed. Credit Union, 1949-72, sec., 1963-72; bd. dirs. Miami League Women Voters, 1952-53. Recipient certificate of merit Fla. Fedn. Womens Clubs, 1964; John Cotton Dana Publicity awards for library, 1952-54. Mem. Am. (past dir., com. chmn., 2d. vice pres. adult services div. 1968-69; now reference and adult services rep. to membership com. promotion task force), Fla. (Nat. Library Week award 66, sect. pres., com. chmn.), Dade County (past pres.) library assns., City Miami Pub. Library Staff Orgn. (past pres.), Nat. League Am. Pen Women (sec., dir., past v.p. Greater Miami br., editor Owls Feather 1970-72, 1st v.p. 1972-74, pres. 1974—, conv. chmn. state orgn. 1972-74, workshop chmn. 1974—), Laramore Rader Poetry Group (pres. 1959-61). Contbr. articles to profl. jours. Home: 152 NE 46th St Miami FL 33137 Office: 1 Biscayne Blvd Miami FL 33132

EASTER, RUFUS BENJAMIN, JR., ednl. adminstr.; b. Hampton, Va., Oct. 5, 1928; s. Rufus Benjamin and Annie (Watts) E.; ed. N.Y. U., Hampton, Inst., Temple U., Piano Technicians Schs.; m. Evelyn Wills, June 8, 1951; children—Rufus Benjamin III, Robert Landon, Russell Alan, Deborah Ann. Adminstr. Hampton Inst., 1950—; curriculum developer, cons. to supt. Va. State Sch. Deaf and Blind, 1954—; founder, exec. dir. Hampton Assn. Arts and Humanities, 1967—; cons. community affairs radio and TV sta. WVEC, 1970—. Bd. dirs. Assn. Coll. and Univ. Concert Mgrs., Peninsula Symphony Orch, Peninsula Community Theatre. Recipient Man of Year award Peninsula Vol. Services Bur. for work arts and humanities, 1969. Mem. Asso. Council Arts, Assn. State and Local History, Assn. Preservation Va. Antiquities. Club: Bachelor Benedict. Home: 1036 Mary Peake Blvd Hampton VA 23677

EASTERDAY, KENNETH EUGENE, educator; b. Kirksville, Ind., June 27, 1933; s. Harvey and Emma (Robison) E.; B.S., Ind. U., 1955, M.A., 1961; Ed.D., Case Western Res. U., 1963; m. Helen Chesrown, Aug. 8, 1959; 1 son, Norman Eugene. Tchr. pub. schs., Norwalk, O., 1957, Columbus, Ind., 1957-59, Parma, O., 1959-63; asso. prof. math. N.Y. State U. at Potsdam, 1963-64; prof. edn. Auburn (Ala.) U., 1964—. Served with M.C., U.S. Army, 1955-57. Eli Lilly research fellow in math., 1958, Gen. Electric fellow in math., 1959. Co-author: Random House Mathematics Program, 1969-70. Home: 1212 Boxwood Blvd Columbus GA 31906 Office: 5064 Haley Center Auburn U Auburn AL 36830

EASTERLING, WILLIAM EWART, JR., physician, educator; b. Raleigh, N.C., Oct. 8, 1930; s. William Ewart and Hannah (Montgomery) E.; A.B., Duke, 1953; M.D., U. N.C., 1956; m. Mary Ellyn Roye, June 7, 1952; children—William Ewart III, David R., R. Bryan, J. Wyatt, Jeffrey T. Intern, N.C. Meml. Hosp., 1956-57, resident, 1957-61; asst. prof. obstetrics and gynecology U. N.C., Chapel Hill, 1964-67, asso. prof., 1967-72, prof., 1972—. Bd. dirs. N.C. div. Am. Cancer Soc., Penich Home for Aged. Served with USAF, 1961-63. Diplomate Am. Bd. Obstetrics and Gynecology. Mem. A.M.A., So. Med. Assn., Endocrine Soc., N.Y. Acad. Scis., Am. Coll. Obstetricians and Gynecologists, Soc. for Gynecologic Investigation, Robert A. Ross Obstet. & Gynecol. Soc. Home address: 2134 N Lakeshore Dr Chapel Hill NC 27514

EASTERWOOD, KENNETH, SR., architect; b. Davilla, Tex., 1910; s. Birch Duggan and Pearl (Barker) E.; student Baylor U., 1930-31, U. Tex., 1931-32; m. Rosalee Pritchett, Oct. 18, 1934; 1 son, Kenneth. Prin. Kenneth Easterwood & Assos., Architects, Ft. Worth, 1932—. Prin. works include 20 bldgs. at Baylor U., also hosp., schs., comml. and indsl. works. Home: 1903 Rockridge St Fort Worth TX 76102 Office: 1319 Summit St Fort Worth TX 76102

EASTLAND, DAVID MEADE, engring. educator; b. Meridian, Miss., Nov. 27, 1922; s. James Oliver and Bess (Remschel) E.; B.S., Miss. State U., 1944, M.S., 1950; m. Hattie Mae Miller, Dec. 14, 1944 (dec. June 1972). Jr. engr. Tenn. Eastman Co., Oak Ridge, 1944-46; mem. faculty Miss. State U., 1946—, prof. mech. engring., 1958—; cons. in field. Registered profl. engr., Miss. Mem. Am. Soc. M.E., Am. Soc. Engring. Edn., Nat., Miss. socs. profl. engrs., Oktibbehe County C. of C.; hon. mem. Pi Tau Sigma, Tau Beta Pi. Republican. Club: Starkville Country. Home: Route 5 Box 408 Starkville MS 39759 Office: Drawer ME Miss State Univ State College MS 39762

EASTLAND, ELIZABETH COLEMAN (MRS. JAMES OLIVER EASTLAND), wife of U.S. senator; b. Doddsville, Miss., Nov. 28, 1909; d. Julian Eugene and Ella (Grider) Coleman; A.B., Sophie Newcomb Coll., 1930; m. James Oliver Eastland (U.S. senator from Miss.), July 6, 1932; children—Nell (Mrs. Culberson Amos), Anne (Mrs. Donald Howdeshell), Susan (Mrs. Champ Terney), Woods Eugene. Mem. Phi Mu. Club: Congressional (Washington). Home: 5116 Macomb St NW Washington DC 20016

EASTLAND, JAMES O., U.S. senator; b. Doddsville, Miss., Nov. 28, 1904; s. Woods Caperton and Alma (Austin) E.; student U. Miss., 1922-24, Vanderbilt U., 1925-26, U. Ala., 1926-27; m. Elizabeth Coleman, July 6, 1932; children—Nell, Anne, Sue, Woods Eugene. Admitted to Miss. bar, 1927, practiced Forest, Miss.; moved to Sunflower County, 1934; apptd. to U.S. Senate to fill vacancy, June-Sept. 1941; elected U.S. senator, 1943—, chmn. senate com. on judiciary, 1956—. Mem. Miss. House of Reps., 1928-32. Democrat. Home: Doddsville, MS 38736 also 5116 Macomb St Washington DC 20016 Office: Dirksen Bldg Washington DC 20510

EASTMOORE, EUGENE LEGARE, judge; b. Jacksonville, Fla., May 22, 1929; s. Theodore Harold and Harriet (Manning) E.; B.A., U. Fla., 1950, J.D., 1952; m. Jeanine Herrington, June 8, 1952; children—Katherine Harriet, Theodore Charles, John Riley. Admitted to Fla. bar, 1952; practiced in Palatka, Fla., 1954-72; atty. City of Palatka, 1956-59, 61-72; judge Circuit Ct. 7th Jud. Circuit, 1973—. Mem. exec. com. Fla. Conf. Circuit Judges. Bd. dirs. Rodeheavers Boys Ranch, Putnam County Blood Bank (pres. 1967-71). Served with AUS, 1951-54; lt. col. Fla. N.G., 1954—. Mem. Am., Putnam County bar assns., Fla. Bar, Am. Legion, Nat., Fla. skeet shooting assns., C. of C., V.F.W. Episcopalian. Elk, Kiwanian (pres. 1963; lt. gov. 1967). Club: Palatka Skeet (pres. 1966). Home: 2210 Palma Ceia Palatka FL 32077 Office: Courthouse Palatka FL 31077

EASTWOOD, RICHARD TRUMAN, med. adminstr.; b. Pawnee County, Neb., Nov. 19, 1912; s. Frank Wesley and Elizabeth (Wilkinson) E.; A.B., Tarkio (Mo.) Coll., 1936; M.A., U. Neb., 1939; Ph.D. in Econs. (Richard T. Ely scholar 1939-40), U. Wis., 1954; m. Elizabeth Comer, Apr. 5, 1942; children—Elizabeth Ann, Barbara Jean. Instr., Maysville (Mo.) High Sch., 1936-38; grad. asst. U. Neb., 1938-39; instr. econs. U. Ala., 1939-43, asst. supr. engring., sci. and mgmt. war tng. program, 1941-43, asst. prof. mgmt., then asso. prof., 1946-54, dir. commerce extension service, 1946-51, prof. econs., 1954-62, dir. Birmingham Center, 1951-58, asso. dean extension div., 1956-58, exec. dir. univ. affairs in Birmingham, 1958-62; exec. v.p. Tex. Med. Center, Houston, 1962—. Cons. NIH, 1961—; mem. nat. adv. council Inst. Gen. Med. Scis.; chmn. Com. Aging Jefferson County, Ala., 1954, 56-60; mem. Gov. Ala. Adv. Com. Planning for White House Conf. Aging, also del., 1961; chmn. Ala. Subcom. Housing Needs for Older Persons, 1960-61; sec., vice chmn., chmn. Regional Med. Programs Tex.; v.p., sec. Tex. Med. Center Housing, Inc. Bd. dirs. Jefferson County Coordinating Council Social Forces, 1956-62; trustee, v.p. Med. Benevolence Found. Served to lt. USNR, 1943-46. Am. Christian Palestine Com. scholar for study tour Middle East, 1955. Mem. Soc. Advancement Mgmt. (pres. Ala. 1953-54), Nat. U. Extension Assn. (sec. eve. div. 1958-59), Am., So. econ. assns., Indsl. Relations Research Assn., Tex. Med. Assn. (com. continuing edn. 1971-74, com. health planning 1974—), Houston C. of C. (dir. 1973), Alpha Kappa Psi, Phi Beta Pi. Presbyn. (permanent theol. com. Gen. Assembly, chmn. candidates and exams. com. Brazos Presbytery 1973-74). Home: 6135 Doliver Dr Houston TX 77027

EAVES, GRADY JYLES, lawyer; b. Louisville, Miss., Nov. 6, 1933; s. William Andrew and Pearl (Rogers) E.; B.A., Miss. State U., 1960; J.D., U. Miss., 1962; m. Juan Dean Herrington, Aug. 25, 1962; 1 dau., Juanita Pearl. Admitted to Miss. bar, 1962, since practiced in Jackson, Louisville, 1964—; sr. mem. Eaves & Eaves, 1963—; dist. atty. Fifth Circuit Ct. Dist. Miss., 1967-72. Vice pres. Louisville-Winston Ednl. Found., Inc. Served with Hosp. Corps, USNR, 1956-57. Mem. Winston County Bar Assn. (past pres.), Am. Legion, Phi Alpha Delta. Democrat. Baptist. Mason (Shriner). Home: East Ridge Dr Louisville MS 39339 Office: 114 S. Columbus Av Louisville MS 39339

EAVES, JOEL HARRY, athletic dir.; b. Copperhill Tenn., June 3, 1914; s. Rufus Harry and Mabel (Puckett) E.; B.S. in Edn., Auburn U., 1937; m. Wealthy Elizabeth Lindsay, Jan. 20, 1946; children—Wealthy Joanne. Basketball coach, asst. in football U. of South, 1937-41, Boys High Sch., Atlanta, 1946-47; basketball coach, head football Murphy High Sch., Atlanta, 1947-49; basketball coach Auburn U., 1949-63, asst. in football, 1949-60; athletic dir. U. Ga., Athens, 1963—. Mem. U.S. Olympic Basketball Com.; mem. basketball tournament com. Nat. Collegiate Athletic Assn. Served to lt. col. F.A., AUS, 1941-45. Named S.E. Conf. Basketball Coach of Year, 1958, 60, 62, Ga. Sports Adminstr. of Year, 1972; named to Ga. Athletic Hall Fame, 1972, v.p., 1973. Presbyn. Author: Basketball's Shuffle Offense, 1960. Home: 550 Forest Rd Athens GA 30601

EAVES, WILLIAM ALFRED, steel co. exec.; b. Chattanooga, Dec. 23, 1925; s. Robert Edwin and Nell (Eldridge) E.; grad. high sch.; m. Iris Shannon Williams, Mar. 31, 1952; children—Martha Jane, William Alfred, Jr. Clk. Vance Iron & Steel, Chattanooga, 1945-55; with O'Neal Steel, Inc., Chattanooga, 1955—, v.p., 1968—. Methodist. Lion (sec. 1973). Home: Mason Dr Ringgold GA 30736 Office: 2500 E 38th St Chattanooga TN 37407

EBAUGH, ELIZABETH BROWN (MRS. FRANK WRIGHT EBAUGH), civic worker; b. Jacksonville, Tex.; d. John Lemuel and Jewel (Newton) Brown; B.A., U. Colo., 1925; M.A., Tchrs. Coll., Columbia, 1927; m. Frank Wright Ebaugh, Feb. 22, 1930; 1 dau., Betty Jane (Mrs. Gordon B. McFarland, Jr.). Kindergarten tchr., Port Arthur, Tex., 1927-30. Mem. bd. Jacksonville (Tex.) Pub. Library, 1944—, pres., 1944-46, curator, organizer Vanishing Texana Mus., 1965—. Mem. Cherokee County Hist. Survey Com., 1964—. Recipient Appreciation plaque Jacksonville Library, 1969. Mem. D.A.R. (charter; registar 1965—), Chi Omega. Presbyn. (historian 1965-66). Home: 428 S Patton St Jacksonville TX 75766

EBAUGH, FRANK WRIGHT, cons. indsl. engr., investments exec.; b. New Orleans, July 31, 1901; s. John Lynn and Mary (Wright) E.; B. in Chem. Engring., Tulane U., 1923; m. Elizabeth Brown, Feb. 22, 1930; 1 dau., Betty Jane (Mrs. Gordon B. McFarland, Jr.). Engr., asso. mgmt. Texas Co., 1923-34; partner retail firm, Jacksonville, Tex., 1934-54; mgr., partner Ebaugh & Brown Investments, Jacksonville, 1955-62; dir. Palestine Savs. & Loan Assn. Pres. Upper Neches River Municipal Water Authority; dir. Tex. Indsl. Devel. Council; vice chmn. Tex. Mapping Adv. Com.; sec. Tex. Coordinating Water Com.; pres. Neches River Devel. Assn.; Mem. panel chmn. Cherokee County (Texas) War Price and Ration Board, 3 years. Mem. regional com. of Girl Scouts Am.; mem. Cherokee County Hist. Survey Com. Bd. dirs. Neches River Conservation Dist. Named Man of Month, East Tex. C. of C., 1953; named Man of Year, Lions Club, 1953; honored as Distinguished Visitor Tex. Senate; Appreciation Plaque erected in Jacksonville Library, 1969. Mem. Nat., Tex. (chmn. Water Com.) socs. profl. engrs., East Texas, Jacksonville (past pres., dir., chmn. water resources com.) C.'s of C., Am. Chem. Soc., A.A.A.S., Tex. Acad. Sci., Tex. Water Conservation Assn., Texas Water Pollution Control Assn. Presbyn. (elder). Clubs: Headliners (Austin); Rotary, Country of Jacksonville (past pres.). Patentee Ebaugh Mixer. Home: 428 S Patton St Jacksonville TX 75766 Office: Box 1031 Jacksonville TX 75766

EBBESSON, SVEN OLOF EBBE, educator; b. Backaby, Sweden, Oct. 14, 1937; s. Ebbe Sven and Ruth (Gota) E.; came to U.S., 1953, naturalized, 1958; A.B., Southwestern Coll., 1957; Ph.D., U. Md., 1964; m. Barbara Penzotti, Oct. 3, 1962; children—Gunnar, Lars, Nils. Asst. in anatomy Tulane U., New Orleans, 1958-60; neuroanatomist dept. neurophysiology Walter Reed Army Inst. Research, Washington, 1962-65; instr. anatomy U. Md., Balt., 1964-65; asst. prof. anatomy U. P.R., San Juan, 1966-69, vis. prof., 1969, 71, 72; sr. scientist USPHS, head comparative neurology sect. lab. perinatal physiology Nat. Inst. Neurol. Diseases and Stroke, San Juan, 1965-69; asso. prof. neurol. surgery and anatomy U. Va., Charlottesville, 1969-72, prof., 1972—. Vis. prof. State U. N.Y., Bklyn., 1971-72, U. Cal. at Berkeley, 1971-72; cons. NASA, 1971-72; pres., dir. Solhem Farm, Inc., North Garden, Va., 1972—. Served to capt. AUS, 1961-65; lt. comdr. to comdr. USPHS, 1965-69. Decorated Army Commendation medal; recipient Career Devel. award Nat. Inst. Neurol. Diseases and Stroke, 1971—. Mem. Am. Assn. Anatomists, A.A.A.S., Internat. Soc. for Stereology, Am. Soc. Zoologists, Biol. Stain Commn., Soc. for Neurosci. (pres. Va. chpt. 1972-74). Home: Solhem North Garden VA 22959 Office: Dept Neurosurgery U Va Charlottesville VA 22901

EBEL, ALAN JOHN, elec. engr.; b. Winston-Salem, N.C., Sept. 9, 1947; s. John Rudolph and Lois Aline (Hardin) E.; B.S. in Elec. Engring., N.C. State U., 1969; m. Julia Margaret Taylor, Nov. 27, 1971. With Duke Power Co., 1969—, dist. engr., High Point, N.C., 1973—. Mem. Greensboro Oritorio Soc. Methodist (mem. choir 1962-65, youth counselor 1968-72, treas. Men's Club 1973, pres. Young Adult Club 1972-73). Home: PO Box 145 Thomasville NC 27360 Office: 233 S Main St High Point NC 27261

EBERHARDT, WILLIAM HENRY, educator; b. Montclair, N.J., Feb. 11, 1920; s. Ernest Theodore and Marian Carver (Vanderhoef) E.; B.A., Johns Hopkins, 1941; Ph.D., Cal. Inst. Tech., 1945; m. Dorothy Burgess, Sept. 28, 1946; children—Kathrine (Mrs. Frank Maguson), Barbara (Mrs. Haven Hodges), Carol. Asst. prof. Ga. Inst. Tech., Atlanta, 1946-50, asso. prof., 1950-56, prof. chemistry, 1956-62, Regents prof., 1962—, asso. dean, 1969—; vis. prof. U. Minn., 1953, U. Ill., 1956, Harvard, 1963; exec. dir. Adv. Council on Coll. Chemistry, 1967. Mem. Am. Chem. Soc., A.A.A.S., Am. Phys. Soc. Home: 2249 Riada Dr NW Atlanta GA 30305

EBERT, MYRL LUA-FRANCES, librarian, educator; b. Louisville, Oct. 20, 1913; d. Clifford William and Ella Mae (Pitt) Ebert; B.S. George Peabody Coll., 1943; B.S. in L.S., George Peabody Library Sch., 1945; M.S., Columbia, 1951. Clerical asst. Vanderbilt U. Med. Sch. Library, also joint univ. libraries, Nashville, 1939-45; reference asst. Columbia U. Sch. Med. Library, N.Y.C., 1945-46; reference asst., asst. reference librarian, periodical librarian N.Y. Acad. Medicine, N.Y.C., 1946-51; library asso. N.Y.U. Bellevue Med. Center Library, N.Y.C., 1951-52; dir., prof. librarianship Health Scis. Libraries, U. N.C., Chapel Hill, 1952—, prof. Sch. Library Sci., 1958-73. Cons. med., hosp. libraries, instns.; med. library cons. U. Saigon Med. Center, 1966-73; cons. medlars program Nat. Library Medicine, 1965-73; bd. dirs. U.S. Book Exchange. Mem. Med. Library Assn. (chmn. so. regional group 1953-54, sec. 1962-64), Spl. Libraries Assn., N.C. Library Assn. (rec. sec. 1957-59), Am. Assn. History Medicine. Author: Introduction to Literature of the Medical Sciences, 3d edit., 1970. Contbr. articles to profl. jours. Home: Route 6 Box 126 Chapel Hill NC 27514

ECHANDI, EDDIE, educator; b. San Jose, Costa Rica, Nov. 21, 1926; s. Jorge and Gladys (Zurcher) E.; B.S., U. Costa Rica, 1951; M.S., IICA, Turrialsba, Costa Rica, 1952; Ph.D., U. Wis., 1955; m. Mildred Saborio de Echandi, July 5, 1952; children—Diana, Ivonne. Came to U.S., 1969. Head dept. plant pathology Ministry of Agr., Costa Rica, 1955; prof. plant pathology, head dept. plant industry and soils IICA, 1967; prof. plant pathology N.C. State U., 1967—. AID fellow, 1952-54. Mem. Am. Phytopath. Soc., Asociacion Latinoamericana de Phytopatologia. Author: Manual de Laboratorio para Fitopatologia General, 1971. Asso. editor of Phytopathology, 1972—. Home: 4908 N Hills Dr Raleigh NC 27607

ECHANIZ, PEDRO ARNULFO, food co. exec.; b. El Paso, Tex., Feb. 7, 1914; s. Pedro and Maria (Reyes) E.; grad. high sch.; m. Dorothy West, July 17, 1938; 1 son, David W. Salesman, Cotera Bros., El Paso, 1932-42; with Seven-Up Bottling Co., El Paso, 1942—, sec., treas., mgr., 1956—. Home: 9905 Honolulu Dr El Paso TX 79925 Office: 7328 Boeing Dr El Paso TX 79925

ECHOLS, DOROTHY JANE HILLE (MRS. JAMES EWELL ECHOLS, JR.), civic worker; b. Collins, Miss., June 4, 1932; d. Hollie Rich and Bessie Mae (McKenzie) Shoemake; B.S., U. So. Miss., 1954, M.S., 1967; m. James Ewell Echols, Jr., Nov. 12, 1970; children—Kimberly, Scott Alan. Counselor, acad. adviser U. So. Miss., 1965-67, asst. dean women, 1967-68, dean of women, 1968-71. Active P.T.A., Cub Scout Am.; chmn. Seoul Officers Wives Club Korean Welfare Com. Recipient Faculty Outstanding Service award U. So. Miss., 1970-71. Mem. Nat. Assn. Women Deans and Counselors, So. U. Student Govt. Assn. (exec. mem.), Am. Assn. U. Women (1st v.p.), Protestant Women of Chapel, Delta Kappa Gamma, Phi Mu. Mem. Order Eastern Star. Club: Officers Wives (pres. 1972-73 Ft. McPherson, Ga.). Home: KRE HQ APO San Francisco CA 96301

ECHTERHOFF, JAMES HENRY, pipeline co. exec.; b. San Antonio, Dec. 31, 1914; s. John Henry and Lela Ethel (Gabbart) E.; B.S., Tex. A. and M. U., 1936; postgrad. Harvard Bus. Sch., 1965; m. Marion Lucille Blanchard, Oct. 11, 1941; children—James Henry, Lawrence B., John T. With United Gas Pipe Line Co., Shreveport, La., 1938—, asst. gen. supt., 1964-67, asst. to pres., 1968-69, v.p., 1969—. Served to capt. C.E., AUS, 1941-45. Mem. Am., So. gas assns. Presbyn. (deacon, elder). Rotarian. Clubs: Shreveport, Shreveport Country. Home: 3929 Maryland St Shreveport LA 71106 Office: 1525 Fairfield St Shreveport LA 71102

ECKBERG, LLOYD ELLSWORTH, orgn. exec.; b. Shinnston, W.Va., Nov. 11, 1929; s. William Quinn and Emma (Rhodes) E.; student, Fairmont State Coll., 1947-50; m. Glenna Maxine Tacy, Aug. 26, 1950; children—Tim Edward, Sharri Ann. Gen. mgr. Burnham Warehouses, Columbus, Ga., 1952-59; life underwriter N.Y. Life Ins. Co., Columbus, 1959-60; exec. dir. Warner Robins (Ga.) C. of C., 1960-63; exec. v.p. Thomasville-Thomas County C. of C., Thomasville, Ga., 1963—. Bd. dirs. Salvation Army. Served with AUS, 1950-52. Mem. Ga. C. of C. Execs. Assn. (pres. 1967-68), Am. C. of C. Execs. Assn., So Assn. C. of C. Execs. (dir. 1964-69), So. Indsl. Devel. Council. Methodist. Club: Optimist. Contbg. editor Ga. Bus. and Securities News. Home: 527 E Jefferson St Thomasville GA 31792 Office: 401 S Broad St Thomasville GA 31792

ECKBERT, WILLIAM FOX, physician; b. New Cumberland, Pa., May 25, 1914; s. Chester Arthur and Angeline (Mapes) E.; student U. Del., 1932-35; M.D., Duke U., 1939; m. Sarah Ann Wilson, Apr. 9, 1939; children—William Fox, Patricia Ann. Intern Balt. City Hosps., 1939-40; resident contagious diseases Sydenham Hosp., Balt., 1940-41; gen. practice medicine Garrett Meml. Hosp., Crossnore, N.C., 1941-42; pvt. practice medicine, Cramerton, N.C., 1946—; mem. staff Gaston Meml. Hosp., chief of staff, 1959-60. Pres. Gaston County Cancer Soc., 1962-63; mem. Cramerton Sch. Bd., 1951-58. Bd. dirs. Gaston County Heart Assn. Served to capt. AUS, 1942-46. Decorated Bronze Star medal. Mem. Am., So. med. assns., N.C. State Med. Soc., Am. Acad. Gen. Practice, Am. Assn. Physicians and Surgeons, Gaston County Med. Soc. (pres. 1955-56), Sigma Nu, Alpha Kappa Kappa. Republican. Presbyn. (trustee, ruling elder). Kiwanian (pres. 1952), Elks. Club: Gaston Country. Home: Box 360 Belvue Terrace Rt 4 Gastonia NC 28052 Office: Box 317 Cramerton NC 28032

ECKELMANN, WALTER ROBERT, research co. exec.; b. Englewood, N.J., May 25, 1929; s. Herman John and Rosa (Schwarz) E.; B.S., Wheaton Coll., 1951; M.A., Columbia, 1953, Ph.D., 1956; m. Barbara Burda, Aug. 25, 1951; children—Robert, Carol, Bryan. Various tech. mgmt. positions Exxon Corp., 1957-72; pres., dir. Esso Prodn. Research Co., Houston, 1972—. Mem. A.A.A.S., Am. Assn. Petroleum Geologists, Am. Chem. Soc., Am. Petroleum Inst., Am. Geophys. Union, N.Y. Acad. Scis., Am. Geophys. Soc., Indsl. Research Inst., Sigma Xi. Clubs: Petroleum, Lakeside Country. Home: 306 N Wilcrest St Houston TX 77024 Office: PO Box 2189 Houston TX 77001

ECKELS, ROBERT Y., county ofcl.; b. Temple, Tex., July 24, 1929; s. Robert Y. and Mildred Louise (Daniel) E.; B.S., Sam Houston State Coll., 1949; M.Ed., U. Houston, 1955; m. Carolyn Bickley, Dec. 20, 1949; children—Robert Allen, Carol Ann. Tchr., Houston Ind. Sch. Dist., 1949-57; ins. agt. Bob Eckels & Assos., 1963-70, gen. agt., 1957-60, co. mgr., 1960-63; pres. Sur-Agts., Inc., Houston, 1970-73; county commr., Harris County, Tex., 1973—; dir. Mark III, Gulf Coast Nat. Bank. Mem. Houston Ind. Sch. Dist. Bd. Edn., 1961-69, pres., 1964-65, 68-69. Mem. Sam Houston Alumni Assn. (pres. 1970-71), P.T.A. Mason (32 deg., Shriner). Home: 32 E Shady Lane Houston TX 77042 Office: Family Law Center Houston TX 77005

ECKERT, ANDREW WILBURN, ednl. adminstr.; b. Galveston, Tex., Nov. 27, 1915; s. Fred Andrew and Cora B. (Northington) E.; A.A., U. Houston, 1935; B.B.A., U. Tex., 1941; M.Ed., Tex. Tech U., 1939; m. Winona Helen Sloan, May 11, 1937; children—Andrea (Mrs. Tom Harold Watters), Andrew Wilburn, Sherry, Maribeth. Bus. mgr. Orange Ind. Sch. Dist. (Tex.), 1947-51; bus. mgr. Lubbock (Tex.) Ind. Sch. Dist., 1951-63; asso. supt. bus. Mpls. Pub. Schs., 1963-70; mgr. ednl. resources Dallas Pub. Schs., after 1970, now mgr. fiscal operations. Vis. instr. U. Wis. Sch. Bus. Workshop, 1968—; cons. Tex. Tech U., U. Tex., 1951-63, vis. lectr. Sch. Bus. Workshop, 1973—. Pres. Camp Fire Girls, 1952-54. Bd. dirs. A.R.C., United Fund. Recipient commendations A.R.C., 1963. Ednl. Facilities Lab. grantee, 1967. Mem. Am. Assn. Sch. Adminstrs., Assn. Sch. Bus. Ofcls., Tex. Assn. Sch. Bus. Ofcls. (pres. 1955), Met. Sch. Facilities Council, Tex. State Tchrs. Assn., Dallas Sch. Adminstrs. Assn., Phi Delta Kappa, Sigma Iota Epsilon. Democrat. Methodist. Rotarian, Kiwanian. Home: 5977 Fox Hill Lane Dallas TX 75232 Office: 3700 Ross St Dallas TX 75204

ECKHARDT, ROBERT CHRISTIAN, congressman; b. Austin, Tex., July 16, 1913; s. Joseph Carl Augustus and Norma (Wurzbach) E.; B.A., U. Tex., 1935, LL.B., 1939; m. Orissa Stephenson (dec.); children—Orissa, Rosalind; m. 2d, Nadine Ellen Cannon, Mar. 8, 1962; children—Sidney, Shelby, Willie, Sarah. S.W. regional dir. Office Coordinator Inter-Am. Affairs, Austin, 1944-46; admitted to Tex. bar, 1939, practice law Austin, 1939-42, 46-48, Dallas, 1948-50, Houston, 1950-67; mem. Tex. Ho. of Reps., Austin, 1958-67; mem. 90th to 93d Congresses from 8th Tex. Dist., mem. interstate and fgn. commerce com., mcht. marine and fisheries com. Served with USAAC, 1942-44. Mem. State Bar Tex. Democrat. Home: 18710 Bamwood St Houston TX 77090 Office: 1741 Longworth House Office Bldg Washington DC 20515

ECKLUND, GEORGE NORMAN, govt. ofcl.; b. Odebolt, Ia., June 7, 1920; s. George Milton and Anna Naomi (Peterson) E.; B.A., Drake U., 1945; M.A., U. Minn., 1953, Ph.D., 1962; m. Dolores Lula Newberg, Mar. 16, 1945; children—Carol, Paula, Valerie. Mem. pub. relations staff Pillsbury Mills, Inc., Mpls., 1946-49; economist CIA, Washington, 1953-69; dir. Office Econ. Research, U.S. Tariff Commn., 1969—. Professorial lectr. econs. Am. U., Washington, 1962-69. Served with USAAF, 1942-45. Recipient certificate of Distinction, CIA, 1969. Mem. Am. Econs. Assn. Club: Tacomis (Washington). Author: Financing the Chinese Government Budget, 1950-59, 1966; contbr. chpt. to China A Handbook, 1973. Home: 4211 Woodlark Dr Annandale VA 22003 Office: United State Tariff Commn Washington DC 20436

ECKOLS, HOWARD LOYD, banker; b. Luling, Tex., Mar. 23, 1930; s. Lewis Vernard and Gladys (Colwell) E.; student Tex. Tech., 1947-48; B.B.A., S.W. Tex. State U., 1954; m. Martha Lynn Wilson, Jan. 24, 1954; children—Timothy, Linda. State auditor State of Tex., Austin, 1954-55; mgr. data processing Shell Oil Co., Houston, 1956-62, Tex. Commerce Bank, 1962-69; mgr. data processing Houston Nat. Bank, 1969—, asst. v.p., 1965—. Served with USNR, 1948-49. Mem. Data Processing Mgmt. Assn. (dir. Houston chpt. 1965—). Home: 7219 Bayou Forest Dr Houston TX 77088 Office: Box 2518 Houston TX 77001

ECROYD, RICHARD JOSEPH, bldg. co. exec.; b. Suffern, N.Y., Mar. 25, 1940; s. William Henry and Angela Rose (Kuzmik) E.; B.A., Southeastern U., Washington, 1970; M.B.A., Loyola Coll., Balt., 1972. Chief accountant Arlington Iron Works (Va.), 1962-65; asst. controller Schwartz Bros. Inc., Washington, 1965-66; controller Colonial Bldg. Supply, Inc., 1966-69; controller, asst. sec. Revere Group, Inc., Silver Spring, Md., 1969-73, also treas. Revere South Inc., controller, sec. Revere Fla., asst. sec., controller Contempo Furniture Co. Inc., Revere Furniture and Equipment Co.; controller Md. Housing Corp., Balt., 1974—. Served with AUS, 1958-61. C.P.A., Md. Mem. Am. Inst. C.P.A.'s, Md. Assn. C.P.A.'s, Sigma Upsilon. Home: 4420 68th Pl Hyattsville MD 20784 Office: 5820 Southwestern Blvd Baltimore MD 21227

EDDIN, M. SHEHAB, educator, adminstr.; b. Cairo, Egypt, July 20, 1932; s. Mohammed Hassan Shehab and Asala (Eltabeiy) E.; B.A., U. Cairo, 1958; M.A., Am. U., Washington, 1963, Ph.D., 1966, postdoctoral research, 1967; postdoctoral research U.N.C., Chapel Hill, 1972-73, Grad. Sch. Dept. Agr., Washington, 1967-68; m. Mary Edna Wright, Oct. 1, 1964; 1 dau., Ahlam. Came to U.S., 1960, naturalized, 1970. Mgr. tannery, Cairo, 1946-50; tchr. English and Arabic, Syria, U.A.R., 1950-60; supr. distbn. World Confn. Orgns. of Teaching Professions, Washington, 1962-65; asst. prof. polit. sci. and econs. Western Carolina U., Cullowhee, N.C., 1967-69; prof. Gardner-Webb Coll., Boiling Springs, N.C., 1969—; on leave for study and research, 1973—; project adminstr. Dept. Parks, Recreation and Tourism, State of S.C., Columbia, 1973—; owner, dir. pvt. evening sch. adult edn., Cairo, 1952-55; adminstrv. asst., asst. dir. Mus. Rokn-Helwan, Cairo, 1955-58; mem. Egyptian Ednl. Mission to Syria, 1958-60, also instr. English civilization and Arabic, Shaabiya Inst., Syria. Mem. Am. Polit. Sci. Assn., Am. Soc. Internat. Law, Am. Acad. Polit. and Social Scis., Internat., So. polit. sci. assns., Middle East Inst., Am. Friends of Middle East, Internat. Platform Assn., Am. Civil Liberties Union, Acad. Polit. Sci., Pi Sigma Alpha. Author: Pan-Arabism and the Islamic Tradition: Ideology and Political Consensus, 1967. Contbr. articles to jours. Rotarian. Home: PO Box 4234 Columbia SC 29240 Office: SC Dept Parks Recreation and Tourism Columbia SC 29202

EDDLEMAN, HENRY LEO, inst. pres.; b. Morgantown, Miss., Apr. 4, 1911; s. Richard Aaron and Lucille (Power) E.; A.B., Miss. Coll., 1932; Th. M., So. Bapt. Theol. Sem. Louisville, 1935, Ph.D., 1942; D.D., Georgetown Coll., 1949; m. Sarah Fox, Sept. 7, 1937; children—Sarah Enfield, Evelyn Lucille. Ordained to ministry Bapt. Ch., 1930; ednl. and religious work, Palestine, 1935-41; tchr. O. T., Hebrew, New Orleans Bapt. Sem., 1941-42; pastor Parkland Ch., Louisville, 1942-52; faculty O. T., Hebrew, So. Bapt. Sem., 1950-54; pres. Georgetown Coll., 1954-59, New Orleans Bapt. Theol. Sem., 1959-70; editorial cons. Sunday Sch. Bd. So. Baptist Conv., 1970-72; pres. Criswell Bible Inst., Dallas, 1972—. Asst. moderator

Gen. Assn. Bapts. Ky., also chmn. state bd., chmn. budget com., chmn. com. for nominations, 1954; bd. mgrs. Western Recorder (Bapt. state paper); mem. hosp. bd., pres. state bd. missions Ky. Bapts., also adv. com. Home for Aged; mem. fgn. mission bd., chmn. com. on ministerial edn, for Negroes, So. Bapt. Conv.; pres. So. Assn. Bapt. Colls., 1958. Bd. dirs. Miss. Coll. Alumni Assn., trustee La. Moral and Civic Found. Mem. Internat. Platform Assn., Nat. Assn. Profs. Hebrew of Am. Author: To Make Men Free, 1954; Teachings of Jesus in Matthew 5-7, 1955; Missionary Task of a Church, 1961; Mandelbaum Gate, 1963; (with others) The Second Coming, 1963; Trustees And Higher Education, 1966; Guidlines to Ecumenicalism, 1967; (with others) Last Things: Eschatology, 1968; Federal Aid, Trustees and Higher Education, 1969. Home: The Manor House Apt 1011 1222 Commerce St Dallas TX 75202

EDDLEMAN, WILLIAM LEE, JR., ins. exec.; b. Houston, Oct. 6, 1943; s. William Lee and Marjorie (Nelson) E.; B.S., U. Houston, 1965; M.B.A., Columbia, 1967; m. Carolyn Faye Archer, Dec. 28, 1966; children—W. Christian, Harry Walter Archer. Financial analyst Winchester Western div. Olin Mathieson Chem. Co., New Haven, 1967-68; asst. trust investment officer Houston Bank & Trust Co., 1968-69; asst. v.p. Gt. So. Life Ins. Co., Houston, 1969—; treas. Securities Mgmt. Corp. Trustee Gt. So. Employees Thrift Plan. C.P.A. Mem. Houston Soc. Financial Analysts, Omicron Delta Epsilon. Methodist. Home: 2024 Dunstan Rd Houston TX 77005 Office: 3121 Buffalo Speedway Houston TX 77001

EDDS, GEORGE TYSON, educator, pharmacologist; b. Heidenheimer, Tex., Jan. 9, 1913; s. John Cleveland and Eunice (Tyson) E.; student U. Tex., 1930-31; B.S., Tex. A. and M., 1936, D.V.M., 1936, M.S., 1938; Ph.D., U. Minn., 1952; m. Lorene Keith, Aug. 30, 1931; children—Charles Mack, Pamela (Mrs. Richard C. West), Cynthia Ann (Mrs. James W. Dumont). Instr., Tex. A. and M., 1936-38, asst. prof. 1938-40, asso. prof. 1940-44, prof. 1944-50; v.p. Fort Dodge (Ia.) Labs., 1950-62; prof. vet. sci. U. Fla., Gainesville, 1962—, chmn. dept., 1962-71. Cons. Health, Edn. and Welfare Vet. Medicine, Health Manpower, 1967-72. Chmn. bd. dirs. Sioux Falls Coll., 1961-62. Gen. Edn. Bd. fellow 1948-49. Mem. Toxicology Soc. Am. (exec. com. 1969-73), U.S. Animal Health Assn. (chmn. pharm. com. 1965-70), Fla. Vet. Med. Assn. Home: 7616 SW 36th Av Gainesville FL 32601

EDELMAN, JOSEPH MARTIN, physician; b. Ft. Worth, July 11, 1920; s. Samuel Lawrence and Rose (Goldberg) E.; B.S., La. State U., 1940, M.D., 1943; m. Frances Greenberg, July 28, 1954; children—Susan Laurie, Ann Marsha. Intern U. Minn. Hosp., Mpls., 1944; resident Charity Hosp., New Orleans, 1947-49, Neurol. Inst., N.Y.C., 1949-50, Lahey Clinic, Boston, 1950-51; practice medicine specializing in neurosurgery, New Orleans, 1951-54, Baton Rouge, La., 1954—; mem. staff Baton Rouge Gen. Hosp., 1954—; instr. La. State U. Med. Sch., Baton Rouge, 1972—; co-founder, pres. Edelman Systems, Inc., Baton Rouge, La., 1970—. Served with M.C., AUS, 1944-46. Mem. Soc. for Computer Medicine (pres. 1973). Home: 1999 Hillside Circle Baton Rouge LA 70808 Office: 244 Peachtree St Baton Rouge LA 70806

EDEN, EDWIN WINFIELD, JR., cons.; b. Highland Park, N.J., June 4, 1911; s. Edwin Winfield and Elizabeth (Malmros) E.; B.S. in C.E., Rutgers U., 1933, B.S., 1940; M.S. in Hydraulics, U. Ia., 1938; M.S. in Conservation, U. Mich., 1962; m. Florence Syble Brown, Sept. 4, 1937; children—Donna (Mrs. Robert Barker), Sandra (Mrs. Lester Hall), Gregory (Mrs. Kathy McNeilly). Commd. ensign U.S. Navy, 1943, advanced through grades to lt. comdr., 1962; chief hydraulic design Upper Miss. Valley div. Corps Engrs., St. Louis, 1942-50; chief hydraulic and hydrologic planning and design C.E., Jacksonville, Fla., 1950-56; chief planning and reports br., 1956-65; chief engr. Interoceanic Canal Studies, Corps Engrs., Jacksonville, 1965-70; cons. water resource design and devel. U.S. Interoceanic Canal Study Commn. and Jacksonville Dist. Corps Engrs., 1970—. Registered profl. engr., Fla. Mem. Nat. Soc. Profl. Engrs., Am. Soc. C.E. (Arthur Wellington prize 1970), Am. Geophys. Union, U.S. Nat. Com. for Irrigation and Drainage, U.S. Com. Large Dams, Internat. Assn. Nav. Congress, Fla. Engring. Soc., Soc. Am. Mil. Engrs. Contbr. numerous articles to tech. jours. Address: 5375 Sanders Rd Jacksonville FL 32211

EDEN, HENRY FRANCIS, phys. scientist; b. Newcastle on Tyne, Eng., Dec. 23, 1934; s. Henry and Ellen (Coney) E.; B.Sc., U. Durham, 1956; Ph.D., U. Newcastle, 1959. Came to U.S., 1962, naturalized, 1971. Sci. officer Nat. Physics Lab., Eng., 1959-60; sr. research asso. physics U. Newcastle, Eng., 1960-62; research asso. geophysics Mass. Inst. Tech., 1962-64; with Arthur D. Little, Inc., Cambridge, Mass., 1964-70; program dir. meteorology NSF, Washington, 1970—. Fellow Royal Meteorol. Soc.; mem. Am. Geophys. Union, Am. Meteorol. Soc. Contbr. articles profl. jours. Home: 4600 S Four Mile Run Dr Arlington VA 22204 Office: 1800 G St Washington DC 20550

EDGAR, CHARLES ERNEST, III, army officer; b. Mobile, Ala., Jan. 15, 1936; s. Charles Ernest and Amelia Lyon (Moore) Edgar; B.S., Va. Mil. Inst., 1958; M.S., Ia. State U., 1962; grad. U.S. Army Command and Gen. Staff Coll., 1969, U.S. Naval War Coll., 1974; m. Mary Elizabeth Brown, June 27, 1964; children—Charles Ernest, Mary Elizabeth, Leverett William. Commd. 2d lt. C.E., U.S. Army, 1958, advanced through grades to lt. col., 1968; engr. group adviser Mil. Assistance Command, Vietnam, 1965-66; chief edn. (engr.), office personnel operations Dept. Army, Washington, 1966-68; comdr. officer 577 Engr. Bd., Vietnam 1969-70; staff officer, office dep. chief staff mil. operations Dept. Army, Washington, 1970-72; asst. dir. civil works lower Miss. Valley, office chief engrs., Washington, 1972-73. Decorated Legion of Merit with 1 oak leaf cluster, Bronze Star medal, Air medal, Army Commendation medal with 1 oak leaf cluster. Mem. Am. Soc. C.E., Kappa Alpha Order. Episcopalian. Home: 2207 N Levert Dr Mobile AL 36607 also 27 Jackson Ct Brenton Village Newport RI 02840 Office: US Naval War Coll Newport RI 02840

EDGAR, JAMES WINFRED, commr. edn.; b. Briggs, Tex., Sept. 15, 1904; s. James William and Sarah (Morris) E.; B.A., Howard Payne Coll., 1928; M.A., U. Tex., 1938, Ed.D., 1948; LL.D., Austin Coll., 1958; D. Litt., Southwestern U., 1967; m. Sue Oaklay, Aug. 22, 1927; children—Frances Ruth, Sarah Elizabeth, Susan Elaine. Tchr., Burnet County, Tex., 1923-27; prin., Heidenheimer, Tex., 1928-29; asst. supt. schs., Victoria, Tex., 1936-39; supt. schs., Mirando City, Tex., 1929-36; Orange, Tex., 1939-47, Austin, Tex., 1947-50; state commr. edn., Tex., 1950—. Nat. com. on scouting in schs. Boy Scouts Am. Mem. Am. Assn. Sch. Adminstrs. (mem. 1950 Yearbook commn.), Tex (pres. 1942-44, chmn. edn. policies com. 1947-48) assns. sch. adminstrs., Tex. Tchrs. Assn. (exec. com. 1947, legislative com. 1947-49), N.E.A., Phi Delta Kappa. Presbyn. (mem. adv. council higher edn. U.S.). Editorial bd. Sch. Execs. mag., 1947-52. Home: 1517 Parkway Austin TX 78703 Office: Tex Edn Agy State Capitol Austin TX 78711

EDGE, GOODE BRYANT, curator; b. Macon, Ga., Mar. 25, 1910; s. John Miller and Blance (Williams) E.; student Centenary Coll., 1928-31; m. DeLeta Iola Turner, Apr. 28, 1930; children—Virginia (Mrs. John Moore), Blanche (Mrs. Dennis McCloskey), Margaret (Mrs. Roger Chalfant). With W.C. Nabors Co., trailer mfg., 1932-63, br. mgr. sales and service, Jackson, Miss., 1936-57, Houston, 1957-63; supt., curator, custodian Mansfield (La.) Battle Park and Mus., La. Parks and Recreation Commn., 1970—. Active Community Chest; life mem. Dads Club So. Meth. U. Recipient Appreciation certificate Boy Scouts Am., 1971. Mem. Kappa Alpha. Methodist. Home: 904 MaryJane Blvd Mansfield LA 71052 Office: Route 2 Box 252 Mansfield LA 71052

EDGECOMB, CLARK RAYMOND III, architect; b. Long Beach, Cal., Nov. 25, 1941; s. Clark Raymond and Virginia (Starkey) E.; B.Arch., Tex. Technol. U., 1966; m. Melinda Kay Sanders, July 31, 1965. Designer firm W. Jackson Wisdom, Houston, 1966-69; project architect firm McKittrick, Drennan, Richardson & Wallace, Houston, 1969-73; architect firm Lloyd, Morgan & Jones, Houston, 1973; dir. design, planning Pilgram Realty & Devel. Corp., Houston, 1973—. Registered architect, Tex. Mem. A.I.A., Tex. Soc. Architects, Houston Jr. C. of C. (welcome com. 1969). Methodist (sec. council on ministries). Home: 2919 Quenby St Houston TX 77005 Office: 6723 Stella Link Houston TX 77005

EDIE, WAYNE PAUL, clergyman; b. Canton, O., Feb. 3, 1942; s. Wayne Arthur and Dora Mae (Hinchliff) E.; student Arlington Coll., 1963-65, Santa Ana Coll., 1960-63; B.A., Anderson Coll., 1968; m. Norma Jean Craddock, Aug. 21, 1965; children—Gregory Paul, Jill Renee. Ordained to ministry 1st Ch. of God, 1969; pastor 1st Ch. of God, Lincoln, Neb., 1968-70, Danville, Ky., 1970—. Mem. Evang. Ministerial Assembly, Lincoln, 1968-70, Neb. Council on Alcohol Edn., 1969-70; com. mem. City-Wide Youth for Christ, Lincoln, 1969-70; mem. Ky. Volunteers in Correction, 1972—; com. chmn. Cub Scouts, 1972—. Bd. dirs. City Mission, Lincoln, 1968-70. Mem. City Ministerial Assn. Republican. Home: 804 Mohawk Trail Danville KY 40422 Office: 400 N 4th St Danville KY 40422

EDINGER, DON BAUER, petroleum engr.; b. Tulsa, Aug. 29, 1919; s. Harry M. and Helen (Bauer) E.; B.S., U. Tulsa, 1949; m. Margarett Wade, Nov. 4, 1944; children—Sara Jane, Margarett Ann. With Prodn. Engring. Labs., Inc., 1949-55, gen. mgr., Oklahoma City, 1953-55; dist. sales engr. Core Labs., Oklahoma City, 1955-59; pres. Corco, Inc., Oklahoma City, 1959-63, Petro-Core, Inc., Oklahoma City, 1963-69; staff engr. Okla. Corp. Commn., Oklahoma City, 1969—, now sr. engr.; pres. Admiral Products Co., Oklahoma City, 1966—. Served to 1st lt. AUS, 1942-46. Registered profl. engr., Okla. Mem. Soc. Petroleum Engrs., Am. Inst. Mining, Metall. and Petroleum Engrs. (bd. sec. 1956). Am. Petroleum Inst., Oklahoma City Geol. Soc., A.A.A.S. Club: Petroleum. Home: 436 Northwest 21st St Oklahoma City OK 73103 Office: Jim Thorpe Bldg Oklahoma City OK 73105

EDINGER, WARD MUNSON, petroleum engr.; b. Elizabeth, N.J., Nov. 5, 1912; s. Harry Munson and Helen (Bauer) E.; B.S., U. Mo., 1935; m. Lucille Hull, Oct. 26, 1940; children—Ronald Ward, Eileen Lucille, Susan (Mrs. Robert Murrill), Robert Dale. Chemist Sinclair Prairie Oil Co., Tulsa, 1935-39; head engring. dept. Core Labs., Inc., Dallas, 1939-46; chief engr. Harper Turner Oil Co., Oklahoma City, 1946-47; pres. prodn. Engring. Labs., Inc., Oklahoma City, 1947-54; pres. Edinger, Inc., Oklahoma City, 1954—; dir. Equity Benefit Life Ins. Co., Blackwell, Okla. Co-chmn. Radio Free Europe fund, 1966-67. Mng. trustee Hales Estate Trust. Served to 2d lt. F.A., AUS, World War II. Mem. Alpha Chi Sigma, Lambda Chi Alpha. Christian Scientist. Club: Downtown Sertoma (pres. 1965-66). Home: 1603 Drakestone St Oklahoma City OK 73120 Office: Hightower Bldg Oklahoma City OK 73102

EDMISON, MARVIN TIPTON, ednl. adminstr.; b. Lincoln, Neb., July 21, 1912; s. Wellington Viscount and Maude (Clemans) E.; B.A., U. Neb., 1933, M.S., 1947; Ph.D., Okla. A. & M. Coll., 1952; m. Ila Fern Hallstrom, Aug. 17, 1939; children—William Robert, Lawrence Ray. Tchr. sci. Shattuck Sch., Faribault, Minn., 1938-41, Wentworth Mil. Acad., Lexington, Mo., 1947-48; mem. faculty U. Ark., Fayetteville, 1951-55; mem. faculty Okla. State U., Stillwater, 1955—, prof. chemistry, 1955—, asst. v.p. acad. affairs, 1968—, dir. Research Found., 1955—. Chmn. Region V Nat. Council Univ. Research Adminstrs., 1970—; mem. conf. com. Nat. Conf. on Adminstrn. Research, 1971—, mem. exec. com., 1974, program chmn., 1974. Mem. sci. adv. com. Okla. SSS, Oklahoma City, 1965—; chmn. coordinating com. Okla. Water Resources Research Inst., Stillwater, 1964—; mem. Govs. Com. Water Resources, Oklahoma City, 1965—; mem. Stillwater Municipal Com. Urban Renewal, 1971—. Chmn., bd. dirs. Okla. Econ. Devel. Found., Norman, 1966—; sec., treas. Council Mid-Am. State Univs. Assn., 1967—; bd. dirs. Okla. State U. Edn. and Research Found., Inc., 1969—, exec. dir., 1972—. Served to col. U.S. Army Res., 1935-38, 41-46, 49-50. Okla. Acad. Sci. fellow, 1967—; Distinguished Service award Okla. Phychol. Assn., 1969. Mem. Res. Officers Assn. (pres. Okla. chpt. 1965-66), Am. Acad. Scis., Ret. Officers Assn., Nat. Assn. Uniformed Services, C. of C. (chmn. mil. affairs com. 1955-57). Methodist. Lion. Club: Golf and Country (Stillwater). Home: 1107 N Skyline Dr Stillwater OK 74074

EDMONDS, BOBBY FRANC, county engr.; b. McCormick, S.C., Apr. 6, 1932; s. Ralph Eugene and Onie Edna (Dillashaw) E.; grad. high sch.; m. Mary Kathryn Gable, Dec. 23, 1954; 1 dau., Bonnie Franc. With S.C. Hwy. Dept., McCormick, 1951—, chief clk., 1968-73, maintenance supt., 1973—. Custodian New Bordeaux Hist. Site, 1954-74; pres. McCormick County Hist. Soc., 1971-73; chmn. McCormick County Hist. Commn., 1972-74, Sec. McCormick County Bd. Edn., 1968-74. Mem. S.C. Profl Photographers Assn., Huguenot Soc. S.C., S.C. Cattlemen's Assn., Am. Tree Farm. Baptist. Mason. Active in restoration of Badwell site hist. home of J.L. Petigru, also Badwell Cemetery, 1973. Home: Cedar Hill McCormick SC 29835 Office: PO Box 266 McCormick SC 29835

EDMONDS, JOHN WILLIS, III, lawyer; b. Richmond, Va., Nov. 9, 1932; s. John Willis and Katharine Holland (Spicer) E.; B.A., U. Richmond, 1953, LL.B., 1956; m. Barbara Louise Bigony, Oct. 20, 1956; children—John Willis IV, David Charlton, Meade Spicer. Admitted to Va. bar, 1956; with legal dept. Va.-Carolina Chem. Co., Richmond, 1956; mem. firm Tucker, Mays, Moore & Reed, Richmond, 1956-66, Mays, Valentine, Davenport & Moore, Richmond, 1967—. Dir. Fairfield Nat. Bank, 1969—. Sec. William Byrd Press, Richmond, 1969—, Va. Indsl. Devel. Corp., Richmond, 1961—; instr. corporate law U. Richmond Sch. Law, 1966. Trustee, U. Richmond, 1971—, pres. alumni council 1969-70; bd. dirs. Va. Inst. for Sci. Research, 1970—. Mem. Am. Bar Assn. (chmn. com. comml. paper, bank deposits and letters of credit 1970—, vice chmn. com. on significant trust and estate legislation 1973—), Kappa Alpha. Baptist. Author: Virginia Practice, Uniform Commercial Code Forms, 1968. Contbr. articles in field to profl. jours. Home: 1315 Careybrook Dr Richmond VA 23233 Office: 1200 Russ Blvd Richmond VA 23219

EDMONDSON, LOCKE FRANKLIN, govt. ofcl.; b. New Edinburg, Ark., Mar. 4, 1921; s. Robert Franklin and Ruth (Bonham) E.; B.S., U. Ark., 1942; M.S., Okla. A. and M. Coll., 1949; Ph.D., U. Cal., 1954; m. Berenice Andrea, Dec. 30, 1944; children—Byron Stanley, Keith Alan, Norma Jean. Instr. dairy dept. Okla. A. and M. Coll., 1949; research specialist U. Cal., 1949-54; chemist to supervisory research chemist Agrl. Research Service, Dept. Agr., Washington, 1954-73. acting chief dairy products lab., 1973—. Instnl. rep., advisor Explorer Scouts, Boy Scouts Am., 1959-62. Served to lt. comdr. USNR, 1942-46; PTO. Recipient Superior Service award Dept. Agr., 1964. Mem. Am. Chem. Soc., Am. Oil Chemists Soc., N.Y. Acad. Scis., Am. Dairy Sci. Assn., Sigma Xi. Presbyn. (elder). Contbr. articles to profl. jours. Patentee in field. Home: 7110 Kempton Rd Lanham MD 20801 Office: Agricultural Research Service Dept of Agriculture Washington DC 20250

EDMONSON, GEORGE HAMPTON, JR., dentist; b. Magee, Miss., Feb. 9, 1937; s. George Hampton and Lanelle (Russell) E.; student Miss. State Coll., 1955-58; B.S., U. Miss., 1961; D.D.S., Emory U., 1969; m. Linda Ray Hartfield, May 8, 1964; children—Mark David, Amy Lynn. Pharmacist, Patterson-Welch Drug Store, Jackson, Miss., 1961-62, Walnut St. Pharmacy, Hattiesburg, Miss., 1962-64, Emory U. Hosp., Ga. Bapt. Hosp., Atlanta, 1965-68; individual practice dentistry, Brookhaven, Miss., 1969—. Organizer, adviser Andrew Jackson Council Boy Scouts Am., 1973-74. Bd. dirs. United Givers Fund Lincoln County. Mem. Am., Miss. (mem. publs. council 1974—) dental assns., Gideons, 6th Dist. Dental Soc. (pres. 1974—), Miss. Pharm. Assn., Xi Psi Phi, Kappa Alpha, Kappa Psi, Phi Eta Sigma. Baptist (deacon). Kiwanian. Club: Exchange (Brookhaven, Miss.). Home: 1200 S Church St Brookhaven MS 39601 Office: 232 W Court St Brookhaven MS 39601

EDMUNDS, GEORGE BEAUREGARD, printer, pub.; b. Augusta, Ga., Apr. 11, 1907; s. William Oscar and Irene (Gray) E.; ed. pub. schs.; m. Madeleine Matilda Lang, Dec. 25, 1928; 1 dau., Gloria Ann (Mrs. Walter Gerald Glover). With art and editorial dept. King Feature Syndicate, Inc., N.Y.C., 1927-34; founder, pres. Dixie-Rush Co., Decatur, Ga., 1937-48; pres., treas. Atlanta Dixie-Rush Bottling Co., 1938-48; founder, owner Mountain City (Ga.) Press, 1961—. Mem. Humanitarian Soc., Nat. Ry. Hist. Soc., Internat. Platform Assn., Gypsy Lore Soc. Methodist. Mason (32 deg.). Home: 357 Electric Av Mountain City GA 30562 Office: PO Drawer E Mountain City GA 30562

EDMUNDS, JAMES TELFORD, lawyer; b. Amsterdam, N.Y., Sept. 12, 1931; s. Allen Telford and Margaret Rhea (Sleight) E.; student U. Richmond, 1949-51, Columbia Coll., 1951-52, Columbia Law Sch., 1952-53; LL.B., U. Richmond, 1955; m. Ellen Louise McLuckie, Dec. 26, 1952; children—Jeanne Louise, Thomas Arthur, Mark Allen, Andrew Griffing. Admitted to Va. bar, 1955, U.S. Supreme Ct. bar; practiced in Kenbridge, 1955—; town atty., Kenbridge, 1966—; mem. Va. Senate from 17th Dist., 1972—, mem. adv. com. on professions and occupations, 1973. Sec.-treas., dir. Kenbridge Industries, Inc.; mem. adv. bd. Fidelity Nat. Bank; guest lectr. Southside Community Coll. Sec., Lunenburg County Planning Commn., 1960-70; Mem. Va. Democratic Central Com. Bd. dirs. Va. Mental Health Found. Named Jaycee Outstanding Young Man of Year, 1966. Mem. Va., 10th Circuit bar assns., McNeill Law Soc., Delta Theta Phi, Phi Gamma Delta. Methodist. Lion. Club: Bull and Bear (Richmond). Home: 305 5th Av Kenbridge VA 23944 Office: 115 5th St Kenbridge VA 23944

EDMUNDS, STEPHEN ORRELL, constrn. co. exec.; b. Gretna, Va., July 17, 1919; s. John Thomas (dec.) and Byrd May (Farmer) E.; B.S. in Archtl. Engring., Va. Poly. Inst., 1941; m. Norma Jeanne Parsons, July 8, 1949; children—Margaret Susan, Robert Stephen. Estimator for several gen. contractors, 1946-50; concrete contractor, estimator Spidel & Hall, Inc., Washington, 1950-52; chief estimator E.L. Daniels, Gen. Contractor, Arlington, Va., 1952-55; gen. mgr. So. Comml. Constrn., Inc., Washington, 1955-58; chief estimator Eugene Simpson & Bros., Inc., Alexandria, Va., 1959-61, v.p., 1961-72, sr. v.p., 1972—. Mem. engring. adv. com. No. Va. Community Coll., Annandale, 1968—; tchr. Fairfax County Adult Edn. Program, 1970—. Vice chmn. Fairfax County Plumbing Bd., 1968—. Bd. dirs. Glen Forest Community Assn., 1963—, Fairfax County Vocational Ednl. Found., 1972—. Served with AUS, 1941-45; PTO. Decorated Legion of Merit. Mem. No. Va. Builders Assn. (dir. 1967—, pres. 1971), Am. Concrete Inst., A.I.M. Baptist (treas. 1972—). Home: 3308 Longbranch Dr Falls Church VA 22041 Office: PO Box 711 Alexandria VA 22313

EDMUNDS, (THOMAS) MURRELL, author, lawyer; b. Halifax, Va., Mar. 23, 1898; s. John Richard and Willie Thurman (Murrell) E.; J.D., U. Va., 1921. Tchr. English, head coach varsity basketball Episcopal High Sch., Va., 1921-22; admitted to Va. bar, 1920; pvt. practice law, asst. commonwealth's atty., 1922-26; author novels, short stories, poetry; playwright. Served with U.S. Army, World War I. Recipient annual poetry award, Ariz. Quar., 1963. Mem. Tilka Soc., Raven Soc., Alpha Tau Omega, Phi Delta Phi. Unitarian. Author: (novels) Sojourn Among Shadows, 1936; Between the Devil, 1939; Time's Laughter in Their Ears, 1942; Behold Thy Brother, 1950; Passionate Journey to Winter, 1962; Beautiful Upon the Mountains, 1966; Shadow of a Great Rock, 1969; (short stories) Red, White and Black, 1945; Laurel for the Undefeated, 1964; (poetry) Dim Footprints Along a Hazardous Trail, 1971; (play) Moon of My Delight, 1961. Home: 936 St Charles Av New Orleans LA 70130

EDMUNDSON, WALTER FLETCHER, dermatologist; b. Pitts., 1917; M.D., Hahnemann Med. Coll., 1941; M.Sc. in Pharmacology, U. Miami (Fla.). Intern Shadyside Hosp., Pitts., 1941-42; asst. resident in dermatology U. Mich. Hosp., Ann Arbor, 1945-46; practice medicine specializing in dermatology, 1946—; staff Venereal Disease Research Lab., also chief dermatology sect. U.S. Marine Hosp., S.I., N.Y., 1946-48; with dermatol. clin. investigations br. Div. Indsl. Hygiene, USPHS, Washington, 1950-51, asso. dir., also chief clin. investigations sect. Venereal Disease Research Lab., Chamblee, Ga., 1952-54, chief Out Patient Dept., USPHS Hosp., San Francisco, 1962-63; med. dir. Inst. Interam. Affairs, Pub. Health Service, Mexico, 1951-52; dir. Okla. Prevention and Control Center, 1954-55; chief tech. services Pesticides Research Lab., FDA, Perrine, 1964-66, with Perrine Primate Research Lab., U.S. Environmental Protection Agy., 1971—. Teaching fellow dermatology Grad. Sch. Pub. Health, U. Pitts., 1948-49, instr. dermatology, also adj. asst. prof. Dept. Epidemiology, 1955-62; asst. prof. Dept. Medicine, U. Miami (Fla.), 1970—. Asst. dir. Community Studies on Pesticides, Dade County (Fla.)-USPHS, Miami, 1966-70. Served to capt. M.C., AUS, 1942-45. Decorated Air medal. Diplomate Am. Bd. Dermatology. Fellow Am. Acad. Dermatology; mem. Am. Pub. Health Assn., A.M.A. Address: 9001 SW 77th Av Miami FL 33156

EDSON, MERRITT AUSTIN, JR., designer, editor; b. Pensacola, Fla., July 2, 1922; s. Merritt Austin and Ethel (Robbins) E.; student Georgetown Sch. Fgn. Service, 1941-43, postgrad., 1954-56; B.S. in Fgn. Service, Villanova Coll., 1943-44. Sub-accountant Nat. City Bank N.Y., 1946-48; co-owner Harding Hill Farm, Mt. Sunapee, N.H., 1949-51; marine display and research cons., 1957—; engr. asst. Alan M. Voorhees & Assos., Inc., McLean, Va., 1966-70; designer Planning Research Corp., McLean Va., 1970, Alan M. Voorhees & Assos., Inc., 1970-72, sr. designer, 1972—; editor Nautical Research Jour., 1965-69, editorial adviser, 1969—, sec., 1972—. Permanent exhibits maritime history Smithsonian Instn. Served to 2d lt., USMCR, 1943-46, to capt., 1st Marine Div., 1951-57. Mem. Naut. Research Guild, Soc. Naut. Research, Nat. Rifle Assn., 1st Marine

Div. Assn. Republican. Conglist. Club: Army and Navy (Washington). Contbr. articles to nautical research publs. Address: 6413 Dahlonega Rd Washington DC 20016

EDWARD, CHARLES E.H., elec. engr.; b. Washington, Mar. 13, 1930; s. Harvey and Frances (Williamson) E.; B.S., U.S. Mil. Acad., 1953; M.S., Purdue, 1959; m. Jessie Hill, June 4, 1953; children—Catherine, Joan. Commd. 2d lt. U.S. Army, 1953, advanced through grades to capt., 1960, resigned 1963; microwave design engr. NASA, Goddard Space Flight Center, Greenbelt, Md., 1963-65; with Harry Diamond labs. Dept. of Army, Washington, 1965—, supervisory engr., 1969—. Mem. I.E.E.E. (chpt. chmn. microwave theory and techniques group 1971-72), A.A.A.S., Def. Preparedness Assn. Home: 3300 Wake Dr Kensington MD 20795 Office: Harry Diamond Labs Dept of Army Conn and Van Ness St Washington DC 20438

EDWARDS, ALFRED LEROY, govt. ofcl.; b. Key West, Fla., Aug. 9, 1920; s. Eddie E. and Kathleen L. (Sands) E.; B.A., Livingstone Coll., Salisbury, N.C., 1948; M.A., U. Mich., 1949; Ph.D., State U. Ia., 1958; m. Willie Mae Lewis, June 4, 1949; children—Beryl Laurette, Alfred Leroy. Instr. econs. dept. social sci. So. U., Baton Rouge, 1949-54; instr. econs. State U. Ia., 1956-57; asst. prof. econs. Mich. State U., 1957-60, 62-63; econs. adviser U. Nigeria, Nsukka, W.Africa, 1960-62; dep. asst. sec. for rural devel. and conservation U.S. Dept. Agr., Washington, 1963-73, spl. asst. to commr. Consumer Product Safety Commn., 1973—; lectr. dept. econs. Howard U. Mem. Nat. Adv. Com. on Vocational Edn., 1964—, D.C. Adv. Com. on Vocational Rehab., 1965—. Bd. mgmt. Met. YMCA. Served with Signal Corps. AUS, 1943-46. Recipient Livingstone Coll. Alumni Achievement award, 1967, Distinguished Service award U.S. Dept. Agr., 1969. Danforth Faculty fellow, summer 1958, Postdoctoral fellow U. Mich., summer 1960, Ford Found. Faculty fellow in econs., 1963-64. Author: A Study of Local Government Debt in Michigan, 1960; The Detroit Income Tax, 1963. Home: 819 6th St SW Washington DC 20024 Office: 1750 K St NW Washington DC 20207

EDWARDS, CHARLES HENRY, educator, commodity broker; b. Relief, N.C., Feb. 10, 1908; s. Elbert Henry and Emily (Peterson) E.; B.S. in Agrl. Edn., U. Tenn., 1939, M.S. in Extension Methods, 1962; postgrad. Cornell U., 1946, U. Ark., 1956; m. Ruby Jewel Grimsley, July 25, 1936; children—Charles Henry, Kenneth Creighton, Linda Ruth (Mrs. Charles Wright Sydnor, Jr.). Asst. county agt., Monroe County, 1939-40; county agrl. agt. Morgan County, Tenn., 1940-46, Greene County, Tenn., 1946-50; sr. agrl. expert Govt. Thailand, 1950-51; agrl. agt. Blount County, Maryville, Tenn., 1952-65, extension leader, 1965-73; commodity speculator, 1973—. Del., Nat. Conf. Econ. Issues in Agr., Washington, 1963. Recipient Gov.'s citation for services as war fund chmn. Morgan County 1945; Outstanding County Agt. award Tenn., 1959, 61; Fed. Civilian Career Service award, 1962; Distinguished Service award Nat. Assn. County Agrl. Agts., 1967. Mem. Nat. chmn. recognition and awards com. 1954-55), Tenn. (sec. 1947-48) county agts. assn., Exchange Club, C. of C., Epsilon Sigma Phi, Alpha Zeta, Phi Epsilon, Biologia, Phi Delta Kappa, Phi Kappa Phi. Methodist (steward, tchr. Sunday sch. supt.). Rotarian. Author: Tobacco Production in Thailand, 1951. Editor Tenn. Farmer Mag., 1938-39. Contbr. over 1,000 articles to newspapers, mags. Home: Route 6 Maryville TN 37801

EDWARDS, CHARLES WESLEY, JR., banker; b. Birmingham, Nov. 23, 1931; s. Charles Wesley and Orlean (Randle) E.; A.B., Harvard, 1954; postgrad., U. Pa., 1957-59; m. Katherine Long Sellers, Mar. 24, 1961; children—Charles Wesley III, James Sellers, William Thompson. Asst. v.p. comml. loan dept. First Nat. Bank Montgomery (Ala.), 1958-64; exec. v.p., trust officer Central Bank & Trust Co., Owensboro, Ky., 1964-66; pres. Shoals Nat. Bank of Florence (Ala.), 1966—, also dir.; dir. Chem. Haulers Inc., Sheffield, Ala., 1968-73, Bileco Inc., Sheffield, 1968-73. Asso. professorial lectr. George Washington U. at Maxwell AFB, 1961-64; instr. U. Ala. at Montgomery, 1959-61. Mem. exec. com. Florence-Lauderdale chpt. United Fund, 1968-73, Jr. Achievement Quad Cities (Ala.), 1971-73, Florence-Lauderdale Indsl. Bd., 1971—, Florence-Lauderdale Indsl. Expansion Com., 1970—, Muscle Shoals Assn. Mental Health, 1970—, Tenn. Valley council Boy Scouts Am., 1968—. Vice chmn. bd. dirs. Salvation Army, Florence area. Served to capt. USAF, 1954-56. Mem. Am. Bankers Assn. (chmn. Ala. pub. relations com. 1970, investment credit com. 1972), Florence C. of C. (past dir.), Am. Legion. Democrat. Methodist (mem. adminstrv. bd.). Elk. Club: Turtle Point Yacht and Country. Home: 530 River Bend Pl Florence AL 35630 Office: 102 N Court St Florence AL 35630

EDWARDS, CLAUDE REYNOLDS, judge; b. Chester, S.C., Aug. 29, 1922; s. Claude R. and Mary (Walsh) E.; A.B., Wofford Coll., 1943; LL.B., Yale, 1949; m. Sarah Chapman Walker, Sept. 27, 1948; children—Sarah, Claude R., James A. Asst. dir. Inst. of Govt., Chapel Hill, N.C., 1949-50; legal cons. to gen. counsel Econ. Stabilization Agy., Washington, 1950; admitted to Fla. bar, 1950; practiced in Deland, 1950-51, Orlando, 1951-68; circuit judge State Fla., Orlando, 1968-73; chief judge 9th Jud. Circuit Ct., 1973—. City councilman, Orlando, Fla., 1955-58; chmn. Orlando Traffic Commn., 1955-58. Mem. Orange County Republican Exec. Com., 1955-67; pres. Orange County Young Republican Club, 1958. Bd. dirs. Orlando Civil Service, 1960-67, chmn., 1967; trustee Orlando Pub. Library, 1958-70, pres., 1969-70. Served with AUS, 1943-46. Mem. Fla., Orange County, Osceola County bar assns., Yale Alumni Assn. (past pres. Central Fla.), Blue Key, Phi Delta Phi, Sigma Alpha Epsilon (past pres. Central Fla. alumni), Pi Gamma Mu. Methodist. Rotarian. Office: 479 Orange County Courthouse Orlando FL 32801

EDWARDS, DANIEL JAMES, economist, govt. ofcl.; b. Washington, Dec. 20, 1928; s. James Daniel and Anna (Lattin) E.; certificate Syracuse U., 1952; B.A., U. Md., 1956, M.A., 1958; (Earhart fellow, Reim fellow), U. Va., 1961; student U.S. Naval Postgrad. Sch., Monterey, Cal., 1966; m. Ruth Knight, Oct. 7, 1952; children—Richard Kenneth, Glenn Steven, Laura Jeanne, Deborah Suzanne, Donna, Patricia. Grad. asst. Bur. Bus. and Econ. Research U. Md., 1956, teaching asst., 1956-57; with the Bur. Mines, summer 1958; part time instructor Univ. Virginia, 1957-59, graduate assistant Bur. Population and Econ. Research, 1959-60; vis. lectr. internat. econs. Sweet Briar Coll., 1959; asst. prof. Western Md. Coll., 1960-61; economist Flow of Funds Fed. Res. Bd., 1961-62; asso. professorial lectr. George Washington U., 1961—; economist Bus. Def. Service Adminstrn., econ. growth staff Commerce Dept., 1962-64; asso. prof. Georgetown U., summer 1963; economist Housing and Home Finance Agy., 1964; sec. treasury's chief economist spl. studies, treasury observer and participant Pres.'s Adv. Com. Supersonic Transport U.S. Treasury, Washington, 1964-67; cons. to Sec. Treasury, 1967-68; chief economist House Banking and Currency Com., 1967-69; econ. cons. to Joint Econ. Com., 1967-69; fiscal-monetary economist Joint Econ. Com., 1967 chief supply demand group Bus. Mines, Washington, 1970—. Cons. sec. natural resources P.R., San Juan, 1973—. Served with USAF, 1951-54. Relm fellow, 1958-59, Earhart fellow, 1957-58. Mem. Bd. U.S. Civil Service Examiners for Economists, Internat. Soc. Tech. Assessment, World Future Soc., Assn. Comparative Econ. Studies, Royal, Am., So. econ. assns., Am. Statis. Assn., Am. Finance Assn., Assn. Study Soviet-Type Econs., Pi Gamma Mu. Editorial asst. Jour. Polit. Economy, Natural Resources Jour. Contbr. articles to profl. publs. Home: 4916 44th St NW Washington DC 20016 Office: 4015 Wilson Bld Arlington VA 22203

EDWARDS, DON RABY, clergyman; b. Tarboro, N.C., June 13, 1931; s. Charles Kenneth and Mabel (Craft) E.; A.B., East Carolina U., 1955; M.Div., Va. Theol. Sem., 1958; m. Jane Mann Credle, June 3, 1957; children—Charles Blount, Nathaniel Carter. Ordained to ministry Episcopalian Ch., 1958; vicar, St. Christopher's Ch., Havelock, N.C., 1958-61; rector, St. Paul's Ch., Wilmington, N.C., 1961-63, St. Stephen's, Goldsboro, N.C., 1963-68, Emmanuel Ch., Athens, Ga., 1968-73, St. Stephens Ch., Richmond, Va., 1973—; mem. Commn. Ministry Diocese Va., 1974—. Pres., Athens Boys Club, 1972-73; v.p. Council on Alcoholism Wayne County, 1965-67. Bd. dirs. Wayne Sheltered Workshop, 1965-68, Mental Healt Assn., Goldsboro, 1966-68, Thompson Orphanage, Charlotte, N.C., 1965-68, St. Christopher's Sch., Richmond, 1974—. Served with USCGR, 1950-52. Fellow Sch. Continuing Edn. Va. Theol. Sem., 1970-71; recipient Distinguished Service award Goldsboro Jr. C. of C., 1966. Home: 311 Clovelly Rd Richmond VA 23221 Office: 6004 Three Chopt Rd Richmond VA 23226

EDWARDS, DONALD BRUCE, mus. ofcl.; b. Pine Bluff, Ark., Oct. 2, 1949; s. Harvey Brown and Betty Jean (Cearley) E.; B.F.A., Ark. State U., 1971. Ednl. dir. S.E. Ark. Arts and Sci. Center, Pine Bluff, 1971—; one-man shows at State Festival of Arts, Little Rock, 1972; exhibited prints, drawings and crafts Ark. Arts Center, 1973; represented in pvt. collections. Mem. Am. Crafts Council, Brush and Palatte Guild. Home: 1901 Laurel St Pine Bluff AR 71601 Office: Civic Center Pine Bluff AR 71601

EDWARDS, DONALD E., educator; b. Osage, Tex., Oct. 19, 1938; s. W.C. and Clarice (Sheffield) E.; B.B.A., North Tex. State U., 1959, M.B.A., 1960; Ph.D., U. Ark., 1966; m. Judy Anne Turner, June 6, 1964; children—William Turner, Erin Elisabeth. Staff accountant Price Waterhouse & Co., Dallas, 1960-62; instr. accounting U. Ark., 1962-65; asst. prof. accounting La. State U., New Orleans, 1965-66; asso. prof. dept. bus. Tarleton State Coll., Stephenville, Tex., 1966-67; prof., dir. grad. div. Coll. Adminstrn. and Bus., La. Tech. U., Ruston, 1967—. Served with U.S. Army, 1960-61. C.P.A., Tex. Mem. Am. Accounting Assn., Alpha Kappa Psi, Beta Alpha Psi. Lion. Contbr. articles to profl. jours. Home: 602 Hundred Oaks St Ruston LA 71270

EDWARDS, EDWIN WASHINGTON, gov. La.; b. Marksville, La., Aug. 7, 1927; s. Clarence W. and Agnes (Brouillette) E.; J.D., La. State U., 1949; m. Elaine Schwartzenburg, Apr. 5, 1949; children—Anna Laure, Victoria Elaine, Stephen Randolph, David Edwin. Admitted to La. bar, 1949; gen. practice in Crowley, La 1949-66; sr. founding partner firm Edwards, Edwards & Broadhurst, 1954—; mem. Crowley City Council, 1954-62, La. Senate from 35th dist., 1964-65; mem. 89-92d congresses 7th dist. La.; gov. of La., 1972—. Served with USNR, World War II. Mem. Internat. Rice Festival, Crowley C. of C., Crowley Indsl. Found., Am. Legion. Democrat. Catholic. Lion. Home: 1226 N Av J Crowley LA 70526 Office: PO Box 44004 Capitol Station Baton Rouge LA 70804

EDWARDS, ELTON, lawyer, state senator; b. nr. Goldsboro, N.C., Aug. 14, 1923; s. Charles Henry and Lillie (Thornton) E.; A.B., U. N.C., 1943, J.D., 1948; m. Jessie Macon Sapp, Mar. 27, 1954; children—Elton Thornton, Ruth Macon. Admitted to N.C. bar, 1948; practiced in Greensboro, 1949—; partner firm Moseley, Edwards & Greeson, Greensboro, N.C., 1954-71, Edwards, Greeson & Toumaras, 1971—; mem. N.C. Ho. of Reps., 1964-68, N.C. Senate, 1968-70. Chmn. Handi-Clean Family Found. Served with AUS, World War II, now lt. col. USAF Res. Mem. Am., N.C., Greensboro bar assns., Res. Officers Assn. (state pres. 1973-74), Air Force Assn. (state pres. 1974—, chmn. J.M. Morehead com.), Phi Alpha Delta. Democrat. Presbyn. (elder). Mason (32deg., Shriner). Home: 309 N Tremont Dr Greensboro NC 27403 Office: PO Box 37 Greensboro NC 27402

EDWARDS, EMMETT WELDON, clergyman, lectr.; b. Fort Worth, Dec. 10, 1924; s. Emmitt Houston and Winley (Box) E.; D.D., Trinity Hall Coll. and Sem., 1956, B.D., 1960; LL.B., LaSalle Extension U., 1969 Joined USAF, 1954, served until 1965; pastor Centeral Bible Temple, Chateauroux, France, 1956-59, Universal Harmony Temple, San Antonio, 1960-63; lectr., Haltom City, Tex., 1962—; pastor Open Door Prayer Chapel, Ft. Worth. Mem. Am. Ministerial Assn., Trinity Hall Coll. and Sem. Alumni Soc., Epsilon Delta Chi. Mason. Author: Faith Healing. 1958. Address: 3317 Azle Av Fort Worth TX 76106

EDWARDS, HAROLD MILLS, lawyer; b. Anson County, N.C., Nov. 20, 1930; s. William H. and Bertha (Baucom) E.; B.S., Wake Forest U., 1953, LL.B., 1959. Admitted to N.C. bar, 1959; since practiced in Charlotte; judge Charlotte Municipal Ct., 1964-68; pres. Keystone Investment Corp. Mem. N.C. Bd. Alcoholic Control, 1970-73. Mem. various bar assns. Home: 7905 Charter Oak Lane Pineville NC 28203 Office: Johnston Bldg Charlotte NC 28281

EDWARDS, JAMES BURROWS, dentists, state senator; b. Hawthorne, Fla., June 24, 1927; s. O. Morton and Bertie (Hieronymus) E.; B.S., Coll. Charleston, 1950; D.M.D., U. Louisville, 1955; postgrad. U. Pa., 1957-58; m. Ann Norris Darlington, Sept. 1, 1951; children—James B., Catherine Darlington. Resident Henry Ford Hosp., Detroit, 1958-60; practice dentistry, specializing in oral surgery, Charleston, S.C., 1960—; clin. asso. oral surgery Med. U. S.C., Charleston, 1968—. Cons. USPHS, Charleston, 1964—; lectr. to profl. groups, U.S., Eng. Vice pres. East Cooper Pvt. Sch. Corp., Mt. Pleasant, S.C., 1966—. Bd. dirs. Coastal Carolina council Boy Scouts Am., 1969-72; trustee Charles County Hosp., 1966-70, Greater Charleston YMCA, 1965-70, East Cooper chpt. Sertoma Internat., 1963-66. Nominee 1st. Congl. Dist. S.C. to U.S. Ho. of Reps., Republican party, 1971; mem. S.C. Senate, 1972—; chmn. Charleston County Rep. Com., 1964-69, also mem. steering com., 1969-72; chmn. 1st Congl. Dist. S.C. Rep. com., 1969-70; mem. steering com. S.C. Rep. com., 1968-70; del. Rep. Nat. Conv., 1968, 72. Served with U.S. Maritime Service, 1944-47, with USNR, 1955-57. Diplomate Am. Bd. Oral Surgery. Fellow Am. Coll. Dentists, Internat. Coll. Dentists; mem. S.C. (past pres., founder, charter mem.), Brit. socs. oral surgeons, Am., S.C. dental assns., Coastal Dist. (past pres.), Charleston dental socs., Chalmers Lyons Acad. Oral Surgery, Internat. Soc. Oral Surgeons, Fedn. Dentaire Internat., Greater Charleston C. of C. Home: 1 Darlington Lane Mount Pleasant SC 29464 Office: 61 Gadsden St Charleston SC 29401

EDWARDS, JAMES DAVIS, recreation cons.; b. Arkadelphia, Ark., Feb. 7, 1933; s. Ben Davis and Ena Elizabeth (Baker) E.; student Henderson State Coll., 1951-53, 60-61; B.S., N. Tex. State U., 1962, postgrad., 1963; m. Martha Ann Eaton, Dec. 21, 1957; children—Kimberly Ann, Robert Davis. Dir. parks and recreation Richardson, Tex., 1963-66; dir. outdoor recreation Ark. Planning Commn., Little Rock, 1966; dep. dir. Ozarks Regional Commn., Little Rock, 1968-73; sr. recreation economist Midwest Research Inst., Kansas City, Mo., 1973—. Mem. S.W. Dist. Adv. Council on Parks and Recreation. Trustee, U.S. Travel Data Center. Served with USAAF, 1953-56. Recipient U.S. Jr. C. of C. Spoke award, Hope, Ark., 1957, 58, 59, Grapevine, Tex., 1961-62. Mem. Nat., Ark. (pres. 1967, 68) Parks and Recreation assns. Home: 5 Wingfield Circle Little Rock AR 72205 Office: 270 Evergreen Pl Little Rock AR 72207

EDWARDS, JAMES EDWIN, lawyer; b. Clarkesville, Ga., July 29, 1914; s. Gus Calloway and Mary Clara (McKinney) E.; student U. Tex., 1931-33; B.A., George Washington U., 1935, J.D., 1946; m. Frances Lillian Stanley, Nov. 22, 1948; children—Robin Anne, James Christopher, Clare (Mrs. Ronald C. Wilkson). Admitted to Fla. bar, 1938, practiced, Cocoa, Fla., 1938-42; divisional asst. Dept. of State, 1945-50; practice law, Ft. Lauderdale, 1951—; mem. firm Bell, Edwards, Coker, Carlon & Amsden, 1956-59; asst. city atty., Ft. Lauderdale, 1961, 63-65; city commr., Coral Springs, Fla., 1970—, mayor, 1972-73; pres., dir. Peninsula Land Co., Ocean Beach Improvement Co. Chmm., Ft. Lauderdale for Eisenhower, 1952; Republican county parliamentarian, 1954-59; pres. Rep. Attys. Club Broward County, 1960-64. Served to lt. USCGR, 1942-45; lt. col. USAF Res. ret. Mem. Am., Fla., Broward County bar assns., Res. Officers Assn. (state judge adv. 1960-61, state v.p. for air, 1961-62), Fla. Sportsmen's Assn. (pres. 1967-68), Delta Sigma Rho, Pi Gamma Mu, Phi Delta Phi, Phi Sigma Kappa. Club: Broken Woods Golf and Country (Coral Springs). Home: 10 Covered Bridge Dr Coral Springs FL 33065 Office: 2822 E Commercial Blvd Fort Lauderdale FL 33308 also 112 Home Center Coral Springs FL 33065

EDWARDS, JOE HARLE, city ofcl.; b. Cleve., Dec. 21, 1943; s. Lea Hanle and Ione (Copeland) E.; C.E., U. Tenn., 1964; B.S., Tenn. Tech. U., 1966; postgrad. Cleve. State Community Coll., 1971, postgrad. U. Tenn. at Chattanooga; m. Nell Green, Aug. 8, 1964; 1 dau., Leslie. With Tenn. Dept. Hwys., Chattanooga, 1964, 66-69; engr., asst. supt. Cleveland (Tenn.) Water System, 1969-72; city engr. City of Cleveland, 1973—. Cons. utilities, site constrn., Cleveland, 1974. Mem: Cleveland Planning Commn., 1972-74; mem. com. on environmental services Tenn. Municipal League, Nashville, 1972-73; mem. Bradley County Utilities Bd., 1974, Hiwassee Utilities Commn., 1974. Registered profl. engr., Tenn. Mem. Am. Water Works Assn., Tenn. Water and Wastewater Assn. Elk. Home: 4475 Mouse Creek Rd Cleveland TN 37311 Office: 90 Church St NE Cleveland TN 37311

EDWARDS, JOHN DIXON, engring. co. exec.; b. Wake County, N.C., Jan. 28, 1933; s. John Dixon and Magnolia (Woody) E.; B.S., N.C. State U., 1956, M.S., 1958; m. Ida Gerlene Hinnant, Sept. 10, 1954; children—Mark D., Alan Bradford. Designer, N.C. State Hwy. Commn., Raleigh, 1956-58; transp. planner City of Cin., 1958-62; with Traffic Planning Asso., Inc., Atlanta, 1962—, pres., 1965—. Lectr. Ga. Inst. Tech., 1965—. Mem. Am. Inst. Planners (chpt. sec. 1962), Inst. Traffic Engrs. (pres. 1964, mem. tech. council 1968-70, internat. dir. 1972—, Herman J. Hoose Distinguished Service award 1973), Hwy. Research Bd. Contbg. author: Urban Design Manual, 1965; Revised Traffic Engineering Handbook, 1973-74, 1973. Home: 3912 Sheldon Dr NE Atlanta GA 30342 Office: 600 W Peachtree St Atlanta GA 30308

EDWARDS, JOSEPH DANIEL, JR., chemist, educator; b. Alexandria, La., Nov. 25, 1924; s. Joseph Daniel and Florence Cora (Hoell) E.; B.S., La. Coll., 1944; M.A., U. Tex., 1948, Ph.D., 1950; postgrad. (fellow) U. Ill., 1950-51; m. Eunice Ray Rike, July 16, 1960; 1 dau., Laurexia Catharine. Chemist, Fercleve Corp., Oak Ridge, 1945; chemist U.S. Naval Research Lab., Phila., 1946; prin. scientist research div. VA, Houston, 1951-59; asst. prof. Baylor U. Sch. Medicine, 1951-59; asso. prof. chemistry Clemson U., 1959; asso. prof. Lamar U., Beaumont, Tex., 1960-65, prof. chemistry, 1965-67; prof. U. Southwestern La., Lafayette, 1967—, head dept. chemistry, 1967-72. Active Heart Fund, Cancer Drive, Cleanest City; student adviser Boys Club, 1960-67. Robert A. Welch Found. grantee, 1962-67, Lamar U. grantee, 1962-67. Fellow Cotton Research Com.; mem. Am. Chem. Soc., Chem. Soc. (London), Phythochem. Soc., Alpha Chi, Phi Lambda Upsilon, Alpha Chi Sigma. Home: 1204 Johnston St Lafayette LA 70501

EDWARDS, MARVIN RAYMOND, investment counsel, econ. forecaster; b. N.Y.C., June 29, 1921; s. Albert H. and Blanche (Gans) E.; B.S., N.Y. U., 1947; m. Helene C. Sirota, Mar. 12, 1955; children—Jeffrey Randell, Douglas Lee, Carolyn Beth. Pres., White Star Sales Corp., Jacksonville, Fla., 1947-58; pres. Edwards & Edwards, Inc., Jacksonville, 1958—. Bd. dirs., v.p. Jacksonville Humane Soc., 1953-56; bd. dirs., pres. Community Service Planning Council, 1955-58, Duval Rehab. Center, 1958, Better Schs. Citizens Com., 1959-65; v.p., bd. dirs., chmn. edn. com. Greater Jacksonville Taxpayers Assn., 1965-71; v.p., bd. dirs. Jacksonville Safety Council, 1949-55; exec. v.p., bd. dirs. Fla. Edn. Research Found., 1970-71; bd. dirs. Sch. Bootstrap Action Com., 1966-68; bd. dirs., mem. exec. com. N.E. Fla. Kidney Found., 1971—. Served to lt. USAAF, 1943-46. Decorated Air medal; recipient commendation for pub. service Duval County Sch. Bd., 1968, community service awards Jacksonville Safety Council, 1949, Jacksonville Jr. C. of C., 1950. Mem. Financial Analysts Fedn., Jacksonville Financial Analysts Soc., Nat. Microfilm Assn., Nat. Assn. Bus. Economists. Address: 1345 Riverbirch Lane Jacksonville FL 32207

EDWARDS, MAX NIXON, lawyer; b. Wichita, Kan., Dec. 4, 1921; s. Walter Lee and Jane (Nixon) E.; A.B., Dartmouth, 1947; LL.B., U. Ariz., 1950; m. Leona Timko, Dec. 2, 1967. Admitted to N.M. bar, 1950; practiced in Hobbs, 1950, 54-60; mem. firm Edwards & Reese, 1954-60; asst. dist. atty. 5th Jud. Dist. N.M., 1951-53; gen. counsel N.M. Senate, 1959; asst. to sec., legislative counsel Dept. Interior, 1961-67, asst. sec. water quality and research, 1967-69; partner Collier, Shannon, Rill & Edwards, Washington, 1969—. Chmn. Presdl. Adv. Bd. Water Pollution Control, 1968; lectr. environmental subjects. Adviser Democratic Nat. Com., 1960. Trustee Environic Found. internat.; vice chmn. Nat. Pollution Control Found. Mem. Bar Assn. D.C., N.M., Ariz. bar assns., Bar Assn. U.S. Supreme Ct., V.F.W. Club: Nat. Golf Links of Am. (Southampton, L.I., N.Y.). Contbr. articles on pollution control to various publs. Home: 2905 P St NW Washington DC 20016 Office: 1666 K St NW Washington DC 20006

EDWARDS, PALMER LOWELL, educator; b. Enterprise, Ala., Mar. 9, 1923; s. Cincinnatus Fernando and Dovie Adele (Pridgen) E.; student Ala. Poly. Inst., 1942-43; B.S., La. State U., 1944; S.M., Harvard U., 1947; Ph.D., U. Md., 1958; m. Dorothy Alice Commons, Mar. 21, 1964. With Naval Ordnance Lab., White Oak, Md., 1944-60, solid state physicist, 1955-60; faculty Tex. Christian U., Ft. Worth, 1960-67; prof. physics, chmn. dept. U. W. Fla., Pensacola, 1967—. Adj. prof. U. Md., College Park, 1958, No. Extension of U. Va., Falls Church, 1959-60. Vice pres. bd. dirs. Fla. State Employees Fed. Credit Union; bd. dirs. Pensacola Arts Council, Inc. Served with USNR, 1945-46. Mem. Am. Phys. Soc., Am. Inst. Physics, A.A.A.S., Am. Assn. U. Profs., Am. Assn. Physics Tchrs., Fla. Acad. Sci., Am. Civil Liberties Union, Sigma Xi, Phi Kappa Phi, Sigma Pi Sigma. Club: Scenic Hills Country (Pensacola). Contbr. articles to profl. jours. Home: 8866 Burning Tree Rd Pensacola FL 32504

EDWARDS, RODERICK YERKES, coast guard officer; b. Phila., Sept. 20, 1909; s. David William and Elizabeth (Yerkes) E.; student Rutgers U., U. N.Y., Am. U., U. San Francisco; m. Rita Thiele, July

10, 1937; children—Roderick Yerkes, David Thiele. With Am. Export Lines, 1927-40; maritime tchr. N.Y. Bd. Edn., 1940-41; insp. hulls Bur. Marine Inspection and Navigation, 1941-42; commd. lt. USCG, 1942, advanced through grades to rear adm., 1967; chief pub. and internat. affairs, 1966—. U.S. del. Internat. Maritime Consultive Orgn., 1966; chmn. Mcht. Marine Council, 1966; vice chmn. IMCO com. Marine Pollution, 1967, chmn. council, 1971—; mem. Nat. Cargo Bur., 1966, Am. Boat and Yacht Council, 1963. Bd. dirs. Nat. Air and Space Museum. Decorated Navy Commendation medal, Legion of Merit; named hon. citizen Antwerp, Belgium. Clubs: Army-Navy, Nat. Aviation, Propellor (Washington); Commercial (San Francisco). Home: 1600 S Eads St Arlington VA 22202 Office: 1625 K St NW Washington DC 20004

EDWARDS, SCOTT SAMUEL, JR., lawyer; b. Atlanta, Apr. 16, 1915; s. Scott Samuel and Maggie (Harris) E., Sr.; LL.B., Woodrow Wilson Coll., 1941; m. Jeanette Victoria Smith, Nov. 14, 1945; 1 son, David Scott. Admitted to Ga. bar, 1941, practiced in Marietta, Ga., 1946—; asst. county atty., Cobb County, 1948-53; atty. City of Marietta, 1948-60, City of Marietta Hosp. Authority, 1948-73; now mem. firm. Edwards, Awtrey & Parker. Served with Signal Corps, AUS, 1941-45; PTO. Mem. Am., Ga., Cobb County (pres. 1955-56) bar assns., Am. Legion. Presbyn. Club: Civitan (pres. 1952-53). Home: 330 S Woodland Dr Marietta GA 30060 Office: 199 Roswell St Marietta GA 30060

EDWARDS, STEVE, educator; b. Quincy, Fla., June 16, 1930; s. Steve and Sarah Frances (Ryan) E.; B.S., Fla. State U., 1952, M.S., 1954; Ph.D. (Gen. Motors fellow), Johns Hopkins, 1960; m. Helen Wallace Carothers, Dec. 17, 1964; children—Ashley Lynn, Leigh Holladay. Grad. asst. Fla. State U. at Tallahassee, 1952-55, asst. prof. physics, 1960-65, asso. prof., 1965-69, prof., 1969—, asso. chmn. physics, 1965-73, chmn. physics, 1973—; jr. instr. Johns Hopkins, 1955-57; bd. dirs. Recon, Inc., Tallahassee, 1960-65, staff coms., 1965-70. Recipient Coyle E. Moore award Fla. State U., 1965. Mem. Am. Assn. Physics Tchrs., Am. Phys. Soc., Order De Molay (chevalier degree 1949, legion of honor 1963), Sigma Xi, Sigma Pi Sigma (zone supr. southeastern U.S. 1962-65), Gamma Alpha, Kappa Sigma, Phi Mu Alpha Sinfonia, Omicron Delta Kappa, Order Omega. Democrat. Episcopalian. Author: Lectures on the Theory of Direct Reactions, 1961; General Physics, 1968; Physics-A Discovery Approach, 1971; also articles. Home: 5026 Barfield Rd Tallahassee FL 32303

EDWARDS, WALLACE HAYWARD, constrn. co. exec.; b. Oakland, Cal., July 26, 1925; s. Donald Robert and Geraldine Amelia (Hayward) E.; student Occidental Coll., Los Angeles, 1943-44; B.S. in Civil Engring., Heald Engring. Coll., San Francisco, 1948; m. Phyllis Mae Robinson, Aug. 30, 1947; children—Robin (Mrs. William T. Maxey), Donald R., Mary (Mrs. John A. Allen). Structural engr., estimator Austin Co., Oakland, 1948-56, project engr., 1956-58, project planner, Dallas, 1958-62, asst. dist. mgr., Houston, 1962-66, v.p., dist. mgr., Houston, 1966—. Bd. dirs. Houston Council on Human Relations, 1971-72, Interface, 1972—. Served with USMCR, 1943-45, 52-53. Mem. Kappa Sigma. Presbyn. (elder). Mason, Rotarian. Home: 13310 Tosca St Houston TX 77024 Office: 2727 Buffalo Speedway Houston TX 77006

EDWARDS, WALTER RAY, wholesale trade exec.; b. Ozark, Ala., Sept. 26, 1917; s. Walter Leroy and Mary Tom (Ray) E.; student U. Va., 1935, U. Ala., 1936; m. Dorothy Fuqua, Dec. 25, 1936; 1 dau., Mary Ann. Operator Edwards Sash Door and Millwork, Ozark, Ala., 1945-49; with Henderson, Black & Greene, Inc., Troy, Ala., 1949—, v.p., dir., 1966—. Owner Edwards Aircraft Repair Service, Troy, 1956—. Served with USNR, 1943-45. Mem. Kappa Sigma. Methodist. Club: Country (Troy). Patentee in field. Home: 919 Murphree St Troy AL 36081 Office: 1 Hanchey St Troy AL 36081

EDWARDS, WALTON MERIDETH, physician, educator; b. Washington, Jan. 29, 1910; s. William Walton and Mary Janet (Donnally) E.; A.B., Stanford, 1933; M.D., Cornell U., 1937; m. Bernice E. French, June 16, 1937; children—Wendy (Mrs. Earl Rust), Margo (Mrs. John Minan), Austin. Intern, D.C. Gen. Hosp., 1937-38; resident Strong Meml. Hosp., Rochester, N.Y., 1938-39, Childrens Hosp., Phila., 1939-40; commd. 1st lt., M.C., U.S. Army, 1940, advanced through grades to col., 1961; pediatrician, allergist out patient service Letterman Army Hosp., San Francisco, 1940-42, chief pediatrics, 1946-49, 52-57; med. officer 3d Inf. Div., 124th Evacuation Hosp., Europe, 1942-45; chief pediatric service Tripler Army Hosp., Honolulu, 1949-52; chief med. service and pediatric sect., communicable disease sect, U.S. Army Hosp., Landstuhl, Germany, 1957-60, also coordinator German intern tng. program; chief pediatric Service Ireland Army Hosp., Ft. Knox, Ky., 1960-62, dir. med. edn., 1962-63; ret., 1963; practice medicine, specializing in pediatrics, Louisville, 1963—; asso. prof. U. Louisville, 1963—, asso. dept. internal medicine, 1966—; physician in chief Children's Hosp., Louisville, 1963—; fellow cardiovascular disease U. Ky., 1970-71; vis. prof. faculty medicine U. Saigon (Vietnam), 1971. Diplomate Am. Bd. Pediatrics, Am. Bd. Internal Medicine. Fellow A.C.P. (asso.); mem. A.M.A., Am. Hosp. Dirs. Med. Edn., Louisville Pediatric Soc. Contbr. articles to med. jours. Home: 3604 Cascade Rd Louisville KY 40222 Office: 226 E Chestnut St Louisville KY 40202

EDWARDS, WENDELL EDWARD, educator; b. Waco, Tex., Aug. 25, 1937; s. William Penn and Florence Helen (Gasaway) E.; B.B.A., Tex. A. and M. U., 1959, M.B.A., 1964; Ph.D., North Tex. State U., 1972; m. Linda Lucille Yeats, Dec. 19, 1964; children—Karen, Kathy. Staff accountant W.O. Ligon & Co., Ft. Worth, 1964-66; asst. prof. accounting East Tex. State U., Commerce, 1969—, asso. prof. accounting, 1973—. Served to 1st lt. USAF, 1959-62. C.P.A., Tex. Mem. Tex. Soc. C.P.A.'s, Am. Inst. C.P.A.'s, Am. Accounting Assn., Beta Alpha Psi, Sigma Iota Epsilon. Home: 2813 McCarley St Commerce TX 75428

EDWARDS, WILLIAM WARREN, landscape architect; b. Oklahoma City, Nov. 28, 1929; s. Warren Hamilton and Pauline Caroline (Mills) E.; student U. Okla., 1947-50; B.S. in Botany, Okla. State U., 1953; B.Landscape Architecture, N.C. State U., 1958; m. Barbara Jean Messenbaugh, Aug. 17, 1965. Landscape architect O'Neil Ford, San Antonio, 1959-60, Lewis Clarke, Raleigh, N.C., 1960-62, 63-64, Richard Bell, Raleigh, 1962-63; pvt. practice landscape architecture, Oklahoma City, 1965—. Instr. landscape architecture Okla. State U., 1969-70. Mem. Hist. Preservation Commn. Oklahoma City, 1971—. Bd. dirs. Oklahoma City Beautiful Inc. Served with USAF, 1953-55. Harvard Bd. Trustees jr. research fellow landscape architecture Dumbarton Oaks, 1958-59. Mem. Am. Soc. Landscape Architects (state chmn. 1967—), Am. Inst. Interior Decorators (design asso.), Okla. Zool. Soc., Phi Kappa Psi. Republican. Presbyn. Mason. Home: 528 NW 18th St Oklahoma City OK 73103 Office: 6100 NW Grand Blvd Oklahoma City OK 73118

EDWARDSON, JOHN RICHARD, geneticist, educator; b. Kansas City, Mo., Apr. 17, 1923; s. George E. and Louise M. (Sundstrom) E.; B.A., Tex. A. and M. U., 1948, M.S., 1949; Ph.D., Harvard, 1954; m. Mickie L. Newbill, Dec. 20, 1969; children—George, Elizabeth, Sarah. Asst. prof. agronomy Fla. Agrl. Expt. Sta., U. Fla., Gainesville, 1953-60, asso. prof., 1960-66, prof., 1966—. Served with AUS, 1942-45. Mem. A.A.A.S., Genetics Soc. Am., Am. Genetics Assn., Bot. Soc. Am., N.Y. Acad. Scis. Democrat. Home: 2721 SW 3rd St Gainesville FL 32607

EFRON, MARVIN, optometrist; b. Aiken, S.C., May 30, 1930; s. Harry H. and Mary (Fadem) E.; student U. S.C., 1947-48, Ohio State U., 1958; Dr. Optometry, So. Coll. Optometry, 1951; M.A., U. S.C., 1965, Ph.D., 1969; m. Sara Lyon Timmerman, June 20, 1956; children—Leslie Kay, Susan Frances. Practice of optometry, Edgefield, S.C., 1952-58, West Columbia, S.C., 1958—. Lectr., U.S.C. Coll. Edn., 1970—; mem. adv. com. programs for edn. of handicapped S.C. Dept. Edn. Trustee S.C. Opportunity Sch., cons. various indsl. concerns, Reading Clinic U. S.C. Chmn. Recreational Needs Survey for areas of West Columbia. Cayce and Springsdale, S.C., 1961-63; past chmn. Lexington County Commn. Higher Edn. Trustee United Community Services Lexington and Richland Counties. Recipient Distinguished Service award, 1966; best Scientific paper on vision in South, 1966, 70; Distinguished Service award S.C. Otometric Assn., 1969, Optometrist of Year award, 1970. Mem. S.C. (past chmn.) Central (pres. 1968-69) optometric assns., So. Council Optometry, Am. Psychol. Assn., Am. Optometric Found., West Columbia-Cayce (pres. 1965-66), Greater Columbia (dir.) chambers commerce, Phi Epsilon Pi. Mason, Woodman of World. Home: 1212 Canary Dr West Columbia SC 29169 Office: 1205 D Av West Columbia SC 29169

EFRON, SAMUEL, lawyer; b. Lansford, Pa., May 6, 1915; s. Abraham and Rose (Kaduchin) E.; B.A., Lehigh U., 1935; LL.B., Harvard, 1938; m. Hope Bachrach Newman, Apr. 5, 1941; children—Marc Fred, Eric Michael. Admitted to Pa. bar, 1938, D.C. bar, 1949; atty. forms and regulations div., also registration div. SEC, 1939-40, Office Solicitor, Dept. Labor, 1940-42; asst. chief real and personal property sect. Office Alien Property Custodian, 1942-43; chief debt claims sect., also asst. chief claims br. Office Alien Property, Dept. Justice, 1946-51; asst. gen. counsel internat. affairs Dept. Def., 1951-53, cons., 1953-54; partner firm Surrey, Karasik, Gould & Efron, Washington, 1954-61, now partner firm Arent, Fox, Kintner, Plotkin & Kahn. Dir. Parsons & Whittemore, Inc., N.Y.C. Served to lt. (s.g.) USNR, 1943-46. Mem. Am., Fed., Inter-Am. bar assns., Am. Soc. Internat. Law, A.I.M. (pres. council 1965), Phi Beta Kappa. Republican. Clubs: Army-Navy, Capitol Hill, Nat. Press, Nat. Lawyers, Harvard (Washington); New York, Harvard, Lotos (N.Y.C.). Author: Creditors Claims Under the Trading with the Enemy Act, 1948; Foreign Taxes on United States Expenditures, 1954; Offshore Procurement and Industrial Mobilization, 1955. Home: 3537 Ordway St NW Washington DC 20016 Office: Arent Fox Kintner Plotkin & Kahn 600 Federal Bar Bldg 1815 H St NW Washington DC 20006

EGAN, M(ARTIN) DAVID, educator; b. Trenton, N.J., Feb. 13, 1941; s. Martin James and Madolyn (Brown) E.; B.C.E., Lafayette Coll., 1962; M.C.E., Mass. Inst. Tech., 1966; m. Dorothy Jean Strong, Aug. 5, 1967. Mech. engr. Shell Oil Co., New Orleans, 1966-68; cons. Bolt, Beranek & Newman, Cambridge, Mass., 1968-69; asst. prof. architecture Tulane U., 1969-72; asso. prof. architecture Clemson U., 1972—; adj. prof. architecture Ga. Inst. Tech., Atlanta, 1973—; cons. archtl. acoustics and noise control, Anderson, S.C.; lectr. in field. Served with AUS, 1962-64. Mem. Nat. Council Acoustical Cons., Acoustical Soc. Am. (sec. tech. com. on archtl. acoustics), Am. Soc. Heating, Refrigerating and Air-Conditioning Engrs. Phi Gamma Delta. Republican. Methodist. Author: Concepts in Architectural Acoustics, 1972; Concepts in Thermal Comfort, 1974. Office: PO Box 365 Anderson SC 29621

EGAN, MICHAEL JOSEPH, JR., lawyer, legislator; b. Savannah, Ga., Aug. 8, 1926; s. Michael Joseph and Elise (Robider) E.; B.A., Yale, 1950; LL.B., Harvard, 1955; m. Donna Cole, Apr. 14, 1951; children—Moira, Michael, Donna, Cole, Roby, John. Admitted to Ga. bar, 1955; partner Sutherland, Asbill & Brennan, Atlanta and Washington, 1960—; mem. Ga. Ho. of Reps., 1965—, minority leader, 1970—. Home: 97 Brighton Rd Atlanta GA 30309 Office: First Nat Bank Tower Atlanta GA 30303

EGAN, ROBERT LEE, physician, educator; b. Morrilton, Ark., May 9, 1920; s. Philip Kearny and Camilla (Roach) E.; student Coll. of Ozarks, Clarksville, Ark., 1935-39; M.D., U. Pitts., 1950; m. Mary Alice Vetterly, Oct. 27, 1950; children—Kathleen Louise, Deborah Ann, Cheryl Lynn, Melissa Jean, Patricia Lea. Intern, U.S. Naval Hosp., Portsmouth, Va., 1950-51; resident Jefferson Med. Coll. Hosp., Phila., 1953-55; practice medicine specializing in radiology, Houston, 1955-62, Indpls., 1962-64, Atlanta, 1964—; asso. radiologist diagnostic radiology U. Tex. M.D. Anderson Hosp. and Tumor Inst., Houston, 1961-62; chief sect. exptl. diagnostic radiology M.D. Anderson Hosp., 1961-62; radiologist dept. radiology Methodist Hosp. of Ind., Indpls., 1962-65; chief mammography sect. Emory U., Atlanta, 1965—, asso. prof. radiology, 1965-68, prof., 1968—. Served to lt. (j.g.) USNR, 1937-38, 44-46, 50-51. Diplomate Am. Bd. Radiology. Fellow Am. Coll. Radiology; mem. A.M.A., Fulton County Med. Soc., Radiol. Soc. N.Am., Ga. Radiol. Soc., Am. Roentgen Ray Soc. Author: Mammography, 1964, 72; Technologist Guide to Mammography, 1968; Egan's Data on Mammography and Breast Cancer, 1972. Home: 1365 Clifton Rd Atlanta GA 30322

EGER, ALBERT BELA, accountant; b. Presov, Czechoslovakia, Apr. 20, 1919; s. Josef and Blanche (Fiserova) E.; student U. Prague (Czechoslovakia), 1938-39, Nat. Conservatory (Prague), 1945; B.B.A., U. Balt., 1954; postgrad. U. Ala., 1968; m. Edie Eva Elefant, Nov. 12, 1946; children—Marianne (Mrs. Robert Engle), Audrey, John. Came to U.S., 1949, naturalized, 1954. With M. Eger & Son, Presov, 1939-41, officer, owner firm, 1946-49; bookkeeper BVD, Inc., Balt., 1950-52; accountant S.L. Silber, C.P.A., Balt., 1952-55, Douplas & Huple, C.P.A.'s, El Paso, 1955-59; owner bookkeeping service, El Paso, 1960-67; owner C.P.A. firm, El Paso, 1967—. Pres. Jewish Family Service, El Paso, 1960-71; mem. exec. bd. Jewish Community Council, 1960—; mem. nat. council Joint Hebrew Aid Immigrant Soc., 1962—; mem. Anti-Defamation League. Active polit. campaigns candidates Democratic party, 1970—; treas. El Paso div. McGovern for Pres. Campaign, 1972. Served to jr. lt. Czechoslovakian Armed Forces, 1939-45; POW, 1940-41; decorated Distinguished Guerilla Medal for Freedom Czechoslovakia. C.P.A., Tex. Mem. Am. Inst. C.P.A.'s, Tex., El Paso socs. C.P.A.'s. Jewish religion. Mem. B'nai B'rith (v.p. 1971-72). Home: 6305 Snowheights Ct El Paso TX 79912 Office: 201 ABC Bank Bldg El Paso TX 79901

EGGEN, DOUGLAS AMBROSE, educator; b. Rushford, Minn., Apr. 30, 1925; s. Ambrose Ingvold and Alma Josefine (Monson) E.; Ph.B., U. Chgo., 1947, S.B., 1955, Ph.D. (NSF fellow), 1957; m. Elsie M. Gertz, Sept. 9, 1950; children—Steven D., Karen J., Susan E. Research asso. Research Inst., U. Chgo., 1955-58; research asso. dept. pathology La. State U. Med. Center, New Orleans, 1958-61, instr., 1961-63, asst. prof., 1963-66, asso. prof., 1966-72, prof. pathology and biometry, 1972—, dir. Biomedical Computer Center, 1972—. Served with USNR, 1943-45. Mem. Biophys. Soc., Am. Soc. Exptl. Pathologists, Am. Heart Assn. (fellow council on arteriosclerosis), Sigma Xi. Contbr. articles to profl. jours. Research on atherosclerosis and cholesterol metabolism in sub-human primates. Office: 1542 Tulane Av New Orleans LA 70112

EGGERS, PAUL WALTER, lawyer; b. Seymour, Ind., Apr. 20, 1919; s. Ernest H. and Ottile (Carre) E.; B.A., Valparaiso U., 1941; LL.B., U. Tex., 1948; m. Frances Kramer, Dec. 29, 1946 (div. July 1973); 1 son, Steven Paul; m. 2d, Virginia McMillin Streeter, Feb. 23, 1974. Admitted to Tex. bar, 1948; practiced in Wichita Falls, 1948-69; mem. firm Eggers, Sherrill & Pace, 1952-69; gen. Counsel U.S. Treasury Dept., Washington, 1969-70; practice, Dallas, 1971—. Pres., Wichita Falls Symphony, 1960-62. Chmn., Wichita County Republican Party, 1966-67; chmn. Rep. State Task Force on Revenue and Fiscal Policy, 1967; Rep. candidate for gov. of Tex., 1968, 70. Commr. Pres. Assay Commn., 1972—. Trustee Episcopal Ch. Bldg. Fund, Dallas Symphony Orch., St. Mark's Sch. of Tex., 1974—; bd. dirs. Student Loan Marketing Assn., 1973—; adv. council St. Paul Hosp., 1974—. Served to maj. AUS, 1941-46. Mem. State Bar Tex., Am. Bar Assn., Am. Judicature Soc. Episcopalian. Home: 15417 Preston Rd Dallas TX 75240 Office: 1407 Main St Dallas TX 75202

EGGERTON, WALTER HAWKINS, elec. engr.; b. Meridian, Miss., Feb. 4, 1924; s. Albert Sidney and Martha Josephine (Hawkins) E.; B.S. magna cum laude, U. S.C., 1944; m. Jacquelyn Lucille Roseberry, Mar. 27, 1954; children—Jennifer, Martha, Walter Hawkins, Max. Engr., RCA, Camden, N.J., 1946-51; project engr. Melpar, Inc., Fairfax, Va., 1951-57; with Martin Marietta Aerospace, Orlando, Fla., 1957—, mgr. seeker design dept., 1972—. Served to lt. (j.g.) USNR, 1944-46. Fellow Am. Inst. Aeros. and Astronautics (asso.); mem. I.E.E.E., Phi Beta Kappa. Home: 2923 Timberlake Dr Orlando FL 32806 Office: PO Box 5837 Sand Lake Rd Orlando FL 32805

EHART, ROSALIE BOSWELL, educator, clubwoman; b. Indpls.; d. John Bruce and Edith K. (Harvey) Boswell; student Barry Coll., 1963-64; B.A., U. Miami, 1965, postgrad., 1969—; M.S. (Nat. Sci. fellow), Colby Coll., 1969; m. William McMein Ehart, Sept. 3, 1944 (div. Aug. 1957); children—Jan Bruce, Penelope Margaret, William McMein. Columnist, Diario las Americas, 1954-55; pres., chmn. bd. Collins Pharmacal Co., 1955-59; tchr. biology Mays Sr. High Sch., Goulds, Fla., 1966-70, Portobello Secondary Sch., Edinburgh, Scotland, 1971-72, Miami Edison Sr. High Sch., 1970, 72—. Mem. Women's Congress on Housing, 1956, 57; dir. Am. Homes Com. for Miami Jr. Woman's Club, 1952, dir. social activities, 1953-54; vol. chmn. Jackson Meml. Hosp. NSF fellow, summers 1966-69; Fulbright fellow, 1971-72. Mem. Dade County Classroom Tchrs. Assn. (mem. human relations commn.), Am. Assn. U. Women, Theosophical Soc., English-Speaking Union, Council Internat. Visitors. Roman Catholic. Home: 1224 Tangier Coral Gables FL 33134

EHLE, JOHN MARSDEN, SR., ins. exec.; b. Morgantown, W.Va., May 5, 1904; s. John F. and Nancy (Marsden) E.; student Bingham Mil. Sch., Asheville, N.C., 1923-24; m. Gladys Starnes, Feb. 21, 1925; children—John, Robert Starnes, Mary Ann, David Bolton, Nancy Elizabeth. With Imperial Life Ins. Co., Asheville, N.C., 1927-57, agt., 1927-28, asst. advt. mgr., 1929, advt. mgr., 1930-40, agy. sec., 1940—, mgr. ordinary dept., 1945-48, v.p., 1949-57; 2d v.p. Western & So. Life Ins. Co., 1957-60; regional mgr. Western N.C., Franklin Life Ins. Co., 1960—; propr. Ehle Ins. Agy., 1970—. Asst. chief aux. police, Asheville civilian def., 1942—; chmn. Christmas Cheer Fund, 1948, 49; chmn. adv. bd. Salvation Army; chmn. Gospel Projects, Inc.; dir. Asheville Jr. Achievement Inc.; publicity chmn, United Appeal. Trustee, mem. exec. com. Asheville Orthopedic Hosp., sec. Orthopedic Hosp. and Rehab. Center; treas. Ben Lippen Sch.; chmn. bd. trustees Eliada Homes, Inc., Faith Cottage. Mem. C. of C., Ins. Agy. Mgmt. Assn., Life Advertisers Assn. (charter mem., past chmn., sec. So. roundtable, mem. nat. exec. com.), Nat., Asheville (past pres., sec.) assns. life underwriters, Carolina Home Office Underwriters (charter mem., past chmn.), Gideons. Mem. Gospel Tabernacle (trustee). Kiwanian (hon.). Club: Men's (past pres.). Editor: The Imperial Indicator (weekly), 1930-55. Contbr. to life ins. publs. Home: 8 Cedarcliff Rd Asheville NC 28803 Office: 217 E Merrimon Av Asheville NC 28801

EHLE, JOHN MARSDEN, JR., author; b. Asheville, N.C., Dec. 13, 1925; s. John M. and Gladys (Starnes) E.; B.A., U. N.C., 1949, M.A., 1953; m. Gail Oliver, Aug. 30, 1952 (div. Apr. 1967); m. 2d, Rosemary Harris, Oct. 22, 1967; 1 dau., Jennifer Anne. Faculty, U. N.C. at Chapel Hill., 1951-63, asst. prof., 1954-57, asso. prof., 1957-64; spl. asst. to Gov. Terry Sanford, Raleigh, N.C., 1963-64; adviser programs Ford Found., N.Y.C., 1964-65, cons., 1966-67; vis. asso. prof. N.Y. U., 1958-59; author novels: Move Over, Mountain, 1957; Kingstree Island, 1959; Lion on the Hearth, 1961; The Land Breakers, 1964 (Sir Walter Raleigh prize); The Road, 1967; Time of Drums, 1970; The Journey of August King, 1971; non-fiction books; The Survivor, 1958, Shepherd of the Streets, 1960; The Free Men (Mayflower Soc. cup) 1965; the Cheeses and Wines of England and France, with Notes on Irish Whiskey, 1972; plays: American Adventure (broadcast) 1954-56; pub. also in several fgn. countries. Mem. U.S. Nat. Commn. for UNESCO, 1965-68, White House Group for Domestic Affairs, 1964-66, Nat. Council Humanities, 1966-70; bd. visitors Appalachian State U., Boone, N.C., 1969—; mem. exec. com. Nat. Book Com., N.Y.C. Bd. dirs. Inst. Outdoor Drama, U. N.C., Chapel Hill, Winston-Salem, Anne C. Stouffer Found., Winston-Salem. Mem. Authors League P.E.N. Club: Century (N.Y.C.). Home: 125 Westview Dr N Winston-Salem NC 27104 Office: care Candida Donadio 111 W 57th St New York City NY 10019

EHLERS, SABINE LILA (MRS. WALTER H. EHLERS), editor; b. Harbin, China, June 26, 1910; d. Joseph and Ann Bardack; B.S., N.Y. U., 1935, postgrad., 1936; m. Walter Henry Ehlers, June 1, 1935; children—Rhea Judith (Mrs. R. John Maxwell), Joyce Reed (Mrs. Joel Esquith), Carol Joan (Mrs. Thomas McMahon). Came to U.S., 1921, naturalized, 1936. Tchr. N.Y. Kindergarten Assn., 1935-37; reporter Mill Valley (Cal.) Record, 1946-50; owner Ideas Promoted, 1951-52; editor, reporter, Honolulu Star-Bull., 1950-52; editor U. Hawaii, Honolulu, 1952-53; exec. editor Pearl Harbor Naval Shipyard, 1953-59; writer, editor Polaroid Corp., Cambridge, Mass., 1959-64, publs. cons., 1959-60; free lance editing Florence Heller Sch., Brandeis U., 1961; free-lance editor, writer, and photographer, Topsfield, Mass., 1964—; owner, dir. E & E Assos., Topsfield, 1964—; owner, mgr. Alsa Jewelry, mail order bus.; women's editor weekly newspaper Capital Canon, Tallahassee; corr. Tampa Tribune, 1970—; writer on assignment Fla. Wildlife Mag., 1971—. Recipient award for editorial excellence Hawaii Employers Council, 1953, West Coast indsl. editors' award for best layout, 1955, award for layout Pacific Coast Indsl. Editors Awards Program, 1957, Superior Accomplishment award Pearl Harbor Naval Shipyard, 1957; award of excellence for creative advt. Tallahassee Advt. Fedn. Mem. Indsl. Editors of Hawaii (pres.), Fla. State U. Women, Internat. Council of Indsl. Editors. Editor: Kauai Guide Book, 1951, rev. edit. 1957. Author: Hawaiian Legends for Boys and Girls, 1958. Contbr. work in photography. Home: 2006 Lee Av Tallahassee FL 32303 Office: E & E Assos Tallahassee FL

EHLERS, WALTER HENRY, educator; b. N.Y.C., May 3, 1912; s. Gustave and Frieda S. (Natusch) E.; B.S., N.Y. U., 1936, M.A., 1942; D.S.W., Brandeis U., 1962; m. Sabine Lila Bardack, June 1, 1935; children—Rhea Judith (Mrs. R. John Maxwell), Joyce Reed (Mrs. Joel Esquith), Carol Joan (Mrs. Thomas McMahon). With YMCA, 1937-52, exec. sec., Ventura Cal. also Kauai, Hawaii, 1942-52; exec.

dir. Palama Settlement, Honolulu, 1952-59; dist. coordinator Action for Boston Community Devel., 1961-62; dir. urban planning dept. United Community Services, Boston, 1962-65; prof. social work Fla. State U., Tallahassee, 1965—. Mem. faculty Northeastern U., 1963-65, Simmons Sch. Social Work, 1964-65, Boston Coll. Sch. Social Work, 1964-65; cons. E. & E. Assos., Tallahassee, 1965—; project dir. improving social work edn. U.S. Dept. Health, Edn. and Welfare, 1969—. Recipient McInerney grant, 1956—. Mem. Nat. Assn. Social Workers, Council Social Work Edn., Am. Assn. U. Profs., Internat. Conf. Social Work, Fla. Conf. Social Welfare, Phi Delta Kappa. Author: Proposal for a Local Planning Organization Within United Community Services, 1964; Mothers of Retarded Children: How They Feel, Where They Seek Help, 1966; (with others) An Introduction to Mental Retardation, 1973. Contbr. chpt. to book, articles to publs. Home: 2006 Lee Av Tallahassee FL 32303

EHNI, FREDERICK MARION, architect; b. Moncks Corner, S.C., Aug. 21, 1935; s. Adolph Gustav and Lula Mae (Metts) E.; B.Arch. with honors, Clemson U., 1964; m. Frances Anne Owens, July 28, 1957. Architect, Beachum & Wood, Greenville, S.C., 1959, Lucas & Stubbs Assos., Charleston, S.C., 1964-68; self-employed as architect, Charleston, 1968—. Chmn. Downtown Council Parking Com., 1971. Mem. Charleston County Zoning Bd. Adjustment, 1971—, chmn., 1971-72; exec. committeeman Democratic party, Charleston County, 1971—. Served with USNR, 1957-59. Recipient Minaret award Clemson U., 1961, award S.C. Concrete Masonry Assn., 1961, Rudolph E. Lee award Clemson U., 1963, award of merit for design excellence AIA, 1967. Mem. A.I.A., Architects' Council Charleston (pres. 1970), Charleston Trident C. of C., Historic Ansonborough Neighborhood Assn. (pres. 1969), Tau Sigma Delta. Club: Exchange. Prin. archtl. works include S.C. Dept. Corrections, Coastal Community Pre-Release Center, Village Shaftsbury (a planned-unit devel.). Address: 66 Society St Charleston SC 29401

EHRHARDT, WILLARD FREDERICK, JR., cons. b. Scranton, Pa., July 27, 1940; s. Willard Frederick and Mary (Swingle) E.; student Western Mich. U., 1958-59, postgrad., 1964-65; B.S., U. Mich., 1963. Indsl. engr. Kellogg Co., Battle Creek, Mich., 1964-67, plant indsl. engr., Memphis, 1968; mem. cons. staff Ernst & Ernst, Memphis, 1969-71, cons. supr., 1972, supr. in charge of cons., Ft. Worth, 1973—. Jr. achievement adviser, Battle Creek and Memphis, 1967-69. Served to 1st lt. AUS, 1965-71. Registered profl. engr., Tenn. Mem. Am. Inst. Indsl. Engrs. (chpt. pres. 1970, dir. 1969-71), Nat. Assn. Accountants Assn. for Systems Mgmt., Hosp. Financial Mgmt. Assn. Clubs: Ft. Worth Ski; Buckneer Sailing (Memphis). Home: 5516 Boca Raton Blvd Apt 324 Fort Worth TX 76112 Office: Fort Worth Nat Bank Bldg Fort Worth TX 76102

EHRLICH, JAMES BURTON, airline exec.; b. Chgo., Nov. 20, 1929; s. Max Charles and Amanda (Palmquist) E.; student Carleton Coll., 1947-49; B.A., Ill. Wesleyan U., 1952; m. Audrey Evans Choate, Sept. 21, 1956; 1 stepdau., Karen Schuyler Choate; children—Andrew Carl, Evan Peter. Intelligence officer C.I.A., Washington, 1956-59; asst. to v.p. fed affairs Air Transport Assn. Am., Washington, 1959-68; dir. civic affairs Trans World Airlines, Inc., Washington, 1968—. Served to lt. (j.g.) USNR, 1952-55. Mem. Sigma Chi. Club: University (Washington). Home: 2116 Belle Haven Rd Alexandria VA 22307 Office: 1000 16th St NW Washington DC 20036

EHRLICH, S(AUL) PAUL, JR., govt. ofcl., physician; b. Mpls., May 4, 1932; s. Sol P. and Dorothy E. (Fiterman) E.; B.A., U. Minn., 1953, B.S., 1955, M.D., 1957; M.P.H., U. Cal., 1961; m. Geraldine McKenna, June 20, 1959; children—Susan P., Paula J., Jill M. Intern USPHS Hosp., S.I., N.Y., 1958; resident epidemiology U. Cal., 1961-63; mem. grants and tng. br. Nat. Heart Inst., Bethesda, Md., 1959-60; chief field and tng. sta. div. chronic diseases Heart Disease Control Program, San Francisco, 1961-65, asst. chief program devel., Arlington, Va., 1966-67; dep. chief Heart Disease Control Program of Nat. Center Chronic Disease Control, Arlington, 1967; asso. dir. bilateral programs Office Internat. Health of USPHS, Washington, 1967; dep. dir. Office of Internat. Health, Office of Sec. Dept. Health, Edn. and Welfare, Washington, 1968-69, acting dir., 1969-70, dir., 1970—, also acting surgeon gen. USPHS, 1973—; lectr. epidemiology U. Cal.; clin. asso. prof. community medicine and internat. health Georgetown U.; adj. prof. internat. health U. Tex. U.S. rep. exec. bd. WHO, 1969-72, 73—, chmn., 1972. Served to lt. USCG, 1958-59. Diplomate Am. Bd. Preventive Medicine. Fellow Am. Coll. Preventive Medicine, Am. Pub. Health Assn., Am. Heart Assn.; mem. A.M.A., A.A.A.S., Am. Geriatrics Soc., N.Y. Acad. Scis., Internat. Epidemiol. Assn., D.C. Pub. Health Assn. Contbr. articles profl. jours. Home: 6512 Lakeview Dr Falls Church VA 22041 Office: 5600 Fishers Lane Rockville MD 20852

EIBENSCHUTZ, JUAN, nuclear engr.; b. Mexico D.F., Mexico, May 26, 1935; s. Eugenio and Barbara (Hartman) E.; Ingeniero Mecanico Electricista, Universidad Nacional Autonoma de Mexico, 1958; Nuclear Engr., Inst. Nat. des Scis. et Techniques Nucleaires, Saclay, Freance, 1960; m. Antinea Gutierrez Zamora, Aug. 28, 1959; children—Antinea Catalina, Barbara, Carla. Asst. to prodn. mgr. Electromotores Mexicanos, 1956; tech. asst. to gen. mgr. Fondicion ABC, 1957; test and design engr. Indsl. Electrica Mexicana SA, 1958; engr. planning dept. Comision Federal de Electricidad, Mexico, 1959-61, engr. operations dept., 1961-62, asst. to dep. dir. gen., 1964-71, dir. research inst., mgr. nuclear div., 1971—; on leave as asso. officer div. nuclear power and reactors Internat. Atomic Energy Agy., Vienna, Austria, 1962-64. Adviser, Secretaria de la Presidencia, Mexico, 1971—. Mem. I.E.E.E., Am. Nuclear Soc., Colegio de Ingenieros Mecanicos Electricitas, Asociacion de Ingenieros Universitarios Mecanicos Electricitas, Canadian Nuclear Assn. Author: (with others) Decision Analysis of Nuclear Plants in Electrical System Expension, 1968. Contbr. articles to profl. jours. Patentee device for direct energy conversion. Home: Cerro Prieto 31 Mexico 21 DF Mexico Office: Rodano 14 Mexico 5 DF Mexico

EICHELBERGER, DEAN AUSTIN, architect; b. Jerome, Ida., Nov. 29, 1911; s. Frank Earl and Anita Bell (Austin) E.; student U. Ida., 1929-33; B.A. in Arch., U. Pa., 1936; m. Kathleen Braden, Nov. 29, 1949; children—Dean Austin, Peter Braden, John Francis, Mary Ann. Chief design br. Army C.E., Philipine Islands, chief engring. div., Guam, 1946-48; pvt. practice architecture, Houston, 1948—. Served to lt. comdr. USNR, 1942-46; to lt. col. USAF, 1950-54. Recipient Religious Archtl. Guild award, 1956. Mem. A.I.A., Am. Soc. C.E., Houston Engring. and Sci. Soc., Army-Navy Assn., Alpha Tau Omega. Kiwanian. Prin. works include Tufuna AFB, Pago Pago, Samoa. Rehab. Downtown Saginaw, Mich., 1972, Navy Hosp., Houston, 1948, St. Joseph Profl. Bldg., Houston, 1963. Home: 18 Stillforest St Houston TX 77024 Office: 2 Chelsea Pl Houston TX 77006

EICHENBAUM, E. CHARLES, lawyer; b. Little Rock, May 30, 1907; s. Ephraim Harris and Sadie (Cohn) E.; J.D., Washington U., St. Louis, 1928; m. Helen Lockwood, July 9, 1933; 1 dau., Peggy (Mrs. Leo Richard Jalenak, Jr.). Admitted to Ark. bar, 1928, since practiced in Little Rock; sr. partner Eichenbaum, Scott, Miller, Crockett & Bryant, 1932—; lectr. regional and nat. tax insts. and seminars. Pres. Capital Av. Bldg. Co., Profl. Bldg. Co.; dir. Sterling Stores Co., Inc., Dillard Dept. Stores, Inc., Little Rock, Boston Store, Ft. Smith, Ark., United Dollar Stores, Inc., Dumas, Ark., Ike Kempner Bros., Inc., 555, Inc., Pfeifer Plumbing & Heating Co., Little Rock. Mem. Ozark Cultural Commn., 1969-73. Trustee Nat. Conf. Christians and Jews, Leo N. Levi Hosp. Fellow Am. Bar Found.; mem. Am. (sub-com. chmn.), Ark. (com. chmn.), Pulaski County bar assns., Am. Judicature Soc., Pralma, Thurntene, Zeta Beta Tau. Jewish religion (trustee temple). Mem. B'nai B'rith, Rotarian. Contbr. articles to profl. jours. Home: Summit House Apts 400 N University St Little Rock AR 72205 Office: Tower Bldg Little Rock AR 72201

EICHORN, PAUL ANTHONY, tobacco co. exec.; b. Boston, Aug. 8, 1916; s. Charles Lawrence and Ruth Katherine (Brown) E.; A.B., Boston Coll., 1938, M.A., 1940, licentiate philosophy, 1942; Ph.D., Fordham U., 1946; m. Margaret Theresa Bohmert, Aug. 6, 1947; children—Robert P., Charles L., Catharine M., Paul J. With Lederle Labs., Pearl River, N.Y., 1947-55, Warner-Lambert Co., Morris Plains, N.J., 1957-66; with Philip Morris Co., Richmond, Va., 1966—, mgr. tech. planning and information, 1966—. Mem. A.A.A.S., Nat. Conf. Adminstrv. Research, N.Y. Acad. Sci., Assn. for Tech. Assessment, Planning Execs. Inst., Inst. for Mgmt. Scis. Roman Catholic. Club: Lake Monticello (Palmyra, Va.). Home: 3411 Traylor Dr Richmond VA 23235 Office: PO Box 26583 Richmond VA 23261

EIDSON, JOHN OLIN, coll. pres.; b. Johnston, S.C., Dec. 10, 1908; s. Olin Marvin and Margaret (Rushton) E.; A.B., Wofford Coll., 1929, Litt.D. (hon.), 1954; M.A., Vanderbilt U., 1930; Ph.D., Duke, 1941; m. Perrin Cudd, Aug. 7, 1952. Faculty U. Ga., Athens, 1936-68, beginning as instr. English, successively dean Coordinate Coll., dir. U. Center in Ga., dean Coll. Arts and Scis., 1957-68; pres. Ga. So. Coll., Statesboro, 1968-71; vice chancellor U. System of Ga., 1971—; vis. prof. Am. lit. U. Freiberg, Germany, 1956. Mem. senate Nat. Assn. State Univs. and Land-Grant Colls., 1963-66. Mem. Atlanta Municipal Edn. Adv. Com., 1971—. Exec. bd. Atlanta area council Boy Scouts Am., 1973—. Served from lt. to maj., inf., AUS, 1942-46; lt. col. Res. Recipient M.G. Michael award for research, 1950. Mem. Am. Studies Assn. (v.p. southeastern 1964-66, pres. 1966-68), Am. Assn. State Colls. and Univs. (mem. grad. com.), Conf. Acad. Deans So. States (pres. 1967-68), Nat. Council Colls. Arts and Scis. (mem. exec. bd. 1965-68), English Assn., Tennyson Soc. Modern Lang. Assn. Am., S. Atlantic Modern Lang. Assn., Newcomen Soc. N. Am., Sphinx, Phi Beta Kappa (chmn. S. Atlantic dist. 1958-61, pres. Coastal Ga.-Carolina 1970-71), Pi Kappa Delta, Phi Kappa Phi, Delta Phi Alpha (nat. sec. 1929-34, mem. nat. council 1969—), Tau Kappa Alpha, Kappa Delta Pi, Phi Delta Kappa, Kappa Phi Kappa. Methodist. Rotarian. Author: Tennyson in America, 1943; Charles Stearns Wheeler: Friend of Emerson, 1951; (with W. W. Davidson) Reading for Pleasure, 1948. Editor: Georgia Review, 1950-57, mem. editorial bd., 1957—. Contbr. articles and revs. to scholastic jours. Home: 362 Valley Green Dr NE Atlanta GA 30342 Office: 244 Washington St SW Atlanta GA 30334

EIDSON, PERRIN CUDD (MRS. JOHN OLIN EIDSON), club woman; b. Spartanburg, S.C., May 19, 1914; d. Alfred Perry and Pleasant (Bishop) Cudd; A.B., Converse Coll., 1932; M.A., Columbia, 1949; m. John Olin Eidson, Aug. 7, 1952. Tchr., counselor Spartanburg Sr. High Sch., 1934-52. Del., Intellectual Life Conf., Pugwash, N.S., Can., 1960. Pres., S.C. Dean of Women Assn., 1952; pres. Woman's Club of U. Ga., Athens, 1959-60, adviser to newcomers, 1967-68; historian Ga. So. Coll. Dames Club, 1969-70. Bd. dirs. Community Concert Assn., Athens; exec. com. Gen. Hosp. Aux. 1967-68. Mem. D.A.R., Athens Hist. Soc., Soc. for Preservation Old Athens, Am. Assn. U. Women, U.D.C. (v.p. chpt. 1959—), Tennyson Soc., Delta Kappa Gamma, Alpha Xi Delta (nat. steering com. 1966—). Clubs: Ga. Tech. Women's, South Carolina (exec. bd. 1973—) (Atlanta). Address: 362 Valley Green Dr NE Atlanta GA 30342

EIGENBROD, WALTER FREDERICK, lawyer; b. New Orleans, Dec. 5, 1912; s. Walter H. and Vivian (Madel) E.; B.A., La. State U., 1935; J.D., Tulane U., 1941; m. Marie Elizabeth Vail, Nov. 7, 1942. Admitted to La. bar, 1941, Ala. bar, 1947; practiced in New Orleans, 1945-46, Huntsville, Ala., 1947—; mem. Arbitration Panel, Fed. Mediation and Conciliation Service, Washington, 1953—; mem. Am. Arbitration Assn. Vol. Labor Arbitration Panel, N.Y.C., 1953—. Dir. South Huntsville Land Development Co., Inc., Ideal Baking Co., Ardmore, Inc. Mem. Presdl. Emergency Bd., 1962. Pres., Madison County Tb Assn., 1947-49; chmn. Madison County March of Dimes, 1950; mem. bd. advisers Huntsville Little Theater, 1958—. Adviser on ofcl. U.S. delegation to 5th Session Trade and Devel. Bd. UN Conf., Geneva, 1967. Mem. Ala. State Democratic exec. com. Served to capt. USAAF, 1941-45. Mem. Am. (co-chmn. labor arbitration and law of collective bargaining agreements 1967—), La., Huntsville-Madison County (pres. 1963-64) bar assns., Nat. Acad. Arbitrators, Ala. State Bar (chmn. local bar activities State Ala.), Assn. U.S. Army (chpt. pres.), Huntsville-Madison County C. of C., Huntsville Indsl. Expansion Com., Am. Legion (past post vice-comdr.), 40 and 8. Democrat. Roman Catholic. Kiwanian (pres. Huntsville 1958). Home: 1009 Cleermont Dr Huntsville AL 35801 Office: Terry-Hutchens Bldg Huntsville AL 35801

EIKER, LARRY EUGENE, county ofcl.; b. Chanute, Kan., Aug. 20, 1938; s. Kenneth George and Alma Elizabeth (Biggs) E.; student Central Mo. State Coll., 1956-58; B.A., Kan. State Tchrs. Coll., 1961, postgrad., 1963, 68-69; postgrad. U. Md., 1962-63, M.A., 1970; postgrad. U. Mo., 1969; m. Peggy Lois Martin, Apr. 13, 1968; 1 son, Jeff Whitney. Secondary tchr. Fairfax (Va.) Bd. Edn., 1963-64; ins. agt. Prudential Ins. Co. Am., Falls Church, Va., 1964-67; secondary tchr. Columbia Station (O.) Bd. Edn., 1967-68; asst. city mgr. City of Gladstone, Mo., 1969-70; city mgr. City Centralia, Ill., 1970; borough mgr., city clk. Borough Washington, N.J., 1971-73; city mgr., Miami Springs, Fla., 1973-74; mem. staff county mgrs.'s office Dade County, Miami, Fla., 1974—. Active Boy Scouts Am. Served with AUS, 1961. Mem. Nat. Recreation and Park Assn., Internat. Inst. Municipal Clks., Internat. City Mgmt. Assn., Fla., Dade County municipal mgmt. assns., Am. Forestry Assn. Fla., Nat. water pollution control assns., Internat. Personnel Mgmt. Assn., Municipal Finance Officers Assn., Fla. Municipal Clks. and Finance Officers Assn., Pi Sigma Alpha. Home: 375 S Royal Poinciana Blvd Miami Springs FL 33166 Office: Dade County Courthouse Miami FL

EISEN, EUGENE J., geneticist, educator; b. N.Y.C., May 14, 1938; s. Abraham and Fay (Hantman) E.; A.A.S., State U. N.Y. at Farmingdale, 1957; B.S. in Agr., U. Ga., 1959; M.S., Purdue U., 1962, Ph.D., 1964; m. Jacqueline Serxner, Aug. 27, 1960; children—Arri, Avram, Andrea. Mem. faculty N.C. State U. at Raleigh, 1964—, asso. prof. animal sci., 1967-73, prof., 1973—. Vis. asso. prof. U. Cal. at Davis, 1970-71. NIH grantee, 1964-68, Sigma Xi research award, 1972. Mem. Biometrics Soc., Genetics Soc. Am., A.A.A.S., Am. Soc. Animal Sci. Mem. B'nai B'rith (pres. lodge 1969-70). Contbr. articles to profl. jours. Home: 308 Northfield Dr Raleigh NC 27609

EISENBERG, JOHN F(REDERICK), zoologist, educator; b. Everett, Wash., June 20, 1935; B.S., Wash. State U., 1957; M.A. (NSF fellow), U. Cal. at Berkeley, 1959, Ph.D. in Zoology (Nat. Acad. Sci. fellow), 1962; m. 2 children. Asst. prof. zoology U.B.C., 1962-64; asst. prof. zoology U. Md., College Park, 1964-65, research asso. prof., 1965—. Resident scientist Nat. Zool. Park, Smithsonian Instn., Washington, 1965—. Research on animal behavior, analysis of social structure, factors responsible for limiting population growth, philosophy of sci. Office: University of Md College Park MD 20742 also Nat Zoological Park Rock Creek Valley Rd NW Washington DC 20009*

EISENBERG, JUDAH MOSHE, physicist, educator; b. Cin., Dec. 17, 1938; s. Azriel and Rose (Leibow) E.; A.B., Columbia, 1958; Ph.D., Mass. Inst. Tech., 1962; m. Marion A. Capriles, Aug. 27, 1961; children—Deborah Ruth, Naomi Tal, Daniel Jacob. Asst. prof. physics U. Va., Charlottesville, 1962-65, asso. prof., 1965-68, prof., 1968—, chmn. dept., 1970—. Mem. program adv. com. Los Alamos Meson Physics Facility, 72. Fellow Am. Phys. Soc. Jewish religion (pres. temple). Author: (with W. Greiner) Excitation Mechanisms of the Nucleus, 1970, Nuclear Models, 1970, Microscopic Theory of the Nucleus, 1972. Contbr. articles to profl. jours. Home: 2514 Hillwood Pl Charlottesville VA 22901

EISENBERG, KENNETH SAWYER, restoration expert; b. Newark, Dec. 30, 1932; s. William C. and Elsie G. (Greenfield) E.; B.S., N.Y. U., 1954, LL.B., 1961; m. Ruth Miller, Aug. 15, 1965. Engaged in devel. plans for hist. restoration programs Universal Engring. Newark, 1961-69; inventor Permo Bond/Dekosit Process for re-creating stone, 1963; founder Universal Restoration Inc., Washington and Copenhagen, Denmark, 1967, pres., chmn. bd., 1969—. Adviser, restoration tech. Nat. Park Service. Served to lt. USAF, 1955-57. Mem. Nat. Trust for Historic Preservation, Nat. Capital Hist. Soc., Soc. for Preservation Ancient Bldgs. (London, Eng.). Clubs: International, Touch Down (both Washington). Restored original Corcoran Gallery of Art (now Renwick Mus.), Washington; restored and preserved Castle Clinton Nat. Monument, N.Y.C., Pioneer Ct. House, Portland, Ore., Independence Hall, Wheeling, W.Va.; restored Lafayette Sq. Hist. Row Houses. Home: 2801 New Mexico Av NW Washington DC 20007 Office: 1750 Pennsylvania Av NW Washington DC 20006

EISENBRAUN, EDMUND JULIUS JOHANNES, educator; b. Wewela, S.D., Dec. 10, 1920; s. Julius and Elizabeth (Hermann) E.; B.S., U. Wis., 1950, M.S., 1951, Ph.D. (Carbide and Carbon Chem. Co. fellow 1954-55), 1955; m. Joyce Marie Abrahamson, Aug. 20, 1949; children—Ellen (Mrs. Michael Fitzgerald), Greta, Ann. Wis. Alumni Research Found. research asst., 1952-54; research chemist Monsanto Chem. Co., Dayton, O., 1955-56; postdoctoral research fellow chemistry Wayne State U., Detroit, 1956-59; sr. research asso. Stanford (Cal.) U., 1959-61; dir. research Aldrich Chem. Co., Milw., 1961-62; prof. chemistry Okla. State U., Stillwater, 1962—, also dir. research project Am. Petroleum Inst. Served with 34th Inf. Div., AUS, 1941-46; ETO. Mem. Am. Chem. Soc., Chem. Soc. London, Sigma Xi, Phi Lambda Upsilon. Contbr. articles profl. jours. Home: 1102 Graham Dr Stillwater OK 74074

EISENBRAUN, JOYCE MARIE (MRS. EDMUND J. EISENBRAUN), radiologist; b. Unity, Wis., Dec. 30, 1926; d. Norman H. and Ella P. (Brehm) Abrahamson; B.S., U. Wis., 1948, M.D., 1951; m. Edmund J. Eisenbraun, Aug. 20, 1949; children—Ellen, Greta, Ann. Intern St. Mary's Hosp., Madison, Wis., 1951-52; resident radiology Wayne State U., Detroit, 1956-59; acting chief, dept. radiology, Palo Alto (Cal.) Stanford VA Hosp., 1960-61; practice medicine specializing in radiology, Milw., 1961-62, Stillwater, Okla., 1962—, Oklahoma City, 1962—; mem. staff Mercy Hosp., Oklahoma City. Mem. Am., Okla. med. assns., Payne County Med. Soc., Am. Coll. Radiology, Okla. Radiologic Soc., Phi Beta Kappa, Alpha Omega Alpha. Baptist. Home: 1102 Graham Dr Stillwater OK 74074 Office: 501 NW 12th Oklahoma City OK 73103

EISENSTADT, HEINZ BERNHARD, physician; b. Berlin, Germany, Dec. 15, 1905; s. Ludwig and Elise (Schmulewitz) E.; M.D., U. Berlin, 1929; m. Ruth Haase, Dec. 12, 1934; 1 dau., Rita Marion (Mrs. David Danziger). Intern, Rudolf Virchow Hosp., 1929-30; resident internal medicine and roentgenology in Berlin, 1930-35, King's Daus. Hosp., Temple, Tex., 1937-38; gen. practice internal medicine Port Arthur, Tex., 1938—; dir. S. Jefferson County Tumor Clinic, 1957-70. Diplomate Am. Bd. Internal Medicine. Fellow A.C.P. (life), Am. Coll. Gastroenterology (life; trustee, v.p.), Am. Coll. Chest Physicians (life), Am. Coll. Cardiology, Am. Coll. Nutrition; mem. Nuclear Soc. (charter), Am., Tex. Socs. internal medicine (charter), Tex. Acad. Medicine. Contbr. to book, articles to profl. jours. Home: 210 4th Av Port Arthur TX 77640 Office: 3030 39th St Port Arthur TX 77640

EISENSTATT, PHILLIP, geologist; b. Omaha, Oct. 16, 1922; s. Harry and Rose (Steinberg) E.; B.Sc., U. Neb., 1943; m. Joann Louise Solomon, Nov. 27, 1949; children—Kay (Mrs. Philip Pollack), Larry, Gerald. With Shell Oil Co., various locations, 1943—, div. geologist, Jackson, Miss., 1952-66, staff geologist, New Orleans, 1966—. Fellow Geol. Soc. Am.; mem. Am. Assn. Petroleum Geologists, Sigma Alpha Mu. Democrat. Jewish religion. Mason. Home: 3721 Nashville Av New Orleans LA 70125 Office: Exploration Dept Shell Oil Box 60193 New Orleans LA 70160

EISENSTEIN, ALFRED, music pub. co. exec.; b. Brody, Poland, Nov. 14, 1899; s. Markus and Louise (Sokol) E.; Degree in Civil Engring., Tech. Hochschule Vienna (Austria), 28; Dipl. Civil Engring., Tech. Hochschule, Berlin, Germany, 1929; m. Marya Brettler, May 14, 1933 (dec. Oct. 1935); m. 2d, Mercedes Malespin Felix, Feb. 21, 1952. Came to U.S., 1939, naturalized, 1948. Mgr. estate, Strupkow, Poland, 1929-33; structural engr., designer Pub. Works Dept., Jerusalem, 1933-37; owner constrn. co., Jerusalem, 1937-39; structural designer, draftsman Badger & Co., W. Kellog, Grace & Co., N.Y.C., 1940-46; structural designer City of Miami (Fla.), 1948-49; owner, mgr. constrn. co., N.Y.C., 1949-63; founding pres. firm Alfred Eisenstein, Inc., N.Y.C., 1963-69, Miami, 1969—, Pops Music Ltd., N.Y.C., 1953—. Performer piano various charities, 1935—; prod. All-Eisenstein Symphonic Concert and Ballet Benefit, Variety Children's Hosp., Miami Beach, Fla. Recipient Bronze Plaque award Queensborough (N.Y.) C. of C., 1968, Spl. Plaque award Audio Soc. N.Y., 1967, Plaque award Greater Miami Variety Club, 1974. Registered profl. engr., Fla., N.Y. Mem. A.S.C.A.P. Mason. Club: Jerusalem (Israel). Composer numerous works, including Life Was Beautiful (song), 1947; Tango of Love, 1950; Adagio Lamentoso, symphonic tone poem, 1964; Petite Suite for Orch., 1964; Romance for Violin and Piano, 1950; Melodic Reflections for cello, 1964; Impromtu, Symphonic tone poem, 1968. Home: 18900 NE 14th Av North Miami Beach FL 33162 Office: 9999 NW 7th Av Miami FL 33150

EISS, ALBERT FRANK, cons. learning systems and curriculum; b. La Fargeville, N.Y., Feb. 2, 1910; s. Albert George and Frances Deborah (Bort) E.; B.A., Houghton Coll., 1933; M.A., St. Lawrence U., 1942; Ph.D., N.Y. U., 1954; m. Grace Elizabeth Rogers, Apr. 24, 1934; children—Roger Lewis, Michael Albert, Kathryn Grace (Mrs. James Dalton Byrd). Tchr. pub. schs. N.Y., 1934-46; instr. Clarkson Coll. Tech., Potsdam, N.Y., 1946-49, Paul Smiths (N.Y.) Coll., 1949-57; prof. Indiana (Pa.) U., 1957-59; coordinator sci. and math. Pa. Dept. Edn., Harrisburg, 1957-64; asso. exec. sec. Nat. Sci. Tchrs. Assn., Washington, 1964-71; pres. Innovations, Inc., Carrollton, Ga., 1971—. Fellow A.A.A.S.; mem. Nat. Soc. Programmed Instrn., Nat.

Sci. Tchrs. Assn., Am. Ednl. Research Assn., Phi Delta Kappa. Democrat. Methodist. Mason (Shriner). Author: The Earth-Space Sciences, 1970; Evaluation of Instructional Systems, 1970; Evaluating Learning, 1973. Home: 118 Alice Lane Carrollton GA 30117 Office: Box 847 Carrollton GA 30117

EKERS, ERIC NORTON, internat. orgn. exec.; b. Essex, Eng., Mar. 30, 1922; s. Ernest William and Winifred Amy (Norton) E.; B. Sc. with honors, U. London (Eng.), 1949; M.A. (Fulbright scholar 1949-51), U. Cal. at Berkeley, 1951, M.P.H. (Dean's scholar), 1962; postgrad. Ecole des Sciences Politiques, Paris, France, 1952; m. Dagmar Hedvika Novakova, 1955 (div. 1962); 1 dau., Viveca Joy. Ins. ofcl., London, 1939-42; economist U.S. Mut. Security Agy., Paris, 1952-54; editor Internat. Bank Reconstrn. and Devel., Washington, 1954-55; tng. officer WHO, Washington, 1956-61, cons. pub. health, Central Am., 1962-65; prof. pub. health edn. WHO/U. Jamaica, 1963-64; dir. Washington center Orgn. Econ. Cooperation and Devel., 1966—. Propr. Norton Properties. Bd. govs. Royal Hosp. and Home for Incurables, London. Served with RAF, 1942-46. Fellow Royal Soc. Tropical Medicine, Am. Pub. Health Assn.; mem. Am. Econ. Assn. Clubs: Fairfax Racquet, Washington Athletic. Editor: Pan Am. Health Quar., 1956-58, now contbr. Contbr. to Chronicle of WHO, also articles to profl. jours. Home: 2475 Virginia Av NW Washington DC 20037 Office: 1750 Pennsylvania Av NW Washington DC 20006

EKEY, DAVID CLIFTON, educator; b. Toronto, O., Feb. 19, 1923; s. Josiah David and Pauline Elizabeth (Goff) E.; B.S. in Engring., Ohio State U., 1950, in Edn., 1950, M.S., 1950, Ph.D., 1955; m. Betty Gatewood Price, Mar. 16, 1947; children—David Price, Maribeth. Chief purchasing clk. Weirton Steel Co. (W.Va.), 1944-45; asst. prof. indsl. engring. Pa. State U., College State, 1951-55; tech. dir. Lebanon Steel Foundry Co. (Pa.), 1955-57; prof. indsl. engring. Ga. Inst. Tech., Atlanta, 1957-61; prof., chmn. dept. indsl. mgmt. U. Richmond (Va.), 1961—. Cons., Reynolds Metals, Va. Dept. Edn., Boeing Aircraft, Glamorgan Pipe & Foundry Co. Mem. Va. Gov.'s Com. on Pub. Edn., 1968, Va. Gov.'s Com. on Civilian Def., 1966—. Faculty mem. bd. trustees U. Richmond, 1970—. Served with USNR, 1943-44. Am. Foundrymen's Soc. fellow, 1950-51. Registered profl. engr., O., Pa., Va. Mem. U. Richmond Men's Faculty Club, Am. Inst. Indsl. Engring. (chpt. v.p. 1956-57, dir. 1956-58, 62-63), Soc. Advancement Mgmt. (dir. 1963-65), Sigma Xi, Tau Beta Pi, Omicron Delta Kappa, Beta Gamma Sigma, Alpha Pi Mu, Epsilon Pi Tau, Sigma Tau. Methodist. Mason. Author: Gray Iron Foundry Practice, 1958; Introduction to Foundry Technology, 1958; The Use of Consultants, 1964. Home: 210 College Rd Richmond VA 23229 Office: Sch Bus Administration Univ Richmond Richmond VA 23173

ELAM, ANDREW GREGORY, II, ins. co. exec.; b. Winchester, Va., Feb. 6, 1932; s. Andrew Gregory and Francis Clayton (Gold) E.; A.B., Presbyn. Coll., 1955; m. Rebecca Rhea Cole, Oct. 26, 1958; children—Andrew Gregory III, Philip Cole, Dawna Francis. Adminstrv. asst. Citizen's and So. Nat. Bank, Columbia, S.C., 1955-56; nat. exec. dir. Pi Kappa Phi, Sumter, S.C., 1956-59; pres. Carolina Potato Co., Inc., West Columbia, S.C., 1959-61; mem. pub. relations staff Kendavis Industries Internat., Inc., Fort Worth, 1961-63; dir. sales promotion Pioneer Am. Ins. Co., Fort Worth, 1963-64, dir. pub. relations and sales promotion, 1964-66, asst. v.p., 1966-68, v.p., mem. exec. com., 1968-71, dir., 1970-71; v.p. pub. relations and sales promotion Gt. Am. Res. Ins. Co., Dallas, 1972—. Mem. pub. relations adv. council Inst. Life Ins., N.Y.C., 1971—; mem. pub. relations com. Tex. Life Conv., 1970—. Mem. pub. information adv. com. Am. Cancer Soc., Tex. div., 1969—, chmn., 1972—; vice-chmn. pub. relations com. Tarrant County United Fund, 1967; campaign leader Community Pride Campaign Performing Arts, 1969. Bd. dirs. Fort Worth Community Theatre, 1971-72; bd. dirs., treas., vice-chmn. Tarrant County unit Am. Cancer Soc., 1963-71, bd. dirs. Dallas County unit, 1972—. Mem. Life Ins. Advertisers Assn. (dir. communications workshop 1970-71, exec. com. 1973—, chmn. So. Round Table 1972), Pub. Relations Soc. Am., Tex. Pub. Relations Assn. (dir. 1966), Indsl. Editors Fort Worth (pres. 1968), So. Round Table (vice-chmn. 1971), Advt. Club Fort Worth, Dallas-Fort Worth Art Dirs. Club, Fort Worth C. of C. (chmn. publ. com. 1970). Presbyn. (deacon 1966-68; ruling elder 1969-71). Lion. Club: Ridglea Country (Fort Worth). Home: 7730 Chattington St Dallas TX 75240 Office: 2020 Live Oak Dallas TX 75221

ELAM, HARPER JOHNSTON, III, city ofcl., textile lawyer; b. Greensboro, N.C., Sept. 30, 1926; s. Harper Johnston and Elizabeth (Martin) E.; B.S. in Commerce, U. N.C., 1950, LL.B., 1952; m. Mary Carolyn Glendinning, Aug. 30, 1947; children—George Martin, John Claibourne, Erin Patricia. Asst. prof. pub. law and govt. U. N.C., Chapel Hill, 1952-54; admitted to N.C. bar, 1952; asst. to city atty. Greensboro, 1954-57, city atty., 1957-61; corp. counsel, asst. sec. Cone Mills Corp., Greensboro, 1961-68, gen. counsel, 1968—. Lectr. Inst. Govt., U. N.C., 1954—, mem. U. N.C. Law Found. Council, 1961—. Mayor pro tem Greensboro, 1965-69, 71—, mayor, 1969-71. Served with USNR, 1944-46; PTO; now comdr. Res. Recipient Bancroft-Whitney award in constl. law, U. N.C. Law Sch., 1952. Mem. U. N.C. Law Alumni Assn. (past pres.), Am. Mgmt. Assn. (seminar chmn. 1962—), Nat. Inst. Municipal Law Officer (past treas.), Am., N.C. bar assns., Lawyers' Assn. Textile Industry (pres.), N.C. League Municipalities (pres.), Textile Lawyers Assn. (bd. govs.), Phi Delta Theta, Phi Delta Phi. Methodist. Mason, Odd Fellow. Home: 110 S Park Dr Greensboro NC 27401 Office: 1201 Maple St Greensboro NC 27405

ELBEIN, ALAN DAVID, chemist, educator; b. Lynn, Mass., Mar. 20, 1933; s. Gersh and Golda (Stryer) E.; A.B., Clark U., 1954; M.S., U. Ariz., 1956; Ph.D. (NIH fellow), Purdue U., 1960; m. Elaine Jean Brooks, June 13, 1953; children—Steven C., Bradley M., Richard C. Research asso., NIH fellow U. Mich., Ann Arbor, 1960-63; asso. research biochemist U. Cal. at Berkeley, 1963-64; asst. prof. biochemistry Rice U., Houston, 1964-67, asso. prof., 1967-69; asso. prof. Med. Sch. U. Tex., San Antonio, 1969-70, prof., 1970—. Research career devel. award, 1967-69. Mem. Alamo Area council Gov. of Tex.'s Lit. Council. Mem. A.A.A.S., Am. Soc. Microbiology, Am. Chem. Soc., (chmn. biochemistry sect. S.W. region 1971 sec. San Antonio sect. 1972-73), Am. Soc. Biol. Chemistry, Sigma Xi. Club: Sierra. Mem. edit. bd. Jour. Bacteriology, 1971—. Contbr. articles to profl. jours. Home: 5325 Callaghan St San Antonio TX 78228

ELDER, SAMUEL THOMAS, psychologist; b. New Orleans, June 11, 1929; s. James Harelson and Katherine L. (Wilson) E.; B.A., U. S.W. La., 1956; M.A., U. Houston, 1958; Ph.D. (USPHS fellow), La. State U., 1962; m. Eleanor A. Shafer, Aug. 5, 1955; children—Alyson Jane, Timothy Martin. Research asso. dept. psychiatry and neurology Tulane U. Med. Sch., New Orleans, 1961-63, asst. prof., 1963-64; asso. prof. La. State U., New Orleans, 1964-66, acting chmn. dept., 1966, chmn., 1966-73, prof., 1970—. Pvt. practice psychology in New Orleans 1968—. Grantee Nat. Inst. Mental Health, 1961-64, 69, A.M.A. Edn. and Research Found. grantee, 1962; NSF grantee, 1965. Mem. Am., La. (pres. 1969-70), S.E. (sec.-treas. 1969-70), S.W. psychol. assns., A.A.A.S., Sigma Xi. Author: (with V.J. Cieutat and L.P. Krimerman) Traditional Logic and the Venn Diagram: A Programmed Introduction. Contbr. articles to profl. jours. Home: 7050 Curran Blvd New Orleans LA 70126

ELDIN, HAMED KAMAL, educator; b. Cairo, Egypt, Dec. 31, 1924; s. Mahmoud Hamed and Saidieh Mahmoud (Enan) E.; B.Sc., Cairo U., 1945; M.Sc., Cal. Inst. Tech., 1948; Ph.D., State U. Ia., 1951; children—Amany, Tania, Mannal. Came to U.S., 1963, naturalized, 1967. With Esso Standard Near East, Cairo, 1952-57; mgr. pub. relations, adminstrv. mgr. Mobil Oil, Cairo, 1957-61; dep. gen. mgr. Gen. Orgn. for Tech. Industries, Cairo, 1961-63; cons. systems and mgmt. sci. Mobil Internat., N.Y.C., 1963-67; prof. indsl. engring. and mgmt. Okla. State U., Stillwater, 1967—. Cons., Ford Found., UN Indsl. Devel. Orgn. NSF grantee, 1973-74. Mem. Am. Inst. Indsl. Engring. (sr.), Operations Research Soc. Am., Am. Soc. Engring. Edn., Inst. Mgmt. Sci. Author: Information Systems-A Management Science Approach, 1974. Home: 1907 Elvin Dr Stillwater OK 74074 Office: Dept Industrial Engineering and Management Okla State Univ Stillwater OK 74074

ELDRIDGE, FRANCIS R., JR., physicist; b. Augusta, Ga., July 21, 1916; s. Francis R. and Kathleen (Sanzo) E.; student N.Y. U., 1933-34, George Washington U., 1934-41, Johns Hopkins, 1949-50; m. Margaret Jeannette Cook, Apr. 18, 1942; 1 son, Francis R. III. Research asst. Carnegie Instn. of Washington, 1938-39; asso. physicist Naval Ordnance Lab., Washington, 1939-43; physicist Jones & Lamson Machine Co., Springfield, Vt., 1943-47; spl. electronics engr. Glenn L. Martin Co., Balt., 1947-48; research scientist Johns Hopkins Inst. for Coop. Research, Balt., 1948-52, dir. Controls Research Lab., 1952-55; phys. sci. and project leader RAND Corp., Santa Monica, Cal., 1955-62; spl. asst. for command, control and communications Dept. Def. OASD, Systems Analysis, Pentagon, Washington, 1962-66; dept. asso. dir. Office Telecommunications Mgmt., Exec. Office Pres., Washington, 1966-67; v.p. Kelly Sci. Corp., Washington, 1967; mem. research council Research Analysis Corp., McLean, Va., 1968-70; mem. div. staff Mitre Corp., McLean, Va., 1971—. Mem. N.Y. Acad. Sci., I.E.E.E., Sigma Xi, Sigma Pi Sigma. Patentee voice response computer devices. Home: 4557 32d Rd N Arlington VA 22207 Office: Mitre Corp Westgate Research Park McLean VA 22101

ELEBASH, HUNLEY AGEE, bishop; b. Pensacola, Fla., July 27, 1923; s. Eugene Perrin and Ann (Agee) E.; B.S., U. of South, 1944, B.D., 1950, D.D., 1969; m. Maurine Ashton, Nov. 2, 1946; children—David Hunley, Brett Randolph. Ordained to ministry Episcopal Ch., 1950; rector in Jacksonville, Fla., 1950-57, Wilmington, N.C., 1957-65; exec. sec. Diocese East Carolina, 1965-68, bishop coadjutor, 1968-73, bishop, 1973—. Sec. Diocese Fla., 1953-57; del. Gen. Conv. Episcopal Ch., 1961, 64, 67. Served to 1st lt. USMCR, 1943-46. Fellow Coll. Preachers, Washington, 1958. Home: 1905 Live Oak Pkwy Wilmington NC 28401 Office: 305 S 3d St Wilmington NC 28401

ELEDGE, WILLIAM WALTER, JR., hosp. adminstr.; b. Englewood, Tenn., Sept. 4, 1916; s. William Walter and Stella Belle (Liner) E.; B.S., Carson-Newman Coll., 1939; postgrad. U. Tenn., 1940-41, U. Pa., 1947-48; m. Pauline Bullard, Jan. 23, 1943; children—Margaret (Mrs. Leonard Taylor Lee), William Walter III. Tchr., coach, prin., McMinn County, Tenn., 1936-41; entered U.S. Army as pvt., 1941, advanced through grades to col. USAF, 1961; ret., 1967; adminstr. Woods Meml. Hosp., Etowah, Tenn., 1967—. Mem. Etowah City Planning Commn., 1969—, Ga.-Tenn. Regional Health Commn., 1970—. Bd. dirs. S.E. Tenn. Area Health Edn. Center, 1972—. Chmn bd. dirs. McMinn County Mental Health Center. Decorated Legion of Merit. Fellow Am. Coll. Nursing Home Adminstrs.; mem. Am. Coll. Hosp. Adminstrs. Democrat. Baptist. Mason, Lion, Rotarian. Home: Route 2 Box 255L Etowah TN 37331 Office: Woods Memorial Hospital Etowah TN 37331

ELEGANT, IRA M., lawyer; b. N.Y.C., July 9, 1942; s. Albert and Betty (Rosen) E.; B.B.A., U. Miami (Fla.), 1963, J.D., 1966; m. Sharon Glickman, Nov. 22, 1967; children—Justin Banning, Adam Trevor. Admitted to Fla. bar, 1966, also bars U.S. Dist. Ct. So. Dist. Fla., 1966, U.S. Ct. Appeals, 5th Circuit, 1966, U.S. Tax Ct., 1968, U.S. Ct. Claims, 1970, U.S. Ct. Appeals for D.C., 1971, U.S. Supreme Ct., 1971; practiced in Miami Beach, 1966—; asso. mem. firm Irving Cypen, Miami Beach, 1966-67; sr. asst. city atty. City of Miami Beach, 1967-70; dir. NVF Co., Yorklyn, Del., Sharon Steel Corp. (Pa.), Nat. Propane Corp., Garden City, N.Y., Pa. Engring. Corp., New Castle, Wilson Brothers, N.Y.C., others; v.p. asst. sec., dir. DWG Corp., Miami Beach, 1970—; v.p., dir. Southeastern Pub. Service Co., Miami Beach, 1971—; trustee, v.p. Universal Housing & Devel. Co., Balt. and Miami Beach, 1971—. Mem. Fla. Bar (mem. appellate ct. rules subcom. 1971—), Fraternal Order Police (asso.), Dade County, Miami Beach bar assns., D.C. Bar, Phi Delta Phi. Clubs: Coral Gables Country; Jockey, Standard (Miami). Home: 122 E 2 Court Hibiscus Island Miami Beach FL 33139 Office: 825 Arthur Godfrey Rd Miami Beach FL 33140 also 6917 Collins Av Suite 1707 Miami Beach FL 33141

ELFE, THOMAS BLANEY, elec. engr.; b. Macon, Ga., Jan. 28, 1926; s. Thomas Blaney and Vallie (West) E.; B.S., Ga. Inst. Tech., 1948; M.S., U. Ill., 1950, A.M., 1951; postgrad. U. Fla., 1956-57; m. Mary Ruth Tate, Dec. 23, 1953; children—Martha, Carolyn, Doris. Accelerator engr. U. Ill., Urbana, 1951-56; sr. devel. engr. Sperry Rand Co., Gainesville, Fla., 1956—. Chmn. Alachua County Republican exec. com., 1970—. Served with USNR, 1944-46. Mem. I.E.E.E. (sect. chmn. 1972-73), Kappa Alpha, Pi Mu Epsilon. Methodist (mem. adminstrv. bd. 1958-74). Home: 3547 NW 32nd Pl Gainesville FL 32605 Office: Waldo Rd Gainesville FL 32601

ELFMON, SAMUEL LEON, ret. physician; b. Russia, Mar. 27, 1911; s. Louis and Sara (Levine) E.; came to U.S., 1921, naturalized, 1927; B.S., U. Richmond, 1932; M.D., Med. Coll. Va., 1935; m. Lillian Shain, Nov. 28, 1938; children—Linda (Mrs. Joel Fleishman), Shila (Mrs. David Elden). Intern, resident Highsmith Hosp., Fayetteville, N.C., 1935-38; gen. practice medicine, 1938-42, specializing in internal medicine, 1945-70; mem. staff Duke, 1945-67. Dir. Andy Griffith Products, So. Nat. Bank, Mid South Ins. Co. Mem. N.C. Bd. Mental Health, 1964-73. Dir. YMCA, 1960-68, hon. mem., 1973—. Served to capt., M.C., AUS, 1942-45; ETO. Diplomate Am. Bd. Internal Medicine. Fellow A.C.P.; mem. N.C., Fayetteville med. socs. Mason; mem. B'nai B'rith. Home: Hound Ears Club Blowing Rock NC 28605 Office: PO Drawer 3925 Fayetteville NC 28305

ELFNER, LLOYD FRANCIS, psychologist, educator; b. Manitowoc, Wis., Sept. 13, 1923; s. Edward Jacob and Julia Mary (Bellin) E.; B.S. cum laude, U. Wis., 1958, M.A., 1960, Ph.D., 1962; m. Elinor Ann Peilstick, Apr. 16, 1963; children—Whitney, Eric, Karen. Asst. prof. psychology Kent (O.) State U., 1962-66, asso. prof., 1966-67; asso. prof. Fla. State U., Tallahassee, 1967-70, prof., 1970—. Served with AUS, 1942-46; ETO. USPHS grantee, 1963-64, 65-68; NSF grantee, 1965-69, 70-72. Mem. N.Y. Acad. Scis., Psychonomic Soc., Am., Southeastern, Midwestern psychol. socs., Acoustical Soc. Am., Internat. Evoke Audiometry Study Group, Sigma Xi, Phi Eta Sigma. Contbr. articles to profl. jours. Home: 2007 Lee Av Tallahassee FL 32303

ELIASON, JON TATE, elec. engr.; b. Menominee, Mich., Mar. 23, 1938; s. Edwin Adolf and Irene Albertyn (Longlais) E.; B.S. in Sci. Engring., U. Mich., 1960; M.S. in Physics, Ore. State U., 1966; m. Barbara Ann Love, July 2, 1960; children—Ellen Artimese, Eric Alan, Eileen Amber. Engr. Gen. Electric Co., Vallecitos Nuclear Lab., Pleasanton, Cal., 1964-66; sr. staff engr., engring. cons. Sperry Rand Corp., Huntsville, Ala., 1966—. Lectr. U. Ala., Huntsville, 1972-73. Registered profl. engr., Ala. Mem. Am. Phys. Soc., I.E.E.E., Sigma Pi Sigma. Home: 6501 Robinhood Lane Huntsville AL 35806 Office: Sperry Rand Corp 716 Arcadia Circle Huntsville AL 35801

ELIEL, LEONARD PAUL, physician, educator; b. Los Angeles, Sept. 14, 1914; s. Paul and Harriet (Judd) E.; B.S., Harvard, 1936, M.D. cum laude, 1940; m. Marjorie Blake, Jan. 14, 1943; children—Alan, Suzanne. Intern, Mass. Gen. Hosp., Boston, 1940-42; pediatric fellow Children's Hosp., Boston, 1946-48; Damon Runyon sr. clin. research fellow, asso. Sloan-Kettering Inst., 1949-51; asst. prof. Cornell Med. Coll., 1950-51; head cancer research sect. Okla. Med. Research Found., Oklahoma City, 1951-64, v.p., dir. research, 1965-70; prof. research medicine U. Okla., Oklahoma City, 1956-66, prof. medicine, 1966—, head endocrinology sect. dept. medicine, 1973—, asso. dir., also asso. dean Grad. Coll. Med. Center, 1970, interim exec. v.p., dir. Health Scis. Center 1970-71, exec. v.p., also dir. Health Scis. Center, 1971-73; exec. dir. Okla. Med. Research Found., 1959-65. Pres. Oklahoma City Symphony Soc., 1968-69. Served to lt. USNR, 1944-46. Fellow A.C.P.; mem. Am. Assn. Cancer Research, Am. Clin. and Climatol. Assn., Am. Soc. Clin. Investigation, Endocrine Soc. Episcopalian. Rotarian. Contbr. numerous articles to sci. jours. Research in cancer endocrinology and parathyroid physiology. Home: 2541 Wilshire Blvd Oklahoma City OK 73116 Office: 800 NE 13th St Oklahoma City OK 73104

ELKIN, BENJAMIN JAMES, bank exec.; b. Lexington, Ky., May 7, 1930; s. Z. F. and Rose (Moller) E.; B.S., U. Ky., 1952; postgrad. La. U., 1965-67, Ohio State U., 1968-69, Okla. U., 1969; certificate Am. Inst. Banking, 1963; m. Nita L. Myers, Jan. 17, 1951; children—Kathleen L., Fielding, Julie C. Trainee First Security Nat. Bank, Lexington, Ky., 1956-58, teller, 1958-59, note teller, 1959-60, asst. cashier operations, 1959-60, credit dept. mgr., 1960-61, asst. cashier comml. lending, 1961-62, asst. v.p. comml. lending, 1962-66, v.p. comml. lending, 1966-73, 1st v.p. comml. lending, 1973—; dir. G. F. Vaughan Tobacco Co. Instr. Ky. Sch. Banking, 1965-67. Chmn. Easter Seals, 1968; vice-chmn. campaign United Community Fund, 1969, campaign chmn. Lexington-Fayette County, 1970; treas. Wilderness Road Girl Scouts, 1973; treas., campaign chmn. Jr. Achievement of Blue Grass, 1973. Bd. dirs. Blue Grass Assn. for Mentally Retarded, 1973. Served with AUS, 1952-54. Mem. Lexington Mortgage Bankers Assn. (sec. 1971-72), Ky., Greater Lexington area C. of C.'s, Delta Tau Delta, Delta Sigma Phi. Rotarian. Home: 1893 Blairmore Rd Lexington KY 40502 Office: 1 First Security Plaza Lexington KY 40507

ELKINS, BILLY BOB, ednl. adminstr. tech. sch.; b. Henrietta, Tex., Mar. 29, 1940; s. Claude C. and Anne Lee (Morrow) E.; B.S., So. Meth. U., 1963; m. Laura Ann Poindexter, July 29, 1966; children—Laura Sue, Lee Ann. With Elkins Inst., Inc., Dallas, 1958—, pres., 1969—; former pres. KEIR Inc., Triple E Enterprises; dir. Elkins Industries, Inc., Elkins Ednl. Research Found. Cons. to U.S. commr. edn. Mem. I.E.E.E., Nat. Rehab. Counciling Assn., Nat. Assn. Radio Engrs., Tex. (dir. 1955-73), Dallas Area rehab. assns., So. Meth. U. Alumni Assn. (dir. 1969-73), Young Pres.'s Orgn., Delta Chi. Home: 5320 Pebblebrook Dr Dallas TX 75229 Office: 2727 Inwood Rd Dallas TX 75235

ELKINS, JAMES ANDERSON, banker, lawyer; b. Huntsville, Tex., Sept. 25, 1879; LL.B., U. Tex., 1901; m. Isabel Mitchell; children W.S., James, Anderson. Sr. partner Vinson, Elkins, Weems & Searls, Houston; sr. chmn. bd. First City Nat. Bank, Houston; chmn. bd. South Main State Bank, Harrisburg Nat. Bank, Houston, dir., Am. Gen. Ins. Co., Gt. So. Life Ins. Co., Houston, Pure Oil Co., Palatine, Ill. Mem. Am., Houston bar assns. Office: First City Nat Bank Bldg Houston TX 77001

ELKINS, JAMES ANDERSON, JR., banker; b. Galveston, Tex., Mar. 24, 1919; s. James Anderson and Isabel (Mitchell) E.; grad. Hill Sch., 1937; B.A., Princeton, 1941; m. Margaret Wiess, Nov. 24, 1945; children—Elise, James Anderson III, Leslie K. With First City Nat. Bank, Houston, 1941—, v.p., 1946-50, pres., 1950-60, chm. bd., 1960—, also dir.; dir. Eastern Airlines, Cameron Iron Works, Am. Gen. Ins. Co., Houston. Trustee U. Houston, Baylor Coll. Medicine, Princeton. Mem. Houston C. of C. (exec. com., dir.). Episcopalian. Home: 101 Farish Circle Houston TX 77024 Office: First City Nat Bank Houston TX 77001

ELKINS, SCOTT WILLIAM, bank exec.; b. Morristown, Tenn., Jan. 15, 1940; s. Frank Shellman and Elizabeth (Brame) E.; B.S., East Tenn. State U., 1962; postgrad. U. Va., 1965, Harvard, 1966, Ind. U., 1974; grad. Banking Sch., Rutgers U., 1974; m. 2d, Kay Carlisle, Jan. 11, 1974; 1 dau., Leigh Anne. With State Nat. Bank of Bethesda (Md.), 1968-70; v.p., sr. loan officer Clarendon Bank & Trust, Arlington, Va., 1973—. Lectr. Indsl. Coll. Armed Forces, 1972-73. Mem. Nat. Assn. Credit Mgmt., Robert Morris Assos., Pi Kappa Alpha. Rotarian. Club: Country of Fairfax (Va.). Home: 4918 Schuyler Dr Annandale VA 22003 Office: 3192 Wilson Blvd Arlington VA 22201

ELKOURI, JIM RAY, librarian; b. Chickasha, Okla., Aug. 7, 1938; s. David and Adel (Elkouri) E.; B.A. with distinction, U. Okla., 1960, M.L.S., 1962; postgrad. Oklahoma City U., 1965-66. Documents cataloger Okla. State U., Stillwater, 1962-63; documents librarian Oklahoma City U., 1963-65, catalog librarian, asst. prof. library sci., 1965-70; sr. cataloger Cal. Inst. Arts, Valencia, 1970-72; circulation librarian Los Angeles City Coll., 1972-73; head catalog dept. U. Tulsa, 1973—. Mem. Am., Okla. library assns., Phi Beta Kappa, Beta Phi Mu, Phi Alpha Theta. Home: 2332 NW 16th St Oklahoma City OK 73107

ELLEDGE, LARRY FRANCIS, editor; b. Poplar Bluff, Mo., May 22, 1941; s. John Elwood and Barbara (Dysinger) E.; B.S., Ark. State U., 1963; m. Ethel Jean Wyatt, June 29, 1963; children—Selena Grace, Amber Dawn. Sports editor Springdale (Ark.) News, 1963-64; asst. sports editor Pine Bluff (Ark.) Commercial, 1964; news editor Mt. Vernon (Ind.) Democrat, 1966-67; editor Piggott (Ark.) Banner, 1967-69; city editor Texarkana (Tex.-Ark.) Gazette and Daily News, 1969, mng. editor, 1969-71; exec. editor Hot Springs (Ark.) Sentinel Record & New Era, 1971—. Mem. Hot Springs C. of C., Tex. United Press Editors Assn. (dir. 1970-71), Ark. Asso. Press Assn., Lambda Chi Alpha. Methodist. Kiwanian. Home: 105 Fernwood Hot Springs AR 71901

ELLEFSON, GEORGE EDWIN, JR., elec. engr.; b. Fort Smith, Ark., June 19, 1929; s. George Edwin and Cecil (Soard) E.; B.S. in E.E., U. Ark., 1954; student U. N.M., 1954-55; m. Dorothy Claire Stannus, Aug. 28, 1952; children—Dorothy Lynn, Jane Ann. Staff engr., Sandia Corp., Albuquerque, 1954-55; engr. Reynolds Metals Co., Jones Mills, Ark., 1955-56; elec. mgr. Erhart, Eichenbaum, Rauch, Blass architects, Little Rock, 1956-60; engr. Leo L. Landauer & Assos., Inc., Little Rock, 1960-61; prin. G.E. Ellefson & Assos., Inc., Little Rock, 1961-70; gen. partner Ecology Dynamics Assos., Ltd., Little Rock, 1970-73; area tech. mgr. Am. Standards Testing Bur., Inc., Little Rock, 1973—. Served with USN, 1947-50. Named

Engr. of Distinction, Engrs. Joint Council, 1974. Mem. I.E.E.E., U.S. (recipient Engring. excellence award 1968), Ark. I.E.S., Am. Cons. Engrs. Council. Presbyn. (elder). Home: 11 Berwyn Dr Little Rock AR 72207 Office: 1200 Summit Av Little Rock AR 72202

ELLEN, JOHN CALHOUN, JR., educator; b. Dillon, S.C., Apr. 4, 1921; s. John Calhoun and Grevelle (Hounshell) E.; B.A., Emory and Henry Coll., 1941; A.B. in Journalism, U. Ga., 1949; M.A., U. S.C., 1954, Ph.D., 1958; m. Dorothy Elizabeth Humphreys, Aug. 20, 1961; children—Elizabeth Delaney, Kathryn Lynn. Grad. teaching asst. U. S.C., 1956-58; asst. prof. history East Carolina Coll., Greenville, N.C., 1959-62, asso. prof., 1962-69, prof, 1969—, dir. Nat. Def. Edn. Act History Inst., summer, 1965, dir. Inst. for Hist. Research in Tobacco, 1973—. Served with AUS, 1942, USAAF, 1943-45. Mem. So., S.C. hist. assns., N.C. Lit. and Hist. Assn., Orgn. Am. Historians, S.C. Hist. Soc. Author: Political Newspapers of the Piedmont Carolinas during the 1850's 1958. Contbr. articles, book revs to hist. publs. Home: 1504 S Brownlea Dr Greenville NC 27834

ELLENBURG, ROBERT BLANTON, elec. engr.; b. Greeneville, Tenn., Feb. 4, 1919; s. Noah Alfred and Martha Ladora (Ottinger) E.; B.S. in Elec. Engring., U. Tenn., 1942; m. Janus Elizabeth Yentsch, Oct. 16, 1943. Elec. draftsman Western Electric Co., Balt., 1946-47; elec. engr., designer TVA, Knoxville, 1942, 47-57; sr. elec. engr. So. Services, Inc., Birmingham, Ala., 1957-66, project engr., 1966-72, elec. project mgr., 1972—. Served from ensign to lt., USNR, 1942-46. Registered profl. engr., Tenn., Ala. Mem. I.E.E.E., Tau Beta Pi. Republican. Episcopalian. Club: Shades Valley Camera (sec. 1958-59, v.p. 1959-60, pres. 1960-61, statis. sec. 1961—). Home: 1133 Lido Dr Birmingham AL 35226 Office: PO Box 2625 Birmingham AL 35202

ELLER, JAMES EDGAR, lumber co. exec.; b. Bristol, Tenn., Aug. 6, 1931; s. Don James and Wilma (Bentley) E.; student U. of South, 1951, U. Tenn., 1952, 54, N.C. State U., 1954; m. Retha Lois Ragan, Sept. 16, 1950; children—Michael Edgar, Deborah Rai; m. 2d, Connie Charlene Wilcox, Apr. 30, 1971; stepchildren—Thomas Brian Wilcox, John Brett Wilcox. With Cortrim Hardwood Parts Co., Bristol, 1947-58, dry kiln technician, 1951-53, mill room supr., 1953-57, sales mgr., 1959-61, gen. mgr., 1961—; sales engr. Harris Mfg. Co., Johnson City, Tenn., 1958-59. Mem. C. of C. (mem. exec. council 1966-67). Methodist. Mason, Moose, Elk. Home: 213 Sparkling Brook Dr Bristol TN 37620 Office: 1320 Georgia Av Bristol TN 37620

ELLETT, EDWIN WILLARD, veterinarian, educator; b. Midlothian, Va., May 21, 1925; s. William Hundley and Alice Olive (Hulce) E.; B.S., Va. Poly. Inst., 1954; D.V.M., U. Ga., 1953; M.S., Tex. A. and M. Coll., 1961; m. Lois Jean Way, Apr. 19, 1958; children—William Ladd. Pvt. vet. practice, Blackstone, Va., 1953-56; asst. prof. vet. sci. Okla. State U., Stillwater, 1956-58; asst. prof. Tex. A. and M. U., College Station, 1958-61, asso. prof., 1961-67, chief small animal clinic, 1961—, prof., 1967—. Dir., chmn. bd. Research Equipment Co., Bryan, Tex. Treas., dir. Companion Animal Research and Ednl. Assn., 1972—. Served with USCGR, 1943-46. Mem. Am. Assn. Vet. Clinicians (v.p. 1967-68), Am. Animal Hosp. Assn. (dir. continuing edn. region 4, 1967-70), Tex. Assn. Companion Animals (pres., chmn. bd. 1972—), Tex. Vet. Med. Assn., Am. Soc. Vet. Ophthalmologists, Phi Zeta, Alpha Psi, Alpha Zeta. Home: Route 4 Box 162B Bryan TX 77801 Office: Small Animal Clinic College Vet Medicine Texas A and M Univ College Station TX 77843

ELLING, LAWRENCE JOHN, civil engr.; b. Riviera, Tex., Mar. 30, 1915; s. Fred John and Clara Teresa (Hertzberg) E.; B.S. in Math., Tex. A. and I. U., 1946, B.S. in Engring., 1952, M.S., 1953; m. Mary Elizabeth Rich, Apr. 20, 1948; 1 son, John Frederick. Surveyor Tex. Hwy. Dept., Kingsville, 1946-49; mem. civil engring. dept. Houston Natural Gas Corp., Corpus Christi, Tex., 1953-57, Houston, 1957—. Instr. mech. drawing Del Mar Jr. Coll., Corpus Christi, 1954-57. Mem. Planning and Zoning Com., Spring Valley, Houston, 1964-68. Served with AUS, 1941-45. Recipient Meritorious Service awards Engrs. Council Houston, 1962, 64. Registered profl. engr., Tex.; registered land surveyor. Fellow Am. Soc. C.E.; mem. Tex. Soc. Profl. Engrs., Engrs. Council Houston (pres. 1961), Houston Engring. and Sci. Soc., Houston C. of C. (mem. water supply and conservation com. 1964—). Home: 8718 Winningham Lane Houston TX 77055 Office: PO Box 1188 Houston TX 77001

ELLINGER, CHARLES WILLIAM, dental educator; b. Lancaster, O., June 8, 1934; s. LeRoy Edward and Mable Bernice (Behrens) E.; D.D.S., Ohio State U., 1959, M.Sc., 1965; m. Janet D. Murphy, Mar. 23, 1958;children—Susan, Stacy Ann, Charles William II. Intern, Fla. Instl. Internship Program, Ocala, 1959-60; individual practice dentistry, Lima, O., 1960-62; mem. staff dept. prosthodontics U. Ky., Lexington, 1965—, now prof., chmn. dept. Cons. VA Hosp., Lexington, Ky., 1967-72, Nat. Inst. Mental Health, Hosp., Lexington, 1971-72. Served to capt. AUS, 1963-64. Mem. Am. Dental Assn., Blue Grass Dental Soc., Am., Carl O. Boucher (mem. nominations com. 1968-69, v.p. 1973-74), Southeastern (mem. membership com. 1969-70) prosthodontic socs., Psi Omega. Lutheran. Author: (with J. H. Rayson, J. A. Terry, A. O. Rahn) Synopsis of Complete Dentures, 1972. Contbr. articles to profl. jours. Home: 1866 Parkers Mill Lexington KY 40504

ELLIOT, DAVIS HASKINS, elec. engr.; b. Fall River, Mass., Jan. 26, 1907; s. Arthur Frank and Edith Emma (Haskins) E.; B.Sc., U. Mass., 1930; m. Elizabeth Flourney Adams, Dec. 15, 1934; 1 son, William Davis. From clk. distbn. dept. to asst. mgr. Appalachian Electric Power Co., Roanoke, Va., 1930-42; chmn. bd. Davis H. Elliot Co., Inc., elec. constrn., Roanoke and Lexington, Ky., 1946—. Pres. Community Fund, 1950-51; v.p. Roanoke Fine Arts Center; pres. Southwestern Va. chpt. Trout Unlimited. Mem. State Apprenticeship Council, 1953—. Served from lt. (j.g.) to lt. comdr., USNR, 1942-46; comdr. Mine Div. 33, 1945. Recipient Savs. Bond program award U.S. Treasury, 1958; McGraw award for advancement elec. industry, 1973. Fellow Acad. Elec. Contracting; mem. I.E.E.E., English-speaking Union (br. pres. 1960—, mem. nat. bd.), Roanoke C. of C. (pres. 1957). Episcopalian (warden). Clubs: Roanoke German, Roanoke Country, Shenandoah (pres. 1952), (Roanoke); Commonwealth (Richmond); Army and Navy (Washington); Norfolk (Va.) Yacht and Country, Anglers (N.Y.); Fly Fishers (London, Eng.). Home: 3266 White Oak Rd Roanoke VA 24014 Office: 1920 Progress Dr SE Roanoke VA 24013

ELLIOT, SIMON, lawyer; b. Wilno, Poland, Feb. 4, 1912; s. Eliakimowicz and Nelkin E.; came to U.S., 1936, naturalized, 1943; LL.B., N.Y. U., 1945, J.D., 1969; m. Dec. 31, 1949; children—Mark, Helen. Admitted to N.Y. bar, 1929; founding partner Maquinaria Minera SA, Motolinia, Mexico, 1947—, Kenaf Mexicano SA, Mesones, Mexico; pres. Industrias Sorel SA, Mexico, 1966—; exec. v.p. Fibras Vitricas Mex SA, Monserrat, Mexico, 1968—. Vice pres. Pre Bar Assn., 1941—; founder, legal counsel New Americans for the Democratic Party, 1945—. Home: Sierra Gorda 39 Mexico 10 DF Mexico

ELLIOTT, CLARENCE WILLARD, educator, accountant; b. Hampton, Ark., Oct. 9, 1936; s. Clarence Willard and Madge (Lyon) E.; B.S., Ark. A. and M. Coll., 1958; M.B.A., U. Ark., 1960, Ph.D., 1964; m. Sherry Carolyn Kennedy, Sept. 3, 1960; children—Clarence Willard III, Erin Gaye. Cost accountant Duracraft Boats, Inc., Monticello, Ark., 1957-58; instr. U. Ark., Fayetteville, 1959-62; asst. prof. accounting St. Josephs Coll., Rensselaer, Ind., 1962-64; asso. prof. accounting La. State U., Baton Rouge, 1964-74, prof., 1974—, also dir. placement Coll. Bus. Adminstrn. Auditor, R.J. Flynn, C.P.A., Rensselaer, 1962-64; cons. internat. div. Ethyl Corp., Baton Rouge, summer 1966; cons. Harbor Banana Distbrs., Inc., Long Beach, Cal., Aluminum Products Co., New Orleans, Basil M. Lee & Co., C.P.A.'s, Baton Rouge; cons. edn. and tng. Arthur Young & Co., 1968-69; mem. faculty Inst. Ins. Marketing. Recipient service award La. LP-Gas Assn., 1968. C.P.A., La. Mem. Am. Inst. C.P.A.s La. Soc. C.P.A.'s (chpt. pres.), Am. Accounting Assn., Alpha Chi, Beta Alpha Psi, Beta Gamma Sigma. Contbr. numerous articles to profl. jours. Home: 3848 N Bluebonnet Rd Baton Rouge LA 70809

ELLIOTT, DONALD RICHARD, data processing exec.; b. Peoria, Ill., Aug. 23, 1914; s. Jesse P. and Ruth (Bowman) E.; student U. Ia., 1932-33; Ph.D. in Bus. Adminstrn., Hamilton State U., Tucson, 1973; m. Marjorie Elizabeth Mackley, July 21, 1934; children—Ruth Ann (Mrs. Robert Lee Schwaner), Roxy Mackley. Profl. musician various name dance bands, Chgo., N.Y.C., 1934-42; IBM technician, supr. Caterpillar Tractor Co., Peoria, 1947-54; asst. sec., data processing mgr. Ins. Co. of Tex., Presdl. Ins. Co., Jacksonville, Fla., 1955-56; v.p., dir. servicing and data processing Fed. Title & Ins. Corp. and Republic Mortgage Corp., Miami, Fla., 1956-64; pres. Doriel, Inc., Computer Service Center, Miami, 1965-66; dir. computer operations Lon Worth Crow Co., mortgage bankers, Miami, 1966-70; dir., v.p. Bank Directory, Inc., Miami, 1964-70; v.p. data processing S.E. Mortgage Co., Miami, 1970-73; data processing cons., Norfolk, Va., 1973—. Served with C.E., AUS, 1943-45. Mem. Mortgage Bankers Assn. (loan adminstrn. chmn. 1964), Data Processing Mgmt. Assn., Nat. Machine Accountants Assn. (pres., nat dir. 1958, 63). Mason. Address: 7861-B Wherry Dr Norfolk VA 23505

ELLIOTT, FLOYD AVERY, bank exec.; b. Chester, S.C., Feb. 14, 1928; s. John Alexander and Minnie Frances (Cassells) E.; B.A., Duke, 1949; M.Banking, La. State U., 1966; m. Ola Wilkerson Matlock, Apr. 23, 1955; children—Floyd Matlock, John Avery, Robert Wilkerson. Asst. cashier Peoples Nat. Bank, Chester, S.C., 1955-60, asst. v.p., asst. trust officer, 1960-68, v.p., asst. trust officer, dir., 1968—. Mem. Chester County Bd. Devel. and Commerce, 1969-72; sec. Chester Metropolitan Sewer Dist., 1964-73. Bd. dirs. United Fund. Served with AUS, 1950-52. Mem. Nat. Asso. Bank Auditors and Comptrollers (dir. S.C. 1967-68), Young Bankers S.C. (dir. 1966-68). Democrat. Baptist (deacon 1964—). Lion. Home: 107 Hillcrest Dr Chester SC 29706 Office: 120 Church St Chester SC 29706

ELLIOTT, FRANKIE JO LEWIS, educator; b. Austin, Tex., Apr. 24; d. John Leeman and Lois (Perry) Lewis; B.A., U. Tex., 1947; M.A., Rice U., 1952; div.; children—John Perry Kirk, Robin Lois Elliott. Teaching fellow Rice Inst., Houston, 1951-52; tchr. English Bellaire high sch., Houston, 1959-61; asst. prof. English and bus. communications downtown sch., U. Houston, 1961-67, asst. prof. communications Coll. Bus., main campus, 1967—. Soloist various chs., social orgns; performer Theatre, Inc., Houston, 1953-56; also active Alley Theatre Guild. Recipient Neiman Marcus Profl. Women of the Week award, 1962. Mem. Am. Bus. Communication Assn. (sec.-treas. S.W. sect. 1967-68), Internat. Soc. gen. Semantics, Acad. Mgmt., S. Central Modern Lang. Assn., Southwestern Social Sci. Assn., Phi Beta Kappa, Alpha Lambda Delta, Chi Omega. Episcopalian. Home: 2423 Wroxton Rd Houston TX 77005 Office: Coll Bus U Houston Houston TX 77004

ELLIOTT, IRVIN WESLEY, JR., chemist, educator; b. Newton, Kan., Oct. 21, 1925; s. Irvin Wesley and Leota Bernice (Jordan) E.; B.S., U. Kan., 1947, M.S., 1949, Ph.D., 1952; postdoctoral (NSF faculty fellow) Harvard, 1957-58; m. Joan Louise Curl, Aug. 27, 1952; children—Derek Wesley, Karen Jean. Instr., So. U., Baton Rouge, La., 1949-50; asso. prof. chemistry Fla. A. and M. U., Tallahassee, 1952-57; prof. chemistry Fisk U., Nashville, 1958—. Cons. coll. chemistry; vis. prof. Howard U., Washington, 1965-66. Bd. dirs. CEMREL Inst., St. Louis. Mem. Am. Chem. Soc. (chmn. Nashville sect. 1970), Nat. Inst. Sci., Chem. Soc. London, Sigma Xi, Omicron Delta Kappa, Beta Kappa Chi. Contbr. research articles on organic chemistry to sci. jours. Home: 2014 Jordan Dr Nashville TN 37218 Office: Fisk University Nashville TN 37203

ELLIOTT, JAMES HOWARD, ophthalmologist, educator; b. Hastings, Neb., Jan. 15, 1927; s. Arthur Elwood and Ivy Jane (Furman) E.; B.A., Phillips U., 1948; M.D. summa cum laude, U. Okla., 1952; m. Janice Juanita Thrower, Aug. 21, 1948; children—James Richard, Janice Elaine, John Thrower, Stephen Scott. Intern Mercy Hosp., Oklahoma City, 1952-53; gen. practice medicine, Nowata, Okla., 1953-60; resident ophthalmology U. Okla. Med. Center, Oklahoma City, 1960-62; fellow ophthalmology Harvard Med. Sch., Boston, 1962-65, instr., 1965-66; asso. prof., head div. ophthalmology Vanderbilt Med. Sch., Nashville, 1966-68, prof., head div., 1968-72, prof., chmn. dept., 1972—; also ophthalmologist in chief Vanderbilt U. Hosp., Nashville, 1968—. Lectr., Harvard, 1967, 69, 68; mem. visual scis. study sect., div. research grants NIH, 1970-74, corneal task force Nat. Eye Inst., 1972; med. adviser Tenn. Nat. Soc. Prevention Blindness, 1969—; spl. ad hoc cons. ophthalmology Sch. Medicine U. Okla., 1972. Mem. Assn. Research and Vision in Ophthalmology (chmn. sect. immunology and microbiology 1972-73), Assn. U. Profs Ophthalmology (trustee 1972-76), Assn. Research and Vision in Ophthalmology (trustee 1974—), Am. Acad. Ophthalmology and Otolaryngology, A.M.A., N.Y. Acad. Scis., Nashville, Tenn. acads. ophthalmology, Tenn., Nashville-Davidson County, So. med. assns. Editorial bd. Archives Ophthalmology, A.M.A., 1973—. Contbr. articles profl. jours. Home: 4300 Estes Rd Nashville TN 37215 Office: Vanderbilt Univ Hospital Nashville TN 37232

ELLIOTT, JIM LYNN, data processing co. engr.; b. Dallas, Nov. 12, 1946; s. Gilbert Myron and Frances (Lynn) E.; Asso. Sci. in Electronics Tech., Okla. State U., 1966, B.S. in Tech. Edn., 1968; postgrad. Ore. State U., 1973—; m. Linda Marie Eskelsen, Nov. 27, 1972—. With Control Data Corp., 1968-72, European tech. support coordinator, Heidelberg, West Germany, 1969-72; staff tech. cons. to Potter Instrument Co. GmbH, Vienna, Austria, 1972-73; independent cons., 1972—. Teaching asst. Ore. State U., Corvallis, 1973—. Mem. Assn. Computing Machinery, I.E.E.E. Mem. Order DeMolay. Home: 4804 N Woodward St Oklahoma City OK 73112

ELLIOTT, JOHN FRANKLIN, clergyman; b. Neosho, Mo., June 11, 1915; s. William Marion and Charlotte Jeanette (Crump) E.; student Maryville Coll., 1933-35; A.B., Austin Coll., 1937; postgrad. Louisville Presbyn. Sem., 1937-38, U. Tenn., 1938, Dallas Theol. Sem., 1939-40; B.D., Columbia Theol. Sem., 1942, M.Div., 1971; D.Litt. (hon.), Internat. Acad., 1954; m. Winifred Margaret Key, July 6, 1939; children—Paul Timothy, Stephen Marion, Andrew Daniel. Ordained to ministry Presbyn. Ch., 1942; founder Emory Presbyn. Ch., Atlanta, 1941, Wildwood Presbyn. Ch., Salem, 1950; pastor Wylam Presbyn. Ch., Birmingham, Ala., 1942-47, Salem (Va.) Presbyn. Ch., 1947-51, Calvary Presbyn. Ch. Ind., Fort Worth, 1952—; founder, pastor Grace Presbyn. Ch. Ind., Roanoke, Va., 1951-52; headmaster Colony Christian Sch., Ft. Worth, 1969—. Founder, dir. Ft. Worth Home Bible Classes, 1954—. Dir. Spanish Publs., Inc., 1969—. Bd. dirs. Ind. Bd. for Presbyn. Home Missions, Collingwood, N.J., 1956-74; dist. committeeman Longhorn council Boy Scouts Am., Ft. Worth, 1960-66; instr., examiner U.S. Coast Guard Aux., Ft. Worth, 1967-72; pilot, chaplain, maj. CAP, Ft. Worth, 1970—; ministerial adviser bd. dirs. Reformed Theol. Sem., Jackson, Miss., 1973—; bd. dirs. Graham Bible Coll., 1966-74. Fellow Philos. Soc. Great Britain (Victoria Inst.), Royal Geog. Soc., Huguenot Soc. of London. Clubs: Ft. Worth, Ridglea Country, Ft. Worth Boat. Home: 3980 Edgehill Rd Fort Worth TX 76116 Office: 4800 El Campo Av Fort Worth TX 76107

ELLIOTT, MORRIS FRANCIS, ret. clergyman; b. Phila., Mar. 26, 1909; s. Matthew and Elizabeth Margaret (Morris) E.; B.A., William and Mary Coll., 1933; B.D., Va. Theol. Sem., 1936; D.D., Daniel Baker Coll., 1953; m. Margaret Ann Miller, May 23, 1938; 1 dau., Barbara Ann. Ordained to ministry P.E. Ch. as deacon, 1936, priest, 1937; asst. rector Galveston, Tex., 1936-38; rector Houston, 1938-41, Lufkin, Tex., 1941-49; rector Emmanuel Ch., San Angelo, Tex., 1949-74, ret., 1974. Mem. Com. State of Ch., 1950-51; chmn. examining chaplains Diocese of N.W. Tex., 1950-60, mem., from 1960, mem. exec. bd., 1960-73; del. Provincial Synod, 1951, 54, 57, 66, 69, 72. Mem. adv. bd. Planned Parenthood, San Angelo, 1959—. Mem. bd. Servicemen's Center, 1964—, pres., 1967-70; adv. bd. Parents Without Partners; president San Angelo Council of Churches, 1968-69; mem. San Angelo Council on Alcoholism, 1966—. Trustee, Daniel Baker Coll., Brownwood, Tex., 1950-51; Sem. of S.W.; bd. dirs. San Angelo Symphony Orch.; 1949-60, San Angelo Art Gallery, 1954. Mem. San Angelo Ministerial Alliance (v.p. 1950, pres. 1951). Mason, Elk, Rotarian. Home: 2228 Waco St San Angelo TX 76901

ELLIOTT, PAUL CHERRY, broadcasting exec.; b. Nashville, Nov. 21, 1941; s. Philip Cherry and Dorthea Lorene (Dobyns) E.; student Maryville Coll., 1959-63; B.S., George Peabody Coll., 1964; M.F.A., U. N.C., 1968; m. Johnnia Ruth Hester, July 29, 1966; children—Keats Leigh, Kiersten Tate. Educator deaf, Nashville Met. Bd. Edn. and Bill Wilkerson Hearing and Speech Center, 1964-67; dir. speech and drama, chmn. performing arts Stratford Coll., Danville, Va., 1968-73; prodn. mgr. TV sta. WTLT, 1973—. Dir. summer stock Danville Little Theatre, 1972-73. Bd. dirs. Broadway Theatre Guild Danville, 1968-72, Danville Little Theatre, 1968-73. Mem. Speech Communication Assn., Ednl. Theatre Assn., Southeastern Theatre Conf., Va. Theatre Conf. Author play Ledge, Ledger, and the Legend, 1972; The Legacy, 1973. Home: PO Box 94 Kingston Springs TN 37082 Office: WTLT Television 38th and Charlotte Sts Nashville TN 37212

ELLIOTT, ROBERT BURL, orthopaedic surgeon; b. Kirksville, Mo., Dec. 30, 1919; s. Burl Dennis and Beatrice (Corbin) E.; A.B., U. Ia., 1941, M.D., 1943; M.S., U. Minn., 1951; m. Georgia Anne Lindley, Aug. 24, 1950; children—Robert Burl, Stephen Corbin, Gregory Taylor. Intern, Md. Gen. Hosp., Balt., 1944; Cole fellowship in orthopaedic surgery U. Minn., Mayo Clinic, 1944-47; practice orthopaedic surgery, Houston, 1948—; instr. orthopaedic surgery Lillie Jolly Sch. Nursing, Meml. Hosp.; chmn. orthopaedic sect., chief surgery, dir. acad. orthopaedics Meml. Bapt. Hosp.; instr. clin. faculty Baylor U. Med. Sch.; asso. prof. U. Tex. Med. Sch. Diplomate Am. Bd. Orthopaedic Surgery, Am. Acad. Orthopaedic Surgery. Fellow A.C.S., Internat. Coll. Surgeons (pres. Tex. 1971-72); mem. Am. Fracture Assn. (pres. 1969-71; bd. govs.), Tex. Orthopaedic Soc., So., Pan-Am. med. assns., Houston Surg. Soc., Am. Soc. Testing Materials (com. F-4 surg. implants; sub.-com. performance and implant application; chmn. implant application com. 1968—), Western Orthopaedic Assn., Houston Orthopaedic Club, Am. Orthopaedic Foot Soc. (ednl. com.), Sam Houston Trail Assn. (bd. dirs. pres. 1971-73), Sociedad Latino-Americana de Ortopedia y Traumatologia, Spectators Orthopaedic Club, Sigma Alpha Epsilon, Phi Rho Sigma. Mason (K.T., Shriner), Elk. Club: International. Home: 10902 Wickwild Dr Houston TX 77024 Office: 1010 Louisiana St Houston TX 77002

ELLIOTT, ROSS LILES, lawyer; b. Breckenridge, Tex., Jan. 7, 1916; s. Ross and Katie Mattie (Liles) E.; student John Tarleton Coll., 1933-35; B.B.A., U. Tex., 1938,J.D., 1940; m. Frances A. Russell, Apr. 17, 1941; children—Janice (Mrs. Edward R. Vice), Linda (Mrs. Harry L. Ledbetter), Mary (Mrs. R. William Whitman, Jr.), Ross Liles, Jr. Admitted to Tex. bar, 1940; practice law, Breckenridge, Tex., 1940-55; v.p., gen. counsel Graridge Corp., Breckenridge, 1955-68; partner firm Elliott & Bevill, Attys., Breckenridge, 1968-73. County atty., Stephens County, Tex., 1941-42, 1947-49. Pres. Tex. High Sch. Football Hall of Fame, 1971—. Chmn. Stephens County Democratic party, 1958-69. Trustee Graridge Corp. and Asso. Cos. Employees Pension Trust, Breckenridge, Tex., 1955—. Served with USAF, 1942-45. Mem. State Bar Tex. Lion. Home: 200 N Harding Av Breckenridge TX 76024 Office: 306 N Breckenridge Av Breckenridge TX 76024

ELLIOTT, VANCE JOHNSON, physician; b. Knoxville, Ia., July 10, 1917; s. Jake and Lena (Johnson) E.; M.D., State U. Ia., 1939; m. Albert J. Mater, Oct. 8, 1932; children—Vancene, Cathy; m. 2d, Jean C. Stubbs, Dec. 31, 1959 (div. Dec. 1969); one son, Vance II. Intern and resident Charity Hosp., La., 1939-40; pvt. practice, Knoxville, Ia., 1945-47, Odessa, Tex., 1947—; staff Collins Meml. Hosp., Knoxville, 1945-47; staff Med. Center Hosp., Odessa, Tex., 1950—, chief of staff, 1955—; pres. V.J.E., Inc., owner chief obstet. and gynecol. service, 1950-56, pres., Profl. Building Clinic; dir. Corp. Gt. S.W., Inter-Continental Corp., Trinity Valley Ranch Corp., Gt. S.W. Life Ins. Co., Big D Devel. (all Dallas); asso. Harding-Elliott ranches of Texas and Ia. Dir. Community Chest, Odessa. Served as flight surgeon, from lt. to maj., USAAF, 1940-45. Decorated Bronze Star medal. Fellow Am. Coll. Obstetrics and Gynecology, Am. Soc. Study of Sterility, Am. Geriatrics Soc., Am. Soc. Abdominal Surgeons, Am. Coll. Geriatrics, Royal Soc. Health; mem. Pan Am. Cancer Cytology Soc., A.M.A. (chmn. polit. action com. 11 Congl. dist.), So., Tex. (chmn. polit. action com. 11th Congl. district) med. assns., Am. Assn. Physicians and Surgeons, Aero. Med. Soc., Tex., W. Tex. surgeons assns., Tex. Cattlemens Assn., Am. Legion, C. of C. U. Ia. Alumni Assn., Phi Gamma Delta. Methodist. Home: 809 W 15th Odessa TX 79760 Office: 313-B N Alleghaney St Odessa TX 79760

ELLIOTT, WILLIAM FLOYD, ednl. adminstr.; b. Tyler, Tex., Aug. 9, 1928; s. Albert R. and Lillian (Jernigan) E.; B.S., E.Tex. State Coll., 1950, M.Ed., 1951; Ed.D., N.Tex. State U., 1964; postgrad. U. Okla., 1957, 60, Cornell U., 1959; m. Vera Joyce Petty, May 28, 1948; children—David Lynn, Susan Ruth. Tchr., adminstr. Overton (Tex.) Ind. Sch. Dist., 1950-62; inst. Kilgore (Tex.) Coll., 1962-64; prof. edn., dir. tchr. edn. div. U. Corpus Christi (Tex.), 1964-65; asso. prof. edn. Tex. Coll. Arts and Industries, Kingsville, 1965-66; asst. to pres., dir. research and devel. Tex. A. and I. U., Kingsville, 1966-68, v.p. for student affairs, 1968—. Ednl. cons. U.S. Office Edn., Tex. Edn. Agy., Ednl. Projects, Inc., S.W. Edn. Devel. Lab., Pub. Sch. Dists. Mem. Am. Assn. U. Profs., Nat. Council U. Research Adminstrs., Tex. Assn. Coll. Tchrs., Phi Delta Kappa. Developer, Elliott Sociometric Scale, 1964, spl. edn. programs for tchrs. of migrant, educationally deprived children, 1965-67. Home: 102 University Blvd Kingsville TX 78363

ELLIOTT, WILLIAM YOUNG, author; b. Leeds, Ala., Apr. 18, 1902; s. James Barnett and Ida Lee (Vann) E.; B.S., Birmingham-So. Coll., 1926; M.A., U. Ala., 1929; postgrad. George Peabody Coll. for Tchrs., summer 1937; m. Laura Emily Bozeman, Feb. 25, 1928; children—William Young, Dorothy Emily, Robert Collier. tchr. pub. schs., Jefferson County, Ala., 1926-29, Tarrant City, Ala., 1929-37, Birmingham, Ala., 1937-42; with pyrometry dept. Tenn. Coal, Iron & Ry. Co. (now known as Fairfield Works, U.S. Steel), Birmingham, Ala., 1942-67. Author: Skylights (poems), Book I, 1951, Book 2, 1954, Book 3, 1958, Most Lovely Lizzie, 1958; Voices, Book I (poems): Voices, Book II (poems): Wings (poems), 1969; works included in Oberfirst's Anthology of Best Short Stories, Volume,4, 1955, Volume 6, 1958, Volume 7, 1959, Vol. 8, 1960; cover poet Scimitar and Song mag., May 1957; also readings, essays, stories. Leader poetry study group Ala. Writers Conclave, 1959, poetry panel leader, 1967, now treas., dean of poetry, 1971. Recipient 1st prize The Prairie Poet mag., Winter issue, 1957-58; Emil Hess award, poetry contest, Birmingham Festival of Arts, 1958, 2d prize, poetry contest, 1963; 1st prize, ann. poetry contest New Work Writers Guild, 1961; prizes short stories, articles, poems Ala. Writers Conclave; 1st prize religious poem Mid-S. Poetry Festival, 1st prize free verse, 1968; 1st prize blank verse, 1969, 2d prize in category, 1971; 1st prize, peace poem contest, Am. Poets Fellowship Soc., 1967; commendable excellence award Cal. Olympiad of Arts, 1968; Distinguished Service citation World Poetry Soc., 1970. Mem. Am. Poetry League (bd. advisers), Am. Poets Fellowship Soc. (1st prize in category 1970), Ala. Poetry Soc. (Poet of Year 1971), Ala. Writers Conclave (dean of poetry 1971), Centro Studi E Scambi Internazionali (Rome), Am. Radio Relay League, Internat. Platform Assn. Methodist. Home: 3516 Mariposa Rd SW Huntsville AL 35805

ELLIOTT, WYLEY J., ednl. adminstr.; b. Camden, Ark., Sept. 16, 1926; s. Wyley Madison and Ruby Irene (Womack) E.; B.S., Ouachita Bapt. U., 1948; M.A., George Peabody Coll., 1951; postgrad. Auburn U., 1958-69, Columbia, 1960; postgrad. (fellow) U. Ark. 1971—; m. Evelyn Gillespie, Dec. 23, 1951; children—Laura, David, Melinda. Biology and sci. tchr. Camden (Ark.) Sr. High Sch., 1948-51; prin. Arkadelphia Sr. High Sch., 1951-56; prin. Camden Sr. High Sch., 1956-66; supt. Camden Pub. Schs., 1966-73. Mem. Gov's. Adv. Council on Community Service and Continuing Edn., 1967—; mem.-at-large Commn. on Secondary Schs. of North Central Assn.; mem. U.S. Sch. Study Mission to Germany and Denmark, 1970. Mem. local adv. council Democratic party, 1969—. Served with AUS, 1945-46; PTO. Recipient Distinguished Service award Arkadelphia Jr. C. of C., 1952, Schoolmen medal Freedoms Found., 1974. Mem. N.E.A. (dir. 1970—), Ark. Edn. Assn. (pres. 1968-69), Ark. Assn. Secondary Sch. Prins. (pres. 1965-66), Camden C. of C., Phi Delta Kappa. Baptist (deacon 1958). Rotarian. Clubs: Camden Country; Little Rock Capital. Home: 280 S Hill St Fayetteville AR 72701 Office: Div Continuing Edn U Ark Fayetteville AR 72701

ELLIOTT, YANCEY CALDONIA, JR., apparel products co. exec.; b. Raleigh, N.C., Nov. 11, 1935; s. Yancey Caldonia and Sarah Lucille (Martin) E.; student N.C. State U., 1954-57; B.S., U. N.C., 1960; M.B.A., East Carolina U., 1969; m. Myrtha LaRue Lockerman, May 15, 1965; 1 son, Yancey Caldonia III. Vice-pres., asst. trust officer Edgecombe Bank & Trust Co., Tarboro, N.C., 1960-68; sec., treas. Runnymede Mills, Inc., Tarboro, N.C., 1968—. Chmn. supervisory devel. com. Edgecombe Tech. Inst., 1969—; chmn. Citizens' Adv. Com., 1970-71; gifts chmn. Friends of the Edgecombe County Meml. Library. Bd. dirs., treas. Edgecombe United Fund; trustee Tarboro Student Aid Assn. Served to 1st lt. USNGR, 1960-67. Mem. Nat. Assn. Accountants, East Carolina Estate Planning Council, Tarboro Mchts. Assn. (pres. 1967-68), Tarboro C. of C., Sigma Chi. Baptist. Home: 1009 Panola St Tarboro NC 27886 Office: 1004 Fountain St Tarboro NC 27886

ELLIS, ANDREW JACKSON, JR., lawyer; b. Ashland, Va., June 23, 1930; s. Andrew Jackson and Sue (Carter) E.; A.B., Washington and Lee U., 1951, LL.B., 1953; m. Dorothy Lichliter, Apr. 24, 1954; children—Elizabeth C., Andrew C., William D. Admitted to Va. bar, 1952; partner Campbell, Ellis & Campbell, Ashland, Va., 1955-70, Mays, Valentine, Davenport & Moore, Richmond, Va., 1970—; substitute Hanover County judge, 1958-63; police justice Ashland, 1958-63; commonwealth atty. Hanover County, 1963-69; county atty. Hanover County, 1970—; dir. Ashland and Montpelier br. First & Mchts. Nat. Bank. Councilman, Ashland, 1956-63; mayor, Ashland, 1958-63. Trustee Hanover Acad., J. Sargeant Reynolds Community Coll. Served to 1st lt., Judge Adv. Gen.'s Corps, AUS, 1953-55. Mem. Am., Va. (mem. council), 15th Jud. (past pres.), Richmond bar assns., Va. Trial Lawyers Assn., Ashland C. of C., S.R., Phi Kappa Sigma, Phi Alpha Delta. Kiwanian. Home: Broomfield Route 2 Box 218 Beaverdam VA 23015 Office: PO Box 1122 Ross Bldg Richmond VA 23219

ELLIS, CAREY JAMES, JR., lawyer; b. New Orleans, July 21, 1920; s. Carey Jay and Innes (Morris) E.; B.A., Tulane U., 1942, LL.B., 1943; m. Linda Annette Hudson, June 3, 1943; 1 son, Carey Jay III. Admitted to La. bar, 1943, U.S. Supreme Ct. bar, 1973; practiced in Rayville, La., 1946—. Dir. Richland State Bank, Rayville Delta Finance Co., Rayville, Econ. Devel. Co., Inc., Rayville. Franklin Loan Co., Inc., Winnsboro, La. Dist. atty. 5th Jud. Dist., 1958-60. Bd. dirs. Richland Parish Library, 1950-58. Served with USNR, 1943-45; PTO. Mem. Am. Trial Lawyers Assn., Am., La. (mem. ho. of dels. 1956-57) bar assns., Am. Legion, V.F.W. Episcopalian (mem. vestry 1970—). Home: 904 Smith St Rayville LA 71269 Office: 105 S Julia St Rayville LA 71269

ELLIS, CHARLES GRANT, museum ofcl.; b. Kingston, N.Y., Oct. 12, 1908; s. Charles George and Mary Lewis (Grant) E.; grad. Blair Acad., Blairstown, N.J., 1926; student Princeton, 1926-30; m. Gretchen Hart Snyder, Sept. 30, 1931; children—Gretchen Anne, John Grant. Research asso. Textile Mus., Washington, 1961—; adviser Ency. Brit. Served with USNR, 1941-45. Club: Hajji Baba. Translator Antique Rugs from the Near East (Bode and Kühnel), 1958, Oriental Carpets (Erdmann), 1960. Contbr. articles to mags., chpts. to books. Home: 186 Fair St Kingston NY 12401 Office: Textile Museum 2320 S St NW Washington DC 20008

ELLIS, DAVID BRADLEY, physician; b. nr. New Albany, Miss., Mar. 29, 1920; s. William Augustus and Della Dee (Teer) Ellis; B.A. in Agr., Miss. State U., 1947, B.S., U. Miss., 1953; M.D., U. Tenn., 1956; m. Nancy Katherine McKinstry, 1948; children—Nancy Margaret (Mrs. Frederick Robbins Rogers), Mary Corinne (Mrs. Samuel Carroll Pace), Elizabeth Ann, Martha Jane, David Bradley, John McKinstry. Asst. county extension agt., Lafayette County, Miss., 1948-49; asso. county extension agt., Prentiss County, Miss., 1949-50; county agt., Clay County, Miss., 1950-51; intern John Gaston Hosp., Memphis, 1955-56; practice medicine specializing in gen. practice, Ripley, Miss., 1956-57, New Albany, 1957—; chief staff Union County Gen. Hosp., New Albany, 1970—; farmer, land owner. Served with USAAF, 1942-46. Mem. Am., Miss. med. assns., Am. Acad. Family Practice, North Miss., Union County med. socs., Alpha Kappa Kappa. Democrat. Presbyn. Home: Hwy 15 N New Albany MS 38652 Office: 701 Hwy 30 W New Albany MS 38652

ELLIS, ELMO ISRAEL, broadcasting exec.; b. Birmingham, Ala., Nov. 11, 1918; s. Samuel B. and Bertha F. (Seletz) Israel; A.B., U. Ala., 1940; M.A., Emory U., 1948; postgrad. Am. Mgmt. Assn., 1959, Emory U., 1965; m. Ruth M. Ballinger, Dec. 26, 1944; children—Janet Faye, William Bryan. Dir. publicity, prodn. mgr. WSB, Atlanta, 1940-42, dir. scripts and prodn., 1947—, prodn. mgr., 1948-52, mgr. programming WSB Radio (AM-FM), 1952-63, v.p., gen. mgr., 1963—; v.p. Cox Broadcasting Corp., 1969—; dir. Citizens & So. Nat. Bank of Sandy Springs; writer-producer network radio programs NBC, ABC, CBS and Mut. Broadcasting System, 1942-46; writer-producer We The People radio program, Great Jury Trials, FBI in Peace and War. CBS Sch. of the Air, Continental Celebrity Club, 1946. Vice pres. Ga. Safety Council, 1968-69; mem. Ga. Industry Adv. Com.; mem. nat. publicity com. Freedoms Found., 1968-69; radio-TV rep. Nat. Heart Assn., 1969; mem. ad hoc com. high blood pressure edn. Ga. Heart Assn.; mem. Gov.'s Com. on Employment Handicapped, 1972, adv. panel Ga. Nutrition Council, 1972; chmn. publicity Ga. Anti-Litter Campaign, 1973; adv. com. Ga. Crime Prevention Month, 1973; mem. S.E. regional adv. bd. Anti-Defamation League, B'nai B'rith; gen. adv. com. Atlanta-Fulton County Schs. Vocational-Tech. and Adult Edn. Asst. to dir. Democratic Nat. Convs., 1952, 56, 60, 64. Vice pres. exec. bd., nat. sponsor Ga. Easter Seal Soc.; bd. dirs. Ga. Safety Council, Jr. Achievement Greater Atlanta, Arthritis Found., Ga. Mental Health Assn., Radio Advt. Bur., Am. Jewish Com.; adv. bd. Consumer Credit Services Greater Atlanta; mem. president's council Oglethorpe Coll. Served to capt. USAAF, 1942-46. Recipient Silver medal award Atlanta Advt. Club, 1965, Peabody award, 1966, Alfred P. Sloan award, 1966; Sch. Bell award Ga. Edn. Assn., 1967; named Citizen of Year, Ga. Assn. Broadcasters, 1965; recipient Distinguished 20-year Service award A.R.C., 1968; Abraham Lincoln award So. Baptist Radio-TV Commn., 1972; Silver Beaver award Boy Scouts Am., 1972; Pioneer Broadcaster Ga. award Di Gamma Kappa, 1972; Meritorious Service award Am. Heart Assn., 1970; Distinguished Alumnus award U. Ala., 1971; Gavin Distinguished Broadcaster award, 1972; Distinguished Service award Nat. Safety Council, 1973; George Washington Honor medal and Distinguished Service award, 1973; named Gavin Mgr. of Year, 1971. Mem. Ga. Asso. Press Broadcasters (chpt. pres.), Nat. Assn. FM Broadcasters (dir.-at-large, past chmn.), Ga. Assn. Broadcasters (dir.), Emory U., U. Ala. alumni assns., Sigma Delta Chi. Mem. B'nai B'rith (bd. dirs.). Clubs: Standard, Commerce. Author: (with others) Radio Station Management; Happiness Is Worth The Effort; Sleepy Hollow Poems. Home: 6345 Aberdeen Dr NE Atlanta GA 30328 Office: 1601 W Peachtree St NE Atlanta GA 30309

ELLIS, GARLAND CECIL, chem. engr.; b. nr. Siler City, N.C., Aug. 27, 1920; s. Grover Cleveland and Mary Fleta (Hayworth) E.; B.S., High Point (N.C.) Coll., 1941; m. Mary Belle Fair, Mar. 28, 1952; children—Charles Garland, Garland Stephen. With Marietta Paint & Color Co., 1941-42; control chemist Allied Chem. Corp., Hopewell, Va., 1942-46, research chemist, 1946-51, sr. research chemist, 1951-60, product mgr. tech. service, 1960-66, Morristown, N.J. product mgr. tech. service, 1966-68; plant tech. mgr. Koch Chem. Co., Orange, Tex., 1968—. Fellow Am. Inst. Chemists; mem. Am. Chem. Soc. Methodist. Contbr. articles to profl. jours. Patentee in field. Home: 950 Columbia Circle Bridge City TX 77611 Office: PO Box 216 Orange TX 77630

ELLIS, GEORGE WASHINGTON, ednl. adminstr.; b. Arcadia, Fla., Jan. 1, 1925; s. George Edward and Gussie (Staley) E.; B.S., Fla. A. and M. Coll., 1947; Ed.M., U. Pitts., 1954, postgrad., 1956-60; postgrad. Columbia U., 1961, Fla. U., 1966-71, U. Miami, 1968, Fla. Atlantic U., 1969-70; m. Alvalia Jones, July 7, 1956; children—George, Ruth, Cheryl, Jean. Tchr. indsl. edn. Alcorn (Miss.) A. and M. Coll., 1947-48, Fla. N and I Coll., St. Augustine, 1948; asst. prin. Carver High Sch., Dothan, Ala., 1948-50; prin. Bayview Jr. High Sch., Bonifay, Fla., 1950-53, Shadeville High Sch., Crawfordville, Fla., 1953-56, Monitor High Sch., Fitzgerald, Ga., 1956-57, Richardson High Sch., Lake City, Fla., 1957-60, Westside High Sch., Valdosta, Ga., 1960-62, Williston (Fla.) High Sch., 1962-63; prin. Center High Sch., Waycross, Ga., 1963-67; asst. prin. Drew Jr. High Sch., 1967-69, prin., 1969; prin. Dorsey Jr. High Sch., Miami, Fla., 1969-70; asst. prin. Riviera Jr. High Sch., Miami, 1970—. Vice pres. N.A.A.C.P., Miami, 1970-73; chmn. polit. action Push, Miami, 1970-73. Bd. dirs. Open Door Care and Tng. Center, Miami, 1971-74. Recipient grants Fla. Dept. Edn., 1956, Ga. Dept. Edn., 1964, Kellogg Study grant, 1961; named Sigma Man of the Year, Fla., 1972. Mem. Republican Exec. Com. Dade County, 1972—; v.p. Northwestern Republican Club, 1971-73. Mem. Nat. Soc. Study Edn., Nat. Assn. Secondary Sch. Prins., Fla. A. and M. Alumni Assn., Minister and Layman Assn. Miami, Kappa Delta Pi, Phi Beta Sigma (v.p. Fla., asso. dir. So. region). Home: 1055 NW 52d St Miami FL 33127 Office: 10301 SW 48th St Miami FL 33165

ELLIS, JAMES BLAIR, mfg. co. exec.; b. Goldsboro, N.C., Jan. 1, 1933; s. John Brantley and Virginia (Earp) E.; student Duke, 1950-51; B.S., East Carolina U., 1954, M.A., 1958; m. Gwendolyn Richardson, Dec. 29, 1953; children—James Blair, John Marshall, Richard Clyde. Reporter, Greenville (N.C.) Reflector, 1956-59; mem. pub. relations staff Am. Textile Mfrs. Inst., Charlotte, N.C., 1959-66; regional information mgr. Celanese Corp., Charlotte, 1966-68; dir. pub. relations Hanes Corp., Winston-Salem, N.C., 1968—. Served with AUS, 1954-56. Mem. Pub. Relations Soc. Am. Methodist. Home: 1301 Abingdon Way Winston-Salem NC 27106 Office: PO Box 5416 Winston-Salem NC 27103

ELLIS, JAMES LEWIS, lawyer, banker; b. Louisville, Ala., Jan. 15, 1892; s. James L. and Pearia (Hobdy) E.; m. Marybel Hixon, Oct. 21, 1939. Admitted to Ga. bar, 1916, since practiced in Americus; city atty., Americus, 1933. Pres. 1st Fed. Savs. & Loan Assn., 1950-56, dir., chmn. bd., chmn. exec. com., exec. mgr., 1950—. Mem. Adv. Com. Naval Affairs, Mem. U.S. Savs. and Loan League (mem. investments and mortgage lending com. 1958-59, dir. Southeastern Conf. 1961-62, mem. com. on fed. home loan bank system 1969—), Navy League U.S., Americus and Sumter County C. of C. (dir. 1961-62), Nat. Rivers and Harbors Congress, Flint River Valley Devel. Assn. (dir., v.p.), Am. Judicature Soc., Am., Ga., Americus bar assns. Methodist. Mason, Elk, Kiwanian (past pres.; lt. gov. Ga. dist. 1922). Club: Commerce (Atlanta). Home: 1301 S Lee St Americus GA 31709 Office: First Federal Savings Bldg Americus GA 31709

ELLIS, JOHN WESLEY, physician; b. Greenfield, Tenn., July 26, 1917; s. Robert Clinton and Brinnie Elinor (Cantrel) E.; student Bethel Coll., 1935-36, Memphis State U., 1948-49; M.D., U. Tenn., 1953; m. Georgia Alton McIlwain, Aug. 16, 1946; children—George Robert, Julie Prudence. Intern, John Gaston Hosp., Memphis, 1953-54; gen. practice medicine with Dyer (Tenn.) Clinic, 1954-64, Doctor's Clinic, Gibson Gen. Hosp., Trenton, Tenn., 1964—. Dir. Bank of Dyer. Served with AUS, 1942-45. Diplomate Am. Bd. Family Practice. Mem. V.F.W. Presbyn. (elder). Mason. Home: PO Box 264 Dyer TN 38330 Office: Doctors Clinic Gibson General Hospital Trenton TN 38382

ELLIS, MARJORIE LOU WHEATLEY (MRS. FRANK B. ELLIS), geographer, educator; b. Plainview, Tex., Feb. 4, 1931; d. Elbert Morris and Edith (Pate) Wheatley; B.S., Kan. State Coll., 1951; M.A., So. Mehtodist U., 1964; postgrad. U. Cal. at Los Angeles, 1964-66; Ph.D. in Geog. Edn., Okla. State U., 1973; m. Frank B. Ellis, Nov. 18, 1965 (dec. Nov. 1969). Tchr. pub. schs., West Plains, Mo., 1951-53, Joplin, Mo., 1954-56, Merriam, Kan., 1957-60, Rockville, Md., 1961-63; teaching fellow U. Cal. at Los Angeles, 1965; faculty East Tex. State U., Commerce, 1970-71; tchr. geography So. Meth. U., Dallas, 1972; instr., coordinator geog. edn. S.W. Tex. State U., San Marcos, 1972—. Mem. Assn. Am. Geographers. Am. Geog. Soc., Southwestern Social Sci. Assn., English Speaking Union, Nat. Council Geog. Edn. (coordinator Tex.), Delta Kappa Gamma, Gamma Theta Upsilon. Republican. Mem. Disciples of Christ Ch. Clubs: Racquet (Palm Springs, Cal.). Research on history of maps Office: Dept Geography SW Tex State U San Marcos TX 78666

ELLIS, MARVIN ELLIOTT, county agr. agt.; b. Cordele, Ga., Feb. 26, 1935; s. George Marvin and Irene (Taylor) E.; B.S., U. Ga., 1956, M.S., 1974; m. Lucile Forehand Busbee, Dec. 22, 1955; children—Michael Elliott, Bradley Phillip, Keith Marvin. Asst. county agt. Harris County, Ga., 1956-57, Spalding County, Ga., 1957-62; county agr. agt. Hancock County, 1962-69, Morgan County, 1969—. Mem. Epsilon Sigma Phi. Baptist. Clubs: American Business of Griffin (past sec.), Kiwanis, Lions (pres. 1967). Home: Lakeview Dr Madison GA 30650 Office: PO Box 413 Madison GA 30650

ELLIS, RAYMOND EARL, accountant; b. Fort Worth, Tex., Feb. 4, 1927; s. Chalmus H. and Myrtle (Shepherd) E.; B.S.C., Tex. Christian U., 1950; m. Joan Aurin, Apr. 17, 1949; 1 son, David Wesley. Partner, W.O. Ligon & Co., Fort Worth, 1950-51, 54-55, 55-65; v.p. E.E. Cloer gen. contractor, Fort Worth, 1951-54, 55; mgr. tax dept. Price Waterhouse & Co., Fort Worth, 1965-67; owner Raymond E. Ellis C.P.A., Fort Worth, 1967-69; partner Sproles, Woodard, Laverty & Ray, C.P.A.'s, Fort Worth, 1969—. Bd. dirs., treas., exec. com. De Cordova Bend Estates Assn., 1973-74, sec.-treas. Ponte Verde Condominium Owners Assn., 1972-74; bd. dirs., treas. bldg. fund Youth Crime Prevention League Am., 1969—. Served with USNR, 1944-46. Named Outstanding Optimist, Fort Worth, 1971-72. Mem. Am. Inst. C.P.A.'s, Tex. Soc. C.P.A.'s (pres. elect Fort Worth chpt.), Fort Worth Bus. and Estate Council. Optimist (sec.-treas. Found., 1969-72). Club: De Cordova Bend Estates Country (Acton, Tex.). Home: Ponte Verde Condo 5 De Cordova Bend Estates Granbury TX 76048 Office: Fort Worth National Bank Bldg Fort Worth TX 76102

ELLIS, RICHARD BASSETT, educator; b. Abilene, Tex., May 12, 1915; s. Amasa Donaldson and Irene Alice (Clarkson) E.; B.A., Vanderbilt U., 1936, M.S., 1937, Ph.D., 1940; m. Martha Victoria Cameron, Aug. 31, 1940; children—Martha Ann (Mrs. Baxter Donald Pair), Dorothy (Mrs. William E. Barkman), Richard Cameron. Analytical chemist Joseph E. Seagram & Sons, Inc., Louisville, 1940-42; research chemist Corning (N.Y.) Glass Works, 1942-46; instr. chemistry U. Fla., Gainesville, 1946-47; asst. prof. chemistry U. Miami, Coral Gables, 1947-51; sr. research chemist So. Research Inst., Birmingham, Ala., 1951-68; prof., head physics dept. Huntingdon Coll., Montgomery, Ala., 1968-70; prof., head sci. dept. Troy State U., Montgomery, 1970—. Asso. prof. chemistry U. Ala., Birmingham, 1962-68. Mem. Am. Chem. Soc., Am. Assn. Physics Tchrs., A.A.A.S., Am. Physics Soc., Phi Beta Kappa. Contbr. articles in field to profl. jours. Patentee in field. Home: 3115 Partridge Rd Montgomery AL 36111 Office: Bldg 625 Maxwell AFB AL 36112

ELLIS, ROBERT RUFUS, III, drug co. exec.; b. Memphis, Apr. 1, 1939; s. Robert Rufus and Martha Jane (Dickinson) E.; B.B.A., U. Miss. Asst. to sales mgr. Ellis-Bagwell Wholesale Drug Co., Memphis, 1961-63, sales mgr., 1963-65, pres., 1965—; pres E-B Data Co., 1968—, Drug Service, Memphis, 1971—; v.p. Henry B. Gilpin Co., Washington. Mem. So. Drug Club (pres. 1972-73), Traveling Men of Tenn. (pres. 1972-73). Kiwanian. Clubs: Memphis Country, Summit. Home: 3564 Lily Lane Memphis TN 38111 Office: 455 S Front St Memphis TN 38102

ELLIS, ROGER ALLEN, public accountant; b. Dekalb, Tex., Nov. 10, 1940; s. Thomas Earl and Cora Lee (Cox) E.; student Dallas Baptist Coll., 1966-69; B.B.A. (Meritorious scholar), N. Tex. State U., 1970; m. Kathryn Vanderpool, Dec. 27, 1966; children—Mitzi Paige, Matthew Roger. Patrolman, Dallas Police Dept., 1964-68; mem. audit staff Arthur Young & Co., C.P.A.'s, Dallas, 1970—; v.p. Quick Foods, Inc., Dallas, 1969—; tchr. Dallas Bapt. Coll., 1970-72. Served with USAAF, 1958-62. Recipient medal of valor Dallas Police Dept., 1965. C.P.A., Tex. Mem. Am. Inst. C.P.A.'s, Tex. Soc. C.P.A.'s, Blue Key, Beta Gamma Sigma. Home: 2003 Wedgewood St Carrollton TX 75006 Office: 3800 Republic Nat Bank Dallas TX 75209

ELLIS, RYAN BRADFORD, mfg. and mgmt. cons.; b. Ayden, N.C., Apr. 17, 1932; s. L. Ryan and Nancy (Arnold) E.; B. Indsl. Engring., Ga. Inst. Tech., 1954; m. Shirley Fullagar, Jan. 30, 1956. Prodn. engr. Raytheon Co., Waltham, Mass., 1954-56, equipment application engr., 1957, Atlanta, 1957-60; asst. v.p. Marketing Sci. Atlanta, Inc., 1960-61; USAF engring. adviser quality control; dept. mgr. plant 6 Lockheed Aircraft, Marietta, Ga., 1961-62; indsl. engr., contracts adminstr. U.S. Army, Dallas, 1962-65; mfg. and mgmt. cons. Syntron, Inc., Dallas, 1965; various mfg., marketing and mgmt. positions TRACOR, Inc., Austin, Tex., 1965-70; cons. engr. and gen. mgmt.; pres. TIE Inc. investments, 1970-73, Brad Ellis & Assos., Inc., 1973—. Chmn. vol. services council Travis State Sch., Austin, 1970-72; vice chmn. vol. services council Tex. Dept. Mental Health and Mental Retardation, 1972-73. Served with USAF, 1954-57, 68-69. Registered profl. engr., Tex. Mem. Am. Inst. Indsl. Engrs., Nat., Tex. socs. profl. engrs. Lion (sec. 1964-65, pres. 1972-73). Home: 2512 Great Oaks Pkwy Austin TX 78756 Office: 4101 Medical Pkwy Austin TX 78756

ELLIS, WALTER LEE, III, dairy mfg. co. exec.; b. Kosciusko, Miss., June 30, 1925; s. Walter Lee and Catherine (McGee) E.; student La. State U., 1943; B.S., Miss. State U., 1949; m. Lucretia Ann Graham, June 22, 1947; children—Claudia Michele, Michaela Rynn, Walter Lee IV. With LuVel Dairy Products, Inc., Kosciusko, Miss., 1949—, treas., 1953—, chmn. bd., 1967—. Chmn. Kosciusko Planning Commn., 1966—, Kosciusko Redevel. Authority, 1969—. Bd. dirs. Andrew Jackson council Boy Scouts Am. Served with Inf., AUS, 1943-45. Decorated Purple Heart with three oak leaf clusters, Bronze Star medal with oak leaf cluster, Silver Star. Mem. Am. Dairy Products (mem. exec. com. 1968—, bd. dirs.), Miss. (mem. exec. com. 1962-72, pres.), Dixie (bd. dirs.) dairy products assns., Am. Legion, V.F.W., Miss. Econ. Council (v.p. 1974), Miss. State U. Alumni Council (dist. pres. 1967-69), Kosciusko-Attala C. of C. (pres. 1963), Miss. Art Assn. (dir.). Methodist (chmn. finance com., long range planning com. 1968-69). Rotarian (bd. dirs.), Moose. Home: 331 E Adams St Kosciusko MS 39090 Office: 926 Hwy 35 South Kosciusko MS 39090

ELLIS, WILLIAM C., nutritionist, educator; b. Clay, La., Apr. 23, 1931; s. James M. and Ledie Eddie (Wilhite) E.; B.S., La. Poly. Inst., 1953; M.S., U. Mo., 1955, Ph.D., 1958; m. Bobbie L. Scroggin, Aug. 7, 1955; children—Linda Louise, Pamela Anne, William Keith. Asst. prof. U. Mo., Columbia, 1958-59; mem. faculty Tex. A. and M. U., College Station, 1960—, asso. prof. animal sci., 1962-70, prof., 1970—. NATO postdoctoral fellow, Rowett Research Inst., Scotland, 1959-60. Mem. Am. Soc. Animal Sci., Am. Inst. Nutrition.

Methodist. Home: 2520 Willowbend St Bryan TX 77801 Office: Dept Animal Science Texas A and M University College Station TX 77843

ELLISON, ARNOLD DANIEL, assn. exec.; b. Charleston, S.C., Mar. 4, 1917; s. Charles and Frances Lillian (Reisman) E.; A.B., U. N.C., 1937, M.A., 1940; m. Anne Witten, Sept. 11, 1943; children—Paula (Mrs. Richard Woolf), Elaine M. (Mrs. Jeffrey Rittenbaum). Research fellow La. State U., 1938; dist. membership dir. Dist. Grand Lodge, B'nai B'rith, Atlanta, 1956-63, exec. sec., 1963-67, exec. dir., 1967-69, exec. v.p., 1969—. Mem. tech. adv. com., Fulton and DeKalb Counties, 1965-68. Trustee Leo N. Levi Meml. Hosp., Hot Springs, Ark., Nat. Jewish Hosp., Denver. Served with inf. AUS, 1941-45; ETO. Mem. Pi Sigma Alpha. Mem. B'nai B'rith. Author: History of Civil Service in North Carolina, 1939. Home: Office: 805 Peachtree St NE Atlanta GA 30308

ELLISON, MARLON LOUIS, biologist, educator; b. Woodbine, Ia., Dec. 18, 1916; s. Russel and Adeline Eliza (Mefford) E.; B.S., Ia. State U., 1940; M.S., Trinity U., San Antonio, 1961; Ph.D., U. Kan., 1964; m. Johnetta E. Perry, Apr. 30, 1949. Commd. 1st lt., U.S. Army, 1940, advanced through grades to lt. col., 1960; ret., 1960; mem. faculty. U. Tampa (Fla.), 1960—, asso. prof. biology, 1967-70, prof., 1970—. Home: 5125 San Jose St Tampa FL 33609

ELLISON, RALPH ARNOLD, elec. engr.; b. San Antonio, June 7, 1909; s. Webster Jennings and Eunice (Arnold) E.; B.S., Auburn U., 1929; m. Alyne Roden, July 7, 1951; children—Jean (Mrs. William W. Arrants), Ralph Arnold. Design engr. TVA, Chattanooga, 1946-52, supr. design sect., 1952-69, ret., 1969. Served to col. AUS, 1941-45. Decorated Bronze Star. Mem. Nat. Soc. Profl. Engrs., I.E.E.E. Club: Sertoma. Home: 3503 Missionaire Av Chattanooga TN 37412

ELLISON, THORLEIF, engr.; b. Lyngdal, Norway, May 13, 1902; s. Andreas Emanuel and Gemalie (Svensen) E.; C.E., Christianie Coll. Tech., 1924; postgrad. George Washington U., U. Va.; m. Reidun Ingeborg Skonhoft, Jan. 1, 1932; children—Earl Otto, Thorleif Glenn, Sonja Karen. Came to U.S., 1928, naturalized, 1933. Supervising engr. Gen. Services Adminstrn., Washington, 1948-57; supervising airport and airways service engr. FAA, 1957-61, chief airways engring. AID, Iran, West Pakistan, Turkey, 1961-67; cons. engr., Washington, Va., 1942—; mission dir. Bethlehem, Israel, Holy Land Christian Mission, Kansas City, 1968-71. Active Christian Bus. Man's Com., Washington, Boy Scouts. Mem. Nat. Soc. Profl. Engrs. (officer), Sons of Norway (pres. Washington chpt.), Norwegian Soc. (treas.). Presbyn. (ruling elder). Home: Svennevik Rosfjord 4580 Lyngdal Norway also 6324 Telegraph Rd Alexandria VA 22310

ELLISTON, LURA DUFF (MRS. FRED ADDISON ELLISTON), club woman; b. Leesville, La., May 28, 1907; d. James Edward and Kate (Williamson) Duff; B.A. summa cum laude, Rice Inst., 1928; m. Fred Addison Elliston, May 21, 1932 (dec. 1970); 1 dau., Lura Elliston Remes. Pres., Jr. Woman's Club, Ft. Worth, 1933-34, Thursday Study Club, Ft. Worth, 1950-51, Friday Lecture Club, Ft. Worth, 1955-56, 61-62; mem. Round Table, Ft. Worth, Tex. Christian U. Fine Arts Found. Guild, Ft. Worth; founder J.E. Duff Fund, Ft. Worth; v.p. Ft. Worth Opera Assn. Bd. dirs. Opera Guild, Ft. Worth, 1950—, Community Theatre, 1963—, Ft. Worth Art Assn., 1967—; bd. dirs. William Edrington Scott Theatre, 1965— (with husband) named patron of arts, 1967, chmn. theater bd., 1968—. Republican. Mem. Christian Ch. Home: 2222 Winton Terrace E Fort Worth TX 76109

ELMORE, CARROLL DENNIS, agronomist; b. Pheba, Miss., Apr. 3, 1940; s. Clarence Wilson and Nadine (Berry) E.; B.S., Miss. State U., 1962; M.S., U. Ariz., 1966; Ph.D. (NSF traineeship), U. Ill., 1970. Research physiologist cotton physiology research lab. U.S. Dept. Agr., Stoneville, Miss., 1970—. Served to lt. AUS, 1962-64. Mem. Genetics Soc. Am., Am. Soc. Agronomy, Am. Soc. Plant Physiologists, A.A.A.S., Am. Inst. Biol. Scis., Sigma Xi, Scabbard and Blade, Blue Key, Alpha Zeta, Phi Eta Sigma, Omicron Delta Kappa. Home: 910 6th St Leland MS 38756 Office: PO Box 225 Stoneville MS 38776

ELMQUIST, KARL ERIK, educator; b. Evanston, Ill., Jan. 7, 1912; s. Axel Louis and Minna Louise (Harter) E.; B.A., So. Meth. U., 1932; postgrad. U. Chgo., 1932-35; M.A., U. Tex., 1939, postgrad. 1948-50; postgrad. U. Mich. Linguistic Inst., summer 1950; m. Anne Marie Siegel, Feb. 23, 1943; children—Judy Angela, Mark Paul, John Peter, James Martin. Instr., YWCA, Dallas, 1931-32; student asst. So. Meth. U., Dallas, 1931-32; fellow dept. English, U. Chgo., 1934-35; instr. English, Tex. A & M U., College Station, 1935-39, asst. prof., 1941-43, 1945-47, asso. prof. English, 1947—, dir. continuing edn. writing clinics, 1969—; dir. writing clinic New Careers U.S. Dept. Labor, Austin, 1971; instr. North Park Coll., Chgo., 1939-40; research analyst U.S. War Dept., Washington, 1941-43; mem. Grad. Faculty Tex. A & M U.; dir. writing workshops Agrl. Stblzn. and Cons. Service, U.S. Dept. Agr., 1970—. Served to capt. AUS, 1943-45. Recipient Battalion student newspaper awards for debate coaching and supervising student publs., 1948, 57. Mem. Linguistic Soc. Am., Nat. Council Tchrs. English, Tex. Council Tchr. English (publs. editor 1967-68), Conf. Coll. Tchrs. English (Tex.), Am. Assn. U. Profs., Tex. Assn. Coll. Tchrs., Phi Kappa Phi, Sigma Delta Chi, Alpha Theta Phi. Editor: Texas Aggie, part-time 1955-66. Contbr. articles to profl. jours. Home: Drawer H College Station TX 77840

ELMS, BILL GEORGE, accountant; b. Savanna, Okla., June 2, 1935; s. Clarence L. and D. Lorene (Key) E.; A.B., Odessa Coll., 1954; m. Anita Childress, Aug. 6, 1953; children—Tracy K., Terri L., Clark C., Steven W. Partner, Faris, Chapman & Marsh, Odessa, Tex., 1961-65, Chapman, Stroka & Elms, C.P.A.'s, Odessa, 1965-68, Bill Elms & Co., C.P.A.'s, Odessa, 1968-71; mng. partner Elms, Faris & Co., C.P.A.'s, 1971—; pres., dir. Panaquad, Inc., Odessa, 1967—; sec.-treas., dir. Cone & Kerley, Inc., Odessa, 1968—, Gibson Products Co., San Angelo, Tex., 1967—; sec.-treas. Panaquad Oil Co.; pres., dir. Gibson Products Co., Monahans, Tex., 1968—, Gibson Products Co., Newnan, Ga., Gibson Products Co., Kermit, Tex. County commr. Ector County, Tex., 1969—; dir. Home Savs. Assn., 1972—. Treas., Permian Playhouse of Odessa, 1967-69; pres. Odessa Beautiful Assn., 1966-67; v.p. Ector County United Fund, 1971—. Bd. dirs., v.p. Odessa Boys Clubs, 1965-69. Mem. Am. Inst. C.P.A.'s, Tex. Soc. C.P.A.'s, Jr. C. of C. (pres. 1965-66), C. of C. (dir. 1965-66, 72—). Rotarian. Home: 3300 Sherbrook Country Club Estates Odessa TX 79763 Office: 1st National Bldg Odessa TX 79761

ELROD, PARKER DAVID, physician; b. Nashville, July 4, 1919; s. Lacy Huffman and Lucy Lillian (Jones) E.; B.A., Vanderbilt U., 1940, M.D., 1943; m. Sammye Louise Malone, Sept. 6, 1943; children—Anita Dawn, (Mrs. Clay Corley Whitelaw), Burton Folk, Walter Malone, Parker David. Intern, U.S. Marine Hosp., Norfolk, Va., 1944; resident thoracic surgery VA Hosp., Oteen, N.C., 1947-48, asst. resident surgery, Nashville, 1948-50; practice medicine specializing in surgery, Centerville, Tenn., 1952—; chief surgeon Hickman County Hosp., Centerville, 1964—, chief of staff, 1965—; chief surgeon Perry County Hosp., Linden, Tenn., 1956; staff Decatur County Hosp., 1960-70 Weathers Hosp., 1956-68, Nautilus Hosp., 1960-70, Goodlark Hosp., 1956-65; instr. surgery Vanderbilt Hosp., Nashville, 1948-60, asst. clin. prof., 1960—. Med. examiner Hickman County, Centerville, 1965—. Served with M.C., AUS, 1945-47. Diplomate Am. Bd. Surgery. Fellow Am. Coll. Surgeons, Southeastern Surg. Congress, Am. Coll. Chest Physicians (asso.); mem. Am., Tenn. med. assns., Buffalo River Med. Soc. Mem. Ch. of Christ (elder 1961—). Contbr. articles to profl. jours. Home: 110 W Swan St Centerville TN 37033 Office: 103 E Swan St Centerville TN 37033

ELSBERG, PAUL, physician; b. Warendorf, Westfalen, Germany, Apr. 9, 1907; s. David and Ricka (Windmueller) E.; student U. Vienna, 1927-28, U. Freiburg/Breisgau, 1928, U. Breslau, 1929-30; M.D., U. Giessen (Germany), 1932; student N.Y.U., 1942; m. Elizabeth M. Swartz, Jan. 30, 1943; children—Betty Lee (Mrs. William F. Hubbard), David Donald. Came to U.S., 1938, naturalized, 1943. Intern, Gen. Barmbeck Hosp., Hosp., Hamburg, Germany, 1933, Gen. Hosp., Saranac Lake, N.Y., 1938-40; intern Emergency Hosp., Washington, 1940-41, resident anesthesiology, 1941-43; pvt. practice medicine, specializing in anesthesiology, Washington, 1943—; chmn. dept. obstetrical anesthesiology Garfield Hosp., Washington, 1954-57; mem. exec. and teaching staff Doctor's Hosp., Washington, 1958—, mem. post-grad. edn. com., 1969—. Bd. dirs., violinist Alexandria (Va.) Symphony Orch. Mem. Royal Soc. Medicine (Eng.), N.Y. Acad. Scis., Am., So. med. assns., Am. Soc. Anesthesiologists, D.C. Med. Soc., D.C. Soc. Anesthesiology, Washington Heart Assn. Club: Old Dominion Boat Club (Alexandria, Va.). Home: 914 Timber Branch Pkwy Alexandria VA 22302 Office: 1815 Eye St NW Washington DC 10005

ELSILA, DAVID AUGUST, editor; b. Detroit, Feb. 2, 1939; s. Edward J. and Sylvia (Mikkola) E.; B.A., Eastern Mich. U., 1960, postgrad., 1962; m. Kathlyn Deutch, July 17, 1965. Tchr. pub. schs., Livonia, Mich., 1960-64; editor-in-chief Livonia Observer, 1964-65; dir. publs., editor Am. Tchr., also Changing Edn., Am. Fedn. Tchrs., Washington, 1965—. Editor ofcl. publs. Am. Civil Liberties Union, Ill., Mich., 1964-67. Recipient Page 1 award Chgo. Newspaper Guild, 1967, 1st awards in Journalism, Internat. Labor Press Assn., 1968, 69, Ednl. Press Assn. Am., 1968. Mem. Washington-Balt. Newspaper Guild (exec. bd.), Ednl. Press Assn. Am. (pres. Washington chpt., 1971, treas. 1968), Am. Civil Liberties Union, Phi Delta Kappa. Home: 1754 Kenyon St NW Washington DC 20010 Office: 1012 14th St NW Washington DC 20005

ELSON, QUIN SAMUEL, judge; b. Washington, Apr. 23, 1935; s. Samuel Jacob and Dorothy Louise (Quinn) E.; B.A., George Washington U., 1956, LL.B., 1959; m. Mary Gretchen Mayers, June 29, 1965; children—Stacie L., Samuel L. Admitted to Va. bar, 1959; practice law, Fairfax, Va., 1959-61; with Commonwealth's Atty. Office, Fairfax County, Va., 1961-64; prosecutor City Fairfax, Va., 1964-68; judge Municipal Ct., Fairfax, 1968-73; judge Gen. Dist. Ct., Fairfax, 1973—. Instr. criminal law Am. U. No. Va. Police Acad., 1967-70. Chmn. City Fairfax Hwy. Safety Commn., 1968; mem. Alcohol Safety Action Project Adv. Com., 1971-73; mem. Criminal Justice Adv. Council No. Va., 1970-73. Chmn. Young Dems. 10th Congl. Dist., 1965-66. Served with AUS, 1959. Named Citizen of Year Fairfax C. of C., 1968, Outstanding Young Man, 1970. Mem. Am., Va., Fairfax County (sec. 1962-63, mem. com. 1973—) bar assns., Nat. Dist. Attys. Assn., Am., No. Va. trial lawyers assns. Club: Corinthian Yacht (Ridge, Md.). Home: 10108 Alice Ct Fairfax VA 22030 Office: 4150 Chainbridge Rd Fairfax VA 22030

ELVOVE, JOSEPH TEVYA, resort and land devel. exec.; b. Washington, Aug. 19, 1914; s. Elias and Etta (Milatiner) E.; B.S., U. Md., 1934, M.A., 1936; postgrad. Harvard, 1940-41. Dep. dir. sugar div. U.S. Dept. Agr., Washington, 1936-50; dept. head W. R. Grace & Co., N.Y.C., 1950-52; exec. v.p. dir. Pacific Molasses Co., San Francisco, N.Y.C., 1952-63; v.p. Savannah Food Industries, Inc. (Ga.), 1963-71; pres. Resort Cons., Harbor Ventures Ltd. (both Hilton Head, S.C.), 1970—; v.p. Calibogue Properties, Inc.; cons. Sea Pines Co., Hilton Head, 1970—; dir. Stevens Shipping & Terminal Co., Atlantic Towing Co., 1968-71. Trustee Historic Savannah Found., Telfair Acad. Arts and Scis. Served with USNR, 1942-45. Republican. Episcopalian. Clubs: Sugar, India House (N.Y.); Oglethorpe; Chatham (Savannah, Ga.); Plantation (Hilton Head Island, S.C.). Home: Sea Pines Plantation Hilton Head Island SC 29928 Office: Sea Pines Co Hilton Head Island SC 29928

ELWOOD, WILLIAM KENT, educator; b. Ashtabula, O., Oct. 15, 1928; s. Price Alonzo and Alta May (MacDowell) E.; B.A., Ohio Wesleyan U., 1950; M.S., Ohio State U., 1953, D.D.S., 1957; Ph.D., Wayne State U., 1965; m. Persis Townsend, Dec. 22, 1956; children—Persis, Holly, Bryan. Research asso. Henry Ford Hosp., Detroit, 1957-65; NIH spl. fellow, guest investigator Rockefeller U., N.Y.C., 1965-66; asst. prof. anatomy Med. Center, U. Ky., Lexington, 1966-72, asst. prof. restorative dentistry, 1966-70, asst. prof. oral biology, 1970-72, asso. prof. anatomy Coll. Medicine, 1972—, asso. prof. oral biology Coll. Dentistry, 1972—. Mem. Am. Assn. Anatomy, Internat. Assn. Dental Research, Am. Soc. Cell Biology, Electron Microscopy Soc. Am., Ky. Dental Assn., Am. Assn. Dental Schs., Bluegrass Dental Soc., Sigma Xi, Alpha Sigma Phi, Delta Sigma Delta, Omicron Kappa Upsilon. Contbr. articles to profl. jours. Home: 755 Bravington Way Lexington KY 40503

ELY, MARICA MCCANN (MRS. NORTHCUTT ELY), interior designer, lectr.; b. Pachuca, Mexico (parents Am. citizens); d. Warner and Mary (Cook) McCann; B.A., U. Cal. at Berkeley, 1929; grad. interior design Pratt Inst. Art, 1931; prof. Ikebana, Sogetsu Sch., Tokyo, Japan, 1969; m. Northcutt Ely, Dec. 2, 1931; children—Michael N., Craig N., Parry Haines. Past pres. Kenwood Garden Club, Md.; art editor Nat. Capital Garden Club League Flower Arrangement Calendar, Washington, 1957-58; lectr. on flower arranging. Bd. dirs. Washington Hearing Soc., 1969-70; co-founder Delta Gamma Found. for Visually Handicapped; bd. dirs. Nat. Library for Blind, Washington. Finalist Jackson Perkins Nat. Silver Bowl Flower Arrangement Competition, 1966. Recipient Order of Delta Gamma Rose, 1968. Mem. Internat. Platform Assn., Bot. Soc. South Africa, Ikebana Internat., Delta Gamma. Clubs: Berkeley Tennis of California; Chevy Chase; Washington Women's Home: 4200 Massachusetts Av Washington DC 20016

ELY, RICHARD EUGENE, mech. engr.; b. Kalamazoo, Mich., Sept. 26, 1922; s. Walter Morley and Mary Adine (Schricker) E.; B.S. in Mech. Engring., U. Ala., 1948, M.S., 1957; m. Mary Ann Funk, Feb. 15, 1946; children—Madelynn A., Melynda A. Test engr. Stewart-Warner Corp., Indpls., 1948-50; intermediate scientist Rohm & Haas Co., Redstone Arsenal, Ala., 1950-54; supervisory research aerospace engr. U.S. Army Missile Command, Redstone Arsenal, 1954—. Instr. mechanics U. Ala., Huntsville, 1956-58. Served with AUS, 1942-45. Mem. Soc. Exptl. Stress Analysis, Am. Soc. M.E. (sectional chmn. 1957-58; vice chmn. 1956-57), Tau Beta P', Pi Tau Sigma, Theta Tau. Contbr. articles to profl. jours. Patentee in field. Home: 1204 Stonehurst Dr Huntsville AL 35801 Office: US Army Missile Command Redstone Arsenal AL 35809

ELY, THOMAS SOUTHGATE, physician; b. Jonesville, Va., June 8, 1914; s. Thomas Bascom and Jennie (Edds) E.; A.B. magna cum laude, Emory and Henry Coll., 1935; M.D., Med. Coll. Va., 1939; m. Barbara Ellen Dixon, Sept. 7, 1940; children—Thomas Harrison, Maria Jane. Intern hosp. div. Med. Coll. Va., 1939-40; practice gen. medicine, Jonesville, 1945—; med. examiner, coroner Lee County, Va. Pres. Jonesville Drug Co., Inc., 1951—; dir. Powell Valley Nat. Bank, Jonesville, Lee Farmers' Tobacco Warehouse, Pennington Gap, Va. Chmn. Jefferson Forest dist. Boy Scouts Am., commr. Wilderness Rd. dist., 1970—, Silver Beaver award, 1972, Pioneer award, 1973. Chmn. Jonesville Town Planning and Zoning Com., Lee County Sch. Electoral Bd.; med. adviser Lee County Selective Service Bd., 1964—. Bd. trustees Holston Conf. Colls., 1961—; exec. com. Emory and Henry Coll., 1962-70. Served to maj. M.C., AUS, 1941-46; ETO, N. Africa. Decorated N. Africa-ETO medal with 7 battle stars; recipient De Molay Legion of Honor, 1970. Fellow Am. Acad. Gen. Practice; mem. Am. Legion (local post positions to dept. comdr., dept. rehab. chmn., nat. med. adv. bd., vice chmn. nat. legislative Commn.; nat. exec. committeeman from Va.), 40 and 8 (life, cheminot nat. 1958-59), Lee County C. of C. (organizer, pres. pro-tem., dir.), Lee County Med. Soc. (past sec.-treas., (past pres.), Med. Soc. Va., A.M.A., Emory and Henry Alumni Assn. (pres. 1963-69), The Cabiri, Blue Key, Tau Kappa Alpha, Pi Gamma Mu, Kappa Phi Kappa, Theta Kappa Psi, Sigma Zeta. Methodist (chmn. bd. stewards, lay leader, chmn. bd. trustees, pres. dist. laymen's orgn. 1959-60, mem. bd. hosps. and instns. Holstein Conf.). Mason (K.T., 32 deg., Shriner, Jester), Odd Fellow, Woodman of World; mem. Order Eastern Star (past patron). Club: Lions (past pres. Jonesville; zone chmn. 1959-60; dist. gov. 1961-62; internat. counsellor 1962—, Lion of Year, Achievement award). Address: PO Box 115 Jonesville VA 24263

EL-ZIK, KAMAL MILAD, geneticist; b. Cairo, Egypt, June 10, 1932; s. Milad L. and Helene T. (Hanna) El-Z.; B.S., Alexandria U., 1952, M.S., 1960; Ph.D., Tex. A. and M. U., 1967; m. Daphne G. Economides, Aug. 27, 1953; 1 dau., Marlene. Came to U.S., 1962, naturalized, 1974. Research asso. Tex. A. and M. U., 1966-68, postdoctoral fellow, 1968-69; v.p. research Lockett Seed Co., Vernon, Tex., 1969—. Mem. Am. Phytopathological Soc., Am. Soc. Agronomy, Crop Sci. Soc. Am., Am. Genetic Assn., Sigma Xi, Gamma Sigma Delta. Rotarian. Contbr. articles to profl. jours. Home: PO Box 1723 Vernon TX 76384 Office: PO Box 1579 Vernon TX 76384

EMBREE, MARTHA LOUISE, organic chem. mfg. co. exec.; b. Houston, Nov. 30, 1936; d. Elisha D. and Alma (Bedell) Embree; B.F.A., U. Houston, 1958. Copy trainee, prodn. mgr. Erwin Wasey Advt., Houston, 1959-60; film mgr., prodn. asst. KPRC-TV, Houston, 1960-62; copy chief R.S. Townsend Advt., Kansas City, Mo., 1962-63; advt. asst. Chemagro, Kansas City, 1963-66; free lance copywriter, 1966-68; marketing asst. Glidden-Durkee div. SCM Corp., Jacksonville, Fla., 1968-70, supr. advt., 1970-71, mgr. communications, 1971—. Mem. N.E. Fla. Bus. Communicators (1st v.p. 1970-71, pres. 1971-72), Advt. Fedn. Jacksonville (chmn. bull. 1971-72, dir. 1972-74). Home: Jacksonville FL 32250 Office: PO Box 389 Jacksonville FL 32201

EMBRY, CARLOS BROGDON, newspaper pub.; b. Baizetown, Ky., Jan. 21, 1906; s. Marion Armstrong and Lola (Albin) E.; A.B., Western Ky. U., 1929; student U. Ariz., 1949-50; m. Zora Romans, June 30, 1940; children—Jane Carroll (Mrs. Morris J. Hardwick, Jr.), Carlos Brogdon. Prin. jr. high sch., Bulloch County, Ga., 1926-27, Lynnvale High Sch., White Mills, Ky., 1928-29; owner-pub. Ohio County Messenger, Beaver Dam, Ky., 1930—; pres. Embry Newspapers, Inc., Beaver Dam; builder, owner Embry's Valley Shopping Center. Beaver Dam; pres. Kentucky Weekly Newspaper Assn., 1967-68, chmn. bd. dirs., 1968-69, v.p. legislation, 1969—. Dir. Ky. Republican Com., 1944; mem. Ky. Senate, 10th dist., 1945-49; mem. Ohio County Bd. Election Commrs., 1973—. Recipient Ky. Statesman award, 1964; Ky. Col. Mem. Beaver Dam Bd. Trade, Ky. Hist. Soc. Baptist. Clubs: Lions (Beaver Dam); Filson. Author: America's Concentration Camps—The Facts About Our Indian Reservations Today, 1956; Beaver Dam and the Green Valley, 1970. Contbr. articles mags. and newspapers. Home: 211 N Main St Beaver Dam KY 42320 Office: 220 N Main St Beaver Dam KY 42320

EMERSON, DAVID EDWIN, chemist; b. Checotah, Okla., May 15, 1932; s. David Ervin and Della Elizabeth (Fennell) E.; B.S. in Chemistry, S.E. State Coll., 1955; m. Ermyne Faith Snodgrass, Aug. 21, 1953; children—Joe David, Sally Gayle, Terry William. Civilian instr. USAF, Amarillo, Tex., 1955-57; chemist U.S. Bur. Mines, Helium Research Center, Amarillo, 1957-59, supr. chemist, 1959-62, chief br. lab. services, 1962-71, chief unit tech. services, 1971—. Dist. distbr. Amway Corp., Amarillo, 1970—; owner and glassblower S.W. Glassblowing Lab., Amarillo, 1965—. Served with AUS, 1956-62. Mem. Am. Chem. Soc., Am. Soc. Mass Spectrometry. Contbr. articles to profl. jours. Patentee in field. Home: Route 2 Box 43V1B4 Amarillo TX 79101 Office: PO Box H4372 Amarillo TX 79101

EMERSON, HORACE MANN III, r.r. exec.; b. Wilmington, N.C., Jan. 22, 1914; s. Horace Mann and Laura Placida (Clark) E.; student pub. and pvt. schs., Sumter, Columbia, S.C.; m. Susan LeRoy Carr, June 1, 1943; children—Susan C. (Mrs. Nicholas H. Bancks), Laura C. Clk., A.C.L. R.R., Wilmington, N.C., 1934-47, gen. agt., Jacksonville, Fla., 1947-51, asst. gen. freight agt., Wilmington, N.C., 1952-57, asst. treas., 1957-58, treas., Wilmington and Jacksonville, 1958-61, asst. v.p. traffic, 1961-67; sr. asst. v.p. traffic Seaboard Coast Line R.R. Co., Jacksonville, 1967-68, v.p. freight traffic, 1968-73; sr. v.p. traffic S.C.L. Industries, 1973—; sr. v.p., dir. S.C.L. R.R., Louisville & Nashville R.R.; chief traffic officer Ga. R.R., A.&W.P. R.R., W. Ry. of A., C.C.&O. R.R., 1973—; dir. Central R.R. Co. S.C., Columbia, Newberry & Laurens R.R., Seacoast Transp. Co., S.C. Pacific Ry. Co. Served to capt. U.S. Army, 1946-52. Mem. Assn. ICC Practitioners, Nat. Freight Traffic Assn., Fla. Traffic Assn., N.Y. Traffic Club, Jackson Area C. of C. Democrat. Episcopalian (mem. vestry 1970—). Clubs: Timuquana Country, River, University, Meninak, Ponte Vedra (Jacksonville, Fla.). Home: 4805 King Richard Rd Jacksonville FL 32210 Office: 500 Water St Jacksonville FL 32202

EMERSON, KARY CADMUS, biologist, govt. ofcl.; b. Sasakwa, Okla., Mar. 13, 1918; s. Earle Evans and Diva (Wilkins) E.; B.S., Okla. State U., 1939, M.S., 1940, Ph.D., 1949; m. Mary Rebecca Williams, Aug. 13, 1939; children—William K., James B., Robert E. Joined U.S. Army, 1940, advanced through grades to col., 1962, instr. U.S. Army Command and Staff Coll., 1955-58, ret., 1966; asst. for research to the asst. sec. of the Army, 1961—, acting dep. asst. sec. for research and devel., 1973—. Adj. prof. Okla. State U., 1971—. Mem. U.N. Mil. Armistice Commn. in Korea, 1958-59. Dir. Biol. Soc. of Washington, Research asso. Smithsonian Inst., 1959—. U.S. mem. NATO Panel for long term Sci. Studies, 1970—. Decorated Bronze Star medal, Purple Heart, Legion of Merit. Recipient Outstanding Civilian award Army Dept., 1973. Fellow Washington Acad. Sci.; mem. Am. Soc. Parasitologists, Am. Soc. Tropical Medicine and Hygiene, Wildlife Disease Assn., Entomol. Soc. Am., Biol. Soc. Wash., Entomol. Soc. Washington, Am. Inst. Biol. Scis., A.A.A.S., Sigma Xi, Alpha Zeta. Club: Cosmos. Contbr articles in field to profl. jours. Home: 2704 N Kensington Arlington VA 22207 Office: Office Sec of the Army Washington DC 20310

EMERSON, MARVIN CHESTER, lawyer, state ofcl.; b. Cromwell, Okla., Dec. 28, 1928; s. Earle Evans and Diva (Wilkins) E.; B.A., U. Okla., 1950, LL.B., 1953; m. George Etta Killingsworth, Feb. 7, 1954;

children—Mary Caroline, George Marvin. Admitted to Okla. bar, 1953; practiced in Coalgate, Okla., 1953-55; county atty. Coal County (Okla.), 1955-56; asst. county atty. Pontotoc County (Okla.), 1956-57; asst. dir. State Soil Conservation Bd., Oklahoma City, 1957-61, exec. dir., 1961-71; first asst. atty. gen., Okla., 1971—. Served with USAAF, 1946-47. Named Outstanding Soil Conservationist in Okla., Okla. chpt. Nat. Wildlife Fedn., 1965. Mem. Okla. Bar Assn. Mason (32deg.).Home: 7216 Comanche Av Oklahoma City OK 73132 Office: Atty Gens Office State Capitol Oklahoma City OK 73105

EMERSON, MAXWELL, ret. army officer, educator; b. Newton Center, Mass., Mar. 25, 1903; s. Howard and Ada (Maxwell) E.; student Dartmouth, 1921-23; B.S.C., Roosevelt U., 1957; M.A., Memphis State U., 1960; m. Mary Byram Millet Aug. 18, 1927; 1 son, David M.; m. 2d, Dorothy Jane Kerr, Aug. 1, 1945; 1 dau., June Alice. Plantation overseer United Fruit Co., Guatemala, 1924-26; store mgr. Loft, Inc., Newark, 1927-32; sales dept. Shell Oil Co., N.Y.C., 1933-38; commd. 2d lt. U.S. Army, 1938; advanced through grades to col., 1950; q.m. worldwide assignments, ret., 1958; asst. prof. mgmt. Memphis State U. Coll. Bus. Adminstrn., 1960-72. Decorated Silver Star, Bronze Star medal, Army Commendation medal with oak leaf cluster. Mem. Def. Supply Assn., Mayflower Soc. (dep. gov. gen. 1973—), S.A.R. (pres. Tenn. 1970-71, pres. Memphis chpt. 1968-69), Descs. Colonial Clergy, Tenn. Soc. Colonial Wars (sec.), New Eng. Hist.-Geneal. Soc., Mil. Order World Wars (nat. staff 1940), Mil. Order Fgn. Wars (comdr. Tenn. commandery 1972—), Descs. Colonial Govs., Tenn. Huguenot Soc., Baronial Order Magna Carta, Order Crown of Charlemagne in U.S., Order Colonial Lords Manors in Am., Adam Hawkes Family Assn., Stetson Kindred, Nat. Soc. Ams. Royal Descent, Delta Sigma Pi, Phi Sigma Kappa. Methodist. Mason. Home: 223 Lorece Lane Memphis TN 38117

EMERSON, O. D., accountant; b. Hillsboro, Tex., June 25, 1909; s. Ollie D. and Sudie (Johnson) E.; B.B.A., Baylor U., 1932; spl. courses LaSalle U., also the N.Y. Univ.; m. Myrtle Mae Hennigan, Feb. 17, 1933; 1 son Philip Edward. Disbursing officer Tex. Relief Commn., 1933-36; agt. U.S. Bur. Internal Revenue, 1936-45; pub. accounting O. D. Emerson, Jr., C.P.A., Hattiesburg and McComb, Miss., 1945-61, Emerson & Emerson, C.P.A.'s, Hattiesburg, Columbia and McComb, Miss., 1961—; sec., treas. Pearl River Land Co.; dir. S. Miss. Oil Corp. Meridian Vendors, Inc. Former lectr. accounting U. So. Miss. Trustee St. Bernard Hosp. Mem. Am. Inst. Accts., Tex., Miss. socs. C.P.A.'s. Methodist. Mason. Club: Metropolitan. Home: Route 3 Box 118 Sumrall MS 39482 Office: 610 W Pine St Hattiesburg MS 39401

EMERSON, ROBERT BISCAL, chemist, physicist; b. Nashville, Mar. 17, 1909; s. Winiford Frank and Roberta (Griffith) E.; M.S., La. State U., 1950; grad. Army Command and Gen. Staff Coll., 1948; m. Opal Lynelle Duke, Nov. 3, 1934; children—Robert B., Jin. Commd. 2d lt. U.S. Army, 1935, advanced through grades to col., 1952; mem. Spearhead Planning Staff, 1944, top secret control officer, 1944-46, G-4 Base sect., ETO, 1944-46, dir. command and gen. staff dept. U.S. Army Res. Sch., 1951-57, instr. or dir. for command and gen. staff subjects, Ft. Sill, Okla., 1953-57, Ft. Sam Houston, Tex., 1957, comdg. officer 4225 Logistical Command (C), 1957-62; ret., 1962; asst. to forensic chemist State of Fla., Tampa, 1926; control chemist Victor Chem. Works, Nashville, 1927; chief chemist Fla. Match Co., St. Petersburg, 1928-29; owner Emerson Testing Labs., St. Petersburg, 1930-38; forensic chemist State of Fla., St. Petersburg, 1930-36; asso. chemist Gable Clin. Labs., St. Petersburg, 1930-38, Hurst Labs., St. Petersburg, 1936-38; owner Emerson Testing Labs., Baton Rouge, 1948—; physics instr. La. State U., 1948-53; sr. research chemist, staff research asso. Chem. Aluminas, Kaiser Chems., Baton Rouge, 1953-74. Decorated Legion of Merit, Bronze Star medal. Mem. Am. Phys. Soc., Am. Chem. Soc., T.A.P.P.I., A.A.A.S., Inst. Fundamental Studies Assn., Internat. Platform Assn., Community Leaders Am., So. Rubber Group, Catalysis Soc., Mil. Order of World Wars, Am. Theosophical Soc., Inst. Psychorientology, Inst. Noetic. Scis., Am. Bicentennial Research Inst., Nat. Ret. Tchrs. Assn., Am. Parapsychology Research Found., Acad. Parapsychology, Am. Soc. Psychical Research, Army Transport Soc., Nat. Assn. Uniformed Services, Nat. Investigations Com. Aerial Phenomena, Phi Eta Sigma, Phi Lambda Upsilon, Phi Kappa Phi, Sigma Pi Sigma. Patentee in field. Home: 1560 Stephens Av Baton Rouge LA 70808 Office: 1560 Stephens Av Baton Rouge LA 70808

EMERY, FRED JOSEPH, govt. ofcl.; b. Buffalo, Oct. 12, 1933; s. Frederick Mead and Frances (Dahlem) E.; A.B., Union Coll., 1954; LL.B., Albany Law Sch., 1957; m. Lola Louise Meyer, Apr. 6, 1958; children—Jean, Alan, Andrew. Admitted to N.Y. bar, 1957; legal cons. Dept. Audit and Control, N.Y. State, Albany, 1958, atty. Bd. Equalization and Assessment, 1959-63; atty. FAA, 1963-67, chief Air Carrier and Ops. br., Gen. Counsel's Office, Washington, 1967-68; dep. asst. gen. counsel for regulations Transp. Dept., 1968-70, dir. sec. adminstrv. com. Fed. Register, Gen. Services Adminstrn., 1970—. Served to 2d lt. USAF, 1957-58, 61-62. Mem. Fed., Am., N.Y. State bar assns. Home: 3526 Quesada St NW Washington DC 20015 Office: Nat Archives Bldg 18th and F Sts NW Washington DC 20408

EMERY, WILLIAM VANDERBILT, III, judge; b. Harrisburg, Pa., May 21, 1936; s. William V. and Gimmie Lu (Ronalder) E.; B. in Engring., Vanderbilt U., 1958; J.D., U. Miami, 1968; m. Carolyn Joyce Crews, Aug. 23, 1958; children—Mark William, Jonathan David, Matthew Denton. Engr. Fla. Power & Light Co., Daytona Beach, 1958-61, Miami, 1961-68; admitted to Fla. bar, 1968; practiced in Daytona Beach, 1968-69, Ormond Beach, Fla., 1969—; mem. firm Gosnay, Emery & Hutcheson, 1968-69, William V. Emery III, 1969—; municipal judge City Ormond Beach, Fla., 1973—. Instr. gen. aviation and aviation law Embry-Riddle Aero. U., Daytona Beach, Fla., 1971-72; dir. Two-Fifty Bldg. Corp., Ormond Beach, Fla., Daytona Beach Track Club, Inc., Daytona Beach Aviation, Inc., Comdr. Aviation, Inc., Ormond Beach. Served with AUS, 1958-59. Registered profl. engr., Fla. Mem. Estate Planning Council Volusia County (v.p. 1972; sec. 1973, 1st v.p. 1974), Am., Fla. (mem. trial lawyers sect., real property, probate and trust sect.), Volusia County bar assns., Fla. Municipal Judge's Assn., Fla. Engring. Soc. (sr.), Nat. Soc. Profl. Engrs., Lawyers' Title Guaranty Fund, Delta Theta Phi. Mem. Christian Ch. Home: 16 Tanglewood Circle Ormond Beach FL 32074 Office: 434 N Halifax Dr Ormond Beach FL 32074

EMMET, RICHARD PERRINS, judge; b. Albertville, Ala., Apr. 13, 1929; s. Joseph H. and Nonna Rose (McMullen) E.; B.S., U. Ala., 1953, J.D., 1956; m. Elizabeth Thigpen, Oct. 22, 1956. Admitted to Ala. bar, 1956; circuit judge 15th Judicial Circuit, Montgomery, Ala., 1960—; organized Family Court Montgomery, 1960. Served with AUS, 1951-53; Korea. Recipient Outstanding Young Man Ala. award Jr. C. of C., 1962. Mem. Am. Legion, V.F.W. Presbyn. (elder). Mason, Lion. Home: 2324 Woodley Rd Montgomery AL 36111 Office: Courthouse 15th Judicial Circuit Montgomery AL 36102

EMMONS, RONALD REECE, accountant; b. Canton, Okla., Feb. 21, 1941; s. William Reece and Gladys (Prigmore) E.; B.S., U. Tulsa, 1963; m. Eleanor Gail Storey, June 1, 1962; children—Kevin Reece, William Bradford, Carrie Kathleen. Tax mgr. Arthur Andersen & Co., Tulsa, 1963-69, tax mgr., 1971—; treas., controller Ednl. Devel. Corp., Tulsa, 1969-71. Adj. prof. acctg. Tulsa U. Mem. Am. Inst. C.P.A.'s, Okla. Soc. C.P.A.'s, Tulsa U. Alumni Assn., Okla. Ofcls. Assn., N.G. Assn. Methodist (ofcl. bd.). Home: 3527 S Joplin Pl Tulsa OK 74135 Office: Fourth Nat Bank Bldg Tulsa OK 74119

EMMONS, WILLIAM REECE, finance ofcl.; b. Arnett, Okla., Feb. 20, 1915; s. Vernon LeRoy and Dollie (Platt) E.; B.S., Southwestern State Coll., Weatherford, Okla., 1938; postgrad. Tulsa U., 1961-64; m. Gladys Prigmore, June 5, 1937; children—Ronald Reece, Peggy Joyce (Mrs. William F. Combs). Tchr. bus. edn. Canton (Okla.) Pub. Schs., 1938-42; accountant Glenn R. Davis, C.P.A., Muskogee, Okla., 1947-54; agt. Internal Revenue Service, Tulsa, 1942-47, 54-60, field audit group supr., 1960-69, large case audit mgr., 1969—. Capt., Community Chest drive, 1967-68. C.P.A., Okla. Mem. Am. Inst. C.P.A.'s, Okla. Soc. C.P.A.'s, Delta Theta Phi. Methodist. Mason. Home: 5045 E Admiral Blvd Tulsa OK 74115 Office: 15 W 6th St Tulsa OK 74119

ENCK, RUDOLPH ROBERT, state ofcl.; b. Seguin, Tex., Jan. 7, 1910; s. Dan Henry and Setma (Weniger) E.; student Tex. Lutheran Coll., 1929-30; m. Myrtle Lorayne Teas, Dec. 25, 1931; 1 dau., Sandra Kay (Mrs. James Joseph West). Bookkeeper, Seguin Cotton Oil Co., 1930-41; with R.R. Commn. Tex., 1941—, dir. records services, Austin, 1963—. Hon. mem. Seguin (Tex.) Fire Dept. Named Boss of Year, Am. Bus. Womens Assn., 1963. Mem. Christian Ch. (bd. elders 1966-68). Home: 2402 Bridle Path Austin TX 78703 Office: Ernest O Thompson Bldg Austin TX 78711

ENDER, MAX WILLIAM, finance co. exec.; b. Odem, Tex., Oct. 22, 1934; s. Reinhold Gottfried and Anita Rose (Poldrack) E.; B.S., student Tex. Lutheran Coll., 1952-53, 55-56; U. Corpus Christi, 1958; m. Carolyn Delores Reeves, Dec. 24, 1958; children—Tanna Lynn, Tammie Laurie, Timothy William. Credit mgr. Universal CIT Credit Corp., Corpus Christi, Tex., 1958-61; br. mgr. Lamesa Fed. Savs. & Loan (Tex.), 1961-64; controller, sec., treas. Corpus Christi Savs. & Loan, 1964-66; examiner Fed. Home Loan Bank, Little Rock, 1966-67; sec., dir. First Fed. Savs. & Loan Assn., Marshall, Tex., 1967-70; v.p., sec. Marshall Fed. Savs. & Loan Assn., 1970-73; mng. officer Town E. Savs. & Loan Assn., Mesquite, Tex., 1973—; dir. First State Bank, Milford, Tex. Pres., United Fund, Seminole, Tex., 1963. Served with USMCR, 1953-54; Korea. Mem. Nat. Accountants Assn., Nat. Assn. Real Estate Appraisers, Am. Savs. and Loan Inst. (gov. 1970—), Seminole (pres. 1964), Seminole Jr. (pres. 1963) chambers commerce. Elk. Club: Marshall Lakeside Country. Home: 4413 Ivy St Mesquite TX 75149 Office: Town East Savings and Loan Assn Mesquite TX 75149

ENDSLEY, FRED ROBERT, educator; b. Moline, Ill., Aug. 17, 1930; s. Matt and Bessie (Erickson) E.; B.A., Grinnell Coll., 1952; M.B.A., Ind. U., 1958; Ph.D., La. State U., 1967; m. Peggy Ann Dupre, Sept. 13, 1953; children—Pamela Dawn, Kim Yvette. Mgr., Reliable Implement Store, Marshalltown, Ia., 1954-57; asst. prof. bus. U. Ga., Athens, 1958-60; asst. prof. mgmt. Eastern Ill. U., Charleston, 1963-64; instr. marketing La. State U., Baton Rouge, 1964-65, asst. prof. mgmt., marketing, 1969—, head corr. study dept., 1965-70, asst. dean Coll. Bus., 1970-72, asso. dean, 1972—, acting chmn. marketing dept., 1972-73. Vice pres. Econ. & Indsl. Research, Inc., 1971-73. Cons. mgmt., marketing. Mem. troop com. Boy Scouts Am., Baton Rouge, 1966-68. Served to 2d lt. USAF, 1952-54. Mem. Am. (faculty adviser 1969-70), So. marketing assns., Sales and Marketing Execs. Internat., Southwestern Social Sci. Assn., Nat. U. Extension Assn. (nat. sec.-treas. ind. study div. 1968-70), Red Red Rose, Delta Sigma Pi, Pi Sigma Epsilon, Beta Gamma Sigma. Methodist. Clubs: Rotary, Baton Rouge Advertising (hon.). Home: 3064 Brandywine Dr Baton Rouge LA 70808

ENELOW, MORTON LEONARD, physician; b. Pitts., Dec. 30, 1925; s. Isadore Maurice and Rose (Kasdan) E.; M.D., U. Louisville, 1948; student W.Va. U., 1943-44; m. Sylvia Solomon, June 21, 1953; children—Richard Ian, Robert Stewart, Thomas, James Morton. Intern, Touro Infirmary, New Orleans, 1948-49; resident medicine Louisville Gen. Hosp., 1949-50; practice medicine, New Orleans, 1950-51; fellow psychiatry Tulanc U., 1951-54, trainee psychoanalysis, 1951-56; practice medicine, specializing in psychiatry, psychoanalysis, New Orleans, 1955—; mem. sr. staff Touro Infirmary; sr. vis. physician Charity Hosp. La.; cons. staff Mercy Hosp., E. Jefferson Gen. Hosps.; asst. prof. clin. psychiatry Tulane U., 1957-64, asso. prof. clin. psychiatry, 1964—, tng. analyst, psychoanalytic tng. program, supervising analyst, 1956—, dir., coordinator psychoanalytic tng. program Grad. Sch. Medicine, 1966—. Dir. Met. Crime Commn., New Orleans, 1959—. Diplomate Nat. Bd. Med. Examiners, Am. Bd. Psychiatry and Neurology. Fellow Am. Psychiat. Assn., Am. Acad. Psychoanalysis; mem. Am. Orthopsychiat. Assn., Am. Psychosomatic Soc., World Fedn. Mental Health, A.A.A.S., A.M.A. Author chpt. in textbook on sexual perversions, chpt. in textbook on dreams in psychoanalysis. Research treatment coll. acad. problems, homosexuality, nature of psychotherapy, dreams in psychotherapy and psychoanalysis. Home: 485 Audubon St New Orleans LA 70118 Office: 4510 St Charles Av New Orleans LA 70115

ENGEL, GERALD LAWRENCE, educator; b. Cleve., July 5, 1942; s. Alvin Ralph and Martha May (Chamberlin) E.; B.S., Hampden Sydney Coll., 1964; M.A., La. State U., 1965; postgrad. Pa. State U., 1971-73; m. Doris Evelyn Smith, Aug. 22, 1964; children—Samantha Emily, Shannon Elliott. Instr. math. Randolph Macon Coll., Ashland, Va., 1965-67; asst. prof., dir. Computer Center, Hampden Sydney (Va.) Coll., 1967-71; instr. computer sci. Pa. State U., University Park, 1971-73; head dept. data processing and statis. services, asso. marine scientist Va. Inst. Marine Sci., Gloucester Point, 1973—. Mem. Assn. Computing Machinery (dir., chmn. coll. computing service, 1973-74), Am. Assn. U. Profs. (chmn. chpt. 1970-71), Nat. Council Tchrs. Math., Math. Assn. Am., Chi Beta Phi, Upsilon Pi Epsilon, Phi Kappa Phi, Pi Mu Epsilon. Home: Box 602 Gloucester Point VA 23062

ENGEL, WALBURGA VON RAFFLER (MRS. A. FERDINAND ENGEL), linguist; b. Munich, Germany, Sept. 25, 1920; d. Friedrich J. and Gertrud (Kiefer) von Raffler; D.Litt., U. Turin (Italy), 1947; M.S., Columbia, 1951; Ph.D., Ind. U., 1953; came to U.S., 1949, naturalized, 1955; m. A. Ferdinand Engel, June 2, 1957; children—Lea Maxine, Eric Robert von Raffler. Faculty, Bennett Coll., Greensboro, N.C., 1953-55, Morris Harvey Coll., Charleston, W.Va., 1955-57, City Coll. of City U. N.Y., Adelphi U., 1957-58, N.Y. U., 1957-59, U. Florence (Italy), 1959-60, Istituto Post Universitario Organizzazione Aziendale, Italy, 1960-61, Bologna Center of Johns Hopkins U., 1964; faculty Vanderbilt U., Nashville, 1965—, asso. prof. linguistics, 1966—; vis. prof. U. Ottawa, 1971-72. Free lance journalist, 1949-58. Mem. Am. Assn. U. Profs., A.A.A.S., Internat. Linguists Assn., Linguistic Soc. Am., Societas Linguistica Europea, Internat. Phonetics Assn., Internat. Child Lang. Assn. (sec.). Author: Il Prelinquaggio Infantile, 1964. Editor: Achievements and Perspectives in Language Acquisition, 1974; Prospects in Child Language, 1974; chmn. bd. editorial advisers Child Lang. Newsletter; adv. bd. Jour. Child Lang. Contbr. articles to profl. publs. Home: 372 Elmington Av Nashville TN 37205

ENGEL, WILLIAM EMANUEL, broadcasting co. exec.; b. New Orleans, Feb. 9, 1948; s. Russell Patrick and Virginia (Legg) E.; B.S. in Bus. Adminstrn., U. Ala., 1972; m. Susan Lee Shepard, Dec. 20, 1969. Dir. marketing radio sta. WSGN, Birmingham, Ala., 1971-73; asst. to pres. So. Broadcasting Co., Winston-Salem, N.C., 1973—. Program coordinator Ala. Catholic Youth Orgn., 1971-73; radio publicity United Appeal of Jefferson County, 1971-73; chmn. pub. relations com. Birmingham Shades Valley YMCA, 1971-73, bd. mgmt., 1972-73. Bd. dirs. Birmingham Jr. C. of C., 1973. Mem. Am. Marketing Assn., U. Ala. Alumni Assn., U. Ala. Commerce Execs. Soc., Phi Kappa Theta. Home: 1441-B Brookwood Dr Winston-Salem NC 27106 Office: PO Box 5176 Winston-Salem NC 27103

ENGLAND, IRA ALBERT, educator, clergyman; b. Ottumwa, Ia., Aug. 8, 1915; s. Ira Albert and Margaret (England) Brown; student Parsons Coll., 1933-37; Ph.B., Carroll Coll., 1939; S.B., Central State Tchrs. Coll., 1940; M.A. in Edn., U. Fla., 1954, Edn. Specialist, 1955, Ed.D., 1957. Ordained to ministry P.E. Ch., 1942; rector, Lincoln, Ill., 1944-49; headmaster St. Johns Parish Day Sch., 1951-53, St. Stephens Episcopal Day Sch., 1961-62; asso. sec. unit evaluation Dept. Christian Edn., Nat. Council Episcopal Ch., 1957-61; prof. anthropology and sociology Miami-Dade Jr. Coll., 1962—. Sec. Diocese of Springfield (Ill.), chmn. dept. Christian edn., 1946-48; asst. in adminstrn., research U. Fla., Gainesville, 1953-55; cons. gen. research, 1957—, cons. Indian work, 1962—. Mem. Am., Fla. anthrop. assns., Religious Edn. Assn., Phi Delta Kappa, Kappa Delta Pi, Alpha Kappa Delta, Phi Alpha Theta. Mason (K.T.), Rotarian (past exec. sec. Lincoln, Ill.), Lion. Author: The Allapattah Study, 1967; A Community in Crisis, Allapattah and Cosmopolis. Home: 9674 NW 10th Av Miami FL 33150

ENGLAND, LONDON THURMAN, radio sales exec.; b. Winters, Tex., May 12, 1919; s. George Floy and Molly Maud (Moore) E.; grad. Tyler Comml. Coll., 1938; m. Mary Anna Seibel, Sept. 25, 1940; children—London Thurman, Judy (Mrs. Steve Fincher). Engr., announcer KIUN Radio, Pecos, Tex., 1938-38, KLUF Radio, Galveston, Tex., 1938-41, KTRH Radio, Houston, 1941-52, Graybar Elec. Co., 1952-56; dist. mgr. radio and FM sales Gates div. Harris Intertype Corp., Houston, 1956—. Served with USNR, 1944-46; PTO. Mem. I.E.E.E. Club: Long Meadows Country (Houston). Home: 5210 Kinglet St Houston TX 77035 Office: 4019 Richmond St Houston TX 77027

ENGLAND, WALTER DONALD, coll. dean; b. Elm Store, Ark., Oct. 10, 1919; s. Marion Nixon and Dora (Hall) E.; B.S. in Edn., Ark. State Coll., 1949; M.S. in Edn., U. Miss., 1953; postgrad. U. Colo., 1956, U. Miss., 1957-63; m. Louise Horner, June 3, 1951; children—Cynthia, Janie, Amber Dawn. Tchr. elementary schs., Couch, Mo., 1941-42, Elm Store, Ark., 1942-45; coach, bus. tchr., Paragould, Ark., 1945-47; prin. schs., Paragould, 1947-50; supt. Cash (Ark.) High Sch., 1950-55, Alton (Mo.) High Sch., 1955-64; dean Ark. State Coll., Beebe, 1964—. Mem. White County Community Action Program. Mem. Orgen County Adminstrs. Assn. (pres. 1960—), Ark. Jr. Coll. Assn. (v.p. 1969-72, pres. 1973—), Beebe C. of C. (dir. 1973—), Kappa Delta Pi. Baptist (deacon; tchr. Sunday sch. and tng. union, mem. ch. pulpit com., bldg. com. 1970—). Kiwanian (pres. 1967, bd. mem. 1968). Home: Center St Beebe AR 72012

ENGLE, SAMUEL DARKE, lawyer; b. Charles Town, W.Va., May 28, 1937; s. Samuel Darke and Ethel (Mercer) E.; A.B., W.Va. U., 1959; LL.B., U. Va., 1962; m. Ann DeLashmutt, Feb. 26, 1972; 1 son, Samuel Darke. Admitted to Va. bar, 1962, practiced in Leesburg, Va., 1965—; mem. firm Hall, Monahan, Engle, Mahan and Mitchell, 1965—. Trustee Loudoun Meml. Hosp., 1968—, Loudoun County chpt. A.R.C., 1965—. Served to capt. AUS, 1962-65. Mem. Am., Va. bar assns., Va. Trial Lawyers Assn. (v.p. 1968-69), W.Va. State Bar (council), Sigma Chi, Sigma Nu Phi. Rotarian. Home: 11 E Cornwall St Leesburg VA 22075 Office: 3 E Market St Leesburg VA 22075

ENGLEBRIGHT, CURTIS LEE, educator; b. nr. Springfield, Ill., Oct. 13, 1928; s. Charles Roy and Anna (Stallings) E.; B.S., So. Ill. U., 1958, M.S., 1959, Ph.D. (Nat. Def. Edn. Act fellow), 1965; m. Alice Clark, Nov. 21, 1956; children—Donna Lee, Jane Dee, Jill Ann. Minor league baseball player, 1947-52; tchr. Wayne County, Ill., 1951-52, Wayne City, Ill., 1953-59; asst. county supt. schs., Wayne County, 1959-63; asst. prof. Bowling Green State U., 1965-67; asso. prof., elementary edn., dir. reading services Western Ky. U., Bowling Green, after 1967, now prof., head dept. reading and spl. edn. Mem. Internat. Reading Assn. (pres. Ky. council), N.E.A., Ky. Edn. Assn., Am. Ednl. Research Assn., Phi Delta Kappa, Kappa Delta Pi. Presbyn. (elder). Home: 1926 Price St Bowling Green KY 42101

ENGLERTH, WILLIAM MOYER, civil engr.; b. Chattanooga, Tenn., Aug. 20, 1930; s. William Basley and Mae (Moyer) E.; student Ga. Inst. Tech., 1948-50; B.S., Tex. Western Coll., 1960; m. Barbara Anne Pruette, Mar. 16, 1952; children—Francis Andrew, William Moyer, Cynthia Lynn. Cons. engr. Hensley-Schmidt, Inc., Chattanooga, 1960-70; v.p. Pressure Concrete Constrn. Co., 1970—. Served with USAF, 1950-54. Registered profl. engr., Tenn. Mem. Am. Soc. C.E., Nat., Tenn. socs. profl. engrs., Chattanooga Engrs. Club: Kappa Sigma. Elk. Home: 1216 Collins Circle Chattanooga TN 37911 Office: 2020 21st Av S Nashville TN 37212

ENGLESMITH, GEORGE, architect, indsl. designer; b. Liverpool, Eng., May 31, 1914; s. George and Agnes Beatrice (Dean) E.; B.Arch., Liverpool U., 1937; m. Lydia Julia Johnson-Briet, Sept. 9, 1939; children—Suzelle, Tejas. Came to U.S., 1920, naturalized, 1962. Chief asst. to archtl. adviser to dir. of works Ministry of Works, U.K., 1938-46; prin. G. Englesmith Asso., 1946-52; project designer J.B. Parkin Assos., 1952-54; partner Kohl & Englesmith, 1954-56; project architect Wyatt Hedrick; 1957-59; project designer Frank Dill, 1960-62; project architect Manned Spacecraft Center, NASA, 1962; asso. Floyd & James, 1962-65; design cons. Rustay, Martin, Vale, Architects, Houston, 1965-68; pvt. practice architect, planning and design cons., Houston, 1968-71; asso. architect Allison Assos., Houston, 1971—. U.S. del. Internat. Council Socs. Indsl. Design, London, Eng., 1969. Sec.-treas. Brit. Benevolent Fund Com., Tex., 1962—; mem. adv. com. U. Houston, 1956—. Coronation medalist, 1953. Registered architect Nat. Council Archtl. Registration Bds. Fellow Royal Soc. Arts (life); mem. Tex. Soc. Architects, Archtl. Assn. London, Soc. Indsl. Artists and Designers, Assn. Canadian Indsl. Designers (hon. life), Royal Inst. Brit. Architects, Royal Archtl. Inst. Can., Tex. Hosp. Assn., Nat. Indsl. Design Council Can. (co-founder). Office: 5959 West Loop South Houston TX 77401

ENGLISH, BRUCE VAUGHAN, environmental cons.; b. Richmond, Va., Aug. 6, 1921; s. Pollard and Lucy (Rice) E.; B.S., Randolph-Macon Coll., 1942; M.S., Ind. U., 1943; postgrad. (Ford Found. fellow) Pa. State U., 1951-52; Ph.D. (Danforth fellow 1956-57; DuPont fellow 1957-58), U. Va., 1958; m. Virginia McCall Shaw, Feb. 6, 1949. Asst. prof. Randolph-Macon Coll., Ashland, Va., 1943-44, asso. prof., 1948-58, prof., chmn. dept. physics, 1958-64; prin. cons. firm Bruce V. English, Ashland, Va., 1964—. Columnist environmental sci. Herald-Progress, Ashland, 1971—; del. Internat. Clean Air Congress, London, Eng., 1966, Washington, 70. Co-founder Richmond Symphony, 1957; bd. dirs. Edgar Allan Poe Found., 1969—, pres., 1973—, mem. Church Hill Model Neighborhood Policy

Adv. Bd., Richmond, 1969-73; mem. Patrick Henry Scotchtown Com., Hanover County, Va., 1958—. Former mem. bd. dirs. Hist. Richmond Found. Served with USN, 1944-45. Recipient Smithey Math. Gold medal Randolph-Macon Coll., 1942. Mem. Nat. Soc. Clean Air (Gt. Britain), Am. Phys. Soc., Air Pollution Control Assn. Pitts., Va. Acad. Sci., Richmond Physics Club, Va. Hist. Soc., Soc. Archtl. Historians, Nat. Trust Hist. Preservation in U.S., Assn. Preservation Va. Antiquities (vice-dir.), A.A.A.S., Sigma Xi, Phi Beta Xappa, Omicron Delta Kappa, Chi Beta Phi, Kappa Alpha. Episcopalian. Clubs: Farmington Country (Charlottesville); City Tavern (Washington). Home: 109 Arlington St Ashland VA 23005 Office: PO Box 267 Ashland VA 23005

ENGLISH, EDWARD NEILL, JR., lawyer; b. Dallas, Apr. 3, 1934; s. Edward Neill and Naida Ruth (Wadsworth) E.; B.B.A., So. Meth. U., 1955, J.D., 1961; m. Dorothy J. Barbour, Aug. 8, 1953; children—Lisa Kay, Christopher Neill, Katharine Ann. Admitted to Tex. bar, 1961; asst. dist. atty. Dallas County, 1961-64; practiced in Irving, 1964—; partner firm English, Deatherage & Boyle, 1970—. Dir. Citizens Bank, Irving. Pres., bd. dirs. Irving Symphony Assn. Mem. Am., Tex., Irving (pres. 1967-68), bar assns., Tex. Criminal Def. Lawyers Assn. (charter), Irving C. of C. (dir. 1969-71, v.p. 1972), Phi Alpha Delta. Republican. Home: 1600 Canyon Oak St Irving TX 75061 Office: 304 Southwest Bank Bldg Irving TX 75061

ENGLISH, GEORGE W., lawyer; b. Vienna, Ill., Feb. 19, 1898; s. George W. and Lillie May (Farris) E.; B.S., U. Ill., 1921; J.D., Harvard, 1924; D.Hum. (hon.), Nova U. Advanced Tech.; m. Alma R. Witt, Sept. 11, 1935; 1 son (by previous marriage), George W. III. Admitted to Fla. bar, 1925; sr. mem. English, McCaughan & O'Bryan; chmn. bd. First Nat. Bank, Ft. Lauderdale, Fla., Guaranty First Nat. Bank, Ft. Lauderdale, 1st Nat. Bank of Sunrise, Ft. Lauderdale; chmn. Landmark Banking Corp. Fla., Inc.; dir. First Fed. Savs. & Loan Assn. of Broward County (Fla.), Plantation 1st Nat. Bank (Fla.), Fla. Power & Light Co., Wright & Putnam, Inc., Harbor Beach Cos., Security 1st Nat. Bank, Union Nat. Bank & Trust Co., St. Petersburg, Fla. State dir. Orange Bowl Com., 1958-68; trustee U. Fla. Found., 1959-69, mem. pres.'s council; hon. trustee Nova U., 1964-69; mem. bd. control Fla. Instns. of Higher Learning, 1952-55; mem. U. Ill. Found. Mem. Ft. Lauderdale Hist. Soc. (trustee), U. Fla. Alumni Assn. (hon.), Newcomen Soc., Sigma Chi, Beta Gamma Sigma. Presbyn. Mason (Shriner), Elk. Clubs: Harvard (Ft. Lauderdale); 100 of Broward County; Lauderdale Yacht; University (N.Y.C.). Home: 1636 SW 15th Av Ft Lauderdale FL 33312 Office: First Fed Bldg Ft Lauderdale FL 33301

ENGLISH, ROBERT GOODRICH, supt. schs.; b. Belton, S.C., Dec. 9, 1932; s. John Waymon and Grace (McAllistor) E.; B.S., Erskine U., 1955; M.Ed., U. S.C., 1964; m. Nancy Juanita Malone, Apr. 29, 1955; children—Patti Darlene, Robert Mark, John Steven. Tchr., Mount Zion High Sch., Winnsboro, S.C., 1958-61, prin., 1961-64; prin. Edito High Sch., Cordova, 1964-69, McCormick (S.C.) High Sch., 1969; supt. Swansea (S.C.) Pub. Schs., 1969—. Served with AUS, 1955-57. Mem. McCormick County Tchrs. Assn. (pres. 1966-67). Lion. Address: Box 128 Swansea SC 29160

ENGLUND, RALPH CALDWELL, constrn. co. exec.; b. Gaffrey, S.C., Mar. 29, 1925; s. Carl G. and Anna (Hall) E.; B.S. in C.E., Ga. Inst. Tech., 1945; m. Sallie Bozier Allen, Nov. 26, 1949; children—John, Susan, Virginia. With Daniel Internat. Corp., Inc., Birmingham, Ala., 1946—, estimator, project mgr., 1946-54, asst. div. mgr., 1954-58, div. mgr., 1958-62, v.p., 1962—; v.p. Daniel Realty Corp., Birmingham, 1970—. Served with USNR, 1943-46. Mem. Am. Mgmt. Assn. Methodist. Kiwanian. Home: 2901 Warrington Rd Birmingham AL 35223 Office: 1900 Daniel Bldg Birmingham AL 35233

ENIX, (AGNES) LUCILLE, mag. editor; b. Drummond, Okla., Jan. 17, 1933; d. James Robert and Alma (Hodges) Enix; B.S., Okla. State U., 1955; M.S., Northwestern U., 1966. Dietetic intern VA Hosp., Los Angeles, 1955-56, staff dietician, 1956-57; nutritionist Dairy Council of Greater Kansas City, Mo., 1957-61; asso. dir. materials devel. dept. Nat. Dairy Council, Chgo., 1961-65; reporter, features writer Chgo. Tribune, 1966-67; copywriter Rogers & Smith Advt. Agts., Dallas, 1967-68; editor Dallas mag. Dallas C. of C., 1968—. Adv. bd. journalism dept. N. Tex. State U., 1974. Recipient Southwest Journalism Forum award, 1970, Journalism award Tex. Med. Assn., 1971. Mem. Am. Dietetic Assn. Theta Sigma Phi (Matrix award 1971), Omicron Nu, Phi Upsilon Omicron, Alpha Delta Pi. Club: Dallas Press (dir., sec.). Home: 2622 Highland Rd Dallas TX 75228 Office: 1507 Pacific Av Dallas TX 75201

ENLOE, JOSEPH, chem. engr.; b. Bloomington, Ind., Nov. 1, 1922; s. John J. and Bessie A. (Sager) E.; B.S., Ill. Inst. Tech., 1952; m. Rose Barnes, Nov. 16, 1945; children—Heather, Ruth, Mary. With TVA, 1973—, now engring. cons., Waynesville, N.C. Served with Chem. Corps, AUS, 1942-47. Decorated Bronze Star. Home and office: PO Box 676 Waynesville NC 28786

ENRIQUEZ, OSCAR ROBERTO ALCALA, elec. engr.; b. Chihuahua, Mexico, Feb. 7, 1915; s. Emiliano and Carmen (Alcala) E.; grad. Engring. Sch. Politecnic Inst. Mexico, 1935; m. Maria Teresa Prieto, Mar. 27, 1940; children—Carlos Federico, Maria Guadalupe (Mrs. Juan R. Herrero), Graciela, Hortensia, Maria Teresa, Rosa Martha, Oscar Roberto. Engr., Flohr Elevators & Demag's, Mexico, 1939-41; asst. cons. engr., chief head hydroelectric dept. Mexico Nat. Commn. Irrigation, Mexico City, 1941-46; cons. engr. Internat. Boundary and Water Commn. between Mexico and U.S., Mexico City, 1943-56; tech. adviser Ministry Economy and to Dir. Gen. Electricity Mexico, 1944-48; head electromech. dept. Ministry Hydraulic Resources, 1947-48; dir. firm Investigaciones y Proyectes S.A., Mexico City, 1948-51; exec. mgr. Tecnica Progreso S.A., Mexico City, 1951—. Mng. partner, dir. Disenos y Construcciones S.A., Mexico City, 1952—; del. to bd. Cierres Alco S.A., Mexico City. Hon. consul Grand Ducy Luxembourg, Mexico, 1970—. Mem. Coll. Mech. and Elec. Engrs. Mexico (founder 1945), Asn. Engrs. and Architects Mexico, Am. Inst. Elec. Engrs. (chmn., 1944-46), Assn. Mech. and Elec. Engrs. Mexico, I.E.E.E. (sr.). Author: Planta Hidroelectrica Temascal, 1953; Estructuras Ligeras Para Torres de Transmission, 1964; Ela provechamiento del carbon Mexicano en la Generacion Electrica, 1969. Patentee in crusibles, transmission towers, prefab concrete elements and non evaporating cooling towers. Home: 146 Chilpancingo Mexico DF 7 Mexico Office: 255 Tehuantepec Mexico DF 7 Mexico

ENSENAT, LOUIS ALBERT, physician; b. Merida, Mexico, Oct. 24, 1916; s. Frank and Guadalupe F. (Ensenat) E.; B.S., Tulane U., 1937, M.D., 1941; M.Sc. in Medicine, U. Pa., 1953; m. Ruth Ogden, July 9, 1943; children—Gloria Louise, Tinita Ruth, Louis Albert, Rita Joan, Barbara Jean, Michael Monroe. Intern, Charity Hosp., New Orleans, 1941-42; resident surgery Charity Hosp., Monroe, La., 1942, Lakeshore Hosp., New Orleans, VA hosp., New Orleans, Batavia, N.Y.; fellow in surg. pathology Tulane U. Sch. Med.; preceptership in surgery Biloxi (Miss.) VA Hosp.; staff surg. VA Hosp., Montgomery, 1946-52; pvt. practice surgery, Pasadena, Tex., 1952-63, New Orleans, 1963—; adminstr. Mercy Hosp. Pasadena, 1954-63, chief surgery, 1954-63. Founder, dir. Gulf Coast Home Bulders, Inc. Trustee Big State Factors Corp. Served from lt. (j.g.) to lt. comdr. USN, 1942-46. Decorated Purple Heart. Diplomate Am. Bd. Surgery, Am. Bd. Abdominal Surgery. Fellow French Soc. Phlebology, Am. Coll. Angiology (v.p.); mem. Hawthorne Surg. Soc., Am. Soc. Abdominal Surgeons, N.Y. Acad. Scis., Am. Med. Writers' Assn. Author articles in field. Home: 7630 Jeannette Pl New Orleans LA 70118 Office: 2839 Gen Pershing New Orleans LA 70115

ENSTAM, RAYMOND ANDERS, lawyer; b. New Britain, Conn., Apr. 1, 1937; s. Reuben Anders and Rita Margaret (Belleveau) E.; student Trinity Coll., 1956-58; B.A., Marietta Coll., 1960; J.D., Duke U., 1963; LL.M., N.Y. U., 1968; m. Mary Elizabeth York, Aug. 6, 1963; 1 dau., Gwendolyn Elizabeth. Admitted to N.Y. State bar, 1964, Tex. bar, 1969; practiced in Dallas, 1971—; atty. investment div. Met. Life Ins. Co., N.Y.C., 1963-68; gen. counsel, sec. Data Automation Co., Inc., 1968-71; chmn. bd., v.p., sec., gen. counsel Worldcom, Inc., Dallas. Mem. Am., Tex. bar assns. Home: 4132 Lomita Lane Dallas TX 75220 Office: 1341 Mockingbird Lane Dallas TX 75247

ENTSMINGER, PHILLIP WALTER, elec. engr.; b. Powersville, Mo., Dec. 1, 1929; s. Walter Chesney and Florence Anna (Pollock) E.; B.S. in Elec. Engring., U. Mo., 1959; m. Betty Jean Bowery, Jan. 22, 1949; children—Debra Jean, Rebecca Elaine, Pamela Rose. Systems engr., program mgr. Collins Radio Co., Richardson, Tex., 1959—. Served with AUS, 1952-54; Korea. Mem. I.E.E.E., Tau Beta Pi, Eta Kappa Nu. Baptist. Home: 511 Worcester Way Richardson TX 75080 Office: 1200 N Alma Rd Richardson TX 75080

EPHRAIM, CHARLES, lawyer; b. Chgo., Sept. 18, 1924; s. Max H. and Margaret (O'Neil) E.; Ph.B., U. Chgo., 1948, J.D., 1951; m. Marguerite Marie Lamont, Dec. 23, 1944; children—Linda Patrice, Charles Lamont. Admitted to D.C. bar, 1951; gen. practice, Washington, 1951—; asso. Posner, Berge, Fox & Arent, 1951-53; mem. firm Layne & Ephraim, 1953-56; gen. practice, 1956-69; mem. firm Ephraim & Clark, 1969—. Sec.-dir. Herner & Co. Served to 1st lt. USAAF, 1943-47. Mem. Am. Bar Assn., Motor Carrier Lawyers Assn., Order of Coif, Phi Beta Kappa. Contbr. articles profl. jours. Home: 5604 Western Av Chevy Chase MD 20015 Office: 1250 Connecticut Av NW Washington DC 20036

EPPERLY, JOHN DAVID, lawyer; b. Floyd, Va., Oct. 14, 1920; s. Isaac Lafayette and Linda (Weddle) E.; B.S.C., U. Va., 1941, LL.B., 1947, J.D., 1970; m. Judy Martin, Oct. 4, 1968; children—Carolyn E. (Mrs. David E. Smith), John David, Jr., Elizabeth R. Admitted to Va. bar, 1947; since practiced in Martinsville; mem. firm Broaddus, Epperly & Broaddus, 1947—. Dir. Southwestern Va. Gas Co., Lester Lumber Co., Inc., Am. Standard Homes Corp. Instr. comml. law U. Va., 1960-64. Mem. Am., Va. bar assns., Raven Soc., Internat. Soc. Barristers, Am., Va. trial lawyers assns., Order of Coif, Omicron Delta Kappa. Elk, K.P. Home: 211 Thomas Hts PO Box 1342 Martinsville VA 24112 Office: 106 E Main St Martinsville VA 24112

EPPS, JAMES HAWS, III, lawyer; b. Johnson City, Tenn., Sept. 15, 1936; s. James H. and Anne (Sessoms) E.; grad. Episcopal High Sch., Alexandria, Va., 1955; B.A. U. N.C., 1959; J.D., Vanderbilt U., 1962; m. Nancy Jane Atkinson, Nov. 30, 1958; children—James Haws IV, Sara Stuart. Admitted to Tenn. bar, 1962, U.S. Supreme Ct., 1967, other fed. cts.; now partner Epps, Powell, Epps & Lawrence, Johnson City, Tenn. City atty. Johnson City, 1967—. Dir. Farmers & Mchts. Bank, Limestone, Tenn. Mem. Tenn. Law Revision Commn., 1970-71. Mem. budget com. United Fund, Johnson City, 1964-68, now mem. bd. dirs.; mem. Appalachian council Girl Scouts Am., legal adviser, 1969—; mem. Civil Def. Adv. Bd. Mem. county exec. com. Democratic party. Bd. dirs. Tenn. Mental Health Assn., Washington County Mental Health Assn., Salvation Army. Mem. Am., Tenn. (mem. continuing legal edn. com.), Washington County (past pres.) bar assns., Am. Judicature Soc., Tenn. Municipal Attys. Assn., Assn. Interstate Commerce Commn. Practitioners (mem. com. profl. ethics and grievances), Motor Carrier Lawyers' Assn. (bd. govs. Transp. Law Jour.), Am. Counsel Assn., Nat. Assn. R.R. Trial Counsel, Nat. Inst. Municipal Law Officers, C. of C. (govtl. affairs com.), Tenn. Taxpayers Assn., Internat. Platform Assn., Nat. Legal Aid Defender Assn., Tipton Haynes Hist. Assn. (dir.), Phi Delta Phi, Phi Delta Theta. Episcopalian (vestryman, 1965-68, 70-71, clk. 1968, 70, 71, layreader). Elk (legal counsel 1963-67). Clubs: North Johnson City Business (dir., pres. 1966-67), Hurstleigh, Johnson City Country; Nat. Lawyers, Unaka Rod and Gun, Highland Stable. Home: 1222 Ridgeway Rd Johnson City TN 37601 Office: 115 E Unaka Av Johnson City TN 37601

EPSTEIN, ARTHUR WILLIAM, physician, educator; b. N.Y.C. May 15, 1923; s. Jacob E. and Anne (Bass) E.; A.B. Columbia, 1944, M.D., 1947; m. Leona Cruce, Mar. 2, 1955; children—David Byron, Nona Kathryn, Emily Vera, James Jacob. Intern, Mt. Sinai Hosp., N.Y.C., 1947-48, resident, 1949-50; clin. asst. Norristown (Pa.) State Hosp., 1948-49; faculty Tulane U., New Orleans, 1954—, asso. prof. psychiatry and neurology, 1959-64, prof., 1964—; pvt. practice medicine, specializing in neuropsychiatry, New Orleans, 1954—; vis. physician Charity Hosp., New Orleans, 1951—; cons. U.S. Army Hosp., New Orleans, 1958-64, VA Hosp., New Orleans, 1969—. Med. adviser Social Security Adminstrn., 1968—. Bd. dirs. Ednl. Research and Treatment Center, New Orleans. Served with M.C., USNR, 1956-58. Fellow Am. Psychiat. Assn. (leisure time and its uses com.), Am. Acad. Psychoanalysis, A.A.A.S., Am. Acad. Neurology; mem. Soc. Biol. Psychiatry (asst. sec. 1973-74), Soc. for Neurosci., Am. Epilepsy Soc., Alpha Omega Alpha. Author: An Anatomist's Dream of Love, 1966. Contbr. articles profl. jours. Home: 1664 Robert St New Orleans LA 70115 Office: 1430 Tulane Av New Orleans LA 70112

EPSTEIN, BARRY RONALD, assn. exec.; b. N.Y.C., Mar. 22, 1942; s. Irving H. and Libby F. (Ertel) E.; B.S., Kent State U., 1964; m. Judy L. Stender, July 19, 1964; children—Larry Marc, Lori Ann. Promotion mgr. White Plains (N.Y.) C. of C., 1964-66; asst. mgr. Ypsilanti (Mich.) C. of C., 1966-67; exec. v.p. Warren County (Pa.) C. of C., 1967-71, Greater Hollywood (Fla.) C. of C., 1971—. Mem. Hollywood Planning and Zoning Bd., Hollywood Bd. Appeals, 1973—. Mem. Am., Fla. assns. C. of C. execs., Am. Retail Assn. Execs. (dir. 1970-72), Am. Indsl. Devel. Council. Office: 330 N Federal Hwy Hollywood FL 33022

ERBELE, LEO ALBERT, physician; b. Mandan, N.D., Jan. 8, 1927; s. Albert Frederick and Anna (Goldmann) E.; student Creighton U., 1944-45; B.A., U. N.D., 1949, B.S., 1950; M.D., Bowman Gray Sch. Medicine, 1952; m. Josephine Phelps Matthews, Apr. 26, 1973; children by previous marriage—John, Olivia, Peter, Mary. Intern City Hosp., Winston-Salem, N.C., 1952-53; gen. practice medicine, Clover, S.C., 1953-54, Marion, N.C., 1954-55; residency tng. Bowman Gray Sch. Medicine, Winston-Salem, 1955-59; asso. pathologist Macon (Ga.) Hosp., 1959-61, dir. labs., 1961-65; now engaged in pvt. practice. Served as sgt. USAAF, 1945-47. Diplomate in anatomic pathology and clin. pathology Am. Bd. Pathology, Am. Bd. Nuclear Medicine. Fellow Am. Soc. Clin. Pathologists, Coll. Am. Pathologists; mem. A.M.A., So. Med. Assn., Soc. Nuclear Medicine. Home: 3379 Osborne Pl Macon GA 31204 Office: 1021 Daisy Park Macon GA 31208

ERBS, HAROLD JOHN, oil drilling and prodn. co. exec.; b. St. Louis, Mar. 31, 1932; s. Oliver F. and Louise Irene (Rolves) E.; B.S. in Accounting, St. Louis U., 1954; m. Marilyn L. Metcalf, Feb. 6, 1954; children—Susan Marie, James, Mary Lou. Accountant, Price Waterhouse & Co., St. Louis, 1956-57; systems analyst Mississippi River Fuel Corp., 1957-58; with Milchem, Inc., Houston, 1958—, v.p., treas., adminstrv. v.p., 1966-73, also dir.; v.p. Goldrus Drilling Co., 1973—. Dir. Oleum, Inc. (formerly Trice Prodn. Co.), Longview, Tex., Galleria Bank, Houston. Chmn. Houston Diocesan Financial Adv. Bd., 1971—. Served with AUS, 1954-56. Mem. Financial Execs. Inst., Mensa. Roman Catholic. Lion (pres. 1966). Clubs: St. Louis University; Westbury Civic (pres. 1961), Meyerland (pres. 1972), Petroleum (Houston). Home: 5130 Braesheather St Houston TX 77035 Office: First City Nat Bank Bldg Houston TX 77002

ERDREICH, BENJAMIN LEADER, state legislator; b. Birmingham, Ala., Dec. 9, 1938; s. Stanley M. and Corinne (Leader) E.; B.A., Yale, 1960; J.D., U. Ala., 1963; m. Ellen Cooper, May 30, 1965; children—Jeremy Cooper, Anna Bethia. Admitted to Ala. bar, 1963; asso. Kaye, Scholer, Fierman, Hays & Handler, N.Y.C., 1965-66; partner Cooper, Mitch & Crawford, Birmingham, Ala., 1967—; mem. Ala. Ho. of Reps., 1970—. Served to 1st. lt. AUS, 1963-65. Mem. Am., Ala., Birmingham bar assns. Home: 4326 Kennesaw Dr Birmingham AL 35213 Office: 409 N 21st St Birmingham AL 35203

ERDRICH, HOWARD IRVING, furniture co. exec.; b. N.Y.C., June 14, 1929; s. Samuel and Gladys (Kaufman) E.; B.S., L.I. U., 1950; m. Bernice Lechowitz, June 14, 1953; children—Gayle, Stewart. Buyer, Ludwig Baumann, N.Y.C., 1951-52; furniture buyer Snellenbergs, Phila., 1955-58; mgr. mdse. A.J. Legom, Norfolk, Va., 1959-66; mgr. mdse., supr. Reliable Stores, Washington, 1966-69; v.p. J. Bain, Inc., Atlanta and Miami, Fla., 1969—. Served with USMC, 1951-53. Democrat. Jewish religion. Home: 9125 SW 77th Av Miami FL 30132 Office: 1200 NW 167th St Miami FL 33156

ERFFT, KENNETH REYNDERS, ednl. adminstr.; b. Chgo., Nov. 14, 1908; s. Victor Athen and Ethel (Reynders) E.; A.B., No. Mich. U.; 1932; M.A., U. Richmond, 1936, D.S.C., 1967; Litt.D., Maclean College, 1947; LL.D., No. Mich. U., 1961; m. Nancy Fontaine Creath, June 8, 1940. Instr. Ironwood (Mich.) High Sch., 1932-34; clk. bd. edn. Petersburg (Va.) pub. schs., 1936-42; bus. mgr. Furman U., Greenville, S.C., 1946-54; comptroller Pa. State U., 1954-57; v.p., treas. Rutgers State U., 1957-62, Thomas Jefferson U., 1962-64; pres. Kenneth R. Erfft Assos., Inc., ednl. cons., Phila. 1964-66; v.p. Duquesne U., Pitts., 1966-72; exec. dir. Nationwide Conf. Edn. Centers, Inc., Atlanta, 1972—. Chmn. bd. dirs. Afuture Fund, Afortress Fund. Mem. adminstrv. com. for Cal. and Western Conf. Cost and Statis. Study, 1955-57. Served from lt. (j.g.) to comdr. USNR, 1942-46. Mem. Eastern Assn. Coll. and U. Bus. Officers (pres.), Am. Assn. U. Profs., Middle States Assn., Delta Sigma Phi, Phi Epsilon, Tau Kappa Alpha, Omicron Delta Kappa, Theta Omicron Rho. Clubs: International Torch, University (Pitts.). Co-author: Administrators in Higher Education, 1962. Editorial com. College and University Business Administration, rev. edits. Home: 2031 Westover Av Petersburg VA 23803

ERICKSON, ANDREW JOHN, mfg. and tech. services cons.; b. N.Y.C., July 2, 1906; s. John Andrew and Tekla Josephine (Brostrom) E.; B.S. in Elec. Engring., Poly. Inst. Bklyn., 1931; grad. student N.Y. U., 1937-38; grad. exec. mgmt. program, Columbia, 1960, Air War Coll., 1965; m. Francenia Ann Cantwell Langley, Oct. 15, 1930; children—Willy Ann (Mrs. John D. Holmgren), William Andrew. With Vitro Corp. Am., Ft. Walton Beach, Fla., 1944—, pres. Vitro Services div., 1951—, v.p. corp., 1966—; v.p. parent corp. Automation Industries, Inc., 1969—; dir. First Peoples Bank, Ft. Walton Beach. Chmn. adv. com. tech. edn. Fla. Dept. Edn., 1960—; v.p. Gulf Coast council Boy Scouts Am., 1968—, bd. dirs., 1965—; pres. Okaloosa County United Fund, 1959-60, bd. dirs., 1961-65, exec. com., 1965—; trustee Okaloosa-Walton Jr. Coll., Valparaiso, Fla., 1965-71, chmn. finance com., chmn. bd., 1966-67. Decorated Red Cross of Constantine; recipient Civic Achievement award Ft. Walton Beach Bd. Realtors, 1959; Boss of Yr. award Nat. Secretaries Assn., 1967; named Outstanding Young Man of Yr., Ft. Walton Beach Jaycees, 1968; recipient Good Citizenship award WFTW radio sta., 1974. Mem. I.E.E.E., Greater Ft. Walton Beach C. of C. (v.p. 1961-63, dir. 1962-64, mem. mil. affairs com 1964—). Democrat. Mason (32 deg., Shriner), Rotarian (pres. 1961-62, dir. 1959-61). Clubs: Krewe of Bowlegs (treas. 1966), Ft. Walton Beach Yacht (commodore 1964). Home: 237 Yacht Club Dr Fort Walton Beach FL 32548 Office: Automation Industries Inc Vitro Services Div Industrial Park Fort Walton Beach FL 32548

ERICKSON, ERIC FREDERICK, wholesale trade exec.; b. Helsingland, Sweden, July 18, 1919; s. Ole and Bertha M. (Michelsson) E.; student Am. Tech. Soc. Sch., 1940-42; m. Judy Schleicher, Dec. 28, 1939; children—Glen, Donna Sue (Mrs. Jerry Parker). Came to U.S., 1924, naturalized, 1944. Mgr. retail food store, Chgo., 1938-40; merchandiser Salerno-Magowen Biscuit Co., 1940-42; sales supr. Consol. Biscuit Co., 1942-45; asst. sales mgr. Schulze-Burch Biscuit Co., 1945-46; gen. sales mgr. Ill. Chem. Co., 1946-47; v.p. sales Wortz Biscuit Co., Fort Smith, Ark., 1947-67; sales dir. Blue Springs Fish Hatchery, Birmingham, Ala., 1967-72; regional mgr. Hartz Mountain Corp., Birmingham, 1973—. Instr. salesmanship Fort Smith Jr. Coll., 1961; lectr. Small Bus. Adminstrn. Inst., 1962; coordinator salesmanship course U. Ala., 1969. Mem. Sales and Marketing Execs. Club (pres. 1956, 61). Lutheran (v.p. ch. council 1964-66). Mason (Shriner), Elk. Club: The Club (Birmingham). Home: 163 Glenview Dr Birmingham AL 35213 Office: 149 Distribution Dr Birmingham AL 35210

ERICKSON, ERIC LEROY, civil engr.; b. Chgo., Oct. 8, 1896; s. John Edwin and Hulda (Magnuson) E.; student Highland Park Coll., 1912-14; student civil engring. State U. Ia., 1914-16; m. Velma Fondren, Jan. 29, 1924; children—Susanne (Mrs. Maurice Chamblee), William M. Bridge designer Ind., N.C. Hwy. Commns., 1919-23; asst. state bridge engr. La. Hwy. Commn., 1923-41; bridge engr. southeastern div. U.S. Bur. Pub. Rds., 1941-46, asst. chief bridge engr., 1946-48, chief bridge engr., 1948-66; cons. Office. Sec. Transp., Washington, 1966—. Cons. Govt. Victoria, Australia, 1962, Govt. Netherlands, 1967; mem. bd. cons. Panama Canal Bridge at Balboa, 1958-63. Mem. research adv. com. U. Ill., Lehigh U. Served with AUS, 1917-19. Recipient Silver Medal award Dept. Commerce, 1956, Gold Medal award, 1964; Charles S. Whitney award Am. Concrete Inst., 1969; Arthur J. Boaze award Reinforced Concrete Research Council Am. Soc. Engrs., 1972. Mem. Am. Soc. C.E. (life), Am. Rd. Builders Assn. (life), Nat. Acad. Sci. (hwy. research bd.), Prestressed Concrete Inst. (hon.). Mason. Home and Office: 501 Dumbarton Dr Shreveport LA 71106

ERICKSON, FREDERICK KENNETH, san. engr.; b. Missoula, Mont., Apr. 11, 1916; s. David William and Elin (Erickson) E.; student Mont. State Coll. 1934-35, 1937; B.S., U. Wash., 1940; SM., Harvard, 1943; m. Esther Mae McGlone, Jan. 29, 1944; children—Elin Katherine, Frederick Kenneth, Diane Marie. Jr. engr. U.S. Army Engrs., Ketchikan, Alaska, 1940-41; san. engr. Pierce County Health Dept., Tacoma, 1941-42; asst. and sr. asst. san. engr.

USPHS, La. Fla., Egypt, Italy, Yugoslavia, Washington, 1943-46; asst. prof. Wash. State Coll., 1946-50, asso. prof. civil engring., head water pollution research, 1950-51; sr. san engr. USPHS, Fed. Civil Def. Adminstrn., 1951-54; prof. san. engring. India Inst. Hygiene, Calcutta, 1954-56; san. engring. dir. Office Engring. Resources, Washington, 1956-61; asso. regional health dir. USPHS Kansas City, Mo., 1961-66; dep. dir. div. of Allied Health Manpower, USPHS, Arlington, Va., 1967-68; asst. commr. tng. and manpower devel. Environmental Control Adminstrn., Rockville, Md., 1968-71; dir. environmental affairs Ryckman, Edgerley, Tomlinson & Assos., 1971-73; environmental engr. Montgomery County, Rockville, Md., 1973—. Recipient Clements Herschel award, 1943. Registered profl. engr., Pa., Wash., Md., Va. Diplomate Am. Acad. San. Engrs. Fellow Am. Soc. C.E., Am. Pub. Health Assn.; mem Am. Soc. Engring. Edn., Nat. Soc. Profl. Engrs. Home: 8016 Falstaff Rd McLean VA 22101 Office: County Office Bldg Rockville Md 20850

ERICKSON, HOWARD HUGH, physiologist; b. Wahoo, Neb., Mar. 16, 1936; s. Conrad Robert and Hannah Laurene (Swanson) E.; B.S., Kan. State U., 1957, D.V.M., 1959; Ph.D., Ia. State U., 1966; m. Ann Elizabeth Nicolay, June 6, 1959; children—James Howard, David Michael. Gen. vet. practice, Wahoo, Neb., 1959-60; commd. lt. U.S. Air Force, 1959, advanced through grades to maj., 1967; area veterinarian U.K., USAF, 1960-63; cardiovascular physiologist, vet. scientist Applied Physiology Br. and Biodynamics br. USAF Sch. Aerospace Medicine, Brooks AFB, Tex., 1966-73; asst. chief biodynamics br., 1973—. Sci. adviser NRC Air Force Systems Command Associateship program, 1971—; clin. asst. prof. U. Tex. Med. Sch., San Antonio, 1972—. Com. mem. Alamo Area council Boy Scouts Am., San Antonio, 1971—. Fellow Royal Soc. Health, Aerospace Med. Assn. (asso.); mem. Am. Vet. Med. Assn., Am. Pub. Health Assn., Am. Physiol. Soc., Am. Heart Assn., N.Y. Acad. Scis., Biomed. Engring. Soc., Instrument Soc. Am., I.E.E.E., Acad. Vet. Cardiology, A.A.A.S. Lutheran (sec. ch. council 1967—). Home: 3210 Canaveral Dr San Antonio TX 78217 Office: Biodynamics Br USAF Sch Aerospace Medicine Brooks AFB TX 78235

ERICSON, JOE ELLIS, educator; b. Throckmorton County, Tex., June 9, 1925; s. Lester Y. and Lena Agnes (Ellis) E.; student U. Tex., 1943-44, postgrad., 1948-51; B.S. in Edn., Tex. Technol. Coll., 1946, M.A., 1948, Ph.D., 1957; m. Carolyn Reeves, July 16, 1955; children—Linda Dianne, Joseph Reeves, John Ellis. Instr. W. Tex. State U., 1951-53; instr. Arlington State Coll., 1955-57; mem. faculty Stephen F. Austin State Coll., Nacogdoches, Tex., 1957—, prof. polit. sci., head dept., 1964—. County chmn. Democratic Party, Nacogdoches, 1972—. Mem. Am. Polit. Sci. Assn., Am. Studies Assn. (pres. Tex. 1971-72), Alpha Chi (hon.), Pi Sigma Alpha, Pi Kappa Alpha. Mason. Home: 1614 Redbud St Nacogdoches TX 75961

ERICSSON, RALPH LOUIS, chem. co. exec.; b. Ridgway, Pa., Sept. 20, 1908; s. Louis F. and Florence (Siggins) E.; B.S. in Chemistry, Carnegie Inst. Tech., 1933; m. Ruth E. Jacobson, Oct. 18, 1941; 1 dau., Carol A. With Westvaco Chlorine Products Corp. (name later changed to FMC Corp.) N.Y.C., 1933-41, chief chemist, Carteret, N.J., 1934-37, mgr. tech. service, N.Y.C. 1937-41; asst. mgr. tech. service Comml. Solvents Corp., Terre Haute, Ind., 1941-44, asst. to v.p. sales, 1944-45, asst. mgr. pharm. div., 1945-48; sales mgr. Sumner Chem. Co., Inc. div. Miles Lab., N.Y.C., 1948-53, v.p. sales, 1951-54, dir., 1952-56, exec. v.p., gen. mgr., 1954-56; sales mgr. Tex. Butadiene & Chem. Corp., N.Y.C. 1957-59, v.p. marketing, 1958-62; v.p., dir. Tex. Butadiene & Chem. Internat., Ltd., Montreal Que., Can., 1958-62; owner, operator Ericsson Chem. Services, Inc., Houston, 1962—. Mem. Sales Assn. Chem. Industry (dir. 1948-51, 52-55), Am. Chem. Soc., Mfg. Chemists Assn. Clubs: Chemists (trustee 1955-56, 60-62), (N.Y.C.); Houston, Petroleum. Contbr. articles to tech. publs. Patentee, fields textile treating, tobacco conditioning, pharm. chems. Home: 11108 Meadowick St Houston TX 77024 Office: 2100 Travis St Houston TX 77002

ERIKSON, SHELTON WILLARD, chem. exec.; b. Pecan Island, La., July 23, 1926; s. John Erik and Veronica (Vaughn) E.; student pub. schs.; m. Theresa Bourgeois, Jan. 1, 1954; children—Shelton Leonard, Sylvia Reed (Mrs. Robert W. Feller). Owner Erikson Chem. Corp., New Iberia, La., 1967—, also Erikson Pollution Control, Inc. Served with AUS, 1944-46. Decorated Purple Heart, 3 Bronze Stars. Mason (Shriner). Home: Route B Box 237 New Iberia LA 70560 Office: PO Box 1424 New Iberia LA 70560

ERMUTLU, ILHAN MEHMET, state ofcl., physician; b. Istanbul, Turkey, June 24, 1927; s. Sami and Ihsan (Emin) E.; M.D., U. Ankara, 1952; came to U.S., 1954, naturalized, 1964; m. Karen Harper, Sept. 9, 1956; children—David Sami, Gary Deniz. Intern, Knickerbocker Hosp., N.Y.C., 1954-55; resident psychiatry Bellevue and Hillside hosps., Glen Oaks, N.Y., 1955-58; resident neurology Goldwater Meml. Hosp., N.Y.C., 1958-59; chief service Eastern State Hosp., Williamsburg, Va., 1959-61; dir. Tidewater Mental Health Clinic, Williamsburg, 1961-63; practice of medicine specializing in psychiatry, Richmond, 1963-64; asst. dir. div. mental health Ga. Dept. Pub. Health, Atlanta, 1964-70; supt. Ga. Regional Hosp., Savannah, 1970-73; asso. in psychiatry Emory U. Sch. Medicine, Atlanta, 1964-73; chief outpatient clinic William S. Hall Psychiat. Inst., Columbia, S.C., 1973—. Served with Turkish Army, 1953-54. Fellow Am. Psychiat. Assn., Am. Pub. Health Assn.; mem. A.M.A., S.C. Pub. Health Assn., Columbia Med. Soc. Home: 2112 Chipmunk Lane West Columbia SC 29169 Office: PO Drawer 119 Columbia SC 29202

ERNST, LARRY MASON, elec. engr.; b. Ridgeland, S.C., July 20, 1946; s. David H. and Edna Lee (Mason) E.; B.S. in Elec. Engring., U. S.C., 1968; M.S. in Elec. Engring., U. Ky., 1972. Jr. elec. engr. IBM Office Products Div., Lexington, Ky., 1968-73, project engr., 1973—. Registered profl. engr., S.C. Mem. I.E.E.E., Ky. (regional v.p. 1973-74), Lexington (dir. 1971-72, v.p. 1972-73) Jaycees, Pi Mu Epsilon, Eta Kappa Nu, Tau Beta Pi, Omicron Delta Kappa, Alpha Phi Omega. Republican. Home: 3465 Milam Lane Lexington KY 40503 Office: IBM Bldg 032 3 New Circle Rd Lexington KY 40505

ERTEL, EDWARD EUGENE, utility co. exec.; b. Maywood, Cal., July 30, 1932; s. Chester L. and Christie M. (White) E.; student Culver-Stockton Coll., 1951-52; B.S., U. Mo., 1955; m. Janice Kay Gibson, May 2, 1953; children—Debra K., Mark E. Asst. dist. engr. Mo. Pub. Service Co., Sedalia, 1955-60; with Ark.-Mo. Power Co., Blytheville, Ark., 1960—, mgr. electric operations and maintenance, 1973—. Bd. dirs. Blytheville (Ark.) YMCA, 1968—, pres. 1971, treas. 1972—. Served with Signal Corps, AUS, 1955-57. Mem. I.E.E.E., Mo. Valley Electric Assn., Southeastern Electric Exchange, Lambda Chi Alpha. Mem. Christian Ch. (bd. trustees 1968-69, 71-72). Kiwanian (dir. 1969-70). Home: 408 Mimosa St Blytheville AR 72315 Office: 405 W Park St Blytheville AR 72315

ERVIN, SAMUEL JAMES, JR., U.S. senator; b. Morganton, N.C., Sept. 27, 1896; s. Samuel James and Laura T. (Powe) E.; A.B., U. N.C., 1917, LL.D., 1951; LL.B., Harvard, 1922; LL.D., Western Carolina Coll. 1955, George Washington U., 1972, Davidson Coll., 1972, St. Andrews Presbyn. Coll., 1972, Boston U., 1973; Dr. Pub. Adminstrn., Suffolk U., 1957, Wake Forest U., 1971; L.H.D., Wilkes Coll., 1973; m. Margaret Bruce Bell, June 18, 1924; children—Samuel James, Margaret Leslie (Mrs. Gerald M. Hansler), Laura Powe (Mrs. William Edward Smith). Admitted to N.C. bar, 1919; licensed to practice before ICC, Tax Ct. of U.S., and U.S. Supreme Ct.; engaged in gen. practice of law, Morganton, N.C., 1922—; rep. from Burke County, N.C. gen. assembly 1923, 25, 31; judge, Burke County Criminal Ct., 1935-37, N.C. Superior Ct., 1937-43; rep. in Congress from 10th N.C. Dist., Jan. 1946-Jan. 1947; asso. justice N.C. Supreme Ct., 1948-54, U.S. senator from N.C., 1954—, chmn. com. on govt. ops., chmn. select com. on presdl. campaign activities, mem. armed sers. com., chmn. status of forces subcom., mem. judiciary com., chmn. sub-com. on codification and revision of laws, subcom. on constl. rights, subcom. on separation of powers. Chmn., Commn. for Improvement of Adminstrn. of Justice in N.C., 1947-49. Trustee Morganton Graded Schs., 1927-30, U. of N.C., 1932-35, 1945-53, Davidson Coll., 1948-58. Served with Co. I, 28th inf., 1st div., France, 18 months (twice wounded in action, twice cited for gallantry in action), World War I. Awarded French Fourragere, Purple Heart with 1 oakleaf cluster, Silver Star, Distinguished Service Cross. Mem. N.C. State Bd. of Law Examiners, 1944-46; N.C. State Dem. exec. com., 1930-37. Mem. Am., N.C. bar assns., N.C. State Bar, Junior Order United Am. Mechanics, Am. Legion, V.F.W., D.A.V., Soc. 1st Div., Legion of Valor, Morganton C. of C., N.C. Literary and Hist. Assn., So. Hist. Assn., Soc. Mayflower Desc. State N.C. (gov. 1950-52), Gen. Alumni Assn. U. N.C. (pres. 1947-48), Am. Judicature Soc., Am., S.C. hist. assns., N.C. Soc. Preservation Antiquities, Soc. Cin. Sons of Am. Revolution, Sigma Upsilon, Phi Delta Phi. Democrat. Presbyterian (elder). Mason (33 deg., K.T., Kiwanian. Home: Morganton NC 28655 Office: Senate Office Bldg Washington DC 20510

ERVIN, SAMUEL JAMES, III, judge; b. Morganton, N.C., Mar. 2, 1926; s. Samuel James and Margaret Bruce (Bell) E.; B.S., Davidson Coll., 1948; J.D., Harvard, 1951; m. Elisabeth Fore Crawford, Oct. 25, 1952; children—Samuel James IV, Elisabeth Fore, Robert Crawford, Margaret Bell. Admitted to N.C. Bar, then practiced in Morganton; mem. firm Patton, Ervin & Starnes, Morganton, 1957-67; judge Superior Ct. N.C., 1967—. Solicitor Burke County (N.C.) Criminal Ct., 1954-56; mem. N.C. Ho. of Reps., 1965-67; former chmn. Burke County Democratic party. Trustee Grace Hosp., Morganton, Lee-McRae Coll.; trustee ex officio Davidson Coll. Served with AUS, 1944-46, 51-52. Named Morganton Young Man of Year, 1954. Mem. Morganton C. of C. (pres. 1958), Davidson Coll. Alumni Assn. (pres. 1973-74), Mayflower Soc., Kappa Alpha. Presbyn. (elder, deacon). Mason, Kiwanian. Home: 4 Woodside Pl Morganton NC 28655

ERWIN, GEORGE MONTAGUE, ins. co. exec.; b. Howell, Mich., Oct. 3, 1917; s. Harold A. and Kittie (Montague) E.; student Bates Coll., 1935-38; m. Ann Ansley, Aug. 20, 1941; children—Diane Elizabeth (Mrs. Peter C. Baxter), Susan Ansley (Mrs. Donald S. Carswell), Kittie Montague. With Atlantic-Richfield Co. (formerly Atlanta Refining Co.), 1939-49, asst. dist. mgr., Worcester, Mass., 1941-49; partner Johnson-Erwin Ins. Agy., Atlanta, 1949-59; pres. Ins. Agts., Inc., Atlanta, 1959-64; founder Am. Agy. Life Ins. Co., Atlanta, 1964, pres., 1964—; pres. Am. Agy. Financial Corp., Atlanta, 1969—. Pres., Ga. Assn. for Mental Health, 1958-59, Atlanta chpt. Multiple Sclerosis Soc., 1960-61. Served to maj. C.E., AUS, 1943-46. Named Ins. Agt. of Year, 1963, recipient Edgar Dunlap award Ga. Assn. Ins. Agts., 1960. Mem. Atlanta C. of C., Mil. Order World Wars (past comdr.), Atlanta Assn. Ins. Agts. (past pres.), Ga. Assn. Ind. Ins. Agts. (past pres.). Episcopalian. Rotarian (past pres.; past dist. gov.). Club: Atlanta Athletic. Home: 2575 Peachtree Rd NE Atlanta GA 30305 Office: 1252 W Peachtree St NW Atlanta GA 30309

ERWIN, HOWELL C., JR., lawyer; b. Athens, Ga., Oct. 14, 1917; A.B., LL.B., U. Ga. Admitted to Ga. bar, 1940, since practiced law, Ga., 1940—. Mem. State Bd. Bar Examiners, 1959-65. Fellow Am. Coll. Probate Counsel, Am. Bar Found.; mem. Am., Athens, Western Circuit bar assns., State Bar Ga. (pres. 1969-70), Phi Beta Kappa, Phi Delta Phi, Phi Kappa Phi. Address: PO Box 1587 Athens GA 30601

ERWIN, JOHN PRESTON, JR., physician; b. Hemphill, Tex., Mar. 16, 1939; s. John Preston and Clemence Eloise (Buckley) E.; B.S., Lamar State Coll., 1960; M.D., U. Tex., 1964; m. Martha Jo Phillips, Jan. 31, 1965; children—John Preston III, Bryan, Mark. Intern John Peter Smith Hosp., Ft. Worth, 1964-65, gen. practice resident, 1964-66; partner Family Diagnostic Center, Hillsboro, Tex., 1968—; chief staff Grant-Buie Hosp., Inc., 1970-72. Vice chmn. Hillsboro Housing Authority, 1970-72; pres. Hill County Cancer Soc., 1970-72; exec. com. Hillsboro Better Schs. Com. Chmn. Hill County Republican Party, 1971—; mem. sch. bd. Hillsboro Ind. Sch. Dist., 1973—. Served to capt. USAF, 1966-68. Recipient Tng. Grant NIH, 1960, 61. Diplomate Am. Bd. Family Practice. Mem. A.M.A., Tex. Acad. Family Practice (mem. membership and credentials com. 1971—), Mu Delta, Phi Rho Sigma. Episcopalian (mem. vestry 1968-69, 73—, treas. 1973—). Mason, Lion (dir.). Home: 112 Mockingbird St Hillsboro TX 76645 Office: 101 Circle Dr Hillsboro TX 76645

ERWIN, ROBERT MONROE, JR., lawyer; b. Laurens, S.C., Aug. 7, 1937; s. Robert Monroe and Isabel (Dunlap) E.; B.S., Clemson U., 1959; LL.B., U. S.C., 1964; m. Martha Woods Twitty, June 11, 1960; children—Robert M., Martha Woods, Isabel Dunlap, Samuel Latimer, John Weldon. Admitted to S.C. bar, 1964, practiced in Greenwood, S.C., 1964—; asso. firm Grier, McDonald, Burns and Bradford, 1964-66; mem. firm Burns, McDonald, Bradford, Erwin and Few, and predecessor, 1966—. Dir. Bankers Trust of S.C., Greenwood. Chmn. City of Greenwood Citizens Adv. Com. on Housing, 1966—. Bd. dirs. Greenwood YMCA, v.p., 1973-74; trustee Self Meml. Hosp., 1973—. Served with Ordinance Corps, AUS, 1959-61. Mem. Am., S.C. bar assns., Greenwood C. of C. (dir. 1968-72), Phi Delta Phi. Presbyn. (chmn. youth div. 1967-74). Kiwanian (dir. 1972—, pres. 1974-75). Home: 201 Creek Rd East Greenwood SC 29646 Office: PO Box 1207 Greenwood SC 29646

ESCARDO, MAURICIO ENRIQUE, educator; b. Montevideo, Uruguay, Sept. 4, 1914; s. Victor and Alicia (Berlan) Escardo y Anaya; B.A., Instituto de Humanidades, Cordoba, Argentina, 1936; Ph.L., Facultad de Filosoffa, San Miguel, Argentina, 1941; M.A., Universidad Nacional del Litoral, Santa Fe, Argentina, 1952; Ph.D., Instituto Libre de Humanidades, Santa Fe, Argentina, 1952; J.D., Loyola U., 1962; diploma Instituto de Derecho Comparado, Universidad Autonoma de Mexico, 1962; m. Margot Gallofre, May 21, 1960. Came to U.S., 1956, naturalized, 1962. Acting dean, prof. law Universidad Iberoamerica, Sch. Law, Mexico City, 1953-56; asso. prof. philosophy Loyola U., New Orleans, 1957-63; asso. prof. theology and philosophy Georgetown U., Washington, 1963-66, lectr. law Sch. Law, 1964-65; prof. philosophy, history of art, modern langs. Coll. V.I., St. Thomas, 1966—, chmn. dept. humanities, 1968-72. Mem. Am. Philos. Assn., Am. Assn. U. Profs., La. Bar Assn. Author: Graficos de Historia de la Filosofia, 1940. Address: Coll VI St Thomas VI 00801

ESCHENBRENNER, GUNTHER PAUL, mech. engr.; b. Hamburg, Germany, Mar. 3, 1925; s. Karl Christian and Lotte (Hepner) E.; diploma engr. mech., Tech. U. Darmstadt (Germany), 1951; M.S., Columbia U., 1955; m. Ellen Sue Spitzer, Oct. 3, 1953; children—Ronald Carl, Sandra Ellen. Came to U.S., 1952, naturalized, 1957. Project engr. Lurgi Gesellschaft fuer Waermetechnick, Frankfurt, Germany, 1951; design engr. Lummus Co., N.Y.C., 1952; with M.W. Kellogg Co., N.Y.C. and Houston, 1952—, dept. mgr., Houston, 1970-72, dir. engring., 1972—. Area chmn. Community Chest, Greenwich, Conn., 1964; asst. scoutmaster Greenwich council Boy Scouts Am., 1966-70. Registered profl. engr., Tex., Conn., N.Y., N.J., Colo., Okla. Fellow Am. Soc. M.E.; mem. Sci. Research Soc. Am. (pres. Kellogg br. 1972-73), Nat., Tex. socs. profl. engrs., Audubon Soc., Wilderness Soc., Sierra Club. Patentee in field. Home: 6 S Cheska Lane Houston TX 77024 Office: 1300 Three Greenway Plaza E Houston TX 67046

ESCOBEDO, MANUEL G(REGORIO), lawyer; b. Zacatecas, Zacatecas, Mexico, May 9, 1896; s. Enrique and Ana Maria Diaz de Leon Escobedo; Ph.B., Licentiate in Law, Instituto Clentificio de Mexico, 1907-14; Nat. U., 1914-15, Law Sch. Mexico City, 1916-20, U. Paris, 1921-22, London U., 1922-25; m. Elsie Fulda, Aug. 22, 1931; children—Elena, Miguel. Prof. comml. law Escuela Libre de Derecho, 1927-37; asso. Basham & Ringe, 1927-34; sr. partner Noriega y Escobedo, Mexico City, 1934—; prof. civil law Nat. U., 1947-62, Escuela Libre de Derecho, 1965—; dir. Asbestos de Mexico, S.A., Banco del Atlantico, S.A., Cinzano de Mexico, S.A., Gen. Motors Acceptance Corp., de Mexico, S.A., Johnson & Johnson de Mexico, S.A., Olivetti Mexicana, S.A., Productos de Maiz, S.A., Reaseguradora Patria, S.A., Sanborn Hermanos, S.A., Sanborn Monterrey, S.A., Cia de Equipo Industrial Acme de Mexico, S.A., Cia Mercantil Internacional, S.A., Steinbock de Mexico, S.A., Garlock de Mexico, S.A., Ascensores Schindler Mexicana, S.A., Sulzer Hermanos, S.A., Becton Dickinson de Mexico, Vitos de Mexico, S.A., Underwood Mexicana, S.A., Norton de Mexico, S.A. de C.V., Quimica Niagara de Mexico, S.A., Electroquimica Mexicana, S.A., Decorated Insignia de Honor Forense (Mexico); Goldbadge of merit (Austria); Knight 1st class Royal Order St. Olav (Norway); Comdr. Order Brit. Empire. Mem. Internat. (past-pres.), Am. Inter-Am. bar assns., Assn. Bar City N.Y., Union Iberoamericana de Colegios y Agrupaciones de Abogados (v.p. 1957—), Nat. Coll. Lawyers, Mexico City Bar, Nat. Acad. Law and Jurisprudence. Home: 23 Historiadores Mexico City 20 Mexico Office: 14 Av Juarez Mexico City 1 Mexico

ESCOBEDO, MIGUEL STUART, lawyer; b. Mexico City, Dec. 12, 1936; s. Manuel Gregorio and Elsie Stuart (Fulda) E.; student Centro Universitario, Mexico, 1952-54; Licenciate in Law, Universidad Nacional Autonoma de Mexico, 1960; m. Maria Guadalupe Conover Lazo, Aug. 26, 1966; children—Maria Beatriz, Manuel Sanitago, Juan Nicolas. Admitted to Mexico bar, 1963; mem. firm Noriega y Escobedo, Mexico City, 1957—, partner, 1961—. Dir. Olivette Mexicana, Massey-Ferguson de Mexico, Reaseguaradora Patria, Interamericana de Arrendamientos. Mem. Mexican Bar Assn. (mem. council 1966-72), Illustre y Nacional Colegio de Abogados (sec. 1967-70). Club: Banqueros de Mexico. Home: 20 Cerrada de San Jeronimo San Jeronimo Lidice Mexico Office: 14 Juarez Av Mexico City Mexico

ESKRIDGE, CHARLES DEWITT, aerospace engr.; b. Walterboro, S.C. Aug. 21, 1937; s. Charles DeWitt and Lois (Lavender) E.; B.S., Va. Poly. Inst. 1959, M.S., 1963, Ph.D., 1964; postgrad. U. Ala., 1971-72, Med. U. S.C., 1972-73; m. Ida Frances Howard, July 20, 1957; children—Charles, James, John, Paul. Instr. engring. mechanics VA. Poly. Inst., Blacksburg, 1959-64; research engr. Douglas Aircraft Co., 1964-66; sr. engr. The Boeing Co., Huntsville, Ala., 1966-72; sr. scientist Sci. Applications, Inc., La Jolla, Cal., 1972—. Instr. engring. U. N.C., Charlotte, 1965-66. Registered profl. engr., N.C. Apollo Achievement award NASA, 1969; named Man of the Year Saturn Engring., 1970. Mem. Am. Astronautical Soc., Northwest Optimist Club (v.p. 1971-72). Home: 1004 Lepley Rd Hanahan SC 29406 Office: 80 Barre St Charleston SC 29401

ESPEY, LAWRENCE LEE, educator; b. Mercedes, Tex., Sept. 5, 1935; s. Harry Woods and Irene Evelyn (Dodson) E.; B.A., U. Tex., 1958, M.A., 1961; Ph.D., Fla. State U., 1964; m. Esther Mae Tetsch, Dec. 26, 1959; children—Richard Andrew, Elaine, Annette. Instr. biology Fla. State U., Tallahassee, 1964; NIH post-doctoral fellow U. Mich. Med. Sch., Ann Arbor, 1965-66; asso. prof. biology Trinity U., San Antonio, 1966-71, asso. prof., chmn. environmental studies, 1972—. Cons. NIH, 1973. Vol. cons. Planned Parenthood, San Antonio, 1972—. Bd. dirs. Citizens for a Better Environment, San Antonio, 1972—. NIH research grantee, 1967—. Contbr. articles to profl. jours. Home: 2515 Greencrest St San Antonio TX 78213

ESPOSITO, VITO MICHAEL, hosp. supply co. exec.; b. Logan, W.Va., Sept. 11, 1940; s. Vito T. and Mary Frances (Lamp) E.; B.S., Marshall U., 1962; M.S., W.Va. U., 1965, Ph.D. (USPHS fellow), 1966; m. Betty Honaker, Jan. 18, 1960; children—Anne Elizabeth, Leslie Christine. Sr. staff fellow immunology NIH, Bethesda, Md., 1969-71; dir. research and devel. DADE div. Am. Hosp. Supply Corp., Miami, Fla., 1971—. Cons. Canadian Specifications Bd. for Blood Bank Reagents, 1973—. Served to lt. comdr. USPHS, 1967-69. NIH Sr. Staff fellow., 1969-71. Mem. Am. Soc. Microbiology, A.A.A.S., Am. Assn. Blood Banks, N.Y. Acad. Sci., Genetics Soc. Am., Am. Soc. Clin. Pathology, Sigma Xi. Contbr. articles to sci. jours. Patentee in field. Home: 8351 SW 156th St Miami FL 33157 Office: PO Box 672 Miami FL 33152

ESPY, ISAAC PUGH, civil engr., lawyer; b. Clarksville, Tenn., Mar. 23, 1939; s. Goodman Basil and Dacy Clyde (Pugh) E.; B.S. in Civil Engring., U. Ala., 1961, postgrad., 1961-62, J.D. (William Hepburn scholar), 1972; m. Carol Janet Carpenter, May 29, 1960; children—Jami Lucretia, Isaac Pugh, Amanda Susan. Part-time instr. U. Ala., 1961-62; profl. engr., land surveyor, Jackson, Ala., 1965-69; partner G. B. Espy Jr. & Son, Jackson, 1965-69; with Gilbreath, Foster & Brooks, Inc., Tuscaloosa, Ala., 1969—, chief structural engr., 1969-70, chief engr., 1971—, v.p., 1971-73, pres., 1973—; admitted to Ala. bar, 1972; partner Crowder & Espy, attys., 1972—. Del. Ala. State Republican Conv., 1966-68. Served with C.E., USNR, 1962-65. Registered profl. engr., Ala., Fla., S.C. Mem. Am. Soc. C.E. (mem. com. 1969-71), Am. Congress on Surveying and Mapping, Ala. Soc. Profl. Land Surveyors (pres. 1974), Ala. Soc. Profl. Engrs. (dir.), Am., Ala. bar assns. Republican. Baptist (deacon 1966-71, chmn. bd. trustees 1972). Mason. Home: 93 Woodland Hills Tuscaloosa AL 35401 Office: PO Box 1966 Tuscaloosa AL 35401

ESSLINGER, WILLIAM GLENN, chemist, educator; b. Huntsville, Ala., Oct. 21, 1937; s. William Holbert and Helen (Scott) E.; B.S. in Chemistry, U. Ala., 1962, M.S., 1964, Ph.D. (NASA fellow) 1966; m. Jacquelyn Randitt, Sept. 15, 1958; children—Nancy Lynn, Bonnie Dianne, Glenda Gayle, William Glenn. Head dept. chemist Union U., Jackson, Tenn., 1966-68; asst. prof. West Ga. Coll., Carrollton, 1968-71, asso. prof., 1971—, chmn. dept. chemistry, 1972—. Cons. to copper industry; research chemist Chemstrand Co., Decatur, Ga., summer 1964. Mem. Am. Chem. Soc., Ga. Acad. Sci., Sigma Xi, Delta Tau Delta. Kiwanian (dir. 1970-72). Club: Exchange. Home: Route 10 Box 111 Carrollton GA 30117

ESSRICK, ABRAHAM JOSEPH, judge; b. Phila., Feb. 8, 1914; s. Jacob and Rachel (Pressman) E.; B.A. in Accounting, George Washington U., 1956; J.D. cum laude, Rutgers U., 1940; post-grad. U. Grenoble, France, 1945; m. Riva Krakuzin, Feb. 14, 1943 (dec. Aug. 1959); children—Helene (Mrs. Feldsher), Carol; m. 2d, Pearl Gibel, May 20, 1972; children—Frances H. Gibel, Bonnie (Mrs. Schneider).

Admitted to D.C. bar, 1941, U.S. Supreme Ct., 1964; atty. adviser SEC, Washington, 1946-53; atty. advisor ICC, Washington, 1953-59. hearing examiner, 1959-72, adminstrv. law judge, 1972—. Mem. Phila. Speakers Council, 1942, Jewish Educators Council, 1958-60; mem. bd. dirs. govt. div. United Jewish Appeal of Greater Washington, Inc., 1958—, mem. exec. com., 1964-65, trustee, 1960-61, 64—, vice chmn. exec. com. govt. div., 1965. Served with Signal Intelligence Div., ETO, 1944-45. Mem. Am., Fed. bar assns., Am. Judicature Soc., Nat. Lawyers Club, Fed. Adminstrv. Law Judges Conf., Smithsonian Assos., Friends John F. Kennedy Center, Internat. Platform Assn. Jewish religion. Mem. B'nai B'rith. Clubs: Rutgers, Gaslight (Washington). Home: 905 Kenbrook Dr Silver Spring MD 20902 Office: ICC 12th and Constitution Av NW Washington DC 20423

ESTABROOK, RONALD WINFIELD, ednl. adminstr.; b. Albany, N.Y., Jan. 3, 1926; s. George Arthur and Lillian Florence (Childs) E.; B.S., Rensselaer Poly. Inst., 1950; Ph.D., U. Rochester, 1954; m. June Elizabeth Templeton, Aug. 23, 1947; children—Linda (Mrs. Stephen Gilbert), Laura (Mrs. Sydney Verinder), Jill, David. Research fellow Johnson Research Found., U. Pa. Sch. Medicine, Phila., 1955-58; research asso. Molteno Inst. Cambridge (Eng.) U., 1958-59; asst. prof. phys. biochemistry U. Pa. Sch. Medicine, 1959-62, asso. prof., 1962-65, prof., 1965-68; prof., chmn. dept. biochemistry U. Tex. Southwestern Med. Sch., Dallas, 1968—, dean Grad. Sch. Biomed. Scis., 1973—. Nat. corr. Fedn. Am. Socs. Exptl. Biology Pub. Affairs Com., Bethesda, Md., 1970-72; mem. adv. com. NIH of USPHS, 1968-71; chmn. basic sci. rev. com. VA, Washington, 1972—; Assn. Am. Med. Colls. rep. Nat. Bd. Med. Examiners, 1972—; spl. cons. Nat. Heart and Lung Inst., Bethesda, 1972. Served with USNR, 1943-46. USPHS Gen. Support grantee, 1968—. Mem. Pan-Am. Assn. Biochem. Socs. (sec., gen. 1972—), Am. Chem. Soc., Am. Soc. Biol. Chemists, Am. Soc. Pharmacology and Exptl. Therapeutics, John Morgan Soc. (pres. 1967-68), Sigma Xi. Episcopalian. Editor: Hemes and Hemoproteins (R.W. Estabrook), 1966; Methods in Enzymology, Vol. 10 (R.W. Estabrook and M. Pullman), 1967. Exec. editor Archives Biochemistry and Biophysics, 1966-73. Contbr. numerous articles to profl. jours. Home: 5208 Preston Haven Dallas TX 75229

ESTEB, ADLAI ALBERT, clergyman, author; b. La Grande, Ore., Nov. 17, 1901; s. Lemuel Albert and Addretta (Koger) E.; B.Th., Walla Walla Coll., 1931; M.A., Cal. Coll., Peiping, China, 1953; Ph.D., U. So. Cal., 1944; m. Florence Edna Airey, Feb. 5, 1923; children—Adeline, Lucille (Mrs. Cleat Laney). Ordained to ministry Seventh Day Adventist Ch., 1923; missionary to China, 1923-37; pastor Seventh Day Adventist Ch., Long Beach, Cal., 1938-40; sec. Home Missionary Dept., So. Cal. Conf. Seventh Day Adventist Ch., 1940-46, Pacific Union Conf. Seventh Day Adventist Ch., Glendale, Cal., 1946-50; editor Go, Jour. for Adventist Laymen, gen. conf. Seventh Day Adventist Ch., Washington, 1950-70; vis. prof., lectr.; Christian ethics Andrews U., Berrien Springs, Mich., 1955—. Cited as poet laureate of denomination by pres. World Conf., 1966. Mem. China Soc. of So. Cal. (pres. 1946-50), Oriental Fellowship (pres. 1963), Phi Beta Kappa, Phi Kai Phi, Phi Kappa Phi. Author: Driftwood, 1947; Firewood 1952; Sandalwood, 1955; Morning Manna, 1962; Rosewood, 1964; Scrapwood, 1967; (poetry) Redwood, 1970; Kindle Kindness, 1971; The Meaning of Christmas, 1972; When Suffering Comes, 1974; Straight Ahead, 1974. Home: 8013 Silgo Creek Pkwy Washington DC 20012 Office: 6840 Eastern Av Washington DC 20012

ESTES, CHARLES EDWIN, trucking co. exec.; b. Chase City, Va., Jan. 23, 1923; s. Webb Wallace and Ruth Gladys (Berry) E.; student U. Va., 1946; m. Dorothy LeeThomasson, Nov. 1, 1947; children—Michael Edwin, Martha Lee. Propr. C.E. Estes Contract Carrier, Richmond, Va., 1948—; pres., owner Great Coastal Express, Inc., Richmond, 1959—; v.p. Garland & Estes Oil Co., Richmond, 1958—; C.E. Estes, Inc., 1958—, owner C.E. Estes Realty, 1959—; founder, dir. Second Nat. Bank, Richmond. Trustee C.E. Estes Contract Carrier Employees Profit Sharing Plan and Trust, Great Coastal Express, Inc. Employees Profit Sharing Plan and Trust. Bd. dirs. Gill Sch., Richmond; trustee Estes Found. Served with USAAF, 1943-44. Mem. Am. Trucking Assn. (dir.), Va. Hwy. Users Assn. (dir.), West Richmond Businessmen's Assn., Richmond Traffic Club, Nat. Right to Work Legal Found. Methodist (trustee 1964, past chmn. coms.). Mason (32 deg., Shriner). Clubs: Richmond Ski, Hermitage Country, Bull and Bear, Bachelor's (Richmond). Home: 8801 River Rd Richmond VA 23229 Office: 501 S 14th St Richmond VA 23224

ESTES, DEWITT OCLE, county agrl. agt.; b. Lafayette, Ala., June 4, 1914; s. Olen J. and Corine (Hamilton) E.; B.S., Ala. Poly. Inst., 1949; m. Sarah Elizabeth Edwards, Oct. 24, 1950. With Extension Service, U.S. Dept. Agr., 1949—, asst. county agt. Monroe County, Ala., 1949-50, Sumter County, Livingston, Ala., 1950-52; asst. county agt. Washington, County, Chatom, Ala., 1952-60, county agt., 1960-66, county extension chmn., 1966—. Adviser, Chatom Indsl. Bd., 1962—. Served with USAAF, 1942-45. Decorated Air medal with bronze oak leaf cluster. Recipient certificate of Achievement for outstanding 4-H work Ala. Assn. County Agts., 1958. Mem. Ala. Assn. County Agrl. Agts., Epsilon Sigma Phi. Baptist (deacon). Mason (32 deg., Shriner). Home: 205 E Pinehurst Dr Chatom AL 36518 Office: Frank Turner Hall PO Box 280 Chatom AL 36518

ESTES, GERALD WALTER, newspaper exec.; b. Memphis, Apr. 21, 1928; s. Edward Leon and Grace Virginia (Knight) E.; student Memphis State U., 1949-50; m. Mary Charlene Owen, Nov. 7, 1953; children—Patricia (Mrs. Roy Brian Tischler), Charles Edward, Susan Lynn, Jacqueline Ann. Research asst. Washington Star News, 1954-56, asst. prodn. mgr., 1956-68; prodn. mgr. Richmond (Va.) Newspapers, S.E. Media, Inc., 1968-69, gen. mgr., 1969-73, v.p., 1969—; v.p. Media Gen., Inc., 1974—. Served with USAF, 1946-49. Mem. Richmond C. of C., Central Richmond Assn., So. Newspaper Pubs. Assn., So. Printing Prodn. Inst. Republican. Methodist. Clubs: Bull and Bear, Salisbury Country, Research in newspaper automation and computerized newspaper prodn. facility. Home: 7505 River Rd Richmond VA 23229 Office: 333 E Grace Richmond VA 23219

ESTES, MOREAU PINCKNEY IV, lawyer, business exec.; b. Nashville, Oct. 10, 1917; s.; Moreau Pinckney and Lillian (Cole) E.; student Vanderbilt U., 1937; LL.B., Cumberland U. Law Sch., 1938; m. Bertha Lewis, Jan. 14, 1941; children—Moreau Pinckney V, Robert Lewis, Victoria Susanne. Admitted to Tenn. bar, 1938; practiced in Nashville, 1938-41; bldg. contractor, Nashville, 1940-42; asst. employees service dir. Vultee Aircraft, Nashville, 1942; bldg. contractor, Nashville, 1946-53; dir. Davidson County Farm Bur., Nashville, 1950-56; v.p. Davidson Farmers Co-Op, 1955-56; gen. mgr. Harpeth Valley Utilities Dist. of Davidson and Williamson Counties, Tenn., 1963-67; now pres. Hillsboro-Harpeth Corp.; v.p. Rivermont Farms, Inc.; property adminstr. State of Tenn., 1964-67, atty. property div., 1962-64; dir. So. Title Guaranty Corp. of Tenn. Del. Democratic State Conv., 1951; sec. Williamson County Dem. Primary Commn., 1967-69. Served as 1st lt., Signal Corps, AUS, 1942-46. Mem. Nashville Home Bldrs. Assn. (pres. 1951, dir. 1952), Tenn. Horsemens Assn., (dir. 1964), Tenn. Hist. Assn., Nashville Tennis Assn. (dir. 1969-72), Tenn., Nashville bar assns., Am. Judicature Soc., Internat. Platform Assn., Davidson County Farm Bur., Am. Legion, Delta Kappa Epsilon. Democrat. Methodist (steward 1940-50). Clubs: Inglewood Sch. Men's (past pres.), Percy Priest Sch. Men's (pres., 1963), Wildwood Swimming and Tennis (founder, 1st chmn. bd.). Home: Beech Creek Rd Route 2 Brentwood TN 37027 Office: Life & Casualty Tower Nashville TN 37219

ESTES, WINSTON MARVIN, author, ret. air force officer; b. Quanah, Tex., Oct. 31, 1917; s. Thomas Marvin and Bertha Grace (Newson) E.; student Tex. Tech. Coll., 1938-39; m. Sarah Hamlin Spears, Feb. 23, 1946; children—Richard Hawley, Elizabeth Meade. Enlisted in U.S. Army Air Force, 1941, advanced through grades to lt. col. U.S. Air Force 1959; pub. affairs officer, edn. and tng. officer, intelligence officer in S.W. Pacific, 1942-45, U.S., 1945-55, 58-69, Germany, 1955-58; ret., 1969. Mem. Authors Guild Am., Ret. Officers Assn., Tex. Hist. Soc. Episcopalian (vestryman 1964, 73). Author; Winston in Wonderland, 1956; Another Part of the House, 1970; A Streetful of People, 1972; A Simple Act of Kindness, 1973. Address: 5302 Ravensworth Rd Springfield VA 22151

ESTEVES, ALBERTO RAUL, lawyer; b. Aguadilla, P.R., Oct. 23, 1926; s.Alberto and Sofia (Marques) E.; B.S.A. cum laude, U. Fla., 1949; LL.B., U. P.R., 1961; LL.M., Columbia U., 1962; m. Ada Rita Vergne, May 22, 1964; children—Alberto Juan, Francisco Javier, Ada Sofia. Admitted to P.R. bar, 1964; since practiced in San Juan; aso. mem. firm Thomas C. Tilley, Hato Rey, San Juan, 1964-66, partner, 1966—. Pres., Gov.'s Com. on Consumer Housing Protection, 1971; mem. State Bd. for Consumer Protection, 1973-74. Bd. dirs. San Juan Anti-Tb Assn., 1972-74. Mem. P.R. (pres. consumer protection commn. 1971-73), Am. bar assns. Roman Catholic. Club: Rock Tennis. Home: RDF 3-43Y Beverly Hills Rio Piedras PR 00928 Office: 401 Teachers Assn Bldg Hato Rey San Juan PR 00918

ESTILL, JOHN STAPLES, JR., lawyer; b. Grapevine, Tex., Jan. 20, 1919; s. John Staples and Ada (Chambers) E.; B.S. in Commerce, Tex. Christian U., 1940; J.D., So. Methodist U., 1948; m. Dorothy Finlayson, Nov. 27, 1940; children—John S. III, James Calloway, Sally Finlayson. Admitted to Tex. bar, 1948, Kan. bar, 1958, Okla. bar, 1966; No. Dist. Tex. bar, 1949; U.S. Circuit Ct. Appeals, 1973; sole practice, Fort Worth, 1948-50; spl. asst. to U.S. atty. No. Dist. Tex., Fort Worth, 1950-53; atty. Sinclair Oil & Gas Corp., Fort Worth, 1953-57, Tulsa, 1965-67; atty. Sinclair Pipe Line Co., Independence, Kan., 1957-64, gen. atty., 1964-65; sr. partner Hall, Estill, Hardwick, Gable, Collingsworth & Nelson, Tulsa, 1967—; sec., counsel Williams Pipe Line Co., 1969—. Served with Supply Corps, USNR, 1942-46. Mem. Am., Tulsa County, Tex., Kan., Okla. bar assns. Elk. Methodist (steward). Clubs: Tulsa, Oaks Country (both Tulsa). Home: 4734 S Delaware St Tulsa OK 74105 Office: 805 Nat Bank Tulsa Bldg Tulsa OK 74103

ESTRELLA, WILLIAM, lawyer; b. Santurce, P.R., Apr. 28, 1935; s. Guillermo and Lucy (Lopez de Victoria) E.; B.S. in Econs., U. P.R., 1957, LL.B. cum laude, 1960; m. Susana Conesa Braun, Oct. 26, 1965; children—William Ricardo, Alberto Guillermo. Admitted to P.R. bar, 1960, U.S. Dist. Ct. P.R., 1963, U.S. Ct. Appeals, 1964; asso. James R. Beverley, San Juan, P.R., 1960-67; partner firm Beverley, Rodriquez, Estrella & Pesquera, 1967-73; individual practice, 1974—; dir. Allied Wholesale Co. P.R. Inc., Cayey-Guayama Devel. Corp.; legal adviser Texaco P.R., Inc., Inter. Am. U. P.R., Presbyn. Community Hosp., San Juan. Served to 1st lt. AUS, 1961-62. Mem. Bar Assn. P.R. (bd. examiners), Am. Bar Assn., Navy League. Elk. Club: Bankers (San Juan). Home: W-1 Jobos St Valle Arriba Heights Carolina PR 00630 Office: PO Box S-4826 San Juan PR 00905

ETCHISON, ANNIE LAURIE, librarian, artist; b. Cana, N.C., Dec. 5, 1908; d. John W. and Nana (Cain) Etchison; A.B., Western Res. U., 1939, B.L.S., 1940. Librarian, Cleve. Pub. Library, 1941-42; chief librarian Langley AFB, Va., 1942-44; supervisory librarian U.S. Army, Hawaii, 1945; chief librarian Armed Forces Western Pacific, Phillipines, Okinawa 1945-46; command librarian 2d Dist. U.S. Army, Europe, 1947-49, U.S. Air Force, Alaska, 1950-52; librarian recruiter U.S. Army, Washington, 1952-54; staff librarian U.S. Army, Korean Communication Zone, 1954-55; librarian Dept. Navy, 1956; dir. libraries, Ft. Bragg, N.C., 1957-63; staff librarian 3d U.S. Army, 1963-72; library dir. Hdqrs. U.S. Army Europe, 1972—. Cons. automation of libraries, library design and facilities, personnel mgmt. Home: RFD 5 Box 58 Mocksville NC 27028 Office: Hdqrs US Army Europe APO New York City NY 09403

ETHEREDGE, ROBERT FOSTER, lawyer, state legislator; b. Birmingham, Ala., July 14, 1920; s. Joel H. and Nell (Cain) E.; A.B., U. Ala., 1946, LL.B., 1949; m. Joanna Carson, Aug. 28, 1948; children—Robert Foster, Carson, Nancy. Admitted to Ala. bar, 1949; since practiced in Birmingham; mem. firm Spain, Gillon, Riley, Tate, & Ansley, and predecessor, 1949—. Mem. Ala. Ho. of Reps., 1963—. Mem. adv. com. Family Ct.; pres. Ala. Soc. Crippled Children and Adults, 1971-73; chmn. profl. div. United Appeal. Bd. dirs. Jefferson County Socs. for Crippled Children and Adults, North Central Ala. Rehab. Facility. Served to 1st lt. AUS, 1943-46. Mem. Am. (mem. state legislative com.), Birmingham bar assns., Ala. State Bar, Am. Legion, V.F.W., Relay House, Ala. Law Inst., Farrah Law Soc., Ala. Def. Lawyers Assn., Internat. Assn. Ins. Counsel, Am. Judicature Soc., Omicron Delta Kappa, Pi Kappa Alpha. Democrat. Methodist. Elk, Eagle, Rotarian. Club: Country of Birmingham. Home: 3748 Locksley Dr Birmingham AL 35223 Office: John A Hand Bldg Birmingham AL 35203

ETHINGTON, GROVER CLEVELAND, JR., state ofcl.; b. Shelby County, Ky., Aug. 24, 1923; s. Grover C. and Samantha G. (Hulker) E.; B.S. in Elec. Engring., U. Ky., 1950; certificate Yale, 1964; m. Virginia M. Watkins, Nov. 22, 1951; children—Jerry Wayne, Candy Marie. Engr., Joe Wakefield, contractor, Shelbyville, Ky., 1950; project engr. Schenley Distillers, Inc., Frankfort, Ky., 1950-54; traffic engr. Ky. Dept. of Hwys., Frankfort, 1954-61, chief traffic engr., 1961-64, asst. dir. traffic, 1964—. Served with AUS, 1942-45, 61-62. Fellow Inst. Traffic Engrs.; mem. Triangle, Scabbard and Blade, Eta Kappa Nu. Democrat. Baptist. Home: 245 Hawkeegan Dr Frankfort KY 40601 Office: State Office Bldg Bureau Hwys Frankfort KY 40601

EUBANK, RAYMOND HENRY, petroleum co. exec.; b. Dallas, Aug. 10, 1927; s. Joseph Henry and Fannie Pearl (Riddle) E.; B.S. in Petroleum Engring., Tex. A. & M. U., 1950; m. Ora May Davis, Nov. 28, 1951; children—Richard Henry, Sheri Janece, Dennis Ray. Petroleum engr. Sun Oil Co., 1950-56, Hunt Oil Co., 1956-65; petroleum cons., Dallas, 1965-67; exec. v.p. Triton Oil & Gas Corp., Dallas, 1967—, also dir. Dir. New Zealand Petroleum Co., Ltd., Electrothermic Co. Served to 1st lt. AUS, 1946-48, 1951-53. Registered profl. engr., Tex. Mem. Soc. Petroleum Engrs. of Am. Inst. Mining Engrs., Petroleum Engrs. Club, Dallas Petroleum Clubs, Engrs. Club (dir. 1973—). Methodist (mem. bd. 1968-69). Club: Royal Oaks Country (dir. 1970-73; v.p. 1971—) (Dallas). Home: 9626 Estate Lane Dallas TX 75238 Office: 2310 Republic Bank Tower Dallas TX 75201

EUBANKS, JEWEL GOLDEN (MRS. J. GROVER EUBANKS), educator; b. Birmingham, Ala.; d. Dowdell D. and Alice (Stone) Golden; B.S. with honors, Auburn U., 1933; M.A., Tchrs. Coll., Columbia, 1941; Ph.D., Fla. State U., 1958; m. J. Grover Eubanks, Feb. 24, 1973; stepchildren—James Grover, Steve, Carol (Mrs. Rentz), Lynne (Mrs. Fust). Tchr. home econs. Billingsley (Ala.) High Sch., 1933-34, Red Leval (Ala.) High Sch., 1934-35, Selma (Ala.) Jr. High Sch., 1935-41; instr. Winthrop Coll., 1941-42; asst. prof. clothing and textiles Tex. Tech. Coll., 1942-43, Auburn U., 1943-54; asso. prof. clothing and textiles U. Md., 1958-59; asso. prof. clothing and textiles U. So. Miss., Hattiesburg, 1960-62, prof., 1962-73, chmn. dept. environmental design, 1971-73. Mem. Am. Assn. U. Women (br. v.p. 1963-65), Am., Miss. (chmn. coll. clubs sect. 1960-61, clothing and textiles sect. 1964-66) home econs. assns., Am. Assn. Textile Chemists and Colorists, Nat., Central Region (adv. com. 1971-72) assns. coll. tchrs. textiles and clothing, Mortar Bd., Phi Kappa Phi, Omicron Nu, Kappa Delta Pi, Alpha Phi Epsilon, Chi Delta Phi, Delta Kappa Gamma (pres. 1970-72), Pi Tau Chi. Presbyn. Home: 2026 Pepperell Pkwy Opelika AL 36801 Office: PO Box 1234 Pepperell Sta Opelika AL 36801

EUBANKS, WILLIAM HUNTER, engr., educator; b. Columbus, Miss., Dec. 13, 1921; s. William Hunter and Pauline (Propst) E.; B.S. in Aero. Engring., Miss. State Coll., 1947; M. Ed., 1952; m. Juanita Patrick, Mar. 5, 1944; children—William H., Kenneth B., Cora Diane. Engr., draftsman Miss. Light & Power Dept., Columbus, 1946-47; instr. Miss. State Coll., 1947-53; engr. estimator U.S. Steel Corp., Birmingham, Ala., 1953-54; asso. prof. Miss. State U., State College, 1953-60, head dept. engring. graphics, 1960—, prof., 1962—. Chmn. bd trustees Oktibbeha County Hosp., 1969—. Served with C.E., AUS, 1943-46; ETO. Registered profl. engr., Miss. Mem. Am. Soc. Engring. Edn. (chmn. Southeastern sect. engring. graphics div. 1965-66), Nat., Miss. socs. profl. engrs. Rotarian (dir. internat. services 1971-72). Home: Route 2 Hwy 82 E Starkville MS 39759 Office: PO Box EG Mississippi State University MS 39762

EUDALY, HAZEL MARIE (PEN NAME MARIA SADDLER DE EUDALY), editor; b. Appleton City, Mo., Dec. 22, 1911; d. Russell Godby and Bertha (Piepmeier) Saddler; student William Jewell Coll., 1929-31; B.S. in Edn., Central Mo. State Tchrs. Coll., 1936; M.R.E., Southwestern Bapt. Theol. Sem., 1939, postgrad., 1956-57, 62-63; m. Nathan Hoyt Eudaly, Nov. 22, 1941; children—Richard Milton, Katharine (Mrs. William George Hart), Nathan Hoyt. Tchr. pub. schs., Amsterdam, Mo., 1931-37; with ednl. sects. Bapt. Ch., 1939—, editor, writer Bapt. Spanish Pub. House, Fgn. Mission Bd. El Paso, 1948—. Curriculum cons. Bapt. World Alliance, 1966. Active local chpts. P.T.A., 1960-68, chmn. life edn. com. dist. XV, 1971—; pres. Austin High Sch. chpt. Am. Field Service, 1969—, host 1971-72. Recipient Life Service award S.W. Bapt. Coll., 1972. Mem. Sigma Delta Pi. Mem. Order Eastern Star. Author: 19 books in Spanish and English, including: Dickie in Mexico, 1949; Chatting With the Chews, 1950; Object Lessons, 1952; My Helpers, 1957; My Friends, 1958; My Family, 1959; Stories of the New Testament, 1970. Address: PO Box 4255 7000 Alabama El Paso TX 79914

EUDALY, NATHAN HOYT, sales exec.; b. Pecos, Tex., Apr. 24, 1913; s. Milton Truman and Katharine (Barber) E.; B.B.A., Tex. Tech. U., 1938; B.D., Southwestern Bapt. Theol. Sem., 1948, M.R.E., 1957, D.R.E. with honors, 1959; m. Marie Saddler, Nov. 22, 1941; children—Richard Milton, Katharine Hart, Nathan Hoyt. Mem. staff Bapt. Home Mission Bd., 1946-48; field evangelism Bapt. Fgn. Missionary So. Bapt. Conv., 1948, field evangelism, Morelia, Mexico, 1948-49; student lang., Medellin, Colombia, 1949-50; prof. Bapt. Theol. Sem., Torreon, Mexico, 1950-52; bus. mgr. Bapt. Spanish Publishing House, El Paso, Tex., 1952-60, dir. distbn. div., 1960-64, sales-distbg. div., 1964-67, dir. sales div., 1967-73, dir. marketing services div., 1973—. Mem. Internat. Com. Christian Edn., 1952-66; participant Latin Am. Missions confs., 1956, 59; mem. Christian Edn. com. Mexican Bapt. Conv., 1959-62. Active Boys Scouts Am., P.T.A., Am. Field Service. Treas. City of Grandfalls, Tex., 1938-41; parliamentarian, rep. county Democratic convs. Mem. Evang. Lit. Overseas, Spanish Evang. Pubs. Assn., Christian Booksellers Assn., Congreso Latinoamericano de Evangelismo. Editor pedagogical and adminstrv. sect. El Promotor de Educaion Cristiana, 1966-71, asso. editor, 1973—; mng. editor Mundo Bautista, 1973—. Contbr. numerous articles to religious jours. Address: Box 4255 7000 Alabama St El Paso TX 79914

EUSTON, ANDREW FRANCIS, JR., govt. ofcl.; b. New Haven, Conn., Sept. 8, 1934; s. Andrew Francis and Kathleen (Holwell) E.; grad. Hotchkiss Sch., 1952; B.A., Yale, 1956, B.Arch., 1959, M.Arch., 1972. Designer A.F. Euston (Sr.), Architect, New Haven, 1956-59; architect firm McLoed, Ferrara & Ensign, Washington, 1962, firm W.H. Metcalf Assos., Washington, 1963-65; urban designer firm Cooper & Auerbach, Washington, 1965-66; dir. urban programs A.I.A., Washington, 1966-68; dir. urban design br. Office Community Devel., Dept. Housing and Urban Devel., Washington, 1968-70, prin. urban design officer Environmental and Land Use Planning div., 1970—; mem. adv. staff Tech. Adv. Panel on Housing, Commerce Dept., 1968; vis. critic Grad. Sch. Design, Harvard, Cambridge, Mass., 1971-72; columnist Capitol Hill News, Washington, 1964-65. Treas. The Seversmith Found., 1966-72; mem. Capitol Hill Community Council, 1962-68, Neighborhood Commons Archtl. Adv. Com., 1964-66, Emergency Recreation Com. for Capitol East, 1966-68; dir. Assn. Study Man-Environment Relations, 1969—, Washington Ethical Soc., 1972—, World Future Soc., 1968—. Bd. dirs. humanist involvement div. Am. Humanist Assn., 1966-68, pres. Washington Chpt. 1962—. Served as 1st lt. M.C., USAF, 1959-62. Loeb fellow in advanced environmental studies, Harvard, 1971-72. Mem. A.I.A. (mem. com. urban design, com. govt. affairs), Am. Soc. Planning Ofcls., Nat. Assn. Housing and Redevel. Ofcls., Nat. Trust for Historic Preservation. Clubs: Yale (Washington); Faculty (Harvard). Author: (with Archibald C. Rogers) Check-list for Cities, 1968; (with others) Socio-Physical Technology: A State-of-the-Art Report, 1971. Home: 1758 T St NW Washington DC 20009 Office: Rm 8212 Dept Housing and Urban Development Washington DC 20410

EVANS, CHARLES HARRISON, supt. schs.; b. Bastrop, Tex., Nov. 23, 1925; s. Charles Harrison and Lilly Ann (Hemphill) E.; B.A., Baylor U., 1949; M.S., Tex. Coll. Arts and Industries, 1956; m. June Marie Hensley, Dec. 24, 1949; children—Marcus Eugene, Keith Byron. Tchr., coach, Marble Falls (Tex.) Ind. Sch. Dist., 1949-50, Port Lavaca Ind. Sch. Dist., 1950-53; prin. high sch. coach Sundeen Ind. Sch. Dist., Corpus Christi, 1953-56; prin. high sch. Agua Dulce Ind. Sch. Dist., 1956-57, supt. schs., 1 57-67; supt. schs. Bastrop (Tex.) Ind. Sch. Dist., 1967—. Served with USAAF, 1944-45. Mem. Phi Delta Kappa. Methodist. Mason (Shriner), Elk, Lion (chmn. 1971-72). Home: Route 2 Box 151A Bastrop TX 78602 Office: 1602 Hill Bastrop TX 78602

EVANS, CHARLES WAYNE, sem. ofcl.; b. Happy, Tex., Jan. 16, 1919; s. Joseph George and Bertie Mae (Mulkey) S.; B.S., Hardin-Simmons U., 1940, LL.D., 1961; studied Tex. Christian U., U. Ky.; m. Zona Elizabeth Horn, June 9, 1940; children—David, Lyn, Jan. Stockman-farmer, Hereford, Tex., 1940-46; dealer Internat. Harvester Co., 1946-53; v.p. bus. affairs Southwestern Bapt. Theol. Sem., Fort Worth, 1954—. Past chmn. budget com. United Fund Fort Worth and Tarrant County; past pres. Ft. Worth Assn. for Retarded Children. Trustee Hardin-Simmons U., 1947-66. Recipient Outstanding Citizen of Year award, Hereford, Tex., 1946, John J.

Keeter Jr. Meml. Alumni award Hardin-Simmons U., 1951. Mem. Nat., So. assns. coll. and univ. bus. officers, Bapt. Gen. Conv. Tex. (exec. bd. 1952-64), Sem. Mgmt. Assn., So. Bapt. Bus. Officers Conf., Hereford-Deaf Smith County C. of C. (past pres.). Baptist (deacon). Mason (32 deg.). Club: Ft. Worth Knife and Fork (gov., 1st v.p.). Home: 1810 W Broadus St Fort Worth TX 76115 Office: PO Box 22000 Fort Worth TX 76122

EVANS, DAVID A., constrn. co. exec.; b. Texas City, Tex., Feb. 4, 1925; s. Adolph Roemer and Augusta (Henderson) E.; student U. Ark., 1943-44; diploma in Bldg. Contracting, Internat. Corr. Schs., 1949; LL.B., LaSalle U., 1965. Owner, operator Evans Constrn. Co., Texas City, 1949—; pres. Evans Asso. Industries, Inc., Texas City; dir. Texas City Hotel Corp., Provident Security Ins. Co., Houston, 1960-62. Sec. bd. pilot commrs. Ports of Galveston and Texas City, 1962—. Chmn. tax equalization bd. Texas City Schs., 1959; dir. Texas City Civil Def., 1961. Bd. dirs. Tex. Lions Camp Crippled Children, Kerrville. Served with AUS, 1943-45; ETO. Recipient Good Neighbor award Continental Oil Co., 1960. Mem. Nat. Tex. (dir.) home builders assns. Methodist (steward, lay del. ann. conf. Meth. Chs.). Lion (internat. pres. 1968-69, presidents award 1960, 62-68). Address: 10043 Cedar Creek Lane Houston TX 77042

EVANS, DAVID STANLEY, astronomer; b. Cardiff, Wales, Jan. 28, 1916; s. Arthur Cyril and Kate (Priest) E.; B.A. (Cantab), Kings Coll., Cambridge, Eng., 1937, M.A., Ph.D. (Cantab), 1941, Sc.D. (Cantab), 1971; m. Betty Hall Hart, Mar. 8, 1949; children—Jonathan Gareth Weston, Barnaby Huw Weston. Came to U.S., 1968. Research asst. Univ. Obs., Oxford, Eng., 1938-46; 2d asst. Radcliffe Obs., Pretoria, South Africa, 1946-51; chief asst. Royal Obs., Cape of Good Hope, South Africa, 1951-68; prof. astronomy U. Tex. at Austin, 1968—. Trustee South African Mus., 1966-68. Recipient Tyson medal, Cambridge U., 1937, Rayleigh prize, 1938, McIntyre award, Astron. Soc. Africa, 1972; NSF sr. vis. scientist fellow, 1965-66; grantee NSF, NASA. Fellow Royal Astron. Soc., Inst. Physics (Brit.), Royal Soc. S. Africa (mem. council); mem. Am. Astron. Soc., Astron Soc. So. Africa (pres. 1953-54), Internat. Astron. Union (commn. pres. 1967-70). Clubs: Western Province Sports (Cape Town), Owl (Cape Town), Town and Gown (Austin). Author: Frontiers of Astronomy, 1946; Teach Yourself Astronomy, 1952; Observation in Modern Astronomy, 1968. Editor; Herschel at the Cape, 1969; The Shadow of the Telescope, 1970; External Galaxies and Quasistellar Objects, 1972; editor of The Obs. Mag., 1941-45; sci. adv. editor of Discovery, 1944-46. Contbr. articles to profl. jours. Home: 6001 Mountainclimb Dr Austin TX 78731

EVANS, EDGAR ERNEST, educator; b. Pittsview, Ala., Jan. 20, 1908; s. Ebenezer Ernest and Mary G. (Day) E.; B.A., Fisk U., 1930; M.A., U. Mich., 1948; m. Zelia V. Stephens, Dec. 25, 1940. Prin., Apopka (Fla.) Jr. High Sch., 1931-34, Winter Garden (Fla.) Jr. High Sch., 1934-38, Starke (Fla.) High Sch., 1938-41, Siluria (Ala.) Jr. High Sch., 1941-42, Rosenwald High Sch., Waynesboro, Va., 1946-48; asso. prof. edn. Ala. State Coll. at Montgomery, 1949—. Pres. Farm & City Enterprises, Inc., 1952-59, 61—. Served with USAAF, 1942-45. Fellow Royal Soc. of Health; mem. Am. Pub. Health Assn., Royal Soc. Pub. Health, N.E.A., Am. Sociol. Assn., Internat. Platform Assn., Am. Assn. U. Profs., Phi Delta Kappa, Phi Beta Sigma (state dir. 1953, pres.). Democrat. Member A.M.E. Ch. (1st v.p. Laymens League, 3d state v.p., mem. state edn. com, 2d v.p. lay orgn.). Mason (33 deg., Shriner), Elk (asso. state dir. edn.). Home: 1433 Cleveland Av Montgomery AL 36108

EVANS, ERNEST COLSTON, chem. co. exec.; b. N.Y.C., July 19, 1920; s. Harold Colston and Violet (White) E.; student Mass. Inst. Tech., 1943-44; B.S. in Engring. Physics, U. Tenn., 1954, M.S. in Physics, 1957; m. Marie Odile Ricci, Dec. 5, 1944; children—Edward, Thomas, Robert. With nuclear div. Union Carbide Corp., Oak Ridge, 1946—, head separation systems dept. biomed. devel., 1960-67, supt. separation systems div., 1967—. Served with AUS, 1942-46. Recipient Elec. Engring. Honors award Mass. Inst. Tech., 1944. Registered profl. engr., Tenn. Fellow Instrument Soc. Am. (pres. 1965-66); mem. Tech. Socs. Joint Council (past pres.), Research Soc. Am., Tenn. Soc. Profl. Engrs. Kiwanian. Patentee in field. Contbr. articles to profl. jours. Home: 139 N Seneca Rd Oak Ridge TN 37830 Office: PO Box P Oak Ridge TN 37830

EVANS, ERNEST PIPKIN, JR., former govt. ofcl.; b. St. Petersburg, Fla., Mar. 6, 1944; s. Ernest P. and Carrie (McLeod) E.; student Jacksonville U., 1963-65; B.A., U. Md., 1970. Exec. dir. Jacksonville (Fla.) Youth Council, 1962-64, Nat. Youth Councils, Washington, 1964-66; profl. staff mem. Urban Am., Inc., Washington, 1966-67, U.S. Senate Select Com. Small Bus., Washington, 1967-74. Recipient citation of merit Reader's Digest, 1965; Service to Mankind award Sertoma Internat., 1964. Mem. Am. Soc. Assn. Execs., Nat. Com. Children and Youth, Capitol Hill Restoration Soc. Clubs: U.S. Senate Staff, Capitol Hill Young Democratic. Home: Route 1 Box 205 Elkton VA 22827

EVANS, FRANK GARRETTSON, judge; b. San Antonio, Jan. 12, 1928; s. Frank G. and Ruth (Faquier) E.; LL.B., U. Tex., 1951; m. Patricia Byrd, Apr. 12, 1951; children—Richard B., Margaret. Admitted to Tex. bar, 1951; partner firm Cox, Evans, Pakenhom & Roady, Houston, 1955-73; asso. justice First Ct. Civil Appeals, Houston, 1973—. Pres., mem. bd. dirs. Concerned Teens, Inc., Houston, 1969—. Served with USMCR, W.W. II, Korean War. Mem. Am., Houston bar assns., State Tex. Bar Assn., Am. Judicature Soc. Home: 2023 Drexel St Houston TX 77027 Office: 6th Floor Civil Ct Bldg Houston 77002

EVANS, GEORGE E(DWARD), JR., coal mining exec.; b. Charleston, W.Va., June 7, 1918; s. George E. and Nell (Harrington) E.; B.S.C., Notre Dame U., 1940; m. Josephine Collins, Feb. 16, 1942; children—Patricia Ellen (Mrs. Neal J. Crowley), Mary Josephine (Mrs. Phillip R. Johnson), Jane Collins. Pres. Nat. Mines Corp. (subsidiary Nat. Steel Corp.); dir. 1st Guaranty Bank, Martin, Ky.; chmn. Bank Lexington (Ky.). Mem. coal mining research com. U. Ky.; sec. Inst. Mining Research, Morehead (Ky.) State U.; mem. bd. Ky. Dept. Mines and Minerals. Dist. chmn. Boy Scouts Am., 1954; mem. Ky. Racing Commn. Bd. dirs., mem. exec. com. Spindletop Research, Lexington; trustee Alice Lloyd Coll., Pippa Passes, Ky., Spindletop Found., Frankfort, Ky. Mem. Am. Inst. Mining and Metall. Engrs., Am. Mining Congress (adv. council), Ky. Coal Assn., Big Sandy Elkhorn Coal Operators Assn., Ky. Mining Inst. Lion (pres. Wayland 1952). Home: 120 Chinoe St Lexington KY 40502 Office: PO Box 8125 Lexington KY 40503 also PO Box 295 Wayland KY 41666

EVANS, GILES LINCOLN, JR., state ofcl.; b. Nov. 30, 1914; s. Giles Lincoln and Georgia Mai (Fly) E.; student Vanderbilt U., 1932-33; B.S., U.S. Mil. Acad., 1937; M.S. in Civil Engring., Mass. Inst. Tech., 1960. Commd. 2d lt. U.S. Army, 1937, advanced through grades to col.; ret., 1960; now mgr. Fla. Canal Authority, Jacksonville. Mason (Shriner). Address: 803 Rosselle St Jacksonville FL 32204

EVANS, H(AROLD) BRADLEY, JR., lawyer; b. Watertown, N.Y., Oct. 12, 1937; s. Harold Bradley and Kathleen (Whearty) E.; grad. Williston Acad., 1955; B.A., Yale, 1959; LL.B., Georgetown U., 1966; m. Allene I. Thompson, July 22, 1967; children—Harold Bradley III, Barrett Allen. Admitted to Va. bar, 1966; law clk. D.C. Ct. Appeals, 1966-67; asso. firm Boothe Dudley Koontz, 1967-69; partner firm Evans & Economou, Alexandria, Va., 1969—. Served to H. USNR, 1960-65. Mem. Fairfax County, Alexandria bar assns., Am., Va., No. Va. (v.p. 1972-73, pres. 1974) trial lawyers assns. Home: 1136 Custis St Alexandria VA 22308 Office: 122 S Royal St Alexandria VA 22314

EVANS, HAROLD LEROY, civil engr.; b. Rockwell, Tex., Nov. 13, 1930; s. George W. and Alice I. (Brewer) E.; B.S., So. Meth. U., 1960; m. Sally M. McGlon, Oct. 4, 1952; children—Scott W., Suzanne, H. Craig. Asst. div. engr. M.-K.-T. R.R., Waco, Tex., 1960-65; engr. Magnolia Pipe Line Co., Houston, 1965-66; chief civil engr. Davis & Assos., Dallas, 1966-68; pvt. practice civil engring. Harold L. Evans, cons. engr., Dallas, 1968-70; v.p. Evans-Robertson, Inc., cons. engrs., Dallas, 1970-73, chmn. bd., 1972—, pres., 1973—. Served with USMCR, 1952-54. Mem. Tex. Soc. Profl. Engrs., Am. Soc. C.E. Democrat. Baptist. Mason, Rotarian. Home: Route 1 Box 7 Forney TX 75126 Office: PO Box 28355 Dallas TX 75228

EVANS, HARRY DEAN, chem. engr.; b. Arcola, Mo., July 10, 1915; s. Robert Roy and Fannie Belle (Diefenderfer) E.; B.S. in Chem. Engring., U. Ill., 1937; M.S. in Chem. Engring. (Am. Petroleum Inst. fellow), Cal. Inst. Tech., 1938; m. May Judson, Oct. 4, 1941; 1 son, Harry Kent. Engr., Shell Devel. Co., Dominguez, Cal., 1938-40, engr., San Francisco, 1940-50, engr., Emeryville, Cal., 1950-53, devel. supr., Emeryville, 1953, 54-55, 56-61, 61-63, devel. supr., Curacao, Netherlands Antilles, 1961, N.Y.C., 1955-56, 63-64, Emeryville, 1964-65, head licensing engring. dept., Emeryville, 1965-68, head process engring. chem. dept., 1968-72, dir. process engring., Emeryville, 1972, Houston, 1972—; with Koningklijk Shell Laboratorium, Amsterdam, Holland, 1953-54. Served from 2d lt. to lt. col., C.E., AUS, 1942-46. Mem. Am. Inst. Chem. Engrs. Home: 12981 Trail Hollow Houston TX 77024 Office: 2525 Murworth St Houston TX 77012

EVANS, HAWTHORNE CLOUGH, JR., coll. pres.; b. Morristown, Tenn., Aug. 18, 1927; s. Hawthorne Clough and Lily (Myers) E.; B.A., Carson-Newman Coll., 1950; M.A., Columbia, 1951; Ed. D., U. Tenn., 1958; postgrad. U. Colo., 1956, Lafayette Coll., 1951; m. Barbara Teagarden, Dec. 18, 1963; 1 son, Mark Richard. Band dir. Morristown (Tenn.) Jr. High Sch., 1951-54; guidance counselor Morristown City Schs., 1954-55; prin. Rose Elementary Sch., Morristown, 1955-56, Roberts Elementary Sch., Morristown, 1958-60; asso. prof. edn., psychology Carson-Newman Coll., Jefferson City, Tenn., 1960-62, placement dir., 1962-63, dir. student teaching, 1963-67, chmn. dept. psychology and edn., dir. tchr. edn., 1966-67; pres. Lees-McRae Coll., Banner Elk, N.C., 1967—. Dir. N.C. Nat. Bank, Banner Elk; adv. bd. Newland br. Watauga Savs. & Loan. Dir. Camp at Buck Hill Falls (Pa.), 1962-67; mem. exec. bd. Daniel Boone council, area chmn. Daniel Boone council Boy Scouts Am.; former chmn. Ky-Tenn. Circle K.; dir. charge organizer Boys Club Jefferson City, Inc., former mem. bd. dirs.; adviser Cherokee Tribe; dir. Blue Ridge Health Council; trustee N.C. Found. Ch. Related Colls.; commr., chmn. Presbyn. survey com. Presbyn. Ch. U.S. Gen. Assembly; bd. govs. Highland U. Served with USAAF, 1946-48; maj. USAF Res. Named Young Man of Year, Morristown Jr. C. of C., 1955; Tenn. Tchr. of Year, Tenn. Fedn. Women's Clubs, 1957; U.S. Airman of Year, USAF Res.; recipient Silver Beaver award Boy Scouts Am., 1958. Mem. Nat. (life mem.), Tenn. (past chmn. guidance sect.), Morristown (past pres.) edn. assns., Nat., Tenn. assns. student teaching, Internat. Platform Assn., Tenn. P.T.A. (life), Phi Kappa Phi, Phi Delta Kappa. Presbyn. (elder, past moderator). Kiwanian (lt. gov. Carolina dist. 1972-73, dist. chmn. gov.'s flying squad, dist. key club com.). Author: (mus. comedy) Tom. Contbr. to mags. and newspapers. Home: Box 35 Banner Elk NC 28604 Office: Lees McRae Coll Banner Elk NC 28604

EVANS, HAZEL ATKINSON, polit. ofcl.; b. Atlanta, Aug. 16, 1931; d. Alex P. and Hazel (Thomas) Robert; student Marjorie Webster Jr. Coll., Washington, 1951; m. W. Reed Talley, Sept. 11, 1951; children—W. Reed Talley, Alex R.; m. 2d, Robert Winfield Evans, Nov. 30, 1968. Mem. State Democratic Com. Manatee, Pinellas County, 1962—; mem. Dem. Nat. Com., 1968—; mem. State Central Com. Dem. Exec. Com., Fla., 1966—; sec. Young Dem. Clubs Fla., 1962-63, v.p., 1963-64; del. Dem. Nat. Conv., 1964, 68, 72, mem.-at-large exec. com., 1976. Mem. Gov.'s Adv. Com. Pinellas County; Commr. Pinellas County Housing Authority, 1972—. Bd. dirs. Fla. Heart Assn., Fla. Mental Health Assn., Ringling Mus. Art, United Fund Manatee, Pinellas County. Recipient Meritorious award Am. Heart Assn., 1960, 64, 66, President's award Young Democrats Fla., 1963, 64. Mem. Beta Sigma Phi. Home: 1146 41st Av NE St Petersburg FL 33703

EVANS, JAMES MIGNON, architect; b. Memphis, May 9, 1938; s. Mignon Kemper and Elizabeth Louise (Fulcher) E.; B.A., Rice U., 1960; M.F.A. in Arch. (Lowell M. Palmer fellow), Princeton, 1962; m. Gayle Dupont, Aug. 20, 1965; children—Virginia, Matthew Moseby, Benjamin. Architect Perkins and Will, Washington, 1965-66; Doxiadis Assos., Washington, 1966-67, Gassner/Nathan/Browne, Memphis, 1968—, also dir., 1971—. Served to 1st. lt. AUS, 1963-65. Mem. A.I.A. Prin. works include Balmoral Sch., 1970, Aquarius Townhouses, 1972, Southwyck Village, 1972 (all Memphis), Phys. Edn. Center, Millsaps Coll., Jackson, Miss., 1973, gymnasium Lane Coll., Jackson, Tenn., 1973. Home: 1604 Vinton Av Memphis TN 38104 Office: 265 Court Av Memphis TN 38103

EVANS, JAMES WILLIAM, JR., crafts exec.; b. Red Bluff, Cal., July 13, 1936; s. James William and Suzanne (Laveley) E.; student Shasta Coll., 1956; B.S., Campbellsville Coll., 1963; M.A., Western Ky. U., 1966; m. Mary Ann Moore, Jan. 31, 1960; children—James William III, Barbara Ann. Asst. sta. mgr. Standard Oil of Cal., Dunsmuir, 1953-56; owner Green Jersey Restaurant, Greensburg, Ky., 1960-63; tchr. Greensburg High Sch., 1963-65; programs coordinator Green County Schs., Greensburg, 1965-68; dir. Green County Vocational Sch., 1968-72; plant mgr. Am. Needlecrafts, 1973—; breeder Appaloosas horses, 1970—. edn. specialist Western Ky. U., 1970. Chmn. bd. West Lake Cumberland Area Devel. Council, 1967-73; chmn. Lake Cumberland Area Devel. Dist., 1969-73. Served with USAF, 1956-60. Mem. Greensburg Hist. Soc. (v.p. 1962-67), C. of C. (v.p. 1965). Republican. Presbyn. (elder). Rotarian (pres. 1966). Home: Route 5 Box 11 Greensburg KY 42743

EVANS, JOHN MARTIN, ednl. adminstr.; b. Whitesville, Ala., Oct. 12, 1916; s. Martin Luther and Naomi Ruth (Duke) E.; student Jones County Jr. Coll., 1940-42; B.A., Miss. Coll., 1947; B.D., Southwestern Bapt. Theol. Sem., 1949; M.A., U. So. Miss., 1953, Ed.D. (teaching fellow 1964-66), 1972; m. Esther McQuagge, June 30, 1944; children—Paul, Ruth (Mrs. Duane Jensen). Tchr. Beat Four High Sch., 1942-43; ordained to ministry Bapt. Ch., 1949; pastor Crystal Springs Bapt. Ch., Tylertown, Miss., 1949-51, McLaurin (Miss.) Bapt. Ch., 1951-56, Sunflower (Miss.) Bapt. Ch., 1956-64; instr. Jones County Jr. Coll., Ellisville, Miss., 1966-68, registrar, 1968—. Mem. Miss. Bapt. Conv. Bd., 1961-63. Served with USAAF, 1943-46. Mem. Am. Personnel and Guidance Assn., Southwestern Bapt. Theol. Sem. Alumni Assn. (chpt. pres. 1958-59), U. So. Miss. Alumni Assn., Phi Delta Kappa, Phi Alpha Theta. Rotarian (pres. 1962). Home: 412 Harrison St Ellisville MS 39437

EVANS, JOHN MCCALLUM, physician, educator; b. Hamburg, N.Y., July 18, 1913; s. George Frank and Daisy (Wells) E.; B.A., Denison U., 1935; M.D., U. Buffalo, 1939; m. Marion Jane Cornwell, Nov. 22, 1941; 1 son, Gregory. Intern, Buffalo Gen. Hosp., 1939-40, resident, 1940-41; resident Peter Bent Brigham Hosp., Boston, 1946-48; practice medicine, specializing in cardiology, Washington, 1948—; instr. medicine U. Buffalo, 1940-41; asst. in medicine Harvard, 1946-48; asst. prof., asso. prof. George Washington U., 1948-60, prof. medicine, 1960—, lectr. Cath. U., 1957—; cons. cardiology N. D. Baker Hosp., Mt. Alto Hosp., Washington Hosp. Center; dir. cardiology George Washington U. Hosp. Served with AUS, 1941-46. Fellow A.C.P., Am. Coll. Cardiology; mem. N.Y. Acad. Scis., Acad. Medicine Washington, Assn. U. Cardiologists, Washington Heart Assn. (dir. 1952—, v.p. 1962-63), Am. Heart Assn. (fellow council clin. cardiology), So. Soc. Clin. Investigation. Contbr. numerous articles profl. jours. Home: 7104 Lenhart Dr Chevy Chase MD 20015 Office: 5480 Wisconsin Av NW Washington DC 20015

EVANS, KEITH WILLIAM, aluminum co. exec.; b. Detroit, Nov. 30, 1920; s. Walter and Ethel (Constable) E.; pre-med. student Mich. State Coll., 1939-41; Chem.E., Mich. Coll. Mining and Tech., 1946; m. Audrey Bowling, July 13, 1959; children—Gerald, Dawn, Linda. Adminstrv. officer Ordnance Tank Auto Command, Detroit, 1950-56; gen. mgr. Fla. Enterprises, Miami, 1956-59; v.p., gen. mgr. Cinco Screens Inc., Miami, 1959-60; pres., gen. mgr. Fla. Aluminum Enterprises, Miami, 1960-71; v.p. Warren Industries, 1971-72; exec. v.p. Advance Metals, 1971—, also dir.; pres., gen. mgr. Fla. Screen Enterprises, Inc., 1972—. Served with USNR, 1942-45. Presbyn. (elder 1965-70). Home: 19540 NW 8th Av North Miami FL 33161 Office: 3650 NW 46th St Miami FL 33161

EVANS, MALCOLM EUGENE, elec. engr.; b. Rayville, La., May 12, 1941; s. Jack and Ella (Woods) E.; student Northeast La. U., 1959-60; B.S., La. Tech. U., 1964; postgrad., La. State U., 1966-69; m. Judy Aulds, Jan. 30, 1965. With South Central Bell Telephone Co., New Orleans, 1964—, supervising engr., 1969—. Mem. I.E.E.E. (chmn. communications soc. 1972-73), Tau Beta Pi. Moose (sec. 1972-73). Club: Diamondhead Country (Bay St. Louis, Miss.). Home: 157 S Park Dr Slidell LA 70458 Office: 3500 N Causeway Blvd Metairie LA 70035

EVANS, MAURICE LEE, clergyman; b. Yates Center, Kan., Oct. 12, 1926; s. William Edward and Sylvia Bernice (Gustin) E.; B.A., Phillips U., 1951; B.D., Tex. Christian U., 1957, M.Div., 1973; Ph.D., U. Okla., 1973. Ordained to ministry Christian Ch., 1951; sr. minister Mt. Auburn Christian Ch., Dallas, 1955-60, 1st Christian Ch., Moore, Okla., 1966-70, Pa. Av. Christian Ch., Oklahoma City, 1970-73. Panel mem. commentator KDLD-TV, Dallas, also WKY-TV, Oklahoma City. Coordinator Christmas Spl. Welfare Program, Oklahoma City, 1970-73. Bd. dirs. Juliette Fowler Homes for Aged and Children, Dallas, 1957-60. Served with USNR, 1944-46, to lt. comdr., 1960-65. Mason, Lion, Toastmaster. Republican. Club: Cosmopolitan. Contbr. to numerous jours. Home: 210 Kenway Dr Rockwall TX 75087 Office: 305 S Fannin St Rockwall TX 75087

EVANS, MELVIN HERBERT, gov. V.I.; b. Christiansted, St. Croix, V.I., Aug. 7, 1917; s. Charles Herbert and Maude (Rogiers) E.; B.S., Howard U., 1940, M.D., 1944; M.P.H., U. Cal. at Berkeley, 1967; m. Mary Phyllis Anderson, Aug. 26, 1945; children—Melvin Herbert, Robert Rogiers, William Charles, Cornelius Duncan. Intern, Harlem Hosp., N.Y.C., 1944-45; physician-in-charge Frederiksted, Govt. V.I., 1945-48, 50-51; sr. asst. surgeon USPHS, Washington, 1948-50; chief municipal physician, St. Croix, 1951-56, 57-59; fellow cardiology Johns Hopkins Hosp., 1956-57; commr. health for V.I., 1959-67; pvt. practice medicine, specializing in internal medicine, St. Croix, 1967-69; gov. V.I., 1969—. Trustee New St. Croix Savs. Bank. Chmn. Bd. Med. Examiners, 1959-67. Mem. Gov.'s Commn. on Civil Def. 1961-66; chmn. Gov.'s Commn. on Human Services, 1962-66; mem. U.S. Selective Service Bd. Appeals, 1967-69. Chmn. bd. trustees Coll. V.I.; bd. dirs. Good Hope Sch., St. Croix; bd. advice St. Dunstan Sch., St. Croix, Island Center St. Croix. Fellow A.C.P.; mem. A.M.A., Nat., Pan Am. med. assns., V.I. Med. Soc. (past pres.), Am. Assn. Pub. Health, Physicians, Am. Pub. Health Assn., St. Croix C. of C., Phi Beta Sigma, Kappa Pi. Methodist. Mason, Rotarian. Club: St. Croix Yacht. Home: La Grande Princesse Christiansted St Croix VI 00820 Office: Govt House Charlotte Amalie St Thomas VI 00801

EVANS, MORTIMER DANIEL, hotel exec.; b. N.Y.C., Feb. 27, 1930; s. Earle and Essie (Applegreen) E.; B.S. in Aeros., St. Louis U., 1951; postgrad. Jacksonville U., 1969-70; children by previous marriage—Stanley Paul, Ilene Claire, Roy Alan; m. 2d, Bobbie Gene Barnett, Aug. 25, 1971. Sales, field engr. Gen. Electric Co., Syracuse, N.Y., 1953-56, Fort Wayne, Ind., 1956-58; chief financial officer Price Co., Inc., Jacksonville, Fla., 1958-66, Atlantic Consol., Inc. (merged with Price Co., Inc. 1966), Jacksonville, 1966-70; pres. 1061 Corp., Mobile Ala., 1971—, Evans Properties, Inc. New Orleans, 1971—. Cons. ind. motel owners, 1968—. Vice pres., bd. dirs. Jacksonville Jewish Center, 1967-70, bd. chmn. bldg. fund, 1968-70; trustee Jacksonville Art Mus., 1969-71; bd. dirs. River Garden Hebrew Home, 1970. Kiwanian, Mason (32 degree, Shriner). Office: PO Box 7781 3030 I-10 Service Rd Metairie LA 70011

EVANS, OVERTON CHENAULT II, constrn. equipment dealer; b. Ancon, C.Z., Feb. 22, 1912; s. Joe Ashby and Minnie (Williams) E.; student Ky. Wesleyan U., 1930; A.B., Morehead State U., 1934; m. Madge Durham, July 6, 1940; children—Peter Chenault, David Overton. Pres., O. C. Evans Equipment Corp., Mount Sterling, Ky., 1934—; partner Oldham and Evans, land developers and home builders, 1964-72; dir. Montgomery Nat. Bank, Mount Sterling. Mem. Mount Sterling Water Commn. 1971-72; mem. Mount Sterling Sch. Bd., 1962-64. Bd. dirs. Mount Sterling Indsl. Found., Mary Chiles Hosp. Served with AUS, 1942-43. Mem. Mount Sterling C. of C. (dir. 1966—), Am. Legion. Baptist (trustee 1960—). Mason, Lion. Club: Mount Sterling Golf and Country (dir. 1960—). Home: 307 Sycamore St Mount Sterling KY 40353 Office: 9 Wilson St Mount Sterling KY 40353

EVANS, PETER KENNETH, advt. exec.; b. Brighton, Eng., Apr. 18, 1935; s. Percy Edward and Doris (McCoy) E.; ed. in Eng.; m. Juana Santana Ramirez, Mar. 31, 1956; children—Luis Miguel, Linda Rosa Del Rocio, Pilar De Los Angeles. Dental technician E.J. Steele, Shoreham, Eng., 1950-51, John Williams, Brighton, Eng., 1951-53, W.G. Hetherington, Salisbury, Eng., 1955-58; art dir. Grant Advt., Toronto, Ont., Can., 1958-61; art dir., writer Goodis, Goldberg & Soren, Toronto, 1961-63; creative dir., v.p. Baker Advt., Toronto, 1963-65; creative dir. Kenyon & Eckhardt, Toronto, 1965-66, Mexico, 1967-68; creative dir., exec. v.p. Vladimir & Evans, Inc., Miami, Fla., 1968-71; pres. Peter Evans Advt., Inc., 1971—. Served with RAF, 1953-55. Recipient numerous medals from advt. orgns. Home: 285 W Mashta Dr Key Biscayne FL 33149 Office: 420 LeJeune Rd N Miami FL 33126

EVANS, RAYMOND, aero. and mech. engr.; b. Pineapple, Ala., Dec. 29, 1925; s. Travis Elmer and Caratee (Barkley) E.; B.S., U. Ala., 1953, Ph.D. in Bus. Adminstrn., 1973; m. Marie Elizabeth Grzymkowski, May 10, 1952; children—Marie Elizabeth, Ann, Barbara, Elizabeth, Catherine, Denise. Research engr. Ford Motor

Co., Dearborn, Mich., 1954-56; design and project engr. Gen. Electric Co., Syracuse, N.Y., 1956-63, Huntsville, Ala., 1963-65; non-destructive testing project engr. Spaco, Inc., Huntsville, Ala., 1965-66; sr. prodn. engr. Raytheon Co., Portsmouth, 1966-70; chief indsl. engr. Lowry AFB, Denver, 1970-71; project engr. Savanna (Ill.) Army Depot, 1971-73; gen. engr. human factor engr. U.S. Army Airborne, Communication and Electronics Bd., Fort Bragg, N.C., 1973—. Served with USNR, 1943-46, 51-52. Decorated 2 Purple Heart medals; recipient Gen. Electric Accent on Value award, 1964. Registered profl. engr. Ala. Mem. Nat., R.I., Ala. (sec. 1966) socs. profl. engrs. V.F.W. Democrat. Roman Catholic. Home: 401 E Donaldson Av Raeford NC 28376 Office: Fort Bragg NC 28307

EVANS, RONALD DALE, educator; b. Lanagan, Mo., Aug. 15, 1933; s. Dwight Taft and Grace (Morris) E.; B.S. in Math., East Central Okla. State Coll., 1956; M.Natural Sci. (NSF fellow) Ariz. State U., 1961, M.S. in Engring. (NSF trainee), 1967, Ph.D. (NSF trainee), 1968; m. Estelle Lee Wood, Nov. 1, 1952; children—Tammy, Paula, Tracy, Rhonda. Engr., Motorola, Inc., Phoenix, 1963; systems engr. Sperry Gyroscope Co., Great Neck, N.Y., 1963-64, RCA Service Co., 1964-65; prof., chmn. dept. mech. engring. and aerospace scis. Fla. Tech. U., Orlando, 1968—. Cons. Central Fla. Engring. Services, Inc., Orlando, 1972—, ITF Leasing Corp., Longwood, Fla., 1971-72. Served with AUS, 1956-58. Registered profl. engr., Fla., Okla., Tex., La. Mem. Am. Soc. M.E. (chmn. Fla. 1971-72), Am. Inst. Aero. and Astronautics, Am. Soc. Engring. Edn., Nat. Soc. Profl. Engrs., Fla. Engring. Soc. Home: 781 Goldwater Ct Maitland FL 32751 Office: PO Box 25000 Orlando FL 32816

EVANS, ROSALEEN MALOOLY, music dir.; b. El Paso, Tex.; d. Elias and Mamie (Coury) Malooly; B.A., Colo. Coll., 1945; M.Music, U. So. Cal., 1949; 1 son, John Anthony. Debut as concert pianist Wilshire Ebel Theater, Los Angeles, 1950; profl. operatic appearances Los Angeles Biltmore Theatre, 1949; supper clubs, 1952-60; musical dir. Dallas Summer Musicales, also O'Keefe Center, Toronto, Ont., Can., 1968, Festival Theatre, 1965-71, others; tchr. voice, theater, piano, Los Angeles, 1950, Dallas, 1955, El Paso, 1965—. Adv. bd. Festival Theater, El Paso. Named Woman of the Year for music El Paso Herald Post, 1968. Mem. Nat. Soc. Arts and Letters (v.p. 1970-71), Am. Assn. U. Women, Am. Ednl. Theatre Assn., Shakespearean Inst., Internat. Platform Assn., Mu Phi Epsilon. Club: MacDowell (El Paso). Home: 116 Sultan Place El Paso TX 79912

EVANS, ROSEMARY KING (MRS. HOWELL DEXTER EVANS), librarian; b. Forsyth, Ga., Nov. 16, 1924; d. Wiley Gwin and Mary (Goggans) King; B.S., Tift Coll., 1957; librarian's certificate Woman's Coll. of Ga., 1963; M. Library Edn., U. Ga., 1972; m. Howell Dexter Evans, June 29, 1945; children—Joseph Williams, Curtis McKenney. Tchr. elementary sch., Forsyth, Ga., 1946-48, 54-62; librarian Mary Persons High Sch., Forsyth, 1962-73; catalog librarian Tift Coll., Forsyth, 1973—. Spiritual edn. chmn. P.T.A., 1960-61. Named Star Tchr., 1966. Mem. Nat., Ga., Monroe County (sec. 1959-60, v.p. 1961-62, pres. 1962-63) edn. assns., Internat. Platform Assn., Ga. Library Assn. (dist. pres. 1965), A.L.A. Methodist (chmn. local edn. bd. 1964-65, chmn. commn. on Christian Vocation 1965—, tchr. adult Bible class). Clubs: Jaycettes, Woman's (1st v.p. 1955-56, chmn. edn. dept. 1959-60, chmn. pub. affairs dept. 1961-62) (Forsyth). Home: Smarr GA 31086 Office: Hardin Library Tift College Forsyth GA 31029

EVANS, RUTHANA WILSON (MRS. LIT PARKER EVANS, JR.), educator; b. Roxie, Miss.; d. James and Luberta (Wade) Wilson; B.S., Tougaloo Coll., 1955; postgrad. (Nat. Def. Edn. Act grantee) U. Ill., 1965, (Nat. Def. Edn. Act grantee) N.C. Coll., 1967; M.S., Delta State Coll., 1971; m. Lit Parker Evans, Jr., Mar. 22, 1957; children—Cedric Glenn, Valerie Denise. Elementary tchr., Shaw, Miss., 1955-57; tchr., curriculum chmn. Nailor Elementary Sch., Cleveland, Miss., 1957-60, tchr., librarian H.M. Nailor Sch., 1960-62, librarian, 1963-64; library supr. Bolivar County Dist. 4 elementary schs., Cleveland, 1965-67; curriculum resources tchr. ednl. TV Jackson, Miss., 1968-70; librarian Parks and Pearman elementary schs., Cleveland, 1968-70; cons. Greenville (Miss.) Elementary Sch., 1970; edn. dir. Miss. Head Start activities, Cleveland, 1970—. Librarian, Presch. Story Hour, 1964-66, Little Rascals kindergarten, 1966-68; organizer elementary sch. library program Bolivar County, 1969; job trainer Neighborhood Youth Corps, Cleveland, 1969; trainer man power program Step, Cleveland, 1970—; cons. Indianola (Miss.) presch. activities, 1971; organizer inventory, classification system Head Start, 1970. Sec., Negro's Citizens Com. Cleveland, 1957-61, P.T.A., Shaw, Miss., 1955; active Boy Scouts Am.; librarian Bapt. Tng. Union, Cleveland, 1972—. Mem. Miss. Personnel and Guidance Assn., Miss., Bolivar County tchrs. assns., N.E.A., N.A.A.C.P., Am. Miss. library assns., Negro Voters League. Democrat. Clubs: East Side High Sch. Band Booster (treas. Cleveland 1972), Athena Social (treas. 1971), Women's (sec. Cleveland 1970). Contbr. articles to profl. jours. Home: 816 Cross St Cleveland MS 38732 Office: 321 S Sharpe St Cleveland MS 38732

EVANS, SELBY HENRY, psychologist, educator; b. Dallas, Nov. 17, 1929; s. Selby Henry and Alice Charlotte (Cunningham) E.; student Columbia, 1948-51; B.A., So. Methodist U., 1956, M.A., 1960; Ph.D., Tex. Christian U., 1964. Asst. prof. psychology Tex. Christian U., Ft. Worth, 1963-66, asso. prof., 1966-72, prof., 1972—, dir. Inst. for Study Cognitive Systems, 1967—. Partner Evans, Dansereau and Fenker, psychol. consultants, 1971—. Served with AUS, 1951-54; Korea. NASA grantee, 1969, Nat. Inst. Mental Health grantee, 1966, Nat. Inst. Neurol. Diseases and Blindness grantee, 1967. Mem. A.A.A.S., Am. Assn. U. Profs., So. Soc. for Philosophy and Psychology, Am. Psychol. Assn., Assn. for Computing Machinery, Electronic Industries Assn. (com. automatic imagery pattern recognition 1971—), I.E.E.E. (cybernetics group 1971—), Pattern Recognition Soc., Sigma Xi. Author: (with Leona Aiken) Systematic Formulations in Human Pattern Perceptions, 1973. Contbr. articles on psychology to profl. jours. Office: Psychology Dept Tex Christian University Fort Worth TX 76129

EVANS, THOMAS ALFRED, architect; b. Buffalo, Apr. 22, 1930; s. John Hugh and Helen Elizabeth (Ryan) E.; B.S., B.Arch. (V.B. Higgins scholar 1956; Lyles Bisset Carlyle and Wolf scholar 1957), Clemson U., 1957; M.Arch., U. Pa., 1959. Project architect Barrows Parks Marin Hall & Brennan, architects, Rochester, N.Y., 1959-62; chief designer Mills Petticord & Mills, architects, engrs., Washington, 1962-64; head design dept. McLeod Ferrara & Ensign, architects, Washington, 1964-68; asso. Thomas E. Stanley & Assos., architects, engrs., Dallas, 1968-72, Warden & Evans, architects, planners, 1972—. Teaching fellow Ga. Inst. Tech., 1958; critic U. Ohio, 1968. Served with USN, USMC, 1948-52. Recipient 1st prize So. Brick and Tile competition, 2d prize Armstrong Tile competition, A.A.S.A. Honor award, 1965-69. Mem. A.I.A. (medal 1957; Honor award 1962, 63), Nat. Council Archtl. Registration Bd., Phi Eta Sigma. Home: Box 19112 Dallas TX 75219 Office: Box 2189 Dallas TX 75221

EVANS, THOMAS PEABODY, govt. ofcl.; b. Wade, N.C., Oct. 9, 1912; s. William and Lillian (May) E.; B.S., U. S.C., 1937; grad-student Duke, 1938; m. Valree Lide, Aug. 8, 1955. Tchr. pub. schs., Columbia, S.C., 1937-41; statistician S.C. Employment Security Commn., Columbia, 1941-46, chief research and statistics, 1946-65; dir. staff service, S.C. Employment Security Commn., 1965-66; dir. statistical research, S.C. Budget and Control Bd., 1966—; mem. com. research and reporting Interstate Conf. Employment Security Agys., 1956-58, 64; cons. U.S. Employment Service, Bur. Employment Security, Washington. Trustee, chmn. Fed. Statistics Users' Conf., 1972-73. Served with USNR, 1942-46; now lt. comdr. ret. Mem. Am. Statis. Assn. (pres. S.C. 1970), S.C. State Employees Assn. Presbyn. Club: Optimist. Author: (with S. M. Derrick) The Cost of Unemployment Insurance in South Carolina, 1954; (with William B. Richey) Benefit Financing in South Carolina, 1959. Home: 1505 Greenhill Rd Columbia SC 29206 Office: R L Bryan Bldg PO Box 11038 Columbia SC 29211

EVANS, TRUMAN, airline exec.; b. San Antonio, Oct. 10, 1917; s. Truman and Lucinda (Latimer) E.; B.S. in C. E., Okla. State U., 1941; m. Henrietta Louise Mackay, Aug. 29, 1952; 1 dau., Marcia Joan (Mrs. Robert William Specht). Control engr. C.E., U.S. Army, Tulsa, Kansas City, Mo., 1941-44; plant indsl. engr. Pitts. Plate Glass Co., Clarksburg, W.Va., Creighton, Pa., 1945-47, divisional controller for window glass, Pitts., 1947-52, mgr. prodn. planning for glass div., 1952-61; dir. inventory control Am. Airlines, Tulsa, 1962-64, dir. mgmt. systems planning, 1964—. Instr. physics Okla. State U., 1944-45. Mem. Mayor's Com. for Joint Systems Devel. for City, County, Sch. Bd., 1968—; mem. Tulsa Govtl. Mgmt. Study Com., 1968-69; mem. Data Processing Adv. Commn. State Okla., 1972—; mem. mgmt. adv. bd. Concentrated Employment Program for Tulsa, 1972—; chmn. Welfare Services Study Com. for Tulsa County, 1969—; mem. Com. on Study of Rehab. Services in Tulsa, 1969—; mem. adv. bd. for curriculum devel. Tulsa Jr. Coll., 1972—. Bd. dirs. Community Service Council Greater Tulsa, 1969—; bd. dirs., exec. com., chmn. health care com. St. John's Hosp., 1972—. Recipient Citation of Recognition Ind. U. and OEEC, 1961. Registered profl. engr., Okla. Mem. Nat., Okla., Tulsa socs. profl. engrs., Am. Inst. Indsl. Engrs., Inst. Mgmt. Scis., Engrs. Council for Profl. Devel. (mem. ethics com. 1968—), Nat. Mgmt. Assn., Am. Prodn. and Inventory Control Soc. (founder, charter mem.), Tulsa C. of C. (vice-chmn. edn. com. 1967-68, mem. com. for Tulsa Jr. Coll. devel. fund 1972—, com. for health care edn. 1972—). Presbyn. (elder 1956—). Mason (32 deg., Shriner). Home: 3614 E 55th St Tulsa OK 74135 Office: 3800 N Mingo Rd Tulsa OK 74151

EVENS, F. MONTE, chemist; b. Herculaneum, Mo., Jan. 21, 1932; s. Robert Waller and Myrtle May (Manning) E.; B.S., Southeast Mo. State Coll., 1955; M.S., Ia. State U., 1959, Ph.D., 1962; m. Alice R. Frowitter, Oct. 25, 1952; children—Cynthia, Elizabeth, Amy, Elaine, Gwyn. Research scientist Ia. State U., Ames, 1954-62; research scientist Procter & Gamble Corp., Cin., 1962-63; with Continental Oil Co., Ponca City, Okla., 1963—, research group leader, 1967—. Active Girl Scouts Am., 1965—. Mem. Am. Chem. Soc., Soc. Applied Spectroscopy. Elk. Home: 2716 Larchmont St Ponca City OK 74601 Office: 1000 S Pine St Ponca City OK 74601

EVERARD, WILLIAM HOWARD, fire protection engr., city ofcl.; b. Washington, Aug. 27, 1941; s. William Phelps and Thelma Lulee (Patterson) E.; student Bucknell U., 1959-62; B.S. in Elec. Engring., George Washington U., 1966; B.S. in Fire Protection, U. Md., 1970. Jr. engr. communications and signals Pa. R.R., 1966; dispatcher, equipment installer Security Assos., Inc., Rockville, Md., 1968-69; fire protection engr. Alexandria (Va.) Fire dept., 1969—. Lectr. fire sci. No. Va. Community Coll., 1970-71; instr. fire protection U. Md., College Park, 1972. Chief, Ballston Vol. Fire Dept., Arlington County, Va., 1965-66. Served with inf., AUS, 1966-68. Mem. I.E.E.E., Soc. Fire Protection Engrs., Am. Soc. for Testing and Materials, Nat. Fire Protection Assn., Internat. Assn. Arson Investigation, Salamander Fire Protection Frat. Home: 903 Ramsey St Alexandria VA 22301 Office: Alexandria Fire Dept Powhatan St and 2d St Alexandria VA 22314

EVERETT, FRED EUGENE, elec. products mfg. co. exec.; b. Norfolk, Va., Oct. 9, 1920; s. Howell Ernest and Freddie Belle (Garraux) E.; B.S., Va. Poly. Inst., 1943; postgrad. U. Pitts., 1946; m. Mary Elizabeth Hortenstine, Apr. 15, 1944; children—John Howell, James Wilson, Joel Campbell. Tchr. algebra and trigonometry Va. Poly. Inst., 1942-43; sales engr. Westinghouse Electric Corp., Washington, 1946-53, dist. sales mgr., 1953-57, hdqrs. marine mgr., Pitts., 1957-60, zone mgr., Washington, 1960—. Vice pres. Hollindale Citizens Assn., 1967-69. Served to maj. USAAF, World War II: PTO. Decorated Air medal. Registered profl. engr., D.C. Mem. Am. Def. Preparedness Assn. (pres.), Nat. Space Club (1st v.p.), Armed Forces Communications and Electronics Assn. (v.p. 1969). Club: Belle Haven Country. Contbr. articles to profl. jours. Home: 1804 White Oaks Dr Alexandria VA 22306 Office: 1801 K St NW Washington DC 20006

EVERETT, GROVER WOODROW, chemist, educator; b. Newton, Miss., Sept. 11, 1912; s. Eugene Bisette and Lena Wallace (Edwards) E.; B.S. in Chemistry, U. Va., 1935; M.A. in Edn., George Washington U., 1939; Ph.D., U. N.C., 1955; m. Nell Louise Clingenpeel, Sept. 1, 1937; children—Grover Woodrow, Sherbourne (Mrs. James Charles McGrath III). Tchr. chemistry E.C. Glass High Sch., Lynchburg, Va., 1935-42, 46; prof. chemistry Lynchburg (Va.) Coll., 1947-55; prof. chemistry East Carolina U., 1955—, also chmn. dept chemistry, 1962-65. Pres. High Sch. P.T.A., 1960. Served to comdr. USNR, 1942-46. NSF grantee, 1964. Mem. Am. Chem. Soc. (chmn. local sect. 1955—), A.A.A.S., Am. Assn. U. Profs., N.C. Acad. Sci. (chmn. chem. sect. 1965-67), N.C. Edn. Assn., Sigma Xi. Democrat. Baptist (deacon 1960—, tchr. 1957—). Kiwanian (pres. 1964, pres.'s award 1971), Moose. Author: Freshman Chemistry Lab. Manual, 1969-73. Home: 122 King George Rd Greenville NC 27834

EVERETT, JOHN WENDELL, educator; b. Ovid, Mich., Mar. 5, 1906; s. Fred Ross and Laura Mae (Grimes) E.; A.B., Olivet Coll., 1928; Ph.D., Yale, 1932; m. Marian Della Eggstaff, Sept. 14, 1932; children—Ronald Wilcox, Janice (Mrs. David E. Rideout). Instr. biology Goucher Coll., Balt., 1930-31; mem. faculty Duke U. Sch. Medicine, Durham, 1932—, asso. prof. anatomy, 1947-50, prof., 1950—. Vis. prof. anatomy summers U. Cal. at Los Angeles, 1952, U. Tenn. at Memphis, 1954. Recipient Fred Conrad Koch medal Endocrine Soc., 1973, Carl G. Hartman Lectureship award Soc. Study Reproduction, 1971. Fellow N.Y. Acad. Sci.; mem. Am. Assn. Anatomists (pres., 1973-74), Am. Physiol. Soc., Endocrine Soc., Soc. Exptl. Biology and Medicine, Soc. Study Reprodn., A.A.A.S., Internat. Soc. Neuroendocrinology, Am. Inst. Biol. Scis., Sigma Xi. Editorial bd. Endocrinology, 1953-56, 59—, Neuroendocrinology, 1966-73, Anatomical Record, 1957-63, Biology of Reproduction, 1968-69. Home: 1105 Woodburn Rd Durham NC 27705

EVERETT, MARK ALLEN, physician; b. Oklahoma City, May 30, 1928; s. Mark Reuben and Alice G. (Allen) E.; B.A., U. Okla., 1947, M.D., 1951; postgrad. Tulane U., 1952. Intern pediatrics U. Mich. at Ann Arbor, 1951-52; resident dermatology, 1954-57; instr. dermatology U. Okla., Oklahoma City, 1957-59, asst. prof., 1959-63, asso. prof., 1963-67, prof., 1967—, chmn. faculty bd., 1974—. Pres., Mark Allen Everett Found., Oklahoma City, 1963—; bd. dirs. Arthritis Found., 1971—. Served to capt. M.C., USAF, 1952-54. Mem. A.M.A., Am. Acad. Dermatology, Am. Assn. Cancer Research, Am. Soc. for Dermatopathology, Am. Dermatol. Assn., N.Y. Acad. Scis., Phi Beta Kappa, Alpha Omega Alpha. Club: Lotus (N.Y.C.). Home: 609 NW 37th St Oklahoma City OK 73118

EVERHART, OSCAR CHARLES, librarian; b. Danville, Ill., July 2, 1909; s. Charles E. and Maud Amy (Chatfield) E.; student U. Md., 1926-28; B.A., Pomona Coll., 1948; M.A. in L.S., Ind. U., 1950. Head librarian Jeffersonville (Ind.) Pub. Library, 1948-51; field cons. extension div. Ind. State Library, Indpls., 1951-53, aquisitions librarian, asst. to dir., 1953-58; asso. librarian Miami Beach (Fla.) Pub. Library, 1958, chief librarian, 1958—. Library rep. A. C. McClurg & Co., Chgo., 1929-46. Served with AUS, 1942-45. Mem. Am., Fla., Southeastern, Dade County library assns. Home: 4490 Royal Palm Av Miami Beach FL 33140 Office: 2100 Collins Av Miami Beach FL 33139

EVERSOLE, ALEX GORDON, supt. schs.; b. Krypton, Ky., Aug. 9, 1932; s. App and Cassie (Pennington) E.; B.S. in Edn., Eastern Ky. U., 1959, M.A. in Edn., 1960; m. Golda Witt, Dec. 26, 1952; children—Dwight, Steven, Alexis Ann. Tchr. M.C. Napier High Sch., Hazard, Ky., 1959-62; prin. D. Wooton Elementary Sch., Hazard, 1962-63; asst. supt. Perry County Schs., Hazard, 1963-67, supt., 1967—. Chmn. bd. Ky. Ednl. Region 12, 1970—; bd. dirs. Ky. ESEA Title III Region 6. Served with USAF, 1952-56. Mem. Perry County Edn. Assn. (pres. 1961-62), Ky. Edn. Assn. (mem. bd. 1969—), N.E.A., Am., Ky. assns. sch. adminstrs., Ky. Assn. Sch. Supts. (dir. 1972-74). Lion (bd. dirs. 1969-71). Home: Rural Route 2 Box 596 Hazard KY 41701 Office: Perry County Schs Hazard KY 41701

EVETTS, EDGAR RAY, retail exec.; b. Moaffet, Tex., Dec. 1, 1915; s. Edgar Roy and Nannie Elizabeth (Evans) E.; grad. Hillsboro (Tex.) Jr. Coll., 1935; m. Mary Juanita Huff, Feb. 13, 1938; children—Robert Craig, Betty Joan (Mrs. John Robert Kuehl). Asst. mgr. S. H. Kress, Inc., Waxahachie, Tex., 1930-36, asst. mgr. all-chain variety stores, 1936-51; with Perry Bros., Mineola, Tex., Mineral Wells, Tex. and Lufkin, Tex., 1940-51; with Winns Stores, Inc., San Antonio, 1951—, exec. v.p., 1969—. Dir., v.p. Winn Western Real Estate, San Antonio, 1957—; pres., dir. S & W Wholesale Corp., San Antonio, 1954-72; rancher, Stockdale, Tex., 1969—. Served with AUS, 1944-45. Home: 215 Hillview Dr San Antonio TX 78209 Office: 1235 Gembler Rd San Antonio TX 78219

EVINS, JOSEPH LANDON, congressman; b. DeKalb County, Tenn., Oct. 24, 1910; s. James Edgar and Myrtie (Goodson) E.; A.B., Vanderbilt U., 1933; LL.B., Cumberland U., 1934, LL.D., 1958; postgrad. George Washington U., 1938-40; m. Ann Smartt, June 7, 1935; children—Joanna (Mrs. Malcolm R. Carnaham), Jane (Mrs. Robert J. Leonard), Mary. Admitted to Tenn. bar, 1934; engaged in gen. law practice, Smithville, 1934-41; atty. FTC, Washington 1935-38, asst. sec., 1938-40; v.p. 1st Nat. Bank, Smithville, Tenn., 1944-54, pres., 1954-63, chmn. bd., 1963—; men. 80th-93d Congresses, 4th Congl. Dist.; mem. com. appropriations, chmn. subcom. pub. works AEC appropriations, mem. former chmn. subcom. housing-space-sci.-vets. appropriations, chmn. select com. small bus. Chmn. Tenn. Democratic Campaign Com., 1964. Served to maj. AUS, 1942-46; ETO. Received Dem. nomination as state senator, 12th Tenn. senatorial dist. (declined to serve during war), 1944. Mem. Am. Legion, V.F.W., Army Res. Corps, 40 and 8, Amvets, Phi Kappa Sigma, Phi Delta Phi. Mason (33 deg., Shriner), Elk. Clubs: Lions, Commodore, Army-Navy. Author: Understanding Congress, 1962. Home: 300 E Main St Smithville TN 37166 also 5044 Klingle St NW Washington DC 20016 Office: Rayburn House Office Bldg Washington DC 20515

EVITT, JAMES EDWARD, JR., telephone co. exec.; b. Ringgold, Ga., Sept. 1, 1912; s. James E. and Annie (Ward) E.; grad. McCallie Sch.; student U. Ga., 1929-33, U. Chattanooga, 1931; 1 dau., Alice Lee. Druggist, Ringgold Drug Co., 1934-53; owner, mgr. Ringgold Telephone Co., 1948-58, pres., 1958—; treas. Catoosa Industries, Inc.; dir. Bank Ringgold. Dir. Chattanooga Area Met. Council; dir. of YMCA of Ga.; chmn. Ga.-Tenn. Regional Health Commn., 1970—; mem. Catoosa County Bd. Health; dir. Coosa Valley Planning Com., Chattanooga Full Employment Com., Inc., 1969—. Dep. clerk of Superior Court of Catoosa County, 1933-44; mem. Ga. Ho. of Reps., 1945-51; pres. Ga. Young Democratic Club, 1945-46. Treas. Hutchison Meml. Tri-County Hosp., Ft. Oglethorpe, Ga., 1947-67, vice chmn., 1967—; pres. Ga. Hosp. Governing Bd. Assn., 1957; mem. Ga. Hosp. Indigent Care Council, 1957-59. Mem. Ga. Telephone Assn. (pres. 1961-62; dir.), Nat. R.E.A. Telephone Assn. (dir.), Greater Chattanooga C. of C. (dir. 1969-71), Ind. Pioneer Telephone Assn. Clubs: Rotary, Quarterback. Died Nov. 15, 1973. Address: Ringgold GA 30736

EVITTS, CHARLES ALLEN, bank exec.; b. Mahanoy City, Pa., Aug. 9, 1931; s. Allen Blair and Ruth Marian (Tregellas) E.; student Armstrong Jr. Coll., 1955-56; m. Ruth Athleen Norris, July 19, 1952; children—Amy Allene, Allen Blair, Charles Tregellas. With Burroughs Corp., Savannah, Ga., 1955-63; with First Nat. Bank, Brunswick, Ga., 1963—, v.p. 1969—. Served with USNR, 1950-54. Mason. Home: 1414 Palmetto Brunswick GA 31520 Office: Gloucester St Brunswick GA 31520

EVJEN, VICTOR HARALD, cons., editor; b. Gettysburg, Pa., Aug. 29, 1906; s. John Oluf and Selma (Kretschmann) E.; B.A., Wittenberg, U., 1926; B.A.S., George Williams Coll., 1929; M.A., U. Chgo., 1930; m. Jessie Barbara Heinl, June 26, 1931. Dir. social work Div. St. YMCA, Chgo., 1926-31; intake supr. Ill. Emergency Relief Commn., 1931-33; probation officer Chgo. Juvenile Ct., 1933-36; probation parole officer U.S. Dist. Ct., Chgo., 1936-40; asst. chief Fed. Probation System, 1940-72, editor Fed. Probation quar., pub. with Fed. Bur. Prisons, 1953-72; now cons. correctional field; lectr. criminology George Washington U., 1953-58; profl. lectr. criminology, Am. U., 1958-72; Chmn. adv. council, established by D.C. govt., Inst. Criminol. Research, 1956-61. Mem. bd. social missions Luth. Ch. in Am., 1950-64, mem. commn. on marriage and divorce, 1953. Served as asst. to dir. Army mil. prison system, sec. Under Sec. of War Bd. Cons. on correctional problems; recorder, alternate mem. War Dept. Adv. Bd. Parole, 1943-46. Recipient Ann. award Health and Welfare Council Nat. Capital area, 1962; distinguished alumnus award, George Williams Coll., 1962, Irving W. Halpern Nat. award Nat. Council on Crime and Delinquency, 1968. Mem. Nat. Conf. Social Welfare (nat. bd.), Nat. Council on Crime and Delinquency (profl. council 1960—). Author: The Presentence Investigation Report, 1943, rev. edit., 1965; The Case Record and Case Recording, 1952; Statistical Study of 24,327 General Prisoners, 1946; cons. Guides for Sentencing, 1957. Editor 650-page report on Army's mil. prison program during World War II, Procs. Pres.'s Nat. Conf. Corrections, 1971. Home: 4401 Glenridge St Kensington MD 20795

EWBANK, WALTER JAMES, mech. engr., educator; b. Lawrenceburg, Ind., Aug. 1, 1914; s. James Henry and Mae (Curtis) E.; B.S., Purdue U., 1936; M.S., Va. Poly. Inst., 1938; m. Kathryn Bauer, Nov. 17, 1939; children—Ann (Mrs. Michael Cowan), James B., Jani (Mrs. Robert Sprinkle), Barbara Jean (Mrs. Robert Crook), John L. Research engr. Briggs Clarifier Co., Bethesda, Md., 1938-47; asst. prof. mech. engring. U. Okla., Norman, 1948-53, asso. prof.,

1953-60, prof., 1960—. Cons. in fuels, lubricants, waste disposal. Recipient Earle prize Nat. Lubricating Grease Inst., 1967. Mem. Soc. Automotive Engrs., Am. Soc. Lubricating Engrs., Am. Assn. U. Profs., Am. Soc. for Engring. Edn. Unitarian. Author: (with C.M. Sliepevich and J.E. Powers) Foundations of Thermodynamic Analysis, 1972. Home: Box 2128 Norman OK 73069

EWERS, JOHN CANFIELD, museum adminstr.; b. Cleve., July 21, 1909; s. John Ray and Mary Alice (Canfield) E.; A.B. Dartmouth, 1931, D.Sc., 1968; M.A., Yale, 1934; LL.D., U. Mont., 1966; m. Margaret Elizabeth Dumville, Sept. 6, 1934; children—Jane (Mrs. Robinson), Diane (Mrs. Peterson). Field curator Nat. Park Service, Wash., Morristown, N.J., Berkeley, Cal., Macon, Ga., 1935-40; curator Mus. Plains Indian, Browning, Mont., 1941-44; asso. curator ethnology U.S. Nat. Mus., Smithsonian Instn., Washington, 1946-56, planning officer, 1956-59, asst. dir. Mus. History and Tech., 1959-64, dir., 1964-65, sr. scientist Office Anthropology, 1965—, now sr. ethnologist Office Anthropology. Museum planning cons. Bur. Indian Affairs, 1948-49, Mont. Hist. Soc., 1950-54; cons. Am. Heritage, 1959. Trustee Mus. Am. Indian, Hoye Found., N.Y.C., 1972—. Served with USNR, 1944-46. Recipient 1st Exception Service award Smithsonian Instn., 1965. Fellow Am. Anthrop. Assn.; mem. Am. Indian Ethnologist Conf. (pres. 1960-61), Am. Assn. Museums, Anthrop. Soc. Washington. Author: Plains Indian Painting, 1940; The Horse in Blackfoot Indian Culture, 1955; The Blackfeet: Raiders on the Northwestern Plains, 1958; Artists of the Old West, 1965, enlarged edit., 1973; Indian Life on Upper Missouri, 1968. Editor: Adventures of Zenas Leonard, Fur Trader, 1959; Crow Indian Medicine Bundles, 1960; Five Indian Tribes of the Upper Missouri, 1961; O-Kee-Pa, A Religious Ceremony and Other Customs of the Mandans (George Catlin), 1967; The Indians of Texas in 1830, 1969. Editor: Jour. Washington Acad. Scis., 1955-56; editorial bd. The American West, 1965—. Contbr. articles to profl. publs. Home: 4432 26th Rd N Arlington VA Office: Smithsonian Instn Washington DC 20560

EWING, ANDREW, lawyer; b. nr. Nashville, Tenn., May 8, 1900; s. Francis McGavock and Eliza McClung (Marshall) E.; student, Hampden-Sydney Coll., 1916; student Vanderbilt U., 1917-18, LL.B., 1927; m. Cornelia Keeble, June 14, 1930; children—Andrew Jr., Emmie Elizabeth. Accountant, traffic engr. Cumberland Telephone & Telegraph Co., Nashville, 1918-24, Memphis, 1923-24; admitted to Tenn. bar, 1926; since practiced in Nashville; clk. firm Manier & Crouch, Attys., Nashville, 1925-26, asso., 1926-34; partner firm Bailey, Ewing & Powell (named changed to Bailey, Ewing, Dale & Bailey, 1944-68, Bailey, Ewing, Dale & Conner, 1968), Attys., Nashville, 1944-71; partner Dearborn & Ewing, Attys., Nashville, 1972—. Instr. law Andrew Jackson U., Nashville, 1933-34; dir. Hart County Creameries, Inc., Horse Cave, Ky., others. Trustee Webb Sch., Bell Buckle, Tenn., 1951—. Mem. Am., Tenn. bar assns., Nashville Bar and Library Assn. Presbyn. (deacon 1957-65). Republican. Presbyn. (trustee ch. 1955—). Clubs: Cumberland, Belle Meade Country (Nashville). Home: 501 E Bellvue Dr Nashville TN 37205 Office: Suite 1912 Parkway Towers 404 James Robertson Parkway Nashville TN 37219

EWING, GEORGE H., business exec.; b. San Antonio, June 11, 1925; s. H. L. and Miriam (Galloway) E.; B.S. in C. E., Tex. A. and M. U., 1948; m. Doris Ann Cannan, May 31, 1947; children—Susan, Beverly, Mary, Bryan. With Tex. Eastern Transmission Corp., Houston, 1948—, supr. plans and research div., 1956-58, supervising engr., 1958-64, v.p., chief engr., 1965-71, v.p. engring. and supplemental fuels and devel., 1971—. Served with USNR, 1943-46. Registered profl. engr., La. Mem. Am. Soc. M.E., Am. Gas Assn., Ind. Natural Gas Assn. Houston. Presbyn. Club: Petroleum (Houston). Home: 502 W Forest St Houston TX 77024 Office: PO Box 2521 Houston TX 77001

EWING, NEILS ORTVED, dairy co. exec.; b. Louisville, Nov. 24, 1936; s. Charles Oscar and Anne Elizabeth (Ortved) E.; A.B., Kenyon Coll., 1958; m. Mary Sue Kinsman, Dec. 16, 1961; children—Niels Christian and Elizabeth Murray (Twins). With Oscar Ewing, Inc., Louisville, 1958—, pres., 1966—. Bd. dirs. Louisville Area Safety Council, 1970-74, pres., 1973-74; bd. dirs. Downtown Louisville YMCA, 1972. Mem. Louisville Zool. Soc. (dir. 1972—). Presbyn. (elder 1970-73). Rotarian. Club: Louisville Country, Pendennis (Louisville). Home: 5607 Apache Rd Louisville KY 40207 Office: PO Box 1017 Louisville KY 40201

EYDE, RICHARD HUSTED, botanist; b. Lancaster, Pa., Dec. 23, 1928; s. Richard H. and Thelma (Somers) E.; B.S., Franklin and Marshall Coll., 1956; M.Sc., Ohio State U., 1957; Ph.D., Harvard, 1962; m. Lorraine Sylvia Dittrich, June 8, 1957; children—Douglas Alan, Dana Everest. Fulbright scholar Birbal Sahni Inst. Palaeobotany, Lucknow, India, 1960-61; research asst. dept. botany Smithsonian Instn., Washington, 1961-62, asso. curator, 1962-69, curator, 1969—. Home: 2400 S Arlington Ridge Rd Arlington VA 22202 Office: Dept Botany Smithsonian Instn Washington DC 20560

EYEINGTON, CHARLES DAVID, city ofcl.; b. Buffalo, Aug. 19, 1919; s. David F. and Mira (Pettit) E.; B.A., Baylor U., 1953; m. Tillie Hejl, Nov. 28, 1946; children—Charlotte (Mrs. John MacClelland), Charles David II, Emily, Thomas, James, Mary Beth, Robert. Plant supt. SWS Mfg. Co., 1951-54; mgr. C. of C., Hughes Springs, Tex., 1954-55, Daingerfield, 1955-58; city mgr. City of Daingerfield, 1958-65, City of Georgetown, 1965-68, City of Mission, 1968—. Served with AUS, 1941-46. Mem. Internat., Tex. city mgrs. assns., Municipal Finance Officers Assn., N.G. Assn. U.S. and Tex. Lion. Home: 1223 Doherty Av Mission TX 78572 Office: 900 Doherty Av Mission TX 78572

EYRES, DEREK EDMUND CRESSWELL, interior decorator; b. Bombay, India, July 1, 1913; s. Charles Lionel and Ethel Vera (French) E.; matriculated Dulwich Coll., London, Eng., 1928-31, Magdalen Coll., Oxford U. (Eng.), 1931-33; m. Kathryne Mary Woodson, July 1, 1958; 1 dau., Kathryne Avon (Mrs. Joseph Alan Towler). Came to U.S., 1950, naturalized, 1962. Owner Derek Eyres, Ltd., London, 1945-50; partner Edwards & Eyres, Ltd., N.Y.C., 1950-53; interior designer W & J Sloane, N.Y.C., 1953-56, Beverly Hills, Cal., 1962-65; owner London Studio Interior Design, Richmond, Va., 1967—. Served with Royal Navy, 1939-45. Decorated Distinguished Service Cross (Eng.). Mem. Am. Inst. Interior Designers. Clubs: Junior Naval and Military Overseas, Royal Automobile (London). Home: Darbytown House 7515 Darbytown Rd Richmond VA 23231 Office: 7515 Darbytown Rd Richmond VA 23231

EZELL, FLOY THOMAS, city mgr.; b. Sanger, Tex., Dec. 30, 1918; s. Floy Henry and Ora Lee (Gentle) E.; B.A., North Tex. U., 1936-41; m. Verdie M. Horst, May 3, 1945; children—James, Kerry. Sta. master Santa Fe Ry., Ft. Worth, 1948-51; city adminstr. City of Sanger, 1957-60; city mgr. City of Grapevine (Tex.), 1960—. Mem. Municipal Finance Officers Assn., Internat., Tex. city mgrs. assns., Internat. City Clks. Assn., Grapevine C. of C. Mason, Lion, Rotarian. Home: 503 Ridge Rd Grapevine TX 76015 Office: 413 S Main St Grapevine TX 76051

EZELL, FRANCIS HAYS, librarian; b. Chapel Hill, Tenn., Jan. 5, 1933; d. Edward Swanson and Sara (Bailey) Ezell; B.S. in Elementary Edn., Middle Tenn. State U., 1954; M. in Library Sci., George Peabody Coll., 1960. Tchr. Muscogee County Sch. System, Columbus, Ga., 1955; library asst. Main Post Library, Ft. Benning, Ga., 1955-59; librarian Free Library Phila., 1960-61; asst. regional librarian Upper Cumberland Regional Library Center, Cookeville, Tenn., 1961-68; sr. librarian Tenn. State Library and Archives, Nashville, 1968-70; dir. Tenn. Library for Blind and Physically Handicapped, Nashville, 1970—. Mem. Tenn., Southeastern library assns., Am. Assn. Workers for the Blind, Bus. and Profl. Women, Am. Assn. U. Women (v.p. 1961-64). Home: 2601 Hillsboro Rd Nashville TN 37212 Office: 5200 Centennial Blvd Nashville TN 37209

EZELLE, SAM, III, labor union exec.; b. Evansville, Ind., July 16, 1920; s. Samuel Wahl and Augusta (Culley) E.; LL.B., Jefferson Law Sch., Louisville, 1948, U. Louisville, 1951; m. Ruby Gordon Layman, Sept. 16, 1939; 1 son, Sam IV; m. 2d, Dorothy W., Dec. 16, 1967; children—Kent, Dale. Began career as a structural ironworker, 1941-46; dir. dept. research and edn. Ky. Fedn. Labor, 1946-52, exec. sec., 1952-58; exec. sec. Ky. AFL-CIO, 1958—; sec.-treas. Ky. Labor News, Inc., 1952-72; v.p. Am. Health Profiles, Inc., 1972—. Labor edn. specialist Mut. Security Agy., 1952; mem. Ky. Atomic Energy Commn., 1961—, U.S. Labor-Mgmt. Manpower Com., 1956—. Bd. regents Western State Coll., Bowling Green, Ky., 1957-59; bd. trustees U. Ky., 1960-68. Served with USAAF, 1942-43. Democrat. Home: 801 Glen Leven Dr Nashville TN 37204 Office: 4304 Harding Rd Nashville TN 37205

EZZARD, GEORGE PIERCE, physician; b. Lawrenceville, Ga., June 7, 1935; s. Webster Pierce and Doris Virginia (Cooper) E.; grad. Emory-at-Oxford Jr. Coll., 1953; B.S., U. Ga., 1955, B.A., 1956; M.D., Emory Med. Sch., 1961; m. Polly Anne Efird, Aug. 15, 1959; children—Mary Anne, Margaret Lynn, Carolyn Marie. Intern Crawford W. Long Hosp., Atlanta, 1961-62; practice gen. medicine, Lawrenceville, 1962—; mem. staff Button Gwinnett Hosp., Lawrenceville. Dir. Gwinnett Comml. Bank, Lawrenceville. Mem. Chattahoochee Med. Soc., Phi Chi. Methodist. Home: Route 3 Lawrenceville GA 30245 Office: Ezzard Bldg Lawrenceville GA 30245

FABER, CHARLES FRANKLIN, educator; b. Moravia, Ia., Dec. 6, 1926; s. Richard Andrew and Inez (McAlister) F.; B.A., Coe Coll., 1948; M.A., Columbia, 1952; Ph.D., U. Chgo., 1961; m. Patricia Jane Utt, June 8, 1947; children—Deborah, Daniel, Melinda. Pub. sch. tchr., adminstr., Ill., 1949-59; asst. prof. edn. Ia. State U., 1961-64; prof. edn., chmn. dept. ednl. adminstrn. Peabody Coll., Nashville, 1964-71; prof. edn., chmn. dept. ednl. adminstrn. U. Ky., Lexington, 1971—; cons. sch. systems and other ednl. agys., Ill., Ia., Mo., Ky., Tenn., Ala., Fla. Served with USNR, 1944-46. Mem. Am. Ednl. Research Assn., Am. Assn. Sch. Adminstrs., Nat. Conf. Profs. Ednl. Adminstrn., Phi Delta Kappa. Author: (with Gilbert Shearron) Elementary School Adminstration: Theory and Practice, 1970. Sect. editor: Educational Administration Abstracts, 1968-71. Contbr. articles to profl. jours. Home: 3569 Cornwall Dr Lexington KY 40503

FABER, SHEPARD MAZOR, educator; b. Bklyn., Aug. 8, 1928; s. Harry and Gertrude (Mazor) F.; B.A., Emory U., 1949; M.A., Columbia, 1950; Ed.D., U. Fla., 1960; m. Mary Ann Harbin, Jan. 1, 1953; children—Shane, Jesse, Samuel, Robin. Tchr. sci. Bradford County High Sch., Starke, Fla., 1953-56; asst. prof. East Carolina Coll., Greenville, N.C., 1959-62; asso. prof. phys. sci. U. Miami, Coral Gables, Fla., 1962-70 prof., 1970—. Served with USAF, 1951-52. Mem. A.A.A.S., Nat. Assn. Research Sci. Tchrs., Am. Assn. U. Profs., Iron Arrow, Sigma Pi Sigma, Omicron Delta Kappa. Home: 4722 SW 89th Ct Miami FL 33165 Office: Physics Dept U Miami Coral Gables FL 33124

FABRE, LOUIS FERNAND, psychiatrist; b. Akron, O., Sept. 13, 1941; s. Louis Fernand and Mary Jane (Tait) F.; B.S., Akron U., 1962; Ph.D., Case Western Res. U., 1966; M.D., Baylor Coll., 1969; m. Karen Willoughby, Oct. 12, 1963. With Tex. Research Inst. Mental Scis., Houston, 1965-73, chief alcoholism research, 1972-73; intern Methodist Hosp., Houston, 1969-70; resident Baylor Affiliated Hosps., Tex. Research Inst. Mental Scis., Houston, 1970-73; practice medicine specializing in psychiatry Houston, 1973—; dir. Crawford Street Clinic, Portland Clinic, Champions Clinic (all Houston); asst. prof. mental scis. U. Tex. Grad. Sch. Biomed. Scis., Houston, 1969—, also asso. prof. psychiatry Med. Sch. Cons. gas chromatography VA Hosp., Houston, 1967-70. Recipient Physicians Recognition award A.M.A., 1972-75; NIH travel fellow. Mem. Internat. Soc. Endocrinology, Endocrine Soc., Am. Fedn. Clin. Research, A.M.A., Am. Physiol. Soc., Am. Psychiat. Assn., Flying Physicians Assn., N.Y. Acad. Scis., Tex. Med. Assn., Harris County Med. Soc., Phi Sigma Alpha. Home: 6227 Coral Gables Houston TX 77069 Office: 120 Portland St Houston TX 77006

FABRY, PAUL ANDREW, internat. assn. exec.; b. Budapest, Hungary, June 19, 1919; s. Andrew and Ilona (Gombos) F.; B.A., Godollo Jr. Coll., 1937; Ph.D., U. Budapest, 1942, J.D., 1943; m. Louise Hitchcock Fair, May 15, 1958 (div. 1968); children—Lydia Louise, Alexa Fair; m. 2d, Angela Andrews Rutledge, May 8, 1971. Came to U.S., 1949, naturalized. War corr. Central European Press Service, Warsaw, Poland, Berlin Germany, Vienna, Austria, Zurich, Switzerland, Budapest, 1943-44; sec. Fgn. Office, Budapest, 1945; head Prime Minister's Cabinet, Budapest, 1945-46; charge d'affaires of Hungary, Ankara, Turkey 1946-47; fgn. corr. Istanbul, Turkey, 1948-49; sect. chief Radio Free Europe, N.Y.C., 1950-53; free lance writer, lectr., N.Y.C., 1954; pub. relations adviser E.I. du Pont de Nemours & Co., Wilmington, Del., 1955-62; mng. dir. Internat. House, New Orleans 1962—. Rep. Internat. Red Cross, Vienna-Budapest, 1945-46; adv. bd. Istanbul U., 1948-49, Internat. Econ. Cooperation Com., N.Y.C.; v.p. Cultural Services, Inc., N.Y.C., 1953-54; moderator Fact and Opinion, WYES-TV, 1965—. Active United Fund, Wilmington, 1955-60. Trustee, mem. exec. com. New Orleans Ednl. TV Found., 1970—. Served as capt. Royal Hungarian Artillery, 1943. Mem. Pub. Relations Soc. Am., Miss. Valley World Trade Council (dir., mem. exec. com. 1963—); World Trade Centers Assn. (v.p., treas. 1969—). Fgn. Press Assn., New Orleans Bd. Trade, C. of C. Home: 1127 Bourbon St New Orleans LA 70116 Office: 607 Gravier St New Orleans LA 70130

FABRYCKY, WOLTER JOSEPH, educator; b. N.Y.C., Dec. 6, 1932; s. Louis L. and Stephanie L. (Wadis) F.; B.S. in Indsl. Engring., Wichita State U., 1957; M.S. in Indsl. Engring., U. Ark., 1958; Ph.D. in Engring. (Ethyl Corp. fellow), Okla. State U., 1962; m. Luba Swerbilow, Sept. 4, 1954; children—David, Kathryn. Design engr. Cessna Aircraft, 1954-57; instr. indsl. engring. U. Ark., 1957-60; asst. prof. indsl. engring. Okla. State U., 1962-64, asso. prof., 1964-65; asso. prof. indsl. engring. and operations research Va. Poly. Inst. and State U., Blacksburg, 1965-66, prof., 1966—, asso. dean engring., 1970—. Cons. Brown Engring., 1962-65, Forest Products Marketing Lab., 1967, Inland Motors, 1967-68, U.S. Army, 1968-70. Mem. Am. Inst. Indsl. Engrs. (chpt. pres. 1967-68, inst. v.p. 1974—), Am. Soc. Engring. Edn. (div. dir. 1971), Operations Research Soc. Am. Author: (with H.G. and G.J. Thoesen) Engineering Economy, 1971; (with J. Banks) Procurement and Inventory Systems, 1967; (with Torgersen and Ghare) Industrial Operations Research, 1972; (with G.J. Thuesen) Economic Decision Analysis, 1974. Home: 1200 Lakewood Dr NW Blacksburg VA 24060

FACKELMAN, ROBERT HENRY, newspaper exec.; b. Ponca, Neb., Oct. 19, 1907; s. Herman Carl and Jeanette (Pomeroy) F.; student Midland Coll., 1923-25; B.J., U. Mo., 1927; postgrad. Harvard, 1941-42; m. Anna Laura Torbert, June 6, 1928; 1 dau., Ann Karen (Mrs. Frank Nixon). Editor, pub. Baxter Springs (Kan.) Citizen, 1927-28, Raymondville (Tex.) Chronicle, 1929-40, Morristown (Tenn.) Sun, 1950-52; editor, gen. mgr. Winter Haven (Fla.) News-Chief, 1943-50; pub. Cleveland (Tenn.) Banner, 1952-54; v.p. So. Newspapers, Inc., 1954-58; pres. Newspaper Service Co., Inc., 1953—; pres. Gulf Coast Newspapers, Inc., 1958—; pres. Ruston (La.) Pubs., Inc., Minden (La.) Newspapers, Inc., Tarpon Springs (Fla.) Leader, Inc. v.p. Slidell Newspapers, Inc.; sec. Panhandle Press Pubs. Served in USAAF, 1941-42. Mem. So. Newspaper Pubs. Assn. (dir. 1970—). Address: 408 S Bonita Av Panama City FL 32401

FADDIS, EDWARD LEROY, architect; b. Mobile, Ala., Nov. 5, 1925; s. LeRoy and Edna Lucille (Hilburn) F.; student Va. Mil. Inst., 1943, U. Ala., 1946-47; B.Arch., Auburn U., 1951; m. Anne Shannon, Aug. 20, 1949; children—Sara Shannon, John Paige. Draftsman, Pearson & Tittle, architects, Montgomery, 1947; draftsman Pearson, Tittle & Narrows, architects, Montgomery, 1951-53, chief draftsman, 1953-56, job capt., 1951-58; job capt. Platt Roberts & Co., architects, Mobile, 1958-59; individual practice architecture, Mobile, 1959; partner Harry Inge Johnstone & Edward L. Faddis, architects, Mobile, 1962-70; prin. Architects Group, Inc., Mobile, 1971—. Mem. archtl. rev. bd. City of Mobile, 1965-70, chmn., 1970. Served with USAAF, 1943-45. Mem. A.I.A. (chpt. treas. 1971), Scarab. Presbyn. (deacon 1969—). Club: Exchange (dir. Mobile 1966-67). Prin. archtl. works include Library Bldg., U. South Ala., 1967, Bus. and Mgmt. Studies Bldg., U. South Ala., 1969, First Fed. Tower, Mobile, 1970. Home: 118 E Ridgelawn Dr Mobile AL 36608 Office: 818 First Federal Tower Mobile AL 36606

FAGALY, WILLIAM ARTHUR, art mus. curator; b. Lawrenceburg, Ind., Mar. 1, 1938; s. William James and Dorothy Rae (Wheeler) F.; A.B., Ind. U., 1962, M.A., 1967. Asst. registrar Ind. U. Mus. Art, 1964-66, registrar, Isaac Delgado Mus. of Art, New Orleans, 1966-67, curator of collections, 1967-72; acting dir. New Orleans Mus. of Art, 1972, 73, chief curator, 1973—; asst. prof. art history Delgado Coll., 1967-69. Mem. Internat. Council of Museums, Am. Assn. Museums, Sigma Chi. Author: Treasures by Peter Carl Fabergé and Other Master Jewelers, 1972. Home: 618 Governor Nicholls New Orleans LA 70116 Office: New Orleans Museum of Art City Park New Orleans LA 70179

FAGAN, MAURICE JAMES, dentist; b. Coventry, R.I., Dec. 4, 1921; s. Maurice James and Ellen Louisa (Albro) F.; B.S., Providence Coll., 1943; student Balt. Coll. Dental Surgery 1944-47; D.D.S., U. Md., 1947; m. Ruth Pearl Mcdonald, June 28, 1947; children—Maurice James III, Malford, Mark, Mitchell, Laurie Anne, Margo Jean. Practice dentistry, Wakefield, R.I., 1947, Atlanta, 1956—; asso. in geriatrics, cons. Malford Thewlis Geriatric Clinic, 1947-56, Dental Masters, Inc.; founder dental health program South Kingston (R.I.) Sch. Dept. 1948, dir., 1948-50; instr. USAF Med. Service, Atlanta, 1959-64; pres. Dental Practice Plan Inc. Founder, 1960, since pres., chmn. bd. dirs., trustee Maurice J. Fagan Meml. Dental Hosp., Dentistry for Aged, Handicapped, Atlanta. Served from pvt. to lt. col., USAF, 1942-72. Fellow Am. Acad. Gen. Dentistry, Internat. Coll. Oral Implantologists (a founder 1972), Royal Soc. Health; mem. So. Acad. Oral Implantology (founder; pres. 1969-70), Am. Acad. Implant Dentistry, Am., Ga. dental assns., No. Dist. Dental Soc., Am. Soc. Dentistry for Children, Acad. Dentistry for Handicapped, Am. Geriatric Soc., Am. Soc. Geriatric Dentistry, Res. Officers Assn., Am. Soc. Clin. Hypnosis, Acad. Gen. Dentistry, Associazone Nazionale Implantoprotesi Orale. Author: Dental Practice Planning; How to Succeed in Dentistry; New Concepts in Implant Dentistry. Home: 5360 Peachtree-Dunwoody Rd NE Atlanta GA 30342 Office: 960 Johnson Ferry Rd NE Atlanta GA 30342

FAGAN, WAYNE STANTON, accountant; b. Nekoosa, Wis., Nov. 3, 1918; s. Ralph R. and Opal (Brower) F.; B.B.A., U. Wis., 1946-48; m. Elizabeth Ann Guill, June 18, 1954; children—Michael Wayne, Patricia Ann. Supervising sr. accountant Touche, Ross, Bailey & Smart, Chgo. and Houston, 1948-53; treas., plant mgr. Bernhard Altmann Tex. Corp., San Antonio, 1953-56; supervisory auditor U.S. Army, San Antonio, 1956-61; sr. price analyst, contract negotiator USAF, San Antonio, 1961-64; asst. regional audit mgr. NASA, Houston, 1964—. Served with USAAF, 1942-45. Decorated Air medal. C.P.A., Ill., Tex. Mem. Am. Inst. C.P.A.'s, Fed. Govt. Accountants Assn., Am. Legion, Phi Beta Kappa, Beta Gamma Sigma. Home: 2214 Lillian St Pasadena TX 77502 Office: NASA Manned Spacecraft Center Houston TX 77058

FAGET, MAXIME ALLAN, govt. ofcl.; b. Stann Creek, British Honduras, Aug. 26, 1921 (parents Am. citizens); s. Guy Henry and Isabelle Marie (LeBlanc) F.; student San Francisco Jr. Coll., 1939-40; B.S. in M.E., La. State U., 1943; D.Eng., U. Pitts., 1966; D.Engr. La. State U., 1972; m. Nancy Carastro, June 21, 1947; children—Ann, Carol, Guy, Nanette. With NASA, 1946—, dir. engring. and devel. Johnson Space Center, Houston, 1960—. Vis. prof. La. State U., 1961-65. Served with USNR, 1943-46. Recipient Arthur S. Fleming award, 1960; Astronautics award Guggenheim Internat., 1973. Fellow Am. Inst. Aeros. and Astronautics (Design award 1970), Am. Astronautical Soc. (Lovelace award 1972); mem. Internat. Acad. Astronautics, Nat. Acad. Engring. Home: 221 W Bayou Dr Dickinson TX 77539 Office: NASA Lyndon B Johnson Space Center Houston TX 77058

FAGIN, DAVID KYLE, petroleum co. exec.; b. Dallas, Apr. 9, 1938; s. Kyle Marshall and Frances Margaret (Gaston) F.; B.S., U. Okla., 1960; postgrad. So. Meth. U., 1968; m. Margaret Ann Hazlett, Jan. 24, 1959; children—David Kyle, Scott Edward. Petroleum engr. W.C. Bednar Petroleum Cons., 1958-62; partner, W.C. Bednar Cons., 1962-65; petroleum appraisal engr. First Nat. Bank Dallas, 1965-68; exec. v.p. Alamo Petroleum Co., Dallas, 1968-71, pres., 1971—; v.p. oil and gas Rosario Resources Co., Dallas, 1968—; dir. Alamo Petroleum Co., Alamo Petroleum Ltd. (Can.), Global Energy Co., Trans Tex Pipe Line Co., Am. Diversified Properties, Inc., Phipps Oil Ltd. (Eng.). Active various community drives. Bd. dirs., chmn. bd. U. Okla., Dallas, 1969-71. Registered profl. engr., Okla., La., Tex. Mem. Am. Inst. Mining, Metall. and Petroleum Engrs. (vice-chmn. Dallas sect. 1971-73), Tex. Ind. Producers and Royalty Owners, Ind. Producers Assn. Am., Petroleum Engrs. Club Dallas (pres. 1968), Dallas Geol. Soc., Engrs. Club Dallas, Petroleum Club Dallas, U. Okla. Alumni Assn., Phi Delta Theta. Republican. Methodist (mem. ofcl. bd. 1963—). Clubs: Captain's Cove Yacht (commodore 1971-72), Rush Creek Yacht (bd. govs. 1967-71), Corinthian Sailing (Dallas). Home: 6218 Sul Ross Lane Dallas TX 75214 Office: 600 One Energy Square Dallas TX 75206

FAHLBERG, WILLSON JOEL, educator; b. Madison, Wis., July 20, 1918; s. Earnest David and Veva Isabel (Willson) F.; Ph.B., U. Wis., 1948, M.S., 1949, Ph.D., 1951; m. Audrey Syse, July 30, 1938;

children—Karen Rae (Mrs. Leonard Laube), Willson Joel, Merrilee Ann (Mrs. Raymond DeAngelis), Lawrence David. Research chemist Universal Oil Products Co., 1938-44; teaching asst. U. Wis., 1948-50; research fellow Polio Found., U. Wis., 1949-51; instr. microbiology Baylor U. Coll. Medicine, Houston, 1951-53, asst. prof. microbiology, 1953-60, asso. prof., 1960—, coordinator Cardiovascular Research and Tng. Center, 1967-68; dir. med. affairs Meml. Hosp. System, 1969—; cons., staff mem. Meth. Hosp., 1952—, St. Joseph's Hosp., 1958—, Tex. Inst. Rehab. and Research, 1966—; dir. labs., cons. Tex. Research Inst. Mental Scis., 1962—; cons. M. D. Anderson Hosp., 1957—, St. Elizabeth's Hosp., 1971—, VA, 1953—. Exec. dir. Conv. and Travel Coordinating Service, Inc., 1968—. Served with M.C., AUS, 1944-45. Diplomate Am. Bd. Microbiology. Fellow Am. Acad. Microbiology, Royal Soc. Health, Doctors Club, Pan Am. Doctors Club. Episcopalian. Club: World Trade (Houston). Contbr. articles to profl. jours. Home: 3746 Darcus St Houston TX 77005 Office: Suite 770 1010 Louisiana St Houston TX 77002 also Baylor Coll Medicine Texas Medical Center Houston TX 77025

FAIL, THOMAS ALLEN, contractor; b. Jackson, Tenn., Nov. 13, 1922; s. Thomas Allen and Nela (Myracle) F.; student Lambuth Coll., 1946-47, Union U., 1947, Vanderbilt U., 1948-49; m. Beverly Townsend, June 3, 1949; children—Beverly Jessica, Sherri Lisa, Allycin Clair. Engr., G., M. & O. R.R. Co., Jackson, Tenn., 1940-44; resident mgr. Townsend Electric Co., Memphis, 1949-56, v.p., Jackson, 1956—; v.p. Townsend Supply Co., Jackson, 1956—, also dir. Served with C.E., AUS, 1944-46: PTO. Mem. I.E.E.E., V.F.W., Elec. Apparatus Service Assn. (co. rep. 1956—), Jackson and Madison County Area C. of C. Methodist (supt. youth dept. 1963—). Mason. Club: Golf and Country (Jackson, Tenn.). Home: 22 Fairfield Pl Jackson TN 38301 Office: 128 Johnson St Jackson TN 38301

FAILE, WILLIAM THOMAS, lawyer; b. Selma, Ala., Apr. 8, 1942; s. Willard T. and Annie Verna (Sherrer) F.; B.S., Livingston U., 1964; LL.B., U. Ala., 1967; m. Carolyn Farrior, Sept. 18, 1971. Admitted to Ala. bar, 1967; since practiced in Selma; mem. firm Lapsley & Berry, 1968-69; dep. dist. atty., 4th Jud. Circuit, Selma, 1969-70, dist. atty., 1970—. Mem. Am., Ala. bar assns., Ala. Peace Officers, Ala. Dist. Attys. Assn. Presbyn. Home: Landline Rd Selma AL 36701 Office: Dallas County Courthouse Selma AL 36701

FAILS, JAMES CLAYTON, lawyer; b. Comanche, Tex., Oct. 19, 1928; s. Reddoch McCullough and Inez (Johnson) F.; B.S. in Chem. Engring., Tex. A. and M. U., 1950, M.S. in Chem. Engring., 1958; J.D., So. Meth. U., 1965; m. Anna Jean Atchison, June 27, 1953; children—Deborah Jean, Sandra Lynn, Sharon Kay. Jr. gas engr. Mobil Oil Corp., Healdton, Okla., 1950-51, plant engr., field engr., reservoir engr., acting dist. engr., 1956-57; engr. in charge underground storage, Vanderbilt, Tex., 1958-59, employee relations asst., Dallas, 1959-60, sr. patent engr., 1960-63, patent agt. and atty., 1963-67; pvt. practice, 1968—. Teaching asst. Tex. A. and M. U., 1957-58; mem. adv. com. S.W. Patent law Inst., 1971. Judge, Sci. Fair, 1959; active United Fund, Big Bros. Am. Served to capt. USAF, 1951-56. Recipient Australian Water Evaporation Retardation Research Grant, 1958. Mem. Am. Inst. Chem. Engrs., Am. Inst. Mining, Metall. and Petroleum Engrs., Am., Tex., Fort Worth-Tarrant County bar assns., Research and Sci. Soc. Am. (high sch. liaison 1959-63), Delta Theta Phi. Baptist. Lion. Patentee in field. Home: 3729 Ashford Av Fort Worth TX 76133 Office: 500 Baker Bldg Fort Worth TX 76102

FAIN, DOUGLAS WILSON, carpet co. exec.; b. Weatherford, Tex., Oct. 1, 1919; s. Douglas Wythe and Mary (Barber) F.; A.A., Weatherford Jr. Coll., 1938; B.B.A., Tex. U., 1942; m. Bette Jane Harder, Jan. 16, 1960; children—Gregorl, Mary Tanya. Cashier, Mchts. & Farmers State Bank, Weatherford, 1946-50; partner Berhard-Fain Carpets, Dallas, 1950—; dir., mem. exec. com. Inwood Nat. Bank. Mem. city council, Dallas, dep. mayor pro tem, 1971—. Served with Mil. Intelligence Corps, AUS, 1942-45; ETO. Decorated Bronze Star. Mem. N. Dallas C. of C. (pres. 1963-64). Mason (32 deg., Shriner), Lion (past pres. Park Cities club.). Home: 4444 Lovers Lane Dallas TX 75229

FAIN, ROBERT CHARLES, coll. dean; b. Santa Rosa, Tex., Oct. 19, 1936; s. Horace Edgar and Ruth Irene (Carroll) F.; B.S., Southwest Tex. State U., 1958, M.A., 1959; Ph.D., U. Tex., 1965; m. Patricia Ann Todd, Aug. 23, 1958; children—Cheryl Lynn, James Robert. Instr. chemistry Southwest Tex. State U., San Marcos, 1959-61; research chemist Celanese Chem. Corp., Summit, N.J., 1965-66; asso. prof. chemistry Tarleton State U., Stephenville, Tex., 1966-68, prof., 1968—, head dept. chemistry, 1968-73, dean Sch. Arts and Scis., 1970—. Bd. dirs. Stephenville United Fund, 1969-72, Comanche Trail council Boy Scouts Am., 1969—. Mem. C. of C. (dir. 1973—), Alpha Chi. Club: Optimist (pres. 1972-73) (Stephenville). Home: 1340 Rose Dr Stephenville TX 76401

FAIN, ROBIN PAULINE, librarian; b. nr. Nicholasville, Ky., Apr. 14, 1912; d. Larkin Davis and Minnie (House) Fain; A.B., U. Ky., 1941, M.A., 1952, postgrad., 1953-58, 69; postgrad. U. Denver, 1962. Elementary tchr. Jessamine County (Ky.) Schs., 1930-45; tchr. English, Wilmore High Sch., 1946-58; librarian Jessamine County High Sch., Nicholasville, 1958—; instr. summer sch. U. Ky., 1961, 63-66. Named Outstanding Ky. Sch. Librarian, Ky. Library Trustees Assn., 1967. Mem. N.E.A. (life), Ky. Edn. Assn., Jessamine County Tchrs. Assn. (past pres.), A.L.A., Southeastern, Ky. library assns., Ky. Assn. Sch. Librarians (past pres.), Ky. Audio-Visual Assn., Delta Kappa Gamma. Republican. Methodist. Home: Route 2 Nicholasville KY 40356 Office: Route 4 Jessamine County High Sch Nicholasville KY 40356

FAIR, HENRY THOMAS, JR., real estate co. exec.; b. Fort Worth, Mar. 30, 1920; s. Henry Thomas and Mabel (Chapman) F.; B.S., Tex. Christian U., 1949; m. Georgia B. McCamey, Mar. 1, 1940; children—Michael, Karen, Thomas. Self-employed as C.P.A., Fort Worth, 1949-51; treas., Reserve Oil & Gas Co., San Francisco, 1951-62; v.p., Sinclair Oil & Gas Co., Tulsa, 1962-65, N.Y.C., 1965-66; pres., Rathborne Land Co., Inc., Harvey, La., 1966—. Served with Signal Corps, AUS, 1941-46. Mem. Petroleum Club New Orleans. Club: Timberlane Country (Gretna, La.). Home: 5635 Sutton Pl New Orleans LA 70114 Office: PO Box 157 Harvey LA 70058

FAIRBANKS, LAURENCE DEE, educator, zoologist; b. Fredonia, Kan., May 23, 1926; s. L. Dee and Laura Leola (Huber) F.; A.A., Independence (Kan.) Jr. Coll., 1947; A.B., U. Kan., 1949, M.A., 1956; Ph.D., Tulane U., 1959; m. Ruth Ellen Edwards, Dec. 19, 1953; children—Laurence Francis, Henry Dee, Sarah Alicia. Grad. asst. teaching and research U. Kan., 1953-55; asst. teaching and grad. research Tulane U., New Orleans, 1955-58, instr. dept. med. and dept. zoology, 1958-67, asst. prof. medicine, instr. dept. phys. edn., 1967-70, asso. prof. medicine, instr. dept. phys. edn., 1970—. Served with AUS, 1950-51. NIH fellow, 1958-62, NIH grantee, 1962-73. Home: 4539 Gen Meyer Av New Orleans LA 70114

FAIRCHILD, BENNIE DARREL, oil producer; b. Camargo, Okla., July 12, 1918; s. Thomas E. and Adell A. (Wood) F.; student No. Okla. Coll., 1935-36, Central State U., Edmond, Okla., 1936-38, Phillips U., 1938-39; m. Hazel A. Wimple, June 28, 1940; 1 dau., Deborah Denise. Tchr. rural sch., Garber, Okla., 1938-40; with Continental Oil Co., Ponca City, Okla., 1940-62, prodn. foreman, 1950-62; pres. Fairchild Well Service, Inc., Tonkawa, Okla., 1962—; dir. Service Bank of Tonkawa. Served with AUS, 1942-45; CBI. Mem. C. of C. (pres. 1969-70), V.F.W., Am. Legion. Methodist. Home: 400 N Frantz St Tonkawa OK 74653 Office: 313 S Main St Tonkawa OK 74653

FAIRCHILD, CLARE E., investment, biog. exec.; b. Marietta, S.D., Dec. 15, 1911; s. Fred Lamont and Eleanor (Stobbs) F.; student U. Wash., 1933-34; m. Eleanore Marie Donoghue, Jan. 27, 1947; children—Linda Jean, Brenda, Mark. Photographer Atlas Photos, N.Y.C., 1935-39; ad man Clovis (Cal.) Tribune, 1939-41; steelworker C.P.N.A.B., Honolulu, Hawaii, 1942-44; insp. Bahrein Petroleum Co., Persian Gulf, 1944-45, treas. Fairchild Bros., Inc., Rutland, Mass., 1945-48; pres., treas. Brentwood Realty Corp., Worcester, 1948—; designer, builder Fairbrook Hotel. Pres., treas. Capital Investors, Inc., Holden, 1954—; pres. C.A. Turner Co. of Florida, 1964—; v.p. U.S. Water Conservation Corp.; developed Brentwood Estates; pres., treas. Fairchild Products Corp., West Palm Beach, Fla., Ofcl. Equipment Co. Bd. dirs. Barker Players, Inc., Worcester Art Mus., Worcester Found. Exptl. Biology; nat. dir. Child Safety Edn. Assn. Inc. Mem. Nat. Assn. Home Builders, Fla. Sheriffs Assn., Palm Beach County Sheriff's Aux., Nat. Assn. Real Estate Bds., Master Home Builders Assn. Worcester County (v.p.), Worcester C. of C. Mason. Clubs: Fairbrook Country (treas.); Quinsigamond Yacht; Nat. Exchange, Holden Country (treas.); Palm Beach Yacht, Palm Beach Athletic. Home: 142 Peruvian Av Palm Beach FL 33480 Office: 512 24th St West Palm Beach FL

FAIRCHILD, WILEY, constrn. co. exec.; b. Covington County, Miss., Sept. 19, 1912; s. William Robert and Susie (Ingram) F.; student pub. schs.; D.B.A. (hon.), William Carey Coll., 1974; m. Marie Ishee, May 21, 1938; children—Redditt Andrew, Wiley Jean (Mrs. Fairchild Commiskey). With W.R. Fairchild Constrn. Co., Hattiesburg, Miss., 1924—, gen. partner, 1945—, gen. mgr., 1948—; an organizer So. Nat. Bank of Hattiesburg, 1965, v.p., dir., 1972—; with Fairchild-Fla. Constrn. Co., Monticello, Fla., 1950—; pres. Fairco Contractors, Inc., Hattiesburg, 1965—; dir. Miss. Valley Cement Industries, Inc., Magna Corp., Pik-A-Pak Delicatessen & Service Co., Inc. Trustee William Carey Coll., Hattiesburg, chmn. trustees, 1972—; bd. dirs. Miss Park Commn., 1973. Clubs: Hattiesburg Country Lamplighters. Home: 114 S 24th Av Hattiesburg MS 39401 Office: PO Box 1609 Hattiesburg MS 39401

FAIRCLOTH, JOSEPH SHERRON, civil engr.; b. Brundidge, Ala., Apr. 5, 1937; s. Pink and Beanie Lee (Mauldin) F.; B.S. in C.E., U. Ala., 1967, M.S. in C.E., 1969; m. Betty Blair Youngblood, May 31, 1963; children—Blair Lea, Beth Ami. Engrs. asst. Ala. Hwy. Dept., 1955-56, 58-61, profl. engr., 1968-71; constrn. and facilities mgr. Ala. Army N.G., Montgomery, 1971—. Served with AUS, 1956-58, 61-62. Registered profl. engr., Ala. Mem. Am. Soc. C.E. (asso. mem., dir. 1973-74), Nat. Soc. Profl. Engrs., Am. Legion, Ala. State Employees Assn. (pres. 1970-71), Montgomery Jr. C. of C. (sec. 1969-70), Sigma Xi. Home: 3555 Lancaster Lane Montgomery AL 36106 Office: PO Box 1311 1720 Federal Dr Montgomery AL 36102

FAIRCLOTH, WAYNE REYNOLDS, educator; b. Whigham, Ga., Jan. 15, 1932; s. G. Henry and Ruby M. (Sanders) F.; B.S., Valdosta State Coll., 1955; M.Ed., U. N.C., 1959; Ph.D., U. Ga., 1971; m. Juanita Jane Norsworthy, Sept. 5, 1966; children—Anna Marjorie, Amy Claire. Instr., chmn. dept. sci. Whigham High Sch., 1951-61; asst. prof. biology Valdosta (Ga.) State Coll., 1961-67, asso. prof. biology, curator herbarium, 1967-71, prof. biology, curator herbarium, 1971—. Mem. Bot. Soc. Am., Am. Fern Soc., So. Appalachian Bot. Club, Assn. Southeastern Biologists, Phi Sigma, Phi Kappa Phi, Omicron Delta Kappa. Home: 2302 White Oak Dr Valdosta GA 31601

FAIRLEY, JAMES ARCHIE, civil engr.; b. Clarksdale, Miss., May 20, 1942; s. Paul V. and Frances R. (Rickman) F.; student U. Tenn., 1964-66; B.S. in C.E., Christian Bros. Coll., 1970; postgrad. LaSalle U., 1971—; m. Lynda Ruth Monroe, June 25, 1960; children—Leigh Ann, Amanda Lynne. Design engr. Pickering Engring. Assos., Inc., 1964-70; engr., planner Thomas Seabrook & Assos., Inc., 1970-71; co-owner, gen. mgr. Fairley, Pickering & Assos., 1971-72; partner, v.p. engring. Seabrook, Lithgow & Kujath, Inc., 1973; owner, pres. Fairley Engring., Inc., Biloxi, Miss., 1972—; dir. Magnolia Plaza, Inc., Biloxi, Miss. Bd. dirs. Boys Club. Recipient Design Recognition Asphalt Inst., 1973. Registered profl. engr., Miss., Ark., Tenn., Ky., La., Ala. Mem. Am. Chem. Soc., Am. Soc. C.E., Nat., Tenn. Miss. socs. profl. engrs., Soc. Am. Mil. Engrs. Profl. Engrs. in Pvt. Practice, Am. Coll. Surveyors, C. of C. (vice-chmn. transp. com. 1972-73), Jr. C. of C. (chmn. distinguished service award 1972—). Republican. Mem. Christian Ch. (deacon 1966-70). Moose, Elk, Kiwanian. Home: 304 S Shore Dr Biloxi MS 39530 Office: 137 Magnolia Mall Biloxi MS 39530

FAIRSTEIN, EDWARD, elec. co. exec.; b. Bklyn., Dec. 14, 1922; s. Sidney Samuel and Katherine (Bader) F.; B.S. in E.E., City Coll. N.Y., 1944; grad. U. Tenn., 1951; m. Helen Chastain, July 9, 1949 (div. Oct. 1971); children—John Elliot, Joel Alan. Trainee, Tenn. Eastman Corp., Oak Ridge, 1945-46; sr. engr. Oak Ridge (Tenn.) Nat. Lab., 1946-59; sec.-treas., chief engr. FairPort Instruments, Inc., 1959-60; chmn. bd., chief engr. Tennelec, Inc., Oak Ridge, 1960—; sec. Research Consultants, Inc., Oak Ridge, 1971—; dir. Tennecomp Systems, Inc., Hamilton First Nat. Bank, Grove Devel. Corp., Oak Ridge. Sec. Indsl. Devel. Bd., Oak Ridge, 1969—. Fellow I.E.E.E. (chpt. dir. 1970), mem. Sci. Research Soc. Am., Am. Phys. Soc., A.A.A.S. Editorial bd. Review Sci. Instruments, 1958-61. Contbr. articles to profl. jours. Patentee in field. Home: 228 Outer Dr Oak Ridge TN 37830 Office: Box D Oak Ridge TN 37830

FAISON, FRANK ALLEN, city mgr.; b. Richmond, Va., Nov. 14, 1929; s. Patrick L. and May (Trusheim) F.; B.S., Va. Poly. Inst., 1951, M.S., 1952; postgrad. U. Chgo., 1959-60; m. Marilyn Roth, Sept. 13, 1958; children—E. Lawrence, David L., Elizabeth L., Patricia L. Adminstrv. asst. City LaGrange Park (Ill.), 1956-59, city mgr., 1961-67; dir. pub. works City of St. Charles (Ill.), 1959-61; city mgr., Danville, Va., 1967-71, Pensacola, Fla., 1971—. Lectr. Va. Commonwealth U., Pensacola Jr. Coll. Bd. dirs. Pensacola United Fund. Served with C.E., U.S. Army, 1952-56, now lt. col. Res. Decorated Bronze Star medal. Mem. Internat. City Mgmt. Assn. (instr. Municipal Adminstrn. Tng. Inst.), Fla. City and County Mgrs. Assn. Omicron Delta Kappa, Chi Epsilon. Lion, Kiwanian, Rotarian. Home: 4745 Howe Av Pensacola FL 32504 Office: City Hall Pensacola FL 32502

FAKLIS, NICK VASILE, dentist; b. Tarpon Springs, Fla., Nov. 28, 1931; s. Vasile George and Dikea (Valsamis) F.; B.S., U. Tampa, 1954; D.M.D., U. Louisville, 1964; m. Anna Marie Athanason, Sept. 11, 1966; 1 children—Theda Marie, Debra Ann. Trainer dental nurses, operator Hillsborough County Dental Research Clinic, 1964-65; individual practice dentistry, Clearwater Beach, Fla., 1965—. Served with AUS, 1954-56. Mem. Am., Fla., Ky., Pinellas County dental assns., Royal Soc. Health, Am. Soc. Geriatric Dentistry, Fedn. Dentaire Internationale, Acad. Gen. Dentistry, Oral Assn. for Research (founder, pres.), Delta Sigma Delta. Democrat. Greek Orthodox. Rotarian. Contbr. to We Like These Ideas, 1970; also articles profl. jours. Home: 331 Leeward Island Clearwater Beach FL 33515 Office: 491 Mandalay Av Clearwater Beach FL 33515

FALK, CHARLES EUGENE, govt. found. ofcl.; b. Hamm, Germany, Oct. 20, 1923; s. Eric J. and Lucy (Kaiser) F.; came to U.S., 1938, naturalized, 1944; B.A., N.Y. U., 1944, M.S., 1946; D.Sc., Carnegie-Mellon U., 1950; m. Lillian Mandel, Dec. 26, 1948; children—Michael K., Gary M., Jeffrey D. Physicist Brookhaven Nat. Lab., Upton, N.Y., 1950-56, 58-66, asst. dir., 1960, asso. dir., 1961-66; physicist AEC, Washington, 1956-58; planning dir. div. sci. resources and policy studies NSF, Washington, 1966-70, dir. div. sci. resources, 1970—. Vis. fellow U. Sussex (Eng.), 1972-73. Served with AUS, 1944-46. Mem. Am. Phys. Soc., A.A.A.S., N.Y. Acad. Scis., Sigma Xi. Home: 8116 Lilly Stone Dr Bethesda MD 20034 Office: NSF 1800 G St NW Washington DC 20550

FALK, HANS LUDWIG, govt. ofcl.; b. Breslau, Germany, Sept. 15, 1919; s. Herman and Gertrude (Raphaelsohn) F.; student U. London, 1938-40; B.Sc. (Maj. Hiram Mills scholar 1943), McGill U., 1944, Ph.D., 1947; m. Gabrielle Clara Fund, June 30, 1950; children—Raymond Walter, Donald Herman, Stephen Thomas. Came to U.S., 1947, naturalized, 1953. Instr. dept. pathology U. Chgo., 1947-52; adj. asst., asso. prof. pathology U. So. Cal., Los Angeles, 1952-62; head chemistry sect. Nat. Cancer Inst., NIH, Bethesda, Md., 1962-63, chief carcinogen studies br., 1963-66, asso. sci. dir. carcinogenesis, 1966-68; asst. dir. lab. research Nat. Inst. Environmental Health Scis., NIH, Research Triangle Park, N.C., 1968-71, asso. dir. program, 1971—. Recipient Superior Service award USPHS, 1968. Mem. A.A.A.S., Am. Assn. Cancer Research, Am. Soc. Cell Biology, Am. Soc. Exptl. Pathology, Soc. Toxicology, Am. Inst. Chemists, Royal Soc. Health, Reticuloendothelial Soc., N.Y. Acad. Scis. Sigma Xi. Co-author: Chemical Mutagens - Environmental Effects on Biological Systems, 1970. Home: 4508 Pitt St Raleigh NC 27609 Office: PO Box 12233 Research Triangle Park NC 27709

FALK, JACK ARNOLD, circuit judge; b. Bridgeport, Conn., Nov. 8, 1927; s. Louis E. and Bessie (Adelman) F.; B.A. cum laude, U. Miami, 1949, J.D. magna cum laude, 1950; m. Corinne Clifton, Oct. 17, 1957; children—Andrew, Jack Arnold, Elizabeth. Admitted to Fla. bar, 1950; practiced law, Miami, 1950-60; dep. commr. Fla. Indsl. Commn., 1958-60; judge Criminal Ct. of Record, Dade County, 1960-66, Circuit Ct. 11th Jud. Circuit, Miami, 1966—. Pres. Dade County (Fla.) U.S.O. Council, 1966-70. Served with AUS, 1946-48. Mem. Am., Dade County bar assns., Fla. Bar (chmn. Dade County grievance com. 1960). Res. Officers Assn. (chpt. sec. 1963-64), U. Miami Law Alumni (v.p. 1964), Phi Kappa Phi. Mason (32 deg, Shriner). Clubs: Optimist (pres. 1958-59). Home: 1835 SW 82d Ct Miami FL 33155 Office: Dade County Courthouse Miami FL 33130

FALK, LESLIE ALAN, physician, educator; b. St. Louis, Apr. 19, 1915; s. Albert F. and Eleanor (Allina) F.; A.B., U. Ill., 1935; D.Phil. (Rhodes scholar), Oxford U., 1940; M.D., Johns Hopkins, 1942; m. Joy Hume, Dec. 29, 1942; children—Gail, Theodore, Donald, Beth. Intern, Johns Hopkins Hosp., Balt., 1942-43; fellow Med. Adminstrn. Service and Com. on Research in Med. Econs., 1943; med. officer UNRRA, Eastern Europe, 1946; med. dir. Migratory Labor Health Assn. USPHS, Atlanta, 1947; mem. staff Med. Group Practice Study div. Pub. Health Methods, Washington, 1948; area med. adminstr. UMWA Welfare and Retirement Fund, Pitts., 1948-67; project co-dir. Meharry Neighborhood Health Center, Nashville, 1967-69; lectr. Am. U. Sch. Pub. Affairs, 1948; lectr. U. Pitts. Sch. Social Work, 1949-67; lectr. med. care adminstrn. U. Mich. Sch. Pub. Health, 1965—; adj. asso. prof. med. and hosp. adminstrn. U. Pitts. Grad. Sch. Pub. Health, 1950—; prof., chmn. dept. family and community health Meharry Med. Coll., 1967—; health cons. food industry health and welfare plan Pub. Sch. Edn., St. Louis. Served with M.C., AUS, 1943-46. Diplomate Am. Bd. Preventive Medicine and Pub. Health. Home: 1476 Clairmont Pl Nashville TN 37215 Office: Meharry Med Coll Nashville TN 37208

FALKENSTEN, RICHARD GEORGE, dentist; b. L.I., N.Y., June 25, 1940; s. Richard Nelson and Lorraine D. (Duerr) F.; student U. Okla., 1958-59, U. Tulsa, 1959-62; D.D.S., U. Mo., Kansas City, 1966; children—Richard Christopher, Michele Marie. Staff doctor Tulsa City-County Health Dept., 1968; pvt. practice dentistry, Tulsa, 1968—; tchr., cons. Tulsa Dental Asst.'s Sch. Vocational Tng.; cons. Tulsa Jr. Coll.; mem. staff Hillcrest Hosp.; founder, mem. staff Charity Dental Clinic at Tulsa Boys Home. City dir., chmn. com. for Explorers, 1970—; sec., treas., dir., trustee Okla. Dental Service Corp.; mem. Okla. Com. Continuing Edn. in Dentistry. Bd. dirs. Okla. Delta Dental Plan, 1973, Tulsa Boys Home; mem. exec. bd. Indian Nations council Boy Scouts Am.; bd. dirs., chmn. Continuing Edn. Found. Served with AUS, 1966-68. Recipient Vol. of Year award Tulsa Boys Home, 1970. Mem. Am., Okla. (mem. peer rev. com., bd. govs. 1972—) dental assns., Tulsa County Dental Soc. (com. chmn. dental health and community service, 1970-71; mem. constn. and by-laws com. 1971-72; dir. edn. 1972-73), Tulsa Endodontic Study Club, Am. Soc. Analgesia, Acad. Gen. Dentistry, Am. Soc. Preventive Dentistry, Psi Omega. Club: Tulsa Optimist. Office: 4515 S Yale Av Tulsa OK 74135

FALL, FREDERICK, comdr.; b. Baden, Austria, July 25, 1899; s. Gustav H. and Fridericke (Moller) F.; B.A., State Acad. Music, Vienna, Austria 1918-23; hon. doctorate Southwestern Conservatory Music and Fine Arts, 1944. Came to U.S., 1937, naturalized 1943. Condr. opera cos., Bremen, Krefeld, Germany, 1924-29; comdr. in chief German Opera, Brno, Chechoslovakia, 1930-32, Volksoper, Vienna, 1932-37; concerts with European orchs., 1925-37, N.Y.C., Boston, Phila., New Orleans, Dallas, 1937—; comdr. Tyler (Tex.) Symphony, 1942-46; dir. Agy. Symphony, 1948-58, Washington Civic Symphony, 1959-65, Washington Civic Opera Assn., 1955—; music tchr., 1937—. Recipient Nat. Music Week award, 1964. Mem. Am. Fedn. Musicians. Composer music for piano, songs, string quartet. Home: 2308 20th St NW Washington DC 20009 Office: Washington Civic Opera Assn 3149 16th St NW Washington DC 20010

FALLS, ANONA JENKINS (MRS. GEORGE E. FALLS), librarian; b. Clarksdale, Miss.; d. James Talmadge and Effie (Turney) Jenkins; student Goucher Coll., Balt., 1922-25; summer study U. Ill., 1938; certificate library sci. Carnegie Library Sch., Carnegie Inst. Tech., 1940. With Carnegie Pub. Library, Clarksdale, Miss., 1936—, successively library asst. children's librarian, asst. librarian, 1936-48, head librarian, 1948—. Mem. sec., bd. commrs. Miss. Library Commn., 1955-58. Mem. A.L.A. (Miss. rep. council 1954-58, mem. recruiting network 1961—, notable books council adult services div. 1970—), Miss. (exec. bd. 1950-59, pres. 1952-53, chmn. adult edn. com. 1960-61), Children's (membership regional chmn. 1944-46, state membership chmn. 1942). Southeastern library assns., Bus. and Profl. Women's Club, D.A.R., Delta Kappa Gamma, Gamma Phi Beta. Home: 229 Maple St Clarksdale MS 38614 Office: Carnegie Pub Library Clarksdale MS 38614

FALLS, LEE WAYNE, statistician; b. Cleve., Mar. 17, 1929; s. George B. and Winifred (Jaycox) F.; student Fenn Coll., 1953; B.S., Kent State U., 1959; M.S., U. Ga., 1965; postgrad. U. Ala., 1966; m. Phyllis Brazo, Aug. 28, 1955 (div. Aug. 1968); children—Tad Lee, David Wayne, Randall Allan. Aerospace engr. George C. Marshall Space Flight Center, NASA, Huntsville, Ala., 1965—. Mem. Am. Statis. Assn. Home: 604 Stella Dr Madison AL 35758 Office: NASA Marshall Space Center R-Aero-YT Huntsville AL 35812

FAN, CHIEN, aerospace scientist; b. Kiang-su, China, Apr. 1, 1930; s. Chin Meng and Shih Ze (Shih); B.S., Nat. Taiwan U., 1954; M.S., U. Ill., 1958, Ph.D., 1964; m. Ning-Sun Chang, May 3, 1958; children—Albert, May, Marie. Came to U.S., 1956, naturalized, 1969. Asst. prof. Fla. State U., Tallahassee, 1961-65; research specialist Lockhead Missiles & Space Co., Huntsville, Ala., 1965—. Asso. prof. U. Ala., Huntsville, 1967-69; vis. scientist Republic China, 1970. Mem. N.Y. Acad. Scis., Sigma Xi, Pi Mu Epsilon. Office: PO Box 1103 Huntsville AL 35807

FANKHAUSER, GLENN HENRY, citrus mgmt. co. exec.; b. Burlington, Okla., Aug. 16, 1910; s. Henry Isaac and Lucy Louise (Schwab) F.; student Tex. A. and M. U., 1928-31; m. Dorothy Woods, Apr. 16, 1936. Hort. foreman Am. Land Co., Harlingen, Tex., 1931-34; agt. Franklin Life Ins. Co., Houston and Mission, Tex., 1935; mgr. Valley Growers Chems., Mission, 1936; constrn. foreman Dodds & Wedegartner, San Benito, Tex., 1936-40; supt. Am. Investment Corp., Mission, Tex., 1940-64; tchr. Farm Hand Gen. fed. program instrn. to farm labor, Edinburg, Tex., 1965; pres., owner Citrus Mgmt. Corp., Mission, 1965-73. Active land and citrus appraiser and broker. Alternate mem. Texas Valley Citrus Com., 1973. Chmn. Democratic Precinct, Hidalgo County, Tex., 1962-72. Bd. dirs. Hidalgo County Water Control and Improvement Dist. 6, 1972—. Mem. Edinburg Citrus Assn. (dir. 1966-72), Tex. Citrus Mut. (dir. 1971-72). Mason (Shriner). Address: Box 965 Mission TX 78572

FANNIN, TROY EDWARD, optometrist, educator; b. Sandy Hook, Ky., Jan. 19, 1925; s. Floyd Mitchell and Elizabeth (Hayes) F.; B.S., U.S. Mcht. Marine Acad., 1945; B.S., Dr. Optometry, Ohio State U., 1952; m. Cecile Mae Owen, Nov. 24, 1949; 1 dau., Heather Fay. Marine engr. Isthmian S.S. Co., 1945-46, Coastwise S.S. Co., 1946-47; instr. U. Houston Coll. Optometry, 1954-56, asst. prof., 1965-68, asso. prof., 1968-73, prof., 1973—; vis. asso. prof. U. Cal. at Berkeley, summer 1969; individual practice optometry, Houston, 1956-65. Served to lt. USNR. Diplomate Nat. Bd. Optometry. Mem. Am. Acad. Optometry (chmn. sect. meetings), Am., Tex., Harris County optometric assns., Am. Assn. U. Profs., Tex. Assn. Coll. Tchrs., Editorial Council Am. Acad. Optometry, Assn. Optometric Educators, Beta Sigma Kappa. Unitarian. Home: 13334 Bretagne Dr Houston TX 77015

FANNING, CHARLES BUCKNER, clergyman; b. Houston, Mar. 13, 1926; s. Charles A. and Beryl (Buckner) F.; B.A., Baylor U., 1949; B.D., So. Bapt. Theol. Sem., 1954; D.D., Howard Payne U., 1962; m. Martha Howell, June 5, 1949; children—Michael Buckner, Stephen Scott, Martha Lisa. Ordained to ministry Baptist Ch., 1948; pres. Buckner Fanning Evangelistic Found., Dallas, 1955-59; pastor Trinity Bapt. Ch., San Antonio, 1959—. Vice pres. Bapt. Gen. Conv. Tex., 1963; speaker before various groups in U.S., overseas 1947—; mem. fgn. mission bd. So. Bapt. Conv. Mem. exec. council Boy Scouts Am., 1961—; mem. Citizens Com. to Provide Treatment Center for Narcotic Addicts, San Antonio, 1965—; bd. dirs. Planned Parenthood; spl. pub. relations cons. Hemisfair '68; chmn. Billy Graham Hemisfair Crusade, 1968; mem. Gov.'s Council Lifetime Sports, Urban Coalition of San Antonio. Trustee Bapt. Meml. Hosp., San Antonio. Served with USMCR, 1943-46. Mem. C. of C. (human resources council). Contbr. articles to religious jours. Home: 2327 Blanton Dr San Antonio TX 78212 Office: 319 E Mulberry St San Antonio TX 78209

FANNING, JAMES COLLIER, educator; b. Atlanta, Nov. 8, 1931; s. James Choice and Lois Mae (Collier) F.; B.S., The Citadel, 1953; M.S., Ga. Inst. Tech., 1956, Ph.D., 1960; m. Sybil Rebecca Smith, Aug. 10, 1957; children—Elizabeth, Kathleen, Rebecca. Asst. prof. Clemson (S.C.) U., 1961-65, asso. prof., 1965-71, prof. chemistry, 1971—. Vis. lectr. U. Ill., 1966-67. Served with AUS, 1960. Postdoctoral fellow Tulane U., 1960-61. Mem. Am. Assn. U. Profs., Am. Chem. Soc. (chmn. Western Carolinas sect. 1971-72), S.C. Acad. Scis. (councilor 1972-75), Sigma Xi. Home: 203 Wren St Clemson SC 29631

FANNING, ROBERT ALLEN, lawyer; b. Dallas, Nov. 3, 1931; s. Charles Allen and Beryl Julia (Buckner) F.; B.B.A., Baylor U., 1953; J.D., So. Meth. U., 1960; m. Carolyn Parker Hedges, Aug. 6, 1960; children—Barry H., Marc H. Admitted to Tex. bar, 1959; since practiced in Dallas; mem. firm Fanning & Harper, Dallas, 1960—; dir. Translinear, Inc., Equity Capital Mgmt., Inc., Townbuilders, Inc. Mem. bd. visitors So. Meth. U. Sch. Law, 1971-72; mem. adv. council Southwestern Bapt. Theol. Sem., 1966-68; mem. devel. council Baylor U., 1965-73. Trustee Annuity Bd. So. Bapt. Conv.; bd. dirs. Nat. Bd. Fellowship Christian Athletes; trustee San Marcos Baptist. Acad. Served to 1st lt. USAF, 1954-56. Recipient Distinguished Service medal, San Marcos Acad., 1970. Mem. Am. Judicature Soc., Am., Tex. State, Dallas bar assns., S.W. Legal Found., Tex. Assn. Defense Counsel, Delta Theta Phi. Mason (32 deg., Shriner). Clubs: Dallas, City, Insurance (Dallas). Home: 3605 Crescent Dr Dallas TX 75205 Office: 4040 First Nat Bank Bldg Dallas TX 75202

FANSHIER, CHESTER, metal products mfg. exec.; b. Wilson County, Kan., Mar. 2, 1897; s. Thomas J. and Nora Belle (Maxwell) F.; m. Ina Muriel Goens, Apr. 12, 1918; 1 dau., Norma Elaine (Mrs. Robert B. Rice). Gen. mgr. Bart Products Co., 1932-39; pres. gen. mgr. Metal Goods Mfg. Co., 1939—. Commr. Tulsa Presbytery to 156th Gen. Assembly, Presbyn. Ch. U.S.A., 1944; pres. Sunday Eve. Fedn. (chs.), 1937-38. Recipient Wisdom award Honor, 1970. Registered profl. engr. Okla. Mem. Am. Soc. M.E., Am. Soc. Testing Materials, Bartlesville C. of C., Am. Def. Preparedness Assn. (life), Nat. Rifle Assn. Am. (life), Nat., Okla. (charter) socs. profl. engrs., Okla. Rifle Assn., Profl. Photographers Am. Presbyn. (elder). Clubs: Rotary (pres. 1956-57), Engineers of Bartlesville (charter mem.; past dir.). Home: 1328 Cherokee Av Bartlesville OK 74003 Office: 309 W Hensley Blvd Bartlesville OK 74003

FANT, ELENA BEDFORD (MRS. GEORGE FANT), bus. exec.; b. nr. Bridgeport, Tex., Aug. 15, 1908; d. John Wesley and Beatrice (Acord) Newsom; student Tex. Bus. Coll., 1925-26; m. George Fant, Apr. 26, 1941 (dec. Sept. 1962). Sec., First Nat. Bank, Weatherford, Tex., 1926-40, asst. cashier, 1941-45, v.p., dir. 1946-49; sec. and clk. Mut. Bldg. & Loan Assn., 1926-40, asst. sec., 1941-49, v.p., 1950-58, pres., 1959—, also dir. Hon. mem. 4-H Club, Parker County. Founder, George Fant Found., George Fant-Stephens Catholic Ch. Found. Trustee E. D. Farmer Relief Fund. Mem. Soc. Savs. and Loan Controllers, Soc. Real Estate Appraisers (asso.), A.I.M. (pres.'s council 1967-69). Baptist. Clubs: Jim Wright Congressional, Weatherford Kangaroo Booster, Live Oak Country. Home: 508 W Baylor St Weatherford TX 76086 Office: 133 College Av Weatherford TX 76086

FANT, FRANCIS RODGERS, JR., lawyer; b. Anderson, S.C., Oct. 28, 1940; s. Francis Rodgers and Josie Lind (Young) F.; B.A., Erskin Coll., 1964; J.D., U. S.C., 1964; m. Dolly Virginia Bosserman, Mar. 26, 1966; children—Maria Moffat, Clair Virginia, Jill Alea. Admitted to S.C. bar, 1964; practiced in Anderson, 1968-69; asso., Fant & Rogers, 1964-67; partner, Doyle, Fant, Vaughan & Palmer, Anderson, S.C., 1970—. Trustee Nevitt Woods Trust, Lebanon Estates Trust, 1968—; v.p., Nevitt Forest, Inc., 1968—. Bd. dirs., vice-chmn. A.R.C., Anderson chpt., 1972-73. Mem. Am. Soc. Phys. Research, Am., S.C., Anderson County bar assns., S.C. State Bar, Anderson C. of C., Phi Delta Phi. Democrat. Unitarian. Club: Tri-State Country (Oconee, S.C.). Home: Westwind Way Lake Hartwell Anderson SC 29621 Office: 122 W Whitner St Anderson SC 29621

FANT, JULIAN EARLE, JR., banker; b. Jacksonville, Fla., Mar. 11, 1939; s. Julian Earle and Nathalie Lorraine (Beville) F.; B.S., U. Fla., 1961; M.B.A., U. Pa., 1962; m. Dorothy Stephenson, Sept. 2, 1966; children—Julian Earle III and Jennifer Lynne (twins). Pres., First Guaranty Bank & Trust Co., Jacksonville, 1962—; vice chmn. Five Points Guaranty Bank; faculty U. Fla., Fla. Sch. Banking. Mem. city council, Jacksonville, 1971—. Bd. dirs. N.E. Fla. Heart Assn., Jacksonville Childrens Hosp. Mem. Fla. Bankers Assn. (dir.), Kappa Alpha. Democrat. Episcopalian. Home: 4415 Pirates Cove Rd Jacksonville FL 32210 Office: 1234 King St Jacksonville FL 32205

FANT, PATRICK CLEBURNE, lawyer; b. Belton, S.C., Jan. 8, 1905; s. Andrew Preston and Ella (Davis) F.; A.B., Furman U., 1927, LL.B. magna cum laude, 1929; m. Mary Elizabeth Carnes, June 30, 1931; children—Patrick Cleburne, Martha Susanne (Mrs. L. R. Hodges, Jr.). Admitted to S.C. bar, 1928; mem. firms Hayworth & Hayworth, 1929-46, Rainey, Fant & McKay, 1950—. Bd. dirs. Greenville. Mem. Greenville Bar Assn. (pres. 1962), Phi Kappa Phi. Club: Greenville Country (mem. bd. 1963) (S.C.). Home: 210 Camile Av Greenville SC 29605 Office: 118 Broadus Av Greenville SC 29003

FARALDO, GEORGE JACOB, airport exec.; b. Key West, Fla., July 22, 1919; s. Jacob Raymond and Amanda (Fletcher) F.; Ph.D., Sunshine U., 1962; postgrad. Auburn U., 1965-73; m. Norma Mary, June 4, 1941; children—Monica (Mrs. Robert Newby), George Alfred. Owner, mgr. Faraldo Flying Service, 1945-55; mgr. Key West Internat. Airport (Fla.), 1948—; owner, mgr. Faraldo Enterprises, 1955—. Bd. dirs. Boy Scouts Am., Center of Hope. Served with USNR, 1942-45. Mem. Am. Legion, D.A.V. (comdr. 1970), Southeastern Airport Mgrs. Assn. (pres. 1970), Fla. Airport Mgrs. (dir. 1962-65). Toastmaster (pres. 1963-66). Home: 1501 17th Terrace Key West FL 33040 Office: Key West Internat Airport Key West FL 33040

FARGARSON, ROBERT MELVYN, lawyer; b. Aransas Pass, Tex., Feb. 23, 1932; s. Melvin Lavone and Bobbie Inez (Lawrence) F.; student So. Meth. U., 1949-52; LL.B., Cumberland U., 1957; m. Jonetta Lovett, July 25, 1953; children—Kim, Dabney, Robert Melvyn, Michael, Angel. Law clk. U.S. Govt., 1957-58; admitted to Tenn. and Tex. bars, 1957; practiced in Memphis, Tenn., 1958—; mem. firm Neely, Green & Fargarson, 1958—; sec., Estes Disposal Co., 1960-63. Lectr. Memphis State Law Sch., 1965-66. Chmn. Memphis Bd. Tax Equalization, 1970-72; chmn. Memphis Civil Service Commn., 1972—. Mem. Tenn. Ho. of Reps., 1963-67. Served with USMCR, 1953-55. Clubs: Summit, Colonial Country, Tennessee (all Memphis). Home: 643 Anderson Pl Memphis TN 38104 Office: 60 N Main St Memphis TN 38103

FARIELLO, ARNOLD SALVATOR, dentist; b. Bklyn., Jan. 17, 1943; s. Arnold and Filippina (DeLuca) F.; student Wake Forest Coll., 1961-62, St. Francis Coll., 1962-64; D.D.S., Georgetown U., 1968; m. Martha Elizabeth Jacobs, July 6, 1968; 1 dau., Elizabeth Wendalyn. Pvt. practice dentistry, Fairfax, Va., 1970—, Arlington, Va., 1969—; pres. Diversified Dental Securities Investment Co., Washington, 1970—. Served to capt. AUS, 1968-70. Mem. Am., No. Va. dental assns., Delta Sigma Delta. Home: 5311 Richardson Dr Fairfax VA 22030 Office: 10720 Main St Fairfax VA 22030

FARIOLETTI, MARIUS, economist; b. Turin, Italy, Apr. 22, 1908; s. Joseph and Josephine (Pasquino) F.; brought to U.S., 1913, naturalized, 1926; B.B.A. cum laude, Chattanooga U., 1932; M.A. in Econs. (fellow), Oberlin Coll., 1933; postgrad. (univ. teaching fellow), Duke, 1933-35; m. Elizabeth Byrd Venable Mar. 28, 1935; children—Mary Jo (Mrs. David Portch), Elizabeth. Economist, A.A.A., 1935-39; economist, asst. dir. tax research U.S. Treas. Dept., 1939-48; tax advisor, asst. dir. plans and policy div. U.S. Internal. Revenue Service, Washington, 1948-65, dir. planning and analysis div., 1966-70, econ. cons. tax and tax adminstrn. systems, 1970—. Lectr., Cath. U., 1937-39, U. So. Cal., 1973; chmn. Equalization Bd., 1951-53, Fiscal Affairs Com., 1958-59 (both Arlington County, Va.). Recipient Superior Work Performance award Internal Revenue Service, 1960, Commr.'s award, 1966; Treasury's Albert Gallatin award, 1970; Treasury's Meritorious Service award, 1970. Mem. Nat. Tax Assn., Nat. Press Club. Home: 4822 3d St N Arlington VA 22203 Office: Nat Press Bldg Washington DC 20004

FARISH, STEPHEN THOMAS, JR., singer, educator; b. Columbia, Va., May 5, 1936; s. Stephen Thomas and Jessie (Jones) F.; B.S., E. Carolina Coll., 1958; MusM., U. Ill., 1959, D.Mus. Arts, 1962; pvt. study Bruce Foote, Paul Ulanovsky, George Reeves, Caro Carapetyn; m. Anna Withers Montgomery, May 31, 1958; children—Stephen David, Virginia Kaye. Singer, 1956—; appearances include tv, radio, recitals, concerts; appeared with Chgo. NBC Symphony, Tex. Boys Choir, W. Coast Symphony, Fort Worth Opera Assn.; faculty N.Tex. State U., Denton, 1962—, asso. prof. music, 1967-72, prof. music, 1972—; vis. asso. prof. Okla. U., summer 1963; contest adjudicator, clinician, Okla., Tex., Mo., La., Ill.; minister music First Meth. Ch., Urbana, Ill., 1961-62, St. Andrew Presbyn. Ch., Denton, 1964-72, Univ. Christian Ch., Ft. Worth, 1972—; mus. dir. Denton Community Chorus. Mem. Phi Mu Alpha Sinfonia, Phi Kappa Phi, Pi Kappa Lambda, Kappa Delta Pi. Mem. Disciples of Christ. Home: 1900 Emerson Dr Denton TX 76201

FARISS, JAMES LEE, JR., hosp. exec.; b. Austin, Tex., July 4, 1934; s. James Lee and Dolores Amelia (Hanson) F.; B.B.A., U. Tex., 1961; m. Mary Earl Adkins, Aug. 21, 1959; children—Joe Leslie, Jill Leigh. Auditor, Peat, Marwick, Mitchell & Co., Houston, 1961-62. Marvin, Henry & Co., Austin, Tex., 1962-63; asst. to controller Brown Schs., Inc., Austin, San Marcos, Tex., 1963-65, asst. controller, 1965-67, controller, 1967-72, controller-treas., 1972—, also dir. Partner Fariss & Fariss, Mellenbruch & Fariss. Active Little League Baseball Program. Precinct chmn. Republican party, Austin, Tex., 1966-69. Served with USN, 1954-58. C.P.A., Tex. Mem. Tex. Soc. C.P.A.'s. Home: 7304 Middlebury Cove Austin TX 78723 Office: 1110 E 32d St Austin TX 78722

FARKASFALVY, DENIS MIKLOS, headmaster; b. Szekesfehervar, Hungary, June 23, 1936; s. Stephen and Maria (Knazoviczky) F.; student Eotvos U., Budapest, 1954-56; D. Th., U. St. Anselm (Rome, Italy), 1962; M.S., Tex. Christian U., 1965. Came to U.S., 1962, naturalized, 1967. Joined Cistercian Order, 1956; ordained priest Roman Catholic Ch., 1961; tchr. theology and math. Cistercian Prep. Sch., Irving, Tex., 1965—, headmaster, 1969—. Home and office: Route 2 Box 1 Irving TX 75062

FARLEY, JACK EMORY, lawyer; b. Pikeville, Ky., Jan. 4, 1939; s. Lewis Clyde and Mary (Emory) F.; B.A., U. Ky., 1962; J.D., Am. U., 1967; m. Margaret Rose Saad, Jan. 26, 1963; children—Aletha Claire, Jennifer Lucille, Dana Rose. Admitted to D.C. bar, 1968, Ky. bar, 1969; analyst Def. Dept., Washington, 1962-67; trial atty. Justice Dept., Washington, 1967-68; exec. dir. Pike County C. Pikeville, Ky., 1968-72; practice law, Pikeville, 1970—. Counsel Pikeville-Pike County Airport Bd., 1969—, Pikeville Urban Renewal Agy., 1970—; chmn. Pike County Headstart Policy Com., 1970-71; v.p. Eastern Highlands Tourism Region, 1970-72. Bd. dirs., v.p. Big Sandy Area Devel. Council, 1970-72. Served with AUS, 1956-64. Named Ky. Col., 1962. Mem. Am. Fed., Ky., Pike County bar assns., Democrat. Methodist. Home: Smith Hill Pikeville KY 41501 Office: PO Box 90 Pikeville KY 41501

FARLOW, E(LBERT) ALLISON, motel exec., lawyer; b. Wilmington, N.C., June 12, 1929; s. Elbert Allison and Lillian Irene (Leath) F.; B.S., The Citadel, 1951; J.D., U. S.C., 1956; m. Patricia Leatherwood, June 12, 1961; children—Elizabeth Allison, Leath Anne, William Allison. Admitted to S.C. bar, 1956, since practiced in Myrtle Beach; owner Waterside Motel, Myrtle Beach, 1959—; pres. The Breakers, Myrtle Beach, 1970—; chmn. bd. Anchor Bank of Myrtle Beach, 1973—. Chmn. S.C. Travel Council, 1968; mem. Myrtle Beach City Council, 1968, 69, 72—, mayor pro-tem, 1973; exec. com. S.C. Municipal Assn., 1973—; vice chmn. Myrtle Beach Planning and Zoning Commn., 1970-71; vice chmn. Horry County Devel. Planning and Tourism Commn., 1967-73, chmn., 1973. Mem. adv. bd. Horry County Salvation Army. Served as lt. arty. AUS, 1951-53. Named Citizen of Yr., Myrtle Beach C. of C. Mem. Am. (chmn. S.C. Jr. Bar Conf. 1959), S.C. (circuit v.p. 1960), Horry County bar assns., S.C. (dir. 1965-66), Greater Myrtle Beach (pres. 1966) chambers commerce, S.C., Horry County (pres. 1970) hist. socs., Long Bay Power Squadron (comdr. 1964), S.A.R. (pres. S.C. 1960), Phi Delta Phi. Democrat. Presbyn. (Sunday sch. supt. 1966-68, chmn. bd. deacons 1969, elder 1970—). Mason, Rotarian (pres. 1971). Club: Dunes Golf and Beach (dir. 1967—, sec. 1967-73, pres. 1973) (Myrtle Beach, S.C.). Home: 4801 N Ocean Blvd Myrtle Beach SC 29577 Office: 2206 N Ocean Blvd Myrtle Beach SC 29577 Mailing address: PO Box 322 Myrtle Beach SC 29577

FARMAN, IRVIN SAMUEL, bank pub. relations exec.; b. L.I., N.Y., Aug. 23, 1921; s. Samuel and Goldie (Elkins) F.; B.J., U. Mo., 1943; m. Rosalyn Graves, June 7, 1947; 1 son, Richard Kent. Sports writer Dallas Morning News, 1946, A.P., 1946; reporter, columnist Fort Worth StarTelegram, 1946-53; with Witherspoon & Assos., Inc., Ft. Worth, 1953-73, exec. v.p., dir., 1960-73; v.p., dir. pub. relations Ft. Worth Nat. Bank, 1973—. Mem. faculty pub. relations course Tex. Christian U. Evening Coll., 1965—. Exec. sec. Greater Ft. Worth Planning Com., 1956-61; commr. Fort Worth Housing Authority, 1965—, vice chmn. 1967-72, chmn., 1972—; bd. dirs. Tarrant County Assn. Mental Health, Friends of Ft. Worth Library. Served to capt. USAAC, 1943-46. Mem. Pub. Relations Soc. Am. (chpt. v.p. 1964—), Ridotto, Newcomen Soc. N.Am., Sigma Delta Chi (chpt. pres. 1955—), Kappa Tau Alpha, Phi Eta Sigma. Republican. Methodist. Clubs: Kiwanis (pres. 1970-71), River Crest Country. Home: 409 Ridgewood Rd Fort Worth TX 76107 Office: PO Box 2050 Fort Worth TX 76101

FARMER, BERKWOOD MALCOLM, univ. adminstr.; b. Danville, Va., Aug. 3, 1938; s. Isham Malcolm and Aubria (Mylum) F.; B.S., N.C. State U., 1960, M.S. (Nat. Def. Edn. Act fellow), 1963, Ph.D., 1970; m. Mariah Anderson, July 14, 1958; children—Donna Louise, Katherine Lynn, Berkwood Malcolm. Instr. dept. econs. N.C. State U., 1963-64; commd. 2d lt. U.S. Army, 1964, advanced through grades to maj., 1968; asst. prof. dept. social scis. U.S. Mil. Acad., 1968-71; asst. prof. econs. U. Richmond, Va., 1971—, asso. dean U. Coll., 1972—. Decorated Bronze Star medal; recipient Wall St Jour. Student Achievement award N.C. State U., 1960. Mem. Am. Econs. Assn., Am. Agrl. Econs. Assn., Lambda Chi Alpha. Baptist. Club: Richmond Country. Contbr. articles to profl. jours. Home: 9402 Midvale Rd Richmond VA 23229 Office: 7 W Franklin St Richmond VA 23220

FARMER, ERIN (MRS. CHARLEY WALTON FARMER), club woman; b. Camden, Ala., Oct. 10, 1900; d. Charles Prescott and Jessie (Laird) Atkinson; A.B., Huntington Coll., 1922; m. Charley Walton Farmer, July 20, 1922; 1 dau., June (Mrs. Harold Everett Causey). Tchr., Samson (Ala.) Schs., 1921, St. Petersburg (Fla.) Schs., 1924-26. Pres. Vineville Garden Club, Macon, Ga., 1939, sec., 1968-70, dir., 1971-73; pres. Shirley Hills Garden Club, 1953, dir., 1951—; dir. Garden Club Ga., 1961—; leader Florence Bernd Jr. Garden Club, 1963-64; accredited judge Am. Camellia Soc., 1955-61; trustee Macon YWCA, 1959—, mem. residence com., 1957—, sec., 1959—. Bd. dirs. Boy's Club, Macon. Mem. D.A.R., Hist. Soc. Methodist (pres. Bible class 1938). Clubs: Macon Idle Hour Country (Macon and Montgomery, Ala.); College (Montgomery, Ala.). Home: 2691 Stanislaus Circle Macon GA 31204

FARMER, JAMES SEBRELL, lawyer; b. Virginia Beach, Va., July 17, 1933; s. Isaac Herbert and Anne Bell (Sebrell) F.; B.A., Lynchburg Coll., 1957; LL.D., Washington and Lee U., 1965; m. Frances Marion Love, June 17, 1961; children—James Sebrell, Robert Harris. Tchr., coach Va. Episcopal Sch., Lynchburg, 1956-62; admitted to Va. bar, 1965, since practiced in Lynchburg; mem. firm Hickson, Davies & Lyle, then Davies, Farmer & Smith, 1965-72; substitute judge Lynchburg Municipal Ct., 1969-71, Bedford County (Va.) Juvenile and Demoestic Relations Ct., 1971—, County Ct., 1971—, Campbell County (Va.) County Ct., 1973—. Instr. bus. law Phillips Bus. Coll., 1966-68; instr. police sci. Central Va. Community Coll., Lynchburg, 1972—. Mem. Lynchburg Democratic Com., 1972—. Bd. dirs. Art Wing, Lynchburg Fine Arts Center, 1966-68, Sheltered Work Shop, Lynchburg, 1972—. Served with USAF, 1950-52. Mem. Va., Lynchburg bar assns., Va. Trial Lawyers Assn., Phi Alpha Delta. Episcopalian. Home: 221 Kensington Av Lynchburg VA 24503 Office: 801 Court St Lynchburg VA 24504

FARMER, JOHN MILBURN, physician; b. Linn Creek, Mo., May 3, 1937; s. Lee Wendall and Abigail (Roach) F.; A.B., U. Mo., 1959, M.D., 1963; m. Carol Sue Dunn, Dec. 22, 1957; children—Rebecca Sue, Teressa Jon, John Milburn III. Intern, St. Louis County Hosp., 1963-64; gen. practice medicine, Magnolia, Ark., 1966—; mem. staff Magnolia City Hosp. Served to capt. USAF, 1964-66. Diplomate Am. Bd. Family Practice. Mem. Am. Acad. Family Physicians (charter), A.M.A., Ark., Columbia County med. socs. Home: 910 Peach St Magnolia AR 71753 Office: 104 E Columbia St Magnolia AR 71753

FARMER, LEON, JR., lawyer, wholesale exec.; b. Athens, Ga., May 23, 1937; s. H.L. and Eloise (Harmon) F.; B.B.A., U. Ga., 1964, J.D., 1967; m. Marilyn Therese Wade, Apr. 26, 1958; children—Terri Leigh, Lisa Rene, Joni Denise, Leon III. Admitted to Ga. bar, 1966, since practiced in Athens, 1966—; exec. v.p., gen. mgr. Premium Distbg. Co., Inc., Athens; mem. Ga. Ho. of Reps., 1967-71. Mem. Ga. Manpower Planning Council, 1971—. Ofcl. del., temp. floor chmn., reg. Ga. delegation Democratic Nat. Conv., 1968; mem. exec. com.

Dem. party Clarke County, 1969-71. Served with USMCR, 1957-59; comdt. Ga. Marine Corps, 1967-71. Mem. State Bar Ga., Am., Athens bar assns., Chi Phi, Phi Alpha Delta. Home: 1000 Old Creek Rd Athens GA 30601 Office: Farmer Bldg 1700 Commerce Rd Athens GA 30601

FARMER, LESTER FRANKLIN, banker; b. Tuckerman, Ark., Feb. 17, 1907; s. Joseph F. and Ann (Butler) F.; Okla. Bapt. U., 1926-27, U. Ark., 1928-29; m. Katchie Jones, Aug. 16, 1929; 1 son, Joseph F. With U.S. Dept. Agr., Newport, Ark., 1933-35; editor Newport Daily Ind., 1935-37; cashier 1st Nat. Bank, Tuckerman, 1937-45, pres., 1945—; dir. 1st Nat. Bank, Newport, Zenith Seed Co., Tuckerman, Citizens Power & Light Co., Tuckerman. Chmn., Jackson County Bd. Edn., 1940-50, Jackson County Welfare Bd., 1936-50; sec. Tuckerman Sch. Bd., 1946-56. Sec., Democratic Central Com., 1935-55. Baptist. Mason (32 deg.). Address: Tuckerman AR 72473

FARMER, RALPH NUCKOLLS, ins. exec.; b. Woodlawn, Va., Aug. 17, 1919; s. James F. and Irena (Worrell) F.; student W.Va. Bus. Coll., 1939, Indsl. Coll. Armed Forces, 1960; m. Ethel Scism, Jan. 17, 1942; children—James Ralph, Harriet Elaine. Pub. accountant, Charlotte, N.C., 1945-48; accountant Thermoid Co., 1949-50; asst. treas. Hardware Mut. Ins. Co. of Carolinas, 1951-55, treas., 1956-59, v.p., 1960-62, exec. v.p., 1963-64, pres., dir., 1965—; pres., dir. Acme Ins. Agy., HMC Corp., Pathway Ins. Agy. Mem. adv. com. Citizens Safety Assn. Served with USAAF, 1941-45. Mem. Charlotte C. of C. Baptist. Clubs: Charlotte Executives; Carmel Country. Home: 4532 Belknap Rd Charlotte NC 28211 Office: 1356 E Morehead St Charlotte NC 28233

FARMER, RICHARD GUERARD, psychiatrist; b. Memphis, Jan. 2, 1937; s. John Byron and Mellie (Guerard) F.; B.S., U. Tenn., 1957, M.D., 1960. Intern, Bethesda (Md.) Naval Hosp., 1960-61; resident U. Cal., U. Tenn., Oakland (Cal.) Naval hosps., 1964-68; practice medicine specializing in psychiatry, Memphis, 1968—; mem. staff Bapt. Meml., City Memphis, Meth., Drs., Brunswick hosps., Memphis. Cons. VA Hosp., Memphis, Suicide and Crisis Service of Memphis; asso. prof. dept. psychiatry U. Tenn., 1968—. Chmn. bd. Doctors Hosp., 1972—. Served to lt. comdr. USN, 1960-66. Home: 4382 Walnut Grove Memphis TN 38118 Office: 899 Madison St Memphis TN 38103

FARMER, THOMAS ALBERT, JR., educator; b. Smithfield, N.C., Jan. 28, 1932; s. Thomas Albert and Oma Martha (Adams) Farmer; student Davidson Coll., 1950-51; B.S., U. N.C., 1953, M.D., 1957; m. Nancy Josephine Nussear, Aug. 25, 1956; children—Thomas Albert III, David Crown, Steven Adams, Kelly Elizabeth. Asst. prof. medicine, asst. dean curriculum matters U. Ala. Med. Center, Birmingham, 1965-67, asso. dean, dir. student affairs and curriculum, 1967-68, asso. prof. medicine, 1967-69, exec. asso. dean, dir. undergrad. med. edn., 1968—, prof. medicine, 1969-72; dean Sch. Medicine, U. Tenn., Memphis, 1972—. Served to capt. AUS, 1961-63. Diplomate Am. Bd. Internal Medicine. Fellow. A.C.P.; mem. Am. Fedn. Clin. Research, Endocrine Soc. Contbr. articles to profl. pubs. Home: 6503 Kirby Woods Dr Memphis TN 38103

FARMER, THOMAS WOHLSEN, physician, educator; b. Lancaster, Pa., Sept. 18, 1914; s. Clarence R. and Laura (Wohlsen) F.; A.B., Harvard, 1935; M.A., Duke, 1937; M.D., Harvard, 1941; postgrad. U. Copenhagen, 1957-58, U. Cal. at San Diego, 1971-72; m. Phyllis McCormick, July 19, 1941; children—Pamela (Mrs. Fred Henderson), Thomas Wohlsen. Intern, Penn. Hosp., Philadelphia, 1941-42; resident, Boston City Hosp., 1942-43, Johns Hopkins Hosp., 1943-44, 46-47; mem. staff N.C. Meml. Hosp., Chapel Hill; instr. medicine Johns Hopkins Med. Sch., Balt., 1947-48; asst. prof. neurology Southwestern Med. Sch., U. Tex., Dallas, 1948-49, asso. prof., 1949-50, prof., 1950-52, prof. medicine, acting chmn., 1951-52; prof. neurol. medicine, head div. neurology U. N.C. Sch. Medicine, Chapel Hill, 1952—. Served with USNR, 1944-46. Mem. Am. Acad. Neurology (sec. nat. 1955-57), Am. Neurol. Assn. (councillor 1962-64), Am. Bd. Psychiatry and Neurology (dir. 1969—), Am. Acad. Neurology, A.C.P., A.M.A., Assn. Research Nervous and Mental Diseases, Am. Epilepsy Soc., Am. Neurol. Assn., Assn. U. Profs. Neurology, Child Neurology Soc. Author: Pediatric Neurology, 1964; Neurologia Pediatrica, 1972. Home: 1304 Mason Farm Rd Chapel Hill NC 27514

FARNHAM, JERRY JOE, city ofcl.; b. Oklahoma City, June 28, 1933; s. John B. and Eva A. (Barns) F.; student East Central State Coll., 1968, U. Okla., 1971—; m. Mamie F. Arney, Oct. 31, 1952; children—Mark Allen, Peggy Jo. Traffic mgr. Evergreen Mills, Inc., Ada, Okla., 1952-63; shipping supr. Ideal Cement Co., Ada., 1963-67; dir. finance City of Ada, 1967—. Mem. State Bd. for Certification of Municipal Clks., Treasurers and Finance Officers. HUD fellow for grad. work in pub. adminstrn., 1971-75. Mem. Municipal Clks., Treasurers and Finance Officers (state pres.). Kiwanian. Home: 2204 Foster Dr Ada OK 74820 Office: 13th and Townsend Sts Ada OK 74820

FARNUM, LEON VERNON, JR., dentist; b. Birmingham, Ala., Dec. 14, 1916; s. Leon Vernon and Rose Lambert (Tyus) F.; B.S., Birmingham So. Coll., 1938; D.D.S., Northwestern U., 1944; m. Martha Reeves McGahee, Dec. 27, 1943; children—Nancy (Mrs. David Alan Calkins), Leon Vernon III. With Tenn. Coal, Iron & R.R. Co., 1939-41; pvt. practice dentistry, Birmingham, 1946—; asst. prof. U. Ala. Dental Sch., 1948-58. Dir. Pacific Am. Corp., Life Ins. Co. Am., Investors Corp. Am., Internat. Resorts, Inc. Asst. commr. Southside Little League Baseball, 1968-69; mem. Colonel's Club, Woodlawn High Sch., 1968—. Bd. dirs. Crestwood Youth Athletic Assn., 1963-69, Community Service Council. Served to lt. Dental Corps, USNR, 1944-46. Mem. Acad. Gen. Dentistry, Am., Ala. (trustee) dental assns., Birmingham Dist. Dental Soc. (pres.), Birmingham Dental Study Group (pres. 1967-68), Xi Psi Phi. Methodist (steward, trustee ch.). Club: The Club (Birmingham). Home: 5721 10th Av S Birmingham AL 35222 Office: 2114 10th Av S Birmingham AL 35205

FARR, MONTY HAROLD, accountant; b. San Angelo, Tex., July 12, 1915; s. John and Ethel Jane (Phillips) F.; grad. Felmmings Bus. Coll., 1938, LaSalle U., 1941; m. Orie Howard, Mar. 9, 1941; 1 son, Monty Harold. Bookkeeper, Kansas City Power & Light, Borger, Tex., 1938-41; sr. auditor H.V. Robertson & Co., Amarillo, Tex., 1941-46; self-employed as C.P.A., Amarillo, Tex., 1947—; owner cattle ranch, N.M., 1951—. C.P.A., Tex. Mem. Am. Inst. Accountants, Tex. Soc. C.P.A.'s. Home: 1301 Beverly St Amarillo TX 79106 Office: 1503 W 10th St Amarillo TX 79105

FARRAR, MILLARD BAKER, fgn. trade cons.; b. Elwood, Ind., Sept. 19, 1906; s. Charles Millard and Grace (Baker) F.; B.S., Clemson U., 1928; m. Thelma Plankinton, Apr. 21, 1933; export mgr. Nat. Carbon div. Union Carbide Corp., 1943-48; mgr. indsl. products div. Union Carbide Europa, Geneva, Switzerland, 1948-51; mng. dir. Kemet Products Ltd., Eng., 1951-56; mgr. sales Kemet Co. Union Carbide Corp., 1956-65; asst. gen. mgr. electronics div. Union Carbide Corp., 1965-67; dir. planning and corporate relations Clemson (S.C.) U., 1968-71; fgn. trade cons., Clemson, 1967—. Mem. Knights Templar Ednl. Found., 1938-73, Harmon Found., 1968-73. Bd. dirs., mem. exec. com. Pickens County United Fund. Mem. Assn. Iron and Steel Engrs. (life), Am. Soc. Testing and Materials, I.E.E.E., Inst. Dirs. (Eng.), Sigma Nu. Rotarian. Clubs: Pickens (S.C.) County Country; Poinsett (Greenville, S.C.); Fort Hill Clemson (pres. 1971-73). Patentee in field. Home: 113 Knight Circle Clemson SC 29631

FARRELL, JAMES DAVID, editor; b. Manhattan, Kan., July 19, 1927; s. Francis David and Mildred Leona (Jensen) F.; Ph.B., U. Chgo., 1948; B.S., Kan. State U., 1951; M.A., U. Chgo., 1955. Fgn. service officer Dept. State, 1955-65; mng. editor Africa Report mag., 1965-69; exec. editor, information editor Brookings Instsn., Washington, 1969—. Office: Brookings Instn 1775 Massachusetts Av NW Washington DC 20036

FARRELL, JOSEPH MICHAEL, shipping co. exec.; b. Yonkers, N.Y., June 7, 1922; s. Joseph Michael and Mary Elizabeth (Powers) F.; B.S. in Econs., U.S. Mcht. Marine Acad., 1943; postgrad. Columbia, 1948-50, Fordham U., 1947-48; m. Cloatta Grace Pennington, Dec. 6, 1945; children—Cloatta M., Anthony J., Christopher J., Janice E. Commd. ensign U.S. Navy, 1944, advanced through grades to capt., 1960; ret. 1960; mgr. Great Lakes Service, States Marine Lines, 1960-62; European mgr., Bremerhaven, Germany, 1962-65; sr. v.p. Waterman S.S. Corp., Washington, 1965—; v.p. Hammond Leasing Corp., Mobile, Ala., 1967—, Waterman S.S. Co. of Del. Mem. Propeller Club U.S. (v.p., bd. govs. 1967-68), Nat. Def. Transp. Assn., Navy League. Clubs: Congressional Country, University, George Town, Army-Navy (Washington). Home: 7010 Armat Dr Bethesda MD 20034 Office: 910 17th St NW Washington DC 20006

FARRELL, KENNETH ROYDEN, govt. ofcl.; b. Ottawa, Ont., Can., Jan. 17, 1927; (came to U.S. 1950, naturalized 1958); s. William R. and Velma V. (Wood) F.; B.S., U. Toronto, 1950; M.S., Ia. State U., 1955, Ph.D., 1958; m. Mary Christine Souter, Sept. 7, 1951; children—Janet, Betty, Deborah, Robert, Patricia, Lisa. Economist, U. Cal. at Berkeley, 1957-69, asso. dir. Gianniai Found., 1969-71; dep. adminstr. Econ. Research Service, U.S. Dept. Agr., Washington, 1971—. Econ. cons. U.S. firms. Mem. Am. Agrl. Econs. Assn., Am. Econs. Assn., A.A.A.S., Gamma Sigma Delta, Phi Kappa Phi. Home: 11312 Handlebar Rd Reston VA 22091 Office: 500 12th St SW Washington DC 20250

FARRELL, PAUL EDWARD, naval dental officer; b. Upper Darby, Pa., Nov. 15, 1926; s. James Patrick and Marie Edythe (Kerk) F.; D.D.S., U. Pa., 1951; postgrad. Naval Dental Sch., Bethesda, Md., 1956-57; m. Romayne A. Farrell, Aug. 23, 1952; children—Anne Marie, Paul Edward. Commd. lt. (j.g.) Dental Corps, U.S. Navy, 1951, advanced through grades to capt., 1968; head naval res. br., dental div. Bur. Medicine and Surgery, 1970-73; dep. dir., comdg. officer Naval Regional Dental Center, Norfolk, Va., 1973—; mem. staff Naval Dental Sch., 1964-67. Decorated Navy Commendation medal with combat V. Fellow Am. Coll. Dentists; mem. Am. Dental Assn., Am. Acad. Gold Foil Operators, Acad. Operative Dentistry, Omicron Kappa Upsilon, Delta Sigma Delta. Republican. Home: 820 Sheraton Dr Virginia Beach VA 23452 Office: Naval Regional Dental Center Norfolk VA 23511

FARRINGER, JOHN LEE, JR., surgeon; b. Bowling Green, Ky., Sept. 4, 1920; s. John Lee and Zora (Lawson) F.; B.A., Vanderbilt U., 1942; M.D., U. Tenn., 1945, M.S., 1950; m. Mary Margaret Smith, Mar. 8, 1947; children—John Lee, III, Janice Ann, Mary Jill. Intern, Harris Meml. Meth. Hosp., Ft. Worth, 1946; resident John Gaston and U. Tenn. Hosp., Memphis, 1949-54; practice surgery, Nashville, 1954—; asst. clin. prof. surgery Vanderbilt U. Sch. Medicine, 1956—; chief surgery Baptist Hosp., Nashville, 1966-69, vice chief staff, 1973—. Coordinator, Battle Nashville Centennial Commemoration, 1964—; chmn. Met. Hist. Commn., Nashville, 1966-73; exec. bd. Middle Tenn. council Boy Scouts Am., 1961—; pres. Davidson County Found. for Med. Care, 1973—. Bd. dirs. Davidson County unit Am. Cancer Soc., Davidson County Council Retarded Children, Police Assistance League, Profl. Systems Nashville, Tenn. Historic Site Fedn.; trustee Parkview Hosp., 1970-73. Served with AUS, 1943-45. Diplomate Am. Bd. Surgery. Fellow A.C.S., Southeastern Surg. Congress, So. Surg. Assn., Am. Geriatric Soc.; mem. Nashville Acad. Medicine (dir. 1970-73), Davidson County Med. Soc. (dir. 1970-73), So. Med. Assn., Nashville Surg. Soc. (pres. 1973), Co. Mil. Historians, Nashville Area C. of C., Alpha Kappa Kappa. Clubs: Richland Country, Nashville City, University (Nashville). Contbr. articles to surg. jours. Home: 2325 Golf Club Lane Nashville TN 37215 Office: 1907 Hayes St Nashville TN 37203

FARRINGTON, JOHN ABBINGTON, JR., elec. engr.; b. Coleanor, Ala., Nov. 9, 1935; s. John A. and Willie Ethel (Simpson) F.; B.S. in E.E., Auburn U., 1957; m. Carolyn Jo Martin, Apr. 1, 1955; children—Mike, Mark, Chris, Jenifer. Lab. engr. Anderson Electric Corp., 1957-59, asso. engr., 1959-60, product engr., 1960-64, mgr., 1964—. Mem. I.E.E.E. Home: 816 Zellmark Dr Birmingham AL 35235 Office: Box 455 Leeds AL 35094

FARRIS, DONN MICHAEL, librarian; b. Welch, W.Va., Nov. 4, 1921; s. Robert Coleman and Aileen (Hutson) F.; A.B., Berea Coll., 1943; M.Div., Garrett Theol. Sem., 1947; postgrad. Northwestern U., Yale; M.S., Columbia 1950; m. Joyce Gwendolyn Lockhart, Nov. 20, 1956; children—Evan Michael, Amy Virginia. Gen. asst. Yale Div. Sch. Library, 1948-49; cataloging asst. Gen. Theol. Sem. Library, N.Y.C., 1949-50; librarian Duke Div. Sch., 1950—, asst. prof. theol. bibliography, 1959-64, asso. prof., 1964-71, prof., 1971—. Mem. Am. Soc. Ch. History, Am. Theol. (v.p. 1961-62, pres. 1962-63, editor Newsletter 1953—), N.C., Southeastern library assns. Democrat. Presbyn. Contbr. articles to profl. jours. Home: 921 Buchanan Blvd Durham NC 27701

FARRIS, FRANK MITCHELL, JR., lawyer; b. Nashville, Sept. 29, 1915; s. Frank Mitchell and Mary Frances (Lellyett) F.; B.A., Vanderbilt U., 1937; student N.Y. Law Sch., 1939; m. Genevieve Baird, June 7, 1941; 1 dau., Genevieve Baird. Admitted to Tenn. bar, U.S. Supreme Ct. bar; mem. firm Clayton & Farris, 1939-40, 40-41; conciliation commr., def. counsel 12th Naval Dist., Treasure Island, Cal., 1944; partner firm Farris, Evans & Evans, Nashville, 1946-71, Farris, Warfield & Samuels, 1972—. Dir., gen. counsel Cherokee Ins. Co., Nashville, 1947—; mem. finance com., dir., counsel 3d Nat. Bank, Nashville; dir. Cherokee Equity Corp. Chmn. commrs. Watkins Inst., Nashville. Trustee, gen. counsel, exec. com. George Peabody Coll.; chmn. bd. dirs. Oak Hill Sch.; asso. Grad. Sch. Vanderbilt U. Served to lt. USNR, World War II. Mem. Bar Assn. Tenn., Beta Theta Pi, Phi Delta Phi. Presbyn. Clubs: Cumberland, Belle Meade Country, City (Nashville). Home: 940 Overton Lea Rd Nashville TN 37220 Office: 3d Nat Bank Bldg Nashville TN 37219

FARRIS, JULIA CAROLYN WAITS (MRS. GEORGE E. FARRIS), sch. adminstr.; b. Greenville, Miss., Jan. 1, 1935; d. Hilton and Mildred (Barnard) Waits; B.A., U. Miss., 1956, M.Ed., 1960, student Sch. Law, 1963-64; m. George E. Farris, Dec. 30, 1972. Field sec. Phi Mu, Memphis, 1957; panhellenic adviser, asst. dean women U. Miss., Oxford, 1957-66, community program planning specialist, U. Extension, Oxford, 1966-67; asst. dean women, La. State U., Baton Rouge, 1967—. Tchr. U. Miss., 1961-63. Vice pres. League Women Voters, Oxford, Miss., 1967. Bd. dirs. A.R.C., Lafayette County. Mem. Am. Assn. U. Women (Miss. treas. 1965), Nat. Assn. Women Deans and Counselors, Mortar Bd. (sect. dir.), Phi Mu. Home: 1100 S Foster Dr Baton Rouge LA 70806

FARST, DON DAVID, veterinarian; b. Wadsworth, O., Feb. 25, 1941; s. Walter K. and Ada K. (Stetler) F.; D.V.M., Ohio State U., 1965; m. Mollye Ann Beale, Dec. 16, 1961; children—Julie, Jenny. Gen. practice vet. medicine, Franklin, Pa., 1965-69; resident veterinarian Columbus (O.) Zoo, 1969-70; faculty Ohio State Coll. Vet. Medicine, 1969-70; asso. dir. Gladys Porter Zoo, Brownsville, Tex., 1970-74, dir., 1974—. Mem. Am. Vet. Med. Assn., Am. Assn. Zoo Veterinarians, Am. Assn. Zoos, Parks and Aquariums. Elk. Editor Jour. of Zoo Animal Medicine. Home: 24 Cowan Terrace Brownsville TX 78520 Office: 500 Ringgold St Brownsville TX 78520

FARST, KENNETH EDSON, land devel. co. exec.; b. Barberton, O., Oct. 19, 1935; s. Walter Kenneth and Ada Kathryn (Stetler) F.; B. Indsl. Engring., Ohio State U., 1958; m. Phyllis Ann Burger, June 10, 1956; children—Douglas Edson, Deborah Kay. Engr., North Electric Co., Galion, O., 1958-67; chief engr. Northwestern Co., Atlanta, 1967-69; v.p., Gt. Am. Corp., Johnson City, Tenn., 1969—. Pres., Galion (O.) Safety Council, 1962-63; cub pack chmn. Johnny Appleseed council Boy Scouts Am., 1965-67. Bd. dirs. Sci. Hill High Sch. Sports Club. Reigstered profl. engr., Ga., Tenn., Ala., S.C., Ky., W.Va., Ohio, Ind., Mich., N.M., Colo., Wyo., Mont. Mem. Am. Inst. Indsl. Engrs., Nat. Rifle Assn., Ohio State U. Assn., Internat. Underwater Explorers Soc., Tenn. Sheriff's Assn., Alpha Pi Mu, Phi Delta Gamma, Texnikoi. Home: 326 Baron Dr Johnson City TN 37601 Office: PO Box 3595 Johnson City TN 37601

FARVER, ALVIN D., dentist; b. Topeka, Ind., Oct. 25, 1893; s. Moses A. and Mary Elizabeth (Hostetler) F.; D.D.S., Ind. U., 1914; m. Marie Ellen Troyer, June 20, 1918; children—Frances Charlene (Mrs. Jack E. Farley), Gloria Jean (Mrs. Richard L. Payton), Patricia Ann (Mrs. Jerry R. Lusk). Practice gen. dentistry, Middlebury, Ind., 1914-27, restorative dentistry, Miami Beach, Fla., 1940—; presented clinics to numerous dental groups, 1945—; instr. gold inlays, crown and bridge group Dade County Dental Research Clinic, 1948—; cons. in restorative dentistry Miami VA, 1954-58. Served to 1st lt. Dental Corps, U.S. Army, 1917-19; AEF. Fellow Am., Internat. colls. dentists; mem. Am. Dental Assn. (1st v.p. 1962-63), Ind., Fla. (pres. 1959-60), East Coast Dist. (pres. 1942-43), Miami (pres. 1940—), Miami Beach, Chgo. dental socs., Dade County Dental Research Clinic (pres. 1952-53), Am. Acad. Restorative Dentistry, Am. Legion, 40 and 8, Xi Psi Phi. Conglist. Mason (Shriner, K.T.). Home: 4291 Nautilus Dr Miami Beach FL 33140 Office: 333 Arthur Godfrey Rd Miami Beach FL 33140

FARVER, FRANCIS FRANKLIN, dentist; b. Middlebury, Ind., Jan. 29, 1899; s. Moses A. and Mary Elizabeth (Hostetler) F.; D.D.S., Ind. U., 1922; m. Mary Celia Wheeler, June 25, 1924. Practice dentistry, South Bend, Ind., 1922-25; practice specializing in restorative dentistry, Miami Beach, Fla., 1925—; asso. mem. Dade County Research Dental Clinic, 1948—. Pres. St. Joseph Dental Soc., 1922-25; mem. Fla. Bd. Exam. to Practice Dentistry and Dental Hygiene, 1956—, chmn., 1960-64, 68-71. Served with U.S. Army, World War I; to comdr. USNR, 1942-45. Fellow Internat. Coll. Dentistry, Am. Coll. Dentistry, S.E. Acad. Prosthodontics; life mem. Am. Dental Assn.; mem. Fedn. Dentaire Internat., E. Coast, Miami, Miami Beach, Chgo. dental socs., Pierre Fauchard Acad., So. Conf. Dental Deans, Am. Legion, Xi Psi Phi. Mason (Shriner). Clubs: La Gorce, Surf (Miami Beach). Home: 5431 Alton Rd Miami Beach FL 33140 Office: 605 Lincoln Rd Miami Beach FL 33139

FASCELL, DANTE B(RUNO), congressman; b. Bridgehampton, L.I., N.Y., Mar. 9, 1917; s. Charles A. and Mary (Gullotti) F.; J.D., U. Miami, 1938; m. Jeanne-Marie Pelot, Sept. 19, 1941; children—Sandra J., Toni F., Dante J. Admitted to Fla. bar, 1938, practiced in Miami, 1938-41, 46—; mem. Turner, Hendrick, Fascell, Guilford, Goldstein & McDonald, and predecessor firms, 1950-71. Legal attache state legislative delegation Dade County, 1947-50; mem. Fla. Ho. of Reps., 1950-54; mem. 84th-92d congresses from 12th dist. Fla. Served as officer U.S. Army, 1942-46. Named one of ten outstanding legislators Fla. Legislature, 1951, 53; one of five outstanding men in Fla., Fla. Jr. C. of C., 1951. Mem. Miami Jr. C. of C. (pres. 1947-48), Am., Dade County, Coral Gables bar assns., Fla. Bar, Am. Legion, Mil. Order World Wars, Kappa Sigma. Democrat. Clubs: Lions, Italian-American (pres. 1947-48), Dade County Young Democratic (pres. 1947-48) (Miami, Fla.). Home: 6300 SW 99th Terrace Miami FL 33156 Office: House Office Bldg Washington DC 20515

FASKEN, DAVID R(OBERT), oil producer; b. Toronto, Ont., Can., Apr. 22, 1915; s. Robert Winstanley and Mae (Farland) F.; student San Rafael Mil. Acad. Jr. Coll., 1932-34, U. San Francisco, 1935. Livestock breeder, Tex., Cal., 1939—; pres. Midland Farms Co., Tex., 1943-44, Palafox Exploration Co., Midland and Laredo, Tex.; ind. oil producer, 1953—. Republican. Episcopalian. Club: Olympic (San Francisco). Home: Circle Dr Ross CA 94957 Office: First Nat Bank Bldg Midland TX 79701

FASOLD, RALPH WILLIAM AUGUST, educator; b. Passaic, N.J., Apr. 8, 1940; s. Ewald Conrad Dietrich and Ruth Evans (Morgan) F.; A.B., Wheaton Coll., 1962; A.M., U. Chgo., 1965, Ph.D., 1968; m. Gae Glenndelle Garman, Aug. 22, 1964; children—Judd Glenn Ayvalt, Ward Bradley Ralph. Research asso. Center Applied Linguistics, Washington, 1967-69, sr. linguist, 1969-70; asst. prof. linguistics Georgetown U., Washington, 1970—. Mem. citizen curriculum adv. com. Alexandria (Va.) Pub. Schs., 1973-74. Nat. Def. Edn. Act fellow, 1962-65, 65-66. Mem. Linguistic Soc. Am., Nat. Council Tchrs. English, S.E. Conf. on Linguistics. Author: Tense Marking in Black English, 1972; (with Walt Wolfram) The Study of Social Dialects in American English, 1974. Editor: (with Roger Shuy) Teaching Standard English in the Inner City, 1970; Language Attitudes: Current Trends and Prospects, 1973. Home: 26 W Spring St Alexandria VA 22301 Office: Georgetown U Washington DC 20007

FASTI, ALBERT JAMES, dentist; b. Wilmington, Del., Jan. 31, 1943; s. Albert James and Evelyn Virginia (Buchanan) Fasti; student U. Del., 1961-63; D.M.D., U. Pa., 1967; m. Irene Doris Greenway, Aug. 8, 1964; children—Christopher Alan, Michelle Lynn. Pvt. practice dentistry, Houston, 1969—. Asst. prof. community dentistry U. Tex. Dental Br., 1969-72; lectr. Tex. Women's U.; bd. dirs. Dental Asst. Tng. Program, 1971-72. Served with Dental Corps, USAF, 1967-69. Mem. Am. Soc. Preventive Dentistry (v.p. 1969-71), Am. Soc. Dentistry for Children, Rocky Mountain Analgesia Soc., Am. Dental Assn., Houston Dist. Dental Assn. (bd. censors), Houston Acad. Gen. Dentistry (dir.). Republican. Roman Catholic. Home: 12442 Briar Forest Dr Houston TX 77042 Office: 14465 Memorial Dr Houston TX 77024

FAUBION, JERRY TOLBERT, fiber and chem. co. exec.; b. Pidcoke, Tex., June 9, 1917; s. Roy Arthur and Lilly (Pendleton) F.; B.S. in Engring. Adminstrn., Tex. A. and M. U., 1940; m. Rena Louise

Derouen, July 20, 1940; 1 son, Roy Michael. Mech. and chem. engr. Dow Chem. Co., Freeport, Tex., 1942-43, supt. prodn. control, 1943-55, mgr. prodn. coordination, 1955-57, mgr. planning and distbn., 1957-63, mgr. organic chems., Midland, Mich., 1963-64, mgr. packaging dept., 1964-65; pres. Dow Badische Co., Williamsburg, Va., 1966—, also dir.; dir. United Va. Bank of Williamsburg, Lurex N.V., Lurex Co., Ltd., Castlecreek Fabrics, Inc., Bentex Mills, Inc., Universal Textured Yarns, Inc.; dir., mem. exec. com., finance com. United Va. Bankshares, Inc., Richmond. Mem. city council City of Freeport (Tex.), 1950-51; mem. Brazosport (Tex.) Ind. Sch. Bd., 1952-57, pres., 1955-57. Trustee Community Hosp., Freeport, Tex., 1960-61; bd. dirs. Williamsburg (Va.) Community Hosp., Carpet and Rug Inst. Registered profl. engr., Tex. Presbyn. (elder). Home: Box BT Williamsburg VA 23185 Office: Dow Badische Co Williamsburg VA 23185

FAUBION, R(OSCOE) MORRIS, automobile dealer, sci. cons.; b. Austin, Tex., Feb. 13, 1937; s. Roscoe H. and Myrtle (Jennings) F.; B.S., Southwestern U., 1959 ; m. Janice Lea Whiteley, Feb 6, 1959; children—Robert Morris, Julia Lea. Research scientist Mil. Physics Research Lab., Austin, 1959-61; asst. chief research and devel. Electro-Mechanics Co., Austin, 1961-64; engr., sci. TRACOR, Inc., Austin, 1964-70; owner, operator cattle ranch, Travis County, Tex., 1961-70; owner Faubion Chevrolet, Mason, Tex., 1970—, J. & R. Co., Mason, 1970—, Faubion Ins. Agy., Mason, 1970—; sci. cons., Mason, 1970—. Treas. Round Mountain Community Club, 1962-67; pres. Lake Travis Assn., 1966-69, Mason County unit Am. Cancer Soc., 1972—; area chmn. Cattlemen's Round Up for Crippled Children, 1972—; commr. Mason Housing Authority, 1973—. Bd. dirs. Highland Lakes Tourist Assn., 1973—. Mem. Assn. of Old Crows, Am. Phys. Soc., Nat., Tex. automobile dealers assns., Tex. and Southwestern Cattle Raisers Assn., Mason C. of C. (dir. 1972—, pres. 1973—); Mason County Hist. Soc. (dir. 1970—), Blue Key, Kappa Alpha. Mem. Ch. of Christ. Mason. Contbr. articles to profl. publs. Home: 208 Rainey Mason TX 76856 Office: 403 San Antonio Rd Mason TX 76856

FAUCETT, HENRY LEWIS, chem. engr.; b. Marietta, Ga., Sept. 27, 1938; s. Omra Lewis and Martha Elizabeth (Hopkins) F.; B.Chem. Engring., Ga. Inst. Tech., 1960; m. Janet Lee Zachary, Sept. 9, 1961. Chem. engr., TVA, Nat. Fertilizer Devel. Center, Muscle Shoals, Ala., 1960—. Instr. engring. and math. Florence (Ala.) State U., 1969—. Bd. dirs. Florence (Ala.) Community Theater. Registered profl. engr., Ala. Mem. Am. Inst. Chem. Engrs. (pres. N. Ala. chpt. 1970), TVA Assn. Profl. Chemists and Chem. Engrs. (pres. 1969). Methodist (steward 1965—). Lion. Home: 1929 Conway Dr Florence AL 35630 Office: TVA Muscle Shoals AL 35660

FAUL, ROBERTA HELLER, mag. editor; b. York, Pa., Dec. 11, 1946; d. Robert Joseph and Olive (Lease) Heller; student Wilson Coll., 1965-67; B.A. with distinction, George Washington U., 1969; m. Jan Walkley Faul, June 27, 1970. Research librarian Gen. Motors Corp., 1969; pub. relations asst. Psychiat. Insts. Am., 1970; asst. editor Museum News of Am. Assn. Museums, Washington, 1970-71, editor, 1971—; v.p. The Lab, Inc. Mem. Museum Edn. Roundtable (dir.). Home: 3409 Ordway St NW Washington DC 20016 Office: 2233 Wisconsin Av NW Washington DC 20007

FAULCONER, HUBERT LLOYD, banker; b. Lynchburg, Va., Aug. 7, 1926; s. Henry Edward and Edna (Bailey) F.; student Sch. Consumer Banking, U. Va., 1954-57; m. Elva Moore, Dec. 20, 1947; children—Sharon Scott, Hubert Lloyd. Shipping clk. Dunlop Tire & Rubber Co., Richmond, Va., 1946; with Fidelity Nat. Bank, Lynchburg, Va., 1946—, asst. cashier, asst. v.p., installment loan officer, 1953-65, v.p. sales finance, 1965-70, v.p. loan adminstrn., 1970-71, v.p. charge liquidations and recovery dept., 1971—. Instr. Am. Inst. Banking; thesis advisor Sch. Consumer Banking, U. Va. Served with USNR, 1943-52. Clubs: Sandusky (treas. 1952-70), Piedmont (Lynchburg); Colonial Hills (Forest, Va.). Home: 720 Chinook Pl Lynchburg VA 24502 Office: 828 Main St Lynchburg VA 24505

FAULCONER, ROBERT JAMIESON, pathologist; b. Sedlescombe, Sussex, Eng., July 11, 1923; s. Robert Hoffman and Gladys Alice (Jamieson) F.; came to U.S., 1925, naturalized, 1932; B.S., Coll. William and Mary, 1943; M.D., Johns Hopkins, 1947; m. Virginia Myrl Davis, Aug. 11, 1945; children—Anne, Elizabeth, Mary Waite, John. Intern. Johns Hopkins, 1948-48, fellow, 1948-49; resident, Presbyn.-U. Pa. Med. Center, Phila., 1949-52; pathologist, DePaul Hosp., Norfolk, Va., 1954—; pathologist, dir. labs., 1965—; clin. prof. pathology Med. Coll. Va., 1972—; cons. pathologist U.S. Naval Hosp., Portsmouth, Va., 1958—, U.S. VA, Hampton, Va., 1956—. Bd. visitors Coll. William and Mary; nat. bd. dirs., mem. exec. com. Am. Cancer Soc. Served with USNR, 1943-46, M.C., AUS, 1952-54. Recipient J. Shelton Horsley award of merit Va. div. Am. Cancer Soc., 1966. Mem. Am. Soc. Clin. Pathologists, Coll. Am. Pathologists, Am. Assn. Anatomists, A.M.A. Episcopalian. Clubs: Commonwealth (Richmond, Va.): Yacht and Country (Norfolk, Va.). Home: 1507 Buckingham Av Norfolk VA 23508 Office: 201 Med Tower Norfolk VA 23507

FAULK, LILLIAN MILDRED TIBBELS (MRS. RAYMOND B. FAULK), ednl. adminstr.; b. Smithville, Ark., Aug. 3, 1912; d. Charles D. and Aurelia J. (Shaver) Tibbels; B.S. Edn., Ark. State Tchrs. Coll., 1940; M.A., George Peabody Coll. Tchrs., 1947; Specialist in Edn., U. Tenn., 1970; m. Raymond B. Faulk, Mar. 19, 1954 (dec. Aug. 1955). Tchr., Black Rock (Ark.) Elementary Sch., 1936-40; tchr. Hulbert (Ark.)-West Memphis Schs., 1940-49, elementary sch. prin., 1949-69; elementary sch. supr. West Memphis Pub. Schs., 1969—; instr. edn. Ark. State Coll., Jonesboro, summer 1956. Chmn. elementary sch. council Ark. Dept. Edn., 1965-68. Named Favorite Tchr. in Ark. and Mo., Memphis Comml. Appeal, 1959; Woman of Year, West Memphis Jr. C. of C., 1966. Mem. N.E.A. (Ark. rep. dept. elementary sch. prins. 1963-69), Ark. Edn. Assn. (mem. com. profl. rights and responsibilities 1965-68), Ark. Assn. Supervision and Curriculum Devel. (pres. 1961-62), Ark. Elementary Sch. Prins. (sec. 1952-53), Pi Gamma Mu, Kappa Delta Pi, Delta Kappa Gamma (state treas. 1965-67), Alpha Tau (pres. 1960-62). Baptist. Mem. Order Eastern Star. Clubs: West Memphis Quota, Beethoven Music. Home: 508 Gibson St West Memphis AR 72301 Office: Adminstrv Annex PO Box 261 West Memphis AR 72301

FAULK, MURL EDMUND, JR., neurosurgeon; b. Columbus, O., May 25, 1922; s. Murl Edmund and Lucile Anna (Worley) Fulk; B.S., Va. Mil. Inst., 1942; M.D., Western Res. U., 1945; m. Catherine Young Cowen, July 15, 1944; children—Stuart Roland, Dean McKenzie. Intern, Franklin Hosp., San Francisco, 1945-46; resident neurology Tulane U. Sch. Medicine, New Orleans, 1948-49; resident neurol. surgery Oschner Clinic, New Orleans, 1949-52; fellow NIH - Montreal (Cal.) Neurol. Inst., 1952-53; instr. neurol. surgery Tulane U., New Orleans, 1953-55, asst. prof., 1955—; practice neurol. surgery, Beaumont, Tex., 1955—; mem. staff St. Elizabeth, Bapt. hosp., Beaumont. Treas., Starr, Rafes, Faulk & Kubala Asso., Beaumont, 1955—. Mem. Beaumont Symphony Soc. Bd. dirs. Beaumont Art Mus., 1970-72, v.p., 1971-72. Served to capt. M.C., AUS, 1943-49. NIH fellow, 1953. Mem. Am. Assn. Neurol. Surgeons, Pan Am. Med. Assn., Houston Neurol. Soc., Beaumont Acad. Medicine. Home: 850 Thomas Rd Beaumont TX 77706 Office: 3260 Fannin St Beaumont TX 77701

FAULK, NILES RICHARD, geologist; b. Canton, O., July 22, 1920; s. Albert Roy and Freda (Sponseller) F.; B.S., Mt. Union Coll., 1944; M.S., Ohio State U., 1948; m. Melba A. Dotson, Oct. 14, 1944. Devel. geologist Cal. Co., Laramie, Wyo., 1948, surface geologist, Farmington, N.M., 1948-49, Meridian, Canton, Forest, Miss., 1949-50, subsurface geologist, New Orleans, 1950-53; div. geologist La. Land and Exploration Co., New Orleans, 1953-55, chief geologist, 1955-63, v.p., 1963—. Served to 1st lt. USAAF, 1943-46. Mem. Am. Assn. Petroleum Geologists, Am. Soc. Oceanography, New Orleans Geol. Soc., Petroleum Club New Orleans, Sigma Alpha Epsilon. Democrat. Methodist. Clubs: Country (Metairie, La.); Plaza (Houston). Home: 3505 James Dr Metairie LA 70003 Office: PO Box 60350 New Orleans LA 70160

FAULKINBERRY, FRANK ALBERT, chem. engr.; b. Decherd. Tenn., Nov. 12, 1921; s. Frank Albert and Margaret Lee (Mabry) F.; B.S., U. Tenn., 1946; m. Dorothy Morris, June 8, 1947; children—Patricia, David. Chem. engr. TVA, Wilson Dam, Ala., 1947-52; project engr. Rust Engring. Co., Birmingham. Ala., 1955-59, project mgr., 1959-66, asst. v.p., 1966-67, v.p., 1967-73, pres., 1973—; v.p. Wheelabrator-Frye, Inc., N.Y.C., 1973—. Adv. bd. Diabetes Hosp. Trust Fund, Birmingham, 1968—; bd. dirs. United Appeal, 1974—. Registered profl. engr., Ala., Tenn., Ga., La. Mem. Am. Inst. Chem. Engrs., Am. Chem. Soc., T.A.P.P.I., Phi Kappa Phi, Tau Beta Pi. Clubs: Duquesne, Alleghany (Pitts.); The Club, Vestavia Country, Downtown, Relay House (Birmingham). Home: 3504 Crestbrook Rd Birmingham AL 35223 Office: PO Box 101 Birmingham AL 35201

FAULKNER, JAMES HERMAN, publisher; b. Lamar County, Ala., Mar. 1, 1916; s. Henry L. and Ebbie (Johnson) F.; B.J., U. Mo., 1936; m. Evelyn Irwin, Apr. 16, 1937; children—James Herman, Henry Wade. Co-owner, co-pub. The Baldwin Times, Bay Minette, Ala., 1936-74, also The Onlooker, Foley, Ala., 1969-74, Fairhope (Ala.) Courier, 1970-74; pres. Faulkner Radio, Inc., Bay Minette Mills, Inc.; owner radio stas. WLBB, WBTR, Carrollton, Ga., WBCA and WWSM, Bay Minette, WGAA, Cedartown, Ga., WAOA and WFRI, Opelika, Ala.; sr. v.p. David Volkert & Assos., architects and engrs., Mobile, Ala., Washington, Baton Rouge, Miami, Fla.; founder, pres. Loyal Am. Life Ins. Co., Mobile, 1955-57; dir. Baldwin Nat. Bank, Robertsdale, 1964—; pres., dir. Gulf Area Ins. Agy., Inc., Bay Minette, 1964—. Mayor, Bay Minette, 1940; mem. Ala. Dem. Com.; del. Dem. Conv. in Phila., 1948; Ala. state senator, 1951-55; candidate gov. Ala. Chmn. Baldwin County Hosp. Bd., Bay Minette Housing Authority, Bay Minette Municipal Airport Com., 1968—, Pub. Edn., Bldg. Com. of Bay Minette, 1967—, Indsl. Devel. Bd. Bay Minette, 1968—; chmn. adv. bd. James H. Faulkner State Coll. Bd. dirs Ala. Safety Council, 1967—, Ala. Crippled Children's Soc.; bd. dirs. Ala. div. Am. Cancer Soc., chmn., 1960-61; state chmn. Cancer Fund Drive, chmn. bd. trustees Ala. Christian Coll., Montgomery. Served with USAAF, World War II. Named Man of Year, Bay Minette, 1965; named Journalist of Year (weekly newspaper), U.S. Steel Corp., 1966. Mem. Ala. Press Assn. (pres. 1939), Ala. (dir. 1947—), Bay Minette (pres.) chambers commerce, Am. Legion, 40 and 8, Sigma Delta Chi. Rotarian. Home: 705 E 5th St Bay Minette AL 36507 Office: Baldwin Times Bay Minette AL 36507

FAULKNER, JAMES HERMAN, JR., real estate exec.; b. Bay Minette, Ala., May 31, 1938; s. James Herman and Evelyn (Irwin) F.; A.A., Marion Mil. Inst., 1958; B.A., U. Ala., 1960; m. Roxie Anne Allen, Aug. 25, 1960; children—James Herman III, Jenny, Mary Jane, Rebecca, Rachel. Co-pub. Baldwin Times, Bay Minette, 1969-74; sec.-treas. Faulkner Radio, Inc., 1961—; co-pub. The Onlooker, Foley, Ala., 1967-74; partner P.R.F. Cons. Co.; co-pub. Fairhope (Ala.) Courier, 1971-74. Past pres. Ft. Pierce Wildlife Assn. Bd. dirs. Mobile Area council Boy Scouts Am. Served with inf. AUS, 1961. Mem. Ala. Press Assn. (past dir.). Mem. Ch. of Christ (deacon). Rotarian (past pres.). Pub.: A History of Baldwin County, 1970. Home: Lee Av Extension Bay Minette AL 36507 Office: 102 W 2d St Bay Minette AL 36507

FAULKNER, JOHN SAMUEL, physicist; b. Memphis, Sept. 30, 1932; s. William Oliver and Willella (Aycock) F.; student Maryville Coll., 1950-52; B.S., Auburn U., 1954, M.S., 1955; Ph.D., Ohio State U., 1959; m. Mary Alice Crouch, June 12, 1957; children—Lee Anne, John Samuel. Asst. prof. U. Fla., Gainesville, 1959-62; physicist Oak Ridge Nat. Lab., 1962—, head theory group in metals and ceramics div., 1965—. Mem. Anderson County Dem. Exec. Com., 1969—; Dem. precinct capt., 1972—. Fulbright scholar, 1968-69. Fellow Am. Phys. Soc. Home: 123 E Morningside Dr Oak Ridge TN 37830 Office: Oak Ridge Nat Lab Oak Ridge TN 37830

FAULKNER, RUSSELL CONKLIN, JR., educator; b. Barbourville, Ky., Jan. 31, 1920; s. Russell C. and Mattie Frances (Kelly) F.; B.S., Lincoln Meml. U., 1948; M.S., U. Okla., 1952, Ph.D., 1958; m. Mary Fern Cravens, Aug. 11, 1954; children—Mary Ann, Russell Conklin III. Asst. prof. biology Lincoln Meml. U., 1948, 50-51, 52; research asst. U. Okla., 1950-53, grad. asst., 1953-55; chmn. dept. biology Okla. Bapt. Coll., 1955-56; asst. prof. biology Tex. Christian U., 1957-61, asso. prof., 1961-67; prof., head dept. biology Stephen F. Austin State U., Nacogdoches, Tex., 1967—. Mem. Angelina-Neches adv. com. Tex. Parks and Wildlife Dept., 1972—. Served with USNR, 1940-46. Mem. A.A.A.S., Am. Microscopical Soc., Am. Soc. Zoologists, Am. Assn. U. Profs., Tex. Acad. Sci., N. Tex. Biol. Soc., Sigma Xi, Phi Sigma, Beta Beta Beta. Methodist. Home: 1816 Sheffield Dr Nacogdoches TX 75961

FAULSTICH, ALBERT JOSEPH, govt. ofcl.; b. New Orleans, May 28, 1910; s. Albert and Mary (Balser) F.; B.S. in Accounting and Econs., Columbus U., Washington, 1938, M.S. in Accounting and Finance, 1948; m. Anna Emily Collignon, June 30, 1940; children—Albert Joseph, Richard Charles. With Treasury Dept., 1939—, dir. salary and wage adminstrn., 1946-53, asst. to dir. personnel, 1954-60, acting dir. personnel, 1960, asst. to under sec. treasury, 1961, dir. Office of Security, 1962, asst. to comptroller of currency, 1962-65, dep. comptroller of currency for FDIC affairs, 1965—, dir. FDIC, 1965—, mem. bd. rev., 1966—, mem. com. on liquidations, loans and purchases of assets, 1966—. Chmn. comptroller currency orgn. for nation-wide campaign for Kennedy Library Fund, 1964. Served to lt. USNR, 1943-46. Decorated Commendation medal; recipient commendation Treasury Dept., 1962, Meritorious award, 1972. Democrat. Roman Catholic. Home 505 Elderwood Rd Silver Spring MD 20904 Office: 550 17th St NW Washington DC 20429

FAUNTROY, WALTER E., congressman; b. Washington, Feb. 6, 1933; s. William T. and Ethel V.F.; A.B. cum laude, Va. Union U., 1955, D.D., 1968; B.D., Yale, 1958, D.D., 1969; LL.D., Muskingum Coll., 1971; m. Dorothy Simms; 1 son, Marvin Keith. Ordained to ministry Baptist Ch.; pastor New Bethel Bapt. Ch., Washington, 1969—; mem. 92d congress from D.C. Coordinator March on Washington for Jobs and Freedom, 1963; coordinator Selma (Ala.) to Montgomery March, 1965; chmn. D.C. Coalition Conscience, 1965-66; nat. coordinator Poor People's Campaign, 1969; former dir. So. Christian Leadership Conf., Washington. Vice chmn. Washington City Council, 1967-69; chmn. D.C. Met. Transit Authority, 1967; del. Democratic nat. conv., 1972. Bd. dirs. Martin Luther King Jr. Center for Social Change, Atlanta; chmn. bd. dirs. Model Inner City Community Orgn. Mem. Inter-religious Com. Race Relations, Leadership Conf. Civil Rights, other civil rights orgns. Address: 326 Cannon House Office Bldg Washington DC 20515*

FAUST, SISTER CLAUDE MARIE, educator; b. San Antonio, Nov. 18, 1917; d. Frederick Herman and Josephine Clotilda (Burger) Faust; B.A., Incarnate Word Coll., 1939; M.A., Cath. U. Am., 1954; M.S., Marquette U., 1955; Ph.D., U. Notre Dame, 1961. Substitute tchr., San Antonio Pub. Schs., 1939-42; geometry instr. Incarnate Word High Sch., 1942-43; elementary sch. tchr., San Angelo, Tex., 1945-46; faculty Incarnate Word Coll., San Antonio, 1946—, prof. math., 1961—. Dir. Minnemast Project, 1963-68; dir. NSF In-Service Insts. in Math. for High Sch. Tchrs., 1963-72. Recipient Sc. Faculty Fellowship, U. Notre Dame, 1956-57, 57-58, NSF Sci. Faculty Fellowship, U. Notre Dame, 1959; named Minnie Stevens Piper prof., 1967. Mem. Am. Math. Soc., Math. Assn. Am., Nat. Council Tchrs. Math., Alpha Lambda Delta, Alpha Chi, Pi Mu Epsilon, Kappa Gamma Pi. Address: 4301 Broadway San Antonio TX 78209

FAUST, JOHN WILLIAM, JR., educator; b. Pitts., July 25, 1922; s. John William and Helen (Crowther) F.; B.S., in Chem. Engring., Purdue U., 1943; M.A., U. Mo., 1949, Ph.D., 1951; m. Mary Claire Barton, June 7, 1947; children—Mary (Mrs. Kenneth Baumert), Elizabeth Wickham, John William III, Charles Barton, Ann Louise, Susan Bosley, Helen Crowther, Thomas McCullough. Research scientist Westinghouse Research Labs., Pitts., 1951-63; mgr. materials characterization lab., 1963-65, project mgr. crystal growth, 1965-67; prof. materials sci. Pa. State U., State College, 1967-69; prof. engring. U. S.C., Columbia, 1969—. Cons. Wright Patterson Air Force Research Center, 1957, Corning Glass Research Labs., 1968-70, Dow Corning Semiconductor Div., 1967-69, Gen. Telephone and Telegraph Labs., 1968, Sylvania, materials div., 1968-70, Langley Air Force Research Labs., 1970. Served with USNR, 1943-46. Mem. Electrochem. Soc. (mem. editorial com. 1971—), Am. Inst. Mining, Metall. and Petroleum Engrs. (mem. electronic materials com. 1967-73), A.A.A.S. (councillor 1967-69), Am. Phys. Soc., Am. Inst. Chemists, Am. Soc. Metals, Am. Chem. Soc., Sigma Xi. Editor: The Surface Chemistry of Metals and Semiconductors, 1960. Cons. editor Marcel Dekker, Inc., 1967—; divisional editor Jour. Electrochem. Soc., 1971—. Contbr. articles to profl. jours. Patentee in field. Home: 2455 Robincrest Dr W Columbia SC 29169

FAUST, JOSEF, geologist; b. Meggen, Germany, Feb. 6, 1902; s. Heinrich and Maria (Hunoldt) F.; Diplom-Engr., Technische Hochschule-Berlin-Charlottenburg, 1927, D.Eng., 1928; m. Irmgard Kamkowski, Apr. 29, 1934; children—Margrete Irma (Mrs. Curtis G. Hookway, Jr.), Mary Jo (Mrs. Harold E. Johnson). Came to U.S., 1929, naturalized, 1942. Mining engr. Wenzeslaus Grube Moeltke, Neder, Silesia, Germany, 1928-29; ingenieur Carnegie Steel Co., Pitts., 1929; geologist Hall & Briscoe, Oklahoma City, 1929-34; cons. geologist, engr., Oklahoma City, 1934—. Registered profl. engr., Okla. Mem. Am. Assn. Petroleum Geologists, Am. Assn. Profl. Engrs., Am. Assn. Petroleum Landsmen, Okla. Geol. Soc., Okla. Landmen's Assn., Soc. Profl. Engrs. Oklahoma City. Rotarian. Home: 2717 Pembroke Terrace Oklahoma City OK 73116 Office: Suite 504 May-Ex Bldg 3022 NW Expressway Oklahoma City OK 73112

FAVALORO, FRANK BOYD, dentist; b. New Orleans, Jan. 30, 1943; s. Frank Angelo and Ellen (Hart) F.; student U. S. Fla., 1962-64, U. Fla., 1964-65; D.D.S., U. Loyola, New Orleans, 1969; m. Paula Kathryn Holten, Aug. 23, 1969; children—Stephen Boyd, Stephanie Anne. Commd. 2d lt. U.S. Army, 1967, advanced through grades to capt., 1969; mem. intern program, Ft. Bragg, N.C., 1969-70; dental surgeon Hunter Leggett Mil. Reservation, Jolon, Cal., 1970-73. Mem. C. Victor Vignes Odontological Soc., Pi Kappa Alpha, Delta Sigma Delta. Roman Catholic. Address: PO Box G Lutcher LA 70071

FAVARO, MARY KAYE ASPERHEIM (MRS. BIAGINO PHILIP FAVARO), pediatrician; b. Edgerton, Wis., Sept. 30, 1934; d. Harold Wilbur and Genevieve Catherine (Hyland) Asperheim; B.S., U. Wis., 1956; M.S., St. Louis Coll. Pharmacy, 1965; M.D., U. Wis., 1969; m. Biagino Philip Favaro, May 31, 1969; children—Justin Peter, Gina Sue. Instr. pharmacology St. Louis U. and St. Mary's Hosp. Sch. Practical Nurses, 1959-64; staff pharmacist U. Hosps., Madison, Wis., 1964-65; intern Albany (N.Y.) Med. Center, 1969-70, resident, 1970-71; resident in pediatrics U. S.C., Charleston, 1971-72, asst. prof. pediatrics, 1973—. Mem. A.M.A., Am. Med. Women's Assn. Roman Catholic. Author: Pharmacology for Practical Nurses, 1963; The Pharmacologic Basis of Patient Care, 1968. Home: 1866 Capri Dr Charleston SC 29407 Office: Medical University of SC 80 Barre St Charleston SC 29401

FAW, DENNIS BOYDE, research chemist; b. nr. Winston-Salem, N.C., Jan. 2, 1921; s. Noah Henry and Mary (Foltz) F.; student Guilford Coll., 1939, Duke, 1948; B.S., High Point Coll., 1949, B.A., 1956. Tchr. high sch., Forsth County, N.C., 1949-50; chemist Carolina Paint & Varnish Co., Greensboro, N.C., 1956-57; chemist Research Lab., Cone Mille Corp., Greensboro, 1957-70; cons. chemist Lockette Corp., Greensboro, 1970-71; cons. chemist, 1971—. Mem. A.A.A.S., Am. Chem. Soc., Am. Assn. Textile Colorists and Chemists. Home: Route 4 Winston Salem NC 27107

FAWCETT, LESLIE CLARENCE, JR., accountant; b. Ft. Davis, Tex., May 12, 1920; s. Leslie Clarence and Estelle Virginia (Bloys) F.; student San Antonio Jr. Coll., 1938-41, St. Mary's U., 1947-48; B.B.A., U. Tex., 1949, M.B.A., 1951. Jr. accountant Fred E. Pflughaupt & Co., C.P.A.'s, San Antonio, 1951-52, sr. accountant, 1953-59, partner, 1960—. Served with Signal Corps, AUS, 1942-45. C.P.A., Tex. Mem. Am. Inst. C.P.A.'s, Tex. Soc. C.P.A.'s. Presbyn. Home: 428 Hammond Av San Antonio TX 78210 Office: 1222 Alamo Nat Bldg San Antonio TX 78205

FAWSETT, EDWARD HARVEY, newspaper exec.; b. Washington, Aug. 1, 1916; s. Clifford Cleveland and Lillie (Peters) F.; B.S., U. Fla., 1939; m. Talulah Frances Doggett, Sept. 5, 1942; children—Judith Chandler (Mrs. James S. Wilder), Robert Hastings, Clifford Carleton, Jane Leslie. Teller, Morris Plan Bank, Washington, 1939-41; fed. govt. bank examiner Fed. Home Loan Bank Bd., Winston-Salem, N.C., 1941-43; auditor, credit mgr. Washington Star, 1943-58, controller, 1958-67, asst. bus. mgr., 1967-69, asst. to pres., 1969—; v.p., treas. Tal-Star Computer Systems, Inc., 1969—; treas. Washington Star Syndicate, 1969—. Recipient Carley award for writing Inst. Newspaper Controller and Finance Officers. Mem. Financial Execs. Inst., Inst. Newspaper Controllers and Finance Officers, Phi Delta Theta. Episcopalian. Contbr. articles to profl. jours. Home: 8520 Durham Ct Springfield VA 22151 Office: 225 Virginia Av SE Washington DC 20003

FAXON, LOUIS HENSLIE, JR., architect; b. Wadena, Minn., July 13, 1930; s. Louis Henslie and Edna Dell (McFall) F.; B.S., La. State U., 1958; m. Martha Anne Hill, Oct. 31, 1970; 1 son (by previous marriage), Louis Henslie III. Designer, A. Hays Town, architect, Baton Rouge, 1958-59; architect B.G. Buquoi, architect, Baton Rouge, 1960-61, Perry L. Brown, Inc., Baton Rouge, 1961-66, v.p., 1964-66;

pres. Louis H. Faxon, Inc., Architects, Baton Rouge, 1966—. Asst. prof. architecture La. State U., Baton Rouge, 1966—. Pres. bd. Baton Rouge Symphony Assn., 1966-67; asst. scoutmaster Istrouma Area council Boy Scouts Am., 1963-64; mem. sch. plants and facilities com. East Baton Rouge Parish Sch. Bd., 1969-71. Bd. dirs. Baton Rouge Symphony Assn., Baton Rouge Community Concert Assn., Baton Rouge Gallery. Served with USAF, 1950-53. Decorated Air medal with oak leaf cluster. Mem. A.I.A., La. Architects Assn., Council Ednl. Facilities Planners, U.S. Power Squadrons, Tau Beta Pi. Methodist. Clubs: Baton Rouge Rifle and Pistol, City, Camelot (Baton Rouge); Southern Yacht (New Orleans). Home: 10436-F Jefferson Hwy Baton Rouge LA 70809 Office: 460 Florida St Suite 14 Baton Rouge LA 70801

FAXON, MARTHA ANNE HILL (MRS. LOUIS HENSLIE FAXON), clubwoman; b. Atlanta; d. Hines LaFayette and Elizabeth (Marsh) H.; student Shorter Coll., 1957-58; A.B., Ga. State U., 1961; M.Ed., U. Ga., 1965, Edn. Specialist, 1972; m. Louis Henslie Faxon, Oct. 31, 1970. Tchr., Fulton High Sch., Atlanta, 1961-64; counselor O'Keefe High Sch., Atlanta, 1965-68; coordinator visitor services Atlanta Pub. Schs., 1968-70; sec.-treas. Louis H. Faxon, Inc., Architects. Publicity chmn. Baton Rouge Newcomers Club, 1972-73; treas. Baton Rouge Symphony Women's Aux., 1972-73, pres., 1973-74; mem. La. Arts and Sci. Center, Com. Formation Baton Rouge Arts Council, Arts and Humanities Council Baton Rouge; v.p. Baton Rouge chpt. La. Council Music and Performing Arts, 1972-73. Bd. dirs. Baton Rouge Gallery, 1971—. Mem. Mental Health Assn. Baton Rouge, Baton Rouge Opera Guild (trustee 1972-74, 1st v.p. 1974—), Am., Ga., La. personnel and guidance assns., Atlanta Area Assn. Personnel Workers, Ga., Atlanta edn. assns., Am. Sch. Counselors Assn., Assn. Measurement and Evaluation in Guidance, Am. Coll. Personnel Assn., Nat. Vocational Guidance Assn., Found. for Hist. La., Baton Rouge Power Squadron Woman's Aux., Alpha Omicron Pi Alumni. Lutheran. Democrat. Club: Baton Rouge Music. Home: 10436-F Jefferson Hwy Baton Rouge LA 70809

FAY, PETER THORP, judge; b. Rochester, N.Y., Jan. 18, 1929; s. Lester Thorp and Jane (Baumler) F.; B.A., Rollins Coll., 1951; J.D., University of Florida, 1956; m. Claudia Pat Zimmerman, Oct. 1, 1958; children—Michael, William, Darcy. Admitted Fla. bar, 1956, U.S. Supreme Ct. bar, 1961; partner, Nichols, Gaither Green, Frates & Beckham, Miami, 1956-61; partner Frates, Fay, Floyd & Pearson and predecessors, Miami, 1961-70; U.S. dist. judge, Miami, 1970—. Prof., Fla. Jr. Bar Practical Legal Inst., 1959-65; lectr. Fla. Bar Legal Insts. Dist. collector United Fund, 1957-70. Served with USAF, 1951-53. Mem. Law Sci. Acad., Nat., Fla. assns. compensation and claimants attys., Fla., Fla. Jr. (gov.), Dade County Jr., John Marshall (pres.) bar assns., U. Fla. Alumni Assn. (dir.), Miami C. of C., Order of Coif, Phi Delta Phi (pres.), Medico Legal Inst., Omicron Delta Kappa (pres.), Pi Gamma Mu (pres.), Phi Kappa Phi, Phi Delta Theta (sec.). Republican. Catholic. Clubs: Miami, University, Riviera Country, Snapper Creek Lakes, Coral Oaks; Wildcat Cliffs Country (Highlands, N.C.). Home: 11000 Snapper Creek Rd Miami FL 33156 Office: US Post Office and Court House Miami FL 33101

FAY, RONALD LYLE, headmaster; b. Proctor, Vt., Nov. 11, 1939; s. Marshall Thorburn and Bernice Mary (Morse) F.; B.A., U. Vt., 1962; M.S., U. Pa., 1967; m. Ann Saari Parker, Aug. 31, 1963; children—Elizabeth, Courtney, Jarrod. Tchr. Chestnut Hill (Pa.) Acad., 1963-65, reading cons., 1965-67, head jr. sch., 1967-70; headmaster Ensworth Sch., Nashville, 1971—. Mem. Ind. Sch. Tchrs. Assn., Nat. Assn. Ind. Schs., Mid-South Assn. Ind. Schs., Club: Exchange. Home: 224 Ensworth Av Nashville TN 37205 Office: Ensworth Sch Ensworth Av Nashville TN 37205

FAZEKAS, GABRIEL ANDREW GEORGE, educator; b. Kalocsa, Hungary, Mar. 16, 1911; s. Leopold Paul and Adrienne (Berger) F.; Dipl. Ing., Fed. Inst. Tech., Zurich, 1934; student London U., 1942-46, Courant Inst., 1962-63; m. Lily Shrager, Apr. 26, 1942; children—Frances Pauline, Paul Anthony. Came to U.S., 1951, naturalized, 1956. Prof. mech. engring. Poly. Inst. Bklyn., 1952-64; mgr. mech. engring. tech. staff Am. Machine & Foundry Co., Greenwich, Conn., 1957-59; prof. mech. engring. U. Houston, 1964. Mem. Am. Soc. M.E., Instn. Mech. Engrs., Sigma Xi, Tau Beta Pi, Pi Tau Sigma. Patentee in field. Home: 26 Knipp Rd Houston TX 77024 Office: Cullen Blvd Houston TX 77004

FEAGANS, ROBERT GEARY, mech. engr.; b. Ashland, Ky., July 5, 1924; s. Guy and Hazel Edna (McIntyre) F.; B.S., U. Ky., 1948; m. Anna Louise McCalvin, Sept. 14, 1924; children—Deborah Louise, Pamella Gaye. Self-employed as mech. contractor, Ironton, O. and Frankfort, Ky., 1948-63; mech. engr. Rust Engring. Co., Calhoun, Tenn., 1965-68; sr. mech. engr. Patchen, Mingledorff & Asso., cons. engrs., Augusta, Ga., 1969—. Pecan grower, Aiken County, S.C., 1971—. Served with U.S. Mcht. Marine, 1944-45. Registered profl. engr., Tenn. Mem. Am. Soc. Heating, Refrigerating and Air-Conditioning Engrs., Ga. Soc. Profl. Engrs. (sec. 1973-74). Home: Route 1 Box 494 Aiken SC 29801 Office: Ga RR Bank Bldg Augusta GA 30902

FEAGIN, ARTHUR HENRY, civil engr.; b. Union Springs, Ala., Apr. 4, 1911; s. Arthur Henry and Irene (Peach) F.; B.S. in Civil Engring., Auburn U., 1932; m. Margaret Stokes, Oct. 8, 1935. Resident engr. Ala. Hwy. Dept., 1932-41; with U.S. Army Engrs., 1948-71, engr. in charge various constrn. operations, 1952-71; self-employed as cons. engr., Birmingham, Ala., 1971—. Served from 2d lt. to lt. col., C.E., AUS, 1941-48. Recipient Sustained Superior Performance certificate Army C.E., 1970. Mem. Am. Soc. C.E., Retired Officers Assn., Phi Delta Theta. Presbyn. Address: 3906 Montevallo Rd Birmingham AL 35213

FEAGIN, ROBERT R., newspaper publisher. Pres., pub. Jacksonville (Fla.) Times-Union/Jour. Office: One Riverside Av Jacksonville FL 32201

FEAREY, MARY ESTILL (MRS. PORTER FEAREY), club woman; b. Corpus Christi, Tex., Mar. 30, 1917; d. Richard Gentry and Mary Henrietta (King) Estill; student Columbia Coll., 1936-37, U. Mo., 1937-39; m. Porter Fearey, May 14, 1944; 1 dau., Mary (Mrs. James McEwen Dewar). With Trans World Airlines, 1941-43. Flower show life judge Nat. Council State Garden Clubs, 1964—, flower show master judge, 1965—; hon. internat. flower show judge, 1963—; instr., demonstrator flower arranging; lectr. mobiles, also cultivation and uses of gourds, Central Tex., 1968—; lectr. pictorial slide programs with emphasis on bot. aspects of internat. travel, 1958—. Co-creator Mary Henrietta King Estill scholarship Columbia (Mo.) Coll., 1970—. Served as pilot Women's Airforce Service, 1943-44. Mem. Nationally Accredited Flower Show Judges (pres. San Antonio 1966-67, v.p. 1970-71), Tex. Garden Clubs (state chmn. judges councils 1965-67, state chmn. pilgrimages 1967-69, state chmn. bonsai 1969-71, state chmn. bonsai and gourds 1971—), Am. Gourd Soc., Am. Horticulture Soc., Nat. Wildlife Fedn., Aircraft Owners and Pilots Assn., Ninety-Nines, Columbia Coll. Alumni Assn., New Braunfels Conservation Soc., Innerwheel, Colonial Dames Am., Dames Mil. Order Loyal Legion U.S. Republican. Episcopalian. Clubs: Sierra (life), Easter Island Exchange (Alexandria, Va.); St. Anthony, University, Argyle (San Antonio). Home: PO Box 633 New Braunfels TX 78130

FEAREY, PORTER, distbg. and sales co. exec.; b. Albany, N.Y., June 17, 1918; s. Porter and Elizabeth B. W. (Martin) F.; student Williams Coll., 1938-39, S.W. Tex. State Coll., 1946-48; m. Mary King Estill, May 14, 1944; 1 dau., Mary King Estill (Mrs. James McEwan Dewar). Salesman, Westchester Pubs., Inc., Noel Macy Chain, Yonkers, N.Y., 1940-41; marketing supr. Gulf Oil Corp., N.Y.C., 1941-45, Tex. Co. (Texaco, Inc.), Houston, 1945-46; owner, pres. Water Service Co., San Antonio, 1948—; pres., dir. Apartimientos S.A., Monterrey, Mexico, 1958-68; owner, pres. Ice Service, Inc., San Antonio. Mem. central exec. com. Episcopal Diocese West Tex., 1960—, mem. finance dept., 1963—, mem. exec. bd., 1963-66, 69-72, mem. central exec. com. Episcopal Advance Fund; del. Tex. Council Chs., 1968; del. Tex. Conf. Chs., 1969-72, 73-74. Del. Tex. State Republican Conv., 1960, 74; del. Comal County (Tex.) Rep. Conv., 1956, 74. Served with USAAF, World War II; ret. Mem. S.W. Found. Research and Edn., Comal County (dir.), New Braunfels (dir.), San Antonio, South Tex. chambers commerce, Good Govt. League (dir.), Episcopal Churchmens Assn., Williams Coll. Alumni Assn., Am. Legion, Mil. Order Loyal Legion U.S. (comdr. Tex. commandery 1965—), Mil. Order World Wars, Res. Officers Assn., Ret. Officers Assn., Armed Forces Communications and Electronics Assn., Am. Ordnance Assn., San Antonio Zool. Soc., Comal County Hist. Soc. (dir.), New Braunfels Conservation Soc. (dir.), Mil. Order Fgn. Wars U.S., St. Nicholas Soc. N.Y.C., N.Y. So. Soc., St. Georges Soc. N.Y., S.R., Soc. Colonial Wars, Vets. Assn. 7th Regiment N.Y. N.G., Assos. Engr. Corps 7th Regiment N.Y. N.G., Mil. Order World Wars, Am. Geog. Soc., Kappa Alpha. Republican. Episcopalian (vestryman, sr. warden); diocesan exec. bd.; del. Rotarian, Elk. Clubs: Explorers (N.Y.C.); San Antonio Press; Williams (N.Y.C.). Home: 100 Paeso Encinal San Antonio TX 78212 Office: care Water Service Co Maverick Bldg San Antonio TX 78205

FEARS, JOHN CARROLL, JR., lawyer; b. Louisville, June 7, 1923; s. John Carroll and Mary Gertrude (Edelen) F.; LL.B., U. Louisville, 1950; m. Mary Rodes Harris, Sept. 5, 1951; children—Mary Ewing, John Allen, Lawrence Edelen. Claims supr. Liberty Mutual Ins. Co., Norfolk, Va., 1951-62; admitted to Ky. bar, 1950, Va. bar, 1955; practiced in Norfolk, Va., 1962—; atty., partner, Parsons, Stant & Parsons, 1962-64, Taylor, Gustin, Harris, Fears & Davis, Norfolk, Va., 1964—; v.p., dir. Kitty Hawk Devel. Corp. (N.C.), Golf View, Inc., Windjammer Motor Lodge, Inc. Served with AUS, 1943-46. Mem. Fed. Bar Assn., Nat. Assn. Criminal Trial Lawyers, Am. Judicature Soc., Am., Va. State bar assns., Va. Trial Lawyers Assn., Va. Defense Trial Counsel, Sigma Chi, Delta Theta Phi. Club: Cavalier Golf and Yacht (v.p. 1971-73) (Virginia Beach, Va.). Home: 1264 Tanager Trail Virginia Beach VA 23451 Office: 1440 Virginia Nat Bank Bldg Norfolk VA 23510

FEBLES-VIZCARRONDO, FRANCISCO, physician; b. San Juan, P.R., Mar. 12, 1929; s. Francisco and Rosalia (Viscarrondo-Llompart) Febles-Martinez; B.S., George Washington U., 1950, M.D., 1955; m. Maria Esther Morales-Yordan, July 26, 1953; children—Mayra Jean, Francisco III, Maria Eugenia, Adrian Febles. Intern, Providence Hosp., Washington, 1955-56; resident in pathology and internal medicine U. P.R., San Juan, 1961-65, asst. prof. internal medicine dept., 1969—; practice medicine, specializing in internal medicine and gastroenterology, Hato Rey, P.R., 1971—. Treas., El Centro Profl. Group, Inc., 1971—. Pres. com. human resources P.R. Dept. Health, 1967-68. Served to lt. comdr. USPHS, 1958-61. Mem. A.M.A. (Med. Achievement award 1971), A.C.P., Am. Soc. Tropical Medicine, Am. Fedn. Clin. Research, Am. Soc. Mil. Surgeons, P.R. Med. Assn., P.R. Soc. Gastroenterology (sec.-gen.), George Washington U. Med. Alumni Assn. (pres. P.R. chpt. 1966-68), Phi Eta Mu, Phi Chi. Roman Catholic. Club: Casino de P.R. Contbr. articles to med. jours. Research on tropical sprue, schistosomiasis, peptic ulcer. Home: 5 Castana Urb San Patricio Guaynabo PR 00657 Office: 500 Munoz-Rivera Av Condominium El Centro I Hato Rey PR 00919

FECHTMANN, FRED, banker; b. Woodhaven, N.Y., Mar. 15, 1916; s. Reinhart and Emily Margaret (Koch) F.; bus. certificate Bob Jones Coll., 1937; m. Dora Elizabeth Cline, Apr. 18, 1944; children—Virginia (Mrs. Thomas R. Coughenour), Freddie Ann (Mrs. James Wood), Elizabeth E. Supr., L.I. Feather Marketing Corp., 1937-41; cashier Harrisonburg Loan & Thrift Corp. (Va.), 1946-56; asst. cashier, mgr. consumer loan dept. First Nat. Bank, Harrisonburg, 1957-62, v.p., comml. loan officer, 1962-68, sr. v.p., chief lending officer, 1968-70; sr. v.p. Va. Nat. Bank, Harrisonburg, 1970—, mgr., 1972—; dir. Friendship Industries, Inc. Served to 1st lt. AUS, 1941-46. Mem. Robert Morris Assos., Am. Inst. Banking, Va. Poultry Fedn., Va. C. of C. Lutheran (v.p., trustee). Club: Exchange (past dist. gov., past pres. Harrisonburg). Home: Box 372 Harrisonburg VA 22801 Office: P O Box 1212 Harrisonburg VA 22801

FEDUCCIA, JOHN ALAN, educator; b. Mobile, Ala., Apr. 25, 1943; s. Joseph Charles F.; B.S., La. State U., 1965; M.A., U. Mich., 1966, Ph.D., 1969. Lectr. zoology U. Mich., 1969; asst. prof. zoology So. Meth. U., 1969-71, research asso. Shuler Mus. Paleontology, 1970-71; asst. prof. zoology U. N.C., Chapel Hill, 1971-74, asso. prof., 1974—. Author: Evolutionary Trends in the Neotropical Ovenbirds and Woodhewers, 1973; Structure and Evolution of Vertebrates, 1974. Address: Dept Zoology U NC Chapel Hill NC 27514

FEFERMAN, DONALD MARK, lawyer; b. Amarillo, Tex., Aug. 6, 1940; s. Abe and Alda Lois (Braunig) F.; student U. Tex., 1958-60; B.S., U. Pa., 1962; J.D., Harvard, 1965; m. Carol Ann Androski, Nov. 13, 1965; children—Andrew Mark, Kery Leigh. Admitted to Tex. bar, 1965; practiced in Corpus Christi, 1967—; partner, Branscomb, Gary, Thomasson & Hall, Corpus Christi, Tex., 1967—. Trustee Jewish Community Council. Served to capt. AUS, 1965-67. C.P.A., Tex. Decorated Bronze Star medal. Mem. Am., Tex., Nueces County bar assns., Am. Inst. C.P.A.'s, Tex. Soc. C.P.A.'s. Jewish religion (trustee temple 1969—). Club: Yacht (Corpus Christi, Tex.). Home: 318 Bermuda St Corpus Christi TX 78411 Office: Hawn Bldg Corpus Christi TX 78401

FEFFER, JAMES JOSEPH, univ. adminstr., physician; b. N.Y.C., Nov. 3, 1913; s. William and Fannie Rose (Senior) F.; A.B., Ind. U., 1935, M.D., 1938; m. Mary Theresa Carroll, May 31, 1941; children—Barbara Joyce (Mrs. Niyazi Al-Sharif), Carol Louise (Mrs. Joseph Wolfer). Intern, Kings County Hosp., N.Y.C., 1938-40; resident internal medicine and pulmonary diseases Kings County Hosp., 1940-41; med. officer Glenn Dale (Md.) Hosp., 1942-44; practice medicine specializing in pulmonary diseases, Washington, 1944-68; dir. pulmonary disease div. George Washington U. Med. Center, Washington, 1944-68, asso. dean clin. affairs, chief staff university hosp., 1968--72, univ. v.p. med. affairs, med. center chief exec. officer, 1972—, clin. instr. medicine, 1944-47, asst. clin. prof., 1947-59, asso. clin. prof., 1959-64, clin. prof., 1964-68, prof., 1968—; cons. Prince George's Gen. Hosp., 1944-68, St. Elizabeth's Hosp., 1964-68, Children's Hosp. Nat. Med. Center, 1950—. Washington VA Hosp., 1950-59, NIH Clin. Center, 1955-70, Newton D. Baker VA Hosp., 1959-68, Washington Hosp. Center, 1968—. Mem. D.C. Gen. Hosp. Gov. Bd., 1970—; mem. dean's com. Washington VA Hosp., 1970-73, chmn., 1971-72. Pres., D.C. Tb Assn., 1955-57. Diplomate Am. Bd. Internal Medicine. Fellow A.C.P., Am. Coll. Chest Physicians; mem. Am. Soc. Internal Medicine (pres. 1967-68, trustee 1962-69), Am. Therapeutic Soc. (v.p. 1968-69), Am. Soc. Clin. Pharmacology and Therapeutics (dir. 1971-72), So. Med. Assn. (chmn. sect. medicine 1967-68), Smith Reed Russell Hon. Soc., Med. Soc. D.C. (mem. liaison com. with med. schs. 1971—), D.C. Soc. Internal Medicine (pres. 1962-63), D.C. Thoracic Soc. (past pres.). Club: Cosmos (Washington). Home: 2700 Virginia Av NW Washington DC 20037 Office: 2300 Eye St NW Washington DC 20037

FEGGANS, EDWARD LELAND, univ. ofcl.; b. Atlantic City, Mar. 5, 1919; s. Edward Leland and Ethel M. (McIntyre) F.; student Suffolk U., 1946-48, Howard U., 1949-51; m. Ozra Young, Feb. 25, 1950; children—James Enoch, Helen Anna. Clk., 1st Nat. Bank of Boston, 1948; teller, asst. auditor Indsl. Bank of Washington, 1949-50; adminstrv. clk. U.S. Navy Yard, Washington, 1951-52; ry. mail clk. U.S. Post Office, 1952-53; regional salesman Sch. Jewelry, Herf Jones Co., 1953-54; asst. sales mgr. Kaplan & Crawford Dodge and Plymouth Agy., Washington, 1954-57; sales mgr. Fuller Products Co., Washington, 1957-64; bus. counselor United Planning Orgn., Washington, 1964-66; trade assn. officer Small Bus. Guidance and Devel. Center, Howard U., Washington, 1966—; owner, pres. Ed Feggans Oldmobile, 1972—; exec. dir. Washington Area Contractors Assn., 1970; dir. Hemisphere Nat. Bank, Washington. Tchr. bus. mgmt. D.C. Pub. Schs., 1964; instr. Washington Tech. Inst. Sec. Nat. Bus. League, 1969; bd. mgmt. YMCA, Washington; vice comdr. USCG Flotilla 75, 5th Dist. Mem. D.C. Republican Com., 1964—, vice chmn., 1971. Bd. dirs. Washington Red Cross, Better Bus. Bur. Washington, Davis Meml. Goodwill Industries, Metro Washington Bus. Resource Center. Mem. D.C. C. of C. (v.p. 1969, dir. 1971). Episcopalian (lay reader). Mason (K.T., Shriner). Clubs: Neptune Yacht (commodore Balt. 1964-67); Seafarers Yacht (vice commodore). Home: 2504 S Dakota Av NE Washington DC 20018

FEHRENBACH, T(HEODORE) R(EED), author; b. San Benito, Tex., Jan. 12, 1925; s. Theodore R. and Mardel (Wentz) F.; A.B. magna cum laude, Princeton, 1947; m. Lillian Breetz, Aug. 22, 1951. Pvt. practice as ins. broker San Antonio, 1956-70, ins. cons., 1970—; mgr. Fehrenbach Trusts; pres. Royal Poinciana Corp., San Antonio. Chmn. adv. com. Inst. Pub. and Internat. Affairs, St. Mary's U. Pres. Republican Citizen's Com. of Bexar County, 1965-66. Served from pvt. to 1st sgt. AUS, 1943-46; served as 1st lt., AUS, 1951-53; ret. lt. col., Res. Mem. Am. Numis. Soc., Tex. Inst. Letters, Authors Guild, Sons Republic Tex., S.A.R., Mil. Order World Wars. Episcopalian. Author: Battle of Anzio, 1962; U.S. Marines in Action, 1962; Crisis in Cuba, 1963; This Kind of War, 1963; This Kind of Peace, 1966; The Swiss Banks, 1966; Crossroads in Korea, 1966; FDR's Undeclared War, 1967; Elkdom USA, 1968; UN in War and Peace, 1968; Lone Star, 1968; Fight for Korea, 1969; Fire and Blood, 1973; Comanches, 1974; also stories and articles in U.S. and European mags., including Sat. Eve. Post, Argosy, Esquire, Atlantic. Home: 131 Mary D Av San Antonio TX 78209 Office: 7078 San Pedro AV San Antonio TX 78216

FEIGHT, JOHN WILLIAM DUNCAN, advt. exec.; b. Millersburg, O., Jan. 16, 1940; s. Henry Baughman and Lois Louise (Duncan) F.; B.A., U. Fla.; m. Linda Lee, July 4, 1964; children—John Scott Duncan, Andrew Lee. Asst. account exec. Batten, Barton, Durstine & Osborne, N.Y.C., 1964-67; account exec. Delehanty Kurnit Geller Advt., N.Y.C., 1967-69; sr. account exec. Marschalk Advt., Atlanta, 1969-70; v.p., Burton, Campbell & Kelley, Atlanta, 1971—. Served with AUS, 1963. Mem. Am. Marketing Assn. (v.p. 1973-74). Home: 230 Hillswick Ct Atlanta GA 30328 Office: 1800 Peachtree St Atlanta GA 30309

FEILD, JAMES RODNEY, physician; b. Memphis, Mar. 12, 1934; s. Roscoe Adam and Georgia (Bledsoe) F.; student Southwestern U. at Memphis, 1952-54; M.D. with honors, U. Tenn., 1957, postgrad. biol. scis., 1966—; m. Nancy Lee Tanner, June 14, 1958; children—Mary Janet, Frederick Duane, Jamie Lee, John Alan, Nancy Glynn. Intern John Gaston Hosp., Memphis, 1958; practice gen. medicine, Albany, Ky., 1959; resident neurosurgery U. Tenn.-Bapt. Meml. Hosp., Memphis, 1960-63; spl. fellow neurology Mayo Clinic, Rochester, Minn., 1964; practice medicine specializing in neurosurgery, Memphis, 1965—; active staff Bapt. Meml. Hosp.; courtesy staff Methodist Hosp., Memphis, St. Joseph Hosp., Memphis; instr. neuroanatomy U. Tenn. at Memphis, 1965-69, asst. prof. anatomy, 1969-72. Mem. health ins. benefits adv. council Medicare, Dept. Health, Edn. and Welfare, 1971—. Mem. Hosp. Authority Shelby County (Tenn.), 1973—. State chmn. Tenn. Physicians Com. for Re-election of the Pres., 1972, Diplomate Am. Bd. Neurosurgery. Fellow Congress Neurol. Surgeons, Internat. Congress Surgeons, A.C.S.; mem. A.M.A., Tenn., Memphis and Shelby County med. assns., Memphis Surg. Soc., U. Tenn. Med. Alumni Assn. (pres. 1973), Sigma Xi, Alpha Omega Alpha. Contbr. articles to profl. jours. Home: 2254 N Parkway Memphis TN 38112 Office: 910 Madison St Suite 922 Memphis TN 38103

FEILD, SAM CLEAGE, JR., electronics engr.; b. Washington, Sept. 17, 1927; s. Sam Cleage and Jacqueline Epes (Pryor) F.; student George Washington U., 1950-60, U. Va., 1953-60, Capitol Radio Engring. Inst., 1946-48; m. Chalene Audrey Freudenberg, July 18, 1947; children—Jacki Lynn, Charon Ann. Tech. writer systems div. Remington-Rand Corp., Washington, 1947-48; engring. technician Melpar div., E-Systems, Inc., Alexandria, Va., 1948-50, jr. engr., 1950-52, engr., 1952-56, sr. engr., 1956-59, prin. engr., 1959-62, project engr., 1962-70, lab. mgr., 1970-71, project mgr., 1971—; pres. M-N Studios, Inc., Annandale, Va., 1965—. Trustee Nat. Capitol Astronomers, Inc., 1962-63. Served with USNR, 1944-46. Mem. I.E.E.E. Home: 7804 Dassett Ct Annandale VA 22003 also 11398 72d Terrace N Seminole FL 33542 Office: 7700 Arlington Blvd Falls Church VA 22046

FEIN, HARVEY LESTER, aerospace engr.; b. Washington, Mar. 4, 1936; s. Ben and Mae (Friedman) F.; B.Chem. Engring. with distinction, Cornell U., 1959; M.S. (Dow Chem. Co. fellow), Mass. Inst. Tech., 1961, Sc.D. (W.R. Grace fellow), 1963. Chem. engr. Atlantic Research Corp., Alexandria, Va., 1963-65, head thermodynamics sect., 1965-68, staff scientist, 1968—. Active Muscular Dystrophy Assn. Mem. Combustion Inst., Am. Inst. Aeros. and Astronautics, Am. Chem. Soc., Sigma Xi, Tau Beta Pi, Phi Lambda Upsilon, Alpha Epsilon Pi. Home: 6444 Elmdale Rd Alexandria VA 22312 Office: 5390 Cherokee Av Alexandria VA 22314

FEINGOLD, S. NORMAN, psychologist; b. Worcester, Mass., Feb. 2, 1914; s. William and Aida (Salit) F.; A.B., Ind. U., 1937; M.A., Clark U., 1940; Ed.D., Boston U., 1948; m. Marie Goodman, Mar. 24, 1947; children—Elizabeth Anne, Margaret Ellen, Deborah Carol, Marilyn Nancy. Dir. vocational service and ednl. and vocational dir. Hecht Neighborhood House, Boston, 1940-43; exec. dir. Boston Jewish Vocational Service and Work Adjustment Center, 1946-58; nat. dir. B'nai B'rith Career and Counseling Services, Washington, 1958—; exec. adviser Rehab. Services. Boston, 1953-58; dir. ednl. and vocational workshop United Cerebral Palsy of Greater Boston, Inc., 1957-58; cons. to Scholarships, Fellowships and Loans News Service to state and fed. govts.; instr., spl. lectr. Boston U., 1951-58; cons. Social Security Adminstrn., 1962—; professorial lectr. Am. U. Rehab. Counseling Adv. Panel, 1963-65; mem. Am. Bd. Counseling Services, 1962-65, 70—; chmn. Washington Bus.-Industry Group, 1963-64. Chmn., Gov.'s Council on Aging, 1956-58; mem. President's Com. on Employment Handicapped, 1950—; mem. adv. com. Nat. Health Council; mem. Nat. Home Study Accrediting Commn. Served from pvt. to 1st lt. AUS., 1943-46; ETO and PTO. Recipient Community Service award B'nai B'rith, 1957, Brotherhood and Americanization award, 1958. Fellow Am. Psychol. Assn.; mem. Greater Boston (pres. 1952-53), Am. (pres.-elect) personnel and guidance assns., Mass., Eastern psychol. assns., Nat. Vocational Guidance Assn. (past pres.), Am. Assn. Adult Edn., A.A.A.S., Am. Coll. Personnel Assn., Am. Gerontol. Assn., Indsl. Relations Assn., Mass. Conf. Social Work, Nat. Council on Measurements Used Edn., Nat. Soc. Study Edn., Nat. Rehab. Assn., Phi Delta Kappa. Clubs: Torch, New Century (dir. 1957-58). Author: Jobs in Unusual Occupations; Scholarships, Fellowships and Loans (5 vols.); How to Choose that Career, Words for Work: How to get College Scholarships: Finding Part-time Jobs; The Job Finder; It Pays to Advertise; Occupations and Careers, 1969; The Vocational Expert in the Social Security Disability Program, 1969, A Counselor's Handbook, 1972. Editor: Counselors Information Service. Home: 9707 Singleton Dr Bethesda MD 20034 Office: 1640 Rhode Island Av Washington DC 20036

FEINMAN, MICHAEL RICHARD, retail furniture co. exec.; b. N.Y.C., Aug. 30, 1944; s. Richard Bert and Elaine Beverly (Galin) F.; student N.Y. U., 1962-64; B.B.A., Hofstra U., 1968; M.B.A., U. N.C., 1972; m. Janice Ellen Popkin, Sept. 4, 1966; children—Phoebe, Joshua. Continuity dir. Westinghouse Broadcasting Co., N.Y.C., 1964-65; mgr. marketing research Berkline Corp., Morristown, Tenn., 1968-70; sec.-treas. Expressway, Inc., Knoxville, Tenn., 1972—; dir. Turning Point Art Prodns., Inc. Cons. East Tenn. League Progressive Bus., 1968-72. Mem. Am. Marketing Assn. Jewish religion (dir. temple 1973—). Home: 8945 Shallowford Rd Knoxville TN 37921 Office: 2401 Dutch Valley Rd Knoxville TN 37918

FEINSTONE, W(OLFFE) HARRY, scientist; b. Pultusk, Poland, Oct. 1, 1913 (naturalized U.S. citizen); B.S., U. Ark., 1936; Sc.D. in Bacteriology (scholar), Johns Hopkins, 1939; m. 1938; 3 children. Asst. chemotherapy Johns Hopkins, 1937-39; research bacteriologist Am. Cyanamid Co., 1939-44; dir. biol. research Pyridium Corp., 1944-47; dir. research Central Pharmacol. Co., 1947-48; sci. dir. C.B. Kendall Co., 1949-58; v.p. sci. adminstrn. Plough, Inc., Memphis, 1958-73, v.p. research and tech. div., 1973—; cons. in field, 1949-58. Mem. A.A.A.S., Am. Chem. Soc., Soc. Exptl. Biology, Soc. Microbiology, Inst. Chemists. Home: 3745 S Galloway Dr Memphis TN 38111 Office: Plough Inc 3033 Jackson Av Memphis TN 38112

FEKETEKUTY, GEZA, govt. ofcl.; b. Budapest, Hungary, June 15, 1940; s. Laszlo and Margit (Von Kern) F.; A.B., Columbia, 1962; M.A., Princeton, 1964. Came to U.S., 1954. Statis. analyst Book of the Month Club, N.Y.C., 1959-62, cons., 1962-65; spl. asst. 1st Nat. City Bank of N.Y., 1965; instr. econs. Princeton, 1965-67; vis. prof. Cornell U., 1967-68; economist, budget examiner Office of Mgmt. and Budget, Exec. Office of Pres., Washington, 1968-72, sr. staff economist for internat. trade and finance Council Econ. Advisers, 1972-74, dir. policy planning and analysis office Spl. Rep. for Trade Negotiations, 1974—. Internat. Finance fellow, 1962-64. Mem. Am. Econ. Assn., Phi Beta Kappa. Editor-in-chief The Am. Economist, 1962-65. Home: 2505 I St NW Washington DC 20037 Office: Office Spl Rep Trade Negotiations Executive Office of the President Washington DC 20500

FELDMAN, ALBERT WILLIAM, educator; b. Gardner, Ill., Aug. 6, 1918; s. Joseph and Ann (Miller) F.; B.S., U. Ill., 1942; M.S., U. N.C., 1944; Ph.D., U. Minn., 1947; m. Helen Louise Taylor, July 21, 1944; children—Michael Ann (Mrs. I. W. Sieffert), William Taylor. Asst. prof. U. R.I., 1947-51; product research mgr. Uniroyal Co., 1951-58; prof. physiological pathology U. Fla., Lake Alfred, 1958—. NATO prof. U. Bari, Italy, 1969; cons. UN FAO, Philippines, 1971. Mem. Am. Phytopath. Soc., A.A.A.S., Physiology Soc., Internat. Orgn. Citrus Virologists, Sigma Xi. Elk. Patentee in field. Office: U Fla Citrus Sta Lake Alfred FL 33850

FELDMAN, ARNOLD HAROLD, dentist; b. Chgo., July 10, 1903; s. Emil and Esther (Gruenwald) F.; student Lewis Inst., 1926-27; D.D.S., Northwestern U., 1931; m. Clara Lolita Michael, May 11, 1934; children—Eleanor (Mrs. John Murphy), David, Daniel. Practice Dentistry, Chgo., 1931-41, DeKalb, Ill., 1946-50; commd. 1st lt. U.S. Army, 1941, advanced through grades to Col., 1963; presented dental clinics U.S., India, Okinawa, Germany, 1939-63; organizer Central Dental Lab. Service, CBI, 1944; cons. Ruyukus Govt., 1952-53; chief hosp. dental service, Ft. Benning, Ga., 1956-57; organized, presented Dental Sci. Health Fair, Germany, 1963; ret. 1963; pub. health dentist Ga. counties, 1964-66; dental cons. LSI Service Corp., 1966; evaluator Headstart Programs LSI Service Corp., 1966. Chmn. Service Corps Ret. Execs., Columbus, Ga., 1966-67. Decorated Army Commendation medal. Mem. Royal Soc. Health, Am. Dental Assn., Ill., Fox River Valley dental socs. Mason (32 deg.), Elk. Home: 1126 E Gore St Orlando FL 32806

FELDMAN, EDWIN BARRY, indsl. engr.; b. Atlanta, Apr. 30, 1925; s. Max Alex and Hannah (Levy) F.; B.Indsl. Engring., Ga. Inst. Tech., 1950; m. Zelda Coplan, Aug. 31, 1947; children—Lindsey Sue, Mitchell Arnold, Bryan David. Plant engr. Puritan Chem. Co., Atlanta, 1950-55, plant mgr., 1956-57, v.p., dir. engring., 1958-60; founder, pres. Service Engring. Assos., Atlanta, 1960—. Served with AUS, 1943-46. Recipient Outstanding Service award Ga. Soc. Profl. Engrs., 1967. Registered profl. engr., Ga. Mem. Am. Mgmt. Assn., Am. Inst. Indsl. Engrs., Am. Inst. Plant Engrs., Nat., Ga. socs. profl. engrs. Author: Industrial Housekeeping, 1963; How to Use Your Time to Get Things Done, 1968; Housekeeping Handbook for Institutions Business and Industry, 1969. Contbg. author Handbook of College and University Business. Contbr. articles to profl. jours. Patentee in field. Home: 1023 Burton Dr Atlanta GA 30329 Office: 3960 Peachtree Rd Atlanta GA 30319

FELDMAN, MARTIN ROBERT, educator; b. N.Y.C., Apr. 23, 1938; s. Michael I. and Ruth D. (Levitt) F.; A.B., Columbia, 1958; Ph.D., U. Cal. at Los Angeles, 1963; m. Janet Steinfeld, Dec. 20, 1959; children—Jonathan, Lisa. Postdoctoral research chemist U. Cal. at Berkeley, 1962-63; asst. prof. chemistry Howard U., Washington, 1963-68, asso. prof., 1968-71, prof., 1971—. Recipient NSF Grad. Fellowship, 1958-62, NSF Sci. Faculty Fellowship, 1969-70. Mem. Am. Chem. Soc., Sigma Xi, Phi Beta Kappa. Home: 116 Hamilton Av Silver Spring MD 20901 Office: Dept Chemistry Howard U Washington DC 20001

FELDMAN, NORMAN JOSEPH, typographer; b. Cherniachov, Russia, Aug. 15, 1907; s. Joseph and Braina (Weinerman) F.; came to U.S. 1935, naturalized 1940; student N.Y. U., 1930-31; m. Claire Ruchlin, July 13, 1935; children—Barbara Joy, Alvin Jay. Compositor, Nat. Printing Co., Toronto, Ont., Can., 1922-28; compositor, proofreader, Sumner Printing & Pub. Co., Windsor, Ont., 1933-35; proofreader Morning Telegraph, N.Y.C., 1935-36; owner Quality Printing Co. Bklyn., 1936-41; composing room foreman Bowling Green Printing Co., N.Y.C., 1941-44; asst. foreman Morris and Walsh Typesetting Co., N.Y.C., 1944-52; foreman Homestead (Fla.) News, 1952-53; dir. Monotype Composition Corp., Miami, Fla., 1953-56; owner Norman Typographic Service, Miami, 1956—; pres. Norman Typographic Service, Inc., Miami, 1962-69, chmn. bd., 1969—; dir. Alphabet Innovations Fla., Inc., AlphaSette Graphics, Inc. Mem. Advt. Typographers Assn. Am. Mason, K.P. Home: 10060 SW 213th Terrace Miami FL 33157 Office: 247 SW 17th Av Miami FL 33135

FELICIANO, HECTOR ANIBAL, physician; b. Maricao, P.R., Dec. 26, 1925; s. Lino V. and Eva R. (Rodriguez) F.; B.S., U. P.R., 1945; M.D., Hahnemann Med. Coll. of Pa., 1953; m. Nereida Mal Donado, June 6, 1946; children—Nereida, Hector, Jose. Intern San Juan (P.R.) City Hosp., 1953-54; gen. practice medicine, Rio Piedras, 1954—; clin. preceptor in family medicine U. P.R. Sch. Medicine, now asst. prof. medicine. Lay dir. Movement for Better World, Cath. Ch. Served with M.C., AUS, 1944-45. Diplomate Am. Bd. Family Practice, Nat. Bd. Med. Examiners. Mem. Alpha Omega Alpha. Rotarian. Home: 213 Rossi St Hato Rey PR 00918 Office: 1124 Vallejo St Rio Piedras PR 00925

FELIX, CHARLES JEFFREY, geologist; b. Lynch, Ky., July 2, 1921; s. Stanley and Jennie (Garland) F.; Student U. Mich., 1948; B.A., U. Tenn., 1949; M.A., Washington U., St. Louis, 1952, Ph.D. (Univ. fellow 1953-54), 1954; postgrad. So. Meth. U., 1969; m. June Ann Alsobrook, June 27, 1957; children—Linda Felix, Lisa, Charlotte. Instr. Sch. Botany, Washington U., St. Louis, 1952-53; paleobotanist, U.S. Geol. Survey, Columbus, O., 1954-56; research scientist Sun Oil Co., Dallas, 1957—, sr. geologist, 1964—. Served with USMC, 1942-46. Decorated Bronze Star medal. NSF fellow, 1954. Mem. Sigma Xi, Phi Beta Phi, Phi Kappa Phi. Republican. Mem. Ch. of Christ. Contbr. articles to profl. jours. Home: 1303 Nantucket St Richardson TX 75080 Office: PO Box 2880 Dallas TX 75221

FELIX, OTIS LEANDER, govt. ofcl.; b. Christiansted, St. Croix, V.I., Nov. 7, 1915; s. James and Sarah (Barnwell) F.; N.Y. Police Acad., 1951; Cin. Police Acad., 1955; Boston Sch. Criminology, 1962; FBI Nat. Acad., 1964; Ph.D. in Pub. Adminstrn., 1968; m. Edna Steele, Aug. 9, 1940; children—Priscilla (Mrs. Adrian Plunkett), Rita, Ramon, Otis. Mem. V.I. police dept., 1941—, chief detectives, 1949-55, chief police, 1955-62, commr. pub. safety, 1962-69, spl. asst. to commr. pub. safety Govt. V.I., 1972—. Vice-pres. Internat. Assn. Identification, V.I. Assn. Criminology. Dir. P.A.L. Served in World War II, 1945-47. Mem. A.C.S., FBI Nat. Acad. Assos. Odd Fellow. Democrat. Home: No 12 Contant St Thomas VI 00801

FELIX, SYLVANUS GEORGE, lawyer; b. Los Angeles, Feb. 25, 1910; s. Sylvanus George and Nettie (Poindexter) F.; A.B., Oklahoma City U., 1935; B.B.A., U. Okla., 1936, J.D., 1939; m. Mary Gay Lyon, June 3, 1945 (dec. 1970); children—Barbara E. (Mrs. Ralph E. Combes), Charles Sylvanus, Sylvanus George III. Admitted to Okla. bar, 1939, Tax Ct. U.S., 1940, U.S. Supreme Ct., 1946; asso. Yancey & Douglass, Oklahoma City, 1939-41; partner Felix, Bowman, McIntyre & McDivitt, and predecessor firms, Oklahoma City, 1941—, specializing in real estate, corporate law, fed. income and estate tax matters; pres. Standard Devel. Co., Inc., Park Estates Investment Co., Inc., Skyline View Land Co., Inc., Casady Heights Developers, Inc., Felix Devel. Co., Inc., Inc.; v.p. Park Estates Devel. Co., Casady Hts. Investment Co., Inc., Okla. Nat. Mortgage Co., Allied Devel. Co. Mem. Am., Okla., Oklahoma County bar assns., Nat. Assn. Home Builders (life dir.), Oklahoma City Home Builders Assn. (past pres.), C. of C. (dir.), Order of Coif, Phi Delta Phi, Kappa Alpha. Mason (Shriner, 32 deg.). Clubs: Oklahoma City Young Men's, Lawyers, Beacon, Oklahoma, Petroleum, Oklahoma City Golf and Country; Lawyers (N.Y.C.); Nat. Lawyers (Washington). Home: 1708 Kingsbury Lane Oklahoma City OK 73116 Office: City National Bank Tower Oklahoma City OK 73102

FELLER, RICHARD TABLER, cathedral adminstr.; b. Fairmont, W.Va., Mar. 14, 1919; s. Richard Roeder and Ethel (Tabler) F.; B.S. in Civil Engring., W.Va. U., 1942; m. Wilma Gertrude Stenger, June 1, 1943; children—Richard Stenger, Nancy Carol (Mrs. James M. Bogart). Supervising engr. Def. Plant Corp., Indpls., 1942-45; v.p. Huber, Hunt & Nichols, Inc., Indpls., 1945-47; gen. mgr. Richard R. Feller Co., Martinsburg, W.Va., 1947-51; engr. Ceco Steel Products Co., Washington, 1952-53; mgr. purchasing and accounting, Washington Cathedral, 1953-57, clk. of works, 1957—. Trustee Stone Cutters and Carvers Welfare Fund, 1965—; dir., treas. Frat. Housing Corp., Washington, 1952-69, exec. v.p., 1969—. Mem. Guild for Religious Architecture, Nat. Sculpture Soc. (patron mem.), Soc. Archtl. Historians, Kappa Alpha (exec. council 1961-71, nat. pres. 1971-73). Episcopalian (sr. warden). Mason. Club: Arts (bd. govs. 1969-71, v.p. 1970-71) (Washington). Author: (with Marshall W. Fishwick) For Thy Great Glory, 1965. Contbr. articles to religious periodicles. Home: 8014 Maple Ridge Rd Bethesda MD 20014 Office: Washington Cathedral Mt St Alban Washington DC 20016

FELLER, WILLIAM FRANK, med. educator; b. St. Paul, Nov. 2, 1925; s. William and Eva Caroline (Nordstrom) F.; B.A. magna cum laude, U. Minn., 1948, B.S., 1952, M.D., 1954, Ph.D., 1962; m. Margareta Helm, Sept. 5, 1964; children—William Frank III, Elizabeth Susan. Intern, U. Minn., Mpls., 1954-55, resident, 1955-60, instr. surgery 1960-62; vis. scientist Nat. Cancer Inst., Bethesda, Md., 1962-64; dir. surg. edn. Sibley Meml. Hosp., Washington, 1964-67; asst. prof. surgery Georgetown U. Med. Sch., Washington, 1964-69, asso. prof., 1969—. Served with USNR, 1944-46. Diplomate Am. Bd. Surgery. Mem. Med. Soc. D.C., Washington Acad. Surgery, Washington Med.-Surg. Soc., Southeastern Surg. Congress, N.Y. Acad. Sci., A.A.A.S., Am. Assn. Cancer Research A.C.S., Am. Scandinavian Found. (chpt. pres. 1969-71). Episcopalian. Contbr. articles to profl. jours. Home: 7028 Barkwater Ct Bethesda MD 20034 Office: 3800 Reservoir Rd NW Washington DC 20007

FELSENFELD, AMBHAN DASANEYAVAJA (MRS. OSCAR FELSENFELD), virologist; b. Dhonburi, Thailand, Oct. 8, 1922; d. Luang Trikitsayanukarn and Imm (Fakmitong) Dasaneyavaja; M.D., Siriraj Hosp. Med. Sch., Bangkok, Thailand, 1950; M.P.H., Johns Hopkins, 1955; m. Oscar Felsenfeld, July 15, 1962. Came to U.S., 1963, naturalized, 1966. Intern, Chulalongkorn Hosp., Bangkok, Thailand, 1950-51; resident, Rockefeller Inst., N.Y.C., 1959-60; instr. Chulahongkorn Hosp. Med. Sch., Bangkok, Thailand, 1955-59, asst. prof. pathology in charge virology, 1959-62; research virologist U.S. Armed Forces Inst. Pathology, Washington, 1963-65; research scientist in virology Tulane U. Research Center, Covington, La., 1965—, chief dept., 1965-71. Lectr. Tulane U., 1965-70; spl. researcher U. Ill., Urbana, 1955-56, Communicable Disease Center, Atlanta, 1956, U. Pitts. Grad. Sch., 1956-57. Recipient Grant, U.S. Army, 1961-62, Rockefeller fellow, 1959-60. Diplomate Am. Bd. Microbiology. Mem. U.S. Assn. Mil. Surgeons, A.A.A.S., Tulane U. Women's Soc. Lion. Home: 123 Magnolia Dr Covington LA 70433

FELTNER, DONALD RAY, ednl. adminstr.; b. Hazard, Ky., Aug. 31, 1933; s. Clarence E. and Dora (Feltner) F.; B.S., Eastern Ky. U., 1956, M.A., 1960; postgrad. U. Ky., intermittently 1963—; m. Marthalyn Holliday, Aug. 25, 1956; 1 son, Derek Ray. Sports corr. Louisville Courier-Jour., 1950-52; staff Eastern Ky. U., Richmond, 1956-57, dir. publicity and publs., 1959-63, coordinator pub. affairs, 1963-66, dean pub. affairs, 1966-70, v.p. pub. affairs, 1970—; adviser weekly student newspaper, univ. yearbook, 1960—. Active various community drives. Served to lt. AUS, 1957-59; capt. Ky. N.G. Named Ky. col. Mem. N.E.A., Ky. Edn. Assn., Assn. for Higher Edn., Columbia Advisers Assn., Ky. Intercollegiate Press Assn. (exec. dir.), Nat. Council Coll. Publs. Advisers (state dir. 1965-67, dist. V chmn., 1967; v.p. 1969—), Am. Coll. Pub. Relations Assn., Phi Delta Kappa. Democrat. Presbn. Club: Madison Country. Editor: Eastern Alumnus, 1961—. Contbr. articles to publs. Home: 406 Barnes Mill Rd Richmond KY 40475

FELTON, JOSEPH DURWOOD, JR., san. engr.; b. Richmond, Va., May 4, 1915; s. Joseph D. and Mary (Hatcher) F.; student Va. Poly. Inst., 1934-36; m. Dorothy D. Davidson, Mar. 14, 1942; children—Joseph Durwood III, David Bryan, Harriott E., Walter D. Prin. engr., C. & O. Ry. Co., 1947-60; self-employed as engr., Richmond, 1960-63; san. engr., U.S. Govt., Richmond, 1963—. Served with Signal Corps, AUS, 1942-46; CBI. Registered profl. engr., Va., W.Va. Mem. Am. Soc. M.E., Nat. Soc. Profl. Engrs., Water Pollution Control Assn. Mason (Shriner). Home: 10261 Maplested Lane Richmond VA 23235 Office: 701 E Franklin St Richmond VA 23219

FELTS, CORNELIUS BUFORD, JR., elevator co. exec.; b. Kansas City, Mo., Mar. 31, 1928; s. Cornelius Buford and Hazel (Vandivier) F.; B.A., U. Mo., 1950; m. Jeannine Troupe, June 7, 1948; children—William Thomas, Mary Michelle, Richard Neal. Pub. accountant Arthur Young & Co., Kansas City, 1950-57; treas., dir. Simpson, Laybourne, Miller & Stark-Colo. Grain Co., Salina, Kan., 1957-59; treas. Grain Mchts., Inc., Topeka, 1959-63; pres. Garvey Elevators, Inc., Ft. Worth, 1963—; dir. Jim Garvey Ranches, JaGee Corp., Rafter-J Ranch, Inc.; corp. officer Jim Garvey Ranches, Inc., Rafter-J Ranch, Inc. Mem. Chgo., Kansas City bds. trade, Ft. Worth Grain Exchange. Sec.-treas. Garvey Tex. Found. Served with USN, 1945-47. Mem. Am. Inst. C.P.A.'s, Financial Execs. Inst., Ft. Worth C. of C., Newcomen Soc. N.Am. Episcopalian. Mason. Clubs: Ridglea Country (Fort Worth), Colonial Country. Home: 4104 Harlanwood Dr Fort Worth TX 76109 Office: PO Box 1688 Fort Worth TX 76101

FELTS, JAMES RONE, JR., trust adminstr.; b. Charlotte, N.C., Aug. 5, 1912; s. James Rone and Alma (Query) F.; student U. N.C., 1930-32; m. Frances Isabelle Miller, Sept. 29, 1945; children—Julian (Mrs. John A. Miller, Jr.), James Rone III. With Duke Power Co., Charlotte, N.C., 1933-37; adminstrv. asst. Charlotte Meml. Hosp., 1940-41; bus. mgr. Cabarrus Meml. Hosp., Concord, 1941-42; with Duke Endowment, Charlotte, 1937-40, 45—, exec. dir. hosp. and child care sect., 1966—, asst. sec., 1961-73, trustee, 1971—. Clin. instr. hosp. adminstrn. Duke U. Med. Center, Durham, 1950—, mem. bd. visitors, 1971—. Dir. City Nat. Bank. Vice pres. United Community Services, Charlotte, 1966-68, 70—, chmn. budget bd., 1966-68; mem. Social Planning Council, Charlotte, 1968-72, chmn., 1970-72, chmn. capital funds bd., 1973—; treas. bd. pensions Western N.C. conf. United Methodist Ch., 1964—; mem. N.C. Med. Care Commn., 1969—; mem. adv. bd. Kate B. Reynolds Health Care Trust; mem. exec. com. N.C. Regional Med. Adv. Bd. Chmn., trustee Eugene M. Cole Found. Served to maj. AUS, 1942-45. Mem. Am., Southeastern, N.C., S.C. hosp. assns. Methodist (chmn. adminstrv. bd.). Rotarian. Club: Carmel Country. Home: 1534 Andover Rd Charlotte NC 28211 Office: NC Nat Bank Bldg Charlotte NC 28202

FELTS, JEAN CAROLE, real estate cons.; b. nr. Yale, Mich., Feb. 16, 1933; d. Ollie James and Jean Madeline (Dafoe) Filbeck; student U. Detroit, 1950-53, U. Chgo., 1964, U. Ga., 1967; m. Roland B. Felts, Oct. 7, 1950 (div. Sept. 1953). Statistician, Ford Motor Co., Dearborn, Mich., 1949-54; salesman Gordon Williamson Co., Detroit, 1954-57; self employed in sales, constrn. mgmt. real estate, Detroit, 1957-61; salesman, mgr., appraiser, v.p. Waguespack, Pratt, New Orleans, 1961-65; v.p., appraiser, cons. Waguespack & DuPree, Inc., New Orleans, 1965-74, Waguespack, DuPree & Felts, Inc., 1974—. Instr. real estate Delgado Coll., New Orleans, 1969-72. Mem. Nat. Assn. Real Estate Bds. (pres. woman's council New Orleans 1970), La. Realtors Assn., Real Estate Bd. New Orleans, Soc. Real Estate Appraisers, Am. Inst. Real Estate Appraisers, Soc. Real Estate Appraisers (chpt. pres. 1969), Am. Soc. Real Estate Counselors. Home: 1468 Calhoun St New Orleans LA 70118 Office: 822 Perdido St New Orleans LA 70112

FELTS, MARCUS RICHARD, cons. engr., mfg. co. exec.; b. Oakland, Fla., June 1, 1911; s. Elmer Barnett and Elizabeth Foss (Moremen) F.; student U. Fla., 1931-32, Columbia, 1942-43, N.Y. U., 1943, Coll. of Conn., 1944; m. Christine Wyatt, Oct. 18, 1952; children—Robert Walter, Nancy Kathleen. Cons. engr. Corrigan, Osborne & Wells, N.Y.C., 1944-45, Stevenson, Jordan & Harrison, Cleve., 1945, War Assets Adminstrn., Washington and Jacksonville, Fla., 1946, Felts & Assos., Atlanta, 1946—; pres., treas. Butters Mfg. Co., Atlanta, 1967—, Airport Land Enterprises, Inc., 1969—; sec.-treas. Pleasant Mobile Homes, Inc.; dir. Stone Mountain Scenic R.R., Photog. Assistance Corp. Chmn. Com. for Merger Atlanta and Fulton County, 1969; pres. Atlanta Humane Soc., 1960. Mem. Atlanta C. of C. (local affairs com. 1954-71). Baptist. Mason (32 deg., Shriner). Home: 60 Palisades Rd NE Atlanta GA 30309 Office: 338 Luckie St NW Atlanta GA 30313

FELTS, WILLIAM JOSEPH LAWRENCE, educator; b. Saginaw, Mich., Dec. 29, 1924; s. Fredrick J. and Mary T. (Regan) F.; A.B., U. Mich., 1948, M.S., 1951, Ph.D. in Anatomy, 1952; m. Anne M. Morehous, Feb. 24, 1946; children—Wayne, Anne Marie, Kurt R. Instr., Ind. U., 1951; asst. prof. Tulane U., 1952-55; asst. prof. U. Minn., 1955-60; asso. prof. 1960-65, prof., 1965-68; prof., dept. chmn. health scis., U. Okla., 1968—. Recipient Research Grants, NIH, 1955-69, NSF, 1959, 62, 70, 73. Mem. Am. Assn. Anatomists, Antarctican Soc., Am. Soc. Zoologists, Sigma Xi. Asso. editor Anatomical Record, 1969—. Home: 5713 Stonewall Dr Oklahoma City OK 73111

FENDLER, OSCAR, lawyer; b. Blytheville, Ark., Mar. 22, 1909; s. Alfred and Rae (Sattler) F.; B.A., U. Ark., 1930, LL.B., Harvard, 1933; m. Patricia Shane, Oct. 26, 1946; children—Tilden P. Wright III (stepson), Frances Shane. Admitted to Ark. bar, 1933; practice in Blytheville, 1933-41, 46—; spl. justice Ark Supreme Ct., 1965. Mem. Ark. Jud. Council, 1959-60; pres. Conf. Local Bar Assn., 1958-60; pres. bd. dirs. Ark. Law Rev., 1961-67. Mem. Miss. County Democratic Central Com., 1948—. Served with USNR, 1941-45. Fellow Am. Coll. Probate Counsel, Am. Bar Found.; mem. Am. (chmn. gen. practice sect. 1966-67, mem. council sect. gen. practice 1964—, mem. ho. of dels. 1968—, chmn. com. on law lists 1973—), Ark. (chmn. exec. com. 1956-57, pres. 1962-63) bar assns., Am. Judicature Soc. (dir. 1964-68), Nat. Conf. Bar Pres.'s (exec. council 1963-65), Blytheville C. of C. (past v.p., dir.), Navy League, Am. Legion. Rotarian (past pres.). Club: Blytheville Country. Home: 1062 W Hearn St Blytheville AR 72315 Office: 104 N 6th St Blytheville AR 72315

FENIMORE, JACK CURTIS, supt. schs.; b. Littlefield, Tex., May 31, 1933; s. Tony Barty and Ima Dean (Clark) F.; B.S., Central State Coll., Edmond, Okla., 1955; M.S., Southeastern State Coll., Durant,

Okla., 1963; Dr. Ednl. Adminstrn., Okla. State U., 1974; m. Winnie Mae DeShazo, July 7, 1952; children—Vivian Sue, Jack Curtis, Vareeda Gale. Jet mechanics instr. Amarillo (Tex.) AFB, 1955-56; tchr. math., coach Collinsville (Okla.) pub. schs., 1956-64; supt. Loyal (Okla.) pub. schs., 1964-66; supt. Drummond (Okla.) pub. schs., 1966—. Chmn. bd. control Garfield County (Okla.) Schs., 1967-70, Okla. Schs., Inc.; mem. nominating com. Okla. Athletic Hall of Fame; mem. seminar team which visited Soviet Union Schs., 1971. Mem. Okla. Edn. Assn., Am., Okla. assns. sch. adminstrs. Baptist (trustee). Home: Box 193 Drummond OK 73735

FENN, HARRY TALBOT, lawyer accountant; b. Battle Creek, Mich., Sept. 22, 1911; s. Frank Edward and Harriet Bernice (Barker) F.; B.C.S., Ga. State Coll., 1949; J.D., Woodrow Wilson Coll. Law, 1955; m. Rachael Elizabeth Grier, June 8, 1946; children—Frank S., Donald, Harriet. C.P.A., Napier & Hamrick, Atlanta, 1954-55, Harry T. Fenn, Chamblee, Ga., 1955-64, Fenn & Gordon, Chamblee, 1964—; dir. C & S Bank Chamblee, 1961—. Served with USAAC, 1942-46. C.P.A., Ga. Mem. DeKalb C. of C. (com. chmn. 1966—, dir. 1968—, v.p. 1971-72), Am. Inst. C.P.A.'s, Ga. Soc. C.P.A.'s (chpt. v.p. 1965-66), Am. (pres.-elect. Ga. chpt.), Ga. socs. attys.-C.P.A.'s, Nat. Assn. Accounting, Tax Inst. Am., Am., Ga., Atlanta bar assn. Lion (pres. 1964-65). Home: 2612 Clairmont Rd Atlanta GA 30329 Office: 2508 Carroll Av Chamblee GA 30341

FENNO, RICHARD MONTGOMERY, physician; b. Milw., Feb. 7, 1918; s. Montgomery Rae and Lillian (Weiss) F.; B.S., U. Wis., 1941, M.D., 1949; M.P.H., Johns Hopkins, 1955; m. Gratia Bettina Witter, Feb. 21, 1942; children—Laura Jean (Mrs. Laura F. Flail), Lillian Lynn (Mrs. James M. Hunt), Lani Louise (Mrs. Dennis Reid). Intern, Queen's Hosp., Honolulu, 1949-50; commd. 1st lt. U.S. Air Force, 1949, advanced through grades to lt. col., 1965, resident aerospace medicine, 1953-57; dir. air medicine Kanto (Japan), 1962-65; dir. communicable disease div. Houston Health Dept., 1965-68, Kelsey Seybold Clinic, Houston, 1968—; also dep. project mgr. occupational and aerospace medicine NASA, Houston, 1968—; mem. courtesy staff Alvin's Gulf Coast Hosp., Alvin, Tex., Clear Lake (Tex.) City Hosp., Space Center Meml. Hosp., Nassau Bay, Tex. Served with AUS, 1942-46. Decorated Purple Heart, Bronze Star medal with oak leaf cluster. Diplomate Am. Bd. Preventive Medicine. Fellow A.C.P., Am. Coll. Preventive Medicine; mem. A.M.A., Tex., Harris County med. assns. Mason. Home: Route 5 Box 426 Alvin TX 77511 Office: NASA Manned Spacecraft Center Houston TX 77058

FENTON, ALBERT B., restaurant chain exec.; b. Centerville, Ia., Mar. 11, 1934; s. A. B. and Edwyna (Payton) F.; B.A., U. Ia., 1952-56; J.D., U. Tex., 1961; m. Janey R. Birdwell, Sept. 19, 1964; children—Susan Elizabeth, Holly Elaine. Admitted to Tex. bar, 1961; asst. city atty., Dallas, 1961-65; asst. gen. counsel Diversa, Inc., holding Co., 1965-67; v.p., gen. counsel, sec., dir. Bonanza Internat., Inc., Dallas, 1967—. Served to lt. AUS, 1956-58. Mem. Am., Tex., Dallas bar assns., Naval Res. Assn. Presbyn. Elk. Home: 3410 White Hall Dr Dallas TX 75229 Office: 1000 Campbell Centre 8350 North Central Expressway Dallas TX 75206

FENTON, EDWARD A., assn. exec.; b. N.Y.C., Nov. 17, 1925; s. Philip and Rose (Poppick) F.; B.Mech. Engring., Coll. City N.Y., 1947; M.Metall. Engring., Poly. Inst. Bklyn., 1951; m. Elaine B. Schlam, June 27, 1953; children—Ellen, Eliot. Various positions in metall. field in shipbldg., r.r., oil refinery, chem. plant, aircraft industry, 1947-54; mem. staff Am. Welding Soc., Inc., N.Y.C., 1954—, tech. dir., 1957-69, exec. dir., sec., 1969—; cons. engr. industry and govt., 1959—. Author: Marks Handbook for Mechanical Engineers, 1967; Index of Standards From 23 Nations, 1968; The AWS Bibliographies, 1968. Contbr. to Book of Knowledge, Ency. Brittanica Jr., World Book, Ency. Internat., also articles to profl. jours. Home: 7190 SW 99th St Miami FL 33156 Office: 2501 NW 7th St Miami FL 33125

FENTRISS, GRAYSON GOLDZIER, ins. co. exec., lawyer; b. Danville, Va., Oct. 1, 1929; s. Robert Bernard and Janie (Thompson) F.; student George Washington U., 1947-48, 51; B.A., U. Va., 1951; J.D., William and Mary Coll., 1969; m. Joan Dorothy Copeland, Oct. 21, 1950; children—Stephen, Laurence, Cynthia. Agt., underwriter Acacia Mut. Ins. Co., Washington, 1951-53; underwriting clk. Prudential Ins. Co., Jacksonville, Fla., 1953-54, underwriting approver, 1954-55, asst. underwriter, 1955-57, life, sickness and accident underwriter, 1957-58; chief underwriter Fidelity Bankers Life Ins. Co., Richmond, Va., 1958-60; state sales mgr. Peoples-Home Life Ins. Co. Ind., 1960-64; organizer Williamsburg Life Ins. Co. (Va.), 1964, pres., 1964-67; pres. Flexibility Unitd., Inc., 1967—, Flexibility Investment Corp. Internat., 1970—. Life Underwriter's Tng. Council chmn., City of Williamsburg, 1965-67. C.L.U. Mem. Internat., Richmond (past pres.) assns. health underwriters, Am. Richmond (past ednl. chmn.) socs. C.L.U., Va., Richmond (dir.) assns. life underwriters, A.I.M. (pres.'s council), Nat. Assn. Life Ins. Cos. (v.p. 1965-68), Richmond Jr. C. of C. (sec. 1959), Am. Fedn. Police (v.p. 1971). Home: 7802 Hillview Av Richmond VA 23229 Office: 11001 Midlothian Pike Richmond VA 23235 also Penniman Rd and Wickre St Williamsburg VA 23185

FEREBEE, CLAUDE WILLIAM, JR., lawyer, trucking co. exec.; b. Vernon, Tex., July 10, 1925; s. Claude William and Anne Belle (Bennett) F.; B.B.A., So. Methodist U., 1948; J.D., Loyola U. of South, 1971; m. Dorothy Jean Smith, June 3, 1948; children—William Curtis, David Warren, Dayna. Self employed in grocery bus., 1948-58; pres., dir. Tom Hicks Transfer Co., Inc., Harvey, La., 1958—; admitted to La. bar, 1971; dir. Plaquimine Loan & Investment Co. Bd. dirs. Juliette Fowler Homes, Inc.; bd. dirs. Jefferson Plaquemine Drainage Dist. Served with USNR, 1943-46; PTO. Mem. Am., La. bar assns., La. Oilfield Haulers Assn. (past pres., dir.), Am. Trucking Assn. (past chmn. oilfield haulers div.), La. Motor Transp. Assn. (dir.), assn. ICC Practitioners, Alpha Sigma Nu. Mem. Christian Ch. (past chmn. bd., pres. Assembly of La. Assn. Christian Chs. 1973). Home: 14 Noble Dr Belle Chasse LA 70037 Office: Box 283 Harvey LA 70058

FERGUSON, ALFRED LEA, physician; b. Kingston, Tenn., Apr. 21, 1936; s. John Alfred and Ruth Lea (Patton) F.; B.S., U. Tenn., 1958, M.D., 1961; m. Mary Robinette, Apr. 4, 1964; 1 son, Alexander Lea. Intern U. Tenn. Meml. Hosp., Knoxville, 1961-62, resident, 1962-64; fellow nephrology Duke Med. Center, Durham, N.C., 1966-69; practice internal medicine and nephrology, Greenville, N.C., 1969—; mem. staff, dir. hemodialysis unit Pitt County Meml. Hosp., Greenville, 1969—; asso. clin. prof. medicine E. Caroline Sch. Medicine, Greenville, 1972—. Founder, operator Greenville Hemodialysis Center, 1972—. Mem. adv. com. to Chronic Renal Disease Div. N.C. Bd. Health, 1970—. Trustee N.C. Kidney Found. Served with USAF, 1964-66. Mem. Internat., Am. socs. nephrology, Med. Soc. N.C. Methodist (mem. adminstrv. bd. 1971-73). Rotarian (dir. 1972—), Home: 215 Dalebrook Circle Greenville NC 27834 Office: 1705 W 6th St Greenville NC 27834

FERGUSON, CHESTER HOWELL, lawyer; b. Americus, Ga., July 1, 1908; s. Sidney Hugh and Barbara (White) F.; student Mercer U., U. Ala.; LL.B., U. Fla., 1930; m. Louise Lykes, Dec. 2, 1939; children—Stella Louise, Howell Lykes. Admitted to Fla. bar, 1930; with Macfarlane, Ferguson, Allison & Kelly, predecessors, Tampa, 1930—, mem. firm, 1935—. Chmn., dir. Lykes Bros., Inc., 1945—; chmn. First Financial Corp., 1st Nat. Bank in Palm Beach; vice chmn. Lykes Youngstown Corp.; dir. First Nat. Bank of Tampa, Lykes Bros. S.S. Co., Inc., Pasco Packing Co., Knight & Wall Co., Bank of Clearwater, Kennesaw Life & Accident Ins. Co. Dir. civil def. Hillsborough County, also Gulf Coast dist. Fla., 1947-63. Trustee U. Tampa, 1950—; mem., former chmn. bd. regents Fla. State U. System. Served from 1st lt. to col., USAAF, 1942-46; asst. chief staff CBI. Decorated Air medal, Legion of Merit, Bronze Star medal, also Chinese decoration. Mem. Fla., Greater Tampa chambers commerce, Am. Legion, Air Force Assn., Mil. Order World Wars, Newcomen Soc., Am., Fla., Tampa bar assns., Am. Coll. Trial Lawyers, Internat. Ins. Counsel Assn., Maritime Law Assn., Am. Coll. Probate Counsel, Blue Key. Phi Delta Theta, Omicron Delta Kappa. Phi Delta Phi. Episcopalian (sr. warden). Rotarian. Clubs: University, Tampa Yacht and Country, Palma Ceia Golf and Country, Merrymakers, Ye Mystic Krewe of Gasparilla (Tampa). Home: 5400 Interbay Blvd Tampa FL 33611 Office: 512 Florida Av Tampa FL 33601

FERGUSON, DALE VERNON, educator; b. Tulsa, Nov. 29, 1943; s. Jack Russell and Goldie Mae (Griffin) F.; B.S., Okla. State U., 1966, M.S., 1967, Ph.D., 1970; m. Barbara Rae Davalt, Aug. 18, 1963; children—Barbara Denise, Thad Vernon. Research microbiologist Armour-Baldwin Labs., 1967-68; prof. dept. biology U. Ark., Little Rock, 1970—. Recipient Fellowship, Nat. Defense Edn. Act, 1968. Mem. Am. Soc. Microbiologists, Am. Assn. Clin. Pathologists, Ark. Acad. Scis., Mo. Valley Br. Microbiologists, Sigma Xi. Author: Basic Principles of Microbiology, 1974. Home: 10305 Milkyway St Mabelvale AR 72103 Office: 33d University Little Rock AR 72204

FERGUSON, GEORGE ROBERT, lawyer; b. Learned, Miss., Aug. 13, 1933; s. George R. and Eugenia (Williams) F.; B.S., Miss. State U., 1955; LL.B., Jackson Sch. Law, 1964; m. Martha Gillespie, July 5, 1959; children—Martha Elizabeth, George Robert, Cade Drew. Admitted to Miss. bar, 1965; sales rep. Procter & Gamble Co., 1958-60; dir. advt., pub. relations Standard Life Ins. Co., 1960-64; v.p. advt., pub. relations L. E. Davis & Assos., 1964-65; pvt. practice law, Raymond, Miss., 1965—; mem. Miss. Ho. of Reps., 1967—; owner, pub. Miss. Valley Stockman-Farmer mag., 1965—; v.p., dir. Statewide Savs. and Loan Assn., 1971-73. Mem. Miss. Classification Commn., 1970-73; chmn. Hinds County Christmas Seal campaign, 1971. Bd. dirs. Hinds County TB Assn., Jackson, Miss., 1969—. Served with AUS, 1956-58. Named among Outstanding Young Men of Am., Nat. Jr. C. of C., 1969. Mem. Am., Miss., Hinds County bar assns. Presbyn. (elder 1963—). Lion (pres. 1969-70, zone chmn. 1970-71), Mason (Shriner), Moose. Home: PO Drawer 89 Oak Street Raymond MS 39154 Office: Main St Raymond MS 39154

FERGUSON, HOWARD, mgmt. cons.; b. Bartlett, Tex., Dec. 10, 1903; s. William Simpson and Annie (Moss) F.; B.B.A., U. Tex., 1925; M.S., Syracuse U., 1927; m. Grace Elizabeth Hourihan, June 29, 1940. Asst. dir. health and welfare, Ft. Worth, 1928-29; exec. sec. Good Govt. League. Ft. Worth, 1929-30; with Griffenhagen & Assos., Chgo., 1930-57, as cons. to pub. ofcls., spl. state commns., various cities and counties, U.S. War Dept., 1942-45, Office chief of Engrs., U.S. Army, 1951, U.S. Dept. Justice, 1952; cons. on reorgn. Ky. Hwy. Dept., 1956-57, personnel adminstrn. State Ohio, 1958, suburban govt. in Milw., 1955-62; prin. cons. Jacobs Co., Chgo., 1959-73; cons. on city adminstrn. Chgo., 1960-67, city orgn. Norfolk, 1966, fiscal affairs Chattanooga-Hamilton County, 1967-68, Davenport, Ia., 1969, law enforcement planning, Ill. counties, 1969, adminstrv. improvements, Panama, 1969, police adminstrn., Birmingham, Ala., 1968, Davenport, Ia., 1969, Springfield, Ill., 1971, Owensboro, Ky., 1972, property tax assessment Va., 1973. Mem. Ill. St. Andrew Soc., Govtl. Research Assn., Am. Soc. Pub. Adminstrn., Am. Polit. Sci. Assn., Nat. Municipal League. Home: 3102 Beverly Rd Austin TX 78703

FERGUSON, JOHN CARRUTHERS, educator; b. Tuscaloosa, Ala., Mar. 2, 1937; s. John Howard and Rosalind Vera (Carruthers) F.; B.A., Duke, 1958; M.A., Cornell, 1961, Ph.D., 1963; m. Rebecca Arletta Folsom, July 15, 1961; children—Katherine, Joellyn, John. Asst. prof. biology Fla. Presbyn. Coll., St. Petersburg, 1963-67, asso. prof., 1967-72; prof. biology Eckerd Coll., St. Petersburg, 1972—. Vis. investigator Marine Biol. Lab., Woods Hole, Mass., 1962, 66, Friday Harbor (Wash.) Labs., 1970. Mem. St. Petersburg Environmental Devel. and Planning Commn., 1972—. NSF grantee, 1964-66, 66-67, 67-69, 69-70, 71-73, Bird Found. grantee, 1971. Mem. A.A.A.S., Am. Soc. Zoologists, Am. Microscopical Soc., Fla. Acad. Sci. (chmn. honors com. 1967-69, mem. exec. council 1967-69), Sigma Xi. Club: Boca Ciega Yacht (St. Petersburg). Home: 2127 Inner Circle S St Petersburg FL 33712 Office: Eckerd Coll Box 12560 St Petersburg FL 33733

FERGUSON, MALCOLM DOUGLAS, former bank; b. Marble Falls, Tex., Sept. 24, 1925; s. William Malcolm and Virginia Maude (Rowney) F.; student U. Tex., 1942-46, B.B.A., 1972; grad. Stonier Grad. Sch. Banking of Rutgers U., 1964; m. Marilyn Joyce Houston, Apr. 19, 1947. With Alamo Nat. Bank, San Antonio, 1946-49; v.p. Tex. State Bank, Austin, 1949-69; sr. v.p., dir. Univ. State Bank, Austin, 1969-71; investments, 1971—. Dir. Arts Council of Austin; treas., dir. All Faiths Chapel Corp. Mem. Robert Morris Assos., Delta Sigma Pi, Beta Alpha Psi. Methodist. Mason (Shriner). Clubs: University Area Kiwanis, Westwood Country (Austin). Home: 7602 Mesa Dr Austin TX 78731 Office: 8024 Mesa Dr Austin TX 78731

FERGUSON, THOMAS CAMPBELL, lawyer; b. Roswell, N.M., Sept. 3, 1906; s. William Marion and Martha Ann (Harvey) F.; grad. high sch.; m. Vera Elizabeth Foster, Apr. 20, 1930. Owner-editor Liberty Hill Index, 1921-23, Blanco Courier, 1923-24; pub. Burnet (Tex.) Bull., 1924-26; floor foreman, advt. mgr. Superior (Ariz.) Sun, 1926-27; dep. dist. clk. Burnet County, 1927-28; admitted to Tex. bar, 1929, U.S. Supreme Ct., 5th Circuit Ct. of Appeals, U.S. Dist. Ct.; practiced in Burnet, 1929—; city atty., Burnet, 1932-36, Marble Falls, Tex., 1930-42, 63-66; spl. counsel County of Burnet, 1932-38; atty. Home Owners Loan Corp.; atty. City of Johnson City, 1963-68. County judge Burnet County, 1945-47; dist. judge 33d Jud. Dist. Tex., 1947-60, ret.; now state jud. officer; chmn. State Bd. Ins., 1961-62; sec.-treas. Burnet Nat. Farm Loan Assn.; dir. First State Bank of Burnet, Moore State Bank of Llano (Tex.), Moursund Abstract Co., Johnson City. Mem. Burnet County Sch. Bd., 1934-41; chmn. Def. Bond sales Burnet County, 1941-42; county officer U.S.O., 1940-42; county chmn. A.R.C., 1946-47; adult scouter Boy Scout program, 1940-72. Chmn. Burnet County Democratic Com., 1928-30; mem. Tex. Ho. of Reps., 1931-32; mem. State Dem. Exec. Com. from 10th Dist., 1933-34; mayor, Burnet, 1939-43. Bd. dirs. Lower Colorado River Authority, 1935-37, 45, 65-71; chmn. adv. bd. to registrants SSS for Burnet County, 1939-47. Served with AUS, 1942-45. Mem. Am., Tex., Hill Country bar assns., Am. Judicature Soc., Tex. Heritage Found. (life), Nat., Tex. hist. assns., Washington-on-the-Brazos Park Assn., Am. Legion, 40 and 8. Mem. Christian Ch. Mason. Home: 208 E Post Oak St Burnet TX 78611 Office: P O Box 38 Burnet TX 78611

FERGUSON, WAYNE JAMES, civil engr.; b. Oklahoma City, Nov. 2, 1923; s. Mannie James and Mammie Pearl (Pulliam) F.; B.S., U. Tulsa, 1958; m. M. Marie Stansberry, Jan. 27, 1942; children—Wayne James II, Rebecca Lea, Craig Thomas. With C.E., Tulsa, 1941—, chief planning br., 1971—. Bd. dirs. Tulsa Fed. Employees Credit Union, 1962—. Served with USAF, 1943-45, 51-53. Decorated D.F.C., Air medal. Elk. Home: 4161 E 43d St Tulsa OK 74135 Office: PO Box 61 Tulsa OK 74102

FERGUSON, WILLIAM LEE, lawyer; b. Charlotte, N.C., May 19, 1937; s. Harry Mason and Lantie (Pannell) F.; A.B., Davidson Coll., 1959; J.D., U. S.C., 1967. Admitted to S.C. bar, 1967; practiced in Rockhill, 1967—; mem. firm Chiles & Ferguson, 1967-68, Spencer & Spencer, Rockhill, S.C., 1968—; asst. solicitor 16th Judicial Circuit, 1970—. Pres., York County Young Democratic Club, 1967-69. Served to capt. AUS, 1960-65. Mem. V.F.W. Elk. Home: 827 Lucas St Rockhill SC 29730 Office: Citizens & Southern Bank Bldg Main Rockhill SC 29730

FERLITA, ERNEST CHARLES, educator; b. Tampa, Fla., Dec. 1, 1927; s. Giusseppe Rosario and Vincenta Rose (Ficarrotta) F.; B.S., Spring Hill Coll., 1950; S.T.L., St. Louis U., 1964; D.F.A., Yale, 1969. Ordained priest Roman Catholic Ch., 1962; asst. prof. drama and religious studies Loyola U., New Orleans, 1969—, chmn. dept. drama and speech, 1970—, chmn. bd. dirs., 1972—. Dir. Jesuit Inst. Arts, 1973—. Served with AUS, 1945-46. Author: The Theatre of Pilgrimage, 1971. Home: 1575 Calhoun St New Orleans LA 70118

FERM, JOHN CHARLES, educator; b. East Liverpool, O., Mar. 21, 1925; s. John Ferdinand and Margaret (Kline) F.; B.S., Pa. State U., 1946, M.S., 1949, Ph.D., 1957; postgrad. U. Mich., 1948-49, U. Ill., 1949-50; m. Doris Lippincott Bye, June 19, 1949; children—Margaret Halverson, John Barclay, Carol Virginia. Instr., Pa. State U., State College, 1951-52; geologist U.S. Geol. Survey, Lexington, Ky., 1952-57; asst. prof. La. State U., Baton Rouge, 1957-62, asso. prof., 1962-67, prof., 1967-69; prof. geology U. S.C., Columbia, 1969—, dir. grad. studies, 1969-74. Mem. adv. com. Richland County Dist. Sch. Bd., 1971-72. Recipient Grants, NSF, 1962-63, 71, 72-73, AEC, 1971, U.S. Bur. Mines, 1973, Environmental Protection Agy., 1973, Westmoreland Coal Co., 1974. Mem. Geol. Soc. Am., Soc. Econ. Paleontologists, Mineralogists, Am. Assn. U. Profs., A.A.A.S., Sigma Xi. Home: 3203 Bratton St Columbia SC 29205

FERMAN, IRVING, lawyer, educator; b. N.Y.C., July 4, 1919; s. Joseph and Sadie (Stein) F.; B.S., N.Y.U., 1941; J.D., Harvard, 1948; m. Bertha Paglin, June 12, 1946; children—James Paglin, Susan Paglin. Admitted to La. bar, 1948; partner Provensal, Faris & Ferman, attys., New Orleans, 1948-52; v.p. Internat. Latex Corp., 1960-66; pres. Piedmont Theatres Corp., 1966-69; adj. asso. prof. mgmt. N.Y.U., 1964-67; prof. law Howard U. Law Sch., Washington, 1968—; vis. prof. law Am. U., 1971—; dir. Washington office Am. Civil Liberties Union, 1952-59, vice chmn. Nat. Civil Liberties Clearing House, 1952-54. Mem. citizens adv. com. U.S. Commn. on Govt. Security, 1957; vice chmn. Pres.'s Com. Govt. Contracts, 1959-60; mem. Am. Com. Cultural Freedom, 1954—, D.C. Health and Welfare Council; bd. dirs. New Orleans Acad. Art, 1948-51; mem. Com. of Arts and Scis. for Eisenhower, 1956; chmn. Washington Police Complaint Rev. Bd., 1965—; mem. Dept. Health, Edn. and Welfare Reviewing Authority, 1969—. Served from cadet to 1st lt. USAF, 1942-46. Mem. Am., La., New Orleans bar assns. Jewish religion. Clubs: Capitol Hill, International (Washington); Harvard, Caterpillar (N.Y.C.). Home: 3818 Huntington St Washington DC 20015 Office: Howard U Law Sch 6th St and Howard Pl NW Washington DC 20001

FERNALD, CHARLES EDWARD, transp. co. exec.; b. Downingtown, Pa., Sept. 28, 1902; s. Joshiah Pennell and Sophia (Weltner) F.; student mech. engring. Drexel Inst. Tech., 1921-24; student Wharton Sch., U. Pa., 1926-30; m. Gertrude Marie Connell, Oct. 17, 1936; 1 son, Charles Edward. With credit dept. Notaseme Hosiery Co., 1919-22; purchasing agt. Haslett Chute & Conveyor Co., Oaks, Pa., 1922-24; sr. partner Fernald & Co., Phila., 1924-63; sec., dir., chmn. finance com. Chem. Leaman Tank Lines, Inc., Downingtown. Active Republican Com. Past pres., trustee Credit Research Found., Inc. Served as lt. (j.g.) spl. assignments USN, USCG Res., World War II. C.P.A., Pa., N.J., N.Y., Ill. Mem. Am. Inst. C.P.A.'s, Pa., N.J., N.Y., Ill. Socs. C.P.A.'s, Nat. Assn. Credit Mgmt. (past nat. pres.). Clubs: Poor Richard, Seaview Country, Union League (Phila.); Union League (Chgo.); PGA Country (Palm Beach Gardens, Fla.). Home: 2600 N Flagler Dr West Palm Beach FL 33407 Office: 1813 Ranstead St Philadelphia PA 19103

FERNANDEZ, ALDO LINO, air conditioning co. exec.; b. Manzanillo, Cuba, Sept. 23, 1929; s. Luis and Magdalena (Soriano) F.; E.E., Havana U., 1955; m. Silvia Recio, Nov. 12, 1960; children—Aldo Luis, Silvia Maria. Came to U.S., 1960, naturalized, 1970. Project engr. Gen. Electric Cubana, S.A., Havana, 1955-60; chief engr. A. Martinez & Co., Inc., P.R., 1961-65, Dublin Engring. Co., Miami, 1965-69; pres., Economy Air Conditioning and Sheet Metal Co., Inc., Miami, 1969—, Economy Air Conditioning Service, Inc., Miami, 1969—. Registered profl. engr., Fla. Mem. Am. Soc. Heating, Refrigeration and Air Conditioning Engrs., Nat. Soc. Profl. Engrs., Fla. Engring. Soc. Club: American (Miami). Home: 9055 SW 48th Terrace Miami FL 33165 Office: 4772 SW 75th Av Miami FL 33155

FERNANDEZ, RAFAEL ANGEL, elec. engr.; b. Havana, Cuba, Mar. 10, 1926; s. Rafael Angel and Elena Laura (Adan) F.; B.S. in E.E., Havana U., 1950; M.S. in E.E., U. So. Fla., 1972; m. Marguerite E. Valdes, May 5, 1951; 1 son, Rafael E. Came to U.S., 1960, naturalized, 1971. Asst. dir. Internat. Tel. & Tel. Cuban Telephone Co., Havana, 1950-60; asst. mgr. Internat. Tel. & Tel. P.R. Telephone Co., San Juan, 1961-62; engring. supr. Gen. Telephone Co. Fla., Tampa, 1962—. Registered profl. engr., Fla. Mem. Nat. Soc. Profl. Engrs., Assn. Cuban Engrs. in Exile, Fla. Engring. Soc. (sec. Tampa chpt. 1973—). Roman Catholic. Home: 720 S Davis Blvd Tampa FL 33606 Office: 610 Morgan St Tampa FL 33601

FERNANDEZ-MARINA, RAMON, physician; b. San Juan, P.R., Sept. 16, 1909; s. Ramon and Sofia (Marina) Fernandez-Abarca; B.S., U. Madrid (Spain), 1930, M.S., 1931, M.D., 1933; m. Luz Petrovich, Aug. 31, 1941; 1 son, Ramon. Intern, San Juan City Hosp., 1933-34; St. Elizabeth's Hosp., Washington, 1945, Chestnut Lodge, Rockville, Md., 1945-47; practice medicine specializing in internal medicine, Bayamon, P.R., 1933-45, specializing in psychiatry and psychoanalysis, Santurce, P.R., 1947—; dir. State Psychiat. Hosp., Rio Piedras, P.R., 1952, P.R. Inst. Psychiatry, Bayamon, 1952—; asst. prof. psychiatry U. P.R. Sch. Medicine, 1952-57, lectr. Sch. Law, 1963-65. Television lectr. sta. WIPR, Santurce, 1961-63; instr. residents in psychiatry P.R. Inst. Psychiatry, 1956—; pres. Mountain Camp Resort, Inc., Rosario, P.R., 1956—. Trustee Camp Rosario Rehab. Center. Recipient several medals, diplomas for poetry, short stories. Diplomate Am. Bd. Psychiatry and Mental Hosp. Adminstrn. Washington Sch. Psychiatry, Washington Psychoanalytic Inst. Fellow Am. Acad. Psychoanalysis, Am. Psychiat. Assn., A.A.A.S., N.Y. Acad. Sci.; mem. Am. Psychoanalytic Assn., P.R. Med. Assn., P.R. Pub. Health Assn. (past pres.), P.R. Psychiat. Sect. (past pres.), Argentine Child and Adolescents Psychiat. Assn. (hon.). Clubs: Caparra Country, Yacht (San Juan). Author (with Ursula von Eckardt) The Horizons of the Mind, 1965; The Sober Generation,

1968; also articles. Patentee diving mask. Home: Box 789 Hato Rey PR 00919 Office: Profl Bldg Santurce PR 00909

FERNANDEZ-MARTINEZ, JOSE, physician; b. San Juan, P.R., Apr. 17, 1930; s. Telesforo and Luisa (Martinez) F.; B.S., Villanova (Pa.) U., 1951; M.D., U. Pa., 1955; m. Carmen Dolores Noya, Dec. 26, 1954. Intern, Hosp. U. Pa., 1955-56, resident internal medicine, 1956-59, fellow in hypertension and cardiovascular diseases, 1956-57; pvt. practice medicine, specializing in internal medicine and cardiovascular diseases, Santurce, P.R., 1961—; attending in internal medicine San Juan City Hosp., 1961—. Served to capt. U.S. Army, 1959-61. Diplomate Am. Bd. Internal Medicine, also splty. cardiovascular diseases. Fellow A.C.P.; asso. fellow Am. Coll. Cardiology; mem. P.R. Med. Assn. (pres. sci. council 1968). Home: 54 King's Ct Santurce PR 00911 Office: Ashford Med Center Ashford and Washington Sts Santurce PR 00907

FERNANE, JAMES, electronics engr.; b. Worcester, Mass., Dec. 11, 1917; s. Garrett Marthimore and Susan Elizabeth (Crowley) F.; E.E., Worcester Poly. Inst., 1942. With FCC, Washington, 1942—, sr. coordinating engr. emergency broadcast system planning, 1957-64, chief communication systems br. Emergency Communications Div., 1973—. Served with USNR, 1944-46. Registered profl. engr., Tex. Mem. I.E.E.E. (sr. mem.), V.F.W., Am. Legion, Am. Radio Relay League, Quarter-Century Wireless Assn. Roman Catholic. K.C., Elk. Home: PO Box 19174 Washington DC 20036 Office: FCC Washington DC 20554

FERRAN, HARRY AVERY, mech. engr.; b. Orlando, Fla., Nov. 28, 1936; s. Edgar Loraine and Laura Fair (Morrow) F.; B.Mech. Engring., U. Fla., 1964; 1 son, Robert Clark. Field sales engr. Trane Co., 1964-67; owner, pres. Ferran Air Conditioning Co., 1967-69, Ward Air Conditioning Co., Orlando, Fla., 1967—, Harry A. Ferran & Assos., cons. engrs., Orlando, Fla., 1969—, Avtech Corp., Orlando, Fla., 1971—. Tchr. vocational courses Orange County Sch. System, 1971-72. Served with USNR, 1956-59. Registered profl. engr., Fla. Mem. Nat. Soc. Profl. Engrs., Fla. Engring. Soc., Refrigeration Service Engrs. Soc., Am. Soc. Heating, Refrigeration and Air Conditioning Engrs., Assn. Bldg. Contractors, Exptl. Aircraft Assn., Antique Aircraft Assn., Air Force Assn., Orlando C. of C. (dir. 1970-73). Democrat. Presbyn. Clubs: Country (mem. membership com. 1972-73), University Cypress Creek Country (Orlando, Fla.). Home: 5228 Cypress Creek Dr Orlando FL 32805 Office: 530 Grand St Orlando FL 32805

FERRARACCIO, FRANCISCO PAOLO, assn. exec.; b. Du Bois, Pa., Jan. 1, 1923; s. Biagio and Grace (DePalma) F.; B.S., Allegheny Coll., 1949, postgrad. econs., 1950; M.B.A., George Washington U., 1960; m. Margaret Louise McCrory, Aug. 27, 1949; children—Blaise Edward, Francis Paul, Christopher Michael. Adminstr. George Washington U. Hosp., Washington, 1950-65; adminstr. Cafritz Hosp., Washington, 1965-68; adminstr. Univ. Clinics George Washington U. Med. Center, Washington, 1968-71; exec. dir. Med. Soc. D.C., 1971—; cons. in field. Exec. bd. dirs. Nat. Capital Med. Care Found.; trustee Med. Service D.C., Nat. Arthritis and Rheumatism Assn. Served with USAAF, 1942-46. Decorated D.F.C., Air medal. Mem. Am. Coll. Hosp. Adminstrs., Am. Assn. Soc. Execs., Am. Hosp. Assn., Phi Delta Theta. Home: 1723 Evelyn Dr Rockville MD 20852 Office: 2007 Eye St NW Washington DC 20006

FERRE, GEORGE FRANS, physician; b. Malmberget, Sweden, Apr. 26, 1904; came to U.S., 1919, naturalized, 1925; s. Frans A. and Maria (Wickman) F.; Th.B., Bethel Theol. Sem., 1923; M.D., Boston U., 1931; postgraduate work in surgery, Vienna, Austria and Stockholm, Sweden, 1937; m. Elna Dagmar Peterson, Aug. 3, 1929; children—Barbara (Mrs. Marion Phillips), George Allen, Paul Gordon. Dir. edn. N.E. Conf. Bapt. Ch., 1923-25; ordained to ministry, Bapt. Ch., 1925; pastor First Ch., Canton, Miss., 1925-27; pastor, Swedish Temple, Boston, 1927-31; intern, resident in surgery Queens Hosp., Honolulu, 1931-33; plantation physician Hamakau Coast, Hawaii, 1934-36; practice gen. surgery, Manchester, N.H., 1938-41, Miami, Fla., 1945-70; surg. cons. Munroe Meml. Gen. Hosp., Ocala, Fla., 1970—. Owner cattle ranch, registered cattle, Ocala, Fla. Trustee Miami Bapt. Hosp., Inc. Served as lt. M.C., AUS, 1939-41; as lt. comdr. M.C., USNR, 1942-45. Mem. Internat. Coll. Surgeons (past regent, mem. bd. govs. 1955—), Am., Fla., Miami med. assns., Mil. Order World Wars, Ry. Physicians Assn. and others. Bapt. Mason (K.T., 32 deg., Shriner), Kiwanian (past pres. Miami Shores). Home: Silver Acres Ranch Route 1 Box 46 Fort McCoy FL 32637

FERRE, JOSE A(NTONIO), corp. ofcl.; b. Ponce, P.R., Sept. 13, 1902; s. Antonio and Mary Aguayo (Casais) F.; B.B.A., Boston U., 1924; M.B.A., U. Miami, 1955; m. Patricia Christensen; children—Maurice, Mary Ann, Jo, Noel, Jose, Emile Christina. Salesman P.R. Iron Works, Inc., 1924-34, v.p., 1934—; exec. v.p. Ponce Cement Corp., 1941—; co-chmn. Puerto Rican Cement Co., Inc.; pres. P.R. Marine Corp., Pan Am. Investment, Inc., P.R. Cement Corp., Cementos Nacionales, S.A., P.R. Drydock & Marine Terminal, Ponce Products, Inc., 1947—; v.p. P.R. Glass Corp., P.R. Clay Corp., P.R. Paper & Pulp Corp., Ferre Export Corp., N.Y.C., 1947—; chmn. Maule Industries, Inc., Miami, Fla., 1956—. Adviser P.R. delegation Caribbean Commn., 1952; hon. consul for Brazil, San Juan, P.R. Pres. Ponce Harbor Bd., 1937-38. Chmn. A.R.C., Ponce, 1943; pres. finance com. Cath. U. P.R.; pres. bd. trustees Dr. Phila.'s Hosp., Ponce, 1955-57; pres. Cancer Hosp. Bldg., Com., San Juan. Trustee Boston U., Pan Am. Hosp., Miami, U. Miami, Catholic U. P.R. Mem. Navy League. Elk, Rotarian. Club: Athletic, Advertising (N.Y.C.); Yacht (Havana, San Juan, Miami); Bankers; Surf; La Gorce. Home: PO Box 1349 Ponce PR 00731

FERRE, MAURICE ANTONIO, mayor Miami; b. Ponce, P.R., June 23, 1935; s. Jose Antonio and Florence (Salichs) F.; grad. Lawrenceville (N.J.) Sch., 1953; B.S. in Archtl. Engring., U. Miami (Fla.), 1957; m. Maria Mercedes Malaussena, Aug. 25, 1955; children—Mary Isabel, Jose Luis, Carlos Maurice, Maurice Raimundo, Francisco, Florence. Pres. Ferre Florida Corp., cement quarrying, Miami, 1960-64, v.p., 1964—; sr. v.p. Maule Industries, Inc., mfr. bldg. materials, Miami, 1961-63, pres., 1963—; mayor Miami, 1974—; dir. P.R. Cement Co., Inc., Empresas Ferre, 1st Nat. Bank of Miami. Mem. Fla. Ho. of Reps., 1967; mem. Miami City Commn., 1967-70; interim mayor, 1973. Chmn. bldg. and constrn. div. Miami United Fund, 1964, trustee; 1st v.p. Miami Com. 21; vice chmn. Inter-Am. Center Authority; mem. Fla. Council of 100 Coll., Miami, Lawrenceville Sch.; bd. dirs. Miami Heart Inst., Community TV Found. S. Fla. Recipient Silver Medallion Nat. Conf. Christians and Jews, 1968; Man of Year award Miami Jaycees, 1968, Outstanding Young Man of Miami, 1970; named Democrat of Year Young Democratic Club Fla., 1969. Mem. Econ. Soc. S. Fla., Miami-Dade County C. of C. (dir.), Young Pres. Orgn. Home: 1643 Brickell Av Miami FL 33129 Office: Office of Mayor City Hall Miami FL

FERRELL, HENRY HASKINS JR., physician; b. Danville, Va., Mar. 4, 1915; s. Henry Haskins and Pattie (Smith) F.; M.D., U. Va., 1940; m. Joan Jamieson Cotter, May 20, 1944; children—Leslie C., Henry Haskins III, Joan P. Intern, resident C.W. Long Hosp., Atlanta, 1940-42, 46-47; practice medicine, specializing in obstetrics and gynecology, Alexandria, Va., 1947—; mem. staff Circle Terrace Hosp., Alexandria, also pres. bd. dirs., 1955—; staff Arlington (Va.) Hosp., Fairfax Hosp., Falls Church, Va.; chief dept. obstetrics and gynecology Alexandria Hosp., 1969-71, chief of staff, 1973; dir. Alexandria Med. Center, Inc. Mem. Friendship Vets. Fire Engine Co., 1965—. Bd. govs. St. Stephens Sch., Alexandria. Served to capt. 28th Inf. Div., AUS, 1942-45. Decorated Bronze Star medal; Croix de Guerre (Luxembourg). Fellow A.C.S.; mem. Alexandria Med. Soc. (pres. 1956-57), No. Va. Obstet. Soc. (pres. 1961), Med. Soc. Va., A.M.A., So. Med. Assn., Royal Soc. Medicine (London), Soc. Colonial Wars D.C., Chi Phi. Episcopalian. Home: 511 Cathedral Dr Alexandria VA 22314 Office: 312 S Washington St Alexandria VA 22314

FERRELL, ORVILLE LEE, hosp. adminstr.; b. Glenalum, W.Va., Mar. 31, 1921; s. Willie and Ava (Carter) F.; student N.C. State U., 1946, Hardbarger Bus. Coll., 1946-47; A.B., Marshall U., 1950; m. Rachel May, Mar. 29, 1945; children—Richard Daniel, William James, Robert Gordon. With Williams & Wall, C.P.A.'s, 1947-49, N.C. Med. Care Commn., 1950-51; asst. adminstr. St. Agnes Hosp., 1951-53, Rowan Meml. Hosp., 1953-58; adminstr. Cherokee County Meml. Hosp., Gaffney, S.C., 1958-61, Meml. Hosp., Waycross, Ga., 1961-69, Riverside Nursing Home, Waycross, 1965-69, Ormond Beach (Fla.) Meml. Hosp., 1969-72, Baldwin County Hosp., Milledgeville, Ga., 1972-73; adminstr. Tifton (Ga.) Gen. Hosp., 1973—. Instr. Waycross (Ga.) Ware Vocational Tech. Sch., 1968—, Daytona Beach (Fla.) Community Coll., 1970; vice chmn. Comprehensive Psycho-Ednl. Services, 1973-74; cons. adminstrn. Southeast council Ga. Hosp. Assn., 1967—. Chmn. Waycross chpt. Am. Cancer Soc., 1968—; bd. dirs. Mental Health Assn., Waycross, United Fund, Waycross. Served to lt. USNR, 1942-46. Fellow Am. Coll. Hosp. Adminstrs.; mem. Ga. Hosp. Assn. (sec.-treas. southwest council 1973-74), Southwest Comprehensive Health Planning Assn. Methodist. Rotarian. Home: 301 Fulwool Blvd Tifton GA 31794

FERRER, EDWIN, architect; b. N.Y.C., Dec. 2, 1928; s. Juan and Rosaura (Lopez) F.; B.S., U. Houston, 1957, B.Arch., 1958; m. Nadene Joan Reinders, Oct. 18, 1961; children—Andrea. Designer, project architect Rustay, Martin & Vale, Houston, 1962-69; project architect Neuhaus & Taylor, Houston, 1969-71, Wyatt C. Hedrick, Houston, 1971-72, Koetter, Tharp & Cowell, Houston, 1973—. Served with AUS, 1946-48. Mem. A.I.A., Tex. Soc. Architects. Home: 3231 Purdue St Houston TX 77005 Office: 1535 W Loop S Houston TX 77027

FERRIE, GEORGE ROBERT, radio broadcasting co. exec.; b. Spirit Lake, Ia., Oct. 11, 1919; s. Clem J. and Bertha Jane (Liddle) F.; B.A., U. Ia., 1941; m. Margaret Louise Weiss, Nov. 20, 1948; children—Louise Marie (Mrs. Douglas Allan Rose), George, Brian. News editor WOI, Ia. State Coll., Ames, 1943-44; announcer, newscaster KABC, San Antonio, 1945-48; newscaster KITE, 1948-61, KONO, 1961-63; news editor KITE, San Antonio, 1963—. Tchr. radio news Trinity U., 1970-71; pub. relations cons. Minnie Stevens Piper Found., San Antonio, 1971—. Mem. Sigma Delta Chi, San Antonio Media Club. Presbyn. (deacon 1968-70, 72—). Mason, Kiwanian. Club: Lost Valley Country (Bandera, Tex.). Home: 403 Hillwood Dr San Antonio TX 78213 Office: 8400 Data Point Dr San Antonio TX 78229

FERRIN, ROBERT WAYNE, constrn. co. exec.; b. Oklahoma City, Apr. 20, 1931; s. Horace Harlan and Lorene Lovinia (Richardson) F.; student U. Okla., 1949-53, Okla. A. and M. U., 1950, Oklahoma City U. Law Sch., 1954, West Tex. State U., 1957; m. Koletyo Belvin, Oct. 8, 1954; children—Robert Sterling, Stephen Craig. With Southwestern Pub. Service Co., Amarillo, Tex., 1956-59; owner Bob Ferrin Constrn. Co., Amarillo, 1959—; pres. Ferrin Enterprises, Inc., Ferrin-Standefer Co.; chmn. bd., dir. 1st Nat. Bank, Rhome, Tex. Pres. Tex. Panhandle Home Builders Assn., 1964. Served with AUS, 1954-56. Recipient Honor Man award USN, 1952. Methodist. Home: 3200 Hawthorne St Amarillo TX 79109 Office: 3213 Western St Amarillo TX 79109

FERRIS, FREDERICK JOSEPH, social work adminstr.; b. Troy, N.Y., June 2, 1920; s. John and Amelia (Deeb) F.; B.A. cum laude, State U. N.Y. at Albany, 1942; M.S., Columbia, 1949, D.S.W., 1968; m. Ellen J. Walsh, June 12, 1965. Head social studies dept. Heatly High Sch., Green Island, N.Y., 1946-47; sec. Information Service, Greater N.Y. Fund, N.Y.C., 1949-51; exec. sec. N. Met. div. United Community Services, Boston, 1951-53, mem. Research div. com., 1953-57; dir. community orgn., asst. prof. Boston Coll. Sch. Social Work, 1953-57; dean, prof. Nat. Catholic Sch. Social Service, Catholic U. Am. 1960-69; asso. dir. planning and research Am. Assn. Ret. Persons and Nat. Ret. Tchrs. Assn. 1972—, A.A.R.P.-N.R.T.A. coordinator White House Conf. on Aging, 1970—. Adj. asso. prof. Fordham U. Sch. Social Service, 1957-60; lectr. Adelphi and Rutgers univs., 1959-60; social planning cons. Am. Found. for Blind, 1958-59; cons. Inst. Community Studies, United Way Am., 1970-71, Psychiat. Inst. Found., 1970. Del. White House Conf. on Aging, 1971; mem. commn. on services to aging Archdiocese of Washington, 1971—; vice chmn. Joint Legislative Com., Boston, 1954-57; mem. exec. com. Nat. Steering Com. Vol. Orgns., 1972—; mem. commn. on aging Nat. Conf. Cath. Charities, 1972—. Bd. dirs. Social Service Exchange, Boston, 1955-57, Child Welfare League Am., 1966-70, Cath. Internat. Union Social Service, 1967—, Christ Child Soc. Washington, 1967—; treas., bd. dirs. Nat. Conf. Catholic Charities, 1971—. Chmn. Washington com. 13th Internat. Conf. Schs. Social Work, 1965-66. Served from pvt. to capt. AUS, 1942-46. Recipient Lasker Doctoral fellowship Columbia, 1957-58. Mem. Nat. (chpt. treas. 1956-57, task force on services to aging 1973—, Am. (chmn. div. pub. policy and social work, exec. com. 1953-55) assns. social workers, Mass. Conf. Social Work (bd. dirs., chmn. nominating com. 1956-57), Am. Acad. Polit. and Social Sci., Alumni Assn. Columbia U. Sch. Social Work (chpt. chmn. 1954-55, dir. 1956-59), United Community Funds and Councils Am. (nat. adv. com. health and welfare services 1955-57, council planning execs. 1957-59), Nat. Assn. Hearing and Speech Agys. (nat. tng. adv. com. 1963-70), Acad. Certified Social Workers, Council Social Work Edn. (deans adv. com. fed. welfare agys. 1962-64, 66-68), Nat. Conf. Social Welfare, Social Welfare History Group, Nat. Council on Aging, Gerontological Soc. Home: 5101 River Rd Washington DC 20016

FERRISS, ABBOTT LAMOYNE, sociologist; b. Jonestown, Miss., Jan. 31, 1915; s. Alfred William O. and Grace Childs (Mitchell) F.; B.J., U. Mo., 1937; M.A., U. N.C., 1943, Ph.D., 1950; m. Ruth Elizabeth Sparks, Dec. 21, 1940; children—John Abbott, William Thomas. Lectr. Berea Coll., 1946; asst. prof. Vanderbilt U., 1949-51; chief human relations div. Air Force Human Resources Research Inst., 1951-54; chief orgn. effectiveness br. Air Force Personnel and Training Research Center, 1954-57; chief health statistics br. Census Bur., 1957-59; statistician, Outdoor Recreation Resources Review Commn., 1959-62; asso. study dir. NSF, 1962-67; research sociologist social indicator project Russell Sage Found., 1967-70; prof., chmn. dept. sociology and anthropology Emory U., Atlanta, 1970—. Cons. RANN program NSF, 1971—; exec. dir. Southeastern Social Scientists, Inc., 1970—; part time instr. U. N.C., 1948-49, George Washington U., 1957-58, U. Md., 1958-59, N. Va. Center, U. Va., 1959-70. Served with USAAF, 1943-46. Mem. Internat. Union Sci. Study Population, Sociol. Research Assn., Am. Statis. Assn., A.A.A.S., Population Assn. Am. (sec.-treas. 1968-71, dir. 1971-72), So. Regional Demographic Group, So. (v.p. 1966-67), D.C. (pres. 1969-70) sociol. socs., Sigma Alpha Epsilon, Phi Eta Sigma. Club: Cosmos (Washington). Author: Indicators of Trends in the Status of American Women, 1971; Indicators of Trends in American Education, 1969; Indicators of Change in the American Family, 1970; National Recreation Survey, 1962. Editor: Research and the 1970 Census, 1971. Contbr. articles to profl. jours. Home: 1273 Oxford Rd NE Atlanta GA 30306

FERSTER, CHARLES BOHRIS, educator; b. Freehold, N.J., Nov. 1, 1922; s. Julius B. and Mollie M. (Madwin) F.; B.S., Rutgers U., 1947; M.A., Columbia, 1948, Ph.D., 1950; m. Elyce Zenoff, May 16, 1964; children—William, Andrea, Sam, Warren. Research fellow Harvard, 1950-55; research scientist Yerkes Lab. Primate Biology, Orange Park, Fla., 1955-57; asso. prof. dept. psychiatry Inst. for Psychol. Research, Ind. U. Sch. Medicine, Indpls., 1957-62; research scientist, exec. dir. Inst. for Behavioral Research, Silver Spring, Md., 1962-66; prof. Georgetown U., Washington, 1966-68; prof., chmn. psychology dept., dir. Univ. Learning Center, Am. U., Washington, 1968—. Served with USAAF, 1943-46. Editor: Schedules of Reinforcement (B.F. Skinner), 1957; Behavior Principles (M.C. Perrott), 1968. Editor Jour. Exptl. Analysis of Behavior, 1958-61. Home: 4708 Linnean Av NW Washington DC 20008

FERTL, WALTER HANS, petroleum engr.; b. Vienna, Austria, Mar. 16, 1940; s. Johann and Anna (Schiegl) F.; Dipl. Ing., U. Mining and Metallurgy, Austria, 1963; Dr. mont., 1971; M.S., U. Tex., 1966, Ph.D., 1968; m. Irma Ilse Szabo, May 11, 1965; children—Dagmar, Tania. Came to U.S., 1965, naturalized, 1970. Asst. mgr. Austrian Petroleum Co., Austria, 1963-65; grader, dept. petroleum enging. U. Tex., Austin, 1967-68; sr. research scientist Continental Oil Co., Ponca City, Okla., 1968—. Lectr., U. Zulia, Maracaibo, Venezuela, 1967, 73, U. Tex. Engring. Found., 1967-72, U. Mining and Metallurgy, Austria, 1971, Tech. U. Istanbul (Turkey), 1971, Geophys. Soc., Budapest, Hungary, 1971, Royal Ministry Industry, Oslo, Norway, 1971. Registered profl. engr., Okla. Mem. Am. Inst. Mining, Metall. and Petroleum Engrs. (mem. tech. com. 1972), Soc. Exploration Geophysicists, Soc. Canadian Well Log Analysts, Soc. Profl. Well Log Analysts (1st v.p. Tulsa chpt. 1972, dir. overseas activities 1972), Sigma Xi, Phi Kappa Phi, Pi Epsilon Tau. Kiwanian. Contbr. articles to profl. jours. Patentee in field. Home: 3235 Whippoorwill St Ponca City OK 74601 Office: Drawer 1267 Ponca City OK 74601

FESHBACH, MURRAY, economist; b. N.Y.C., Aug. 8, 1929; s. Benjamin and Lilly (Harfenist) F.; A.B., Syracuse U., 1950; M.A., Columbia, 1951; Ph.D., Am. U., 1974; m. Muriel Joan Schreiner, Dec. 30, 1956; children—Michael L., David S. Research asst. Nat. Bur. Econ. Research, N.Y.C., 1955-56; analyst fgn. demographic analysis div. Bur. Census, 1957-67, chief USSR br., 1967-68, chief USSR/East Europe br., 1969-72; supervisory economist, chief USSR/East Europe br., fgn. demographic analysis div. Bur. Econ. Analysis, Washington, 1972—. Research asso., bibliog. cons. NSF projects, 1963-71; guest lectr. Indsl. Coll. Armed Forces, 1962-71, Am. U., 1968, Syracuse U., 1970, Pa. U., 1971, George Washington U., 1973; mem. Fgn. Area Research Coordination Group, USSR and Eastern Europe subcom., U.S. Dept. State, 1969—. Served with AUS, 1951-55. Mem. Am. Econ. Assn., Assn. for Study Soviet-Type Econs. (mem. exec. com. 1970-71), Am. Assn. Advancement Slavic Studies (mem. nat. bibliog. and documentation com. 1971—), Omicron Delta Epsilon. Author: Manpower in the USSR, U.S. Congress Joint Econ. Com., New Directions in the Soviet Economy, 1966; (with others) Labor Constraints in the Five-Year Plan, 1973. Contbr. articles to profl. jours. Home: 11403 Fairoak Dr Silver Spring MD 20902 Office: FDAD 24M Annex Dept Commerce Washington DC 20230

FESMIRE, FRANCIS MILLER, physician; b. Baxter, Tenn., July 21, 1933; s. William J. and Eulu (Hoy) F.; student U. of South, 1951-53; M.D., U. Tenn., 1957; postgrad. Oak Ridge Inst. Nuclear Studies, 1959; m. Carolyn Block, Nov. 9, 1957; children—Carolyn Lee, Francis Miller, Mary Ann. Intern, U. Ala. Hosp., 1957; resident 3d U.S. Army Med. Lab., 1958-61; trainee in clin. pathology Kennedy VA Hosp., Memphis, 1962-64; asst. pathologist Meth. Hosp., Memphis, 1964; pathologist Rutherford Hosp., Murfreesboro, Tenn., 1964-71; asso. pathologist Baroness Erlanger Hosp., Chattanooga, 1971—. Mem. adv. com. Tenn. Mid-S. Regional Med. Program, 1968—. Bd. dirs. Nat. Regional Red Cross Center, Nashville. Served to capt. M.C., AUS, 1958-61. Diplomate in anatomical and clin. pathology Am. Bd. Pathology. Fellow Coll. Am. Pathology, Am. Assn. Clin. Pathology; mem. Am. Assn. Blood Banks, Am. Nuclear Soc., A.M.A., Alpha Tau Omega. Methodist (mem. ofcl. bd.). Rotarian. Contbr. articles to med. jours. Home: 13 Fairhills Dr Chattanooga TN 37403 Office: Erlanger Hospital Chattanooga TN 37403

FESMIRE, HAROLD LUNN, banker; b. Lexington, Tenn., Mar. 1, 1929; s. Thompsie Wesley and Pauline (Lunn) F.; student Okaloosa Walton Jr. Coll., 1961; m. Eva Ruth Jones, May 19, 1950; 1 dau., Sharon Lynn. Dep. sheriff, counselor Juvenile Ct., Okaloosa County, Fla., 1956-59; owner A & W Root Beer franchise, 1957-71; dir. 1st Nat. Bank, Ft. Walton Beach, Fla., 1964—; adv. council A & W Corp., 1966-69. Co-sponsor Jamaica Mission Program, Isle of Jamaica, 1971. Bd. dirs. Mental Health Assn. Okaloosa County, 1961, Ala. Christian Coll., Wiregrass Youth Camp, Enterprise, Ala.; bd. dirs., officer Okaloosa div. West Fla. Heart Assn. Served with USNR, 1950-52. Mem. Ft. Walton Beach C. of C. Mem. Ch. of Christ (deacon, treas.). Home: 583 Mooney Rd Fort Walton Beach FL 32548 Office: 55 Eglin Pkwy Fort Walton Beach FL 32548

FESTA, SALVATORE ANTONIO, ednl. adminstr.; b. Vineland, N.J., Nov. 23, 1921; s. Anthony Joseph and Mary Anna (Tomasello) F.; A.B., Elon Coll., 1943; M.Ed., U. N.C., Greensboro, 1953; postgrad. Duke, 1960, U. N.C., Chapel Hill, 1965; m. Helen Deanne Yarborough, Oct. 18, 1947; children—Anita Marie, Donna Cecilia, Carmella Anne. Purchase service clk., expeditor Western Electric Co., Burlington, N.C., 1946-50, tech. asst. engr., summers 1956-57; sci. instr. Bessemer High Sch., Guilford County, N.C., 1950-53; prin. Brightwood Elementary Sch., 1953-55; dir. pub. relations audio-visual and sci. Burlington (N.C.) city schs., 1955-62; prin. Broad St. Jr. High Sch., 1962-66, dir. instructional materials services, 1966—. Night prin. Tech. Inst. of Alamance, 1958-60, speed reading instr., 1960-61; speed reading instr. Forsyth Tech. Inst., 1961; vis. instr. U. N.C., Greensboro, 1967, 69; tchr. grad. courses in extension U. N.C., 1966-70, U. Va., 1968-71; mem. Almanance County Human Relations Council, 1972—; instr. Media Inst. for N.C. Dept. Pub. Instrn. at Burlington, summer 1970; cons. Durham County Schs., Audio-Visual Workshop, 1967, Montgomery County Schs., Audio-Visual Workshop, Troy, N.C., 1969, State Adv. Council on Tchr. Edn.; mem. adv. coms. N.C. Dept. Pub. Instrn. NDEA-Audio-Visual and Sci. Civil def. coordinator, 1955-60; mem.-at-large Alamance County Community Council, 1955—; mem. Burlington City Traffic Commn., 1973—; capt. United Fund, 1971—; instnl. rep. Boy Scouts Am., 1966—, leadership tng. chmn. dist. com., 1968—; pub. relations chmn., treas. Parents League, 1965; mem. alumni exec. com. Elon Coll., 1968-70. Precinct del. State Conv. Democratic party, 1964.

Served with Med. Dept., AUS, 1943-46. Mem. N.E.A. (life), N.C. Assn. Edn. (pres. ednl. media assn. 1972—), Am. Assn. Sch. Adminstrs., Assn. for Ednl. Communications and Tech. (dir. 1959-60, state legislative chmn. 1971—), N.C. Acad. Sci. (pres. Guilford County sci. com. 1950-53), N.C. Dept. Audio-Visual Edn. (pres. 1959-60). Roman Catholic. K.C. (master 1972-74), Moose. Home: 2914 Amherst Av Burlington NC 27215 Office: 217 Union Av Burlington NC 27215

FETTER, BERNARD FRANK, educator; b. Balt., Jan. 21, 1921; s. Joseph William and Elizabeth Madelin (Levy) F.; A.B., Johns Hopkins, 1941; M.D., Duke, 1944; m. Anna Lee Hinton, Mar. 12, 1945; children—Kathryn, Richard, Edward, Mary. Intern, Duke Hosp., Durham, N.C., 1944-45, resident, 1951-53; resident, Vets. Adminstrn. Hosp., Ft. Howard, Md., 1947-48; mem. staff Duke U. Med. Center; instr., Duke U. Sch. Medicine, Durham, N.C., 1951-53, asst. prof., 1955-59, asso. prof., 1957-67, prof. pathology, 1967—. Cons. VA Hosp., Durham, N.C., 1960—, Watts Hosp., Durham, N.C., 1962—, Womack Army Hosp., Ft. Bragg, N.C., 1958—. Served to capt., M.C., AUS, 1945-47. Recipient Golden Apple award Student Am. Med. Assn., 1970. Mem. A.M.A., Am. Soc. Dermatology, Coll. Am. Pathologists, Am. Soc. Clin. Pathologists, Am. Acad. Dermatopathlogy, Alpha Omega Alpha. Home: 3836 Somerset Dr Durham NC 27707

FETTER, WILLIAM HUTCHINSON, oil refining co. exec.; b. Jenkintown, Pa., Dec. 1, 1916; s. A. Leroy and Elizabeth H. (Smith) F.; B.S., Pa. State U., 1938; m. Jean C. Agster, Aug. 6, 1940; children—Lee (Mrs. Lee Anderson), Sally (Mrs. John Winslow), Lynn (Mrs. Dudley Smith). With Atlantic Oil Co., Phila., 1938-39; mgr. petroleum Pa. Farm Bur., Harrisburg, 1939-51; pres. Texas City Refining, Inc. (Tex.), 1951—; dir. Bank of the Mainland, LaMarque, Tex. Bd. dirs. United Fund, Region IV Ednl. Service, Galveston County Research Council; past pres. bd. trustees LaMarque Ind. Sch. Dist. Served with AUS, 1942-44. Recipient certificate of merit LaMarque Pub. Schs., 1966, Distinguished Service award LaMarque Jr. C. of C., 1970; named Sr. Citizen of LaMarque, 1970. Registered profl. engr., Tex., Pa. Mem. Nat. Petroleum Refiners Assn., Am. Petroleum Inst., Texas City/LaMarque C. of C. (v.p.), Sigma Alpha Epsilon. Presbyn. (trustee, pres.). Home: 2215 Carriage Lane LaMarque TX 77568 Office: Box 1271 Texas City TX 77590

FETTERMAN, JOHN, journalist; b. Danville, Ky., Feb. 25, 1920; s. John Lawrence and Zora (Goad) F.; B.S., Murray State U., 1948; postgrad. U. Ky., 1949-51; Litt.D. (hon.), U. Louisville, 1974; m. Evelyn Alline Maner, Nov. 2, 1944; children—Phyllis Lee (Mrs. John Terry), Mindy Nelle. Editor, Ledger & Times, Murray, Ky., 1945-46; writer Nashville Tennessean, 1950-56; writer-photographer Louisville Courier-Jour., 1957—. Served with USNR, 1942-45; PTO. Co-recipient Pulitzer prize, 1967; recipient Pulitzer prize, 1969, Nat. Headliner award, 1969; named Distinguished Alumnus, Murray State U., 1971. Methodist. Author: Stinking Creek, 1967. Home: 4425 Greenbriar Rd Louisville KY 40207

FETZER, CARL STEPHAN, JR., agr. exec.; b. Lakewood, O., Jan. 13, 1927; s. Carl Stephan and Bessie (Haffemeister) F.; student Western Res. U., 1946-48; m. Martha Jeanne Smith, June 21, 1949; children—Carl Stephan III, Mark, Gayle. Distbr. for Scott & Fetzer Co., Cleve., 1949-59; pres. Sefco, Inc., Vero Beach, Fla., 1959—; div. mgr. Blue Goose Growers, Inc., 1974—, Sefco, Inc., 1973—; dir. Comml. Bank Vero Beach. Vice chmn. Indian River Grapefruit Com., 1971-72, chmn., 1973-74. Bd. dirs. Indian River Citrus League. Served with USAAF, 1944-46. Republican. Christian Scientist (dir.). Home: 917 Lady Bug Lane Vero Beach FL 32960 Office: P O Box 2226 Vero Beach FL 32960

FETZER, HOMER DONALD, educator; b. San Antonio, Oct. 19, 1932; s. William J. and Gertrude L. (Lamm) F.; B.S., St. Mary's U., 1954; M.S., U. Tex., 1959, Ph.D., 1965; m. Laura Sue Gorrell, June 19, 1954; children—Donald, Jeffrey, Susan, Patrick, Mark. Teaching asst. U. Tex., 1957-59; asst. prof. physics St. Mary's U., San Antonio, 1959-62, asso. prof., 1962-68, prof., 1970—, chmn. dept. physics, 1965-69, 73—. Active Boy Scouts Am., 1967-70. Served to 1st lt. AUS, 1954-57. Recipient Sci. Faculty Fellowship, NSF, 1963-65. Mem. Am. Assn. Physics Tchrs., Nat. Sci. Tchrs. Assn., Research Soc. Am. Home: 4231 Havenview St San Antonio TX 78228 Office: 2700 Cincinnati St San Antonio TX 78284

FICHANDLER, ZELDA DIAMOND (MRS. THOMAS C. FICHANDLER), theater producer, dir.; b. Sept. 18, 1924; d. Harry and Ida (Epstein) Diamond; B.A., Cornell U., 1945; M.A., George Washington U., 1950; L.H.D. (hon.), Hood Coll., 1962; m. Thomas C. Fichandler, Feb. 17, 1946; 2 sons. Founder, producer, dir. Arena Stage; mem. exec. com. Theatre Communication Group. Recipient ann. award Nat. Theater Conf., 1971, Margo Jones award, 1971. Mem. Phi Beta Kappa. Home: 3120 Newark St NW Washington DC 20008 Office: Arena Stage 6th and M Sts SW Washington DC 20024*

FICHTER, GEORGE SIEBERT, author; b. Hamilton, O., Sept. 17, 1922; s. Matthew and Hazel Evelen (Siebert) F.; A.B., Miami U., 1947; M.S., N.C. State U., 1948; postgrad. U. N.C., 1948-49; m. Nadine Kay Warner, Feb. 10, 1945; children—Susan Kay, Thomas Matt, Jane Ann. Instr. zoology and conservation Miami U., Oxford, O., 1948-50; zoology editor Jour. Sch. Sci. and Math., Chgo., 1949-50; v.p., editor-in-chief Fisherman Press, Inc., Oxford and N.Y.C., 1950-55; asst. exec. v.p. Sport Fishing Inst., Washington, 1955-57; dir. Golden Guides, Western Pub. Co., N.Y.C., 1967-68; free lance writer and editor of pubs. in area of natural history. Mem. A.A.A.S., Am. Entomol. Soc., Am. Littoral Soc., Sigma Xi, Phi Kappa Phi. Author of numerous nature books including Insect Pests, 1966, Animal Kingdom, 1968, Snakes and Other Reptiles, 1968, Airborne Animals, 1969, Your World--Your Survival, 1970, Birds of Florida, 1971, Bicycling, 1972; Cats, 1973; (with others) Ecology, 1973; The Florida Cookbook, 1973. Contbr. articles, and papers to profl. pubs. Editor: Golden Encyclopedia of Natural History, 1962, Golden Bookshelf of Natural History, 1963, and numerous other nature books. Address: P O Box 1368 Homestead FL 33030

FICKLING, WILLIAM ARTHUR, JR., health care co. exec.; b. Macon, Ga., July 23, 1932; s. William Arthur and Claudia Darden (Foster) F.; B.S. cum laude, Auburn U., 1954; m. Neva Jane Langley, Dec. 30, 1954; children—William Arthur III, Jane Dru, Julia Claudia, Roy Hampton. Exec. v.p. Fickling & Walker, Inc., Macon, 1954—; chmn. bd., chief exec. officer Charter Med. Corp., 1969—; chmn. bd. Atlanta Nat. Real Estate Trust; dir. Ga. Power Co., C & S Nat. Bank, Macon, Family Fed. Savs. & Loan Assn., S. Ga. Ry. Co., Riverside Ford, Handshaker Ford, Lakeside Ford. Mem. Macon Bd. Realtors. Trustee, Wesleyan Coll., Macon. Mem. Young Pres.'s Orgn., Kappa Alpha, Delta Sigma Phi, Phi Kappa Phi. Methodist. Home: 4918 Wesleyan Woods Dr Macon GA 31204 Office: 577 Mulberry St Macon GA 31201

FIDLER, DONALD HENRY, lawyer; b. Aurora, Ill., Jan. 19, 1928; s. Nicholas P. and Susan A. (Leick) F.; B.S. in Mech. Engring., U. Notre Dame, 1949; J.D. with distinction, George Washington U., 1956; m. Patricia Booth, Apr. 19, 1953; children—Donald H., Pattie Anne. Engr., Creamery Package Co., Ft. Atkinson, Wis., 1949-50, Fairbanks-Morse Co., Beloit, Wis., 1950-53; patent examiner U.S. Patent Office, Washington, 1953-56; admitted to Va. bar, 1956, Tex. bar, 1957; atty. Varo Mfg. Co., Garland, Tex., 1957-58, Schlumberger, Ltd., Houston, 1958-70; pvt. practice in Houston, 1970—. Dir. Sivco, Inc., Splty. Bindery Services, Inc. Councilman, Bunker Hill Village, Tex., 1973—. Served with USAF, 1950-53. Mem. Am. (ho. dels. 1971—), Va., Houston bar assns., State Bar Tex. (exec. com.), Am. Patent Law Assn. (pres. Houston, mem. nat. council). Catholic. K.C. (past grand knight). Club: Houston Racquet. Home: 87 Williamsburg St Houston TX 77024 Office: Houston Bar Center Bldg Houston TX 77002

FIDLER, RAYMOND WILLIAM, electronic engr.; b. Miami Springs, Fla., July 17, 1933; s. Mildred May Fidler; student U. Akron, 1955-56, U. Miami, 1958-59; B.E.E. (with honors), U. Fla., 1963, M.E.E., 1964, postgrad., 1964-68; m. Marilyn Ardeth Jackson, Nov. 28, 1953; 1 dau., Gayle Janiece. Research and devel. technician Goodyear Aircraft Corp., Akron, O., 1955-56; field engr. AC Spark Plug div. Gen. Motors Corp., Milw., 1956-57; test technician Milgo Electronics, Inc., Miami, Fla., 1957; meter reader, City of Hialeah, Fla., 1958-59; grad. teaching asst. U. Fla., 1963-67, research asso., 1967-68; electronic engr. Naval Coastal Systems Lab., Panama City, Fla., 1968—; v.p., dir. Safety Devices, Inc., 1971—. Cons., Gov.'s Council on Criminal Justice, Region 1, 1971. Served with USN 1951-55, USNR, 61-62. Recipient Superior Achievement award Naval Coastal Systems Lab., 1968. Mem. I.E.E.E. (chmn. Panama City sect. 1973—, sec.-treas. 1972-73), U.S. Power Squadron. Democrat. Methodist (trustee). Mason. Home: 1819 Carolina Av Lynn Haven FL 32444 Office: Naval Coastal Systems Lab Panama City FL 32401

FIDLER, WALTHER BALDERSON, lawyer; b. Sharps, Va., Apr. 18, 1923; s. Peyton Joseph and Gladys Ellen (Balderson) F.; B.A., Randolph-Macon Coll., 1944; J.D., U. Richmond, 1949; m. Martha Elizabeth Spencer, June 10, 1950; children—Kathleen McCray, Frances O., Jane E., Mrs. James Robert II. Admitted to Va. bar, 1949; mem. firm Ryland & Fidler, Warsaw, Va., 1950—; counsel, dir. pub. affairs Va. Mfrs. Assn., Warsaw, 1974—. Gen. counsel Standard Products Co., Inc., 1963—, also dir.; dir. Va. Savs. & Loan Assn. Chmn., No. Neck Regional Planning Commn., Warsaw, 1966-68; mem. Va. Ho. of Dels., 1960-74. Served to lt. (j.g.) USNR, 1943-46. Decorated Navy Commendation ribbon. Recipient Outstanding Citizen award Richmond County, Va., 1968. Mem. Farm Bur., Phi Delta Theta, Delta Theta Phi, Omicron Delta Kappa, Pi Delta Epsilon. Presbyn. (elder 1958—). Club: Ruritan (Warsaw). Home: Sharps VA 22548 Office: 3 Main St Warsaw VA 22572

FIEDOTIN, ARNOLDO, physician; b. Parana, Argentina, May 25, 1936; s. Aaron Adolfo and Paulina (Spector) F.; B.A. cum laude, Coll. Nac Nicolas Avellaneda, Buenos Aires, Argentina, 1954; M.D., U. Buenos Aires, 1961; m. Rosa L. Ludner, June 9, 1961; children—Diana Sylvia, Richard Alan, Norma Alexandra. Came to U.S., 1961, naturalized, 1967. Intern, Pontiac (Mich.) Gen. Hosp., 1961-62; resident St. Joseph's Hosp., Pontiac, 1962-65; NIH fellow N.J. Coll. Medicine, 1965-66; fellow in cardiology Cleve. Clinic, 1966-67; practice of medicine, specializing in cardiology, Atlanta, 1967—; dir. cardiac services St. Joseph's Infirmary, Atlanta, 1967—; asst. clin. prof. medicine Emory U., 1968—. Cons. cardiology Office Vocational Rehab., Ga. Dept. Edn., 1968—. Mem. Am. Coll. Cardiology (asso. fellow), A.C.P. (asso. fellow, life mem.), A.M.A., Am. Heart Assn., Am. Soc. Internal Medicine, Ga. Med. Assn., Med. Assn. Atlanta, Atlanta Forum Cardiology. Home: 1818 W Wesley Rd NW Atlanta GA 30327 Office: 265 Ivy St NE Atlanta GA 30303

FIELD, HENRY, anthropologist; b. Chgo., Dec. 15, 1902; ed. in Eng.; student Eton Coll., 1916-21, New Coll., Oxford, 1921-26; B.A., Oxford U., 1925, Diploma in Anthropology, 1926, M.A., 1929, D.Sc., 1937; research U. Heidelberg, 1926; research Peabody Mus., Harvard, 1936-37; m. Julia Rand Allen, Feb. 6, 1953; 1 dau., Juliana Lathrop Sweeney; (by previous marriage), Mariana Hoppin. Anthropologist Field Mus. Natural History, 1926-41, asst. curator of phys. anthropology, 1926-36, curator, 1937-41; govt. adviser Pres. F.D. Roosevelt, Pres. Harry S. Truman, Washington, 1941-45. Mem. archaeol. expdn. in Europe, Africa and Southwestern Asia; leader Marshall Field Archaeol. Expdns. to Europe, North Arabian Desert, Iraq, and others; mem. Harvard expdns. Research fellow phys. anthropology Harvard 1950-69, hon. asso. in phys. anthropology, 1969—; adj. prof. U. Miami, 1966—; Forbes Hawkes lectr. U. Miami, Lowell Inst., Boston, 1952. Trustee Am. Sch. Prehistoric Research; hon. mem. Glasgow Archaeol. Soc.; corr. mem. several fgn. scientific socs. Mem. U.S. and fgn. profl. and scientific socs. and assns., anthropol., archaeol., and other spl. orgns. Fellow A.A.A.S., Royal Geog. Soc., Royal Central Asian Soc., Royal Asiatic Soc., Royal Anthrop. Inst. of Gt. Brit. and Ireland, Geol. Soc., Zool. Soc., Prehistoric Soc., and others; mem. Acad. Arts and Scis. Ams. (pres. 1964—). U.S. del. to internat. congresses and sci. confs. Mem. U.S. mission to Moscow and Leningrad for 220th anniversary of Acad. Scis. USSR, 1945, Internat. Congress, Moscow, 1964, Internat. Geog. Congress, Eng., 1964. Club: Explorers (pres. Fla. chpt. 1973) (N.Y.). Author books on S.W. Asia including: Useful Plants and drugs of Iran and Iraq (with David Hooper), 1937; The Anthropology of Iraq, 1939, 40, 48, 51, 52; Contbns. to the Anthropology of the Caucasus, 1953; The Track of Man, 1953; Los Indios de Tepoztlan, Morelos, Mexico, 1954; Ancient and Modern Man in S.W. Asia, I, 1956, II, 1961; Bibliographies on S.W. Asia I-VII, 1953-61; Anthropological Reconnaissance in West Pakistan, 1959; North Arabian Desert Archaeological Survey, 1925-50, 1960; M Project for F.D.R., Studies on Migration and Settlement, 1962; Physical Anthropology of India, 1970. Editor Peabody Mus. Russian Translation Series, 1959-72. Home: 3551 Main Highway Coconut Grove Miami FL 33133 Office: Peabody Museum Cambridge MA 02138

FIELD, JULIA ALLEN, environmental planner, writer; b. Boston, Jan. 5, 1937; d. Howard Locke and Julia (Wright) Allen; A.B. cum laude, Harvard, 1960; postgrad. Pius XII Art Inst., Florence, Italy, 1961, Harvard Grad. Sch. Design, 1964-65. Founder, v.p. Black Grove Inc., Fla., 1970—, Amazonia 2000, Colombia, S.Am., 1971—; asso. cons. Environment Cons., Inc., Dallas. Preparator Exhbn. for internat. conf. Cities in Context, U. Notre Dame, 1968; mem. Symposium Tropical Biology, Leticia, Colombia, 1969; cons. to forestry dept. Simla, Himachal Pradesh, N. India, 1969; mem. Presdl. Adv. Group of Year 2000, Republic of Colombia, 1972; del. from Amazonia 2000 to Nat. Seminar on Ecology and Urbanization, Bogota, Colombia, 1973. Author: Essays on American Culture, 1961; (film) Man Against Nature, 1966. Editor: Game and Wild Life Preserves in the USSR, 1965. Home: 3551 Main Hwy Coconut Grove FL 33133

FIELD, RICHARD LANE, editor; b. Balt., Sept. 12, 1897; s. Charles Carter and Mary Virginia (Lane) F.; A.B., Johns Hopkins, 1920; m. Camilla L. Chewning, June 25, 1932; children—Richard Lana, William Carter. Reporter, Balt. Sun, 1920-23, night city editor, 1923-24; swing editor Balt. Am., 1925; asst. make-up editor N.Y. Herald-Tribune, 1926, asst. editor Sunday Mag., 1926-35; article editor This Week Mag., 1935-45; asso. editor Holiday mag., 1945-47, mng. editor, 1947-57, prodn. dir. Holiday mag., 1957-64; city editor High Springs (Fla.) Herald, 1966; cons., part-time editor The Floridian, Sunday mag. of St. Petersburg (Fla.) Times, 1966-69. Participant founding Herald Tribune Sunday mag., 1926, This Week mag., 1935, Holiday mag., 1945, The Floridian, 1966. Dir. mag. information OPA, Washington, 1945. Served as pvt. U.S. Army, 1918. Mem. Kappa Alpha. Clubs: Dutch Treat, Johns Hopkins, P.E.N. (New York). Contbr. articles to nat. mags. Home: Ivanhoe House Apt #202 5955 30th Av S Gulfport FL 33707

FIELD, ROBERT JOSEPH, petroleum co. exec.; b. Langdon, N.D., May 24, 1924; s. William Hansford and Florence Esther (Quick) F.; B.S., Colo. Coll., 1948, M.A., 1951; m. Freddie Jean Morgan, Jan. 26, 1952; children—James, Murray, Laurie. Engr., Eastman Oil Well, Long Beach, Cal., 1949-50; geologist Deep Rock Oil Co., Denver, 1951-54; div. geologist Sohio Petroleum Co., Houston, 1954-61; exploration mgr. Morgan Drilling Co., Oklahoma City, 1961-63, An-Son Corp., 1963-65; pres. Morgan Petroleum Co., 1965—. Served with USMCR, 1943-45. Mem. Am. Assn. Petroleum Geologists., Okla. City Geol. Soc., Kappa Sigma. Club: Petroleum (Oklahoma City). Office: 2000 Liberty Tower Oklahoma City OK 73102

FIELD, STANLEY, govt. ofcl.; b. Ukraine, May 20, 1911; s. Henry and Nina (Cibulsky) F.; brought to U.S., 1914, naturalized, 1924; B.A., Bklyn. Coll., 1934; m. Joyce Stillman, Dec. 7, 1935; children—Jeffrey Michael, Constance Elyse. Program dir. Radio sta. WLTH, N.Y.C., 1935-37, writer NBC, 1937-38; copywriter Emil Mogul Advt. Agy., 1939-40; free lance writer, Washington, 1941—; information specialist Dept. Army, Washington, 1941—. Instr. Bklyn Coll., 1938-40, Grad. Sch. Dept. Agr., 1969—. Adult Edn. div. Arlington County, Va., 1967—; adj. prof. Am. U., 1953-67. Recipient Emmy award Acad. TV Arts and Scis., spl. award YMCA Internat, 1947. Mem. The Author's Guild, Assn. Profl. Broadcasting Edn., Nat. Assn. Ednl. Broadcasters. Author: Television and Radio Writing, 1958; Guide to Opportunities in the Sciences, 1968; Bible Stories for Adults, 1969; Professional Broadcast Writer's Handbook, 1972; The Mini-Documentary, 1974; also numerous TV and radio documentary and dramatic scripts, articles and short stories Home: 3520 Duff Dr Falls Church VA 22041 Office: Broadcast Pictorial Branch US Army Command Information Unit Washington DC 20315

FIELDEN, GEORGIA FREEMAN (MRS. C. FRANKLIN FIELDEN, JR.), interior designer, residential and comml. cons.; b. Alexandria, La., Aug. 3, 1919; d. John D. and Landis (Barton) Freeman; student fine arts Ward-Belmont, 1932-37, Blue Mountain Coll., 1937-38; B.S., George Peabody Coll., 1941; postgrad. N.Y. Sch. Interior Design, 1953; m. Clarence Franklin Fielden, Jr., July 16, 1942; children—Clarence Franklin III, Landis Michaux. Head dept. arts and crafts Camp Bon Air, Sparta, Tenn., 1939-42; asst. instr. fine arts demonstration sch. Peabody Coll., 1940-41; instr. fine arts Jackson (Miss.) Pub. Schs., 1941-42; lectr., interior designer, Colorado Springs, Colo., 1942-67; design cons., Denver, 1968—. Local pres. P.T.A., 1954-56. Mem. Am. Assn. U. Women, Am. Inst. Interior Designers (Rocky Mountain publicity dir. 1957-58, sec. 1959-60, nat. com. pub. relations 1959-61), Constrn. Specifications Inst., D.A.R., Illuminating Engring. Soc. (asso.), Internat. Platform Assn., English Speaking Union, Huguenot Soc. of Founders Manakin in Colony Va. Presbyn. Clubs: Rotaryann (local v.p. 1959-60), Soroptomist. Contbr. articles to profl. jours. Home: Box 27503 Atlanta GA 30327 Office: Denver Mdse Mart Denver CO 80216

FIELDS, HUBERT, dentist; b. London, Ky., May 20, 1923; s. Hubert and Mary Eileen (Warner) F.; certificate Sue Bennett Jr. Coll., London, 1943; student U. Wis., 1943-44; D.M.D., U. Louisville, 1947; m. Jean Elizabeth Sheets, June 15, 1950; 1 son, Douglas Scott. Asst. dental surgeon USPHS, 1947-49, sr. asst. dental surgeon, 1949-53; asst. prof. prosthodontics U. Louisville, 1953-57, asso. prof., 1957-60, prof., 1960—, chmn. dept. prosthodontics, 1972—, dir. clinics, 1973—; cons. Ky. Bd. Dental Examiners, 1968-70. Mem. Fed. Dental Service Com., 1963-65, chmn., 1965. Leader troop Boy Scouts Am., 1964-65. Served with AUS, 1943-44. Fellow Am. Coll. Dentists (sec. Ky. sect.); mem. Am., Ky. (ho. of dels. 1966—), Louisville (dental trade and dental lab. relations com. 1969-71) dental assns., Am. Prosthodontic Soc., Southeastern Acad. Prosthodontics, Am. Assn. Dental Schs., Omicron Kappa Upsilon, Delta Sigma Delta, Phi Delta. Mason. Contbr. articles to profl. jours. Home: 4325 Foeburn Lane Louisville KY 40207

FIELDS, JAMES ODELL, physician, surgeon; b. Milan, Tenn., Sept. 1, 1916; s. Eric Odell and Mildred Love (George) F.; M.D., U. Tenn., 1940; m. Cecille Williams, Aug. 29, 1942; 1 son, Thomas Dudley. Rotating intern Charity Hosp. of La., New Orleans, 1940-41; gen. practice medicine and surgery, Milan, 1946—; chief of staff City of Milan Hosp. Mem. W. Tenn. council Boy Scouts Am., 1948-68. Served to maj. USAAF, 1942-46. Decorated Air Combat medal with 4 bronze stars. Hon. col. staff Gov. Tenn. Fellow Am. Acad. Family Practice. Mem. A.M.A., So. (sec. gen. practice sect. 1967), Tenn. med. assns., Tenn. Acad. Gen. Practice, W.Tenn. Consol. Med. Assembly, Mid-South Med. Assembly, Milan C. of C., W.Tenn. Heart Assn. (dir.), Sigma Chi, Phi Chi. Democrat. Presbyn. (elder). Mason (Shriner). Home: Route 4 Jackson Hwy Milan TN 38358 Office: 123 Hospital Dr Milan TN 38358

FIELDS, WILBERT OSBORNE, JR., state ofcl.; b. nr. Selma, N.C., Sept. 12, 1928; s. Wilbert Osborne and Mary Eliza (Worrell) F.; B.S., U. N.C., 1950, M.Ed., 1957, Ph.D., 1962; m. Jean Mozelle Kirby, Dec. 22, 1951; children—Sara, Frank. Elementary and secondary sch. tchr., Johnston County, N.C., 1953-56; elementary and secondary sch. prin., Bertie County, N.C., 1956-61; exec. sec. N.C. State Sch. Buss. Assn., Chapel Hill, 1961-63; asst. supt. Rocky Mount, N.C., 1963-66, supt. schs., 1966-70; asst. supt. State Dept. Pub. Instruction, Raleigh, 1970—. Mem. N.C. State Adv. Com. Vocational Edn., 1969-72; mem. Gov.'s Commn. to Study Pub. Schs., 1968. Bd. dirs. Rocky Mount United Fund, Nash Edgecombe Manpower Devel. Commn., Nash County Cancer Soc. Served with AUS, 1950-52. Mem. Am. Assn. Sch. Adminstrs., N.E.A., N.C. Assn. Educators (pres. unit 1959-60, 65-66), So. Assn. Colls. and Schs. (mem. state com. 1967-71), Methodist. N.C. Conf. Bd. Laity, N.C. Conf. Bd. Edn., N.C. Conf. Bd. Coll. Visitors, N.C. Conf. Bd. Commn. on Higher Edn.). Home: 3917 Quail Hollow Dr Raleigh NC 27609 Office: N C Dept Public Instruction Raleigh NC 27602

FIFE, HAROLD EUGENE, chem. co. exec.; b. Gallipolis, O., Dec. 26, 1920; s. Forrest H. and Sarah Elizabeth (Reese) F.; B.S., Ohio State U., 1947; m. Jeanne C. Kenyon, July 11, 1948; children—Barbara (Mrs. Ronnie Day), Gregory, Pamela. Prodn. engr. Drackett Co., 1947-50; project, process and prodn. mgr. Am. Cyanamid Co., Wallingford, Conn., 1950-60; mgr. polystyrene, tech. mgr., prodn. mgr., gen. works mgr. Rexall Drug & Chem. Co. (now Rexene Polymers div. Dart Industries), Odessa, Tex., 1960—. Served with USAAF, 1942-46. Mem. Tex. Chem. Council (dir.), Tex. C. of C. (v.p.). Club: Exchange (Odessa). Home: 4224 Kirkwood St Odessa TX 79762 Office: PO Box 554 Odessa TX 79762

FIFE, JOSEPH RAY, broadcasting exec.; b. Marion, Ind., Mar. 23, 1919; s. Joseph Ray and Maude Estelle (Day) F.; A.B., U. Kan., 1944; postgrad. Ind. U., 1946, Mich. State U., 1954; m. Melba Louise Grove, Apr. 23, 1944 (div. Oct. 1952); children—Patricia, Diane, Sarah, Marjorie; m. 2d, Johnnie Harper. Vice pres. radio sta. **KYOK,**

Houston, New Orleans, Memphis, 1959-68; editor, pub. Tri-State Comet, Evansville, Ind., 1964-68; gen. mgr. radio sta. WGRD, Chgo., 1968-71, radio sta., WGO, Atlanta, 1971—; pres. Broadcast Sales Motivation, Atlanta, 1971—. Mem. Gov.'s Com. on Crime, 1973; mem. Mayor's Adv. Com., Houston, 1960-61. Bd. dirs. Atlanta Black Charities, 1972—. Served with AUS, 1938-42. Named Houston Man of Yr., Houston Citizens C. of C., 1961; recipient editorial award A.P., 1971. Mem. Nat., Ga. (Broadcaster-Citizen of Year 1974) assns. broadcasters. Mason (32 deg., Shriner). Home: 7438 Twin Hill Way Austell GA 30001 Office: 659 Peachtree St NE Atlanta GA 30383

FIGG, ROBERT MCCORMICK, JR., lawyer; b. Radford, Va., Oct. 22, 1901; s. Robert McCormick and Helen Josephine (Cecil) F.; grad. Porter Mil. Acad., Charleston, S.C., A.B., Coll. of Charleston, 1920, Litt.D., 1970; student law Columbia, 1920-22; LL.D., U. S.C., 1959; m. Sallie Alexander Tobias, May 10, 1927; children—Robert McCormick III, Emily (Mrs. Richard A. Dalla Mura), Jefferson Tobias. Admitted S.C. bar, 1922, practiced in Charleston, 1922-61; circuit solicitor 9th Jud. Circuit of S.C., 1935-47, spl. circuit judge, 1957; dean Law Sch., U.S.C., 1959-70; sr. counsel firm Robinson, McFadden, Moore & Pope, Columbia, 1970—. Dir. Palmetto State Life Ins. Co., Home Fed. Savs. & Loan Assn. Mem. S.C. Ho. of Reps., 1933-35; mem. S.C. Reorgn. Commn., 1948—, chmn., 1951-55, 71—. Pres., Coll. Charleston Found., 1970—. Fellow Am. Coll. Trial Lawyers; mem. Am., Inter-Am., Charleston County (pres. 1953) bar assns., Am. Law Inst., Am. Judicature Soc., Inst. Jud. Adminstrn., S.C. State Bar (pres. 1970-71), Blue Key, Phi Beta Kappa, Phi Delta Phi. Mason (grand master S.C. 1972—). Home: 1522 Deans Lane Columbia SC 29205

FIGUEROA, MIGUEL, JR., physician; b. San Lorenzo, P.R., Nov. 19, 1922; s. Miguel and Maria Luisa (Mangual) F.; B.S., Fordham U., 1943; M.D., N.Y. Med. Coll., 1948; m. Lillian Grossberg, July 26, 1949. Intern, Fordham Hosp., Bronx, N.Y.C., 1948-49; gen. practice medicine, San Juan, P.R., 1949-51; resident anesthesia San Juan City Hosp., 1951-53; practice medicine, specializing in anesthesiology, 1954, Miami, Fla., 1957—; trustee Abbey Hosp. Med. Center and Found., Coral Gables, Fla.; mem. bd. dirs. Palmetto Gen. Hosp., Hialeah, Fla.; clin. prof. anesthesiology U. Miami, 1970—; chief div. anesthesiology Parkway Gen. Hosp., North Miami Beach, Fla., Palmetto Gen. Hosp., Hialeah, Fla. Served to capt. USAF, 1954-56. Mem. Am., So., Fla. med. assns., Am., Fla. (pres. 1969-70, bd. dirs. 1966-71), P.R. (pres. 1953-54) socs. anesthesiologists, Am. Heart Assn. Home: 11111 Biscayne Blvd Miami FL 33161 Office: 16800 NW 2d Av Suite 207 Miami Beach FL 33169

FIKE, HAROLD LESTER, research dir.; b. Toledo, Jan. 30, 1926; s. James Lester and Laura Augusta (Sterner) F.; B.S., U. Toledo, 1950; M.B.A., Northwestern U., 1963; m. Nancy Jane Trueblood, Mar. 10, 1956; children—Laura Marie, David Warren, Lisa Jane, Lawrence Andrew. Chemist, Internat. Minerals & Chem. Corp., Skokie, Ill., 1952-63, economist, 1963-68; dir. research Sulfur Inst., Washington, 1968—. Patentee in field. Home: 1894 Milboro Dr Potomac MD 20854 Office: 1725 K St NW Washington DC 20006

FILER, THEODORE HENRY, JR., plant pathologist; b. Galveston, Tex., Aug. 15, 1928; s. Theodore Henry and Thersia Grace (Barrak) F.; B.S., Tex. A. and M. U., 1951, M.S. (DuPont Chem. fellow), 1958; Ph.D., Wash. State U., 1963; m. Mary Lorena (Moseley), Dec. 30, 1950; children—Theodore Henry III, Janet Lynn. Instr., Wash. State U., 1962-63; research plant pathologist U.S. Forest Service, Stoneville, Miss., 1963—. Served to 1st lt. AUS, 1952-54. Mem. Am. Phytopath. Soc., Am. Mycology Soc., Internat. Poplar Council (chmn. protection com.). Elk. Clubs: Toastmasters International (lt. gov. Dist. 43 1972), National Exchange (Greenville, Miss.). Home: 118 Forest St Greenville MS 38701 Office: Box 227 Stoneville MS 38776

FILERMAN, GARY LEWIS, assn. exec.; b. Mpls., Nov. 16, 1936; s. Joseph H. and Bonnie D. (Dickerman) F.; B.A., U. Minn., 1959, M.H.A. (Phillips Found. fellow), 1961, M.A. (W.K. Kellogg fellow), 1963, Ph.D., 1970; m. Jane K. Harding, Sept. 15, 1962; children—Amy, Joseph, Suzanne. Dir., World Univ. Service Hungarian Student Center, 1956-57; adminstrv. resident Johns Hopkins Hosp., 1960-61; guest scholar Brookings Instn., 1962; fellow Nat. Health Service of Chile, 1964; project dir. Minn. Hosp. Assn., 1965; exec. dir. Assn. U. Programs in Health Adminstrn., Washington, 1965—; exec. sec. Accrediting Com. on Grad. Edn. for Hosp. Adminstrn., Washington, 1968—. Adj. instr. Washington U. Sch. Medicine, 1973—; cons. Dept. Health, Edn. and Welfare, WHO, Mexico, Colombia, Chile, Argentina, W.K. Kellogg Found.; vice chmn. Council Specialized Accreditation Agys., 1973-75. Mem. Am. Council Edn. Commn. Ednl. Credit, 1973-76. Recipient King Gustav award B'nai B'rith, 1959, Silver medal Leuven U., Belgium, 1972—. OAS fellow, 1964; Milbank Fund fellow, 1964. Fellow Am. Pub. Health Assn., Inst. for European Health Services Research; mem. Royal Soc. Health (London), Am. Coll. Hosp. Adminstrs., Assn. Am. Med. Colls., Fedn. Assns. Schs. of Health Profs. (chmn. 1971-72), Common Cause, Nat. Audubon Soc., Wilderness Soc. Democrat. Jewish religion. Edn. editor Teke Life, 1958-60; editor Assn. U. Programs in Health Adminstrn. Program Notes, 1965—; editorial bd. Health Adminstrn. Press, 1973—. Contbr. articles to profl. jours. Home: 1322 Banquo Ct McLean VA 22101 Office: One Dupont Circle Washington DC 20036

FILLHART, JON EDWARD, landscape architect; b. Butler, Pa., Dec. 13, 1943; s. Edward Sylvester and Leona Harriet (Croup) F.; B.S. summa cum laude, Pa. State U., 1965; M. Landscape Arch., U. Mich., 1967, Ph.D., 1970. Sr. designer Crane & Gorwic, Detroit, 1968; dir. landscape architecture Victor Shrem & Assos., Detroit, 1969; prin., partner Edward D. Stone Jr. & Assos., Ft. Lauderdale, Fla., 1970—. Lectr., research asso. dept. landscape arthitecure U. Mich., Ann Arbor, 1967-68. Mem. Am. Soc. Landscape Architects, Scarab, Phi Kappa Phi, Pi Gamma Alpha, Pi Alpha Xi. Home: 501 NE 23d Av Fort Lauderdale FL 33301 Office: 2400 E Oakland Park Blvd Fort Lauderdale FL 33306

FIMMEL, GUSTAV ADOLF, III, civil engr.; b. Milltown, N.J., Oct. 3, 1922; s. Gustav A. and Olga (Harmel) F.; B.S. in Civil Engring., Newark Coll. Engring., 1943; B.S., Pelman Inst., 1940; m. Bonny I.C. Bitthien, Apr. 18, 1942; 1 son, Jon Ernest. Various engring. positions Bethlehem Steel Co., Elizabethport, N.J., Yara Engring. Co., Elizabeth, N.J., A.P. & R.K. Michaels, Orlando, Fla., George M. Brewster & Son, Inc., Bogota, N.J., Berger Assos., Harrisburg, Pa., 1943-54; self-employed in engring. and surveying, Orlando, Fla., 1954-57; sr. engr. Reynolds, Smith & Hills, Jacksonville, 1957-58; engr.-programmer Martin Co., Orlando, 1958; field engr. R.F. Ball Constrn. Co., Pinecastle, Fla., 1959; city engr. City of Melbourne (Fla.), 1960-61, City of Cocoa (Fla.), 1961-63; pres. The Cape Seminole Co., Inc., Forest City (Orlando) Fla., 1963—. Mem. Fla. Engring. Soc. (sr. life), Fla. Sheriffs Assn. (hon.), Nat. Soc. Profl. Engrs. (life), Forest City Community Assn. (life), Tau Beta Pi (life). Home: Route 2 Box 712 Maitland FL 32751

FINCH, HEBER, JR., lawyer, state legislator; b. Dresden, Tenn., Nov. 15, 1916; s. Heber and Bertha (Templeton) F.; B.A., Okla. U., 1937, LL.B., 1939; m. Lillian Waldean Autry, Oct. 11, 1943; children—Dwayla Dean, Lillian. Admitted to Okla. bar, 1939; partner firm Finch & Finch, Sapulpa, Okla., 1939—; mem. Okla. Ho. of Reps., 1954—. Served with AUS, 1941-45. Mem. Okla. Bar Assn. Home: 1225 S Adams St Sapulpa OK 74066 Office: Security Bldg Sapulpa OK 74066

FINCH, HUGH EDSEL, real estate and ins. exec.; b. Spartanburg, S.C., June 21, 1928; s. Robert Lewis and Rosalee (Wyatt) F.; A.B., Wofford Coll., 1952; m. Sharon K. Smith, 1971; 1 dau., Alice Michelle; children by previous marriage—Deborah Elaine, Susan Denise. Newspaper reporter Spartanburg (S.C.) Herald Jour., 1952-54; tchr. Pacolet (S.C.) High Sch., 1955-56; operator, owner Hugh E. Finch Agy., ins. and real estate, Spartanburg, 1958. Mem. S.C. Ho. of Reps., 1956-66, 69-72. County chmn. March of Dimes, 1968. Mem. Nat., S.C., Spartanburg County ins. assns. Methodist. Mason (Shriner), Lion. Club: Ruritan (past pres.). Home: 1517 Rutherford Rd Landrum SC 29356 Office: Asheville Hwy Spartanburg SC 29303

FINCH, JERALD ALLEN, newspaper editor; b. Huntington, W.Va., June 17, 1927; s. Plynn Jerald and Annabelle Virginia (Allen) F.; A.B. with high distinction, U. Ky., 1950; m. Nancy Tynes St. Clair, Nov. 30, 1963; children—Jerald Kelly, Laura Plynn, Allen St. Clair, Thomas Tynes. Reporter, sports writer, asst. sports editor Lexington (Ky.) Leader, 1948-55; with Richmond (Va.) News Leader, 1955—, successively copy editor, makeup editor, asst. city editor, asso. city editor, city editor, exec. city editor, now mng. editor. Served with USAAF, 1944-46. Home: 923 Cowan Rd Bon Air VA 23235 Office: 333 E Grace St Richmond VA 23219

FINCH, ROBERT MACON, physician; b. Little Rock, Dec. 19, 1933; s. Joe E. and Beulah Ann (Jernigan) F.; student E. Tex. State Tchrs. Coll., 1951-52, Ouachita Bapt. Coll., 1952-54, Hendrix Coll., 1958-60; B.S., U. Ark., M.D., 1964; m. Myra Sue Beasley, Aug. 27, 1961; 1 dau., Laura Lee. Intern, Ark. Bapt. Hosp., Little Rock, 1964-65; gen. practice medicine, Forrest City, Ark., 1965-66, Caraway, Ark., 1966-67, Paragould, Ark., 1967—; mem. staff Community Meth. Hosp. Bd. dirs. Crowleys Ridge council Girl Scouts Am. Served with USAF, 1954-58. Mem. Ark., Greene-Clay County med. socs. Home: Finch Rd Paragould AR 72450 Office: 1001 Kingshighway Paragould AR 72450

FINCH, THOMAS AUSTIN, JR., furniture mfg. co. exec.; b. Thomasville, N.C., Aug. 12, 1922; s. Thomas Austin and Ernestine (Lambeth) F.; grad. Woodberry Forest Sch., 1940; B.S. in Engring., Princeton, 1943; m. Meredith Clark Slane, June 4, 1949; children—Thomas Austin III, John Lambeth, David Slane, Sumner Slane, Meredith Kempton. With Thomasville Furniture Industries, Inc., 1946—, pres., 1961—; sr. v.p. parent co. Armstrong Cork Co., 1968—, also dir.; dir. Wachovia Bank and Trust Co., Winston-Salem, N.C., Carolina and Northwestern R.R., Washington Integon Corp. Winston-Salem. Trustee Duke, 1963—, Davidson County Pub. Library, Woodberry Forest Sch., 1967—, Community Gen. Hosp., Thomasville, 1964-72. Served to lt. (j.g.) USNR, World War II. Named Furniture Man of Year, Am. Furniture Mart Corp., 1963. Mem. Phi Beta Kappa. Methodist (past chmn. ofcl. bd.). Rotarian (pres. Thomasville 1958). Home: Pine Needle Lane Thomasville NC 27360 Office: 401 E Main St Thomasville NC 27360

FINCHER, CAMERON LANE, educator; b. Douglas County, Ga., Nov. 4, 1926; s. Andrew Jackson and Ada (Swafford) F.; B.C.S., Ga. State U., 1950; M.A., U. Minn., 1951; Ph.D., Ohio State U., 1956; m. Mary Frances Cutts, June 15, 1957; children—Marcelle, Matt, Mandy, Melissa. Dir. testing and counseling Ga. State Coll., Atlanta, 1956-65; asso. dir. Inst. Higher Edn., U. Ga., Athens, 1965-69, dir. Inst. Higher Edn., 1969—, prof. higher edn., psychology, 1965—. Cons. various indsl. and comml. cos., also colls. and univs. Served to USNR, 1944-46. Mem. Am. Psychol. Assn., Am. Ednl. Research Assn., Am. Assn. for Higher Edn., Assn. for Instnl. Research, Nat. Council on Measurement in Edn., Alpha Kappa Psi, Phi Delta Kappa. Author: A Preface to Psychology, 1972. Contbr. articles to profl. jours. Office: Inst Higher Edn Candler Hall U Ga Athens GA 30602

FINCHER, CHARLIE ERNEST, JR., govt. ofcl.; b. Arlington, Ga., Nov. 16, 1917; s. Charlie Ernest and Clyde (Jordan) F.; B.C.S., Columbus U., 1944; m. Liliana Palma, Apr. 4, 1966; children—Romina Liliana, Deborah Charlene, Anastasia Josephine. Cost accountant U.S. Mint, 1945-51; systems accountant U.S. Gen. Accounting Office, Washington, 1951-56; dep. comptroller U.S. Govt. Printing Office, Washington, 1956-58; chief finance div. U.S. Bur. Pub. Rds., Washington, 1958-63; finance officer UN FAO, Rome, Italy, 1963-67; self employed C.P.A., Savannah, 1967-69; chief accounting systems staff Bur. Mint, Washington, 1969—. Served with USMCR, 1942-45. Named lt. col., aide-de-camp gov. Ga. C.P.A., Ga. Mem. Am. Inst. C.P.A.'s, Ga. Soc. C.P.A.'s, Fed. Govt. Accountants Assn. Mason (Shriner). Home: 8315 Garfield Ct Springfield VA 22152 Office: US Treasury Dept Bur Mint Washington DC 20220

FINCHER, DORSEY RAY, cons. engr.; b. Rosston, Ark., July 1, 1927; s. Earl and Helen Gould (Murry) F.; B.S., Tex. A. and M. U., 1948; m. Bette Corrinne Pyland, Nov. 29, 1946; children—Stephen Ruell, David Bruce. Engr. Getty Oil Co., 1948-70; cons. engr., mfr. splty. instruments and devices Fincher Engring. Co., Houston, 1970—. Registered profl. engr., Tex. Mem. Nat. Assn. Corrosion Engrs. (dir.), Am. Petroleum Inst., Nat. Gas Processors Assn., Am. Inst. Mining, Metall. and Petroleum Engrs., Am. Inst. Chem. Engrs. Mason. Contbr. articles to tech. jours. Patentee in field. Home: 13306 Havershire Houston TX 77024 Office: 6826 Addicks-Fairbanks Rd Route 9 Box 909 Houston TX 77040

FINCKE, DALE EUGENE, army officer; b. San Antonio, Apr. 21, 1944; s. Eugene Julius and Opal Faye (Thornsberry) F.; B.S., Trinity U., 1966; M.S., Lamar U., 1968; m. Susan Gaye Fitzgerald, June 15, 1968; children—Dale Eugene, Christopher Stephen. Elec. engr. U.S. Steel Corp., Fairless Hills, Pa., 1966-67; commd. 2d lt. U.S. Army, 1966, advanced through grades to capt., 1968; co. comdr. 57th Signal Bn., Ft. Hood, Tex., 1969; radio officer ADSO 4th Inf. Div., Vietnam, 1969-70; signal officers advance course, Ft. Monmouth, N.J., 1970-71; research and devel. electronic engr. U.S. Army Tactical Data Systems, 1971-73; operations officer 123d Signal Bn., 3d Inf. Div., Wurzburg, Germany, 1973—. Teaching fellow Sch. Engring., Lamar U., 1966-68. Decorated Bronze Star medal with 2 oak leaf clusters, Air medal. Mem. I.E.E.E. Mason. Home: 722 Avant St San Antonio TX 78210 Office: HHC 123d Signal Bn APO New York City NY 09036

FINDLAY, ROBERT CLYDE, real estate exec.; b. Springfield, Mo., Aug. 17, 1920; s. Clyde P. and Lettie Mae (St. Clair) F.; B.S., magna cum laude, Abilene Christian Coll., 1943; M.B.A., Harvard Bus. Sch., 1947; m. Carole Dale, Nov. 3, 1973; children—Steven, Bruce, Elaine, Linda, Laura. Pres., Brazosport Savs. & Loan Assn., Freeport, Tex., 1953-65; owner Findlay Enterprises, Arlington, Tex., 1965—. Mem. exec. com. Ft. Worth chpt. A.R.C. Served to 1st lt. AUS, World War II. Named Citizen of Year, Brazosport C. of C., 1958; Arlington Realtor of Year, 1971; Builder of Year, Builders Assn. Ft. Worth, 1972. Mem. Arlington C. of C. (v.p.), Urban Land Inst., Nat. Assn. Homebuilders (chmn. land use com.), Builders Assn. Ft. Worth (past pres.), Tex. Assn. Builders. Home: 6505 Kingswood Dr Fort Worth TX 76133 Office: 2201 Smith-Barry Rd Arlington TX 76013

FINDLEY, GERALD WILLIAM, govt. ofcl.; b. Evergreen, Ala., Mar. 1, 1933; s. Hamon Murray and Bernice (Jackson) F.; B.S., Troy State Coll., 1958; M.S., Fla. State U., 1959; m. Meritta Carter, Nov. 5, 1955; children—Lynn, Phillip. Mathematician, Vitro Corp. Am., Eglin AFB, Fla., 1955-58; programmer analyst Union Carbide Co., Oak Ridge, 1959-62, CEIR, Arlington, Va., 1962-64; mem. tech. staff Bellcomm, Inc., Washington, 1964-66; dept. mgr. TRW Systems, Inc., Washington, 1966-71; mgr. Gen. Services Adminstrn., Washington, 1971—; faculty U. Tenn., 1960-62, Luther Rice Coll., 1969-70. Cons. U.S. Govt. Precinct chmn. Republican party, 1966-70. Mem. Assn. Computing Machinery. Home: 5316 Neville Ct Alexandria VA 22310

FINE, GERALD THOMAS, indsl. controls co. exec.; b. Oklahoma City, July 7, 1936; s. Charles Thomas and Clara Ethel (Reed) F.; B.S., Okla. State U., 1959; M.B.A., Oklahoma City U., 1966; m. Alice Yvonne Scally, Aug. 18, 1956; children—Gregg Dowel, Joe Thomas. With Western Electric Co., Oklahoma City, 1959-66; mgr. indsl. engring., Corken Pump Co., Oklahoma City, 1966-73; dir. mfg., Fife Corp., Oklahoma City, 1973—. Registered profl. engr., Okla. Mem. Soc. Mfg. Engrs. (regional chmn. 1973-74). Home: Route 2 Box 137 Edmond OK 73034 Office: PO Box 18815 Oklahoma City OK 73118

FINE, J(AMES) ALLEN, ins. co. exec.; b. Albemarle, N.C., May 2, 1934; s. Samuel Lee and Ocie (Loflin) F.; student Pfeiffer Coll., 1957-58; B.S., U. N.C., 1961, M.B.A., 1965; m. Marie Nan Morris, Sept. 1, 1957; children—James A(llen), William Morris. Sr. accountant Haskins & Sells, C.P.A.'s Charlotte, N.C., 1961-62, Watson, Penry, & Morgan, Asheboro, N.C., 1962-64; instr. U. N.C., Chapel Hill, 1964-65; asst. prof. Pfeiffer Coll., Misenheimer, N.C., 1965-66; treas., v.p. adminstrn. Nat. Lab. for Higher Edn. (formerly Regional Edn. Lab. Carolinas and Va.), Durham, N.C., 1966-72; organizer, pres., treas., dir. Investors Title Ins. Co., Inc., Chapel Hill, 1972—; chmn. bd., pres. treas. Investors Title Ins. Co. S.C., Columbia, 1973—. Lectr. accounting U. N.C., Chapel Hill, 1967-70. Area officer ann. alumni giving U. N.C., Chapel Hill, 1968-69, 71, 72, 73. Served with USN, 1953-57. Recipient Haskins & Sells Found. award for excellence in accounting, 1961; N.C. Assn. CPA's award for most outstanding accounting student U. N.C., 1961. Mem. Am. Inst. C.P.A.'s, N.C. Assn. C.P.A.'s, Am. Accounting Assn., CEDAR Bus. Mgrs. (chmn. nat. exec. com. 1971), Phi Beta Kappa, Beta Gamma Sigma (treas. 1961). Home: 112 Carolina Forest Chapel Hill NC 27514 Office: University Sq Chapel Hill NC 27514

FINE, ROBERT STANLEY, electronics engr.; b. San Pedro, Cal., June 17, 1939; s. Ben J. and Jean B. (Goldenburg) F.; B.S., U. Cal. at Los Angeles, 1962; M.E., U. Fla., 1968; m. Barbara G. Foshee, June 11, 1960; children—Robin, Ronald. Electronics designer McDonnell Douglas Corp., Los Angeles, 1962-65, missile test and evaluation engr., Cape Kennedy, Fla., 1965—. Mem. I.E.E.E., Nat. Soc. Profl. Engrs. Home: 527 Indian River Av Titusville FL 32780 Office: PO Box 21007 Kennedy Space Center FL 32899

FINERAN, JOHN STEPHEN, realtor; b. New Orleans, Jan. 8, 1918; s. John Stephen and Louisa Theresa (Everett) F.; student Notre Dame Sem., New Orleans, 1937-40, Loyola Sch. Law, Los Angeles, 1946-47; M.A.I., Notre Dame U., 1957; m. Carol Mary Hardebeck, Aug. 18, 1944; children—Maureen (Mrs. Floyd B. Bringle), Kathleen T., John Stephen III. Salesman, Pangborn Realty Co., Arcadia, Cal., 1945; agt. New York Life Ins. Co., Pasadena, Cal., 1948; real estate agt. Texaco, Inc., New Orleans, 1951-63; real estate appraiser, broker, Memphis, 1963—. Guest lectr. U. Tenn./Memphis State U.; independent fee appraiser FHA, VA, FAA, City of Memphis, Internal Revenue Service, Tenn. State Hwy. Dept., TVA. Active Shelby United Neighbors, 1963-65. Served to maj. USAAF, 1941-45. Decorated Air medal with 8 oak leaf clusters. Mem. Am. Inst. Real Estate Appraisers, Memphis Bd. Realtors, Nat. Assn. Realtors. Roman Catholic. Clubs: Legion of Mary, Civitan. Home: 5095 Whiteway Dr Memphis TN 38117 Office: Commerce Title Bldg Memphis TN 38103

FINGAR, WALTER WIGGS, educator; b. Nashville, Jan. 14, 1934; s. Julian Russell and Murphy (Vaden) F.; student Middle Tenn. State U., 1952-54; D.D.S., U. Tenn., 1957; M.S., U. Ia., 1965; m. Mildred Annette Heinz, July 15, 1955; children—Mildred Elizabeth, Linda Elaine, Walter Brian, William Russell, Amy Jo, Rachel Lynn. Practice dentistry, Nashville, 1959-63; USPHS fellow, instr., asst. prof. U. Ia., Iowa City, 1963-67; asst. prof. U. Tenn., Memphis, 1967-68; asso. prof. operative dentistry Med. S.C., Charleston, 1968—, chmn. dept. operative dentistry-endodontics, 1971—; mem. staff Med. U. S.C. Hosp. Served to capt. Dental Corps, AUS, 1957-59. Mem. Am., S.C., Coastal dental assns., Am. Assn. U. Profs. Am. Assn. Dental Schs., Am. Acad. Operative Dentistry, Am. Acad. Gen. Dentistry. Home: 766 Norfolk Dr Charleston SC 29401

FINGER, HOMER ELLIS, JR., bishop; b. Ripley, Miss., Oct. 8, 1916; s. Homer Ellis and Bertha (Rogers) F.; A.B., Millsaps Coll., Jackson, Miss., 1937; student Emory U., 1938-39; B.D., Yale, 1941; student Union Theol. Sem., N.Y.C., 1946; D.D. (hon.), Centenary Coll. La., 1954; m. Mamie Lee Ratliff, Oct. 6, 1942; children—Homer Ellis, William Ratliff, Elizabeth Ellen. Math. tchr. Aberdeen (Miss.) high sch., 1937-38; ordained to ministry Methodist Ch., 1941; pastor, Coldwater, Miss., 1941-43, Oxford, Miss., 1946-52; pres. Millsaps Coll., 1952-64; resident bishop Meth. Ch., Nashville, 1964—. Mem. commn. on colls., exec. council So. Assn. Colls. and Secondary Schs.; mem. univ. senate Meth. Ch.; mem. Southeastern Jurisdictional Council, 1956—; chmn. United Meth. Commn. on Chaplains and Related Ministries, 1968-72; mem. exec. com. World Meth. Council, mem. bd. Christian social concerns. Served as chaplain USNR, Air Sta., Pensacola, Fla., 1944-45, with 75th constrn. bn., Philippines, 1945-46. Mem. Jackson C. of C. (dir.), Pi Kappa Alpha, Omicron Delta Kappa, Eta Sigma Phi (past nat. pres.). Rotarian (dir. Jackson). Home: 301 Hillwood Dr Nashville TN 37205 Office: 95 White Bridge Rd Nashville TN 37205

FINK, DONALD ALFRED, economist; b. Hammond, Ind., Jan. 16, 1930; s. Lee Edward and Jane (Dye) F.; B.A., Yale, 1952, M.A., 1955; postgrad. Am. U., 1963-65; m. Beatrice C. Freeman, June 11, 1955; children—Alan Lee, Marc Louis. Research asso. Carnegie Inst. Tech., 1959-62; cons. Govt. of Columbia, 1962-63; sr. economist Pan Am. Union, Washington, 1963—, chief Andean countries, 1965-67, chief Caribbean countries, 1967-68; economist Nat. Assn. Wool Mfrs., 1968-71; sec., treas. McLean Products Internat., Inc., 1971—, also dir.; dep. mng. dir. Skoko Ltd., 1971—, also dir.; dir. UNCO, Inc. Econ. cons. Latin Am. Iron and Steel Inst., Latin Am. Free Trade Assn. Bd. dirs. Springfield Boys Club. Served with USN, 1955-59; now comdr. Supply Corps Res. Mem. Am. Econ. Assn., Royal Econ. Soc. Eng., Am. Finance Assn. Home: 6111 Madawaska Rd Bethesda MD 20016 Office: Suite 838 815 15th St NW Washington DC 20005

FINK, ELI HARRY, lawyer; b. Jacksonville, Fla., June 18, 1909; s. Harry and Sophie (Starr) Finkelstein; A.B., Washington and Lee U., 1932, LL.B., J.D., 1935; m. Emily Morgenstern, Feb. 14, 1946; children—Elizabeth Sue, Eli Harry, Edward Lawrence. Admitted to Fla. bar, 1935; practiced in Jacksonville, 1935—; asst. city atty., 1937-42; city solicitor, 1946; counsel Kent, Sears, Durden & Kent, 1973—. Pres., chmn. bd. So. Indsl. Bank, Jacksonville. Past pres., bd. dirs., mem. exec. com. St. Lukes Hosp.; past pres., bd. dirs.

Jacksonville Civic Music Assn.; bd. regents Fla. Bd. Control, 1949-53. Served to lt. comdr. USNR, World War II. Mem. Am., Fla., Jacksonville bar assns., Omicron Delta Kappa, Zeta Beta Tau. Jewish religion. Clubs: River, University, Beauclerc Country (Jacksonville). Home: 1205 Jean Ct Jacksonville FL 32207 Office: Fla Nat Bank Bldg Jacksonville FL 32202

FINK, JOHN BERNARD, newspaper advt. exec.; b. N.Y.C., Apr. 6, 1935; s. Edward Bernard and Kathryn (Long) F.; student pub. schs.; m. Cheryl Dorothy Hurst, Mar. 28, 1969; 1 son, Glen Patrick. Police officer, Hallandale, Fla., 1961-66; classified salesman Miami Herald, 1966-69, classified office mgr., 1969-70; classified advt. mgr. Tallahassee (Fla.) Democrat, 1970—. Disaster chmn. Leon County A.R.C., 1970-71. Served with USMC, 1953-57. Mem. Tallahassee Advt. Fedn. (pres. 1971), Tallahassee Auto dealers Assn. Tallahassee Builders Assn., Tallahassee Realtors Assn., Tallahassee C. of C. (mem. pres.'s council 1970-71). Mem. Fraternal Order Police. Elk. Home: 828-4 Ingleside St Tallahassee FL 32303 Office: 277 N Magnolia Dr Tallahassee FL 32302

FINKNER, ALVA LEROY, research co. exec.; b. Akron, Colo., May 8, 1917; s. A. Ed G. and Iona A. (Roszell) F.; B.S., Colo. State U., 1938; M.S., Kan. State U., 1940; Ph.D., N.C. State U., 1950; m. Betty Jane Rabeler, Feb. 17, 1946; children—Patricia (Mrs. Rodney Boyette), Stephen Glen, Judith Lynn. With statis. reporting service U.S. Dept. Agr., Raleigh, N.C., 1940-50, agrl. statistician, head Raleigh research office, 1946; asso. prof. N.C. State U., Raleigh, 1950-55, prof., 1955-60, adj. prof., 1960—; with Research Triangle Inst., Research Triangle Park, N.C., 1960—, sr. statistician, dir. statistics research div., 1964-71, v.p. for social scis. and human resources, 1971—. Served to maj. AUS, 1942-46. Decorated Bronze Star. Fellow Am. Statis. Assn.; mem. Inter-Am. Statis. Inst. (asso.), Am. Farm Econs. Assn., (mem. joint com. agrl. statistics with Am. Statis. Assn.), Sigma Xi, Phi Kappa Phi, Gamma Sigma Delta, Alpha Zeta. Author: (with Robert Monroe) Principles of Test Design, 1955; (with John Monroe) Handbook of Area Sampling, 1959. Home: 3909 Arrow Dr Raleigh NC 27612 Office: PO Box 12194 Research Triangle Park NC 27709

FINLAYSON, BIRDWELL, physician, educator; b. Pocatello, Ida., Oct. 28, 1932; s. Birdwell and Jessie Leon (Smith) F.; student, U. Utah, 1951-53, Ida. State Coll., 1950-51; M.D., U. Chgo., 1957, Ph.D., 1967; m. Carol Jean Deaton, Sept. 20, 1955; children—Deborah Ann, Jon Camille. Intern, U. Chgo. Clinics, 1957-58, resident, 1958-67; asst. prof. urology U. Fla., Gainesville, 1967-69, asso. prof., 1969-71, prof., 1971—. USPHS fellow, 1960-63, 63-67; Fla. Med. Found. grantee, 1967-69; NIH grantee, 1969—. Diplomate Am. Bd. Urology, Nat. Bd. Med. Examiners. Fellow A.C.S., Surgeons; mem. Am. Urol. Assn., Soc. of Univ. Urologists, Alachua County Med. Soc. Contbr. articles in field to profl. jours. Home: 815 NW 36th Dr Gainesville FL 32601 Office: Shands Teaching Hospital Gainesville FL 32610

FINLEY, GEORGE PARKEY, lawyer; b. Aspermont, Tex., Dec. 28, 1915; s. George Parkey and Ethel Frances (Ferrell) F.; student, Tex. Tech., 1932-34; B.B.A. with honors, Tex. U., 1948, LL.B., 1950; m. Wilma Terry, May 8, 1941; children—Mary Kay. Admitted to Tex. bar, 1950; since practiced in Kermit; mem. firm Roberson, Finley & Duncan, 1953-57, Finley & Scogin, 1957—; county atty., 1953-57. Served with USNR, 1942-45. Mem. State Bar Tex., Tex. Bar Found., Am. Tex. trial lawyers assns., Am. Coll. Probate Counsel, Tex. Soc. C.P.A.'s, Delta Sigma Pi, Beta Gamma Sigma, Phi Delta Phi, Beta Alpha Psi. Home: 215 S Av H Kermit TX 79745 Office: PO Box 920 211 N Oak St Kermit TX 79745

FINLEY, JOHN BROWNING, educator; b. Crowley, La., July 18, 1919; s. John Armen and Bess Opal (Browning) F.; B.S., U. Southwestern La., 1941, B.S. in Chem. Engring., 1942, M.S., 1960; Ph.D., Okla. State U., 1963; m. Agnes Katherine Baumback, July 25, 1943; children—Jane (Mrs. Belve Dansby Marks III), Karl, Forrest, Deborah (Mrs. Jerry Wayne Bravenec). Research chem. engr. Humble Oil Co., Baytown, Tex., 1942-47; retail automobile dealer, Crowley, La., 1947-54; chem. engring. cons., Lafayette, La., 1954-56; gen. mgr. rice mill, Crowley, 1956-58; prof. chem. engring. Tex. A. and I. U., Kingsville, 1963—. Precinct chmn. Republican Party, 1965-66. Registered profl. engr., Tex., La. Mem. Am. Inst. Chem. Engrs. (asso.), Am. Soc. Engring. Edn., Am. Chem. Soc., Sigma Psi, Omega Chi Epsilon. Mason, Rotarian. Home: 1776 Santa Maria St Kingsville TX 78363

FINLEY, WILLIAM WALTER, JR., civil and environmental engr.; b. nr. Charlottesville, Va., Jan. 24, 1928; s. William Walter and Milissa (Hoover) F.; B.S., Va. Poly. Inst., 1953, M.S., 1968; m. Mae Elliott, Aug. 7, 1953; children—John Weldon, Walter Gordon, Martha Sharon, James Edward, William Eugene. Civil engr. TVA, Knoxville, Tenn., 1953-55; structural engr. Burns & Roe, Inc., N.Y.C., 1955-59; sr. civil engr., chief div. of waste treatment City of Richmond, Va., 1959-63; partner Blue & Finley, cons. engrs., Charlottesville, 1965-66; san. engr., chief planning and reports Chesapeake Bay-Susquehanna River Basins project Fed. Water Pollution Control Adminstrn., 1966-68; project mgr. WHO Master Plans Waste Disposal and Drainage, UNDP Spl. Fund Project Ibadan, Nigeria, 1968-72; internat. dir. Research and Devel. of Environmental Pollution Control Programs, Sao Paulo, Brazil, 1972—; instr. civil engring. Va. Poly. Inst., 1964-65; lectr. civil engring. U. Va., 1965-66. Served to 1st lt. AUS, 1946-47. Registered profl. engr. Diplomate Am. Acad. Environmental Engrs. Mem. Water Pollution Control Fedn., Va. Soc. Profl. Engrs. Baptist (deacon). Address: Free Union VA

FINN, DANIEL FRANCIS, ednl. assn. exec.; b. Norwich, Conn., Aug. 15, 1922; s. Daniel Francis and Elizabeth Ann (Elliott) F.; A.B. cum laude in Econ., Brown U., 1943; postgrad. U. Me., 1944, U. Nancy (France), 1945, Purdue U., 1957; m. Gabrielle LaFayette Beausoleil, Aug. 26, 1948; children—Daniel, Mark, Chad, Beth, Bart. Asst. purchasing agt. Brown U., Providence, 1946-48, purchasing agt., 1948-55; purchasing agt. Purdue U., Lafayette, Ind., 1955-61, bus. mgr., asst. treas., 1961-69; exec. v.p. Nat. Assn. Coll. and Univ. Bus. Officers, Washington, 1969—. Instr. extension course Brown U., Providence, 1954. Chmn. nat. adv. panel Nat. Center Higher Edn. Mgmt. Systems, Boulder, Colo., 1969-72; parish chmn. Bishop's Appeal, Washington, 1972—. Exec. bd. Tippecanoe Council, Boy Scouts Am., 1963-69, Lafayette Symphony Orch., 1965-69; bd. dirs. Center for Research Libraries, Chgo., 1961-69, pres., 1966; bd. dirs. Coop. Coll. Registry, 1973. Served with Q.M.C. and inf. AUS, 1943-45. Decorated Croix de Guerre (France). Mem. Nat. Assn. Ednl. Buyers (hon. life), Ind. Assn. Coll. and Univ. Bus. Officers (hon. life), Assn. Phys. Plant Adminstrn. (hon. life), Phi Beta Kappa. Democrat. Roman Catholic. Rotarian. Mem. adv. bd. Coll. and Univ. Bus. mag., Chgo., 1950-60. Home: 8517 Warde Terrace Potomac MD 20854 Office: One Dupont Circle Suite 510 Washington DC 20036

FINN, DAVID LESTER, educator; b. Memphis, Mar. 30, 1924; s. Romer Carl and Kate (Holt) F.; B.S., Purdue U., 1948, M.S., 1950, Ph.D., 1952; m. Celia Taylor, Apr. 4, 1948; children—Katherine, Bette, Ruth. Prof. elec. engring. Ga. Inst. Tech., Atlanta, 1952—. Served with USAAF, 1943-46. Mem. Am. Assn. U. Profs. Home: 646 Longwood Dr Atlanta GA 30305

FINNEGAN, MARCUS BARTLETT, lawyer; b. Morristown, N.J., Sept. 15, 1927; s. George Bernard and Elisabeth (Morgan) F.; B.S., U.S. Mil. Acad., 1949; LL.B., U. Va., 1955; LL.M., George Washington U., 1957; m. Betsy Neil Hummer, June 3, 1950; children—Nancy Lee, Susan Bartlett, Katharine Elisabeth. Admitted to Va., D.C. bars, 1955, U.S. Supreme Ct., N.Y. bars, 1960; U.S. patent adviser to Japan, Tokyo, 1957-59; atty. firm Morgan, Finnegan, Durham & Pine, N.Y.C., 1959-63, Irons, Birch, Swindler, & McKie, Washington, 1963-65; sr. partner Finnegan, Henderson, Farabow & Garrett, Washington, 1965—. Professorial lectr. law George Washington U., 1971—; lectr. various profl. groups; invited expert tech. licensing, group meeting experts UNIDO, Vienna, Austria, 1972; cons. licensing and tech. transfer Govt. Mexico, 1973—. Served to capt. U.S. Army, 1949-59. Mem. Raven Soc., Bar Assn. D.C., Am. (chmn. patent law com., adminstrv. law sect. 1974), Fed., Va., Inter-Am., Internat. bar assns., Am. (bd. mgrs. 1974—), N.Y., N.J. patent law assns., U.S. C. of C. (antitrust and trade regulation com.), N.Y. County Lawyers Assn., Assn. Bar City of N.Y., Am. Soc. Metals, U. Va. Law Sch. Found., Inst. Mil. Law, Internat. Legal Soc. Japan, Va. State Bar, Am. Judicature Soc., Assn. Grads. U.S. Mil. Acad., West Point Soc. O.C., Army Athletic Assn., Licensing Execs. Soc. U.S.A. (v.p. Eastern region 1971-72, pres. 1973-74), Licensing Execs. Soc.-Internat. (pres. elect), Am. Mgmt. Assn., Internat. Patent and Trademark Assn., World Peace Through Law Center, Patent and Trademark Inst. Can., Order of Coif, Phi Delta Phi, Omicron Delta Kappa. Episcopalian. Clubs: Touchdown (Washington); Army and Navy, Nat. Lawyers, International, George Washington University (Washington); Tokyo (Japan) Am.; Army Navy Country, Washington Golf and Country (Arlington, Va.); Congressional Country, Kenwood Country (Bethesda, Md.); Metropolitan. Author: (with Richard W. Pogue) Federal Employee Invention Rights-Time to Legislate, 1957; co-author: Patent-Antiturst: Compliance and Confrontation, 1972. Contbg. editor Les Nouvelles Internat. Licensing Jour. Home: 9017 Clewerwall Dr Bethesda MD 20034 Office: 1775 K St NW Washington DC 20006

FINNELL, WILLIAM CONRAD, lawyer; b. Cleve., Nov. 20, 1938; s. William Theodore and Beatrice Ellen (Presswood) F.; B.S., U. Tenn., 1959, LL.B., 1962; m. Warnie Elizabeth Dooly, June 4, 1960; 1 dau., Jennifer Ellen. Salesman, Southwestern Co., Nashville, 1955-62; admitted to Tenn. bar, 1962; practice law, Cleveland, Tenn., 1962—; sr. partner law firm. Finnell, Thompson, Scott & Logan, 1962—; prin. Travena Grammar Sch., Cleveland, Tenn., 1958; partner Finnell, Thompson & Cannon Apartments, Cleveland, Tenn., 1968—; dir. Founders Security Life Ins. Co., Memphis. Pres. Cleveland Bradley County Citizens for Better Schs., 1964-65; boxing coach YMCA, 1962-63. Bd. dirs. Cleveland Bradley County March of Dimes Campaign, 1965. Recipient Man of the Year award Cleveland (Tenn.) Jr. C. of C. Mem. Am., Tenn. bar assns., Am., Tenn. (bd. govs.) trial lawyers assns., Am. Judicature Soc., Cleveland Jr. C. of C., V.F.W., Lambda Chi Alphi (pres.). Republican Lion. Home: 2620 Springplace Rd Cleveland TN 37311 Office: 213 Broad St Cleveland TN 37311

FINNERAN, RICHARD JOHN, educator; b. N.Y.C., Dec. 19, 1943; s. Edward George and Maude Florence (Rudden) F.; B.A., N.Y. U., 1964; Ph.D., U. N.C., 1968. Instr., U. Fla., 1967-68, N.Y. U., 1968-70; asst. prof. English Newcomb Coll., Tulane U., 1970—. Mem. Internat. Assn. Study Anglo-Irish Lit. (mem. exec. com. 1973—), Modern Lang. Assn. (chmn. Celtic group 1972), Am. Assn. U. Profs., Am. Com. for Irish Studies, South Atlantic Modern Lang. Assn., South Central Modern Lang. Assn. (chmn. Anglo-Irish sect. 1972). Author: The Prose Fiction of W.B. Yeats 1973; Editor: John Sherman and Dhoya (W.B. Yeats), 1969; William Butler Yeats: The Byzantium Poems (W.B. Yeats), 1970; Letters of James Stephens, 1974. Contbr. articles to profl. jours. Home: 1024 Lowerline St New Orleans LA 70118

FINNERTY, HUGH JAMES, investment co. exec.; b. St. Louis, Sept. 29, 1918; s. Hugh Joseph and Lena (Schultz) F.; student St. Louis U., 1936-37, U. Minn., 1942; m. Kathryn Joy Mutz, Nov. 28, 1946; children—Mark Hugh, Danny James. Sports dir. KOTV, tv. sta., Tulsa, 1953-56, regional sales mgr., 1956-59; sales mgr. KTUL-TV, 1959-61; gen. mgr. Tulsa Baseball Club, 1961-65; pres. Tex. Baseball League, 1965-69; v.p. Ada Securities Corp., Houston, 1969—; pres. bd. Tulsa Speedway, Inc., 1971—. Vice-pres. bd. Tulsa YMCA, 1967. Served with AUS, 1941-45. Mem. Sales and Marketing Execs. of Tulsa (pres. 1961), Sales and Marketing Execs. Inst. (council pres. 1970-71). Clubs: Coat of Arms (pres. 1968—), Petroleum (Tulsa). Home: 4625 S Lewis St Tulsa OK 74105 Office: Box 4196 Tulsa OK 74104

FINNEY, JOSEPH CLAUDE JEANS, educator; b. Urbana, Ill., Mar. 18, 1927; s. Claude Lee and Margaret Ellen (Boillin) F.; B.A., Vanderbilt U., 1946; postgrad. U. Notre Dame, 1947; M.D., Harvard, 1949; postgrad. U. Cal. at Berkeley, 1950-51, 52-53; Ph.D., Stanford, 1959; LL.B., LaSalle U., 1972; m. Mary Littlefield, Jan. 21, 1955; children—Carol, Michael, John, Ellen. Med. intern Johns Hopkins Hosp., Balt., 1949-50; resident physician U.S. VA Hosp., Palo Alto, 1953-56; dir. Champaign County Mental Health Center, 1956-60; chief research State Mental Health System, Hawaii, 1960-63; asso. prof. psychiatry U. Ky., 1963-67, prof. ednl. psychology, 1967—. Cons. U.S. Dept. Justice, 1966—; vice-chmn. Joint Nat. Liaison Com. Law and Psychiatry, 1973-74. Leader, Blue Grass Council Boy Scouts Am., 1970—. Served to lt. (j.g.) USPHS, 1951-53. Recipient Research Grants, U.S. Nat. Inst. Mental Health, 1966-68, U.S. Social and Rehab. Services, 1967-70. Fellow Am. Psychiat. Assn., Am. Coll. Legal Medicine, Am. Anthropol. Assn.; mem. Am. Bar Assn., Am. Psychol. Assn., Linguistic Soc., Am., Assn. Research in Nervous and Mental Disease, Am. Personnel and Guidance Assn., Polynesian Soc., Soc. Sci. Study Sex, V.F.W., Ky. Assn. Profl. Psychologists (pres. 1973), Phi Beta Kappa. Kiwanian. Author: Culture Change, Mental Health and Poverty, 1969. Home: 821 Cahaba Dr Lexington KY 40502

FINNEY, THOMAS DUNN, JR., lawyer; b. Idabel, Okla., Jan. 20, 1925; s. Thomas D. and Bettie (Higgs) F.; A.B., U. Okla., 1945, LL.B., 1948; m. Sally Van Horn, June 25, 1945; children—Susan Deuell (Mrs. Richard Ford), Kathleen, Deirdre, Thomas. Admitted to Okla. bar, 1948, D.C. bar, 1963; with Finney & Finney, Idabel, 1948-51; polit. officer U.S. Fgn. Service embassy Copenhagen (Denmark), 1952-55; with Foliart, Hunt & Shepherd, Oklahoma City, 1955-57; adminstrv. asst. to U.S. Senator A.S. Mike Monroney, 1957-63; with Clifford, Warnke, Glass, McIlwain, & Finney (formerly Clifford & Miller) Washington, 1963—. Dep. spl. asst. to pres. for fgn. trade policy, 1962; spl. counsel to credentials com. Democratic Nat. Conv., 1964. Served to lt. (j.g.) USNR, 1943-46. Mem. Phi Gamma Delta, Phi Delta Phi, Delta Sigma Rho. Home: 9000 McDonald Dr Bethesda MD 20034 Office: 815 Connecticut Av Washington DC 20006

FIORELLA, BARBARA CLAIRE TOHMS, social worker; b. Chgo., July 15, 1927; d. Clifton and Frances (Byrnes) Tohms.; B.S., Pa. State U., 1959; M.S.W. (Nat. Inst. Mental Health fellow), Fla. State U., 1962; postgrad. Fla. Atlantic U., 1968; m. Theodore Joseph Fiorella, June 12, 1948 (div. Oct. 1958); children—Stephen Ward, Mark John, Theodore Jeffry, Barbara Lynn. Caseworker, Children's Service Bur., Miami, Fla., 1962-64; psychiat. caseworker Jackson Meml. Hosp. Psychiat. Inst., Miami, 1964—; mem. clin. faculty Barry Coll. Grad. Sch. Social Work, Miami, 1972—; instr. dept. psychiatry U. Miami Med. Sch., 1964—; vis. lectr. Fla. Internat. U., Miami, 1974—. Bd. dirs. Big Sisters of Greater Miami, 1969-71, v.p., 1970-71. Mem. Fla. Juvenile Officer's Assn., Assn. Agy. Field Instrs., Acad. Certified Social Workers, Fla. Soc. Clin. Social Work (charter). Home: 10235 SW 106th St Miami FL 33156 Office: 1700 NW 10th Av Miami FL 33132

FIRESTONE, GEORGE, investments exec., state senator; b. N.Y.C., May 13, 1931; s. Benjamin and Sally (Gollon) F.; student pub. schs., Miami, Fla.; m. Helene A. Eiserman, Aug. 28, 1952. Ins. broker Berkshire Life Ins. Co., 1952-56, Guardian Life Ins. Co., 1956-61; with Gray Security Service, Miami, Fla., 1961-72; sec., treas. Investco, Inc., Miami, 1972—; mem. Fla. Ho. of Reps., 1966-71; mem. Fla. Senate, 1971—. Pres., N.W. Miami Property Owners Assn., 1957; v.p. Dade County Council Civic Orgns., 1957; chmn. Miami Econ. Adv. Bd., 1962, Dade County Personnel Adv. Bd., 1965. Bd. dirs. Here's Help. Served with AUS, 1948-52. Mem. Nat. Soc. State Legislators (pres.), Greater Miami Jr. C. of C. (pres. 1960). Home: 630 SW 8th Av Miami FL 33130 Office: 2424 S Dixie Hwy Miami FL 33133

FISCHER, ERNEST FREDERICK, JR., researcher, investment exec.; b. Houston, Feb. 11, 1940; s. Ernest Fredrick and Margaret Louise (Fitzgerald) F.; B.A., Gustavus Adolphus Coll., 1962; M.A., U. Tex., 1964; m. Jeanne Serur, Apr. 4, 1964; children—Charlotte Jean, Jason Frederick. Asst. prof. U.S. Army-Baylor U. program health care adminstrn., San Antonio, 1966-69, also asst. prof. San Antonio Coll., 1966-70, and lectr. St. Mary's Grad. Sch. Bus., San Antonio, 1969-70; research asso. A.M.A., Chgo., 1969-70, also project dir. Hosp. Research and Ednl. Trust, Chgo., 1969-73; health economist U. Ill. Coll. Medicine, 1973; pres., dir. Urban Am. Corp., Austin, Tex., 1968-74; pres., dir. Urban Am. Investments, Inc., 1970-74. Adminstrv. asst. Rep. Nat. Comitteeman of Tex., 1965. Served to capt. M.S.C., AUS, 1966-69. Mem. Chgo. Assn. Bus. Economists, Am. Econs. Assn. Republican. Lutheran. Author: Houston—Site for Industrial Location, 1967; Annotated Bibliography on the Sharing, Centralization and Consolidation of Clinical Laboratory and Related Diagnostic Facilities, 1971. Office: P O Box 731 Austin TX 78767

FISCHER, GEORGE HERMAN, utility exec., lawyer; b. Jacksonville, Fla., June 27, 1923; s. George H. and Florence Lucille (Lawson) F.; LL.B., U. S.C., 1949; LL.M., Duke, 1950; m. Dorothy Virginia Flory, Dec. 23, 1947; children—George, Cindy, Karen, David, Susan. Admitted to S.C. bar, 1949; editor, Lawyers Coop. Publ. Co., Rochester, N.Y., 1950-53; mem. firm Nelson, Mullins & Grier, Columbia, S.C., 1953-59; v.p., gen. counsel S.C. Electric & Gas Co., Columbia, 1959—; trustee Bankers Trust S.C., Columbia. Pres., United Community Services, 1970, campaign chmn., 1968. Served to 1st lt. USAAF, 1943-46: PTO. Decorated Air medal with oak leaf cluster. Mem. Am., S.C., bar assns., Fed. Power Bar Assn., Edison Electric Inst., Columbia C. of C. (v.p. 1967). Presbyn. (deacon). Clubs: Army Navy (Washington); Carolina Yacht (Charleston, S.C.; Palmetto, Forest Lake (Columbia). Home: 4737 Lockewood Lane Columbia SC 29206 Office: PO Box 764 Columbia SC 29218

FISCHER, MABEL JULIA THOMAS (MRS. THEODORE C. FISCHER), librarian; b. Reading Pa.; d. Costa and Katharine Irene (Kalbach) Thomas; A.B., Albright Coll.; M.A., Temple U.; M.L.S., Tex. Woman's U.; m. Theodore C. Fischer. Br. librarian Reading Pub. Library, 1944-48; children's asst. Tulsa Pub. Library, 1949-50; dept. head Ft. Worth Pub. Library, 1950-62, asst. dir., 1964-70, dir., 1970—; br. head Dallas Pub. Library, 1963-64. Mem. summer faculty Tex. Woman's U., 1962-70. Mem. audit com. Fort Worth City Employees Credit Union, 1968—, chmn., 1972. Bd. dirs. YWCA, Ft. Worth. Mem. A.L.A., Tex. (pres., sec.-treas. pub. library div., chmn. dist. planning com), S.W. library assns., Am. Assn. U. Women, Ft. Worth Bus. and Profl. Women's Club. Club: Altrusa. Home: Route 1 Box 132 Roanoke TX 76262 Office: Ft Worth Public Library 9th and Throckmorton Sts Fort Worth TX 76102

FISCHLSCHWEIGER, WERNER, educator; b. Bremen, Germany, May 4, 1932; s. Hermann and Martha (von Ahsen) Schwiebert; certificate Tchrs. Tng. Coll., Graz, Austria, 1952; Ph.D., U. Graz, Austria, 1957; m. Karin Groeger, Apr. 29, 1960; children—Hagen, Thomas. Came to U.S., 1963, naturalized, 1973. Dir. tissue culture lab. Austrian Cancer Research Inst., Vienna, 1958-61; asst. prof. U. Graz Med. Sch., 1962-63; asst. prof. dept. anatomy St. Louis U., 1963-65; asso. prof. U. Md. Dental Sch., 1965-69; prof. dept. basic dental scis. U. Fla. Coll. Dentistry, Gainesville, 1969—. Troop com. N. Fla. Council Boy Scouts Am., 1972—. Home: 804 NW 36th Terrace Gainesville FL 32605

FISCHMAN, LEONARD LIPMAN, economist; b. Bklyn., Jan. 23, 1919; s. Murray M. and Sarah G. (Link) F.; A.B., N.Y. U., 1937; M.A., Am. U., 1939; m. Evelyn R. Kay, Apr. 18, 1958. Asst. operation head U.S. Bur. Census, Washington, 1940-41; chief statistics spl. studies br. program coordination div. UNRRA, Rome, Italy, 1946-47; internat. trade economist, acting chief Mediterranean sect. Office Internat. Trade U.S. Dept. Commerce, Washington, 1948-50; internat. economist, editor Minerals Yearbook, U.S. Bur. Mines, Washington, 1950-53; cons. P.R. Econ. Devel. Adminstrn., San Juan, 1953-58; econ. cons., dir. Econ. Assos., Inc., Washington, 1958—, pres., 1962—. Served with AUS, 1941-46. Mem. Am. Econ. Assn., Am. Statis. Assn., A.A.A.S., Nat. Planning Assn., Nat. Economists Club, Nat. Assn. Bus. Economists, Assn. Evolutionary Econs., Soc. Internat. Devel. Club Internat. (Washington). Home: 520 22d St NW Washington DC 20037 Office: 1730 K St NW Washington DC 20006

FISH, JOHN HAROLD III, elec. engr.; b. Lake Village, Ark., Apr. 13, 1940; s. John Harold and Edith Gail (Nelson) F.; B.E., Vanderbilt U., 1963; M.S. in E.E., U. Tenn., 1971. With TVA, Chattanooga, 1963—, elec. engr. planning for transmission system expansions. City bldg. inspector, Jasper, Tenn., 1969-73. Registered profl. engr., Tenn. Mem. I.E.E.E., Delta Kappa Epsilon. Home: 217B Baxter St Chattanooga TN 37415 Office: Chattanooga Bank Bldg Chattanooga TN 37401

FISH, STEWART ALLISON, physician, educator; b. Benton, Ill., Nov. 4, 1925; s. Floyd Hamilton and Mary Vivian (Fish) F.; student Va. Poly. Inst., 1943-44, U. Va., 1944-45; M.D., U. Pa., 1949; m. Patsy June Patterson, Apr. 24, 1957; children—Jayne, Jeffrey, Carolyn, Mary. Intern, Hosp. U. Pa., 1949-50; resident obstetrics-gynecology Columbia-Presbyn. Med. Center, N.Y.C., 1950-53; chief resident gynecology Free Hosp. Women, Boston, 1953-54; asst. prof. obstetrics and gynecology Southwestern Med. Sch., U. Tex., 1954-56; practice medicine specializing in obstetrics and gynecology, Dallas, 1956; asst. prof. obstetrics and gynecology U. Ark., Little Rock, 1962; prof., chmn. obstetrics and gynecology U. Tenn., Memphis, 1966—; obstetrician, gynecologist in chief City of Memphis Hosps.; mem. active staff Bapt. Meml. Hosp; cons. U.S. Naval, St. Joseph, Meth. hosps., Memphis, Tenn. Served with USNR, 1943-46. Recipient Golden Apple award U. Ark., 1965-66, Bicentennial Silver medal Columbia Coll. Phys. and Surg., 1968. Fellow A.C.S., Am. Coll. Obstetricians and Gynecologists; mem. Am., Central assns. obstetricians and gynecologists, Tenn. State Obstet. and Gynecol.

Soc. (pres. 1972-73), Sigma Xi, Sigma Chi, Phi Chi. Episcopalian. Mem. editorial bd. Tenn. Med. Alumnus, 1970. Home: 1507 Massey Rd Memphis TN 38138

FISHBACK, ELLA SCOTT, wholesale trade co. exec.; b. Lexington, Ky., July 30, 1918; d. Robert Edward and Bessie Mae (Scott) Fishback; student U. Ky., 1935-37. Clk. dairy and poultry plant Swift & Co., Inc., Lexington, Ky., 1939-41, chief clk., 1941-55; office mgr. Ky. Ignition Co., Inc., Lexington, 1955-67, sec., 1963—, controller, dir., Louisville, 1967—; sec., dir. S.E. Gasket & Parts Warehouse, Atlanta. Mem. Am. Soc. Women Accountants (dir., past treas.). Club: Altrusa (dir.) (Louisville). Home: 4834A Westport Rd Louisville KY 40222 Office: 737 S 3d St Louisville KY 40202

FISHBEIN, GERSHON WILLIAM, editor; b. Washington, Oct. 9, 1921; s. Abraham and Anna (Scheer) F.; B.A., George Washington U., 1943; postgrad. U. Paris Ecole Libre des Sciences Politiques, 1945-46; m. Phyllis Shapiro, Nov. 21, 1948; children—Alan, Lawrence, Jeffrey, Janice. Sports writer Washington Post, 1938-40, asst. city editor, 1949-52; reporter and rewrite Asso. Press, Washington, 1941-43; writer Office Pub. Affairs, State Dept., Washington, 1946-49; asso. editor TV Digest, Washington, 1952-57; chief Washington bur. Med. Tribune, 1957-65; founder, editor, pub. Environmental Health Letter, Washington, 1961—, Occupational Health and Safety Letters, Washington, 1971—. First v.p. Montgomery County (Md.) Soc. for Crippled Children and Adults, 1954-60. Served with AUS, 1943-46. Contbr. articles to various publs., including Sat. Eve. Post, Parade, Changing Times. Mem. D.C. Pub. Health Assn. (governing council 1972—). Home: 408 Neale Ct Silver Spring MD 20901 Office: 1097 National Press Bldg Washington DC 20004

FISHBURNE, FRANK BEATTY, hydraulic press mfg. co. exec.; b. Columbia, S.C., July 13, 1915; s. Frank Beatty and Anita L. (Bellinger) F.; grad. high sch.; m. Mary Alice Whitton, Mar. 18, 1938; children—Frank Beatty III, Willard B., Carolyn A., Mary Janette. Plant engr. Pacific Iron & Steel Co., Los Angeles, 1942-45; pres. Standard Designers, Inc., Ashville, N.C., 1946-54; engr. Engring. Assos., Inc., Asheville, N.C., 1955-59; pres. Fishburne Equipment Co., Ashville, 1960—; pres. Asheville (N.C.) Ceramic Equipment Co., Fishburne Internat., Inc. Bd. dirs. N.C. World Trade Assn. Patentee in field. Home: 24 Summit Dr Arden NC 28704 Office: Airport Rd Arden NC 28704

FISHBURNE, JUNIUS RODES, JR., state ofcl.; b. Charlottesville, Va., Jan. 1, 1940; s. Junius Rodes and Ora Lewis (Davis) F.; grad. Epsicopal High Sch., Alexandria, Va., 1958; B.A., U. Va., 1962; postgrad. Coll. William and Mary, 1963-64, U. Nottingham (Eng.), 1962-63; M.A., Tulane U., 1967, Ph.D., 1971; m. Eleanor Gwathmey Lane, June 1, 1974. 1 son, Junius Rodes III. Mem. staff Va. Historic Landmarks Commn., Richmond, 1967—, exec. dir., 1972—. Mem. English Speaking Union (treas. Richmond), Delta Kappa Epsilon, Omicron Delta Kappa. Home: 203 N Allen Av Richmond VA 23220 Office: Morson's Row 221 Governor St Richmond VA 3219

FISHEL, CLARK RAMSEY, airport exec.; b. East Orange, N.J., Feb. 28, 1921; s. Newell Herbert and Muriel Elizabeth (Bush) F.; B.S., U. Ill., 1942; m. Iva Wilma Simmer, Dec. 20, 1947; children—Clark, Mark, Dawn, Dallas, Parke. Sales promotion and advt. copywriter Gen. Electric Co., Milw., 1946-49; indsl. advt. coordinator Allis-Chalmers, Milw., 1949-53; corp. information mgr. Tex. Instruments, Dallas, 1953-66, personnel activities mgr., 1966-73; marketing v.p. Dallas-Fort Worth Regional Airport, 1973—. Heavy industry unit chmn. Dallas United Fund, 1966-70; savs. bond chmn. Tex. Instruments, 1966-69; mem. Goals for Dallas, Greater Dallas Community Council. Served with USAAF, 1942-46. Mem. Assn. Indsl. Advertisers, Soc. Profl. Journalists, Smithsonian Instn., China-Burma-India Vets. Assn. (adj. 1970, historian 1972), Nat. Rifle Assn., Chili Appreciation Soc., Am. Quarter Horse Breeders Assn., Nat. Indsl. Recreation Assn. (nat. dir. 1972—), Pi Kappa Phi, Sigma Delta Chi (v.p. 1966). Republican. Christian. Clubs: Dallas Press, Dallas Woods and Waters, Texins Rod and Gun, Texins Texoma. Home: 201 Greenville Av Allen TX 75002 Office: 3303 Lee Pkwy Dallas TX 75219

FISHER, ALLAN CARROLL, JR., editor, writer; b. Cumberland, Md., Feb. 17, 1919; s. Allan C. and Ella (Rees) F.; A.B., U. Md., 1941; m. Mary Alice Michael, Jan. 20, 1944; children—Suzanne de Cessna (Mrs. Roger A. Eichholz), Martha Rees. Staff writer Washington Post, 1941, Balt. Sun, 1941-43; editorial staff N.Y. bur. A.P., 1943-47; N.Y. pub. relations rep. Kaiser-Frazer Corp., 1947-48; v.p. Booke & Fisher, Inc., pub. relations, Houston, 1948-49; asso. Hammond Assos., pub. relations, Balt., 1949-50; mem. staff Nat. Geog. Mag., 1950—, asst. editor charge articles, 1963-65, sr. asst. editor, 1965—. Recipient James J. Strebig Meml. award Aviation Writers Assn., 1956, 60. Mem. Aviation/Space Writers Assn., Nat. Assn. Sci. Writers, Nat. Aero. Assn., A.A.A.S. Democrat. Episcopalian. Clubs: Nat. Space (bd. govs. 1961-62), Nat. Press. Nat. Aviation, Aero, Cosmos (Washington); Pups (Melbourne, Australia); Annapolis Yacht. Author: America's Inland Waterway: Cruising the Atlantic Seaboard, 1973. Contbr. numerous articles Nat. Geog. Mag. Home: Beaumaris Bywater Rd Annapolis MD 21401 Office: Nat Geog Soc 17th and M Sts N W Washington DC 20036

FISHER, BEN COLEMAN, assn. exec., educator; b. Webster, N.C., May 27, 1915; s. Ben Franklin and Amy (Long) F.; A.B., Wake Forest U., 1938, D.D., 1971; B.D., Andover-Newton Theol. Sch., 1942; LL.D., Campbell Coll., 1968; m. Sara Gehman, Dec. 27, 1940; children—David Lincoln, Hugh Robert. Ordained to ministry Bapt. Ch., 1938; pastor Bapt. chs., Nashville, 1942-45, Newton, N.C., 1945-47; chmn. English dept. Gardner-Webb Jr. Coll., 1947-48, exec. asst. to pres., dir. pub. relations, 1948-52; asso. sec. Edn. Commn. So. Bapt. Conv., exec. sec. dept. Christian edn. Gen. Assn. Bapts. in Ky., 1952-54; chmn. pub. relations adv. com., 1959-60, chmn. edn. commn., 1968-70; asso. editor Educator, 1952-54; adminstrv. asst. to pres., dir. pub. relations Southeastern Bapt. Theol. Sem., 1954-62; exec. sec. Council on Christian Higher Edn., Bapt. State Conv. N.C., Raleigh, 1962-70; exec. sec.-treas. edn. commn. So. Bapt. Conv., Nashville, 1970—. Mem. New Eng. Town and Country Ch. Commn., 1941-42; mem. ednl. survey team Bapt. Colls. in Miss. and Ga., 1952; mem. N.C. Bd. Higher Edn. adv. com. on inter-instl. cooperation, 1967, mem. adv. com. on role pvt. higher edn., 1968, cons., 1968-70; coordinator N.C. Assn. Ind. Colls., 1969-70; mem. N.C. Commn. on Study of Statutes Relating to Vis. Speakers at State-supported Instns., 1965; chmn. bd. Bibl. Recorder; trustee Campbell Coll. Recipient citation merit Trustees Gardner-Webb Jr. Coll., 1953; Tar Heel of Week award News and Observer, 1963, Distinguished Alumni award Wake Forest U., 1966, gov.'s citation for contbns. to devel. of N.C., 1967. Mem. Am. Coll. Pub. Relations Assn., Am. Alumni Council, So. Bapt. Pub. Relations Assn. (past pres.), Grange. Democrat. Lion, Rotarian. Author: Public Relations Manual for Church Related Colleges, 1954; Communications Manual, 1961; A Manual for College Trustees, 1965; Duties and Responsibilities of College Trustees, 1969; An Orientation Manual for College Trustees, 1971. Editor: Outlook, Southeastern Bapt. Theol. Sem., 1954-62, Educator, 1970—. Home: 3415 West End Av Nashville TN 37203 Office: 460 James Robertson Pkwy Nashville TN 37219

FISHER, BILLY LEE, mortgage banker; b. Gladewater, Tex., Aug. 30, 1943; s. Loral Lee and Bessie (Mackey) F.; B.S., Abilene Christian Coll., 1965; J.D., U. Houston, 1974; m. Patricia Lynn Dorrell, Aug. 29, 1964; children—Stacy, Sheri. With Robert D. Mouser & Co., C.P.A., Abilene, 1964-65, Masquelette, Bruhl & Co., C.P.A.'s, Houston, 1965-66, 68-70, Davis & Mosher, C.P.A.'s, Pasadena, 1970-71; asst. sec., mortgage servicing supr. First Mortgage Co. of Tex., Inc., Houston, 1971—. Served with AUS, 1966-68. C.P.A., Tex. Mem. Am. Inst. C.P.A.'s, Tex. Soc. C.P.A.'s, Am. Bar Assn., Tex. Jr. Bar Assn. Mem. Ch. of Christ (deacon 1969—). Home: 5809 Birdwood St Houston TX 77036 Office: 1919 Allen Pkwy Houston TX 77019

FISHER, CHARLES FREDERICK, ednl. adminstr.; b. Oak Park, Ill., Mar. 20, 1936; s. Frank Theodore and Helen Annabelle (Davis) F.; B.A., Lawrence Coll., 1958; M.A. (Delta Alpha Pi scholar, N.Y. State Regents, scholar), Columbia, 1966, Ed.D., 1973. Asst. to pres. Lawrence U., 1962-65; research asst. Inst. Higher Edn., Columbia, N.Y.C., 1965-67; asst. dir. Acad. Adminstrn. Intership Program, Am. Council on Edn., Washington, 1967-68, dir. tng. programs for coll. and univ. pres., 1969—, program dir. Inst. Coll. and Univ. Adminstrs., 1969-73, dir., 1974—. Dir. tng. programs for acad. deans U.S. Office Edn., 1969-70; lectr. Program for Internat. Visitors to U.S., Washington Internat. Center, 1969—; lectr. Fulbright-Hayes Fgn. Scholars Program, 1971—. Del. White House Conf. on Youth, 1971; chmn. United Charities, 1957-58; coordinator Council on Religion and Internat. Affairs, 1962-65. Bd. dirs., v.p. Lawrence U. Alumni. Served to lt. USNR, 1958-62. Recipient Sci. award Bausch & Lomb, 1954, award Phi Beta Kappa, 1954, Distinguished Grad. award Lawrence Coll., 1958, People-to-People award USN, 1962. Mem. Am. Assn. Higher Edn., Res. Officers Assn. U.S., Washington Higher Edn. Soc., Internat. Platform Assn., Phi Delta Kappa, Beta Theta Pi pres. 1957-58, alumni pres. 1962-65). Episcopalian. Home: 1545 18th St NW Washington DC 20036 Office: 1 Dupont Circle Washington DC 20036

FISHER, DONALD DALE, educator; b. Spokane, Wash., Dec. 20, 1929; s. Albert and Lelia Belle (Buckner) F.; B.A., Wash. State U., 1951, M.A., 1953; Ph.D., Stanford, 1962; m. Shirley Florence Bissett, Apr. 21, 1951; children—Kristy Lee, Kerry Ann, David Burton. Math. analyst Douglas Aircraft, 1953-54; grad. asst. Stanford, 1954-58; applied sci. rep. IBM, 1958-60, math. analyst, 1960-62; research asso. Stanford, 1962-65; asso. prof., dir. med. research computation center Ind. U. Med. Center, 1965-69; prof., head dept. computing and information scis. Okla. State U., Stillwater, 1969-73, prof., dir. Sch. Math. Scis., 1973—. Mem. Assn. Computing Machinery, Soc. Indsl. and Applied Math., Sigma Xi, Phi Eta Sigma, Phi Beta Kappa, Phi Kappa Phi. Mason.

FISHER, FRANCENIA ELEANORE, plant pathologist; b. Green Cove Springs, Fla., Sept. 23, 1924; d. Roy Dexter and Daisy (Sparkman) Fisher; B.S., Fla. State U., 1945; postgrad. U. Chgo., 1945; M.S., Mich. State U., 1946. Plant pathologist Citrus Expt. Sta., U. Fla., Lake Alfred, 1946—; researcher, cons., 1946—; cons. U. Cal. at Berkeley, 1972-73. Mem. A.A.A.S., Soc. Econ. Botany, Am. Phytopath. Soc., Internat. Soc. Plant Pathology, Fla. Hort. Soc., Internat. Soc. Plant Pathology, Smithsonian Assos., Internat. Congress Plant Protection, Internat. Orgn. Citrus Virologists, Seminarium Botanicum (hon.), Ancient Order Ranales (hon.), Sigma Xi. Democrat. Episcopalian. Club: Lake Region Yacht and Country (charter mem.). Editor, pub.: World Directory of Plant Pathologists. Contbr. articles on citrus diseases caused by fungi, chem. control, biol. control, fungus diseases of insects and mites attacking citrus to profl. jours. and trade mags. Home: 1507 W Lake Cannon Dr PO Box 242 Winter Haven FL 33880 Office: U Fla Agricultural Research and Education Center Lake Alfred FL 33850

FISHER, GUY DALE, savs. and loan exec.; b. Killeen, Tex., Feb. 3, 1936; s. Andy Guy and Lois (Haynes) F.; Nixon Clay Bus. Coll., 1954-57; m. Emma Louise-Marie Jost, Nov. 8, 1958; children—Rory Dale, Sabrina Juliana. Bookkeeper, Fisher Bros. Elec. Co., Killeen, 1957; teller Killeen Savs. & Loan Assn., 1957-58, v.p., 1960—, mgr. Copperas Cove (Tex.) Br., 1970—. Cattle rancher, 1960—. Chmn., Am. Cancer drive, Killeen, 1969, 70. Served with USAF, 1958-60. Mem. C. of C. Copperas Cove (treas. 1973), Found. Beefmaster Assn. Lutheran (pres. 1970-71). Mason. Home: Route 2 Box 133 Killeen TX 76541 Office: PO Box 279 Copperas Cove TX 76522

FISHER, IRVING SANBORN, educator; b. Augusta, Me., May 21, 1920; s. Franklin and Marion Rae (Sanborn) F.; B.A., Bates Coll., 1941; postgrad. Dartmouth, 1941-42; M.A., Harvard, 1948, Ph.D., 1952; m. Virginia Stockman, June 16, 1945; children—Lawrence, Beth, Charles. Prof. geology U. Ky., Lexington, 1949—. Served to lt. USNR, 1941-45. Decorated Bronze Star medal. Fellow Geol. Soc. Am., Meteoritical Soc., A.A.A.S.; mem. Nat. Assn. Geol. Tchrs., Mineral. Soc. Am., Ky. Geol. Soc. (pres. 1962-63), Sigma Xi. Home: 1844 McDonald Av Lexington KY 40503

FISHER, JAMES HERSCHEL, architect; b. Greenville, Tex., July 19, 1914; s. Virgil Harper and Jewell Olive (Durham) F.; B.Arch., U. Tex., 1936; M.Arch., Mass. Inst. Tech., 1940; m. Betty Belle Richardson, Dec. 29, 1940; children—Jeffie Jean (Mrs. Arden Ristau), James Herschel, Hunter Lee. Archtl. designer Arthur Thomas, 1938-40; partner, Wiltshire & Fisher, 1943-50, Fisher & Jarvis, 1950-60; chmn. bd. Fisher & Spillman Architects, Inc., Dallas, 1971—. Teaching cons. U. Tex., 1945-46, Tex. A. and M. U., 1950-54, Tex. U., Arlington, 1965-68. Mem. adv. bd. Perkins Sch. Theology, So. Meth. U., Dallas, 1970-73. Trustee Dallas Meth. Hosp., 1956-60; bd. dirs., chmn. bd. Dallas Theol. Sem., 1960-73. Served to lt. USNR, 1941-43. Decorated Purple Heart. Fellow A.I.A. (pres. Dallas chpt. 1950-51); mem. Sphinx, Tau Sigma Delta. Prin. archtl. works include Callier Hearing & Speech Center, Southland Corp. Hdqrs., Coll. Fine Arts and Performing Arts Center, U. Tex., Austin. Home: 1630 Nob Hill Dallas TX 75208 Office: 3204 Fairmount St Dallas TX 75201

FISHER, JOHN MILLER, JR., constrn. engr.; b. Roanoke Rapids, N.C., July 19, 1926; s. John Miller and Cassie (Sadler) F.; B.C.E., N.C. State Coll., 1951; m. Betty J. Harper, June 23, 1969; children—Victor H., John Miller, Betty Melissa. Engr. aide Alaska Rd. Commn., Anchorage dist., 1951-52; with Ebasco Services, Inc., N.Y.C., 1952-54, 56—, field and office engr., Mt. Gilead, N.C., 1959-61, office engr., Farmington, N.M., 1961-64, office engr., purchasing agt., constrn. engr., Elderton, Pa., 1964-67, resident engr., constrn. supt., project supt., New Florence, Pa., 1967-72, constrn. supt., project supt., Hutchinson Island, Fla., 1972—. Fallout Shelter analyst U.S. Dept. Def., 1966—. Registered profl. engr., Vt., N.C., N.M., Pa. Served with USNR, 1944-46; PTO. Mem. Am. Soc. Civil Engrs., A.A.A.S., Nat., N.M. socs. profl. engrs., Am. Soc. for Testing and Materials, A.I.M., Mensa, Internat. Platform Assn., Nat. Constructors Assn. (sec. tri-state com. 1969, vice chmn. 1970, co-chmn. 1971), Am. Arbitration Assn. (panel arbitrators). Home: 601 N Fork Rd Stuart FL 33494 Office: 1117 Jensen Beach FL 33457

FISHER, JOHN MORRIS, assn. ofcl., educator; b. Fairhaven, O., Apr. 20, 1922; s. Marion Hays and Bessie (Morris) F.; A.B., Miami U., Oxford, O., 1947; postgrad. Bklyn Law Sch., 1950-51, Northwestern U., 1954-55; LL.D., Masson Coll., 1972; m. Thelma Ison, Feb. 2, 1947; children—Steven Roger, Linda Lucille. With Belden Mfg. Co., Richmond, Ind., 1941; spl. agt. FBI, 1947-53; exec. trainee Sears Roebuck & Co., Chgo., 1953, exec. staff asst. to v.p. personnel and employee relations, 1953-57, chmn. security com., 1957-61; operating dir. Am. Security Council, 1956-57, pres., chief exec. officer, 1957—; pres. Am. Research Found., 1961—; pres., chief exec. officer Inst. Am. Strategy, 1962—; pres. Communications Corp. Am., 1972—; organizer, pres. Fidelifax, Inc., 1956-57; chmn. merc. div. Nat. Safety Council, 1959-60, 1st vice chmn. trades and services sect., 1961—. Chmn. Chgo. Retail Safety Conf., 1959-60; spl. adviser Ill. Supt. Pub. Instrn., 1963-64; cons. to Gov. Fla.; cons. to chmn. com. cold war edn. Nat. Gov.'s Conf., 1962-65, Ill. Civil Def. Adv. Council, 1965-68; pres. Am. Council World Freedom, 1971-72; mem. exec. com. Nat. Captive Nations Com., 1968—. Bd. visitors Freedoms Found., 1964-65. Served to 1st lt. USAAF, 1943-45. Decorated Air medal with clusters; recipient 10th Anniversary medal and scroll Assembly Captive European Nations, Order Lafayette Freedom award, 1973. Mem. Am. Soc. Indsl. Security (dir. 1959-62), Phi Kappa Tau. Republican. Presbyn. Mason. Clubs: Tower; Culpeper (Va.) Country; Army Navy, Capitol Hill (Washington). Home: Pleasant Hill Boston VA 22713 Office: Boston VA 22713

FISHER, JOSEPH FRANKLIN, physician; b. Clinton, N.C., Aug. 3, 1926; s. Walter Harrison and Lossie Salena (Herring) F.; student Wake Forest Coll., 1943-45; M.D., Bowman Gray Sch. Medicine, 1949; m. E. Jean Wilson, June 9, 1951; children—Joseph Franklin, Andra Harrison, Walter Clark. Intern, Nashville Gen. Hosp., 1949-50; gen. practice medicine, Sparta, Tenn., 1950-52, Arlington, Tex., 1952-55, McMinnville, Tenn., 1957—. Chmn. bd. dirs. Plateau Mental Health Clinic, Cookeville, Tenn. Trustee Warren County Hosp., 1973. Served to capt. USAF, 1955-57. Recipient Distinguished Service award Mental Health Assn., 1973. Mem. A.M.A., Tenn., Warren County med. assns. Methodist. Club: McMinnville Flying. Home: Oak Hill Dr McMinnville TN 37110 Office: Plaza Shopping Center McMinnville TN 37110

FISHER, KING, marine contracting co. exec.; b. Port Lavaca, Tex., Jan. 14, 1916; s. Charles Everett and Kittie (Moss) F.; student pub. schs., Port Lavaca; m. Jewel Tanner, Aug. 13, 1937; children—Ann (Mrs. Waymon Boyd), Linda (Mrs. LaQuay). Pres. King Fisher Marine Service, Inc., Port Lavaca, 1941—; treas. Fisher Channel & Dock Co., Port Lavaca, 1954—; dir. First Nat. Bank of Flour Bluff, Corpus Christi. Mem. Tex. Mid-Coast Water Devel. Assn., Port Lavaca C. of C. Home: Hillcrest Chocolate Bay Port Lavaca TX 77979 Office: PO Box 108 Port Lavaca TX 77979

FISHER, MARION LEROY, JR., educator, clergyman; b. Detroit, Nov. 20, 1925; s. Marion LeRoy and Clela Mae (Smith) F.; B.A., Defiance Coll., 1947; M.Div., Duke, 1950; M.Ed., Bowling Green State U., 1959; Advanced Certificate, East Carolina U., 1974; m. Mary Frances Alsbrook. Ordained to ministry Meth. Ch., 1951; minister Harmony (N.C.) Meth. Ch., 1950-52; instr. chemistry, physics Holgate (O.) High Sch., 1952-58, prin., 1958-60; supervising prin. Poynor Jr. High Sch., Florence, S.C., 1964-67, Moore Jr. High School, 1964-66; instr. U. S.C., 1966-67; dir. fed. programs and adult edn. Florence Sch. Dist. 1, from 1967; supt. schs. Weldon (N.C.) City Schs., 1969—. Dir. S.C. State Sci. Fair, 1962-64, regional sci. fair, 1961-65. Mem. Council of Del., Florence County, 1963-66, del. Ohio Edn. Assn., 1959. Scoutmaster, Boy Scouts Am., chmn. Moratock dist., 1972-73. Named Sci. Tchr. of the Year, O. Acad. Sci., 1960. Mem. Nat., S.C., Edn. Assn., A.A.A.S., N.C. Assn. Educators, N.C. Assn. Sch. Adminstrs., Travelers Protective Assn. Am., Phi Delta Kappa. Mason, Rotarian. Contbr. articles to jours. Home: 600 W 2d St Roanoke Rapids NC 27870 Office: PO Box 31 Weldon NC 27890

FISHER, MILTON NATHAN, mfg. co. exec.; b. Newark, Nov. 25, 1921; s. Davis and Maria (Rapaport) F.; B.S. in Bus. Adminstrn., U. Fla., 1946; m. Berna Braunstein, June 9, 1946; 1 son, Jerome Peter. Pres., dir. Panelfab Internat. Corp., Miami, Fla., 1951—; pres., dir. Decor Internacional de Cuba, 1958-59; pres., dir. Dicoa Corp., 1958—; pres., dir. Panelfab Pacific, Inc., 1965—, Panelfab P.R., Inc., 1967—; dir. Nihon Panelfab, Ltd., Japan, 1967—, Panelfab Europe, Ltd. Mem. regional export expansion council U.S. Dept. Commerce; sec.-treas., dir. Fla. Council Internat. Devel. Bd. dirs. Internat. Trade, now pres.; pres., bd. dirs. Internat. Center, Greater Miami, Fla.; bd. dirs. Dade County chpt. A.R.C. Served to maj. USAAF, 1942-45. Decorated D.F.C., Air medal with 3 oak leaf clusters. Mem. Tau Epsilon Phi, Beta Alpha Psi, Beta Gamma Sigma. Mason. Club: Kings Bay Yacht (Coral Gables, Fla.). Home: 535 Reinante Av Coral Gables FL 33156 Office: 1600 N W Le Jeune Rd Miami FL 33126

FISHER, O. CLARK, congressman; b. nr. Junction, Tex., Nov. 22, 1903; s. Jobe B. and Rhoda (Clark) Fisher; student U. Tex.; LL.B., Baylor U., 1929; m. Marian DeWalsh, Sept. 12, 1927; 1 dau., Rhoda. Admitted to Tex. bar, 1929; county atty., Tom Green County, 1931-35; state rep., 1935-37; dist. atty., 51st Jud. Dist., 1937-43; mem. 78th-93d U.S. Congresses from 21st Tex. Dist. Democrat. Mem. Acacia. Mason; mem. Order Eastern Star; K.P., Rotarian. Author: It Occurred in Kimble, 1937; The Texas Heritage of the Fishers and the Clarks, 1963; King Fisher, his Life and Times; co-author: Great Western Indian Fights, 1960. Home: San Angelo TX 78206 Office: Rayburn Office Bldg Washington DC 20515

FISHER, PAUL, economist; b. Vienna, Austria, July 9, 1908; s. Ernst and Irma (Loebl) Fischer; student U. Paris (Sorbonne), 1926-27; J.D., U. Vienna, 1930; m. Susan Schwarz, June 5, 1948. Came to U.S., 1938, naturalized, 1944. Instr. dept. econs. William and Mary Coll., Williamsburg, Va. 1938-40, U. Me. at Orono, 1941-43; asst. prof. dept. econs. Clark U., Worcester, Mass., 1943-46, Dartmouth Coll., Hanover, N.H., 1946-51; chief labor econ. br., dep. dir. div. planning assistance Agy. for Econ. Devel., Washington, 1952-63; chief internat. staff Social Security Adminstrn., Dept. Health, Edn. and Welfare, Washington, 1963—; sr. research economist ILO, Geneva, Switzerland, 1968-69; adj. prof. econs. Am. U., Washington, 1952—. Mem. Am. Econ. Assn., Indsl. Relations Research Assn. Contbr. numerous articles in field to profl. jours. Home: 7024 Bybrook Lane Chevy Chase MD 20015 Office: 1875 Connecticut Av NW Washington DC 20009

FISHER, ROBERT DALE, economist; b. Memphis, July 30, 1924; s. Hollis Welton and Anna Sue (Parrish) F.; student Tex. Christian U., 1940-44; B.A., Am. U., 1959; m. Joy Lee Chandler, Mar. 30, 1946. Commd. ensign USN, 1944, advanced through grades to comdr., 1963; served with various ships and stas.; tng. officer Polaris Missile program, 1956-59; comdr. U.S.S. McCaffery, 1960-63; ret., 1963; now with duPont Glore Forgan, Inc., mem. N.Y. Stock Exchange, Washington. Mem. Internat. Platform Assn., Am. Econ. Assn., Naval Inst. Methodist. Kiwanian (pres. Falls Church). Clubs: Army-Navy, Navy League (Washington). Contbr. articles to profl. jours. Home: 6033 Chesterbrook Rd McLean VA 22101 Office: 1211 Connecticut Av NW Washington DC 20036

FISHER, ROBERT HENRY, yacht broker; b. Boston, May 20, 1925; s. Milton and Mae (Gurson) F.; student Mass. Inst. Tech., 1948, Boston U., 1948; m. Peggy von Lindenmayer, Aug. 3, 1954. Vice pres., gen. mgr. Gloucester Marine Railways Corp., Rocky Neck Shipyards, Inc., Gloucester, Mass., 1950-59; v.p. Breen-Fisher & Assos., yacht brokers, Ft. Lauderdale, Fla., 1960-64; pres., chief exec. officer Northrop & Johnson, Inc., yacht brokers, Ft. Lauderdale, 1964—. Pvt. marine cons. Bd. dirs., mem. marine adv. com. Fla. Atlantic U.; bd. dirs. Fla. Ocean Scis. Inst.; chmn. marine adv. com. Johns Hopkins. Served with USN, 1941-46. Mem. North Am. Yacht Racing Union, So. Yacht Brokers Assn. (pres. 1964-65), Soc. Am. Yacht Brokers (pres. 1971-74). Clubs: Storm Trysail (fleet capt. So. sta.), Coral Reef Yacht (Miami, Fla.); Royal Norwegian Yacht (Oslo); Propellor, Gulfstream Sailing (Ft. Lauderdale); Boston Yacht (Marblehead, Mass.). Home: 2629 Clematis Pl Fort Lauderdale FL 33301 Office: 2190 SE 17th St Fort Lauderdale FL 33316

FISHER, STANLEY MILTON, ins. co. exec.; b. Mansfield, O., Dec. 23, 1921; s. Joseph Clarence and Mildred Lucille (Van Antwerp) F.; J.D., Wayne State U., 1949; m. Joan Pauline Frederiksen, Mar. 27, 1943; children—Richard Brage, Peter Jay. With Abstract & Title Guaranty Co., Detroit, 1940-51, office mgr., to 1951; admitted to Mich. bar, 1949; individual practice law, Lincoln Park, Mich., 1951-55; pres. Am. Title Co. of Mich., Detroit, 1955-59; sr. v.p. Am. Title Ins. Co., Detroit, 1959-69, exec. v.p., Miami, 1969—; dir. Attys. Title Guaranty Fund, Inc., Denver. Served to 1st lt. USAAF, 1942-45. Decorated Air medal with 12 oak leaf clusters. Mem. State Bar Assn. Mich., Detroit, Macomb, Am., Down River bar assns., Mich. Real Estate Assn., Detroit Real Estate Bd., Nat. Assn. Real Estate Bds., Mortgage Bankers Assn. Mich. Club: Detroit Yacht. Home: 68 Greenbriar Lane Grosse Pointe Shores MI 48236 Office: 150 S E 3d Av Miami FL 33131

FISHER, WAYNE, lawyer; b. Cameron, Tex., June 22, 1937; s. George N. and Mary J. (Diver) F.; B.B.A. with honors, Baylor U., 1961, J.D. with honors, 1961; m. Patsy Ruth Mullinax, July 25, 1958; children—Terri Layne, Bryan H. Admitted to Tex. bar, 1961; since practiced in Houston; asso., Fulbright, Crooker & Jaworski, Houston, 1961-66; partner, Fisher, Roch, McLendon & Gallagher, Houston, 1966—. Mem. Am. Judicature Soc., Am., Houston bar assns., State Bar Tex. (dir. 1972-74), Tex. Bar Found. (sec. bd. dirs. 1973), Tex. (dir., pres.-elect 1973), Houston (pres. 1971) trial lawyers assns., Delta Theta Pi. Club: Athletic (Houston). Home: 14963 Bramblewood St Houston TX 77024 Office: 610 Houston Bar Center 723 Main St Houston TX 77002

FISHER, WILLIAM LAWRENCE, geologist; b. Marion, Ill., Sept. 16, 1932; s. Henry Adam and Madge Lenora (Moore) F.; B.S., So. Ill. U., 1954; M.S., U. Kan., 1958, Ph.D. (Shell fellow), 1961; m. Marilee Booth, Dec. 18, 1954; children—Leah, Karl, Peter. Research scientist Tex. Bur. Econ. Geology, Austin, 1960-68, asso. dir., 1968-70, dir., 1970—. Prof. dept. geol. scis. U. Tex., Austin, 1960—. Mem. geology asso. bd. U. Kan., 1972-74. Served with AUS, 1954-56. Recipient Haworth Grad. award U. Kan., 1956. Fellow Geol. Soc. Am.; mem. Am. Inst. Profl. Geologists, Am. Assn. Petroleum Geologists, Austin Geol. Soc. (pres. 1973-74), Austin C. of C. (mem. energy research com. 1973). Rotarian. Clubs: Headliners, Citadel (both Austin). Author: Mineral Resources of East Texas, 1964; Depositional Systems in the Wilcox Group, 1969; Delta Systems in the Exploration for Oil and Gas, 1969; Environmental Geologic Atlas of Texas Coastal Zone, 1972. Home: 8705 Ridgehill Dr Austin TX 78759 Office: University Sta Box X Austin TX 78712

FISHKIN, ROBERT EARL, cons. engr.; b. Galveston, Tex., Sept. 6, 1935; s. Abraham Earl and Iva Lee (Mintz) F.; B.S. in Archtl. Engring., U. Tex., 1959; m. Karen Suzanne Luginbill, Dec. 26, 1964; children—Christopher Earl, Donna Sue, Dayna Kae. With Davis & Foster, architects, El Paso, 1954-56, Nesmith-Lane-Kuykendall, architects, El Paso, 1956, C.L. Reeves, contractor, Austin, 1957-59; structural engr. Nesmith & Lane, architects, El Paso, 1959-65; owner Fishkin Engring., cons. engr., El Paso, 1965-69, 70—; regional structural engr. S.E. region Portland Cement Assn., Birmingham, Ala., 1969-70. Served with USNR, 1953-61. Registered profl. engr., Tex., Ariz., N.M., Colo., Wyo., Okla., Kan., Ala., Fla., Tenn., S.C., N.C., Ga., Miss., Ore., Wash. Mem. Cons. Engrs. Council, Am. Soc. C.E., Am. Concrete Inst., Prestressed Concrete Inst., Constrn. Specifications Inst., Am. Welding Soc., Ramshorn Soc. Methodist. Home: 7116 Tierra Alta El Paso TX 79912 Office: 444 Executive Center El Paso TX 79902

FISHMAN, JACOB ROBERT, psychiatrist, educator; b. N.Y.C., Aug. 6, 1930; s. Samuel and Fannie (Goldin) F.; A.B., Columbia, 1952; M.D., Boston U., 1956; m. Tamar Hendel, June 1, 1958; children—Marc Judah, Risa Esther, Zalman Schneur, Rebecca Anne. Intern, medicine Einstein Coll. Medicine, Bronx, N.Y., 1956-57, resident psychiatry, 1957-59; research psychiatrist Nat. Inst. Mental Health, Washington, 1959-62; prof. psychiatry Howard U. Coll. Medicine, Washington, 1962-71; dir. Howard-D.C. Comprehensive Mental Health Center, 1966-68; chmn. bd., pres. Univ. Research Corp., Washington, 1968—, Am. Health Services, Inc.; pres. Center for Human Services, 1968—, Human Service Group, 1971—. Cons. various govt. agys. including U.S. Dept. Labor, numerous pvt. corps. Bd. dirs. Webster Coll., Washington, 1971—, Center for Human Services, 1967—, DePaul Hosp., New Orleans, 1973—, St. Elizabeth's Hosp., Richmond, Va., 1971—, Cin. Mental Health Inst., 1971—, Nat. Capital Day Care Assn., 1966-68; mem. D.C. Pub. Health Adv. Council, 1966-68; attending psychiatrist Freedman's Hosp., Washington Vets. Hosp., D.C. Gen. Hosp., 1962-68. Served with USPHS, 1959-61. Fellow Am. Pub. Health Assn.; mem. Am. Psychiat. Assn., D.C. Psychiat. Soc., A.A.A.S., D.C. Pub. Health Assn. Author numerous profl. articles and books. Bd. editors Nat. Jour. Research on Crime and Delinquency, 1965-71. Home: 1717 Poplar Lane NW Washington DC 20012 Office: 5530 Wisconsin Av NW Washington DC 20015

FISHMAN, ROBERT JACK, pub., editor; b. Memphis, Nov. 1, 1934; s. Saul Jack and Katherine (Little) F.; B.S., Memphis State U., 1955; postgrad. U. N.C. Inst. for Orgn. Mgmt., 1958-61, U. Okla. Indsl. Devel. Inst., 1963-65; m. Nancy Allen, Nov. 25, 1955; children—Jeffrey Daniel, Robert Michael. Mgr. Jesup-Wayne County C. of C., Jesup, Ga., 1956-59, Morristown (Tenn.) C. of C., 1959-65, pres., 1973—; exec. dir. Middle Tenn. Indsl. Devel. Assn., Nashville, 1965-66; editor, pub. Citizen Tribune, Morristown, Tenn., 1966—. Tchr. bus. mgmt. clinic Carson-Newman Coll., 1962, Environmental Health Clinic, Cin., 1962-63, Southeastern Inst. for Orgn. Mgmt., U. Ga., 1963-65. Sec. bd. trustees Morristown Hamblen Hosp. Chmn. 2d dist. Gov.'s Citizens Commn. on Compensation; chmn. Tenn. Indsl. and Agrl. Devel. Commn., Tenn. Indsl. Finance Com., Morristown Indsl. Devel. Bd.; vice chmn. Gov.'s Econ. Study Com.; mem. Gt. Smoky Mountain council, finance chmn. Cherokee dist. Boy Scouts Am. Named Tenn. Young Man of Year, 1964. Bd. dirs. Smokey Mountain Passion Play. Mem. Tenn. (past pres.), Am., So. assns. chambers commerce execs., So., Am., E. Tenn. (pres. 1962), indsl. devel. councils, Holston River Devel. Assn. (v.p. 1963-65), Gov. Tenn. Travel and Tourist Promotion Council, Pi Delta Epsilon, Kappa Sigma, Theta Kappa Omega (nat. pres. 1955-56). Episcopalian. Elk, Kiwanian (pres.-elect). Home: 2114 Collins Av Morristown TN 37814 Office: 1609 W 1st at North St Morristown TN 37814

FISHWICK, JOHN PALMER, r.r. exec.; b. Roanoke, Va., Sept. 29, 1916; s. William and Nellie (Cross) F.; A.B., Roanoke Coll., 1937; LL.B., Harvard, 1940; m. Blair Wiley, Jan. 4, 1941; children—Ellen Blair, Anne Palmer, John Palmer. Admitted to Va. bar, 1939; asso. Cravath, Swaine & Moore, N.Y.C., 1940-42; asst. to gen. solicitor N. & W. Ry., Roanoke, Va., 1945-47, asst. gen. solicitor, 1947-51, asst. gen. counsel, 1951-54, gen. solicitor, 1954-56, gen. counsel, 1956-58, v.p., gen. counsel, 1958-59, v.p. law, 1959-63, sr. v.p., dir., then pres., chief exec. officer, dir., 1963—; former chmn., chief exec. officer Erie Lackawanna Ry. Co.; former pres., chief exec. officer Del. and Hudson Ry. Co., Dereco, Inc., now dir.; dir. Trailer Train Co., Akron, Canton & Youngstown R.R., Va. Commonwealth Corp., Pocahontas Land Corp., Va. Holding Corp. Pres., United Fund of Roanoke Valley, 1960, dir., 1959-62, campaign chmn. 1959. Trustee Roanoke Coll., Salem, Va.; bd. dirs. Roanoke Fine Arts Center. Served as lt. comdr. USNR, 1942-45. Mem. Am., Va. (exec. com. 1959-62), Roanoke bar assns., Am. Law Inst., Newcomen Soc. N.Am., Va. (dir. 1959-62, 65—), Roanoke (pres. 1958) chambers commerce, Kappa Alpha, Tau Kappa Alpha. Episcopalian. Clubs: City Tavern Assn. (Georgetown); Commonwealth, Shenandoah (Roanoke); Duquesne (Pitts); Metropolitan (Washington). Home: 535 Market St Salem VA 24153 Office: 106 N Jefferson St Roanoke VA 24011

FITE, WALLACE ARMSTRONG, savings and loan exec.; b. Washington Court House, O., June 28, 1914; s. Edward and Susan Pearl (Cockerill) F.; student Northwestern U., 1951-53, U. Fla., 1957-58; grad. U.S. Savs. and Loan Inst., 1968; m. Virginia Lee Traylor, Mar. 14, 1969. Real estate salesman and real estate broker Aldredge Realty Co., Bradenton, Fla., 1957; real estate broker, mortgage financer Garden Homes, Inc., 1959-60; asst. v.p. mortgage loan dept. Palmetto (Fla.) Savs. & Loan, 1961-66; asst. v.p. mortgage loans Sarasota (Fla.) Fed. Savs. & Loan, 1966-69; v.p., mgr. mortgage loan dept. Manatee Fed. Savs. & Loan, Bradenton, Fla., 1969-72; v.p., chief underwriter mortgage loans First Fed. Savs. & Loan, Sarasota, Fla., 1972—. Served with USN, 1931-57. Mem. Mortgage Officers Soc. (regional dir. 1962-73), Bd. Realtors, Manatee County C. of C. Baptist. Home: 220 47th St West Bradenton FL 33505 Office: PO Box 1478 Sarasota FL 33578

FITTS, JAMES WALTER, educator; b. Ft. Riley, Kan., July 17, 1913; s. Josiah Burt and Eva Rose (Freeman) F.; B.S., Neb. State Tchrs. Coll., 1935; M.S., U. Neb., 1937; Ph.D., Ia. State U., 1952; m. Mary M. Kocher, June 4, 1935; children—Jerry Burt, Dorothy Louise (Mrs. J.H. Johnson), Donald James. Asst. prof. soil sci. U. Neb., 1937-48; asst. prof. soil sci. Ia. State U., 1948-52; prof. soil sci. N.C. State U., Raleigh, 1952—, head soil dept., 1956-65, dir. internat. soil fertilizer evaluation project, 1964—; pres., Agrl. Environmental Systems, Inc., 1973—. Recipient Research award Soil Sci. Soc. N.C., 1966. Fellow Am. Soc. Agronomy; mem. Soil Sci. Soc. Am. (pres. 1960), Internat. Soil Sci. Soc. (div. vice-chmn. 1960-64), Sigma Xi, Gamma Sigma Delta. Contbr. articles to profl. jours. Home: 1021 Gardner St Raleigh NC 27067

FITZGERALD, ROBERT DEMARS, ins. co. exec.; b. Hartford, Conn., May 11, 1923; s. John Joseph and Viola Helen (DeMars) F.; B.A., U. Conn., 1948; diploma in mgmt. Am. Coll. Life Underwriters, 1965; m. Glenna Gibbs Cady, July 14, 1951. Second v.p. Fed. Life & Casualty Co., Battle Creek, Mich., 1965-67; v.p. Bankers Security Life Ins. Soc. (N.Y.), Washington, 1967-68; exec. v.p. Bankers Financial Life Co. (Okla.), Washington, 1968-71; exec. v.p., sec. Consumers United Ins. Co. (Del.), Washington, 1971—; dir. Consumer Credit Ins. Assn. Served with USAAF, 1943-45. C.L.U. Mem. Nat. Assn. Life Underwriters, Gen. Agts. and Mgrs. Conf., Am. Soc. C.L.U.'s, Hartford Alumni Assn. (pres. 1957-59), Sigma Alpha Epsilon. Home: 620 Bennington Dr Silver Spring MD 20910 Office: 1611 N Kent St Arlington VA 22209

FITZMORRIS, JAMES E., JR., lt. gov. of La.; b. New Orleans, Nov. 15, 1921; student Loyola U., New Orleans; m. Gloria Lopez; 1 dau., Lisa Marie. With K.C.S. Ry., New Orleans, 1940-72, v.p., until 1972; lt. gov. State of La., Baton Rouge, 1972—. Active numerous civic activities, including mem. La. Bd. Pub. Welfare, 1952-54, Regional Planning Commn., 1965-66; mem. citizen adv. com. New Orleans Recreation Dept.; regional v.p. Nat. Municipal League, 1966-71; pres. Mississippi Valley World Trade Council, 1968; nat. nat. adv. bd. Small Bus. Adminstrn., 1966-72; pres. Culbural Attractions Fund Greater New Orleans, 1971; mem. Nat. Def. Exec. Res., Office Emergency Transp.; mem. President's Hwy. Safety Com., 1957-63; La. chmn. March of Dimes, 1968-69. Mem. New Orleans City Council, 1954-66. Bd. dirs. New Orleans Bd. Trade, 1967-69, Internat. House, New Orleans Philharmonic Symphonic Soc., Youth Concerts Assn., New Orleans chpt. Nat. Conf. Christians and Jews, 1967-71, Camp Fire Girls, 1967-71; trustee Delgado Art Mus., 1958-62, United Fund for Greater New Orleans Area, 1965-70, Leukemia Soc., Nat. Cystic Fibrosis Research Found., 1967-68. Served from pvt. to maj., AUS, 1942-46. Recipient deLesseps S. Morrison Meml. award, 1965, Distinguished Citizens award Nat. Municipal League, 1968, various others. Mem. New Orleans Area C. of C. (hon. life, v.p. 1966-68), Young Men's Bus. Club Greater New Orleans (hon. life, past pres.), World Trade Club Greater New Orleans (hon. life), Nat. Def. Transp. Assn. (nat. v.p. 1968-69). KC (4 deg.). Home: 700 Emerald St New Orleans LA 70124 Office: State Capitol Bldg Baton Rouge LA 70804*

FITZPATRICK, HUGH, physician; b. Richmond, Va., Dec. 6, 1921; s. Hugh and Ruby Amoretta (Gilliam) F.; B.S., Hampden Sydney Coll., 1943; M.D., Med. Coll. Va., 1950; m. Rachel Anne Lewis, Dec. 21, 1948; children—Hugh E., Stuart L., Julia L., Anne L. Intern, U.S. Naval Hosp., Phila., 1950-51; practice medicine, Asheboro, N.C., 1951-70; emergency room physician High Point (N.C.) Meml. Hosp., 1970—, chief emergency dept. staff, 1973—; health dir. Randolph County, N.C., part-time, 1970—; mem. staff High Point Meml. Hosp.; mem. courtesy staff Randolph Hosp., Asheboro; county coroner, 1954-58. Pres. bd. Randolph County Tb. and Health Assn., 1956-58; mem. Asheboro City Sch. Bd., 1962-68. Bd. dirs. Randolph Center for Exceptional Children, United Fund. Served to lt. (j.g.) USNR, 1943-46, 50-51. Mem. N.C., Randolph County (pres. 1957) med. socs., Am. Acad. Gen. Practice, Am. Coll. Emergency Physicians, Theta Chi, Alpha Kappa Kappa. Presbyn. (ruling elder 1957). Democrat. Kiwanian (bd. dirs. 1956-58). Home: 117 S Main St Asheboro NC 27203

FITZPATRICK, JOE WARREN, educator; b. Waco, Tex., Mar. 18, 1925; s. Frank M. and Winnie (Warren) F.; B.S., Baylor U., 1948; M.A., U. Tex., 1950; m. Donna P. Davis, Nov. 3, 1951; children—Wynn Davis, Scott Warren. Research physicist Monsanto Chem. Co., Texas City, Tex., 1950-54; faculty Trinity U., San Antonio, 1956-66, prof. math., 1960-66; prof. math U. Tex., El Paso, 1966—. Active Yucca council Boy Scouts Am., troop com. chmn., 1973. Mem. Math. Assn. Am., Soc. Indsl. and Applied Math., Nat. Council Tchrs. Math., A.A.A.S., Tex. Acad. Sci., Internat. Platform Assn., Sigma Pi Sigma. Home: 5813 Viewmont St El Paso TX 79912

FITZPATRICK, JOHN J., clergyman; b. Trenton, Ont., Can., Oct. 12, 1918; ed. Propaganda Fide Coll. (Italy), Our Lady of Angels Sem. (U.S.) Ordained priest Roman Catholic ch., 1942; named titular bishop of Cenae and aux. of Miami (Fla.), 1968, consecrated, 1968; named bishop of Brownsville, 1971, installed, 1971. Address: PO Box 2279 Brownsville TX 78520

FITZPATRICK, RAY ERLAN, realtor; b. Gardner, Ill., June 25, 1912; s. Ray Harvey and Pearl Adele (Jeffers) F.; student Crane Coll., 1930; m. Stella Marie Baker, July 21, 1945; 1 dau., Susan Adele. With U.S. Govt. Civil Service, 1935-66, indsl. specialist U.S. Dept. Commerce, Washington, 1951-66; realtor Tucker Agy., Abingdon, Va., 1969—. Asso. prof. mil. sci. and tactics Va. Poly. Inst., 1944. Served to maj. AUS, 1942-46. Mem. Res. Officers Assn., Ret. Officers Assn., Nat. Assn. Ret. Civil Employees, Va. State (dir. 1972—), Washington-Smyth (pres. 1971) bds. realtors. Kiwanian. Home: 136 Hill Dr Abingdon VA 24210 Office: Box 206 Abingdon VA 24210

FLACKE, WERNER ERNST, physician, educator; b. Recke, Westphalia, West Germany, July 14, 1924; s. Josef and Alwine (Bremm) F.; Abitur, Gymnasium Carolinum, Osnabrueck, 1942; postgrad. Ludwigs U., Muenster, 1942, Philipps U., Marburg, 1945-47; M.D., Medizin Akademie, Duesseldorf, 1950; m. Jean Klella Wareham, Aug. 7, 1957; children—Christopher, Gerhard, Timothy. Came to U.S., 1954, naturalized, 1963. Asst. in pharmacology Medizin Akademie, Duesseldorf, 1951-52; asst. in pathology Koblenz, 1952-53; resident medicine St. Elisabeth Hosp., Essen, 1953-54; research fellow, dept. pharmacology Harvard Med. Sch., Boston, 1954-55, instr., 1955-57, asso., 1957-62, asst. prof., 1962-69, asso. prof., 1969-70; German Pharmhungsgemeinschaft Sr. research asso., dept. physiology Homburg/Saar, 1960-61; faculty U. Ark. Sch. Medicine, 1970—, prof. dept. pharmacology, 1970—, chmn. dept., 1970—; cons. Peter Bent Brigham Hosp., Boston, 1964-70. Mem. exec. bd. Joing Grad Program in Toxicology, Nat. Center Toxicology Research, 1973; mem. research and edn. com. VA Hosp., Little Rock and North Little Rock, Ark., 1971. Mem. sci. adv. bd. Ark. Heart Assn., 1973. Served with German Air Force, 1942-45. Recipient Career Research award NIH, 1963-70, Teaching award Student Am. Med. Assn., 1970. Mem. Am. Soc. Pharm. and Exptl. Therapeutics, German Pharmakologische Gesellschaft, Biophys. Soc., A.A.A.S., Am. Assn. Advancement Med. Instrumentation. Pavlovian Soc. Contbr. articles to profl. jours. Editorial bd. Jour. Pharm. and Exptl. Therapeutics, 1970. Office: U Ark Sch Medicine 4301 W Markham St Little Rock AR 72201

FLAGG, ROGER HOLMES, dentist; b. Buffalo, Aug. 7, 1930; s. Lloyd Eugene and Luella (Breed) F.; D.D.S., U. Buffalo, 1954; m. Nancy Jane Mabee, Dec. 10, 1954; children—David Kenneth, Peter Wesley, Mark Holmes, Susan Carroll. Commd. lt. (j.g.) U.S. Navy, 1954, advanced through grades to Capt., 1971; intern U.S. Naval Hosp., Camp Pendleton, Cal., 1954-55; staff dental officer Comdr. Constrn. Battalions, U.S. Atlantic Fleet, 1963-64; sr. dental officer U.S.S. Grand Canyon, 1964-66; Clin. supr., prosthodontist Naval Dental Clinic, Washington, 1966-70; dental officer U.S.S. Intrepid, 1970-72. Guest lectr. U. Philippines, and U. Far East, Manilla, 1960-61, Kent County (R.I.) Dental Soc., 1971. Awards chmn., treas. troop Cub Scouts Am., Vienna, Va., 1967-69. Recipient certificate of appreciation Philippines Dental Assn., 1961, certificate of recognition R.I. Dental Soc., 1962. Mem. Am. Dental Assn., Am. Acad. Oral Medicine. Methodist (v.p. men's club 1968-69). Home: 8401 Stonewall Dr Vienna VA 22180 Office: Arlington Annex BR US Naval Dental Clinic Washington DC

FLAHERTY, BERNARD EDWARD, psychiatrist; b. Peru, Ind., Aug. 1, 1917; s. John Edward and Hazel Mary (Moyer) F.; B.A., Ind. U., 1941, M.D., 1944. Intern U.S. Marine Hosp., New Orleans; resident psychiatry Sawtelle, Brentwood Hosp., W. Los Angeles, 1947-49, Langley-Porter Neuropsychiat. Inst., San Francisco, 1956-57; commd. 1st lt. USAF, 1945, advanced through grades to col., 1966, ret., 1967; practice medicine specializing in psychiatry, Washington, 1967—; mem. staff Washington Psychiat. Inst.; cons. U.S. Civil Service Commn., Washington, 1969—, Fed. Aviation Agy., Washington, 1968-72, Potomac Found., Bethesda, 1970—. Decorated Airman's medal, Commendation medal. Diplomate Am. Bd. Psychiatry and Neurology. Mem. A.M.A., Am. Psychiat. Assn., Aerospace Med. Assn., D.C. Med. Soc., Washington Psychiat. Soc. Editor: Psychophysiologic Aspects of Space Flight, 1967. Contbr. numerous articles to various publs. Address: 617 G St SW Washington DC 20024

FLAHERTY, DAVID THOMAS, state ofcl.; b. Boston, Dec. 9, 1928; s. Thomas Patrick and Mabel (Seely) F.; B.S. in Bus. Adminstrn., Boston U., 1955; m. Nancy Ann Hamill, Dec. 6, 1952; children—David Thomas, Stephen F., Deborah A., Jon E. Sales rep. Broyhill Furniture Factories, Lenoir, N.C., 1955-56, jr. exec., 1956-58, asst. sales mgr., 1958-60, gen. mgr. Broyhill Plastics, Inc. (div. Broyhill Industries), 1960-72; sec. N.C. Dept. Human Resources, Raleigh, 1972—. Del. NATO Youth Conf., Bonn, Germany, 1963; dist. chmn., council tng. chmn. Boy Scouts Am.; founder, pres. Bunny Maynard Midget Football League. Mem. N.C. Republican Exec. Com., 1949-52; nat chmn. Young Rep. Com., 1965; nat. committeeman Nat. Fedn. Young Reps., 1964, 65, state chmn., 1963, vice chmn. pub. relations, 1962, nat. co-chmn. campaign com., 1966; mem. N.C. Senate, 1969-72, mem. appropriations com., hwy. safety com., mental health com., ins. com., mfg., labor and commerce com., edn. com. Recipient Scouters key Boy Scouts Am., 1961, Council Pres.'s trophy, 1968, Silver Beaver award Boy Scouts Am., 1968; named Outstanding Young Republican N.C., 1964. Mem. Scarlet Key, Lock, D.A.V. (comdr. Lenoir chpt.), Alpha Kappa Psi. Optimist (bd. govs., chmn. oratorical contest, 1957, 60). Clubs: Lenoir Golf, Cedar Rock Country. Home: 1207 Barcroft Pl Raleigh NC 27609 Office: 325 N Salisbury St Raleigh NC 27602

FLAIG, FRANK JOSEPH, ins. co. exec.; b. St. Louis, Mar. 9, 1916; s. Frank Henry and Emma (Bates) F.; student Hadley Bus. Sch., 1933-34; m. Jean Mary Genovese, Nov. 14, 1942; children—Lawrence William, Linda Jean. Shipping clk. Advance Sales Co., St. Louis, 1933-34; merchandise control mgr. Sears Roebuck & Co., St. Louis, 1934-69, ret., 1969. With Coastal Bonded Title Ins. Co., New Port Richey, Fla., 1972—, dir., 1973—. Pres. Southside Corkball League, St. Louis, 1959-60. Comdr. Coast Guard Aux., Richey, Fla., 1973—. Served to capt. AUS, 1941-46. Decorated Purple Heart. Clubs: Gulf Harbors Yacht (commodore 1971-73) (New Port Richey, Fla.); Toastmaster (pres. 1958) (St. Louis). Home: 15 Harbor Ct S New Port Richey FL 33552 Office: 706 N Main St New Port Richey FL 33552

FLAIGG, NORMAN GAIL, govt. ofcl.; b. Deadwood, S.D., July 14, 1918; s. Louis Rudolph and Rena Louise (Nelson) F.; B.S., S.D. Sch. Mines, 1939, C.E., 1948; B.S. in San. Engring., U. Ill., 1945; M.C.E., U. Okla., 1952; m. Lillian Latimer, Sept. 4, 1970; 1 son, Don A. Diamond drill insp. Bur. Mines, Tinton, S.D., 1939; with Bur. Reclamation, Austin, Tex., 1940—, planning officer, 1964—. Served with AUS, 1944-45. Mem. Am. Soc. C.E., Sigma Tau, Theta Tau. Home: 3403 Santa Monica St Austin TX 78741 Office: Box 1946 Austin TX 76767

FLANDERS, DONALD HARGIS, mfg. co. exec.; b. Memphis, Apr. 26, 1924; s. Henry Jackson and Mae (Hargis) F.; student Tex. Christian U., 1943; B.B.A., Baylor U., 1947; m. Phala Katherine Davis, Dec. 15, 1946; children—Donald Hargis, Dudley Kennedy, Phala Katherine. Purchasing agt., cost accountant McCoy-Couch Furniture Mfg. Co., Benton, Ark., 1947-50; dir. cost accounting and purchasing Garrison Furniture Mfg. Co., Ft. Smith, Ark., 1950-54;

pres., gen. mgr. Flanders Mfg. Co., Ft. Smith, 1954-70; pres. Flanders Industries, Inc., 1970—; dir., chmn. exec. com. City Nat. Bank Ft. Smith, 1960-71; dir. 1st Nat. Bank, 1974—. Chmn. exec. com. Ft. Smith Freight Bur., 1960-61; chmn. furniture bd. govs. Dallas Market Center, 1968; mem. exec. com. Ark. Council on Econ. Edn., 1964-67; mem. Small Bus. Adv. Council, Ark., 1966-68, 73—. Chmn. Ft. Smith United Fund, 1962; dist. chmn. Boy Scouts Am., Ft. Smith, 1960-62, pres. Westark area council, 1963-65, mem.-at-large nat. council, 1963—, regional exec. com., 1964—, vice chmn. Region 5, 1967-69, chmn. Region 5, 1969-71, rep. nat. council, 1968—, mem. nat. exec. bd., 1969—, Silver Antelope, Silver Beaver, Silver Buffalo, Distinguished Eagle Scout awards; mem. Com. of 100, 1965—. Trustee Sparks Regional Med. Center, Hendrix Coll. Served from apprentice seaman to lt. (s.g.) USNR, 1943-46. Named Industrialist of Year, Ft. Smith Realtors Bd., 1965; recipient Free Enterprise award, 1964. Mem. Southwestern Furniture Marketing Assn. (pres. 1963), Ft. Smith C. of C. (dir. 1961-63). Ark. Retail Furniture Assn. (dir. 1960), Ark. Wood Products Assn. (dir. 1965-68), Delta Sigma Pi. Methodist (trustee conf.). Mason (K.T., 33 deg., Shriner). Home: 20 Berry Hill Rd Fort Smith AR 72901 Office: 1901 Wheeler Av Fort Smith AR 72901

FLANDERS, HENRY JACKSON, JR., educator; b. Malvern, Ark., Oct. 2, 1921; s. Henry Jackson and Mae (Hargis) F.; B.A., Baylor U., 1943; B.D., So. Bapt. Theol. Sem., 1948, Th.D., 1950; postgrad. U. Tenn., 1943, Union Theol. Sem., 1963, Hebrew Union Coll., 1948; m. Tommie Lou Pardew, Apr. 19, 1944; children—Janet, Jack III. Ordained to ministry Bapt. Ch., 1940; prof., chmn. dept. religion, chaplain Furman U., 1950-62; pastor First Bapt. Ch., Waco, Tex., 1962-69; prof. religion Baylor U., Waco, 1969—. Chaplain, Tex. Rangers Commn. Trustee Baylor U., Hillcrest Bapt. Hosp.; chmn. bd. Golden Gate Bapt. Theol. Sem.; mem. exec. bd. Bapt. Gen. Conv. Tex.; pres. bd. dirs. Econ. Opportunity Advancement Corp.; bd. dirs. Heart of Tex. Red Cross. Served with USAAF, 1943-45. Decorated Air medal with clusters. Mem. Baylor Ex-students Assn. (pres.), Waco Bapt. Ministerial Assn. (pres.), Assn. Bapt. Profs. Religion (pres.), Soc. Bibl. Lit., Am. Assn. U. Profs. (chpt. pres. 1971—), Am. Acad. Religion. Mason, Rotarian. Club: Western S.C. Torch (Greenville, S.C.). Author: People of the Covenant, 1963; Introduction to the Bible, 1973. Home: 3820 Chateau St Waco TX 76710

FLANIGEN, JOHN M., ret. elec. engr., city ofcl.; b. Athens, Ga., Nov. 25, 1895; s. Cameron Douglas and Mary (Nevitt) F.; B.S. in Elec. Engring., Ga. Sch. Tech., 1917; m. Hannah Scofield, Oct. 15, 1924; children—John M., Anna (Mrs. Edwin Scott), Charlotte (Mrs. Bruce E. Paine), William Scofield. Engr. in tng. Cities Service Co., 1919-20, engr., supt. various utility properties, Conn., Md., Ohio, 1920-27; asst. supt. distbn. Ga. Power Co., 1927-39, plant engr., 1939-60. Alderman City of Atlanta, 1962-73. Served to 1st lt. U.S. Army, 1917-19; AEF in France. Registered profl. engr., Ga. Fellow I.E.E.E. (dir. 1945-48); mem. Beta Theta Pi. Episcopalian. Mason. Address: 245 3d Av SE Atlanta GA 30317

FLANNAGAN, BENJAMIN COLLINS, IV, lawyer; b. Richmond, Va., Sept. 7, 1927; s. Benjamin Collins and Virginia Carolyn (Gay) F.; B.A., U. Va., 1947, M.A., 1948, J.D., 1951; LL.M., Georgetown U., 1956. Admitted to Va. bar, 1951; trial atty. Internal Security div. and Criminal div. Justice Dept., 1955—. Served as 1st lt. Judge Adv. Gen.'s Corps, 1952-55; maj. Res. Mem. Va. Bar Assn., Beta Gamma Sigma. Clubs: Country of Virginia, Deep Run Hunt (Richmond). Episcopalian. Book rev. editor Va. Law Rev., 1950-51. Home: 4000 Massachusetts Av NW Washington DC 20016 Office: US Dept Justice Washington DC 20530

FLANNAGAN, FRANCIS WILLS, lawyer; b. Clintwood, Va., Apr. 30, 1919; s. John William and Francis Deal (Pruner) F.; B.A., King Coll., 1940; postgrad. Am. U., 1941; J.D., Washington & Lee U., 1947; m. Florine Bibbe, Dec. 18, 1943; 1 dau., Florine (Mrs. Richard Tallman). Admitted to Va. bar, 1947; since practiced in Bristol; partner Flannagan & Flannagan, 1947-66, Woodward, Miles & Flannagan, Bristol, Va., 1966—. Vice pres. Huff-Cook Mut. Ins. Co., Bristol, 1966—. Arbitrator Fed. Mediation and Conciliation Service, Washington, 1952—. Pres. Bristol Mental Health Assn., 1953. Served with USAAF, 1941-45. Mem. Am., Va. bar assns., Internat. Assn. Ins. Counsel, Am. Trial Lawyers Assn. Elk. Home: 102 Flannagan Dr Bristol VA 24201 Office: 115 Johnson St Bristol VA 24201

FLASHING, DONALD JOSEPH, dentist; b. Chgo., Feb. 19, 1937; s. Michael Joseph and Evelyn (Tansley) F.; student Tex. A. and M. U., 1956, Arlington State Coll., 1960-63; D.D.S., Baylor U., 1967; m. Patricia Ann Campbell, Nov. 26, 1964. Pvt. practice dentistry, Garland, Tex., 1967—; mem. staff Meml. Hosp., Speegle Clinic, Garland Clinic, Garland. Bd. dirs. Garland Welfare Bd., 1968-69. Served with USAF, 1956-60. Mem. Am., Tex. dental assns., Acad. Gen. Dentistry, Internat. Assn. Orthodontists, Dallas County Dental Soc., Phi Kappa Theta, Zi Psi Phi (pres. 1966-67), Garland Jr. C. of C. (bd. dirs. 1968). Kiwanian (bd. dirs. 1969-71). Patentee crown and splint remover, 1971. Home: 1821 Meadowcrest St Garland TX 75042 Office: Forest Tower Bldg Garland TX 75042

FLATT, MURRAY ATHLYN, mech. contracting co. exec.; b. Newbern, Tenn., Mar. 30, 1917; s. James Madison and Clara Sue (Gibbons) F.; grad. high sch.; m. Johnnie Clyde Wilson, Mar. 30, 1935; children—Van Wilson, John Murray, Nika Athlyne, Jannice Lee. With E.I. duPont de Nemours & Co., Inc., 1939-43; founder Murray Flatt Electric Co., Newbern, 1946, pres., 1970—; dir. Bank of Yorkville (Tenn.). Mem. Tenn. Commn. on Aging, 1971—; del. White House Conf. on Aging, 1971; mem. nat. council Fla. Coll., 1965—. Alderman, City of Newbern, 1954—, mayor, 1967—; dir. Newbern Planning Commn., 1967—. Bd. dirs. Newbern Indsl. Devel. Corp., N.W. Tenn. Econ. Devel. Council. Served with USNR Air Force, 1944-45; PTO. Mem. Greater Dyersburg Dyer County C. of C. (dir., pres.). Mem. Ch. of Christ (elder 1955—). Rotarian. Club: Tenn. Capitol (Nashville). Address: PO Box 237 US Hwy 51 S Newbern TN 38059

FLATT, WELDON PIERCE, banker; b. Hamilton, Tex., Mar. 5, 1936; s. Cortis Leonard and Iola Ivena (Newton) F.; student Alvin Jr. Coll., 1965-66, Galveston Coll., 1966-68, So. Meth. U., 1969-71; m. Nell Battle, Apr. 25, 1957; children—Steve, Robert, Lisa. With First Hutchings-Sealy Nat. Bank, Galveston, Tex., 1964-71; with First Nat. Bank, Dothan, Ala., 1971—, v.p., 1972—, trust officer, 1971—. Mem. Dothan Citizens Supervisory Council, Dothan Interclub Council, 1972-73. Bd. dirs. Dothan chpt. A.R.C., 1972—, United Fund, 1973—. Served with AUS, 1956-57. Mem. Ala. Bankers Assn. (edn. com., trust div. 1971-73), Dothan Assn. Life Underwriters. Mem. Ch. of Christ (deacon 1972—). Clubs: Toastmasters (pres. 1972), Exchange (pres. 1973) (Dothan). Home: 1504 Buena Vista Dr Dothan AL 36301 Office: 101 E Main St Dothan AL 36301

FLATT, WILLIAM PERRY, univ. adminstr.; b. Newbern, Tenn., June 17, 1931; s. Carl Hadley and Evelyn Inez (Kelso) F.; student Bethel Coll., 1948-49; B.S., U. Tenn., 1952; Ph.D., Cornell U., 1955; postgrad. Rowett Research Inst. (Scotland), 1967-68; m. June Nesbitt, Apr. 9, 1949; children—Melynda Claire, Katherine Ann. Dairy cattle nutritionist, head energy metabolism lab. Agrl. Research Services, U.S. Dept. Agr., Beltsville, Md., 1956-68, asst. dir. animal husbandry research div., 1968-69; prof. animal sci., head animal sci. div. U. Ga., Athens, 1969-70, dir. agrl. expt. stas. Coll. Agr., 1970—. Recipient NSF fellowship, Cornell U., 1953-55, Presidential Citation, U.S. Dept. Agr., 1965. Superior Service award, 1968, award Am. Feed Mfrs. Assn., 1965, Hoblitzelle Nat. award Tex. Research Found., 1968. Mem. A.A.A.S., Am. Soc. Animal Sci., Am. Dairy Sci. Assn., Am. Inst. Nutrition. Rotarian. Contbr. articles to profl. jours. Home: 110 Broomsedge Trail Athens GA 30601

FLAWN, PETER TYRRELL, univ. pres.; b. Miami, Fla., Feb. 17, 1926; s. Stanley Charles and Laura Carolyn (Rotz) F.; B.A., Oberlin Coll., 1947; M.S. (Cooksey fellow), Yale, 1948, Ph.D. (Binney fellow), 1951; m. Priscilla Bernice Pond, June 28, 1946; children—Tyrrell (Mrs. Graham Hill), Laura. Jr. geologist mineral deposits br. U.S. Geol. Survey, 1948; research scientist, geologist Bur. Econ. Geology, U. Tex. at Austin, 1949-60, spl. mem. Grad. Faculty, 1958-60, dir. Bur. Econ. Geology, prof. geology, 1960-70, dir. div. natural resources and environment, prof. geol. scis. and pub. affairs, 1970-73, v.p. acad. affairs, 1970-72, exec. v.p., 1972-73; pres. U. Tex. at San Antonio, 1973—; vis. lectr. geology Northwestern U., 1960; vis. prof. geology, research geologist Instituto de Geologia, La Universidad Nacional Autonoma de Mexico, summer 1964; pvt. cons. econ. geology, 1954—. Mem. Tex. Mapping Adv. Com., 1960-70; chmn. Tex. Adv. Com. on Conservation Edn., 1967-68; mem. Tex. Interagy. Council on Natural Resources and Environment, 1969-73. Mem. adv. bd. Gulf Univs. Research Corp., 1968-73, U. Tex. rep., 1970-73, mem. sci. planning council, 1970-72; adv. trustee S.W. Found. for Research and Edn., 1973—; trustee Tex. Mil. Inst., San Antonio. Served with USAAF, 1944-45. Recipient Am. Fedn. Mineral. Socs. award, 1972; NSF research grantee, 1963. Mem. Am. Inst. Mining, Metall. and Petroleum Engrs. (dir. Tex. Coast mining and metals sect. 1961-63), Am. Inst. Profl. Geologists (mem. exec. com. Tex. sect. 1969-70), Am. Assn. Petroleum Geologists (trustee group ins. program 1967-68), Assn. Am. State Geologists (pres. 1969-70), Soc. Econ. Geologists (found. trustee 1973), Sociedad Geologica Mexicana, Am. Geol. Inst. (dir. 1967-70), Geol. Soc. Am. (councilor 1971-74), Scholia. Rotarian. Clubs: Headliners, Town and Gown Citadel, (Austin); Argyle, St. Anthony (San Antonio); Cosmos (Washington). Contbr. articles to profl. jours. Home: 209 Sir Arthur Ct San Antonio TX 78213 Office: 4242 Piedras Dr E San Antonio TX 78284

FLAX-JAFFE, HERMAN JACOB, physician; b. Richmond, Va., Mar. 31, 1917; s. Bernard Nathan and Jennie (Jaffe) F.; B.S., U. Richmond, 1936; M.D., Med. Coll. Va., 1940; M.Med. Sci. in Phys. Medicine, U. Pa., 1952; m. Josefina Guarch, Sept. 13, 1940; children—Hjalmar, Judith, Jennifer. Intern, Stuart Circle Hosp., Richmond, 1940-41; resident surgery Charity Dist. Hosps., Bayamon, Arecibo, P.R., 1941; fellow phys. medicine and rehab. Workmens Compensation Bd., Rehab. Center, Toronto, Ont., Can., 1947, Malton, Ont., 1948-51, Inst. Phys. Medicine and Rehab., N.Y.C., 1951; practice medicine specializing in phys. medicine and rehab., San Juan, P.R., 1951—; dir. pub. charities, Manati, P.R., 1941-44; med. insp., chief phys. medicine and rehab. State Inc. Fund, San Juan, 1945-51; chief phys. medicine and rehab. San Juan VA Center, Clinica Dr. E. Fernandez Garcia, 1951— (all San Juan); attending U. Hosp., Municipal Hosp.; cons. Auxillo Med. Mutuo, Clinica Mimiya, Drs. Hosp., Presbyn. Hosp., Dept. Vocational Rehab., 1952— (all San Juan); from asst. prof. to prof. phys. medicine and rehab. U. P.R. Sch. Medicine, 1952—. Med. cons., organizer P.R. chpt. Crippled Children and Adults Assn., 1950—; mem. Pres.'s Com. on Hiring Physically Handicapped, 1956-60; mem. med. research study section Social Security Agy., Dept. Health, Edn. and Welfare, 1969-72. Diplomate Am. Bd. Phys. Medicine and Rehab. Fellow A.C.P.; mem. Internat. Soc. Rehab. Disabled (dir., med. cons. U.S. com. 1960-72), P.R., Ind. med. assns., A.M.A., Am. Congress Rehab. Medicine (pres. 1970-71), Am. Acad. Phys. Medicine and Rehab., Assn. Phys. and Mental Rehab., Assn. Med. Rehab. Dirs. and Coordinators, Assn. Mil. Surgeons U.S., Am. Assn. Electromyography and Electrodiagnosis, Am. Acad. Cerebral Palsy, Nat. Rehab. Assn., Am. Soc. Med. Hydrology, Internat. Rehab. Medicine Assn., Phi Sigma Delta, Phi Delta Epsilon, Sigma Pi Sigma. Contbr. numerous articles to sci. jours. Home: Luhn 2 Urb Victor Braegger Villa Caparra Bayamon PR 00619

FLAXMAN, FRED, broadcasting co. exec.; b. N.Y.C., May 9, 1940; s. Philip and Helen (Sinn) F.; B.A. with honors in Journalism, U. Mich., 1962; Certificate in French lang., U. Paris, 1962; M.A. in Govt., Stanford, 1964; m. Annick Story, Sept. 10, 1963; children—Michel, Tana. Asso. editor Changing Times Mag., Washington, 1966; asst. dir. pub. relations New Town Reston, Va., 1966-67; asst. to gen. mgr. WETA-TV, Washington, 1968-70, dir. radio WETA, Washington, 1970—. Asst. dir. pub. relations Prentice-Hall, Inc., Englewood Cliffs, N.J., 1963-64; reporter The Record, Hackensack, N.J., 1964-65; asst. editor Scholastic Mags., 1965-66. Del. Va. Dem. Conv., 1968. Recipient Emmy award for TV writing, prodn. of membership spots, 1968. Mem. Nat. Assn. Ednl. Broadcasters. Contbr. articles to various mags. and newspapers. Home: 11535 Maple Ridge Rd Reston VA 22090 Office: 5217 19th Rd N Arlington VA 22207

FLEETWOOD, JOSEPH ANDERTON, physician; b. Jackson, N.C., Jan. 27, 1894; s. Robert Wilson and Harriet Rebecca (Burnette) F.; B.S., Wake Forest Coll., 1919; M.D., Tulane U., 1921; m. Caroline Lane, Dec. 27, 1924; 1 son, Joseph Anderton. Intern, St. Vincent Hosp., Norfolk, Va., 1921-22, City Hosp., Macon, Ga., 1922, Walker Meml. Hosp., Wilmington, N.C., 1922-23; physician Atlantic Coast Line Hosp., Atlantic Coast Line R.R., Rocky Mount, N.C., 1923; practice medicine, Conway, N.C., 1923—; mem. staff Roanoke Rapids Hosp. Examiner, Selective Service, 1942-46. Mem. Conway Sch. Bd., 1934-42, town council, 1942-50. Mem. Am. Acad. Gen. Practice, A.M.A., N.C., Northampton-Halifax County med. socs., Seaboard Coastline R.R. Surgeons, N.C. Hist. Soc. Baptist. Mason (32 deg.). Address: Main St Conway NC 27820

FLEISCHAKER, JERRY JEROME, psychiatrist; b. Louisville, Mar. 15, 1931; s. Alvin and Rose Mary (Ermann) F.; B.A., U. Louisville, 1951; M.D., U. Louisville Med. Sch., 1955; m. Billie Dove Thibodeaux, May 30, 1959; children—Jack Henry, Marc Eric, Melissa Leah. Intern Good Samaritan Hosp., Lexington, Ky., 1955-56; resident in psychiatry Duke U., 1956-57, 59-61; dir. Hillsborough Community Mental Health Center, Tampa, Fla., 1961—; part-time pvt. practice medicine, specializing in psychiatry, Tampa, 1961—; mem. staff Tampa Gen., Hillsborough County, Tampa Heights hosps. Chmn., Fla. Council Mental Health Clinics, 1965. Served with USAF, 1957-59. Fellow Am. Orthopsychiat. Assn., Am. Psychiat. Assn., Fla. Psychiat. Soc. Home: 4206 Cleveland St Tampa FL 33609 Office: 5707 N 22d St Tampa FL 33610

FLEISCHMAN, SOL JOSEPH, television broadcasting exec.; b. Hawkinsville, Ga., Sept. 12, 1910; s. Joseph Simon and Alma (Rockman) F.; hon. degree, U. Tampa (Fla.), 1954; children—Sol Joseph, Martin Paul. Profl. musician Am. Fedn. Musicians, Tampa, 1926-32; announcer, control operator WDAE Radio, Tampa, Fla., 1928, chief announcer, 1950-57; sports dir., outdoor editor Tampa (Fla.) Daily Times, 1946-57; asst. to gen. mgr. L.S. Mitchell, 1956-57; sports, dir., pub. relations dir. WTVT Television, Tampa, 1957—. Mem. Fla. Gov.'s Conservation Com., 1969-72; mem. Tampa Mayor's Bd. Pub. Recreation, Pub. Relations and Conv. Centers, 1968—. Trustee Land's For You, Inc. Served with USCG, 1942-46. Named Tampa's Outstanding Citizen, Tampa Sports Club, 1969-70. Mem. Outdoor Writers Am., Fla. Outdoor Writers Assn., Fla. League Outdoor Writers, Fla. Lunkers Assn., Fla. Sportscasters Assn. (mem. bd. 1970-73), Greater Tampa C. of C., Sigma Delta Chi. Mason (Shriner), Rotarian. Clubs: Palma Ceia Golf and Country, Sword and Shield, Tampa University Quarterback, Touchdown (Tampa). Home: 3909 Cleveland St Apt 104 Tampa FL 33609 also 798 Northshore Dr Anna Maria FL 33501 Office: PO Box 22013 Tampa FL 33622

FLEMING, BENTON SCOTT, savs. and loan exec.; b. Houston, Apr. 12, 1922; s. Earl Hampton and Lorena Oklahoma (Stapler) F.; student Tex. U., 1940-43; LL.B., South Tex. Sch. Law, 1951; postgrad. U. Houston, 1952-53; m. Narcille Busch, Dec. 1, 1951; children—Scott, Joan, Guy, Diane. Admitted to Tex. bar, 1951; mortgage loan atty. First Am. Life Ins. Co., Houston, 1951-52; atty., specializing in mortgage loans, Houston, 1952-55; pres. Tex. Investment Corp., La Porte, 1955—; chmn. bd., pres. First State Bank, Point, Tex., 1961-68; pres. United Bus. Capital, Inc., La Porte, 1963—; pres. Bayshore Savs. Assn., La Porte, 1967—, chmn. bd., 1967—; dir. Bayshore Nat. Bank, La Porte; adv. dir. Tex. Nat. Bank of Baytown. Aderman City of Shoreacres, 1973—. Served to lt. (j.g.) USNR, 1943-46. Mem. Tex. State Bar Assn., La Porte C. of C. (1st v.p. 1972-74, dir. 1972-74), Alpha Tau Omega. Episcopalian. Rotarian. Club: Houston Yacht. Home: 626 Baywood St La Porte TX 77571 Office: 1102 S Broadway La Porte TX 77571

FLEMING, EDWARD STITT, physician; b. San Diego, Apr. 11, 1930; s. Robert Walton and Emma Scott (Stitt) F.; B.A. in Psychology, U. N.C., 1951; M.A. in Psychology, U. Tex., 1952; M.D. cum laude, George Washington U., 1957; m. Mariana Moran; children—Edward Stitt, Edith Page, Richard B. Intern, U. N.C. Sch. Medicine, 1957-58; resident in psychiatry Yale Sch. Medicine, 1958-61, instr. psychiatry, 1961-63, also physician-in-charge psychiat. outpatient clinic Yale-New Haven Hosp., 1961-63; career tchr. Nat. Inst. Mental Health, 1963-65; dir. inpatient psychiat. services George Washington U. Hosp., Washington, 1963-67; asst. prof. psychiatry George Washington U. Sch. Medicine, 1963-65, asso. clin. prof., 1965—; postgrad. med. tng. Washington Psychoanalytic Inst., 1963-67; founder Psychiat. Inst. Washington, 1966, pres., 1966-73; founder, pres. Psychiat. Insts. Am., 1967—; founder, bd. dirs. Psychiat. Inst. Found., 1968—; bd. dirs. Tidewater Psychiat. Inst., Norfolk, Va., 1970—, Virginia Beach, Va., 1972—, Elmcrest Psychiat. Inst., Portland, Conn., 1971—, Commonwealth Psychiat. Centre, Richmond, 1972—. Psychiat. Southwood Mental Health Centers San Diego, 1972—, Banyan Psychiat. Inst., Palm Beach, Fla., 1973—, Cedarbrook Psychiat. Hosp., Las Vagas, 1973—. Served to capt. USAF, 1951-53. Fellow Am. Psychiat. Assn.; mem. A.M.A., D.C. Med. Soc., World, Washington psychiat. socs., N.Y. Acad. Scis., Alpha Omega Alpha. Episcopalian. Clubs: Internat. (Washington); Gibson Island; Princess Anne. Home: 5017 Tilden St NW Washington DC 20016 Office: Psychiatric Insts America 1825 K St NW Washington DC 20006

FLEMING, ELDRIDGE ERASTUS, health complex adminstr.; b. Smithdale, Miss., Sept. 19, 1936; s. Ervin Erastus and Hellen Ruth (Palmer) F.; B.A., Miss. Coll., 1958; M.Div., Midwestern Bapt. Theol. Sem., 1962; M.A., Miss. State U., 1971; postgrad. U. Miss., 1973—; m. Martha W. Dupuy Wackerfuss, Aug. 12, 1972; children (by previous marriage)—Janet Susan, Timothy E., Kenneth Patrick; stepchildren—Pamela J., Barbara G. 2d Richard W. Wackerfuss. Ordained to ministry Christian Ch., 1963; minister First Christian Ch., Kansas City, Kan., 1963-65, Tupelo, Miss., 1965-69; dir. alcohol programs Mental Health Complex, Tupelo, 1969—; summer instr. Miss. State U., 1973—. Cons. State Bd. Edn. Drugs, 1969—; chmn. Tupelo Drug Abuse Com., 1971—. Mem. Alcohol and Drug Problems Assn. N.Am., Miss. Alumni Assn. Schs. Alcohol and Drug Studies (pres. 1971-73). Lion. Home: 2307 Lafayette St Tupelo MS 38801 Office: 830 S Gloster St Tupelo MS 38801

FLEMING, GEORGE CLAYTON, elec. engr.; b. St. Louis, Aug. 3, 1919; s. Clarence Brandon and Maud Alice (Mueller) F.; student Washington U., St. Louis, 1937-39; B.S., U.S. Coast Guard Acad., 1942; M.S., Mass. Inst. Tech., 1956; m. Mary Jane Lange, Nov. 19, 1946; children—Dorothy, JoAnne, James. Commd. ensign U.S. Coast Guard, 1942, advanced through grades to capt., 1964; chief electronics engring. div. Coast Guard Hdqrs., Washington, 1965-68; ret., 1968; systems engr., elec. engring. mgr., engring. support services project, aerospace services div. Pan Am. World Airways, Inc., Kennedy Space Center, Fla., 1968—. Mem. U.S. exec. com. Internat. Radio Consultative Com., 1965-68. Mem. I.E.E.E. (sr.), Naval Inst., Inst. Nav., Sigma Xi. Home: 403 Aruba Ct Satellite Beach FL 32937 Office: Engring Support Services Project Aerospace Services Div Pan American World Airways Inc Kennedy Space Center FL 32899

FLEMING, JAMES FURMAN, assn. exec.; b. Conway, S.C., Mar. 31, 1937; s. Irvin McLaurn and Martha (Denton) F.; A.A., N. Greenville Jr. Coll., 1960; student St. Bernard Coll., 1969; m. Martha Ann Capps, July 12, 1958; children—James Furman, William Keith. Partner, Fleming Bros. Photo Service, Conway, S.C., 1955-56; news editor Georgetown Times (S.C.), 1956-58, 60-61; staff mem. Greenville News (S.C.), 1958-60; field rep. S.C. Farm Bur., Columbia, 1962-64, dir. dept. promotions, 1964-66; exec. v.p. Ala. Poultry Industry Assn., also sec.-treas. Ala. Poultry and Egg Council, 1966-70; dir. pub. and govtl. relations United Egg Producers, Atlanta, 1970—. Recipient Outstanding Leadership award in poultry industry Poultry and Egg Nat. Bd., 1963. Mem. Am. Soc. Assn. Execs. (Mgmt. award 1970), State Poultry Exec. Secs. Assn. (dir. 1966-67, sec.-treas. 1967-70). Baptist (deacon). Home: 4184 Idlevale Dr Tucker GA 30084 Office: 1001 International Blvd Atlanta GA 30354

FLEMING, JULIAN DENVER, JR., lawyer; b. Rome, Ga., Jan. 12, 1934; s. Julian Denver and Margaret (Mangham) F.; student U. Pa., 1951-53; B.Chem. Engring. with highest honors, Ga. Inst. Tech., 1955, Ph.D., 1959; J.D. with distinction, Emory U., 1967; m. Sidney Mack Howell, June 28, 1960; 1 dau., Julie Adrianne. Research asst., instr. Ga. Inst. Tech., Atlanta, 1955-59, research asso., asst. prof., 1959-61, research engr., asso. prof., 1961-66, research engr., prof. chem. engring., 1966-67; admitted to D.C. and Ga. bars; now practicing in Atlanta. Research project dir. for programs of U.S. Army, USN, AEC; engring. cons. Oak Ridge Nat. Lab., Rayonier, Inc., Glasrock Products, Inc., Buckman Labs., Bd. dirs. Ga. Mental Health Assn., Met. Atlanta Mental Health Assn. Registered profl. engr., Ga., Cal. Fellow Am. Inst. Chemists; mem. Am., Ga. bar assns., Sigma Xi, Tau Beta Pi, Omicron Delta Kappa, Phi Lambda Epsilon, Phi Kappa Phi, Phi Delta Theta. Republican. Author profl. papers, govt. and pvt. research reports. Editor-in-chief Jour. Pub. Law, 1966-67. Patentee in field. Home: 2238 Hill Park Ct Decatur GA 30033 Office: 1st Nat Bank Bldg Atlanta GA 30303

FLEMING, JULIAN ROANE, san. engr.; b. Grand Junction, Tenn., Jan. 25, 1912; s. Walter Roane and Allie Hall (Smith) F.; B.S., U. Tenn., 1934, M.S., 1935; M.S., U. Ia., 1942; postgrad. U. Wis., 1936-38; m. Clara Kirkpatrick, Oct. 23, 1937; 1 dau., Allie Ann (Mrs. Aubrey Baxter Book). Instr. U. Tenn. at Knoxville, 1937-40, asst. prof., 1941-48, asso. prof., 1949-55; san. engr. Greeley & Hansen, Chgo., 1945-46; pvt. practice as cons. engrs., Knoxville, 1950-55;

hydraulic engr. TVA, Knoxville, 1941-44; dir. div. san. engring. Tenn. Dept. Pub. Health, Jackson, 1955-72, asst. dir. div. san. engring., 1972-74. Fellow Am. Soc. C.E.; mem. Am. Water Works Assn. (life, Fuller award 1958), Water Pollution Control Fedn. (hon., Arthur Sidney Bedell award 1971), Conf. State San. Engrs. (chmn. 1969-70), Tau Beta Pi, Phi Kappa Phi. Presbyn. Contbr. articles to profl. jours. Home: 65 Woodhaven Dr Jackson TN 38301 Office: 201 Peoples Protective Life Bldg Jackson TN 38301

FLEMING, SAMUEL LAFAYETTE, clergyman; b. Hot Springs, N.C., Dec. 25, 1916; s. Harvey James and Julia (Parker) F.; B.A., Johnson Bible Coll., 1940; B.D., Butler U., 1946; Th.D., Washington Profl. Coll., 1951; M.Div., Christian Theol. Sem., 1952; m. Irene Thompson, June 26, 1943; children—Helen Elizabeth, Mary Ann, Samuel Lafayette, Jr. Ordained to ministry Christian Ch., 1941; minister First Christian Ch., Asheville, N.C., 1950-56, New Castle, Pa., 1956-64, Donelson Christian Ch., Nashville, 1964-71, First Christian Ch., Crossville, Tenn., 1971—. Conductor various radio programs, 1940—; pres. Pa. Christian Ministers Assn., 1960-61; mem. internat. recommendations com. Christian Ch., 1954; v.p. Christmount Christian Assembly, Inc., 1955; originator Christ Child Festival, 1956. Mem. Internat. Platform Assn. Mason, Kiwanian (pres. 1973—). Author: What Must I Do to Be Saved?, 1942; Debates of Alexander Campbell, 1946. Home: Route 8 Hamby Lane Crossville TN 38555 Office: Box 264 Crossville TN 38555

FLEMING, STANLEY LOUIS, dentist; b. Johnson City, Tenn., Oct. 21, 1933; s. Smith George and Vivian Cecile (Richardson) F.; student U. Denver, 1951-52, Wayne State U., 1955-58; D.D.S., Howard U., 1962; M.S. in Physiology, Georgetown U., 1972 children—Stanley Louis, Ron D., Lovie T., Tanya R. Instr., Coll. Dentistry, Howard U., 1963-66, asst. prof., 1966-69; dentist Dental Health Clinic, Washington, 1963-67; individual practice dentistry, Washington, 1963—; asst. prof. Coll. Dentistry, Howard U.; NIH postdoctoral research fellow Georgetown U., 1969-71. Vol. dentist Resurrection City, Washington, 1968; dentist Head Start Program and Med. Assistance Program. Served with USAF, 1951-55. Mem. Am., Nat. dental assns., D.C. (dental health com.), Robert T. Freeman dental socs., Washington, Nat. Negro golf assns., Chi Delta Mu, Omega Psi Phi. Methodist. Home: 4000 Tunlaw Rd NW Washington DC 20007 Office: 231 Atlantic St SE Washington DC 20032

FLEMING, WALTER CLARK, JR., farm mgmt. cons.; b. Greensboro, N.C., Mar. 20, 1907; s. Walter C. and Mary Lee (Clark) F.; student pub. schs., Guilford County, N.C.; m. Olive Stebbins, May 22, 1938. Herd mgr. Butler Island Plantation, Brunswick, Ga., 1934-39, Dinsmore Farms, Jacksonville, Fla., 1939-40; supt. dairy cattle, creamery, swine dept. Eleutheria Ltd., Hatchett Bay, Eleutheria, Bahamas, B.W.I., 1940-43; mgr. Model Dairy, Opa Locka, Fla., 1943-44; gen. mgr. Bayville Farms, Virginia Beach, Va., 1944-72, pres., gen. mgr., 1961-72; head farm services William E. Wood & Assos., Virginia Beach, Va., 1972—; dir. Virginia Beach br. Va. Nat. Bank. Ofcl. judge Guernsey Cattle Club, 1936-72; mem. subcom. dairying Va. Industry Agr., 1966-69; mem. com. land assessment and taxation Commn. Industry Agr. Va., 1970-71; mem. adv. com. Sch. Agr., Va. Poly. Inst., 1960-64; mem. Va. Forest Industries on Timber Valuation and Taxation, 1972—. Mem. Virginia Beach Devel. Council, 1962—, pres., 1968-69; dir. Virginia Beach Beautification Commn., 1962—; mem. pres.'s adv. com. Va. Wesleyan Coll., 1970—; mem. Personnel Bd., Virginia Beach, 1970—; mem. Virginia Beach Wetlands Bd., 1972—, vice chmn.; dir. Va. Dare Soil and Water Conservation Dist., 1972—. Co-campaign mgr. Robert Daniel to Congress, Virginia Beach, 1973. Recipient Achievement award Va. Poly. Inst. Dairy Sci. Club, 1967, Certificate of Honor, Va. Guernsey Breeders Assn., 1965; named Man of Year in Agr., Virginia Beach C. of C., 1968. Mem. Am. Guernsey Cattle Club (dir., mem. exec. com. 1967-72), Golden Guernsey Inc. (mem. com. 1967-72), Dairy Shrine Club (dir. 1963-65), Am. Dairy Sci. Assn., Va. (pres., dir. 1950-72), Southeastern (pres., dir. 1946-65), Eastern (v.p. 1961-64) guernsey breeders assns., Va. State Dairymens Assn. (dir. 1950-62), Va. Dairy Products Assn. (dir. 1969-72), Dairy Council Tidewater (pres., dir. 1967-68), Virginia Beach C. of C. (chmn. agr. com. 1967-68, dir. 1965-67, 71-73), Princess Anne Farm Bur. (dir. 1971-72), N.C. Soc. Farm Mgrs. and Rural Appraisers. Methodist (mem. ofcl. bd. 1964—). Home: PO Box 5506 Virginia Beach VA 23455 Office: 5633 Princess Anne Rd Virginia Beach VA 23462

FLEMING, WILLIAM MARVIN, JR., judge; b. Winston-Salem, N.C., Oct. 20, 1924; s. William M. and Effie Lee (Neville) F.; LL.B., U. Ga., 1950; m. Marilyn Meehan, Aug. 14, 1965; children—William Meehan, Brendan Neville. Admitted to Ga. bar, 1951; mem. firm Nicholson & Fleming, Augusta, 1951-68; judge Superior Ct., Augusta Jud. Circuit, 1968—. Mem. Ga. Ho. of Reps., 1958-68. Served with USAF, 1942-45. Mem. Am., Augusta, Augusta Circuit (pres. 1964-68) bar assns. Home: 615 Scotts Way Augusta GA 30904 Office: 305 City County Bldg Augusta GA 30902

FLETCHER, DAVID RICHARD, land devel. exec.; b. Greenwood, S.C., May 25, 1936; s. Elton Freeman and Frances (Chewning) F.; B.S., Fla. So. Coll., 1962; m. Sonya Ennis, Dec. 23, 1961; 1 dau., Kara Suzanne. Pres. David R. Fletcher & Assos., Inc., St. Petersburg, Fla., 1968-72; with Am. Housing & Devel. Corp., St. Petersburg, 1972—, exec. v.p., 1974—. Mem. publicity com. Fla. div. Am. Cancer Soc., 1972-73. Bd. dirs. Big Bros. Pinellas County, 1973-74. Served with USAF, 1954-58. Recipient 1st place winner Assn. Category, Fla. Pub. Relations Assn., 1971. Named pub. relations Man of the Year Gasparilla chpt. Fla. Pub. Relations, 1970. Mem. Pub. Relations Soc. Am., Sigma Chi. Author: How to Sell Your Unlisted Company to the Financial Community, 1971. Home: 7319 4th Av N St Petersburg FL 33710 Office: 3333 Pasadena Av S St Petersburg FL 33707

FLETCHER, LUTHER DUDLEY, clergyman; b. Brandon, Tex., Aug. 21, 1913; s. James Washington and Pauline Maze (Howe) F.; B.A., Austin Coll., 1936, M.A., 1937; M.Th., Union Theol. Sem., Richmond, Va., 1939; grad. Command and Staff Coll., 1954; m. Nora Mae Atkinson, Aug. 23, 1939; 1 dau., Jeann (Mrs. Lua R. Blankenship). Ordained to ministry Presbyn. Ch., 1939; bus. mgr. Presby. of South mag., Richmond, Va., 1938-39; commd. 1st lt. USAF, 1942, advanced through grades to lt. col., 1962; staff chaplain 18th Air Force, Greenville, S.C.; instr. chaplain Command and Staff Coll., Acad. Instrs. Sch., Air U., 1959-62; ret., 1967; asso. dir. Tex. Presbyn. Found., Dallas, 1967-72; evangelist Presbytery of Covenant, Presbyn. Ch. U.S., Dallas, 1973—. Recipient USAF Commendation awards for humanitarian work in Korea, 1954, for ministry to wounded, 1966, for counseling, 1967; decorated Bronze Star medal with oak leaf cluster; recipient Nat. Freedoms Found. awards, 1959, 62, 66, 68, Austin Coll. Alumni award, 1961. Mason, Kiwanian. Home and office: 7118 Joyce Way Dallas TX 75225

FLETCHER, RILEY EUGENE, lawyer; b. Eddy, Tex., Nov. 29, 1912; s. Riley Jordan and Lelih (Gill) F.; B.A., Baylor U., 1950, J.D., 1950; m. Hattie Inez Blackwell, June 11, 1954. Admitted to Tex. bar, 1950; asst. county atty. Navarro County, Tex., 1951-52, county atty., 1952-54; pvt. practice law, Corsicana, Tex., 1955-56; asst. atty. gen. Tex., 1956-62, chief law enforcement div., atty. gen.'s dept., 1958-61; chief taxation div., atty. gen.'s dept., 1961-62; asst. gen. counsel Tex. Municipal League, Austin, 1962-63, gen. counsel, 1963—. Lt. col. AUS ret. Mem. Am., Travis County bar assns., State Bar Tex., Am. Judicature Soc., Res. Officers Assn., Assn. U.S. Army (chpt. pres. 1965-66), Am. Legion, Judge Advs. Assn. Baptist. Mason. K.P. Home: 8100 Balcones Dr Austin TX 78759 Office: 1020 Southwest Tower TX 78701

FLICKINGER, CHARLES JOHN, educator; b. Bethlehem, Pa., July 13, 1938; s. Wilbur James and Verna (Diehl) F.; A.B., Dartmouth Coll., 1960; M.D., Harvard, 1964; m. Agnes Elizabeth Dickel, Feb. 23, 1963; children—Laura Jill, David Paul. Research fellow dept. anatomy U. Colo., Denver, 1964-65, Harvard Med. Sch., Boston, 1965-66; research asso. Inst. Developmental Biology, U. Colo., Boulder, 1966-67, asst. prof., 1967-70; asso. prof. dept. anatomy Sch. Medicine, U. Va., Charlottesville, 1971—. NIH research career devel. award grantee, 1968-70. Mem. Am. Soc. Cell Biology Am. Assn. Anatomists, Phi Beta Kappa, Alpha Omega Alpha. Asso. editor: Anatomical Record jour. Am. Assn. Anatomists, 1972—. Home: 2009 Meadowbrook Rd Charlottesville VA 22901

FLICKINGER, W(ALTER) GARRETT, lawyer, educator; b. Erie, Pa., July 9, 1928; s. Carlton Phillip and Kathleen (Garrett) F.; A.B. with high honors, Yale, 1950; J.D., U. Mich., 1953; postgrad. Columbia, 1967-68 Admitted to N.Y. bar, 1956, Ky. bar, 1969; asso. White & Case, N.Y.C., 1953, 55-60; asst. prof. law Boston U., 1960-63; vis. asso. prof. law U. Ky., 1963-64, asso. prof., 1964-67, prof., 1967—. Bd. govs. Citizens Assn. for Planning, Lexington, 1964-70; trustee LSAC Council, 1969-71, 72-74. Served with AUS, 1953-55. Mem. Am. Bar Assn. (mem. com. on successions 1966—), Assn. Bar City N.Y., Phi Beta Kappa, Delta Theta Phi, Order of Coif, Omicron Delta Kappa. Democrat. Episcopalian. Home: 1416 Cochran Rd Lexington KY 40502

FLIEGER, HOWARD WENTWORTH, editor; b. Denver, Oct. 11, 1909; s. Sterling N. and Florence (Milliken) F.; student pub. schs.; m. Dorothy Kathryn James, Apr. 7, 1927; children—Howard Wentworth, Kenneth Hugh. Reporter, city editor Shawnee (Okla.) Morning News, 1929-33; with A.P.; St. Louis, 1933-35, night news editor, Kansas City, Mo., 1935-37, bur. chief, Jefferson City, 1937-43, White House corr., Washington, 1943-45; mng. editor World Report, Washington, 1945-48; directing editor world staff U.S. News and World Report, 1948-58, asst. exec. editor, 1958-65, asso. exec. editor, 1965-69, exec. editor, 1969-72, editor, sr. v.p., 1972—. Mem. White House Corrs. Assn. Clubs: Nat. Press. F Street (Washington). Home: 6818 Selkirk Dr Bethesda MD 20034 Office: US News and World Report Washington DC 20037

FLINN, WILLIAM ADAMS, educator; b. Atlanta, May 11, 1912; s. Richard Orme and Anna (Emery) F.; B.A., Davidson Coll., 1933; M.B.A., Harvard, 1936; Ph.D., Ohio State U., 1959; m. Caroline Elizabeth Blackshear, Apr. 20, 1940; children—William Adams, David Lynnfield, Richard Orme III, Perry Blackshear. Clk., Gulf Oil Co., Atlanta, 1934; with sales dept. Reynolds Metals Co., N.Y.C., San Francisco, 1936-38; supt. Rich's, Inc., dept. store, Atlanta, 1938-41; purchasing agt., gen. mgr. subsidiary trucking co. Irvindale Farms, Inc., Atlanta, 1946-47; sec.-treas., gen. mgr. Spacarb Distbrs., Inc., Atlanta, 1948; instr. Emory U. Sch. Bus., Atlanta, 1949; asst. prof. Ga. Inst. Tech., Coll. Indsl. Mgmt., Atlanta, 1949-58, asso. prof., 1959-68, prof., 1969-72, coordinator marketing, 1953-72; lectr. U. Md., Univ. Coll., Europe, Italy, Germany, Eng., Turkey, Spain, 1972—. Dir. Specialized Investments, Inc., Miami, Fla. Trustee Basic Values Found. Served with AUS, 1941-46. NSF grantee, 1967-68. Mem. Am. (chpt. pres. 1964-65), So. marketing assns., Sales and Marketing Execs. Internat., Am. Assn. U. Profs. (chpt. pres. 1962-63), Kappa Alpha Order, Omicron Delta Kappa. Presbyn. (ruling elder). Club: Ansley Golf (Atlanta). Home: 145 Avery Dr NE Atlanta GA 30309 Office: U Md APO New York City NY 09403

FLINT, CORT RAY, clergyman, author, cons.; b. Leedey, Okla., Mar. 17, 1915; s. Corties Ray and Kathryn (Logan) F.; B.A., Southwestern State Coll., 1935; postgrad. U. Okla., summers 1937, 39; Th.M., So. Bapt. Theol. Sem., 1943, Th.D., 1952; m. Wilma Ilene Moore, Nov. 24, 1920; children—Sue Ann, Cort Ray. Tchr. pub. schs., Okla., 1935-40; ordained to ministry, Bapt. Ch., 1940; pastor, New Haven, Ky., 1941-43, Pleasant Grove Ch., Hodgenville, Ky., 1941-42, 46-47; asst. pastor Southside Bapt. Ch., Birmingham, Ala., 1947-48; pastor First Ch., Olney, Tex., 1948-50, Lynn Acres Ch., Louisville, 1951-53; adminstrv. asst. So. Bapt. Theol. Sem., Louisville, 1952-55; pastor First Ch., Anderson, S.C., 1955—; interim pres. Anderson Coll., 1957—; pastor Meadows of Dan Bapt. Ch., Va.; dir., pres. Anderson Sch. Theology for Laymen; vice chmn. bd. PACA. Various offices Bapt. convs., Tex., Ky., 1948-53; chmn. stewardship com. S.C. Bapt. Conv., 1957-58, gen. bd., 1957—; finance com. Saluda Bapt. Assn. S.C., 1955-58. Active YMCA, Anderson County Tb Assn.; exec. bd. Blue Ridge council Boy Scouts Am. Vice chmn. bd. trustees So. Bapt. Theol. Sec., Louisville; trustee Furman U. Served as lt., chaplain, USNR, 1943-46; PTO. Mem. Anderson Ministerial Assn. (pres. 1956-57), Internat. Platform Speakers Orgn. Mason, Odd Fellow. Clubs: Rotary, Kiwanis. Author: Grief's Slow Wisdom; To Thine Own Self Be True; Better Men or Bitter Men; Grief Is Love; The Best Is Yet To Be; The Purpose of Love. Editor: The Quotable Dr. Crane; The Quotable Billy Graham. Home: The Recluse Route 2 Box 174 Hillsville VA 24343

FLINT, FRANKLIN FORD, educator; b. Victoria, Va., Aug. 4, 1925; s. Lloyd Granville and Delia Jefferson (Hammock) F.; B.S., Lynchburg Coll., 1949; M.S., U. Va., 1950, Ph.D., 1955; m. Dona Joan Cook, June 5, 1948; children—Kathryn, Roger, Julie. Faculty, Randolph-Macon Woman's Coll., Lynchburg, Va., 1951—, prof. biology, 1966—; research prof. George Washington U., 1968-69. Staff biologist Com. Undergrad. Edn. in Biol. Sci., 1968-69. Bd. dirs. R.E. Lee Soil and Water Conservation Dist., 1973—. Served to comdr. USNR, 1942-46. Am. Philos. Soc. grantee, 1957-58; Am. Acad. Arts and Sci. grantee, 1957-58; Fulbright-Hays sr. research scholar to Portugal, 1964-65. Mem. Am. Inst. Biol. Scis. (gov. 1971—), A.A.A.S. (council 1973), Va. Acad. Sci. (pres. 1972-73). Kiwanian. Home: 2427 Indian Hill Rd Lynchburg VA 24503 Office: Biology Dept Randolph-Macon Woman's Coll Lynchburg VA 24504

FLIPPEN, JAMES HOWARD, JR., lawyer; b. Richmond, Va., Nov. 14, 1929; s. James Howard and Anne Evelyn (Tucker) F.; B.A., Va. Mil. Inst., 1950; LL.B., Washington & Lee U., 1953; m. Nancy Virginia Shults, July 3, 1955; children—James Howard, III, John Brooks, Mary Virginia. Admitted to Va. bar, 1953; practiced in Norfolk, 1955—; partner Breeden, Howard & MacMillan, 1955—. Substitute judge Juvenile and Domestic Relations Ct., City Norfolk, Va., 1968—. Served with USAF, 1953-55. Mem. Am., Va., Norfolk bar assns., Kappa Alpha, Phi Delta Phi. Kiwanian. Clubs: Yacht and Country, Harbor (Norfolk, Va.). Home: 1402 Trouville Av Norfolk VA 23505 Office: 1530 Virginia Nat Bank Bldg Norfolk VA 23510

FLIPPEN, LLEWELLYN TUCKER, dentist; b. Richmond, Va., July 8, 1933; s. James Howard and Evelyn (Tucker) F.; B.A., U. Richmond, 1954; D.D.S., Va. Commonwealth U., 1958. Rotating dental intern Wilford Hall Hosp., San Antonio, 1958-59; pvt. practice dentistry, Richmond, 1961—; asst. clin. prof. restorative dept. Sch. Dentistry, Va. Commonwealth U., 1961—. Dir. Westhampton Savs. & Loan Assn., 1973—. Mem. alumni interfraternity council U. Richmond, 1966-69. Served to capt. USAF, 1958-61. Mem. Met. Acad. Dentistry (treas. 1969), Richmond Dental Soc. (bd. dirs., sec., ho. of dels. 1973), Va. Assn. professions, Am. Profl. Practice Assn., S.A.R. (chpt. pres. 1966, bd. mgrs. 1964-69), Omicron Kappa Upsilon, Kappa Alpha, Delta Sigma Delta, Alpha Sigma Chi, Sigma Zeta. Presbyn. (chmn. bd. deacons 1971-72, elder 1972—). Club: Bull and Bear. Home: 4310 Old Brook Rd Richmond VA 23227 Office: 4100 Brook Rd Richmond VA 23227

FLOCKS, KARL W., lawyer; b. N.Y.C., Apr. 27, 1910; B.E. in Mech. Engring., Johns Hopkins U., 1930; J.D., George Washington U., 1934. Admitted to D.C. bar, 1933, U.S. Ct. Customs and Patent Appeals bar, 1934, U.S. Supreme Ct. bar, 1955; patent examiner U.S. Patent Office, 1930-37; now with Karl W. Flocks and Assos., Washington. Mem. Am. Bar Assn., Bar Assn. D.C. (council sect. patent, trademark and copyright law 1960), Am. Trial Lawyers Assn., Am. Patent Law Assn., Tau Beta Pi. Home: 4848 Loughboro Rd NW Washington DC 20016 Office: Munsey Bldg Washington DC 20004*

FLOOD, WALTER ALOYSIUS, educator; b. N.Y.C., Apr. 27, 1927; s. Walter Aloysius and Lillian Edna (Peterson) F.; student Queens Coll., 1943-44, Syracuse U., 1944-45; B.E.E., Cornell U., 1950, M.E.E., 1952, Ph.D., 1954; m. Joan C. Cruthers, Sept. 6, 1954; children—Peter, Amanda, Timothy. Asso. engr. Cornell Aeronautical Lab., Buffalo, 1954-55, research engr., 1956-62, prin. engr. staff scientist, 1962-67; exchange prof. Cornell U., Ithaca, N.Y., 1965-66; prof. elec. engring. N.C. State U., Raleigh, 1967—. Cons. Gen. Electric Tempo, Santa Barbara, 1968—, Stanford Research Inst., Menlo Park, Cal., 1968—, Research Triangle Inst., 1967-72; dir. Applied Sci. Assn., Raleigh, N.C., 1973—. Served with AUS, 1945-46. Mem. I.E.E.E., A.A.A.S., Internat. Radio Sci. Union, Sigma Xi, Eta Kappa Nu. Home: 5808 Winthrop Dr Raleigh NC 27612

FLOREA, HAROLD ROBERT, mech. engr.; b. N.Y.C., July 24, 1914; s. Maurice and Anna (Yankowicz) F.; M.E., Stevens Inst. Tech., 1937; m. Margaret Dawn Dickinson, Sept. 12, 1947. With U.S. Naval Tng. Device Center, Orlando, Fla., 1950-72, head lab. services dept., 1960-64, head audio-visual engring. dept., 1964-72; pvt. tech. cons., tng. devices, Winter Park, Fla., 1972—. Pres. Orange County Democratic Club, 1973—. Mem. Engrs. and Scientists Assn. (pres. 1960-61), Middle Mgmt. Assn. (pres. 1972-73). Clubs: Maitland Tennis, Maitland Bridge (Fla.). Patentee in field. Home: 2912 Ambergate Rd Winter Park FL 32789

FLOREN, MARVIN JOHN, dentist; b. Chulumami, Bolivia, S.A., Sept. 3, 1941 (parents Am. citizens); s. Roger Chevalier and Pearl Marvie (Hubbard) F.; student Andrews U., 1960-61; D.D.S., Loma Linda U., 1967; m. Carol Conard Morgan, July 31, 1966; children—John Wesley, Jeffery Dean. Research asst. restorative dept. Loma Linda U., 1965, 66; clin. instr. crown and bridge dept. Emory U., Atlanta, 1969—; clinician Ben Massell Dental Clinic, 1969-70. Mem. north dist. com. Emergency Dental Service for City of Atlanta, 1973. Active United Way, 1973. Recipient awards Loma Linda U. Dental Clinic, 1966, Ben Massell Dental Clinic, 1970. Mem. Am., Ga. dental assns., S.A.R. Mem. Ch. of Seventh Day Adventist. Home: 826 John Aldon Rd Stone Mountain GA 30083 Office: 3312 Piedmont Rd NE Atlanta GA 30305

FLORENTZ, ALFRED NILS, ins. co. exec.; b. Little Rock, Nov. 4, 1905; s. Alfred Nichols and Nellie Louise (Boylston) F.; student Drake U., 1928-29; LL.D., U. Ark., 1962; m. Margaret Frances Hill, Apr. 4, 1931; 1 dau., Eleanor Louise. Br. officer cashier Cotton States Life Ins. Co., Memphis, 1924-25, salesman, 1925-26; asst. mgr. Ind. Life Ins. Co., Memphis, 1926-28; conservation mgr. Central Life Assurance Soc., Des Moines, 1928-29, traveling auditor, 1929, chief accountant Union Life Ins. Co., Little Rock, 1929-32, asst. sec., 1932-44, v.p., comptroller, 1944-45, v.p., sec. dir., to 1970, now dir.; asst. trust officer First Nat. Bank & Trust Co., Mountain Home, Ark., 1973—; treas. Home-Bound Industries of Pulaski County. Past chmn. bd. Ark. Children's Colony. Mem. Life Underwriters Assn. (past dir.), Life Office Mgmt. Assn. (past dir.), Chartered Life Underwriters (past local pres.), Ark. Assn. for Crippled (dir.), Exceptional Children's School Assn. (organizer, 1948, pres. 1948-53), C. of C. Episcopalian Home: 1302 E 9th St Mountain Home AR 72653 Office: First Nat Bank Bldg Mountain Home AR 72653

FLORES, ADOLPH ANTHONY, JR., physician; b. Mansfield, La., Oct. 16, 1921; s. Adolph Abnard and Kathleen Garland (Rambin) F.; B.S., La. State U., 1942, M.D., 1944. Intern Charity Hosp., Shreveport, La., 1944-45; gen. practice medicine, Pleasant Hill, La., 1946-50; resident in medicine Charity Hosp. La., New Orleans, 1950-53, asst. dir., 1955-59; practice medicine specializing in internal medicine, New Orleans, 1959—; asst. cardiologist So. Bapt. Hosp., New Orleans; mem. staff So. Bapt. Hosp., Hotel Dieu Sisters Hosp.; clin. prof. medicine La. State U. Sch. Medicine, New Orleans, 1971—. Chief med. div. New Orleans Civil Def., 1965—; mem. La. Med. Adv. Bd. Bd. dirs. La. Med. Polit. Action Com., 1964-68; charter mem. Greater New Orleans Area Wide Health Planning Council; trustee HEAL; bd. govs. OPMS; charter mem., v.p. Vis. Nurses Assn. Greater New Orleans. Served with USNR, World War II, Korea. Diplomate Am. Bd. Internal Medicine. Mem. A.M.A., A.C.P.; mem. Assn. Am. Physicians and Surgeons, Am. Soc. Internal Medicine, So. Med. Assn., La. State Med. Soc., New Orleans Acad. Internal Medicine (pres. 1967-68), Orleans Parish Med. Soc. (dir. 1970-72), Phi Chi. Roman Catholic. K.C. Home: 1737 Milan St New Orleans LA 70115 Office: 4500 Magnolia St New Orleans LA 70115

FLORES, BENITO EUSEBIO, educator; b. Saltillo, Coahuila, Mexico, Oct. 19, 1937; s. Benito F. and Ernestina (Sandoval) F.; B.S., Tex. A. and M. U., 1960; M.S., U. Houston, 1964, Ph.D., 1969; m. Kathryn Meath, Aug. 26, 1960; children—Benito, Adriana, Laura. Indsl. engr. B.F. Goodrich, Mexico City, 1960-61; instr. indsl. engring. U. Houston, 1962-67; prof. indsl. engring. Monterrey Inst. Tech., Monterrey, Mexico, 1967—. Cons. to pvt. industry and govt. Mem. Am. Inst. Indsl. Engrs., Am. Prodn. Inventory Control Soc., Inst. Mgmt. Scis., Am. Inst. Decision Scis., Asociacian Mexicana de Ingeinieros Industriales. Contbr. articles to profl. jours. Home: 410 Rio Elba Pte Col del Valle NL Mexico

FLORY, DAVID PAUL, communications engr.; b. Phillipsburg, O., Aug. 3, 1919; s. David Chleo and Della (Fox) F.; B.A., Denison U., 1941; m. Virginia Ruth Knox, Mar. 20, 1943; children—Katharine Knox (Mrs. Winston Michael Fox), Carol Wallace (Mrs. Harold H. Wingerd, Jr.), David Paul. Engr., Western Electric Co., Chgo., 1946-49; partner D.C. Flory & Sons, Gen. Contractors, Dayton, O., 1949-52; engr. So. Bell Tel. & Tel. Co., Charlotte, N.C., 1952-63, supervising engr., 1963—. Sec. treas. Carolinas Memory Fund. Served to 1st lt. USAF, 1941-46; now ltd. col. Res. ret. Registered profl. engr., N.C. Mem. Nat. Soc. Profl. Engrs., Phi Gamma Delta. Episcopalian. Home: 3301 Eastburn Rd Charlotte NC 28210 Office: PO Box 240 Charlotte NC 28230

FLORY, ROBERT ALLAN, chemist; b. Sullivan, Ind., Nov. 12, 1924; s. James Ivan and Winnie (McCain) F.; B.S., Ball State U., 1951; m. Aletha M. Ammerman, Dec. 4, 1945; children—Michele Lynn (Mrs. James E. Hardie), Craig Alan; m. 2d, Callie F. Cox, Apr. 7, 1973. Chemist, Ball Bros. Co., Muncie, Ind., 1951-53; chemist

Hawkeye Rubber Co., Cedar Rapids, Ia., 1953-60; plant mgr. H. B. Egan Mfg. Co., Muskogee, Okla., 1960—. Active YMCA, Muskogee, Okla., 1963—. Republican precinct chmn., 1964. Served with AUS, 1942-45. Decorated Purple Heart, Bronze Star medal (U.S.); Belgian Fourragere. Mem. Am. Chem. Soc. Presbyn. Mason. Address: Route 2 Webbers Falls OK 74470

FLOURNOY, EDWIN ELLIOTT, JR., physician; b. Jackson, Miss., Nov. 30, 1935; s. Edwin Elliott and Josephine (Cotten) F.; B.S., Millsaps Coll., 1956; M.D., U. Miss., 1960; m. Mary Beth Brandon, June 29, 1957; children—Elizabeth Lynn, Katherine Elliott. Intern, Womack Army Hosp., Ft. Bragg, N.C., 1960-61; resident gen. practice Lafayette (La.) Charity Hosp., 1964-65; practice medicine specializing in family practice, 1965—; mem. med. staff Phoebe Putney Meml. Hosp., Albany, Ga., Palmyra Park Hosp. Served with USAF, 1960-64. Mem. Am. (program com.), Ga. (pres.) acads. family physicians, Am., So. med. assns., Med. Assn. Ga., Dougherty County Med. Soc. Baptist. Elk. Home: 508 Dr Albany GA 31705 Office: 1009 N Monroe St Albany GA 31701

FLOWERS, BYRON LAYFELT, bakery exec.; b. nr. Brundiage, Ala., Jan. 13, 1931; s. Clarence Albert and Rebecca (Connor) F.; student LaSalle Extension U., 1964; m. Eleanor Joyce Lee, Jan. 9, 1954; 1 dau., Carmen Camille. With Eagle-Phoenix Cotton Mill, Columbus, Ga., 1948-50, signal dept. Atlantic Coast Lines, 1953-54; with traffic dept. Sunshine Biscuits, Inc., Columbus, 1954—, traffic mgr., 1968—. Served with USMC, 1950-53. Club: Traffic (1st v.p. 1973—) (Columbus). Home: 4008 Lakewood Dr Phoenix City AL 36867 Office: PO Box 1660 Columbua GA 31902

FLOWERS, CHARLES ELY, JR., physician; b. Zebulon, N.C., July 20, 1920; s. Charles Ely and Carmen, (Poole) F.; B.S., The Citadel, 1941; M.D., Johns Hopkins, 1944; m. Juanita Bays, Nov. 23, 1944 (dec.); children—Charles Ely III, Carmen Eva; m. 2d Juanzetta Shew, Sept. 25, 1972. Intern, Johns Hopkins Hosp., Balt., 1944, resident, 1945-50; instr. State U. N.Y., 1950-51, asst. prof., 1951-53; asso. prof. U. N.C., 1953-61, prof., 1961-66; prof., chmn. dept. obstetrics and gynecology Baylor U., Houston, 1966-69; prof., chmn. dept. obstetrics and gynecology U. Ala. Sch. Medicine, Birmingham, 1969—; obstetrician and gynecologist-in-chief U. Ala. Med. Center. Cons. NIH; asso examiner Am. Bd. Obstetrics and Gynecology; gen. chmn. 6th World Congress Obstetrics and Gynecology; adv. com. oral contraceptives Internat. Planned Parenthood; mem. nat. clin. adv. com. Nat. Found. Served to capt. M.C., AUS, 1946-48. Recipient Teaching award Baylor Coll. Medicine, 1968; Distinguished Service award U. N.C. Mem. A.M.A., Continental Gynecol. Soc., Am. Gynecol. Soc., Am., Central assns. obstetricians and gynecologists, A.C.S. (obstetrics and gynecology council), Am. Coll. Obstetricians and Gynecologists (chmn. com. obstetric anesthesia and analgesia), Internat. Coll. Anesthetists. Mem. editorial bd. Obstetrics and Gynecology, 1970. Research in obstet. anesthesia, analgesia, population control and toxemia of pregnancy, physiology of endometrium. Home: 3757 Rockhill Rd Birmingham AL 35223 Office: U Ala Sch Medicine Univ Sta Birmingham AL 35294

FLOWERS, ELLIOTT GALETIN, lawyer; b. Houston, Mar. 10, 1913; s. Louis Irwin and Hazel (Lawshae) F.; B.A., Rice U., 1934; LL.B., Tex. U., 1937; m. Elizabeth Sinclair, Jan. 22, 1957; children—Leigh (Mrs. L.F. Bonner, Jr.), Elliott Galetin, Lynn Zarr, Lucy (Mrs. A.J. Foyt, Jr.). Admitted to Tex. bar, 1937; practiced Houston, 1939-41, 47—; gen. counsel McCarthy Oil & Gas Corp., Houston, 1947-52; asso. counsel Allied Chem. Corp., Houston, 1952-71, asst. gen. counsel, 1971—; exec. asst. to pres. Union Tex. Petroleum, Houston, 1952—. Served to lt. comdr. USNR, 1942-47. Mem. Am., Tex. bar assns., Fed. Power Bar Assn., Ind. Petroleum Assn. (v.p. 1963-66, dir. 1966—), Mid-Continent Oil and Gas Assn. (mem. exec. mgmt., legis., legal coms. 1964— finance com. 1964-68, dir. 1970—), So. Gas Assn. (adv. council 1962-63), Houston Bar Assn. (finance and budget com. 1963-64). Author: Municipal Officials in Texas, 1939. Contbr. articles on municipal law to profl. jours. Home: 3330 Del Monte Houston TX 77019 Office: 3000 Richmond Av Houston TX 77006

FLOWERS, NEAL STEWART, physician; b. Pensacola, Fla., Nov. 27, 1926; s. Kyrie Neal and Annie Laurie (Stewart) F.; B.S., U. Ala., 1949; M.D., Tulane U., 1952; m. Helen Marie Scott, June 12, 1948; children—Jeaneal Marie, Kevin Neal; m. 2d, Ruby Reyes Flowers, Sept. 30, 1973. Intern Piedmont Hosp., Atlanta, 1952-53; resident radiology Hurley Hosp., Flint, Mich., 1953-56; radiologist Mobile (Ala.) Gen. Hosp., 1956-60, Mobile Infirmary, 1956-62, Monroe County Hosp., 1962—. Cons. radiologist USPHS, 1957-62, USAF Hosp., Brookley, 1963-64. Served with USNR, 1944-46. Diplomate Am. Bd. Radiology. Mem. Internat. Congress Radiology, Am., So. med. assns., Am. Coll. Radiology, Radiol. Soc. N.A., So. Radiologic Conf., Ala. Radiologic Soc. (pres. 1960-61), Med. Soc. Mobile County (pres. 1967), South Ala. Radiol. Soc. (sec.-treas.), Phi Beta Kappa, Alpha Omega Alpha, Congress County Med. Socs. (trustee 1967-68), Tb and Health Assn. Mobile (pres.). Lion. Home: 7049 Dickens Ferry Rd Box 7349 Mobile AL 36607 Office: 130 Louiselle St Mobile AL 36607

FLOWERS, WALTER, congressman; b. Greenville, Ala., Apr. 12, 1933; s. Walter W. and Ruth (Swaim) F.; A.B., U. Ala., 1955, LL.B., 1957; Rotary Found. fellow, U. London, 1957-58; m. Margaret V. Pringle, Aug. 21, 1958; children—Vivian Victoria, Walter Winkler III, Victor Woodley. Admitted to Ala. bar, 1957, Miss. bar, 1960; sr. partner firm Flowers and Shelby, Tuscaloosa, Ala., 1961-68; mem. 91st-93d Congresses, 7th Dist. Ala. Past mem. Black Warrior council Boy Scouts Am., Tuscaloosa YMCA; former mem., chmn. Tuscaloosa Civil Service Bd.; past pres. Tuscaloosa County Mental Health Assn.; past bd. dirs. Tuscaloosa County chpt. A.R.C., Tuscaloosa Tb Assn. Served to 1st lt. AUS, 1958-59. Mem. Am., Miss., Ala., Tuscaloosa County bar assns., U. Ala. Alumni Assn. (past pres. Tuscaloosa County), Phi Beta Kappa, Omicron Delta Kappa, Jasons Soc., Phi Delta Phi, Sigma Alpha Epsilon. Democrat. Episcopalian. Rotarian. Home: 31 University Circle Tuscaloosa AL 35401 Office: House of Representatives Washington DC 20515

FLOYD, CARLISLE, composer, educator; b. Latta, S.C., June 11, 1926; s. Carlisle Sessions and Ida (Fenegan) F.; Mus.B., Syracuse U., 1946, Mus. M., 1949; m. Kay Reeder, Nov. 28, 1957. Mem. faculty Sch. Music, Fla. State U., Tallahassee, 1947—, now prof. music; composer Slow Dusk (mus. play), 1949, Susannah (mus. drama), 1954, Pilgrimage, 1955, Sonata For Piano, 1957, Wuthering Heights (mus. drama), 1958, The Mystery, 1960, The Passion of Jonathan Wade (mus. drama), 1962, The Sojourner and Mollie Sinclair (comedy-drama), 1963; Markheim (mus. drama), 1965, Of Mice and Men (mus. drama), 1970; Flower and Hawk (monodrama), 1972. Recipient Citation of Merit, Nat. Assn. Am. Composers and Conductors, 1957, N.Y. Music Critics Circle award, 1957; named one of ten Outstanding Young Men, U.S. Jr. C. of C., 1959; Guggenheim fellow, 1956. Mem. A.S.C.A.P., Am. Guild Mus. Artists, Pi Kappa Lambda, Phi Mu Alpha, Delta Omicron. Democrat. Episcopalian. Home: 806 Middlebrook Circle Tallahassee FL 32303

FLOYD, ELDRA MOORE, JR., lawyer; b. Fairmont, N.C., July 19, 1920; s. Eldra Moore and Sarah Augusta (Blake) F.; B.A., Wake Forest U., 1950; J.D., U. S.C., 1948; m. Eugenia Chandler, Oct. 31, 1942; children—Michael H., Cindy M., Eldra Moore III, Eugenia, Ruth H. Admitted to S.C. bar, 1948, since practiced in Hartsville; partner Floyd & Craig, Hartsville, 1958—. Commr., Darlington County, 1961-64; mem. Darlington County Bd. Edn., 1968—; mem. Darlington County Democratic Exec. Com., 1962—. Served as lt. comdr. USNR, 1940-45; PTO. Mem. Am., S.C. (mem. exec. com. 1973—), Darlington County (pres. 1973) bar assns., Am. Judicature Soc. Episcopalian. Mason (Shriner), Lion. Home: 411 Kenwood Dr Hartsville SC 29550 Office: 125 W Home Av PO Box 909 Hartsville SC 29550

FLOYD, ERNEST HAZEL, educator; b. Aiken County, nr. Belvedere, S.C., Apr. 5, 1914; s. John Lincoln and Katie Susan (Fontaine) F.; B.S., Clemson U., 1937; M.S., La. State U., 1939; postgrad. Ohio State U., 1940; m. Marine Gertrude Brown, Apr. 14, 1938; 1 dau., Marine Anne. Mem. faculty La. State U., Baton Rouge, 1940—, prof. entomology, 1954—. Served with AUS, 1943-46. Decorated Bronze Star. Mem. Entomol. Soc. Am., La. Entomologists (pres. 1971). Baptist. Contbr. articles to sci. jours. Home: 1962 Stuart St Baton Rouge LA 70808

FLOYD, HENRY BASCOM, III, indsl. engr.; b. Floyd Dale, S.C., Sept. 6, 1927; s. Henry Bascom and Isabelle (Sanders) F.; B.S. in C.E., The Citadel, 1949; M.S. in Indsl. Mgmt., Ga. Tech., 1966; m. Rubie Mae Fore, Mar. 27, 1948; children—Rebecca Anne (Mrs. Alan H. Arrington), Henry Bascom IV, Jennette Isabelle, Tina Fore. Constrn. engr. DuPont, Camden, S.C., Martinsville, Va., Pensacola, Fla., 1950-54; cons. engr. Townsend Builder's Supply, Whiteville, N.C., 1954-55; plant engr. Serv-Air Aviation Corp., Kinston, N.C., 1955-57; dep. base engr. USAF, Seymour Johnson AFB, Goldsboro, N.C., 1957-62; tech. mgr. NASA, Marshall Space Flight Center, Huntsville, Ala., 1963-66, mgr. facilities and logistics Saturn program, 1966—, dep. project mgr. Skylab Expt. project, 1971—, also project mgr. Skylab student project. Founding dir. Boy's Home Inc., Lake Waccamaw, N.C. Served with USNR, 1945-46; PTO. Registered profl. engr., Ala., N.C. Methodist. Mason. Clubs: Civitan, Greenwyche Community Club and Pool, Valley Inc. Home: 4017 Dobbs Dr Huntsville AL 35802 Office: Marshall Space Flight Center Huntsville AL 35812

FLOYD, JOHN LEWIS, clergyman; b. Gasburg, Va., Nov. 27, 1911; s. Buford Tillman and Hattie Lucy (Lynch) F.; B.A., Duke, 1938; B.D., Tex. Christian U., 1941; postgrad. Tex. Tech. Coll., 1961-62; m. Ona Lee Reid, July 31, 1939; children—Melvita, John Lewis. Ordained to ministry Christian Ch., 1941; minister The Christian Ch., Wapanucka, Okla., 1939-40, Fort Worth, 1940-41, Donna, Tex., 1941-47, Gulfport, Miss., 1947-49, Purcell, Okla., 1949-52, Spur, Tex., 1952-61, Slaton, Tex., 1962-65, Kermit, Tex., 1965—. Mem. resolutions com. Christian Ch., 1969-72. Bd. dirs. Salvation Army, Kermit. Mem. Winkler County Ministerial Alliance (pres. 1970—). Mason, Lion. Home: 215 E Bryan St Kermit TX 79745 Office: PO Box 1181 Kermit TX 79745

FLOYD, LOUIS CARL, physician; b. Malakoff, Tex., Nov. 22, 1914; s. Marion Avery and Minnie Ada (Payne) F.; student Tex. Christian U., 1931; B.A., Rice U., 1938; M.D., U. Tex., 1942; m. Aera Margaret Allsup, Sept. 20, 1938 (dec. 1952); children—Marilyn Jo, Louis Carl; m. 2d, Margery Francis Johnson, June 8, 1957; stepchildren—Martha Jo, Barbara Lynn. Commd. asst. surgeon, 1st lt., USPHS, 1943; advanced through grades to col., 1961, ret., 1964; intern USPHS Hosp., Balt., 1942-43; resident USPHS Hosp., Boston, 1945-47; chief med. officer various fed. prisons, 1952-63; dep. chief surgery USPHS Hosp., Chgo., 1963-64, ret.; pvt. practice medicine specializing in geriatrics and surgery, Yukon, Okla., Bella Vista, Ark., 1964—. Pres. Floyd Enterprises Okla., Inc., 1965—. Charter mem. Am. Bd. Family Practice. Mem. A.M.A., Okla. Med. Assn., Am. Acad. Family Practice, Nu Sigma Nu, Alpha Omega Alpha. Democrat. Baptist. Mason, Moose. Home: 703 S Holly Yukon OK 73099 Office: 800 W Main PO Box D Yukon OK 73099 also Concordia Med Center Bella Vista AR 72712

FLOYD, PICOT DE BOISFEUILLET, city mgr.; b. Savannah, Ga., Aug. 18, 1931; s. Marmaduke Hamilton and Marie Dolores (Boisfeuillet) F.; A.A., St. Bernard Coll., 1951; A.B., St. Mary's Coll., Balt., 1953; M.A. in Govt., George Washington U., 1965; postgrad. in pub. adminstrn. U. Ga., 1965-66; m. Mary Mullarky Keating, Dec. 26, 1959; children—Geoffrey Keating, John Adam Fendin, Picot de Boisfeuillet. Staff writer Savannah Morning News, 1959-60; asst. city mgr. City of Savannah, 1960-62, city mgr., 1967-71; asst. city mgr. City of Alexandria (Va.), 1962-65; area coordinator Ala.-Miss. community action programs U.S. Office Econ. Opportunity, 1965-66; dir. field services program Inst. of Govt., U. Ga., Athens, 1966-67; sr. v.p., corporate sec. Pub. Tech., Inc., state and local govt. research and devel. orgn., Washington, 1971-73; city mgr., Clearwater, Fla., 1973—. Former mem. Chatham County-Savannah Met. Planning Commn. Served to lt. (j.g.) USCGR, 1955-59. Mem. Internat. City Mgmt. Assn., Am. Soc. for Pub. Adminstrn., Am., So. polit. sci. assns., Assn. for Systems Mgmt., Urban and Regional Information Systems Assn., Ga. Hist. Soc. (curator). Roman Catholic. Contbr. articles to profl. jours. Home: 515 Hobart Av Clearwater FL 33515 Office: Office of City Mgr PO Box 4748 Clearwater FL 33518

FLOYD, W.C., county judge; b. Conway, S.C., Oct. 4, 1904; s. William Thomas and Charlotte (Johnson) F.; student pub. schs., S.C.; m. Ruth Smith, Sept. 16, 1923; children—Eugene C. Mozelle, Billie Roy Nichols, Sidney T. Farmer, Horry County, 1923-34; owner Floyd Supply Co., Conway, S.C., 1934-58; probate judge Horry County, Conway, S.C., 1959—. Mason, Lion. Home: 411 Beaty St Conway SC 29526 Office: Court House Conway SC 29526

FLUGRATH, JAMES MARION, audiologist; b. St. Joseph, Mich., Sept. 23, 1934; s. Ralph and Helen (Bischoff) F.; A.B., U. Mich., 1961; M.A., Wayne State U., 1963, Ph.D., 1965; m. Nancy Louise Sharp, May 30, 1962. Adult aphasic counselor U. Mich., 1961; speech pathologist St. Clair Shores (Mich.) pub. schs., 1961-62; audiologist Wayne State U., 1962-65, Eastern Ill. U., 1965-68; dir. clin. audiology Memphis State U. Speech and Hearing Center, 1968-71; chief audiology and speech pathology Mountain Home (Tenn.) VA Center, 1971—. Cons. audiologist, Memphis, 1968-71. Served with AUS, 1953-56. Mem. Am. Speech and Hearing Assn. (recipient certificates in basic hearing 1961, basic speech 1961, clin. competence in audiology 1968, in speech pathology 1969), Acoustical Soc. Am., Volta Bur., Mt. Empire Tenn. speech and hearing assns., Nat. Assn. Hearing and Speech Agys., Soc. Audiologists of South, Am. Audiology Soc. Contbr. articles to profl. jours. Home: 1812 McClellan Dr Johnson City TN 37601 Office: VA Center Mountain Home TN 37684

FLUKER, WILLIAM GORDON, civil engr.; b. Birmingham, Ala., Sept. 17, 1938; s. William David and Ila Gertrude (Reach) F.; B.C.E., Auburn U., 1963; m. Nancy Louise Wallace, Nov. 26, 1958; children—Kathryn Denise, Deborah Ellen. Field engr. J.M. Keel & Assos., Birmingham, Ala., 1956-68; sr. design engr. Rust Engrng. Co., Birmingham, 1968—. Mason (32 deg., Shriner). Home: 909 19th Ct Birmingham AL 35215 Office: PO Box 101 Birmingham AL 35201

FLUNO, JOHN ARTHUR, cons. entomologist; b. Appleton, Wis., July 21, 1914; s. Arthur Swetland and Elsie (Younger) F.; B.S., Rollins Coll., 1937; M.S., Ohio State U., 1939; m. Ruth Margaret Johnson, Aug. 15, 1942; children—Ruth Adaire, Jo Anne. Field aide U.S. Dept. Agr., Orlando, Fla., 1937-38, entomologist, Orlando, Fla., Beltsville, Md., 1946-72; asst. Ohio Biol. Survey, Columbus, 1938-40; instr. Rollins Coll., Winter Park, Fla., 1941; jr. entomologist USPHS, 1941-46; now cons. Served with AUS, 1943-46. Mem. Am. Mosquito Control Assn., Entomol. Soc. Am., Entomol. Soc. Washington, Rollins Coll. Alumni Assn. (past pres.). Home and office: 1234 Lakeview Dr Winter Park FL 32789

FLY, JOHN WESLEY, city ofcl.; b. Zellwood, Fla., Aug. 17, 1915; s. E. W. and Leila (King) F.; B.S., U. Fla., 1937; M.S., U. Ill., 1941; m. Bessie Faye Mires, Sept. 3, 1938; children—John Wesley, Walter Mires, James Lawrence. Asst. prof. accounting U. Fla., 1938-41; partner Pribble, Wells & Fly, C.P.A.'s, Orlando, Fla., 1946-48; exec. in gas and equipment cos., Orlando, 1948-64; dir. finance City of Orlando, 1965—; dir. Plaza First Nat. Bank. Sec. Fla. State Racing Commn., 1954. Trustee Fla. Meth. Childrens Home. Served to maj. USAAF, 1942-45. C.P.A., Fla. Mem. Blue Key, Theta Chi, Beta Alpha Psi, Phi Kappa Phi. Methodist (trustee). Kiwanian. Club: Country (Orlando). Home: 2050 Fawsett Rd Winter Park FL 32789 Office: 400 S Orange Av Orlando FL 32801

FLY, WILLIAM STONER, lawyer; b. Victoria, Tex., Mar. 15, 1920; s. Benjiman Watt and Janie (Stoner) F.; LL.B., U. Tex., 1942; m. Betty Dickson Clements, Dec. 7, 1946; 1 dau., Laura Neal. Admitted to Tex. bar, 1943; mem. firm Hutchins & Fly, 1946-50, Fly & Moeller, 1954-64, Fly, Cory & Moeller, 1964-70, Fly, Moeller & Stevenson, all Victoria, 1970—; sec., gen. counsel S. Tex. Water Co., Rosharon, Tex., 1960-73; v.p., trust officer Am. Bank of Commerce, Victoria, 1960—; v.p., gen. counsel S. Tex. Savs. Assn., Victoria, 1950—. Mem. Tex. Ho. of Reps., 1947-53, Tex. Senate, 1954-60, Victoria County Airport Commn., 1972—. Served with USNR, 1942-46. Named Outstanding Young Man, Jr. C. of C., 1951. Rotarian. Home: 307 E Buena Vista Victoria TX 77901 Office: Americana Bank of Commerce Bldg Victoria TX 77901

FLYNN, GEORGE QUITMAN, educator; b. New Orleans, Feb. 12, 1937; s. George Quitman and Dorothy (Schneider) F.; B.S., Loyola U. South (New Orleans), 1960; M.A., La. State U., 1962, Ph.D., 1966; m. Mary Ann Reising, Sept. 3, 1960; children—Sean, Kathleen, Margaret. Asst. prof. dept. history Seattle U., 1966-69; asso. prof. U. Miami, Coral Gables, Fla., 1971-73; asso. prof. Tex. Tech. U., 1973—; vis. asso. prof. Ind. U., Bloomington, 1969-71. Mem. Am. Hist. Assn., Orgn. Am. Historians, Nat. Geographic Soc. Roman Catholic. Author: American Catholics and the Roosevelt Presidency, 1932-36, 1968. Home: 5601 Geneva Av Lubbock TX 79413 Office: Dept History Tex Tech U Lubbock TX 79409

FLYNN, RICHARD JAMES, lawyer; b. Omaha, Dec. 6, 1928; s. Richard T. and Eileen (Murphy) F.; student Cornell U., 1944-46; B.S., Northwestern U., 1950, J.D., 1953; children—Richard McDonnell, William Thomas, Kathryn Eileen, James Daniel. Admitted to D.C. bar, 1953, Ill. bar, 1954; law clk. to Chief Justices Vinson and Warren, 1953-54; asso. Sidley, Austin, Burgess & Smith, Chgo., 1954-63, partner, Washington, 1963-66, Sidley & Austin, 1967—. Served with USN, 1946-48. Mem. Am. (chmn. subcom. transp. antitrust sect. 1971-73), Chgo. (antitrust com. 1961-63), Fed. Power bar assns., Bar Assn. D.C., Nat. Lawyers Club, ICC Practioners, Washington Lawyers Commn. Civil Rights Under Law (exec. com.), Order of Coif, Phi Beta Kappa, Phi Delta Phi, Sigma Chi. Republican. Presbyn. (deacon, elder). Clubs: Metropolitan (Washington), Economic of Chicago, Legal, Kenwood Golf and Country. Contbr. articles to profl. jours. Home: 5000 38th St NW Washington DC 20016 Office: 1730 Pennsylvania Av NW Washington DC 20006

FLYNT, JOHN JAMES, JR., congressman; b. Griffin, Ga., Nov. 8, 1914; s. John James and Susan Winn (Banks) F.; student Ga. Mil. Acad.; A.B., U. Ga., 1936; postgrad. Emory U., 1937-38; J.D., George Washington U., 1940; grad. Command and Gen. Staff Sch., Air Corps Advanced Flying Sch., Brooks Field, Tex.; m. Patricia Irby Bradley; children—Susan Banks, John James III, Crisp Bradley. Admitted to Ga. bar, 1938; asst. U.S. atty. No. Dist. Ga., 1939-41, 45-46; mem. Ga. Ho. of Reps., 1947-48; solicitor gen. Griffin Jud. Circuit, 1949-54; mem. 83d-88th congresses, 4th Ga. Dist.; mem. 89th-93d congresses, 6th Ga. Dist. Bd. visitors U.S. Air Force Acad., Colo.; trustee LaGrange (Ga.) Coll., Woodward Acad. Served in U.S. Army, 1936-37, 41-45, col. Res. Decorated Bronze Star medal. Mem. Ga. (pres.), Am. (com. jud. selection, tenure, compensation) bar assns., Am. Legion, V.F.W., Phi Delta Phi, Sigma Alpha Epsilon. Democrat. Methodist (chmn. bd. stewards). Mason (Shriner). Home: Griffin GA 30223 Office: House Office Bldg Washington DC 20515

FLYTHE, SIMON SUTTON, banker; b. Jackson, N.C., Mar. 15, 1907; s. Jesse Thomas and Acree (Lassiter) F.; student Trinity Coll., Duke; m. Virginia White, Sept. 6, 1926; children—Walter W., Simon Sutton, Margaret F. (Mrs. Francis B. Teague, Jr.), James Thomas. Vice pres., cashier Bank of Fieldale, Va., 1928-47; exec. v.p. First Nat. Bank of Martinsville and Henry County, Martinsville, Va., 1947-54, pres., 1954—, also dir.; dir. Fieldale Ins. Agy., Inc., Bassett-Walker Knitting Co., Inc., Bassett, Va., Martinsville Novelty Corp., Martinsville Cablevision, Inc. Mem. State Hwy. Commn., 1954-65, sec., 1963-65; mem. nat. council Boy Scouts Am. Mem. Henry County Sch. Bd., 1953-54. Bd. dirs. Martinsville Med. Center, Va. Dept. Welfare and Instns., 1968-71; trustee Martinsville-Henry County Meml. Hosp., Va. Found. Ind. Colls.; mem. adv. bd. Patrick Henry Coll.; bd. visitors Med. Coll. Va., 1966-67. Mem. Am. (mem. exec. com. Va.), Va. (pres. 1965-66) bankers assns. Kiwanian. Club: Chatmoss Country. Home: 1101 Sam Lions Trail Martinsville VA 24112 Office: PO Box 4911 Martinsville VA 24112

FOARD, SUSAN LEE, editor; b. Asheville, N.C., Aug. 1, 1938; d. Carson Cowan and Anne (Brown) Foard; A.B., Salem Coll., 1960; M.A., William and Mary Coll., 1966. Asst. editor Inst. Early Am. Hist. and Culture, Williamsburg, Va., 1961-66, asso. editor, 1966; editor U. Press of Va., Charlottesville, 1966—. Active League of Women Voters. Office: Box 3608 University Station Charlottesville VA 22903

FODOR, GEORGE EMERIC, chemist; b. Mako, Hungary, Feb. 13, 1932; s. Imre and Ilona (Messinger) F.; came to U.S., 1956, naturalized, 1962; dipl. chemist, U. Scis., Szeged, Hungary, 1955; Ph.D. (fellow 1960-62, Robert A. Welch Found. fellow 1962-65), Rice U., 1965; m. Marjory Ann Byrne, Feb. 13, 1965; children—Cara Anne, John Emeric. With Hungarian Oil and Natural Gas Research Inst., Veszprem, Hungary, 1956, Pontiac Refining Corp., Corpus Christi, Tex., 1957-60; asst. Rice U., Houston, 1960-62; with photo products dept. E.I. duPont de Nemours & Co., Inc., Parlin, N.J., 1965-66; sr. research chemist Southwest Research Inst., San Antonio, 1966—. Mem. Am. Chem. Soc., Sci. Research Soc. Am., N.Y. Acad. Scis. Club: Canyon Creek Country (San Antonio). Home: 10323 Red

Quill Dr San Antonio TX 78213 Office: PO Drawer 28510 San Antonio TX 78284

FOELKER, HENRY EDWARD, elec. engr.; b. Rio Hondo, Tex., Apr. 1, 1927; s. Walter Edward and Rose Mary (Kindinger) F.; student St. Mary's U., 1948; B.S. in Elec. Engring., Tex. Arts & Industries, 1950; M.S., Tex. Agr. and Mech. Coll., 1951; m. Retta Belle Stanford, June 6, 1953; children—Lor, Jim, Gwen, John, Margie, Emily. With Central Power & Light Co., 1950—, engring. asst., San Benito, Tex., 1950-54, elec. engr., Corpus Christi, Tex., 1954-57, distbn. coordination engr., Corpus Christi, 1957—. Instr. U. Corpus Christi, 1961-63, Del Mar Tech. Inst., Corpus Christi, 1969-71. Served with USNR, 1945-46. Recipient Scholastic scholarship St. Mary's U., 1944-48. Registered profl. engr., Tex. Mem. I.E.E.E., Tex. Soc. Profl. Engrs., Serra International (pres. 1963). Home: 4005 Pope Dr Corpus Christi TX 78411 Office: PO Box 2121 Home Office Engring 120 N Chaparral St Corpus Christi TX 78401

FOERSTER, EDWARD LEROY, SR., chem. engr.; b. Chgo., Sept. 17, 1919; s. Arthur Henry and Lillian Henrietta (Behm) F.; B.S., U. Ill., 1941; Chem. E., U. Va., 1942; m. Lois Mason Claybrook, Dec. 30, 1948; children—Gerald Claybrook, Jean (Mrs. Frank W. Gearing, II), Edward LeRoy, Jr. Engr. Merck & Co., Inc., Elkton, Va., 1942-58; mgr., Danville, Pa., 1958-59; cons. engring. and chemistry, Harrisonburg, Va., 1960—. Registered profl. engr., Penn., Va. Mem. Am. Chem. Soc., Am. Inst. Chem. Engrs., Water Pollution Control Fedn., Am. Inst. Chemists, Nat. Soc. Profl. Engrs. Lutheran (treas. 1964-66). Elk, Lion. Patentee in field. Home: 1230 Moffett Terrace Harrisonburg VA 22801 Office: Box 779 Harrisonburg VA 22801

FOGARTIE, JAMES EUGENE, clergyman; b. Brookhaven, Miss., June 20, 1924; s. Arthur Finley and Eugenia Elizabeth (Vance) F.; B.A., U. Tex., 1945, M.A., 1948; B.D., Austin Presbyn. Theol. Sem., 1948; Th.M., Union Theol. Sem., 1954; D.D., Austin Coll., 1969; m. Ruth Ann Douglass, Aug. 30, 1946; children—Ann Douglass, Elizabeth Vance, Arthur Ford, James Eugene. Ordained to ministry Presbyn. Ch., 1948; minister First Presbyn. Ch., Marianna, Ark., 1948-52, Ft. Smith, Ark., 1952-55, Myers Park Presbyn. Ch., Charlotte, N.C., 1955—; supply minister St. Andrews Presbyn. Ch., Wembley, London, Eng., summer 1952. Vice pres. Mecklenburg County council Boy Scouts Am., Charlotte, N.C., 1971—. Recipient Silver Beaver award Boy Scouts Am., 1971. Sec. bd. trustees Queens Coll., Charlotte, N.C., 1958; trustee Stillman Coll., Tuscaloosa, Ala., 1956-59, Johnson C. Smith U., Charlotte, N.C., 1973—; bd. regents Barium Springs (N.C.) Home for Children, 1971. Rotarian (dir. 1973—). Club: Philosophers (Charlotte). Home: 2146 Roswell Av Charlotte NC 28207 Office: 2501 Oxford Place Charlotte NC 28207

FOGEL, BERNARD J., physician, univ. dean; b. N.Y.C., Nov. 30, 1936; s. Isadore and Shirley Edith (Golden) F.; student Emory U., 1954-56; M.D. (Nat. Allergy Found. fellow 1958-59), U. Miami, 1961; m. Judith Ann Abbott, June 8, 1958; children—Lori, Wendy Amy. Intern pediatrics Jackson Meml. Hosp., Miami, 1961-62, resident, 1962-63; chief resident pediatrics Sinai Hosp., Balt., 1963-64; fellow dept. pediatrics Johns Hopkins U. Sch. Medicine, Balt., 1964-66; researcher dept. serology div. communicable diseases and immunology Walter Reed Army Inst. Research, Washington, 1964-66; asst. chief dept. pediatrics Walter Reed Gen. Hosp., Washington, 1964-66; fellow Am. Cancer Soc., Miami, 1966-69; mem. faculty U. Miami Sch. Medicine, Miami, Fla., 1966—, asst. prof. pediatrics, 1966-69, co-dir. newborn nursery, 1966-72, dir. birth defects center, 1966—, asst. dean curriculum affairs, 1967-69, asso. dean med. edn., 1970—, asso. prof. pediatrics, 1970—, acting asso. dean for research adminstrn., 1971—; practice medicine specializing in pediatrics, Miami, 1966-73; mem. staffs Jackson Meml. Hosp., U. Miami Hosp. and Clinics. Cons. to various orgns., 1971—. Chmn. com. career motivation for black students Greater Miami Coalition, Inc., 1971-73. Bd. trustees Mus. Sci., Miami, 1962-73; med. dir. Nat. Found., 1967-73. Served with AUS, 1966. Decorated Army Commendation medal; recipient Outstanding Tchr. award U. Miami Sch. Medicine, 1968, Iron Arrow, 1972. Diplomate Nat. Bd. Med. Examiners, Fla. State Bds. Mem. So. Soc. Pediatric Research, Fla. Pediatric Soc. (program dir. 1969-72), Assn. Am. Med. Colls. (mem. com. 1972—), Phi Delta Epsilon. Editorial cons. Jour. Fla. Med. Assn., 1970-73. Home: 9240 SW 120th St Miami FL 33153 Office: PO Box 875 Biscanyne Anex Miami FL 33156

FOGELMAN, MORRIS JOSEPH, physician; b. Chgo., Feb. 27, 1923; s. Joseph and Tillie (Schwartz) F.; B.A., U. Ill., 1941, M.D., 1944, M.S., 1948; children—Evan, Joe, Margo. Intern Wayne County Gen. Hosp., Eloise, Mich., 1944-45; resident Parkland Hosp., Dallas, 1948-51; research fellow dept. clin. sci. U. Ill. Coll. Medicine, Chgo., 1947-48, asst. physiology, 1947-48; asst. in physiology and pharmacology Southwestern Med. Sch., Dallas, 1948-50, fellow in surgery, 1948-52, instr. surgery, 1952-53, asst. prof. surgery, asst. prof. surgery, 1952-53, asso. prof. surgery, 1953, prof. surgery, 1954-57, clin. prof. surgery, 1957—; practice medicine specializing in surgery, Dallas, 1952—; sr. attending surgeon Parkland Meml. Hosp., Dallas, 1953; cons. physician in surgery VA Hosp., Dallas, 1954; attending surgeon Baylor Hosp., 1957, Parkland Meml. Hosp., 1952, Presbyn. Hosp., Dallas; pres. med. staff Presbyn. Hosp., Dallas, 1973, Morris J. Fogelman, MD & Assos., Dallas, 1972—; dir. surgery Baylor Med. Center, 1972—. Served to capt. M.C., AUS, 1945-47. Diplomate Am. Bd. Surgery. Fellow Am. Assn. for Surgery of Trauma; mem. Am. Assn. for History of Medicine, A.C.S., A.A.A.S., A.M.A., Dallas County Med. Soc., Dallas Soc. Gen. Surgeons, Dallas So. Clin. Soc., N.Y. Acad. Sci., Tex. Med. Assn., Tex. Traumatic Surg. Soc., Sigma Xi. Contbr. articles to various publs. Home: 6921 Norway Pl Dallas TX 75231 Office: 8210 Walnut Hill Lane Suite 513 Dallas TX 75231

FOGLEMAN, JOHN ALBERT, justice Ark. Supreme Ct; b. Memphis, Nov. 5, 1911; s. John Franklin and Julia (McAdams) F.; student U. Ark., 1927-31; LL.B., U. Memphis (now Memphis State U.), 1934; m. Annis Adell Appleby, Oct. 24, 1933; children—John Albert. Annis Adell (Mrs. Henry M. Rector), Mary Barton (Mrs. Charles L. Williams, Jr.). Admitted to Ark. bar, 1934; dep. circuit ct. clk. Critenden County, 1933-34; pvt. practice law, 1934-44; partner Hale & Fogleman, West Memphis, Ark., 1944-66; dep. pros. atty., Crittenden County, 1946-57; asso. justice Ark. Supreme Ct., 1967—. Mem. State Bar Examiners, 1960-63; chmn. Ark. Jud. Commn., 1963-65; mem. Ark. Constl. Revision Study Com., 1967, Ark. Criminal Code Revision Com., 1972—. Active Ark. and Crittenden County Democratic central com. Served to 1st lt. AUS, 1944-45, Fellow Am. Coll. Trial Lawyers; mem. Ark. (past pres.), N.E. Ark. (past pres.), Crittenden County (past pres.) bar assns. Mason, Rotarian. Home: 67 Cherry St Marion AR 72364 Office: Justice Bldg State Capitol Grounds Little Rock AR 72201

FOLDEN, DEWEY BRAY, JR., educator; b. Charleston, W.Va., Dec. 2, 1923; s. Dewey Bray and Mabel Lenna (Vaughan) F.; B.S., Morris Harvey Coll., 1947, A.B., 1948; M.S., W.Va. U., 1949; postgrad. U. Md., 1956; m. Geneva Pearl Nicely, Sept. 14, 1949. Instr. biology Memphis State Coll., 1949-55, Dickinson Coll., 1955-57; asst. prof. biology Memphis State U., 1958-60, asso. prof., 1961—. Served with USNR, 1944-46. Recipient grants Am. Physiol. Soc., 1958, NIH, 1960. Mem. A.A.A.S., Tenn. Acad. Sci., Tenn. Edn. Assn., Sigma Xi, Chi Beta Phi. Methodist. Home: 2349 Culloden Cove Memphis TN 38138 Office: Dept Biology Memphis State U Memphis TN 38152

FOLEN, VINCENT J., physicist; b. Scranton, Pa., Jan. 17, 1924; s. Joseph William and Josephine (Maldonate) F.; B.A., LaSalle Coll., 1949; M.A., U. Pa., 1954; Ph.D., Am. U., 1972; m. Doris Ruth Braun, Feb. 14, 1954. Physicist, U.S. Naval Research Lab., Washington, 1954-59, head ferromagnetism sect., 1959—. Served with USAAF, 1943-46. Recipient award for outstanding performance U.S. Naval Research Lab., 1962; Research Publs. award U.S. Naval Research Lab., 1968, 70; Pure Sci. award Sci. Research Soc. Am., 1971. Fellow Am. Phys. Soc.; mem. Research Soc. Am., Philos. Soc. Washington, Alpha Epsilon. Contb. articles profl. jours. Co-founder magnetoelectric effect, 1961. Home: 203 Tecumseh Dr Washington DC 20021 Office: US Naval Research Lab Washington DC 20375

FOLEY, LESTER WILLIAM, lumber exec.; b. Mpls., Aug. 13, 1903; s. J. S. and Marie (Scanlon) F.; student Ga. Inst. Tech., 1920; A.B., U. Notre Dame, 1924; m. Edith Klug, Apr. 20, 1926; children—Jerry S. III, Patricia F. Stedeford. Pres. Foley Lumber Industries, Jacksonville, Fla., Beiswenger-Hoch & Assos. Mem. adv. bd. U. Notre Dame. Mem. Soc. Am. Mil. Engrs., Navy League U.S. (dir.), Friars. Roman Catholic. Clubs: Florida Yacht, Seminole, Deerwood, Ponce de Leon, Quarterback, Timuguana Country, Ponte Vedra, River. Home: 3626 Richmond St Jacksonville FL 32207 Office: Gulf Life Towers Jacksonville FL 32207

FOLEY, MARY ALICE DODD (MRS. LAWSON EDGAR FOLEY), piano tchr., civic worker; b. Roanoke, Va., Dec. 24, 1912; d. Cubert Bosworth and Fannie (Hale) Dodd; student St. Louis Inst. Music, 1932, 37, U. Va., 1939-53, Hollins Coll., 1953-55, U. Richmond, 1960-62, U. N.C., summers 1965-67; m. Lawson Edgar Foley, Apr. 12, 1933. Tchr. piano, 1933—. Mem. Roanoke (parliamentarian 1969-71), Va. (state parliamentarian 1969-71, 1st v.p., 1968-70, chmn. bd. certification 1971—) music tchrs. assns. Nat. Guild Piano Tchrs., Am. Piano Tchrs. Assn., Music Tchrs. Nat. Assn., Inc. (del. People-to-People travel program), Daus. of Confederacy (pres. 1966-68), Magna Charta Dames, Soc. Descendants Knights of Most Noble Order Garter, Nat., Va. (councilor 1971—) socs. daus. colonial wars, Huguenot Soc. Va. (rec. sec. 1971-73), Nat. Soc. Daus. Am. Colonists, Roanoke Hist. Soc., Colonial Dames XVII Century (chpt. pres. 1971-73, chmn. heraldry and coats of arms 1973-75), Blue Ridge Forum (v.p. 1961-62), D.A.R. (chpt. regent 1968-71, dir. Dist. VII Va. 1971—), Soc. Daus. Colonial Wars, Huguenot Soc. Va. (rec. sec. 1971-73, Councilor 1973-75), Wythe County, New River (charter mem. drama com.) hist. socs., Alpha Pi Mu (past pres.). Methodist. Home: 6630 Laban Rd Roanoke VA 24019

FOLGER, JOHN KENNETH, state ofcl.; b. Atlanta, Mar. 13, 1924; s. Dagnall Frank and Vivian (Rowland) F.; student W. Ga. Coll., Carrollton, 1940-42; A.B., Emory U., 1943; M.A., U. N.C., 1950, Ph.D., 1951; m. Marjorie Bullock, July 27, 1947; children—Karen, John Kenneth, Carol Anne; m. 2d, Mary J. Harrison, May 10, 1958; children—Susan, Dagnall, James. Chief tech. services Human Resources Research Inst., U.S. Air Force, Montgomery, Ala., 1951-53; research asso. So. Regional Edn. Bd., Atlanta, 1953-57, asso. dir., 1957-61; dean Grad. Sch., Fla. State U., Tallahassee, 1961-65, 67-68; dir. Tenn. Commn. Higher Edn., 1968—; dir. Commn. Human Resources, Nat. Acad. Scis., 1965-67. Mem. tech. adv. com. 1960 and 1970 Census. Served lt. (j.g.) USNR, 1944-46. Fellow Am. Sociol. Assn.; mem. Am. Statis. Assn., Population Assn. Am. Author: Education of the American Population, 1967; Human Resources and Higher Education, 1969. Home: 5437 Camelot Rd Brentwood TN 37027

FOLGER, LEE MERRITT, investment co. exec.; b. Washington, May 5, 1934; s. John Clifford and Mary Kathrine (Dulin) F.; A.B., Harvard, 1956; m. Nancy Sue McElroy, Feb. 11, 1961; children—Neil, Peter, Nicholas. With Folger Nolan Fleming Douglas, investments, Washington, 1959—, v.p. sales and sales mgmt., 1962—; pres. Cumberland Trust Co., Knoxville, Tenn., 1962—; v.p. Piedmont Mortgage Co., Washington, 1960—. Chmn. D.C. chpt. A.R.C., 1971—. Bd. govs. St. Albans Sch., Washington; trustee Corcoran Gallery of Art.; v.p. The Folger Fund, Washington, 1958—. Served to lt. (j.g.), USNR, 1956-58. Mem. Nat. Assn. Securities Dealers (dist. com. 1971—), The Downtown Assn. Clubs: The Book (N.Y.C.); Chevy Chase, Metropolitan (Washington). Home: 2918 33d Pl Washington DC 20008 Office: 725 15th St NW Washington DC 20005

FOLK, EARL DONALD, biostatician; b. Corpus Christi, Tex., Mar. 16, 1939; s. Joe Washington and Louise Helen (Bartos) F.; B.S., Okla. State Coll., 1961; M.S., Kan. State U., 1962, U. Wis., 1964; Ph.D., U. Okla., 1970; m. Patti Ann Hansen, Sept. 3, 1960 (dec. Aug. 1969); children—Ann Louise, Nancy Lynne. Research asst. dept. neurology U. Wis., Madison, 1962-66; chief biostatis. staff Civil Aeromed. Inst., FAA, Dept. Transp., Oklahoma City, 1968—. Tng. grantee NIH, 1966-67. Mem. A.A.A.S., Am. Statis. Assn., Biometric Soc., Statisticians in Okla. (sec. 1973—), Pi Mu Epsilon. Home: 2825 NW 117 Oklahoma City OK 73120 Office: PO Box 25082 Oklahoma City OK 73125

FOLK, EMERSON DEWEY, printing co. exec.; b. Dayton, O., Apr. 25, 1898; s. John Henry and Agnes Lillian (Witwer) F.; ed. pub. schs., Dayton, various higher instns.; m. Berdena Brown, June 19, 1943; 1 dau., Sharon Lynn. Pres., chmn. bd. dirs. Standard Bus. Forms, Inc., Gastonia, N.C., 1947-56, Nat. Bus. Forms, Inc., Greeneville, Tenn., 1959-72, Nat. Forms Co., Inc., Gastonia, 1968-72. Mem. Personnel Assn. Greeneville. Republican. Methodist. Rotarian. Home: Rural Route 4 Greeneville TN 37743 Office: PO Box 31 Greeneville TN 37743

FOLK, ROBERT LOUIS, educator; b. Cleve., Sept. 30, 1925; s. George Billmyer and Marjorie Marshall (Kinkead) F.; B.S., Pa. State Coll., 1946, M.S., 1950, Ph.D., 1952; m. Marjorie Thomas, Sept. 7, 1946; children—Robert T., Jennifer Louise, Charles Marshall. Research geologist Gulf Oil Co., Houston, 1951-52; mem. faculty U. Tex., Austin, 1952—, prof. geology, 1960—. Vis. tchr. Australian Nat. U., Canberra, 1965; vis. researcher Universita degli Studi, Milano, Italy, 1973. Fellow Geol. Soc. Am.; mem. Soc. Econ. Paleontologists and Mineralogists. Methodist. Club: Friends of the Microscope. Author: Petrology of Sedimentary Rocks, 1968. Contbr. articles to sci. publs. Home: 1107 Bluebonnet St Austin TX 78704

FOLSOM, JAMES CANNON, psychiatrist, govt. ofcl.; b. Sweetwater, Ala., Oct. 11, 1921; s. Douglas L. and Lillian McMillan (Hart) F.; student Livingston State Coll., 1939-41, U. Ariz., 1941, U. Ala., 1942, U. Ala. Med. Coll., 1942-44; M.D., Wash. U. Sch. Medicine, 1946; m. Ruth Becton, Aug. 1947 (div. 1950); m. 2d, Geneva Scheihing, Dec. 29, 1958; children—Ivy (Mrs. John E. Gary Simpson), Lisa Kay. Intern, Jefferson-Hillman Hosp., Birmingham, Ala., 1946-47; spl. course neurology and psychiatry U. Vienna, summer 1948; resident in psychiatry Timberlawn San., Dallas, 1950-52; resident physician, fellow Menninger Sch. Psychiatry VA Hosp., Topeka, 1952-53; psychiatrist Hill Crest San., Birmingham, 1949; staff psychiatrist Timberlawn San., Dallas, 1952; admission physician VA Hosp., Topeka, 1953-55, chief phys. medicine and rehab., 1955-60; clin. dir. Mental Health Inst., Mt. Pleasant, Ia., 1960-62; chief staff VA Hosp. Tuscaloosa, Ala., 1962-66, dir. hosp., 1966-71; dep. commr. hosps. Ala. Dept. Mental Health, 1971—; mem. faculty Menninger Sch. Psychiatry, 1953-60; asso. clin. prof. psychiatry Med. Coll. U. Ala., 1963—. Mem. Interagy. Bd. U.S. Civil Service Examiners N. Ala., 1966-71; mem. central bd. mgmt. Tuscaloosa County YMCA, 1966; mem. adv. com. Planning a Program for Overcoming Deprivation in Aesthetic Experiences, Tuscaloosa County, 1967; mem. steering com. Tuscaloosa County Comprehensive Community Mental Center, 1967; mem. Assn. Regional Planning Dirs. and Adminstrs. Ala. Regional Med. Program, 1968; mem. adv. bd. Tuscaloosa County Salvation Army, 1967; mem. Ala. Gov.'s Com. on Employment of Handicapped, 1967; mem. adv. bd. Ala. Jaycees Mental Health-Mental Retardation Com., 1967; chmn. Ala. State White House Conf. on Aging, 1971. Bd. dirs. Ala. Assn. for Mental Health, Tuscaloosa County Assn. for Mental Health, Boys' Club Tuscaloosa County, United Fund Tuscaloosa County; trustee The Menninger Found. Served to 1st lt. M.C., AUS, 1947-49. Recipient William C. Porter award in psychiatry Assn. Mil. Surgeons U.S., 1971. Fellow Am. Coll. Psychiatrists, Am. Psychiat. Assn. (1st editor Kan. Dist. br., Ala. Dist. br. Newsletter), Am. Geriatric Soc.; mem. A.M.A., Assn. Med. Supts. Mental Hosps. (pres. elect 1971, council), Ala. Acad. Neurology and Psychiatry (pres. 1968-69), Tuscaloosa County Med. Soc., Menninger Sch. Psychiatry Alumni Assn. (pres. 1958-59, editor Alumni Bull. 1954-57, mem. nat. alumni adv. com. 1969), Am. Hosp. Assn. (governing council psychiat. hosp. sect. 1969—, mem. spl. adv. panel assn. type I mental health instns. and services 1968-69), Tuscaloosa C. of C. (state-fed. hosps. action com. 1966). Kiwanian (pres. 1965). Editorial bd. Staff Mag. Contbr. articles to med. jours. Home: Bryce Hosp Tuscaloosa AL 35401

FOLWELL, WILLIAM HOPKINS, clergyman; b. Port Washington, N.Y., Oct. 26, 1924; s. Ralph Taylor and Sara Ewing (Hopkins) D.; B.C.E., Ga. Inst. Tech., 1947; B.D., Seabury-Western Theol. Sem., 1953, D.D., 1970; D.D., U. of South, 1970; m. Christine Elizabeth Cramp, Apr. 22, 1949; children—Ann (Mrs. David Stanford), Mark, Susan. Engr., Miami, Fla., 1947-49; ordained to ministry Episcopal Ch.; vicar St. Peter's Ch., Plant City, Fla., 1952-55; priest-in-charge St Luke's Ch., Mulberry, Fla., 1954-55; chaplain St. Martin's Sch., New Orleans, 1955-56; rector St. Gabriel's Ch., Titusville, Fla., 1956-59; rector All Saints Ch., Winter Park, Fla., 1959-70; bishop Central Fla., Winter Park, 1970—. Served with USNR, 1943-46. Home: 458 Virginia Dr Winter Park FL 32789 Office: Diocese Central Fla PO Box 790 Winter Park FL 32789

FONG, HENRY, govt. ofcl.; b. Widener, Ark., Oct. 4, 1935; s. Edward H. and Wong (Wong) F.; B.A., Hendrix Coll., 1958; M.B.A., U. Ark., 1959; postgrad. (Princeton fellow) Princeton U., 1971; m. E. Fay Elenberg, Dec. 21, 1962. With accountancy staff USAF, various locations, 1959—, systems accountant, Washington, 1965-68, Denver, 1968-72; chief accounting concepts and policy Hdqrs. USAF, Washington, 1972—. Dir., v.p. Dynahealth, Inc., Denver, 1972—. C.P.A., Ark. Mem. Am. Soc. Mil. Comptrollers, Am. Soc. C.P.A.'s. Home: 9428 Goshen Lane Burke VA 22015 Office: AF/ACFB Pentagon Washington DC 20330

FONG, PETER, physicist, educator; b. Tungshang, Chekiang, China, Sept. 3, 1924; s. Pin-Lan and Han-Yin (Mao) F.; B.S., U. Chekiang, 1945; M.S., U. Chgo., 1950, Ph.D., 1953; m. Teresa Wai, Jan. 17, 1959; children—Nora Lillian, Karen Elizabeth, William Peter. Came to U.S., 1947, naturalized, 1967. Physicist Inst. Nuclear Studies U. Chgo., 1954; mem. faculty Utica Coll. of Syracuse U., Utica, 1954-66, prof. physics, 1962-66; vis. prof. physics Cornell U., Ithaca, 1963-64, Lawrence Radiation Lab. U. Cal., Berkeley, 1965-66; prof. physics Emory U., Atlanta, 1966—. Fellow Am. Phys. Soc.; mem. Biophys. Soc., Sigma Xi, Sigma Pi Sigma. Author: Elementary Quantum Mechanics, 1962; Foundations of Thermodynamics, 1963; Statistical Theory of Nuclear Fission, 1969; Understanding China-Perspectives in Sinology, 1972. Contbr. articles to profl. jours. Office: Physics Dept Emory U Atlanta GA 30322

FONTAINE, ROBERT ELLERY, physician, USPHS officer; b. Boston, Feb. 8, 1947; s. Russell Edgar and Vera (Clifton) F.; B.S., U. Cal. at Davis, 1968, M.D., 1972. Intern USPHS, Balt., 1972-73; commd. USPHS, 1972, EIS officer, Atlanta, 1973—. Home: 707 N Parkwood Rd Decatur GA 30030 Office: Center for Disease Control USPHS 1600 Clifton Rd Atlanta GA 30333

FONTANA, MARIO HERBERT, mech. engr.; b. West Springfield, Mass., Mar. 30, 1933; s. Remo and Sabina (DeAngelis) F.; B.S., U. Mass., 1955; M.S., Mass. Inst. Tech., 1957; postgrad. Oak Ridge Sch. Reactor, 1958; Ph.D., Purdue U., 1968; m. Sue Janeway, Apr. 12, 1958; children—Richard, Edward. Tech. staff Oak Ridge (Tenn.) Nat. Lab., 1957-61, 1962-63, 1965-68, asst. dir. nuclear safety program, 1968-73, mgr. fast breeder reactor safety and core systems programs, 1973—; sr. scientist High Temp. Materials, Inc., Boston, 1961; Avco Research and Advanced Devel., Inc., Wilmington, Mass., 1963-64; instr. Purdue U., Lafayette, Ind., 1964-65. Cons. in reactor safety Atomic Energy Commn., Washington, 1973—. Registered profl. engr., Tenn. Committeeman Boy Scouts Am., Oak Ridge, 1971—. Mem. Am. Nuclear Soc. (mem. exec. com. 1971—; vice chmn. tech. group 1971-73), Am. Soc. Mech. Engrs. (sect. chmn. 1971-72), A.A.A.S., Nat., Tenn. socs. profl. engrs., Scientists and Engrs. for Appalachia. Club: Country (Oak Ridge, Tenn.). Contbr. articles to various publs. Patentee in field. Home: 106 Caldwell St Oak Ridge TN 37830 Office: Oak Ridge Nat Lab PO Box Y Oak Ridge TN 37830

FOOKS, JACK HERBERT, san. engr.; b. Wilmington, Del., Sept. 11, 1917; s. Reginald Herbert and Lolita (Walker) F.; B.C.E., U. Del., 1941; M.S. in San. Engring., U. N.C., 1948; M.P.H., Johns Hopkins, 1960; m. Lucille Grace Palese, Nov. 29, 1941; children—Jack Herbert, Andrew David. Civil engr. Wilmington Water Dept., 1941, Inst. Inter-Am. Affairs, Victoria, Brazil, 1946-47, USPHS, Chgo., 1949-54, Denver, 1955-59, Washington, 1960-68; internat. san. engring. cons., 1968—. Cons. sterility control Spacecraft NASA; cons. on water supplies to mcpl. govts.; cons. radiol. and nuclear control problems to state govts. served with AUS, 1940-45. Decorated Purple Heart with cluster. Recipient Apollo Achievement award NASA, 1969, USPHS Commendation medal with cluster. Diplomate Am. Acad. San Engrs. Fellow Am. Soc. C.E. Baptist (trustee). Clubs: Punta Gorda Isles Yacht and Racquet, Councilors Point Sail. Research on water supply systems, petroleum refinery waste treatment, amebiasis, fluoridation, radiol. health, iodine in child thyroid, fission prodn. in milk. Address: 2550 NE 8th Av Pompano Beach FL 33064

FOOTE, GUY MYRPH, mfg. co. exec.; b. Nacogdoches, Tex., Jan. 31, 1922; s. James Burton and Clyde (Locke) F.; B.S., Stephen F. Austin State U., 1942; postgrad. So. Meth. U., 1947-49; m. Mary Nell Taylor, Feb. 3, 1946; children—Guy Myrph, Jr., Kenneth Taylor. C.P.A. Dranquet, Foote & Co., Dallas, 1947-60, Haskins & Sells, Dallas, 1960-72; pres., dir. Weil-McLain Co., Inc., Dallas, 1972—. Bd. dirs. Goodwill Industries, Dallas, 1970-73; active United Fund, Dallas, 1960-73; vice chmn. Dallas chpt. Cancer Soc. 1968. Served with USAAF, 1942-46. C.P.A., Tex., Okla., N.M. Mem. Am. Inst. C.P.A.'s. Democrat. Methodist. Clubs: Northwood, Petroleum, Preston Trail Golf (all Dallas); University (Washington). Home:

11586 Ricks Circle Dallas TX 75230 Office: PO Box 31349 Dallas TX 75231

FOOTE, WILLIAM ENGENE, JR., banker; b. Hamburg, Ark., Nov. 16, 1912; s. William Eugene and Lydia W. (Stock) F.; student U. Ark., 1930-31, Taylor Comml. Coll., 1932; m. Mildred D. Sawyer, July 3, 1935; children—Bill, Jeff, Joe. Pres. Footes Grocery, Inc., Hamburg, Ark., 1935-73; with Farmers Bank, Hamburg, Ark., 1953—, pres., 1970—. Mem. Ark. Bankers Assn. (mem. governing bd. 1973-74). Home: 424 S Cherry St Hamburg AR 71646 Office: 111 N Mulberry St Hamburg AR 71646

FORBES, HENRY WILLIAM, govt. ofcl.; b. Vienna, Austria, Nov. 9, 1918; s. Isidor and Ida (Loewy) F.; came to U.S., 1941, naturalized, 1942; A.A., U. Cal. at Los Angeles, 1948, B.A., 1949; Ph.D. in Internat. Relations, Georgetown U., 1959; grad. Army War Coll., 1970; m. Alice Berger, Oct. 23, 1959; children—Evelyn, Monica, Jessica. Chief logistics div. Ordnance Tech. Intelligence Agy., Dept. Army, Washington, 1951-63, chief econ. br. Def. Intelligence Agy., 1963—. Lectr. George Washington U., 1959-66, U. Va., Richmond extension, 1967—. Served to capt. arty., AUS, 1942-45. Mem. Am. Econ. Assn., Am. Def. Preparedness Assn., Am. Goethe Soc. Lutheran. Author: The Strategy of Disarmament, 1962. Home: 3208 Annandale Rd Falls Church VA 22042 Office: Def Intelligence Agy Washington DC 20301

FORBES, SARAH ELIZABETH, physician; b. Currituck, N.C.; d. Dexter Thomas and Mary (Brock) Forbes; B.A. U. Rochester, 1949; M.D., Med. Coll. Va., 1954. Intern, Norfolk (Va.) Gen. Hosp, 1954-55, resident, 1956-58; resident Johnston-Willis Hosp., Richmond, Va., 1955-56; practice medicine specializing in obstetrics and gynecology, Newport News, Va., 1958—; mem. staff, teaching staff Riverside Hosp. Pres., Soc. for Prevention Cruelty to Animals, 1967—; pres. Cancer Soc., 1960-69; chmn. Research for Cancer Soc., 1961-69, now pres. mem. bd. Family Planning Council, 1969—. Fellow Am. Coll. Obstetrics and Gynecology; mem. Tidewater Obstet. and Gynecol. Soc., Va. Peninsula Acad. Medicine (pres.), Newport News Med. Soc., Va. Med. Soc., A.M.A. Home: 5 Merry Point Terrace Newport News VA 23606 Office: 12420 Warwick Blvd Newport News VA 23606

FORBIS, JAMES EDWIN, lawyer; b. Ft. Worth, Dec. 4, 1931; s. Tommy Tillman and Sarah Jane (McKinnis) F.; student Arlington State Coll., 1950-51; B.B.A., U. Tex., 1953, J.D., 1955; m. Althea Clara Nielsen, Jan. 20, 1962; children—Christopher, Nancy; stepchildren—Thomas Nielsen Long, Jana (Mrs. Martin Bennett Woodruff). Admitted to Tex. bar, 1955; mem. firm Sewell & Forbis, Decatur, 1957—. Trustee Decatur Ind. Sch. Dist., 1966—, pres., 1971—; bd. dirs., sec. Decatur Hosp. Authority, 1967—. Served with USAF, 1955-57. Mem. Am., Tex. trial lawyers assns., Wise County Bar Assn., State Bar Tex., Tex. Criminal Def. Lawyers Assn., Decatur C. of C. (pres. 1966-67), Phi Alpha Delta. Episcopalian. Lion. Address: Box 534 102 W Walnut St Decatur TX 76234

FORCE, CARLTON GREGORY, chemist; b. Gouverneur, N.Y., Aug. 5, 1926; s. Leon Henry and Christina (Hampton) F.; B.S. with honors, Clarkson Coll. Tech., 1952, Ph.D., 1965; M.S., U. Ill., 1957; m. Rosalie Marie Gotham, June 20, 1953; children—Gregory, Jeffrey, Stuart, Ralph. Research chemist Merck & Co., Rahway, N.J., 1952-56, Esso Research and Engring. Co., Linden, N.J., 1957-59; research chemist Latex Fiber Industries, Inc., Beaver Falls, N.Y., 1959-61, sr. research chemist, 1963-67; with Westvaco Corp., Charleston, S.C., 1967—, sr. research chemist, 1969—. Asst. scoutmaster Boy Scouts Am., 1960-61, 67—, scoutmaster, 1964-67; Webelos leader Cub Scouts Am., 1965-66, 69-71. Served with AUS, 1945-47. Mem. Am. Chem. Soc., Am. Inst. Chemists. Presbyn. (deacon 1968-71). Club: Hobcaw Yacht (exec. bd. 1972—) (Mt. Pleasant, S.C.). Patentee in field. Home: 239 Hobcaw Dr Mt Pleasant SC 29464 Office: Westvaco Corp PO Box 5207 N Charleston SC 29406

FORD, BENNIE RUFUS, parasitologist; b. Wichita Falls, Tex., May 8, 1936; s. Printess F. and Maggie E. (Harris) F.; B.S. in Biology, William Carey Coll., 1962; M.S., U. Okla., 1964, Ph.D. in Zoology, 1967; m. Jeanette Stewart, May 29, 1960; children—Alan, Lynn. Research asst. U. Okla., Norman, 1962-65; asst. prof. biology Samford U., Birmingham, Ala., 1966-70; asst. prof. zoology U. No. Colo., Greeley, 1969; with T.A. Lawson State Jr. Coll., Birmingham, Ala., 1971—, chmn. div. scis. and math., 1972—. Served with U.S. Corps Engrs., 1955-58. Recipient Research Fund grant Samford U., 1969-70; Biol. Sta. Summer Grant, U. Okla., 1962. Mem. Am. Soc. Parasitologists, Helminthological Soc. Washington, Am. Inst. Biol. Scis., Sigma Xi. Home: Route 1 Chelsea AL 35043 Office: TA Lawson State Jr Coll Birmingham AL 35221

FORD, BLANCHARD FRED, JR., physician; b. Florence, S.C., Sept. 19, 1913; s. Blanchard Fred and Vera (Ratcliffe) F.; B.S., U. S.C., 1933; M.D., Med. Coll. S.C., 1938; m. Marjorie Nell Wells, July 6, 1940; children—Diane, Blanchard Fred III. Intern Roper Hosp., Charleston, S.C., 1940-41; resident McLeod Infirmary, Florence, S.C., 1941-42; practice medicine, Maxton, N.C., 1946-68, Shallotte, N.C., 1968—; chief staff Scotland County Meml. Hosp., 1955-56; health dir. Horry and Georgetown counties, S.C., 1957-64. Served to lt. comdr. M.C., USNR, World War II. Mem. Am., So. med. assns., New Hanover, Scotland County (pres. 1956-57) med. socs., Am. Legion. Mason, Lion. Home: Copa Shores Shallotte NC 28459 Office: N Main St Shallotte NC 28459

FORD, CHARLES EDWARD, banker; b. Batesville, Ark., Jan. 5, 1944; s. Walter Alvin and Christine Clyde (Hess) F.; B.A. in Bus. and Econs., Ark. Coll., Batesville, 1969; postgrad. Sch. Banking of South, La. State U.; m. Martha Jewell Vinson, Aug. 26, 1967; children—Christopher Kyle, James Brent. With Worthen Bank & Trust Co., Little Rock, 1967-70, Bank Dept. State of Ark., Little Rock, 1970-71; exec. v.p. 1st State Bank, Lonoke, Ark., 1971—. So. Regional Edn. Bd. grantee, 1969. Mem. Bank Adminstrn. Inst., Bank Marketing Assn., Lonoke C. of C. (dir.), Tau Kappa Epsilon. Methodist. Mason. Home: 320 College St Lonoke AR 72086 Office: 101 E Front St Lonoke AR 72086

FORD, D. WAYNE, tax adminstr.; b. Lipan, Tex., June 22, 1933; s. Ira Buck and Betty (Lewis) F.; B.A., Howard Payne Coll., 1960, M.Ed., 1964; student Tex. Christian U., 1965, Hardin-Simmons U., 1963-64, Abilene Christian Coll., 1967-72, Tex. A. and M. U., 1969; m. Melda Joyce Allen, Mar. 22, 1952; children—Donna Kay, Kelly Dianne, Russell Wayne. Tchr. Cross Plains (Tex.) Ind. Sch. Dist., 1960-63, prin. secondary sch., 1963-66, supt., 1966-74; tax adminstr. Stephenville (Tex.) Ind. Sch. Dist., 1974—. Instr. English Howard Payne Coll., Brownwood, summers 1962, 63, Cisco Jr. Coll., summers, 1965—. Ordained to ministry So. Bapt. Ch., 1958; minister, Shiloh, Tex., 1958, Patillo, Tex., 1959-60, Cross Cut, Tex., 1960-63. Served with AUS, 1954-56. Mem. Tex. Tchrs. Assn. (pres. Callahan County unit 1967-68), N.E.A., Tex. Assn. Sch. Adminstrs., Tex. Assn. Sch. Bds., Cross Plains C. of C. (pres. 1968-69), Phi Delta Kappa, Kappa Delta Pi. Home: 1350 N Charlotte St Stephenville TX 76461 Office: Box 62 Stephenville TX 76401

FORD, EDSEL WILLIAM, psychiat. social worker; b. Muskogee, Okla., Nov. 4, 1930; s. Robert Lee and Florence (Detherage) F.; B.S. in Edn., Northeastern State Coll., 1955; M.S.W., U. Okla., 1961; m. Ruth Stark, Dec. 17, 1953; children—Edsel William, Kelly Carl. With Okla. Dept. Pub. Welfare, 1955-62, field rep., 1960-62; with Family Service Center, Oklahoma City, 1962-64; with Okla. Dept. Mental Health, Oklahoma City, 1964—, regional supr. of after care, 1966—. Mem. profl. adv. bd. Okla. State Council on Crime and Delinquency, 1966-70. Bd. dirs., past pres. Okla. Health and Welfare. Served with USN, 1948-52; capt. Civil Air Patrol, USAF Aux., 1970—. Mem. Nat. Assn. Social Workers (chpt. chmn. 1965-67, mem. exec. bd. 1967—), Okla. Health and Welfare Assn. (bd. mem., pres. 1970-71). Baptist (dept. supt. 1964-68). Mason. Home: 11221 Jeffords St Nicoma Park OK 73066 Office: 1615 N Lincoln Blvd Oklahoma City OK 73104

FORD, ELIZABETH BLOOMER (MRS. GERALD R. FORD), wife of Pres. of U.S.; b. Chgo., Apr. 8, 1918; d. William Stephenson and Hortence (Neahr) Bloomer; student Bennington Sch. Dance, 1936-38; m. William Warren, 1942 (div. 1947); m. 2d, Gerald R. Ford (38th Pres. U.S.), Oct. 15, 1948; children—Michael Gerald, John Gardner, Steven Meigs, Susan Elizabeth. Dancer, Martha Graham Concert Group, N.Y.C., 1939-41; model John Powers Agy., N.Y.C., 1939-41; fashion dir. Herpolsheimer's Dept. Store, Grand Rapids, Mich., 1943-48; dance instr., Grand Rapids, 1932-48. Formerly active Cub Scouts Am.; formerly program chmn. Alexandria (Va.) Cancer Fund Drive; chmn. Heart Sunday, Washington Heart Assn., 1974; pres. Red Cross Senate Wives Club; patron Salvation Army Aux. Ann. Fashion Show Luncheon; active benefits Hosp. for Sick Children, Washington. Dir. League Republican Women, D.C. Episcopalian (Sunday sch. tchr. 1961-64). Home: White House 1600 Pennsylvania Av Washington DC 20500

FORD, ERNEST LESLIE, clergyman; b. Trimble, Ky., Apr. 7, 1894; s. John Chesney and Sarah Frances (McBeath) F.; A.B., Transylvania U., 1922; B.D., Coll. Bible, 1922; m. Mary Oneita Shewmaker, Aug. 16, 1917; children—Leslie Porter, Kenneth Chesney. Ordained to ministry. Christian Ch.; pastor Parkland Christian Ch., 1922-29, Central Christian Ch., Dayton, O., 1929-37, First Christian Ch., Shelbyville, Ind., 1937-53, First Christian Ch., Portsmouth, O., 1953-62. Pres., United Way, 1960, chmn. commn. on edn., 1955-60. Mem. Nat. Hist. Soc. Kiwanian. Address: 241 Delmar Av Lexington KY 40508

FORD, GERALD R., JR., pres. U.S.; b. Omaha, July 14, 1913; s. Gerald R. and Dorothy (Gardner) F.; A.B., U. Mich., 1935; LL.B., Yale, 1941; LL.D., Mich. State U., Aquinas Coll., Spring Arbor Coll., Albion Coll., Grand Valley State Coll., Belmont Abby Coll., Western Mich. U.; m. Elizabeth Bloomer, Oct. 15, 1948; children—Michael Gerald, John G., Steven M., Susan Elizabeth. Admitted to Mich. bar, 1941, practiced in Grand Rapids, 1941-49; asso. firm Butterfield, Amberg, Law & Buchen, Grand Rapids, 1946-51; mem. firm Amberg, Law, Buchen & Fallon, 1951-59; former mem. firm Buchen & Ford; mem. 81st to 93d Congresses, 5th Mich. Dist., mem. appropriations com., minority leader, 1965-73; vice pres. U.S., 1973-74; pres. U.S., 1974—. Served to lt. comdr. USN, 1942-46. Recipient 1948 Grand Rapids Jr. C. of C. Distinguished Service award; Distinguished Service award as one of ten outstanding young men in U.S., U.S. Jr. C. of C., 1950, Sports Illustrated Silver Anniversary All-Am. award, 1959, Congl. Distinguished Service award Am. Polit. Sci. Assn., 1961; George Washington award, Am. Good Govt. Soc., 1966; Gold Medal award Nat. Football Found., 1972. Mem. Am., Mich., Grand Rapids bar assns., Delta Kappa Epsilon, Phi Delta Phi. Republican. Episcopalian. Mason. Clubs: University, Peninsular (Kent County). Co-author: Portrait of the Assassin. Home: White House 1600 Pennsylvania Av NW Washington DC 20500 also 1624 Sherman St SE Grand Rapids MI 49506 also 425 Cherry St SE Grand Rapids MI 49502

FORD, GORDON BUELL, accountant; b. Greenville, Ky., Sept. 27, 1913; s. Otha and Mattye (Newman) F.; B.S., Western Ky. U., 1934; m. Rubye Ann Allen, Sept. 1, 1935; children—Gordon, Gayle (Mrs. Robert W. Greene, III). Partner Coopers & Lybrand, C.P.A.'s, Louisville, 1934—. Dir. Louisville Central Area, Inc., 1973—. Bd. trustees City Mockingbird, Valley, Ky., 1950—, Gorjim Found., Louisville, 1960—. C.P.A., Ky., Tenn., N.D. Mem. Am. Inst. C.P.A. (mem. council 1965-71; v.p. 1972-73), Ky. Soc. C.P.A.'s (pres. 1949-50). Rotarian. Clubs: Country (Louisville); Pendennis (Louisville); Delray Dunes Country (Delray Beach, Fla.). Author: (with L.C.J. Yeager) History of the Professional Practice of Accounting in Kentucky 1875-1965, 1967. Home: 315 Venetian Dr Delray Beach FL 34444 Office: 3500 First Nat Tower Louisville KY 40202

FORD, HARRY W., educator; b. Maumee, O., June 21, 1922; s. Wilbur H. and Josephine (Wogaman) F.; B.S., Ohio State U., 1946, M.S., 1947, Ph.D., 1950; m. Margaret Gladys Zimola, Sept. 4, 1948; children—William Harry, Donald Wilbur. Mem. faculty U. Fla., Lake Alfred, 1950—, asst. prof., 1950-56, asso. prof., 1957-62, prof. horticulture, 1963—. Cons. Hancor, Findlay, O., 1973—. Served with AUS, 1943-46; ETO. Recipient Annual Research award Fla. Fruit and Vegetable Assn., 1965; Faculty Devel. award U. Fla., 1969, 73. Mem. Am. Soc. Hort. Sci., Fla. State Hort. Soc., Soil and Crop Sci. Soc. Fla., Sigma Xi, Gamma Sigma Delta. Contbr. articles to sci. jours. Home: 160 S Seminole St Lake Alfred FL 33850

FORD, HOMOR TAYLOR, JR., govt. ofcl.; b. Springfield, Mo., Nov. 6, 1911; s. Homor Taylor and Eugenia (Morice) F.; student S.W. Mo. State Coll., 1929-30; B.S. in E.E., Mo. Sch. Mines, 1934; m. Rosemary McKenna, Nov. 21, 1935; children—Judith Anne (Mrs. Ronald J. Groeger), Homor Taylor III, Rosemary Vicki (Mrs. Gary A. Arndt). Vice pres. Ford Electric Co., Springfield, 1934-38; engr., contractor Springfield, 1938-40; with VA Hosps., 1946—, engr. officer, Springfield, 1946-51, asst. mgr. trainee, Hines, Ill., 1951-52, asst. dir., 1962-63, asst. mgr., Memphis, 1952-55, asst. dir., St. Louis, 1955-62, dir. engring. service VA Dept. Medicine and Surgery, Washington, 1964-71, dir. VA Hosp., Fayetteville, N.C., 1971-73; dir. VA Hosps., Little Rock, Ark., 1973—. Served with AUS, 1941-46. Registered profl. engr., Mo. Fellow Am. Coll. Hosp. Adminstrs.; mem. Mo., Nat. socs. profl. engrs., Soc. Am. Mil. Engrs., Am. Legion, Lambda Chi Alpha. Roman Catholic. Rotarian. Home: Quarters 40 VA Hosp North Little Rock AR 72114 Office: 300 E Roosevelt Rd Little Rock AR 72206

FORD, J. CLARK, physician; b. Ruston, La., Oct. 29, 1930; s. Amos W. and Elizabeth (Clark) F.; B.S. magna cum laude, La. Poly. Inst., 1953; M.D., La. State U., 1955; m. Mildred Mae Weatherly, Dec. 19, 1956; m. Elizabeth Ann, Richard Clark, Joe Edward. Intern Charity Hosp., New Orleans, 1955-56, resident, 1956-59; practice medicine, specializing in internal medicine, Davidson's Clinic, Lake Worth, Fla., 1961—; chief medicine John F. Kennedy Hosp., Atlantis, Fla., 1968-70; mem. staff John F. Kennedy Hosp., Bethesda Meml. Hosp., Boynton Beach, Fla. Served with USNR, 1959-61. Diplomate Am. Bd. Internal Medicine. Fellow Am. Coll. Cardiology; mem. Fla. Heart Assn., Am. Soc. Internal Medicine, A.C.P., Fla., Palm Beach County med. assns., A.M.A. Baptist. Home: 457 N Country Dr Atlantis FL 33460 Office: 601 S Fed Hwy Lake Worth FL 33460

FORD, JON CHARLES, journalist; b. Cushing, Tex., Nov. 27, 1920; s. John Charles and Monterie (Swearingen) F.; B.J., U. Tex., 1942; m. Marian Benson Colley, June 17, 1942; children—Jon Michael, Mary Jane, Charles Colley, Ann Shelley. Reporter Honolulu Advertiser, Hawaii, 1945; mng. editor Odessa Am., Tex., 1946-48; reporter San Antonio Express and News, 1948-49, successively mng. editor, 1949-51, asso. editor, 1952-54, state capital bur. chief, 1955-60, 63-73; chief state capital bur. Harte-Hanks Newspapers, 1970-73; polit. editor Newspapers Inc., 1974—. Adminstrv. asst. Gov. Price Daniel of Tex., 1960-62. Tex. writer C.S. Monitor; Tex. delegation reporter Republican and Democratic nat. convs. NBC News, 1968. Bd. dirs. Gonzales (Tex.) Warm Springs Found. Served with AUS, 1942-45; PTO. Recipient citation for distinguished writing Headliners Club, Austin, Tex., 1957. Mem. Sigma Delta Chi. Home: 13 Peak Rd Austin TX 78746

FORD, LESLIE ALMERON, milling co. exec.; b. Shawnee, Okla., Feb. 22, 1914; s. John Lloyd and Frances (Sims) F.; student Okla. Bapt. U., 1934-35; B.S. in Bus. Adminstrn., U. Okla., 1937; m. Margaret Anne Long, May 28, 1938; children—Edith Anne (Mrs. William C. McCurdy, III), William L., Robert L., Margaret Frances (Mrs. James Elder). With Shawnee Milling Co., 1937—, v.p., 1939-46, pres., 1946—. Dir. Am. Corn Millers Fedn., Washington, Millers Nat. Fedn., Chgo., First Fed. Savs. & Loan, Shawnee, Okla. Natural Gas Co., Tulsa. Bd. trustees Okla. Pub. Expenditures Council, 1965—, mem. exec. com., 1972—; mem. exec. com. Okla. Health Scis., Oklahoma City, 1969—. Mem. Okla. U. Alumni Assn. (life), Okla. U. Dad's Assn., Okla. Zool. Soc., Assn. Industries Okla., Game Conservation Internat., Sigma Alpha Epsilon. Democrat. Baptist. Mason (32 deg., Shriner). Club: Nat. Quail (Enid, Okla.). Home: 2205 N Broadway Shawnee OK 74801 Office: 401 S Broadway Shawnee OK 74801

FORD, L(ESTER) HARLAN, ednl. adminstr.; b. Troy, Tex., Mar. 27, 1929; s. Ben F. and Pearl A. (Dockray) F.; B.S., S.W. Tex. State Coll., 1950, M.Ed., 1955; Ed.D., Colo. State Coll., 1960; m. Jo Ann Cravens, Dec. 26, 1950; children—Robert Harlan, William Harlan. Tchr., Junction (Tex.) Pub. Schs, 1947-50; dean San Marcos (Tex.) Mil. Acad., 1951-59; ednl. cons., Greeley, Colo., 1959-60; prof. secondary edn. Howard Payne Coll., Brownwood, Tex., 1960-61; dir. tchr. edn. Sul Ross State Coll., Alpine, Tex., 1961-63, dean of coll., 1963-67, interim pres., 1964-65; exec. dir. region XIX Edn. Service Center, El Paso, Tex., 1967-68; asst. commr. tchr. edn. and instrn. Tex. Edn. Agy., Austin, 1968—. Dir. W. Tex. Innovative Edn. Center, 1965-66; vis. prof. U. Alta., Edmonton, Can., 1964. Chmn., Big Bend Community Action Com., 1965—, Boy Scouts Am., 1965—, Salvation Army, 1964— (all Alpine); mem. City Planning Com., Alpine, 1965—, State Planning Council for Tex. Ednl. Devel., 1967—. Trustee, Mary Hardin Baylor Coll., Belton, Tex., 1972—. Served with AUS, 1951-53. Recipient Distinguished Service award Alpine Jr. C. of C., 1966; Educator of Month award Tex. Sch. Bus. Pubis., 1971; Meritorious award Tex. Indsl. Arts Assn., 1972; Meritorious award Tex. Assn. Health, Phys. Edn. and Recreation, 1970. Mem. Tex. State Tchrs. Assn. (dist. pres. 1966—), Nat. Assn. Drs. U.S., N.E.A., Phi Delta Kappa, Kappa Delta Pi, Phi Alpha Theta. Democrat. Baptist. Lion (dir.). Author: History of San Marcos Academy, 1960; Guide for Administrative Interns, 1964: Ideas. Resources. Results, 1965. Home: 801 Country Club Rd Georgetown TX 78626 Office: Tex Edn Agy 11th and Brazos Austin TX 78711

FORD, RUTLEDGE FREDERICK, agronomist; b. Crossett, Ark., Nov. 17, 1926; s. Frederick Rice and Pauline Ester (Dunn) F.; student Ark. A. and M. Coll., 1949-50; B.S., U. Ark., 1953, M.S., 1961; m. Alma Lucille Orr, Sept. 1, 1957; children—Rebecca Suzanne, Jonathan Jeffrey. Asst., asso. county agrl. agt. Ark. Agrl. Extension Service, Pine Bluff, 1958-64, county agrl. agt., DeWitt, 1964-66, area agonomist for cotton, Jonesboro, 1966-68; area agronomist cotton and cotton agronomist, agronomy dept. U. Ark., Jonesboro, 1968—. Cons. Wheeler Crop Conditioning, Inc., Leachville, Ark., Brycot Seed Co., Jonesboro. Served with AUS, 1945-46. Recipient research grant Nationwide Chem. Co., 1969. Mem. County Agrl. Agts. Assn. (retirement ins. chmn. 1963-66), Ark. Pesticide Assn., Farm Bur. (dri.-at-large 1964-66), Epsilon Sigma Phi. Methodist (adminstrv. bd. 1965-71). Mason (Shriner), Rotarian (chmn. interact com. 1968-69, chmn. classification com. 1973—); mem. Order Eastern Star. Home: PO Box 1405 1832 Rosemond St Jonesboro AR 72401 Office: PO Box 1405 Federal Bldg Jonesboro AR 72401

FORD, THOMAS JEFFERS, indsl. developer; b. Charleston, S.C., Sept. 9, 1930; s. Rufus and Mildred (Jeffers) F.; A.B., Wofford Coll., 1952; postgrad. U. N.C., 1956-58, 59-61, U. Okla., 1965-67; m. Barbara Jean Jackson, Dec. 28, 1954; children—Thomas Jeffers, Edward Rufus. Asst. mgr. Albany (Ga.) C. of C., 1956; mgr. Rock Hill (S.C.) C. of C., 1957-58; dir. trade devel. Greenville (S.C.) C. of C., 1959-60, dir. bus. and indsl. relations, 1961; exec. dir. Marlboro County Devel. Bd., Bennettsville, S.C., 1962-65, Lakeland (Fla.) Indsl. Bd., 1966-67; dir. Chesterfield-Marlboro Tech. Edn. Center, Cheraw, S.C., 1968-72; dir. area devel. dept. 6th Congl. Dist. S.C., Florence, 1973—. Served with USN, 1952-53. Fellow Am. Indsl. Devel. Council (past mem. internat. certified indsl. devel. bd.); mem. S.C. Indsl. Developers Assn. (founder, dir., 1st pres. 1965), So. Indsl. Devel. Council (past dir.), S.C. Assn. C. of C. Execs. (past officer, dir.), Blue Key, Sigma Alpha Epsilon. Methodist. Rotarian (past pres. Cheraw club). Club: Cheraw Country. Home: 15 Hamden Circle Cheraw SC 29520 Office: PO Box 1660 Florence SC 29501

FORD, WENDELL HAMPTON, gov. Ky.; b. Owensboro, Ky., Sept. 8, 1924; s. Ernest M. and Irene (Schenk) F.; student U. Ky., 1942-43; grad. Md. Sch. Ins., 1947; m. Jean Neel, Sept. 18, 1943; children—Shirley Jean (Mrs. Shirley Ford Dexter), Steven. Partner Gen. Ins. Agy., Owensboro, 1959-67; chief asst. to gov. (Ky.), 1959-61; mem. Ky. Senate, 1965-67; lt. gov. Ky., 1967-71, gov., 1971—. Chmn. Legislative Research Commn., Ky., mem. Ky. Property and Bldgs. Commn., Ky. Turnpike Authority; chmn. Nat. Democratic Gov.'s Caucas; chmn. com. on law enforcement, justice and pub. safety So. Gov.'s Conf.; vice chmn. natural resources and environmental com. Nat. Gov.'s Conf. Mem. adv. council Nat. Dem. Com. Served with AUS, 1944-46; Ky. Nat. Guard, 1949-62. Mem. U.S., Ky. (pres. 1954-55) jr. chambers commerce (nat. pres. commerce (pres. 1956-57), Jr. C. of C. Internat. (v.p. N.Am. 1958-59), U.S. C. of C. (bd. dirs.). Democrat. Baptist. Elk. Home: 2017 Fieldrest Dr Owensboro KY 42301 Office: Executive Mansion Frankfort KY 40601

FORD, WILLIAM LAMONTE, dentist; b. Ardmore, Okla., Feb. 4, 1941; s. Lester Bill and Peggy Mary (Ford) F.; B.S., Baylor U., 1963, D.D.S., 1967; m. Jaqueline Ann Jordan, June 6, 1964; 1 dau., Kerri Elaine. Practice dentistry, Hamilton, Tex., 1967—; dir. 1st Nat. Bank, Classic Candles, Inc., Hamilton, 1969-70. Chmn., City Planning Commn., Hamilton, 1970-71, 72. Mem. Tex. Soc. Dentistry for Children, Am. Dental Assn., Central Tex. Dist. Dental Soc., Psi Omega, Hamilton C. of C. (pres. bd. 1970-71), Hamilton Jr. C. of C. Baptist (deacon, chmn. stewardship com. 1967-71, ch. bldg. com. 1970-71). Lion. Club: Hamilton Country. Home: Navajo Trail Hamilton TX 76531 Office: 310 E Main St Hamilton TX 76531

FORDE, CLIFTON DOUGLAS, JR., lawyer; b. Nashville, Dec. 23, 1921; s. Clifton Douglass and Elizabeth Marshall (Zarecor) F.; B.A., Vanderbilt U., 1943; J.D., So. Meth. U. Sch. Law, 1948; m. Mary Ellen Haughton, Sept. 8, 1945; children—Clifton D., III (dec.), Ellen Alice. Admitted to Tex. bar, 1948; atty. legal dept. Sun Oil Co., Dallas, 1948-50; pvt. practice law, San Angelo, Tex., 1950-52; gen. atty. Domestic Div. Seaboard Oil Co., Dallas, 1952-58; partner Dalton, Moore, Forde, Joiner & Stollenwerck, Dallas, 1965—. Served with USMCR, 1941-45. Mem. Am., Dallas bar assns., State Bar Tex., Sigma Alpha Epsilon, Delta Theta Phi. Clubs: Petroleum, T-Bar-M Racquet (both Dallas). Home: 3601 Haynie St Dallas TX 75205 Office: 2110 Republic Nat Bank Tower Dallas TX 75201

FORDICE, DANIEL KIRKWOOD, constrn. co. exec.; b. Russellville, Ind., Dec. 27, 1901; s. Morton William and Ella (Guilliams) F.; student Purdue U., 1921, 23, U. Tenn., 1938, 39; m. Clara Aileen Augustine, Dec. 31, 1929; children—Grace Aileen (Mrs. William M. Holt), Daniel K. Engr., U.S. Army Corps of Engrs., Memphis, 1922-42; partner Fordice Constrn. Co., Memphis, 1946—; pres. Abraham & Fordice, Inc., 1956-69. Served with AUS, 1942-46. Mem. Asso. Gen. Contractors of Am. (dir.), Cons. Constructors Council Am., Soc. Am. Mil. Engrs., Asso. Gen. Contractors Miss. Valley Flood Control (br. pres. 1957). Republican. Address: 3350 Highland Park Pl Memphis TN 38111

FORDICE, DANIEL KIRKWOOD, JR., constrn. co. exec.; b. Memphis, Feb. 10, 1934; s. Daniel Kirkwood and Clara Aileen (Augustine) F.; B.S., Purdue U., 1956, M.S., 1957; m. Patricia Louise Owens, Aug. 13, 1955; children—Angela Leigh, Daniel Kirkwood III, Hunter Lloyd, James Owens. Engr., Humble Oil & Refining Co., Baton Rouge, La., 1956-62; partner Fordice Constrn. Co., Delta, 1962—; pres. Fordice Constrn. Co., Inc., Vicksburg, Miss., 1970—, dir., 1970—; pres. Vicksburg Quality Edn., Inc., 1971—. Chmn. Warren County (Miss.) Republican Com., 1972—. Served to 1st lt. C.E., AUS, 1957-59. Recipient Distinguished Service award Vicksburg Jr. C. of C., 1969. Mem. Am. Inst. Constructors, Am. Soc. C.E., Aircraft Owners and Pilots Assn., Pilots Internat. Assn., Asso. Gen. Contractors Am. (nat. bd. dirs. 1970—, pres. Miss. Valley flood control br. 1970), Sigma Chi, Tau Beta Pi, Chi Epsilon. Republican. Clubs: Army Navy, Engineers (Vicksburg, Miss.). Home: 1457 Parkside Dr Vicksburg MS 39180 Office: PO Box 37 Delta LA 71233

FORDYCE, EDWARD CLYDE II, architect, engr.; b. Cheswick, Pa., Nov. 9, 1941; s. Kent Conrad and Leila L. (Swann) F.; B.Arch. (ROTC scholar 1959-63), Pa. State U., 1964; M.Urban Design, Va. Poly. Inst. and State U., 1974; m. Rachel Allene Poole, July 19, 1969; 1 son, Ehren Conrad. Architect L.D. Schmidt & Son, Fairmont, W.Va., 1966-68, 1970-71, Paul Schweikher, Pitts., 1969-70, Wilmot-Porter, Washington, 1968-69; with Sci. Mus. Va., Richmond, 1973—, also dir. planning. Pres. Resource Systems, Inc., Fairmont, W.Va., 1971—; instr. arch. Va. Poly. Inst. and State U., Blocksburg, Va., 1971-72. Recipient Thesis fellowship Nat. Endowment for the Arts, 1972-73, Environmental Awareness Stipend fellowship Assn. of Collegiate Schs. Arch., 1972-73, A.I.A. Mem. Internat. Solar Energy Soc. Contbr. articles to bldg. jours. Home: 1721 Grove Av Richmond VA 23220 Office: 217 Govenor St Richmond VA 23219

FORDYCE, PHILLIP RANDALL, educator; b. Lyons, Ind., May 28, 1928; s. Russell and Agnes (Fulk) F.; B.S., Butler U., 1951, M.S., 1954; m. Lois Marilyn Lamb, Dec. 27, 1947; children—Deborah, Natalie, Marilyn, Kerry, Timothy. Asst. prof. sci. edn. Fla. State U., Tallahassee, 1963-67, asso. prof., 1967-70, prof., 1970—, asst. dean Coll. Edn., 1965-67, asso. dean, 1967-69, dean, 1969-74, provost Profl. Schs. and Colls., 1974—. Cons. U.S.-AID Sci. Edn. in India Program, summer 1964; dir. 38 NSF-US Dept. Edn. Grant projects; edn. cons., Zaire, Korea, Turkey, Australia, Colombia. Bd. dirs. Council Internat. Edn. Exchange. Fellow A.A.A.S.; mem. Assn. for Edn. Tchrs. in Sci., Phi Delta Kappa, Kappa Delta Pi. Co-author sci. texts. Contbr. articles to profl. jours. Home: 2805 St Leonard Dr Tallahassee FL 32303

FORDYCE, SAMUEL WESLEY, electronic engr.; b. Jackson, Miss., Feb. 28, 1927; s. Samuel Wesley and Polly Adams (White) F.; B.S. in Physics, Harvard Coll., 1949; M.S. in E.E., Washington U., 1953; m. Sally Gillespie, Apr. 9, 1970; children—Katherine, Deborah, Wesley. Project engr. Emerson Electric, St. Louis, 1949-58; mem. tech. staff Space Tech. Labs., Los Angeles, 1958-60; mgr. communication and tracking dept. Aeronautics div. Ford Motor Co., Newport Beach, Cal., 1960-61; mem. tech. staff Gen. Electric, Santa Barbara, Cal., 1961-62; with Office Manned Space Flight, NASA, Washington, 1962—, electronic engr. Dir. Robertson Aircraft Co., St. Louis, 1957. Served with USNR, 1944-46. Registered profl. engr., Mo. Mem. I.E.E.E., Am. Inst. Aeros. and Astronautics. Clubs: Metropolitan, University (Washington); Country (St. Louis). Home: 3528 Water St Washington DC 20007 Office: 600 Independence Av SW Washington DC 20502

FOREMAN, BARNEY SIMPSON, retail trade exec.; b. Lake Charles, La., June 26, 1917; s. Homer and Aldea (Bushnell) F.; B.A., U. Southwestern La., 1939; m. Fleurette Emile Kahn, Apr. 1, 1942; children—Julian Brian, Glenn Barney. Tchr., coach, Crowley (La.) High Sch., 1939-42, Lake Charles (La.) High Sch., 1942-44; with Mefvine Kahn Co., retail trade, Rayne, La., 1944—, sec.-treas., mgr. hardware and appliance dept., 1944—. Chmn. Rayne Youth Program, 1962-69; active Little League Football, Boy Scouts Am. Mem. Rayne Council, 1946-50, mayor pro-tem, 1946-50. Baptist. Mason (Shriner). Home: 309 E Jeff Davis St Rayne LA 70578 Office: PO Box 29 Rayne LA 70578

FOREMAN, KENNETH JOSEPH, JR., found. exec., clergyman; b. Princeton, N.J., Dec. 28, 1921; s. Kenneth Joseph and Susan Allison (Lewis) F.; grad. Mt. Hermon Sch., 1938; B.S., Haverford Coll., 1942; B.D., Union Theol. Sem., Richmond, Va., 1945; Th.M. with distinction, Louisville Presbyn. Theol. Sem., 1953; postgrad. Princeton Theol. Sem., 1964—; m. Mary Frances Ogden, June 7, 1945; children—Carol, Frances Ogden (Mrs. Paul Leslie Garber, Jr.), Samuel Lewis, Joseph Lapsley. Ordained to ministry Presbyn. Ch. U.S., 1945; home missionary pastor Presbyn. Ch. U.S., Ashe County, 1945-48; fgn. mission evangelist, tchr. U.P. Ch. U.S.A., China, 1948-53, Korea, 1954-65, Ch. of Christ in China, 1949-52, Presbyn. Ch. in Korea, 1954-64, Korea Mission of Australian Presbyn. Ch., 1963-64; exec. dir. Hist. Found. Presbyn. and Ref. Chs., Montreat, N.C., 1969—. Clk., Bd. of Adjustments Town of Montreat, 1971—. Bd. dirs. Tien Nan Middle Sch., Kunming, Yunnan, Ch. of Christ in China Yunnan Mission com. Kienshui Hosp., Pusan (Korea) Presbyn. Theol. Sem.; moderator Presbytery of Concord, Presbyn. Ch. U.S., 1972. Mem. Am. Soc. Archivists, Am. Soc. Ch. History, Am. Radio Relay League, Aircraft Owners and Pilots Assn., Phi Beta Kappa. Author: Leaves From Behind the Bamboo Curtain, 1953; Speak Yunnanese, 1952. Editor: Yearbook of Prayer of Christian Work in Korea, 1958. Editor, contbr. Study Papers Korea 1953, 1953. Asso. editor Ashe Presbyn., 1945-48; editor Hist. Found. News, 1969—; mem. editorial bd. Jour. Presbyn. History, 1969—. Home: Box 488W Montreat NC 28757 Office: Box 847W Montreat NC 28757

FOREMAN, RICHARD JESSE, truck leasing co. exec.; b. Augusta, Ga., Jan. 16, 1918; s. Simkins and Gertrude (Baker) F.; grad. high sch.; m. Claudine M. Bentley, Aug. 13, 1939; children—Gertie (Mrs. William W. McElmurray), Richard Jesse Foreman. Owner, pres. R.J. Foreman Trucking Co., Jackson, S.C., 1935—; v.p., dir. First State Nat. Bank. Mem. Aiken County Planning and Devel. Bd., 1960-68, Aiken County Sch. Bd., 1958-64. Baptist. (Mason (32 deg., Shriner), Lion. Club: Silverton Agriculture (pres. 1962-63) (Jackson). Address: Route 1 Jackson SC 29831

FOREMAN, WILMER LOUIS, advt. agy. exec.; b. Eden, Miss., June 8, 1912; s. Daniel Henry and Bessie Belle (Faulk) F.; student Delta State Coll., Cleve., Miss., 1932, B.A., U. Ala., 1937-40; m. Virginia Sims, Apr. 4, 1941; 1 dau., Laura Virginia. Editor, Atmore (Ala.) Advance, 1941-42; asso. editor Huntsville (Ala.) Times, 1946-47; editor Comml. Dispatch, Columbus, Miss., 1947-48; pub. relations staff Nat. Cotton Council, Memphis, 1948-53, pub. relations mgr., 1953-70, dir. pub. relations and promotion, 1970-72; dir. pub. relations and promotion John Malmo Advt., Memphis, 1973—. Vol. exec. Internat. Exec. Service Corps, Thailand, 1972. Served to comdr. USNR, 1942-46. Mem. Pub. Relations Soc. Am. (mem. nat. exec. com. 1958), Agrl. Relations Council (pres. 1961), Lambda Chi Alpha. Republican. Methodist. Author: Cotton From Field to Fabric, 1966. Contbr. articles to profl. publs. Home: 297 Mary Ann Dr Memphis TN 38117 Office: Commerce Title Bldg Memphis TN 38103

FORESMAN, HENRY JOYCE, lawyer; b. East Liberty, Pa., Nov. 9, 1919; s. Robert All and Helen (Joyce) F.; B.A., Va. Mil. Inst., 1941; student Tulane U. La. Coll. Law, U. Colo. Sch. Law, 1947; J.D., Washington and Lee U., 1948 ; m. Helen Tilden Williamson, Apr. 19, 1952; children—Henry Joyce, Lee Gephart, Robert Holmes, George Williamson. Admitted to Va. bar, 1949, practice law, Buena Vista, Va, 1949-59, Lexington, Va., 1959—; town atty. Glasgow, Va., 1951—; city atty. Buena Vista, 1952-55, atty. for commonwealth, 1952-56; sec. Lexington Electoral Bd., 1966-69; spl. asst. to supt. Va. M.I. Inst., 1971—. Mem. Buena Vista City Democratic Com., 1952-59; del. State Dem. Convs., 1952, 56, 60, 64. Trustee Kappa Alpha Scholarship Fund, 1965-71. Served to capt. AUS, 1941-45; PTO. Decorated Bronze Star medal, Air medal, Purple Heart. Recipient George Washington Honor Medal award Freedoms Found., 1967. Mem. Am., Va., Lexington-Buena Vista-Rockbridge (pres. 1952-53) bar assns., Virginia State Bar (council 1953-56), Nat. Inst. Municipal Law Officers, Am. Judicature Soc., Kappa Alpha Order (nat. pres. 1965-67). Phi Delta Phi. Episcopalian. Home: 408 Highland Rd Lexington VA 24450 Office: 20 W Washington St Lexington VA 24450

FORGOTSON, EDWARD HERMAN, lawyer; b. Albuquerque, May 10, 1934; s. James Morris and Selma (Miller) F.; B.A., U. Tex., 1953, J.D., 1960; M.D., Washington U. Sch. Medicine, 1957; LL.M., U. Mich., 1963; m, Judith Hood, Aug. 25, 1962 (div.); children—Elizabeth Nell, Edward Herman, Jr. Admitted to Tex. bar, 1960; atty. U.S. Atomic Energy Commn. Staff, Washington, 1960-62; dir. program analysis U.S. Dept. Health Edn. and Welfare, Washington, 1963; dep. spl. asst. staff White House, Washington, 1964-65; asso. firm Worsham, Forsythe & Samples, Dallas, 1973—. Asso. prof. health systems planning U. Cal. Sch. Pub. Health, Los Angeles, 1965-69; dir. legal research Nat. Adv. Council Health Manpower, Washington, 1966-67. Recipient Ford Grant, 1968, Cook fellowship U. Mich., 1962-63. Mem. Am. Bar Assn. (chmn. com. 1972), State Bar of Tex., State Bar Cal. Club: Rush Creek Yacht (Heath). Home: 6016 Gaston Av Dallas TX 75214 Office: Suite 2500 2001 Bryan Tower Dallas TX 75201

FORKNER, CLAUDE ELLIS, physician; b. Stevensville, Mont., Aug. 14, 1900; s. Allen F. and Lucy Adeline (Irvine) F.; B.A. cum laude, U. Cal. at Berkeley, 1922, M.A., 1923; M.D., Harvard, 1926; m. Marion Sturges DeBois, Sept. 3, 1927; children—Claude E., Helen (Mrs. David Farley), Lucy (Mrs. Thomas A. Greene). Asst. anatomy U. Cal., Berkeley, 1922-23; teaching fellow in histology Harvard Med. Sch., 1924-26; intern internal medicine Johns Hopkins Hosp., 1926-27; asst. pathology and bacteriology Rockefeller Inst. Med. Research, N.Y.C., 1927-29; NRC fellow pathology and clin. investigation, Freiburg, Germany, Nat. Hosp., London, 1929-30; first Francis Weld Peabody fellow in medicine Thorndike Lab., Harvard Med. Sch., 1930-32; practice medicine, specializing in internal medicine, Boston, 1930-32, Peking, China, 1932-37, N.Y.C., 1937—, DeLand, Fla., 1970—; asso. prof. medicine Peking Union Med. Coll. (China), 1932-36, hon. lectr. medicine, 1936-37; asst. prof. clin. medicine Cornell U., Med. Coll., 1937-43, asso. prof., 1943-53, clin. prof. medicine, 1953-66, clin. prof. emeritus, 1966—; asst. attending physician N.Y. Hosp., 1937-45, asso. attending physician, 1945-50, attending physician, 1950-66, cons. medicine, 1966—; attending physician Roosevelt Hosp., 1946-51; cons. internal medicine Roosevelt Hosp., 1951-69, U.S. Naval Hosp., St. Albans, N.Y., 1952-53; cons. N.Y. Infirmary, 1950-69; cons. medicine Bronx VA Hosp., 1956-69. Dir., prof. medicine China Med. Bd., Rockefeller Found., 1943-45; hon. prof. medicine Cheeloo U. Med. Coll., Chengtu, China, 1943-45, Nat. Shanghai Med. Coll., Chengtu, China, 1943-45; civilian cons. to surgeon gen. Army, CBI, 1943-45; mem. med. adv. com. Unitarian Service Com., 1961-67; mem. panel advisers N.Y. State Com. on Med. Edn., 1962. Bd. dirs. C.T. Loo, Chinease Ednl. Fund, 1947-69; trustee Iran Found., Inc., 1953-65, pres., 1955-58, chmn. bd., 1958-61; trustee Tchrs. Coll., Columbia, 1954-69, emeritus, 1969—; founder, exec. dir. Med. Passport Found., 1957—, pres., 1973—. Served to 1st lt. U.S. Army, 1918, 1st lt. Res., 1922-27. Decorated companion Royal Order Homayun (Iran); recipient Medal of Honored Merit, Republic China, 1942, Gold Medal, Harvard Med. Alumni Assn., 1965. Diplomate Nat. Bd. Med. Examiners, Am. Bd. Internal Medicine. Fellow N.Y. Acad. Scis.; mem. A.M.A., A.A.A.S., Am. Soc. Clin. Investigation, Assn. Am. Physicians, Internat. Soc. Hematology, Blood Club (pres. 1954), Pan Am. Med. Assn. (pres. sect. on internal medicine 1962-65), Royal Soc. Health London, Am. Clin. and Climatological Assn., Assn. Health Records, Soc. Computer Medicine, A.C.P. (life), Assn. Advancement Med. Instrumentation, Soc. Advanced Med. Systems (dir. 1972—), N.Y. County Med. Soc. (life), N.Y. State Med. Assn. (life), N.Y. Acad. Medicine (life; v.p. 1953-54), N.Y. Soc. Study Blood (pres. 1951-52), N.Y. Med. and Surg. Soc. (pres. 1966), N.Y. Cancer Soc. (pres. 1960-61), N.Y. Acad. Sci., Harvard Med. Soc. N.Y. (pres. 1958-60), A Program for Harvard Medicine (nat. alumni chmn. 1962-65), Sigma Xi. Presbyn. Clubs: Century Assn., Harvard (N.Y.C.); Harvard of Central Fla. Author: Leukemia and Allied Disorders, 1938; also numerous sci. articles. Editor: Practitioners Conferences, Vols. 1-6, 1955-57. Home: PO Box 820 DeLand FL 32720 Office: 704 N Kansas Av DeLand FL 32720 also 115 E 61st St New York City NY 10021

FORMAN, FRANK (SHANE, III), govt. ofcl.; b. Kansas City, Mo., Oct. 28, 1944; s. Frank Shane, Jr., and Dorothy Jean (Roberts) F.; B.A., U. Va., 1966, M.A. (Ford Found. U. Scholar and fellow 1964-67; NSF grad. fellow 1966-68), 1968; m. Sarah Stirling Banks, Feb. 2, 1968. Research economist CAB, Washington, 1969—. Contbr. articles to profl. jours., bulls. Home: 2205 California St NW Washington DC 20008 Office: Civil Aeronautics Board Washington DC 20428

FORMAN, HAMILTON COLLINS, banking and nursery co. exec.; b. Ft. Lauderdale, Fla., Apr. 3, 1919; s. Hamilton Mc Lure and Blanche (Collins) F.; student U. Tenn., 1939-43; m. Doris Marie Davis, Jan. 7, 1945; children—Miles Austin, Hamilton Collins. Owner, mgr. Forman's San. Dairy, 1945-55; dir., v.p. Fern Crest Quarries, 1955-62; owner, mgr. Forman's Palm Nursery, Fern Crest Village, Fla., 1955—; dir., v.p. United Fed. Savs. & Loan Assn., Ft. Lauderdale, 1965—. Pres., Hamilton M. and Blanche C. Forman Christian Found., 1955—; commr., treas., chmn. bd. North Broward Hosp. Dist., 1961—; mem. nat. adv. bd. Berea in Korea Found. and Sch., 1960—; mem. nat. adv. council Lynchburg (Va.) Coll., 1967—; commr., treas., town clk. Fern Crest Village, 1955—; pres., dir. Fern Crest Improvement Dist., 1957—; mem. Gov.'s Com. Interstate Land Sales of Fla., 1963, Ft. Lauderdale Opera Guild; commr. Tindall Hammock Irrigation and Soil Conservation Dist.; mem. Fla.-Columbia Alliance, Taxpayers League Broward County, Broward County Narcotics Guidance Council, Gov.'s Com Tax Reform. Trustee Bethany (W. Va.) Coll., Nova U. Advanced Tech.; bd. dirs. Nova Gold Key Assn. Served with USAAF, World War II. Mem. Fla. Hosp. Commrs. and Trustees Assn. (vice chmn., dir.), S.A.R., Phi Eta Sigma, Kappa Sigma. Democrat. Mem. Christian Ch. (Elder, chmn. bd.). Kiwanian (award Ft. Lauderdale 1966), Gideon. Clubs: Fort Lauderdale Yacht, Rolling Hills Golf and Country (dir., treas. 1960—), Gold Coast Rotunda, Tiger Bay (Ft. Lauderdale). Home: 1524 Coral Ridge Dr Fort Lauderdale FL 33304 Office: 3600 N Federal Hwy Fort Lauderdale FL 33308

FORMAN, WADE KULENKAMPFF, forging co. exec.; b. Kansas City, Mo., Dec. 14, 1913; s. Joseph F. and Alida M. (Kulenkampff) F.; B.S., N.Y. U., 1939; M.B.A., Harvard, 1941; m. Joan Brewster, Mar. 1, 1942; children—Kathleen, Judith, Merry, Jane, Patricia. With Lone Star Gas Co., Fort Worth, 1946-51; dist. mgr. W. Pat Crow Forge Co, 1951-56; co-founder Trinity Forge, Inc., Mansfield, Tex., 1957, chmn. bd., pres., 1957—. Instr. bus. mgmt. and marketing Tex. Christian U., 1947-52. Trustee Forging Industry Ednl. and Research Found., 1968—, pres., 1972-73. Served to lt. comdr. USNR, 1941-46. Mem. Forging Industry Assn. (dir. 1966-70). Home: 1931 Westview St Arlington TX 76013 Office: 947 Trinity Dr Mansfield TX 76063

FORREST, HERBERT EMERSON, lawyer; b. N.Y.C., Sept. 20, 1923; s. Jacob K. and Rose (Fried) F.; B.A., George Washington U., 1948, J.D., 1952; student Coll. City N.Y., 1941, Ohio U., 1943-44; m. Marilyn Lefsky, Jan. 12, 1952; children—Glenn Clifford, Andrew Matthew. Admitted to Va., D.C. bars, 1952, Md. bar, 1959; law clk. Bolitha J. Laws, Chief Judge U.S. Dist. Ct., Washington, 1952-55; practiced in Washington, 1952—; mem. firm Welch & Morgan, 1955-65, Steptoe & Johnson, 1965—. Chmn. D.C. Criminal Justice Act Adv. Bd., 1972—; mem. com. on admissions and grievances U.S. Ct. Appeals D.C. Served with AUS, 1943-46. Mem. Am. Judicature Soc., Am. (mem. council adminstrv. law, chmn. com. on reports), Va. State, Fed., Fed. Commn. (chmn. legal aid com., mem. publs. com.) bar assns., Bar Assn. D.C., D.C. Unified Bar (chmn. Govt. Equal Employment Referral Center com.), N.A.M. (telecommunications com.), Washington Council Lawyers, Order of Coif, Phi Beta Kappa, Pi Gamma Mu, Artus, Phi Eta Sigma, Phi Delta Phi. Democrat. Mem. B'nai B'rith. Book editor Fed. Commn. Bar Jour. Contbr. articles to profl. jours. Bd. advisers Duke Law Jour. Home: 7001 Whittier Blvd Bethesda MD 20034 Office: 1250 Connecticut Av Washington DC 20036

FORREST, HUGH SOMMERVILLE, educator; b. Glasgow, Scotland, Apr. 28, 1924; s. Archibald and Margaret Wilson (Peden) F.; B.S. with honors, U. Glasgow, Scotland, 1944; Ph.D., U. London, 1947; Ph.D., U. Cambridge, 1951; Sc.D., U. London, 1970; m. Rosamond Scott Baker, June 12, 1953; children—Eleanor Scott, Anne Sommerville, Hugh Watson. Came to U.S., 1951. Research scientist Med. Research Council Gt. Britain, 1947-51; research fellow Cal. Inst. Tech., Pasadena, 1951-54, sr. research fellow, 1954-55; research scientist U. Tex., Austin, 1955-56; asso. prof. U. Tex., Austin, 1956-63, prof. zoology, 1963—. Recipient Carnegie scholarship, 1944-45; Dept. Sci. and Indsl. Research fellowship, Gt. Britain, 1948-51; USPHS Research fellow, 1951-53; Spl. Research fellow, 1973; numerous Research grants from NIH, USPHS, and Robert A. Welch Found., 1954—. Fellow Royal Chem. Soc. (Gt. Britain); mem. Am. Chem. Soc., Soc. Gen. Physiologists, Soc. Biol. Chemists. Editor: (with R.P. Wagner) Biochemical Genetics, 1971—. Contbr. articles to profl. jours. Home: 3302 River Rd Austin TX 78703

FORREST, PHILIP RYDER, JR., banker; b. N.Y.C., July 25, 1919; s. Philip Ryder and Marie (Shannon) F.; A.B., Spring Hill Coll., 1942; m. Anne Martina Dermeranville, Feb. 14, 1942; children—Philip Ryder III, Marie S. (Mrs. Douglas Perryman), Helena P., Anne H. Reporter, feature writer Mobile (Ala.) Press Register, 1940-42; mem. staff indsl. personnel and pub. relations Ala. Drydock & Shipbldg. Co., 1942-44; with A.P., N.Y.C., 1944-46; owner Shoppers Delivery Service, Mobile, 1946-48; with Morris Timbes Advt. Agy.-Howard Barney Advt. Agy., 1948-50; promotion mgr., program dir. WABB Radio, 1950-57; promotion dir., news dir. WALA-TV, 1957-59; owner Phil Forrest Advt. Agy., 1959-63; pub. relations dir. Am. Jr. Miss Pageant, Inc., 1963-69; dir. advt. and pub. relations Mchts. Nat. Bank of Mobile, 1969—. Pres. St. Catherine Sch. P.T.A., 1966-68. Campaign dir. Young Republicans for Eisenhower, 1952-56. Recipient Exceptional Achievement award Pub. Relations Council Ala., 1970, 73. Mem. Overseas Press Club Am., Am., Ala. pub. relations socs., Pub. Relations Council Ala. (dir. 1972—), Pub. Relations Council Mobile (pres. 1972), Am. Bankers Assn., Bank Marketing Assn., Spring Hill Coll. Alumni Assn. K.C. (4 deg.). Clubs: International Trade, Athelstan. Home: 412 W Ridgelawn Dr Mobile AL 36608 Office: PO Box 2527 106 St Francis St Mobile AL 36622

FORREST, WILLIAM A., JR., bussiness exec., b. 1929; U. Va., 1951, LL.B., 1956; married. Admitted to Va. bar, 1956; atty. McGuire, Woods, King, Davis & Patterson Assos. (name now McGuire, Woods & Battle), 1956-61, partner, 1961-66; asst. gen. counsel, asst. sec. A.H. Robins Co., Inc., Richmond, Va., 1966-67, sec., asst. gen. counsel, 1967-69, sec., gen. counsel, 1969—, v.p., 1974—; dir. Capital Savs. and Loan Assn., Va. Trust Co. Former chmn. finance com. Va. Republican Com. Trustee Crippled Chidren's Hosp.; bd. dirs. Team of Progress, 1970—, Senior Center, 1966-69. Served to 1st lt. AUS, 1951-53. Mem. Richmond Tennis Patrons Assn. (pres. 1969-71), U. Va. Alumni Assn. (pres. Richmond chpt. 1968-70). Address: 1407 Cummings Dr Richmond VA 23220

FORRESTAL, DANIEL JOSEPH, III, investment co. exec.; b. St. Louis, Dec. 6, 1941; s. Daniel Joseph and Esther (Witte) F.; B.A. in Econs., Holy Cross Coll., 1963; M.B.A., Washington U., 1970; m. Pamela Duchesne Coy, Feb. 19, 1966; children—Amy Katharine, Molly Coy. Security analyst Boatmen's Nat. Bank, St. Louis, 1964-68; investment officer St. Louis Union Trust Co., 1968-70; portfolio mgr. First Nat. Bank, Dallas, 1970-73; pres. 1st Internat. Investment Mgmt., Inc., 1974—. Instr. Southwestern Grad. Sch. Banking, Dallas, 1970-74. Served with AUS, 1963-69. Mem. Tex. Bankers Assn., Dallas Soc. Investment Analysts, Financial Analysts Fedn., Beta Gamma Sigma. Club: Brookhaven Country (Dallas). Home: 13210 Roaring Springs Dallas TX 75240 Office: PO Box 6031 Dallas TX 75222

FORRESTER, EUGENE NORWOOD, physician; b. Jacksonville, Fla., July 1, 1924; s. Vinson T. and Mary Alice (Moore) F.; A.B., Duke U., 1949, M.D., 1954; m. Mary Frances Hickman, Jan. 28, 1947; children—Cynthia Patrice, Eugene Norwood, John Vinson, David

Kevin. Intern U.S. Naval Hosp., St. Albans, L.I., N.Y., 1954; pvt. practice medicine, Clayton, N.C., 1956-58, Winter Park, Fla., 1958—. Dir. Atlantic Bank, Casselberry, Fla., 1972—. Served with USNR, 1943-45, 1953-55. Mem. Fla., So., Am. med. assns., Orange County Med. Soc. Home: 719 Kiwi Circle Winter Park FL 32789 Office: 2035 Glenwood Dr Winter Park FL 32789

FORRESTER, JOEL WILLIAM, city ofcl.; b. Meridian, Miss., Nov. 9, 1916; s. Henry Collier and Daisy (Bearce) F.; B.S., U. Miss.; postgrad. Colo. U., 1943; m. Peggy Moss, Sept. 7, 1949; children—Joellyn, Joel William. Mgr., L.L. Maprise, Inc., 1938-41; mgr. Wright Constrn. Co., 1946-49; city clk. City of Meridian, 1949-55, city treas., 1955-59, city mgr., 1959—. Served with USAAF, 1942-46; PTO. Mem. C. of C. Presbyn. (elder), Kiwanian. Club: Northwood Country (Meridian). Home: 2917 28th St Meridian MS 39301 Office: City Hall Meridian MS 39301

FORRESTER, MILLARD LEE, JR., city ofcl.; b. Jacksonville, Fla., Mar. 1, 1939; s. Millard Lee and Nellie Belinda (Stewart) F.; A.A., Jacksonville U., 1958; m. Shirley Ann Rhoden, Sept. 6, 1958; children—Corlleen England, Barkley Scot. With Stevens Enterprises, Jacksonville, 1959-65; gen. mgr. So. States Utilities Jacksonville, 1965-71; utilities planning officer City of Jacksonville, 1971—; water and sewer utilities adminstrv. cons. Mem. Am. Water Works Assn., Am. Pub. Works Assn., Water Pollution Control Fedn., Fla. Pollution Control Assn. Home: 2331 Ardmore Court Jacksonville FL 32211 Office: Room 400 City Hall 220 E Bay St Jacksonville FL 32202

FORSYTHE, PETER, state conservation engr.; b. Bozeman, Mont., Aug. 23, 1932; s. W.L. Evans and Jane Aurel (Westermann) F.; B.S., Mont. State U., 1955; m. Evelyn Sandsness, Mar. 17, 1956; children—Richard, Melainie, Stephen. Work unit engr. Soil Conservation Service, Livingston, Mont., 1955-56, area engr., Miles City, Mont., 1956-64, Missoula, Mont., 1964-66, asst. state engr., Indpls., 1966-71, state conservation engr., Jackson, Miss., 1971-73. Registered profl. engr., Mont., Ind., Miss. Mem. Am. Soc. Agrl. Engrs., Soil Conservation Soc. Am., Sigma Nu. Contbr. articles to profl. jours. Home: 1209 Foxhill Dr Clinton MS 39056 Office: Box 410 Jackson MS 39205

FORT, ARTHUR TOMLINSON, III, physician, educator; b. Lumpkin, Ga., Sept. 24, 1931; s. Thomas Morton and Gladys (Davis) F.; student N. Ga. Coll., 1948-50; B.B.A., U. Ga., 1952; student Memphis State U., 1957-58; M.D., U. Tenn., 1962; m. Jane Wilmer McClelland, June 15, 1957; children—Abby Lucinda, Arthur Tomlinson Jr., Juliana Melody, Ernest Arlington II. Intern, Bapt. Meml. Hosp., Memphis, 1962-63; resident obstetrics and gynecology U. Tenn., 1963-66, asst. prof., 1966-70; prof., head dept. gynecology and obstetrics La. State U. Med. Sch., Shreveport, 1971-73; prof. maternal and child health and family planning Tulane U. Med. Center, 1973—, dir. family health program Sch. Pub. Health and Tropical Medicine, 1973—; pvt. practice obstetrics and gynecology, Memphis, 1966-70. Mem. med. com., bd. dirs. La. Family Planning Program, Caddo Parish, 1971—; mem. nat. adv. council Nat. Center Family Planning Program Devel.; pres. Family Health Found. Served with USAF, 1952-57. Recipient Student Golden Apple award A.M.A., 1969. Diplomate Am. Bd. Obstetrics and Gynecology. Fellow Am. Coll. Obstetrics and Gynecology; mem. Am. Fertility Soc., Am., So. med. assns., S.-Central Obstet. and Gynecol. Soc., Soc. for Study Reprodn., Nat. Assn. Family Planning Program Dirs., Nat. Planning Forum. Democrat. Presbyn. Home 6016 Pitt St New Orleans LA 70118 Office: 136 S Roman St New Orleans LA 70112

FORT, WILLIAM LAPHAM, publishing co. exec.; b. Bklyn., Sept. 19, 1904; s. William Lapham and Elsie Knox (Pearson) F.; grad. Rome Acad., 1922; student various Harvard Sterling Forest seminars; m. Margaret M. McKenney, Sept. 8, 1925 (dec. Aug. 1968); 1 dau., Barbara Pearson (Mrs. John David Dorsey); m. 2d, Doris Alford Preston, Nov. 8, 1969. Reporter, copywriter, 1922-25; bus. devel. mgr. Citizens Trust Co., Utica, N.Y., 1925-28, asst. v.p., 1928-30; mem. advt. sales staff McFadd 1931-32, A.E. Blackett, Sample, Hummert, 1933-34; advt. mgr. Rural Progress mag., 1934-36; mem. staff Am. Weekly mag., 1936-47; advt. dir. Coronet mag., 1947-49; exec. Life mag., N.Y.C., 1949-67; cons. Time, Inc., 1967—. Dep. fire commr., Utica, 1927-28. Mem. So. Vt. Artists Assn. (trustee), S.A.R., S.R., New Eng. Soc., Soc. Colonial Wars, Huguenot Soc., Empire State Soc., St. Nicholas Soc. Episcopalian Clubs: Metropolitan, N.Y. Yacht (N.Y.C.); Internat. (Washington), Ekwanok Country (Manchester, Vt.); Royal Thames Yacht, American (London, Eng.); Mid-Ocean (Bermuda); La Coquille (Palm Beach, Fla.); Fla. Yacht (Jacksonville). Home: 139 E 63d St New York City NY 10021 also Manchester VT 05254 also Ponte Vedra FL 32082

FORTENBERRY, JOHN LAMAR, supt. schs.; b. Sumrall, Miss., Sept. 11, 1922; s. William Edward and Pearlie (Wilks) F.; B.S., Southeastern La. Coll., 1948; M.A., U. So. Miss., 1950; Ed.D., U. Miss., 1956; m. Mary Margaret Mosal, Sept. 10, 1964; children—Lisa Mosal, John Lamar, William Parrish. Asst. prof. edn. U. Miss., 1950-52; prin. high sch., Bay St. Louis, Miss., 1952-55; state supr. edn. State Dept. Edn., Jackson, Miss., 1956-65; supt. schs., Canton, Miss., 1965—; instr. extension classes U. Miss., Miss. State U., U. So. Miss. Served with USNR, 1942-47. Mem. Am. Assn. Sch. Adminstrs., Miss. Ednl. Assn., Am. Legion, Phi Delta Kappa, Kappa Delta Pi. Mason (32 deg.). Rotarian. Author: Fortenberry's Mississippi School Guide, 1958. Home: 226 Rebecca Dr Canton MS 39046 Office: 403 E Lincoln St Canton MS 39046

FORTEY, JOSEPH WILLIAM, educator; b. Birmingham, Eng., Sept. 18, 1925; s. Joseph Alfred and May (Deer) F.; B.S., U. London, 1958; M.S., Rice U., 1960; Doctorat (Robert Blair fellow), U. Toulouse, 1966; m. Hazel May Pritchard, Aug. 14, 1957; children—Nicholas, Martine. Came to U.S., 1966, naturalized, 1973. Lectr., U. Aston, 1949-58; Fulbright vis. prof. Rice U., Houston, 1958-60; lectr. U. Birmingham (Eng.), 1964-66. prof. sch. architecture U. Tenn., Knoxville, 1966—. Cons. TVA, other engring. orgns. NATO fellow, 1969. Fellow Am. Soc. C.E.; mem. Instn. Structural Engrs. (Gt. Britain), Am. Soc. Engring. Edn., Internat. Assn. Bridge and Structural Engrs., Internat. Assn. for Hydraulic Research, Sigma Xi, Phi Kappa Phi. Home: 4712 Florence Rd Knoxville TN 37920

FOSBERG, IRVING ARTHUR, psychologist; b. N.Y.C., Jan. 22, 1916; s. Albert and Julia (Greenfield) F.; B.S., N.Y. U., 1937 Ph.D., 1940; M.A., Columbia, 1938; m. Betty Pearlman, Feb. 11, 1945; children—Ben, Orin, Barry. Cons. psychologist, N.Y.C., 1940-41; asst. prof. psychology Farragut Coll., Farragut, Ida., 1946-47; dir. Bur. Psychol. Service, Tulane U., New Orleans, asst. prof. psychology, 1947-48; chief psychologist VA Hosp., New Orleans, 1952-57; pres. Psychol. Service Center New Orleans, Inc., 1955—; asso. prof. Loyola U. Sch. Bus. Adminstrn., New Orleans, 1960-67, prof., 1967—. Cons. psychologist Cerebral Palsy Clinic, Civil Service Commn. New Orleans; vocational cons. U.S. Dept. Health, Edn. and Welfare. Served with USNR, 1941-68; now comdr. ret. Fellow Am. Psychol. Assn., A.A.A.S., Rorschach Inst.; mem. So. Soc. Philos. Psychology, Am. Assn. U. Profs., La. Psychol. Assn. (past pres.). Contbr. articles to profl. jours. Home: 6020 Freret St New Orleans LA 70115 Office: 8116 Hampson St New Orleans LA 70118

FOSCO, PETER, labor union ofcl.; b. Russia, May 13, 1892; s. Vincent and Antonio Fosco; student, U. Ill.; m. Carmela Santucci, Dec. 3, 1916; children—Angelo, James. Came to U.S., 1913. Financial sec. local union #2 Laborers' Internat. Union N. Am., Chgo., 1916-20, pres., 1920-38, mgr. Chgo. regional office, 1936-68, gen. sec.-treas., Washington, 1950-68, gen. pres., Washington, 1968—; v.p. AFL-CIO, 1st v.p. Bldg. and Constrn. Trades dept. Democratic ward committeeman, Chgo.; commr., Cook County, Ill., 1936-46. Named Man of Year Amerita Soc., 1972. Mem. Italian Soc. Chgo. K.C. Home: 1757 N Nordica Av Chicago IL 60635 Office: 905 16th St NW Washington DC 20006

FOSDICK, FRANKLIN LAWRENCE, aircraft exec.; b. Ansonia, Conn., Sept. 12, 1919; s. Horace George and Maude Percy (Buck) F.; student New Haven Coll., 1946-48; B.B.A. with highest honors, So. Meth. U., 1962; m. Bette H. Burns, Sept. 19, 1940; 1 son, Franklin Lawrence, Jr. With LTV Aerospace Corp., 1946—, mgr. material services, purchasing and operations control, Mich. div., Warren, 1963-70, chief traffic, transp. and shipping, Vought Systems div., Dallas, 1970—. Chmn. liability and claims task force, mem. exec. com. traffic service div. Aerospace Industries Assn. Am., 1970—. Pres., prin. owner Bali Hi Apts., Dallas, 1958—; dir., sec. LTV Missiles & Space Credit Union, Warren, 1964-70. Mem. freight adv. bd. Am. Airlines, N.Y.C., 1970—. Served to 1st lt. AUS, 1944-46. Mem. Purchasing Mgmt. Assn. Detroit (dir. 1969), Nat. Assn. Purchasing Mgmt. (dist. vice chmn. pub. relations 1970), Dallas Apt. Assn. Methodist (chmn. adminstrv. bd. 1973—). Mason (32 deg., Shriner). Club: Village Players (Birmingham, Mich.). Home: 1639 Whitedove St Dallas TX 75224 Office: LTV Aerospace Corp PO Box 6114 Dallas TX 75222

FOSDICK, RICHARD JOHN, fertilizer co. exec.; b. Keota, Ia., Dec. 9, 1918; s. Charles Alphonse and Eva Anna (Palm) F.; grad. high sch.; m. Betty Jean Holmes, July 20, 1941; children—Sharon (Mrs. John R. Byrne), Peggy (Mrs. Paul R. Terry, Jr.), Linda (Mrs. Thomas C. Abbott). Laborer, Streit Feed Store, Keota, 1937; mgr. Streit Feed Co., Cedar Rapids, Ia., 1938-42; feed salesman Archer-Daniels-Midland Co., Mpls., 1946-52; sales supr. Smith-Douglass div./Borden, Inc., Texas City, Tex., 1952-59, asst. sales mgr., 1959-62, sales mgr., 1962-67, br. mgr., 1967—; v.p., dir. Sun-Vue Fertilizers, Inc., Lockney, Tex., 1970—, Caddo County Farm Supply, Inc., Carnegie, Okla., 1970—, Sanner's Farm Supply, Inc., Zimmerdale, Kan., 1970—, Crop Service, Inc., Garwood, Tex., 1970—. Pres., Jr. Achievement Mainland, Inc., Texas City, 1971-72, 72-73, chmn., 1973—; gen. chmn. Southwest Fertilizer Conf., Houston, 1972; vice chmn. Galveston County Research Council, Inc., 1971-72, chmn., 1972-73. Bd. dirs. Mainland Communities United Fund, Texas City, Served with USNR, 1942-45. Named Texas City Outstanding Sr. Citizen, Jr. C. of C., 1972. Mem. Texas City-LaMarque C. of C. (pres. 1973). Rotarian (pres. 1973—). Roman Catholic. Home: 515 6th Av N Texas City TX 77590 Office: PO Box 1571 Grant Av Texas City TX 77590

FOSGATE, OLIN TRACY, educator; b. Peru, N.Y., May 14, 1918; s. Cecil and Lila (Harrington) F.; student Eastern Mich. U., 1935-36; B.S., U. Wis., 1950, M.S., 1954, Ph.D., 1956; m. Grace J. Alverstrom, Aug. 17, 1946; children—Heather, Kevin, Brian. Instr. U. Wis., Madison, 1948-56; asst. prof. animal husbandry W.H. Miner Research Inst., Chazy, N.Y., 1956-57; asst. prof. U. Ga., Athens, 1957-62, asso. prof., 1962-68, prof. dairy sci., 1968—. Internat. cons. for dairying, 1970-73. Recipient Outstanding Tchr. award U. Ga., 1969-70. Home: 230 Valley Brook Dr Athens GA 30601 Office: Dairy Sci Dept U Ga Athens GA 30602

FOSHEE, DONALD PRESTON, educator; b. Albertville, Ala., Jan. 8, 1931; s. Byrd Preston and Ruby (Hooten) F.; student Snead Jr. Coll., 1954-56; B.A., Birmingham So. Coll., 1959; M.A., Vanderbilt U., 1958, Ph.D., 1962; m. Grace E. Coley, Mar. 5, 1931; children—Vicky, Kay, Steve, David. Postdoctoral in neurophysiology U. Miss. Med. Sch., Jackson, 1961-62, chief Lab. Exptl. Behavior, 1962-65; asso. prof., asst. chmn. psychology dept. Auburn (Ala.) U., 1965-69, prof. psychology, 1969—. Cons. VA Hosp., Tuskegee, Ala., 1971; pres. East Ala. Co-operative Housing, Inc., Auburn, 1969-73, bd. dirs., 1969-73. Served with USAF, 1950-54. Recipient USPHS Predoctoral fellowship, 1959-61, USPHS Postdoctoral fellowship, 1961-63. Mem. Lee County Mental Health Assn. (pres. 1971), Miss. (pres. 1964), Southeastern psychol. assns., A.M.A. Contbr. articles to profl. jours. Home: 355 Gardner Dr Auburn AL 36830

FOSHEE, WAYNE OTIS, constrn. co. exec.; b. Hot Springs, Ark., Jan. 17, 1937; s. Otis B. and Greta Edna (Smith) F.; student U. Va., 1955-56, U. So. Cal., 1957, Santa Monica City Coll., 1958-59; B.A. in Philosophy, U. Cal. at Los Angeles, 1961; m. Dorothy Lee Westerman, May 31, 1957; children—Michael Wayne, Kevin Otis. Tchr. social studies secondary schs., 1961-63; co-founder Brown & Foshee Constrn. Co., Hot Springs, 1963, partner, 1963—; profl. draftsman, 1957—; co-founder, dir. Stagecoach Junction, Inc., Hot Springs, Toolmakers, Inc., Doniphan, Mo., Wayne Foshee, Ltd., Shelter, Inc., Hot Springs, Trails Inn, Inc., Hot Springs; founder, pres., dir. Wayne O. Foshee, Inc. Homebuilders, Indsl. Marketing Corp., Hot Springs; dir. Trail's Inn, Inc., Shelter, Inc., Gt. Western Land Corp., Southeast Land Corp., Valley Lumber & Supply Co., Inc.; founding partner, dir. Am. Letter, Inc.; co-founder, partner Paul Wayne Devel. Co., Nat. Realty Developers & Investment Co. Pres. Garland County Property Owners Assn., 1964. Recipient Am. Legion Citizenship award, 1955, D.A.R. Citizenship award, 1952. Mem. Nat. Assn. Homebuilders (dir.), Ark. (past pres., dir.), Hot Springs (past pres., dir.) homebuilders assns. Republican. Methodist. Home: 1003 Prospect St Hot Springs AR 71901 Office: PO Box 1217 Hot Springs AR 71901

FOSS, ARTHUR HAZEN, educator; b. Haverhill, Mass., Jan. 23, 1930; s. Hazen Arthur and Lillian (Thompson) F.; A.B., Boston U., 1951, M.A., 1959; postgrad. U. Fla., 1964-65. Tchr. Wamogo Regional High Sch., Litchfield, Conn., 1955-57; Edgewater High Sch., Orlando, Fla., 1957-60; instr. Jr. Coll. Broward County, Ft. Lauderdale, Fla., 1960—, head dept. math., 1963-69, pre-profl. math. program coordinator, 1967-68. Mem. Fla. Task Force in Math. Articulation, 1965—; pres. Fla. Jr. Coll. Council Tchrs. Math., 1972. Served with USNR, 1951-54. Mem. Math. Assn. Am., Am. Assn. U. Profs., Phi Beta Kappa, Phi Delta Kappa, Alpha Phi Omega. Democrat. Baptist. Kiwanian. Home: 5007 SW 88th Terrace Ft Lauderdale FL 33314

FOSSETT, ROBERT OWEN, editor; b. Falmouth, Ky., Jan. 26, 1907; s. Elmer Esta and Anna (Haufler) F.; ed. Ohio Mechanics Inst., Cin., Miller's Bus. Coll., Cin.; m. Ruth Hilda Beason, Dec. 23, 1927; children—Wallace Lee, Lennie Wayne. With Ft. Thomas Hardware & Paint Co. (Ky.), 1925; 26, Sherwin Williams Co., various locations, 1927-50; with Signs of Times Pub. Co., Cin., 1953—, editor Screen Printing mag., 1953-73, cons. editor, 1973—. Adv. council Youth Screen Printing, Inc., Dayton, O.; former bd. dirs. Screen Printing Assn. Nigeria. Served with U.S. Army, World War I, USNR, World War II. Recipient Elmer G. Voight award Edn. Council Graphic Arts, 1960. Mem. Screen Pringing Assn. Internat. (internat. chmn. ednl. and vocational devel. com. 1958-59, mem. ednl. com. 1970—; Howard Parmele award 1960, hon. life), Acad. Screen Printing Tech., Midwest Screen Printing Assn. (sec.-treas. 1969—), Cin. Graphic Arts Assn. Baptist (tchr. men's Bible class). Author: Photography for the Screen Printer, 1959. Home: 3231 Riggs Av Erlanger KY 41018 Office: 407 Gilbert Av Cincinnati OH 45202

FOSTER, BRUCE PARKS, educator; b. Mussoorie, V.P., India, June 27, 1925 (parents Am. citizens); s. Robert Alexander and Aurel Lenore (Anderson) F.; student Westminster Coll., 1946-47; B.S., Baldwin Wallace Coll., 1948; M.S., Yale, 1951, Ph.D., 1953; m. Gertrude Lilias Martin, June 14, 1947; children—Kathryn Ann, Robert Anderson, Gregory Martin. Faculty physics N. Tex. State U., Denton, 1953—. With Oak Ridge Nat. Lab., summer 1955-56; research participant Tex. Inst., Inc., Dallas, 1954, 60, 65; Fulbright lectr. Peshawar (West Pakistan) U., 1960-61; physics lectr. Punjab U., Lahore, West Pakistan, 1961-63; research work Livermore (Cal.) Nat. Lab., 1969. Served with AUS, 1943-46. Home: 1106 Hillcrest Denton TX 76201

FOSTER, CHARLES BRADFORD, JR., civil engr.; b. Hope, Ark., Aug. 27, 1915; s. Charles B. and Nancy (Lightle) F.; B.S. in Civil Engring., Tex. A. and M. U., 1938; postgrad. Tex. U. Water Utility Mgmt. Inst., 1962; m. Cecile L. Gatlin, Sept. 23, 1944; children—Charles Bradford III, Nancy Lightle II. Civil engr. Tex. Hwy. Dept., Childress, 1938-39; with Dept. Water Utilities, Shreveport, La., 1939-71, gen. supt. dept., 1962-71; dir. sch. plant Caddo Parish (La.) Schs., 1971—. Comdg. officer U.S. Army Reserve Sch., 1966-71; col. Res. Decorated Legion of Merit. Registered profl. engr., La., Tex., Ark. Fellow Am. Soc. C.E.; mem. Nat. Soc. Profl. Engrs., Engrs. Joint Council, La. Engring. Soc., Am. Water Works Assn. Episcopalian (ch. sch. tchr. 1953—). Lion, Elk. Club: Shreveport Tex. A. and M. Home: 736 Monrovia St Shreveport LA 71106 Office: Caddo Parish Schs Shreveport LA 71108

FOSTER, DANIEL W., physician, educator; b. Marlin, Tex., Mar. 4, 1930; B.A., Tex. Western Coll. of U. Tex., 1951; M.D., U. Tex. Southwestern Med. Sch. at Dallas, 1955; m. 3 sons. Intern in internal medicine Parkland Meml. Hosp., Dallas, 1955-56, asst. resident, 1956-58, chief resident, 1958-59; USPHS Postdoctoral fellow U. Tex. Southwestern Med. Sch., Dallas, 1959-60; sr. asst. surgeon USPHS, 1960-62; investigator Intermediary Metabolism sect. Nat. Inst. Arthritis and Metabolic Diseases, NIH, Bethesda, Md., 1960-62; instr. medicine U. Tex. Med. Sch., Dallas, 1962-63, asst. prof., 1963-68, asso. prof. internal medicine, 1968-70, prof. internal medicine, 1970—; attending physician Parkland Meml. Hosp.; cons. internal medicine and research VA Hosp., Dallas. Mem. metabolism study sect. NIH, 1968-70, chmn., 1970-72. Mem. Dallas Bd. Edn., 1969-72. Recipient Career Devel. award Nat. Inst. Arthritis and Metabolic Diseases, NIH, 1963. Mem. Am. Fedn. for Clin. Research, Dallas County Med. Soc., Am., Tex. med. assns., Am., So. socs. for clin. investigation, Am. Soc. for Biol. Chemists, Assn. Am. Physicians, Sigma Xi, Alpha Omega Alpha. Presbyn. (ruling elder; moderator N.E. Tex. presbytery 1968). Mem. editorial bd. Metabolism, Clin. and Expt.; asso. editor Jour. Clin. Investigation. Office: 5323 Harry Hines Blvd Dallas TX 75235

FOSTER, DAVID DEVARD, architect; b. Decatur, Tex., Nov. 7, 1941; s. Henry Grady and Gladys (Collier) F.; student Midwestern U., 1960-62, U. Houston, 1970; m. Sharon Kay Morphis, June 22, 1962. With Robert Hussman, architect, Houston, 1965-70, Joel Brand, architect, Houston, 1970-72, Joel Brand & David Foster, Houston, 1972-73; pvt. archtl. practice, Houston, 1973—. Partner, Grace & Foster Investments, Houston, 1971—. Bd. dirs. Garden Oaks Subdiv., 1970—. Mem. A.I.A., Tex. Soc. Architects. Home: 714 W 42nd St Houston TX 77018 Office: 2910 Ferndale Houston TX 77006

FOSTER, EARL MASTERS, banker; b. Boston, May 28, 1940; s. John Jacob and Etta (Masters) F.; A.B., Tufts U., 1962; M.B.A., Boston U., 1964; Ph.D., N.Y. U., 1969; m. Nancy Ruth Hall, Sept. 20, 1964; children—Tamar, Elana, Dara. Instr., Grad. Sch. Bus. Adminstrn., Pace Coll., N.Y.C., 1967-68; asst. prof. Coll. Bus. Adminstrn., Boston U., 1968-72; sr. investment analyst, trust officer First Nat. Bank Miami, 1972-73, v.p., dir. investment div., 1974—. Cons., Data Edn., Inc., N.Y. Port Authority; editorial reviewer Allyn & Bacon, McGraw-Hill, Jour. Financial and Quantitative Analysis, Quar. Rev. Econs. and Bus. Mem. Am. Econ. Assn., Am. Finance Assn., Financial Analysts Soc. Miami, Omicron Delta Epsilon, Beta Gamma Sigma. Author: Common Stock Investment, 1974. Contbr. articles to profl. jours. Home: 14522 SW 75th St Miami FL 33143 Office: First Nat Bank Miami 100 S Biscayne Blvd Miami FL 33131

FOSTER, EDITH LENORE, librarian, educator; b. Carrollton, Ga., Mar. 6, 1906; d. Robert Ellis and Margaret (Byrom) Foster; A.B., La Grange Coll., 1926; A.B. in L.S., Emory U., 1944, postgrad.; postgrad. West Ga. Coll., U. Ga., Milw. U., Fla. State U. Tchr. Buena Vista (Ga.) High Sch., 1926-27; drama coach Wayne P. Sewell Producing Co., 1927-28; head English Dept. Choctaw County High Sch., Butler, Ala., 1928-33, Trion (Ga.) High Sch., 1933-40, Tallapoosa (Ga.) High Sch., 1940-41, Gordon meml. High Sch., Chickamauga, Ga., 1941-43; dir. West Ga. Regional Library, Carrollton, 1944—; instr. English West Ga. Coll., Carrollton, summers 1944-45, asst. prof. library edn., 1958—. Cons. Fla. State U. Adult Edn. Inst., summer 1955; library cons. for Carroll, Douglas, Haralson, Heard, Paulding counties, Ga., 1944—. Mem. Carrollton City Hall Bldg. Com., 1955-57; chmn. Carroll County Sesquicentennial Com., 1976. Bd. dirs. Carroll Service Council. Recipient Betty Crocker award of honor, 1950, Nat. Library Week awards 1960, 61; Distinguished Service award Carrollton C. of C., 1969; named Carroll County's Outstanding Citizen, 1952; Carroll County's Outstanding Woman in Edn., 1964. Mem. Am. (pres. adult edn. sect. 1955, mem. Ga. assembly adult edn. 1956, chmn. operation nat. library project 1958-59, council 1960-63), Ga. (pres. 1961-63, chmn. library devel. com. 1964, chmn. intellectual freedom com. 1965-67; handbook com., govt. relations com., chmn. Nix-Jones distinguished service award, manual com. 1969-71), Southeastern (chmn. recruitment com. 1952-56) library assns., Ga. Sch. and Coll. Library Assn. (mem. adv. bldg. com. 1969-71), Carroll Hist. Soc. Democrat. Methodist (mem. council ministries 1974, adminstrv. bd. 1973—). Author: Beside the Wishing Well, 1937; To Wind a Chain, 1951; A Librarian's Memorial Tribute to Lucile Nix. Contbr. articles to profl. jours. Home: 219 E Sims St Carrollton GA 30117 Office: Rome St at Spring St Carrollton GA 30117

FOSTER, E(LTON) GORDON, chem. engr.; b. Milw., Feb. 4, 1919; s. Percy and Edith (Elton) F.; B.S., U. Wis., 1941, M.S., 1942, Ph.D., 1944; m. Lois Thomson, June 23, 1941; 1 dau., Cynthia. Group leader, DuPont Co., Wilmington, Del., 1944-51; asst. prof. U. Louisville, 1951-52; engr., Shell Devel. Co., Emeryville, Cal., 1952-54; supr., 1954-65; mgr. process devel. Indsl. Chems. div. Shell Chem. Co., N.Y.C., 1965-68; mgr. process engring., licensing Shell Devel. Co., Emeryville, 1968-72, Houston, 1972—. Mem. Cal. Legis. Council for Profl. Engrs., 1962-64. Fellow Am. Inst. Chemists; mem. Am. Chem. Soc., Am. Inst. Chem. Engrs. Patentee in chem. processing. Home: 2034 Dryden Rd Houston TX 77025 Office: 2525 Murworth Dr Houston TX 77094

FOSTER, JAMES HENRY, race track operator; b. Winston-Salem, N.C., Jan. 25, 1927; s. Henry Shuford and Mary (Corcoran) F.; B.A., Catawba Coll., 1950; m. Barbara Jean Spillman, May 10, 1954. Sports editor Winston-Salem Sentinel, 1944; sports reporter Winston-Salem Jour., 1946; pub. relations dir. Catawba Coll., 1946-50; sports and telegraph editor Salisbury (N.C.) Post, 1950-53; golf editor Greensboro (N.C.) Record, 1954-57; sports editor Spartanburg (S.C.) Herald-Jour., 1957-65; So. News Bur. mgr. Chrysler Corp., 1966-67; asst. to pres. Nat. Assn. Stock Car Auto Racing, 1968-71; v.p., dir. corporate communications Internat. Speedway Corp., Daytona Beach, Fla., 1971—; partner Pine Korner Gift Shop, Spartanburg. Served with USNR, World War II; PTO. Home: 182 Riverside Dr Ormond Beach FL 32074 Office: PO Box S Daytona Beach FL 32015

FOSTER, J(OHN) EDWIN, ednl. administr.; b. Stoughton, Sask., Can., Jan. 6, 1917; s. Gloyd and Lydena (Scott) F.; B.A., U. Sask., 1939, B.Ed., 1942; M.S., Ind. U., 1948, Ed.D., 1950; m. Marjorie Kathleen Currie, Aug. 22, 1942; 1 son, Scott Percy. Prin., Radisson (Sask.) High Sch., 1939-41; supr. Aux. War Services Overseas, Canadian Army, 1942-46; field rep. Nat. Film Bd. Can., 1946-47, supr., 1950-52; dir. Med. Film Inst., Chgo., 1952-57; audio visual dir. Am. Heart Assn., N.Y., 1957-61; exec. dir. Ednl. Media Council, N.Y., 1961-65; dir. learning systems Howard U., Washington, 1965—. Cons. U.S. Office Edn., 1965. Mem. Nat. Assn. Ednl. Broadcasters, Phi Delta Kappa. Patentee in field. Home: 6012 Namakagan Rd Washington DC 20016 Office: 2400 6th St NW Washington DC 20001

FOSTER, LAWRENCE, music dir.; b. Los Angeles, 1941; pupil Fritz Zweig; student Bayreuth Festival Masterclasses. Debut as orch. condr. Young Musicians' Found. Debut Orch., 1960, condr., mus. dir., 1960-64; asso. condr. San Francisco Ballet, 1964-65; asst. condr. Los Angeles Philharmonic Orch., 1965-68; chief guest condr. Royal Philharmonic Orch., Eng., 1969—; guest condr. Houston Symphony, 1970-71, condr.-in-chief, 1971-72, now music dir.; guest condr. orchs. U.S., Europe. Recipient Koussevitsky Meml. Conducting prize, 1966, Eleanor R. Crane Meml. prize Berkshire Festival, Tanglewood, Mass., 1966. Office: 615 Louisiana Av Houston TX 77002

FOSTER, WILLIAM BELL, JR., clothing co. exec.; b. Washington, June 27, 1923; s. William Bell and Jennie May (Hardwick) F.; B.A., Cornell U., Ithaca, N.Y., 1947, M.B.A., 1948; m. Martha Elizabeth Walker, Jan. 25, 1953; children—Dorothy, Nancy. Dir., Hardwick Clothes, Inc., Cleveland, Tenn., 1948—, sec., 1951—, v.p. marketing, 1966—. Trustee, Cleveland (Tenn.) Day Sch. Served to capt. AUS, 1942-46; now col. Res. Mem. Soc. Mayflower Descs., Res. Officers Assn., Assn. of U.S. Army, Mil. Order of World Wars, Am. Legion, V.F.W., Pilgrim John Howland Soc., Kappa Sigma. Methodist. Elk. Clubs: Cleveland Country (pres. 1953); Cornell (N.Y.C.). Home: 2701 Highland Dr Cleveland TN 37311 Office: 445 Church St Cleveland TN 37311

FOSTER, WILLIE STEPHEN, pub., lawyer; b. Crockett, Tex., Aug. 7, 1896; s. Thomas Jefferson and Dora (Hollingsworth) F.; A.B., Baylor U., 1921; m. Vera Alberta Chadwick, Aug. 28, 1921; children—Beverly Jean, Barbara Dell, Brady McCall, Bill Chadwick. Asso., Corpus Christi (Tex.) Crony, 1912, Corpus Christi Printing Co., 1913-14, Baylor U. Press, 1915-16; mng. editor, editor Baylor Lariat, 1917, 1920; prin. coach West High Sch., 1921-22; pub. Quanah Observer, 1922-23; asso. Donna News, 1923, McAllen Daily Press, 1924; owner, pub. Valley Morning Telegram, McAllen, Tex., 1924; with Corpus Christi Caller, San Antonio Express, 1925; owner, pub. Brady Dailey Sentinel, 1926-27; with Waco News-Tribune, 1928; mng. editor Waco Am., 1928-29; organizer, operator Waco Press Record, Overton News, Foster Pub. Co., Inc., Waco, 1930-33; pres. Foster Petroleum Co., Overton, 1932-39; active practice law, 1934—; owned Brady Herald, McCullough County News, DeLeon Free Press, 1946; with Dallas Times Herald, 1948-50; owner pub. Victoria County Mirror, Rogers News, Waco Citizen, 1942—; partner Roy Craig, stamford Am. Leader; an organizer Bellmead State Bank; also real estate owner. Active in civic improvements, urban renewal and model cities plans. Mem. Tex. Legislature, 1945-47. Served in 1st O.T.C., Leon Springs, Tex., 1917, North Sea Mine Sweeping Fleet, U.S. Navy, 1918-19. Mem. Typpog. Union, Am. Legion (pas C. of C. V.F.W. (past comdr., dist. comdr.), Am., Tex., Waco-McLennan County bar assns., Texas Press Assn., Baylor Ex-Student Assn., 40 et 8, Mil. Order Cooties (past grand seam squirrel), Sigma Delta Chi. Methodist (steward, trustee). Mason (Shriner); mem. Order Eastern Star (past worthy patron), Red Man. Clubs: Lion, Advertising; Rotary (organizer Quanah, Brady, Donna, Tex.). Home: 2616 Old Robinson Rd Waco TX 76706 Office: 1020 N 25th St Waco TX 76707

FOUNTAIN, BENJAMIN EAGLES, JR., ednl. adminstr.; b. nr. Rocky Mount, N.C., July 20, 1929; s. Benjamin Eagles and Emmie (Green) F.; A.B., U. N.C., 1950, M.Ed., 1952, Ph.D. (Kellogg fellow 1957-58), 1958; m. Norma Fagan, Apr. 9, 1955; children—Stephanie, Claire, Benjamin Eagles III, Susan. Tchr., prin. Rocky Mount (N.C.) Schs., 1950-55; sec. N.C. Sch. Bds. Assn., Chapel Hill, 1955-57; prof. U. N.C., 1958-61; supt. schs., Elizabeth City, 1961-65; pres. Lenoir Community Coll., Kinston, 1965-71; state pres. N.C. Dept. Community Colls., Raleigh, 1971—. Dir. Raleigh Bd. Br. Banking & Trust Co. Named Citizen of Year, Kinston C. of C., 1970. Mem. N.E.A., N.C. Assn. Educators, N.C. Assn. Community Coll. Presidents (chmn. 1967-68). Democrat. Presbyn. Club: MacGregor Downs Country (Cary, N.C.). Chmn. editorial bd. Community Coll. Rev. Home: 212 Annandale Dr Cary NC 27511 Office: Dept Community Colls State Bd Edn Raleigh NC 27602

FOUNTAIN, L. H., congressman; b. Leggett, N.C., Apr. 23, 1913; s. Lawrence H. and Sallie (Barnes) F.; A.B., U. N.C. (Wiley P. Mangrim Oratorial medal), 1934, LL.B. (Mary D. Wright Debate medal 1935), 1936; m. Christine Dail, May 14, 1942; 1 dau., Nancy Dial. Admitted to N.C. bar, 1936; reading clk. N.C. Senate, 1936-41; sec., treas. Coastal Plains Broadcasting Co., radio sta. WCPS, Tarboro, now exec. v.p.; mem. 83d-93d Congresses, 2d Dist. N.C., mem. com. fgn. affairs, chmn. Near East sub. com. of govt. operations com.; chmn. inter-govtl. relations sub-com.; del. to UN, 1967. Mem. exec. com. E. Carolina council Boy Scouts Am. Trustee St. Andrews Coll. Mem. N.C. State Senate from 4th Senatorial Dist., 1947-52; pres. Edgecombe Young Dem. Club, 1940; eastern organizer, past chmn. 2d dist. exec. com. Young Dem. Clubs N.C. Enlisted AUS as pvt., 1942, disch. as maj. J.A.G.O., O.R.C., 1946. Elected Tarboro's Man of Year, 1948. Mem. Am., N.C., Edgecombe County bar assns., N.C. Farm Bur., N.C. Grange, Am. Legion. Democrat. Presbyn. (elder). Elk, Kiwanian (past pres., lt. gov. 6th N.C. div.). Home: 1102 Panola St Tarboro NC 27886 also 4000 Cathedral Av Washington DC 20016 Office: House Office Bldg Washington DC 20515 also US Post Office Tarboro NC 27886

FOUNTAIN, (PETE) PETER DEWEY, JR., clarinet player; b. New Orleans, July 3, 1930. Played clarinet in sch. band, 1942; with Jr. Dixieland Jazz Band, 1948-49, Phil Zito, 1949-50, Basin Street Six, 1950-54; appeared New Orleans, also Jazz Ltd. and Blue Note, Chgo., 1949-53; formed group Pete Fountain and His Three Coins, 1954-57; leader Dixieland combo Lawrence Welk Orch., ABC-TV series, 1957-59. Address: Lake Vista LA 70124

FOUNTAIN, SILAS DAVID, osteo. physician; b. Wild Cherry, Ark., Oct. 29, 1915; s. Alfred Wesley and Mary (Locke) F.; D.O., Kansas City Coll. Osteopathy and Surgery, 1937; m. Lillian Grey McLamb, Nov. 25, 1936; children—Henry Mac, Mary, David, Nellie, John. Intern Conley Clin. Hosp., Kansas City, Mo., 1938; practice osteopathic medicine specializing in surgery, Noel, Mo., 1938-73; mem. staff McDonald County Osteo. Hosp., Cardwell Meml. Hosp. Pres. bd. dirs. Cardwell Meml. Hosp., Inc. Mem. Am. Osteo. Assn., Mo. Assn. Osteo. Physicians and Surgeons, S.W. Mo. Assn. Osteo. Physicians and Surgeons (v.p.), Am. Acad. Osteo. Surgeons (bd. govs.), Am. Med. Soc. Vienna (life). Methodist (sec. bd. dirs.). Died June 29, 1973. Home: Sulphur Springs AR 72768 Office: Noel MO 64854

FOURIER, ARTHUR ERNEST, educator; b. Chgo., Nov. 2, 1917; s. Arthur Ernest and Rose (Buske) F.; B.S., U. Ill., 1940; postgrad. Chgo. Tchrs. Coll., 1940-41; M.A., George Peabody Coll., 1949, Ph.D., 1954; m. Mary Ruth Gasser, Sept. 30, 1944; children—Arthur Ernest, Barbara Renee. Asst. football coach Foreman High Sch., Chgo., 1940-41; tchr. University High Sch., Columbia, S.C., 1945; instr., asst. prof. U. S.C., Columbia, 1945-61; prof., head dept. health, phys. edn. and recreation Auburn (Ala.) U., 1961—. Served to ensign USNR, 1941-44. Mem. A.A.H.P.E.R., N.E.A., Nat. Recreation and Parks Assn., Am. Assn. U. Profs., Nat. Coll. Phys. Edn. Assn. for Men, Phi Delta Kappa. Home: 477 Cary Dr Auburn AL 36830

FOURNET, JOHN BAPTISTE, ret. judge; b. St. Martinville, La., July 27, 1895; s. Louis Michel and Marcelite (Gauthier) F.; grad. La. State Normal, 1915; LL.B., La. State U., 1920, LL.D., 1956; m. Rose M. Dupuis, Feb. 1, 1921 (div.); children—Lela Mae Ann (Mrs. Roger Vincent), John Dupuis; m. 2d, Sylvia Ann Fournet. Admitted to La. bar, 1920; practice law, St. Martinville, 1920, Baton Rouge, 1921-22, Jennings, 1922; mem., speaker La. Ho. of Reps., 1928-32; lt. gov. of La., 1932-35; asso. justice Supreme Ct. La., 1935-49, chief justice, 1949-70; retired. Served as pvt. U.S. Army, 1918. Mem. Am., La. bar assns., Am. Judicature Soc., Conf. Chief Justices, Order of Coif, Blue Key, Gamma Eta Gamma, Phi Alpha Delta, Pi Lambda Beta, Pi Gamma Mu. Democrat. Mason (32 deg., Shriner). Clubs: Lamplighters; New Orleans Country. Home: 2100 St Charles Av New Orleans LA 70140

FOURNET, LEON FRANCIS, dentist; b. New Orleans, June 9, 1940; s. Earl Joseph and Lucia Marie (Cuccia) F.; D.D.S., Loyola U., New Orleans, 1964; m. Sandra Fonseca, June 5, 1961; children—Leslie, Kevin and Keith (twins), Monique. Intern oral surgery Charity Hosp., New Orleans, 1964-65; resident Ochsner Found. Hosp., New Orleans, 1967-70; pvt. practice dentistry specializing in oral surgery Suburban Med. Plaza, Metairie, La., 1970—; part time asst. clin. prof. oral surgery Charity Hosp., La. State U. Med. Center, New Orleans, 1971—; chief dental sect. East Jefferson Gen. Hosp., 1973-74. Served to capt. AUS, 1965-67. Recipient Dean Echoles award Ochsner Found. Hosp., 1969. Diplomate Am. Bd. Oral Surgeons. Mem. Am., New Orleans chmn. membership com. 1972-73) dental assns., Am., Southeastern socs. oral surgeons, Psi Omega. Democrat. Roman Catholic. Home: 5021 Folse Dr Metairie LA 70002 Office: 4324 Veterans Blvd Metairie LA 70002

FOURNIER, WINSTON CARROLL, pub. relations exec.; b. Ypsilanti, Mich., Feb. 13, 1920; s. C. Wallace and Gladys Ellen (Lutz) F.; student Purdue U., 1937-39; A.B. in Journalism, Ind. U., 1946; m. Mary Ann Jones, June 11, 1949; children—Charles Winston, Mark Melson. Telegraph editor St. Joseph (Mo.) Gazette, 1946; copy editor Schenectady Union-Star, 1946-47; copy editor, reporter, bur. chief Wall St. Jour., N.Y.C., Chgo., Dallas, St. Louis, 1947-57; account exec. Fleishman-Hillard, Inc., St. Louis, 1958-60; pres. Winston Fournier & Assos., Inc., Dallas, 1960—; lectr. financial pub. relations U. Dallas. Served with USAAF, 1942-45. Mem. Pub. Relations Soc. Am. (pres. Dallas chpt. 1967, nat. assemblyman 1970-72, S.W. judicial panel 1968-70, 73), Nat. Investor Relations Inst. (pres. Dallas chpt. 1973), Press Club of Dallas, Sigma Delta Chi. Methodist. Home: 4056 Willow Ridge St Dallas TX 75234 Office: 2425 First Nat Bank Bldg Dallas TX 75202

FOURRIER, BROTHER FELICIAN, supt. schs.; b. Baton Rouge, Sept. 17, 1914; s. J.D. Lawrence and Felicie Marie (Landry) F.; B.S. in Chemistry, Loyola U., New Orleans, 1945; M.S. in Edn., Fordham U., 1951. Headmaster, prin., U.S., Can., Kenya, Uganda; asst. supt. schs. Archdiocese of New Orleans, 1967-69; supt. schs. Diocese of Baton Rouge, 1969—. Dir. studies Bros. of Sacred Heart. Home: 2021 Terrace Ave Baton Rouge LA 70806 Office: PO Box 2028 Baton Rouge LA 70821*

FOUSHEE, ROGER BABSON, pub. rep.; b. Haw River, N.C., July 29, 1938; s. Joseph Baxter and Elsie Bellwood (Jenkins) F.; A.B., U. N.C., 1960, postgrad., 1960-64. Serials asst. Wilson Library, U. N.C., 1960-62; research asst. Gov.'s Commn. Edn. Beyond High Sch., 1962; research asso., inst. of govt. U. N.C., 1963; pubs. rep. George Scheer Assos., Chapel Hill, N.C., 1964—. Mem. Central Bus. Dist. Com. of Chapel Hill, 1973; chmn. Orange County Am. Revolution Bicentennial Commn. Chmn. Orange County Dem. Com., 1968-72; mem. N.C. Dem. Exec. Com., 1970—. Named one of 10 outstanding young Dems. in N.C., 1969, 72. Mem. Chapel Hill Hist. Soc. (pres.), L.Q.C. Lamar Soc., Phi Eta Sigma, Phi Alpha Theta. Mem. Order of Golden Fleece; Rotarian. Home: 735 Raleigh Rd Chapel Hill NC 27514 Office: Box 1145 Franklin St Sta Chapel Hill NC 27514

FOUSS, JAMES LAWRENCE, agrl. engr.; b. Warsaw, O., Feb. 22, 1936; s. Raymond Lawrence and Hazel (Sergent) F.; B.Agrl. Engring., Ohio State U., 1959, M.S., 1962, Ph.D., 1971; m. Judith Lysle Theiss, Dec. 28, 1957; children—JoAnna Patricia, James Michael. Agrl. engr. soil and water conservation research div. Agrl. Research Service, U.S. Dept. Agr., Ohio State U., Columbus, 1960-72, Coastal Plains Soil & Water Research Center, Florence, S.C., 1972—. Troop asst. scoutmaster Pee Dee Area council Boy Scouts Am., 1972-73; vice pres. Florence Parent-Tchr.-Student Assn., 1972—. Recipient Spl. Service, 1962, Outstanding Performance, 1968, 72, Superior Service Commendation, 1972 awards U.S. Dept. Agr. Mem. Am. Soc. Agrl. Engrs. (recipient young designer award 1972), Soil Conservation Soc. Am., Sigma Xi, Gamma Sigma Delta, Alpha Epsilon. Contbr. profl. jours. Home: 1319 3d Loop Rd Florence SC 29501 Office: PO Box 3039 Florence SC 29501

FOWINKLE, EUGENE W., physician; b. Memphis, Sept. 2, 1934; student Southwestern at Memphis, 1952-55; M.D., U. Tenn., 1958; M.P.H., U. Mich., 1962; m. Ruby Fowinkle; children—Greta, Frieda, Brenda. Intern City Memphis Hosps., 1959; resident neurosurgery Bapt. Meml. Hosp., 1960; resident pub. health Tenn. Dept. Pub. Health, 1962-64; pub. health physician Memphis and Shelby County Health Dept., 1961, dir. communicable disease control, 1962-65, asst. dir. dept., 1965-66, dir., 1966-69; commr. pub. health State Tenn., 1969—; asst. preventive medicine U. Tenn., 1963-64, asst. prof., 1965—; asso. clin. prof. Vanderbilt U., 1969—. Mem. Milbank Found. Commn. Higher Edn. Needs in Pub. Health; mem. project policy adv. com. Assn. State and Territorial Health Officers. Diplomate Am. Bd. Preventive Medicine. Fellow Am. Pub. Health Assn. (governing council 1969; Charles G. Jordan Meml. award 1972), Am. Coll. Preventive Medicine; mem. A.M.A., Tenn. Med. Assn., Tenn. Pub. Health Assn., Nashville and Davidson County Med. Soc., Am. Assn. Pub. Health Physicians (trustee 1970—; pres. 1972-73), Alpha Omega Alpha. Contbr. numerous articles to profl. jours. Office: Cordell Hull Bldg 436 6th Av Nashville TN 37219

FOWLER, CALVIN DENNIS, elec. mfg. co. exec.; b. Abbeville, S.C., Aug. 1, 1928; s. James Edward and Alma Iris (Gable) F.; B.S., U. Wis., 1955; M.S., Fla. State U., 1967; m. Joyce Marilyn Winefeld, Mar. 26, 1949; children—Dennis Edward, Yvonne Frances. Asst. base mgr. Convair, Cheyenne, Wyo., 1960-61, launch comdr. at Cape Canaveral, Fla., 1961-65; base mgr. Gen. Electric Co., Kennedy Space Center, Fla., 1965—. Chmn. 11th Space Congress, 1974. Bd. dirs. United Way for Brevard County, Fla. Served with USNR, 1946-49, 50-52. Recipient NASA Pub. Service Group Achievement award for Apollo Program, 1973. Mem. Am. Inst. Aeros. and Astronautics, Aircraft Owners and Pilots Assn. Presbyn. (elder, past trustee, deacon). Home: 409 Thomas Av Cocoa FL 32922 Office: PO Box 21067 Kennedy Space Center FL 32922

FOWLER, CRAIG MATHEW, lawyer; b. Ft. Wayne, Ind., July 3, 1941; s. Hanes Mathew and Bonsilene Adele (Craig) Fowler; B.B.A., Tex. Christian U., 1963; LL.B., U. Houston, 1965; m. Robin Irene McKinnon, Jan. 26, 1963; children—Michael Mathew, John McKinnon. Admitted to Tex. bar, 1965; law clk., Fed. Judiciary, Dallas, 1965-66; asso. Strasburger, Price, Kelton, Martin & Unis, Dallas, 1966-69; partner Tabor & Fowler, Irving, Tex., 1969—. Democratic Election Judge, Dallas County, 1972—. Bd. dirs. Physicians and Surgeon's Hosp., Irving, Tex., 1970; mem. bd. trustees Dallas Cardiac Inst., 1973. Mem. State Bar Tex., Sigma Chi, Phi Alpha Delta. Rotarian. Club: Las Colinas Country (Irving). Home: 3209 Coronado Irving TX 75062 Office: 303 Irving Bank Tower Irving TX 75060

FOWLER, GEORGE PALMER, educator; b. Marietta, O., Aug. 1, 1909; s. George Edward and Mary E. (Palmer) F.; B.Sacred Lit., Butler U., 1933; B.D., Vanderbilt U., 1943; Ph.D., Yale, 1954; m. Lorene McClure, Apr. 16, 1931; children—Jo Anne (Mrs. Theron D. Oxley), Janet (Mrs. Richard Ross). Ordained to ministry Christian Ch., 1933; minister Christian Chs., Ind., Ky., Tenn., 1933-43; faculty Tex. Christian U., Ft. Worth, 1947—, prof. religion and Greek, 1957—. Mem. Am. Acad. Religion, Soc. Bibl. Lit., Am. Schs. Oriental Research. Author: Our Religious Heritage-A Guide to the Study of the Bible, 1969, rev. edit., 1972; Fundamentals of Grammar of the Greek New Testament, rev. edit. 1971. Home: 2616 Rogers Av Fort Worth TX 76109

FOWLER, GORDON, brokerage co. exec.; b. Texas City, Tex., Oct. 10, 1913; s. Raymond Foster and Josephine (Syndenham) F.; B.S., U.S. Naval Acad., 1936; postgrad George Washington U., 1959-61; m. Elaine Wootten Meekins, June 5, 1938; children—Gordon, Terry (Mrs. Terry Fabrizio Fiumi), Eric Raymond. Commd. ensign, USN, advanced through grades to capt., 1954; ret., 1961; account exec. Merrill Lynch Peirce Fenner & Smith, Inc., Washington, 1961—. Dir. Watergate West, Inc., 1972—, v.p., 1974. Decorated D.F.C., Air medal. Mem. Assn. Investment Brokers Met. Washington (pres. 1969-71), Washington Soc. Investment Analysts. Clubs: Army Navy, Army Navy Country. Home: 2700 Virginia Av NW Washington DC 20037 Office: 1100 Connecticut Av NW Washington DC 20036

FOWLER, HAMMOND, lawyer, savs. and loan assn. exec.; b. Rockwood, Tenn., Apr. 6, 1901; s. Hammond and Zoe (Leland) F.; student U. Tenn., 1918-19, 21-22, Maryville, Coll., 1919; LL.B., Cumberland U., 1929; m. Netha McCorkle, Apr. 26, 1952. Pres., Times Printing Co., also pub. Rockwood Times, 1922-42; admitted to Tenn. bar, 1929; practice law, Rockwood, 1931—; atty. City of Rockwood, 1933-53; dir. Rockwood Fed. Savs. & Loan Assn., 1934—, v.p., 1946—; v.p., atty., dir. Tenn-Val Realty, Inc., Rockwood, 1973—; gen. counsel Tenn. Dept. Employment Security, 1939-47. Mem. Tenn. Pub. Service Commn., 1948-72; dir. indsl. devel. bd. City of Rockwood, 1964—. Mem. Tenn. Senate, 1934-36; mem. Roane County Democratic Exec. Com., 1922—. Served from lt. to lt. comdr. USNR, 1942-45. Mem. Tenn., Am., Roane County bar assns., Am. Legion, V.F.W., S.A.R. (pres. Tenn. Soc. 1971-72), Soc. Colonial Wars, Mil. Order World Wars, Lambda Chi Alpha. Rotarian (hon.). K.P. Clubs: Civitan, Rockwood Golf and Country. Home: 421 S Douglas Av Rockwood TN 37854 Office: 104 S Front Av Rockwood TN 37854

FOWLER, HAROLD HENDERSON, banker; b. Montgomery, Pa., Sept. 20, 1914; s. Harold Sherman and Mary Helen (Henderson) F.; B.S., Temple U., 1936; m. Marian Annette Shuman, Jan. 8, 1943; 1 dau., Marian Elizabeth (Mrs. Harry Landon Pearce). Supr. audit div. Westinghouse Electric Corp., East Pittsburgh, Pa., 1944-45; comptroller, office mgr. Campbell Chain Co., York, Pa., 1946-50; auditor Western Nat. Bank, York, 1951-58; auditor Broward Nat. Bank, Ft. Lauderdale, Fla., 1958-67, v.p., cashier, 1967—. Served with AUS, 1942-44. Mem. Nat. Office Mgmt. Assn. (past pres.), Nat. Assn. Cost Accountants (past dir.). Mason (Shriner). Home: 3496 NE 19th Av Fort Lauderdale FL 33306 Office: 25 S Andrews Av Fort Lauderdale FL 33302

FOWLER, HOWLAND AUCHINCLOSS, govt. ofcl.; b. N.Y.C., Jan. 25, 1930; s. Robert Henry and Caroline (Auchincloss) F.; grad. Phillips Exeter Acad., 1947; A.B., Princeton, 1952; M.Sc. (Socony-Vacuum research fellow), Brown U., 1955, Ph.D. (Corinna Borden Keene research fellow), 1957; m. Shirley Joyce Boers, May 5, 1962; children—Joanna Louise, Amy Auchincloss. With Nat. Bur. of Standards of U.S. Dept. Commerce, Washington, 1957—, postdoctoral asso., successively physicist, project leader atomic physics div., project leader electricity div., 1957-71, sci. asst. to dir. Inst. Basic Standards, 1971—. Mem. Philos. Soc. Washington, Am. Phys. Soc., I.E.E.E., Sigma Xi. Presbyn. (bd. ushers). Research and publs. on electron scattering and ultraviolet optical constants in metals, superconducting-tunneling. Home: 5413 Albermarle St Bethesda MD 20016 Office: Physics Bldg National Bureau of Standards Washington DC 20234

FOWLER, KEITH FRANKLIN, theatre dir.; b. San Francisco, Feb. 23, 1939; s. Jack Franklin and Jacklyn Lucille Dorothy Hocking (Montgomery) F.; B.A. magna cum laude, San Francisco State U., 1960; certificate Shakespeare Inst., Stratford-upon-Avon, Eng., 1961; D.F.A., Yale, 1969; m. Janet Bell, June 16, 1962; 1 son, Jeremy Clay. Dir. Casino Playhouse, Holyoke, Mass., 1963, San Francisco Shakespeare Festival, 1964; asst. prof., dir. exptl. theatre Williams Coll., Williamstown, Mass., 1964-68; dir. Asolo State Theatre Fla., Sarasota, 1968; producing dir. Va. Museum Theater, head theatre arts div. Va. Mus., Richmond, 1969—, also founder VMT Repertory Co., 1972—. Fulbright grantee, U.K., 1960; Woodrow Wilson fellow, 1961; John Shubert Meml. scholar, 1963-64. Mem. Actors Equity Assn., Am. Theatre Assn., Revels Office (pres. 1972), Alpha Psi Omega. Producer, dir. Macbeth starring E.G. Marshall, 1973. Home: 2119 Stuart Av Richmond VA 23221 Office: Va Museum Theatre Repertory Boulevard and Grove Sts Richmond VA 23221

FOWLER, RICHARD EDMOND LEE, physician, educator; b. Marion, Miss., Dec. 20, 1923; s. Robert Edward Lee and Charlotte Augusta (Morrow) F.; B.A., U. Miss., 1943; M.D., Duke, 1945; m. Margaret Marlene Sekelsky, Aug. 13, 1947 (dec. 1964); children—Robert Joseph, Cynthia Gayle, Richard Lee, Carol Lynne,

William Edmond; m. 2d, Rosemarie Brozman Adams, Dec. 22, 1972. Intern Charity Hosp., New Orleans, 1945, resident pediatrics, La. State U. unit, 1948-50, pediatrician in chief, 1955—; resident pediatrics Birmingham (Ala.) Childrens Hosp., 1946; Nat. Heart Inst. fellow in pediatric cardiology La. State U. Med. Sch., New Orleans, 1950-51, instr. pediatrics, 1953, asst. prof., 1954, prof., head dept. pediatrics, 1955—; practice medicine, specializing in pediatric cardiology, New Orleans, 1953—; sr. asst. surgeon USPHS, 1951-52. Served from 1st lt. to capt., M.C., AUS, 1946-47. Research grantee La. Heart Assn., 1955-60. Diplomate Am. Bd. Pediatrics (ofcl. examiner 1966—). Mem. Am., So. socs. pediatric research, Am., La., Orlean Parish pediatric socs., Am. Acad. Pediatrics (com. med. edn. 1970—), Am. Coll. Cardiology, Am., La. (pres. 1962-63) heart assns., A.M.A., La., Orleans Parish med. socs. Contbr. articles to profl. jours. Home: 2416 Lake Oaks Pkwy New Orleans LA 70122 Office: 1542 Tulane Av New Orleans LA 70122

FOWLER, ROBERT DOBBS, newspaper pub.; b. Marietta Ga., Sept. 1, 1930; s. Ralph W. and Irma (Dobbs) F.; B.A., U. South, Sewanee, Tenn., 1952; m. Judith Knox Lidstone, Sept. 8, 1956; children—Nancy Adair, Elizabeth Louise. Editor, Cobb County Times, Marietta, 1956-58, Marietta Daily Jour., 1958-64; pub. Gwinnett Daily News, Lawrenceville, Ga., 1964—; v.p. N. Ga. Radio, Inc., Dalton, 1961—, also dir.; pres. Gwinnett Pub. Co., Lawrenceville, 1964—, also dir. Dir. Ga. Newspaper Service. Trustee Ga. Press Ednl. Found., Atlanta, Atlanta Crime Commn. Served to 1st lt. USAF, 1952-56. Mem. Ga. Press Assn. (pres. 1966-67), Gwinnett (Ga.) C. of C., Kappa Alpha, Sigma Delta Chi. Episcopalian. Kiwanian. Home: 174 Maplewood Dr Lawrenceville GA 30245 Office: 394 Clayton St NE Lawrenceville GA 30245

FOWLER, WILMA SIM (MONK), business exec.; b. Gustine, Tex., Jan. 10, 1920; s. William Sim and Nettie Vera (Estis) F.; student John Tarleton Coll., 1939-40; B.S., U. Tenn., 1948; postgrad. in ins. marketing La. State U.; m. Sarah Frances Livingston, Dec. 20, 1947; children—Sarah Frances, William Hilary. Athletic dir., head coach pub. high schs., Lexington, Tenn., 1948, Corinth, Miss., 1949-50; pres., gen. mgr. Dr. Pepper Seven-Up Bottling Co., Kosciusko, Miss., 1951-67; sr. v.p. Dixie Nat. Life Ins. Co., Jackson, Miss., 1966-69, also dir., mem. exec. com.; sec.-treas., dir. Natchez-Trace Savs. & Loan, Kosciusko, 1965—; mgr. Kosciusko-Attala Airport, Kosciusko, 1956-60; dir. Jackson Savs. & Loan, Attala Bank, Kosciusko, Fisher Oil Guard, Dixie Nat. Life Ins. Co., Dixie Nat. Corp. Chmn., Heart Fund Attala County, 1957. Bd. dirs., pres. Miss. YMCA, mem. Columbia YMCA. Served to comdr. AC, USNR, 1941-46. Decorated Silver Star medal, D.F.C. with Gold Star, Order of Red Star, others. Mem. Naval Air Mus. Found., Nat. Football Hall of Fame Found. (charter), Am. Legion (comdr. 1955), V.F.W., V-5 Assn., Tarleton Ex-Students Assn. (life), T Club Tarleton State Coll., Internat. Platform Assn., T Club U. Tenn., Columbus C. of C., Pi Kappa Alpha. Independent. Presbyn. Mason (Shriner), Old Timer (pres., dir.). Clubs: Nat. Exchange (dist. gov. 1953-54), Kosciusko Exchange (past pres.), Columbus Exchange Columbus Tennis. Established Earl Rudder Scholarship Fund. Home: Liberty Hall PO Box 309 Columbus MS 39701 Office: 1st Columbus Nat Bank Bldg Columbus MS 39701

FOX, BAYNARD FRANCIS, clergyman; b. Stephensport, Ky., Dec. 13, 1910; s. Louis Deedrich and Georgia Ann (McCubbins) F.; A.B., Georgetown (Ky.) Coll., 1958; M.B.A., U. Louisville, 1961; m. Thelma Pearl Shaw, Aug. 27, 1931; children—Baynard L., Randall L., Rebecca Jean (Mrs. Robert W. Jakoby). Ordained to ministry Baptist Ch., 1936; pastor Stephensport Bapt. Ch., 1935-37, Shirley Meml. Bapt. Ch., Prospect, Ky., 1937-42, Macedonia Bapt. Ch., Rockvale, Ky., 1942-43, Elkton (Ky.) Bapt. Ch., 1943-46; area rep. Annuity Bd., So. Bapt. Conv., Dallas, 1946-64, dir. ins. div., 1964-68, v.p. devel. div., 1968-73, v.p. devel. research and tng., 1973—. Home: 5707 Fox Hill Lane Dallas TX 75232 Office: 511 N Akard Bldg Dallas TX 75201

FOX, EDWARD MARK, paper co. exec.; b. Montreal, Que., Can., Apr. 8, 1924; s. George James and Sarah Lucida (Blakely) F.; B.Commerce, McGill U., Montreal, 1950; m. Marilyn Adrienne Huguenin, July 17, 1954; children—Jeffrey Numa, Jorja-An Dubois. Came to U.S., 1954, naturalized, 1960. Sales mgr. Celanese Plastics Co., Newark, 1956-63; marketing mgr. Weyerhaeuser Co., N.Y.C., 1963-66; v.p. marketing Perfect Fit Industries N.Y.C., 1966-67; dir. marketing services Standard Packaging Corp., N.Y.C., 1967-68; v.p. marketing and sales fine papers Eastern Fine Paper Inc. div. Eddy Paper Co. Ltd., Brewer, Me., 1968—, also dir., mem. exec. com.; dir., v.p. parent co., 1970—. Served with Royal Canadian Navy, 1943-45. Mem. McGill U. Alumni Assn., Delta Sigma Phi. Clubs: Canadian of N.Y., Paper (N.Y.C.); Royal Ottawa (Fla.) Golf; Montreal Amateur Athletic. Home: 613 Citrus Ct Melbourne Beach FL 32951 Office: Eastern Fine Paper Inc PO Box 129 Brewer ME 04412

FOX, GERALD GEORGE, city mgr.; b. Chgo., Nov. 11, 1932; s. John E. and Dolores (Chess) F.; B.A., Beloit Coll., 1954; M.P.A., U. Kan., 1963; m. Dolores Condon, Sept. 27, 1958; children—Stephen Edward, Gerald George, Carol Elizabeth. Administrv. asst. to city mgr., San Antonio, 1957-59; city manager, Ennis, Tex., 1959-62, Camden, Ark., 1963-66, Fayetteville, Ark., 1966-69, Wichita Falls, Tex., 1969—. Mem. state and local govt. adv. commn. Office Econ. Opportunity; mem. information and statistics task force to Nat. Adv. Commn. on Criminal Justice Standards and Goals, Dept. Justice. Served with AUS, 1954-56. Mem. Internat. (v.p., dir.), Tex. (bd. dirs., chmn. scholarship com.) city mgmt. assns., Am. Soc. Pub. Adminstrn., Municipal Finance Officers Assn., Tex. Municipal League (mem. human resources com., com. on future), Urban and Regional Information Systems Assn. (pres., dir.), Phi Kappa Psi, Omicron Delta Kappa. Roman Catholic. Rotarian. Contbr. articles to profl. jours. Office: City Manager City Hall Wichita Falls TX 76307

FOX, HARRISON WILLIAM, savs. and loan exec.; b. Galway, N.Y., Aug. 6, 1919; s. Harrison Edgar and Frances Belle (Brown) F.; B.C.E., N.C. State Coll., 1941; B.S., Cal. Inst. Tech., 1945; postgrad. Ind. U., 1964; m. Ruth Pirtle, Nov. 8, 1941; children—Harrison William, Mary (Mrs. Charles Franckle), Charlotte. Partner, Fox & Fox Bldg. Contractor, St. Petersburg, Fla., 1946-56; asst. project engr. Hamilton Standard, St. Petersburg, 1956-58; project engr. Fla. Builders, St. Petersburg, 1958; v.p. Home Fed. Savs. & Loan Assn., St. Petersburg, 1959-63; sr. v.p. Fla. Fed. Savings & Loan Assn. (formerly 1st Fed. Savs. and Loan), St. Petersburg, 1963-73, exec. v.p., 1973—, pres., dir. subsidiary First St. Petersburg Service Corp., 1970—, chmn. bd. subsidiaries Glanville Mortgage Co., 1972—, Southeastern Real Estate Appraisal Corp., 1974—. Mem. Fed. Home Loan Bank Bd. Task Force, 1970-71. Chpt. chmn. constrn. div. United Fund Pinellas County, 1966; mem. gen. contractors exam. bd. City of St. Petersburg, Fla., 1951-56; mem. blue ribbon zoning com. City of St. Petersburg, Fla., 1965-67; mem. Fla. selection com. R.O.T.C., 1971; chmn. Carpenters Joint Apprenticeship Com., St. Petersburg, 1950-53. Bd. dirs., treas., chmn. adv. bd. St. Petersburg Salvation Army. Served as comdr. USNR, 1941-46. Mem. St. Petersburg Home Bldg. Assn. (charter sec., dir. 1946), Contractors and Builders Assn. Pinellas County (charter pres. 1949), St. Petersburg C. of C. (gov. 1968-71), Mortgage Loan Officers Soc. West Coast Fla. (pres. 1965, dir. 1961-66), Am. Orchid Soc., Assn. Gen. Contractors (mem. nat. com. apprenticeship 1952), Suncoasters, Engr. Council, Blue Key, Pine Burr, Scabbard and Blade, Tau Beta Pi, Theta Tau, Navy League (v.p. St. Petersburg 1969-72). Presbyn. (elder, deacon 1951). Mason. Clubs: Yacht, Commerce (St. Petersburg); Tower (Tampa); Citrus (Orlando, Fla.). Home: 3230 Walnut St NE St Petersburg FL 33704 Office: PO Box 1509 St Petersburg FL 33731

FOX, HERBERT ADOLF, oil co. exec.; b. Houston, June 19, 1934; s. Herbert A. and Doris M. (McCulland) Fuchs; B.S. Tex. A. and M. U., 1956; m. Lanatter M. Gabriel, July 29, 1956; children—Jill M., Keith L. Process engr. Signal Oil and Gas Co., Los Angeles, 1960-64, tech. supr., 1964-68; project mgr. Murphy Oil Corp., El Dorado, Ark., 1968-73, mgr. Crude Oil Supply and Transportation Div., 1973—. Served to capt. USAF, 1957-61. Registered profl. engr., Tex., La., Ark., Wis. Mem. Am. Petroleum Inst., Am. Inst. Chem. Engrs., Houston Engr. Sci. Soc., Shreveport Petroleum Club. Club: El Dorado Golf and Country. Home: 1528 West Cedar El Dorado AR 71730 Office: 200 Jefferson El Dorado AR 71730

FOX, HOMER MCGRADY, chemist; b. Batesville, Ark., Apr. 15, 1920; s. Homer William and Alta Mae (Baker) F.; A.B., Hendrix Coll., 1941; postgrad. Ga. Sch. Tech., 1941-42; m. Doris Mae Snow, July 31, 1948; children—Kendall Mark, Lisa Lynn. Engr., E.I. duPont de Nemours & Co., Charleston, W.Va., 1942-43; with Phillips Petroleum Co., Bartlesville, Okla., 1946—, group leader combustion, 1949-52, research project mgr., 1952-72, br. mgr. petroleum products, 1972—. Served to comdr. USNR, 1943-46; PTO. Mem. Soc. Automotive Engrs., Am. Inst. Aeros. and Astronautics, Electrochem. Soc. Methodist. Contbr. articles profl. jours. Patentee in field. Home: 728 Winding Way Bartlesville OK 74003 Office: Phillips Research Center Bartlesville OK 74004

FOX, JACK LEE, food co. exec.; b. Balt., Nov. 29, 1932; s. Martin and Lillian Mae (Scherr) F.; B.S. in Indsl. Engring., Lehigh U., 1957; m. D. Beverly Cole, Feb. 4, 1954; children—Linda A., Steven I., Jeffry H. With Austin Biscuit Co., Balt. (now div. Fairmont Foods Co.), 1957—, v.p., gen. mgr., 1969—; dir. Stauffer Biscuit Co., York, Pa.; lectr. in field. Mem. Biscuit and Cracker Mfrs. Assn. (dir.), Nat. Peanut Council (dir.), Am. Inst. Indsl. Engrs. (pres. Balt. 1962), Toastmasters Internat. (lt. gov. Md. 1964-65). Home: 300 Edinburgh Dr Cary NC 27602 Office: PO Box 2536 Raleigh NC 27602

FOX, JOHN NIXON, educator; b. Crescent, Okla., Sept. 18, 1932; s. John N. and Maude (Wells) F.; B.S., U. Okla., 1955, M.Engring., 1962; Ph.D., U. Cal. at Los Angeles, 1967; m. Evelyn Louise Conley, June 28, 1955; children—Kathleen Sue, Caroline Louise, John Nixon III, Connie Leigh. Engr., U. Okla., 1960-62; sr. specialist in engring. mgmt. N. Am. Rockwell, 1962-68; prof. engring. U. Tex. at Arlington, 1968—. Dir. Data Tab Computer Corp., Dallas; cons. LTV. Mgr., coach Little League Baseball, Arlington, 1968—. Served with USAF, 1955-58; now capt. Res. Fellow Nat. Safety Found., 1965-67. Registered profl. engr., Tex., Okla. Mem. Am. Inst. Aeros. and Astronautics, Air Force Assn., Human Factors Soc., Am. Soc. Engring. Edn., Sigma Xi, Alpha Sigma Phi, Alpha Phi Omega, Mason (32 degree). Club: Optimist. Home: 1804 Winewood St Arlington TX 76010

FOX, LAURA (MRS. VERNON B. FOX), educator; b. Albion, Mich., July 5, 1916; d. Arthur Holmes and Grace (Fellows) Ellerby; A.B., Fla. State U., 1955, M.S., 1958; student Albion Coll., 1938-40; m. Vernon B. Fox, Mar. 22, 1941; children—Karen M., Vernon B., Loraine G. Tchr. biology Leon High Sch., Tallahassee, 1955—. Mem. Am. Assn. U. Women. Nat. Assn. Biology Tchrs., Nat. Assn. Sci. Tchrs., Nat., Fla. edn. assns., Kappa Delta Pi. Home: 644 Voncile Av Tallahassee FL 32303

FOX, LESTER IRVING, physician; b. Lawrence, Mass., Aug. 19, 1912; s. James L. and Ethel (Hacker) F.; student Bates Coll., 1930-31; A.B., Johns Hopkins, 1934; M.D., U. Md., 1938; m. June White, Apr. 29, 1946; children—Susan Scott, William Peyton, Elizabeth Forrest. Commd. 1st lt. M.C., U.S. Army, 1938, advanced through grades to maj., 1945; intern Quincy City Hosp., 1939-40; active duty, 1940-42; Japanese prisoner of war, 1942-45; resident physician VA Hosp., Richmond, Va., 1947-48; resident allergist, instr. medicine Med. Coll. Va., 1948-49; chief medicine, 1949-63, chief profl. services U.S. Army Health Clinic, Fort Monroe, Va., 1949-73; ret., 1973. Decorated Silver Star medal, Purple Heart. Diplomate Am. Bd. Internal Medicine. Fellow A.C.P., Am. Geriatric Assn.; asso. fellow Am. Coll. Cardiology; mem. Am. Acad. Allergy, Am., Peninsula (2d v.p.) heart assns., Peninsula Acad. Medicine, Briarcliffe Acres Assn. Clubs: Army-Navy (Washington); Beachwood Golf (N. Myrtle Beach, S.C.). Home: 150 Briarcliff Acres PO Box 2426 North Myrtle Beach SC 29582

FOX, LOUIS JOHN, city mgr.; b. St. Louis, Sept. 22, 1943; s. Everett John and Bernice (Gromp) F.; A.A., Harris Tchrs. Coll., 1963; B.S. in Pub. Adminstrn., U. Mo., 1965; M.Pub. Adminstrn., U. Kan., 1967; m. Jean Marie Starnes, Feb. 17, 1968; 1 dau., Sarah Beth. Adminstrv. analyst City of Wichita (Kan.), 1966-68; asst. city mgr. City of Overland Park (Kan.), 1968-72; city mgr. City of Orange (Tex.), 1972—. Served with USMCR, 1967-68. Mem. Internat. City Mgmt. Assn., Am. Soc. Pub. Adminstrn., Municipal Finance Officers Assn. Rotarian. Home: 2418 Fairway St Orange TX 77630 Office: PO Box 520 Orange TX 77630

FOX, MARK, accountant; b. N.Y.C., Apr. 28, 1923; s. Abraham and Rose (Rosenbaum) F.; B.B.A., Coll., City N.Y., 1943; m. Del Franklin, Jan. 15, 1951; children—Andrew Eric, Steven Alan. Sr. accountant Samuel Fischman & Co., C.P.A.'s, 1948-51; mgr., supr. J.K. Lasser & Co., C.P.A.'s, 1951-59; gen. practice pub. accounting, tax cons., mgmt. cons., Sarasota, Fla., 1959—. Served with AUS, 1943-46. Mem. Am., Fla. insts. C.P.A.'s, N.Y. State Soc. C.P.A.'s. Mason (32 deg. Shriner), Elk. Club: University. Home: 4634 Higel Av Sarasota FL 33581 Office: 1272 N Palm Av Sarasota FL 33577

FOX, PETER FRANKLIN, JR., theater exec.; b. Sweetwater, Tex., May 1, 1939; s. Peter Franklin and Corese Clair (Hembree) F.; B.B.A., So. Meth. U., 1962, M.F.A., 1969; m. Sheila Kay Young, Apr. 14, 1963; children—Peter Franklin, Fleur Diane. Intern dir. Midlane (Tex.) Community Theatre, 1968-69; mng. dir. Amarillo (Tex.) Little Theatre, 1969—. Founder, pres. Tex. Non-Profit Theatres, Inc., 1970. Adviser, High Sch. Inter-Act Club; mem. adv. bd. Nat. Youth Project Using Minibikes. Bd. dirs. Amarillo Dance Theatre. Served to 1st. lt. USAF, 1962-66. Mem. Am. Theatre Assn., Southwest Theatre Conf., Amarillo Fine Arts Assn. (dir.), Delta Sigma Pi, Lambda Chi Alpha. Democrat. Presbyn. Rotarian. Home: 5303 Berget Amarillo TX 79106 Office: 2019 Civic Circle Amarillo TX 79105

FOX, RICHARD CHARLES, educator; b. Athens, Mich., Sept. 5, 1925; s. Marion Allison and Mary Ruth (Snyder) F.; B.S., Mich. State U., 1948, M.F., 1949, Ph.D., 1958; m. Barbara Eileen Wright, Mar. 22, 1947; children—James R., Bruce A., Joel S. Instr. botany, Oxford, O., 1949-51; forest entomologist Mich. Conservation Dept., 1951-55; instr. entomology Mich. State U., 1955-58; prof. entomology Clemson U., 1958—; square dance caller. Served with AUS, 1943-45. Mem. Entomol. Soc. Am., S.C. Entomol. Soc., Entomol. Soc. Washington, Ga. Entomol. Soc., Sigma Xi, Phi Sigma, Xi Sigma Phi, Gamma Sigma Delta. Republican. Home: PO Box 888 Clemson SC 29631

FOX, SAMUEL MICKLE, III, physician, assn. exec.; b. Andalusia, Pa., 1923; M.D., U. Pa., 1947. Intern Pa. Hosp., Phila., 1947-48, resident in medicine 1950; resident fellow gastro-enterology U. Pa. Hosp., 1948-49, resident in pathology, 1949; acting chief gastro-enterology Nat. Naval Med. Center, Bethesda, Md., 1950-51, chief cardiological services, 1954; head Dept. Clin. Investigation, U.S. Naval Med. Research Unit 3, Cairo, Egypt, 1954-56; chief cardiological services, U.S. Naval Hosp., Portsmouth, Va., 1956-57; sr. staff Nat. Heart Inst., NIH, 1957-59, co-chief cardiodynamics, 1959-61, asst. dir., 1961-62; cons., NASA, 1959-63, mem. research adv. com. for bio-tech. and human research, 1963-68; dep. chief Heart Disease Control Program, USPHS, 1963-64, chief, 1965-70. Asst. instr. medicine U. Pa., 1948-49, instr. pathology, 1949, instr. medicine, 1950; vis. prof. medicine Ein Shams U., also Kasr-el-Aini Faculties Medicine, Cairo, 1955-56; clin. asst. prof. medicine Georgetown U., 1959-70; prof. medicine George Washington U., 1970—. Served to comdr. M.C., USNR, 1950-57. Diplomate Am. Bd. Internal Medicine. Fellow Am. Coll. Cardiology (pres. 1972-73), A.C.P.; A.A.A.S.; mem. A.M.A., Am. Heart Assn. Address: 7400 Fairfax Rd Bethesda MD 20014

FOX, THEODORE BERT, educator; b. Jacksonville, Ala., Oct. 25, 1912; s. Cass and Jennie Magnolia (Taylor) F.; student Selma U., 1929-30, Gen. Motors Inst., 1935-36; certificate Ala. State U., 1954, Allen Electric Co. Sch., 1950, Ala. A. and M. U., 1956; m. Agnes Marshall Watley, Apr. 7, 1933; children—Sydney (Mrs. Eugene Reid, Jr.), June (Mrs. J. Mason Davis), Barbara (Mrs. Franklin Todd), Sandra (Mrs. Thomas Sudduth). Supr., Anniston (Ala.) Army Ordnance Depot, 1940-46; vocational instr. Anniston City Bd. Edn., 1946—, tchr. Anniston Area Vocational Tech. Sch. Mem. City Council, Jacksonville, Ala., 1968—; bd. dirs. Ala. Democratic Com., 1970—. Pres. Jacksonville Civic League; bd. dirs. Jacksonville Child Care Center; mem. exec. bd. Choccolocco council Boy Scouts Am.; bd. dirs. Cottaquilla council Boy Scouts Am. Recipient Silver Beaver award Boy Scouts Am., 1962. Mem. N.E.A., Anniston Edn. Assn. (pres.), N.A.A.C.P. Baptist. (pres. Sunday sch., Bapt. tng. Union Congress). Home: 157 Spring St Jacksonville AL 36265 Office: Anniston Area Vocational Tech Sch Anniston AL 36201

FOX, VERNON BRITTAIN, educator, criminologist; b. Boyne Falls, Mich., Apr. 25, 1916; s. John Lorenzo and Ethel (Hamilton) F.; A.B., Mich. State U., 1940, certificate in social work, 1941, M.A., 1943, Ph.D., 1949; m. Laura Grace Ellerby, Mar. 22, 1941; children—Karen, Vernon, Loraine. Dir. case work, coach Starr Commonwealth, Albion, Mich., 1941-42; psychologist State Prison So. Mich., 1942-46, dep. warden, 1949-52; psychologist Cassiday Lake Tech. Sch., Mich. Dept. Corrections, 1946-49; prof. criminology Fla. State U., 1952—, also dir. delinquency control inst. Mem. Fla. Adv. council on Adult Corrections and Prison Industries; mem. Gov.'s Adv. Council Law Enforcement Edn. Bd. visitors U.S. Army Mil. Police Sch., Fort Gordon, Ga. Served with AUS, 1945-46. Named Outstanding Prof. of Yr., Fla. State U., 1960, 68, Alumni Prof. of Yr., 1970; personal papers and publs. in Archive of Contemporary Hist., U. Wyo. Mem. Am. Correctional Assn., Am. Sociol. Soc., Fla. Psychol. Assn., C. of C., Omicron Delta Kappa, Delta Tau Kappa (chancellor Southeastern U.S.). Clubs: Capital City Country, Tallahassee Exchange. Author: Violence Behind Bars 1956; Guidelines for Education in Corrections in Community and Junior Colleges, 1969; Introduction to Corrections, 1972; Handbook for Volunteers in Juvenile Courts, 1973; co-author: Introduction to the Criminal Justice System, 1974. Mem. internat. bd. editors Exerpta Criminologica; bd. editors Internat. Behavioral Scientist. Home: 644 Voncile Av Tallahassee FL 32303

FOY, THOMAS JOSEPH, JR., banker; b. Charleston, S.C., Oct. 6, 1925; s. Thomas Joseph and Ethel Vivian (Purse) F.; student Coll. Charleston, 1942-43, The Citadel, 1946-48, U. Wis. Sch. Banking, 1956-58; m. Nona Willette Snipes, June 4, 1949; children—Barry Joseph, Thomas Patrick, Lee Ann, Janice Maureen, Thomas Joseph. With Citizens and So. Nat. Bank of S.C., Columbia, 1948—, v.p., 1965—, adv. bd., 1965—. Instr., Columbia chpt. Am. Inst. Banking, 1966-67. Treas. Spartanburg County Heart Fund, 1958-59. Bd. dirs. Salvation Army, Spartanburg, 1957-58, United Cerebral Palsy, Spartanburg, 1957-58. Friendship Center Columbia, Central Tb Assn. Served with USNR, 1944-46. Mem. Am. Inst. Banking (pres. chpt. 1959-60, bd. govs. chpt. 1960-61), Nat. Assn. Bank Auditors and Comptrollers (pres. conf. 1957-58, nat. program commn. 1966), Internat. Adminstrv. Mgmt. Soc. (v.p. 1971-72), Bank Adminstrn. Inst. (chmn. nominating com. 1970), Columbia C. of C. Lion (bd. dirs. 1970-71). Clubs: Citadel (treas. 1956-57) (Spartanburg); Columbia (S.C.) Country (bd. dirs. 1970—, treas. 1970—). Home: 3835 Rockbridge Rd Columbia SC 29206 Office: PO Box 727 Columbia SC 29202

FOYE, LAURANCE V., JR., physician, govt. ofcl.; b. Seattle, 1925; M.D., U. Cal., 1952. Intern San Francisco Gen. Hosp., 1952-53; resident in internal medicine VA Hosp., San Francisco, 1953-55, 56-57, attending physician in medicine, 1957-58, asst. chief med. services, 1958-66, chief Cancer Chemotherapy Sect., 1960-66; resident in internal medicine Stanford Hosp., 1955-56; chief Cancer Therapy Evaluation Br., Nat. Cancer Inst., 1966-68, chief Clin. Investigation Br., 1968-70; dir. ednl. services VA Central Office, Washington, 1970-73, asst. chief med. dir. for acad. affairs, 1973-74, dep. chief med. dir., 1974—. Research asso. Cancer Research Inst., also asst. clin. prof. medicine U. Cal., 1962-66. Diplomate Am. Bd. Internal Medicine. Fellow A.C.P.; mem. Am. Soc. Clin. Oncology. Office: VA Central Office Vermont at H St NW Washington DC 20420

FRACHTMAN, HIRSH JULIAN, physician; b. Houston, Sept. 2, 1913; s. Henry and Sophia (Mesinger) F.; B.A. with distinction, Rice U., 1933; M.D., U. Tex., 1937; m. Marijane Lowenstein, July 27, 1941; children—Richard, Robert, Michael. Intern, Touro Infirmary, New Orleans, 1937, resident, 1938; fellow in medicine Tulane Med. Coll., 1939; practice medicine, specializing in internal medicine and cardiology, Houston, 1946—. Asso. clin. prof. medicine Baylor U., Houston, 1964. Served to col. M.C., AUS, 1940-46. Decorated Bronze Star medal. Diplomate Am. Bd. Internal Medicine. Fellow Am. Coll. Cardiology; mem. Am. Soc. Internal Medicine, Phi Beta Kappa, Alpha Omega Alpha. Contbr. articles to profl. jours. Home: 5334 Paisley Lane Houston TX 77035 Office: Hermann Profl Bldg Houston TX 77025

FRAISER, RONALD DOUGLAS, broadcaster; b. Yazoo City, Miss., Sept. 1, 1941; s. Paul D. and Ruby M. (Morales) F.; student Hinds Jr. Coll., 1958-59, So. Ill. U., 1962-63; m. Mary Bankston, July 28, 1968; children—Dawn, Michelle. With WNOE, New Orleans, 1963-64, WABB, Mobile, Ala., 1964-66, WHOO, Orlando, Fla., 1966-67, WLEE, Richmond, Va., 1968; program dir. WNOR, Norfolk, Va., 1969, WPOP, Hartford, Conn., 1969-71, WKKE, Asheville, N.C., 1971-72, WZUU, Milw., 1972, WYOO, Mpls., 1972-73, WRBC, Jackson, Miss., 1973—; announcer Balt. Orioles AA Farm Club, Asheville, 1971-72; singer and composer. Mem. Midwest Sportscasters Assn. (sec.-treas.). Composer: Summer Skies, 1961; A Wish for Love, 1961; Send Me a Little Girl, 1963; I'm Not Lonely Anymore, 1963; Anytime at All, 1965; Dianne, 1965; Summer With

You, 1967; Another Girl, 1967. Home: Rt 8 Box 194 Jackson MS 39213 Office: PO Box 9801 Jackson MS 39206

FRALISH, MARVIN LEWIS, JR., ednl. adminstr.; b. High Wycombe, Eng., Nov. 6, 1943; came to U.S., 1947, naturalized, 1953; s. Marvin Lewis and Brenda G. (Smith) F.; student U. Ga., 1962-63; A.B., Ga. State Coll., 1966; M.Ednl. Adminstrn., Ga. State U., 1970; m. Mildred Christine Sorrow, Sept. 27, 1963; children—Marcus Paul, Stephan David, Gregory Brian. With Atlanta (Ga.) Jour., 1961-62; shipping clk. Grinnell Co., Atlanta, 1962-64; English asst. Ga. State Coll., 1964-66; secondary tchr. Cobb County Bd. Edn. (Ga.), 1966-67; secondary tchr. DeKalb County Bd. Edn., 1967-69, elementary tchr., 1969-70; prin. Oakcliff Sch., Doraville, Ga., 1970—. Mem. DeKalb County Bicentennial Com., 1974. Recipient Achievement in Edn. award Jr. C. of C., Atlanta, 1970. Mem. Ga. (rep. 1971), DeKalb County (rep. 1968-71, pres. 1973-74) edn. assns., DeKalb Classroom Tchrs. Assn. (sec. 1970), DeKalb Elementary Prins. Assn. (rep. 1971-72, del. to N.E.A. 1973-74), Ga. Assn. Educators (legislative com. 1974), Improvement Assn. (publicity chmn. 1971-72), P.T.A., Assn. Supervision and Curriculum Devel., Ga. Dept. Elementary Prins., Ga. State U. Alumni Assn., Pi Kappa Alpha Alumni Assn. (v.p. 1974—), Sigma Tau Delta. Club: Civitan (chmn. jr. civitan com. 1971-72). Home: 4348 Tucker North Court Tucker GA 30084 Office: 3150 Willow Oak Way Doraville GA 30340

FRAMPTON, WILLIAM WALLACE, headmaster; b. Charleston, S.C., Jan. 18, 1934; s. William Horlbeck and Grace Pauline (Haltiwanger) F.; B.S. in Edn., Ga. Tchrs. Coll. at Statesboro, 1958; postgrad. Appalachian State U. at Boone, N.C., 1962-63; m. Elizabeth Garden Pringle Haigh, Dec. 29, 1960; children—William Wallace, Alexander Chisolm, Elizabeth Garden. Tchr. Riverland Terrace Elementary Sch., James Island, S.C., 1958-59; tchr. Chicorn Grade Sch., Charleston Heights, S.C., 1959-61, asst. prin., 1961-63; prin. Alice Birney Elementary Sch., North Charleston, S.C., 1963-70; headmaster Charleston Day Sch., 1970—. Mem. Tri County Mental Health Bd., 1969-71; mem. exec. bd. Charleston Area Mental Health Assn., 1970, Cooper River Council P.T.A.'s, 1965-68; bd. dirs. Reading Clinic Charleston, 1969-70. Mem. Nat. Assn. Elementary Sch. Prins., Preservation Soc. Charleston. Clubs: Carolina Yacht, St. Cecilia Soc., Lets Dance, Lords Proprietors Ball Assn. Home: 98 King St Charleston SC 29401 Office: 51 State St Charleston SC 29401

FRANCE, ROGER JAMES, electronic co. exec.; b. Bismarck, N.D., Feb. 8, 1930; s. Oscar J. and Rebecca (Neuman) F.; B.S., Jamestown Coll., 1952; student George Washington U., 1960. Exec. v.p. Control Sci. Corp., Alexandria, Va., 1962-64, pres., 1964—, dir., 1962; pres., dir. Aquarius Enterprises, Inc., Alexandria, 1969—; treas., dir. Spectra Research Corp., Alexandria, 1969—; dir. Amron, Inc., Alexandria, Va. Served with AUS, 1953-55. Mason. Home: 10904 Ambleside Ct Reston VA 22070 Office: 4810 Beauregard St Alexandria VA 22312

FRANCIS, EUGENE A., educator; b. Christiansted, St. Croix, V.I., Oct. 27, 1927; s. Alfred and Leona (Williams) F.; B.A., Poly. Inst. P.R., 1949; M.A., Columbia, 1951; postgrad. Pa. State U., 1959-60; m. Antonia P. Martinez Rivera, Sept. 4, 1955. Faculty, U. P.R., Mayaguez, 1951—, prof. math., 1966—, chmn. math. dept., 1967-72, asso. dean studies, 1972—. Spl. lectr. math. Interamerican U. P.R., 1951, 56; pres. Commn. on Math., CEEB, P.R. Office, 1966-68; math. cons. Dept. Edn. P.R., 1964—. Served with AUS, 1954-56. Mem. Am. Math. Soc., Math. Assn. Am., N.Y. Acad. Scis., A.A.A.S., Nat. Council Tchrs. Math., Asociación Puertorriqueña de Maestros de Matemáticas (pres. 1970-72), Pi Mu Epsilon, Phi Kappa Phi. Reviewer, Math. Tchr., 1970—.

FRANCIS, HORACE, supt. schs.; b. Stockman, Tex., Dec. 18, 1920; s. Eugene A. and Medie (Murray) F.; B.S., Stephen F. Austin State Coll., 1941, M.A., 1950; m. Johnnie Williams, Feb. 21, 1942; children—Horace Francis, David Anthony. Prin. pub. schs., Stockman, Tex., 1941-43, Garrison, Tex., 1948-51; supt. pub. schs., Garrison, 1951—. Postmaster, Stockman, Tex., 1942-52. Mem. Nat., Tex. edn. assns., Tex. Assn. Sch. Adminstrs., Tex. Small Schs. Assn. (past pres.), Univ. Interscholastic League (legislative council), Phi Delta Kappa. Methodist. Mason. Lion. Home: PO Box 510 Garrison TX 75946

FRANCIS, JAMES HARRIS, physician; b. Memphis, Tex., Feb. 14, 1928; s. Roy N. and Zephyr Lee (Wills) F.; B.A., Tex. U., 1956, M.D., 1959; m. Bera Meade Miller, May 5, 1951; children—Alan Kirk, Marsha Ann. Intern Orange County (Cal.) Gen. Hosp., 1959-60; individual practice medicine, Fullerton, Cal., 1959; practice medicine specializing in family practice, Garland, Tex., 1961—; chief staff Garland Clinic & Hosp., 1965-66, now mem. staff; mem. staff Meml. Hosp. of Garland. Pres. HFC Corp., Garland, 1963—; adviser med. asst. program Dallas County Jr. Coll., 1972, 73; student preceptor instr. Southwest Med. Sch., U. Tex., 1971—. Bd. dirs. Garland (Tex.) YMCA, 1967-68; bd. dirs. Garland Clinic and Hosp., 1967-73, vice moderator bd., 1973—; bd. dirs. Dallas County Med. Assts., 1973—. Diplomate Am. Bd. Family Practice. Mem. C. of C., Dallas County Med. Soc., Am. Acad. Family Practice (v.p. 1971—, pres. 1974—), Tex. Med. Assn., Dallas County Med. Soc., A.M.A. (Physicians Recognition award 1970—). Mem. Ch. of Christ. Home: 3106 Ridgedale St Garland TX 75041 Office: 325 N Shiloh Rd Garland TX 75042

FRANCIS, JAMES WALLACE, real estate and ins. broker; b. Ballinger, Tex., Aug. 21, 1895; s. James Wallace and Kate (Fentress) F.; student Tex. A. and M. U., 1918; m. Roberta Beryl May, Feb. 28, 1924; 1 dau., Beryl Kathryn (Mrs. Beryl F. Ponton). Equipment engr. Tex. Hwy. Dept., 1919-25; owner James W. Francis Co., 1925-33, James W. Francis Truck Co., 1927-33, Motor Equipment Corp., 1930-57, Delphian Devel. Corp., 1927-33; bonds, ins. rec. agt. and real estate broker, San Antonio, 1958—; dir. Valley-Hi Nat. Bank. Served as 1st lt. Signal Corps, Aviation Sect., U.S. Army, 1917-18, from capt. to lt. col. ordnance, AUS, 1942-45. Mem. San Antonio Safety Council (pres. 1957-58), U.S. Hwy. 87 Improvement Assn. (pres. 1960, 71), San Antonio C. of C. (1st v.p. 1957, dir. 1955-57), Tex. Good Roads Assn. (dir.). Presbyn. (chmn. bd. deacons, mem. bench elders). Mason (32 deg., Shriner). Clubs: Quarterback (pres. 1951), Conopus (dir. 1936), San Antonio (1st v.p. 1953), San Antonio Country. Home: 214 Terrell Rd San Antonio TX 78209

FRANCIS, JOHN HUBERT, JR., electric utility exec.; b. Meridian, Miss., Apr. 27, 1928; s. John H. and Mary (Stevenson) F.; student Miss. State Coll., 1945-46; B.A., U. Ala., 1952; M.A. La. State U., 1966; Ph.D. (hon.), Hamilton Coll., 1973; m. Carolynne B. Vann, Jan. 23, 1949; 1 dau., Kathryn Alayne. Staff asst. U. (Ala.) Press Bur., 1952; employee information supr. So. Bell Tel. & Tel. Co., Atlanta, 1953-54; sr. dist. rep. Am. Petroleum Inst., 1955-59; asso. dir. La Petroleum Council, 1959-67; Southwest pub. relations mgr. Humble Oil & Refining Co., 1967-73; dir. corporate communications Fla. Power & Light Co., 1973—. Pres., La. Travel Council, 1967; mem. adv. com. La. Tourist Devel. Commn.; lectr. Sch. Communications, U. Houston, 1970-73. Served from pvt. to staff sgt. AUS, 1946-48, capt., 1950-52; lt. col. Res. ret. Recipient Inter Frat. Congress publ. award 7 times, 1950-56, 59, Citation for Service, La. Oil and Gas Industry, Distinguished Service to Journalism award; Distinguished Service award Tex. Tourist Council. named Man of the Year, 1959, 1960; named Friend of Tex. Press, 1971; hon. Lifetime Mem., Gulf Coast Press Assn. Mem. Inter Frat. Congress (pres. 1958-59), C. of C., Res. Officers Assn., Pub. Relations Soc. Am., Tex. Bur. Econ. Understanding, Assn. Petroleum Writers, Fla. Press Assn., Internat. Platform Assn., Fla. Assn. Broadcasters, Assn. Edn. Journalism, Sigma Delta Chi (pres. 1960-61; Distinguished Service award), Omicron Delta Kappa, Theta Kappa Omega (nat. pres. 1950-56), Kappa Alpha. Kiwanian. Clubs: Bankers, Unicorn. Home: 8265 SW 114th St Miami FL 33156 Office: PO Box 3100 Miami FL 33101

FRANCIS, LEON WALTER, dentist; b. Prescott, Ark., Mar. 17, 1926; s. John Ricks and Mary Ada (Still) F.; student Ark. A. and M. Coll., 1944-46; B.S., U. Ark., 1947; D.D.S., U. Tenn., 1962; m. Esther Lougene Thornton, May 22, 1948; children—Jacquelyn Ruth, Lee Thornton. High sch. tchr. math. and sci., Altheimer, Ark., 1947-50; cotton farmer, Altheimer, 1950-59; practice dentistry, Pine Bluff, Ark., 1963—; farm operator, 1967—. Pres. Pine Bluff Bd. Edn., 1969-71. Bd. dirs. Teen Town, pres., 1967, 68. Served with USNR, 1944-46. Mem. Am., Ark. dental assns., S.E. Ark., Jefferson County dental socs., Aircraft Owners and Pilots Assn., Am. Farm Bur. Fedn., Omicron Kappa Upsilon. Mason (32 deg., Shriner), Kiwanian (dir. 1964-66). Club: Pine Bluff Country. Home: 25 Longmeadow Pine Bluff AR 71601 Office: 1616 Cherry St Pine Bluff AR 71601

FRANCIS, LEWIS, physician; b. Troy, O., Dec. 16, 1921; s. Jesse Bernard and Joy Louise (Miller) F.; B.A., Ohio State U., 1943, M.D., 1945; m. Jean Davis, June 14, 1941; children—Carol (Mrs. Stephen Little), Patricia (Mrs. Kenneth McAshan), Joy. Intern Harris Hosp., Ft. Worth, 1945-46; resident Mass. Gen. Hosp., Boston, 1948-50; instrn., asst. anesthesia Harvard U. Med. Sch., Boston, 1950; practice medicine, Oakland, Cal., 1950-51; instr. anesthesia Stanford Med. Sch., San Francisco, 1952; dir. anesthesia Central Bapt. Hosp., Lexington, Ky., 1954—; asst. prof. clin. anesthesia U. Ky. Med. Sch., Lexington, 1962—; cons. anesthesia USPHS, Lexington. Mem. Fayette County Republican Adv. Com., 1967-71, Ky. Ednl. Med. Polit. Action Com., 1965-72. Bd. dirs. Central Ky. Youth Music Symphony, 1964-65, Lexington YMCA, 1963—; chmn. bd. trustees Sayre Sch., 1963. Served with AUS, 1942-46, USPHS, 1946-48. Recipient Community Service to Youth award YMCA, Lexington, 1965. Diplomate Am. Bd. Anesthesiology. Fellow Am. Coll. Anesthesiologists; mem. Am., Ky. (pres. 1959) socs. anesthesiologists, Internat. Anesthesia Research Soc., A.M.A., Ky., Fayette County med. socs., Assn. Am. Physicians and Surgeons, Phi Chi. Presbyn. (deacon 1961-64, trustee 1964-66). Lion (dir. 1965-66). Club: Lansdowne (Lexington,). Home: 3022 Breckenwood Dr Lexington KY 40502 Office: 300 Nunn Bldg Lexington KY 40507

FRANCIS, RICARDO HUGH, lawyer; b. San Juan, P.R., July 4, 1935; s. Hugh Richard and Mercedes (Lajara) F.; B.A., Harvard, 1955, LL.M., 1962; LL.B., U. P.R., 1958; m. Vanessa Vassallo, June 27, 1958; children—Valerie, Hildren. Admitted to P.R. bar; partner firm Trias, Saldana & Francis, Hato Rey, P.R.; prof. taxation, corp. law and bus. planning U. P.R. Law Sch., 1962—. Dir. Boricua Broadcasting Corp., Mercantile Investment Co., Enterprising Realty Corp., P.R. Auto Corp., Hato Rey Supply, Inc. Mem. adv. council to Gov. P.R. Mem. Am., P.R. bar assns., Am. Assn. Trial Lawyers, Nat. Assn. Mfrs., Nu Sigma Beta. Clubs: San Juan Yacht; Metropolitan Shooting. Home: 603 Condominio San Luis San Juan PR 00609 Office: 1900 Popular Center Bldg Hato Rey PR 00609

FRANCIS, WILLIAM SAMUEL, JR., lawyer; b. Atlanta, July 24, 1941; s. William Samuel and Alice Wathern (Wood) F.; A.B., Coll. William and Mary, 1964, J.D., 1967; m. Carolyn Gray Andrews, Mar. 31, 1962; children—William Samuel III, Marh Catherine. Admitted to Va. bar, 1967; asso. Bowles & Boyd, Richmond, Va., 1967-70; partner Bowles & Boyd, Richmond, 1971-73; partner Francis & Hubard, Richmond, 1973—. Mem. staff Richmond Legal Aid, 1969-71; legal counsel Richmond Youth Emergency Service of Richmond Area Community Council, 1971—. Area chmn. William and Mary Fund, Boy Scouts Am., Mem. Am., Va., Richmond bar assns., Va. State Bar, Va. Trial Lawyers Assn., Am. Judicature Soc., William and Mary Alumni Assn., Marshall-Wythe Sch. Law Alumni Assn. Home: 1010 Dinwiddie Av Richmond VA 23229 Office: 1203 E Main St Richmond VA 23219

FRANCO, JOHAN (HENRI GUSTAVE), composer; b. Zaandam, Netherlands, July 12, 1908; s. S. Franco and Margaretha J. E. C. (Gosschalk) F.; grad. First Coll., The Hague; studied composition with Willem Pijper, Amsterdam, 4 yrs.; m. Eloise Lavrischeff, Mar. 28, 1948. Came to U.S., 1934, naturalized, 1942. Entire program of his compositions was presented at Town Hall, N.Y., 1938; collaborated with Oscar Thompson on Sect. on Contemporary Dutch composers in the Cyclopedia of Music and Musicians, 1938. Served with AUS, 1942-43. Mem. Broadcast Music Inc., Am. Composers Alliance, Southeastern Composers League. Prin. works: 5 symphonies; Divertimento for Flute and Strings, 1946; many songs, 2 cello sonatas, 1 viola sonata 6 partitas piano, 10 partitas and other compositions for carillon, classical guitar, flute, saxophone; As the Prophets Foretold (cantata); Fantasy for cello and orch.; The Stars Look Down (oratorio); The Prodigal string quartet; Songs of the Spirit for soprano and woodwind quintet; The Song of Life (for mixed chorus a cappella); Concerto Lirico No. 1 for violin and orch.; Concerto Lirico No. 2 for cello and orch.; Concerto Lirico No. 3 for piano and orch.; Concerto Lirico No. 4 for percussion and orch.; Concerto Lirico No. 5 for guitar and orch.; incidental music for the Book of Job, Romans by St. Paul; the Pilgrim's Progress, Electra and the Tempest for the Everyman Players produced and directed by Orlin Corey; Supplication-Revelation-Triumph for orch.; also recs. Home: 403 Lake Dr Virginia Beach VA 23451

FRANDSEN, HENRY, educator; b. Chgo., May 21, 1933; s. Henry and Catherine Anna (Hansen) F.; B.S., U. Ill., 1957, M.S., 1959, Ph.D., 1961; m. Jean M. Dading, Nov. 7, 1953; children—Peter T., Karen M., Wendy J. Asst. prof. math. Clark U., Worcester, Mass., 1961-66, dir. NSF Summer Inst., 1966; asso. prof. math. Wheaton Coll., Norton, Mass., 1966-67; asso. prof. math. and edn. U. Tenn., Knoxville, 1967-71, prof., 1971—, dir. Prospective Tchr. Fellowship Program, 1968-70. Cons., Mitre Corp., Bedford, Mass., 1963-67. Served to lt. (j.g.) USNR, 1952-56; ETO. Mem. Am. Math. Soc., Am. Assn. U. Profs., A.A.A.S., Nat. Council Tchrs. Math., Sigma Xi, Pi Mu Epsilon, Kappa Delta Pi, Phi Delta Kappa. Episcopalian. Contbr. chpt. to Second Handbook of Research on Teaching, 1973. Home: 7912 Bennington Dr Knoxville TN 37919

FRANK, EUGENE MAXWELL, bishop; b. Cherryvale, Kan., Dec. 11, 1907; s. Ade W. and Emma W. (Maxwell) F.; B.S., Kan. State Tchrs. Coll., 1930; B.D., Garrett Bibl. Inst, 1932; D.D., Baker U., 1947; LL.D., Central Coll., 1957; D.D., DePaw U., 1959, St. Paul Sch. Theology, Methodist, 1962; m. Wilma A. Sedoris, June 20, 1930; children—Wilmagene (Mrs. Lewis C. Noonan), Gretchen (Mrs. J. Harrison Beal), Susan, Frank (Mrs. Michael Pomcrantz), Thomas Frank. Ordained to ministry Methodist Ch., 1932; pastor, Tonganoxie, Kan., 1932, Americus, Kan., 1933-36, Olathe, Kan., 1936-42, Kansas City, Kan., 1942-48, Topeka, Kan., 1948-56; consecrated bishop, 1956; bishop of Mo., St. Louis, 1956-72; bishop of Ark., 1972—. Pres., Council Bishops, United Methodist Ch., 1968-69; mem. bd. global missions, bd. ch. and soc. Mem. Kappa Delta Pi, Pi Kappa Delta, Phi Mu Alpha. Tau Kappa Epsilon. Address: 3909 S Lookout Rd Little Rock AR 72205

FRANK, JOHN NATHANIEL, pottery mfr.; b. Chgo., Jan. 31, 1905; s. Adam Henry and Marie Katherin (Letter) F.; B.A., Chgo. Art Inst., 1932; m. Grace Lee Bowman, Sept. 4, 1928; children—Donna (Mrs. August LeBoeuf), Joniece. Instr. art U. Okla., 1927-36; designer, mgr., lectr. ceramic mfg. Frankoma Pottery, Inc., Sapula, Okla., 1933-73. Past chmn. Library Bd.; dir. Emergency Planning for Okla.; active Salvation Army. Bd. dirs. Youth for Christ. Named Outstanding Small Businessman of Okla., 1971, Outstanding Small Businessman in U.S.A., 1971, Outstanding Marketing Man, Tulsa Area, 1972; recipient other awards. Mem. Am. Ceramic Soc. (past pres. S.W. div.), Okla., Sapulpa chambers commerce, Am. Patriots League, Nat., Okla. assns. mfrs. Methodist. Rotarian. Home: 1300 Luker Lane Sapulpa OK 74066 Office: 2400 Frankoma Rd Sapulpa OK 74066 Died Nov. 10, 1973

FRANK, STEVEN ALLAN, govt. ofcl.; b. Bklyn., Apr. 15, 1942; s. Sigfried and Flora Frieda (Winter) F.; B.B.A., U. Pitts., 1963; M.B.A., N.Y. U., 1965; postgrad. George Washington U., 1965-70; m. Regina Nancy Uliss, June 21, 1964; children—Scott David, Marcia Beth. Operations research analyst Inst. Mgmt. Sci. and Engring. of George Washington U., 1965-69; operations research analyst and statistician, chief program rev. div. Econ. Devel. Adminstrn. of U.S. Dept. Commerce, Washington, 1969—; tchr. bus. policy and bus. statistics N.Y. U., 1963-65. Del., chmn. environmental com., mem. exec. com. Allied Civic Group; pres. Forest Glen Citizens Assn., 1969-71; mem. bd. mgmt. YMCA Camp Letts. Bd. dirs. Montgomery Environmental Coalition, Montgomery Recycling Orgn., Sensible Citizens Against Throwaways. Recipient certificate of commendation for superior performance U.S. Dept. Commerce, 1970. Mem. Operations Research Soc. Am., Inst. Mgmt. Sci., Am. Statis. Assn., A.A.A.S., Sigma Alpha Mu. Home: 6215 Stoneham Rd Bethesda MD 20034 Office: US Dept Commerce Washington DC 20230

FRANKENBERG, DIRK, educator; b. Woodsville, N.H., Nov. 25, 1937; s. Charles Henry and Patricia Edith (Smith) F.; A.B. (Henry Francis Burrows Meml. fellow), Dartmouth, 1959; M.S., Emory U., 1960, Ph.D. (NIH fellow), 1962; m. Susan Alice Campbell, June 25, 1960; children—Elizabeth Alice, Eben Whitfield. Asst. prof. zoology, research asso. Marine Inst., U. Ga., 1962-66, asso. prof., research asso., 1967-72, prof., research asso., 1972—, coordinator grad. studies dept. zoology, 1968-69, acting head dept. zoology, 1969-70, dir. Biol. Oceanography Program, NSF, 1970-71; adj. lectr. dept. biol. scis. Dartmouth, 1965-69; asst. prof. dept. biol. scis. U. Del., 1966-67. Mem. biol. oceanography adv. panel NSF, 1970-72; mem. ocean sci. com. Nat. Acad. Scis., 1973; cons. NSF, Duke. Recipient research grants NSF, 1963-66, 68-70, 70—, U.S. Coast Geodetic Survey, 1964, Dept. Commerce, 1970—. Fellow A.A.A.S.; mem. Assn. Southeastern Biologists, Am. Soc. Limnology and Oceanography (chmn. nominating com. 1970-71), Ecol. Soc. Am., Sphinx, Sigma Xi, Phi Sigma. Contbr. articles to profl. jours. Home: 115 Tillman Lane Athens GA 30601

FRANKLAND, WALTER LESLIE, JR., assn. exec.; b. Jackson, Tenn., June 4, 1924; s. Walter Leslie and Sarah (Moore) F.; B.S., U.S. Mil. Acad., 1946; M.A. in Journalism, U. Fla., 1955; m. Carol Elizabeth Armstrong, June 20, 1946; children—Walter, Mary Elizabeth. Commd. 2d lt. Inf., U.S. Army, 1946, advanced through grades to lt. col., 1963; served in Japan, 1947-49; with 10th Tng. Div., Ft. Riley, Kan., 1950-51; assigned to Armored Sch., 1951-52; 2d Inf. Div., Korea, 1952-53, U.S. Mil. Acad., 1955-58, French Army Staff Coll., 1958-59, Am. embassy, Paris, 1959-63, Armed Forces Staff Coll., Norfolk, 1963; officer Office Chief Information, Dept. Army, Washington, 1964-66; ret., 1966; exec. sec. Silver Users Assn., Washington, 1966, exec. dir., 1967-71, exec. v.p., 1971—; exec. v.p. Nat. Tax Equality Assn., 1972-73; exec. v.p., dir. Nat. Asso. Businessmen, 1971-73; partner Scott & Frankland, mgmt. cons., 1971-73; pres. Frankland's/Washington, cons., 1973—. Pres., Arlington-Forest (Va.) Citizens Assn., 1970, Washington-Lee High Sch. Boosters Club, 1971-72. Decorated Combat Inf. badge, Bronze Star medal, Commendation medal; French Croix de Guerre Otre Mere (Korea). Mem. Pub. Relations Soc. Am. (v.p., dir. Nat. Capital chpt.), Am. Soc. Assn. Execs., West Point Soc. D.C. (treas., dir.), Nat. Press Club, Stockholders of Am. (dir.), Fla. State Soc., Tenn. State Soc. (v.p. 1971-73), Sigma Delta Chi. Clubs: Nat. Press, Army-Navy (Washington); Army-Navy Country (Arlington, Va.). Home: 2674 Marcey Rd Arlington VA 22207 Office: 1717 K St NW Washington DC 20006

FRANKLIN, CHARLES BOB, diversified industry exec.; b. Dallas, May 4, 1928; s. Arlie H. and Mary Ann (Edwards) F.; Asso. Aero. Engring., Spartan Coll. Engring., Tulsa, Okla., 1951; m. Jeannine Hart, Mar. 19, 1949; children—Judith Elaine, Donna Carol, Kenneth Bob. Chief project engr. LTV Aerospace Corp., Dallas, 1961-62, dir. vehicle programs, 1963-67; v.p., gen. mgr. engring. systems div. Service Tech. Corp., subsidiary LTV Aerospace Corp., 1968-69, pres., 1970-72; chmn. bd., pres. Childres Canvas Products, Inc., Dallas, 1972—, Foamspray Chems., Inc., Dallas, 1972—. Served with AUS, 1946-49. Home: 6940 Heatherknoll Dallas TX 75240 Office: 10414 Harry Hines Blvd Dallas TX 75220

FRANKLIN, DONALD WAYNE, govt. ofcl.; b. Fountain Run, Ky., Aug. 21, 1944; s. McDonald and Thelma Jewell (Bullington) F.; B.S., Western Ky. U.; m. Carla Sue Dotson, Aug. 20, 1966; children—Patricia Michelle, David Michael. Tax auditor Internal Revenue Service, Louisville, 1967—. Mem. Am. Blind Bowling Assn. (v.p. 1973—), Alpha Phi Omega, Delta Sigma Pi. Baptist (asso. deacon 1974—). Home: 135 N Vernon Av Louisville KY 40206 Office: PO Box 306 Louisville KY 40201

FRANKLIN, J. STUART, JR., civil engr.; b. Richmond, Va., May 2, 1920; s. James Stuart and Gaynelle (Phillips) F.; B.S., Va. Poly. Inst.; m. Margaret Elizabeth May, June 12, 1948. Field engr. Mason & Hanger, Dublin, Va. and Baraboo, Wis., 1941-42; insp. Fred Bur. Rds., Blue Ridge, Parkway, Va., 1946-47; civil engr., structural design for numerous schs., chs., hosps., indsl. bldgs., Eubank & Caldwell, Inc., Roanoke, Va., 1948-55; structural designer Am. Bridge div. U.S. Steel Corp., 1955-58; v.p., gen. mgr. Cates Bldg. Spltys., Inc., 1958-60; partner Eubank, Caldwell & Assos., architects and engrs., 1961-66, Eubank, Caldwell, Dobbins, Sherertz & Franklin, 1966-70, Sherertz & Franklin, 1970—. Served as staff sgt. C.E., AUS, Africa, Hawaii, 1942-46. Registered profl. engr., Va. Fellow Am. Soc. C.E. (pres. Roanoke br. 1955-56, pres. Va. sect. 1968, mem. nat. com. on student chpts.); mem. Va. Assn. Professions, Va. Soc. Profl. Engrs. (sec.-treas. Roanoke chpt. 1955, v.p. 1956), Va., Roanoke chambers commerce, Tau Beta Pi, Chi Epsilon. Baptist (deacon). Mason, Kiwanian (pres. 1967, lt. gov. 1970-71, pres. found.), Elk. Club: Hunting Hills Country. Home: 3256 Woodland Dr SW Roanoke VA 24015 Office: First Fed Bldg Roanoke VA 24011

FRANKLIN, MARY ANNE GUY, tv ednl. exec.; b. Columbia, S.C.; adopted dau. Lynn Trimble and Roberta (Mitchell) Guy; B.A., U. Richmond, 1935; M.A., U. Va., 1943; m. Samuel Howell Franklin Jr., Oct. 16, 1946 (div. Nov. 1952). Tchr. pub. schs., Richmond Va.,

1936-58, ednl. TV cons., 1956-64; v.p., program dir. ednl. WCVE/WCVW-TV, Richmond, 1964-71; dir. ednl. TV, Va. Dept. Edn., 1971—; tchr. English evening sch. Richmond Profl. Inst., 1960-64, summer insts. U. Mich., Ann Arbor, 1955; Madison Coll., Harrisonburg, Va., 1962, U. Richmond, 1963. Cons. ednl. TV workshops Del. 1965, W. Va., 1968; field cons. Nat. Project for Improvement TV Instrn., Nat. Assn. Ednl. Broadcasters, 1966—. Mem. State Bd. Community Colls., 1966—, Regional Council for Continuing Edn., Richmond, 1967—, steering com. for ednl. TV, State Council Higher Edn., 1967—. Bd. dirs. Va. Ednl. TV, Inc. Winifred Cullis lecture fellow. Eng., Scotland, 1953; Fulbright fellow, Thailand, 1958-59; exchange tchr., London, Eng. 1948-49. Mem. Am. Assn. U. Women (past pres. Richmond), English Speaking Union (past v.p. Va. chpt.), Phi Beta Kappa (past pres. Richmond chpt.). Republican. Baptist. Club: Willow Oaks Country. Home: 1829 Hanover Av Richmond VA 23220 Office: 9th St Office Bldg Richmond VA 23216

FRANKLIN, PHILIP EARLE, economist; b. Detroit, Jan. 11, 1928; s. Edward Earle and Minnie (Evans) F.; B.A., George Washington U., 1949, M.A., 1955; Ph.D., Am. U., 1968; m. Jacqueline Jo Rogers, Dec. 28, 1949; children—Debora, Janice, Stephanie, Diana, Jennifer. Bus. economist Office Bus. Econs., Dept. Commerce, 1950-51; indsl. analyst Govt. Patents Bd., Exec. Office Pres., 1952-55; gen. economist Bur. Fgn. Commerce, Dept. of Commerce, 1955-56; transp. specialist Commodity Stblzn. Service, Dept. Agr., 1956-57; transp. economist Maritime Adminstrn., Dept. Commerce, 1957-60, gen. economist Office of Area Devel., 1960-61, transp. economist Office of Under Sec. of Commerce for Transp., 1961-62, internat. economist Bur. Internat. Commerce, 1962-64, gen. economist Office Undersec. Transp., 1964-67; coordinator for water resources Office of Sec., Dept. Transp., 1967-70, chief econs. and spl. project div., 1970-73, chief, organizer internat. trans. div., 1973—; fellow Center for Internat. Affairs, Harvard, 1972-73; transp. cons. UN, 1965. Pres. Eastpines Citizens Assn., Riverdale, Md., 1955-57. Served with USAAF, 1945-47. Served as 1st lt. AUS, 1951-52. Mem. Am. Econ. Assn., Council on Fgn. Relations, Am. Water Resources Assn., Soc. Govt. Economists, Regional Sci. Assn., Econ. History Assn., A.A.A.S., Am. Soc. Pub. Adminstrn., Am. Acad. Polit. Social Sci., Delta Phi Epsilon (pres. Washington alumni assn. 1965-66). Home: 3734 Northampton St NW Washington DC 20015 Office: Office of Sec Dept Transp Washington DC 20590

FRANKS, MILAS DOYLE, city ofcl.; b. Coeburn, Va., Aug. 7, 1942; s. Thomas Doyle and Rosa Ann (Carico) F.; ed. pub. schs., Internat. Corr. Schs.; m. Hazel Ann Bevins, July 14, 1962; children—William Doyle, Elizabeth Ann. Inspector hwy. constrn. Va. Dept. Hwys., Fredericksburg, 1961-64, Christiansburg, 1964-69; city engr. City of Norton (Va.), 1969-71, city mgr., 1971—. Mem. City of Norton Welfare Bd. Named outstanding young man Norton-Wise Jr. C. of C., 1972. Mem. Internat. City Mgrs. Assn., Va. Govtl. Employees Assn. Mem. Ch. of God (treas.). Mason, Kiwanian (pres. 1972-73). Home: 406 Chestnut St Norton VA 24273 Office: PO Box 618 Norton VA 24273

FRANTZ, JOSEPH FOSTER, chem. engr.; b. McComb, Miss., Feb. 21, 1933; s. Elmer Joseph and Corinne (Bevill) F.; B.S., La. State U., 1955, M.S., 1956, Ph.D., 1958; m. Etta Sue Murphy, May 14, 1960; children—Marjorie Corinne, Joseph Foster II, Susan Elizabeth. Research chem. engr. Monsanto Co., El Dorado, Ark., St. Louis, Texas City, Tex., 1958-65; mgr. devel. South Hampton Co., Houston, 1965-68; pres. Frantz Chem. Cons., Houston, 1968—. Mem. S.Ark. Symphony, 1958-61, Houston Civic Symphony, 1968—. Mem. Am. Chem. Soc., Am. Inst. Chem. Engrs. (Publ. award S.Tex. sect. 1963-64). Methodist (trustee). Club: Whitehall. Composer: Uncle Charlie's March, 1951. Contbr. articles to profl. jours. Patentee in field. Home: 6410 Tam O'Shanter Houston TX 77036 Office: 7255 Clarewood St Houston TX 77036

FRANZ, ROBERT MANFRED, clergyman; b. Ft. Lauderdale, Fla., Oct. 10, 1946; s. Manfred and Elizabeth Mary (Boffi) F.; student DePauw U., 1964-66; B.A., Transylvania U., 1968; M.Div., Lexington Theol. Semn., 1972; m. Sandra Kay Naylor, June 18, 1972. Ordained to ministry Christian Ch. (Disciples of Christ), 1972; minister Monterey (Ky.) Christian Ch., 1970-72, Crofton (Ky.) Christian Ch., 1972-74; asso. minister First Christian Ch., Hopkinsville, Ky., 1974—. Counselor-adviser Listening Post (Crisis Intervention Telephone Service); dist. coordinator Ky. Disciples of Christ Stewardship Program, 1972-74, youth dir. dist. program, 1974—. Pack leader Boy Scouts Am., 1972-74; mem. Vol. Fire Dept., 1972-74. Mem. Christian County Ministerial Assn., Delta Upsilon. Club: North Christian County Booster. Address: Box 44 Hopkinsville KY 42240

FRANZMATHES, JOSEPH EDWARD, lawyer; b. Beloit, Kan., Dec. 8, 1907; s. Joseph W. and Grace (Shafer) F.; student Kan. Wesleyan Coll., 1927-29; LL.B., U. Mo., 1937; m. Elizabeth M. Lutz, July 1, 1950. Admitted to Mo. bar, 1937; accountant Am. Service Co., 1931-39; atty., auditor Consumers Pub. Service Co., 1939-42; atty. passport office State Dept., Washington, 1945—. Served with CIC, AUS, 1942-45. Mem. Am., Fed., Mo. bar assns., Am. Legion (vice comdr. 1959-60). Home: 5415 Connecticut Av NW Washington DC 20015 Office: McPherson Bldg 1425 K St Washington DC 20524

FRASER, DONALD HINES, U.S. atty.; b. Hinesville, Ga., Feb. 27, 1906; s. Donald and Beulah Lee (Hines) F.; student Mercer U., 1923-25; LL.B., U. Fla., 1927; m. Evelyn Hughey Green, July 13, 1933; 1 dau., Jane Evelyn (wife of Lt. William E. Bowen). Admitted to Ga. and Fla. bars, 1928; judge city ct., Darien, Ga., 1943-45, Hinesville, Ga. 1933-49; solicitor gen. Atlantic Jud. Circuit, 1950-51; pvt. practice law, Hinesville, 1951—; asst. U.S. atty. So. Dist. Ga., 1951-61, U.S. atty., 1961—. Mem. Ga. Gen. Assembly from Liberty County, 1930-31, 70—; mem. Hinesville City Council, 1931-33. Mem. Ga. Bar Assn. (bd. govs. 1950), St. Andrews Soc. Savannah, S.A.R. Democrat. Methodist. Club: Exchange. Home: 503 Oglethorpe Hwy Hinesville GA 31313 Office: PO Box 472 Hinesville GA 31313

FRASER, THOMAS AUGUSTUS, JR., bishop; b. Atlanta, Apr. 17, 1915; s. Thomas Augustus and Lena Lee (Connell) F.; B.A., Hobart Coll., 1938, S.T.D., 1965; B.D., Va. Theol. Sem., 1941, D.D., 1960; special student U. Jena (Germany), 1937; D.D., U. of South 1960, Wake Forest Coll., 1961; m. Marjorie Louise Rimbach, May 29, 1943; children—Thomas Augustus III, Constance Louise Fraser. Ordained to ministry Episcopal Ch. as deacon, 1941, priest, 1942, bishop, 1960; missionary Diocese L.I., N.Y., 1941-42; sec., chaplain Bishop of L.I., 1942; sr. asst., N.Y.C., 1942-44; rector in Alexandria, Va., 1944-51, Winston-Salem, N.C., 1951-60; bishop coadjutor Diocese of N.C., Raleigh, 1960-65, diocesan bishop, 1965—. Mem. edn. com. Anglican Cong., Toronto, Can., 1963; chmn. joint commn. on edn. Holy Orders Am. Episcopal Ch.; sec. commn. on priesthood Lambeth Conf., 1968. Mem. Community Nursing, Alexandria, Va., 1944-50, Winston-Salem, N.C., 1951-60, Alcoholic Rehab., Winston-Salem, 1954-59; United Fund, Winston-Salem, 1957-60, Family and Child Welfare, Winston-Salem, 1955-57, Children's Psychol. Clinic, Winston-Salem, 1955-57. Trustee, U. of South, Sewanee, Tenn., St. Mary's Jr. College, Raleigh, N.C.; chmn. bd. trustees St. Augustine's Coll., Raleigh. Mem. exec. com. Gov.'s Commn. on Piedmont Crescent, 1964—. Mem. Tau Kappa Alpha, Sigma Chi. Home: 1200 Glen Eden Dr Raleigh NC 27609 Office: Diocesan House 201 St Albans Dr Raleigh NC 27609

FRASER, WHITMAN, physician; b. Wichita Falls, Tex., Oct. 24, 1926; s. Wallace Winn and Jen (Whitman) F.; student Okla. A. and M. U., 1944, Va. Poly. Inst., 1945, Midwestern U., Wichita Falls, 1947, Rice Inst., 1947-50; B.A., U. Tex., 1952, M.D., 1956; m. Mary Lou Snead, Mar. 23, 1951; children—Sherry Lynn, Mary Gwynn, Clint. Sr. asst. surgeon USPHS Hosps., New Orleans, 1956-57, Savannah, Ga., 1957-58; individual practice gen. medicine, Hinesville, Ga., 1958—; chief of staff Liberty Meml. Hosp., 1961—. Chmn. Liberty County Bd. Health, 1963—; organizer, speaker Liberty County Com. on Drug Abuse, 1970—. City councilman, Hinesville, 1963-67; del. Republican State Conv., 1964; county chmn. Rep. Party, 1968—. Trustee Rabun Gap-Nacoochie Sch. Served with AUS, 1944-47; PTO. Mem. Am. Assn. Physicians and Surgeons, Savannah Presbytery Men of the Ch. (pres. 1968). Presbyn. (elder). Address: PO Box 406 Hinesville GA 31313

FRASHER, JAMES HOWARD, petroleum exploration co. exec.; b. Gardner, Colo., Mar. 28, 1919; s. Jonah J. and Susan C. (Simms) F.; student Colo. State U., 1936-41; m. Venna Singleton, Nov. 19, 1946; children—James Howard, Linda S., Barbara A. With Nat. Geophys. and Teledyne Exploration, geophysicists, Houston, 1946—, pres., 1970—. Served with USAAF, 1942-45. Decorated Bronze Star. Mem. Soc. Exploration Geophysicists, Am. Assn. Petroleum Geologists, European Soc. Exploration Geophysicists, Internat. Assn. Geophys. Contractors (dir. 1971-73, treas. 1971-72), Houston C. of C., Houston World Trade Assn. Club: Lakeside Country. Home: 14751 Quail Grove St Houston TX 77024 Office: 5825 Chimney Rock Rd Houston TX 77036

FRASIER, RALPH KENNEDY, lawyer, bank exec.; b. Winston-Salem, N.C., Sept. 16, 1938; s. LeRoy Benjamin and Katheryn O. (Kennedy) F.; B.S. in Bus. Adminstrn., N.C. Central U., 1962, J.D., 1965; m. Annie Mae Spaulding, Sept. 16, 1961; children—Karen Denise, Gail Spaulding, Ralph Kennedy, Jr., Keith Lowery. Admitted to N.C. bar, 1965; legal asst. Wachovia Bank & Trust Co., Winston-Salem, 1965-66, asst. sec., 1966-68, asst. v.p., 1968-69, v.p., mgr. legal dept., 1969-70; v.p., asso. gen. counsel Wachovia Corp. (parent co. Wachovia Bank & Trust Co.). 1970. Bd. dirs. Family Services, Inc., 1966—, asst. sec., 1967-68, chmn. pub. relations com., 1968-69, sec., 1973-74, v.p., 1974—; vice chmn. Winston-Salem Transit Authority, 1968-74, chmn., 1974—; bd. dirs. Research for Advancement Personalities, Inc., 1968-71, N.C. United Community Services, Inc., 1970—; bd. dirs., sec. Winston-Salem Citizens for Fair Housing, 1969-72; trustee Appalachian State U., 1973—, Appalachian State U. Found., 1973—; mem. citizens adv. com. Winston-Salem/Forsyth County Sch. Bd., 1973—. Served with AUS, 1958-60. Mem. N.C., Forsyth County bar assns., Southeastern Lawyers Assn., Am. Bar Assn., Greater Winston-Salem C. of C., N.A.A.C.P. (mem. exec. bd. 1966-67), Alpha Pi Lambda, Alpha Phi Alpha. Home: 3222 Pennington Lane Winston-Salem NC 27106 Office: PO Box 3099 301 N Main St Winston-Salem NC 27102

FRAZER, JOHN STANLEY, state ofcl.; b. Furman, Ala., Aug. 1, 1911; s. George Stanley and Mary Elizabeth (Williams) F.; student Southwestern Coll., 1928-30; B.A., U. Fla., 1932; M.A., U. N.C., 1933; m. Eleanor Beatrice Carlton, May 19, 1944; 1 dau., Beatrice Carolyn. Sr. personnel technician Ala. Personnel Dept., Montgomery, 1939-41, dep. dir., 1945-53, dir., 1954—; sr. examiner La. Dept. State Civil Service, Baton Rouge, 1941-42; mem. field staff Pub. Adminstrn. Service, Sao Paulo. Brazil, 1953-54. Served from ensign to lt. USN, 1942-45; now lt. comdr. Res. ret. Mem. Pub. Personnel Assn. (chmn. So. Regional Conf. 1959-60, mem. exec. council 1960-64). Democrat. Methodist. Home: Route 1 Box 399 Millbrook AL 36054 Office: State Adminstrv Bldg Montgomery AL 36104

FRAZIER, CHALMER HAYNES, hosp. adminstr.; b. Martin, Ky., Sept. 28, 1911; s. Noah Melvin and Laura (Maggard) F.; B.A., Berea Coll., 1934; M.A., U. Ky., 1939; m. Kathryn Stumbo, Apr. 11, 1935; children—Kay Anne (Mrs. Stephen Wilborn), Elizabeth Lynn (Mrs. John W. Sutherland), William C. Tchr. high sch., 1934-40, prin., 1940-48; supt. schs., Prestonsburg, Ky., 1948-58; adminstr. Prestonsburg (Ky.) Gen. Hosp., 1958-73; Highlands Regional Med. Center, 1973—. Recipient Silver Beaver award Boy Scouts Am., 1965. Mem. Am. Coll. Hosp. Adminstrs., Ky. (pres. 1970-71), Bluegrass (pres. 1968-69) hosp. assns. Kiwanian (local pres. 1965-66, lt. gov. div. 1967-68). Home: 102 E Court St Prestonsburg KY 41653 Office: US 23 N Prestonsburg KY 41653

FRAZIER, GRIFFIN GUY, ret. dentist; b. Reading, Pa., May 24, 1889; s. Charles Cooper and Ida (Faries) F.; D.D.S., George Washington U., 1916, A.A., 1951; D.D.S., U. Pa., 1923; m. Bernice Frances Peck, Jan. 3, 1918; 1 son, Griffin Peck. Pvt. practice gen. dentistry, Washington, 1923-56. Served to lt. comdr. Dental Corps USN, 1917-21. Recipient Confederate Stamp Alliance trophy, 1956. Mem. Am. Dental Assn. (life), Soc. Colonial Wars, S.A.R., Soc. War 1812, Naval Order U.S., Psi Omega. Republican. Mason. Club: Aztec of 1847 (past sec.) (Washington). Researcher, compiler, pub. James Frazier, Kent County, Delaware, and Descendants, 1965. Home: 2001 N Adams St Arlington VA 22201

FRAZIER, RUSSELL WAYNE, athletic dir., educator; b. Youngsville, N.C., Oct. 11, 1932; s. Grover Haywood and Goldie Geneva (Hagwood) F.; B.S., N.C. State U., 1958; M.S., U. N.C., 1959; m. Virginia Clara Wright, Sept. 4, 1954; children—Russell Wayne III. Baseball coach, athletic dir., tchr. Louisburg (N.C.) Coll., 1960—. Served with U.S. Army, 1954-56. Named Regional Coach of Year, 1971, Dist. Coach of Year, 1971, Conf. Coach of Year, 1971. Mem. Am. Assn. Coll. Baseball Coaches. Home: Route 1 Youngsville NC 27596 Office: Louisburg Coll Louisburg NC 27549

FRAZIER, SAMUEL DAVID, coll. pres.; b. Blaine, Tenn., July 18, 1931; s. William Dewey and Nancy (Jarvis) F.; A.B., Carson-Newman Coll., 1953; M.S., U. Tenn., 1956; Ph.D., Fla. State U., 1962; m. Bobbye Jeane Frazier, June 3, 1956; children—Nelson David, DeAnne Lynn. Tchr. high sch., 1953; sch. counselor, Jacksonville, Fla., 1956-58; prin. Minta (Tenn.) Sch., 1958-59; admissions counselor U. Ga., 1959-61; dean of students and admissions Young Harris (Ga.) Coll., 1962-65; pres. Peace Coll., Raleigh, N.C., 1965—. Bd. dirs. United Fund; dir. Raleigh Concert Music Assn., 1960. Served with AUS, 1953-55. Mem. N.C. Jr. Coll. Assn. (pres. 1968-70), N.C. Assn. Ind. Colls. (treas., mem. exec. com.), N.C. Assn. Colls. and Univs. (pres. elect 1971-72). Presbyn. (elder). Kiwanian. (dir.). Home: 2017 St Marys St Raleigh NC 27608

FREAS, ANNIE BELLE HAMILTON (MRS. MAURICE HENRY FREAS), constrn. co. exec.; b. Delrose, Tenn.; d. James N. and Emma (McLaughlin) Hamilton; grad. Martin Jr. Coll., Pulaski, Tenn., 1923; m. Maurice Henry Freas, June 6, 1931. Sec. law firm Bass, Berry & Sims, 1923-24; coml. tchr., bookkeeper Martin Coll., 1924-25; bookkeeping machine operator, head accounting dept., asst. comptroller T. L. Herbert & Sons, W. G. Bush & Co., Sangravl Co., Nashville, 1925-58; bookkeeper, co-owner M. H. Freas, gen. contractor, Nashville, 1958-63; sec., gen. bookkeeper Freas & Houghland Gen. Contractors, Inc., Nashville, 1963-67; sec.-treas. Freas Constrn. Co., Inc., 1967—; office mgr. Pres. Women of Ch. Downtown Presbyn. Ch., 1961-63, recipient life membership pin, 1964. Mem. Ladies Hermitage Assn., Cheekwood YWCA, Assn. for Preservation Tenn. Antiquities, Tenn. Bot. Gardens and Fine Arts Center. Recipient medal Underwood Typewriter Co., 1923. Mem. Women in Constrn. (pres. Nashville 1964-66, regional dir. 1966-68, mem. nat. bd. dirs. 1966—, named WIC of Year 1965, nat. orgn. and extension chmn. 1973-74, chmn. friendship com. 1973-74, mem. finance, standing rules, decorating coms.; recipient certificate 1972), Internat. Platform Assn., Centro Studi's for Arts, Letters, Speeches (hon. v.p.). Club: Zonta (treas. 1973-74, v.p. 1969, program chmn. 1969, dist. chmn. pub. affairs S. and S.W.; chpt. pres. 1970, chmn. GROW 1972-73). Address: 3003 Natchez Trace Nashville TN 37215

FREDERICK, CAROLYN HALL ESSIG (MRS. HOLMES W. FREDERICK), state legislator; b. Atlanta; d. Philip Martin and Lillian (Hall) Essig; A.B., Agnes Scott Coll., 1928; m. Holmes Walter Frederick, Oct. 1, 1933; children—Lynn (Mrs. John Grant Williamson), Rosa Margaret (Mrs. Glen Clayton Smith). Asso., Rich's, Atlanta, 1928-29; advt., promotion dir. Burdine's, Miami, Fla., 1931-33, Jordan Marsh, Boston, 1934; asso. dir. Greenville (S.C.) County Community Chest and Council, 1950-53; pub. relations cons., Greenville, 1954—; mem. S.C. Ho. of Reps., 1967—, sec. Greenville delegation, 1967, 68. Mgr. Greenville (S.C.) Symphony Assn., 1954-70; S.C. state rep. to U.S. com. for UNICEF, 1963-65; mem. masters art teaching program com. Converse Coll., 1961-66; initiator, exec. dir. Arts Festival Greenville, 1963-65; pub. relations dir. Greenville YWCA 1958-64, bd. dirs.; vice chmn. State-Wide Master Planning Com. Nursing Edn., 1971—; mem. S.C. Higher Edn. Tuition Grants Com., 1972—; adv. com. arts John F. Kennedy Center for Performing Arts, 1970—. Named Outstanding Woman in Community Service, Greenville Piedmont, 1963; Career Woman of Yr., Greenville Zonta, 1967; S.C. Woman of Yr., S.C. Conf. Status Women, 1970. Mem. Nat. League Am. Penwomen, Am. Assn. U. Women (br. pres. 1944-45, 57-58, mem. nat. mass media com. 1958-63, S.C. state pres. 1959-61, mem. nat. nominating com. 1963, Carolyn Frederick Fellowship grant established 1971, mem. nat. topic com. 1973, 74), Aux. S.C. Soc. Profl. Engrs. (charter pres. 1956). Presbyn. (mem. ch. long-range planning com. 1972—). Home: 326 Chick Springs Rd Greenville SC 29609

FREDERICK, LAFAYETTE, educator; b. Friarspoint, Miss., Mar. 19, 1923; s. James Davis and Ellen (Johnson) F.; B.S., Tuskegee Inst., 1943; M.S., U. Rhode, 1950; Ph.D., Wash. State U., 1952; m. Antoinette Arlene Reed, Dec. 24, 1950; children—Lewis Reed, Karla Mae, David Warren. Asso. prof., prof. biology So. U., Baton Rouge, 1952-62; prof. biology Atlanta U., 1962—, chmn. dept. biology, 1963—. Commr., Commn. on Undergrad. Edn. Biol. Scis., 1970-71; mem. biology achievement test com. Ednl. Testing Service, 1971—. Mem. Southeastern Forestry Research adv. com.; mem. gen. support adv. com. NIH. Trustee Ga. Conservancy. Served with USNR, 1944-46. Recipient 2d Ann. Trustees award for excellence in teaching, 1964. Fellow Ga. Acad. Sci.; mem. A.A.A.S., Bot. Soc. Am., Mycol. Soc. Am., Am. Phytopathol. Soc., Assn. Southeastern Biologists, So. Appalachian Bot. Club, Am. Inst. Biol. Scis., Sigma Xi, Phi Sigma, Beta Beta Beta, Phi Kappa Phi. Presbyn. Home: 672 Beckwith St SW Atlanta GA 30314 Office: 223 Chestnut St SW Atlanta GA 30314

FREDERICK, PHILIP, JR., physician; b. Atlanta, Ga., Aug. 11, 1929; s. Philip and Mary Ella (Arnold) F.; B.S., U. Richmond, 1950; M.D., Med. Coll. Va., 1954; m. Margaret Ann Peery, June 21, 1958; children—Mary Helen, Clair Peery, Philip III. Intern, U. Minn., 1954-55; resident internal medicine Med. Coll. Va., 1957-59; fellow gastroenterology Ochsner Clinic, New Orleans, 1959-60; practice medicine, specializing in internal medicine and gastroenterology, Richmond, Va., 1960—; mem. staff Med. Coll. Va., Johnston-Willis Hosp., Richmond. Served to lt. USNR, 1955-57. Diplomate Am. Bd Internal Medicine. Fellow A.C.P.; mem. Phi Beta Kappa, Omicron Delta Kappa, Alpha Omega Alpha. Home: 4108 Cambridge Rd Richmond VA 23221 Office: 2208 Monument Av Richmond VA 23220

FREDERICKSON, EVAN LLOYD, physician, educator; b. Spring Green, Wis., Mar. 1, 1922; s. Edward and Rebecca Lloyd (Jones) F.; B.S., U. Wis., 1947, M.D., 1950; M.S., U. Ia., 1953; m. Ruth Evans Murphey, Sept. 17, 1946; children—Mary Evans (Mrs. Clinton H. Joiner), Helen Lloyd, Edward Dent. Intern, Walter Reed Army Hosp., Washington, 1950-51; resident State U. Ia. Hosps., 1951-53; practice medicine, specializing in anesthesiology, Atlanta, 1965—; instr., asst. prof. U. Kan. Med. Sch., 1953-56, prof., 1959-65; asst. prof., asso. prof. U. Wash. Sch. Medicine, 1956-59; prof., dir. anesthesia research Emory U. Sch. Medicine, Atlanta, 1965—; vis. prof. U. Rochester Sch. Medicine, U. Mo. Sch. Medicine, U. Miami Sch. Medicine, U. Tex. Sch. Medicine, San Antonio. Dir. Computer Dynamics; mem. tng. com. NIH, 1969-73; mem. adv. com. Food and Drug Adminstrn. Bd. dirs. Immunologic Cancer Research Fund. Served with AUS, 1943-46, 50-51. Diplomate Am. Bd. Anesthesiology. Fellow Am. Coll. Anesthesiologists; mem. Am. Soc. Anesthesiologists, A.M.A., A.A.A.S., Pan Am. Med. Assn. Asso. editor Surveys of Anesthesiology, 1964-73, Clin. Anesthesia, 1967-70. Contbr. articles profl. jours. Home: 961 Castle Falls Dr NE Atlanta GA 30329

FREDERICKSON, HARRY GRAY, oil co. exec.; b. Oklahoma City, Apr. 5, 1904; s. George and Mary (Brownlee) F.; B.S., Princeton, 1925; m. Dorothy McBride, June 12, 1930; 1 son, Gray. With Security First Nat. Bank, Los Angeles, 1925-28; real estate developer, 1928-31; partner Fain Drilling Co., Oklahoma City, 1931-36; v.p., treas., dir. Dual Parking Meter Co., Oklahoma City, 1936-41; ind. oil and gas producer, Oklahoma City, 1941—. Served to lt. comdr. USNR, 1941-45. Mem. Sigma Chi. Clubs: Oklahoma City Golf and Country; University (Los Angeles); Cannon (Princeton, N.J.). Promoter, mgr. Wiley Post's round the world record flight, 1933. Home: 2612 Lancaster Lane Oklahoma City OK 73116 Office: 6421 Avondale St Oklahoma City OK 73116

FREDERIKSEN, RICHARD ALLAN, educator; b. Renville, Minn., Aug. 9, 1933; s. Oscar Frice and Sylvia Josephine (Anderson) F.; student Gustavus Adolphus Coll., 1951-52; B.S., U. Minn., 1955, M.S., 1957, Ph.D., 1961; m. Phyllis Darlene Krinke, July 19, 1958; children—Jonathan Karl, Kristin Jo. Research plant pathologist Dept. Agr., St. Paul, 1961-63; asst. prof. Tex. A. and M. U., College Station, 1963-70, asso. prof., 1970-73, prof. plant pathology, 1973—. Served with AUS, 1957-58. Mem. Am., Internat., Indian phytopathol. socs., Tex. Acad. Sci., Sigma Zi, Gamma Sigma Delta, Alpha Zeta. Home: 1308 Leacrest Dr College Station TX 77840

FREDRICH, RUSSELL LEROY, broadcasting co. exec.; b. Merrick, L.I., N.Y., Nov. 29, 1930; s. Robert Miller and Anna Helen (Clarimont) F.; student, Armstrong State Coll., 1958; m. Anne Daniels, Feb. 18, 1961; children—Jennifer, Russell Miller, Leigh Ann. Advt. bus. and sales mgr. for various radio stas., 1958-69; pres. Regency Broadcasting, Inc., Savannah, Ga., 1969—. Chmn. March of Dimes, Savannah, 1965-66; charter mem. German Heritage Soc., 1964—; mem. Jewish Edn. Alliance, Savannah, 1964—. Served with USMC, 1951-53. Mem. Nat., Ga. assns. of broadcasters. Baptist.

Home: 36 Jameswood Av Savannah GA 31406 Office: PO Box 9705 Savannah GA 31402

FREDRICKSON, ARTHUR ALLAN, newspaper exec.; b. Grand Island, Neb., May 30, 1923; s. Edmond Russell and Jeannette (Burlingame) F.; student Doane Coll., 1940-42; m. Joyce Meredith Walls, June 3, 1949; children—Jeannette Walls, Arthur Allan. Mng. editor Blytheville (Ark.) Courier News, 1950-54, city editor, 1947-49, sports editor, 1946-47, asso. editor, 1949-50; copy editor, state news desk Times Union, Jacksonville, Fla., 1954-60, women's news editor, 1960-67, asst. exec. editor Fla. Pub. Co., Jacksonville, 1967—. Served with USNR, 1942-46. Mem. Fla. Soc. Newspaper Editors. Democrat. Episcopalian. Home: 2918 Princeton Av Jacksonville FL 32210 Office: 1 Riverside Av Jacksonville FL 32202

FREE, ANN COTTRELL, writer; b. Richmond, Va.; d. Emmett Drewry and Emily (Blake) Cottrell; grad. Collegiate Sch. for Girls, Richmond, 1934; student Richmond div. Coll. William and Mary, 1934-36; A.B., Barnard Coll., Columbia, 1938; m. James Stillman Free, Feb. 24, 1950; 1 dau., Elissa. Reporter Richmond Times Dispatch, 1938-40; Washington corr., Newsweek, 1940-41, Chgo. Sun, 1941-43, N.Y. Herald Tribune, 1943-46; pub. information dir. UNRRA China Mission, Shanghai, 1946-47; corr. Middle and Nr. East and Europe, 1947-48; writer-photographer Marshall Plan, Washington and Western Europe, 1949-50; contbr. N.Am. Newspaper Alliance Syndicate, Washingtonian Mag. Founding mem. Friends Nat. Zoo, Eleanor Roosevelt Meml. Commn.; mem. adv. com. Council Livestock Protection; mem. editorial bd. Potomac Valley Conservation and Recreation Council; assembly mem. Inst. Ecology. Bd. govs., v.p. Montgomery County Humane Soc.; bd. dirs. Rachel Carson Trust for Living Environment. Recipient Dodd Mead-Boys' Life Writing award, 1963, Albert Schweitzer medal, Animal Welfare Inst., 1963, Jr. Book award certificate Boys Clubs of Am., 1964; Humanitarian of Yr. awards Washington Animal Rescue League, 1971, Montgomery County Humane Soc., 1971. Episcopalian. Clubs: Am. Newspaper Women, Washington Press. Author: Forever the Wild Mare, 1963. Home: 4700 Jamestown Rd (Westmoreland Hills MD) Washington DC 20016

FREE, JAMES, newspaper corr.; b. Gordo, Ala., Nov. 5, 1908; s. James S. and Nettie (Bell) F.; A.B., U. Ala., 1929; B.Litt., Columbia, 1930; m. Ann Cottrell, Feb. 24, 1950; 1 dau., Elissa. With Tuscaloosa (Ala.) News, Birmingham (Ala.) News, Richmond (Va.) Times-Dispatch, Washington Star, Chgo. Sun (Washington bur.), 1930-47; Washington corr. Birmingham News, 1947—, Newhouse Nat. Service, 1962—. Served as lt. USNR, World War II, Carribean Sea Frontier and Amphibious Forces, Pacific Ocean Area; capt. Res., now ret. Chmn. Standing Com. of Correspondents, U.S. Capitol, 1959. Mem. Omicron Delta Kappa, Phi Kappa Sigma, Sigma Delta Chi. Democrat. Clubs: Nat. Press, Gridiron, Internat. (Washington. Contbr. to nat. mags., newspaper syndicates. Home: 4700 Jamestown Rd Washington DC 20016 Office: 1750 Pennsylvania Av NW Washington DC 20006

FREED, ABBYE LIPPER, JR., retail store exec.; b. Houston, Aug. 29, 1925; s. Abbye Lipper and Elsa (Schwartz) F.; B.S., La. State U., 1948; m. Anne Louise Lawrence, Apr. 2, 1949; children—Ellan (Mrs. Edward Dellon), Lauren (Mrs. Steven Wessinger). Partner, Ike L. Freed Co., Houston, 1949; with Goldstein-Migel Co., Waco, Tex., 1950—, pres., 1965—. Active various civic orgn. Urban Renewal Commr., Waco, 1972-74. Served to 1st lt., inf. AUS, 1943-46. Bd. dirs. Tex. Retail Fedn. 1970-73. Mem. C. of C. (dir. 1966-74). Jewish religion (pres. congregation 1963-65). Mem. B'nai B'rith (pres. 1956-58). Home: 2500 Arroyo Rd Waco TX 76710 Office: Box 890 Waco TX 76703

FREED, SAMUEL WELLS, investment co. exec.; b. Washington, Jan. 7, 1926; s. Samuel and Della (Wells) F.; B.A., U. N.C., 1949, M.S., 1951; m. Shirley Ann Weber, Sept. 7, 1955; children—Deborah Ann, David Alan. Research, Fort Detrick, Md., 1951-59; entered brokerage bus., 1959; v.p., dir. Pressman, Frohlich & Frost, Inc., Washington, 1966—; dir. Sentinel Resources Corp. Allied mem. N.Y. and Am. stock exchanges, 1966; mem. Phila., Balt. stock exchanges, 1971. Served with USNR, 1943-46. Mem. Bond Club Washington, Mut. Fund Council Million Dollar Producers, Zeta Beta Tau. Mason (Shriner). Club: Touchdown (Washington). Home: 9019 LeVelle Dr Chevy Chase MD 20015 Office: 1100 17th St NW Washington DC 20036

FREEDLAND, JACOB BERKE, dentist; b. Wilmington, N.C., Mar. 19, 1913; s. Morris and Molly (Burke) F.; student U. N.C., 1930-32; D.D.S., Emory U., 1936; m. Charlotte Soble, Sept. 7, 1939; children—Martin Berke, Leslie Ann (Mrs. Malcolm Frederick Locke, Jr.). Individual practice gen. dentistry, Charlotte, N.C., 1938-41, 46-63, specializing in endodontics, Charlotte, 1963—; cons., lectr. USN Dental Corps, U.S. Army Dental Corps, Naval Dental Sch., Nat. Naval Med. Center, Bethesda, Md., U.S. Naval Hosp., Portsmouth, Ft. Knox, Ky., Ft. Benning, Ga., Ft. Bragg, N.C., U.S. Army Inst. Dental Research; cons. Am. Dental Assn. Council on Dental Edn.; prof. dept. endodontics U. N.C. Sch. Dentistry. Bd. dirs. Charlotte Symphony, Jr. Achievement Am., Mecklenburg County chpt. A.R.C., Blood Bank, Am. Assn. Endodontists Endowment and Meml. Found., Dental Found. N.C., John Motley Morehead Found. Selection Com. Served to maj., Dental Corps, AUS, 1941-46; ETO. Recipient Thomas P. Hinman medallion for meritorious service, 1964, Charlotte Dental Soc. award, 1965, Am. Assn. Endodontists Appreciation award, 1967, Thomas P. Hinman Appreciation award, 1969. Diplomate Am. Bd. Endodontics. Fellow Am. Coll. Dentists; mem. Internat. Coll. Dentists, Am. Assn. Endodontists (past pres.), Am. Dental Assn., N.C. 2d Dist. Dental Soc. (past pres.), Am. Acad. Dental Medicine (past v.p.), Am. Acad. Dental Practice (past dir., editor), Am. Inst. Oral Scis. (past chmn.), Am. Acad. Oral Pathology, Internat. Assn. Dental Research, Omicron Kappa Upsilon. Mem. editorial bd. Jour. of Oral Surgery, Oral Medicine and Oral Pathology, 1964—. Contbr. articles to profl. jours. Home: 811 Hempstead Pl Charlotte NC 28207 Office: Doctors Bldg 1012 Kings Dr Charlotte NC 28207

FREEDMAN, BEN, physician, state ofcl.; b. Wilmington, Del., Apr. 11, 1905; s. David and Henrietta (Kiel) F.; student Loyola U., New Orleans, 1926-28; M.D., Tulane U., 1935; postgrad. Vanderbilt U., 1937, La. State U., 1938; M.P.H., Johns Hopkins, 1940; postgrad. U. Mich., 1943-44; m. Miriam Katz, Aug. 17, 1931. Intern Hotel Dieu, New Orleans, 1935-36, resident, 1936; with La. Dept. Health, New Orleans, 1936—, dir. pub. health tng., 1946—, dir. Bur. Health Conservation, chief handicapped children's sect., head div. spl. services, 1954—; prof. pub. health adminstrn. dept. tropical medicine and pub. health Tulane U. Med. Sch., New Orleans, 1949—; lectr. Northwestern State U. Sch. Nursing. 1951—, U.S. Children's Bur., 1955—. Chmn. La. Gov.'s Com. Rehab. Mentally Retarded Children and Adults, 1959-60; mem. White House Conf. Children and Youth, 1965; chmn. health com. La. Commn. Aging, 1964-65. Served with AUS, 1942-44. Recipient Medal of Freedom (Norway), Alfed E. Clay award Children's Bur. New Orleans, 1973. Fellow Am. Pub. Health Assn. (exec. com., governing council 1950-58, past pres. So. br., governing council 1948—, chmn. com. pub. health history); mem. A.A.A.S., A.M.A., Am. Acad. Polit. and Social Scis., Nat. Assn. Sanitarians (citation 1960, Mangold award 1969), La. State, Orleans Parish med. socs., Am. Assn. for History Medicine, Assn., State Maternal and Child Health and Crippled Children Dirs. (exec. com., pres. elect), Assn. Research Health Depts. (pres.), Am. Assn. Pub. Health Physicians (past pres., editor Bull. 1958—, Distinguished Service awards, 1962, 66 plaque distinguished service, 1967), La. Pub. Health Assn. (past pres., Dr. C. B. White Meml. award 1954, Dr. Edward Hall Barton Meml. award 1958), La. Assn. for Retarded Children, La. Heart Assn., Philosophy Sci. Assn., Fedn. Am. Scientists, Delta Omega (chmn. publs. com. 1959—). Author: Sanitary Inspector's Manual, 1942; Sanitarians's Handbook: Theory and Administrative Practice, 1957. Contbr. numerous articles to pub. health and med. jours. Home: 1321 Frankfort St New Orleans LA 70122 Office: State Office Bldg 325 Loyola Av New Orleans LA 70112

FREEDMAN, JOEL IRWIN, shoe co. exec.; b. Dallas, Dec. 29, 1945; s. Morty and Margaret Ann (Bloom) F.; student North Tex. State U., 1963-65, U. Houston, 1965; m. Judith Catherine Gist, Oct. 24, 1970. Vice pres. apparel marketing M & B Mfg. Co., Dallas, 1969-70; pres. Dentex Shoe Corp., Laredo, Tex., 1970—. Served to 1st lt. AUS, 1965-69. Decorated Army Commendation medal. Jewish religion. Rotarian. Home: 2517 Villa Way Laredo TX 78040 Office: PO Box 1774 Laredo TX 78040

FREEDMAN, JOSEPH, internat. finance agy. ofcl.; b. Brighton, Mass., Oct. 16, 1923; s. Edwin Arkiva and Fanny (Wine) F.; B.S. in Pub. Health Engring., Ga. Sch. Tech., 1943; M.S. in San. Engring. (fellow), U. N.C., 1945; S.M. in San. Engring., Harvard, 1955; groundwater devel. certificate U. Minn., 1959; m. Emily Ann Feltman, Nov. 4, 1959; 1 dau., Susan Alexandra, Jr. san. engr. Holmes & Narver Co., Okinawa, 1946-48; chief san. engr. Mariannas Bonins Command Dept. Army, Guam, 1948-49; exec., partner Continental Devel. Co., Mexico, 1949-50, 51-52; designer Charles T. Main., Inc., Boston, 1950-51, 52-53; san. engr. adviser to Govt. Honduras, WHO, Tegucigalpa, 1955-61; san. engr., adviser Govt. of Bolivia AID, 1961-63; san. engring adviser Govt. of Paraguay, AID, 1963; sr. specialist project analysis div. Interam. Devel. Bank, 1964-73; engr. projects div. Latin Am. and Caribbean region Internat. Bank for Reconstruction and Devel., 1973—. Registered profl. engr., Mass. Mem. Am. Soc. C.E., Inter-Am. Soc. San. Engrs. (charter), Royal Soc. Health, Am. Water Works Assn., Am. Pub. Works Assn., Sigma Xi, Phi Kappa Phi, Phi Eta Sigma. Home: 6504 Elgin Lane Bethesda MD 20034 Office: 1818 H St NW Washington DC 20433

FREEDMAN, WALTER, lawyer; b. St. Louis, 1914; A.B., Washington U., 1937, LL.B., 1937; LL.M., Harvard, 1938. Admitted to Mo. bar, 1947, U.S. Supreme Ct. bar, 1940, D.C. bar, 1946; atty. SEC, 1938-41; chief legal research sect. Bituminous Coal div., 1941-42; chief counsel Office Export Control, 1942-43; dep. dir., then dir. export control Fgn. Econ. Adminstrn., 1943-45; now mem. firm Freedman, Levy, Kroll & Simonds, Washington. Mem. Bar Assn. D.C., Fed., Am. bar assns., Am. Law Inst., Order Coif, Phi Beta Kappa, Omicron Delta Kappa. Editor-in-chief Washington U. Law Quar., 1936-37. Address: Freedman Levy Krolls & Simonds 1730 K St NW Washington DC 20006

FREEMAN, BERNICE, educator; b. LaGrange, Ga., Aug. 8, 1909; d. Thomas Norman and Everette (Jenkins) Freeman; A.B., Tift Coll., 1930; M.A. in English, U. N.C., 1932; Ed.D. in English, Columbia, 1952. Tchr. math. pub. schs., Dublin, Ga., 1930-31; tchr. social studies pub. schs., La Grange, Ga., 1932-42; tchr. social studies, English Peabody Demonstration Sch., Ga. State Coll. Women, 1942-48, prin., tchr. 1948-51; dir. curriculum Troup County Schs., La Grange, 1951-67; asso. prof. edn. West Ga. Coll., Carrollton, Ga.; 1967-69, prof. edn., 1969—, coordinator secondary edn. 1969-73, chmn. dept. secondary edn., 1973—. Del. Washington Conf. Academically Talented, 1958, White House Conf. Children and Youth, 1960; chmn. English curriculum guide com., Ga. Pub. Schs., 1960-64, mem. steering com., English curriculum guide com., 1965-68; pres. Ga. Dept. Instructional Supervision, 1961-62, co-dir. English Study in Ga., 1951-52. Bd. dirs. Troup-Harris-Cowetta Regional Library. Mem. League Women Voters (pres. Carrollton br. 1970-72), Am. Assn. U. Women (pres. Ga. div. 1957-59), Ga. Council Tchrs. English (pres. 1947-48), Ga. Writers Assn., Ga. Acad. Social Scis., Nat. Council Tchrs. English, Pi Lambda Theta, Kappa Delta Pi, Pi Gamma Mu, Delta Kappa Gamma. Preparation ednl. materials (with Lydia A. Thomas) The Reader's Digest, N.E.A. (exec. com. dept. rural education 1965-69), Reading Skill Builder, Grade 5, Part 3, 1960. Home: 305 Park Av LaGrange GA 30240 Office: West Ga Coll Carrollton GA 30117

FREEMAN, DONALD WILFORD, financial exec.; b. Brooksville, Fla., Sept. 25, 1929; s. Fred Maxwell and Dovie (Keef) F.; B.S., U. Ala., 1953, LL.B., 1953; LL.M., N.Y. U., 1957; m. Ruby Jane Lewis, Aug. 6, 1931; children—Clifton Lewis, Susan Anne. Accountant Ernst & Ernst, Atlanta, 1953-55; admitted to Ala. bar, 1953; tax atty. Office Chief Counsel, U.S. Treasury Dept., N.Y.C., 1955-57, West Point Mfg. Co. (Ga.), 1957-58; asst. treas. Ryder System, Inc., Miami, Fla., 1958-61; v.p., dir., Henderson's Portion Pak, Inc., 1961-63; pres. Biscayne Capital Corp., 1963-66; asso. Lazard Freres & Co., N.Y.C., 1967-69; pres. James A. Ryder Corp., Miami, 1969—. Served with AUS, 1946-48; PTO. C.P.A., Ga. Mem. Fla. Inst. C.P.A.'s, Phi Kappa Sigma, Beta Gamma Sigma. Episcopalian. Home: 13026 Nevada St Coral Gables FL 33156 Office: 2701 S Bayshore Dr Miami FL 33133

FREEMAN, EDWIN, realtor, state senator; b. nr. Harrodsburg, Ky., Dec. 10, 1921; s. Wheeler and Dora (Robinson) F.; grad. high sch.; m. Elsie Kirkland, Nov. 21, 1940; 1 dau., Ann Harriet (Mrs. William Dedman). Realtor, Harrodsburg, Ky., 1954—; auctioneer, owner tobacco warehouse, 1956—; mem. Ky. Senate, 1970—; dir. Mercer County Nat. Bank, Mercer Savs. & Loan Assn. Mem. Ky. Ho. of Reps., 1956-57, 62-63; county judge, Mercer County, 1965-69. Democratic chmn. Mercer County, 1965-69. Mason. Home: 505 Beaumont Av Harrodsburg KY 40330 Office: 300 Chiles St Harrodsburg KY 40330

FREEMAN, EUGENE ERNEST, JR., veneer mfg. co. exec.; b. Lexington, Ky., Sept. 10, 1929; s. Eugene Ernest and Laura (Tomlinson) F.; B.A., Washington and Lee U., 1951; M.S., N.Y. Coll. Forestry, 1953; m. Talitha Reid, Apr. 2, 1955; children—Laura Ann, Eugene Reid, George Tomlinson. With Freeman Corp., Winchester, Ky., 1953—, pres., 1955—; chmn. bd. Winchester Bank, 1974—. Bd. dirs. Ky. Forest Industries Com., 1958—, chmn., 1963-64; bd. dirs. Asso. Industries Ky., 1966-68, Clark County Hosp., Winchester. Mem. Am. Walnut Assn. (dir.), Fine Hardwoods Assn. (dir.), Phi Beta Kappa, Phi Delta Theta, Alpha Kappa Psi, Phi Eta Sigma. Rotarian (pres. 1962-63). Clubs: Union League (Chgo.); Keeneland, Idle House Country, Lafayette (Lexington); Winchester Country, Iroquois Hunt (Winchester). Home: PO Box 543 Winchester KY 40391 Office: PO Box 96 Winchester KY 40391

FREEMAN, GEORGE CLEMON, JR., lawyer; b. Birmingham, Ala., Jan. 3, 1929; s. George Clemon and Annie Laura (Gill) F.; B.A. magna cum laude, Vanderbilt U., 1950; LL.B., Yale, 1956; m. Anne Colston Hobson, Dec. 6, 1958; children—Anne Colston, George Clemon III, Joseph Reid Anderson. Admitted to Ala. bar, 1956, Va. bar, 1958; law clk. to Justice Black, U.S. Supreme Ct., 1956; asso. firm Hunton, Williams, Gay, Powell & Gibson, Richmond, Va., 1957-62, partner, 1962—. Cons. Va. Outdoor Recreation Study Commn. Va. Gen. Assembly, 1964-65, gov's. spl. com. on water resources, 1966. Mem. Richmond Democratic Com., 1964—, chmn., 1969-72. Bd. dirs. Richmond Symphony, 1958-64, sec., 1960-64; trustee Am. the Beautiful Fund. Served to lt. (j.g.) USNR, 1951-54. Mem. Am. (chmn. standing com. on facilities Law Library of Congress 1967-73, sec. continuing legal edn. com. sect. corporate banking and bus. law 1966—, chmn. trade assn. com. 1969—), Va., Richmond bar assns., Am. Law Inst., Nature Conservancy (chmn. Va. chpt. 1962-64), Phi Beta Kappa, Phi Delta Phi, Omicron Delta Kappa. Episcopalian. Clubs: Country, Deep Run Hunt (Richmond); Knickerbocker (N.Y.C.). Contbr. articles to profl. jours. Home: 10 Paxton Rd Richmond VA 23226 Office: 700 E Main St Richmond VA 23226

FREEMAN, GEORGE LESTER, assn. exec.; b. Detroit, Feb. 16, 1928; s. Jasper W. and Marie Lester F.; B.A., Vanderbilt U., 1951; m. Mary Roderick; children—Tom, Helen, Martha. Successively directory advt. salesman, office mgr., customer services, pub. relations staff, mem. exec. adminstrn., v.p. South Fla. area operations So. Bell Telephone Co., 1952-68; exec. v.p. Greater Miami (Fla.) C. of C., 1968—. Chmn. agy. operations com. United Fund Dade County, 1966-68, now adv. bd. Vol. Action Center; now mem. Fla. Gov.'s Adv. Com. Tourism, Manpower Area Planning Council, Gov.'s Task Force Coordinating Polit. Convs.; mem. vocational adv. com. Dade County (Fla.) Schs.; mem. com. Orange Bowl; Mem. exec. com. 3d Century U.S.A. Corp. Trustee Greater Miami Progress Found., Inc., Fla. Agrl. and Mech. U. Found.; bd. dirs. Fla. Internat. U. Mem. Nat. Alliance Businessmen (met. dir.). Clubs: Miami, Bankers, Aviation Executives. Home: 7350 S W 108th Terrace Miami FL 33156 Office: Greater Miami C of C 1200 Biscayne Blvd Miami FL 33132

FREEMAN, JAMES POLK, JR., dentist; b. Knoxville, Tenn., Mar. 31, 1929; s. James Polk and Dovie Mae (Jones) F.; student E. Tenn. State Coll., 1950; D.D.S., U. Tenn., 1954; m. Joyce Joan Leinart, June 26, 1955; children—James Polk III, Daniel, Joyce. Asso., Glen A. Bibee, Fountain City, Tenn., 1954-55; practice dentistry, LaFollette, Tenn., 1958—; mem. dental staff E. Tenn. Bapt. Hosp., 1954-55, 57—, chief surg. dental dept., 1960; mem. dental staff LaFollette Community Hosp., 1959—. Committeeman, troop 23 Boy Scouts Am., LaFollette, 1960—; chmn. Campbell County Indsl. Com., 1966-67. Vice mayor, chmn. finances City of LaFollette, 1967-71, mayor, 1971—. Bd. dirs. Clinch Powell River Valley Assn.; bd. dirs. LaFollette Housing Authority, 1964—. Served with USAF, 1955-57. Mem. Campbell County Health Dept. Mem. Am., Tenn., 2d Dist. (v.p. 1962, mem. exec. council 1963, 65-68) dental assns., Bapt. Brotherhood (sec. 1965-66), Powells Valley Conservation League, Pierre Fauchard Acad. Dentistry, LaFollette C. of C. (pres. 1966-67, dir. 1969—), Delta Tau Delta, Xi Psi Phi. Baptist (trustee 1961—, chmn. bd. trustees 1962-64). Mason (32 deg. Shriner). Clubs: Optimist (charter mem., past dir., pres. 1962-63, chmn. membership and attendance com. dist. 11 1963-64, lt. gov. Tenn. dist. 1965-66). Home: 312 W Central Av LaFollette TN 37766 Office: Davis Clinic Bldg LaFollette TN 37766

FREEMAN, MILTON V., lawyer; b. N.Y.C., Nov. 16, 1911; s. Samuel and Celia (Gelfand) F.; A.B., Coll. City of N.Y., 1931; LL.B., Columbia, 1934; m. Phyllis Young, Dec. 19, 1937; children—Nancy Lois (Mrs. Gans), Daniel Martin, Andrew Samuel, Amy Martha. Admitted to N.Y. bar, 1934; D.C. bar, 1946, U.S. Supreme Ct. bar, 1943; with gen. counsel's office, S.E.C., 1934-42, asst. solicitor, 1942-46; with securities div., F.T.C., 1934; practice with firm Arnold & Porter and predecessor firms, Washington, 1946—. Lectr. law schs. Trustee, Inst. for Internat. and Fgn. Trade Law, Georgetown U. Mem. Am., D.C., Fed. bar assns. Contbr. articles to legal jours. Home: 3405 Woolsey Dr Chevy Chase MD 20015 Office: 1229 19th St NW Washington DC 20036

FREEMAN, RALPH NEPTUNE, petroleum co. exec.; b. Barberton, O., Mar. 31, 1923; s. Oscar Neptune and Maude (Henderson) F.; B.Sc., Ohio State U., 1948; M.Sc. (Anne Voorheim Higgin scholar 1948-50), U. Ky., 1951; m. Grace Fisher Barrier, Sept. 12, 1948; children—Kathryn (Mrs. Carl A. Yakabowskas), Gretch S., Barbara L. Geologist, Magnolia Petroleum Co., 1950-57; with Pauley Petroleum Co., 1957-62, chief geologist, Mexico City, 1959-62; geologist Delhi Australian Petroleum Co., Adelaide, 1962-64; cons. geologist, Adelaide, 1964-67, Johannesburg, South Africa, 1967-68; gen. mgr. Ada Oil Co., Guayaquil, Ecuador, 1968-70; v.p. petroleum div. OKC Corp., Dallas, 1970—. Mem. sch. bd. Anglican Mission Sch., Amman, Jordan. Served with AUS, 1943-45. Mem. Am. Assn. Petroleum Geologists, Geol. Soc. Am., Am. Geol. Inst., Geol. Soc. South Africa, Geol. Soc. Australia, Royal Soc. South Australia, Australian-New Zealand Assn. Advancement Sci. Clubs: Petroleum, Engineers, Brookhaven Country (Dallas). Contbr. articles to profl. jours. Home: 2508 Grandview St Plano TX 75074 Office: 1949 N Stemmons Freeway Suite 100 Dallas TX 75207

FREEMAN, RICHARD WEST, JR., soft drink co. exec.; b. Chgo., May 15, 1938; s. Richard West and Montine (McDaniel) F.; grad. Culver Mil. Acad., 1956; B.B.A., Tulane U., 1960; m. Sandra Draughn, Jan. 4, 1964; children—Richard West III, Adair Draughn, Sarah Goodrich. Exec. asst. La. Coca-Cola Bottling Co. Ltd., New Orleans, 1963-69, exec. v.p., 1969-70, pres., 1970—. Chmn., Vieux Carre Commn., 1970—. Bd. dirs. Bur. Govtl. Research, 1970, Met. New Orleans Safety Council, 1966-70, Longue Vue Gardens, 1971—; trustee Delgado Mus., United Fund Greater New Orleans Area, Alton Ochsner Med. Found., Nat. Trust for Historic Preservation. Served to lt. (j.g.) USNR, 1960-63. Mem. Greater New Orleans Area C. of C., Soc. Colonial Wars in La. Presbyn. (elder). Rotarian. Clubs: Boston, La., La. Landmarks, Pickwick, Stratford. Home: 1640 State St New Orleans LA 70118 Office: 1050 S Jefferson Davis Pkwy New Orleans LA 70150

FREEMAN, THOMAS GENE, lawyer; b. Springfield, Ill., Oct. 24, 1937; s. Thomas Gene and Dorothy (Chodera) F.; A.B., U. Ill., 1960; J.D., U. Fla., 1965; m. Beverley Pride, Aug. 12, 1960; children—Nancy Sue, Melanie Elaine. Admitted to Fla. bar, 1965; partner Stenstrom, David & McIntosh, Sanford, 1966-72; pvt. practice, Altamonte Springs, 1973—. Instr., Police Standards Council; instr. bus. law Seminole Jr. Coll.; legal counsel Fla. Jr. C. of C., 1970-71. Municipal judge, Winter Springs, 1971-72. Pres., United Cerebral Palsy of Fla. Bd. dirs. Childrens Home Soc. Served with USNR, 1963. Named Municipal Judge of Year, 1971-72, One of Five Outstanding Young Men in Fla., 1971. Mem. Fla. (bd. govs. young lawyers sect.), Seminole County (v.p.) bar assns., Fla. Municipal Judges Assn. (pres. 1972), Fellowship Christian Athletes. Mason (32 deg.), Rotarian, Lion. Home: 2319 Castlewood Rd Maitland FL 32751 Office: 1007 Hwy 436 Altamonte Springs FL 32701

FREEMAN, WILLIAM M., educator, govt. ofcl.; b. Selma, Ala.; B.S., U. Denver, also M.A., Ph.D.; M.R. Ed., Dever Sch. Religion; postgrad. (So. Fund fellow) U. So. Cal. Mem. faculty So. U., Baton Rouge, 1957—. Goodwill ambassador U.S. Dept. State, 1959; now rep. State Dept. Confs. Internat. Relations Far East and Middle East. Mem. Omega Psi Phi (life, scholarship dir.). Baptist. Mason (33 deg.). Home: 1755 79th Av Baton Rouge LA 70807

FREESE, SIMON WILKE, civil engr.; b. Blossom, Tex., Dec. 4, 1900; s. Wilke Harm and Novella (Hancock) F.; student So. Meth. U., 1917-19; B.S., Mass. Inst. Tech., 1921; postgrad. Trinity Coll., Cambridge U., 1923-24; m. Eunice Elizabeth Brooks, June 30, 1927; children—Eunice (Mrs. Robb H. Rutledge), John Wilke, Lee Brooks. Partner, Hawley & Freese, cons. civil engrs., Ft. Worth, Tex., 1927-28, Hawley, Freese & Nichols, cons. civil engrs., Ft. Worth, 1928-38, Freese & Nichols, Ft. Worth, 1938—. Pres., Ft. Worth Bd. Edn., 1931-41. Served from maj. to lt. col., AUS, 1943-46. Mem. Am. Soc. C.E., Am. Water Works Assn., Nat. Soc. Profl. Engrs., Sigma Alpha Epsilon, Chi Epsilon. Mason. Club: Fort Worth. Home: 3318 Avondale St Fort Worth TX 76109 Office: 811 Lamar St Fort Worth TX 76102

FREGLY, MELVIN JAMES, physiologist, educator; b. Patton, Pa., May 26, 1925; s. Frank and Nellie May (Wellings) F.; B.S., Bucknell U., 1949, M.S., 1949; Ph.D., U. Rochester, 1952; m. Marilyn Sumner Southwick, May 30, 1956. Instr. physiology Harvard Med. Sch., Boston, 1952-56; asst. prof. physiology U. Fla. Coll. Medicine, Gainesville, 1956-60, asso. prof., 1960-65, prof. physiology, 1965—, asst. dean, 1966-72. Cons., Strasenburgh Pharm. Co., Rochester, N.Y., 1965-67. Served with AUS, 1943-46; PTO. Am. Physiol. Soc. Travel fellow to XXth Internat. Physiol. Congress, Brussels, 1956, Nat. Acad. Sci. Travel fellow XXIst Internat. Physiol. Congress, Buenos Aires, 1959, Internat. Union Physiol. Sci. Travel fellow to XXIId Internat. Physiol. Congress, Leiden, 1962. Mem. Am., Canadian physiol. socs., Endocrine Soc., Soc. Zoologists, N.Y. Acad. Scis., A.A.A.S., Soc. Exptl. Biology and Medicine (editorial bd. Proceedings 1966-69), Am. Thyroid Assn., Council on High Blood Pressure, Am. Heart Assn., Am. Soc. Nephrology, Sigma Xi. Editor: Oral Contraceptives and High Blood Pressure, 1974. Mem. editorial bd. Am. Jour. Physiology, 1972—. Contbr. articles to profl. jours., chpts. to books. Home: 6581 NW 20th Pl Gainesville FL 32605

FREIBURGER, E. ALLEN, marketing cons.; b. Chgo., Sept. 21, 1920; s. Emil Herman and Eleanor (Beringer) F.; student Northwestern U., 1939, 45, Lake Forest Coll., 1940, 41; m. Dolores Ruth Brant, June 15, 1946; children—Gary Allen, Gail Ann. Flight radio engr./cryptographer Intercontinental div. TWA, 1942-43; semi sr. engr. John M. Thorne, Inc., Washington, 1943-45; sales engr. Indsl. Condenser Corp., Chgo., 1946-48; regional sales mgr. Midwest region, govt. and indsl. div., dist. rep. radio and TV div. Philco Corp., Phila., 1948-53; regional mgr. Admiral Corp., Chgo., 1953-56; mdse. mgr. RCA Victor Div., Camden, N.J., 1956-57; gen. mgr. Concertapes, Inc., Wilmette, Ill., 1957-59; mgr. central-south region, communications systems div. ITT, Chgo., 1959-60; govt. relations mgr., videograph div. A.B. Dick Co., Chgo., 1960-63; Washington rep., mgr. NASA programs, mgr. aerospace programs, mgr. advanced tech. UNIVAC Def. Systems div. Sperry Rand Corp., St. Paul, 1963-67; dir. program devel. CEIR subsidiary Control Data Corp., Mpls., 1967; mgr. NASA programs, mgr. civil agys., space and def. div., mgr. NASA programs, advance systems marketing, sr. marketing cons., Control Data Corp., Mpls., 1967-72; marketing cons., dir. govt. marketing, dir. marketing, analytical services div. Tesdata Systems Corp., McLean, Va., 1972-73; owner Sr. Marketing Engrs., electronic engring. reps. and cons., Falls Church, Va., 1973—. Served with USNR, 1941-42. Mem. I.E.E.E., Am. Inst. Aeros. and Astronautics Sigma Pi Sigma (sustaining). Home: 3718 Tollgate Terrace Falls Church VA 22041

FREIDSON, MORRIS, retail drug co. exec.; b. Mpls., July 20, 1919; s. Michael and Freda (Rothman) F.; B.S., George Washington U., 1945; comml. certificate Strayer Coll., Washington, 1936; m. Shirley Fortunoff, Aug. 22, 1948. With Drug Fair, Inc., Alexandria, Va., 1957—, v.p. adminstrn., 1971-73, sr. v.p. adminstrn., 1973—, also mem. exec. com., chmn. mgmt. adv. com. Chmn. combined mgmt. research analysis Drug Fair-IBM Corp., 1973—. Mem. Crystal City (Va.) Civic Assn. Served with USAAF, 1942-45. Mem. Va., Potomac pharm. assns., Va. C. of C. Mem. B'nai B'rith. Club: Chantilly (Va.) Nat. Golf and Country. Home: 2111 Jeff Davis Hwy Arlington VA 22202 Office: 6295 Edsall Rd Alexandria VA 22314

FREIS, EDWARD DAVID, research physician; b. Chgo., May 13, 1912; s. Roy Joel and Rose (Goldstein) F.; B.S., U. Ariz., 1936; M.D., Columbia, 1940; m. Willa Irene Hussey, Aug. 12, 1936; children—S. Richard, Susan (Mrs. Ronald Ezell), Martha (Mrs. Charles Bramhall). Intern, Mass. Meml. Hosps., Boston, 1940-41; resident Boston City Hosp., 1941-42; research on drug treatment of hypertension Mass. Meml. Hosps., Boston, 1946-49; research on drug treatment of hypertension VA Hosp.-Georgetown U., Washington, 1949—, sr. med. investigator, 1957—. Served to maj. M.C., USAAF, 1942-45. Recipient Distinguished Achievement award Modern Medicine, 1970; Albert Lasker award in clin. medicine, 1971. Mem. Am. Soc. for Clin. Investigation, Am. Heart Assn., Am. Coll. Cardiology, Council for High Blood Pressure Research (mem. Dripps com. 1972—, mem. internat. exec. council 1970-73). Club: Crofton (Md.) Country. Editorial bd. Annals of Internal Medicine, 1973—. Home: 1201 Woodside Pkwy Silver Spring MD 20910 Office: VA Hospital Washington DC 20422

FREIXEDO, SALVADOR, clergyman, author; b. Spain, Apr. 23, 1923; s. Salvador and Maria (Tabares) F.; Licenciado in Philosophy and Theology, U. Comillas, Spain, 1953; Spl. degree in Theology, Alma Coll., Cal., 1954; degree in Asthetics, Montlaurier, Can., 1955; postgrad. Loyola U., Los Angeles, Fordham U., N.Y.C., 1956-57. Ordained priest Roman Catholic Ch., 1953; vice-nat. chaplain Young Christian Workers in Cuba, 1958; founder, nat. chaplain Young Christian Workers in P.R., San Juan, 1959-68; archdiocesan chaplain lay apostolate Diocese of San Juan, 1968—. Mem. Jr. C. of C. of San Juan (hon.). Author: 40 Casos de Injusticia social, 1958; My Church is Asleep, 1969; When UFOs Land, Dogmas Fly Away, 1970; The Diabolical Unconscious, 1973; The Rotten Authority, 1973. Office: Box 11155 Caparra Heights San Juan PR 00922

FRENCH, SHELBY RAY, accountant; b. Killeen, Tex., Nov. 26, 1937; s. Claude Thomas and Mavon Bell (Blair) F.; B.B.A., So. Meth. U., 1966; m. Nelda Adelle Tucker, June 20, 1958; children—Maria Denice, Michael Rene, Shelby Tyrone. Mgr. corporate accounting Varo, Inc., Garland, Tex., 1966-72; consol. accountant Tex. Instruments, Inc., Dallas, 1972-73; pvt. practice as C.P.A., Dallas, 1973—. C.P.A., Tex. Mem. Am. Inst. C.P.A.'s, Tex., Dallas socs. C.P.A.'s, Dallas Estate Planning Council. Mem. Ch. of Christ (treas. mission com. 1969—). Address: 9530 Ash Creek Dr Dallas TX 75228

FRENCH, W(ILLIAM) CHIPLEY, mining and elec. constrn. co. exec.; b. Miami, Fla., Oct. 31, 1940; s. Robert Mansfield, Jr., and Elizabeth (Jones) F.; B.S., B.A., U. Fla., 1963; m. Marion Phillips, Aug. 7, 1962; 1 son, Price Chipley. Ins. adjuster Crawford & Co., West Palm Beach, Fla., 1963-64; sales rep. Howe E. Moredock Co., Miami, Fla., 1964-65; product mgr. Canaveral Indian River Groves, 1965-68; dir., v.p., product mgr. Lake Byrd Citrus Packing Co., 1968-71; v.p. Goldfield Corp., Melbourne, Fla., 1970—; v.p., dir. Sebastian River Groves, 1966-70, Fla. Orange Growers, Inc., 1967-71, Oak Hammock Groves, Inc.; dir. Citrus Growers of Fla., Inc. Mem. Planning and Zoning Bd., Palm Bay, Fla., 1972—, Recreation Bd., Palm Bay, 1973—. Mem. Melbourne Area C. of C. Republican. Episcopalian. Rotarian. Club: Port Malabar Country (Palm Bay). Home: 565 Knecht Rd Palm Bay FL 32905 Office: 65 E NASA Blvd Melbourne FL 32901

FRENKEL, EUGENE PHILLIP, physician; b. Detroit, Aug. 27, 1929; s. David Eugene and Eva (Antin) F.; B.S., Wayne State U., 1949; M.D., U. Mich., 1953; m. Dr. Rhoda Smilay, Dec. 18, 1958; children—Lisa Michelle, Peter Alan. Intern Wayne County Gen. Hosp., Eloise, Mich., 1953-54; resident Boston City Hosp., 1954-55, U. Mich. Med. Center, 1957-59, research asso., 1959-62; asst. prof. internal medicine Southwestern Med. Sch. of U. Tex., 1962-64, asso. prof., 1964-69, prof., 1969—, Am. Cancer Soc. prof. oncology, 1973—; cons. VA Hosp., Dallas, Brooke Army Hosp., San Antonio, Baylor, Presbyn., Meth. hosps., Dallas. Served with USAF, 1955-57. Diplomate Am. Bd. Internal Medicine (subsplty. hematology and med. oncology. Fellow A.C.P.; mem. Am., Internat. socs. hematology, Am. Fedn. Clin. Research, So. Soc. Clin. Research, Am. Assn. Cancer Research, Am. Soc. Clin. Oncology, Am. Cancer Soc. (pres. Dallas County unit 1970-71), Am. Soc. Clin. Investigation. Contbr. articles to profl. jours. Home: 4028 Shady Hill Dr Dallas TX 75229 Office: 5323 Harry Hines Blvd Dallas TX 75235

FRESHOUR, JON DANNING, mus. ofcl.; b. Jackson Hole, Wyo., July 13, 1938; s. Beryl Harry and Dorothy Emma (McCain) F.; B.F.A., Alfred U., 1967. Research asst. Nat. Portrait Gallery, Smithsonian Instn., Washington, 1968-69, registrar, 1969—. Mem. Am. Assn. Museums. Served with USNR, 1961-65. Office: F St at 8th NW Washington DC 20560

FRETZ, EUGENE CAMP, newspaperman; b. Knoxville, Tenn., Jan. 23, 1922; s. Eugene Camp and Elizabeth (Sprankle) F.; B.A., U. Tenn., 1943; LL.B., U. Va., 1948; m. Llewellyn Bane Sprigg, Feb. 11, 1950; children—Elizabeth Llewellyn (Mrs. Kent G. Murdick), Thomas Robertson. Reporter, copy editor Knoxville Jour., 1941-45; copy editor Portland (Ore.) Oregonian, 1945-46; copy editor Tulsa World, 1948; copy editor, Sunday mag. editor, book revs. Ark. Gazette, Little Rock, 1949-59, advt., pub. relations, 1959-73, mem. staff, 1973—. Mem. Phi Gamma Delta. Democrat. Episcopalian. Clubs: Country of Little Rock; Cherokee Country (Knoxville). Home: 305 Crystal Ct Little Rock AR 72205

FREUDENTHAL, ERNEST GUENTHER, corp. exec.; b. Mannheim, Germany, July 22, 1920; s. Leopold and Selma (Rosenthal) F.; came to U.S., 1937, naturalized, 1944; B.A. in Econs., Vanderbilt U., 1948, M.A., 1971; m. Stephanie R. Karlsruher, Dec. 26, 1948; children—Pamela Diane (Mrs. Charles H. Lusthaus), Joan Connie. With Werthan Industries, Nashville, 1942—, v.p. mfg. operations, 1969-70, sr. v.p. corp. devel., 1970—; dir. Check Printers, Inc., House Boating Corp. Am.; adj. asso. prof. engring. mgmt. Vanderbilt U. Pres. Council Community Services Nashville, 1970-72, Jewish Community Center Nashville, 1965-67; mem. Nashville Mayor's Adv. Com. Housing and Urban Devel., 1970-73, Met. Nashville/Davidson County Area Manpower Planning Council, 1973—; pres. Jewish Fedn. Nashville and Middle Tenn., 1974—. Bd. dirs. South St. Community Center, Nashville, 1962-68. Served with AUS, 1944-46. Sr. mem. Am. Inst. Indsl. Engrs., Am. Soc. Quality Control; mem. Textile Quality Control Assn. (past pres.), Am. Assn. Textile Chemists and Colorists, Phi Beta Kappa. Jewish religion (trustee temple). Club: University (Nashville). Author papers in field. Home: 4406 Sunnybrook Dr Nashville TN 37205 Office: PO Box 1268 Nashville TN 37202

FREUND, RUDOLF JAKOB, statistician, educator; b. Kiel, Germany, Mar. 3, 1927; s. Rudolf Ernst and Susanne Herta (Ascher) F.; came to U.S., 1939, naturalized, 1945; M.A., U. Chgo., 1951; Ph.D., N.C. State U., 1955; m. Margaret Minor Caskie, June 27, 1948; children—Susanne (Mrs. Nicholas Dalio), Karl, Jaquelin. Asso. prof. statistics Va. Poly. Inst., 1955-62; prof., asso. dir. Inst. Statistics, Tex. A. and M. U., College Station, 1962—. Served with AUS, 1945-46. Mem. Am. Statis. Assn. Lion. Home: 1508 Dominik Dr College Station TX 77840

FREY, GERARD LOUIS, bishop; b. New Orleans, May 10, 1914; s. Andrew and Maria Therese (DeRose) F.; D.D., St. Joseph's Sem. at St. Benedict's La., 1933; D.D., Notre Dame Sem., New Orleans, 1933. Ordained priest Roman Cath. Ch., 1938; asst. pastor, Taft, La., 1938-46; asst. dir. Confraternity Christian Doctrine, Archdiocese New Orleans, also asst. St. James Ch., New Orleans, dir. Confraternity Christian Doctrine, Archdiocese New Orleans, also asst. pastor St. Leo the Great Paris, 1946-67; founding pastor St. Francis Cabrini Ch., New Orleans, 1942-63; pastor St. Frances de Sales Parish, Houma, La., 1962-67; clergy rep. 2d Vatican Council, 1964; dir. Diocesan Friendship Corps, New Orleans, 1966; bishop of Savannah, Ga., 1967-73, of Lafayette, La., 1973—; Episcopal moderator Theresians Am., 1968—. Recipient Bishop Tracy Vocation award St. Joseph's Sem. Alumni Assn., 1959. Address: PO Box 3387 421 Lippi Blvd Lafayette LA 70501

FREY, LOUIS, JR., congressman; b. Rutherford, N.J., Jan. 11, 1934; s. Louis and Mildred (Engel) F.; B.A. cum laude, Colgate U., 1955; J.D. with honors, Mich. Law Sch., 1961; m. Marcia Turner, Nov. 1956; children—Julie, Lynne, Louis, Lauren, Chris. Admitted to Fla. bar, 1961; practice in Orlando; asst. county solicitor, 1963; mem. 91st-93d Congresses from 5th and 9th dists. Fla. Served to lt (j.g.) USNR, 1955-58; comdr. Res. Mem. Order of Coif, Phi Gamma Delta, Phi Delta Phi. Lutheran. Home: 139 Genius Dr Winter Park FL 32789 Office: 214 Cannon House Office Bldg Washington DC 20515

FRICK, FRED GENTRY, accountant; b. Dallas, May 27, 1932; s. Fred Henry and Opal Geraldine (Gentry) F.; B.B.A., Stephen F. Austin State U., 1954; m. Sue Ann Alley, Jan. 24, 1953; children—Paul, Michael, Scott. With Price Waterhouse & Co., Dallas, 1955-65, Seattle, 1965-68, partner in charge Nashville office, 1968—. C.P.A., Tenn., Tex., others. Mem. Am. Inst. C.P.A.'s, Nat. Assn. Accountants, Tenn. Soc. C.P.A.'s. Baptist. Elk. Clubs: Cumberland, Hillwood Country, Nashville City, Exchange (Nashville). Home: 1151 Gateway Lane Nashville TN 37220 Office: 3d Nat Bank Bldg Nashville TN 37219

FRICKE, ARTHUR LEE, educator; b. Huntington, W.Va., Mar. 6, 1934; s. Arthur Henry and Anna Agnes (Turley) F.; Ch.E., U. Cinn., 1957; M.S., U. Wis., 1959, Ph.D., 1961; m. Alice Faye Saunders, Mar. 14, 1954; children—Alice Kaye, Marsha Lee, Arthur Christian. Instr. chem. engring. U. Wis., Madison, 1959-60; research engr. Shell Devel. Co., Emeryville, Cal., 1961-63, group leader, 1963-65; asst. dept. mgr., lab. tech., market devel. unit, mgr. market devel. unit Shell Chem. Co., Martinez, 1965-66, sr. technologist, N.Y.C., 1966-67; asso. chem. engring. Va. Poly. Inst. and State U., Blacksburg, 1967-71, asst. prof., 1971—; v.p. research, dir. Polytron Corp. of Va., Christiansburg, 1968-70. Shell fellow, 1958-59, Esso fellow, 1960-61. Mem. Am. Inst. Chem. Engrs. (sect. vice chmn. 1971-73), Soc. Plastics Engrs., Am. Chem. Soc., Sigma Xi, Tau Beta Pi, Alpha Chi Sigma. Lutheran (mem. ch. council 1963-65, 72—). Patentee in field. Home: 906 Elliott Dr Blacksburg VA 24060

FRIDAY, JOHN ROBERT, chem. engr.; b. Dallas, Jan. 14, 1935; s. Earnest E. and Robbye (Douthit) F.; B.S., Okla. State U., 1957; Ph.D. (NSF fellow 1960-62), Purdue U., 1963; m. Jane Wilson, Mar. 9, 1958; children—John D., Janet, Ellen. Asso. engr., tech. service Humble Oil, Baytown, Tex., 1957-59; with Continental Oil Co., Ponca City, Okla., 1963—, dir. processing lab., 1970—. Patentee in field. Home: 1118 El Camino St Ponca City OK 74601 Office: Process Lab Continental Oil Co Ponca City OK 74601

FRIDAY, WILLIAM CLYDE, univ. pres.; b. Raphine, Va., July 13, 1920; s. David L. and Mary E. (Rowan) F.; student Wake Forest Coll., 1937; B.S., N.C. State Coll., 1941; LL.B., U. N.C., 1948; LL.D., Belmont Abbey Coll., Wake Forest Coll., 1957, Duke, Princeton, 1958, Elon Coll., 1959, Davidson Coll., 1961, U. Ky., 1970; m. Ida Howell, May 13, 1942; children—Frances H., Mary H., Ida Elizabeth. Admitted to N.C. bar, 1948; asst. dean student U. N.C., 1948-51, asst. to pres., 1951-55, sec. of univ., 1955-56, acting. pres., 1956, pres., 1956—. Past pres. N.C. div. Am. Cancer Soc.; past chmn. Am. Council on Edn.; past mem. central adv. council Marshall Scholarship Scheme; chmn. Pres.'s Task Force on Edn., 1966-67; vice chmn. So. Regional Edn. Bd., 1967-69, mem. exec. com., 1969—; mem. nat. council Boy Scouts Am. Trustee Carnegie Found. for Advancement Teaching; bd. visitors Davidson Coll.; mem. Carnegie Commn. on Higher Edn. Served as lt. USNR, World War II. Mem. Assn. Am. Univs. (pres. 1971). Democrat. Baptist. Home: 402 E Franklin St Chapel Hill NC 27514

FRIDOVICH, IRWIN, educator; b. N.Y.C., Aug. 2, 1929; s. Louis and Sylvia (Applebaum) F.; B.S., Coll. City N.Y., 1951; Ph.D., Duke, 1955; m. Mollie D. Finkel, Sept. 7, 1952; children—Sharon E., Judith L. Faculty, Duke U. Med. Center, Durham, N.C., 1956—, prof. biochemistry, 1969—. Mem. biochemistry study sect. NIH, 1967-71. Mem. Nat. Bd. Med. Examiners, Am. Soc. Biol. Chemists, N.C. Acad. Scis., Sigma Xi. Contbr. articles to profl. jours. Home: 3517 Courtland Dr Durham NC 27707

FRIEDBERG, FELIX, educator; b. Kopenhagen, Denmark, Apr. 3, 1921; s. Abram and Lina (Schwartz) F.; brought to U.S., 1938; naturalized, 1944; B.S., U. Denver, 1944; Ph.D., U. Cal. at Berkeley, 1947; m. Gladys Chester, Aug. 16, 1971. Research fellow U. Cal., Berkeley, 1947-48; instr. Coll. Medicine, dept. biochemistry Howard U., Washington, 1948-52, asst. prof., 1953-57, asso. prof., 1957-61, prof. biochemistry, 1961—; vis. lectr. Cath. U. Am., Washington, 1950-52. Recipient Lederle Med. Faculty award, 1956. Mem. Am. Soc. Biol. Chemists, Wash. Acad. Scis., Phi Lambda Upsilon, Phi Beta Kappa, Sigma Xi. Author: Thoughts About Life, 1954. Contbr. articles to various pubs. Office: Coll Medicine Dept Biochemistry Howard U Fifth and W Sts NW Washington DC 20001

FRIEDHEIM, JERRY WARDEN, govt. ofcl.; b. Joplin, Mo., Oct. 7, 1934; s. Volmer Havens and Billie Alice (Warden) F.; B.J., U. Mo., 1956, A.M., 1962; m. Shirley Margarette Beavers, Oct. 17, 1956; children—Daniel Volmer, Cynthia Dianne, Thomas Eric. Reporter, editor, editorial writer Neosho (Mo.) Daily News, Joplin (Mo.) Globe, Columbia Missourian, 1956-61; instr. U. Mo. at Columbia, 1961-62; mem. staff Ho. of Reps., Washington, 1962; legislative asst., press sec., exec. asst. U.S. Senator John Tower, Washington, 1963-69; dep. asst. sec. Def. for pub. affairs, Washington, 1969-73, asst. sec. Def., 1973—. Served to capt. AUS, 1956-58. Congressional fellow Am. Polit. Sci. Assn.; mem. Sigma Delta Chi. Author: Where Are the Voters, 1968. Home: 3412 Old Dominion Blvd Alexandria VA 22305 Office: The Pentagon Washington DC 20301

FRIEDHEIM, STEPHEN BAILEY, assn. exec.; b. Joplin, Mo., Nov. 13, 1934; s. Robert Wray and Virginia Grace (Bailey) F.; student U. Ark., 1952-56; m. Maureen E. Kulpin Mauck, Sept. 16, 1972; children by previous marriage—Neenah Marie, Stephen Bailey II, Robert William, Juli Ann, Rene, Paul Adam. Announcer Radio Sta. KBRS, Springdale, Ark., 1956-57; newsman Radio Sta. KFSB, Joplin, 1957; dir. pub. relations Am. Personnel and Guidance Assn., Washington, 1961-66; exec. dir. Am. Soc. for Med. Tech., Houston, 1966—. Bd. govs. Nat. Econ. Council Allied Health Professions. Served with AUS, 1957-61. Recipient Freedom Found. award, 1960, 62; American Legion Aux. award, 1961; Nat. Safety Council award, 1961. Fellow Australasian Coll. Biomed. Scientists; mem. Am. Soc. Assn. Execs. (bd. editors and pubs.), Acacia. Episcopalian. Home: 10627 Inwood St Houston TX 77042 Office: 5555 W Loops St Bellaire TX 77401

FRIEDLANDER, HERBERT NORMAN, research co. exec.; b. Chicago Heights, Ill., Mar. 12, 1922; s. Harry and Bertha (Tartak) F.; B.S., U. Chgo., 1942, Ph.D., 1947; m. Sophie Thoness, Oct. 10, 1943; children—Miriam (Mrs. Neil Fisch), Carl, Ira. Dir. new products research and devel., mgr. polymer sci. Chemstrand Research Center, Inc., Durham, N.C., 1962-67, v.p., dir. tech. operations, 1967—. Chmn. Gordon Research Conf. on Polymers, 1966; dir. Goldsworthy Engring. Co., 1967-70. Dir. N.C. Engring. Found., Raleigh, 1966—; bd. dirs. Wake County Community Council, Raleigh, 1969-72; trustee United Fund, Wake County, N.C., 1967—. Mem. Soc. Aerospace Material and Process Engrs., Am. Chem. Soc., A.A.A.S., Fiber Soc., Phi Beta Kappa, Sigma Xi. Mem. B'nai B'rith. Club: Racquet (Raleigh, N.C.). Contbr. articles to various pubs. Patentee in field. Home: 2409 Rock Ridge Ct Raleigh NC 27612 Office: PO Box 731 Durham NC 27702

FRIEDMAN, ABRAHAM SOLOMON, govt. ofcl.; b. N.Y.C., Oct. 25, 1921; s. Israel Hyman and Sarah Golda (Cohen) F.; B.A., Bklyn. Coll., 1943; diploma chem. engring. Pa. State U., 1944; Ph.D., Ohio State U., 1950; m. Diana Elena Scott, July 4, 1952; children—Danielle Suzanna, Rebecca Lea, Abigail Sarah, Michelle Miriam. Chemist, engr. Manhattan Project, Decatur, Ill., Oak Ridge, Tenn., Chgo., 1944-46; mem. research faculty Ohio State U., Columbus, 1950-51, U. Amsterdam (Netherlands), 1951-52; research scientist Nat. Bur. Standards, Washington, 1952-56; sr. chemist U.S. AEC, Washington, 1956-62, sci. rep. Am. Embassy, Paris, France, 1962-65, dir. div. internat. programs, Washington, 1966—. Served with AUS, 1943-46. Recipient Distinguished Alumni award Bklyn. Coll., 1969. Mem. Am. Phys. Soc., Am. Chem. Soc., A.A.A.S., Netherlands Phys. Soc., N.Y., Washington acads. scis., Philos. Soc. Washington. Author: (with Haar and Beckett) Ideal Gas Thermodynamic Functions and Isotope Exchange Functions, 1961. Home: 6305 Phyllis Lane Bethesda MD 20034 Office: US AEC Washington DC 20545

FRIEDMAN, BEN IGNATIUS, physician, educator; b. Cin., Oct. 18, 1926; s. Ben and Ruth (Mueller) F.; M.D., U. Cin., 1948, postgrad., 1948; m. Ruth Reinhart, Jan. 24, 1954; 1 son, Richard. Intern Cin. Gen. Hosp., 1948-49, resident, 1949-50; resident Duke Hosp., 1950, 1952-53; fellow hematology and nutrition Cin. Gen. Hosp., 1953-55; practice medicine, specializing in internal medicine and hematology, Cin., 1955-67; attending phys. City Memphis Hosps., 1968; mem. staff Memphis VA Hosp.; mem. faculty U. Cin., 1953-68, asst. prof. radiology, 1964-68, asso. prof. medicine, 1965-68; prof. medicine Coll. Medicine, U. Tenn., Memphis, 1968—, prof. radiology, 1968-73, acting chmn. dept. radiology, 1971-73, prof. nuclear medicine, 1973—, dir. div. radiation scis., 1973—. Served to capt. M.C. USAF, 1950-52. Diplomate Am. Bd. Internal Medicine, Am. Bd. Nuclear Medicine. Fellow A.C.P.; mem. Soc. Nuclear Medicine, Shelby County Med. Soc., A.M.A., Am. Soc. Hematology, Tenn. Radiol. Soc., C. of C. (culture com. 1971—). Contbr. articles to profl. jours. Home: 4541 Shady Grove Memphis TN 38117 Office: 865 Jefferson St Memphis TN 38163

FRIEDMAN, EPHRAIM RICHARD, optometrist; b. Youngstown, O., Sept. 19, 1918; s. Martin Benjamin and Flora (Klein) F.; O.D., Ill. Coll. Optometry, 1939; m. Ruth Baird, Dec. 13, 1943; children—Carol (Mrs. Donald Reiser), Diane (Mrs. Paul Capehart), Paula (Mrs. Dan Spigel). Optometrist, Dallas. Mem. Tex. Optometry Bd., 1973—; chmn. enforcement div. Dallas Hist. Soc., 1966-73. Served with USNR, 1941-45. Fellow Am. Acad. Optometry, Southwest Contact Lens Soc. (treas. 1967-70); mem. Tex. Optometric Assn. (pres. 1969-71), North Tex. Optometric Soc. (pres. 1952-54). Jewish religion. Mem. B'nai B'rith, Lion. Home: 7240 Yamini Dr Dallas TX 75230 Office: 2550 Redbird Lane Dallas TX 75237

FRIEDMAN, SAMUEL JOHN, research co. exec.; b. Cleve., Jan. 25, 1918; s. Adolph Jacob and Margaret Helen (Smith) F.; B.S., Case Western Res. U., 1939, M.S., 1941; m. Saralee Long, Oct. 21, 1950; children—Alden James, Brion David. Chem. engr. E.I. duPont de Nemours & Co., Wilmington, Del., 1941-47, indsl. engr., Parlin, N.J., 1947-48, chem. engr., Wilmington, 1948-50, sr. engr., Camden, S.C., 1950-52, group leader, 1952-53, research supr., Waynesboro, Va., 1953-57, sr. tech. supr., 1957-62, research mgr., Wilmington, 1962-63, tech. supt., 1963-69, lab. dir., Old Hickory, Tenn., 1969—. Mem. A.A.A.S., Am. Inst. Chem. Engrs., Am. Chem. Soc., Am. Soc. M.E., Nashville C. of C., Phi Kappa Tau, Gamma Phi, Tau Beta Pi, Sigma Xi. Club: Hillwood Country (Nashville). Patentee in field. Contbr. articles to profl. pubs. Home: 708 Summerly Dr Nashville TN 37209 Office: Textile Fibers Dept Old Hickory TN 37138

FRIEDMAN, SUZANNE LOIS NEUMAN (MRS. THEODORE FRIEDMAN), social worker, educator, b. Cleve., Dec. 14, 1931; d. Bertram Morton and Gertrude (Miller) Neuman; A.B., U. Ky., 1953; M.S., Case Western Res. U., 1958; m. Theodore Friedman, Apr. 12, 1959; children—Greta Ruth, Aron David. Field dir., camp dir. Dayton (O.) Girl Scout Council, 1953-56; with Eastern State Hosp., Lexington, Ky., 1958-73, program dir. community placement program, 1969-72; asst. prof. social work Eastern Ky. U., 1973—. Pres., Jewish Community Assn., 1970-71. Bd. dirs. Sarah Fox Ades Nursery Sch., 1969-72, Lexington. Mem. Nat. Assn. Social Workers, Phi Sigma Sigma. Jewish religion (synagogue trustee, chmn. edn. com. 1968-70). Home: 307 Lakeshore Dr Lexington KY 40502 Office: Dept Anthropology Sociology and Social Work Eastern Kentucky U Richmond KY 40475

FRIEDRICH, OTTO MARTIN, JR., elec. engr., educator; b. Austin, Tex., Jan. 29, 1939; s. Otto Martin and Lillie Louise (Stark) F.; B.S. in E.E., U. Tex., 1961, M.S. in E.E., 1962, Ph.D. in E.E., 1965. Research engr. U. Tex., Austin, 1961-65, mem. faculty, 1965—, research engr.-faculty, 1969—, asst. dir. Electronics Research Center, 1971—. Cons. profl. engring. to industry, Fed., State and local govtl. agys., profl. engring. socs. Mem. president's com. Am. Christian Coll., Tulsa, 1973—. Recipient Dr. Charles Stark Draiper award Instrument Soc. Am., 1972. Registered profl. engr., Tex. Mem. I.E.E.E. (sr.) (chmn. working group nat. security 1973—), Instrument Soc. Am., Am. Phys. Soc., A.A.A.S., Am. Inst. Aeros. and Astronautics, Am. Geophys. Soc., Optical Soc. Am., Nat., Tex. socs. profl. engrs., Tex. Acad. Sci., Eta Kappa Nu, Tau Beta Pi, Sigma Xi, Phi Kappa Phi. Contbr. articles to various publs. Home: 1125 Shady Lane Austin TX 78721 Office: ENS #114B U Tex Austin TX 78712

FRIEMEL, JEROME LOUIS, feed co. exec.; b. Canyon, Tex., Dec. 9, 1932; s. Herbert Joseph and Josephine Teresa (Wieck) F.; student West Tex. State U., Canyon, 1970; m. Romilda Mary Gerber, Apr. 24, 1957; children—Rebecca Marie, John Barry, Anna Beth, Karen Teresa, Randall Louis. Ind. agr. businessman, Deaf Smith, Oldham, Dallam and Carson Counties, Tex. and Otero County, N.M., 1957—; sec., dir. Latigo Co., Inc., Westway Feeders, Inc.; sec.-treas., dir. Tularosa Farms, Inc.; dir. Hereford Grain Corp., S.W. Feed Yards, Inc. Chmn. judges panel N.M. Maid of Cotton Pageant, 1971; mem. Vets. Land Bd., 1968-74. Dir. Deaf Smith County Farm Bur. Served with U.S. Army, 1953-55. Mem. Deaf Smith County Water Assn., Grain Sorghum Producers Assn., Tex. Wheat Growers Assn., Tex.-N.M. Sugar Beet Growers Assn. K.C. Patentee in field. Home: Route 4 Hereford TX 79045 Office: Box 87 Hereford TX 79045

FRIEND, AARON DAVID, elec. engr.; b. El Dorado, Ark., Oct. 8, 1921; s. Ralph Jacob and Sophrona Elizabeth (Gregory) F.; student Okla. State U., 1944, LeTourneau Coll., 1959-62; m. Barbara Ann Hensley, June 21, 1941; children—Reginald David, Terrye Gale (Mrs. Frank Montes), Dennis Mark, Sherry Beth, Vicki Carol. Constrn., maintenance supr. R.G. LeTourneau, Inc., Longview, Tex., 1946-55, plant engr., 1955-58, elec. test engr., 1958-61, elec. design engr., 1961-67; pres. Allied Armature Works, Harvey, La., 1967-68; chief elec. engr. Marathon LeTourneau Co., Longview, 1968—. Cons. offshore drilling rig power systems, 1967—. Served with USAF, 1943-46. Decorated Presidential citation. Mem. I.E.E.E., Christian and Missionary Alliance (trustee 1960-72; elder 1965-73). Clubs: Civitan, Longview (pres. 1972-73; dist. lt. gov. 1973-74) (Longview, Tex.). Patentee in field. Home: 1515 Auburn St Longview TX 75601 Office: PO Box 2307 Longview TX 75601

FRIEND, EDWARD MALCOLM, lawyer; s. Edward M. and May (Gusfield) F.; A.B., U. Ala., 1933, LL.B., 1935; m. Hermione Frances Curjel, Sept. 22, 1938; children—Ellen (Mrs. Frederick John Elsas), Edward M. Admitted to Ala. bar, 1935; individual practice law, Birmingham, 1935—. Mem. bd. Nat. Legal Aid and Defender Assn., 1959-62; gen. co-chmn. Jefferson County (Ala.) United Fund, 1959; pres. Legal Aid Soc., Birmingham, 1954-55; pres. Family Counseling Assn., Jefferson County, 1958-59; pres. Ala. Law Sch. Found., 1969-71. Trustee Ala. Law Sch. Found., Children's Hosp., Meth. Hosp., Birmingham Symphony Orch.; bd. dirs. Jefferson County A.R.C.; mem. nat. bd. Nat. Conf. Christians and Jews, 1969-71. Served with AUS, 1941-45; brig. gen. Res. ret. Decorated Legion of Merit, Bronze Star medal with cluster (U.S.); Croix de Guerre with palm (France); recipient Daniel J. Meador Outstanding Alumnus award U. Ala. Law Sch., 1971; Outstanding Service award U.S. Army. Mem. Ala. State Bar Assn. (co-chmn. joint com. lawyers and interested citizens to study Ala. correctional instns. and procedures 1973), Birmingham Bar Assn. (v.p. 1970, pres. 1971), Birmingham C. of C. (bd. dirs.), Phi Beta Kappa, Omicron Delta Kappa, Zeta Beta Tau. Rotarian (Birmingham pres. elect). Home: 22 Woodhill Rd Birmingham AL 35223 Office: First Fed Bldg 2030 1st Av N Birmingham AL 35203

FRIEND, RALPH EDWARD, accountant; b. Satanta, Kan., Sept. 17, 1934; s. Raymond E. and Julia (Stidd) F.; B.S., U. Southwestern La., 1956; m. Beverly Castille, Apr. 6, 1958; 1 son, Brian E. Staff accountant Peat, Marwick, Mitchell & Co., C.P.A.'s, New Orleans, 1960-64, Paul Crochet, C.P.A., New Iberia, La., 1965-66; partner Crochet, Dressel & Friend, C.P.A.'s, New Iberia, 1966-70, Crochet, Friend & Co., C.P.A.'s, New Iberia, 1970-72; sole proprietor Ralph Friend CPA, New Iberia, 1972—. Mem. Am. Inst. C.P.A.'s, La. Soc. C.P.A.'s (treas. Lafayette chpt. 1968-69, sec. 1969-70, v.p. 1970-71, pres. 1971-72) Methodist (treas. 1971-73). Rotarian (pres. 1972-73). Home: 618 Myra St New Iberia LA 70560 Office: 1919 E Main St New Iberia LA 70560

FRIES, EDWARD DAVID, physician; b. Chgo., May 13, 1912; s. Roy Joel and Rose (Goldstein) F.; B.S., U. Ariz., 1936; M.D., Columbia, 1940; m. Willa Irene Hussey, Aug. 13, 1934; children—S. Richard, Susan (Mrs. Ronald Ezell), Martha (Mrs. Bramhall). Intern Mass. Meml. Hosp., Boston, 1940-42; asst. resident Evans Meml. Hosp., Boston, 1946-47; practice medicine, specializing in internal medicine, 1949—; instr. medicine Boston U., 1946-49, research fellow, 1947-49; adj. prof. Georgetown U., Washington, 1949-54, chief Hypertension Clinic, 1950, prof. medicine, 1957—, dir. Cardiovascular Research Lab., 1949—; asst. chief med. service VA Hosp., Washington, 1949-54, chief med. service, 1954-59, sr. med. investigator, 1959—. Served with M.C., USAAF, 1942-46. Recipient Silver Medalion, Alumni Assn. Columbia U. Coll. Physicians and Surgeons, 1967, Distinguished Achievement award Modern Medicine mag., 1970, Vicennial medal Georgetown U., 1971, Albert Lasker award for clin. research, 1971. Diplomate Am. Bd. Internal Medicine. Fellow A.M.A., A.C.P.; mem. Mass. Med. Soc., Am. (vice chmn. council on high blood pressure research 1960, chmn. 1961), Washington (pres. 1963-64) heart assns., So. Soc. Clin. Research (v.p. 1953), Am. Soc. Clin. Investigation, Soc. Exptl. Biology and Medicine, Am. Soc. Pharmacology, Am. Soc. Study Arteriosclerosis, Biophys. Soc., Am. Soc. Pharmacology and Exptl. Therapeutics, Instrument Soc. Am., Am. Fedn. Clin. Research., Am. Physiol. Soc. Club: Crofton Country. Contbr. articles in field to profl. jours. Home: 1201 Woodside Pkwy Silver Spring MD 20910 Office: 50 Irving St NW Washington DC 20422

FRIES, HELEN SERGEANT HAYNES (MRS. STUART G. FRIES), civic leader; b. Atlanta; d. Harwood Syme and Alice (Hobson) Haynes; student Coll. William and Mary, 1935-38; m. Stuart G. Fries, May 5, 1938. Bd. mem. Community Ballet Assn., Huntsville, Ala., 1968—; mem. nat. nurses aid com. A.R.C., 1958-59; dir. A.R.C. Aero Club, England, 1943-44; supr. A.R.C. Clubmobile, Europe, 1944-46. Bd. dirs. Madison County Republican Club, 1969-70; mem. nat. council Women's Nat. Rep. Club N.Y., 1963—, chmn. hospitality com., 1963-65; bd. dirs. League Rep. Women, 1952-61. Mem. Nat. Soc. Colonial Dames Am., D.A.R., Nat. Trust for Historic Preservation, Va., Valley Forge (Pa.), Eastern Shore Va., Huntsville hist. socs., Assn. for Preservation of Va. Antiquities, Greensboro Soc. for Preservation, Tenn. Valley Geneal. Soc., English Speaking Union, Nat. Symphony Orch. (women's com.). Clubs: Washington, Capitol Hill, Army-Navy Country (Washington); Garden (Redstone Arsenal), Redstone (Ala.) Yacht; Army-Navy (D.C.). Home: care Col Stuart G Fries TUSLOG Det 193 Box 1604 APO New York City NY 09289

FRIES, HERBERT CHRISTIAN, engring. exec.; b. Vienna, Austria, Jan. 19, 1917; s. Egon and Rosa Renee Fries; chem. engring. diploma Tech. U. Vienna, 1940; postgrad. Universidad Nacional de Ingenieria, Lima, Peru, U. Tulsa; m. Helga Fischer, Sept. 12, 1942; children—Christiane, Margaret Rose, Norbert Christian. Came to U.S., 1957, naturalized, 1962. Engr., Nova Refinery, Vienna, 1940-44; mgr. Ebensee Refinery, Austria, 1944-48; mgr. Eastern div. Empresa Petrolera Fiscal, Lima, 1948-57; v.p. Portable Gasoline Plants, Inc., Tulsa, 1957—; dir. Pressurre Vessel Handbook Pub., Inc., Tulsa. Chmn. internat. relations Internat. Petroleum Exposition, 1976. Troop chmn. outdoor activities Boy Scouts Am., 1974. Mem. Nat., Okla. socs. profl. engrs., Nat. Oil Equipment Mfrs. Soc. (pres. 1967, regent 1968-70), Natural Gas Processors Assn. Clubs: Kiwanis (chmn. internat. relations Tulsa), University, Internat., Philcrest Hills Tennis. Contbr. articles on oil and gas industries. Home: 4308 S Braden Av Tulsa OK 74135 Office: Beacon Bldg Tulsa OK 74103

FRIESE, HARRISON LEONARD, city ofcl.; b. L.I., N.Y., July 17, 1904; s. Herman A. and Marie Louise (Elcholtz) F.; grad. St. Paul's Sch., 1923; A.B. in Econs. and Banking, Colgate U., 1927; m. Grace M. Fellows, May 6, 1933 (dec. Oct. 1966); children—Harrison Leonard, John F.; m. 2d, Bette H. Hinsdale, June 29, 1968. With Fellows Engring. & Constrn., Hollis, N.Y., 1934-37; v.p. Fellows and Friese Constrn., 1938-42; planning Grumman Aircraft, Bethpage, L.I., 1942-47; owner, operator Sunrise Nursery, landscape constrn. and design, Fort Lauderdale, Fla., 1948-68; vice mayor, Fort Lauderdale, 1967-69; city commr. Fort Lauderdale, 1963-71. Vice chmn. Fort Lauderdale Planning and Zoning Bd., 1961-63; mem. Fort Lauderdale-Hollywood Internat. Airport Zoning Bd,, 1965-67; mem. area planning bd. Community Shelter Com. Broward County, 1969-71; mem. Broward County Erosion Prevention Bd., 1967-71; mem. Ft. Lauderdale Little Yankee Stadium Com. Republican precinct committeeman, Ft. Lauderdale, 1961-63. Bd. dirs. Fort Lauderdale Mus. Arts, Fort Lauderdale Symphony Orch., N. Central Fla. Community Mental Health Center; trustee Ft. Lauderdale Parker Play House, 1967-69; bd. dirs., hon. alumnus Nova. U. Recipient V.I.P. award Little League Baseball League, 1970. Mem. Fla. League Municipalities (legislative com. 1967-69), Taxpayers League Broward County (v.p. 1960), Fla. Nurserymen and Growers Assn. (charter), Gilchrist County C. of C. (v.p. 1972), Fla. Planning-Zoning Assn., Broward County Traffic Assn., U.S. Power Squadron, Phi Kappa Psi. Episcopalian. Mason (Shriner), Elk, Rotarian. Clubs: Colgate Gold Coast Alumni (pres. 1962), Harbor Beach Surf (pres. 1963-65); Gainesville (Fla.) Golf and County. Home: Rt 2 Box 185 Trenton FL 32693 also 4900 Bay View Dr Fort Lauderdale FL 33308

FRINGS, CHRISTOPHER STANTON, chemist, toxicologist; b. Birmingham, Ala., Aug. 10, 1940; s. Raymond Francis and Norvelle Virginia (Norman) F.; B.S., U. Ala., 1961; Ph.D., Purdue U., 1966; m. Roberta Elizabeth Alfrey, Aug. 7, 1965; children—Michael Christopher, Mary Elizabeth. Research asst. Mayo Clinic and Mayo Grad. Sch. Medicine, Rochester, Minn., 1966-67; dir. clin. chemistry, toxicology Med. Lab. Assos., Birmingham, 1967—. Clin. asso. prof. clin. pathology U. Ala. Sch. Medicine, Birmingham, 1967—. Mem. Jefferson County Drug Abuse Coordinating Com., 1972—. Mem. Am. Assn. Clin. Chemists (sect. chmn. 1972), Am. Acad. Clin. Toxicology, Am. Chem. Soc., Sigma Xi. Author: Clinical Chemistry Procedures of Medical Laboratory Associates, 1972. Contbr. articles to various publs. Home: 633 Winwood Dr Birmingham AL 35226 Office: 1025 S 18th St Birmingham AL 35205

FRISBIE, WILLIAM MORRIS, lawyer; b. Sturgeon, Mo., Apr. 4, 1929; s. Haden Reed and Linnie Francis (Morris) F.; J.D., U. Mo., 1956; postgrad. Internat. Accountants Soc., 1960-62; m. Janet Lynell Pruitt, June 10, 1961; 1 dau., Joellyn Elizabeth. With Continental Casualty Co., Chgo., 1957-61; with Space div. Chrysler Corp., New Orleans, 1961-62; admitted to Miss. bar, 1964; practiced law, Bay St. Louis, 1964—; with Gen. Electric Co., Bay St. Louis, Miss., 1969; instr. U. So. Miss. Extension Service; commr. pub. utilities, Bay St. Louis, 1969-73. Trustee Christ Episcopal Day Sch., Inc., CEDS Coast Episcopal High Sch. Served with AUS, 1951-53. Mem. Am., Miss., Ill., Mo. bar assns., Am. Legion, V.F.W., Bay St. Louis C. of C., Sigma Chi, Phi Delta Phi. Episcopalian. Mason (32 deg., Shriner), Rotarian. Home: 106 Carroll Av Bay St Louis MS 39520 Office: 140 Main St Bay St Louis MS 39520

FRITH, CHARLES EDWARD, architect; b. Shreveport, La., May 19, 1941; s. Dennis C. and P. Frances (Holmes) F.; B.Arch., Tex. A. and M. U., 1964; m. Karen Jane Williams, Sept. 3, 1966; 1 son, David Williams. Asso., Huddleston-Emerson-Stiller & Assos., architects, Shreveport, La., 1964-66, Wilson/Crain/Anderson, architects, Longview, Tex., 1966—. Mem. budget com. Greater Longview United Fund, 1973-74. Trustee Longview Museum and Arts Center. Mem. A.I.A. (chpt. sec.-treas. 1973-75), Ducks Unlimited (chpt. trustee). Rotarian. Home: 507 Coleman Dr Longview TX 75601 Office: 222 E Tyler St PO Box 352 Longview TX 75601

FRITH, DOUGLAS KYLE, lawyer; b. Henry County, Va., Sept. 2, 1931; s. Jacob Ewell and Sally Ada (Nunn) F.; A.B., Roanoke Coll., 1952; J.D., Washington and Lee U., 1957; m. Ella Margaret Tuck, Sept. 10, 1960; children—Margaret Waller, Susan Elaine. Admitted to Va. bar, 1957; since practiced law in Martinsville; asso. firm Taylor & Young, Martinsville, 1959-60; partner Young, Kiser & Frith, 1960-71, Frith & Gardner, 1973—. Dir. Va. Nat. Bank of Henry County, Frith Constrn. Co., Inc., Frith Equipment Corp. Substitute judge 21st Gen. Dist. Ct., 21st Juvenile and Domestic Relations Dist. Ct., 1969—. Chmn., March of Dimes, 1960, Brotherhood Week, 1960; capt. profl. div. United Fund, 1971. Served with AUS, 1952-54. Mem. Va. (com. torts and ins. 1971), Martinsville-Henry County (pres. 1970-71) bar assns., Va. Trial Lawyers Assn. (dist. v.p. 1970-71, del.-at-large 1971—). Baptist (deacon). Kiwanian (dir. Martinsville). Home: 1409 Whittle Rd Martinsville VA 24112 Office: 58 W Church St Martinsville VA 24112

FRITH, JAMES BURNESS, constrn. co. exec.; b. Va., Jan. 29, 1916; s. Jacob Ewell and Sally Ada (Nunn) F.; B.C.S., Nat. Bus. Coll., Roanoke, Va., 1937; m. Mary Kathryn Nininger, Aug. 21, 1947; children—Shelley Anne (Mrs. Wayne A. Kenas), Jacob Ewell II, James Burness. Gen. bldg. contractor, 1945—; pres., treas. Frith Constrn. Co., Inc., Martinsville, Va., 1956—; pres. Frith, Inc., Martinsville; sec.-treas. Frith Equipment Corp.; dir. Graves Supply Co., Piedmont Trust Bank. Bd. dirs. Patrick Henry Coll. Scholarship Found., Va. Coll. Fund, Richmond, 1973—; county and city adv. bd. Salvation Army. Served with USAAF, 1942-45. Mem. Asso. Gen. Contractors Am. (state bd. dirs. 1967-72, state exec. com. 1972—), Martinsville-Henry County C. of C. (dir. 1973, sec. 1972—). Kiwanian (pres. 1952, lt. gov. 1955), Elk, K.P. Clubs: Shenandoah (Roanoke, Va.); Chatmoss Country, Forest Park Country (Martinsville). Home: 1127 Cherokee Trail Martinsville VA 24112 Office: PO Box 5028 Martinsville VA 24112

FRITON, JOHN FRANCIS, mfg. co. exec.; b. N.Y.C.; s. George and Nellie J. (Danaher) F.; B. Mech. Engring., N.Y. U., 1938; m. Bernice H. Jagareski, Nov. 20, 1943; children—John E., Joan B. Plant mgr. Cluett Peabody, Troy, N.Y., 1948-59; indsl. engr. Sears Roebuck & Co., Chgo., 1959-66; pres., dir. Longview Mfg. Co. (Tex.), 1966—. Served to maj. C.E., AUS, 1942-46. Registered profl. engr., Ill. Clubs: Cherokee, Pinecrest Country (Longview). Home: 19 Brownwood Pl Longview TX 75601 Office: 205 Gum Springs Rd Longview TX 75601

FRITZ, CARL GEORGE, mech. engr.; b. Poughkeepsie, N.Y., Sept. 8, 1923; s. Carl VerValin and Katherine (Robb) F.; B.M.E., Villanova U., 1946; M.S. in M.E., Purdue U., 1963; m. Grace Eileen Musker, June 16, 1948. Test engr. Stratos Corp., Babylon, L.I., N.Y., 1948-50; head mechanics dept. Musker Engring. Inst., Winnipeg, Man., Can., 1950-53; asst. prof. U. Man., Winnipeg, 1953-60; chief thermodynamics and heat transfer Marshall Space Flight Center, NASA, Huntsville, Ala., 1960—. Mem. Am. Soc. M.E. (mem. nat. bd. energitics 1967-69), Soc. Automotive Engrs., Am. Soc. Engring. Edn. Elk. Club: Burning Tree Country (Decatur, Ala.). Home: Route 3 Box 681 Huntsville AL 35806 Office: NASA Marshall Space Flight Center Huntsville AL 35812

FRITZE, JULIUS ARNOLD, marriage counselor; b. Albuquerque, Dec. 30, 1918; s. Martin Herman and Mary (Staerkel) F.; student St. Paul's Jr. Coll., 1937-39; diploma Concordia Sem., 1944; B.A., in Edn., U. N.M., 1943; M.S., Central Mo. State Coll., 1969; m. Marion Caroline Becker, June 4, 1944; children—Christine, Timothy; m. 2d, Anita Carol Dozier, May 18, 1973. Ordained to ministry Lutheran Ch., 1944; pastor in Corpus Christi, Tex., 1944-48, Higginsville, Mo., 1948-57; exec. dir. Marriage and Parenthood Center, Dallas, 1957-59; pvt. practice marriage counseling, Dallas, 1959—. Cons. Mo. Snyod, Luth. Ch., St. Louis, 1961; lectr. to profl. and laymen's insts., 1956—; lectr. Dallas County Jr. Coll. Mem. Am. Assn. Marriage Counselors, Am. Personnel and Guidance Assn., Nat. Vocational Guidance Assn., Nat. Council Family Relations Am., Southwestern, Tex. psychol. assns., Internat. Platform Assn. Author: The Essence of Marriage, 1969. Contbr. series of articles to nat. mags. Home: 5517 W Hanover St Dallas TX 75209 Office: Suite 112 2919 Welborn Dallas TX 75219

FRIZZELL, WILLIAM RAYMOND, architect; b. Punta Gorda, Fla., Sept. 29, 1929; s. Roy Stanley and Sarah Lee (Thompson) F.; B.S., Ga. Inst. Tech., 1952, B.Arch., 1953; m. Margaret Morrow, Jan. 3, 1953; children—Leigh, Roy Tyler. With Lockheed Aircraft Corp., Marietta, Ga., 1951, Toombs & Co. Architects, Atlanta, 1952, Finch & Barnes Architects, Atlanta, 1953, Mark Hampton Architect, Tampa, Fla., 1954, McBryde & Frizzell Architects, Fort Myers, Fla., 1955-65; pres. W.R. Frizzell Architects, Inc., Fort Myers, 1965—; pres. Frizzell/Vickrey Architects/Planners, Inc.; sec. Sanibel Devel. Corp.; dir. 1st Fed. Savs. & Loan Assn. Bd. dirs. S.W. Fla. council Boy Scouts Am. Mem. A.I.A., Council Ednl. Facility Planners, Fort Myers C. of C. (dir.), Phi Delta Theta. Democrat. Presbyn. Rotarian, Elk. Clubs: Cypress Lake Country, Royal Palm Yacht (commodore). Important works include South Fla. Jr. Coll., Edison Jr. Coll., Fort Myers City Hall, Riverdale High Sch. Home: 1601 Llewellyn Dr Fort Myers FL 33901 Office: Lee County Motor Bank Fort Myers FL 33901

FRODYMA, MICHAEL MITCHELL, found. exec.; b. Holyoke, Mass., Mar. 3, 1920; s. Michael and Katherine (Bloniasz) F.; B.S., U. Mass., 1942; M.A., Columbia U., 1947; M.S., U. Hawaii, 1949; Ph.D. (Teaching fellow 1949-52), George Washington U., 1952; m. Martha Wynona Jackson, Mar. 31, 1951; 1 son, Michael Mitchell, III. Asst. in chemistry dept. U. Hawaii, Honolulu, 1947-49, asst. prof., 1952-58, asso. prof., 1958-67, prof., 1967; exchange asst. prof. Vassar Coll., Poughkeepsie, 1957-58, lectr., 1958; program dir., mgr. pre-coll. edn. in sci. NSF, Washington, 1967—. Served with AUS, 1942-46. Recipient NSF Sci. Faculty fellowship, 1958-61. Mem. Am. Chem. Soc., Chem. Soc. (London), Am. Inst. Chemists, A.A.A.S., Phi Kappa Phi, Sigma Xi, Kappa Delta Pi, Phi Delta Kappa. Home: 4242 East West Hwy Chevy Chase MD 20015 Office: NSF Washington DC 20550

FROHBERT, JOHN HENRY, city ofcl.; b. Gillisonville, S.C., Sept. 26, 1907; s. Henry Nicholas and Emma Florence (Moore) F.; student U. Ga., 1926-27; m. Julia Cheshire, Feb. 1, 1934; 1 dau., Julianne (Mrs. Clarence Saxby Chambliss). Freight clk. Atlantic Coast Line Railroad, Thomasville, Ga., 1927-35; office mgr. Kirby Evans Material Co., Thomasville, 1935-40, sec.-treas., 1940-62; treas. City of Thomasville, Ga., 1962—. Bd. dirs. YMCA, Thomasville, 1956-59. Mem. Ga. Finance Officers Assn. (bd. dirs. 1968-69), C. of C. (bd. dirs. 1956-58). Methodist (chmn. bd. stewards 1958). Rotarian (pres. 1959). Club: Glen Arven Country (Thomasville). Home: 909 E Washington St Thomasville GA 31792 Office: 144 E Jackson St Thomasville GA 31792

FROHLICH, EDWARD DAVID, educator, physician; b. N.Y.C., Sept. 10, 1931; s. William and May Ruth (Zneimer) F.; B.A. cum laude, Washington and Jefferson Coll., 1952; M.D., U. Md. Sch. Medicine, 1956; M.S. in Physiology, Northwestern U., Chgo., 1963; m. Sherry Linda Fine, Nov. 1, 1959; children—Margie, Bruce, Lara. Intern D.C. Gen. Hosp., Washington, 1956-57; resident Georgetown U. Med. Center, Washington, 1957-60; asso. in medicine Northwestern U. Med. Sch., Chgo., 1963-64; clin. investigator, chief hypertension clinic VA Research Hosp., Chgo., 1962-64; mem. staff research div. Cleve. Clinic, 1964-69; asso. prof. medicine U. Okla. Health Scis. Center, Oklahoma City, 1969-71, prof. medicine and physiology and biophysics, dir. div. hypertension, 1974—; cons. VA Hosp., Oklahoma City, 1969—, Nat. Heart and Lung Inst., Bethesda, 1972—, Food and Drug Adminstrn., Washington, 1971—; mem. VA Co-op. Study on Hypertension, 1969—. Served to capt. AUS, 1960-62. Recipient Honors Achievement award Angiology Research Found., 1964; Distinguished Faculty award U. Okla. Med. Sch., 1970; So. Med. Assn. award U. Louisville, 1971. Fellow Am. Coll. Cardiology, A.C.P.; mem. Okla. Heart Assn. (bd. dirs. 1972—), Am. Soc. Clin. Pharmacology and Therapeutics (pres. 1973-74), Am. Heart Assn. (mem. exec. com. 1972—), A.M.A., Am. Soc. Clin. Investigation, Central Soc. Clin. Investigation, So. Soc. Clin. Investigation, Am. Physiol. Soc., Am. Soc. Exptl. Pharmacology and Therapeutics. Editor: Pathophysiology 1972; editor-in-chief Jour. Lab. and Clin. Medicine, 1974—. Contbr. articles to various publs. Home: 1725 Dorchester Dr Oklahoma City OK 73120 Office: PO Box 26901 Oklahoma City OK 73190

FROHMAN, ALICE PATRICIA, lawyer; b. Washington, Mar. 16, 1930; d. Philip Hubert and Olivia (Avery) Frohman; student George Washington U., 1948-49; J.D., 1955; A.B., Wellesley Coll., 1952. Admitted to D.C. bar, 1955; atty. Lawyers Title Ins. Corp., Washington, 1955-57; law clk. Judge Burnita S. Matthews, U.S. Dist. Ct., Washington, 1957-63; asst. U.S. atty., Washington, 1963—. Chmn. dist. fund-raising Wellesley Coll., 1965-67. Treas., Washington Forum, 1969-70; trustee Legal Aid Soc., Washington, 1968-72; mem. D.C. Commn. on Status of Women, 1973—. Recipient Young Lawyer of the Year award D.C. Bar Assn., 1966. Mem. Women's Bar Assn. D.C. (pres. 1963-64, dir. 1966-69), D.C. Bar Assn. (dir. 1967-69, sec. 1968-69, treas. 1973-74), Chevy Chase Bus. and Profl. Womens Club (pres. 1964-65), State Fedn. Bus. and Profl. Womens Clubs D.C. (corr. sec. 1968-69, treas. 1969-70, pres. 1973-74), Order of Coif, Kappa Beta Pi, Delta Gamma. Republican. Roman Catholic. Home: 5245 43d St NW Washington DC 20015 Office: US Attys Office US Court House Washington DC 20001

FROHOCK, FRED CLIFTON, civil engr.; b. Lake Jackson, Fla., May 15, 1909; s. Luther Russell and Weltha (Cowart) F.; B.S. in C.E., U. Fla., 1934; m. Marie Domenech, Dec. 22, 1935; children—Fred Manuel, Patrick Anthony. Engr., C.E., Jacksonville, Fla., 1938-41; dir. engring. div. U.S. Navy Dept., Key West, Fla., 1941-52, dir. tech. div., Port Lyautey, French Morocco, 1952-53; chief engr. Paul Smith Constrn. Co., Miami, Fla., 1953-55; engr. Maurice H. Connell & Assos., Miami, 1955-66; former dir. U.S. Navy Aqueduct, Key West, 1966; now with Luddvici & Orange Cons. Engrs., Miami. Chmn. S. Fla. Tech. Socs. Council, 1961. Registered profl. engr., Fla., S.C. Mem. Nat. Soc. Profl. Engrs., Soc. Am. Mil. Engrs., Am. Soc. C.E., Fla. Engring. Soc. (chpt. pres. 1959, state dir. 1965), Am. Water Work Assn.,-Sigma Tau. Home: 1854 SW 23d Terrace Miami FL 33145

FROMHERZ, FRANK C(HARLES), civil san. engr.; b. New Orleans, Sept. 5, 1921; s. Alvin M. and Alice (Spetz) F.; B.E., Tulane U., 1943; S.M., Harvard, 1947; m. Jocelyn Nyland, Sept. 12, 1946; children—Frank Charles II, Martha Joanne. Stress analyst Goodyear Aircraft Corp., 1943-45; with USPHS, 1945-46; pub. health engr. La. Dept. Health, 1947-48; partner Fromherz Engrs., cons. civil, mech. elec. and municipal engrs., 1948—. Mem. Water Pollution Control Fedn., Am. Soc. C.E. (past pres. La. sect.), Am. Water Works Assn., La. Engring. Soc., Nat. Soc. Profl. Engrs., Am. Assn. Port Authorities, Am. Cons. Engrs. Council, Sigma Chi. Contbr. articles profl. jour. Home: 1327 Pine St New Orleans LA 70118 Office: 1539 Jackson Av New Orleans LA 70130

FROMMHOLD, LOTHAR WERNER, educator; b. Wurzburg, Germany, Apr. 20, 1930; s. Walter Karl Otto and Karolina (Bernhardt) F.; diplom-phys, U. Hamburg, Germany, 1954, Ph.D., 1960, Dr. habil, 1964; m. Margareta Mercedes Benz, May 3, 1959; children—Sebastian, Caroline. Came to U.S., 1964, naturalized, 1971. Research scientist, instr. U. Hamburg, Germany, 1954-64; vis. prof. U. Pitts., 1964-66; mem. faculty U. Tex., Austin, 1966—, prof. physics, 1968—. Recipient Fulbright Travel fellowship, 1964, various Research grants, 1967-73. Fellow Am. Phys. Soc. Contbr. articles to profl. jours. Home: 4706 Ridge Oak Dr Austin TX 78731 Office: Physics Dept U Tex Austin TX 78712

FROOM, GEORGE ALLEN, banker; b. Pomeroy, Ia., Sept. 22, 1922; s. George Vitalis and Signe Amanda (Larson) F.; B.S., U. Richmond, 1949; m. Frances Beverly Bowles, Nov. 27, 1943; 1 son, Dana Allen. Credit Supr. Gen. Motors Acceptance Corp., Richmond, Va., 1949-55; v.p., cashier First Nat. Bank Harrisonburg, 1955-68; sr. v.p. Shenandoah Valley Nat. Bank of Winchester, 1968-73, pres., 1973—. Vice pres. Shenandoan Apple Blossom Festival, Inc., 1971—, United Fund Winchester-Frederick County, 1969—. Bd. dirs. Shenandoah council Boy Scouts Am., 1972—; bd. dirs., treas. Northwestern Workshop, Inc., 1969—. Served to 1st lt. AUS, 1942-46. Mem. Va. Bankers Assn. (com. on state legislation 1973—), Winchester-Frederick C. of C. (dir. 1973—), Phi Beta Kappa. Methodist. Rotarian. Home: 319 Walker St Winchester VA 22601 Office: PO Box 1000 Winchester VA 22601

FROOMKIN, JOSEPH NATHAN, economist; b. Harbin, China, Feb. 7, 1927; s. Nathan and Rachel (Sineikin) F.; came to U.S., 1947, naturalized, 1953; B.A., St. John's U., 1946; M.B.A., U. Chgo., 1947, Ph.D., 1950; m. Maya Pines, Dec. 12, 1959; children—A. Michael, Daniel P. Research asso. Law Sch., Harvard, 1953-54; economist Aeronautical Research Found., Cambridge, Mass., 1954-55; mgr. marketing planning IBM Corp., White Plains, N.Y., 1956-65; asst. commr. Dept. Health Edn. and Welfare, U.S. Office Edn., 1965-68; planner, IBM Corp., Washington, 1968-69; pres. Joseph Froomkin, Inc., cons., Washington, 1969—. Served with Transp. Corps, AUS, 1953-54. Mem. Am. Econ. Assn., Am. Statis. Assn., Beta Sigma. Author: (with A. J. Jaffe) Technology and Jobs, 1968; Aspirations Enrollments and Resources, 1969. Home: 4724 32d St NW Washington DC 20008 Office: 1015 18th St NW Washington DC 20036

FROSCH, CURTIS EUGENE, banker; b. Lexington, Tex., Nov. 1, 1936; s. Herbert Otto and Lena Anna (Winkler) F.; pre-standard certificate Am. Inst. Banking, 1959; m. Mary Ann Urban, May 6, 1956; 1 dau., Deborah Gail. Bookkeeper, teller Austin Nat. Bank (Tex.), 1956-60; with First Nat. Bank of Giddings, Tex., 1960—, cashier, 1961-63, v.p., 1963—. Chmn. Salvation Army drive, 1967, Boy Scouts Am. drive, 1969; co-chmn. Giddings Centennial Com., 1971, Lee County Centennial Com., 1974. Bd. dirs. Lee County Recreation Assn., 1974—. Mem. Giddings C. of C. (dir. 1962-65, 74—, v.p. 1974—). Lutheran (elder, chmn. congregation). Clubs: Cummins Creek Country (dir. 1974—); Lions (dep. dist. gov. 1969-70, treas. 1968—). Home: 413 S Williams Av Giddings TX 78942 Office: Box 269 Giddings TX 78942

FROSH, STANLEY B., lawyer, banker; b. Denver, Jan. 9, 1919; s. Joseph and Anna (Wabeck) F.; B.S., Northwestern U., 1939, J.D., 1942; m. Judith Lee Wirkman, May 7, 1943; children—Brian Esten, Robin Dale, Wendy Joan. Admitted to D.C. bar, U.S. Supreme Ct. bar, also state and fed. cts.; practiced in Washington, 1945—, Montgomery County, Md., 1949—; partner firm Frosh, Lane & Edson, Washington; chief rent atty. Chgo. regional office OPA, 1942-43; sr. litigation atty. OPA, Washington, 1945-47; lectr. internat. law Am. U., Washington, 1947-49; lectr. as Am. specialist in polit. sci. and internat. law USIA and Dept. State in Africa, 1964, Asia, 1966. Chmn. bd., gen. counsel State Nat. Bank Bethesda (Md.). Assn., 1962-68, Montgomery County Arts Found.; mem. nat. panel arbitrators Am. Arbitration Assn.; mem. Montgomery County Council, 1958-62, pres. pro-tem, 1961-62. Bd. dirs. Washington met. area Community Chest and Council, 1948-57, Montgomery County, 1949-57; bd. govs. Dag Hammerskjold Coll.; bd. dirs. Washington Housing and Planning Assn., 1962-68, Montgomery County Arts Found. Served with AUS, 1942-45; ETO. Decorated Bronze Star. Mem. Am., Md. Montgomery County bar assns., Bar Assn. D.C. Mem. B'nai B'rith (pres. met. Washington council, 1950-52, chmn. Montgomery County Am. Civil Liberties Union). Club: Internat. (dir. and gen. counsel 1962—) (Washington). Home: 6100 Bradley Blvd Bethesda MD 20034 Office: 1025 Connecticut Av NW Washington DC 20005 also Nat Bank Bldg Bethesda MD 20014

FROST, JUANITA C. CORBITT, orgn. exec.; b. Rockford, Ill., Aug. 4, 1926; d. Mervin Charles and Eva Marie (Moberg) Corbitt; student Little Rock U., 1959-61; m. Thomas Tapenden Frost, Jan. 3, 1954 (dec. Oct. 1966); children—Annemarie, Thomas Tapenden. Med. sec., asst. clin. pathology lab. VA Hosp., Whipple, Ariz., 1951-54; exec. dir. Camp Fire Girls, Temple, Tex., after 1967; now exec. sec. to dir. Nursing Service Scott and White Hosp., also Sherwood and Brindley Found., Temple. Den mother Cub Scouts, 1969; mem. Community Concert Assn., 1954—. Mem. Bell County Med. Aux., Phi Sigma Alpha (charter pres. 1966). Episcopalian. Clubs: Central Texas Dinner, Stillhouse Sailing (sec. 1974). Home: 3001 Las Moras Dr Temple TX 76501 Office: 2401 S 31st St Temple TX 76501

FROST, LAURENCE LEONARD, psychologist; b. North Platte, Neb., Feb. 18, 1925; s. Leonard Laurence and Agnes (Greenwood) F.; B.A., U. Denver, 1949, Ph.D., 1952; m. Alice Louise Cecil, Apr. 14, 1956; children—Laurence Leonard III, Amy Louise. Clin. psychologist div. psychosomatic medicine U. Colo. Med. Center, 1952-53; chief sect. clin. psychology Nat. Inst. Neurol. Diseases and Blindness, NIH, Bethesda, Md., 1953-57; dir. Child Guidance Clinic, D.C. Juvenile Ct., 1957-64; supervising psychologist St. Elizabeths Hosp., Washington, 1964—. Mem. Am., D.C., Md. psychol. assns., A.A.A.S., Am. Acad. Neurology, Am. Orthopsychiatric Assn. Home: 11214 Ashley Dr Rockville MD 20853 Office: St Elizabeths Hosp Washington DC 20032

FROST, SYLVIA KRAFT (MRS. HERRICK EDWARD FROST JR.), banker; b. Geneva, Ill., Aug. 18, 1936; d. Melvin L. and Ruth (McArthur) Kraft; grad. cum laude Manatee Jr. Coll. Sch. Nursing, 1964; m. James Gilkey, Aug. 31, 1952 (dec. Apr. 1961); children—Laura, Timothy, Cheryl; m. 2d, David L. McNulty, June 30, 1962 (dec. Dec. 1962); 1 dau., Melissa; m. 3d, Herrick Edward Frost, Jr., May 6, 1964; 1 dau., Victoria. Dir. McNulty Group of Banks, Haines City, Fla., 1962-67, 1st Fla. Bancorp., Tampa, Fla., 1967-74, Bank of Zephyrhills, Fla., DeSoto Nat. Bank, Arcadia, Fla.; adv. dir. Flagship Banks of Fla. Fund raiser Am. Cancer Soc., United Fund, Morton F. Plant Hosp. Assn. Del., Pinellas County Republican Exec. Com., 1968—. Mem. Fla. Hist. Soc., Fla. Gulf Coast Fine Arts Soc. Methodist. Home: 301 Lotus Path Clearwater FL 33516

FRUEH, WILLIAM DEAN, city ofcl.; b. Afton, Pa., Mar. 3, 1935; s. John William and Ethyl May (Heine) F.; B.S. in Civil Engring., Ia. State U., 1958; m. Judith Ann Fahrenkrog, Oct. 10, 1959; children—Mark, Patricia, John, Thomas, James. Hwy. engr. Ia. State Hwy. Commn., Council Bluffs. 1958-61; partner Mann, Hager & Frueh, Cons. Engrs., Council Bluffs, 1961-62; city engr. City of Council Bluffs, 1962-68, dir. pub. works, 1965-68, asst. city mgr., 1967-68; city mgr., Newton, N.J., 1968-70, Shawnee, Okla., 1970—. Bd. dirs. Shawnee council Campfire Girls, 1972-73. Registered profl. engr., Ia., Okla. Named Young Man of Year Council Bluffs, 1967. Mem. Internat., Okla. city mgmt. assns., Shawnee C. of C. Home: 12 Chickasaw St Shawnee OK 74801 Office: City Hall Shawnee OK 74801

FRUGE, J. CLEVELAND, judge; b. nr. Basile, La., Oct. 17, 1900; s. Augustine and Alice (Reed) F.; student St. Charles Coll., Grand Coteau, La., 1914-16, St. Paul's Coll., Covington, La., 1916-18; LL.B., Loyola, New Orleans, 1922; m. Georgiana Tate, June 30, 1919 (dec. July 1963); children—Jack C., James F.; m. 2d, Heloise Boudreaux, Aug. 17, 1964. Admitted to La. bar, 1922, practiced in Ville Platte, 1922-35; asst. dist. atty., 13th Jud. Dist. La., 1930-35, dist. judge, 1935-60, presiding judge La. Ct. Appeal, 3d Circuit, 1960—; justice Supreme Ct. La., 1949. Mem. La. Legislature, 1928-30. Past pres. Evangeline area council Boy Scouts Am. Recipient first Hebert Lincoln Harley award Am. Judicature Soc., 1973; named Hon. Alumnus La. State U. Law Sch., 1973. Mem. La. Bar Assn. K.C. (4 deg., state retreat chmn. La. State). Rotarian (past pres.). Home: 204 Hi-School Dr Ville Platte LA 70586 Office: PO Box 3000 Lake Charles LA 70601

FRY, DAVID DONALD, civil engr.; b. Canton, O., Oct. 4, 1924; s. Don David and Mary J. (Petch) F.; student Kan. State Coll., 1943-44; B.C.E., Case Inst. Tech., 1949; m. Ann Selden Nicholson, Apr. 25, 1958; 1 dau., Constance Louise. Engr. Ohio Dept. Hwys., Ravenna, 1949-53; engr. Peter Kiewit Sons Co., Portsmouth, O., 1953-54; area engr. Arabian Am. Oil Co., Dhahran, S.A., 1954-56; design engr. M. H. Connell & Assoc., Inc., Miami, 1956-60; asst. dir. pub. works City Coral Gables, Fla., 1960-67; v.p. charge Fla. Office Brighton Engring. Co., 1967-69; project engr. Clarkeson, Kononoff & Smith, Inc., Coral Gables, 1970-71; chief engr. Pavlo Engring. Co., Inc., Coral Gables, 1971—. Registered profl. engr., Ohio Fla. Mem. Theta Chi. Presbyn. Home: 6001 SW 81st St South Miami FL 33143 Office: 2012 Ponce de Leon Blvd Coral Gables FL 33134

FRY, HENRY DEWEY, mech. engr.; b. Kansas City, Kan., Mar. 18, 1943; s. Charles Edward and Nellie Pearl (Thoele) F.; B.S. in Mech. Engring., U. Kan., 1966; m. Patricia Ray Alexander, Aug. 2, 1964; children—Heather Kathleen, Jason Dewey. Design engr. Internat. Harvester Co., Hinsdale, Ill., 1966-68; design engr. Gardner-Denver Co., Dallas, 1968-72, project engr., 1972—. Coach Garland (Tex.) Girls Softball Assn., 1971-73. Registered profl. engr., Tex. Mem. Am. Soc. Mech. Engrs., Nat., Tex. socs. profl. engrs. Home: 1025 Mill River Dr Garland TX 75041 Office: 4400 Hatcher St Dallas TX 75226

FRY, JOHN CRAIG, govt. ofcl.; b. Salem, Ore., Dec. 11, 1926; s. Orris J. and Bernice O. (Craig) F.; B.S., U.S. Naval Acad., 1947; M.S., U. Cal. at La Jolla, 1952, postgrad., 1959-60; m. Tanya A. Ojeda, Sept. 3, 1949; children—John Craig, David, Matthew. Sr. staff mem. Nat. Council on Marine Resources and Engring. Devel., Exec. Office of Pres., 1967-69; v.p., dir. Ocean Data Systems, Inc., Washington, 1969-71; dep. dir. Office Sci. and Tech., AID, Washington, 1971—. Recipient Superior Honor award AID, Dept. State, 1973. Mem. Am. Geophys. Union, U.S. Naval Inst., Sigma Xi. Clubs: Edgemoor (Bethesda, Md.); Army Navy (Washington). Contbr. articles to profl. jours. Home: 7200 Fairfax Rd Bethesda MD 20014 Office: AID Washington DC 20523

FRY, RAY DANIEL, computer scientist; b. Cleve., Feb. 7, 1929; s. Fred W. and Ellen Elizabeth (Brenton) F.; student Miami U., 1947-49; B.A. in Math., Western Res. U., 1962; m. Evelyn Jean MacFadyen, Jan. 20, 1967; 1 dau., Mimi Elizabeth. Pres., Gt. Western Oil Co., Cleve., 1951-54; corporate mgr. systems and data processing Hanna Mining Co., Cleve., 1959-66; mgr. Price Waterhouse & Co., Cleve., 1966-69; pres. Computer Assistance Corp., Clearwater, Fla., 1969-71; v.p. 1st Fed. Savs. & Loan Assn., Tampa, Fla., 1971-72; mgr. computer services Univ. Community Hosp., Tampa, 1972—. Computer cons., 1954-59; lectr. summer series Mass. Inst. Tech., 1959-60; instr. systems analysis Cuyahoga Community Coll., 1964-69; cons. field data system U.S. Army, 1965. Chmn. Republican Finance Com. Cuyahoga and Lake Counties, O., 1962-66; mem. Zoning Bd. Appeals, Mentor-on-the-Lake, O., 1965-67, Charter Commn., 1966-67. Served with USAF, 1951-53. Mem. Data Processing Mgmt. Assn. (internat. dir. 1970-71), Assn. for Systems Mgmt. (v.p. 1964-65), Inst. Mgmt. Sci., Am. Soc. Certifield Data Processors, Lambda Chi Alpha. Presbyn. Clubs: Clearwater Evening Sertoma (v.p. 1971-72); Bath (Redington Beach, Fla.). Developed Echo-Plex data transmission technique. Home: 4194 Harbor Hills Dr Largo FL 33540 Office: 13505 N 31st St Tampa FL 33512

FRYBURGER, L(AWRENCE) BRUCE, lawyer; b. Cin., Apr. 7, 1933; s. Lawrence W. and Norma C. (Hunsicker) F.; B.A., (Sutphin law scholar), U. Cin., 1956, LL.B., U. Tex., 1958; m. Ann Elizabeth Plankey, June 24, 1961; children—Craig William, Lawrence Kent. Admitted to Tex. bar, 1959; specialist in labor relations law for mgmt., San Antonio, 1959—; spl. prof. on labor relations law San Antonio Coll., 1968—. Originator Ann. Tex. Young Lawyers Inst., 1964. Chmn. lawyers div. United Fund, San Antonio and Bexar County, 1967-68; mem. Bd. Adjustment, City of San Antonio, 1969-72. Bd. dirs. March of Dimes, San Antonio. Served with USAF, 1958-59. Recipient Outstanding Young Lawyer of San Antonio award, 1967. Mem. State Bar of Tex., Am., Tex. Jr. (bd. dirs. 1964-66), San Antonio, San Antonio Jr. (pres. 1963-64) bar assns., Phi Delta Phi, Sigma Chi. Presbyn. (bd. deacons). Club: San Antonio German. Contbr. articles to profl. jours. Mem. editorial bd. Tex. Lawyers Practice Guide, 1964. Office: 1661 Frost Bank Tower San Antonio TX 78205

FRYE, ALVA LEONARD, chem. co. exec.; b. Gray, Okla., July 19, 1922; s. John Leonard and Flora (Appling) F.; student John Tarleton A & M Coll., 1940-41; B.S. in Chem. Engring., Ia. State U.; m. Evelyn Mae De Booy, Dec. 9, 1943; children—Katherine (Mrs. Howard Ellstrom), Susan (Mrs. Vincent Melashenko). With 3M Co., 1944-69; v.p. research and devel. Inmont Corp., 1969-70; with Aladdin Industries, Inc., Nashville, 1970—, v.p. research and devel. Mem. Am. Chem. Soc., Am. Inst. Chem. Engrs., Am. Mgmt. Assn. (mem. council 1970—). Home: Route 2 Bridlewood Lane Brentwood TN 37027 Office: 703 Murfreesboro Rd Nashville TN 37210

FRYE, DOLAN BRUCE, textile co. exec.; b. Albemarle, N.C., Oct. 26, 1918; s. David Alexander and Nellie S. (Staton) F.; B.S., N.C. State U., 1950; m. Eva Louise Webb, July 26, 1947; children—Richard Dolan, Mark Reid. Overseer, supt. Wiscassett Mills Co., Albemarle, N.C., 1950-60; gen. mgr., 1960-65; mgr. Kendall Co., Albertville, Ala., 1965-69, mgr. Pelzer (S.C.) upper plant, 1969, mgr. Pelzer plants, 1970—. Pres., United Givers Fund, Albertville, 1969, Tri-Cities Med. Services, 1974; chmn. Marshall County dist. Boy Scouts Am., Albertville, 1969; v.p. Wiscassett YMCA, Albemarle, 1962-65. Bd. dirs. Stanly County Hosp., Albemarle, 1965, Piedmont Health Care Corp., 1974—; trustee Wiscassett YMCA, 1962-65. Served with USNR, 1942-45. Mem. C. of C. (bd. dirs. 1968-69). Methodist (trustee 1963-65). Lion (pres. 1962, 71), Rotarian (dir. 1967-69). Home: 18 Lebby St Pelzer SC 29669 Office: PO Box 396 Pelzer SC 29669

FRYE, JAMES MARION, JR., food co. exec.; b. nr. Mount Airy, N.C., Oct. 3, 1930; s. James M. and Thelma R. (Williamson) F.; B.S. in Bus. Adminstrn., U. Richmond, 1953, M.B.A., 1959; postgrad. Brookings Inst. Advanced Study, 1965; m. Virginia Nash, Nov. 24, 1962. With Philip Morris, Inc., Richmond, Va., 1953—, mgr. community relations, Richmond, 1964-68, dir. corporate relations, N.Y.C., 1968-69, dir. community relations, Richmond, 1969—. Mem. Richmond Indsl. Devel. Authority. Pres. U. Richmond Alumni Council, 1968; v.p. United Givers Fund, 1970—, bd. dirs., 1970—; bd. dirs. Va. Council Health and Med. Care, 1964-67, Richmond Boys Club, 1969-70, Press Club Va., 1965—, Big Brothers, Nat. Tobacco Festival, Va. Thanksgiving Festival, Va. Coll. Fund. Served with AUS, 1953-55. Mem. Pub. Relations Soc. Am. (dir. 1970—), Richmond Pub. Relations Assn. (pres. 1973), Richmond Indsl. Personnel Club (pres. 1959), Richmond C. of C., Va. C. of C. Rotarian. Clubs: Capitol Hill (Washington); Country of Va., Westwood Racquet, Downtown (Richmond, Va.). Home: 109 S Wilton Rd Richmond VA 23226 Office: 4001 Commerce Rd Richmond VA 23234

FRYE, JOHN H., JR., metall. engr.; b. Birmingham, Ala., Oct. 1, 1908; s. John H. and Helen (Mushat) F.; B.A. (with honors), Howard Coll., 1930; M.S., Lehigh U., 1934; D.Phil., Oxford (Eng.) U., 1942; m. Helen Lewis Johnston, Sept. 21, 1935; children—John H., III, Helen (Mrs. Grant Van Siclen Parr), Kathleen (Mrs. Walter T. Woods, Jr.). Asst. prof. metallurgy Lehigh U., 1937-40, asso. prof. metallurgy, 1940-44; civilian employee Office Sci. Research and Devel., 1944; research engr. Bethlehem Steel Co., 1944-48; dir. metals and ceramics div. Oak Ridge Nat. Lab., (Tenn.), 1948-73; lectr. U. Tenn. Grad. Sch., 1950-73; hon. adj. prof. U. Ala. Coll. Engring., 1964-67, prof. metall. engring., 1973—. Dir. Bank Oak Ridge, 1956—. Tech. adviser on U.S. delegation to 2d Internat. Conf. on Peaceful Uses Atomic Energy, Geneva, Switzerland, 1958. Fellow A.A.A.S., Am. Soc. for Metals (mem. handbook com. 1969-72); mem. Am. Inst. Mining, Metall. and Petroleum Engrs. (exec. com. inst. metals div. 1959-60), Sigma Xi. Episcopalian. Clubs: Oak Ridge Country, Indian Hills Country. Editorial adv. bd. Jour. Less-Common Metals, 1962—. Contbr. articles to profl. jours. Home: 69 High Forest Tuscaloosa AL 35401

FRYE, OZRO EARLE, JR., state ofcl.; b. Petersburg, Tenn., Oct. 8, 1917; s. Ozro Earle and Mabel (Wooten) F.; B.S., U. Fla., 1939, M.S., 1941, Ph.D., 1954; postgrad. Tex. A. and M. Coll., 1941-42; m. Barbara Ann Landstreet, Oct. 8, 1949; children—Scott Walton, Leslie Ann. Research asst. Ala. Coop. Wildlife Research Unit, Auburn, 1940; Tex. A. and M. Coll., College Station, 1941-42; research biologist Fla. Game and Fresh Water Fish Commn., Tallahassee, 1944-48, chief wildlife biologist, 1948-51, asst. dir., 1951-65, dir., 1965—. Chmn., Atlantic Waterfowl Council, 1970—, Land Acquisition Commn., 1957-64, Nat. Waterfowl Council, 1960-61. Pres., Tallahassee Little Theater, 1954-55. Served to lt. USNR, 1942-46. Decorated Air medal with two gold stars; recipient Conservation award Am. Motors Corp., 1966, Fla. Conservation award Ft. Myers Rod and Gun Club, 1966.

Mem. Wildlife Soc. (award 1957), Southeastern Assn. Game and Fish Commrs. (pres. 1968-69), Audubon Soc., Ecol. Soc. Am., Wilderness Soc., Wilson Ornithol. Club, Fla. Acad. Scis. (past pres.), Internat. Assn. Game, Fish and Conservation Commrs. (chmn. exec. com. 1971, pres. 1973-74). Home: 758 DuParc Circle Tallahassee FL 32303 Office: Fla Game and Fresh Water Fish Commn 620 S Meridian St Tallahassee FL 32304

FRYE, WILBUR WAYNE, educator; b. Finger, Tenn., Aug. 6, 1933; s. Alfred Dewey and Lela Elizabeth (Rouse) F.; B.S., U. Tenn., 1961, M.S., 1964; Ph.D., Va. Poly. Inst. and State U., 1969; m. Martha Hoskins, Apr. 20, 1957; children—Thomas Wayne, John Davis. Asst. controller Fed. Aviation Agy., Memphis Air-Route Traffic Control Center, Memphis, 1957-58; asst. prof. agronomy Tenn. Technol. U., Cookeville, 1963-67, asso. prof., chmn. dept. agronomy, 1970-72, prof., chmn. dept. plant and soil sci., 1972—. Bd. dirs. Wesley Found., Cookeville, Tenn., 1973—. Served with USAF, 1953-57. Recipient NSF Sci. Faculty fellowship, 1966. Mem. Am. Soc. Agronomy, Soil Sci. Soc. Am., Clay Minerals Soc., Soil Conservation Soc. Am. (chpt. pres. 1966-67), Am. Forestry Assn., Internat. Soil Sci. Soc., Nat. Assn. Colls. and Tchrs. Agr., Tenn. Edn. Assn., Sigma Xi, Phi Kappa Phi, Alpha Zeta. Rotarian. Home: 122 Adams Av Algood TN 38501 Office: Box 5102 Tenn Technological University Cookeville TN 38501

FRYER, THOMAS WAITT, SR., clergyman; b. Chadbourn, N.C., Jan. 14, 1908; s. Matthew Alexander and Frances Etta (Parker) F.; student Roanoke Coll., 1927-30, D.D., 1954; student So. Bapt. Theol. Sem., 1931-32; m. Pauline Harp, July 8, 1931; children—Thomas Waitt, Laura Frances, Mary Ann. Ordained to ministry Baptist Ch., 1932; pastor chs. in Clintwood, Va., 1932-34, Scottsburg, Va., 1934-36, Starling Av. Ch., Martinsville, Va., 1936-40, First Bapt. Ch., Dunn, N.C., 1940-42, First Bapt. Ch., New Bern, N.C., 1942-49, West End Ch., Suffolk, Va., 1949-51, Moffett Meml. Chm., Danville, Va., 1951-54, Stanton Meml. Ch., Miami, Fla., 1954-59, Immanuel Bapt. Ch., Florence, S.C., 1959-63, College Park Bapt. Ch., Florence, 1963-73. Moderator Blue Ridge (Va.) Bapt. Assn., 1938, Atlantic Bapt. Assn., N.C., 1948. Trustee, treas. Harnett County Hosp., Dunn, N.C.; trustee N.C. Bapt. Hosp. Mem. 0 x 5 Club of Am. Mason (32 deg.). Rotarian (past pres. New Bern N.C.), Lion. Home: 2128 S Converse Dr Florence SC 29501

FRYER, WILLIAM NEAL, psychologist; b. Cin., Mar. 10, 1920; s. Roy Charles and Alice (Carson) F.; B.A., Harding Coll., 1948; M.A., Columbia, 1953, Ed.D., 1965; m. Dorothy Elizabeth McClain, May 11, 1942; children—Bonnie Jean, Debra Lynn. Aircraft painter Aero. Corp. Am., Cin., 1937-39; salesman Sears, Roebuck & Co., Covington, Ky., 1940-41; minister Bklyn. Ch. of Christ, 1948-56; asst. prof. psychology Abilene (Tex.) Christian Coll., 1956-65, asso. prof., 1965-68, part-time tchr. psychology, 1968-70; chief psychologist Abilene State Sch., 1968—. Mem. Mayor's Com. on Mental Retardation, Abilene, 1964-65; mem. exec. com., profl. adviser Abilene Suicide Prevention Service. Bd. dirs., mem. profl. adv. com. Abilene Assn. for Mental Health, pres., 1958-59; past bd. dirs. Tex. Assn. for Mental Health. Served to capt. USAAF, 1941-46. Mem. Am., Southwestern, Tex., Abilene (past pres.) psychol. assns., A.A.A.S., N.Y. Acad. Sci., Am. Assn. Mental Deficiency, Phi Delta Kappa, Kappa Delta Pi. Mem. Ch. of Christ. Kiwanian. Author: (with Orval Filbeck, Max Leach) College, Classroom, Campus, and You, 1959. Home: 833 NE 10th St Abilene TX 79601 Office: Box 451 Abilene TX 79604

FRYER, WOODRING MANN, real estate broker; b. Henderson, Ky., Jan. 1, 1923; s. Charles Alvin and Rebekah (Mann) F.; grad. high sch.; m. Vonda Lee Moore, Dec. 6, 1941; children—Rebekah Virginia, Charles Herman, William Mann, Vonda Suzanne, Juli Anne, Patricia Kae. Pres., mgr. Fryer Realty Co., Henderson, Ky., 1945—; mgr. Property Sales Corp., 1964—; pres. Appraisers Asso., Inc.; sec. Lively Homes, Evansville, Ind. Pres., dir. Grantwood Hills, Inc., Melwood Developments, Inc., Eastgate Center, Inc. (all Henderson). Served with USN, 1943-45. Named Ky. col. Mem. Henderson Bd. Realtors (past pres.), Nat. Assn. Ind. Fee Appraisers (nat. dir. 1972, nat. treas. 1974, mem. nat. edn. com., chmn. nat. membership com., past pres. Greater Evansville chpt.), Nat. Assn. Real Estate Bds., Nat. Inst. Real Estate Brokers, Soc. Real Estate Appraisers, Henderson C. of C., Nat. Inst. Real Estate Bds., Nat. Assn. Real Estate Bds., Evansville Bd. Realtors. Mason (32 deg., Shriner). Club: Internat. Traders. Home and office: 1 S Main St Henderson KY 42420

FRYREAR, DONALD WILLIAM, agr. engr.; b. Haxtun, Colo., Dec. 8, 1936; s. Willie A. and Marjorie A. (Adams) F.; A.A., Northeastern Jr. Coll., 1956; B.S., Colo. State U., 1959; M.S., Kan. State U., 1962; m. Sherry Janice Watson, Sept. 16, 1956; children—Debra Lou, Kenneth William. With Agrl. Research Service, U.S. Dept. Agr., 1959—, engr., Akron, Colo., 1959, engr., Manhattan, Kan., 1960-62, research engr., Temple, Tex., 1962-65, research engr., location leader, Big Spring, Tex., 1965—. Adj. asso. prof. Tex. Tech. U., Lubbock, 1972-73. Dist. explorer chmn. Boy Scouts Am., Big Spring, 1970-73. Mem. Am. Soc. Agronomy, Am. Geophys. Union, Am. Soc. Agrl. Engrs. (chmn. com. 1971-73), Soil Conservation Soc. Am. (chpt. pres. 1970). Baptist. Lion. Club: Toastmasters International (Temple, Tex.). Home: Route 1 Box 319 Big Spring TX 79720 Office: PO Box 909 Big Spring TX 79720

FUCHS, LASZLO, mathematician, educator; b. Budapest, Hungary, June 24, 1924; s. David Raphael and Theresia (Rosenberg) F.; diploma U. Budapest, 1947, Ph.D., 1947; venia legendi L. Eotvos U., Budapest, 1951; D. Math. Scis. Hungarian Acad. Scis., 1954. Came to U.S., 1966, naturalized, 1973. Tchrs. Tng. Inst., Budapest, Hungary, 1947-49; asst. L. Eotvos U., Budapest, 1949-52, docent, 1952-54, prof., 1954-66; prof. U. Miami, Coral Gables, Fla., 1966-68; prof. math. Tulane U., New Orleans, 1968—. Vis. prof. Tulane U., New Orleans, 1961-62, U. New South Wales, Kensington, Australia, 1965, U. Montpellier, France, 1968, U. Ariz., Tucson, 1972; head algebra sect. Math. Research Inst., Budapest, Hungary, 1963-66. Recipient Kossuth Prize Hungarian govt., 1953. Mem. Bolyai Math. Soc. (treas. 1951-63, sec. gen. 1963-66), Deutsche Math. Vereinigung, Am. Math. Soc., Math. Assn. Am. (sect. v.p. 1967-68). Author: Abelian Groups, 1958; Partially Ordered Algebraic Systems, 1963; Teilweise Geordnete Algebraische Strukturen, 1966; Infinite Abelian Groups I-II, 1970-73. Contbr. articles to profl. jours. Home: 4504 Laudun St Metairie LA 70002 Office: Dept Math Tulane U New Orleans LA 70118

FUELSCH, DON JAMES, editor, pub.; b. St. Louis, Jan. 16, 1921; s. Arthur George and Verna (Kamler) F.; m. Lerah Mae Moreland, May 27, 1945; m. 2d, Janet Williams Griffin, Dec. 30, 1968. Editor Outdoor Field, Hot Springs, Ark., 1950—, pub., 1960—. Cons. advt. sales, design of outdoor products. Served as liaison pilot USAAF, 1942-43. Mem. Outdoor Writers Assn. Am. Author: Southern Angler's and Hunter's Guide, 1961, rev. edit., 1962, 63, 64, 65, 67. Office: PO Box 2188 Hot Springs AR 71901

FUERTES, RAFAEL RODRIGUEZ, lawyer, savs. and loan assn. exec.; b. Naguabo, P.R., Feb. 1, 1914; s. Jose R. and Mercedes (Garzot) F.; B.A., U. P.R., 1936, LL.B., 1938; m. Evangelina Thillet, June 12, 1948; children—Roberto, Felix Rafael. Admitted to P.R., bar, 1938; practiced in San Juan, P.R., 1938-40, 44-45; chief legal div. P.R. Planning Bd., 1945-56; with Caguas Fed. Savs. & Loan Assn. (P.R.), 1959—, sr. v.p., 1968—, dir., 1959—. Territorial dep. P.R., 1958-62. K.C. (grand knight 1952-54). Office: Caguas Fed Savs and Loan Assn Box 666 Caguas PR 00625

FUERTES, RAUL ARMANDO, sch. adminstr.; b. Havana, Cuba, Nov. 4, 1940; s. Raul and Luisa Elvira (Pichardo) F.; Baccalaureate in Letters, U. Havana, 1961; B.A., U. Miami, 1967, B.Edn., 1968; M.S., Barry Coll., 1972. Came to U.S., 1961, naturalized, 1971. Sales mgr. Radio Movil Service, Havana, 1959-61; head cashier Grand Way Co., Miami, Fla., 1961-67; dir. admissions Miami Mil. Acad., 1967-71, dir. guidance, 1973—. Chmn. United Fund, Miami Mil. Acad., 1972—. Mem. Am. Personnel and Guidance Assn., Nat. Assn. Soccer Coaches (Fla. chmn. 1972—), Nat. Assn. Sch. Psychologists. Republican. Roman Catholic. Home and office: 10601 Biscayne Blvd Miami FL 33138

FUGATE, DOUGLAS BROWN, hwy. adminstr.; b. Reed Island, Va., Aug. 14, 1906; s. Jesse Honaker and Elizabeth (Brown) F.; B.S., Va. Mil. Inst., 1927; m. Mary Addison Latham, June 15, 1940 (dec.); 1 son, Douglas Brown; m. 2d, Emma Stimson Reed, July 7, 1973. Civil engr. Va. Dept. Hwys., Richmond, 1927-42, asst. chief engr., chief engr., dep. commr., 1956-64, commr., 1964—; dir. toll facilities State of Va., Norfolk, 1946-56. Chmn., Elizabeth River Tunnel Commn., 1964-73; mem. Va. Outdoor Recreation Commn., 1965—; mem. exec. com. Hwy. Research Bd. Served to lt. col. C.E., AUS, 1942-46. Recipient Exceptional Service award Am. Road Builders Assn., 1970; Thomas H. McDonald award for exceptional service in hwy. engring. Am. Assn. State Hwy. Ofcls., 1971, Distinguished service award VMI Found., 1972. Fellow Am. Soc. C.E. (past pres. Va. sect); mem. Nat. Soc. Profl. Engrs., Am. (past pres.), Southeastern (past pres.) assns. state hwy. ofcls., Am. Rd. Builders Assn. (regional v.p.). Episcopalian. Home: 102 Portland Pl Richmond VA 23221 Office: 1221 E Broad St Richmond VA 23219

FUGUA, DON, congressman; b. Jacksonville, Fla., Aug. 20, 1933; s. J. D. and Lucille (Langford) F.; B.S. in Agrl. Econs., U. Fla., 1957; m. Doris Akidakis, Dec. 20, 1955; children—Laura, John. Mem. Fla. House of Reps. from Calhoun County, 1958-62; mem. 88th-92d Congresses, 2d Dist. Fla. Served with M.C., AUS, Korean War. Named one of five outstanding young men in Fla., Fla. Jr. C. of C., 1963. Mem. Future Farmers Am. (state pres. 1950-51), Am. Legion, Fla. Blue Key, Fla. Gold Key, Alpha Gamma Rho, Gamma Sigma Delta. Presbyn. (elder). Mason (32 deg., Shriner, Jester), Elk, Woodman of World, Rotarian. Home: Altha FL 32421 Office: House Office Bldg Washington DC 20515

FUJII, TERUO, educator; b. Magna, Utah, Mar. 25, 1932; s. Masaru Daijiro and Shigeno (Yamada) F.; student U. Utah, 1949-51, B.S. in Elec. Engring., 1958, M.S. in Elec. Engring., 1960, Ph.D. in Telecommunication, 1970; m. Catharine Esther Crary, June 10, 1961; children—Cindy Arlene, Blair Alan, Carla Rochelle, Bryce Darin. Mem. tech. staff Hughes Aircraft Co., Culver City, Cal., 1958-59, 60-62; scientist Northrop Corp., Anaheim, 1962-64; mem. tech. staff Hughes Aircraft Co., Fullerton, 1964-70; asst. to dir. Sci. and Engring. Computer Center Kennecott Copper Co., Salt Lake City, 1970-72; asst. prof. U. Ky., Lexington, 1972—. Served with AUS, 1951-54. Mem. I.E.E.E., Optical Soc. Am., Soc. Mining Engrs. Sigma Xi. Author: Non-Interactive, Color TV Conversion Circuit for X-Ray Protection, 1970. Asso. editor: A Decade of Digital Computing in the Mineral Industry, 1969. Contbr. to sci. jours. Home: 194 Elm St Versailles KY 40383 Office: Dept Telecommunications U Ky 322 McVey Hall Lexington KY 40506

FULBRIGHT, GARLAND W., state ofcl.; b. nr. Hillsboro, Tex., Nov. 30, 1909; s. Edward H. and Maude B. (Barnes) F.; student Southwestern Jr. Coll., 1926-27; m. Marjorie Ruth Trimble, Apr. 27, 1935; children—Donald G., Larry Ray, Linda Jean. With San Antonio Fire Dept., 1929-42, 47-71, fire marshall, 1952-63, 1st asst. fire chief and exec. officer, 1963-71; exec. dir. Tex. Commn. on Fire Protection Personnel Standards and Edn., Austin, 1971—; 1st asst. chief in charge crash fire fighting Kelly AFB, San Antonio, 1942-47; dir. 8th Service Command Crash Fire-fighting Sch., 1942; instr. Tex. A. and M. College Fire Sch., 1939—; mem. fire ins. rate study com. Tex. Municipal League, San Antonio; pres. bd. dirs. Tex. Arson Conf., Inc., Austin, 1958-68; fire cons. for Hemisfair, 1967-68. Dir., treas. San Antonio Fed. Credit Union, 1948-70, pres., 1971; pres. Highland Park Little League Stadium, Inc., San Antonio, 1950-64; safety chmn, Bob Hill dist. Boy Scouts Am., 1951-53, advancement chmn., 1953-57; chmn. formation and control Fiesta Flambeau, San Antonio, 1948-71; pres. Northwood Elementary Sch. P.T.A., 1960-62; coordinator San Antonio Civil Def., 1958-60, chief staff, 1960-71. Bd. dirs. Nat. Found., San Antonio (exec. com. county chpt., chmn. ednl. com.), Firemen's Benevolent Fund, San Antonio; Bexar County campaign dir. March of Dimes. Recipient various awards San Antonio Civil Def., 1958, Tex. Civil Def., 1958, Tex. A. and M. Coll., 1958, Treasury Dept., 1944; Guy Cude award for fireman making most outstanding contbn. to community and civic projects. Exchange Club, 1961; named Outstanding Fireman of Year, 1962. Mem. Internat. Assn. Firefighters, Nat. Fire Protection Assn. (chmn. subcom. useful statistics 1963—, mem. fire reporting com., mem. steering com.), Fire Marshalls' Assn. N.A., Tex. Firemen's and Fire Marshall's Assn. (pres. 1970-71), San Antonio C. of C. (mem. fire prevention com. 1947-71, certificate of merit 1951), Hermann Sons Tex., San Antonio Power Squadron. Methodist (mem. ofcl. bd. 1949-61). Mason (Shriner). Developer fire demonstration equipment. Home: 8404 Stillwood Lane Austin TX 78758 Office: Suite B 2209 Hancock Dr Austin TX 78756

FULBRIGHT, JAMES WILLIAM, U.S. Senator; b. Sumner, Mo., Apr. 9, 1905; s. Jay and Roberta (Waugh) F.; A.B., U. Ark., 1925; B.A., Oxford (Eng.) U., 1928, M.A., 1931; LL.B., George Washington U., 1934; m. Elizabeth Williams, June 15, 1932; children—Elizabeth Williams (Mrs. John Lowrie Winnacker), Roberta Waugh (Mrs. Edward Thaddeus Foote II). Admitted to D.C. bar, 1934; spl. atty. Anti-Trust Div., U.S. Dept. of Justice, 1934-35; instr. in law, George Washington U., 1935-36; lectr. in law, U. Ark., 1936-39, pres., 1939-41; Mem. 78th Congress, 3d Dist. Ark., 1943-45; U.S. Senator from Ark., 1945-75, mem. finance com., chmn. com. fgn. relations. Mem. Sigma Chi. Democrat. Mem. Disciples of Christ Ch. Rotarian. Home: Fayetteville AR 72701 also 2527 Belmont Rd NW Washington DC Office: New Senate Office Bldg Washington DC 20510

FULGENZI, JOHN ALFRED, civil engr.; b. Madrid, Spain, Jan. 19, 1930; s. Ben and Cecilia Pearl (Ridgeway) F. (parents Am. citizens); B.S. in Civil Engring., Okla. State U., 1952; postgrad. U. N.M., 1961-63; m. Kay Charlotte Lofley, July 29, 1966; stepchildren—Stephen Faulkner, John Faulkner. Div. engr. marketing Continental Oil Co., Albuquerque, 1954-58; dist. engr. Continental Pipeline, Wichita Falls, Tex., 1958-59; constrn. supt. Blumenthal Bros. Constrn. Co., Albuquerque, 1960-61; pres. Fulgenzi Engring., Santa Fe, N.M. and Amarillo, Tex., 1962—; v.p. Panhandle Engrs. and Contractors, Inc., 1971-74; pres. Tex. Engring. & Developers, 1974—. Coach Kids, Inc., Amarillo, 1968-71, bd. govs., 1971—; active YMCA. Commr., Randall County, Tex., 1971—. Served to 1st lt. USAF, 1952-53; maj., liaison officer U.S. Air Force Acad., 1953—. Registered profl. engr., N.M., Tex., Colo., Ariz. Mem. Nat. Soc. Profl. Engrs., Am. Soc. C.E. Methodist. Editor West Tex. sect. Am. Soc. C.E. paper, 1971. Home: 6704 Dreyfuss St Amarillo TX 79106 Office: 216 S Lipscomb St Amarillo TX 79105

FULKS, LEWIS L., educator; b. Burkburnet, Tex., Feb. 11, 1926; s. Millard Filmore and Bertha Paralee (Bower) F.; B.A., Abilene Christian Coll., 1948; M.A., U. So. Cal., 1950, postgrad., 1959-61; m. Jerelene Warren, Dec. 15, 1949. Designer theatre, asso. dir. theatre, tchr. drama Abilene Christian Coll. (Tex.), 1949-58, dir. theatre, designer, 1961-73, asso. prof. drama, 1963—; dir. theatre, designer Pepperdine Coll., Los Angeles, 1958-61. Designer, dir. Oklahoma, South Pacific, Abilene Philharmonic Orch., 1965-66. Mem. Am. Assn. U. Profs., Am. Theatre Assn., Blue Key, Alpha Psi Omega. Mem. Ch. of Christ. Home: 525 College Dr Abilene TX 79601

FULLAGAR, PAUL DAVID, educator; b. Ft. Edward, N.Y., Dec. 19, 1938; s. William Alfred and Evelyn Louise (Hoyt) F.; B.A. (Columbia Nat. scholar, Gen. Motors scholar), Columbia, 1960; Ph.D. (University fellow, Shell Co. fellow), U. Ill., 1963; m. Patricia Ann Kelley, June 6, 1959; children—Scott David, Eric Craig. Asst. prof. geology Old Dominion Coll., Norfolk, Va., 1963-67; asst. prof. geology U. N.C., Chapel Hill, 1967-69, asso. prof. geology, 1969-73, prof. geology, 1973—. Analytical geochemist Goddard Space Flight Center, Greenbelt, Md., part-time, 1964-68; asst. chmn. geology U. N.C., Chapel Hill, 1969—. NSF research grantee, 1964-67, 1967-70, 1970-72, 1972—. Fellow Geol. Soc. Am.; mem. Elisha Mitchell Sci. Soc. (sec., treas. 1970-72), Am. Assn. U. Profs., A.A.A.S., Am. Geophys. Union, Nat. Assn. Geology Tchrs., Geochem. Soc., Carolina Geol. Soc., Internat. Assn. Geochemistry and Cosmochemistry, Sigma Xi. Home: 354 Wesley Dr Chapel Hill NC 27514

FULLEN, EUGENE FRANCIS, oil well service co. exec.; b. Duluth, Minn., Feb. 2, 1914; s. Ferman F. and Alice (Crane) F.; student pub. schs., Robinson, Ill.; m. Mildred Chapman, Feb. 28, 1934; children—Phyllis Anne (Mrs. L.W. Lewis), Alice Ruth (Mrs. Tom Hull). Began career as truck driver for Fred S. Endsley, Robinson, 1932-36; roughneck D.D. Feldman, Jennings, La., 1936-37; roustabout, foreman Pan Am. Prodn. Co., Houston area, 1937-46; supt. Pan Am. Prod. Co. Houston area, 1946-52; mgr. expln. and devel. Columbia Carbon Co., Monroe, La., 1952-53; owner, pres. Mallard Well Service, Lafayette, La., 1952—, Drake Rentals Inc., 1968—; v.p. petroleum services div. Crutcher Resources Corp., 1971—; chmn. La. Gulf Coast Oil Expn., Lafayette 1972-73. Mem. Am. Assn. Oilwell Drilling Contractors, Am. Petroleum Inst. Mining, Metall. and Petroleum Engrs., Greater Lafayette C. of C. (past chmn. oil industry com.). Methodist. Mason (Shriner). Club: Oakbourne Country (pres. 1968). Home: PO Box 53002 OCS 101 Crescent Ridge Pl Lafayette LA 70501 Office: 331 Heymann Blvd Lafayette LA 70501

FULLENWEIDER, DONN CHARLES, lawyer; b. Milw., Jan. 25, 1935; s. Russell Charles and Anne Mae (Murphy) F.; B.S., U. Houston, 1957, J.D., 1958; m. Jerrie Rabon, June 23, 1962; 1 son, Keith Rabon. Admitted to Tex. bar, 1958; asso. law firm with Fred Parks, Houston, 1958-65; partner Haynes & Fullenweider, Houston, 1965—. Adj. asso. prof. law U. Houston Bates Coll. Law, 1972-74. Mem. 43d Joint Civilian Orientation Conf., 1973. Bd. dirs. Post Oak Am. Little League Assn. Fellow Tex. Bar Found.; mem. Am., Houston (1st v.p., 1970-73) bar assns., State Bar Tex. (dir.), Am., Houston (v.p. 1971) trial lawyers assns., Def. Orientation Conf. Assn., Houston C. of C., Sigma Chi, Phi Delta Phi. Clubs: River Oaks Country, Houston. Home: 1568 Kirby Dr Houston TX 77017 Office: 711 Fannin St Suite 610 Houston TX 77002

FULLER, EARL HOUSTON, textile co. exec.; b. Columbia, S.C., Mar. 23, 1916; s. Linzey Thurmond and Sue Ethel (Stover) F.; B.S., Clemson U., 1938; m. Claudia Marian Wallace, Mar. 30, 1937; children—Judith (Mrs. Drew C. Smith), Claudia (Mrs. Marshall F. Thompson, Jr.), Earl Houston. Various positions to supt. Simmons Co., 1939-55; supt., plant mgr. J.P. Stevens & Co., Inc., 1956-66, group gen. mgr., 1966-70, group v.p., Roanoke Rapids, N.C., 1970-73; exec. v.p., mfg. head domestics and allied products div., Greenville, S.C., 1973—. Chmn. Halifax County Draft Bd., 1949-54, Roanoke Rapids Recreation Commn., 1953-55; mem. Roanoke Rapids Bd. Edn., 1961-67. Served to maj. AUS, 1942-46; ETO. Decorated Bronze Star medal with oak leaf cluster, Purple Heart; named Young Man of Year, Roanoke Rapids Jr. C. of C., 1951. Presbyn. (elder). Home: 206 Redcliffe Rd Greenville SC 29607 Office: J P Stevens & Co Inc Greenville SC 29202

FULLER, EDGAR, educator; b. La Crosse, Wis., Mar. 23, 1904; s. Ernest Edgar and Mary (Wise) F.; A.B., Brigham Young U., 1927; J.D., U. Chgo., 1932; Ed.D., Harvard, 1940; m. Alta Pamela Call, Sept. 10, 1926 (dec. 1972); children—Mary Margaret, Kathryn Jean (Mrs. L.S. Reid, Jr.), Carol Yvonne (Mrs. John H. Hinrichs, Jr.); m. 2d, Blanche E. Crippen, 1973. Laborer in timber woods and mills, 1919-23; mucker and miner, 1923-27; supt. schs., Virden, N.M., 1929-31, 32-33; pres, Gila Jr. Coll., Thatcher, Ariz., 1933-39; lectr. on ednl. adminstrn. Harvard, 1940-42; prin. educationist and acting chief aviation edn. div. U.S. CAA, Washington, 1942-46; commr. edn. State of N.H., 1946-48; exec. sec. Council Chief State Sch. Officers, 1948-69, exec. sec. emeritus, 1969—. Mem. Pres.' Nat. Com. for Devel. Scientists and Engrs.; mem. various ednl. bds. and commns. Recipient Brewer trophy Nat. Aeros. Assn. for outstanding contbn. to air youth edn. Mem. N.E.A., Am. Assn. Sch. Adminstrs., Nat. Joint Com. Ednl. TV, Horace Mann League (pres. 1959; chmn. com. constnl. law 1962-73). Unitarian. Author, Editor numerous books and articles on pub. law, ednl. finance and adminstrn. and aviation edn.; contbr. to Harvard Law Rev., Harvard Ednl. Rev., Am. Sch. Bd. Jour., Nat. Aeros., and similar periodicals; also bulls. and pamphlets on these subjects, 1932—; Evidence for Administrative Changes in Federal-State-Local Education, 1971. Editor: Education in the States, 2 vols., 1969. Died Aug. 4, 1973. Home: 12904 Mt Royal Lane Fairfax VA 22030

FULLER, LAWRENCE LEE, lawyer; b. Tucson, Nov. 13, 1926; s. Lawrence L. and Anna Marie (Mullaney) F.; B.B.A., U. Tex., 1950, LL.B., 1957; m. Peggy Bogard, June 2, 1967; children—Pam (Mrs. Jay Holland), Debra (Mrs. Ron Little), Patricia. Admitted to Tex. bar, 1957, U.S. Supreme Ct., 1968; asst. county atty., El Paso, 1957-59; asst. U.S. atty. Western Dist. Tex., 1959-61; partner Turpin, Smith, Dyer, Hardie & Harman, Midland and Odessa, 1961-70; individual practice law, Monahans, 1970—; dist. atty. Ward, Reeves and Loving counties, 1973—. Pres. Monahans Indsl. Found., 1972-73. Served with USNR, 1944-46. Fellow Tex. Bar Found.; mem. Nat., Tex. dist. attys. assns., State Bar Tex., Ward County Bar Assn., Tex. Assn. Def. Counsel, Trans-Pecos Bar Assn. (pres. 1973—). Democrat. Rotarian. Home: 1403 S Ike St Monahans TX 79756 Office: PO Box 1208 Monahans TX 79756

FULLER, MAYNARD GERALD, civil engr.; b. Ft. Cobb, Okla., Apr. 21, 1907; s. Martin Luther and Christina Barbara (Patten) F.; B.S. in Civil Engring., Okla. U., 1930; m. Ethel Mae Munson, June 6, 1931 (dec. Feb. 1973); children—Maynard Gerald, Alen Munson,

Ingrid Ellen (Mrs. Michael Hogue); m. Bonnie Hartley Wade, June 2, 1973. Surveyor, Gypsy Oil Co., Tulsa, 1928; resident engr. Okla. Hwy. Dept., 1930-38, 40-41; constrn. engr. Holway & Neuffer, cons. engr. Grand River Dam Authority, 1938-40; sr. engr. C.E., Tulsa Dist., 1941-44, Hdqrs. 8th Service Command, Dallas, 1944-46; sr. engr., chief rds., r.r.'s runways-engr. sect. hdgrs. 4th Army, San Antonio, 1946-54; sr. engr., civilian asst. post engr. U.S. Army, Ft. Sill, Okla., 1954-58; contractor hwy. and heavy Freeman, Inc., Lawton, Okla., 1958-61; co-founder, partner Dambold & Fuller, Cons. Engrs., 1961-64; cons. civil engr., founder, owner M.G. Fuller and Assos., Inc., Cons. Engrs., Lawton, Okla., 1964—. Co-promoter registration law for profl. engrs. in Okla., 1934-35. Co-founder Christian Serviceman's Center, San Antonio, dir., 1951-54; co-founder Christian Serviceman's Center, Lawton, Okla., dir., 1959—, pres. bd., 1959. Recipient certificate appreciation for civilian war service with war dept. Sec. War, 1946; certificate achievement U.S. Army Arty. and Missile Center, 1958. Registered profl. engr., Okla., Tex., Ark., Kan., Pa., Va. Mem. Okla. Soc. Profl. Engrs. (co-founder, charter mem., dir., sec.-treas. 1942, v.p. 1943, pres. 1944), Am. Soc. Planning ofcls., Am. Congress Surveying and Mapping, Am. Water Works Assn., Frontiers Sci., Profl. Soc. Nuclear Def. (charter), U.S. Com. Dams, Sigma Tau. Democrat. Baptist (deacon 1944—, tchr. bible 1945—). Author: Focal Paths of Revelation, 1969. Contbr articles to profl. jours. Home: 3011 E Gore Apt 227 Lawton OK 73501 Office: 1313A Av Lawton OK 73501

FULLER, PARRISH, lumber mfr.; b. Madison, Wis., May 21, 1892; s. William Wilson and Minnie Lora (Parrish) F.; student Wabash Coll., 1910-11, M.A., 1949, LL.D., 1954; m. Hester Porter, Oct. 18, 1919; children—Mary Margaret (Mrs. James D. Voorhees), William Porter. Gen. mgr. J. O. Parish Lumber Co., Shelbyville, Ind., 1914-18; asst. to pres. Hillyer Deutsch Edwards, Inc., Oakdale, La., 1919-20, v.p., gen. mgr., 1920-68; v.p. Hillyer Edwards Fuller, Inc., Glenmora, La., 1923-40; gen. partner King Edwards-Fuller Co., St. Francisville, La., 1940-47, Avoyelles Timber Co., Bordelonville, La., 1940-64; v.p. King Lumber Industries, Canton, Miss., 1946-50, Canton (Miss.) & Carthage R.R. Co., 1946-53, Heflands, Inc., 1961-68, Porter Steel Specialties, Inc., Shelbyville, Ind., 1946-51; dir., chmn. forest lands and products Celotex Corp., Chgo., 1946-66; pres. J. O. Parrish Lumber Co., Shelbyville, Ind.; gen. partner Fuller Farms, Shelbyville, 1930-72, Edwards & Fuller, Oakdale, La., 1938-70; former dir. Nat. Bank of Commerce, New Orleans, South Shore Oil and Devel. Co., New Orleans, Lower Coast R.R. Chmn., Citizens Adv. Com. on La. Edn., 1964. State Salvage chmn. 1942-45, United War Fund, 1943-45; pres. Pub. Affairs Research Council La., Inc., 1958; mem. Coordinating council La. State Colleges and La. State U., 1948-52; mem. La. State Bd. Edn., 1929-52, pres., 1952; vice chmn. La. Commn. Higher Edn., 1955-56. Bd. visitors Tulane U., 1953; bd. govs. Ochsner Med. Found., New Orleans; trustee Wabash Coll. Served as 2d lt. aviation sect. O.R.C., 1919. Received Citizenship Citation, La. div. V.F.W. (14th Good Citizenship medal for pub. service in a vital war effort); pub. service citations So. U., 1952, La. Council Coll. Pres., 1953; award merit Wabash Coll., 1960; named Humanitarian of Yr., Abbeville, La., 1960. Mem. Sigma Chi. Presbyn. Clubs: The Chicago; Boston, International House, Plimsoll (New Orleans). Address: Box 663 Oakdale LA 71463

FULLERTON, CHARLES GORDON, astronaut; b. Rochester, N.Y., Oct. 11, 1936; s. Charles Renwick and Grace (Sherman) F.; B.S., Cal. Inst. Tech., 1957, M.S. in M. E., 1958; m. Marie Jeanette Buettner, July 6, 1968. Commd. 2d lt. U.S. Air Force, 1958, advanced through grades to maj., 1969; completed pilot tng., 1959; bomber pilot SAC, Davis-Monthan AFB, Tucson, 1960-64; completed aerospace research pilot sch. Edwards AFB, 1965; bomber flight test pilot, 1966; astronaut USAF Manned Orbiting Lab., 1966-69, NASA Manned Spacecraft Center, Houston, 1969—. Decorated USAF Commendation medal, Outstanding Unit award, Nat. Def. Service medal. Mem. Soc. Exptl. Test Pilots (asso.), Tau Beta Pi. Home: 16006 Torry Pines Rd Houston TX 77058 Office: Astronaut Office NASA Manned Spacecraft Center Houston TX 77058

FULLERTON, SAMUEL BAKER, constrn. co. exec.; b. St. Louis, July 10, 1931; s. Samuel Baker and Mary (Styron) F.; grad. Lawrenceville Sch., 1950; student Duke U., 1950-51; B.S., B.A., U. Ark., 1955; m. Tomme Fairfax Triplett, July 31, 1953; children—Samuel Baker III, Fairfax Triplett, Arthur King. Accounting trainee Bradley Lumber Co., Warren, Ark., 1954-55, asst. to pres., 1956-58; incorporator Moro Gravel Co., Warren, Ark., 1959-63; pres., treas. Moro, Inc., constrn., 1961—; dir. First Nat. Bank. Served to capt. USAF, 1955-56; now capt. Res. ret. Mem. Asso. Gen. Contractors Am., Asso. Gen. Contractors Ark. (bd. dirs. 1967-68), Kappa Sigma. Presbyn. (deacon 1961—). Rotarian. Clubs: Warren Country, Pine Bluff (Ark.) Country, Little Rock Country, Capitol, Little Rock. Home: 416 S Myrtle St Warren AR 71671 Office: Box 232 Warren AR 71671

FULLINGTON, RICHARD WAYNE, curator; b. Dallas, Jan. 12, 1942; s. Richard Clinton and Jimmie Anita (Dodson) F.; B.S., So. Meth. U., 1967, M.S., 1969; m. Gail Frances Grafflin, Aug. 3, 1962 (div. May 1972); 1 son, Richard Steven. Curator invertebrate zoology dept. Dallas Mus. Natural History, 1969—. Sci. cons. Dallas Ind. Sch. Dist., 1971—, Dallas Community Jr. Colls., 1970—; vis. lectr. So. Meth. U., 1973—. Served with USNR, 1960-62. Research land and fresh water mollusca of Tex. Home: 7170 Gaston Av Dallas TX 75214 Office: PO Box 26193 Fair Park Station Dallas TX 75226

FULLMER, HAROLD MILTON, dental educator; b. Gary, Ind., July 9, 1918; s. Howard and Rachael Eva (Tiedge) F.; B.S., Ind. U., 1942, D.D.S., 1944; m. Marjorie Lucile Engel, Dec. 31, 1942; children—Angela Sue, Pamela Rose. Intern, Charity Hosp., New Orleans, 1946-47, resident, 1947-48, vis. dental surgeon, 1948-53; instr. Loyola U., New Orleans, 1948-49, asst. prof., 1949-50, asso. prof. gen. and oral pathology, 1949-53; cons. pathology VA hosps., Biloxi and Gulfport, Miss., 1950-53; asst. dental surgeon Nat. Inst. Dental Research, NIH, Bethesda, Md., 1953-54, dental surgeon, 1954-56, sr. dental surgeon, 1956-60, dental dir., 1960-70, chief sect. histochemistry Nat. Inst. Dental Research, 1967-70, chief exptl. pathology, 1969-70; dir. Inst. Dental Research, prof. pathology, prof. dentistry, asso. dean Sch. Dentistry, U. Ala. Med. Center, Birmingham, 1970—. Served to capt. AUS, 1944-46. Recipient Isaac Schour award for outstanding research and teaching in anat. scis., Internat. Assn. Dental Research, 1973. Fulbright grantee, 1972. Diplomate Am. Bd. Oral Pathology. Fellow Am. Coll. Dentists, Am. Acad. Oral Pathology, A.A.A.S.; mem. Am. Dental Assn., Internat. Assn. Dental Research (v.p. 1974-75), Internat. Assn. Pathologists, Histochem. Soc., Biol. Stain Commn., Am. Coll. Dentists, Commd. Officers Assn. Club: Exchange (pres. New Orleans 1952-53) (Birmingham). Editor: (with R.D. Lillie) Histopathologic Technic and Practical Histochemistry, 1975. Editor Jour. Oral Pathology, 1972—; asso. editor Jour. Cutaneous Pathology, 1973—, Oral Surgery, Oral Medicine, Oral Pathology, 1970—. Home: 3514 Bethune Dr Birmingham AL 35223

FULTON, RICHARD HARMON, congressman; b. Nashville, Jan. 27, 1927; s. Lyle Houston and Labina (Plummer) F.; student U. Tenn., 1946-47; m. Jewel Simpson, Dec. 23, 1945; children—Richard, Michael, Barry, Donna, Linda. Real estate broker Fulton & Riddle Realty Co.; mem. Tenn. Senate 1959-60; mem. 88th-93d Congresses, 5th Tenn. Dist. Served as seaman USNR, 1945-46. Democrat. Methodist. Mason (Shriner). Home: 911 Preston Dr Nashville TN 37206 also 104 Schott's Ct NE Washington DC Office: Rayburn House Office Bldg Washington DC 20515

FULTON, ROBERT EARLE, civil engr.; b. Dothan, Ala., Jan. 23, 1931; s. Fitzhugh Lee and Manilla (Thompson) F.; student Jacksonville State U., 1948-49; B.S., Auburn U., 1953; M.S. (Grad. scholar), U. Ill., 1958, Ph.D., 1960; m. Autumn Bernice Cook, Dec. 27, 1953; children—David Earle, Robert Bruce, Lori Leeanne. Structural designer Chgo. Bridge & Iron Co., Birmingham, Ala., 1953-54; research asst., dept. civil engring. U. Ill., Urbana, 1957-60, asst. prof., 1960-62; research engr. NASA Langley Research Center, Hampton, Va., 1962-65, research supr., 1965—. Adj. prof. U. Va., 1962-67, George Washington U., Washington, 1967—, N.C. State U., 1971. Mem. York County (Va.) Sch. Bd., 1970—, chmn., 1973—. Bd. dirs. Hampton Rds. Ednl. TV Assn., 1971—, chmn. bd., 1973—. Served to 1st lt. USAF, 1954-57. Recipient Algernon Sydney Sullivan award Auburn U., 1953. Mem. Am. Soc. C.E. (chmn. com. electronic computation 1970—), Am. Inst. Aeronautics and Astronautics, Am. Soc. M.E., Sigma Xi, Lambda Chi Alpha, Tau Beta Pi, Phi Kappa Phi, Chi Epsilon. Contbr. articles to profl. jours. Editorial adv. bd. Jour. Computers and Structures. Home: 121 Will Scarlet Lane Williamsburg VA 23185 Office: Structures and Dynamics Div NASA Langley Research Center Hampton VA 23665

FULTON, WARREN CRIGLER, banker; b. Stuart, Va., June 20, 1912; s. James Wayte and Mary Ward (King) F.; student Danville Community Coll., 1938, Am. Inst. Banking, 1939-40; m. Barbara Bancroft, Pratt, Oct. 3, 1942; children—Warren Jr., Truxton King, Phyllis Jean. Teller, head bookkeeper First Nat. Bank, Danville, Va., 1934-42; with Bank Va., Danville, 1945—, head teller, 1945-48; operations mgr., 1948-59, loan officer, 1959-64, mgr. Ballou Park br., 1964-69, v.p., cashier, 1969-71, sr. v.p., 1971—. Pres. First Va. Conf., Bank Adminstrn. Inst., Richmond, 1954. Bd. dirs. A.R.C., Danville, 1963-73, Hughes Meml. Sch., 1955-73, Basil Browder Health Found., 1965-72, United Fund, 1968-72; mem. gifts div. com. Meml. Hosp. Expansion Fund, Danville, 1971-72. Served with AUS, 1942-45. Decorated Bronze Star medal. Named Father of Year Danville Exchange Club, 1954. Presbyn. (treas. 1947—; trustee 1948-73; elder 1947-73). Club: Exchange (bd. dirs. 1972-73) (Danville, Va.). Home: 169 Confederate Av Danville VA 24541 Office: 530 Main St Danville VA 24541

FUNDERBURK, SAPP, cons.; b. Columbia, S.C., Sept. 12, 1916; s. Virgil F. and Virginia (Sapp) F.; student Furman U., 1939; m. Frances Norwood, Mar. 2, 1940; children—George Norwood, Sapp. Asst. v.p., asst. treas. Auto Finance Co., Greenville, S.C., 1939-61, asst. treas., 1958-61, asst. v.p., 1955-61, also asst. v.p. Am. Discount Co., Greenville, 1955-61; v.p. installment loan dept. Citizens and So. Nat. Bank S.C., Greenville, 1961-67, adv. bd., 1958-67; mem. 5th Fed. Res. Dist. Adv. Bd.-Installment Credit, 1961—. Adv. Com. S.C. Tech. Tng. Com. Chmn. United Fund campaign, 1959; mem. Greenville County Planning and Devel. Bd., 1961—. Bd. dirs. Carolinas United Community Services, 1961—; chmn. bd. dirs. Broner Home; bd. dirs. Greenville YMCA; chmn., trustee Greenville County Found.; mem. adv. council Furman U., St. Francis Hospital; campaign chmn. Furman U. Devel. Fund; bd. dirs. Greenville County chpt. A.R.C., 1959-62; Served to maj. USAAF, World War II. Decorated Bronze Star medal. Recipient Distinguished Alumni award Furman U., 1963. Mem. Greenville C. of C. (past pres., dir., chmn. indsl. com., chmn. Better Bus. div.), Furman U. Alumni Assn. (pres.), Furman U. Athletic Council (past chmn.), Kappa Alpha (ct. of honor). Methodist. Mason, Elk, Rotarian (past pres., dir.). Clubs: Touchdown (past pres.), Greenville Cotillion, Poinsett (all Greenville). Address: 417 Belmont Av Greenville SC 29601

FUNKE, FRANCIS JOSEPH, educator; b. Indpls., June 11, 1915; s. Anthony and Caroline A. (Reimer) F.; A.B. magna cum laude (Liberal Arts scholar 1936-37), Butler U., 1937; M.A. (Legislative scholar 1937-38), U. Wis., 1938; postgrad. U. Pa., 1940, George Washington U., 1953-54; Ph.D., Fla. State U., 1964; m. Bertha Julia Sainz, Aug. 20, 1941; 1 son, John Anthony (dec.). Tchr. modern lang. Riverside Mil. Acad., Gainesville, Ga., 1938-41; Spanish tchr. Reitz High Sch., Evansville, Ind., 1941-43; tchr., Culver (Ind.) Mil. Acad., 1943-45; pharm. translator Eli Lilly Internat. Corp., Indpls., 1945-50; translator, interpreter U.S. Govt., Washington, 1950-55; adult edn. tchr. Good Neighbor Sch., Washington, 1951-53; tchr., North Miami High Sch., 1955-60; prof. Spanish-French Miami-Dade Community Coll., 1960—. Vice pres. Institut de Cultura Hispanica de Miami. Mem. Am. Assn. Tchrs. Spanish and Portuguese, Am. Assn. Tchrs. French, Modern Lang. Assn., Am. Dialect Soc., So. Atlantic Modern Lang. Assn., Dade County Spanish Tchrs. Assn. (pres. 1960-61), Fla. State Alumni Assn. (sec. bd. Dade County 1967—), Kappa Delta Pi (pres. Miami alumni chpt.), Phi Kappa Phi, Sigma Delta Pi, Pi Delta Phi, Alpha Mu Gamma. Home: 6700 Brookline Dr Country Club Miami Hialeah FL 33015

FUNKHOUSER, JOHN WILLIAM, educator; b. Beaverdam, Va., Aug., 28, 1926; s. Joseph Alfred and Mary Gordon (Redd) F.; B.A. magna cum laude, Washington and Lee U., 1948; Ph.D. (Atomic Energy fellow), Stanford, 1951, postgrad., 1953-54; student Richmond Profl. Inst., 1966-67; m. Anne Black, July 8, 1950; children—Susan (Mrs. Donald Peterson), William. Instr. Stanford (Cal.) U., 1951-52, research asso., 1952-54; research geologist Jersey Prodn. Research Co., Tulsa, 1954-63; sr. paleontologist Int. Petroleum, Ltd., Bogota, Colombia, 1963-66; asst. mgr. Concurso de Chivor Emerald Mines, Bogota, Colombia, 1966; mem. faculty John Tyler Community Coll., Chester, Va., 1967—, prof. geology, 1971—. Lectr. on environment to clubs, schs., others, 1969—. Mem. Internat. Com. Bot. Nomenclature, Netherlands, 1959—. Served with USNR, 1945-46. Recipient Robinson award, 1948, Herndon library award 1948 (both Washington & Lee U.). Mem. Va. Acad. Sci. (sect. chmn. 1973-74), Geol. Soc. Am., Am. Inst. Biol. Sci., Inter-Am. Philatetic Soc., Internat. Assn. Plant Taxonomy, Internat. Assn. Paleobotanists, A.A.A.S., Smithsonian Assos., Sigma Xi, Phi Beta Kappa, Tau Kappa Iota, Phi Eta Sigma. Clubs: Sierra (San Francisco); Camera (Richmond, Va.). Home: 12221 Chestertown Rd Chester VA 23831

FUQUA, BENJAMIN THOMAS, savs. and loan assn. exec.; b. Dickson, Tenn., Apr. 1, 1922; s. Benjamin Franklin and Ethel (Baker) F.; diploma Bowling Green Bus. U., 1946. Payroll clk. fuel dept. N. & W Rwy., Williamson, W.Va., 1946-50; personnel dir. Red Jacket Coal Co., Red Jacket, W.Va., 1952-55; with First Fed. Savs. & Loan Assn., Dickson, Tenn., 1955—, exec. v.p., mng. officer, 1966-71, pres., 1971—. Dist. chmn. Boy Scouts Am., 1958-62, mem. exec. bd. Middle Tenn. Council, 1958-73; chmn. Dickson County Adv. Com., Dept. Pub. Welfare, 1958. Bd. dirs. Tenn. Savs. and Loan League, 1972-73. Served with AUS, 1942-45, 51. Decorated Bronze Star medal; recipient Silver Beaver award Boy Scouts Am., 1963, Long Rifle award, 1971. Mem. Dickson County C. of C. (pres. 1969), V.F.W., Am. Legion. Methodist (chmn. adminstrn. bd. 1966-69; treas. 1966-73). Kiwanian (sec. 1956-58, pres. 1959). Home: Box 432 Route 1 Dickson TN 37055 Office: 611 E College St Dickson TN 37055

FUREY, FRANCIS JAMES, bishop; b. Summit Hill, Pa., Feb. 22, 1905; s. John and Anna (O'Donnell) F.; student St. Charles Sem., Overbrook, Pa., 1920-24; Ph.D., Pontificio Seminario Romano, Rome, 1926, S.T.D., 1930; LL.D., La Salle Coll., Phila., 1944, St. John's U., Bklyn., 1946, Villanova U., 1947, St. Joseph's Coll., Phila., 1949. Ordained priest Roman Catholic Ch., 1930; pvt. sec. to Cardinal Dougherty, 1930-36; pres. Immaculata (Pa.) Coll., 1936-46; rector St. Charles Sem., 1946-58, St. Helena's Parish, Phila., 1958-63; consecrated bishop, 1960; auxiliary bishop Phila., titular bishop Temnus, 1960-63; bishop San Diego, Cal., 1963, now bishop, San Antonio. Dir. Cath. Charities Appeal, Phila., 1958. Bd. dirs. Misericordia Hosp., Phila., St. Joseph Hosp., Phila., Ravenhill Acad., Germantown, Pa.; trustee Roman Cath. High Sch., Phila. Named Domestic Prelate by Pope Pius XII, 1947; knight comdr. Legion Cedars Lebanon. Mem. Nat., Pa. Cath. ednl. assns., Assn. Coll. Presidents Pa., John Henry Newman Soc. Address: PO Box 32648 San Antonio TX 78284

FURMAN, WALTER LAURIE, educator; b. Charlotte, N.C., Nov. 30, 1913; s. Henry Sylvester and Edna Earl (Jenkins) F.; B.S., The Citadel, 1933; M.S., U. Fla., 1941, Ph.D., 1961. Ordained priest Roman Cath. Ch., 1950; asst. in physics U. Fla., Gainesville, 1934-36, 1953-55; instr. Spring Hill Coll., Mobile, Ala., 1943-46, 1951-53, asst. prof., 1957-59, 1960-63, asso. prof., 1963-67, prof., chmn. dept. math., 1967—, dir. Co-op. Sch.-Coll. Sci. project, 1966-70; instr. U. Fla., Gainesville, 1955-57. Recipient Fellowship for fgn. study Universidad Javeriana, 1959-60. Mem. Am. Math. Soc., Math. Assn. Am., Soc. Indsl. and Applied Math., A.A.A.S. Address: Spring Hill Coll Mobile AL 36608

FURMAN, WILLIAM MICHAEL, banker; b. Tullulah, La., May 10, 1937; s. Gwyn Gould and Mary Elizabeth (Beyhan) F.; B.A. in Bus., Tex. Western Coll., B.A. in Geology; LL.B., U. Tex. Sch. Law; m. Charlotte Ann Walker, Aug. 18, 1961; children—Michael Scott, Susan Elaine, Stacy Ann. Admitted to Tex. bar, 1966; with First Nat. Bank, Midland, Tex., 1966-68, First State Bank, Odessa, Tex., 1968-73; pres., chief exec. officer, dir. Odessa Savs. & Loan Assn., 1973—. Dir. McVean & Barlow Pipeline Co., Odessa, Model Shop, Odessa; lectr. Odessa Coll., 1968-69. Mem., chmn. spl. berquests Cancer Crusade, Odessa, 1971; chmn. profl. div. United Fund, Odessa, 1973—. Regent Odessa Coll., 1973—. Bd. dirs. Presdl. Mus., 1971-72, YMCA, 1972, Salvation Army, 1968-73, Boys Club, 1968-71, Midland-Odessa Symphony, 1970-71, Cancer Soc., 1971-72, Permian Basin Estate Council, 1965-73. Served to capt. AUS, 1963-65. Mem. Am., Tex., Ector County bar assns., Mem. Christian Ch. Rotarian. Home: 2909 E 17th St Odessa TX 79760 Office: 7th and Texas Sts Odessa TX 79760

FURNAS, WENDELL JESS, naval officer; b. Wichita, Kan., July 27, 1917; s. Edgar Allen and Dottie (Scoggins) F.; A.B. in English History, U. Cal. at Berkeley, 1939; m. Esther Helen Hyde, July 11, 1943; children—Mary (Mrs. Tammi), Christine. Commd. ensign USN, 1943, advanced through grades to capt., 1964; comdg. officer Naval Intelligence Processing System Support Activity, 1965-69; comdt. Def. Intelligence Sch., Washington, 1971—. Prof., U. Shanghai, 1941-42. Mem. Phi Beta Kappa. Republican. Clubs: Army Navy Country, Internat. Sportsmans. Contbr. articles to nat. mags. Home: 3403 Cameron Mills Rd Alexandria VA 22305 Office: Defense Intelligence School Washington Navy Yard Anacostia Annex Washington DC 20374

FURR, AARON KEITH, educator; b. Salisbury, N.C., Mar. 5, 1932; s. Carl Albert and Sue Thomas (Howell) F.; A.B., Catawba Coll., 1954; M.S., Emory U., 1955; Ph.D., Duke U., 1962; m. Dora Anne Mondon, Mar. 22, 1958; children—Elizabeth Anne (adopted), Julia Ellen, Joel Keith, Robin Stuart. Faculty, dept. physics Va. Poly. Inst. and State U., Blacksburg, 1960-70, prof. nuclear engring., dept. mech. engring., 1970—. Mem. Am. Nuclear Soc. Home: Route 1 Box 448A Blacksburg VA 24060

FURR, CARTER BRANHAM SNOW, lawyer; b. Norfolk, Va., Oct. 30, 1932; s. Carlton Harris and Marion Carter (Snow) F.; B.S. magna cum laude, Hampden-Sydney Coll., 1954; J.D., U. Va., 1957; m. Caroline Ann Huffstutler, July 7, 1962; 1 son, Carter Branham, Jr. Admitted to Va. bar, 1957; pvt. practice law, Norfolk, Va.; asso. Gordon H. Campbell, Norfolk, Va., 1958, Seawell, McCoy, Winston & Dalton, Norfolk, 1958-62; asso. Jett, Sykes & Berkley, Norfolk, 1962-63; partner Jett, Berkley, Furr & Heilig, Norfolk, Va., 1963—. Mem. Republican City Com., Norfolk, Va., 1966—. Dir. Norfolk Hist. Soc., 1967-73, pres., 1970-72, 1st v.p., 1973—. Served with AUS, 1957. Mem. Fed., Am., Va., Norfolk, Portsmouth bar assns., Maritime Law Assn., Va. Trial Lawyers Assn., Elizabeth River Power Squadron (lt. 1971-73), Order of Coif, Phi Alpha Delta, Lambda Chi Alpha, Chi Beta Phi. Episcopalian (mem. vestry 1970-72; sr. warden 1971-72). Clubs: German, Yacht and Country, Virginia (Norfolk, Va.); Princess Anne Country (Virginia Beach). Home: 1418 Graydon Pl Norfolk VA 23507 Office: 801 Bank of Virginia Bldg Norfolk VA 23510

FURR, ROBERT EARL, dentist, air force officer; b. Greenville, N.C., Mar. 27, 1929; s. James Elisha, Sr., and Viola (Carpenter) F.; student Wake Forest Coll., 1947-50; D.D.S., U. N.C., 1954; certificate postgrad tng. prosthetics U. Ala., 1960-62; m. Danny Marie Hayes, Sept. 12, 1953. Individual practice dentistry, Wilmington, N.C., 1956-57; commd. 2d lt. U.S. Air Force, 1954, advanced through grades to col., 1973; chief prosthetics Maxwell AFB, Ala., 1971—. Dir. J.E. Furr, Inc. Decorated Bronze Star medal. Mem. Am. Dental Assn., Delta Sigma Delta. Baptist. Home: 408 East Dr Maxwell Air Force Base AL 36113 Office: Maxwell Regional Hospital Maxwell Air Force Base AL 36113

FUSARO, BERNARD ALEXANDER, educator; b. Charleston, W.Va., Aug. 9, 1924; s. Joseph A. and Charlotte (Santoro) F.; B.A., Swarthmore Coll., 1950; M.A., Columbia, 1954; Ph.D., U. Md., 1965; m. Elizabeth June Lazzara, Aug. 3, 1966; 1 dau., Amelia Rebecca. Instr. U. Md., College Park, 1957-61; vis. asst. prof. U. Okla., Norman, 1961-62; asst. prof. U. South Fla., Tampa, 1962-67; mem. faculty Queens Coll., Charlotte, N.C., 1967—, prof., chmn. dept. math., 1967—. Served with USMC, 1943-46. Mem. Am. Math. Soc., Math. Assn. Am., Soc. Indsl. and Applied Math. Home: 2100 Brandon Circle Charlotte NC 28211 Office: Dept Math Queens Coll Charlotte NC 28207

FUSELIER, LOUIS ALFRED, lawyer; b. New Orleans, Mar. 26, 1932; s. Robert Howe and Monica (Hanemann) F.; B.S., La. State U., 1953; LL.B., Tulane U., 1959; m. Eveline Gasquet Fenner, Dec. 27, 1956; children—Louis Alfred, Henri de la Claire, Elizabeth Fenner. Admitted to La. bar, 1959, Miss. bar, 1964, U.S. Supreme Ct. bar 1965; trial atty. NLRB, 1959-62 (all New Orleans); partner law firm Fuselier, Ott, McKee & Flowers and predecessors, Jackson, Miss. Served as pilot USAF, 1953-56. Mem. Am., La (past chmn. labor law sect.), New Orleans, Miss., Hinds County, Fed. bar assns., Miss. Bar Found., Jackson C. of C., Am. Judicature Soc. Rotarian. Clubs: Round Table, Boston (New Orleans); Country, Capital City Petroleum (Jackson, Miss.). Office: 1600 Standard Life Bldg PO Box 95 Jackson MS 39205

FUZEK, JOHN FRANK, chemist; b. Knoxville, Tenn., Dec. 21, 1921; s. John and Maria (Pucher) F.; B.S., U. Tenn., 1943, M.S., 1945, Ph.D., 1947; m. Bettye Lynn Bean, May 31, 1943; children—Mary Ann, Margaret Elizabeth, Martha Lynn. Chemist Hercules Powder Co., Wilmington, Del., 1943-44; research chemist North Am. Rayon Corp. subsidiary Beaunit, Elizabethton, Tenn., 1948-55; head physics lab. Beaunit Fibers, Elizabethton, 1956-66; sr. research chemist Tenn. Eastman Co., Kingsport, 1966-70, research asso., 1970—. Recipient Hercules Powder Co. Research fellowship, 1944-47; Office Naval Research Postdoctoral fellowship, 1947-48; Oak Ridge Inst. Nuclear Studies Sci. Research award, 1950. Fellow Am. Inst. Chemists (state pres. 1971-72; chmn. com. 1972—), A.A.A.S.; mem. Am. Chem. Soc. (sec., treas. 1955-56; sect. chmn. 1957-58; nat. councilor 1964-66), Am. Soc. Testing Materials (subcom. chmn. 1972—), Fiber Soc., Am. Assn. Textile Chemists and Colorists, Am. Crystallographic Assn., N.Y. Acad. Sci., Sigma Xi (sec., treas. 1973—), Phi Eta Sigma, Phi Kappa Phi, Tau Beta Pi, Alpha Chi Sigma. Presbyn. (deacon 1949-62; elder 1963-66). Home: 4603 Mitchell Rd Kingsport TN 37664 Office: Tenn Eastman Co Kingsport TN 37662

GABBARD, TOM LEMUEL, supt. schs.; b. Newport, Ky., Jan. 15, 1925; s. Houston B. and Lou Etta (Creech) G.; B.S. U. Cin., 1949; M.A., Xavier U., 1952; Ph.D., Burton Coll. and Sem., 1961; m. Dorothy Rechtin, June 5, 1948; children—Cathy Lou, Susan Lee, Nanci Lynn, Tom Lemuel. Tchr. ind. schs., Silver Grove, Ky., 1949-50, supt. schs., 1950-69; supt. schs., Newport, 1969—. Asst. prof. air sci. U. Cin., 1951-63; liaison officer U.S. Air Force Acad., 1957—. Mem. adv. council Ky. Dept. Surplus Property, 1951-59; mem. Ky. Regional Crime Commn., 1971—; mem. Community Action Exec. Bd., Edn. and Community Devel. Bd., 1971. Named Man of the Year, Jr. C. of C. Campbell County, Ky., 1950; nat. award Edn. of the Handicapped Program, 1971. Distinguished Service award Midway Jr. Coll., 1969. Mem. Am., Ky., Newport assns. sch. adminstrs., No. Ky. C. of C. (edn. com. 1971—), Christian Enlistment Bd., Early Childhood Edn. Bd., Mem. United Ch. of Christ (ch. council 1960-63, deacon 1964-68). Mason. Home: 37 Sweetbriar St Fort Thomas KY 41075 Office: 8th and Washington Av Newport KY 41071

GABLE, JAMES JACKSON, JR., physician; b. Oklahoma City, Apr. 3, 1918; s. James Jackson and Naomi (Jones) G.; B.S., U. Okla., 1940, M.D., 1942; m. Joan Rice, June 8, 1941; children—Diane, Robert Phillips, Susan, Howard Yeilding, Rebecca, Ann, James Jackson III. Intern Good Samaritan Hosp., Portland, Ore., 1942-43; resident internal medicine San Diego County Hosp., 1945-46, VA Hosp., U. Okla. Med. Center, 1946-48; practice medicine specializing in internal medicine and cardiology, Oklahoma City, 1948—; partner, trustee Oklahoma City Clinic, 1948—; mem. active staff, trustee Wesley, Presbyn. hosps., 1948—; attending physician VA Hosp., 1950—; asso. prof. medicine U. Okla. Sch. Medicine and U. Hosps., 1961-72, clin. prof. medicine, 1972—; trustee Oklahoma City Clinic Bus. Trust; dir. Oklahoma City Clinic Bldg. Corp.; chief med. service Presbyn. Hosp., 1964, 68. Trustee Presbyn. and Wesley Hosp. Found. Served with AUS, 1943-45, 50-52. Decorated Bronze Star medal with cluster. Diplomate Am. Bd. Internal Medicine. Fellow A.C.P.; mem. A.M.A., Am. Heart Assn., Osler Soc., Diabetes Assn., N.Y. Acad. Scis. Club: Golf and Country, Mayfair (Oklahoma City). Contbr. articles to profl. jours. Home: 829 NW 41st St Oklahoma City OK 73118 Office: 301 NW 12th St Oklahoma City OK 73103

GABLE, ROBERT ELLEDY, coal and lumber co. exec.; b. N.Y.C., Feb. 20, 1934; s. Gilbert E. and Paulina (Stearns) G.; grad. Deerfield (Mass.) Acad.; B.S., Stanford, 1956; m. Emily Brinton Thompson, July 5, 1958; children—James, Elizabeth, John. With Stearns Coal & Lumber Co. Inc. (Ky.), 1958—, asst. to pres., 1958-60, sec., 1960-70, treas., 1961-62, v.p., 1962-70, chmn. bd., 1970—, also dir.; chmn. bd., dir. Ky. & Tenn. Ry., Stearns; chmn. bd. Stearns Mining Co.; v.p., dir. King Lumber Co., Inc., Stearns; dir. McCreary County Bank. Commr. Ky. Dept. Parks, 1967-70; mem. pub. lands com. Interstate Oil Compact Commn., 1968-70; mem. adv. com. Ky. Ednl. TV, 1971—. Dir. Ky. Blue Shield Plan. Past pres., past dir. McCreary County Indsl. Devel. Corp.; trustee Stearns Recreational Assn., Inc., sec., 1962-68; bd. dirs. Ky. Mountain Laurel Festival Assn.; mem. McCreary County Air Bd., 1967—; mem. adv. bd. U. Ky. for Somerset Community Coll., 1965-73. Republican candidate for U.S. Senate from Ky., 1972; Ky. co-chmn. Finance Com. for Relection of Pres., 1972; mem. Rep. Nat. Finance Com., 1971—; state finance chmn., mem. Ky. Rep. Central Com., 1974—. Trustee George Peabody Coll. for Tchrs.; bd. dirs., pres. Ky. Council on Econ. Edn., Inc. Served to lt. (j.g.) USNR, 1956-58. Named Ky. Col., Mr. Coal of Ky., 1970. Mem. Ky. Hotel-Motel Assn. (dir. 1968-70), Ky. Travel Council (dir. 1969-70), Nat. Assn. State Park Dirs., Nat. Recreation and Park Assn., Assn. Southeastern State Park Dirs. (v.p. 1969-70), Res. Officers Assn. U.S., Ky. Coal Assn. (dir. 1972—), Ky. Hist. Soc., Ky. C. of C. (regional v.p. 1971-72, dir. 1971—), McCreary County Devel. Assn., McCreary County Jaycees (past pres.), Tau Beta Pi, Alpha Kappa Lambda (past chpt. pres.). Episcopalian. Clubs: Lions (Whitley City, Ky.); Stearns (Ky.) Golf; Frankfort (Ky.) Country; Franklin County Lincoln (dir.). Home: 1 Stearns Lane Stearns KY 42647 also 290 Leawood Dr Frankfort KY 40601 Office: Stearns Coal & Lumber Co Stearns Ky 42647 also McClure Bldg Frankfort KY 40601

GABLE, WILBURN CARROL, JR., lawyer; b. Asheville, N.C., May 23, 1930; s. Wilburn Carrol and Margaret D. (Murdock) G.; B.A., The Citadel, 1950; J.D., U. S.C., 1958; m. Betty J. Kelly, Mar. 4, 1953; children—Carol Francis, Elizabeth Kaye. Admitted to S.C. bar, 1958; law clk. U.S. Ct. Appeals, 4th Circuit, 1957-58; partner Grisso & Gable, Anderson, S.C., 1958-64, Watkins, Wandiver, Kirven, Long & Gable, Anderson, S.C., 1965—. Commr. Anderson County Alcohol and Drug Abuse Commn., 1974—. Served to 1st lt., inf., AUS, 1951-53. Mem. Am., S.C. (v.p. 1968—), Anderson County (pres. 1973) bar assns., S.C. Def. Attys. Assn. Elk. Club: Anderson Country. Home: 805 Camfield St Anderson SC 29621 Office: 500 S McDuffie St Anderson SC 29621

GABRIEL, HENRY, devel. engr.; b. Berlin, Germany, Apr. 28, 1914; s. Maximilian and Adele (Ascher) G.; came to U.S., 1926; naturalized, 1935; B.S. cum laude, L.I. U., 1934; M.S. in Chemistry, George Washington U., 1949; Ph.D. in Phys. Chemistry, Stanford, 1951; m. Virginia Newson Gabriel, May 8, 1938. Prof., Berlitz Sch. Langs., Washington, 1936-42, asst. dir., 1936-42; asso. in chemistry George Washington U., Washington, 1946-48; instr. U. Santa Clara, Cal., 1949-50, asst. prof., 1950-51; asst. prof. Fisk U., Nashville, 1951-53; asso. prof. Siena Coll., Loudonville, N.Y., 1953-56; mem. tech. information staff Phillips Petroleum Co., Bartlesville, Okla., 1952-63, devel. engr. research and devel., 1963—. Pres., Community Concert Assn., Bartlesville, 1962-64, dir. 1957-65. Served with AUS, 1942-45. Carnegie grantee Fisk U., 1952. Mem. Am. Chem. Soc., A.A.A.S., Am. Philatelic Soc., Okla. (pres. 1962-64, dir. 1962—), Washington County (pres. 1961, 74) philatelic socs., Am. Legion. Republican. Methodist. Patentee in field. Home: 1948 S Santa Fe St Bartlesville OK 74003 Office: Phillips Petroleum Co Bartlesville OK 74003

GABRIEL, OTHMAR RUDOLF, educator; b. Vienna, Austria, Jan. 10, 1925; s. Othmar and Rosa (Fellner) G.; Ph.D., U. Vienna, 1954; m. Rachelle Rothenberg, Aug. 5, 1965; children—Annamaria, Harriet. Came to U.S., 1958, Naturalized, 1963. Research asst. U. Vienna, 1954-58; asso. Columbia Med. Center, N.Y.C., 1958-60; vis. scientist NIH, Bethesda, Md., 1960-64, research chemist, 1964-65; asso. prof. dept. biochemistry Georgetown U. Schs. Medicine and Dentistry, Washington, 1965-70, prof., 1970—. Cons. chemist K.K.S. Preparate, Vienna, 1956-58; vis. biochemist, biol. chemistry Harvard Med. Sch., Boston, 1973. Mem. Am. Soc. Biol. Chemists, Am. Chem. Soc., Am. Assn. U. Profs., Am. Soc. Microbiology, Brit. Biochem. Soc., N.Y. Acad. Scis., Soc. Exptl. Biology and Medicine, Sigma Xi. Contbr. articles to profl. jours. Home: 5802 Linder Lane Bethesda MD 20034 Office: 3900 Reservoir Rd Washington DC 20007

GABRIEL, PAT (MRS. GENE F. GABRIEL), club woman; b. Rock Island, Ill., May 2, 1922; d. Max Voyle and Faye (Crist) Wolfe; grad. Canterbury Sch. Fine Arts, 1939; m. Gene Floyd Gabriel, Mar. 8, 1941; 1 dau., Patricia Gene. Society columnist, drama critic Coral Gables Times-Guide. Drama chmn. Morgan Park Jr. Woman's Club, Chgo., 1952-54, 3d Dist Jrs., 1952-54; children's theatre dir. Beverly Hills Jr. Woman's Club, Chgo., 1954; dist. coordinator Mothers March of Dimes, Chgo., 1952-55, Coral Gables, Fla., 1956-61; publicity chmn. woman's com., pres. woman's com. Variety Children's Hosp., pres. women's com., 1968-70; pres. Theatre Arts League, Inc., 1971-73; pres. Dade County Com. for Project Hope, 1973-74; chmn. Com. of Allied and Performing Arts of City of Coral Gables; 2d v.p. Dade County Women's Com. Project Hope. Women's campaign mgr. Senator Doyle Carlton, Jr. for Gov., Coral Gables, 1960. Mem. D.A.R. (rec. sec. 1962-64), Fla. Fedn. Women's Clubs (drama co-chmn. 1960-62), Women in Communications. Methodist. Club: Coral Gables Senior Women's (1st v.p. 1962-64). Home: 3915 Monserrate St Coral Gables FL 33134

GABRILES, GEORGE ANTONIO, mech. engring. co. exec.; b. Barcelona, Spain, June 24, 1926; s. Demitrius and Mary (Cohen) G.; brought to U.S., 1937, naturalized, 1949; B.M.E., U. Houston, 1954; m. Delphia Reeder, Nov. 10, 1947; children—Glenda, Gary, Jerel, Lorie. Gen. supervising engr. Monsanto Co., Texas City, Tex., 1954-67, maintenance supt., Trenton, Mich., 1968-69; v.p. Mallay Freeport Corp., Freeport, Tex., 1969—, dir., 1969—; v.p. Mono Valve Corp.; pres. Brazoria Aviation Enterprises Corp., Mallay Corp., Mallay Freeport Corp., Cam-Lock Fasteners, Inc. Instr. Dale Carnegie Leadership Course, Dale Carnegie Supervisory and Mgmt. Course; maintenance engring. cons. Tng. dir. Explorers, Boy Scouts Am. Bd. dirs. Lake Jackson (Tex.) United Fund, Bay Area chpt. Am. Heart Assn. Served with USNR, 1944-46. Mem. Am. Inst. Plant Engrs. (regional v.p. 1964-65), U. Houston Alumni Assn. Texas City C. of C. v.p.). Lion, Rotarian. Home: 53 Willow Ct Lake Jackson TX 77566 Office: PO Box 2890 Freeport TX 77541

GABY, WILLIAM LAURENCE, educator; b. Hot Springs, N.C., June 15, 1917; s. Edward Lee and Frances Bertha (Rufty) G.; B.A., U. Tenn., 1939, M.S., 1940; Ph.D., St. Louis U., 1946; m. Virginia Cox, June 1, 1940; children—Nancy Sue, Virginia Lee (Mrs. Kenneth W. Holt); Frances Ann. Sr. bacteriologist Tenn. Dept. Pub. Health, Nashville, 1940-41; bacteriologist Winthrop Chem. Co., Albany, N.Y., 1941-42; sr. bacteriologist Bristol Labs., Inc., Syracuse, N.Y., 1946-48; asso. prof. Hahnemann Med. Coll., Phila., 1949-64; faculty E. Tenn. State U., Johnson City, 1964—, prof. dept. health scis., chmn. dept., 1964—. Diplomate Am. Bd. Microbiology. Fellow Am. Acad. Microbiology; mem. Am. Soc. Microbiologists, Am. Assn. Immunologists, Am. Soc. Biol. Chemists, Sigma Xi, Phi Kappa Phi. Contbr. articles to profl. jours. Home: 1408 College Heights Dr Johnson City TN 37601

GACHET, THOMAS HUGH, cons. engr.; b. Clio, Ala., Apr. 11, 1938; s. Hugh Chalmers and Mary Olive (Massengale) G.; B.S., U. Ala., 1960; m. Judith Annette Reeves, July 15, 1961; children—Thomas Randall, Melissa Gayle. Research engr. Am. Cast Iron Pipe Co., Birmingham, Ala., 1960-61; design engr. Walter Schoel Engring. Co., Inc., Birmingham, 1961-68; pres. Paragon Engring., Inc., Leeds, 1968—. Trustee, 1st v.p. Rocky Ridge Fire Dist., 1970-74. Served with AUS, 1961. Named Young Engr. of Yr., Birmingham Engring. Council, 1972. Mem. Am. Soc. C.E., Ala. Soc. Profl. Land Surveyors, Am. Congress Surveying and Mapping, Prestress Concrete Inst., Archtl. Precast Assn., So. Bldg. Code Congress. Baptist (deacon). Elk. Home: 2209 Lynncrest Lane Birmingham AL 35216 Office: PO Box 555 Leeds AL 35094

GADDIE, GEORGE NATHAN, univ. adminstr.; b. Louisville, July 18, 1938; s. Horace N. and Mayme Ethel (Johns) G.; B.S., Ky. Wesleyan Coll., 1962; postgrad. Vanderbilt U., Peabody Coll., Miss. State U., Scarritt Coll.; m. Patricia Ann Sanders, Jan. 2, 1972. Dir. student activities Lindsey Wilson Coll., Columbia, Ky., 1965-72, asso. dir. admissions, Columbia, 1972-73, dean student affairs, 1972-73; dir. preadmissions U. Ky., Lexington, 1973—. Bd. dirs. Wesley Found., Western Ky. U., Bowling Green, Ky., 1973—. Mem. Ky. Assn. for Promotion Coll. Admissions (pres. 1973), Ky. Personnel and Guidance Assn. (dir. 1973), Ky. Assn. Collegiate Registrars and Admissions Officers. Methodist. Home: 527 Greenbriar St Nicholasville KY 40356 Office: Administration Annex University of Kentucky Lexington KY 40506

GADSDEN, RICHARD HAMILTON, educator; b. Denver, June 30, 1925; s. Paul Hamilton and Ellen Theresa (Page) G.; B.S., Coll. Charleston, 1950; M.S., Med. Coll. S.C., 1952, Ph.D., 1956; m. Emily Anne Mercer, June 20, 1953; children—Judith G., Richard Hamilton, Frank McC., Phillip E., Ellen L.A., Johnathan C.M. Teaching fellow Coll. of Charleston (S.C.), 1949-50; instr. Med. U. S.C., Charleston, 1954-56, asst. prof., 1956-65, asso. prof., 1965-68, prof. biochemistry and clin. pathology, 1968—. Cons. biochemistry VA Hosp., Charleston, 1967—; cons. transp., food products Am. Bar Assn., 1973—. Dir. N.C. Warehouse Corp., Charleston. Trustee Coll. of Charleston, 1969-71. Served with USNR, 1943-46. Fellow A.A.A.S., Assn. Clin. Scientists, Am. Inst. Chemists; mem. S.C. Inst. Chemists (pres. 1971-72), Charleston Symphony Assn. (pres. 1972-73), Coll. Charleston Alumni Assn. (pres. 1967-68), Med. U. S.C. Alumni Assn. (pres. elect 1973-74), Soc. of Cincinnati, Sigma Xi. Episcopalian. Editor Clinical Toxicology, Selected Methods in Clinical Chemistry. Contbr. to publs. in field. Home: 544 Sweetbay Rd Charleston SC 29412

GAEKE, GOTTLIEB CHARLES, JR., chemist; b. Goose Creek, Tex., Sept. 11, 1928; s. Gottlieb Charles and Ida Louise (Ludwig) Gaeke; B.S., U. Houston, 1950; M.S., La. State U., 1956; m. Rosemarie Theresa Gibson, Sept. 7, 1952; children—Charles Gibson, Diane Marie. Gen. mgr. Kem-Tech Labs., Baton Rouge, 1956-60; asst. prof. La. State U., Alexandria, 1960-61; research asso. Ethyl Corp., Baton Rouge, 1961—. Fellow Am. Inst. Chemists; mem. Am. Chem. Soc., Sigma Xi. Home: 581 College Hill Dr Baton Rouge LA 70808 Office: PO Box 341 Baton Rouge LA 70821

GAFFORD, FRANK HALL, univ. dean; b. Afton, Okla., Jan. 11, 1903; s. Benjamin Ford and Elizabeth Newman (Payne) G.; B.A., U. Tex., 1925, M.A., 1927, Ph.D., 1940; m. Anita Marguerite Engerrand, Dec. 28, 1926; children—Eleanor Marguerite (Mrs. Ernest Owen Bransford, Jr.), Frank Hall, Jeanne Engerrand. Instr. history U. Miss., 1927-29, asst. prof., 1929-31; asst. prof. history Coll. of Charleston, S.C., 1931-32, asso. prof., 1932-41, prof., 1941-49; asso. prof. history North Tex. State U., 1949-51, prof., 1951—, chmn. dept., 1951-52, dir., 1952-65, dean Coll. Arts and Scis., 1953—; summer instr. U. of South, 1944, Tulane U., 1949. Mem. Am. Hist. Assn., Am. Assn. U. Profs., Phi Alpha Theta, Pi Sigma Alpha, Pi Kappa Alpha. Home: 2520 Royal Lane Denton TX 76201

GAGE, FRED FENNER, broadcast exec.; b. Battle Creek, Mich., Sept. 8, 1931; s. William Caleb and Margaret Helen (Baker) G.; B.S. in Bus. Adminstrn., Ohio State U., 1956; m. Janet A. Stewart, Dec. 18, 1953; children—Cynthia Ann, Frederick William, Mary Elizabeth. Announcer, WHCK, WTVN, WRFD, Columbus, O., 1953-58, WBBM, Chgo., 1958-61, WGR, WYSL, Buffalo, 1961-65; salesman WYSL, WWOC, Buffalo, 1965-69; gen. sales mgr. WNOR, Norfolk, Va., 1969—, v.p., 1973-74, exec. v.p., gen. mgr., 1974—; instr. div. continuing edn. Old Dominion U., 1971-74. Bd. dirs. United Cerebral Palsy, 1971; mem. adv. com. dept. spl. edn. Norfolk City Schs.; mem. exec. com., South group chmn. Tidewater Soap Box Derby. Recipient Individual Achievement award Exptl. Aircraft Assn., 1966. Mem. Sales and Marketing Execs. (dir.), Va. Assn. Broadcasters (chmn. utilities rates and tariffs com.). Club: Civitan (Norfolk). Home: 4617 Player Lane Virginia Beach VA 23452 Office: 252 W Brambleton Av Norfolk VA 23510

GAGE, GEORGE RAYMOND, JR., physician; b. Bklyn., Feb. 13, 1919; s. George R. and Mary A. (Green) G.; B.A., Columbia, 1938, M.D., 1942; m. Mildred Jeanne Cahill, Nov. 15, 1947 (div.); children—Mary, Joanne, Janice, Kathleen, Margaret, George III, Richard; m. 2d, Doris Jean Robbins, Aug. 25, 1972. Practice obstetrics and gynecology, Coral Gables, Fla., 1950-72; asst. prof. obstetrics and gynecology U. Miami. Served lt. M.C. USNR, 1943-47. Diplomate Am. Bd. Obstetrics and Gynecology. Fellow A.C.S., Am. Coll. Obstetricians and Gynecologists, South Atlantic Assn. Obstetrics and Gynecology, Internat. Coll. Surgeons; asso. Royal Soc. Medicine; mem. Fraternal Order of Police Assos. K.C. Office: 365 Alcazar Av Coral Gables FL 33134

GAGLIANO, NICHOLAS CHARLES, med. educator; b. New Orleans, Apr. 5, 1927; s. Charles M. and Pauline (Galliano) G.; B.S., Loyola U. of South, New Orleans, 1948; M.D., La. State U., 1952; m. Evangeline Guillory, June 13, 1951; children—David, Gina. Intern, Charity Hosp., New Orleans, 1952-53, resident, 1953-55; practice medicine, specializing in pediatrics, New Orleans, 1955-60; faculty dept. pediatrics La. State U. Med. Sch., New Orleans, 1960—, prof. pediatrics, 1972—, faculty dept. preventive medicine, 1962—, prof. preventive medicine, 1972—, acting head dept. preventive medicine, 1972—. Served with USNR, 1945-46. Diplomate Am. Bd. Pediatrics. Mem. Am. Acad. Pediatrics, Assn. Tchrs. Preventive Medicine, New Orleans Pediatric Soc., La., Orleans Parish, med. socs. Home: 49 Hawk St New Orleans LA 70124 Office: 1542 Tulane Av New Orleans LA 70112

GAGLIARDI, FRANK JOSEPH, bus. exec.; b. N.Y.C., June 26, 1933; s. Biagio and Mary (Iraldi) G.; grad. Gettysburg (Pa.) Coll., 1956; m. Suzanne Lee Wickman, Dec. 27, 1958; children—Marylee, Laura, Ellen, Gail, Caroline. Tchr., Neptune (N.J.) High Sch., 1958-59; rep. Field Enterprises Edn. Corp., Chgo., 1959, dist. mgr., 1960, regional mgr., 1961, sales mgr. home office, 1962-63, Australian mgr., 1964-65, v.p., gen. sales mgr., 1966-70; pres. Field Creations subsidiary Field Enterprises, 1970—. Served with AUS, 1956-58; Korea. Named 1 of 10 Outstanding Young Men Chgo., 1966. Mem. Phi Kappa Psi. Club: Atlanta County. Home: 320 Pine Valley Rd Marietta GA 30060 Office: 2759 Delk Rd Marietta GA 30060

GAINER, RUBY JACKSON (MRS. HERBERT P. GAINER), educator, civic leader; b. Buena-Vista, Ga.; d. William B. and Lovie (Jones) Jackson; student Miles Meml. Coll.; B.S., Ala. State Tchrs. Coll.; M.A. in English and Social Studies, Atlanta U.; postgrad. Fla. A. and M. Coll., Western Wash. State Coll., U. Conn., Okla. State U.; Dr. Humanities (hon.) Selma U., Daniel Payne Coll., 1971; LL.D., Birmingham Bapt. Coll.; Ph.D. (hon.), Colo. State Christian Coll., 1973; m. Herbert P. Gainer; children—Ruby Paulette, James H., Cecil F. Tchr. J.B. Turner High Sch., Milton, Fla., pub. schs., Birmingham, Ala., Washington Jr. High Sch., Pensacola, Fla., prior to 1968; guidance counselor Wedgewood Jr.-Sr. High Sch., Pensacola; English tchr. Woodham High Sch., Pensacola. Brought 2 successful legal cases against Jefferson (Ala.) County Sch. Bd. for equalization of Negro tchr. salaries, 1946-47, re-instatement Negro tchrs. under Tchr. Tenure Act in 1960's; organized 1st tchrs. union, Birmingham; also organized local high sch. chpt. Future Tchrs. Am., local tchr. aide and teen service groups, local and county assns. edn.; local capt. Heart Fund, Mothers March of Dimes, Cancer Fund; active local P.T.A., chmn. Fla. P.T.A. Workshop; participant Gov. Fla. Conf. Edn., Tallahassee, Nat. conf. Profl. Rights and Responsibilities, Arlington, Tex.; participant chmn. numerous profl. ednl. confs. So. U.S.; mem. Escambia County Guidance Council; mem., past officer Fla. Guidance Council; mem., bd. dirs. Partners for Progress. Bd. dirs. Escambia County Tb Assn. Recipient Tchr. of Year Award Dist. 1 Fla. State Tchrs. Assn., also award meritorious service, Distinguished Service award, 1966, DuShane Outstanding Service award; recipient DuShane Outstanding Dir. award Escambia County Tchrs. Assn., 1967, Distinguished Service award civil, human, profl. rights, 1965; recipient Outstanding Tchr. and Leader award Fla. Edn. Assn., honor award N.E.A. and Fla. State Tchrs. Assn., 1966, also numerous awards distinguished service youth, community orgns.; cited newspapers, NAACP. Mem. Jefferson County (past sec., past pres.), Escambia County (past sec., past pres.), Fla. State (past bd. dirs. dist. 1, past pres. dist. 1, mem. tchr. edn. and profl. standards commn. and evaluation com., bd. advisers dept. classroom tchrs.), Ala. (past chmn. secondary sch. tchrs.), Am. tchrs. assns., Am. Assn. U. Women, Jefferson County Tchrs. Union (past pres.), N.E.A., Assn. Classroom Tchrs. (v.p. 1969), Nat. Council English Tchrs., Nat. Council Social Studies Tchrs., Escambia County League Justice, Future Tchrs. Am. Advisers Council, City-Wide Fedn. Women's Clubs (past officer), League Women Voters, Alpha Kappa Alpha. Baptist (mem., pres. Bd. Ushers). Democrat. Mem. Order Eastern Star. Clubs: Mary M. Bethune (officer); New Idea Art and Study (officer). Composer: God Planted You Here, Talking to the Moon, It Is Better Not to Know, In the Quiet of the Day. Contbr. articles, poems, publs. Address: 1516 W Gadsden St Pensacola FL 32501

GAINES, JAMES EDWIN, JR., librarian; b. Dalton, Ga., Feb. 21, 1938; s. James Edwin and Olivia (McCarty) G.; A.B., Emory U., 1961, M. Librarianship, 1964; postgrad. Fla. State U., 1974—; m. Sally Nichols Martin, Nov. 27, 1965; children—Thomas Martin, Robin Jeannette. English tchr. Marist Coll. High Sch., Atlanta, 1961-62; library asst. Emory U., 1962-64; service librarian U. Cin., 1964-65; asst. librarian tech. services Antioch Coll., 1965-66, dir. reclassification project, 1966-68; dir. library Birmingham-So. Coll., 1968-74. Mem. A.L.A., Southeastern (exec. bd. coll. and univ. sect. 1970-72), Ala. library assns., Kappa Phi Kappa. Democrat. Methodist. Home: 1903 Nanticoke Circle Tallahassee FL 32303

GAINES, SYDNEY APPEL, air conditioning co. exec.; b. N.Y.C., Mar. 30, 1895; s. Roy Grundy and Henrietta (Appel) G.; student Dallas pub. schs.; m. Betty Trobett, Aug. 17, 1921 (dec. Oct. 1950); children—Jodelle (Mrs. Maurice W. McCall), Craig T.; m. 2d, Ethel Pack, Sept. 24, 1951. Circulation mgr. Dallas Times Herald, 1914-17; sec.-treas. Gaines Motor Sales, Wichita Falls, Tex., 1919-28; v.p.

Wichita Falls Wholesale Drug Co., 1928-32; co-owner United Elec. Co., Wichita Falls, 1932-64, pres. 1964—. Chmn., Wichita County Crippled Children's Com., 1932-58; v.p. Tex. Soc. Crippled Children, 1937-46; mem. adv. com. Tex. Crippled Children's div., 1941; mem. planning com. A.R.C., 1949, adv. bd. Salvation Army, 1947-51; v.p. YMCA, 1950; chmn. Wichita Falls Park Planning Com., 1949-51; adv. council Citizens Com., 1950-53; adv. bd. vocational tng. Wichita Falls Sr. High Sch., 1949-54; mem. adv. commn. on vocational edn. So. Schs. and Univs., 1972—. chmn. Wichita County Employ the Handicapped, 1953-54; v.p. N. Tex. Cerebral Palsy Treatment Center, 1951-61; chmn. area devel. com. N.W. Tex., S.W. Okla. Devel. Assn., 1955; arrangements chmn. nat. security seminar United States Armed Forces, 1967. Precinct chmn. Democratic party, 1952; del. state conv., 1952. Served with U.S. Army, 1917-18. Named Citizen of Yr., Lions Club, 1969, Man of Year, Altrusa, 1964, Distinguished Salesman's award Sales and Marketing Execs., 1973. Distinguished Layman in Edn., Phi Delta Kappa, 1973. Mem. C. of C. (pres. 1961), Wichita Falls Indsl. Found. (pres. 1953-54), Tex. Mfrs. Assn., Am. Soc. Refrigeration Engrs., Air Force Assn. Episcopalian. Mason (Shriner, K.T., 33 deg.). Clubs: Kiwanis (charter mem.), Rotary (dist. gov. 1956-57, several awards), Wichita, Wichita Falls Country. Home: 2615 Chase Dr Wichita Falls TX 76308 Office: 501-17 Kell Blvd Wichita Falls TX 76307

GAIO, RAYMOND LEE, architect; b. Springfield, Ill., May 3, 1938; s. Americo and Edith E. (Bloom) G.; student Millikin U., summer 1960; profl. architecture degree U. Notre Dame, 1961. Designer, draftsman Spangler, Beall, Salogga & Bradley, Decatur, Ill., 1961-62; designer, planner, draftsman, client relations Leo A. Daly Co., Omaha, 1962-63; schematic design draftsman Perkins & Will, Washington, 1963-64; dir. Dept. of State, chpt. and student affairs A.I.A., Washington, 1964-69; mgr. client relations Vincent G. Kling & Assos., Phila., 1969-70; pres., chief exec. officer, treas. Gaio Assos., Ltd., Washington, also Los Angeles, 1970—; pres. Bldg. Industry Devel. Services, Washington, 1973—; dir. corporate devel. Gruen Assos., Los Angeles, N.Y.C., Washington, Vienna, Teheran, 1970. Lectr. various univs.; archtl. orgn. mgmt. cons. Resource Mgmt. Corp., Bethesda, Md., also Santa Monica, Cal. Adviser, Jr. Achievement, Omaha, 1962-63; mem. Royal Ct. of Ak-Sar-Ben, 1962-63; adviser, lectr. Heights Study House, Washington, 1965; mem. joint engring. council Notre Dame U., 1958-59, 60-61. Licensed architect, V.I. Mem. A.I.A. (corporate, nat. student pres. 1960-61; co-chmn. nat. task force on student action programs), Coral Gables Jr. C. of C. Notre Dame Alumni Assn. Republican. Roman Catholic. Author: A.I.A. Organizational Guidelines Manual; A.I.A. Student Chapter Handbook; The State Organization; Chapter Organization. Contbr. articles to profl. jours. Office: Gaio Assos Ltd 1301 20th St NW Suite 104 Washington DC 20036 Offices: Seattle WA also San Francisco CA also Denver CO also Boston MA also New York City NY

GAITHER, ROSCOE B., lawyer; b. El Paso, Tex., Aug. 25, 1894; B.S., U. Va., 1917; LL.B., 1923, J.D., 1971; postgrad. Sorbonne U. Paris, 1919. Admitted to N.Y. bar, 1924; now practice law, Mexico City. Mem. Assn. Bar City N.Y., Am. Bar Assn., Academia Mexicana de Legislacion y Jurisprudencia, Correspondiente a la de Espana. Author: Expropriation in Mexico, 1940. Address: Reforma 51-706 Mexico 1 DF Mexico*

GALANE, IRMA ADELE BERESTON, electronic engr.; b. Balt., Aug. 23, 1921; d. Arthur and Sarah (Hillman) Bereston; B.A., Goucher Coll., 1940; postgrad. Johns Hopkins, 1940-42, Mass. Inst. Tech., 1943, George Washington U., 1945, U. Md., 1958, Army Mgmt. Sch., 1964; 1 dau., Suzanne Felice. Physicist, Naval Ordnance Lab., 1942-43; electronic engr. Navy Bur. Ships, 1943-49, Army Office Chief Signal Officer, 1949-51, Navy Bur. Aeros., 1951-56, Air Research and Devel. Command, USAF, 1956-57, FCC, 1957-60, NASA, 1960-62; supervisory electronic engr. USCG Hdqrs., 1962-64; sci. specialist, engring. Scis. Library of Congress, Washington, 1964-65; project engr., advanced aerial fire support system Army Materiel Command, 1965-66; gen. engr. Navy Dept., 1966-71; electronic engr. Spectrum Mgmt. Task Force, FCC, 1971—. Registered profl. engr., D.C. Mem. A.A.A.S., I.E.E.E. (sr.), Am. Inst. Aeros. and Astronautics, Nat. Soc. Profl. Engrs. (chmn. publs. com. 1959-60), Soc. Women Engrs. (sr. mem.; nat. membership chmn. 1952, nat. dir. 1953, mem. nat. scholarship awards com. 1958), Armed Forces Communications and Electronics Assn., Fedn. Profl. Assn., Am. Ordnance Assn., U.S. Naval Inst., Marine Tech. Soc., Smithsonian Instn. (asso.), Johns Hopkins Alumni Assn. Editor: The Met. Washington Profl. Engr., 1958-60. Home: 4201 Cathedral Av NW Washington DC 20016

GALANTY, IRVING MAX, synagogue exec.; b. Bklyn., Apr. 30, 1906; s. Ellis Hyman and Dina Dora (Reiskind) G.; student pub. schs.; m. Fannye Heiman, Aug. 3, 1933; children—Ellen H., Renee L. Organizer, editor Atlanta Jewish News, 1921-22; owner, operator variety stores, Atlanta, 1937-53; exec. dir., campaign dir. Ahavath Achim Congregation, Atlanta, 1955—. Mem. Nat. Assn. Synagogue Adminstrs. (mem. governing bd. 1962—). Mason (32 deg., Shriner). Home: 1766 Johnson Rd NE Atlanta GA 30306 Office: 600 Peachtree Battle Av NW Atlanta GA 30327

GALE, EDWIN MORRIS, mfg. co. exec.; b. Beaumont, Tex., Mar. 16, 1924; s. Lawrence David and Marie (Boulwate) G.; B.B.A., U. Tex., 1947. With Warren Refrigeration Co., Inc., Beaumont, Tex., 1947—, pres., 1965—; with Warren Mfg. Co., Inc., Beaumont, Tex., 1947—, pres. 1965—. Dir. Citizens Nat. Bank, Beaumont, Tex., 1965-74. Mem. Chancellors Council, U. Tex. at Austin 1966-74, Art and Scis. Council, 1968-74. Served with USNR, 1942-46. Mem. Beaumont Jewish Fedn. (pres. 1970—). Home: 2275 Long St Beaumont TX 77701 Office: Box 3928 Beaumont TX 77704

GALIANO, AUGUST, newspaper exec.; b. Beaumont, Tex., Jan. 14, 1927; s. Augustine and Ida (Hillman) G.; B.B.A., U. Houston, 1955; m. Elizabeth Willis, June 9, 1952; children—Margaret, Elizabeth, Allison August. With Houston Chronicle, 1955—, research and promotion dir., 1971—. Lectr. marketing research U. Houston, 1965—. Served with AUS, 1946-49, 50-51. Mem. Internat. Newspaper Promotion Assn. (pres. So. region 1971—), Am. Marketing Assn. (pres. Houston chpt. 1971). Home: 1011 Cheshire St Houston TX 77018 Office: 801 Texas Av Houston TX 77001

GALINDO, DESIDERIO LEO, physician; b. Allende, Mexico, Feb. 6, 1919; s. Arnulfo F. and Maria (Lozano) G.; came to U.S., 1919, naturalized, 1940; B.S., U. Tex., 1940; M.D., Baylor U., 1947; m. Emma Flores, June 11, 1947; children—Denis Leo, Jonathan. Intern, Santa Rosa Hosp., San Antonio, 1947-48, resident, 1948-49; resident Baylor U., Houston, 1949-51; dir. labs. King's Daughters Clinic and Hosp., 1953-54; asst. pathologist St. John's Hosp., Tulsa, 1954-56; dir. labs. R. B. Green Hosp., San Antonio, 1956-66; cons. M. D. Anderson Hosp., 1957—; dir. lab. Luth. Gen. Hosp., 1967—, pres. med. staff, 1969; pres. Pathology Assos., Galindo & Thuss, 1970; pres. med. staff Park North Gen. Hosp., San Antonio, 1972—; clin. prof. pathology U. Tex., S. Tex. Med. Sch. Mem. San Antonio Urban Renewal Adv. Com., 1961—; vice chmn. San Antonio Pub. Library Bd., 1958-64, pres., 1964-66; trustee San Antonio City Water Bd., 1968-74, vice chmn., 1972-74, chmn., 1974. Bd. dirs. U.S.O., San Antonio. Served with AUS, 1942-46, 51-53, Diplomate Am. Bd. Pathology. Fellow Am. Coll. Pathologists; mem. Am., Tex. med. assns., Bexar County Med. Soc. (sec.), Am. Soc. Clin. Pathologists, San Antonio Soc. Pathologists (sec.-treas. 1960—), Am. Cancer Soc., Cerebral Palsy, Sembradores de Amistad (charter), Mexican C. of C. Methodist. Home: 338 Club Hill Dr San Antonio TX 78228 Office: Med Arts Bldg San Antonio TX 78205

GALL, JAMES WILLIAM, chemist; b. Taylorville, Ill., Apr. 22, 1942; s. Joseph James and Veronica Margaret (Gottsacher) G.; B.S., U. Ill., 1964; Ph.D., Ohio State U., 1969; m. Bonnie Hope Leonard, Aug. 20, 1966; children—Michelle, Leslie, Kristin. Research asst. Kaiser Chem. Co., San Leandro, Cal., 1964; research chemist Phillips Petroleum Co., Bartlesville, Okla., 1969—. Nat. Air Pollution Control Adminstrn. spl. fellow, 1965-69. Mem. Am. Chem. Soc., Soc. Petroleum Engrs., Phi Lambda Upsilon. Elk. Patentee in field. Home: 3600 Dana Dr Bartlesville OK 74003 Office: Phillips Petroleum Co 267 RB1 Bartlesville OK 74004

GALLAGHER, BERNARD THOMAS, govt. ofcl.; b. N.Y.C., Jan. 28, 1922; s. Bernard A. and Helen L. (Kelly) G.; ed. U. Ala.; diploma Command Staff Coll., Air U., 1962; diploma nuclear weapons def. Atomic Support Agy., 1963; diploma U.S. Army Dugway Proving Ground, 1964, Indsl. Coll. Armed Forces, 1969; m. Stanley Ernestine Partin, Feb. 1, 1951; children—Shawn Leah, Marta JoAnn. Commd. 2d Lt. USAAF, 1942, advanced through grades to col. U.S. Air Force, 1965; comdr. 2857th test squadron Olmstead AFB, Pa., 1958-62; chief spl. flight br. USAF hdqrs., Washington, 1963-64; advanced agt. for pres., 1963-64; USAF disaster control officer, Washington, 1964-65; ret. 1965; chief plans and programs br. Office Emergency Preparedness, Exec. Office Pres., 1965-66, dep. chief spl. operations div., 1966-68, chief div. Office Emergency Preparedness, 1968—; cons. in nuclear, biol. and chem. Warfare. Chmn. Quadrapartite Standardization Coordinating Com., 1964—; tech. adviser to U.S. rep. to NATO, 1964—; mem. NATO Interservice NBC Warfare procedures working party, 1964—. Home: 112 Sydnor Dr Route 2 Leesburg VA 22075 Office: Exec Office of Pres Washington DC 20504

GALLAGHER, EDWARD FELIX III, pub. co. exec.; b. Asheville, N.C., Dec. 13, 1932; s. Edward Felix and Iva Lea (Graybeal) G.; student Belmont Abbey Coll., 1947-50, Benedictine Coll., 1950-51, Alexander Hamilton Inst. Bus., 1951-53; m. Iris June Crayton, Aug. 31, 1957; children—Lisa LaVerne, Edward Felix IV, Barbara June, Susan Lea. Jr. salesman Good Will Pubs., Inc., Chgo., 1951, sr. salesman, trainer, Springfield, Mass., 1951, Phila., 1951, area mgr., New Orleans, 1952, dist. mgr., St. Louis, 1952, office mgr. Gastonia, N.C., 1953, Canadian dir., Montreal, Que., Montreal, 1954-55, asst. v.p., Charlotte, 1956-64, v.p., 1964-70, v.p. research, marketing, 1970—, dir., 1970—. Cons. fund-raising World Vision Internat., Monrovia, Cal., 1972—; dir. pub. relations Piedmont council Boy Scouts Am., 1965-68. State co-chmn. primary elections Republican gubernatorial campaign, 1964, state dir. research for gen. election, 1964. Recipient various appreciation award Boy Scouts Am., 1967, medal pub. relations program, 1968; Voice of Am. and Voice of Democracy award V.F.W., 1964. Mem. Direct Selling Assn., Direct Mail Advt. Assn., Internat. Platform Assn. Eagle (local pres. 1962-63, state pres. 1963-64), Rotarian. Home: 601 Owens Dr Gastonia NC 28052 Office: 1520 York Rd Gastonia NC 28052

GALLAGHER, JOHN GEORGE, engr.; b. Pitts., May 15, 1935; s. Edward Francis and Margaret (Clifford) G.; B.S., Cath. U., 1959; m. Anne Mary Baroody, Sept. 12, 1959; children—Catherine Anne, Anne Miriam, Mary Theresa, Rebecca Anne, John Joseph, Judith Elizabeth. Engr. radar lab. staff Melpar, Inc. (now a div. of E-Systems, Inc.), Falls Church, Va., 1959-64, sr. elec. engr., 1964-67, sr. elec. engr. night vision lab. support br., 1967-72, prin. engr. electronic warfare dept., 1972—. Mem. Acoustical Soc. Am., Am. Inst. Physics, I.E.E.E., A.A.A.S. Home: 14042 Mathews Dr Woodbridge VA 22191 Office: 7700 Arlington Blvd Falls Church VA 22046

GALLAHER, ART, JR., coll. dean; b. Duncan, Okla., Mar. 22, 1925; s. Art and Mildred (Dunaway) G.; B.A., U. Okla., 1950, M.A., 1951; Ph.D., U. Ariz., 1956; m. Dixie Ann Clower, June 6, 1950; children—Brynn, Kell. From instr. to asso. prof. anthropology and sociology U. Houston, 1956-62; vis. lectr. Rice U., 1961-62; asso. prof. anthropology U. Neb., 1962-63; prof. dept. anthropology, dept. behavioral sci., dep. dir. Center for Developmental Change, U. Ky., Lexington, 1963-70, chmn. dept. anthropology, 1970-72, dean Coll. Arts and Scis., 1972—. Served with USCGR, 1943-46. Fellow Am. Anthrop. Assn., Soc. for Applied Anthropology (sec.-treas.); mem. Am. Ethnol. Soc., Am. Assn. U. Profs., Alpha Kappa Delta, Phi Delta Kappa. Author: Plainville Fifteen Years Later, 1961; Perspectives in Developmental Change, 1968. Home: 3167 Roxburg Dr W Lexington KY 40503

GALLANT, DONALD MARVIN, psychiatrist; b. Bklyn., Aug. 9, 1929; s. Herman and Ann (Chasnoff) G.; B.S., Tulane U., 1951, M.D., 1955; m. Joyce Cooper, Dec. 26, 1954; 1 dau., Dianne Hillary. Intern, Charity Hosp., New Orleans, 1955-56, resident, 1956-59; med. dir., psychiat. cons. Alcoholism Inpatient Treatment Service S.E. La. Hosp., also New Orleans Alcoholism Clinic, 1962—; med. dir., psychiat. cons. drug research ward East La. State Hosp., Jackson, 1961—; dir. group therapy tng. and edn., dept. psychiatry and neurology Tulane U. Sch. Medicine, New Orleans, 1968—, prof. psychiatry and neurology, 1969—; dir. psychiatry and counseling Tulane U. Health Center, 1970—; program dir. Algiers-Fischer Community Action Mental Health Center, 1970-72. Prin. investigator psychopharmacology research grant program of Nat. Inst. Mental Health at Tulane Med. Sch., 1965—; Mem. La. Commn. on Law Enforcement and Adminstrn. Criminal Justice, Alcoholism, Dangerous Drugs and Mental Health, 1969-72; cons. adv. panel system FDA, 1972—; mem. Juvenile Ct. Vol. Program Adv. Com., 1973—. Served to capt. USAF, 1959-61. Diplomate Am. Bd. Psychiatry and Neurology. Fellow Am. Coll. Neuropsychopharmacology, Am. Psychiat. Assn.; mem. Am. Group Psychotherapy Assn. (La. pres. 1964-65), La. Psychiat. Assn. (chmn. com. on alcoholism and drug addiction, 1968—, chmn. com. on social issues 1973—), A.M.A. (cons. council on drugs for drug evaluations 1970—), Assn. for Group Psychoanalysis and Process (charter), La Sociedad Latinoamericana de Farmacologia (U.S. rep.), Sigma Pi Sigma. Contbr. articles to profl. jours. Office: Dept Psychiatry and Neurology Tulane Med Sch 1430 Tulane Av New Orleans LA 70112

GALLANT, THOMAS GRADY, state ofcl.; b. Gadsden Ala., June 14, 1920; s. Thomas Grady and Louise (Ralls) G.; student Emory U., 1939-41, 46-47; m. Micheal Ann Snider, Mar. 18, 1946; children—Lacy (Mrs. John Campbell-Orde), Thomas Grady III, Scott. Editor, Cleveland (Tenn.) Daily Banner, 1947-48; reporter Chattanooga News Free Press, 1948-63; columnist Chattanooga Times, 1963-67; columnist, city editor Chattanooga Post, 1966-70; city editor News and Observer, Raleigh, N.C., 1970-71; chief polit. writer, columnist Nashville Banner, 1971-74; information officer Tenn. Office Comptroller Treasury, Nashville, 1974—. Publicity dir. Cherokee (N.C.) Hist. Assn., 1959-61; mem. museum adv. panel Tenn. Arts Commn. Served with USMC, 1941-45. Episcopalian. Author: On Valor's Side, 1963; The Friendly Dead, 1964. Contbr. Marine Corps Gazette. Home: 3314 West End Av Nashville TN 37203 Office: State Capitol Nashville TN 37202

GALLANT, WADE MILLER, JR., lawyer; b. Raleigh, N.C., Jan. 12, 1930; s. Wade M. and Sallie (Jones) G.; B.A. summa cum laude, Wake Forest Coll., 1952, LL.B. cum laude, 1955; m. Nona Hanes Porter, June 15, 1963 (div. Oct. 1969); m. 2d, Margaret Legette, Nov. 27, 1970. Admitted to N.C. bar, 1955; asso. Womble, Carlyle, Sandridge & Rise, Attys. and Counselors at Law, Winston-Salem, N.C., 1955-63, partner, 1963—. Chmn., dir. Cayman Reef Devel. Co. Ltd.; dir. Wacayman Bank & Trust Co., Wacayman Banking Corp. Ltd. (both Grand Cayman), Life Assurance Co. Carolina, Brenner Industries, Inc., Thomas Built Buses, Inc., Piece Goods Shops, Inc., Fomento de Inversiones, S.A., Duque, S.A. (both Mexico City). Pres., Forsyth County Legal Aid Soc., 1963-67, Asso. Family and Child Service Agy., Winston-Salem, 1962-65, Winston-Salem Symphony Assn., 1965-66. Bd. dirs., v.p. N.C. Mental Health Assn., 1973—. Lectr. continuing legal edn. program N.C. Bar Found., 1966—. Mem. Am., N.C., Forsyth County bar assns., Internat. Fiscal Assn., Am. Judicature Soc., Am. Counsel Assn. (hon.), Phi Beta Kappa, Omicron Delta Kappa, Phi Delta Phi. Clubs: Old Town, Twin City (Winston-Salem); Dunes (Atlantic Beach, N.C.). Home: 224 Roslyn Rd Winston-Salem NC 27104 Office: 2400 Wachovia Bldg Winston-Salem NC 27101

GALLASPY, JOHN NORMAN, lawyer; b. Pelican, La., Nov. 8, 1932; s. Francis Norman and Hazel (Weeks) G.; B.A., La. State U., 1952, LL.B., 1958; m. Dixie Nell Yates, June 14, 1958; children—John Whithurst, Gardner Weeks, Leland Redding. Admitted to La. bar, 1958; practiced in Lake Charles, La., 1958-61, Bogalusa, La., 1961—; asst. dist. atty. 22d Jud. Dist., 1969—. Chmn. City of Bogalusa Bd. of Adjustments, 1963-69, Bogalusa Community Affairs Com., 1965. Dir. Milltown Players, 1964-66. Served to 1st lt. AUS, 1952-54. Recipient Distinguished Service award Bogalusa Jr. C. of C., 1966. Mem. Am. Judicature Soc., Am., La. State bar assns., C. of C. (dir. 1964-66), Sigma Chi, Gamma Eta Gamma. Methodist (chmn. adminstrv. bd. 1968-70). Rotarian (dir. 1962-65). Home: 1737 Gaylord Dr Bogalusa LA 70427 Office: 327 Memphis St Bogalusa LA 70427

GALLAWAY, BOB MITCHELL, educator; b. Kosciusko, Miss., Oct. 14, 1916; s. William Franklin and Lieura (Williams) G.; B.S., Tex. A. and M. U., 1943, M.S., 1946, M.Eng., 1956; m. Emily Susan Dillehay, Feb. 1, 1941; children—Robert M., Suzanne (Mrs. George Huebner), Mary Cay. Corrosion engr. Magnolia Petroleum Refinery, Beaumont, Tex., 1943-44; instr. civil engring. Tex. A. and M. U., College Station, 1945-46, asst. prof., asst. research engr., 1947-57, asso. prof., asso. research engr., 1957-59, prof., research engr., 1959—; pres. Cons. and Research Services, Inc., Bryan, Tex., 1965—. Bd. dirs. Jr. Museum Natural History, Bryan, 1967—. Recipient Engr. of Yr. award Brazos chpt. Tex. Soc. Profl. Engrs., 1969, Distinguished Faculty Achievement award for research Tex. A. and M. U., 1971. Registered profl. engr., Tex. Mem. Nat., Tex. (chpt. pres. 1969) socs. profl. engrs., Am. Assn. Engring. Edn., Am. Assn. U. Profs., Am. Concrete Inst., Assn. Asphalt Paving Technologists (dir.-at-large 1972—, 2d v.p. 1973, 1st v.p. 1974), Am. Soc. Testing and Materials (sec. E-17, 1970—), Sigma Xi, Tau Beta Pi, Phi Kappa Phi, Chi Epsilon. Author: (with W.A. Goodwin) Engineering Materials, 1958; (with W.A. Dunlap) Handbook for Building Homes of Earth, 1965. Contbr. articles to profl. jours. Patentee in field. Home: 200 Redbud St Bryan TX 77801 Office: Civil Engring Dept Tex A and M U College Station TX 77843

GALLEMORE, JOHNNIE L., JR., psychiatrist; b. Macon, Ga., July 3, 1939; s. Johnnie L. and Eloise (Graham) G.; student Harvard, summer 1959; B.A., Emory U., Atlanta, 1960, M.D., 1964; J.D., Duke, 1974; m. Gail Hurd, Aug. 23, 1964; children—John Lawrence, Thomas Wilson Ira. Intern, Duke Hosp., Durham, N.C., 1964-65, resident, 1965-68; practice medicine specializing in psychiatry, Durham, 1968—; instr. dept. psychiatry Duke U. Med. Center, 1968-69, asso., 1969-71, asst. prof., 1971-74, asso. prof., 1974—, asso. dir. med. edn., 1971—. Psychiat. cons. N.C. Dept. Corrections, 1968—, VA Hosp., Durham, 1970—. White House fellow, 1973-74. Mem. A.M.A., So. Med. Assn. (sec. sect. on neurology and psychiatry 1970-74), Am., So. psychiat. assns., N.C. Neuropsychiat. Assn., Am. Acad. Psychiatry and the Law. Contbr. articles to profl. jours. Home: 2945 Friendship Rd Durham NC 27705 Office: PO Box 3005 Duke Hosp Durham NC 27710

GALLETTE, RUSSELL F., banker; b. Toledo, Nov. 4, 1918; s. Russell C. and Ora Ada (Harmon) G.; B.S., U. Toledo, 1942; m. Lucille Elinora Rupley, May 10, 1956; 1 son, Russell F. Vice-pres. First Nat. Bank, Lake Worth, Fla., 1959-63; v.p., Litchfield State Savs. Bank, (Mich.), 1963-68; exec. v.p., sec. Citizens Trust Co., Portsmouth, Va., 1968—; pres., chmn. bd. Portsmouth Local Devel. Co., Inc., 1970—; sec., dir. Citizens Trust Co., 1968—. Chmn. Hillsdale County (Mich.) chpt. Office Econ. Opportunity, 1964-65. Council mem., finance dir., fire commr. Village of Palm Springs, Fla., 1959-61; mem. Portsmouth Planning Commn., 1973, Portsmouth TV Cable Study Commn., 1973. Bd. dirs. United Fund, Portsmouth, treas. 1970-71, exec. com. 1970-71, v.p. 1973. Served with USAAF, 1943-46. Mem. Am. Inst. Banking, Bank Adminstrn. Inst., C. of C. (state and local legislation com.), Aircraft Owners and Pilots Assn., Clubs: Cedar Point, Elizabeth Manor Golf and Country (Portsmouth). Home: 135 Yorkshire Rd Portsmouth VA 23701 Office: 355 Crawford St Portsmouth VA 23704

GALLIANO, ALBERTO M., physician; b. Sancti-Spiritus, Las Villas, Cuba, Sept. 8, 1927 (came to U.S. 1958, naturalized 1963); s. Domingo and Enriqueta Maria (Galliano) G.; B.S., Instituto de Segunda Ensenanza de Sancti-Spiritus, Las Villas, Cuba, 1945; M.D., Havana (Cuba) Med. Sch., 1953; m. Maria Rosa Mendiboure, July 9, 1951; children—Rosa Maria, Alberto Enrique, Carlos Enrique. Rotating intern Ga. Bapt. Hosp., Atlanta, 1959-60, resident gen. surgery, 1960-62; resident gen. practice Halifax Dist. Hosp., Daytona, Beach, Fla., 1962-64, now mem. staff; practice medicine specializing in family practice, Daytona Beach and Ormand Beach, Fla., 1964—; mem. staff Ormond Beach Meml. Hosp., mem. exec. com. 1968-70. Diplomate Am. Bd. Family Practice. Fellow Am. Acad. Family Physicians; mem. Am., Fla., Volusia County med. assns., Am., Fla. acads. gen. practice, Fla. Diabetes Assn., Ormond Beach C. of C. Roman Catholic. Home: 220 John Anderson Dr Ormond Beach FL 32074 Office: 722 S Atlantic Av Ormond Beach FL 32074

GALLIANO, VERNON FREDERICK, univ. pres.; b. Cut Off, La., Apr. 26, 1923; s. Emile D. and Josephine (Vega) G.; B.S. (Univ. acad. scholar), U. Southwestern La., 1947; M.S., La. State U., 1954, Ph.D. (Univ. fellow), 1960; m. Josephine Bennett, Apr. 13, 1945; children—Vernon Frederick, Timothy, Gregory, Jonathon. Tchr. Vocational agr. Larose-Cut Off High Sch., Lafourche Parish, La., 1947-54; supervising tchr. Southwestern La. Inst. (now U. Southwestern La.), Lafayette, 1948-54, prof. agrl. edn., dir. tchr. tng., 1954-60; dean edn. Nicholls State Coll., Thibodaux, La., 1960-63, pres. Nicholls State U., Thibodaux, 1963—. Dir. Citizens Bank & Trust Co., Thibodaux; trustee Gulf S. Research Inst. Mem. adv. com. La. State Supt. Edn., 1965-66; chmn. adv. council for vocational and tech. edn. La. Bd. Edn., 1969-72; mem. adv. council for federally assisted programs La. Dept. Edn., 1967-72; mem. La. Gov.'s Legislative Com. Study Coordination Higher Edn., 1968-69, La. Indsl. Adv. Com., 1968-69, Council for Devel. French-Speaking La., 1968—. Dist. finance campaign chmn. Boy Scouts Am., 1965; mem. La. Sci. Found., 1964-70, v.p., 1967-68, pres., 1969-70; mem. com. community action and crime La. Commn. Law Enforcement and Adminstrn. Criminal Justice, 1968—, citizens adv. com. Greater Lafourche Port Commn., 1969, adv. com. Lafourche Parish Airport Dist., 1964-65; chmn. St. Charles-St. John the Baptist Bridge and Ferry Authority, 1968-70; mem. So. Regional Edn. Bd., 1972—, La. Sea Grant Adv. Council, 1974—. Bd. dirs. St. Joseph Hosp., Thibodaux, 1965-69; past mem. bd. advisers St. Joseph Sem., St. Benedict, La.; bd. commrs. Hosp. Service Dist. 3 Lafourche Parish; mem. adv. bd. Nat. Ocean Industries Assn. Served to lt. USNR, 1943-45, 61-62; lt. comdr. Air Res. ret. Recipient Hon. State Farmer degree La. Assn. Future Farmers Am., 1955, commendation Houma-Terrebonne C. of C., 1966; Best Educator award River Parishes Chem. Indsl. Council, 1972. Mem. So. Educators Corp. (bd. govs. 1968—), Gulf S. (Athletic) Conf. (pres. 1971-72), Am. Assn. State Colls. and Univs. (environment com. 1970—, com. on sea grant programs 1969-70), La. State Colls. and Univs. Presidents' Council (chmn. 1964-66), La. Tchrs. Assn. and Dept. Higher Edn., Thibodaux C. of C., Am. Legion, V.F.W., John Henry Cardinal Newman Hon. Soc., Blue Key, Phi Kappa Phi, Phi Delta Kappa, Delta Tau Alpha. Democrat. Roman Catholic. K.C., Rotarian (pres. Thibodaux club 1966-67). Club: Propeller of the U.S. (Port of Orleans). Contbr. articles to ednl. jours. Home: President's Home Nicholls State University Thibodaux LA 70301 Office: Box 2001 Nicholls University Station Thibodaux LA 70301

GALLIEN, JOHN HURST, dentist; b. Waynesboro, Tenn., Dec. 10, 1937; s. Glenn S. and Mary Belle (Hurst) G.; D.D.S., U. Tenn., 1960; m. Shelby Webb, July 13, 1957; children—Mary Susan, Jean Anne, Jane Ellen. With Tenn. Dept. Pub. Health, 1960; pvt. practice dentistry, Savannah, Tenn., 1961—. Pres., dir. Hardin County Bank, Savannah; magistrate Hardin County Ct. Mem. Savannah Zoning and Planning Commn.; mem. Southwest Tenn. Health Planning Com.; chmn. bd. commrs. Hardin County Gen. Hosp. Mem. Hardin County Bd. Health. Bd. dirs. Hardin United Givers Orgn. Mem. Am., Tenn. (ho. dels.) dental assns., Seventh Dist. Dental Soc. (chmn. dental health com., pres. 1973-74), Am. Endodontic Soc., Pierre Fauchard Acad., Savannah C. of C. (pres. 1971-72), Xi Psi Phi. Methodist. Mason (32 deg.), Lion (pres. Savannah club 1971-72). Home: 1016 Church St Savannah TN 38372 Office: 903 College St Savannah TN 38372

GALLOWAY, FRANK AMEND, indsl. engr.; b. Tulsa, Nov. 12, 1938; s. Frank H. and Odessa M. (Amend) G.; B.S. in Indsl. Engring., Okla. State U., 1961, M.B.A., 1962; m. Verna C. Mason, June 4, 1960; children—Mary Catherine, Linda Kay. Systems engr. IBM, Oklahoma City, 1962-69, staff engr., Washington, 1969—. Mem. Am. Inst. Indsl. Engrs. (chpt. pres. 1968-69). Kappa Sigma. Democrat. Presbyn. (deacon 1967-69). Elk. Home: 4918 Gadsen Dr Fairfax VA 22030 Office: 1801 K St NW Washington DC 20006

GALLOWAY, GRADY RANSOM, state ofcl.; b. Whittier, N.C., Apr. 13, 1919; s. Elbert Daniel and Sarah (Ward) G.; B.S., Western Carolina U., 1941, M.A., 1961; m. Irene Graham, Oct. 20, 1950; children—Karen, Neal, Mark. Rehab. counselor, Asheville, N.C., 1946-55; dist. rehab. supr., Asheville, 1955-65; asst. dir. div. vocational rehab., Raleigh, N.C., 1965; exec. dir. N.C. Commn. for Blind, Raleigh, 1965-70; asst. dir. Vocational Rehab. Agy., N.C. Dept. Human Resources, 1970—. Mem. Gov.'s Council on Comprehensive Health Planning, 1968-70. Bd. dirs. Raleigh Lions Clinic; past trustee Am. Printing House for Blind; past mem. adv. com. on rehab. U. N.C., E. Carolina U. Served with USCGR, 1942-46. Decorated Silver Star medal. Mem. Am. Assn. Workers for Blind (past (chpt. pres.), Am. Legion, Naval League (past sec.-treas.), N.C. Rehab. Assn. (past. pres.), Rehab. Counseling Assn. (past regional pres.), N.C. Assn. for Blind (past dir.), Soc. for Prevention Blindness (chpt. dir.). Baptist. Lion. Home: 104 Shirley Dr Cary NC 27511 Office: 620 N West St Raleigh NC 27602

GALLOWAY, LOUIE ALTHEIMER, III, educator; b. Pine Bluff, Ark., Feb. 3, 1936; s. Louie Altheimer and Jessie Nina (Laws) G.; A.B., Hendrix Coll., 1958; M.S., Case Inst. Tech., 1961, Ph.D., 1966; m. Harriett Allen Laws, June 7, 1958; children—Nina Victoria, Louie Altheimer IV, Mack Laws. Asst. prof. William and Mary U., 1963; asso. prof. physics Centenary Coll. of La., Shreveport, 1966-69, prof., 1969—, chmn. dept., 1967—, Keen prof., 1972, dir. Computing Center, 1968—; pres. Foremost Cons., Shreveport, 1966—, Legal Data Systems, Shreveport, 1972-74; aerospace technologist NASA Manned Spacecraft Center, Houston, 1967. NSF fellow, 1967-68, NASA grantee, 1968. Mem. Am. Phys. Soc., Am. Assn. Physics Tchrs. Republican. Methodist (adminstrv. bd. 1973). Elk. Club: Optimist (Shreveport). Home: 3606 Reily Lane Shreveport LA 71105 Office: Dept Physics Box 4188 Centenary Coll Shreveport LA 71104

GALLOWAY, PAUL VERNON, bishop; b. Mountain Home, Ark., Apr. 5, 1904; s. James Jesse and Ella (Burkhead) G.; student Hendrix Coll., 1921-22, D.D., 1951; A.B., Henderson-Brown Coll., 1926; student So. Meth. U., 1926-27, LL.D. (hon.), 1964; B.D., Yale, 1929; student U. Chgo., 1933; LL.D., Ark. A. and M. Coll., 1947; L.H.D., Oklahoma City U., 1960; Litt.D., McMurray Coll.; m. Elizabeth Boney, June 14, 1932; 1 son, Paul Vernon. Ordained to ministry Meth. Ch., 1929, consecrated bishop, 1960; pastor in Ark., 1925-50, Okla., 1950-60; bishop of San Antonio-North West Texas area, 1960-64; bishop Ark. area, 1964—; pres. Gen. Bd. Health and Welfare Ministries, 1968-72, now ret.; visitor to mission fields abroad, 1947, 54, 58, 59, 61, 62. Chmn. conf. hosps. and homes Meth. Ch., 1939-48, chmn. commn. world service and finance, 1952-60, program chmn., also chmn. commn. entertainment, 1952-60, chmn. commn. camp activities, 1964—, chmn. campus commn., mem. Com. on Christian Vocations; mem., v.p. nat. div. of Bd. Missions. Mem. Gov. Ark. Com. to Study Vocational Tng., 1939; rep. Ark. A. and M. Coll. on Ednl. Com. Colls. and Higher Edn., 1936-50. Trustee Meth. Hosp., Memphis, Meth. Childrens Home, Little Rock; bd. dirs. So. Meth. U., Lydia Patterson Inst., El Paso, McMurry Coll., Southwestern U., Ark. A. and M. Coll.; bd. mgrs. Ark. Indsl. Schs. Mem. Delta Chi, Pi Kappa Delta (pres. 1925-26; Diamond key 1926). Mason (32 deg., grand chaplain Ark.). Home: 200 Center Plaza Tulsa OK 74119 Office: 723 Center Little Rock AR 72201

GALLOWAY, RICHARD THOMAS, physicist; b. Hartford, Ala., July 20, 1923; s. Fletcher and Johnnie Mary (Brannon) G.; B.S., Auburn U., 1949; M.S., Fla. State U., 1950; m. Lois Straughn, June 15, 1952; children—Sharon Elaine (Mrs. Dock Mitchell Taylor), Patti Lynn, Margaret Anna. Electronics mechanic Army Air Force Air Depot, Mobile, Ala., 1941-43; instr. math. State Tchrs. Coll., Florence, Ala., 1950-51; project leader Naval Coastal Systems Lab., Panama City, Fla., 1951-67, div. head, 1967—. Served with USAAF, 1943-46. Recipient Superior Accomplishment award USN, 1961, 1965. Mem. Inst. Nav. Baptist (deacon). Patentee in field. Home: 1615 Grant Av Panama City FL 32401 Office: Naval Coastal Systems Lab Panama City FL 32401

GALLY, ROBERT SAMUEL, state ofcl.; b. Phila., July 13, 1938; s. Samuel and Elizabeth Dewhurst (Day) G.; B.A., Morehead State U., 1967; M.A., U. Ky., 1968. Med. counselor U.S. Peace Corps, Brazil, 1962-64; instr. sociology Morehead (Ky.) State U., 1969-71; supt. Frenchburg (Ky.) Delinquent Instn., Ky. Dept. Child Welfare, 1971-73, dept. social service supr., Hopkinsville, 1973—. Officer for grounds Menifee County Fair, Frenchburg, 1973—. Served with USN, 1955-59. Decorated Bronze medal of merit (Brazil). Mason, Lion. Home: Briarwood Apts #7 Prestonburg KY 41653 Office: PO Box 447 Prestonburg KY 41653

GALPHIN, BRUCE MAXWELL, writer; b. Tallahassee, Aug. 11, 1932; s. Lawrence Tatum and Helen (Hoskins) G.; A.B., Fla. State U., 1954. With Atlanta Constn., 1954-69, polit. corr., 1956-60, race relations specialist, 1960-62 editorial asso., 1963-69; Atlanta bur. chief The Washington Post, 1969-70; mng. editor Atlanta mag., 1971—. Nieman fellow, Harvard, 1962-63; named Outstanding Young Man in Professions, Atlanta Jr. C. of C., 1967. Mem. Atlanta Press Club (pres. 1968). Author: The Riddle of Lester Maddox, 1968. Contbr. articles to various mags. including Saturday Rev., N.Y. Times mag., Gentleman's Quar., New Republic, Nation. Contbg. editor Atlanta mag., 1963-71. Home: 217 Westminstr Dr NE Atlanta GA 30309 Office: Commerce Bldg Atlanta GA 30303

GALT, BARRY JACK, lawyer; b. Ardmore, Okla., Dec. 14, 1933; s. Monroe S. and Ethelyn (Barry) G.; B.A. (Naval ROTC scholar), U. Okla., 1955, LL.B., 1960; m. Mary Kathryn Moore, Aug. 14, 1954; children—Terri Kathryn, Carol Ann, Gayle Lyn. Research asst. to dean Law Sch. U. Okla., 1959-60; admitted to Okla. bar, 1960; asso. Conner, Winters, Ballaine, Barry & McGowen and predecessor firm, Tulsa, 1960-65, partner, 1966—. Dir. Cotton Petroleum Corp., Ednl. Devel. Corp., Fadler Co., Inc., Community State Bank. Com. chmn. 52d PGA Championship, 1969-70. Bd. dirs. Salvation Army, Hillcrest Med. Center Assos. Served to lt. USNR, 1955-58. Mem. Am., Okla., Tulsa County bar assns., Order of Coif, Phi Delta Theta, Phi Alpha Delta. Presbyn. (elder). Clubs: Southern Hills Country, Tulsa. Editor Okla. Law Rev. Case, 1959-60. Home: 6730 S Evanston St Tulsa OK 74136 Office: First Nat Tower Tulsa OK 74103

GAMBATESE, JOSEPH MICHAEL, profl. assn. exec.; b. Cleve., Mar. 13, 1912; s. Joseph and Concetta (Vaccariello) G.; student Miami U., Oxford, O., 1929-30; A.B., Western Res. U., 1933; m. Betty Antonelli, Sept. 8, 1934; children—Roger, Richard. Reporter, Cleve. Plain Dealer, 1934-42; information dir. press sect. Nat. War Labor Bd., Washington, 1943-45; information dir. Nat. Wage Stablzn. Bd., Washington, 1945; reporter Washington bur. McGraw-Hill, 1946-53; communications cons. Gen. Electric Co., N.Y.C., 1953-54; asso. editor Nation's Business, Washington, 1953-65; mgr. news dept. C. of C. of U.S., Washington, 1965-71, communications gen mgr., 1971—. Mem. Indsl. Relations Research Assn., Pub. Relations Soc. Am., Washington Soc. Assn. Execs. Clubs: Advertising, Nat. Press (treas. 1965) (Washington). Editor: Golf Guide, 1963—. Home: 7119 Exfair Rd Bethesda MD 20014 Office: 1615 H St NW Washington DC 20006

GAMBEL, CHARLES LANGE, mfg. co. exec.; b. Lakeland, La., Mar. 23, 1909; s. William and Anna (Alraum) Lange; B.S. cum laude in Math. and Physics, Spring Hill Coll., 1929; postgrad. Tulane U., 1929-31, Loyola U., New Orleans, 1932-33; m. Helen Lorraine Nalty, June 30, 1934; children—Charles Lange, Ellen (Mrs. E.K. Simon), William C., Raymond H., Gregory F. Pres. Colonial Coffee Corp., New Orleans, 1932-38; sales promotion mgr. Blue Plate Foods div. Wesson Oil Co., New Orleans, 1940-42; night supt. Gulf Engring. Co., New Orleans, 1942, supt. for navy repairs, 1943-45, supt. engr., chief estimator, 1945-47; asst. gen. mgr. Charles Ferran & Co., New Orleans, 1948-54; distbr. prin. air-conditioning div. Gen. Electric Co., New Orleans, 1954-60; pres. Gen. Heating and Air-Conditioning Co., Inc., New Orleans, 1960—; pres. Climate Control New Orleans Co., 1955—, Creative Speciality Distbrs., Inc., New Orleans, 1967—. Trustee Lorraine Nalty Gambel Ednl. Fund. Mem. Am. Soc. Naval Engrs., Am. Soc. Heating, Refrigerating and Air-Conditioning Engrs., N.Am. Yacht Racing Union (area rep. jr. sailing activities 1971—). Club: Southern Yacht (commodore 1956-58, hon. life mem.) (New Orleans). Patentee in field. Home: 511 Hector Av Metairie LA 70005 Office: 3500 Monticello Av New Orleans LA 70118

GAMBLE, ALFRED JAMES, retail co. exec.; b. Lansing, Mich., July 18, 1921; s. Alfred F. and Rebecca B. (Woodward) G.; student Mich. State U., 1939-42; children—Alfred T., Ernest Mark. Exec. v.p. Hartley Boiler Works, 1946-61; pres. Gamble's, Montgomery, Ala., 1957—; dir. Trinity Industries, Inc. Served to 1st lt. USAAF, 1941-45. Mem. Sales and Marketing Execs. of Montgomery, So. Assn. Steel Fabricators (past pres.), Montgomery C. of C. (dir.), Men of Montgomery (dir.), Ala. Roadbuilders Assn. (dir.). Republican. Episcopalian. Elk, Mason (Shriner). Clubs: Montgomery Country, Quarterback (Montgomery). Home: 5020 Yellow Pine Dr Montgomery AL 36111 Office: 1401 N Decatur St Montgomery AL 36102

GAMBLE, CONNOLLY CURRIE, JR., educator, assn. exec.; b. Hickory, N.C., Oct. 24, 1921; s. Connolly Currie and Rachel (Pugh) G.; A.B., Lenoir Rhyne Coll., 1942; B.D., Union Theol. Sem. Va., 1945, Th.M. (Moses D. Hoge and Salem Ch. fellow 1949-51), 1950, Th.D., 1952; B.S. in L.S., U. N.C., 1952; m. Melba Lucille Burgess, Mar. 16, 1945; children—Susan Rainey (Mrs. Thaddeus George Dankel, Jr.), Melanie Holden (Mrs. Robert Cosmo Walker, Jr.), Sallie Burgess. Ordained to ministry Presbyn. Ch., 1945; pastor Presbyn. Ch., Whitmire, S.C., 1946-49; asst. librarian Union Theol. Sem., Richmond, Va., 1952-56, asso. prof. bibliography, 1956—, dir. continuing edn., 1956—; pres. Soc. for Advancement Continuing Edn. for Ministry, 1967-69, exec. sec., 1969—. Moderator, Presbyn. Synod of Va., 1970-71; pres. Korean Ministers' Continuing Edn., Washington, 1965—. Served as lt. (j.g.) USNR, 1945-46. Author: The Continuing Theological Education of the American Minister, 1960; Continuing Education and the Church's Ministry, 1967. Home: 3218 Chamberlayne Av Richmond VA 23227

GAMBLE, JESS FRANKLIN, hematologist; b. Pollock, Mo., Feb. 14, 1914; s. Shelby Vale and Jessie Alma (Garrett) G.; student U. Omaha, 1936; B.S., U. Neb., 1938, M.D., 1940; m. Eleanor Winifred McNulty, Mar. 30, 1942; children—John Franklin, Eleanor Ann, William Raymond. Intern, Walter Reed Gen. Hosp., Washington, 1940-41; resident internal medicine and hematology Ohio State U. Hosps., Columbus, 1946-49; instr. Ohio State U., 1948-49; asst. chief medicine VA Hosp., Houston, 1949-52, chief medicine, 1952-53; asst. prof. clin. medicine Baylor U. Coll. Medicine, Houston, 1949-65; practice medicine specializing in hematology and internal medicine, Houston, 1954-65; asso. internist, asso. prof. medicine U. Tex.-M.D. Anderson Hosp., Houston, 1965—. Served to col. M.C., AUS, 1941-46. Decorated Bronze Star medal. Mem. Internat. Soc. Exptl. Hematology, S.W. Oncology Group, Am. Assn. Cancer Research, Am., Tex., Houston socs. internal medicine, Am., Tex., Harris County med. assns., So. Med Assn. Home: 5118 Queensloch St Houston TX 77035 Office: 6723 Bertner St Houston TX 77025

GAMBLE, MOSES HOUSTON, JR., lawyer; b. Maryville, Tenn., July 20, 1914; s. Moses H. and Nancy Martha (Caldwell) G.; B.A., Maryville Coll., 1936; LL.B., U. Mich., 1939; m. Mary Neal Wilson, Oct. 5, 1940; children—Gale Cooper, Robert Houston, Nancy (Mrs. Marcus Bromley). Admitted to Tenn. Bar, 1939; since practiced in Maryville; mem. firm Goddard & Gamble, 1939—. Republican del. to Tenn. Constitutional Conv., 1953. Bd. dirs. Laurel Lake Youth Camp, 1969-73, Blount Meml. Hosp., 1973—. Served with AUS, 1942-45. Mem. Am., Blount County (pres. 1968-69), Tenn. bar assns. Club: Green Meadow Country. Home: 1505 Court St Maryville TN 37801 Office: Bank of Maryville Bldg Broadway St Maryville TN 37801

GAMBLE, ROBERT ALAN, librarian; b. Duncan, Okla., June 1, 1940; s. Maurice Dean and Cleta Mae (Sharp) G.; B.A., Okla. State U., 1963; postgrad. U. Kan., 1963; M.L.S., U. Okla., 1965. Govt. documents librarian Oakland U., Rochester, Mich., 1965-67; govt. documents librarian U. Tex. at Arlington, 1967-69, dir. div. archives, 1969—. Mem. Soc. Am. Archivists, Western History Assn. Home: 605 Mullins Dr Apt A Arlington TX 76014 Office: Library Room 65 Texas Arlington TX 76019

GAMBLE, ROY JACKSON, forester; b. nr. Hanceville, Ala., June 5, 1924; s. Ota K. and Ivela (Parsons) G.; B.S., Auburn U., 1951; m. Mary Jane Duren, Apr. 18, 1953; children—David Jackson, Steven Roy, Julia Dale, John Neil, Barbara Jane. Asst. forester Gulf States Paper Corp., 1951-52, asst. dist. forester, 1952-54, dist. forester, 1954-61, dist. supt., 1961-66; intermittent cons.-dist. chmn. Ala. Tree Farm Com., 1962-66; now pulpwood dealer, Cullman, Ala. Active Boy Scouts Am. Vice chmn. Bibb County Republican Com., 1964—. Served with USMCR, 1944-46. Mem. Soc. Am. Foresters, Forest Farmers Assn., Ala. Registered Foresters. So. Methodist. Mason (Shriner). Contbr. articles to co. jours. Home: 741 Scenic Dr NE Cullman AL 35055 Office: PO Box 253 Hanceville AL 35077

GAMBLE, WILLIAM BELSER, JR., physician; b. Andrews, S.C., Apr. 17, 1925; s. William Belser and Anna (Moyd) G.; B.S., U. S.C., 1945; M.D., Med. Coll. S.C., 1948; M.P.H., U. N.C., 1972; m. Margaret Florence DuBose, June 7, 1947; children—William Belser III, Richard Ervin, Heather Moyd. Intern, Roper Hosp., Charleston, S.C., 1948-49; resident pediatrics, teaching fellow Med, Coll. S.C., Charleston, 1953-56, asso. prof. pediatrics; practice medicine specializing in pediatrics and allergy, Charleston, 1956-71; state epidemiologist State Bd. Health, Columbia., S.C., 1972—; mem. staffs Med. Coll., Roper, St. Francis hosps., Charleston. Pres., Coastal Carolina Tb. and Health Assn. Dist. dir. S.C. Bd. of Health, 1972. Bd. dirs. Charleston County Mental Health Assn., Charleston County Tb Assn., Charleston. Served with M.C., AUS, 1951-53. Diplomate Am. Bd. Pediatrics, Am. Bd. Clin. Allergy and Immunology. Mem. A.M.A., Am. Acad. Pediatrics, Am. Acad. Allergy, Phi Beta Kappa, Alpha Kappa Kappa, Kappa Sigma, Alpha Omega Alpha. Methodist (mem. ofcl. bd.). Rotarian (past pres.). Contbr. articles to profl. jours. Address: 5 Guerard Rd Charleston SC 29401

GAMBRELL, BARMORE P., lawyer; b. Belton, S.C., Jan. 27, 1894; s. Enoch Pepper and Macie (Latimer) G.; B.A., Furman U.; Washington and Lee U.; LL.B., Georgetown U. Clk. office of sec. of U.S. Senate, 1 1/2 years; in practice of law, Atlanta, 1920—; mem. law firm Arnold, Arnold & Gambrell, 1930-33, Arnold, Gambrell & Arnold, 1933-52, Arnold & Gambrell, 1952-57; pvt. practice, 1957—. Served with U.S. Navy, World War I. Recipient Distinguished Alumnus award Furman U., 1968. Fellow Am. Coll. Trial Lawyers, Am. Bar Found.; mem. Am., Atlanta bar assns., State Bar Ga., Am. Judicature Soc., Lawyers Club, Am. Legion (comdr. Atlanta post 1922-23). Democrat. Baptist. Clubs: Capital City, Piedmont Driving (Atlanta). Home: 2025 Peachtree St NE Atlanta GA 30309 Office: 1512 William-Oliver Bldg Atlanta GA 30303

GAMBRELL, HERBERT, historian; b. Tyler, Tex., July 15, 1898; s. Joel Halbert Gambrell; B.A., M.A., So. Meth. U.; postgrad. U. Nacional de Mexico; Ph.D., U. Texas; m. Virginia Leddy, Aug. 4, 1940. Mem. faculty So. Meth. U., chmn. dept. history, 1948-64; hist. dir. Tex. Centennial, 1936; dir. museum Tex. Hall of State, Dallas Hist. Soc., Dallas, 1938-48, hist. dir., 1948—. Decorated officer Acad. France; recipient Collins award Tex. Inst. Letters, 1948; Faculty Achievement award So. Methodist U. Alumni Faculty, 1958. Fellow Royal Soc. Arts; mem. Tex. Inst. Letters (sec., editor, pres. 1950-52), Newcomen Soc. New Eng., Philos. Soc. Tex. (sec., editor, pres. 1968-69), French Council History and Heraldry (corr.), Soc. Am. Historians, Tex. State Hist. Assn. (pres. 1950-52), Phi Beta Kappa. Author: Texas Yesterday and Today; Mirabeau Buonaparte Lamar, Troubadour and Crusader; Anson Jones, the Last President of Texas; (with Virginia Gambrell) A Pictorial History of Texas (Summerfield G. Roberts award for best Tex. book of year Sons of Rep. of Tex., 1960), 1960. Address: Tex Hall of State Fair Pk Dallas TX 75226

GAMBRELL, SAMUEL CHESTER, JR., educator; b. Owings, S.C., Sept. 15, 1935; s. Samuel Chester and Mary Belle (Hood) G.; B.S., Clemson U., 1957, M.S. 1961; Ph.D., W.Va. U., 1965; m. Dorothy Anne Rogers, Nov. 23, 1957; children—Leslie, Anne, Sam. Instr., Clemson (S.C.) U., 1959-61, asst. prof., 1961-62; instr. W.Va. U., Morgantown, 1962-63; asst. prof. aerospace engring., mech. engring. and engring. mechs. dept. U. Ala., University, 1965-67, asso. prof., 1967-73, prof., 1973—, dir. solid mechanics div., 1969—. Served to 1st lt. air def. arty., AUS, 1957-59; now maj. Res. NSF Sci. Faculty fellow, 1963-64, NASA fellow, 1964-65. Registered profl. engr., Ala. Mem. Am. Soc. Engring. Edn., Soc. Exptl. Stress Analysis, Am. Soc. M.E., Sigma Xi, Phi Kappa Phi, Phi Eta Sigma, Tau Beta Pi. Presbyn. Home: 71 Coventry Tuscaloosa AL 35401 Office: Box 2908 University AL 35486

GAMBRELL, VIRGINIA LEDDY (MRS. HERBERT GAMBRELL), museum dir.; b. Greenville, Tex., Aug. 7, 1910; d. Charles A. Leddy; B.A., U. Tex., 1933; postgrad. So. Meth. U., 1934; m. Herbert Gambrell, Aug. 4, 1940. Archivist, Dallas Hist. Soc., 1934-48, dir. Museum Tex. Hall of State, 1948—. Mem. Tex. Library and Hist. Commn., 1944-51, chmn., 1949-51. Fellow Royal Soc. Arts; mem. Am. Assn. State and Local History (v.p. 1948-68), Soc. Am. Archivists (mem. council 1945-48), Phi Beta Kappa. Author: (with Herbert Gambrell) A Pictorial History of Texas, 1960 (Summerfield G. Roberts award for best Tex. book of year Sons of Rep. of Texas, 1960). Address: Tex Hall of State Fair Pk Dallas TX 75226

GAMMON, JOSEPH A., mgmt. and finance co. exec.; b. 1921; div.; 1 son, John Scott. Pres., dir. So. Cab Corp., 1956—, Yellow Cab Co. of Louisville, 1960—; v.p., dir. So. Atlantic Co., 1963-66; v.p. Nat. Industries Inc., Louisville, 1966-71, exec. v.p., 1971—, also dir. Served with USNR, 1944-45. Office: Nat Industries Inc 510 W Broadway Louisville KY 40202*

GAMMON, JOSEPH ALLEN, conglomerate exec.; b. Bowling Green, Ky., Apr. 13, 1922; s. Lelie S. and Lela (Bray) G.; ed. pub. schs., Bowling Green; 1 son from previous marriage, John Scott. Propr. retail liquor bus., Indpls., 1944-47; pres., part owner Service Transport Co., Bowling Green, 1948-52; exec. v.p. Gasoline Transport Co., Louisville, 1953-56; pres. So. Tank Lines, Louisville, 1957-66; pres., stockholder Ala. Tank Lines, Birmingham, Ala., 1957-64; pres., stockholder Yellow Cab-Louisville, 1957—, Yellow Cab-Birmingham,

1957-66, Yellow Cab-Memphis, 1957—, Yellow Cab-Atlanta, 1957-66, Yellow Cab-Tampa (Fla.), 1957-66; exec. v.p. South Atlantic Co., Tampa, 1962-66; v.p. transp. Nat. Industries, Louisville, 1967-70, exec. v.p., chief operating officer, 1971—; pres., dir. Cott Corp., Nat. Recreation Products Inc. Mem. Ky AEC, 1960-66; chmn. Louisville Tourist Council, 1972; dir. Louisville Area Safety Council, 1973. Served with USNR, 1942-44. Named Ky. Col. Mem. Nat. Tank Truck Carriers Assn. (dir. 1958-66), Internat. Taxicab Assn. (dir. 1970), Ky. Motor Transp. Assn. (pres. 1963-65, chmn. 1966-67, dir. 1961-65). Mason. Clubs: Standard Country, Pendennis, Jefferson (Louisville). Home: 3215 Orchard Manor Circle Louisville KY 40220 Office: 510 W Broadway Louisville KY 40202

GAMMON, NATHAN, JR., educator; b. Cheyenne, Wyo., June 22, 1914; s. Nathan and Mabel Agnes (Fair) G.; B.S., U. Md., 1936, M.S., 1938; Ph.D., Ohio State U., 1941; m. Dorothy Verna Allen, Mar. 25, 1941; children—Nathan Allen, Penelope Gay. Asst. in agronomy U. Md., College Park, 1936-38; asst. in corn investigations Ohio Agrl. Exptl. Sta., Wooster, 1938-42; faculty dept. soil sci. U. Fla., Gainesville, 1946—, prof. soil chemistry, 1946—. Served to lt. USNR, 1942-46. Fellow A.A.A.S.; mem. Am. Chem. Soc., Am. Soc. Agronomy, Soil Sci. Soc. Am., Soil and Crop Sci. Soc. Fla. (pres. 1955-56, asso. editor procs. 1972—), Fla. Hort. Soc., S.E. Pecan Growers Assn., Gainesville Rose Soc., Sigma Xi, Alpha Chi Sigma, Phi Lambda Upsilon, Phi Upsilon Phi, Gamma Alpha, Gamma Sigma Delta. Presbyn. (deacon). Contbr. articles to profl. jours. Home: 1403 NW 11th Rd Gainesville FL 32605

GAMMON, WILLIAM HOWARD, educator, computer specialist; b. Danville, Va., Mar. 9, 1910; s. William Edward and Nannie Ellen (Fallin) G.; B.A., George Washington U., 1941, D.B.A., 1971; M.A., Am. U., 1956; m. Martha Winters, Sept. 3, 1937; children—Robert Winston, Richard Harriss, Lawrence Edward, Philip Lee. With Fed. civil service, 1930-70, orgn. and methods examiner U.S. Bur. Budget, Washington, 1945-55; automatic data processing systems analyst Office Sec. Def., Washington, 1955-63; asst. to dir. Nat. Bur. Standards, Washington, 1963-66, asst. to dir. Center for Computer Scis. and Tech., 1966-70; asst. prof. Center for Tech. and Adminstrn., Am. U., Washington, 1970—. Served to lt. (j.g.) USNR, 1944-46. Recipient Evening Star trophy Arlington Civic Fedn., 1956. Mem. Assn. for Computing Machinery, Am. Soc. Pub. Adminstrn., I.E.E.E., Harvard Bus. Sch. Club Washington, Acad. Mgmt., Soc. for Mgmt. Information Systems, A.A.A.S., Am. Assn. U. Profs., Am. Mgmt. Assn. Home: 5740 N 18th St Arlington VA 22205 Office: Center for Tech and Adminstrn Am U Washington DC 20016

GAMMON, WILLIAM HUGH, oil co. exec.; b. St. Louis, Mar. 8, 1926; s. James Blakely and Floy Mabel (Randolph) G.; B.S., U. Mo., 1949, Chem.E., 1968; m. Dorothy L. Scheips, Nov. 25, 1948; children—Nancy (Mrs. Peter Dienna), Janice Lynn, William Hugh. Pilot plant engr. Sinclair Research Labs., Harvey, Ill., 1949-55; devel. supr. Ashland Oil, Inc. (Ky.), 1955-60, asst. dir. research and devel., 1960-63, mgr. research and devel. united carbon div., Houston, 1963, dir. research and devel., 1964; pres. united carbon div., 1964-68, v.p., 1966; sr. v.p. Ashland Chem. Co., Columbus, O., adminstrv. v.p., Ashland, Ky., 1970—, also dir. Chmn. bd. Spindle Top Research, Lexington, Ky. Pres. P.T.A., 1961-62. Served with USMCR, 1944-46. Decorated Purple Heart. Kiwanian. Clubs: Bellefonte Country (Ashland); Lakeside Country (Houston). Home: 1718 Oaks Dr Ashland KY 41101 Office: PO Box 391 Ashland KY 41101

GANDER, GEORGE WILLIAM, educator; b. Hamilton, Mont., June 27, 1930; s. Loren Dwight and Blanche Lenore (Mackey) G.; B.S., Mont. State U., 1953; M.S., Cornell U., 1955, Ph.D., 1959; m. Elizabeth Karen Brand, Feb. 1, 1958; children—Joseph Loren, Nicholas B., Sarah Elizabeth. Teaching and research asst. Cornell U., Ithaca, N.Y., 1953-59; research asso. dept. dairy industries U. Conn., Storrs, 1959-61; research asso. dept. pathology Albany (N.Y.) Med. Coll., 1961-63; asst. prof. exptl. pathology, dept. pathology Med. Coll. Va., Va. Commonwealth U., Richmond, 1963-67, asso. prof., 1967-74, prof., 1974—. Bd. dirs. Roslyn Hills Civic Assn., 1971-73, v.p. social affairs, 1973. Mem. Am. Chem. Soc., Am. Soc. Exptl. Pathology, N.Y. Acad. Scis., Va. Acad. Sci., Reticuloendothelial Soc., Sigma Xi (v.p. Va. Commonwealth U. chtp. 1973-74, pres. 1974—). Contbr. articles to profl. jours. Home: 211 Roslyn Hills Dr Richmond VA 23229

GANDY, THOMAS WHITNEY, coll. dean; b. Foley, Ala., Oct. 18, 1919; s. John William and Amye (Daniel) G.; B.S., Berry Coll., 1942; B.S., Auburn U., 1947, M.S., 1950; Ed.D., U. Ill., 1953; m. Theodora H. Nettles, Oct. 25, 1944; 1 dau., Suzanne Nettles. Tchr. vocational agr., Opelika, Ala., 1945-46, 47-50; instr. agrl. edn. Auburn (Ala.) U., 1950-51, asso. prof., 1953-61; research asst. U. Ill., Urbana, 1951-53; adminstrv. asst. to pres. Womans Coll. Ga., Milledgeville, 1961-63; v.p. Berry Coll. and Berry Acad., Mt. Berry, Ga., 1963-69, acad. dean Berry Coll., 1969-71; dean Sch. Edn., Valdosta (Ga.) State Coll., 1971-73, dir. pub. services, 1971—. Pres. Lee County (Ala.) Mental Health Assn., 1958-59; drive dir. Auburn Community Chest, 1959-61. Trustee, Berry Coll., 1954-56; devel. dir. Found. Womans Coll. Ga., 1961-63. Served with USNR, 1942-45. Mem. Berry Alumni Assn. (nat. pres. 1954-56), Ala. Vocational Assn. (sec.-treas. 1959-61), Phi Kappa Phi, Gamma Sigma Delta, Phi Delta Kappa, Kappa Delta Pi. Rotarian. Editor: The Agrl. Edn. Mag., 1961-62. Address: 115 High St Valdosta GA 31601

GANGI, ANTHONY FRANK, educator; b. Newark, Feb. 19, 1929; s. Frank Paul and Sarah Lucille (Cozenza) G.; student Glendale Coll., 1948-49; B.S., U. Cal. at Los Angeles, 1953, M.S., 1954, Ph.D. (Shell fellow), 1960; m. Enrichette DeGange, Jan. 26, 1961; 1 son, John Darerl; stepchildren—Robert F. Grove, Theresa A. Rice, Stephen J. Grove. Mem. tech. staff Space Electronics Corp., Glendale, Cal., 1959-61, mgr. antenna techniques dept., El Monte, 1961-64; asso. prof. geophysics Mass. Inst. Tech., 1964-67; asso. prof. dept. geophysics Tex. A. and M. U., College Station, 1967-70, prof., 1970—. Served with AUS, 1946-48. Recipient various grants NSF and U.S. Air Force. Mem. Am. Geophys. Union, Seismol. Soc. Am., I.E.E.E., Soc. Exploration Geophysicists, Am. Assn. U. Profs., N.Y. Acad. Scis., Sigma Xi, Sigma Pi Sigma. Home: 3804 Sunnybrook Lane Bryan TX 77801 Office: Dept Geophysics Texas A and M U College Station TX 77843

GANN, VICTOR DOW, civil engr.; b. Hamilton, Ala., May 15, 1937; s. Allsie Dow and Z. Cuple (Taylor) G.; B.S., U. Ala., 1960, postgrad., 1968-71; m. Judith Patricia Perkinson, Aug. 26, 1960; children—Victor Dow, Leslie D. Missile engr. Apollo program Brown Engring. Co., Huntsville, Ala., 1962-66; engr. Army missile systems U.S. Army Missile Command, Redstone Arsenal, Ala., 1966-71; test engr. ABM missiles U.S. Safeguard System Command, Huntsville, 1971—. Mem. unit com. Boy Scouts Am., 1971—, treas., 1971-73; vol. coach sports program YMCA, Huntsville, 1972—; treas. Mount Gap Sch. P.T.A., Huntsville, 1973-74. Served with AUS, 1961-62. Registered profl. engr., Ala. Baptist (deacon). Home: 12117 Chicamauga Trail SE Huntsville AL 35803 Office: US Army Safeguard System Command Huntsville AL 35807

GANS, JOHN DAVID, diversified mfg. co. exec.; b. Milw., Apr. 10, 1928; s. Thomas S. and Ruth Renee (Rubens) G.; B.A., Amherst Coll., 1949; M.S., Columbia, 1951; m. Marcia Cummings, Oct. 17, 1953; children—Thomas Cummings, Timothy Hunt, Patrick Winslow. With Rubbermaid, Inc., Wooster, O., 1956—, v.p. marketing, 1965—, mem. corporate council, 1963—, pres. Rubbermaid Comml. Products, Inc., Winchester, Va., 1970—; dir. RCP, Inc., Winchester, Farmers Mchts. Nat. Bank. Finance chmn. United Fund. Bd. dirs. Shenandoah Coll., Meml. Hosp. of Winchester, Winchester-Frederick Devel. Corp., Boys Clubs Am. Mem. Va. (dir.); Winchester chambers commerce, Beta Theta Pi. Served as 1st lt. USAF, 1943-46. Decorated Flying medal. Presbyn. Rotarian. Clubs: Winchester Golf, Menauhaut Yacht (East Falmouth, Mass.). Home: Shockey Dr Route 6 Winchester VA 22601

GANSLEN, RICHARD VICTOR, city ofcl.; b. Newark, Feb. 15, 1917; s. Charles and Bertha (Baum) G.; B.S., Columbia, 1939; M.Ed., Springfield Coll., 1940; Ph.D., U. Ill., 1952; m. Helen Olivia Milne, Aug. 21, 1941; children—Vickie (Mrs. Bruce Saunders), Bruce Eric, Kim Milne, Wendy Astride, Brian Charles. Instr. physiology Rutgers U., New Brunswick, N.J., 1946-48; asst. prof. U. Ill., 1948-52; asso. prof. physiology U. Ark. at Fayetteville, 1952-62; vis. prof. U. Cal. at Los Angeles, 1963; sr. physiologist Aerospace medicine McDonnell Aircraft Corp., St. Louis, 1963-67; prof. Tex. Woman's U., Denton, 1967-71; dir. health edn., tng. and pub. information City of Dallas Health Dept., 1971—. Cons. Finnish Olympic Assn., 1949, Cuban Olympic Assn., 1954, 55; cons. devel. of sports equipment. Chmn. Ft. Worth Regional Adv. Council on Alcoholism, 1972-73; chmn. research grants North Tex. Council Govts., 1973-74. Chmn. bd. Denton County Council on Alcoholism, 1971-74. Served to capt. AUS, 1944-46; now lt. col. Res. ret. Decorated Order of Cloud and Banner (China). Recipient research grant NIH, 1960, 61-62. Mem. Aerospace Med. Assn., Am., Tex. pub. health assns., Federacion Aeronautique de Internationale, Sigma Mu. Author 12 books. Contbr. numerous articles to various publs. Home: 1204 Windsor Dr Denton TX 75201 Office: 1936 Amelia Ct Dallas TX 75235

GANT, DUPLAIN RHODES, govt. ofcl.; b. Washington, June 24, 1924; s. Wallace Porter and Carrie (Rhodes) G.; A.B., Dillard U., 1948; M.S.W., Howard U., 1951; D.S.W., Catholic U., 1958; m. Lois Alva Williams, July 24, 1949; children—Adrienne Cecelia, Duplain Rhodes. Supervisory social worker Pub. Assistance Div., D.C. Dept. Pub. Welfare, Washington, 1958-62, chief research sect. planning and research div., 1964-67, chief Bur. Spl. Services, 1967—. Spl. cons. Pres.'s Commn. on Crime in D.C. Chmn. Foundry-Met. Community Council, Inc., 1968-69. Trustee United Planning Orgn., 1969-74. Served with AUS, 1943-46. Mem. Nat. Assn. Social Workers, Am. Pub. Welfare Assn., D.C. Pub. Health Assn., Am. Pub. Health Assn. Home: 6308 16th St NW Washington DC 20011 Office: 1875 Connecticut Av NW Washington DC 20009

GANT, FRED ALLEN, educator; b. Howard, Ala., Aug. 7, 1936; s. James Allen and Stella (Thompson) G.; A.A., Walker Jr. Coll., 1957; B.S., U. Ala., 1962, M.S., 1965, Ph.D., 1967; m. Noma Carol Meeker, Dec. 19, 1970. Chemist, Swift & Co. Research Lab., Atlanta, 1960-61; research asst. U. Ala., summer 1963; asst. prof. chemistry Mobile (Ala.) Coll., 1967-68; faculty dept. chemistry Jacksonville (Ala.) State U., 1967—, asso. prof. phys. chemistry, 1968—. Tchr. gymnastics Anniston (Ala.) YMCA, 1971—, asst. gymnastics coach, 1972—; Southeastern chmn. gymnastics Amateur Athletic Union Jr. Olympics, 1972—. Recipient Outstanding Service award Anniston YMCA, 1972. Mem. Am. Chem. Soc. (Ala. treas. 1972-73), Sigma Xi. Club: Exchange (Jacksonville). Home: Route 2 Box 3 Jacksonville AL 36265

GANT, JAMES QUINCY, JR., physician; b. Detroit, May 26, 1906; s. James Q. and Alice (Black) G.; A.B., Ohio State U., 1930, M.S., 1931; M.D., Med. Coll. Va., 1935; m. Irene S. Ellis, May 21, 1938 (dec. Feb. 1962); m. 2d, Helen Relic Fentress, June 30, 1962; stepchildren—William George, Carole Ann, Janet Marie Fentress. Interne, Stuart Circle Hosp., Bellevue Hosp.; with USPHS, 1939-46; pvt. practice, 1946—, practice ltd. to dermatology; chmn. skin and allergy service U.S. Vets. Hosp., Washington, 1946-66; emeritus prof. clin. dermatology and syphilology George Washington U. Sch. Medicine. Pres., Assn. Res. Officers USPHS, 1962-65, bd. govs., 1966—. Med. dir. USPHS ret. reserves, 1946-71; active duty D.C. Civil Def., 1959—. Diplomate Am. Bd. Dermatology, Am. Bd. Immunology and Clin. Allergy. Fellow Am. Acad. Dermatology and Syphilology, Am. Acad. Allergy; mem. A.M.A., Med. Soc. D.C., British Astron. Soc., Royal Astron. Soc. Can., Internat. Lunar Soc. (pres. 1958-62, sec. gen. 1963—), Washington Acad. Scis., Assn. Lunar and Planetary Observors (lunar recorder Eastern U.S.), Med. Arts Soc. Greater Washington (pres. 1960-61), Va. Med. Soc., Va. Acad. Sci., Richmond Acad. Medicine, So. Med. Assn., Am. Venereal Disease Assn., Assn. Mil. Surgeons, Washington Acad. Sci., Am. Geophys. Union, Internat. Assn. Planetology. Club: Cosmos (Washington). Author articles. Episcopalian. Home: 4349 Klingle St NW Washington DC 20016 Office: 1835 I St NW Washington DC 20006

GANTT, AUBREY DOYLE, physician; b. Pelion, S.C., Feb. 9, 1924; s. Grover and Blanche (Holley) G.; student Clemson Coll., 1940-43; M.D., Med. Coll. S.C., 1946; m. Jane Henricks Jones, Dec. 22, 1948; children—Rebecca (Mrs. John W. White Jr.), Aubrey Doyle, George Grover. Intern Roper Hosp., Charleston, S.C., 1946-47; gen. practice medicine, Williston, S.C., 1950—; mem. staff Barnwell County Hosp. Mem. adv. bd. Am. Bank & Trust Co. Mem. dist. com. health Boy Scouts Am., 1963-72. Mayor pro-tem, Williston, 1947-59; Councilman, Williston, 1953-55. Trustee Williston Schs., 1958-67; bd. visitors Clemson U., 1968. Served with USNR, 1943-50. Fellow Am. Acad Family Practice; mem. A.M.A., S.C., So., Barnwell County med. assns., Assn. So. Ry. Surgeons. Baptist. Mason, Elk, Woodman. Home: 701 Springfield St Williston SC 29853 Office: 101 W Main St Williston SC 29853

GANTT, FRED, JR., educator; b. Foreman, Ark., Nov. 12, 1922; s. Fred and Margaret Elizabeth (Taaffe) G.; A.A., So. State Coll., 1941; B.A., So. Meth. U., 1943, M.A., 1948; Ph.D., U. Tex., 1962. Instr. So. Meth. U., Dallas, 1947-51; teaching fellow U. Tex., 1951-52; adminstrv. asst. to personnel dir. Lone Star Ordnance Plant, Texarkana, Tex., 1952-55; instr., dir. evening sch. Texarkana (Tex.) Coll., 1955-58; teaching fellow U. Tex., 1958-60; instr. Tex. A. and M. U., College Station, 1961-62; faculty North Tex. State U., Denton, 1962—, prof. polit. sci., 1966—, chmn. dept., 1969—. Vis. prof. U. Tex., Austin, 1968, research asso. Inst. Pub. Affairs, 1969; vis. prof. L.B.J. Sch. Pub. Affairs, U. Tex., 1973; cons. Tex. Constl. Rev. Commn., 1967, Com. on Reorgn. Exec. Br., Nat. Govs. Conf., 1968, Commrs. Ct., Dallas County, Tex., 1972-73. Del. Tex. State Democratic Conv., 1964. Served with AUS, 1944-46. Mem. Am. Assn. U. Profs., Am. Soc. Pub. Adminstrn., Am., Southwestern (pres. 1970-71), Midwest, So. polit. sci. assns., Tex. Assn. Coll. Tchrs., Pi Sigma Alpha, Phi Theta Kappa, Psi Chi. Democrat. Methodist. Author: The Chief Executive in Texas, 1964; (with I. O. Dawson and L. G. Hagard) Governing Texas, 1966, rev. edit., 1970; (with J.T. Thompson and A.W. Jamison, Jr.) The Use of Land Resources in Dallas County, Texas, 1973; The State Executive in Texas: A Background Paper for the Texas Constitutional Revision Commission, 1973. Home: 1900 Westminster Dr Denton TX 76201

GANTT, MELVIN SPENCER, communications engr.; b. Salisbury, N.C., July 27, 1917; s. Melvin Lee and Myrtie Lee (Misenhiemer) G.; student Lenoir Rhyne Coll., 1940, N.C. State U., 1940-41; m. Dorothy A. Brown, July 17, 1942; children—Judith, Rebecca (Mrs. Robert Joe Eddins), Lynn. With So. Bell Tel.&Tel. Co., 1940—, supervising engr., Charlotte, N.C., 1951-55, Winston-Salem, N.C., 1955-56, dist. engr., Winston-Salem, 1956—. Mem. agr. com. Winston-Salem Leaf Tobacco Market. Vice chmn. N.W. N.C. Devel. Assn.; mem. Social Services Bd. Forsyth County, Young Life Adv. Com.; pres. Winston-Salem chpt. Internat. Municipalities Coop., 1969; mem. Citizens Action Com. for Corp. Freeway, Forsyth County adv. bd. Agrl. Extension Service; regional dir. Family and Child Services, 1971. Bd. dirs. Children's Center Physically Handicapped. Served with Signal Corps, AUS, World War II; ETO. Mem. Winston-Salem C. of C., Telephone Pioneers Am. (pres. N.C. chpt. 1969-70), I.E.E.E. (vice chmn. N.C. sect. 1962-63), Armed Forces Communications and Electronics Assn. Lutheran. Mason (Shriner), Kiwanian (gov. Carolinas dist.). Home: 720 Wilshire Rd Winston-Salem NC 27106 Office: 2150 Country Club Rd Winston-Salem NC 27104

GARB, FORREST ALLAN, petroleum engring. cons.; b. San Antonio, Dec. 15, 1929; s. Julius and Sada (Pullen) G.; B.S., Tex. A. and M. U., 1951, M.S., 1963; m. Janelda Duke, Feb. 7, 1959; children—David Forrest, Kara Lee. Petroleum engr. Mobil Oil Co., 1953-57; engr. H.J. Gruy & Assos., Dallas, 1957-61, exec. v.p., 1961-73, pres., 1973—, also dir. Active rep. Boy Scouts Am., 1969—. Served to 1st lt. USAF, 1951-53. Registered profl. engr., Tex. Mem. Soc. Petroleum Engrs., Nat. Soc. Profl. Engrs., Am. Assn. Petroleum Geologists, Assn. Computing Machinery, Model A Ford Club Am. Jewish religion (pres. congregation brotherhood 1970-71). Club: Dallas Corinthian Yacht (commodore 1970-71). Home: 2973 Sunbeck Circle Dallas TX 75234 Office: 2501 Cedar Springs Rd Dallas TX 75201

GARCIA, CLOTILDE PEREZ, physician; b. Victoria, Mexico, Jan. 11, 1917; d. Jose Garcia and Faustina (Perz) Garcia; A.A., Edinburg Jr. Coll., 1936; B.A., U. Tex., 1938, M.Ed. 1950, M.D., 1954; m. Hipolito Canales, May 25, 1943; 1 son, Jose Antonio. Tchr. pub. schs. Mercedes, Tex., 1944-50; intern Meml. Hosp., Corpus Christi, Tex., 1954-55, now mem. staff; practice medicine, specializing in family practice, Corpus Christi, 1954—. Founding mem. Parents and Friends Club, Carmelite Day Nursery, Corpus Christi, 1968; mem. nat. program rev. com. Nurse Tng. Act, Dept. Health, Edn. and Welfare, 1967—; mem. adv. com. on aging to U.S. Senate, 1971—, to Gov. Tex., 1971—; mem. Tex. Rehab. Assn., 1971—; Tex. dir. for health, mem. com. aging Am. GI Forum Ladies Aux., 1971-72; mem. Tex. Constl. Revision Commn., 1973. Nat. bd. dirs. Service, Employment and Devel. Com. Office Econ. Opportunity and Manpower Dept. Labor; bd. dirs. Nueces County Anti-Poverty Community Com., Nueces County Cerebral Palsey Assn.; mem. bd. regents Del Mar Coll., Corpus Christi. Mem. A.M.A., Nueces County (mem. disaster com.), Tex. med. socs. Nueces County Hist. Socs. and Geneology, Tex. Hist. Assn. Home: 3017 Ocean Dr Corpus Christi TX 78405 Office: 2601 Morgan St Corpus Christi TX 78405

GARCIA, ENRIQUE REGINALDO, elec. engr.; b. El Paso, Tex., Oct. 1, 1936; s. Mariano Baltier and Maria del (Refugio) G.; B.S. in Elec. Engring., U. Tex. at El Paso, 1963, M.S. in Elec. Engring., 1969; m. Graciella Paredes, Jan. 7, 1967; children—Inez, Oscar, Rebecca. Engr. autonetics div. N.Am. Aviation, Anaheim, Cal., 1963-66; electronic engr. Lockheed Elec. Co., White Sands Missile Range, N.M., 1966-68; elec. engr. U.S. Army Safeguard Systems Evaluation Agy., White Sands Missile Range, 1968—. Served with USMC, 1954-58; Mem. I.E.E.E. Home: 4705 Tumbleweed Av El Paso TX 79924 Office: US Army Safeguard Systems Evaluation Agency White Sands Missile Range NM 88002

GARCIA, ULPIANO RODRIGUEZ DEL VALLE, merchant; b. Aviles, Spain, July 18, 1926; s. Ulpiano R. DelValle and Maria (Garcia) Abril; E.E., Oviedo U., Spain, 1950; m. Maria Herminia Madera, Apr. 12, 1958; children—Carlos, Marina, Gonzalo. Came to U.S., 1959. Engr., Miguel Pascual & Co., Oviedo, Spain, 1950-55; gen. mgr. Elecsa Corp., Aviles, Spain, 1955-59; pres. Spanish Am. Trading Co. Inc., San Juan P.R., 1959—. Vice pres. Instituto Puertorriqueno Cultura Hispanica, 1967—, Spanish House, 1969—, Auxilio Mutuo Hosp., Hato Rey, P.R., 1966-68; pres. Asturian Center, San Juan, 1965-68. Decorated Knight Corpus Christi; Officer Civil Merit. Mem. Asociacion Nacional Ingenieros Industriales, I.E.E.E., P.R. C. of C. (dir. 1966-72), Spanish C. of C. (pres. 1966—; Gold Medal 1972). Home: PO Box 332 San Juan PR 00902 Office: PO Box 777 Carolina PR 00630

GARCIA-GONZALEZ, EFRAIN, physician; b. Lares, P.R., Mar. 21, 1932; s. Pablo and Emilia (Gonzalez) Garcia; B.S., U. P.R., 1951, M.D., 1955; m. Rosemary Kendrigan, Aug. 20, 1958; children—Margarita, Rosanne, Alicia, Sara, Carmen. Intern Med. Coll. Va. Hosp., 1955-56, resident internal medicine, 1957-59; resident cardiovascular diseases Brooke Gen. Hosp., 1960, asst. chief cardiology, 1962-65; dir. cardiac catheterization lab. VA Hosp., Houston, 1966; cardiologist Kelsey Seybold Co., 1965-71; asst. med. dir. Tex. Heart Inst., Houston, 1971—; clin. asso. prof. medicine Baylor U.; cons. Tex. Children's Hosp., Kelsey Seybold Clinic, Center Pavillion Hosp. Served with AUS, 1955-65. Fellow A.C.P., Am. Coll. Cardiology; mem. Am. Heart Assn. (fellow council clin. cardiology). Home: 7603 Meadowvale St Houston TX 77042 Office: 6720 Bertner St Houston TX 77025

GARCIA-KUTZBACH, ABRAHAM, physician; b. Guatemala City, Guatemala, Mar. 22, 1940; s. Abraham and Elena (Kutzbach de Garcia) Garcia; B.A., Colegio Salesiano Don Bosco, Guatemala City, 1957; M.D., Universidad de San Carlos de Guatemala, 1966; m. Lissette Girlinger, Feb. 19, 1966; children—Lissette, Ursula Elena. Came to U.S., 1967. Intern, St. Francis Hosp., Trenton, N.J., 1967-68; fellow in medicine Johns Hopkins U., Balt., 1968-69; resident medicine, fellow rheumatology U. Tenn., Memphis, 1969-73, clin. instr. medicine, 1973—; jr. staff City of Memphis Hosp., Bapt. Meml. Hosp., Memphis, Meth. Hosp., Memphis. Diplomate Am. Bd. Internal Medicine. Mem. A.C.P., Am. Rheumatism Assn., Johns Hopkins Med. and Surg. Assn. Home: 3542 Acacia Dr Memphis TN 38116 Office: 1734 Madison Av Memphis TN 38103

GARCIA-MATIENZO, FEBIO, wholesale co. exec.; b. Santurce, P.R., Dec. 21, 1943; s. Fabio and Maria Cristina (Matienzo) Garcia-Castillo; B.S., U. Dayton, 1964, M.B.A., 1966; m. Sylvia M. Passalacqua, June 8, 1968; children—Fabio, Ana Sylvia, Carlos Manuel. Marketing cons. Econ. Devel. Adminstrn., 1966-68; marketing dis. Gen. Foods, Inc., 1968-69, Ufferman, Shoemaker & Domenech Advt., Inc., 1969; marketing cons. Touche Ross & Co., 1967-70; exec. v.p. V. Suarez & Co., Inc., San Juan, P.R., 1971—. Prof. marketing Grad. Sch. Bus., U. P.R., 1967-70, Inter Am. U., 1967-70. Mem. adv. com. consumer protection Gov.'s Adv. Council; developer P.R. Consumer Protection Agy. Mem. Sales and Marketing Exec. Assn., Am. Mgmt. Assn., Am. Marketing Assn. Home: 49 Hicaco St Urb Milaville Rio Piedras PR 00926 Office: GPO Box 4588 San Juan PR 00936

GARCIA-MENDEZ, MIGUEL A., lawyer, industrialist, polit. party ofcl.; b. Aguadilla, P.R., Nov. 17, 1902; s. Juan Garcia-Figueroa and Carmen Mendez-Elias; LL.B., U. P.R., 1922; diploma in constl. law, Princeton, 1922; m. Fredeswinda Ramirez de Areliano, June 25, 1926; children—Ileana (Mrs. Leonard B. Carr), Fredeswinda (Mrs. Antonio Frontera). Pres., Mayaguez Ins. Service, Inc., 1942-52, Super-A Fertilizer Works, Inc., 1942-52, Western Distilling & Devel. Co., Inc., 1942-52, Western Fed. Savs. & Loan Assn., 1968—; chmn. bd. Central Eureka, Inc., Atlantic Quality Constrn. Corp., Mayaguez Motors Corp., Western Realty, Inc., Mayaguez Realty Corp., Integrated Industries, Inc., Publicaciones Editorial, Inc. (El Impareial; mem. adv. bd. Banco Mercantil de P.R.; dir. Lincoln Finance Mortgage; judge Ct. of San German, P.R., 1923-24; mem. P.R. Ho. of Reps., 1929-33, speaker, 1933-41; mem. P.R. Constl. Conv., 1951-52; senator-at-large, P.R. Legislative Assembly, 1953-69, also floor leader; mem. Commn. on Status of P.R.; pres., state chmn. Statehood Republican Party, P.R., 1952-68; chmn. delegation Republican Nat. Conv., 1952-68. 1968. Mem. Am. Bar Assn., Lawyers' Assn. P.R., Assn. of U.S. Army, Ateneo Puertorriqueno, Sociedad de Periodistas, Assn. Sugar Producers of P.R. Roman Catholic. Lion. Clubs: Bankers (P.R.); Congressional (Washington). Address: PO Box 599 Cerro Las Mesas Mayaguez PR 00708

GARCIA-PALMIERI, MARIO RUBEN, physician, educator; b. Adjuntas, P.R., Aug. 2, 1927; s. Rafael Garcia-Borregon and Mercedes (Palmieri-Ferri) G.-P.; B.S. magna cum laude, U. P.R., 1947; M.D., U. Md., 1951. Intern, Fajardo (P.R.) Dist. Hosp., 1951-52, head dept. med., 1955-56; resident in medicine Bayamon (P.R.) Dist. Hosp., 1952-53, cons., 1953—; resident in medicine San Juan VA Hosp., asst. in medicine U. P.R. Sch. Medicine, San Juan, 1953-54, Nat. Heart Inst. fellow in cardiology, 1954-55, instr. medicine, 1955-56, asso. in medicine, 1956-58, asst. prof., 1958-60, asso. prof., 1960, prof., head dept. medicine, chief sect. cardiology, 1961-66, 68—, prof., chief sect. cardiology, 1967-68, lectr. cardiovascular epidemiology, 1968—; head dept. medicine and sect. cardiology U. Hosp., San Juan, 1961-66, 67—; sec. health of P.R., 1966-67; pres. bd. dirs. P.R. Med. Center, 1966-67; cons. Presbyn., San Jorge, San Juan City, Auxilio Mutuo, Drs., Tchrs. hosps. Vis. prof. Seton Hall Coll. Medicine, 1963, U. Fla. Sch. Medicine, 1963, N.Y. Med. Coll., 1971, Downstate Med. Center Sch. Medicine, Bklyn., 1971; vis. lectr. Ind. U. Sch. Medicine, 1963, Bklyn. Jewish Hosp., 1964, Central U. Venezuela, 1964; guest lectr. U. Md., 1965; lectr. Postgrad. Course on Adminstrn. Med. Care Services, Dominican Republic, 1966, 68. Recipient certificate of merit Fajardo Dist. Hosp., 1965, certificate of distinction Associacion de Hospitales de P.R., 1970. Diplomate Am. Bd. Internal Medicine. Fellow A.C.P., Am. Coll. Cardiology (gov. P.R. chpt. 1966-69); mem. Am. Heart Assn. (fellow council clin. cardiology, council on epidemiology, editorial bd. Jour. 1965-70), Internat. (dir. 1964-68, v.p. 1968-72, founder, mem. sci. council on epidemiology and prevention 1968—), P.R. (pres. 1968-69), Dominican (hon.) socs. cardiology, Pan. Am. (Latin Am. v.p. sect. cardiovascular diseases 67—), P.R. (editor Bull. 1960-66, pres. sect. cardiology 1968-69, certificate of merit 1965) med. assns., A.A.A.S., Am. Fedn. for Clin. Research, Am. Soc. Tropical Medicine and Hygiene, Assn. Am. Med. Colls., Am. Soc. Internal Medicine, Am., P.R. pub. health assns., Royal Soc. Health, Soc. for Epidemiologic Research, Assn. Univ. Cardiologists, Assn. Am. Physicians, Soc. Soc. Clin. Investigation, P.R. Soc. Gastroenterology, P.R. Acad. Arts and Scis., Alpha Omega Alpha. Author: (with R.C. Rodriguez and C. Girod) The Electrocardiogram and Vectorcardiogram in Congenital Heart Disease, 1965. Mem. bd. advisers Buhiti. Contbr. numerous articles to med. jours. Home: Box DG Caparra Heights Sta San Juan PR 00922 Office: Dept of Medicine University of PR Medical Sciences Campus Box 5067 San Juan PR 00936

GARCIA-SERRA, ALBERTO JORGE, savings and loan assn. exec.; b. Havana, Cuba, Nov. 9, 1946; s. Roberto Felipe and Olga Ramona (Segurola) G.-S.; B.S., U. Fla., 1968; postgrad. U. Miami, 1968-69; m. Brenda Rodriguez, June 22, 1968; children—Brenda Marie, Allie Marie. Mgmt. trainee Compton Advt., N.Y.C., 1967; media buyer Hume-Smith-Mickelberry, advt., Miami, 1969-70, media dir., 1969-70, jr. account exec., 1970; advt. and pub. relations officer Flagler Fed. Savs. & Loan Assn., Miami, 1970—, marketing officer, 1972-73, asst. v.p. marketing, 1973—. Advt. cons. Miami Latin market. Mem. Savs. and Loan Inst. (dir. 1970), Savs. and Loan Marketing Soc. (pres. 1974), Advt. Fedn. Miami, Alpha Delta Sigma. Home: 9821 SW 164th St Miami FL 33157 Office: 101 NE 1st Av Miami FL 33132

GARDEA, RAYMOND ANGEL, physician; b. El Paso, Jan. 23, 1922; s. Juan and Luz (Soto) Gardea; B.A., U. Tex., 1951, M.D., 1955; m. Eleanor Covell, Dec. 27, 1954; children—Ann Marie, Elena, Louise, Raymond Angel, Margaret. Intern, R. E. Thomason Gen. Hosp., El Paso, 1955-56; gen. practice medicine, El Paso, 1956—; mem. staff Hotel Dieu, Sun Towers, Providence, Thomason Gen. hosps., El Paso; v.p. Paisano Med. Clinic, El Paso, 1969—. Mem. Nat. Adv. Council to Surgeon Gen. on Med., Dental, Optometric and Podiatric Edn., 1966-67; mem. Regional Health Adv. Commn., 1968-73; v.p. S.W. Ednl. Devel. Lab., 1971-72, pres. 1972-73; adviser Project Head Start, El Paso Sch. System, 1968-72. Bd. dirs. Urban Coalition, mem. exec. com., 1971-73. Served with USAAF, 1942-46. Named Outstanding Ex-Student, U. Tex. at El Paso, 1971. Mem. Am. Acad. Gen. Practice, A.M.A., Am. Cancer Soc. (pres. El Paso chpt. 1966-67, dir. Tex. div. 1966-67), El Paso County Med. Soc., Theta Kappa Psi. Elk. Club: El Paso Tennis. Home: 625 E Kerbey St El Paso TX 79902 Office: 5301 Alameda Av El Paso TX 77515

GARDINE, JUANITA CONSTANTIA FORBES (MRS. CYPRIAN A. GARDINE), sch. adminstr.; b. St. Croix, V.I., Aug. 6, 1912; d. Alphonso Sebastian and Petrina (Actien) Forbes; B.A., Hunter Coll., 1934; M.A., Columbia, 1940; postgrad. U. Chgo., 1950, N.Y. U., 1960-66; m. Cyprian A. Gardine, Apr. 23, 1942; children—Cyprian A., Vicki Maria Camilla, Letitia Theresa, Richard Whittington. Tchr. elementary schs., 1934-35; tchr. math. high sch., 1935-41, 48-49; acting asst. high sch. prin., 1941; jr. high sch. prin., 1941-47; substitute tchr. math., physics, Montclair, N.J., 1947-48; asst. supt. edn., 1949-55; asso. dean Community Colls., 1955-57; high sch. prin., 1957-58; supr. ednl. statistics, 1958-62; social worker Dept. Welfare, 1962-63; prin. Christiansted (St. Croix) Pub. Grammar Sch., 1963-74; tchr. math. evening session extension classes Cath. U. P.R. Sec. bd. dirs. St. Croix Fed. chpt. A.R.C., chmn. supervisory com. St. Croix Fed. Credit Union; sec. St. Croix Sch. Health Com.; past mem. St. Croix (V.I.) Mental Health Assn.; active Girl Scouts. Pres., Tchrs. Assn., 1940, Municipal Employees Assn., 1942. Mem. Am. Statis. Assn., Nat. Assn. Elementary Sch. Prins., V.I. Fedn. Bus. and Profl. Womens Clubs (past sec.). Episcopal Ch. Women of V.I. (past chmn. world affairs com.), Christiansted Bus. and Profl. Women's Club (pres.), Daus. King (sec.), Hunter Coll. Alumni Assn. Episcopalian (past pres. women's group). Home: 142 Whim St Frederiksted St Croix VI 00840

GARDINER, DONALD ANDREW, statistician, educator; b. Buffalo, Feb. 2, 1922; s. Andrew and Bertha Johanna (Kruger) G.; B.S., U. Buffalo, 1943, M.B.A., 1948; Ph.D., N.C. State U., 1956; m. Marie Abigail Tropman, Dec. 4, 1943; children—Ellen (Mrs. Tommy Edmonds Morgan), Andrew Donald, Kathryn Abilgail. Instr., U. Buffalo, 1946-48; faculty U. Tenn., Knoxville, 1948-51, 64—, prof. math., 1973—; with Oak Ridge Nat. Lab., 1956-73, asst. dir. math. div., 1967-73; head math. and statistics research dept. computer scis. div. Nuclear div. Union Carbide Corp., Oak Ridge, 1973—. Vis. prof. Fla. State U., Tallahassee, 1966-67. Served with USNR, 1943-46, 51-53. Fellow Am. Statis. Assn.; mem. Inst. Math. Statistics, Internat. Assn. for Statistics in Phys. Scis., Biometric Soc., Sigma Xi, Phi Kappa Phi. Mason. Editor: Technometrics, 1972—. Home: 108 Mason Lane Oak Ridge TN 37830 Office: Union Carbide Corp PO Box Y Oak Ridge TN 37830

GARDINER, PETER WHITTON, restaurant exec.; b. Niagara Falls, N.Y., Sept. 25, 1934; s. William Cecil and Anne Charlotte (Hicks) G.; B.A., Wesleyan U., Middletown, Conn., 1956; M.B.A., Harvard, 1958; m. Janet Williams Patton, Dec. 20, 1958; children—Jennifer Williams, Catherine Stuart, Pamela Andrews. Financial analyst Union Carbide Corp., N.Y.C., 1958-63; cost analyst McGraw-Hill, Inc., N.Y.C., 1963-64; div. controller Diamond Crystal Salt Co., Wilmington, Mass., 1964-66; v.p. adminstrn. and finance Venus Esterbrook Corp., N.Y.C., 1966-68; mgmt. cons. McKinsey & Co., Inc., N.Y.C., 1968-69; v.p. adminstrn. and finance Candy Corp. Am., Bklyn., 1970-71; v.p. finance, dir. Royal Castle System, Inc., Miami, Fla., 1971—. Served with AUS, 1958, 61-62. Decorated Meritorious Service award. Mem. Wesleyan U. Alumni Assn. (class reunion chmn. 1956). Club: Harvard (N.Y.C.). Home: 14803 SW 74th Pl Miami FL 33158 Office: 3800 NW 62d St Miami FL 33147

GARDNER, BILLY DEAN, univ. ofcl.; b. Wellington, Tex., Sept. 29, 1936; s. Troy William and Grace (Johnson) G.; B.B.A., West Tex. State U., 1960, M.B.A., 1970; m. Jewell Carline Uselton, Sept. 4, 1955; children—Kathy Lynn, Jeffery Douglas. Accountant Leon L. Hoyt & Co., C.P.A.'s, Amarillo, Tex., 1960-63; adminstrv. staff West Tex. State U., 1963-73; partner firm Holcomb & Gardner, C.P.A.'s, Canyon, Tex., 1973; comptroller Tex. A. & I. U. at Corpus Christi, Tex., 1973—. Former bd. dirs. Randall County Little League; bd. dirs. Randall County Kids, Inc. C.P.A., Tex. Mem. Tex. Soc. C.P.A.'s, Am. Inst. C.P.A.'s. Kiwanian (past dir.). Home: 123 Carmel St Portland TX 78374 Office: 6300 Ocean Dr Corpus Christi TX 78412

GARDNER, CHARLES BRUCE, elec. engr.; b. Knoxville, Tenn., Oct. 6, 1923; s. Horace Alexander and Martha Grace (Carmichael) G.; B.S., U. Tenn., 1950; m. Marjorie Meredith Gamble, Sept. 7, 1945; children—Bruce Lynn, Frederick Lee, David Charles, Carolyn Marie. Elec. engr. Knoxville Utilities Bd., Knoxville, 1950-51; elec. engr. TVA, Norris, 1951—, supr. instrument engring. sect., 1971—. Pres. Heiskell P.T.A., 1962. Served with AUS, 1943-45, 51-52. Registered profl. engr., Tenn. Mem. Powell Alumni Assn. (pres. 1970). Republican. Methodist. Home: Route 1 Box 438 Heiskell TN 37754 Office: TVA Engring Lab PO Drawer E Norris TN 37828

GARDNER, CLARENCE ELLSWORTH, JR., surgeon; b. Bucyrus, O., Feb. 27, 1903; s. Clarence Ellsworth and Anna (Startzman) G.; A.B., Wittenberg U., 1924, D.Sc., 1950; M.D., Johns Hopkins, 1928; m. Beatrice Ina Lockwood, June 8, 1928; 1 dau., Jane Lockwood. Intern, asst. resident surgery Johns Hopkins Hosp., also instr. surgery Johns Hopkins Sch. Medicine, 1928-30; resident surgery Duke Hosp., asso. surgery Duke Sch. Medicine, Durham, N.C., 1928-30, ast. prof. surgery, 1930-34, asso. prof., 1934-37, prof., 1937—, chmn. dept. surgery, 1960-64, emeritus prof. surgery, 1968—. Served to col. M.C., AUS, 1942-45. Diplomate Am. Bd. Surgery. Fellow A.C.S.; mem. A.M.A., So., Orange, Durham med. assns., So., Am. surg. assns., Soc. U. Surgeons, Internat. Surg. Soc., Phi Beta Kappa, Alpha Omega Alpha. Contbr. articles to surg. lit. Home: Route 1 Box 72 Astor FL 32002

GARDNER, DALLAS ADAMS, JR., financial co. exec.; b. Orangeburg, S.C., Oct. 12, 1920; s. Dallas Adams and Ruth Wallace (Sanderlin) G.; B.A., Citadel, 1941; m. Mary Kate Smith, Sept. 9, 1944; children—Julie A., Dallas Adams III. Gen. mgr. Bamberg Lumber Co., Fairfax, S.C., 1941-42, pres., treas., gen. mgr., Orangeburg, S.C., 1946-57; U.S. Marshal, Charleston, S.C., 1957-61; pvt. practice accounting and tax cons., Orangeburg, S.C., 1961-65; with First Fed. Savs. & Loan Assn., Orangeburg, S.C., 1965—, exec. v.p., 1971—, dir., 1966—. County chmn. Rep. party, Orangeburg, S.C., 1961-65, state committeeman, 1962-64. Served to capt. USAAF, 1942-46; lt. col. USAF, 1959-68. Mem. U.S. (com. mem. 1969-73), S.C. (com. mem. 1971-73) savs. and loan leagues. Methodist. Elk (exalted ruler 1957-58). Home: 861 Evergreen St Orangeburg SC 29115 Office: PO Box 997 Orangeburg SC 29115

GARDNER, EARL WILLIAM, JR., educator; b. Houston, July 31, 1928; s. Earl William and Louise (Muhl) G.; B.S., Baylor U., 1950; M.A., U. Tex. at Austin, 1954, Ph.D., 1958; m. Anita Sue Brown, Aug. 31, 1962; children—James William, Martha Louise, Jennifer Sue. Asst. prof. biology Tex. Christian U., 1958-62, asso. prof., 1962-68, prof., 1968—, chmn. sci. div., 1973—; cons. Gen. Dynamics, Ft. Worth, Tex., 1965—; health scientist adminstr. Nat. Inst. Health, 1970-72. Am. Soc. for Microbiology Pres.'s fellow, 1956-63; Sigma Xi research grantee, 1964; Welch Found. grantee, 1969; NIH research grantee, 1960-69. Recipient USPHS High Performance award, 1972. Mem. Am. Soc. Microbiology, N.Y. Acad. Scis., A.A.A.S., Internat. Assn. Dental Research, Sigma Xi. Author: (with others) Elementary Microbiology, 1963. Asso. editor Tex. Jour. Sci., 1962—. Contbr. articles to sci. jours. Home: Rt 1 Box 32A Santo TX 76472 Office: Tex Christian U Dept Biology Ft Worth TX 76129

GARDNER, ELIZABETH ANN HUNT (MRS. VERNON EVERETT GARDNER), artist; b. Chgo., Aug. 8, 1916; d. William Luther and Elizabeth (Miller) Hunt; student Wilson Tchrs. Coll., Washington, 1934-35; m. Vernon Everett Gardner, Mar. 25, 1950. Art instr. Studio 6624, Falls Church, Va., 1968—; vol. arts tchr. Anderson Orthopedic Hosp., Arlington, Va., 1958-66; certified flower judge Nat. Capital Garden Club League; one-woman show dried flower arrangements, 1974; exhibited in all important area art shows and flower shows. Mem. Arts Club Washington, Arlington Arts Craft Club, Palette Club, Emerald Shillelagh, Am. Hort. Soc. Unitarian. Clubs: Travel, Washington Figure Skating. Address: 6624 Kirby Ct Falls Church VA 22043

GARDNER, GEORGE PERCY, JR., motel exec.; b. Jackson, Tenn., Nov. 26, 1914; s. George Percy and Helen Ruth (Kesselus) G.; student Memphis State Coll., 1934-35, Bowling Green Bus. U., 1935-36; m. Ardis Margaret Worthington, June 18, 1938 (dec.); children—George Percy III, John Worthington; m. 2d, Nell Henderson Portis, June 27, 1971. With George Anna Motel, Jackson, 1927—, mgr., 1936-41, partner, 1941, pres., gen. mgr., 1963—; dir. Jackson State Bank, Superior Motels, Inc. Active United Fund drives. Bd. dirs. Jackson area Council Alcoholism and Drug Abuse, treas., 1969-72. Mem. Am. Motor Hotel Assn. (dir. 1950-68, gov. bd. 1959-60), Tenn. Motel Assn. (founder, pres. 1950), Jackson C. of C. (dir. 1954-56, v.p. 1955-56). Mason (Shriner), Elk, K.P., Moose. Baptist (supt. jr. dept. 1954-57, supt. young peoples dept. 1957-59). Club: Exchange (dir. 1959-60). Home: 423 Airways Blvd Jackson TN 38301

GARDNER, JAMES CRESWELL, utility co. exec.; b. Shreveport, La., June 17, 1924; s. Arville Pitts and Marie Pleasants (Creswell) G.; A.B., La. State U., 1947; m. Mary Ella Buchanan, Oct. 14, 1944; children—Ellen Buchanan (Mrs. Samuel W. Caverlle), James Creswell. With Southwestern Electric Power Co., Shreveport, La., 1959—, v.p., 1971—, also dir. Dir. La. Bank & Trust Co., Shreveport, La. Mem. La. Ho. of Reps., 1952-54; mayor, City of Shreveport, La., 1954-58. Trustee Centenary Coll., 1963—. Served with AUS, 1943-46. Mem. Am., La., Shreveport bar assns., Shreveport C. of C. (pres. 1971). Rotarian (pres. 1965). Clubs: Shreveport, Shreveport Country; City of Baton Rouge. Home: 550 Elmwood Shreveport LA 71104 Office: 428 Travis St Shreveport LA 71156

GARDNER, JAMES MADISON, lawyer; b. Wynne, Ark., Apr. 4, 1925; s. Menta G. and Mable R. (Eubanks) G.; J.D., U. Ark., 1949; m. Martha Ann Lintzenich, Oct. 19, 1950; children—Charles Jefferson, Marsha Gail. Admitted to Ark. bar, 1949; practice law, Blytheville, Ark., 1949—; mem. firm Gardner & Steinsiek, 1960—. Spl. chancellor 12th Chancery Dist., 1954, 59. Mem. Ark. Bd. Pardon and Paroles. Trustee Ark. Bapt. Hosp., 1953-59. Served with AUS, 1943-46. Mem. Am., Ark., Blytheville (pres. 1955-56) bar assns., Bar Assn. Ark., Blytheville C. of C. (pres. 1961-62), Blue Key, Delta Theta Phi, Pi Kappa Alpha. Baptist (chmn. bd. deacons 1967-69, trustee 1961—). Home: 1700 Eastgate Lane Blytheville AR 72315 Office: 118 W Walnut St Blytheville AR 72315

GARDNER, JOHNNY BERTEN, chemist; b. Shamrock, Tex., Aug. 31, 1928; s. Coin Cyril and Clara Anna (Bowden) G.; A.B., Bethany Nazarene Coll., 1951; M.S., Tex. A. and M. U., 1958; m. Frankie Moore, Aug. 19, 1950; children—Jeryl Ray, John Randyl, Gay Lynn, Kevin Jay. Chemist, Pan Am So. Corp., El Dorado, Ark., 1951-53; with Dow Chem. Co., Freeport, Tex., 1953—, sr. research chemist, 1960—. Scoutmaster, Boy Scouts Am., Lake Jackson, Tex., 1960-68, commr., 1956-60. Mem. Am. Chem. Soc. (sec. 1967). Mem. Ch. of Nazarene. Patentee in field. Home: 520 Circle Way Lake Jackson TX 77566 Office: Dow Chemical Bldg B-2601 Freeport TX 77541

GARDNER, JOYCE THRESHER (MRS. RUSSELL MENESE GARDNER), club women, travel cons.; b. Glen Ridge, N.J., Nov. 19, 1922; d. Harold Hayward and Hilda (Gillet) Thresher; student Arlington Hall Jr. Coll., 1939; A.B., Duke, 1944; m. Russell Menese Gardner, Mar. 7, 1946; children—Winthrop Gillet, Page Stansbury, June Thresher. Guest editor Mademoiselle mag., N.Y.C., 1943; asst. promotion mgr. Sta. WGBS, Miami, Fla., 1945-46; editor house organ Sta. WDNC, Durham, N.C., 1947-48; columnist Personally Speaking, Miami Herald, 1952-54; owner Joyce Gardner Travel Cons., 1968—. Pub. relations dir. Ft. Lauderdale (Fla.) Garden Club, 1951; Children's radio chmn. Jr. League, Miami, 1945-48; pres. Jr. League Sustainers, 1967-68; moderator monthly panel on current issues Miami Herald; radio-TV chmn. Ft. Lauderdale Mus. Arts, 1958-59, lecture chmn., 1960-61, co-chmn. spl. gifts com., 1960-61, bd. dirs., 1959-68, mem. exec. com., 1961-62, rec. sec. 1961-62, founder, corr. sec. Beaux Arts of Ft. Lauderdale, Inc., 1960-61, rec. sec., 1961-62, pres., 1964-66, asso. rep., 1971—; adv. bd. Fort Lauderdale Library, 1963—. Mem. A.L.A., Am. Assn. Museums, Soc. Mayflower Descs. (lt. gov. John Alden colony 1972-74), Phi Beta Kappa, Alpha Delta Pi. Democrat. Presbyn. Clubs: Ft. Lauderdale Yacht, Coral Ridge Country (Ft. Lauderdale); Le Club International. Home: 2412 NE 14th St Ft Lauderdale FL 33304 Office: 2400 E Las Olas Blvd Ft Lauderdale FL 33301

GARDNER, RALPH WEBB, lawyer; b. Shelby, N.C., Jan. 9, 1912; s. O. Max and Fay (Webb) G.; A.B., U. N.C., 1935; LL.B., Yale, 1938; m. Carrie Horn Derby, Sept. 14, 1950. Admitted to N.C. bar, 1938, D.C. bar, 1941; asso. Gardner, Morrison, Sheriff & Beddow, Washington, 1938-73; practice law, Shelby, 1964—. Pres., dir. Gardner Land Co., Shelby, 1942—; dir. Piedmont Aviation, Inc., Winston-Salem, N.C.; mem. bd. advisers U. N.C. Press, 1971—. Mem. Shelby Revitalization Com., 1964-70. Pres. Young Democrats Club N.C., 1938; mem. N.C. Senate, 1939-41. Trustee O. Max Gardner Found., 1947—, pres., 1969—; trustee Gardner-Webb Coll., Boiling Springs, N.C. Served to maj. AUS, 1942-46. Mem. Am., N.C. bar assns., Bar Assn. D.C., Soc. of Cincinnati, S.A.R., Phi Beta Kappa, Phi Delta Phi, Delta Kappa Epsilon. Clubs: Charlotte (N.C.) City; Cleveland Country; North Lake. Breeder purebred Aberdeen-Angus cattle. Home: 1340 E Marion St Shelby NC 28150 Office: 403 S Washington St Shelby NC 28150

GARDNER, RICHARD JACOB, lawyer; b. Quincy, Fla., Apr. 10, 1912; s. Ignatz N. and Olga (Fischl) G.; B.A., U. Fla., 1933, J.D., 1935; m. Lila M. Strouse, June 30, 1945 (dec. June 1968); children—Richard Jacob, Charles Robert, Jane, David Alan. Admitted to Fla. bar, 1935; practiced in Quincy, 1937—; mem. firm Gardner & Lines, 1937-68, individual practice, 1968—. Dir. Quincy State Bank, 1st Fed. Savs. & Loan Assn. Mem. Fla. Jud. Council, 1953-59; legislative counsel Gov. Leroy Collins, 1955-57; pres. Suwannee River Area council Boy Scouts Am., 1953-54, Fla. State U. Found., Inc., 1967—; vice chmn. Fla. Bd. Bar Examiners, 1967-68, chmn., 1968-69. Trustee Fla. State U. Found., 1964—, chmn., 1968-69; trustee So. Acad. Letters, Arts and Scis., 1971—. Served to capt. USAAF, 1942-46. Fellow Am. Coll. Probate Counsel; mem. Am. Legion, Blue Key, Phi Kappa Phi, Phi Alpha Delta. Mason, Rotarian. Home: 905 Myrtle Av Quincy FL 32351 Office: 4 E Washington St Quincy FL 32351

GARDNER, ROBERT JACK, utilities exec.; b. Dowagiac, Mich., Nov. 13, 1928; s. Dick B. and Gennette (Pixley) G.; B.S., U. Mich., 1950, LL.B., 1953; m. Susan Crecraft, June 13, 1952; children—Robert, Joseph, James, Susan. Admitted to Fla. bar, 1955; with Fla. Power & Light Co., Miami, 1954—, v.p., 1971—. Mem. Am. Soc. M.E., Fla. Bar Assn. Club: Biscayne Bay Yacht (Miami). Home: 4401 University Dr Coral Gables FL 33146 Office: 4200 Flagler St Miami FL 33101 Mailing Address: PO Box 013100 Miami FL 33101

GARDNER, ROBIN PIERCE, educator; b. Charlotte, N.C., Aug. 17, 1934; s. Robin Brem and Margaret (Pierce) G.; B.Ch.E., N.C. State U., 1956, M.S., 1958; Ph.D., Pa. State U., 1961; m. Martha Ball Miller, May 31, 1958. Scientist, Oak Ridge Inst. Nuclear Studies, 1961-63; research engr., asst. dir. measurement and controls lab. Research Triangle Inst., Research Triangle Park, N.C., 1963-67; research prof. nuclear engring. and chem. engring. N.C. State U., 1967—. Cons. Oak Ridge Inst. Nuclear Studies, Research Triangle Inst., Oak Ridge Nat. Lab., Internat. Atomic Energy Agy., NASA, AEC. Served to lt. AUS, 1956. Mem. Am. Nuclear Soc., Am. Inst. Chem. Engrs., Sigma Xi, Phi Kappa Phi, Phi Lambda Upsilon. Author: (with Ralph L. Ely, Jr.) Radioisotope Measurement Applications in Engineering, 1967. Contbr. numerous articles to sci. jours. Home: 4206 Azalea Dr Raleigh NC 27612 Office: Dept Nuclear Engring NC State U Raleigh NC 27607

GARDNER, RUSSELL MENESE, lawyer; b. High Point, N.C., July 14, 1920; s. Joseph Hayes and Clara (Flynn) G.; A.B., Duke, 1942, LL.B., 1948; m. Joyce Thresher, Mar. 7, 1946; children—Winthrop Gillet, Page Stansbury, June Thresher. Admitted to Fla. bar, 1948; asso. McCune, Hiaasen, Crum, Ferris & Gardner, and predecessor firms, 1949-50, partner, 1950—. Dir. Thellian Co., Inc. Charter revision com. City of Fort Lauderdale, 1957; mem., chmn. information and edn. subcom. Ft. Lauderdale Citizens Adv. Com. Pres., chmn. bd. Jack and Jill Nursery, Inc. Bd. dirs. United Fund Broward County; trustee Ft. Lauderdale Museum Arts, pres. bd.,

1964-67; bd. dirs. Boys Clubs of Broward County Cultural Council Greater Ft. Lauderdale, Inc. Served from ensign to lt. Supply Corps, USNR, 1942-46. Mem. Fla. Bar (mem. grievance com.), Am., Broward County (chmn. cts. com.) bar assns., Am. Judicature Soc., Ft. Lauderdale Hist. Soc. (trustee), U.S. Navy League (dir. Ft. Lauderdale council), Phi Delta Phi, Omicron Delta Kappa. Democrat. Presbyn. (trustee, deacon, elder). Kiwanian. Clubs: Hundred of Broward County; Drummer; Coral Ridge Country; Lauderdale Yacht (dir.); le Club International. Home: 2412 NE 14th St Fort Lauderdale FL 33304 Office: Broward Nat Bank Bldg Fort Lauderdale FL 33301

GARDNER, THOMAS VINCENT, JR., dentist, army officer; b. Kansas City, Mo., Aug. 5, 1931; s. Thomas Vincent and Francois Tiffany (White) G.; B.S., U. Pitts., 1955, D.D.S., 1955; M.S., Georgetown U., 1965; m. Constance Eileen Campbell, Apr. 14, 1954; children—Thomas Lee, Tiffany Eileen. Commd. 1st lt. Dental Corps, U.S. Army, 1955, advanced through grades to col., 1972; practice dentistry Schofield Barracks, Hawaii, 1955-58; chief hosp. dental service Ft. Dix, N.J., 1958-61; practice gen. dentistry Walter Reed Gen. Hosp., 1962-63; mem. faculty asst. chief dept. dental material U.S. Army Inst. Dental Research, 1965-68; comdg. officer 40th Med. Detachment, Vietnam, 1968-69; dir. dental edn. Ft. Sill, Okla., 1969—. Sponsor South Central Dist. Dental Assts. Soc. Recipient Fairbanks medal Med. Field Service Sch., 1962; decorated Bronze Star with oak leaf cluster, Air medal. Mem. Am. Dental Assn., Acad. Gen. Dentistry, Dental Materials Group, Internat. Assn. Dental Research, Assn. U.S. Army, Rathskeller Dental Study Club, Delta Sigma Delta. Republican. Presbyn. Mason. Club: Artillery Hunt (pres.) (Ft. Sill). Home: 531 Lindsay St Ft Sill OK 73503 Office: Dental Detachment Ft Sill OK 73503

GARDNER, VERNON EVERETT, govt. ofcl., elec. engr.; b. Alkabo, N.D., Dec. 7, 1913; s. Timothy William and Julia Olgina (Hillestad) G.; student N.D. Sch. Forestry, 1934-36; B.S. in Elec. Engring., U. N.D., 1938; postgrad. U. Pitts., 1940; m. Elizabeth Ann Hunt, Mar. 25, 1950. Instr. elec. engring. U. N.D., Grand Forks, 1939; elec. engr. Westinghouse Electric Co. East Pittsburg, 1940; elec., electrochem. engr. Navy Dept., Washington, 1941—. Registered profl. engr., D.C. Mem. I.E.E.E. (chmn. reliability group Washington sect. 1970-71), Assn. Sr. Engrs. (Outstanding service award 1972), Electrochem. Soc., Sigma Xi, Sigma Tau, Phi Theta Kappa. Unitarian. Clubs: Washington Figure Skating, Arts, Shillelagh Flying. Home: 6624 Kirby Ct Falls Church VA 22043 Office: Naval Ship Systems Command 2531 J D Hwy Arlington VA 22202

GARDNER, WILLIAM LEONARD, ret. mil. sch. supt.; b. nr. Jefferson, S.C., Nov. 22, 1902; s. Benjamin F. and Rosa (Ogburn) G.; A.B., The Citadel, 1928; postgrad. Cornell U., 1931, Yale, 1943; M.Ed., U. Va., 1953; m. Mabel Marguerite Stott, Sept. 10, 1930; children—Margaret Lee (Mrs. Manley Patton Caldwell, Jr.), Nancy Alice (Mrs. Coleman DeLynne Carter). Tchr., Staunton (Va.) Mil. Acad., 1928-30, Howe (Ind.) Mil. Acad., 1930-32, Fork Union (Va.) Mil. Acad., 1939-41; comdg. officer Civilian Conservation Corps Camps, N.C., S.C., 1933-39; prof. mil. sci. and tactics The Citadel, 1945; tchr., supt. Augusta Mil. Acad., Ft. Defiance, Va., 1945—, now supt. emeritus. Corporator Kings Daus. Hosp., Staunton. Dir. Ind. Sch. Fund, 1965-66. Active A.R.C., United Fund. Served to lt. col. AUS, 1941-46; ETO. Mem. Va. Edn. Assn., S.C. Tchrs. Assn. (life), Ret. Officers Assn., Kappa Delta Pi. Baptist (deacon). Mason, Kiwanian. Author: Progress in Reading, 1959. Home: 20 Orchard Rd Staunton VA 24401

GARDNER, WILLIAM ROBERT, physician; b. Oklahoma City, June 16, 1931; s. Stearns H. and Mary L. (Venable) G.; B.A., Oklahoma City U., 1955; M.D., Baylor U., 1959; children—Mary Catherine, Russell Morgan, Laurie Ann, Amy Lynn, John Randolph. Intern, then resident John Peter Smith Hosp., Ft. Worth, 1959-61; pvt. practice medicine, Mansfield, Tex., 1961—; owner, adminstr. Cedars Hosp., Mansfield, 1965—; health officer, Mansfield, 1966—. Vice pres., dir. Gardner Kirk & Cowden Oil Co., Denver Oil Co., Gilmore Gardner & Kirk Oil Co. Trustee Mansfield Ind. Sch. System, 1964—. Served with AUS, 1952-54. Diplomate Am. Bd. Family Practice. Fellow Am. Acad. Family Practice, Royal Soc. Health; mem. Am., Tex. med. assns., Mansfield C. of C. (pres. 1963). Presbyn. (elder, trustee). Lion. (pres. Mansfield 1963). Club: Ft. Worth. Home: Route 2 Mansfield TX 76063 Office: 106 Cedars St Mansfield TX 76063

GARDSBANE, HYMAN JACOB, optometrist; b. Shreveport, La., Feb. 18, 1924; s. Joseph and Annie (Dorfman) G.; student Centenary Coll., 1941-42, La. State U., 1942-43; Dr. Optometry, So. Coll. Optometry, 1945; m. Salome Heiman, Sept. 12, 1951; children—Karen Jean (Mrs. Robert Gordon), Diane Ruth, Arlene Fay. Pvt. practice optometry, Shreveport, 1948—. Vice pres. Developmental Vision Assos., Inc.; clin. asso. Optometric Extension Program; cons. USAF Hosp., Barksdale AFB, Leadership Tng. Inst. in Learning Disabilities U. Ariz., 1971-72, U.S. Office Edn., 1971—. Vice pres. 4-C Com., Community Child Care Council, 1971—; del. White House Conf. on Children, 1970; mem. La. Adv. Council on Learning Disabilities, 1973; chmn. bd. Heritage Sch. for Children with Learning Disabilities; pres. Shreveport Council for Children with Learning Disabilities, 1966-68, now v.p. Bd. dirs. Shreveport Community Council, Nat. Reading Center. Named La. Optometrist of Year, 1970. Mem. Am., La., Shreveport (pres. 1965-66) optometric assns., Internat. Reading Assn., Nat. Assn. for Children with Learning Disabilities (pres. 1970-71, v.p., dir., govtl. affairs adviser), Nat. Reading Council, Caddo-Bossier Assn. for Retarded Children, Caddo-Bossier Day Care Assn. (dir.). Mason (Shriner), Elk, Lion; mem. B'nai Zion Brotherhood (v.p.). Home: 165 Bruce Av Shreveport LA 71105 Office: 2950 Hearne Av Shreveport LA 71103

GARIKES, ARTHUR GEORGE, ednl. adminstr.; b. Chgo., Sept. 13, 1928; s. George Thomas and Assimo (Tsakiris) G.; student Wilson Jr. Coll., 1947-49; B.S. in Architecture, U. Ill. at Urbana, 1956; m. Betty Jean Tansor, Sept. 27, 1953; children—Sandra Lee, George Charles, Ronald Wayne. Designer, Milw. R.R., Chgo., 1956; asso. Perkins & Will, architects, Chgo., 1956-65; dir. clin. facilities planning, asst. to v.p. health affairs U. Ala., Birmingham, 1965-72, faculty mem. Sch. Community and Allied Health Resources, 1967-72; partner Moss, Garikes & Assos., Architects, Inc., 1972—. Mem. project rev. com. Health Planning Commn.; mem. Birmingham Com. for Employment of Handicapped; mem. Pres.'s Com. on Employment of Handicapped. Trustee Jefferson Health Found.; bd. dirs. Univ. Credit Union. Served with AUS, 1951-53. Registered architect, Ala., Ill., Ohio, Mass. Mem. Nat. Council Archtl. Registration Bds., A.I.A. (treas. chpt. 1969), Nat. Assn. Power Engrs., Inc., Am. Hosp. Assn., Am. Legion, U. Ill. Alumni Assn., Gresham Athletic Assn. (v.p. 1970-71), Cahaba Heights (pres. 1968), Shades Valley (v.p. 1973) athletic assns. Mem. Greek Orthodox Ch. (chmn. bldg. com. 1969—). Clubs: Civitan, Altedena Valley Golf and Country (Birmingham). Bd. editors Ala. Jour. Med. Scis. Home: 2917 Christopher Ct Birmingham AL 35243 Office: 2305 Arlington Av Birmingham AL 35205

GARLAND, MICHAEL MCKEE, educator; b. Clarksville, Tenn., Jan. 12, 1939; s. Charles Richard and Frances (Wolf) G.; B.A., Austin Peay State U., 1961; Ph.D., Clemson U., 1965; m. Rebecca Jean Drescher, Sept. 16, 1957; children—Michael McKee, Paul Geoffrey. With dept. physics Memphis State U., 1965—, asso. prof., 1969-73, prof., 1973—. E.B. Shepherd scholar, 1957-61; Clemson U. Alumni fellow, 1962-65; Research Corp. grantee, 1969. Mem. Am. Assn. Physics Tchrs., S.E. sect. Am. Phys. Soc., Memphis Geol. Soc., Sigma Pi Sigma. Contbr. articles to sci. jours. Home: 444 Meadowcrest Memphis TN 38117 Office: Dept Physics Memphis State U Memphis TN 38111

GARLAND, WALTER BROOKS, judge; b. Strawn, Ill., Oct. 18, 1917; s. Pierce N. and Eva (Brooks) G.; B.S., E. Tenn. State U., 1939; LL.B., U. Tenn., 1945; m. Edith Elsie Bradley, June 7, 1939; children—Walda Carole (Mrs. Louis Whitney), Wayne Bradley, Kent Winston. Tchr. Tenn. High Sch., Bristol, 1939-41; admitted to Tenn. bar, 1945; asst. prof. law U. Tenn., Knoxville, 1945-49; practiced law, Erwin, Tenn., 1949-66; mem. firm Garland & Garland, 1949-66; judge Ct. Gen. Sessions, Unicoi County, 1960-66; circuit ct. judge First Jud. Dist., State of Tenn., Erwin, 1966—. Bd. dirs. Erwin Utilities (Tenn.). Chmn. United Fund Campaign, Erwin, 1950, bd. dirs., 1950—; pres. Unicoi County Indsl. Com., 1960-62, bd. dirs., 1957—. Chmn. Unicoi County Republican Party, 1956-62. Mem. Bar. Assn. Tenn., Am., Unicoi County bar assns., Tenn. Jud. Conf., Order of Coif, Unicoi County Hist. Soc. (pres. 1972—), Phi Delta Phi. Methodist. Mason. Club: Civitan (Erwin pres. 1953-54, dist. lt. gov. 1954-55, bd. dirs.). Home: 453 Ash St Erwin TN 37650 Office: Municipal Bldg Erwin TN 37650

GARLICK, NORMAN LEE, educator; b. Tacoma, Wash., Apr. 11, 1916; s. Lee Sherman and Norma Claire (Roberts) G.; B.S., Washington State U., 1940, D.V.M., 1941; postgrad. Med. U.S.C., 1951-52; m. Helen Alberta Frantz, July 3, 1938; children—Marilyn (Mrs. David Wesley Reid), Marvin. Pvt. practice vet. medicine, Tacoma, Wash., 1941-51; with U.S. Dept. Agr., Washington, 1955-68, chief staff veterinarian, cattle diseases, 1963-68; faculty U.S.C., Charleston, 1968—, prof., chmn. dept. lab. animal sci., 1968—. Chief, research in lab. animal medicine, sci. and tech. VA Hosp., Charleston, S.C., 1968—. Served as capt. Vet. Corps, AUS, 1952-54. Fellow Am. Coll. Vet. Toxicologists (mem. exec. council 1971—); mem. Am., Wash. (pres. 1948), S.C. vet. med. assns., Am. Assn. for Lab. Animal Sci., Am. Soc. Lab. Animal Practitioners, Internat. Acad. Pathology, A.A.A.S., N.Y. Acad. Sci., Soc. for the Prevention of Cruelty to Animals (mem. exec. bd. 1970—, 2nd v.p. 1973—). Club: Ft. Johnson Estates Civic (Charleston, S.C.). Home: 439 Trapier Dr Charleston SC 29412

GARNER, EARL RAY, county ofcl.; b. Varnado, La., May 3, 1920; s. Mike Robert and Rozella (Seal) G.; B.S. in Mech. Engring., U. Ark., 1942; postgrad. U. Pitts., 1954-55; grad. student Bell System Mgmt. Tng. Program, 1949-50; m. Josephine Massaro, July 26, 1945; children—Robert Earl, William Louis, Deborah Ann (Mrs. Robert Lee Burton, Jr.) Cythia Seal (Mrs. David W. House), John Dupont. Supervising engr. Bell System, 1946-56, 60-64; constrn. engr. Mellon Bank, Pitts., 1956-60; cons. Middle West Service Co., Chgo., 1964-65; asst. dir. phys. plant U. Fla., Gainesville, 1965-66; dir. Dept. Inspections and Licenses Fulton County, Atlanta, 1967—. Chief exam. engr. State of Ga. for Nat. Inst. for Uniform Licensing of Power Engrs. Served to capt. AUS, 1942-46. Registered profl. engr., Pa., Ga., Fla. Mem. Ga. Archtl. and Engring. Soc., Bldg. Ofcl. Conf. Am., Ga. Conservancy, So. Bldg. Code Congress, Nat. Acad. Code Aminstrs., Met. Atlanta Insps. Assn. (pres. 1973). Home: 4007 Gladney Dr Atlanta GA 30340 Office: 165 Central Av Atlanta GA 30303

GARNER, JACKIE BASS, educator; b. Jonesboro, La., Aug. 21, 1934; s. James J. and Arrelia (Tumlin) G.; B.S., La. Inst. Tech., 1955; M.S., Auburn U., 1957, Ph.D., 1960; m. Shirley Hightower, Sept. 1, 1957; children—Tina, Dawn. Instr. math. La. Inst. Tech., 1957-58, asst. prof. dept. math, 1958-62, asso. prof., 1962-65, prof., 1965—. Mem. Am. Math. Soc., Math. Assn. Am., Sigma Xi, Pi Mu Epsilon. Kiwanian. Contbr. articles to math. jours. Home: 200 Hundred Oaks Ruston LA 71270 Office: Math Dept La Tech U Ruston LA 71270

GARNER, JOHN MICHAEL, lawyer, banker; b. Miami, Fla., July 17, 1935; s. James Geston and Alberta (Willis) G.; B.A., Washington and Lee U., 1957, LL.B., 1960; m. Beatrice Marie Keep, Apr. 5, 1958; children—John Michael, Mary Elizabeth. Admitted to Fla. bar, 1960, since practiced in Miami. Pres., dir. Garner Mortgage Co., Miami, 1960—, First State Bank of Miami, 1972—; exec. v.p., dir. 1st State Banking Corp.; pres. Garner & Assos., Inc., Miami, 1968—; dir. Airport First State Bank, Hialeah-Miami Springs First State Bank, North Hialeah First State Bank, Miami Lakes First State Bank, State Mut. Ins. Co. Pres. Dade County Crippled Children's Soc., 1965-67, bd. dirs., 1961—; mem. Fla. Crippled Children's Commn., 1968-71. Trustee Eckerd Coll., St. Petersburg. Mem. Am. Bar Assn., Fla. Bar, Sigma Chi, Phi Alpha Delta. Democrat. Presbyn. (deacon 1967-70). Clubs: University, Bath, LaGorce Country, Rod and Reel, Ocean Reef, Key Largo Anglers, Com. of 100; Chub Cay (Bahamas). Home: 4621 Lake Rd Miami FL 33137 Office: 8017 NE 2d Av Miami FL 33138

GARNER, REUBEN JOHN, environmental scientist; b. Oundle, U.K., Feb. 4, 1921; s. John Henry and Alice (Horsley) G.; B.A. with honors, Cambridge (Eng.) U., 1942, M.A. with honors, 1945; M.R.C.V.S., Royal Vet. Coll. London (Eng.) U., 1942, F.R.C.V.S., 1945; M. Vet. Sci., Liverpool (Eng.) U., 1952, D. Vet. Sci., 1961; m. Daphne Muriel Gascoyne, June 12, 1942; children—Karen Lesley, Julian Guy. Came to U.S., 1965, naturalized, 1971. Lectr. vet. biochemistry Liverpool U., 1950-53; sr. lectr. chem. pathology Bristol (Eng.) U., 1953-57; head radiobiology lab. Inst. Research Animal Disease, Agrl. Research Council, Compton, Eng., 1957-60; head pub. health sect. Health, Safety br. U.K. Atomic Energy Authority, Harwell, Eng., 1960-65; prof. radiation biology and biochemistry, dir. collaborative radiol. health lab. Colo. State U., Fort Collins, 1965-72; dir. exptl. biology lab. Nat. Environmental Research Center, Environmental Protection Agy., Research Triangle Park, N.C., 1972—. Churchill Found. fellow, 1956. Mem. Health Physics Assn., Radiation Research Soc., Biochem. Soc., Brit. Vet. Assn., Vet. Research Club, A.A.A.S., N.Y. Acad. Sci., Sigma Xi. Author: Garner's Veterinary Toxicology, 1957. Home: 3238 Pickett Rd Durham NC 27705 Office: Research Triangle Park NC 27711

GARNER, ROBERT FRANK, investment co. exec.; b. Toccoa, Ga., Oct. 19, 1918; s. Robert Frank and Ella Margaret (Cooper) G.; student North Ga. Coll., 1936-38; B.S., U. Ga., 1938-40; postgrad. Duke U. and U. N.C., 1948-49, George Washington U., 1951, U. Omaha (Carnegie fellow), 1961-62, Armed Forces Staff Coll., 1956-57; m. Virginia Nell Bogue, May 30, 1942; children—Robert Frank III, James R., Margaret J. Vice-pres. bus. affairs Fla. Presbyn. Eckerd Coll., St. Petersburg, 1960-67; pres. Cee Bee Income Properties, 1967—; sec.-treas., dir. R.J. Financial Corp., 1967—; sr. v.p., sec., treas. Raymond, James & Assos., St. Petersburg, 1967—; pres. Planning Corp. Am., 1972—. Ednl. bus. cons. Sec., Fla. Boxing Commn., 1940-42. Active Boy Scouts Am.; mem. Mayor's Goals Com. Mem. devel. bd. Fla. Presbyn. Coll., Clearwater Christian Coll., 1968-71. Served to lt. col. USAF, 1940-60. Decorated Bronze Star. Mem. Am. Ordnance Assn. (charter pres. Fla. chpt.), Symphony Soc. (pres. elect, dir. 1964-68), Lambda Chi Alpha. Republican. Presbyn. (deacon 1947-62, elder 1963-71). Mason, Kiwanian (pres. 1968). Clubs: Toastmasters (Norfolk, Va. and St. Petersburg); Civic Association (St. Petersburg). Home: 5030 39th St S St Petersburg FL 33711 Office: 6090 Central Av St Petersburg FL 33707

GARNSEY, CLARKE HENDERSON, artist, historian; b. Joliet, Ill., Sept. 22, 1913; s. Charles Bushniell and Sibyl Mary (VanPelt) G.; grad. Cleve. Inst. Art, 1947; B.S., Western Res. U., 1947, M.A., 1948, Ph.D., 1962; postgrad. U. Colo., W. Tex. State; m. Jean Sharpless Shoemaker, Oct. 21, 1943. Ednl. staff Cleve. Mus. Art, 1947-49, 57-59; instr. Cleve. Inst. Art, 1957-59; dept. chmn. art. Amarillo Coll., Tex., 1949-63; prof., chmn. dept. art Wichita State U., 1963-66; chmn. dept. art U. Tex., El Paso, 1966—; cons. El Paso Div. Upward Bound. Bd. dirs. Wichita Art Mus. Served with USAAF, 1941-46. Mem. Coll. Art Assn. Am., Soc. Archtl. Historians. Home: 221 Carnival Dr El Paso TX 79912

GARRARD, JEANNE (MRS. GARRARD EBERSOLE), editor, educator, writer; b. Birmingham, Ala., Apr. 9, 1923; d. Oscar and Jeanne (Holoman) Garrard; Stetson U., 1940-42; postgrad. Lindsey Hopkins Hotel Sch., 1959; m. Huber S. Ebersole, Oct. 1, 1957 (div. Nov. 1960). Radio dir., writer, commentator radio sta. WDBO, WLOF, Orlando, Fla., 1942-43; columnist Sentinel-Star, Orlando, 1943; radio commentator, writer for Burdine's, Palm Beach, Fla., 1943, Miami, Fla., 1943-44, radio Sta. WKAT, Miami Beach, 1944-45; commentator Sta. WIOD, Miami, 1944, commentator, writer Sta. WGBS, 1945; program dir. Melody, Inc., Miami Beach, 1945-48; writer Grant Advt., Inc., 1946; columnist Miami Beach Sun Star, 1946; writer for sta. WVCG, Coral Gables, Fla., 1949-50; columnist Miami Beach, 1950, Riviera-Times, Coral Gables, 1950, Miami Daily News, 1950-51; writer for Sta. WIOD, Miami, 1951; feature editor Miami Visitor Publ. Co., Miami Beach, 1952-55, mng. editor, 1955-56, editor, 1956-58; free-lance writer, photographer with work appearing in various publ. including Am. Home mag., Stag mag., numerous newspapers; scout asst. to Better Homes & Gardens, Des Moines, 1959—; asst. mgr., housekeeper Anson Hotel, Surfside, Fla., 1959; asst. to editor, photographer Meredith Pub. Co., Des Moines, 1961; instr. writing adult edn. North Miami (Fla.) High Sch., 1956—; editorial asst. Ortho Garden Guide, Cal. Chem. Co., San Francisco, 1964; became exec. editor Beach and Town, Visitor Pub. Co., Miami Beach, 1964, now cons. editor, bus. mgr. Visitor Pub. Co., until 1971; freelance writer, Miamian, Miami Pictorial, Palm Beach Life, 1971—; also sometime lectr. Bd. dirs. Miami Beach Garden Center and Conservatory. Mem. S. Fla. Orchid Soc., Met. Miami Flower Show Assn., Theta Sigma Phi (chpt. pres. 1966-67), Pi Beta Pi. Club: Miami Beach Garden (pres. 1966-68). Author: Growing Orchids for Pleasure (Nat. Lit. Horticulture award Nat. Council Garden Clubs, 1967); Potted: Flowers of Bermuda, 1970; Tropical Flowers of Florida, 1970; Flowers of Caribbean, 1970; Flowers of Bahamas, 1970; Fairchild Tropical Garden, 1972; Tropical Flowers, 1973. South Fla. editor Flower and Garden mag. Home: 5768 Pine Tree Dr Miami Beach FL 33140

GARRETT, ALBERT EARLE III, lawyer; b. Danville, Va., July 3, 1934; s. Albert Earle and Evelyn (Steele) G.; A.B., U. N.C., 1956; J.D. (Goodwin Meml. scholar), William and Mary Coll., 1963; m. Sara Scott Harman, Oct. 24, 1964; children—Albert Earle IV, Scott Freeman. Admitted to Va. bar, 1963; mem. firm Garrett, Garrett & Smith, Danville, 1963—; U.S. commr., 1965-71, magistrate, 1971—. Instr. Danville Community Coll., 1968—. Mem. Danville Planning Comm., 1972—; mem. City Council Airport Com., 1973—; mem. Bldg. Bd. of Appeals, 1970. Bd. dirs. Hope Harbor Alcoholic Rehab. Services, Inc., Danville Va., 1972—; bd. dirs. Goodwill Industries, Danville, 1970—, v.p. 1972, pres., 1973; bd. dirs. Fitzgerald-White, Inc., 1973—, Carolinas Region PCA, Inc., 1965—. Bd. dirs., sec., treas. Danville Theater Prodns., Inc., 1969—. Served with USNR, 1956-59, 60-61; lt. Res. Mem. Am., Va., Danville bar assns., Kappa Alpha Order, Phi Alpha Delta, C. of C., Southside Pilots Assn., Internat. Motor Sports Assn., Aircraft Owners and Pilots Assn. Clubs: Danville Young Men's, Porsche of Am., Sports Car of Am. Home: 129 Wilton Av Danville VA 24541 Office: 824 Masonic Bldg Danville VA 24541

GARRETT, FRANKLIN MILLER, historian; b. Milw., Sept. 25, 1906; s. Clarence Robert and Ada (Kirkwood) G.; LL.B., Woodrow Wilson Coll. Law, 1941; L.H.D., Oglethorpe Coll., 1970; div.; children—Patricia Abbott, Franklin Miller. Br. mgr. Western Union Telegraph Co., Atlanta, 1934-38; salesman Ward Wight & Co., Atlanta, 1939-40; mem. exec. staff pub. relations, historian, Coca-Cola Co., Atlanta, 1940-68. Chmn., Fulton County (Ga.) Civil Service Bd., 1955-72. Bd. dirs. Children's Center Met. Atlanta, 1958-70. Served with AUS, 1942-45. Mem. Nat. Ry., Va., Ga., Atlanta (chmn. bd. trustees 1967-68, dir. 1968—), DeKalb County hist. socs., Newcomen Soc. N.Am., Atlanta Art Assn., Atlanta Civil War Round Table, Grand Jurors Assn. Fulton County, Ga. Geneal. Soc. Presbyn. Clubs: Rotary, Commerce, Piedmont Driving, Atlanta City. Author: Atlanta and Environs I-III, 1954, rev. edit., 1969. Home: 3433 Roxboro Rd NE Atlanta GA 30326 Office: 3099 Andrews Dr NW Atlanta GA 30305

GARRETT, JAMES LAMAR, city engr.; b. Topton, Miss., Jan. 24, 1933; s. James Robert and Louise (Hooks) G.; student Meridian Jr. Coll., 1951; B.S., Miss. State U., 1954; m. Barbara P. Merrill, Nov. 12, 1955; children—Jimmy, Robby, Keith. Project engr. Metal Landing Mats. Project, U.S. Army Engrs., Waterways Experiment Station, Vicksburg, Miss., 1954-60; asst. city engr., planning dir. City of Meridian, Miss., 1960-62, city engr., dir. pub. works, 1962—. Registered profl. engr., Miss. Mem. Meridian Municipal Employees Assn. (v.p. 1971-72), Miss. Soc. Profl. Engrs. (chmn. engrs. in govt. sect. 1971-72), Pvt. Sch. Ofcl. Assn., Phi Kappa Phi, Tau Beta Pi, Phi Delta Kappa (pres. 1966-69). Democrat. Baptist. Moose. Club: Briawood Country (Meridian). Home: 4519 30th St Meridian MS 39301 Office: PO Box 1430 Meridian MS 39301

GARRETT, JAMES LOWELL, constrn. co. exec.; b. Stillwater, Okla., Dec. 29, 1946; s. Calvin Lee and Jetta Lee (Hubble) G.; B.S., Okla. State U., 1970 1 dau., Kristina Dawn. With The Atlas Orgn., Inc., gen. constrn., and devel., Oklahoma City, 1970—, v.p., 1971—; partner Garrett-Andersen, real estate devel. and investments, Dallas; partner Shiver-Garrett; land acquisition agt. Nat. Community Builders, Inc.; partner apt. devel. co. Adviser capital devel. div. Transfinancial of Okla., 1971—. Mem. loyalty fund Okla. State U., 1970-71. Mem. Oklahoma City C. of C., Okla. State U. Alumni Assn., Lambda Chi Alpha. Club: Athletic. Home: 2424 Arroyo Apt 206 Dallas TX 75219 Office: 7321 N Broadway Oklahoma City OK 73116 also Suite 100 1720 Regal Row Dallas TX

GARRETT, JOHN MAXWELL, JR., retail trade exec.; b. Greensboro, N.C., Sept. 14, 1924; s. John Maxwell and Nellie Victoria (Leonard) G.; B.A., Elon Coll., 1948; m. Jean Marie Abell, Dec. 25, 1949; children—Victoria Marie, John Keith. Asst. mgr. Western Auto Supply Co., Knoxville, 1948-49, mgr., 1949-50, Raleigh, N.C., 1950-51, Winston-Salem, N.C., 1951-52, retail sales mgr., Atlanta, 1952-57; mgr. Lowe's Cos., North Wilkesboro, N.C., 1957-73, regional v.p., 1973—. Mem. Profit Sharing Investment Com., 1970—. Bd. dirs. Alcoholic Beverage Control, 1971—. Served with AUS, 1943-45. Decorated Bronze Star. Mem. Alpha Phi Delta. Democrat. Presbyn. (deacon 1970—). Elk. Club: Oakwoods Country. Home:

1114 Brookwood Dr Wilkesboro NC 28697 Office: Lowes Hardware Box 1111 North Wilkesboro NC 28659

GARRETT, MARVIN STUART, food co. exec.; b. Booneville, Ky., Jan. 2, 1919; s. George Washington and Lucy Susan (Moyers) G.; student Eastern Ky. U., 1938-39; B.S., Purdue U., 1942; m. Charlotte Thurston Stocker, June 20, 1942; children—Jennifer Jean (Mrs. Ronald S. Eddy), Laurel Lynton (Mrs. John G. Brooks), George Whitlock. Surveyor Clark, Stewart & Woods, Richmond, Ky., 1946; home builder, 1946; project and indsl. engr. Schenley Distillers, Frankfort, Ky., 1946-52; successively indsl. engr., plant engr., plant mgr., v.p. prodn. Paramount Foods, Louisville, 1952—. Trustee, dist. vice chmn. Mohawk dist. Old Ky. Home Boy Scouts Am. Served to lt. USNR, 1942-45; PTO. Mem. Am. Inst. Indsl. Engrs. (pres. Louisville chpt. 1957), Theta Xi. Republican. Mem. Disciples of Christ (elder). Clubs: Audubon Kiwanis of Louisville (pres. 1968), Cardinal Toastmasters (Louisville). Home: 3303 Thrush Rd Louisville KY 40213 Office: PO Box 13025 Louisville KY 40213

GARRETT, NORMAN HESSON, JR., physician; b. Mount Kisco, N.Y., Jan. 10, 1927; s. Norman Hesson and Mary (Mellow) G.; M.D., Duke, 1950; m. Anne Rebecca Honeycutt, Mar. 19, 1950; children—Elizabeth Ann, Linda Carol, Mary Katherine, Norman Hesson III. Intern medicine Duke, 1950, Cin. Gen. Hosp., 1951; resident pathology Cin. Gen. Hosp., 1952; resident medicine Duke Hosp., 1953, instr. medicine, 1954; practice medicine specializing in internal medicine, Greensboro, N.C., 1954—; chief staff Moses Cone Hosp., Greensboro, 1968-69, chmn. dept. medicine, 1974—; clin. asso. prof. medicine, U. N.C. Medicine, 1967—. Served with AUS, 1945-46. Mem. Am. Soc. Internal Medicine (chmn. membership com. 1968—), N.C. Diabetes Assn. (pres. 1969-70), N.C. Soc. Internal Medicine (pres. 1970-71), Greensboro Acad. Medicine (pres. 1967-68), Alpha Omega Alpha. Presbyn. (elder 1963-66, 68-71, 73—). Home: 3932 Madison Av Greensboro NC 27410 Office: 1038 Profl Village Greensboro NC 27401

GARRETT, RICHARD EDWARD, educator; b. Roanoke, Va., Feb. 17, 1922; s. James Paul and Elizabeth Marie (Craig) G.; B.S., Roanoke Coll., 1942; M.S., Ga. Inst. Tech., 1950; Ph.D. (Dupont fellow), U. Va., 1953; m. Gene Alice Harvath, June 4, 1947. Instr. to asst. prof. physics, math. Roanoke Coll., 1942-43, 46-48; instr. physics Ga. Inst. Tech., 1948-50, U. Va., 1950-53; asso. prof. physics Hollins Coll., 1953-63; research asso. U. Va., 1962-63; asso. prof. physics U. Fla., 1963-70, prof., 1970—. Vis. lectr.; editorial cons. to pubs. Served with USNR, 1943-46; PTO. Mem. Am. Phys. Soc., Am. Assn. Physics Tchrs. (sec.-treas. Fla. sect. 1966-70), A.A.A.S., Fla. (pres. 1971-73), Va. (chmn. 1961) acads. sci., Sigma Xi, Sigma Pi Sigma. Home: Route 1 Box 381 Melrose FL 32666 Office: U Fla Gainesville FL 32611

GARRETT, WILLIAM ALLAN, lawyer; b. Danville, Va., Aug. 17, 1925; s. Albert Earle and Susie W. (Blackwell) G.; A.B., U. N.C., 1947; J.D., Washington and Lee Law Sch., 1950; m. Anne Martin, Sept. 7, 1946; children—William Allan, Martin, Jack, Joe, Jin Jin. Admitted to Va. bar, 1950, since practiced in Danville; mem. firm Garrett & Wheatley, 1950-58, Garrett & Garrett, 1958-63, Garrett, Garrett & Smith, 1963—. Served with USNR, 1944-46; lt. Res. Mem. Danville Bar Assn. (pres. 1973—). Methodist. Lion (pres. 1960). Clubs: German, Young Men's (Danville), Danville Golf. Home: 153 Hawthorne Dr Danville VA 24541 Office: 824 Masonic Bldg Danville VA 24541

GARRETT, WILLIAM RAY, physicist; b. Warrior, Ala., Oct. 17, 1937; s. Lawrence H. and Gladys C. (Mann) G.; B.S., U. Ala., 1960, M.S. (NSF fellow), 1962, Ph.D. (NSF fellow), 1963; m. Jo Ann Sanders, Oct. 19, 1957; children—Laurel, Lawrence, Susan. Grad. asst. U. Ala., Huntsville, 1960-63, research asso., 1963-65, asst. prof. physics, 1965-66; theoretical physicist Oak Ridge Nat. Lab., 1966—. Mem. Am. Phys. Soc. Home: 101 Windham Rd Oak Ridge TN 37830 Office: PO Box X Oak Ridge TN 37830

GARRETT, WILLIAM TARRANT, plastic co. exec.; b. Dallas, May 11, 1925; s. Wilburn T. and Ella Mae (Miles) G.; student U. Pickton, 1950; m. Betty B. Kretchmer, Jan. 25, 1945; children—William T. III, Glenn Herbert, Raymond Wayne. Coordinator, Stanford Univ. Press, 1946-49; sales mgr. A & A Plastic Supply Co., Dallas, 1950-58; pres., gen. mgr. A-1 Plastic Supply Co., Dallas, 1959—. Mem. Circle 10 council Cub Scouts, Boy Scouts of Am., 1954-57; coach Little League Baseball, 1954-56, Midget League Basketball, 1955-57. Served with AUS, 1944-46. Mem. Soc. Plastic Engrs. (sr.), Dallas C. of C. Home: 2534 Crest Ridge Dallas TX 75228 Office: 13700 Gamma Rd Dallas TX 75240

GARRIGO, JOSE RAMON, banker; b. Havana, Cuba, June 3, 1936; s. Faustino Buenaventura and Esther (Pita) G.; B.C.S., U. Villanova, Havana, 1960; postgrad. Rutgers U., 1972; m. Silvia Ondina Duran, Apr. 7, 1959; children—Jose Ramon, Silvia Maria, Jorge Ignacio. Came to U.S., 1960, naturalized, 1970. With Central Nat. Bank of Richmond, Va., 1953-54; with Banco Garrigo, Havana, 1954-60, asst. mgr., 1957-60; trainee Chem. Bank New York Trust Co., 1956; asst. v.p. Met. Bank of Miami, Fla., 1960-64; v.p. Pan Am. Bank of Miami, 1964-71; exec. v.p. Bank of Miami, 1971—; lectr. internat. banking Central Am. Sch. Banking, 1970—. Organizer, pres. St. James the Apostle Council, Cuban Catholic Action, Santiago de las Vegas, Cuba, 1948-52; trustee 3d Century U.S.A., Greater Miami Bicentennial Orgn.; mem. bd. Catholic Service Bur., Archdiocese of Miami; bd. dirs. Christian Commitment Found., Inc. Recipient Lincoln-Marti award for distinguished service Dept. Health, Edn. and Welfare, Washington, 1969. Mem. Assn. Pub. and Pvt. Accountants of Cuba in Exile, De La Salle Alumni Assn., Am. Inst. Banking, Interamerican Businessmens Assn. (pres., dir.), Cursillos in Christianity, Greater Miami C. of C., Am. Bankers Assn. Clubs: American (dir.), Big Five (sec., dir.) (Miami); Cuban American Sertoma (Coral Gables). Home: 7751 SW 29th Terrace Miami FL 33155 Office: 110 E Flagler St Miami FL 33131

GARRIOTT, OWEN K., astronaut; b. Enid, Okla., Nov. 22, 1930; B.S. in Elec. Engring., U. Okla., 1953; M.S., Stanford, 1957, Ph.D., 1960; m. Helen Mary Walker; children—Randall O., Robert K., Richard A., Linda S. NSF fellow Cambridge (Eng.) U., Radio Research Sta., Slough, Eng., 1960-61; instr. electronics, electro-magnetic theory, ionospheric physics Stanford, 1961-65; astronaut Johnson Space Center, Houston, 1965—, sci. pilot Skylab-3, 1973, dep. dir. Sci. and Applications Directorate, 1974—. Served with USNR, 1953-56. Recipient Distinguished Service medal NASA, 1973. Mem. Am. Geophys. Union, I.E.E.E., Am. Astron. Soc., Internat. Sci. Radio Union, Sigma Xi, Tau Beta Pi. Former regional editor Planetary and Space Scis. Address: Johnson Space Center Houston TX 77058

GARRIS, HOWARD FRANKLIN, supt. schs.; b. Round, O., Sept. 6, 1906; s. William B. and Minnie (Dodd) G.; B.S. in C.E., The Citadel, 1929; C.E., U.S.C., 1930, M.A., 1938; m. Julia Crider, Aug. 17, 1932; 1 dau., Julia Helen. Testing engr. S.C. Hwy. Dept., 1930-32; tchr., prin. St. George (S.C.) High Sch., 1932-41; supt. Bethune (S.C.) Schs., 1941-43, Blackville (S.C.) Schs., 1943-47; supt. St. Matthews (S.C.) Schs., 1947-72. Mem. Fed., S.C. edn. assns., Am., S.C. assns. sch. adminstrs. Baptist. Mason. Lion. Address: Route 2 Box 265B St Matthews SC 29135

GARRISON, ARTHUR WAYNE, chemist; b. Greenville, S.C., Sept. 9, 1934; s. Preston Maxwell and Lois (Walker) G.; B.S., The Citadel, 1956; M.S., Clemson U., 1958; Ph.D., Emory U., 1966; m. Rosevelyn Collins, June 16, 1956; children—Arthur Wayne, Bonnie Leigh. Analyt. chemist div. water supply and pollution control USPHS, Atlanta, 1961-65, chemist S.E. Water Lab., Athens, Ga., 1965-66; research chemist S.E. Environmental Research Lab., U.S. Environmental Protection Agy., Athens, Ga., 1966-73, supervisory research chemist, chief pollutant identification sect., 1973—. Served to 1st lt. Ordnance Corps, AUS, 1958-60. Mem. Am. Chem. Soc. (sec. N.E. Ga. sect. 1969-71), Sigma Xi. Presbyn. (elder 1971-74, Sunday sch. teacher 1971-73). Contbr. articles to tech. jours. Home: Hardin Hill Rd Watkinsville GA 30677 Office: EPA-SERL College Sta Rd Athens GA 30601

GARRISON, CHARLES CLAYTON, ednl. adminstr.; b. Slocum, Tex., July 6, 1927; s. Emmett Riall and Cora Dell (Skidmore) G.; B.B.A., N. Tex. State U., 1949; M.Ed., Stephen F. Austin State U., 1956; m. Bonnie Faye Roberts, Feb. 3, 1950; children—John Thomas, Frank Anthony. Tchr., Kirbyville Sch. Dist., 1949-62, prin., 1952-53, tax-assessor-collector, bus. mgr., 1954-58; tchr. Deer Park (Tex.) Ind. Sch. Dist., 1962-63, asst. bus. mgr., 1963-68, asst. supt. for bus., 1968—; dir. Nat. Bank Deer Park. Served with USNR, 1945-46. Mem. Assn. Sch. Bus. Ofcls. U.S. and Can., Gulf Coast Sch. Bus. Ofcls. (pres. 1969-70), Tex. State Tchrs. Assn., Deer Park C. of C. (dir. 1970-71), Phi Delta Kappa. Kiwanian. Home: 814 Mark St Deer Park TX 77536 Office: 203 Ivy St Deer Park TX 77536

GARRISON, JAMES EUNICE, dairy exec.; b. Pontotoc, Miss., July 5, 1924; s. Basil E. and Mamie (Cruse) G.; B.S., Miss. State U., 1949; m. Edith Archer, May 12, 1950; children—Beth, David, Nancy. Sales rep. Johnson & Johnson, Chgo., 1949-53; asst. to mgr. Pontotoc Dairy, 1953-56; gen. mgr. Ryan Milk Co., Murray, Ky., 1956-60, pres., 1960—; dir. Nat. All Jersey, Ky. Dairy Products Assn., Bank of Murray. Pres., Dairy Council of Mid-South, Inc., 1973-74. Chmn., Murray Airport Bd., 1967. Bd. dirs. Murray Hosp. Bd., Murray Indsl. Found. Served with USAAF, 1943-46. Decorated Air medal. Mem. Murray C. of C. (dir.). Methodist. Home: 303 Oakdale Dr Murray KY Office: East Chestnut Murray KY 42071

GARRISON, RICHARD NEIL, sculptor; b. Ft. Bidwell, Cal., Nov. 26, 1912; s. John Henry and Vera (Bell) G.; student Visalia Jr. Coll., 1930-31; m. Jeanne C. Trimble, Oct. 12, 1968. One man shows at Long Boat Key Art Center, Friends Gallery, Sarasota, Fla.; two-man shows Art League Manatee County, Artisan Shop, Cortez Gallery, Boca Grande; exhibited in group shows at Art League Manatee County, Sarasota Art Assn., Contemporary Gallery, St. Petersburg, Fla., Venice Art Assn,, Cortez Art Sch. and Galleries, Compass Galleries, Nantucket, Mass., Artisan Shop, Cortez Gallery, Latin Quarter Gallery, Magellan House, Tampa; represented in permanent collections at Edison Jr. Coll., Ft. Myers, Fla., also pvt. collections; instr. sculpture, dir. Art League of Manatee County, 1964-70. Pres. Fla. Craftsmen, 1971-73. Mem. Art League Manatee County, Sarasota Art Assn., Am. Craftsmans Council, Fla. Craftsmen, Long Boat Key Art Assn. (instr. 1971-74). Home and studio: 5911 Shore Acres Dr NW Bradenton FL 33505

GARRISON, THOMAS ALEXANDER, banker; b. Jackson, Tenn., Aug. 29, 1918; s. Thomas Alexander and Frances Lucile (Hicks) G.; student pub. schs., Memphis; m. Gean Koberlein, Oct. 16, 1945; 1 dau., Linda (Mrs. John W. Ellwood). With Union Planters Nat. Bank, Memphis, 1937—, now exec. v.p., mgr. banking group; dir. Bus. Music Corp. Chmn. adv. com. Opportunities Industrialization Center. Bd. dirs. Memphis Boys Town, Inc., St. Joseph Hosp., St. Joseph Hosp. East. Served with AUS, World War II; ETO. Decorated Silver Star medal, Bronze Star medal. Rotarian. Home: 8187 Cherryfield Lane Germantown TN 38138 Office: 67 Madison St Memphis TN 38147

GARRISS, PHYLLIS WEYER (MRS. W. P. GARRISS), educator; b. Hastings, Neb., Dec. 25, 1923; d. Frank Elmer and Mabelle (Carey) G.; A.B., Hastings Coll., 1945, Mus.B., 1945; Mus.M., Eastman Sch. Music, U. Rochester, 1948; m. William Philip Garriss, Aug. 28, 1954; children—Daniel Weyer, Meredith Carey, Margaret Elizabeth. Instr. mus. theory, violin DePauw U., Greencastle, Ind., 1948-51; vis. prof. violin Ball State Coll., Muncie, Ind., summers, 1951, 53; asst. prof. violin, advanced theory Meredith Coll., Raleigh, N.C., 1951—. Mem. Tri-City Chamber Symphony, 1951—, Roanoke Symphony, 1954—, Duke U. Symphony, 1954—; tchr. Cannon Music Camp, Appalachian State U., Boone, N.C., summers 1971—. Mem. Raleigh Civic Council, 1958-60. Mem. Raleigh Chamber Music Guild (dir.), N.C. Art Soc., N.C. Fedn. Music Clubs, Nat. Assn. Amateur Chamber Music Players, Am. Assn. U. Women, Am. Assn. U. Profs. (sec. chpt. 1961), Am. String Tchrs. Assn. (corr. sec. 1950-54), Music Educators Nat. Conf., Music Tchrs. Nat. Assn., Raleigh Concert Music Assn. (dir.), Am. Fedn. Musicians (dir. local), P.E.O., Mu Phi Epsilon, Pi Kappa Lambda. Presbyn. Home: 3400 Merriman Av Raleigh NC 27607

GARTH, WINSTON FEARN, warehouse co. exec.; b. Huntsville, Ala., Mar. 14, 1913; s. William Willis and Mary Louise (Dodsworth) G.; B.S., Dartmouth Coll., 1935; postgrad. Harvard Bus. Sch., 1936-37; m. Emily Hails Thornton, Apr. 27, 1940; children—Winston Fearn, Robert D., J. Thornton, Thomas F., Emily, John F., Frederick D. With Mills Asso., Deering Milliken, Inc., textile mfg., Ala., S.C., Ga., 1942-61; owner, mgr. Southeastern Freezer Corp., cold storage warehouse, Gainesville, Ga., 1963—; dir. Gainesville Midland R.R., Home Fed. Savs. and Loan Assn. Bd. dirs. Brenau Coll. Mem. Nat. Frozen Foods Assn., Phi Kappa Psi. Episcopalian (sr. warden 1958-59). Elk, Rotarian. Clubs: Chattahoochie Country. Home: 1090 Dixon Circle Gainesville GA 30501 Office: P O Box 1212 Gainesville GA 30501

GARTON, ANTHONY VOLLRATH, arts adminstr.; b. Sheboygan, Wis., Dec. 30, 1944; s. Robert Edmund and Mary Elizabeth (Vollrath) G.; B.Mus., U. Wis., 1967; postgrad. Tanglewood Inst., Berkshire Music Center, 1967; M.A., Columbia U., 1968; m. Jane Ellen Dwyre, Aug. 9, 1970; children—Johanna Elenore, Britt Mary. Dir. promotions Ann Arbor (Mich.) Jr. Light Opera, 1971-72; dir. Kingsport (Tenn.) Fine Arts Center, 1972—. Tchr. pub. schs., Lansing, Ia., 1969-71. Vol., Community Crisis Center, Kingsport, 1973—; chmn. coordinated arts adv. panel Tenn. Arts Commn., 1973-74. Bd. dirs. Tri-Cities Arts Council, 1973—. Mem. Asso. Councils Arts, Am. Theatre Assn., Am. Assn. Museums, Assn. Coll. and Univ. Concert Mgrs., Am. Symphony Orch. League. Home: 3308 Ridge View St Kingsport TN 37664 Office: Kingsport Fine Arts Center Church Circle Kingsport TN 37660

GARVAN, JOSEPH BOND, textile co. exec.; b. Hartford, Conn., Oct. 28, 1925; s. John S. and Louise (Bond) G.; grad. The Gunnery, Washington, Conn., 1943; B.A., Yale, 1951; m. Catherine Wheeler, Aug. 26, 1950; children—Stephen B. Gregory L., Melissa W. Pres., P. Garvan, Inc., Spartanburg, S.C., 1957—; dir. Am. Cotton Waste Exchange, First Citizens Bank & Trust Co. Bd. dirs. Broad River Tb-Respiratory Disease Assn., Spartanburg YMCA, Spartanburg Salvation Army, Spartanburg Animal Shelter, S.C. Arthritis Found.; trustee John S. Garvan Found., Wofford Coll., Spartanburg Day Sch. Served with USAAF, 1943-46. Republican. Episcopalian. Clubs: Wofford Eleven (dir.), Piedmont-Yale (alumni bd. rep.). Home: 35 Montgomery Dr Spartanburg SC 29302 Office: PO Box 1492 Spartanburg SC 29301

GARY, NATHAN BENNETT, JR., lawyer; b. Sherman, Tex., May 25, 1934; s. Nathan Bennett and Nadyne Coy (Shumate) G.; student Rice Inst., 1951-52, Tex. Christian U., 1952-54; B.A., U. Tex., 1956; J.D., So. Meth. U., 1966; m. Rebecca Fay Orton, Aug. 12, 1961; children—James Bennett, Sydney Catherine, Marcus Orton. Exec. v.p. Waples-Painter Co., Gainesville, Tex., 1960-63, v.p., 1966—; v.p., Gary-Nees Lumber Co., Bowie, Tex., 1966—; admitted to Tex. bar, 1966; practiced in Bowie, 1966—; dir. First Nat. Bank, Bowie. City atty., Bowie, 1967—. Trustee Bowie Hosp. Authority. Served to lt. comdr. USNR, 1956-59; comdr. Res. Mem. Naval Res. Assn., State Bar Tex., Lumbermen's Assn. Tex. (dir. 1971—), Phi Delta Phi. Methodist. Home: 4 Creekwood Bowie TX 76230 Office: PO Box 1282 Bowie TX 76230

GARY, ROLAND THACHER, educator; b. Locker, Tex., Apr. 29, 1916; s. William Evans and Rhoda de Lana (West) G.; B.S., S.W. Tex. State U., 1940, M.A., 1946; Ph.D., George Peabody Coll. for Tchrs., 1953; m. Nawona Adelle Taylor, Nov. 9, 1949; children—Nawona (Mrs. Walter Louis Crenwelge), Albadelana (Mrs. Gary Waynam Daniel). Tchr. pub. schs., Tex., 1938, 40, 41; faculty biology dept. S.W. Tex. State U., San Marcos, 1946—, prof. biology, 1957—. Tchr., cons. ednl. TV, TEMP, San Marcos, 1959-70; mem. Tex. Adv. Com. on Conservation Edn., 1946-73. Served to capt. AUS, 1942-45; PTO. Jesse Jones fellow, 1949-50, Algernon Sydney Sullivan fellow, 1950-51; Ford Found. grantee, 1959-61, Tex. Organized Research grantee, 1973-74. Mem. Conservation Edn. Assn., Nat. Assn. Biology Tchrs., Tex. Coll. Classroom Tchrs. Assn. Author lab. and curriculum manuals. Home: Route 1 Box 327C San Marcos TX 78666

GASKINS, LOSSIE LEONARD, ednl. adminstr.; b. nr. Sparks, Ga., May 25, 1925; s. Joseph Leonard and Sallie Mae (Thornton) G.; diploma Middle Ga. Coll., 1946; B.S., Ga. Tchrs. Coll., 1954; M.A., Ga. Peabody Coll. for Teachers, 1962; m. Eleanor Hambrick, June 11, 1967. Tchr.-coach Nashville (Ga.) High Sch., 1946-51; prin. New River Jr. High Sch., Nashville, 1951-54; tchr. English dept. head Berrien County High Sch., 1954-59; asst. prof. Abraham Baldwin Coll., Tifton, 1959-64; county sch. supt. Berrien County, Nashville, 1964—. Active Boy Scouts Am. Served with USNR, 1944. Mem. N.E.A., Ga., Berrien County assns. educators, Ga. Assn. Sch. Supts. Baptist (deacon; Sunday Sch. supt.). Clubs: Civitan (past sec.), Rotary (past pres.). Home: South Dogwood Dr Nashville GA 31639 Office: PO Box 625 Nashville GA 31639

GASPERONI, ELLEN JEAN LIAS (MRS. EMIL GASPERONI), auto wash exec.; b. Rural Valley, Pa.; d. Dale S. and Ruth (Harris) Lias; student Youngstown U., 1952-54, John Carrol U., 1953-54, Westminster Coll., 1951-52; grad. Am. Inst. Banking; m. Emil Gasperoni, May 28, 1955; children—Sam, Emil, Jean Ellen. Bd. dirs. Fill-Up-Up Auto Wash Co., Inc., Ft. Lauderdale, Fla., 1968—, sec., 1968—. Mem. Jr. Business Womens Club (dir. 1962-64). Presbyn. Clubs: Le Club Internat., Coral Ridge Country (Ft. Lauderdale). Home: 4201 NE 25th St Fort Lauderdale FL 33308

GASSMANN, ALBERT HENRY, golf equipment mfg. co. exec.; b. Elmhurst, N.Y., July 8, 1922; s. Albert Charles and Anna Marie (Kurz) G.; B.S. in M.E., U. Wis., 1946; B.S. in Bus. Adminstrn. summa cum laude, Rutgers U., 1952; m. Emily Theresa Prufer, Mar. 23, 1946; children—Janet Lynn, Lorraine Joan, Ellen Annmarie. Mfg. engr. heating and air conditioning equipment Gen. Electric Co., 1950-53; mgr. new products Mergenthaler Linotype Co., 1953-60; dir. operations Amfare div., AMF Inc., 1960-67; v.p. mfg. Ben Hogan Co., Fort Worth, 1967—. Served with USNR, 1942-46. Mem. Am. Soc. Tooling and Mfg. Engrs., Soc. Am. Value Engrs., Am. Mgmt. Assn. Mason. Club: Wisconsin Alumni and Nat. "W". Patentee in field. Home: 3904 Stonehenge Rd Fort Worth TX 76109 Office: 2912 W Pafford St Fort Worth TX 76110

GASTON, JAMES ELMER, ins. co. exec.; b. El Dorado, Ark., Apr. 1, 1938; s. Elmer Word and Jeroline Floy (Halsey) G.; B.S., U. Ark., 1961; m. Betty Sue Darby, Mar. 31, 1959; children—Maurine, James, William, Richard. With Equitable Securities Corp., Nashville, 1961; with Nat. Old Line Ins. Co., Little Rock, 1961—, treas., 1966-72, v.p., 1972—, dir. 1965—; treas. Equity Nat. Life Ins. Co., Little Rock, 1971—, dir. 1973—. Mem. Ark. Govtl. Efficiency Study Commn., 1967-68. Bd. dirs. Little Rock Boy's Club, Razorback Letterman's Club. Mem. Ark. Soc. Financial Mgrs. (pres. 1973—, dir. 1971—), Dallas Assn. Financial Analysts, Financial Analysts Fedn., Sigma Nu. Methodist (mem. bd. stewards 1972—). Club: Pleasant Valley Country (Little Rock). Home: 13 Pinehurst Circle Little Rock AR 72207 Office: 501 Woodlane Little Rock AR 72203

GATES, CHARLES EDGAR, educator; b. Rapid City, S.D., Mar. 6, 1926; s. Edgar Ashley and Marguerite M. (McCain) G.; B.S., Ia. State U., 1950; M.S., N.C. State U., 1952, Ph.D., 1954; m. Eleanor Louise Breckenridge, July 28, 1951; children—Greta Louise, Gail Esther, Glenda M. Instr. U. Louisville, 1955-56; statistician Agrl. Expt. Sta. of U. Minn., 1956-66; prof. statistics Tex. A. and M. U., 1966—; cons. Kennecott Copper Corp., SCI Systems, Inc. Bd. dirs. Bryan City Mission, 1971—. Served with USNR, 1944, AUS, 1955-56. Recipient distinguished faculty achievement award Tex. A. and M. U., 1973. Mem. Am. Statis. Assn., Biometrics Soc., Royal Statis. Soc., Sigma Xi, ALpha Zeta. Presbyn. (elder, deacon). Contbr. articles profl. jours. Home: 1002 Pershing Dr College Station TX 77840

GATES, ERNEST PLEASANTS, circuit ct. judge; b. Chesterfield, Va., June 16, 1924; s. Ordway Benjamin and Ida (Heath) G.; B.S., Hampden-Sydney Coll., 1947; LL.B., Washington and Lee U., 1950; m. Virginia Yonce, Aug. 18, 1951; children—William Mayo, Ernest Pleasants, David Heath, Elizabeth Williams, Virginia Morehead, Thomas Bass. Admitted to Va. bar, 1950; commonwealth atty., Va., 1954-66; additional judge 37th Jud. Circuit, Va., 1966-68, sr. judge, 1968—. Served to lt. (j.g.) USNR, 1946. Decorated Purple Heart. Mason. Home: 4701 Bruce Rd Chester VA 23831 Office: Courthouse Chesterfield VA 23832

GATES, GRIFFITH GRANVILLE, mus. curator; b. Newark, Nov. 20, 1921; s. Rupert Granville and Anne (Williams) G.; B.S., U. Tex., 1951; m. Bobbie Jane Atchley, Feb. 19, 1960; 1 son, Paul Atchley. Dir. arts and crafts div. spl. services U.S. Army, Ft. Sam Houston, Tex., 1959-63, Ft. Sill, Okla., 1963-66, asst. dir. U.S. Army Field Arty. Mus., 1966—. Pres., Lawton-Ft. Sill Art Council (Okla.), 1968-71; scoutmaster Boy Scouts Am., Lawton-Ft. Sill Art Council (Okla.), 1968-71; scoutmaster Boy Scouts Am., Lawton, Okla., 1972—. Bd. dirs. Lawton Heritage Assn., Inc., 1973—. Served with USNR, 1943-46. Mem. Am. Assn. Museums, Okla. Hist. Soc., S.W. Watercolor Soc. Home: 5108 NW Elm Av Lawton OK 73501 Office: US Army Field Artillery Museum Fort Sill OK 73503

GATES, HOWARD MARION, coll. adminstr.; b. Huntington, Tex., May 3, 1920; s. Davis Beauregard and Cora Stella (Richardson) G.; B.B.A., Stephen F. Austin State U., 1943; M.S., Tex. A. and M. U.,

1944; m. Maggie Hazel McKeown, Dec. 26, 1955. Claim investigator Mo. Pacific R.R., Palestine, Tex., 1945-56; accountant, Tex. A. and M. U. System, College Station, 1956-65; bus. mgr. Tex. State Tech. Inst., Waco, 1965-68; bus. mgr. Angelina Coll., Lufkin, Tex., 1968—. Served with AUS, 1945. Mem. Tex. Assn. Pub. Jr. Coll. Bus. Officers (pres. 1973-74), Tex. State Tchrs. Assn., Nat. Assn. Accountants (sec. chpt., charter mem.). Methodist (mem. adminstrv. bd.). Home: 1404 Sleepy Hollow Lufkin TX 75901 Office: PO Box 1768 Lufkin TX 75901

GATES, MAC STUART, clergyman, sch. adminstr.; b. Romeo, Mich., June 24, 1914; s. Ernest E. and Mary (Stuart) G.; student Moody Bible Inst., 1942-44; B.A. cum laude, Ouachita Bapt. U., 1948; student U. Ark., 1950, 53; M.S. in Edn., Henderson State Tchrs. Coll., 1956; m. Mary E. Brown, Jan. 21, 1949; step-children—Mary P. (Mrs. William L. Parker), Rual T. Lee. Ordained to ministry Bapt. Ch., 1945; pastor-evangelist, 1940-48; pastor Glenwood (Ill.) United Ch., 1944-45, 1st Bapt. Ch., Bingen, Ark., 1945-49, Walnut Valley Ch., 1950-56, Riverside Ch., Donaldson, Ark., 1956-59; adminstr. Malvern (Ark.) pub. schs., 1948—; mission pastor 1st Bapt. Ch., Malvern, 1959-65; prin. Malvern Jr. High Sch.; pastor 2d Bapt. Ch., Bryant, Ark., Salem Bapt. Ch., Benton, Ark., 1970-72, Mountain Valley Bapt. Ch., Hot Springs, Ark., 1972—; lectr. series, Edn., Now, 1965—. Mem. Hot Spring County Library Bd., 1955-57; sec., publicity dir. Malvern City Planning Commn., 1952-65; mem. State Com. Guidance and Selection Audio-Visual Materials; chmn. Malvern Housing Authority, 1966-74; chmn. Malvern Civil Service Commn., 1973. Mem. Photographers Internat. Assn., Nat., Ark., Hot Spring County (pres. 1956-57) edn. assns., Ark. Hist. Assn., Ouachita Valley Schoolmasters Assn. (past pres.), Ams. United for Separation of Ch. and State (Malvern pres. 1973), Phi Delta Kappa (historian Henderson State Coll. chpt. 1970). Home: 2017 Wilson Malvern AR 72104 Office: 1910 Roosevelt St Malvern AR 72104

GATES, WILLIAM FRED, JR., bishop; b. Lexington, Va., Mar. 29, 1912; s. William Fred and Edna (Brundige) G.; student Hobart Coll., 1931-32; A.B., U. Chattanooga, 1934; B.D., Va. Theol. Sem., 1937, D.D., 1967; D.D., U. of South, 1967; m. Jane Gregory Dillard, Apr. 25, 1938; children—Anne Gregory, Susan Wenrick. Ordained priest Episcopal Ch., 1938; asst. minister Calvary Episcopal Ch., Memphis, 1937-38; priest-in-charge St. John's Ch., Old Hickory, Tenn., 1938-42; rector St. Peter's Ch., Columbia, Tenn., 1943-66; suffragan bishop Episcopal Diocese Tenn., Memphis, 1966—, also mem. bishop and council, standing com., bd. examining chaplains. Chmn. Maury County chpt. A.R.C., 1947-49; pres. Maury County United Givers Fund, 1965-66. Mem. Kappa Alpha. Club: Memphis Country. Home: 5302 Southwood Dr Memphis TN 38117 Office: 692 Poplar Av Memphis TN 38105

GATEWOOD, MAUD F., artist; b. Yanceyville, N.C., Jan. 8, 1934; d. J. Yancey and Mary Lea (Florance) Gatewood; A.B., U. N.C. Woman's Coll., 1954; M.A., Ohio State U., 1955; postgrad. Harvard, summer 1957, U. Vienna, Acad. of Applied Arts Vienna, 1962-63. Instr. art Huntingdon Coll., 1956-58, Tex. Christian U., 1959-62; faculty U. N.C. at Charlotte, 1964-73; one man shows at Heath Gallery, Atlanta, U. N.C. at Greensboro, Mint Mus. Art, Winston-Salem Gallery Fine Arts; exhibited in group shows at N.C. Mus. Art, Library of Congress, Dallas Mus. Fine Arts, Denver Mus., many others; represented in permanent collections Mint Mus., N.C. Nat. Bank, pvt. collections. Fulbright grantee, 1962-63. Home: 2309 Pender Pl Charlotte NC 28209

GATLIFF, BEN FRANKLIN, physician; b. Macon, Ga., Jan. 19, 1922; s. Benjamin and Mellie (Corley) G.; B.S., U. Ga., 1948; M.D., Med. Coll. Ga., 1952; m. Marion Hays, Aug. 19, 1950; children—Gary Edwin, Eda Marie, Laural Francis. Intern, Orange Meml. Hosp., Orlando, Fla., 1952-53; pvt. practice medicine specializing in gen. practice, Plant City, Fla., 1953—; staff mem. South Fl. Bapt. Hosp., Plant City, chief of staff, 1959-60. Served from pvt. to T/5, AUS, 1943-45. Mem. A.M.A., Fla. Med. Assn., Theta Kappa Psi. Episcopalian. Named Ky. col. Home: 716 Pinedale Dr Plant City FL 33566 Office: 402 Dort St Plant City FL 33566

GATTIS, ELVIS FRANKLIN, sheet metal contractor; b. Jacksonville, Tex., Aug. 21, 1932; s. Arnett M. and Bertha A. (Yancy) G.; student U. Houston, 1972-73; m. Annie Joyce Ermel, June 20, 1953; children—Elvera, Gary, Lera, Jerry. With Straus-Frank Co., Houston, 1951-53, 1954-58, A & M Sheet Metal, Houston, 1958-59; owner E.F. Gattis Sheet Metal, Houston, 1959-66; pres. Gattis Inc., Houston, 1966—. Mem. Houston Sheet Metal Contractors Assn. (dir. 1969-70), Am. Soc. Heating, Refrigerating and Air-Conditioning Engrs., Nat. Assn. Sheet Metal and Air-Conditioning Contractors, Tex. Environmental Balancing Bur. Baptist. Woodman of the World. Home: 746 Suebarnett Houston TX 77218 Office: 1615 Keene Houston TX 77009

GATTIS, JOHN EDWARD, electronic engr.; b. Paris, Ark., Mar. 29, 1934; s. Clark Edward and Jewell Linda (Titsworth) G.; student Ark. Tech. Coll., 1953-54; B.S. Elec. Engring., U. Ark., 1961; m. Alma Dean Dorrough, Mar. 13, 1955; 1 dau., Pamela Kay. Electronic engr. Western Electric Co., Inc., Winston-Salem, N.C., 1961-63; aerospace engr. Saturn IB, Saturn V, Apollo and Skylab space programs NASA, Marshall Space Flight Center, Huntsville, Ala., 1963—. Served with AUS, 1954-57. Recipient Apollo achievement award NASA, 1969, Outstanding Performance award, 1972. Registered profl. engr., Ala. Baptist. Home: 10117 Dunbarton Dr SE Huntsville AL 35803 Office: S & E ASTR C Marshall Space Flight Center AL 35812

GATTO, DAVID KEITH, savs. and loan exec.; b. L.I., N.Y., Sept. 23, 1940; s. Lucio Ernest and Janice (Sedorchuk) G.; B.A., Tulane U., 1962; m. Jean Owens Jeffers, June 9, 1962; children—David Keith, Alexander Owens, Gregory Jeffers. Real estate appraiser, mortgage loan underwriter New Orleans office Equitable Life Assurance Soc., 1962-67; dir., exec. v.p., pres. New Orleans Fed. Savs. & Loan Assn., 1967—; dir., exec. v.p. Capital Funds, Inc. Comml. and indsl. real estate cons. Panel chmn. com. on agy. relations United Fund of New Orleans, 1969—; mem. men's adv. com. YWCA, New Orleans, 1969—, New Orleans Home for Incurables, 1971—; treas. La. Hist. Soc., 1971-73. Bd. dirs. Sara Mayo Hosp. Mem. Internat. Wine and Food Soc. London (sec. New Orleans chpt.), Guild of Sommeliers, Soc. Bacchus, Phi Kappa Sigma. Clubs: Metairie Country, Plimsoll, Round Table; City (Baton Rouge). Home: 345 Walnut St New Orleans LA 70118 Office: 4948 Chef Menteur Hwy New Orleans LA 70126

GATTON, ROBERT LAURENCE, headmaster; b. Ft. Wayne, Ind., Sept. 21, 1937; s. James Walter and Virginia Evelyn (Geyer) G.; B.A., Union Coll., 1960, M.A. (Nat. Def. Edn. Act fellow), 1963; postgrad. U. Ky., 1964-65; Ed.D. (U.S. Office Edn. fellow, W.K. Kellogg Found. fellow), U. Fla., 1971; m. Christine Dale Banks, Jan. 22, 1960; children—Robert Earl, Melissa Anne. Tchr. English and social studies Cumberland (Ky.) High Sch., 1960-61, Whitesburg (Ky.) High Sch., 1961-64; tchr., prin. Eolia (Ky.) Consol. Sch., 1966-69; dean Brenau Acad., Gainesville, Ga., 1971-72; headmaster Wilkes Acad., Washington, Ga., 1972—. Dir. Washington-Wilkes Youth Center. Mem. Am. Assn. Sch. Adminstrs. (life) N.E.A., Jaycees, Pi Gamma Mu, Kappa Delta Pi, Phi Delta Kappa. Home: 201 W Robert Toombs Av Washington GA 20673

GATTON, T(HOMAS) HARRY, banking assn. exec.; b. Harmony, N.C., Mar. 10, 1918; s. Thomas Lee and Freddie Cornelia (Moore) G.; A.B., U. N.C., 1940; m. Mary Louise Gordon, Sept. 12, 1942. Newspaper reporter Statesville (N.C.) Daily Record, 1941-42; engaged in broadcasting sta. mgmt., 1946-50; charge radio savs. bond. div. Treasury Dept., 1951-53; administrv. asst. to U.S. Senator Lennon, 1953-54; exec. sec. to U.S. Senator Ervin, 1954-60; exec. dir. N.C. Bankers Assn., 1960-67, exec. v.p., 1967—, also editor, mgr. Tarheel Banker mag. Mem. Am. Battle Monuments Commn., 1961-69, Statesville Civil Service Commn., 1947-48. Chmn. bd. trustees Sch. Banking of South, La. State U.; registrar-treas. N.C. Sch. Banking, U. N.C.; mem. exec. bd. N.C. Dept. Archives and History, vice chmn., 1965-72, chmn., 1972-73; chmn. N.C. Hist. Commn., 1973—; mem. George Washington Statue Commn., 1968-71; mem. presdl. adv. bd. Campbell Coll., N.C., 1968—; mem. bus. adv. council Peace Coll., chmn., 1971—; bd. dirs. Southeastern Trust Sch., Campbell Coll. Alternate del. Democratic Nat. Conv., 1956; dir. orgn. Young Dem. Clubs N.C., 1950; pres. N.C. Dem. Club, 1958-59. Served with USNR, 1942-45; lt. comdr. Res. Mem. N.C. Lit. and Hist. Soc., Civil War Round Table D.C., Am. Bankers Assn. (bd. dirs. 1971-72, chmn. state assn. div. 1971-72), Conf. So. Banking Assn. Execs. (pres. 1964-65), N.C. Soc. for Preservation of Antiquities (v.p. 1965-66, pres. 1967-70), N.C. Soc. Assn. Execs. (pres. 1973-74), Wake County Hist. Soc. (pres. 1967-68), Order Golden Fleece, U.S. Senate Adminstrv. Assts. and Secs. Club, Newcomen Soc. Methodist. Mason, Rotarian (pres. 1971-72). Home: 3012 Eton Rd Raleigh NC 27608 Office: 3709 National Dr Raleigh NC 27612

GATZKE, DELMAR ERWIN, housewares mfg. co exec.; b. Auburn, Wis., Nov. 29, 1929; s. Norbert H. and Laura (Backhaus) G.; B. in M.E., Marquette U., 1965; m. Anita C. Brinkmann, Oct. 17, 1953; children—Jean, Paul, David, Diane. Prodn. worker The West Bend Co. (Wis.), 1949-54, indsl. engr., 1954-59, indsl. engring. coordinator, 1959-62, indsl. engring. supr., 1962-65, resident mgr. Sheridan (Ark.) div., 1965—. Sec., dir. Grant County Bank, 1972—. Vice pres. dist. Quapaw council Boy Scouts Am., 1967-68, 73—; mem. Grant County Health Adv. Council, 1970-72, pres., 1972; mem. Sheridan City Planning Commn., 1967—; chmn. Bd. Zoning Adjustment, 1968—; mem. Grant County Family Planning Com., 1972—. Bd. dirs. Grant County Indsl. Devel. Commn., 1966—. Served with AUS, 1951-53. Mem. Soc. Advancement Mgmt., Am. Soc. M.E., Grant County C. of C. (1st v.p. 1968-69, pres. 1970, dir. 1973—), Grant County Wildlife Fedn. (pres., dir. 1971-72). Lutheran. Rotarian (v.p. club). Club: Sheridan Golf and Country (dir. 1973—) Home: Route 1 Box 4G Sheridan AR 72150 Office: Route 1 Box 291B Sheridan AR 72150

GAUB, MARGARET LUISE, physician; b. Guatemala City, Guatemala (parents Am. citizens); d. William H. and Margaret (Lattelle) Gaub; B.S. cum laude, U. Wash., 1954, M.D. (Ethel Young Phillips scholar, Group Health Coop. scholar, Nat. Found. Infantile Paralysis fellow, Nat. Inst. Mental Health grantee), 1960. Research asst. zoology dept. U. Wash., 1951, asst. poliomyelitis lab., 1953, research asst. microbiology dept., 1953-54, research asst. for U.S. Army, pharmacology dept., 1959; bacteriologist Seattle-King County Dept. Health, 1954-56; intern surgery Jackson Meml. Hosp., Miami, Fla., 1960-61, resident surgery, 1961-63; research fellow anesthesiology U. Miami Sch. Medicine, 1963-65, resident anesthesiology, 1965-66, instr. anesthesiology, 1966-70, asst. prof. anesthesiology, 1970—; practice medicine specializing in pediatric anesthesiology, 1966—. Mem. Dade County Opera Guild, Greater Miami Philharmonic Soc., 1965—. Recipient Anna C. Dunlap prize Soroptomist Club, 1958-59. Diplomate Am. Bd. Anesthesiology. Fellow Am. Coll. Anesthesiologists; mem. Phi Beta Kappa, Sigma Xi, (asso.) Phi Sigma, Alpha Epsilon Delta, Iota Sigma Pi, Sigma Epsilon Sigma, Alpha Xi Delta. Contbr. articles to profl. jours. Home: 2451 Brickell Av Apt 21-S Miami FL 33129

GAUCHER, DONALD HOLMAN, pub. affairs exec.; b. Port Arthur, Tex., Aug. 2, 1931; s. Leon Philip and Hattie Lu (Holman) G.; B.A., Rice Inst., 1953, B.S., 1954; postgrad. Oak Ridge Sch. Reactor Tech., 1955-56; J.D., U. Houston, 1963; m. Jane Peel Heyck, June 15, 1957; children—Susan Heyck, Beverly Jane. Research engr. Humble Prodn. Research Co., Houston, 1958-61; corporate planner Humble Oil & Refining Co., Houston, 1961-65, Standard Oil of N.J., N.Y.C., 1965-68; pub. affairs planner Exxon Co. U.S.A., Houston, 1968—. Home: 5561 Bordley St Houston TX 77027 Office: PO Box 2180 Houston TX 77001

GAUDIN, HOMER CHARLES, judge; b. New Orleans, July 14, 1930; s. Regis B. and Inez C. (Grenier) G.; B.A., U. Southwestern La., 1952; LL.B., Loyola U., New Orleans, 1958; postgrad. La. State U., 1950, U. Pa., 1967, U. Nev., 1970; m. Myra Elizabeth Altman, June 8, 1956; children—Melanee Anne, Monique Grenier, Charles Altman. Head football and basketball coach St. Paul's Coll., Covington, La., 1954-55; sports columnist New Orleans States-Item newspaper, 1956-66; admitted to La. bar, 1958; practiced in New Orleans and Gretna, La., 1958-66; dist. judge 24th Jud. Dist. Ct., Gretna, 1966—. State pres. Nat. Cystic Fibrosis Research Found. Served with USAF, 1952-54. Mem. Am., La., Jefferson Parish bar assns., La. Dist. Judges Assn. (dir.), Am. Judicature Soc., N. Am. Judges Assn., Fourth Circuit Judges Assn. (pres.), V.F.W., Amvets, Delta Theta Phi. Roman Catholic. Clubs: Lions, Timberlane Country (dir. 1964—). Home: 28 Farnham Pl Metairie LA 70005 Office: New Parish Courthouse Gretna LA 70053

GAUGH, FAY MERTON, army officer; b. Springfield, O., Aug. 4, 1910; s. Lee and Mellie (Campbell) G.; M.A., George Peabody Coll., 1955; D.D., Am. Bible Coll., 1943; m. Jessie Studebaker, Oct. 25, 1934; children—Joanna (Mrs. Robert Swyers), Brenda (Mrs. Harold Stout, Jr.), Jon Lee. Regional supr. USO, 1941; asst. prin. Sch. for Officers' Tng., 1963; city comdr. Salvation Army, Birmingham, 1964-71, Tulsa, 1971—. Brig. gen. on staff Tenn. Gov. Mem. Nat. Assn. Social Workers, Acad. Certified Social Workers. Author: Social Work Practice, 1962. Address: 2329 Westfield Rd Charlotte NC 28207

GAUNT, WILBUR MARTIN, JR., dairy products assn. adminstr., b. Berryville, Va., Jan. 11, 1918; s. Wilbur Martin and Carmen (Pierce) G.; B.S. in Agr., Va. Poly. Inst., Blacksburg, 1939; m. Phyllis Jeanette Morris, Sept. 26, 1942; children—Sharon Jeanette, Carmen Annette (Mrs. Cary Breckinridge Bowen). Supr. for U.S. Dept. Agr., five counties in Va., 1939-41; mng. dir. Southeastern & Va. Chain Store Council, Richmond, 1946-65, also exec. v.p., 1952-65; exec. v.p. Va. Dairy Products Assn., Richmond, 1965—. Dir. Va. Agrl. Bus. Council, Inc. Mem. Adv. Com. Va. Poly. Inst. Coll. Agr., 1961-62. Pres. Va. Food Council, 1957-63; mem. Richmond Dem. Com., 1967—. Bd. dirs. United Givers Fund, Richmond, 1957-64. Served from 2d lt. to lt. col., inf., AUS, 1941-46; ETO. Recipient Virginia Pub. Relations award, 1952; named Businessman of Year Va. Assn. Distributive Edn. Clubs Am., 1957. Mem. Va. Soc. Execs., Richmond Pub. Relations Assn., Va. Press Assn., Va. C. of C., Internat. Assn. Ice Cream Mfrs., Dairy Assn. Execs. Conf., Am. Soc. Execs. Clubs: Willow Oaks Country, Commonwealth. Home: 3416 Northview Place Richmond VA 23225 Office: Suite 1520 700 E Main St Richmond VA 23219

GAUSMAN, HAROLD WESLEY, physiologist; b. Morris, Minn., Dec. 23, 1921; s. Emil Henry and Kate Emma (Heick) G.; B.S. with distinction, U. Me., 1949; M.S., U. Ill., 1950, Ph.D., 1952; m. Laura Ellen Davis, Feb. 3, 1945; 1 son, Donald Harris. Research asst. U. Ill., Urbana, 1949-52; scientist Tex. A. and M. U., College Station, 1952-54; research specialist Rutgers U., New Brunswick, N.J., 1954-55; faculty U. Me., Orono, 1955-67, prof. soil chemistry, 1957-67; plant physiologist U.S. Dept. Agr., Agrl. Research Service, Weslaco, Tex., 1967—. Radiation protection officer U. Me., Orono, 1956-60, chmn. grad. faculty, Coll. Agrl., 1965-66. Served with USAAF, 1942-45. Recipient NSF Research fellowship, 1964. Mem. Am. Soc. Agronomy, Am. Inst. Biol. Scis., Am. Soc. Plant Physiology, A.A.A.S., Societas Physiologiae Plantarum Scandinavia, Sigma Xi, Phi Kappa Phi, Alpha Zeta, Gamma Sigma Delta, Phi Sigma. Contbr. articles in field to profl. jours. Home: 502 W 11th St Weslaco TX 78596 Office: Box 267 Weslaco TX 78596

GAUTIER, NEWTON PERRY, supt. schs.; b. Gautier, Miss., Mar. 16, 1926; s. Newton Houston and May Omega (Golden) G.; student Perkinston Jr. Coll., 1948, Miss. State U., 1948-49; B.S., U. So. Miss., 1951, M.Ed., 1961; m. Dixie Ann Wieder, Jan. 2, 1953; children—Choyce Mayo, Elizabeth Ann. Tchr., Vancleave Consol. Sch., 1949-52, Pascagoula High Sch., 1952-53; tchr. Ocean Springs High Sch., 1953-54, prin., 1954-59, 65-66; supt. edn. Jackson County, 1960-64; supt. schs. Pascagoula (Miss.) Municipal Separate Sch. Dist., 1966—. Chmn. Jackson County chpt. A.R.C., 1964; pres. Jackson County Heart Fund, 1969. Trustee Miss. Gulf Coast Jr. Coll., 1960-64. Served with USNR, 1944-46. Mem. Am. Assn. Sch. Adminstrs. (state membership chmn. 1970-71), Council Pub. Schs. (pres. 1971-72, v.p. 1970-71, sec.-treas. 1967-70), Miss. Assn. Sch. Adminstrs., Miss. Supts. Assn. (exec. dir.), Miss. (resolutions com. 1967-68, credentials com. 1969-70, dir. 1973), Pascagoula (pres. 1968-69) edn. assns., Pascagoula-Moss Point Area C. of C., Phi Delta Kappa. Rotarian. Methodist (mem. adminstrv. bd. 1953). Home: PO Box 237 Gautier MS 39553 Office: PO Box 250 Pascagoula MS 39567

GAVAZZI, ALADINO A., govt. hosp. adminstr.; b. Exeter, Pa., July 24, 1922; s. Guido and Ambrozina (O'Brien) G.; B.S., Columbia, 1953, M.H.A., 1955; m. Nancylee Ray, June 21, 1958; children—William A., Alan Lee, Michael Joseph, Ann Marie, Lisa Kathryn. Adminstrv. officer VA, N.Y.C., 1946-50, med. adminstrv. officer VA Hosp., Bklyn. and Bronx, N.Y., 1950-53, hosp. adminstr. VA Hosp., Hampton, Va., 1955-57, Chgo., 1957-59, Dwight, Ill., 1960-62, Mt. Alto, Wash., 1963-64, asso. dir. hosp. constrn., Washington, 1964-65, dir. center, Martinsburg, W. Va., 1965-68, exec. asst. to chief med. dir. VA Dept. Medicine and Surgery, 1958-70, exec. dir. adminstrn. Dept. Medicine and Surgery, 1970-73, now adminstr. dir. VA Hosp., Washington; hosp. adminstrn. resident Bronx, Beth Israel and Presbyn. hosps., N.Y.C., 1953-54; profl. lectr. health care adminstrn. George Washington U. Served with AUS, 1950-55; col. Res. Fellow Am. Coll. Hosp. Adminstrs., Royal Soc. Health London; mem. Am. Hosp. Assn., Am. Assn. Hosp. Planners, Assn. Am. Med. Colls., Assn. Mil. Surgeons U.S., Fed. Execs. Inst. (chmn.), Exec. Adminstrn. Alumni Assn. (v.p.). Home: 16541 Dahlia Ct McLean VA 22101 Office: 50 Irving St NW Washington DC 20422

GAW, JAMES RICHARD, auditorium mgr.; b. Owensboro, Ky., July 12, 1926; s. James William and Josephine (Thompson) G.; student Owensboro Bus. Coll., Brescia Coll.; m. Alma Irene Knott, Aug. 16, 1952; children—Stephen Thomas, Barbara, Monica, James Gerard, Angela, Theresa. Prodn. mgr. Murphy-Miller, Inc., Owensboro, 1947-48; asst. mgr. Owensboro Sportscenter, 1949-52, mgr., 1958—; partner Elite Cigar Co., Owensboro, 1952-57, Magistrate, Daviess County, Owensboro, 1958-61. Pres. Young Democrats Daviess County, 1955; sec. exec. com. Daviess County Dem. Com., 1960-64. Bd. dirs. Spastic Home and Sch., Owensboro, 1956—, chmn., 1959-60. Named Ky. col., 1955. Mem. Internat. Assn. Auditorium Mgrs., Ky. Parks Soc., Ky. Magistrates Assn. (pres. 1960-61), Owensboro Jr. C. of C. (pres. 1954), Ice Skating Inst. Am. (dir.). Democrat. Roman Catholic. K.C., Elk, Moose. Home: 1810 Cecelia Ct Owensboro KY 42301 Office: Owensboro Sportscenter 12th St and Hickman Av Owensboro KY 42301

GAWARECKI, STEPHEN JEROME, geologist; b. Newark, July 31, 1929; s. Stephen and Bertha (Lapinski) G.; student Seton Hall U., 1946-49; B.S., Rutgers U., 1951, M.S., 1952; Ph.D., U. Colo., 1963; m. Carolyn Ann Grosse, Apr. 3, 1954; children—Susan Lynn, Cathy Ann. Geologist N.J. Zinc Co., Gilman, Colo., Friedensville, Pa., 1952-53; geologist Doeringsfeld, Amuedo & Ivey, Denver, 1953-62; geologist U.S. Geol. Survey, Washington, 1962—, now staff geologist remote sensing activities Office Internat. Geology. Treas., Holmes Run Valley Citizens Assn., 1971. Served to lt. USNR, 1953-57. Mem. Am. Soc. Photogrammetry, Geol. Soc. Washington, A.A.A.S., Sigma Xi. Club: Rutgers (pres. 1967-69) (Washington). Home: 7018 Vagabond Dr Falls Church VA 22042 Office: 12201 Sunrise Valley Dr Reston VA 22092

GAXIOLA, FRANCISCO JOSE, lawyer; b. Mexico City, D.F., Mex., Apr. 21, 1942; s. F. Jorge and Eloina (de Haro) G.; law degree Escuela Libre de Derecho, 1967; LL.M., Nat. U. Mexico, 1969; m. Cecilia Cuevas, Oct. 5, 1967; children—Cecilia, Francisco Jose, Diego, Lorena. Admitted to Mexican bar 1967; atty. Treasury Dept., Mexico City, 1965-69, Instituto Mexicano del Seguro Social, 1967-69; gen. counsel Union Carbide Mexicana, S.A., 1969-73; mem. firm Ogarrio, Narro y Gaxiola, Mexico City, 1973—. Prof., Escuela Libre de Derecho, Mexico City, 1968-69. Mem. Mexican, Interam. bar assns., Asociacion Nacional de Abogagos de Empresa. Author: Los Altos Funcionarios Publicos, 1967. Home: 18 Cerrada Hda de los Morales 10 Mexico Office: Lucerna 80 Piso 5 Mexico 6 D F Mexico

GAY, BIRDIE SPIVEY, librarian; b. Atlanta, Mar. 13, 1918; d. Charlie Warren and Bertha (Harris) Spivey; A.B., Morris Brown Coll., 1939; M.S. in L.S., Atlanta U., 1962; m. Howard Donald Gay, Nov. 24, 1943. Mem. staff, faculty E.R. Carter Elementary Sch., Atlanta, 1946—, librarian, 1959-70, media specialist, 1970—. Mem. com. on adminstrn. YWCA, Atlanta, 1969-72; neighborhood chmn. fund drive Easter Seal Drive, 1968-71. Named Tchr. of Year, E.R. Carter Elementary Sch., 1961. Mem. Am. Bus. Women's Assn., Beta Phi Mu, Sigma Gamma Rho. Club: Nancy Bridge (Atlanta). Home: 1874 Penelope Rd NW Atlanta GA 30314 Office: 80 Ashby St NW Atlanta GA 30314

GAY, JACOB DOUGLAS, JR., business exec.; b. Lexington, Ky., Apr. 4, 1910; s. Jacob Douglas and Lucy Field (Graddy) G.; B.S., Trinity Coll., 1934; m. Elizabeth Caldwell, 1936 (dec. 1968); children—Monnie (Mrs. Joseph Owens), Elizabeth (Mrs. William J. Wood), Juliet (Mrs. Steve Sivils); m. 2d, Corrine Norton, Sept. 5, 1970. Owner, Brookview Farms, Pine Grove, Ky., 1934—; partner Sphar & Gay Seed Co., Pine Grove, 1937—; pres. Gay-Bell Corp., Paris, Ky., 1946—. Dir. WLEX-TV, Lexington, 1955—, Am. Livestock Ins. Co., Geneva, Ill., 1952—, First Security Nat. Bank & Trust Co., Lexington, 1941—; mem. exec. com. Bankers Land Corp., Lexington, 1960—. Mem. Bluegrass Seed Com., Lexington, 1966-68. Bd. govs. Transylvania U., Lexington, 1946—, bd. curators, 1958—, mem. exec. com., 1948—. Mem. Am. (dir. 1950-56, pres. 1954-55), Ky. (dir. 1947—) Hereford assns., Nat. Cattlemen's Assn. Mem. Christian Ch. Clubs: Lexington (dir. 1960—), Idle Hour Country,

Lafayette, Iriquois Hunt (Lexington); Naples Yacht, Royal Poinciana Golf, (Naples, Fla.); Mountain Brook (Birmingham, Ala.). Home: Brookview Farms Pine Grove KY 40470 Office: WLEX-TV Inc PO Box 1457 Lexington KY 40501

GAY, JAMES FERBEE, pharm. co. exec.; b. Norfolk, Va., Dec. 9, 1942; s. Milton F. and Thelma (Henderson) G.; B.S., Norfolk State Coll., 1965; J.D., U. Va., 1968. Admitted to Va. bar, 1968; market analyst, legal officer Allied Chem. Internat., N.Y.C., 1968-69; asst. to pres. Nat. Bus. League, Washington, 1969, adv. counsel, 1973—; pres. Coastal Pharm. Co., Inc., Norfolk, Va., 1970—; pres. Ghent Arms Corp., Aqua Dynamics, Ltd., Global Dynamica Ltd. Pres., Va. Coll. Young Democrats, 1967. Pres., Tidewater Area Bus. League, 1971. Bd. dirs. United Cancer Assn., Planned Parenthood, Norfolk Soc. for Prevention Cruelty to Animals; trustee Norfolk State Coll. Found., Coastal Pharm. Edn. Found. Recipient Pres.'s award Tidewater Area Bus. League, 1972; Phi Beta Lambda Bus. Leadership award, 1973. Mem. Va., Old Dominion, Norfolk-Portsmouth bar assns., Alpha Phi Alpha. Mem. Ch. of Christ (trustee). Co-author: Rhodes Directory of Black Dentists in the U.S., 1973. Home: 1232 Westover Av Norfolk VA 23507 Office: 2509 Granby St Norfolk VA 23517

GAY, LEONARD OMAR, retail furniture exec.; b. Georgetown, Ga., Mar. 13, 1919; s. Lee Omar and Emmelle (Hammack) G.; B.B.A.; Emory U., 1941; m. Augusta Hixon, June 10, 1942; children—Emily June, Leonard O. Sr. accountant Ernst & Ernst, Atlanta, 1941-47; v.p., treas. Haverty Furniture Cos., Inc., Atlanta, 1947—, dir., 1961—. Dir. Atlanta Better Bus. Bur., 1974-76. Bd. dirs. Atlanta council Camp Fire Girls, Inc.; trustee Tift Coll.; mem. parents adv. council Wofford Coll., Spartanburg, S.C. Served as ensign USNR, 1941. Mem. Financial Execs. Inst. (treas. 1966-67), Ga. Soc. C.P.A.'s, Nat. Assn. Cost Accountants (asso. dir.), Nat. Home Furnishings Assn. (dir. 1970—, chmn. govtl. affairs com. 1972—, mem. mgmt. devel. faculty Northwestern U. 1972, 73), Atlanta Tax Club, C. of C., DeKalb County Grand Jurors Assn., Alpha Kappa Psi. Baptist (chmn. bd. deacons 1967). Home: 1534 Victoria Falls Dr NE Atlanta GA 30329 Office: 866 W Peachtree St NW Atlanta GA 30308

GAY, WILLIAM WALLACE, telephone co. exec.; b. Meridian, Miss., Jan. 18, 1928; s. William Raymond and Lula Mae (Lucy) G.; B.S., U. So. Miss., 1951, M.A., 1953; m. Mary Elizabeth Trussell, Aug. 21, 1949; 1 son, William Alan. Tchr., Forrest County (Miss.) Schs., 1951-52; instr. extension dept. U. So. Miss., 1951-53; jr. engr. So. Bell Telephone Co., Jackson, Miss., 1953-55, statis. accountant, Atlanta, 1955-59, staff statistician, 1959-65, supervising statistician, 1965-68; bus. research mgr. S. Central Bell Telephone Co., Birmingham, Ala., 1968—. Precinct leader DeKalb County (Ga.) Republican Party, 1966-68; mem. DeKalb County Rep. Exec. Com., 1967-68; mem. 4th Congl. Dist. Ga. Rep. Exec. Com., 1967-68. Served with USAAF, 1945-48. Mem. Am. Marketing Assn. (v.p., dir. Birmingham chpt.). Club: Optimist of Shades Valley (pres. Homewood, Ala. 1971-72). Home: 3273 Brashford Rd Birmingham AL 35216 Office: PO Box 532 Birmingham AL 35201

GAY, WILTON CARLYLE, banker, pub. relations exec.; b. Rocky Mount, N.C., Oct. 7, 1923; s. Oliver Lee and Deborah Ruth (Worsley) G.; B.S. in Bus. Adminstrn., U. N.C., 1948; m. Mary Elizabeth Peirson, May 14, 1955; children—Wilton Carlyle, Deborah Elizabeth. Pub. relations officer Planters Nat. Bank & Trust Co., Rocky Mount, 1954-56, asst. v.p., 1956-58, v.p. advt., 1958—. Bd. dirs. Edgecombe County ABC, 1969—, Braswell Pub. Library, 1968-70, Rocky Mount Arts Center Bd., 1968-70, N.C. Wesleyan Coll. Area Found., 1966-70. Served with USNR, 1943-46. Recipient various advt. awards. Mem. Bank Marketing Assn. Kiwanian. Presbyn. Home: 956 Tarboro St Rocky Mount NC 27801 Office: 131 N Church St Rocky Mount NC 27801

GAYHARTT, HOMER, aerospace exec.; b. Hardburley, Ky., Mar. 30, 1920; s. Curtis and Martha (Williams) G.; diploma, Coyne Elec. Sch., 1938; student Brevard Jr. Coll., 1965, 68-69; m. Dorothy McAdam, Mar. 1, 1947; children—Mary Anne, James Curtis. Joined USN as elec. supr., 1939, advanced to chief warrant officer, 1952; tech. adviser Turkish Navy, 1948-49; spl. weapons assembly officer atomic, Albuquerque, 1952-54; ret., 1959; field insp. Titan Missile, Martin Co., Cocoa Beach, Fla., 1960; supr. Minuteman Launch Complexes, aerospace div. Pan Am. World Airways. Cape Canaveral Air Force Sta., 1960-71; supr. Unmanned Launch Vehicle Complexes, Aerospace div. Pan Am. World Airways, Cape Canaveral Air Force Sta., 1972-73, supr. Polaris, Poseidon, Trident Launch Complexes, Aerospace div., 1973—. Mem. Ret. Officers Assn. Club: Indian River Yacht (commodore) (Cocoa, Fla.). Home: 42 Scott Lane Rockledge FL 32955 Office: Pan Am World Airways Aerospace Div Patrick AFB FL 32931

GAYLORD, EDWARD KING, pub. co. exec.; b. Muscotah, Kan., Mar. 5, 1873; s. George Lewis and Eunice M. (Edwards) G.; student Colo. Coll., 1894-97, LL.D., 1936; studied law at Cororado Springs, 1900-02; m. Inex Kinney, Dec. 29, 1914; children—Edith Kinney, Edward Lewis, Virginia Elizabeth. Clerk of Dist. Court. Colorado Springs and Cripple Creek, 1897-1900; telegraph editor, editorial writer Colorado Springs Telegraph, 1901; bus. mgr. St. Joseph Gazette 1902; gen. mgr. Daily Oklahoman, Oklahoma City Times, Okla. Farmer-Stockman, 1903—; pres. Oklahoma Pub. Co., 1918—, pub. editor The Daily Oklahoman, Oklahoma Times; pres. Mistletoe Express Co., chmn. bd. WKY Television Systems, Inc.; dir. Southland Paper Mills, Inc., Lufkin, Tex. Mem. commn. in charge constrn. Okla. State Capitol, 1916. Pres. Oklahoma City C. of C., 1915. Mem. A.P., Am., So. Newspaper editors assns. Democrat. Conglist. Mason. Home: 6907 Avondale Av Oklahoma City OK 73116 Office: 500 N Broadway Oklahoma City OK 73102

GAYLORD, WILLIAM STANDISH, JR., investment co. exec.; b. N.Y.C., July 20, 1907; s. William Standish and Mary Ellen (Coonley) G.; grad. Kent. Sch., 1925; B.A., Yale, 1960; M.B.A., Harvard, 1932; m. Mary Tuttle Simmons, Aug. 29, 1947; stepchildren—Lester F. Simmons, Rachel (Mrs. John W. Henderson). Employed in plastics industry, 1932-47; prodn. control mgr. Gen. Precision Equipment, Newark, 1947-50; renegotiation Def. Prodn. Adminstrn. and Renegotiation Bd., Washington, 1951-54; security analyst Babson's Reports, Wellesley, Mass., 1955-66; security analyst Chase Investment Counsel Corp., Charlottesville, Va., 1966—, v.p., 1967—. Mem. Investment Counsel Assn. Am., Richmond Soc. Financial Analysts, Soc. Mayflower Descs. (state treas. 1971—). Episcopalian. Club: Farmington Country (Charlottesville). Home: 1916 Blue Ridge Rd Charlottesville VA 22903 Office: 415 4th St NE Charlottesville VA 22901

GAYNOR, JAY IRVIN, dentist; b. Chgo., May 13, 1924; s. Sam and Frieda (Dorman) G.; student Theodore Herzl Jr. Coll., 1941-42; B.S., U. Ill. at Urbana, 1943; D.D.S., U. Ill. at Chgo., 1947; m. Elaine Ruth Shure, Oct. 12, 1947 (dec. Dec. 1965); 1 son, Richard, Mitchell; m. 2d, Barbara Legrande Beene, May 15, 1968; stepchildren—Gordon Beene, Debra (Mrs. Ricky White Hamby). Pvt. practice dentistry, Chgo., 1947-56, Hale Center, Tex., 1956-64, Plainview, Tex., 1964—; mem. staff Hi-Plains Hosp., Hale Center, Tex., 1956—, Central Plains Gen. Hosp., Plainview, 1964—. Mem. Hale Center (Tex.) City Council, 1959-63. Trustee, Tex. Tech. U. Dads Assn. Served with AUS, 1942-45. Mem. Acad. Gen. Dentistry, Am., Tex. dental assns., Internat. Assn. Orthodontia, European Orthodontic Soc., Soc. Dentistry for Children, Internat. Assn. Begg Study Groups. Lion. Home: 1106 Holiday Dr Plainview TX 79072 Office: 701 Houston St Plainview TX 79072

GEARHISER, CHARLES JOSEF, lawyer; b. Dyersburg, Tenn., Aug. 14, 1938; s. Charles Josef and Mary Josephine (Plant) G.; LL.B., U. Tenn., 1961; B.S., Austin Peay State U., 1965; m. Joy Edwards, June 4, 1959; children—Charles Josef, Laura, Christy. Admitted to Tenn. bar, 1962; with Strang, Fletcher, Carriger & Walker, 1961-63; law clk. to Judge Frank W. Wilson, 1963-64; asst. U.S. atty., 1964-66; trial atty. Stophel, Caldwell & Heggie, Chattanooga, 1966—, also U.S. magistrate, 1967—. Chmn. bd. Golden Gloves Assn. of Chattanooga, 1973-74. Dir. Young Dems. Club Hamilton County. Mem. Am., Tenn., Chattanooga (pres. 1973-74) bar assns., Am., Tenn., Chattanooga trial lawyers assns., Order of Coif, Phi Delta Phi. Home: 12 N Crest Rd Chattanooga TN 37404 Office: Maclellan Bldg Chattanooga TN 37402

GEAUQUE, EDWIN PRESTON, publishing co. exec.; b. Phila., Jan. 28, 1901; ed. U. Cal. at Berkeley, Stanford. Formerly reporter San Francisco Chronicle, corr., Europe and Far East; with govt. intelligence staff, World War II; founder Wake-Brook House, Ft. Lauderdale, Fla., 1946, now exec. dir. Founder, exec. dir. Fine Arts Found. Home: Ft Lauderdale FL summer Hyannis MA Office: Wake-Brook House 3038 North Federal Hwy Times Sq Fort Lauderdale FL 33306

GEBER, WILLIAM FREDERICK, JR., educator; b. Rahway, N.J., Oct. 26, 1923; s. William Frederick and Margaret (Babel) G.; A.B., Dartmouth Coll., 1947; M.S., Ind. U., 1950, Ph.D., 1953; m. Joan Rezny, June 29, 1946; 1 dau., Sharron Ruth. Teaching asso. Ind. U., 1952-53; research asso. U. Minn., 1953-54; asst. prof. physiology St. Louis U.,1955-58; asso. prof. U. S.D., 1958-64; asso. prof. pharmacology Med. Coll. Ga., 1965-70, prof., 1971—; narcotics lectr. Bur. Narcotics and Dangerous Drugs; U.S. Army Officer and Mil. Police Schs. Vice-pres. Augusta City-County Alcohol-Drug Abuse Council, 1969-72. Served with USNR, 1942-46. Mem. Am. Soc. Pharmacology and Exptl. Therapeutics, Am. Physiol. Soc., Am. Chem. Soc., N.Y. Acad. Sci., Soc. Exptl. Biology and Medicine, Sigma Xi. Contbr. numerous articles to sci. jours. Home: 1319 Martinique Dr Augusta GA 30904 Office: Med Coll Ga Augusta GA 30902

GEDA, STANLEY RICHARD, landscape architect; b. N.Y.C., Mar. 3, 1932; s. Stanley and Waclawa (Serfinska) G.; ed. State U. N.Y. at Syracuse, 1950-54; m. Sally A. Stearns, Aug. 21, 1954; children—Karen, Mark, Donald. Asso. in charge establishing landscape architecture dept. Morton S. Fine & Assos., Bloomfield, Conn., 1958-63; exec. v.p. design, promotion and mgmt. Currier, Andersen & Geda, Inc., Avon, Conn., 1963-73; v.p., dir. environmental design and landscape architecture, Hudgins, Thompson, Ball & Assos., Tulsa, 1973—; dir. Devel. Coordinators, Inc., Farmington, Conn.; vis. critic Hartford (Conn.) Tech. Inst., 1967, Wesleyan U., Middletown, Conn., 1968, Okla. State U., 1974; judge design New Orleans awards excellence program, 1974. Served to capt. USAF, 1955-58. Mem. Am. Soc. Landscape Architects (officer Conn. chpt. 1966), Kappa Sigma. Roman Catholic. Club: Indian Springs Country (Broken Arrow, Okla.). Contbr. works to profl. jours. Home: 304 Fairway Dr Broken Arrow OK 74012 Office: PO Box 3289 Tulsa OK 74101

GEDDIE, EDGAR MCPHAIL, power and light co. exec.; b. Fayetteville, N.C., Jan. 3, 1912; s. Edgar Chestnut and Lottie (Bullard) G.; student Campbell Coll., 1929-30; B.S., N.C. State Coll., 1934; m. Katie Lee Ward, Apr. 2, 1938; children—Edgar McPhail, Kathryn Ward, Donald Thomas. Electrician, Erwin Mills (N.C.), 1934-35; jr. engr. Carolina Power & Light Co., Raleigh, N.C., 1935-39, div. dist. engr., 1939-48, div. supt., 1948-62, supt. lines and motor vehicles, 1962-68, asst. v.p. transmission and distbn. dept., 1968-69, v.p. transmission and distbn. dept., 1969—, v.p. div. operations, 1972—. Bd. dirs. Wake County Tb Assn., 1965-70. Mem. Raleigh Engrs. Club, Raleigh C. of C. Methodist (mem. ofcl. bd. 1964-68). Kiwanian. Home: 316 Forsyth St Raleigh NC 27609 Office: 336 Fayetteville St Raleigh NC 27602

GEDDIE, HENRY LAWRENCE, pub. relations exec.; b. Colfax, Tex., Jan. 2, 1920; s. Henry N. and Hermie A. (Lawrence) G.; ed. Tyler Comml. Coll., U. Tex.; m. Martha Frazier Baldwin, Dec. 14, 1944; children—John Baldwin, Anna (Mrs. Jeffrey S. Stanley), Barbara Lawrence. Asso. editor Grand Saline Sun, 1935-37; reporter Tyler (Tex.) Courier Times, 1937-38, Am. Statesman, Austin, Tex., 1938-42; account exec. Julius G. Berens, 1945-48; founder Southwestern Builder mag., 1948; counselor Henry L. Geddie Co., Ft. Worth, 1948—. Alternate del. Democratic Nat. Conv., 1940. Served with USAAF, World War II. Mem. Home Builders Assn. Ft. Worth, Am. Legion, Ex-Students Assn. U. Tex. Mason (K.T., Shriner). Club: Press of Ft. Worth. Author: Geddie & McPhail Genealogy, Colfax, Southern Pollard Families Of the Colorful Free State. Home: 7500 Oxley Dr Ft Worth TX 76118 Office: Trans American Bldg Ft Worth TX 76102

GEE, ROBERT SANFORD, lawyer; b. Oklahoma City, Feb. 24, 1932; s. Robert Lee and Vernice (Doughty) G.; A.A., Muskogee Jr. Coll., 1951; A.B., U. Okla., 1953, LL.B., 1955; m. Nancy Neil, Aug. 23, 1953; children—Robert Neil, Catherine Ann, Elizabeth Ruth, James Kenneth. Admitted to Okla. bar, 1955; asst. county atty. Ottawa County, Okla., 1955-59, county atty., 1960-64, dist. atty., 1972-73; partner law firm Wallace & Owens, Miami, Okla., 1965—; mem. Okla. State Senate, 1965-69, chmn. jud. com. 1st and 2d session, 1967-68, senate adminstr., 1969-72. Vice chmn. Grand Lakes dist. Boy Scouts Am., 1963-65, chmn. orgn., extension com., 1965-67; chmn. Constrnl. Revision Commn. of Okla. Mem. Okla. (mem. adminstrn. justice com. 1967-74, chmn. adminstrn. justice com. 1970-71), Am., Ottawa County bar assns., Miami Jr. C. of C. (pres. 1959-60), Miami C. of C. Presbyn. (elder 1960-64, mem. adv. council Ch. and Society United 1973—). Home: 421 G NW Miami OK 74354 Office: Savs & Loan Bldg Miami OK 74354

GEE, THOMAS GIBBS, judge; b. Jacksonville, Fla., Dec. 9, 1925; s. James Gilliam and Cecile (Gibbs) G.; student The Citadel, 1942-43; B.S., U.S. Mil. Acad., 1946; LL.B., U. Tex. Law Sch., 1953; m. Barbara Ann Green, Apr. 11, 1970; children—Jennifer Gee (Mrs. Andrew Hurst) John Christopher, Mary Cecile, Thomas Gibbs. Admitted to Tex. bar, 1953; asso. law firm Baker & Botts, Attys. at Law, Houston, 1953-54; asso. law firm Graves Dougherty, Gee, Hearon, Moody & Garwood, Attys. at Law, Austin, Tex., 1954, partner, 1955-73; judge U.S. Circuit Ct., Austin, 1973—. Served with USAF, 1946-50. Mem. Am. Law Inst., Am. Bar Assn., Am. Judicature Soc., Tex. Bar Found., Order of Coif. Contbr. articles to profl. jours., publs. Editor-in-chief Texas Law Review, 1952-53. Home: 4603 Ridge Oak Austin TX 78731 Office: US Courthouse 200 W 8th St Austin TX 78701

GEENTIENS, GASTON PETRUS, JR., constrn. engring. exec.; b. Garfield, N.J., Apr. 6, 1935; s. Gaston Petrus and Margaret (Piros) G.; B.S. in Civil Engring., The Citadel, 1956; m. Barbara Ann Chamberlain, Oct. 14, 1960; children—Mercedes Frith, Faith Piros. Plant engr. Western Elec. Co., Inc., Kearny, N.J., 1956-58, owner's rep., N.Y.C., 1960-64; v.p. Gentyne Motors, Inc., Passaic, N.J., 1958-60; project engr. Ethyl Corp., Baton Rouge, 1964-65; mgr. Timothy McCarthy Constrn. Co., Atlanta, 1965; asst. to v.p. A.R. Abrams, Inc. and Columbia Engring., Inc., Atlanta, 1965-66; supr. engring. and constrn. Litton Industries, N.Y.C., 1966-71; pres. G.P. Geetiens, Jr., Inc., Charleston, S.C., 1971—. Mem. Ramapo (N.Y.) Republican Com., 1961-64. Served to 1st lt. C.E., AUS, 1956-58. Registered profl. engr., 13 states. Mem. Am. Soc. C.E., Soc. Profl. Engrs. Kiwanian. Home: 7 Fort Royal Dr Charleston SC 29407 Office: 10 Gillon St Charleston SC 29401

GEER, DANIEL EARL, textile co. exec.; b. Orme, Tenn., Mar. 13, 1918; s. Henry Clay and Mary Lee (Sparkman) G.; student U. Chattanooga, 1935-37, Internat. Accountants Soc., Massey Coll., Chattanooga State Tech. Inst.; m. Mary Elizabeth Moore, Aug. 28, 1949; children—Daniel Earl, Michael Sparkman. Ship clk. Davenport Hosiery Mills, Inc., Chattanooga, 1938-39; accounting clk. U.S. TVA, Chattanooga, 1939-41; accountant A.W. Taber, 1941-46; city auditor City of Chattanooga, 1947-51; controller E-Z Mills, Inc., Cartersville, Ga., 1951-64, Magic Chef, Inc., Cleveland, Tenn., 1964-68; asst. controller Coats & Clark, Inc., 1968-70, asst. treas., 1970, mgr. finance dept., Atlanta, 1971—; treas. Coats & Clark Sales Corp., 1973—. Tchr. McKenzie Sch. Bus., Chattanooga; adv. bd. Chattanooga State Tech. Inst. Served with AUS, 1946-47. C.P.A. Tenn. Mem. Am. Inst. C.P.A.'s, Ga. Soc. C.P.A.'s, Nat. Assn. Accountants, Data Processing Mgmt. Assn., Financial Execs. Inst. Mem. Ch. of Christ. Home: 2658 Meadow Mere E Chamblee GA 30341 Office: PO Box 48266 Atlanta GA 30340

GEER, SAMUEL LEE, banker; b. Sparta, Tenn., May 24, 1921; s. Thomas Beecher and Martha Elizabeth G.; student U. Ala., 1943-44; grad. La. State U. Sch. Banking, 1967; m. Mary Esther Bryant, Dec. 30, 1944; children—Martha Gwendolyn (Mrs. David Edward Krebs), Beth (Mrs. Jerold Jennings). Asst. cashier Bank of Cowan, Tenn., 1946-47; teller, asst. cashier, asst. v.p. and cashier, v.p. and cashier, v.p., sr. v.p. Pompano Beach (Fla.) Bank & Trust Co., 1947—; sec.-treas. Fla. Bancorp. Inc., 1972—. Mem. personnel com. Fla. Bankers Assn., 1966-69. Treas., bd. dirs. 4-H Found. Broward County. Trustee Pompano Beach Pension Plan, 1972-73. Served with USAF, 1943-45. Mem. Am. Inst. Banking (past v.p. Broward County), Greater Pompano Beach C. of C. (past treas., dir.). Mem. Ch. of Christ. Kiwanian (1st v.p.). Home: 1003 S W 4th Terrace Pompano Beach FL 33060 Office: 1101 Atlantic Blvd Pompano Beach FL 33060

GEESLIN, DORINE HAWK (MRS. ROBERT JONES GEESLIN), educator; b. Priceville, Ky., June 22, 1918; d. Benjamin Franklin and Rosa (Avery) Hawk; B.A., Western Ky. U., 1938; M.Ed., U. Louisville, 1959; D.Ed., Fla. State U., 1967; m. Robert Jones Geeslin, May 19, 1938; children—Robert Hawk, Franklin Andrew, Melanie Rose. Tchr., Versailles (Ky.) City Schs., 1950-52, Jefferson County Schs., Louisville, 1952-56; supr. of instrn. Elizabethtown (Ky.) City Schs., 1956-64; research asst. Fla. State U., Tallahassee, 1964-65; dir. reading inst. N. Fla. Jr. Coll., Madison, summer 1965; asst. prof. edn. and human devel. Valdosta (Ga.) State Coll., 1965-67; reading cons. DeKalb County Schs. Reading Center, Clarkston, Ga., 1967-70; instr. dept. psychology, asst. prof. edn. Western Ky. U., Bowling Green, 1970—. Mem. Am. Assn. U. Women, Am. Assn. U. Profs., Delta Kappa Gamma (pres. 1972—), Phi Kappa Phi, Kappa Delta Pi. Presbyn. Democrat. Home: Upton KY 42784 Office: Dept Edn Western Ky U Bowling Green KY 42101

GEHRING, DONALD MCGLASHAN, pub. relations exec.; b. Lakewood, O., Apr. 19, 1913; s. Carl Walter and Mabel Mary (McGlashan) G.; A.B., Cornell U., 1935; m. Catherine Margaret Sutter, May 18, 1946. Radio broadcaster, Ohio, Mich., 1935-39, 46-51; advt., pub. relations dir. Wire Reinforcement Inst., Washington, 1953-67; propr. Don Gehring Pub. Relations, Alexandria, Va., 1967—. Served to capt., inf., AUS, World War II, 1951-52. Mem. Alexandria C. of C., Constrn. Writers Assn. (past pres.), Road Gang, Am. Rd. Builders Assn., Hwy. Research Bd. (past chmn. spl. com. information), Sigma Nu. Club: Nat. Press. Home: 502-A Woodland Terrace Alexandria VA 22302

GEIGER, JAMES EDWARD, elec. engr.; b. Chattanooga, Jan. 2, 1931; s. Winfield Homer and Sally (Barger) G.; student U. Chattanooga, 1948-50; B.S., U. Tenn., 1954; m. Jeanne Sexton, Dec. 18, 1954; children—James Edward, Gregory E., Melissa Christine. Owner, cons. engr. James E. Geiger & Assos., Knoxville, Tenn., 1960—. Lectr., U. Tenn. Sch. Architecture, Knoxville, 1967—. Active United Fund. Bd. dirs. Knoxville Young Set, Inc., 1962—. Served with USMC, 1950-52. Reigstered profl. engr., 12 states. Mem. Nat. Soc. Profl. Engrs., Tenn. Soc. Profl. Engrs., Constrn. Specifications Inst. (pres. 1966-67), Lambda Chi Alpha. Methodist. Clubs: Sertoma, Faculty (Knoxville). Home: 2000 Velmetta Circle Knoxville TN 37920 Office: 9100 Kingston Pike Knoxville TN 37919

GEIGER, SYDNEY, steel co. exec.; b. Jacksonville, Fla., Dec. 21, 1923; s. Sydney and Bertha (Jacobs) G.; B.S. in Civil Engring., The Citadel, 1948; m. Joan M. Nirenberg, Dec. 21, 1947; children—Beverly, Susan, Steven, Mindy. Engr., Va. bridge plant U.S. Steel Co., Birmingham, Ala., 1948-51; steel engr. Howell Steel Co., Jackson, Miss., 1951-55; pres. Delta Steel Co., Inc., Jackson, 1955—. Mem. social action com. Union Am. Hebrew Congregations, 1964-74, mem. exec. bd., 1970-74. Bd. dirs. Council Human Relations, Urban League, Goodwill Industries, 1960-72. Served with AUS, 1945-48; ETO. Mem. Am. Inst. Steel Constrn., Am. Soc. C.E., Am. Soc. Profl. Engrs. Jewish religion (pres. congregation, trustee, nat. bd. mem.). Mem. B'nai B'rith. Club: North Jackson Civitan (past dir.). Home: 2246 Greenbriar Dr Jackson MS 39211 Office: P O Box 9266 Jackson MS 39206

GEIGERMAN, CLARICE FURCHGOTT, pub. relations, ins. and real estate agt.; b. Charleston, S.C., Sept. 24, 1916; d. Melvin and Doreta (Brown) Furchgott; student Draughon Sch. Commerce, 1934-35, U. Ga., 1935-36, Am. Inst. Banking, 1936-41; m. Henry David Geigerman, July 4, 1941 (dec. Nov. 1967); children—Henry David, Robert M. Sec. to v.p. investment dept. Citizens & So. Nat. Bank, Atlanta, 1935-41; personnel dir., payroll chief Atlanta Ordnance Dept., 1941-43; pub. relations counselor, 1944—; agt. Nat. Life Ins. Co. Vt., Atlanta, 1968—; agt. First Atlanta Equity Corp., 1972—. Bd. dirs. So. Regional Opera, 1969—, chmn. women's com., 1969—, v.p. exec. com., 1972—; pres. Atlanta Civic Ballet Assos., 1962-64; adv. bd. Muscular Dystrophy Assn., 1968—; bd. sponsors Atlanta Symphony Guild, 1969—, v.p. women's bd., 1966-68, mem. policy bd., 1966—; bd. dirs. Active Voters, 1965—, Youth Symphony Met. Atlanta; mem. High Mus. Art; mem. women's com. Brandeis U., Alliance Theatre; mem. Atlanta Fund Appeals Rev. Bd.; pres. Atlanta Playhouse Theatre. Mem. Am. Women in Radio and TV, Pub. Relations Soc. Am. Women's C. of C., English-Speaking Union, Italian Cultural Soc., Victorian Soc. Am. Nat. Council Jewish Women, Atlanta Music Club (dir., co-editor newsletter). Jewish religion. Clubs: Atlanta Press, Georgia Writers, Standard, Oaks (Atlanta). Contbg. editor Arts mag., So. Israelite, TV Guide, Seydell Quar., Nat. Messenger. Home: 620 Peachtree St NE Atlanta GA 30308 Office: 151 Ellis St Atlanta GA 30308 also 100 Peachtree St NW Atlanta GA

GEIS, CLARENCE HUGH, ret. ednl. adminstr.; b. Huntington, Ark., July 2, 1907; s. Peter and Nola (Hart) G.; B.S. in Edn., U. Ark., 1930, M.S., 1952; m. Hazel Dawson Baucum, Dec. 26, 1930; children—William Peter, Susan Elaine (Mrs. John Ellerbe Sanford), John Perry. Coach high schs., Jonesboro, Ark., 1930, 39-41, 46-48, Minden, La., 1931-36, Texarkana, Ark., 1936-39, Central High Sch., Little Rock, 1941-44; adminstr. Jonesboro Pub. Schs., 1949-73. Served with USNR, 1944-45. Mem. N.E.A., Ark. Edn. Assn. Secondary Sch. Prins. (past pres.), Am., Ark. assns. sch. adminstrs., Ark. Congress Parents and Tchrs. (life), Ark. Sch. Study Council (pres. 1967-68), Ark. Activities Assn. (exec. com.), Phi Delta Kappa. Methodist. Rotarian. Home: 524 W Oak St Jonesboro AR 72401

GEISBERG, HARRY, textile co. exec.; b. Anderson, S.C., Oct. 27, 1918; s. Harry and Sadie (Cohen) G.; B.S. in Textile Engring., Clemson U., 1938; m. Carol Rosenbaum, Nov. 30, 1940; 1 son, Harry Irvin. With Louisville Textiles, Inc., 1938—, pres., 1967—; sec. Cane Run Lanes, Inc., 1954—. Served to capt. AUS, 1943-46. Decorated Army Commendation medal. Jewish religion (pres. temple). Mason, Kiwanian. Home: 415 Country Lane Louisville KY 40207 Office: 1318 McHenry St Louisville KY 40217

GEISER, MARVIN DOYLE, JR., utility exec.; b. San Antonio, Dec. 29, 1931; s. M.D. and Anna (Wise) G.; B.S., Tex. Agrl. and Indsl. U., 1959; m. Rosa Lee Dennis, Aug. 29, 1958; children—Karen Lee, Cheryl Lynn, James Doyle. Utilization engr. Lone Star Gas Co., Ft. Worth, 1959-65, air conditioning sales supr., 1965-67, mdse. sales mgr., 1967-68, promotion projects mgr., 1968-69, dist. mgr., Cleburne, Tex., 1969, gen. supt., Ft. Worth, 1969-71, regional mgr. San Angelo, Tex., 1971—. Loaned exec. Tarrant County United Fund, 1960-69; adviser Jr. Achievement, 1961-63. Served with Signal Corps, AUS, 1954-56. Registered profl. engr., Tex. Mem. Tex. Soc. Profl. Engrs. (chpt. treas. 1964), Tarrant County Home Builders Assn. (dir. 1969), Tarrant County Apt. Assn. (dir. 1969). Republican. Baptist. Mason (K.T.), Rotarian. Clubs: Optimist (v.p. and dir. 1969) (Ft. Worth, Tex.). Home: 2738 Chimney Rock Lane San Angelo TX 76901 Office: 111 W Twohig St San Angelo TX 76901

GELBAND, STEPHEN L., lawyer; b. N.Y.C., Feb. 13, 1931; A.B., Yale, 1952; J.D., Harvard, 1955. Admitted to N.Y. bar, 1955, D.C. bar, 1961, U.S. Ct. Appeals bar, 1963; atty. Office U.S. Atty. So. Dist. N.Y., 1955; legal assistance adviser, Ft. Myer, Va., 1956-57; trial atty. Bur. Econ. Regulation, CAB, 1957-60; now mem. firm Fisher & Gelband, Washington. Mem. Bar Assn. D.C. (mem. internat. law com.), Am., Fed. bar assns. Address: Fisher & Gelband 1522 K St NW Washington DC 20005

GELLER, IRVING, behavioral pharmacologist; b. Boston, Oct. 26, 1925; s. Benjamin and Nellie (Siegle) G.; B.A., George Washington U., 1949, M.A. in Psychology, 1951; Ph.D. in Psychology, Am. U., 1957; m. Ruth Boose, Feb. 15, 1951; children—David, Diane, Robert, Leslie Ann. Aviation psychologist Naval Research Lab., Washington, 1951-54; research psychologist Walter Reed Army Inst. Research, Washington, 1952-57; sr. research scientist, head dept. psychopharmacology Wyeth Labs., Inc., Phila., 1957-64; asso. prof. pharmacology N.Y. Med. Coll., N.Y.C., 1964-66; chmn. dept. exptl. pharmacology S.W. Found. for Research & Edn., San Antonio, 1966-73; prof. dept. psychiatry Tex. Tech. U., Lubbock, 1973—. Lectr., Villanova (Pa.) U., 1963, San Antonio Coll., 1967-69; adj. asso. prof. U. Tex. Med. Br., Galveston, 1968—; prof. Trinity U., San Antonio, 1969-72. Served with AUS, 1944-46. Fellow Am. Psychol. Assn.; mem. Eastern, Southeastern, Southwestern Psychol. assns., Psychonomic Soc., Am. Soc. for Pharmacology and Exptl. Therapeutics, A.A.A.S., Sigma Xi. Reviewer: Physiology and Behavior, 1969—, Psychopharmacologia, 1968—, Pharmacology, Biochemistry, and Behavior, 1973—. Office: Texas Tech University School Medicine Gaston Hall Lubbock TX 79409

GELLINEK, CHRISTIAN JOHANN G., educator; b. Potsdam, Germany, May 11, 1930; s. Christian and Margaretha (Lorenzen) G.; came to U.S., 1961, naturalized, 1966; B.A., U. Toronto, 1959; M.A., Yale, 1963, Ph.D., 1964. Instr., Yale, New Haven, 1964-66, asst. prof., 1966-68, asso. prof., 1968-70; prof. Conn. Coll., New London, 1970-71; prof. dept. German and Slavic, U. Fla., Gainesville, 1971—, chmn., 1973—. Mem. Modern Lang. Assn. Author: Koenig Rother, 1968; Programmed German Dictionary, 1968; Die deutsche Kaiserchronik, 1972. Home: 507-241 39th Rd Gainesville FL 32607 Office: Dept German and Slavic U Fla Gainesville FL 32601

GEMBERLING, ROBERT PERRY, govt. ofcl.; b. Emden, Ill., Oct. 12, 1922; s. Robert Clyde and Georgia Marie (Perry) G.; secretarial certificate Peoria (Ill.) Inst. Bus., 1941; student Springfield (Ill.) Jr. Coll., 1946-47; B.S., Northwestern U., Chgo., 1949; postgrad. DePaul U., Chgo., 1950; m. Virginia Lee Best, June 12, 1948; 1 dau., Gail Ann. With FBI, 1941—, spl. agt., Detroit, 1950-51, Indpls., 1951-54, Honolulu, 1954-56, Dallas, 1956—. Served with USMCR, 1943-46. Decorated Purple Heart; recipient 30 Year Active Service award FBI, 1973. C.P.A., Ill., Tex. Mem. Tex. Soc. C.P.A.'s. Coordinated investigation of assassination Pres. Kennedy, 1963. Home: 7106 Clemson Dr Dallas TX 75214 Office: 1810 Commerce St Dallas TX 75201

GEMMER, HIRAM ROBERT, civic worker, clergyman; b. Indpls., Apr. 4, 1923; s. Hiram Conrad and Edith May (Miller) G.; B.S., Ind. U., 1944; certificate Yale Sch. Alcohol Studies, 1945; B.D., Chgo. Theol. Sem., also U. Chgo., 1947; postgrad. Christian Theol. Sem., 1950; M.A., Western Res. U., 1960; m. Myrna Jean Flory, June 11, 1949; children—David Robert, Jean (Mrs. Larry J. McCutchan). Ordained to ministry Christian Ch. (Disciples of Christ), 1947; asst. minister, dir. youth activities First Friends Ch., Indpls., 1948-49; pastor First Ch. of Brethren, Cleve., 1951-55; asst. to dir. student activities and guidance Fenn Coll. (now Cleve. State U.), 1955-56, acting dir. student activities, 1956-57; dir. social welfare dept. Cleve. Area Ch. Fedn., 1957-63; exec. dir. Council Chs. Mohawk Valley Area, Utica, N.Y., 1963-67, Council Chs. Greater St. Petersburg (Fla.), 1967-70; salesman Wholesale Tours Internat. N.Y., 1972—. Dean, Bapt. Disciples Brethern Sch. Christian Living, 1954, 55; mem. adv. com. WLCY-TV, 1968—, commentator, 1967-70. Pres. Council Human Relations of Greater St. Petersburg, 1968—; sec. Religions United in Action for Community, 1968-69, mem. exec. com., 1969-70; mem. Minority Relations Goals Com., St. Petersburg, 1970—; mem. adv. com. Pinellas County Charter Commn., 1971-72; chmn. Pub. Health Council, Utica, 1966-67; treas. Suncoast Progress, 1968, Pinellas Opportunity Council, 1969; v.p. Lakewood Property Owners Assn., 1972, pres., 1974—; mem. Nat. Ch. Commn. on Scouting, 1963-70; pres. H.C. Gemmer Family Christian Found., 1956—; edn. chmn., bd. dirs. St. Petersburg br. N.A.A.C.P., 1969—; mem. UN Day Com., St. Petersburg, 1969—; active numerous other orgns. Republican candidate Pinellas Sch. Bd., 1968; ofcl. observer Pinellas County Sch. Bd., 1971—, chmn. bi-racial adv. com., 1969-70, sec.-treas., 1970-71, alternate, 1971—; non-partisan candidate St. Petersburg City Council, 1970. Bd. dirs. Found. Religious Studies Indpls., Baptist Children's Home, Oneida, N.Y., 1965-67, St. Petersburg chpt. UNA-U.S.A., 1969—, Suncoast Goodwill Industries, 1969-72, numerous others. Recipient citation U.S. Sec. Health, Edn. and Welfare, 1962. Mem. Acacia. Contbg. editor Peace Action, 1955-68. Contbr. articles to mags. Address: 1863 Lakewood Dr S St Petersburg FL 33712

GENCAY, FERIDUN FIKRET, elec. engr.; b. Sivas, Turkey, Aug. 29, 1924; s. Ali Recep Riza and Emine Fatima G.; student Istanbul Tech. U., 1945-47; B.S., U. Tenn., 1954, postgrad., 1954-55; postgrad. U. Cin., 1956-58; m. Lou Ella Miller, Dec. 22, 1951; children—Feride Denise, Jeffry Feridun, David Riza, Lloyd Levent. Came to U.S., 1949, naturalized, 1958. Elec. engr. TVA, Knoxville, 1954-55, 58-67, supr. powerhouse elec. equipment sect., elec. engring. br., project devel. group, 1967-73, supr. elec. equipment and lighting sect., thermal power engring. design projects Sequoyah and Watts bar nuclear plants design, 1973—; designer H.K. Ferguson, Cin., 1955-56, Chem. & Indsl. Corp., Cin., 1956-58. Mem. I.E.E.E., Eta Kappa Nu. Club: Cricket (v.p., co-chmn. maintenance com. (Powell, Tenn.). Home: 2820 Staffordshire Blvd Powell TN 37849 Office: 302 LB-K TVA Knoxville TN 37902

GENDEL, BENJAMIN ROBERT, physician; b. N.Y.C., Apr. 29, 1911; s. Aaron and Fannie (Litt) G.; B.S., Tulane U., 1931, M.D., 1935; m. Rena Spector, Aug. 1, 1937. Intern Greenpoint Hosp., Bklyn., 1935-37; practice medicine specializing in internal medicine, New Haven, 1937-42, Atlanta, 1955-71, Memphis, 1971— vis. prof. pediatric research unit Guy's Hosp. Med. Sch., London, Eng., 1968-69; chief med. service VA Hosp., Memphis, 1971—; cons. internal medicine and hematology Grady Meml. Hosp. and VA Hosp., Atlanta, 1956-71; prof. medicine Emory U. Sch. Medicine, 1955-71; prof., asso. chmn. dept. medicine U. Tenn. Coll. Medicine, 1971—. Served with AUS, 1942-46. Diplomate Am. Bd. Internal Medicine. Fellow A.C.P., Internal Soc. Hematology; mem. Am. Fedn. Clin. Research, Am. Soc. Human Genetics, Am. Soc. Hematology, A.M.A., Phi Beta Kappa, Alpha Omega Alpha. Home: 435 N Highland St Memphis TN 38122 Office: 1030 Jefferson Av Memphis TN 38104

GENOWAYS, HUGH HOWARD, curator; b. Scottsbluff, Neb., Dec. 24, 1940; s. Theodore Thompson and Sarah Louise (Beales) G.; B.A., Hastings Coll., 1963; postgrad. U. Western Australia, 1964; Ph.D., U. Kan., 1971; m. Joyce Elaine Cox, July 28, 1963; children—Margaret Louise, Theodore Howard. Research asso. Tex. Tech. U. Mus., Lubbock, 1971-72, curator of mammals, 1972—, adj. asst. prof. vet. and zool. medicine, 1973—, adj. asst. prof. biol. scis., 1973—. Fulbright grantee, 1964. Mem. A.A.A.S., Am. Soc. Mammalogists, Am. Soc. Naturalists, Ecol. Soc. Am., Soc. Systematic Zoologists, Soc. for Study Evolution, Biol. Soc. Washington, Sigma Xi. Mng. editor Jour. of Mammalogy, 1974—. Contbr. articles to profl. jours. Home: 3702 28th St Lubbock TX 79410

GENTLE, JIMMIE LYNN, clergyman; b. Prosper, Tex., Mar. 24, 1936; s. Roscoe C. and Lucille Fay (Coplen) G.; A.B., Phillips U., 1959; M.Div., Tex. A. and M. Coll., 1955, Ph.D., 1973; m. Connie Kay Roberts, June 14, 1959; children—Stephen Wayne, Donald Lynn, Jimmie David. Ordained to ministry Christian Ch., 1959; asso. pastor Crown Heights Christian Ch., Oklahoma City, 1962-63, First Christian Chs., Seminole, Okla., 1963-64, Newkirk, Okla., 1964-66, Alva, Okla., 1966—; instr. Northwestern State U., Alva, 1966—. Moderator elect Christian Ch. in Okla., 1973—; mem. gen. bd. Christian Ch. U.S.A., 1973—. White House Conf. Children and Youth del. World and Nat. Mental Health Assembly, 1970. City councilman, Alva, 1971—; chmn. Woods County Democratic Central Com., 1972—; mem. Okla. Dem. Central Com., 1972—. Bd. dirs. Share Hosp., Alva Municipal Airport; mem. exec. com. Okla. Mental Health Assn. Rotarian. Contbr. articles to profl. publs. Home: 1215 Flynn St Alva OK 73717 Office: 821 College St Alva OK 73717

GEOFFREY, LLOYD EDSON, JR., oil and gas producer; b. Borger, Tex., July 25, 1950; s. Lloyd Edson and Maedean (Maeberry) G.; student West Tex. State U., 1968-72; m. Doris June Mixon, May 21, 1971; 1 dau., Michelle Leigh. Vice pres., gen. mgr. Tex. Energies, Inc., Amarillo, Tex., 1967—; v.p. Republic Natural Gas Co. Home: 904 N Houston St Amarillo TX 79107 Office: 306 Bank of SW Amarillo TX 79109

GEORGE, CHARLES REDGENAL, educator; b. Faison, N.C., July 21, 1938; s. Noah and Lucille (Hicks) G.; B.S., N.C. A. and T. Coll., 1960; M.S. (NSF fellow), Okla. State U., 1965; Ph.D. (NIH fellow), Cornell U., 1970; m. Willia Robinson, Mar. 5, 1961; children—Sonia, Yvette. Instr. biology E.E. Smith High Sch., Kenansville, N.C., 1960-64; instr. biology Fayetteville (N.C.) State Coll., 1964-65; prof. biology N.C. Central U., Durham, 1970—. Recipient NIH grant N.C. Central U., 1972—. Mem. N.C. Acad. Sci., Soc. Invertebrate Pathology, Entomol. Soc. Am., Am. Soc. Parasitologists, Beta Kappa Chi. Contbr. articles profl. jours. Home: 3501 Suffolk St Durham NC 27707

GEORGE, DIMITRA STEVE, state ofcl.; b. N.Y.C., Jan. 26, 1925; d. Steve and Amelia (Petalas) George; A.B. in Sociology, U. N.C., Greensboro, 1946; M.A., U. Chgo., 1954. Caseworker, Welfare Dept., Wilmington, N.C., 1946-50; supr. Welfare Dept., Concord, N.C., 1950-52; chief psychiat. social worker Richland Mental Health Clinic, Columbia, S.C., 1954-64; mental health cons. S.C. Dept. Mental Health, Columbia, 1964—. Instr. sociology and psychology U. S.C., Columbia, 1958—; cons. mem. adult edn. adv. com. Columbia (S.C.) Sch. Dist. 1, 1960—. Mem. Nat. Assn. Social Workers (mem. leadership tng. program 1969-71), So. Community Execs. Inst. Blue Ridge (mem. exec. com. 1964-69), S.C. Council Family Relations (pres. 1969-71), Chief Social Workers in State Mental Health Programs (mem. exec. com. 1968-69), League Women Voters, Daus. of Penelope. Club: Soroptimist. Home: 1509 Brennen Rd Columbia SC 29206 Office: 2414 Bull St Columbia SC 29202

GEORGE, JAMES COLLIN, II, surgeon; b. Tampa, Fla., June 20, 1917; s. Sawnie McKinney and Lula (McDougal) G.; student Tex. Southmost Coll., 1933-35, U. Tex., 1935-38; M.D., Baylor U., 1942; m. Jane Jarvis, June 1, 1942; children—Jane Elizabeth, James Collin III, Robert Jarvis. Intern, Robert B. Green Meml. Hosp., San Antonio, 1942-43, resident in surgery AAF Regional Hosp., Salt Lake City, 1943-44, Baylor U. Hosp., Dallas, 1946-47, Ball Meml. Hosp., Muncie, Ind., 1947-48; practice medicine specializing in surgery, Brownsville, Tex., 1948—; mem. staff Mercy Hosp., 1948—, chief surgery, chief staff; county health officer Cameron County, Tex., 1963—. Dir., v.p. Nat. Bank of Commerce, Brownsville. Founder, organizer City County Health Clinic, 1951, chmn., 1951-52; founder, organizer Brownsville Soc. Crippled Children, 1950, med. dir., 1950-58. Chmn. Brownsville Bd. City Devel., 1955-56; mem. Brownsville Indsl. Commn., 1960-61; organizer Cameron County Community Project, Nat. Econ. Opportunity Act, 1966, chmn., 1966-67; mayor City of Brownsville, 1959-61; mem. Brownsville Pub. Utility Bd., 1960-61. Served with USAAF, World War II. Fellow A.C.S.; mem. Am., Tex. med. assns., Southwestern, Pan Pacific med. socs., Am. Bd. Abdominal Surgeons, Internat. Acad. Medicine, Internat. Coll. Proctology, Skull and Key, Sigma Alpha Epsilon, Phi Chi. Episcopalian. Home: 285 Calle Cenizo Brownsville TX 78520 Office: 705 W Jefferson St Brownsville TX 78520

GEORGE, LILA-GENE PLOWE KENNEDY (MRS. RICHARD PAINTER GEORGE), composer; b. Sioux City, Ia., Sept. 25, 1918; d. Eugene Preston and Lila Mae (Pickle) Plowe; B.A., U. Okla., 1939, Mus.B., 1940; postgrad. Northwestern U., 1950, Columbia, 1963-65; pvt. study piano with Egon Petri, Silvio Scionti, Herbert Ricker, Edward Steuermann, 1942-63; pvt. study composition with Nadia Boulanger, Fountainebleau, summers 1971, 72, 73; m. Richard Painter George, Sept. 11, 1941; children—Eugenia (Mrs. Edward N. Haley), Richard Painter. Solo pianist Okla. Little Symphony, 1935-37, Houston Symphony, 1956; pvt. piano tchr. Latin Am., 1948-52, N.Y., 1961-65, Houston, 1955-60, 71—. Adjudicator contests, Okla., 1940. Recipient Composers award Sigma Alpha Iota Okla., 1969. Mem. Am. Music Center, Am. Musicological Soc., Tuesday Mus. Club (pres. 1960), Pan Am. Round Table, D.A.R., Sigma Alpha Iota, Chi Delta Phi. Episcopalian. Composer: Horn Trio, 1963; Violin and Piano Sonata, 1964; Madrigals, 1966; Children's pieces, 1964, 73; Organ Preludes, 1965, 73. Home: 2301 Reba Dr Houston TX 77019

GEORGE, MILDRED A. MILLER (MRS. SAMUEL F. GEORGE), assn. exec.; b. Tiffin, O., Sept. 17, 1916; d. Grover A. and Clara (Dellinger) Miller; grad. Tiffin U., 1937; ed. Am. Savs. & Loan Inst., 1951; m. Samuel F. George, Feb. 11, 1956. Sec., teller Citizens Savs. & Loan Assn., Tiffin, O., 1937-44, bookkeeper, 1944-50; bookkeeper Anacostia Fed. Savs. & Loan Assn., Washington, 1950-56, asst. treas., 1951-56; asst. controller Perpetual Bldg. Assn., Washington, 1956-68; asst. v.p., mgr. s.w. br., Perpetual Bldg. Assn. in L'Enfant Plaza, Washington, 1968—. Mem. Ft. Washington Estates Citizens Assn., 1958—, sec., 1959-60, v.p., 1971-72. Mem. Nat. Soc. Controllers and Financial Officers of Savs. Instns., Kappa Delta Phi. Methodist. Soroptomist. Home: 13503 Reid Circle Oxon Hill MD 20022 Office: 965 L'Enfant Plaza N Washington DC 20024

GEORGE, RONALD BAYLIS, physician; b. Zwolle, La., Nov. 17, 1932; s. Ronald Lee and Theodora Virginia (Baylis) G.; B.A., U. Ala., 1954; M.D., Tulane U., 1958. Intern Charity Hosp., New Orleans, 1958-59, resident internal medicine, 1959-60, 62-64; fellow pulmonary diseases Tulane U., New Orleans, 1964-66, chief inhalation therapy and emphysema sect. VA Hosp., New Orleans, 1966-71; asso. prof. medicine, head pulmonary diseases sect. La. State U. Med. Center, Sch. Medicine, 1972—; chief physician inhalation therapy Confederate Meml. Med. Center, Shreveport, 1972—. Served to capt. USAF, 1960-62. Diplomate Am. Bd. Internal Medicine. Fellow Am. Coll. Chest Physicians, A.C.P.; mem. Am. Thoracic Soc., Alpha Omega Alpha. Home: 208 Villa Contessa Shreveport LA 71106 Office: 3730 Blair St Shreveport LA 71130

GEORGE, THEODORE ALEXANDER, aero. engr.; b. Detroit, Nov. 1, 1926; s. Alexander T. and Nada (Braun) G.; B.A., George Washington U., 1950; B.M.E., Cath. U., 1959, M.Aero. Engring., 1960; m. Lillian C. Clark, Nov. 14, 1953. Aero. engr. Dept. Army, Washington, 1950-58; mgr. project discoverer Office Sec. Def., Washington, 1960-61; dept. dir. nuclear test detection, 1961-64; prin. engr. Office Manned Space Flight, NASA, Washington, 1964-67, mgr. Earth Resources Tech. Satellite, 1967-70; asst. to water quality commr. Environmental Protection Agy., 1970-71; mgr. earth observing advanced programs NASA, 1971-72; asst. for arms control ODDR&E Office Sec. Def., 1972—. Guest lectr. applied math. U. Va., Fairfax. Served with AUS, 1946-47. Registered profl. engr., Md., D.C. Mem. Soc. for Indsl. and Applied Math., Am. Inst. Aeros. and Astronautics, N.Y. Acad. Sci., Nat. Soc. Profl. Engrs., Tau Beta Pi. Author: Principles of Atmospheric Reentry, 1961. Home: 4132 N River St Arlington VA 22207 Office: Pentagon Bldg Washington DC 20301

GERAN, RUTH IRIS, biologist; b. Middletown, O., Nov. 27, 1922; d. Harry Clayton and Ethel Lacy (Kinney) Geran; B.A., Am. U., 1944; M.S., George Washington U., 1954, M. Phil., 1969, Ph.D., 1971. Biologist drug evaluation br. Nat. Cancer Inst., Bethesda, Md., 1958—. Mem. A.A.A.S., Am. Forestry Assn., Am. Inst. Biol. Scis., Am. Soc. Animal Sci., Am. Soc. Zoologists, Found. for Advanced Edn. in Scis., Nat. Cancer Inst. Assembly of Scientists, Mortar Bd., Kappa Delta, Sigma Delta Epsilon. Home: 420 N Oakland St Arlington VA 22203 Office: National Cancer Inst Bethesda MD 20014

GERARD, CLEVELAND JOSEPH, educator; b. Milton, La., Sept. 27, 1924; s. Ix Joseph and Noemie (Breaux) G.; B.S., U. Southwestern La., 1948; M.S., Kan. State U., 1950; Ph.D., Tex. A. and M. U., 1955; m. Frances Marie Dyer, Nov. 17, 1963; children—Ginger Gail, Ann Marie. Soil scientist Ore. State U., Corvallis and U.S. Dept. Agr., Pendleton, Ore., 1953-57; faculty Tex. Agrl. Expt. Sta., Tex. A. and M. U., Weslaco, 1957—, prof. soil physics, 1957—. Served with USNR, 1943-46. Mem. Internat. Soil Sci. Soc., Am. Soc. Agronomy, Soil Sci. Soc. Am., Sigma Xi, Phi Kappa Phi, Gamma Sigma Delta. Home: 804 S Illinois St Weslaco TX 78596

GERBER, ISRAEL J., clergyman, educator, author; b. N.Y.C., July 30, 1918; s. Max and Sadie (Shuster) G.; B.A., Yeshiva U., 1939; M.S., City Coll. N.Y., 1940; Ph.D., Boston U., 1950; m. Sydelle Reba Katzman, Jan. 9, 1943; children—Barbara J., Sharon M., Wayne S. Tchr. N.Y.C. schs., 1941-42; prof. of O.T. Livingstone Coll., Hood Sem., Salisbury, N.C., 1960—; prof. psychology Johnson C. Smith U., Charlotte, N.C., 1969—; rabbi Beth Jacob Synogogue, Plymouth, Mass., 1943-44, Congregation Agudath Achim, Fitchburg, Mass., 1944-53, Temple Emanu-El, Dothan, Ala., 1953-59, Temple Beth El, Charlotte, 1959-72; lectr. U. N.C., Charlotte, 1968-71; dir. Inst. Jewish Studies, Charlotte, 1972—. Chaplain Boston Psychopathic Hosp., 1948-50; cons. psychologist Southeast Ala. Gen. Hosp., 1956-59. Mem. Charlotte-Meckenburg Council on Human Relations, Multiple Sclerosis Soc., Citizens Safety Assn.; v.p. Mental Health Assn. Charlotte and Mecklenburg County; pres. Mecklenburg County Soc. for Crippled Children and Adults, 1956-59, chmn. Hearthstone Half-Way House; chmn. Charlotte chpt. Nat. Conf. Christians and Jews; trustee Florence Crittendon Home. Bd. govs. Inst. Pastoral Care. Served as chaplain, AUS, 1951-52. Recipient Award in Religion, Charlotte Jr. Womens Club, 1962. Mem. Central Conf. Am. Rabbis, New Eng. Zionist Region, Southeast Assn. Reform Rabbis (sec.-treas. 1956-59), B'nai B'rith (lodge pres. 1956-58), Am., Southeastern, N.C., Ala., Mecklenburg County psychol. assns., Am. Assn. U. Profs., Am. Acad. Religion, Soc. Sci. Study Religion, Nat. Assn. Biblican Instrs., Jewish Chaplains Assn., Acad. Religion and Mental Health; hon. mem. Internat. Mark Twain Soc. Mason, Rotarian, Elk, Kiwanian. Author: The Psychology of the Suffering Mind, 1951; Man on a Pendulum, 1956; Immortal Rebels, 1963; Rabbinical Counseling, 1966. Contbr. articles to religious mags. Home: 5727 Riviere Dr Charlotte NC 28211 Office: 5727 Riviere Dr Charlotte NC 28211

GERBETH, JOHN, merchandising co. exec.; b. Germany, July 7, 1930; s. Albin and Margaret (Smith) G.; came to U.S., 1949, naturalized, 1952; grad. Advanced Mgmt. Program, Harvard, 1959; m. Dorothy Collette Herman; 1 dau., Deirdre Catherine. Plant mgr. Popular Club Plan, Passaic, also Fairlawn, N.J., 1955-59; controller Carr's Dept. Store, West Orange, N.J., 1959-60; mgr. diversification Popular Merchandising Co., Inc., Passaic, 1961-62, corporate comptroller, 1962-68; v.p. finance Popular Services, Inc., 1968-72; exec. v.p. Stuart McGuire, Salem, Va., 1972—; mem. adv. bd. Bank of Passaic & Clifton. Served with USAF, 1951-52. Mem. Passaic Area C. of C. (dir. 1972—). Home: 3002 Avenham Av Roanoke VA 24014 Office: Brand Rd Salem VA 24153

GEREAU, MARY M. CONDON, labor assn. exec.; b. Winterset, Ia., Oct. 10, 1916; d. David Joseph and Sarah Rose (Stack) Condon; student Mt. Mercy Jr. Coll., 1935-37; B.A. in English, State U. Ia., 1939, M.A., in U.S. History, 1941, postgrad., 1948—; m. Gerald R. Gereau, Jan. 14, 1961. Tchr. English, history high sch., Colo., Ia., 1941-42, Creston, Ia., 1942, 43; program dir. A.R.C., India, 1943-45, field cons. Mont., N.D., S.D., 1945-46; dean students Eastern Mont. Coll. Edn., 1946-48; supt. pub. instrn. Mont., Helena, 1949-57; specialist U.S. Senate Com. Interior Affairs, Washington, 1957; adviser Pa. Council Edn., Harrisburg, 1957; asst. dir. rural services N.E.A., 1957-61, legislative cons., 1961-73, pres. staff orgn., 1961; dir. legislation Nat. Treasury Employees' Union, 1974—. Sec. Mont. Bd. Edn., 1949-57; vice-chmn. Mont. Land Bd., 1949-57; chmn. Mont. Tchrs. Retirement System, 1949-57, council chief state sch. officers, dir., 1953-55, pres., 1956; chmn. nat. com. sch. savs. U.S. Treasury Dept., 1950-56; chmn. Mont. Conf. Children and Youth, 1950; del. White House Conf. Edn., 1955; mem. profl. staff White House Conf. Edn., 1965. Del. Democratic Nat. Conv., 1956; mem. platform com. Mont. Dem. Party; exec. dir. Educators for Johnson-Humphrey, 1964, Educators for Humphrey-Muskie 1968; chmn. Women's Joint Congl. Com., 1969-72; nat. chmn. Equal Rights Amendment Ratification Council, 1972. Recipient spl. citation V.F.W., 1954; named Conservationist of Year, Mont., 1950; recipient Distinguished Service award Council of Chief State Sch. Officers, 1956; made hon. princess Blackfeet Indian Tribe. Mem. N.E.A. (life), Mont. Edn. Assn. (life), Am. Assn. Sch. Adminstrs. Democrat. Roman Catholic. Home: 1234 Massachusetts Av NW Washington DC 20005 Office: 1730 K St NW Washington DC 20006

GERGEN, JOHN ANDREW, psychiatrist; b. Cambridge, Mass., Aug. 7, 1932; s. John Jay and Aubigne (Lermond) G.; B.S. magna cum laude, Yale, 1953; M.D. (Earl H. Kirkland fellow), Harvard, 1957; m. Jacqueline Dunn, Aug. 1, 1970; children by previous marriage—Peter, Mark, James, Michael, Constance; stepchildren—Elizabeth Kennedy, James Kennedy, Susan Kennedy, Stephanie Kennedy. Intern Duke, 1957-58, resident neurology, 1958-59, resident psychiatry, 1968-71, asst. prof. psychiatry, 1971-72; asst. prof. physiology Bowman Gray Sch. Medicine, Winston-Salem, N.C., 1962-67, asso. prof., 1967-68, lectr. 1968-70; med. examiner Durham County, N.C., 1969-72; cons. psychiatrist Durham County Community Mental Health Center, Durham, N.C., 1971-72; asso. prof. psychiatry, dir. div. community and liaison psychiatry U. Ala., Birmingham, 1972-74; dir. Comprehensive Community Mental Health Center, 1973-74. Served with USPHS, 1959-62. Diplomate Am. Bd. Med. Examiners, Am. Electroencephalographic Soc. Mem. Am. Psychiatric Assn., A.M.A., Ala. Acad. Neurology and Psychiatry, Am. Physiol. Soc., Phi Beta Kappa, Sigma Xi. Contbr. articles in field to profl. jours. Home: 4269 Sharpsburg Dr Mountain Brook AL 35213 Office: Dept Psychiatry U Ala University Station Birmingham AL 35294

GERMANY, EUGENE WILSON, petroleum mining exec., mayor; b. Grand Saline, Tex., Mar. 11, 1916; s. Eugene Benjamin and Maggie Lee (Wilson) G.; B.S., So. Meth. U., 1937; m. Jennie Margaret Blackman, Jan. 17, 1940; children—Wesley H., Joan Lee. Partner, E. B. Germany & Sons, Dallas, 1937—; partner Germany Investment Co., 1948—; pres. Calto Oil Co., 1956—; dir., vice chmn. bd. Preston State Bank; dir. Southwestern Gen. Life Ins. Co.; mayor, University Park, Tex., 1970—. Mem. City Commn., University Park, 1959-70. Pres. Dallas YMCA; bd. dirs. Meth. Hosp. Dallas; trustee So. Meth. U. Mem. Am. Assn. Petroleum Geologists, Am. Assn. Petroleum Landmen, Petroleum Assn. Am., Dallas Petroleum Club, Phi Delta Theta, Alpha Kappa Psi. Methodist (trustee). Mason. Clubs: Dallas Country, Preston Trail Golf, Northwood (Dallas). Home: 3508 Wentwood St Dallas TX 75225 Office: 8111 Preston Rd Dallas TX 75225

GERMANY, JAMES HORACE, coll. pres.; b. Union, Miss., Feb. 9, 1914; s. Mack Henry and Lenora (Reagan) G.; Th.B., Anderson (Ind.) Coll., 1944; m. Janetta Marie Smith, June 16, 1939; children—Sondra (Mrs. Alton J. Hayostek), James Michael, Ruth (Mrs. Stanley V. Hill), Mary Jane (Mrs. Donald Lorfing). Ordained to ministry Ch. of God, 1941; pastor, Ind. and Miss., 1938-60; founder, pres. Bay Ridge Christian Coll., Kendleton, Tex., 1960—. Mem. publ. bd. Warner Press, Anderson, 1956—. Mem. sch. bd., Kendleton, 1965-73. Address: PO Box 726 Kendleton TX 77451

GERRISH, ROBERT GRANT, investment banking co. exec.; b. Boston, Feb. 9, 1921; s. John Jordan and Alice (Grant) G.; student Tufts Coll., 1938-39; Boston U., 1939-42; children—Grant T., Gail V., Conrad J., Thomas R. Salesman, Whiting Weeks & Stubbs, Boston, 1945-50; mgr. syndicate and municipal bond depts. G.H. Walker & Co., Providence, 1950-59; partner Oscar E. Dooly & Co., Miami, Fla., 1959-64; pres. Dooly, Gerrish & Co., Inc., 1964-70; account exec. Reynolds Securities Inc., Miami, 1970—. Past pres. United Way of Fla., Inc. Mem. R.I. Pub. Expenditures Council, Providence, 1956-59, Com. State Budget, 1957-59, Taxation Com., 1957-59, Met. Govt. Com., 1957-59. Trustee, R.I. United Fund, 1955-59; bd. dirs. Big Brothers of Greater Miami, Hearing and Speech Center of Dade County, United Way of Dade County, Crime Commn. Greater Miami. Served with USNR, 1942-45. Mem. Investment Bankers Assn. Am. (edn. com.), N.Y. Stock Exchange (investors information com.). R.I. Assn. Investment Firms (founder 1959), Nat. Security Traders Assn. (edn. com.), Fla. Security Dealers Assn. (past pres.), Security Dealers Assn. Greater Miami (past pres.). Clubs: Boston Investment (founder 1946, pres. 1946-48); Country (Coral Gables, Fla.); Miami. Home: 1525 S Miami Av Miami FL 33129 Office: 444 Brickell Av Miami FL 33131

GERTZ, JOSEPH BARRY, investments exec.; b. Detroit, May 7, 1942; s. Harold Morris and Geneva Rice (Skirvin) G.; A.B., Stanford, 1964; M.B.A., U. Cal. at Los Angeles, 1966, C.Phil., 1970. Investment analyst Bank of Am., Los Angeles, 1961-63; officer tng. program Shearson Hammill & Co., Los Angeles, 1965; research asso. finance U. Cal. at Los Angeles, 1966-68; asst. prof. finance U. Tex., 1968-71; pres. J.B. Gertz & Co., Austin, Tex., 1969—, No. Trust Co., Panama, 1973—, Am. Land Investors Co., N.Y.C., 1973—, Combined Deposits Fund, Inc., Los Angeles, 1974—; owner Faubion Ranch, Leander, Tex., 1970-73; Town Lake Apts., Austin, 1971-73; cons. Competitive Capital Corp., 1968-69; editorial cons. on investments to pubs.; lectr. investment banking and portfolio mgmt.; dir. Innovation Research Assos. of Prescott (Ariz.) Coll. Trustee Endowment for Commonwealth, Gertz Found. Mem. Econometric Soc., Am. Econ. Assn., Am. Finance Assn., Am. Mgmt. Assn., Inst. Mgmt. Sci., Hon. Order Ky. Cols., Beta Gamma Sigma, Delta Sigma Pi. Club: Los Angeles Athletic. Home: 5232 Los Adornos Way Los Angeles CA 90027 Office: PO Box 5370 Austin TX 78763 also 150 E 77th St New York City NY 10021

GERUGHTY, RONALD MILLS, pathologist, dentist; b. San Francisco, Aug. 9, 1932; s. Stanley Charles and Eleanor Rosalie (Meadows) G.; A.A., City Coll. San Francisco, 1957; D.D.S., U. Cal. at San Francisco, 1961, Ph.D., 1965; m. Sybil Grae Murphy, May 23, 1955; children—Cheryl Ann, Denise Michelle, Jeanine Louise, Shannon Marlene. Instr., asst. dir. clinics U. Cal. Sch. Dentistry, 1961; prof., chmn. dept. oral pathology, head div. head and neck pathology Med. U. S.C., Charleston, 1966—; cons. pathology VA Hosps., Charleston and Columbia, St. Francis Hosp., Roper Hosp., Charleston. State chmn. vol. edn. tng. S.C. div. Am. Cancer Soc., 1973-74, bd. dirs. Charleston County unit and S.C. div. Served with USN, 1951-55. Diplomate Am. Bd. Oral Pathology. Fellow Am. Acad. Oral Pathology; mem. Am., S.C., Charleston dental socs., Tissue Culture Assn., Internat. Acad. Pathology, Am. Assn. U. Profs. (pres. Med. U. S.C. chpt.), Am. Bronchoesophogological Assn. (asso.). Club: Sertoma Internat. (sec. Charleston). Home: 1076 Ripley Dr Charleston SC 20412

GERWE, RODERICK DANIEL, chemist; b. Cin., Jan. 5, 1938; s. Dr. Raymond Daniel and Florence (Cary) G.; B.S., Duke, 1960; Ph.D., Fla. State U., 1965; postdoctoral Tech. U. Karlsruhe (West Germany), 1965-67; m. Barbara Jean Williams, Feb. 20, 1940; children—David Roderick, Elizabeth Aimee, Caroline Elise. Chemist devel. labs. Tenn. Eastman Co., Kingsport, 1967-70, sr. chemist in prodn., 1970—. Sec., dir. Kingsport Concert Assn., 1972—. NIH fellow, 1963; NATO postdoctoral fellow, 1965; Alexander von Humboldt postdoctoral fellow, 1966. Mem. Am. Chem. Soc., Sigma Xi. Presbyn. Research on dealkylation on amine oxides. Home: 601 Meadow Lane Kingsport TN 37663 Office: Tennessee Eastman Co Kingsport TN 37660

GESUND, HANS, educator; b. Vienna, Austria, Sept. 18, 1928 (came to U.S. 1940, derivative citizen); s. Carl and Else (Sternberg) G.; B.E. with honors, Yale, 1950, M. Engring., 1953, D. Engring., 1958; m. Irmgard Orth, Jan. 28, 1951; children—Peter J., Ann M. Instr. civil engring. Yale, 1954-58; asst. prof. structural engring. U. Ky., Lexington, 1958-60, asso. prof., 1960-64, prof., 1964—. Served from lt. to capt. AUS, 1950-52, 61-62, now maj. Res. ret. Registered profl. engr., Conn., Ky. Fellow Am. Soc. C.E., Am. Concrete Inst.; mem. Am. Soc. Engring. Edn., Am. Soc. Testing and Materials, Internat. Assn. Bridge and Structural Engring., Internat. Assn. Shell Structures, Sigma Xi, Tau Beta Pi, Chi Epsilon. Jewish religion (trustee 1965—, pres. congregation 1971-73). Mem. B'nai B'rith (dir. lodge). Home: 844 Celia Lane Lexington KY 40504

GETTER, THEODORE ARTHUR, elec. engr.; b. Bklyn., May 19, 1916; s. William Frederick and Mary (Schultheiss) G.; student Pratt Inst., 1934-37; m. Lois Lucille Bellis, Aug. 8, 1943; 1 son, Ray Lee. Elec. engr. Bur. Yards and Docks, Naval Facilities Engring. Command, Charleston, S.C., 1941-43, 49—; elec. engr. Toole-Woodward Engring. Co., Charleston, 1946-48. Registered profl. engr., S.C. Mem. Nat. Soc. Profl. Engrs., I.E.E.E. (editor state publ.). Editor: Southern Corona. Home: 121 Lambert St Charleston SC 29406 Office: PO Box 10068 Charleston SC 29411

GETTIG, CARL WILLIAM, optometrist; b. Cleve., June 15 1928; s. Edmund Elmer and Arlie (Williams) G.; O.D., No. Ill. Coll. Optometry, 1949; student U. Ala., 1952-53, Spring Hill Coll., 1957; A.B., Oberlin Coll., 1962, B.M., 1962; attended Mozarteum, Salzburg, Austria, 1959-60. Individual practice optometry, Norwalk, O., 1949-50, Mobile, Ala., 1952-58, Foley, Ala., 1963—; part-time music tchr., Foley and Robertsdale, Ala., 1955—. Co-founder Performing Arts Assn., Foley, 1967, pres., 1968-69, 72-73. Served with AUS, 1950-52. Mem. Am. Optometric Assn., Am. Optometric Found., Coll. Optometrists in Vision Devel., Am. Pub. Health Assn., Am. Guild Organists, A.L.A., Am. Forestry Assn. Composer piano sonata, 1961. Home: 1515 N McKenzie St Foley AL 36535 Office: 1517 N McKenzie St Foley AL 36535

GETTINGS, ROBERT MICHAEL, assn. exec.; b. Peckville, Pa., Jan. 15, 1940; s. Theodore Roosevelt and Evelyn (Austin) G.; A.B., Bucknell U., 1961; M.P.A., Pa. State U., 1966; m. Karin Eva Karlsson, Sept. 3, 1966; children—Michael Edward, Kathryn Ann. Asst. for govt. affairs Nat. Assn. Retarded Children, N.Y.C., 1965-68; mgmt. officer Pres.'s Com. on Mental Retardation, Washington, 1968-70; exec. dir. Nat. Assn. Coordinators State Programs for Mentally Retarded, Inc., Arlington, Va., 1970—. Mem. adv. bd. Developmental Disabilities Tech. Assistance Project, U. N.C. Served as 1st lt. Adj. Gen.'s Corps, U.S. Army, 1963-65. Named Outstanding Young Man of Am., 1970. Mem. Am. Assn. Mental Deficiency (chmn. com. on social and legislative issues 1972—). Author: After Planning - What?, 1966; The 92d Congress: A Summary of Legislation Affecting the Mentally Retarded and Other Handicapped Persons, 1973. Home: 7106 Hundsford Lane Springfield VA 22153 Office: 2001 Jefferson Davis Hwy Arlington VA 22202

GETTY, JAMES RAHN, railroad exec.; b. Oaks, Pa., Sept. 26, 1914; s. Claude W. and Lorene (Stadon) G.; B.R., U. Pa., 1936; m. Jean Hutchison, Apr. 14, 1956; 1 son, James Hutchison; 1 stepson, Winfield A. Worth III. Tour agt. Am. Express Co., Chgo., San Diego, summers 1934, 35; ticket agt. Pa. R.R., Wilmington, Del., 1936; passenger agt., Seaboard R.R., Phila., 1937-40, dist. passenger agt., 1940-43, gen. passenger agt., Miami, Fla., 1943-48, passenger traffic mgr., Norfolk, Va., 1948-52, head gen. passenger traffic mgr., Richmond, Va., 1952; v.p. passenger traffic Seaboard Coast Line, R.R., Richmond, 1967—; v.p. passenger traffic Louisville & Nashville R.R., 1972—; dir. Nat. Ry. Publ. Co., N.Y.C., Richmond Terminal Ry. Co. Mem. travel adv. com. U.S. Dept. Commerce, Richmond bd. Bank of Va. Decorated order of So. Cross (Brazil); Distinguished Transp. Service award Costa Rica. Mem. Am. Assn. Passenger Traffic Officers (pres. 1962-63), Nat. Assn. Travel Orgns. (former dir.), Nat. Def. Transp. Assn. (life). Episcopalian. Kiwanian (past dir. Richmond). Home: 9808 St Julians Lane Richmond VA 23233 Office: PO Box 27581 3600 W Broad St Richmond VA 23261

GETTYS, THOMAS SMITHWICK, congressman; b. Rock Hill, S.C., June 19, 1912; s. John E. and Maud (Martin) G.; student Clemson U., 1929-30; A.B., Erskine Coll., 1933; postgrad. Duke, Winthrop Coll.; m. Mary Phillips White, Dec. 9, 1947; children—Julia Martin (Mrs. Burchett), Sara Elizabeth. Tchr., coach Rock Hill High Sch., 1933-35; prin. Central Sch., Rock Hill, 1935-41; sec. to Congressman Richards, 1941-51, postmaster, Rock Hill, 1951-54: admitted to S.C. bar, 1953; practice in Rock Hill, 1954-64; mem. 88th to 93d congresses from 5th S.C. Dist., mem. banking and currency com., house adminstrn. com. Pres. Rock Hill YMCA, 1960; chmn. Rock Hill United Fund campaign, 1955; chmn. trustees Rock Hill Sch. Dist. 3. Served with USNR, World War II; PTO. Mem. Am., S.C., York County bar assns., Am. Legion, V.F.W., Rock Hill C. of C. (past pres.). Democrat. Presbyn. (elder). Elk, Rotarian (past pres. Rock Hill). Home: Rock Hill SC 29730 Office: House Office Bldg Washington DC 20515

GEWERTZ, IRVING DAVID, architect, educator; b. N.Y.C., Jan. 4, 1923; s. Morris Aaron and Hannah (Gross) G.; student, Corpus Christi Jr. Coll., 1941-42, Kan. City Art Inst., 1946; B.Arch., Tex. A. and M. U., 1947; m. Anita Rose Indin, Dec. 25, 1946; children—Martin Anson, Jay Alan. With, Tatum, Alexander & Quade, Dallas, 1947-53, Roscoe DeWitt, Dallas, 1953-64, Pratt, Box & Henderson, Dallas, 1965-66, Goodwin & Cavitt, Dallas, 1966-68, Manuel Morris, Kansas City, Mo., 1968-71; instr. architecture Dallas County Community Coll., 1971—. Feature artist, real estate sect. Dallas Times-Herald, 1964-73; art instr. Julius Schepps Community Center, Dallas, 1972-73. Served with inf. AUS, 1943-46; ETO. Jewish religion. Home: 7125 Northaven Rd Dallas TX 75230

GHOLSON, HUNTER MAURICE, lawyer; b. Columbus, Miss., Feb. 19, 1933; s. Leon Carter and Marie (McDoniell) G.; B.A., U. Miss., 1954, LL.B., 1955, J.D. 1968; m. Hortense Jones, June 3, 1961; children—Emily Jones, William Webster. Admitted to Miss. bar, 1955; since practiced in Columbus; mem. firm William G. Burgin, 1955-56, Burgin, Gholson, Hicks & Nichols, and predecessor firm, 1959—; dir. Nat. Bank Commerce Miss. Sec., dir. Realty Rentals Corp., Meml. Leasing Co., Quality Products, Inc., Egger's dept. store. Chmn., Lowndes County Republican Party, 1960-64. Pres., dir. Columbus Ednl. Found., 1965-70; founder, dir. Stephen D. Lee Found. Served to lt. USNR. 1956-59. Mem. Am., Miss., Lowndes County (pres. 1973-74) bar assn., Lowndes County Hist. Soc. (pres. 1964-65), Columbus C. of C. (dir. 1969—), Ole Miss. Alumni Assn. (chpt. pres. 1964-65), Claiborne Soc., Phi Delta Theta, Phi Delta Phi. Episcopalian. Kiwanian (v.p. 1964, dir. 1960-64). Home: 1100 N 6th St Columbus MS 39701 Office: 516 N 2d Av Columbus MS 39701

GHUMAN, GIAN SINGH, educator; b. Barchuhi, Punjab, India, July 7, 1929; s. Hazara and Mahon (Kaur) Singh; B.S., Punjab U., 1952, M.S., 1955; Ph.D. (Dry Land Research fellow), U. Cal. at Davis, 1967; m. Sital Kaur, June 2, 1948; children—Tarlochan Singh, Jaspaul Singh, Mintoo. Came to U.S., 1963. Research asst. Punjab Agr. Dept., Nawanshahar, India, 1955-57; asst. prof. Coll. of Agr., Jaipur, Rajasthan, India, 1957-62; asso. prof. Savannah (Ga.) State Coll., 1967-71, prof. earth scis., 1971—. Cons., Kiah Mus., Savannah, 1969-71. Chmn. entertainment com. India Assn. of Savannah, 1971-73, v.p., 1973-74. Bd. dirs. Student Loan Fund, Savannah State Coll., 1971—. NSF grantee, 1973—. Mem. Am. Soc. Agronomy, Am. Soc. Soil Sci., A.A.A.S., Clay Minerals Soc. Home: 8510 Kent Dr Savannah GA 31406

GIAMMITTORIO, GEORGE MARVIN, judge; b. Alexandria, Va., May 6, 1921; s. David and Rosina (Recchiuti) G.; LL.B., George Washington U., 1941, LL.M., 1942; m. Mary Lucy Parrish, Nov. 9, 1946; children—Eugene Robert, David Carrington, Rosemary Parrish, Ruthanne Miller, Gregory Mark. Admitted to Va. bar, 1942; practiced in Alexandria, 1946-64; judge Corp. Ct., Alexandria, 1964-73. Pres., chmn. bd., dir. Peoples Bank & Trust Co. of Fairfax. Chmn. Alexandria council Boy Scouts Am., 1955-56; life mem. Friendship Fire Co. Co-founder, pres., regent Ascension Acad., pres. Parents Orgn. U. Richmond, 1969-70; 70-71. Served with USNR, 1942-46. Recipient Outstanding Citizenship award Order of Eagles, 1965. Mem. Am., Fed., Va. bar assns., Am. Legion (past post comdr.), Sigma Delta Kappa. Roman Catholic. K.C. Died Oct. 3, 1973. Home: 2416 Ridge Road Dr Alexandria VA 22302

GIBBES, WILLIAM HOLMAN, lawyer; b. Hartsville, S.C., Feb. 25, 1930; s. Ernest Lawrence and Nancy (Watson) G.; student Coker Coll., 1947-48; B.S., U. S.C., 1952, LL.B., 1953; postgrad., U. Va., 1954; m. Frances Virginia Hagood, May 1, 1954; children—Richard H., William Holman, Lynn. Admitted to S.C. bar, 1953; asst. atty. gen. S.C., Columbia, 1957-62; mem. firm Berry, Lightsey & Gibbes, Columbia, 1962-71; pvt. practice law, Columbia, 1971—. Sec., gen. counsel S.C. Credit Ins. Assn., Columbia, 1963—. Chmn., trustee U. S.C. YMCA, Columbia, 1958-62. Served as 1st lt. AUS, 1954-57; now col. Res. Mem. Am., S.C. (exec. com. 1961-62), Richland County bar assns., Euphradian Soc., U. S.C. Alumni Assn. (counselor-at-large 1959-60), Columbia C. of C., Omicron Delta Kappa, Kappa Sigma Kappa, Pi Kappa Alpha. Democrat. Episcopalian. Kiwanian (dir.). Clubs: Young Lawyers (pres. 1960-61); German; Forest Lake; Tarentella; Caprician (all Columbia). Home: 1360 Sinkler Rd Columbia SC 29206 Office: 1518 Washington St Columbia SC 29201

GIBBON, SAMUEL YOUNG, investment banker; b. Phila., Apr. 8, 1905; s. John Heysham and Marjorie Gwendolyn (Young) G.; B.A., Princeton, 1924; m. Virginia Newbold, Apr. 29, 1930; children—Samuel Young, Virginia G. (Mrs. J. Daniel Nyhart). With Am. Tube & Stamping Co., Bridgeport, Conn., 1924-26, Battles & Co., investment bankers, Phila., 1926-32; with W.H. Newbold's Son & Co., mem. N.Y. Stock Exchange, Phila., 1933-42, partner in charge trading and investment counsel div., 1936-42, ltd. partner, 1967—; founder, pres., chmn. Air-Shields, Inc., Hatboro, Pa., 1946-66. Mayor Town of Longboat Key (Fla.), 1969—, mem. Longboat Key Town Commn., 1968—. Served to capt. USAAF, 1942-45. Clubs: Princeton (N.Y.C.); Philadelphia; Sarasota (Fla.) Yacht, University (Sarasota). Patentee in field infant incubators, other breathing equipment. Home: 641 Rountree Dr Sarasota FL 33577 Office: 10 S Adams Dr PO Box 908 Sarasota FL 33578

GIBBONS, CELIA VICTORIA TOWNSEND (MRS. JOHN SHELDON GIBBONS), editor, publisher; b. Fargo, N.D. d. Harry Alton and Helen (Haag) Townsend; student U. Minn., 1930-33; m. John Sheldon Gibbons, May 1, 1935; children—Mary Vee (Mrs. Kenneth E. Ellenberg), John Townsend. Advt. mgr. Hotel Nicollet, Mpls., 1933-37; contbg. editor children's mags., 1935—; partner Youth Assos. Co., Mpls., 1942—; pub., art dir. Mines and Escholier mags., 1954—; founder Bull. Bd. Pictures, Inc., Mpls., 1954, pres., 1954—; founder Periodical Litho Art Co., Mpls., 1962, pres., 1962—. Republican chairwoman Golden Valley, Minn., 1950; alternate del. Hennepin County Rep. Conv., 1962. Mem. Mpls. Inst. Arts, Ft. Lauderdale Mus. Arts, Art Guild of Boca Raton, Delta Zeta. Clubs: Woman's, Minikahda. Home: 1416 Alpine Pass Tyrol Hills Minneapolis MN 55416 Office: 1057 A1A Hillsboro Beach FL 33062

GIBBONS, SAM MELVILLE, congressman; b. Tampa, Fla., Jan. 20, 1920; s. Gunby and Jessie Kirk (Cralle) G.; LL.B., U. Fla., 1947; LL.D., U. So. Fla., 1969; m. Martha Hanley, Sept. 14, 1946; children—Clifford, Mark, Timothy. Admitted to Fla. bar, 1947; mem. Fla. Ho. of Reps. from Hillsborough County, 1952-58, Fla. Senate, 1958-62; mem. 88th-89th U.S. congresses, 10th Dist. Fla., 90th-92d congress, 6th dist. Fla. Bd. dirs. Hillsborough County Heart Assn., Hillsborough County Guidance Center, Fla. Mental Health Assn.; founder, 1st pres. U.S. Fla. Found., 1958. Served to maj. AUS, 1941-45; ETO. Decorated Bronze Star medal; named Outstanding Young Man, Tampa Jr. C. of C., 1954; recipient President's award Tampa C. of C., 1955. Mem. Tampa (dir.), Hillsborough (dir.) bar assns., Greater Tampa C. of C. (dir.), Democrat. Presbyn. (deacon). Home: 940 S Sterling Av Tampa FL 33609 Office: House Office Bldg Washington DC 20515

GIBBS, FREDERICK H., educator; b. Knoxville, Tenn., Mar. 31, 1902; s. William Aaron and Lena Margaret (Durham) G.; student U. Tenn., 1920-21; B.S., U. Md., 1958; M.H.A., U. Minn., 1959; m. Ivy Lois Brooks, May 1, 1931; children—Frederick William, Thomas Cecil, Helen Lois (Mrs. John J. Justy), Mary Barbara (Mrs. Thomas Keith Treichel). Salesman, asst. supt. Cosmopolitan Life Ins. Co., Nashville, 1921-25; joined U.S. Army, 1925, advanced through grades to col.; with Transport Service, 1930-32, hosp. insp. 4th Service Command, 1943-45, exec. office surgeon Far East Command, 1945-48, exec. officer plans and operations Div. Surgeon Gen., 1948-52, organizer Surgeon Gen.'s Hosp. Mgmt. Research Program, 1948-52, dir. dept. adminstrn. Army Med. Service Sch., San Antonio, 1952-56; ret., 1957; dir. grad. program in hosp. adminstrn. Baylor U., 1952-56; Found. Adminstrs., Washington, 1956-70; prof. hosp. adminstrn., coordinator-dir., chmn. dept. health care adminstrn. George Washington U., Washington, 1959-67, Gordon A. Friesen prof. health care adminstrn., 1969-72, emeritus, 1972—; ednl. cons.

1957—; cons., Cath. Hosp. Assn., 1956-57, Office Def. Moblzn., 1960-61, Columbia U.'s Health Care Continuation Studies, 1956-67; vis. prof. U. San Paulo, 1964, Trinity U., San Antonio, 1973. Pres. Assn. Univ. Programs in Hosp. Adminstrn., 1964-65, mem. long term care task force, 1965-72; cons. chief med. dir. VA, 1961-68; mem. adv. council Med. Service Internat., 1966-71. Recipient awards for outstanding ednl. contbns. Surgeon Gen., Fed. Med. Service, 1965, 1970. Fellow Am. Coll. Hosp. Adminstrs. (book awards com., policy com. 1960-68, adv. editorial bd. 1970—), chmn. on long term care 1972—), Am. Coll. Nursing Home Adminstrs. (hon., com. on ethics 1970-71, chmn. jour. com. 1971-73, cons. editor 1973—); mem. Inter-Agy. Insts. Alumni Assn. (pres. 1953, distinguished service award 1968), Am. Hosp. Assn. (council on adminstrv. practice 1951-55, chmn. com. on methods improvement 1954-55), Am. Nursing Home Assn. (hon.; trustee ednl. trust, Better Life award for lasting contbns. to instns. for health care of aged, 1970), Am. Assn. U. Profs., Am. Pub. Health Assn. Contbr. to mags. Address: Box 29 Deale MD 20751

GIBBS, JAMES ALANSON, geologist; b. Wichita Falls, Tex., June 18, 1935; s. James Ford and Clovis (Robinson) G.; B.S., U. Okla., 1957, M.S., 1962; m. Judith Walker, June 18, 1966; children—Ford W., John A. Geologist, Cal. Co., New Orleans, 1961-63, Lafayette, La., 1963-64; cons. geologist, oil producer, Dallas, 1964—. Served with USNR, 1957-59. Certified profl. geologist. Mem. Dallas Geol. Soc., Am. Assn. Petroleum Geologists, Am. Inst. Profl. Geologists, Geol. Information Library of Dallas (v.p.), Soc. Ind. Profl. Earth Scientists, Sigma Xi, Sigma Gamma Epsilon, Phi Delta Theta, Petroleum Engrs. Club: Dallas. Republican. Methodist. Home: 6223 Park Lane Dallas TX 75225 Office: One Energy Sq Dallas TX 75206

GIBBS, JESSE, elec. engr.; b. Grove, Ky., Aug. 31, 1925; s. Ancil and Mary (Ellison) G.; diploma Cumberland Coll., 1948; B.S. in Elec. Engring., U. Tenn., 1950; m. Nina Margaret Wattenbarger, Nov. 9, 1946; children—Jesse Edward, Patricia Diann (Mrs. Kelton Levell Owen), Randal Ray. Elec. engr. TVA, Watts Bar Dam, Tenn., 1951—, Charter mem. Rhea County Rescue Squad, 1964—. Bd. dirs. Watts Bar TVA Employees Credit Union; sec. bd. assos. Hiwassee Coll., Madisonville, Tenn., 1970—. Served with USAAF, 1943-46; PTO. Mem. I.E.E.E., Am. Legion, Eta Kappa Nu. Methodist (trustee). Home: PO Box 185 Spring City TN 37381 Office: Watts Bar Engring Unit Watts Bar Dam TN 37395

GIBBS, RICHARD HENRY, social worker exec.; b. Richmond, Va., Mar. 2, 1925; s. Herbert P. and Lillian (Crew) G.; B.S., Va. Commonwealth U., 1946, M.S.W., 1948; children—Richard H., Robert, Betsy. Dir. teen age activities YWCA, Richmond, 1948-50; child welfare worker State Dept. Welfare, Richmond, 1950-51; casework supr. VA Hosp., Richmond, 1951-56; chief med. assistance div. Dept. Pub. Welfare, Norfolk, Va., 1956-57; med. social cons. State Dept. Health, Richmond, 1957-64, dir. social work, 1964—. Pres. Va. Council Social Welfare, 1971—; bd. dirs. Blue Ridge Inst. So. Community Service Execs., 1966-69; adv. com. Sch. Social Work Va. Commonwealth U., 1970—. Served with USNR, 1942-45. Mem. Nat. Assn. Social Workers, Phi Delta Theta. Home: 7602 Foxhall Lane Richmond VA 23228 Office: 109 Governor St Richmond VA 23219

GIBBS, SAMUEL JULIAN, dental educator; b. Amory, Miss., Apr. 1, 1932; s. Samuel John and Inez (McCarity) G.; student U. Ala., 1950-52; D.D.S., Emory U., 1956; Ph.D., U. Rochester, 1969; m. Emily Jane Starnes, Feb. 15, 1958; children—Samuel Phillip, Stephen Julian, Julie Ann. Pvt. practice dentistry, Vernon, Ala., 1959-63; fellow dentistry and dental research U. Rochester (N.Y.), 1963-68, asst. prof. radiology and dental research, 1968-70; asst. prof. radiology and dentistry Vanderbilt U., Nashville, 1970—, asso. dir. div. dentistry, 1972—, dir. dental hygiene program, 1971-73; cons. dentistry Nashville VA Hosp., 1970—; cons. Council on Dental Edn., Am. Dental Assn., 1971—, Bur. Radiol. Health, USPHS, 1971—. Served with Dental Corps, USAF, 1956-59. Mem. Internat. Assn. Dental Research (sec. Nashville 1972-74), A.A.A.S., Internat. Assn. Maxillofacial Radiology, Am. Assn. Dental Schs. (sec. council of advanced edn. 1973-74, sec. sect. grad. edn. 1973-74), Radiation Research Soc., Am. Acad. Dental Radiology (councillor 1973-74, chmn. radiation protection com. 1973-74), Am., Tenn. dental assns., Nashville Dental Soc. Home: 784 Greeley Dr Nashville TN 37205

GIBSON, ALLYN DOUGLAS, social worker; b. Lakeland, Fla., Jan. 26, 1932; s. Horace Wood and Elizabeth (Sneed) G.; A.A., Gardner-Webb Coll., 1952; B.A., Wake Forest U., 1956; M.S.W., Fla State U., 1961; spl. certificate U. Chgo., 1968. Social worker Fla. Dept. Pub. Welfare, Lakeland, 1957-59; sr. caseworker, supr. Family Service Agy., Ft. Lauderdale, Fla., 1961-67; instr., field instr. Barry Coll. Sch. Social Work, Miami, Fla., 1967-69, asst. prof., 1969-74, asso. prof., 1974—; field work instr. Fla. State U., 1963-67; adj. asst. prof. Fla. Atlantic U., Boca Raton, 1971—. Social work cons. Plantation Nursing Home, Fla., 1969-70. Served with AUS, 1953-55, Mem. Nat. Assn. Social Workers (chpt. pres. 1966-68, chpt. del. 1966-73), Am. Assn. U. Profs., Acad. Certified Social Workers, Council on Social Work Edn. Home: 3550 Galt Ocean Dr Fort Lauderdale FL 33308 Office: 11300 NE 2d Av Miami Dr Fort Lauderdale FL 33308 Office: 11300 NE 2d Av Miami Shores FL 33161

GIBSON, BEN TERRELL, JR., ins. and real estate co. exec.; b. Union S.C., July 26, 1929; s. Ben Terrell and Marie (Garner) G.; B.S. in Bus. Adminstrn., Davidson Coll., 1951; m. Amelia Ann Douglass, Oct. 16, 1954; children—Ben Terrell III, Preston D. Partner, Gibson Agy., Union, 1951-53, owner, mgr., 1955—; treas., mgr., dir. Cherokee Estates, Inc., Union, 1954—; pres. Cedarbrook, Inc., Union; pres., dir. Aimco., Inc., Union; chmn. bd. Consol. Bldg. Systems, Inc. Served with USNR, 1948-49. Mem. Pi Kappa Alpha. Methodist. Elk, Rotarian. Home: 1 Cherokee Pl Union SC 29379 Office: 105 S Gadberry St Union SC 29379

GIBSON, C. A. NEAL, JR., land surveyor; b. Sherman, Tex., Dec. 12, 1925; s. C.A. Neal and Annie Lea (McBride) G.; B.S., Tex. A. and M. U., 1947; m. Bobbie J. Petty, Nov. 25, 1965; children—Phillip, Patricia (Mrs. William Cobb). With Haidt-Templeton, Inc., Mobile, Ala., 1955-70; pres. chmn. bd. Neal Gibson & Assos., Inc., Mobile, 1970—. Served with AUS, 1943-45, 49-50. Mem. Am. Soc. C.E. (affiliate), Am. Water Works Assn., Am. Congress Surveying Mapping, Ala. Well Drillers Assn., Ala. Soc. Profl. Surveyors (dir. 1972-74). Club: Skyline Country (Mobile). Home: 401 Ridge Crest Ct Mobile AL 36609 Office: 3304 Old Shell Rd Mobile AL 36607

GIBSON, CHARLES ARCHIE, educator; b. Greenville, Miss., Feb. 11, 1931; s. Prentiss Eugene and Laura Belle (McDonald) G.; B.S., Miss. State U., 1957, M.S., 1959; Ph.D. (Ford Found. fellow), U. Fla., 1964; m. Jeanette Mosley, June 29, 1952; children—Michael Lynn, Jane Dianne, Laura Ruth, Jack Arnold. Instr., Miss. State U., Starkville, 1958-59; asst. prof. elec. engring. U. Ala., University, 1959-64, asso. prof., 1964-71, prof., 1971—; devel. engr. So. Services, Inc., Birmingham, 1971-72. Cons. to local electric utility, pvt. industry, govt. agys. Served with USNR, 1951-54. Registered profl. engr., Ala. Mem. I.E.E.E. (sr.), Am. Soc. Engrs. Edn., Tau Beta Pi, Eta Kappa Nu. Baptist. Home: 19 Valley View Tuscaloosa AL 35401 Office: PO Box 6169 University AL 35486

GIBSON, DAVID BAILEY, electronic devel. co. exec.; b. N.Y.C., Aug. 9, 1913; s. David Derrick and Florence Anna (Bailey) G.; B.S., Auburn U., 1936; postgrad. Syracuse U., 1955-56; m. Sally Estelle Watson, Dec. 23, 1936; children—David Bailey, Kirkwood W., Charlotte E. Pres., chief exec. officer Unitron Corp., Dade City, Fla., 1954—. Registered profl. engr., Fla. Mem. Nat. Soc. Profl. Engrs. (sr.), Fla. Engring. Soc., Auburn U. Alumni (life). Methodist. Patentee in field. Home: 1607 Fort King Hwy Dade City FL 33525 Office: PO Box 235 Dade City FL 33525

GIBSON, EDWARD GEORGE, astronaut; b. Buffalo, Nov. 8, 1936; s. Calder Alexander and Geraldine (Shannon) G.; B.S., U. Rochester, 1959, D.Sc. (hon.), 1974; M.S., Cal. Inst. Tech., 1960, Ph.D. in Engring. and Physics, 1964; D.Sc. (hon.), Wagner Coll., 1974; m. Julie Anne Volk, Aug. 22, 1959; children—Jannet Lynn, John Edward, Julie Ann, Joseph Michael. With Aronutronic research lab. Philco Corp., Newport Beach, Cal., 1964-65; astronaut Johnson Spacecraft Center, Houston, 1965—, pilot, 3d manned Skylab mission. Solar physics Subcom. NASA. Mem. Am. Astron. Soc., Inst. Physics, Am. Inst. Aeros. and Astronauts, Sigma Xi, Tau Beta Pi, Theta Chi. Author: The Quiet Sun. Home: 18611 Martinique Dr Nassau Bay Houston TX 77058 Office: Code (CB) Johnson Spacecraft Center Houston TX 77058

GIBSON, GARY LEON, elec. engr.; b. Borger, Tex., Nov. 25, 1941; s. Lee H. and Anna (Stiles) G.; B.S. in Elec. Engring., Tex. Technol. U., 1964; postgrad. West Tex. State U., 1970—; m. Cheryl Ann Harmon, Dec. 24, 1962; children—Jeffery Lee, Angela Lynn. With Southwest Pub. Service Co., Amarillo, Tex., 1964—, div. elec. engr., 1969-72, power sales engr., 1972—. Vocational instr. Amarillo Coll., 1967—. Registered profl. engr., Tex., Mem. I.E.E.E. (dir.), Tex. Soc. Profl. Engrs. Toastmaster. Home: 5711 W 49th St Amarillo TX 79109 Office: PO Box 1261 Amarillo TX 79105

GIBSON, HENRY WRIGHT, physician; b. Batesburg, S.C., June 18, 1924; s. William Thornwell and Kate Bates (Wright) G.; B.S., Wofford Coll., 1946; M.D., Med. U. S.C., 1950; m. Janet Yvonne Gilliland, June 6, 1953; children—Yvonne Kinsley, Amy Susan, Rosalyn Bates, Katherine Wright. Intern Columbia Hosp. Richland County, 1950-51; gen. practice medicine, Barnwell, S.C., 1951—; chief staff Barnwell County Hosp.; surgeon So. Ry. System, Seaboard-Coastline R.R.; med. dir. Shuron-Continental; mem. adv. bd. Am. Bank and Trust Co.; med. dir. Barnwell Woolen Mills. Trustee Barnwell County Hosp. Served with USAAF, 1943-45. Decorated Air medal with four oak leaf clusters. Mem. A.M.A., Am. Acad. Gen. Practice, S.C., So. Barnwell County (pres. 1972—) med. assns., Am. Legion, Kappa Sigma, Alpha Kappa Kappa. Methodist (bd. stewards 1952—). Home: 2015 Simms Av Barnwell SC 29812 Office: 1802 Wren St Barnwell SC 29812

GIBSON, JOE WALLACE, banker; b. Durant, Okla., Dec. 16, 1916; s. Hade and Anne George (Mason) G.; B.S., Southeastern U., 1938; m. Vivian Dee Crutcher, Sept. 10, 1940; 1 dau., George Ann. With 1st State Bank, Caddo, Okla., 1939-41; with 1st Nat. Bank in Durant, 1941-42, 45-58, 62—, exec. v.p., 1962-72, pres., 1972—, dir., 1962—; exec. v.p. 1st State Bank of Caddo, 1958-59; bank examiner State of Okla., 1959-62. Active Heart Assn., Tb Assn., Boy Scouts Am., Campfire Girls. Mem. Durant City Council; pres. Durant Sch. Bd. Served as lt., USNR, World War II. Mem. D.A.V., Am. Legion, V.F.W. Wars. Methodist. Mason (Shriner), Elk, Rotarian (pres. Durant 1972). Club: Durant Country. Home: Route 2 Durant OK 74701 Office: First National Bank Durant OK 74701

GIBSON, JOHN CLIFTON, savs. and loan exec.; b. Charleston, Ark., Nov. 4, 1939; s. John Virgil and Vivian Christine (Minnis) G.; student U. Ark., 1957-58, Texarkana Jr. Coll., 1962-63; B.S., Ark. Poly. Coll., 1966; m. Nan McCarrell, Dec. 20, 1958; children—Clifton McCarrell, Christine Johnette. Sr. accountant Peat, Marwick, Mitchell & Co., C.P.A., Little Rock, 1966-71; v.p., dir. First Fed. Savs. & Loan Assn. of Morrilton (Ark.), 1971—; dir. River Valley Service Corp., Morrilton. Bd. dirs. Conway County Indsl. Devel. Commn., 1973-74, Conway County Community Services, 1973-74, Wesley Found., Ark. Poly. Coll., 1973-74. Served with USNR, 1958-62. C.P.A., Ark. Mem. Am. Inst. C.P.A.'s, Ark. Soc. C.P.A.'s, Morrilton (dir. 1973-74), Morrilton Jr. chambers commerce. Methodist (asso. dist. lay leader for lay life and work 1973-74, sec.-treas. Men's Club 1971-73). Mason. Club: Morrilton Golf and Country (pres. 1974). Home: 10 Winthrop Dr Morrilton AR 72110 Office: 309 E Broadway Morrilton AR 72110

GIBSON, JOSEPH WOODWARD, water mgmt. cons.; b. Carson, La., Dec. 24, 1917; s. Myron Ellis and Theodosia Ernestine (Woodward) G.; B.S., Ouachita Bapt. U., 1939; postgrad. Northwestern U., 1946-48; m. Mary Elizabeth Mabile, Oct. 31, 1942; children—Richard David, Donna (Mrs. Steven Michael James). Instr. organic chemistry Ouachita Bapt. U., Arkadelphia, Ark., 1938-39; tech. rep. D.W. Haering & Co., Inc., water cons., Memphis, 1940-42, asst. service dir., Chgo., 1946-49, service dir., chief chemist, San Antonio, 1949-64; field cons. Wright Chem. Corp., Shawnee Mission, Kan., 1964-69, dist. mgr., Houston, 1969—. Fellow Am. Inst. Chemists; mem. Am. Chem. Soc. (sr.), Nat. Assn. Corrosion Engrs. Baptist (deacon). Home: 10515 Huntington Dale Dr Houston TX 77072 Office: 5715 Navigation Blvd Houston TX 77011

GIBSON, ROBERT FISHER, bishop; b. Williamsport, Pa., Nov. 22, 1906; s. Robert F. and Harriet (McKenney) G.; A.B., Trinity Coll., Hartford, Conn., 1928; A.M., U. Va., 1932; B.D., Va. Theol. Sem., 1940, D.D., 1948; m. Alison Morice, June 1, 1935; children—Robert Fisher III, John V. M., Margaret Alison, Peter McKenney. Ordained priest Protestant Episcopal Ch., 1940; held business and teaching positions, P.I., Dutch East Indies, Balt., also N.Y.C., 1928-38; asso. prof. church history Va. Theol. Sem., 1940-46; liaison officer P.E. Ch. in Mexico, 1946-49; dean Sch. Theology, U. of South, 1947-49; suffragan bishop P.E. Ch., Diocese of Va., 1949-54, bishop coadjutor, 1954-61, diocesan bishop, 1961—. Chmn. Joint Commn. on Ecumenical Relations. Episcopal Ch. Home: 8737 River Rd Richmond VA 23229 Office: 110 W Franklin St Richmond VA 23220

GIBSON, WALLACE CLIFTON, SR., judge; b. Pinson, Ala., Dec. 21, 1914; s. James Turner and Harriett Christina (Leeper) G.; student Birmingham-So. Coll., 1935-37; J.D., U. Ala., 1940; m. Gladys Mabel Allen, May 5, 1943; children—Lynn Jett (Mrs. Stephen Walker Brown), Wallace Clifton, James Turner III. Admitted to Ala. bar, 1940; with Jim & Wallace Gibson Attys., 1940-46, Gibson, Hewitt & Gibson, Attys., 1946-55, Jim & Wallace Gibson & Charles M. Hewitt; judge Jefferson County Criminal Ct., Birmingham, 1955-57; circuit judge 10th Jud. Circuit of Ala., Birmingham, 1957—. Mem. Ala. Ho. of Reps., 1947-51. Served to lt. comdr. USNR, 1941-45. Mem. Ala. State Bar, Birmingham Bar Assn., Ala. Circuit Judge Assn. Home: 1907 Shades Cliff Terrace Birmingham AL 35216 Office: 613 Court House Birmingham AL 35203

GIBSON, WILLIAM ARTHUR, mfg. co. exec.; b. Morgantown, W.Va., Aug. 8, 1933; s. John Arthur and Eleanor Willard (Reynolds) G.; A.B., W.Va. U., 1954; Ph.D., U. Rochester, 1960; m. Mary Alene Conner, June 12, 1965; children—Michael, John. Physicist, Oak Ridge Nat. Lab., Oak Ridge, Tenn., 1960-67; v.p., gen. mgr. Tennecomp Systems, Inc., Oak Ridge, 1967—, also dir. Cons. Oak Ridge Nat. Lab., 1968-69. Vice pres. Oak Ridge Symphony Orch., 1972. Mem. Phi Beta Kappa, Sigma Xi, Sigma Pi Sigma. Home: Gallagher Ferry Dr Route 5 Lenoir City TN 37771 Office: 795 Turnpike Oak Ridge TN 37830

GIBSON, WILLIAM EDWIN, mining engr.; b. Weeksbury, Ky., Sept. 16, 1930; s. Edwin Joseph and Irene (Depew) G.; B.S. in Mining Engring., Va. Poly. Inst., 1955; m. Gwenda Jean Wicker, Dec. 15, 1954; children—James Edwin, Barbara Ann, Deborah Irene. Indsl. engr. U.S. Steel Co., Lynch, Ky., 1956-62; mining engr. Evans Elkhorn Coal Corp., Wayland, 1964-66; indsl. engr. Eastern Coal Corp., Stone Ky., 1962-64, mining engr., 1966-70; mining engr. Ky. Carbon Corp., Phelps, 1970—. Registered profl. engr. Mem. Nat., Ky., W.Va. socs. profl. engrs., Am. Inst. Mining Metall. and Petroleum Engrs. Mason. Home: Star Route W Box 31-1A Phelps KY 41553 Office: Ky Carbon Corp Phelps KY 41553

GIDDEN, NORMAN L., ins. co. exec., 1916; A.B., Coll. City N.Y., 1937. Prodn. mgr. Gaston de Paris, 1937-39; self-employed ins. broker, 1939-40; with Govt. Employees Ins. Co., Washington, 1946—, v.p. adminstrn., 1954-63, 1st v.p., 1963-64, exec. v.p., 1964-66, pres., 1966—, vice chmn. bd., 1973, chmn. bd., 1973—; dir. Riggs Nat. Bank of Washington, Western Pacific Industries, Inc., Western Pacific R.R. Bd. govs. Ins. Inst. Am.; trustee Am. Inst. Property and Liability Underwriters; mem. Washington bd. trustees Fed. City Council. Served to maj. USMCR, 1940-46. Address: 1705 L St NW Washington DC 20036

GIDDENS, CLARENCE J., city ofcl.; b. Perry, Fla., Oct. 16, 1925; s. Jessie O. and Essie L. (Knight) G.; student Fla. State U., 1946-48; m. Belle Hunter, May 20, 1950; children—Theresa Diane, Clarence J., Kathy Annette. City clk., mgr. City of Perry, 1948—. Exec. sec., treas. Taylor County Recreation Bd., Perry-Taylor Employees Fed. Credit Union. Mem. Gov.'s Adv. Com., 1971-74. Mem. Taylor County Democratic Exec. Com., 1950-51. Recipient Outstanding Service award Municipal League Cities, 1965; Solid Citizen award Jaycees, 1970, Leadership and Tng. award, 1963; Friend of Forestry award Perry C. of C., 1967; Conservation award Woodmen of World, 1952; Water Conservation award Taylor County, 1972. Mem. Fla. Municipal Finance Officers Assn., Perry C. of C. Baptist (deacon). Mason (Shriner), Kiwanian, Elk. Home: 816 W Bay St Perry FL 32347 Office: PO Drawer 109 Perry FL 32347

GIDDENS, JOEL EDWIN, educator; b. Eastman, Ga., Feb. 11, 1917; s. Benjamin Franklin and Annie Maud (Mullis) G.; student Abraham Baldwin Agrl. Coll., 1936-38; B.S., U. Ga., 1940, M.S., 1942; Ph.D. (Gen. Edn. Bd. fellow), Rutgers U., 1950; m. Elizabeth Annette Williamson, Oct. 31, 1942; children—Charles Edwin, Ann Gladys, Dale Joel. Jr. chemist So. Regional Research Lab., U.S. Dept. Agr., New Orleans, 1942-45; research asso. U. Ga., Athens, 1946-48, asst. prof. agronomy, 1950-52, asso. prof., 1952-58, prof., 1958—. Instnl. rep. Boy Scouts Am., 1959-61. Served with AUS, 1945-46. Co-recipient prize for best paper Am. Soc. Plant Taxonomists, 1960. Mem. Am. Soc. Agronomy (Ga. chmn. 1961), Am. Chem. Soc., Am. Soc. Microbiology, Soil Conservation Soc. Am., Ga. Plant Food Soc., Ga. Acad. Sci., Sigma Xi, Phi Kappa Phi, Alpha Zeta, Gamma Sigma Delta. Baptist (deacon). Co-author: Principles of Soils Laboratory, 1967. Contbr. articles to profl. jours. Home: 315 Parkway Dr Athens GA 30601

GIDDIS, WILLIAM JAMES, educator; b. Coopersville, Mich., Aug. 28, 1927; s. Joseph Anthony and Sarah (Van Belkum) G.; B.S., Western Mich. U., 1951, M.A., 1952; Ed.D., Mich. State U., 1964; m. Donna Mae Charboneau, Sept. 9, 1954; children—Rayanne, Kevin Howard. Tchr., Dowagiac, Mich., 1953-56; sch. adminstr., Niles, Mich., 1956-62; asso. prof. Miami U., Oxford, O., 1966-70; prof. Hope Coll., Holland, Mich., 1970-71; faculty U. West Fla., Pensacola, 1971—, prof. edn., 1974—, chmn. dept., faculty of profl. edn., 1971—. Mem. Nat., Mich. edn. assns., Am., Mich., Ohio assns. sch. adminstrs., Nat., Mich., Ohio assns. secondary sch. prins., Assn. for Supervision and Curriculum Devel., Am. Ednl. Research Assn., Fla. Assn. Childhood Edn., Nat. Community Sch. Edn. Assn., Nat. Community Resource Workshop Assn. (pres. 1968-71). Home: 605 Poinciana Ct Gulf Breeze FL 32561 Office: Faculty Profl Edn U West Fla Pensacola FL 32561

GIDEON, RUSSELL ARTHUR, editor; b. Catoosa, Okla., Apr. 20, 1908; s. Arthur Burton and Laura (Bradshaw) G.; student U. Kan., 1927-28, U. Tulsa, summer 1930; B.A., U. Okla., 1931; m. Helen Belt, June 22, 1935 (dec. Oct. 1945); children—Lee Burton, Robert Wesley; m. 2d, Louisa Brown Lovell, Jan. 1, 1949 (div. Aug. 1951); m. 3d, Dorothy Naylor Bowen, Feb. 22, 1957. With Tulsa World, 1932—, asst. sports editor, news reporter, asst. city editor, 1932-45, Sunday editor, 1945—. Mem. Am. Assn. Sunday and Feature Editors (pres. 1964), Okla., Tulsa County (past v.p., dir.) hist. socs., Tulsa Press Club (pres. 1944-45), Kappa Sigma. Home: 2013 S Canton Av Tulsa OK 74112 Office: Tulsa World Box 1770 Tulsa OK 74102

GIDUZ, ROLAND, journalist; b. Fall River, Mass., July 24, 1925; s. Hugo and Edith May (Baker) G.; A.B. in Journalism, U. N.C., 1948; M.S. in Journalism, Columbia, 1949; m. Helen Frances Jeter, Dec. 25, 1949; children—William Roland, Robert Baker, Thomas Tracy. Migrant field rep. Home Missions Council N.Am., 1949-50; staff writer Chapel Hill (N.C.) Weekly, Durham (N.C.) Herald & Sun, 1950-54; state editor N.C. Jr. C. of C., 1951-54; editor Chapel Hill News Leader, 1954-58, News of Orange County (N.C.), 1960-66; editor, pub. Triangle Pointer, Chapel Hill, 1960—. Editor Alumni Rev., U. N.C. at Chapel Hill, 1966—, Univ. Report, 1969—, asso. sec. Gen. Alumni Assn., 1970—; founder Visitor Information Publs., Chapel Hill, 1970, pres., 1970-73. Mem. Chapel Hill Bd. Aldermen, 1957-69; mayor pro-tem, Chapel Hill, 1964-69; mem. Orange County Democratic Party Exec. Com., 1964-69. Served as pvt. 399th Inf. Regiment, 100 Div., AUS, 1943-45; ETO. Decorated Purple Heart. Mass Media fellow Fund Adult Edn. Harvard, 1958-59. Mem. Chapel Hill-Carrboro C. of C. (dir. 1969-71). Presbyn. Mason (K.T., Shriner), Toastmaster, Rotarian (pres. Chapel Hill 1972-73). Home: Box 44 Chapel Hill NC 27514 Office: Gen Alumni Assn U N C Chapel Hill Box 660 Chapel Hill NC 27514

GIESE, JAMES WILLIAM, educator; b. Twin Falls, Ida., Aug. 30, 1925; s. Herman A. and Ella (Buchanan) G.; B.A., U. Wash., 1947; M.S., U. Ill., 1959, Ph.D., 1962; m. Jean Cameron, Sept. 10, 1949; children—Jon Mark, Katherine Marie, William Timothy, Jeffery Herman. Prof. accounting North Tex. State U., Denton, 1966—, chmn. dept. accounting, 1967-69. Mem. exec. com. Denton Citizens for Improved Correction System, 1973-74. C.P.A., Tex. Mem. Tex. Assn. Coll. Tchrs. (v.p. chpt. 1973-74), Am. Inst. C.P.A.'s, Tex. Soc. C.P.A.'s (pres. Ednl. Found. 1970-72, trustee found. 1968—), Beta Alpha Psi, Beta Gamma Sigma, Phi Kappa Phi. Author: (with B.A. Coda and H.M. Anderson) Basic Account Concepts, 1974. Home: Route 2 Box 611A Denton TX 76201

GIESE, ROBERT PAUL, mathematician; b. Green Bay, Wis., June 23, 1936; s. Paul Richard and Meta Ernstenia (Boettcher) G.; B.S., U. Wis., 1961; M.A., U. Mo., 1968; Ph.D., U. Houston, 1974. Cartographer, Aero. Chart & Information Center, St. Louis, 1962-65;

computer programmer, instr. math. U. Mo., Columbia, 1965-68; systems analyst Cal. Computer Products, Houston, 1968-69; mem. sr. research staff Ray Geophys. div. Ampex Corp., Houston, 1969-71; computer programmer U. Tex.-M.D. Anderson Hosp., Houston, 1971-73; self-employed math. and computer cons., Houston, 1971—. Served with USAF, 1955-57. Mem. Math. Assn. Am., Sierra Club, Gamma Theta Upsilon. Mem. Universal Life Ch. (ordained to ministry 1972). Clubs: Houston Bicycle (pres. 1969-70), Seabreeze Sailing (Houston). Home and office: 4710 Benning Dr Houston TX 77035

GIESELMAN, ELMER JAMES, food co. exec.; b. St. Louis, May 4, 1917; s. Elmer Jacob and Blanche Van Stan (Schulz) G.; student Westminster Coll., 1934-35, Washington U., St. Louis, 1936-37; m. Benedette Texada Barker, Dec. 30, 1943; children—Benedette (Mrs. Thomas Edward Reh), Martha Jane (Mrs. Conrad Meyer IV), James Frederick. Sales rep. Deere & Co., St. Louis, 1937-42; sales rep. Consol. Cos., Inc., New Orleans, 1945-47, whole sale food distbrs., Plaquemine, La., 1947-49, br. mgr., New Orleans, 1949-65, sales v.p., 1965—. Pres., Azalea Grocery, Mobile, Ala., 1968, chmn. bd., 1969—; v.p., dir. Code, Inc., Pitts., 1969—, mem. exec. com., 1973—. Served to 2nd lt. USAAF, 1943-45. Decorated Air medal with clusters, D.F.C. with cluster. Mem. Beta Theta Pi. Republican. Club: Plimsoll. Office: 8130 Halmetto St New Orleans LA 70125

GIESEN, BERNARD WILLIAM, II, accountant; b. Houston, Jan. 22, 1945; s. Bernard William and Catherine Miriam (Flint) G.; B.A., Rice U., 1967; M.B.A., U. Pa., 1970; m. Karen Gaye Nelson, June 10, 1967; children—Bernard William III, Nelson Matthew. Accountant, Haskins & Sells, C.P.A.'s, Houston, 1970—. Class of '67 chmn. Rice U. Fund drive, 1973-74; county adviser Jr. Achievement, 1970-71. Served to 1st lt. AUS, 1967-69. Recipient Sam W. Becker award Res. Officers Tng. Corps, 1967, Nat. Transp. award Ret. Officers Assn., 1967. C.P.A., Tex. Mem. Am. Inst. C.P.A.'s, Tex. Soc. C.P.A.'s, Wharton Grad. Sch. Alumni Assn. (dir. 1973-74), Jr. C. of C. Clubs: Wharton (pres. 1973-74), Brazos (Houston). Home: 2226 South Blvd Houston TX 77006 Office: Haskins & Sells 1200 Travis St Houston TX 77002

GIESEN, FRANK HARTMAN, civil engr.; b. Superior, Wis., Oct. 5, 1932; s. Irving W. and Tracy (O'Donnel) G.; B.S., Marquette U., 1955; m. Mary Margaret Girouard, Aug. 13, 1955; children—David, Stephen, Robert, Tracy, Mary Patrice, Francis Gregory. Mgr., project engr. Consoer, Towsend & Assos., Cons. Engrs., Nashville, 1955-71, partner, 1966—. Dir. Plumbing Examiners and Appeals, City of Nashville, 1965—. Mem. Am. Soc. C.E., Tenn. Soc. Engrs. (treas. 1970, dir. 1966-68), Water Pollution Control Fedn. Club: Civitan (pres. Hendersonville, Tenn. 1963). Home: 513 Freda Villa Madison TN 37115 Office: 404 James Robertson Pkwy Nashville TN 37219

GIETZEN, ARTHUR WILLIAM, JR., civil engr.; b. Beaumont, Tex., Jan. 13, 1927; s. Arthur William and Pauline (Andrus) G.; B.S., Lamar State Coll. Tech., 1961; m. Patsy Page, Mar. 3, 1956; children—Karen Denise, John Eric. Engring. asst. Tex. Hwy. Dept., Silsbee, 1961-65, resident engr., 1965-67; project engr. Eastex, Inc., Silsbee, 1967—. Served with AUS, 1946-49. Mem. Am. Soc. C.E. (chpt. pres. 1964), Tex. Soc. Profl. Engrs. (pres. 1969). Roman Catholic. Home: 105 Read St Silsbee TX 77656 Office: PO Box 816 Silsbee TX 77656

GIFFEN, JAMES KELLY, lawyer; b. Knoxville, Tenn., Nov. 30, 1942; s. Lowell Lorimer and Mary Hartley (James) G.; B.S., U. Tenn., 1966, J.D., 1967; m. Joan Phyllis Meyer, Sept. 4, 1965; children—James Eric, John Gregory. Admitted to Tenn. bar, 1967; asso. Fowler, Rowntree, Fowler & Robertson, Knoxville, 1967-68, partner, 1968—. Bd. dirs., treas. Knoxville Housing Corp. of Kappa Sigma, 1972—. Mem. Am., Tenn., Knoxville bar assns., Knoxville Jr. C. of C. (treas. 1968-69), Phi Delta Phi, Kappa Sigma, Omicron Delta Kappa, Phi Kappa Phi, Beta Gamma Sigma. Clubs: Knoxville City; Fox Den Country (dir., sec. Concord Tenn. 1970—); Carolina Caribbean (Banner Elk, N.C.). Presbyn. (deacon 1969-72). Home: 12428 Hound Ears Point Concord TN 37720 Office: Hamilton Bank Bldg Knoxville TN 37902

GIFFORD, GEORGE EDWIN, educator; b. Mpls., Dec. 6, 1924; s. Ernest Wilbur and Hulda Victoria (Widen) G.; B.A. cum laude, U. Minn., 1949, M.S., 1953, Ph.D., 1955; m. June Marie Pirila, Dec. 29, 1956; children—Charles Stephen, Sheryl Diane. Instr. dept. bacteriology and immunology U. Minn., Mpls., 1955-56; asst. prof. dept. immunology and med. microbiology U. Fla. Coll. Medicine, Gainesville, 1957-64, asso. prof., 1964-68, prof., 1968—, acting chmn., 1965-66, 72-73, departmental grad. coordinator, 1968—; USPHS spl. fellow, research scientist Nat. Inst. for Med. Research, London, Eng., 1962-63. Served with USNR, 1943-46. Fellow Am. Acad. Microbiology, A.A.A.S. Contbr. articles to profl. jours. Home: 1013 NW 91st Terrace Gainesville FL 32601

GIFFORD, MARIE BATTEY (MRS. JOSEPH GIFFORD), radio sta. exec.; b. Cordell, Okla., Jan. 12, 1917; d. John William and Mary (Yoder) Battey; B.F.A., U. Okla., 1937; m. Joseph Gifford, Sept. 2, 1948 (dec. Dec. 1960). Account exec. Sta. KOME, Tulsa, Okla., 1941-44; instr. Baylor U. Sch. Radio, 1944-45; asst. program dir. Sta KWKH, Shreveport, La., 1945-57; account exec. Sta. KTBS, 1947-55, sales mgr., 1955-57; sales mgr. Sta. KEEL, Inc., 1957-62, gen. mgr., 1962—, v.p., 1964-69, pres., 1969—; v.p. Lin Broadcasting, 1966—. Exec. asst. Shreveport Summer Theatre, 1954-60. Bd. dirs. Community Action Program, Caddo-Bossior Parishes, 1969-71. Recipient Broadcaster of Yr. award La. Assn. Broadcasters, 1970. Mem. Shreveport Advt. Club (pres, 1964-65), Advt. Fedn. Am. (dir. 10th dist. 1964-66), La. Assn. Broadcasters (former officer), Shreveport C. of C. dir. 1968-71), Chi Omega. Club: Ambassadors (Shreveport). Home: 3818 Akard St Shreveport LA 71105 Office: 710 Spring St Shreveport LA 71120

GIFFORD, WILLIAM LEO, govt. ofcl.; b. Weston, Conn., Aug. 30, 1930; s. Rolland Wyckoff and Margaret (Clifford) G.; B.A., Fordham U., 1952; student U. Conn., 1952-55; m. Marion Frances Miletti, Oct. 27, 1956; children—Margaret Rose, William Leo, David Wyckoff. Polit. reporter Jamestown (N.Y.) Post-Jour., 1957-59; adminstr. asst. Rep. Charles E. Goodell of N.Y., Washington, 1959-68, Rep. James F. Hastings of N.Y., 1969; spl. asst. Sec. of Labor for Legislative Affairs, Washington, 1969-70; spl. asst. to Pres., 1970-72; dep. under-sec. Dept. of Treasury, 1972—. Mem. Nat. Press Club, Am. Polit. Sci. Assn. Republican. Home: 3908 Terry Pl Alexandria VA 22304 Office: Dept of Treasury Washington DC 20220

GIGICOS, THEODORE DEAN, clergyman; b. Troy, O., Feb. 15, 1941; s. George Chris and Anna (Kiriakou) G.; B.A., Holy Cross Greek Orthodox Theol. Sch., Brookline, Mass., 1965; m. Elaine Papageorge, Jan. 2, 1966; children—George, Ann. Lay asst., youth dir., Denver, 1965; ordained priest Greek Orthodox Ch., 1966; minister Greek Orthodox Chs., Waterloo, Ia., 1966-68, Honolulu, 1968-70, Pensacola, Fla., 1970—; tchr. Greek, Ch. Sch. Kiwanian.

GILBERT, ARCH BURTON, lawyer; b. Fairfax, Okla., Nov. 21, 1933; s. Raymond Donald and Thelma Eleanor (Williams) G.; B.A., U. Okla., 1955, LL.B., 1957; LL.M., So. Meth. U., 1963; m. Jo Anne Dollins, June 16, 1957; children—Shannon Gilbert, Devon. Admitted to Tex. bar, 1960; atty. Brooks, Tarlton, Gilbert, Penner, Douglas & Dressler, Fort Worth, 1962—; sec., dir. U.S. Bancshares, Inc., Dallas, Global Gas Corp., Fort Worth. Trustee Camp Crucis, 1973—. Served with USAF, 1957-60. Mem. Am., Tarrant County bar assns., State Bar Tex., Order of Coif, Phi Beta Kappa, Phi Alpha Delta. Author: (with Arthur Mitchell), Texas Methods of Practice, 5 vols., 1970. Clubs: Petroleum, Century II, Colonial Country, River Crest Country (Fort Worth). Home: 3616 Park Hill Dr Fort Worth TX 76109 Office: 2902 Fort Worth National Bank Bldg Fort Worth TX 76102

GILBERT, CLARENCE MITCHELL, physician; b. Chester, Pa., Dec. 30, 1931; s. Clarence M. and Leila G. (Wilson) G.; B.A., U. Pa., 1953, M.D., 1957; m. Barbara Patterson, Mar. 28, 1953; children—Clarence Mitchell III, Ronald S. Rotating intern Hosp. U. Pa., Phila., 1957-58, asst. resident medicine, 1958-59, resident medicine, 1961-62; asst. instr. medicine, dept. medicine U. Pa., 1958-59, 61-63, instr., 1963-64, fellow in cardiology Robinette Dept., 1962-64; practice medicine specializing in cardiovascular diseases, Orlando, Fla., 1964—; mem. active staff Orange Meml. Hosp., mem. cardiology staff Holiday Hosp., Lucerne Gen. Hosp.; med. dir. dept. cardiopulmonary therapy Orange Meml. Hosp., 1971—; clin. prof. allied health scis., Fla. Tech. U., 1970, Valencia Community Coll. Served to capt. M.C., USAF, 1959-61. Diplomate Am. Bd. Internal Medicine, Nat. Bd. Med. Examiners. Fellow Am. Coll. Chest Physicians, Am. Heart Assn., Am. Coll. Cardiology, Am. Coll. Angiology, A.C.P.; mem. A.M.A., Am. Fedn. Clin. Research, So., Pa., Fla. med. assns., Fla., Central Fla. (pres. 1970) heart assns., Orange County Med. Soc. (v.p. 1971, 73, pres. elect 1974), Med. Study Club Orlando. Rotarian. Home: 1020 Terrace Blvd Orlando FL 32803 Office: 15 W Columbia St Orlando FL 32806

GILBERT, HAROLD STANLEY, warehousing co. exec.; b. Fort Worth, Jan. 22, 1924; s. Sydney Ralph and Reba Samuels (Lever) G.; B.A., U. Tex., 1947, M.Ed., 1949; grad. Air Command and Staff Coll., 1961, Air War Coll., 1970, Indsl. Coll. Armed Forces, 1970; m. Jeanne Schwarz, Apr. 6, 1950; children—Marsha, Mark S., John L. Sci. tchr., coach Houston Ind. Schs., 1949-51; asst. prin., head sci. dept., athletic dir., coach USAF Dependents Sch. System, Germany, 1953-55; v.p. Coastal Bag and Bagging Corp., Houston, 1968-71; v.p. gen. mgr. Coastal Storehouse, Houston, 1968—. Mem. def. strategy seminar Nat. War Coll., 1973. Served with AUS, 1943-45, USAF, 1951-53. Decorated Bronze Star, Purple Heart with oak leaf cluster. Mem. Air Force Assn., Res. Officers Assn. (v.p. chpt. 1973-74, pres. chpt. 1974-75), Nat. Fedn. Temple Brotherhoods (dir. 1964-72, regional asso. dir. 1972—), Jewish Chautauqua Soc. (chmn. S.W. region 1964-72), T Assn. U. Tex., Houston C. of C. (mil. affairs com. 1969—), Houston, S.W. warehouse and transfer assns., Phi Delta Kappa, Sigma Alpha Mu. Elk, Rotarian (pres. club activities Houston and Harris County 1969-70). Home: 476 N Post Oak Lane Houston TX 77024 Office: PO Box 3207 Houston TX 77001

GILBERT, HAROLD WENDELL, record co. exec.; b. Murray, Ky., Jan. 24, 1939; s. Vernon and Martha (Walls) G.; student Miss. Vocational Coll., 1956-58, Wayne State U., George Peabody Coll., Austin Peay State U.; B.S., Tenn. A. and I. U., 1958-62; m. Jean Farley, Sept. 7, 1958; children—Kenneth, Keith, King, Kim, Kleetha. Tchr. Hampton High Sch., Dickson, Tenn., 1960-65; pres. Hitsburgh Music Co. & Rec. Co., Gallatin, 1964—; chmn. bd. Hal and Jean Enterprises, Inc.; pres. So. City Records; staff songwriter Cape Ann Music Co., 1971-72, Moss Ross Music Co., 1963, Tree Pub. Co., 1962-63; resource specialist Clarksville-Montgomery Sch. System, Clarksville, Tenn. Work Adjustment coordinator Tenn. Div. Vocational Rehab. Served with USAF, 1958-60. Named Mid-Tenn. High Sch. Band Dir. of Yr., 1969. Mem. Nat., Tenn., Clarksville Montgomery edn. assns., Council for Exceptional Children, U.S. Olympic Soc. Club: Mystery Men Society (treas.). Author: A History of Black American Music. Home: 157 Ford Av Gallatin TN 37066 Office: Hitsburgh Music Bldg Ford Av Gallatin TN 37066

GILBERT, JOSEPH GATLIFF, clin. psychologist; b. Pineville, Ky., Nov. 21, 1920; s. Thomas Joseph and Eva (Gatliff) G.; B.A. cum laude, U. S.C., 1951, M.A., 1952; Ph.D. in Clin. Psychology, U. Tenn., 1954; m. Katherine Armida Jennings, Aug. 30, 1948; children—Armida Jennings, Arthur Herbert, Robert Joseph, Katherine Elizabeth. Clin. psychologist Regional Office VA, St. Petersburg, Fla., 1954-55; chief clin. psychologist VA Mental Health Clinic, Pensacola, Fla., 1955-59, VA Gen. Med. and Surg. Hosp., Fayetteville, N.C., 1959-60; clin. and research psychologist State Hosp., Yankton, S.D., 1960-61; chief clin. psychologist Richland County Mental Health Clinic, Columbia, S.C., 1961-63, Child Devel. Center, S.C. Med. Coll. Hosp., Charleston, 1963-64; chief clin. psychologist Mental Health Center, Anderson, 1964-66; clin. psychologist VA Hosp., Charleston, 1966-69, S.C. State Hosp., Columbia, 1969—. Served with U.S. Mcht. Marine, 1942-46. Mem. Phi Beta Kappa. Author: Clinical Psychological Tests in Psychiatric and Medical Practice, 1969. Research and publs. in field. Home: 14 S Washington St Sumter SC 29150 Office: SC State Hosp Columbia SC 29201

GILBERT, NORMAN SUTCLIFFE, physician, med. sch. adminstr.; b. Butte, Mont., July 8, 1919; s. Norman Sutcliffe and Naomi (Robinson) G.; B.S., La. State U., 1939; M.D., 1943; m. Andrea Armbruster, Apr. 23, 1949; children—Andrea Naomi, Carolyn Sutcilffe. Intern, Charity Hosp., New Orleans, 1943-44, asst. vis. physician in internal medicine, 1946-47, vis. physician, 1950, sr. vis. physician, 1958—; resident internal medicine Shreveport (La.) Charity Hosp., 1958; staff physician Murray Hosp., Butte, 1948-50; instr. La. State U., New Orleans, 1950-51, asst. prof., 1951-57, asso. prof. rehab. medicine, 1958-65, prof., 1965—, asso. dean Sch. Medicine, 1964—, med. dir. Vocational Rehab. Inst., 1966—. Served from 1st lt. to capt. M.C., AUS, 1944-46. Diplomate Am. Bd. Internal Medicine. Mem. Orleans Parish, La. State med. socs., New Orleans Acad. Internal Medicine. Home: 3120 Coliseum St New Orleans LA 70115

GILBERT, PERRY WEBSTER, educator; b. North Branford, Conn., Dec. 1, 1912; s. Scott Warren and Hester (Weatherwax) G.; A.B., Dartmouth Coll., 1934; Ph.D. (Cramer fellow), Cornell, 1940; m. Claire Rachel Kelly, Sept. 3, 1938; children—Ann (Mrs. Bradley McDonald), David, Stephen, John, Mary (Mrs. Andrew Seyfried), Lois, Christopher, Philip. Asst. in zoology Cornell U., Ithaca, N.Y., 1937-40, instr., 1940-43, asst. prof., 1943-46, asso. prof., 1946-52, prof., 1952—, dir. Mote Marine Lab., Sarasota, Fla., 1967—. Mem. panel on biol. and med. scis. Polar Research Com., 1959-63; leader Tahiti-Tikehau Expdn., 1964; chief scientist Brit. Honduras Expdn. Shark, 1969; research asso. Lerner Marine Lab., Bimini, Bahamas, 1964—. Carnegie fellow, 1949-50, Guggenheim fellow, 1957, 63. Fellow A.A.A.S.; mem. Am. Inst. Biol. Scis. (chmn. shark research panel 1958—), Am. Soc. Zoologists, Am. Assn. Anatomists, Institut International d'Embryologie, Marine Biol. Assn. India, Am. Soc. Ichythyologists and Herpetologists, Am. Soc. Mammalogists, Am. Ornithologists Union, Am. Littoral Soc., Soc. Study Evolution, Animal Behavior Soc., Sigma Xi. Author: Sharks and Survival, 1963; Sharks, Skates and Rays, 1967. Asso. editor Jour. Morphology, 1954-58. Contbr. articles to profl. jours. Home: 852 Siesta Dr Sarasota FL 33581

GILBERT, RICHARD DEAN, educator; b. Winnipeg, Man., Can., Mar. 14, 1920; s. James W.B. and Florence A. (Sargeant) G.; B.S., U. Man., 1942, M.S., 1944; Ph.D., U. Notre Dame, 1950; m. Alma Louis Baldwin, Oct. 20, 1944; 1 dau., Laura Louise. Came to U.S., 1951, naturalized, 1957. Chief chemist Man. Sugar Co., Winnipeg, 1943-46; research chemist Polymer Corp., Sarnia, Ont., Can., 1946-47; research scientist Def. Research Bd. of Can., Sarnia, 1950-51; research chemist Am. Synthetic Rubber Corp., Louisville, 1951-55; sect. mgr. Synthetic Rubber & Latex Research and Devel., Uniroyal Chem. Corp., Naugatuck, Conn., 1955-66; asso. prof. textile chemistry N.C. State U., Raleigh, 1966-68, prof. textile chemistry, 1968—. Cons. Borg-Warner Chems., 1969—, Wica Chems., 1973-74. Mem. Cheshire (Conn.) Dem. Com., 1963-65; del. N.C. Dem. State Conv., 1972; sec. Planning Commn., Cheshire, 1965. Mem. Am. Chem. Soc. (chmn. New Haven, 1962, alternate councillor N.C. 1972—), N.Y. Acad. Sci., Sigma Xi, Phi Kappa Phi. Patentee in field. Home: 713 Dartmouth Rd Raleigh NC 27609

GILBERT, TED CURTIS, ednl. administr.; b. Arjay, Ky., Feb. 11, 1917; s. Roland and Cora (Hayslett) G.; A.B., Eastern Ky. U., 1939, M.A., 1947; postgrad. U. Ky., 1948; LL.D., Georgetown Coll., 1962; m. Eva Marie Neal, Feb. 6, 1944; 1 dau., Jane. Tchr., Bell County (Ky.) Elementary Schs., 1937, Breathitt County (Ky.) High Sch., 1939-40; prin. Pineville Elementary Schs., 1940-42, New Albany (Ind.) Jr. High Sch., 1946-49; supt. schs., London, 1949-50, Maysville, 1950-56; head bur. adminstrn. and finance Ky. Dept. Edn., 1956-58, asst. supt. pub. instrn., 1958-60; exec. sec. Ky. Council Pub. Higher Edn., Frankfort, 1960-62, exec. dir., 1964-72; staff asst. Office of Pres., U. Ky., 1972—; asst. supt schs., Louisville, 1962-64. Chmn., Christian edn. com. Ky. Bapt. Conv., 1958-65; mem. exec. com. So. Bapt. Conv., 1966-73; mem. adv. com. Ky. Ednl. TV Authority, 1968—. Bd. dirs. Ky. Child Welfare Research Found., Frankfort, 1964-71. Served to capt. AUS, 1942-46. Recipient Outstanding Alumnus award Eastern Ky. U., 1963. Mem. Nat. Assn. State Higher Edn. Exec. Officers (pres. 1971), Am. Assn. Higher Edn., Am. Assn. Sch. Adminstrs., Ky. Edn. Assn. (1st v.p. 1952-53), Nat. Assn. Chief State Sch. Officers (mem. study commn. 1958-60). Baptist (deacon). Rotarian (pres. 1955). Home: 1214 Richmond RD Lexington KY 40502

GILBERTSON, VIRGINIA MABRY (MRS. WALLACE CORNELL GILBERTSON), piano tchr.; b. Memphis, Dec. 2, 1914; d. Edgar Duval and Ina (Woods) Mabry; student Memphis State U., 1932-34; B.M., De Shazo Coll. Music, 1936; studied with Edwin Hughes, N.Y.C., 1944-64; m. Wallace Cornell Gilbertson, Apr. 21, 1935; children—Jon Wallace, Virginia Mabry, Cynthia Anne. Asso. tchr. De Shazo Coll. Music, Memphis, 1936-41; pvt. piano tchr., Wilmington, N.C., 1941-42, Charlotte, N.C., 1942-49, Fremont, O., 1949-57, New Canaan, Conn., 1957-60, Kinnelon, N.J., 1960-72, Tarboro, N.C., 1973-74; dir. music Charlotte Country Day Sch., 1944-46; accompanist Silvermine Guild Artists, New Canaan, Conn., 1957-60, New Canaan Town Players, 1957-60, Westport (Conn.) Community Theatre, 1958-63, Westport Madrigal Singers, 1958-59. Bd. dirs. Smoke Rise Players, 1970, Friends of Library, Edgecombe County, N.C. Recipient 1st prize Tenn. contest Nat. Fedn. Music Clubs, 1930. Mem. A.S.C.A.P., Am. Guild Authors and Composers, Edgecombe County Hist. Soc. (sec.), Internat. Platform Assn., D.A.R., Pi Mu. Club: Women of Smoke Rise (Kinnelon). Composer, co-author Next to Heaven, 1960; One Bronze Fealther (for N.J. tricentennial), 1964; several songs, 1955-65. Home and Office: Tarboro NC 27886

GILBREATH, CHARLES HARBIN, civil engr.; b. Double Springs, Ala., Jan. 10, 1932; s. Leldon Clifford and Isabell (Bufford) G.; B.S., U. Ala., 1961; m. Dorothy Marlyn Wilson, Mar. 8, 1952; children—Daphne (Mrs. David Allen Goodman), Julia Lynn, Marsha Dale (Mrs. Nathaniel Carlos Kennedy), Dotty Beth. Tool design detailer Chance Vought Aircraft, Grand Prairie, Tex., 1953-54; hwy. designer Ala. Hwy. Dept., 1954-56; design engr. A.C. Parker & Son, engrs., Tuscaloosa, Ala., 1956-68; chmn. bd. dirs. Gilbreath, Foster & Brooks, Inc., cons. engrs. and land surveyors, 1968—. Chmn. bd. dirs. Linnie Oden Boys Home, 1969-71. Mem. Am. Water Works Assn., Am. Soc. C.E., Cons. Engrs. Council, Am. Soc. Profl. Engrs., Tuscaloosa C. of C., Tuscaloosa Home Builders Assn. Mem. Assembly of God Ch. Clubs: Civitan. Home: 18 Riverdale St Tuscaloosa AL 35401 Office: 610 24th Av Tuscaloosa AL 35401

GILBRETH, HAROLD BRITE, coll. adminstr.; b. Bowling Green, Ky., Dec. 20, 1908; s. Wiley Smith and Eulah (Brite) G.; A.B., Western Ky. U., 1930, Bowling Green Coll. Commerce, 1931; M.A., U. Ky., 1935; Ed.D., N.Y., U., 1940; m. Georgia Mary Lecroy, Dec. 24, 1938. Tchr. pub. high sch. Rome, Ga., 1931-35, Winthrop Coll., Rocky Hill, S.C., 1935-37; teaching fellow N.Y. U., N.Y.C., 1937-38, Western Ill. U., Macomb, 1938-40; chmn. dept. bus. Winthrop Coll., 1940-67, dean Grad. Sch., 1967—. Vis. prof. U. N.C. at Greensboro, summer 1946. Recipient distinguished prof. award, Winthrop Coll., 1960; Found. for Econ. Edn. fellow, 1951. Mem. So. (past pres.), S.C. (past pres.), Ga. (past pres.) bus. edn. assns., S.C. Acad. Sci., Phi Kappa Phi, Delta Pi Epsilon, Pi Gamma Mu. Service editor Bus. Edn. Forum, 1947-52; asst. editor Modern Bus. Edn. Contbr. articles to profl. jours. Home: 616 Guilford Rd Rock Hill SC 29730

GILCHRIST, RALPH EDWARD, petroleum engr.; b. Milw., Dec. 17, 1926; s. Ralph Towns and Anna (Eggert) G.; student Lawrence Coll., 1944-46, Cornell Coll., summer 1945, Colo. Sch. Mines, summer 1946; B.A., Denver U., 1947; B.S., U. Tex., 1950, M.S., 1951; Ph.D., Penn. State U., 1957; m. Mary Ann Gill, Jan. 8, 1955; children—Gayle Lee, Jeffery Towns, Andrew McCord. Research engr., Texaco, Bellaire, Tex., 1951-52; research asst. Pa. State U., University Park, 1954-57; project engr. Sinclair Oil Co., Tulsa, 1957-59; sr. research engr. Phillips Petroleum Co., Bartlesville, Okla., 1959-66; dir. prodn. research Tenneco Oil Co., Houston, 1966-71; mgr. exploration and prodn. research, dept. applied physics Southwest Research Inst., Houston, 1971-73; dean Coll. Sci. and Tech., prof. sci. Tex. A. and I. U., Corpus Christi, 1973—; lectr. U. Tulsa, 1958-59. Served to 1st lt. AUS, 1952-54. Mem. Am. Inst. Mining Engrs., Soc. Petroleum Engrs. (founding mem., 1st chmn. Bartlesville Sect. 1962-63), Am. Soc. for Oceanography, S.A.R., Sigma Xi, Sigma Gamma Epsilon, Pi Epsilon Tau, Beta Theta Pi. Republican. Lutheran. Patentee in field. Home: 310 Cape Cod St Corpus Christi TX 78412

GILDEN, ROBERT OREN, govt. ofcl.; b. Anacortes, Wash., Dec. 4, 1922; s. Elmer John and Janie Maria (Lovelace) G.; B.S. in Agrl. Engring., Wash. State Coll., 1947, M.S., 1951 divorced; children—Jack, Ronald, Leanne. Instr. Wash. State Coll., 1947-51; prof. U. Wyo., 1951-56; extension agrl. engr., extension service Dept. Agr., 1956-71, exec. sec. Com. on Safety in Agr., 1971—; coordinator Agrl. Engrs. Internat. 1967—. Served with USAAF, 1942-45. Decorated Purple Heart, Air medal with 2 oak leaf clusters. Mem. Am. Soc. Agrl. Engrs. (chmn. structures and environmental div. 1970-71, chmn. Washington-Md. sect. 1971), Am. Geophys. Union, A.A.A.S., Sigma Tau, Epsilon Sigma Phi. Mason. Home: 1111 Army Navy Dr Arlington VA 22202 Office: ES-USDA Washington DC 20250

GILES, CARL HOWARD, educator; b. Big Stone Gap, Va., Mar. 13, 1935; s. William Carl and Thelma (Fields) G.; B.S., Fla. So. Coll., 1962; M.S., W.Va. U., 1965; m. Shelby Jean Ball, Nov. 24, 1956; 1 son, Sheldon. Tchr., Terry Parker High Sch., Jacksonville, Fla., 1962-64; asst. prof. journalism U. Tenn. at Martin, 1965—. Newspaper Fund fellow, 1963, Assn. for Edn. in Journalism mag. fellow, 1965. Mem. Assn. for Edn. in Journalism, Nat. Council Coll. Publ. Advisers (state chmn. 1972-74), Sigma Delta Chi, Kappa Tau Alpha. Author mystery documentaries, history, media textbooks, including: 1927: The Picture Story of a Wonderful Year, 1972; Writing Right—To Sell, 1970; Journalism: Dateline, the World, 1973; others. Contbr. numerous articles to mags., including True, Holiday, Adam, Man-to-Man. Office: English/Communications Dept U Tenn at Martin Martin TN 38237

GILES, HERMAN HASCAL, newspaper exec.; b. Big Stone Gap, Va., July 30, 1922; s. Harrison Oliver and Clara (Rose) G.; grad. pub. high sch.; m. Ruth Miller, Sept. 21, 1942; children—Kay, Eric, Amanda. With Bristol Virginia-Tennessean newspaper, Bristol, Va., 1949-50, 53—, asso. pub., 1961-64, pub., 1969—; asst. news editor Nashville Tennessean, 1950-51; make-up editor Louisville Times, 1951-53; v.p. Bristol Newspaper Printing Co., 1953; sr. v.p. Worrell Newspapers, Bristol, 1969—; v.p., Daily Corinthian, Corinth, Miss., 1958—, dir. Suffolk (Va.) News Herald, 1964—, Lenoir (N.C.) News-Topic, 1965—, Blacksburg (Va.) Sun, 1970—, Florence (Ala.) Times Tri-Cities Daily, 1970—, Sun-News, Las Cruces, N.M., 1970—, Sun Herald, Winter Park, Fla., 1970—, Greensburg (Ind.) Daily News, 1973—, The Messenger, Madisonville, Ky., 1970—, Princeton (W.Va.) Times, 1969—, several others. Chmn. Bristol (Tenn.) Indsl. Devel. Commn., 1969—. Recipient N.W. Ayer award Kingsport News, 1944; news writing award Va. Press Assn., 1954. Mem. Bristol C. of C. (pres. 1963). Baptist. Author: Kansas Trail, 1956; also adventure stories in popular publs. Home: 100 Stonecroft Circle Bristol TN 37620 Office: 320 Morrison Blvd Bristol VA 24201

GILES, JESSE ALBION, III, chemist; b. New Kensington, Pa., June 2, 1931; s. William Everette and Zora Ann (Matthews) G.; B.S., U. N.C., 1953; M.S., U. Ala., 1954; m. Alberta Ratledge, Jan. 3, 1953; children—Everette, Alan, Elease. Research chemist R. J. Reynolds Tobacco Co., Winston-Salem, N.C., 1954-67, head research sect., 1967—. Mem. Am. Chem. Soc., Sigma Xi, Alpha Chi Sigma, Phi Kappa Sigma. Patentee in field. Home: 2626 Village Trail Winston-Salem NC 27106 Office: Research Dept RJ Reynolds Tobacco Co Winston-Salem NC 27102

GILES, LAWRENCE ELMER, educator; b. Sunset, Wash., Aug. 23, 1914; s. Luther and Kittie (Wear) G.; B.A., Wash. State U., 1936, B.Ed., 1939; M.A., U. Minn., 1948, Ph.D., 1950; m. Margaret Sinclair Smith, Apr. 7, 1942; children—Mary (Mrs. John Clinton McClain, Jr.), Catherine Lynn, Carol Ann, Margaret Sinclair. Instr., U. Minn., 1948-50; asst. prof. U. Ill., 1950-52; prof. social sci. Territorial Coll. of Guam, 1952-54; mem. faculty U. S.C., Columbia, 1954—, prof. edn., 1960—, chmn. psychol. services, 1956-62, chmn. secondary edn., 1962-70, dir. Univ. M.A. in Teaching, 1970—. Served to comdr. USNR, 1942-45. Mem. Am. Psychol. Assn., Assn. Supervision and Curriculum Devel. (past pres. S.C.), Nat. Council Social Studies, Phi Delta Theta, Sigma Delta Chi. Rotarian. Democrat. Presbyn. (elder). Home: 4218 St Clair Dr Columbia SC 29206

GILKESON, JAMES WILLIAM, JR., constrn. co. exec.; b. Fisherville, Va., Oct. 9, 1925; s. James William and Zania Julia (Winchester) G.; B.S. in Civil Engring., Va. Poly. Inst., 1950; m. Emily Thomas Scott, June 27, 1953; children—J. Scott, Julia R., David T., Emily Page. Foreman, Va. Asphalt Paving Co., Inc., 1950-55, mgr. no. dist., 1955-56; v.p. engring., safety dir. Nielsen Constrn. Co., Inc., Harrisonburg, Va., also dir.; dir. Shen Valley Corp., 1968-71. Mem. gen. adv. com. Massenutten Vocation Tech. Center, 1970—; mem. exec. com. bldg. div., constrn. sect. Indsl. Dept., Nat. Safety Council, 1970—; chmn. activities com., dir. Stonewall Jackson Area council Boy Scouts Am., 1970—; mem. local Price Stabilization Bd., 1970—; mem. Christian edn. com. Lexington Presbytery, Va., 1959-67, pres. ch. sch. supts., 1961-62, with Christian edn. com. Synod of Va. Presbyn. Ch., 1961-63; commr. Gen. Assembly Presbyn. Ch. U.S., 1965; missions leader Desmios Community House Ch., 1972-73, pastoral leader, 1973—; mem. corrections adv. com. Va. State Crime Commn., 1973—. Mem. Planning Commn., City of Harrisonburg, Va., 1969—, vice-chmn., 1971-72, chmn., 1973—. Bd. dirs. Va. Safety Assn., Inc., 1970—. Bd. dirs. Homes Found. Served with USNR, 1943-46. Recipient dist. award merit Stonewall Jackson area council Boy Scouts Am., 1971, Silver Beaver award, 1973. Mem. Am. Soc. C.E. (asso. mem.; mem. exec. council, program chmn. Blue Ridge chpt. Va. sect. 1971), Asso. Gen. Contractors Am. (co-chmn. safety com. Va. br. 1967), Harrisonburg Rockingham C. of C. (chmn. safety com. 1968-73), Va. Poly. Inst. Alumni Assn. (v.p. Massanutten chpt. 1967-68), Order Arrow Boy Scouts Am. (Vigil honor 1972). Presbyn. (elder 1961—). Home: 1048 S Dogwood Dr Harrisonburg VA 22801 Office: Route #1 PO Box 591 Harrisonburg VA 22801

GILL, EUGENE LAVERNE, accountant; b. Kansas City, Kan., Jan. 2, 1929; s. Carl and Anna (Sambol) G.; student La. State U., 1953-59, U. Ala., 1960; m. Mary Alita Williams, Sept. 9, 1967; children—Alita Ann, Carla Gene. Partner firm Carl Gill & Son, Mercantile, New Roads, La., 1950-63; pub. accountant Eugene L. Gill, C.P.A., New Roads, 1962-66; partner Gill & Kendrick, New Roads, 1966—; pres. 104 West End Drive, Inc., Ben Morgan Furniture Co., Poor Boy's Friend, Inc., Gill Land Co., Ltd. Chmn. bd. dirs. Pointe Coupee Gen. Hosp., 1969-70. Conferee, La. Regional Citizens Conf. on Criminal Justice, 1973. C.P.A., La., Miss., Ark. Mem. Am. Accounting Assn., Nat. Assn. Accountants, Am. Inst. C.P.A.'s. Soc. La. C.P.A.'s (mem. com. to secure C.P.A. problems 1962-69, chmn. 1963-66, vice chmn. consultation com. 1966-67, mem. profl. devel. council 1967-71), La. Civil Service League, Am. Bus. Law Assn., Am. Judicature Soc., Pub. Affairs Research Council La. (trustee 1968—), Nat. Sourjourners, Farm Bur. Fedn., Am. Radio Relay League. Democrat. Episcopalian (warden, vestryman, lay reader). Mason (32deg., Shriner), Lion (past pres., past treas. New Roads); mem. Order Eastern Star. Clubs: Executive, Shrine (Baton Rouge); False River Country. Contbr. articles to profl. jours. Home: Waterloo Pl Ventress LA 70783 Office: 104 W End Dr New Roads LA 70760

GILL, HARRY WILLIAM CYRIL, educator; b. Gillingham, Eng., May 31, 1902; s. Harry and Katherine (Wallace) G.; B.A., U. London, 1923, M.A., 1925; m. Kathleen R. Williams, Apr. 28, 1927; children—Sheila Margaret (Mrs. Donald A. Maser), Barbara Elaine (Mrs. Malcolm Templeton), Humphrey G. Came to U.S., 1943. Asst. prof. Georgetown U., 1946-50; headmaster Fla. Mil. Acad., Ft. Lauderdale, 1953-57; asst. prof., then asso. prof. St. Leo (Fla.) Coll., 1957-66, prof. polit. sci. and history, 1966-69, distinguished prof. polit. sci., 1969—; vis. prof. U. Scranton, 1967. Mem. Am. Assn. U. Profs., Am. Polit. Sci. Assn., So. Polit. Sci. Assn., Polynesian Soc. Roman Catholic (diocesan historian). K.C. (4 deg., dep. jr. knight). Home: PO Box 2301 Saint Leo FL 33574

GILL, JOHN PAUL, educator; b. Warrior-Run, Pa., Jan. 7, 1910; s. John and Hedwig (Ryto) G.; student Pa. State Coll., 1929-31; A.B., U. Ala., 1932, M.A., 1934; Ph.D., U. Tex., 1950; m. Bernice Victoria Alman, May 24, 1932; 1 son, John Paul. Asst. instr. Sch. Bus. Adminstrn., U. Ala., 1932-34, comml. math., 1934-42, instr. bus. statistics, statistician Bur. Bus. Research, 1942-43, asst. prof., 1945-46; head math. dept. John E. Brown Coll., summers 1934-35; research statistician, dept. research Fed. Res. Bank, Dallas, 1943-45; chief research and progress analysis div. Houston regional office, War Assets Adminstrn., 1946-47; instr. U. Tex., 1947-49; asst. prof. Fla. State U., 1949-51; prof. econ. statistics, dir. div. research, also editor Atlanta Econ. Rev., Sch., Bus. Adminstrn., Atlanta div. U. Ga., 1951-54, prof. econs., dir. Bur. Bus. Research, coordinator grad. studies, also editor Ga. Bus., Coll. Bus. Adminstrn., U. Ga., 1954-60; prof. Sch. Commerce and Bus. Adminstrn., U. Ala., 1960—, head dept. bus. statistics, 1960-71. Mem. Am. Assn. U. Profs., Am. Statis. Assn. (pres. Ala. chpt. 1965-66), So. Econs. Assn., Pi Mu Epsilon, Alpha Kappa Psi, Beta Gamma Sigma (nat. exec. com. 1958-61). Author booklet on indexes of retail sales, also chpt. 1953-54 Credit Mgmt. Year-Book; numerous articles in field. Editor Southeastern Resources Handbook, Vols. I, II, III. Home: 10 C Northwood Northport AL 35476

GILL, JOSEPH PETER, JR., broadcast engr.; b. Plains, Pa., Feb. 23, 1928; s. Joseph Peter and Mary (Jukniewicz) G.; Asso. Sci., Central Tech. Inst., Kansas City, Mo., 1949; student Ohio State U., 1950-53; B.S., U. S.C., 1971; m. Margaret E. McNulty, Feb. 27, 1954; children—Michael Edward, Christopher Francis. Chief engr. WRDW-TV, Augusta, Ga., 1953-62; chief engr. WIS-TV, Columbia, S.C., 1962-68, chief engr., 1968—, also dir. engring. Cosmos Broadcasting Co., Columbia, 1968—. Treas. Dentsville Boys Baseball, Football and Basketball Assn., Columbia, 1967—; pres. Spring Valley Booster Club, Columbia, 1973—. Chmn. St. Peter's Sch. Bd., Columbia, 1970—; mem. exec. com. Diocese Charleston (S.C.) Sch. Bd., 1973—, pres., 1974. Bd. dirs. Asso. Social Agy. Served with USNR, 1945-47. Mem. I.E.E.E., Soc. Motion Picture and TV Engrs. Rotarian. Home: 3926 Rockbridge Rd Columbia SC 29206 Office: 1111 Bull St Columbia SC 29201

GILLASPY, JAMES EDWARD, educator; b. Bartlett, Tex., Oct., 15, 1917; s. Arthur Porter and Mae Lou (Mitchusson) G.; B.S., Tex. A. and M. U., 1940; postgrad. Ohio State U., 1941; Ph.D., U. Cal. at Berkeley, 1954; m. Maude Dorene Lannen, Aug. 3, 1948; children—Cathy (Mrs. E.R. DeLeon), Zena (Mrs. Eric Gibson), Kyna Dorene. Entomologist, War Dept., Camp Shelby, Miss., 1941-42; with Plant Quarantine Div., U.S. Dept. Agr., Laredo, Tex., 1946-48; salesman Cal. Spray-Chem. Corp., Twin Falls, Ida., 1954-55; research asso. Mus. Comparative Zoology, Cambridge, Mass., 1961-63; faculty Mankato (Minn.) State Coll., 1963-66; asso. prof. biology Tex. A. and I. U., Kingsville, 1966—. Served from pvt. to 1st lt. USAAF, 1942-46. Mem. A.A.A.S., Entomol. Soc. Am., Sigma Xi. Home: 719 W Av A Kingsville TX 78363

GILLEN, MARY-MARGARET D., lawyer; b. Poughkeepsie, N.Y., May 17, 1941; B.A. magna cum laude, Trinity Coll., 1962; J.D., Georgetown U., 1965, LL.M., 1966. Admitted to D.C. bar, 1966, U.S. Ct. Appeals bar, 1966; now mem. firm Bergson, Borkland, Margolis & Adler, Washington. Mem. Bar. Assn. D.C., Am. Bar Assn. Editor Georgetown Law Rev., 1964-65. Address: Bergson Borkland Margolis & Adler 21 DuPont Circle NW Washington DC 20036

GILLENWATER, JAY KING, chem. co. exec.; b. Esserville, Va., Mar. 3, 1907; s. J. A. and Nannie (Slemp) G.; student Lincoln Meml. U., 1921-25, U. Va., 1925-28; m. Anne Young, Dec. 21, 1931; children—Jay Young, Joyce (Mrs. J. W. Mottern), John K. Salesman, Tenn. Eastman Co. div. Eastman Kodak Co., 1931-34, asst. sales mgr., 1934-42, purchasing agt., 1942-53, dir. purchases, 1953-61, dir. purchases and traffic, 1961-68, dir. supply and distbn., 1968-69, v.p. supply and distbn., 1969—. Mem. Am. Chem. Soc., Nat. Assn. Purchasing Mgmt., Inc., Tenneva Assn. Purchasing Agts., C. of C., Alpha Chi Sigma. Club: Ridgefields Country (Kingsport, Tenn.). Home: 2221 Charsley St Kingsport TN 37660 Office: PO Box 511 Kingsport TN 37662

GILLESPIE, HAROLD EDWIN, state ofcl.; b. Minto, N.D., Aug. 12, 1907; s. Alexander G. and Rosa (Engebretson) G.; student U. Mont., 1924-27; B.A., B.S., B.M., U. Minn., 1932, M.D., 1933; m. Mary Miller Kress, June 29, 1940; children—Angus Kress, Mary Sabra, Cameron Alexander. Commd. lt. (j.g.) U.S. Navy, 1932, advanced through grades to capt., 1945; intern USN Hosp., Mare Island, Cal., 1932-33, St. Francis Hosp., San Francisco, 1933; hosp. comdr. Naval Air Stations, various locations, 1947-59; with Mil. Air Transport Services, 1959-63; ret., 1963; health dir., Williamsburg, Va., 1964-66; dep. commr. health Va. Dept. Health, Richmond, 1966—. Diplomate Am. Bd. Preventive Medicine. Fellow Am. Coll. Preventive Medicine; mem. Iron Wedge, Incus. Home: 1827 Grove Av Richmond VA 23220 Office: 109 Governor St Richmond VA 23219

GILLESPIE, JAMES WILLIAM, engr.; b. Choctaw, Okla., Jan. 30, 1935; s. James William and Gladys Bernice (Smith) G.; B.S., Okla. State U., 1957, M.S., 1958, Ph.D., 1961; m. Barbara Sue Mattern, Aug. 9, 1960; children—John Michel, James Edward. Asst. prof. Okla. State U., Stillwater, 1960-64; mgr. U.S. Steel Corp., Pitts., 1964-68; with Cities Service Co., Tulsa, 1968—, chief tech. adviser, 1968—. Recipient Instl. fellowship, 1953-54; Roberson Steel Co. fellow, 1958-60. Mem. Am. Soc. Civil Engrs., Nat. Soc. Profl. Engrs., Am. Soc. for Engring. Edn., Okla. Soc. Profl. Engrs., Sigma Xi, Phi Kappa Phi, Omicron Delta Kappa, Sigma Tau, Chi Epsilon, Phi Eta Sigma, Acacia. Home: 3177 E 38th Place Tulsa OK 74105 Office: Box 300 Tulsa OK 74102

GILLESPIE, JESSE SAMUEL, JR., research inst. exec.; b. Lynchburg, Va., Dec. 20, 1921; s. Jesse Samuel and Norna Brenda (Wright) G.; B.S., Va. Mil. Inst., 1943; Ph.D. (Tenn. Eastman fellow), U. Va., 1949; m. Nancy Vaughn Blackburn, Sept. 1, 1950; children—Samuel Harrison, Leonard Blackburn, William Wright, Nan Walker. Asst. prof. chemistry U. Richmond (Va.), 1949-51; sr. chemist, group leader, research dept. Va.-Carolina Chem. Corp., Richmond, 1951-54, asst. div. mgr. fiber div., 1954-56, sales mgr., 1956-58; partner Cox and Gillespie, Richmond, 1958-62; sr. research chemist Va. Inst. Sci. Research, Richmond, 1962-68, dir., 1968—. Vis. prof. chemistry Randolph-Macon Coll., 1960-61; adj. prof. chemistry U. Richmond, 1969—; advanced sci. tchr. St. Christopher's Sch., 1964-68; mem. library adv. com. State Council Higher Edn., 1968-71. Mem. Richmond Air Pollution Control Appeals Bd., 1971—; mem. Selective Service State Adv. Com. on Sci., Engring. and Specialized Personnel, 1969-71; regional v.p. Nat. Kidney Found., 1960-63. Served to 1st lt. AUS, World War II. Decorated Purple Heart; recipient Jackson-Hope medal Va. Mil. Inst., 1943. Mem. Am. Chem. Soc. (exec. com. local sect. 1965—), Va. Acad. Sci., Soc. Va. Creepers, Raven Soc., Sigma Xi, Alpha Chi Sigma, Omicron Delta Kappa, Kappa Alpha. Republican. Episcopalian. Rotarian. Club: Country of Va. (Richmond). Contbr. articles to profl. jours. Home: 22 Maxwell Rd Richmond VA 23226 Office: 6300 River Rd Richmond VA 23229

GILLESPIE, ROBERT GILL, chief justice Miss. Supreme Ct.; b. Madison, Ala., Sept. 17, 1903; s. Philander M. and Flora (Gill) G.; student Huntsville Jr. Coll., 1923-24; law student U. Ala., 1924-26; m. Margaret Griffith, June 30, 1930; children—Robert Gill, Virgil Griffith. Admitted to Miss. bar, 1927, practiced in Meridian, 1927-33; spl. agt. FBI, 1934-35; partner Bailey & Gillespie, 1939-43, Gillespie & Minniece, 1945-48, Gillespie, Huff & Williams, 1948-54; chancellor 2d Chancery Ct. Dist. of Miss., 1939; justice Miss. Supreme Ct., 1954-66, presiding justice, 1966-71, chief justice, 1971—. Mem. Miss. Council State Govts., 1944-48. Bd. dirs. Southwestern Coll., 1952-60. Mem. Am. Bar Assn., Miss. State Bar, Am. Judicature Soc., Delta Tau Delta. Presbyn. Home: 432 Dunbar St Jackson MS 39216 Office: Miss State Supreme Ct New Capitol Jackson MS 39201

GILLETT, GROVER, JR., educator; b. Whitewright, Tex., June 22, 1927; s. Grover Cleveland and Gertrude (Holland) G.; B.B.A., Tex. Technol. U., 1949; M.B.A., U. Tex., 1951; postgrad. Columbia, 1953, So. Meth. U., 1964-65; m. Mary Margaret Landress, Aug. 16, 1963. Accountant, Sproles & Woodard, Midland, Tex., 1951-53; auditor Lumbermans Mut., Dallas, 1954-56; auditor U.S. Army Audit Agy., Dallas, 1956-58; self-employed as C.P.A., Dallas, 1958-64; asst. prof., div. bus. McMurry Coll., Abilene, 1964-66; sr. internal auditor Ling-Temco-Vought Aerospace Corp., Dallas, 1966-67; instr. div. bus. El Centro Coll., Dallas, 1967—. Served as lt. (j.g.) USNR, 1945-46. C.P.A., Tex. Mem. Am. Accounting Assn., Nat., Tex. bus. edn. assns., Am. Inst. C.P.A.'s, S.W. Social Sci. Assn., Tex. Soc. C.P.A.'s. Author: (with others) Personnel Policites of Public Accounting Firms in Texas, 1951. Home: 7119 Rutgers Dr Dallas TX 75214

GILLETT, JOHN SHACKLEFORD, supt. schs.; b. George West, Tex., Sept. 4, 1909; s. Henry Pleasants and Mabel Cordia (Crawford) G.; B.A., Tex. A. and I. U., 1934, M.A., 1938; m. Lela Jo Merideth, July 30, 1945. Tchr. Kingsville (Tex.) pub. schs., 1934-37, prin., 1937-42, 47-52, asst. supt., 1952-56, supt. schs., 1956—. Pres. Community Concerts Assn., Kingsville, 1960-67. Bd. dirs. Kingsville Pub. Library. Served to lt. comdr. USNR, 1942-46. Mem. Tex. State Tchrs. Assn., N.E.A., Tex., Am. assns. sch. adminstrs., Phi Delta Kappa. Home: Box 988 Kingsville TX 78363 Office: Box 871 Kingsville TX 78363

GILLEY, WILSON CLEON, accountant; b. Cleveland, Tex., Dec. 9, 1944; s. William Francis and Nola Ellen (Bartlett) G.; student Massey Bus. Coll., 1964; B.B.A., Sam Houston State U., 1970; m. Marcia Kay Nelson, Dec. 9, 1964. With Byford Bates Bookkeeping & Tax Service, Cleveland, Tex., 1964-67; with Hereford Lynch & Co., C.P.A.'s, 1967—, tax dept., Conro, Tex., 1973—. Bd. dirs. Cleveland (Tex.) Livestock Show and Rodeo, 1972. C.P.A., Tex. Recipient Standard Oil of Tex. award and scholarship, 1969. Mem. Tex. Soc. C.P.A.'s. Rotarian. Home: 1510 Odd Fellow 5 Conroe TX 77301 Office: 509 N Main St Conroe TX 77301

GILLIAM, DARRELL KAY, physician; b. Wise, Va., Nov. 11, 1928; s. Franklin William and Mary Virginia (Bevins) G.; student Marshall U., 1946-48; B.A., U. Richmond, 1950; M.D., Med. Coll. Va., 1959; m. Nancy Evelyn Giannotti, Mar. 25, 1951; children—Darrell Kent, Shelley Lynn, William Anthony. Rotating intern Stuart Circle Hosp., Richmond, Va., 1959-60, now mem. staff; gen. practice medicine, Richmond, Va., 1960—, mem. staff St. Luke's Hosp., Richmond, Retreat for the Sick, Richmond, Johnston-Willis Hosp., Richmond, Grace Hosp., Richmond, Chippenham Hosp., Richmond; clin. instr. dept. family practice, health sci. div. Va. Commonwealth U., 1970-71. Pres., owner Broad Rock Bldg. Corp. Served with AUS, 1951-53; ETO. Diplomate Am. Bd. Family Practice. Fellow Am. Acad. Family Physicians; mem. A.M.A., Med. Soc. Va., Va. (del. 1971, sec. 1973) Richmond (pres. 1969-70) acads. family physicians, Richmond Acad. Medicine (sec. 1968-70), Manchester Med. Soc., Alumnus U. Richmond, Theta Kappa, Sigma Phi Epsilon. Methodist (chmn. bd. trustees 1966-71). Club: Beulah Recreation Assn. (Richmond). Home: 5110 Monza Ct Richmond VA 23234 Office: 3315 Broad Rock Rd Richmond VA 23224

GILLIAM, GEORGE HARRISON, lawyer; b. Alexandria, Va., July 26, 1942; s. Robert Skelton and Delia Bryan (Harrison) G.; student Princeton, 1960-61; B.S., Columbia, 1965; LL.B., U. Va., 1968; m. Sara Wilson Brown, May 29, 1964; children—Louise Bell, Sara Carter. Admitted to Va. bar, 1968; asst. commonwealth's atty., Charlottesville, Va., 1968-70; asso. Paxson, Marshall & Smith, Carlottesville, 1968-70: mem. firm Paxson, Smith, Boyd, Gilliam & Gouldman, Charlottesville, 1970—. Sec., treas. Titlesearch, Inc., Charlottesville, 1969—; sec. O'Neill Realty & Mortgage Co., Charlottesville, 1969—. Pres., Family Service of Charlottesville-Albemarle, Va., 1970-71; Charlottesville-Albemarle Mental Health Assn., 1968-70; treas. Va. Assn. for Mental Health, 1970; pres. Camp Holiday Trails, Charlottesville, 1971-74. City councilman City of Charlottesville, 1972—; mem. Charlottesville Dem. Com., 1969-73. Recipient Distinguished Service award Charlottesville-Albemarle Jaycees, 1972. Mem. Va., Charlottesville-Albemarle bar assns., Phi Alpha Delta. Episcopalian. Club: Farmington Country (Charlottesville). Home: 1409 Foxbrook Lane Charlottesville VA 22901 Office: PO Box 1151 Charlottesville VA 22902

GILLIAM, JOSEPHINE CALDWELL (MRS. RAYMOND A. GILLIAM), oil co. exec.; b. Bowie, Tex., June 8, 1912; d. John Walter and Josephine (Ribble) Caldwell; student Trinity U., 1929-30; m. Raymond Arnold Gilliam, June 3, 1932. Typist, Elliot & Waldron Abstract Cos. Inc., Athens, Tex., 1932-35, titleman, 1935-40; mgr. Elliott & Waldron, Quitman, Tex., 1940-42; staff fiduciary trust suit Shell Oil Co., Houston, 1942-43, sr. title clk. land dept., 1943-50; mgr. land dept., corporate asst. sec. J. Ray McDermott & Co., Houston, 1951-68; mgr. land dept., corporate asst. sec. TransOcean Oil Inc., Houston, 1968-74, spl. adviser, 1974—. Trans Ocean Oil Can. Ltd., 1971—, Trans Ocean Oil (U.K.) Ltd., 1971—, Trans Ocean (U.K.) Inc., 1971—, corporate asst. sec. brs. J. Ray McDermott Can., Ltd., 1967-71. Mem. Am. Bus. Women's Assn. (pres. 1967-68, Woman of Year 1965-66, editor Shamrock chpt. monthly mag. Blarney Stone 1970—). Home: 10626 Chevy Chase Houston TX 77042 Office: 1700 First City East Bldg Houston TX 77002

GILLIAM, LESLIE DON, data processor; b. Ardmore, Okla., Oct. 18, 1934; s. Don Lacy and Anna Corine (Hutson) G.; Asso. Sci., Murray State Coll., 1954; B.S., Okla. State U., 1956; postgrad. Tex. Christian U., 1958; m. Martha Jane Dobbins, Aug. 31, 1956; children—Dan, Julie, Cynthia. Computation engr. Chance Vought Aircraft, Dallas, 1956-61; with Continental Oil Co., Ponca City, Okla., 1961—, dir. computer planning and services div., 1969—. Lectr. computer installation mgmt. Okla. State U., 1970. Mem. Assn. for Computing Machinery, Ponca City Computer Assn. Baptist (trustee 1968-69, deacon 1963—). Home: 1124 South 7th St Ponca City OK 74601 Office: 1000 South Pine Ponca City OK 74601

GILLIAM, ROBERT LINDSAY, III, lawyer; b. Lynchburg, Va., Dec. 13, 1937; s. Robert Lindsay and Kathaleen Kimball (Snyder) G.; student U. Miss., 1955-58; LL.B. summa cum laude, Washington and Lee U., 1961; m. Marie Annette Whitaker, May 29, 1957 (div. June 1973); children—Marie Kimball, Robert Lindsay IV. Admitted to Va. bar, 1961; asso. Wilbur C. Hall, Leesburg, Va., 1961-62; partner firm Hill, Dizerega & DeButts, Leesburg, 1961-64; asso. firm Cohen, Cox & Kelly, Richmond, Va., 1964; practiced in Montross, Va., 1964—; Commonwealth's atty. Westmoreland County (Va.), 1964. Fund dr. chmn. Red Cross, Westmoreland County, 1965. Sec., Westmoreland Dem. County Com., 1964—. Bd. dirs. Woodland Acad., 1970—, chmn. 1971—. Served with USAF, 1961-62. Mem. Am., Va., No. Neck bar assns., Order of Coif. Home: Box 277 Montross VA 22520

GILLIARD, JOSEPH WADUS, educator; b. Taylors, S.C., Nov. 23, 1914; s. Josephus and Anna (Durant) G.; B.S., Hampton Inst., 1941, M.A., 1952; m. Bertha Holder, Mar. 19, 1943; children—Bernard O., Brenda L. Faculty, Hampton (Va.) Inst., 1941—, asst. prof. art, 1949-71, asso. prof. art, 1971—. Ceramic art exhibited at Ceramic Nat., Syracuse Mus. Fine Arts, Richmond Mus. Fine Arts. Instnl. rep., dist. commr. Peninsula council Boy Scouts Am. Served with USNR, 1942-44. Recipient Merit award 2d biennial showing of Chesapeake Craftsmen, Norfolk Museum, 1954; Meritorious award Peninsula Jaycees, 1958; Walter R. Brown award Gamma Ita chpt. Alpha Phi Alpha; Outstanding Achievement award Gamma Epsilon chpt. Omega Psi Phi, 1964; Silver Beaver award Boy Scouts Am., 1966; Outstanding Achievement award Alpha Delta Mu Honor Soc., Hampton Inst., 1965-66. Mem. Am. Ceramic Soc., Am. Indsl. Arts Assn., Am. Assn. U. Profs. Baptist (trustee). Home: 108 W County St Hampton VA 23363

GILLILAND, BOBBY EUGENE, coll. dean; b. Epps, La., Aug. 6, 1936; s. Otho Clyde and Vivian Margaret (Smith) G.; B.S., La. Tech. U., 1958; M.S. (Ga.-Pacific Corp. fellow), U. Ark., 1964, Ph.D. (Instrument Soc. of America's Found. for Instrumentation and Edn. fellow), 1968; m. Sara Frances Matkins, Sept. 12, 1959; 1 dau., Sara Clair. Asst. prof. elec. and computer engring. Clemson (S.C.) U., 1967-69, asso. prof., 1969—, asst. to the dean Coll. of Engring., 1973—. Partner, BBZ Enterprizes, Clemson, S.C. Mem. S.C. Gov's. Nuclear Adv. Council, 1973—. Served to capt. AUS, 1959-62. Registered profl. engr., La. Mem. Nat. Soc. Profl. Engrs., Am. Soc. Engring. Edn., I.E.E.E., Instrument Soc. Am., Sigma Xi. Club: Sertoma Internat. (Clemson). Home: 411 Shorecrest Dr Clemson SC 29631

GILLILAND, FRANK MARSHALL, JR., lawyer; b. Memphis, Nov. 27, 1927; s. Frank Marshall and Elizabeth (Jordan) G.; B.A., Vanderbilt U., 1949, LL.B., 1951; m. Tandy A. Jones, Dec. 27, 1958; children—Tandy Elizabeth, Mary Josephine, Carol Jordan, Frank Marshall III. Admitted to Tenn. bar, 1951, since practiced in Memphis; law clk. U.S. Dist. Judge, Memphis, 1955-56; mem. firm Frank M. Gilliland, 1956-69, Pittman, Clay, Morgan, Cole & Gilliland, 1959—. Pres. Gilliland Co.; sec.-treas. Gilliland Farms; sec.-treas. DeSoto Properties, Inc. Gen. counsel Memphis Cotton Carnival Assn., 1959—. Trustee Webb Sch., Bell Buckle, Tenn., 1961—. Served to lt. (j.g.) USNR, 1951-54. Mem. Vanderbilt Law Rev., Navy League U.S., Order of Coif, Phi Beta Kappa, Omicron Delta Kappa, Phi Delta Theta, Phi Delta Phi. Clubs: Memphis Country, Memhis Univ. Home: 4008 N Galloway Dr Memphis TN 38111 Office: Sterick Bldg Memphis TN 38103

GILLILAND, HAROLD EUGENE, chem. engr.; b. Duncan, Okla., Sept. 9, 1937; s. Lonnie and Lillian Otelia (Baade) G.; S.B., Mass. Inst. Tech., 1959, S.M., 1961, Ph.D. (Nat. Sci. Coop. fellow), 1965; postgrad. (Fulbright scholar) U. Bristol (Eng.), 1959-60. Sloan teaching fellow Mass. Inst. Tech., Cambridge, 1960, instr. chem. engring., 1962-63; with Continental Oil Co., Ponca City, Okla., 1964—, research group supr., 1968—. Mem. Soc. Petroleum Engrs. (chmn. No. Okla. sect. 1970-71), Sigma Xi, Tau Beta Pi, Phi Lambda Upsilon. Republican. Club: Mass. Inst. Tech. Club of Okla. (bd. govs. 1973—). Home: 13 Pioneer Place 715 Monument Ponca City OK 74601 Office: PO Drawer 1267 Ponca City OK 74602

GILLILAND, JOHN ALVIN, real estate co. exec.; b. Hartselle, Ala., Nov. 11, 1911; s. John Alvin and Lena Marguerite (Boyce) G.; B.S.C., U. Miss., 1933; m. Marion Russell McCrory, Oct. 21, 1940; children—John Alvin, Louisa Christina, Marion Russell. Exec. v.p., dir. Knight Orr and Co., Inc., Jacksonville, Fla., 1945-62; pres., dir. Stockton, Whatley, Davin & Co., Jacksonville, 1962—; dir. State Bank Jacksonville, Title and Trust Co. Fla., Jacksonville, Security Fed. Savs. and Loan Assn., Jacksonville, Investors Central Mgmt. Corp., Computer Power, Inc.; trustee Barnett Mortgage Trust, Jacksonville. Bd. dirs. Children's Home Soc. Fla., Jacksonville Children's Hosp.; trustee Bolle Sch., Jacksonville; lay adv. bd. St. Vincent's Hosp., Jacksonville; corporator Riverside Hosp. Served to lt. comdr. USNR, 1942-45. Mem. Mortgage Bankers Assn. Am. (pres. 1967), U. Miss. Alumni Assn. Episcopalian (sr. warden). Clubs: Florida Yacht, Deerwood (Jacksonville); Ponte Vedra. Home: 3089 Doctors Lake Dr Orange Park FL 32073 Office: 100 W Bay St Jacksonville FL 32202

GILLILAND, JOHN WESLEY, ednl. adminstr.; b. Springfield, Mo., June 12, 1905; s. William Greene and Laura Etta (Wade) G.; A.B., S.W. Mo. State U., 1927; M.A., U. Mo., 1931; Ed.D., N.Y.U., 1949; postgrad. Columbia, 1935—, Northwestern U., 1940-41, Washington U., St. Louis, 1945; m. Ruth L. Stice, Dec. 24, 1928; children—Marlene (Mrs. Robert Z. Fowler), Gene, Richard. Supt. city schs., Mo., 1927-40; secondary prin., Aurora, Mo., 1931-32; instr. edn. S.W. Mo. State U., 1933; elementary sch. prin., Clayton, Mo., 1940-46; prof. edn., dir. sch. planning lab. U. Tenn., 1951-70; dir. ednl. facility planning U. Fla., Gainesville, 1970—. Mem. Am. Assn. Sch. Adminstrs., Council Ednl. Facility Planners, Phi Delta Kappa. Methodist (trustee 1941—). Author: Selection and Care of Carpet for Schools, 1971. Home: 10819 NW 11th Av Gainesville FL 32601

GILLILAND, LUKIN, lawyer; b. San Antonio, Mar. 1, 1927; s. Taylor and Mary (Lukin) G.; LL.B., U. Tex., 1951; m. Ruth Harsh, Dec. 28, 1950; children—Lukin, Kip, John. Admitted to Tex. bar, 1951; practiced in San Antonio, 1951-63; mem. firm Gilliland, McNeel & Garwood, San Antonio, 1963—. Councilman City of Alamo Heights, Tex., 1964-71, mayor, 1971—. Served with USNR, 1945-46. Mem. State Bar Tex., Am. Bar Assn., Delta Kappa Epsilon. Home: 219 Argyle San Antonio TX 78209 Office: D-123 Petroleum Center San Antonio TX 78209

GILLILAND, WILLIAM ELTON, lawyer; b. Hood County, Tex., May 8, 1919; s. Albert Floyd and Rosa Lee (Wood) G.; student Tex. Technol. Coll., 1937-39, U. Tex., 1939-41; LL.B., U. Tex., 1947; m. Garlan Nita Thomas, May 17, 1947; children—Chloe Ella, John Marshall. Admitted to Tex. bar 1947; county atty. Martin County, Tex., 1947-48, Howard County, Tex., 1948-49; dist. atty. 118th Jud. Dist. Tex., 1949-54; mem. firm Little & Gilliland, Big Spring, Tex., 1954-59, firm McDonald, Shafer & Guilliland, Odessa, Tex., 1959-62, Shafer, Guilliland, Davis, Bunton & McCollum, Odessa, 1962—. Served to capt. Signal Corps, AUS, 1942-46. Mem. Am. Coll. Trial Lawyers, Am. Law Inst., Tex. Bar Found., State Bar Tex., Am. Bar Assn., Internat. Assn. Ins. Counsel, Am. Judicature Soc., Tex. Assn. Def. Counsel. Home: 2600 E 17th St Odessa TX 79761 Office: First Nat Bank Bldg Box 1552 Odessa TX 79760

GILLIN, CAROLINE JULIA, govt. ofcl.; b. Alpena, Mich., Sept. 16, 1932; d. Thomas F. and Frances (Kendziorski) Gillin; B.A. magna cum laude, Mercy Coll. Detroit, 1960; M.Ed., Wayne State U., 1964; Ed.D., 1969, Tchr. parochial schs., Detroit, Lansing and Ia., 1952-62; faculty, adminstr. tchr. edn. Mercy Coll. Detroit, 1962-70; sr. program specialist U.S. Office Edn., Tchr. Corps, Washington, 1970—. Research asst. Mt. Clements (Mich.) Community Sch. Dist., 1967; Project REMIDY Wayne County Intermediate Sch. Dist., 1968-69. Bur. Research grantee; U.S. Office Edn. fellow. Mem. Am. Assn. for Higher Edn., Assn. Tchr. Educators, Am. Edn. Research Assn., Lambda Iota Tau, Delta Epsilon Sigma, Kappa Delta Pi, Phi Delta Kappa. Democrat. Roman Catholic. Home: 1100 6th St SW Washington DC 20024 Office: US Office Edn Tchr Corps Washington DC 20202

GILLIOM, RICHARD D., educator; b. Bluffton, Ind., June 25, 1934; s. Andrew and Roberta Aldine (Dowty) G.; student, Centenary Coll., 1952-54; B.S., Southwestern at Memphis, 1956; Ph.D. (Sun Oil fellow), Mass. Inst. Tech., 1960; m. Patricia Ann Hastings, Mar. 7, 1958; children—Laura Rhea, Andrea Lee, Bruce Hastings. Chemist, Esso Research Labs., Baton Rouge, 1960-61; asst. prof. chemistry Southwestern U. at Memphis, 1961-64, asso. prof., 1964-71, prof., 1971—. Fulbright Hays lectr., Skopje, Yugoslavia, 1968-69. NSF research grantee, 1970-73. Mem. Am. Chem. Soc., Sigma Xi. Methodist. Club: Delta Sailing (Memphis). Author: Introduction to Physical Organic Chemistry, 1970. Contbr. articles to profl. jours. Home: 3017 Dumbarton Rd Memphis TN 38128

GILLIS, JAMES HILL, newspaperman; b. Poydras Plantation, La., July 2, 1908; s. Gary Eldridge and Stella May (Taylor) G.; B.A., Tulane U., 1931; m. Isadora Bright Myers Wilson, Jan. 25, 1940; 1 dau., Stella Elizabeth (Mrs. Franklin Ronald Waller Diemont); stepchildren-David C. Wilson, Oren C. Wilson, Jack M. Wilson. Reporter, New Orleans Times-Picayune, 1931-40, ships news reporter and marine editor, 1932-39, city hall reporter, polit. columnist, 1945—, state legislature corr., 1960—. Served to lt. comdr. USNR, 1940-45; PTO. Mem. S.A.R., Press Club of New Orleans, Alpha Tau Omega. Republican. Episcopalian. Home: 5111 Dryades St New Orleans LA 70115 Office: 3800 Howard Av New Orleans LA 70140

GILLIS, RICHARD SAMUEL, JR., assn. exec.; b. Lawrenceville, Va., Sept. 10, 1915; s. Richard Samuel and Janie (Wilkins) G.; student U.S. Mil. Acad., 1935; B.A., Randolph-Macon Coll., 1940; m. Margaret Crawford Shelton, July 10, 1948; 1 dau., Margaret Kimbrough. News editor Herald Progress, Ashland, Va., 1940-41; adminstrv. asst. Randolph-Macon Coll., 1945-51; exec. dir. Va. C. of C., Richmond, 1951—; mil. staffs Govs. Mills Godwin and Linwood Holton, Richmond Export Expansion Council; 1966—. Mem. Va. regional adv. council Small Bus. Administrn.; chmn. Mental Health and Mental Retardation Bd. Trustee Jamestown Found., Common Glory Found.; vice chmn. Pamunkey Regional Library, Hanover, Va. Served to capt. AUS, 1941-45. Recipient Distinguished Service awards Randolph-Macon Coll., 1960, Am. Cancer Soc., 1960. Mem. Richmond Pub. Relations Soc. (past pres.), Va. Assn. C. of C. Execs. (past pres.), Am. Legion (past comdr.), Export-Import Club (past pres.). Baptist. Kiwanian. Home: Route 1 Box 2A Hanover VA 23069 Office: 611 E Franklin St Richmond VA 23219

GILLQUIST, PETER EDWARD, author; b. Mpls., July 13, 1938; s. William Parker and Louise Ethel (Blitsch) G.; B.A., U. Minn., 1960; postgrad. Dallas Theol. Sem., 1960-61, Wheaton Coll., 1961-62; m. Marilyn Joyce Grinder, May 14, 1960; children—Wendy Jo, Gregory, Ginger Ann, Terri Beth, Heidi Lou, Peter Jon. Regional dir., editor Campus Crusade for Christ, Inc., Evanston, Ill., 1960-68; dir. devel. Memphis State U., 1969-72, exec. v.p. Memphis State U. Found., 1969-72. Cons. Tenn. Sheriffs Youth Town, 1972-74. Program dir. Memphis Drug Commn., 1970-72. Mem. Sigma Alpha Epsilon. Author: Love is Now, 1970; Handbook for Spiritual Survival, 1971; Let's Quit Fighting About the Holy Spirit, 1974. Home: Paupers Alley Grand Junction TN 38039 Office: same

GILMAN, LAUREN CUNDIFF, educator; b. Bozeman, Mont., Nov. 24, 1914; s. Ralph Webster and Pearl (Cundiff) G.; A.B., Baker U., 1936; Ph.D., Johns Hopkins U., 1940. Asst. prof. zoology U. S.D., Vermillion, S.D., 1946-47; asso. prof. zoology U. Miami, Coral Gables, 1947—. Mem. corp. Marine Biol. Lab., Woods Hole, Mass., 1949—. Served from pvt. to capt. AUS, 1941-46. Fellow A.A.A.S. (council 1967-73); mem. Am. Inst. Biol. Scis., Am. Genetic Assn., Am. Assn. U. Profs., Assn. Southeastern Biologists, Soc. Protozoologists (mem. exec. com. 1957-62), Phi Beta Kappa (pres. Greater Miami assn. 1964), Sigma Xi (treas. Miami chpt. 1959-65), Alpha Delta Sigma, Beta Beta Beta, Gamma Alpha. Democrat. Research in mating types and syngens in Paramecium caudatum; morphol. and physiol. differences among syngens. Home: 423 Majorca St Coral Gables FL 33134

GILMAN, LEE ATTERBURY, pub. relations counselor; b. Chgo., Jan. 17, 1926; s. Victor Boughton and Beulah (Fisk) G.; B.A. in English, U. Tex., 1951; postgrad. U. Cal. at Berkeley, 1951; m. Virginia R. Dana, Oct. 1, 1966. City editor Hillsboro (Tex.) Daily Mirror, 1951; asst. publicity dir. Tex. Ind. Producers and Royalty Owners Assn., Austin, 1952-54; pvt. practice as pub. relations cons., 1954-56; pub. relations asst. Southwestern Life Ins. Co., Dallas, 1956-60; gen. mgr. Gilman & Co., 1960-61, pres., 1961-65; dir. pub. relations Interstate Life & Accident Ins. Co., 1968—. Served with USNR, 1944-46. Mem. Pub. Relations Soc. Am., Life Ins. Advertisers Assn., Chattanooga Ad Club, Alpha Phi Omega. Republican. Episcopalian. Home: 724 Bacon Trail Chattanooga TN 37412 Office: Interstate Life Bldg Chattanooga TN 37402

GILMARTIN, FRANCIS THOMAS, JR., museum ofcl.; b. Palmer, Mass., Aug. 6, 1940; s. Francis Thomas and Dorothy Mary (Diamond) G.; student Sch. Worcester Art Museum, 1960-63; B.A., Goddard Coll., 1973. Resident artist Penland Sch. Crafts, Penland, N.C., 1965-66; ednl. supr. crafts program, spl. services br. U.S. Army, 1966-68; edn. dir. So. Highland Handicraft Guild, Asheville, N.C., 1968-70; team supr. Army Artist Team XI, Thailand, 1970-71; tchr. pub. schs., Newport News, Va., 1971-72; tchr. Asheville Art Museum, 1968-70, dir. museum, 1973—. Designer exhbn. series Eastern Cherokee Indians; cons. Vols. in Tech. Assistance, Mt. Ranier, Md., 1970-74. Served with AUS, 1963-65. Study grantee Babcock Found., 1965-66. Mem. Am. Civil Liberties Union. Author: Cherokee Indians. Home: 98 N Holland St Asheville NC 28801 Office: 152 Pearson Dr Asheville NC 28801

GILMORE, HUGH REDLAND, govt. ofcl.; b. Bristol, Vt., Aug. 13, 1916; s. John R. and Rubie (Rathbun) G.; Ph.B. magna cum laude, U. Vt., 1937; J.D., Columbia, 1941; m. Marjorie V. Havens, May 8, 1942; children—Douglas H., Anne C., Joan L. Admitted to Vt. bar, 1946, N.Y. State bar, 1948; asso. firm Sylvester & Ready, St. Albans, Vt., 1946-47; atty.-adviser Office Gen. Counsel Air Force, Office Sec. Air Force, Washington, 1949-54, asst. gen. counsel Air Force for personnel and adminstrn., 1954—. Served to maj. AUS, 1942-46, 47-49; col. Air Force Res. Decorated Asiatic-Pacific ribbon with 3 bronze stars, Phillippine Liberation ribbon with 1 bronze star; recipient Exceptional Civilian Service award U.S. Air Force 1965; certificate of spl. recognition Sec. Air Force, 1969. Mem. Fed. Bar Assn., Phi Beta Kappa, Pi Gamma Mu. Mason. Clubs: Overlee Community Assn., Arlington Forest (past dir.). Home: 3020 N Nottingham St Arlington VA 22207

GILMORE, JERRY CARL, lawyer; b. Memphis, Dec. 29, 1933; s. Hugh Bailey and Gladys Herd (Jones) G.; B.A., U. Tex., 1955, J.D., 1957; m. Martha Niendorff, Dec. 1, 1956; children—Daniel, Susan, Charles. Admitted to Tex. bar, 1957; mem. firm Green, Gilmore, Crutcher, Rothpeltz & Burke, Dallas, 1957—. Pres., N. Tex. Found. for Human Resources Devel., Dallas, 1972—; mem. exec. bd. N. Central Tex. Council of Govts., 1973-74. Mem. Dallas City Council, 1971—. Recipient Oak Cliff Civitan Outstanding Community Service award, 1972; Mem. Am., Dallas, Dallas Jr. (Outstanding Young Lawyer of City of Dallas, 1971, pres. 1962-63) bar assns., State Bar Tex., Oak Cliff C. of C. (dir.), Delta Theta Phi. Baptist (deacon 1959—). Mason (Shriner, K.T., 32 deg.), Lion. Club: High Noon (Dallas). Home: 1608 W Colorado St Dallas TX 75208 Office: 1307 Pacific Suite 400 Dallas TX 75202

GILMORE, MARJORIE HAVENS (MRS. HUGH REDLAND GILMORE), lawyer, club woman; b. N.Y.C., Aug. 1, 1918; d. William Westerfield and Elsie (Medl) Havens; A.B., Hunter Coll., 1938; J.D., Columbia, 1941; m. Hugh Redland Gilmore, May 8, 1942; children—Douglas Hugh, Anne Charlotte, Joan Louise. Admitted to N.Y. bar, 1941, Va. bar, 1968; research asst. N.Y. Law Revision Comm., 1941-42; asso. firm Spence, Windels, Waiser, Hotchkiss & Angell, N.Y.C., 1942, Chadbourne, Wallace, Parke & Whiteside, N.Y.C., 1942-43; atty. U.S. Army, Washington, 1948-53. Sec., Thomas Jefferson Jr. High Sch. P.T.A., 1956-58; parliamentarian Wakefield High Sch. P.T.A., 1959-60, chmn. citizenship com., 1960-61; publicity chmn. Patrick Henry Sch. P.T.A., 1963-64, sec., 1964-65; parliamentarian Nottingham P.T.A., 1966-69; troop leader Girl Scouts U.S.A., 1963-70; mem. extra-curricular activities com. Arlington County Sch. Bd.; area chmn. fund drive Cancer Soc., 1955-56. Recipient Constl. Law award Hunter Coll., 1938. Mem. Columbia Law Sch. Alumni Assn., Alpha Sigma Rho. Presbyn. Club: Williamsburg Women's (publicity chmn. 1969-70, corr. sec. 1970-72, 1st v.p. 1972-74, pres. 1974—). Home: 3020 N Nottingham St Arlington VA 22207

GILMORE, ROBERT JAMES, communications engr.; b. Tulsa, Aug. 18, 1925; s. James Harvey and Velma (Goforth) G.; student So. Meth. U., 1943, Ga. Tech. U., 1944-45; B.S., U. Tulsa, 1949; postgrad. Washington U., 1965; m. Mary Lee Jenkins, Aug. 30, 1947; children—Gayle, Robert James. Computer, Petty Geophys. Engring. Co., Tulsa and Minot, N.D., 1947-49; with Southwestern Bell Tel. Co., 1950—, sr. engr., Oklahoma City, 1958-66, spl. services engr., 1966-71, equipment maintenance engr., 1971-72, equipment engr. spl. service, 1972—; cons. income tax, 1952-64. Cub scoutmaster, 1966-67; instnl. rep. Boy Scouts Am.; coach jr. baseball YMCA, 1962-67. Served with USNR, 1943-46. Mem. Nat., Okla. socs. profl. engrs., Armed Forces Communications and Electronics Assn., Am. Legion, Okla. Sports Assn. (dir.), Lambda Chi Alpha. Mem. Disciples of Christ. Optimist (pres. club 1972-73, dir. 1973-74). Home: 3220 NW 54th St Oklahoma City OK 73112 Office: 707 N Robinson St Oklahoma City OK 73102

GILMORE, WILLIAM CAMPBELL, JR., banker; b. Rome, Ga., Mar. 11, 1919; s. William Campbell and Susan Glen (Watts) G.; grad. Darlington Sch., 1936; B.S., Davidson Coll., 1940; M.S., Vanderbilt U., 1941; m. Elizabeth Anne McMichael, Dec. 20, 1945; children—Susan Dorsey (Mrs. George R. McSwain), William Campbell, Elizabeth Anne. City traffic mgr. Delta Air Lines Inc., Atlanta, 1946-47; mgr. heating and air conditioning I.W. Phillips & Co., Tampa, Fla., 1947-62; mgr. indsl. Dept. Greater Tampa C. of C., 1962-66; v.p. First Nat. Bank, Tampa, 1966-69, sr. v.p. 1969—. Served to lt. col. USAAF, 1941-46. Mem. Greater Tampa C. of C., Com. of 100, Am. Meteorol. Soc., So. Indsl. Devel. Council, Am. Inst. Banking, Fla. Bankers Assn. Phi Delta Theta, Sigma Phi Sigma. Democrat. Presbyn. (ruling elder 1962—). Clubs: University of Tampa, Tampa Yacht and Country, Tower. Home: 715 South Blvd Tampa FL 33606 Office: PO Box 1810 Tampa FL 33601

GIMARC, BENJAMIN MAURICE, chemist, educator; b. Nogales, Ariz., Dec. 5, 1934; s. John and Virgie D. (Ringo) G.; B.A., Rice U., 1956; Ph.D., Northwestern U., 1962; m. Jerry Dell Watts, June 27, 1959. Postdoctoral fellow and lectr. Johns Hopkins, 1962-64; asst. prof. Ga. Inst. Tech., Atlanta, 1964-66; asst. prof. chemistry U. S.C., Columbia, 1966-71, asso. prof., 1971—, chmn. chemistry dept., 1973—. Served to lt. (j.g.), USNR, 1956-58. Mem. Am. Chem. Soc., Am. Phys. Soc., A.A.A.S., Sigma Xi. Contbr. articles to profl. jours. Home: 316 Wateree Av Columbia SC 29205

GINGER, LYMAN VERNON, state ofcl.; b. nr. Wickliffe, Ky., June 21, 1907; s. Grover Cleveland and Emma (Abell) G.; A.B., Ky. Wesleyan Coll., 1929; M.A., U. Ky., 1942, Ed.D., 1950; m. Elizabeth Gardner Sudduth, June 7, 1932; children—Leslie Thomas, William Wesley. Tchr., athletic coach Winchester High Sch., 1929-39; prin. Owingsville Consol. Sch., 1939-42; prin. Univ. High Sch., Lexington, Ky., 1942-43, acting dir., 1943-46, dir., chmn. div. instrn. and placement, 1946-54; dean Coll. Adult and Extension Edn., U. Ky., 1954-56, became dean Coll. Edn., acting dean Coll. Adult and Extension Edn., 1956, then asso. dean tchr. edn. and certification; now supt. pub. instrn. State of Ky., Frankfort. Mem. Ky. High Sch. Athletic Bd. Control, 1944-53, Nat. High Sch. Football Rules Com., 1945-52; chmn. Gov.'s Commn. Pub. Edn., 1960-61; mem. Ky. Council So. Regional Edn., 1954-60, Ky. White House Conf. Com., 1955-56. Dir. Lexington YMCA. Ky. col. Mem. Ky. High Sch. Athletic Assn. (pres. 1948-53), Ky. Edn. Assn. (pres. 1952-54), N.E.A. (pres. 1957-58, treas. 1960—), Phi Delta Kappa, Kappa Delta Pi. Presbyn. Mason. Office: Ky State Dept Edn Frankfort KY 40601

GINGRICH, DOROTHEA LOHOFF, journalist; b. Lane County, Kan., May 7, 1911; d. Paul and Emma (Thon) Lohoff; student Washington U., 1927-29; B.J., U.Mo. (outstanding woman journalism student), 1931, M.A., 1941; m. R. G. Schlegel, Aug. 29, 1933 (div.); 1 dau., Sandra Kay (Mrs. Tucker Hollamon); m. 2d, Jack Edward Gingrich, July 27, 1941; 1 son, Paul Schuyler. Editor West Plains (Mo.) Jour., 1931-33; dir. journalism and publicity Mary Hardin-Baylor Coll., Belton, Tex., 1936-41, dir. Centennial pub. relations, 1944-45; mem. journalism faculty Tex. Christian U., 1947-49; asso. editor Seguin (Tex.) Enterprise, 1951-53, woman's page, 1953-55, featured columnist, 1954—; corr. San Antonio Light, 1951-68; head journalism dept. Tex. Luth. Coll. Girl Scout commr., Robstown, Tex., mem. council Ft. Worth, Seguin; pres. Seguin Friends of Library, 1961, hon. life mem.; trustee County Library, 1961—, chmn. bd. 1965—. Region V mem. Women's Civil Def. Council. Recipient Headliner award Theta Sigma Phi, San Antonio, 1956; 1st place award for column South Tex. Press Assn., 1957; distinction in journalism Tex. Centennial Rangerette Commn., 1936; 1st place award in state for newspaper column Tex. Women's Press Assn., 1960, 61, 63, 65, 66, 67, 69; 1st place Tex. Press Assn., 1960; 3d place Nat. Fedn. Press Women's contest, 1960; Outstanding Community Service award Seguin and Guadalupe County C. of C., 1970; Devoted Service plaque Library Bd., 1970; named Library Trustee of Year, Tex. Library Assn., 1965, chmn. Trustee, Round Table, 1970. Mem. Women's Soc. Christian Service (pres. 1957), Tex. Press Women, Inc. (pres. 1968-69), Nat. Fedn. Press Women (2d v.p. 1969-70, nat. historian 1973—), Am. Assn. U. Women (state bd. mem., past pres.), Am. Coll. Pub. Assn. (pres. Tex.-Okla. dist. 1941), Tex. Fedn. Women's Clubs (dist. chmn. edn. dept. 1961-64, pres. Alamo dist. 1968-70, state div. chmn.), Conservation Soc., Tex. Assn. Coll. Jour. Tchrs. (pres. 1959), Theta Sigma Phi (past nat., sec., v.p., regional dir.; distinguished service award 1962), Delta Delta Delta (nat. pub. relations chmn.), Beta Sigma Phi (hon.; order Rose degree 1970), Kappa Tau Alpha, Delta Kappa Gamma. Methodist (steward). Clubs:

Seguin Shakespeare (pres. 1965—), Delphian (pres.). Home: 1120 N King St Apt 210 Seguin TX 78155 Office: Seguin Enterprise N Austin St Seguin TX 78155

GINN, RONALD (BO), congressman; b. Morgan, Ga., May 31, 1934; student Abraham Baldwin Agrl. Coll., 1951-53, Ga. So. Coll., 1953-56; m. Gloria Averitt, 1956; children—Kacy, Julie, Bryan. Tchr.; businessman; farmer; adminstrv. asst. to Rep. G. Elliott Hagan, 1961-66, Sen. Herman E. Talmadge, 1967-71; mem. 93d Congress from 1st Dist. Ga. Democrat. Baptist (deacon). Address: 508 Cannon House Office Bldg Washington DC 20515

GINN, VALORAN NILE, fertilizer co. exec.; b. Tollesboro, Ky., Oct. 23, 1930; s. Forrest R. and Helen L. (McDaniel) G.; student U. Ky., 1951, Chgo. Inst. Mgmt., 1953-55; m. Dottie Faul, July 29, 1950; children—Deborah (Mrs. Samuel Hampton), Larraine, Troy, Samantha. Chief exec. officer Ohio Valley Fertilizer, Inc., Maysville, Ky., 1955—, Ky. Plating and Polishing Co., 1970—; sec.-treas. Ohio Valley Fertilizer Corp., 1964—. Exec. dir. United Appeal, 1959-62. Served with USNR, 1951-53. Mem. Chem. Engring. Soc., Ky. Plant Food Council. Democrat. Presbyn. Odd Fellow, Lion. Home: Route 4 Box 405 Maysville KY 41056 Office: PO Box 36 Maysville KY 41056

GINSBURG, MERRILL STUART, geophysicist; b. Chgo., July 20, 1935; s. William Joseph and Ethel (Geller) G.; B.S., Mass. Inst. Tech., 1959, M.S., 1960; Ph.D., U. Utah, 1963; m. Margaret Patricia Myers, Apr. 9, 1971; 1 son, Jason Ross. Sr. geophys. engr. Mobil Oil Corp., Dallas, 1963-70, asso. geophysicist, 1970—. Mem. Am. Geophys. Union, Soc. of Exploration Geophysicists, European Assn. Exploration Geophysicists, Dallas Geophys. Soc., N.Y. Acad. Scis., Sigma Xi, Phi Kappa Phi. Mem. B'nai B'rith. Home: 6211 W Northwest Hwy Apt 2807 Dallas TX 75225 Office: Mobil Oil Corp Exploration Services Center Box 900 Dallas TX 75221

GIOVANELLA, BEPPINO CARLO, biologist; b. Merano, Italy, June 12, 1932; s. Clemente and Maria Francesca (Felicelli) G.; Laurea in Biol. Scis. magna cum laude, U. Rome (Italy), 1956; postgrad. (post doctoral fellow), U. Wis., 1960-62; m. Wendy Ann Lohman, June 18, 1971; 1 son, Corrado Francesco. Came to U.S., 1960, naturalized, 1973. Research fellow Regina Elena Cancer Inst., Rome, 1956-60; research asso. McArdle Lab. for Cancer Research, Madison, Wis., 1962-70; lab. dir. Stehlin Found. for Cancer Research, Houston, 1970—. Clin. asst. prof. oncology, dept. obstetrics and gynecology Baylor U. Coll. Medicine, Houston, 1970—. Internat. fellow, USPHS, 1960; Damon Runyon Found. fellow, 1960, Libera Docenza in gen. pathology, Rome, 1962. Mem. Am. Assn. Cancer Research, A.A.A.S. Home: 8711 Twisting Vine Lane Houston TX 77040 Office: St Joseph Profl Bldg Houston TX 77002

GIPSON, WILEY KAYE, finance exec.; b. Knoxville, Tenn., Aug. 11, 1918; s. Claude Elvie and Elizabeth Forrest (Kauerz) G.; B.S., U. Tampa, 1939; m. Frances Russo, June 29, 1944. Chief authorizer Maas Bros., Tampa, 1939-40; mgr. Time Finance Co., Louisville, also Time Loan Co., Cin., 1940-46; organizer Term Finance Co., Cynthiana, Ky., 1947, gen. mgr., sec., treas., 1947-53, pres., gen. mgr., 1953—; sec. treas. Term Thrift Plan, Inc., 1959—; founder, pres., dir. F & W Investors Financial Corp., 1971—; Adv. com. Ky. commr. banking, 1956-57; mem. com. to draft consumer finance law Ky., 1960-61; mem. Ky. Consumer Affairs Commn., 1968—, Ky. Consumer Affairs Legislative Subcom., 1968—. Bd. dirs. Harrison County chpt. Nat. Found. Served with USAAF, 1942-45. Mem. Ky. Consumer Finance Assn. (past pres., dir.), Cynthiana-Harrison C. of C. (past pres.). Rotarian (past pres. dir. Newport, Ky.). Home: 218 Beechwood Rd S Fort Mitchell KY 41017 Office: PO Box 223 Fort Thomas KY 41075

GITTESS, RONALD MARVIN, dentist; b. Nyack, N.Y., Nov. 10, 1937; s. David and Mildred (Levin) G.; B.S., Columbia, 1959, D.D.S., 1963; postgrad. U. Pa., 1964-66; m. Carol May Block, Apr. 6, 1963; children—Robert Andrew, Leslie Ellen. Intern, Mt. Sinai Hosp., Miami, Fla., 1963-64, now attending dental surgeon; pvt. practice dentistry, specializing in edodontics, Miami, 1966—; mem. staff Variety Children's Hosp., VA Hosp., Miami, Mt. Sinai Hosp.; cons. Dade County Dental Research Clinic. Asst. coordinator dental div. United Fund Campaign, 1968. Recipient certificate of recognition Jarvie Honor Soc., 1961. USPHS fellow, 1962-63. Diplomate Am. Bd. Endodontics. Mem. Am. Dental Assn., Am. Assn. Endodontics, A.A.A.S., Fedn. Dentaire Internationale, Fla., Miami, Miami Beach, South Dade, East Coast dental socs., So. Endodontic Study Group. Alpha Omega. Home: 14520 SW 84th Av Miami FL 33158 Office: 7400 N Kendall Dr Miami FL 33156

GIVHAN, THOMAS BARTRAM, lawyer, state legislator; b. Lexington, Ky., Sept. 24, 1926; s. Thomas Holman and Eva Mae (Beck) G.; student Ia. State Coll., 1947; LL.B., U. Ky., 1951; m. Sharon Rose Richard, June 11, 1949; children—Elise Charles, Ellen Foster, Aaron Todd. Admitted to Ky. bar, 1951; practice law, Shepherdsville, Ky.; mem. firm Givhan & Porter; city atty., Shepherdsville, 1953-58; county atty. Bullitt County, 1959-62, 66-73. Mem. Ky. Ho. of Reps., 1974—. Dir. Echo Telephone Co., Shepherdsville. Served with USMC, 1945-46. Mem. Ky. Bar Assn., Am. Bar Assn., Am. Trial Lawyers Assn., Sigma Chi. Baptist. Mason. Clubs: Louisville Boat, Jefferson Club (Louisville). Home: 5406 East Hwy 44 Shepherdsville KY 40165 Office: Professional Bldg Shepherdsville KY 40165

GJERNES, OSCAR, psychologist; b. Oklee, Minn., Aug. 24, 1914; s. Ellef K. and Borghild (Gjeldaker) G.; B.A., Concordia Coll., 1941; M.S., N.D. State U., 1954; postgrad. U. Minn., 1958, U. N.D., 1965; m. Myrdith L. Kronschandbel, Apr. 13, 1941; children—Marylou Diane. Counseling psychologist VA, N.D., 1946-49; with N.D. Employment Service, 1941-65; supr. tech. services, Bismarck, 1957-65; employment service adviser Manpower Adminstrn., Dept. Labor, Washington, 1965—. Served with AUS, 1942-45, 1951-52. Mem. Nat. Vocational Guidance Assn., Nat. Employment Counselor Assn. (pres. 1969-70), N.D. Assn. Personnel in Employment, N.D. Personnel and Guidance Assn. (past pres.), N.D. Vocational Guidance Assn. (past pres.). Lutheran (deacon). Research in psychol. field. Home: 9039 Sligo Creek Pkwy Silver Springs MD 20901

GLADDEN, JAMES WALTER, educator; b. Dunbar, Pa., Nov. 3, 1912; s. T. Milton and Hattie (Rowley) G.; A.B., Waynesburg Coll., 1933; M.Div., Wesley Theol. Sch., 1936; M.Ed., U. Pitts., 1943, Ph.D., 1946; m. Cynthia E. Hales, June 22, 1935 (dec. June 1971); children—Peg (Mrs. C. F. Hermann); James Walter; m. 2d, Helen J. Baur, Mar. 17, 1973. Ordained to ministry Meth. Ch., 1938; pastor Meth. chs., Pa., 1935-46; head dept. sociology Mt. Union Coll., Alliance, O., 1946-49; prof. sociology U. Ky., Lexington, 1949—. Mem. Am., So., Ohio Valley sociol. socs., Nat. (Osborne award for outstanding teaching 1972), Regional, councils on family relations. Democrat. Kiwanian. Contbr. numerous articles in field to profl. jours. Home: 3401 Bellefonte Dr Lexington KY 40502

GLADSON, WILLARD BENSON, mfg. co. exec.; b. Snyder, Tex., Oct. 13, 1916; s. Earl and Hettie Louticia (Carden) G.; grad. high sch.; m. Flora Holley, Dec. 18, 1937; children—Royce, Judith Rousseau, Elvin Rousseau, Janis Page, George Page, Gayna Cowan, Cecil Cowan, Ronal. With Odstreil Drilling Co., Snyder, Tex., 1944-50, drilling supr., 1950-55, partner, 1955-63; owner Willard Gladson Oil Field Contracting Co., Snyder, 1963—. Bd. dirs. Synder unit Boys Club Am. Baptist. Address: 2705 35th St Snyder TX 79549

GLASGOW, CLARENCE OGDEN, mfg. co. exec.; b. Fairview, Okla., Sept. 26, 1908; s. Arthur W. and Floy (McCowan) G.; B.S. in Mech. Engring., Okla. State U., 1934; m. Elizabeth McClung, Feb. 15, 1938; children—Edsel, Melvin. With Nat. Tank Co., Tulsa, 1934-61, v.p., dir., 1949-61; pres. Custom Engring. & Mfg. Corp., Tulsa, 1961—; dir. Tulsa Rubber Co.; owner Spring Valley Ranch, Locust Grove, Okla., 1948—. Bd. regents Oral Roberts U., Tulsa. Mem. Am. Soc. M.E., Okla. Inventors Congress (bd. mem.), Tulsa C. of C. Methodist. Club: Petroleum. Patentee in field. Home: 2620 S Yorktown St Tulsa OK 74114 Office: 1073 N Owasso St Tulsa OK 74150

GLASGOW, JAMES MONROE, lawyer; b. nr. Dresden, Tenn., Feb. 17, 1920; s. William Ayers and Mary Catherine (Dismukes) G.; J.D., U. Tenn., 1948; m. Jo Evelyn Burkeen, Sept. 17, 1943; children—Carol Ann (Mrs. Ronald Kirkland), James Monroe, Linda Sue. Admitted to Tenn. bar, 1947; gen. practice, Dresden, 1948-52; asst. atty. gen. Tenn., 1952-60; asst. gen. counsel Nat. Life & Accident Ins. Co., Nashville, 1961-63; mem. firm Elam, Glasgow, Tanner & Acree, Union City, 1964—. Pres., Obion County United Fund, 1969. Mem. U. Tenn. at Martin Devel. Council, 1972—. Served to capt. USAAF, 1941-45. Mem. Am., Tenn., Obion County bar assns., Union City C. of C. (pres.). Democrat. Methodist. Rotarian, Elk, Moose. Home: Armstrong Rd Union City TN 38261 Office: W Church St Union City TN 38261

GLASGOW, JOSEPH LELAND, physician; b. DeQueen, Ark., Nov. 7, 1931; s. John Leland and Minnie Venus (Martindale) G.; B.S., Ouachita Coll., 1953; M.D., U. Ark., 1959; m. Jeanne Rae Bonar, May 30, 1960; children—Leslie Ann, David Leland, John Bonar. Chief nuclear medicine VA Hosp., Jackson, Miss., 1965—, chief med. service, 1970—; asst. prof. medicine U. Miss., 1967-69, asso. prof., 1969—. Served with USMC, 1953-55. Diplomate Am. Bd. Internal Medicine, Am. Bd. Nuclear Medicine. Fellow A.C.P., Am. Coll. Chest Physicians; mem. Soc. Nuclear Medicine, A.M.A., Am. Diabetes Assn., A.A.A.S., Sigma Xi. Home: 4730 N Hampton Dr Jackson MS 39211 Office: Veterans Administration Hospital Jackson MS 39216

GLASGOW, LESLIE LLOYD, univ. adminstr.; b. nr. Portland, Ind., Mar. 29, 1914; s. James S. and Margaret Ann (Hogg) G.; B.S., Purdue U., 1942; M.S., U. Me., 1948; Ph.D., Tex. A. and M. U., 1958; m. Garnet L. Confer, May 13, 1942; children—Vaughan L., Hugh R., Robert B. Prof., asst. dir. Sch. Forestry and Wildlife, La. State U., Baton Rouge, 1971—; dir. La. Wildlife and Fisheries Commn.; asst. sec. Dept. Interior Fish, Wildlife and Parks. Pvt. cons. environmental problems. Served with USAF, 1944-46. Mem. Xi Sigma Pi, Omicron Delta Kappa, Gamma Sigma Delta. Home: 663 Sunset Blvd Baton Rouge LA 70808 Office: Sch Forestry and Wildlife La State U Baton Rouge LA 70803

GLASGOW, ROBERT SAMUEL, JR., lawyer; b. Adamsville, Ala., July 3, 1907; s. Robert Samuel and Louise (Maxwell) G.; A.B., Birmingham-So. Coll., 1928; J.D., U. Ala., 1933; m. Thelma Thompson, Nov. 7, 1935; 1 dau., Gloria Elaine (Mrs. G. Preston Bryant). Admitted to Ala. bar, 1933; pvt. law practice, 1933—; owner Home Supply Co., 1936-41; v.p. Davidson-Pratt Mining Co., Inc., 1943-44; partner Blossburg Mining Co., 1944; chief area atty. Office of Housing Expediter, 1945-51; mayor, Adamsville, Ala., 1953-55, city atty., 1955-56; title agt. Ala. Power Co., Birmingham, 1955-62; partner Glasgow & Sides Devel. Co.; atty. for Town of Brookside (Ala.), 1954-56. Gen. and trial atty. Office Price Stblzn., 1951-52; hearing examiner Bur. Hearings and Appeals, Social Security Adminstrn., Birmingham, 1962-73; U.S. adminstrv. law judge, 1973—. Mem. Am. Ala., Birmingham bar assns., Fed. Adminstrv. Law Judges Conf., Tenn., Ala., Newberry (S.C.) hist. assns., Sons of Confederate Vets., Theta Chi, Sigma Upsilon, Phi Alpha Delta. Methodist (chmn. council on ministries, trustee). Mason, Lion (past pres., past sec., past zone chmn.) Club: The Club (Birmingham, Ala.). Home: Adamsville AL 35005 Office: Room 420 11 W Oxmoor Rd Birmingham AL 35209

GLASKE, PAUL EDWARD, heavy machinery mfg. co. exec.; b. Benton Harbor, Mich., Aug. 31, 1933; s. Herman John and Ella Martha (Prillwitz) G.; B.S., Bob Jones U., 1957; m. Jacqueline Brolin, Aug. 20, 1955; children—Randall Paul, Laura Lynn, Caryn Louise. Auditor, Standard Oil Co., Chgo., 1957-63; v.p. bus. affairs LeTourneau Coll., Longview, Tex., 1963-68; v.p. adminstrn. R.G. LeTourneau, Inc., Longview, 1968-71; v.p. Marathon Mfg. Co., 1970—, pres. Longview div., 1971—. Organizing chmn. East Tex. council Boy Scouts Am., 1971-72; mem. LeTourneau Coll. Council, 1971—; counselor Jr. Achievement, Chgo., 1958-59; dir. U.S. Savs. Bond Program for E. Tex., 1973-74. Committeeman Rich Twp. Republican Com., Ill., 1960-63. Bd. dirs. Good Shepherd Hosp., Longview, United Fund, YMCA. Named Jr. C. of C. Boss of Year, Longview, 1973. Mem. Tex. Mfrs. Assn. (chmn. East Tex. chpt. 1971-72, 1972-73, dir.), Longview C. of C. (dir. 1971-73), Christian Bus. Men's Com. (adviser 1972-73). Club: Civitan. Baptist. Home: 5 Cherrywood Circle Longview TX 75601 Office: PO Box 2307 Longview TX 75601

GLASS, ALBERT JULIUS, psychiatrist, educator; b. Balt., June 16, 1908; s. Simon Barry and Jennie (Miller) G.; Ph.G., U. Md., 1928, B.S., 1928, M.D., 1932; m. Loretta Marie Lesnau, Aug. 6, 1936; children—Susan (Mrs. David Pithkethly), David, Richard, Judith. Intern Gouverneur Hosp., N.Y.C., 1933-34; resident specializing in neurology Central Neurol. Hosp., N.Y.C., 1934-35, Riverside Hosp., N.Y.C., 1936; practice of medicine, Balt., 1936-41; commd. maj. U.S. Army, 1946, advanced through grades to col., 1950; chief psychiatry Far East command, 1950-56, Walter Reed Gen. Hosp., Washington, 1951-56; cons. psychiatry U.S. Surgeon Gen., 1956-61; ret., 1963; dir. Okla. Dept. Mental Health, Oklahoma City, 1963-70; dir. Ill. Dept. Mental Health, 1970-73; prof. psychiatry Okla. Health Scis. Center, 1973—. Served with AUS, 1941-45. Decorated Bronze Star medal, Legion of Merit with oak leaf cluster. Recipient Gorgas medal Assn. Mil. Surgeons, 1959. Fellow Am. Psychiat. Assn.; mem. Group for Advancement Psychiatry. Rotarian. Contbr. chpts. to books, also articles to profl. publs. Home: 2305 NW 57th St Oklahoma City OK 73112

GLASS, JAMES GERBER, pipeline co. exec.; b. N.Y.C., Oct. 12, 1928; s. Joseph and Bessie (Gerber) G.; B.S., U. Tex., 1950; m. Geraldine Eisenberg, Sept. 3, 1950; children—Randall, Joseph, Amy Lyn, Robert, Brett, Bart, Kimberly. Petroleum engr., chief reservoir engr. Midstates Oil Corp., Tulsa, 1953-58, N.Y.C., 1955-56, dir. Middle States Petroleum Corp., La.; N.W.R.R., 1956-58; cons. petroleum engr. Glass & Moove Co., Tulsa, 1958-64; gen. mgr., Bigheart Pipe Line Corp., Tulsa, 1964-72, v.p., 1967-71, sr. v.p., 1971—; gen. mgr. Bigheart Crude Oil Corp., Tulsa, 1969-72, v.p., 1969-71, sr. v.p., 1971—; gen. mgr. Bigheart Transport Co., Tulsa, 1968-72, v.p., 1968-71, sr. v.p., 1971—. Trustee Tulsa Edn. Found., 1963-64. Served with USCGR, 1951-53. Registered profl. engr., Okla. Mem. Am. Inst., Mining, Metall. and Petroleum Engrs., Am. Assn. Petroleum Geologists, Internat. Oil Scouts Assn., Tulsa Engrs. Club, Petroleum Club Tulsa. Office: Amoco E Bldg Tulsa OK 74101

GLASS, POWELL, JR., publisher; b. Lynchburg, Va., Feb. 21, 1917; s. Powell and Ann (Cleghorn) G.; B.A., Washington and Lee U., 1938; student London Sch. Econs., 1938-39; postgrad. N.Y. U., 1939-40, U. Pa., 1956; LL.B., U. Va., 1947; m. Marianna Rhett duPont, June 18, 1940 (div. Jan. 1956); children—Anne Cleghorne, Marianna Rhett, Alicia Middleton; m. 2d, Joan Marilyn de Sardon, Nov. 24, 1958. Admitted to Va. bar, 1947; law clk. Isaac W. Diggs, N.Y.C. 1939-40, firm Davies, Auderbach & Hardy, N.Y.C., 1940; co-pub. Lynchburg News, Lynchburg Daily Advance, 1946-50, 51-56, v.p. Lynchburg News, Inc., 1959-72; v.p. Daily Advance, 1959-72; editorial dir. Lynchburg News, also Lynchburg Daily Advance, 1969; dir. Carter Glass & Sons, Inc., 1959—, v.p., 1972-74, pres., 1974—; editor-pub. Sea Coast Echo, Bay St. Louis, Miss., 1958-68; pres. MTO Publicity Corp., 1964—. Instr. law U. Va., 1947-48; asso. prof. law Mercer U., 1956-58. Served with USMC, 1940-46, 50-51. Fellow Internat. Conf. Newspaper Editors; mem. Order Coif, Raven Soc., Hancock County C. of C. (past pres.), Nat. Conf. of Editorial Writers, Omicron Delta Kappa, Kappa Sigma. Rotarian. Contbr. articles to legal jours. Home: 1509 Clayton Av Lynchburg VA 24503 Office: 857 Church St Lynchburg VA 24505

GLASS, THOMAS EDGAR, JR., ednl. adminstr.; b. Tarboro, N.C., July 15, 1928; s. Thomas Edgar and Lilly Mae (Smith) G.; student Campbell Coll., 1947-48; A.B., U. N.C., 1954, M.Ed., 1957; m. Jean Ball DeWitt, Dec. 26, 1953; children—Thomas Edgar III, Janet. Tchr., athletic dir. Charlotte (N.C.) City Schs., 1954-60; self-employed as salesman, 1960-64; evening dir. Durham (N.C.) Tech. Inst., 1964-66, bus. mgr., 1966—. Served with AUS, 1951-53. Mem. N.E.A., Am. Assn. Sch. Adminstrs., Assn. Sch. Bus. Ofcls. U.S. and Can. (state chmn. 1968-70), N.C. Edn. Assn., N.C. Classroom Tchrs. Assn., N.C. Assn. Community Coll. Bus. Ofcls. (charter, exec. com. 1971-74, pres. 1974). Club: Willowhaven Country (Durham). Home: 1030 Evergreen Dr Durham NC 27705 Office: 1637 Lawson St Durham NC 27703

GLASS, WILLIAM A., petroleum co. exec.; B.S. in Petroleum Engring., U. Okla., 1959. With Big Chief Drilling Co., Oklahoma City, 1959—, drilling engr., Oklahoma City, 1962, then project engr. AEC project, named chief drilling engr., 1964, mgr. drilling operations, 1966, v.p., mgr. drilling, 1967, now v.p. Mem. com. Scripps Inst. Oceanography. Mem. Am. Petroleum Inst., Am. Inst. Mining Engrs., Mid Continent Oil and Gas Assn., Oklahoma City Petroleum Club. Address: Big Chief Drilling Co 601 N E 63d St Oklahoma City OK 73144

GLASSCOCK, CHARLES GUS, JR., rancher; b. San Antonio, Feb. 19, 1918; s. Charles Gus and Lucille (Freeman) G.; student Baylor U., 1935-38; m. Bonnie Dell Smith, Jan. 25, 1947; children—Charles Gus III, John Donley, James Thomas. Owner 2 G Cattle Ranches, Columbus, Tex., Glenderey, Colo., 1960—; chmn. bd. Bell Western Corp.; pres. Coral Pines, Ltd., Freeport, Bahamas. Trustee Houston Bapt. Coll. Mem. Tex., Southwestern, Am. cattlemens assns., Aircraft Owners and Pilots Assn., Baylor U. Alumni Assn. (past v.p.), Tex. Mid-Continent Oil and Gas Assn. Club: Cherry Hills Country (Denver). Home: Route 2 Box 84 Columbus TX 78934 Office: 2016 Main St Houston TX 77002

GLASSMAN, MICHAEL, educator; b. Fastov, Russia, Oct. 12, 1899; s. Meyer Joseph and Frieda (Kaganovsky) G.; brought to U.S., 1908, naturalized, 1924; B.A. (Tremaine scholar 1921), Coll. City N.Y., 1923, M.S. in Edn., 1932; J.D., N.Y. U., 1926; m. Miriam Frantz, Aug. 24, 1935; children—Rhoda (Mrs. Paul Norehad), Judith M. Admitted to N.Y. bar, 1927; tchr., adminstr. N.Y.C. Bd. Edn., 1923-69, asst. examiner personnel dept., 1944, prin. Benjamin Franklin Jr. High Sch., 1955-60, prin. Parsons Jr. High Sch., 1960-69; adj. instr. edn. Bklyn. Coll., 1944-47; adj. asst. prof. edn. emeritus Pace Coll., 1970—. Ednl. adviser, journalist N.Y. Herald Tribune, N.Y.C., 1955-58. Mem. Audubon Soc., Smithsonian Instn., Wildlife Fedn., N.Y. Tchrs. Guild (co-organizer; mem. exec. bd.), Am. Fedn. Tchrs. (del. nat. conv. 1934), Jr. High Sch. Prins. Assn., Council Suprs., Adminstrs. N.Y.C., Retired Tchrs. Assn. Independent. Jewish religion. Author: New York State: Its History and Its Constitution, 1949, rev. title New York State: Geography, History, Government, 1965; Barron's Social Studies Regents series, 1949-70; Pollution of the Environment: Can We Survive, 1974. Address: 2666 Emory Dr East West Palm Beach FL 33406

GLAVE, JAMES MILLARD, architect; b. Chgo., May 13, 1933; s. Harold Ernest and Lavona (Millard) G.; student Randolph-Macon Coll., Ashland, Va., 1950-51; B.Arch., U. Va., 1955; M.Arch., U. Pa., 1959; m. Patricia McKenna, June 14, 1958; children—Clark, Kenna, Olivia. Architect, Marcellus, Wright & Son, Richmond, Va., 1961-65; partner Glave & Newman, architects, Richmond, 1966-69, Glave, Newman & Anderson, 1969-72; pres. Glave Newman Anderson & Assos., Inc., 1972—. Mem. Maymont Found., 1968—, Richmond City Planning Commn., 1969—, City Recreation and Parks Adv. Bd., 1969-72. Served to lt. (j.g.) USNR, 1955-58. Mem. A.I.A. (pres. Richmond sect. 1969, nat. com. urban design. Home: 1725 Park Av Richmond VA 23220 Office: 209 W Franklin St Richmond VA 23220

GLAVIN, W(ILLIAM) RICHARD, cons.; b. Mahanoy City, Pa., Nov. 30, 1903; s. David Emmett and Sophia (Molichan) G.; B.C.S., Southeastern U., 1928; m. Edith Ann Williams, June 26, 1926; children—Ann (Mrs. C.W. Johnson, Jr.), Richard. Asst. div. accountant Internat. Tel. & Tel., 1927-31; civil and criminal accounting investigations, 1929-31; spl. agt. FBI, N.Y.C., Phila., Washington, 1931-34, insp., asst. dir. in charge budget and personnel mgmt., 1934-54; lectr. FBI Nat. Acad., 1935-54; asst. sec. East Volusia Mosquito Control Dist., Daytona Beach, Fla., 1957-62; exec. sec. Fla. State Bd. Architecture, Ormond Beach, 1962-70. Alternate mem. adv. staff U.S. Senate Civil Service Com. on Personnel Matters, 1954; chmn. FBI U.S. Civil Service Appeals Com., 1950-54; tax. cons. Daytona Beach (Fla.) C. of C., 1955-56; mem. finance com. Continuing Council for Edn., Volusia County, 1955-57; personnel and budget cons. Halifax Dist. Hosp., 1956-57; mem. Gov's. Tax Study Com. for Volusia County, 1956; cons. personnel budget and finance N.Y. State Police, 1960-62; pres. Halifax area Boys' Clubs Am., 1969—. Served with USMC, 1922-27. Mem. Soc. Former Spl. Agts. FBI (chmn. Southeastern chpt. 1965), Fla. Anti-Mosquito Assn. Kiwanian (dir. Ormond Beach 1965—). Clubs: Riviera Country, Oceanside Country. Home: 461 Pinewood St Ormond Beach FL 32074

GLAZE, ROBERT PINCKNEY, univ. adminstr.; b. Birmingham, Ala., Apr. 14, 1933; s. Andrew Lewis and Mildred (Ezell) G.; B.S., U. of South, 1955; Ph.D., U. Rochester, 1961; postdoctoral fellow Johns Hopkins U. Sch. Medicine, 1961-64; m. Barbara Catherine Malloy, Aug. 23, 1958; children—David, Jennifer. Asst. prof. biochemistry U. Ala. at Birmingham, 1964-72, coordinator research grants, 1967-73, asst. dean Med. Coll. Ala. and Sch. Dentistry, 1967-69, asso. dean Schs. Medicine and Dentistry, 1969-72, dir. Instnl. Study Program, 1972-73, asst. to pres., 1973—. Mem. Citizen's Adv. Bd. on Health and Environmental Quality Ala. Commn. on Intergovtl. Cooperation, 1972—. Trustee Gorgas Scholarship Found. Inc. Predoctoral trainee USPHS, 1955-58, predoctoral fellow, 1958-61, fellow, 1962-63; recipient NSF grant, 1966-68. Mem. Ala., N.Y. acad. sci., A.A.A.S., Am. Chem. Soc., Nat. Council U. Research Adminstrs., Soc. Research Adminstrs., So. Assn. Colls. and Schs. (cons. 1971—), Birmingham Area C. of C. (mem. edn. information services com. 1971—). Home: 906 Sheridan Dr Birmingham AL 35213

GLAZNER, VICTOR WALLIS, architect; b. Baton Rouge, Oct. 27, 1941; s. Charles Elmer and Orma Lee (Maddox) G.; B.Arch., La. State U., 1964; m. Sandra Irene Stromei, July 22, 1967; Asso. architect Woods-Steber Assos., Mobile, Ala., 1964-68; prin. architect Victor W. Glazner, Mobile, 1968—. Mem. Mobile Hist. Devel. Commn. Mem. A.I.A. (Mobile chpt. treas. 1970, sec. 1971, v.p. 1972, pres. 1973, state code chmn.). Home: 6527 Old Shell Rd Mobile AL 36608 Office: PO Box 6184 Mobile AL 36606

GLEASON, JAMES GORDON, educator; b. Hammondsport, N.Y., Mar. 24, 1915; s. Donald Irving and Elizabeth (Gardner) G.; student N.Y. State Merchant Marine Acad., 1934; B.S. in Aero. Engring., Ala. Poly. Inst., 1938; M.S. in Mech. Engring., U. Ark., 1954; m. Natalie Creel, July 4, 1940; 1 son, Donald Crawford. Lab technician Ala. Poly. Inst., 1938-40; prof. mech. engring. U. Ark., 1940—; research engr. Boeing Airplane Co., Seattle, summers, 1951, 1952, 1957; research engr. Boeing Airplane Co., Wichita, Kan., summers 1955-56, 58-60; asst. project engr. Pratt & Whitney Aircraft Co., East Hartford, Conn., summers, 1961-67; research engr. Beech Aircraft Corp., Wichita, summers 1968-69; engr. Forest Park Canning Co., Johnston, Ark., summer 1970; cons. machine designs, testing, and refrigeration projects. Registered profl. engr., Ark., Kan. Mem. Am. Soc. M.E., Am. Soc. Engring. Edn., Soc. Automotive Engrs., Nat. Soc. Profl. Engrs. Elk. Home: 1139 Sunset St Fayetteville AR 72701

GLEASON, WILLIAM HENRY, lawyer, judge; b. Eau Gallie, Fla., Jan. 9, 1928; s. William Lansing and Carol (Hurlburt) G.; student Ga. Inst. Tech., 1944-47; J.D., Vanderbilt U., 1950; m. Angela Gleason; 1 dau., Jane Carey. Admitted to Fla. bar, 1951; practiced in Brevard County, Fla., 1953—; mem. firm Gleason, Walker, Pearson & Shreve, Indialantic, Fla., 1964—; city judge, Indian Harbour Beach, 1955—, West Melbourne, Fla., 1968—, Indialantic, 1971—. Organizer, v.p., dir. 1st Nat. Bank, Satellite Beach, Fla., 1963-69; organizer, dir. Harbor City Nat. Bank, Eau Gallie, 1963—; organizer, dir. 1st Fed. Savs. and Loan Assn., Eau Gallie, 1959—, pres., 1966-68. Commr. Indian Harbour Beach, 1961-64, mayor, 1964-66. Bd. dirs. Brevard Heart Fund, 1954—, pres., 1965-66. Served with AUS, 1951-53; Korea. Decorated Bronze Star. Mem. Am., D.C., Brevard County bar assns., Fla. Bar, V.F.W., Phi Delta Phi. Rotarian, Mason (Shriner, 32 deg.). Clubs: Eau Gallie Yacht. Home: 200 Poinciana Dr Indian Harbour Beach FL 32937 Office: 121 5th Av Indialantic FL 32901

GLEAZER, EDMUND JOHN JR., assn. exec.; b. Phila., Aug. 24, 1916; s. Edmund John and Jane Hunter (Laurie) G.; A.A., Graceland Coll., 1936; A.B., U. Cal. at Los Angeles, 1938; Ed.M., Temple U., 1943; Ed.D., Harvard, 1953; m. Charlene A. Allen, Apr. 14, 1940; children—Allen, Sandra Jo, John, Susan. Minister, Reorganized Ch. of Jesus Christ of Latter Day Saints, Phila., 1938-43, pres. So. Iowa dist., 1943-46; pres. Graceland Coll., Lamoni, Ia., 1946-57; exec. dir. Am. Assn. Jr. Colls., Washington, 1958—. Mem. nat. adv. com. for asso. degree programs in nursing Nat. League Nursing; mem. U.S. Tech. Edn. Delegation to USSR, 1961, edn. survey team AID, Kenya, 1962; chmn. Def. Adv. Com. on Edn. in Armed Forces, 1962; mem. vis. com. Stanford U., Sch. Edn., 1962. Mem. North Central Jr. Colls. (pres. council 1954), North Central Assn. (commn. colls. and univs. 1955-57), Am. Assn. Jr. Colls. (pres. 1957), Am. Council on Edn. (sec.), Phi Delta Kappa. Rotarian. Clubs: Harvard, Cosmos (Washington). Author: This is The Community College, 1968. Editor: American Junior Colleges, 1960, 63, 67. Home: 8208 Woodhaven Blvd Bethesda MD 20034 Office: 1 DuPont Circle NW Washington DC 20036

GLEIT, CHESTER EUGENE, chemist, educator; b. N.Y.C., Apr. 26, 1933; s. Reuben Eliot and Helen Eleanor (Madfes) G.; A.B., U. Chgo., 1952, M.S., 1955; Ph.D., Mass. Inst. Tech., 1958; m. Carol Joyce Hansen, Jan. 22, 1956; children—Ruth Ellen, Natalie Joan, Robert Theodore, Nathan Roy. Sr. scientist Bettis Atomic Power Lab., Pitts., 1958-60; dir. research and devel. Tracerlab. div. Lab. for Electronics, Richmond, Cal., 1960-64; asso. prof. chemistry N.C. State U., Raleigh, 1964—, chmn. drug edn. com., 1973. Cons., Perkin-Elmer Corp., Hilemn Labs., Inst. Med. Tech., Research Triangle Inst., N.C. Bd. Tech. Dir., Bay Area Scientist's Information Com., 1963-64; tng. dir. Hopeline, Inc., 1973. Bd. dirs. Found. for Med. Tech. Recipient grants from AEC, 1962-64, Dept. Def., 1961-64; Union Carbide fellow, 1954-55. Mem. Am. Assn. Contamination Control (research dir. 1970-72), N.C. Acad. Scis. (Poteat award 1972), A.A.A.S., Am. Chem. Soc., Microchem. Soc., Fedn. Am. Scientists (del. 1962, 64), Sigma Xi. Contbr. articles profl. jours. Patentee in field. Home: 1428 Dixie Trail Raleigh NC 27607

GLEMBOCKI, RAYMOND THOMAS, airline market research dir.; b. Hamtramck, Mich., Mar. 10, 1940; s. Zygmund and Clara (Bzdal) G.; B.S., Mich. Tech. U., 1963; M.B.A., Pepperdine U., 1968; m. Cecilia Mary Hichwa, Aug. 8, 1964; children—Christopher, Carolyn, Cathy. With Asso. Spring Corp., Bristol, Conn., 1963-65, Douglas Aircraft, Long Beach, Cal., 1966-68; market research dir. Nat. Airlines, Miami, Fla., 1968—; adj. prof. marketing Fla. Internat. U.; prof. mgmt. Emery Riddle U. Mem. Am. Marketing Assn., Travel Research Assn. Home: 15341 SW 82d Av Miami FL 33157 Office: Box 2055 Airport Mail Facility Miami FL 33159

GLENDINNING, RICHARD (EDWIN), writer; b. Elizabeth, N.J., Oct. 10, 1917; s. Richard Edwin and Alice May (Summers) G.; A.B., Dartmouth, 1940; m. Sara Helena Wilson, Dec. 27, 1941; 1 dau., Elizabeth Ann (Mrs. Alan Burrell). Writer, Vogue Mag., 1940-41; pub. relations Balt. Mus. Art, 1941; author short stories and articles in nat. publs., radio dramas, novels, hist. non-fiction, 1945—. Mem. Sarasota (Fla.) Library Bd., Sarasota County Library Adv. Bd.; chmn. Sarasota County Hist. Commn.; mem. adv. council Myakka River State Park. Served as lt. comdr. USNR, World War II. Mem. Soc. Am. Historians, Mystery Writers Am. Methodist. Club: Forest Lakes Country (Sarasota). Home: 1638 South Dr Sarasota FL 33579

GLENN, ALFRED HILL, meteorology and oceanography cons.; b. Yonkers, N.Y., June 3, 1921; s. Earl Rouse and Mary Elizabeth (Easley) G.; student Ind. U., 1938-39, Cal. Inst. Tech., 1939-40; B.S. in Civil Engring., U. Wis., 1942; M.S. in Meteorology, N.Y. U., 1943; postgrad. in oceanography, U.C.L.A., 1943, in math. Tulane U., 1950; m. Gladys Norris Glenn, Sept. 12, 1947. Engr., Chgo. Bridge and Iron Co., 1942; meteorologist USAAF, Washington, 1946; pres. A.H. Glenn Assos., New Orleans, 1946—. Served to capt., USAAF, 1943-45; PTO. Decorated Air medal; recipient Applied Meteorology award, Am. Meteorol. Soc., 1962, Outstanding Service to Meteorology award, 1970, Distinguished Alumnus citation, N.Y. U., 1955. Registered civil engr., La., Tex. Fellow Am. Soc. C.E., Royal Meteorol. Soc.; mem. Soc. Petroleum Engrs., Am. Soc. Limnology and Oceanography, A.A.A.S., Am. Geophys. Union, N.Y. Acad. Scis., Tau Beta Pi. Contbr. articles in field to profl. jours. Home: 60 Wren St New Orleans LA 70124 Office: New Orleans Lakefront Airport New Orleans LA 70126

GLENN, HELEN IRENE, univ. adminstr.; b. Atlanta, Aug. 17, 1918; d. Harry James and Edna (Montanye) Glenn; A.B., Mercer U., 1938; M.A., Ind. U., 1942. Tchr. pub. schs. Porterdale, Ga., 1938-40; dir. pub. relations, asso. prof. journalism Brenau Coll., Gainesville, Ga., 1946-48; grand sec., treas. Alpha Delta Pi, Berkeley, Cal., Kansas City, Mo., Atlanta, 1948-57; dir. pub. relations asso. prof. journalism Wesleyan Coll., Macon, Ga., 1957-61; dean of women, asst. prof. journalism Mercer U., Macon, 1961-70; adviser to married students Auburn (Ala.) U., 1970-71; dir. financial aids Jacksonville (Fla.) U., 1971—. Nat. Panhellenic Conf. del. Alpha Delta Pi, 1959-62; pres. Macon Council Women's Civic Clubs, 1962-64; mem. membership com. YWCA, 1969-70. Served to maj. WAC, AUS, 1942-46. Mem. Am. Assn. U. Women, Assn. Edn. in Journalism, So. Coll. Personnel Assn. (state membership chmn., chmn. job opportunities service; pres. 1969), Nat. Assn. Student Financial Aid Adminstrs., So., Fla., Nat., Ga. (pres. 1967-69) assns. women deans and counselors, Jacksonville City Panhellenic Assn. (corr. sec. 1974—), Am. Legion, Women in Communications, Kappa Delta Epsilon, Alpha Delta Pi, Delta Kappa Gamma. Club: Quota (past dist. gov.; past pres. Macon). Home: 3830 University Blvd S Apt 49 Jacksonville FL 32216

GLENN, JACK FITTEN, investment banker; b. Atlanta, Nov. 16, 1910; s. William Harper and Anne (Fitten) G.; B.S., Ga. Inst. Tech., 1932; m. Anne Amanda Alston, Dec. 18, 1935; children—Jack Fitten, Philip Alston, Robert James, James Lewis. Various positions Coca-Cola Co., Atlanta, 1932-35; salesman unlisted securities, head trading dept. and underwriting dept. Courts & Co., Atlanta, 1936-42, gen. partner, 1942-50, charge br. office operations, 1945-50; became asst. pres. Citizens & So. Nat. Bank Ga., Atlanta 1951-67, chmn. bd., 1967-73; mng. dir. Lehman Bros. Inc., Atlanta, 1973—. Active United Appeal Community Chest; commr. Atlanta Housing Authority. Trustee Ga. Tech. Found. Served as lt. USNR, 1942-45. Mem. Phi Delta Phi. Clubs: Piedmont Driving (past v.p., pres., dir.), Capital City (past dir.), Peachtree Golf (pres.), Nine O'Clocks (past pres., dir.), Commerce (past dir., treas.), Homosassa Fishing (past v.p., bd.) (Atlanta). Home: 8 Cherokee Rd NW Atlanta GA 30305 Office: 1st Nat Bank Tower 2 Peachtree St Atlanta GA 30303

GLENN, JAMES FRANCIS, surgeon; b. Lexington, Ky., May 10, 1928; s. Cambridge Francis and Martha (Morrow) G.; student U. Ky., 1947-48; B.A., U. Rochester, 1949; M.D., Duke, 1952; m. Gale Brooke Morrison, Dec. 29, 1948; children—Cambridge Francis II, Sara Brooke, Nancy Carrick, James Morrison Woodworth. House officer gen. surgery Peter Bent Brigham Hosp., Boston, 1952-54; resident urology Duke Med. Center, Durham, N.C., 1956-59; asst. prof. urology Yale, 1959-61; asso. prof. Bowman Gray Med. Sch., Winston-Salem, N.C., 1961-63; prof., chmn. urology dept. Duke, 1963—; practice medicine specializing in urologic surgery, New Haven, 1959-61, Winston-Salem, 1961-63, Durham, 1963—; mem. staff Duke, Watts, Lincoln, VA hosps. (all Durham). Cons. U.S. Army, USAF, VA, Nat. Acad. Scis., NRC; mem. sci. adv. bd. Nat. Kidney Found., 1964-69. Served to capt. M.C., USAF, 1954-56. Mem. Soc. Univ. Urologists (sec., pres.), A.C.S., Am. Assn. Genito-Urinary Surgeons, Am. Urologic Assn., Am. Fertility Soc., Internat. Urologic Soc. Sigma Xi, Delta Kappa Epsilon, Phi Chi, Alpha Omega Alpha. Author: Diagnostic Urology, 1964; Ureteral Reflux in Children, 1967; Urologic Surgery, 1969. Mem. editorial bd. Urology Digest, 1965—, Human Sexuality, 1967—, Urological Survey, 1968—. Home: 27 Oak Dr Durham NC 27707

GLENN, WILLIAM LAURENCE, JR., elec. engr.; b. Decatur, Ga., July 5, 1931; s. William Laurence and Marie (Pearce) G.; B.E.E., Ala. Poly. Inst., 1957; children—William Laurence III, Patricia Kathleen, Karen Ann, James Patrick. Powerplant installation engr., base operations mgr. Pan Am. World Airways, Grand Turk, B.W.I., 1958-59, asst. supt. range operations, program specialist, 1959-61; Saturn operations engr. Douglas Aircraft Co., Cocoa Beach, Fla., 1961-70; pres. Glenn-Terrill Devel. Corp., 1970—. Served with USCG, 1951-54. Mem. I.E.E.E., Phi Delta Theta. Republican. Roman Catholic. Lion. Home: 201 Harbor City Pkwy Indian Harbour Beach FL 32937 Office: 600 Royal Palm Blvd Vero Beach FL 32960

GLICK, EDWARD MAURICE, found. exec., author; b. Cleve., May 23, 1920; s. Philip and Lillian (Levin) G.; B.A., cum laude, Ohio State U., 1943; M.A., Western Reserve U., 1947; Ph.D., Ohio State U., 1960; m. Florence Goldman, Sept. 22, 1946; children—Linda Ruth (Mrs. Samuel Drewen), Ellen Adrienne. Dir. pub. relations Ohio Bur. Unemployment Compensation, 1947-50; chief publs. and reports State and Health, Edn. and Welfare Depts., Washington, 1951-57; pres. Glisand Corp., Washington, 1957-60; editor, pub. Med.-Hosp. Research Digest, Washington, 1957-60; spl. corr. Times of London, 1960-62; cons. Senate Judiciary Com., U.S. Congress, Washington, 1963-64; mng. dir. Am. Inst. for Polit. Communication, Washington, 1965—. Prof. polit. sci. George Washington U., 1964-65, Md. U., 1965-66; prof. journalism Am. U., 1962-63. Pres., dir. Am. Inst. for Polit. Communication, 1965. Served with AUS, 1943-45. Decorated Purple Heart. Mem. Am., So. polit. sci. assns., Am. Acad. Polit. and Social Sci., Phi Beta Kappa, Sigma Delta Chi. Club: Nat. Press (Washington). Author: The New Methodology: A Study of Political Strategy and Tactics, 1967; The Federal Government-Daily Press Relationship, 1968; Media and Non-Media Effects on Formation of Public Opinion, 1969; The Credibility Problem, 1972; co-author Television Station Ownership, 1971; co-author, editor Media Monopoly and Politics, 1973. Contbr. to profl. jours. Home: 5401 Westbard Av Bethesda MD 20016 Office: Prudential Bldg Washington DC 20005

GLICKSTEIN, JOSEPH M(ORRIS), lawyer; b. Jacksonville, Fla., Feb. 26, 1899; s. Harry and Fannie B. (Shorr) G.; LL.B., Washington and Lee U., 1920; m. Myra M. Grunthal, Jan. 8, 1924; children—Joseph Morris, Hugh S. Admitted to Fla. bar, 1920, U.S. Supreme Ct. bar, 1933; practiced in Jacksonville; 1920—; now sr. partner Glickstein, Crenshaw, Glickstein, Fay & Block; atty. City of Neptune Beach (Fla.); gen. counsel So. Indsl. Corp., Fulton Distbg. Co. of Fla., Universal Marion Corp; spl. counsel Merrit-Chapman & Scott Corp.; counsel Bapt. Meml. Hosp., B.B. McCormick & Sons, Inc., Ace Electric Supply Co., Harbor View Farm, Daylight Industries, Inc., John Deihl Chevrolet Co.; sr. adviser Barnett Bank of Jacksonville, N.A. Mem. staff govs. Fla., 1937-39, 49—; mem. Duval County Civil Service Commn., 1937-38; mem. registrants adv. bd., No. 3, Jacksonville, World War II. Mayor Town of Neptune Beach, 1945-47, councilman, 1937-45. Trustee Jacksonville Baptist Hosp., 1950—. Mem. Am. Judicature Soc., Am. Legion, Nat. Geographic Soc., Am., Fla. and Jacksonville bar assns., C. of C., Union Am. Hebrew Congregations (past trustee), Robert E. Lee Assos. (charter), Zeta Beta Tau, Omicron Delta Kappa. Democrat. Jewish. Clubs: University (charter), River (charter), Ponte Vedra. Author article. Home: 1008 Ocean Front Neptune Beach FL 32233 Office: Universal Marion Bldg Jacksonville FL 32202 also PO Box 1086 Jacksonville FL 32201

GLIEBER, (JOHN) FRANK, sportscaster; b. Milw., Apr. 5, 1934; s. John and Mary (Augenstein) G.; B.S. in Speech, Northwestern U., 1956; m. Mary Frances Kuhn, Mar. 26, 1961; children—Lynne, Jon, Robin, Craig, Mitchell. Sports dir. KRLD-AM-FM-TV, Dallas, 1959-66, 67-73; sports dir. WJW, Cleve., 1966-67; sportscaster CBS-TV, 1962—, Hughes Sports Network, 1967—. Mem. Am. Fedn. TV and Radio Artists, Nat. Sportscasters and Sportswriters Assn. (Sportscaster of Yr. 1965-67, 69-72). Club: T Bar M Racquet (Dallas). Home: 13430 Forestway Dr Dallas TX 75240 Office: 7901 Carpenter Freeway Dallas TX 75247

GLISPIN, VERNON LEE, accountant; b. Houston, Nov. 19, 1923; s. Frank Amell and Pearl (Williams) G.; B.B.A., U. Houston, 1950; m. Agnes Pauline McKenzie, Apr. 8, 1951; children—Joanna Lyn, Melissa Lee, Sharla Suzanne. Pub. accountant, Pasadena, Tex., 1952-59, 66—; partner Spain, Glispin & Co., Pasadena, 1959-66; v.p., dir., charter sec. Southmore Savs. Assn., Pasadena, 1959—; dir., sec.-treas. Smith's Appliances, Inc., Pasadena, 1955—, Petro-Chem. Suppliers, Inc., Houston, 1968—; dir., v.p. A-B Distbg. Co., Inc., Harlingen, Tex., 1959—; dir., treas. H & H Apts., Inc., Pasadena, 1967—. Chmn. dist. orgn. and extension com. Sam Houston Area council Boy Scouts Am., 1970-71. Served with USNR, 1943-46, ensign, 1950-55. Mem. Tex. Soc. C.P.A.'s, Am. Inst. C.P.A.'s, Pasadena C. of C., Pasadena Livestock and Rodeo Assn., Nat. Rifle Assn. (life) Optimist (treas. Pasadena 1970-72). Club: Exchange (charter sec. Pasadena 1953-66, charter mem. S.E. Houston). Home: 1311 Jefferson St Pasadena TX 77502 Office: 825 E Southmore St Pasadena TX 77502

GLISSON, LOUISE HILTON (MRS. DANIEL BEVERLY GLISSON), city ofcl.; b. Trenton, Fla., Apr. 3, 1922; d. William Forrest and Inez Melinda (Hughes) Hilton; student Wall Bus. Coll., 1939, 40, Fla. So. Coll., 1964-65, Polk community Coll., 1970—; m. Daniel Beverly Glisson, Feb. 13, 1944; children—Daniel Beverly, Deidre. Sec. to city clk., Bradenton, Fla., 1940-45; sec. Meth. Ch., Auburn, Ala., 1945-47; employed with City of Lake Wales (Fla.), 1959—, city clk.-treas., 1971—. Mem. Internat. Municipal Finance Officers, Municipal Finance Officers of Fla., Bus. and Profl. Women's Club. Methodist. Home: Route 1 Box 196 Lake Wales FL 33853 Office: PO Box 1320 Lake Wales FL 33853

GLOCKER, THEODORE WESLEY, JR., lawyer; b. Knoxville, Tenn., Aug. 10, 1925; s. Theodore W. and Julia (McClarty) G.; student U. of South, 1943-44, U. Tex., 1944-45; B.S., U. Tenn., 1947; J.D., Harvard, 1950; m. Eleanor Julia Glocker, Nov. 30, 1950; children—Theodore William, Margaret McClarty, Eleanor Julia, David Hansen. Admitted to N.M. bar, 1951, D.C. bar, 1953, Fla. bar, 1956; practiced in Albuquerque, 1950-51, Jacksonville, Fla., 1956—; mem. firm Buck & Drew, 1956-57, Buck, Drew & Glocker, 1958—; trial atty., lands div. Dept. of Justice, Washington, 1952-53; atty. Tax Ct. of U.S., 1953-56. Mem. Spl. Liaison Tax Com. Southeastern Region, Jacksonville, 1956-57, 59-60, 65-67. Chmn. bd. Duval County Beaches Hosp., 1959-63; v.p., bd. dirs. Riverside Presbyn. House, Inc., 1970—. Served with USNR, 1943-46. Mem. Am., N.M., Jacksonville bar assns., Bar Assn. of D.C., Fla. Bar (chmn. tax sect. 1963-64). Sigma Chi, Tau Beta Pi, Beta Gamma Sigma, Phi Kappa Phi. Presbyn. Home: 949 Elder Lane Jacksonville FL 32204 Office: Fla Title Bldg Jacksonville FL 32202

GLOSTER, HUGH MORRIS, coll. pres.; b. Brownsville, Tenn., May 11, 1911; s. John and Dora (Morris) G.; student LeMoyne Coll., 1927-29; B.A., Morehouse Coll., 1931; M.A. (Univ. fellow), Atlanta U., 1933; Ph.D. (Gen. Edn. Bd. fellow), N.Y. U., 1943; Hon. Doctorate, U. Haiti, 1968, N.Y. U., 1971; m. Louise Elizabeth Torrence, June 1, 1935 (div.); children—Alice Louise, Evelyn Elaine; m. 2d, Beulah Victoria Harold, Sept. 9, 1957; 1 son, Hugh Morris Jr. Instr., asso. prof. English, LeMoyne Coll., 1933-41; prof. English, Morehouse Coll., 1941-43; program dir. USO, Ft. Huachuca, Ariz., 1943-44, asso. regional exec., Atlanta, 1944-46; prof. English, chmn. dept. lang. and lit. Hampton Inst., 1946-67, dir. summer session, 1952-62, dean of faculty, 1963-67; pres. Morehouse Coll., Atlanta, 1967—; prof. English, Atlanta U., summers 1942, 43; guest prof. English, N.Y. U., summers 1949, 62; Fulbright prof. English, Hiroshima U., Japan, 1953-55; lectr. Orientation Center Fgn. Grad. Students, Coll. William and Mary, summer 1955; vis. prof. Am. lit. U. Warsaw, Poland, 1961-62; lectr. tours, 1933-55, 56, 59; summer faculty various univs. and colls. Bd. dirs. Nat. Assn. for Equal Opportunity in Higher Edn., United Bd. for Coll. Devel., Council Protestant Colls. and Univs.; bd. dirs., trustee United Negro Coll. Fund; trustee Atlanta U., Morehouse Coll., Interdenominational Theol. Center, Inst. Ednl. Devel., Martin Luther King Jr. Meml. Center, Ednl. Testing Service, So. Christian Leadership Conf. Alpha Phi Alpha research grantee, summer 1940; research grantee Carnegie Found., 1950-51; distinguished contbns. award Coll. Lang. Assn., 1958; Alumnus of Year, LaMoyne Coll., 1967. Mem. Assn. Pvt. Colls. and Univs. Ga. (v.p.), Am. Assn. U. Adminstrs. (dir.), Coll. Lang. Assn. (founder, pres. 1937-38, 49-50, trustee), Assn. Am. Colls. (commn. coll. adminstrn.), Nat. Collegiate Athletic Assn. (long-range planning com., Theodore Roosevelt award Jury), Inst. European Studies, (pres.'s council), Am. Assn. Higher Edn. (exec. com. 1967-69), Nat. Reading Council (dir.), Com. on Econ. Devel. (dir.), Phi Beta Kappa, Sigma Pi Phi, Alpha Phi Alpha, Rotarian. Author: Negro Voices in American Fiction, 1948. Co-Editor: The Brown Thrush: An Anthology of Verse by Negro College Students, 1935; My Life-My Country-My World: College Readings for Modern Living, 1952. Contbg. editor Phylon: The Atlanta U. Review of Race and Culture, 1948-53; adv. editor Coll. Lang. Assn. Jour., 1957—. Home: 900 Flamingo Dr SW Atlanta GA 30311

GLOVER, EDWARD BRUCE, digital system design exec.; b. Brunswick, Ga., Mar. 29, 1927; s. Alver Sterling and Bessie Loretta (Decker) G.; B.S., Ga. Inst. Tech., 1951; S.M., Mass. Inst. Tech., 1957; M.S. (NSF fellow), U. Mich., 1965; m. Levie Dorothy Newman, Feb. 9, 1947; 1 dau., Mary Michele. Instrument engr. E.I. duPont de Nemours & Co., Oak Ridge, 1951-52, Aiken, S.C., 1952-54; staff mem. Mass. Inst. Tech. Lincoln Lab., Lexington, 1954-57; with Radiation, Inc., Melbourne, Fla., 1957—, asso. prin. research engr., 1962-63, sect. head systems sect., 1963-64, prin. research engr., 1964-73, sect. head data processing, 1973—; lectr. math. and elec. engring. Fla. Inst. Tech. Served to sgt. AUS, 1945-46. Mem. I.E.E.E., Sigma Xi, Sigma Chi. Baptist (deacon). Patentee in field. Home: 508 Hibiscus Trail Melbourne Beach FL 32951 Office: PO Box 37 Melbourne FL 32961

GLOVER, HARRY DOLPHIN, dentist; b. Chautauqua, Kan., Aug. 16, 1906; s. Edward Bruce and Dora (Anderson) G.; D.D.S., U. Kansas City, 1928; m. Edyth Berniece Parker, Aug. 10, 1925; children—Cyntha (Mrs. Richard F. Ward), Shirley (Mrs. James T. Hoke, Jr.), Rhoda (Mrs. Billy G. McGuire), Michael. Practice dentistry, Stillwater, Okla., 1928—. Mem. Am., Okla., Stillwater dental assns., Am. Inst. Oral Biology, So. Med. Assn., Psi Omega. Democrat. Presbyn. Rotarian (past pres.). Home: 3614 S Husband St Stillwater OK 74074 Office: 1604 W 8th St Stillwater OK 74074

GLOVER, LYNN III, geologist, educator; b. Washington, Nov. 29, 1928; s. Lynn and Winifred (Mears) G.; B.S., Va. Poly. Inst. and State U., 1952, M.S. in Geology, 1953; Ph.D. in Geology, Princeton, 1967; m. Ellen Fielder Waters, Nov. 4, 1950. Geologist, U.S. Geol. Survey, southeastern U.S. and P.R., 1953-70; prof. geology Va. Poly. Inst. and State U., Blacksburg, 1970—. NSF grantee, 1971, 73. Fellow Geol.

Soc. Am.; mem. Am. Assn. Petroleum Geologists, Am. Geophys. Union, Soc. Econ. Petrologists and Mineralogists, Sigma Xi. Contbr. articles on geology of Caribbean and Appalachian regions to sci. jours. Home: 914 Mason Dr Blacksburg VA 24060

GLOVER, WENDELL JOE, supt. schs.; b. Okmulgee, Okla., Mar. 6, 1931; s. Blain E. and Joyce Mabel (Reed) G.; B.S., E. Central State Coll., Ada, Okla., 1952; M.S., Okla. State U., 1956, Ed.D., 1968; m. Wilma Jean King, July 16, 1954; children—Deborah, David, Daniel, Derald. Tchr., coach Eram Schs., Boynton, Okla., 1952-57; prin. Twin Hills Sch., Okmulgee, 1957-59, Beggs (Okla.) Jr. High Sch., 1959-62; supt. Beggs Pub. Schs., 1962-65; grad. asst. univ. placement services Okla. State U., Stillwater, 1965-66; supt. schs. Stillwater Schs., 1966-69, Woodward (Okla.) Pub. Schs., 1969—; tchr. pub. sch. finance Okla. State U., Stillwater, summer 1968, tchr. extension class in sch. finance, 1969. Mem. manpower planning council Dist. II, Okla. Econ. Devel. Assn., 1971-72. Bd. dirs. Woodward Kids, Inc., Plains Indian Mus. Found. Mem. Am., Okla. (v.p. 1970-71) assns. sch. adminstrs., N.E.A., Okla., Woodward County edn. assns., N.W. Okla. Adminstrs. Orgn. (pres. 1970), Okla. Assn. Sch. Bus. Ofcls., Woodward C. of C. (dir. 1969-72), Phi Delta Kappa. Home: Route 3 Box 94 M Woodward OK 73801 Office: PO Box 668 10th and Main Woodward OK 73801

GLUCK, FRANCIS WILCOX, JR., physician; b. Balt., Oct. 19, 1938; s. Francis Wilcox and Jean Harvey (Anderson) G.; B.A., Williams Coll., 1961; M.D., Johns Hopkins, 1965; m. Judith Aileen Hughes, Oct. 12, 1968; 1 son, Robert Francis. Intern, Vanderbilt Hosp., Nashville, 1965-66, resident, 1966-67, 69-71; practice medicine, specializing in internal medicine, Nashville, 1971—; asst. prof. medicine Vanderbilt U., 1971—. Served with USNR, 1967-69. Mem. A.C.P. Home: Route 3 Murry Lane Brentwood TN 37027 Office: Vanderbilt Clinic B-1105 Nashville TN 37232

GLYNN, EMMETT MARTIN, realtor; b. Arbroth, La., Aug. 9, 1912; s. Alexander A. and Felicia (Supple) G.; B.S., La. State U., 1936, postgrad., 1938-40; m. Natalie Jones, Apr. 27, 1946; children—Christine Supple, Martin Alex. Cattle farmer, 1945-53; salesman J. T. Doiron Realtor, Baton Rouge, 1945-49; gen. sales mgr. Anhydrous Ammonia div. Gen. Gas Corp., Baton Rouge, 1954-56; v.p. Glenrich, Inc., 1960-69; pres. Schriever Devel. Co., Inc., 1958-69, Broadmoor Heights, Inc., 1965-69, E.M. Glynn, Inc., Houma, La., 1957—. Mem. La. State U. Alumni Council, 1936-42, chmn. exec. com., 1939-40. Served with A.C., AUS, 1942-45. Roman Catholic. K.C., Elk. Clubs: Bayou Country, R.O.T.C. Parents (Thibodaux, La.). Home: 605 St Philip St Thibodaux LA 70301 Office: 705 Lafayette St Houma LA 70360

GLYNN, WILLIAM ALLEN, mathematician, educator; b. Nowata, Okla., Jan. 21, 1935; s. Roy Burnard and Ethel Faye (Lane) G.; B.S. in Math. Edn., Northeastern Okla. State Coll., 1960; M.S. in Math. (NSF fellow), Okla. State U., 1962, Ph.D. in Math., 1965; m. Mary Ann Turner, Jan. 15, 1953; children—Timothy Allen and Kym (Mrs. Vincent J. Ramseur). Asst. prof. math. Western Ill. U., Macomb, 1965-68; asso. prof. Va. Commonwealth U., 1968-73, chmn. dept. of math. scis., 1968—, prof., 1973—. Mem. Math. Assn. Am., Am. Math. Soc., Ill., Greater Richmond councils tchrs. math. Home: 10108 A Palace Way Richmond VA 23233 Office: 901 W Franklin St Richmond VA 23284

GOBER, HENRY FRED, lawyer; b. Gainesville, Ga., Apr. 30, 1917; s. John Y. and Leila (Johnson) G.; A.B., Columbia, 1939, LL.B., 1942; m. Margaret Carolyn Maddox, Feb. 19, 1948; children—Henry Fred, James Alan, Carolyn Jean, Elisabeth Ann. Admitted to Ga. bar, 1942; asso. Dunaway, Riley & Howard, Atlanta, 1946-50; gen. counsel Atlanta Legal Aid Soc., 1950-55; asso. Arnall, Golden & Gregory, 1955-58, partner, 1959—; lectr. in law Emory U., 1950—; v.p., dir. Am. Frozen Foods, Inc. Mem. Fulton County Ct. Revision Commn. Bd. dirs. YMCA, 1959. Served from pvt. to staff sgt., CIC, AUS, 1942-46. Mem. Am. Ga. (legal aid com. chmn. 1959), Atlanta bar assns., Lawyers Club of Atlanta, Am. Judicature Soc., Legal Aid Assn. (chmn. com. on policies standards and statistics 1955-56); Southeastern Law Tchrs. Assn., P.T.A. (chmn. edn. com. 1959), Phi Alpha Delta, Sigma Chi. Methodist (ofcl. bd.). Mason (Shriner) Clubs: East Lake Civic (pres. 1958), Atlanta Social Workers (dir. 1954-56). Editor: Supplement Code of the City of Atlanta, 1949; (Ga. sect.) Compendium of Laws-Armed Forces, 1954. Home: 4358 Northside Dr NW Atlanta GA 30327 Office: Fulton Fed Bldg Atlanta GA 30303

GOCKEL, ASHFORD RAVENSCROFT, petroleum co. exec.; b. Tulsa, Okla., Dec. 10, 1925; s. Edward and Eugenia Jane (Graves) G.; B.E. with high honors, Yale, 1945, LL.B., 1948; m. Gladys Darnell, July 29, 1950; children—Ashford Ravenscroft, Dencie E. Asst. instr. dept. civil engring. Yale, 1945-48; dir. sales adminstrn. Deep Rock Oil Corp., Tulsa, Okla., 1948-53, bulk sales mgr., 1953-55; dir. sales adminstrn. and marketing research Kerr-McGee Corp., Oklahoma City, 1955-63, gen. mgr. petroleum supply and transp., 1963-67, gen. mgr. corp. purchasing and transp., 1967-68, v.p., 1968—; pres. Kerr-McGee Pipeline Corp.; pres., dir. White Shoal Pipeline Corp. Mem. Am. Petroleum Inst. (mem. gen. com. div. refining 1968—), Ind. Petroleum Assn. Am., Nat. Petroleum Refiners Assn., Soc. Advancement Mgmt., Okla. Bar Assn., Oklahoma City Petroleum Club, Sigma Xi, Tau Beta Pi. Republican. Presbyn. (ruling elder 1960). Home: 1208 Glenwood Av Oklahoma City OK 73116 Office: Kerr McGee Bldg Oklahoma City OK 73102

GODARD, LOUIE D., dist. judge; b. Mobile, Ala., Aug. 16, 1908; s. Louie J. and Beulah Emma (Sossman) G.; LL.B., J.D., U. Tex., 1936; m. Glennis Jeannette Birket, Oct. 10, 1946; children—Jeanette, (Mrs. William R. Livesay, Jr.), Tom. Admitted to Tex. bar, 1936; atty. Office Tex. Atty. Gen., 1936-37; with firm Beasley & Beasley, Beeville, Tex., 1937-38, Thornton, Markwell & Godard, Texas City, 1938-40, Godard & Dazey, Texas City, 1940-59; judge 122d Jud. Dist. of Tex., Galveston, 1959—. Dir. Mainland Bank, Texas City. Mem. Tex. Ho. of Reps., 1947-51. Served with AUS, 1942-46. Mem. Am., Tex. bar assns., Am. Judicature Soc. Rotarian (v.p., dir. Texas City 1957), K.C. Home: 1721 Oleander Rd Dickinson TX 77539 Office: Court House Galveston TX 77550

GODBEE, BARRON WHITEHEAD, JR., theatre circuit mgr.; b. Vidalia, Ga., Oct. 6, 1926; s. Barron Whitehead and Julia (Jenkins) G.; student Emory Coll., 1943, N. Ga. Coll., 1944; diploma in sound engring. Capitol Radio Engring. Inst., 1950. With Pal Theatre, Vidalia, 1941-43, asst. mgr., 1946-47, mgr., 1950-60; asst. engr., purchasing agt. Pal Amusement Co., Vidalia, 1950-63, supr., 1960-63, booker, buyer, gen. mgr., 1963—. Crusades chmn. Toombs County Cancer Soc., 1971-72, edn. chmn., 1971-72, v.p., 1972-73; finance chmn. Vidalia YMCA, 1971-73; past pres. Vidalia High Sch. Band Boosters. Served with USNR, 1944-46. Named Citizen of Year, civic clubs Vidalia, 1971. Mem. Vidalia C. of C. (v.p. 1970-71, pres. 1970-71), Nat. Assn. Theatre Owners Ga. (v.p. 1969—). Elk, Lion (Lion of Year 1968-69, Zone chmn. 1960-62). Home: 101 Brumette St SE Vidalia GA 30474 office: PO Box 750 Church St Vidalia GA 30474

GODBEY, JOHN KIRBY, research engr., b. Cisco, Tex., Nov. 14, 1921; s. Josiah Jernigan and Emma Lee (Taylor) G.; B.S. in Elec. Engring. with honors, So. Meth. U., 1944; M.S. in Elec. Engring., U. Tex., 1947; m. Jo Fay Harrison, Nov. 20, 1943; children—John Kirby, Gayle Harrison (Mrs. Daniel Arthur Morgan III). Teaching fellow U. Tex., Austin, 1946-47; research technologist field research lab. Magnolia Petroleum Co., Dallas, 1947-58; sr. research engr. in petroleum prodn. Mobil Research & Devel. Corp., Dallas, 1958—. Served to lt. (j.g.) USNR, 1944-46. Registered profl. engr., Tex. Mem. Dallas-Ft. Worth Council Sci. Soc., Tex. Mid-Continent Oil and Gas Assn. (Outstanding Performance award 1964, chmn. oil information com. 1961-69), League for Ednl. Advancement in Dallas, I.E.E.E. (chmn. Dallas-Ft. Worth sect. 1952-53), Soc. Petroleum Engrs., Measurements and Data Soc., U.S., Tex. socs. profl. engrs., Dallas Petroleum Engrs.' Club. Contbr. articles to profl. jours. Patentee in field petroleum prodn., exploration. Home: 4339 Hockaday Dr Dallas TX 75229 Office: PO Box 900 Dallas TX 75221

GODBEY, LUTHER DAVID, architect; b. Friend, Neb., May 28, 1938; s. Luther Dobbs and Ruth (Thomas) G.; B.Arch., U. Neb., 1961; m. Priscilla White, Oct. 6, 1963; children—Emily, Patrick David. Draftsman, Benjamin Votava & Assos., Omaha, 1960-61; designer Selmer A. Solheim & Assos., Lincoln, Neb., 1961-63; partner Golemon & Rolfe, Architects, Houston, 1963—. Bd. dirs. Billboards Ltd., 1965-66. Mem. A.I.A., Tex. Soc. Architects. Rotarian. Clubs: Tejas Breakfast (pres. 1971), Cotillion (pres. 1970). Prin. works include Fire Sta. Houston Intercontinental Airport, River Oaks Country Club, U. Tex. at El Paso, Edn. and Engring. Teaching Center, Diagnostic Clinic, Deer Park High Sch. Home: 2203 University Blvd Houston TX 77025 Office: 5100 Travis St Houston TX 77002

GODBOLD, CLYDE EVERETT, dentist; b. Rains, S.C., Sept. 16, 1923; s. Fred Monroe and Frances Leona (Grice) G.; student U. S.C., 1946-49; D.D.S., Med. Coll. Va., 1953; postgrad. Dewey Sch. Orthodontics, N.Y. U., 1964, 69, U. Pitts., 1965, 69; m. Elizabeth Arlene Branham, Apr. 10, 1955; children—Sarah, Cheryl, Debbie, Rhett, Walter. Practice gen. dentistry, Myrtle Beach, S.C., 1953—, gen. dentistry and orthodontics, 1963—. Chmn. Horry County Heart Fund Campaign, 1974. Served with USNR, 1944-46; PTO. Mem. S.C., Am. dental assns., Internat. Assn. Orthodontics, Acad. Gen. Dentistry, Civitan Club (dir. 1970-72). Methodist. Mason (Shriner), Elk. Home: 3916 Pine Lakes Dr Myrtle Beach SC 29577 Office: 3409 N Kings Hwy Myrtle Beach SC 29577

GODBOLD, JOHN COOPER, U.S. judge; b. Coy, Ala., Mar. 24, 1920; s. Edwin Condie and Elsie (Williamson) G.; B.S., Auburn U., 1940; J.D., Harvard, 1948; m. Elizabeth Showalter, July 18, 1942; children—Susan, Richard, John C., Cornelia, Sally. Admitted to Ala. bar, 1948; with firm of Richard T. Rives, Montgomery, (Ala.,) 1948-49; partner firm Godbold, Hobbs & Copeland, and predecessors, 1949-66; U.S. circuit judge Ct. of Appeals, 5th Circuit, Montgomery, 1966—. Served with F.A., AUS, 1941-46. Mem. Montgomery County Bar Assn., Ala. State Bar, Alpha Tau Omega, Omicron Delta Kappa, Phi Kappa Phi. Club: Montgomery Country. Home: 3590 Thomas Av Montgomery AL 36111 Office: Federal Bldg Montgomery AL 36102

GODBOLD, PERCY ELLIS, JR., banker; b. Pine Hill, Ala., Feb. 5, 1913; s. Percy Ellis and Kathleen (Davie) G.; B.S., U. Ala., 1933; m. Grace Fuller, Sept. 16, 1937; 1 son, Leonard William. Agt. Internal Revenue Service, Birmingham, Ala., 1945-50; partner Kirkland, Godbold & Smith, C.P.A.'s, Birmingham, 1951-63; self-employed mgmt. cons., Anniston, Ala., 1964-73; chmn. bd. Comml. Bank, Douglasville, Ga., 1961—, Bank of Pine Hill (Ala.), 1972—; chmn., pres. Peoples Bank, Anniston, 1973—. Trustee Stringfellow Meml. Hosp., Anniston. Served with AUS, 1943-45. C.P.A., Ala. Mem. Am. Bankers Assn. Baptist. Kiwanian. Club: Country (Anniston) Home: 2105 Henry Rd Anniston AL 36201 Office: PO Box 1176 Douglasville GA 30134 also PO Box 1366 Anniston AL 36201

GODCHAUX, CHARLES RAGLAND, food co. exec.; b. Abbeville, La., Dec. 27, 1930; s. Frank Area and Mary Lawrence (Ragland) G.; B.A., Vanderbilt U., 1952; m. Wilma Polk Monypeny, Mar. 21, 1953; children—Theresa Polk, Rebecca Ragland. With La. State Rice Milling Co., Inc (now Lastarmco Inc.), Abbeville, La., 1954—, v.p., 1956—, mem. exec. com., 1964—, also dir.; v.p., dir. Riviana Foods, Inc. Pres. Vermilion Parish Library Bd. Control, 1967-72. Served to lt. (j.g.) USNR, 1952-54. Mem. Phi Delta Theta. Episcopalian. Home: Homeplace Abbeville LA 70510 Office: PO Box 269 Abbeville LA 70510

GODDARD, FREDERICK PERCY, bishop; b. Seymour, Conn., Dec. 8, 1903; s. Frederick and Louisa (Marshall) G.; Ph.B., Yale, 1924; B.D., Berkeley Div. Sch., 1927, S.T.D., 1950; D.D., U. South, 1954; m. May Selena Bennett, Sept. 8, 1928 (dec. Apr. 1965); children—Marie Louise (Mrs. John Bullard), Gladys Emily (Mrs. Roger Rishel); m. 2d, Hazel Bennett Falconer, Nov. 17, 1968. Ordained to ministry Episcopal Ch. as deacon, 1927, as priest, 1928; rector St. John's Episcopal Ch., Marlin, Tex., 1927-55; suffragan bishop Diocese of Tex., Tyler, 1955—. Sec., Diocese of Tex., 1939-46; del. gen. conv. Episcopal Ch., 1934, 37, 43, 46, 49, 53; pres. standing com. Diocese of Tex., 1950-55. Chmn. ARC, Falls County, Tex., 1934-42, Community Welfare, Falls County, 1932-48. Trustee U. of South, Sem. of Southwest. Recipient Silver Beaver award Boy Scouts Am. Mem. Tex. Archeol. Soc. Club: Yale (Houston). Editor: Texas Churchman, 1930-39. Home: 615 Perry St Marlin TX 76661

GODDARD, RUTH, publishing co. exec.; b. Ballinger, Tex., Dec. 5, 1911; d. John Eugene and Dora Ruth (Elder) Gressett; grad. high sch.; m. John H. Hunnicut, Nov. 18, 1927 (dec. Oct. 1948); children—Joann (Mrs. John P. Taylor), Dolores (Mrs. A.L. Delaney, Jr.), Carolyn (Mrs. Charles Scarborough); m. 2d, Walter C. Goddard, Oct. 12, 1952 (dec. Sept. 1971). Script writer U. Tex., 1946-52; copy writer KNOW, Austin, Tex., 1954-60, KTBC, Austin, 1963-67; now asso. editor, pub. relations Jenkins Pub. Co., Austin; writer radio series Tex. Sch. Air. Recipient of 5 nat. awards for radio plays; Theta Sigma award, 1971. Mem. Christian Ch. Author: Live and Help Live, 1953; Ralph Ogden and The Seven Mustangs, 1970. Home: 1108 West 9 Austin TX 78703 Office: 6929 S Interregional P O Box 2085 Austin TX 78767

GODEAU, DON LOUIS, shipbuilding co. exec.; b. Eunice, La., July 25, 1935; s. Don Louis and Odill (Fruge) G.; student Lamar State Coll., 1954-56; m. Helen Stanley, Oct. 10, 1953; children—Randy, Jodi. Marine draftsman Todd Shipyards, Houston, 1954-60, project engr., 1960-65; mgr. prodn. Port Houston Shipyard, Houston, 1965-67, v.p., gen. mgr., 1967—. Served with USNR, 1953-60. Mem. Soc. Naval Architects. Home: 18646 Prince William Lane Nassau Bay Houston TX 77058 Office: 819 S 80th St Houston TX 77012

GODFREY, RICHARD HENRY, lawyer; b. Fairview, Okla., May 20, 1914; s. J. Nile and Mary (Every) G.; student Oklahoma City U., 1933-34, LL.B., 1938; m. Marcella Hill, Jan. 1, 1941; 1 son, Richard Henry. Admitted to Okla. bar, 1937; practiced in Oklahoma City, 1937-40; with investment firm, Levelland, Tex., 1940-42; pvt. practice, Oklahoma City, 1946-60; pres., dir. Am.-First Title & Trust Co., Oklahoma City, 1960—, Capitol Corp., 1962—; dir. Village Bank, Oklahoma City, 1962-74. Mem. Oklahoma World's Fair Adv. Council; vice chmn. Mercy Hosp. Heart Sta., 1958-60; dir. Frontiers of Sci. Found., treas., 1965-74; adv. dir. Salvation Army, 1969-74, mem. finance com., 1971-74. Bd. dirs. YMCA, 1974—. Served from pvt. to capt. USAAF, 1942-45. Mem. Am., Okla. bar assns., Okla. Land Title Assn. (pres. 1966-67), Am. Land Title Assn. (gov. 1968-70), Oklahoma City Bd. Realtors, Oklahoma City Home Builders Assn., Mortgage Bankers Am., Better Bus. Bur. (pres. 1967-68, dir. 1967-72), Oklahoma City C. of C. (dir. 1965-74). Presbyn. (pres. trustees 1968, sec.-treas. 1971-74). Clubs: Revelers (pres. 1964-65), Economic of Oklahoma, Lawyers, Beacon (pres. 1958-60), Quail Creek Golf and Country, Men's Dinner. Home: 6401 N Hillcrest Av Oklahoma City OK 73116 Office: 219 Park Av Oklahoma City OK 73102

GODFREY, WILLIAM AUBREY, JR., physician; b. Dallas, Dec. 9, 1931; s. William Aubrey and Mary Sue (Sherman) G.; student Baylor U., 1948-51; M.D., Southwestern Med. Sch., U. Tex., 1955; m. Mary Elizabeth Heffington, Sept. 21, 1963; children—Martha Sue, Mary Catherine. Intern, VA Hosp., Dallas, 1955-56, resident, 1956-57, 59-62; practice medicine specializing in internal medicine and diagnosis, Dallas, 1962—; partner, Physicians and Surgeons Clinic, Dallas, 1962—; mem. sr. attending staff Parkland Meml. Hosp.; mem. staff Meth. Hosp. Dallas; asso. clin. prof. internal medicine U. Tex. S.W. Med. Sch., 1970-71. Served with USAF, 1957-59. Diplomate Am. Bd. Internal Medicine. Fellow A.C.P.; mem. Am., Tex. socs. internal medicine, Tex. Acad. Internal Medicine, North Tex. Diabetes Assn. (chmn. bd. dirs. 1973-74), Phi Chi. Home: 1547 Cedar Hill Av Dallas TX 75208 Office: 1511 N Beckley St Dallas TX 75203

GODFREY, WILLIAM MELVIN, state ofcl.; b. Lakeland, Fla., July 7, 1927; s. William Edwin and Nettie (Terry) G.; B.C.E., U. Fla., 1950; m. Charlotte Arthur Laird, July 2, 1949; children—Douglas Alan (dec.), James Kenneth. Draftsman, Fla. Rd. Dept., Tallahassee, 1950-51, designer, 1951-56, sr. designer, 1956-62, asst. engr. bridge design, 1962-66, dep. engr. traffic and planning, 1966-69, chief bur. planning, 1969-70, dep. dir. div. planning and programming, 1970—. Mem. com. Suwannee River Area council Boy Scouts Am., 1965—. Served with USNR, 1952-55. Registered profl. engr., Fla. Home: 2010 Wahalaw Nene Tallahassee FL 32301 Office: Haydon Burns Bldg 605 Suwannee Tallahassee FL 32304

GODRIDGE, JOSEPH EDWARD, JR., securities broker; b. Flushing, N.Y., Oct. 29, 1926; s. Joseph Edward and Dorothy (Anderson) G.; B.S., U. Va., 1949; m. Barbara L. Krauss, June 19, 1948; children—Joseph Edward III, Victoria Anne. Sales rep. Burroughs Corp., Roanoke, Va., 1949-50, Charlottesville, Va., 1950-55, Washington, 1955-56; broker Ferris & Co., Washington, 1956-66, sales mgr., 1966-68, gen. partner, 1969-71, sr. v.p., dir., 1971—; pres. Pola Corp., Arlington, Va., 1971—; instr. investments Arlington County (Va.) Adult Edn., 1956—. Served with USNR, 1945-46. Mem. Wash. Soc. Investment Analysts, Met. Washington Bd. Trade, Nat. Economists Club, Kappa Sigma. Clubs: Exchange of Washington (pres. 1974), Columbia Country (Chevy Chase, Md.). Home: 8018 Glendale Rd Chevy Chase MD 20015 Office: 1720 I St NW Washington DC 20006

GODSEY, CARL WAYNE, broadcast journalist; b. Lynchburg, Va., Aug. 5, 1946; s. Carl Dodge and Frances (Keesee) G.; B.A. in English, Lynchburg Coll., 1968; m. Barbara Lynn Borneman, Aug. 24, 1968. Reporter, assignment editor, news dir. WSOC-AM-FM-TV, Charlotte, N.C., 1969-74; reporter, producer Newsweek, N.Y.C., 1974—. Mem. Mayor's Com. Better Charlotte, 1972—, environmental pollution task force Charlotte C. of C., 1971—; mem. publicity com. United Negro Coll. Fund, 1972—. Mem. Radio-Television News Dirs. Assn. (regional dir.), N.C. Asso. Press Broadcasters Assn. (dir.), Sigma Delta Chi, Alpha Phi Omega. Republican. Home: 1037 Archdale Dr Charlotte NC 28210 also Apt 1B 147 W 78th St New York City NY Office: 444 Madison Av New York City NY 10022

GODSEY, FRANK WALDMAN, cons.; b. Beaumont, Tex., Sept. 14, 1906; s. Frank Waldman and Martha Evelyn (Wilkerson) G.; B.S., Rice U., 1927; M.S., Yale, 1929, E.E., 1933; m. Helen Anita Kjoss, Dec. 12, 1929; children—Anne (Mrs. Robert J. Stinnett), Sally (Mrs. Richard T. Goshen), Frank Waldman III, William J. Devel. engr. safety car H & L Co., New Haven, 1928-34; chief elec. engr. Sprague Electric Co., North Adams, Mass., 1934-40; v.p. Westinghouse Electric Co., Pitts. and Balt., 1940-56; pres. Electronic Communications, Inc., St. Petersburg, Fla., 1956-61; owner, pres. Advanced Tech. Corp., Towson, Md., 1964-68; cons. in mgmt. and tech. cons., Washington and St. Petersburg, 1961—; cons. NASA, 1961-71, Dept. Transp., 1969-72. Fellow I.E.E.E.; mem. Nat. Security Indsl. Assn. (life), Sigma Xi. Author: Gas Turbines for Aircraft, 1949. Patentee in field. Home: 311 Cordova Blvd St Petersburg FL 33704

GODSHALL, ARTHUR RAY, lawyer; b. Union, S.C., July 19, 1906; s. Leslie Byron and Lillie Belle (Jones) G.; B.A., U.S.C., 1928, J.D., 1932; m. Rachel Elizabeth Pridmore, June 14, 1934; children—Alyce Kathleen (Mrs. Robert Henry Hileman), Evelyn Belle (Mrs. Charles DePass Cathcart). Admitted to S.C. bar, 1932; practiced in Gaffney, S.C., 1932—; chmn. S.C. Pardon Bd., 1935-39; sec. U.S. Senator Olin D. Johnston, 1945; city atty., Gaffney, S.C., 1943—; atty., Cherokee County Sch. Dist., 1960—, United Cities Gas Co., 1945—; pres., gen. counsel Radio Sta. WFGN, Gaffney, S.C., 1948—; dir., gen. counsel Bank of Gaffney; dir. Gaffney Devel. Co. Mem. adv. bd. Salvation Army, 1969-73. Mem. Cherokee County (pres. 1959-60), S.C., Seventh Circuit (pres. 1953-54) bar assns., S.C. Trial Lawyers Assn., Blue Key, Phi Delta Phi, Sigma Phi Epsilon. Lion. Home: 609 S Limestone St Gaffney SC 29340 Office: 415 1/2 N Limestone St Gaffney SC 29340

GODSY, JAMES DAVID, civil engr., city ofcl.; b. Fremont, Mo., Apr. 4, 1932; s. Ira Howard and Opal (O'Dell) G.; B.S. in Civil Engring., Mo. Sch. Mines, 1959; m. Mary Wendolyn Coates, Sept. 27, 1957; children—Jay David, Mary Alice, Naida Louise. Rodman, U.S. Geol. Survey, Texarkana, Ark., 1951-52, Barnesville, Minn., 1952; engr. Boeing Co., Wichita, Kan., 1959-62, New Orleans, 1962-65, Seattle, 1970-71, Huntsville, Ala., 1965-70; asst. engr. City of Huntsville, 1970—. Registered profl. engr., Ala. Baptist. Home: Rural Route 1 Box 691 Harvest AL 35749 Office: PO Drawer 308 Huntsville AL 35508

GODWIN, ADOLPHUS PILSTON, JR., judge; b. Gatesville, N.C., Oct. 6, 1912; s. Adolphus Pilston and Mabel C. (Hayes) G.; LL.B., Wake Forest Coll., 1937;; m. Mildred Vann, Aug. 10, 1940; children—Adolphus Pilston, Gretchen Vann. Admitted N.C. bar, 1937; mem. firm Godwin & Godwin, Gatesville, 1937-65; spl. agt. FBI, 1942-45; v.p. Tarheel Bank & Trust Co., 1954-65, pres., 1965-66, also dir. Judge N.C. Superior Ct., 1967—. Mem. N.C. Senate, 1953-57, gen. statutes com., 1953-55, 61-62; commr. N.C. Dept. Motor Vehicles, 1965-67. Mem. State Dem. Exec. Com., 1948-66. Mem. 1st Jud. Dist. Bar (pres. 1953-54). N.C. State Bar Inc., N.C. Bar Assn. (gov. 1957-61, 63-64, pres. 1965-66). Baptist. Mason (past master). Address: 2706 Fairview Rd Raleigh NC 27608

GODWIN, MILLS EDWIN, JR., gov. Va.; b. Nansemond County, Va., Nov. 19, 1914; s. Mills Edwin and Otelia (Darden) G.; LL.B., U. Va., 1938; LL.D. (hon.), Elon (N.C.) Coll., 1954, Coll. William and Mary, 1966, Roanoke Coll., 1969, Washington and Lee U., 1970, Elmira Coll., 1972, Hampden-Sydney Coll., 1973; m. Katherine Beale,

Oct. 26, 1940; 1 dau., Becky (dec.). Admitted to Va. bar 1937; practice in Suffolk, 1938-62, 70-73; spl. agt. FBI, 1942-46; mem. Va. Ho. Dels. from Suffolk-Nansemond County, 1947-52, senate, 1952-61; lt. gov. Va., 1962-66; gov. Va., Richmond, 1966-70, 73—. Dir. Va. Nat. Bank, N. & W. Ry., Standard Brands, Inc., Union Camp Corp., Dan River, Inc., Va. Real Estate Investment Trust. Chmn. So. Regional Edn. Bd., 1968-69; chmn. Appalachian Govs. Council, 1968-69; vice chmn. So. Govs. Conf., 1968-69; exec. com. Nat. Govs. Conf., 1968-69. Trustee Elon Coll., Va. Wesleyan Coll. Named Suffolk and Nansemond County First Citizen, 1956, 59. Mem. Raven Soc., Omicron Delta Kappa, Phi Delta Phi. Republican. Mem. Christian Ch. K.P., Mason (33, Shriner), Rotarian, Moose, Ruritan (nat. pres. 1952). Home: Governor's Mansion Richmond VA also Cedar Point Crittenden VA 23342 Office: State Capitol Richmond VA

GODWIN, WELDON, mfg. co. exec.; b. Lou Ann, Ark., Apr. 12, 1927; s. William Armor and Bertha Olivia (DeFee) G.; student U. Houston, 1948-49; m. Ernestine Marie Bedford, June 5, 1947; children—Marolea (Mrs. Joe E. Adams Jr.), Craig Weldon. With South Tex. Tool Co., Houston, 1953—, pres. 1965—; pres. United Machine Works, New Waverly, Tex., 1972—. Served with USNR, 1944-45. Republican. Baptist. Home: PO Box 367 New Waverly TX 77358 Office: 3004 April Lane Houston TX 77018

GODWIN, WINSTON YUVAWN, physician; b. Summerton, S.C., Nov. 5, 1928; s. Chalmers Luke and Anna Snow (Huggins) G.; B.S., Clemson U., 1949; postgrad. The Citadel, 1955-56; M.D., Med. U. S.C., 1959; m. Mary Hodge, June 3, 1950; children—Winston Yuvawn, Paul L., Michael L., Mary L., David A., Roger T. Self-employed in farm machinery and supplies, ins. agy., automobile sales and repair, 1949-53; intern Med. U.S.C. teaching hosps., 1959-60; practice medicine specializing in family practice, Cheraw, S.C., 1969—; chief staff Chesterfield County Meml. Hosp.; pres., med. dir. Cheraw Nursing Home, Inc., 1965—. Mem. exec. com. S.C. State Bd. Health, 1970—. Mem. Chesterfield County Sch. Bd., 1962—. Served to 1st lt. USAF, 1953-55. Diplomate Am. Bd. Family Practice. Mem. Internat. Flying Farmers, Am. Legion, A.M.A., S.C. Acad. Family Practice (chmn. membership com. 1970—), S.C., Cheraw med. assns., Alpha Omega Alpha. Baptist (trustee 1969-72). Mason. Club: Civitan (dir. 1970—) (Cheraw). Home: Hwy 9 Cheraw SC 29520 Office: 207 Marion St Cheraw SC 29520

GOEHRING, JOHN BROWN, chemist, educator; b. Pitts., Apr. 24, 1935; s. James Lindsay and Dorothy Westlake (Brown) G.; B.S. Davidson Coll., 1956; Ph.D. (NSF fellow), U. N.C., 1962; m. Ouida Lee Reaves, Aug. 28, 1960; children—Dorothy Lee, Patricia Reaves, Alexander Brown. Instr. U. N.C., Chapel Hill, 1960-63; asst. prof. chemistry Washington and Lee U., Lexington, Va., 1963-66, asso. prof., 1966-70, prof., 1970—. NSF faculty fellow, 1969-70. Mem. Am. Chem. Soc., The Chem. Soc. London, A.A.A.S., Va. Acad. Sci., Sigma Xi, Phi Beta Kappa, Phi Mu Alpha, Gamma Sigma Epsilon. Presbyn. Composer operatta Isadora, 1952. Office: Dept Chemistry Washington and Lee Univ Lexington VA 24450

GOERITZ, MATHIAS, artist; b. Danzig, Germany, Apr. 4, 1915; s. Ernst and Hedwig (Bruenner) G.; Ph.D., U. Berlin (Germany), 1940; m. Ida Rodriguez Prampolini, Dec. 9, 1960; 1 son, Daniel. Came to Mexico, 1949. Prof. U. Guadalajara (Mexico), 1949-54; prof. Nat. U. Mexico, Mexico City, 1954—; painter, sculptor, architect; founder, dir. Indsl. Design Sch. Ibero Americana U., Mexico City, 1957-60; artist-in-residence Aspen (Colo.) Inst. Humanistic Studies, summers, 1970, 71, 72; lectr. in field. Artist adviser Organizing Com. Olympic Games, Mexico City, 1966-68. Mem. Acad. Arts Berlin. Author, illustrator several books. Editor art sect. Arquitectura, 1959—. Works include design Exptl. Museum Mexico, Mexico City; executed murals, sculpture Tower of Satellite City, Mexico City. Address: 58 Jalapa San Angel Tizapan Mexico 20 DF Mexico

GOERTZ, JOHN WILLIAM, mammalogist, educator; b. Hackensack, N.J., Aug. 25, 1929; s. William and Rose Francis (Scheldorfer) G.; A.A., Sierra Jr. Coll., 1954; B.S., Ore. State U., 1957, M.S. (Sci. Adv. fellow), 1959; Ph.D. (Coop. Wildlife fellow 1960, Nat. Wildlife Fedn. fellow 1960, NIH fellow 1961-62), Okla. State U., 1962; m. Lorna Bernice Edwards, Dec. 19, 1953; children—Dona Diane, Thomas William, Peter Edwards. Prof. zoology La. Tech. U., Ruston, 1962—. Served with USN, 1948-52. Mem. Am. Soc. Mammalogists, Ecol. Soc. Am., Am. Ornithologists Union, Wildlife Soc., Southwestern Assn. Naturalists, Nat. Geog. Soc., Sigma Xi, Phi Kappa Phi. Author: Laboratory Exercises in Zoology, 2d edit., 1971. Contbr. articles to profl. jours. Home: 1402 Caddo St Ruston LA 71270

GOETHALS, HENRY WEBB, newspaper corr.; b. Boston, Mar. 16, 1922; s. Thomas Rodman and Mary (Webb) G.; grad. Roxbury Latin Sch., 1940; B.A., Harvard, 1947. Reporter, editor El Paso (Tex.) Herald Post, 1948-50; night editor Mexico City (Mexico) News, 1951-55; corr. McGraw-Hill, Havanna, Cuba, 1956-60; corr. Mexico, Central Am., Copley News Service, Mexico City, 1960-64, mem. news service bur., Washington, 1964—. Served with USAAF, 1943-46. Home: 1801 Clydesdale Pl NW Washington DC 20009

GOETHALS, PAUL LAWRENCE, physician; b. Rock Island, Ill., Oct. 21, 1933; s. Otto A. and Barbara L. (Biasig) G.; B.S., Loyola U., Chgo., 1956, M.D., 1958; M.S. in Otolaryngology, U. Minn., 1963; m. Judith Arlene Albrecht, Apr. 11, 1964; children—Cynthia Marie, Patricia Lynn, Andrea Lee, Paul Lawrence, James, Lisa. Intern Mound Park Hosp., St. Petersburg, Fla., 1958-59; resident Mayo Clinic, Rochester, Minn., 1959-63; practice medicine specializing in otolaryngology, Winter Park, Fla., 1965—. Served to lt. comdr., M.C., USNR, 1963-65. Diplomate Am. Bd. Otolaryngology. Fellow Am. Acad. Ophthalmology and Otolaryngology, A.C.S.; mem. Am., So., Fla. med. assns., Orange County Med. Soc., Mayo Alumni Assn., Am. Council Otolarynology. Republican. Roman Catholic. Rotarian. Club: University (Winter Park). Home: 727 Kiwi Circle Winter Park FL 32789 Office: 255 N Lakemont Av Winter Park FL 32789

GOETTEE, JAMES HENRY, ret. ednl. adminstr.; b. Carmona, Tex., July 18, 1907; s. Francis Marion and L. Catherine (Welch) G.; B.S., Sam Houston U., 1933; M.Ed., U. Tex., 1937; D.Ed., U. Houston, 1959; m. Edna Mae Survant, Aug. 23, 1933; 1 son, James Lee. Teaching prin. county schs., Trinity County, Tex., 1927-30; teaching prin. Field's Store Sch., Waller, Tex., 1930-33; supt. Spring (Tex.) Ind. Sch. Dist., 1933-38; tchr. Oates Jr. High Sch., Houston, 1938-42, acting prin., 1942-44; asst. prin. Stephen F. Austin Sr. High Sch., Houston, 1944-49, prin., 1949-66; dir. secondary edn. Houston Ind. Sch. Dist., 1966-68, asst. supt., 1968-72. Mem. Tex. Tchrs. Assn. (past v.p.), Houston Council Edn. (past pres.), Houston Assn. Sch. Adminstrs. (past pres.), So. Assn. Coll. and Schs. (Tex. com.), Nat. (life), Tex. (life) congresses parents and tchrs., Nat. Assn. Drs. in U.S., S.A.R., San Houston State Coll. Ex-Students Assn. (past pres.), Nat. Assn. Secondary Sch. Prins., Phi Delta Kappa, Delta Kappa Pi. Democrat. Baptist. Mason (33deg., Shriner); mem. Order Eastern Star (past grand patron Tex.), Clubs: Knife and Fork (Houston), Southeastern Houston Kiwanis (past pres. Contbr. to profl. publs. Home: 8106 Beverly Hill Lane Houston TX 77042

GOFF, FREDERICK RICHMOND, cons. Library of Congress; b. Newport, R.I., Apr. 23, 1916; s. Francis Shubael and Amelia Richmond (Seabury) G.; A.B., Brown U., 1937, A.M., 1939, Litt.D., 1965 Asst. to editor Incunabula in Am. libraries, 1937-40, editor 3d census, 1964; asst. to curator, 1940-41, acting chief, 1941-45, chief rare book div. Library of Congress, 1945-72, hon. cons. in early printed books, 1972—; Feldman lectr. U. Tex., 1968; vis. com. Hunt Bot. Library, Pitts.; com. mgmt. Annmary Brown Meml., Providence; mem. adv. com. rare book library Washington Cathedral. Mem. Bibliog. Soc. Va., Am. Antiquarian Soc., A.L.A. (chmn. rare book sect. 1960), Bibliog. Soc. Am. (council, pres. 1968-70), Bibl. Soc. (London), Internat. Bibliophile Assn., Lit. Soc. Washington, Manuscript Soc., Phi Beta Kappa, Theta Delta Chi. Unitarian. Clubs: Grolier (N.Y.); 1925 F Street (Washington). Author: (monograph) The Dates in Certain German Incunabula; Catalog of recent additions to the Lessing J. Rosenwald Collection in the Library of Congress, 1947; Early Belgian Books in the Rosenwald Collection, 1948; Early Music Books in the Rare Book Div. of Library of Congress, 1948; Fifteenth Century Books in the Library of Congress, 1950; The Rare Books Division-A Guide to the Collections and Services, 1950, rev. 1965. Editor: Essays Honoring Lawrence C. Wroth, 1951; The Rosenwald Collection, a Catalogue of Manuscripts, Illustrated Books, Books from Celebrated Presses, and Maps, 1150-1950, 2d edit., 1974; The Hersholt Collection of Anderseniana, 1954; Early Printed Books from the Low Countries, 1958; The Primordia of Bishop White Kennett, 1959; 3rd Census of Incunabula in American Libraries, 1964, supplement, 1973; The Permanence of Johann Gutenberg, 1970. Contbr. to Library of Congress Quar. Jour.; articles and reviews to various periodicals. Home: 5034 Sherrier Pl NW Washington DC 20016 Office: Library of Congress Washington DC 20540

GOFF, GERALD KENNETH, educator; b. Apache, Okla., June 26, 1925; s. Orville Hix and Justin Ruth (Dudley) G.; B.A., Phillips U., 1950, M.Ed., 1953; Ed.D., Okla. State U., 1962; m. Esther Louise Thomas, May 5, 1951; children—Kathy Lynn, Kelly Don. Tchr., Verden (Okla.) High Sch., 1950-55; tchr., prin. Garber (Okla.) High Sch., 1955-56; prof. math. Southwestern State Coll., Weatherford, Okla., 1957-65; prof. math. Okla. State U., Stillwater, 1965—; Fulbright lectr. Uruguay, summer 1968; vis. prof. Universidad de Carabobo, Valencia, Venezuela, 1970. Bd. examiners basic scis. State of Okla., 1973—. Served with USNR, 1943-46. Decorated Orden de Andres Bello, Venezuela. Mem. Math. Assn. Am., Okla. Council Tchrs. Math., Okla. Edn. Assn. (chmn. local unit), N.E.A., Okla. Jr. Coll. Math. Assn. Author: (with Berg) Basic Mathematics, 1968. Home: 2803 N Lincoln St Stillwater OK 74074

GOFF, JAMES FRANKLIN, research physicist; b. Louisville, Ky., Aug. 1, 1928; s. James Robert and Mary Louise (Kubaugh) G.; B.S., Mass. Inst. Tech., 1950; M.S., Purdue U., 1953, Ph.D., 1962; m. Barbara Louise Kral, June 20, 1959; children—Sidra Denise, Alexander. Grad. research asst. Purdue U., 1955-61; research physicist materials U.S. Naval Ordnance Lab., Silver Spring, Md., 1961—. Served with AUS, 1953-55. Mem. Am. Phys. Soc., Sigma Xi. Club: Cosmos. Research field transport properties of semiconductors and transition metals. Home: 3405 34th Pl NW Washington DC 20016 Office: US Naval Ordnance Lab Silver Spring MD 20910

GOFF, KENNETH HAROLD, lawyer; b. Spring Lick, Ky., Nov. 1, 1926; s. Tom and Beulah (Carter) G.; A.B. in History, Western Ky. State U., 1949; LL.B., U. Ky., 1951; m. Florene Shain, Aug. 1, 1956; children—Kenneth Harold, Thomas H., Laura Jane, John H., Tracy Lynn. Admitted to Ky. bar, 1951, since practiced in Leitchfield; mem. firm Goff & Meredith; judge pro tem Grayson County, Ky., 1951-54, county atty., 1954-66; mem. Ky. Workmen's Compensation Bd., 1968-69; commonwealth's atty. 46th Jud. Dist. Ky., 1968—. Chmn. Caney Creek Watershed Conservancy Dist., 1956-63; sec.-treas. Grayson County Fair, 1956-68; vice chmn. Lincoln Trail Econ. Devel. Dist.; past chmn. Lincoln Trail Comprehensive Health Planning Commn. Del. Republican Nat. Conv., 1960, 64. Bd. dirs. Grayson Housing; past sec.-treas. Grayson County Hosp. Found. Mem. Leitchfield-Grayson County C. of C. (pres. 1968-72). Mason. Home: Route 3 Leitchfield KY 42754 Office: 62 Court Sq Leitchfield KY 42754

GOFF, WAYNE HULEN, educator; b. Imboden, Ark., May 1, 1922; s. Washington Esro and Ruth Etta (Abee) G.; B.S. in Physics and Math., U. S.W. La., 1955; M.A. in Pub. Adminstrn., U. Okla., 1967; Ph.D. in Mgmt., N. Tex. State U., 1972; m. Julia Elizabeth Sanford, Sept. 2, 1943; children—Sandra Janice, Larry Wayne, Ronald Keith, Susan Lynn, Elizabeth Ann, Rebecca Kay. Electronics specialist CAA, Lafayette, La., 1947-58; dep. dist. supr. FAA, 1958-59, dist. supr., 1959-63, chief tech. staff, Ft. Worth, 1963-65, chief engring. br., 1965-67, chief plans and programs br., 1967-68, chief facilities and equipment br., 1968-70, chief electronics engring. br., 1970-72; prof. mgmt. Ark. State U., 1972—. Instr. physics U. S.W. La., also Centenary Coll., 1958-59. Served with USNR, 1940-46. Mem. Am. Inst. for Decision Scis., Am. Soc. for Pub. Adminstrn., Soc. for Gen. Systems Research. Home: 1620 Dupwe Jonesboro AR 72401 Office: Ark State U Coll Bus State University AR 72467

GOFORTH, JAMES ALTON, civil engr.; b. Asheville, N.C., July 17, 1915; s. James Alton and Elizabeth (Savage) Goforth; student Berea Coll.; B.S., U. Ky., 1938; m. Charline Adams, Sept. 13, 1940; children—Betty (Mrs. James M. Horton), James Adams, John L. Project engr., FSA Western Ky., 1938-42; stress engr. Bristol Aircraft Div. (Va.), 1942-43; constrn. engr. Clinchfield R.R. Co., Erwin, Tenn., 1943-48, maintenance engr., 1951-68, chief engr., 1968-73; city engr., Johnson City, Tenn., 1973—; pvt. practice as consulting engr., Erwin, 1948-51; cons. city engr., Erwin, 1947-65. Bd. dirs. Tenn. Conservation League. Registered profl. engr. Mem. Nat., Tenn., socs. profl. engrs., Am. Ry. Engring. Assn., (chmn. engring. div. com. roadway and track), Assn. Am. Railroads (Tenn. chmn. grade crossing com.), Am. Ry. Bridge and Bldg. Assn. (pres. 1970). Presbyn. (deacon, elder). Clubs: Erwin Kiwanis (past pres.), Unicoi County Rod and Gun (Distinguished Service award 1962, past pres.). Home: 743 N Elm St Erwin TN 37650 Office: Municipal Bldg Johnson City TN 37601

GOFORTH, JOHN LAWRENCE, physician; b. 1897; M.D., Johns Hopkins, 1923. Practice medicine specializing in pathology, Dallas. Cons. pathology Dallas City Health Lab., Med. Arts Hosp., St. Paul Hosp. Mem. Am. Assn. Pathologists and Bacteriologists, A.M.A., A.C.P., Coll. Am. Pathologists, Am. Soc. Clin. Pathologists. Office: Med Arts Bldg 1717 Pacific Av Dallas TX 75201

GOGGINS, HORACE, dentist; b. Hodges, S.C., May 14, 1929; s. Ulysses and Mattie Lou (Butler) G.; B.S., S.C. State Coll., 1950; D.D.S., Howard U., 1954; m. Juanita Willmon, May 13, 1961; 1 son, Horace Willmon. Individual practice dentistry, Rock Hill, S.C., 1956—. Mem. Mayors' Citizens Adv. Com., So. Regional Council, 1965-71. Bd. dirs. Carolina Community Actions, 1965-67. Served to capt., Dental Corps, AUS, 1954-56. Mem. N.A.A.C.P. (sec. Rock Hill br. 1960-67), Am. Soc. Analgesia, Nat., Palmetto dental assns., Beta Kappa Chi, Alpha Phi Alpha. Democrat. Baptist. Home: Route 1 Box 465 Rock Hill SC 29730 Office: 425 S Trade St Rock Hill SC 29730

GOING, ROBERT ERNEST, dentist, educator; b. Parma, Mo., Apr. 15, 1928; s. Arthur Ernest and Grace (Smith) G.; A.B., Valparaiso U., 1948; B.S., U. Ill., 1951, D.D.S., 1953, M.S., 1959; m. Carol Ione; children—Robert E., Kimberly Kay, David Louis, Timothy Kendall, Karin Kirsten. Practice dentistry, Denver, 1959-64; asst. prof. operative dentistry Northwestern Dental Sch., Chgo., 1965-66; clin. investigator VA, San Francisco, 1966-69; prof., chmn. div. biomaterials U. Fla. Coll. Dentistry, Gainesville, 1969—. Cons. VA., Naval Grad. Dental Sch., Bethesda, Md., 1970—; lectr. Coach Gainesville Recreational Program, 1969-71. Active North Fla. council Boy Scouts Am., 1970-73. Served with USAF, 1953-56. Fellow Am. Coll. Dentists; mem. Am., Fla. dental assns., Central Dist. Dental Soc., Am. Assn. Dental Schs., Acad. Operative Dentistry, Internat. Assn. for Dental Research, Sigma Xi, Omicron Kappa Upsilon, Delta Sigma Delta. Author: Penetration of Dental Restorations, 1959. Contbr. articles on dentistry to profl. publs. Home: 1916 NW 27th Terrace Gainesville FL 32601

GOINS, TRUMAN, gen. engr.; b. Peason, La., Nov. 14, 1920; s. John Henry and Elizabeth (Pantalion) G.; B.S., La. State U., 1950; M.S., Ohio State U., 1954, postgrad., 1955-58; m. Mary Beatrice, Aug. 18, 1943; 1 son, Neal Rodney. Asst. prof. Ohio Agrl. Expt. Sta., Columbus, 1950-58; engr. adviser ICA, Tegucigalpa, Honduras, 1958-61; engr. adviser, regional dir. AID, Guayaquil, Ecuador, 1961-63, water resources engr., Vientiane, Laos, 1966-67, Washington, 1967-68; research engr. Agrl. Research Service, Norfolk, Va., 1963-66; civil engr. U.S. Dept. Housing and Urban Devel., Washington, 1968—. Rep. tech. and coordinating coms. Water Resources Council. Asst. scoutmaster Tidewater council Boy Scouts Am., 1964. Served with USCG, 1939-46; ETO. Decorated Bronze Star (3). Mem. Am. Soc. Agrl. Engrs. (past pres., sec.-treas. Ohio sect.), Nat. Soc. Profl. Engrs., Soil Sci. Soc. Am., Am. Soc. C.E., Res. Officers Assn. (pres. Washington dept. 1973-74), Phi Eta Sigma, Alpha Zeta, Tau Beta Pi, Phi Kappa Phi, Gamma Sigma Delta. Home: 11610 Hickory Dr Oxon Hill MD 20022 Office: Dept Housing and Urban Devel Washington DC 20410

GOIZUETA, ROBERTO CRISPULO, soft drink co. exec.; b. Havana, Cuba, Nov. 18, 1931; s. Crispulo Domingo and Aida (Cantera) G.; B.S., Yale, 1953; m. Olga T. Casteleiro, June 14, 1953; children—Roberto S., Olga M., Javier C. Chemist, Coca-Cola Co., Havana, 1954-56, tech. dir., 1956-60; asst. to v.p. Coca-Cola Export Co., Nassau, 1961-64; asst. to v.p. Coca-Cola Co., Atlanta, 1964-68, v.p., 1968-74, sr. v.p., corporate tech. dir., 1974—, also mem. corporate mgmt. com. Mem. Am. Inst. Chem. Engrs., Inst. Food Technologists, Soc. Soft Drinks Technologists, Am. Soc. Profl. Engrs. (Ann. award corp. engring. dept. 1971), Tau Beta Pi. Club: Capital City (Atlanta). Home: 4620 Jettridge Dr NW Atlanta GA 30327 Office: 310 North Av Atlanta GA 30301

GOKEE, DONALD LEROY, clergyman; b. Lansing, Mich., Aug. 8, 1933; s. Richard Alden and June (Colenso) G.; student Mich. State U., 1951-52; B.A., Temple Coll., Chattanooga, 1958; postgrad. (A. Morehouse and William Walker scholar, 1962) George Washington U., 1960-64, Washington Sch. Psychiatry, 1964, Va. Theol. Sem., 1965; m. Maxine Pawlik Adkins; children—Douglas Richard, Charles Jeffrey, Mary Beth. Ordained to ministry Presbyn. Ch., 1965; dir. edn. Presbyn. chs., Chattanooga, 1958-59, Alexandria, Va., 1959-65; asso. pastor Pine Shores Presbyn. Ch., Sarasota, Fla., 1966-69; pastor Conway Presbyn. Ch., Orlando, Fla., 1969—. Chaplain Juvenile Ct. System, Orlando, 1969-72; mem. council Synod Fla., 1972—. Mem. Citizens' Adv. Commn. Edn. Fla., 1968-69, Drug Abuse Council Orange County, 1969—. Mem. Ministerial Assn. (pres.). Home: 3026 Carmia Dr Orlando FL 32806 Office: 4300 Lake Margaret Dr Orlando FL 32806

GOLAND, MARTIN, research inst. exec.; b. N.Y.C., July 12, 1919; s. Herman and Josephine (Bloch) G.; M.E., Cornell U., 1940; LL.D., St. Mary's U., San Antonio; m. Charlotte Nelson, Oct. 16, 1948; children—Claudia, Lawrence Jon, Nelson Stuart. Instr. mech. engring. Cornell U., 1940-42; sect. head structures dept. Research Lab., Curtiss-Wright Corp., research lab. Airplane div., Buffalo, 1942-46; chmn. div. engring. Midwest Research Inst., Kansas City, Mo., 1946-50, dir. for engring. scis., 1950-55; v.p. S.W. Research Inst., San Antonio, 1955-57, dir., 1957-59, pres., 1959—; pres. Southwest Found. for Research and Edn., San Antonio, 1973—; prof. research (honoris causa) St. Mary's U., San Antonio. Mem. sci. adv. com. Harry Diamond Labs., 1955—; mem. Nat. Commn. on Libraries and Information Sci., 1971—; mem. missile adv. group Army Missile Command; mem. sci. adv. panel Dept. Army; chmn. U.S. Army Weapons Command Adv. Group; mem. materials adv. bd. NRC; mem. research and tech. adv. com. on aeronautics NASA, 1967-71; mem. sci. adv. com. Gen. Motors, 1971—; chmn. lab. adv. bd. on undersea warfare Dept. Navy, 1970—; mem. adv. bd. on mil. personnel supplies Nat. Acad. Scis., 1973—. Pres. San Antonio Symphony Soc., 1968-70, chmn. bd., 1971—. Bd. govs. St. Mary's U., San Antonio. Recipient Spirit of St. Louis Jr. award Am. Soc. M.E., 1945, Jr. award, 1946; Alfred E. Noble prize Am. Soc. M.E., 1947. Fellow A.A.A.S., Am. Inst. Aeros. and Astronautics (pres. 1971, dir. 1972—); mem. Nat. Acad. Engring. (council 1969—), Am. Soc. M.E. (hon.), Am. Ordnance Assn., Sigma Xi, Tau Beta Phi. Editor: Applied Mechanics Rev., 1952-59, editorial advisor, 1959—. Home: 211 Five Oaks Dr San Antonio TX 78209 Office: 8500 Culebra Rd San Antonio TX 78284

GOLD, ALLEN JAY, apparel co. exec.; b. Newark, Aug. 23, 1927; s. Bernard Leon and Shirley (Brodofsky) G.; student So. Meth. U., 1945-47. Partner, Nardis of Dallas, 1948-65; pres. Nardis of Dallas, Inc., 1965—, also dir. Bd. dirs. Dallas Civic Opera. Served with USCGR, 1945-46. Mason (32 deg., Shriner). Home: 5205 Royal Lane Dallas TX 75229 Office: 1300 Corinth St Dallas TX 75215

GOLD, BURTON MALCOLM, carpet co. exec.; b. N.Y.C., Apr. 7, 1929; s. William and Mildred (Heidenreich) G.; B.C.E., Cornell U., 1951; m. Lenore Joan Elis, Aug. 30, 1953; children—Joanne Meredith, Lauren Elizabeth, Janice Hilary, Pamela Alison. Pres., William Gold, Inc., N.Y.C., 1953-67, Stratton Industries, Inc., Atlanta, 1963—, Celestial Carpet Mills, Inc., Atlanta, 1966—; dir. William Gold, Inc., N.Y.C. Mem. auction com. Arts Festival Atlanta, 1970-72. Served to 1st. lt. Ordnance Corps, AUS, 1951-53. Mem. Cornell Soc. Engrs., The Temple, High Mus. Art, Mus. Modern Art, Cartersville C. of C., Carpet and Rug Inst., Chi Epsilon, Phi Sigma Delta, Zeta Beta Tau. Clubs: Cornell (N.Y.C.); Standard (Atlanta); Dalton (Ga.) Golf and Country; Cartersville (Ga.) Country. Home: 3550 Rembrandt Rd NW Atlanta GA 30327 Office: Cartersville GA 30120

GOLDBERG, ALFRED, historian, govt. ofcl.; b. Balt., Dec. 23, 1918; s. David and Jeanette (Goldstein) G.; A.B., Western Md. Coll., 1938; Ph.D., Johns Hopkins, 1950; m. Gertrud K. Kannova, June 28, 1949; children—Paul F., Alan D., Marian J. Sr. historian USAF, Washington, 1950-65; sr. staff mem. Rand Corp., Santa Monica, Cal., 1965-73; historian Office Sec. of Def., 1973—. Vis. fellow Kings Coll., U. London, Eng., 1962-63. Served from pvt. to capt. AUS, 1942-46. Decorated Bronze Star medal. Social Sci. Research Council grantee, 1962. Mem. Am. Hist. Assn., Am. Mil. Inst., Internat. Inst. Strategic Studies. Author: (with Craven and Cate) Army Air Force in World

War II, 7 vols., 1948-56. Editor: A History of U.S. Air Force, 1957. Home: 3842 N 26th St Arlington VA 22207 Office: Office of Secretary of Defense Washington DC 20301

GOLDBERG, DOROTHY K. (MRS. ARTHUR J. GOLDBERG), artist, author; b. St. Louis; B.A., U. Chgo.; student Art Inst. Chgo., various pvt. tchrs.; m. Arthur J. Goldberg; children—Robert, Barbara (Mrs. David A. Cramer). Exhibited in numerous one-man shows; vol. recruiter for programs to combat juvenile delinquency, Washington; active Counsellors Aides Program, Art Enrichment Programs, Widening Horizons Program, founder Friends of Juvenile Ct., 1964; responsible for numerous meetings U.S. Mission to UN Am. women's group clubs, including Congl. wives' tours; mem. Pres.'s Task Force Internat. Edn., Pres.'s Commn. Employment Handicapped; lectr. Bd. dirs. UN Assn., Nat. Sch. Vol. Program. Author: The Creative Woman, 1963. Contbr. articles to mags. Home: 2801 New Mexico Av Washington DC 20007

GOLDBERG, HERBERT SIDNEY, elec. engr.; b. Asheville, N.C., Oct. 30, 1925; s. Ezen C. and Mildred (Jacobs) G.; B.S. in Elec. Engring., N.C. State Coll. at Raleigh, 1950; m. Helen T. Lipman, Oct. 15, 1950; children—Alan D., Cheryl D., Susan R. With Charleston Nav. Shipyard (S.C.), 1950—, supr. electronics engr., 1964—. Vice pres. Charleston Estates Civic Club, 1967—. Served with USNR, 1943-46; PTO. Mem. I.E.E.E. (sr. mem.; past chmn.), Jewish War Vets. (past comdr.). Jewish religion (pres. temple brotherhood 1962-63). Mason. Home: 1308 Coleridge St Charleston SC 29407 Office: Code 193-1G Charleston Nav Shipyard Charleston SC 29408

GOLDBERG, IVAN BAER, corp. exec.; b. Newport News, Va., Apr. 20, 1939; s. David and Sara (Levy) G.; student U. Va., 1957-58, Coll. William and Mary, 1958-60; m. Linda Caffee, Oct. 27, 1969; 1 son, Stephen Morris. Exec. v.p., dir. Bedding Supply Co., Inc., Newport News, 1961—, Goldkress Corp., 1968—, Goldkress Investment Co., 1970—. Served with USCGR, 1962. Mem. Hampton Roads Jr. C. of C., Def. Supply Assn., Va. Mfrs. Assn. Jewish religion. Elk. Home: 120 Tipton Rd Newport News VA 23606 Office: 524-2628 25th St Newport News VA 23607

GOLDBERG, MOSES HAYM, educator, theatre dir.; b. New Orleans, May 25, 1940; s. Leon and Celia (Draisen) G.; student Univ. Coll., London, 1959-60; B.S., Tulane U., 1961; M.A., Stanford, 1963; M.A., U. Wash., 1965; Ph.D., U. Minn., 1969; m. Patricia Davis, Dec. 27, 1964; children—Ruth Deborah, Joel Ari. Instr. Southwest Tex. State Tchrs. Coll., 1967-69; dir. children's theatre Asolo State Theatre, Sarasota, Fla., 1969; asso. prof. theatre Fla. State U., 1969—; cons. editor young audience scripts; judge play contests. Fla. Arts Council grantee, 1970. Mem. Children's (gov.), Am. theatre assns., Internat. Assn. Theatre for Children and Youth (vice chmn. U.S. delegation), Alpha Epsilon Pi. Author: Children's Theatre: A Philosophy and a Method, 1974. Contbr. to New Plays for Children, 1972, articles to profl. jours. Home: Route 3 Box 76 Tallahassee FL 32303

GOLDBERG, STANLEY IRWIN, real estate exec.; b. Newport News, Va., May 13, 1934; s. David and Sara (Levy) G.; student Coll. William and Mary, 1952-54, U. Va., 1954-55; m. Marilyn Levin, Nov. 22, 1963 (dec. Oct. 1970); 1 son, Andrew Garfield; m. 2d, Carol Firestone, May 27, 1973. With Bedding Supply Co., Inc., Newport News, 1956-73, v.p., 1956-59, exec. v.p., 1960-61, pres. 1962-73; now real estate exec.; dir. Goldkress Corp. Served with USAF, 1957-58. Mem. Va. Mfrs. Assn., Def. Supply Assn. Jewish religion (trustee temple). Elk. Home: 19 Hopemont Dr Newport News VA 23606 Office: 1 Regency Sq Newport News VA 23601

GOLDEN, HARRY, editor, publisher, author; b. N.Y.C., May 6, 1903; s. Leib and Anna (Klein) Goldhirsch; student Coll. City N.Y., 1919-22; m. Genevieve Gallagher, Apr. 20, 1926; children—Richard, Harry, William, Peter. Editor, pub. Carolina Israelite, 1942—. Named Man of Year, Carver Coll., 1957, Johnson C. Smith Coll., 1958, Temple Emanu-El, N.Y.C., 1958. Mem Am. Jewish Congress (mem. bd.), N.A.A.C.P. (life), Shakespeare Soc. Am., Catholic Inter-racial Council. B'nai B'rith. Author: Only in America, 1958; For 2 cents Plain, 1959; Enjoy, Enjoy. 1951; Life of Carl Sandburg, 1961; Five Boyhoods, 1962; You're Entitle, 1962; Forgotten Pioneer, 1963; Mr. Kennedy and the Negroes, 1964; So What Else is New?, 1965; A Little Girl is Dead, 1966; Ess Ess Mein Kindt, 1967; The Best of Harry Golden, 1968; Autobiography of Harry Golden, 1969; The Israelis, 1970; So Long as You're Healthy, 1970; Golden Book of Jewish Humor, 1972; The Greatest Jewish City in the World, 1972. Home: 1701 E 8th St Charlotte NC 28204

GOLDFINGER, GEORGE, chemist, educator; b. Budapest, Hungary, Dec. 24, 1911; s. Oscar and Regina (Haiman) G.; student U. Berlin, U. Gottingen, U. Vienna, U. Liége; Docteur de l'Universite de Paris, 1937; m. Herta Sokal, Aug. 4, 1934. Came to U.S., 1940, naturalized, 1949. Research asso. Poly. Inst. Bklyn., 1941-43; research chemist G.L. Cabot, Inc., Boston, 1943-45; prof. U. Buffalo, 1945-56; sr. sci. adviser Armour Research Found., Chgo., 1956-57; sr. scientist Uniroyal Chem. Co., Naugatuck, Conn., 1957-67; prof. N.C. State U., Raleigh, 1967—. Fellow N.Y. Acad. Scis.; mem. Am. Chem. Soc., Intersociety Colour Council, Sigma Xi. Author: Clean Surfaces, 1970. Contbr. articles profl. jours.

GOLDGAR, ANSEL NATHAN, elec. engr.; b. Dallas, May 20, 1943; s. J. Morris and Sara (Goldblatt) G.; B.S. in Elec. Engring., U. Tex. at Arlington, 1967; M.S. in Elec. Engring., So. Methodist U., 1974; m. Sharon Ann Barton, Aug. 7, 1965; children—Gary Morris, David Samuel. Jr. electronics engr. Continental Electronics Mfg. Co., Dallas, 1967-69; sr. electronic systems engr. E-Systems Inc., Garland, Tex., 1969—. Jewish religion. Clubs: Rex Breeders United; North Texas Cat, Lone Star Cat (Dallas). Office: PO Box 6118 Dallas TX 75222

GOLDMAN, MARVIN ISRAEL, drug co. exec.; b. Cleve., Sept. 11, 1924; s. Samuel Harry and Dena Zachariah (Sands) G.; student U. Miami, 1940-44; m. Carol Milberg, June 25, 1950; children—Howard, Marjorie, Andrea. Pres. Gulf Drug Co., Hialeah, Fla., 1949—. Chmn. drug div. Combined Jewish Appeal Miami, 1965-71; chmn. gen. med. div. United Fund Dade County, 1971—. Bd. dirs. Greater Miami Jewish Fedn. Served with AUS, 1942-46. Home: 4207 University Dr Coral Gables FL 33146 Office: 425 E 10th Ct Hialeah FL 33011

GOLDMAN, MAX, lawyer; b. N.Y.C., Dec. 19, 1916; s. Samuel and Pauline (Ackerhalt) G.; B.S. cum laude, Coll. City N.Y., 1936; J.D., Columbia, 1940; m. Victoria Scardino, May 29, 1954; children—Ann Shirley, Jeanne Louise. Admitted to N.Y. bar, 1940, P.R. bar, 1956, U.S. Supreme Ct. bar, 1945; law clk. Judge Learned Hand, Chief Judge U.S. Ct. of Appeals, 1944-45; asst. gen. counsel FCC, Washington, 1949-52; dir. Office of Indsl. Tax Exemption of P.R., 1952-59; pvt. practice law, Santurce, P.R., 1959—; partner firm Goldman, Antonetti, Barreto, Curbelo & Davila, San Juan, P.R., 1965—; prof. law ad honorem U. P.R. Law Sch., 1964-65. Mem. Civil Rights Commn., Commonwealth of P.R., 1965-69; v.p. Amigos de Calle de Cristo, 1964—. Mem. Am., Fed., P.R. bar assns. Contbr. articles and book revs. to legal jours. Home: 2001 Flamboyan (Monteflores) Santurce PR 00915 Office: PO Box 13486 Santurce PR 00908

GOLDSMITH, ADOLPH OLIVER, educator, journalist; b. Kennett, Mo., Dec. 20, 1908; s. James Nathaniel and Susan Jane (Elliott) G.; B.A. in Journalism, La. State U., 1949, M.A., 1951; Ph.D. in Mass Communications, U. Ia., 1967; m. Josephine Bristol, Dec. 10, 1941; children—James R., Nathan Kent, Sarah Sue (Mrs. Ray R. Thorpe, Jr.). Printer, reporter, editorial writer Dunklin Democrat, Kennett, 1926-36; columnist, feature writer Ark. Democrat, Little Rock, 1936-42; editor Want Ad Builder, Baton Rouge, 1951-53; mgr. prodn., promotion Univ. Press, La. State U., Baton Rouge, 1950-55, instr., 1953-55, asst. prof., 1955-58, asso. prof., 1958-67, prof. journalism, 1967—, also dir. Sch. Journalism. Vice-chmn. La. Commn. Govtl. Ethics, Baton Rouge, 1969-73. Served with AUS, 1942-45. Mem. Assn. Edn. in Journalism, Assn. Am. Schs. and Depts. Journalism, S.W. Journalism Congress (pres. 1960-61), Nat. Press Photography Assn., La. News Photography Assn. (pres. 1968-69), Phi Kappa Phi, Kappa Tau Alpha, Sigma Delta Chi. Democrat. Presbyn. Author: Dust That is a Little Gilt (poems), 1954. Home: 2213 Ovid St Baton Rouge LA 70808

GOLDSMITH, MORTIMER, retail co. exec.; b. N.Y.C., Nov. 28, 1902; s. Marcus and Fannie (Marx) G.; student N.Y. U. Sch. Retailing, 1926-28; m. Jane Straus, June 30, 1930; children—Marc Bernard, Susan G. (Mrs. Cary Dennen). With Levy Bros., Inc., Louisville, 1943—, now sec.-treas., controller; lectr. retailing U. Louisville Sch. Bus. Adminstrn. Chmn. Jefferson County Citizens Adv. Com., 1962-66, State Adv. Com. on Met. Govt., 1959, Speakers Bur., Constn. Revision Com., 1966, Morton-Wyatt Commn., 1970. Mayor, Brownsboro Village, 1956-60, trustee, 1961-65; mem. Jefferson County Republican Exec. Com., 1964-72. Bd. dirs. Louisville Hebrew Home, Jewish Community Center, Jewish Vocational Service, Conf. Jewish Orgns.; bd. dirs., past pres. Bur. Jewish Edn.; bd. dirs., vice chmn. exec. and finance coms. Sts. Mary and Elizabeth Hosp.; past chmn. exec. com. Jefferson County Govt. Conf. Hon. master Belle of Louisville, hon. citizen City of Louisville. Mem. Nat. Retail Mchts. Assn. (dir., past chmn. conv. com.), Menswear Retailers Am. (dir.), Bluegrass Retail Controllers Assn. (past chmn.), Am. Mgmt. Assn., Am. Inst. Mgmt., Soc. for Information Systems Mgmt., Adminstrv. Mgmt. Soc. (past pres.), Louisville Area C. of C. (com. chmn.), Hon. Order Ky. Cols. Jewish religion (trustee, past pres. congregation). Home: 303 Sprite Rd Brownsboro Village KY 40207 Office: Market at 3d St Louisville KY 40202

GOLDSMITH, ROBERT HILLIS, educator; b. East Lansing, Mich., Sept. 3, 1911; s. Robert and Edith (Darrow) G.; B.A., Pa. State U., 1936; M.A., Columbia, 1943, Ph.D., 1952; m. Mary Alice Glass, June 1, 1942; children—Alice Darrow, Robert Glass. Instr. dept. English, Temple U., Phila., 1946-52, U. Md., College Park, 1952-55; asso. prof. Emory (Va.) and Henry Coll., 1955-60, prof., 1960—, chmn. dept., 1971—, Henry Carter Stuart prof. English, 1974—. Reader Folger Library, Washington, 1959; intern S.E. Renaissance Inst., U. N.C. at Chapel Hill, 1965, humanities fellow, 1966-67. Served with USAAF, 1942-46. Recipient 1st prize playwriting Cal. Western U., San Diego, 1963. Mem. Am. Assn. U. Profs. (pres. chpt. 1964-65), Modern Lang. Assn., Shakespeare Assn. Am., Southeastern Renaissance Conf. (pres.), Phi Kappa Phi. Author: Wise Fools in Shakespeare, 1955; Survey of English Literature, vol. I, 1974. Contbr. articles to profl. jours. Home: PO Box 55 Emory VA 24327

GOLDSTEIN, HERMAN BERNARD, chem. co. exec.; b. Providence, June 19, 1917; s. Morris and Minnie (Hirsch) G.; A.B., Brown U., 1940; m. Myrtle B. Abedon, June 7, 1942; children—Lawrence B., Caila B. Chief chemist Providence Textile Chem. Co., 1940-44; research dir. Warwick Chem. Co., Wood River Junction, R.I., 1944-47; gen. mgr. chem. div. Sun Chem. Corp., Chester, S.C., 1968-72, v.p. planning, 1973—. Cons. So. Regional Lab., U.S. Dept. Agr., 1964-68. Fellow Am. Inst. Chemists; mem. Am. Chem. Soc., Am. Assn. Textile Chemists and Colorists (Olney medal 1973), T.A.P.P.I., Internat. Textile Club, Phi Beta Kappa, Sigma Xi. Contbr. articles to profl. jours. Patentee in field. Home: 138 Park Dr Chester SC 29706 Office: Sun Chem Corp 72 By-Pass Chester SC 29706

GOLDSTEIN, IRVING SOLOMON, educator; b. Bronx, N.Y., Aug. 20, 1921; s. Jacob and Jennie (Rathsprecher) G.; B.S., Rensselaer Poly. Inst., 1941; M.S., Ill. Inst. Tech., 1944; Ph.D., Harvard, 1948; m. Helen Haft, Dec. 16, 1945; children—Ardath Ann, Darra Jane, Jared Haft. Research chemist N.Am. Rayon Corp., 1948-51; sr. research chemist, mgr. wood chemistry research Koppers Co., Inc., Pitts., 1951-63; sr. research scientist Nalco Chem. Co., Chgo., 1963-66; mgr. paper research Continental Can Co., Chgo., 1966-68; prof. forest sci. Tex. A. and M. U., 1968-71; prof. wood and paper sci., head dept. N.C. State U., Raleigh, 1971—. Served to lt. USNR, 1942-46. Teaching fellow Harvard, 1946-48. Mem. Am. Chem. Soc., A.A.A.S., Forest Products Research Soc., T.A.P.P.I., Soc. Wood Sci. and Tech., Sigma Xi, Zeta Beta Tau, Phi Lambda Upsilon, Xi Sigma Pi. Jewish religion (trustee temple). Contbr. articles to profl. jours. Patentee in field. Home: 209 Glasgow Rd Cary NC 27511 Office: Biltmore Hall NC State U Raleigh NC 27607

GOLDSTEIN, LIONEL, mfg. co. exec.; b. Bklyn., Oct. 19, 1932; s. Alexander and Ruth (Spitzer) G.; student Tex. A. and M. U., 1950-52, So. Meth. U., 1960-65; children—Alex, Sharon; m. Judy Ruth Calk, May 19, 1973. Accountant, Arrow Industries, Inc., Carrollton, Tex., 1965, office mgr., 1966-68, controller, 1968-69, v.p., 1969—, also dir.; dir. Ark. Charcoal Co., Forest Products Charcoal Co., Campfire Charcoal Co., Polyprint, Inc. Bd. dirs. Keller Springs-Two Worlds; trustee Rosenberg Brothers Found. Served with C.E., AUS, 1952-54. Mem. Nat. Assn. Accountants, Data Processing Mgmt. Assn., Financial Mgmt. Assn., Am. Soc. Ins. Mgrs., N.W. C. of C. Jewish religion. Club: Brookhaven Country. Home: 2645 Via Catalina Carrollton TX 75006 Office: 2625 Belt Line Rd Carrollton TX 75006

GOLOD, WILLIAM HERSH, coll. dean; b. N.Y.C., June 28, 1933; s. David and Sarah M. (Millner) G.; B.S., Fordham U., 1954; M.S., St. Louis Coll. Pharmacy, 1955; Ph.D., Purdue U., 1958; m. Marsha Berebitsky, June 24, 1961; children—Lisa Helene, Jill Diane, David Andrew. Asst. prof. Med. U. S.C., Charleston, 1958-63, asso. prof., 1963-67, prof., 1967—, dean Coll. Pharmacy, 1965—. Chmn., Charleston County Drug Abuse Control Commn., 1972-73. Bd. dirs. Health Sci. Found. Med. U. S.C.; mem. S.C. Pharm. Found. Mem. Am. Pharm. Assn., Am. Soc. Hosp. Pharmacists, Sigma Xi, Rho Chi. Home: 14 Nuffield Rd Charleston SC 29407 Office: Sch Pharmacy Med U SC 80 Barre St Charleston SC 29401

GOMES, NORMAN VINCENT, indsl. engr.; b. New Bedford, Mass., Nov. 7, 1914; s. John Vincent and Georgianna (Sylvia) G.; B.S. in Indsl. Engring. and Mgmt., Okla. State U., 1950; M.B.A. in Mgmt., Xavier U., 1955; m. Carolyn Moore, June 6, 1942. Asst. chief engr. Leschen div. H.K. Porter Co., St. Louis, 1950-52; staff mfg. cons. Gen. Electric Co., Cin., 1952-57; lectr. indsl. mgmt. U. Cin., 1955-56; vis. lectr. indsl. mgmt. Xavier U. Sch. Bus. Adminstrn., 1956-57; staff indsl. engr. Gen. Dynamics, Ft. Worth, 1957-60; chief operations analysis Ryan Electronics, San Diego, 1960-64; sr. engr., Jet Propulsion Lab. Cal. Inst. Tech., Pasadena, Cal., 1964-67, mgr. mgmt. systems, 1967-71; indsl. rep. Commn. Govt. Procurement, 1970-71, cons., 1971—. Served as 2d lt. to maj., C.E., AUS, 1941-46; engring. adviser to War Manpower Bd., 1945. Registered profl. engr., Mo., Tex., Cal. Mem. Am. Inst. Indsl. Engrs. (nat. chmn. prodn. control research com., 1951-57; nat. dir. community services 1969-73; bd. dirs. Cin., Fort Worth, San Diego, Los Angeles chpts. 1954-71, v.p. Los Angeles chpt. 1970, pres. 1970-71; nat. pres. award 1969), Nat. Soc. Profl. Engrs., Soc. Am. Mil. Engrs., Nat. Mgmt. Assn., Ret. Officers Assn. U.S. (chpt. pres. 1968, nat. certificate of merit 1968), Mil. order world wars, Nat. Security Indsl. Assn. (mgmt. systems subcom. 1967-69). Republican. Roman Catholic. K.C. Home: Buchanan House 2301 S Jefferson Davis Hwy Arlington VA 22202 Office: Suite 927 1717 H St NW Washington DC 20006

GÓMEZ, JOSUÉ, auditor; b. Crystal City, Tex., Sept. 4, 1940; s. Gregorio Castillo and Evangelina (Reyes) G.; B.B.A., Tex. Western Coll., 1962; M.B.A., U. Houston, 1969; m. Mary Yolanda Bolaños, June 11, 1966. Financial accountant Bemis Co., Inc., Mpls., 1967-69; asst. to controller Internat. Systems & Control Corp., Houston, 1969-73; dir. internat. auditing Anderson, Clayton & Co., food processors, Houston, 1973—; mng. partner Mexipan Co., Houston, 1973—. Mem. lay adv. council Perkins Sch. Theology, So. Meth. U., Dallas, 1972—. Served to 1st lt. AUS, 1962-65. Decorated D.F.C., Air medal with 13 oak leaf clusters, Purple Heart, Army Commendation medal. C.P.A., Tex. Mem. Am. Inst. C.P.A.'s, Tex. Soc. C.P.A.'s. Methodist (sec. council on finance and adminstrn. Rio Grande conf. 1972—).

GONCE, ROBERT EUGENE, orthodontist; b. Haileyville, Okla., Nov. 20, 1927; s. Thompson A. and Abbie R. (Reed) G.; student Okla. U., 1944-46; B.S., Central State U., 1950; D.D.S., U. Mo., 1954, M.S., 1964; m. Geraldine Ethel Lund, Aug. 7, 1954; children—Debra, Robert, Mark, Mike. Pvt. practice dentistry, Oklahoma City, 1954-64, pvt. practice orthodontics, Oklahoma City, 1964—. Asst. prof. surgery Okla. Sch. Medicine, 1965—. Served with AUS, 1946-48. Mem. Am. Orthodontic Soc., Am. Dental Assn., Okla. State, Okla. County dental socs., Southwestern, Okla. State socs. orthodontists, Okla. County Orthodontic Soc. (pres. 1968-70), Oklahoma City C. of C. Democrat. Baptist. Club: Quail Creek Golf and Country (Oklahoma City). Home: 12909 Cedar Springs Rd Oklahoma City OK 72120 Office: 3333 NW 63d St Oklahoma City OK 73116

GONG, EDMOND JOSEPH, lawyer, former state senator; b. Miami, Fla., Oct. 7, 1930; s. Joe Fred and Fayline G.; A.B. cum laude, Harvard, 1952, student Sch. Law, 1954-55; J.D., U. Miami, 1960; m. Sophie Vlachos, July 25, 1957; children—Frances Fayline, Peter Joseph, Madeleine, Joseph Fred II, Edmond Joseph. Spl. writer Hong Kong Tiger Standard, 1955-56; staff writer Miami Herald, 1958-59; admitted to Fla. bar; asso. firm Helliwell, Melrose & De Wolf, 1960-61; practice law, Miami, 1962—; mem. Fla. Senate, 1966-72. Trustee Fla. Gulf Realty Trust; pres. Inflahedge Resources Fund; chmn. Fla. Land Sales Adv. Council. Asst. U.S. Atty. So. Dist. Fla., 1961-62; mem. Fla. Ho. of Reps., 1963-66. Fellow Inst. Politics John Fitzgerald Kennedy Sch. Govt., Harvard, 1969-70, asso. dir., 1971-72. Mem. Am., Dade County, Fed. bar assns., Assn. Harvard Alumni (dir.-at-large). Methodist. Home: 7751 S W 78th Ct Miami FL 33143 Office: 8585 Sunset Dr Miami FL 33143

GONSOULIN, DEWEY JUDE, lawyer; b. Houston, Dec. 27, 1929; s. Robert Frederic and Elma (Bourgeois) G.; B.A. with distinction, Rice Inst., 1951; LL.B. with honors, U. Tex., 1954; m. Jean E. Johnson, Apr. 25, 1959; children—Jean E., Anne C., Dewey J. Admitted to Tex. bar, 1954; asso. firm Mehaffy, Weber, Keith & Gonsoulin, Beaumont, 1956-62, partner, 1962-72, shareholder employee 1972—. Mem. Beaumont Civil Service Commn., 1971—; dir. Beaumont council Camp Fire Girls, Inc., 1964-70. Served with AUS, 1954-56. Mem. Jefferson County (pres. 1973—), Am., Tex. bar assns., Tex. Assn. Def. Counsel (dir. 1971-73), Phi Beta Kappa, Delta Tau Delta, Phi Delta Phi. Roman Catholic. Club: Knife and Fork Club of Beaumont (pres. 1964-65). Asso. casenote editor Tex. Law Review, 1953-54. Home: 8185 Evangeline Lane Beaumont TX 77706 Office: 1400 San Jacinto Bldg Beaumont TX 77701

GONZALES, BROTHER ALEXIS (JOSEPH M. GONZALES), educator, drama dir.; b. Santa Fe, Oct. 1, 1931; B.A., Coll. Santa Fe, 1957; M.Ed., U. S.W. La., 1960. Mem. teaching order Christian Bros., 1949—; acad. dean Catholic Coll., Negros Occidental, Philippines, 1960-66; tchr. English and religion, drama coach, film producer Antonian High Sch., San Antonio, 1967-70, also organizer amateur theater group; Univ. prof. theatre and communications Loyola U., New Orleans, 1970—. Organizer internat. film festival HemisFair, San Antonio, 1967; dir. summer Creative Arts Festival, San Antonio; organizer Center Social Communications, seminars on media, San Antonio, 1968; mem. planning council Coll.-Community Creative Arts Center, Model Cities, San Antonio, 1969—; bd. consultors Mexican-Am. Social Communications Inst., San Antonio, 1971-72; dir. premier The Serpent, Mexico City; vis. prof. theatre dept. U. Mexico, 1971-72; vis. lectr. Latin Am. Center, Institute Latinoamericano de Investigaciones Pedagogicas y Antropologicas, Mexico, City, 1971-72. Rockefeller Found. grantee cultural center P.I. Mem. ANTA, Am. Ednl. Theatre Assn., Nat. Cultural Theatre Conf., N.E.A., Tex. Audio Visual Assn., Internat. Fine Arts Council S.W., Jesuit Inst. for Arts. Produced, exhibited films An Investigation of All the Lonely People; The Black and White Checkerboard Society, others. Address: Loyola U New Orleans LA 70118

GONZALES, ELWOOD JOHN, JR., chemist; b. New Orleans, Oct. 19, 1927; s. Elwood John and Sarah (Vicari) G.; B.S., Loyola U., New Orleans, 1953; M.S. (Research Corp. fellow), Tulane U., 1955, Ph.D. (Am. Cyanamid fellow), 1958; m. Rose Marie Hargis, Feb. 9, 1963; children—Lisa Marie, Elwood John III, Guy Joseph, Eric Henry. Research chemist Dept. Agr., New Orleans, 1957—. Mem. Terrytown Civic Assn., Gretna, La. Fellow Am. Inst. Chemists (sec.-treas. 1973—), Research Soc. Am., A.A.A.S.; mem. Am. Chem. Soc. (Outstanding Student award La. chpt. 1953), Am. Assn. Textile Chemists and Colorists, La. Hist. Soc., Sigma Xi, Alpha Chi Sigma. Club: Christ the King Dad's. Contbr. articles to profl. jours. Patentee in field. Home: 2137 Graham Dr Gretna LA 70053 Office: 1100 Robert E Lee Blvd New Orleans LA 70179

GONZALEZ, CELSO MIGUEL, lawyer; b. Havana, Cuba, Dec. 1, 1935; s. Celso G. and Isabel E. (Falla) Gonzalez-Hierro; Doctor en Derecho Civil, Universidad Catolica de Santo Tomas de Villanueva, 1958; m. Marylis Rodriguez, Oct. 11, 1959 (dec. Aug. 1964); children—Celso M., Jose I., Marylis, Christine, Julie, Susana, Barbara; m. 2d, Michelle Clemons Perry, June 23, 1968. Came to U.S., 1961, naturalized, 1966. Vice pres. Cia Ganadera El Palmar S.A., Cuba, 1958-61; landman Coastal States Gas Producing Co., 1961-66; admitted to Tex. bar, 1967; v.p., gen. counsel Cattle Land Oil Co., Corpus Christi, Tex., 1966-69; partner Porter, Taylor, Gonzalez, Thompson & Rogers, Corpus Christi, 1969—. Dir. Bank of Commerce, Guaranty Nat. Bank & Trust Co., Corpus Christi. Trustee Corpus Christi Osteo. Hosp. Mem. Am., Tex. (chmn. Tex. corporate system) bar assns. Clubs: Corpus Christi Country, Corpus Christi Yacht, Bay Yacht. Home: 249 Cape Henry Corpus Christi TX 78412 Office: Guaranty Bank Plaza Corpus Christi TX 78401

GONZALEZ, HENRY B., congressman; b. San Antonio, May 3, 1916; s. Leonides and Genevieve (Barbosa) G.; student San Antonio Jr. Coll.; B.A., U. Tex.; grad. St. Mary's Law Sch., St. Mary's U., San Antonio; m. Bertha Cuellar, 1940; children—Henry Thomas, Rosemary, Charles A., Bertha, Stephen, Genevieve, Francis, Anna Maria. Tchr. citizenship adult vocational class Ladies Garment Workers Union; slum clearance projects San Antonio Housing Authority; translator; pub. relations counselor for ins. co., San Antonio; chief probation officer Bexar County, Tex., 1946; exec. sec. Jr. Deputies of Am. (predecessor Pan Am. Progressive Assn.); councilman, San Antonio 1953-56, mayor pro-tem, 1955-56; mem. Tex. Senate, 1956-61; mem. 87th to 93d Congresses from 20th Tex. Dist.; chmn. subcom. on internat. finance Banking and Currency Com., 1972—. Past civilian cable and radio censor Mil. and Naval Intelligence, World War II. Home: 238 W King's Hwy San Antonio TX 78212 Office: Rayburn House Office Bldg Washington DC 20515

GONZALEZ, JOSE, assn. exec.; b. Lagos, Jalisco, Mexico, Sept. 15, 1917; s. Jose Madrigal and Maria Asuncion (Mora) G.; B.S., U. Mexico, 1934, M.D., 1943; M.H.A., Northwestern U., 1946; m. Helen Miller, Oct. 18, 1947; children—Jean G. (Mrs. Charles Veneable), Joseph Miller. Came to U.S., 1948, naturalized, 1950. Intern, Univ. Hosp., Mexico City, 1944; rotating intern Charity Hosp. of La., New Orleans, 1945, resident urology, 1945; adminstrv. resident hosp. adminstrn. St. Luke's Hosp., Chgo., 1947; dir. Hosp. Fajer de Mexico, 1948; field staff surveyor Hosp. Standardization Program, A.C.S., Chgo., 1949-52; field staff surveyor Joint Commn. on Accreditation Hosps., Am. Hosp. Assn., 1953-54, dir. Latin Am. Program under contract with U.S. ICA, Washington, 1954-58, dir. Latin Am. Program under grant W.K. Kellogg Found., 1958-59, dir. Internat. Hosp. Program under contract with U.S. AID, 1959—. Recipient Order of Merit Bernardo O'Higgins in rank of officer Chilean Govt., 1968. Fellow Am. Pub. Health Assn.; mem. World Med. Assn., Am. Acad. Polit. and Social Sci., Nat. Council Internat. Health, Internat. Hosp. Fedn. (sec.), Inter-Am. Hosp. Assn. (exec. sec.); hon. mem. Brazilian, Paraguayan, Costa Rican hosp. assns., Pan Am. Med. Assn. (pres. sect. hosp. adminstrn. 1960-62), Panamanian Pub. Health Assn., Brazilian Coll. Hosp. Adminstrs. Contbr. articles profl. jours. Home: 2021 Cascade Rd Silver Spring MD 20902 Office: 1 Farragut Sq Washington DC 20006

GONZALEZ, JOSE LOZANO, pub. health engr.; b. Laredo, Tex., June 16, 1924; s. Jose G. and Concepcion (Lozano) G.; B.S. in Civil engring., Notre Dame U., 1950; M.P.H., Johns Hopkins, 1964; m. Maria Margarita Verduzco, Nov. 18, 1961; children—Alejandra, Gabriela. Asso. resident engr. Tex. Hwy. Dept., Laredo and San Benito, 1950-56; pub. health engr. adminstr. Laredo-Webb County Health Dept., 1956—. Civil def. dir. City of Laredo, 1961—; cons. engr. WHO, 1961—; mem. Gov.'s Adv. Manpower Council, also Tex. Adv. Council for Constrn. Mental Health Centers; mem. Tex. Health Adv. Com. Campaign chmn. A.R.C., 1959, chmn. Laredo Internat. Bridge Ceremony, 1960—; past vice chmn., sec. health com. Internat. Good Neighbor Council. Bd. dirs., campaign chmn. Laredo United Fund, Washington's Birthday Assn. Served with USAAF, 1942-46; lt. (j.g.) USNR. Registered profl. engr., Tex. Mem. Tex. Soc. Profl. Engrs., U.S.-Mexico Border (v.p.), Am., Tex. pub. health assns. Roman Catholic. Rotarian. Contbr. articles to nat. mags. Home: 2105 Guatemozin St Laredo TX 78040 Office: 2600 Cedar Av Laredo TX 78040

GOOCH, JOHN PHILLIP, chem. engr.; b. N.Y.C., June 6, 1941; s. Durward Belmont and Ruth (Alexander) G.; B.S., Auburn U., 1963, M.S., 1964; Ph.D., U. Ala., 1971. Asso. chem. engr. So. Research Inst., Birmingham, Ala., 1964-68, research chem. engr., 1970-73, head chem. engring. sect., 1973—; reserach asst. U.S. Bur. Mines, Tuscaloosa, Ala., 1968-70. Registered profl. engr., Ala. Mem. Am. Inst. Chem. Engrs. (asso.), Phi Kappa Phi, Tau Beta Pi, Phi Lambda Upsilon. Sigma Pi Sigma, Omega Chi Epsilon. Home: 3560 Stonehenge Pl Birmingham AL 35210 Office: Southern Research Inst 2000 9th Av S Birmingham AL 35205

GOOD, ANNE LEEPER (MRS. JOHN CARTER GOOD), civic worker; b. Jackson, Tenn., Nov. 10, 1923; d. Robert Allen and Ola (Crittenden) Leeper; A.B., B.S. cum laude, Lambuth Coll., 1944; m. John Carter Good, Oct. 28, 1945; children—John Robert, Carter Crittenden, William Allen. Co-chmn. Introduction to Washington com. THIS, the Hospitality and Information Service, 1968-71, treas., 1971—; membership chmn. Spanish Portuguese Study Group, 1968-69, v.p., 1969-70, pres., 1970-71; mem. women's bd. House of Mercy, 1970—, treas., 1972—. Bd. dirs D.C. br. Nat. Capitol Area YWCA, 1970—, mem. area planning and priorities com., 1971-73, bd. dirs., 1973—, also mem. Hannah Harrison Sch. Com.; bd. dirs. Rosemount Infant Day Care Center, 1972—, Met. Washington chpt. Achievement Rewards for Coll. Scientists, 1971-72. Mem. Nat. Council of Women, Alliance Francaise, Club d'Amitie Franco-Internationale. Clubs: St. Albans School Mothers (pres. Washington 1964-65), Air Force Officers Wives (mem. bd. Washington 1959-61). Home: 3712 Fordham Rd NW Washington DC 20016

GOOD, EDGAR CLIFTON, JR., pub. relations exec.; b. Washington, May 11, 1939; s. Edgar and Alma Mae (Dunn) G.; A.B., George Washington U., 1961; postgrad. Boston U., 1962; m. Patricia Jeanette Sullivan, Dec. 26, 1961; children—John Clifton, Wendy Marie. Editorial asst. Dow Jones Pub. Co., Washington, 1957-59; dir. news bur. George Washington U., Washington, 1965-67; editor Red Cross Youth Publs., Am. Nat. Red Cross, Washington, 1967-71, dep. dir. Office Pub. Relations, 1971—. Served to capt. USAF, 1961-65. Recipient awards Am. Coll. Pub. Relations Assn., Ednl. Press Assn. Am. Mem. Pub. Relations Soc. Am., Edn. Writers Assn. Republican. Episcopalian. Club: Evergreen Hunt (Mt. Falls, Va.). Home: 900-A Mt Vernon Av Alexandria VA 22301 Office: 18th and D Sts NW Washington DC 20006

GOOD, GEORGE MERLIN, JR., chem. co. purchasing exec.; b. Welford Wharf, Va., Oct. 25, 1918; s. George Merlin and Lucy (Elliott) G.; B.S., Heidelberg Coll., 1940; student U. Cal. at Berkeley, 1940-42; m. Ida Ellen Sherck, May 28, 1941; children—David Stanley, Kay (Mrs. Gerald Kuehner), Carol (Mrs. Patrick Patterson), Susan. Chemist Shell Devel. Co., Emeryville, Cal., 1942-52, research supr., 1952-55, with Koninklijke-Shell Lab., Amsterdam, 1952-53, tech. asst. to pres., N.Y.C., 1955-57, research supr., Emeryville, Cal., 1957-60, sr. engr. Shell Oil Co., San Francisco, 1960-61, spl. engr., N.Y.C., 1961-65, mgr. prod. application dept. Shell Chem. Co., N.Y.C., 1965-69, staff buyer purchasing Shell Oil Co., N.Y.C. also Houston, 1969-73, sr. staff buyer, Houston, 1973—. Mem. Am. Chem. Soc. Clubs: Pine Forest Country, Summit. Patentee U.S., Fgn. patents chem. industry. Contbr. articles to tech. jours. Home: 4906 Clift Haven Houston TX 77018 Office: 1 Shell Plaza Houston TX 77001

GOOD, IRVING JOHN, educator; b. London, Eng., Dec. 9, 1916; s. Morris Edward and Sophia (Polikoff) G.; M.A., Cambridge U., 1943, Ph.D., 1941, Sc.D., 1963; D.Sc., Oxford U., 1964. Came to U.S., 1967. With Brit. Fgn. Office, 1941-45; lectr. math., electronic computing Manchester U. (Eng.), 1945-48; statistician Govt. Communication Hdqrs., Cheltenham, Eng., 1948-59; spl. merit dep. chief sci. officer Admiralty Research Lab., Teddington, Eng., 1959-62; communications research div. Inst. Def. Analysis, Princeton, N.J., 1962-64; sr. research fellow Sci. Research Council Atlas Computer Lab., Trinity Coll., Oxford, 1964-67; prof. statistics Va. Poly. Inst. and State U., 1967—, univ. prof., 1969—, mem. adv. bd. Center for Study of Pub. Choice, 1970—. Fellow Inst. Math. Statistics, Am. Statis. Assn.; mem. Internat. Statis. Inst., Crypto-Math. Inst., London Math. Soc., Cambridge Philos. Soc., Mind Assn., Royal Statis. Soc., Brit. Soc. Philosophy of Sci., Brit. Assn., Math. Assn. Am., Gen. Systems Soc., Classification Soc., Am. Statis. Assn., A.A.A.S., Am. Math. Soc., Computer Arts Soc., Biometric Soc., Brain Research Assn., Pi Mu Epsilon. Author: Probability and the Weighing of Evidence, 1950; The Estimation of Probabilities, 1965. Gen. editor The Scientist Speculates, 1962; mem. editorial bd. Internat. Jour. Theoretical Physics, 1968—, Research Jour. Philosophy and Social Scis., 1963—, Jour. Statis. Computation and Simulation, 1970—. Home: 707 Terrace View Blacksburg VA 24060 Office: Dept Statistics Va Poly Inst and State U Blacksburg VA 24061

GOOD, JACOB WARREN, JR., realtor; b. Mt. Jackson, Va., Apr. 20, 1919; s. Jacob Warren and Fannie (Dellinger) G.; grad. high sch.; m. Lucille Virginia Fawley, June 25, 1944; 1 son, Jacob Warren III. Farmer, Mt. Jackson, 1941-50; salesman Valley Fertilizer & Chem. Co., Mt. Jackson, 1950-61; real estate salesman, developer, Woodstock, Va., 1961—; pres., dir. Planaway Inc., Woodstock, 1964—; pres., dir. Mid-Valley Devel. Co., Woodstock; dir. Shenandoah Recreation and Trail Riders Inc., R.J. Clower Ins. Agy. Chmn. Shenandoah County chpt. Am. Cancer Soc., 1973-74. Mem. Massanutten Bd. Realtors (sec.). Mem. Ch. of Brethren (deacon). Lion.

GOODALE, FAIRFIELD, educator; b. Framingham, Mass., May 4, 1923; s. Fairfield and Anna (Perkins) G.; grad. Milton Acad., 1941; student Harvard, 1941-42; student Western Res. U., 1945-46, M.D., 1950; m. Mary Margaret Lyman, Aug. 19, 1945; children—Tad, Nan (Mrs. David W. Witt), John, Susan, Tim. Intern, Mt. Auburn Hosp., Cambridge, Mass., 1950-51; resident pathology Mass. Gen. Hosp., Boston, 1951-54, chief resident pathology, 1954-55, USPHS research fellow, asst. in pathology, 1957-58; teaching fellow Harvard Med. Sch., Cambridge, Mass., 1954-55, asst. in pathology, 1957-58; USPHS research fellow St. Mary's Hosp., London, 1955-56; research fellow U.S. Pub. Health Dept., Oxford, 1956-57; asst. prof. pathology Dartmouth Med. Sch., also asso. dir. labs. Mary Hitchcock Meml. Hosp. and Clinic, Hanover, N.H., 1958-60; asst. prof. pathology Albany (N.Y.) Med. Coll., 1960-63; prof., chmn. dept. pathology Med. Coll. Va., Richmond, 1963—, asst. dean for curriculum, 1972—. Served with USAAF, 1942-45. Diplomate Am. Bd. Pathology. Fellow Coll. Am. Pathologists; mem. Internat. Acad. Pathologists, A.M.A., Am. Soc. Clin. Pathologists, Am. Assn. Pathologists and Bacteriologists, Am. Soc. for Exptl. Pathology, Assn. Pathology chmn., New Eng., Va. socs. pathologists, Soc. for Exptl. Biology and Medicine. Contbg. author Etiology of Myocardial Infarction, 1963; also articles. Research on causes of fever, atherosclerosis; isolated protein released from white blood cells which produces fever. Home: Contention Crozier VA 23039 Office: Medical College Virginia Box 817 Richmond VA 23298

GOODALL, LEON STEELE, ins. co. exec.; b. Lebanon, Tenn., Aug. 24, 1925; s. William Thomas and Effie (Steele) G.; student U. Tenn., 1943; B.S., U. S.C., 1947, LL.B., 1950; m. Billie Rice, Sept. 9, 1949; children—David Christian, Katherine Stuart. Spl. agt. FBI, 1950-52; sr. auditor S.C. Tax Commn., Columbia, 1952-53; sales devel. mgr. Allstate Ins. Co., Charlotte, N.C., 1953-59; agy. v.p. Colonial Life & Accident Ins. Co., Columbia, S.C., 1959-70, pres., 1970—; dir., 1964—; mem. Columbia adv. bd. Am. Bank & Trust Co. Trustee, Columbia Coll. Served with USNR, 1943-47. Mem. S.C. State Bar Assn., Sales Marketing Execs. Club, Soc. Former FBI Agts. Methodist. Club: Sertoma. Home: 6328 Eastshore Rd Columbia SC 29206 Office: 1612 Marion St Columbia SC 29201

GOODALL, MCCHESNEY, physician, educator; b. Staunton, Va., Nov. 10, 1916; s. McChesney and Julia (Ellison) G.; B.A., U. Va., 1939; M.D., Med. Coll. Va., 1948; Ph.D., Karolinska Institutet, Sweden, 1951; m. Wayne Stokes, Feb. 27, 1953; children—Bettine Marshall, Eugenia Ellison, McChesney, Pendleton, William Stokes. Asso. prof. physiology Yale Med. Sch., New Haven, 1951-53; prof. physiology and surgery Duke Med. Sch., Durham, N.C., 1953-58; med. dir. U. Tenn. Meml. Research Center and Hosp., Knoxville, 1958-66; prof. physiology, also research dir. Burns Inst., 1966-67; prof. pharmacology, physiology and surg. research U. Tex. Med. Br., Galveston, 1966-72; prof. clin. pharmacology Duke Sch. Med., 1972—. Chmn. bd. Ecological Sci. Corp., Miami, Fla., 1972—; dir. Va. Trout Co., Monterey, Cal., Calibiochem, Los Angeles. Established investigator Am. Heart Assn., 1954—. Served with AC, USNR, 1940-46. Mem. Am. Physiol. Soc., Sigma Xi. Author: Studies of Adrenaline and Noradrenaline in Mammalian Heart and Suprarenals, 1951. Contbr. articles on adrenaline and noradrenaline to profl. jours. Research on sympathetic nervous system, adrenal medulla, biosynthesis, others; discoverer L-DOPA and dopamine in mammalian tissue. Home: 618 Morgan Creek Rd Chapel Hill NC 27514 Office: Burroughs Wellcome Co Research Triangle Park NC

GOODALL, VAN DOREN, physician; b. Valley Mills, Tex., July 21, 1909; s. William George and Ethel (Barnett) G.; student Baylor U., 1927-29; M.D., U. Tex., 1933; m. Valorie Birdie Shaw, June 10, 1933; children—Valorie Shaw (Mrs. William Piatt Mooney), Van Doren. Intern, Providence Hosp., Waco, Tex., 1933-34; practice medicine, specializing in internal medicine, Clifton, Tex., 1934—; co-founder, sr. staff mem. Goodall-Witcher Hosp. Found., 1939—, Clifton Med. and Surg. Clinic, 1939—; dir., v.p. Farmers State Bank, Clifton, Tex. Mem. Tex. Hosp. Licensing Bd., 1959—, chmn., 1970. Bd. dirs. Tex. Good Rds. Assn., Am. Heart-Tex. Affiliate Assn., 1973—. Mem. A.M.A., Am. Soc. Internal Medicine, Tex. Acad. Gen. Practice (pres. 1958), Tex. Pvt. Clinics and Hosp. Assn. (pres. 1961), Tex. Med. Assn., Bosque-Hamilton County Med. Soc., Clifton C. of C. (v.p. 1970), Baylor U. (pres. 1960), U. Tex. Med. Br. (pres. 1971) ex-students assns. Presbyn. (elder 1945—). Lion. Clubs: Ridgewood Country (Waco); Bosque Valley Country (Meridian, Tex.). Home: 1415 W Hackberry St Clifton TX 76634 Office: 201 S Av T Clifton TX 76634

GOODE, MONROE JACK, plant pathologist, educator; b. Whitney, Ala., Feb. 15, 1928; s. Paul and Lila Mae (Puckett) G.; diploma, Meridian Jr. Coll., 1950; B.S., Miss. State Coll., 1952, M.S., 1954; Ph.D., N.C. State U., 1957; m. Ethel Lorene Carter, May 27, 1950; children—Dana Faye, Paula Carol, Monroe Carter. Asst. prof. dept. plant pathology Sch. Agr. and Agrl. Expt. Sta., U. Ark., Fayetteville, 1957-61, asso. prof., 1961-66, prof., 1966—; guest lectr. Tex. A. and M. U., U. Mo.; mem. So. Regional Vegetable Task Force. Served with AUS, 1946-49. NSF Research grantee, 1961, NSF Teaching Equipment grantee, 1967. Mem. Am. Phytopathol. Soc., Sigma Xi, Gamma Sigma Delta, Phi Kappa Phi, Alpha Zeta, Beta Beta Beta. Lion. Author: (with others) Laboratory Manual Plant Pathology, 1960. Contbr. articles profl. jours. Home: 1525 Hefley St Fayetteville AR 72701

GOODE, MORTON JACOB, dentist; b. Washington, Feb. 3, 1924; s. Julius and Sadie (Fleisher) G.; B.S., Georgetown U., 1942; D.D.S., Temple U., 1946; m. Amy Lou Harris, Dec. 23, 1945; children—Scott, Robert, Jill. Intern Glendale (Md.) Sanitarium, 1946; asso. Dr. Jack Goldblatt, Washington, 1947-49; individual practice gen. dentistry, Washington, 1949-51, 52-59, gen. dentistry, crown bridge and rehab., 1959—. Pres. Budget Rent-a-Car, (Miami Beach, Fla.); dir. Beverage Control, Inc.; v.p. Derma-Hair; lectr.; staff adviser dental dept. Children's Hosp., Hebrew Home for Aged. Dir. Boy Scouts Am., 1961-62. Served as p.f.c., AUS, 1943-44, as capt. Dental Corps, USAF, 1950-51. Mem. Am. Dental Assn., D.C. Dental Soc. (dir. dental program for treatment of mentally retarded children), Acad. Gen. Dentistry, D.C. Dental Sci. Club (past pres.). Jewish religion (dir. congregation). Kiwanian. Contbr. articles to profl. jours. Home: 5504 Uppingham St Chevy Chase MD 22015 Office: 7723 Alaska Av NW Washington DC 20012

GOODE, RILEY RAY, county ofcl.; b. Pineville, W.Va., Feb. 21, 1937; s. Walter G. and Lillie (Meadows) G.; B.A., Morris Harvey Coll., 1960; M.P.A., Pa. State U., 1962; m. Casandra Brackin, Jan. 26, 1964; children—Deborah, Donna. Budget analyst Office of Gov. Pa., 1961-62; adminstrv. asst. Office County Mgr., Dade County, Fla., 1962-63; welfare dir. Met. Dade County, 1963-66, budget dir., 1966-68, county mgr., 1970—; exec. v.p. Greater Miami Coalition, 1968-70; instr. pub. mgmt. and govt. finance Miami Dade Jr. Coll. Chmn. Gov.'s Council on Criminal Justice, 1972—, Govt. div. United Fund of Dade County, 1971—. Trustee, Nat. Urban Coalition; bd. advisers Fla. Internat. U. Recipient Outstanding Civilian Service medal U.S. Dept. Army, 1972; named County Man of Action, Greater Miami C. of C., 1971. Mem. Am. Soc. Pub. Adminstrn. (past nat. bd. dirs.), Internat. City Mgmt. Assn. Baptist. Home: 7240 SW 146th Terrace Miami FL 33158 Office: 73 W Flagler St Miami FL 33130

GOODING, JESSIE JEWELL SIMS (MRS. ARTHUR RAY GOODING), clubwoman; b. Hartshorne, Okla., May 9, 1902; d. William Poley and Leola (Sullivan) Sims; student Okla. Coll. Women, 1921-22; m. Arthur Ray Gooding, Aug. 16, 1925; children—Jack Bascom, Arthur Gene. Shipping clk. William Volker Wholesale Co., Oklahoma City, 1942-43; bookkeeper, sales clk. Seela Windowshade Co., 1944-51; sales clk. John A. Brown Co., 1957. Recipient Torch award Am. War Mothers, 1966. Mem. Bus. and Profl. Women's Club, Am. War Mothers (charter, chpt. pres. 1955-56, chpt. treas. 1956-62, state treas. 1958-60, chpt. corr. sec. 1963-68, chpt. historian 1969-74, state pres. 1968-70; state alternate rep. in Vets. Voluntary Service 1969-71), World War One Aux. (jr. v.p. 1973-74), Am. War Dads. Aux. (pres. 1965-66, nat. council woman, Okla. historian, state parliamentarian 1971-74; life mem.), Am. Assn. Ret. Persons. Baptist. Mem. Order Eastern Star. Clubs: Flower (v.p. 1965—), Home Demonstration, Merry Modern Mothers (past v.p.). Home: 508 SW 35th St Oklahoma City OK 73109

GOODLET, JAMES HARRIS, city ofcl.; b. Columbus, Ga., Sept. 10, 1922; s. Hiram O. and Nona (Harris) G.; B.S., Samford U., 1946; m. Thelma I. Moon, Sept. 17, 1944; children—Janice Gail, Gloria Jean. Asst. to bus. mgr. Howard Coll., Birmingham, Ala. 1946-48; agt. Life Ins. Co. of Ga., Miami, Fla., 1948-49; city clk., treas., personnel dir. City of Hialeah (Fla.), 1949—. Trustee, treas. City of Hialeah Employees Retirement System. Served to lt. USAAF, 1943-45. Decorated Silver Star, Air medals with two oak leaf clusters, Purple Heart. Mem. Fla., Dade County (past pres.) finance officers assns., Fla. Assn. Personnel Agencies (past pres.), Internat. Inst. Municipal Clks. Baptist. Home: 951 E 37th St Hialeah FL 33013 Office: 501 Palm Av Hialeah FL 33010

GOODLOE, HERBERT HAMILTON, electronic engr.; b. El Paso, Tex., Dec. 31, 1939; s. Herbert Hamilton and Estelle Catherine (Belmont) G.; B.S. in E.E., U. Tex. at El Paso, 1961, postgrad. 1968—; m. Diane Carol Stahlhuth, Jan. 20, 1968. Electronic engr., U.S. Civil Service, White Sands Missile Range, N.M., 1961-65, ACD Computer div., 1968—. Served with USAF, 1966-68. Registered profl. engr., Tex. Mem. I.E.E.E. Baptist (deacon). Home: 10821 Vista Alegre El Paso TX 79935 Office: NR-A Computer Div White Sands Missile Range NM 88002

GOODMAN, ADOLPH WINKLER, educator; b. San Antonio, July 20, 1915; s. William Wolf and Hannah (Winkler) G.; B.Sc., U. Cin., 1939, M.A., 1941; Ph.D., Columbia, 1947; m. Betty Posman, Dec. 6, 1947; children—Dianne E., William L., Sheila L., Glenn David. Faculty, Rutgers U., 1947-49, U. Ky., 1949-64; faculty U. South Fla., Tampa, 1964—, distinguished prof. math., 1966—. Recipient Alumni Assn. award for outstanding research U. Ky., 1958. Mem. Am. Math. Soc., Math. Assn. Am., Indian Math. Soc., Soc. Math de France. Clubs: Tampa Chess, Tampa Coin. Author: Analytical Geometry and the Calculus, 1963; (with J.S. Ratti) Finite Mathematics, 1971; Mainstream of Algebra and Trigonometry, 1973; also research articles. Reviewer: Math. Revs., 1947—. Home: 11321 Carrollwood Dr Tampa FL 33618

GOODMAN, GEORGE JONES, botanist, educator; b. Evanston, Wyo., Nov. 5, 1904; s. Arthur Duane and Mary Elizabeth (Jones) G.; A.B., U. Wyo., 1929; M.S., Washington U., St. Louis, 1930, Ph.D., 1933; m. Marcia McCay, Dec. 19, 1948. Instr. U. Okla., Norman, 1933-34, asst. prof. botany, 1934-36; asst. prof. botany Ia. State Coll., Ames, 1936-44, asso. prof., 1944-45; prof. botany U. Okla., Norman, 1945—, Regents prof. botany, 1967—, curator Herbarium, 1950—, curator of botany Stovall Mus., 1949—. Plant Taxonomist Okla. Biol. Survey, Norman, 1956—. Mem. A.A.A.S., Am. Soc. Plant Taxonomists, Bot. Soc. Am., Southwestern Assn. Naturalists (pres. 1956), Okla. Acad. Sci. (pres. 1958). Author: Spring Flora of Central Oklahoma, 1958. Contbr. articles to sci. publs. Home: 1229 Avondale Dr Norman OK 73069 Office: 770 Van Vleet Oval Norman OK 73069

GOODMAN, JAMES FLATT, computer co. exec.; b. Champaign, Ill., May 27, 1923; s. Willard Gaddis and Nell Irene (Flatt) G.; B.S., U. Ill., 1943, J.D., 1948; M.B.A., U. Tex., 1950; m. Ann Catlett, Apr. 5, 1944; children—John Catlett, James Jefferson, Nancy Nell (Mrs. Loyd Dalton Jr.). Admitted to Tex. bar, 1950; prof. accounting and bus. law Baylor U., Waco, Tex., 1948-53; sr. partner firm Goodman, Nielsen & Pakis, Waco, 1952-62; real estate developer, investor, Waco and Houston, 1963-71; pres., chmn. bd. DataMate Computer Systems, Inc., Houston, 1972—; dir. First Capital Corp., 1961—. Del., Tex. Republican State Conv., 1970. Trustee Salvation Army, 1958-60, Campus Crusade for Christ, 1966-69. Served to 1st lt. AUS, 1942-46; ETO. C.P.A., Tex. Mem. State Bar Tex., Beta Theta Pi, Beta Alpha Psi. Mem. Linolean Ch. Clubs: Hedonia (pres. 1954-55) (Waco); Huisache (Houston). Author: Successful Estate Planning, 1951. Home: 9940 Memorial Dr Houston TX 77024 Office: 5400 Memorial Towers Houston TX 77007

GOODMAN, JAMES JACOB, psychiatrist; b. Boston, Mar. 31, 1922; s. Morris and Rosa (Wolfsen) G.; B.A., Boston U., 1943; M.D., Middlesex U., 1945; m. Janice Annabel Stenson, July 11, 1951; 1 dau., Ann Rosalind. Intern St. Mark's Hosp., Salt Lake City, 1946-47; resident St. Vincent's Sanitarium, St. Louis, 1947-48, Western State Hosp., Ft. Steilacoom, Wash., 1948-50; staff psychiatrist VA Hosp., American Lake, Wash., 1950-51; asst. attending physician dept. psychiatry and neurology Jackson Hosp., Miami, Fla., 1954—, also clin. dir. Miami Med. Center; practice medicine specializing in psychiatry, Miami, 1954-65; staff psychiatrist VA Hosp., Indpls., 1966-69, VA Hosp., Miami, Fla., 1969—. Instr. psychiatry U. Miami,

1955-57, clin. asst. prof. neurology, 1957-59, clin. instr. psychiatry, 1969-72, clin. asst. prof. Sch. Medicine, 1972-73, asst. prof. dept. psychiatry, 1973—; instr. psychiatry Ind. U. Sch. Medicine, 1967-69. Bd. dirs. P.L. Dodge Found. and Meml. Hosp., Miami. Served to capt. M.C., AUS, 1951-54. Mem. Am. Psychiat. Assn. A.M.A. (So., Fla., Dade County med. assns. Assn. Am. Med. Colls., Am. Assn. U. Profs., Nat. Assn. for Mental Health, Mental Health Soc. S.E. Fla., Assn. Mil. Surgeons, Am. Soc. for Group Psychotherapy and Psychodrama, Acad. Religion and Mental Health, Fla. Council on Aging, Fla. Soc. Neurology and Psychiatry, World Med. Assn. (U.S. com.), Nat. Com. on Alcoholism, N.Y. Acad. Scis., Am. Geriatrics Soc., Am. Acad. Forensic Scis. Home: 6818 Corsica St Coral Gables FL 33146 Office: 1201 NW 16th St Miami FL 33125

GOODMAN, WILLIAM WOLF, lawyer; b. Memphis, June 26, 1900; s. Abe and Bobye (Wolf) G.; ed. Memphis U. Sch., Culver Mil. Acad.; B.A., U. Pa., 1920; J.D., Harvard U., 1923; grad. student St. Johns Coll., Cambridge (Eng.) U., 1923-24; Barrister, Lincoln's Inn (London), 1926; m. 1942; 5 children. Sec. Tenn. Planning Commn., 1932-40; chmn. bd. treas. Am. Finishing Co.; chmn. Memphis Cold Storage Warehouse Co., Mid-South Refrigerated Warehouse Co., McCall & Dermon Bldgs. Co.; chmn. Commerce Title Guaranty Co.; pres. Madison Oil & Devel. Co. Pres. commr. Goodwyn Inst.; pres. Lausanne Sch., Memphis. Served with U.S. Army, 1918, World War I; col. USAAF, 1942-45. Decorated Legion of Merit. Army Commendation Ribbon, Royal Yugoslav Aviator's Wings, Honoris Causa; Spl. Breast Award Order of Yun Hui (Cloud and Banner) (China); knight comdr. Order Orange-Nassau (Netherlands); knight comdr. Royal Order St. Olaf (Norway); chevalier Legion of Honor (French); officer Order of Brit. Empire (Eng.). Mem. Am., Tenn. bar assns., Assn. Bar City N.Y., Brit. Barrister, Memphis and Shelby County bar assns., Memphis Freight Bur. (pres. 1951-60). Clubs: Harvard (N.Y.C.); Army and Navy (Washington); University, Ridgeway Country (Memphis). Home: 159 E Parkway N Memphis TN 38104 Office: Commerce Title Bldg Memphis TN 38103

GOODNER, ARMEL HOYT, hosp. adminstr.; b. Boles, Ark., June 24, 1934; s. Orval Kern and Effie Hanna (Taylor) G.; student Ark. Tech. Coll., 1951-53, State Coll. Ark., 1953, Okla. State U., 1966; m. Linda Jean Davis, July 30, 1960; children—Karan Lynn, Gregory Todd. Asst. mgr. Waldron Furniture Factory, Ark., 1954-56; asst. parts mgr. Dewitt Oldsmobile Co., Ft. Smith, Ark., 1959; comml. rep. S.W. Bell Tel. Co., Stillwater, Okla., 1959-70; adminstr. Scott County Hosp., Waldron, 1970—. Served with AUS, 1956-58. Mem. Waldron C. of C. Lion. Home: Box 81 Waldron AR 72958 Office: Box Q Waldron AR 72958

GOODNER, DWIGHT BENJAMIN, educator; b. What Cheer, Ia., Aug. 15, 1913; s. William Clifford and Myrtle E. (Harbour) G.; B.A. with honors, William Penn Coll., 1934; M.A. (T.Wistar Brown fellow), Haverford Coll., 1935; Ph.D. (Univ. fellow), U. Ill., 1949; m. Mildred E. Wilson, June 29, 1936. Instr. S.D. State Coll., Brookings, 1937-41, asst. prof., 1941-46; faculty Fla. State U., Tallahassee, 1949—, prof. math., 1954—, asso. dean grad. sch., 1953-58. Cons. Commn. on Accreditation of Armed Services Ednl. Experiences, 1950-59, Ednl. Testing Service, Princeton, N.J., 1965-70. Served with USNR, 1942-46. Mem. Am., London, Edinburgh, Indian math. socs., Math. Assn. Am. (gov. 1967-71, cons. 1971—), Sigma Xi, Phi Beta Kappa, Phi Kappa Phi, Pi Mu Epsilon, Phi Delta Kappa, Chi Gamma Iota, Phi Eta. Presbyn. (ruling elder 1957—). Math. editor: Jour. of Communication, 1959-61. Contbr. articles in field to profl. jours. Home: 1317 Lemond Tallahassee FL 32303

GOODNER, ORVAL KERN, banker; b. Boles, Ark., June 19, 1910; s. William Robert and Louisa (Walls) G.; student Ark. Poly. Inst., 1931-33; m. Effie Hanna Taylor, Sept. 6, 1933; children—Hoyt, Harland, Oleta (Mrs. Harrell Lewis). Tchr. Boles High Sch., 1933-40; with Bank Waldron (Ark.), 1941—, exec. v.p., 1964—, also sec. bd. Treas., recorder City of Waldron, 1942-72. Sec. Scott County Democratic Com., 1942—. Bd. dirs. Farm Bur., Scott County Devel. Assn. Mem. C. of C. Waldron (dir.). Baptist (deacon). Lion. Home: 950 S Main St Waldron AR 72958 Office: 910 Washington St Waldron AR 72958

GOODPASTURE, BENTON CORDELL, publisher, editor; b. Livingston, Tenn., Apr. 9, 1895; s. John Jefferson and Elora (Thompson) G.; B.A., David Lipscomb Coll., 1918; LL.D., Pepperdine Coll., 1955, Magic Valley Coll., 1955; Litt.D., Harding Coll., 1955; m. Cleveland Cliett, Sept. 3, 1918 (dec. Nov. 1964); children—Benton Cordell, Eleanor Pauline (Mrs. Myron L. King), John Cliett; m. 2d, Freddie Joan Goetz, Nov. 11, 1965. Ordained to ministry Ch. of Christ, 1912; minister Main St. Ch. of Christ, Shelbyville, Tenn., 1918-19, West End Ch. of Christ, Atlanta, 1920-27, Poplar St. Ch. of Christ, Florence, Ala., 1927-28, Druid Hills Ch. of Christ, Atlanta, 1927-39, Hillsboro Ch. of Christ, Nashville, 1939-51; editor Gospel Advocate Co., Inc., Nashville, 1939—, pres., 1950—. Bd. dirs. Potter Orphan Home, Atlanta Christian Schs., B.C. Goodpasture Christian Sch. Author: Sermons and Lectures, 1964; (with W.T. Moore) Biographies and Sermons of Pioneer Preachers, 1954, Great Preachers of Today, 1967. Home: 932 Caldwell Lane Nashville TN 37204 Office: 1006 Elm Hill Pike Nashville TN 37210

GOODRICH, BERNARD ARTHUR, pub. relations exec.; b. Saranac Lake, N.Y., Oct. 7, 1929; s. Frederick T. and Eva Mildred (Lesperance) G.; B.A., George Washington U., 1958; m. Margaret Phoebe Sheppard, Sept. 14, 1957; 1 dau., Christine Margaret. Reporter Washington Evening Star, Washington, 1947-55; chief press relations Am. Trucking Assos., Washington, 1955-65; dir. pub. relations Nat. Rural Electric Co-op Assn., Washington, 1965-67; dir. news services Internat. Tel. & Tel. Corp., Washington, 1967—. Served with USMCR, 1950-52. Recipient Profl. Excellence award Pub. Relations Soc., 1969. Mem. Nat. Press Club, Pub. Relations Soc. Am. Clubs: Columbia Country, George Town. Home: 5008 Cathedral Av NW Washington DC 20016 Office: 1707 L St NW Washington DC 20036

GOODRICH, GEORGE HERBERT, judge; b. Charleston, W.Va., June 19, 1925; s. Edgar Jennings and Beulah Etta (Lenfest) G.; B.A., Williams Coll., 1949; LL.B., U. Va., 1952; m. Nancy Ann Needham, Sept. 3, 1949; children—George Herbert, Craig N., Thomas A. Admitted to D.C. bar, 1953, Md. bar, 1958; practiced in Washington, 1953-69; asso. firm Guggenheimer, Untermeyer & Goodrich, 1953-62, Burton, Heffelfinger, McCarthy & Kendrick, 1962-67; mem. firm Heffelfinger, Schweitzer & Goodrich, 1967-69; asso. judge Superior Court D.C., 1969—. Law instr. Bus. Sch., Am. U., 1969—. Pres. Homemaker Service Nat. Capitol Area, 1966; v.p. Hillcrest Children's Center, 1969; mem. community adv. com. Jr. League D.C., 1969—. Bd. dirs. A.R.C. Served with USNR, 1943-46. Mem. Am., D.C. bar assns. Club: Chevy Chase (Md.); Metropolitan (Washington). Home: 6003 Corbin Rd Washington DC 20016 Office: 4th and E Sts NW Washington DC 20001

GOODRICH, NANCY ANN NEEDHAM (MRS. GEORGE HERBERT GOODRICH), ednl. tape producer; b. Cleve., Nov. 10, 1927; d. Delos N. and Florence (Duval) Needham; B.A. in Polit. Sci., Mt. Holyoke Coll., 1948; m. George Herbert Goodrich, Sept. 3, 1949; children—George Herbert, Craig Needham, Thomas Abrams. Mem. jr. exec. tng. course Time Inc., N.Y.C., 1948-49; broadcaster, dir. women's program radio sta. WCHV, Charlottesville, Va., 1949-52; moderator, producer program The 25th Hour sta. WTOP-TV, Washington, 1957-62; v.p., exec. producer Washington Tapes Inc., Washington, 1965—. Founding pres. Jr. Goodwill Guild, Washington, 1952-54; sec. Jr. League, Washington, 1957, pres., 1962-64. Vice chmn. D.C. com. arts Nixon-Agnew campaign, Washington, 1968; mem. Inaugural Ball Com., 1968-69. Episcopalian. Producer curriculum-keyed audio-tapes for sr. high schs. and colls. Home: 6003 Corbin Rd NW Washington DC 20016 Office: 5540 Connecticut Av NW Washington DC 20015

GOODRICH, ROBERT BRUCE, phys. sci. adminstr.; b. Portland, Conn., June 19, 1914; s. Frederick Rossiter and Bertha Manie (Wilson) G.; B.A., Wesleyan U., Middletown, Conn., 1936, M.A., 1937; postgrad. U. Tenn. at Knoxville, 1947; m. Beatrice Blacky, July 29, 1937; children—Mary Jane Jugl, Welles B. Chemist, Dewey & Almy Chem. Co., Cambridge, Mass., 1937-39; materials engr. Conn. State Hwy. Dept. Lab., Portland, 1939-43; research chemist SAM Labs. (Manhattan Project), N.Y.C., 1943-46; sr. scientist Oak Ridge Nat. Labs., 1946-48; br. chief Nat. Bur. Standards, Washington, 1948-53; div. chief Diamond Ordnance Fuze Labs., Washington, 1953-63; phys. sci. adminstr. U.S. Govt., Washington, 1963—. Mem. Phi Beta Kappa, Sigma Xi. Mason. Home: 3905 Huntington St NW Washington DC 20015

GOODRICH, ROY GORDON, educator; b. Dallas, Sept. 17, 1938; s. Hale C. and Flora Virginia (Forehand) G.; B.S., La. Poly. Inst., 1960; M.S., U. Cal. at Riverside, 1962, Ph.D., 1965; m. Doris Ann Hendrickson, Nov. 21, 1959; children—Laurann E., Katherine H., Andrew G. Instr. dept. physics U. So. Miss., Hattiesburg, 1960-61; asst. prof. La. State U., Baton Rouge, 1965-67, asso. prof., 1967-72, prof., 1972—, chmn. dept. physics and astronomy, 1973—. Cons. Gulf South Research, New Orleans, 1969-70. Recipient Frederick Gardner Cottrell grant Research Corp., 1967, NSF grants, 1969, 71, 73. Mem. Am. Phys. Soc., Kappa Alpha. Contbr. articles to profl. jours. Home: 6025 Chandler Dr Baton Rouge LA 70808

GOODSON, EDWARD LEE, hosp. adminstr.; b. Leeds, Ala., Feb. 9, 1927; s. Roy E. and Bernice (Lee) G.; B.A., Ala. Poly. Inst., 1950; m. Mary Lou Mitchell, May 6, 1948; children—Stephen E., William Lee, David Lynn. Rep., Ala. Dept. Pub. Welfare, Montgomery, 1950-60; adminstr. Leeds Hosp., 1960—, sec. bd. dirs., 1960—. Mem. Leeds Planning and Zoning Commn., 1962—, Jefferson County Planning and Zoning Commn., 1961-64; mem. Jefferson County Assn. Mental Health, 1969—; chmn. Leeds Indsl. Devel. Bd., 1969—. Bd. dirs. Leeds Housing Authority, 1968—. Served with USAAF, 1946-47. Mem. C. of C. (dir. 1962-69). Presbyn. (elder). Clubs: Terry Walker Country, Civitan (pres. 1962-63), Quarterback (pres. 1958). Home: 107 Greenbrier Acres Leeds AL 35094 Office: 100 Parkway Dr Leeds AL 35094

GOODSON, RAYMOND LYLE, JR., civil engr.; b. Burkburnett, Tex., Dec. 11, 1918; s. Raymond Lyle and Gretchen (Brooks) G.; B.S. in Civil Engring., So. Meth. U., 1941; M.C.E., N.Y.U., 1949; m. Ann Clark Meriwether, Aug. 22, 1947; children—James Lyle, David Meriwether, Sarah Ann. Design engr. Myers & Noyes & Assos., cons. engrs., 1941, 46-48; asst. prof. So. Meth. U. Engring. Sch., 1949-51; project engr. Myers & Noyes, 1951-53; owner, Raymond L. Goodson, Jr., Inc., cons. engrs., Dallas, 1953—. Mem. Greater Dallas Planning Council, 1967-71; bd. devel. Engr. Sch., So. Meth. U., 1970-71. Served to lt. comdr. USNR, 1941-46. Named Civil Engr. Year, Dallas chpt., Nat. Soc. Profl. Engrs., 1971. Registered profl. engr., Tex. Mem. Cons. Engrs. Council U.S.A. (dir. 1965-67), Am. Soc. C.E. (pres. Dallas br. 1967), Nat. Soc. Profl. Engrs., Cons. Engrs. Council Tex. (pres. 1963), Engrs. Club Dallas. Episcopalian. Club: Lakewood Country (bd. govs. 1970-72) (Dallas). Home: 3708 Alderson St Dallas TX 75204 Office: 2909 Lemmon Av Dallas TX 75214

GOODSON, WALTER KENNETH, bishop; b. Salisbury, N.C., Sept. 25, 1912; s. Daniel Washington and Sarah (Peeler) G.; A.B., Catawba Coll., 1934; postgrad. Duke Div. Sch., 1934-37, D.D., 1960; D.D., High Point Coll., 1951, Athens Coll., Birmingham-So. Coll., Shenandoah Coll., 1973; L.H.D., St. Bernard Coll., 1968; LL.D., U. Ala., 1968; m. Martha Ann Ogburn, July 12, 1937; children—Sara Ann (Mrs. Larry M. Faust), Walter Kenneth, Nancy Craven (Mrs. Thomas S. Johnson). Ordained to ministry Methodist Ch., 1939; pastor in Western N.C. Conf., 1935-64; bishop Birmingham (Ala.) area, 1964-72, Richmond, Va. area, 1972—. Del. World Conf. Meth. Ch., Oxford, Eng., 1951, Lake Junaluska, N.C., 1956; mem. Mission Team to Gt. Britain, 1962, study team to France and Berlin, 1962. Pres. J.B. Cornelius Found., 1946-64. Trustee Brevard Coll., Randolph-Macon Coll., Va. Wesleyan Coll., Shenandoah Coll., Duke U., Randolph-Macon Acad. Methodist (pres. gen. bd. discipleship). Rotarian, Mason (32 deg.). Home: 211 Massie Rd Richmond VA 23221 Office: 4016 Broad St Richmond VA 23230

GOODSPEED, WOODIE DENSON, financial co. exec.; b. San Antonio, Aug. 3, 1939; s. William Gardner and Hazel LaVerne (Lindsey) G.; student San Antonio Coll., 1958-59; B.S., Trinity U., 1961; grad. diploma Am. Savs. and Loan Inst., 1971; m. Patricia Anne Dunkin, Aug. 6, 1960; children—Douglas, Melissa. With, Bexar County Nat. Bank, San Antonio, 1959-62; with First Fed. Savs., San Antonio, 1962—, v.p., sec. 1971—. Tex. vice chmn. Com. to Re-elect the Pres., 1972. Mem. Am. Savs. and Loan Inst. (chpt. pres. 1972-73), Controllers Soc. for Savs. Insts. Club: Optimist (treas. 1972-73, dir. 1973—) (San Antonio). Home: 1746 Deer Run San Antonio TX 78232 Office: 800 Navarro San Antonio TX 78286

GOODWIN, BRUCE KESSELI, educator; b. Providence, R.I., Oct. 14, 1931; s. Thomas William and Lizetta Christina (Kesseli) G.; A.B., U. Pa., 1953; M.S., Lehigh U., 1957, Ph.D., 1959; m. Joan Marilyn Horton, June 9, 1956; children—Stephen B., Susan J., Jennifer Anne. Grad. asst. Lehigh U., Bethlehem, Pa., 1956-59; instr. U. Pa., Phila., 1959-63; faculty Coll. William and Mary, Williamsburg, Va., 1963—, prof. geology, 1971—, chmn. dept., 1970—. Troop committeeman Boy Scouts Am., Williamsburg, 1969-71. Served to cpl. AUS, 1953-55. Recipient Thomas Jefferson Teaching award Coll. William and Mary, 1971. Fellow Geol. Soc. Am.; mem. Nat. Assn. Geology Tchrs., A.A.A.S., Va. Acad. Sci., Sigma Xi. Contbr. articles to profl. jours. Home: 103 Wake Robin Rd Williamsburg VA 23185

GOODWIN, HAROLD LELAND, govt. ofcl.; b. Ellenburg, N.Y., Nov. 20, 1914; s. Frank Elmer and Imogene (Van Arman) G.; student Elliot Radio Sch., 1934-35; m. Elizabeth I. Swensk, Apr. 12, 1947; children—Alan C., Christopher R., Derek V. White House corr. Transradio News, Washington, 1942; press. attache Fgn. Service, Dept. State, Manila, Philippines, 1947-50; dir. atomic test operations FCDA, 1951-58; sci. adviser USIA, 1958-62; spl. asst. to adminstr. NASA, 1962-67; asso. dir. Office Sea Grant Programs, NSF, Washington, 1967-70; dep. dir. sea grant and program mgr. aquaculture Nat. Oceanic and Atmospheric Adminstrn., Dept. Commerce, 1970—. Served to 1st lt. USMCR, 1942-45. Decorated Air medal; recipient Silver medal Dept. Commerce, 1972; Arthur S. Flemmming award U.S. Jr. C. of C., 1952. Mem. Am. Littoral Soc. (Dusan award 1974), Marine Tech. Soc. (sec. for profl. and student sects. 1970-72), Am. Oceanic Orgn. (dir. 1970-73), Antarctic Soc., Am. sci. Film Assn. (nat. v.p. 1965-67), Underwater Soc. Am., Boston Sea Rovers, Profl. Assn. Diving Instrs. (internat. bd. dirs. 1972—). Methodist. Author: All about Rockets and Space Flight, 1962; Space Frontier Unlimited, 1964; Images of Space, 1965; Rick Brant Science Adventure series Challenge of Seven Seas, 1966, others. Home: 6212 Verne St Bethesda MD 20034 Office: Sea Grant 425 13th St Washington DC 20006

GOODWIN, JACK HOWARD, librarian; b. Columbus, O., Mar. 9, 1921; s. Ernest S. and Lucy Rebecca (Hart) G.; B.A., Olivet Nazarene Coll., 1948; M.L.S., U. Ill., 1949; postgrad. U. Edinburgh (Scotland), 1951-52; m. Mary Ellen Wilson, July 25, 1943; children—James Wilson, Jeremy Philip. Librarian, Va. Theol. Sem., Alexandria, 1954—. Served with AUS, 1942-46. Mem. Am. Theol Library Assn. Home: Box 12111 Alexandria VA 22304

GOODWIN, JAMES MONROE, ins. co. exec.; b. Forest, Miss., Sept. 29, 1937; s. Wilbur R. and Thelma (Spillman) G.; B.S. in Edn., Miss. Coll., 1959; m. Katherine Elizabeth Attridge, Apr. 16, 1959; children—Angela Lynne, Katherine Elizabeth. Coach, tchr., Biloxi (Miss.) Schs., 1959-60; agr. Morris Ins. Agy., Forest, 1960-61; pres. Forest Ins. Agy., Inc., 1961—; dir. Farmers & Merchants Bank, Forest, Mid-Miss. Devel. Corp. Housing officer, Forest, 1963-73, alderman-at-large, 1974—. Vice chmn., bd. dirs S.E. Lackey Meml. Hosp., Forest; alderman-at-large, Forest, 1973—. Mem. Miss. Mut. Ins. Agts. Assn. (bd. dirs., pres. 1972-73), Forest C. of C. (v.p. 1965, 71, dir. 1964-66, 71-72). Baptist. Mason (Shriner), Lion (sec.-treas. Forest 1965-68). Club: Forest Country (pres. 1970-71). Address: 104 Sunset Dr Forest MS 39074

GOODWIN, JAMES RANDALL, ins. exec.; b. Trinity, Tex., Apr. 4, 1933; s. Dan Frank and Ollie (Atkinson) G.; student U. Louisville, 1955; B.S., La. State U., 1956; m. Margaret Ann Lee, June 6, 1959; children—James Randall, Lee Ann, Margaret Lynn, Garland Katherine. Pres., gen. mgr. Goodwin-Gauthier Ins. Agy., Baton Rouge, 1955—. Mem. City-Parish Planning and Zoning Commn., Baton Rouge, 1963-64, Recreation and Planning Commn., 1963-64; mem. East Baton Rouge Parish Sch. Bd., 1962-71, v.p., 1968-70, pres., 1971—. Bd. dirs. Baton Rouge Symphony, 1966-67; Baton Rouge Sci. Found. Mem. Nat. Assn. Casualty and Surety Agts. (fed. liaison com. 1966—), Sales and Marketing Execs. Baton Rouge (bd. mem., 2d v.p. 1962), Baton Rouge Ins. Exchange (pres. 1964), Fellowship Christian Athletes (chpt. charter mem.), Baton Rouge C. of C., Better Bus. Bur., Kappa Alpha, Eta Sigma Pi. Presbyn. (elder). Clubs: Audubon Kiwanis (dir., chmn. vocational guidance com. 1968—), L, Baton Rouge Country. Home: 1134 W Lakeview Dr Baton Rouge LA 70810 Office: 3968 North Blvd Baton Rouge LA 70806

GOODWIN, JAMES WILLIAM, utility co. exec.; b. Birmingham, Ala., Nov. 4, 1905; s. Pinkney Ollie and Willie Elizabeth (Butler) G.; B.S. in Civil Engring., Auburn U., 1927; m. Virginia Mabry, Dec. 28, 1949; 1 dau., Joy Elizabeth. Pres., J. W. Goodwin Engring. Co., Birmingham, 1933-63, chmn. bd. dirs., 1933-63; chmn. bd. dirs., chief exec. officer Carolina Pipeline Co., Columbia, S.C., 1957—, S.C. Pub. Utility, 1957—. U.S. Army and Navy on airbases and camps, 1940-50. Bd. dirs. Birmingham Boys Club, 1954—, Birmingham Girls Club, 1956—. Recipient Man and Boy award Boys Club Am., 1960, Silver Keystone medallion, 1961. Mem. Auburn U. Alumni Assn. (life, named Outstanding Alumni 1972), Am. Gas Assn. Methodist (dir.). Mason (Shriner). Clubs: Vestiva Country, The Club, Downtown (pres. 1955); Coral Ridge Country (Fort Lauderdale, Fla.). Home: 3248 E Briarcliff Circle Birmingham AL 35223 Office: 201 Office Park Circle 6 Birmingham AL 35223

GOODWIN, ROBERT ARCHER, JR., physician; b. Kuling, China, Aug. 3, 1914; s. Robert Archer and Emily (Gravatt) G.; B.S., U. Va., 1936; M.D., Johns Hopkins U., 1940; m. Jean Moulton, Oct. 2, 1944; children—Robert A., Jane C., Anne M. Intern, Johns Hopkins, Balt., 1940-41; asst. resident Thorndike Meml. Lab., Boston, 1941-42; asst. resident Vanderbilt U. Hosp., Nashville, 1946, resident physician, 1946-47; trainee chest service Bellevue Hosp., N.Y.C., 1947; chief tb sect. Thayer VA Hosp., Nashville, 1947-52, chief pulmonary disease service, 1952—; instr. medicine Harvard Med. Sch., 1941-42; instr. clin. medicine Vanderbilt U., Nashville, 1947-51, asst. prof., 1951-56, asso. clin. prof., 1956-62, asso. prof. medicine, 1962—. Served to maj. M.C., AUS, 1942-46. Diplomate Am. Bd. Internal Medicine. Fellow Am. Coll. Physicians; mem. Am. Thoracic Soc., A.M.A., Nashville Soc. Internal Medicine, Sigma Xi, Phi Beta Kappa, Alpha Omega Alpha. Home: 3720 Benham St Nashville TN 37215 Office: Veterans Administration Hospital Nashville TN 37203

GOODWIN, RONALD RAY, lawyer; b. Phillips, Tex., Jan. 9, 1941; s. Aaron Nathaniel and Paula Anna (Earl) G.; B.B.A., Baylor U., 1963, LL.B., 1968; m. Sharon Wynne Tripp, Mar. 27, 1964; children—Ronald Brad, Kristi Anna Lyn. With First Nat. Bank, Odessa, Tex., 1969; admitted to Tex. bar, 1969; practiced in San Angelo, Tex., 1970—; mem. firm Kerr, Gayer, Gregg & Goodwin, 1972—. Dir. San Angelo Abstract Co., Composite Metering, Inc. Mem. Civil Service Bd. San Angelo, 1971—. Bd. dirs. March of Dimes, 1971—, campaign chmn. 1970-71; bd. dirs. Concho Valley Estate Planning Council, 1971-72, Angelo State U. Ram Club, 1972-73. Mem. Am., Tom Green County bar assns., State Bar Tex., Baylor U. Law Sch. Alumni (dir. 1973—), Omicron Delta Kappa. Mem. Christian Ch. (deacon 1970—). Kiwanian (dir. 1970-71). Home: 3702 Sul Ross St San Angelo TX 76901 Office: PO Box Drawer 31 San Angelo TX 76901

GOODWYN, JACK RAY, chem. products co. exec., chemist; b. Center, Tex., June 28, 1934; s. Armon G. and Ell (Lout) G.; B.A. cum laude, Baylor U., 1956, Ph.D. Phys. Chemistry, 1960; m. Eloise McKinley, Aug. 19, 1955; children—Cynthia, Thomas, David. Chemist devel. dept. Tex. Eastman Co., Longview, Tex., 1960-64, sr. chemist, 1964-68, sr. chemist plastics lab., 1968-73, asst. to mgr., 1973—. Mem. Am. Chem. Soc., Soc. Plastics Engrs. Presbyn. Home: 2308 Kentucky Longview TX 75601 Office: PO Box 7444 Longview TX 75601

GOOLSBY, THOMAS MORRIS, JR., educator, psychologist; b. Wetumpka, Ala., Apr. 3, 1932; s. Thomas Morris and Lottie Mae (Collier) G.; B.S., U. Ala., 1954; M.Ed., Auburn U., 1960; Ph.D., U. Ia., 1963. Tchr. sci. Robert E. Lee High Sch., Montgomery, Ala., 1958-59, Ramey Base Schs., P.R., 1959-60; research asst. psychol. measurement U. Ia., 1960-63; prof. ednl. psychology, measurement and statistics U. So. Cal., 1963-64; prof. Fla. State U., Tallahassee, 1964-68, dir. univ. test service, 1965-68; prof. U. Ga., Athens, 1968—, asso. dir., research and devel. center in ednl. stimulation, 1969. Measurement and research cons. pub. schs., govtl. agys. and pvt. enterprise. Served to 1st lt. AUS, 1955-57. Mem. Am. Psychol. Assn., Am. Ednl. Research Assn., Am. Acad. Polit. and Social Sci., A.A.A.S., Nat. Soc. Study Edn., Nat. Council Measurement Edn., U.K. Reading Assn., Theta Chi. Episcopalian. Club: Civitan. Contbr. articles to publs. Home: 20 Glenn Forest Athens GA 30603

GORDLEY, METZ TRANBARGER, artist, educator; b. Cedar Rapids, Ia., May 24, 1932; s. Clyde Metz and Martha (Tranbarger) G.; B.F.A., Washington U., St. Louis, 1956; M.F.A., U. Okla., 1957; postgrad. Ohio State U., 1957-58, U. N.C. at Chapel Hill, 1964; m.

Marilyn F.M. Classe, Aug. 25, 1956; children—Scott Tran, Lillian Claire. Mem. faculty Sch. Art, East Carolina U., Greenville, 1959—, asso. prof., 1960-62, prof., 1963—, also asso. dean Sch. Art, 1966—; exhibited in one-man shows at Garden Gallery, Raleigh, N.C., 1969, Louisburg (N.C.) Coll., 1967; exhibited in group shows Ball State U., Muncie, Ind., 1973, N.C. Mus. Art, Raleigh, 1973-74, numerous others. Art competition judge, 1971—. Served with AUS, 1953-55. Mem. Coll. Art Assn., Assn. Artists N.C. (dir.). Home: 105 Dalebrook Circle Greenville NC 27834

GORDON, DOUGLAS LITTLETON, physician; b. Baton Rouge, Mar. 15, 1924; s. Amos Kilgore and Irma Ruth (John) G.; student La. State U., 1941-43; M.D., Tulane U., 1946; m. Betty Pauline Bishop, Nov. 29, 1947 (dec. Sept. 1960); children—Douglas Littleton, Pamela Gayle; m. 2d, Florence Cecilia Vine, Dec. 30, 1961; children—Stephen Vine, Stewart Thomas. Intern Charity Hosp., New Orleans, 1946-47; fellow in internal medicine Ochsner Clinic, 1947-49; clin. asso. Endocrine Research Lab., Alton Ochsner Med. Found., 1949-51, 53-57; practice medicine specializing in internal medicine and endocrinology, Baton Rouge, 1954—; instr. medicine Tulane U. Sch. Medicine, 1949-51, 53-57; mem. staff sect. endocrinology Ochsner clinic, 1949-51, 53-57; asst. vis. physician Charity Hosp., Tulane unit, 1951; vis. physician, 1953-57, vis. physician La. State U. unit, 1957-61, sr. vis. physician, 1961—; vis. staff Baton Rouge Gen. Hosp., 1954—, chief staff, 1967; vis. staff Our lady of Lake Hosp., Baton Rouge, 1954—; cons. internal medicine East La. State Hosp., Jackson, 1961-63; dep. coroner East Baton Rouge Parish, 1955-70; mem. staff sect. medicine Baton Rouge Clinic, 1959—; clin. asst. prof. medicine La. State U. Sch. Medicine, 1957-62, clin. asso. prof. medicine, 1962-67, clin. prof. medicine, 1967—. Served to capt., M.C., USAF, 1951-53. Diplomate Am. Bd. Internal Medicine. Fellow A.C.P.; mem. A.M.A., Am. Fedn. Clin. Research, Endocrine Soc., A.A.A.S., Am. Diabetes Assn., So. Med. Assn., So. Soc. Clin. Research, N.Y. Acad. Scis., La. State, East Baton Rouge Parish med. socs., New Orleans Acad. Internal Medicine, Baton Rouge Acad. Internal Medicine (pres. 1962), Sigma Xi, Alpha Omega Alpha. Episcopalian. Contbr. articles to profl. jours. Home: 4534 Woodside Dr Baton Rouge LA 70808 Office: 134 N 19th St Baton Rouge LA 70808

GORDON, EVERETT JULIUS, orthopaedic surgeon; b. Washington, July 23, 1914; s. Solvin William and Freda (Weiss) G.; A.B., George Washington U., 1933; M.A., Catholic U., 1937; M.D., Jefferson Med. Coll.; m. Marian Ruth Kressin, Dec. 23, 1951; children—Solvin William, Stuart Leon, Elissa Anne. Intern, Emergency Hosp., D.C., 1937, Sinai Hosp., Balt., 1938, City Hosp., N.Y.C., 1939; orthopaedic surgery Children's Hosp., Gen. Hosp., Cin., 1945-46; practice medicine specializing in orthopaedic surgery, Washington, 1946—; chief orthopaedic surgery Hadley Meml. Hosp., Washington, Jefferson Meml. Hosp., Alexandria, Va.; sr. attending orthopaedic surgeon Cafritz Hosp., Sibley Hosp., Doctors Hosp., Children's Hosp.; asso. prof. orthopaedic surgery Georgetown U. Sch. Medicine, Washington, 1965—; cons. U.S. Civil Service Commn., 1963—, Md. and D.C. Vocational Rehab., 1963—. Med. dir. Boys Clubs Met. Police, Washington, 1950—, pres., 1972—. Pres., Gordon Found., 1950—. Served to maj. M.C., U.S. Army, 1941-46. Diplomate Am. Bd. Orthopaedic Surgery. Fellow Am. Acad. Orthopaedic Surgery, A.C.S., Internat. Coll. Surgeons; mem. Alpha Omega Alpha. Jewish religion. Mem. B'nai B'rith (pres. local lodge 1952, mem. exec. com. anti-defamation league 1960—); Clubs: Army and Navy, George Washington Alumni, Woodmont Country (Washington). Author: A Practical Medico-Legal Guide for the Physician, 1973. Contbr. numerous articles in field to profl. jours. Home: 2916 Ellicott Terrace NW Washington DC 20008 Office: 730 24th St NW Washington DC 20037 also 9401 Indian Head Hwy Oxon Hill MD 20022

GORDON, FRANK HUGH, elec. engr.; b. Caddo, Tex., Aug. 6, 1925; s. Charlie Thomas and Florice (Houghton) G.; B.S. in Elec. Engring., Tex. A. and M. U., 1950; m. Helen Marie Harding, June 10, 1949; children—Renee Mignon, Craig Hugh. Elec. engr. Bovay Cons. Engrs., Houston, 1953-55; project engr. Ethyl Corp., Pasadena, Tex., 1955—. Instr. Houston Community Coll., 1971—. Served with AUS, 1943-46; ETO. Mem. I.E.E.E. Registered profl. engr., Tex. Mem. Tau Beta Pi. Mason. Home: 7735 Wilmerdean St Houston TX 77017 Office: PO Box 472 Pasadena TX 77501

GORDON, HAMILTON ADAIR, JR., assn. exec.; b. East Orange, N.J., Feb. 24, 1912; s. Hamilton Adair and Caroline (Cochrane) G.; student Newark Sch. Fine Arts, 1931-33, N.Y.U., 1934, C. of C. Insts., 1948-63; m. Margaret C. Morris, Mar. 3, 1938; children—Nancy Cora, Thomas Kipp, Jane Adair. With Catlin-Farish Co., Inc., N.Y.C., 1932-33; bus. mgr. Crow Rock Ranch, Miles City, Mont., 1934-47; exec. v.p. Miles City C. of C., 1948-56; owner, operator motel, Ocala, Fla., 1957-60; exec. v.p. Putnam County C. of C., Palatka, Fla., 1961—. Mem. Mont. Gov.'s State Land Com., 1944-45. Bd. dirs. Rocky Mountain Isnt., 1955-56. Mem. Am., Fla. (dir.) C. of C. execs., Fla. Crown Council of Chambers Commerce (past pres.). Elk. Home: 123 Crestwood Av Palatka FL 32077 Office: Box 550 Palatka FL 32077

GORDON, HUGH WESCOTT, JR., constrn. co. exec.; b. Houston, Sept. 25, 1926; s. Hugh Wescott and Hattie Florence (Tate) G.; student Rice U., 1943-44; B.B.A., U. Tex., 1948; m. Ann Holmes Gordon, Oct. 7, 1956; children—Michael Wescott, William Edward, Raleigh Ann. With Brown & Root, Inc., Houston, 1951—, exec. v.p., 1971—, also dir.; v.p., dir. Brown & Root subsidiary cos.; v.p., dir. Jackson Marine Co., Taylor Diving & Salvage Co., Locher Constrn. Co. Served with USNR, 1944-46. Mem. Kappa Alpha. Clubs: Petroleum, Racquet, Houston Country (Houston). Home: 930 Briar Ridge Rd Houston TX 77027 Office: PO Box 3 Houston TX 77001

GORDON, M. MICHAEL, judge; b. San Francisco, Dec. 21, 1911; s. Rudolph and Sarah (Mesinger) G.; B.A., St. Ignatius Coll., 1931; LL.B., U. San Francisco, 1935. Admitted to Tex. bar, 1935, since practiced in Houston; now mem. firm M. Michael Gordon; judge Houston Municipal Ct., 1962—; dir., gen. counsel Sterling Electronics, Inc., Houston. Founder, Teenage Jury System, 1964, judge, 1964—. Pres. Juvenile Delinquency and Crime Commn., Houston 1958-59. Mem. bd. Houston Bd. Pub. Welfare, 1948-56; Bd. dirs. Am. Acad. Jud. Edn., 1970—, Nat. Center for State Cts., 1971—. Served to capt., USAAF, 1942-46. Recipient Disneyland trophy for achievement in reducing juvenile delinquency in U.S. and Can., Nat. Assn. Municipal Judges, 1965. Mem. N.Am. Judges Assn. (gov. 1965—, treas. 1965-66, pres. 1969-70), Am., Houston bar assns., State Bar Tex. Am. Judicature Soc. (dir. 1969-70, Centennial jud. award 1972), Am. Acad. Jud. Edn. (pres. 1972—) Mason (Shriner). Home: 2014 Southgate Houston TX 77025 Office: 5017 Fanin St Houston TX 77004

GORDON, MARSHALL, educator; b. Paducah, Ky., Sept. 1, 1937; s. Ollie J. and Dora Ellen (Everett) G.; B.A., Murray State U., 1959; Ph.D., Vanderbilt U., 1963; m. Annette Waters, Mar. 17, 1962; 1 dau., Mary Ann. Prof. chemistry Murray (Ky.) State U., 1963—. Mem. zoning bd. City of Murray, 1972—. Mem. Internat. Assn. Water Pollution Research, Am. Chem. Soc., Sigma Xi. Contbr. articles to profl. jours. Home: 1310 Doran Rd Murray KY 42071

GORDON, RICHARD F., JR., profl. football club exec., former astronaut; b. Seattle, Oct. 5, 1929; s. Richard F. and Angela Gordon; B.S. in Chemistry, U. Wash., 1951; postgrad. U.S. Naval Post Grad Sch., Monterey; m. Barbara Jean Field; children—Carleen Elizabeth, Richard F. III, Lawrence Joseph, Thomas Alan, James Edward, Diane Marie. Entered U.S. Navy, 1951, advanced through grades to capt., grad. All-Weather Flight Sch., Test Pilot Sch.; astronaut NASA Manned Spacecraft Center, Houston; pilot Gemini XI, 1966; command module pilot Apollo XII, 1969; ret., 1972; exec. v.p. New Orleans Saints Profl. Football Club, 1972—. Winner Bendix Trophy Race from Los Angeles to N.Y., 1961. Mem. Soc. Exptl. Test Pilots. Office: 944 St Charles Av New Orleans LA 70130

GORDON, ROBERT WILLARD, banker; b. Rochester, N.Y., Oct. 1, 1916; s. Nicholas and Evelyn (Lazarus) Gordon; A.B., Harvard, 1938; m. June Elaine Mailman, June 17, 1945; children—Spencer Bruce, Jonathan Richard, Jill Mia. Free lance radio and mag. writer, 1938-42; pres. Robert Gordon Co., Ltd., Montreal, Can., 1946-52; pres. Miramar Corp., real estate devel., Hollywood, Fla., 1952-60; sr. v.p. Barnett Bank of Hollywood, 1960—, also dir. Mem. Hollywood Planning Bd., 1962-64; pres. Mental Health Assn. Broward County, 1963-68; Jewish Welfare Fedn., 1969-70; mem. planning bd. S. Broward Hosp. Dist., 1971-72. Mayor, City of Miramar, Fla., 1955-59. Bd. dirs United Fund Broward County, 1965-67. Served with AUS, 1942-46. Mem. Jewish Religion. Clubs: Harvard (Boston) (Broward County, Fla.); Ocean Reef Yacht (Key Largo, Fla.), Hollywood Yacht. Writer and dir. scripts on network radio, 1939-41. Contbr. articles and short stories Saturday Evening Post, 1936-45. Home: 800 Washington St Hollywood FL 33020 Office: 1900 Tyler St Hollywood FL 33022

GORDON, RONALD NOLAN, data processor; b. Waterville, Kan., Dec. 5, 1935; s. Foster A. and Florence Hazel (Hull) G.; B.S., U. Ky., 1957. Teaching fellow U. Ky., Lexington, 1957-59; programmer Ky. Dept. Hwys., Frankfort, 1958-59; mathematician Nat. Security Agy., Washington, 1962-66; mgr. computer center Scope Electronics, Inc., Reston, Va., 1966-73; system programmer, analyst Dimension, Inc., Reston, 1973—. Served with AUS, 1959-62. Mem. Assn. for Computing Machinery, Am. Recorder Soc. Home: 11627 Vantage Hill Reston VA 22090 Office: 1860 Michael Faraday Dr Reston VA 22090

GORDON, RONNIE DREW, chemist; b. Waxahachie, Tex., Sept. 25, 1941; s. John Daniel and Myrtle Louise (Gee) G.; B.S., U. Tex., 1963, Ph.D. (Robert E. Welch fellow), 1968; m. Mary Virginia Allerton, Dec. 18, 1965; children—Christopher Mead, Eric Daniel. Sr. research scientist Continental Oil Co., Ponca City, Okla., 1968-71; research chemist Lone Star Gas Co., Dallas, 1971—. Mem. Am. Chem. Soc., Am. Inst. Chem. Engrs., A.A.A.S. Patentee in field. Home: 906 Redwood Dr Richardson TX 75080 Office: 301 S Harwood Dallas TX 75201

GORDON, ROY IRVING, govt. ofcl.; b. Peekskill, N.Y., Jan. 7, 1921; s. Samuel and Leah (Blaine) G.; B.A., L.I. U., 1941; M.A., N.Y. U., 1942; m. Ethel J. Shonet, Aug. 26, 1951; children—Frederick E., Elizabeth J. Reporter, suburban news editor, columnist Ossining (N.Y.) Citizen Register, 1947-50; religious news, ednl. news editor Mt. Vernon (N.Y.), Daily Argus, 1950-53; editor Fall River (Mass.) Transcript, 1953-54; news bur. chief Yankee Mut. Radio Sta. WALE, Fall River, Mass., 1954-55; copy editor N.Y. World Telegram and Sun, 1955-57; with Pub. Affairs office C.E., U.S. Army, Washington, 1958—, asst. for policies, 1961—. Prof. journalism U. Md., part-time, 1966—; adj. prof. Journalism Georgetown U., Washington, 1970—. Vice pres. Alexandria Council P.T.A., 1966-69; sec. Govt. Information Orgn., 1970-71. Served to lt. col. AUS, 1942-45, 60-62. Decorated Bronze Star, Silver Star, Purple Heart. Mem. Pub. Relations Soc. Am., Assn. Edn. Journalism. Clubs: Nat. Press; Tantallon Country; Tantallon Yacht; Nat. Potomac Yacht. Contbr. articles, stories to mags. Home: 601 Prospect Pl Alexandria VA 22304 Office: Forrestal Bldg Army Corps Engrs Washington DC 20314

GORDON, THOMAS CHRISTIAN, JR., lawyer; b. Richmond, Va., July 14, 1915; s. Thomas Christian and Ruth (Robins) G.; grad. Episcopal High Sch., Alexandria, Va., 1932; B.S., U. Va., 1936, LL.B., 1938. Admitted to Va. bar, 1937; asso. firm Parrish, Butcher & Parrish, Richmond, 1938-40; asso. firm McGuire, Woods & Battle and predecessor, Richmond, 1940-48, partner, 1949-65, 72—, asso. justice Supreme Ct. Va., Richmond, 1965-72. Lectr., U. Va. Law Sch. Trustee, mem. exec. com. Crippled Children's Hosp., 1948—, pres., 1954-59. Served from pvt. to maj., AUS, 1941-45. Decorated Bronze Star with oak leaf cluster. Fellow Am. Bar Found.; mem. Am., Va. State (pres. 1963-64), Richmond bar assns., Am. Law Inst., Va. State Bar. Episcopalian (vestryman). Contbr. articles to law revs. Home: 300 W Franklin St Richmond VA 23220 Office: 1400 Ross Bldg Richmond VA 23219

GORDON, THOMAS EDWIN, JR., dentist; b. Orlando, Fla., Sept. 12, 1925; s. Thomas Edwin and Lillian (Stover) G.; D.D.S., Emory U., 1948; m. Jeanne Love, Nov. 19, 1949; children—Tina Lynne, Thomas Gary, Karen Anne. Pvt. practice dentistry Decatur, Ga., 1948-50, Orlando, Fla., 1951-53, 1955—; cons. dentistry in space; attending staff Orange Meml. Hosp., chief laser lab. Bd. dirs. Orange County unit Am. Cancer Soc; trustee Central Fla. Mus. and Planetarium, sec. bd. trustees, 1960-61, chmn. finance com., 1963—; trustee Constantine Found. Served from 1st lt. to capt. USAF, 1953-55. Fellow Royal Soc. Health; mem. Internat. Soc. Dental Research, Am. Dental Assn., Am. Acad. Implant Dentistry, Soc. Occlusion and Oral Physiology, Am. Acad. Maxillo Facial Prosthesis, Sigma Xi (hon.), Sigma Chi. Author articles publ. profl. jours. Research laser in dentistry and med. research; developer 1st laser welding system and technique for dentistry. Home: 1410 N Westmoreland Dr Orlando FL 32804 Office: 550 N Bumby Av Orlando FL 32803

GORDON, WILLIAM HYATT, JR., neurologist, educator; b. Balt., Dec. 2, 1934; s. William Hyatt and Cornelia (Burford) G.; B.A., Rice U., 1956; J.D., U. Tex., 1959; M.D., Baylor U., 1963; m. Simone Zaniowka, Mar. 2, 1967; children—William Hyatt III, David Charles. Intern, Vanderbilt Hosp., Nashville, 1963-64; resident Neurol. Inst. N.Y., N.Y.C., 1964-67; asst. in neurology Columbia Coll. Phys. and Surgs., 1968-69; instr. neurology Baylor Coll. Medicine, Houston, 1969-70, asst. prof. neurology, 1970-71; practice medicine, specializing in neurology, Lubbock, Tex., 1971—; clin. prof., chmn. depts. neurology and forensic medicine Tex. Technol. U. Sch. Medicine, 1972—. Served to lt. comdr. USNR, 1967-69. Mem. Am. Acad. Neurology, A.M.A., Tex., Lubbock-Crosby-Garza med. assns., Tex. Bar Assn., Muscular Dystrophy Assn. Am. (South Plains chpt.), Lubbock County Assn. Mental Health, Multiple Sclerosis Assn. (South Plains chpt.). Rotarian. Home: 4607 16th St Lubbock TX 79410 Office: 3801 19th St Lubbock TX 79410

GORE, BUDD, publishing co. exec.; b. La Grange, Ill., July 1, 1913; s. Edward Everett and Amanda (Burgdorff) G.; student U. Chgo., 1932-33; Aero. U., Chgo., 1940-41; m. Margaret Ellen Masterson, Apr. 22, 1938; children—James, Judith, Cary, Ann. Pub., La Grange Messenger, 1933-34; police reporter City News Bur. of Chgo., 1934-35; sale promotion mgr. Chgo. Daily News, 1935-39; mgr. out-of-town promotion, sign bur. direct mail bur., asst. to advt. mgr. Marshall Field & Co., Chgo., 1939-43, asst. to sales promotion mgr., 1945-46, advt. mgr., 1947-52; chief adminstrv. officer Metall. lab. Manhattan Project, U. Chgo., 1943-45; sales promotion mgr. H & S Pogue Co., Cin., 1946-47; owner Budd Gore & Co., Chgo., 1952-53; asst. to exec. editor, Chgo. Sun-Times, 1953-54; publicity dir. Halle Bros. Co., Cleve., 1954-56; retail advt. mgr., advt. mgr., asst. to gen. mgr. Chgo. Daily News, 1956-61; sales promotion and pub. relations mgr. L.S. Ayres & Co., Indpls., 1961-64; v.p., sales promotion mgr. Halle Bros. Co., Cleve., 1964-65; v.p. Ralf Shockey & Assos., N.Y.C., 1965-66; v.p. marketing Finance Mag., N.Y.C., 1966-67; v.p., mgr. sales promotion div. Nat. Retail Mchts. Assn., N.Y.C., 1968-69; pres. Budd Gore & Co., Scarsdale, N.Y., 1969-73, Gainesville, Ga., 1973—; dir. marketing Times Pub. Co., Gainesville, 1973—. Co-founder, Retail Advt. Conf., Chgo., 1952, co-dir., 1952-65; pub. relations counsel A.R.C., 1958—. Nat. chmn. U. Chgo. Alumni Found., 1959-61. Recipient citation U.S. sec. of war, 1946. Mem. Nat. Retail Mchts. Assn. Author: The Name of the Game is Sell, 1968; How to Sell the Whole Store as Fashion, 1969. Contbr. articles to trade mags. Mng. editor radio and TV advt. edits. Retail Broadcaster Newsletters, 1969-74; editor, pub. Retail Marketing Newsletter, 1971—, Newspaper Advertising Newsletter, 1972—, Pure Gore Newsletter, 1973—. Home: 639 Crestview Terrace Gainesville GA 30501 Office: 345 Green St PO Box 838 Gainesville GA 30501

GORE, CHARLES MINOR, lawyer; b. Johnson City, Tenn., Oct. 26, 1910; s. Benjamin Stone and Helen (Hayward) G.; A.B., Venderbilt U., 1933; postgrad. Harvard Law Sch., 1933-34; LL.B., U. Tenn., 1936; m. Mildred Anne Smith, June 20, 1937; children—Charles Smith, Anne Hayward. Admitted to Tenn. bar, 1936; mem. firm Gore & Gore, Bristol, Tenn., 1937-54, 63-65, Gore, Gore & McIntyre, Bristol, 1954-63, Gore, Gore and Ladd, Bristol, 1965-68, Gore, Ladd and Gillenwater, Bristol, 1968—. Asst. sec., dir. Appalachian Broadcasting Corp., WCYB-TV, 1946—; sec., dir. Strong-Robinette Bag Co., Inc., 1953—; dir. Gen. Shale Products Corp., Johnson City. Mem. Tenn. Democratic exec. com., 1970—. Bd. dirs. United Fund., 1957-59. Served from lt. (j.g.) to lt., USNR, 1943-46. Mem. Am., Tenn., Bristol bar assns., Jud. Conf. Sixth Dist. (life). Presbyn. Democrat. Home: 101 Lick Branch Rd Bristol TN 37620 Office: Central Bldg Bristol TN 37620

GORGES, HEINZ AUGUST, research engr.; b. Stettin, Germany, July, 22, 1913; s. Gustav and Marga (Benda) G.; M.E., Tech. U. Dresden (Germany), 1938; Ph.D., Tech. U. Hannover, Germany, 1946; m. Sapienza Teresa Coco, Sept. 2, 1957. Came to U.S., 1959. Group leader LFA Aero Research Establishment, Braunschweig, Germany, 1940-45; with Royal Aircraft Establishment, Farnborough, Eng. 1946-49; prin. sci. officer Weapons Research Establishment, Adelaide, South Australia, 1949-59; sci. asst. George C. Marshall Space Flight Center, NASA, Huntsville, Ala., 1959-61; dir. advanced projects Cook Technol Center, Morton Grove, Ill., 1961-62; scientific adviser Ill. Inst. Tech. Research Inst., Chgo., 1962-66; prin. scientist, dir. research Tracor, Inc., Austin, Tex., 1966—, asst. v.p. Environmental and Phys. Scis. div., 1970-72, v.p. Tracor-Jitco, Rockville, Md., 1972—. Prof. Redstone extension U. Ala., 1960. Registered profl. engr., D.C. Fellow Am. Inst. Aeros. and Astronautics (asso.); mem. Am. Geophys. Union, Am. Soc. M.E., Acoustical Soc. Am. Research on thermodynamics, indsl. engring., resource mgmt., system engring. and analysis. Home: 3705 Sleepy Hollow Rd Falls Church VA 22041 Office: 1300 E Gude Dr Rockville MD 20851

GORMAN, ARTHUR PAUL, constrn. co. exec.; b. Bartlesville, Okla., Feb. 23, 1930; s. Charles Rankin and Etta Sue (Simpson) G.; B.S., U. Okla., 1954; postgrad. U. Tulsa, 1957-58; m. Carolyn Krizer, Aug. 4, 1967; children—Thomas Arhtur, John Simpson. With Gorman Constrn. Co., Bartlesville, Okla., 1957—, owner, mgr., 1967—. Served with C.E., AUS, 1955-57. Mem. Nat. Assn. Home Builders (nat. dir. 1964—), Nat. Real Estate Bds. Assn., Okla. State Home Builders Assn. (pres. 1973—), Okla. Soc. Profl. Engrs., U.S., Bartlesville chambers of commerce, Phi Delta Theta. Club: Hillcrest Country (Bartlesville). Home: 1720 Cherokee Place Bartlesville OK 74003 Office: PO Drawer C Bartlesville OK 74003

GORMAN, (MIKE) THOMAS FRANCIS, reporter, writer; b. N.Y.C., Dec. 7, 1913; s. Frank and Mary (Naughton) G.; A.B., N.Y.U., 1934, postgrad. 1934-36; m. Ernestine Brown, June 3, 1946 (dec. June 1958); children—Michael, Patricia. Advt., free-lance writer, 1936-41; reporter, cover gen. med. run Daily Oklahoman, 1945; writer numerous news stories and editorials in mental hosp. campaign; pioneered in establishment mental hygiene clin. in Okla., also mental hygiene orgn.; chief writer, dir. pub. hearings President's Commn. on Health Needs of Nation, 1950-53; exec. dir. Nat. Com. Against Mental Illness, Washington, 1953—. Mem. Menninger Found. Nat. Com. Mental Hygiene; exec. bd. Okla. Com. Mental Hygiene. Served with USAAF, 1942-45. Recipient spl. Lasker award 10 outstanding young men U.S. Jr. C. of C., 1949; Edward A. Strecker Meml. medal, 1962, William C. Menninger Meml. medal, 1971. Fellow Am. Pub. Health Assn., Am. Psychiat. Assn. (hon.), Royal Soc. Health (Eng.), N.Y. Acad. Scis.; mem. Nature Conservancy, Phi Beta Kappa. Clubs: Federal City, City Tavern, Nat. Press (Washington). Author: Oklahoma Attacks its Snake Pits, 1948; Every Other Bed, 1956; co-author Impressions of Soviet Psychiatry, 1969. Contbr. articles on psychiat. subjects to mags. Home: 1230 30th St NW Washington DC 20007 Office: 1101 17th St NW Washington DC 20036

GORMAN, WILLIAM DONALD, systems analyst; b. Italy, Tex., Dec. 20, 1934; s. Elliott Owen and Kathryn Falsom (Wolverton) G.; B.S., U. Tex., 1958; M.S., So. Meth. U., 1962; Ph.D., Tex. A. and M. U., 1969; m. Carolyn Porter, Jan. 25, 1958; children—John William, James Eric, Michael Elliott. Electronics engr. Temco, Dallas, 1958-60; instr. elec. engring., mem. grad. faculty So. Meth. U., 1960-65; instr. elec. engring. Tex. A. and M. U., 1965-69; systems analyst Tex. Instruments, Inc., Dallas, 1969—. Cons. Southwestern Med. Sch., Dallas Eye Found. Mem. Goals for Austin Assembly; election judge, 1973. Served with USNR, 1953-54. Mem. I.E.E.E., Sigma Tau, Eta Kappa Nu. Methodist (trustee, mem. adminstrv. bd.) Home: 9206 Collinfield St Austin TX 78758 Office: Tex Instruments Inc Dallas TX 75222

GORODETZKY, CHARLES WILLIAM, physician; b. Boston, May 31, 1937; s. Saul and Rose (Leavit) G.; B.S., Mass. Inst. Tech., 1958; M.D., Boston U., 1962; postgrad. U. Ky., 1965-68; m. Barbara Labovich, June 18, 1961; children—Amy Lynne, Mark Steven, David Barry, Theodore Alan. Intern, Boston City Hosp., 1962-63; commd. sr. asst. surgeon USPHS, 1963, advanced through grades to sr. surgeon, 1969; med. officer Addiction Research Center, Nat. Inst. Mental Health, Lexington, Ky., 1963-65, 68, chief sect. on drug metabolism and kinetics, 1969—. Mem. adj. vol. faculty dept. pharmacology U. Ky. Sch. Medicine, 1966-71; cons. on drug abuse Fayette County (Ky.) Pub. Schs., 1971—; mem. adv. com. on drug detection spl. action Office of Drug Abuse Prevention, Washington, 1972—. Bd. dirs. Jewish Community Assn. Central Ky., 1969—, pres. 1971—. Mem. A.A.A.S., A.M.A., Am. Soc. Pharmacology and Exptl. Therapeutics, Am. Soc. Clin. Pharmacology and Therapeutics, N.Y. Acad. Scis., Soc. Neurosci., Sigma Xi. Republican. Jewish religion (trustee 1971—, sec. 1973—). Author: (with S.T. Christian) What You Should Know About Drugs, 1970. Contbr. articles to profl. jours.

Home: 3418 Brookhaven Dr Lexington KY 40502 Office: PO Box 2000 Lexington KY 40507

GORRELL, FRANK C., lawyer, state senator; b. Russellville, Ky., June 20, 1927; s. Lilburn and Mrs. G.; A.B., Vanderbilt U., 1949, LL.B., 1952; m. Bette Jamison; children—Frank C. III, Jamison Richter. Admitted to Tenn. bar 1952, since practiced in Nashville; former mem. Tenn. senate, former speaker; lt. gov. State of Tenn., 1967-71. Mem. Tenn. council Boy Scouts Am.; chmn. Tenn. Cancer Crusade, 1967-69. Trustee Aquinas Jr. Coll.; bd. dirs. YMCA, Muscular Dystrophy Assn. Mem. Am., Tenn., Nashville (dir.) bar assns., Am. Judicature Soc., Nat. Conf. Lt. Govs. (exec. com.), Nat. Soc. State Legislators (dir.), Vanderbilt Alumni Assn. (dir.). Elk. Clubs: Nashville Vanderbilt; Woodmont School Men's (dir.). Office: State Capitol Bldg Nashville TN 37219

GORSLINE, GEORGE WILLIAM, educator; b. Battle Creek, Mich., Dec. 19, 1923; s. James M. and Lora (Gates) G.; B.S., Va. Poly. Inst., 1948; M.S., Pa. State Coll., 1957, Ph.D., 1959; m. Anne Bonner, Aug. 9, 1947; children—George William, Gary B., Cynthia Suzanne. County extension agt. Pa. State U., University Park, 1948-56, instr., asst. prof. agronomy, 1956-65, customer cons. Computation Center, 1963-65; dir. Computer Center, U. Ohio, Athens, 1965-67; faculty Va. Poly. Inst., Blacksburg, 1967—, prof. computer sci., 1969—, head computer sci. dept., 1967-72. Served with AUS, 1943-45. AEC grantee 1961-64, NSF grantee, 1965-67, State of Va. grantee, 1969—. Fellow A.A.A.S.; mem. Am. Assn. U. Profs. (chpt. pres. 1973—), Assn. for Computing Machinery, Crop Sci. Soc. Am., Am. Soc. Agronomy, Sigma Xi, Gamma Sigma Delta. Contbr. articles to profl. jours. Home: 624 Watson Blacksburg VA 24060

GORTNER, WILLARD AUSTIN, stock broker; b. Morris, Ill., Jan. 25, 1926; s. Peter Franklin and Emma Rachel (Ream) G.; B.S. in Bus. Adminstrn., Northwestern U., 1950; m. Satie Elizabeth Broyhill, Oct. 12, 1968; children—Terri Leigh, Harvey Franklin; stepchildren—Jan E., Kenneth M., Michael H., Robert B. Investigator, Retail Credit Co., St. Petersburg, Fla., 1950-51; spl. agt. FBI, 1951-53; owner, mgr. Gortner Ford & Mercury Sales, Inc., Keyser, W.Va., 1954-60; broker A.G. Edwards & Sons, St. Petersburg, Fla., 1961-62; v.p. Harris, Upham & Co., Inc., St. Petersburg, 1963—. Chmn. Mineral County (W.Va.) United Fund, 1958. Bd. dirs., treas. St. Petersburg Symphony, 1961-68; bd. dirs. Potomac Valley council Boy Scouts Am., 1954-58; trustee, chmn. investment com. Eckerd Coll.; trustee Tusculum Coll., Greenville, Tenn. Served with AUS, 1944-46. Presbyn. (chmn. trustees 1966-70). Mason (Shriner). Clubs: Yacht, Lakewood Country (St. Petersburg); Commerce (Pinellas County, Fla.). Home: 500 Bluff View Dr Belleair Bluffs FL 33540 Office: 6666 22d Av N St Petersburg FL 33710

GORTON, FRANK HENRY, banker; b. Alameda, Cal., Apr. 27, 1926; s. Ralph Lindley and Ursa Dorthea (Prindle) G.; student Am. Inst. Banking, 1958-63, Sch. Banking, So. Methodist U., 1963. File clk., bookkeeper First Nat. Bank, Brownfield, Tex., 1949-50, proof clk., 1951-52, teller, 1953, asst. cashier, 1953-59, cashier, 1960-66, v.p., cashier, 1967—, auditor, security officer, 1968—. Unit treas. South Plains council Boy Scouts Am., 1954; treas. Terry County (Tex.) Cancer Soc., 1954; treas. Terry County United Fund, 1965, 70-72, v.p., 1966-67. Precinct chmn. Terry County Republican Party, 1970-74. Bd. dirs. Terry County March of Dimes. Recipient numerous awards. Mem. Terry County Tb. Assn. (dir. 1960), Brownfield Jr. C. of C. (sec.-treas. 1958-59, pres. 1960-61, Distinguished Service award 1960, Jaycees of Month award 1960), Brownfield Optimist Club (sec. 1966-67, pres. 1967-68, Achievement award, 1967), Brownfield Credit Mgrs. Club (pres. 1961-62), Terry County Young Farmers (Distinguished Service award, 1966), Bank Adminstrn. Inst. Presbyn. (elder, Sunday sch. supt., jr. class tchr., sec. Sunday sch., bd. Christian edn.) Home: 320 E Hill St Brownfield TX 79316 Office: Box 1067 Brownfield TX 79316

GOSHEN, CHARLES ERNEST, med. educator; b. Altoona, Pa., Sept. 2, 1916; s. Charles W. and Pearl (Rice) G.; A.B., Columbia Coll., 1938, M.D., 1942; m. Patricia McGuire, Sept. 22, 1940; children—C. Robert, Anne (Mrs. Bruce Hubbard). Intern, Boston City Hosp., 1942-43; resident, Mitchell Field A.F. Hosp., 1943-44, Bronx V.A. Hosp., 1946-48; dir. Nassau (N.Y.) Neuropsychiatric Service, 1948-57; research dir. Am. Psychiatric Assn., Hempstead, N.Y., 1957-59; profl. asso. Nat. Research Council, Washington, 1959-61; asso. prof. psychiatry U. W.Va., Morgantown, 1961-67; faculty Vanderbilt U., Nashville, 1967—, prof. psychiatry, prof. mgmt., 1971—. Treas., Houseboat Corp. Am., 1971—. Field rep. Joint Commn. on Accrediation of Hospitals, Chgo., 1972—. Served to capt. M.C., AUS, 1943-46. Diplomate Am. Bd. Psychiatry. Fellow Am. Psychiatric Assn.; mem. Am. Acad. Mgmt., Am. Soc. Engring. Edn., Sigma Chi. Author: Drinks, Drugs and Do-Gooders, 1972; Language of Mental Health, 1972; Society of Youthful Offenders, 1973. Home: 6029 Ashland Dr Nashville TN 37215 Office: Station B Box 1729 Vanderbilt University Nashville TN 37203

GOSHORN, DONALD HANAFORD, clergyman; b. Charleston, W. Va., Mar. 8, 1911; s. Donald W. and Lucy (Hansford) G.; student U. Mich., 1930-31, Hampton-Sydney Coll., 1931-32, 36; B.A., So. Meth. U., 1938; M.Div., Union Theol. Sem. (Va.), 1941, postgrad. (Tower scholar), 1960; m. Jane Larus Reed, Nov. 8, 1941; children—Jane (Mrs. Cyrus Arthur Smith), Donald Hansford. Ordained to ministry Presbyn. Ch., 1941; pastor, Kenova, W.Va., 1946-48, Westminster, Charleston, W. Va., 1948-53, Byrd, Hebron, Goochland, Va., 1956-60; pastor Holmes Presbyn. Ch., Cheriton, Va., 1960—. Served as chaplain USCGR, USNR, 1942-46. Rotarian. Contbr. articles to profl. jours. Address: PO Box 225 Cherrystone Rd Cheriton VA 23316

GOSNELL, AUBREY BREWER, chemist, educator; b. Provo, Ark., Sept. 1, 1929; s. Leffel Aubrey and Ivah Kitty (McWhorter) G.; student Ouachita Bapt. Coll., 1947-48; B.S., Henderson State Coll., 1951; M.S., U. Ark., 1962; postgrad. Duke, 1962-63; Ph.D., N.C. State U., 1967; m. Tommy Sue Parsons, Sept. 4, 1948; children—Charles, Steven, Paul. High sch. tchr., Mansfield, Ark., 1949-51; lab. tester Am. Oil Co., El Dorado, Ark., 1951-57, refinery operator, 1957-60; research chemist Research Triangle Inst., Durham, N.C., 1962-67; prof. chemistry Henderson State Coll., Arkadelphia, Ark., 1967—. Active HSC-Clark Community Drug Analysis Program, 1972-73. Recipient Ann. Research grant Henderson State Coll., 1969—. Mem. Am. Chem. Soc. (sec.-treas., chmn. elect, Ark. regional rep. polymer div.), Am. Inst. Chemists, Sigma Xi. Democrat. Mem. Ch. of Christ (elder). Contbr. articles to profl. jours. Home: 2075 Elaine Circle Arkadelphia AR 71923

GOSNELL, HAROLD CORNELIUS, clergyman; b. Syracuse, N.Y., July 17, 1908; s. Cornelius Parsons and Carrie (Fawcett) G.; B.A., Syracuse U., 1930; B.D., Episcopal Theol. Sch., Cambridge, Mass., 1930-33; D.D., U. of South, 1956; m. Marjorie O. Adams, Aug. 29, 1932; children—Judith (Mrs. James M. Cavender III), Harold Cornelius. Ordained to ministry Episcopal Ch., 1933; rector St. John's Ch., Marcellus, N.Y., 1933-36, All Saints Ch., Fulton, N.Y., 1936-38, Holy Trinity Ch., Lincoln, Neb., 1938-48, St. Mark's Ch., San Antonio, 1948-68; consecrated bishop coadjutor Diocese W. Tex., 1968; bishop of West Tex., 1968—. Mem. exec. bd., trustee Diocese of West Tex.; mem. Nat. Commn. Ch. in Human Affairs; mem. Armed Forces Commn. Episcopal Ch.; mem. bd. Gen. Commn. on Chaplains and Armed Forces Personnel; dep. Episcopal Gen. convs., 1940, 43, 46, 49, 52, 55, 58, 61, 64, 67; mem. exec. council Episcopal Ch., 1970—. Pres. Allied Children's Services, 1958-64, San Antonio Council of Chs., 1963-64. Bd. dirs. United Fund (pres. 1962-63), Community Chest, also Good Govt. League, 1952— (all San Antonio); trustee St. Mary's Hall, San Antonio; regent U. South, Sewanee, Tenn. Served with USNR, 1943-46; ret. capt. Reserve. Mem. Psi Upsilon. Mason (33 deg., Shriner), Rotarian (past pres. San Antonio). Club: Oak Hills Country (San Antonio). Home: 342 E Terra Alta San Antonio TX 78209 Office: 111 Torcido Dr San Antonio TX 78209

GOSWICK, CARL RAYMOND, JR., computer co. exec.; b. nr. Wilkesboro, N.C., May 23, 1939; s. Carl Raymond and Katherine (McNeill) G.; B.S. in Elec. Engring. N.C. State U., 1961; m. Gretchen Eleanor Mehulka, Dec. 22, 1964; children—Daniel Alan, Julia Alanne. Supr./systems programmer McDonnell Douglas Co., Huntington Beach, Cal., 1961-69; systems programming mgr. PRC Computer Center Inc., McLean, Va., 1969—. Cons. computer scis. dept. U. Cal. at Los Angeles, 1967-69. Office: 7670 Old Springhouse Rd McLean VA 22101

GOTAUTAS, VITO ADOLPH, cons. geologist; b. Chgo., Dec. 6, 1928; s. John Dominic and Anele (Markevich) G.; A.B., Miami U., 1950; M.S., 1951; postgrad. Yale U., 1955-56; m. Mary Jane Dean, Oct. 4, 1952; children—Jane, Patricia, Anita. Exploration geologist Atlantic Refining Co., Lake Charles and Lafayette La., 1956-61; v.p., exploration mgr., Century Mineral Corp., 1961-63; independent cons. geologist, 1963—. Served with USNR, 1951-55. ETO. Certified profl. geologist. Mem. Am. Assn. Petroleum Geologists, Am. Inst. Mining Engrs., Soc. Exploration Geophysicists, Am. Inst. Profl. Geologists (nat. membership chmn. 1969-71, pres. La. sect. 1965, nat. sec.-treas. 1973), Soc. Econ. Mineralogists and Paleontologists, Am. Assn. Profl. Well Log Analysts, Lafayette Geol. Soc. (past sec.), Houston Geol. Soc., Lafayette Geophysical Soc., Sigma Xi, Sigma Gamma Epsilon. Clubs: Toastmasters (pres. 1971), Civitan of Lafayette (charter pres. 1959-60, gov. La. dist. 1964), Lafayette Chess (pres. 1967). Petroleum of Lafayette; Oakbourne Country. Contbr. articles in field to profl. jours. Home: 133 Maurice Lafayette LA 70501 Office: PO Box 51788 OCS Lafayette LA 70501

GOTHARD, NICHOLAS, air pollution control exec.; b. Pecs, Hungary, Dec. 12, 1933 (came to U.S. 1960, naturalized 1966); s. Jozsef and Margit (Schweiczer) G.; Elec. Engr., Budapest Tech. U., 1956; M.S., Mass. Inst. Tech., 1962; Ph.D. (NASA fellow), Cornell U., 1965; m. Julianna Erdesz, Dec. 21, 1957; children—Anita, Monica. With RCA Victor Co. Ltd., Montreal, Que., Can., 1958-60; research asst. Mass. Inst. Tech., Cambridge, 1960-62; research cons., 1962-63; asst. prof. Pa. State U., University Park, 1965-66; asst. prof. Tex. A. and M. U., College Station, 1967; co-founder Filtronics Corp., (name now Filteron Internat. Inc.) 1967, v.p., 1967-72; founder Gothard Industries Corp., Garland, Tex., 1972, owner, 1972—, also dir. Contbr. numerous articles to profl. jours. Patentee in field. Home: 4424 Ridge Rd Dallas TX 75221 Office: 333 Kirby St Garland TX 75042

GOTHIA, SISTER BLANCHE, media coordinator; b. Port Arthur, Tex., Oct. 27, 1930; d. Elton Joseph and Blanche (Landry) Gothia; B.A., Dominican Coll., 1960; M.L.S., Tex. Women's U., 1973. Joined Dominican Sisters, 1948; tchr. elementary, secondary schs., 1950-69; tchr. St. Anthony's Cathedral Sch., Beaumont, Tex., 1964-67, prin., 1965-67; audio-visual dir. St. Agnes Acad., Houston, 1967-69, media coordinator, 1969—. Mem. Am., Tex., Catholic (vice-chmn. unit 1973-75) library assns., Assn. Ednl. Communications and Tech. (co-chmn. Tex. legislative com. 1970—), Tex. Assn. Ednl. Tech., Am. Film Inst. Home and office: 9000 Bellaire Blvd Houston TX 77036

GOTT, CLYDE MORRIS, supt. schs.; b. Anahuac, Tex., Sept. 21, 1912; s. James William and Stella (Palmer) G.; B.S., S.W. Tex. State U., 1934; M.Ed., U. Tex., 1940, Ed.D., 1966; m. Louise Marie Kneuper, Jan. 23, 1937; 1 son, Carroll Deene. Athletic coach, tchr. Hull-Daisetta (Tex.) High Sch., 1934-38, Smithville (Tex.) High Sch., 1938-40; athletic coach, tchr. Burbank High Sch., San Antonio, 1940-41, asst. prin., 1942-52; supt. Smithville (Tex.) Ind. Sch. Dist., 1941-42; asst. prin. Thomas Jefferson High Sch., San Antonio, 1952-56, prin., 1956-60; prin. Thomas Jefferson High Sch., Port Arthur, Tex., 1960-66; supt. Port Arthur Ind. Sch. Dist., 1966—. Mem. Tex. Commn. on Sch. and Coll. Relations, 1965, Tex. Commn. on Sch. Accreditation, 1965. Pres. CavOilcade, Port Arthur, 1968-69; pres. YMCA, 1967. Mem. N.E.A., Am. Assn. Sch. Adminstrs., Tex. Assn. Sch. Adminstrs., Tex. Tchrs. Assn. (dist. chmn. 1957, 71-72), Tex. Congress Parents and Tchrs., Phi Delta Kappa (chpt. pres. 1966-67). Methodist (chmn. bd. stewards 1966-67, lay leader 1967-68). Mason (Shriner), Lion (pres. Part Arthur 1967). Home: 3049 Bryan Av Groves TX 77619 Office: 733 5th St Port Arthur TX 77640

GOTT, PORTER HASTINGS, oral surgeon; b. Akron, O., July 9, 1921; s. Philip Porter and Ethel (Hastings) G.; student Oberlin Coll., 1939-42; D.D.S., Georgetown U. Sch. Dentistry, 1945; postgrad. U. Pa. Grad. Sch. Medicine, 1946-47; m. Ernestine Hudson, July 21, 1945; children—Philip Hudson, Leslie Lorinda. Individual practice oral surgery, Washington, 1948-49, Ft. Lauderdale, Fla., 1949—. Served with USNR, 1944-46, 1951-52. Diplomate Am. Bd. Oral Surgery. Fellow Internat. Coll. Dentists; mem. Fla. Acad. Dental Practice Mgmt., Broward County Dental Assn. (pres. 1955-56), East Coast Dist. Dental Soc. (pres. 1967-68), Am. (del. 1970-71), Fla. (sec. 1960—) socs. oral surgeons, Fla. Dental Assn. Mason. Club: Tennis (Fort Lauderdale, Fla.). Home: 1711 Middle River Dr Fort Lauderdale FL 33305 Office: 906 NE 26th Av Fort Lauderdale FL 33304

GOTTEN, WILLIAM MONROE, lawyer; b. Memphis, June 9, 1942; s. Nicholas and Mary Meredith (Whitaker) G.; A.B., Washington and Lee U., 1965; J.D., Memphis State U., 1968; m. Camille Lane, July 16, 1966; 1 son, William Monroe. Admitted to Tenn. bar, 1968; asso. Nelson, Norvell, Wilson, McRae, Ivy & Farmer, Memphis, 1968-69; mem. firm Lane, Wages & Gotten, Memphis, 1969-72, Lane, Wages, Gotten & Lane, Memphis, 1972—. Mem. Am., Memphis, Shelby County bar assns., Bar Assn. Tenn., Am. Trial Lawyers Assn., Kappa Sigma, Phi Alpha Delta. Republican. Presbyn. Rotarian. Home: 6426 Kirby Oaks Dr Memphis TN 38138 Office: 850 Commerce Title Bldg Memphis TN 38103

GOTTLIEB, BERTRAM, research adminstr.; b. N.Y.C., Feb. 9, 1921; s. Samuel and Bessie (Halpern) G.; B.S., Ill. Inst. Tech., 1949, M.S., 1950; postgrad. U. Wis., 1950-54; m. Phyllis Virginia Jacobson, Mar. 24, 1940; children—Richard Allan, Deborah Ann, Lisa Susan. Instr. econs. Ill. Inst. Tech., 1948-50; instr. labor relations U. Wis., 1950-54, 56-57; research prof. assigned to U. Phillipines, U. Conn., 1954-56; indsl. engr. AFL-CIO, 1957-66, asst. dir. research, 1967-68; prof. bus. adminstrn., U. Ia., 1966-67; dir. research Transp. Inst., Washington, 1968—. Indsl. engring. cons., 1950-54, 56-57, 68—; labor arbitrator Fed. Mediation and Conciliation Service and Am. Arbitration Assn.; mem. tech. adv. bd. U.S. Dept. Commerce, 1967—; mem. adv. com. Dept. Labor, 1957—; mem. central com. to standardize indsl. engring. terminology Am. Nat. Standards Inst., 1964—; mem. maritime transp. research bd. Nat. Acad. Sci.; speaker, lectr. various univs., profl. socs., radio, tv. Served with USAAF, 1943-46. Fellow Am. Inst. Indsl. Engrs. (editorial bd. 1960, nat. dir. div. indsl. and labor relations 1968-70, chpt. dir. 1968—), A.A.A.S., Indsl. Relations Research Assn. (gov. 1966-68), Sigma Iota Epsilon. Contbr. articles to profl. jours., textbooks. Home: 703 Hillsboro Dr Silver Spring MD 20902 Office: 923 16th St NW Washington DC 20005

GOTTO, ANTONIO MARION, JR., med. educator; b. Nashville, Oct. 10, 1935; s. Antonio Marion and Reatha Gray (Hardison) G.; B.A., Vanderbilt U., 1957, M.D., 1965; Ph.D. (Rhodes scholar 1957-59, USPHS fellow 1959-61), U. Oxford, 1961; m. Anita Louise Safford, July 31, 1959; children—Jennifer Gwenyth, Gillian Elizabeth, Teresa Anne. Intern, Mass. Gen. Hosp., 1965-67; med. house officer Mass. Gen. Hosp., Boston, 1965-67; mem. staffs Meth. Hosp., VA Hosp., Ben Taub Hosp., Houston; chief, sect. on molecular structure Nat. Heart and Lung Inst., NIH, Bethesda, Md., 1969-71; prof. medicine and biochemistry, chief, div. atherosclerosis and lipoprotein research Baylor Coll. Medicine-Meth. Hosp., dir. Nat. Heart and Lung Inst., Lipid Research Clinic-Nat. Heart and Lung Inst. Specialized Center of Research in Arteriosclerosis, Baylor Coll. Medicine-Meth. Hosp., Houston, 1971—; scientific dir. Cardiovascular Research and Tng. Center, Baylor Coll. Medicine, 1973—. Cons. on hypolipodemic drugs U.S. Food and Drug Adminstrn., 1972—; chmn. adv. com. stroke center Baylor Coll. Medicine, 1972—; prin. investigator John A. Hartford Found. grant, 1971—. Mem. metabolism study sect. Pub. Adv. Panel, NIH, Houston, 1972—. Served as surgeon USPHS, 1967-69. Recipient Research scholarship Am. Cancer Soc., 1963-65; Albert Weinstein award for proficiency in internal medicine Vanderbilt U., 1965. Mem. Am. Soc. Clin. Investigation, Am. Soc. for Biol. Chemists, Am. Heart Assn. (dir. Houston chpt. 1973—), Biophys. Soc., Tex. Heart Assn., Sigma Xi, Phi Beta Kappa, Omicron Delta Kappa. Mem. Ch. of Christ (deacon 1973—). Club: Huntwick Bath and Racquet Assn. (Houston). Contbr. articles in field to profl. jours. Home: 5307 Westminster Court Houston TX 77069 Office: Baylor College of Medicine The Methodist Hospital 6515 Bertner Blvd B280 Houston TX 77025

GOTTSEGEN, JACK JACOB, govt. ofcl.; b. Bklyn., Mar. 4, 1907; s. Leopold and Rose (Moskovitz) G.; B.A., Amherst Coll., 1928; M.B.A., Harvard, 1930; Ph.D., Columbia, 1940; m. Annette Sherman, Aug. 19, 1937; 1 son, Daniel. Accountant, Klein, Hinds & Finke, N.Y.C., 1931-35; instr. Coll. City N.Y., 1931-41; chief chem. fuels and paper, price div. U.S. Bur. Statistics, Washington, 1941-47; chief chem. rubber and metallic products U.S. Bur. Census, Washington, 1947-58, chief, commodity and material data br., industry div., 1958-64; asst. to chief interindustry div. Bur. Econ. Analysis, U.S. Dept. Commerce, Washington, 1964—; cons. to Office of Minority Bus., 1970. Mem. Phi Beta Kappa, Beta Gamma Sigma. Home: 3001 Veazey Terrace NW Washington DC 20008 Office: Bur Econ Analysis 51 US Dept Commerce Washington DC 20233

GOUGE, SUSAN CORNELIA JONES (MRS. JOHN OSCAR GOUGE), microbiologist; b. Chgo., Apr. 18, 1924; d. Harry LeRoy and Gladys (Moon) Jones; student Am. U., Washington, 1942-43, La. Coll., 1944-45; B.S., George Washington U., 1948; postgrad. Georgetown U., 1966-70; m. John Oscar Gouge, Aug. 7, 1943; children—John Ronald, Richard Michael, Claudia Renee. Med. technician Children's Hosp. Research Lab., Washington, 1948-49; bacteriologist George Washington U. Research Lab., D.C. Gen. Hosp., 1950-53; med. microbiologist Walter Reed Army Inst. Research, Washington, 1953-61; research asst. Dental Research, Walter Reed Med. Center, 1961-62; microbiologist antibiotics div. FDA, 1962-63; supr. quality control John D. Copanos Co., Pharms., Balt., 1963-64; research tng. asst. infectious diseases and tropical medicine Howard U. Med. Sch., 1964-65; research asso. Georgetown U. Lab. Infectious Diseases, D.C. Gen. Hosp., 1966-69; mycologist Georgetown U. Hosp. Lab., 1969-70; microbiologist The Research Found. of The Washington Hosp. Center, 1971-73; dir. quality control Bio-Medium Corp., Silver spring, Md., 1973—. Sec. to exec. bd. Bethesda Project Awareness, 1970-71; vol. lead poisoning detection testing project, D.C. Office Vols. Internat. Tech. Assistance, 1970-71. Recipient medal community service. Mem. Nat. Capital Harp Ensemble, 1941-65. Mem. Women's Suburban Democratic Club. Mem. A.A.A.S., Am. Soc. for Microbiology, Am. Assn. Clin. Chemists, Am. Astronautical Soc., Albertus Magnus Guild, Capital Bus. and Profl. Women's Club (rec. sec. 1973-74, 1st v.p. 1974—), Pi Kappa Delta. Roman Catholic. Home: 4101 Maryland Av Washington DC 20016 Office: Bio-Medium Corp 8841 Brookville Rd Silver Spring MD 20910

GOUGH, JESSIE POST (MRS. HERBERT FREDERICK GOUGH), educator; b. Nakon Sri Tamaraj, Thailand, Jan. 26, 1907 (parents Am. citizens); d. Richard Walter and Mame (Stebbins) Post; B.A., Maryville Coll., 1927; M.A. in English, U. Chgo., 1928; Ed.D., U. Ga., 1965; m. Herbert Frederick Gough, June 30, 1934; children—Joan Acland (Mrs. Alexander Reed), Herbert Frederick. Tchr. English, Linden Hall, Lititz, Pa., 1930-32; tchr. Fairyland Sch., Lookout Mountain, Tenn., 1955-64; research asst. English curriculum studies center U. Ga., 1964-65; prof. elementary edn. LaGrange (Ga.) Coll., 1965—. Prof., N.W. Ga. area tchr. edn. services, 1969-71. Mem. Walker County (Ga.) Curriculum Council, 1959-61, Walker County Ednl. Planning Bd., 1958-60. Mem. Am. Ednl. Research Assn., Nat. Soc. Study Edn., Nat. Council Social Studies, East Tenn. Hist. Soc., Nat., Ga. edn. assns., Delta Kappa Gamma, Kappa Delta Pi. Home: 401 Ridley Av LaGrange GA 30240

GOUGH, ORAN DEAN, broadcasting-advt. exec.; b. Detroit, Apr. 3, 1937; s. Henry Dean Gough and Gertrude (Schutz) Gough Kidd; m. Sharon Ann Beals, Dec. 12, 1955 (dec. Feb. 1972); children—Laura Ellen, Oran Dean, Frank Dixon II, Juliann Michelle; m. 2d, Joyce A. Ondo-Southrey, Apr. 12, 1972. Program dir. WIRK-TV, Palm Beach, Fla., 1953-56; pres., gen. mgr. Eloral Assos., Inc., Pub., 1957-59; prodn. mgr., TV dir. Florino Advt., 1960-62; mgr. Palm Coast Shopping Center, 1963; program dir. WEAT-TV, West Palm Beach, Fla., 1943-66, prodn. mgr., 1966-70, dir. operations, mem. mgmt. com. WEAT-AM-FM-TV, 1970-73; pres. Oran D. Gough and Assos., Inc., Advt., 1974—; pres. Color Communications Corp., 1967-70. Pub. relations counsel Palm Beach County Republican Exec. Com. Bd., 1968-70. Bd. dirs. Big Bros., 1971-72; trustee Better Bus. Bur. Palm Beach County, 1972-73, bd. dirs., 1974—. Recipient Outstanding individual Achievement award 4th dist. Am. Advt. Fedn., 1969. Mem. Palm Beaches Advt. Club (v.p., sec., dir. 1961-64, 69-71, pres. 1972). Home: Apt C-17 1500 N Congress Av West Palm Beach FL 33407 Office: Suite 301 711 S Flagler Dr West Palm Beach FL 33401

GOULD, HOWARD ROSS, geologist; b. Adrian, W.Va., Nov. 10, 1921; s. Sidney Ross and Grace (Harris) G.; B.A., U. Minn., 1943; postgrad. Scripps Inst. Oceanography, U. Cal. at San Diego, 1946-47; Ph.D., U. So. Cal., 1953; m. Marilyn Bradley, Feb. 14, 1948; children—Bradley H., Suzanne E. Marine geologist div. war research, U. Cal. at San Diego, 1943-46; geologist U.S. Geol. Survey, Washington, 1947-53; asst. prof. marine geology and oceanography U.

Wash., Seattle, 1953-56; research geologist Humble Oil & Refining Co., Houston, 1956-63, mgr. Geologic Research, 1964; mgr. Stratigraphic Geology div. Esso Production Research Co., Houston, 1965-67; research scientist, 1967—. Mem. Am. Assn. Petroleum Geologists (Distinguished Service award 1972, Distinguished Lectr. award 1966-67), Am. Petroleum Inst., A.A.A.S., Soc. Econ. Paleontologists and Mineralogists (v.p. 1968), Geol. Soc. Am., Am. Geophys. Union, Marine Tech. Soc., Houston Geol. Soc. Clubs: Briar; University (Houston). Contbr. articles to profl. jours. Home: 5231 Piping Rock Houston TX 77027 Office: Box 2189 Houston TX 77001

GOULD, PHILLIP, mech. engr.; b. N.Y.C., Feb. 19, 1940; s. Isaac and Blanche (Handler) G.; B.M.E., City Coll. N.Y., 1961; M.S., Mass. Inst. Tech., 1963, D.Sc., 1965; m. Joanna Grugeon, Apr. 17, 1964; children—David Elliot, Jessica Ann. Asst. prof. mech. engring. Mass. Inst. Tech., Cambridge, 1965-67; mem. Inst. for Def. Analyses, Arlington, Va., 1967—. Fellow A.A.A.S.; mem. Am. Soc. M.E., N.Y. Acad. Scis., Operations Research Soc. Am., Am. Inst. Aeros. and Astronautics, Sigma Xi. Home: 415 S Lee St Alexandria VA 22314 Office: 400 Army-Navy Dr Arlington VA 22202

GOULD, ROBERT ALBERT, city ofcl.; b. Cresent City, Fla., Sept. 29, 1926; s. Albert W. and Anna (Richards) G.; student Orlando Jr. Coll., 1950-53, Stetson U., 1953-54; m. Evelyn Joyce Walker, Dec. 30, 1953; children—Mary Elizabeth, Leila Catherine. With City of Orlando (Fla.), 1947—, asst. supt., 1957-62, supt., 1962—, mgr. city auditorium, 1957—. Commr. Amateur Softball Assn., Orlando, 1971—. Served with USNR, 1945-46. Baptist (deacon). Home: 903 Silver Dr Orlando FL 32804 Office: 649 W Livingston St Orlando FL 32801

GOULD, ROBERT WILLIAM, educator; b. Shanghai, China, Feb. 5, 1934; s. Moses Joseph and Ruth Virginia (Colledge) G.; B.S., U. Fla., 1955, M.S., 1962, Ph.D., 1964; m. Marcia Rodes, Aug. 27, 1955; children—Robert W., Patricia, Stephanie, Thomas. With Am. Cynamid Co., Brewster, Fla., 1957-58, Kaiser Aluminum Co., Permanente, Cal., 1958-59; research engr. U. Fla., Gainesville, 1959-62, prof. materials sci. and engring., 1964—. Vice pres. Materials Cons., Inc.; cons. engr., Fla. Mem. Am. Soc. Metals, Am. Soc. Testing Materials, Phi Beta Kappa, Sigma Nu. Mem. Evang. Free Ch. Editor: Characterization of Ceramics, 1972. Contbr. articles to profl. jours. Home: 11103 NW 11th Av Gainesville FL 32601

GOULD, STEPHEN, paper mfg. exec., author; b. N.Y.C., Dec. 25, 1909; s. Jacob and Fannie (Schwartz) G.; D.F.A., Geneva Theol. Coll., 1969; D.Integral Philosophy, World U., 1969, D.F.A., 1972; m. Marlene Ossias, Aug. 24, 1941; children—Phyllis Jane Miller, Roberta Louise Herman, Debra Elaine Rhonheimer. Columnist Port & Terminal publs., L.I., N.Y., 1931-36; dir., cons. Stephen Gould Paper Co., Inc. N.J., Bayonne, Stephen Gould Corp. N.J., Bayonne, Stephen Gould Ohio Inc., Cleve., Stephen Gould Mass. Inc., Needham, Stephen Gould Conn., Orange, Stephen Gould Pa. Inc., Phila., Stephen Gould Fla. Inc., Coral Gables, Gould So., Atlanta. Fellow Am. Assn. Humanistic Psychology; mem. Indsl. Packaging and Handling Engrs., Soc. N.Y. Acad. Sci. (life), Nat. Soc. Arts and Letters (life), Royal Soc. Arts (life). Mason. Clubs: Sabal Palms Country (Tamarac, Fla.). Home: 6350 NW 63d St Apt 101 Tamarac FL 33313

GOULD, SYD S., publisher; b. Boston, Dec. 16, 1912; s. Charles M. and Cecelia (Duke) G.; student Coll. William and Mary, 1934; m. Grace Leich, May 22, 1938; 1 dau., Nancy Hamilton (Mrs. Lucien M. Gex, Jr.). Radio bus., Buenos Aires, Argentina, 1934, 36; advt. dept. Call-Chronicle Newspapers, Allentown, Pa., 1936-42; v.p., adv. dir. Baytown (Tex.) Sun, 1943-55; pub.-owner Cleveland (Tenn.) Daily Banner, 1955—; pres. Cleveland Newspapers, Inc., 1956-67; exec. v.p. Southern Newspapers, Inc., 1963-69; pres. Syd S. Gould Assos., 1966—, Bolivar Newspapers, Inc., 1967—, Ironton Tribune Corp. (O.), Franklin Newspapers, Inc. (La.), Comet-Press Newspapers, Thibodaux, La., Milton Newspapers, Inc. (Fla.). Mem. Regional Small Bus. Adv. Council. Sec., Bradley County (Tenn.) Indsl. Devel. Bd., 1961—; pres. Bradley County Heart Assn., 1960-61. Served with USNR, World War II. Mem. Newspaper Advt. Execs. Assn., Tenn. Press. Assn., Bur. Advt., Am. Newspaper Pubs. Assn., USCG Aux., Sigma Delta Chi. Episcopalian. Clubs: Bayou Country, Mobile Big Game Fishing, Isle Dauphine Country Capitol Hill, Yachting of Am., Internat. Trade, Athelstan. Home: Route 1 Box 146 Theodore AL 36582 Office: 5464 Government Blvd Mobile AL 36609

GOULDING, CLARENCE EUGENE, JR., anesthesiologist; b. Memphis, Nov. 9, 1931; s. Clarence Eugene and Bertha Maude (Tomlinson) G.; student East Tenn. State U., 1949-51; M.D., U. Tenn., 1954; m. Melba Jean Leonard, Dec. 21, 1952; children—Amelia Ann, Clarence Eugene III, Karen Jean, Richard Leonard. Intern, Knoxville (Tenn.) Gen. Hosp., 1955-56; gen. practice medicine Elizabethton, Tenn., 1956-57; resident anesthesiology U. Tenn. Meml. Research Center and Hosp., Knoxville, 1959-61; practice medicine specializing in anesthesiology, Johnson City, Tenn., 1961—; mem. staffs Johnson City Meml. Hosp., chmn. med. staff, 1968-69. Vice chmn. Daniel Boone Dist., Boy Scouts Am., Johnson City, 1967-68. Bd. dirs. Watauga Hist. Assn., 1962-73. Served to lt. comdr. M.C., USNR, 1957-59. Named Kiwanian of the Year, 1966. Diplomate Am. Bd. Anesthesiology. Mem. Am., Tenn. med. assns., Washington, Carter, Unicoi county med. socs., So. Med. Assn., Am. Philatelic Soc., Am., Tenn. State Socs. anesthesiologists, Internat. Anesthesia Research Soc. Methodist (lay leader 1967-69). Mason, Kiwanian (pres. 1971). Clubs: Met. Dinner (dir. 1972-73); Holston Stamp (Johnson City). Home: 1600 Crystal Springs Dr Johnson City TN 37601 Office: Anesthesia Office Memorial Hospital Johnson City TN 37601

GOURAS, PETER, physician, govt. scientist; b. N.Y.C., Apr. 15, 1930; s. James and Julia (Crowley) G.; A.B., Johns Hopkins, 1951, M.D., 1955; m. Ute Keppler, Aug. 29, 1959; children—Eckhart, Gunnar, Roswitha. Surg. intern Johns Hopkins Hosp., 1955-56; research scientist Physiol. lab. Cambridge, (Eng.) U., 1958-59; instr. physiology dept. U. Pa. Med. Sch., 1959-60; research asso. neurosurgery NIH, Bethesda, Md., 1956-57, research asso. ophthalmology, 1957-58, sr. investigator ophthalmology physiology, 1960-68, chief sect. ophthalmology, physiology, 1968—. Humboldt vis. prof. Freiburg (Germany) U., 1974-75. Nat. Found. March of Dimes fellow, 1958. Recipient citation Nat. Council To Combat Blindness, 1961. Mem. Am. Physiol. Soc., Soc. Gen. Physiologists, Optical Soc. Am., N.Y. Acad. Sci., A.A.A.S., Phi Beta Kappa. Hon. editorial adv. bd. Vision Research; editorial bd. Investigative Ophthalmology. Contbr. papers to sci. lit. Home: 6309 Crathie Lane Washington DC 20016 Office: NIH Bethesda MD 20014

GOURDOUZE, FRANK REX., basketball coach; b. Bicknell, Ind., Dec. 20, 1920; s. Arthur and Madelene (Janssaud) G.; B.S., Ind. State U., 1943, M.S., 1950, Dir. Recreation, 1953; m. Grace Oyer, Nov. 20, 1949; children—Randall, Robbyn, Richelle. Coach, Ind. High Schs., 1946-69; dir. athletics, basketball coach So. Union State Jr. Coll., Wadley, Ala., 1969—. Served with USNR, 1943-46. Lion (dist. chmn. Ind. Hall of Fame 1961-62). Contbr. articles to profl. jours. Patentee in field. Office: Southern Union State College Wadley AL 36276

GOURLEY, JAMES LELAND, editor, columnist; b. Mounds, Okla., Jan. 29, 1919; s. Samuel O. and Lodema (Scott) G.; B. Liberal Studies, U. Okla., 1963; m. Billie Jo Simpson, Apr. 11, 1943; children—James Leland II, Janna Lynn. Editor, pub., pres. Oklahoma City Friday; Henryetta (Okla.) Free-Lance, 1946-73; pres. radio sta. KHEN and KHEN-FM, Henryetta, 1955-71; pres. Hugo (Okla.) Daily News, 1953-63; chief asst. gov. Okla., 1959-63; pres. State Capitol Bank, 1962-67, chmn. bd., chmn. exec. com., 1962-68; chmn., pres. State Capitol Bldg. Corp.; treas. radio sta. KJEM, Oklahoma City, 1963-67; v.p. radio sta. KXOJ, Sapulpa, Okla., 1972—. Mem. Pres. Nat. Pub. Adv. Com. to Sec. of Commerce, 1963-66; mem. Nat. Council State Govts., 1960-63; dir. So. Regional Edn. Bd., 1959-67; exec. dir. Gov.'s Commn. on Higher Edn., 1960-61; chmn. Okla. Lake Redevel. Authority, 1960-63; mem. Okla. Bicentennial Commn., 1971—. Dist. chmn. Boy Scouts Am., 1962-64. Chmn. adult edn. subcom. U. Okla., 1967-68. Vice chmn. Nat. Finals Rodeo, 1966-68. Democratic candidate for gov. Okla., 1966. Served to maj. AUS, 1941-46. Decorated Bronze Star; recipient 13 Best Small Town Daily Newspaper Okla. awards, Marshall Gregory award for distinguished journalism in edn., 1971. Mem. Nat. Newspaper Assn., Okla. Press Assn., (Newspaper Community Service award 1973), Nat. Assn. Broadcasters, Mil. Order World Wars, Oklahoma City C. of C. (dir.), Sigma Delta Chi, Pi Kappa Alpha. Democrat. Mem. Disciples of Christ Ch. (pres. Okla. laymen 1964-65). Rotarian. Home: 7511 N Country Club Dr Oklahoma City OK 73116 Office: PO Box 20340 Oklahoma City OK 73120

GOVAERTS, KENNETH CHARLES, ednl. adminstr.; b. Sargent, Neb., Sept. 18, 1939; s. Donald Duane and Betty Ruth (Moore) G.; B.S., Okla. State U., 1963; postgrad. U. Mo., 1964, Tex. A. and M. U., 1967; M. Pub. Works Adminstrn., U. Pitts., 1969; M.C.E., U. Okla., 1967, D.C.E., 1972; m. Kathryn Ann Murphy, Aug. 27, 1961; children—Timothy, Elizabeth. Pub. health engr. State of Neb., Lincoln, 1963-65; city engr. City of Seward, Neb., 1965-66; faculty Okla. State U., Oklahoma City, 1966—, dir. community and alumni affairs, 1973—; grad. asst. fellow U. Pitts., 1969. Cons. State of Okla., 1970-71, U. Okla., 1973—. Coach, Little League Baseball, Norman, 1972-73. Mem. Moore-Norman Vocational-Tech. Sch. Bd., 1972-73. AEC fellow, 1967, NSF fellow, 1964. Mem. Nat. Soc. Profl. Engrs., Am. Soc. Engring. Edn. (membership chmn. 1971-72), Am. Soc. C.E., Am. Vocational Assn. Kiwanian. Home: Rural Route 1 Box 149M Norman OK 73069 Office: 900 N Portland Oklahoma State U Oklahoma City OK 73107

GOWEN, BARNEY ALEXANDER, banker; b. Camden County, Ga., Apr. 2, 1902; s. George Rhoan and Courtney (Littlefield) G.; grad. Ga.-Ala. Bus. Coll., 1923; m. Ethel Veale, June 28, 1932; children—Anne, B. Alex. Asst. bookkeeper Brandon Lumber Co., White Oak and Rickmond Hill, Ga., 1924-25; machine bookkeeper D.P. Davis Properties, Tampa, St. Augustine, Fla., 1926-27; owner, Gowen's Gen. Mdse., Woodbine, Ga., 1928-56; vice chmn. bd. State Bank of Kingsland (Ga.); dir. Am. Nat. Bank, Brunswick, Ga., 1971-73, Exco, Inc., Woodbine, Ga. Commr., Camden County, 1930-34; councilman, Woodbine, 1934-40; mem. sec. treas. Camden County Democratic Exec. Com., 1948-60; chmn. Camden County Bd. Edn., Woodbine, Ga., 1955-62; mem. Camden County Ind. Com., 1959-74, mem. govs. staff, 1959-60; mem. Ga. Indsl. Devel. Commn., 1962—; chief register Camden County, Ga., 1965—. Mem. area exec. com. Boy Scouts Am. Mem. Woodbine C. of C. (pres. 1966). Methodist. Mason. (Shriner), Lion (pres. Woodbine 1966). Home: 4th St Woodbine GA 31569

GOYER, ROBERT ANDREW, educator; b. Hartford, Conn., June 2, 1927; s. Andrew and Cecelia (Castonguay) G.; B.S., Holy Cross Coll., 1950; M.D., St. Louis U., 1955; m. Mary Ellen Wilke, Feb. 5, 1955; children—Barbara, John, Peter, Ellen. Intern, St. Francis Hosp., Hartford, 1955-56; asst. resident obstetrics and gynecology St. Louis U. Hosp., 1956-57, resident in pathology, 1957-61; Nat. Found. fellow St. Louis U., 1959-61, asst. prof. pathology Sch. Medicine, 1962-65; research fellow Univ. Coll. Med. Sch., London, 1961-62; dir. labs. Cardinal Glennon Hosp. for Children, St. Louis, 1962-65; faculty U. N.C., Chapel Hill, 1965—, prof. pathology, 1971—; vis. scientist Nat. Inst. Environmental Health Scis., Research Triangle Park, N.C., 1971-72. Served with USNR, 1945-47. Home: 3 Iris Lane Chapel Hill NC 27514

GOYETTE, LEWIS EDWARD, chem. co. exec.; b. Kansas City, Mo., July 22, 1924; s. Lewis Edward and Clare Rose (Miller) G.; A.B., U. Kan., 1947, Ph.D., 1951; m. Alleyne Boyd McDowell, Sept. 3, 1946; children—Edward, Clare, Susan. Research botanist Va. Carolina Chem. Corp., Richmond, Va., 1951-54, sr. scientist, 1954-55, group leader, 1955-57, profl. mgr. agrl. chemistry, 1957-64; v.p. Dragon Chem. Corp., Roanoke, Va., 1964-73; v.p. Carlyle Chem. Co., Roanoke, 1973—; pres. Country Garden Industries, Inc., 1973—. Served with AUS, 1944-46. Mem. So. Agrl. Chem. Assn. (pres. 1972). Patentee in field. Home: 3806 Winding Way Rd Roanoke VA 24015 Office: 1501 Cleveland Av Roanoke VA 24015

GRABEN, HENRY WILLINGHAM, educator; b. Talladega, Ala., Nov. 9, 1934; s. Eral Ross and Violet Cleo (Willingham) G.; B.S., Birmingham-So. Coll., 1957; M.S., (So. fellow), U. Tenn., 1961, Ph.D., 1962; m. Harriet Ann Mason, Aug. 19, 1961; children—Ellen Hartsfield, Eric Knox. Physicist, Oak Ridge Nat. Lab., 1962-63, cons., 1965—; faculty Clemson (S.C.) U., 1963—, prof. physics, 1971—. NSF fellow, 1961-62. Mem. Am. Phys. Soc., Phi Beta Kappa, Phi Kappa Phi. Contbr. articles to profl. jours. Home: PO Box 848 Clemson SC 29631

GRABER, CHARLES DAVID, scientist, educator; b. Pomeroy, O., Dec. 19, 1917; s. Charles Peter and Julia Agnes (Hennessey) G.; B.S., Ohio State U., 1939, Ph.D., 1957; M.S., U. Colo., 1954; m. Agnes Terry Teachey, Feb. 28, 1944; children—Charles Scott, David R., Ellen R. Commd. 2d lt. M.C., U.S. Army, 1941, advanced through grades to lt. col., 1959, ret. 1962; asst. prof. pathology Baylor Med. Sch., Houston, 1963-66; faculty Med. U. S.C., Charleston, 1966—, prof. microbiology-immunology, 1971—. Cons. NASA Johnson Space Center, 1963-66, VA Hosp., Charleston, S.C., 1966—. Diplomate Am. Bd. Microbiology. Mem. Am. Acad. Microbiology, Am. Assn. Immunologists, Am. Soc. for Microbiology, Soc. Exptl. Biology and Medicine, Societe Immunologie Francaise, Sigma Xi, Sigma Delta Chi. Author: Rapid Methods in Medical Diagnostic Microbiology, 1970. Contbr. articles to profl. jours. Home: 436 Trapier Dr Charleston SC 29412

GRABOW, GARY LOUIS, savs. & loan assn. exec.; b. Loyal, Okla., July 19, 1935; s. Alfred D. and June (Shearer) G.; student Okla. State U., 1955-57; m. Regina W. Garrison, June 1, 1957; children—Gary Lynn, Geoffrey Louis. With Kingfisher (Okla.) Fed. Savs. & Loan Assn., 1960—, asst. sec., 1963-65, asst. treas., 1966-70, v.p., mgr., dir., 1970—. Served with AUS, 1958-59. Mem. U.S. Savs. and Loan League (mem. exec. com. smaller city instns. 1973-74), Kingfisher C. of C. (sec. 1967-68). Baptist (asst. treas. 1971-73). Rotarian (v.p. 1967-68, sec., 1965-66, treas. 1963-64). Home: 4 Meadowlark Dr Kingfisher OK 73750 Office: 213 N Main St Kingfisher OK 73750

GRACE, CHARLES C(LYDE), physician; b. Belleville, Ark., May 23, 1905; s. William H. and Edna (Harkness) G.; student Hendrix Coll., 1922-24; B.S., U. Ark., 1928, M.D., 1928; m. May H. Clarke, Dec. 26, 1931; children—Charles Clyde, Marilyn. Intern, resident Greenville City Hosp., 1928-30; resident Pitts. Eye and Ear Hosp., 1930-31; ophthalmologist, otolaryngologist, chief staff Flagler Hosp. Dir., Exchange Bank of St. Augustine. North Fla. cons. Council for Blind, 1944-66. Mem. com. otolaryngology Fla. Mid Winter Seminar; dir. Fla. Midwinter Seminar Ophthalmology and Otolaryngology. Diplomate Am. Bd. Otolaryngology. Fellow A.C.S., Internat. Coll. Surgeons; mem. Fla. Med. Assn. (pres.), Fla. Soc. Ophthalmology and Otolaryngology, Am. Laryngol. Rhinol. and Otolog. Soc. (v.p.), Am. Acad. Ophthalmology and Otolaryngology, A.M.A. Democrat. Presbyn. Mason (K.T., Shriner), Kiwanian. Contbr. articles to med. jours. Home: 22 E Park Av St Augustine FL 32084 Office: Doctors Bldg St Augustine FL 32084

GRACE, MICHAEL FRANCIS, mfg. co. exec.; b. Huntsville, Ala., May 5, 1921; s. Clarence M. and Mary F. (Coyle) G.; B.S., Auburn U., 1947; m. Anna Catharine Kidd, Sept. 5, 1946; children—Jon, Roger, Laura, Courtnay. Dist. sales mgr. Robertshaw Controls, Los Angeles, Dallas, Chattanooga, 1947-59, nat. sales mgr. Grayson Controls div., Long Beach, Cal., 1959-69; chmn. bd., pres. APCOM, Inc., Franklin, Tenn., 1969—. Served to capt. C.E., AUS, 1942-46, 50-52. Mem. Guild of Ancient Supplers, So-What-Club Inc. of Nashville (pres. 1973). Club: Brentwood (Tenn.) Country. Home: 105 Meadow Lake Rd Brentwood TN 37027 Office: Box 687 Franklin TN 37064

GRACEY, HUGH CATRON, lawyer; b. Mooresville, Tenn., Aug. 19, 1913; s. Clarence Brainard and Mary Elizabeth (Orr) G.; B.S., Davidson Coll., 1937; J.D., Duke U., 1940; m. Sarah Esther Dyer, Nov. 8, 1941; children—Hugh Catron, Sarah Dyer, Susan Orr. Admitted to Tenn. bar, 1940; sr. partner Gracey, Buck, Maddin & Cowan, 1958—. Prof. law Cumberland Sch. Law, Lebanon, Tenn., 1946-49. Served to capt. AUS, 1942-45. Mem. Am., Nashville (v.p. 1964-65, dir. 1962-65), bar assns., Bar Assn. Tenn., Tenn. Defense Lawyers Assn. (pres. 1973-74), Fedn. Ins. Counsel (v.p. 1970-71), Phi Delta Phi, Kappa Sigma. Presbyn. Mason (32 deg., Shriner). Clubs: Hillwood Country (dir. 1968-70, v.p. 1969-70), Cumberland (Nashville). Home: 930 Tyne Blvd Nashville TN 37220 Office: 500 Court Sq Bldg 300 James Robertson Pkwy Nashville TN 37201

GRACIA, VALENTIN, surgeon; b. Panuco, Veracruz, Mexico, May 5, 1929; s. Valentin and Maria (Sanchez) G.; B.S., U. Mexico, 1946, M.D., 1952; m. Joan Oltmann, Mar. 13, 1954; children—Linda Joan, Valentin, Walter Dietrich, Maria, Rita Lynn, Phillip, Irene, Carlos. Came to U.S., 1952, naturalized, 1960. Rotating intern Monmouth Meml. Hosp., Long Branch, N.J., 1952-53; surg. resident St. Luke's Hosp., Bethlehem, 1953-54, Scott & White Clinic, Temple, 1954-57; resident plastic surgery Baylor Med. Center, Dallas, 1957-59; gen. practice medicine specializing in plastic surgery, Ft. Worth, 1959—; mem. staffs All Saints Episcopal, Harris, St. Joseph's, John Peter Smith, Arlington Meml., Fort Worth Children's Glenview, Cook's Blvd. hosps.; cons. plastic surgeon USPHS Hosp., Ft. Worth. Diplomate Am. Bd. Plastic Surgery. Fellow A.C.S., Internat. Coll. Surgeons; mem. Am. Soc. Plastic Surgery, A.A.A.S., N.Y. Acad. Scis., Am., Tex. Soc. Plastic Surgeons, Ft. Worth Surg. Soc., Internat. Good Neighbor Council, So., Tex., Tarrant County med. assns., Am. Burn Assn., Internat. Soc. Burn Injuries, Internat. Soc. Plastic Surgeons. Mason (K.T., Shriner), Rotarian. Contbr. articles to profl. jours. Home: 2013 Jenson Rd Fort Worth TX 76112 Office: 1001 W Rosedale PO Box 2476 Fort Worth TX 76101

GRACY, ROBERT WAYNE, educator; b. McKinney, Tex., Dec. 30, 1941; s. William C. and Ruby L. (Cantrell) G.; B.S., Cal. State Poly., 1964; Ph.D. (Nat. Def. Edn. Act fellow), U. Cal. at Riverside, 1968; m. Lynne Hitchcock, Dec. 28, 1963; children—Kimberly Noelle, Delaney Kristan. Damon Runyon Cancer Found. fellow Albert Einstein Coll. Medicine, N.Y.C., 1968-70; asst. prof. N. Tex. State U., Denton, 1970-73, asso. prof. chemistry and basic health scis., 1973—. Bd. dirs. Denton (Tex.) unit Am. Cancer Soc., 1971—. NIH Career Devel. grantee 1972—; Nat. Inst. Arthritis and Metabolic Disease grantee, 1971-73; Research Corp. fellow, 1972; R.A. Welch Found. fellow, 1972—. Mem. Am. Chem. Soc., Am. Soc. Biol. Chemists, Am. Assn. U. Profs., A.A.A.S., Sigma Xi. Contbr. articles in field to profl. jours. Home: 1414 Windsor Dr Denton TX 76201

GRADY, JAMES MARTIN, computer exec.; b. Horatio, Ark., July 2, 1935; s. Paul Elmo and Annie Laurie (Martin) G.; B.A., Rice U., 1958; B.A. in Econs., U. Houston, 1966-67. With Tenneco, Inc., Houston, 1961—, systems mgr. pipeline group, 1971—. Instr. Naval Res. Officers Sch., Houston, 1967—. Explorer service chmn. Sam Houston Council, Boy Scouts Am., 1972—. Served to lt. USNR, 1958-60. Mem. Assn. for System Mgmt., Data Processing Mgmt. Assn., Res. Officers Assn., (mem. mil. affairs com. 1973—), Naval Res. Assn. Methodist. Home: 6307 Spruce Forest Houston TX 77018 Office: 1010 Milam Houston TX 77001

GRADY, JOHN EDWARD, JR., real estate co. exec.; b. Boston, June 15, 1935; s. John Edward and Catherine Agnes (Connolly) G.; A.B., Harvard, 1956, M.B.A., 1965; m. Angela Loretta McDonnell, July 10, 1965; children—John Edward III, Robert Emmet McDonnell, Douglas Anderson. Account exec. Merrill Lynch, Pierce, Fenner & Smith, N.Y.C., 1960-63; sr. asso. Cresap, McCormick and Paget, N.Y.C., 1965-69; v.p., Investment Mgmt. and Research, Inc., St. Petersburg, Fla., 1969-70; v.p. finance, treas. Suncoast Highland Corp., Largo, Fla., 1970—, also dir. Commr. Highlands Road and Bridge Dist., Pasco County, Fla., 1973—, Lake Grady Road and Bridge Dist., Hillsborough County, Fla., 1973—. Regional chmn. Harvard Bus. Sch. Fund, 1971—; mem. pres. roundtable Eckerd Coll., 1971—. Trustee, treas. bd. trustees Canterbury Sch. Fla. Served to lt. (j.g.) USNR, 1956-60. Clubs: Lakewood Country, Harvard West Coast (sec.-treas. 1973-74), St. Petersburg Yacht (St. Petersburg, Fla.); Harvard Business School (sec. 1969) (N.Y.C.) Home: 1640 N Dakota Av NE St Petersburg FL 33703 Office: 1180 Jasper St Largo FL 33540

GRAF, G(OTTFRIED) C(HRISTIAN), educator; b. Louisville, Jan. 23, 1911; s. Gottfried and Anna (Dapp) G.; B.S., Mich. State U., 1934; M.S., U. Minn., 1940, Ph.D., 1951; m. Gwendolyn Evans, June 14, 1938. Instr. vocational agrl. Bay Port (Mich.) High Sch., 1934-35; supr. dairy herd U. Conn., Storrs, 1935-41, instr. dairy sci., 1941-43, asst. prof., 1943-45; asso. prof. dairy sci. Va. Poly. Inst., Blacksburg, 1945-52, prof., 1952—, head, dept. dairy sci., 1952-64. Cons. mgmt. practices Beatrice Foods Co., 1963-65. Mem. A.A.A.S., Am. Assn. U. Profs. (pres. 1969-70), Am. Dairy Sci. Assn., Am. Soc. Animal Sci., Dairy Shrine, Sigma Xi, Epsilon Sigma Phi, Va. Acad. Sci. Gamma Sigma Delta. Home: 1308 Oak Dr Blacksburg VA 24060

GRAF, JAMES WILLIAM, apparel co. exec.; b. Hamilton, O., Sept. 20, 1931; s. Paul Emil and Florence Cecilia (Custer) G.; B.S., U. Ark., 1960; m. Marion Henry McAmis, Dec. 28, 1956; children—Thomas Paul, Lelia Ann. Asst. buyer M.M. Cohn Co., Little Rock, 1956-60, buyer, mgr., 1960-63, buyer, 1963-66, merchandiser, 1966-68, v.p., 1968—; v.p., dir. Mchts. Realty Co., Little Rock, 1972—, West Mchts. Realty Co., 1972—. Mem. budget com. United Fund, Little

Rock, 1971-72. Served to 1st lt. USAF, 1952-55. Mem. Specialty Stores Assn. (com. chmn. 1973—). Rotarian. Club: Little Rock Racquet (dir. 1970—). Home: 12 Bugle Ct Little Rock AR 72207 Office: 510 Main St Little Rock AR 72203

GRAF, JOSEPH CHARLES, petroleum co. exec.; b. Jersey City, Sept. 10, 1928; s. John Bernard and Margaret Cecilia (Toomey) G.; B.S., Seton Hall U., 1949; M.B.A., U. Pa., 1954; m. Lauretta Marie Sanfacon, Nov. 26, 1955; children—Claire, Joseph Charles, Michelle, Mary Ellen, Thomas, Richard. Trainee, Prudential Ins. Co., Newark, 1954-55, systems analyst, 1955-56, asst. research analyst, 1956-58, research analyst, 1958-61, investment analyst, 1961-63, sr. investment analyst, 1963-64, Houston, 1964-67; v.p. So. Nat. Bank, Houston, 1967-69; financial analyst Quintana Petroleum Corp., Houston, 1969—. Dir. Terrain King Corp., Tapco Internat., Inc., White Mfg. Co., Diversified Plastics, Inc. Cons. research com. Houston C. of C., 1966-71. Served with AUS, 1951-53. Mem. Houston Financial Analysts (pres. 1973—). Clubs: Houston, Houston Racquet. Home: 8 Pine Tree Lane Houston TX 77024 Office: 500 Jefferson Bldg Houston TX 77002

GRAFF, HOMER LEVESQUE, physician; b. Texla, Tex., Nov. 2, 1925; s. Homer Levesque and Bessie Lee (Bridges) C.; student Tex. Christian U., 1943-44; M.D., Baylor U., 1951, B.S., 1948; m. Dora Villafane, Dec. 18, 1949; children—Mark, Philip, Laura, Paul, Hans. Intern, Gorgas Hosp., C.Z., 1951-52; resident Ind. U. Med. Center, Indpls. and Baylor U. Hosp. Group, 1953-56; gen. practice medicine, C.Z., 1952-53; specializing in otolaryngology, Houston, 1956—; mem. staff Meml. Bapt., St. Lukes, Tex. Childrens hosps.; clin. instr. Baylor U. Coll. Medicine, 1956—. Served to lt. (j.g.) USNR, 1943-46. Mem. A.M.A., Tex. Harris County med. socs., Tex. Otolaryngol. Soc., Royal Soc. Medicine (Eng.). Home: 11335 Bothwell Way Houston TX 77024 Office: 6565 Demoss St Houston TX 77036

GRAGG, ANNETTE GANO (MRS. HUGH E. GRAGG), architect; b. Tulsa, Oct. 28, 1925; d. Richard Chilton and Margaret (Doherty) Gano; B.A., Rice U., 1947, B.S. in Architecture, 1948; m. Hugh E. Gragg, June 23, 1948; 1 dau., Julie Katherine. Draftsman, Wirtz, Calhoun & Tungate, Architects, Houston, 1947-49, Page, Southerland & Page, Austin, 1953-54, Hamilton Brown, Architect, Houston, summers 1954, 55, Thompson McCleary, Architect, Houston, 1956-57; asso. Hugh E. Gragg, Architect, Houston, 1957—. Mem. Womens Aux. A.I.A. (pres. 1972—), Rice U. Archtl. Alumni Assn., Soc. Rice U. Women. Unitarian. Rotary Ann. (pres. 1969-70). Home: 2249 Pelham Dr Houston TX 77019 Office: 2727 Kirby Dr Houston TX 77006

GRAGG, HUGH ERNEST, architect; b. Dallas, Sept. 28, 1919; s. Joe Lee and Clara (Henderson) G.; student John Tarleton Coll., 1936-38; B.A., Rice Inst., 1941, B.S., 1942, M.A., 1947; m. Annette Gano, June 23, 1948; 1 dau., Julie (Mrs. William Robert Thomas). With Wilson, Morris & Crain, architects, Houston, 1946-48, Stayton, Nunn, Milton & McGinty, Houston, 1948-50; asst. prof. architecture U. Tex., Austin, 1951-53; prin. Hugh E. Gragg, Architect, Houston, 1954—. Mem. exec. com. Citizens Adv. Com. on Housing, Houston, 1969; mem. citizens adv. com. Tex. Constn. Revision Commn., 1973—, chmn. land use com., 1973—. Served with USNR, 1942-46. Mem. A.I.A. (chpt. pres. 1969), Tex. Soc. Architects, Houston Philos. Soc. (pres. 1971-72), Rice Inst. Alumni Assn., Houston C. of C. (mem. cultural affairs com. 1969). Rotarian (sec. 1967-69). Home: 2249 Pelham Houston TX 77019 Office: 2727 Kirby Dr Houston TX 77006

GRAHAM, CLARENCE R., librarian; b. Louisville, Feb. 28, 1907; s. Samuel J. and Lillian Ellen (Paris) G.; student U. N.C., 1924-27; A.B., U. Louisville, 1934; B.S. in L.S., Western Res. U., 1935; postgrad. Northwestern U., 1937-38; m. Esther Charlotte Lothman, Feb. 28, 1930; 1 dau., Carolyn. Student asst. U. N.C. Library, 1925-27; field rep. N.C. Dept. Health, Raleigh, 1924-25; with dept. statistics Brown & Williamson Tobacco Co., Louisville, 1929-30; librarian Parkland Jr. High Sch., 1930-34; asst. to librarian Louisville Free Pub. Library, 1935-36, librarian 1942—. Vis. asso. prof. dept. library sci. U. Ky.; dir. Nat. Coll. Edn. Library Evanston, Ill., 1936-42; instr. in library scis. U. Louisville, 1946-51. Mem. Louisville Labor-Mgmt. Com. Bd. dirs. Jr. Art Gallery, Louisville Theatrical Assn., Childrens Theatre. Mem. A.L.A. (pres. 1950-51, audio-visual bd.), Ky., (1st v.p. 1946, pres. 1947), Southeastern (pres. 1948-50) library assns., Art Center Assn. (dir.). Adult Edn. Assn. U.S.A. (del. assembly), Arts Club (dir.), Newcomen Soc. N.A., Louisville Urban League. Rotarian. Clubs: Louisville Library (pres. 1948-49), Filson. Co-founder, 1947, and cons. to free neighborhood colls. in br. libraries sponsored by U. Louisville, Free Pub. Library. Author: First Book of Public Libraries, 1959. Contbr. articles to profl. jours. Home: 1028 Cherokee Rd Louisville KY 40204 Office: 301-333 Library Pl Louisville KY 40203

GRAHAM, DANIEL ROBERT, cattle producing co. exec., state senator; b. Coral Gables, Fla., Nov. 9, 1936; s. Ernest R. and Hilda Elizabeth (Simmons) G.; B.A., U. Fla., 1959; LL.B., Harvard, 1962; m. Adele Khoury, Feb. 2, 1959; children—Gwendolyn Patricia, Glynn Adele, Arva Suzanne, Kendall Elizabeth. Vice pres. Graham Co. various locations in Fla., Albany, Ga., 1962—; v.p., sec. Sengra Devel. Corp., Miami Lakes, Fla., 1962—; mem. Fla. Senate, 1970—; admitted to Fla. bar, 1962. Mem. Fla. Ho. of Reps., 1966-70. Mem. So. Regional Edn. Bd.; mem. Edn. Commn. of States. Named Outstanding Young Man, Fla. Jr. C. of C., 1970-71, Most Valuable Mem. Fla. Senate, St. Petersburg Times, 1972. Mem. Blue Key, Phi Beta Kappa. Mem. United Ch. Home: 16141 Aberdeen Way Miami Lakes FL 33014 Office: 14420 NW 60th Av Miami Lakes FL 33014

GRAHAM, EDWARD, JR., elec. engr.; b. Lebanon, Tenn., June 18, 1919; s. Edward and Jessie Bonner (Campbell) G.; student Va. Poly. Inst., 1937-38; B.A., U. Tenn., 1949; m. Carolyn Tate Breeding, Dec. 11, 1942; children—Edward, Carann (Mrs. William Randolph Turner III), John, Carolyn. Engr. Radio Sta. WROL, Knoxville, Tenn., 1945-49, WSM, WSM-TV, Nashville, 1950-56; dir. engring. WGTV, U. Ga., Athens, 1956—. Mem. engring. com. Pub. Broadcasting Service. Bd. dirs. Recording for Blind, Athens. Served with Signal Corps, AUS, 1940; to 1st lt. USAAF, 1942-45. Decorated D.F.C., Air medal with 3 oak leaf clusters. Mem. I.E.E.E., Soc. Motion Picture and Television Engrs., Internat. Radio Standards Orgn., Soaring Soc. Am. Episcopalian. Club: Athens Country. Office: 139 Ga Center Athens GA 30602

GRAHAM, EDWARD UNDERWOOD, state govt. ofcl., engr.; b. Washington, Sept. 27, 1943; s. Henry Underwood and Doris Louise (McIntire) G.; B.S. in Elec. Engring., Mass. Inst. Tech., 1964; M.S. in Elec. Engring., Carnegie-Mellon U., 1965, Ph.D. in Systems and Communications Sci., 1969; m. Barbara Janet Bramble, June 23, 1967. Engr. Auerbach Assos., information sci. cons., Washington, 1968-72; environmental planner water resources planning Montgomery County (Md.) Rockville, 1972—. Mem. I.E.E.E., Soc. for Computer Simulation. Home: 2434 39th St NW Washington DC 20007 Office: 100 S Perry St Rockville MD 20850

GRAHAM, FREDERICK BOLLES, banker; b. Wallace, N.C., Mar 2, 1906; s. Benjamin R. and Edith (Bolles) G.; B.S., U. N.C., 1928; postgrad. Wilmington Law Sch., 1931-33; grad. Stonier's Grad. Sch. Banking, Rutgers U., 1947; m. Katherine Carr, Oct. 20, 1934; children—Katherine (Mrs. John Daughtridge), Benjamin Robinson III, Frederick Bolles. Bookkeeper, Wilmington Savs. & Trust Co. (N.C.), 1928-32, asst. trust officer, 1932-37, asst. cashier, 1937-50, v.p., 1950-58, dir., 1953-58, pres., 1958; sr. v.p. Wachovia Bank & Trust Co. (merger Wilmington Savs. & Trust Co. and Wachovia Bank & Trust Co. 1958), Wilmington, 1958—, also mem. bd. mgrs. Past v.p., dir. Cape Fear Holding Co., Wilmington. Chmn., Wilmington-New Hanover County Charter Commn., 1970-71. Pres., dir. Southeastern N.C. Devel. Assn., 1955-64. Mem. bd. aldermen, Wrightsville Beach, N.C., 1945-47, mayor pro tem, 1946-47. Chmn., Wilmington chpt. A.R.C., 1968-69; chmn. exec. com., trustee Wilmington Coll., 1964-68, chmn. bd., 1968-69; a founder, trustee Univ. Found., U. N.C. at Wilmington, 1962-68. Mem. N.C. Bankers Assn. (pres. trust div. 1939), Lower Cape Fear Hist. Soc., Sigma Alpha Epsilon, Episcopalian. Clubs: L'Ariosa German, Cape Fear, Cape Fear Country (Wilmington); Surf, Caroline Yacht (Wrightsville Beach). Home: 1411 Live Oak Pkwy Wilmington NC 28401 Office: PO Box 1422 Wilmington NC 28401

GRAHAM, JACK HAROLD, elec. engr.; b. Oklahoma City, Mar. 16, 1937; s. Oscar Lee and Lillian Iona (Shelton) G.; B.S., Okla. State U., 1959; M.B.A., Oklahoma City U., 1974; m. Josephine Ann Lacy, 1955; children—Cynthia Denise, Darrell William, Karen Lynn. Field engr. Sperry Gyroscope Co., Great Neck, N.Y., 1959-64; elec. system research engr. Saturn V/Apollo program Boeing Co., Huntsville, Ala., 1964-65; sr. staff engr., group leader Saturn V/Apollo program Space Support div. Sperry Rand, Huntsville, 1966-68; sr. design engr. elec./electronics classified spl. def. program LTV Missile & Space Co., Dallas, 1968-70; cons. engr. Carnahan, Thompson & Delano, Oklahoma City, 1970—. Registered profl. engr., Okla., Ala. Mem. Nat., Okla. (membership chmn.) socs. profl. engrs. Mem. Christian Ch. (deacon). Lion. Home: 11150 Colechester Ct Yukon OK 73099 Office: Classen Bldg Oklahoma City OK 73106

GRAHAM, JACKSON, transp. exec., govt. ofcl.; b. Mosier, Ore., June 27, 1915; s. A.E. and Nada (Clark) G.; B.S. in Civil Engring., Ore. State U., 1936; postgrad. Mass. Inst. Tech., 1939-40; Nat. War Coll., 1958-59; m. Mabel Lee Dowlin, July 4, 1943; children—Ona Lee, Jackson Reade. Commd. 2d lt. C.E., U.S. Army, 1936, advanced through grades to maj. gen., 1963; comdr. combat engr. regt., ETO. World War II; comdr. all aviation engrs., Korea, 1954; dir. civil works Army Engrs., 1963-66, ret., 1967; gen. mgr. Washington Met. Area Transit Authority, 1967—. Decorated D.S.M., Legion of Merit, Commendation medal; Medal of Merit (Brazil). Mem. Sigma Phi Epsilon. Mason. Home: 2836 Fort Scott Dr Arlington VA 22202 Office: 600 5th St NW Washington DC 20001

GRAHAM, LOUIS SPARKMAN, JR., pathologist; b. Washington, Dec. 29, 1920; s. Louis Sparkman and Hortense (Meyer) G.; B.A., U. Va., 1942, M.D., 1945; m. Madelyn Borden, Dec. 20, 1943; children—Louis Sparkman III, Roy Steven. Intern, Touro Infirmary, New Orleans, 1945-46; resident in pathology U. Va., Charlottesville, 1947-50; fellow pathology Meml. Center for Cancer and Allied Diseases, N.Y.C., 1951-52; instr. pathology U. Va., 1952-53; asst. prof. U. Ala., Birmingham, 1954-55, asso. prof. pathology, 1955-56; asso. pathologist Druid City Hosp., Tuscaloosa, Ala., 1956-62, St. Thomas Hosp., Nashville, 1962—. Served to capt. M.C., AUS, 1946-47. Mem. Am. Soc. Cytology, A.M.A., Am. Soc. Clin. Pathologists, Coll. Am. Pathologists. Home: 4724 Benton Smith Rd Nashville TN 37215 Office: 2000 Hayes St Nashville TN 37203

GRAHAM, OLIVER CROMWELL, printing co. exec.; b. Laurel, Miss., Sept. 16, 1931; s. Joseph A. and Jessie M. (Tisdale) G.; B.S., Carnegie-Mellon U., 1960; M.B.A., Samford U., 1966; m. Gala Collins, Nov. 6, 1949; children—Joel Dante, Mauri Shane. Asst. supt. Oxmoor Press, Birmingham, Ala., 1961-65, v.p., mgr. customer service, 1965-73, v.p., gen. mgr., 1973—. Mason (Shriner), Rotarian. Home: 2433 Jamestown Dr Birmingham AL 35226

GRAHAM, ROBERT DUKE, savs. and loan assn. exec.; b. Greensboro, N.C., Sept. 8, 1900; s. John Buie and Emma (Fowler) G.; grad. high sch.; m. Edith Brown, Aug. 20, 1937. Pres. C.W. Lampkin Hotels, Bowling Green, Ky., 1926-60; v.p. Fidelity Fed. Savs. & Loan Assn., Bowling Green, 1965—; mayor Bowling Green, Ky., 1959-64, 1968-72. Chmn. Democratic County Com., 1940-52; chmn. City Bd. Pub. Works, 1953-59. Bd. dirs. Bowling Green Indsl. Found., 1940-71. Presbyn. Lion. Home: 1716 Normal Dr Bowling Green KY 42101 Office: City Hall 10th and College Sts Bowling Green KY 42101

GRAHAM, RONALD WILLIAM, educator, clergyman; b. Kempsey, Australia, Aug. 31, 1918; s. Ewan Duncan and Nella Margaret (Espuler) G.; B.A., U. Melbourne (Australia), 1948; M.A., Drake U., 1957, B.D., 1958; Ph.D., U. Ia., 1966; m. Elsie Gwendoline Bills, Dec. 29, 1943; children—Beth (Mrs. Mark H. Smith), Jan (Mrs. Dennis J. Easter), Kerry. Came to U.S., 1954. Ordained to ministry Christian Ch. (Disciples of Christ), 1944; minister Christian Chs. in Australia, 1942-54, Ia., 1954-60; prof. N.T., Drake Div. Sch., 1960-68, Lexington (Ky.) Theol. Sem., 1968—. Home: 3536 Cornwall Dr Lexington KY 40503 Office: 631 S Limestone St Lexington KY 40508

GRAHAM, WALTER ALEXANDER, lawyer; b. Pembroke, Ky., Aug. 24, 1907; s. Douglas and Erma (Alexander) G.; A.B., Ky. Wesleyan U., 1929; LL.B., Yale, 1935; LL.D., Elon Coll., 1958; m. Martha Juanita Boswell, Sept. 30, 1929; children—Walter Alexander, Ermaleen (Mrs. Donald Dunn), Lounita Elaine (Mrs. Rodney Wells), Carol Sue (Mrs. Phil Key) and Doris Ann (twins). Admitted to D.C. bar, 1937, Ky. bar, 1946; with U.S. Dept. Commerce, Washington, N.Y.C. also San Juan, P.R., 1935-45; practice law, Pembroke, Ky., 1946—; dir. laymen's work Bd. Home Mission, United Ch. Christ, hdqrs. Pembroke, 1946-57; pres. So. Union Coll., 1958-70; pres. Peoples Bank of Pembroke, 1967—. City atty., Pembroke, Ky., 1946—; dir. Nat. Council Ind. Jr. Colls., Washington, 1970-72; treas. Gideons Internat. Camp, Hopkinsville, 1973—. Named Ky. Col., 1969; Ala. Col., 1973. Mem. D.C., U.S. Supreme Ct. bar assns. Kiwanian. Club: Pembroke Ruritan (sec. 1974). Home: PO Box 79 Pembroke KY 42266 Office: Peoples Bank of Pembroke Pembroke KY 42266

GRAHAM, WILLIAM KARR, editorial cartoonist; b. Coshocton, O., Dec. 14, 1920; s. Lorenzo Karr and Zola (McGinnis) G.; B.S. in Social Sci., Centenary Coll., 1942; m. Wilma Lea Been, Oct. 19, 1945; children—Walter, Joseph. Reporter, cartoonist Coshocton Tribune, 1946-48; editorial cartoonist Ark. Gazette, Little Rock, 1948—. Traveling exhbns. Nat. Cartoonists Soc., Assn. Am. Editorial Cartoonists; represented in collections U. Kan., Wayne State U., Va. Mil. Inst., U. Mo., Syracuse, U. Cin., L.B.J. Library, U. Tex. Served with AUS, 1942-46. Mem. Nat. Cartoonists Soc., Assn. Am. Editorial Cartoonists, Kappa Sigma. Mem. Ch. of Christ. Mason. Home: 5208 W 24th St Little Rock AR 72204 Office: Ark Gazette Little Rock AR 72203

GRAHAM, WILMER ALLEN, accountant; b. Ft. Stockton, Tex., Jan. 15, 1914; s. Joel Allen and Mattie (Pullen) G.; student West Tex. State U., 1946-48; m. Mary A. Fields, Mar. 19, 1938; children—Betty J. (Mrs. David Hinton), Donald A. With U.S. Dept. Agr., 1938-45; partner Russell, Graham & Brown, Amarillo, Tex., 1948-57, Glover, Graham & Brown, C.P.A.'s, Tulia, Tex., 1957-72; pres. Brown, Graham & Co., 1973—. Vis. prof. Sch. Bus., West Tex. State U., Canyon, 1950-67. Bd. dir., treas. Tulia (Tex.) Indsl. Found. Served with USNR, 1945-46. C.P.A., Tex. Mem. Ch. of Christ. Rotarian (pres. 1963-64, 69-70). Home: 45 Fannin Dr Tulia TX 79088 Office: 125 N Maxwell St Tulia TX 79088

GRAHLMAN, FRANK WILSON, ednl. adminstr.; b. Omak, Wash., Oct. 6, 1932; s. Frank Cloud and Mabel Francis (Wilson) G.; B.A., Eastern Washington State Coll., 1957, M.Ed. (fellow), 1961; postgrad. Sacramento State Coll., 1965; m. Dixie Lee Marsh, Aug. 17, 1971; children by previous marriage—Debbie (Mrs. Michael Kellenberger), Richard Grahlman. Tchr., Bellevue (Wash.) Schs., 1957-61, spl. counselor, 1961-63; tchr. Folsom Cordova Schs., Rancho Cordova, Cal., 1963-65, vice prin., 1965-71; prin. Wilbur Jr. High Sch., Palo Alto, Cal., 1971-73; grad. asst. Okla. State U., Stillwater, 1973—. Served with USNR, 1953-55. Mem. Scarlet Arrow, Toastmasters. Home: 1901 W Arrowhead Dr Stillwater OK 74074

GRAINE, GEORGE NATHAN, govt. ofcl.; b. Bklyn., Mar. 4, 1934; s. Allen Robert and Rosalind Schancupp (Goldberg) G.; B.A., Alfred U., 1955, M.A., 1956; m. Gwendolyn Whiting, Nov. 13, 1958; children—Steven, Robin. Counselor Wiltwyck Sch. Boys, Esopus, N.Y., 1956-57; research psychologist Human Resources Research Office, Ft. Benning, Ga., 1957-59; research psychologist, 1959-67; head anti-submarine warfare weapons br. Personnel Research Lab., Washington, 1967-68, asst. for human factors coordination Naval Ship Systems Command, Washington, 1968-73, program mgr. command support program, 1974—. Bus. mgr. Holmes Run Acres Civic Assn., Falls Church, Va., 1967; publs. mgr. Holmes Run Acres Recreation Assn., 1968-69, 72, 73. Served with AUS, 1957-59. Mem. Human Factors Soc., Am., Eastern, D.C. psychol. assns. Contbr. articles to profl. jours. Home: 7604 Westminster Ct Falls Church VA 22042 Office: Naval Ship Systems Command SHIPS 047C12 Washington DC 20362

GRAINGER, DAVID ALAN, dentist; b. Sydney, Australia, Sept. 25, 1934; s. William Alan and Sybil Wahl (Baxter) G.; B.D.S. with honors, Sydney U., 1956; D.D.S., Northwestern U., 1957; 4 children. Came to U.S., 1956, naturalized, 1968. Asst. in dental medicine Harvard-Forsyth, Boston, 1957-59; pvt. practice dentistry, London, Eng., 1959-60, Sydney, 1961-64; instr. Tufts Dental Sch., Boston, 1964-65, asst. prof., 1965-68, asso. prof., 1968-69; prof., chmn. operative dentistry U. Fla., Gainesville, 1969—. Cons. Vets. Adminstrn. Hosp., Gainesville, 1969—. Served with Australian Nat. Service, 1952-55. Fellow Internat. Coll. Dentists, Australian Coll. Dental Surgeons. Author: (with Bruce Bell) Basic Operative Dentistry Procedures, 2d. edit., 1971. Office: Coll Dentistry U Fla J Hillis Miller Health Center Gainesville FL 32601

GRAMLEY, DALE H(ARTZLER), found. exec.; b. Loganville, Pa., Sept. 23, 1905; s. Andrew D. and Ada Laura (Meals) G.; A.B., Albright Coll., 1926, Litt.D., 1949; S.M., Columbia, 1929; LL.D., Moravian Coll. and Theol. Sem., 1950; Litt.D. (hon.), Wake Forest Coll., 1955; LL.D. (hon.), Davidson Coll., 1960; m. Caroline Lois Illick, Dec. 27, 1929; children—Hugh Andrew, William Eugene, Dale Illick, Stephan Edward. Reporter, asst. editor U. York (Pa.) Dispatch, 1926-28; copy-reader N.Y. Jour. of Commerce, 1929; instr. journalism Lehigh U., 1929-33, asst. prof., 1933-35, asso. prof., 1935-42, dir. of courses in journalism, 1931-42, editor of Univ. News, 1936-42; asst. to pres. Moravian Coll. and Theol. Sem., 1942-44; editor Bethlehem (Pa.) Globe-Times, 1944-49; v.p. and dir., Bethlehem Globe-Times, WGPA Charities, Inc., 1947-49; v.p. Old Salem Inc., 1950-68; pres. Salem Acad. and Coll. Winston-Salem, 1949-71; exec. dir., sec.-treas. Z. Smith Reynolds Found., 1971—; dir. Triangle Broadcasting Co. Alumnus trustee Albright Coll., 1931-40; trustee Moravian Coll. and Theol. Sem., 1947-50; v.p. Moravian Music Found., 1956-71; bd. dirs. Reynolda House, Inc., 1967-71; pres. Piedmont U. Center of N.C., 1964-69. Mem. Winston-Salem C. of C. (pres. 1968, chmn. bd. 1969), Pi Delta Epsilon. Democrat. Moravian, Rotarian. Clubs: Forsyth Country; Winston-Salem Automobile (dir.). Home: 331 S Main St Winston-Salem NC 27101

GRAMLICH, CHARLES VINCENT, city ofcl.; b. Ft. Smith, Ark., Dec. 5, 1947; s. Charles Edward and Frances Christine (Rothgerber) G.; B.S. in Econs., Northeastern State Coll., 1970; postgrad. Okla. State U., 1965-66, 68. Adminstrv. asst. City of McAlester (Okla.), 1970-71, asst. city mgr., 1971-72, city mgr., 1972—. Chmn. P.T.A. Safety Council, 1972—. Vice chmn. 3d dist. Okla. Municipal League, 1972-73. Bd. dirs. Boys Club, 1972—, United Fund; trustee McAlester Parking Authority. Served with AUS, 1970-71. Mem. Internat., Okla. city mgrs. assns., Beta Theta Pi. Home: 1215 E Miami St McAlester OK 74501 Office: PO Box 578 McAlester OK 74501

GRAMLICH, EDWARD MARTIN, govt. ofcl.; b. Rochester, N.Y., June 18, 1939; s. Jacob Edward and Harriet (Williams) G.; B.A., Williams Coll., 1961; M.A., Yale, 1962, Ph.D., 1965; m. Ruth Ann Brown, Aug. 29, 1964; children—Sarah Becker, Robert Edward. Mem. staff Fed. Res. Bd., 1965-70; with Monash U., Australia, 1970; dir. policy research div. Office Econ. Opportunity, Washington, 1970-73; with Brookings Instn., Washington, 1973—. Mem. econs. adv. bd. NSF, 1973—. Recipient Abramson award Nat. Assn. Bus. Economists, 1970. Editorial bd. Nat. Tax Jour., 1971—. Home: 11529 Links Dr Reston VA 22090 Office: Brookings Instn Washington DC 20036

GRAMLING, ELIZABETH B., clubwoman; b. Carp, Tenn., Mar. 2, 1910; d. James Rhea and Cynthia (Smith) Bogart; R.N., James M. Jackson Hosp. Sch. Nursing, Miami, Fla., 1931; m. William Sanders Gramling, Sept. 11, 1935; 1 son, Frank Robert. Nurse, 1931-35. First vol. instr. home nursing A.R.C., Dade County, 1941, organizer nurses aide corps, 1941, chmn., 1941-42, 44, vice chmn. vol. spl. services Dade County chpt., 1944, bd. dirs., 1949-50; sec. Miami Beach Garden Center and Conservatory Com., 1958-68, treas., 1969-72. Mem., sec. bd. trustees Jackson Meml. Hosp., 1938-42; trustee Opera Guild Greater Miami. Recipient certificates of appreciation for civic work. Mem. U.D.C. (chpt. pres. 1957-60, chmn. state by-laws com. 1959-60, chmn. nat. by-laws com. 1960—), So. Dames of Am. (founding mem.). Episcopalian. Clubs: Bath, Miami Beach Garden (pres. 1950-52), Coast Guard Officers Wives. Home: 251 E San Marino Dr Miami Beach FL 33139

GRAMMER, JOHN COLQUITTE, physician; b. Brenham, Tex., June 20, 1925; s. John Colquitte and Elizabeth (Miller) G.; student Tex. A. and M. Coll., 1942-43; M.D., Southwestern Med. Sch., 1947; student U. Pa. Grad. Sch. Medicine, 1953-54; m. Jessica Turpin, May 11, 1956; children—John Miller, Robert Turpin. Intern, City-County Hosp., Ft. Worth, Tex., 1947-48; resident Gen. Hosp., Kansas City, Mo., 1948-50; practice medicine, specializing in internal medicine, Midland, Tex., 1954-66; fellow cardiovascular diseases Scripps Clinic and Research Found., La Jolla, Cal., 1966-67; cons. cardiologist, dir. coronary care unit St. Paul Hosp., Dallas, 1967—, also dir. tng. courses nurses and physicians. Served with M.C., USMC, 1951-53; lt. USNR Res. Diplomate Am. Bd. Internal Medicine. Fellow Am. Coll. Cardiology, Am. Coll. Chest Physicians; mem. A.C.P., Tex. Acad. Internal Medicine, Am. Soc. Internal Medicine, Tex. Club Internists,

Sigma Nu, Phi Chi. Home: 3809 Stratford St Dallas TX 75205 Office: 5909 Harry Hines St Dallas TX 75235

GRANATA, SAM, city ofcl.; b. San Antonio, Mar. 26, 1923; s. Sam and Lena (Granato) G.; B.S., Tex. A. and M. U., 1948; m. Florence Ammerman, Oct. 7, 1945. With City of San Antonio, 1949—, city mgr., 1973—. Served to 1st lt. C.E., AUS, 1943-47. Named Pub. Works Man of Yr., Kiwanis Internat. and Am. Pub. Works Assn., 1965. Mem. Nat., Tex. pub. works assns., Soc. Profl. Engrs., Tex. Municipal League, Nat., Tex. (Engr. of Yr. award Bexar County chpt. 1968) socs. profl. engrs., Christopher Columbus Soc. Democrat. Roman Catholic. Contbr. articles to profl. jours. Home: 3306 Yorktown Dr San Antonio TX 78230 Office: City Hall PO Box 9066 San Antonio TX 78285

GRANATIR, WILLIAM LOUIS, psychoanalyst; b. Phila., Apr. 1, 1916; s. Jacob and Anna (Stein) G.; B.A., U. Pa., 1936; M.D., Hahnemann Med. Coll. Phila., 1941; m. Mildred Silver, July 4, 1941; children—John R., Joseph P., Thomas A., Charles E. Intern, Mt. Sinai Hosp., Phila., 1941-42; resident St. Elizabeth Hosp., Washington, 1946-48; dir. Washington Inst. Mental Hygiene, 1948-50; practice medicine, specializing in psychiatry and psychoanalysis, Washington, 1950—; tng. and supervising analyst Washington Psychoanalytical Inst., 1964—. Cons. Jewish-Social Service Agy., Washington, 1951—; cons. adult psychiatry br. Nat. Inst. Mental Health, 1968—. Served with USAAF, 1942-46. Fellow Am. Psychiat. Assn.; mem. Washington Psychoanalytic Soc. (pres. 1973—). Home: 3572 Appleton St NW Washington DC 20008 Office: 4545 Connecticut Av NW Washington DC 20008

GRANBERRY, GEORGIA LOU, ednl. therapist; b. Wesson, Miss., Dec. 25, 1939; d. George Richmond and Lou (Meadows) Granberry; student Millsaps Coll., 1958-59; B.S., U. So. Miss., 1962, M.S., 1966, certificate in corrective therapy, 1974. Tchr. spl. edn. program Kuhn Meml. State Hosp., Vicksburg, Miss., 1963-64, recreation dir. for the blind Div. State Rehab. Dept., 1963; head resident U. So. Miss., 1964-66; resident counselor Fla. State U., 1966-67; residence hall counselor, Panhellenic adviser La. Tech. U., Ruston, 1967-72; deaf-blind tchr., 1972-73; corrective therapist Miss. Deaf-Blind Program, Ellisville State Sch., 1973—. Mem. Am. Corrective Therapy Assn., Am. Assn. U. Women (1st v.p. Ruston br. 1971), U. So. Miss. Alumni Assn., Phi Delta Gamma, Cwens. Methodist. Club: F, Fla. State University (Tallahassee). Home: 4103 Lur Lane Laurel MS 39440

GRANER, STANLEY, corp. exec.; b. Dallas, Dec. 4, 1925; s. Walter and Marie (Weaks) G.; student So. Methodist U., 1943-44; B.S., U. Tex., 1947, M.B.A., 1948; m. Ann Elizabeth Carnathan, Aug. 13, 1949; children—Ann, Lane, Stanley, Jane. With U.S. Cold Storage Corp., 1948—, salesman, Dallas, 1948-51, adminstrv. asst., Kansas City, Mo., 1951, adminstrv. asst., asst. treas., Chgo., 1951-53 asst to pres., Kansas City, Mo., 1953-54, sales mgr., Ft. Worth, 1954-58, v.p., mgr., 1958-71, exec. v.p., 1971—. Councilman, mayor pro tem North Richland Hills, Tex., 1958-61. Served to lt. (j.g.) USNR, 1943-46. Mem. Nat. Assn. Refrigerated Warehouses (chpt. past pres., dir. 1970—), Refrigeration Research Found. (past gov.). Republican. Methodist. Clubs: Rotary, Diamond Oaks Country. Home: 5929 Diamond Oaks Dr Fort Worth TX 76117 Office: 5150 Pulaski St Dallas TX 75247

GRANGER, GILBERT LOFTON, accountant; b. Charleston, S.C., June 25, 1935; s. Warren B. and Dorothy Lofton (Gilbert) G.; A.B., Coll. William and Mary, 1957; m. Ann Cornelia Hill, Sept. 25, 1958; children—Gilinda Dawn, Gray Ann, Gregory Hill. Partner Granger, Lent & Hawthorne, C.P.A.'s, Williamsburg, Va., 1961—; pres. G-Square, Inc., Williamsburg, 1965—; columnist Va. Gazette, 1969—. Mem. Sch. Bd., Williamsburg, 1973—. Bd. dirs. Williamsburg Area Recreation Assn., 1964-72, pres., 1969; bd. dirs. Williamsburg Area Day Care Center, 1968—. Recipient Service award Nat. Found., 1965, Jaycee of Year award, 1963, Distinguished Service award, 1966, Outstanding State Chmn. award Va. Jaycees, 1971. Mem. Am. Inst. C.P.A.'s, socs. C.P.A.'s, Williamsburg Jaycees (pres. 1967-68), James City County (dir. 1963-68, pres. 1966-67), Williamsburg chambers commerce, St Andrew's Soc., Mensa, William and Mary Alumni Soc., Lambda Chi Alpha. Presbyn. (deacon 1970-71, chmn. 1971). Elk (pres. 1965-66), Kiwanian (dir. 1967, 71-74, pres. 1973-74). Home: 302 Harrison Av Williamsburg VA 23185 Office: 1005 Richmond Rd Williamsburg VA 23185

GRANT, BRUCE SHERWOOD, educator, geneticist; b. N.Y.C., Apr. 17, 1942; s. William Threlked and Cornelia Joan (Zeueney) G.; B.S., Bloomsburg State Coll., 1964; M.S. (NIH fellow), N.C. State U., 1966, Ph.D., 1968; m. Mary Catherine Lesevich, June 14, 1964; 1 dau., Megan Elizabeth. Instr. genetics N.C. State U., Raleigh, 1968; asst. prof. biology Coll. William and Mary, Williamsburg, Va., 1968-72, asso. prof., 1972—. Speaker various civic groups, socs., and polit. orgns. Faculty Research grantee, 1969, 71; AEC fellow, 1970. Mem. Nat. Wildlife Fedn. (asso.), Genetics Soc. Am., Soc. for Study of Evolution, Va. Acad. Sci., Phi Sigma, Phi Kappa Phi. Club: Bagpipe Band (Williamsburg). Contbr. articles in field to profl. jours. Home: 222 Colony Point Rd Williamsburg VA 23185

GRANT, DAVID ALAN, physician; b. Mart, Tex., Nov. 28, 1926; s. Walter Lee and Emma (Reichert) G.; student Tex. Christian U., 1944-45; B.A., U. Tex., 1947, M.D., 1951; m. Alice Louise Inskeep, Dec. 23, 1949; children—Cynthia Lynn, Karen Ann. Intern, Emory U., 1951-52; resident U. Tex. Med. Br., 1954-60; practice medicine, specializing in plastic surgery, Ft. Worth, 1960—; mem. staffs St. Joseph's, All Saints Episcopal. Ft. Worth Children's, W. I. Cook Childrens', Glenview hosps.; chief div. surgery Harris Hosp., 1971-73; chief div. plastic surgery John Peter Smith Hosp., 1969-74; spl. lectr. Harris Coll. Nursing, Tex. Christian U., 1963; hon. cons. Carswell Air Force Hosp. Pres. bd. dirs. Tarrant County Easter Seal Soc. for Crippled Children and Adults, 1971-72. Served to lt. (j.g.) M.C., USNR, 1952-54. Diplomate Am. Bd. Surgery, Am. Bd. Plastic Surgery. Fellow A.C.S.; mem. A.M.A., Tex., So. med. assns., Tarrant County Med. Soc., Southwestern Surg. Congress, Ft. Worth Acad. Medicine, Tex., Ft. Worth, Singleton (1st v.p. 1965) surg. socs., Am. Burn Assn., Tex. Soc. Plastic Surgery (v.p. 1969-70, pres. 1971), Am. Soc. Plastic and Reconstructive Surgery, Am. Assn. for Hand Surgery, Am. Assn. Physicians and Surgeons, Sigma Xi, Phi Beta Pi, Alpha Epsilon Delta, Alpha Phi Omega. Rotarian (dir. 1964-66). Home: 2736 Colonial Pkwy Fort Worth TX 76109 Office: 800 8th Av Fort Worth TX 76104

GRANT, ELIZABETH BRUBAKER (MRS. BEN J. GRANT), artist; b. St. Paul, Apr. 3, 1917; d. Delmer Dawson and Maude (Spear) Brubaker; student Sarah Lawrence Coll., 1934-37; m. Ben J. Grant, Aug. 9, 1938; children—William Dowman, Richard Martin, Martha Watts (Mrs. Mark A. Bedner). Exhibited in one-man shows Down East Gallery, Washington, Port Royal Inn, Hilton Head, S.C., 1970, Red Piano Art Gallery, Hilton Head, 1973; exhibited in group shows at Nat. Press Club Ann. Art Shows, Washington Soc. Artists Show, 1962. Recipient First Popular prize Washington Religious Art Exhibit, 1962, 65, Congl. Club Art Show, 1964, St. Andrews Religious Art Exhibit, 1964, 65, Best of Show Nat. Capital Garden Club Show, 1956, 62. Mem. Nat. Capital Area Fedn. Garden Clubs, Artists Equity Assn. Conglist. Clubs: Kenwood Golf and Country (Bethesda, Md.); Plantation (Hilton Head, S.C.). Home: 7000 Orkney Pkwy Bethesda MD 20034 also North Sea Pines Dr Hilton Head Island SC 29928

GRANT, EMORY BRYAN, coll. adminstr.; b. Griffin, Ga., July 14, 1917; s. Joseph Franklin and Martha Ethel (Weldon) G.; B.S., Ga. Inst. Tech., 1949; m. Lina Beatrice Poteet, July 23, 1937; children—Lyna (Mrs. John L. Taylor) Jim Bryan. Asst. regional dir. U.S. Bur. Census, Atlanta, 1949-52; comptroller Middle Ga. Coll., Cochran, Ga., 1953-66, Dalton (Ga.) Jr. Coll., 1967—. Mem. evaluation coms. So. Assn. Colls. and Schs. Trustee, treas. Dalton Jr. Coll. Found. Served with AUS, 1942-46. Methodist (chmn. trustees 1965-66, mem. ofcl. bd. 1967—, mem. Ga. commn. higher edn.). Rotarian (pres. Cochran 1959-60). Home: 1021 E Lakeshore Dr Dalton GA 30720 Office: Dalton Junior Coll Dalton GA 30720

GRANT, GEORGE CLIFFORD, biologist, educator; b. Medford, Mass., Aug. 13, 1929; s. George Arland and Beatrice (Chadwick) G.; student Amarillo Jr. Coll., 1952-53; B.S., U. Mass., 1956; M.A., Coll. William and Mary, 1962; Ph.D. (Nat. Def. Edn. Act fellow), U. R.I., 1967; m. Eileen M. O'Connor, Apr. 20, 1952; children—Shelley Ann (Mrs. Dennis M. Robins), George Charles. Fishery research biologist U.S. Fish and Wildlife Service, Millville, Del., 1956-60; asso. marine scientist, asst. prof. marine sci. Va. Inst. Marine Sci., Gloucester Point, Va., 1967—; asst. prof. marine sci. Coll. William and Mary, Williamsburg, 1967—, U. Va., Charlottesville, 1967—. Served with AUS, 1948-52. Mem. Am. Fisheries Soc., Am. Soc. Limnology and Oceanography, Soc. Systematic Zoology, Estuarine Research Fedn., Am. Soc. Ichthyologists and Herpetologists, Sigma Xi. Home: Route 3 Box 264 Gloucester VA 23061 Office: Virginia Inst Marine Science Gloucester Point VA 23062

GRANT, GEORGE THOMAS, optometrist; b. Chgo., Oct. 17, 1937; s. George Merton and Juanita (Battistoni) G.; student Ill. State U., 1956-58, Thornton Jr. Coll., 1958-59; D.Optometry, Ill. Coll. Optometry, 1962; m. Kathryn Lucille Racanelli, May 9, 1959; children—Jeffrey Thomas, Matthew Thomas, Brynn Elizabeth. Practice optometry, Perry, Ga., 1962-63, Hinesville, Ga., 1964-71, Cartersville, Ga., 1972—. Mem. Liberty County Bd. Health Hinesville, 1964-71; Liberty County rep. Comprehensive Health Planning, 1968-71; mem. Liberty County Title I Adv. Com., 1968-71, Liberty County Recreation Commn., 1970-71; pres. Coastal Areawide Comprehensive Health Planning Council, 1970-71; mem. Ga. Comprehensive Health Planning Council, 1972—; chpt. chmn. Liberty County chpt. A.R.C., 1964-66, mem. Bartow County chpt., 1972—. Liberty County campaign chmn. Jimmy Carter for Gov., 1970. Recipient award of appreciation A.R.C., 1966; commd. adm. Ga. Navy, 1971. Fellow Am. Acad. Optometry (sec.-treas. Ga. chpt. 1970-72, chpt. pres. 1972—); mem. Am., Ga. (pres. 1974—) optometric assns., Ga. Vision Services (dir. 1971—), So. Council Optometrists, 1st Dist. (pres. 1965-66), 7th Dist. optometric socs., C. of C. (past pres. Liberty County, v.p., dir. Cartersville-Bartow County), Tomb and Key, Beta Sigma Kappa. Rotarian. Home: 216 Pioneer Trail Cartersville GA 30120 Office: 310 N Tennessee St Cartersville GA 30120

GRANT, JAMES MARSE, editor; b. High Point, N.C., Sept. 13, 1920; s. Lon L. and Elsie (Warren) G.; A.B. with honors, High Point Coll., 1941, L.H.D., 1972; m. Marian Gibbs, June 16, 1942; children—Susan (Mrs. Robert Rawls), Marcia (Mrs. Kenneth Hungate), Carol. With personnel dept. Firestone Textiles, 1943-47; editor Ecusta Paper Corp. (now Olin Mathieson), Pisgah Forest, N.C., 1947; editor Lincoln County News, Lincolnton, N.C., 1948, News-Herald, Morganton, N.C., 1949; editor Charity and Children for Bapt. Children's Homes, Bapt. State Conv. N.G., Thomasville, N.C., 1950-60, editor Bibl. Recorder, Raleigh, 1960—. Mem. N.C. Good Neighbor Council, 1963-71, exec. com., 1963-71; N.C. chmn. March of Dimes, 1964-67. Mem. N.C. Gov.'s Com. Jobs for Ex-Offenders, 1970—, Raleigh Mayor's Com. Employment of Handicapped, 1970—, N.C. Adv. Com. Pub. Edn., 1970-72. Com. to Study N.C. Liquor Laws, 1973—. Mem. So. Bapt. Radio and TV Commn., So. Bapt. Press Assn. (pres. 1970). Author: Whiskey at the Wheel, 1970. Home: 1428 Ridge Rd Raleigh NC 27607 Office: Biblical Recorder PO Box 26568 Raleigh NC 27611

GRANT, JAMES RICHARD, JR., govt. ofcl.; b. Fayetteville, Ark., Sept. 16, 1914; s. James Richard and Gracey (Sowers) G.; student Ark. Tech., 1930-32; B.A., U. Ark., 1934; postgrad. Ia. State U., 1941, 43-44; m. Mary Louise Keller, Oct. 3, 1936; 1 son, James Richard III. Asst. agrl. statistician Ark. Fed. State Crop Reporting Service, Little Rock, 1938-43; asso. agrl. statistician Statis. Lab., Ia. State U., 1943-44; statis. analyst Office of Chief, Bur. Agrl. Econs., Washington, 1944-52; agrl. statistician FAO, UN, 1952; dept. clearance officer Agrl. Marketing Service, Washington, 1953-61, Statis. Reporting Service, Dept. Agr., Washington, 1962—. Recipient Superior Service award Dept. Agr., 1956. Fellow Am. Statis. Assn.; mem. Am. Agrl. Econs. Assn. Democrat. Baptist. Home: 3425 N Emerson St Arlington VA 22207 Office: Statis Reporting Service Dept Agr 14th and Independence SW Washington DC 20250

GRANT, LORENZO HALE, civil engr.; b. Greenville, Ala., Dec. 11, 1936; s. Ralph Lorenzo and Mary Alice (Rhodes) G.; grad. high sch.; m. Carolyn Lucille Pemberton, Dec. 21, 1958; children—Philip Lorenzo, Lisa Carol. Engring. asst. Ala. Hwy. Dept., Alexander City, 1954-63, civil engr., 1963-71, profl. civil engr., 1971—. Served with AUS, 1957. Mem. Ch. of Christ (treas. 1973-74). Home: Route 5 Box 241-A Alexander City AL 35010 Office: PO Box 432 Alexander City AL 35010

GRANT, MILTON, broadcasting exec. Vice pres. WDCA-TV, Washington. Address: 5202 River Rd Washington DC 20016*

GRANT, WILLIAM ALEXANDER, JR., coal co. exec.; b. Richmond, Va., Nov 7, 1918; s. William Alexander and Louise (Hooper) G.; B.A., U. Richmond, 1941; m. Marion Louise Bankhead, Aug. 27, 1945; children—William Alexander III, Blossom Grant, Walter Bankhead. Sec.-treas. Bankhead Mining Co. Inc., 1953—; sec. Tri W Broadcasting, Inc., Jasper, 1965—, Bankhead Broadcasting Fayette, Inc., Jasper, 1970—, Franklin Broadcasting Inc., Russellville, Ala., 1965—, Bankhead Devel. Inc., Jasper, 1960—, Live Line Inc., Jasper, 1968—; chmn. bd. Gatorland Broadcasting Inc., St. Augustine, Fla., 1969—; gen. partner Pinewood Devel. Ltd., 1973; mng. partner Cobb Coal Co., Jasper, Automated Accounting Systems, Jasper, 1973; owner Easy Clean Center, Jasper, 1964—; dir. Viking Oil Co., Jasper. Chmn. March of Dimes, 1955. Served as lt. (s.g.) USNR, 1942-46. Decorated Navy Cross, D.F.C., Air Medal with gold star. Mem. Nat. Assn. Accountants, Theta Chi, C. of C. (dir. 1956). Clubs: Downtown (Birmingham); Musgrove Country, Rotary. Home: 912 9th Av Jasper AL 35501 Office: Box 16 29 Jasper AL 35501

GRANT, WILLIAM FRANKLIN, JR., banker; b. Marion, N.C., May 4, 1921; s. William Franklin and Mary Ellen (Allison) G.; student Brevard Jr. Coll., 1938-40, E. Carolina Tchrs. Coll., 1940-42, U. N.C., 1950-54, La. State U., 1962-65; m. Mildred Lenore Ragan, Nov. 16, 1946; children—William Franklin III, Michael Ragan, David Allison. Vice pres., First Nat. Bank, Hickory, N.C., 1950-66; v.p., cashier Alexandria Nat. Bank (Va.), 1966-68, Peoples Nat. Bank, Chester, S.C., 1968—. Tchr. Am. Inst. Banking, 1954-55. Sec.-treas. Hickory Community Found., Inc., 1960-66. Bd. dirs., chmn. United Fund; bd. dirs., treas. Chester County Mental Health Assn.; bd. dirs., vice chmn. S.C. Mental Health Assn.; chmn. bd. dirs. York, Chester, Lancaster Mental Health Center, Rock Hill, S.C., 1972—. Served with USNR, 1942-46. Recipient Distinguished Service award Nat. Polio Found., 1957, Nat. Heart Assn., 1960, United Fund, 1970; named Civitan of the Year, 1970. Mem. Am. Inst. Banking (chpt. pres. 1955-56), N.C., Va., S.C. bankers assns., Am. Legion, Democrat. Baptist. Moose. Club: Civitan (lt. gov. S.C. dist.) (Chester, S.C.). Home: Hill Top Acres Chester SC 29706 Office: Church St Chester SC 29706

GRANT, W(ILLIAM) VANCE, JR., govt. ofcl.; b. Gainesville, Ga., Sept. 3, 1924; s. W. Vance and Myrtle (Haynes) G.; A.B., Piedmont Coll., 1943; B.B.A., U. Ga., 1947; M.A., Columbia, 1948; M.S., Fla. State U., 1951; Ph.D., U. Md., 1968; postgrad. U. London, 1957; m. Earlynn Vance, Aug. 23, 1952; children—James, Jean. Psychometrist, Fla. State U., 1951-52; statistician, test technician State of Fla., Tallahassee, 1952-54; research psychologist U.S. Dept. Army, Washington, 1954-55; specialist ednl. statistics U.S. Office Edn., Washington, 1955—. Served with USNR, 1944-45. Mem. Am. Polit. Sci. Assn. Baptist. Author: (with others) Biennial Survey of Education in the United States, 1957, 59, 62; (with Kenneth A. Simon) Digest of Educational Statistics, 1962-71, 2d edit. (with C. George Lind), 1973; (with others) Progress of Public Education in the United States of America, 1967-1968, 1968. Contbr. to Historical Statistics of the United States, Colonial Times to 1957, 1960. Contbr. articles to profl. jours. Home: 211 W Columbia St Falls Church VA 22046 Office: 400 Maryland Av SW Washington DC 20202

GRASER, MERLE LAWRENCE, banker; b. Toledo, July 18, 1929; s. Ottomar and Irene Olga (Frommer) G.; student U. Miami, 1955-56; B.S. in Bus. Adminstrn., U. Fla., 1959; m. Lila Patricia Woodburn, Nov. 6, 1948; children—Shaun Douglass, Cathleen Patricia. Asst. v.p. City Nat. Bank Coral Gables, Fla., 1960-63; with First Nat. Bank Venice, Fla., 1963—, exec. v.p., 1970-72, pres., 1970-72, chmn. bd., 1972—, Instr. Am. Inst. Banking, 1960-71; dir. Charlotte County Nat. Bank, Port Charlotte, Fla. Bd. dirs. Golden Beach Assn., Venice, Fla., 1964—, Loveland Sch. for Retarded Children, 1964—. Served with USCG, 1951-54. Mem. Delta Sigma Pi. Lion (pres. 1969-70), Rotarian, Elk. Club: Yacht (Venice, Fla.). Home: 612 Hibiscus Dr Venice FL 33595 Office: 200 Nokomis Av S Venice FL 33595

GRASSI, RICHARD JOSEPH, electronics co. exec., realtor; b. Bklyn., Apr. 16, 1939; s. Anthony John and Elva (Highfill) G.; student Pratt Inst., Bklyn., 1957-59; B.S., U. So. Cal., 1963; postgrad. U. Ala., 1966-67, So. Meth. U., 1968-69; m. Linda Ann Highfill, June 6, 1964; children—Ralph Richard, Todd Raymond, Marion Elizabeth. Engr., Autonetics, Inc., Anaheim, Cal., 1959-63; circuit design engr. Electronic Communications, Inc., St. Petersburg, Fla., Lockheed Aircraft Co., Huntsville, Ala., 1963-67; sr. engr. Tex. Instruments, Inc., Dallas, 1967-72, financial adminstr. advanced design br., 1972—; owner Dick Grassi Realtors, Plano, Tex. Mem. Plano Capital Water and Sewerage Improvement Bd., 1973, Plano Bldg. Code Appeal Bd., 1972—. Precinct chmn. Collin County (Tex.) Republican Com., 1970-71. Bd. dirs. Plano Home Owners Assn. Mem. Nat. Assn. Real Estate Brokers. Roman Catholic. K.C. Home: 365 Willow Wood Rd Plano TX 75074 Office: PO Box 6015 Dallas TX 75222

GRAUGNARD, FORTUNE ANTOINE, sugar co. exec.; b. St. James, La., May 31, 1916; s. Fortune Antoine and Denise (Schexnayder) G.; student La. State U., 1932-34; m. Mary Ann Delaune, Mar. 2, 1916; s. Anne (Mrs. Bourg), Denise (Mrs. Jerry J. St. Pierre), Susan (Mrs. Melvin). Mgr., Graugnard Farms, St. James, 1935-45; pres. St. James Sugar Coop., Inc., 1945—; dir. Miss. Chem. Co., Washington Life Ins. Co., Farm Credit Bank New Orleans, Farm Land Bank New Orleans, Fed. Intermediate Credit Bank, New Orleans Bank for Coops. Mem. La. Ho. Reps., 1952-58. Mem. La. State U. Found. Democrat. Elk, K.C. Clubs: Boston, Plimsoll (New Orleans). Address: St James LA 70086

GRAVEL, CAMILLE F(RANCIS), JR., lawyer; b. Alexandria, La., Aug. 10, 1915; s. Camille F. and Aline (Delvaille) G.; student Notre Dame U., 1931-35, La. State U., 1935-37, Catholic U. Am., 1937-39; m. Katherine Yvonne David, Nov. 26, 1939; children—Katherine Ann, Mary Eileen (Mrs. Richard B. Cappell), Martha Louise (Mrs. Thomas A. Antoon), Camille F. III, Grady David, Eunice Holloman (Mrs. Joseph A. Mitchell), Virginia Maureen (Mrs. Charles L. Carbo, Jr.), Margaret Lynn, Mark Alan, Charles Gregory. Mem. U.S. Capitol Police Force, 1937-39; admitted to La. bar, 1940, U.S. Supreme Ct. bar, U.S. 5th Circuit Ct. Appeal bar, U.S. Dist. Cts. of La.; practiced in 1940—; sr. partner firm Gravel, Roy & Burnes; asst. dist. atty. Rapides Parish, La., 1942, atty. for inheritance tax collector, 1943-45; asst. atty. city of Alexandria, 1946-48. Atty., La. Workmen's Compensation Laws and Tax Laws, 1964-65; spl. counsel on medicare to gov. of La., 1966-67, on health, 1967; mem. La. Interdepartmental Health Policy Commn., 1967-68; gen. counsel La. Labor-Mgmt. Commn. on Inquiry, 1967. Mem. Nat. Citizen's Com. for Community Relations, 1964-68, La. Adv. Com. on Civil Rights, 1965-67, Nat. Adv. Bd. on Community Relations, 1965-67; founding mem. Com. on So. Progress; mem. adv. bd. Catholic Youth Orgn., Diocese of Alexandria. Mem. La. Democratic Central Com., 1948-64; Dem. nat. committeeman for La., 1954-60; rep. on exec. com. Dem. Nat. Com., 1955-60; chmn. La. delegation Dem. Nat. Conv., 1956, chmn. site selection com., co-chmn. credentials com., mem. arrangements com., 1960, del., 1964; mem. Nat. Adv. Council of Dem. Party, 1956-60; co-chmn. La. Lawyers for Johnson-Humphrey Presdl. Campaign, 1964; founding mem. So. Com. on Polit Ethics, So. Polit. Edn. Action Com. Bd. dirs. La. Council on Human Relations, 1965-68, Catholic Charities, Diocese of Alexandria. Decorated Knight of St. Gregory; recipient citation for outstanding achievement in field of politics Catholic U. Am., 1962. Fellow Internat. Acad. Trial Lawyers (dir. 1960-69); mem. Am., La. (gov. 1969-71, chmn. criminal law sect. 1971—), Alexandria (pres. 1949-50) bar assns., Notre Dame Law Assn. (dir. 1960-66, pres. 1962-63), Law Sci. Acad., Internat. Soc. Barristers, Am. Trial Lawyers Assn., Nat. Assn. Compensation Claimant's Attys. (asso. editor Law jour. 1954-68, state v.p. 1958-59), Alexandria-Pineville C. of C., Pub. Affairs Research Council, La. Civil Service League, Am. Legion, Internat. Platform Assn., L.Q.C. Lamar Soc., Catholic U. Am. Alumni Assn. (nat. gov. 1963-67, 71—, past pres. Alexandria chpt.), Phi Delta Phi, Kappa Sigma. K.C. (4 deg.), Elk (past exalted ruler Alexandria). Club: City (Baton Rouge). Home: 3214 Carol Ct Alexandria LA 71301

GRAVELY, SAMUEL LEE, JR., naval officer; b. Richmond, Va., June 4, 1922; s. Samuel Lee and Mary George (Simon); student Va. Union U., 1938-40, 46-48, B.A. in History, 1948; student U. Cal. at Los Angeles, 1943-44, Columbia, 1944; postgrad. U.S. Naval War Coll., 1963-64, George Washington U., 1964; m. Alma Bernice Clark, Feb. 12, 1946; children—Robert Michael, David Edward, Tracey Ernestine. Commd. ensign U.S. Navy, 1944, advanced through grades to rear adm., 1971; asst. bn. comdr. Naval Tng. Center, Great Lakes, Ill., 1944-45; communications officer, electronics officer, exec. officer, personnel officer USS PC-1264, 1945-46; communications watch officer Fleet Tng. Group, Norfolk, Va., 1946; asst. to officer in charge for recruiting Naval Recruiting Sta. and Officer Procurement, Washington, 1949-51; radio officer U.S.S. Iowa, 1952-53;

communications officer U.S.S. Toledo, 1953-55, also asst. operations officer, 1953-55; asst. dist. security officer Hdqrs. 3d Naval Dist., N.Y., 1955-57; operations officer U.S.S. Seminole, 1957-59; mem. staffs Comdr. Destroyer Squadrons Seven and Five, 1959-60; exec. officer U.S.S. Theodore E. Chandler, 1960-61, comdg. officer, 1961, exec. officer, 1961-62; comdr. U.S.S. Falgout, Pearl Harbor, Hawaii, 1962-63; nat. emergency airborne command post programmer. Def. Communications Agy., Arlington, Va., 1964-66; comdg. officer U.S.S. Taussig, 1966-68; coordinator Navy Satellite Communications Program Office Asst. Chief Naval Operations, 1968-70; comdr. U.S.S. Jouett, San Diego, 1970-71; comdr. Naval Communications Command, dir. Naval Communications Div. Chief Naval Operations, Washington, 1971-73; comdr. Cruiser Destroyer Group Two, 1973—; ry. postal clerk Richmond (Va.) office. Decorated Bronze Star, Meritorious Service Medal, Joint Services Commendation Medal, Navy Commendation Medal with bronze star and combat V, Nat. Def. medal with 1 bronze star, China Service medal, Korean Service medal with 2 bronze stars, UN Service medal, Armed Forces Expeditionary medal, Vietnam Service medal with 6 Bronze stars, Vietnamese Campaign medal, others. Mem. Armed Forces Electronics Assn. (v.p. 1971—), I.E.E.E., Alpha Phi Alpha. Kiwanian (hon.). Home: 7211 Idylwood Ct Falls Church VA 22043 Office: Comdr Destroyer Group Two FPO New York City NY 09501

GRAVER, RICHARD BYRD, chem. engr.; b. Cambridge City, Ind., Apr. 5, 1932; s. Orie Otto and Mary Caroline (Byrd) G.; B.S. (Alcoa scholar), Purdue U., 1954; M.S., U. Mich., 1955, Ph.D., 1958; m. Doris Evelyn White, June 29, 1952; children—Bruce, Jeanne, Mark, Jay, Timothy. Project leader ADM Chems., Mpls., 1957-60, resin group leader, 1960-67; mgr. polymer research Celanese Coatings Corp., Louisville, 1967-73, tech. mgr. powder coatings div., 1973—. Finance dir. Louisville Regional Sci. Fair, 1970—. ADM fellow, 1954-57, Trigg fellow, 1956-57. Mem. Am. Chem. Soc., Louisville Paint Soc., Sigma Xi, Tau Beta Pi, Omega Chi Epsilon. Kiwanian (pres. 1972). Patentee in field. Home: 108 Dorsey Lane Anchorage KY 40223 Office: 9800 Bluegrass Pkwy Louisville KY 40299

GRAVES, CHARLES CARLETON, educator; b. New Haven, Nov. 28, 1922; s. Charles Lewis and Helen Mary (Hughes) G.; B.E., Yale, 1944, M.E., 1947, D.Eng., 1952; m. Teresa Marie Murphy, June 25, 1949; children—Charles C., Eileen M., John M., Richard B., James P. Aero. research scientist NACA, 1947-53, asst. sect. head Lewis Flight Propulsion Research Lab., 1953-56; sci. adviser to chief research United Nuclear Corp., White Plains, N.Y., 1956-65; prof., chmn. dept. nuclear sci. and engring. Cath. U., Washington, 1965—. Spl. cons. AEC, pvt. industry. Served with AUS, 1943-44, USNR, 1944-46. Mem. Am. Nuclear Soc., Am. Soc. M.E., Sigma Xi. Contbr. articles to profl. jours. Home: 13125 Collingwood Terrace Silver Spring MD 20904 Office: B-19 Pangborn Cath U Washington DC 20017

GRAVES, CRANOR FRANKLIN, marriage counselor; b. Kinston, N.C., Oct. 26, 1926; s. Charles Franklin and Sarah (Barker) G.; student U. N.C., 1943-44; S.T.B., St. Mary's Sem., Balt., 1950; m. Rita Catherine Gassman, Aug. 6, 1971. Ordained priest Roman Catholic Ch., 1950; editor N.C., Cath., 1954-57; nat. dir. Movement for a Better World, 1965-67; chmn. priests senate, Diocese of Raleigh, N.C., 1968-69; vocational rehab. counselor, 1971-73; marriage counselor, 1973—. Mem. Raleigh Community Relations Com., 1969-72. Asso. mem. Am. Assn. Marriage and Family Counselors. Home: 1109 E Morgan St Raleigh NC 27610

GRAVES, DOROTHY LOU IRISH (MRS. BRUCE B. GRAVES), banker; b. Hurley, N.M., Feb. 10, 1925; d. R. Levon and Lucretia Alice (Dunbar) Irish; student Meadows-Draughn Bus. Sch., 1945-46; m. Paul Organ Barron, Apr. 5, 1942 (dec. Oct. 1961); children—Charlotte L., Linda K., Paul Levon; m. 2d, Bruce B. Graves, Aug. 29, 1962. Sec. Samuel G. Wiener Co., Shreveport, La., 1946-47; bookkeeper Haslam Lumber Co. (Tex.), 1950-52; bookkeeper Tex. State Bank, Joaquin, 1952-55, asst. cashier, 1955-67, cashier, 1967—. Bd. dirs. Joaquin Cemetery Perpetual Fund Com. Presbyn. Mem. Order Eastern Star. Home: Box 95 Joaquin TX 75954 Office: Box 98 Texas State Bank Joaquin TX 75954

GRAVES, EMORY LEA, developing co. exec.; b. New Orleans, Sept. 2, 1923; s. Emory and Esther (Lea) G.; B.A., Tulane U., 1942; postgrad. La. Polytech. Inst., 1942, La. Normal Coll., 1943; U. Ga., 1943; Southeastern La. Coll., 1950-51, La. State U., 1951, Loyola U. Law Sch., 1951-52; m. 2d, Sylvia Acosta; children—Emory Lea, Christy, Ann Elizabeth, Julie. Sales mgr. William B. Reily & Co., Inc., New Orleans, 1946-48; pres. Christy Ann Lea Inc., 1948—, Crestmont Devel. Corp., 1964—, Slidell Ford Tractors, Inc., 1972—; owner Emory L. Graves Realty Co., 1950—, Emory L. Graves Enterprises, 1950— (all Slidell, La.). Served with USNR, 1943-46. Mem. Nat. Inst. Farm and Land Brokers, St. Tammany Bd. Realtors (past pres., dir. 1965-68; realtor of year 1964); Am. Legion V.F.W., Res. Officers Am. Episcopalian (vestryman, treas., lay reader). Mason (Shriner). Home: Treasure Cove on Bayou Liberty Slidell LA 70458 Office: 520 Rigolets Rd Slidell LA 70458

GRAVES, HENRY THEODORE NORTHCOTT, corp. exec.; b. Luray, Va., Nov. 10, 1922; s. Henry Walton and Katherine (Northcott) G.; grad. Lawrenceville Sch.; student U. Miami; B.S., U. Va.; m. Rebecca Beall Jackson, Nov. 29, 1944; children—Rebecca (Mrs. John R. Hudson, Jr.), Henry Theodore Northcott II, Katherine Murchison, Elizabeth Duval, Cornelia Walton, John Howard Hershey, James Roderick Oughton. Pres. Luray Caverns Corp. (Va.), 1952—, Car & Carriage Caravan, Inc., Luray, 1957—, Luray Service Co., Inc., 1962—, Carillon Properties, Inc., Luray, 1965—, Luray Mfg. & Distbg. Co., Inc., 1963—; Historic Stoners Store, Fredericksburg; dir. Page Valley Nat. Bank, Va. Sky-Line Co., Inc. Richmond. Mem. Gov.'s Travel Adv. Com., Page County Sch. Bd.; mem. Upper Valley Regional Park Authority, Harrisonburg, Va. Mem. adv. com. New Market Battlefield Meml., Woodrow Wilson Found. Served with USAAF, 1942-45. Mem. Va. Travel Council (past pres.), So. Highland Attractions (past pres.), Nat. Caves Assn. (past pres.), Am. Soc. Travel Agts., Sovereign Colonial Soc. Ams. Royal Descent, Kappa Sigma. Conservative Democrat. Episcopalian. Mem. Order Magna Carta Barons; Mason, Rotarian. Clubs: National Press (Washington); Commonwealth (Richmond). Home: PO Box 389 Luray VA 22835

GRAVES, JAMES CLEVE, railroad equipment co. exec.; b. Melissa, Tex., Nov. 3, 1930; s. Glen L. and Nina (Hendricks) G.; student So. Meth. U., 1953-58; Accounting Certificate, N.Tex. Bus. Coll., 1949; m. Barbara Sharber, May 3, 1951; children—Elizabeth (Mrs. Gary Brandon), Paul, Shirley, Glen. With traffic dept. Mobil Oil Corp., Kansas City, Mo., 1952-64, supr. rail equipment, 1958-64; mgr. operations Celtran, Inc., Corpus Christi, Tex., 1964—. Served with USNR, 1948-49, 50-52. Mem. Mfg. Chemists Assn. Home: 215 Hampton Hall Lane Conroe TX 77301 Office: 777 S Post Oak Rd Houston TX 77027

GRAVES, JERRY BROOK, educator; b. Tylertown, Miss., Feb. 28, 1935; s. Jesse Brook and Mamie Ellen (Dillon) G.; B.S., Miss. State U., 1955, M.S., 1958; Ph.D. La. State U., 1962; m. Mary Ellen Brumfield, Dec. 25, 1960; 1 dau., Kathryn Shannon. Research asst. Miss. State U., State College, 1957-58; research asst. entomology La. State U., Baton Rouge, 1958-61, research asso., 1961-63, asst. prof., 1963-66, asso. prof., 1966-71, prof. entomology, 1971—. Served to 1st lt. AUS, 1955-57. Research grantee U.S. Dept. Agr., 1961—. Mem. Entomol. Soc. Am. (sec., treas. Southeastern br. 1972—), Sigma Xi, Gamma Sigma Delta, Phi Kappa Phi. Baptist. Contbr. articles to profl. jours. Home: 650 Rodney Dr Baton Rouge LA 70808

GRAVES, KENNETH MARTIN, architect; b. Beaumont, Tex., July 6, 1943; s. Ernest Leroy and Margaret Louise (Hillyer) G.; B.Arch., Okla. State U., 1967; m. Patricia Ann Edwards, Aug. 28, 1965. Asso. Ford, Powell & Carson, architects and planners, San Antonio, 1969-73; partner Tuggle & Graves, San Antonio, 1973—. Bd. dir. First Repertory, 1972—. Served to 1st lt. Ordnance Corps, AUS, 1967-69. Decorated Army Commendation medal. Mem. Nat. Inst. Architects, Nat. Council Archtl. Registration Bds., A.I.A., Tex. Soc. Architects. Republican. Episcopalian. Home: 7500 Callaghan Rd San Antonio TX 78229 Office: 404 E Mulberry St San Antonio TX 78212

GRAVES, QUINTIN BRANSON, educator; b. Fairview, Okla., Oct. 23, 1905; s. Will James and Sarah Prescott (Cowgill) G.; student Washburn U., 1924-25; B.S., U. Kan., 1930; M.S., U. Ia., 1933; m. Elletha Kathryn Haines, Sept. 6, 1932; 1 dau., Mary Kathryn Harber. Grad. asst. U. Ia., Iowa City, 1930-33; instr. U. Tenn., Knoxville, 1933-35; hydraulic engr. TVA, Knoxville, 1935-37; instr. U. Tex., Austin, 1937-41, asst. prof., 1941-45, asso. prof. civil engring., 1945-46; acting dir. div. san. engring. S.D. Bd. Health, Pierre, 1945-46; asso. prof. civil engring. Okla. State U., Stillwater, 1946-47, prof., 1947-71, prof. emeritus, 1971—. Cons. Okla. State U. Water Supply Pipe Line, 1948-50, supt. water plant, 1950-56; cons. USPHS, 1965; mem. regional review com. on health grants USPHS, 1967-69. Recipient James R. Croes medal Am. Soc. C.E., 1940; Arthur Sidney Bedell award Water Pollution Control Assn., 1953; George Warren Fuller award Am. Water Works Assn., 1965. Diplomate Am. Acad. Environmental Engring.; Fellow Am. Soc. C.E.; mem. Am. Soc. for Engring. Edn., Am. Water Works Assn. (sect. pres. 1957-58), Okla. Water and Pollution Control Assn., Sigma Xi, Chi Epsilon. Kiwanian. Home: 607 N Bellis Stillwater OK 74074 Office: School Civil Engineering Oklahoma State University Stillwater OK 74074

GRAVES, ROY WILLIAM, JR., editor; b. Ada, Okla., Dec. 29, 1915; s. Roy William and Rosalie Christina (Haak) G.; B.S., Tex. A. and M. U., 1939; M.S., U. Mo. at Rolla, 1941; Ph.D., U. Tex. at Austin, 1949; m. Kathleen Marie Wasmuth, Nov. 8, 1942; children—Sandra (Mrs. Edwin F. Kagin), Michael David, Terrill Kent. Research geologist Standard Oil Co. of Cal., LaHabra, 1949-54, exploration geologist, 1954-60; sr. geologist Monsanto Chem. Co., Denver, 1960-63; adj. asso. prof., dept. information services U. Tulsa, 1963—, editor Petroleum Abstracts, 1963—. Served to lt. col. AUS, 1941-46. Fellow Geol. Soc. Am.; mem. Am. Assn. Petroleum Geologists, Geosci. Information Soc. (pres. 1972), Am. Geol. Inst. (mem. governing bd. 1973), Assn. Earth Sci. Editors, Am. Soc. Information Scis., Sigma Xi. Home: 6864 E 57th St Tulsa OK 74145 Office: 1133 N Lewis Av Tulsa OK 74110

GRAVES, WILLIAM LAVAN, architect; b. Wichita Falls, Tex., Jan. 6, 1937; s. William LaVan and Lela Lou (Harber) G.; B.Arch., Tex. Technol. U., 1960; m. Marian Virginia Salinas, Aug. 19, 1969; children—William LaVan III, Angela Nicole, Gillian Michelle. Draftsman, Boone & Pope, architects and engrs., Abilene, Tex., 1960-64, Tittle & Luther, architects, Abilene, 1964-65; designer, Preston Geren, architect, Ft. Worth, 1966-67; chief designer, v.p. Gordon Sibeck & Assos., Inc., Dallas, 1967—. Served with AUS, 1960-61. Mem. A.I.A., Tex. Army N.G. Assn. Roman Catholic. Prin. archtl. works include: territorial office bldg. Sears, Roebuck & Co., Dallas, 1971, Amigoland Mall Shopping Center, Brownsville, Tex., 1972, Cielo Vista Mall Shopping Center, El Paso, 1973. Home: 11032 Eastview Circle Dallas TX 75230 Office: 1407 Main St Dallas TX 75202

GRAVITT, T(HUR) O(DELL), telephone co. exec.; b. Apperson, Okla., July 10, 1923; s. Miles C. and Winnie C. (Harris) G.; student U. Kan., 1943-44, U. Tulsa, 1947-49; m. Oleta Maye, July 23, 1943; children—Michael T., Patrick D. With Southwestern Bell Telephone Co., 1947—, gen. comml. mgr., Topeka, Kan., 1964-69, v.p. staff, 1969-70, v.p., gen. mgr. San Antonio area, 1970-73, v.p. Tex. area, Dallas, 1973—; dir. 1st Nat. Bank, Dallas, Met. Savs. and Loan, Southwestern Life Ins. Co. Bd. dirs. A.R.C., Dallas Citizens Com., Tex. Research League. Clubs: Northwood, City, Chaparral (Dallas); Austin. Home: 7124 Lupton Dr Dallas TX 75225 Office: PO Box 5521 Dallas TX 75222

GRAY, BLAINE EDWARD, electric co. exec.; b. North Charleston, S.C., Feb. 2, 1922; s. Bailey Hendrix and Ruth (Spaulding) G.; B.E.E., Clemson Coll., 1943; postgrad. Internat. Corr. Schs., 1953; m. Edith Paris Shouf, Feb. 18, 1949; children—Blaine Edward, Patrick H., M. Anne, Susan C., James R., Robert S. Engr. mfg. div. Western Electric Co., Inc., Greensboro, N.C., 1946—, engring. mgr. quality reliability and safety, 1967—, asst. dir. engring. Engring. Research Center, N.J., 1960. Com. chmn. Boy Scouts Am., Flemington, N.J., 1964-65. Served with AUS, 1944-46. Registered profl. engr., N.C. Mem. I.E.E.E. (sr.), Am. Soc. Quality Control, Nat. Soc. Profl. Engrs. Presbyn. (deacon). Home: 3011 Magazine Dr Winston-Salem NC 27106 Office: PO Box 20046 Greensboro NC 27420

GRAY, CHARLES DOWD, SR., brokerage exec.; b. Gastonia, N.C., Aug. 21, 1890; s. George A. and Jennie (Withers) G.; student Trinity Coll., 1907-09, Washington and Lee U., 1909-10; m. Clarice Poff, July 9, 1912; children—Charles D., David G., Betty Claire (Mrs. L. S. Summey), Catherine Demaris (Mrs. H. Chapin Jackson). Pres. Gray Cotton Co., 1914-31, Priscilla Spinning Co., 1921-27; salesman Textiles, Inc., 1931-36, dir., 1933—; pres. Gray & Daniel, Inc. 1936—; incorporator Rex Spinning Co., Priscilla Spinning Co., Parkdale Mills. Inc., Ranlo Mfg. Co., Arkray Mills, Inc., Myrtle Mills, Inc. Past chmn. adv. council Belmont Abbey Coll.; past mem. N.C. State Ports Authority. Mem. Kappa Sigma. Mason (Shriner). Clubs: Kiwanis, Gastonia Country, Biltmore Country. Home: 1805 Country Club Rd Gastonia NC 28052 Office: Box 1238 Gastonia NC 28052

GRAY, CHARLES WEBSTER, mgmt. cons., cons. engr.; b. nr. Clinton, Mo., Sept. 9, 1914; s. Harvey Gant and Mary (Lay) G.; student Central Coll., 1931-33, U. Mo., 1933-36; Pittsburg (Kan.) State Coll., 1949-50; m. Frances Louise Thomas, Sept. 6, 1936; children—Mary Elizabeth (Mrs. James E. Bolin, Jr.), Charles Webster. Jr. engr., supr., asst. state planning engr. WPA, Jefferson City, Mo., 1936-40; design engr., field engr., asst. maintenance supt. Hercules Powder Co., Radford, Va., Wilmington, Del., 1940-46; maintenance and engring cons., Carthage, Mo., 1946; engr., sr. engr., projects supt. Spencer Chem. Co., Quaker Valley Constructors, Inc. subsidiary, Pittsburg and Kansas City, 1947-53; sr. maintenance engr., maintenance supt. Am. Cyanamid Co., New Orleans, 1953-59; maintenance cons., pres. Gray Equipment, Inc., Metairie, La., 1959-61, chmn. bd., 1959—; resident engr. Barnard and Burk, Baton Rouge, Seneca, S.C., 1961-62; chief planner, project supt., project mgr., cons. Catalytic Inc., Orange, Tex., Toledo, Phila., 1962—; mgmt. and engring. cons. on maintenance, constrn. chem. and petroleum industries and critical path method planning for chem. processing cos., oil refining cos., govt. agys., others, 1961—. Recipient numerous commendations, certificates for distinguished service in engring. planning and mgmt. achievements. Registered profl. engr., Mo., La., Kan. Mem. Internat. Platform Assn., Am. Mgmt. Assn., Nat., Mo. socs. profl. engrs., La. Engring. Soc., Am. Welding Soc. (dir. 1954-55). Democrat. Methodist (ofcl. bd.). Elk. Home: 121 N Livingston Pl Metairie LA 70005 Office: 121 N Livingston Pl Metairie LA 70005 also 1908 Dana Dr Adelphi MD 20783 also care Haskins-Sharp-Ordelheide 1009 Baltimore Kansas City MO 64105 also 613 S Patterson St Gibsonburg OH 43431 also 1528 Walnut St Philadelphia PA 19102

GRAY, CLARENCE JONES, educator, dean; b. Red Bank, N.J., June 21, 1908; s. Clarence J. Sr. and Elsie (Megill) G.; A.B., U. Richmond, 1933; M.A., Columbia U., 1934; postgrad. Centro de Estudios Historicos, Madrid, Spain, summer 1935; Ed.D., U.Va., 1962; m. Jane Love Little, Aug. 25, 1934; children—Frances Elizabeth (Mrs. Harry B. Mark Jr.), Kenneth Stewart. Underwriter Aetna Life Ins. Co., 1925-30; instr. Spanish, Columbia U., 1934-38; gen. sec., mem. exec. council Instituto de las Espanas en los Estados Unidos, 1934-39; instr., sec. dept. Romance langs. Queens Coll., N.Y.C., 1938-46 (on mil. leave 1943-46); dean students U. Richmond (Va.), 1946-68, asso. prof. modern langs., 1946-62, prof., 1962—, dean administrv. services, 1968-73, dean adminstrn., 1973—, editor bull., 1968—, moderator U. Richmond-WRNL Radio Scholarship Quiz Program. Cons., Commn. on Colls., So. Assn. Colls. and Schs. Trustee' Inst. Mediterranean Studies. Served from lt. to lt. comdr., USNR, 1943-46. Mem. Modern Lang. Assn., N.E.A., Am. Assn. Tchrs. Spanish, Am. Assn. for Higher Edn., Phi Beta Kappa, Phi Delta Kappa, Kappa Delta Pi, Omicron Delta Kappa (nat. sec. gen. council 1966-72, Distinguished Service key 1968, nat. chmn. scholarship awards 1972—), Alpha Psi Omega, Phi Gamma Delta, Alpha Phi Omega. Baptist. Mason. Mem. Legion of Honor, Order of De Molay. Clubs: Country of Va., Colonnade. Contbr. to profl. jours. Home: 1 Bostwick Lane U Richmond Richmond VA 23173

GRAY, CLINTON W., veterinarian; b. Wilmington, Del.; D.V.M., Mich. State U., 1943. Veterinarian, Md. Livestock San. Service, 1943-46; gen. practice vet. medicine, 1946-48; supr. Vaccine Prodn. Unit, Dept. Agr., Mexico City, 1948-50; staff biology dept. Norden Labs., Lincoln, Neb., 1950-55; with dept. Agr., S.Am., 1955-58; with Dept. Pub. Health S.Am., 1958-63; head animal health dept. Nat. Zool. Park, Washington, 1963—. Mem. Am., Md. vet. med. assns., Am. Animal Hosp. Assn., D.C. Acad. Vet. Medicine, Am. Assn. Zoo Veterinarians (sec.-treas. 1970-71, 73-74). Office: Nat Zool Park Rock Creek Park Washington DC 20009

GRAY, EARL HOWARD, chem. engr.; b. Spokane, Wash., May 28, 1916; s. Earl Howard and Magdalene (Cortesy) G.; B.S., Wash. State U., 1939; M.S., Washington U. at St. Louis, 1948; m. Verna Lee Venneberg, July 9, 1943; children—Robert M., Thomas A., Richard J., Virginia A. Engr., Mo. Portland Cement Co., St. Louis, 1940-41, research dir., 1946-48; research engr. Phillips Petroleum Co., Bartlesville, Okla., 1949—. Served with AUS, 1941-46. Decorated Bronze Star. Mem. Am. Inst. Chem. Engrs. Elk. Home: 1329 Rockdale Rd Bartlesville OK 74003 Office: Bldg 94G PRC Phillips Petroleum Bartlesville OK 74004

GRAY, GEORGE WILLIAM, soft drink co. exec.; b. Akron, O., July 8, 1933; s. C. Audley and Verena (Commerson) G.; B.A., Haverford Coll., 1955; M.B.A., Harvard, 1959; m. Margaret Brubaker, Dec. 7, 1963; children—Christina Anne, Caroline Courtright. Successively auditor, audit mgr., cost mgr. Harbison-Walker Refractories div. Dresser Industries, Inc., Pitts., 1959-68; gen. mgr. project Massey-Ferguson, Inc., Des Moines, 1968-70; treasury project mgr. Massey-Ferguson, Ltd., Toronto, Can., 1970-71; controller Royal Crown Cola Co., Columbus, Ga., 1971—. Served with AUS, 1955-57. Mem. Nat. Assn. Accountants. Republican. Lutheran. Mason (Shriner), Kiwanian. Club: Columbus Country. Home: 2401 Craigston Dr Columbus GA 31906 Office: 1000 10th Av Columbus GA 31902

GRAY, GUY LINCOLN, mfg. co. exec.; b. Cadiz, Ky., Feb. 13, 1909; s. Joe Nathan and Docia H. (Cook) G.; student pub. schs., Paducah, Ky.; m. Gladys Marie Lee, Apr. 9, 1932 (dec. Nov. 1967); children—Judith Lee, Joseph William; m. 2d, Eula Anderson Spradling, Nov. 23, 1968. With Henry A. Petter Supply Co., Paducah, 1925-47; pres. Ohio Valley Supply Co., Inc., Paducah, 1947-66, Guy Gray Mfg. Co., Inc., Paducah, 1958—, A-G Products, Inc., Paducah, 1961—, Lone Oak (Ky.) Recreation Corp., 1964—; formed Guy Gray Supply Co., 1966. Nat. bd. dirs. Boy Scouts Am. Mem. Travelers Protective Assn. (dir. post A). Methodist. Lion (past pres.). Home: Route 1 S Friendship Rd Paducah KY 42001 Office: PO Box 771 Paducah KY 42001

GRAY, HAROLD, lawyer; b. Ottawa, Ill., May 14, 1926; s. John E. and Mildred (Grady) G.; Ph.B., Ill. Westleyan U., 1949; summer student U. Cal. at Los Angeles, 1947; law student U. Ill., summer 1950; J.D., Valparaiso (Ind.) U., 1951; m. Judith Maddox; children—Nora Alison, Jeffrey John. Admitted to Fla. bar, 1955; established claims dept. State Farm Mut. Automobile Ins. Co., West Palm Beach, Fla., 1951-54; practiced in Miami, Fla., 1955—; of counsel Bolles, Goodwin and Ryskamp; trial counsel for So. Indemnity Ins. Co., Miami, 1959. Trustee Unitarian Fellowship of Palm Beach County, Fla., 1957-58. Served with USAAF, 1944-46. Mem. Palm Beach County Claim Men's Assn. (pres. 1952), West Palm Beach Jr. C. of C., Fla. Bar Assn., Sigma Chi, Phi Alpha Delta (past justice Halleck chpt., Vaiparaiso U.). Unitarian. Clubs: Surf (Miami Beach); Beach (Palm Beach).

GRAY, HARRY GORDON, civil engr.; b. Brookline, Mass., May 13, 1908; s. David Smith and Mary (Bell) G.; B.C.E., Northeastern U., 1928; m. Beatrice G. Churchil, Sept. 24, 1932; 1 son, Robert Norman. Project and resident engr. Mass. Dept. Pub. Works, Boston, 1932-42, chief engr., exec. asst., 1953-61; project mgr. Metcalf & Eddy, engrs., Boston, 1961-63; dir. Pinellas County Pub. Works & Engring,, Clearwater, Fla., 1963—. Mem. Planning Bd., Beverly, Mass., 1960-63. Served with Civil Engr. Corps, USNR, 1942-46, USNR, 1947-48, to capt. Civil Engr. Corps, 1951-53. Registered profl., engr. Mass., N.Y., Fla., Me., N.H., Vt. Fellow Am. Soc. C.E. (br. pres. 1970-71); mem. Fla. Engring. Soc. Home: 1438 Monte Carlo Dr Clearwater FL 33516 Office: 315 Haven St Clearwater FL 33516

GRAY, HERBERT HAROLD, JR., elec. co. exec.; b. Graysville, Ala., Sept. 20, 1919; s. Herbert H. and Dorothy R. (Jones) G.; B.S., U. Ala., 1943; postgrad. Ga. Inst. Tech., 1961, Stanford Bus. Sch., 1966; m. Mary Ellen Parsons, June 17, 1944; children—Herbert Harold III, Thomas Parsons. Asst. sales engr. Westinghouse Electric Co., Nashville, 1947-50, sales engr. Chattanooga, 1950-54, area sales mgr., Atlanta, 1954-57, asst. to indsl. mgr. Pitts., 1957-58, mgr., marine, aviation and transp. sales, 1958-60, dist. mgr., Birmingham, Ala., 1960-62, S.E. Zone mgr., elec. utility sales, Atlanta, 1962-67, nat. field sales mgr. power systems, Pitts., 1967-72, Southeastern regional v.p., Atlanta, 1972—. Dir. Southeastern Electric Exchange. Mem. Fla. Council 100. Bd. dirs. Ga. div. Am. Cancer Soc. Served to capt. AUS, 1943-46, ETO, PTO. Registered profl. engr. Tenn. Mem. I.E.E.E. Conf. Bd., Ga., Atlanta chambers commerce, Theta Tau. Presbyn. Clubs: Capitol City, Commerce (Atlanta); University (Pitts.); The Club (Birmingham Ala.) Author: (with E.G. Fischer)

Shockproofing For Hardened Bases, 1959. Office: Westinghouse Electric Co 1299 Northside Dr PO Box 4808 Atlanta GA 30302

GRAY, JAMES PEYTON, elec. engr.; b. Los Angeles, June 4, 1943; s. Lawrence Lenoir and Evelyn Ruth (Buss) G.; B.Engring., Yale, 1965, Ph.D. (NSF fellow), 1970; m. Laura Carol Henry, Sept. 7, 1962; children—Richard Lawrence, Cynthia Carolyn. With IBM, Research Triangle Park, N.C., 1970—, adv. engr., 1971—. Mem. I.E.E.E., Assn. for Computing Machinery. Club: Chapel Hill (N.C.) Tennis. Home: 904 Emory Dr Chapel Hill NC 27514 Office: PO Box 12275 E97/B192 Research Triangle Park NC 27709

GRAY, JOHN EDMUND, energy cons.; b. Woonsocket, R. I., Apr. 13, 1922; s. John Joseph and Alice (Naylor) G.; B.S. in Chem. Engring., U. R.I., 1943; m. Mary Lightbody, Dec. 3, 1944; children—Jane Elizabeth (Mrs. Peter W. Redmond), John Carlton, Jeffrey Naylor. Research engr. Westinghouse Electric Corp., 1943-46; sr. design engr. Engring. div. Gen. Electric Co., Hanford, Wash., 1946-47, head materials sect. atomic power dept. Gen. Engring. and Cons. Lab., Schenectady, 1948-49; materials adminstr. naval reactors br. AEC, U.S. Navy, 1949-50; dir. tech. and prodn. div. AEC, Savannah River Operations Office, 1950-54; project mgr. for Shippingport atomic power sta. Duquesne Light Co., Pitts., 1954-60; pres., chief exec. officer NUS Corp., Rockville, Md., 1960-69, chmn. bd., chief exec. offcer, 1969-72; chmn. bd. Neutron Products, Inc., Rockville, 1962-72. Consultec, Inc., Rockville, 1967-72; dir. Gourdine Systems, Inc., 1968-72; dir. Inst. Pub. Transp., N.Y.C., 1972—; cons. energy policy project Ford Found., 1972-73; mgr. enriched uranium supply program Edison Electric Inst., 1973; cons. energy research and devel. study Mass. Inst. Tech., 1973. Served with AUS, 1945-46. Mem. Am. Inst. Chem. Engrs. (mem. ad hoc com. on energy), Am. Nuclear Soc. Clubs: University (Washington); Belle Haven Country (Alexandria, Va). Author: Decision Making in the Energy Industry. Contbr. articles to profl. publs., Mark's Standard Handbook for Mech. Engrs. Home and office: 2007 Windsor Rd Alexandria VA 22307

GRAY, JULES, architect, oil co. exec.; b. Haralson, Ga., June 5, 1907; s. Lattimer and Willie (Hodnett) G.; B.S. in Architecture, Ga. Inst. Tech., 1927; m. Ellen Southwell, Sept. 5, 1939; children—James Southwell, Elizabeth (Mrs. David Jamison), Judith Ellen. Draftsman, Hentz, Adler & Shutze, Atlanta, 1930-31; designer Chrysler Bldg. Corp., N.Y.C., 1931-36; asst. to mdse. mgr. Sinclair Co., Atlanta, 1936, field merchandiser, Fayetteville, N.C., 1937, field constrn. engr., 1937-45; Southeastern constrn. engr. Pure Oil Co., Atlanta, 1945-65; div. constrn. mgr. Union Oil Co., Atlanta, 1965-68, regional constrn. mgr., 1968-72. Recipient Gold Certificate, Hall of Fame award Petroleum Council Ga., 1965, Service to Chpt. award A.I.A., 1960, Leadership award A.I.A., 1969, Ivan Allen award, 1970. Mem. A.I.A. (dir. Atlanta chpt. 1964, 68-70), Am. Petroleum Inst. (mem. com. on pub. affairs so. region 1967-72), Atlanta Petroleum Engrs. (chmn. 1961), Alpha Tau Omega. Presbyn. Prin. archtl. works include Sinclairs Nat. Biltmore Type Service Sta., Atlanta, Varsity Drive-In, Atlanta, Daytona Speedway-Nascar Office Bldg., J.H. Williams Oil Co., Butterfly Roof Service Sta., Tampa, Fla., Miller Bookstore Interiors, Atlanta, Jobber Non-Interstate Truck Stop, Columbus, Miss. Home: 515 W Paces Ferry Rd NW Atlanta GA 30305

GRAY, MAY HARRIS (MRS. THOMAS VIRGIL GRAY), writer; b. Canton, Ky.; d. James Robert and Mary Priscilla (Bridges) Harris; student Northeastern La. Bus. Coll., Fort Smith, Ark., 1917-18; m. Thomas Virgil Gray, June 19, 1920; children—Jean (Mrs. Louis H. Peer), Dorothy (Mrs. Joseph Beech Edwards), Thomas Virgil. Co-owner COIN-Stores, Fort Smith, Ark. and Oklahoma, Tex., 1946—. Mem. womans bd. Sparks Meml. Hosp., Fort Smith, 1936—. Recipient John Gould Fletcher Poetry award, 1964, 68; Jesse Stuart award, 1967; Dylan Thomas award, 1968; Poet Laureate's citation, 1966; Southwest Times Record award Poets Roundtable Ark. Mem. Ft. Smith Poets Roundtable Group (co-founder), Acad. Am. Poets, Nat. Fedn. State Poetry Socs., Nat. League Am. Pen Women (treas. 1968-69), Poetry Soc. Am., Poets Roundtable Ark., University City Poetry Club, P.E.O. (chpt. pres. 1960-61), D.A.R. Baptist. Club: Explorers. Author: In the Garden, 1935; The Voice of the Sea, 1963; Moment Before Summer, 1970; poems pub. in various mags., anthologies, newspapers; lectr. on poetry. Home: 1315-55 Terrace Fort Smith AR 72901 Office: 2300 Rogers Av Fort Smith ARK 72901

GRAY, MURRAY DANIEL, JR., banker; b. Columbus, Ga., Dec. 1, 1933; s. Murray Daniel and Martha (Martin) G.; student Auburn U., 1952-54, W.Ga. Coll., 1954-55; B.S., Auburn, 1957; m. Janet Pulliam, June 11, 1955; children—Roxann Malsby, Murray Daniel III. Jr. accountant Leonard, West, Favors, Columbus, 1955-57; v.p., trust officer Columbus Bank & Trust Co., 1958—, head trust dept., 1970—; dir. United Oil Corp., Columbus, Ga. Treas. Little League Football Columbus, 1970. Bd. dirs. Columbus Opportunity, Inc., 1970—, Columbus Mus., 1970—, Boys Club, Orphans Home, Muscogee council Boy Scouts Am., 1971—. Served with AUS, 1957; maj. Res. Mem. Ga. Bankers Assn. (pres. trust div. 1973-74), Estate Planning Council Columbus, Columbus Life Underwriters Assn. Baptist. Lion. Club: Country Columbus. Home: 2835 Roswell Lane Columbus GA 31906 Office: PO Box 120 Columbus GA 31902

GRAY, OSCAR SHALOM, lawyer; b. N.Y.C., Oct. 18, 1926; s. Samuel Zavl and Esther Malke (Grynberg) G.; grad. Mercersburg Acad., 1944; B.A., Yale, 1948, J.D., 1951; m. Sheila Hafter, Apr. 8, 1967. Admitted to Md. bar, 1951, D.C. bar, 1952; atty.-adviser Legal Adviser's Office, U.S. Dept. State, Washington, 1951-57; sec. Nuclear Materials & Equipment Corp., Apollo, Pa., 1957-64, treas., 1957-67, v.p., 1964-71, dir. 1964-67; spl. counsel Pres.'s Task Force on Communications Policy, Washington, 1967-68; cons. telecommunications policy U.S. Dept. Transp., Washington, 1967-68; acting dir. Office Environmental Impact, 1968-70; adj. prof. environmental law Georgetown U. Law Center, lectr. Cath. U. Am. Sch. Law, Washington, 1970-71; asso. prof. law U. Md. Sch. Law, Balt., 1971-74, prof., 1974—; practice law, Washington 1970—, Balt., 1971—. Served with USNR, 1945-46. Mem. Md. Bar Assn., Assn. Trial Lawyers Am., Order of Coif, Phi Beta Kappa. Clubs: Harvard-Yale-Princeton (Pitts.). Author: Cases and Materials on Environmental Law, 1970, 2d edit., 1973. Office: 1225 19th St NW Washington DC 20036 also 500 W Baltimore St Baltimore MD 21201

GRAY, RICHARD EDWIN, elec. engr.; b. Tulsa, Nov. 26, 1937; s. Richard Edwin and Naida Rue (Acton) G.; B.S., Okla. State U., 1961; postgrad. Wichita State U., 1961-62, U. Tulsa, 1965-66; m. Alice Joann Romshe, Oct. 16, 1965; children—Gregory Edwin, Brian Edwin, Jennifer Joann. Asso. engr. Boeing Aircraft Co., Wichita, Kan., 1961-63; engr. Pub. Service Co. Okla., Tulsa, 1963-66; engr. Avco Corp., Tulsa and Cin., 1966-67; with Williams Bros. Engring. Co., Tulsa, 1967-72; sr. elec. engr. Butler Assos., Inc., Tulsa, 1972—. Registered profl. engr., Okla. Mem. I.E.E.E. (chpt. treas. 1973—), Instrument Soc. Am. (sr.). Home: 9426 E 49th St Tulsa OK 74145 Office: 4815 S Harvard St Tulsa OK 74135

GRAY, ROBERT ALTON, sch. supt.; b. Stokes, N.C., Nov. 23, 1926; s. Henry Abram and Lucy Elizabeth (Carrington) G.; B.S., East Carolina U., 1949, M.A., 1950; Advanced Adminstrs. Certificate, U. N.C., 1965; m. Marie Whitford, Sept. 1, 1950; children—Robert Alton, Diane Marie. Tchr. sci. Bethel (N.C.) High Sch., 1949-51; prin. Magnolia (N.C.) High Sch., 1951-52, Faison (N.C.) High Sch., 1952-55, Mingo High Sch., Dunn, N.C., 1955-56, Boone Trail Sch., Mamers, N.C., 1956-63; asst. supt. Harnett County Schs., Lillington, N.C., 1963-66, supt., 1966—. Chmn. Lee-Harnett Mental Health, 1963-65, 73-74, bd. dirs., Harnett County Health Dept.; chmn. bd. Harnett County Library, 1970-74. Served with USNR, 1944-46. NSF, grantee, 1960-61. Mem. N.E.A. (life), N. C. Assn. Educators (life, div. state dir. 1970-71, dist. pres. 1961-62), Am. Assn. Sch. Adminstrs., Nat. Rural Supts. Presbyn. (deacon, elder). Mason, Rotarian. Club: Ruritan (Mamers). Home: PO Box 26 Lillington NC 27546 Office: PO Box 1027 Lillington NC 27546

GRAY, ROBERT STEELE, publishing co. exec.; b. Beaumont, Tex., Oct. 6, 1923; s. Fred and Ruth Louise (Lewelling) G.; B.S. in Journalism, U. Houston, 1952; m. Nellie Frances McGuinness, July 3, 1945; children—Robert Steele, Laura Elizabeth, Ruth (Mrs. Paul Lindholm). Newsman radio sta. KPRC, Houston, 1947-48; radio news dir. sta. KNUZ, Houston, 1948-49, KXYZ, Houston, 1949-50; staff writer Citizen Weekly Newspapers, Houston, 1949-50, Houston Post, 1956-59; founder Cordovan Corp., Houston, 1959, pub., gen. mgr., 1959—; tchr. TV news reporting U. Houston, 1954. Service with USMCR, 1942-46, 51-52. Mem. Am. Horse Publs. (pres. 1972-73), Sigma Delta Chi (v.p. Gulf Coast chpt. 1973). Author or co-author 5 books on horses and horse tng. Home: Route 2 Box 225 Cypress TX 77429 Office: 5314 Bingle Rd Houston TX 77018

GRAY, ROBERT WINSTON, security analyst; b. Austin, Tex., July 20, 1938; s. Hob and Mary (Tanner) G.; B.S. in Petroleum Engring., U. Tex., 1960; M.B.A., Harvard, 1963; m. Patricia Wadlington, Aug. 5, 1961; children—Susan Patricia, Lauren Ashley. Petroleum engr. Continental Oil Co., Sweetwater, Tex., 1960-61; accountant Arthur Young & Co., Houston, 1963-65; security analyst Underwood Neuhaus & Co., Houston, 1965-70, Rauscher Pierce Securities Corp., Dallas, 1970—. C.P.A., Tex. Mem. Am. Inst. C.P.A.'s, Tex. Soc. C.P.A.'s, Financial Analysts Fedn., Inst. Chartered Financial Analysts, Dallas Assn. Investment Analysts, Harvard Bus. Sch. Club (dir. 1969-70), Phi Gamma Delta, Tau Beta Pi. Home: 825 Teakwood Pl Richardson TX 75080 Office: 1200 Mercantile Dallas Bldg Dallas TX 75201

GRAY, ROBIN BRYANT, aerospace engr., educator; b. Statesville, N.C., Dec. 4, 1925; s. James Perry and Annie (Hartsell) G.; B. Aero. Engring., Rensselaer Poly. Inst., 1946; M.S. in Aero. Engring., Ga. Inst. Tech., 1947; Ph.D. Princeton U., 1957; m. F.R. Thompson, Apr. 30, 1949; children—Robin, William Carl. Research engr. Ga. Inst. Tech., Atlanta, 1947-49; research asst. then research assos. Princeton, 1949-56; asso. prof. Ga. Inst. Tech., Atlanta, then Regents prof., asso. dir. Sch. Aerospace Engring., 1956—. Councilman, North Atlanta, Ga., 1963-64, councilman, vice-mayor, 1964-65. Served to ensign, USNR, 1943-46. Mem. Am. Helicopter Soc., Am. Inst. Aeros. and Astronautics, Sigma Xi, Tau Beta Pi. Presbyn. (deacon 1961-63, 66-68, treas. trustee 1965—). Contbr. tech. articles and reports on aerospace engring. to profl. publs. Home: 1077 Spring Mill Lane NE Atlanta GA 30319

GRAY, ROY COOPER, JR., cattle co. exec.; b. Flemingsburg, Ky., June 4, 1928; s. Roy Cooper and Alice Kerr (Hood) G.; B.S., U. Ky., 1956, M.S., 1957; Ph.D., Auburn U., 1964; m. Norma Jean Wright, June 12, 1954; children—Susan, Roy Cooper, Steven. Farmer, Flemingsburg, Ky., 1947-50; staff mem. Auburn U., 1957-64; U. Ky., 1964-70; pres. Purebred Herds of Am., Inc., 1970-71, also dir.; pres., owner Modern Cattle Mgmt. Inc., Lexington, Ky., 1971—; dir. Profl. Services, Inc., Cattle Herds, Inc., Westbrook Cattle, Inc. Served with AUS, 1950-53, 61-62. Decorated Bronze Star medal. Mem. Am. Soc. Animal Prodn., Res. Officers Assn., Am. Legion, Sigma Xi, Gamma Sigma Delta. Kiwanian. Home: Route 5 Nicholasville KY 40356 Office: Box 866 Lexington KY 40501

GRAY, STEPHEN WOOD, educator; b. Oakland, Cal., Apr. 27, 1915; s. Roy Barnett and Ethel (Graham) G.; B.A., Lake Forest Coll., 1936; M.A. (Univ. fellow), U. Ill., 1937, Ph.D., 1939; m. Betty Fountain Edwards, June 16, 1973. Instr. physiology U. Ill., Champaign, 1939-42, asst. prof. zoology, 1945; postdoctoral study Harvard U., Cambridge, Mass., 1945; asst. prof. anatomy Emory U., Atlanta, 1945-48, asso. prof., 1948-61, prof., 1961—, mem. sci. staff Emory U. Hosp., 1957—. Cons. Piedmont Hosp., 1972—, NASA, 1968-69. Served as capt. USAAF, 1942-45. Carnegie Found. grantee, 1949-50, USPHS grantee, 1959-63, Assn. Aid Crippled Children grantee, 1961-62, NASA grantee, 1963-69. Mem. Am. Physiol. Soc., Am. Assn. Anatomy, Am. Soc. Zoology, So. Soc. Anatomy, Ga. (pres. 1964-65), N.Y. acads. sci., Found. Study of Cycles, Sigma Xi. Author: Smooth Muscle Tumors of Alimentary Tract, 1962; Embryology for Surgeons, 1973. Contbr. articles in field to profl. jours. Home: 1191 Oakdale Rd Atlanta GA 30307

GRAY, THOMAS IRA, meteorologist; b. Blytheville, Ark., Dec. 4, 1918; s. Thomas Ira and Laura (Hardy) G.; B.S., Ark. State Coll., 1940; student (Weather Bur.-Civil Aeros. Adminstrn. scholar), U. Chgo., 1940-41; m. Jane Kathryn Fuller, Oct. 19, 1943; children—Nancy Jean, Rand Lee, Christopher Alan, Patti Sue. Asst. observer Weather Bur. Office, Little Rock, Ark., 1941; with Weather Bur. Central Office, Washington, 1941-57; supervising meteorologist Antarctic Weather Central, Internat. Geophys. Year, U.S. Nat. Com., Little Am., 1957-59; U.S. rep. Internat. Antarctic Analysis Center, Australia, 1959-62; research meteorologist Meteorol. Satellite Lab., Nat. Environmental Satellite Service, Nat. Oceanic Atmospheric Adminstrn., Washington, 1962—. Meteorol. adviser U.S. mem., Spl. Com. Antarctic Research, Canberra, Australia, 1959, Wellington, N.Z., 1961; mem. Civil Service Bd. Examiners, 1963—; instr. U.S. Dept. Agrl. Grad. Sch., Washington, 1950-56. Mem. Am. Meteorol. Soc., Am. Geophys. Union, N.Y. Acad. Scis. Methodist. Home: 6721 Botetourt Dr SE Washington DC 20022 Office: Suite World Weather Bldg 5200 Auth Rd SE Washington DC 20031

GRAY, THOMAS TURNER, distillery exec.; b. Topeka, Apr. 24, 1927; s. Ben Foster and Catherine (Turner) G.; B.A., U. Louisville, 1950; postgrad. Ky. Indsl. Devel. Inst., 1966; m. Cynthia Ann Sloane, May 27, 1961; 1 dau., Catherine Lynn. Staff corr. U.P.I., Louisville, 1952-63; pub. relations specialist Dept. Pub. Information, Commonwealth of Ky., Frankfort, 1963-66; mgr. external communications Brown-Forman Distillers Corp., Louisville, 1966-73, mgr. pub. relations, 1973—. Mem. pres.'s award com. Ky. Derby Festival, 1973. Served with AUS, 1945-47. Mem. Pub. Relations Soc. Am. (accredited, chpt. treas. 1971, dir. 1972, pres. Blue Grass chpt. 1974, mem. nat. awards com. 1973), Louisville C. of C. (tourist council 1971-74). Club: Plantation Country (Louisville). Home: 404 Sprite Rd Louisville KY 40207 Office: 850 Dixie Hwy Louisville KY 40210

GRAY, VIRGIL CLAYTON, city ofcl.; b. Brady, Tex., Feb. 10, 1934; s. Elmer L. and Lois E. (Turner) G.; grad. Brownwood Bus. Coll., 1959; m. Emily Grace Lancaster, Mar. 23, 1957; children—Lisa Gaye, Clayton Louis. City sec. City Brownwood, Tex., 1957-62, asst. city mgr., city sec., 1967—; office mgr. Tex. Brick Co., Brownwood, 1962-67. Trustee Tex. Municipal Retirement System, 1968—. Served with USAF, 1953-57. Mem. Municipal Finance Officers U.S. and Tex., Internat. City Clks. and Secs., Tex. City Mgrs. Assn. Kiwanian (pres. 1967). Home: 2502 Belmeade St Brownwood TX 76801 Office: 110 S Greenleaf St Brownwood TX 76801

GRAY, WALTER, JR., dir. Community Workshop; mem. exec. com. Adult Edn. Assn. of U.S.; vice chmn. Am. Inst. Discussion. Author: Manual for Discussion Moderators. Address: Oklahoma County Libraries 131 NW 3d St Oklahoma City OK 73102

GRAY, WILLIAM DOUGLAS, lawyer; b. Orangeburg County, S.C., Apr. 24, 1941; s. Charles Ally and Louise (Kearse) G.; A.B., U. S.C., 1963, J.D., 1966; m. Charlotte Stribling, June 29, 1963; children—Christopher Douglas, David Myers. Admitted to S.C. bar, 1966; asso. Watkins, Vandiver, Kirven, Long & Gable, Anderson, S.C., 1966-71, partner, 1971—. Vice chmn. Anderson chpt. A.R.C., 1971-72. Bd. dirs. Anderson Community Found., 1972—, Anderson Crippled Children's Soc., 1967-70. Mem. Am., S.C., Anderson bar assns., Pi Kappa Phi, Omicron Delta Kappa, Kappa Sigma Kappa. Rotarian. Home: 2810 Echo Trail Anderson SC 29621 Office: 500 S McDuffie St Anderson SC 29621

GRAY, WILLIAM PAUL, physician; b. Batesville, Ark., Aug. 14, 1912; s. Frank Alexander and Mary Melissa (Laman) G.; B.A., Ark. Coll., 1934; M.D., U. Ark. Sch. Medicine, 1938; m. Dorothy Hope Landis, Dec. 30, 1950; 1 dau., Mary Ann. Intern Church Home and Infirmary, Balt., Balt. City Hosp.; pvt. practice gen. medicine, Batesville, Ark., 1940—; adminstr. Dr. Gray's Hosp., Batesville, Ark., 1940—. Mem. Ark. (counselor 1960-75), Independence County med. socs., A.M.A., Am. Coll. Chest Physicians, Am. Acad. Gen. Practice. Home: 589 College St Batesville AR 72501 Office: 477 E Main St Batesville AR 72501

GRAYBEAL, HENRY CLAY, educator; b. Damascus, Va., Feb. 1, 1889; s. David and Lydia Florence (Mock) G.; B.A., Emory and Henry Coll., 1913, L.H.D., 1966; postgrad. Vanderbilt U., summer 1916; M.S., Cornell U., 1923; m. June Evangeline McCornell, June 15, 1916; children—David, Charlton, William, Clare (Mrs. Roland Houghton), Burke, Patrick. Prin. high sch., Rogersville, Tenn., 1913-15, Damascus, Va., 1915-18; faculty U. Tenn., 1921-24, Emory and Henry Coll., 1924-32, Radford Coll., 1932-42; supr. secondary edn. Va. Dept. Edn., 1942-58, chmn. Secondary Sch. Evaluation Com., 1955-56; pres. New River Hist. Soc., 1967—; chmn. Bi-Centennial Commn., Radford, Va., 1972—; chmn. Radford Recreation Commn., 1941-50. Trustee, Emory and Henry Coll., Tenn. Wesleyan Coll., Hiwassee Jr. Coll., 1960-72. Served with U.S. Army, World War I. Recipient Distinguished Service award Emory and Henry Coll. Alumni Assn., 1964, Meritorious Service award Country Life Commn., 1965, Silver Beaver award Boy Scouts Am., 1944. Mem. Va. Council Chs. (v.p.), Ret. Tchrs. Va. (pres. 1972—), Am. Legion (chpt. comdr.), World War I Vets. (chpt. comdr.), Phi Delta Kappa. Methodist. Rotarian. Home: Gilbert and Sullivan Sts Radford VA 24141

GRAYBEAL, JACK DANIEL, chemist, educator; b. Detroit, May 16, 1930; s. Paul Herman and Polly Dale (McClintic) G.; B.S. (Bd. Govs. scholar), W.Va. U., 1951; M.S., U. Wis., 1953, Ph.D., 1955; m. Evelyn Alice Nicolai, June 13, 1954; children—Daniel Lee, David Eugene, Dale Kevin. Mem. tech. staff Bell Telephone Labs., Holmdel, N.J., 1955-57; asst. prof. W.Va. U., Morgantown, 1957-62, asso. prof., 1962-68; asso. prof. chemistry Va. Poly. Inst. and State U., Blacksburg, 1968-69, prof., 1969—. Treas. Gilbert Linkous P.T.A., 1971-72, v.p., 1962-73, pres., 1973—. Mem. Am. Chem. Soc. (sec. No. W.Va. sect. 1967-68), Am. Phys. Soc., Sigma Xi, Phi Lambda Upsilon, Sigma Pi Sigma. Mason. Contbr. articles to profl. jours. Home: 312 Apperson Dr Blacksburg VA 24060

GRAYBEAL, WILLIAM SAMUEL, educator; b. Emory, Va., Nov. 7, 1924; s. Henry Clay and June (McConnell) G.; B.S., Emory and Henry Coll., 1947; M.S., Va. Poly. Inst., 1953; Ed.D., George Peabody Coll., 1962; m. Kathryn Sellers, Mar. 21, 1970. Tchr. Wills (Va.) High Sch., 1947-49; asst. prin. Pearisburg (Va.) High Sch., 1949-50; prin. Speedwell (Va.) High Sch., 1950-51; asst. to supt., vis. tchr. Wythe County Schs., Wythsville, Va., 1951-52; high sch. supr., 1952-54; dir. secondary edn. Fairfax County Schs., Fairfax, Va., 1956-60; research asst. div. surveys and field services George Peabody Coll., 1960-62, asst. prof. edn., asso. dir. div. surveys and field services, 1962-63; supr. ednl. research Va. State Dept. Edn., Richmond, 1963-65; asst. dir. research div. N.E.A., Washington, 1965—. Served with USNR, 1944-46. Mem. N.E.A., Nat. Soc. Study Edn., Am. Edn. Research Assn., Assn. Supr. and Curriculum Devel., A.A.A.S., Am. Assn. Sch. Adminstrs., Blue Key, Phi Delta Kappa, Kappa Delta Pi. Methodist. Home: 1700 Fox Run Ct Vienna VA 22180 Office: NEA 1201 16th St NW Washington DC 20036

GRAYBILL, JACK SHELTON, securities co. exec.; b. Columbia, S.C., Jan. 22, 1928; s. Cecil Eugene and Lucy Ellen Pearl (Kennedy) G.; B.S., U. S.C., 1949; m. Susan Tennent McElveen, June 2, 1951; children—Susan Tennent, Lucy Kennedy, Margaret Powers, Elizabeth Shelton. Salesman, Sewell Mfg. Co., Bremen, Ga., 1949-61; securities salesman Furman Co., Columbia, 1961-65; securities salesman, br. mgr., v.p. Robinson Humphrey Co., Columbia, 1965—. Chmn., U. S.C. Gen. Fund, 1972-73; bd. dirs. Asso. Agys.; trustee United Community Services; mem. adv. bd. Salvation Army. Mem. Nat. Traders Assn., Security Dealers Ga., Security Dealers Carolinas, St. Andrews Soc., Sigma Alpha Epsilon. Presbyn. (elder). Clubs: Richland Sertoma (dir.); Cotillion, Tarantella, Columbia Ball, Forest Lake Country. Home: 4334 Chicora St Columbia SC 29206 Office: 1316 Main St Columbia SC 29201

GRAYSON, ERNEST CARSON, sch. supt.; b. Evansville, Ind., Mar. 2, 1926; s. Ernest Clay and Ruby (Tapp) G.; B.S., U. Louisville, 1950, M.B.A., 1956; m. Patsy Sipes, Oct. 1, 1949; children—Deborah, Carson, Amy. Marketing asst. Standard Oil Co., Louisville, 1949-55; asso. supt., treas. Jefferson County Schs., Louisville, 1955—. Treas. WKPC-TV, Louisville, 1969—. Bd. dirs. Am. Jr. Red Cross, U.S.O., Jefferson County Assn. for Children with Learning Disabilities, Boy Scouts Am. Served to capt. USNR, 1944-46, 1950-52; Korea. Decorated Presidential Unit Citation. Mem. Internat. (pres. 1969), Ky. (pres. 1964) assns. sch. bus. ofcls. Methodist (mem. edn. commn. 1965—, chmn. adminstrv. bd. 1973). Mason. Home: 9204 Tiverton Way Louisville KY 40222 Office: 3332 Newburg Rd Louisville KY 40218

GRAYSON, JAMES PAYNE, lawyer; b. Mountain City, Tenn., Nov. 23, 1937; s. John Luke and Bess Mae (Payne) G.; B.S., E. Tenn. State U., 1959; LL.B., Cumberland U., 1961. Admitted to Tenn. bar, 1961; mem. firm Caldwell, Johnson, Winston, Haynes, Grayson & Massengill, Bristol, Tenn., 1968—. Served with USAF, 1961-65. Mem. Tenn., Bristol (sec. 1972-73) bar assns., Am. Legion. Republican. Methodist. Address: PO Box 745 Bristol TN 37620

GRAYSON, PATRICK HAROLD, JR., lawyer; b. Greenville, S.C., Mar. 8, 1934; s. Patrick Harold and Eloise (Alexander) G.; B.S., U. S.C., 1956, LL.B., 1958; m. Harriet Ann Estridge, Dec. 22, 1957; children—Patrick Harold III, Neil Estridge, Elizabeth Ann, Nancy Letitia. Admitted to S.C. bar, 1958; practice law, Greenville, S.C., 1958—; partner law firm Earle, Bozeman & Grayson, 1960—. Sec. bd.

dirs. Goodwill Industries; treas. bd. dirs. Legal Services; bd. dirs. Vocational Rehab. Agy. Mem. Greenville Jr. C. of C. (dir. 1958-60), Phi Delta Theta. Presbyn. (deacon 1964-66, elder 1966-69, trustee 1972—). Club: Sertoma (Pres. 1964-65). Home: 106 Ramblewood Ln Greenville SC 29607 Office: 2 Hampton St Greenville SC 29602

GRAZIANO, ROBERT MICHAEL, transp. exec.; b. Rockville Centre, N.Y., May 26, 1940; s. Michael and Virginia Helen (Lanigan) G.; student Villanova U., 1958-60, Acad. Advnaced Traffic, 1968-69; m. Kathryn Clare Carroll, Mar. 3, 1962; children—Robert, Kathryn. With Bur. Explosives, Washington, 1968—, spl. rep., 1969-70, dir., 1970—. Mem. Am. Soc. for Testing Materials, Nat. Fire Protection Assn., Nat. Def. Transp. Assn., Nat. Cargo Bur., Traffic Club Washington. Author: Transportation of Hazardous Materials, 1973; co-author: Emergency Handling of Hazardous Materials in Surface Transportation, 1973. Home: 5494 Lighthouse Lane Burke VA 20015 Office: 1920 L St NW Washington DC 20036

GRECCO, WILLIAM LOUIS, educator; b. Brockway, Pa., Aug. 28, 1924; s. Cosimo Cola and Mary (Seroskie) G.; B.S., U. Pitts., 1947, M.S., 1951; Ph.D., Mich. State U., 1962; m. Patricia Margaret Sullivan, Sept. 13, 1947; children—Karen (Mrs. Michael Cornell), Michael, Kathryn (Mrs. William Garner), Nancy, Martha, Mary Margaret, Daniel, Paul, Amy. Mem. faculty U. Pitts., 1947-52, 58-62, asso. prof., 1956-62; traffic cons. firm Donald M. McNeil, Pitts., 1952-58; prof. Purdue U., West Lafayette, Ind., 1962-72; prof., chmn. dept. civil engring. U. Tenn., Knoxville, 1972—; transp. economist Brown & Root, S.A. Honduras, C.Am., Tegucigalpa, 1965-69. Mem. hwy. research bd. Nat. Acad. Scis., 1958—. Bd. dirs. Purdue Calumet Devel. Found., East Chicago, Ind., 1965-72. Served with USNR, 1944-46. Fellow Am. Soc. C.E., Inst. Traffic Engrs.; mem. Am. Soc. Engring. Edn., Am. Inst. Planners, Sigma Xi, Chi Epsilon, Phi Delta Theta. Editor: Jour. Urban Planning and Devel. Div. Am. Soc. C.E., 1967-70. Contbr. profl. jours. Home: 7935 Corteland Dr Knoxville TN 37919 Office: 118 Perkins Hall Univ Tenn Knoxville TN 37916

GRECO, CHARLES P., clergyman; b. Rodney, Miss., Oct. 29, 1894; s. Frank P. and Carmela (Testa) G.; student Jesuit Coll., New Orleans, 1904-07; Jefferson Coll., Convent, La., 1908; St. Joseph Sem., St. Benedict, La., 1907-13; Am. Coll., Louvain, Belgium, 1910-14; U. of Fribourg, Switzerland, 1914-18. Ordained priest Roman Cath. Church, 1918; asst. pastor, Houma, La., 1918-23, vice chancellor and chancellor of New Orleans, 1923-26, adminstr. and pastor of St. Maurice Ch., 1926-45, bishop of Alexandria, 1946—. Sec., Defender of Marriage Bond, presiding judge of Matrimonial Court, 1923-46; vicar gen. of New Orleans, 1944-46. Editor-in-chief Cath. Action of South, 1944-46. Address: PO Drawer 191 Alexandria LA 71301

GRECO, DICK A., JR., mayor; b. Tampa, Fla., Sept. 14, 1933; s. Dick A. and Evelyn (Cotarella) G.; student U. Fla.; B.S., U. Tampa, 1956; m. Dana Hepinstall, Apr. 3, 1953; children—Richard L., Dana L., Darcy L. Councilman, City of Tampa, 1963-67, mayor, 1967—. Vice pres. King-Greco Hardware Co., Inc. Pres. Travelers Aid Soc.; v.p. Davis Islands Civic Center. Bd. dirs. MacDonald's Tng. Center, Fla. League Municipalities. Named Outstanding Young Man of Year, Jr. C. of C., 1965; mem. Nat. Skeet Champion-All Am. Skeet Team, 1950-51. Mem. C. of C. (dir.). Home: 112 Lodoga St Tampa FL 33606 Office: City Hall Florida Av and JF Kennedy Blvd Tampa FL 33602

GRECO, EDWARD CARL, research scientist; b. Marsala, Italy, Nov. 2, 1911; s. Camelo L. and Domenica (LoGacano) G.; came to U.S., 1914, naturalized, 1941; B.A., Northwestern State Coll., 1934; D.Sc., Centenary Coll., 1963; m. Marcia Scott Dudley, Apr. 20, 1938; children—Edward Carl, Marcia Scott. With Lone Star Ordnance Plant, U.S. Army Ordnance, Texarkana, Tex., 1942-43, E.I. du Pont, Millington, Tenn., 1943-45; with United Gas Corp., Shreveport, La., 1945-67, sr. research asso.; dir. research Supplementary Edn. Center, Northwestern State Coll., Nachitoches, La., 1967-70; coordinator sci. and tech. Northwestern State U., Nachitoches, 1970-73, dir. Inst. Sci. Research, 1969-73, lectr. chemistry; sr. corrosion engr. Olive Corrosion Control, Inc., Shreveport, 1973—. Pres., 2d Internat. Congress on Metallic Corrosion, 1963-66, v.p. 4th internat. congress; speaker various colls. and univs. Fellow Am. Inst. Chemists, A.A.A.S.; mem. Nat. Assn. Corrosion Engrs. (pres. 1962-63), La. Acad. Scis. (pres. 1955-56), Shreveport C. of C. (v.p. 1967), Am. Chem. Soc. Editor: Materials Protection, 1966—; adv. editor Protection of Metals, 1965—. Contbr. prefaces, chpts. to tech. books articles to publs. Home: 1406 Captain Shreve Shreveport LA 71105

GREEAR, PHILIP FRENCH-CARSON, educator; b. Troutdale, Va., Aug. 25, 1918; s. John Fields and Carrie Cleo (Cox) G.; student Young Harris Jr. Coll., 1939; B.S., U. Ga., 1949, M.S., 1959, Ph.D., 1967; m. Mildred White, June 4, 1943; children—Carol Britt (Mrs. Bruce Carstarphen), Delbert, Virginia, Margaret, Teressa. Entered USAAF, 1941, advanced through grades to capt. USAF, 1945, ret., 1954; tchr. White County (Ga.) Pub. Schs., 1956-59; county surveyor White County, Ga., 1955-60; farmer, nr. Helen, Ga., 1954-60; biology tchr. Cartersville (Ga.) High Sch., 1960-61; prof. dept. biology and earth sci. Shorter Coll., Rome, Ga., 1961—. Ecol. cons. to various civic and comml. devels. Bd. dirs. Ga. Concervancy, 1971—, Save Ams. Vital Environment, 1970—, Ga. League Environmental Voters, 1972—, Ga. Environmental Edn. Council, 1970-73. Decorated Bronze Star. Recipient Conservation award Am. Motors, 1973. Fellow Ga. Acad. Sci. (pres. elect 1973-74); mem. A.A.A.S., Ga. Bot. Soc., Phi Sigma, Beta Beta Beta. Contbr. articles to profl. jours. Home: 330 Mount Alto Rd Rome GA 30161 Office: Box 2 Shorter College Rome GA 30161

GREEMAN, NELSON WILLIAM LINTON, JR., optometrist; b. San Antonio, Mar. 26, 1923; s. Nelson William Linton and Edith Mae (Crow) G.; D. Optometry, Ohio State U., 1948; postgrad. U. Houston, 1959-62, Purdue U., 1957; m. Dorothy Ruth Trimble, Dec. 22, 1946 (dec. July 1970); children—Janice (Mrs. Dennis Bryant), Nelson William Linton III; m. 2d, Patsy Ruth Seiler, Oct. 16, 1971; 1 dau., Laura Lee. Pvt. practice optometry, San Antonio, 1948—. Extern, Gesell Inst. Child Devel., New Haven, 1958; vis. lectr. Coll. Optometry, U. Houston, 1964-65; guest lectr. U. Miss., 1965; clinics chmn. S.W. Congress Optometry, 1960—; lectr. various groups and profl. orgns. Pres. San Antonio Better Bus. Bur., 1957. Served to 2d lt. USAAF, 1943-45. Named Optometrist of Yr., Tex. Optometric Assn., 1972. Fellow Am. Acad. Optometrists; Coll. Optometrists in Vision Devel. Internat. (chmn. bd. 1971-72), S.W. Contact Lens Soc. (pres. 1972-74); mem. S.W. Developmental Vision Soc. (pres. 1969-70), Am. Acad. Optometry (pres. Tex. chpt. 1960-61), Bexar County Dist. Optometric Soc. (past pres.), Am. Legion (post comdr. 1968). Methodist (mem. adminstrv. bd. 1958-64, 70-74). Club: Optimist (San Antonio). Home: 208 Wyanoke St San Antonio TX 78209 Office: 249 E Hildebrand St San Antonio TX 78212

GREEN, ALEX EDWARD SAMUEL, educator; b. N.Y.C., June 2, 1919; s. Joseph Marvin and Celia (Kahn) G.; B.S., Coll. City N.Y., 1940; M.S., Cal. Inst. Tech., 1941; Ph.D., U. Cin., 1946; m. Freda Kaplowitz, June 2, 1946; children—Bruce, Deborah, Marcia (Mrs. Kenneth Lockhart), Linda, Tamara. Asso. prof. U. Cin., 1946-53; acting chmn. physics dept. Fla. State U., Tallahassee, 1953-59; mgr. space sci. lab. Gen. Dynamics, San Diego, 1959-63; grad. research prof. dept. physics U. Fla., Gainesville, 1963—. Dir. Interdisciplinary Atmospheric Center, 1970-73. Chmn. subcom. on air and noise Fla. Dept. Pollution Control, Gainesville, 1973—. Served with USAAF, 1944-45. Fellow Am. Phys. Soc.; mem. Am. Inst. Aeros. and Astronautics, Am. Rocket Soc., Am. Assn. Physics Tchrs., Am. Geophys. Union, Nat. Acad. Scis. (mem. NATO postdoctoral selection com. 1965-67), Optical Soc. Am., Sigma Xi, Pi Beta Kappa. Home: 2900 NW 14th Place Gainesville FL 32601

GREEN, ALLEN LELDON, aircraft co. ofcl.; b. Hanceville, Ala., Feb. 15, 1938; s. Onis Leldon and Stella Magnolia (Day) G.; B.S. in Mech. Engring., U. Miss., 1961; children—Cooper Alan, Elizabeth Nicole and Kimberly Kelly (twins). Engr. aide TVA Power Prodn., New Johnson, Tenn., 1960; punter, field goal kicker, line backer Dallas Cowboys, 1961-62, design engr. Chgo. Bridge & Iron Co., Birmingham, Ala., 1962-63, field engr., 1963; punter, field goal kicker Green Bay Packers, 1964; structures engr. B, Chrysler Corp./Space Div., Huntsville, Ala., 1963-64, test, devel. engr. B, 1964-65, test, devel. engr. A, 1965-67, test engr. sr., 1967, test engr. sr. mgmt., 1967-68; organized Tide Corp., Birmingham, 1969, v.p., 1969—; adminstr. program planning Martin-Marietta Corp., Huntsville, 1969—; owner Allen Green Golf Driving Range, Huntsville, 1969—. Mem. exec. com. Tenn. Valley Boy Scouts Am., 1967. Named Hon. Col., Miss. Gov., 1961. Mem. Nat. Football League Players Assn., Am. Soc. M.E., Am. Soc. Weights Engrs., Chrysler Basketball League, Chrysler Golf League and Tournaments (award 1968). Club: Alabama Hawks Professional Football (award 1967) (Huntsville). Home: 203 Al Ridgely Huntsville AL 35806 Office: Martin Marietta Corp PO Box 1107 Huntsville AL 35807

GREEN, ARTHUR GEORGE, accountant; b. Midland, Tex., June 2, 1937; s. Lymond Darrel and Viona (Grant) G.; Asso. Applied Sci., Odessa Coll., 1960; B.B.A., U. Tex., 1962; m. Margaret Hash, June 1, 1959; children—Shane Ann, Sabrina Kay, Amy Suzanne, William Wade. Estimator, Boing Co., New Orleans, 1962-63; staff accountant Main, Lafrentz & Co., Odessa, Tex., 1963-65, Will Faris & Co., Odessa, 1965-67; partner Faris, Sims & Green, Odessa, 1968-73, Griffin & Green, Odessa, 1973—. Govs., treas. Globe of Gt. S.W., 1969—; bd. dirs. Tex. Tech. U. Tax Inst., 1967-70; bd. regents Odessa Coll., 1972—. Served with USAF, 1954-58. Mem. Am. Inst. C.P.A.'s, Tex. Soc. C.P.A.'s (chpt. v.p. 1969—), Data Processing Mgrs. Assn. (chpt. treas. 1970), Odessa Jr. C. of C. Mem. Christian Ch. (dir.) Mason (K.T., Shriner). Home: 1700 Redbud Odessa TX 79760 Office: 2101 N Grandview St Odessa TX 79761

GREEN, BEN LAMAR, JR., supt. schs.; b. Monroe, La., Feb. 28, 1921; s. Ben Lamar and Lorraine (Lowe) G.; B.A., La. State U., 1954, M.Ed., 1956; Ed.S., George Peabody Coll. Tchrs., 1964; Ed.D., U. So. Miss., 1973; m. Maxine Boyd, Jan. 6, 1946; children—Ben Lamar III, Terry Boyd, Penny Maxine. Tchr., coach Vidalia (La.) High Sch., 1954-55; tch. bus. edn., coach Ferriday (La.) High Sch., 1956-57; supr. instrn. Concordia Parish Schs., Vidalia, 1958-60; prin. Ferriday Elementary Sch., 1961-69; supt. Concordia Parish Schs., Vidalia, 1969—. Mem. Selective Service Bd., Concordia Parish, 1967—. Served with USMCR, 1942-45. Decorated Purple Heart, Bronze Star. Mem. Phi Delta Kappa. Mason (Shriner), Rotarian (pres. 1970-71). Address: Box 548 Vidalia LA 71373

GREEN, BERNARD CLAY, lawyer; b. Shelby County, Ky., Oct. 11, 1904; s. Clarence Evans and Fanny (Baker) G.; student Centre Coll., 1922-25; student Jefferson Sch. Law, 1927-29; LL.B., U. Louisville, 1930; m. Clara Ellen McCammon, Aug. 6, 1936; children—Wanda Mae, Suzette Clay, Earl Mac. Admitted to Ky. bar, 1929; dept. supt. United Merc. Agys., Louisville 1930-36; practiced in Louisville, 1936-40, Owensboro, Ky., 1940—; asst. county atty. Daviess County, Ky., 1953; city prosecutor, Owensboro, 1954-58. Mem. Am., Ky. State, Daviess County (pres. 1970) bar assns., Am. Trial Lawyers Assn., Comml. Law League Am., Am. Judicature Soc., Internat. Acad. Law and Sci., Ky. Hist. Soc. Mem. Christian Ch. (elder, mem. ofcl. bd., past chmn.). Kiwanian (pres. Owensboro 1970-71). Home: 1030 College Dr Owensboro KY 42301 Office: 700 Frederica St Owensboro KY 42301

GREEN, DAVID SPENCER, architect; b. Dallas, Jan. 22, 1943; s. Herbert Spencer and Delma Dorothy (Stephenson) G.; student Arlington State Coll., 1961-63; B.Arch., Tex. A. and M. U., 1968; m. Janet Sue Allen, May 30, 1963; children—Derek Scott, Lamar Allen. Draftsman, George E. Christenson, Dallas, 1960-63; facilities design specialist, 1970-72; project architect Army and Air Force Exchange Service, Dallas, 1972—. Vice chmn. Dallas Area Block Partnership Program. Prin. works: concept planning for shopping centers Ft. Jackson, S.C., Ft. Benning, Ga., Ft. Knox, Ky.; Amusement Center, Rome Inn, Ft. Riley, Kan.; amusement center Pease AFB, N.H. Home: 408 E Scotland St Irving TX 75062 Office: 3911 Walton Walker Blvd Dallas TX 75222

GREEN, ELEANOR BROOME (MRS. LEON GREEN, JR.), mus. dir.; b. Covina, Cal.; d. Charles Samuels and Eleanor Broome; A.B., Vassar Coll., 1949; M.A., George Washington U., 1971, Ph.D., 1973; m. Leon Green, Jr. Curator Washington Gallery Modern Art, 1964-67; curator contemporary art Corcoran Gallery Art, Washington, 1967-71; dir. U. Md. Art Gallery, 1972—. Art critic. Mem. Am. Assn. Museums, Jr. League of Washington. Episcopalian. Club: Porto Cervo Yacht. Contbr. articles to profl. publs. Home: 5140 Westpath Way Washington DC 20016 also Villa Green Porto Cervo Sardegna Italy Office: Art Dept U Md College Park MD 20742

GREEN, FRANKLIN A., JR., bus. exec.; b. Selma, Ala., Apr. 13, 1931; s. Franklin A. and Louis (Webb) G.; B.S. in Agr., Auburn U., 1954; m. Frances Fuller Green, Apr. 7, 1957; children—Elizabeth, Franklin, Frances Ann, Cary. With Ring Around Products, Inc., and predecessor, Pratville, Ala., 1956—, v.p., 1968—. Served with AUS, 1954-56. Mem. So., Ala. seedsmens assns., Am. Seed Trade Assn. Baptist. Kiwanian. Home: 3906 Rouse Ridge Ct Montgomery AL 36111 Office: PO Box 589 Montgomery AL 36111

GREEN, FRED WILLIAM, cons.; b. Springfield, Ill., May 31, 1935; s. John Walker and Ruth (Foor) G.; B.S., Washington U., St. Louis, 1957; M.B.A., U. Chgo., 1968; m. Merian Jalane Thiele, June 16, 1957; children—Karen Lynne, Sharon Anne. Mfg. trainee R.R. Donnelley & Sons, Crawfordsville, Ind., 1957-61; mgmt. engr. Decatur (Ill.) Meml. Hosp., 1961-64; adminstrv. asso. dept. med. edn. A.M.A., Chgo., 1964-67; dir. mgmt. services Chgo. Hosp. Council, 1967-69; v.p., hosp. computer cons., exec. v.p. Med. Sci. Internat., Clearwater, Fla., 1969-70; health systems cons. Fred W. Green & Assos., Clearwater, Fla., 1970—. Instr. Sch. Industrial Engring., Ill. Inst. Tech., Chgo., 1968-69. Registered profl. engr., Ill., Cal., Fla. Recipient Hosp. Mgmt. Systems Soc. Annual Lit. award Am. Hosp. Assn., 1969. Mem. Am. Inst. Indsl. Engrs. (nat. dir. hosp. div. 1963-68, pres. chpt. 1963-64, dir. chpt. 1964-65), Hosp. Mgmt. Systems Soc. (pres. 1966-67, dir. 1967-69). Contbr. articles in field to profl. jours. Home: 731 Snug Island Clearwater FL 33515 Office: 410 S Lincoln Av Clearwater FL 33516

GREEN, GEORGE, dentist; b. Nathalie, Va., Dec. 31, 1925; s. John Collins and Frances (Oliver) G.; student Mars Hill Coll., 1942-44; D.D.S., Med. Coll. Va., 1948; certificate in periodontology, Columbia, 1961. Gen. practice dentistry, Brookneal, Va., 1948—; clin. cons. Columbia U. Dental Sch. Instr. Campbell County chpt. Va. Cancer Soc., 1956-59. Served with USN, 1944-45, 51-53. Mem. Am., Va. dental assns., Piedmont Dental Soc., Am. Legion, 40 and 8, Brookneal C. of C., Delta Sigma Delta. Democrat. Baptist. Mason (Shriner), Elk, Moose, Lion. Clubs: Piedmont, German, Cotillion, Country. Home: Forest St Brookneal VA 24528 Office: Rush St Brookneal VA 24528

GREEN, GEORGE FRANKLIN, physician; b. Bostwick, Ga., Sept. 27, 1924; s. Rice Burkitt and Rubye (Riden) G.; B.S., N. Ga. Coll., 1948; M.D., Med. Coll. Ga., 1951; m. Helen Montine Maxwell, June 4, 1944; children—George F., Helen Claudia, Wallace Maxwell. Intern Brooke Army Med. Center, 1951; pvt. practice, gen. practitioner, Sparta, Ga., 1953—; chief staff Hancock Meml. Hosp.; asso. prof. clin. medicine Duke; asso. prof. clin. and ambulatory medicine U. Ala. Pres. Oconee Valley Investment Corp.; dir. Bank of Hancock County; pres. Hancock Redevel. Corp., Sparta Med. Clinic. Mayor, Sparta, Ga., 1966-70; commr. Hancock County Bd. Rds. and Revenue; past chmn. Oconee Area Planning and Devel. Commn. Bd. dirs. local council Boy Scouts Am. Served as capt. inf. AUS, 1943-46; capt. M.C. AUS, 1951-53. Fellow Am. Geriatrics Soc., Am. Acad. Family Physicians (charter); mem. Am., So., Ga. med. assns., Oconee Valley Med. Soc., Ga. Acad. Family Practice (past dir. 6th dist.), V.F.W., Gridiron Soc., Am. Legion, Delta Sigma Pi (hon.) Baptist (deacon). Mason (Shriner, K.T.), Lion (pres. 1961-62). Club: Civitan (past pres. Sparta br., past lt. gov. Ga. dist.). Home: 333 Parkway Dr Sparta GA 31087 Office: 325 E Broad St Sparta GA 31087

GREEN, GEORGE MARVIN, lawyer; b. Tampa, Fla., Sept. 22, 1904; s. William Truman and Maude (Powell) G.; LL.B., U. Fla., 1930; m. Mary Bentley, May 22, 1958; 1 dau., Linda. Admitted to Fla. bar, 1930; partner firm Carlton, Fields, Ward, Emmanuel, Smith & Cutler, Tampa. Mem. Hillsborough County Bd. Pub. Instrn., 1947-67, chmn., 1959-62, vice chmn., 1965. Served to lt. col. USAAF, 1941-46. Mem. Am., Tampa, Hillsborough County bar assns., Fla. Bar, Am. Judicature Soc., Am. Legion, 40 and 8 (chef de gar passe), Sigma Nu, Phi Delta Phi. Mason (Shriner). Home: 3707 Obispo St Tampa FL 33609 Office: Exchange Nat Bank Bldg Tampa FL 33602

GREEN, HAROLD, lawyer; b. Camden, N.J., Apr. 2, 1923; s. Harold and Elizabeth (Sharp) G.; student Clemson U., 1944; B.A., Baylor U., 1949, LL.B., 1951, J.D., 1969; m. Bettye Jane Richardson, Mar. 22, 1946; children—Richard Harold, Laura Beth. Admitted to Tex. bar, 1951, since practiced in Tahoka; atty. Lynn County, 1955-65; acting dist. judge, 1967-68. Asso. govt. appeal agt. SSS, 1964-71. Organizer, Little League Baseball, Tahoka, 1955, sec., 1955-65; counsellor Baylor U. Sch. Law; lay adviser Perkins Sch. Theology, So. Meth. U. Bd. dirs. Fed. Housing Authority. Served with AUS, 1943-45. Mem. Tex., South Plains (pres. 1957-58) bar assns., Tahoka C. of C. (pres. 1974-75), Phi Delta Phi, Alpha Chi. Methodist (pres. ofcl. bd., pres. Meth. Men). Rotarian. Home: 1916 N 6th St Tahoka TX 79373 Office: 1929 Av K Tahoka TX 79373

GREEN, HAROLD RUGBY, educator; b. Hallettsville, Tex., Feb. 19, 1926; s. Joseph Franklin and Nell Vesta (Kilby) G.; B.A., Tex. Wesleyan Coll., 1946; M.A., Tex. Christian U., 1948; postgrad. U. Ark., 1955, U. Ala., 1960; M.S., N.Tex. State U., 1961; m. Charlotte Larue Shannon, May 30, 1953. Tchr., Tex. Pub. Schs., 1946-55; prof. math. McNeese State Coll., 1959-60; prof. math. U. Tex., Arlington, 1955-59, 60—. Mem. Tex. Assn. Coll. Tchrs., Guardians of Golden Shears, Alpha Chi. Baptist. Home: 715 White Oak Lane Arlington TX 76012

GREEN, HARRY GEORGE, bus. coll. pres.; b. Harbor Springs, Mich., Aug. 28, 1908; s. Judson Burrows and Ella Agnes (Burdge) G.; Ph.C., U. Wash., 1930, B.S., 1931; m. Martha Jane Hart, Dec. 28, 1935; children—Richard B., Harry George, Rogers H., Barbara (Mrs. H. Murrell McLeod), Judy (Mrs. Claude D. Foster). With Delta Tau Delta Frat., N.Y.C., 1931-33, field sec., editor, asst. to controller, Indpls., 1933-37; bus. mgr. Phillips Bus. Coll., Lynchburg, Va., 1937-44, pres., 1944—. Pres. Lynchburg Met. YMCA, 1968-72. Mem. Lynchburg Sch. Bd., 1948-58, chmn., 1951-58; mem. Lynchburg Interracial Commn., 1960-72, sec., 1962-72. Mem. Assn. Ind. Colls. and Schs. (pres. 1967-68), Va. Council Bus. Colls. (pres. 1971-73), Nat. Secs. Assn. (hon.). Methodist (lay leader 1964—). Lion (local pres. 1946-47, dist. gov. 1950-51), Mason. Home: 1020 Federal St Lynchburg VA 24504 Office: 1112 Church St Lynchburg VA 24505

GREEN, HOLLIS LYNN, religious assn. exec.; b. Rhea County, Tenn., Jan. 6, 1933; s. Herbert Barton and Grace Irene (Curton) G.; student Beckley Coll., 1952-54, U. Cin., 1957-58, Miami Christian U., 1961-62; B.D., Luther Rice Sem., 1965, Th.D., 1968; m. Peggy Jean Lane, Dec. 8, 1951 (div. 1972); children—Barton Lynn, Brian Lane; m. 2d, Gloria Gail Parks, 1974. Ordained to ministry, 1959; pastor various churches Ohio, S.C., Ind., Fla., 1958-64; state dir. Christian edn. W.Va., 1952-58; mem. gen. youth and Christian Edn. Bd., Ch. of God, 1958-62; dir. pub. relations Ch. of God Exec. Offices, 1964-72; pres. Aid, Ltd., Atlanta, 1966—; dir. Ch. Funding, Inc., Hialeah, Fla., 1971—; founder, pres. New L.I.F.E. Ministries, Atlanta, 1973—; dir. Provident Investment Corp., Atlanta. Cons., Time Life Books, Protestant Armed Forces Field Rep. Mem. U.S. Postal Forum II, III, 1968-69, Inter-Racial Study Commn. of the South, 1962-64, Dr. King's List of 200, 1966-68. Trustee Luther Rice Sem., 1968—, v.p., 1974—. Served as res. chaplain (maj.) CAP, USAF, 1964-74. Recipient pub. service award U.S. Postal Service, 1968. Fellow Program and Platform Techniques div. Internat. Platform Assn.; mem. Pub. Relations Soc. Am., Religious Pub. Relations Council, Evangelical Press Assn., Soc. Pentecostal Scholars, Nat. Sunday Sch. Assn. (bd. dirs. 1958-62), Internat. Pub. Relations Assn. Republican. Baptist. Kiwanian. Author: Hitching Your Star to a Wagon, 1958; Dynamics of Christian Discipleship, 1962, Christian Education Cyclopedia, 1965; Marchings As to War, 1969; Understanding Pentecostalism, 1970; Where in the World are you Going, 1971; Why Churches Die, 1972. Home: 5555 Roswell Rd Apt A-4 Atlanta GA 30342 Office: Box 28355 Atlanta GA 30328

GREEN, HOWARD LEMUEL, county judge; b. Swenson, Tex., Jan. 24, 1921; s. Thomas Lemuel and Della (Hall) G.; B.S., McMurry Coll., 1943; m. Betty Bratton, Jan. 6, 1950; children—Leslie Carole, Howard Lemuel. Sports writer Abilene Reporter-News, 1939-47; pres. Longhorn Baseball League, 1947-48, Gulf Coast Baseball League, 1950-52, Big State Baseball League, 1951-55; mem. Tex. Ho. of Reps., 1957-67; judge Tarrant County, Tex., 1967—. Served with USAAF, 1943-45. Decorated Air medal. Democrat. Methodist. Home: 7316 Oakland Lane Fort Worth TX 76118 Office: Tarrant County Courthouse Fort Worth TX 76102

GREEN, JOSEPH LEE, writer; b. Compass Lake, Fla., Jan. 14, 1931; s. Francis Marion and Mattie (Carlyle) G.; A.A., Brevard Jr. Coll., 1967; m. Juanita Henderson, Mar. 3, 1951; children—William Merrit, Rose-Marie (Mrs. Douglas Clark). Technician's supr. Boeing Co., Seattle, 1959-62, sr. supr., 1962-63; tech. writer LTV Aerospace Corp., Kennedy Space Center, Fla., 1965-71, Boeing Co., Kennedy Space Center, 1971—; instr. creative writing Brevard Community Coll., Eve. Sch., 1972. Mem. Sci. Fiction Writers Am. (elections com. chmn. 1973). Author: The Loafers of Refuge, 1965; An Affair with Genius, 1969; Gold the Man, 1971, pub. in U.S. as Mind Behind the

Eye, 1972; Conscience Interplanetary, 1973. Contbr. numerous stories and articles to mags. Home: 1390 Holly Av Merritt Island FL 32952 Office: MS BOFG-36 Kennedy Space Center FL 32889

GREEN, JOSHUA, lawyer; b. Jackson, Miss., Nov. 12, 1922; s. Garner Wynn and Winifred (Calhoon) G.; B.A. magna cum laude, Vanderbilt U., 1946, J.D., 1949; m. Myra Louise Allison Hamilton, Apr. 10, 1947; 1 dau., Lynn Hamilton. Admitted to Miss. bar, 1949, U.S. Supreme Ct. bar, 1963; partner firm Green, Cheney, Jones and Hughes (formerly Green, Green and Cheney), Jackson, Miss., 1949—. Dir., Old Trace Marina, Inc., 1970. Trustee St. Andrews Day Sch., Jackson, 1961-65; pres. Allison Art Colony, Way, Miss., 1953; treas. Jackson Civic Art Council, Inc., 1958, v.p., 1961, pres., 1963, dir. 1956-70; bd. dirs. Miss. Art Assn., 1959—, pres., 1958. Served from pvt. to sgt. AUS, 1943-46. Mem. Miss. State Bar, Am., Hinds County bar assns., Comml. Law League Am., Phi Beta Kappa, Phi Alpha Delta, Phi Delta Theta. Episcopalian. Clubs: Capital City Petroleum, Jackson Yacht (sec.-treas. 1964, commodore 1966, editor Mainsheet, 1970). Home: 154 Glen Way Jackson MS 39216 Office: 800 Electric Bldg Jackson MS 39205

GREEN, JOYCE HENS (MRS. SAMUEL GREEN), judge; b. N.Y.C., Nov. 13, 1928; d. James Stanley and Hedy (Bucher) Hens; B.A., U. Md., 1949; LL.B., George Washington U., 1951; m. Samuel Green, Sept. 25, 1965; children—James Harry, Michael Timothy, June Heather. Admitted to D.C. bar, 1951, Va. bar, 1956; practiced in Washington, 1951-68, Arlington, Va., 1956-68; partner (with husband) Green & Green, Washington, until 1968; asso. judge D.C. Ct. Gen. Sessions, 1968-71, Superior Ct. of D.C., 1971—. Trustee D.C. div. Am. Cancer Soc., 1963—. Recipient certificate of merit for outstanding profl. achievement D.C. Profl. Panhellenic Assn. Fellow Am. Acad. Matrimonial Lawyers; mem. Am., Va., Arlington County, D.C. Women's (pres. 1960-62) bar assns., Bar Assn. D.C., Unified Bar of D.C., Va. State Bar, Nat. Lawyers Club, Va. Assn. Trial Attys., U. Md. Alumni Assn., Kappa Beta Pi Home: 1714 N Glebe Rd Arlington VA 22207 Office: Superior Court of DC 4th and E Sts NW Washington DC 20001

GREEN, MYRA HAMILTON, artist; b. Fayetteville, Tenn., Nov. 28, 1929; d. Herbert Reid and Sallye (Kelly) Hamilton; certificate Va. Intermont Coll., 1946; B.A., Miss. Coll.; student Art Students League; pvt. study painting; m. Joshua Green, Apr. 10, 1947; 1 dau., Lynn Hamilton. Portrait painter; tchr. pvt. studio, Jackson, 1947—; one-man shows at Wolfe Gallery, 1949, Miss. Coll., Clinton, 1965, Miss. State U., 1965, Washington Street Gallery, Amarillo, Tex., 1967, numerous others; two-man shows at Alison's Gallery, 1952, Jackson Municipal Gallery, 1953, 64; three-man show Municipal Art Gallery, 1964; group shows at Miss. Art Assn., Miss. Watercolor Soc., New Orleans Art Assn., Brooke Meml. Gallery, Memphis, Ann. Southeastern exhibit, Atlanta. Recipient 1st prize Alison Art Colony, 1953; 2d prize Miss. Art Colony, 1967, LaFont Workship, 1967. Mem. Miss. Art Assn., Alison Art Colony, Jr. League. Episcopalian. Address: 154 Glenway St Jackson MS 39216

GREEN, RALPH TILLMAN, banker; b. Paxton, Tex., Apr. 10, 1922; s. Ralph Eugene and Nettie Ann (Cammack) G.; B.A., Tex. A. and M. U., 1942, M.S., 1947; Ph.D., Duke, 1954; m. Mary Lou Malone, June 20, 1945; children—Meslissa Ann, Susan Kimberly, Nancy Alison. Financial economist Fed. Res. Bank of Dallas, 1949-55, v.p., 1962—; prof., chmn. dept. econs. Baylor U., 1955-56; exec. dir. Tex. Commn. Higher Edn., 1956-62. Mem. So. Regional Edn. Bd., 1956-62; cons. Va. Council Higher Edn., 1961, So. Regional Edn. Bd., 1958-60, Tex. Coordinating Bd. Higher Edn., 1971; mem. research adv. com. Fed. Res. System; lectr. univs. Mem. tech. adv. com. Goals for Dallas, 1967-70. Bd. dirs. Tex. United Fund, 1968-72. Served to lt., USNR, 1942-46; PTO. Fellow Found. Econ. Edn., Irvington-on-Hudson, N.Y., 1948. Mem. Am., So. econ. assns., Am. Finance Assn., S.W. Social Sci. Assn., Dallas C. of C., Dallas Economists Club (pres. 1967). Home: 4017 Northview Lane Dallas TX 75229 Office: 400 S Akard St Dallas TX 75222

GREEN, ROBERT HAMILTON, engring. co. exec.; b. Bridgeport, Conn., July 3, 1935; s. Albert Arthur and Mary Elizabeth (Hansen) G.; B.S. in Engring., U. Fla., 1958, B.Indsl. Engring., 1959; postgrad. Ga. Inst. Tech., 1963; m. Paula Hathaway Anderson, Sept. 6, 1958; children—Lydia Anne, Edith Hathaway, Elizabeth Anderson, Cecilia Hamilton. Flight test engr. Mercury Program, Gen. Dynamics Co., Cape Canaveral, Fla., 1958-61; project engr. airlift containerized freight L.I.P., Atlanta, 1961-68; scientist asso. graphite fiber composite materials Lockheed Ga. Co., Marietta, 1968-70. Mem. Sandy Springs Planning Commn., Atlanta, 1967—. Registered profl. engr., Ga., Fla., Ala. Mem. Nat., Ga. socs. profl. engrs., Am. Inst. Indsl. Engrs., Soc. Plastics Engrs., Ga. Cons. Engrs. Council, Engrs. Joint Council, Tau Beta Pi, Lambda Chi Alpha. Episcopalian. Clubs: Atlanta Yacht (past fleet capt.); U. Fla. Alumni (Gainesville). Contbr. articles to profl. jours. Patentee in field. Home: 550 High Point Lane NE Atlanta GA 30342 Office: RH Green Engineering Co Inc Atlanta GA 30342

GREEN, THOMAS ROBERT, aviation co. exec.; b. Columbus, O., Aug. 15, 1922; s. Charles William and Reba (Maxwell) G.; student Kenyon Coll., 1940-42; m. Nilda Lopez, Oct. 12, 1945; children—Stephanie, Timothy, Thomas R., Melissa, Juan. Jr. sta. mgr. Pan Am. Airways, 1944-46; area operations mgr., chief dispatcher Transportes Aeroes Central Americanos, 1946-47; pres. Dispatch Services, Inc., 1947—; Air Acgy., Inc., 1949—; Fla. Aviation Fueling Co., Inc., 1952—; Pan African Airlines (Nigeria) Ltd., 1961—; Freeport Flight Services, Ltd., 1965—; Safari Air Services, Ltd., Nairobi, 1968—; dir. Fla. Nat. Bank & Trust Co., Miami, Dania Jai Alai. Served with AUS, 1943-44. Mem. C. of C. of Miami, Aviation Exec. Club (dir.), Quiet Birdman. Lion. Clubs: Lucaya Beach Country, Bahama Reef Country (Freeport, Bahamas); Calusa Country; Coral Reef Yacht. Home: 3500 Granada Blvd Coral Gables FL 33134 Office: PO Box 2034 Miami FL 33159

GREEN, VICTOR EUGENE, JR., educator; b. DeRidder, La., Sept. 3, 1922; s. Victor Eugene and Laura Mae (Harris) G.; B.S., La. State U., 1947, M.S., 1948; Ph.D., Purdue U., 1951; m. Ada Ruth Hellert, June 5, 1945; children—Judy Ellen (Mrs. David Louis Brewer), Philip Martin. Asst. prof. La. State U., 1947-49; asso. prof. U. Fla., Gainesville, 1951-56, asso. prof., 1956-65, prof. agronomy, 1965—. Adviser in agr. Costa Rican Govt., 1965-68. Served to col. AUS, 1942-46; PTO. Recipient only diploma ever presented to fgn. scientist by Costa Rican Ministry Agr., 1968. Mem. Soil Sci. Soc. Fla. (pres. 1965), Sigma Xi, Alpha Zeta, Gamma Sigma Delta, Lambda Chi Alpha. Lion. Home: 3915 SW 3d Av Gainesville FL 32607

GREEN, WILLIAM HARRIS, lawyer; b. Gainesville, Fla., July 23, 1943; s. Robert Alexis and Bessie Lucile (Harris) G.; B.S., U. S.C., 1963, Ph.D., 1967; J.D., Georgetown U., 1973; m. Diane Sue Viglione, Apr. 27, 1968; 1 dau., Amber Wren. Nat. Acad. Scis.-NRC postdoctoral fellow Naval Research Lab., Washington, 1967-68, research chemist, 1967-73, acting head chem. spectroscopy sect., 1973-74; admitted to Fla. bar, 1973; asso. firm Mahoney, Hadlow, Chambers & Adams, Jacksonville, Fla., 1974—. Mem. Am. Bar Assn., Am. Chem. Soc., A.A.A.S., Coblentz Soc., Sigma Xi. Democrat. Baptist. Research and publs. on molecular energy transfer and chem. lasers. Office: Barnett Bank Bldg 100 Laura St Jacksonville FL 32201

GREEN, WILLIAM LAWRENCE, C.P.A.; b. Tulsa, June 15, 1942; s. Robert Lee and Dorothy Sue (Porter) G.; B.B.A., U. Houston, 1966; m. Patricia Ann Ellis, Aug. 6, 1965. Staff accountant Arthur Young & Co., Houston, 1966-68; with Weller, Jeffery & Green, Inc., C.P.A.'s Houston, 1968—, v.p., sec., 1971—. Capt., Pin Oak Charity Horse Show, Houston, 1972—. Mem. dean's adv. bd. U. Houston Coll. Bus., 1974-77. Served with AUS, 1960-63. Mem. Am. Inst. C.P.A.'s. Tex. Soc. C.P.A.'s, U. Houston Coll. Bus. Alumni Assn. (dir. 1971—, pres. 1973—), Beta Alpha Psi. Rotarian. Home: 3106 Lawrence St Houston TX 77018 Office: 717 First City National Bank Bldg Houston TX 77002

GREEN, WILLIAM WELLS, civil engr.; b. Sioux City, Ia., Nov. 26, 1911; s. Thomas William and Jessie Eadie (Wells) G.; B.S., U. Notre Dame, 1934; m. Patricia Cecille Gregory, Jan. 10, 1944; children—William Joseph, Mary Teresa. Asst. engr. Ia. Hwy. Commn., Cherokee, 1935-40; asst. engr. City Corpus Christi, Tex., 1940-44; asst. office county surveyor, Nueces County Tex., 1944-54, county surveyor, 1955—. Mem. Tex. Bd. Registration Pub. Surveyors. Bd. dirs. Carmelite Day Nursery. Fellow Am. Soc. C.E.; mem. Am. Congress Surveying Mapping, Tex. Surveyors Assn. (past dir.). Democrat. Roman Catholic. K.C. Home: 3149 Topeka St Corpus Christi TX 78404 Office: 206 Courthouse Annex 409 Mann St Corpus Christi TX 78401

GREENAWALT, JACK ORMOND, engring. co. exec., civil engr.; b. Princeton, Kan., Oct. 10, 1924; s. Frank Ralph and Marie (McCall) G.; B.S. in Elec. Engring., Kan. State U., 1950, B.S. in Bus. Adminstrn., 1950; m. Phyllis M. Fine, May 29, 1949; children—Larry N., Kirk D., Scott C., Todd M. Spl. agt. Aetna Ins. Co., Chgo., 1950-55; corrosion engr. Phillips Petroleum Co., Bartlesville, Okla., 1955-72; prin. Greenawalt-Armstrong Engring. Co., cons. engrs., Bartlesville, 1972—. Pres. Little League Baseball, Bartlesville, 1950—; active Boy Scouts Am., 1960—; dist. adminstr. Little League, Okla., 1970—. Served with AUS, 1943-46. Registered profl. engr., Okla. Mem. Bartlesville Homebuilders Assn., Nat., Okla. socs. profl. engrs., Nat. Assn. Corrosion Engrs., Okla. Soc. Land Surveyors, Am. Congress of Surveying and Mapping, Bartlesville C. of C. Mason, Lion. Home: 229 SE Madison Blvd Bartlesville OK 74003 Office: 1656 Washington Blvd Bartlesville OK 74003

GREENAWAY, DONALD, hotel exec.; b. Frankfort, Mich., Apr. 14, 1911; s. George Henry and Mary Elizabeth (Orr) G.; B.A., Mich. State U., 1934; m. Louise Constance Wadsworth, June 27, 1936; 1 dau., Jeanne Elizabeth (Mrs. Robert Mattice); m. 2d, Lorraine Muellenbach, July 6, 1958; 1 dau., Karen. Engaged in hotel adminstrn. and mgmt., 1934-41; food service exec. Trans World Airlines, 1946-47; prof. hotel adminstrn. Coll. Bus., Wash. State U., 1947-51; prof., adminstr.-dir. Sch. Hotel, Restaurant and Instl. Mgmt., Coll. Bus., Mich. State U., 1951-58; exec. v.p. Nat. Restaurant Assn., Chgo., from 1958—; now asso. dean Conrad Hilton Sch. Hotel and Restaurant Mgmt. Mem. Gov. Wash. Com. Devel. State Wash., 1950-51; pres., founder Nat. Council Hotel and Restaurant Edn., 1946; bd. dirs. Govs. Confs. Tourism Pacific N.W., 1947-49, Pacific-N.W. Trade Assn., 1947-48; adviser USPHS, USAF World-Wide Food Service; mgmt. cons. Soc. Advancement Food Service Research; mem. U.S. Travel Service, also trade assn. adv. com. U.S. C. of C.; trade missions to Europe auspices Dept. Commerce. Dir. Wilkensburg Hotel Co. (Pa.), Hotel Elkhart (Ind.). Served to capt. USAAF, 1942-46. Mem. Am. Assn. U. Profs., Am. Soc. Assn. Execs., Execs. Forum, Mich. Resort Assn., Mich., Pa. hotel assns., Food Execs. Assn., Fifth Internat. World Food Congress, Internat. Ho-Re-Ca. Confrerie de la Chaine des Rotisseurs, Theta Chi, Alpha Kappa Psi. Rotarian. Author: Manual for Resort Operations, 1950; also monographs, papers, articles. Home: 5580 Longmont St Houston TX 77027 Office: 925 Caroline St Houston TX 77002

GREENBAUM, MYER LOUIS, govt. ofcl.; b. Toledo, O., Aug. 23, 1921; s. Arthur Abraham and Helen Lenore (Mechler) G.; B.Engring., U. Toledo, 1943, postgrad., 1952; postgrad. Yale, 1943, Cornell U., 1960; m. Isabel Goldwater, May 2, 1948; 1 son, Arthur Franklin. Prodn. engr. Atlas Brazing Co., Toledo, 1947-48; asst. chief engr. Peters Stamping Co., Perrysburg, O., 1949-50; chief indsl. engr. Rossford (O.) Ordnance Depot, 1951-61; chief indsl. engr. Brookley AFB, 1961-64; chief warehousing materials handling U.S. Army Supply and Maintenance Command, Washington, 1964-66; cons. indsl. engring. U.S. Army Materiel Command, Washington, 1966-69, chief storage br., 1969—; instr. USAF, 1957-58. Del. D.C. Council Archtl. and Engring. Socs., 1968-70. Pres. Hillview P.T.A., Sylvania O., 1959. Served to 1st lt. USAAF, 1943-46. Registered profl. engr., Ohio, Ala. Sr. mem. Am. Inst. Indsl. Engrs. (pres. Mobile chpt. 1962, dir. Nat. Capitol chpt. 1968-70, mem. govt. div. and mgmt. div. 1961—), Am. Ordnance Assn. (mem. adv. group 1969—, vice-chmn. Army packaging bd. 1971—), Lambda Chi. Mason. Home: 5422 Richenbacher Av Alexandria VA 22304 Office: US Army Materiel Command 5001 Eisenhower Av Alexandria VA 22304

GREENBAUM, SAMUEL MEYER, lawyer; b. Washington, July 15, 1916; s. Samuel M. and Estelle (Ball) G.; J.D., Georgetown U., 1939, LL.M., 1942; m. Helen L. Marx, Feb. 15, 1942; children—Steven M., Marcia E. Admitted to D.C. bar, 1939; practiced in Washington, 1939—. Alternate chmn. Commn. on Mental Health, U.S. Dist. Ct. for D.C., 1962-72; instr. Catholic U. Columbus Sch. Law, 1965-73; adj. prof. creditor's rights in bankruptcy Georgetown U. Law Center, 1971; professorial lectr. creditor's rights in bankruptcy Am. U., 1971-74. Sec., dir. Lady Hamilton, Inc., Arlington, Va. Mem. Am., Fed. (chmn. com. on bankruptcy law 1971-72), D.C. (chmn. subcom. on bankruptcy) bar assns., Comml. Law League. Author: Plenary, Summary and Concurrent Jurisdiction under the Bankruptcy Act, 1942. Home: 2840 Brandywine St NW Washington DC 20008 Office: 1000 Connecticut Av Washington DC 20036

GREENBERG, BENJAMIN EDWIN, radiologist; b. N.Y.C., Aug. 25, 1907; s. Samuel and Edith (Goodman) G.; B.A., Columbia, 1929; M.D., N.Y. State U., 1932; m. Mollie Weinstein, June 5, 1932; 1 dau., Barbara J. Intern Beth-Eli Hosp., Bklyn., 1932; practice medicine specializing in radiology, 1933-42; with VA, 1946—, chief radiology service VA Hosp., Memphis, 1950—; prof. radiology U. Tenn., 1965—. Served from 1st lt. to maj., M.C., AUS, 1942-46. Diplomate Am. Bd. Radiology. Fellow Am. Coll. Radiology; mem. Memphis Roentgen Soc. (pres. 1956-57). Home: 294 Aurora Circle Memphis TN 38111 Office: VA Hosp Memphis TN 38104

GREENBERG, DANIEL SHELDON, publisher; b. N.Y.C., May 5, 1931; s. Max and Bertha (Rosenberg) G.; A.B., Columbia, 1953; m. Polly Hoben, June 6, 1953; children—Julie, Margaret, Cathryn, Elizabeth. Reporter, Wilmington (Del.) Jour., 1955-57, Washington Post, 1957-60; news editor, fgn. editor Sci. Mag., A.A.A.S., Washington, 1961-70; research fellow dept. history of sci. Johns Hopkins, Balt., 1965-67; regents lectr. U. Cal. at Santa Barbara, 1971; pub. Sci. and Govt. Report Newsletter, Washington, 1970—. Vis. fellow Sussex (Eng.) U., 1973. Served to lt. (j.g.) USNR, 1953-55. Congl. fellow Am. Polit. Sci. Assn., 1961. Recipient Distinguished Alumni award Columbia, 1971. Author: Politics of Pure Science, 1968. Address: 3736 Kanawha St NW Washington DC 20015

GREENBERG, DAVID BERNARD, chem. engr., educator; b. Norfolk, Va., Nov. 2, 1928; s. Abraham David and Ida (Frenkil) G.; B.S. in Chem. Engring., Carnegie Inst. Tech., 1952; M.S. in Chem. Engring., Johns Hopkins, 1959; Ph.D. in Chem. Engring., La. State U., 1964; m. Helen Muriell Levine, Aug. 15, 1959; children—Lisa, Jan, Jill. Process engr. U.S. Indsl. Chems., Balt., 1952-55; project engr. Food Machinery & Chem. Corp., Balt., 1955-56; asst. prof. U.S. Naval Acad., Annapolis, Md., 1958-61; instr. La. State U., Baton Rouge, 1961-64, asst. prof., 1964-67, asso. prof., 1967-72, prof., 1972—. Program dir. engring. div. NSF, Washington, 1973. Served with USNR, 1947-49. NSF research fellow, 1961, Esso fellow, 1964-65. Registered profl. engr., La. Mem. Am. Inst. Chem. Engrs., Am. Chem. Soc., Am. Soc. for Engring. Edn., Simulation Councils, Sigma Xi, Phi Lambda Upsilon. Asso. editor Jour. of Simulation, 1970—; editor CEP Symposium Series, 1968. Home: 305 Daventry Dr Baton Rouge LA 70808 Office: PO Box 19900-A Baton Rouge LA 70803

GREENBERG, MICHAEL JOHN, educator; b. N.Y.C., Sept. 28, 1931; s. Abraham S. and Lena (Kirsch) G.; A.B., Cornell U., 1953; M.A., Fla. State U., 1955; Ph.D., Harvard, 1958; m. Rima Robbins, June 10, 1954; children—Peter A., John K., Karl P. Instr. zoology U. Ill., Urbana, 1958-60, asst. prof., 1960-64; asso. prof. biol. scis. Fla. State U., Tallahassee, 1965-73, prof., 1973—. Instr. exptl. invertebrate zoology Marine Biol. Lab., Woods Hole, Mass., summers 1969-73. Mem. Gov.'s Task Force on Narcotics, Dangerous Drugs and Alcohol Abuse, 1970-72; mem. United Fund Com. Fla. State U., 1972-73. Recipient grants Fla. State U. Research Council, 1965-67, AEC, 1967-72, Am. Cancer Soc., 1967, Nat. Heart and Lung Inst. NIH, 1960-75; NSF sr. postdoctoral fellow U. Melbourne (Australia), 1964-65, Misaki Marine Lab., Japan, 1965. Mem. Am. Soc. Zoologists (div. program officer 1969-70), Am. Physiol. Soc., Soc. Gen. Physiologists, A.A.A.S., Marine Biol. Lab. Woods Hole, Tallahassee, Sopchoppy and Gulf Coast Marine Biol. Assn. (pres. 1967—), Sigma Delta Chi. Mem. editorial bd. Jour. Drug Issues, 1971—, Jour. Exptl. Zoology, 1974—, Comparative Gen. Pharmacology, 1970—. Home: 3210 Brookforest Dr Tallahassee FL 32303

GREENBERG, SANFORD DAVID, realty and constrn. co. exec.; b. Buffalo, Dec. 13, 1940; s. Carl and Sarah (Fox) G.; A.B., Columbia, 1962, M.B.A., 1966; M.A., Ph.D. (Woodrow Wilson fellow) Harvard, 1965, postgrad. Law Sch., 1965-66; postgrad. (Marshal scholar) Oxford U. (Eng.), 1964-65; m. Susan Beth Roseno, Aug. 12, 1962; children—Paul Eric, James Albert. Mng. partner Compressed Speech Found., 1961—; asst. prof. govt. Columbia; N.Y.C., 1965; research asso. Center for Internat. Affairs, Harvard, 1966; asst. to Pres.'s sci. adviser White House, Washington, 1966-67; dir. corporate devel. Systems Devel. Corp., Washington, 1967-68; chmn. bd. ED-TECH Corp., Washington, 1968-71; chmn. bd. Am. Metals and Alloys, 1970; vice chmn. bd. KMS Industries, Inc., Washington, 1971—; dir., financial adviser Tishman Realty and Constrn. Co. Inc., 1973—, Capital Centre, 1974—, Washington Hockey Partnership, 1974—. Univ. Research prof. U. Md., 1971-73. Trustee Nat. Braille Press, Boston, Charles River Acad., Cambridge, Mass., Opera Soc. Washington; bd. dirs. Nat. Com. on U.S.-China Relations; bd. govs. Ben Gurion U. of Negev. Named One of 10 Outstanding Young Mem. of Am., U.S. Jaycees, 1966, One of 4 Outstanding Young Men of Mass., Mass. Jaycees, 1966, One of 10 Outstanding Young Men, Boston Jaycees, 1966. Mem. Young Pres.'s Orgn. (Man of Year award 1974). Am. Polit. Sci. Assn., Am. Hist. Assn., Oxford Union Soc., Assn. for Computing Machinery, Newcomen Soc. N. Am., Phi Beta Kappa, Zeta Beta Tau (trustee Found.). Clubs: Harvard (N.Y.C.); Federal City, Harmonie, International (Washington); Bay. Editor: (with T. Cronin) The Presidential Advisory System, 1969. Patentee device for compression and expension of speech. Home: 700 New Hampshire Av NW Apt 106 Washington DC 20037 Office: 600 New Hampshire Av NW Washington DC 20037

GREENE, BARNET, accountant; b. N.Y.C., May 8, 1916; s. Harry and Ceilia (Myerson) G.; B.S., Am. U., 1952; m. Rosalie Maletz, May 29, 1949; children—Ellyn Bailey (Mrs. Steven Allen Stark), Barbara Lynn. Mgmt. analyst Rural Electrification Adminstrn., Washington, 1948-53; with Forrest E. Ferguson, C.P.A., 1953, Burke, Lansburg & Gerber, C.P.A.'s, 1954, Marinus Koster, C.P.A., 1955-58 (all Washington); accountant Bernet Greene, C.P.A., Washington and Silver Spring, Md., 1958—. Instr., Am. U., Washington, 1958-62. Treas., Connecticut Estates Civic Assn., Silver Spring, Md., 1955-56, Parkland Pool Assn., 1965-66. Served with AUS, 1942-46. Mem. Am., D.C. insts. C.P.A.'s Md. Assn. C.P.A.'s (chpt. treas. 1969-70, sec. 1970-71, v.p., pres.-elect 1971-72, pres. 1972-73), Accounting Research Assn. Home: 11300 Gilsan St Silver Spring MD 20902 Office: 3408 Wisconsin Av NW Washington DC 20016

GREENE, DALLAS WHORTON, JR., city ofcl.; b. Shreveport, La., June 29, 1923; s. Dallas Whorton and Eunice (Lester) G.; student Centenary Coll., 1941; m. Alice Whittington, Oct. 4, 1947; 1 dau., Valerie (Mrs. David Randall Rockett). With La. Fire Dept., Shreveport, 1942—, fire chief, 1965—. Mem. Shreveport Assn. for Blind, 1966—; YMCA. Mem. governing com. Arthritis Found., 1968—. Served with C.E., AUS, 1943-45. Recipient Friendship award Fraternal Order Police; Dictograph Salutes award Internat. Assn. Fire Chiefs, 1973. Mem. Internat. Assn. Fire Chiefs (pres. Southwestern div. 1971-72, dir. 1972—), La. State Fire Chiefs Assn. (dir.), La. Firemens Assn. (life), Fraternal Order Fire Fighters (hon.), 40 and 8, Nat. Fire Protection Assn., Am. Legion (post comdr.), V.F.W., Am. Ordnance Assn. Mem. Christian Ch. Lion. Home: 8826 Stonelake Pl Shreveport LA 71108 Office: PO Box 1143 Shreveport LA 71163

GREENE, E(RNEST) LONZO, architect; b. Greenville, S.C., Apr. 8, 1931; s. Ernest W. and Gertrude P. (Pitts) G.; B.S., Clemson U., 1952; children—Lon, Lynn. Co-owner, A/E, Inc., Greenville, S.C., 1965-70, exec. v.p., 1965-70; partner Greene, Bankes & Lee, Greenville, S.C., 1970-72; owner E. Lonzo Greene Architect, Greenville, S.C., 1972; pres. Greene & Lee Assos., Greenville, S.C., 1972—. Served with AUS, 1953-55. Mem. A.I.A., Greenville Council of Architects (pres. 1968-69). Baptist (deacon 1964-71). Rotarian (dir. 1969-70). Architectural works include K-Mart Shopping Centers, Kannapolis, N.C., Anderson, S.C., and Montgomery, Ala., Greenville (S.C.) Jr. High Sch., Sans Souci Jr. High Sch., Greenville, S.C., Presbyn. Ch., Baptist Ch., Ranch House Restaurant, Greenwood, S.C., Masonic Temple, Baptist Book Store (both Greenville), others. Home: 109 Howell Circle Greenville SC 29607 Office: PO Box 5559 Greenville SC 29606

GREENE, HAROLD HERMAN, judge; b. Frankfurt, Germany, Feb. 6, 1923 (came to U.S. 1942, naturalized 1944); s. Irving and Edith (Spandau) G.; student George Washington U., 1948-52, J.D. with distinction, 1952; student Biarritz Am. U., 1946; m. Evelyn Schroer, Sept. 19, 1948; children—Michael D., Stephanie A. Admitted to D.C. bar, 1952; asst. U.S. atty., Washington, D.C., 1953-57; atty. Office Legal Counsel, U.S. Dept. Justice, Washington, 1957-58, chief appeals sect. Civil Rights div., 1958-65; judge D.C. Ct. Gen. Sessions, 1965-66, chief judge, 1966-71; chief judge Superior Ct. D.C., 1971—. Served with AUS, 1944-47. Recipient Isaiah award for pursuit of justice, 1971; Distinguished Alumnus award George

Washington U. Law Sch., 1969. Mem. Am., Fed. bar assns., Bar Assn. D.C. (Distinguished Service award 1970), Am. Judicature Soc., World Peace Through Law Assn., Order of Coif, Phi Delta Phi. Jewish religion. Asso. editor George Washington U. Law Rev., 1951. Contbr. articles to profl. jours. Home: 6417 Tone Dr Bethesda MD 20034 Office: Superior Court Dist Columbia 4th and F Sts NW Washington DC 20001

GREENE, JACK CARPER, govt. ofcl.; b. Roundup, Mont., June 3, 1921; s. John Carper and Estelle Sarah (Haney) G.; B.S., Mass. Inst. Tech., 1947; M. in Engring. Adminstrn., George Washington U., 1971; m. Leslie Call, Aug. 2, 1953; children—Cherie, Daune Carroll Carter. With AEC, Washington, 1947-51, Def. Civil Preparedness Agy. and predecessors, 1951—. Mem. sci. adv. com. NATO, 1956-61. Served with AUS, 1943-47. Mem. Nat. Acad. Sci. (mem. adv. com. civil def. 1955-73). Home: 7600 Whittier Blvd Bethesda MD 20034 Office: Deputy Assistant Director for Research Defense Civil Preparedness Pentagon 1E536 Washington DC 20301

GREENE, JAMES ALLEN, psychiatrist; b. Sneedville, Tenn., Mar. 15, 1939; s. Ambrose Kyle and Martha Argelene (Surgenor) G.; B.S., U. Tenn., 1959, M.D., 1963; m. Rebecca O'Connor, Sept. 18, 1970. Intern, U. Tenn. Hosp., Knoxville, 1963-64; resident Dorothea Dix Hosp., Raleigh, N.C., 1964-67, asst. dir. forensic unit, 1968-69; asso. med. dir. Oak Ridge (Tenn.) Regional Mental Health Center, 1969-70; practice medicine specializing in psychiatry, Birmingham, Ala., 1970—; mem. staff Hillcrest Hosp., Birmingham, Ala., pres. 1973—; clin. instr. psychiatry U. Ala., Coll. Medicine, Birmingham, 1970—. Mem. profl. activities com. Salvation Army Hosp., Birmingham, Ala., 1973—. Served with USAF, 1967-68. Recipient Physicians Recognition award A.M.A., 1969, 72. Fellow Acad. Psychosomatic Medicine; mem. Am., So. psychiatric assns., Am., Ala. (vice chmn. reference com. 1973—, del. 1973), So. med. assns., Ala. Acad. Neurology, Birmingham Acad. Medicine, C. of C. Kiwanian. Home: 4213 Shiloh Dr Birmingham AL 35213 Office: 7005 5th Av S Birmingham AL 35212

GREENE, LEON NORMAN, physician; b. Bklyn., May 1, 1910; s. Max and Fannie (Kaplan) G.; A.B., Columbia Coll., 1931, M.D., 1935; m. Gloria Kaufman, Nov. 9, 1962. Intern, Mt. Sinai Hosp., N.Y.C., 1935-36, resident, 1936-40; resident in obstetrics and gynecology French Hosp., N.Y.C., 1940-41, Bellevue Hosp., N.Y.C., 1941-42, Queen's Gen. Hosp., N.Y.C., 1942-43; practice medicine specializing in obstetrics and gynecology, 1943—; instr. obstetrics and gynecology N.Y. U. Coll. Medicine, 1946-49, U. Miami Sch. Medicine, 1950—; dir. dept. obstetrics and gynecology Mt. Sinai Med. Center, Miami, Fla., 1962-64, also mem. staff; mem. staff Miami Heart Inst., South Shore Hosp., Miami Beach. Served to maj. MC AUS, 1943-46. Diplomate Am. Bd. Obstetrics and Gynecology. Mem. Miami Obstet. and Gynecol. Soc. (pres. 1962-63), Fla. Obstet. and Gynecol. Soc., A.C.S., Phi Beta Kappa, Alpha Omega Alpha. Home: 1200 W 21st St Miami Beach FL 33140 Office: 1431 N Bayshore Dr Miami FL 33132

GREENE, MILTON J., mortgage banker; b. N.Y.C., Dec. 21, 1919; s. A. and Belle (Costa) G.; B.S., N.Y. U., 1940; m. Barbara Huntley, May 15, 1949; children—Richard, Douglas, Virginia. With Touche, Niven & Co., N.Y.C., 1946-49; with So. Trust & Mortgage Co., Dallas, 1950-71, pres., 1965-71; vice chmn. bd. Ryan Mortgage Co., Arlington, Tex., 1971—. Served with AUS, 1941-45. Mem. Tex. Mortgage Bankers Assn. (pres. 1971-72), Mortgage Bankers Assn. Am. (regional v.p. 1968—). Home: 4635 Park Lane Dallas TX 75220 Office: Ryan Mortgage Co 611 Ryan Plaza Dr Arlington TX 76012

GREENE, R. GLENN, physician; b. Nashville, Oct. 16, 1929; s. Albert Reams and Annie Lois (Atkins) G.; B.A., Vanderbilt U., 1951, M.D., 1954, postgrad., 1954-57; m. Lexie Dell Daugherty, Mar. 6, 1955; children—Ginger Clay, Dierdre Clay. Intern, Vanderbilt U. Hosp., Nashville, 1954-55, resident, 1955-57; resident Barnes Hosp., St. Louis, 1959-60; practice medicine, specializing in internal medicine, Owensboro, Ky., 1960—. Mem. Ky. State Bd. Health, 1972-73. Served with M.C., AUS, 1957-59. Diplomate Am. Bd. Internal Medicine. Mem. A.C.P., Ky. Med. Assn. (program dir. 1970-74), Flying Physicians Assn. Home: 1635 Griffith Av Owensboro KY 42301 Office: Mayfair Sq Owensboro KY 42301

GREENE, RICHARD ELTON, savs. and loan exec.; b. Sandpoint, Ida., Aug. 17, 1942; s. Hollis Elton and Mary Elizabeth (Winter) G.; B.S. in Bus. Adminstrn., N.E. La. U., 1965; m. Sylvia Lorena Pritcher, Aug. 25, 1964; children—Richard Brian, Stacey Lynne. Asst. v.p. First Fidelity Mortgage Co., Monroe, La. and Arlington, Tex., 1965-69; v.p. Arlington Savs. Assn., 1969, exec. v.p., 1970, pres., 1971—, also dir.; v.p., dir. Affiliated Capital Corp., Houston; adv. dir. State Savs. & Loan Assn., Lubbock, Tex. Guest lectr. Arlington Bd. Realtors and Homebuilders Assn. Chmn. bus. div. Cancer Crusade, 1973-74. Pres., bd. dirs. Young Men for Arlington; v.p., bd. dirs. Arlington chpt. Am. Cancer Soc.; bd. dirs. Tarrant County chpt. A.R.C. Mem. Arlington C. of C. (dir., chmn. Arlington Night 1973, Friday Forum 1973), Scabbard and Blade, Pi Sigma Epsilon. Baptist (deacon). Home: 2114 Cross Creek Ct Arlington TX 76015 Office: 200 E Abram St Arlington TX 76010

GREENE, ROBERT THOMAS, clergyman, writer; b. Vance County, N.C., Aug. 28, 1919; s. Edward Jones and Iola (Gooch) G.; B.A., Wake Forest Coll., 1944; B.D., So. Baptist Theol. Sem., Louisville, 1948; spl. grad. studies Syracuse U., summer 1963; m. Grace Carolyn Bailey, Dec. 24, 1939; children—Ruth Adams, Robert Thomas. Ordained to ministry Bapt. Ch., 1942; pastor Bapt. Center Bapt. Ch., Clayton, N.C., 1942-44, Olive Branch Bapt. Ch., Dillsboro, Ind., 1945-48, Beech Grove Bapt. Ch., Owenton, Ky., 1948-49, Riverside Bapt. Ch., Merry Hill, N.C., 1949-52; missionary for West Chowan Bapt. Assn., Ahoskie, N.C., 1952-53, Cabarrus Bapt. Assn., Concord, N.C., 1953-60; dir. retirement Bapt. State Conv. N.C., 1960-61, sec. dept., stewardship devel., 1963-70, dir. coop. program promotion, 1971—, dir. dept. stewardship, 1973—; sec. Christian Education Advance, 1962-63. Pub. relations dir. for denominational work in Bapt. assns. in N.C., 1957-58; writer Bible. Column for newspapers called Biblical Series, 1952-57; regular writer for Bibl. Recorder, other Bapt. mags. Active in A.R.C. Recipient citation from Editorial Conf. of N.C., 1953. Democrat. Co-author: How To Write and Use a Few Words for an Effective Harvest, 1967. Contrbr. over 1000 articles to Bapt. publs., over 300 to jours. and newspapers. Home: 2700 St Marys St Raleigh NC 27609 Office: PO Box 26508 Raleigh NC 27611

GREENE, WALTER EARL, educator; b. Elwood, Ind., Sept. 11, 1929; s. Walter E. and Nellie Ethel (Redman) G.; B.S., U. Md., 1959; M.S., U. N.D., 1967; postgrad. U. Ark., 1970—; m. Ruth Violet Vincent, Dec. 30, 1949; children—Donna Mae, Donald Michael, Diane Sue, David Allan. Joined USAAF, 1947, advanced through grades to capt. USAF, 1962, ret., 1967; bus. mgr. Mt. Senario Coll., Ladysmith, Wis., 1967-68; prof. bus. adminstrn. S.E. Mo. State U., Cape Girardeau, 1968-71; instr. U. Ark. at Fayetteville, 1971—. Dist. commr. Swanee council Boy Scouts Am., 1970-71. Bd. dirs. Adminstrs. Coop., St. Louis, 1968-73. Mem. Acad. Mgmt., Soc. Advancement Mgmt., Midwest Bus. Adminstrs. Assn., Am. Marketing Assn., Am. Inst. Decision Scis., Am. Assn. U. Profs., Assn. Sch. Bus. Ofcls., Ark. Sch. Adminstrs. Assn., Alpha Kappa Psi, Alpha Phi Omega, Sigma Iota Epsilon, Delta Nu Alpha. Mason (K.T., Shriner). Club: Cape Shrine (co-founder, trustee 1970-73). Author: Plant Location Factors, 1969. Home: 1618 E 5th St Fayetteville AR 72701 Office: Box 2384 Univ Ark Fayetteville AR 72701

GREENE, WILDA WITT (MRS. WALLACE S. GREENE, JR.), author; b. Falkville, Ala.; d. Frank Thomas and Ida Dixie (Lovelady) Witt; student pub. schs.; m. Wallace S. Greene, Jr., Mar 2, 1936; 1 dau., Donna (Mrs. William T. Miller). Author: Visitation Evangelism, 1955; The Disturbing Christ: A Devotional Study of Hebrews, 1968; numerous articles in field for religious publs. Mem. Nat. League of Am. Pen Women, Authors Guild, Internat. Platform Assn. Clubs: Tenn. Woman's Press and Authors; Nashville Womans' Press and Authors'. Co-author: Broadman Devotional Annual, 1973. Address: 5020 Dovecote Dr Nashville TN 37220

GREENFIELD, CHARLES THOMAS, mfg. co. exec.; b. Toronto, Ont., Can., Jan. 9, 1920; s. Albert Edgar and Emily (Smith) G.; came to U.S., 1920, naturalized, 1946;; student U. Cin., 1951-52; m. Martha Jeannetta Connor, June 29, 1941; children—Janet Kay (Mrs. Ronald Hanock), Richard Duane, Susan Carol (Mrs. Michael Julius), Judith Ann (Mrs. Thomas Ward). Tool maker Union Carbide & Carbon Co., 1941-48, Fostoria Machine & Tool Co., 1948-51; tooling supr. Gen. Tire & Rubber Co., 1951-52; chief tool engr. Aerojet-Gen. Corp., Cin., 1952-54; gen. foreman Ex-Cell-O Corp., Lima, O., 1954-57, plant supt., New Breman, O., 1957-60, asst. plant mgr., Elwood, Ind., 1960-63, div. project mgr., Lima, 1963-64, gen. mgr., Black Mountain, N.C., 1964-66; dir. mfg. Duff-Norton Co., Charlotte, N.C., 1966-70; plant mgr. Kay Mfg. Corp., High Point, N.C., 1970—. Served with USAAF, 1942-45. Decorated Air medal. Mem. Am. Ordnance Assn., Am. Rocket Soc., Am. Soc. Tool Engrs., Am. Inst. Aeros. and Astronautics. Republican. Address: 1422 Grantham Dr High Point NC 27260

GREENFIELD, JOSEPH CHOLMONDELEY, cardiologist; b. Atlanta, Ga., July 20, 1931; s. Joseph Cholmondeley and Agnes (Game) G.; A.B., Emory U., 1954, M.D., 1956; m. Mary Ruth Fordham, Aug. 13, 1955; children—Mary, Ruth Ann, Susan Lee. Intern, Duke U. Med. Center, Durham, N.C., 1956-57, resident medicine, 1957-59, faculty, 1962—, prof. medicine, 1970—; with Nat. Heart Inst., Bethesda, Md., 1954-62; practice medicine, specializing in cardiology, Durham, 1962—; mem. staff VA Hosp., Durham. Served with USPHS, 1959-62. Recipient Career Devel. award NIH, 1965—. Fellow A.C.P., Am. Coll. Cardiology, Soc. Univ. Cardiologists; mem. Am. Heart Assn., Am., So. socs. clin. investigation, Assn. Am. Physicians. Contbr. articles to profl. jours. Home: 1212 Virginia Av Durham NC 27005 Office: Box 3246 Duke University Hospital Durham NC 27710

GREENFIELD, LEO, lawyer; b. Middletown, N.Y., Dec. 25, 1923; s. Alex and Helen (Klein) G.; B.B.A., U. Miami, 1950, J.D., 1948; m. Barbara Merritt, May 2, 1959; children—Jacqueline Beth, Helen Heidi. Admitted to Fla. bar, 1948; partner firm Street & Greenfield, North Miami, Fla., 1948-71; pres. Comutrix Corp., Miami, Fla., 1968-70; instr. law U. Miami, 1952-54; past dir. Capital Nat. Bank of Miami, Mercantile Nat. Bank; past gen. counsel Am. Agronomics Corp. Served with USAAF, 1943-45. Decorated Purple Heart medal, Air medal with four oak leaf clusters, Fourragere (Belgium). Mason (32 degree, Shriner). Club: U. Miami Century. Home: 2040 NE 194th Dr North Miami Beach FL 33162 Office: 1680 NE 135th St North Miami FL 33161

GREENFIELD, LEONARD JULIAN, educator; b. N.Y.C., May 18, 1926; s. David and Esther (Friedman) G.; B.S., Coll. City N.Y., 1949; M.S., U. Miami, 1951; Ph.D., Stanford, 1959. Asst. prof. marine sci. U. Miami, Coral Gables, 1960-63, asso. prof., 1963-70, chmn. marine sci. dept., 1964-66, asso. dean Grad. Sch., 1966-70, prof., chmn. dept. biology, 1970—. Adviser, Dade County master plan Dade County High Sch. Sci. Programs, Miami, 1960—. Served with AUS, 1945-47. Mem. A.A.A.S., Am. Inst. Biol. Scis., Marine Biol. Assn. Plymouth (Eng.), Sigma Xi. Editor: Ecology of the Everglades Conf., 1969. Contbr. articles to profl. jours. Home: 503 Anastasia Av Coral Gables FL 33134

GREENFIELD, MELVIN C., family counselor; b. Spring Lake, N.J., July 24, 1928; s. Joseph and Gussie (Bassin) G.; B.S., Rutgers U., 1960; M.S., Barry Coll., 1970; LhD., Evangelistic Assn., 1971; m. Nancy Lee Reis, Mar. 8, 1958; children—Gloria, Jacqueline, Johnathan. Adminstrv. asst. personnel dept. Jackson Meml. Hosp., Met. Dade County, 1965-70; pvt. practice family counselor Lennar Center, Miami, Fla., 1970—. Served with cav. AUS, 1946-49. Mem. Orthopsychiat. Assn., Council for Exceptional Children, Nat. Alliance for Family Life. Office: 8740 N Kendall Dr Miami FL 33156

GREENFIELD, NANCY LEE (MRS. MELVIN C. GREENFIELD), physician; b. Newark, Oct. 10, 1936; d. Hubert J. and Ethel (Haskin) Reis; B.A., Barnard Coll., 1958; M.D., State U. N.Y., 1962; m. Melvin C. Greenfield, Mar. 8, 1958; children—Glenn Neal, Gloria Haskin, Jacqueline Louise, Johnathan C. Intern U. Miami (Fla.) Sch. Medicine, Jackson Meml. Hosp., 1962, resident pediatrics, 1963-65, resident psychiatry, 1965-68; dir. psychiatry Variety Children's Hosp., Coral Gables, Fla., 1968—; clin. instr. dept. pediatrics, dept. psychiatry U. Miami, 1968—; dir. adolescent unit Montanari Clin. Sch. and Residential Treatment Center, Hialeah, Fla., 1968—. Psychiat. cons. Cystic Fibrosis Assn. Mem. Am., Fla. women's med. assns., Dade County Med. Soc., Am., South Fla. psychiat. socs., Greater Miami Pediatric Soc., Alpha Omega Alpha. Office: 8740 N Kendall Dr Miami FL 33156

GREENGLASS, BERT, indsl. engr., govt. ofcl.; b. N.Y.C., Mar. 16, 1932; s. Morris and Hannah (Stark) G.; B.Indsl Engring., N.Y.U., 1955; m. Anne Goldstein, Jan. 30, 1955; children—Gwen Esther, Felice Joy, Leslie Beth. Time and motion study analyst for various cos., N.Y.C., 1950-55; valuation engr. Pub. Service Commn. N.Y. State, 1955-56; prodn. engr. Ideal Toy Corp., N.Y.C., 1956; indsl. engr., program coordinator Army Ballistic Missile Agy., Huntsville, Ala., 1957-60; chief resources office, launch operations center NASA, Cape Kennedy Fla., 1961-65; chief Apollo Program Control, Kennedy Space Center, Fla., 1965-68; dep. dir. mgmt. systems div. NASA, 1968-69; dir. mgmt. information and program control systems Office Research and Tech., Dept. Housing and Urban Devel., Washington, 1969-71, dir. Office of Adminstrn., Program Planning and Control, Office Policy and Research, 1972—. Cons. resource control techniques; v.p. for operations Am. Med. Bldg. Guild, Madison, Wis., 1971-72. Served with AUS, 1956-57. Registered profl. engr., Ala. Mem. Nat., Ala. socs. profl. engrs., Am. Inst. Indsl. Engrs. (local chpt. pres.; past dir. North Ala. chpt.). Home: 2517 Farrier Lane Reston VA 22070 Office: Dept Housing and Urban Devel 451 7th St SW Washington DC 20410

GREENHILL, JOE R., state justice; b. Houston, July 14, 1914; s. Joe Robert Jr. and Violet (Stanuell) G.; B.A., U. Tex., 1936, B.B.A., 1936, LL.B., 1939; m. Martha Shuford, June 15, 1940; children—Joe Robert IV, William Duke. Admitted to Tex. bar, 1938; partner firm Bryan, Suhr, Bering and Bell, Houston, 1939-41, Graves, Dougherty & Greenhill, Austin, 1950-57; briefing atty. Supreme Ct. of Tex., Austin, 1941-42, 46, asso. justice, 1957-72, chief justice, 1972—; asst. atty. gen. of Tex., 1947-48, 1st asst. gen. of Tex., 1948-50. Served from ensign to lt., USNR, 1942-46. Mem. Am. Bar Assn., State Bar Tex. (chmn. mineral sect. 1957-58, mem. coms. adminstrn. of justice, rules and statutes, water law, chmn. jud. sect. 1970-71), Am. Judicature Soc. (dir.), Philos. Soc. Texas, Order of Coif, Phi Beta Kappa, Phi Delta Theta. Episcopalian. Mason (33 deg.). Lion (past pres. Austin). Home: 3204 Bridge Path Austin TX 78703 Office: Supreme Court of Texas Austin TX 78711

GREENLAW, ROBERT KING, physician; b. St. Stephen, N.B., Can., July 24, 1930; s. Harold E. and Ruby (Thorne) G.; M.D., C.M., Dalhousie U., Halifax, N.S., Can., 1958; M.Sc., McGill U., Montreal, Que., Can., 1961; Ph.D. in Anatomy, Queen's U., Kingston, Ont., Can., 1973; m. Dorothea E. Wallis, July 13, 1957; children—Terry Lea, John Douglas, Beverly Lynn, Roderick King, Pamela Ann. Intern St. John (N.B.) Gen. Hosp., 1957, Victoria Gen. Hosp., Halifax, 1958; resident surgery Royal Victoria Hosp., Montreal, 1958-59; research fellow McGill U., 1959-60; resident orthopaedic surgery U. Cal. at San Francisco, 1960-63; lectr. dept. anatomy Dalhousie U., Halifax, N.S., Can., 1964-65, asst. prof. surgery, 1968; instr. orthopedics Queen's U., Kingston, Ont., Can., 1966-67; asso. prof. orthopedics, dept. surgery U. Man., Winnipeg, 1968-72; asso. prof. orthopedics dept. orthopedic surgery Sch. Medicine, asso. prof. dept. biomed. engring. U. Va., Charlottesville, 1972—; mem. staff U. Va. Hosp. Recipient Frederick C. Bost award U. Cal., 1963; Orthopedic Research and Edn. Found. fellow Armed Forces Inst. Pathology, Washington, 1965; Canadian Arthritis and Rheumatism Soc. fellow, 1966-67, Med. Research Council Can. grantee, 1971-72. Fellow A.C.S., Royal Coll. Physicians and Surgeons Can.; mem. Canadian Orthopedic Assn., Canadian Orthopedic Found., Canadian Orthopedic Research Soc., Leroy C. Abbott Orthopedic Soc., Pan Pacific Surg. Assn., Canadian Assn. Anatomists, Can. Med. and Biol. Engring. Soc., N.S., Albemarle County med. socs., Internat. Soc. Prosthetics and Othotics, Royal Soc. Medicine (London). Home: Hickory Ridge Farm Earlysville VA 22936 Office: Dept Orthopedic Surgery Univ Va Hosp Charlottesville VA 22903

GREENMAN, ANDREW BURT, advt. agy. exec.; b. N.Y.C., Aug. 5, 1934; s. Charles and Helen (Rosenberg) G.; B.A., Washington and Lee U., 1956; m. Brenda Ellen Reshefsky, June 29, 1958; children—Jeffrey Saul, Jennifer Lynn. With Newman, Stern & Mandell, Miami Beach, Fla., 1957; founder Gross, Greenman Advt., Hollywood, Fla., 1958, pres., 1958-62; pres. Greenman Advt. Assos., Greenman Corporate Cons., Inc., Hollywood, Fla., 1963—; dir. Finance Ins. Premium, Inc. Served to 1st lt. Transp. Corps, AUS, 1957-58. Mem. Miami, Ft. Lauderdale advt. clubs, Hollywood Jr. C. of C. (past dir.), Sigma Delta Chi. Jewish religion (past dir. temple). Mason; mem. B'nai B'rith. Home: 910 Jefferson St Hollywood FL 33020 Office: 307 S 21st Av Hollywood FL 33020

GREENMAN, JACK NORMAN, co. exec.; b. Kansas City, Mo., July 30, 1912; s. Jack Norman and Josephine (Hershfield) G.; grad. pub. schs.; m. Elise Schoenberg, Dec. 28, 1935; children—Jack Norman, Richard A., Robert L. Clk. Uhlmann Grain Co., Kansas City, Mo., 1929-35, mgr., Amarillo, Tex., 1935-37; pres. Uhlmann Elevators Co., Ft. Worth, 1937-65; pres. Richland Warehouse Co., Ft. Worth, 1954—, Flour Mills of Am., Inc., Ft. Worth, 1965—; pres. dir. Chickasha Cotton Oil Co., Ft. Worth, 1970—; dir. Bank of Commerce, Ft. Worth & Denver Ry. Mem. Chgo. Bd. Trade. Pres., Ft. Worth Jr. Achievement, 1959-61. Bd. dirs. Trinity Improvement Assn., 1959, A.R.C., 1960—. Crippled Children's Soc., 1959—; trustee Mt. Olivet Cemetery Assn., Ft. Worth Children's Hosp. Mem. Nat. Grain Dealers Assn. (dir.), Newcomen Soc. N.Am., Nat. Grain Trade Council (dir.). Home: 3905 Monticello Dr Fort Worth TX 76107 Office: 2109 S Main St Fort Worth TX 76101

GREENWAY, CHARLES RADFORD, civil engr.; b. Ruston, La., June 11, 1931; s. Charles Radford and Lyla Anne (Carter) G.; B.S., U. Ark., 1958; m. Julia Maxine Leak, Mar. 7, 1958; children—Charles Arlis, Glenn Alan, Elizabeth Anne. Engr. trainee C.E., Little Rock, 1958-60, office engr. Dardenelle (Ark.) Resident Office, 1960-65, chief engring. br. Ozark (Ark.) Resident Office, 1965-72, project engr. Lake Whitney Project, Clifton, Tex., 1972—. Pres. Ozark P.T.A., 1970. Served with USMCR, 1951-54. Registered profl. engr., Ark. Mem. Am. Soc. C.E., Nat., Tex. socs. profl. engrs., V.F.W. Methodist. Home: 919 S Av M Clifton TX 76634 Office: PO Box 38 Laguna Park Rural Sta Clifton TX 76634

GREENWAY, ZELMAR CARVEY, fire chief; b. Swainsboro, Ga., Nov. 16, 1919; s. Arlie Thomas and Mattie (Davis) G.; student Tampa Bus. Coll., 1938, St. Petersburg Jr. Coll., 1961, 68-69; m. Donnie Mae Thomas, Mar. 12, 1943; 1 dau., Donnie Jean (Mrs. Alan C. Brown). With St. Petersburg (Fla.) Fire Dept., 1946—, fire capt., 1957, tng. officer, 1958-61, fire chief, 1962—. Dir. rescue Pinellas County, 1961; exec. dir. St. Petersburg Civil Def., 1969. Pres. Greater Sun Coast chpt. Muscular Dystrophy Assn. Am.; mem. adv. council Medic Alert. Served with USNR, 1942-45. Recipient Pub. Service citation of merit Muscular Dystrophy Assn., 1963-68; Service Appreciation award A.R.C., 1961. Mem. Internat., Southeastern, Fla. assns. fire chiefs. Democrat. Methodist. Rotarian. Home: 4574 8th Av N St Petersburg FL 33713 Office: 150 14th St N St Petersburg FL 33705

GREENWOOD, EL CAROL VOIGHTMAN, lawyer; b. Seward, Neb., Oct. 2, 1920; s. James Charles and Ella (Voightman) G.; A.B., Hastings Coll., 1941; postgrad. in econs. U. Neb. 1941-42; J.D., U. Mich., 1949; m. Wilma Ernestine Hopson, Nov. 19, 1945; 1 son, Richard Hopson. Admitted to Tex. bar, 1950, since practiced in Houston; mem. firm Fulbright & Crooker, 1949-63, partner, 1963—. Served with USNR, 1942-46. Mem. Maritime Law Assn. (exec. com. 1970-73), Am. Judicature Soc., Am., Houston bar assns., State Bar Tex., Propeller Club U.S., Phi Delta Theta. Methodist (steward, trustee). Clubs: Champions Golf, Plaza (Houston). Home: 6223 Rolling Water Dr Houston TX 77069 Office: Bank of Southwest Bldg Houston TX 77002

GREENWOOD, JOSEPH ALBERT, govt. scientist; b. Breckenridge, Mo., Sept. 18, 1906; s. Charles Sumner and Lucy (Umstott) G.; A.B., U. Mo., 1927, M.A., 1929, Ph.D., 1931; m. Neva Louise Garner, Aug. 28, 1930; children—Nancy Lee (Mrs. Frederick Phillips Brooks, Jr.), Joseph Richard, Neva Elizabeth. Asst. prof. math. Duke, 1930-42; math. statistician Bauer Navy Dept., Air Force Intelligence Center, Armed Forces Radiobiology Research Inst., Washington, 1946-65; math. statistician Food and Drug Adminstrn., Drug Enforcement Adminstrn., Washington, 1966—. Mem. math. dept. No. Va. extension U. Va., 1948-62. Served to lt. comdr. USNR, 1942-46. Fellow Am. Soc. for Quality Control, A.A.A.S.; mem. Parapsychology Assn., Inst. Math. Statistics, Am. Statis. Assn. Statis. editor Jour. Parapsychology, 1946—. Home: 430 Great Falls St Falls Church VA 22046 Office: 1405 Eye St Washington DC 20537

GREENWOOD, SAMUEL ROSS, banker; b. Speegleville, Tex., Sept. 1, 1921; s. Samuel Tillian and Rosa (Oliver) G.; student Okla. A. and M. U., Stillwater, City Coll., Los Angeles; postgrad. So. Meth. U.; m. Clara Hejl, Feb. 6, 1943; children—Gayle (Mrs. Richard Edwin Pitts), Samuel T., Fletcher Hejl. Pres., dir. Temple Nat. Bank (Tex.), 1967—, also dir.; dir. Am. Income Life Ins. Co.; pres. Investors

Diversified Devel. Corp., Inc., 1965—. Mem. Nat. Mortgage Sch. Faculty, Ohio State U., 1961-69; Mem. exec. com., chmn. finance com. Wesleyan Homes, Inc., 1959—; chmn. Gov.'s State Com. on Aging, 1965—; mem. nat. adv. com. White House Conf. on Aging, 1971; pres. Temple Lions Crippled Children's Found., 1962; mem. Temple Law Enforcement Commn., 1970—; mem. regional adv. group, exec. com., task force allied health sci. Regional Med. Program Tex., 1969—; mem. Tex. United Community Services, 1970-72. Bd. dirs. Tex. Soc. on Aging; bd. dirs., treas. Bell County Mental Health and Mental Retardation Center; trustee, pres. bd. Central Tex. Regional Med. Edn. Found.; mem. lay adv. council So. Meth. U., 1972. Recipient Outstanding Citizen award Temple Jr. C. of C., 1969, Distinguished Service award Tex. Soc. Aging, 1969. Mem. V.F.W., Am. Legion, D.P.T. & D. Hunting Soc., Am. (panel moderator, seminar leader mortgage finance com. 1959-68, mem. nat. mortgage finance com. 1961-66, chmn. com. on housing and urban devel. 1965-66), Tex. (chmn. mortgage finance com. 1968-70) bankers assns., Temple C. of C. (pres. 1966, chmn. transp. and hwy. div. 1971-72, Boss of Yr. award 1973). Methodist (chmn. bd. stewards 1957-58). Mason (Shriner), Elk, Lion (pres. Temple 1961). Clubs: Country (Temple); Stagecoach Country (Salado, Tex.); City (Waco, Tex.); Admirals, Lancers (Dallas). Home: 3005 Las Cruces St Temple TX 76501 Office: PO Box 809 Temple TX 76501

GREER, ALFRED EDGAR, supt. schs.; b. Snyder, Tex., June 3, 1929; s. Fred T. and Mable (Houston) G.; A.A., Decatur Bapt. Coll., 1949; B.S., N. Tex. State U., 1951; M.S., 1954; postgrad. Tex. Tech. U., 1962-66; m. J. Elaine Calloway, Dec. 20, 1952; children—Gerry D., Cheryl L. Elementary prin. pub. schs., Era, Tex., 1951-53, high sch. prin., 1953-54; prin. high sch. Rockwall (Tex.) Ind. Sch. Dist., 1954-55; supt. schs., Ponder, 1955-58, Errant, Tex., 1958-62, Anton, Tex. 1962-66, Memphis, Tex., 1966-67; supt. schs. Bridgeport (Tex.) Ind. Sch. Dist., 1967—. Mem. Bridgeport Park Bd., 1967-71. Bd. dirs. Denton County Tchr. Credit Union, 1973-74. Mem. Tex. Tchrs. Assn., N.E.A., Tex. Assn. Sch. Adminstrs., Hockley County Tchrs. Assn. (v.p. 1966), Bridgeport C. of C. (dir. 1968-71, 3d v.p. 1969-70), Phi Delta Kappa. Mason (Shriner), Lion (dir. 1971, v.p. 1973-74, pres. 1974—). Home: 123 Nottingham Circle Bridgeport TX 76026 Office: 1407 Carpenter St Bridgeport TX 76026

GREER, DAVID MCKAY, civil engr.; b. Whangarei, New Zealand, Nov. 2, 1908; s. Dane Manson and Mary Elizabeth (McKay) G. (parents Am. citizens); came to U.S., 1910; B.A., Stanford U., 1929; M.S., Harvard, 1939; m. Louise Blan Saunders, Nov. 26, 1939; children—Dane Malcolm, Gail McKay. With U.S. Corps Engrs., Little Rock and Galveston, Tex., 1939-45; partner Greer & McClelland, cons. soil and found. engrs., Houston, 1946-52, Montclair, N.J., 1952-55; propr. Greer Engring. Assos., Montclair, 1955-59, merged with Woodward-Clyde-Sherard & Assos., Clifton, N.J. and N.Y.C., 1959, partner, 1959-68. Fellow Am. Soc. C.E.; mem. Am. Cons. Engrs. Council. Editor, co-author Drilled Pier Foundations, 1972. Home: 30 E Cleburn St Fayetteville AR 72701

GREER, DOROTHY LUCILLE LEECH (MRS. THOMAS KEISTER GREER), bus. exec.; b. Fort Morgan, Colo., Nov. 5, 1921; d. Laurence Blakely and Lucille Otis (Gill) Leech; student Mills Coll., 1939-40; B.A., San Diego State Coll., 1943; m. Thomas Keister Greer, Jan. 9, 1943; children—Nancy Taliaferro (Mrs. William Nelson Alexander II), Giles Carter, Celeste Claiborne. Tchr., Franklin County Schs., Rocky Mount, Va., 1944-45, 48-49, Roanoke (Va.) City Schs., 1949-51; dir., sec.-treas. Franklin County Times, Inc., Rocky Mount, 1968—. Mem. central com. Assistance League So. Cal., Los Angeles, 1952-54; mem. patrons com. Internat. Debutante Ball, 1969-71. Mem. D.A.R. Christian Scientist. Clubs: Willow Creek Country (sec.-dir. Rocky Mount 1962-64); Roanoke Country; San Diego Yacht. Home: The Grove Rocky Mount VA 24151

GREER, EARL VINCENT, educator; b. Kechi, Kan., Mar. 27, 1912; s. Thomas Shadrach and Carrie (Crismond) G.; A.B., Olivet Nazarene Coll., 1932; M.A., U. Ill., 1934; student U. Mich., summers 1945-47; Ph.D., U. Okla., 1951; m. Myrtle Margaret Thompson, July 24, 1935; children—Vincent Allan, Marilyn Lou (Mrs. William Edward Stanford), Marcia Kay, Melinda Sue. Instr., Bresee Coll., Hutchinson, Kan., 1934-36, dean coll., 1936-40, merged into Bethany (Okla.) Nazarene Coll., 1940, asst. prof. math., 1940-48, asso. prof., 1948-50, prof., 1950—, head dept. math., 1940—; part time instr. U. Okla., 1948-50; lectr. NSF Inst., Kan. State Tchrs. Coll., summer 1960, Southwestern State Coll., Durant, Okla., summers 1961-72. NSF fellow, 1959. Mem. Okla. Council Tchrs. Math. (dir. 1961-65), Nat. Council Tchrs. Math., Math. Assn. Am., Sigma Xi, Phi Delta Lambda. Mem. Ch. Nazarene. Home: 4700 N Donald St Bethany OK 73008 Office: 6729 NW 39th Expwy Bethany OK 73008

GREER, ELDON GERALD, JR., county extension dir.; b. Enid, Okla., May 10, 1937; s. Eldon Gerald and Matilda Evangeline (Taborsky) G.; Asso. Sci., Connor's Jr. Coll., 1957; B.S., Okla. State U., 1960, M.S., 1971; m. Judith Sue White, Apr. 3, 1965; children—Diana Sue, Brenda Dawn, Marek Tavis. Farmer, Enid, Okla., 1955-61; wage employee Soil Conservation Service, 1961-62; supt. Agr. Research Agronomy Sta., Okla. State U., Cherokee, 1962-69; extension agt. Coop. Extension Service, Watonga, 1969-72, county extension dir., Hollis, 1972—. Neighborhood chmn. Salt Plains council Boy Scouts Am., 1964-66; chmn. Sight Conservation, 1970-72. Served with AUS, 1961. Mem. Am. Soc. Agronomy, Am. Soc. Crop Sci., Am. Soc. Soil Sci., Reserve Officers Assn., Okla. County Extension Agts. Assn. (mem. 4-H and youth com. 1962—), Defense Supply Assn., Okla. Farm Bur., Higher Edn. Alumni Assn. Okla., Okla. State U. Alumni. Methodist. Lion. Home: Agriculture Bldg Hollis OK 73550

GREER, JAMES EDWARD, chemist; b. Greer, S.C., Apr. 30, 1912; s. Edward Garrison ar l Pearle Virginia (James) G.; B.S., Presbyn. Coll., 1933; postgrad. Clemson U., 1934, Mass. Inst. Tech., 1952; m. Nellie Law, June 1, 1940; children—Phyllis L. (Mrs. William Mossburg), Kathleen (Mrs. William Gailey), Carolyn (Mrs. Kenneth Melton). Chemist, Pacific Mills, Lyman, S.C., 1933-38; chemist Piedmont Print Works, 1939; dyestuff chemist Am. Aniline Products, Inc., 1939-48; textile chemist Burlington Industries, Greensboro, N.C., 1948—. Alumni dir. Presbyn. Coll., Clinton, S.C. Served to maj. AUS, World War II; ETO. Decorated Order St. George (Greece). Mem. Am. Chem. Soc. (chmn. Central N.C. sect. 1962), Am. Assn. Textile Chemists and Colorists (chmn. No. Piedmont sect. 1952). Patentee in field. Home: 912 Forest Hill Greensboro NC 27410 Office: 3330 W Friendly Av Greensboro NC 27410

GREER, JOHN KEEVER, mus. adminstr., educator; b. Topeka, Kan., July 8, 1930; s. William Jeffries and Dorothy Dean (Jones) G.; B.A., U. Kan., 1955; M.S., Mich. State U., 1960, Ph.D., 1965; m. Marjorie Bedell, Oct. 5, 1959; children—Jeff, John. Asst. dir. U. Okla. Biol. Sta., Willis, 1965-66, dir. Stovall Mus., Norman, 1966—, asso. prof. zoology, 1966—. Mem. Mayor's Adv. Council on Historic Preservation, Norman, 1972—; Okla. rep. Am. Assn. Museums, also past pres. Served with USMCR, 1948-49. Recipient Civic award City of Norman. Fellow Okla. Acad. Sci., mem. Mt. Plains Mus. Conf. (treas., sec. edn.), Okla. Museums Assn. (past sec.-treas.), Okla. Wildlife Soc. Contbr. articles on mammals and ecology to profl. jours. Home: 735 S Lahoma Norman OK 73069

GREER, JOHN ONLY, univ. adminstr.; b. Henderson, Tex., Oct. 21, 1933; s. Dolphus Only and Sarah Flonelle (Brison) G.; B.Arch., A. and M. Coll. Tex., 1957; M.Arch., Tex. A. and M. U., 1964; m. Wanda Faye Knight, June 5, 1954; children—Gregg Only, Valorie Ann. Project architect Matthews & Assos., architects and engrs., Bryan, Tex., 1964-66; partner Maynard & Greer, architects, Nacogdoches, Tex., 1966-71; mgmt. services dir. Archtl. Research Center, Tex. A. and M. U., College Station, 1971-72, asst. dean Coll. Architecture and Environmental Design., 1972—. Pres. Nacogdoches County United Fund, 1969-70. Served to 1st lt. AUS, 1957-59, 61-62. Recipient 2d prize design competition Tex. Soc. Architects, 1956. Mem. A.I.A. (sec. Brazos chpt. 1971, state dir. 1972-74, v.p. 1974), Tex. Soc. Architects (chmn. archtl. edn. com. 1974), Nacogdoches Jr. C. of C. (pres. 1968-69). Prin. archtl. works include (with Carl Victor Maynard) Commercial Nat. Bank, Drive-In Facility, Christ Episcopal Ch. Daysch. Bldg., First Methodist Ch., Sanctuary, Nettie Marshall Elementary Sch. Addition, Baseball-Family Park, Meml. Hosp. Playground, Community Center Park (all Nacogdoches). Home: 506 Brookside St Bryan TX 77801 Office: Coll Arch and Environmental Design Tex A and M U College Station TX 77843

GREER, MACK VARNEDOE, physician; b. Valdosta, Ga., July 29, 1927; s. Lloyd Barton and Julie Winn (Varnedoe) G.; A.B., Emory U., 1951; postgrad. Valdosta State Coll., 1955-56; M.D., Med. Coll. Ga., 1960; m. Betty Dame English, Dec. 27, 1951; children—Betty June, Mack Varnedoe. Adjuster, Crawford & Co., ins. adjusters, Atlanta, 1951-52; high sch. math. and sci. tchr., football coach Clinch County (Ga.) and Waycross (Ga.) High Sch., 1952-55; rotating intern Bapt. Meml. Hosp., Jacksonville, Fla., 1960-61; gen. practice medicine and surgery, Homerville, Ga., 1961-72; mem. staff South Ga. Med. Center; high sch. athletic physician; coll. physician, also asso. prof. biology Valdosta State Coll., 1972—. Served with USMCR, World War II, Korean Conflict. Mem. A.M.A., So., Ga. med. assns., S.Ga. Med. Soc., Clinch County Bd. Health, Clinch County Athletic Assn., Am. Coll. Emergency Physicians, Pi Kappa Alpha, Alpha Kappa Kappa. Methodist. Club: Valdosta (Ga.) Touchdown, Exchange. Home: 213 W Dame Av Homerville GA 31634 Office: 106 W Dame Av Homerville GA 31634

GREER, SHELDON, educator; b. N.Y.C., July 11, 1928; s. Hyman and Ida (Katz) G.; B.A., Bklyn. Coll., 1950; M.A., Columbia U., 1952, Ph.D., 1957; m. Ina Ludwig, June 30, 1956; children—Brian, Corinne, Abbe, Glenn. Research asso. Columbia Coll., N.Y.C., 1957-61; asso. prof. microbiology U. Miami, Miami, Fla., 1961-74, prof., 1974—; molecular geneticist, asso. prof. biochemistry, 1967—, adj. dean Grad. Sch., 1973—. Bd. dirs. Leonardo DaVinci Humanities Club, 1972—. Mem. Soc. Life Scis. (dir. 1968—, assn. dir. life scis. program 1973—), Am. Soc. Biol. Chemists, Phi Beta Kappa, Sigma Xi. Author: Discovery of Chemical Sensitization of Cells to Radiation, 1957; Discovery of Depurination, A New Mechanism of Mutagenesis, 1961. Research on selective chemotherapy Herpes viruses. Home: 8320 SW 86th Terrace Miami FL 33143

GREER, THOMAS KEISTER, lawyer; b. Premier, W.Va., Sept. 28, 1921; s. Moses Theodrick and Goldie (Shaw) G.; B.A. with honors, U. Va., 1947, B.Laws, 1948; m. Dorothy Lucille Leech, Jan. 9, 1943; children—Nancy Taliaferro (Mrs. William N. Alexander), Giles Carter, Celeste Claiborne. Admitted to Va. bar, 1948; practiced in Rocky Mount, Va.; asst. U. S. atty. So. Dist. Cal., 1951-54; pub. Franklin County Times, Rocky Mount, 1968-73; asst. judge, Franklin County, Va.; 1958—; gen. counsel Salyer Land Co., Corcoran, Cal., 1957—. Served to capt. USMC, World War II. Mem. Va., Cal. bars, Va. Hist. Soc., Raven Soc., Order of Coif, Phi Delta Phi. Democrat. Christian Scientist. Clubs: Roanoke (Va.) Country; Willow Creek Country (Rocky Mount); San Diego Yacht. Home: The Grove Rocky Mount VA 24151 Office: 110 Maple Av Rocky Mount VA 24151

GREER, VIRGINIA BRADFORD (MRS. JOHN GREER), writer; b. Atlanta, Mar. 30, 1919; d. John and Floy (Jarrett) Bradford; diploma corr. course in journalism Newspaper Inst. Am., 1952; m. John Greer, Dec. 23, 1936; children—Kitty, John, Lynn. Reporter, Mobile (Ala.) Press Register, 1955; free-lance writer, 1951—. Bd. dirs. Mobile Mental Health Center, A.R.C. Recipient nat. 1st pl. award for outstanding journalism in field home laundry, 1962, other service awards. Mem. Nat. League Am. Pen Women (v.p.). Baptist. Club: Octavia LeVert Toastmistress. Author: Give Them Their Dignity, 1968. Address: Route 5 Box 267TG Mobile AL 36608

GREESON, GEORGIANA WHITE, librarian; b. Capps, Ark., Mar. 26, 1921; d. James L. and Agnes (Calvert) White; student Hendrix Coll., 1939-40; B.A., Ark. State Tchrs. Coll., 1943; B.S. in L.S., La. State U., 1951; m. William H. Greeson, Jan. 16, 1946 (div. 1953); 1 dau., Patricia Evlin. Tchr., English jr. high sch., Harrison, Ark., 1943-44; library asst., librarian North Ark. Regional Library, Harrison, 1944-53; children's librarian Los Angeles Pub. Library, 1954; librarian Phillips County Library, Helena, Ark., 1955-57, St. Charles Parish Library, Hahnville, La., 1958—. Mem. Am., La. library assns. Home: Route 2 Box 34C Luling LA 70070 Office: St Charles Parish Library Hahnville LA 70057

GREGG, JACK RAYMOND, family planning exec.; b. Clarksdale, Miss., Aug. 4, 1936; s. James Frank and Hallie (Jenkins) G.; B.E.E., Vanderbilt U., 1959; postgrad. Ala. A. and M. U., 1970-71, Tulane U., 1972-73; m. Betty Marie Cobb, June 29, 1962; 1 dau., Carrah Leigh. Project engr. NASA-Marshall Space Flight Center, Huntsville, Ala., 1959-65; chief engr. Saturn/Apollo program office N.Am. Rockwell Corp., Huntsville, 1965-71; dir. program planning, control family planning clinics Family Health Found., New Orleans, 1971—; sec., treas. Tech. Utilization Corp., Huntsville, 1970—; mem. faculty Tulane U. Sch. Pub. Health, 1972—. Cons. So. Regional Edn. Bd. Hon. col.-aide-de-camp governor's staff Gov. Albert Brewer, Ala., 1969-71, Gov. Edwin Edwards, La., 1972—. Registered profl. engr., Ala., La. Mem. La. Engring. Soc., Am. Pub. Health Assn., Population Assn. Am. Home: Apt C 7250 Cannonbury Dr New Orleans LA 70126 Office: The Family Health Found 136 S Roman St New Orleans LA 70112

GREGG, PERCIVAL PORCHER, civil engr.; b. Florence, S.C., Sept. 28, 1916; s. Percival Porcher and Constance (Ashby) G.; B.C.E. with honors, N.C. State U., 1940; m. Constance Ruth Weiser, Dec. 31, 1960; children—Janet Porcher, Percival Porcher III. Beginning engr. Pitts.-Des Moines Steel Co., 1941; design engr. Seaboard Airline R.R. Co., Norfolk, Va., 1946-51; constrn. positions, 1951-55; asso. John M. Baldwin & Assos., 1955-60; partner, Baldwin & Gregg, Norfolk, Va., 1960-69, pres., 1969—. Bd. dirs. Cape Henry Sch., 1970-73, v.p., 1972-73; bd. dirs. Virginia Beach, Va. Served with AUS, 1941-46, now lt. col. Res. ret. Registered profl. engr., Va., D.C., N.C., S.C., Fla., La., Ohio. Fellow Am. Soc. C.E.; mem. Soc. Am. Mil. Engrs., Nat., Va. (chmn. profl. engrs. pvt. practice functional sect. 1965-67) socs. profl. engrs., Va. Assn. Surveyors (pres. 1965), Am. Legion. Episcopalian. Clubs: Virginia (dir. 1970-73, v.p. 1973) Harbor (Norfolk); Princess Anne Country (dir. 1967-70) (Virginia Beach, Va.). Home: 1421 N Bay Shore Dr Virginia Beach VA 23451 Office: PO Box 5783 Norfolk VA 23516

GREGG, ROBERT QUINLY, physicist; b. Independence, Mo., May 21, 1916; s. Stanley E. and Daisy M. (Quinly) G.; A.B., Central Meth. Coll., 1938; Ph.D., U. Mo., 1944; m. Wilma Louise McCollum, June 10, 1942; children—Susan (Mrs. David B. Stevens), Wallace, James, Louise, Frank. Physicist, Monsanto Chem. Co., Dayton, O., 1943-46; asst. prof. U. Mo., Columbia, 1946-48; with Phillips Petroleum Co., Bartlesville, Okla., 1948—, sect. mgr., 1967—. Mem. Am. Crystall. Assn., Electron Microscopy Soc., Sigma Xi. Home: 3207 Henrietta Bartlesville OK 74003 Office: 234A Research Bldg 1 Bartlesville OK 74004

GREGG, ROGER ALLEN, metall. engr.; b. Lenoir, N.C., July 19, 1938; s. William Leonard and Bessie May (Warren) G.; B.S., N.C. State U., 1960, M.S., 1962; Ph.D., U. Fla., 1968; m. Susan Elizabeth Davis, July 22, 1961; children—Cynthia Marie, Helen Carol. Instr. N.C. State U., Raleigh, 1961-62; research engr. Pratt & Whitney, North Haven, Conn., 1962-63; research engr. E.I. DuPont Co., Inc., Aiken, S.C., 1968-70, sr. research supr., 1970—. Mem. Am. Inst. Metall. Engrs., Am. Soc. Metals (chpt. chmn. 1972—), Sigma Nu. Republican. Baptist. Home: 805 Spring Dr Aiken SC 29801 Office: Savannah River Laboratory Aiken SC 29801

GREGORY, DALE ROGERS, chem. engr.; b. Lake Village, Ark., Aug. 1, 1934; s. Shelby Gilmore and Ina Mae (Overton) G.; B.S. (Union Carbide fellow 1954, Monsanto fellow 1955), Va. Poly. Inst., 1956, Ph.D. (Shell fellow), 1966; m. Carol Eileen Bushee, Jan. 13, 1956; children—Shelby James, Raymond Duane, Diane Mae. Prodn. supr. Union Carbide, S. Charleston, W.Va., 1956, 59-60; process engr. E.I. duPont Co., Martinsville, Va., 1960-62; with Tenn. Eastman Co. Kingsport, 1965—, research asso., 1974—. Served to 1st lt. AUS, 1956-59. Mem. Am. Inst. Chem. Engrs., Tri-Cities Swimming Assn. Sigma Xi, Tau Beta Pi, Phi Lambda Upsilon, Phi Kappa Phi. Moose. Contbr. articles in field to profl. jours. Home: 3638 Hemlock Park Dr Kingsport TN 37663 Office: Tennessee Eastman Company Kingsport TN 37660

GREGORY, EDWARD MEEKS, clergyman; b. Richmond, Va., Sept. 30, 1922; s. George Craghead and Constance (Heath) G.; grad. St. Christopher's Sch., Richmond, 1941; A.B., U. Va., 1947; S.T.B., Episcopal Theol. Sch., Cambridge, Mass., 1954; postgrad. George Washington U., 1950. Ordained to ministry Episcopal Ch., 1954; instr. Staunton (Va.) Mil. Acad., 1947-48; master Episcopal High Sch., Alexandria, Va., 1948-51; curate St. Mark's Episcopal Ch., Richmond, Va., 1954-69; vicar St. Peter's Episcopal Ch., Richmond, 1969—; dean East Richmond, 1974—; diocesan youth dir., 1956-60; diocesan del. Va. Council Chs., 1967—. Mem. Diocesan Dept. on Social Relations, 1970—, Diocesan Lit. Commn.; 1973—; pres. Religious Edn. Council, Richmond, 1961-62, Richmond Episcopal Clericus, 1972-73. Bd. dirs. Vol. Service Bur., Richmond, 1960-63, Ednl. Therapy Center, 1964—, Multiple Sclerosis, 1961-66, Va. Community Devel. Orgn., 1968—, Va. Am. Civil Liberties Union, 1970-71, Internat. Council; bd. dirs. Va. Council on Human Relations, 1965-70, treas., 1972—; bd. dirs. Planned Parenthood, 1969—, Richmond chpt. A.R.C., 1973—; pres. Richmond Council Human Relations, 1960-62; pres. Friends' Assn. for Children, 1967-70; mem. Richmond Area Community Council; mem. adv. bd. Richmond Model Neighborhood, 1971—. Served with M.C., AUS, 1942-46. Mem. Richmond Clergy Assn., Jamestown Soc. (gov. 1951-54), Mayflower Soc. (elder Va. co. 1963—), Va. Hist. Soc., Episcopal Soc. Cultural and Racial Unity (chmn. Richmond 1964-66), Assn. for Preservation Va. Antiquities, Va. Mus. Fine Arts, Chi Phi. Clubs: Torch Internat. Home: St Peter's Vicarage 1907 N 23d St Richmond VA 23223 Office: St Peter's Episcopal Ch 1719 N 22d St Richmond VA 23223

GREGORY, HERBERT WAYNE, ednl. adminstr.; b. Pittsboro, Miss., Apr. 18, 1921; s. Leonard C. and Leona (Wagner) G.; B.A.E., U. Miss., 1942, M.Ed., 1952, Ed.D., 1954; m. Jeannette Spainhour, June 11, 1955; children—Wayne Porter, Anne Hazel. Tchr., Miss. Pubs. Schs., 1947-50; faculty, chmn. dept. edn. Tift Coll., Forsyth, Ga., 1954-57; faculty, head dept. edn. La. Coll., Pineville, 1957-60; dir. tchr. edn. Southeastern La. Coll., Hammond, 1960-67, asst. to pres. Office of Dean, 1967-68, head dept. student teaching, 1968—. Mem. La. Adv. Com. Tchr. Edn. and Certification, 1958-64. Mem. So. Council Tchrs. Edn., La. Tchrs. Assn. (nat. commn. internships in teaching 1964—), Assn. Student Teaching, La. Assn. Student Teaching (pres. 1964-65), N.E.A., Am. Assn. U. Profs., Kappa Delta Pi, Kappa Phi Kappa, Phi Delta Kappa (La. coordinator 1961—). Rotarian. Home: 126 College Dr Hammond LA 70401

GREGORY, LOWELL DEAN, aerospace co. exec.; b. Chickasha, Okla., Feb. 19, 1918; s. Simeon Roscoe and Pearl (Robinson) G.; B.A. in English, U. Okla., 1940, M.A. in Math., 1950; Ph.D. in Math. Statistics (Ling-Temco-Vought fellow), So. Meth. U., 1968; m. Marian Gavin, May 27, 1939; children—Gavin George, Lynn. Instr. math. U. Okla., Norman, 1947-51; sr. analyst Chance Vought Aircraft, Dallas, 1951-55, devel. project engr., 1955-57, supr. advanced weapon systems analysis, 1957-59, chief reliability astro. div., 1959-62; mgr. reliability engring. astro. div. Ling-Temco-Vought Dallas, 1962-64, supr. operations analysis, 1964—. Spl. lectr. Nat. War Coll., 1972. Served to 1st lt. F.A., AUS, 1940-42, to capt. USAAF, 1942-45. Mem. Aerospace industries Assn. (mem. reliability com. 1964—), Am. Astronautical Soc. Assn. (sr.), Operations Research Soc. Am., North Tex. Operations Research Soc. (dir.), Sigma Xi, Pi Mu Epsilon. Home: 1300 W 2d St Arlington TX 76013 Office: PO Box 5907 Dallas TX 75222

GREGORY, SCOTT SMITH, county ofcl.; b. Tomkinsville, Ky., Sept. 15, 1932; s. Marvin Geers and Lucy Catherine (Smith) G.; B.S. in C.E., U. Ky., 1956; m. Ruth Ann Eyl, Oct. 3, 1959; children—Scott Smith, Steven Clark, Julia Ann. With Ky. Dept. Hwys., 1948-68, dist. planning engr., 1963-65, dist. operations engr., 1965-68; chief engr. Raymond Constrn. Co., Louisville, 1968-70; dir. pub. works Jefferson County (Ky.), 1970—. Vice pres. Capital Projects Corp., Louisville, 1972—; tech. adviser Riverport Authority, Louisville, 1971—; mem. Louisville and Jefferson County Planning Commn., 1971—. Served with AUS, 1956-58. Mem. Nat., Ky. socs. profl. engrs., Am., Ky. pub. works assns. Democrat. Baptist. Home: 2328 Saratoga Dr Louisville KY 40205 Office: 401 Fiscal Court Bldg Louisville KY 40202

GREGORY, THORNE, banker, state legislator; b. Halifax, N.C., Dec. 25, 1928; s. Fletcher Harrison and Boyd (Thorne) G.; grad. Fisburne Mil. Sch., 1946; A.B. in History, U. N.C., 1952; grad. U. N.C. Sch. Banking, 1960; m. Hester Lockett, Feb. 23, 1957; children—Hester Elizabeth, Boyd Wynn, Ann Harrison, Thorne Gregory. Vice pres., dir. Bank of Halifax (N.C.), 1960-68; sr. v.p., dir. Branch Banking & Trust Co., 1968-73, pres., 1973—; mem. N.C. Ho. of Reps., 1959—, chmn. com. on fed. and interstate cooperation, 1961—, also chmn. com. banks and banking, chmn. com. on finance. Mem. Nat. Hwy. Policy, N.C. Com. on Aviation, N.C. Adv. Budget Com., N.C. Bd. Higher Edn., Rex Hosp. Found. Bd. dirs. Roanoke River Valley Basin Assn.; mem. Atlantic States Marine Fisheries Commn., Nat. Highway Policy Com. Served as 1st lt. USAF, 1952-56. Mem. N.C. Bankers Assn. (mem. adv. bd. Group II), Wilson C. of C. (dir.), Order of Gimghoul, Zeta Psi. Democrat. Episcopalian. Clubs: Country of N.C. (Pinehurst); Carolina Country (Raleigh); Wilson

Country, Kiwanis. Home: 1200 Brookside Dr Wilson NC 27893 Office: Branch Banking & Trust Co Wilson NC 27893

GREGORY, WESLEY WRIGHT, JR., entomologist, educator; b. Camden, S.C., Sept. 9, 1942; s. Wesley Wright and Mildred Carolyn (Wilson) G.; B.S., Wofford Coll., 1964; M.S., Clemson U., 1966, Ph.D. (NIH fellow), 1969; NSF fellow, Duke, 1969; m. Anne Byron Rogers, July 31, 1965; children—Wesley Wright III, Juliana Byron. Asst. prof. entomology U. Ky., Lexington, 1969-72, asso. prof. entomology, leader extension entomology sect., 1972—. Mem. A.A.A.S., Entomol. Soc. Am. (chmn. com. on local arrangements N.Central br. 1972), Assn. Southeastern Biologists, Ky. Acad. Scis., YMCA Indian Guides, Sigma Xi, Phi Kappa Phi, Gamma Sigma Delta, Pi Kappa Alpha. Methodist. Club: Toastmasters International (sec. Lexington). Contbr. articles to profl. jours. Home: 1011 Celia Lane Lexington KY 40504

GREGORY, WILLIAM THADIOUS, JR., broadcasting engr.; b. Portsmouth, Va., Oct. 6, 1935; s. William Thadious and Ruth Virginia (Wommack) G.; diploma radio communications Devry Tech. Inst., 1956; m. Dorothy Ann Elder, Aug. 14, 1957; children—William, James, Kevin, David. Studio engr. WRNL AM-FM, Richmond, Va., 1956-57; studio and transmitter engr. WXEX-TV, Petersburg, Va., 1957-63; transmitter engr. WAVY-TV, Portsmouth, 1963-69; chief engr. WYAH-TV, Christian Broadcasting Network, Portsmouth, 1969-73, dir. engring., 1973—. Served with USCGR, 1953-55. Home: 3809 Westcott Rd Portsmouth VA 23703 Office: 1318 Spratley St Portsmouth VA 23704

GREIF, LAWRENCE, B., osteo. physician, surgeon; b. Bklyn., Jan. 15, 1922; s. Samuel and Rose (Scalettar) G.; B.S., Queens Coll., 1942; grad. A.S.T.P. adv. phase physics, Ore. State Coll., 1943; D.O., Phila. Coll. Osteopathy, 1950; m. Maxine Sims, Mar. 14, 1969; children by previous marriage—Douglas Eric, Rose Venus, James Samuel. Individual practice gen. med., surgery Bklyn., 1951-56, Fort Worth, 1956—; chief staff White Settlement Hosp., 1971—. Served with Signal Corps AUS, 1942-46. Mem. Am. Osteo. Assn., Am. Coll. Gen. Practitioners Osteo. Medicine and Surgery, N.Y. State Osteo. Soc., Tex. Assn. Osteo. Physicians and Surgeons, Internat. Platform Assn., Lambda Omicron Gamma. Clubs: Ridglea Country, Civitan (charter pres. 1961—). Inventor pneumotokodynonometer, an external device to measure and record intrauterine pressures. Home: 4016 Shadow Dr Fort Worth TX 76116 Office: 701 S Cherry Lane Fort Worth TX 76108

GREIFENSTEIN, FERDINAND ERNEST, med. educator; b. Newark, Jan. 9, 1915; s. Leopold Henry and Emma Louiss (Wasscibach) G.; B.S., Spring Hill Coll., 1937; M.S., St. Louis U., 1944; m. B. Margaret Lamphear, Dec. 28, 1963; children—Charles Bradford, Jane Louise. Intern, Flower-Fifth Av. Hosps., N.Y.C., 1944-45; resident Met. Hosp., N.Y.C., 1945-46, Hosp. U. Pa., 1948-51; practice medicine, specializing in anesthesiology, Detroit, 1952-63, Little Rock, 1964-73, San Antonio, Tex., 1973—; mem. staff Bexar County, VA hosps., San Antonio; faculty Wayne State U., Detroit, 1952-63, prof. anesthesiology, chmn. dept.; prof. anesthesiology U. Ark., Little Rock, 1964-73, U. Tex. Med. Sch., San Antonio, 1973—. Served to capt. AUS, 1946-48. Mem. Am. Soc. Anesthesiologists, Acad. Anesthesiology, Assn. U. Anesthesiologists, Sigma Xi. Rotarian. Contbr. articles to profl. jours. Home: 207 Wyndale Dr San Antonio TX 78209

GREINER, JAMES ARNOLD, mfg. co. exec.; b. Toledo, Jan. 24, 1923; s. Alfred Henry and Clara Belle (Kanous) G.; student Franklin Inst., 1943; B.C.E., U. Toledo, 1950; m. Gloria Alice Haney, Aug. 31, 1946; children—James Craig, John Elliott, Beverly Jo, Peggy Jean. Structural engr. MaComber, Inc., Canton, O., 1950-52; mem. staff Richards, Bauer & Moorhead, Toledo, 1952-60; with Marolf, Inc., Clearwater, Fla., 1960—, v.p., treas., 1965—, also dir. Mem. Toledo Zool. Soc., 1961-65, Civil Def., Toledo, 1957-60; mem. Fla. Sheriff's Assn., 1966—; mem. Morton Plant Hosp. Assn. Served with USAAF, 1943-46. Registered profl. engr., Ohio, Mich., Fla. Mem. U. Toledo Alumni Assn., Am. Soc. C.E., Nat. Soc. Profl. Engrs., Fla. Engring. Soc., Soc. Am. Mil. Engrs., Royal Soc. Health. Republican. Methodist (pres. trustees; chmn. bd. adminstrn.). Contbr. articles waste treatment jours. Patentee precast concrete bldg. components. Home: 1263 Flushing Dr Clearwater FL 33516 Office: Marolf Inc 15500 49th St N Clearwater FL 33520

GREMILLION, EFFIE GILLIS, clin. social worker; b. Excelsior, La., Nov. 9, 1906; d. Joseph Benjiman and Ada Helen (Phillips) Gillis; student La. Coll., 1949-50; B.A., Tex. U., 1950-53; M.S.W., Wordens Sch. Social Service, 1958; m. Wiley J. Gremillion, Feb. 4, 1928 (div. Mar. 1947); children—Barbara Margaret (Mrs. Linton Bowman, III), Dona Madrice (Mrs. William Weaver Harris), Effie Jeanne (Mrs. Michael Dennis O'Callaghan). Social worker Austin State Hosp., 1954-57; clin. social worker VA Hosp., Shreveport, La., 1958-65, mem. intensive psychiat. staff, 1965—, dir. psychodrama, 1968—. Treas., Austin-Travis County Assn. Mental Health, 1956-57. Bd. dirs. Cadd-Bossier chapt. La. Assn. Mental Health, 1958—. Mem. Nat. Assn. Social Workers, Acad. Certified Social Workers, Moreno Acad. World Center Psychodrama, Sociometry and Group Psychotherapy. Methodist. Home: 2829 Doles Pl Shreveport LA 71104 Office: VA Hosp 510 E Stoner St Shreveport LA 71101

GRENDER, GORDON CONRAD, educator; b. Wakefield, Mich., Jan. 1, 1930; s. Obed Lester and Vera Leona (Conrad) G.; student Denison U., 1947-48; B.S., Ind. U., 1951, A.M., 1952; postgrad. (Whitney fellow), Mass. Inst. Tech., 1956-57; Ph.D. (NSF fellow), Pa. State U., 1960; m. Marilyn Cook, Dec. 24, 1952; children—Anders Eric, Ian Alan. Geologist, Standard Oil Co., Cal., Bakersfield, 1952-56, 61-62; NATO fellow U. Oslo (Norway), 1960-61; research geologist Esso Prodn. Research Co., Tulsa, 1962-64, Houston, 1964-65; asst. prof. Allegheny Coll., Meadville, Pa., 1965-66; asst. prof. Va. Poly. Inst. and State U., Blacksburg, Va., 1966-68, asso. prof., 1968-74, prof., 1974—, head dept. geol. scis., 1971—. Cons. Esso Math. and Systems, Inc., also Esso Prodn. Research Co., 1966-70. Recipient Sporn Teaching award Va. Poly. Inst. and State U., 1970, Wine Teaching award Alumni Found., 1973. Fellow Geol. Soc. Am.; mem. Internat. Assn. Math. Geologists, Va. Acad. Sci., Sigma Xi. Home: 602 Rainbow Ridge Dr SE Blacksburg VA 24060

GRENE, ROBERT, indsl. engr., constrn. co. exec.; b. N.Y.C., Jan. 13, 1915; s. Henry and Rachel (Gordon) G.; student indsl. engring. Pratt Inst., 1938-40, George Washington U., 1940-41; m. Helen Josephs, Oct. 29, 1940; children—Jeffrey Alan, Leslie Gordon, Amy Lynn; m. 2d, Mimi Arnold, 1973. Owner Robert Grene & Co., broker large estates and comml. devels., Washington, 1948—; pres. Bankers Realty & Securities Corp., Washington, 1953; pres. Great Eastern Constrn. Corp., 1948—; builder, owner operator Gregory Estates, Inc., Seat Pleasant, Md., 1954-55; dir. constrn. bridges Bonwit Constrn. Co., N.Y.C., 1955-57; pres. Palmer Park Corp., Washington, 1955-57; builder, owner, operator Deauville Hotel Corp., Havana, Cuba, 1957-58; chmn. bd. Bank Tangier (Morocco), 1957-58; dir. constrn. Caribbean Constrn. Corp., Coral Gables, Fla., 1958-67; exec. dir. Atlanta Cabana Hotel, 1967-68; co-owner Circus Circus, Inc., Las Vegas, Nev., 1968-72; co-owner, developer Travelodge at Amigoland, Brownsville, Tex., 1973—, The Cloisters, Inc., Brownsville, 1973—. Col., aide-de-camp Gov. N.M., 1972. Mem. Am. Mil. Engrs., Am. Inst. Mgmt., U.S. Lawn Tennis Assn., Tex. Tennis Assn., Brownsville Internat. Tennis Assn. (pres.). Democrat. Address: PO Box 1869 Brownsville TX 78520

GRENINGER, EDWIN THOMAS, educator; b. Montoursville, Pa., Apr. 12, 1918; s. Fred R. and Martha (Cutler) G.; student Susquehanna U., 1936-38; A.B., Gettysburg Coll., 1941; M.A., Temple U., 1947; Ph.D., U. Pa., 1958; m. Jane Torbert, June 26, 1948 (dec. Mar. 1963); m. 2d, Gem Kate Taylor, Oct. 26, 1968. Instr. history Valparaiso U., 1948-49, Pa. State U., Ogontz, 1950, 52-53, Wilkes Coll., 1951-52; asst. prof. history E. Tenn. State U., Johnson City, 1958-61, asso. prof. 1961-64, prof. history, 1964—. Mem. com. on higher edn. Synod Va., United Luth. Ch. Am., 1959-63, Southeastern Synod, 1963—. Served with AUS, 1942-46. Mem. So. Hist. Assn. (European sect.), Lexington Group, Am. Assn. U. Profs. (chpt. v.p. 1969-70, pres. 1970-72), Pi Kappa Alpha, Pi Gamma Mu (treas. local chpt. 1961—). Author: Fifteen Days in Russia, 1966. Book rev. editor: Social Science, 1961-62. Home: 2210 Wyndale Rd Johnson City TN 37601

GRESHAM, EARL THOMAS, contractor; b. Galveston, Ind., Nov. 12, 1892; s. William Watkins and Claudia Beatrice (Thomas) G.; student Richmond Acad., 1908-09; m. Katheryn Wells, July 5, 1916 (dec. Dec. 1942); children—Earl Thomas, Wells; m. 2d, Ada Dozier Garrett, Dec. 21, 1946 (dec. July 1964); m. 3d, Elizabeth Graves Plack, May 30, 1969. With Wyatt Coal Co., 1913-16; founder E.T. Gresham Co., Inc., Norfolk, Va., 1916, now chmn. bd.; chmn. Norfolk bd. Va. Nat. Bank, 1963—; dir. Intercoastal Steel Co., Portsmouth Gas Co., Va. Mut. Ins. Co. Bd. dirs., past pres. Norfolk Gen. Hosp.; trustee Tidewater (Va.) Devel. Council; bd. dirs. Eastern Va. Med. Sch., Norfolk Found., Old Dominion U., Kings Daus. Children's Hosp., Florence Crittenten Home, Boys' Club Am. Served with Va. N.G., 1913-16. Recipient Hon. award Cosmopolitan Club, 1951; Silver Keystone award Boys' Club Am., 1962; E award World War II, Navy Acona, 1957; named Norfolk's First Citizen, 1951. Mem. Norfolk Engrs. Club (dir., past pres.), Va. Hwy. Users Assn. (dir., past pres.), Hampton Roads Engring. Soc. (dir., past pres.), Norfolk C. of C. (dir.). Republican. Baptist. Mason. Clubs: Harbor, Cedar Point, Norfolk Yacht and Country. Home: 6063 River Crescent Norfolk VA 23505 Office: 1038 W 26th St Norfolk VA 23517

GRESHAM, SPARKMAN BOOTHE, banker; b. Ashland, Miss., May 10, 1932; s. Marvin and Elizabeth (Johnson) G.; grad. Sch. Banking of South, La. State U., 1964; m. Frances McGill, May 11, 1954; children—Greg, Steve, Anita. With Bank of Holly Springs (Miss.), 1955—, cashier, 1964—, v.p., 1966-73, pres., 1973—, also dir. Served with USAF, 1951-55. Recipient Marshall County Distinguished Service award, 1961. Mem. Holly Springs Jaycees. Baptist. Rotarian (pres. Holly Springs). Home: 710 College St Holly Springs MS 39635 Office: PO Box 250 Holly Springs MS 38635

GRESKY, ALAN TOLSTOY, chemist; b. Piper, Ala., Sept. 29, 1917; s. John Leon and Luda Catherine (Harper) G.; student Ala. Coll., 1936; A.B., U. Ala., 1939; postgrad. Ala. Med. Sch., U. Tenn.; m. Charlotte Ruth Almgren, Nov. 26, 1938; children—Frederic Paul, Ruth Alane (Mrs. Donald Ray Privett), Mary Lou. With Tenn. Coal & Iron Co., ore div. U.S. Steel Co., Birmingham, Ala., 1939-42; with DuPont Chem. Co., Ordnance Works, Childersburg, Ala., 1942-45; chemist Carbide & Carbon Chem. Co., Oak Ridge, Tenn., 1945-46; with Monsanto Chem. Co., Clinton Labs., Oak Ridge, Tenn., 1946-48; with chem. tech. div. Oak Ridge (Tenn.) Nat. Lab., 1948—, tech. asst. to the dir. in long range planning, 1953—. Lectr. nuclear fuel cycle Oak Ridge (Tenn.) Sch. of Reactor Tech., 1958-65. Mem. Am. Chem. Soc., Am. Soc. for Testing and Materials. Author: New Laws of Nature, 1964; (with others) Process Chemistry, 1970. Contbr. articles in field to encys. and profl. jours. Home: 113 Kingsley Rd Oak Ridge TN 37830

GRESSETTE, LAWRENCE MARION, lawyer, state senator; b. nr. St. Matthews, S.C., Feb. 11, 1902; s. J. T. and Rosa (Wannamaker) G.; J.D., U. S.C., 1924; m. Florence Howell, Aug. 18, 1927; 1 son, Lawrence Marion. Practiced in St. Mathews; partner firm Gressette & Gressette; mem. S.C. Senate, 1937—, chmn. jud. com., 1953—, chmn. rules com., 1959—, pres. pro tem, 1972—, chmn. hwys. com., 1972—. Chmn., S.C. Sch. Com., 1951-64. Mem. S.C. Democratic Exec. Com., 1948—, chmn., 1953-54; mem. S.C. Ho. of Reps., 1925-28, 31-32. Fellow Am. Coll. Trial Lawyers; mem. Blue Key, Phi Kappa Phi. Baptist. Mason. Home: PO Box 346 St Matthews SC 29135 Office: State House Columbia SC 29201

GRIBBLE, CHARLES WILLIAM, graphic arts co. exec.; b. Houston, Aug. 16, 1944; s. Charles William and Clara Frances Louise (Cook) G.; B.A., Stephen F. Austin State Coll., 1966, M.A., 1968. With Gribble Stamp & Stencil Co., Houston, 1968—, v.p., 1970-71, pres., 1971—. Mem. Houston Jr. C. of C., 1968-70. Presbyn. (deacon). Rotarian. Office: 121 St Emanuel St Houston TX 77002 also PO Box 4068 Houston TX 77014

GRICE, BENNING MOORE, chief justice Supreme Ct., Ga.; b. Hawkinsville, Ga., Sept. 16, 1909; s. Justice Warren and Clara (Rumph) G.; A.B., Mercer U., 1931, LL.B., 1932; m. Mary Calhoun, Oct. 18, 1941; children—Benning Moore, Ann Victoria, Warren C. Admitted to Ga. bar, 1932, pvt. practice, Macon, 1933-60; asso. justice Supreme Ct. of Ga., 1961—, presiding judge, 1972-74, chief justice, 1974—. Mem. Ga. Bd. Bar Examiners, 1957-60. Trustee YMCA, 1948-67, Ga. Indsl. Home., 1937-42, 47-49; pres. Central Ga. council Boy Scouts Am., 1955-58. Mem. Ga. Ho. of Reps., 1939-42. Served from lt. (j.g.) to lt. comdr., USNR, 1942-45. Named Macon's Outstanding Young Man by civic clubs, 1940. Mem. Am., Ga., Macon Circuit (pres. 1953-54), Atlanta, Macon bar assns., Mercer U. Alumni Assn. (pres. law chpt. 1950-51). Baptist (deacon). Mason, Kiwanian (pres. 1951). Clubs: Idle Hour Golf and Country (Macon); Capital City (Atlanta). Home: 3065 High Point Dr Macon GA 31204 Office: State Judicial Bldg State Capitol Atlanta GA 30334

GRIDER, KELLY VERNON, aerospace engr.; b. Scottsboro, Ala., May 28, 1933; s. Kelly Thomas and Mildred Anna (Morris) G.; B.S. in Elec. Engring., U. Ala., 1958, M.S. in Engring., 1965, Ph.D. in Elec. Engring., m. Lula Frances Smith, Mar. 17, 1952; children—Donna Denee, Lisa Susanne, Kelly Vernon. Aerophysics engr. Gen. Dynamics Convair, Ft. Worth, 1958-59; systems engr. Martin Marietta Corp., Orlando, Fla., 1959-61, sr. engr., 1961-62; aerospace engr. Engring. and Missile Systems Lab., Army Missile Command, Directorate of Research, Redstone Arsenal, Ala., 1962-65, research aerospace engr., 1965-69, supervisory aerospace engr., 1969—, chief guidance and control systems analysis, 1967—; instr. elec. engring. U. Ala. at Huntsville, 1968—. Served to staff sgt. USAF, 1951-54. Mem. I.E.E.E., Control Systems Soc., Assn. U.S. Army. Profl. Group Automatic Control (chmn. Huntsville chpt. 1968-69), Tau Beta Pi, Pi Mu Epsilon, Eta Kappa Nu, Phi Eta Sigma, Theta Tau. Baptist. Mason. Contbr. numerous articles tech. jours. Home: 2100 Gladstone Dr Huntsville AL 35811 Office: Army Missile Command Redstone Arsenal AL 35809

GRIEBEL, GAIL ALAN, mech. engr.; b. Clinton, Ia., Aug. 24, 1936; s. George Davis and Nona Margaret (Kenneberg) G.; B.S. in M.E., Ia. State U., 1958; M.S. in System Mgmt., Fla. Inst. Tech., 1974; m. Norma Lee Morrison, June 15, 1958; children—Geoffrey Alan, Glenda Lee. Jr. design engr. Air Preheater Corp., Wellsville, N.Y., 1958-59; project engr. Armstrong Rubber Co., Des Moines, 1961-65; launch complex engr. Pan Am. Airways, Patrick AFB, Fla., 1965-67; lead engr. Boeing Co., aerospace div., Kennedy Space Center, Fla., 1967—. Served to 1st lt. AUS, 1959-61. Recipient Pub. Service Group Achievement award NASA, 1972. Registered profl. engr., Fla., Ia. Mem. Am. Soc. M.E. Lutheran (elder 1973-75). Patentee in field. Home: 220 June Dr Cocoa Beach FL 32931 Office: Boeing Co Kennedy Space Center FL 32815

GRIER, EDNA CATHERINE GOSSETT, social worker; b. nr. Spartanburg, S.C., Jan. 9, 1897; d. James Hadden and Lillie (Thompson) Gossett; student Draughons Bus. Coll., 1918; student U. S.C., 1942-44, Converse Coll., summers 1966-68; m. James Edward Grier Sr., Oct. 16, 1919 (dec. Dec. 1959); children—James Edward, Galen Marion (Mrs. Wilmot Heinitsh Mitchell, Jr.). Tchr. pub. schs. Georgetown County, S.C., 1916-18; office mgr. Hwy. Dept., Aiken, S.C., 1927-29; dist. supr. WPA projects Union, Cherokee and Spartanburg Counties, S.C., 1938-40; chief counselor Spartanburg Family Ct., 1942-69, vol., 1969—. Chmn. exchange com. Council for Spartanburg County, 1955-57; sec.-treas. Mental Health Clinic Bd., Spartanburg, 1946—; sec. Spartanburg Safety Council, 1964-68, State Bd. Juvenile Corrections, 1946-66; mem. Area Manpower Planning Bd., 1972; mem. fact finding com. S.C. Status of Women Conf., 1968—; mem. adv. com. Pub. Health Nursing, Spartanburg, 1968—. Bd. dirs. S.C. Children's Bureau. Named Career Woman of Year, 1967; recipient certificate appreciation City of Spartanburg, 1969; named Radio Woman of Month, June, 1972. Mem. Spartanburg Social Service Assn. (pres. 1959-60), Spartanburg C. of C. (dir. 1948-50), S.C. Bus. and Profl. Women's Clubs (pres. 1957-59), S.C. Welfare Forum, Nat. Assn. Juvenile Agys., Am. Assn. Ret. Persons (v.p. Spartanburg chpt.), Spartanburg Women's Club (sec. 1960, 65). Methodist. Club: Zonta Internat. Address: 103 Windsor Av Spartanburg SC 29301

GRIER, PAUL LIVINGSTON, librarian; b. Clover, S.C., May 26, 1914; s. William Pressly and Nellie Brownlee (Bigham) G.; A.B., Erskine Coll., 1936; A.B. in L.S., U. N.C., 1938; A.M., U. Mich., 1947; m. Eleanor Jane Meacham, Aug. 16, 1947. Library asst., Washington Pub. Library, 1936-40; librarian Hampden-Sydney (Va.) Coll., 1940-42, 46—. Mem. evaluating coms. So. Assn. Schs. and Colls. Served from ensign to lt., USNR, 1942-46. Mem. A.L.A., Southeastern, Va. library assns., Assn. for Preservation Va. Antiquities, Assn. Am. Museums, English-Speaking Union, Sigma Upsilon, Omicron Delta Kappa. Presbyn. (elder). Home: Hampden-Sydney VA 23943

GRIERSON, IRAN JAN, architect; b. Odessa, Tex., Feb. 14, 1940; s. Ray Harold and Myrtle (Seal) G.; B.Arch., Tex. U., 1965; m. Diantha Davis, Sept. 4, 1965; children—Greg, Eric. Architect, Pratt, Box & Henderson, 1965, Tom Stanley, 1966, Lundgren & Maurer, 1967-69; individual practice, Austin, Tex., 1969—. Mem. A.I.A., Nat. Assn. Home Builders. Author: The City Crisis, 1967. Home: 3605 Summit Bend Austin TX 78759 Office: 5840 Balcones St Austin TX 78731

GRIFFEN, WARD ORIN, JR., educator; b. New Orleans, July 21, 1928; s. Ward Orin and Dorothea (Rosenberg) G.; A.B., Princeton, 1949; M.D., Cornell U., 1953; Ph.D., U. Minn., 1963; m. Margaret Mary Taylor, Dec. 27, 1952; children—Peter, Mary Ellen, Steven, Colleen, Timothy, Margaret, Leah. Intern, Bellevue Hosp., N.Y.C., 1953-54; resident, U. Minn. Hosp., Mpls., 1957-62; instr. surgery U. Minn., 1961-63, asst. prof., 1963-65; practice medicine, specializing in gen. and thoracic surgery, Lexington, Ky., 1965—; asso. prof. surgery, asso. prof. physiology and biophysics U. Ky., 1965-67, prof., chmn. dept. surgery, prof. physiology and biophysics, 1967—; surgeon, chief U. Ky. Med. Center; mem. med. edn. staff St. Joseph's, Good Samaritan, Gen. Bapt. hosps., Lexington; cons. Lexing and Huntington VA Hosp., 1965—. Served with USNR, 1955-57. USPHS fellow, 1960-62; Markle scholar, 1962-67. Mem. Am. Gastroenterol. Assn., Assn. Acad. Surgery Assos. (pres. 1970), Soc. Univ. Surgeons, Am., So., Central surg. assns. Contbr. articles to profl. jours. Editor: Archives Surgery, Jour. Surg. Research, 1972—. Home: 3405 Nantucket St Lexington KY 40502 Office: 800 Rose St Lexington KY 40506

GRIFFENHAGEN, GEORGE BERNARD, pharm. assn. exec.; b. Portland, Ore., June 9, 1924; s. Richard Bernard and Clara (Schoenian) G.; B.S., U. So. Cal., 1949, M.S., 1950; m. Joan Helen Houston, June 26, 1946; children—Gary Bernard, Gordon Wesley, Barbara Clare. Dir. research Nion Corp., Hollywood, Cal., 1950-52; curator Smithsonian Instn., Washington, 1952-59; asso. exec. dir. communications Am. Pharm. Assn., Washington, 1959—. Lectr. U. So. Cal. Sch. Pharmacy, 1950-52; sec.-gen. 4th Pan Am. Congress Pharmacy and Biochemistry, Washington, 1957; sec. organizing com. 31st Internat. Congress Pharm. Scis., Washington, 1971; pres. Am. Inst. History Pharmacy, 1960-61, mem. council, 1961—; pres. Friends Hist. Pharmacy, 1957-58; founding pres. Nat. Coordinating Council Drug Edn., 1968-69, trustee, 1969-72; mem. Nat. Action Com. Drug Edn., Office Edn., 1970-71; mem. Va. Gov.'s Council Narcotic and Drug Abuse Control, 1970-72. Mem. Fairfax County (Va.) Republican Com., 1960—; conv. coordinator Va. State Rep. Com., 1969-72. Served with AUS, World War II. Recipient award Pan Am. Pharm. and Biochem. Fedn., 1963, Pfizer Merit award U.S. Civil Def. Council, 1964, Meritorious Service citation Am. Nat. Red Cross, 1964, Edward Kremers award Am. Inst. History Pharmacy, 1969, Jere Hess Barr award Am. Philatelic Congress, 1969, Outstanding Alumnus award U. So. Cal. Sch. Pharmacy, 1969, award Nat. Coordinating Council Drug Edn., 1970, Distinguished Topical Philatelist award Am. Topical Assn., 1970, Distinguished Service award Pharm. Wholesalers Assn., 1971; Cestoni medal Italian Acad. History Pharmacy, 1973. Mem. Am. Pharm. Assn. (pres. Washington chpt. 1958-59), Am. Topical Assn. (1st v.p. 1972-75, pres. med. subjects unit 1969-72), Pan Am. Fedn. Pharmacy and Biochemistry (1st v.p. 1963-72), World Union Pharmacy Hist. Socs. (v.p. 1970—), Internat. Acad. History Pharmacy (treas. 1970—), Am. Philatelic Soc., Soc. Philatelic Ams., Am. Revenue Assn., Philatelic Lit. Assn., Sigma Xi, Rho Chi, Phi Kappa Phi, Kappa Psi. Editor, Scalpel and Tongs, 1972-73, Jour. Am. Pharm. Assn., 1959—. Home: 2501 Drexel St Vienna VA 22180 Office: 2215 Constitution Av NW Washington DC 20037

GRIFFEY, EARLE BARTLETT, physician, mayor; b. Houston, Oct. 1, 1927; s. Edward W. and May (Bartlett) G.; student Rice U., 1944-45; Ph.B., U. Chgo., 1951, B.S., 1951; M.D., U. Tex., 1956; postgrad. U. Mich., 1956-58; m. Rogene Larsen, Dec. 31, 1962; children—William Earle, Lynn, Anne, Edward Sykes. Intern U. Mich. Hosps., 1956-57, resident 1957-58; gen. practice medicine, Brownsville, Tex., 1958—; mem. staff, exec. com. Mercy Hosp.; city health officer, Brownsville, 1959—; mayor city of Brownsville, 1971—. Dir. Pan Am. Bank. Pres. Am. Cancer Soc., Brownsville, 1965-67, dist. dir., 1967-69. City commr., Brownsville, 1967-69. Bd. dirs. Crippled Childrens Clinic. Served with M.C., USNR, 1945-46.

Mem. Cameron County Med. Soc. (v.p. 1968-69), Delta Upsilon, Zeta Phi Chi, Mu Delta. Home: 1144 Belthair St Brownsville TX 78520 Office: 825 Lakeside St Brownsville TX 78520

GRIFFIES, ELMER GERALD, materials research engr.; b. Huffman, Ala., Feb. 24, 1935; s. Elmer Murphy and Mary Winifred (Bailey) G.; B.S. in Mech. Engring., Auburn U., 1957, M.S. in Mech. Engring., 1959; postgrad. U. Tex., 1959-61; m. Anna Louise Carver, June 18, 1955; children—Jerry Murphy, Barbara Ann. Jr. engr. pressure vessel design Chgo. Bridge & Iron Co., Birmingham, Ala., 1956; instr. mech. engring. Auburn (Ala.) U., 1957-59; engr. Sturm and O'Brien, Inc., cons., Auburn, 1957-59; research engr., instr. mech. engring. U. Tex. at Austin, 1959-61; sr. project engr. space craft design, analysis and testing Brown Engring. Co., 1961-67, sr. research engr. anti ballistic missile studies Stanford Research Inst., 1967-71, engr.-scientist tactical weapons systems Northrop Corp., 1971-72 (all Huntsville, Ala.); research engr. non-metal materials So. Research Inst., Birmingham, Ala., 1972—; asst. prof. engring. mechanics U. Ala. at Huntsville, 1962—. Owner Jerry's Flowers and Gifts, Birmingham, 1973—. Mem. indian guide program Southeast Huntsville YMCA, 1966-67, chief, 1967, coach football program, 1968, 69, 70; coach Little League Baseball, 1967, 68, 69; scoutmaster Boy Scouts Am., 1969—; mem. Jones Valley Elementary Sch. P.T.A., 1967—, chmn. legislative com., 1969-70. Registered profl. engr., Ala. Mem. Am. Soc. M.E. (faculty adviser Auburn U. 1958-59; PVRC terminal strength subcom. 1966—), Phi Kappa Phi, Pi Mu Epsilon, Pi Tau Sigma, Tau Beta Pi. Baptist (tchr. Sunday sch. adult men's class). Home: 1130 Mountain Oaks Dr Birmingham AL 35226 Office: So Research Inst 2000 9th Av S Birmingham AL 35205

GRIFFIES, HIRAM FARRELL, retail exec.; b. Flint, Mich., Oct. 28, 1932; s. Hiram Franklin and Mary Ruth (McClanahan) G.; B.A., Gen. Motors Inst., 1955; M.B.A., U. Detroit, 1958; m. Barbara Lucille Edwards, Aug. 22, 1959; children—Todd Edward, Trayce Drake. Sr. cons. Fry, Inc., 1967-69; head indsl. services br. Ga. Inst. Tech., 1963-67; exec. v.p. Munford, Inc., Atlanta, 1968—. Precinct chmn. Republican Com., 1969-74. Bd. dirs. Jr. Achievement Greater Atlanta, Mem. Atlanta C. of C. (mem. edn. task force 1966-74). Methodist. Club: Chattahouchie Plantation (Atlanta). Home: 4649 Canyon Creek Trail Atlanta GA 30342 Office: 68 Brookwood Dr Atlanta GA 30309

GRIFFIN, CHARLES HENRY, educator, accountant; b. Blooming Grove, Tex., July 3, 1922; s. Lindsay Ira and Fay Dorothy (Pruitt) G.; B.B.A., U. Tex., 1942, M.B.A., 1948, Ph.D., 1953. Staff accountant Peat, Marwick, Mitchell & Co., C.P.A.'s, Dallas office, 1949-50; instr.-lectr. U. Tex., 1950-53; asst. prof. accounting U. Cin., 1953-54, asso. prof., 1954-57; asso. prof. accounting U. Ill., 1957-60, prof., 1960-62, vis. Arthur Young Distinguished prof., 1972-73; prof. accounting U. Tex., Austin, 1962—; vis. prof. U. Birmingham (Eng.), spring 1972. Served as lt. (j.g.) USNR, 1942-46. C.P.A., Tex., Ill. Mem. Am. Accounting Assn., Am. Inst. C.P.A.'s, Nat. Assn. Accountants, Tex., Ill. socs. C.P.A.'s, Beta Alpha Psi, Beta Gamma Sigma, Phi Kappa Phi, Delta Sigma Pi, Phi Kappa Psi. Author: (with T.H. Williams) The Mathematical Dimension of Accounting, 1964; (with Williams, K.D. Larson) Advanced Accounting, rev. edit., 1971; (with Williams) Management Information: A Quantitative Accent, 1967. Editor: Accounting Rev., 1967-70, book rev. editor, 1966-67. Home: 1801 Lavaca Austin TX 78701

GRIFFIN, DANA GOVE III, educator; b. Fort Worth, Nov. 9, 1938; s. Dana Gove and Jessie Caldwell (Carter) G.; B.S., Tex. Tech. Coll., 1961, M.S., 1962; Ph.D., U. Tenn., 1965; m. Nancy Claire Wilson, Dec. 20, 1964; 1 son, Dana Gove IV. Asst. prof. U. Tenn., 1966-67; asst. prof. U. Fla., Gainesville, 1967-72, asso. prof. botany, 1972—. Fulbright lectr. biol. scis. Peru, 1965-66. Mem. Internat. Assn. Plant Taxonomy, Bot. Soc. Am. (sec.-treas. Southeastern sect. 1970-73), Sociedad Botanica de Mexico, Am. Bryological and Lichenological Soc., Am. Soc. Plant Taxonomists, Assn. Tropical Biology, Torrey Bot. Club, Fla. Acad. Scis. Home: 3425 NW 7th Pl Gainesville FL 32607

GRIFFIN, EDWARD LEE, electronics engr.; b. Salisbury, Md., May 24, 1934; s. Fulton Everett and Flora Belle (Hoffman) G.; B.S., N.D. State U., 1965, M.S., 1966; m. Donna Lou Anderson, July 25, 1958; children—Kristine Louise, Karen Lou, Steven Fulton. Commd. 2d lt. U.S. Air Force Res., 1955, advanced through grades to maj., 1969; ret., 1974; system engr. Collins Radio Co., Cedar Rapids, Ia., 1966-69; staff engr. Martin Marietta Co., Orlando, Fla., 1969—. Pres., Winter Park Pines Community Assn., 1971-72, Winter Park Swim Club, 1972-73. Registered profl. engr., Fla. Mem. Nat. Soc. Profl. Engrs., Fla. Engring. Soc., I.E.E.E., Phi Kappa Phi, Tau Beta Pi, Eta Kappa Nu, Lambda Chi Alpha. Republican. Methodist. Home: 2914 Banchory Rd Winter Park FL 32789 Office: PO Box 5837 Orlando FL 32803

GRIFFIN, EDWARD LEGRANT, clergyman, town ofcl.; b. Stockton, Ala., Oct. 1, 1905; s. George and Millie (Kennedy) G.; A.A., Mt. Beulah Coll., 1930; B.S., Alcorn Coll., 1951; M.A., Tuskegee Inst., 1965; m. Luberta B. Jones, June 19, 1934; 1 son, Edward E. Ordained to ministry Christian Ch., 1933, pastor 6th St. Christian Ch., Pensacola, Fla., 1931-36, Shaw (Miss.) Christian Ch., 1937-70; tchr. pub. schs., Alligator, Miss., 1936-40, Duncan, Miss., 1940-43, Shelby, Miss., 1944-70. Mem. bd. Gen. Assembly Christian Ch., 1968-73; pres. Shelby Fed. Credit Union, 1955-74. Alderman, Town of Shelby, 1969—. Mason. Home: Box 281 Shelby MS 38774

GRIFFIN, FLORENCE ANNA TRIDLE (MRS. VICTOR ROBERT GRIFFIN), ret. ednl. adminstr.; b. Indpls., Nov. 8, 1906; d. Chrles B. and Minnie P. (Newby) Tridle; student Tchrs. Coll., Indpls., 1925-26, Ball State Tchrs. Coll., 1928; B.S., Butler U., 1935; M.S., No. Ill. U., 1955; m. Victor Robert Griffin, July 29, 1934; children—Charles Victor, Floronne Leah (Mrs. D. Ray Kerchal). Tchr., Manatee, Fla., 1926-27, Marion County, Ind., 1927-40, Monroe Center, Ill., 1946-51, DeKalb, Ill., 1951-58, Joliet, Ill., 1958-62; dir. student teaching Pestalozzi Froebel Tchrs. Coll., Chgo., 1962-70, Nat. Coll. Edn. Urban Campus, Chgo., 1970-73; ret., 1973. Program chmn. P.T.A., Joliet, 1959-61. Mem. Am. Assn. U. Women (pres. Batavia-Geneva-St. Charles br. 1968-70), N.E.A., Assn. for Student Teaching, Internat. Reading Assn., Assn. for Childhood Internat., Ill. Edn. Assn., Ill. Assn. for Student Teaching (state membership com.), Ill. Assn. for Supervision and Curriculum Devel., West Suburban Assn. for Other Child, Panhellenic, Delta Zeta. Conglist. Mem. Order Eastern Star (past matron, grand lectr.). Home: 1605 Country Club Pkwy Lehigh Acres FL 33936

GRIFFIN, FLOYD SILAS, JR., electronics engr.; b. Bainbridge, Ga., May 28, 1930; s. Floyd Silas and Ethel (Drinkwater) G.; B.S. in Elec. Engring., Ga. Inst. Tech., 1956; m. Laharon Ezell, Sept. 13, 1953; children—Brian Keith, Barbara Wren. Project Engr. Radiation Inc., Melbourne, Fla., 1956-61; lab. dir. Aero Geo Astro, Ft. Walton Beach, Fla., 1961-66 ; pres. Ordnance Research, Inc., Ft. Walton Beach, 1966-71, sec.-treas., 1971—; dir., 1966—; owner United Rent-Alls, Ft. Walton Beach, 1964-69. Served with USN, 1948-52. Mem. Am. Ordnance Assn., I.E.E.E. Baptist (deacon, pres. Mens Brotherhood). Lion. Home: 5 Carlyle Court Ft Walton Beach FL 32548 Office: PO Box 1426 Ft Walton Beach FL 32548

GRIFFIN, GARY WALTER, educator; b. Pasadena, Cal., Nov. 12, 1931; s. Gail W. and Mary Rita (Kiggins) G.; B.A. in Organic Chemistry, Pomona Coll., 1953; Ph.D. in Organic Chemistry, U. Ill. at Urbana, 1956; m. Carol Lee Zuerlein, June 10, 1961; children—Michael Jon, Mark Reed, Cheryl Lee, Sean Robert. Research chemist Humble Oil and Refining Co., Baytown, Tex., 1956-58; instr. Yale, 1958-59; asst. prof., 1959-63; asso. prof. chemistry Tulane U., 1963-66; asso. prof. La. State U., New Orleans, 1966-67, prof., 1967—; vis. prof. U. Ill. at Urbana, summer 1965, Inst. Lipid Research Baylor Coll. Medicine Tex. Med. Center, Houston, 1971-72; cons. So. New Eng. Ultraviolet Co., Middletown Conn., 1962—, 3M Co., St. Paul, 1963—; chmn. Photochem. Symposium Columbia U., 1964; participant numerous others seminars and congresses; lectr. in field. Bd. dirs. Huntington Park Protection Assn., New Orleans, 1970-73. Recipient numerous govtl. and pvt. grants, awards. Fellow Research Inst. Chemists; mem. Am. Chem. Soc., Chem. Soc. (London), Am. Assn. U. Profs., Internat. Assn. Heterocyclic Chemists, Am. Soc. Mass Spectrometry, A.A.A.S., Yale Chemists Assn., Phi Beta Kappa, Sigma Xi, Phi Lambda Upsilon. Contbg. author: Carbenes, 1973; Organic Photochemistry, 1973; Photochemistry of Heterocyclic Compounds, 1974. Contbr. numerous articles to profl. jours. Patentee in field. Home: 7156 Parkside Ct New Orleans LA 70122

GRIFFIN, GEORGE THOMAS, govt. ofcl.; b. Waco, Tex., Mar. 20, 1921; s. George and Elsie A. (Lemon) G.; B.B.A., So. Meth. U., 1949; m. Nell Evelyn King, Apr. 12, 1941; children—Linda Evelyn (Mrs. Frank D. Bollman), Steven Wayne, Vicki Crews. Internal revenue agt. U.S. Govt., 1949-52; sec.-treas. Crest Drilling, Inc., 1952-60; self-employed as C.P.A., Tyler, Tex., 1960-67; financial analyst Small Bus. Adminstrn., 1967-72; adviser financial mgmt. Dept. Health, Edn. and Welfare, Dallas, 1973—. Tchr. eve. sch. Tyler Jr. Coll., 1950-65. Served with AUS, 1940-45. Decorated Bronze Star medal, Purple Heart. C.P.A., Tex. Methodist (treas. 1960-66). Home: 1419 Wolfe City Dr Greenville TX 75401 Office: 1114 Commerce St Dallas TX 75219

GRIFFIN, HERMAN STATHAM, supt. schs.; b. Deport, Tex., June 27, 1905; s. William Statham and Mary Margaret (Grant) G.; B.A., Austin Coll., 1930, M.A., 1939; postgrad. East Tex. State U., 1943-44, North Tex. State U., 1947-48, So. Meth. U., 1947, U. Colo., 1939-40, U. Tex., 1952-53; m. Mary Evelyn Etchison, Aug. 29, 1931; children—Robert Statham, Mary Elizabeth. Tchr., coach Childress (Tex.) High Sch., 1930-33; prin., coach Sonora (Tex.) High Sch., 1933-34; tchr., bus. mgr. Sherman (Tex.) High Sch., 1934-39; tchr. W.H. Adamson High Sch., Dallas, 1939-48; prin. Dallas Schs., 1948-68; asso. supt. Dallas Ind. Sch. Dist., 1968—. Mem. Tex. State Bd. Pub. Accountancy. Recipient Meritorious Service award Austin Coll., 1972. Mem. Dallas Sch. Adminstrs. Assn. (pres. 1962-63), Austin Coll. Alumni Assn. (pres. 1973—). Methodist. Mason, Lion. Home: 610 W Greenbriar St Dallas TX 75208 Office: 3700 Ross Av Dallas TX 75204

GRIFFIN, JOHN ROBERT, chem. engr.; b. DuQuoin, Ill., Apr. 21, 1936; s. Marion Lyle and Agda Victoria (Moline) G.; B.S., U. Ill., 1959; Ph.D., Purdue U., 1963; m. Becky Bush, Jan. 20, 1968; children—Paul Beauman, Julia Victoria, Ann Elizabeth, John Forrest. Inst., Purdue U., Lafayette, Ind., 1962; research chem. engr. Humble Oil & Refining Co., Baytown, Tex., 1963-65; sr. research chem. engr. Esso Research & Engring. Co., Baytown, Tex., 1965-66, research specialist, 1966-67, research asso., 1967—. Recipient A.M. White award Am. Inst. Engrs., 1959, Best Instr. award Tau Beta Pi, Purdue U., 1962. NSF fellow, 1960-62; Am. Oil Found. fellow, 1962-63. Mem. Am. Inst. Chem. Engrs., Theta Chi. Republican. Lutheran. Patentee in field. Home: 225 Pin Oak Dr Baytown TX 77520 Office: PO Box 4255 Baytown TX 77520

GRIFFIN, JOHN WALLACE, museum dir.; b. Connersville, Ind., Nov. 8, 1919; s. Harry Milton and Lona Elizabeth (Zengel) G.; student U. Fla., 1937-39; M.A., U. Chgo., 1946, postgrad., 1966-67; m. Patricia Ann Conaway, Sept. 4, 1945; children—Douglas, Bruce, Lona, Elizabeth. Archaeologist Fla. Park Service, 1946-53; asst. prof. Fla. State U., 1953-54; exec. historian St. Augustine (Fla.) Hist. Soc., 1954-58; regional archaeologist Nat. Park Service, Richmond, Va., 1958-67; chief S.E. Archaeol. Center of Nat. Park Service, Macon, Ga., 1967-71; dir. Historic St. Augustine Preservation Bd., 1971—. Recipient Excellence of Service award U.S. Dept. Interior, 1966. Fellow A.A.A.S., Am. Anthrop. Assn.; mem. Soc. Am. Archaeology, Fla. Anthrop. Soc. (pres.), Fla. Hist. Soc. (dir.), Lambda Chi Alpha. Rotarian. Author: (with M.F. Boyd and H.G. Smith) Here They Once Stood, 1951; Investigations in Russell Cave, 1974. Editor: The Florida Indian and His Neighbors, 1949. Home: Route 5 Box 19 St Augustine FL 32084 Office: PO Box 1987 St Augustine FL 32084

GRIFFIN, LLOYD HUNTER, savings and loan exec.; b. Norfolk, Va., Aug. 26, 1934; s. Rossie Spurgeon and Alethia Virginia (Goodwin) G.; A.B., Trevecca Nazarene Coll., 1965; postgrad. U. Ga., 1966, Ind. U., 1971; m. Clarice Jeanette Spruill, Aug. 25, 1955; children—Sandra June, Kimberly Faye. Vice pres., asst. to pres. Fidelity Fed. Savings & Loan Assn., Nashville, 1957-73; pres. Adahm Corp., Nashville, 1973—; exec. v.p. Vol. Fed. Savings & Loan Assn., Nashville, 1973—, also dir. Chmn. adv. com. Nashville State Tech. Inst., 1970-72; mem. adv. com. Masters in Bus. Adminstrn. Program, U. Tenn., Nashville, 1971-72. Bd. mgrs., chmn. Downtown YMCA; trustee, mem. exec. com. United Givers Fund; trustee Trevecca Nazarene Coll., 1968-70. Served with AUS, 1953-55. Mem. Nat. Assn. Bus. Economists, Nashville Area C. of C. (chmn., mem. speakers bur. 1971-73). Democrat. Methodist. Home: 2046 Hickory Hill Lane Hermitage TN 37076 Office: PO Box 2565 Nashville TN 37219

GRIFFIN, MARY RUFFIN ROBERTSON (MRS. ORMOND BISHOP GRIFFIN), educator; b. Stoneville, N.C., Aug. 24, 1915; d. Samuel Ruffin and Daisy (Joyce) Robertson; R.N., Roanoke Rapids (N.C.) Hosp. Sch. Nursing, 1938; B.S. in Pub. Health Nursing, Peabody Coll. for Tchrs., 1947; M.P.H., U. N.C., 1965; postgrad. East Carolina U., 1962-63; m. Ormond Bishop Griffin, Dec. 28, 1947. Sch. nurse Roanoke Rapids (N.C.) high sch., 1938-41; field health supr. U.S. Govt. Nat. Youth Adminstrn., Kinston, N.C., 1941; mem. infirmary nursing staff East Carolina U., Greenville, 1941-42; pub. health nurse Chatham County Health Dept., Pittsboro, N.C., 1942-46, Greensboro Health Dept., 1947, Halifax County (N.C.) Health Dept., 1953-62; nurse Dr. K. Mathiesen, Pittsboro, 1948; pvt. duty Mathiesen Clinic, Pittsboro, 1949-52; instr. pub. health nursing East Carolina U., 1962-65; asst. prof. East Tenn. State U., Johnson City, 1965-69, prof., 1969—. Tchr. home nursing A.R.C., 1942-44; chmn. nursing adv. com., bd. dirs. Tenn. Tb and Respiratory Disease Assn. Precinct chmn. Haw River Twp. Democratic Com., Moncure, N.C. Mem. Blountville Bus. and Profl. Women's Club, Am., Tenn. pub. health assns., Am., N.C. (dist. pres. 1964) nurses assns. Nat., Am. leagues for nursing, Tenn., East Tenn. edn. assns., Am. Assn. U. Profs. Baptist. Home: Rural Delivery 4 Blountville TN 37617 Office: East Tenn State U Johnson City TN

GRIFFIN, NEWTON BRAMBLETT, obstetrician, gynecologist; b. Nashville, June 7, 1932; s. George Allen and Della Evangeline (Bramblett) G.; B.A. magna cum laude, Vanderbilt U., 1954, M.D., 1957; m. Betty Caroline Stroud, Apr. 9, 1960. Intern surgery Vanderbilt U. Hosp., 1957-58, resident obstetrics and gynecology, 1960-63; practice medicine specializing in obstetrics and gynecology, Nashville, 1965-66, Raleigh, N.C., 1968—; asst. prof. obstetrics and gynecology Vanderbilt U., 1966-68; chief service obstetrics and gynecology Metropolitan Nashville Gen. Hosp., 1966-68; instr. obstetrics and gynecology Vanderbilt U., 1962-63. Served to capt. USAF, 1958-60. Recipient Physicians Recognition award A.M.A., 1969, 72; Advanced Clin. fellow in Gynecology Am. Cancer Soc., M.D. Anderson Hosp. and Tumor Inst., Houston, 1963-64. Diplomate Am. Bd. Obstetrics and Gynecology. Fellow Am. Coll. Obstetrics and Gynecology, Am. Fertility Soc.; mem. A.M.A., So. Med. Assn., N.C., Wake County med. socs., Raleigh Acad. Medicine, Phi Beta Kappa. Baptist. Lion. Home: 3910 Stratford Ct Raleigh NC 27609 Office: 3803 Computer Dr Raleigh NC 27609

GRIFFIN, ROBERT LEWIS, ednl. adminstr.; b. Washington, Ga., Feb. 1, 1926; s. Edward Moore and Linnie Ruth (Johnson) G.; A.B., Olivet Nazarene Coll., 1950, Th.B., 1951; M.A., Butler U., 1959; Ed.D., Okla. State U., 1965; m. Dorothy Maxine Hollingsworth, Oct. 29, 1944; children—Katherine Mary, Timothy Alan, Robert Paul. Ordained to ministry Ch. of Nazarene, 1952; pastor, Logansport, Highland and Crawfordsville, Ind., 1950-59, Cushing and Bartlesville, Okla., 1959-67; prof. philosophy and religion Wesleyan Coll., part-time, 1962-67; asst. prof. philosophy Kan. State Coll., 1963-65; prof., acad. dean, dir. grad. studies Bethany (Okla.) Nazarene Coll., 1967—. Dist. youth pres. Ch. of Nazarene, 1952-66. Served with USAAF, 1944-46. Mem. S.W. Philosophy Edn. Assn., Stillwater Acad. Deans Assn. Conf., Phi Delta Lambda. Kiwanian (chmn. internat. com. 1970-71). Home: 2801 Meridian Court Oklahoma City OK 73127 Office: Bethany Nazarene Coll Bethany OK 73008

GRIFFIN, SAMUEL MARVIN, JR., editor, ednl. adminstr.; b. Bainbridge, Ga., Feb. 12, 1936; s. Samuel Marvin Griffin; B.S. in Indsl. Mgmt., Ga. Inst. Tech., 1958; m. Mary Ann Hill; children—Samuel Marvin III, Virginia Ann. Editor, Bainbridge Post-Searchlight, 1963—. publisher, 1970—. Mem. Ga. Bd. Edn., 1970—, vice chmn., 1971—; past chmn. Decatur County Indsl. Devel. Authority. Served with USNR, 1958-63. Mem. Bainbridge C. of C. (past dir.), Bainbridge Jaycees (past dir.), Ga. Press Assn. (past pres.), Gridiron Secret Soc., Sigma Alpha Epsilon. Presbyn. (elder). Rotarian (past dir.). Office: 301 N Crawford St Bainbridge GA 31717

GRIFFIN, TENNENT LOMAX, real estate broker; b. Montgomery, Ala., Oct. 24, 1902; s. Virgil C. and Mary Lee (Besson) G.; B.S., U. Ala., 1923; m. Catherine Hobbie, Sept. 2, 1924; children—Anne Catherine (Mrs. Ralph Denny Wright), Tennent Lee (Mrs. William Henry Slack, III). Pres. Staples-Pake-Griffin, Inc., Mobile, Ala., 1973—; chmn. bd. adv. bd. dirs. First Nat. Bank of Mobile. Mem. Ala. Bd. Edn., 1st Congl. Dist., 1950-51; U.S. collector of customs, dist. 19, 1961-66; mem. Ala. Savs. and Loan Bd., 1968—. Chmn. Mobile County Bd. Tax Equalization, 1951-54; judge Probate Ct., Mobile County, 1954-56; del. Democratic Nat. Conv., 1956. Mem. Am. Inst. Real Estate Appraisers, Soc. Residential Appraisers (sr. mem.), Nat. Inst. Real Estate Brokers, Mortgage Bankers Assn., C. of C., Downtown Mobile Unltd. (pres. 1967-68), Phi Delta Theta. Presbyn. Clubs: Athelstan, Bienneville, Internat. Trade, Mobile Country (Mobile). Home: 273 Park Terrace Mobile AL 36604 Office: 100 N Royal St Box 333 Mobile AL 36601

GRIFFIN, WILBURN SCOTT, state ofcl.; b. Mantee, Miss., Oct. 15, 1913; s. Virgil Homer and Martha Elizabeth (Davis) G.; B.A., U. Miss., 1941, M.A., 1947; m. Sarah Myrtle Oswalt, Mar. 14, 1941; children—Susan, Georgia. Prin., athletic coach Woodland (Miss.) High Sch., 1936-38, Wathall (Miss.) Elementary Sch., 1938-42; asst. registrar U. Miss., 1945-49; supt. Springhill Consol. Sch., Eupora, Miss., 1950-52; supr. sch. lunch program Miss. Dept. Edn., Jackson, dir. adminstrn. and finance, 1958—. Served with USNR, 1942-45. Mem. Am., Miss. assns. sch. adminstrs., Am. Sch. Food Service Assn. (dir. 1954-55), Miss. Edn. Assn. (dir. 1951-52), Phi Delta Kappa., Am. Legion. Mason. Home: 5051 Canton Heights Jackson MS 39211 Office: PO Box 771 Jackson MS 39205

GRIFFING, GEORGE WARREN, physicist; b. Smith Center, Kan., Feb. 28, 1921; s. George Gilbert and Bessie (Logan) G.; B.S., Fort Hays, Kan. State Coll., 1946, A.B., 1946; M.A., U. Kan., 1948; Ph.D., Queen's U., Belfast, North Ireland, 1954; m. Roberta Jean Brown, Juen 2, 1946; children—George Thomas, John Warren. Asst. prof. physics E. Tenn. State Coll., Johnson City, 1950-51; chief ionospheric reactions sect. Air Force Cambridge Research Center, Boston, 1951-56; sr. physicist Ida. Nuclear Corp., Idaho Falls, 1956-70; phys. scientist Environmental Protection Agy., Raleigh, N.C., 1970—. Adj. prof. physics U. Ida., 1958-68. Served to maj. USAAF, 1942-45, USAF, 1951-56. Home: 1709 Su John Rd Raleigh NC 27607 Office: Meteorology Lab Nat Environmental Research Center Research Triangle Park NC 27711

GRIFFIS, CLARENCE ALTON, assn. exec.; b. Waycross, Ga., Oct. 10, 1927; s. Clarence A. and Trudy (King) G.; B.A., Stetson U., 1951; LL.B., Woodrow Wilson Law Coll., 1958; postgrad. Yale, 1959; m. Rose Whitten, Aug. 15, 1953; children—Miriam (Mrs. Lawrence W. Simon), Ronald W., Mark Alton and Michael Allen (twins). With research dept. Pillsbury Mills Inc., 1953-55; with U.S. Brewers Assn., Inc., Atlanta, 1955—, state dir., 1963-69, So. regional dir., 1969-73, v.p., 1973—. Mem. Peach and Bowl Com. Trustee Found. Visually Handicapped Children, Atlanta. Served to 1st lt. AUS, 1945-47, 51-53. Recipient Excellence award Ga. Press, 1967, Newspaper citation, 1966. Mem. Ga. Press Assn., Ga. Municipal Assn., Ga. Radio-TV Broadcasters Assn., County Commrs. Assn., Ga. Soc. Assn. Execs., Atlanta C. of C., So. Govs. Conf. Clubs: Atlanta Press, Leafmore. Home: 2544 Tanglewood Rd Decatur GA Office: 1655 Tully Circle NE Atlanta GA 30329

GRIFFIS, FLETCHER HUGHES, JR., army officer, engr.; b. Wauchula, Fla., Apr. 22, 1938; s. Fletcher Hughes and Eva Lee (Murphy) G.; B.S., U.S. Mil. Acad., 1960; M.S. in Civil Engring., Okla. State U., 1966, Ph.D., 1971, M.S. in Indsl. Engring., 1972; postgrad. U.S. Army Command and Gen. Staff Coll., 1969-70; m. Nancy Pauline Inch, Oct. 16, 1960; children—Hugh, Greg. Commd. 2d lt. U.S. Army, 1960, advanced through grades to maj., 1967; engr. constrn. troop command, 1961-64; asst. prof. math. U.S. Mil. Acad., 1966-68; chief constrn. mgmt. br. U.S. Army Engr. Constrn. Agy., Vietnam, 1968, operations officer 36th engring. bn., Vietnam, 1969; v.p. Constrn. Data Systems, Inc., Stillwater, Okla., 1970—; program mgr. dredged material research program U.S. Army Engrs. Waterways Expt. Sta., Vicksburg, Miss., 1972—. Adj. prof. Miss. State U.; pvt. constrn. cons. Coach, Little League basketball and football, Vicksburg, 1972-73. Decorated Legion of Merit, Bronze Star; Honor medal 1st class (Vietnam). Registered profl. engr., Okla. Mem. Vicksburg Art Assn. (v.p.), Am. Soc. C.E., Nat. Soc. Profl. Engrs., Project Mgmt. Inst., World Dredging Assn., Assn. Grads. U.S. Mil. Acad., Sigma Tau, Chi Epsilon. Contbr. articles to profl. jours. Home: Quarters 10 WES Vicksburg MS 39180 Office: Office Dredged Material Research USAE Waterways Expt Sta Vicksburg MS 39180

GRIFFIS, JAMES TRUMAN, educator; b. Bonham, Tex., Aug. 1, 1909; s. James Arthur and Minnie (Magouirk) G.; B.A., Austin Coll., 1941; B.S., U. Corpus Christi, 1952; M.A., Tex. Coll. Arts and Industry, 1950; Ed.D., U. Houston, 1955; m. Billye Florine Snow, June 5, 1931; 1 son, Bill J. Tchr., prin. rural schs., Fannin County, Tex., 1937-41; field exec. Boy Scouts Am., Corpus Christi, Tex., 1941-48; elementary prin. Flour Bluff Schs., Corpus Christi, 1948-52; instr., research asst. U. Houston, 1953-55; asst. supt. N.E. Houston schs., 1955-59; prof., head dept. edn., dean men Coll. Ozarks, Clarksville, Ark., 1961-64; prof., head dept. elementary edn. Panhandle State Coll., Goodwell, Okla., 1964—. Summer sch. faculty Troy (Ala.) State Coll., 1963-65, Okla. State U., Stillwater, 1966; research cons. Hugoton (Kan.) Schs., 1966—, Okla. Commn. on Tchr. Edn. and Certification, 1965—. Participant 1st World Congress on Reading, Paris, 1966, 2d congress, Copenhagen, 1968. Recipient Hornaday award for distinguished service to wild life, 1940. Mem. Phi Delta Kappa, Kappa Delta Pi. Presbyn. (elder). Mason (Shriner, 32 deg.), Kiwanian (past pres.), Author monograph: Education at Three Cost Levels, 1955. Home: 426 1st St Goodwell OK 73939

GRIFFITH, BRODIE SHEPPARD, ret. newspaper editor; b. Saluda, S.C., Mar. 14, 1899; s. John Franklin and Elizabeth (Keziah) S.; student Erskine Coll., 1916-17; LL.D., Davidson Coll., 1966, Erskine Coll., 1967; m. Thelma Cobb Wilkinson, Dec. 18, 1920; children—Gail Elizabeth (Mrs. W.C. Dowd, II), Myra Elise (Mrs. Norman L. Moore). Reporter, Greensboro (N.C.) Record, 1919-21, Greensboro Daily News, 1921-23; state editor Charlotte (N.C.) News, 1923-25; mng. editor, 1929-48, exec. editor, 1948-55, gen. mgr., 1955-59, editor, gen. mgr., 1959-65, asso. pub., 1965-66; became v.p., sec., gen. mgr. Charlotte News Pub. Co., Inc., 1955; v.p., treas., dir. Knight Pub. Co., v.p., asso. pub. 1968—, gen. mgr. Charlotte Observer and Charlotte News, 1966-72, now ret.; treas., dir. Observer Transp. Co.; editor N.C. Legion News, 1937—; dir. Knight Newspapers, Inc., Bank of Charlotte. Chmn. N.C. Urban Affairs Com. Mem. Charlotte Zoning Bd. Adjustment, 1949-50, mem. and chmn. Planning Bd., 1950-51. Served as sgt. 118th Inf., 30th Div., 1917-19. A.E.F., 1918-19. Mem. Am., So. newspaper pubs. assns., N.C. Press Assn. (v.p.), Am. Legion 40 and 8, Newcomen Soc., Sigma Delta Chi. Baptist. Mason (32 deg. K.T., Shriner). Club: Charlotte City. Home: 330 Ridgewood Av Charlotte NC 28209

GRIFFITH, JERRY LYNN, librarian; b. George West, Tex., Aug. 29, 1938; s. Ray Septimus and Flossie (Stevens) G.; A.A., Wharton County Jr. Coll., 1958; B.A., N. Tex. State U., 1960; M.S. in Library Sci., E. Tex. State U., 1966. Librarian Ganado (Tex.) High Sch., 1960-66; br. librarian Fort Polk, La., 1966-68; librarian 2d Inf. Div., Korea, 1967-68; adminstrv. librarian Army Spl. Services Library Service Center, Fort Polk, La., 1968-74; reference librarian Waterways Expt. Sta., Vicksburg, Miss., 1974—. Mem. Jaycees (treas.), Am., Southwestern, La. library assns., Internat. Platform Assn., Assn. U.S. Army. Democrat. Methodist. Home: 2916 F Confederate Av Vicksburg MS 39180 Office: Waterways Expt Sta Vicksburg MS 39180

GRIFFITH, JOHN DORLAND, psychiatrist, pharmacologist, educator; b. Jellico, Tenn., Mar. 22, 1931; s. Boyce Taylor and Frances (Baird) G.; student Temple U., 1948-49; B.S. in Engring. Physics, U. Chattanooga, 1951, M.D., 1955; m. Margaret Alice Wilson, Feb. 9, 1962; 1 dau., Frances Alida. Intern VA Hosp., Atlanta, 1955-56; resident U. Tenn. Med. Units, Memphis, 1956-59; dir. Harriett Cohn Guidance Center, Clarksville, Tenn., 1961-63, Mental Health Planning, Oklahoma City, 1963-65; asst. prof. psychiatry and pharmacology Vanderbilt U., Nashville, 1965-70, asso. prof., 1970-71; asso. prof. U. Cal. at San Diego, 1971-72; asso. clin. prof. psychiatry U. Ky., Lexington, 1973—; chief stimulant unit Nat. Inst. Mental Health Addiction Research Center, Lexington, 1971—. Mem. Gov.'s Commn. on Youth, 1964—, Gov.'s Commn. on Alcoholism, 1964-65. Served to capt. USAF, 1959-61. Diplomate Am. Bd. Psychiatry. Mem. A.M.A., Am. Psychiat. Assn., Am. Soc. Clin. Research, A.A.A.S., Sigma Xi. Contbr. articles on clin. pharmacology to profl. jours. Home: 2934 Montavesta Dr Lexington KY 40502 Office: National Inst Mental Health Addiction Research Center Box 2000 Lexington KY 40507

GRIFFITH, JOHN EDWARD, mech. engr., educator; b. Easton, Pa., Mar. 14, 1927; s. Harold Price and Dorothea (Fackenthal) G.; B.S. in Physics, Pa. State U., 1950, M.S. in Engring., 1952, Ph.D. in Engring. (DuPont fellow), 1955; m. Suzanne Hoffman, June 17, 1950; children—Joan, Anne Mary. Asst. prof. civil engring. Yale, 1955-58; asst. prof. engring. mechanics U. Fla., Gainesville, 1958-62; asso. prof. engring. mechanics N.C. State U., Raleigh, 1962-64, prof., chmn. dept. structures, materials and fluids U. South Fla., Tampa, 1964—. Cons. aerospace industries, 1962-65; vice chmn. Southeastern Conf. on Theoretical and Applied Mechanics, 1968-70, exec. chmn., 1970-72. Served with USNR, 1944-45. NSF grantee, 1967-68, U.S. Dept. Def. grantee, 1966-73. Mem. Am. Inst. Aero. and Astronautics, Am. Soc. Engring. Edn., Soc. Rheology, Soc. Exptl. Stress Analysis, Am. Soc. M.E., N.Y. Acad. Scis., Players, Sigma Xi, Sigma Pi Sigma, Alpha Nu, Phi Delta Theta. Contbr. articles to profl. jours. Home: 208 Wollowick Av Temple Terrace FL 33617 Office: SMF Engineering University South Florida Tampa FL 33620

GRIFFITH, KENNETH EARL, clergyman; b. Marshall, Tex., Nov. 2, 1925; s. Russell Egbert and Alma Lucille (Plemons) G.; student Centenary Coll., 1964, So. Meth. U., 1966; B.D., Felix Adler Meml. U., 1967; L.H.D. (hon.), Mt. Sinai Theol. Sem., 1971; m. Dorothy Sue Mason, Feb. 11, 1951; children—Randall Russell, Kenneth Wayne. Letter carrier U.S. Post Office, 1943-45; salesman La. Paper Co., 1947-54; bill auditor, chief clk. Southwestern Elec. Power Co., Shreveport, La., 1955—; pastor So. Meth. Ch. of Haughton, 1968—; founder Cartwright Christian Coll., 1972; ordained to ministry So. Meth. Ch., 1971. Chmn. Conf. Bd. Edn. of So. Meth. Ch., 1971—; poet, hymn writer. Dir. So. Meth. Coll., Orangeburg, S.C. Mem. Caddo-Bossier Poetry Soc. (pres. 1960), Gamma Chi Epsilon. Mason. Club: Bossier City Civitan (pres. 1970-72, dist. chaplain 1969). Author: Seasons and Times, 1969. Contbr. poetry to various publs. Home: 116 Alta Dr Haughton LA 71037 Office: PO Box 1062 Shreveport LA 71163

GRIFFITH, LUTHER BAILEY, accountant; b. Mansfield, La., June 25, 1901; s. William Jasper and Elizabeth (Bailey) G.; student Soule Coll., 1922; B.C.S., YMCA Coll., 1931; m. Louie Barnard, Apr. 25, 1931; children—Emelia Gay, Louie. Vice pres. Griffith Lumber Co., Mansfield, 1922-27; clk. La. Oil Co., Shreveport, 1927-34; bookkeeper Haynes Oil Corp., Shreveport, 1934-41; sr. accountant Colbert & Pasquier, C.P.A.'s, 1935-41; partner Griffith and Hettler, C.P.A.'s, Shreveport, 1941—. Mem. La. Soc. C.P.A.'s, Am. Inst. C.P.A.'s, Internat. Lightning Class Yachting Assn. (life; v.p. 1960-61, co chmn. selection 1st site yacht races 1960-61, commodore So. dist. 1963-64), De Soto Parish Hist. Soc., S.A.R., Ga. Geneological Soc. Episcopalian (vestryman). Mason. Clubs: Shreveport Country, Shreveport Yacht; Northwood Country. Home: 3255 Old Mooringsport Rd Shreveport LA 71107 Office: Ray P Oden Bldg Shreveport LA 71101

GRIFFITH, MARY IRENE, physician; b. Ruffin, N.C., July 1, 1909; d. Harry and Nannie (Dameron) Griffith; student Woman's Coll., U. N.C., 1926-29, U. N.C., 1932-33; M.D., U. Tenn., 1942. Intern, N.C. Bapt. Hosp., Winston-Salem, N.C., 1942, obstetrics gynecology staff, 1942, now mem. staff; intern Johns Hopkins Hosp., 1942-43, asst. resident 1943-44, resident obstetrics, 1944-45; asst. resident pathology Boston Lying-In Hosp., 1945, Free Hosp. for Women, 1945-46; practice medicine, specializing in obstetrics, gynecology, Winston-Salem, N.C., 1946—; mem. staff Forsythe Meml. Hosp.; instr. obstetrics, gynecology Bowman Gray Sch. Medicine, 1946, now asso. prof.; med. cons. Nigeria, Ire Welfare Center, W. Africa, 1954, 62, Bapt. Hosp., Paraguay, 1956. Bd. dirs. Friendship House. Diplomate Am. Bd. Obstetrics and Gynecology. Fellow Am. Coll. Obstetricians and Gynecologists; mem. A.M.A., Am. Med. Women's Assn., World, Pan Am. med. assns. Alpha Epsilon, Iota, Alpha Omega Alpha, C. of C. Baptist. Club: Altrusa. Author articles in field. Home: 419 S Hawthorne Rd Winston-Salem NC 27103 Office: 207 S Hawthorne Rd Winston-Salem NC 27103

GRIFFITH, MELVIN EUGENE, govt. ofcl.; b. Lawrence, Kan., Mar. 24, 1912; s. George Thomas and Estella (Shaw) G.; A.B., U. Kan., 1934, A.M., 1935, Ph.D. (fellow in entomology), 1938; postgrad. U. Mich., summers, 1937-40; m. Pauline Sophia Bogart, June 23, 1941. Instr. zoology N.D. Agrl. Coll., Fargo, 1938-39, asst. prof., 1939-41, asso. prof., 1941-42; malaria control entomologist US PHS, La., 1942-43, Okla. 1943-46; Okla. communicable disease center entomologist US PHS-Okla. Dept. Health, 1946-50; communicable disease center rep. Ark.-White-Red River Basins investigations USPHS, Ark., Colo., Kan., La., Mo., N.M., Okla., Tex., 1950-51; chief malariologist ICA, USPHS, Thailand, 1951-60; asso. dir. Malaria Eradication Tng. Center, Jamaica, 1960; regional malaria adviser S.E. Asia, Agy. Internat. Devel., USPHS, New Delhi, India, 1960-62, regional malaria adviser Near East and So. Asia, 1962-64, dep. chief malaria eradication br., Washington, 1964-67, chief, 1967-71; ret., 1971; cons. Office of Health, AID, Washington, 1971—. Asso. prof. zool. scis. U. Okla., Norman, 1946-52, prof., 1952-56. Recipient citation for distinguished service, U. Kan., 1962. Mem. A.A.A.S., Am. Pub. Health Assn., Am., Royal socs. tropical medicine and hygiene, Am. Mosquito Control Assn., Am. Soc. Limnology and Oceanography, Entomol. Soc. Am., USPHS Commd. Officers Assn., Siam Soc., Phi Beta Kappa, Sigma Xi. Club: Bangkok Sports (Bangkok, Thailand). Contbr. articles and monographs on entomology, malaria control, pub. health, Alconeura of U.S. Address: PO Box 1688 Rockville MD 20850

GRIFFITH, THOMAS JEFFERSON, lawyer; b. Ackerman, Miss., Dec. 12, 1923; s. Thomas Jefferson and Ara Ethel (Stephenson) G.; B.A., U. N.C., 1943; J.D., U. Miss., 1948; m. Nancy Ward, Dec. 1, 1951; children—Sara, Susanna, Thomas Ward. Admitted to Miss. bar, 1948, Tex. bar, 1950; practiced in Columbus, Miss., 1949-50, Lubbock, Tex., 1951—; mem. firm Griffith & Brister, 1970—. Chmn. Democrats Miss. for Truman-Barkley, 1948. Served to col. USMCR, 1943-46, 51-53. Mem. Am. Trial Lawyers Assn., Am., Miss., Lubbock County (pres. 1967) bar assns., State Bar Tex., Beta Theta Pi, Eta Sigma Phi, Phi Alpha Delta. Home: 4405 14th St Lubbock TX 79416 Office: Lubbock Nat Bldg Lubbock TX 79401

GRIFFITH, WILLIAM HOWARD, electric co. exec.; b. Huntingdon, Pa., Aug. 8, 1925; s. Howard Sidney and Gladys Flora (Prindle) G.; B.S., Pa. State U., 1951; postgrad. Northeastern U., 1952-55; m. Patricia Ruth Carney, May 22, 1948; 1 son, Michael John. Engring. supr. Gen. Electric Co., Knolls Atomic Power Lab., Schnectady, 1955-60; v.p. operations Alloy Freitag Mfg. Co., subsidiary Salem-Brosius, Inc., 1960-61; gen. mgr. Salem-Brosius, Inc., alloy mfg. div., Pitts., 1961-62; project mgr. Westinghouse Atomic Equipment and Atomic Fuel divs., Cheswick, Pa., 1962-64; mfg. projects mgr. atomic equipment div., 1966, naval nuclear project mgr., 1966-67; gen. mgr. Westinghouse Electric Corp., Pensacola (Fla.) div., 1967—; dir., chmn. bd. Charter Nat. Bank Pensacola (Fla.). Mem. adv. bd. Bapt. Hosp., 1968—, Sacred Heart Hosp., 1968-72. Bd. dirs. United Fund Greater Pensacola, Fla., Charter Bankshares, Inc. Served with USAF, 1951-55. Mem. Navy League U.S., Atomic Indsl. Forum, Asso. Industries Fla., Fla. State (dist. dir. 1970—), Pensacola chmabers commerce. Mason, Rotarian. Home: 257 Sabine Dr Pensacola Beach FL 32561 Office: PO Box 1313 Pensacola FL 32596

GRIFFITH, WILLIAM KIRK, agronomist, agrl. research inst. exec.; b. Henry, Ill., May 25, 1929; s. Burdette and Mable Alice (Glenn) G.; B.S. in Agrl. Edn., Western Ill. U., 1951; M.S. in Agronomy, U. Ill., 1952; Ph.D. in Crop Physiology, Purdue U., 1960; m. Dorothy Francis Dunsworth, Apr. 14, 1951; children—Jann Louise, Kirk Matthew. Asst. county agt. U. Ariz., 1956-58; research asst. Purdue U., 1958-60; Eastern agronomist Potash Inst. North Am., Washington, 1960-66, asst. to pres., 1966-68, regional dir., 1968—. Served with USNR, 1952-56; PTO. Mem. Am. Soc. Agronomy (Industry award 1972, pres. Northeast br. 1974), Soil Sci. Soc. Am., Crop Sci. Soc., Del.-Md. Plant Food Assn. (pres. 1970), Am. Forage and Grassland Council (dir. 1970—, Merit Certificate award 1969),editorial com. 1960-67). Contbr. articles on agronomy to farm mags. and other publs. Address: 865 Seneca Rd Herndon VA 22070

GRIGGS, JACK ALLEN, banker; b. Brownfield, Tex., July 22, 1942; s. Thomas Jackson and Ruth (Allen) G.; B.S. cum laude, Abilene Christian Coll., 1964; M.B.S., U. Tex. at Austin, 1967. Ph.D., 1971; m. Martha Ann Faubus, Aug. 9, 1963; children—Angela, Julianne. Mem. auditing staff Arthur Andersen & Co., Fort Worth, 1964-66; asst. to dean U. Tex. at Austin, 1967-69; asst. prof. finance Tex. Tech U., 1971-73; v.p. First Nat. Bank San Antonio, 1973—; financial cons., 1967-73. Trustee Abilene Christian Coll., 1974—. Recipient Wall St. Jour. award, 1964. C.P.A., Tex. Mem. Tex. Soc. C.P.A.s, Am. Finance Assn., Financial Mgmt. Assn., Blue Key, Beta Gamma Sigma (pres. chpt. 1972-73). Club: Exchange (San Antonio). Home: 3535 Red Oak Lane San Antonio TX 78230 Office: PO Box 2479 San Antonio TX 78298

GRIGGS, WADE GARNEY, JR., lawyer; b. Jasper, Tex., Nov. 13, 1943; s. Wade Garney and Faye (Frazer) G.; B.A., U. Tex., Austin, 1966, LL.B., 1968; m. Janita Pamela Frye, May 29, 1965; children—Wade Garney, John Bronson. Admitted to Tex. bar, 1968, since practiced in Houston; asso. firm Blades, Crain, Slator, Winters and Ross, 1968-69; mem. firm Ross, Griggs and Harrison, 1969—. Vice pres. Fleeting Service, Inc., Houston, 1970—. Mem. Houston Mus. Fine Arts Found., Zool. Soc. Houston, State Bar Tex., Am., Houston bar assns., Maritime Law Assn. U.S., Phi Alpha Delta, Delta Kappa Epsilon. Republican. Methodist. Clubs: Mariners of Houston, Propeller; Harborview of N.Y. Home: 218 Big Hollow Houston TX 77042 Office: Chamber of Commerce Bldg Houston TX 77002

GRIGGS, WALTER STALEY, JR., electronics engr.; b. Suffolk, Va., Dec. 13, 1926; s. Walter Staley and Beulah (Odom) G.; student Coll. William and Mary, 1944-45; B.S., Va. Poly. Inst., 1948; postgrad. U. Va., 1951-52; m. Mildred Audrey Melvin, Jan. 26, 1952; children—Walter Staley III, James Melvin. Electronics Project engr. Norfolk Naval Shipyard, Portsmouth, Va., 1948-56, head engr. ship radio div., 1956-57; head engr. shore electronics Fifth Naval Dist., Portsmouth, 1957-58, chief electronics engr. for indsl. mgr. USN, 5th Naval Dist., 1958-66; tech. dir. Naval Electronics Systems Command, Atlantic div., Portsmouth, 1966—. Served with USNR, 1945-46. Recipient Superior Work Performance award, 1960, 71. Mem. Armed Forces Mgmt. Assn., I.E.E.E. (sr.), Aircraft Owners and Pilots Assn., Soc. Profl. Naval Engrs. Baptist. Home: 4739 Rivershore Rd Portsmouth VA 23703 Office: Box 55 Portsmouth VA 23705

GRIGSBY, CHESTER POOLE, JR., oil and investments co. exec.; b. Ruston, La., Mar. 4, 1929; s. Chester Poole and Vera Aura (Lamkin) G.; B.S., La. Tech. U., 1951; postgrad. U. Ariz., 1953-54; m. Audrey Jane Tombrink, Mar. 27, 1954; children—Jayne, Chester Poole III, Julia, Diana. Accountant, Hudson Gas & Oil Corp., 1955-61; gen. accounting supr. San Jacinto Gas Processing Corp., 1961-63; v.p., treas., dir. Kinsey Corps., Shreveport, La., 1964—, Kinsey Interests, Inc., N. Shreveport Devel. Co., Enkay Corp., D & W Properties, Inc., Norman Corp. Caddo, Inc.; partner, Freestate Warehouse Co., 1972-73. Bd. dirs., asst. treas. Shreveport-Bossier Youth Services, Inc. Served with USAF, 1951-55. C.P.A., La. Mem. Am. Inst. C.P.A.'s, Soc. La. C.P.A.'s (mem. taxation and mgmt. coms. 1969-71), U.S. Power Squadron, Am. Legion. Elk. Home: 5721 River Rd Shreveport LA 71105 Office: 1407 Petroleum Tower Shreveport LA 71101

GRIGSBY, RONALD DAVIS, educator; b. Tulsa, Feb. 28, 1936; s. Logan Charles and Helen Dorothy (Davis) G.; student Okla. State U., 1954-56; B.S., U. Okla., 1958, B.S. in Chemistry, 1959, Ph.D., 1966; m. Nancy Jane Hampton, Apr. 20, 1962; children—Lynn E., Brian P., Debra C., David R., Steven A., Jonathan C. Research chemist Continental Oil Co., Ponca City, Okla., 1964-68; asst. prof. biochemistry and biophysics Tex. A. and M. U., College Station, 1968—; pres., Mass Spectrometer Accessories, 1972—. Vis. scientist NRC Can., Halifax, N.S., 1973-74. Mem. Am. Chem. Soc., Am. Soc. Mass Spectrometry, N.Y. Acad. Scis., Sigma Xi, Alpha Chi Sigma, Phi Lambda Upsilon. Home: 3707 Warren Circle Bryan TX 77801 Office: Dept Biochemistry and Biophysics Tex A and M U College Station TX 77843

GRIMBALL, BERKELEY, headmaster; b. Charleston, S.C., Nov. 25, 1922; s. Berkeley and Anne (Strohecker) G.; B.A., U. of South, 1943, D.C.L., 1969; M.A., Duke U., 1951; m. Emily-Lawton Kirkland, June 25, 1949; children—Berkeley, Lawton Kirkland, Meta Morris. Owner, headmaster Gaud Sch. for Boys, 1948-63, headmaster, Porter-Gaud Sch., 1963—. Mem. Charleston Playground Commn., 1962-69; trustee Charleston Library Soc., U. of South. Served with AUS, 1943-45. Mem. Nat. Assn. Episcopal Schs. (governing bd. 1971—), St. Cecilia Soc. Episcopalian. Clubs: Rotary (dir. 1973—). Carolina Yacht. Home: 205 Albermarle Rd Charleston SC 29407

GRIMBALL, WILLIAM H., lawyer; b. Charleston, S.C., Feb. 6, 1917; A.B., Coll. Charleston, 1938; LL.B., U. Va., 1941. Admitted to S.C. bar, 1941; now mem. firm Grimball & Cabaniss, Charleston. Mem. S.C. Ho. of Reps., 1953-58, chmn. Charleston County dels., 1956-58; alderman, Charleston, 1960-72, mayor pro tem, 1969. Served to lt. comdr. USNR, 1942-45. Fellow Am. Coll. Trial Lawyers; mem. Charleston County (pres. 1968-69), S.C., Am. bar assns., Coll. Charleston Alumni Assn. (pres. 1953), Order Coif, Phi Alpha Delta. Address: Grimball & Cabaniss 39 Broad St Charleston SC 29402*

GRIMES, RUSSELL NEWELL, educator; b. Meridian, Miss., Dec. 10, 1935; s. Newell Cleveland and Marion Esther (Zehner) G.; B.S. (Alumni scholar 1953-57), Lafayette Coll., 1957; Ph.D., U. Minn., 1962; m. Nancy Farrow Hall, Sept. 21, 1962; children—Susan, David. Postdoctoral research Harvard, 1962, U. Cal. at Riverside, 1962-63; asst. prof. chemistry U. Va., Charlottesville, 1963-68, asso. prof., 1968-73, prof., 1973—. U. Va. Sesquicentennial research fellow, 1974; Fulbright research scholar, 1974. Mem. Am. Chem. Soc., Assn. Harvard Chemists, A.A.A.S. Author: Carboranes, 1970. Contbr. articles to profl. jours. Home: 1401 Foxbrook Lane Charlottesville VA 22901

GRIMLAND, JOHN MARTIN, JR., accountant, orgn. ofcl.; b. Clifton, Tex., May 11, 1917; s. John Martin and Mayme (Gollihar) G.; B.S. in Commerce, Tex. Christian U., 1939; m. Phyllis Montgomery, Nov. 1, 1947; children—Diane, Donna Jean, Norma Gayle. With Universal C.I.T. Corp., 1940-42, Internal Revenue Service, 1946-47; pub. accountant, Midland, Tex., 1947-51, C.P.A., 1951—; partner Main Lafrentz & Co., 1968—. Mem. Optimist Internat., 1949—, gov. Dist. 7, 1957-58, v.p., 1958-59, chmn. pub. relations com., 1959-62, internat. pres., 1962-63, chmn. internat. community service com., 1966-69; treas. High Sky Girls Ranch, 1961-62; treas. Midland Symphony Assn., 1960-62, pres. 1963-65; pres. Midland United Fund, 1969, Indsl. Found. of Midland, 1971—. Trustee Tex. Christian U., 1972—. Served to lt. USNR, World War II. C.P.A., Tex. Mem. Am. Inst. C.P.A.'s, Tex. Christian U. Alumni Assn. (pres. 1965-66), Midland C. of C. (pres. 1970). Methodist (chmn. bd. 1961-62). Home: 1605 Country Club Dr Midland TX 79701 Office: Gihls Tower East Midland TX 79701

GRIMM, DEAN FRANKLIN, aero. engr.; b. Argonia, Kan., May 28, 1930; s. Ralph Albert and Laura MayBelle (McIntyre) G.; B.S., U. Kan., 1958; m. Eunice M. Mull, Nov. 22, 1955; children—Deana Lynne, Gregory Scott. Flight test engr. Convair-Gen. Dynamics, Ft. Worth, 1958-60; aerodynamic engr. Boeing Co., Renton, Wash., 1960-61; flight test engr. FAA, Oklahoma City, 1961-63; chief flight crew integration div. NASA Johnson Space Center, Houston, 1963-74, chief expt. systems div., 1974—. Asst. scout master Boy Scouts Am., Nassau Bay, Tex., 1973—. Bd. dirs. All Play Football, Nassau Bay. Served with USAF, 1950-54. Recipient Exceptional Service medal NASA, 1973. Registered profl. engr., Okla. Mem. Am. Inst. Aeros. and Astronautics. Presbyn. Mason (32 deg.). Home: 18638 Prince William Lane Houston TX 77058 Office: NASA Johnson Space Center (ED) Houston TX 77058

GRINER, ELSIE HIGGS, JR., journalist, entertainer; b. Nashville, Ga., July 15, 1932; d. George and Elsie (Higgs) Griner; student pub. schs., Nashville; m. Hugh D. Alderman, July 20, 1952 (div.); 1 dau., Pandora Dee. Gospel concert singer, song writer Hill & Range, Inc., N.Y.C., 1955-61; recorded with RCA Victor, 1955-61; editor-pub. Nashville (Ga.) Herald, 1962-66; polit. satirist, recording with Lowery Music, Atlanta, 1966—. Mem. Fulton County Democratic Exec. Com., 1970—. Recipient Salvation Army awards, 1964, 66; named Georgia's First Weekly Editorial Columnist, Ga. Press Assn., 1964, 66. Mem. Mensa. Home: 1315 Fairview Rd NE Atlanta GA 30306

GRINER, JOHN F., labor union ofcl.; b. Camilla, Ga., Aug. 7, 1907; s. Will and Dollier (Shiver) G.; LL.B., Columbus U., Washington; m. Claranell Nicholson, Nov. 27, 1936; children—John F., Remer Will. With various railroads, 1925-36; adjudicator, liaison officer, labor relations officer U.S. Railroad Retirement Bd., 1936-62; nat. pres. Am. Fedn. Govt. Employees, 1962—. Mem. Order R.R. Telegraphers, Am. Train Dispatchers Assn.; hon. mem. Brotherhood R.R. Trainmen, R.R. Yardmasters Am., Brotherhood R.R. Signalmen. Democrat. Baptist. Mason (Shriner). Home: 10225 Kensington Pkwy Kensington MD 20015 Office: 400 1st St NW Washington DC 20001

GRISCOM, JOHN HOOPER, physician; b. Nashville, Dec. 30, 1929; s. James Thomas and Rachel (Hooper) G.; B.A., Vanderbilt U., 1951, M.D., 1954; m. Ednyna Howard, Nov. 23, 1955; children—John Hooper, James Thomas, Edwyna Lee. Intern, Vanderbilt U. Hosp., Nashville, 1954-55, resident, 1955-56, 57-59, chief resident, 1958-59; resident Columbia-Presbyn. Hosp., N.Y.C., 1956-57; practice medicine, specializing in internal medicine, Nashville, 1961—; asst. prof. medicine Vanderbilt U., 1964—. Served to lt. comdr. USNR, 1959-61. Diplomate Am. Bd. Internal Medicine. Mem. Middle Tenn. Heart Assn. (pres. 1972-73). Home: 910 Westview St Nashville TN 37205 Office: Med Arts Bldg Nashville TN 37212

GRISE, JERRY WADE, radiologist; b. Ft. Smith, Ark., Apr. 25, 1933; s. Strauther Wade and Mary Beth (Thurman) G.; B.S., E. Tenn. State U., 1953; M.D., U. Tenn., 1956; m. Betty Lunati, Feb. 14, 1959; children—Jeffrey Wade, John David. Intern, D.C. Gen. Hosp., Washington, 1957; resident radiology Strong Meml. Hosp., Rochester, N.Y., 1958-60; practice medicine specializing in radiology Bapt. Hosp., Nashville, 1964-65, Meth. Hosp., Memphis, 1965—. Served to capt. M.C., USAF, 1960-64. Mem. Am., Tenn. med. assns., Radiol. Soc. N.Am., Am. Roentgen Ray Soc., Tenn. Radiol. Soc., Memphis Roentgen Soc. (pres. 1971-72). Home: 4822 Fleetview Memphis TN 38117 Office: Dept Radiology Meth Hosp 1265 Union Av Memphis TN 38104

GRISET, HENRY EDWIN, civil engr.; b. Bklyn., Feb. 24, 1912; s. Gustavus B. and Veronica (Mock) G.; B.S. in Civil Engring., N.Y.U., 1934; M.C.E., Bklyn. Poly. Inst., 1945; m. Iona Jacobi, Mar. 13, 1931; children—Arlene (Mrs. Cletus Waynick), Bruce Henry, Kurt Barron; m. 2d, Ursula Williams, Dec. 29, 1967. Asst. engr. Henry I. Mock, Contractor, Bklyn., 1932-35, N.Y.C. Park Dept., 1935-36; surveyman U.S. Army Engrs., 1936-37; structural engr., appraiser Mortgage Corp. of N.Y., N.Y.C., 1937-40; stress analyst Republic Aviation Corp., Farmingdale, N.Y., 1940-41; structural engr. J. G. White Engring. Corp., N.Y.C., 1941-42; instr. Bklyn. Poly. Inst., 1941-43. Coll. City N.Y., 1943-44; asst. prof. Sch. Civil Engring. Cornell U., 1944-47; part time appraiser Equitable Life Assurance Soc. of U.S., 1944-47; asso. prof. N.C. State Coll., Raleigh, 1947-52, prof. in charge constrn. curriculum, 1950-52; owner Allied Engring. Services, Raleigh, N.C., 1952—. Registered profl. engr. N.Y., N.C., Fla. Mem. Am. Soc. C.E., Am. Concrete Inst., Internat. Assn. Bridge and Structural Engrs., Am. Soc. for Engring. Edn., Nat. Soc. Profl. Engrs., Cornell Soc. Engrs., N.Y. Acad. Scis., N.C. Assn. Professions, N.Y. Acad. Scis., Beta Theta Pi, Tau Beta Pi, Chi Epsilon. Home: 1623 Dixie Trail Raleigh NC 27607 Office: PO Box 10532 Raleigh NC 27605

GRISHAM, DONALD MCFERRIN, civil engr.; b. Altheimer, Ark., Mar. 16, 1937; s. Theodore Vernon and Muda (Morris) G.; ed. Internat. Corr. Schs., U. Ark.; m. Rosemary Hall, Mar. 22, 1969; children by previous marriage—Donald McFerrin, Larry Dean, Natalie Kim. Chief engr. Cooper Communities, Inc., Bella Vista, Ark., 1959-71; pres. Ark. Consultants, Rogers, 1971-72; v.p. Crafton, Tull & Assos., Inc., Rogers, 1972—; v.p. S.W. Properties, Inc., Benton County Communications, Inc. Pres. Boys Club Rogers. County surveyor Benton County, 1972—; sec. Benton County Planning Bd. Served with USAF, 1955-56. Registered profl. engr., Ark., Mo., Kan., Okla., Tex.; registered surveyor, Ark., Kan., Okla. Mem. Nat. Soc. Profl. Engrs., Am. Congress Surveying and Mapping, Ark. Assn. Registered Land Surveyors, Photog. Soc. Am., Urban Land Inst., Aircraft Owners and Pilots Assn. Kiwanian. Home: 2703 Kathy Lane Rogers AR 72756 Office: PO Drawer 549 Rogers AR 72756

GRISMER, RAYMOND LEONARD, educator, author; b. Schenectady, N.Y., Mar. 30, 1895; s. Charles Valentine and Luna M. (Leonard) G.; A.B., U. Vt., 1916; Rhodes Scholar, Oxford U., Eng., 1916-17; M.A., Ohio State U., 1922; Ph.D., U. Cal., 1930; m. Mildred Best, Aug. 20, 1919; children—Jean, Raymond, William. Tchr., Mercersburg Acad., Pa., 1917-18, The Hill Sch., Pottstown, Pa., 1919-20; instr. romance langs. Ohio State U., 1920-24; head modern lang. dept. Oklahoma City U., 1924-27; asso. Spanish, U. Cal., 1927-31; asst. prof. U. Minn., 1931-34, asso. prof. 1934-49, prof. romance langs., 1949-66, prof. emeritus Romance langs., 1966—. Served with O.T.S., Brit. Army, Oxford, Eng., 1917; lt. inf. O.T.C., U.S. Army, Camp Gordon, Ga., 1917-18; capt. arty. Okla. N.G., Ft. Sill, 1925-27. Mem. Am. Assn. Tchrs. Spanish, Modern Lang. Assn. Am., Phi Beta Kappa, Tau Kappa Epsilon. Author: Pageant of Spain (with D.K. Arjona), 1939; Reference Index to Twelve Thousand Spanish-American Authors, 1939; Sailing the Spanish Main, 1940; New Bibliography of the Literatures of Spain and Spanish America (with M.B. Grismer, J. Magraw; 7 vols.), 1941-46; A Brief Spanish Grammar for Beginners, 1942; Spanish Short Stores (with R.H. Olmsted), 1943; Buenos Vecinos, Buenos Amigos (with C.I. Arroyo), 1943; Short Spanish Review Grammar (with D.K. Arjona), 1943; Tales of Spanish America (with N.R. Adams), 1944; Influence of Plautus in Spain Before Lope de Vega, 1944; Easy Spanish-American Reader (with M.W. Molinos, E.D. Corbett), 1945; Elementary Spanish Conversation (with L. C. Keating), 1946; Cervantes: A Bibliography, Vol I, 1946, Vol. II, 1963; Liberatadores y Defensores (with Roy and Margarita Mills), 1953; Bibliography of Lope de Vega, Vols. I and II, 1964-65; Bibliography of the Drama of Spain and Spanish America, Vols. I and II, 1967; and others. Contbr. articles jours. Home: Town Apts South 101 1847 Shore Dr South Pasadena FL 33707

GRISSETT, WALLACE EDWARD, JR., lawyer; b. Clearwater, Fla., Apr. 24, 1926; s. Wallace Edward and Grace (Clark) G.; student Jacksonville U., 1946-47; B.A., Stetson U., 1950, LL.B., 1953; m. Bonnie Tapley, Apr. 14, 1962; children—David Arthur, Stephen Edward Parks, Elizabeth Helen. Admitted to Fla. bar, 1953; practiced in Green Cove Springs, Fla., 1953-55, Jacksonville, 1957—; mem. firm Scott & Cox, 1957-60, Cox, Grissett & Webb, 1960-66, W. E. Grissett, Jr., 1966-69, Grissett, Humphries & Danese, 1969-70, Grissett and Humphries, 1970—; adjuster State Farm Mut. Auto Ins. Co., Tallahassee, 1955-56. Vice chmn. Local Govt. Study Commn. of Duval County, 1965-67; Mem. City Council Consol. City Jacksonville, 1968-71, pres., 1968-69; mem. Fla. Law Revision Commn., 1968—, chmn., 1974—. Bd. dirs. Gateway Girl Scout Council, 1966-72; bd. dirs. Jacksonville Symphony Assn., 1968—, pres., 1973-74; bd. dirs. Gator Bowl Assn., 1968-70. Served with USNR, 1944-46. Mem. Am., Jacksonville (pres. 1970) bar assns., Fedn. Ins. Counsel, Internat. Assn. Ins. Counsel, Am. Judicature Soc., Maritime Law Assn. U.S., Nat. Assn. R.R. Trial Counsel, Inter-Am. Bar Assn., Fla. Bar (bd. gov. 1964-68), Jacksonville U. Alumni Assn. (pres. 1959), Omicron Delta Kappa, Phi Alpha Delta, Sigma Nu. Home: 5720 Cherry Laurel Dr Jacksonville FL 32210 Office: 231 E Forsyth St Jacksonville FL 32202

GRISSOM, JOE BRYAN III, educator; b. Houston, June 13, 1943; s. Joe Bryan and Mary Elizabeth (Askins) G.; B.B.A., Baylor U., 1966, M.B.A., 1967; m. Vicki Terry, Aug. 4, 1967; 1 son, Bryan Terry. Asst. prof. bus. adminstrn. Tarrant County Jr. Coll., Fort Worth, 1967—, dept. chmn., 1972—. C.P.A., Tex. Mem. Beta Alpha Psi, Beta Gamma Sigma. Home: 7516 Yolanda Dr Fort Worth TX 76112

GRISSOM, TERRY HAMILTON, wholesale food chain exec.; b. Glasgow, Ky., June 7, 1918; s. Robert Hamilton and Verla Jewell (Oliver) G.; grad. high sch.; m. Willa Belle Penn, Dec. 20, 1936; 1 son, Robert Hamilton. Store mgr. Glass Food Stores, chain store, Lexington, Ky., 1934-41; with Nat. Life and Accident Ins. Co., Lexington, 1941-42; dist. mgr. Libby, McNeill & Libby, food mfrs., Lexington, 1946-50, Indpls., 1949-50; with Cupples Co., brokers, Lexington, 1950-52; with W.T. Sistrunk & Co., wholesale retail food voluntary chain, Lexington, 1952—, v.p. marketing, 1960—. Cons. food industry activities. Sales contest judge, cons. Jr. Achievement, 1966-71; sales and marketing judge Distributive Edn. Clubs Am., 1970. Served with USCGR, 1942-45. Recipient Most Valuable Member award Lexington Salesmen's Club, 1957. Mem. Nat. Am. Wholesale Grocers Assn. (bd. govs. 1966-68), Nat. Sales Mgmt. Task Force (conf. chmn. 1973), Nat. Advt. Adv. Council. Mason (Shriner). Clubs: Lexington Salesmen's (pres. 1954, 65), Bluegrass Sales and Marketing Executives (dir. 1973-74), Optimist (sec. Lexington 1971-73, 1st v.p. 1973-74, pres. 1974-75). Home: 707 Pasadena Dr Lexington KY 40503 Office: 2155 Young Dr PO Box 1020 Lexington KY 40501

GRISWOLD, KENNETH EDWIN, JR., lab. adminstr.; b. Ruston, La., Oct. 22, 1943; s. Kenneth Edwin and Ella Juanita (Witherington) G.; B.S., La. Tech. U., 1965, M.S., 1967; Ph.D., U. S.C., 1971; m. Bonnie Jo Newcomer, Aug. 26, 1967; children—William, Natalie. Crop entomologist Micro Chem. Co., 1964; entomologist Hercules Powder Co., Winnsboro, La., 1965; news dir., announcer KRUS Radio, Ruston, La., 1962-67; research supt. NIH Grant, La. Tech. U., 1965-67; instr. Coll. Gen. Studies U. S.C., Columbia, 1969-71; asst. prof. biochemistry and pathology La. State U. Med. Center, Shreveport, 1971—; dir. chemistry labs. VA Hosp. and Confederate Med. Center, Shreveport, La., 1972—. Recipient Grants, NIH, 1965, U. S.C., 1969, Kiwanis Club, 1961. Mem. Genetic Soc. Am., Am. Assn. Clin. Chemists, A.A.A.S., Am. Assn. Clin. Lab. Suprs., Sigma Xi, Beta Beta Beta, Omicron Delta Kappa. Home: 319 Wickford St Shreveport LA 71105 Office: 510 E Stoner St Shreveport LA 71130

GRITZ, JACK LINTON, clergyman, editor; b. Okmulgee, Okla., Dec. 31, 1916; s. Harry Vernon and Katie (Houston) G.; student Phillips U., 1935-37; A.B., Okla. Bapt. U., 1939; Th.M., Southwestern Bapt. Theol. Sem., 1942; Th.D., So. Sem., Louisville, 1947; m. Veva Chloe Hammack, June 29, 1947; 1 son, Paul Linton. Asso. sec. dept. religious edn. Bapt. Gen. Conv. Okla., 1944-47; pastor First Bapt. Ch., Tahlequah, Okla., 1947-49; editor Bapt. Messenger, Oklahoma City, 1949—. Mem. So. Bapt. Press Assn. (pres. 1968-69). Home: 1419 N Drexel St Oklahoma City OK 73107 Office: 1141 N Robinson Oklahoma City OK 73103

GRIVET, PAUL EDWARD, electronics engr.; b. St. Louis, Oct. 13, 1906; s. Edward Francis and Etta Pearl (Davis) G.; B.S. in Elec. Engring., Washington U., St. Louis, 1931. Various positions teaching elec., electronic maintenance, 1931-42; elec. engr. CAA, 1947-53, Patchen & Zimmerman, 1953-54; electronics engr. Army Missile Command, Redstone Arsenal, Ala., 1954—. Served with Signal Corps, USAAF, 1942-47; maj. Res. ret. Registered prof. engr., Ala. Mem. I.E.E.E., Nat. Soc. Profl. Engrs. Home: 407 Green Acres Dr Huntsville AL 35805 Office: Army Missile Command Bldg 5400 Redstone Arsenal AL 35809

GRIVSKY, EUGENE MICHAEL, chemist; b. Pskov, Russia, Dec. 20, 1911; s. Michael Theodore and Alexandra Yakovlevna (Gemchuzhina) G.; M.S. summa cum laude, Brussels U., 1938, D.Sc. summa cum laude, 1940; m. Helen Vlassova, Oct. 27, 1935; children—Michael Eugene, Tatiana (Mrs. R.E. Berls, Jr.). Came to U.S., 1957, naturalized, 1962. Research fellow Internat. Bur. Standards, Brussels U., 1938-40; group leader Organic Research Labs., Union Chimique Belge, Brussels, 1941-57; sr. research chemist Wellcome Research Labs., Burroughs Wellcome Co., Tuckahoe, N.Y., 1957-70, Research Triangle Park, N.C., 1970—. Served with Estonian Army, 1931-33. Fellow Am. Inst. Chemists; mem. Am. Chem. Soc., Soc. Chimique Belgique, Soc. Chimique de France, Pharm. Soc. Japan, Chem. Soc. Eng., Gesellschaft Deutscher Chemiker, N.Y. Acad. Scis. Research, publs. in organic and medicinal chemistry, mechanism of reactions, syntheses of new chemotherapeutic and medicinal agts. Patentee in field. Home: Linden Rd PO Box 2571 Chapel Hill NC 27514 Office: 3030 Burrough-Wellcome Co Cornwallis Rd Research Triangle Park NC 27709

GRIZZARD, JOHN LINWOOD, air force officer; b. Drewryville, Va., Dec. 18, 1930; s. Henry Ezelle and Virginia Bell (Norfleet) G.; B.S., Va. Poly. Inst. and State U., 1953; m. Gyneth Cleo Arthur, Aug. 8, 1954; 1 son, John Arthur. Indsl. engr. Richmond Dairy Co., 1953; commd. 2d lt., USAF, 1953, advanced through grades to lt. col., 1973; indsl. engring., facility maintenance and mgmt., 1954-58; indsl. engr. Lynchburg Foundry Co. (Va.), 1958-60; chief indsl. engr. H.K. Porter Co., 1960-61; chief facility maintenance and indsl. engring. Keesler AFB, Miss., 1962-64, Thule AFB, Greenland, 1964-65; chief indsl. engring. Air Force Acad., 1965-69; comdr. constrn. squadron, Vietnam, 1969-70; chief indsl. engring. and data automation Hdqrs. USAF, Pentagon, 1970-72; chief operations and maintenance Bolling AFB, Washington, 1972—. Vice pres. Waynewood P.T.A., 1972-73; scoutmaster Cub Scouts, 1972-73; player, dir. Lee-Mt. Vernon Soccer Assn.; mgr. Ft. Hunt Little League Baseball. Bd. dirs. Ft. Hunt Youth Assn. Decorated Bronze Star Medal, Meritorious Service medal, Pentagon Commendation medal. Mem. Am. Inst. Indsl. Engrs. (pres. Pikes Peak chpt. 1967), Nat. Capitol Plant Engrs. Soc., No. Va. Soc. Profl. Engrs., Soc. Am. Mil. Engrs., Ft. Hunt Sportsmen's Assn., Ft. Hunt Athletic Assn. (dir.). Home: 1106 Croton Dr Alexandria VA 22308 Office: 1100th Civil Engineering Squadron/DEO Bolling Air Force Base DC 20332

GRIZZLE, JAMES ENNIS, educator; b. Herald, Va., Apr. 20, 1930; s. Joseph Jackson and Jeanette Ellen (Bise) G.; B.S., Berea Coll., 1951; M.S., Va. Poly. Inst., 1954; Ph.D., N.C. State U., 1960; m. Barbara Ann Huntsman, Aug. 18, 1951; children—William Joseph, Linda Jean, Thomas Bruce. Research asst. dept. biostatistics Sch. Pub. Health, U. N.C., 1957-60, asst. prof., 1960-64, asso. prof., 1964-67, prof., 1967—, head dept., 1972—. Cons. NIH, 1960—, WHO, 1969-70; vis. prof. U. Exeter (Eng.), 1973, cons. NRC, 1970—. Served with AUS, 1954-56. Fellow Am. Statis. Assn., Am. Pub. Health Assn., Am. Heart Assn., A.A.A.S., Biometric Soc. (pres. Eastern N.Am. region 1972-73); mem. Inst. Math. Statistics, Elisha Mitchel Soc., Sigma Xi. Asso. editor Jour. Am. Statis. Assn., 1970-72, Psychophysiology, 1969-72, Jour. Chronic Disease, 1968—, Jour. Elisha Mitchel Soc., 1965—. Home: 904 Woodbine Dr Chapel Hill NC 27514

GROAH, WILLIAM JENNINGS, JR., assn. exec.; b. Harrisonburg, Va., May 28, 1931; s. William Jennings and Jean Stuart (Nicholas) G.; B.S., Va. Poly. Inst., 1955; M.S. in Wood Technology, N.C. State U., 1956; m. Helen Virginia Gibbs, Dec. 17, 1960; children—William Michael, Suzanne Lynn. Tech. dir. Hardwood Plywood Mfrs. Assn., Arlington, Va., tech. dir., 1970—. Served with USNR, 1956-57. Mem. Am. Soc. for Testing and Materials Forest Products Research Soc., Soc. of Wood Sci. and Tech. Xi Sigma Pi, Phi Sigma. Home: 11233 S Shore Rd Reston VA 22090 Office: 2310 S Walter Reed Dr Arlington VA 22206

GROB, LOUIS WILLIAM, fgn. service officer; b. Cohoes, N.Y., Aug. 27, 1934; s. Louis and Noreen Mary (Lesson) G.; student RCA Insts., 1957-59, FAA U., 1960-61; m. Margaret Mary Burke, Aug. 16, 1959; children—William Scott, Christopher Louis. Staff officer U.S. Fgn. Service, Beirut, Lebanon, also Frankfurt, Germany, Bucharest, Rumania, Pretoria, S.Africa, 1963-72, State Dept., Washington, 1972—. Adviser, cons. tech. security problems. Asst. den leader Mt. Vernon council Boy Scouts Am., 1973—. Served with AUS, 1953-56; ETO. Mem. I.E.E.E., Amateur Radio Relay League. Moose. Home: 7012 Leesville Blvd Springfield VA 22151 Office: US Dept State 21st and Virginia Av NW Washington DC 20520

GROCHAU, HENRY BOYD, radiologist; b. Huntsville, Ala., Feb. 9, 1929; s. Earl Henry and Minnie Lee (Doolittle) G.; M.D., U. Tenn., 1958; m. M. Rachel Dye, May 22, 1956; children—Rebecca Anne, Deborah Lee, Earl Henry. Intern Baptist Meml. Hosp., Memphis, 1958-59; resident Methodist Hosp., Memphis, 1960-63; practice medicine specializing in radiology, Greenville, Miss., 1963—; chief radiologist Kings Daughters Hosp., Greenville, Miss., 1963—, mem. exec. com., 1974—; dir. Sch. Radiol. Tech., Kings Daus. Hosp., Gamble Bros. Clinic, 1968—; affiliated with Miss. Delta Jr. Coll., 1971—. Served with inf. AUS, 1951-53; Korea. Decorated Bronze Star medal. Diplomate Am. Bd. Radiology. Mem. A.M.A., Miss. Med. Soc., Radiol. Soc. N. Am., Am. Coll. Radiology, Am. Coll. Nuclear Medicine, Delta Med. Soc. Home: Route 2 Lake Lee Rd Greenville MS 38701 Office: 339 Arnold Greenville MS 38701

GRODNER, ROBERT MAYNARD, food scientist, educator; b. Bklyn., June 22, 1925; s. Murray S. and Dorothy S. (Goldstene) G.; A.B., Brown U., 1949; M.S., U. Tenn., 1950; postgrad. Duke, 1950-54; Ph.D., La. State U., 1959; m. Mary L. Laslie, Aug. 22, 1959; children—Robert Marshall, Mark William. Instr., Berea (Ky.) Coll., 1950; asst. prof. biology Otterbein Coll., Westerville, O., 1959-62, asso. prof. biology 1963; asso. prof. food sci. La. State U., Baton Rouge, 1963-69, prof. food sci., 1969—. Served with USNR, 1941-43. AEC grantee, 1964-68; U.S. FDA, USPHS grantee 1968-72. Mem. A.A.A.S., Inst. Food Technologists, Sigma Xi, Gamma Sigma Delta, Phi Tau Sigma, Sigma Phi Epsilon. Contbr. articles to profl. jours. Home: 5466 N College Hill Dr Baton Rouge LA 70808

GROEBER, JOHN EDWARD, accountant; b. Springfield, O., Apr. 4, 1919; s. John Harry and Mary Louise (Berry) G.; B.S. in Commerce, Xavier U., 1941; m. Johann Marie McCarthy, Jan. 31, 1942; children—Nancy (Mrs. Robert L. Fedders), Alice (Mrs. John Atkins), Ronald. Staff accountant Gano & Cherrington, Cin., 1946-52; controller Ficks Reed Co., Cin., 1953-63; with Interlake, Inc., Newport, Ky., 1963—, chief accountant, 1969—. Served to capt. AUS, 1941-46. Decorated Purple Heart. C.P.A., Ky. Mem. Ind. Order of Foresters (treas. 1970—). Home: 1415 Amsterdam Park Hills KY 41011 Office: Ninth and Lowell Newport KY 41072

GROGAN, HIRAM JOHN, lawyer, psychologist; b. Ball Ground, Ga., Aug. 21, 1925; s. Paul and Lila (Stamper) G.; student Oglethorpe U., 1942-43, Ga. So. Coll., 1946; A.B. cum laude, Piedmont Coll., 1948; M.Ed., U. Ga., 1949, Ed. S., 1972; J.D., Woodrow Wilson Coll., 1958; m. Ruth Carney, Oct. 2, 1948. Tchr., prin. Etowah Sch., Cherokee County, Ga., 1950-51; tchr., coach Blackwell Sch., Cobb County, Ga., 1951-52; accountant Ga. Hwy. Dept., Atlanta, 1952-56; chief probation officer, Marietta, Ga., 1956-69, area probation supr., 1969-73, psychologist, 1973—; admitted to Ga. bar, 1958; since practiced in Marietta. Part-time instr. sociology Marietta Center, U. Ga., 1964. Apptd. lt. col. gov.'s staff, 1967. Served with USNR, 1944-46. Mem. Am., Ga., Cobb bar assns., Nat. Council on Crime and Delinquency, Ga. Probation and Parole Assn., So. States Corrections Assn., Ga. Psychol. Assn. Clubs: Civitan, Marietta Art. Author: Modern Bow Hunting, 1958; also monographs numerous articles in profl. jours., mags. Home: 3400 Lee St Smyrna GA 30080 Office: 3A King-Williams Bldg Smyrna GA 30080

GROH, NORMAN DANIEL, hotel exec.; b. Balt., May 28, 1929; s. Louis and Frieda (Meyer) G.; student U. Va., 1946-48, Purdue U., 1948-49; m. Laura Barbara Clements, June 1, 1957; children—Steven Clay, Blair Sayling, Alan Jefferson. Asst. v.p. Louis Groh & Son, Inc., 1949-52, v.p., 1952-57, pres., 1957-63; asst. v.p. S.L. Nusbaum Co., Inc., 1963-64, v.p., 1964-66; developer, owner, operator Holiday Inn Motels, Norfolk, Va., 1966—. Served with AUS, 1950-53. Mem. Internat. Assn. Holiday Inns, Nat. Assn. Real Estate Brokers, Va. Hotel Motel Assn., Norfolk C. of C., Downtown Norfolk Assn. Clubs: Cavalier Golf and Yacht (Virginia Beach, Va.); Harbor (Norfolk, Va.); Ocean Reef (Key Largo, Fla.). Home: 1321 N Bay Shore Dr Virginia Beach VA 23451 Office: 700 Monticello Av Norfolk VA 23510

GRONER, FRANK S(HELBY), hosp. adminstr.; b. Stamford, Tex., Sept. 25, 1911; s. Frank S. and Laura (Wyatt) G.; B.A., Baylor U., 1934; LL.D., Tex. Bapt. Coll., 1946, Union U., 1952, Baylor U., 1969; m. Daisy Amanda McFearin, Dec. 12, 1936. Dean sch. bus. Coll. of Marshall (Tex.), 1934-36; asst. adminstr. So. Bapt. Hosp., New Orleans, 1936-43, adminstr., 1943-46; adminstr. Bapt. Meml. Hosp., Memphis, 1946—. Cons. USPHS; cons. Div. Hosp. and Med. Facilities, also Bur. Family Services on Med. Matters, U.S. Dept. Health, Edn. and Welfare; exec. dir. Health, Edn. and Research Found. Mem. Surgeon Gen.'s adv. com. on Nat. Health Survey. Bd. govs., exec. com. Blue Cross; bd. dirs. A.R.C., Am. Cancer Soc. Memphis Community Chest. Dollar-a-Year Man, Washington, 1942-45. Recipient Justin Ford Kimball award, 1964, Distinguished service award Am. Hosp. Assn., 1966, Memphis and Shelby County Med. Soc. Distinguished Service award, 1967, gold medal Am. Coll. Hosp. Adminstrs., 1968. Mem. Am. (pres. chmn. council hosp. planning and plant operation, chmn. hosp. architects qualifications, trustee, past pres.) La. (past pres.), Tenn. (past pres,) hosp. assns., Southeastern Hosp. Conf. (past pres.), Southwide Bapt. Hosp. Assn. (past pres.), So. Inst. Hosp. Administrs. (dir.), Am. Coll. Hosp. Administrs. (pres., dir.), Internat. Hosp. Fedn. (del.) Baptist. Home: 3170 Southern Av Memphis TN 38111 Office: 899 Madison Av Memphis TN 38146

GRONER, PAT NEFF, hosp. adminstr.; b. Dallas, Dec. 21, 1920; s. Frank Shelby and Laura (Wyatt) G.; A.B., Baylor U., 1941; m. Louise Mary Rugg, May 5, 1944; children—Josephine Louise, Frank Shelby III. Pilot, Colonial Airlines (now Eastern Airlines), N.Y.C., 1946-47; asst. adminstr. Mary Fletcher Hosp., Burlington, Vt., 1947-48; adminstr. Barre (Vt.) City Hosp., 1948-50; adminstr. Baptist Hosp., Pensacola, Fla., 1950-67, exec. dir., 1967—. Dir. Mutual Fed. Savs. & Loan Assn. Pres. Hosp. Research and Devel. Inst.; exec. com. Blue Cross of Fla.; bd. dirs. U. W. Fla. Found. Served with USNR, 1941-42; USMC, 1942-45. Recipient Liberty Bell award Soc. Bar for 1st Jud. Circuit State of Fla., Good Govt. award Pensacola Jr. C. of C., award of merit Fla. Hosp. Assn. Fellow Am. Coll. Hosp. Adminstrs. (bd. regents 1966-70); mem. Am. (trustee 1967-70), Fla. (past pres.), Southeastern (past pres.), hosp. assns. Rotarian (pres. 1966-67). Home: 2200 Banquo's Trail Pensacola FL 32503 Office: 1000 W Moreno St Pensacola FL 32501

GRONHOLZ, LEROY FREDERICK, chem. products co. exec.; b. Redfield, S.D., July 10, 1922; s. Fred and Clara Augusta (Muhs) G.; B.A., U. S.D., 1943, M.A., 1948; Ph.D., Carnegie-Mellon U., 1952; m. Marilyn C. Nelson, Mar. 21, 1944; children—Margot (Mrs. Richard C.B. Bittenbender II), Deborah. Research chemist E.I. duPont de Nemours & Co., Wilmington, Del., 1952-53, Buffalo, 1953-60, research supr., Richmond, Va., 1960—. Served with USNR, 1943-46. Mem. Am. Chem. Soc., Navy League, Sigma Xi, Lambda Chi Alpha. Club: Meadowbrook. Home: 2808 Bicknell Rd Richmond VA 23235 Office: PO Box 27222 Richmond VA 23219

GRONLUND, ROBERT BERNARD, univ. exec.; b. Duluth, Minn., May 2, 1926; s. Bernard and Lena J. (Manske) G.; student Ia. State Coll., 1943-44, Duluth Jr. Coll., 1944-47; U. Minn., 1946-47; B.A., Wartburg Coll., 1949; B.D., Wartburg Sem., 1953; postgrad. U. So. Cal., 1954-59; Litt.D., Thiel Coll., 1973; m. Dorothy M. Dahlstrom, June 2, 1951; children—Gaye, Robin, Gregg, Jamie. Ordained to ministry Luth. Ch., 1953; pastor Newport Harbor Luth. Ch., Newport, Cal., 1953-56; campus pastor Los Angeles City Coll., 1956-59; asst. to pres. Cal. Luth. Coll., Thousand Oaks, 1959-62; exec. dir. Am. Luth. Ch. Found., Mpls., 1962-63; v.p. devel. and pub. relations Capital U., Columbus, O., 1963-69, U. Tampa (Fla.), 1969—. Cons. fund raising and pub. relations to colls. and other charitable orgns.; lectr. various colls. Pres., Tampa Bay Art Center, 1971-72. Regent Augustana Acad., 1968-71. Served with AUS, 1944-46. Decorated Bronze Star. Mem. Am. Pub. Relations Assn., Pub. Relations Soc. Am. (chpt. pres. 1973, Silver Anvil award 1973), Nat. Soc. Fund Raisers. Republican. Rotarian. Clubs: University, Yacht and Country (Tampa). Contbr. articles to mags. Home: 2808 Samara Dr Tampa FL 33618

GROOM, DALE, educator, physician; b. Tulsa, Nov. 6, 1912; s. Fernando Hooker and Mary (Dale) G.; A.B., Hiram Coll., 1936; M.D., Med. Coll. Va., 1943; M.S., U. Minn., 1948; m. Marjorie Ruth Tweed, Jan. 26, 1944; children—Shelley Ann, Lincoln Dale, Randall Tweed. Intern, Northwestern U. Passavant Hosp., Chgo., 1943; fellow in medicine Mayo Clinic, 1945-49; practice medicine, specializing in internal medicine, Miami, 1949-53; asso. prof. medicine Med. Coll. S.C., 1953-68; prof. medicine, asso. dean for continuing edn. U. Okla. Med. Center, Oklahoma City, 1968—; mem. staff Univ. Hosp.; cons. Oklahoma City VA Hosp.; nat. cons. cardiology USAF, 1965—, FAA, 1970—. Bd. dirs. Ednl. Resources Found. Served to lt., M.C., USNR, 1944-45. Fellow A.C.P. (regent 1968—), Am. Coll. Cardiology, Council Clin. Cardiology, Am. Heart Assn.; mem. A.M.A. (council on sci. assembly 1965—), Mayo Cardiovascular Soc. (pres. 1971-73), Mayo Alumni Assn. (pres. 1969-71), Sigma Xi, Alpha Omega Alpha. Author: Clinics in Electrocardiography, 1961. Contbr. articles to profl. jours. Home: 3004 Red Oak Rd Oklahoma City OK 73120 Office: U Okla Med Center 800 NE 13th St Oklahoma City OK 73190

GROOM, THEODORE RICHARD, lawyer; b. Wichita, Kan., June 14, 1934; s. John Fuller and Carrie (Leggitt) G.; A.B., Bucknell U., 1956; LL.B., cum laude, Harvard, 1960; m. Virginia Woodard Miller, June 19, 1956; children—Catherine Martin, John Fuller, Theodore Warren. Admitted to Va. bar, 1960, D.C. bar, 1961; law clk. to chief judge U.S. Dist. Ct., Balt., Md., 1960-61; asso. firm Hedrick & Lane, Washington, 1961-67, mem., 1968—. Chmn., Citizens Police Com., Arlington, 1966; vice chmn. legislation com. Adminstrn. Justice, Washington, 1967-70; chmn. Arlington Fiscal Affairs Adv. Com., 1971, Criminal Justice Adv. Com., 1971, Arlington Criminal Justice Adv. Commn., 1972-73. Bd. dirs., finance chmn. Alcoholic Rehab., Inc., Arlington, 1966-69; chmn. Arlington Health and Welfare Council, 1969-70, No. Va. Recreation Authority, 1969-71; mem. Arlington Task Force on Drug Abuse. Finance chmn. various individual polit. campaigns, 1967. Served from lt. to capt., AUS, 1956-57, 60-61. Mem. Am. Va., D.C. bar assns., Phi Gamma Delta, Phi Sigma Alpha. Methodist (dir.). Contbr. articles to legal publs. Home: 4901 N 35th Rd Arlington VA 22207 Office: 1001 Connecticut Av Washington DC 20036

GROSCH, DANIEL SWARTWOOD, educator; b. Bethlehem, Pa., Oct. 25, 1918; s. Edgar Samuel and Laura Francis (Hoodmaker) G.; B.S., Moravian Coll., 1939; M.S., Lehigh U., 1940; Ph.D., U. Pa., 1944; m. Edith Dudley Taft, Mar. 27, 1944; children—Laura (Mrs. Herbert Jackson), Barbara (Mrs. M. Glenn Morris), Douglas Taft, Robert Levers, Gustav. Instr. zoology dept. U. Pa., 1941-44; asst. prof. zoology N.C. State U., Raleigh, 1946-51, asso. prof. genetics, 1951-57, prof., 1957—. Co-investigator U.S. Biosatellite Flights I and II, 1966-67. Served with AUS, 1944-46. Research grantee AEC, 1951-63, NASA, 1964-72, USPHS, 1964—. Mem. A.A.A.S., Am. Inst. Biol. Scis., Am. Soc. Naturalists, Entomol. Soc. Am., Genetics Soc., Radiation Research Soc., Am. Assn. U. Profs., N.C. Acad. Scis., Sigma Xi, Phi Kappa Phi. Mem. Moravian Ch. Author: Biological Effects of Radiations, 1965. Contbr. articles to profl. jours. Home: 1222 Duplin Rd Raleigh NC 27607

GROSCHEL, DIETER HANS MAX, physician, educator; b. Wurzburg, Germany, May 13, 1931; s. Friedrich Wilhelm and Anne (Burger) G.; med. grad. U. Wurzburg, Erlangen and Cologne, 1957; Dr. med., U. Cologne, 1958; m. A. Margarete Pustelny, June 9, 1958; children—Anne, Henrike. Came to U.S., 1963, naturalized, 1969. Intern, U. Cologne, 1957-59, resident, 1959-60, asso., instr. Inst. Hygiene, 1960-63; asso. Wistar Inst., Phila., 1963-65; asso. prof. microbiology Temple U., 1965-68; dir. microbiology and infectious diseases Springfield (Mass.) Hosp., 1968-71; asso. prof. pathology U. Tex. M.D. Anderson Hosp. and Tumor Inst., Houston, 1971—; asso. prof. medicine and pathology U. Tex. Med. Sch., Houston, 1973—; mem. staff Hermann Hosp., Houston. Served with Deutscher Volkssturm, 1945. Fulbright/Scholar U. Colo., 1954-55. Diplomate Am. Bd. Med. Microbiology. Fellow Am. Acad. Microbiology; mem. German Soc. Hygiene and Microbiology, Am. Soc. Microbiology, Am. Assn. Hist. Medicine, Reticuloendothelial Soc., Am. Fedn. Clin. Research, Fedn. Am. Scientists, Am., Mass., Tex. med. assns., Sigma Xi. Home: 17 Valley Forge Dr Houston TX 77024 Office: 6723 Bertner Dr Houston TX 77025

GROSECLOSE, FRANK SNIDER, stock broker; b. Houston, June 4, 1935; s. Frank Edwin and Katherine (Snider) G.; B.B.A., So. Meth. U., 1956; m. Carol Jean Conkle, July 14, 1964; children—Laura Jean, Christine Michelle. Trader, mgr. underwriting dept. E.F. Hutton & Co., Dallas, 1958-65; v.p., mgr. Godnick & Son, Inc., Dallas, 1965-71, Filer, Schmidt & Co., Dallas, 1971—; tchr. corporate seminars. Served with USAF, 1958-64. Mem. Dallas Assn. Security Dealers (pres. 1972), Delta Sigma Pi, Sigma Alpha Epsilon. Home: 3409 Centenary St Dallas TX 75225 Office: First National Bank Bldg Dallas TX 75202

GROSS, DONALD, educator; b. Pitts., Oct. 20, 1934; s. Frank and Marion (Horovitz) G.; B.S., Carnegie Mellon U., 1956; M.S., Cornell U., 1959, Ph.D., 1962; m. Alice Gold, Sept. 20, 1959; children—Stephanie, Joanne. Operations research analyst Atlantic-Richfield Co., Phila., 1961-65; asst. prof. George Washington U., Washington, 1965-67, asso. prof. dept. operations research Sch. Engring. and Applied Sci., 1967—. Cons. Inst. Defense Analyses, 1965-66, Research Analysis Corp., 1967-70, Univ. Research Forum, 1973—, U.S. Govt., 1969—. Mem. Alexandria (Va.) Beautification Com., 1972-73. Served to 1st lt., Signal Corps, AUS, 1962-63. IBM fellow, 1956-58. Mem. Operations Research soc. Am., Inst. Mgmt. Scis., Am. Inst. Indsl. Engrs., Washington Operations Research Council (pres. 1974—), Sigma Xi, Tau Beta Pi, Phi Kappa Phi, Pi Tau Sigma. Home: 3530 N Rockingham St Arlington VA 22213 Office: Dept Operations Research Sch Engring and Applied Sci George Washington U Washington DC 20006

GROSS, JOHN C(HARLES), broker, industrialist; b. N.Y.C., Apr. 2, 1904; s. Edward H. and Anna Catharine (Muelhaus) G.; student pub. schs. N.Y.C.; m. Helen Victoria Newman, Sept. 26, 1926; 1 dau., Jean Anne. Pres., treas., dir. John C. Gross, Inc.; treas., dir. Gen. Automation of Del., Gen. Automation Fla., Metrodynamics Corp.; pres., treas., dir. Yacht Club Island. Corp., Yacht Club Island Apts.; pres., treas. Ponce de Leon Corp., Artifacts Recovery Corp.; pres., dir. New Smyrna Subcontractors Corp. Mem. Com. of 100 of New Smyrna Beach; mem. Edgewater (Fla.) Planning Bd.; chmn. S.E. Volusia Area Devel. Council. Mem. Nat. Assn. Security Dealers, New Smyrna Beach C. of C. Lutheran (council). Rotarian. Home: 404 N Riverside Dr Edgewater FL 32032 Office: 316 Canal St New Smyrna Beach FL 32069

GROSS, JOHN HENRY, ret. physician; b. Fairy Hill, Can., Nov. 18, 1910; came to U.S. 1949, naturalized 1954; s. Phillip and Eva (Armbruster) G.; B.S., U. Sask., 1935; M.D., U. Man., Winnipeg, 1940; m. Margaret MacDonald, July 31, 1937 (dec. Sept. 1969); 1 son, David Ian, m. 2d, Jimmie N. Gunter, Nov. 26, 1970. Staff physician Sask. Anti-TB League, Fort San, Sask., 1940-49; resident Matson Meml. Hosp., Milwaukie, Ore., 1948; staff physician and asst. chief Battey State Hosp., Rome, Ga., 1949-57, chief of all white treatment wards and asst. to supt., 1957-64, dir. outpatient services dept., co-ordinator med. services, 1964-70, clin. dir. div. Tb Control Service Tb Br. State Ga., 1970-71. Charter mem. bd. dirs. Boy's Club of Rome. Served as maj. M.C., AUS, 1950-52; lt. col. Res. Licentiate Med. Council Canada. Fellow Am. Coll. Chest Physicians; mem. Am. Thoracic Soc. (past pres. Ga. chpt.), Coll. Physicians and Surgeons of Sask., Am., Ga. med. assns., Floyd County Med. Soc. Contbr. articles to profl. jours. Home: 10 Elizabeth St Rome GA 30161

GROSS, MAX SIDNEY, brokerage exec.; b. Trenton, Apr. 13, 1928; s. I. Irving and Hildred A. (Ehrlich) G.; student N.Y. Inst. Finance, 1956; m. Cora Lee Kaufmann, May 22, 1955; children—Caren, James, Gary, Steven. Dist. mgr. Reeds Stores Corp., Trenton, 1946-56; registered rep. Ungerleider & Co., N.Y.C., 1952-58; with Bache & Co. Inc., N.Y.C., 1958—, br. mgr., 1965-69, 70-72, dist. v.p., 1971, regional 1st v.p., 1969-70, 72-74, sr. v.p. charge domestic and Canadian offices, dir., 1974—. Vice pres., dir. Md. Diamond & Jewelry Exchange. Bd. dirs., treas. Jewish Community Center, Washington. Mem. Washington Soc. Financial Analysts, Washington Bd. Trade, Security Traders Assn. Washington (co-founder, past v.p.), Bond Club Washington (treas.), Nat. Economists Club. Jewish religion (bd. mgrs. congregation). Club: Woodmont Country. Home: 6405 Kennedy Dr Chevy Chase MD 20015 Office: 1000 16th St NW Washington DC 20036

GROSS, SAMSON RICHARD, biochemist, educator; b. N.Y.C., July 27, 1926; s. Isidor and Ethel (Mermelestein) G.; B.A., N.Y. U., 1949; A.M., Columbia, 1951, Ph.D. (USPHS fellow), 1953; m. Helen Hudi Steinmetz, Sept. 16, 1952; children—Deborah Ann, Michael Robert, Eva Elizabeth. Asst. prof. genetics Stanford, 1956-57, Rockefeller U., N.Y.C., 1957-60; asso. prof. dept. microbiology and immunology Duke, Durham, N.C., 1960-65, dir. grad. studies dept. biochemistry, 1963-65, prof. genetics and biochemistry, 1965—, dir. div. genetics dept. biochemistry 1965—, dir. univ. program in genetics, 1967—. Bd. dirs. Cold Spring Harbor (N.Y.) Lab. Quantitative Biology, 1967-72. USPHS Spl. fellow Weizmann Inst., 1969-70. Mem Genetic Soc. Am., Am. Genetic Assn., A.A.A.S., Am. Soc. Microbiology, Am. Soc. Biol. Chemists, Phi Beta Kappa. Home: 2411 Prince St Durham NC 27707

GROSSBERG, MARC ELIAS, lawyer; b. Houston, Dec. 26, 1940; s. Sylvester Harold and Leah (Hochman) G.; B.S., U. Houston, 1961; J.D. with honors, U. Tex., 1965; m. Pepi Stern, Sept. 5, 1962; children—Lee Ann, Toni Helene. Admitted to Tex. bar, 1965, Cal. bar, 1966; law clk. to Judge Walter Ely, U.S. Ct. Appeals, 9th Circuit, Los Angeles, 1965-66; atty. Fulbright & Crooker, Houston, 1966-71; gen. counsel BH&L Industries, Inc., Houston, 1973—, also dir.; gen. counsel Peden Industries, Inc., Houston, 1973—; individual practice law, Houston, 1971—; dir. Star Furniture Co., Houston. Pres., Tex. Bill of Rights Found., 1972-74; vice chmn. Houston chpt. Am. Jewish Com., 1973—. Advance man, speech writer for Hubert H. Humphrey, 1968 Presdl. Campaign. Bd. dirs. Jewish Family Service, Houston Legal Found., Peaceable Kingdom Found.; founding trustee Harris County Pretrial Release Agy. C.P.A., Tex. Mem. Am. Bar Assn., Tex. Soc. C.P.A.'s, Snake River Soc., Order Coif. Clubs: Coronado, Tejas Breakfast (Houston). Home: 629 Wellesley St Houston TX 77024 Office: PO Box 53089 Houston TX 77052 also 608 N San Jacinto Houston TX 77002

GROSSBERG, ROBERT HENRY, stock broker; b. Bklyn., July 29, 1936; s. Harry M. and Ann (Kinsbrunner) G.; grad. high sch.; m. Patricia Madison, Dec. 29, 1955; children—Nadine, Andrea. With H. Hentz & Co., 1963—, asst. v.p., 1968—; asst. v.p. Hayden Stone, Inc., Miami, 1973—. Exec. dir. U.S. Amateur Jai-Alai Players Assn., 1966—. Served with AUS, 1955-57. Home: 770 NW 197th Terrace Miami FL 33169 Office: 100 SE 2d Av Miami FL 33131

GROSSEL-ROSSI, MARION NICHOLAS, lawyer; b. New Orleans, June 22, 1931; s. Arthur and Helen G. (Troyanovich) G-R; B.S., Tulane U., 1955, LL.B., 1962. Geologist, Forest Oil Corp., Lafayette, La., 1955-59; admitted to La. bar, 1962; with firm Jackson & Hess, New Orleans, 1962-63; partner firm Leach & Grossel-Rossi, New Orleans, 1963-68, Leach, Grossel-Rossi & Paysse, 1968—; sec.-treas. Elisan Corp., New Orleans. Bd. govs. Southeastern Admiralty Law Inst. Mem. Am., La. bar assns., Maritime Law Assn. U.S., Am. Judicature Soc., New Orleans Assn. Def. Counsel, La. Hist. Soc., Upper Audubon Assn. (pres. 1971-72), Audubon Soc., Nat. Rifle Assn., Internat. Oceanographic Found., La. Bromeliad Soc., Def. Research Inst., Am. Arbitration Assn. (panel arbitrators), La. Assn. Def. Counsel. Clubs: Essex, Sports Car of America (pres. Delta region 1965), South Louisiana Gun, Delta Rifle and Pistol. Home: 282 Audubon St New Orleans LA 70118 Office: 1 Shell Sq New Orleans LA 70130

GROSSER, ELMER JOSEPH, ednl. adminstr.; b. Dayton, Ky., Aug. 31, 1922; s. Albert Joseph and Rose Mary (Wiegand) G.; B.A., St. Gregory Sem., 1943; postgrad. Mt. St. Mary Sem., 1943-46; M.A., U. Toronto, 1949, Ph.D., 1953. Ordained priest Roman Catholic Ch., 1946; missionary, N.D., 1947; dir. Newman Club, U. Ky., Lexington, 1947-49; prof. philosophy Holy Cross Sem., Lacrosse, Wis., 1954-56; founder Sem. St. Pius X, Erlanger, Ky., 1955, rector, 1955-71, pres., 1971—; pastor Ch. Blessed Sacrament, Fort Mitchell, Ky., 1971—. Domestic prelate, 1956; consultor Diocese Covington, 1958. Address: 2415 Dixie Hwy Ft Mitchell KY 41017

GROSSKREUTZ, DORIS C., physician, educator; b. Moline, Ill., 1918; M.D., U. Ill., 1942. Intern Wis. Gen. Hosp., Madison, 1942-43; resident anesthesiology Hartford (Conn.) Hosp., 1949-51; mem. staff gen. practice Protestant Deaconess Hosp., Evansville, Ind. and St. Mary's Hosp., Evansville, 1943-49; mem. staff anesthesiolgy Grace-New Haven Community Hosp., 1951-54, N.C. Meml. Hosp., 1954-56, 59; chief dept. anesthesiology VA Hosp., Durham, N.C., 1956-57, San Antonio State Chest Hosp., 1968—; instr. anesthesiology Yale, 1951-54; asst. prof. U. N.C., 1954-57, asso. prof., 1959-62; clin. prof. anesthesiology U. Tex. Med. Sch. at San Antonio, 1965—. Diplomate Am. Bd. Anesthesiology. Fellow Am. Coll. Anesthesiologists; mem. A.M.A., Am. Soc. Anesthesiology, Internat. Anesthesiology Research Soc. Address: 4306 Forest Green San Antonio TX 78222

GROSSMAN, LAURENCE ABRAHAM, physician; b. Nashville, Tenn., Sept. 21, 1916; s. Henry and Etta (Rothstein) G.; B.A., Vanderbilt U., 1938; M.D., 1941; m. Dorothy Ruth Huffine, Oct. 17, 1942; children—Diana Gail (Mrs. Robert L. Officer), Linda Marie, Susanne, J. Anne. Intern, Vanderbilt U. Hosp., Nashville, 1941-42, resident, 1946-47, now staff; practice medicine, specializing in internal medicine and cardiology, Nashville, 1947—; mem. staff St. Thomas, Bapt. hosps.; clin. prof. medicine Vanderbilt U., Meharry Med. Coll., 1960—; med. dir. Am. Health Profiles, 1971—. Served from 1st lt. to maj. AUS, 1942-45. Diplomate Am. Bd. Internal Medicine. Fellow A.C.P., Am. Coll. Chest Physicians, Am. Coll. Cardiology; mem. Nashville Acad. Medicine, Tenn. Med. Assn. (dist. councillor 1959-63), Tenn. Soc. Internal Medicine (pres. 1957-58), Middle Tenn. (pres. 1956-57), Tenn. (pres. 1965-66) heart assns. Home: 4300 Lillywood Rd Nashville TN 37205 Office: 1816 Hayes St Nashville TN 37203

GROSSMAN, MAURICE SIDNEY, physician; b. Corpus Christi, Tex., June 1, 1927; s. Edward and Sarah (Mushlin) G.; B.A., U. Tex., 1948, M.D., 1952; m. Lois Ruth Rosen, May 20, 1957; children—Carla, Daryl, Sandor. Intern medicine, asst. resident internal medicine St. Louis City Hosp., 1953-54; sr. resident internal medicine New Eng. Center Hosp., Boston, 1954-55; chief fellow gastroenterology Lahey Clinic, Boston, 1955-56; mem. staff New Eng. Bapt. Hosp., also New Eng. Deaconess Hosp., Boston, 1955-56; pvt. practice internal medicine and gastroenterology, Corpus Christi, 1957—; chief dept. medicine Spohn Hosp.; mem. staff Meml. Hosp.; lectr. med. groups. Served to maj., AUS Res., 1965-61; served with USNR, 1945-46. Diplomate Am. Bd. Internal Medicine. Fellow A.C.P., Am. Coll. Gastroenterology (exec. council 1973); mem. A.M.A., So. Med. Assn., Am. Soc. Internal Medicine, Am. Gastroenterol. Assn. (asso.), Tex. Acad. Internal Medicine, Corpus Christi Acad. Internal Medicine (pres. 1969), Sigma Alpha Mu, Alpha Epsilon Delta. Jewish religion. Contbr. articles profl. jours. Home: 321 Bayshore Dr Corpus Christi TX 78412 Office: 1001 Louisiana Pkwy Corpus Christic TX 74804

GROSSMAN, MAX R., pub. affairs cons. editor; b. Odessa, Russia, April 21, 1904; s. Abraham and Celia (Tocman) A.; B.B.A., Boston U., 1926, M.B.A., 1930, Ed.M., Sch. Edn., 1929; Harvard, 1935; m. Manya Kaufman, Mar. 26, 1931; children—Lysbeth R., Michael Baruch. Reporter, Pawtucket (R.I.) Times, 1926-28; feature writer Boston Sunday Post, 1929-43; news commentator sta. WEEI, Boston, 1938-40; instr. journalism, Boston U., 1929-31, asst. prof., 1931-35, asso. prof., 1935-39, prof. and head dept., 1939-47; provost Brandeis U., 1947-50; mem. Civic Edn. Project, Cambridge, 1950-51; pub. affairs officer USIA, Frankfurt am Main, Germany, 1951-57, Washington, 1957-61; cultural attache Am. Embassy, Quito, Ecuador, 1961-62; cultural affairs officer, Am. Embassy, London, Eng., 1964-68; forum editor for Voice of Am., USIA, 1962-64, 68-71; pub. affairs cons., 1971—; Washington corr. Finance mag., 1971—; exec. dir. Inst. Certified Travel Agts., 1972—. Writers sect. OWI, 1944-45; sect. chief journalism Biarritz American (France), 1945-46; mng. editor Biarritz Daily Banner, 1945-46; roving corr. The Stars and Stripes (Germany), 1946; lectr. various Brit. univs. and pub. schs. Mem. Fulbright Commn., Quito and London. Mem. Am. Assn. Tchrs. Journalism, English Speaking Union, Am. Assn. Schs. and Depts. of Journalism (pres. 1944-45), Am. Assn. U. Profs., Beta Gamma Sigma, Kappa Tau Alpha (nat. pres. 1944-45), Kappa Omega Sigma. Mason (32 deg.). Clubs: Mass. Press Association; Nat. Press (Washington); Overseas Press (N.Y.C.); Frankfurt Press (Germany); Savile (London). Contbr. articles to mags., newspapers. Address: 603 G St SW Washington DC 20024

GROSSMAN, ROBERT GEORGE, physician, educator; b. N.Y.C., Jan. 24, 1933; s. Ferenc and Vivian (Isenberg) G.; B.A., Swarthmore Coll., 1953; M.D., Columbia, 1957; m. Ellin Friedman, June 26, 1955; children—Amy, Kate, Ruth. Intern, Strong Meml. Hosp., Rochester, N.Y., 1957-58; resident Presbyn. Hosp., Columbia, 1960-63; practice medicine specializing in neurol. surgery, Galveston, Tex., 1973—; instr., asso. prof. neurosurgery U. Tex. S.W. Med. Sch., 1963-68; asso. prof., prof. neurol. surgery Albert Einstein Coll. Medicine, 1969-73; prof., chmn. div. neurol. surgery U. Tex. Med. Br., Galveston, 1973—. Chmn. neurology B study sect. USPHS, NIH, 1972—. Served with AUS, 1958-60. Mem. Am. Assn. Neurol. Surgeons, A.C.S. Author: (with W.D. Willis) Medical Neurobiology, 1973. Home: 18723 Point Lookout Dr Nassau Bay TX 77058 Office: U Tex Med Br Galveston TX 77550

GROSVENOR, DONNA KERKAM (MRS. GILBERT M. GROSVENOR), journalist; b. Washington, July 16, 1938; d. John Freeman and Eleanor (Beck) Kerkam; B.A., Sweet Briar Coll., 1960; m. Gilbert Melville Grosvenor, June 16, 1961; children—Gilbert Hovey, Alexandra Rowland. Various assignments Nat. Geog. mag. and Nat. Geog. Sch. Bull., Egypt. East Africa, Ceylon, Monaco, Indonesia, Washington, 1961—. Sec., Jr. League, Washington, 1966-67; mem. Smithsonian Assos. Ladies Com., 1967-69; mem. bd. Friends Nat. Zoo, 1968—, Child Health Center of Childrens Hosp., 1965—; mem. exec. com. Project Hope, 1967-68; mem. governing bd. Nat. Cathedral Sch., 1972—. Mem. Soc. Woman Geographers, Nat. Cathedral Sch. Alumni Assn. (exec. bd. sec. 1965-68). Clubs: Sulgrave, Washington. Author: Pandas. Home: 1259 Crest Lane McLean VA 22101

GROSVENOR, GILBERT MELVILLE, magazine editor; b. Washington, May 5, 1931; s. Melville Bell and Helen (Rowland) G.; grad. Deerfield Acad., 1950; B.A., Yale, 1954; m. Donna C. Kerkam, June 16, 1961; children—Gilbert Hovey II, Alexandra Rowland. With Nat. Geog. Soc., 1954—, trustee, v.p., 1966—, asso. editor, 1967-70, editor, 1970—. dir. Am. Security & Trust Co., Washington, Ferris & Co., Inc. Bd. dirs. D.C. Soc. for Crippled Children, Alexander Graham Bell Assn. for Deaf; trustee N.Y. Zool. Soc., Conservation Found.; trustee, sec.-treas. African Wildlife Leadership Found.; trustee, treas. Mt. Vernon Jr. Coll.; bd. overseers Sweet Briar Coll.; ann. corp. mem. Children's Hosp. D.C. Served with AUS, 1954-56. Mem. Soc. Am. Geographers, Newcomen Soc. Clubs: Alfalfa, Yale, Overseas Writers; Metropolitan (Washington); Explorers (N.Y.C.); Chevy Chase (Md.) (gov.). Home: 1259 Crest Lane McLean VA 22101 Office: Nat Geographic Soc 17th and M Sts NW Washington DC 20036

GROSVENOR, MELVILLE BELL, editor; b. Washington, Nov. 26, 1901; s. Gilbert Hovey and Elsie May (Bell) G.; B.S., U.S. Naval Acad., 1923; Sc.D., U. Miami (Fla.), 1954; LL.D., George Washington U., 1959; Litt.D., Boston U., 1970; m. Helen North Rowland, Jan. 4, 1924; children—Helen Rowland (Mrs. Richard Lemmerman), Alexander Graham Bell, Gilbert Melville; m. 2d, Anne

E. Revis, Aug. 12, 1950; children—Edwin Stuart, Sara Anne. Asst. chief illustrations div. Nat. Geog. mag., 1924-35, asst. editor, 1935-54, asso. editor, 1954-57, editor, 1957-67, editor in chief, 1967—; adv. dir. Riggs Nat. Bank. Trustee Nat. Geog. Soc., v.p., 1954-57, pres., editor, 1957-67, chmn. bd., 1967—. Trustee U. Miami, George Washington U., Jackson Hole Preserve, Inc. Decorated Mil. Order of Christ (Portugal); commendatore del ordine al Merito della Republica Italiana; recipient Nat. Park Service Conservation award, Horace Albright Conservation award, Eisenhower medal People to People, Inc., 1970. Clubs: Cosmos, Metropolitan, National Press, Chevy Chase, Overseas Writers, Gibson Island, Bath (Miami, Fla.), Cruising Club of Am. Author numerous articles in Nat. Geog. Mag. Editor-in-chief: America's Wonderlands-The National Parks; Wild Animals of North America; America's Historylands; Men, Ships and the Sea; Great Adventures; Birds of North America, Vol. I, Song and Garden, Vol. II, Water, Prey and Game, Wondrous World of Fishes; National Geographic Atlas of World; Indians of the Americas; Man's Best Friend; This England; Life in Bible Times; Greece and Rome: Builders of World; Age of Chivalry. Home: 5510 Grosvenor Lane Bethesda MD 20014 Office: Nat Geog Soc 17th and M Sts NW Washington DC 20036

GROTE, CARL AUGUST, JR., physician; b. Huntsville, Ala., Oct. 19, 1928; s. Carl August and Willie (Barrier) G.; A.B., Vanderbilt U., 1950, M.D., 1954; m. Carole Buzbee, Mar. 26, 1964; children—Mary Eleanor, Carl August, Jane Elizabeth, Charles David. Intern Butterworth Hosp., Grand Rapids, Mich., 1954-55; resident H.P. Long Hosp., Pineville, La., 1957-58; practice gen. medicine, Huntsville, 1958—; mem. exec. com. staff Huntsville Hosp., 1966—, also pres. staff, 1969—. Mem. Madison County Bd. Health and Bd. Censors, 1967-70, chmn., 1971—. Bd. dirs. Ala. Polit. Action Com. Served to capt. M.C., AUS, 1955-57. Diplomate Am. Bd. Family Practice. Mem. Am. Acad. Gen. Practice (Ala. bd. dirs.), Med. Assn. Ala. (Coll. Counselors), A.M.A. Editors Ala. Family Physician Jour., 1967-69. Home: 1807 Mt Brook St Huntsville AL 35801 Office: 700 Green St SE Huntsville AL 35801

GROTEFEND, MARY EMERY, nursing educator, sociologist; b. Wetmore, Kan., Dec. 1, 1910; d. Edward Henry Herbert and Lucy (Ward) Emery; R.N., Bethany Hosp. Sch. Nursing 1931; B.A., Baker U., 1934; M.S., Catholic U. Am., 1944; postgrad. U. Md., 1948-51; Ph.D. in Sociology, Am. U., 1966; m. Ralph L. Grotefend, July 1, 1937 (dec. Mar. 1963); 1 son, Edward Emery. Sci. instr. Jameson Hosp. Sch. Nursing, New Castle, Pa., 1934-35, Columbia Hosp. Sch. Nursing. Milw., 1935-37; ednl. dir. Burge Hosp. Sch. Nursing, Springfield, Mo., 1938-40; sci. instr., asst. dir. Sch. Nursing and Nursing Service. W. Balt. Gen. Hosp., 1941-47; social sci. instr., asst. prof. pub. health nursing U. Md., College Park and Balt., 1947-65, asso. prof. pub. health nursing, 1965-68; project dir. Facilitation of Student Learning through Meaningful Use of Community Resources, also asso. prof. Med. Coll. Ga., Augusta, 1968-71; asso. prof., chmn. nursing div. South Ga. Coll., Douglas, 1971-73. Chmn. social sci. com. Md. Bd. Examiners of Nurses, 1946-47. Mem. Am., Md. (sec. dist. 2, 1946-48), (mem.-at-large exec. com. pub. health sect. 1958-60), Mo. (pres. dist. 4, 1940) nurses assns., Nat., Md. (chmn. membership com. 1945-47) leagues for nursing, Am. Sociol. Assn., Am. Assn. U. Profs., Am. Assn. U. Women, Mental Health Assn., Am. Pub. Health Assn., Women's Soc. Christian Service (pres. 1969-71), League Women Voters, Zeta Tau Alpha, Sigma Theta Tau (organizer, counselor Pi chpt., faculty adviser 1957-60). Methodist (local bd. stewards 1956-59, chmn. commn. on missions 1956-60). Clubs: Augusta Kennel, Dalmatian of America. Contbr. articles profl. jours. Home: Green Acre Farms PO Box 1022 Douglas GA 31533

GROUPE, VINCENT, biologist; b. Phila., Sept. 13, 1918; s. Andrew V. and Georgia (Paterson) G.; B.A., Wesleyan U., 1939; Ph.D., U. Pa., 1942; m. Gerry Finley Nash, Mar. 30, 1942; children—David Vincent, Lawrence Nash. Research asst. Children's Hosp., Phila., 1941-42; bacteriologist E. R. Squibb & Sons, New Brunswick, N.J., 1942-44; research asso. Squibb Inst. Med. Research, New Brunswick, 1944-47; asso. prof. Storrs (Conn.) Agrl. Expt. Sta., 1947-49; asso. prof. microbiology Rutgers U., New Brunswick, N.J., 1949-54, prof. virology, 1954-68, vis. prof., 1968-70; v.p. Life Scis., Inc., St. Petersburg, Fla., 1968—, pres. Life Scis. Research Labs. Cons., Nat. Cancer Inst., Bethesda, Md., Carter-Wallace Labs., Cranbury, N.J. Trustee Princeton Group Arts, New Life Found., The Science Center. Recipient citation for Outstanding Achievement as Tchr. and Scholar Wesleyan U., 1959. Fellow Am. Acad. Microbiology, N.Y. Acad. Medicine, N.Y. Acad. Scis., A.A.A.S.; mem. C. of C., Com. of 100, Pinellas Mfrs. Assn., Am. Assn. Cancer Research, Soc. Exptl. Biology and Medicine, Am. Assn. Immunologists, Soc. Protozoologists. Research in cancer viruses, virus chemotherapy. Home: 444 Bath Club Blvd N St Petersburg FL 33708 Office: 2900 72d St N St Petersburg Fl 33710

GROVAS, RAFAEL, clergyman; b. San Juan, P.R., Nov. 26, 1905; s. Jose and Marcelina (Felix) G.; student Seminario de San Ildefonso, San Juan, 1917-20, Pontificio Collegio Pio Latino Americano, Rome, Italy, 1920-28; Ph.D., Pontificia Universita Gregoriana, Rome, 1923; S.T.D., 1927, licentiate canon law, 1928. Ordained priest Roman Catholic Ch., 1928; chancellor Diocese San Juan, 1933-60; named domestic prelate, 1942, protonotary apostolic, 1954; consecrated 1st bishop, Caguas, P.R., 1965. Mem. Academia de Artes y Ciencias de P.R. Address: Bishop's House Box 698 Caguas PR 00625

GROVE, EDWARD RYNEAL, artist, sculptor; b. Martinsburg, W.Va., Aug. 14, 1912; s. Harry Muth and Bertha Mae (Sigler) G.; art studies Nat. Sch. Art, Washington, 1933-34, Corcoran Sch. Art, Washington, 1934-37, 40-45, Robert Brackman, 1946; m. Jean Virginia Donner, June 24, 1936; children—David Donner, Eric Donner. Die sinker, 1936-40; vignette and portrait engraver Bur. Engraving and Printing, Washington, 1940-47, Security-Columbian Banknote Co., Phila., 1947-62; sculptor-engraver U.S. Mint, Phila., 1962-65; free lance artist, West Palm Beach, Fla., 1965—; works exhibited one man shows Nat. Philatelic Mus., Phila., 1954, Phila. Art Alliance, 1960, Norton Gallery Art, West Palm Beach, 1971; works exhibited Cayuga Mus. History and Art, Auburn, N.Y., 1964, Episcopal Acad. Gallery, Phila., 1966, nat. and regional annual exhibits; works rep. permanent collections U. Pa. Div. Grad. Medicine, Pangborn Corp., Hagerstown, Md., Pa. Hist. Soc., Phila., Am. Bag & Paper Corp., Phila., U.S. Dept. Navy, Smithsonian Instn., Rehab. Inst. Chgo., The Citadel, Washington Cathedral, Ch. of Bethesda-by-the-Sea, Palm Beach, Fla., Coventry (Eng.) Cathedral; instr. drawing and portraiture Flagler Art Center, West Palm Beach, 1972-73; works include Congl. gold medal for Bob Hope, 1963, World War II medal series, 1966-70, mural Ch. of Holy Comforter, Drexel Hill, Pa., 1952-58, four coin set for Knights of Malta, 1965. Recipient bronze medals Washington Landscape Club, 1945, 53, Grumbacher watercolor award Cumberland Valley Art Exhibit, Hagerstown, 1965, Lindsey Morris meml. prize Nat. Sculpture Soc., 1967, Bennett meml. prize, 1971, gold medal Am. Numismatic Assn., 1969, Alphabet medal Soc. Medalists, 1973. Fellow Nat. Sculpture Soc.; mem. Artists Equity Assn. (nat. v.p. 1965-67), Soc. Washington Artists, Engravers Guild, Steel and Copper Plate Engravers League Phila. (pres. 1957-59), Phila. Art Alliance, Phila. Sketch Club, Am. Numismatic Assn., Art Mus. Palm Beaches, Soc. Four Arts, English Speaking Union, Mensa. Republican. Episcopalian (vestryman). Mem. Knights of Malta. Club: Palm Beach Yacht. Contbr. articles to profl. jours. and books. Home and studio: Sea Lake Studio 3215 S Flagler Dr West Palm Beach FL 33405

GROVE, ERNEST WILSON, economist; b. New Kensington, Pa., June 14, 1910; s. Edward Thomas and Adelaide (Wilson) G.; A.B., U. Cal. at Berkeley, 1932, Ph.D., 1948; m. Esther Elizabeth Krewson, Mar. 8, 1947; children—Kathryn Frances, Daniel Edward. Agrl. economist Bur. Agrl. Econs., U.S. Dept. Agr., 1936-41, 46-53, head farm income estimates sect. Agrl. Econs. Div., editor The Farm Income Situation, Washington, 1954-60; staff economist Agrl. Stabilization and Conservation Service, 1960—. Chmn. Citizens Com. for Sch. Improvement Arlington, Va., 1961-62; mem. Arlington Pub. Utilities Commn., 1963-64; chmn., 1964. Served from 2d lt. to lt. col. Control Div., Hdqrs. Army Service Forces, AUS, 1942-45. Decorated Legion of Merit. Fellow A.A.A.S.; mem. Am. Econ. Assn., Am. Agrl. Econs. Assn., Am. Statis. Assn., Conf. on Research in Income and Wealth, Internat. Conf. Agrl. Economists, Nat. Economists Club, Internat. Platform Assn., Phi Beta Kappa, Delta Sigma Rho, Omicron Delta Epsilon. Author jour. articles. Home: 5429 S 5th St Arlington VA 22204 Office: Dept of Agr Washington DC 20250

GROVE, JAMES ROBERT, welding equipment co. exec.; b. Larned, Kan., May 1, 1931; s. James and Marie (Purcell) G.; B.S. in Mech. Engring., Kan. State U., 1954; m. Beverly Ann Jones, May 31, 1952; children—Hollice K., Jay Robert, Jeffery Jones, James Andrew. Sales engr. Union Carbide Corp., Kansas City, Mo., 1954-55, Amarillo, Tex., 1955-57, Houston, 1957-60, mgr., Houston, 1960-63; v.p. Indsl. Welding Equipment Co. and Indsl. Welding Equipment Co. Rentals, Inc., Houston, 1963-67; pres. Alloy Weld Supply Co., 1967—, Indsl. Welding Equipment Co., Inc., So. Welding Supply, Indsl. Welding Equipment Co. Rentals, Inc., (all Houston), 1969—, IWECO, Inc., IWECO of Houston, Cryo Equipment Co., S.W. Welding Equipment Co., 1970—; v.p. Reilco Corp., Houston, 1969—; v.p., sec-treas. Alltea Welding Supply, Clute, Tex., 1970—. Mem. Pi Tu Sigma, Phi Delta Theta. Presbyn. (deacon 1960, elder 1962—). Rotarian (mem. com. 1969—). Club: Brae Burn Country (Houston). Home: 343 Knipp Forest Houston TX 77024 Office: 8350 Moseley St Houston TX 77034

GROVE, RICHARD EDWARD, educator; b. Winchester, Va., Dec. 20, 1926; s. Maynard Edward and Eva Grace (Anderson) G.; B.S., Randolph Macon Coll., 1947; M.A., Johns Hopkins, 1950; Ph.D. (So. Fellowship Fund fellow), Syracuse U., 1959; m. Leatrice Ann Voorhees, Apr. 13, 1957; children—Elizabeth Virginia, Richard Edward. Instr. physics Susquehanna U., Selinsgrove, Pa., 1950-53; asst. prof. physics Randolph-Macon Coll., Ashland, Va., 1953-57, prof. physics, 1957-68, dir. computer center, 1963-70, chmn. dept. physics, 1964-68, prof. computer sci., 1968-70; dir. univ. computer center Va. Commonwealth U., Richmond, 1970-73, dir. computing activities, 1973—. Mem. Assn. for Computing Machinery, Phi Beta Kappa, Omicron Delta Kappa. Home: 607 Glendale Dr Richmond VA 23229 Office: 1015 Floyd Dr Richmond VA 23284

GROVES, IVOR DURHAM, JR., physicist, govt. ofcl.; b. Bowling Green, Ky., Dec. 30, 1919; s. Ivor Durham and Jane Robinson (Atkinson) G.; B.S., Rollins Coll., 1948, M.B.A., 1964; student Oak Ridge Inst. Nuclear Studies, 1949-50; m. Marjorie Louise Lee, Aug. 5, 1944; children—Ivor D., Carol (Mrs. Richard Noland), Gail. Engr. Orlando (Fla.) Broadcasting Co., Inc., 1941-42, 45-48; electronic engr. Union Carbide Co., Oak Ridge, Tenn., 1948-51; physicist Naval Research Lab. underwater sound reference div., Orlando, 1951—. Guest lectr. Tex. A. and M. U., College Station, 1973, U. Fla., Orlando, 1970. Served to capt. USAF, 1943-45. Recipient Sec. Navy Cost Reduction Program award, 1971, Naval Research Lab. Ann. Research Publ. award, 1971. Mem. Acoustical Soc. Am. (mem. tech. com. engring. acoustics 1969-74), Fla. Acoustical Soc. (treas. 1973), Delta Chi. Baptist (deacon 1952—). Home: 518 Baxter St Orlando FL 32806 Office: PO Box 8337 Orlando FL 32806

GROVES, SIDNEY KEPLER, elec. engr.; b. Rome, Ind., Jan. 26, 1917; s. Sidney Kepler and Dessa (Ramsey) G.; B.S. with distinction, Purdue U., 1937 m. Virginia Leonore Lehman, June 14, 1941; 1 dau., Anne Leonore. Tchr. sci. and mathematics Cannelton (Ind.) High Sch., 1937-42; factory engr. Ken-Rad and Gen. Elec. Co., Tell City, Ind., 1942-51; sect. engr. Gen. Elec. Co., 1951-56; specialist process engring., 1956-60, sr. engr. product design, Owensboro, Ky., 1960—. Registered profl. engr., Ind., Ky. Mem. Nat., Ky. socs. profl. engrs., I.E.E.E., Nat. Rifle Assn., Sigma Pi Sigma. Republican. Home: 1612 Ford Av Owensboro KY 42301 Office: 316 E 9th St Owensboro KY 42301*

GROVES, SIGRID MARCZOCH, editor; b. Osnabruck, Germany, Jan. 24, 1937; d. Fritz and Erna (Haselroth) Marczoch; student Alliance Francaise, Paris, 1958-60, West London Coll. Commerce, 1960-61; m. Philip E. Groves, Dec. 24, 1968. Came to U.S., 1961, naturalized, 1966. Asst. editor The Pharmacologist, Bethesda, Md., 1962-64, Profl. Engr. mag., Washington, 1964-68; editor Nat. Candy Wholesaler mag., Washington, 1968—. Mem. Vols. for Internat. Tech. Assistance, Washington, 1967—, sec., 1967-68. Mem. Soc. Nat. Assn. Publs. Home: 2127 California St NW Washington DC 20008 Office: 1430 K St NW Washington DC 20008

GROVES, WILLIAM ERNEST, educator; b. Flint, Mich., Sept. 8, 1935; s. Marion Frederick and Bernice Lois (Truitt) G.; B.S., So. Meth. U., 1957; M.S., U. Ill., 1959, Ph.D. (USPHS fellow), 1962; postgrad. Purdue U., 1972; m. Jamesina Withers, June 25, 1962; children—Janet Louise, Anne Fiona, James Frederick. Research biochemist NIH, Bethesda, Md., 1962-64, St. Jude Children's Research Hosp., Memphis, 1964-71; asst. prof. clin. pathology, dir. Data Center, Med. U. S.C., Charleston, 1971—. Served with USPHS, 1962-64. USPHS fellow, 1959-62, NSF spl. fellow, 1972. Mem. Soc. Cell Biology, A.A.A.S., Am. Chem. Soc., Endocrine Soc., Sigma Xi. Methodist. Club: Scenic Hills Recreation (bd. dirs. 1970-71) (Memphis). Home: 1821 Huntington Dr Charleston SC 29407

GROWALD, MARTIN CHANDLER, architect; b. Salem, Mass., Aug. 21, 1930; s. Henry Kurt and Edith (Chandler) G.; B.S. in Architecture, U. Va., 1954; M.A., Harvard, 1955; m. Monika Bange, Oct. 6, 1962; children—Olaf Martin, Chandler Kurt, Emma Bange. Instr. architecture N.C. State Coll., Raleigh, 1955-56, U. Mich., Ann Arbor, 1957-58; designer Skidmore, Owings & Merrill, N.Y.C., Chgo., San Francisco, Portland, Ore., 1958-63, participating asso., 1963-66, asso. partner, 1966-72; partner firm Growald/Schutts Architects, Inc., Ft. Worth, 1972—. Vis. archtl. critic Sch. Architecture, U. Va., Charlottesville, 1966; prof. archtl. design U. Tex. at Arlington, 1972-73. Served with AUS, C.E., 1956-57. Recipient Sparks Meml. medal Chi Phi, 1952, 53, 54, Alpha Rho Chi medal, 1954. Mem. A.I.A., Archtl. League N.Y. (exec. com. 1967—, chmn. membership com., sec.), Chi Phi. Clubs: Harvard of New York; River Crest Country, Century II, Fort Worth (Ft. Worth). Patentee shell form structure. Sr. designer Chase Manhattan Bank, N.Y.C. 1958-60, Royall Nat. Bank, Tex., 1961, Pennsylvania Av. Commn., Washington, 1962, Main Place, Dallas, 1963, Ford Motor Credit Co. Bldg., Dearborn, Mich., 1965, Mt. Sinai Med. Sch. Lab., N.Y.C., 1966, Blue Hill Office Park, Orangetown, N.Y., 1968, Olympic Tower, N.Y., 1972, Dept. Housing and Urban Devel. Operation Break-Through, Jersey City, 1972, Perry R. Bass Hdqrs., Ft. Worth, 1973, Seatrain Lines, various cities, 1960-73. Home: 2705 Simondale St Fort Worth TX 76109 Office: 515 Fort Worth Nat Bank Bldg Fort Worth TX 76102

GRUBB, CLARENCE EDWARD, elec. engr.; b. Knoxville, Tenn., Dec. 22, 1932; s. Ralph Meyers and Mary Katherine (Brantley) G.; B.S. in E.E., U. Tenn., 1956; m. Jean Juanita Heuther, Feb. 4, 1961; children—Rachel Elaine, Stephen Edward, David Eugene, Elizabeth Jane. Elec. engr. Fla. Power & Light Co., Miami, 1956-67; dir. High Point (N.C.) Electric System, 1967—. Registered profl. engr., Fla. Mem. I.E.E.E., Profl. Engrs. N.C., N.C. Assn. Municipal Electric Systems (pres. 1971-72), Am. Bus. Clubs (dist. gov. 1973), Eta Kappa Nu. Presbyn. (ch. sch. supt. 1972-73). Home: 306 Pineridge Dr High Point NC 27260 Office: PO Box 230 High Point NC 27261

GRUBB, WILLIAM CLAY, data processing engr.; b. Morristown, Tenn., July 4, 1916; s. Robert Miller and Eva Pearl (Reaves) G.; B.S. in Mech. Engring., Ga. Inst. Tech., 1940; postgrad. Lehigh U., 1941; m. Frances Moore Boozer, Aug. 3, 1946; children—Gipsy Hall, William Clay. Jr. engr. Newport News Shipbldg. & Drydock Co. (Va.), 1940-41; engr. Sonoco Products Co., Hartsville, S.C., 1946-48; owner, mgr. Royal Crown Bottling Co., Dothan, Ala., 1948-66, Grubb Coal Co., Dothan, 1948-66; data processing engr. Southeastern Surveyors Inc., Dothan, 1966—. Served from ensign to lt. comdr. USNR, 1941-46. Registered profl. engr., Ala., Fla. Mem. Am. Soc. M.E., Dothan-Houston County C. of C. Home: 519 Girard Av Dothan AL 36301

GRUBBS, FRANK LESLIE, JR., educator; b. Lynchburg, Va., June 21, 1931; s. Frank L. and Grace Louise (Smith) G.; B.A. cum laude, Lynchburg Coll., 1959; M.A., U. Va., 1960, Ph.D., 1963; m. Carolyn Barrington, July 31, 1965; children—Thomas Ashby, Robert B. Lab. technician Mead Corp., Lynchburg, Va., 1949-54; grad. instr. U. Va., 1960-63; prof. history dept. Meredith Coll., Raleigh, N.C., 1963—, dir. Am. civilization program, 1970—. Served with AUS, 1952-54. Francis DuPont fellow, 1960, Dandridge fellow, Nat. Humanities grantee, 1971. Mem. Orgn. Am. Historians, Am. Assn. U. Profs. (mem. watchdog com. N.C. 1965-69), Smithsonian Assos., So. Hist. Soc. Club: Torch (sec. Raleigh 1973). Author: The Struggle for Labor Loyalty, 1968. Contbr. articles to profl. jours. Home: 1706 Baker Rd Raleigh NC 27606

GRUBE, HERMAN CHRISTIAN, architect; b. Charleston, S.C., Feb. 22, 1923; s. Herman Christian and Mary Chloe (Normoyle) G.; grad. high sch.; m. Frances Bevis, Oct. 15, 1947; children—Mary (Mrs. Thomas Joseph Eckenrode), William Herman, Carol (Mrs. Virgil Bruce McClearen), Ellen Catherine and Elaine Margaret (twins), Teresa Lynn, Martin Christian. Architect, Conyers, Ga., then Virginia Beach, Va.; prin. firm Herman C. Grube, Norfolk, Va., 1969—; cons., dir. architecture Econo-Travel-Motor-Hotel Corp., Norfolk, 1972—. Mem. A.I.A. (govtl. affairs com. 1973—). Home: 2220 Sedgwick Dr Virginia Beach VA 23454 Office: Suite 103 Koger Exec Center Bldg No 3 Norfolk VA 23502

GRUBEN, JOHN HENRY, JR., ins. co. exec.; b. Terrell, Tex., Apr. 17, 1909; s. John Henry and Jennie Cecil (Scott) G.; student Tex. A. and M. U., 1928-30; student journalism, Columbia, 1932, Sorbonne, U. Paris (France), 1944; m. Dorothy Barbara Walton, Feb. 11, 1933; 1 dau., Barbara Antoinette (Mrs. Edwin Conway Barker). With Am. Nat. Ins. Co., Galveston, Tex., 1934—, v.p., 1971—, writer, editor Star Bull., 1946—, co. conv. histories, 1946—. Pres. Galveston Little Theatre, 1950-52. Served with AUS, 1944-46; ETO. Decorated Meritorious Service citation (France); recipient Journalism award Freedom's Found., Galveston, 1954, 55, 56, 57; Nat. Editors award Life Insurers Conf., Galveston, 1956, 57; also many leadership awards. Mem. Tex., Harrison County hist. assns., East Tex. Hist. Soc., Galveston Hist. Found. Methodist (ordained minister 1954). Clubs: Galveston Rifle, Gun (pres. Galveston 1958-59, Galveston County Press. Author: Fabulous Colonel Buck, Home: 5210 Av U Galveston TX 77550 Office: Am Nat Ins Co Moody Av at Market St Galveston TX 77550

GRUEBEL, ROBERT LEE, elec. engr.; b. Providence, R.I., May 29, 1946; s. Robert William and Eleanor Jane (Perry) G.; B.S. in Elec. Engring., U. Ark., 1968; postgrad. So. Methodist U., 1972—; m. Margaret Ann McAllister, May 29, 1968. Mgr. product engring Advanced Circuits div. Tex. Instruments, Inc., Sherman, 1968-69, 72—. Coach Little League Baseball, 1973, 74. Served with USAF, 1969-72. Mem. I.E.E.E., Eta Kappa Nu. Baptist. Home: 1710 Ridgeway Sherman TX 75090 Office: Texas Instruments Inc Sherman TX 75090

GRUIS, EDWARD GEORGE, lawyer; b. Chgo., Jan. 20, 1924; s. Edward George and Helen (Bruce) G.; B.S., Purdue U., 1949, M.S., 1951; Dr. en Droit, U. Lyon (France), 1950; J.D. with honors, George Washington U., 1954, LL.M., 1955; postgrad. Georgetown Law Sch., 1960; m. Rosemary Nottingham, Apr. 3, 1948; children—Leslie Nottingham, Tracy Nottingham. Admitted to D.C. bar, 1954, Ind. bar, 1954, also U.S. Supreme Ct. bar; trial atty. antitrust div. U.S. Dept. of Justice, Washington, 1954-59; private practice law, Washington, 1959; trial atty. FTC, Washington, 1960-70; dep. gen. counsel FMC, Washington, 1970—. Pres. Capitol Hill Restoration Soc., 1957, 58, 67; gen. counsel Nat. Conf. State Socs., 1966-68, 3d v.p., 1969-70, Bd. dirs., treas. Indiana Soc, Washington, 1966-73; bd. dirs., vice chmn. Christ Child Settlement House, Washington, 1968-70. Served with AUS, 1943-46. Mem. Am., Fed., Ind. bar assns., Lambda Chi Alpha, Delta Theta Phi. Republican. Episcopalian. Home: 326 2d St SE Washington DC 20003 Office: FMC Washington DC 20573

GRULA, EDWARD ALAN, educator; b. Johnstown, Pa., July 27, 1926; s. Adam J. and Susan M. (Frederick) G.; B.S., Bethany Coll., 1950; M.S., U. Ky., 1952; Ph.D., Purdue U., 1956; m. Mary Rae Muedeking, Feb. 16, 1951; children—John, Margie, Thomas, Lori. Asst. prof. microbiology Okla. State U., Stillwater, 1956-61, asso. prof., 1961-63, prof., 1963—. Pres., P.T.A., 1959-60, 68-70; leader Will Rogers council Boy Scouts Am., 1963-65; coach, Little League, 1962-65. Served with USAAF, 1944-47; PTO. Recipient Career Devel. award NIH, 1961-71. Mem. Am. Soc. Microbiology, Okla. Acad. Scis., Sigma Xi, Phi Lambda Upsilon, Beta Beta Beta. Elk. Contbr. articles to profl. jours. Home: Route 2 Stillwater OK 74074

GRUND, CLARENCE B., JR., elec. utility exec.; b. Portland, Ore., July 31, 1925; s. Clarence B. and Frances (Eckert) G.; B.E.E., Ala. Poly. Inst., 1951, M.E.E., 1952; m. Marilyn Grace Hornsby, May 2, 1948. Engr. system planning Ala. Power Co., Birmingham, 1953-58; engr. rate dept. So. Services, Inc., Birmingham, 1958-63; supr. research rate dept., 1964-67, asst. mgr. rate dept., 1967-69, mgr. rate dept., 1969-72, asst. v.p., 1972—; instr. Ala. Poly. Inst., 1951-52, extension center U. Ala., 1952. Pres., Rocky Ridge Vol. Fire Dept., 1957-58, bd. dirs., 1956-62. Served with USAAF, World War II. Registered profl. engr., Ala., Miss. Mem. I.E.E.E., Nat. Soc. Profl. Engrs., Birmingham Soc. Engrs., Newcomen Soc. N.Am., Internat. Platform Assn., Am. Legion, Phi Kappa Phi, Tau Beta Pi, Eta Kappa Nu. Contbr. articles profl. jours. Home: 3421 Cruzan Dr Birmingham

AL 35243 Office: Southern Services Inc 64 Perimeter Center E PO Box 720071 Atlanta GA 30346

GRUNER, VIRGINIA SHAW (MRS. GEORGE JOHN GRUNER), club woman; b. Chgo., Feb. 19, 1912; d. Neil John and Rose (Tenwick) Shaw; grad. Chgo. Tchrs. Coll., 1931; B.S., Northwestern U., 1932; Ph.D. (hon.), Colo. State Christian Coll., 1973; m. George John Gruner, Nov. 6, 1935 (dec.); children—Valerie Dale, Diane Rae. Tchr., Parker Practice Sch. of Chgo., Chgo. Tchrs. Coll., 1935-40. Active Girl Scouts Am., 1949-53; v.p. Factotums, Scarsdale (N.Y.) Woman's Club. 1953. Recipient Civic Achievement award City of Chgo. Mem. Internat. Platform Assn., High Mus. Art Members Guild, Pi Lambda Theta, Cui Bono, Alpha Omicron Pi. Republican. Presbyn. Clubs: Scarsdale Golf (chmn. women's golf assn. 1954-56), American Yacht (Rye, N.Y.), Coral Ridge Country (Ft. Lauderdale, Fla.). Home: 140 Maison Pl Cross Creek NW Atlanta GA 30327

GUANDOLO, JOHN, lawyer; b. Conway, Pa., Sept. 11, 1919; s. Vincent and Tommasina (Meta) G.; A.B. in Econs., U. Ill., 1940; J.D., U. Md., 1943; transp. courses Northwestern U., 1962; m. Elizabeth Wade, Aug. 13, 1942; 1 son, Joseph Wade. Admitted to bar D.C., 1944, Md., 1952, Ill., 1956, Mo., 1962, U.S. Supreme Ct., 1949; trial atty. Justice Dept., 1948-56; gen. atty. Rock Island R.R., 1956-57; practice law, specializing in transp. and antitrust law, Washington, 1957-62, 63—; commerce atty. M.P. R.R., 1962-63; mem. firm Macdonald & McInerny, Washington, 1963—. Lectr., Am. U., 1967—. Mem. Am., Fed., D.C. bar assns., Assn. ICC Practitioners, Motor Carrier Lawyers Assn., Am. Soc. Traffic and Transp. Club: University (Washington). Author: Federal Procedure Forms, 1949, 3 vols., 1961, also supplements; (with Fair) Regulation of Transportation, 1964, Transportation Regulation, 1973; Transportation Law, 1965; (with others) Coordinated Transportation; Problems and Requirements, 1969; also articles. Editor-in-chief: ICC Practitioners' Jour., 1959—. Home: 10905 Rosemont Dr Rockville MD 20852 Office: 1000 16th St NW Washington DC 20036

GUBBINS, KEITH EDMUND, educator; b. Southampton, Eng., Jan. 27, 1937; s. Albert Edmund and Joyce Lucy (Elmes) G.; B.Sc., Queen Mary Coll., U. London, 1958; Ph.D. (Leverhulme research fellow), King's Coll., U. London, 1962; m. Pauline Margaret Payne, 1960; 1 son, Nicholas Peter. Came to U.S., 1962. Vis. lectr. U. London, 1960-62; postdoctoral fellow U. Fla., Gainesville, 1962-64, asst. prof., 1964-68, asso. prof., 1968-72, prof. chem. engring., 1972—. Vis. cons. U.K. Atomic Energy Authority, Harwell, 1971; vis. prof., Eppley Found. fellow Imperial Coll., London, 1970-71; vis. prof. U. Guelph (Ont., Can.), 1971-73, asso. grad. faculty mem., 1972—. Mem. Am. Chem. Soc., Am. Inst. Chem. Engrs., Chem. Soc. (London), Instn. Chem. Engrs. (London). Author: (with T.M. Reed) Applied Statistical Mechanics, 1973. Contbr. articles to profl. jours. Home: 615 NW 28th St Gainesville FL 32607

GUBERMAN, REUBEN, editor; b. N.Y.C., Aug. 21, 1926; s. Leon and Clara (Tobolsky) G.; student Bklyn. Coll., 1943-45; m. Tamara Frances Sherman, Feb. 21, 1960; children—Leon, Ira, Nanette. Free lance writer children's cartoons, award-winning documentary The Hitachi Symphony, English dialogue motion pictures, actor, dir., Miami, Fla., 1948-68; personality radio shows, Miami, 1965-68; editor Non-Foods Merchandising, Atlanta, 1968—. Mem. B'nai B'rith Youth Orgn. Bd., Miami, 1967. Mem. Am. Soc. Bus. Press Editors. Jewish religion. Author: 52 Retail Promotions, 1968. Contbr. articles to bus. mags. Home: 2695 Terratim Lane Decatur GA 30034 Office: Non-Foods Merchandising United Pub Co 1372 Peachtree St NE Atlanta GA 30309

GUDNASON, HALLDOR VICTOR, physician; b. Reykjavik, Iceland, July 16, 1932; s. Gudni Emil and Kristin (Ingibsartar) K.; student Menntaskoli Reykjavik, 1950-54; M.D., U. Iceland Med. Sch., 1954; m. Drofn Markusdottir, Sept. 4, 1952; children—Haukur Markus, Ingi Valdimar, Gudbjorg Helga, Kristin Halldora. Came to U.S., 1965. Rotating intern U. Hosp. Iceland, 1962-63, St. Joseph Hosp., Chgo., 1965-66; resident anesthesiology U. Va. Hosp., Charlottesville, 1966-69; gen. practice medicine, Olafsfsordur, Iceland, 1963-65; staff physician Rehab. Center for Rheumatic Patients, Hveragerdi, Iceland, 1965; pvt. practice medicine specializing in anesthesiology, Falls Church, Va., 1969—; mem. staff, chief dept. anesthesiology Culpeper (Va.) Meml. Hosp., 1971—; mem. staff Fairfax Hosp., Falls Church, Fauquier Hosp. Recipient NIH Grant, 1969. Mem. Iceland, Va., Fairfax County med. socs., A.M.A., Am., Va. socs. anesthesiologists. Lutheran. Address: 8917 Lynnhurst Dr Fairfax VA 22030

GUERRA, HUMBERTO RUBEN, dentist; b. Mission, Tex., Dec. 19, 1929; s. Cipriano F. and Bertha (Pena) G.; B.S. in Pharmacy Loyola U. of South, 1955, D.D.S., 1962; m. Gail Coons, Aug. 22, 1965; children—Stephen, Thomas, Karen, Gregory, Peter, Elizabeth. Asst. mgr. Walgreens, New Orleans, 1957-62; pvt. practice dentistry, New Orleans, 1962—. Prof. pharmacology Loyola U., New Orleans, 1966—; pres., dir. Aero-Dent, Inc., New Orleans, 1971—. Served with AUS, 1955-57. Mem. Am., New Orleans, La. dental assns., Acad. Gen. Dentistry. Inventor spl. dental spray Detex. Home: 4800 Marque Dr New Orleans LA 70127 Office: 8339 Chef Menteur Hwy New Orleans LA 70127

GUERRERO, JOAQUIN EUGENE, cons. engr.; b. Durango, Durango, Mex., Aug. 20, 1910; s. Laureano and Guadalupe (Reyes) G.; B.S., So. Meth. U., 1934; m. Sara Erwin, June 20, 1941; children—Joaquin Eugene, Jeanne Marie (Mrs. Charles Gore), Kathi Anne, David Blythe. Came to U.S., 1925, naturalized, 1942. Partner, Landauer & Guerrero, cons. engrs., Dallas, 1945-53, Blum & Guerrero, cons. engrs., Dallas, 1954-59, Toombs, Amisano & Wells, architects and engrs., Atlanta, 1959-64; pvt. practice J.E. Guerrero Cons. Engr., Dallas, 1964—. Home: 5910 Woodland Dr Dallas TX 75225 Office: 2909 Lemmon Av Dallas TX 75204

GUESS, GORDON BLUE, banker; b. Princeton, Ky., June 18, 1936; s. Neil Gordon and Virginia (Blue) G.; B.A., Vanderbilt U., 1958; m. Mary Carole Naber, Aug. 8, 1970; 1 son, Neil Gordon II. Trainee, Louisville Trust Co., 1961, programmer, 1962-64, mgr. data processing div., 1965-69, asst. v.p. money mgmt. and investment div., 1969-73; asst. mgr. computer dept. Fla. Nat. Bank of Jacksonville, 1965; exec. v.p., cashier Peoples Bank, Marion, Ky., 1973-74, pres., 1974—, also dir.; pres., dir. Marion Foods, Inc. Co-founder, dir. The Ky. Republican, 1964; vice chmn. Young Rep. Clubs Ky., 1966; nat. committeeman Young Rep. Nat. Fedn., 1969-71; mem. Louisville-Jefferson County Rep. Exec. Com., 1970-71; mem. Rep. State Central Com., 1970-71; chmn. Ky. 3d Dist. Young Reps., 1970-71; treas. Ky. Finance Com. to Re-elect Pres., 1972, Ky. Com. to Re-elect Pres., 1972; mem. Crittenden County Budget Commn., Marion-Crittenden County Planning Commn. Bd. dirs. Pennyrile Area Devel. Dist. Served to capt. AUS, 1959-60, 61-62. Mem. Am. Inst. Banking, Systems and Procedures Assn., Crittenden County C. of C. (dir.), U. Louisville Assos., Delta Kappa Epsilon. Methodist. Clubs: Louisville Quarterback, Lincoln (Louisville, Ky.). Home: Route 2 Marion KY 42064 Office: 116 S Main St Marion KY 42064

GUESS, ISLA MIXSON (MRS. JACKSON CAUTHEN GUESS), banker; b. Hampton, S.C., June 11, 1921; d. Atticus and Rosalie (Ulmer) Mixon; grad. high sch., Yemassee, S.C.; m. Jackson Cauthen Guess, Dec. 30, 1947; children—Sandra (Mrs. Aubrey Lyons), Barbara (Mrs. C.E. Stafford, Jr.) and Janice (Mrs. Strat Stavrou) (twins). Sec. to prin. Yemassee High Sch., 1940-41; co-owner dress shop, 1945-47; with Bank of Yemassee (name later changed to 1st Carolina Bank), 1957—, asst. cashier, 1969—, br. mgr., 1974—. Chmn. fund drives various local charitable orgns.; sec. Limestone Coll. Parents Adv. Council, 1969. Home: PO Box 95 Yemassee SC 29945 Office: PO Box 368 Yemassee SC 29945

GUEST, KENNETH RAY, lawyer; b. nr. Harrisburg, Ill., July 27, 1939; s. Jesse Clayton and Lela (Schroll) G.; B.S., Washington U., St. Louis, 1962; J.D., So. Methodist U., 1965; m. Patsy Lou Reed, June 29, 1968; 1 dau., Kimberly Ann. Admitted to Tex. bar, 1965, since practiced in Dallas; mem. firm Matthews & Matthews, 1965-69; partner firm Schroeder, Guest & Hoffmeyer, 1969—. Mem. adv. council Small Bus. Adminstrn. Republican precinct chmn., 1965-66; del. Rep. Senatorial and State Convs., 1966—, permanent chmn. Senatorial Conv., 1968-70; mem. Tex. Rep. Exec. Com., 1972—. Mem. Am., Dallas bar assns., State Bar Tex., Comml. Law League Am., Dallas County Criminal Bar, Oak Cliff C. of C. Mem. Ch. of God. Club: Oak Cliff Country. Home: 2418 Club Manor Dr Dallas TX 75237 Office: Mercantile Securities Bldg Dallas TX 75201

GUEYDAN, JAMES EDMOND, stockbroker; b. New Orleans, Sept. 6, 1916; s. Robert Lee and Margaret Mary (Riordan) G.; B.B.A., U. Minn., 1938; M.B.A., Harvard, 1952; m. Mary Venette McManus, Apr. 21, 1942; children—Sandra (Mrs. Paul Hickey), Pamela Jeanne. Office mgr. St. Paul Cos., 1938-41; cadet USAAF, 1941, advanced through grades to col., 1961; ret., 1968; v.p. Howard, Weil, Labouisse, Friedrichs Inc., New Orleans, 1968—. Decorated Legion of Merit. Mem. New Orleans C. of C. (mems. council 1971—), Internat. House (mems. com.), Delta Sigma Pi (life). Democrat. Clubs: So. Yacht, Pendennis, Plimsoll, Harvard. Home: 2374 Beck St New Orleans LA 70114 Office: 211 Carondelet St New Orleans LA 70130

GUGLIELMINO, PAUL JOSEPH, advt. and pub. relations cons.; b. Bklyn., May 19, 1942; s. Carl and Rose (Loreto) G.; B.A., The Citadel, 1964; M.A., U. Ga., 1970; m. Lucy Margaret Madsen, July 31, 1965. Marketing analyst Shell Chem. Co., N.Y.C., 1966-67; asst. dir. pub. relations The Citadel, Charleston, S.C., 1967-69; grad. asst. U. Ga., 1970; advt., pub. relations cons., Savannah, Ga., 1970—. Chmn. pub. relations Charleston County Heart Fund, 1969, Chatham County Heart Fund, 1971. Served to 1st lt. AUS, 1964-66. Mem. Pub. Relations Soc. Am. Address: 208 Winchester Dr Savannah GA 31404

GUIBERTEAU, JAMES JOSEPH, dentist; b. Houston, Sept. 10, 1934; s. Milton Joseph and Dorothy (Porter) G.; B.S., Tex. A. and M. U., 1956, postgrad., 1957-58; D.D.S., U. Tex., 1962; m. Naurene Alece Hall, June 2, 1957; children—James Joseph, Peggy Jean, John Joseph. Grad. teaching asst. Tex. A. and M. U., 1957-58; pvt. practice dentistry, Houston, 1964—; staff dentist VA Hosp., Houston, 1967; dental dir. Richmond State Sch., Tex. Dept. Mental Health and Mental Retardation, 1968-74, chief dental service San Antonio State Chest Hosp., 1974—; mem. med. staff Meml. Baptist Hosp. System, Houston, 1966—; clin. instr. Sch. Dental Hygiene, Wharton County Jr. Coll., 1970—. Welbelos leader, Eagle Scout adviser Sam Houston Area council Boy Scouts Am., 1967—; mem. Candlelight Plaza Civic Club, 1967—. Served to capt. Dental Corps., AUS, 1962-64; maj. Res. Recipient certificates of recognition Sam Houston Area council Boy Scouts Am., 1967. Mem. Am., Tex. dental assns., Houston Dist. Dental Soc., Assn. Mil. Surgeons of U.S., Tex. Acad. Pub. Health and Instl. Dentists (exec. sec. 1972—), So. Assn. for Instl. Dentists, U. Tex. Dental Br. Alumni Assn., Tex. A. and M. U. Former Students Assn. Episcopalian. Mason. Home: 1002 Bethlehem Houston TX 77018

GUIDA, FLORIGIO ANTONIO, banker; b. Ship Bottom, N.J., June 16, 1934; s. Emilio and Antonietta (Fedullo) G.; B.S., Villanova U., 1956. With Ernst & Ernst, C.P.A.'s, Washington, 1954-58, Callaway, Carpenter & May, C.P.A.'s, West Palm Beach, Fla., 1958-64; v.p., treas. Internat. Gen. Industries, Internat. Bank, Washington, 1959—. Served to lt. USNR, 1956-58. Mem. Am., Fla., D.C. insts. C.P.A.'s. Home: 1723 Corcoran St NW Washington DC 20009 Office: 1701 Pennsylvania Av NW Washington DC 20006

GUILLAUME, BERNARD GEORGE, realtor; b. Guernsey, Channel Island, July 11, 1910; s. Stephen Osmond and Jessie May (LePage) G.; student LaSalle Extension U., 1940, Loyola U., Chgo., 1941, Northwestern U., 1942; m. Ethylle Marie Perkins, Aug. 27, 1938; 1 son, Stephen B. Owner, mgr. Ebb Tide Motel, Treasure Island, Fla., 1954-70; controller Pickard, Inc., Antioch, Ill., 1945-54; real estate broker Guillaume Realty Co., Seminole, Fla., 1958—. Pres., Holiday Isles Devel. Council, 1973—. Mem. City Commn., Treasure Island, 1960-70; mem. Pinellas County Planning Council, 1964-71, chmn. council, 1968; mem. Pinellas County Charter Commn., 1971-73; pres. Republican Club Greater Seminole, 1972—. Mem. Gulf Beach-Seminole Bd. Realtors (pres. 1968, v.p., dir. 1969—), Greater Seminole C. of C. (dir. 1972—). Republican. Methodist. Mason (32 deg.). Home: 11120 54th Av N St Petersburg FL 33708 Office: 6701 Seminole Blvd Seminole FL 33542 also 18001 Gulf Blvd Redington Shores FL 33708

GUILLIAMS, GEORGE CORNELIOUS, ednl. supr.; b. Rocky Mount, Va., Feb. 22, 1922; s. Thomas Cornelious and Callie Ruth (Agee) G.; B.S., Va. Poly. Inst., 1942, M.S., 1950; m. Mabel Elnora Conner, Sept. 14, 1943; children—Steven Morris, Sue Ellen (Mrs. Robert Warren Thacker). Tchr. vocational agr. Auburn High Sch., Riner, Va., 1942-66; gen. supr. Montgomery County Schs., Christianburg, Va., 1966-67, county supr. vocational edn., 1967—; supr. student tchrs. Va. Poly. Inst., Riner, 1942-66. Organized Livestock Registry Assn. Va., 1956. Treas. Community Action Agy., 1968-70; mem. Montgomery County Pub. Service Authority, 1970—, vice chmn., 1970-72. Bd. dirs. Montgomery County Tb Assn. Mem. Nat., Va., Montgomery County (v.p. 1963-65) edn. assns., Blue Ridge Vocational Agr. Tchrs. (treas. 1960-68), Va. Assn. Future Farmers Am. (hon.), Young Homemakers Va. (hon.). Methodist. Pioneer in planning of water system for Riner area. Home: Route 3 Box 648 Riner VA 24149 Office: 200 Junkin St Christianburg VA 24073

GUILLORY, TROY TILLMAN, bank exec.; b. Sikes, La., Mar. 27, 1920; s. Gill Gilbert and Grace Mae (Burks) G.; student La. State U., 1938-39; B.S., Omaha U., 1960; M.B.A., George Washington U., 1961; postgrad. Indsl. Coll. Armed Forces, 1960-61; m. Mary Joe Standley, Dec. 20, 1941; children—Troy Tillman, Jr., Barbara (Mrs. Noel Mulhearn), Mary Margaret. Commd. ensign U.S. Navy, 1941, advanced to capt., 1961, ret., 1968; with Central Savs. Bank & Trust Co., Monroe, La., 1968—, sr. v.p., 1969—. Crusade chmn. Am. Cancer Soc., 1968-69, pres. 1970-71. Decorated D.F.C., Air medals (2). Mason, Lion. Home: 417 Lakeshore Dr Monroe LA 71201 Office: Central Bank PO Box 5020 Monroe LA 71201

GUINN, DAVID CRITTENDEN, cons. engr.; b. Port Arthur, Tex., Nov. 29, 1926; s. Leland Lee and Corrie Andrews (Avery) G.; A.A., Lamar Inst. Tech., 1948; B.S. in Petroleum Engring., U. Tex. at Austin, 1951; m. Marguerite V. Guinn, Oct. 7, 1966; children—Susan, David, Jay, Jeffrey. Engr. trainee Dowell, Inc., Alice, Tex., 1949; petroleum engr. Cal. Co., Lafayette, La., 1951-52, area prodn. and drilling engr., Venice, La., 1952-54, evaluation engr., New Orleans, 1954-55; dist. engr. Republic Natural Gas Co., 1955-56, div. drilling engr., 1956-57; div. engr. Shaffer Tool Works, Inc., 1957-63, sales mgr., Midcontinent div., Beaumont, 1963-65; div. mgr. Mid-Continent-Gulf Coast div., 1965-67; pvt. practice as cons. petroleum engr., New Orleans, 1957, Houston, 1967—; owner of Guinn and Assos., Engrs., Guinn Internation, Inc.; founder Internat. Subsea Devel. Corp., Atlantic Ocean Service Center, Inc., Mission Drilling and Exploration Corp., Tropic Drilling and Exploration Co. Served from pvt. to cadet USAAF, 1943-46. Registered profl. engr., La., Tex. Mem. Nat., Tex. socs. profl. engrs., Am. Soc. M.E., Am. Inst. Mining Metall. and Petroleum Engrs., Internat. Drilling Contractors, Houston Engring. and Sci. Soc., Am. Mgmt. Assn., Marine Tech. Soc., Am. Soc. Oceanology, Nomad, Internat. Oceanographic Found., S.A.R. Contbr. articles to profl. jours. Home: 7910 Beverly Hill Lane Houston TX 77042 Office: PO Box 1126 Houston TX 77001

GUINN, WOODROW WILSON, traffic mgr.; b. Camp Hugh, Ala., Aug. 30, 1916; s. Thedore Gaither and Ven Zula (Hickman) G.; student U. Ala., 1938, LaSalle Extension U., 1945, U. Houston, 1962; m. Gladys Vashti Fourakre, June 6, 1937; children—Linda (Mrs. William D. Campbell), Carol (Mrs. Richard W. Peters). Traffic analyst Gulf States Paper Corp., Tuscaloosa, Ala., 1941-46; with S.P. R.R., 1946-69, asst. to gen. traffic mgr., Houston, 1963-69; gen. traffic mgr. Sid Richardson Carbon & Gas Co., Ft. Worth, 1969—; dir. Tex. & N.M. R.R. Co. Pres. Beaumont (Tex.) chpt. Nat. Def. Transp. Assn., 1957. Mem. Dallas, Ft. Worth traffic clubs, Delta Nu Alpha. Mason (Shriner). Home: 1736 Westridge St Hurst TX 76053 Office: 1105 Fort Worth Nat Bank Bldg Fort Worth TX 76102

GUITON, DONALD KARL, govt. ofcl.; b. Cleve., Sept. 18, 1927; s. John J. and Matilda (Karl) G.; student Case Inst. Tech., 1945; B.A., Oberlin, 1951; m. Mary Clare Spelic, Feb. 2, 1963; children—Gregory K., Todd J., Renee C. With Nat. Park Service, Dept. Interior, various locations, 1953—, asst. supt. Big Horn Canyon Nat. Recreation Area, Mont., 1968-69, supt. Chickamauga and Chattanooga Nat. Mil. Park, Fort Oglethorpe, Ga., 1969—. 1st v.p. Chattanooga Convs. and Visitors Bur., 1973-74; mem. Greater Chattanooga Bicentennial Commn., 1973-74; mem. Tenn. Gov.'s Tourist Adv. Council; mem. adv. council N.W. Ga. Mental Health Unit. Bd. dirs. Chattanooga Audubon Soc., 1970-74. Served with AUS, 1948-50. Mem. Chattanooga Hist. Assn., Ft. Oglethorpe C. of C. (dir. 1974-75). Kiwanian (pres. Ft. Oglethorpe club 1971-72). Home: Box 2045 Fort Oglethorpe GA 30742 Office: Chickamauga and Chattanooga Nat Military Park Fort Oglethorpe GA 30742

GUITTARD, CLARENCE ALWIN, appeals ct. judge; b. Waco, Tex., Mar. 17, 1917; s. Francis Gevrier and Mamie (Welhausen) G.; student U. Colo., 1937; A.B., Baylor, 1940, L.B., 1940; postgrad. U. Tex., 1941; m. Mary Lou Kee, Aug. 30, 1940; children—Charles F., John R., Mary Louise. Admitted to Tex. bar, 1940; asso. firm Lloyd & Lloyd, Alice, Tex., 1940-41, briefing atty. Tex. Supreme Ct., 1941-43; partner firm Burford, Ryburn & Ford, Dallas, 1943-61; judge 14th Dist. Ct., County, Dallas County, Dallas, 1961-71; asso. justice Ct. Civil Appeals 5th Supreme Jud. Dist., Dallas, 1971—. Lectr., Insts. Eminent Domain, Southwestern Legal Found., 1957—. Mem. Dallas County Democratic Exec. Com., 1956-61, Tex. Dem. Exec. Com., 1960-61. Bd. dirs. Dallas Theatre Center, 1962-69. Served with AUS, 1943-44. Mem. Am., Dallas bar assns., State Bar Tex. (inst. lectr. eminent domain and appellate practice), Am. Judicature Soc. Methodist. Club: Northwood. Contbr. articles to legal publs. Home: 6306 Desco Dr Dallas TX 75225 Office: Ct Civil Appeals Dallas County Courthouse 600 Commerce St Dallas TX 75202

GULDEMANN, EUGENE JOSSLYN ALLIE, constrn. co. exec.; b. Bowman, N.D., Oct. 23, 1913; s. Josslyn E. and Lillian (Allie) G.; B.S., N.D. State U., 1942; M.S., Ore. State U., 1946; m. Joy Clement, June 15, 1945; children—Jolyn G. (Mrs. John W. Mikow), John L. Guldemann. Supt., Megarry Bros., St. Claude, Minn., 1935-42; asso. prof. S.C. State Coll., 1946-48, Tex. Western Coll., 1948-53; pres. Guldemann Constrn. & Engring., Inc., El Paso, 1956—. Chmn., Pub. Service Bd., El Paso, 1964—. Served to lt. AUS, 1942-44. Fellow Am. Soc. C.E.; mem. Nat. Soc. Profl. Engrs., El Paso History Assn., Land Marks, Inc., Tex. Soc. Profl. Engrs. Presbyn. (elder). Rotarian. Home: 315 Country Club Rd El Paso TX 79932 Office: 1918 Bassett Av El Paso TX 79901

GULIHUR, DONALD LEON, broadcasting engr.; b. Purcell, Okla., Oct. 9, 1912; s. Oria Glenn and Ida Belle (Frizzell) G.; B.S. in Physics and Math., Sam Houston State Coll., Huntsville, Tex., 1951; m. Lois Lee Charles, Feb. 28, 1931; children—Monna Lee (Mrs. Hoyt Smith), Donald Leroy, William Glenn, Ida Nell (Mrs. Robert L. Wilkins), James Shawn. Engr. sta. KTHT, Houston, 1951-61; dir. engring. McLendon Broadcasting Co., Jackson, Miss., 1961-62; chief engr. sta. WNOE, New Orleans, 1962—. Served to maj. AUS, 1940-46. Sr. engr. I.R.E. Mason, Lion. Home: PO Box 86 Belle Chasse LA 70027 Office: WNEO 529 Bienville St New Orleans LA 70130

GULLATT, E(NNIS) MURRAY, oil corp. exec.; b. Ada, Okla., Jan. 14, 1935; s. Ennis Murray and Flora Mae (Rainbolt) G.; B.S., Okla. U., 1957, M.S., 1958; M.B.A., Stanford, 1960; m. Nancy Bronaugh, July 23, 1955; children—John Michael, Deborah Leigh. Staff petroleum engr. Delhi-Taylor Oil Corp., Dallas, 1960-63; petroleum engr. Whitney Engring. Co., Tulsa, 1963; chief engr. Livingston Oil Co., Tulsa, 1963-65, v.p., 1965-67; exec. v.p. LVO Corp., Tulsa, 1967-71, pres., 1971—, also dir. Bd. dirs. Tulsa Sci. Found., 1968-71. Mem. Ind. Petroleum Assn. Am., Soc. Petroleum Engrs., Am. Petroleum Inst., Young Pres.'s Orgn., Pi Epsilon Tau. Methodist. Home: 5809 E 63d St Tulsa OK 74136 Office: PO Box 2848 522 S Boston St Tulsa OK 74101

GULLETT, B. B., lawyer; b. Manchester, Tenn., Dec. 9, 1905; A.B., Cumberland U., 1927, L.B., 1927; postgrad. Vanderbilt U., 1928-29. Admitted to Tenn. bar, 1927; chief clk. Tenn. Senate, 1939-41; spl. asst. to atty. gen. State of Tenn., 1941-54; now mem. firm Gullett, Steele, Sanford, Robinson & Merritt, Nashville. Mem. Jud. Conf. 6th Circuit. Mem. Am. Judicature Soc., Nashville (pres. 1959-60), Tenn. (pres. 1967-68), Am. (ho. of dels. 1968—) bar assns. Address: Gullett Steele Sanford Robinson & Merritt 23d Floor Life and Casualty Tower Nashville TN 37219

GULLEY, PETER MALCOLM, accountant; b. San Antonio, Oct. 5, 1943; s. Joseph Lightfoot and Ruth Mae (Finch) G.; B.B.A., U. Tex., 1966; m. Saralyn Marie Overby, Mar. 26, 1965; children—Cameron L., Candice L. Staff accountant Joe L. Gulley, C.P.A., 1966-71; partner Gulley & Gulley, Kenedy, Tex., 1971—. Mem. Tex. Soc. C.P.A.'s, Kenedy C. of C. (pres., dir.). Mem. Ch. of Christ. Rotarian. Home: 202 Graham Rd Kenedy TX 78119 Office: 100 S 2d St Kenedy TX 78119

GULLEY, WILLARD QUENTIN, plastics co. exec.; b. Bulls Gap, Tenn., July 27, 1918; s. William Calvin and Etta Elizabeth (Berry) G.; B.S. in Chem. Engring., U. Tenn., 1943; m. Mazelle Holleman, Oct. 9, 1940; children—John Quentin, Jean Elizabeth. Engr. E.I. duPont de Nemours, 1942-46; v.p. Carolina Indsl. Plastics, Mt. Airy, N.C., 1946-52; sec.-treas. to pres., treas., dir. Vinylex Corp., Knoxville, Tenn., 1952—; dir. Extron Corp., Vinylex Corp. of Fla., Vinylex Corp. of Tex., Formall Plastics. Knox County Rep. finance chmn. for Gov. Winfield Dunn, 1970; mem. Gov.'s Study Com. for Econ. Devel., 1971-72. Baptist. Home: Cove Point Lane Concord TN 37720 Office: 3600 Pleasant Ridge Rd Knoxville TN 37921

GULLO, JOHN JOSEPH, adminstrv. services cons.; b. Shreveport, La., July 4, 1939; s. Robert A. and Mildred (Pizzolato) G.; B.S., Centenary Coll. of La., 1962; M.S., La. State U., 1964; m. Bobbie Moore, June 4, 1960; children—Jeffrey, Gregory, Kristy. With Arthur Andersen & Co., Houston, 1964—, now adminstrv. services mgr. Mem. Assn. Systems Mgmt., Am. Inst. C.P.A.'s, Tex. Soc. C.P.A.'s, Houston Soc. C.P.A.'s. Home: 13731 Taylorcrest St Houston TX 77024 Office: 910 Travis St Houston TX 77002

GUMM, JAMES DONALD, security co. exec.; b. Waco, Tex., Aug. 28, 1939; s. Alfred Boyce and Orvia Normalee (Fields) G.; B.S., Sam Houston State Coll., 1961; m. Elizabeth Ann Hawes, May 27, 1961; children—Melissa Ann, Stephen Mark. With Fed. Security Service, Houston, 1964-70; Guardsmark, Inc., 1970—. Mem. Sigma Chi. Methodist. Club: Pine Forest Country (Houston). Home: 1060 Cheshire St Houston TX 77018

GUMP, RICHARD ANTHONY, lawyer; b. Tulsa, Nov. 22, 1917; s. Harry Allen and Mary Louise (Hanrahan) G.; B.B.A., U. Tex., 1939, LL.B., 1940; m. Billie Louise Nail, Feb. 18, 1941; children—Marilyn (Mrs. Charles L. Stewart), Richard Anthony. Spl. agt. FBI, 1940-45; admitted to Tex. bar, 1940, practiced in Dallas, 1945—; partner firm Akin, Gump, Strauss, Hauer and Feld, 1945—. Mng. dir. Pipe Line Contractors Assn., 1947—. Mem. Dallas, Am. bar assns., State Bar Tex., Serra Club, Pi Kappa Alpha. Clubs: Dallas, Northwood, Chapparral, Salesmanship. Home: 4616 Alta Vista Lane Dallas TX 75229 Office: 2800 Republic Bank Bldg Dallas TX 75201

GUNN, EDWARD MANSFIELD, physician, med. cons.; b. Providence, Oct. 25, 1913; s. Stanley Morton and Emily (Mansfield) G.; student R.I. State Coll., 1935; M.D., Syracuse U., 1939; m. Audrey R. Hopson, May 30, 1936; children—Wendy (Mrs. Herbert Arthur John Wickenden), Edward Mansfield. Physician-educator Civil Service, Dept. Army, 1946-52; intern Charles V. Chapin, Providence Lying-In, R.I. hosps., Providence, 1939-40; med. dir. Sonoco Products Co., 1952-55; cons. occupational medicine, 1955—. Served from 1st lt. to col. M.C., AUS, 1940-46. Mem. Am. Acad. Occupational Medicine, Indsl. Med. Assn., Mil. Surgeons Assn. U.S., A.A.A.S., Am. Soc. Indsl. Security, Internat. Assn. Chiefs Police, Inc. (asso.), Am. Fedn. Police. Travelled in Africa, Near, Middle and Far East. Home: 11 Marsh Wren Rd Sea Pines Plantation Hilton Head Island SC 29928

GUNN, WILLIAM SCHUYLER, investment co. exec.; b. Harvey, Ill., July 1, 1931; s. Harry E. and Irma (Zatkalik) G.; B.A., Beloit Coll., 1953; M.P.A., U. Kan., 1955; m. Diana Gaile Metts, June 12, 1954; children—Jeffrey, Susan, Karen. Adminstrv. asst., City of Janesville, Wis., 1954-55; asst. city mgr., Pompano Beach, Fla., 1957-60; account exec. Lee Higginson, Boca Raton, Fla., 1960-63; v.p., Walston & Co., Inc., Boca Raton, Fla., 1963-73; v.p. Blyth Eastman Dillon & Co. Inc., 1974—. Mem. Civil Service Bd., 1962-64. Bd. dirs., treas. Internat. Found. Gifted Children, 1968—; bd. dirs., pres. United Fund, Boca Raton; bd. dirs. Neighborhood Center of Boca Raton. Served with USN. Mem. Boca Raton C. of C. (pres., dir. 1963-67), Sigma Pi, Pi Sigma Alpha. Unitarian-Universalist (pres., treas. 1962-68). Kiwanian. Home: 360 E Alexander Palm Rd Boca Raton FL 33432 Office: 514-16 Via de Palmas Boca Raton FL 33432

GUNNIN, BILL LEE, structural engr.; b. Dallas, Jan. 19, 1943; s. Royce Gerald and Mary Estelle (Morrow) G.; B.S., Tex. Technol. Coll., 1965; M.S., U. Tex., 1967, Ph.D., 1970; m. Virginia Loree Murphy, June 5, 1965; children—Michael Murphy, Christopher Lee. Sr. project engr. Ellisor Engrs., Inc., Houston, 1970-71; sr. project engr. Ellisor & Tanner, Inc., Dallas, 1971-72, v.p., 1972—. Instr. civil engring. U. Tex., Austin, 1970; vis. indsl. prof. So. Meth. U., Dallas, 1971-72. NSF trainee, 1965-69. Registered profl. engr., Tex. Mem. Am. Soc. C.E. (asso.), Am. Concrete Inst., Sigma Nu. Contbr. articles to profl. jours. Office: 6116 N Central Expressway Suite 800 Dallas TX 75206

GUNTER, MAURY BAYNE, profl. engr.; b. Union, Miss., Oct. 1, 1941; s. Aubrey Harold and Nealie (Williamson) G.; A.A., E.Central Jr. Coll., 1961; B.S., Miss. State U., 1965; m. Mary Ann Loper, Sept. 3, 1961; children—Joycelynn, Julianna. Outside plant engr. S. Central Bell Telephone Co., Jackson, Miss., 1965-66; quality control engr. Gen. Electric Co., Jackson Lamp Plant, 1966-67; pres. Engrs. & Surveyors, Inc., cons. engrs., Newton, Miss., 1967—. City engr., Brandon, Miss., 1968—; county engr. Newton County, 1968—. Recipient Newton's Distinguished Service award, 1972; named Miss. Outstanding Young Engr., 1972. Mem. Newton Jaycees (pres. 1971-72), Newton C. of C. (dir. 1971-72), Miss. Engring. Soc. (pres. Meridian chpt. 1971-72), Nat. Soc. Profl. Engrs., Am. Water Works Assn., Miss. Water Pollution Fedn., I.E.E.E., Tau Beta Pi, Eta Kappa Nu. Baptist (deacon). Mason. Clubs: Newton Country, Newton Booster (pres.). Home: 101 Hamilton Dr Newton MS 39345 Office: 300 Decatur St Newton MS 39345

GUNTER, WILLIAM D., JR., congressman; b. Jacksonville, Fla., July 16, 1934; s. William D. and Ruth (Senterfitt) G.; B.S.A. with high honors, U. Fla., 1956; postgrad. U. Ga., 1957-58; m. Teresa Anne Arbaugh; children by previous marriage—Bartlett David, Joel Stephen. Tchr., Orange County, Fla., 1958-59; ins. agt. State Farm Ins. Co., 1959-61, agy. mgr., 1961-72; mem. Fla. Senate, 1966-72; mem. 93d Congress, from Fla. Mem. Orlando (Fla.) Rehab. and Devel. Adv. Com., 1966. Bd. dirs. Central Fla. Fair. Served with AUS, 1956-58. Mem. Central Fla. Assn. Life Underwriters, Gen. Agts. and Mgrs. Assn., U. Fla. Alumni Assn. (past v.p.). Democrat. Baptist. Home: 1638 Morrill Ct McLean VA 22101

GUNTUR, SEETHAPATHI RAO, shipbldg. co. engr.; b. Vijayawada, India, Nov. 18, 1943; s. Ranga Rao and Ratnavati (Solasa) G.; B.Sc., Andhra U., India, 1962; B.E., Gujarat U., India, 1965; M. Tech., Indian Inst. Tech., 1967; Ph.D., U. Tex., Austin, 1970; m. Purita Garcia, May 15, 1971; 1 dau., Sharaan Rani. Came to U.S. 1967. Research engring. asst. U. Tex., Austin, 1967-70; engring. analyst Engg-Tech. Analysts, Houston, 1971-73; sr. structural analyst Zapata Off-Shore Co., Houston, 1973—. Mem. Am. Soc. C.E., Am. Concrete Inst. Home: 1919 W Main St Apt 36 Houston TX 77006 Office: Houston Club Bldg Houston TX 77002

GUP, BENTON EUGENE, economist, educator; b. Reading, Pa., Mar. 5, 1936; s. Abe L. and Germaine (Bloch) G.; B.A., U. Cin., 1961, M.B.A., 1963, Ph.D., 1966; m. Joanne Greenwold, June 23, 1963; children—Lincoln, Andrew, Jermery. Prof. econs. U. Cin., 1966-67; economist Fed. Res. Bank of Cleve., 1967-70; prof., chmn. banking and finance U. Tulsa, 1960—. Pres. Gen. Econ. Research Corp.; treas. Financial Decision Systems, Inc. Served with USAF, 1954-58. Office: Dept Finance U Tulsa Tulsa OK 74104

GUPTA, YOUDHISHTHIR PRASHAD, research co. exec.; b. Barrod, India, Oct. 5, 1934; s. Badri Prashad and Kala Devi (Rustgi) G.; B.Sc. in Physics with honors, U. Delhi, India, 1953, M.S., 1955; D.I.I.Sc., Indian Inst. Sci., 1957; Sc.D. in Materials, Mass. Inst. Tech., 1963; m. Lisbeth Margareta Hallberg, Dec. 12, 1964; children—Nisha Kiran, Renu Kumari, Maya Devi, Mona Elisabeth. Came to U.S., 1958; naturalized, 1965. Asst. prof. U. Minn., Mpls., 1963-67; dir. materials scis. lab. Northrop Corp. Labs., Hawthorne, Cal., 1967-70, staff asst. to v.p. research and devel., 1970; pres. Centec Co., Los Angeles, 1970-71; mgr. structural mechanics and materials program Advanced Tech. Center, Inc. subsidiary LTV Aerospace Corp., Dallas, 1971-74; corporate dir. energy programs E-Systems, Inc., Dallas, 1974—. Cons. Nat. Co., Malden, Mass., 1960-61, Synnertech., Inc., Van Nuys, Cal., 1971; mem. tech. adv. council So. Meth. U., Dallas, 1972—. AEC grantee, 1965-67; NASA grantee, 1965-67; NSF grantee, 1967; USAF grantee, 1969-70; Tata scholar, 1956; Mahindra and Mahindra scholar, 1958; Ford Found scholar 1962; Mich. State U. scholar, 1961. Asso. fellow Am. Inst. Aeros. and Astronautics (mem. structural dynamics tech. com.), mem. Am. Inst. Mining and Metall. Engrs., Sigma Xi, Tau Beta Pi. Contbr. articles to profl. jours. Home: 1707 Kingsborough Dr Arlington TX 76015 Office: PO Box 6030 Dallas TX 75222

GURLEY, MAX LYNN, dentist; b. Sardis, Tenn., Aug. 29, 1931; s. Alton Isom and Allie (Scott) G.; B.S., Middle Tenn. State Coll., 1958; D.D.S., U. Tenn., 1961; m. Sarah Kate Conrad, Apr. 3, 1954; children—Sarah Alisa, Cynthia Lynn, Lydia Annette, Amy Elizabeth, Timothy Isom. Dental intern Hillsborough County Hosp., Tampa, Fla., 1961-62; pvt. practice dentistry, 1962—. Served with USAF, 1951-55. Mem. Am., West Coast dental assns., Hillsborough County Dental Soc., Brewster Research Clinic, Internat. Assn. Orthodontics. Democrat. Baptist. Club: Cigar City Gun. Home: 11508 Carrollwood Dr Tampa FL 33618 Office: 10552 Florida Av Tampa FL 33612

GURLEY, ROY EARL, lawyer; b. Clinton, Okla., Oct. 6, 1938; s. Earl Thomas and Opal (Rose) G.; B.B.A., North Tex. State U., 1961; J.D., U. Houston, 1968; m. Judy Elaine Blackburn, June 6, 1964; children—Lorie, Leigh Ann. Admitted to Tex. bar, 1968; partner law firm Gassaway & Gurley, Attys., Borger, Tex., 1969—. City atty., Borger, Tex., 1973—; city atty., Fritch, Tex., 1969—. Chmn. Hutchinson County Cancer Crusade, 1971. Bd. dirs. Hutchinson County Cancer Soc. Served with USAF, 1961-62. Mem. Lambda Chi Alpha, Phi Alpha Delta. Rotarian (dir. 1971—). Home: 2005 Hemlock St Borger TX 79007 Office: Box 1709 Borger TX 79007

GURTLER, MARTIN MATHIAS II, civil engr.; b. New Orleans, May 3, 1916; s. Martin Mathias and Louisa Benedicta (Rieth) G.; B.S. in Civil Engring., Tulane U., 1937; m. Audrey May Salzer, Apr. 15, 1944; children—Martin Mathias III, Linda Anna, Friedrich W. L., Michael K. A. Indsl. engr. Engring. Splty. & Mfg. Co., New Orleans, 1937-39; chief engr. LeMieux Bros., Inc., foresters and piledriving contractors, 1939-41; constrn. engr. Doullut & Ewin, Inc., civil engrs., gen. contractors, 1944-46; v.p. Bernard & Byrd, Inc., gen. contractors, 1946-51; pres. Gurtler, Hebert & Co., Inc., civil engrs., gen. contractors, New Orleans, 1951—; pres., dir. Am. Thrift & Finance Plan, Inc.; partner K.W. Salzer & Co., City Park Av. Floral Co. Bd. dirs. New Orleans Opera House Assn.; bd. dirs., mem. exec. com. Information Council of Americas; trustee Geneal. Research Soc. New Orleans, Mem. La. Engring. Soc., Nat. Soc. Profl. Engrs., Nat. Geneal. Soc., Swiss Am. Soc. New Orleans, France-Amerique de la Louisiane, Tau Beta Pi. Roman Catholic. Clubs: Pendennis, Round Table, International House, Paul Morphy (New Orleans); Metairie (La.) Country; City (Baton Rouge). Home: 1320 Second St New Orleans LA 70130 Office: 4334 Earhart Blvd St New Orleans LA 70185

GUSEMAN, JOHN LEE, state ofcl.; b. Boise, Ida., July 5, 1910; s. Staley Lee and Villa Elizabeth (Clevidence) G.; student Fed. Bur. Investigation Nat. Acad., 1953, Municipal Police Adminstrn., Internat. City Mgrs. Assn., 1957; m. Helen Woods, Jan. 7, 1933; children—Robert, Patricia (Mrs. William L. Pelfrey). Chief police, Harlingen, Tex., 1952-58; asst. chief police, Bryan, Tex., 1961, police chief, 1961; dir. police Victoria, Tex., 1961-72; regional adminstr. Tex. Gov.'s Office Traffic Safety, 1972—. Instr. Police Acad., San Antonio, 1947-51, Victoria Police Acad., 1962-71; guest instr. Tex. A. and M. U., 1953-63, Victoria Coll., 1970-71. Commr. Tex. Urban Devel. Commn., 1970-71, vice chmn. law enforcement com., 1970-71. Bd. dirs. Tex. Inst. Children and Youth, 1957-58, FBI Nat. Acad. Assos. Tex., 1953—. Served with USNR, 1941. Mem. Tex. Assembly on State and Urban Crisis, Internat. Assn. Chief Police, Tex. Police Assn. (dir. 1962-63), Internat. Assn. Identification (div. pres. 1958-59). Mason (Shriner), Rotarian. Club: Toastmaster (pres. 1955-56) (Harlingen, Tex.). Home: 2213 E Van Buren St Harlingen TX 78550 Office: PO Box 2743 Harlingen TX 78550

GUSSOW, MILTON, ednl. publishing co. exec.; b. Newark, Sept. 19, 1924; s. Israel and Minnie (Finkelstein) G.; B.S., U.S. Naval Acad., 1949; B.S. in Elec. Engring., U.S. Naval Postgrad. Sch., 1956; M.S., Mass. Inst. Tech., 1957; m. Libbie Gloria Kaye, Dec. 24, 1951; children—Myra Lynn, Susan Adele. Commd. ensign U.S. Navy, 1949, advanced through grades to comdr., 1964; ret., 1967; acad. v.p. Capitol Radio Engring. Inst. div. McGraw-Hill Inc., Washington, 1968-71; sr. v.p. McGraw-Hill Continuing Edn. Center, Washington, 1971—, also dir.; past professorial lectr., adj. prof. Am. U., George Washington U. Sr. mem. I.E.E.E.; mem. Am. Soc. Engring. Edn., Data Processing Mgmt. Assn., Nat. Home Study Council (vice chmn. ednl. com. 1971), Sigma Xi, Sigma Gamma Tau. Club: Lakewood Country (chmn. tennis com. 1973-74) (Rockville, Md.). Author texts in field, also articles. Home: 6609 Lybrook Ct Bethesda MD 20034 Office: 3939 Wisconsin Av Washington DC 20016

GUSTAFSON, ALFORD VINCENT, JR., ins. agt., educator; b. Birmingham, Ala., Jan. 17, 1927; s. Alford Vincent and Ruth (Hamblin) G.; B.S., U. Louisville, 1951; m. Joan Lee, Dec. 17, 1949; children—Virginia, Susan, Barbara, Laura. Owner ins. agy., Louisville, 1951—; instr. ins. course U. Louisville Sch. Bus., 1963—. Pres., Louisville Bd. Independent Ins. Agts. Past pres. Ky. Amateur Athletic Union; past pres., treas. Men's Municipal Softball Assn. Served with AUS, 1945-47. Mem. Ky. State Agts. (dir.). Episcopalian. Clubs: Louisville Boat, Bonnycastle. Home: 2416 Douglass Blvd Louisville KY 40205 Office: 3415 Bardstown Rd Louisville KY 40218

GUSTAFSON, JOEL KARL, lawyer; b. New Haven, May 24, 1937; s. J. Arthur and Jane (Thompson) G.; A.B., Lafayette Coll., 1960; LL.B., Tulane U., 1963; m. Judyth F. Field, Sept. 2, 1961; children—Kimberly Ann, Scott Evan, Stacey Lynn. Admitted to Fla. bar, 1964; prosecuting atty. City of Ft. Lauderdale, Fla., 1964-67; atty. Ft. Lauderdale (Fla.) Bd. of Adjustment, 1964-67, Ft. Lauderdale Planning and Zoning Bd., 1964-67; practiced in Ft. Lauderdale, Fla., 1964—; mem. firm Gustafson, Caldwell & Stephens, 1968—; mem. Fla. Ho. of Reps., 1967-72. Mem. Broward County Narcotics Guidance Council, 1969-72, Fla. Law Revision Commn., 1969-72; chmn. exec. com. Nat. Hwy. Safety Adv. Com., 1971—. Recipient award for meritorious pub. service, 1969. Mem. Am., Fla., Broward bar assns., Kappa Sigma, Republican. Presbyn. Home: 1636 SE 12th Ct Fort Lauderdale FL 33316 Office: Internat Bldg 2455 E Sunrise Blvd Fort Lauderdale FL 33304

GUSTAFSON, JOHN CONRAD, engring. mgr.; b. N.Y.C., Dec. 13, 1936; s. Axel Conrad and Hedvig (Lorentson) G.; student Upsala Coll., 1955-56; B.S., U. Conn., 1960; m. Helen Elaine Parson, Aug. 16, 1958; children—Carl William, Carolyn Elaine, John David. Mech. engr., asst. project engr. Kearfott div. Gen. Precision, Inc., 1960-72; aerospace technologist NASA, Langley Research Center, Hampton, Va., 1972—, mech. and thermal engring. mgr. Viking 75 gas chromatograph mass spectrometer expt., also entry pressure measurements mgr. Viking 75 spacecraft. Mem. Am. Soc. M.E., Nat. Soc. Profl. Engrs., Sigma Pi Sigma. Lutheran. Home: 883 Cascade Dr Newport News VA 23602 Office: NASA Hampton VA 23365

GUSTIN, HARRY NELSON II, lawyer; b. Woodstock, Ont., Can., June 18, 1921; s. Earle Frank and Eddie Mae (Avery) G.; came to U.S., 1921, naturalized, 1937; B.S., Va. Poly. Inst. and State U., 1943; LL.B., U. Va., 1948; m. Esther Grace Callaham, Nov. 4, 1950; children—Harry Nelson III, James Wilson, Thomas Avery. Admitted to Va. bar, 1948; asso. atty. Preston, Phillips & Taylor, Norfolk, 1948-54; partner Taylor, Gustin, Harris, Fears & Davis and predecessor firm, Norfolk, 1954—. Pres., sec. Investment Realty, Inc.; partner, dir. Old Dominion Real Estate Investment Trust. Mem. Norfolk Citizens Adv. Com., 1968-69; vice chmn. Norfolk City Sch. Bd., 1969-72. Mem. Norfolk City Democratic Exec. Com., 1966-72. Pres., bd. dirs. Norfolk Safety Council; bd. dirs. Va. Safety Assn., Va. Sch. Bds. Assn. Served to 2d lt. AUS, 1943; to capt. USAAF, 1944-46; PTO. Mem. Va. State Bar, Norfolk-Portsmouth Bar Assn., Internat. Assn. Ins. Counsel, Phi Alpha Delta, Alpha Kappa Psi, Omicron Delta Kappa. Baptist (deacon, trustee). Mason (Shriner). Clubs: Virginia, Harbor, Norfolk Yacht and Country. Author: Better Law Practice in Virginia, 1973. Home: 416 Sinclair St Norfolk VA 23505 Office: 1440 Virginia Nat Bank Bldg Norfolk VA 23510

GUTERMUTH, CLINTON RAYMOND, conservationist, naturalist; b. Fort Wayne, Ind., Aug. 16, 1900; s. Henry Christian and Alice Virtue (Zion) G.; student Notre Dame, 1918-19; grad. Am. Inst. Banking, 1927, post grad. work, 1927-28; D.Sc., U. Ida., 1972; m. Ila Bessie Horm, Mar. 4, 1922. Asst. cashier St. Joseph Valley Bank, Elkhart, Ind., 1922-34; dir. div. of edn., Ind. Dept. of Conservation, Indianapolis, 1934-40, dir. div. fish and game, 1940-42; Ind. rent dir. O.P.A., Indpls., 1942-45; exec. sec. Am. Wildlife Inst., Washington, 1945-46; v.p. Wildlife Mgmt. Inst. 1946-71. Sec., trustee N.A. Wildlife Found., Inc., 1946—; v.p., trustee Stronghold, Inc., 1947—; former chmn., hon. mem. Natural Resources Council Am., 1946-72; hon. pres., dir. World Wildlife Fund (U.S.), 1963—; trustee, mem. exec. council World Wildlife Fund (Internat.), 1971—; exec. com. Am. Com. Internat. Wildlife Protection, Citizens Com. for Natural Resources. Recipient Leopold medal Wildlife Soc., 1957; Albright medal Am. Scenic and Historic Preservation Soc., 1971; Order Golden Ark, Netherlands, 1973. Fellow A.A.A.S.; mem. Fishing Hall of Fame, Nat. Rifle Assn. (life mem., pres., dir. 1963—), Izaak Walton League Am. (life), Outdoor Writers Assn. Am., Wildlife Soc. (trustee), Am. Forestry Assn. (life mem.), Am. Soc. Range Mgmt., Nat. Audubon Soc., Nat. Parks Assn., Wilderness Soc. (life), Am. Fisheries Soc., Internat. Assn. Game, Fish and Conservation Commrs., Soil Conservation Soc. (hon. life mem.), Arctic Inst. N.Am., Am., Zool. Soc. (N.Y.), Mason (32 deg., K.T.). Clubs: Cosmos, Nat. Press (Washington); Explorers, Boone & Crockett, Camp Fire (N.Y.C.): (hon.) Booneville (Ind.) Press. Elkhart (Ind.) Conservation. Miami (Fla.) Sailfish. Tanana Valley (Alaska) Sportsmen's. Author: Where to Go in Indiana, Official Lake Guide, 1938; Quips and Queries page on natural history, Outdoor Indiana, 1934-42; W.M.I. bi-weekly Outdoor News Bull., 1947-50; co-author: The Fisherman's Encyclopedia; The Standard Book of Fishing. Author numerous articles on natural resource restoration. Home: 4801 Connecticut Av NW Washington DC 20008 Office: Wire Bldg Washington DC 20005

GUTH, PAUL SPENCER, pharmacologist, educator; b. N.Y.C., May 29, 1931; s. Harry Samuel and Hattie (Braun) G.; B.S., Fordham U., 1953; M.S., Phila. Coll. Pharmacy and Sci., 1955; Ph.D., Hahnemann Med. Coll., 1958; m. Judi Papiroff, June 28, 1953; children—Douglas Matthew, Gregory David, Bradley Owen, Derek Adam. Asso. in pharmacology Hahnemann Med. Coll., 1959-60; asst. prof. Tulane U. Sch. Medicine, New Orleans, 1960-63, asso. prof., 1963-66, prof. pharmacology, 1966—; vis. prof. La. State U. Med. Sch., 1973—. Wellcome sr. hon. research fellow U. Birmingham (U.K.) Med. Sch., 1972-73; cons. pharmacology I.C.I. Am. Mem. med. bd. dirs. Open Door. Recipient First Distinguished Alumnus award Hahneman Med. Coll., 1970; NIH research grantee 1960—; Smith, Kline & French Found. fellow, 1955-58, Nat. Paraplegia Found. fellow, 1958-59, Wellcome Trust fellow, 1972-73. Mem. Am. Soc. Pharmacology and Exptl. Therapeutics, N.Y. Acad. Scis., A.A.A.S., Soc. for Neuroscis., Sigma Xi, Rho Chi. Democrat. Jewish religion. Club: New Orleans Yacht. Contbr. articles profl. jours. Home: 4935 Cardenas Dr New Orleans LA 70127 Office: 1430 Tulane Av New Orleans LA 70112

GUTHRIE, FRANK EDWIN, entomologist, educator; b. Louisville, Jan. 14, 1923; s. Blaine and Lera May (Waller) G.; B.S., U. Ky., 1947; M.S., U. Ill., 1949, Ph.D., 1952; m. Bernice Button, Dec. 26, 1947; children—Janet, Caroline. Asst. prof. entomology U. Fla., Quincy, 1952-54; asst. prof. entomology N.C. State U., Raleigh, 1954-59, asso. prof., 1959-62, prof., 1962—, asst. dean Grad. Sch., 1962-64, dir. research and tng. programs in pesticide toxicology, 1964—. Served with USMCR, 1943-46, 51-52. Mem. Entomol. Soc. Am., Am. Chem. Soc., Soc. Toxicology. Co-author: Concepts of Pest Management, 1970. Contbr. articles to profl. jours. Home: 600 Beaver Dam R Raleigh NC 27607 Office: Dept Entomology North Carolina State Univ Raleigh NC

GUTHRIE, KENNETH BERNARD, newspaper editor; b. Jasper, Ala., Aug. 9, 1931; s. Elliott Bernard and Esther (Blevins) G.; B.S. with honors in Journalism, U. Fla., 1953; m. Rita Locy, Aug. 8, 1958; children—Richard Bernard, Susan Yvonne. Editor, Jasper (Ala.) Mountain Eagle, 1955-56; reporter Palatka (Fla.) Daily News, 1956-57, editor, 1960-61; reporter Daytona Beach (Fla.) News-Jour., New Smyrna Beach bur., 1957-58, Palatka bur., 1958-60; state editor Pensacola (Fla.) News-Jour., 1961-65; state editor Orlando (Fla.) Sentinel-Star, 1966-69; editor Osceola (Fla.) Sun., 1969-70, editor, pub., 1970—, dir., 1969—. Served with AUS, 1953-55. Home: 708 Robert St Kissimmee FL 32741 Office: 700 W Vine St Kissimmee FL 32741

GUTHRIE, MARION PHILIP III, med. products co. exec.; b. Vicksburg, Miss., Mar. 26, 1945; s. Marion Philip and Aileen Luton (Perry) G.; B.S. summa cum laude, La. Poly. U., 1967; M.B.A. (Paton fellow), U. Mich., 1968; m. Beverly Alice Blackmon, June 2, 1966; children—Todd, Tait. Cons. financial planning and control Price Waterhouse & Co., C.P.A.'s, Houston, 1968-72; financial v.p. Vicra Sterile, Inc., Dallas, 1972—. Lectr., Am. Mgmt. Assn. C.P.A., La., Tex. Mem. Am. Inst. C.P.A.'s, Tex. Soc. C.P.A.'s, Nat. Assn. Accountants (asso. dir. Houston chpt. 1970), N.Am. Soc. Corporate Planning, Delta Sigma Pi, Phi Kappa Phi, Omicron Delta Kappa, Beta Gamma Sigma, Beta Alpha Psi. Home: 7123 Hillwood Lane Dallas TX 75240

GUTHRIE, NORMAN EUGENE, state ofcl.; b. Salisbury, N.C., Oct. 16, 1930; s. Thomas Ralph and Gene Irene (Deal) G.; B.C.E., N.C. State U., 1957; m. Joyce Elizabeth Teal, Sept. 6, 1956; 1 dau., Deborah Anne. Design engr. Fraioli-Blum-Yesselman, Cons. Engrs., Norfolk, Va., 1957-58; project engr. HSM & M, Architects and Engrs., Roanoke, Va., 1958-63; chief civil engr. Office State Property and Constrn., N.C. Dept. Adminstrn., Raleigh, 1963—. Served with AUS, 1952-54. Mem. Nat. Soc. Profl. Engrs., Am. Soc. C.E. Home: 4100 Spruce Dr Raleigh NC 27612 Office: NC Dept Adminstrn 116 W Jones St Raleigh NC 27602

GUTHRIE, W(ILLIAM) NELSON, ret. clergyman; b. Walker County, Ala., Aug. 5, 1903; s. William Eual and Alice (Adkins) G.; student Birmingham So. Coll., 1921-26; spl. student Emory U.; D.D., Athens Coll., 1942; m. Jessie Lucille Welch, Nov. 5, 1927; children—Carolyn Jayne, William Nelson. Ordained to ministry Meth. Ch., 1929; pastor Meth. churches Tarrant, Ala., 1928-32, Birmingham, Ala., 1933-35, 45-49, Albertville, 1936-38, Sheffield, 1938-40, Tuscaloosa Dist., 1941-45, Decatur (Ala.) Central Meth. Ch., 1949-50; exec. sec., supt. Meth. homes, 1951-57; exec. sec. Meth. Home for Aging, Birmingham, 1957-59; exec. sec. Superannaute Homes, Birmingham, 1959—, now ret. Mem. Mayor's Com. Settle Racial Troubles, 1943, Gov.'s Com. on Phonography. Mem. Gen. Conf. Meth. Ch., 1956, 60, 64, 66, 68, Jurisdictional Conf., 1944, 48, 56, 60, 64, 67, 68; chmn. pensions com. No. Ala. Conf. Meth. Ch., 1968-72; mem. bishop's spl. com. on pensions; mem. Tri-Conf. Com. on Merger, dir. Area IV Conf. Council. Trustee Huntington Coll. Clubs: Civitan, Lions, Rotary, Kiwanis. Pioneered establishment homes for ret. Meth. ministers' widows. Address: 2048 Kentucky Av Birmingham AL 35216

GUTIERREZ, ENRIQUE HIRAM, architect; b. Havana, Cuba, May 20, 1931; s. Enrique and Ana Maria (Rodriguez) G.; architect, U. Havana, 1955; m. Marta Saavedra, Sept. 26 1952; children—Ana Teresa, Fernando. Partner, Alvarez & Gutierrez, Havana, Cuba, 1955-57; partner, head archtl. dept. Saenz, Cancio, Martin, Alvarez & Gutierrez, Havana, Cuba, 1957-59, 1960-65; asst. prof. design U. Havana, 1955-59; prin. partner E. H. Gutierrez & Assos., San Juan, P.R., 1965—; chmn. bd. EHG Enterprises, Inc., 1969—; dir. Barnett Bank, Miami. Hon. consul Costa Rica in San Juan, P.R., 1970—. Recipient Nat. award Colegio Nacional de Arquitectos de Cuba, 1960; Golden Plate award Am. Acad. Achievement, 1972; gold medal Colegio de Arquitectos de Cuba en el Exilio, 1972. Mem. A.I.A., Colegio de Ingenieros, Arquitectos y Agrimensores de P.R. Clubs: Nautico (San Juan, P.R.); N.Y. Athletic (N.Y.C.); Cay Cay (Bahamas); Ocean Reef (Cayo Largo, Fla.); Crown Colony (Berry Islands, Bahamas); Kings Bay, Riviera Country (Miami). Home: Cond Torre del Mar Av Ashford 1477 Santurce PR 00907 also 4745 SW 80th St Miami FL 33143 Office: Box 13171 Santurce PR 00908

GUTIERREZ, JOSE SANTOS, agrl. exec.; b. Alamos, Sonora, Mexico, June 12, 1916; s. Alberto and Argella Garcia Gutierrez; grad. Heriberto Aja, 1934; m. Elsa Luken, Oct. 29, 1942; children—Elsa (Mrs. Hector Amavizca), Jose Santos, Lupita, Juan Alberto, Javier, Monica. Accountant in bank, 1934-40; pres. Gutierrez Hermanos S.A., Hermosillo, Mexico, 1947—, Industrias Avicolas, S.A., Hermosillo, 1947—, Molinos Mezquitel del Oro, Hermosillo, 1966—, Lacteos de Sonora, S.A., Hermosillo, Incuberdoras Mezquital del Oro, Hermosillo, Frigorifica y Empscadora, S.A., Mezquital del Oro, Hermosillo. Gen. treas. State of Sonora, Mexico, 1955-58. Trustee U. Sonora. Clubs: Old Pueblo (Tucson); Casino de Hermosillo. Home: 700 Alatoree St Hermosillo Sonoro Mexico Office: PO Box 138 Hermosillo Sonoro Mexico

GUTIERREZ, ROMAN, lawyer; b. Nuevo Laredo, Tamaulipas, Mexico, Mar. 27, 1936; s. Bernardo and Juanita (Garza) G.; came to U.S., 1940; naturalized, 1957; B.A., E. Tex. State U., 1958; J.D., U. Tex., 1962; m. Carlota Oralia Mejia, July 15, 1961; children—Carlotta Romaynne, Roman G., Letitia Janel. Admitted to Tex. bar, 1962; practiced in Laredo, 1962-68, Edinburg, Tex., 1968—; mem. firms Ligarde, Wilson & Gutierréz, 1962-64, Pena, McDonald & Gutierrez, Edinburg, 1968-73; atty. Laredo Dist. Atty. Office, 1964-66. Dir. Laredo Legal Aid Clinic, 1967-68; dir., pres. Tex. Rural Legal Aid, 1970-73; mem. steering com. Met. Nat. Bank, 1971—. Mem. Edinburg Parks Bd., 1971-73; chmn. Muscular Dystrophy drive, 1964-67. Bd. dirs. Edinburg Pub. Library, San Juan Nursing Home. Served with USMCR, 1959-60. Mem. Hidalgo County Bar Assn. Roman Catholic. Kiwanian (sec. Edinburg chpt. 1969-72). Club: 20-30 (pres.). Home: 1506 Cedar Dr Edinburg TX 78539 Office: 712 S Closner St Edinburg TX 78539 Died July 18, 1973.

GUTIERREZ-PELAEZ, FRANCISCO ALBERTO, physician; b. Pinar del Rio, Cuba, Aug. 7, 1918; s. Francisco Gutierrez Fonte and Vicenta Pelaez Mila; M.D., Havana U. Med. Sch., 1943; m. Maria E. Rissett Mazorra Vega, Aug. 22, 1943; children—Juan Francisco, Jorge Martin, Alberto Alejandro, Maria Eugenia. Intern, U. Havana, 1944-45, surgical resident, 1945-46; asso. gynecology Havana U., 1946-50; anesthesiologist Havana Municipal Maternity Hosp., 1950-61; dir. Anesthesia Institute de Cirugia Cardiovascular ydel torax, Havana, 1961-62; clin. asso. anesthesiology Boston City Hosp., 1962-63; asst. prof. surgery, anesthesia U. W.Va., 1963-68; asso. prof. U. Ala., Birmingham, 1968-72, prof. anesthesia, 1972—; chief anesthesia VA Hosp., Birmingham, 1972—; cons. VA Hosp., Tuskegee, Ala. Diplomate Am. Soc. Anesthesiologists. Fellow Am. Coll. Anesthesiologists. Home: 3512 S Woodridge Rd Birmingham AL 35223

GUTSCHLAG, JOHN PAUL, graphic arts co. exec.; b. Council Bluffs, Ia., Mar. 3, 1940; s. Paul C. and Faye G. (Speer) G.; B.S., U. Neb., 1962; B.S., So. Meth. U., 1962; m. Barbara K. Chandler, Dec. 30, 1961; children—Tracy Linn, Kelly Beth, John Derek. Data processing mgr. Taylor Pub. Co., Dallas, 1961-66; pres. Affiliated Computer Systems, Dallas, 1966-71; pres. graphics div. Herff Jones Co., Indpls., 1971—. Cons. Mgmt. Information Systems. Mem. Phi Gamma Delta, Mu Epsilon Nu. Lutheran. Home: Route 1 Box 41A Sprague AL 36076 Office: 2800 Selma Hwy Montgomery AL 36111

GUTWALD, EDWARD JOHN, civil engr.; b. Davenport, Ia., Jan. 20, 1933; s. Paul Francis and Mildred Ruth (Colcman) G.; B.S. in Civil Engring., The Citadel, 1954; m. Elise Alston Mehrlich, June 14, 1954; children—Elizabeth, Frances. With U.S. Army C.E., 1954—, civil engr., automatic data processing coordinator, Savannah, Ga. and Balt., 1962-70, civil engr., div. automatic data processing coordinator, Atlanta, 1970—. Mem. Fed. Automatic Data Processing Council, Fed. Exec. Bd. Served to 1st lt. AUS, 1954-58. Registered prof. engr., Vt. Mem. Soc. Am. Mil. Engrs., Ga. Numis. Assn. Club: Doranville (Ga.) Coin (bd. dirs.). Home: 3958 Central Dr Clarkston GA 30021 Office: US Army Corps Engrs 510 Title Bldg 30 Pryor St Atlanta GA 30303

GUY, ALBERT GLASGOW, metallurgist, educator; b. Chgo., May 27, 1917; s. Samuel Kerr and Nellie Ellen (Glasgow) G.; B.S., U. Chgo., 1938; M.S., Ohio State U., 1941; D.Sc., Carnegie-Mellon U., 1946; m. Ingeborg von der Bruggen, Apr. 29, 1964; children—Penny Virginia, Nancy Jean. Engr. research lab. Gen. Electric Co., 1944-47; asso. prof. metallurgy N.C. State Coll., 1947-51; prof. metallurgy Sch. Metall. Engring., Purdue U., 1952-60; prof. dept. materials sci. and engring. U. Fla., Gainesville, 1960—. Am. Philos. Soc. grantee, 1964. Lord fellow, 1940-41. Mem. Am. Soc. Metals, Am. Inst. Mining and Metall. Engrs., Brit. Inst. Metals, Sigma Xi. Author: Physical Metallurgy for Engineers, 1962; Introduction to Materials Science, 1972; Elements of Physical Metallurgy, 1974. Home: 1027 NW 11th Av Gainesville FL 32601

GUYTON, JOSEPH WARREN, cons. engr.; b. Vicksburg, Miss., Mar. 24, 1933; s. Joseph Owen and Alice Irene (Potts) G.; B.S., U. Ill., 1955, M.S., 1957; m. Carolyn Ann Owens, Dec. 29, 1956; children—Mark Owen, Paul Warren, Timothy Lee. Transp. planning engr. Harland Bartholomew & Assos., St. Louis, 1959-60, resident engr., Fayetteville, N.C., 1960-61, transp. planning engr., Memphis, 1962-63, asso. partner, Memphis, 1964-70, partner 1971—. Tchr., guest lectr. U. Ill., 1955—, U. Miss., 1963—, U. Tenn., 1965—, Memphis State U., 1967—, U. Ala., 1968-69, U. Tex., 1971—, U. Ky., 1973—. Served with C.E., AUS, 1957-59; ETO. Recipient C. C. Wiley Traveling award hwy. engring. U. Ill., 1955. Registered profl. engr., Fla., Ill., Ind., Ky., O., Mich., Tenn. Mem. Am. Soc. C.E., Hwy. Research Bd., Soc. Am. Mil. Engrs., Inst. Traffic Engrs., Chi Epsilon, Alpha Kappa Lambda. Presbyn. (elder, chmn. bd. deacons). Memphis Athletic. Home: 2085 Firefly Cove Memphis TN 38138 Office: 188 Jefferson Av Memphis TN 38103

GUYTON, PERCY LOVE, economist; b. Kosciusko, Miss., Sept. 29, 1905; s. Thomas Percy and Annie D. (Love) G.; B.S., Miss. State U., 1927; M.B.A., Northwestern U., 1932; postgrad. U. Ill., 1933, U. Ia., 1942; Ph.D., Duke, 1952; m. Margaret Heath Ames, June 26, 1930; children—Jean Love (Mrs. Albert Sidney Newton), Ames Lee. Asst. to gen. mgr. Potts-Oliver Co., Kosciusko, 1922-25; instr., asst. prof. history and econs. Miss. State U., 1928-36; grad. asst. Duke, 1936-38, Duke-Brookings fellow, 1938-39; head dept. econs. and bus. adminstrn. Simpson Coll., 1939-43; with Miss. Dist. and Atlanta Regional OPA, 1943-45; interim instr. econs. Northwestern U., 1945-46; head dept. econs. and bus. adminstrn. King Coll., Bristol, Tenn., 1946-54; prof. econs. Memphis State U., 1954-60; dir. materials devel. Joint Council on Econ. Edn., 1960-66; chmn. div. bus. adminstrn., dir. Center for Econ. Edn., Jacksonville (Fla.) U., 1966-72; cons. to econ. edn. project So. States Work Conf., 1961-65; adviser Jacksonville Indsl. Manpower Center, 1969-70; treas. Fla. Council Econ. Edn., 1970—. Dir. University Heights Civic Club, Memphis, 1958-60; pres. Memphis Campus Christian Life Bd., 1958-60; chmn. program com., chmn. br. council, pres. Friendship Club, Grand Central YMCA, 1964-66. Recipient Distinguished Service awards N.Y.C. Grand Central YMCA, 1966, Kiwanis Club, N.Y.C., 1966. Mem. Am., So. econ. assns., Alpha Kappa Psi. Democrat. Presbyn. (elder). Co-editor: Economic Education Experiences of Enterprising Teachers, 1962-65; Our Growing America, 1963; Teachers Guide to Economics in the Business Education Curriculum, 1963; Teachers Guide to DEEP, 1964; Suggestions for a Basic Economics Library, 1965; Money and You, 1967. Home: 931 Overlook Dr Jacksonville FL 32211

GWALTNEY, CORBIN, editor, pub.; b. Balt., Apr. 16, 1922; s. Howell Corbin and Margaret (Bell) G.; B.A., Johns Hopkins, 1943; L.H.D., L.I. U., 1970; m. Jean Caryl Wyckoff, June 20, 1973; children by previous marriage—Jean, Margaret, Thomas. Indsl. relations Western Electric Co., Gen. Electric Co., 1946-49; editor Johns Hopkins mag., 1950-59; exec. dir., editor Editorial Projects for Edn., Washington, 1959—, pres., 1971—, also trustee; editor Chronicle Higher Edn., 1966—. Served with AUS, 1943-45. Decorated Purple Heart; recipient Distinguished Service to Edn. medal Columbia Alumni Fedn., 1964, award for distinguished service to higher edn. Am. Coll. Pub. Relations Assn., 1971. Club: Johns Hopkins (Balt.). Mem. editorial bd. Tech. Rev., Mass. Inst. Tech., 1972—. Home: 5104 Brookview Dr Bethesda MD 20016 Office: 1717 Massachusetts Av NW Washington DC 20036

GWALTNEY, JACK MERRIT, JR., phsycian; b. Norfolk, Va., Dec. 24, 1930; s. Jack Merrit and Mary Gordon (Weck) G.; B.A., U. Va., 1952, M.D., 1956; m. Sarah Bullock Parrott, June 26, 1954; children—Elizabeth Cromwall, Jack Merrit III. Rotating intern Univ. Hosps., Cleve., 1956-57, resident internal medicine, 1957-59; chief resident internal medicine U. Va. Hosp., Charlottesville, 1959-60; profl. asst. respiratory virus research U. Va. Sch. Medicine, 1962-63, research fellow preventive medicine and medicine, 1963-64, instr. preventive medicine and medicine, 1964-66, asst prof., 1966-70, asso. prof. internal medicine, 1970—, head sect. epidemiology and virology, 1970—; asso. mem. Commn. Acute Respiratory Diseases Armed Forces Epidemiological Bd., 1968-73; mem. adv. panel infectious disease therapy U.S. Pharmacopeia, 1970-75. Served to capt. U.S. Army, 1960-62. Postdoctoral fellow Nat. Inst. Allergy and Infectious Diseases NIH, 1963-64; Edward Livingston Trudeau fellow Am. Thoracic Soc. 1964-67; recipient Research Career Devel. award NIH, 1969-73. Diplomate Am. Bd. Internal Medicine, also subsplty. in infectious diseases. Fellow A.C.P.; mem. Am. Type Culture Collection (trustee 1972-74), Am. Epidemiological Soc., Albemarle County Med. Soc., Am. Fedn. Clin, Research, Am. Soc. Microbiology, Am., Va. (sec.-treas. governing council 1973—) thoracic socs., Am. Assn. U. Profs., A.A.A.S., Infectious Diseases Soc. Am., Med. Soc. Va., So. Soc. Clin. Investigation, Am. Assn. Immunologists, Soc. Epidemiologic Research, Sigma Xi. Editorial bd. Antimicrobial Agents and Chemotherapy. Contbr. numerous articles to profl. jours. Home: 1454 Rugby Rd Charlottesville VA 22903

GWALTNEY, MARION LEWIS, lawyer; b. Dothan, Ala., Jan. 3, 1918; s. Alvin W. and Bernice (Warrick) G.; student in bus. adminstrn., U. Ala., 1937-39, J.D., 1942; m. Mary Estelle Creel, Sept. 14, 1946; children—Marion Lewis, Kathy Creel. Admitted to Ala. bar, 1942; atty. Chief Atty.'s Office, VA, Ala., 1945-46; asso. Maurice F. Bishop, Birmingham, Ala., 1947-52; asst. U.S. atty. for No. Dist. of Ala., 1952-57; with firm Levine and Fulford, Birmingham, Ala., 1957-70, partner, 1958-69; practice law, Birmingham, 1970; exec. dir. Legal Aid Soc. Jefferson County, Ala., Birmingham, 1970-73; faculty, Cumberland Sch. Law, Samford U., Birmingham, 1970—, asso. prof. law, 1973—. Served with USAAF, 1942-45; ETO. Mem. Ala., Birmingham bar assn., Farrah Law Soc., Phi Alpha Delta. Home: 571 Shades Crest Rd Birmingham AL 35226 Office: 800 Lakeshore Dr Birmingham AL 35209

GWATHMEY, ROBERT RYLAND, III, lawyer; b. Richmond, Va., Dec. 21, 1917; s. Robert Ryland and Mary Lewis (Vaden) G.; B.A., Randolph-Macon Coll., 1941; LL.B., U. Va., 1942; m. Bonnie Marek, Sept. 8, 1973; children by previous marriage—Mary, Robin, Robert Ryland IV. Admitted to Va. bar 1941; Commonwealth atty. for Hanover County, Va., 1948-56; asso. county judge, Hanover County, 1956-57; practiced in Richmond, Va., 1942-73; Mechanicsville, Va., 1973—; mem. firm Rogers, Cudlipp & Gwathmey, 1965-73; Mem. Va. Ho. of Dels., 1958—. Served with USNR, 1942-46. Mem. Kappa Alpha, Tau Kappa Alpha. Democrat. Episcopalian. Clubs: Ruritan, Country Va., Downtown Richmond. Home: Hanover VA 23069 Office: 5808 A Mechanicsville Pike Mechanicsville VA 23111

GWATNEY, HAROLD LLOYD, owner automobile agy., banker; b. North Little Rock, Ark., Aug. 17, 1929; s. John Jackson and Bertha Alberta (Chenault) C.; grad. Draughon Sch. Bus., 1950; student Ark. State U., 1968; m. Syble Everee Whitworth, Dec. 16, 1948; children—John Russell, William Alan. Employed in various positions, 1944-57; owner Harold Gwatney Chevrolet Co., Jacksonville, Ark., 1958—; chmn. bd. Citizens Nat. Bank of Jacksonville, 1965—. Alderman, City of North Little Rock, 1956-58. Pres., Young Democrats of Ark., 1957. Mem. Army N.G., 1948—, now brig. gen. Named Outstanding Young Man of Year, North Little Rock Jr. C. of C., 1956. Mem. Ark. Auto Dealers Assn., N.G. Assn. U.S., Jacksonville C. of C. Mason (32 deg., Shriner), Rotarian. Home: 1300 N James St Jacksonville AR 72076 Office: Main and James St Jacksonville AR 72076

GWIN, JAMES BEVERLY, JR., architect; b. Palm Springs, Cal., Feb. 6, 1945; s. James Beverly and Carol (Boone) G.; B.A., Rice U., 1968, B.Arch., 1968; m. Linda Ann Thompson, July 4, 1970. Designer, Sorey-Hill-Binnicker, architects, Oklahoma City, 1968-69; project architect, designer Goleman & Rolfe, Houston, 1970—. Mem. A.I.A. (Houston chpt.), Houston C. of C. Important works include Neurosensory Center for Methodist Hosp., Baylor Coll. Medicine. Home: 2131 Bartlett St Houston TX 77006 Office: 5100 Travis St Houston TX 77002

HAACK, DAVID ARNO, geologist; b. St. Louis, Dec. 21, 1931; s. Arno John and Florence (Reppert) H.; A.B., Washington U., St. Louis, 1954, M.A., 1955; m. Katherine Ann Vanston, June 6, 1953; children—William James, Robert David. Teaching asst. Washington U., 1954-55; geologist, dist. devel. supr. Texaco, Inc., Corpus Christi, Tex., 1957-67, div. staff geologist, well log analyst, devel. supr., Houston, 1967-69; dist. geologist Clark Oil Producing Co., Corpus Christi, 1969-71; chief geologist Normandy Oil and Gas Co., Corpus Christi, 1971-72; sr. exploration geologist Mitchell Energy & Devel. Corp., Houston, 1972—. Served to 1st lt. AUS, 1955-57. Mem. Am. Assn. Petroleum Geologists, Houston, Corpus Christi geol. socs., Sigma Xi, Tau Kappa Epsilon. Clubs: Imperial Point Civic (exec. bd. 1967-69), Alief Band Boosters (v.p. 1968-69) (Houston). Home: 12003 Chessington Dr Houston TX 77071 Office: Mitchell Energy & Devel Corp 3900 One Shell Plaza Houston TX 77002

HAAN, CHARLES THOMAS, educator; b. Muncie, Ind., July 10, 1941; s. Charles Leo and Dorothy (Smith) H.; B.S., Purdue U., 1963, M.S., 1965; Ph.D., Ia. State U., 1967; m. Janice Kay Johnson, June 3, 1967; children—Patricia Kay, Christopher Thomas, Pamela Lynn. Grad. asst. Purdue U., West Lafayette, Ind., 1963-64; research asso. Ia. State U., Ames, 1964-67; asst. prof. agrl. engring. U. Ky., Lexington, 1967—; vis. prof. civil engring. Colo. State U., 1973-74. Cons. Dept. Def., 1970—, Natural Resource Cons., Lexington, 1970—. Recipient Paper award Am. Soc. Agrl. Engrs., 1969. Registered profl. engr., Ky. Mem. Am. Soc. Agrl. Engrs., Am. Geophys. Union, Sigma Xi, Tau Beta Pi, Phi Kappa Phi, Gamma Sigma Delta, Alpha Epsilon. Home: 3509 Berwyn Ct Lexington KY 40503

HAAS, CHARLES DAVID, dentist; b. N.Y.C., Jan. 3, 1941; s. Milton Harold and Elizabeth Ester (Newman) H.; A.B., Boston U., 1962; D.M.D., Tufts U., 1966; m. Sheila Carole Greenberg, July 26, 1964; children—Andrew Scott, Gary Adam. Dental health coordinator Migrant Health Program, Commonwealth of Mass., 1965; intern Montefiore Hosp. and Med. Center, N.Y.C., 1966-67; individual practice dentistry, Miami Beach, Fla., 1969—. Served to capt. U.S. Army, 1967-69. Mem. Internat. Assn. Dental Research, Royal Soc. Health (London), Am. Dental Assn., Alpha Epsilon Pi, Alpha Omega. Author: (with others) Year Book of Dentistry, 1969. Home: 100 Kings Point Dr North Miami Beach FL 33160 Office: 1688 Meridian Av Miami Beach FL 33139

HAAS, GARRY, optometrist; b. El Dorado, Ark., Oct. 7, 1941; s. J.J. and Gwen (Holmes) H.; B.A., Hendrix Coll., 1964; O.D., So. Coll. Optometry, Memphis, 1967. Optometrist, Alford Eye Clinic, Little Rock, 1969-73; owner, optometrist Sherwood (Ark.) Optometric Clinic, 1973—. Served to capt. AUS, 1967-69; capt. Res. Mem. Ark. Optometric Assn., Am. Optometric Found., Visual Research, Am. Optometric Assn., So. Coll. Optometry Alumni Assn., Optometric Center N.Y., Ark. Real Estate Assn., C. of C., Omega Delta. Methodist. Lion. Home: 5901 John F Kennedy Blvd North Little Rock AR 72116 Office: 203 Country Club Rd Sherwood AR 72116

HAAS, THELMA ROBERTS SUMNER(MRS. CHARLES ELMER HAAS), ednl. adminstr.; b. Dade City, Fla., Feb. 28, 1910; d. Jefferson Davis and Mittie (Roberts) Sumner; B.A., Fla. State U., 1931; postgrad. Duke, summers 1935-36; M.Ed. in Personnel Services, U. Fla., 1963; m. Charles Elmer Haas, June 11, 1938; children—Donald Victor, Edith Douglas (Mrs. Stanley W. Hill). Tchr. English and history Benjamin Franklin Jr. High Sch., Tampa, Fla., 1931-34, Andrew Jackson Sr. High Sch., Jacksonville, Fla., 1939-45; tchr. English, H. B. Plant Sr. High Sch., Tampa, 1934-38; tchr. sci. and health North Shore Elementary-Jr. High Sch., Jacksonville, 1954-57; tchr. history Andrew Jackson Sr. High Sch., Jacksonville, 1957-61, guidance counselor, 1961-69, dean girls, 1970—; dean of girls Oceanway Jr. High Sch., Jacksonville, 1969-70. Sec. Marigold Circle Garden Club, 1953-54, v.p., 1954-55; mem. Civic Music Assn., Friends of Pub. Library, Jacksonville, Fedn. Garden Clubs, 1952-56. Mem. N.E.A., Fla. Edn. Assn., Am. Personnel and Guidance Assn., Fla. Deans and Counselors Assn., Am. Assn. U. Women (pres. Tampa br. 1936-38, pres. Jacksonville br. 1939-40, Fla. treas. 1936-37), Mortar Bd., Delta Kappa Gamma (chpt. pres. 1966-68, chmn. coordinating council 1968-70), Alpha Chi Alpha, Pi Lambda Theta, Kappa Delta Pi (corr. sec. 1968-70), Phi Mu. Democrat. Baptist. Home: 332 W 69th St Jacksonville FL 32208 Office: Andrew Jackson Sr High Sch 3816 Main St Jacksonville FL 32206

HABAN, MARY FRANCES, librarian, educator; b. Columbus, O., Jan. 6, 1935; d. Stephen P. and Frances (Zollner) Haban; B.A. magna cum laude, Coll. Mt. St. Joseph, 1956; M.L.S., Carnegie Inst. Tech., 1959; postgrad. Inst. for Sch. Librarians, U. Denver, 1965; Ph.D., U. Pitts., 1971. Tchr. English and math. high sch., Cin., 1956-58; librarian Carnegie Library of Pitts., 1960-62, 70; librarian Central Dist. Catholic High Sch., Pitts., 1962-66; asst. prof., dir. library sci. edn. Duquesne U., Pitts., 1966-68; asso. prof., head library sci. dept. Madison Coll., Harrisonburg, Va., 1970—. Recipient Distinguished Research award Pi Lambda Theta, 1971-72. Mem. A.L.A., N.E.A., Va. Edn. Assn., Va. Library Assn., Va. Assn. for Ednl. Communications and Tech., Am. Assn. U. Profs., Beta Phi Mu, Alpha Beta Alpha. Contbr. articles to profl. jours. Address: Dept of Library Science Madison College Harrisonburg VA 22801

HABEGGER, JAMES HOWARD, physician; b. Indpls., July 30, 1931; s. Myron Lester and Elizabeth Case (Largent) H.; B.S., Ind. U., 1953; M.B.A., Ohio State U., 1956; M.D., McGill U., 1964; m. Phinetta Jane Copeland, Apr. 4, 1952; 1 dau., Etta Ellen. With standards dept. Warner Bur. Div. Bd., Warner Corp., Muncie, Ind., 1953-54; job study engr. Proctor and Gamble Co., Cin., 1956-59; intern Tampa (Fla.) Gen. Hosp., 1964-65; pvt. practice medicine, Rockledge, Fla., 1966—; mem. staff Wuesthoff Hosp.; pres., dir. Rockledge Pharmacy, Inc., Rockledge Med. Arts Bldg., Inc. Served with USAF, 1954-56. Mem. Am., Fla., Indsl. med. assns., Brevard County Med. Soc., Am. Acad. Family Practice. Democrat. Mem. Disciples of Christ Ch. Mason. Home: 815 Rockledge Dr Rockledge FL 32955 Office: 9 Orange Av Rockledge FL 32955

HABER, PAUL ADRIAN LIFE, physician; b. N.Y.C., Feb. 14, 1920; s. Benjamin Walter and Gussie Esther (Schnur) H.; B.A., U. Tex., 1941; M.A., Columbia, 1942; M.D., U. Tex., 1949; M.S., George Washington U., 1968; m. Mary Agatha Crolley, Oct. 25, 1959; 1 son, Peter William. Research chemist Calco Chem. Co., Bound Brook, N.J., 1942-43; intern, Los Angeles County Gen. Hosp., 1949-50; resident VA Hosp., Los Angeles, 1950-52; practice medicine, specializing in internal medicine, Long Beach, Cal., 1952-53; dir. extended care VA Central Office, Washington, 1963-70, dep. asst. chief med. dir., 1970—; asst. clin. prof. medicine U. Cal. at Los Angeles, 1959-63, George Washington U., Washington, 1965-72. Bd. dirs. Nat. Council on Aging, 1972—; mem. adv. council NIH Nat. Inst. Child Health and Human Devel., Dept. Health, Edn., Welfare, 1972—. Mem. Los Angeles County Council on Aging, 1960-63. Served with M.C., USAF, 1953-55. Decorated Air Force Commendation medal; recipient exceptional service medal VA, 1967, commendation medal, 1955. Fellow A.C.P., Am. Geriatrics Soc.; mem. Phi Beta Kappa. Home: 7501 Honeywell Lane Bethesda MD 20014 Office: 810 Vermont St Washington DC 20420

HABERER, PHILLIP COWSERT, civic worker; b. Dimmitt, Tex., Nov. 8, 1924; s. Roy Earl and Ruth (Cowsert) H.; grad. high sch.; m. Nora Jean Wilson, Jan. 1, 1947; children—Daniel Ray, Sharla Sue, Kleta Kay. Farmer, Earth, Tex., 1952—; dir. Dimmitt Agrl. Industries, Inc. (Tex.); dir. Earth Co-op Gin (Tex.), 1971—. Chmn. drive A.R.C., Earth, 1969—. Trustee Earth Meml. Cemetery, 1965-70, pres., 1970-72. Served with AUS, 1944-46. Mem. Castro County Farm Bur. (dir. 1954-56), Earth C. of C. (dir. 1965), Agrl. Stblzn. and Conservation Community (Castro county community committeeman 1960-62, Lamb County, 1970—). Baptist. Lion (pres. 1971-72). Home: Box 17 Earth TX 79031

HABERER, WALTER JOSEPH, JR., county ofcl.; b. Dayton, O., Feb. 4, 1914; s. Walter Joseph and Eva (Smith) H.; student U.S. Army War Coll., 1959, Army Mgmt. Sch., 1962; B.S. in Elec. Engring., U. Dayton, 1935; m. Marcella Dickason, June 3, 1938; children—Marsha (Mrs. Shannon Holsinger), Monica (Mrs. John F. Blaine), Walter Joseph III. Commd. 2d lt. U.S. Army, 1940, advanced through grades to col., 1955; exec. officer VII Corps Arty., Germany, 1953-56; with Joint Chiefs of Staff, 1961-63; chief provincial affairs MACV, Vietnam, 1963-64; div. chief Def. Intelligence Agy., 1964-65; ret., 1965; exec. dir. Reservoirs Regional Planning Commn., Chatham, Va., 1967-68; exec. sec. Campbell County, Va., 1968—. Bd. dirs. Piedmont Tb Assn. Decorated Legion of Merit, Bronze Star medal (2); Spl. Breast Order Yuuh Hui (China); others. Mem. Assn. Virginia County Adminstrs., Internat. City Mgmt. Assn., Am. Legion, Ruritan. Home: Route 1 Box 452 Rustburg VA 24588 Office: Courthouse Rustburg VA 24588

HACK, FREDERICK COURTLAND, land devel. co. exec.; b. Walthourville, Ga., Feb. 16, 1914; s. George Byron and Ethel (Davis) H.; m. Will Davis Stebbins, Mar. 28, 1942; children—Martha Avary, Frederick Courtland, Orion Byron. With Family Land Mgmt., Hinesville, Ga., 1931-38, Ga. Hwy. Dept., 1938-41, land acquisition and div. cartography U.S. Dept. Agr., Washington, 1941-46; lumber operator, Hinesville, 1946-49; exec. v.p., gen. mgr. The Hilton Head Co. (merged with Island Devel. Corp. and Port Royal Plantation, Inc. 1971), Hilton Head Island, S.C., 1950-61, pres., 1961-71, chmn. bd., 1971—; pres. Island Devel. Corp., Hilton Head Island, 1960-71; chmn. bd. Port Royal Plantation, Inc., Hilton Head Island, 1967-71; co-trustee Honey Horn Plantation Properties, Hilton Head Island, 1957—; adv. dir. Bank of Beaufort (S.C.), 1967—; dir. Oxford First Corp., Phila., 1971—, mem. exec. com., 1972-73. Mem. Toll Bridge Authority, James F. Byrnes Crossing, Hilton Head Island, 1955-62; vice chmn. Beaufort County Bd. Commrs., 1952-62. Bd. dirs. Am. Cancer Soc., Beaufort County; adv. dir. Presbyn. Home, Summerville, S.C., 1968—. Mem. Midway Soc. (bd. selectman 1970—). Presbyn. (elder 1956—, commr. 105th gen. assembly 1965). Lion. Address: Honey Horn Plantation Hilton Head Island SC 29928

HACKBARTH, WINSTON PHILIP, botanist, educator; b. Iowa Falls, Ia., June 30, 1924; s. Earl Amos and Irma Porter (Capellen) H.; B.A., State U. Ia., 1946; B.S., Ida. State U., 1947; M.S., U. Denver, 1949; Ph.D., Ia. State U., 1956; m. Dorothy Mae Mussig, June 16, 1956; children—Deborah Lore, Gregory Winston. Teaching asst. Ia. State U., 1950-55; asst. prof. biology Drake U., Des Moines, 1955-56; asst. prof. biology Augustana Coll., Sioux Falls, S.D., 1956-59; asso. prof. La. Tech. U., Ruston, 1959-70, prof. botany, 1970—. Grad. research cons., 1961—, radiobiology cons., 1965—. Clarinet player Ruston Civic Symphony, 1970-74. Served with M.C., AUS, 1943-45. Mem. Ecol. Soc. Am., A.A.A.S., Am. Inst. Biol. Scis., Nature Conservancy, Am. Soc. Plant Physiologists, La., Ia. acads. sci., Sigma Xi, Beta Beta Beta, Phi Sigma, Phi Mu Alpha Sinfonia. Mason. Author: Competition Between Weeds and Corn, 1956. Home: 1419 Brewster Av Ruston LA 71270

HACKER, CARL SIDNEY, educator; b. Newport News, Va., July 22, 1941; s. Charles William and Jeanne Mewborne (Andrews) H.; B.S., Coll. William and Mary, 1963; Ph.D. (fellow) Rice U., 1968; postgrad. (fellow) Cornell U., 1965-67; m. Pierrette Marie Gabrielle Dayhaw, Sept. 3, 1966; 1 dau., Monica Jeanne. Research asso. U. Notre Dame (Ind.), 1968-71; asst. prof. med. zoology U. Tex. Sch. Pub. Health, Houston, 1971—, also adj. prof. math. scis. Rice U., Houston, 1973—. State Va. Sci. scholar, 1959-63; NIH postdoctoral fellow, 1969-71; NSF research grantee, 1972-74, EXXON Edn. Found. Research grantee, 1973-75. Mem. A.A.A.S., Am. Ornithol. Union, Am. Soc. Parasitologists, Ecol. Soc. Am., Am. Soc. Tropical Medicine and Hygiene, Sigma Xi, Pi Delta Epsilon. Home: 12130 Meadowdale Dr Stafford TX 77477 Office: Population Studies Module Univ Tex School Public Health Houston TX 77025

HACKERMAN, NORMAN, univ. pres., chemist; b. Balt., Mar. 2, 1912; s. Jacob and Anna (Raffel) H.; A.B., Johns Hopkins, 1932, Ph.D., 1935; m. Gene Allison Coulbourn, Aug. 25, 1940; children—Patricia Gale, Stephen, Sally, Katherine. Asst. prof. Loyola Coll., Balt., 1935-39; research chemist for Colloid Corp., 1936-40; chemist U.S. Coast Guard, S.I. 1939-41; asst. prof. Va. Poly. Inst., Blacksburg, 1941-43; research chemist Kellex Corp., 1944; asst. prof. chemistry U. Tex., 1945-46, asso. prof., 1946-50, prof., 1950-70, chmn. dept., 1952-61, dir. corrosion research lab., 1948-61, dean research and sponsored programs, 1960-61, v.p., provost, 1961-63, vice chancellor acad. affairs, 1963-67, pres., 1967-70; prof. chemistry Rice U., Houston, 1970—, pres., 1970—. Chmn. Gordon Corrosion Research Conf., 1950; cons. in corrosion, 1946—; chmn. Inter Soc. Corrosion Com., 1956-58; chmn. Gordon Research Conf. on Chemistry, 1959; mem. nat. sci. bd. NSF, 1968—. Recipient Whitney award Nat. Assn. Corrosion Engrs., 1956; Joseph J. Mattiello Meml. lectr. Fedn. for Socs. of Paint Tech., 1964. Fellow A.A.A.S.; mem. Am. Chem. Soc. (bd. editors, 1956-62, exec. com. colloid div. 1955-58, 1965 S.W. Regional award), Electrochem. Soc. (pres. 1957-58, Palladium medal 1965), Faraday Soc., Nat. Corrosion Engrs. (dir. 1952-55, chmn. com. on edn. Corrosion Research Council 1957-60, Argonne Univs. Assn. (chmn. bd. trustees 1969-73), Nat. Acad. Scis., Am. Philos. Soc., Sigma Xi, Phi Lambda Upsilon, Alpha Chi Sigma, Phi Kappa Phi. Editor Jour. Electrochem. Soc., 1969—; mem. editorial bd., mem. adv. edn. bd. Corrosion Sci., 1969-73; mem. editorial bd. Catalysis Rev. Home: President's House Rice Univ PO Box 1892 Houston TX 77001

HACKETT, CHARLES WILSON, JR., educator; b. Austin, Tex., Oct. 26, 1921; s. Charles Wilson and Jean (Hunter) H.; B.A., U. Tex., 1942, M.B.A., 1948; Ph.D., U. Wash., 1955; m. Ruby E. Bloomquist, July 25, 1953; children—Jean Elizabeth, Ruth Christina. Instr., Air Activities Tex., Corsicana, 1942-44, Schreiner Inst., Kerrville, Tex., 1946; mgmt. engr. Gulf Oil Corp., Port Arthur, Tex., 1948-50; instr., research bus. adminstr. U. Wash., Seattle, 1950-55; asst. prof. bus. orgn. Ohio State U., Columbus, 1955-56; industry financial analyst, credit rep. U.S. Steel Corp., Pitts., 1956-64; asst. dist. credit mgr., Houston, 1964-66; asst. prof. finance U. Tex. at Austin, 1966-69, asso. prof., 1969—. Trustee St. Andrew's Episcopal Sch., Austin. Served with USAAF, 1944-46. Recipient Exec. award Dartmouth Coll. Grad. Sch. Credit and Financial Mgmt., 1964. Mem. Am. Finance Assn., Acad. Mgmt., Phi Beta Kappa, Beta Gamma Sigma, Phi Kappa Sigma, Alpha Kappa Psi, Sigma Iota Epsilon, Pi Sigma Alpha, Sigma Delta Pi, Phi Eta Sigma. Episcopalian. Author: A Techno-Fundamental Portfolio Management Simulation with Computer Applications, 1967. Home: 102 W 33d St Austin TX 78705 Office: Dept Finance U Tex Austin TX 78712

HACKETT, DONALD FRED, coll. adminstr.; b. Wakefield, Mich., Nov. 8, 1918; s. Fred Hamilton and Cunnie Agnes (Kraft) H.; B.S., U. Ill., 1940; M.Ed. U. Mo., 1947, Ed.D., 1953; m. Mary Ann Hynes, June 6, 1942; children—Ann, Michael, Mary, David. Tchr. indsl. arts, physics Wellston (Mo.) Jr. Sr. High Sch., 1940-41; tchr. drafting Leyden Community High Sch., Franklin Park, Ill., 1941; tchr. indsl. arts Tulelake (Cal.) High Sch., 1946; asst. prof. indsl. arts, supt. bldgs. and grounds Murray (Ky.) State Tchrs. Coll., 1947-48; chmn. indsl. tech. div. Ga. So. Coll., Statesboro, 1948—. Cons. tech. curriculum, Ala., Miss., Fla., Ill., S.C., N.C., Ga., P.R.; vis. prof. State U. Coll. at Oswego, N.Y., 1965. Served to lt. USNR, 1942-46. Mem. Am. Indsl. Arts Assn. (pres. 1974—), Am. Soc. Engring. Edn., Soc. Mfg. Engrs. (sr.), Soc. History of Technology, Ga. Indsl. Arts Assn., Ga. Edn. Assn., N.E.A., Epsilon Pi Tau. Club: Forest Heights Country. Author: (with Spielman) Modern Wood Technology, 1968. Home: 405 Donehoo St Statesboro GA 30458

HACKETT, EARL RANDOLPH, educator; b. Moulmein, Burma, Feb. 16, 1932 (parents Am. citizens); s. Paul Richmond and Martha Jane (Lewis) H.; B.S., Drury Coll., 1953; M.D., Western Res. U., 1957; m. Shirley Jane Kanghl, May 25, 1953; children—Nancy, Raymond, Susan, Sheryl, Laurie, Richard, Alicia. Intern Charity Hosp., New Orleans, 1957-58, resident, 1959-62; resident VA Hosp., New Orleans, 1958-59; mem. faculty La. State U. Sch. Medicine, New Orleans, 1962—, asso. prof. neurology, 1968-73, prof., 1973—. Diplomate Am. Bd. Psychiatry and Neurology. Mem. A.M.A., La. Med. Soc., Orleans Parish Med. Soc., Am. Acad. Neurology, Am. Assn. U. Profs., A.A.A.S., New Orleans Neurol. Soc. (pres. 1968-69), Soc. Clin. Neurologists. Home: 10125 Suzanne Dr New Orleans LA 70123 Office: 1542 Tulane St La State Univ New Orleans LA 70112

HACKETT, RAYMOND LEWIS, educator; b. White River Junction, Vt., Oct. 30, 1929; s. L.R. and Doris (Miner) H.; B.A., U. Me., 1951; M.D., U. Vt., 1955; m. Mary Elizabeth Benton, June 6, 1955; children—Bruce, Wayne, Laura. Intern Colo. Gen. Hosp., Denver, 1956; resident U. Colo., Denver, 1959, New Eng. Deaconess Hosp., Boston, 1961; research trainee clin. pathology Mass. Meml. Hosp., Boston, 1961-62; mem. faculty U. Fla., Gainesville, 1962—, asso. prof. pathology, 1968-72, prof., 1972—; chief lab. service VA Hosp., Gainesville, 1971—. Served as psychiatrist AUS, 1956-58: Japan. Diplomate Am. Bd. Pathology. Mem. Fla. Soc. Pathologists, Fla. Med. Assn., Internat. Acad. Pathology, Internat., Am. socs. nephrologists, Am. Assn. Pathologists and Bacteriologists, Am. Soc. Exptl. Biology, Fedn. Socs. Biologists and Pathologists. Home: 1814 NW 31st Terrace Gainesville FL 32605 Office: Dept Pathology College Medicine Univ Fla Gainesville FL 32610

HACKETT, ROBERT MOORE, educator; b. Carthage, Tenn., Feb. 10, 1936; s. William Arlis and Bartie Hart (Moore) H.; B.S., Tenn. Technol. U., 1960; M.S., Carnegie-Mellon U., 1966, Ph.D., 1968; m. Barbara Jean Highers, July 26, 1957 (div. Apr. 1973); children—Kimberly Elizabeth, William David, Leigh-Ann. Engr., bridge div. Tenn. Hwy. Dept., Nashville, 1960; civil engr. steam-concrete div. TVA, Knoxville, 1960-62; engr. facilities and criteria br. Brown Engring. Co., Inc., Huntsville, Ala., 1962-64; NSF trainee Carnegie-Mellon U., Pitts., 1964-67; asst. prof. civil engring. and engring. mechanics Vanderbilt U., Nashville, 1967-70, asso. prof., 1970-72, asso. prof. civil engring., dir. program in engring. sci., 1972—. Mem. Structural Analysis and Investigations, 1973—. Dir. sch. community breakfast program Episcopal Ch., 1969-70, chmn. sch. bd. com. on breakfast program implementation, 1970-71; mem. com. on hunger and nutrition Council Community Services, 1970-71, mem. agy. revs. com., 1971—; mem. allocations com. budget panel United Givers Fund, 1971-72. Chmn. bd. dirs. Downtown Assn. Chs., 1971-73. Registered profl. engr., Pa. Mem. Am. Soc. C.E., Am. Soc. Engring. Edn., Am. Acad. Mechanics, Assn. Chmn. Depts. Mechanics, Sigma Xi, Kappa Mu Epsilon, Tau Beta Pi, Chi Epsilon. Democrat. Episcopalian. Author: (with others) Computer Methods of Structural Analysis, 1970. Editor: (with W.H. Rowan, Jr.), Application of Finite Element Methods in Civil Engineering, 1969. Home: 2020 Beech Av Nashville TN 37204

HACKNEY, JAMES ACRA, III, motor vechicle co. exec.; b. Washington, N.C., Sept. 27, 1939; s. James Acra and Margaret Dunston (Hodges) H.; B.S. in M.E., N.C. State U., 1961, B.S. in Indsl. Engring., 1962; m. Constance Garrenton, June 5, 1961; children—Kenneth Ross, Jane Mather. Chief engr. J.A. Hackney & Sons, Inc., Washington, N.C., 1961-63, asst. gen. mgr., 1963-65, exec. v.p., gen. mgr., 1965-70, pres., corporate gen. mgr., 1970—; dir. Wachovia Bank & Trust Co., 1971—. Pres. Coastal Plain Devel. Assn., 1969; v.p. Suppliers div. Va. Soft Drink Assn., 1973-74; chmn. bus. adv. com. Beaufort Tech. Inst., 1969-72; chmn. Beauhywaty dist. East Carolina Council Boy Scouts Am., 1970—; mem. engring. adv. bd. N.C. State U., 1973—. Mem. zoning bd. adjustment, Washington, N.C., 1965-66; mem. zoning and planning commn., Washington, 1966-73. Served to 1st lt. Ordnance Corps, AUS, 1963-65. Recipient Distinguished Service award Jr. C. of C., Washington, 1970; named N.C. Small Businessman Man of Yr., U.S. Small Bus. Adminstrn., 1971; Young Engr. of Yr., Profl. Engrs. N.C., 1970-71; Nat. Young Engr. of Yr., Nat. Soc. Profl. Engrs., 1971. Registered profl. engr., N.C., Kan. Mem. Truck Body and Equipment Assn. (dir. 1970-72), Beverage Body Mfrs. Assn. (pres. 1969-70), Am. Inst. Indsl. Engrs. (pres. Eastern N.C. chpt. 1967-68), Profl. Engrs. N.C. (pres. Eastern N.C. chpt. 1971-72), N.C. Soc. Engrs., Washington C. of C. (v.p. 1971-72, pres. 1972-74). Methodist (bd. stewards 1965-68, 70-73). Clubs: Yacht and Country (Washington, N.C.); Brook Valley Country (Greenville, N.C.). Home: Macswoods Route 4 Box 554 Washington NC 27889 Office: 400 Hackney Av Washington NC 27889

HADDEN, ARTHUR ROBY, U.S. dist. atty.; b. San Antonio, Feb. 13, 1929; s. William Alexander and Kathleen Cranston (Westerman) H.; B.B.A., U. Tex., 1952, LL.B., 1957; m. Marellyn Frances Denton, June 23, 1956; children—Neilson Denton, Lynne Loise, Robert Wesley, Arthur Roby. Admitted to Tex. bar, practiced in Tyler, 1957-70; U.S. dist. atty. for eastern Tex., Tyler, 1970—. Served with USAF, 1952-54. Mem. Smith County, Tex., Fed., Am. bar assns., Am. Judicature Soc. Evang. Methodist. Rotarian. Home: 3335 Heines Dr Tyler TX 75701 Office: PO Box 1049 Tyler TX 75701

HADDOCK, R(EYBURN) PHILIP, lawyer; b. Astoria, Ore., Jan. 8, 1919; s. Walter Hill and Jamie (Wilson) H.; A.B., Coll. William and Mary, 1942, student law sch., 1945-46, J.D., Stetson U., 1947; m. Doris Helen Hussell, June 12, 1948; 1 son, Randolph Reyburn. Admitted to Fla. bar, 1947, since practiced in Lakeland; atty. City of Mulberry, 1950-61; municipal judge, Lakeland, Fla., 1963-64. Dir. Attys. Title Services, 1971—. Trustee Polk County Law Library; bd. dirs. Polk County Blood Center, pres., 1962—; bd. dirs. Fla. Assn. Blood Banks, Lakeland Boys Club. Chmn. Polk County Draft Bd. Served as sgt. inf. AUS, 1942-45. Decorated Bronze Star medal. Mem. Am., Fla., 10th Jud. Circuit (pres. 1957-58), Lakeland (pres. 1960) bar assns., Acad. Fla. Trial Lawyers, Am. Trial Lawyers Assn., Lake Region Audubon Soc. (dir.), C. of C. (pres. 1962), Stetson Alumni Assn. (past pres. Polk County chpt.), Am. Legion, V.F.M., 36th Div. Assn., Phi Alpha, Delta Kappa Alpha. Democrat. Methodist (bd. stewards; pres. bd. trustee Fla. Conf. 1966-68). Kiwanian (pres. 1957), Mason (32 deg.). Home: 2734 Fairmount Av Lakeland FL 30803 Office: 601 E Lime St Lakeland FL 33802

HADDOCK, WILLIAM SPRONG, JR., elec. engr.; b. Fort Worth, Feb. 16, 1945; s. William Sprong and Mary Katherine (Settegast) H.; B.S., U. Houston, 1968; m. Jo Lee Pimlott, June 14, 1968; 1 son, William Pimlott. Jr. engr., Houston Lighting & Power, 1968-69, engr., 1969—. Mem. Tex., Nat. (chmn. pub. relations com. 1973-74, recipient outstanding service certificate 1972) socs. profl. engrs., Jr. C. of C. (project chmn. environmental improvement com. 1969), I.E.E.E., Am. Radio Relay League. Presbyn. Club: Briar. Home: 2340 Bluebonnet St Houston TX 77025 Office: 611 Walker St Houston TX 77002

HADEN, CHARLES MCINTYRE, lawyer; b. Timpson, Tex., Aug. 6, 1923; s. Charles Clinton and Cecil (McIntyre) H.; B.A., Rice U., 1949; LL.B., U. Tex., 1949; m. Cynthia Suzanne Tracy, Dec. 20, 1944; children—Sharon Dianne (Mrs. Gordon Anthony Gabbert, Jr.), Susan Carol, Charles McIntyre. Admitted to Tex. bar, 1949; legal counsel and spl. rep. to pres. Trans-Tex. Airways, 1949; law clk. U.S. Dist. Ct., So. Dist. Tex., 1950; asst. dist. atty. Harris County, Houston, 1950-52; trial lawyer Fulbright, Crooker, Freeman & Bates, Houston, 1952-63; partner Fulbright, Crooker, Freeman, Bates & Jaworski, Houston, 1963-70, Brown & Haden, Houston, 1970—. Mayor, City Hunter's Creek Village, Tex., 1956-58. Chmn., Republican Party Harris County, Houston, 1964; del. Rep. Nat. Conv., 1964. Bd. dirs. Tex. Bar Found., 1973—. Served as lt. (j.g.) USNR, World War II. Mem. Am., Houston bar assns., Am., Tex. (dir.) trial lawyers assns., State Bar Tex. (dir. 1973—), Nat. Assn. R.R. Trial Counsel, Am., Modern Greek Studies Assn. C. of C. (vice-chmn. govtl. affairs com.). Presbyn. (elder). Club: Memorial Drive Country. Contbr. articles to profl. jours. Home: 10709 Old Coach Lane Houston TX 77024 Office: 2d Floor 609 Fannin St Houston TX 77002

HADGOPOULOS, GEORGE JOHN, educator; b. Lamia, Greece, June 29, 1935; s. Ioannis G. and Maria (Tsipnis) H.; B.A., with distinction, Am. U. (Beirut, Lebanon), 1962; M.A., Emory U., 1964; A.B.D., N.Y. U., 1967; m. Saralyn DeHaven Poole, Nov. 23, 1963; 1 son, John George DeHaven. Rep., Case Farm Machinery, Lamia, Greece, 1952-53; interpreter CARE, Inc., Greece, 1954-55; instr. Lamiaki Sch. Mcht. Marine Mechanics, Lamia, 1955-57, Inst. Fgn. Langs., Lamia, 1956-57; instr. English mil. terminology Greek Army Officers, Greece, 1955-59; grad. teaching asst. Emory U., Atlanta, 1962-64; asst. prof. English, Slippery Rock (Pa.) State Coll., 1967-69; prof. English Tidewater Center, George Washington U., Hampton, Va., 1972—, coordinator Program for Afloat Coll. Edn. (PACE), 1973—. Served with Greek Army, 1957-59. Fellow Inst. Linguists (London, Eng.), mem. Modern Lang. Assn. Am., Linguistic Soc. Am., Nat. Hist. Soc., Nat. Council Tchrs. English, Archaeol. Inst. Am., Modern Greek Studies Assn. Address: PO Box 5582 Bayside Sta Virginia Beach VA 23455

HADGOPOULOS, SARALYN POOLE (MRS. GEORGE JOHN HADGOPOULOS), educator, author; b. Atlanta, Aug. 31, 1931; d. George Grady Poole and Sarah (Wimberly) Shaw; student Vassar Coll., 1949-51, Sorbonne, Paris, 1951, U. Ga., 1952; B.S., Columbia, 1955; M.A., N.Y. U., 1961; Ph.D., Emory U., 1965; m. George John Hadgopoulos, Nov. 23, 1963; 1 son, John George de Haven. Promotion asst. TV Programs Am., N.Y.C., 1955-56; asst. to fashion and beauty editor Am. Weekly Mag., N.Y.C., 1956-57; tchr. Miami Edison Sr. High Sch., Fla., 1958-60; asso. prof. English, Slippery Rock (Pa.) State Coll., 1967-69; asso. prof., lectr. George Washington U. Tidewater Center, Hampton, and Norfolk, Va., 1972—. Mem. Inst. Linguists London (Eng.), Modern Lang. Assn. Am., Modern Greek Studies Assn., Oceanographic Soc., Nat. Council Tchrs. English, Archaeol. Inst. Am. Author: Poems of North Africa, 1973. Home: PO Box 5582 Bayside Sta Virginia Beach VA 23455

HADLER, JACQUES BAUER, naval architect; b. Arndt, N.D., June 27, 1918; s. Bernhard Herman and Mable Lyle (Jacques) H.; B.S., U.S. Naval Acad., 1941; M.S., Mass. Inst. Tech., 1947; m. Caryl Loggins, Feb. 21, 1942; children—Jacques Bauer, James, Stephen, Susan. Commd. ensign U.S. Navy, 1941, advanced through grades to lt. comdr., 1945; engring. duties various naval shore establishments; ret., 1949; head full-scale trial br. David Taylor Model Basin, Washington, 1949-51, head surface ship powering br., 1951-53, head ship powering div., 1953-70; acting head advance ship concepts Naval Ship Research and Devel. Center, Bethesda, Md., 1965-66, head spl. study group, 1968, head ship dynamics div., 1970—; cons. naval architect to pvt. shipbuilding co., 1960—. Recipient Letter of Commendation, Chief Bur. Ships, 1944, Joseph Linard award Soc. Naval Architects and Marine Engrs., 1966, U.S. Navy Meritorious Civilian Service award, 1969. Mem. Soc. Naval Architects and Marine Engrs. (com. chmn.), Royal Inst. Naval Architects (Eng.), Japanese Soc. Naval Architects and Marine Engrs., Internat. Towing Tank Conf. (com. chmn.), Am. Towing Tank Conf., Sigma Xi. Contbr. articles to profl. jours. Patentee in field. Home: 6425 Dahlonega Rd Washington DC 20016 Office: Bethesda MD 20034

HAEDICKE, THOMAS ARTHUR, physician; b. Bisbee, Ariz., July 10, 1917; s. George Ernest and Lou (Dysinger) H.; student Port Huron Jr. Coll., 1935-37; B.S., Wayne U., 1939, M.D., 1943; m. Jean Gramling, Apr. 5, 1947; children—George Joseph, Anne Chandler. Rotating intern Harper Hosp., Detroit, 1943-44; commd. 1st lt. U.S. Army 1944, advanced through grades to col., 1966; med. service Lawson Gen. Hosp., Atlanta, 1944-45, Walter Reed Gen. Hosp., 1945-50; spl. lectr. tropical medicine Georgetown U., 1946-48; spl. lectr. pharmacology George Washington U., 1947-48; chief med. sect. area med. office VA, 1952-55; instr. medicine Emory U., 1953-55; internist and gastroenterologist Med. Service VA Center, Jackson, Miss., 1955-60; med. service VA Center, Montgomery, Ala., 1960-70; dep. chief profl. div. Med. Services Adminstrn., Ala. Dept. Pub. Health, Montgomery, 1970-72, med. dir. Med. Services Adminstrn., 1972—; clin. instr. medicine U. Miss., 1955-60; clin. asst. prof. dept. pub. health and epidemiology U. Ala. in Birmingham, Med. Center, 1970—. Diplomate Am. Bd. Internal Medicine. Fellow A.C.P.; mem.

A.M.A., Central Med. Soc. Methodist (steward). Mason. Author articles in med. jours. Home: Route 1 Box 16-C Pike Road AL 36064 Office: Med Services Adminstrn 304 Dexter Av Montgomery AL 36104

HAFFER, LOUIS PAUL, lawyer, assn. exec.; b. Boston, May 19, 1914; s. George and Laura (Yager) H.; LL.B. cum laude, Boston U., 1937; m. Hilda Elizabeth Thompson, Aug. 8, 1941; children—Laura S. (Mrs. J.P. Demombynes), Douglas P. Admitted to Mass. bar, 1937, U.S. Supreme Ct. bar, 1945, D.C. bar, 1949; sec. to justices Mass. Supreme Jud. Ct., 1937-39; atty. Wage and Hour Adminstrn., 1939-42, FDA, 1942; trial atty. Dept. Justice, 1942-48; practiced in Washington, 1948—; exec. v.p., counsel Air Freight Forwarders Assn., Washington, 1956—. Lectr., Catholic U. Sch. Law, 1955-64, Am. Inst. Banking, 1953-54. Mem. consumer adv. bd. CAB, 1970-72. Recipient John Ordronaux prize Boston U., 1937. Mem. Am. Bar Assn. (anti-trust com., adminstrv. law com.). Democrat. Editor-in-chief Boston U. Law Rev., 1937. Home: 4711 MacArthur Blvd NW Washington DC 20007 Office: 1730 Rhode Island Av NW Washington DC 20036

HAFFNER, GEORGE LESLIE, optometrist; b. Pittsfield, Mass., Oct. 8, 1932; s. Harold Richard and Maude (Barnum) H.; A.A., U. Fla., 1953; B.S., So. Coll. Optometry, 1958, Dr. Optometry, 1958; m. Marjorie Newsom, Dec. 30, 1956; children—Marjorie Gail, April Charlene, Kimberlee Anne, George Leslie. Practice optometry, Tampa, Fla., 1959—. Sec., dir. Vision Care, Inc. of Fla., 1969—; mem. Fla. Health Manpower Council, 1969—; mem. profl. staff Easter Seal Soc. Crippled Children, 1967-69; mem. adv. staff optometric assistance course Hillsborough County Sch. System, 1971—. Chmn. optometry div. United Fund, 1966, 70-71. Trustee Hillsborough Vision Care Found., 1964—; mem. Pres.'s council Fla. So. Coll. Served to capt. AUS, 1954-56. Recipient Distinguished Service award Key Club Internat., 1967, Outstanding Service certificates and awards Greater Tampa Lions Sight Fund, Inc., 1961—. Fellow Am. Acad. Optometry; mem. Am. (chmn. career guidance com. 1972-74, Outstanding Service pin 1970), Fla. (trustee 1971-73, chmn. career guidance 1965—, sec.-treas. 1973-74, v.p. 1974-75) optometric assns., Hillsborough Soc. Optometrists (pres. 1964-66). Democrat. Methodist (lay speaker). Mason (32 deg.), Kiwanian (lt. gov. Div. 8 Fla. dist. 1973-74; trustee Fla. dist. Kiwanis Internat. 1973-74). Home: 408 Lakewood Av Tampa FL 33612 Office: 4515 S Manhattan Av Tampa FL 33611

HAGAN, GEORGE SYLVESTER, JR., cons. civil engr.; b. Owensboro, Ky., July 8, 1919; s. George Sylvester and Ruth (Wathen) H.; student Passionist Sem., St. Louis, 1939-41, Internat. Corr. Schs., 1946-48; m. Lillian Nell Tanton, Jan. 20, 1943; children—George Sylvester III, Michael, Stephen, Beverly (Mrs. William Earl Freeman, Jr.), John, James, Christopher, Thomas. Asso. Johnson Depp & Quisenberry, Owensboro, 1946-53, partner, 1953—. Mem. exec. bd. Audubon council Boy Scouts Am., 1970—. Served to maj. AUS, 1941-46. Decorated Bronze Star. Registered profl. engr., Ky. Roman Catholic. Home: 1801 Cherokee Dr Owensboro KY 42301 Office: 2625 Frederica St Owensboro KY 42301

HAGAN, RALPH SEMANS, chemist; b. Uniontown, Pa., May 22, 1931; s. Ralph Semans and Sara Frances (Minehart) H.; B.S., Bucknell U., 1953; m. Carol Lee Childress, Nov. 3, 1969; children (by previous marriage)—Mark, Phillip Stuart; children—Kara, Kristi. Personnel interviewer, mfg. tng. program Gen. Electric Co., Louisville, 1956-58, plastics evaluation chemist, Louisville, 1958-62, polymer rheologist, 1962-64, mgr. polymer research, 1964-68, mgr. plastice lab., 1968—. Lectr., U. Louisville, Stevens Inst. Tech. Served with AUS, 1953-56. Mem. Soc. Plastics Engrs. (chmn. Kentuckiana sect. 1965-66, mem. exec. council 1968-70, chmn. internat. awards com. 1972—), Soc. Rheology, Appliance Engrs. Soc., Sigma Xi. Contbr. articles to profl. jours. Patentee in field. Home: 7112 Cross Creek Blvd Louisville KY 40228 Office: Appliance Park Bldg 1113 Louisville KY 40225

HAGEN, RAOUL O'NEIL, army officer; b. Sioux Falls, S.D., Aug. 24, 1934; s. Albert O. and Theresa (Haugo) H.; B.A., U. Ia., 1955; M.D., U. Ia., 1958; m. Doris J. Foster, Dec. 21, 1957; children—Steve, Mike, Mark, Susan, Elizabeth. Intern, St. Benedict's Hosp., Ogden, Utah, 1958-59; commd. 1st lt. M.C., U.S. Army, 1959, advanced through grades to col., 1973; resident radiology Tripler Gen. Hosp., Honolulu, 1963-65, Walter Reed Gen. Hosp., Washington, 1965-66; chief profl. services 93d Evacuation Hosp., Vietnam, 1968-69; chief dept. radiology Brooke Army Med. Center, Fort Sam Houston, 1970—. Clin. prof. radiology U. Tex. Med. Sch., San Antonio, 1973—. Coach, commr. many youth baseball and basketball teams Fort San Houston, 1967—. Diplomate Am. Bd. Radiology. Mem. Am. Coll. Radiology, Radiol. Soc. N.Am. (Magna Cum Laude award 1971), San Antonio Mil. Civilian Radiology Soc. (pres. 1971-72), Bexar County Med. Soc., Long Binh Radiol Soc. Club: Fort Sam Houston Officers. Home: 178 Artillery Post Fort Sam Houston TX 78234 Office: Brooke Army Med Center Fort Sam Houston TX 78234

HAGEN, VERNON DONOHUE, ednl. adminstr.; b. nr. Waycross, Ga., Jan. 27, 1936; s. Robert Fulton and Emma Lou (Hall) H.; student Berry Coll., 1954-56; B.S., U. Ga., 1958, M.Ed., 1964, postgrad., 1967-68; m. Edith Lane Murphy, June 21, 1959; children—Kim Hugh, Karen Leigh, Kenda Lynn. Tchr., Fairmont (Ga.) High Sch., 1958-61; tchr. Hiram (Ga.) High Sch., 1961-67; prin. Hiram Elementary Sch., 1967—. Councilman, Post 2, Powder Springs, Ga., 1969-71. Named Star Tchr. Hiram High Sch. and Paulding County, 1967. Mem. N.E.A., Ga. Assn. Edn., Ga. Elementary Sch. Prins., Nat. Assn. Elementary Sch. Prins., Paulding County Edn. Assn. (pres.), Paulding County Prins. Assn. (pres.), Phi Kappa Phi. Baptist. Club: Civitan (treas.). Home: 4003 LaFayette Dr Powder Springs GA 30073 Office: Seaboard Av Hiram GA 30141

HAGENS, LOYCE DAWSON, psychologist, educator; b. Henderson, Tex., May 31, 1920; d. Edwin H. and Ada (Hollingsworth) Dawson; student McMurry Coll., 1937-38; B.S., U. Tex., 1941, M. Ed., 1950, Ph.D., 1965; m. Jerome F. Mc Gehearty, July 15, 1948 (div. Oct. 1958); children—Michael Jerome, Patrick Fabian; m. 2d, R.C. Hagens, July 24, 1971. Dir. recreation, Houston, 1941; dir. religious edn. Tyler St. Meth. Ch., Dallas, 1945; psychometrist Ind. Sch. Dist., Austin, 1947-48, counselor, 1948-49; counselor Ind. Sch. Dist., Corpus Christi, Tex., 1954-60; counseling supr. ednl. psychology U. Tex., 1960-63; coordinator demonstration centers child behavior cons. Interprofl. Relations Commn. on Pupil Personnel Services, Austin, Tex., 1963-66; asst. prof. ednl. psychology S.W. Tex. State Coll., San Marcos, 1965-66; prof. psychology, dir. guidance service U. Corpus Christi, 1966-73; psychologist Psychol. Service Center, Corpus Christi, 1973—; dir. Nat. Def. Edn. Act Counseling and Guidance Inst. and Edn. Professions Devel. Act project, Corpus Christi, summers 1967-69; lectr. in field; adj. prof. Tex. A and I. Bd. dirs. Parents without Partners, Corpus Christi, 1969-71, Coastal Bend Mental Health Assn., Corpus Christi, 1969-71, Family Counseling Service, 1970-71, Inst. Child Devel., 1969—. Mem. Am., Southwest, Tex. psychol. assns., Am. Tex. personnel and guidance assns., Am Coll. Personnel Assn., Assn. Counselor Educators and Suprs., Assn. Measurement and Evaluation in Guidance. Editor, columnist Elementary Guidance and Counseling Jour.; asst. editor TPGA Jour. Contbr. articles profl. jours. Home: 313 Meldo Park Corpus Christi TX 78411

HAGER, JOHN STEWART, lawyer; b. Owensboro, Ky., Apr. 3, 1927; s. Lawrence White and Augusta (Brown) H.; grad. Phillips Exeter Acad., Exeter, Mass., 1945; A.B., Princeton, 1950; J.D., U. Mich., 1954; m. Marjorie McManus, Apr. 4, 1953; children—Laura Susan, Sarah Marjorie, John Stewart, Bruce William. Admitted to Ky. bar, 1954; asso. firm Byron, Sandidge, Holbrook, Owensboro, 1954-60; partner firm Sandidge, Holbrook, Craig & Hager, Owensboro, 1960-73; pres., dir. Owensboro Pub. Co.; v.p., dir. radio sta. WOMI, Owensboro; dir. Owensboro Nat. Bank, 1969-71. Chmn. Commn. Missions Meth. Ch., 1960-63, chmn. work area ecumenical affairs, 1969-70, ex-officio mem. Council Ministries, 1969-70. Bd. dirs. Family Y Bd., Jr. Achievement, Salvation Army. Served with USNR, 1945-46. Mem. Am., Ky. (chmn. sect. taxation 1965-66), Daviess County bar assns. Home: 1920 Eaton Av Owensboro KY 42301 Office: 1401 Frederica St Owensboro KY 42301

HAGER, WALTER ELLSWORTH, educator; b. Bellwood, Neb., Mar. 29, 1896; s. Birt Ellsworth and Lona Lenora (Barnum) H.; B.Sc., U. Neb., 1916; A.M., Columbia, 1927, Ph.D., 1931; m. Gertrude Squires, Aug. 27, 1918; children—Richard Ellsworth, Ruth (Mrs. Marion B. Petcher). Tchr. high sch., Pender, Neb., 1916-17; instr. physics Sch. Agr., U. Neb., 1917-18; supt. schs., Adams, Neb., 1919-24, Cozad, Neb., 1924-28; asst. sec. Columbia, 1928-36, sec., 1936-41, asso. dir. student personnel, 1938-41, asst. prof. edn., 1939-41; pres. Wilson Tchrs. Coll., Washington, 1941-55, D.C. Tchrs. Coll., 1955-58; vis. lectr. pedagogical insts., Esslingen and Heidelberg, Germany, 1958-59; vis. lectr. edn. U. Cin., 1959-61; vis. lectr., curriculum cons. Springfield (Mass.) Coll., 1961-62; exec. sec. Am. Assn. State Colls. and Univs., Washington, 1962-65. Pres. Eastern States Assn. Profl. Schs. Tchrs., 1945-46; pres. Am. Assn. Colls. Tchr. Edn., 1948-49; chmn. Council Coop. in Tchr. Edn., 1951-55; sec. Am. Council Edn., 1953-56; cons. workshop tchr. edn. for Wuerttemberg-Baden, Esslingen, 1949; mem. Nat. Commn. Accrediting, 1951-58; Am. delegation 4th Internat. Conf. Health Edn., Duesseldorf, Germany, 1959, Internat. Univs. Conf., Nice, France, 1950, world assembly Internat. Council Edn. for Teaching, Nairobi, Kenya, 1973; mem. adv. com. pub. edn. Nat. Found. Infantile Paralysis, 1948-53. Bd. dirs. Columbia Heights (D.C.) Boys Club, 1955-58, 62-73, chmn., 1956-58; chmn. Am. Found. for Sang Myung Women's Tchrs. Coll., Korea, 1973—; trustee Springfield Coll., 1963-65. Served as 2d lt., inf. U.S. Army, 1918-19. Recipient citation D.C. Fedn. Civic Assns., 1955, Am. Assn. Health, Phys. Edn. and Recreation, 1958. Mem. N.E.A., Phi Beta Kappa, Kappa Delta Pi, Phi Delta Kappa; hon. mem. Am. Assn. State Colls. and Univs. Democrat. Unitarian. Mason. Editorial bd. Ednl. Forum, 1954-65. Home: 4625 S Chelsea Lane Bethesda MD 20014 Office: Suite 700 1 Dupont Circle Washington DC 20036

HAGGARD, CLYDE FRANKLIN, JR., auditor; b. Columbus, Miss., Apr. 15, 1944; s. Clyde Franklin and Naomi (Millard) H.; B.A., Arlington State Coll., 1966; B.B.A., U. Tex., 1967; M.B.A., N. Tex. State U., 1968; m. Sharon Lee Penker, May 26, 1967. Staff accountant Peat, Marwick, Mitchell & Co., Dallas, 1968-70; auditor First Security Nat. Bank, Beaumont, 1970-72, First Security Nat. Corp., Beaumont, 1973—. Adviser Jr. Achievement, 1970-73; financial rep., dist. com. Camp Fire Girls, 1971-73. C.P.A., Tex. Mem. Am. Inst. C.P.A.'s, Tex. Soc. C.P.A.'s, Am. Accounting Assn., Assn. for Computing Machinery, Inst. Internal Auditors, Am. Inst. Banking, Beaumont Heritage Soc. (trustee 1973). Baptist (trustee 1973). Home: 1510 Edson Dr Beaumont TX 77706 Office: PO Box 7348 Beaumont TX 77706

HAGGARD, CURTIS ANDREW, dentist; b. Brooklyn, Ala., July 6, 1913; s. William Andrew and Estelle (Avinger) H.; B.S., U. Fla., 1936; D.M.D., U. Louisville, 1941; m. Marjorie Tumlin, Sept. 2, 1937; children—Patricia (Mrs. Darrel J. Mase, Jr.), William Andrew. Practice dentistry, Miami, Fla., 1941-55, Coral Gables, 1957—. Chmn. bd. Sun Bank, Coral Gables. Cons. Ritter Dental Mfg. Co., Rochester, N.Y., 1960—; mem. adv. com. U. Fla. Dental Sch., Gainesville, 1962—. Chmn. Fla. State Racing Commn., 1953-55. Served as maj., Dental Corps, USAF, 1955-57. Named Dentist of Year Fla. Dental Assn., 1970. Mem. Am. (1st v.p., 1954-55), Fla. dental assns., E. Coast Dist. Dental Soc. (past pres.), Am. Acad. Restorative Dentistry, Nat. Assn. Racing Commrs. (treas., 1953-54), Pi Kappa Alpha. Democrat. Presbyn. Mason (Shriner, Jester), Kiwanian (pres.). Club: Riviera Country. Home: 4301 Santa Maria St Coral Gables FL 33146 Office: 385 Alhambra Circle Coral Gables FL 33134

HAGGARD, PAUL WINTZEL, educator; b. Bennington, Okla., Aug. 31, 1933; s. Francis Taft and Cora Lou (Henderson) H.; B.S., Southeastern State Coll., 1953; M.S., N.Tex. State U., 1960; postgrad. U. Tex., 1961-63; m. Doris Jean Gloff, May 14, 1960; children—John Paul, Robert Francis. Tchr., Madill (Okla.) High Sch., 1955-56; instr., N.Tex. State U., Denton, 1957-58, Lamar U., Beaumont, Tex., 1958-61, U. Tex., 1962-63; asso. prof. math. E.Carolina U., Greenville, N.C., 1963—. Served with AUS, 1953-55. Mem. Am. Assn. U. Profs., Math. Assn. Am., N.C. Acad. Sci. (chmn. math. sect. 1972-73). Democrat. Episcopalian. Author: Elements of Trigonometry, 1968; Modern Analytic Geometry, 1970; Basic Linear Algebra, 1972. Home: 1805 Rosewood Dr Greenville NC 27834

HAGGARD, THEODORE MERRILL, ednl. adminstr.; b. Bowling Green, Ky., Apr. 8, 1926; s. Gerstle Merrill and Violet Estelle (Marsh) H.; A.B., U. Ky., 1949, M.A., 1950; B.D., Emory U., 1959, Ph.D., 1971; m. Ann Elizabeth Sageser, Aug. 21, 1949; children—Elizabeth Ann, Kathryn Louise, Melissa Merrill. Prin., Am. Inst., Cochabamba, Bolivia, South Am., 1951-55; ordained deacon United Methodist Ch., North Ga. Methodist Conf., 1958, elder, 1959; pastor Wesley Chapel Meth. Ch., Decatur, Ga., 1956-58, Salem Meth. Ch., Covington, Ga., 1958-60, Silvertown Ch., Thomaston, Ga., 1960-62, Bethesda Meth. Ch., Lawrenceville, Ga., 1962-65, Palmetto (Ga.) Meth. Ch., 1965-66; dean Reinhardt Coll., Waleska, Ga., 1966-72; dir. devel. Pfeiffer Coll., Misenheimer, N.C., 1972—. Served with USNR, 1944-46. Mem. Am. Soc. Ch. History, Am. Acad. Religion. Rotarian, Lion. Home: Box 206 New London NC 28127 Office: Dir Devel Pfeiffer Coll Drawer 915 Misenheimer NC 28109

HAGGARD, WILLIAM HENRY, meteorologist; b. Woodbridge, Conn., Nov. 20, 1920; s. Howard Wilcox and Josephine Cecilia (Foley) H.; B.S., Yale, 1942, certificate profl. meteorologist Mass. Inst. Tech., 1942; M.S., U. Chgo., 1946; postgrad. Fla. State U., 1959-60; m. Martina Wadewitz, Oct. 1, 1967; children—William Henry, Robert H. Instr., N.C. State U., 1946-47; meteorologist, U.S. Weather Bur., 1947-51, 54-61; dep. dir., dir. Nat. Climatic Center, Asheville, N.C., 1961—. Lectr., U. N.C., Asheville, 1964—. Vice-pres. United Fund, 1971-72, A.R.C., 1971-72. Served to capt. USNR, 1942-45, 51-54. Recipient award Carolinas United Community Service, 1966, award United Appeal Pub. Service, 1967, Program Adminstrn. and Mgmt. award Environmental Sci. Services Adminstrn., 1970. Mem. Am. Meteorol. Soc., Am. Geophys. Union, A.A.A.S. Republican. Presbyn. Rotarian. Asso. editor Jour. Applied Meteorology, 1969—. Contbr. articles to profl. jours. Home: 386 Kimberly Av Asheville NC 28804 Office: Fed Bldg Asheville NC 28801

HAGGART, ROBERT IRA, real estate co. exec.; b. Sulphur, La., Mar. 17, 1930; s. Burns Archie and Allie Josephine (Baker) H.; B.A., Centenary Coll. La., 1951; postgrad. So.Meth. U., 1951-52; m. Vivian Janell Spear, July 8, 1961; children—Robert David, Duncan Kent. Vice-pres. Holly Corp., Dallas, 1959-61, Azusa, Cal., 1961-62; adminstrv. asst. to pres. Daga Co., Dallas, 1962-65; financial asst. Centex Corp., Dallas, 1965-67, controller, 1967-68, treas., 1968-70, v.p. finance, 1970—. Bd. dirs. C.C. Young Home, Dallas. Served with USAF, 1952-58. Mem. Kappa Sigma. Republican. Methodist. Home: 3605 Marquette St Dallas TX 75225 Office: 4600 Republic Nat Bank Tower Dallas TX 75201

HAGGERTY, JAMES JOSEPH, writer; b. Orange, N.J., Feb. 1, 1920; s. James Joseph and Anna (Morahan) H.; student pub. schs.; m. Marian Smith Mitten, Nov. 20, 1962; children—Karin, James Joseph, Brian (by previous marriage). Reporter Orange (N.J.) Daily Courier, 1938-40; mil. editor Am. Aviation Publs., 1948-53; aviation editor Collier's, 1953-56; free lance writer on sci. and aerospace subjects, 1956—; editor Aerospace Year Book, 1957—; aerospace cons. Served with USAAF, 1942-48. Decorated D.F.C., Air medal with clusters. Mem. Aviation Space Writers Assn. (past pres.), Nat. Press Club, A.A.A.S., Air Force Assn. Clubs: Bethesda Country; Touchdown (Washington). Author: First of the Spacemen, 1960; Spacecraft, 1961; Flight, 1964; The U.S. Air Force: A Pictorial History in Art, 1965; Spacecraft II, 1965; Food and Nutrition, 1966; Apollo Lunar Landing, 1969; Hail To The Redskins, 1973, Aviation's Mr. Sam, 1973. Address: 502 H St SW Washington DC 20024

HAGGERTY, PATRICK EUGENE, instrument mfg. exec.; b. Harvey, N.D., Mar. 17, 1914; s. Michael Eugene and Lillian (Evenson) H.; B.S. in Elec. Engring., Marquette U., 1936, LL.D., 1960; LL.D., St. Mary's U., 1959, U. Dallas, 1964, Catholic U., 1971; D.Engring., Poly. Inst. Bklyn., 1962, Rensselaer Poly. Inst., 1972; D.Sc., N.D. State U., 1967; m. E. Beatrice Menne, Feb. 26, 1938; children—Sheila Margaret (Mrs. Martin C. Kelsey, Jr.), Kathleen (Mrs. Robert Moossy), Patrick Eugene, Teresa Ann, Michael Gamble. Asst. gen. mgr. Badger Carton Co., Milw., 1935-42; with Texas Instruments, Inc. (and predecessors), Dallas, 1945—, exec. v.p., dir., 1951-58, pres., 1958-66, chmn. bd., 1967—; mem. internat. adv. com. Chase Manhattan Bank; dir. A.H. Belo Corp. Gov., U.S. Postal Service, 1971-73; mem. Pres.'s Sci. Adv. Com., 1969-72; chmn. Nat. Council Ednl. Research. Nat. fund co-chmn. com. on mems. and funds Am. Nat. Red Cross, 1972-73. Trustee Rockefeller U.; trustee mem. exec. com. U. Dallas; mem. Bus. Council; Served as lt. USNR, Bur. Aero. Washington, 1942-45. Decorated Knight comdr. Holy Sepulchre; recipient Distinguished Service award U. Wis., 1964, Distinguished alumnus award Marquette U., 1966, Electronics Industries Assn. medal Honor, 1967, medal Indsl. Research Inst., 1969, Alumnus of Year Marquette U., 1972, WEMA Medal of Achievement, 1972. Fellow I.E.E.E. (Founders award 1968, John Fritz medalist 1971, past pres., dir.), Tex. Acad. Sci.; mem. Nat. Security Indsl. Assn., Nat. Acad. Engring., Nat. Indsl. Conf. Bd. (past trustee), Sigma Phi Delta, Tau Beta Pi, Alpha Sigma Nu, Eta Kappa Nu (eminent mem.). Clubs: Cosmos, Dallas Petroleum; N.Y. Yacht; Cruising of America. Home: 5455 Northbrook Dallas TX 75220 Office: PO Box 5474 Dallas TX 75222

HAGLER, JOHN CARROLL, III, iron works exec.; b. Augusta, Ga., Feb. 14, 1923; s. John Carroll and Susan (Barrett) H.; B.S., U. Ga. 1946; m. Mary Anne Tyler, Oct. 16, 1948; children—Mary Anne, John Carroll IV, Richard Belton, Katharine Waterman, Elizabeth Tyler. Chmn. bd. Ga. Iron Works Co., 1947—; chmn. bd. GIW Industries, Inc., pres., treas. H & T Brass & Aluminum Foundry, Inc., Evans, Ga., 1965—, Winfield Hills, Inc., Augusta, Ga., 1967—; exec. v.p. Paga Molds, Inc., Augusta, Greenville, Pa., 1961—; v.p., dir. Broad Oaks, Inc., Augusta, 1967—; dir., chmn. bd. Ga.-Carolina Brick and Tile Co. Mem. Augusta Aviation Commn., 1962-72. Trustee, pres. Historic Augusta, Inc.; bd. dirs. Augusta Museum, Richmond County Hist. Soc., Augusta Art Assn. Served with A.C., AUS, 1943-45. Mem. Am. Foundrymen's Soc., Am. Inst. Mining, Metall. and Patroleum Engrs., Am. Soc. for Testing and Materials. Am. Soc. for Metals, Nat. Assn. Mfgrs., Aircraft Owners and Pilots Assn., Quiet Birdmen, Ducks Unltd. (former chmn. Augusta area), Sigma Alpha Epsilon. Republican. Roman Catholic. Rotarian. Clubs: Augusta Country, The Pinnacle. Home: 999 Highland Av Augusta GA 30904 Office: PO Box 626 Grovetown GA 30813

HAHN, DAVID BEECHER, elec. engr.; b. Willimantic, Conn., Oct. 17, 1924; s. Ray Lester and Elizabeth Alice (Steer) H.; B.S., U. Conn., 1949; m. Patricia Louise Kingsley, Jan. 30, 1973; children by previous marriage—Scott Temple, Dawn Michele, Jeffrey Kingsley, Andrew David. Application engr. Westinghouse Electric Corp., N.Y.C., 1949-51; engr., Layne Tex. Co., Dallas, 1953-58; pres. Beecher Co., Inc., Dallas, 1958-60; owner Hahn Engring. Co., Dallas, 1961-67, 73—; regional mgr. Nalgene Piping Systems Div. Nalge Co., Sybron Corp., 1967-72. Lectr., Tex. A. and M. U., 1955-57, U. Tex. at Arlington, 1958-73; gen. chmn. Nat. Engrs. Week, Dallas, 1963. Del., Tex. State Republican Conv., 1964, 68, 72. Served to 1st lt. AUS, 1942-46, 51-53. Registered profl. engr., Tex. Mem. A.A.A.S., Am. Water Works Assn., I.E.E.E., Am. Soc. Testing and Materials, Nat., Tex. socs. profl. engrs., Sigma Chi. Republican. Presbyn. Mason (Shriner). Club: Technical (pres. 1959) (Dallas). Home: 1182 Tranquilla Dr Dallas TX 75218 Office: PO Box 18412 Dallas TX 75218

HAHN, RAYBURN EDGAR, accountant; b. Wilson, Tex., Aug. 9, 1925; s. John Ludwig and Lillie (Umlang) H.; B.A., Tex. Tech. Coll., 1949, M.B.A., 1954; m. Elizabeth Anne Vanhala, Nov. 28, 1953; children—Pamela, Rayburn, Tanya, Melissa. Govt. auditor, 1951-53, 54-55; accountant Chance Vaught Aircraft, 1956-59; partner Craven & Millican, C.P.A.'s 1959-71, Alford, Meroney & Co., C.P.A.'s, 1971—; part-time instr. accounting So. Meth. U., 1956-66. Br. sec. Aid Assn. for Lutherans, 1960-70. Bd. dirs. Tex. dist. Luth. Ch.-Mo. Synod. Served with USNR, 1943-46; to 1st lt. USAF, 1951-53. C.P.A., Tex. Mem. Am. Inst. C.P.A.'s, Tex. Soc. C.P.A.'s, Petroleum Accountants Soc., Luth. Vets. of Japan (pres. 1967-69). Editor: The Lay Voice, 1974—. Home: 2012 W Colorado Blvd Dallas TX 75208 Office: 3500 1st Nat Bank Bldg Dallas TX 75202

HAILE, WILLIAM FERGUSON, dentist; b. San Marcos, Tex., Feb. 24, 1902; s. Milton Fanin and Margaret (Crews) H.; student U. Tex., Baylor U.; D.D.S., Tex. Dental Coll. (now Dental Sch., U. Tex.), 1930; m. Ethel Meier, Mar. 10, 1928; 1 dau., Josephine (Mrs. Nations) (dec.). Practice gen. dentistry, Austin, 1930—. Recipient certificate appreciation, for service to Selective Service System Pres. Franklin Roosevelt, 1945, from Pres. Harry Truman, 1947. Fellow Royal Soc. Health; mem. Tex. (life), Austin dental socs. (past pres.), Tex. (life; recipient Good Fellowship award 1963), Am. (life) dental assns. Mem. Christian Ch. (elder). Club: Civitan (Austin). Home: 501 Honeycomb St Austin TX 78701 Office: 500 W 15th St Austin TX 78701

HAILEY, JOHN PHILLIP, foam mfg. co. exec.; b. Scooba, Miss., Nov. 11, 1924; s. Thomas D. and Christine (West) H.; student, Ohio State U., 1946-48, U. Tampa, 1943-44; married; children—Mark Steven (dec.), Jason T. Field rep. Goodyear Tire & Rubber Co., Akron, O., 1951-53; br. mgr. Merry Weather Foam Latex Co., Akron,

1953-55; dir. sales Dryden Rubber Co., Keokuk, Ia., 1955-58; pres. Phillips-Foscue Corp., High Point, N.C., 1958—. Served with M.C., AUS, 1943-46. Mem. N.C. Wildlife Fedn., Young Presidents Orgn. Clubs: Willow Creek Country; String and Splinter; Southern Furniture (High Point). Home: 1631-B W Rotary Ct High Point NC 27260 Office: PO Box 2024 High Point NC 27261

HAIMAN, ROBERT, newspaper co. exec.; m. Elizabeth Royce Greenlaw; 1 son, Robert Greenlaw. Mng. editor Times, St. Petersburg, Fla.; dir. Times Pub. Co., Semit Broadcasting Co. Bd. dirs. Fla. Gulf Coast Symphony; mem. Pres.'s Roundtable Eckerd Coll. Mem. A.P. Mng. Editors Assn. (dir.), Am. Soc. Newspaper Editors. Presbyn. (elder). Kiwanian. Clubs: Bath, Racquet, University, St. Petersburg Yacht. Home: 3275 Walnut St NE St Petersburg FL 33731 Office: Times PO Box 1121 St Petersburg FL 33731

HAINES, BERTRAM WILLIAMS, statistician; b. Rochester, Minn., Sept. 6, 1924; s. Samuel F. and Emily (Williams) H.; B.S., Ariz. State Coll., 1949; Sc.D., Johns Hopkins, 1956; m. Mary Ann Johnson, July 3, 1953. Dir. Bur. Med. Care Research, Balt. City Health Dept., 1956-60; statistician Army Biol. Lab., Ft. Detrick, Md., 1960-62, chief exptl. design br., 1962-65; staff statistician U.S. Naval Aviation Safety Center, Norfolk, Va., 1965-67, head statistics and math. dept., 1967—. Instr., Frederick Community Coll., 1961-65; instr. U. Va. extension, 1969-70, George Washington U. extension, 1973—. Served with USAAF, 1943-46. Mem. Biometric Soc., Am. Statis. Assn. Contbr. articles to profl. jours. Home: 4055 Heutte Dr Norfolk VA 23518 Office: Naval Safety Center NAS Norfolk VA 23511

HAINS, FRANK WOODRUFF, JR., newspaperman; b. Parkersburg, W.Va., July 7, 1926; s. Frank Woodruff and Earlena (Meyer) H.; A.B., Marietta Coll., 1951. Announcer, WPAR, Parkersburg, 1947-51; asst. mgr. WVIM, Vicksburg, Miss., 1951-54; spl. programmer WQBC, Vicksburg, 1954-55; amusements editor, lit. editor, columnist Jackson (Miss.) Daily News, 1955—. Guest dir. U. So. Miss., summer 1961-68, Belhaven Coll., 1962; guest dir. Vicksburg Little Theatre, 1967, U. Miss., 1969; set designer Millsaps Coll., 1963, 70, Miss. Coll., 1963, Belhaven Coll., Jackson Opera Guild, 1965. Vice pres., founding mem. bd., designer New Stage Theatre, Jackson, Miss., 1966—; instr. in theatre Millsaps Coll., 1972—, bd. dirs. Arts and Lecture Series. Served with AUS, 1945-46. Recipient Nat. Pop Warner Conf. award for service to youth, 1958; Rust Coll. Shield, 1970; Distinguished Service award Miss. Authority Ednl. TV, 1971. Mem. Jackson Little Theatre (mem. staff of dirs. 1955-70, v.p. 1956-65). One man theatrical photography show Jackson Art Gallery, 1960; dir. Miss. Arts Festival, 1965; writer, producer, dir. ednl. Miss. Ednl. TV program A Season of Dreams, winner 1st pl. award So. Ednl. Communications Assn. competition, 1971, Ohio State award, 1972. Office: 311 Pearl St Jackson MS 39201

HAIR, PAUL EUGENE, plastics co. exec.; b. Columbia, S.C., Aug. 29, 1928; s. James T. and Lula (Ballentine) H.; grad. high sch.; m. Betty Jean Smith, June 11, 1949; 1 son, Donald E. With So. Plastics Co., Columbia, 1949—, customer services mgr., 1961-71, v.p. sales, 1971—; also dir. Mem. Soc. Plastics Engrs. Club: Exchange (dir. 1960-66). Home: Route 1 Box 383 Chapin SC 29036 Office: PO Drawer 39 Columbia SC 29202

HAIRE, BILLY GRAY, electronics co. exec.; b. Goldsboro, N.C., Aug. 14, 1925; s. Purlie Highsmith and Susan Estelle (Barwick) H.; student N.C. State U., 1945; certificate of completion Capital Radio Inst., 1946; student Pacific Internat. U., 1955; m. Evelyn Cutler, June 26, 1955; children—William David, Gary Highsmith, Evelyn Lorraine. Engr., Radio Sta. WGBR, 1940-42, Radio Sta. WHIT, 1945-49; chief engr. Coastal Electronics, Inc., New Bern, N.C., 1949—. Served to maj. USAAF, 1945. Mem. I.E.E.E., N.C. Soc. Engrs., East Carolina Engrs. Methodist (chmn. com. finance 1971-74). Mason (32 deg., Shriner), Elk, Lion. Club: Country (New Bern). Home: 3627 Wedgewood Dr New Bern NC 28560 Office: 3300 Trent Rd New Bern NC 28560

HAIRE, JOHN DANIEL, oil co. exec.; b. Mt. Sterling, Ill., Jan. 26, 1897; s. Sylvester and Flora (Homberg) H.; m. Marie Finnegan, Apr. 5, 1926; 1 son, John Daniel, Jr. Agt. Sinclair Oil, Chgo., 1918-26; mgr. Akron Oil Co., 1926-30; asst. mgr. nat. accounts Shell Oil, St. Louis, 1937-39; with Delta Oil Co., 1939—, now exec. officer, vice chmn.; vice chmn., chief exec. officer Realty Investments, Inc., Petersburg, Va., City Point Oil Terminal Co., Hopewell, Va., Delta Realty Co., Petersburg, Colonial Oil Co., Colonial Heights, Va., Delta Materials, Hopewell Delta Properties; v.p. Willow Oaks Farms, Hickory Hill Farms. Dir. Petersburg Indsl. Devel. Authority, Appomatox Basin Indsl. Devel. Corp. Past chmn. Richmond-Petersburg Turnpike Authority, Petersburg, Va. Mem. Nat. Council U.S.O. Served with USNR, 1918. Recipient many awards including Outstanding Citizens award Petersburg B'nai B'rith. Mem. Petersburg C. of C. (dir. 1969-72), Petersburg U.S.O. (dir. 1945), Hopewell C. of C., Nat. Oil Marketers Assn., Va. Oil Men's Assn., Va. Oil Jobbers Assn., U.S. Army Assn. (chpt. pres. 1961-62). Rotarian. Clubs: Country (Petersburg, Va.); Fort Lee Officers' and Golf (Va.). Home: 1801 Westover Petersburg VA 23803 Office: 801 Bollingbrook Petersburg VA 23803

HAISE, FRED WALLACE, JR., astronaut; b. Biloxi, Miss., Nov. 14, 1933; s. Fred Wallace and Lucille (Blacksher) H.; A.A., Perkinston Jr. Coll., 1952; B.S. in Aero Engring., U. Okla., 1959; D.Sc. (hon.), Western Mich. U., 1970; m. Mary Griffin Grant, June 4, 1954; children—Mary Margaret, Frederick Thomas, Stephen William, Thomas Jesse. Naval aviation cadet U.S. Navy, 1952-54; fighter pilot U.S. Marine Corps, 1954-56, Air N.G., Okla., Ohio, 1957-63; capt. U.S. Air Force, 1961-62; research pilot NASA Lewis Research Center, Cleve., 1959-63, NASA Flight Research Center, Edwards AFB, Cal., 1963-66; astronaut NASA Manned Spacecraft Center, Houston, 1966—, lunar module pilot Apollo 13, Apr. 1970. Active Indian Guides YMCA, Lancaster, Cal. 1965—. Recipient AB Honts trophy USAF Aerospace Research Pilot Sch., Edwards AFB, 1964; Presdl. Medal of Freedom, 1970; City of Houston Medal for valor, 1970; Jeff Davis award, Biloxi, Miss., 1970; Gold medal City N.Y., 1970; Distinguished Civilian Service medal State of Miss., 1970. Mem. Soc. Exptl. Test Pilots, Phi Theta Kappa, Tau Beta Pi, Sigma Gamma Tau. Office: Code (CB) NASA Manned Spacecraft Center 2101 NASA Rd Houston TX 77058

HAISLIP, DAVID THOMAS, navigational scientist; b. Nanjemoy, Md., May 18, 1920; s. Thomas Henry and Dorothy Ella (Eaton) H.; student USCG Acad., 1944; m. Victorie Leona Sipe, Jan. 19, 1944; children—David Thomas, Katherine L. (Mrs. Steven Barth), Jon N. Commd. ensign, USCG, 1944, advanced through grades to comdr., 1967; electronics engr., Miami, 1948-49, Site Survey, Can./Greenland, 1951, Juneau, Alaska, 1953-56, Miami, 1958-59, Site Survey, No. Europe, 1959; radionavigation system dir. Am. Embassy, Copenhagen, Denmark, 1963-66; navigational scientist USCG, Washington, 1967—. Chmn. subcom. Radio Aids to Navigation Internat. Assn. Lighthouse Authorities, Paris, 1968—; mem. marine council Inst. Navigation, Washington, 1971—. Troop com. chmn. Nat. Capitol area Council Boy Scouts Am., 1967-69. Recipient Citation, Radio Tech. Com. for Maritime Affairs, 1970. Mem. I.E.E.E. (sr. mem.). Episcopalian (sr. warden 1954-55). Club: Army and Navy (Washington). Home: 6302 Stratford Rd Chevy Chase MD 20015 Office: 400 7th St SW Washington DC 20590

HAITHCOCK, WILLIE MERLE, ret. supt. schs.; b. Estelline, Tex., Jan. 30, 1901; d. Francis Marion and Salina Arris (Duncan) Trapp; B.S., W. Tex. State Tchrs. Coll., 1941; postgrad. U. Tex., 1943-44; M.Ed., Tex. Technol. Coll., 1951; m. Riley Columbus Haithcock, July 5, 1928; 1 dau., Carolyn (Mrs. William Randolph Hale). Tchr. elementary sch., Tex., 1918-20; tchr. English, history high schs., Tex., 1920-46; county sch. supt. Hale County Schs., Plainview, Tex., 1947-70. Mem. Hale County Tchrs. Assn. (pres.), Nat. Assn. County Intermediate Unit Supts. (dir.), Tex. Assn. County Supts. (sec.), C. of C. (women's com.), Delta Kappa Gamma (chpt. pres., state v.p.). Clubs: Plainview Women's (mem. bd.), As You Like It Study (pres.), Altrusa (pres., dir. Plainview). Baptist. Mem. Order Eastern Star. Home: 1205 Houston St Plainview TX 79072 Office: County Courthouse Plainview Tx 79072

HAJJ, HATIM MOHAMMAD, traffic engr.; b. Safad, Palestine, Feb. 12, 1944; s. Mohammad Ali and Rasmyeh Ismail (Faour) H.; B.E. with distinction, Am. U. Beirut, 1964; M.Engring., U. S.C., 1966; M.A., Memphis State U., 1971; postgrad. U. S.C., 1973—; m. Linda S. Moffitt, July 14, 1973. Came to U.S., 1965, naturalized, 1974. Constrn. engr. Trans Arabian Pipe Line Co., Beirut, Lebanon, 1964-65; traffic engr. Wilbur Smith & Assos., Columbia, S.C., 1965-66; project mgr. Harland Bartholomew & Assos., Memphis, 1966-72; asso. research engr. U. S.C., Columbia, 1972—. Pres., Arab Orgn. Memphis, 1971-72. Registered profl. engr., S.C., Tenn. Mem. Am. Soc. C.E., Inst. Traffic Engrs., Hwy. Research Bd., Nat., S.C., Tenn. socs. profl. engrs., Omicron Delta Epsilon. Club: Internat. (Memphis). Home: 1421 Waterwood Dr Columbia SC 29210

HALBKAT, JAMES EVERETT, JR., transp. co. exec.; b. Denver, Dec. 19, 1934; s. James Everett and Eleanor Ware (Baldwin) H.; B.S., Yale, 1957; m. Sandra Gordon Hartshorn, June 14, 1957; children—James Everett III, Lucinda, Amanda, Stanley, Sarah. Investment banker Alex. Brown & Sons, Balt., 1959-65; mgr. diversification planning Continental Can Co., Inc., 1965-69, asst. treas., 1969; v.p. corporate devel., mem. mgmt. com. Liberty Corp., Greenville, S.C., 1969-72; pres., Intertruck Corp., Greenville, S.C., 1972—; dir., mem. audit com. Rowe Price New Horizons Fund, Balt. Bd. dirs. Greenville (S.C.) Symphony. Served with USNR, 1957-59. Mem. Financial Analysts Assn. Wilmington, Del. Episcopalian. Clubs: PeQuot Yacht (Southport, Conn.); Green Valley Country (Greenville, S.C.); Poinsett (Greenville, S.C.); Merchants (Balt.); Yale (N.Y.C.). Home: RFD 7 Foothills Rd Greenville SC 29609 Office: PO Box 6999 Greenville SC 29606

HALBOUTY, MICHEL THOMAS, geologist, petroleum engr., ind. producer, operator; b. Beaumont, Tex., June 21, 1909; s. Tom Christian and Sodia (Monnelly) H.; B.S., Tex. A. and M. Coll., 1930. M.S., 1931, Profl. Degree in Geol. Engring., 1956; E.D., Mont. Coll. Mineral Sci. and Tech., 1966;; m. Fay Renfro, June 22, 1945. Geologist, petroleum engr. Yount-Lee Oil Co., Beaumont, Tex., 1931-33, chief geologist, petroleum engr., 1933-35; v.p., gen. mgr., chief geologist and petroleum engr. Glenn H. McCarthy, Inc., Houston, 1935-37; owner firm of cons. geologists and petroleum engrs. in Houston, 1937—; discoverer numerous oil fields La. and Tex.; pioneer ind. to discover gas field Alaska. Chmn. bd. North Side State Bank, Houston, First Nat. Bank, West Side Nat. Bank, both San Angelo, Tex., First Nat. Bank, Paris, Tex., First Nat. Bank, Deport; dir. Continental-Bank of Tex., Post Oak Bank, Houston. Served as lt. col. AUS, 1942-45. Mem. many tech. and sci. socs. Episcopalian. Clubs: Houston, Petroleum, River Oaks Country (Houston); Eldorado Country (Palm Desert, Cal.); Dallas Petroleum; New Orleans Petroleum; Broadmoor Golf (Colorado Springs, Colo.); Cosmos (Washington). Author: Petrographic and Physical Characteristics of Sand from Seven Gulf Coast Producing Horizons, 1937; Salt Domes—Gulf Region, United States and Mexico, 1967; co-author: Spindletop, 1952, The Last Boom, 1972; also numerous tech. and sci. papers on geology and petroleum engring. Home: 3630 Willowick Rd Houston TX 77019 Office: The Halbouty Center 5100 Westheimer Rd Houston TX 77027

HALBROOK, WILLIAM MARCUS, state ofcl.; b. Zion, Ark., May 9, 1926; s. Dalton Clyde and Vera O. (Haywood) H.; B.S., U. Ark., 1948; LL.B., Ark. Law Sch., 1952; m. Marilyn R. Perkins, Apr. 18, 1970; 1 dau., Emily Lynne. Research statistician, asst. dir. Ark. Legislative Council, 1949-53, dir. research dept., exec. sec., 1953—. Mem. bd. mgrs. Council State Govts., 1963-64; v.p. Nat. Legislative Conf., 1962-63, pres., 1963-64. Mem. Am., Ark. bar assns., Pi Sigma Alpha. Democrat. Baptist. Home: 7404 L St Little Rock AR 72207 Office: State Capitol Bldg Little Rock AR 72201

HALDERSON, MAXWELL HAYES, elec. engr.; b. Newman Grove, Neb., July 1, 1912; s. Helmer and Gertrude (Kenagy) H.; B.S. in E.E., U. Neb., 1934, M.S. in physics, 1936; m. Louise Marcella Skrable, Nov. 30, 1935; children—Joanne Lee (Mrs. Thomas E. Black, Jr.), Clark Allen, Dean Warren. With Phillips Petroleum Co., various locations, 1936—, asst. to chief engr., Bartlesville, Okla., 1951-64, dir. prodn. engring., 1964-74, mgr. spl. projects engring., 1974—. Dir., chmn. tech. adv. com. Sucker Rod Pumping Research, Inc., Bartlesville, 1954-65. Asst. master Cub Scouts, Bartlesville, 1952-55, instl. rep., 1955-56; v.p. Central High Sch. P.T.A., Bartlesville, 1955-56; pres. McKinley P.T.A., 1957-58; mem. Am. for Constl. Action, 1954-74. Mem. Okla. Republican Com., 1964-74. Recipient Appreciation certificates Am. Inst. Elec. Engring., 1958, Am. Petroleum Inst., 1959, 65, I.E.E.E., 1967; J.C. Slonneger award, 1974. Registered profl. engr., Okla. Mem. Okla., Nat. socs. profl. engrs., Am. Petroleum Inst. (chmn. com. oil field belting 1958-62, com. standardization of prodn. equipment 1962-67), I.E.E.E., Am. Inst. Mining and Metall. Engrs., Ind. Petroleum Assn. Am., Sigma Xi, Sigma Tau, Pi Mu Epsilon. Republican. Methodist. Club: Hillcrest Country. Patentee in field. Home: 1529 S Dewey St Bartlesville OK 74003 Office: 450-A FPB Phillips Petroleum Co. Bartlesville OK 74004

HALE, CECIL HARRISON, chem. co. exec.; b. Kilgore, Tex., June 12, 1919; s. Mancel Elder and Bessie May (Rogers) H.; B.S., Trinity U. Tex., 1938; M.S., La. State U., 1940; postgrad. U. Tex. at Austin, 1945; Ph.D., Purdue U., 1948; m. Margie May Nornhausser, May 6, 1945; children—Bryan M., Connie M., Chris A. Analytical chemist, Esso Labs. Standard Oil Devel. Co., Baton Rouge, 1940-45, research chemist, 1948-50; owner Southwestern Analytical Chems., Austin, Tex., 1950-65, pres., 1965—; dir. William H. Gross Co., Austin. Owner, Austin Formulating Co., 1958-65. Bd. dirs. Wesley Found. U. Tex. at Austin. Fellow Am. Inst. Chemists; mem. Am. Chem. Soc., Sigma Xi, Phi Lambda Upsilon. Methodist (trustee). Club: Headliners. Patentee in field. Contbr. articles to profl. jours. Home: 1300 Windsor Rd Austin TX 78703 Office: 821 E Woodward St Austin TX 78704

HALE, CHARLES HERBERT, forester; b. Hobgood, N.C., Mar. 28, 1915; s. George Herbert and Annie Lane (Thigpen) H.; C.E., N.C. State Coll., 1937; m. Margaret Quinn Coates, July 10, 1952; children—Geneva Quinn, Charles Herbert. Forester, True Temper Corp., Plymouth, N.C., 1937-40, Am. Package Corp., Murfreesboro, N.C., 1946-65, Ga. Pacific Corp., Scotland Neck, N.C., 1965—. Mem. Good Neighbor Council, Halifax County, N.C., 1969-70. Democratic precinct chmn., 1965-70. Trustee, sec. Our Community Hosp., Scotland Neck. Served with AUS, 1941-46; ETO. Mem. Soc. Am. Foresters, Am. Congress on Surveying and Mapping, Am. Legion, Am., N.C. forestry assns., N.C. Soc. Surveyors, N.C. Lumber Mfg. Assn., Halifax County Hist. Assn., Lambda Chi Alpha. Episcopalian (vestryman). Mason (Shriner). Clubs: Scotfield Country, Holly Oak Gun (Scotland Neck, N.C.). Home: 1918 Clarksville Dr Scotland Neck NC 27874 Office: 711 Vance St Murfreesboro NC 27855

HALE, DOUGLAS VAN, mech. engr., state legislator; b. Birmingham, Ala., Jan. 1, 1942; s. Willard Douglas and Marion Wilamina (Meeter) H.; B.S. in Mech. Engring., Auburn U., 1964; M.S. in Nuclear Engring. (AEC fellow), Mass. Inst. Tech., 1965; now student Cumberland Sch. Law; m. Joanne Tyus, June 29, 1963; 1 dau., Holly Anne. Mech. engr. Lockheed Co., Huntsville, Ala., 1965-71; systems engr. Computer Scis. Corp., Huntsville, Ala., 1971-72; mem. Ala. Ho. of Reps., 1970-74. Dir. Huntsville Indsl. Expansion Com., 1970—. Active numerous civic orgns. Mem. County Exec. Com. Republican Party, 1966—, State Exec. Com., 1971—. Mem. Huntsville Jr. C. of C., Tau Beta Pi, Pi Tau Sigma, Pi Mu Epsilon, Phi Delta Kappa, Phi Kappa Phi, Pi Kappa Alpha. Baptist (deacon). Home: 2105 Clubview Ct NW Huntsville AL 35810

HALE, FRANCIS JOSEPH, educator; b. Manila, Philippine Islands, Oct. 24, 1922; s. Harold Francis and Teresa Mary (Vaughan) H.; B.S., U.S. Mil. Acad., 1944; S.M., Mass. Inst. Tech., 1952, Sc.D., 1963; m. Frances Eugenia Keller, Apr. 23, 1949; children—Francis Joseph III, Olin Thomas, Margaret Anne. Commd. 2d lt. C.E. U.S. Army, 1944, transferred to USAF, 1948, advanced through grades to col., 1961; dep. dir. THOR and Minuteman weapon systems, 1956-59; head dept. astronautics Air Force Acad., 1962-63; div. chief research and devel. plans Hdqrs., Washington, 1963-65; ret., 1965; prof. mech. and aerospace engring. N.C. State U., Raleigh, 1965—. Vis. prof. mech. engring. Middle E. Tech. U., Ankara, Turkey, 1972-73; professorial lectr. math. George Washington U., Washington, 1964-65; cons. U.S. and N.C. govt. agys., industry, 1966—. NSF grantee, 1973-74. Asso. fellow Am. Inst. Aeros. and Astronautics; mem. S.A.R., Am. Soc. Engring. Edn., A.A.A.S., Order Daedalians, Sigma Xi, Sigma Gamma Tau. Clubs: Army and Navy (Washington); Wilson Country (N.C.). Author: Introduction to Control System Analysis and Design, 1973. Home: 2601 Kinglsey Rd Raleigh NC 27612

HALE, HERBERT DEAN, civil engr.; b. Crowder, Okla., Sept. 30, 1927; s. Granville Newton and Leola (Goodman) H.; B.S. in Civil Engring., U. Okla., 1952; m. Dean Roberts, Aug. 25, 1946; children—Sharon (Mrs. Mike McGregor), Deborah (Mrs. Eddie Proctor), Herbert Dan. Pres., Star Builders, 1951-53; owner, H.D. Hale Bros., Owasso, Okla., 1953-59; owner, Hale Bros. Constrn. Engrs., Owasso, Okla., 1959—, Owasso Builders Supply Co. (Okla.), 1959—; pres., chief exec. officer Hale Investments, Inc., 1963—, Hale Bowl, Inc., 1963—, Hale Sr. Citizens, Inc., 1963—; dir. Admiral State Bank, Tulsa. Served with USNR, 1945-46, 50-51. Mem. V.F.W., Am. Soc. Testing Materials, Owasso C. of C. Baptist (chmn. bd. trustees 1951-70). Odd Fellow, Lion. Home: 710 N Atlanta St Owasso OK 74055 Office: 708 N Main St Owasso OK 74055

HALE, MARGIE NORNHAUSSER, chem. co. exec.; b. Carlsbad, N.M., Oct. 20, 1921; d. Muryl Marshall and Lena Florence (Witthauer) N.; B.S. U. Texas, 1942, M.S. Purdue U., 1948; m. Cecil Harrison Hale, May 6, 1945; children—Bryan M., Connie M., Chris A. Analytical chemist Esso Labs., Standard Oil Devel. Baton Rouge, 1942-45, patent contact, 1948-49, research chem. 1949-50; teaching asst. U. Tex., 1945-46, Purdue U., 1946-48; owner Southwestern Analytical Chems. Austin, Tex., 1950-65; v.p. Southwestern Analytical Chems., Inc. Austin, 1965—. Mem. Am. Chem. Soc. (exec. com., reporter Central Tex. sect. 1972-73); A.A.A.S., Sigma Xi., Methodist (steward 1960-70). Contbr. articles to prof. jours. Home: 1300 Windsor Rd Austin TX 78703 Office: 821 E Woodward Austin TX 78704

HALE, OTHO MARION, educator; b. Frisco City, Ala., July 15, 1921; s. Clarence B. and Mary Louise (Petty) H.; B.S., Auburn U., 1948, M.S., 1950; Ph.D., Ore. State U., 1953; m. Rose Amelia Krpan, Oct. 8, 1944; children—Stephen Lee, Marty M., Marilyn. Asst. prof. Ga. Coastal Plain Expt. Sta., Tifton, 1953-58, asso. prof., 1958-67, prof. animal nutrition, 1967—. Served with USAAF, 1942-46. Mem. Am. Soc. Animal Sci., Ga. Entomol. Soc., Gamma Sigma Delta, Sigma Xi, Phi Kappa Phi. Baptist. Home: 214 Carolina Dr Tifton GA 31794

HALE, SHADRACH PAYNE, real estate lawyer; b. Trenton, Ga., Jan. 13, 1912; s. Shadrach Jerome and Clara (Street) H.; LL.B., Chattanooga Coll. Law, 1931, LL.M., 1934; m. Margaret Virginia Ashworth, Apr. 16, 1937; children—S. Jerome II, Patricia Elaine (Mrs. Herbert William Sams, Jr.). Admitted to Ga. bar, 1931, Tenn. bar, 1936; mem. firm Hale & Hale, Trenton, 1931-36; mem. firm McClure, McClure & Hale (formerly McClure & McClure), Chattanooga, 1936-41, Hale & Ellis, 1941—; sec. Milligan-Reynolds Guaranty Title Agy., Inc., 1941—, dir., 1944—. Mem. Am., Tenn., Chattanooga bar assns., Chattanooga Bd. Realtors (asso.), Home Builders Assn. Chattanooga (asso.), Sigma Delta Kappa. Methodist. Kiwanian. Clubs: Valleybrook Golf and Country, Mountain City. Home: 703-E Mansion Circle Chattanooga TN 37405 Office: 722 Cherry Chattanooga TN 37402

HALES, EVERETT B(URTON), elec. engr.; b. Columbia Station, O., Oct. 22, 1914; s. Burton Edwin and Elva (Stacey) H.; A.B., Miami U., Oxford, 1936; M.S., U. Ill., 1938, Ph.D., 1942; m. Dorothy Elizabeth Wood, Oct. 11, 1942; 1 son, David Gordon. Staff mem. Mass. Inst. Tech. Radiation Lab., Cambridge, 1942-46; staff engr. Gen. Precision Inc., Pleasantville, N.Y., 1946-51, dept. mgr., 1951-57, chief system engr., 1958-60, program mgr., 1960-62; sect. chief Martin-Marietta, Orlando, Fla., 1963—. Teaching asst. dept. physics U. Ill. at Urbana, 1936-42; tech. program mgr. data processing and control system for Air Traffic Control Nat. Expltl. System, Pleasantville, 1960-62. Mem. Hawthorne, N.Y. Sch. Bd., 1954-58. Mem. Am. Phys. Soc., I.E.E.E. (chmn. chpt. computer group 1967-68, aero. and electronic systems group 1973-74). Contbr. articles to Mass. Inst. Tech. Radion Lab. Series, 1945-46. Home: 2121 Thunderbird Trail Maitland FL 32751 Office: MP 297 Martin-Marietta PO Box 5837 Orlando FL 32805

HALEY, GEORGE KIRBY, naval officer; b. Weldon, Tex., Nov. 29, 1932; s. George Worley and Iva Esta (Dent) H.; B.S. in Elec. Engring., U. Tex. at Austin, 1956; B.S. in Communications Engring., U.S. Naval Postgrad. Sch., 1965; M.S., George Washington U., 1972; m. Shirley Dean Knibbe, June 2, 1956; children—Kirby Dean, William Scott, Tamara Marie. Commd. ensign, U.S. Navy, 1956, advanced through grades to comdr., 1970; combat carrier pilot, 1965-68; air operations officer U.S.S. Constellation, 1970-71; jet. tng. officer Naval Air Tng. Command, 1971-74; comdg. officer Tng. Squadron Two Three, 1974—; community speaker and lectr., youth leader, Cal., 1961-63, 66-71, Tex., 1973. Decorated D.F.C., 15 air medals, Navy Commendation medal (U.S.), Cross of Gallantry (Vietnam). Mem. I.E.E.E., Am. Soc. Internat. Law, Scabbard and Blade. Baptist (deacon). Home: 6214 Boca Raton Dr Corpus Christi TX 78413 Office: Training Squadron Two Three NAS Kingsville TX 78363

HALEY, HERBERT PRESTON, bottling co. exec.; b. Albany, Ga., May 27, 1912; s. William Banks and Vernon (Shelley) H.; B.S. in Mech. Engring., Ga. Sch. Tech., 1933; M.S. in Mech. Engring., Mass. Inst. Tech., 1935, Sc.D., 1938; m. 2, Helen Marian Peacock, Mar. 6, 1953; 1 dau., Stella LeVan. Vice pres. Albany (Ga.) Coca-Cola Bottling Co., 1938-50, pres., 1950—; chmn. 1st State Bank & Trust Co., Albany, Ga.; chmn. 1st State Bank of Cordele (Ga.), Fort Gaines Banking Co. (Ga.), 1956—; dir. Fulton Nat. Bank, Atlanta. Past pres. Dougherty County Bd. Edn. Trustee Wesleyan Coll., Macon, Ga., Albany YMCA. Served to lt. comdr. USNR, 1942-46. Mem. C. of C. Methodist (trustee). Rotarian (past pres. Albany club). Home: 1207 Pinecrest Dr Albany GA 31707 Office: PO Box 47 Albany GA 31702 also 925 Pine Av Albany GA 31701

HALEY, JAMES ANDREW, congressman; b. Jacksonville, Ala., Jan. 4, 1899; s. Andrew Jackson and Mary Lee (Stevenson) H.; student U. Ala., 1919-20; m. Aubrey B. Ringling. Accountant, Sarasota, Fla., 1925-33; gen. mgr. John Ringling estate, 1933-43; 1st v.p. Ringling Circus, 1943-45, pres., 1946-48; dir. Ringling Bros. Barnum & Bailey Circus, Sarasota, 1943-48; mem. Fla. Ho. of Reps., 1948-52; mem. 83d-92d Congresses from 7th Fla. Dist., 8th Fla. Dist. 93d Congress. Chmn. Sarasota Democratic Exec. Com., 1935-52. Served with U.S. Army, World War I. Mem. S.A.R., Am. Legion, 40 and 8, V.F.W. Democrat. Methodist. Mason, Elk. Clubs: Sarasota Yacht, Sun and Surf. Home: 4211 S Shade Av Sarasota FL 33581 Office: Longworth Bldg Washington DC 20515

HALEY, JOHN HARVEY, lawyer; b. Hot Springs, Ark., May 29, 1931; s. Harvey H. and Anne (Tanner) H.; A.B., Emory U., 1952; LL.B., U. Ark., 1955; m. Maria Luisa Mabilangan, Sept. 11, 1971; children (by previous marriage)—John Stuart, Susan Downs, David Costen. Admitted to Ark. bar, 1955; law clk. Ark. Supreme Ct., 1955-56; asso. Rose, Meek, House, Barron, Nash & Williamson, Little Rock, 1956-58, partner, 1959-70; mem. firm Haley, Young, Bogard & Gitchel, 1971-73, Laser, Sharp, Haley, Young & Boswell, 1973—. Mem. Ark. Bd. Law Examiners, 1959-65, chmn., 1960-65. Chmn., Election Research Council, 1964-68; pres. Morgan Owens Found. Deaf Coll. Students, 1962-67; mem. State Bd. Pardons and Paroles, 1967-68; chmn. State Bd. of Correction, 1968-72. Bd. dirs. Ark. Council on Human Relations, 1972—. Mem. Am., Ark., Pulaski County bar assns., Sigma Chi. Presbyn. Home: Pine Burro Hwy 10 Little Rock AR 72207 Office: One Union Nat Plaza Little Rock AR 72201

HALEY, POPE ALLEN, editor; b. Elberton, Ga., Mar. 19, 1908; s. George Walton and Sarah (Arnold) H.; A.B. magna cum laude, U. Ga., 1929; m. Joy Elizabeth Bailey, Nov. 30, 1937; 1 dau., Melissa Arnold. Reporter, U.S. Daily, Washington, 1929-31; reporter, editor A. P., Richmond Va., 1931-36, Washington, 1936-46; nat. news editor Pathfinder News Mag., Washington, 1946-50, pub. relations, 1950-58; asst. Sunday editor Nashville Tennessean, 1958-62; asso. editor editorial page. Fla. Times-Union, Jacksonville, 1962-74. War corr., 1943. Mem. Sigma Delta Chi. Methodist. Contbr. Music reviews and columns to various publs. Home: 2560 Oak St Jacksonville FL 32204 Office: 1 Riverside Av Jacksonville FL 32202

HALEY, WILLIAM ROBERT, govt. ofcl.; b. Heflin, Ala., Mar. 22, 1912; s. Andrew Duke and Bessie (Coggin) H.; student pub. schs.; m. Sarah Lee Jones, Mar. 29, 1936; children—William R., Sara Ann. Sect. labor So. Ry. Co., Heflin, Ala., 1934-38; machinist Monasanto Chem. Co., Anniston, Ala., 1938-44; plumber W. R. Haley, Heflin, Ala., 1944-60; clk. U.S. Post Office, Heflin, Ala., 1960—; exec. dir. Heflin Housing Authority, 1959—. Capt., sec.-treas. Cleburne County Rescue Squad, 1960—; capt. Heflin City Fire Dept. Baptist. Mason, Lion. Home: 301 Brockford Rd Heflin AL 36264

HALFACRE, ROBERT GORDON, educator; b. Newberry, S.C., June 22, 1941; s. Edwin Harvey and Lela Mae (Ruff) H.; B.S., Clemson U., 1963, M.S., 1965; Ph.D., Va. Poly. Inst. and State U., 1968; M.L.A., N.C. State U., 1973; m. Mary Carolyn Folk, Jan. 24, 1963; children—Angela Carolyn, Gordon Robert. Asst. prof. dept. horticultural sci. N.C. State U., Raleigh, 1968-71, asso. prof., 1971-74; asso. prof. horticulture Clemson (S.C.) U., 1974—. Recipient research award Sigma Xi, 1968, Julian C. Miller research award Am. Soc. Hort. Sci., 1968, Charles Carter Newman award Clemson U., 1963, outstanding tchr. award N.C. State U., 1970. Mem. Blue Key, Sigma Xi, Phi Kappa Phi, Alpha Zeta, Phi Sigma, Pi Alpha Xi, Gamma Sigma Delta. Lutheran. Author: Carolina Landscape Plants, 1971; Keep 'Em Growing, 1972; Fundamentals of Horticulture, 1975. Home: 206 Kingsway Clemson SC 29631

HALFF, ALBERT HENRY, civil engr.; b. Midland, Tex., Aug. 20, 1915; s. Henry M. and Rosa (Wechsler) H.; B.S. in Civil Engring., So. Meth. U., 1937; M.S. in Civil Engring., Ill. Inst. Tech., 1942; D.Eng., Johns Hopkins, 1950; m. Lee Benson, Aug. 24, 1940; children—Henry M., Albert L. Civil engr. Koch & Fowler, cons. engrs., Dallas, 1937; asst. prof. engring. So. Meth. U., 1946-47; owner Albert H. Halff, san. engr., Dallas, 1950-53, Hundley & Halff, cons. engrs., Dallas, 1953-60; pres. Albert H. Halff Assos., civil engring., Dallas, 1960-70, Albert H. Halff Assos., Inc., cons. engrs., Dallas, 1970—. Cons., Frito-Lay, Inc., 1965—, Southland Corp., 1971-72, W.J. Smith Wood Preserving Co., 1969—, Samuels & Co., Dallas, 1968-70. Mem. Townlake Study Group, 1972. Served with USAAF, 1943-46. Registered profl. engr., Tex., Okla., Ill. Mem. Am. Soc. C.E. (past pres. Dallas chpt.), A.A.A.S., Nat. Soc. Profl. Engrs., Water Pollution Control Fedn., N.Y. Acad. Scis., Dallas C. of C., Sigma Xi, Sigma Tau, Chi Epsilon. Patentee in field. Home: 3514 Rock Creek Dr Dallas TX 75204 Office: 3636 Lemmon Av Dallas TX 75219

HALFHILL, CURTIS SELBY, civil engr.; b. Corydon, Ia., May 23, 1915; s. Clyde Peter and Grace Winifred (Ayres) H.; B.S., Ia. State U., 1946; m. Maude H. Hamlett, Oct. 18, 1945 (dec. Feb., 1968). With Walter Hook & Assos., architects, engrs., Charlotte, N.C., 1946-47; with J.N. Pease Assos., architects, engrs., planners, Charlotte, N.C., 1947—, head structural engring. dept., 1951-73, cons., 1973—. Mem. Charlotte Bldg. Standards Bd., 1964-67, 73—, chmn., 1967, 73—; chmn. Charlotte Mecklenburg Architects and Engrs. Liason Com., 1970—. Served to lt. col. AUS, 1941-45. Decorated Silver Star medal. Fellow Am. Soc. C.E., Profl. Engrs. N.C. (chmn. scholarship com. 1969—), Nat. Soc. Profl. Engrs., N.C. Soc. Engrs., Am. Concrete Inst., Prestressed Concrete Inst. Optimist. Home: 4535 Bradbury Dr Charlotte NC 28209 Office: 2925 E Independence Blvd Charlotte NC 28205

HALL, BENJAMIN FRANKLIN, educator; b. Wilmington, N.C., Feb. 26, 1908; s. John and Katherine Boger (Hoke) H.; A.B., Davidson Coll., 1929; B.D., Union Theol. Sem. Va., 1932, Th.M., 1933, Th.D., 1936; D.D. (hon.), Westminister Coll. Mo., 1942; m. Adelaide Peiffer, Oct. 10, 1933; children—John Tannahill, Michal Hoke, Frank Peiffer. Ordained to ministry Presbyn. Ch., 1932; minister Morehead City and Wildwood (N.C.) Presbyn. chruches, 1933-37; minister Central Presbyn. Ch., St. Louis, 1938-48, Pearsall Meml. Presbyn. Ch., Wilmington, N.C., 1949—; prof. philosophy Wilmington Coll., 1963-69; chmn. dept. philosophy and religion U. N.C. at Wilmington, 1969—. Columnist Wilmington Star, 1954—; pres. St. Louis Ch. Fedn., 1946, Mo. Council Churches, 1947. Charter mem., Lower Cape Fear Hist. Soc., 1957—, pres., 1958-60; pres. Wilmington Community Council, 1957, New Hanover Council on Alcoholism, 1961—. Trustee Westminster Coll., Fulton, Mo., 1940-48, Louisville Presbyn. Theol. Sem., 1942-48, Flora Macdonald Coll., Red Springs, N.C., 1949-61, St. Andrews Coll., Laurinburg, N.C., 1955-66, Davidson (N.C.) Coll., 1956-71. Recipient Keever award for Community Service Exchange Clubs of Wilmington. Mem. Am. Assn. U. Profs., Phi Beta Kappa, Sigma Upsilon, Pi Kappa Phi. Democrat. Author: This Company of New Men, 1965. Contbr. articles to mags. Home: 2819 Chestnut St Wilington NC 28401

HALL, BILLY MIKE, dentist; b. Oklahoma City, June 29, 1925; s. Cleveland G. and Bertha M. (Cassidy) H.; B.S., East Central State Coll., 1946-47; D.D.S., Kansas City Sch. Dentistry, 1947-51; m. Elizabeth Ann Huddleston, Feb. 7, 1944; children—Patrick M., Jerry C., Jeffrey L. Individual practice dentistry, Oklahoma City, 1951—. Bd. dirs. Young Men's Club, 1954-70, 2d v.p., 1968-69; pres. dental div. United Appeal, Oklahoma City, 1964. Bd. dirs. B. Mike Hall Trust, Oklahoma City. Served with M.C., AUS, 1943-46. Home: 3220 NW 35th Pl Oklahoma City OK 73112 Office: 2408 N Geraldine St Oklahoma City OK 73107

HALL, C(HARLES) WILLIAM, physician; b. Gage, Okla., Feb. 8, 1922; s. Cecil A. and Helen (Greene) H.; A.B., Kan. U., 1950, M.A., 1952, M.D., 1956; m. Betty Arlene Woodring, June 6, 1943 (div. Apr. 1962); children—Daniel C., Kendall W., Gregory A., Patrick C., Conan L.; m. 2d, Shirley Anne Thompson, Oct. 20, 1962. Rotating intern Kan. U. Med. Center, 1956-57, resident surgery, 1957-62; fellow cardiovascular surgery Baylor U. Sch. Medicine, 1962-64, project dir. artificial heart program, 1964-68, asst. prof. surgery and physiology, 1964-68; cons. Southwest Research Inst., San Antonio, 1966-68, mgr. artificial organs dept. bioengring., 1968-70, dir. dept. bioengring., 1970—; clin. asst. prof. surgery U. Tex. Med. Sch. at San Antonio, 1969—; mem. clin. staff Bexar County Hosp. Dist., San Antonio, 1969—; mem. biomaterials research nat. adv. bd. Clemson U., 1971—; prof. honoris causa Catholic U. Cordoba (Argentina). Recipient Houston Surg. Soc. 1st Place Essay Contest, 1963; Southwestern Surg. Soc. Essay Contest 1st Place, 1964. Mem. Soc. Surgery of Rosario (Argentina), A.A.A.S., Am. Burn Assn., Am. Assn. Lab. Animal Sci., Am. Coll. Cardiology, Am. Coll. Chest Physicians, Am. Hosp. Assn., A.M.A., Am. Soc. Artificial Internal Organs, Assn. Advancement Med. Instrumentation, Biomed. Engring. Soc., Inst. Soc. Am., Internat. Cardiovascular Soc., Internat. Biomed. Materials Research, Sci. Research Soc. Am., Sigma Xi. Mason. Club: The Torch. Author: Mechanical Devices to Assist the Failing Heart, 1966; Heart Substitutes, 1966; Yearbook of General Surgery, 1967; Research in the Service of Man: Biomedical Knowledge, 1967; Advances in Biomedical Engineering, 1968; Harvard Conference on Organ Preservation, 1968; Second National Conference on Prosthetic Heart Valves, 1968. Editor: Bioceramics-Engineering in Medicine, 1972. Contbr. numerous articles to profl. jours. Home: Route 2 Box 144-M Boerne TX 78006 Office: PO Drawer 28510 San Antonio TX 78284

HALL, CLARENCE WINDLEY, judge; b. Newport, N.C., May 3, 1904; s. James S. and Bettie (Garner) H.; A.B., U. N.C., 1926, J.D., 1928; m. Inez Abernethy, Apr. 27, 1940; children—Ramsey Windley (dec.), Beatrice Avery. Admitted to N.C. bar, 1927; practiced in Durham, N.C., 1928-53; judge Superior Ct. N.C., Durham, N.C., 1953—. Served to col. Judge Advocate Gen. Corps, AUS, 1942-46. Mem. Am., N.C. bar assns. Democrat. Methodist. Home: 1402 Ward St Durham NC 27707

HALL, DANIEL GEORGE, newspaper exec.; b. Bar Harbor, Me., July 22, 1917; s. Ernest M. and Alice Watson (Tracy) H.; A.B., U. Fla., 1938; m. Frances Hardy Harrison, July 7, 1946; children—Daniel George, Jessica Lee, Frances Tracy. Asst. sports editor St. Petersburg (Fla.) Times, 1938-41, sports editor, 1945-51, day editor, 1953-56, personnel dir., 1956-66; personnel dir. Hackensack (N.J.) Record, 1967-71; personnel mgr. Orlando (Fla.) Sentinel Star, 1971—. Served with USAAF, 1941-45, USAF, 1951-52. Decorated Air medal. Mem. Newspaper Personnel Relations Assn. (pres. 1962-63). Democrat. Methodist. Home: 2406 Seabreeze Ct Orlando FL 32805 Office: Box 2833 Orlando FL 32802

HALL, DAVID, gov. Okla.; b. Oklahoma City, Oct. 20, 1930; B.A., U. Okla., 1952; LL.B., U. Tulsa, 1959. Admitted to Okla. bar, 1959, U.S. Supreme Ct. bar, 1965; asst. dist. atty., Tulsa County, Okla., 1959-62, dist. atty., 1962-67; mem. firm Hall & Williams, Tulsa; gov. Okla., 1971—. Lectr. U. Okla. Sch. of Law, 1965-66; lectr. U. Tulsa Sch. of Law, 1963-65, adj. prof., 1969—. Served with USAF. Mem. Am. (adv. com. Nat. Criminal Def. Manual 1966—), Fed., Okla. (chmn. criminal law sect. 1964-65), Tulsa County (exec. com. 1963-65) bar assns., Bar Assn. D.C., Phi Beta Kappa, Phi Alpha Delta. Office: State Capital Bldg Oklahoma City OK 73105

HALL, DONALD MYERS, lawyer; b. Negritos, Peru, June 7, 1934; s. John Dale and Ruby Garnet (Parsons) H.; B.A., U. Miami (Fla.), 1955; LL.B., Tulane, 1958; m. Belen Valentin, Sept. 23, 1966; children—John Dale, Christopher Lee, Layne Allender, Rachel Jennifer, Sarah Amanda. Admitted to La. bar, 1958, Fla. bar, 1960, P.R. bar, 1964; mem. firm Fowler, White, Gillen, Humkey & Trenam, Tampa and Miami, 1959-62, Kullman & Lang, New Orleans, 1962, McConnell, Valdes, Kelley, Sifre, Griggs & Ruiz Suria, San Juan, P.R., 1962—, partner, 1966—. Home: 1797 Diamela St Santa Maria Rio Piedras PR 00927 Office: GPO Box 4225 San Juan PR 00936

HALL, ESTHER JANE WOOD (MRS. JULIAN KENNIS HALL), educator; b. Gadsden, Ala., Sept. 18, 1911; d. Henry William and Emma Virginia (Crowe) Wood; B.S., Samford U., Birmingham, Ala., 1939; M.S., U. Tex., 1953, Ph.D., 1957; m. Julian Kennis Hall, Jan. 13, 1949; 1 dau., Virginia Ann. Pharmacist, Fairview Pharmacy, Birmingham, 1929-39; prodn. control mgr., statistician Warren-Teed Products Co., Columbus, O., 1939-44; label cons., dir., asst. prodn. control mgr. S.E. Massengill Co., Bristol, Tenn., 1944-46; asst. prof. Howard Coll., Birmingham, 1946-47; asst. prof. Coll. Pharmacy, U. Tex., Austin, 1947-61, asso. prof., 1961—; distinguished lectr. history Mercer U., 1964; cons. Am. Pub. Health Assn., Washington, 1961; spl. research Walgreen Co., Chgo., 1960; dir. Tex. Prescription Survey, Abbott Labs., Chgo.; chmn. surveys Tex. Pharm. Assn., 1965-69, Gosselin Rx Surveys, Dedham, Mass., 1961-70, chmn. med. market research, 1970-71. Participant Pharmacy Industry Forum, Princeton, 1959, Pharmacy Adminstrv. Seminar, Walgreen Co., Chgo., 1953, 60, 68. Del., participant Pan Am. Congress Pharmacy and Biochemistry, 1957; participant N.A.B.P. Law Seminar, 1971-73. Chmn. manpower com. The Pharm. Found., U. Tex. Coll. Pharmacy, 1956—. Mem. coordinating bd. Tex. Pharmacy Edn. Study, 1973-74. Faculty fellow Am. Found. for Pharm. Edn., 1953-57; recipient Lederle Lab. faculty award, 1961, 64. Fellow A.A.A.S.; faculty fellow Am. Coll. Apothecaries (chmn. com. on edn., mem. hosp. com.); mem. Am. Assn. Colls. of Pharmacy (chmn. sect. of tchrs. of pharmacy adminstrn., mem. com. on curriculum; mem. com. visual aids 1967-68), Am. Pub. Health Assn., Am. Assn. Indsl. Engrs., Nat. Assn. Retail Druggists, Am. Soc. Hosp. Pharmacists, Friends History Pharmacy Med. Coll. Va., Am. Coll. Apothecaries (sec. Tex. 1967-69), Am. (sec. hist. sect.; state historian Texas 1965-67), Tex. (com. edn. and research 1970-71, 74), Austin, Capital Area pharm. assns., Am. Inst. History of Pharmacy (council), Royal Soc. Health (London, Eng.), Rho Chi, Kappa Epsilon (grand council editor, Tex. sec.), Sigma Iota Epsilon, Phi Mu (adviser). Episcopalian. Club: University (Austin). Author: (with A. H. Chute) The Pharmacist in Retail Distribution, 1953, 55, 60; Teachers Guide, 1960; Study Guide for Pharmaceutical Jurisprudence, 1951, 56, 59, 61, 67; (with Henry M. Burlage) Pharmaceutical Abstracts, 1959-68; also various manuals. Contbr. to Am. Profl. Pharmacist, Am. Jour. Pharmacy Edn., Prac. Edition, Am. Pharm. Assn. Jour., So. Pharm. Jour., Tex. Druggist, Tex. Jour. Pharmacy, Tex. Pharmacy, Am. Druggist, Drug Standards, Dissertation Abstracts, Jour. Am. Hosp. Assn., Texas Pharmacy, Pa. Med. Jour., 1959—. Contbr. articles and tech. papers to profl. jours. Home: The Westgate 1122 Colorado St Austin TX 78701

HALL, FRANK FOY, chemist; b. Seymour, Tex., Apr. 2, 1940; s. Jack and Florence (Styles) H.; B.S., Tex. A. and M. U., 1962, Ph.D., 1966; m. Judith Ann Brom, Feb. 23, 1963; children—Julie Diane, Susan Denise, Kathleen Alice, Thomas Jacob. Chief lab. scientist Scott and White Clinic, Temple, Tex., 1968-74; asso. prof. biochemistry Sch. Medicine, Tex. Tech. U., Lubbock, 1974—. Adj. asst. prof. chemistry Baylor U., Waco, Tex. Pres., St. Vincent de Paul Soc., Temple. Served to capt. AUS, 1966-68. USPHS, NIH grantee. Diplomate Am. Bd. Clin. Chemistry. Fellow Am. Inst. Chemists, Am. Assn. Clin. Chemists; mem. Am. Chem. Soc., A.A.A.S., Central Tex. Research Soc. (pres.), Am. Gastroenterol. Assn. Contbr. articles to profl. jours. Home: 5501 80th St Lubbock TX 79424 Office: PO Box 4569 Lubbock TX 79409

HALL, GEORGE RAY, elec. engr.; b. Whitwell, Tenn., Dec. 1, 1931; s. Robert Herman and Ella Marie (Grayson) H.; B.S., Tenn. Technol. U., 1961; m. Reva Jo McDonough, Apr. 25, 1953; children—Rhonda Gail, Regina Jo. With TVA, Knoxville, 1961—, elec. design project engr., 1973—. Served with USAF, 1953-57. Mem. I.E.E.E. Democrat. Methodist (chmn. council on ministries 1973-74). Mason. Home: Route 4 Betenia Rd Powell TN 37849 Office: Design Dept TVA 300 CCB Knoxville TN 37901

HALL, HAZEL P. PITTMAN (MRS. JULIUS FURMAN HALL), educator; b. Travelers Rest, S.C.; d. William L. and Berta (Fleming) Pittman; A.A., Wingate Jr. Coll., 1936; B.A., Furman U., 1942, M.A., 1950; m. Julius Furman Hall, Apr. 23, 1949. Prin., Travelers Rest Elementary Sch., Greenville, S.C., 1942-47; tchr. Parker High Sch., Greenville, 1947-56, sr. counselor, 1956-66; tchr. Vets. Sch. Greenville County, S.C., evenings 1946-59; tchr. Freshman English, Furman U., Greenville, 1959-62; dean adult edn. Greenville Tech. Edn. Center, 1966-73, dean student devel. services, 1973—. Cons. programmed instrn. Williamsburg County Schs. Mem. N.E.A., Nat. Assn. Women Deans and Counselors, Nat. Adult Edn. Assn., Nat. Soc. for Programmed Instrn., Soc. Edn. Assn., S.C. Assn. Women Deans and Counselors, Greenville County Edn. Assn. (sec.-treas. 1959-62), Alpha Delta Kappa. Club: Zonta. Baptist. Home: Box 12 Travelers Rest SC 29690 Office: Box 5616 Sta B Greenville SC 29606

HALL, HORACE CURLIN, III, lawyer; b. Laredo, Tex., Jan. 2, 1930; s. Horace Curlin, Jr. and Mary Paul (Goldman) H.; B.A., U. Tex., 1950, LL.B., 1955; postgrad. Columbia, 1959; m. Nancy Louise Black, Aug. 7, 1954; children—Martha Ann, Mary Birge, Melle Elizabeth, Molly, Margaret. Admitted to Tex. bar, 1954; atty. Hall & Hall, Laredo, 1954-58; mem. legal staff Texaco, Inc., Houston and N.Y.C., 1958-60; partner Hall & Zaffirini and predecessor firms, Laredo, 1960—. Dir. City Nat. Bank of Laredo. Spl. hearing officer Dept. Justice, 1961-64. Served to 1st lt. arty., U.S. Army, 1951-54. Mem. Am., Tex. bar assns., Sigma Chi, Phi Delta Phi. Episcopalian. Kiwanian. Home: 2204 Musser St Laredo TX 78040 Office: PO Box 207 Laredo TX 78040

HALL, HOWARD RALPH, JR., dentist; b. Cin., May 1, 1919; s. Howard Ralph and Juanita (Coleman); B.S., Wilberforce U., 1943; D.D.S., Meharry Med. Coll. Sch. Dentistry, 1947; m. Dorothy Lillian Johns, Oct. 2, 1948; children—Lillian (Mrs. Lawrence Hawkins, Jr.), Howard Ralph III, Juanita R. Intern Del. State Bd. Health, 1947-48, Cin. Bd. Health Dental Dept., 1948-68; pvt. practice dentistry, Covington, Ky., 1943—; dir. Covington Model City Dental Program, 1970—. Mem. com. mgmt. Melrose Br. YMCA, 1969-70. Bd. dirs. Cin. chpt. A.R.C., 1971-72. Served with Dental Corps USNR, 1949-52. Decorated Bronze Star medal. Mem. Ohio Valley (pres. 1960-61), North Eastern dental socs., Nat. Dental Assn. (asst. publicity chmn. 1970—, mem. house dels. 1968—), Am. Dental Assn., Kappa Alpha Psi. Club: Fenwick (Cin.). Home: 3969 Zinsle St Cincinnati OH 45213 Office: Coppin Bldg Covington KY 41011

HALL, HUGH DAVID, dentist; b. Henryetta, Okla., May 15, 1931; s. Hugh Colford and Mary Isabelle (Sadler) H.; B.S., U. Okla., 1953; postgrad. U. Kansas City Sch. Dentistry, 1952-53; D.M.D. cum laude, Harvard, 1957; m. Katherine Ayers Suydam, Feb. 20, 1960; children—Steven David, Andrew Durland, Brian Sadler. Practice oral surgery, Birmingham, Ala., 1961-68, Nashville, 1968—; mem. faculty U. Ala. Sch. Dentistry, Birmingham, 1961-68, asso. prof. oral surgery, 1964-68, chmn. dept., 1965-68; prof., head div. oral surgery Vanderbilt U. Sch. Medicine, Nashville, 1968—; chief oral surg service VA Hosp. Bd. dirs. Am. Cancer Soc., 1970—. Research Career Devel. grantee Nat. Inst. Dental Research NIH, 1962-64; USPHS research grantee, 1960-68, tng. grantee, 1965-68. Diplomate Am. Bd. Oral Surgery. Fellow Am. Assn. U. Profs., Internat. Assn. Oral Surgeons; mem. Am. Dental Assn., Am. Soc. Oral Surgeons, Southeastern Soc. Oral Surgeons, Am. Physiol. Soc., Internat. Assn. Dental Research, A.A.A.S., Sigma Xi, Omicron Kappa Upsilon. Editorial bd. Jour. Oral Surgery, 1973—. Contbr. articles to profl. jours. Research salivary gland physiology. Home: 4212 Estes Rd Nashville TN 37215 Office: Vanderbilt Hospital Nashville TN 37232

HALL, J. FLOYD, educator; b. Langdale, Ala., Aug. 11, 1925; s. William Clyde and Eunice (Colley) H.; student U. Tenn., 1944, B.S., Auburn U., 1948, M.S., 1951, Ed.D., 1957; m. Martha Bell Snider, Mar. 20, 1947; children—Michael Benton, Reginald Snider. Tchr. sci. Sr. High Sch., Lanett, Ala., 1948-51; asst. prin. elementary Jr. High Sch., Fairfax, Ala., 1951-52; supt.-prin. schs., Fairfax, Ala., 1952-58; supt. Ramey AFB Schs., P.R., 1958-60; asst. Evanston (Ill.) Twp. High Schs., 1960-67; supt. Oak Park (Ill.) and River Forest High Sch., 1967-70; supt. Greenville County (S.C.) Sch. Dist., 1970—; ednl. cons. on sch. orgn. Bloomington (Ill.) City Sch. Bd., 1965-66; visited and evaluated schs. for children mil. personnel, Germany, 1966. Active Boy Scouts Am. Served with USAAF, 1943-45. Named Young Man Of The Year in Chambers County, Ala., 1955. Recipient John Hay fellowship at Colo. Coll., 1963; Silver Beaver award from Boy Scouts of Am., 1965. Mem. Nat. Assn. Secondary Sch. Prins. (life), N.E.A., Assn. Supervision and Curriculum Devel., Am. Assn. Sch. Adminstrs., Midwest Assn. Sch. Supts. (pres.). Baptist (deacon). Rotarian (past pres. Oak Park club). Contbr. articles in field to profl. jours. Home: 100 Hunting Hollow Greenville SC 29607 Office: Box 5575 Station B Greenville SC 29607

HALL, JAMES WILLIAM, JR., univ. adminstr.; b. Montgomery, Ala., Dec. 23, 1931; s. James William and Hazel (Kemp) H.; student Huntington Coll., 1950; B.A., U. Ala., 1958, M.A., 1968; postgrad.

Tulane U., 1964; m. Martha Faye George, Aug. 31, 1958. Gen. assignment reporter Montgomery Advertiser, 1956-57; with So. Bell Telephone Co., New Orleans, 1958-66, directory compilation mgr., 1963-64, pub. relations mgr., 1965-66; exec. dir. Ala. Press Assn., University, 1966-74; asst. to pres. Troy (Ala.) State U., 1974—. Lectr. journalism dept. U. Ala., Tuscaloosa, 1966-72; pres. Quest. Inc., Tuscaloosa, 1968-71; v.p. Ala. News Service, Tuscaloosa, 1969-71. Mem. Ala. Safety Coordinating Com., 1968—, Ala. Farm-City Week Com., 1970—; 2d v.p. New Orleans Floral Trail, 1966; chmn. Nat. Newspaper Week, 1973. Sec. Ala. Press Assn. Journalism Found., 1968-74. Served with USAF, 1951-54. Named Outstanding Indsl. Editor, Greater New Orleans Area United Fund, 1966; Hon. Blind Man Ala. Sch. for Deaf and Blind, 1967; Distinguished Alumnus, U. Ala. Dept. Journalism, 1972. Mem. Ala. Council Assn. Execs., Am. Soc. Assn. Execs., Phi Beta Kappa, Omicron Delta Kappa, Chi Phi, Sigma Delta Chi (pres. 1970), Newspaper Assn. Mgrs. Presbyn. Clubs: Indian Hills Country, Birmingham Press. Mason (32 deg.). Editor Ala. Pub., 1966—. Home: The Albatoir Troy AL 36081

HALL, JOHN GREGORY, librarian; b. Sherman, Tex., July 28, 1936; s. John Clayton and Gladys Maudie (Gregory) H.; B.A., So. Meth. U., 1958; M.L.S., U. Tex., 1960. Reference librarian Dallas Pub. Library, 1960; reference librarian Austin Coll., Sherman, Tex., 1962-67, coll. librarian, 1968-70; reference librarian Borough Barnet, London, Eng., 1967-68; vol. Peace Corps, Meshed (Iran) U., 1970-72; dir. Fondren Library So. Meth. U., Dallas, 1973—. Served with AUS, 1960-62. Mem. Tex. Library Assn., Phi Beta Kappa. Democrat. Methodist. Home: Lantern Yard Ravenna TX 75476 Office: Fondren Library Southern Methodist U Dallas TX 75275

HALL, JOHN PATRICK, lawyer; b. Dallas, Oct. 11, 1936; s. John Patrick and Maurine (Still) H.; student U. Tex., 1954-55; B.B.A., So. Methodist U., 1959, LL.B., 1960; postgrad. U. Brussels (Belgium), 1963-64, Hague Acad. Internat. Law, 1964; Diploma Internat. Faculty for Study of Comparative Law (Strasbourg, France), 1964; m. Carol Anne Fraser, May 5, 1962; children—John Patrick III, Jessica Elizabeth. Admitted to D.C. bar, 1965; Tex. bar, 1960; atty. Corp. Finance div. SEC, Washington, 1960-63; practiced in Brussels, Belgium, 1963-64, Dallas, 1964—; partner firm Stroud & Smith, Dallas, 1964—; dir. Interstate Tel. & Electronics Inc.; dir. Werner Industries Inc. Mem. Environmental Quality Com. City of Dallas, 1971—. Bd. dirs. Dallas chpt. Nat. Conf. Christians and Jews. Mem. Am., Tex., D.C., Dallas bar assns., Sigma Chi, Delta Theta Phi, Beta Alpha Psi. Clubs: City, Brook Hollow Golf, Idlewild, Terpsichorean (Dallas). Home: 6032 DeLoache St Dallas TX 75225 Office: 1407 Main St Dallas TX 75202

HALL, JOHN RANDOLPH, JR., physician; b. Napton, Mo., June 20, 1913; s. John Randolph and Ferda (Roberts) H.; A.B., Central Mo. Meth. Coll., 1935; B.S. in Medicine, U. Neb., 1938; M.D., Washington U., St. Louis, 1939; M.S. in Pharmacology, U. Chgo., 1949; M. Pub. Health, Johns Hopkins, 1954; m. Josephine Miles, Nov. 24, 1938; children—John Randolph III, Sarah (Mrs. William Thompson Garcelon), M. Bruce, Rogers. Commd. lt. M.C., U.S. Army, 1934, advanced through ranks to col., 1946, retired, 1964; intern St. Louis City Hosp., 1939-40; partner Kelsey-Seybold Clinic, Houston, 1964-69, chief occupational medicine, 1964-69; pres. Space Center Med. Assos., Houston, 1969—; mem. staffs Space Center Meml., Meml. Baptist, Methodist, St. Lukes, Galveston County Meml. hosps.; acting dean, organizer Sch. Pub. Health, U. Tex., Houston, 1968-69, adj. prof., 1969—. Bd. dirs. Houston Community Welfare Assn., 1964-70, mem. exec. com., 1968-70; bd. dirs. Family Service Centers, Houston, 1971—. Decorated Silver Star, Legion of Merit, Bronze Star medal (3), Air medal, Purple Heart; recipient Andreas Vesalius medal Augsburg Fortbilding, Augsburg, Germany, 1969. Diplomate Am. Bd. Preventive Medicine. Fellow A.C.P., Am. Coll. Preventive Medicine, Indsl. Med. Assn., Am. Pub. Health Assn.; mem. Assn. Mil. Surgeons U.S., A.M.A., Tex. Med. Assn., Harris County Med. Soc., C. of C. Clear Lake (dir. 1971—), C. of C. Dickinson, Nu Simga Nu. Mason (32 deg., K.T., Shriner). Club: Doctors (Houston). Contbr. to publs. in field. Home: 309 Ivy Lane Dickinson TX 77539 Office: Space Center Med Assos 907 Bay Area Blvd Houston TX 77058

HALL, KENNETH ELLIOTT, lawyer; b. Lubbock, Tex., Aug. 4, 1940; s. Albert Thomas and Willie Marie (McGuire) H.; student Tex. Technol. U., 1959-60; J.D., U. Tenn., 1964; m. Margaret Jane Lambert, Aug. 22, 1959; children—Margaret Jane, Catherine Marie, Patricia Ann, Christine Lambert. Admitted to Tenn. bar, 1965; with firm Lee, McGee & Garrett, Knoxville, 1964-67; partner Egerton, McAfee, Armistead, Davis & McCord, Knoxville, 1967—. Part owner Lambert Materials Inc. rock products, Childersburg, Ala., 1971—; owner K & J Farms Maryville, Tenn., 1974—; a founder, part owner Citizens Bank Blount County; v.p., part owner Cookeville Bowling Corp., McMinnville Bowling Corp., 1970—. Tchr., Legal Aid Clinic, U. Tenn., 1966. Mem. Democratic Exec. Com., Knoxville, 1969-70. All Am. diver, 1956-58. Mem. Am., Tenn. (bd. govs. 1968) trial lawyers assns., Knoxville, Tenn., Am. bar assns., Am. Acad. Polit. and Social Sci. Club: President's Univ. Tenn. Elk. Home: Christy Hill Rd Maryville TN 37801 Office: PO Box 2047 Knoxville TN 37901

HALL, LARRY EUGENE, mech. engr.; b. Coweta, Okla., Jan. 31, 1931; s. William Andrew and Jessie Louella (Hoffman) H.; student N.M. Western Coll., 1949-50; B.S., Okla. State U., 1959, M.S., 1960; m. Rilla Fay Hall, Dec. 28, 1952; children—Alan Dale, Deborah Diane, Stefan Andrew, Joel Brett. Research engr. Boeing Co., Wichita, Kan., 1960-61; with Charles Machine Works, Perry, Okla., 1961—, design and project engr., 1961—. City councilman City of Perry, 1964-70; chmn. Rep. Central Com., Noble County, 1971-73. Bd. dirs. Central Okla. Christian Camp, Guthrie, 1972-74. Served with USNR, 1950-55. Registered profl. engr., Okla. Mem. Nat., Okla. socs. profl. engrs. Mem. Disciples of Christ Ch. Lion. Home: PO Box 822 Perry OK 73077 Office: PO Box 66 Perry OK 73077

HALL, LELAND FRANK, engring. co. exec.; b. Corning, N.Y., Sept. 23, 1924; s. Edward Earl and Edna Augusta (Christen) H.; B.S., N.C. State U., 1950, postgrad., 1967; m. Geraldine Elizabeth Shunk, Aug. 9, 1944; 1 dau., Carla Elaine. Project mgr., mech. installations Rowe-Goodin-Jones, Durham, N.C., 1950-57, profl. mech. engr. Piatt & Davis & T.C. Cooke, Durham, 1957-62; research mech. engr. Chemstrand Research Center, Research Trangle Park, N.C., 1962-68; v.p. John D. Latimer & Asso., Durham, 1968—. Instr. Durham Tech. Inst., 1967-69. Dir. intelligence sect. Durham City-County Civil Def., 1966-67. Served with USAAF, 1943-46. Registered profl. engr., 17 states. Mem. Am. Soc. M.E., Am. Soc. Heating, Refrigerating and Air-Conditioning Engrs., Nat. Soc. Profl. Engrs., Profl. Engrs. N. C. (dir. 1964), N. C. Soc. Engrs., N. C. Assn. Professions, Durham Engrs. Club (sec. treas. 1962-65, dir. 1960-64). Presbyn. (deacon 1968-69). Patentee in field. Home: 3608 Hope Valley Rd Durham NC 27707 Office: PO Box 177 Durham NC 27702

HALL, MICHAEL GRAYSON, physician; b. Havana, Fla., Nov. 9, 1938; s. Raimond Beldwin and Lillie Mae (Odom) H.; A.B., Asbury Coll., 1960; M.D., U. Louisville, 1965; m. Marjorie Jane Lloyd, Aug. 18, 1962; children—Sandra Mae, Michael Grayson. Intern Lakeland (Fla.) Gen. Hosp., 1965-66; gen. practice medicine Brooksville, Fla., 1968—; mem. staff Lykes Meml. Hosp., Brooksville, 1968—, v.p., 1972-73, chief of staff, 1973-74. Served with USAF, 1966-68. Mem. Tri-County Med. Soc., Fla. Med. Assn., A.M.A. Home: 221 Alpine Circle Brooksville FL 33512 Office: 621 W Jefferson St Brooksville FL 33512

HALL, MILES LEWIS, JR., lawyer; b. Ft. Lauderdale, Fla., Aug. 14, 1923; s. Miles Lewis and Mary Frances (Dawson) H.; A.B., Princeton, 1947; LL.B., Harvard, 1950; m. Muriel M. Fisher, Nov. 4, 1950; children—Miles Lewis III, Don Thomas. Admitted to Fla. bar, 1951, since practiced in Miami; partner Hall & Hedrick, 1953—; admitted to U.S. Supreme Ct. bar, 1959. Mem. nominating com. Dade County Met. Ct., 1969-72; chmn. nominating council Dist. Ct. Appeals., 3d Dist. Fla., 1972—. vice pres. Orange Bowl Com., 1961-63, pres., 1964-65, dir., 1966—; vice chmn. Fla. Council of 100, 1961-62, mem., 1971-72, 73—; exec. bd. S. Fla. council Boy Scouts Am., 1966-67; vice chmn., dir. Dade County chpt. A.R.C., 1961-62, chmn., 1963-64, dir., 1967-73, nat. fund cons., 1963, 66-68; mem. adv. bd. Salvation Army, 1968—; bd. dirs. Coral Gables War Meml. Youth Center, 1967—, v.p., 1968-69, pres., 1969-72; mem. citizens bd. U. Miami, 1961-66; pres. Ransom Sch. Parents Assn., 1966; chmn. S. Fla. Gov.'s Scholarship Ball, 1966. Served to 2d lt. USAAF, 1943-45. Mem. Am. (Fla. co-chmn. membership com., sect. corp. banking and bus. law), Dade County (dir. 1964-65, v.p. 1966-67, pres. 1967-68) bar assns., Fla. Bar, Am. Judicature Soc., Miami-Dade County C. of C. (v.p. 1962-64, dir. 1966-68), Harvard Law Sch. Assn. Fla. (dir. 1964-66), Alpha Tau Omega. Methodist (steward). Kiwanian, Clubs: Princeton Southern Fla. (past pres., dir.); Harvard of Miami; Cottage; The Miami. Author: Titles, Ejectment and Election of Remedies, Vol. VIII, Fla. Law and Practice, 1958. Home: 2907 Alhambra Circle Coral Gables FL 33134 Office: 150 SE 2d St Miami FL 33131

HALL, MONTAGUE COCRAM, contracting stevedoring exec.; b. McComb, Miss., Aug. 28, 1907; s. James Thomas and Emmie Gertrude (Guyton) H.; grad. accounting Chenier Bus. Coll., Beaumont, Tex., 1932; m. Wilma Olive Little, June 25, 1937; 1 dau., Frances Anne (Mrs. Bair Clyde Stoker). Salesman, So. Drug Specialty Co., McComb, Miss., 1925-30; asst. dist. auditor Lykes Brothers Steamship Co., Inc., Beaumont, Tex. and Lake Charles, La., 1932-37; payroll and prodn. clk. Stanolind Oil Co., Lake Charles, 1937-39; mem. staff traffic and pub. relations Port of Lake Charles, 1939-41; supt., 1941-42, 47-49; v.p. Lake Charles Stevedores, Inc. and Lake City Stevedores, Inc., 1949—, also dir. both. Treas., Lake Charles Dock Bd., 1971—; commr. La. Pilots Fee Commn., 1967—. Bd. dirs. Campfire Girls, 1952-56. Served as maj., Transp. Corps, AUS, 1942-46. Mem. Nat. Assn. Stevedores (nat. dir. 1974—), Lake Charles Pilots Assn. (commr. 1964—), Lake Charles Maritime Assn. (pres. 1967—). Presbyn. (elder). Mason. Clubs: Lake Charles Traffic, Pioneer, Lake Charles Country; Port Sabine Propeller (dir.); Kiwanis, Lions. Home: 3916 Buccaneer Lane Lake Charles LA 70601 Office: Port Lake Charles Lake Charles LA 70601

HALL, PALMER L., coll. adminstr.; b. McDowell, Ky., May 3, 1910; s. James Emory and Minda (Moore) H.; student Alice Lloyd Jr. Coll., 1928-29; A.B., Tusculum Coll., 1931; postgrad. Coll. Law U. Ky., 1936-39, M.A., 1952, Ed.D., 1955; m. Oval Geneva Bingham, Sept. 20, 1940; 1 dau., Pamalea (Mrs. George Carlos Hill). With Floyd County (Ky.) Sch. System, 1926-52, asst. supt., 1945-46, supt., 1946-52; dean coll. W.Va. Inst. Tech., Montgomery, 1955-57; dir. grad. study Morehead (Ky.) State U., 1957-66, coordinator grad. study Coll. Edn., 1966-73, asst. dean grad. programs, 1973—. Served with 42d Inf. Div., AUS, 1943-45; POW, 1945. Mem. Floyd County Hall of Fame, 1956—. Mem. N.E.A., Ky. Edn. Assn. (pres. higher edn., 1970-71), Phi Delta Kappa. Methodist. Clubs: Morehead Mens, Ky. Long Rifles. Home: 503 N Wilson Av Morehead KY 40351

HALL, REBECCA EDNA LAWRENCE (MRS. JOHN H. HALL, JR.), extension agt.; b. Durham, N.C., Jan. 20, 1922; d. Charlie Mangumn and Mary (Pratt) Lawrence; B.S., Bennett Coll., 1942; postgrad. N.C. Central U., 1946, N.C. State U., 1957, 60, 63, 67, Southeastern Community Coll., 1968; m. John H. Hall, Jr., Sept. 24, 1949; 1 son, Charles B. Home econs. extension agt., Wilmington, N.C., 1944—; home econs. tchr., Forest City, N.C., 1943-44. Condr. daily radio program, monthly TV program. Program dir. Turnkey III Home Ownership Program, 1971—. Sec., YWCA, 1948, bd. dirs., 1974—. Merit badge leader Cape Fear council Girl Scouts U.S.A., 1946. Bd. dirs. Area Mental Health Bd., Sencland Crafts, New Hanover County Drug Abuse. Named Woman of the Year, Wilmington Jour., 1954, Omega Psi Phi, 1969. Mem. Am. Home Econs. Assn., Links, Jack and Jill, Am., Nat., N.C. assns. extension home economists, Alpha Kappa Alpha, Epsilon Psi Phi. Episcopalian. Contbr. weekly columns to newspapers. Home: 389 S Kerr Av Wilmington NC 28401 Office: 222 Division Dr Wilmington NC 28401

HALL, ROBERT BRUCE, bishop; b. Wheeling, W. Va., Jan. 27, 1921; s. Kent Bruce and Mary Ellen (Hazlett) H.; B.A., Trinity Coll., Hartford, Conn., 1943, D.D., 1967; S.T.B., Episcopal Theol. Sem., Cambridge, Mass., 1949; D.D., Seabury Western Theol. Sem. 1966, Va. Theol. Sem., 1967, Kenyon Coll., 1969; m. Dorothy Varner Glass, Jan. 26, 1949; children—Ellen Lynn, Kent Bruce II, Elizabeth Hazlett, Anne Louise, Susan Glass. Ordained to ministry Episcopal Ch., 1949; asso. minister, Huntington, W. Va., 1949-53; rector, Huntington, 1953-58, Chgo., 1958-66; bishop coadjutor Episcopal Diocese Va., Richmond, 1966-73, bishop, 1974—. Mem. corp. Seabury Western Theol. Sem., 1964—; trustee Va. Theol. Sem., 1967—, St. Paul's Coll., Lawrenceville, Va., 1968—, Blue Ridge Sch., Dyke, Va., 1968—, United Charities, Chgo., 1965-66. Served with AUS, 1943-46. Fellow Coll. of Preachers, Delta Phi, Pi Gamma Mu. Clubs: Racquet (Chgo.); Rotunda (Richmond, Va.). Home: 11 River Rd Richmond VA 23226 Office: 110 W Franklin St Richmond VA 23220

HALL, ROBERT JOSEPH, physician; b. Buffalo, June 4, 1926; s. Joseph Mathew and Florence C. (Kirst) H.; student Canisius Coll., 1943-45; M.D., U. Buffalo, 1948; m. Dorothy Nowak, Aug. 28, 1948; children—Thomas, Kathleen, Mary Jeanne, Michael, Steven. Commd. lt. U.S. Army, 1948, advanced through ranks to col., 1966, ret., 1969; intern Mercy Hosp., Buffalo, 1948-49; resident Walter Reed Gen. Hosp., Washington, 1949-52; chief cardiology Brooke Gen. Hosp., San Antonio, 1961-66, Walter Reed Gen. Hosp., Washington, 1966-69; med. dir. Tex. Heart Inst., Houston, 1969—; dir. cardiology St. Lukes Episcopal Hosp., Houston, 1969—, co-chief medicine, 1969—; cons. cardiology to Surgeon Gen. U.S. Army, also VA Hosp., Houston; clin. prof. medicine Baylor U. Coll. Medicine, 1969—. Mem. Pres.'s Panel on Heart Disease, 1972; mem. subspecialty bd. on cardiovascular disease Am. Bd. Internal Medicine, 1969—. Decorated Commendation Ribbon (2), Legion of Merit. Diplomate Am. Bd. Internal Medicine, subsplty. bd. cardiovascular disease. Fellow A.C.P., Am. Coll. Cardiology (gov. Tex., chmn. bd. govs. 1973); mem. A.M.A., Am. (fellow council clin. cardiology), Houston (pres. 1974-75) heart assns. Contbr. articles to profl. jours. Home: 5504 Sturbridge Dr Houston TX 77027 Office: Texas Heart Inst PO Box 20269 Houston TX 77025

HALL, SAM BLAKELEY, JR., lawyer; b. Marshall, Tex., Jan. 11, 1924; s. Sam B. and Valerie (Curtis) H.; A.A., Coll. Marshall, 1942; student U. Tex., 1942-43; LL.B., Baylor U., 1948; m. Madeleine Segal, Feb. 9, 1946; children—Linda Rebecca (Mrs. W.F. Palmer), Amanda Jane, Sandra Blake. Admitted to Tex. bar, 1948; since practiced in Marshall; asso. firm Hall & Huffman, Marshall, 1972—. Chmn. exec. com. Harrison County Hosp. Assn., 1969. Chmn. Marshall Bd. Edn., 1974. Bd. dirs. E. Tex. Area council Boy Scouts Am., 1959-60. Served with USAAF, 1943-45. Recipient Richard W. Blalock award Marshall Jaycees, 1953, Boss of Yr. award Harrison County Legal Secs. Assn., 1965, Marshall's Outstanding Citizen award Marshall News Messenger and C. of C., 1970. Mem. Am., N.E. Tex., Harrison County (pres. 1950-51) bar assns., State Bar Tex., Am. Bd. Trial Advocates, Marshall C. of C. (pres. 1964-65, dir. 1964-65), Am. Legion. Mem. Ch. of Christ (deacon). Mason (32 deg.), Kiwanian (pres. 1958-59, dist. lt. gov. 1959-60). Home: 501 Shadywood Rd Marshall TX 75670 Office: PO Drawer M Marshall TX 75670

HALL, THOMAS LIVINGSTON, educator; b. Great Barrington, Mass., Aug. 14, 1931; s. Livingston and Elizabeth (Blodgett) H.; student Reed Coll., 1949-51; A.B., Harvard Coll., 1953, M.D., 1957, M.P.H., 1961; Dr.P.H., Johns Hopkins, 1967; m. Marie-Francoise Puvrez, Dec. 22, 1955; children—Eric Livingston, Tefel Alan, Rachel Francoise. Intern, Royal Victoria Hosp., Montreal, Que., Can., 1957-58; med. dir. Castaner (P.R.) Gen. Hosp., 1958-60; dir. research and tng. Teaching Health Center, U. P.R. Sch. Medicine, 1961-62; instr. to asso. prof. Johns Hopkins Sch. Hygiene and Pub. Health, 1963-71; acting dir. Carolina Population Center, U. N.C. Sch. Pub. Health, 1971—, asso. prof. dept. health adminstrn., 1971-73, prof., 1974—. Cons., WHO, 1965, 70-71, 73. Trustee Margaret Kendrick Blodgett Found. Fellow Am. Pub. Health Assn.; mem. A.A.A.S., Nat. Family Planning Assn., Population Assn. Am., Soc. Internat. Devel., Delta Omega. Author: Health Manpower in Peru: A Case Study in Planning, 1969; (with T. Bacon, D. Horvitz, M. Smallegan) Family Planning Manpower: Problems and Priorities, 1974; prin. author Professional Health Manpower for Community Health Programs, 1973. Contbr. articles to profl. jours., chpts. to books. Home: 126 Fern Lane Chapel Hill NC 27514 Office: Carolina Population Center University Square Chapel Hill NC 27514

HALL, THOR, educator; b. Larvik, Norway, Mar. 15, 1927; s. Jens Martin and Margit Elvira (Petersen) H.; diploma theology Scandinavian Meth. Sem., 1950; postgrad. Selly Oak Colls., Birmingham, Eng., 1950-51, M.R.E., Duke, 1959, Ph.D., 1962; m. Gerd Hellstrom, July 15, 1950; 1 son, Jan Tore. Came to U.S., 1957, naturalized, 1973. Ordained to ministry Meth. Ch., 1952; minister Kongsvinger-Odal Meth. Ch., Galterud, Norway, 1951-53; exec. sec. youth dept. Meth. Ch. Norway, 1953-57; minister Ansonville (N.C.) Meth. Ch., 1958-59; asst. minister 1st Presbyn. Ch., Durham, N.C., 1960-62; asst. prof. preaching and theology Duke, 1962-68, asso. prof., 1968-72; distinguished prof. religious studies U. Tenn., Chattanooga, 1972—. Mem. Gen. Bd. Evangelism Meth. Ch., 1968-72; cons. Ecumenical Prayer Seminars, 1967—, U.S. Army, Navy, Air Force Chaplains Corps, 1967, 68, 71, 72; James Sprunt lectr., Union Theol. Sem., Richmond, Va., 1970. World Council Chs. scholar, 1950-51; Crusade scholar, 1957-59; Gurney Harris Kearns fellow, 1959-60; Angier Duke Meml. fellow, 1960-61; James B. Duke fellow, 1961-62; Am. Assn. Theol. Schs. faculty fellow, 1968-69. Mem. Soc. Sci. Study Religion, Am. Acad. Religion, Soc. Philosophy of Religion. Author: A Theology of Christian Devotion, 1969; A Framework for Faith, 1970; The Future Shape of Preaching, 1971; Whatever Happened to the Gospel, 1973. Editor: Var Ungdom, 1953-57, The Unfinished Pyramid (Charles P. Bowles), 1967. Contbr. articles to profl. jours. Home: 1102 Montvale Circle Signal Mountain TN 37377 Office: Dept Philosophy and Religion U Tenn Chattanooga TN 37401

HALL, VERNON LLOYD, ecologist; b. Fayetteville, Ark., Apr. 23, 1918; s. William Louis and Ruth Russell (Kesterson) H.; B.S., U. Ark., 1940, M.S., 1948; m. France Louise Elizabeth Rose, Aug. 2, 1941; children—Kathleen (Mrs. Donald Meistrell), Steven, Russell, Thomas, Linda, Norman. With Dept. Agr., Fayetteville, 1940-42, 46-50, Davis, Cal., 1950-51; agronomist Chipman Chem. Co., Inc., Palo Alto, Cal., 1951-55, Houston, 1955-56; faculty U. Ark., 1956-66; Ford Found. rice cons. to New Delhi, India, 1966-72; project ecologist Dames & Moore, Cin., 1972—. Cons., Harza Engring. Co., Chgo., Rice Land Reclamation in Republic of Guinea, West Africa. Served to sgt. AUS, 1942-46. Mem. Am. Soc. Agronomy, Am. Assn. Cereal Chemists, Sigma Xi, Alpha Zeta, Phi Sigma, Gamma Sigma Delta. Contbr. articles to profl. jours. Patentee in herbicide field. Home: 1713 N Garland St Fayetteville AR 72701 Office: 1150 W 8th St Cincinnati OH 45203

HALL, WILLIAM LLOYD, surgeon; b. Wichita Falls, Tex., Aug. 25, 1925; s. Lloyd Lorenso and Frankie (Hodges) H.; M.D., Southwestern med. Coll., 1947; student N. Tex. State U., 1942-44; m. Ann Carolyn Short, July 11, 1947; children—Marc William, Michael Steven, Lisa Meredith, Jay Jonathan; m. 2d, Ann Lee Gilley Gunn, Feb. 26, 1971; 1 dau., Jennifer Gunn. Intern George Washington U. Hosp., 1947-48; resident Gt. Lakes Naval Hosp., 1948-49, Baylor U. Hosp., 1953-56; practice medicine specializing in surgery, Dallas, 1956—; mem. staff Meth. Hosp.; chief of surgery Kessler Hosp., 1961-62. Served at lt. M.C., USN, 1948-53, Diplomate Am. Bd. Surgery. Mem. Am., Tex. med. assns., Dallas County Med. Soc. Rotarian. Home: 4509 S Crown Knoll Circle Dallas TX 75232 Office: 122 W Colorado Dallas TX 75208

HALLMAN, ELEANOR HANCOCK (MRS. ROBERT R. HALLMAN), civic and religious worker; b. Warm Springs, Ga.; d. Royan Thomas and Addie (Simmons) Hancock; student U. Ga. 1927-28; m. Robert R. Hallman, Apr. 15, 1926; 1 son, Robert Richard. Sec.-treas., dir. Hallman Bros. Constrn. Co., 1972—. Vol. A.R.C., Ga. Bapt. Hosp., 1966—, chmn. vols., 1972; bd. dirs. Warren Meml. Boys' Club Am., 1965—; bd. dirs. Home Mission Bd., So. Bapt. Conv., 1965—, chmn. Christian Social Ministries com., 1965—, adminstrv. com., 1968—, 2d v.p. bd., 1968—; mem. exec. com. Womans Missionary Union, Atlanta Bapt. Assn., 1952—, dist. sec., 1953-56, v.p., 1956-60, pres., 1960-64, treas. youth orgn., 1966—; trustee Atlanta Bapt. Coll., 1971—. Mem. Northside Library Assn., Met. Atlanta Better Films Council, Atlanta Symphony Guild, Women in Constrn. Atlanta, Ga. Fedn. Womens Clubs. Clubs: Atlanta Womans, Atlanta Music. Home: 1040 Lindridge Dr NE Atlanta GA 30324

HALLMAN, GRADY LAMAR, JR., physician; b. Tyler, Tex., Oct. 25, 1930; s. Grady Lamar and Mildred (Kennedy) H.; B.A., U. Tex., 1950; M.D., Baylor U., 1954; m. Martha Suit, June 7, 1953; children—Daniel S., David L., Charles H. Intern, Chgo. Wesley Meml. Hosp., 1954-55; resident Baylor U. Coll. Medicine Hosps., 1955-56, 58-62; practice medicine specializing in surgery, Houston, 1962—; mem. staff St. Luke's, Tex. Children's, Meth. hosps.; instr. dept. surgery Baylor U. Coll. Medicine, 1962-63, asst. prof., 1963-67, asso. prof., 1967-69, clin. asso. prof., 1969—; cons. cardiovascular surgery Brooke Army Hosp., also Lackland Air Force Hosp. Served with M.C., AUS, 1956-58. Diplomate Am. Bd. Surgery; Am. Bd. Thoracic Surgery. Fellow A.C.S., Am. Coll. Cardiology, Am. Coll Chest Physicians; mem. Soc. U. Surgeons, Am. Assn. for Thoracic Surgery, Soc. Thoracic Surgeons, Internat. Cardiovascular Soc., Soc. for Vascular Surgery, A.M.A., Internat. Soc. Surgery, Am. Geriatric Soc., Southwestern Surg. Congress, Tex., Houston surg. socs., Pan-Am. Med. Assn., Royal Soc. Health, So. Surg. Assn., Am. Surg.

Soc., So. Thoracic Surg. Assn., Internat. Soc. Surgery. Author: Surgical Treatment of Congenital Heart Disease, 1966. Home: 3443 Inwood St Houston TX 77019 Office: 6621 Fannin PO Box 20345 Houston TX 77025

HALLMAN, JOHN ROLAND, educator; b. Barnesboro, Pa., Oct. 25, 1923; s. Norman Edwin and Mildred Gwen (Roland) H.; student U. Pitts., 1941-42, 46; B.S. in Chem. Engring., Pa. State U., 1948; M.S., U. Mich., 1952; Ph.D., U. Okla., 1971; m. Florence Edna Rieger, Sept. 2, 1950; children—Norman, John Leslie. Pilot plant engr. Warner G. Smith Co., Wyandotte, Mich., 1948-50; sr. design engr. Gen. Dynamics/Convair, San Diego, 1952-66; prof., head dept. chem. engring. tech. Nashville State Tech. Inst., 1970—. Spl. cons. Univ. Engrs., Norman, Okla., 1966-70. Chmn. City Library Bd., Chula Vista, Cal., 1962-66. Served with AUS, 1943-45. Decorated Combat Inf. badge, Purple Heart with oak leaf cluster; recipient Silver Beaver award, Bronze Palm Eagle award, Order of Arrow, Boy Scouts Am. Mem. Am. Inst. Chem. engrs. (nat. chmn. com. for technologists and technicians affairs), Nat., Tenn. socs. profl. engrs., Am. Chem. Soc., Am. Soc. Engring. Edn., Order of Foresters, Sigma Xi. Contbr. articles profl. jours. Home: 3719 Richland Av Nashville TN 37205 Office: 120 White Bridge Rd Nashville TN 37209

HALLMARK, BRUCE CULLEN, lawyer; b. Shamrock, Tex., May 23, 1932; s. Archie Cullen and Amy J. (Kutch) H.; B.B.A., U. Tex., Austin, 1955, J.D., 1956; m. Martha Ann Rosborough, Aug. 19, 1955; children—Bruce Cullen, Elizabeth Fears, Suzanna Rosborough, James Burleson. Admitted to Tex. bar, 1956; trial atty. Internal Revenue Service, Oklahoma City Regional Counsel's Office, 1961-65; partner Goodman & Hallmark, El Paso, 1965—. Pres., dir. Goodman, Hallmark & Akard; dir. Billy the Kid, Inc. Pres. El Paso Estate Planning Counsel, 1970. Bd. dirs. Family Service of El Paso, 1967-71, v.p., 1971. Mem. Am., El Paso bar assns., State Bar Tex., Phi Delta Phi, Phi Kappa Sigma. Methodist (chmn. bd.). Mason. Clubs: El Paso, Coronado Country. Author: Partnership Basis and Basis Adjustments, 1972. Home: 5720 Burning Tree Dr El Paso TX 79912 Office: 333 E Missouri St Bldg PO Box 2900 El Paso TX 79901

HALLOCK, DANIEL LEROY, educator; b. Madison, Wis., Jan. 10, 1921; s. Hulett and Ethlyn Maud (Herrick) H.; B.S., U. Wis., 1949, Ph.D., 1952; m. Ellen Ermadean Story, May 28, 1946; children—Jean (Mrs. Lawrence Doyle), James Leroy, Joan Kay. Asso. prof. agronomy Va. Poly. Inst. and State U., Tidewater Research Sta., Suffolk, Va., 1952—. Mem. Nansemond City Sch. Bd., 1972—. Served with AUS, 1942-45. Mem. Am. Soc. Agronomy, Am. Peanut Research and Edn. Assn., Sigma Xi. Club: Ruritan. Mem. United Ch. of Christ. Home: Suffolk VA 23457 Office: Tidewater Research and Continuing Edn Center Suffolk VA 23437

HALMOS, EUGENE ERWIN, JR., editor; b. N.Y.C., Aug. 24, 1916; s. Eugene Erwin and Rose (Gyory) H.; student Coll. City N.Y., 1931-33; m. Elizabeth Ann Cummings, Feb. 14, 1938. With newspapers, North Platte, Neb., Twin Falls, Ida., Salt Lake City, N.Y.C., 1933-38; news editor McGraw-Hill Pub. Co., 1939-41, mng. editor, 1946-54, sr. editor Engring. News Record, 1954-58; Washington editor Progressive Architecture, Civil Engring. and others, 1958—. Cons. AEC, 1971-72, Nat. Acad. Scis., 1970—. Vice pres. Montgomery County chpt. Md. Municipal League, 1970-71, pres., 1971-72. Pres. commrs., mayor Town of Poolesville, Md., 1963—. Served with USAAF, 1942-45; ETO. Decorated Purple Heart, Air medal. Mem. Am. Soc. C.E., Road Gang, Assn. Petroleum Writers, Constrn. Writers Assn. (pres. 1957-58; Silver Hardhat award Constrn. Writers Assn., 1969). Presbyn. (elder 1958—). Elk. Club: Nat. Press. Home: PO Box 132 Poolesville MD 20837 Office: 601 13th St NW Washington DC 20005

HALPERIN, DON AKIBA, educator; b. Cleve., Jan. 22, 1925; s. Moses Phillips and Sara (Allen) H.; B.S. in C.E., Case Inst. Tech., 1945; B.S. in Archtl. Engring., U. Ill., 1948, M.S., Va. Poly. Inst., 1957, Ph.D., 1960; m. Elsa Mildred Paul, June 18, 1949; children—Philip M., Kenneth M. Civil engr., U.S. Navy, Washington, 1945-46; architect Braverman & Halperin, Cleve., 1948-53; prof. U. Fla., Gainesville, 1953—, chmn. dept. bldg. constrn., 1973—. Cons. architecture, United Synagogues Am., 1970—, Easter Seal Soc., 1971-73. Mem. Pres.'s Com. to Employ Handicapped, 1969-71, Bur. Standards Modular Coordination, Washington, 1971-73; chmn. Gov.'s Com. on Archtl. Accessibility, 1968-70. Served with AUS, 1948-49. Am. Philos. Soc. grantee, 1967, Wolfson Found. grantee, 1968. Mem. Assn. Schs. Constrn. (nat. chmn. grad. study and research 1966-72), Assn. Gen. Contractors (nat. edn. com.). Mem. B'nai B'rith. Author: Building with Steel, 1967; Ancient Synagogues of Iberia, 1969. Home: 745 NW 18th St Gainesville FL 32603

HALPERIN, SAMUEL, univ. adminstr.; b. Chgo., May 10, 1930; s. Herman and Bertha (Kleban) H.; A.B., A.M., Washington U., St. Louis, 1952, Ph.D., 1956; postgrad. Ill. Inst. Tech., 1948-49, Columbia, 1954; m. Marlene Epstein, Aug. 29, 1954; children—Elan, Deena. Prof. polit. sci. Wayne State U., 1956-60; research asst. com. on edn. and labor U.S. Ho. of Reps., 1960-61, legislative asst. Rep. Cleveland M. Bailey, 1961; cons. subcom. on edn., com. on labor and pub. welfare U.S. Senate, 1961; specialist, dir. legislative services br. U.S. Office Edn., 1961-64, asst. commr. edn. for legislation, dir. Office Legislation and Congl. Relations, 1964-66; dep. asst. sec. for legislation Dept. Health, Edn. and Welfare, Washington, 1966-69; dir. Ednl. Staff Seminar, George Washington U., 1969-74, dir. Inst. Ednl. Leadership, 1974—; professorial lectr. Am. U., 1962-63; adj. prof. Tchrs. Coll., Columbia, 1966-68; guest lectr. Harvard, U. Cal., Berkeley, Ohio State U., Syracuse U., Cornell U., Claremont Coll. Cons. Carnegie Found. Study Fed. Govt. and Higher Edn., White House Conf. on Edn., 1965. Recipient Superior Service awards Dept. Health, Edn. and Welfare, 1964, 67, Distinguished Service award, 1968, award of merit Nat. Assn. for Pub. Sch. Adult Edn., 1966. Faculty Research grantee AFL-CIO, Wayne State U., 1959; Am. Polit. Sci. Assn. Congl. fellow, 1960-61, Alfred N. Whitehead fellow for advanced study in edn. Harvard, 1969-70. Mem. Phi Beta Kappa, Pi Sigma Alpha. Author: A University in the Web of Politics, 1960; Political World of American Zionism, 1961. Contbg. editor Ency. Judaica, 1960. Contbr. to Dictionary of Political Science, 1960. Contbr. articles to profl. jours. Home: 3041 Normanstone Terrace NW Washington DC 20008 Office: 2000 L St NW Washington DC 20036

HALPERN, CHARLES ROBERT, lawyer; b. Buffalo, Nov. 16, 1939; s. Philip and Goldene (Friedman) H.; B.A. cum laude, Harvard, 1961; LL.B., Yale, 1964; m. Susan Palter, Sept. 12, 1960; children—Ruth N., Philip L., Robert E. Admitted to N.Y. bar, 1964, D.C. bar, 1966; law clk. Judge George T. Washington, U.S. Ct. of Appeals, D.C. Circuit, 1964-65; att. firm Arnold & Porter, Washington, 1965-69; co-founder, dir. Center for Law and Social Policy, Washington, 1969-72; atty. Center for Law and Social Policy and Mental Health Law Project, Washington, 1972—; cons. Pres.'s Commn. on Mental Retardation; dir., sec. Pub. Law Edn. Inst., publisher Selective Service Law Reporter, Washington, 1968-69; mem. Com. on Pub. Justice, N.Y.C. Sec. Inst. for Policy Studies, Washington, 1967-69; mem. Acad. Contemporary Problems, Columbus, O., 1972—; mem. profl. adv. panel Nat. Assn. for Mental Health, 1972—. Trustee Mental Health Law Project; trustee Center for Law and Social Policy. Fellow U. Pa. Law Sch., 1973. Mem. Bar of N.Y., D.C., U.S. Supreme Ct., Inst. Medicine of Nat. Acad. Scis. Contbr. articles to profl. jours. Home: 2616 Colston Dr Chevy Chase MD 20015 Office: 1751 N St NW Washington DC 20036

HALPERN, KATHERINE SPENCER (MRS. ABRAHAM HALPERN), educator; b. Reading, Mass.; d. Carl Mason and Bertha (Beaudry) Spencer; B.A., Vassar Coll., 1935; M.A., U. Chgo., 1944, Ph.D., 1952; m. Abraham Halpern, in 1968. Social Science Research Council fellow 1941; consultant to A.R.C., Alaska, 1942-44; social sci. analyst OWI, Washington, 1944-46; research asst., dept. social relations Harvard, 1946-50, asso. dir. Community Health Project, 1953-57; asst. prof. N.Y. Sch. Social Work, Columbia, 1950-52; asso. prof. Boston U. Sch. of Social Work, 1954-64, prof., 1964-70, lectr. dept. sociology and anthropology, 1960-70; prof. anthropology Am. U., Washington, 1970—; research associate in social anthropology at McLean Hosp., 1958-65; research asso. dept. psychiatry Harvard 1960-65; cons. div. Indian Health USPHS, 1964-71. Fellow Am. Anthropology Assn., Soc. for Applied Anthropology; mem. A.A.A.S., Soc. Med. Anthropology, Nat. Assn. Social Workers, Phi Beta Kappa, Sigma Xi. Author: Reflections of Social Life in the Navaho Origin Myth (U. N.M. Publs. in Anthropology No. 3), 1947; Mythology and Values, an Analysis of Navaho Chantway Myths (Memoir of the Am. Folklore Soc. No. 48), 1957. Home: 4100 W St NW Washington DC 20007

HALPERT, HAROLD PAUL, mental health,cons.; b. N.Y.C., Apr. 22, 1913; s. Joseph L. and Lillian (Nagelberg) H.; B.A. magna cum laude, N.Y. U., 1932; M.A., U. Ill., 1933; M.P.H., Johns Hopkins, 1964, D.P.H., 1966; m. Sylvia Sidransky, Apr. 27, 1937. Writer, edn. specialist bur. naval personnel Dept. of Def., also U.S. Office Edn., Washington, 1941-52; chief publs. and reports Nat. Inst. Mental Health, Dept. Health, Edn. and Welfare, Washington, 1952-61, cons. on mental health edn. and communications, 1961-66, chief, systems research program, 1966-73, research cons. in mental health, 1973—. Instr. English, George Washington U., Washington, 1943-48; vis. scholar, dept. sociology Columbia, 1971-72. Fellow Am. Orthopsychiat. Assn.; mem. Am. Pub. Health Assn., Soc. for Gen. Systems Research, Phi Beta Kappa. Contbr. articles to profl. jours. Home: 4606 Bayard Blvd NW Washington DC 20016

HALPERT, SYLVIA SIDRANSKY (MRS. HAROLD P. HALPERT), social worker, educator; b. N.Y.C., Feb. 16, 1914; d. Morris and Elizabeth (Katz) Sidransky; B.A., Bklyn. Coll., 1937; M.S., Cath. U. Am., 1945, Dr. Social Welfare, 1965; certificate psychiatry Washington Sch. Psychiatry, 1949; m. Harold P. Halpert, Apr. 27, 1937. Psychiat. social worker Washington Inst. of Mental Hygiene and Hillcrest Children's Center, Washington, 1945-62; asst. prof. research Howard U. Sch. Social Work, Washington, 1965-68; psychiat. social worker Marriage and Family Inst., Washington, 1966—; pvt. practice psychiat. social work, Washington, 1950—. Cons. Head Start Program, 1968—; mem. profl. adv. bd. D.C. Inst. Mental Hygiene, 1968—. Nat. Inst. Mental Health fellow, 1962-64. Fellow Am. Orthopsychiat. Assn.; mem. Council on Social Work Edn., Acad. Certified Social Workers, Nat. Assn. Social Workers, Am. Sociol. Assn. Address: 4606 Bayard Blvd Washington DC 20016

HALPRIN, KENNETH M., educator; b. Bklyn., Mar. 19, 1931; B.A., U. Chgo., 1950, M.D., 1955. Intern, U. Chgo. Clinics, 1955-56, resident, 1956-59; asst. prof. U. Chgo., 1963-64; asso. prof. U. Ore. Med. Sch., Portland, 1964-68; prof. dermatology U. Miami (Fla.), 1968—; chief dermatology Miami VA Hosp. NSF fellow St. John's Hosp. for Diseases of Skin, London, Eng., 1961-62. Served as capt. USAF, 1959-61. Recipient Taub award for psoriasis research, 1971. Mem. Am. Dermatol. Assn., Am. Acad. Dermatology, Soc. Investigative Dermatology, A.A.A.S. Contbr. profl. jours. Office: 1201 NW 16th St Miami FL 33152

HALTER, SAMUEL HENRY, city ofcl.; b. Hamilton, O., Sept. 19, 1939; s. Samuel L. and Helen (Olds) H.; B.S., Miami U., Oxford, O., 1961; M.P.A., Syracuse U., 1962; m. Claire DeBaecke, Nov. 16, 1963; 1 son, Samuel Henry. Adminstrv. analyst City of Phila., 1962-64; research and budget dir. City of Savannah (Ga.), 1964-68, asst. city mgr., 1971—; city adminstr. Miami Springs, Fla., 1968-71. Mem. Internat. City Mgmt. Assn., Am. Soc. Pub. Adminstrn. Home: 1455 Dale Dr Savannah GA 31406 Office: PO Box 1027 Savannah GA 31402

HALTOM, THOMAS BRANSON, physician; b. Nashville, Jan. 16, 1920; s. William Coleman and Katie Pool (Foster) H.; B.A., Vanderbilt U., 1939, M.D., 1942; m. Martha Anne O'Connor, Apr. 12, 1947; children—Helen F. (Mrs. Charles Ousley), Katherine A., Barbara A., Mary L. Intern, Grady Meml. Hosp., Atlanta, 1942-43, asst. resident medicine, 1946-47; asst. resident medicine Thayer VA Hosp., Nashville, 1947-48, sr. resident medicine, 1948-49, tng. diseases of chest, 1949-54, asst. chief Tb service, 1949-54; practice medicine, specializing in internal medicine, Nashville, 1954—; cons. VA Hosp., Nashville; faculty Vanderbilt U., Nashville, 1948—, asst. prof. clin. medicine, 1961—. Served with AUS, 1943-46. Diplomate Am. Bd. Internal Medicine. Fellow Am. Coll. Chest Physicians; mem. A.C.P., A.M.A., Am., Nashville socs. internal medicine, Tenn. Thoracic Soc. (sec.-treas. 1969-71, pres. 1971-73), Nashville Acad. Medicine, Davidson County Anti-Tb Assn. (pres. 1969-71. Contbr. articles in field to profl. jours. Home: 728 Darden Pl Nashville TN 37205 Office: 2122 West End Av Nashville TN 37203

HAM, BERTRAM LAMAR, hwy. constrn. co. exec.; b. Kingston Springs, Tenn., Feb. 6, 1910; s. James Davis and Ida Lura (Fulghum) H.; student pub. schs.; m. Loretta Susan Robinson, May 27, 1939. Partner, J.D. Ham & Sons, Nashville, 1929-32; employed with various bridge and bldg. contractors, 1932-37; bridge foreman Rea Constrn. Co., Charlotte, N.C., 1937-40; with Oman Constrn. Co., Inc., Nashville, 1940—, project mgr., 1945-54, gen. supt. hwy. and r.r. constrn., 1955—, v.p., 1971—. Home: 5813 Robert E Lee Dr Nashville TN 37215 Office: Oman St Nashville TN 37202

HAM, CLARENCE EDWARD, supt. schs.; b. Wink, Tex., Dec. 27, 1936; s. Clarence Joseph and Edwina Olive (Brantley) H.; student Baylor U., 1955-56, B.A., 1959; student Tex. Technol. U., 1956-58, M.Ed., 1965; NSF fellow N.M. State U., 1963; Ph.D. (NDEA Title IV Grad. fellow 1966-69), Tex. U., 1969; m. Joyce Suzella Travis, Apr. 20, 1962; children—Patricia Lynn, John Joseph, Duane Michael. Tchr. Perrin (Tex.) Ind. Sch. Dist., 1960-62, Cotton Center (Tex.) Ind. Sch. Dist., 1962-66; bus. mgr. Orange (Tex.) Ind. Sch. Dist., 1967; supt. Orange County Sch. Dist., 1967-68, Bay City (Tex.) Ind. Sch. Dist., 1969—. Bd. dirs. Matagorda County Econ. Action Com., 1969—, Wharton-Matagorda County Child Welfare Bd., 1971—, Youth Services Bur., 1973—. Mem. N.E.A., Tex. State Tchrs. Assn., Nat., Tex. assns. sch. adminstrs., Tex. Assn. Curriculum Devel., Phi Delta Kappa. Baptist. Rotarian. Home: 2909 Del Monte Av Bay City TX 77414 Office: 1301 Live Oak St Bay City TX 77414

HAM, GOLDIE SUTTLE (MRS. GORDON BELL HANSON), ret. physician; b. Atlanta, Sept. 29, 1896; d. Eugene Gatewood and Edna (Bell) Ham; B.A., Agnes Scott Coll., 1919; M.D., Tulane U., 1923; m. Gordon Bell Hanson, Nov. 11, 1932 (dec. Apr. 1968); children—Ann Louise (Mrs. Ernest Anthony Merklein, Jr.), Elizabeth Bell (Mrs. Wolfgang Christian Durr). Intern, Charity Hosp., New Orleans, 1923-24; resident St. Joseph Hosp., Houston, 1924-26; practice medicine, specializing in obstetrics and gynecology, Houston, 1924—; mem. obstet. teaching staff Jefferson Davis Charity Hosp.; mem. staff St. Joseph, Meth., St. Luke's, Herman hosps. Clin. instr. obstetrics Baylor U. Med. Sch., 1943-60, mem. cons. staff, 1960—. Mem. Houston Bd. Health, 1937-38; mem. bd. Sheltering Arms, 1964-66, 68-71. Diplomate Am. Bd. Obstetrics and Gynecology. Mem. A.M.A., Am. Coll. Obstetricians and Gynecologists, Tex. Med. Assn., Mortar Bd., Alpha Omega Alpha, Alpha Delta Pi. Republican. Presbyn. Home: 2929 Buffalo Speedway Lamar Tower Houston TX 77006

HAM, TIBOR, physician; b. Rakos Palota, Hungary, June 8, 1914 (came to U.S. 1951, naturalized 1956); s. Janos and Marget (Papp) H.; M.D., U. Pazmany, Budapest, Hungary, 1938; m. Margaret Diener, Feb. 28, 1943; children—Andrew, Tibor, Eugene, Christine, Christopher. Asst. physician City Hosp., Budapest, 1939-41, dep. chief physician, 1941-45; intern Doctor's Hosp., Washington, 1951-52, mem. staff, 1953—; gen. practice medicine, Budapest, 1939-48, Vienna, Va., 1953—; owner Vienna Med. Clinic, 1953—; mem. staff Fairfax (Va.) Hosp., N.Va. Doctor's Hosp., Arlington, 1959—, Jefferson Hosp., Alexandria, Va., 1967—. Pres. Bernard Notes, Vienna, 1957. Pres. Am-Hungarian Cultural Center, Washington, 1966—. Lord lt. Province of Sopron, Hungary, 1945-46; majority whip Hungarian Parliament, 1946-47. Leader Youth Resistance Group, Hungary, World War II. Decorated Achievement in Underground Activities award Hungarian Govt., 1945. Fellow Royal Soc. Health (Eng.); mem. Am. Acad. Gen. Practice, A.M.A., Fairfax, Arlington med. socs., Piarist Alumnea Soc. (N.Y.C.). Home: 7016 Green Oak Dr McLean VA 22101 Office: 135 Center St Vienna VA 22180

HAM, WAYNE ALBERT, educator; b. Toronto, Ont., Can., May 13, 1938; s. Albert Alfred and Edna Frances (Dempster) H.; B.A., Graceland Coll., 1959; M.A., Brigham Young U., 1961; postgrad. Coll. of Siskiyous, 1962; M.Div., St. Paul Sch. Theology Meth., 1969; postgrad. Central Mo. State Coll., 1969-70; m. Marliene Margaret Miller, Dec. 24, 1959; children—Terry Russell, Brian Neal. Tchr. langs. Dunsmuir (Ca.) High Sch., 1961-62; asst. prof. English, U. Valle, Cali, Colombia, 1962-63; dir. Adult Materials dept. religious edn. The Auditorium, Independence, Mo., 1963-70; curriculum dir. Wildwood (Fla.) Middle Sch., 1970—; faculty Sch. of Restoration, Independence, 1964-69. Ordained to ministry Reorganized Ch. of Jesus Christ of Latter Day Saints, 1956; dir. religious edn. Santa Fe Stake, 1965-68. Mem. United Teaching Profession, Nat. Council Tchrs. English, Civitan. Author: Enriching Your New Testament Studies, 1965; Man's Living Religion, 1965; Faith and the Arts, 1968; The Call to Covenant, 1969; Publish Glad Tidings, 1970; The First Century Church, 1971; Where Faith and World Meet, 1972; Listening for God's Voice, 1973; On The Growing Edge, 1973. Editor, founder Dimensions, jour. young leadership devel.; editorial bd. Courage, A Jour. of Thought and Action. Home: Route 1 Box 174T Wildwood FL 32785

HAMADA, MOKHTAR MOHAMMAD, chem. engr.; b. Belbase, Egypt, Sept. 21, 1935; s. Mohamad H. and Amina A. (Abdulla) H.; B.Sc., Alexandria (Egypt) U., 1957; M.S., Colo. Sch. Mines, 1963, D.Sc., 1965; m. Sohair A. Tantawi, Apr. 7, 1960; children—Ahmad Tarek, Lobna. Came to U.S., 1960, naturalized, 1974. Instr. chem. engring. Alexandria U., 1957; operation engr. Suez Oil Processing Co., Suez, Egypt, 1958-68; process engr. Bechtel Engring., London, Eng., 1968-69; process devel. engr. Monsanto, Pensacola, Fla., 1969—. Mem. Am. Inst. Chem. Engrs., Am. Chem. Soc. Home: 4921 Woodcliff Dr Pensacola FL 32504 Office: Monsanto Co Pensacola FL 32504

HAMANN, CARL L., JR., environmental engr.; b. Hemple, Mo., Nov. 26, 1937; s. Carl L. and Evelyn (Pickett) H.; B.S. in Civil Engring. (N.T. Veatch scholar 1961-63; Harry A. Jordan scholar Am. Water Works Assn. 1963), U. Kan., 1963, M.S., 1969; m. Sharon Cowing, June 22, 1957; children—Mark Allen, Michael Evan. Draftsman, firm Black & Veatch, Kansas City, Mo., 1958-61, project engr., 1964-72; dir. water, advanced wastewater treatment Eastern region firm Cornell, Howland, Hayes & Merryfield/Hill, Reston, Va., 1972—. Diplomate Am. Acad. Environmental Engrs. Mem. Am. Soc. Civil Engrs., Am. Water Works Assn. (recipient publs. award 1966), Am. Inst. Chem. Engrs., Water Pollution Control Fedn. Home: 1312 Westhills Lane Reston VA 22090 Office: 1930 Isaac Newton Sq E Rm 202 Reston VA 22090

HAMBLEN, LAPSLEY WALKER, JR., lawyer; b. Chattanooga, Dec. 25, 1926; s. Lapsley Walker and Libbie (Shipley) H.; B.A., U. Va., 1949, LL.B., 1953; m. Martha O'Hegan Murdock, Apr. 15, 1950 (div. Oct. 1970); children—Lapsley Walker III, Allen Murdock, William Shipley; m. 2d, Claudia R. Terrell, Mar. 20, 1971. Admitted to W. Va. bar, 1954, Ohio bar, 1955, Va. bar, 1957; law asso. Spilman, Thomas, Battle & Klostermeyer, Charleston, W. Va., 1953-54; asso. Smith, Schnacke & Compton, Dayton, O., 1954-55; trial atty. Office Chief Counsel, Internal Revenue Service, Atlanta, 1955; atty.-adviser to judge Tax Ct. U.S., 1955-56; partner Caskie, Frost, Davidson & Hobbs, 1957-69, Caskie, Frost, Davidson, Hobbs & Hamblen, 1969—. Vice pres., gen. counsel Carter Glass & Sons Pubs., Inc., Lynchburg, 1974—; dir. Staunton Foods, Inc.; organizer, dir. Jefferson Nat. Bank (now Va. Nat. Bank), Lynchburg; co-dir. U. Va. Ann. Conf. Fed. Taxation, 1970—. Trustee So. Fed. Tax Inst., Atlanta, 1973—. Served with USNR, 1945-46. Mem. Am., Fed., Va., Lynchburg bar assns., Va. State Bar, U. Va. Alumni Assn., Greater Lynchburg C. of C. (pres., dir. 1971-72), Raven Soc., Order of Coif, Omicron Delta Kappa. Contbr. articles to profl. jours. Home: 3708 Manton Dr Lynchburg VA 24503 Office: 2306 Atherholt Rd Lynchburg VA 24501

HAMBLEY, WILLIAM ARTHUR, JR., govt. ofcl.; b. Creighton Mine, Ont., Can., July 16, 1925 (parents Am. citizens); s. William Arthur and Almira (Bullock) H.; B.S., U. Wis., 1950; M.A., U. Minn., 1953, postgrad., 1957-66; m. Sharon Lee Robinson, Sept. 10, 1965; 1 dau., Gwyneth Ellen. Indsl. engr. Proctor & Gamble Co., Cin., 1952-53; research asst. Office Sec. Def., Washington, 1953-54; comml. officer, asst. attache Am. embassy, Seoul, Korea, 1954-55; intelligence officer CIA, Washington, 1955-56; staff asst. Sen. Patrick V. McNamara, Washington, 1956-57; mgmt. analyst mgmt. office Govt. D.C., 1957; teaching asst., instr. polit. sci. U. Minn., Mpls., 1957-60; instr. Macalester Coll., St. Paul, 1960; adminstrv. fellow Bur. Student Loans and Scholarships, U. Minn., 1961-62, asst. to v.p. for ednl. relationships and devel., 1962-63, research asso. dean Coll. Med. Scis., 1965-66; asst. prof. No. Mich. U., Marquette, 1963-64; mgmt. intern Office Chief Staff Army, Washington, 1966-67; dir. mgmt. improvement and work simplification programs Army Work Simplification Program, Office Army Comptroller, Washington, 1967—, editor Army Mgmt. Practices Letter, 1967—, Armed Forces Comptroller mag., 1970—. Chmn. 2d ward Democratic Com. Mpls., 1958-59; mem. 3d Congl. Dist. Exec. Com., 1958-61, Central Com. Hennepin County, 1958-62; del. Minn. Conv., 1960, 62. Served with AUS, 1943-46. Citizenship Clearinghouse Nat. fellow, 1961-62; Tozer fellow, 1963. Recipient North Star award U. Minn., 1959. Mem. Am. Polit. Sci. Assn., Am. Soc. for Performance Improvement (nat. dir.), Am. Soc. Pub. Adminstrn., Assn. U.S. Army, Mil. Police Assn., Am.

Vets. Com., Alpha Tau Omega, Theta Tau. Democrat. Unitarian. Home: 2514 Pinoak Lane Reston VA 22091 Office: Office Comptroller Army Washington DC 20310

HAMBLIN, ROBERT LEE, clergyman; b. Hamilton, O., June 29, 1928; s. Millard Fillmore and Rhoda (Muncy) H.; B.A., Union U., 1950; B.D., Southwestern Bapt. Theol. Sem., 1954, Th.D., 1959; m. Mary Ruth Miller, Aug. 27, 1948; children—Bobbie Ruth, Karis Jan, Mary Carole. Ordained to ministry Bapt. Ch., 1947; pastor Elliston Av. Bapt. Ch., Memphis, 1956-58, Harrisburg Bapt. Ch., Tupelo, Miss., 1958—. First v.p. Miss. Bapt. Conv., 1973, mem. bd., 1967—, pres. exec. com., 1969, pres. bd., 1970-73: vice chmn. exec. com. Brotherhood Commn., 1969. Bd. dirs. Lee United Neighbors; trustee Clarke Meml. Coll., Newton, Miss., 1962-67. Kiwanian (pres. 1965). Author: Studies in Galatians, 1972. Home: 210 Hancock Dr Tupelo MS 38801 Office: 1800 W Main St Tupelo MS 38801

HAMBLY, DEREK OWEN, govt. ofcl.; b. Houston, June 22, 1930; s. Frank and Helen Esther (Litherland) H.; B.Sc., Cal. Poly. Coll., 1957; m. Agnes Christine Kurtnaker, July 8, 1951; children—Kathleen Ann, Karen Lynn. With Nat. Park Service Dept. Interior, various locations, 1958—, chief naturalist Colo. Nat. Monument, Fruita, 1963-66, Padre Island Nat. Seashore, Corpus Christi, 1966-71; supt. Fort Davis (Tex.) Nat. Historic Site, 1971—. Ex-offico mem. advanced degree com. biol. scis. Tex. A. and I. U., 1968-71. Served with AUS, 1951-53. Lion (pres., 1973-74). Home and office: Box 1456 Fort Davis TX 79734

HAMBY, DAME SCOTT, educator; b. Macon, Ga., July 8, 1920; s. G. T. and Emma (Scott) H.; B.S., Auburn U., 1946; m. Edna Estelle Johnson, Jan. 20, 1943; children—Michael, Barbara. With Goodyear Tire & Rubber Co., Atco, Ga., 1937-42, Celanese Corp. Am., 1943-45, B.F. Goodrich Co., 1947-48; prof. Sch. Textiles, N.C. State U., Raleigh, 1948-65, head dept. textile tech., 1965-70, dir. textiles extension and continuing edn., 1970—. Dir. Tuscarora Mills, Oakboro Mills. Cons. to numerous textile cos.; mem. field testing com., adv. bd. q.m. research and devel. Nat. Acad. Scis., 1964-70. Recipient Distinguished Service award, textile div. Am. Soc. Quality Control, 1966. Fellow Textile Inst., Am. Soc. Quality Control (chmn. publs. com. textile div. 1957-60), A.A.A.S.; mem. Am. Assn. Textile Technologists (vice chmn. Piedmont sect. 1960-61), Am. Standards Assn. (chmn. com. internat. standardization of textile testing 1961-66), Am. Soc. Testing and Materials (chmn. com. D-13, 1966-72, dir. 1967), Sigma Xi, Phi Kappa Phi, Sigma Tau Sigma. Author: Handbook of Textile Testing and Quality Control, 1960. Editor: The American Cotton Handbook, vols. 1 and 2, 1965. Home: 319 Golf Course Dr Raleigh NC 27610

HAMDY, MOSTAFA KAMAL, educator; b. Cairo, Egypt, May 27, 1921; s. Hamid Alimobark and Nefisa Mohamed (Sultan) H.; B.Sc., Cairo U., 1944, M.Sc., 1949; Ph.D., Ohio State U., 1953; m. Kathryn Ann Russell, May 29, 1954; children—David Hamed, Kathryn Ann. Came to U.S., 1950, naturalized, 1958. Instr., Alexandria U., 1944-48; instr. Cairo U., 1944-49, lectr., 1948-49; Muelhaupt postdoctoral fellow Ohio State U., 1953-54, postdoctoral fellow, 1954-58; asst. prof. food sci. U. Ga., Athens, 1958-62, asso. prof., 1962-65, prof., 1965—. Vice pres. P.T.A., Clarke Middle Sch., 1972-73, Timothy Estate Assn., Athens, 1972-73. Recipient Sears Roebuck Found. award, 1963, Distinguished Research Faculty award Coll. Agr. U. Ga., 1968, Distinguished Research award Sigma Xi, 1967. Fellow Acad. Microbiology; mem. Soc. Exptl. Biology and Medicine (pres. S.E. br. 1973-74), Am. Soc. Microbiology, N.Y. Acad. Scis., So. Assn. Agrl. Scientists (sec.-treas. food sci. and tech. sect. 1973—), Inst. Food Technologists, Sigma Xi, Phi Kappa Phi, Phi Sigma, Gamma Sigma. Clubs: Stamp; Chess. Contbr. profl. jours. Home: 200 Devonshire Dr Athens GA 30601 Office: Dept Food Science Univ Ga Athens GA 30601

HAMEL, GEORGE FELIX, ednl. adminstr.; b. Worcester, Mass., Nov. 26, 1919; s. John B. and Beatrice (Charbonneau) H.; B.S., U. Mass., 1941; M.S., U. Wis., 1966; m. Arline Elizabeth Rainey, Apr. 19, 1952; children—Cynthia, Janet, George, James, William, Sally, Molly. Commd. 2d lt. U.S. Army, 1941, advanced through grades to col., 1964; with 10th Armored div., World War II; grad., instr. U.S. Army Command and Gen. Staff Coll., 1958-61; comdr. 3d Armored div., Germany, 1961-64; dir. community relations Office Sec. Def., Washington, 1966-69; ret., 1969; dir. sch.-community relations Fairfax (Va.) County Pub. Schs., 1969—. Tchr. Norwich U., Northfield, Vt., 1950-53, U. Md., 1967-68, Southeastern U. at Washington, 1966-68. Decorated Legion of Merit, Bronze Star medal with 1 oak leaf cluster. Mem. Nat. Sch. Pub. Relations Assn., D.A.V., Assn. U.S. Army, Ret. Officers Assn., Lambda Chi Alpha. Home: 1500 Twisting Tree Lane McLean VA 22101 Office: 10700 Page Av Fairfax VA 22030

HAMER, JAN, educator, chemist; b. Gombong, Indonesia, May 2, 1927; s. Gerard Pieter and Wijke (de Boer) H.; Candidaat, U. Leiden (The Netherlands), 1948, doctorandus, 1955, doctorate, 1956; m. Millicent May, Mar. 10, 1956; children—Elizabeth May, Hilary Halsey. Research asso. Tulane U., New Orleans, 1956-57, asso. prof., 1960-65, asso. prof. chemistry, 1965—; asso. prof., chmn. dept. chemistry Dillard U., New Orleans, 1958-60. Cons. So. Regional Research Lab., U.S. Dept. Agr.; chmn. Organic Discussion Group, New Orleans, 1965-66, 73-74. Served to 1st lt. Royal Netherlands Army, 1949-51. Mem. A.A.A.S., Am. Assn. U. Profs., Chem. Soc. (London), Royal Netherlands, Am. (sect. exec. com. 1965-68) chem. socs., Sigma Xi, Alpha Chi Sigma. Club: Round Table. Home: 299 Walnut St New Orleans LA 70118

HAMES, LUTHER CLAUDE, JR., judge; b. Marietta, Ga., Nov. 18, 1917; s. Luther C. and Patience (Owen) H.; LL.B., Woodrow Wilson Coll. of Law, Atlanta, 1938; m. Kathryn Johnson, May 6, 1942; children—Dorothy Kay Coker, Lucia Ann Phillips, Patricia Lee. Admitted to Ga. bar, 1939; individual practice 1939-68; judge superior ct., spl. asst. atty. gen. Ga., 1965; dir. Comml. Bank Cobb County. City councilman; mayor pro tem, City of Marietta, 1948-50; solicitor gen., 1953-67; chmn. Marietta Housing Authority, 1950-59; sec., treas. Cobb County Democratic Exec. Com., 1948-60; mem. contest com. Ga. State Conv., 1954. Served from 2d lt. to capt. AUS, 1942-45. Mem. C. of C. (past pres.), Solicitors Gen. Assn. of Ga. (pres. 1956), Am., Ga., Cobb County (pres. 1964-65) bar assns., Council of Trial Judges, Sigma Delta Kappa. Democrat. Baptist. Mason. Home: RFD 4 Old Trace Rd Marietta GA 30060 Office: Cobb Judicial Bldg Marietta GA 30060

HAMILL, WILLARD DEARING, investment broker; b. Roanoke, Va., Mar. 9, 1932; s. Willard Robert and Helen (Hogan) H.; B.S., Va. Polytech. Inst., 1958; m. Jeanette Martin. Seasonal park ranger Blue Ridge Pkwy., Roanoke, Va., summers 1957-58; investment broker Cash, Shoaf & Co., Inc., 1958—, sec., 1960—, pres., treas., 1971—. Served with AUS, 1953. Decorated Bronze Star. Mem. Nat., Va. christmas tree growers assns., Alpha Kappa Psi. Presbyn. Club: Sertoma. Home: 3121 King St NE Roanoke VA 24012 Office: 7 W Campbell Av Roanoke VA 24011

HAMILTON, CHARLES GRANVILLE, clergyman; b. Homestead, Pa., July 18, 1905; s. Augustus William and Mary Catherine (Frey) H.; A.B., Berea Coll., 1925; B.D., Columbia Sem., 1928, M. Div., 1971; D.D., Ministerial Coll., 1941; M.A., U. Miss., 1947; Ph.D., Vanderbilt U., 1958; postgrad. U. S.C., Butler U., Columbia, Emory U., Ind. U., Miss. State U., Temple U., Tulane U., U. Wis., others; m. Mary Elizabeth Casey, May 23, 1939. Ordained to ministry Episcopal Ch., 1929; rector Mid-South field, 1928—; chaplain, prof. religious edn. Okolona Coll., 1933-40, prof. Wood, Furman, Memphis State, Vanderbilt and other univs., 1942—; Danforth fellowships, 1955-60; fellowships St. Augustine's, Canterbury, England, 1961, Ford, 1962, Truman Library, 1963, Bell Telephone 1964, Am. Philos. Soc., 1969; minister Quiet Hour radio broadcast, 1942—; commentator The World Goes On, 1934—; pres., v.p., sec. Miss. Council for Christian Social Action, 1938—; v.p., dir. Rural Fellowship, 1955-63; sec., dir., pres. Crossroads Fellowship, 1964—; columnist Aberdeen (Miss.) Examiner, 1933-47. Del. Province of Sewanee, 1935, 36, 38, 39, 53, 54; sr. reporter Episcopal Convs., 1937—, World Council Chs., 1963. Mem. Miss. Ho. of Reps., 1940-44, floor leader, 1942; del. Democratic Nat. Convs. 1940, 48, 52, 56, 60, 64, 68, 72, mem. credentials com. 1952; chmn. Miss. Vols. for Stevenson, 1952, 56, for Humphrey, 1968; pres., sec., sponsor Young Democrats, 1944-60; mem. White House Traffic Safety Commn., Tenn. Constn. Conv. Commn. Bd. dirs. Family Protection League. Served as 1st lt., chaplain AUS, 1940-42. Named Miss. Minister of Year, 1953; recipient research award Acad. Sci., 1955, Distinguished Alumnus of Year award Berea Coll., 1972; Ky. col. Mem. Am., So., Miss. hist. socs., Am., So. polit. sci. socs., Eugene Field Soc., Soc. Sacred Songwriters, Sons Confederate Vets. (chaplain gen.), Order Stars and Bars (chaplain gen.), New Orleans Civil War Roundtable (sec.), Pi Sigma Alpha, Phi Kappa Phi. Author many works, 1936—, including: Within Whose Memories Abide, 1935; South, 1935; There Came One Running, 1937; Mississippi I Love You, 1941; These United States, 1942; The Prophet in Wartime, 1947; Negro Education in Mississippi, 1952; Lincoln and the Know Nothings, 1954; 48 in '48, 1956; Democratic America, 8th edit., 1969; You Can't Steal First Base, 1971; also booklets. Editor: Brave Voyage, 1936; Lyric Monroe, 1937; Basic Relationships of Science, 1939; Those Precious Years, 1941; Preaching is Flame, 1961; Singing Spirit, 1962; Moments of Meditation, 1963; Music of Eternity, 1964; Grass on the Mountains, 1966; God of the Years, 1968; Our Yesterdays (Mary C. Hamilton), 1969; Christianity in 52 Words, 1970; Life is Benediction, 1971; The North Wind Comes, 1972; Afterglow, 1973; Contbr. Poems of Justice, Master of Men, Poems for Life, others. Editor Jour. Miss. History, 1941-52. Editor: Crossroads, 1957—, Churchman, 1958—. Home: S Meridian Monroe and Maple Aberdeen MS 39370

HAMILTON, CLYDE H., lawyer; b. Edgefield, S.C., Feb. 8, 1934; s. Clyde Henry and Edwina (Odom) H.; B.S., Wofford Coll., 1956; J.D. cum laude, George Washington U., 1961; m. Mary Elizabeth Spillers, July 20, 1957; children—John C., James W. Reference asst., U.S. Senate Library, 1958-61; admitted to S.C. bar, 1961; asso. firm J.R. Folk, Edgefield, 1961-63; asso. mem. Butler, Means, Evins & Browne, Spartanburg, S.C., 1963-65, partner, 1966—. Gen. counsel, asst. sec., dir. Synalloy Corp., Am. Stock Exchange, Spartanburg, S.C., 1969—. Pres., Spartanburg County Arts Council, 1971-73; mem. steering com., undergrad. merit fellowship program Converse Coll., Spartanburg, 1971—. Chmn. trustees Spartanburg Day Sch., 1972—. Served to 1st lt. AUS, 1956-58. Mem. S.C., Am. bar assns., Sigma Alpha Epsilon, Delta Phi Alpha. Methodist (past chmn. adminstrv. bd.). Rotarian (past dir.). Clubs: Piedmont, Spartanburg Cotillion (past dir.). Editorial bd. George Washington Law Rev., 1959-60; editorial staff Cumulative Index of Congressional Com. Hearings, 1955-58, 1959. Home: 422 S Fairview Av Ext Spartanburg SC 29302 Office: PO Drawer 451 Spartanburg SC 29301

HAMILTON, DEWITT CLINTON, JR., educator; b. Eufaula, Okla., Dec. 4, 1918; s. DeWitt Clinton and Jessie May (Patterson) H.; B.S., U. Okla., 1941; M.S. U. Cal. at Berkeley, 1946; Ph.D. (Westinghouse fellow), Purdue U., 1949; m. Elizabeth Angeline Moore, Jan. 17, 1942. Instr. mech. engring. Purdue U., Lafayette, Ind., 1948-49, asst. prof., 1949-51; head devel. engr., reactor div. Union Carbide Nuclear Co., Oak Ridge, 1951-56; lectr. reactor engring. Oak Ridge Sch. Reactor Tech., 1956-65; prof., head dept. mech. engring. Tulane U., New Orleans, 1965—. Vis. lectr. nuclear engring. Ga. Inst. Tech., 1962-63; cons. Union Carbide, 1965-67. Served to maj. USAAF, 1941-46. Mem. Am. Nuclear Soc. (charter), Am. Soc. M.E. (chmn. New Orleans sect. 1973-74, vice chmn. dept. heads com. region X 1973-75), Am. Soc. Engring. Edn. (dir. council grad. and continuing edn. 1973—), Sigma Xi, Tau Beta Pi, Sigma Tau, Pi Tau Sigma, Sigma Pi Sigma. Home: 261 Jules Av Apt 50 New Orleans LA 70114

HAMILTON, EUGENE LEVERETT, newspaperman; b. Staunton, Ind., Aug. 13, 1917; s. Leverett John and Floy Mae (Stout) H.; grad. high sch.; m. Mary Frances Hammons, July 31, 1942 (dec. Mar. 1974); children—Mary Alice, Betty Jean. Clk., Houser Bros. Grocery, Jasonville, Ind., 1937-39; tank wagon salesman Shell Oil Co., Clearwater, Fla., 1939-40; advt. exec. Myers Dept. Store, Clearwater, 1945-47; advt. exec. Clearwater Sun, 1947-51; advt. mgr. Tuscaloosa (Ala.) News, 1951-53, bus. mgr., 1953, v.p., 1954—, gen. mgr., 1966-70, cons., adviser, 1970—. Active United Fund, YMCA, Tuscaloosa Citizens Sch. Com., Warrior Tombigbee Waterways Devel. Assn. Served with AUS, 1941-45; PTO. Mem. Am. Legion, Tuscaloosa C. of C. Presbyn. Kiwanian. Club: Tuscaloosa Country. Home and office: 25 Lakeshore Dr Tuscaloosa AL 35401

HAMILTON, EUGENE NOLAN, judge; b. Memphis, Aug. 24, 1933; s. Thomas E. and Barbara (Blakey) H.; B.A., U. Ill., 1955, LL.B., 1959; m. Virginia David, June 16, 1956; children—Barbara Jane, John Steven, James Poole, Eric Eugene, David Nolan, Rachel Olivette. Admitted to Ill. bar, 1959; sr. trial atty. U.S. Dept. Justice, Washington, 1961-70, asso. judge Superior Ct. D.C., Washington, 1970—. Bd. dirs. Bethany House, Rockville, Md. Served with Judge Adv. Gen. Corps, AUS, 1959-61. Mem. Am. Bar Assn., Phi Delta Phi. Home: 15305 Sweetridge Rd Silver Spring MD 20904 Office: 613 G St NW Washington DC 20001

HAMILTON, HOLMAN, historian, educator; b. Ft. Wayne, Ind., May 30, 1910; s. Dr. Allen and Helen (Knight) H.; A.B., Williams Coll., 1932; Ph.D., U. Ky., 1954; L.H.D., Franklin Coll., Ind., 1966; LL.D., Lincoln Meml. U., 1973; m. Suzanne W. Bowerfind, Oct. 7, 1939; 1 dau., Susan C. Reporter, Ft. Wayne Journal-Gazette, 1932-34; editorial writer, 1935-42, 46, 47-50; asst. prof. history U. Ky., Lexington, 1954-57, asso. prof., 1957-65, prof., 1965—, Hallam prof., 1969-71; Guggenheim fellow, 1946; Fulbright prof. U. Chile, Santiago, 1966. Trustee Lincoln Meml. U., 1957-63. Served from pvt. to maj. AUS, 1942-46. Recipient Pelzer prize Miss. Valley Hist. Assn., 1954; faculty research award U. Ky., 1965, Great Tchr. award, 1968, Distinguished Prof. award Coll. Arts and Scis., 1971. Mem Am., So. hist. assns., Orgn. Am. Historians, Soc. Am. Historians, Ind., Ky. hist. socs. Clubs: Nat. Press (Washington); Idle Hour (Lexington); Williams (N.Y.C.). Author: Zachary Taylor: Soldier of the Republic, 1941; Zachary Taylor: Soldier in the White House, 1951; White House Images and Realities, 1958; Prologue to Conflict, 1964. Co-author: The Democratic Experience, 1963, rev. edit., 1973. Contbr. to Dictionary of American History, 1940; Major Crises in American History, 1962; Notable American Women, 1971; History of American Presidential Elections, 1971. Co-editor: Indianapolis in the Gay Nineties, 1964. Editor: Three American Frontiers, 1968. Home: 220 Barrow Rd Lexington KY 40502

HAMILTON, RAY V., broker; b. Eden, Ia., Aug. 11, 1904; s. Albert J. and Sarah Margaret (Cox) H.; student U. Ia., 1926-29; m. Susanne Fjelstad, Apr. 5, 1931. Gen. mgr. St. Louis Star-Times Radio Stas., 1933-40; account exec. NBC, 1940-42; dir. English lang. propaganda U.S. Dept. State, 1942-44; exec. v.p. Asso. Broadcasters, San Francisco, Los Angeles, Seattle, 1944-46; chmn. bd., owner Hamilton-Landis & Assos., Inc., brokers, Chgo., Dallas, Washington, San Francisco, 1946—; pres., dir. Blackburn-Hamilton Co., Inc., Broadcast Realty Co., Tulsa Industries, Inc., others; chmn. Round The World Shops, Inc. Clubs: Press, Broadcasters of Washington, University, Georgetown (Washington); Press (San Francisco); Circumnavigator; Chicago Athletic. Author (with others) Advertising for the High School Journalist. World traveler. Home: Carlton Towers St Petersburg FL 33701 also 4740 Connecticut Av NW Washington DC 20008 Office: 1730 K St NW Washington DC 20006 also Tribune Tower Chicago IL 60611 also 111 Sutter St San Francisco CA 94104

HAMILTON, THEODORE JAY, pub. relations co. exec.; b. Fremont, O., June 1, 1923; s. Wilson E. and Pauline (Townsend) H.; B.Chem. Engring., Ohio State U., 1947; m. Laura Bowers, June 8, 1948; children—Carol Ann, Philip Wilson. Dist. mgr. Union Carbide Chems. Co., 1947-59; with Wilson E. Hamilton & Assos., Washington, 1959—, pres., 1966—; v.p., treas. Computer Control Corp., Rockville, Md. Treas. Crusade for a Cleaner Environment, Washington. Served with AUS, 1943-45. Home: 7117 Darby Rd Bethesda MD 20034 Office: 2000 L St NW Washington DC 20036

HAMILTON, THOMAS EARLE, educator; b. Savannah, Ga., June 10, 1905; s. Homer Francis and Catherine (Langford) H.; A.B., So. Meth. U., 1927, M.A., 1929; Ph.D., U. Tex., 1940; m. Juanita Vivian Adams, Aug. 2, 1933; children—Earle Hartwell, Charles Lee, Helen Catherine (Mrs. Paul A. Anthony). Instr., Garland (Tex.) High Sch., 1927-29, Highland Park High Sch., Dallas, 1929-37; instr. Tex. Tech. U., Lubbock, 1940-43, asst. prof., 1943-45, asso. prof., 1945-55, prof. Spanish and classics, 1955-71, prof. emeritus, 1971—; vis. prof. Spanish, Tex. Women's U., Saltillo, Mex., summer 1945; vis. prof. Spanish and classics Austin Coll., 1962-63. Mem. Modern Lang. Assn. (life emeritus mem.), Tex. Fgn. Lang. Assn. (pres. 1958, hon. life mem.), Am. Assn. Tchrs. Spanish and Portuguese, Assn. Coll. Honor Socs. (chmn. com. on standards and definitions), Eta Sigma Phi, Sigma Delta Pi (nat. v.p. 1950-59, nat. pres. 1959-68, 72—). Methodist. Editor, S. Central Modern Lang. Assn. Bull., 1954-56, asso. editor, 1965-67; founder, 1st editor Tex. Fgn. Lang. Assn. Bull., 1953-57. Contbr. articles to profl. jours. Home: Route 1 Box 596 Kingsland TX 78639

HAMIT, HAROLD FRANCIS, physician; b. Stockton, Kan., Dec. 29, 1913; s. Claude Charles and Maude Leota (Laurie) H.; A.B., N.Y. U., 1942, M.D., 1945; M.S., U. Colo., 1955; m. Ethel Cordelia Granger, Sept. 6, 1935; children—Francis Granger, Elaine Marie. Commd. 1st lt., M.C., U.S. Army, 1946, advanced through grades to col., 1963; regtl. surgeon 43d Inf., Luxon, P.I., 1946-47; post surgeon Tokyo Q.M. Depot, 1947-48; resident surgery Oliver Gen. Hosp., Augusta, Ga., 1949-50, Brooke Gen. Hosp., San Antonio, Tex., 1950-51, Fitzsimons Gen. Hosp., Denver, 1953-55, Letterman Gen. Hosp., San Francisco, 1960-62; comdr. Army Hosp., Camp Leroy, Johnson, La., 1951-53; chief gen. surgery Army Hosp., Ft. Hood, Tex., 1955-56; postgrad. tng. Walter Reed Army Inst. Research, Washington, 1956-57; chief surg. br. Army Research and Devel. Command, 1957-60; comdr. 121st Evacuation Hosp., Korea, 1962-63; chief gen. surgery Brooke Gen. Hosp., 1965-67; dir. div. surgery Walter Reed Army Inst. Research, 1967-68; ret., 1968; asso. dir. clin. research Travenol Labs., Morton Grove, Ill., 1968-70; asso. chmn. dept. gen. surgery Charlotte (N.C.) Meml. Hosp., 1970—. Research asso. prof. surgery Baylor U. Coll. Medicine, Houston, 1963-65; lectr. Northwestern Sch. Medicine, Chgo., 1968-70. Decorated Legion Merit. Diplomate Am. Bd. Surgery, Am. Bd. Thoracic Surgery. Fellow Am. Assn. Surgery Trauma, A.C.S.; mem. A.M.A., Mil. Surgeons U.S., A.A.A.S., Royal Med. Soc. (affiliate), Am. Trauma Soc. (founding mem.), Internat. Platform Com., Mil. Order Carabao. Contbr. profl. jours. Home: 1309 Providence Rd Charlotte NC 28207 Office: Charlotte Memorial Hosp Charlotte NC 28201

HAMITER, JOHN CECIL, hosp. administr.; b. Carrollton, Ala., Aug. 28, 1919; s. John Tyler and Emma (Corder) H.; B.S., U. Ala., 1952; M.H.A., U. Minn., 1954; m. Miriam Elise Doughty, Dec. 27, 1947; children—John Cecil, Margaret Ann, Miriam Anita. Administrv. resident Jefferson Hillman Hosp. (now U. Hosp.), Birmingham, Ala., 1953-54; asst. adminstr. Carraway Meth. Hosp., Birmingham, 1954-57; adminstr. Bapt. Meml. Hosp., Gadsden, Ala., 1957-69, pres., 1969—; adminstr. Etowah-Cherokee-DeKalb Counties Mental Health Center, 1967—. First v.p., dir. East Gadsden Bank; dir. Rainbow Med. Equipment Co. Vis. faculty Sch. Hosp. Services Adminstrn., U. Ala., preceptor course in hosp. adminstrn. Pres. Health Careers Council Ala.; dir. Southeastern Hosp. Conf. Bd. dirs. Etowah County chpt. A.R.C., Southeastern Hosp. Conf., Etowah County Mental Health Assn.; chmn. bd. dirs. Gadsden-Etowah Area Redevel. Commn.; mem. Gadsden Indsl. Devel. Bd.; chmn. bd. Etowah County Dept. Pensions and Security; bd. dirs. Blue Cross-Blue Shield Ala., Holy Comforter House. Mem. adv. bd. Gadsden State Jr. Coll., Gadsden State Tech. Trade Sch., Ida V. Moffett Sch. Nursing, Birmingham, Lurleen B. Wallace Sch. Nursing, Jacksonville State U.; chmn. profl. adv. com. Home Health Agy. Etowah County. Served with AUS, 1940-45. Fellow Am. Coll. Hosp. Adminstrs. (regent Ala.); mem. Ala. Assn. Hosp. Execs. (pres. 1967—), Ala. Assn. Pub. Welfare Bds,, Birmingham Regional Hosp. Council (pres. 1957), N.E. Ala. Hosp. Council (pres. 1966), N.E. Ala. Health Planning Assn. (dir.), Am., Protestant, Ala. (pres. 1964), Baptist (pres. elect) hosp. assns., Gadsden C. of C. Home: 1428 Monte Vista Dr Gadsden AL 35901 Office: 1007 Goodyear Av Gadsden AL 35903

HAMLIN, OMER, JR., med. librarian; b. Tollesboro, Ky., July 16, 1930; s. Omer and Anna Will (Teager) H.; A.B., Milligan Coll., 1956; postgrad. Lexington Theol. Sem., 1957-58, Morehead State U., summer 1958; M.S. in L.S., U. Ky., 1959; m. Evon Thompson, Aug. 1, 1959; children—David Omer, Stephen Alan. Head librarian Milligan Coll., 1959-62; serials librarian U. Ky. Med. Library, Lexington, 1962, reference and circulation librarian, 1962, asst. med. librarian, 1963, acting med. librarian, 1963, dir. med. library, 1963-70, dir. Med. Center Library and Communication Systems, 1970—. Named Outstanding Spl. Librarian Ky., 1965. Mem. A.L.A., Med. (pres. So. group 1965-66), Ky. (pres. 1968), Lexington library assns., Health Sci. Communication Assn. Home: 3405 Westridge Circle Lexington KY 40502

HAMM, DELBERT LEE, clergyman; b. Stillwater, Okla., July 15, 1931; s. Berton F. and Ethel Mae (Fitzpatrick) H.; B.A., Phillips U., 1954; B.D., 1957; m. Dolores Ann Townsend, Nov. 28, 1953; children—Kyle Kevin, Lee Ann, Terry Lee. Ordained to ministry Christian Ch., 1953; asso. minister Central Christian Ch., Wichita, Kan., 1960-63; minister Hillcrest Christian Ch., Oklahoma City,

1963—. Mem. Christian Ch. Commn. Oklahoma City, 1970—. Served as chaplain USNR, 1957-60. Contbr. articles to mags. Home: 6605 S Barnes St Oklahoma City OK 73159 Office: 1501 SW 59th St Oklahoma City OK 73119

HAMM, DONALD IVAN, educator; b. Wellington, Kan., Jan. 11, 1928; s. Cecil Randolph and Galys (Barker) H.; Student Southwestern Tex. U., 1945-46; B.S., U. Okla., 1949, Ph.D., 1956; M.S., Purdue U., 1951; m. Jean Ann Ewing, Aug. 19, 1950; children—Jeffrey Lloyd, Cheryl (Mrs. Gary Mack Leonard), Deona (Mrs. Aaron Miles Sauer), David Ewing, James Ritchie. Asst. prof. dept. chemistry Southwestern State Coll., 1951-56, asso. prof., 1956-58, prof., 1958—, chmn. dept. chemistry, 1970—; vis. prof. Mich. State U., 1969-70. Mem. Weatherford (Okla.) Bd. Edn., 1960-65, pres., 1965. Served with USNR, 1945-46. Mem. Am. Chem. Soc. (chmn. Okla. sect. 1973), Okla. Acad. Sci., Am. Inst. Chemists, Alpha Chi Sigma, Sigma Pi Sigma, Phi Lambda Upsilon, Sigma Xi. Mem. Ch. Christ (deacon 1968—). Rotarian (pres. 1959-60). Author: Chemistry: An Introduction to Matter and Energy, 1965; Fundamental Concepts of Chemistry, 1969. Home: Box 196 Rural Route 2 Weatherford OK 73096 Office: Southwestern State Coll Weatherford OK 73096

HAMMERSCHMIDT, JOHN PAUL, congressman; b. Harrison, Ark., May 4, 1922; s. Arthur Paul and Junie (Taylor) H.; student The Citadel, 1938-39, U. Ark., 1940-41, Okla. State U., 1945-46; m. Virginia Sharp, Oct. 11, 1948; 1 son, John Arthur. With Hammerschmidt Lumber Co., Harrison, 1946—, pres., 1959—; dir. Harrison Fed. Savs. & Loan Assn.; mem. Harrison City Council, 1948, 60, 62; mem. 90th-93d Congresses, 3d Dist. Ark. Chmn. Ark. Republican Com., 1964-66; mem. Rep. Nat. Finance Com., 1960-64. Served as pilot USAAF, World War II; CBI. Decorated Air medal with 4 oak leaf clusters, D.F.C. with 3 oak leaf clusters. Mem. Ark. Lumber Dealers Assn. (past pres.), Southwestern Lumbermens Assn. (past pres. Kansas City), Harrison C. of C. (named Man of Yr. 1965), Am. Legion, V.F.W. Presbyn. (elder). (deacon). Mason (32 deg., Shriner), Elk, Rotarian (past pres. Harrison). Home: 1710 Kent St Arlington VA 22209 Office: Cannon House Office Bldg Washington DC 20515

HAMMES, JOHN ANTHONY, educator; b. Sault Ste. Marie, Mich., Nov. 1, 1924; s. Roman Burchart and Daisy (Martin) H.; B.A., Duquesne U., 1948; M.A., Cath. U., 1950; Ph.D., Pa. State U., 1953; m. Dorothy Janelle Perkins, Feb. 22, 1964; children—John, Paul, Penny. Research asso. Human Resources Research Office, Washington, 1953-56; asst. prof. U. Ga., 1956-62, asso. prof., 1962-68, prof. psychology, 1968—, dir. Civil Def. Research, 1962—, asso. head dept. psychology, 1969—. Mem. Athens-Clarke County Shelter Plan Steering Com., 1965-66. Served with USNR, 1943-46. Mem. Am., Southeastern, Ga. psychol. assns., Contemporary Authors, A.A.A.S., Cardinal Newman Hon. Soc., Sigma Xi, Psi Chi. Home: 235 Davis Estates Rd Athens GA 30601

HAMMET, BEN HAY, coll. publ. dir.; b. Allendale, S.C., Feb. 13, 1922; s. Benjamin Joseph and Nelleen (Hay) H.; B.A., Presbyn. Coll., 1943; postgrad. Columbia, 1946; B.J., U. Mo., 1948; m. Florence Jane Jenkins, Apr. 29, 1949; children—Ben Hay, Jr., Lewis Jenkins, Errol Scott. Southeastern night editor Internat. News Service, Atlanta, 1948; bur. mgr., 1948-49; dir. alumni and pub. relations, dir. publs., editor coll. mag. Presbyn. Coll., Clinton, S.C., 1949—. Served with AUS, 1943-46. Recipient Outstanding Service award Presbyn. Coll. Bd. Visitors, 1966, Alumni Gold P Presbyn. Coll. Alumni Assn., 1971, Alumni Giving Incentive award U.S. Steel Found., 1967. Mem. Am. Coll. Pub. Relations Assn., Am. Alumni Council, Pub. Relations Soc. Am. (chpt. sec. treas. 1970—), Blue Key, Kappa Tau Alpha. Presbyn. (deacon 1967-74). Kiwanian (pres. 1964). Home: 110 E Maple St Clinton SC 29325 Office: Presbyn Coll S Broad St Clinton SC 29325

HAMMETT, ARTHUR BENJAMIN JOHN, banker; b. nr. Marysville, Kan., Nov. 23, 1900; s. Benjamin J. and Rena Mae (Neal) H.; student mil. and pvt. schs.; m. Alice Neeley, July 19, 1925 (div. July 1935); children—Jo Ann (Mrs. Morgan Huff), Jacqueline Lee (Mrs. S. J. Gaylord, Jr.). With Exchange Bank of Schmidt & Koester, Marysville, Kan., 1917-20; with legal dept. Belt Rwy. Chgo., 1920-23; with Fulsom Wheeler & Co., investment bankers, Kansas City, Mo., 1922-25; exec. mfg. div. Marshall Field & Co., N.Y.C., 1932-37; pres. Village Bus. Center, Inc., 1953—, A.B.J. Hammett Investment Banking Co., 1953—, Victoria Profl. Office Bldg. Corp. (Tex.), 1955—, Kimberlite Diamind Mining Co.; pub. Victoria Mirror Daily News Newspaper, 1958—; chmn. bd. Comml. Nat. Bank, Victoria, 1963—. Active in civic affairs. Served to comdr. naval aviation USNR, 1942-46. Commd. adm. Tex. Navy, 1958. Mem. Tex. Mfrs. Assn., So. Tex. C. of C., V.F.W., Petroleum Club, Mason (32 1/2, Shriner), Elk. Clubs: Victoria Country, Beverley Hills (Cal.); Albany (London, Eng.); Yachting of Am. (charter). Author: Texas Prison Story: Miracle Within the Walls; The Rise and Fall of a Golden Empire—The History of Gold; Merrily We Spend and Spend; the Empresario, also other hist. books. Designed and constructed complete new modern city for Victoria, Tex. Home: 701 N Washington St Victoria TX 37393 Office: Village Office Bldg Victoria TX 37393 also Commercial National Bank Victoria TX 37393

HAMMETT, BOBBY LYNN, data processor; b. Sherman, Tex., Mar. 16, 1935; s. William Henry and Leola (Gurley) H.; student various IBM Data Processing Schs., 1960-73; m. Dorene Yvonne Gantt, June 6, 1958; children—Susan Alysia, Deena Marque. With Levingston Shipbuilding Co., Orange, Tex., 1953—, planner, 1961-65, mgr. data processing, 1965—. Cons. computer installations. Councillor, Jr. Achievement, 1967-72; master Three Rivers Council Boy Scouts, Am., 1954-55. Mem. data processing com. Lamar U., 1971-73. Mem. COMMON, HASU (computer users groups), Am. Numismatic Assn., Data Processing Mgrs. Assn., Citizens Radio Assistance Corp. Home: 3106 Western Av Orange TX 77630 Office: PO Box 968 Orange TX 77630

HAMMON, GARY LEE, data processing coordinator; b. St. Louis, Apr. 2, 1932; s. Floyd David and Bessie Marie (Schatz) H.; student Harris Jr. Coll., 1950-52; U. Mo. at Columbia, 1955; B.S. in B.A., Washington U. at St. Louis, 1956; m. Janice Lynn Beeson, June 26, 1955; children—Cheryl Lynn, David Lee, Holly Jean. Dir. Service Computation Center U. Tex. Med. Br., Galveston, 1961-67, dir. Data Processing div., Austin, 1967-68, data processing coordinator U. Tex. System, Austin, 1968—. Served with AUS, 1952-54. Mem. Electronic Computing Health Oriented (pres. 1971-73, dir. 1970-71), Am., Tex. hosp. assns. Home: 3204 Hyclimb Circle Austin TX 78723 Office: 210 W 6th St Austin TX 78701

HAMMOND, ARTHUR BARKSDALE, retail furniture exec.; b. Graycourt, S.C., Nov. 5, 1921; s. Arthur Wasmansky and Elizabeth (Barksdale) H.; B.S., Wofford Coll., 1942; m. Ann Goolsby, June 3, 1943; children—Arthur Cullen, Robert Wesley. With Hammond-Brown Jennings & Co., Spartanburg, S.C., 1942, salesman, 1945-49, dir., 1949-52, sec., 1952-59, v.p., 1959-66, sr. v.p., 1966—; dir., treas. Eagle Furniture Co., Anderson, S.C., 1969—. Chmn., Spartanburg Housing Authority, 1966—. Bd. dirs. Vis. Nurses Assn., 1963-68. Served to 2d lt. AUS, 1942-43; to capt. USAAF, 1943-45; col. USAF Res. Decorated Air medal with 3 oak leaf clusters, D.F.C. Mem. So. (pres. 1963-64), Nat. (dir. 1964) retail furniture assns., C. of C. (dir. 1965-69), Pi Kappa Phi, Scabbard and Blade, Pi Gamma Mu. Methodist. Mason. Club: Sertoma. Home: 1530 Barberry Lane Spartanburg SC 29302 Office: PO Box 1050 Spartanburg SC 29301

HAMMONDS, WILLIAM HANSON, clergyman; b. Crofton, Ky., May 6, 1932; s. George William and Ruby Edity (Alexander) H.; A.A., Bethel Coll., 1956; B.A., U. Ga., 1963; M.Div., Vanderbilt U., 1968; m. Carolyn J. Carter, June 12, 1955; children—Catherine, Laurie, Amy, Matthew. Ordained to ministry Christian Ch., 1956; minister Crockett Mills, Tenn., 1956-58, 1st Christian Ch., Newport, Ark., 1958-61, Watkinsville, Ga., 1961-64, Central Av. Christian Ch., Humboldt, Tenn., 1968-71, 1st Christian Ch., Athens, Ga., 1970—; also bd. mgrs. Ark. Christian Missionary Soc., 1959, dir. Christian Churches Tenn., 1968, v.p. Christian Ch. in Ga., 1973-74. Columnist, Newport Ind., 1959-61. Served with USAF, 1951. Trustee Christian Coll. Ga., Athens, 1973-74. Named Community Leader of Am., 1970, Outstanding Toastmaster, 1973. Republican. Toastmaster (pres., 1972-73). Home: 156 Valleywood Dr Athens GA 30601 Office: 268 W Dougherty St Athens GA 30601

HAMMONS, DONALD RAY, indsl. research engr.; b. Frederick, Okla., Mar. 16, 1922; s. Phillip Hayden and Cecile Lee (Stewart) H.; B.S., Tex. Technol. U., 1951; m. Genevieve Sophia Litteken, Nov. 9, 1943; children—Carolyn (Mrs. Curtis Lee Nolen), Katherine (Mrs. Gary Earl Adams), Donald Ray II, Brenda Ann, Phillip Martin. Indsl. engr. Red River Arsenal, Texarkana, Tex., 1952-54, Redstone Arsenal, Huntsville, Ala., 1954-56; indsl. engr. meats research U.S. Dept. Agr. at Tex. A. and M. U., College Station, 1956-62, research leader meats industry engring. research Okla. State U., Stillwater, 1962—. Cons. meat plant design and requirements, 1962—. Served with AUS, 1942-46. Registered profl. engr., Tex., Okla. Mem. Nat., Okla. socs. profls. engrs., Inst. Food Technologists. Democrat. Elk. Home: 624 N Grandview St Stillwater OK 74074 Office: PO Box 1193 Stillwater OK 74074

HAMMONS, PAUL EDWARD, educator; b. Bogalousa, La., June 16, 1925; s. James Clifford and Norma Beatrice (Booty) H.; B.S., Northwestern State Coll., Natchitoches, La., 1949; M.S., U. Ark., 1951; D.D.S., Loyola U., New Orleans, 1954; m. Doris Nell Denham, Sept. 3, 1950; children—Bruce Clifford, Mark Denham. Pvt. practice dentistry, Crosset, Ark., 1954-55; mem. faculty U. Ala. Sch. Dentistry, Birmingham, 1955—, prof., 1964—, dir. aux. research, 1963-69, prof., chmn. dept. operative dentistry, 1968—. Cons., VA Hosp., 1960-65, 72—. Served with AUS, 1943-46. Recipient Fuller award, 1973. Fellow Royal Soc. Health; mem. Am. Assn. Dental Schs., Delta Sigma Delta, Omicron Kappa Upsilon, Beta, Beta Beta. Home: 2220 Pine Crest Dr Birmingham AL 35216 Office: Sch Dentistry Univ Ala Birmingham AL 35294

HAMNER, LEWIS HERSCHEL, JR., lawyer; b. Camp Hill, Ala., Feb. 21, 1928; s. Lewis H. and Lillian (Rodgers) H.; LL.B., U. Ala., 1950; m. Marion Pinnell, Nov. 17, 1950; children—Lewis H. III, Jodie Pinnell, Lee Rodgers. Admitted to Ala. bar, 1950; pvt. practice law, Camp Hill, Ala., 1950, Roanoke, Ala., 1952—. Exec. dir. Roanoke (Ala.) Housing Authority, 1955—. Recorder, Municipal Ct. Judge, Roanoke, 1960-68, 72; chmn. Roanoke Bd. Edn., 1965—. Served with Judge Advocate Gens. Corps, AUS, 1950-52. Mem. Am., Ala. bar assns., Am. Trial Lawyers Assn., Am. Legion, V.F.W., Delta Chi, Phi Alpha Delta. Lion. Home: 452 Bullock St Roanoke AL 36274 Office: 29 Main St Roanoke AL 36274

HAMNER, MARTIN ELLIS, univ. dean; b. Castor, La., July 28, 1918; s. Houston H. and Lillian Virginia (Rigdon) H.; B.S., U. Colo., 1949, M.S., 1951, Ph.D., 1955; postgrad. U. Fla., 1951-53; m. Barbara M. Wren, Mar. 30, 1946; children—Barbara Eyleen (Mrs. Jeffrey Farmer), John, Bryan. Lab. asst. U. Colo., 1949-51, instr., 1954-55; practicing pharmacist, 1950-54; instr. U. Fla., 1951-53; asso. prof. Southwestern State Coll., Weatherford, Okla., 1955-59; prof., chmn. dept. pharms. U. Tenn., Memphis, 1959-62, asso. dean Coll. Pharmacy, 1962—. Served with USNR, 1942-45. Mem. Am. Bd. Diplomates in Pharmacy, Am., Tenn. pharm. assns., Rho Chi. Contbr. articles to profl. jours. Home: 4806 Craigmont St Memphis TN 38128 Office: 874 Union St Memphis TN 38163

HAMNER, REGINALD TURNER, assn. exec.; b. Tuscaloosa, Ala., June 4, 1939; s. Raiford Samuel and Ellie Wells (Turner) H.; B.S., U. Ala., 1961, LL.B., 1965; m. Anne Ellen Young, Nov. 8, 1969; 1 son, Patrick Turner. Admitted to Ala. bar, 1965; law clk. Supreme Ct. Ala., Montgomery, 1965; dir. legal-legislative affairs Med. Assn. Ala., Montgomery, 1968-69; exec. sec. Ala. State Bar, Montgomery, 1969—. Served with Judge Adv. Gen., USAF, 1966-68; capt. Res. Mem. Am., Bar Assn., Ala. State Bar, Am. Soc. Assn. Execs., Am. Judicature Soc., Nat. Assn. Bar Execs., Phi Alpha Delta, Alpha Epsilon Delta, Delta Tau Delta. Democrat. Episcopalian. Editor Ala. State Bar Found. Bull., 1969—. Home: 3362 Wilmington Rd Montgomery AL 36105 Office: 415 Dexter Av Montgomery AL 36103

HAMON, RICHARD GRADY, lawyer; b. Corpus Christi, Tex., Dec. 30, 1937; s. Richard Paul and Dorothy Ileen (Norris) H.; A.A., Del Mar Jr. Coll., 1957; B.B.A., Baylor U., 1959, J.D., 1962; m. Mary Lynn Farmer, Mar. 2, 1963; children—Leigh Ann, Clark Everett. Admitted to Tex. bar, 1962, since practiced in Dallas; mem. firm Blanchette & Shelton and predecessor firms, 1962-70; mem. firm Blanchette, Shelton & James, 1970—. Mem. State Bar Tex., Am., Dallas bar assns. Baptist (deacon). Rotarian. Home: 9619 Brentgate Dr Dallas TX 75238 Office: 4000 1st National Bank Bldg Dallas TX 75202

HAMPTON, JAMES WILBURN, physician, educator, researcher; b. Durant, Okla., Sept. 15, 1931; s. Hollis Eugene and Ouida (Mackey) H.; student Southeastern State Coll., Durant, Okla., 1950; B.A., U. Okla., 1952, M.D., 1956; m. Carol C. McDonald, Feb. 22, 1958; children—Jaime Jennifer, Clayton C., Diana E., Neal M. Intern Univ. Hosps., Oklahoma City, 1956-57; resident Univ. Hosps. and VA Hosp., Oklahoma City, 1957-59; NIH research trainee, spl. fellow U. Okla. Sch. Medicine, Oklahoma City, 1959-61, clin. asst. medicine, 1960-61, instr. medicine, 1961-62, asst. prof., 1962-67, asso. prof. medicine, 1967-71, prof. medicine, head hematology-oncology sect., 1971—; mem., head hematology research lab. Okla. Med. Research Found., 1972—; vis. research asso. dept. pathology U. N.C. Sch. Medicine, Chapel Hill, 1966-67; vis. prof. dept. blood coagulation research Karolinska Inst. Stockholm, Sweden, 1967; mem. staff VA Hosp., Central State Hosp. Cons. hematology Tinker AFB Hosp., 1965—; asso. coordinator Med. Edn. for Nat. Def. Program Okla., 1963-68. Pres. Okla. chpt. Nat. Hemophilia Found., 1965-66, nat. trustee, 1964-65; mem. Nat. Adv. Council on Thrombosis Nat. Heart and Lung Inst., 1972-75. Recipient Career Devel. award Nat. Heart Inst., 1966—; Honors Achievement award Angiology Research Found., 1968. Fellow A.C.P.; mem. Am. Assn. Pathologists and Bacteriologists, Am. Physiol. Soc., Am. Genetic Assn., Am. Coll. Angiology, A.C.P., Am. Hematological Soc., A.A.A.S., Am. Psychosomatic Soc., Am. Fedn. Clin. Research (councilor midwestern sect. 1965-68, chmn. 1969-70), So. Soc. for Clin. Investigation, Internat. Soc. on Hemostasis and Thrombosis, Central Soc. for Clin. Research, N.Y. Acad. Sci., S.E. Oncology Group, Alpha Omega Alpha (chpt. historian 1964—), Sigma Xi (pres. local chpt. 1972-73), Sigma Tau Delta, Phi Alpha Theta. Democrat. Episcopalian. Clubs: Oklahoma City Golf and Country, Faculty House. Contbr. articles to sci. jours. Research in hematology and oncology. Office: Okla Med Research Found 825 NE 13th St Oklahoma City OK 73104

HAMPTON, LEE ROYAL, JR., dentist; b. Ocala, Fla., Aug. 27, 1923; s. Lee Royal and Effie Carrie (Mitchell) H.; B.S., Fla. A. and M. U., 1949; D.D.S., Howard U., 1953; m. Miriam Patricia Campbell, Nov. 6, 1945; children—Lee Royal III, Kerry LaRue, Ronald Mitchell, Gwendolyn Alice. Pvt. practice dentistry, Ocala, Fla., 1954—; pres. L.R.H. Co. Ocala, Inc., 1954—. Mem. staff Munroe Meml. Hosp., 1963. Mem. Ocala Housing Authority. Trustee, chmn. bd. Hampton Jr. Coll. Served from 2nd lt. to 1st lt. AUS, 1943-46. Mem. Fla. Med., Dental and Pharm. Assn. (pres. 1971—), N.A.A.C.P. (treas. Marion County br. 1961—), Ocala Marion County C. of C., Nat. Guardsmen Club, Sertoma Club Inc., Alpha Phi Alpha. Mason. Home: 2646 SW Broadway Ocala FL 32670 Office: 124 SW Broadway St Ocala FL 32670

HAMPTON, WADE LEE, realty co. exec.; b. Vida, Ala., Dec. 2, 1928; s. Wade Vanderbilt and Bertie Lee (Crider) H.; B.S. in Bus. Adminstrn., U. Ala., 1953; m. Anne Celeste Koger, Oct. 12, 1962; children—Wade McKissick, Peter Winthrop, Celeste Koger. With So. Bell Tel. & Tel., 1955-65, Fla. tng. supr., Jacksonville, 1959-62, gen. mechanization accountant, Atlanta; v.p. Koger Properties, Orlando, Fla., 1965-70, Jacksonville, 1970—. Gen. mgr. Orlando Area Exec. Center, 1965-70; pres. C&W Hampton Co. investments, Jacksonville, 1972-74, Solarium, Inc., Jacksonville, 1973-74; dir. Barnett Bank Orlando, Gen. Services Inc. Adviser to bd. Central Fla. Civic Theatre, 1968-69; mem. Com. 200 Orlando, 1969—; pres., chmn. Peso. Bd. dirs. Met. YMCA, Jacksonville, Jacksonville U. Council, Loch Haven Art Center, Orlando, 1970, Fla. Symphony Assn., 1968-70; chmn. bd. Central Fla. Heart Assn., 1969. Served to 1st lt. AUS, 1953-55. Mem. Sales and Marketing Execs. Club. Republican. Presbyn. Clubs: Florida Yacht, River Jacksonville; University (Orlando). Home: 2127 River Rd Jacksonville FL 32207 Office: 3986 Blvd Center Dr Jacksonville FL 32207

HAMRICK, FITZHUGH NICHOLSON, dentist; b. Fountain Inn, S.C., Apr. 13, 1926; s. Clarence Thomas and Myrtle Esma (Hamrick) H.; student Coll. Charleston, 1943-44; D.M.D., U. Louisville, 1947; m. Nancy Hart Miller, Nov. 8, 1952; children—Nancy Hart, Margery Elizabeth, Druid Meriwether, Fitzhugh Nicholson. Intern, U. Louisville, 1947-48; pvt. practice dentistry, Charleston, S.C., 1952—. Clin. asso. community dentistry Med. U. S.C. Sch. Dentistry, 1970—. Pres. Charleston Symphony Orch. Assn., 1970. Bd. dirs. Charleston County Hosp., 1969-71, Charleston Concert Assn., 1969-72. Served to lt. USNR, 1968-69, 70-72. Fellow Internat. Coll. Dentists; mem. Am., S.C. dental assns., Charleston Dental Soc. (pres. 1968). Baptist (deacon, bd. dirs. 1957—). Home: 2235 Ashley River Rd Charleston SC 29407 Office: 115 Wentworth St Charleston SC 29401

HAMRICK, JOSEPH THOMAS, research co. exec.; b. Carrollton, Ga., Mar. 20, 1921; s. James Mayfield and Mattie Almon (Gaston) H.; B. Mech. Engring., Ga. Inst. Tech., 1946, M.S., 1948; m. Dorothy Elizabeth Jones, June 19, 1948; children—Jane Elizabeth, Nancy Ann, Thomas Mayfield. Aeronautical research scientist, NASA Lewis Lab., Cleve., 1948-55; chief research engr. TRW Inc., Euclid, O. 1955-61; pres. Aerospace Research Corp., Roanoke, Va. 1961—, also dir. Served to 1st lt. AUS, 1943-46. Mem. Am. Soc. M.E. (chmn. controls and aux. 1970-72), Pi Tau Sigma. Republican. Unitarian (pres. congregation 1967, 68). Contbr. articles to profl. jours. Patentee in field. Home: 6364 JAE Valley Rd SE Roanoke VA 24014 Office: 5454 JAE Valley Rd SE Roanoke VA 24014

HANCOCK, FRANK ARNOLD, theatre dir.; b. Crossett, Ark., July 7, 1933; s. Frank Askew and Doris (Noble) H.; B.S., State Coll. Ark., 1955; M.S. (fellow), Purdue U., 1957; children—Michael Kelley, Mark Kennon. Music and theatre dir. Army Recreation Services, Orleans, France, 1959-64, Stuttgart, Germany, 1964-65, Ft. Stewart and Hunter Army Airfield, Savannah, Ga., 1965-71, Ft. Sheridan, Ill., 1971-72, Ft. Stewart, Ga., 1972—. Served with AUS, 1957-59. Mem. Am. Theatre Assn., Army Theatre Arts Assn. Office: Bldg 396 Recreation Services Fort Stewart GA 31313

HANCOCK, HORACE HOLLOWAY, newspaper exec.; b. Tampa, Fla., Aug. 5, 1924; s. Horace B. and Juanita (Johnston) H.; student pub. schs.; m. Margaret Vogel, Dec. 4, 1943; children—Lynda Lee, Carole Elaine, Richard Douglas, Cynthia Diane. State circulation mgr. Fla. Times-Union, Jacksonville, 1949-54; circulation mgr. Tampa Times, 1954-58, Lakeland (Fla.) Ledger, 1958-63, Tampa Tribune, 1963-64, Atlanta Times, 1964-65; gen. mgr. Hunstville (Ala.) News, 1965-66; exec. v.p. Courier News Corp., 1966-69, pres., 1969—; pub. Plant City (Fla.) Courier, 1966—, Brandon (Fla.) News, 1966—, Palmetto (Fla.) Press, 1966—. State dir. Little Boys Baseball, 1963-64; pres. Babe Ruth Baseball, 1963-64; mem. Plant City Library Bd., Chamber Edn. Com.; bd. dirs. Blood Bank; v.p. United Fund; bd. dirs. S. Fla. Bapt. Hosp. Served with USN, 1942-45. Named Citizen of Yr., Plant City. Mem. Internat., So. (pres. 1965-66, dir. 1967-68) circulation mgrs. assns., Plant City C. of C. (pres. 1968). Baptist (deacon). Kiwanian. Home: 122 W Beacon Rd Lakeland FL 33803 Office: 101 N Thomas St PO Box K Plant City FL 33566

HANCOCK, JAMES DAWSON, JR., town ofcl.; b. Dallas, June 13, 1913; s. James Dawson and Anna Marye (Haynie) H.; B.S., So. Meth. U., 1935; M.B.A., Harvard, 1937; m. Margaret Claiborne Fox, Nov. 14, 1938; children—Margaret (Mrs. Decker Wade), James Dawson III, Randolph F. Salesman Continental Supply Co., Dallas, 1937-42; supr. scheduling N. Am. Aviation Co., Dallas, 1942-45; ind. oil operator Ledge Petroleum Co., Inc., Dallas, 1945-64; town adminstr. Highland Park, Tex., 1964—. Mem., sec. adv. bd. Southwestern Law Enforcement Inst., 1964—. Mem. Highland Park Town Council, 1960-64. Mem. Internat., Tex. city mgmt. assns., Mcpl. Finance Officers Assn., Tex. Assn. Assessing Officers, Alpha Kappa Psi, Lambda Chi Alpha. Episcopalian. Club: Dallas Country (bd. govs. 1970-73, pres. 1972). Home: 4339 Versailles Av Dallas TX 75205 Office: 4700 Drexel Dr Dallas TX 75205

HANCOCK, JAMES EDWARD, radiation therapist; b. Ripley, Tenn., Mar. 7, 1927; s. William Christopher and Mary Isabel (Gilmore) H.; B.S., U. Tenn., 1952, M.D., 1961. Intern Methodist Hosp., Memphis, 1961-62, resident, 1964-66; resident Oak Ridge Inst. Nuclear Studies, 1963; radiation therapist St. Jude Childrens Research Hosp., Memphis, 1968, Bapt. Meml. Hosp., Memphis, 1968—; cons. staff Meth. Hosp., Memphis. Asst. clin. prof. Coll. Medicine U. Tenn., Memphis, 1968—. Bd. dirs. Am. Cancer Soc., 1971—. Served with USNR, 1945-46. Fellow, U. Tex. M.D. Anderson Hosp., 1967-68. Diplomate Am. Bd. Therapeutic Radiology. Mem. A.M.A., Am. Coll. Radiology, Mid South Med. Soc., Tenn. Radiologic Soc., Sports Car Club Am. Home: 3928 Springfield Dr Memphis TN 38128 Office: 899 Madison Av Memphis TN 38146

HANCOCK, JOHANNA BERTHA, speech pathologist and audiologist; b. Louisville, June 1, 1935; d. James Duffy and Marie (Seelbach) Hancock; student Coll. of Notre Dame, Md., 1953-54, Loyola U., Los Angeles, summer 1956; B.S. in Speech, Marquette U., 1957; M.A. in Speech Pathology, Cath. U. Am., 1959; postgrad.

Western Res. U., summer 1957, U. Md., spring 1958, George Washington U., fall 1958; M.A. in Psychology, U. Louisville, 1967. Speech pathologist and audiologist, Louisville, 1959—; part-time therapist Rehab. Center, Inc., Louisville, 1957, United Cerebral Palsy of Greater Louisville, 1959-60, Louisville Deaf-Oral Sch., 1959; instr. dept. speech and communications Bellarmine Coll., Louisville, 1959-61, chmn. dept., 1961-62. Vol. cons. therapist Cleft Palate Clinic, Ky. Commn. for Handicapped Children, 1959-62. Bd. dirs. Jefferson County Med. Soc. Woman's Aux.; mem. Younger Woman's Club of Louisville, Spinsters Cotillion. Recipient certificate appreciation A.R.C.; Distinguished Alumni Achievement award in speech therapy Marquette U., 1966. Mem. Am. (certificates of competence in speech pathology and audiology), Ky. (exec. council) speech and hearing assns., Internat. Council for Exceptional Children, Speech Assn. Am., Alexander Graham Bell Assn. for Parents and Tchrs. of Deaf, Am. Assn. U. Profs., Am. Hearing Assn., Am. Acad. Pvt. Practitioners in Speech Pathology and Audiology, Am. Cleft Palate Assn., Psi Chi, Tau Kappa Alpha (hon.), Sigma Alpha Eta (hon.). Mem. Queen's Daus. Contbr. articles to profl. jours. Home: 80 Valley Rd Louisville KY 40204 Office: 3412 Med Arts Bldg 1169 Eastern Pkwy Louisville KY 40217

HANCOCK, LUCILE R. MUSSELMAN (MRS. WILLIAM S. HANCOCK), banker; b. Waynoka, Okla., Oct. 13, 1915; d. Mahlon M. and Mamie (McGee) Musselman; student Northwestern State Coll., summer 1935, Fla. State Coll. for Women, 1935-36; A.B., Fla. So. Coll., 1939; m. William S. Hancock, May 15, 1966; 1 stepdau., Sandra (Mrs. James B. Wilmot). Head bookkeeper Pasco Packing Co., Dade City, Fla., 1939-44; supr. bookkeeper Bank of Pasco County, Dade City, 1946-65, asst. cashier, auditor, 1960—. Treas., Cancer Cursade East Pasco County, Dade City, 1967—. Served with WAVES, 1944-46. Mem. Nat. Assn. Bank Women, Delta Zeta. Methodist. Home: Route 4 3110 S 301 Dade City FL 33525 Office: PO Box 127 Corner Meridian and 7th Sts Dade City FL 33525

HANCOCK, QUINLAN HARRIS, lawyer; b. Richmond, Va., Apr. 15, 1926; s. Hert Lee and Swaney D. (Harris) H.; A.A., George Washington U., 1947, LL.B., J.D., 1950; m. Viola L. Rhine, Oct. 4, 1944; children—Robyn Lee (Mrs. James Richard Taylor), Paula Sue. Admitted to Va. bar, 1951; atty. FBI, Washington, 1951; settlement atty. Davis & Ruffner Title Corp., Alexandria, Va., 1951-53; partner Howard, Morris & Hancock, Alexandria, 1953-68; individual practice law, Alexandria, 1968—. Served with USNR, 1943-45. Mem. Am., Va., Alexandria (past pres.) bar assns., Va., No. Va. trial lawyers assns., George Washington U., Duke alumni assns., Izaak Walton League, Ducks Unltd., Nat. Rifle Assn., Internat. Platform Assn., Delta Theta Phi. Club: Old Dominion Boat. Home: 825 Timberbranch Pkwy Alexandria VA 22302 Office: 421 King St Alexandria VA 22314

HANCOCK, RICHARD LEO, utilities exec.; b. Austin, Tex., Feb. 18, 1926; s. Louis Melbourne and Bertha Ann (Winke) H.; B.S., U. Tex., 1950; m. Dorothy Nell Reichenau, Sept. 4, 1949; children—Rebecca (Mrs. Scott Davis Sandahl), Richard Craig. With City of Austin Electric Dept., 1949—, asst. supt. transmission and distbn., 1954-67, asst. dir. electric utility, 1967-71, dir., 1971—. Vice pres., bd. dirs. Tex. Municipal League. Served with USAAF, 1944-45. Registered profl. engr., Tex. Mem. I.E.E.E. (chmn. S.Tex. sect. 1962, sec. Dist. 15, 1963). Lutheran. Home: Route 7 Box 932AB Austin TX 78703 Office: PO Box 1088 Austin TX 78767

HANCOCK, V(ERNON) RAY, educator; b. Balt., July 10, 1926; s. Wheeler K. and Rebecca (Helm) H.; B.S., Va. Poly. Inst., 1949; M.A., Johns Hopkins U., 1951; Ph.D., Tulane, 1960; m. Ruth A. Farnham, June 17, 1950; children—Dale K., Clark T. Mem. faculty Va. Poly. Inst., Blacksburg, 1952-63, asst. prof. math., 1955-62, asso. prof., 1962-63; prof. math. Emory and Henry Coll., Emory, Va., 1963—, chmn. math. dept., 1963-74. Cons., U.S. Naval Research Lab., 1955-58. Asst. scoutmaster, explorer adviser Boy Scouts Am., Balt., 1947-52; cubmaster, Blacksburg and Emory, 1961-67; commr. Cub Roundtable Sequoyah council Boy Scouts Am., 1965—; program staff Nat. Jamboree Moraine State Park, Pa., 1973. Served with AUS, 1944-46. Recipient Silver Beaver award Boy Scouts Am., 1969. Mem. Am. Math. Soc., Math. Assn. Am., Nat. Council Tchrs. Math, Nat. Geog. Soc., Am. Heritage Soc., Alpha Phi Omega. Republican. Methodist. Club: Automobile of Va. Home: Box Y Emory VA 24327 Office: Dept Math Emory and Henry Coll Emory VA 24327

HAND, JOHN ELEMUAL, elec. engr.; b. Elkhart, Ind., Sept. 9, 1930; s. Charles Elemual and Minnie (Helbing) H.; B.S., Purdue U., 1953; postgrad. Butler U., 1959-60; m. Shirley Ann Stebbins, Feb. 19, 1957; children—Jeanette Elaine, John Gregory. Sect. head research and devel. P.R. Mallory & Co., Indpls., 1956-64; chief engr. Syncro Corp., Hicksville, Ind., 1964-65; research and devel. engr. Sangamo Electric Co., Springfield, Ill., 1962-65; mgr. engring. Cornell Dubilier, Sanford, N.C., 1965—. Bd. dirs. Lee County Industries, Inc., Sanford, 1969-73. Served with AUS, 1953-55. Korea. Mem. I.E.E.E., Sanford Engrs. Club (pres. 1973), Electrochem. Soc., V.F.W. Elk, Mason. Patentee in field. Home: Route 4 Box 1368 Sanford NC 27330 Office: 2652 Dairymple St Sanford NC 27330

HAND, PERRY ALBERT, cons. civil engr.; b. Heflin, Ala., May 28, 1945; s. Joseph Noel and Mary Harriet (Moon) H.; B.C.E., Auburn U., 1969; m. Joan Marylon Hunt, Aug. 24, 1968; children—Thomas Albert, Marylon Bernice. Surveyor, Frank Boyd & Assos., Powder Springs, Ga., 1958-63, Ala. Hwy. Dept., Montgomery, 1964-69; design engr. David Volker & Assos., Mobile, 1967-70; founder, pres., dir. Perry Hand Assos., Inc., Gulf Shores, Ala., 1972—, also founder, pres., dir. Perry A. Hand Surveying Co., Inc., 1970—; founder, sec-treas., dir. Environmental Cons. Internat., Gulf Shores, 1973—; founder, dir. Samuel Peter Acton, Jr., architect Gulf Shores, 1973—. Registered profl. land surveyor Ala., Fla., Ga., Miss. Mem. Ala. Soc. Land Surveyors, Am. Soc. C.E., Am. Soc. Photogrammetry, Am. Congress Surveying and Mapping. Methodist. Address: PO Box 478 Gulf Shores AL 36542

HANDLER, FRANCES CLARK (MRS. FRANK STEVENSON HANDLER), educator, writer, assn. exec.; b. Maplewood, N.H., Feb. 28; d. Frank J. and Marie (Jamia) Clark; B.S. in Bus. Machine Teaching, Boston U., B.B.S. in Accounting, A.B. in Banking and Finance; Litt. D., Internat. Research Socs., U. Asia, Pakistan, 1968; m. Frank Stevenson Handler, Sept. 21, 1946. Instr. accounting Burroughs Sch., Boston, later collaborating writer poetry books, hist. novels, autobiographies, children's books. Lectr. on women's vocations Barry Coll., Miami, Fla., 1965—; founder, nat. dir. Fla. Nat. Poetry Day Com., 1965—. Named hon. poet laureate UN Day, Philippines, 1967; recipient over 100 awards and prizes, including King Journalism award, 1972. C.P.A., Mass. Mem. United Poets Laureate Internat. (award, 1967, membership chmn. 1968—), World (internat. dir.), Fla. (founder, sec., treas. 1965—, editor, pub. Flamingo 1969), Nev. (hon. life) poetry socs., Fla. Arts Council, Ia. Poetry Day Assn. (hon. life). Nat. League Am. Pen Women (treas. Coral Gables, Fla. br. 1963—), Hotel Accountants Assn. (pres. 1947-51). Author: Reina Mercedes, 1956; Canberra, 1957; Turns On The Spiral, 1971; Beyond The Silent River, 1972; Nobel Goes To Heaven, 1972; Nurses Notes, 1973; Devastators, 1973. Contbr. to Ency. of Jazz, 1955, Selected Poems, 1969-71, Memorial Award Books, 1966-71. Editor, designer International Hall of Fame Poets, 4 books, 1969-72, Governor's Book, 1971-72, 9 Muses I and 9 Muses II, 1971. Home: 1110 N Venetian Dr Miami Beach FL 33139

HANDMAKER, STUART ALLEN, lawyer; b. Louisville, May 27, 1930; s. Sidney David and Ethel Gertrude (Baron) H.; A.B., Stanford, 1952, J.D., 1953; m. Muriel Beton, Aug. 30, 1953; children—Ellen, David, William, Robert. Admitted to Ky. bar, 1953; practiced in Louisville, 1956—; mem. firm Handmaker, Weber & Meyer, attys.-at-law, Louisville, 1956—; sec., dir. Union Trust, Inc., Continental Nat. Bank Ky., Executone Systems Co.; dir. Modern Loan Co. Pres. U.S.O., Jewish Welfare Bd. Armed Services Com., 1961; nat. chmn. leadership devel. Council Jewish Fedn. and Welfare Funds, 1963; pres. Art Center Assn., Inc., Louisville Sch. Art, 1970-73; chmn. community relations council Jewish Community Fedn. of Louisville, 1973—. Served with AUS, 1953-56. Mem. Am., Ky., Louisville bar assns., Order of Coif, Phi Beta Kappa, Phi Alpha Delta. Democrat. Jewish religion. Mem. B'nai B'rith. Club: Standard Country (Louisville). Home: Glenview KY 40025 Office: 2307 Citizens Plaza Louisville KY 40202

HANDY, ALGERNON LEE, JR., lawyer; b. Arlington, Va., Sept. 28, 1914; s. Algernon Lee and Annie Moffett (Coyner) H.; B.C.S., Southeastern U., Washington, 1934, LL.B., 1935; m. Mary Patricia Franks, June 14, 1947; children—Nancy Patricia, Russell Lee, Barbara Lynn. Admitted to D.C. bar, 1937, Va. bar, 1942; practiced law, Arlington, 1945—. Dir., treas. Met. Savs. & Loan Assn., Arlington, 1955—. Commr. accounts Circuit Ct. Arlington County, 1949—. Mem. S.A.R., Arlington County, Am. bar assns., Izaak Walton League Am. Optimist. Home: 2015 N Quantico St Arlington VA 22205 Office: 1515 N Court House Rd Arlington VA 22201

HANDY, RUSSELL PHIPPS, govt. ofcl.; b. Grassy Creek, N.C., Aug. 13, 1917; s. Troy Curtis and Belle (Phipps) H.; B.S., N.C. State U., 1939, postgrad., 1940-47; m. Charlotte Virginia Parleir, Apr. 12, 1941; children—William Russell, Barbara Lynn. Statistician Dept. Agriculture, Raleigh, N.C., also Trenton, N.J., 1939-42; statistician in charge W.Va. Crop Reporting Service, Charleston, W.Va., 1950-58, Columbus, Ohio, 1958-61; asst. adminstr. Statist. Reporting Service, Washington, 1961-70; statistician in charge N.C. Crop Reporting Service, Raleigh, N.C., 1970—. Served with AUS, 1943-45. Recipient USDA Certificate of Merit, 1973. Mem. Am. Statist. Assn., Am. Agrl. Economic Assn., Alpha Zeta, Phi Kappa Phi. Club: Optimist (pres. 1955-56). Home: 4305 Oak Park Rd Raleigh NC 27612 Office: Agrl Bldg Raleigh NC 27611

HANEBRINK, EARL LEE, educator; b. Cape Girardeau, Mo., Mar. 24, 1924; s. Harry H. and Augusta (Fornkohl) H.; B.S. in Edn., S.E. Mo. State U., 1948; M.S., U. Miss., 1955; Ed.D., Okla. State U., 1965; m. Vernelia A. McCrady, Dec. 26, 1956; children—Lisa Ann, Kay Lynn. Tchr. sci., high schs. Parma and Kennett, Mo., 1948-57; mem. faculty Ark. State U., State University, 1958—, asso. prof., 1965-69, prof. biology, 1969—. Environmental cons. U.S. Corp Engrs., 1972-73. Served with AUS, 1944-46: PTO. Mem. Ark. Acad. Sci., Am. Ornithologists Union, Wilson Ornithol. Soc., Soc. S.W. Naturalists, Am. Birding Assn., Ark. (v.p. 1973-74), N.E. Ark. (pres. 1970-72), Tenn. Audubon socs., Nat. Pigeon Assn., Midwest Benthological Soc., Sigma Xi, Phi Sigma, Phi Delta Kappa, Beta Beta Beta. Methodist. Author: Flora of Southeast Missouri, 1958. Contbr. profl. jours. Home: 266 Oakhill Lane Jonesboro AR 72401 Office: Dept Biology Ark State Univ State University AR 72467

HANES, FRANK BORDEN, author; b. Winston-Salem, N.C., Jan. 21, 1920; s. Robert March and Mildred (Borden) H.; grad. Woodberry Forest Sch. (Va.), 1938; B.A., U. N.C., 1942; m. Barbara Mildred Lasater, Dec. 3, 1942; children—Frank Borden, Nancy (Mrs. Sydnor Montgomery White), Robin March. Columnist, feature writer, reporter, copy editor Winston-Salem Jour. & Sentinel, 1946-49; vice chmn., dir. Mchts. Devel. Co., shopping center, Winston-Salem, 1964—; dir. Chatham Mfg. Co., Elkin, Hanes Dye & Finishing Co., Winston-Salem. Chmn. Com. for Endowed Professorships, U. N.C., 1965-67, Friends of U. N.C. Library, 1966-68, Old Salem, Inc., 1968-70; pres. Winston-Salem Operetta Assn., 1949-50, Winston-Salem Arts Council, 1955-56. Trustee Morehead Found., Chapel Hill, N.C., John W. and Anna Hodgin Hanes Found.; bd. visitors U. N.C. Press. Served with USNR, 1942-45. Recipient first Roanoke Chowan award for poetry N.C. Literary and Hist. Assn., 1953, Sir Walter Raleigh award for fiction, 1961, award Winston-Salem Arts Council, 1957. Mem. P.E.N., N.C. Writers' Conf. (chmn. 1951-52), N.C. Literary and Hist. Assn. (pres. 1973), Order of Gimghoul (pres. 1940-41), Order of Minotaur (pres. 1941-42), Sigma Alpha Epsilon. Rotarian. Clubs: Old Town (Winston-Salem, N.C.); Roaring Gap (N.C.), Cane River (Pensacola, N.C.); Rainbow Springs (Macon County, N.C.). Author: Abel Anders, 1951; The Bat Brothers, 1953; The Fleet Rabble, 1961; Journey's Journal, 1958; Jackknife John, 1964. Home: 2020 Buena Vista Rd Winston-Salem NC 27104

HANES, GRAYSON POLLARD, lawyer; b. Washington, Nov. 1, 1937; s. Grayson B. and Elizabeth (Hillsman) H.; B.A., U. of South, 1960; J.D., George Washington U., 1963; m. Esther Mae Rollins, June 11, 1960; children—Grayson S., Chad F. Admitted to Va. bar, 1963; partner law firm Smith, Harrison and Hanes, Arlington, Va., 1963-66; partner law firm Hazel, Beckhorn and Hanes, Fairfax, Va., 1966—; lectr. law No. Va. Savs. & Loan Inst., 1965. Substitute judge Town of Herndon, Va., 1965, town atty., 1965—; mem. No.Va. Criminal Justice Adv. Council, 1970-73. Bd. dirs. Fairfax Legal Aid Soc. Mem. Va. State (mem. com. criminal law 1971—), Am. bar assns., Va., Am. trial lawyers assns., Am. Judicature Soc., No.Va. Bldrs. Assn., Fairfax County C. of C., Herndon Jr. C. of C. Rotarian. Home: 330 Grant St Herndon VA 22070 Office: 10409 Main St Fiarfax VA 22030

HANES, JOHN CHISMAN, lawyer; b. Pine Hall, N.C., May 26, 1909; s. John Lewis and Eliza Pescud (Chisman) H.; A.B., Duke, 1930, LL.B., 1933; student Harvard Law Sch., 1930-31; m. Laura L. Reeves, May 4, 1940; 1 son, John Chisman. Admitted to N.C. bar, 1933, D.C. bar, 1947; gen. practice law, Raleigh, N.C., 1933-34; mem. legal div. R.F.C., 1934-36, 37-42; asst. to chmn. Atty. Gen's. Adv. Com. on Crime, Dept. Justice, 1936-37; spl. asst. to exec. dir. Office of Def. Plants, R.F.C., 1945-46; practice law, Washington, 1946—. Chmn. nat. council Duke, 1967-68; trustee Episcopal Theol. Sem. Va. Served to maj. USAAF, 1942-45. Mem. Am. (mem. council administrv. law sect. 1966-69), D.C., N.C. bar assns., Am. Judicature Soc., Am. Arbitration Assn. (nat. panel arbitrators), Phi Delta Theta, Phi Delta Phi, Omicron Delta Kappa. Episcopalian. Clubs: Army-Navy, National Lawyers (Washington); Belle Haven Country (Alexandria, Va.). Contbr. articles to profl. jours. Home: 1319 Bishop Lane Alexandria VA 22302 Office: Ring Bldg Washington DC 20036

HANES, LEIGH B., JR., U.S. atty.; b. Roanoke, Va., Apr. 4, 1918; s. Leigh Buckner and Lillian Lee (Thompson) H.; B.A. cum laude, Hampden-Sydney Coll., 1940; LL.B., U. Md., 1948; m. Frances H. Hilton, Nov. 1, 1945; children—Katherine Whitney (Mrs. Mark E. Feldmann), Leigh Thompson, David Hilton. Admitted to Va. bar, 1951, Supreme Ct. bar, 1970; spl. agt. FBI, 1943-49; partner firm Hanes & Hanes, Roanoke, 1951-56; asst. U.S. atty., Roanoke, 1956-59; clk. U.S. Dist. Ct., Western dist. Va., Roanoke, 1960-69; U.S. atty., 1969—. Tchr., Va. Western Community Coll., 1967-69; lectr. Am. Inst. Banking, Roanoke, 1951-56. City councilman, vice mayor, Roanoke, 1953-56. Served with AUS, 1944-46. Mem. Am., Fed., Roanoke bar assns., Am. Judicature Soc., Va. State Bar, Omicron Delta Kappa, Kappa Alpha, Tau Kappa Alpha, Chi Beta Phi, Sigma Upsilon. Republican. Presbyn. (elder). Mason (Shriner). Home: 2814 S Jefferson St Roanoke VA 24014 Office: 222 Federal Bldg Roanoke VA 24008

HANES, R. PHILIP, JR., textile dyeing and finishing co. exec.; b. Winston-Salem, N.C., Feb. 25, 1926; s. Ralph Philip and Dewitt (Chatham) H.; grad. Woodberry Forest Sch. 1944; student U. N.C., 1944-46; B.A., Yale, 1949; m. Joan Audrey Humpstone, Jan. 14, 1950. Vice pres. Hanes Dye & Finishing Co., Winston-Salem, 1962-63, exec. v.p., 1963-65, pres., 1965-68, chmn. bd., 1968—; chmn. bd. Bunch-Kelly Co., Conover, N.C., 1973—; dir. Wachovia Bank & Trust Co. Mem. adv. com. Kennedy Center for Performing Arts, Washington, 1962-65; mem. Nat. Council Arts, 1965-70; mem. N.C. Recreation Commn., 1962-65; bd. dirs. Moravian Music Found., Winston-Salem, 1963-65, Roger L. Stevens Fedn., 1972—; vice chmn. Winston-Salem Community Center Fund Drive, 1957, Salem Coll. Arts Center Drive, 1962-63, N.C. Sch. for Arts Drive, 1964-65; vice chmn. Winston-Salem Total Devel. Commn. 1960-62; Bd. dirs. Forsyth Econ. Devel. Corp., 1969-71, Winston-Salem Symphony, 1956-66, Winston-Salem Arts Council Endowment Fund, Film Friends; trustee Sparta Hosp., 1956, Elkin Hosp., Chatham Meml. Hosp., 1956, Salem Coll., 1961-64; trustee Salem Coll., 1961-64; trustee, mem. exec. com. N.C. Sch. for Arts; bd. visitors Barter Theatre, State Theatre Va., 1967—, 1966—; bd. dirs. Winterhur, 1972—; chmn. com. music sch. Yale U. Council. Served to lt. USNR, 1950-52. Recipient Arts Council award, 1960; named Young Man of Yr., N.C., Winston-Salem Jaycees, 1958; Gov.'s award for preservation natural areas, 1969. Asso. fellow Jonathan Edwards Coll., Yale. 1971—. Life fellow Royal Soc. Arts; mem. Boston Mycol. Soc., Arts Councils Am. (pres. 1964-66), Nat. Council on Arts (mem. adv. music panel 1970-72), Tri-States (pres. 1959-61), N.C. (chmn. 1964-67), Winston-Salem (v.p. 1963-64) arts councils, N.C. Arts Soc., N.Y. Classical Guitar Soc., Wilderness Soc., Newcomen Soc. N. Am., Asso. Artists N.C., Ducks Unltd., Sierra Club, N.C. Collectors, Trout Unltd., ANTA, Young Pres. Orgn. (arts dean 1967, 70), Am. Crafts Council (nat. adv. com. 1970—), Jargon Soc. (pres. 1968—), Internat. Platform Assn., Walpole Soc., Am. Assn. Museums, Am. Symphony Orch. League (dir. 1958-61), Nat. Audubon Soc. (dir. 1972—), Delta Kappa Epsilon. Methodist (steward 1960). Rotarian. Clubs: Piedmont, Appalachian Trail (nat. adv. com. 1970—) (Greensboro, N.C.); Currituck (Jarvisburg, N.C.); Cane River (Burnsville, N.C.); Yale (N.Y.C.); Twin City, Old Town (Winston-Salem); Roaring Gap (N.C.). Home: Box 749 Winston-Salem NC 27102 Office: Hanes Dye & Finishing Co Buxton St Winston-Salem NC 27102

HANGER, BOB GRANT, pub. relations exec.; b. Huntington, W.Va., May 18, 1934; s. Theodore Otis and Percie Lee (Tucker) H.; student Marshall U., 1951, U. Va., 1962-64; m. Ruth Ann Suiter, Nov. 24, 1960; children—Pamela Diane, Robert, Connie Sue, Robbie Lee, Rhonda Lynn, Roni Lea. Broadcaster, exec. WINA radio-TV, Charlottesville, Va., 1960—; sales and pub. relations exec. Charlottesville Broadcasting Corp., 1960—; rep. Nat. Chemsearch Corp.. 1974—; group talent mgr. Bee-Gee Enterprises, Charlottesville, 1961—; nat. sales mgr. Bee-Gee Prodns., Charlottesville, 1961—; pres. Bee-Gee Records Div., 1963—, Music Div., 1962—; cons. Dogwood Festival, 1962-65, Hillbilly Pub. Co., 1964—; dir. Bee-Gee Prodns. Talent Agy., Cottonhill Pub. Co. Cons. Cherry River Festival, Richwood, W.Va., 1969—. Nat. sec. U. Hard Knocks, Inc., 1965-68. Named Ky. Col. Mem. East Coast Talent Soc. (dir. 1964—), Va. Soc. Country and Folk Music, Nat. Assn. Broadcasters, Am. Soc. Notaries. Republican. Presbyn. Kiwanian (dir. 1963—). Club: Ruritan (pub. relations dir. Earlysville 1972). Home: 4010 Tompkins Dr Charlottesville VA 22901 Office: Jefferson Village Route 4 Charlottesville VA 22901

HANIG, JOSEPH PETER, pharmacologist; b. N.Y.C., Apr. 29, 1941; s. Israel and Sophie (Ackerman) H.; B.S., Rutgers U., 1962; M.S., N.Y. Med. Coll., 1965, Ph.D., 1968; m. Jill Schwartz, June 29, 1969. Nat. Acad. Sci.-NRC postdoctoral resident research asso. Food & Drug Adminstrn., Washington, 1968-70; pharmacologist, group leader, 1970—; cons. neuropharmacology; neurotoxicology. NSF Predoctoral traineeship, 1966-68; NIH postdoctoral fellow, 1968; adj. asst. prof. pharmacology N.Y. Med. Coll., 1974—. Fellow Am. Inst. Chemists; mem. Am. Soc. Pharmacology and Exptl. Therapeutics, Am. Chem. Soc., A.A.A.S., Soc. Exptl. Biology and Medicine, Sigma Xi. Research neuropharmacology; neurotoxicology; permeability of blood-brain barrier; effects of psychoactive drugs on behavior and brain chemistry; neurotoxicity of hexachlorophene and its antagonism; alcohol and DMSO alteration of blood-brain barrier permeability; new method for analysis of adrenaline and noradrenaline. Home: 822 Eden Ct Alexandria VA 22308 Office: 200 C St SW Washington DC 20204

HANKINSON, JOHN CRIMMINS, JR., banker; b. Waynesboro, Ga., Oct. 14, 1933; s. John Crimmins and Sara (Blount) H.; B.S., Clemson U., 1955; grad. Sch. Banking of South, La. State U., 1964, S.C. Bankers Sch., 1965; children—Mona Lane, Ann Crimmins. Mgmt. trainee S.C. Nat. Bank, Greenville, 1957-59, adminstrv. asst., Sumter, 1959-60, asst. cashier, Cheraw, 1960-63, asst. v.p., sr. officer, Bennettsville, 1963-67, v.p. internat. banking div., Columbia, 1967-71, v.p. adminstrn. nat. banking div., 1971—. Pres., Bennettsville Parking and Devel. Co., 1965-67. Chmn. Pee Dee Area chpt. Nat. Found. March Dimes, 1966-67; chmn. S.C. edn. funds crusade S.C. div. Am. Cancer Soc., 1969-70, treas. S.C. div., 1970-74; vice chmn. S.C. Regional Export Expansion Council, 1969-73. pres. Young Bankers div. S.C. Bankers Assn., 1973-74. Served with AUS, 1956. Presbyn. Home: 1825 St Julian Pl Middleborough Apts Apt 3G Columbia SC 29204 Office: 1241 Main St Columbia SC 29202

HANKINSON, RISDON WILLIAM, chem. engr.; b. St. Joseph, Mo., Dec. 11, 1938; s. William Augusta and Rose Mary (Thompson) H.; B.S., U. Mo., Rolla, 1960, M.S., 1962; Ph.D. (Am. Oil fellow), Ia. State U., 1972; m. Lyla Pollard, June 4, 1960; children—Kenneth, Michelle, Michael. Instr. chem. engring. U. Mo., Rolla, 1960-62; instr. chem. engring. Ia. State U., 1964-67; engr. Phillips Petroleum Co., Bartlesville, Okla., 1967-69, group leader, 1969-70, cons., 1970—; adj. prof. math. Okla. State U., 1967—, Bartlesville Wesleyan Coll., 1969-71. Vice pres. Tech. Careers Adv. Com., 1972-73, pres., 1973—; v.p. Vol. Okla. Overseas Mission Bd., 1970-71. Served from 2d lt. to 1st lt. AUS, 1962-63. Recipient Outstanding Alumnus Achievement award Ia. State U., 1971; named Outstanding Young Engr. in Okla., 1970. Registered profl. engr., Okla. Mem. Am. Inst. Chem. Engrs. (dir., past pres. Bartlesville sect.), Soc. Profl. Engrs. (Young Engr. of Year Bartlesville chpt. 1970). Episcopalian. Elk. Contbr. articles to profl. jours. Home: 701 Sooner Park Dr Bartlesville OK 74003 Office: Adams Bldg Phillips Petroleum Co Bartlesville OK 74004

HANKO, CHARLES WILLIAM, real estate exec.; b. McKeesport, Pa., Aug. 3, 1920; s. Charles William and Alice Elizabeth (Lang) H.; B.S., Mt. Union Coll., 1946; Ed.M., U. Pitts., 1949; LL.B., LaSalle Law Sch., 1951; J.D., Blackstone Sch. Law, 1953; Th.B., Burton Theol. Sem., 1954; Th.M., Free Protestant Episcopal Sem., 1956; postgrad. Duquesne U., 1953-54; hon. degrees: D.D., Clarkesville

Sch. Theology, 1964, Trinity So. Bible Coll., 1963; Th.D., Maranatha Bible Sem., 1969; Litt.D., Sequoia U., 1965; Ed.D., Burton Coll., 1965, U. Aruba, 1972; LL.D., St. Andrews Coll., London, 1957; m. Julia E. Bachisin, June 30, 1956. Ordained to ministry Free Protestant Episcopal Ch., 1958, Pa. Assn. Conglist. Christian Churches, 1963; tchr. history and govt., pub. schs. Pa., 1946-54; instr. history and econs. Poly. Inst. Bklyn., 1954-56; prof. philosophy Transylvania Bible Coll., Freeport, Pa., 1950-51; interim pastor Grace Lutheran Ch., Leechburg, Pa., 1951, 1st Conglist. Ch., Neosho, Mo., 1956; pastor United Conglist. Ch., Sharon, Pa., 1962-64, Greater Musselshell Parish Conglist. Christian Churches, Roundup, Mont., 1964-66; rector Ch. of Our Saviour, West Palm Beach, Fla., 1966-67; adminstrv. asst. to pres., also head pub. relations Marshall Wells Real Estate, Inc., Palm Beach, 1968-70; tchr. King's Acad., West Palm Beach, 1971-72; adminstr. Laurelton Hall Pvt. Sch., West Palm Beach, 1972—; mem. faculty external degree program and internat. adv. council U. Aruba, Oranjestad, 1972—. Pres., Pitcairn (Pa.) Tchrs. Assn., 1945-46, McKeesport Social Studies Council, 1951-52, Armstrong County (Pa.) Social Studies Council, 1957-58. Sec., N. Versailles Twp. Republican Com., 1948-50; candidate Pa. Legislature, 1947, U.S. Congress from 33d Dist. Pa., 1951; city auditor Freeport, Pa., 1960-62. Econs. in action fellow Case Inst. Tech., 1954. Mem. Pa. Assn. Conglist Christian Churches (moderator 1963-65), Am. Legion, Nat. Assn. Conglist. Christian Churches (commn. ministry 1963-66. Mason (Shriner), Lion (dir. 1970-72). Author: Christianity Mobilizing, 1955; The Evangelical Protestant Movement, 1955; The Life of John Gibson: Soldier, Patriot, Statesman, 1954; Persecuted for Service, 1951; Economic Threats to America, 1956; Suarez and Western Civilization, 1972; The Plight of the American Railroads, 1973; The Rise and Decline of the Free Church, 1972; America's Prestige Abroad, 1972; Christians Hate Christ?, 1972; The Relevance of the Church, 1973; Roberto Franceso O. Bellamino: The Master of Controversy, 1974; and others; weekly columnist Freeport (Pa.) Hour., 1955-56, Palm Beach Outlook (translated into Spanish for La Prensa), 1968-69. Contbr. mags. Home: Box 773 Palm Beach FL 33480

HANKS, BERLIN GLENN, clergyman; b. Woodlawn, Va., Nov. 7, 1931; s. Steward and Altia Hans (Coulson) H.; B.A., Lynchburg Coll., 1954-58; M.Div., Lexington Theol. Sem., 1965-68; m. Opal J. Brewer, Aug. 30, 1958; children—Angela Carol, Jonathan Glenn. Ordained to ministry, Christian Ch., 1960; minister Sylvatus Christian Ch., Sylvatus, Va., 1957-58, Oak Grove Christian Ch., WOodlawn, Va., 1955-58, Boones Mill (Va.) Christian Ch., 1958-65, Ewing (Ky.) Christian Ch., 1965-68, Snow Creek Christian Ch., Martinsville, Va., 1968—. Mem. So. Piedmont Conv. Christian Chs., Martinsville, 1968—, pres., 1972. Mem. Snow Creek Vol. Fire Dept. 1968—, Snow Creek Rescue Squad, 1973—. Served with AUS, 1952-54. Mem. Franklin County Ministerial Assn. (v.p. 1965, pres. 1966, 69), Snow Creek Young Farmer Assn. Mason. Home: Route 5 Martinsville VA 24112

HANKS, HAROLD WAYNE, aircraft parts co. exec.; b. Van Wert, Ia., Aug. 18, 1926; s. Harold H. and Martha Ann (Craft) H.; B.A., Los Angeles State Coll., 1951; m. Virginia Lee Craig, Mar. 3, 1956; children—Gregory, Linda, Martha, Jayne. With Am. Machine & Foundry Co., Buffalo, 1962-67; marketing mgr., mfg. programs Aeronca, Inc., Middletown, O., 1965-67; pres., chmn. bd. Control Products Corp., Grand Prairie, Tex., 1967—. Planning and zoning commr. City of Grand Prairie, 1970—. Served with USNR, 1944-46. Mem. Blue Key. Mem. Christian Ch. (deacon 1971—). Elk. Home: 1909 Westminister Grand Prairie TX 75050 Office: 1801 W Jefferson Grand Prairie TX 75050

HANLIN, RICHARD THOMAS, educator; b. Hammond, Ind., May 10, 1931; s. Arthur McKinley and Mary Elizabeth (Hedges) H.; B.S., U. Mich., 1953, M.S., 1955, Ph.D., 1960; m. Elba Isabel Bueno-Clavijo, Aug. 15, 1955; children—Maria E., Janath A., Richard Allen. Asst. prof. Ga. Expt. Sta., Experiment, Ga., 1960-66; asso. prof. plant pathology U. Ga., Athens, 1967-72, prof., 1972—. Mem. Bot. Soc. Am., Mycol. Soc. Am., A.A.A.S., Am. Inst. Biol. Scis., Am. Phytopathol. Soc., Torrey Bot. Club, British Mycol. Soc., Sociedad Mexicana de Micologia, Mycol. Soc. Japan, Sigma Xi, Phi Sigma. Chmn. edit. com. Mycologia Memoirs, 1970—. Home: 235 Valleywood Dr Athens GA 30601

HANN, JOHN ROBERT, oral surgeon, army officer; b. Maryville, Mo., Nov. 3, 1933; s. John Ramsy and Wilda (Jones) H.; B.A., Baker U., 1955; D.D.S., U. Kansas City, 1959; postgrad. Georgetown U., 1966-67; m. Dorothy Lou Kochan, June 8, 1956; children—John Michael, Karen Lea, Matthew Lawrence. Dental intern Womack Army Hosp., Ft. Bragg, N.C., 1959-60; commd. 2d lt. U.S. Army, 1958, advanced through grades to lt. col., 1968; dental officer, Ft. Lawton, Wash., 1960-62, Hawaii, 1962-66; resident oral surgery Inst. Dental Research Walter Reed Army Med. Center, Washington, 1966-67, Womack Army Hosp., 1967-69; oral surgeon, chief dept. dentistry 121th Evacuation Hosp., Korea, 1969-70; oral surgeon, chief dept. dentistry, Ft. Gordon, Ga., 1970—, also dir. dental edn.; asst. prof. dept. Oral Surgery Med. Coll. of Ga.; cons. in field. Diplomate Am. Bd. Oral Surgery. Mem. Am. Dental Assn., Am. Soc. Oral Surgeons, Omicron Kappa Upsilon, Xi Psi. Home: 3103 Shelley Ct Augusta GA 30904 Office: Dept Dentistry USA Med C Fort Gordon GA 30905

HANNAN, PHILIP MATTHEW, archbishop; b. Washington, May 20, 1913; s. Patrick F. and Lillian Louise (Keefe) H.; student St. Charles Coll., 1931-33; A.B., Cath. U., 1935, M.A., 1936, J.C.D., 1949; student North Am. Coll., 1936-40; S.T.B., S.T.L., Gregorian U., Rome, 1940. Ordained priest Roman Catholic Ch., 1939; clerical appointment St. Thomas Aquinas Ch., Balt., 1940-42; student Cath. U., 1946-49, vice chancellor, 1948-51, chancellor, 1951-62, vicar gen., 1960-65; archbishop of New Orleans, 1965—; adminstr. St. Patrick's Ch., Washington 1951-56, pastor, 1956-65; aux. bishop Archdiocese of Washington, 1956-65; editor-in-chief Cath. Standard, 1951-65. Mem. administrv. bd. U.S. Cath. Conf., chmn. dept. communications. Mem. White House Conf. on Children and Youth. Chmn. bd. trustees Cath. U. Am., 1973—; trustee United Fund New Orleans. Served as chaplain USAAF, 1942-46. Address: 7887 Walmsley Av New Orleans LA 70125

HANNON, RAYMOND EDWARD, computer co. exec.; b. Youngstown, O., Oct. 25, 1935; s. John Michael and Opal Lorena (Reitz) H.; B.Sc., McGill U., 1955. Research asst. Canadian Pacific Ry., Montreal, 1955-59; asst. pub. Calgary Albertan, 1959-61; pub. relations officer Burroughs Corp., Pasadena, Cal., 1961-63; dir. communication C-E-I-R, Inc., Washington, 1963-66; v.p. Univ. Computing Co. (now Wyly Corp.), Dallas, 1966-73, asst. to the chmn., 1973—. Mem. Pub. Relations Soc. Am., Nat. Assn. Passenger Traffic Officers, Nat. Assn. R.R. Passengers. Home: 4716 Westchester Mall Dallas TX 75219 Office: UCC Tower 7200 Stemmons Freeway Dallas TX 75247

HANOR, EUGENE BERTRAM, artist; b. Hot Springs, Ark., Oct. 26, 1905; s. Sebastian Montague and Jennie Bell (Cook) H.; student Chgo. Acad. Art, 1925-27, Chgo. Art Inst., 1930-31, Am. Acad. Art, 1935; m. Muriel Louise Tourssen, Mar. 23, 1932; children—Jeffrey S., John B. Illustrator, Chgo. Studio, 1928-29; illustrator, art editor Dog World Mag., Chgo., 1930-35; illustrator Am. Research Corp., 1935-40; illustrator, art dir., buyer Buchen Advt., Inc., Chgo., 1940-68; one-man shows at So. Artists Galleries, Hot Springs, Ark., Ark. State Festival of Arts, 1972; exhibited in group shows at Chgo. Daily News, So. Artists Assn., Ark. Art Center Little Rock Ark. Pub. Library; represented in numerous pvt. collections. Art dir., bd. dirs. So. Artists Galleries, Hot Springs, Ark., 1969-71, Fine Arts Council, Hot Springs, 1971—. Recipient 1st awards Ark. State Festival Arts, 1969, 70, 71; 1st award S.E. Ark. Arts & Sci. Center, 1970. Mem. Jamestowne Soc., S.A.R., So. Artists Assn., Mid-So. Water Colorists. Contbr. hist. articles, illustrations Garland County His. Soc. Record, 1972, 73, 74. Designer ofcl. seal and flag City of Hot Springs. Address: 101 Terryland Dr Hot Springs AR 71901

HANRY, CAROLYN KAY OWENS (MRS. ROBERT EARL HANRY), banker; b. El Dorado, Ark., Dec. 8, 1947; d. Clinton Willie Owens and Maurice (Pepper) Ayers; student pub. schs.; m. Robert Earl Hanry, June 31, 1966; children—Lesia Kay, Kimberly Carol. With Union State Bank, Junction City, Ark., 1965—, asst. cashier, 1966-68, cashier, 1968—. Baptist. Home: 707 S Main St Junction City AR 71749 Office: Box F Junction City AR 71749

HANS, IRLINE COEN (MRS. CLIFFORD J. HANS), oil producing co. exec.; b. Sunflower County, Miss., June 7, 1919; d. Claudius C. and Mary Ann (Hooker) Coen; student Copiah-Lincoln Jr. Coll., 1938-39, Blue Mountain Coll., 1939-40; m. Clifford J. Hans., Oct. 18, 1957. Sec., Nat. Def. Office, Tupelo, Miss. 1941; bookkeeper Crippled Children's Service, sec. Vocational Ednl. Dept., Miss. Dept. Edn., Jackson, 1941, sec. high sch. supr., 1942; sec. Vaughey & Vaughey Ind. Oil Producers, 1942-47, tax accountant, 1944-47, office mgmt., personnel supr., 1947-57, exec. sec. to mgmt., 1957—; participating partner, exec. sec. Vaughey, Blackburn & Vaughey Pipeline Co., 1958—; sec.-treas. Sonora Devel. Corp., 1959—, also dir. Comml. inst. Nat. Youth Adminstrn., Tupelo, 1941. Dist. chmn. Oil Industry Information Com., 1957-58; state chmn. for women Natural Gas and Oil Resources Com., 1955-56. Mem. U.D.C., Exec. Secs., Inc. (charter mem. Jackson, dir. 1957). Methodist. Clubs: Jackson Country, Desk and Derrick (pres. 1951-52). Home: 1565 E Meadowbrook Rd Jackson MS 39211 Office: 1616 Capital Towers Jackson MS 39201

HANSEN, ALICE MCBRIDE, med. librarian; b. Pitts., June 6, 1898; d. Homer James and Victoria (Vaughan) McBride; A.B., Vassar Coll., 1919; B.L.S., Columbia, 1920; Ed.M., Harvard, 1932; m. Robert Arthur Hansen, Oct. 13, 1923; 1 son, Wilbur Vaughan. Cataloger for Columbia U. Library, 1922-24; current periodicals asst. N.Y. Pub. Library, 1922-24; tchr., librarian Irwin (Pa.) High Sch., 1925-27, Munhall High Sch., 1927-28; librarian Slippery Rock State Tchrs. Coll., Pa., 1928-42. Pa. Coll. Women, 1942-51, Rollins Coll., 1951-69; med. librarian Winter Park (Fla.) Meml. Hosp., 1969—. Mem. Am., Fla., Southeastern library assns., Fla. Med. Librarians, Pi Gamma Mu, Sigma Tau Delta. Methodist. Clubs: Vassar of Central Florida; Zonta, Central Florida Harvard. Home: 1551 Lasbury Av Winter Park FL 32789

HANSEN, DONALD VERNON, govt. ofcl.; b. Seattle, Jan. 18, 1931; s. Vernon Arthur and Dolores (Wahl) H.; B.S., U. Wash., 1954, M.S., 1961, Ph.D., 1964; m. Eva Busemann, Aug. 23, 1958; children—Peter, Norman, Christa. Engr., Boeing Airplane Co., Seattle, 1956-57; tchr. Seattle Pub. Schs., 1957-58; research asst. prof. U. Wash. at Seattle, 1964-65; writer Earth Sci. Curriculum Project, Boulder, Colo., 1965-66; oceanographer Environmental Sci. Services Adminstrn., U.S. Dept. Commerce, Silver Spring, Md., 1966-67, Miami, Fla., 1967-69, dir. Phys. Oceanographic Lab., Atlantic Oceanographic and Meteorol. Labs., Nat. Oceanic and Atmospheric Adminstrn., Miami, 1969—; adj. prof. U. Miami, 1970—. Served with AUS, 1954-56. Mem. Am. Soc. Limnology and Oceanography, Am. Geophys. Union, Sigma Xi. Asso. editor Jour. Geophys. Research, 1966-68. Home: 5900 SW 104th St Miami FL 33156 Office: US Dept Commerce 15 Rickenbacker Causeway Miami FL 33149

HANSEN, HOWARD JAMES, pub. co. exec.; b. Chgo., Mar. 12, 1909; s. Harry John and Selma (Fick) H.; B.S. in Engring., Purdue U., 1930; C.E., Tulane U., 1939; m. Harriet O'Neill, Sept. 16, 1931; children—Jennifer (Mrs. David Derbyshire), Gretchen (Mrs. Alvin King). Prof. engring. mechanics U. Fla., Gainesville, 1946-49; pres. Howard Hansen, Inc., Covington, La., 1959—. Cons. civil engr., 1965—. Served to lt. USNR, 1943-46. Registered profl. engr., La., Fla., Ill. Fellow Am. Soc. C.E. Episcopalian. Author: Modern Timber Design, 1942; Timber Engineers Handbook, 1948. Home and office: PO Box 243 Covington LA 70433

HANSEN, NILES MAURICE, educator; b. Louisville, Jan. 2, 1937; s. Kristian and Alma (Jensen) H.; B.A., Centre Coll. Ky., 1958; M.A., Ind. U., 1959, Ph.D., 1963; m. Josephine Drescher, Aug. 22, 1959; children—Karen, Eric, Laura. Mem. research staff Center for Regional Econs., Ghent (Belgium) U., 1961-62; asst. prof. econs. U. Tex. at Austin, 1963-65, prof. econs., dir. center for econ. devel., 1969—; prof. econs. U. Ky. at Lexington, 1967-69; dir. research project Dept. Labor and Econ. Devel. Adminstrn., Dept. Commerce, 1967—. NSF fellow U. Paris (France), 1965-66. Mem. Am., So. econ. assns., Assn. Comparative Econs., Regional Sci. Assn., Assn. French Speaking Regional Economists. Author: French Regional Planning, 1968; France in the Modern World, 1969; Rural Poverty and the Urban Crisis, 1970; Intermediate-Size Cities as Growth Centers, 1971; Growth Centers and Regional Devel., 1972; Location Preferences, Migration and Regional Growth, 1973; The Future of Nonmetropolitan America, 1973; Public Policy and Regional Development, 1974. Contbr. articles to profl. jours. Home: 4003 Tablerook Dr Austin TX 78731 Office: Dept Econs U Tex Austin TX 78712

HANSEN, NILS ERLING, cons. engr.; b. New Orleans, July 28, 1931; s. Hans Trygve and Hanna (Hansen) H.; B.S., Tulane U., 1953; m. Johanna Reinetta Writsers, May 13, 1960; children—Norman Trygve, Helen Reinetta, Jon Erling. Chief engr. T. Hansen Constrn., Inc. New Orleans, 1956-62; design engr. Prescott Follett & Assos., New Orleans, 1962-66; prin. N. E. Hansen & Assos., Cons. Engrs., New Orleans, 1966-70; chief engr. Petro-Marine Engring., Inc., 1970-73; gen. mgr. Ocean Oil Internat. Engring. Corp., 1974—; pres. T. Hansen Constrn., Inc., New Orleans, 1962—. Chmn. bd. trustees Norwegian Seamen's Mission, New Orleans. Served to lt. (j.g.) USCG, 1953-56; capt. Res. Decorated St. Olav's medal (Norway); recipient Achievement medal U.S. Coast Guard, 1970, Commendation medal, 1973. Mem. Am. Soc. C.E., Am. Soc. Mil. Engrs., Mil. Order World Wars, U.S. Naval Inst., Am. Scandinavian Found., Norwegian Am. Hist. Assn., USCG Acad. Alumni Assn., Norwegian Am. Sesquicentennial Assn., U.S. Coast Guard Officers Assn., Norseman's League, Sons of Norway, Soc. Tulane Engrs., La. Engring. Soc., Res. Officers Assn. (pres. 1969-71). Club: Army-Navy (Washington). Home: 6707 Canal Blvd New Orleans LA 70124 Office: 3019 Mercedes Blvd New Orleans LA 70114

HANSING, FRANK DETLEFF, govt. ofcl.; b. Bonfield, Ill., Nov. 25, 1919; s. John Henry and Anna (Krueger) H.; student Ill. State U., 1937-40; B.S., U. Ill., 1941, M.S., 1947, Ph.D., 1954; m. Frances B. Koch, Apr. 25, 1943; children—Kenneth E., David F. Tchr. high sch. Hinckley, Ill., 1941-42; with U.S. Dept. Agr., Va. Poly. Inst., 1948-55, U. Del., 1955-56, Agr. Research Service, Washington, 1956-62; with NASA Hdqrs., Washington, 1962—, chief tng. div. Office Grants and Research Contracts, 1962-68, dir. sustaining univ. program Office Univ. Affairs, 1968-71, dir. Office Univ. Affairs, 1971—. Active Boy Scouts Am., 1955-65. Served with USNR, 1942-46. Recipient Scouters Key, 1961. Mem. Gamma Sigma Delta. Methodist. Contbr. profl. jours. Home: 9701 Cedar Lane Bethesda MD 20014 Office: Office of Univ Affairs NASA Hdqrs Washington DC 20546

HANSON, CLARENCE BLOODWORTH, JR., publisher; b. Augusta, Ga., Nov. 7, 1908; s. Clarence Bloodworth and Harriet (Pinkham) H.; student Richmond Acad., Augusta, Ga., 1921-25, B.S., U. Va., 1930; m. Elizabeth Fontaine Fletcher, Sept. 9, 1929; 1 son, Victor Henry II. Advt. dept. Indpls. Star, 1929-30; with advt. dept. Birmingham (Ala.) News, 1930-34, nat. advt. mgr., 1934-37, asst. advt. dir., 1937-42, pub., 1945; pres., dir., mem. exec. com. The Birmingham News Co. (pubs. Birmingham News, Huntsville Times, Agent, Birmingham Post-Herald); v.p., dir. Mercury Express, Inc.; dir., mem. exec. com. First Nat. Bank Birmingham, Ala. Bancorp.; chmn. exec. com., dir. Royal Crown Cola Co. Bd. dirs. Birmingham Mus. of Art; trustee Alabama Mus. Natural History, Eye Found. Hosp. Served as maj. AC, AUS, 1942-45. Mem. Asso. Press (v.p. 1953-56), Am., So. (pres. 1950) newspaper pubs. assns., Ala. Press Assn. (pres. 1951), Phi Gamma Delta. Episcopalian. Clubs: Mountain Brook County, Birmingham Country, Relay House (Birmingham); Hon. Co. of Edinburg Golfers (Muirfield, Scotland). Home: 4055 Old Leeds Rd Mountain Brook Birmingham AL 35213 Office: 2200 4th Av N Birmingham AL 35203

HANSON, DORIS ELIZABETH, home economist, assn. exec.; b. Bowbells, N.D., Mar. 29, 1928; d. Fred and Laura (Finke) Hanson; B.S., Wash. State U., 1949; M.A., Columbia, 1958, Ed.D., 1964. Home demonstration agt. Colo. Extension Service, Akron, 1949-51; asso. editor household equipment McCalls mag., N.Y.C., 1951-59; adviser Okla.-Pakistan Home Econs. Project Ford Found., Dacca, Bangladesh, 1959-62; asst. dean Purdue U. Sch. Home Econs. 1964-67; exec. dir. Am. Home Econs. Assn., Washington, 1967—. Instr., Columbia, 1958-64. Bd. dirs. Sears Found. Mem. Am. Home Econs. Assn., Am. Nat. Metric Council, Nat. Council Family Relations, Am. Mgmt. Assn., Omicron Nu, Pi Lambda Theta, Kappa Delta Pi. Home: 2727 29th St NW Washington DC 20008 Office: 2010 Massachusetts Av NW Washington DC 20036

HANSON, MORGAN ALFRED, educator; b. Wowan, Australia, Jan. 28, 1930; s. Alfred Sigurd and Catherine (Driver) H.; B.S., U. Queensland, 1952; M.S., U. Melbourne, 1954; Ph.D., U. New South Wales, 1964; m. Lillian Eva Cheesley, Jan. 3, 1954; children—Rosemary, Morgan, Glenda, Carolyn, Gail. Came to U.S., 1968. Physicist, mathematician Imperial Chem. Industries, Melbourne, Australia, 1955; operations research analyst Australian Gas Light Co., Sydney, 1956-58; lectr. U. New South Wales, 1959-65; vis. asso. prof. Fla. State U., 1965; asso. prof. Queen's U., Kingston, Ont., Can., 1966-67; prof. operations research Fla. State U., 1968—; cons. Aerospace Research Labs., 1968. Recipient Can. Nat. Research Council Research grants, 1967-68, Air Force Office of Sci. Research grants, 1972-73. Mem. Am. Math. Soc., Inst. Math. Statistics, Soc. Indsl. and Applied Math., Math. Programming Soc. Contbr. articles to applied math. and statis. jours. Home: 5583 Pimlico Dr Tallahassee FL 32303 Office: Dept Statistics Fla State U Tallahassee FL 32306

HANSON, WILLIAM BERT, educator; b. Warroad, Minn., Dec. 30, 1923; s. Bert and Viola May (Carlquist) H.; B.S., U. Minn., 1944; M.S., U. Minn., 1949; Ph.D., George Washington U., 1954; m. Wenonah Ann Dahlquist, Mar. 14, 1946; children—Bryan, Craig, David, Karen. Physicist, Nat. Bur. Standards, Washington, 1949-54, Boulder, Colo., 1954-56; research scientist Lockheed Missiles & Space Co., Palo Alto, Cal., 1956-57; head atmospheric density and composition, physics dept., 1957-59, head ionospheric physics sect., 1959-62; mem. faculty U. Tex. at Dallas (formerly S.W. Center for Advanced Studies), 1962—, prof. physics, 1962—, dir. Inst. Phys. Scis., 1969—. Bd. dirs. Planned Parenthood, Dallas, 1964-70, nat. orgn., 1969-70. Served with USNR, 1944-46. Erskine fellow, U. Canterbury, Christchurch, New Zealand, 1969. Fellow Am. Geophys. Union; mem. Internat. Sci. Radio Union. Contbr. profl. jours. Research in low temperature physics and space physics. Home: 7831 La Sobrina Dr Dallas TX 75240 Office: Dept Physics Univ Tex Dallas TX 75230

HANSROTE, CHARLES JOHNSON, JR., educator; b. Bowling Green, Md., Nov. 22, 1930; s. Charles Johnson and Hazel Loretta (Groves) H.; B.S., Va. Mil. Inst., 1952; M.S., U. Richmond, 1955; Ph.D., U. Va., 1958; m. Melva Irene Hardinger, June 12, 1953; 1 son, Charles Johnson III. Asst. instr. chemistry Va. Mil. Inst., 1952-53; research chemist Benger Lab., E.I. duPont, Waynesboro, Va., 1958-62; asso. prof. chemistry Frostburg State Coll., 1962-63, prof. chemistry, 1963-64, head chemistry dept., 1964-65; prof. chemistry Lynchburg (Va.) Coll., 1965—, head chemistry dept., 1970-71, 72—; prof. chemistry Va. Commonwealth U., summer 1968. Instr. first aid A.R.C., 1972—; troop committeeman Blue Ridge Mountains council Boy Scouts Am., 1969-70, asst. scoutmaster, 1970-73, scoutmaster, 1973—. Served with AUS, 1952-64. Puryear teaching fellow U. Richmond, 1953-54; Tenn. Eastman fellow U. Va., 1957-58. Mem. Am. Chem. Soc., Sigma Xi, Gamma Sigma Epsilon, Sigma Zeta, Chi Beta Phi, Blue Key. Mason. Club: Bird of Lynchburg. Home: 24 Greenwell Ct Lynchburg VA 24502 Office: Lynchburg Coll Lynchburg VA 24502

HANST, KENNETH FREDERICK, JR., life ins. exec.; b. Woodbury, N.J., May 16, 1920; s. Kenneth Frederick and Kathleen (Elliott) H.; B.S., U.S. Mil. Acad., 1942; m. Barbara Lois Gnau, Dec. 19, 1942; children—Kenneth Frederick III, Susan E. With Army Mut. Aid Assn., Arlington, Va., 1947—, exec. v.p., 1957-71, pres., 1971—. Bd. dirs. Army Distaff Found., West Point Alumni Found. Served with AUS, 1942-47; CBI. Decorated Bronze Star (2). C.L.U. Mem. West Point Soc. D.C. (pres. 1963-64, Benjamin F. Castle award 1967), Chartered Life Underwriters (D.C. chpt. pres. 1964-65), Nat. Assn. Uniformed Services (dir.), D.C. Life Underwriters, Assn. Grads. U.S. Mil. Acad. (trustee). Home: 5597 Seminary Rd #610 Falls Church VA 22041 Office: Fort Myer Arlington VA 22211

HANTHORN, GEORGE WILMOT, mech. engr.; b. Cadams, Neb., Oct. 10, 1913; s. Walter Allyn and Anna Orpha (Ellison) H.; B.S., U. Neb., 1948; m. Ruby Arline Jensen, Oct. 28, 1945; children—George Wilmot, Steven Wesley. Sr. design engr. Phillips Petroleum Co., Bartlesville, Okla., 1948—. Mem. Dewey Sch. Bd. Edn., 1962-67. Served to lt. comdr. USNR, 1940-45. Decorated Air medal. Mem. Okla. Soc. Profl. Engrs., Bartlesville Engrs. Club, S.A.R. Methodist. Patentee fractionator feed control. Home: Route 1 Box 39 Dewey OK 74029 Office: 8B-4 PB Bartlesville OK 74003

HAPP, STAFFORD COLEMAN, geologist; b. Sparrow Bush, N.Y., Sept. 16, 1905; s. Conrad and Hattie A. (Coleman) H.; A.B. (cum laude), Marietta Coll., 1931; student Wesleyan U., 1926-27; Ph.D., Columbia U., 1939; m. Inez Ellen Hale, Dec. 26, 1935; 1 dau., Ellen (Mrs. Kenneth W. Hill). Head stream and valley sedimentation research Soil Conservation Service, Washington, 1935-43; head geology soils sect. Army Engrs., Ocala, Fla., 1943-44; head geology and underground investigations Army Engrs., Kansas City, Mo., 1944-55; chief geologic reports and information sect. AEC, Grand Junction (Colo.) Office 1955-56, asst. chief geologic br., 1957-58, chief prodn. services br., 1959-64; research geologist U.S. Geol. Survey, 1964-65; research geologist Agrl. Research Service, Oxford, Miss., 1965—. Fellow Geol. Soc. Am. (chmn. engring. div. 1960); mem. Am. Inst. Mining, Metall. and Petroleum Engrs., A.A.A.S., Am. Geophys. Union, Am. Soc. C.E., Phi Beta Kappa, Sigma Xi. Contbr. to profl. jours. Office: USDA Sedimentation Lab PO Box 1157 Oxford MS 38655

HAPPEL, RALPH, ret. hist. researcher; b. Fredericksburg, Va.. Apr. 12, 1911; s. John and Margaret (Reiser) H.; B.S., 1932, M.S., 1934; m. Martha Louise Williams, Jan. 1, 1940. With Nat. Park Service, Fredericksburg, Va., 1936-72, hist. research, interpreter. Bd. dirs. Historic Fredericksburg Found.; bd. dirs., v.p. Fredericksburg Cemetery Co. Mem. Soc. for Preservation Va. Antiquities, Confederate Meml. Lit. Soc., others. Presbyn. Home: 1011 Caroline St Fredericksburg VA 22401

HARA, SABURO, educator, pediatrician; b. Yamanashi-shi, Japan, Feb. 16, 1928; s. Riei and Taki (Ogawa) H.; M.D., Tokyo Med. U., 1953; m. Marjorie E. Lyle, Dec. 8, 1958; 1 dau., Mary Katheryn. Came to U.S., 1953, naturalized, 1960. Intern, Bronson Meth. Hosp., Kalamazoo, 1953-54; pediatric resident U. Ill., 1956-59; practice medicine, specializing in pediatrics, Nashville, 1959—; dir. Diagnostic and Tng. Lab., Meharry Med. Coll., Nashville, 1968—, prof. dept. pediatrics, 1971—; chmn. dept. pediatrics Nashville Meml. and Madison hosps., 1970-72; med. cons. Tng. and Habilitation Center, Nashville, 1973—; pres. med. and dental staff G.W. Hubbard Hosp., 1973—. Recipient Golden Apple award Student A.M.A., 1972. Diplomate Am. Bd. Pediatrics. Fellow Am. Acad. Pediatrics; mem. Am. Soc. Human Genetics. Home: 2623 Air Park Dr Nashville TN 37206

HARADON, VIRGINIA ELIZABETH INGLES (MRS. CLAYTON BARTLETT HARADON), ednl. therapist; b. Redfield, S.D., July 27, 1913; d. Thomas Jefferson and Della May (Hooker) Ingles; B.A., U. Omaha, 1946, M.A., 1948; postgrad. research U. Neb. Med. Sch., 1946; M.Ed., Trinity U., 1959; M.S.W. in psychiatric social work (USPHS grantee), Worden Sch. Social Service, Our Lady of Lake Coll., 1961; m. Alvin James Maes, June 1, 1936 (dec. 1944); m. 2d, Clayton Bartlett Haradon, May 10, 1946; children—John Bartlett, Susan. Newspaper reporter suburban Los Angeles, 1933, 36; research asst. on relocation Japanese-Ams. sociology dept. U. Cal. at Los Angeles, 1944; psychol. testing, retarded and disturbed children, psychiat. clinic U. Omaha, also psychodiagnostic testing, family therapy A.E. Bennett Neuropsychiat. Found., Omaha, 1945-47; instr. Marriage and Family, U. Omaha, 1947-48; certified psychologist schs. Locust Valley and Bethpage (both N.Y.), sch. cons. Nassau County (N.Y.) Probation Dept., 1956-58, also marriage and family counselor Family Welfare Assn. Nassau County, summer 1957; psychol. interne Valley Stream (N.Y.) Summer Reading Sch. (study of dyslexia), summer 1958; pvt. practice counseling, ednl. therapy, San Antonio, 1962—; instr. marriage and family Our Lady of the Lake Coll., San Antonio, 1970; cons. San Antonio Lit. Council, YWCA, Juvenile Intervention Program. Mem. Community Com. for Mental Health Clinic, Glen Cove, N.Y., 1958. Bd. dirs. Beautify San Antonio Assn., Arts Council San Antonio. Mem. Nassau County Psychol. Assn., Am. Assn. Marriage and Family Counselors, Am. Personnel and Guidance Assn., Assn. Children with Learning Disabilities, Nat. Assn. Social Workers, N.E.A., Acad. Religion and Mental Health (sec., treas. San Antonio chpt. 1966), A.S.C.A.P., Nat. Acad. Popular Music, San Antonio Group Psychotherapy and Group Process Soc. (exec. council 1973-74), Acad. Certified Social Workers, Internat. Transactional Analysis Assn., A.A.A.S., Family Therapy Assn. Tex., Delphian Soc., Alpha Kappa Delta. Composed, pub. When Are You Comin' Home, Joe (also RCA rec.) 1955; Welcome to Texas, 1968; In Tribute to Trinity; others. Contbr. articles to profl. publs. Home: 614 Fresno Dr San Antonio TX 78212 Office: Suite 4 Kelly Bldg 2003 San Pedro Av San Antonio TX 78212

HARANG, WARREN JOSEPH, JR., sugar cane farmer; b. Thibodaux, la., Aug. 18, 1921; s. Warren Joseph and Winifred (Foret) H.; student Tulane U., 1939-40, La. State U., 1940-42; m. Bernice Peltier, May 24, 1945; children—Mary Margaret (Mrs. Brandt Dufrene), Warren Joseph III, Bernice Ellen, Sarah Alida Ann, Jane Frances, Bryan Harvey, Thomas Benton, Susan Elizabeth, Carolyn Ann. Owner, sugar cane farm, Labadieville, La., 1946—; pres., Cameco, Inc., 1965—, Cameco Sales Corp., 1965—, Tex-Emma, Inc., 1969—, Harang Farms, Inc., 1956—; dir. Lafourche Sugar Corp. Chmn. sugar cane com. Parish Agrl. Extension Service, 1948—. Founder, Jr. Police Force, 1967—, pres., 1967—; v.p. La. Municipal Assn., 1968-69; chmn. Commn. Fed. Housing, City of Thibodaux, La., 1952—; sec.-treas. Lafourche-Terrebonne Soil Conservation Dist. Bd. Suprs., 1952—; mem. State Anhydrous Ammonia Commn., 1960-72; mem. Thibodaux Fire Dept., 1947—, grand marshal, 1952; grand marshal Labadieville Vol. Fire Dept., 1964; mem. Lafourche Parish Fresh Water Dist., 1969—; mem. State Mineral Bd., 1956-60. Bd. dirs. A.R.C., Lafourche Parish chpt. Served to 2d lt. USAAF, 1942-45. Mem. Lafourche Parish Sch. Bd., 1962-68; mayor, City of Thibodaux, La., 1966—. Recipient Durel award V.F.W., 1968, award Boy Scouts Am., 1969, Conservation award Woodmen of World, 1973, Silver Medal of Merit, V.F.W., 1973. Mem. Nat. Rifle Assn., V.F.W., Am. Legion (bd. mem. 1945—), Am. Sugar Cane League (pres. 1952-55), Am. Sugar Cane Technologists (pres. 1968-70), La. State Assn. Soil Conservation Dist. Suprs. (v.p. 1965-66), La. Peace Officers Assn., Thibodaux C. of C., Lafourche Parish C. of C. (pres. 1966—), Lafourche Parish Farm Bur. (pres. 1952-56), La. Farm Bur. (mem. state bd. 1948—). Rotarian. Clubs: Nicholls Colonel, Thibodaux College Cardinal (pres. 1952-56) (both Thibodaux, La.). Home: 128 Elder St Thibodaux Lafourche LA 70301 Office: PO Box 166 Thibodaux Lafourche LA 70301

HARB, JOSEPH WADIE, physician; b. Knoxville, Tenn., Oct. 25, 1934; s. Wadie Joseph and Alice Marie (Makla) H.; B.A., U. Tenn., 1956, M.D., 1960; m. Mary Louise McClelland, Sept. 17, 1967; children—William Joseph, Michelle Louise. Intern, Duval Med. Center, Jacksonville, Fla., 1960-61; resident Los Angeles County Gen. Hosp., 1961-62, U. Okla. Med. Center, 1964-65, Los Angeles County Hosp., 1966-67; practice medicine, specializing in internal medicine, Knoxville, Tenn., 1967—; chief staff St. Mary's Meml. Hosp., 1974. Served with USAF, 1962-64. Diplomate Am. Bd. Internal Medicine. Mason. Home: 1909 Scalybark Lane Knoxville TN 37920 Office: 717 W Cumberland Av Knoxville TN 37902

HARBERT, BILL LEBOLD, constrn. co. exec.; b. Indianola, Miss., July 21, 1923; s. John Murdock and Mae (Schooling) H.; B.S., Auburn U., 1946; grad. Advanced Mgmt. Program, Harvard, 1966; m. Mary Joyce Patrick, June 28, 1952; children—Anne, Elizabeth, Bill LeBold. Exec. v.p., dir. Harbert Constrn. Corp., Birmingham, Ala., 1948—, Montin-Harbert Pipeline Co., Oklahoma City, 1959—, Harbert & Cargile Co., Birmingham, 1952—; v.p., dir. Harbert-Distral Co., Birmingham, 1968—, Carrez Internat., Inc., 1968—. Co-chmn., trustee Laborers Central and So. States Pension Fund, 1968—. Mem. sch. bd. Vestavia Hills Sch., 1968—. Trustee Constrn. Advancement Program of Ala. Served with inf. AUS, 1945. Mem. Pipeline Contractors Assn. (dir. 1968—). Methodist (mem. bd. 1972—). Club: Vestavia Country (pres. 1971) (Birmingham, Ala.). Home: 205 Vestavia Circle Birmingham AL 35216 Office: 2900 Cahaba Rd PO Box 1297 Birmingham AL 35201

HARBIN, WAYNE DEWITT, mfg. co. exec.; b. Donna, Tex., Apr. 29, 1925; s. Jesse Mathuews and Lela (Bettes) H.; B.B.A., U. Tex., 1949; grad. Advanced Mgmt. Program, Harvard, 1962; m. Elinor Victoria Tolish, Apr. 17, 1946; children—Kenneth Wayne, Richard Wayne. With Arthur Young & Co., C.P.A.'s, N.Y.C. and Houston, 1949-68, adminstrv. partner, 1959-68; pres., chmn. bd. Marathon Mfg. Co., fabricated metal products, Houston, 1968-73; chmn. bd., chief exec. officer Richmond Tank Car Co., 1973—; dir. Crutcher Resources Corp., Houston, 1971—, C.H.M., Inc. Mem. adv. council U. Tex. Bus. Sch., 1963—, also mem. chancellor's com.; mem. pres.'s council U. Baylor. Served with USN, 1942-46. Recipient Distinguished Alumni award U. Tex. Bus. Sch. Mem. Tex. Mfrs. Assn. (dir.), Tex. Soc. C.P.A.'s (dir.), Am. Inst. C.P.A.'s. Baptist. Mason. Clubs: River Oaks Country, Petroleum, Coronado (Houston); Harvard Business (Cambridge, Mass.). Home: 3994 Inverness St Houston TX 77019 Office: Richmond Tank Car Co 777 S Post Oak St Houston TX 77027

HARB KARAM, JOSE NASIP, lawyer; b. Monclova, Coahuila, Mexico, July 4, 1944; s. Nasip Mtanous and Angelique (Karam) Harb; degree internat. law summa cum laude, U. Nat. Autonoma de Mexico, 1966; S.J.D., Sorbonne, 1968; m. Noha Kallab Aucar, Nov. 20, 1968; children—Jose Nasip, Veronica. Admitted to Mexico bar, 1966; prof. internat. law U. Nat. Autonoma de Mexico, 1969; dir. Bufete Harb Karam, law firm, Mexico City, 1968—. Gen. dir. Compania Mexicana de Exportaciones e Importaciones, S.A., 1972—. Permanent Mexico counsel UN Orgn., 1967—. Mem. Barra Mexicana de Abogeados, Colegio de Abogados, Inst. Mexicano de Relaciones Internacionales (sec.), Assn. Diplomatiqus Internat., Assn. des Elves Etrangers a la Sorbonne, Assn. Internat. de Droit Comparado. Author: Foreign Investments in Mexico; The Fideicomiso; Limitacioned Al Poder Contituyente en las Re-Formas y Adiciones Constitucionales, 1966; also articles. Home: 506-201 Seneca Col Polanco Mexico City Mexico Office: 445 PB Paseo de la Reforma Mexico City 5 DF Mexico

HARBOR, JAMES GOLDMAN, prison supt.; b. Grenada, Miss., June 3, 1934; s. Timothy B. and Willie Elizabeth (Powell) H.; extension student U. Tenn., 1954; m. Lillie Mae Bevis, May 2, 1953; 1 dau., Deborah Lynn (Mrs. Michael Dee Crossnine). Clk., Mid-South Title Co., Memphis, 1951-62; office mgr. Shelby County Assessor's Office, Memphis, 1962-65; adminstrv. asst. Shelby County Bd. Commnrs., 1966-71; supt. Shelby County Penal Farm, 1971—. Pres. Memphis Jaycees, 1966-67; pres. Assistant's Assn., 1968; v.p., pres. Memphis-Shelby County Safety Council, 1968; vice chmn. Shelby County-Memphis Cystic Fibrosis campaign, 1968. Named Boss of Year, Frayser Jaycees, 1971. Mem. Ch. of Christ. Mason (32 deg., Shriner). Clubs: Gavel (pres. 1968), S.E. Exchange (pres. 1970-71) (Memphis); Germantown Optimist. Home: 5384 Wythe Cove Memphis TN 38134 Office: 1045 Mullins Station Memphis TN 38134

HARBOUR, MACK DAVE, hosp. adminstr.; b. Viola, Ark., June 5, 1937; s. Roy D. and Nona (Snelgrooes) H.; B.A., U. Ark., 1958, M.Ed., 1959, postgrad., 1960-62; postgrad. Ark. State U., 1966-67; m. Greta E. Martin, Jan. 31, 1958; children—Mark, Rebecca, Sarah. Tchr. Vila and Newark (Ark.) High Schs., 1958-60; sch. adminstr. Viola High Sch., 1960-62; adminstr. Fulton County Hosp., Salem, Ark., 1962-65, Community Meth. Hosp., Paragould, Ark., 1965—. Chmn. Parks and Recreation Commn. and Housing Authority, Paragould, Ark.; pres. Greene County Community Fund, Inc.; v.p. East Ark. Council Boy Scouts Am. Bd. dirs. Ark. Arthritis Found. Mem. Am., Ark. (dir.) hosp. assns., C. of C. (pres.), Am. Coll. Hosp. Adminstrs., Blue Key. Baptist (deacon). Mason, Rotarian. Author books on hosp. mgmt. Contbr. articles to profl. jours. Home: 316 N 4th St Paragould AR 72450 Office: 900 W Kings Hwy Paragould AR 72450

HARDBERGER, FLORIAN MAX, educator; b. Atlanta, La., Dec. 18, 1914; s. Willis Otis and Tamar Eugenie (Wilson) H.; B.S., Northwestern State Coll., 1942; M.S., La. State U., 1950; postgrad. U. Ala., 1960-61; m. Dorris Mildred Windham, Jan. 7, 1944; children—Florian Max, Karl Wesley, Dorris Wyolene. Fifth grade tchr., Oakdale, La., 1936-37; social worker Grant Parish Dept. Pub. Welfare, Colfax, La., 1937-41; dental technician Eighth Army, Hot Springs, Ark., 1943-46; block setter Sly Park Saw Mill, Placerville, Cal., 1946-47; biology and chemistry tchr. Nicholls State Jr. Coll. (name now changed to Nicholls State U.), Thibodaux, La., 1950—, head dept. biol. scis., 1959-73. Troop biology adviser Boy Scouts Am., 1952-65, 72-73. Served with AUS, 1943-46. Mem. Pi Delta Epsilon, Sigma Gamma Epsilon, Pi Mu Epsilon. Methodist. Mason. Home: 1706 Lynn Av Thibodaux LA 70301

HARDEE, HOWARD DAVIS, physician; b. Fernandina, Fla., Oct. 20, 1922; s. John Richardson and Ella (Davis) H.; B.S., Fla. So. Coll., 1942; B.S., Tulane U., 1943, M.D., 1946; student Hartford (Conn.) Sem. Found., 1948-49, Prince Leopold Inst. Tropical Medicine, Antwerp, Belgium, 1949-50; m. Ruth Piper, Jan. 24, 1952; children—Dorothy Ann, Ruth Ann. Intern Charlotte (N.C.) Meml. Hosp., 1946-47; resident Tampa (Fla.) Gen. Hosp., 1947-48; med. dir. Meth. Mission, Kapanga, Belgian Congo, Africa, 1950-52, Hillsborough County Welfare Bd., Tampa, 1953-54; gen. practice medicine, Tampa, 1954—. Served as 2d lt. AUS, World War II. Diplomate Nat. Bd. Med. Examiners, Mem. A.M.A., World, Fla., Hillsborough County med. assns., Am. Acad. Gen. Practice, Am. Geriatric Soc. Home: 2823 Samara Dr Carrollwood Tampa FL 33618 Office: 4809 Central Av Tampa FL 33604

HARDEN, ROSS ULLMAN, lawyer; b. Rockford, Ala., Apr. 20, 1909; s. James Elzie and Eunice (Ward) H.; A.B., Mercer U., 1929, LL.B., 1931; m. Annie Mandell Bates, Dec. 12, 1938; children—Sydney (Mrs. Anthony Smith Wynne), Annette (Mrs. Joseph Daniel, Jr.). Admitted to Ga. bar, 1931; practiced in Cairo, 1933-35, Waynesboro, 1947—; law clk. Supreme Ct. Ga., Atlanta, 1936-42; asst. atty. gen. State of Ga., Atlanta, 1943-44, 45-47; solicitor State Ct. Burke County, 1965—. Mem. Burke County Democratic Exec. Com., 1950—, chmn., 1961—. Served with USMCR, 1944-45. Mem. Am. Judicature Soc., State Bar Assn. Ga., Blue Key, Pi Kappa Phi, Phi Alpha Delta. Baptist. Home: 901 Waters St Waynesboro GA 30830 Office: 221 E 6TH St Waynesboro GA 30830

HARDER, LOIS MAYBELLE, cons.; b. Berwyn, Ill., Aug. 30, 1932; d. Clarence Louis and Rose (Johnson) Harder; B.S., Mary Washington Coll., 1953; M.S., MacMurray Coll., 1954; postgrad. N.Y. U., 1960-61. Instr. asst. prof. phys. edn. MacMurray Coll., 1953-60; asst. prof. Goucher Coll., Towson, Md., 1963-69. Riding dir. Camp. Illahec, N.C., 1953; instr. Mary Washington Coll., summer 1961; mem. div. girls and womens sports Nat. Riding Com., 1970—. Instr. life sav. and swimming A.R.C., 1953-67. Mem. Am. Bicentennial Research Inst. Mem. Am. Assn. U. Profs., Am. Assn. U. Women, A.A.H.P.E.R., Am., Va. horse shows assns. Republican. Presbyn. Home: 715 Deacon Rd Fredericksburg VA 22401

HARDESTY, JERRY WARREN, county agrl. agt.; b. nr. Elizabeth City, N.C., Aug. 2, 1935; s. Benjamon T. and Lena Pearl (Cannor) H.; B.S., N.C. State U., 1957, M.A., 1970; m. Mary Ann Jones, Sept. 4, 1955; children—Sheryl, Donna, Randal. Tchr., Great Bridge High Sch., Chesapeake, Va., 1957-58; asst. farm agt. Currituck County, N.C., 1958-63, county extension chmn., 1963—. Sec., Currituck Resources Council, 1963-65; chmn. Currituck Planning Bd., 1966—, chmn. exec. com., 1973; mem. Congress Nat. Rivers. Mem. N.C. County Agt. Assn. (pres., dist. 1971-72), N.C. Farm Markets Assn. (dir. 1971—). Baptist. Club: Ruritan (dist. gov. 1964-65; chmn. planning bd. 1966—). Address: Currituck NC 27929

HARDGRAVE, HOWARD DAVID, elec. engr.; b. Altus, Ark., Feb. 19, 1921; s. Archibald Harrison and Effie O. (Hightower) H.; B.S. in Elec. Engring., Tulane U., 1950; m. Vinita Gray, Oct. 16, 1942; children—David Howard, Sally Ann. With Buckeye Cellulose Corp., Memphis, 1950—, mech. supt., 1955-71, engring. design supt., 1972—. Served with USNR, 1942-45. Registered profl. engr., Tenn. Mem. Tau Beta Pi, Engrs. Club Memphis. Baptist. Home: 5367 Knollwood Dr Memphis TN 38117 Office: 2899 Jackson Av Memphis TN 38112

HARDIE, VIRGINIA SMITH (MRS. NEWTON GARY HARDIE), psychologist, educator; b. nr. Sycamore, Ga., June 12, 1907; d. Wilbur Riddick and Pearl (Fields) Smith; student Agnes Scott Coll., 1925-27; A.B., LaGrange Coll. 1929; M.A., U. Ga., 1933; postgrad. Columbia U. and N.Y. U., 1948-49, U. N.C., 1951; Ed.D., U. Colo., 1955; m. Newton Gary Hardie, Apr. 14, 1936 (dec. Nov. 1958). Tchr. Columbus (Ga.) High Sch., 1935-40, Atlanta and Fulton County high schs., 1940-43; supr., coordinator counseling and rehab. U.S. Army Hosp. Service, 1943-48; owner, dir. pvt. counseling offices N.Y.C. and Augusta, Ga., 1948-54; dir. counseling and placement Atlanta and Fulton County Schs., Atlanta, 1948-50; dir. guidance Richmond County Schs., Augusta, 1950-54; counselor trainer Colo. Dept. Vocational Edn., Denver, 1954-55; acting asst. prof. edn. U. Colo., 1954-55; prof. gerontology adult continuing edn. center Clemson (S.C.) Coll. 1957, 58; asso. prof. ednl. psychology U. Tenn., 1959-62; counseling psychologist, dir. counseling Clemson U., 1962—; vis. prof. various univs. and colls.; vocational cons.; psychol. cons. Dir. S.C. Nat. Bank. Bd. dirs. Presbyn. Coll., Clinton, S.C. Recipient Colo. Bus. and Profl. Women fellowship grant, 1954. Mem. Am., S.C. (tri-county pres. 1963-64) personnel and guidance assns., Am., Southeastern, S.C. psychol. assns., S.C. Mental Health Assn. (pres., mem. exec. bd.), Am. Assn. U. Profs., Am. Assn. U. Women (pres. Columbus 1937-38, 1st v.p. Ga. chpt. 1940-41, 1st v.p. Clemson chpt. 1955-56), Bus. and Profl. Women, League Women Voters, Pi Lambda Theta, Kappa Delta Pi, Kappa Alpha Theta (chpt. pres. 1928-29). Author: Women at Work. Club: Altrusa. Contbr. articles profl. jours. Home: PO Box 86 Pendleton SC 29670

HARDIMAN, RICHARD LAWRENCE, oil co. ofcl.; b. Cheviot, O., May 16, 1912; s. Randolph Lawrence and Bertha Celesta (Henderson) H.; A.A., Ashland Jr. Coll., 1948; B.S., Morehead State U., 1972; m. Ella Louise Stafford, May 18, 1941; children—Jane (Mrs. Charles E. Patterson), Martha (Mrs. George M. Prout). With Ashland Oil Co., Inc. (Ky.), 1933—, tech. service engr. product application dept., 1958—. Served with USNR, 1944-46. Mem. Am. Soc. Lubrication Engrs., Soc. Automotive Engrs., Presbyn. (deacon 1955-57, treas. 1955-57, 69-70, ruling elder 1959-61, 64-66, trustee 1965—). Home: 108 Bellefonte Dr Ashland KY 41101 Office: Ashland Oil Inc 21st and Front Sts Ashland KY 41101

HARDIN, EDWARD REEL, lawyer; b. Wadesboro, N.C., Sept. 26, 1936; s. Paul and Dorothy Elizabeth (Reel) H.; A.B., Duke, 1958, LL.B., 1960, J.D., 1970; m. Elizabeth McAshan Crawford, July 1, 1967. Admitted to N.C. bar, 1960; asso. James B. Lovelace, atty., High Point, N.C., 1961-62; partner Lovelace, Hardin & Bain, High Point, 1962-74; individual practice law, Banner Elk, N.C., 1974—; officer, dir. numerous corps.; sec. So. Film Extruders, Inc., High Point, 1966—; v.p. Cardinal Industries, Inc., High Point, 1969—; pvt. real estate developer, High Point, 1961—. Mem. Gov.'s com. Constl. Amendments, 1968-69; active A.R.C., Salvation Army Boys Club, United Appeal. Pres., Young Democrats Club, 1962-63, active many campaigns. Bd. dirs., pres. Youth Unltd., 1970-72. Served to capt. U.S. Army Res., 1961-69. Mem. Am. (del. 1967-69), N.C. (chmn. young lawyers sect. 1968-69), High Point (pres. elect 1973) bar assns., High Point Community Concert Assn. (pres. 1965-68), High Point C. of C. (hon. life mem.; dir. 1966—; pres. 1973), High Point Arts Council. Rotarian (v.p. 1973-74, pres. elect 1974-75). Address: Banner Elk NC 28604

HARDIN, EDWIN MILTON, civil engr.; b. Birmingham, Ala., June 11, 1926; s. Kyle Felton and Ella Ruth (Ferguson) H.; B.S. in C.E., U. Ala., 1956; m. Edith Loraine Williams, May 1, 1948; children—Judith, Jenny. Jr. structural engr. Rust Engring. Co., Birmingham, Ala., 1956-58; office engr. Walter Sch. Engring. Co., Birmingham, Ala., 1958-63; sr. design engr. Rust Engring. Co., Birmingham, Ala., 1963-68, chief structural engr., 1968-70, chief design engr., 1970—. Served with AUS, 1944-47, 50-52. Mem. Am. Soc. C.E. (pres. Birmingham br. 1970-71), Am. Ry. Engring. Assn., Tau Beta Pi, Chi Epsilon, Theta Tau, Phi Eta Sigma. Baptist. Mason (Shriner). Home: 916 Rockingham Rd Birmingham AL 35235 Office: PO Box 101 Birmingham AL 35201

HARDIN, GEORGE CECIL, JR., petroleum co. exec.; b. Oakwood, Tex., Oct. 6, 1920; s. George Cecil and Pearl (Moore) H.; B.S. in Geology and Petroleum Engring., Tex. A. and M. U., 1941; Ph.D. in Geology (Van Hise fellow 1941), U. Wis., 1942; m. Virginia Howard, Nov. 21, 1942; children—George Howard, Susan. Mining engr. Victory Fluorspar Mine, Cave in Rock, Ill., 1942; geologist U.S. Geol. Survey, 1942-45, party chief, 1944-45; geologist Carter Gragg Oil Co., Palestine, Tex., 1945-46; geologist, petroleum engr. M. T. Halbouty Cons. Firm, Houston, 1946-51; exploration and prodn. mgr. M.T. Halbouty Oil and Gas Interests, Houston, 1951-59, gen. mgr., 1959-61; exec. v.p. Halbouty Alaska Oil Co., 1957-61, dir., 1957—; pres. Ada Exco; v.p. Ada Oil Exploration Co., 1970-71; pres. Ashland Exploration Co., 1971—; sr. v.p. Ashland Oil, Inc., 1971—; partner Hardin and Hardin, cons. geologists, Houston, 1961-64; mgr. oil and gas exploration Kerr-McGee Oil Ind., Inc., 1964-65; v.p. N.Am. Oil & Gas Exploration, 1965-67, v.p. oil, gas and minerals exploration, 1967-68, group v.p. exploration, 1968; v.p. Kerr-McGee Argentina, 1967-68, Kerr-McGee Can., Ltd., 1967-68, Kerr-McGee Australia, Ltd., 1967-68; pres., chief exec. officer Royal Resources Corp., Houston, 1968—; dir. Continental Bank of Tex., Houston, 1956—, mem. exec. com., 1956-62, chmn. auditing com., 1962—; dir. North Side State Bank, Houston; owner Poverty Ridge Farm, Okla. City, 1966—. Registered profl. engr., Tex., Okla. Fellow Geol. Soc. Am., A.A.A.S.; mem. Houston Geol. Soc. (pres. 1961-62), Soc. Econ. Paleontologists and Mineralogists, New Orleans, South Tex. geol. socs., Gulf Coast Assn. Geol. Socs. (pres. 1959), Am. Assn. Petroleum Geologists (sec.-treas. 1964-66; chmn. house dels. 1971-72), Asn. Mexicana de Geologos Petroleros, Soc. Exploration Geophysicists Am. Inst. Profl. Geologists. Clubs: Petroleum (dir. 1956-58), Terra (dir. 1958-59); Brazos River Hunting and Fishing (dir. 1961-64),

Columbia Lakes Country (West Columbia, Tex.); River Oaks Country, Plaza (Houston). Author articles in field. Home: 204 Arborway Houston TX 77027 Office: PO Box 1503 Houston TX 77002

HARDIN, HILLIARD FRANCES, microbiologist; b. Columbia, S.C., Dec. 12, 1917; d. Lawrence Legare and Addria (Chreitzberg) Hardin; A.B., Duke, 1939, M.A., 1949, Ph.D., 1953. Microbiologist, Atomic Bomb Casualty Commn., Hiroshima, Japan, 1950-51; instr. U. Ark., 1953-57; research asso. Duke Med. Center, 1957-62, instr., 1962-63; supervisory microbiologist USPHS, 1963; chief mycology tng. unit Communicable Disease Center, Atlanta, 1963-68; chief microbiology lab. VA Hosp., Little Rock, 1968—; asso. prof. microbiology U. Ark. Med. Center, 1968—. Served with WAVES, USNR, 1942-45. Mem. Am. Thoracic Soc., N.Y. Acad. Sci., Med. Mycology Soc. Am., Sigma Xi, Pi Beta Phi. Home: Quapaw Towers Little Rock AR 72202 Office: Microbiology Lab VA Hosp 300 E Roosevelt Rd Little Rock AR 72206

HARDIN, IRA HAMILTON, constrn. co. exec.; b. Atlanta, Aug. 10, 1902; s. Lewis Sage and Zoe Daughtry (Lansing) H.; B.S. in M.E., Ga. Inst. Tech., 1924; m. Bessye Allen, Feb. 14, 1928; children—Allan Sage, Sandra (Mrs. Charles B. Bottoms, Jr.), Daughtry (Mrs. Richard R. King). Timekeeper, estimator, project exec. A.K. Adams Co., 1924-37; partner Hardin & Ramsey, 1937-46; pres. Ira H. Hardin Co., Atlanta, 1946-68, chmn. bd., chief exec. officer, 1968—; pres., Atlanta-DeKalb Indsl. Park, 1961-67; dir. Comml. Devel. Co. Bd. dirs. Fernbank, Inc., Druid Hills Civic Assn.; trustee Ga. Tech. Found., 1964—, Meth. Children's Home, Ira H. Hardin Found. Fellow Am. Inst. Constructors (dir. 1971—); mem. Cons. Constructors Council Asso. Gen. Contractors Am. (dir. Ga. br. 1946—, pres. 1948, nat. pres. 1965-66), Ga. Soc. Profl. Engrs., Atlanta, Ga. State, DeKalb chambers commerce, Ga. Tech. Nat. Alumni Assn. (pres. 1962), Delta Tau Delta, Ga. Tech. Anak Soc. Methodist (chmn. bd. stewards 1959-61). Clubs: Greater Atlanta Ga. Tech (pres. 1957), Atlanta Athletic (dir. 1953-63, pres. 1957-58, chmn. bd. 1959-60), Breakfast, Commerce, Capital City, Optimist (Atlanta); Royal Poinciana (Naples, Fla.). Home: 330 Blackland Rd NW Atlanta GA 30342 Office: 1380 W Paces Ferry Rd NW Atlanta GA 30327

HARDIN, SIDNEY LANIER, lawyer, lectr., commentator; b. Prairie Hill, Tex., Nov. 16, 1894; s. Lee P. and Clementine (Mitchell) H.; grad. Sam Houston State Coll., 1914; student U. Tex., summers 1914-19; Columbia U. seminar, 1920; U. Cal. at Berkeley, seminars, 1921-22, U. Tex. Law Sch., summer 1929; m. Lucille Mason, Oct. 12, 1935 (dec.); children—Sidney Lee, Margaret Francis, John C.; m. 2d, Lucile Hill. Supt. city schs., Mission, Tex., 1917-32; admitted to Tex. bar, 1930; dist. atty., Edinburg, Tex., 1932-35; pvt. practice law, Edinburg, 1935—; city atty., Edinburg, 1950-54, radio commentator covering Southwestern States, 1940—; lectr., after-dinner speaker, 1924—. Polit. speaker nat. campaigns, 1940— mem. speakers staff of Lifeline Seminars, N.C., Washington. Bd. dirs. Pan-Am. Cancer Found., San Antonio. Recipient Congress of Freedom Liberty award Alcalde of San Antonio (hon. mayor for life), 1963; Silver medal award S.A.R.; George Washington Honor Medal award Freedoms Found., 1970. Mem. Inter-Am. Bar Assn., State Bar Tex., Internat. Platform Assn., U.S. C. of C. Democrat. Baptist. Rotarian (gov. 47th dist., hon. life mem.). Home: 121 Austin Blvd Edinburg TX 75839 Office: First State Bank Bldg Edinburg TX 78539

HARDIN, THOMAS JARREAU, newspaper pub. co. exec.; b. Dallas, Apr. 4, 1928; s. Thomas Anderson and Minnie Lou (Jarreau) H.; student So. Meth. U., 1946-48, diploma Southwestern Sch. Banking, 1960; m. Betsy Boyer, Apr. 12, 1969; children—Cristin Gay, Julia Key, Beverly Jean, Thomas A.J. Bookkeeper-teller Hillcrest State Bank, Dallas, 1948-51; communications engr. Southwestern Bell Telephone Co., 1951-55; asst. v.p., asst. cashier Hillcrest State Bank, Dallas, 1955-58; v.p., cashier N.W. Nat. Bank, 1958-60, pres., 1960-61; v.p., cashier, dir. Park Cities Bank & Trust Co., Dallas, 1960-65; bus. mgr. Dallas Cowboys Football Club, Dallas, 1965-71; sec.-treas., gen. mgr., advt. dir. McCormick & Co., Inc., pub. Daily Town Talk, Alexandria, La., 1971—. Trustee Pub. Affairs Research Council La. Mem. Alex-Pineville Area C. of C. (v.p. 1972-73). Rotarian, Lion. Home: 4309 Wendover Alexandria LA 71301 Office: PO Box 7558 Alexandria LA 71301

HARDING, CHARLES TAYLOE, design, engring. and distbn. cons.; b. Washington, N.C., Dec. 15, 1901; s. Charles Edwin and Sarah Pauline (Whitehurst) H.; student Internat. Corr. Schs., 1924, hon. diploma, 1965; m. Maude Meekins, Apr. 30, 1923 (dec. July 1954); children—Sally (Mrs. L.B. Hasty), Maude (Mrs. J.R. Blakely); m. 2d, Mary Alice Moncure, June 2, 1956; children—Mary Moncure, Charles Tayloe. With Mobil Oil Co. (formerly Va. Carolina Chem. Corp.), 1917-67, pres. Va. Carolina, 1959-63, group v.p. Mobil, 1963-66; v.p., cons. Davy Powergas Inc., Lakeland, Fla., 1967—. Clubs: Lakeland Yacht and Country, Lone Palm Golf (Lakeland). Home: 2402 Newport Av Lakeland FL 33803 Office: PO Box 2436 Lakeland FL 33803

HARDING, HENRY KNOWLES, architect; b. Dedham, Mass., Dec. 20, 1904; s. Charles Lewis and Harriet Appleton (Knowles) H.; grad. St. Georges Sch., 1924; B.S., Princeton, 1928; B. Architecture, U. Pa., 1930; postgrad. Fontainbleu Sch., Paris, 1930, N.Y.U., 1935; m. Lynn Saul, Oct. 17, 1953; children—Florence Harding, Priscilla, Katherine, Susan, Henry Knowles. Owner, Henry K. Harding, architect, Palm Beach, Fla., 1936—. Mem. town council, Ocean Ridge, Fla., 1960, mem. zoning and planning bd., 1967. Served to lt. comdr. USNR, 1941-44. Club: Ivy (Princeton). Home: Dolphin Rd Ocean Ridge FL 33444 Office: 318 Royal Poinciana Plaza Palm Beach FL 33480

HARDING, JACK, chem. mfg. co. exec.; b. LaPorte, Ind., Feb. 7, 1914; s. John Egbert and Sadie Jo (Rogers) H.; B.S. in Elec. Engring., Tex. A. and M. U., 1934; m. Lela Loudder, Dec. 27, 1946; children—Jacqueline (Mrs. David T. Blake), Jill (Mrs. William N. McDonald III), Benjamin Rogers, Jane (Mrs. R.T. Srader), John Philip. Designer, Kelvinator Corp., Detroit, 1934-37; div. sales mgr. Canada Dry Ginger Ale Co., Dallas, 1937-40; gen. mgr. Skillern Drug Stores, Dallas, 1946-50; v.p. marketing Southland Corp., Dallas, 1950-56; account exec. Tracy-Locke Advt. Agy., Dallas, 1956-58; self-employed as lectr., sales, training and mgmt. cons., Dallas, 1958-67; chief exec. Big "D" Chem. Co., Oklahoma City, 1967—, also dir. Served with AUS, 1940-46. Recipient Annual award Nat. Pet Assn., 1967. Mem. Internat. San. Supply Assn. (dir. 1973-75), Nat. Pet Assn. (exec. sec. 1960-67). Republican. Mem. Christian Ch. (lay minister 1954—). Rotarian. Author: Retail Selling Is Fun, 1970. Patentee in field. Home: 6401 N Sterling Dr Oklahoma City OK 73132 Office: 1708 W Main St Oklahoma City OK 73106

HARDING, JAMES LOMBARD, oceanographer; b. Harvey, Ill., Aug. 4, 1929; s. Herbert Paine and Ida Mae (Wissell) H.; B.S., U. South Miss., 1956; M.S., U. Tenn., 1957; Ph.D., Tex. A. and M. U., 1964; m. Meredith Janett Reese, Aug. 28, 1954. Asst. prof. geology U. South Miss., 1959-60; research scientist Tex. A. and M. U., 1963-64; v.p., Oceanonics, Inc., 1964-71; geologic oceanography cons. Marine Resources Center, Savannah, Ga., 1971—; dir. Engring. Enterprises, Houston, 1966-68. Cons. Oceaneering Internat., Houston, 1971—. Served with AUS, 1951-53. Fellow Geol. Soc. Am.; mem. Am. Inst. Profl. Geologists, Sigma Xi. Home: 1708 Stillwood Dr Savannah GA 31406 Office: Skidaway Inst Oceanography PO Box 13987 Savannah GA 31406

HARDING, JOHN ELDON, indsl. engr.; b. New Castle, Ind., Feb. 19, 1919; s. Ambrose O. and Lillie (Means) H.; C.E., U. Cin., 1943; m. Charlotte Thompson, Sept. 2, 1945; children—Susan (Mrs. Stephen Craft), John T. With nuclear div. Union Carbide Corp., Oak Ridge, 1946—, dept. head, 1964—. Mem. Oak Ridge Town Council, 1947; mem. Oak Ridge Planning Commn., 1962—, chmn., 1970—. Served with AUS, 1943-46. Mem. Am. Inst. Indsl. Engrs. (named outstanding engr. 1971), Tenn. Soc. Profl. Engrs. Registered profl. engr., Tenn. Mason. Home: 108 Dana Dr Oak Ridge TN 37830 Office: Union Carbide Corp Box Y Oak Ridge TN 37830

HARDISON, JOSEPH HAMMOND, printing co. exec.; b. Wadesboro, N.C., Jan. 31, 1897; s. William Cameron and Harriet Eleanor (Bennett) H.; student U. N.C., 1913-16; m. Katherine Clark Smith, June 7, 1918; children—Katherine Smith (Mrs. Robert Vaughn Lamb), Sarah Locke (Mrs. Paul Frederick Hoch), Joseph Hammond. With Coxe-Bennett Lumber Co., Wadesboro, 1916-18; mng. partner Hardison-Coxe Lumber Co., Wrightsville, Ga., 1919-23; v.p. Edwards & Broughton Co., Raleigh, N.C., 1923-60, pres., 1960-69, chmn. bd., 1969—. Mem. Draft Bd. 93, 1958-72, chmn., 1971. Bd. dirs. Raleigh United Fund, 1954, Carolina United Fund, 1955, Rex Hosp. Found., 1966; trustee Rex Hosp., 1955-66. Served to 2d lt. AUS, 1918-19. Recipient Distinguished Citizen award City of Raleigh, 1970. Mem. Kappa Sigma, Omicron Delta Kappa. Episcopalian (sr. warden 1957-58). Clubs: Civitan (pres. 1946-47), Carolina Country, Executives (pres. 1954-55) (Raleigh). Home: 915 Holt Dr Raleigh NC 27608 Office: 1821 North Blvd Raleigh NC 27611

HARDLEY, GARY KAYE, social work exec.; b. Pontiac, Mich., Dec. 30, 1931; s. Walter Arnold and Virginia (Gaynor) H.; B.S., Wheaton Coll., 1956; M.S.W., Fla. State U., 1960; postgrad. Miss. So. U., 1960-61, Fla. State U., 1966, U. Va., 1970—; m. Wilma Elizabeth Culpepper, Aug. 8, 1939; children—Kay Marie, William Arnold, Brenda June, David Jonathan, Gary Paul. Tchr. Buckley (Mich.) High Sch., 1956-57; mgr. Clark Oil & Refining Co., Glen Ellyn, Ill., 1957-58; psychiat. social worker VA Center, Gulfport, Miss., 1960-61; casework supr. Evang. Child Welfare Agy., Chgo., 1961-64; dir. social service Woodstock (Ill.) Children's Home, 1964-65; field work instr. Fla. State U., 1965-67; exec. dir., marriage counselor Community Counseling Center Inc., Columbus, Ga., 1967-70; exec. dir., marriage and family counselor Family Service, Charlottesville, Va., 1970—; instr. devel. program academically retarded Columbus Coll., 1968-70; instr. marriage and family Madison Coll., Harrisonburg, Va., 1973—; instr. contemporary living Lane High Sch., Charlottesville, Sch. Continuing Edn. U. Va. Mem. adv. bd. Youth Counseling Service. Mem. Am. Assn. Marriage and Family Counselors, Acad. Certified Social Workers, Nat. Alliance For Family Life (charter), Nat. Council Family Relations, Am. Assn. Sex Educators and Counselors. Home: 1035 Locust Av Charlottesville VA 22901 Office: 116 W Jefferson St Charlottesville VA 22902

HARDWICK, CHARLES VINCENT, judge; b. Kinsale, Va., Sept. 1, 1910; s. Vincent Branson and Willie (Unruh) H.; student U. Va., 1929-32; LL.B., George Washington U., 1937; m. Mary Elizabeth McBirney, July 3, 1937; children—Charles Vincent, Ann McBirney. Admitted to Va. bar, 1937; practice law, Tappahannock, Va., 1937-58; judge, county, juvenile and domestic relations cts., Essex, Richmond and Westmoreland counties, Tappahannock, 1958-72; judge 11th Regional Juvenile and Domestic Relations Ct., 1972-73, 15th Dist. Juvenile and Domestic Relations Cts., 1973—. Served to 2d lt. inf. AUS, 1945. Mem. Va., No. Neck bar assns., Delta Upsilon. Democrat. Methodist. Lion. Club: Ruritan. Home: Hwy 17 Tappahannock VA 22560 Office: 215 Queen St Tappahannock VA 22560

HARDWICK, GALLY JEFF, JR., architect; b. Little Rock, Oct. 25, 1922; s. Gally Jeff and Charlotte Elizabeth (Barber) H.; student Ark. Poly. Coll., 1940-42, U. Ark., 1942, 46-47; m. Flo E. Parchman, May 15, 1944; children—Jeff Norman, John C. Sr. draftsman Swaim & Allen, architects, 1947-59; asso., Swaim-Allen-Wellborn & Assos., architects, Little Rock, 1959-73; partner Swaim-Allen-Welborn & Assos., architects, Little Rock, 1974—. Mem. Spl. Com. on Edn., North Little Rock, Ark., 1966-67. Served to maj. USAAF, 1943-46; ETO, PTO. Mem. A.I.A., Constrn. Specifications Inst. (dir. Little Rock chpt. 1967-70), Little Rock, North Little Rock chambers commerce. Democrat. Baptist (mem. planning com. 1970-73). Clubs: Optomist (dir. 1956-57) North Hills Country (both North Little Rock, Ark.). Prin. archtl. works include Park Hill Bapt. Ch., North Little Rock, Ark., Vocational-Music Bldg. Ark. Sch. for the Blind, Little Rock, addition to St. Vincent Infirmary, Little Rock. Home: 923 E H Av North Little Rock AR 72116 Office: 215 Louisiana St Little Rock AR 72201

HARDWICK, JON EASTMAN, accountant; b. Baird, Tex., Jan. 15, 1932; s. Eastman Lane and Nell (Cox) H.; B.B.A., W.Tex. State U., 1957; m. Betty Zoe Cunningham, Nov. 8, 1957; children—Crecia, Lydia. Self employed as C.P.A., Baird, 1959—; dir. Carmichael Oil Co., Inc.; owner Hardwick Ins. Agy., 1964—. Chmn., Housing Authority, Baird, 1962-73; Presdl. elector, 1968; city councilman, City of Baird, Tex., 1973—. C.P.A., Tex. Mem. Tex. Soc. C.P.A.'s, Tex. Assn. Ins. Agts., Baird C. of C. (pres. 1969-71). Democrat. Methodist (trustee, treas. 1964—). K.P., Lion. Home: 613 Cherry St Baird TX 79504 Office: 322 Market St Baird TX 79504

HARDY, DERRICK, assn. exec.; b. Mafeking, South Africa, Jan. 31, 1931; s. George Spencer and Rose Nelly (Somers) H.; student architecture U. Natal (South Africa), 1948-52; m. Valerie Rodliffe, Sept. 5, 1953; children—Carol, George Derrick. Came to U.S., 1959, naturalized, 1966. Mgr., Central Agencies & Import Co., Durban, South Africa, 1953-59; v.p. Jacksonville Tile Co. (Fla.), 1959-65; exec. sec. Nat. Terrazzo & Mosaic Assn., Inc., Alexandria, Va., 1965—. Vice pres. Strawberry Hills Estates Civic Assn., Bryans Road, Md., 1971-72; chmn. troop com. Nat. Capital Area council Boy Scouts Am., 1972—. Mem. Constrn. Specifications Inst. Presbyn. (elder). Club: Strawberry Hills Swim and Racquet (trustee). Author: Terrazzo Design Data Book, 1972; Terrazzo Technical Data Book, 1973. Home: Route 1 Box 67 Round Hill VA 22141 Office: 716 Church St Alexandria VA 22314

HARDY, FLORENCE C. (MRS. WILLIAM G. HARDY), city ofcl.; b. Pawtucket, R.I.; d. William E. and Mary Baker (Burns) Calland; student Brown U., 1919, U. Fla., 1958; m. William Guthrie Hardy, Jan. 8, 1920; children—Abigail Walker (Mrs. Paul Rust), William Guthrie. Statistician Providence Dist. Nursing Assn., 1915-25; asst. sec. C. of C., Fort Lauderdale, Fla., 1925-26; sec. to pres. First Nat. Bank, 1927-28; asst. acting city mgr. Fort Lauderdale, Fla., 1928—, acting personnel dir., 1946-51, exec. asst. to commn., 1955, city auditor, 1937-39, clk., 1957-63, ret., 1963. Mem. Ft. Lauderdale City Charter Com., 1964-66. Trustee Stranahan Found. Fund. Named Woman of Yr., Bus. and Profl. Woman's Club, 1954; recipient Distinguished Service award Rotary Club, 1959. Kiwanis Club, 1966; Rosicrucian award, 1963; Florence C. Hardy Park dedicated, 1963. Mem. Ft. Lauderdale Hist. Soc. (a founder, pres., acting dir.). Episcopalian. Club: Zonta. Home: 325 SE 9th Av Fort Lauderdale FL 33301 Office: 850 NE 12th Av Extension Holiday Park Fort Lauderdale Fl 33304

HARDY, FRANK LEWIS, constrn. co. exec.; b. Columbus, Ind., July 30, 1910; s. Frank Lewis and Eunice (Kirk) H.; B.S., Auburn U., 1933; m. Margaret Wood, July 30, 1935; children—Mary Margaret (Mrs. David Phillips), Susan Henderson. Jr. engr. West Point Foundry & Machine Co., 1933-34; engring.-contracting trainee York Corp., Pa., 1934-36, zone mgr., Birmingham, Ala., 1936-39; v.p. Rushton Equipment Co., 1940-52; pres., chmn. Hardy Corp., Birmingham, 1953— and affiliates Marwood Corp. and Marsue Realty Co., Inc.; dir. Central Bank & Trust Co., Birmingham, Diversified Foundries, Inc., Birmingham, Thomas Foundries, Inc.; Birmingham, Pollution Control Walther Co. Am. Soc. Heating, Refrigeration and Air Conditioning Engrs., Blue Key, Omicron Delta Kappa, Phi Delta Theta. Clubs: Birmingham Country, Mountain Brook Country (Birmingham). Home: 45 Ridge Dr Birmingham AL 35213 Office: Hardy Corp 430 12th St S Birmingham AL 35233

HARDY, GEORGE FRANCIS, JR., hosp. adminstr.; b. Boston, Aug. 29, 1913; s. George Francis and Ida May (Kenney) H.; B.B.A., Bentley Coll., 1937; m. Eileen Corwin, June 13, 1943; 1 son, David. Pub. accountant Scovell Wellington Co., Boston, 1930-38; office mgr. Sawyer Constrn. Co., 1938-48; asso. adminstr. Good Samaritan Hosp., West Palm Beach, Fla., 1948-67; adminstr. Coral Ridge Psychiat. Hosp., Ft. Lauderdale, Fla., 1967—. Sec.-treas. Broward County area Planning Council, Ft. Lauderdale, 1971—. Served with AUS, 1942-44. Fellow Am. Coll. Hosp. Adminstrs.; mem. Am. Hosp. Assn. Home: 5200 N Ocean Blvd Fort Lauderdale FL 33308 Office: 4545 N Federal Hwy Fort Lauderdale FL 33308

HARDY, HARVEY LOUCHARD, lawyer; b. Dallas, Dec. 2, 1914; s. Nat L. and Winifred (Fouraker) H.; student San Antonio Coll., 1932-33; m. E. Vivian Bedell, Feb. 14, 1948; children—Victoria Elizabeth, Alice Anne. Admitted to Tex. bar, 1936; since practiced San Antonio; 1st asst. dist. atty. Bexar County, Tex., 1947-51; city atty. San Antonio, 1952-53, Castle Hills, 1959—, Leon Valley, 1967—. Served as 1st lt. Inf., AUS, 1941-45. Decorated Bronze Star medal with cluster. Fellow State Bar Tex.; mem. Am., San Antonio bar assns., Am. Judicature Soc. Methodist. Home: 215 Atwater St San Antonio TX 78213 Office: GPM Life Bldg San Antonio TX 78216

HARDY, ROBERT CARLISLE, financial cons., broker; b. Buffalo, Nov. 8, 1904; s. Robert C. and Alicia (Carlisle) H.; B.S., Dartmouth, 1925; J.D., Columbia, 1928; m. Hilda Carswell Hardy, May 12, 1956. Admitted to N.Y. bar, 1928; mem. firm Wilkie, Owen, Farr, Gallagher & Walton, 1937-49; financial cons., 1949-58; chmn. bd., dir. Hardy, Hardy & Assos., Inc., 1958—; mem. Phila.-Balt.-Wash. Stock Exchange; asso. mem. Boston Stock Exchange, Pitts. Stock Exchange, 1959—; mem. Montreal Stock Exchange, 1961—, Cin. Stock Exchange, 1969—; dir. James T. White & Co. Mem. Whitfield-Ballentine Zoning Commn. Mem. Sarasota C. of C., Whitfield-Ballentine Manor Estates Assn., So. Srs. Golf Assn., Am., N.Y., N.Y. County bar assns., Delta Tau Delta, Phi Delta Phi. Clubs: Sara Bay Country, Sarasota Yacht, Ivy League, Dartmouth of Sarasota, Field, 200, World Seniors. Home: 1130 Whitfield Av Sarasota FL 33580 Office: 3640 S Tamiami Trail PO Box 15447 Sarasota FL 33579

HARE, BRUCE EDWARD, lawyer; b. Amarillo, Tex., Nov. 10, 1941; s. Edward and Lahoma Juanita (Groom) Baumel; B.B.A., U. Okla., 1965, J.D., 1968. Admitted to Tex. bar, 1968; asst. to pres. Nunn Electric, Lubbock, 1968-71, sales mgr., 1971-72, legal counsel, 1972—. Bd. dirs., trustee Nunn Electric Profit Sharing Plan, 1969—. Firm chmn. United Fund, 1973. Mem. State Bar Tex., Phi Alpha Delta. Office: PO Drawer 1947 1817 4th St Lubbock TX 79408

HARE, OTHELLO OSCAR, JR., banker; b. Houston, Mar. 11, 1930; s. Othello Oscar and Ora Dell (Harvey) H.; B.B.A., U. Tex., 1952; m. Nelwyn Joyce Gramling, June 14, 1952; children—Candice Lynn, Rebecca Ann, Susan Beth, Maralyn Carol. With Arthur Andersen & Co., C.P.A.'s, Houston, 1954-63; with North Side Bank, Houston, 1963—, pres., 1971—, chief exec. officer, 1967—, also dir.; dir. Crosby State Bank (Tex.). Served with USMCR, 1952-54. C.P.A., Tex. Mem. Am. Bankers Assn., Am. Inst. Banking, Am. Inst. C.P.A.'s, Tex. Soc. C.P.A.'s. Clubs: Houston Racquet, Houston. Home: 11827 Wink St Houston TX 77024 Office: 2010 N Main St Houston TX 77009

HARE, ROY ALLEN, physician; b. Sanford, N.C., Apr. 2, 1921; s. Simpson Turner and Halsie (Holleman) H.; B.S., Wake Forest Coll., 1942; M.D., Bowman Gray Sch. Medicine, 1945; m. Myrtle Frances Brandon, June 20, 1945; children—Joyce (Mrs. Lowell Hugh Mallard), Roy Allen, George Brandon, Ellen Penny. Intern Hartford (Conn.) Hosp., 1945-46; resident in internal medicine Bapt. Hosp., Winston-Salem, N.C., 1949-51; practice medicine specializing in internal medicine, Durham, N.C., 1951—; mem. staff Watts Hosp., Durham, 1951—; cons. N.C. Meml. Hosp., Chapel Hill, 1956—. Served with USAF, 1947-49. Mem. A.C.P., N.C., Durham-Orange County med. socs., U.S. Power Squadron (comdr. Durham 1973-74). Baptist. Kiwanian. Club: Hope Valley Country (Durham). Home: 3828 Somerset Dr Durham NC 27707 Office: 731 Broad St Durham NC 27705

HARE, WILLIAM ROSS, lawyer; b. Chester, S.C., Aug. 6, 1934; s. Robert Lee and Maggie Mobley (Yongue) H.; A.B., U. S.C., 1956, J.D., 1958; m. Elizabeth Rudell Maffett, Aug. 25, 1956; children—Elisa Moffett, William Ross. Admitted to S.C. bar, 1958; practiced in Chester, 1963—; mem. firm Hemphill, Hemphill & Hare, Chester, 1971—; solicitor 6th Circuit, 1970—. Campaign chmn. United Fund, 1965; mem. Tri-County Mental Health Commn., 1966-69. Pres. Chester County Airport Commn., 1965-68; dir. Chester County Devel. Bd., pres. elect, 1974. Served with USAF, 1958-63. Mem. U. S.C. Alumni Assn. (circuit v.p. 1974), Am. Legion. Moose, Rotarian. Home: Center St Chester SC 29706 Office: Drawer 838 Chester SC 29706

HARGIS, LOUIS LANE, civil engr.; b. Bartlett, Tex., Oct. 19, 1936; s. Jewell Bryan and Sarah Louisa (Lane) H.; student Arlington State Coll., 1955-59; B.S. in C.E., Tex. A. and M. U., 1962, M.S., 1963; m. Mary Ann Mosby, Dec. 8, 1956; children—Holly Ann, Julie Michele. Soils and materials engr. Forrest & Cotton, Inc., Dallas, 1962-65, HNTB Engrs., 1965-69; constrn. engr., project mgr. Dahlstrom Corp., Dallas, 1969-72; with Mitchell & Assos., Dallas, 1972—, chief engr., 1972—, gen. mgr., exec. v.p., 1973—. Registered profl. engr., Tex., La., Okla Mem. Nat., Tex. socs. profl. engrs., Constrn. Specifications Inst. Club: Cordelier of Tex. Home: 1705 Windchime St Dallas TX 75224 Office: 11462 Harry Hines St Dallas TX 75229

HARGRAVE, WILLIAM LOFTIN, bishop; b. Wilson N.C., Nov. 10, 1903; s. Benjamin Worthington and Frances (Daniel) H.; LL.B., Atlanta Law Sch., 1924; B.D., Va. Theol. Sem., 1932, D.D., 1962; S.T.M., U. of South, 1952, D.D., 1962; m. Minnie Frances Whittington, Feb. 13, 1939; children—Frances, Elizabeth, Sarah, William. Admitted to Ga. bar, 1925; asst. trust officer Miami Bank &

Trust Co. (Fla.), 1924-26; asso. firm Shutts & Bowen, Miami, 1926-27; ordained to ministry Episcopalian Ch., 1932; rector in Cocoa, Fla., 1932-43, Ft. Pierce, Fla., 1943-45, Holy Comforter Ch., Miami, 1945-48, Holy Communion Ch., Charleston, S.C., 1948-53; exec. sec. Diocese of South Fla., Winter Park, 1953-61, bishop 1961-69; bishop Diocese of S.W. Fla., St. Petersburg, 1969—. Pres. Wuesthoff Hosp. Cocoa, Fla., 1941-43, Porter Mil. Acad. Charleston, 1952. Pres. Fla. Council Chs., 1957-58, Fla. Migrant Ministry, 1963-66; mem. gen. bd. Nat. Council Chs. Christ, 1964-69. Clubs: Rotary (pres. Cocoa 1937); Orlando (Fla.) Country; St. Petersburg Yacht. Home: 1701 Brightwaters Blvd NE St Petersburg FL 33704 Office: Box 20899 St Petersburg FL 33742

HARGREAVES, MARY WILMA MASSEY (MRS. HERBERT WALTER HARGREAVES), editor, educator; b. Erie, Pa., Mar. 1, 1914; d. Albert Edward and Bess (Childs) Massey; A.B., Bucknell U., 1935; M.A., Radcliffe Coll., 1936, Ph.D., 1951; fellow Brookings Instn., 1939-40; m. Herbert Walter Hargreaves, Aug. 24, 1940. Research editor Harvard Grad. Sch. Bus. Adminstrn., 1937-39; asso. editor Papers of Henry Clay, U. Ky., Lexington, 1952-72, co-editor, 1972—, asst. prof. history, 1964-69, asso. prof., 1969-73, prof., 1973—. Mem. Am. Assn. U. Women (chpt. pres. 1957-59, state dir. 1957-64, 66-71), Am. Assn. U. Profs., Am., So. hist. assns., Orgn. Am. Historians, Agrl. History Soc., Phi Beta Kappa (chpt. sec. 1964-70, pres. 1970-71), Phi Alpha Theta, Sigma Tau Delta. Author: Dry Farming in the Northern Great Plains, 1957. Contbr. articles to profl. jours. Home: 237 Cassidy Av Lexington KY 40502 Office: Office Tower U Ky Lexington KY 40506

HARGROVE, FRED LEONARD, lawyer; b. Bonham, Tex., Aug. 15, 1896; s. Oswald L. and Nettie (Leonard) H.; student U. Tex., 1913-14, La. State U., 1915-16; m. George Josephine Southerland, Nov. 29, 1919; 1 dau., Nettie (Mrs. William Edward Jobron). Admitted to La. bar, 1917; mem. law dept. Standard Oil Co. La., Shreveport and New Orleans, 1919-35; mem. firm Wilkinson, Lewis & Wilkinson, 1935-37; sr. mem. firm Hargrove, Guyton, Ramey & Barlow, Shreveport, La., 1946—; dir. Comml. Nat. Bank, Shreveport. Exec. v.p., Norton Oil Co., Shreveport, 1953—. Pres., Shreveport Goodwill, 1950. Vice pres. bd. control R.W. Norton Art Found., 1946—. Served to sgt. U.S. Army, 1918-19. Recipient (with another) United Fund Annual award for distinguished service, 1956. Mem., Am., La., Shreveport bar assns., Am. Judicature Soc. Presbyn. (elder, trustee). Clubs: Shreveport (past pres.), Petroleum. Home: 847 Prospect St Shreveport LA 71104 Office: PO Drawer B Shreveport LA 71161

HARKESS, JAMES WILSON, physician; b. Edinburgh, Scotland, June 26, 1925; s. John Wilson and Catherine Sinclair (Martin) H.; M.B., Ch.B., U. Edinburgh, 1948; m. Janice Beecher, Mar. 20, 1954; children—John R., James W., Jane Catherine. Came to U.S., 1952, naturalized, 1959. Intern St. Martin's Hosp., Bath, Somerset, Eng., 1948-49, 50-51; resident, Princess Margaret Hosp., Edinburgh, 1951, Albany (N.Y.) Hosp., 1952-55, Guis Hosp. and Eastern N.Y. Rehab. Hosp., 1955-56; instr. orthopaedics and anatomy Albany Med. Coll., 1953-56; asst. chief orthopedics Eugene Talmadge Meml. Hosp., Augusta, Ga., 1958-67; instr. surgery Med. Coll. Ga., 1958-60, asst. prof. surgery, 1960-62, asso. prof., 1962-64, prof., 1964-67; Kosair prof. orthopaedic surgery U. Louisville, 1967—; practice medicine, specializing in orthopaedic surgery, 1952—; orthopaedic cons. Jewish Hosp., VA Hosp.; chief orthopaedic service Louisville Gen. Hosp., 1967—. Served to capt. Royal Army Med. Corps, 1949-50, AUS, 1956-58. Mem. Am. Acad. Orthopaedic Surgeons, A.M.A., Assn. Bone & Joint Surgeons, Ky. Med. Assn., Ky. Orthopaedic Soc. (sec.-treas. 1970-73), Louisville Orthopaedic Soc. (sec.-treas. 1972—), Louisville Medico-Chirugical Soc. (pres. 1972—), Assn. Orthopaedic Chmn. (sec.-treas. 1971—), Am. Soc. Surgery Trauma, Lamplighters' Orthopedic Soc., Am. Rheumatism Assn., Clin. Orthopedic Soc. Home: 3011 Lightheart Rd Louisville KY 40222 Office: 982 Eastern Pkwy Louisville KY 40217

HARKEY, JOHN DANIEL, feed co. exec.; b. Brady, Tex., Sept. 7, 1933; s. Audie Mann and Hattie Emily (Hasse) H.; student Tex. A. and M. U., 1950-51; B.S., Tex. Technol. Coll., 1954; m. Lucy Love Wallace, May 4, 1959; 1 son, John Daniel. Dist. sales mgr. Moorman Mfg. Co., Mason, Tex., 1957-60; product mgr. Am. Cyanamid Co., Princeton, N.J., 1960-66; gen. mgr. Lamkin Bros., Inc. div. Nat. Chemsearch Corp., Dallas, 1966-68; pres. Triple F Feeds, Brownwood, Tex., 1968—; pres. S.W. Livestock Co., Brownwood, 1973—; dir. A.M. Harkey Inc., Mason. Trustee Brownwood Sch. Bd. Served to capt. USAF, 1954-58. Mem. C. of C. Methodist. Home: 4107 Glenwood St Brownwood TX 76801 Office: Box 429 Brownwood TX 76801

HARKEY, PAUL, lawyer; b. Idabel, Okla., Mar. 4, 1920; s. John Paul and Jessie (Elliott) H.; B.A., Southeastern State Coll., 1950; J.D. U. Okla., 1961; m. Lucille Roy, June 1, 1942; children—Cheryl Annette, Roy Lee, John Paul. Admitted to Okla. bar, 1948; practice law, Idabel, 1948-55; atty. DeLeuw Cather Engrs., 1955-59; atty. Okla. Hwy. Dept., 1959-64; adminstrv. law judge U.S. Dept. Health, Edn. and Welfare, Dallas, 1964—. Mem. Okla. Legislature, 1946-54; chmn. So. regional edn. bd. Council on Mental Health and Tng., 1955-59. Served with USNR, 1940-46; ETO, PTO; capt. Res. Named to Okla. Med. Scis. Hall of Fame, 1958. Mem. Am. Judicature Soc., Am., Fed., Dallas, Okla. bar assns., State Bar Tex., Am. Soc. Trial lawyers, Nat. Conf. Trial Examiners, Order of Coif, Phi Delta Phi. Mason (Shriner). Home: Box 22122 Dallas TX 75222 Office: 1512 Commerce St Dallas TX 75202

HARKINS, CARL GIRVIN, educator; b. Colorado City, Tex., June 14, 1939; s. Carl Gracey and Victoria Marie (Girvin) H.; B.A. cum laude, McMurry Coll., 1960; M.A., Johns Hopkins, 1962, Ph.D., 1964; m. Elizabeth Ann Stone, Sept. 7, 1960; children—Carl Girvin, Paul Channing, Kimberly Ann. Asst. prof. phys. chemistry, acting dir. materials research Southwest Center for Advanced Studies, Dallas, 1966-68; sr. research chemist, dir. stress corrosion research, adj. asst. prof. materials sci. Rice U., Houston, 1968—. Research dir., Harkins Tech. Services, Houston, 1972—. Postdoctoral fellow, U. Cal. at Berkeley, Stanford, and Lawrence Radiation Lab., 1964-65, Rice U., 1965-66. Fellow Am. Inst. Chemists, Chem. Soc. Britain; mem. Nat. Assn. Corrosion Engrs. (chmn. edn. 1972—), Am. Chem. Soc., Catalysis Soc., A.A.A.S., Sigma Xi, Phi Lambda Upsilon, Alpha Chi. Clubs: Houston Underwater, Internat. Underwater Explorers Society. Methodist. Contbr. articles to profl. jours.

HARKINS, HERSCHEL SPRINGFIELD, lawyer, state rep.; b. Asheville, N.C., Mar. 22, 1917; s. Thomas J. and Roxy (Seevers) H.; student Davidson Coll., 1933-35; A.B., U. N.C., 1938, LL.B., 1940; m. Mary Anne Koonce, Dec. 23, 1968; children—(by previous marriage) Jane (Mrs. Larry M. Cairnes), Spring, Hope. Admitted to N.C. bar, 1940; practiced in Asheville, 1940—; mem. firm Harkins, Van Winkle and Walton, 1940-49, Herschel S. Harkins, 1949—; mem. N.C. Ho. of Reps., 1967—. Mem. N.C. Cts. Commn., 1969-71; chmn. Army Adv. Com. 1949-54; mem. N.C. Local Govt. Study Commn., 1967-71, N.C. Child Care Study Commn., 1967-69. Pres., Asheville Community Theater, 1949. Pres. Buncombe County Young Democratic Club, 1963. Bd. dirs., sec. Victoria Hosp., 1952-54; bd. govs. Sports Car Club of Am., 1964, 66-67. Served to maj. USAAF, 1942-46. Decorated D.F.C., Air medal with twelve oak leaf clusters, Silver Star medal. Mem. Am., N.C., Buncombe County (v.p. 1954) bar assns., Am. Judicature Soc., Asheville C. of C., Phi Delta Theta. Democrat. Episcopalian. Mason (32 deg.). Clubs: Asheville Country, Mountain City (sec. 1954). Home: 5 Griffing Blvd Asheville NC 28804 Office: PO Box 7266 Asheville NC 28807

HARKINS, RALPH DOUGLAS, govt. ofcl.; b. Ponca City, Okla., Apr. 29, 1939; s. Floyd L. and Wilma (Mieir) H.; B.S., Central State Coll., Edmond, Okla., 1962; M.S., U. Okla., 1964, Ph.D., 1967; m. Judy M. Mosley, Aug. 12, 1960; children—Linda, Joe, Karen. Computer programmer U. Okla., 1962-63; math. statistician Fed. Water Pollution Control Adminstrn., Ada, Okla., 1965-67, chief pollution surveillance br., 1967-71; chief tech. and adminstrv. data support br. Environmental Protection Agy., Dallas, 1971-72; facility mgr. region 6 Environmental Protection Agy., Ada, Okla., 1972—. Served with USMC, 1959-65. Mem. Am. Statis. Assn., Biometric Soc. Home: Route 3 Ada OK 74820 Office: PO Box 1198 Ada OK 74820

HARLAN, JAMES CLARKE, banker; b. Charlottesville, Va., May 1, 1928; s. John Frederick and Myrtle (Clarke) H.; B.A., U. Va., 1950, M.A., in Polit. Sci., 1952; certificate Stonier Grad. Sch. Banking, Rutgers U., 1964; m. Betty Anne Blakey, Apr. 16, 1955; children—James Clarke, Sally Blakey. With State-Planters Bank (name changed to United Va. Bank 1971), Richmond, Va., 1954—, v.p., 1965-71, sr. v.p., 1971—. Lectr. banking courses Univ. Coll., U. Richmond, 1959—; instr. Va.-Md. Bankers Sch., Charlottesville, 1964—, Stonier Grad. Sch. Banking, Rutgers U., 1970—. Served to 1st lt. AUS, 1952-54; capt. Res. ret. Mem. Am. Inst. Banking, Robert Morris Assos., Delta Upsilon. Presbyn. Clubs: Farmington Country (Charlottesville); Richmond Host Lions (pres.). Home: 8705 Shadow Lane Richmond VA 23229 Office: 9th and Main Sts Richmond VA 23219

HARLAN, JOHN DENORMANDIE, JR., clergyman; b. New Kensington, Pa., Nov. 18, 1946; s. John DeNormandie and Nancy E. (Rorabaugh) H.; student Grove City Coll., 1964-65; B.A., U. Miami, 1970; M.Div., Eastern Baptist Theol. Sem., 1971; m. Patricia McLendon, Nov. 20, 1971. Ordained to ministry Am. Baptist Ch., 1971; minister Baptist Ch., Phoenixville, Pa., 1970-71, Univ. Christian Ch., Miami, Fla., 1971—. Mem. S.W. Fellowship of Christian Concern (chmn. parish div. 1972-73), So. Cross Astron. Soc., U. Miami Alumni Assn., Eastern Baptist Theol. Sem. Alumni Assn. Home: 12941 SW 17th Terrace Miami FL 33165 Office: 6750 Sunset Dr Miami FL 33143

HARLAN, MONAS OSCAR, educator, tenor; b. New Castle, Pa., Feb. 19, 1912; s. Benjamin Victor and Edith (Cunningham) H.; student Westminster Coll., 1931-33, 36-38, B. Pub. Sch. Music, 1938; postgrad. (scholar) Juilliard Grad. Sch. Music, 1939-42; Mus.M., U. So. Cal., 1950; m. Vivianne Elaine Hodge, Dec. 28, 1962; stepchildren—Laura (Mrs. Eran Buckley), Maribeth Turner, Janis Turner, Charles Turner. Ch. soloist various chs., 1931—, soloist First Ch. Christ Scientist, Shreveport, La., 1959—; mem. faculty U. Louisville, 1953-56, Mont. State U., 1956-59, Centenary Coll., Shreveport, 1959—; world premiers include Volpone, 1953, The Transposed Heads, 1954, Double Trouble, 1954, Sch. for Wives, 1955, Nora, 1967; soloist Los Angeles Philharmonic Orch., 1949, San Francisco Symphony, 1950, Radio Free Europe, 1958, choral groups, Europe, 1956-60; also performer in numerous operas and recitals; dir. Centenary Coll. Opera Workshop, 1964—; judge Met. Opera Auditions, 1962—, voice festivals and talent contests. Served to 1st lt. AUS, 1942-46; PTO. Decorated Bronze Star medal. Mem. Nat. Assn. Tchrs. of Singing, La. Music Tchrs. Assn. (chmn. voice sect. 1961-65), Pi Kappa Lambda. Home: 141 Atkins St Shreveport LA 71104

HARLAN, ROSS EDGAR, utility co. exec.; b. Poteau, Okla., July 11, 1919; s. Edgar L. and Leola (Carter) H.; student Southeastern State Coll., Durant, Okla., 1937-38, Eastern Okla. A. and M. Coll., 1938-39; B.S., Okla. State U., 1941; m. Margaret Burns, May 31, 1942; children—Raymond Carter, Rosemary, Marvin Allen, Scott Lee. Bus. instr. Poteau (Okla.) Jr. Coll., 1946; with Okla. Gas & Electric Co., 1946—, v.p., Oklahoma City, 1964—. Bd. dirs. Oklahoma City area Campfire Girls, Okla. Council Econ. Edn., Variety Health Center, Oklahoma City. Served to lt. col. USAAF, 1941-46. Recipient George Washington Honor medal Freedoms Found., Valley Forge, Pa., 1969. Mem. Oklahoma City C. of C., Beta Gamma Sigma. Methodist. Kiwanian. Club: Beacon (Oklahoma City). Author: Strikes, 1947. Home: 2639 Eagle Lane Oklahoma City OK 73127 Office: 321 N Harvey St Oklahoma City OK 73101

HARLAN, THOMAS JOHN, JR., lawyer; b. Karachi, Pakistan, Dec. 17, 1930; s. Thomas John and Doris May (Palmer) H. (parents Am. citizens); B.A., U. Richmond, 1953, S.J.D., 1961; m. Barbara Ruth Rawling, Apr. 11, 1959; children—T. Keith, Karen L. Admitted to Va. bar, 1961; partner firm Doumar, Pincus, Knight & Harlan, Norfolk, 1961—. Served with USN, 1954-57; now comdr. Res. Mem. Am., Va. bar assns., Va. State Bar, Va. Trial Lawyers Assn., Def. Research Inst., Nat. Assn. Criminal Def. Lawyers. Club: Harbor (Norfolk). Home: 4505 Kelley Ct Virginia Beach VA 23462 Office: 1350 Virginia Nat Bank Bldg Norfolk VA 23510

HARLAN, VERNON ELIJAH, farm implement co. exec.; b. Batesville, Miss., Nov. 14, 1904; s. Luther Montgomery and Jessie Lawrence (Legge) H.; student Warren Bus. Coll., 1929, LaSalle Extension U., 1932; m. Sarah Elizabeth Watson, Oct. 15, 1933; children—Dowell Brooks, Carolyn Drew (Mrs. Cecil Knight Province, Jr.), Ronald Kent (dec.). Prodn. clk. Bradley Lumber Co., Warren, Ark., 1923-29; payroll clk. Lee Wilson & Co., Wilson, 1929-32; office mgr. Keiser Supply Co., Keiser, 1932-37, Lee Wilson & Co., Victoria, 1937-40; treas. Missco, Inc., Osceola, Ark., 1940—, Missco Implement Co., Inc., Monette, 1951—; Missco Implement Co. of Blytheville, Inc., 1941—; registered rep. Consumer-Investor Planning Corp., St. Louis, 1960-71. Treas. Osceola chpt. A.R.C., 1942-45. Mem. C. of C. Osceola. Baptist (treas. 1953-66, sec. bd. deacons 1971). Mason. Home: 404 E Johnson Av Osceola AR 72370 Office: 501 S Walnut St Osceola AR 72370

HARLEY, WILLIAM GARDNER, assn. exec.; b. Madison, Wis., Oct. 9, 1911; s. Joel Alva and Elizabeth (Gardner) H.; B.A., U. Wis., 1935, M.A., 1940, LL.D. (hon.), 1972; m. Jewell Bunnell, June 15, 1940; children—Cynthia (Mrs. Kenwood Foster), Linda (Mrs. John Settle), Gratia, Gail (dec.). Instr. dept. radio-television edn. and staff Sta. WHA, U. Wis., 1936-42, asst. prof., 1942-53, asso. prof., 1953-57, prof., 1957-60; chief announcer Wis. Broadcasting System, 1935-40, program dir., 1940-44, acting dir., 1944-46; program coordinator Ford-Nat. Assn. Ednl. Broadcasters Adult Edn. Radio Project, 1950-52; pres. Nat. Assn. Ednl. Broadcasters, Washington, 1960—; mem. nat. industry adv. com. FCC, 1960-72; del. Internat. Conf. on Schs. Broadcastings, Rome, 1961, Tokyo, 1964, Paris, 1967; bd. dirs. U.S.-Japan Television Program Exchange Center, 1964-68; dir. Joint Council Ednl. Telecommunications, 1960—, pres., 1973—; pres. Ednl. Media Council, 1966-68; chmn. screening com. for Radio-TV Fulbright Scholarships, 1966-72; mem. U.S. Nat. Commn. UNESCO, 1962-68, 70—; chmn. Mass Communications Com., 1967-68, 70—; del. UNESCO Conf. Use Space Broadcasting, Paris, 1971, Internat. Broadcasting Unions Conf. Communications Satellites, 1972; mem. U.S. Nat. Commn. team USSR, 1973. Cons. Rothschild Found., AID, Com. for Econ. Devel., USPHS. Recipient Distinguished Citizen award Creighton U., 1965, Distinguished Alumnus award Wis. Alumni Assn. of Washington, 1966, Distinguished Service in Journalism award U. Wis., 1973. Mem. Nat. Assn. Ednl. Broadcasters, Broadcast Pioneers, Nat. Broadcasters Club, Phi Eta Sigma, Beta Theta Pi. Club: Congressional, International, Cosmos, Broadcasters (Washington); University (N.Y.). Contbr. articles profl. jours. Home: 5301 Boxwood Ct Washington DC 20016 Office: 1346 Connecticut Av Washington DC 20036

HARLING, HUGH WHITMAN, JR., civil engr.; b. Columbia, S.C., Feb. 20, 1943; s. Hugh Whitman and Hester Elaine (Bonnette) H.; B.S., U. Fla., 1966; M.B.A., Fla. State U., 1972; m. Vergie Lorraine Puffinburger, Jan. 23, 1970; children—Candice Lorraine, George Ralph, Gerald Bryan, Hugh Whitman III. Engr., A.E. O'Neall & Assos., Orlando, Fla., 1966-67; engr. Black, Crowe & Eidsness, Gainesville, Fla., 1967; dir. utilities City of Titusville, Fla., 1967-72; pres. Innovation, Tech. & Implementation, Inc., cons. engrs., Orlando, 1972—. Chmn. Brevard County Utilities Policy Com., 1969-72, Orange County Underground Utilities Exam. Bd., 1974. Mem. Am. Soc. C.E. (chmn. speaker com.), Fla. Engring. Soc., Nat. Soc. Profl. Engrs., Am. Water Works Assn., Fla. Pollution Control Assn., Fla. Water and Pollution Control Operators Assn., Fla. Planning and Zoning Assn., Am. Pub. Works Assn., Home Builders Assn. Mid-Fla., Orlando Area C. of C. Home: 3960 Irma Shores Dr Orlando FL 32807 Office: 3319 Maguire Blvd Lexington Bldg Orlando FL 32803

HARLOW, RICHARD FESSENDEN, biologist; b. Boston, Dec. 16, 1919; s. William Bleakie and Harriet (Lailer) H.; B.S., U. Me., 1947, M.S., 1948; M.S., Va. Poly. Inst., 1971; m. Margaret Findlay, Feb. 14, 1942; children—William, David, Dana. Game technician Me. Inland Fisheries and Game, Brewer, 1948-49; soil conservationist Soil Conservation Service, Ebensburg, Pa., 1950-52; asst. chief, game mgmt. div. Fla. Game and Fresh Water Fish Commn., Tallahassee, 1952-66; research wildlife biologist Southeastern Forest Exptl. Sta., U.S. Forest Service, Blacksburg, Va., 1966—. Acting asso. prof. U. Fla., Gainesville, 1972. Served with USCGR, 1941-45. Mem. Kappa Sigma. Contbr. profl. jours. Home: 1617 Kennedy Sf Blacksburg VA 24060 Office: 104 Hubbard St Blacksburg VA 24060

HARMAN, ALEXANDER M(ARRS), judge; b. War, W.Va., Feb. 7, 1921; s. Alexander M. and Rose Sinclair (Brown) H.; student Concord Coll., 1938-41; LL.B., Washington and Lee U., 1944, Nat. Coll. State Trial Judges, 1965. Admitted to Va. bar. 1943; partner Gilmer, Wysor & Gilmer, 1947-52, Gilmer Harman & Sadler, 1952-64; judge 21st Jud. Circuit, 1964-69; justice Supreme Ct. Va., 1969—. Town atty., 1944-46; substitute trial justice, 1945-47. Chmn. Pulaski County Development Authority, 1962-64; chmn. bd. zoning appeals, 1958-64. Chmn. State Bd. Elections of Va., 1955-64; chmn. Pulaski County Dem. Com. 1960-64; mem. finance com. Dem. State Central Com. 1956-64; sec. 19th Dist. Dem. Senatorial Com., 1956-64; mem. Va. Commn. Constnl. Revision, 1968; chmn. Battle for Gov. Com. for Pulaski County, 1949. Pres. New River Valley Indsl. Found., Inc., 1963—. Mem. Am., Va. (v.p. 1949-51), Pulaski County bar assns., Phi Delta Phi, Omicron Delta Kappa, Pi Kappa Alpha. Mason, Elk (Va. pres. 1963-64). Home: 1303 Prospect Av Pulaski VA 24301 Office: Municipal Bldg Pulaski VA also Supreme Ct Bldg Richmond VA 23219

HARMAN, CHARLES MORGAN, educator; b. Cannonsburg, Pa., July 25, 1929; s. Charles Nash and Mildred (Barker) H.; B.S., U. Md., 1954; M.S., U. N.D., 1957; Ph.D., U. Wis., 1961; m. Althea Ann Ahston, June 12, 1956; children—Ruth Ann, Charles Morgan, Samuel Stuart. Asst. prof. mech. engring. Duke U., Durham, N.C., 1961—, asso. dean Grad. Sch., 1970—. Engring. cons. Douglas Aircraft Co., 1961-64, Army Research Office, Durham, 1964-73. Served with USNR, 1949-51. Recipient Profl. Achievement citation Douglas Aircraft Co., 1964. Ford Found. fellow, 1960-61. Registered profl. engr., Wis., N.C. Mem. Am. Soc. M.E., Am. Soc. Engring. Edn. Asso. editor High Speed Groung Transp. Jour., 1970—. Contbr. profl. jours. Home: 2620 McDowell St Durham NC 27705 Office: Dept Mech Engring Duke Univ Durham NC 27706

HARMAN, JAMES WILLIAM, JR., lawyer; b. Richmond, Va., Sept. 29, 1922; s. James William and Coralie (Laird) H.; student Lynchburg Coll., 1940-41; B.S. in Bus. Adminstrn., Washington and Lee U., 1947, LL.B., 1949; m. Evelyn R. Herring, Mar. 29, 1949; children—James William III, Jonathan H.; m. 2d, Joan Brown, Dec. 6, 1972. Partner Harman & Burgess Co., Tazewell, Va., 1946—; admitted to Va. bar, 1949; since practiced law in Tazewell; partner Harman & Harman 1949-70; sr. partner Harman & Campbell, 1970—; atty. Town of Tazewell, 1956-61; commonwealth's atty. Tazewell County, 1952-56; sec., treas., dir. Coal Creek Coal Co., Tazewell, 1951—; partner Edwards & Harman, Welch, W.Va., 1959—; gen. counsel S.W. Va. Nat. Bank, Bluefield, 1963—. Recorder Town of Tazewell, 1949-51, mayor, 1961-67. Pres., bd. dirs. Tazewell Community Hosp., 1968-72. Served with AUS, 1943-46. Mem. Am., Va. (dist. com. 1957-60, chmn. 1960), Tazewell County (pres. 1960-61) bar assns., Phi Beta Kappa, Omicron Delta Kappa, Phi Delta Phi. Republican. Episcopalian. Rotarian (pres. Tazewell club 1962-63). Club: University (Bluefield). Home: Sunset Hills Tazewell VA 24651 Office: 116 W Main St Tazewell VA 24651

HARMAN, JEANNE PERKINS (MRS. HARRY ELLIOTT HARMAN III), author; b. Baxter Springs, Kans.; d. Enoch and Maude (Himes) P.; B.A. magna cum laude, Smith Coll., 1939; m. Harry Elliott Harman III, Mar. 28, 1949; 1 dau., Jeanne Anne. Staff writer Life mag., N.Y.C., 1942-49; corr. Time, Life, Sports Illus. mags., Charlotte Amalie, St. Thomas, V.I., 1949—; tchr. journalism U. Miami (Fla.), 1953-54; corr. N.Y. Times, 1956—; editor, pub. Here's How mag., St. Thomas, 1958—; author spl. articles for various mags. Mem. Am. Soc. Travel Writers, Internat. Platform Assn., Phi Beta Kappa, Kappa Kappa Gamma. Author: The Love Junk, 1951; Such Is Life, 1956; The Virgins: Magic Islands, 1961; Fielding's Guide to the Caribbean and the Bahamas, 1969-73, 74-75. Harman's Official Guide to Cruise Ships, 1971. Address: 2014 Wood Valley Dr Valdosta GA 31601

HARMAN, MARY BROOKS (MRS. SIDNEY ELIJAH HARMAN), librarian; b. Tazewell, Va., May 28, 1912; d. Rees Sylvester and Mollie Randolph (Wyatt) Brooks; B.S., Va. Poly. Inst., 1950, postgrad., 1951; postgrad. U. Utah, 1960, U. Chgo., 1961, U. N.C., 1962, U. Va., 1962-63, 69, U. Ark., 1964, U. Tenn., 1970; m. Sidney Elijah Harman, Feb. 16, 1935; children—Sidney Elijah, Kirk Dennis, Robert E. Lee. Tchr., Pocahontas High Sch., Tazewell, 1931-49, librarian, 1949—. Active Head Start program, 1960-68; pres. P.T.A., Pocahontas, 1948. Pres., Democratic Club, 1964-65. Mem. Nat. Va. edn. assns., Am., Va., Tazewell library assns., Am. Assn. U. Women, Nat. Council Tchrs. English. Baptist (clk. 1942-47). Club: Home Demonstrations (sec. 1948-50) (Bluefield, Va.). Home: Route 1 Box 359 Bluefield VA 24605 Office: Box 308 Pocahontas VA 24635

HARMAN, WILLIAM BOYS, JR., lawyer; b. Newport News, Va., June 5, 1930; s. William Boys and Helen (Conner) H.; A.B., Coll. William and Mary, 1951, B.C.L., 1956; LL.M., Georgetown U., 1960; m. Claudia Carrington Richmond, Dec. 21, 1952; children—Susan

Carol, Thomas Scott, Ann Carrington. Tax atty. Gen. Motors Corp., Detroit, 1956-58; atty. Office of Chief Counsel, Internal Revenue Service, Washington, 1958-59; atty. Office of Tax Legislative Counsel, U.S. Treasury Dept., Washington, 1959-61; atty. Cummings & Sellers, Washington, 1961-62; asso. gen. counsel Am. Life Conv., Washington, 1962-67, gen. counsel, 1968-72; v.p. law Am. Life Ins. Assn., 1973—. Served with USCGR, 1952-54. Mem. Am., Fed. bar assns., Va. State Bar, Bar Assn. D.C., Assn. of Life Ins, Counsel, Am. Law Inst., S.A.R., William and Mary Law Sch. Assn., Phi Beta Kappa, Phi Alpha Delta, Sigma Alpha Epsilon. Clubs: Washington Golf and Country, University, Metropolitan. Home: 4905 N 35th Rd Arlington VA 22207 Office: 1730 Pennsylvania Av NW Washington DC 20006

HARMAN, WILLIAM MARTIN, ins. co. exec.; b. Spring Valley, Ill., Sept. 9, 1924; s. William and Della (Link) H.; B.S., Northwestern U., 1949; m. Carolyn Herd Larson, Mar. 26, 1949. Draftsman, Ebasco Services, Inc., N.Y.C., 1949-50; engr. Nat. Bd. Fire Underwriters, Chgo., 1950-51; with Ins. Services office of Ark., Little Rock, 1951—, mgr., 1966—. Mem. bd. appeals Bldg. Code, City of Little Rock, 1970—. Served with AUS, 1943-46. Registered profl. engr., Ark. Mem. Nat. Fire Protection Assn. Mem. Internat. Order of Blue Goose. Clubs: Little Rock; Western Hills Country (Little Rock), Maumelle Country (North Little Rock, Ark.). Home: 1115 Loretta Lane Little Rock AR 72207 Office: 600 Tower Bldg Little Rock AR 72201

HARMON, ALFRED EUGENE, physician; b. Crowley, La., Oct. 13, 1942; s. Warren Walter and Rita Lucille (Burgin) H.; B.S., U. So. La., 1965; M.D., La. State U., 1967; m. Maudrey Ann Trahan, Jan. 18, 1974; children from previous marriage—Alfred Eugene II, Stephen Kindred, Christine Marie, Mary Catherine. Intern Charity Hosp., New Orleans, 1967-68; resident Lafayette (La.) Charity Hosp., 1968-69; practice medicine specializing in family medicine, Crowley, 1969—. Mem. Crowley Jr. C. of C., Acadia Parish Med. Soc. (sec.-treas., 1971), Phi Beta Phi. Home: 325 E 8th St Crowley LA 70526 Office: PO Box 920 Crowley LA 70526

HARMON, CHARLES CALVIN, ednl. cons.; b. LaJunta, Colo., Mar. 14, 1920; s. Charles George and Elizabeth (Foreman) H.; B.S., U. Tex., 1950, M.Ed., 1953; Ph.D., East Tex. State U. of Commerce, 1969; m. Bonnie Grace Harmon, Apr. 25, 1942; children—Winona, Charles Calvin II, Marsha (Mrs. Karl Harman), Kathleen, Nathan, Beverly, Sterling. Prin., Hart (Tex.) Elementary Sch., 1950-51; prin., coach Kelton (Tex.) Independent Sch. Dist., 1951-52, supt. schs., 1952-55; supt. schs. Vega (Tex.) Ind. Sch. Dist., 1955-61; Nat. Defense Edn. Act. Inst. fellow U. Tex., 1961-62; supt. schs., Hawkins, Tex., 1962-73; ednl. cons. counselors Region VIII Ednl. Service Center, Mt. Pleasant, Tex., 1973—. Chmn. exec. council East Tex. Sch. Study Council, 1971-72; mem. exec. council Region VII Service Center, 1970-71; mem. exec. dist. Region VII council Boy Scouts Am., 1962-72. Served with AUS, 1941-45; PTO Decorated Bronze Star medal with palm. Mem. N.E.A., Am. Assn. Sch. Adminstrs., Tex. Tchrs. Assn. (county pres. 1964-65), Congress of Parents and Tchrs., Phi Delta Kappa. Methodist (chmn. finance com. 1965-72). Lion (pres. 1964-65), Kiwanian (pres. 1957-58). Club: Quarterback, University of Texas T Assn. Home: 104 E Cross Mount Pleasant TX 75455 Office: Region VIII Edn Service Center 100 N Riddle St Mount Pleasant TX 75455

HARMON, FREDERICK INGERSOLL, engring. and equipment co. exec.; b. Waukesha, Wis., Feb. 15, 1923; s. John Neal and Louise (Ingersoll) H.; B.S., U. Tex., 1946; m. Marjorie Elfreda Hanna, Dec. 27, 1944; children—Scott Ingersoll, Keith Hanna, Cynthia Lynn. Process engr. Gasoline Plant Constrn. Corp., Corpus Christi, 1945-56; v.p., chief engr. Gulf Engrs., Houston, 1946-49; founder Southwestern Engring & Equipment Co., Dallas, 1949, v.p., 1949-64, owner, pres., 1964—; v.p. Hanna Devel. Co.; dir. Analytica, Inc. Judge, Sci. Fairs, 1971-73. Mem. adv. council Engring. Found., U. Tex., Austin; mem. adv. council, sci. div. Skyline Tex. Center, Dallas. Served as 2d lt. USAAF, World War II. Registered profl. engr., Tex., N.M. Mem. I.E.E.E., Am. Inst. Aeros. and Astronautics, Inst. Environmental Scis., A.A.A.S., Nat., Tex. socs. profl. engrs., Instrument Soc. Am. Home: 1009 Waterford Dr Dallas TX 75218 Office: 6260 E Mockingbird Lane Dallas TX 75214

HARMON, LOREN FOSTER, art dealer; b. Judsonia, Ark., Nov. 5, 1912; s. Alfred Roscoe and Mae (Foster) H.; student Ind. U., 1930-32, Ohio U., 1932-33; B.A., State U. Ia., 1935, M.A., 1936; m. Martha Foster, July 25, 1943. Dir. Univ. and Exptl. Theatre, Ind. U., Bloomington, 1936-42; pub. relations mgr. WKBN Broadcasting Corp., Youngstown, O., 1943-48; owner, dir. Pine Shores Park, Sarasota, Fla., 1950-54 v.p., dir. Players, Sarasota, 1955-57; pub. relations dir. Ringling Mus. Art, 1958-59; dir. Oehlschlaeger Galleries, Sarasota, Fla., 1961-70; v.p. Vandium Tool Co., Athens, O., 1954-64; owner, dir. Harmon Gallery, Naples, Fla., 1964—. Adviser, Baker Center Collection Am. Art, Ohio U. Bd. dirs. Ringling Mus. Mems. Council, 1957—; corp. mem. Naples Community Hosp., 1966—. Recipient Certificate of Merit, Ohio U., 1970. Mem. Am. Ednl. Theatre Assn. (founder), Am. Fedn. Arts, Sarasota Art Assn. (pres. 1959-60), Fla. League Arts, St. Armands Assn. (pres. 1957-58). Methodist. Clubs: Sarasota Yacht, University. Home: 117 S Polk Dr Lido Sarasota FL 33577 Office: Harmon Gallery 1258 3d St S Naples FL 33940 also PO Box 6187 Sarasota FL 33578

HARMON, ROGER Q., JR., physician; b. Texarkana, Tex., Aug. 31, 1919; s. Roger O. and Clyde Madiline (Perry) H.; student Texarkana Coll., 1939, N. Tex. State U., 1940-41, Kings Coll., Cambridge, England, 1942, Centenary Coll., 1945; grad. La. State U., 1946; M.D., U. Tex., 1951; m. Alma Faye Hall, June 21, 1947; 1 dau., Kay Madelon. Intern, Confederate Meml. Hosp., Shreveport, La., 1951-52; practice medicine specializing in gen. practice, Marshall, Tex., 1952—; mem. staff Meml. Hosp., v.p., 1954, chief med staff, 1972; pres. Pinecrest Med. Center, 1954—; city health officer City of Marshall, 1952-64. Bd. dirs. Cancer Found., 1953. Served with USAAF, 1941-45. Mem. E. Tex. Show Horse Assn. (bd. dirs. 1965-68), C. of C., Tex. Camelia Soc. (pres. 1964-65), Marshall Camelia Soc. (pres. 1959-60), Sigma Alpha Epsilon, Delta Sigma, Theta Kappa Psi. Club: Long Island Ocelot (pres. southwestern br. 1970—). Home: 606 Lansdowne St Marshall TX 75670 Office: 401 E Pinecrest Dr Marshall TX 75670

HARMON, ROY FRANKLIN, JR., surgeon; b. Houston, Miss., Apr. 8, 1929; s. Roy Franklin and Grace Olivia Harmon; B.A., U. Miss., 1951, M.S., 1953, M.D., 1959; m. Bess Moore, Feb. 1, 1957; children—Roy Franklin III, Emily, A.G. Gen. practice medicine, Houston, Miss., 1960-61, specializing in gen. surgery, Houston, Columbia, Tenn., 1965—; chief of surgery Maury County Hosp. Served with AUS, 1953-55. Home: Route 7 Columbia TN 38401 Office: 1510 Hatcher Lane Columbia TN 38401

HARMS, HAROLD HARVEY, physician; b. Cordell, Okla., Sept. 16, 1916; s. John Henry and Margaret Ruth (Kliewer) H.; B.A., Bethel Coll., 1939; B.S., U. Okla. Sch. Medicine, 1939, M.D., 1941; m. Ruth Maydell James, June 7, 1941; children—Karen Marie (Mrs. Wayne Foster), Linda Jayne (Mrs. Dwight A. Lee), Mary Frances. Intern U. Neb. Hosp., Omaha, 1941; resident Shurly Hosp., Detroit, 1946-47, Wayne County Gen. Hosp., 1947-49; ophthalmologist Green Clinic, Ruston, La., 1949—; mem. staff Lincoln Gen. Hosp., Ruston. Clin. instr. ophthalmology La. State U. Sch. Medicine, Shreveport, 1971—. Served from 1st lt. to maj. M.C., AUS, 1942-45. Decorated Bronze Star medal. Diplomate Am. Bd. Ophthalmology. Fellow Am. Acad. Ophthalmology and Otorhinolarynology, La.-Miss. Ophthal. and Otol. Soc., PanAm. Ophthalmology Soc., A.C.S., mem. North Central Parishes, La. State med. socs., A.M.A., Assn. Research Ophthalmologists, Soc. Cryosurgery. Methodist. Kiwanian (pres. 1955). Home: 407 Pinecrest Dr Ruston LA 71270 Office: Green Clinic Ruston LA 71270

HARMS, LOUISE IVIE (MRS. WILLARD DANIEL HARMS), librarian; b. Birmingham, Ala., June 25, 1924; d. Henry J. and Lola (Hicks) Ivie; B.S., U. Ala., 1944; B.S. in L.S., George Peabody Coll. for Tchrs., 1946; m. Willard Daniel Harms, Oct. 17, 1955; children—Dennis Leon, Daniel Lee, Willard Daniel. Asst. librarian Coll. Edn. Library, U. Ala., 1944-45; night reference asst. George Peabody Coll. Tchrs., Nashville, 1945-46; cataloger Allegheny Coll. Library, Meadville, Pa., 1946-47; 1st asst. cataloging dept. U. Ark. Library, Fayetteville, 1947; head cataloger Coll. Edn. Library, U. Ala., 1948-51; spl. services librarian U.S. Army, Europe, 1951-55, library adminstr. spl. activities div., 1958-63; tchr. English, Sweetwater (Tenn.) High Sch., 1963-64; asst. librarian Merner-Pfeiffer Library, Tenn. Wesleyan Coll., Athens, 1964-65, head librarian, 1965—. Mem. A.L.A., Southeastern, E. Tenn., Tenn. library assns., N.E.A., Am. Assn. U. Profs., Alpha Beta Alpha. Presbyn. Home: 20 Hickory Lane Sweetwater TN 37874 Office: Tenn Wesleyan Coll Athens TN 37303

HARMS, ROBERT HENRY, educator; b. Dover, Ark., Sept. 27, 1923; s. Charles W. and Stella (Moore) H.; B.S., U. Ark., 1953, M.S., 1954; Ph.D. (Ralston Purina fellow), Tex. A. and M. U., 1956; m. Kathryn McAllister, Apr. 4, 1944 (dec. Nov. 1962); children—Carolyn (Mrs. Elwin R. Thrasher, Jr.), Robert Henry; m.2d, Mary Bryan, June 22, 1966. Asst. prof. U. Tenn., Knoxville, 1955-57, asso. prof., 1957; asso. prof. U. Fla., Gainesville, 1957-62, prof., 1962-63, chmn. dept. poultry sci. Inst. Food and Agrl. Sci., 1963—. Served with AUS, 1945-46. Recipient Jr. Faculty award Fla. chpt. Gamma Sigma Delta, 1962; Am. Feed Mfrs. Assn. award, 1966. Mem. Am. Inst. Nutrition, Soc. Exptl. Biology and Medicine, Poultry Sci. Assn., World Poultry Sci. Assn., Sigma Xi, Alpha Zeta, Gamma Sigma Delta. Home: 1421 NW 28th St Gainesville FL 32601

HARNER, CHARLES EMORY, editor; b. N.Y.C., Aug. 27, 1901; s. Lloyd Charles and Anna (Webster) H.; A.B., U. Ill., 1923; m. Zofia Wasilewska, July 27, 1935; 1 son, Michael James. Reporter, Hinsdale (Ill.) Doings, 1917-19, Ill. State Jour., Springfield, 1923-24, Chgo. Tribune, 1924-25, Champaign (Ill.) News-Gazette, 1925-28; editor A.P., Chgo., Washington, S.Am., N.Y.C., 1928-41; pub. relations counselor N.W. Ayer & Son, Hill & Knowlton, N.Y.C., 1944-48; dir. pub. relations Nat. Retail Mchts. Assn., N.Y.C., 1944-48; owner, operator advt. agy., Oceanside, Cal., 1948-52; pub. affairs officer Am. embassies, San Salvador, El Salvador, 1952-56, La Paz, Bolivia, 1956-60, Caracas, Venezuela, 1960-64; asso. editor Fla. Trend Mag., Tampa, 1965—. Served from capt. to maj. USAAF, 1942-44. Mem. Tau Kappa Epsilon, Sigma Delta Chi. Episcopalian. Mason (32 deg.). Author: Florida's Promoters: The Men Who Made It Big; Ybor City Intima; Florida's Jazz Age-the Boom and the Bust. Home: 669 Avenida de Mayo Sarasota FL 33581 Office: Box 2350 Tampa FL 33601

HARP, CHARLES ESTLE, educator; b. Kremlin, Okla., Feb. 4, 1910; s. Guy Estle and Blanche Ethel (Fisher) H.; A.B., Phillips U., 1932; M.S., U. Oka., 1938; m. Ona Marie Hollander, Sept. 5, 1935; children—John Charles, Charla Marie. Sci. tchr., Hooker, Okla., 1935-37; physics tchr. Oklahoma City, 1938-43; dir. research Black, Sivalls & Bryson, Inc., Oklahoma City, 1944-48; mem. faculty U. Okla., Norman, 1948—, asso. prof. elec. engring., 1953—. Asst. scoutmaster Gt. Salt Plains council Boy Scouts Am., 1928-29, scoutmaster, 1929-33, scoutmaster Panhandle council, 1934-37, com. mem. Last Frontier council, 1939-43, neighborhood commr., 1943-53, dist. commr., 1953-58, cubmaster, 1959-60, committeeman, 1960-63, recipient Silver Beaver award, 1953. Mem. I.E.E.E. (sect. pres. 1964-65, internat. dir. I.R.E. 1960-62), Am. Inst. E.E. (pres. Oklahoma City sect. 1958-59), Sigma Pi Sigma, Alpha Phi Omega, Sigma Tau, Eta Kappa Nu. Methodist. Home: 524 Macy St Norman OK 73069 Office: 202 W Boyd St Norman OK 73069

HARPER, CHARLES FLOYD, architect; b. Bonham, Tex., Nov. 15, 1929; s. Charles Floyd and Donna Gertrude (Coonrod) H.; B.Arch., Tex. Tech. U., 1955; m. Catherine Elysabethe Fonville, July 1, 1955; children—Charles Martin, Jon Mark. Apprentice architect Harris & Killebrew, architects and engrs., Wichita Falls, Tex., 1955-57; chief designer Butler-Kimmel Co., architects and engrs., Lubbock, Tex., 1957-61; asso. James R. Killebrew & Assos., architects and engrs., Wichita Falls, Tex., 1961-62; partner Harper, Martin & Assos., architects, engrs., Wichita Falls, 1962-69; prin. architect Charles Harper & Assos., architects, programmers, planners, Wichita Falls, Tex., 1969—. Pres., Concern, 1969-70; treas. Concerned Ams. for Responsible Edn., 1971; chmn. Wichita Falls Common Cause. Vice-chmn. Wichita Falls Planning Commn., chmn. Downtown subcom.; del. Democratic state conv., 1972. Bd. dirs. Southside Girls' Club, 1962, Golden Cross Found., McCutcheon Day Nursery. Mem. A.I.A. (pres. Wichita Falls chpt. 1967), Human Resources Council, Tex. Soc. Architects (v.p. 1972), Tech. Execs. Assn. (dir. Wichita Falls 1964-72, pres. 1972), Guild Religious Architects. Methodist (dist. treas. 1970-71). Mason (Shriner). Club: Red Raider (Wichita Falls). Prin. archtl. works include Classroom/Office Bldg. Tex. Tech. U., Evans Elementary Sch., Bonham, Tex., Bethania Hosp., Wichita Falls, Univ. United Meth. Ch., Wichita Falls, Electra Meml. Hosp. Home: 4632 Sierra Madre Dr Wichita Falls TX 76310 Office: 4724 Old Jacksboro Hwy Wichita Falls TX 76302

HARPER, CLYDE WALLACE, physician; b. Greer, S.C., July 23, 1929; s. Clyde Austin and Cecil Stella (Mayfield) H.; student Wofford Coll., 1946-48; A.B., Duke, 1950; M.D., Med. Coll. S.C., 1956; m. Paula Dew, July 23, 1965; children—Susan Elizabeth, Sarah Dew. Intern, St. Louis (Mo.) City Hosp., 1956-57; resident, Med. Center Hosp., Charleston, S.C., 1957-60; fellow in clin. hematology Emory U. Sch. Med., 1960-61; practice medicine specializing in internal medicine, Greenville, S.C., 1961—; sr. asso. in medicine Greenville (S.C.) Gen. Hosp.; asso. clin. prof. medicine Med. U. of S.C., 1973—; cons. medicine Shriner's Hosp. for Crippled Children, Greenville. Mem. council assos. Wofford Coll., Spartanburg, S.C., 1970—. Diplomate Am. Bd. Internal Medicine. Mem. A.C.P., A.M.A., S.C. Med. Assn., Greenville County Med. Soc. Methodist. Club: Greenville Country. Home: 2 Petiver Lane Greenville SC 29605 Office: 24 Vardry St Greenville SC 29601

HARPER, EDWARD JOHN, clergyman; b. Bklyn., July 23, 1910; s. John Edward and Josephine Teresa (Realander) H.; ed. St. Mary's Coll., 1933, Mt. St. Alphonsus Maj. Sem., 1940. Ordained priest Roman Catholic Ch., 1939; missionary priest, P.R., 1941-46, Dominican Republic, 1946-50; dean, Mayaguez, P.R., 1950-56; provincial of vice province P.R., 1956-60; consecrated bishop, 1960; prelate V.I., 1960—. Charter mem., pres. Citizens for Drug Edn., Inc.; mem. V.I. Econ. Devel. Council. K.C. Home: Estate Eliabeth #9 St Thomas VI 00801 Office: Box 1825 St Thomas VI 00801

HARPER, JAMES COLQUITT, oil field service co. exec.; b. Shreveport, La., Mar. 11, 1931; s. George Colquitt and Ruth (Shannon) H.; B.S., La. Tech. U., 1953; m. Jerry Viola Jackson, Feb. 22, 1952; children—Jerry Douglas Rayburn, Pamela, Jamie Michelle, Sandra Lynn, Rebecca Ann; m. 2d, Glenda Bailey Hardy, Jan. 13, 1973; 1 dau., Paige Ann Hardy. Petroleum engr. Humble Oil & Refining Co., New Orleans, 1953-59; mgr. drilling and prodn. J. Ray McDermott & Co., Inc., Houston, 1959-66; v.p., gen. mgr. Dresser Offshore Services, Inc., oil field services, Houston, 1966-71; owner, pres. Services Equipment & Engring., Houma, La., 1971—. Cons. engr. Mem. Am. Assn. Oilwell Drilling Contractors (dir.), Am. Inst. Mining Engrs, Am. Petroleum Inst. Mason (Shriner). Clubs: Ellendale Country (Houma); Conroe Country, Conroe; Lamplighter (bd. dirs. 1969-70) (New Orleans). Patentee in field. Address: Route 2 Box 59 Houma LA 70360

HARPER, JAMES CUNNINGHAM, band dir.; b. Lenoir, N.C., Feb. 17, 1893; s. George Finley and Frances (Cunningham) H.; student Culver Naval Sch.; B.S., Davidson Coll., 1915, L.H.D., 1965; M.A., U. N.C., 1916; postgrad. Duke, 1928, Lenoir Rhyne Coll., 1930, Columbia, 1932; m. Charlotte Critz, Mar. 19, 1927 (dec.); children—Lucy (Mrs. L.A. Grier, Jr.), James Cunningham, George F., Charlotte C. (Mrs. George E. Stone). Band dir. Lenoir (N.C.) High Sch., 1924-58, emeritus, 1958—; v.p., dir. Fairfield Chair Co., Lenoir, N.C.; tchr. summer sch. Appalachian State Tchrs. Coll., 1955, Davidson Coll. Trustee Caldwell Meml. Hosp. Served with O.T.C., 1917, commd. 2d lt., promoted capt., 1918, S.A.T.C., 1918-19. Mem. Am. (pres. 1955, chmn. bd. dirs. 1956), N.C. (pres. 1943-44) bandmasters assns., Am. Sch. Band Dirs. Assn., Music Educators Nat. Conf. (hon. life mem. N.C. assn.), Am. Legion (chaplain 1950), Phi Mu Alpha Sinfonia Soc., Phi Beta Mu. Presbyn. (elder). Club: Lenoir Country. Contbr. articles to sch. mags. and jours. Home: 203 Norwood St Lenoir NC 28645

HARPER, JAMES SHIELDS, retail trade, real estate exec.; b. Clover, S.C., Jan. 16, 1923; s. Carl Brown and Nannie (Dickson) H.; grad. pub. high sch.; m. Edna Marie Wilson, June 14, 1947; children—Susan (Mrs. John D. Hornaday), James Shields. Loan, br. mgr. Comml. Credit Corp., Fayetteville, and Durham, N.C., 1946-49; partner Vann Motor Finance Co., Fayetteville, 1949-55; partner Highland Lumber Co., Fayetteville, 1949-55, sec., 1955-69; pres. Brookwood Water Corp., Fayetteville, 1963—; v.p. Mobile Home Sales Corp., Fayetteville, 1962—; sec. Little Giant Food Mart Inc., Fayetteville, 1970—, and others. Chmn. bd. trustees Cape Fear Valley Hosp., Fayetteville, 1966; sec. bd. trustees Cumberland County Hosp. System Inc., Fayetteville, 1967—. Presbyn. (elder). Kiwanian. Club: Highland Country (Fayetteville). Address: 2306 Raeford Rd Fayetteville NC 28305

HARPER, JOHN PRESTON, judge; b. Portsmouth, Va., Jan. 12, 1921; s. Wilson B. and Bertie (Turner) H.; A.B., Coll. William and Mary, 1941; J.D., U. Va., 1946; m. Dorothy Leigh Hogshire, Oct. 10, 1942; children—John Preston, Penelope Anne. Admitted to Va. bar, 1942; gen. practice Norfolk, Va., 1946-68; gen. counsel Norfolk, Balt. & Carolina Line, Inc., 1960-68, sec., 1965-68; asst. U.S. atty. Eastern Dist. Va., 1947-51; judge Civil Justice Ct., 1968-69, Ct. Law and Chancery, 1969-73, Circuit Ct., Norfolk, 1973—. Mem. Ho. of Dels., Gen. Assembly Va., 1955-60. Mem. alumni bd. Coll. William and Mary, 1958-60, bd. visitors, 1960-68, vice rector, 1966-68. Served with USNR, 1942-46; capt. Res. Mem. Am. Judicature Soc., Pi Kappa Alpha. Presbyn. Clubs: Virginia, Norfolk Yacht and Country. Home: 1501 Eleanor Ct Norfolk VA 23508 Office: 100 St Pauls Blvd Norfolk VA 23510

HARPER, MONTER BLAINE, banker; b. Frenchton, W. Va., June 4, 1920; s. Monter Arnol and Lola Anna (Cutright) H.; student Benjamin Franklin U., 1940-43, Carolinas Sch. Banking, U. N.C., 1946-52; m. Mary Elizabeth Shaw, June 14, 1945; children—Mary Lou (Mrs. James Franklin Lowery, Jr.), Anna Katherine, Sarah Helen. Asst. cashier Central Nat. Bank, Buckhannon, W.Va., 1937-40; files analyst FBI, Washington, 1940-43; with the Carolina Bank, Sanford, N.C., 1946—, exec. v.p., 1965—, also dir. Instr. Carolinas Sch. Banking, 1971-72; cons. Personnel Commn., Bank Adminstrn. Inst., 1969-72. Chmn., Indsl. Devel. Com., Sanford, 1964-70. Served with AUS, 1943-46. Recipient Order of Long Leaf Pine by Gov. N.C., 1971, distinguished service award Sanford Lions Club, 1970. Mem. C. of C. (pres. 1969-70); (distinguished citizen award 1969). Presbyn. Mason (Shriner), Elk, Moose. Home: Route 3 Box 735 Sanford NC 27330 Office: P O Drawer 2100 Sanford NC 27330

HARPER, SPENCER EARL, JR., lawyer; b. Little Rock, Oct. 17, 1933; s. Spencer Earl and Eleanor (Rieder) H.; B.A., U. Louisville, 1955, J.D. cum laude, 1957; m. Clarice Carol Sharpe, July 1, 1955; children—Spencer Earl III, Grafton Sharpe. Admitted to Ky. bar, 1958; practiced in Louisville, 1961—; partner firm Grafton, Ferguson, Fleischer & Harper, 1961—. Trustee, Louisville Law Alumni Found.; mem. exec. com. Louisville Central Area, Inc. Served to capt., Judge Adv. Gen. Corps, USAF, 1958-61. Mem. Am., Fed., Ky., Louisville (mem. exec. com.) bar assns., Am. Judicature Soc., Arnold Air Soc., Phi Kappa Phi, Pi Kappa Phi, Delta Theta Phi, Omicron Delta Kappa. Democrat. Presbyn. Clubs: Pendennis, Tavern, Jefferson, Harmony Landing Country, Fincastle Beagles. Home: 3309 Green Hill Lane Mockingbird Valley Rd Louisville KY 40207 Office: 310 W Liberty St Louisville KY 40202

HARPOLE, TONY HESS, merchant; b. Clinton, Ky., Feb. 26, 1926; s. Homer Hess and Sarah (Cunningham) H.; grad. pub. schs.; m. Margaret Elizabeth Costello, June 23, 1946; children—Jan Hess, Mark Aden. Mgr., owner Harpole Supply Co., Clinton, Ky., 1946—. Asst. fire chief Clinton Fire Dept., 1953-68, chief, 1968—; dir. Hickman County Civil Def., 1956-70; safety services chmn. Clinton chpt. A.R.C., 1968—; mem. Ky. Pub. Safety Adv. Com., 1971-72. Bd. dirs. Four Rivers council Boy Scouts Am. Served with AUS, World War II. Mem. Nat. Assn. Fire Investigators, Am. Legion, I.E.E.E., Am. Radio Relay League, Clinton C. of C. Mem. Christian Ch. (deacon 1968—). Club: Brigadier. Home: 407 N Washington St Clinton KY 42031 Office: 115-119 N Washington St Clinton KY 42031

HARPSTER, JAMES ERVING, lawyer; b. Milw., Dec. 24, 1923; s. Philo E. and Pauline (Daanen) H.; Ph.B., Marquette U., 1950, LL.B., 1952. Admitted to Wis. bar, 1952, Tenn. bar, 1953; dir. information services, Nat. Cotton Council Am., Memphis, 1952-55; dir. pub. relations, Christian Bros. Coll., 1956; mgr. govt. affairs dept. Memphis C. of C., 1956-62; exec. v.p. Rep. Assn. Memphis and Shelby County, 1962-64; individual practice law, Memphis, 1964-67; partner Rickey, Shankman, Blanchard, Agee & Harpster, and predecessor firm, Memphis, 1967—. Mem. Shelby County Tax Assessor's Adv. Com., 1960-61; editor, asst. counsel Memphis and Shelby County Charter Comm., 1962; mem. Shelby County Election Commn., 1968-70; mem. Tenn. State Bd. Elections, 1970-72, sec., 1972, mem. Tenn. State Election Commn., 1973—, chmn., 1974—. A founder Lions Inst. for Visually Handicapped Children, 1954, chmn. E. H. Crump Meml. Football Game for Blind, 1956; pres. Siena Student Aid Found., 1960; bd. dirs. Memphis Pub. Affairs Forum; mem. Civic Research Com., Inc., Citizens Assn. Memphis and Shelby County. Republican candidate Tenn. Gen. Assembly, 1964; v.p. Nat. Council

Republican Workshops, 1967-69; pres. Rep. Workshop Shelby County, 1967, 71, Rep. Assn. Memphis and Shelby County, 1966-67. Chmn. St. Michael the Defender chpt. Catholics United for the Faith, 1973-74. Served as sgt. USAAF, 1942-46. Mem. Am., Tenn., Wis. bar assns., Navy League U.S., Am. Conservative Union, Cardinal Mindszenty Found., Am. Legion. Roman Catholic. Lion (dir. Memphis 1955-62). Clubs: Executives, Press (Memphis). Home: 3032 E Glengarry Rd Memphis TN 38128 Office: Suite 3500 100 North Main Bldg Memphis TN 38103

HARR, KARL GOTTLIEB, JR., lawyer, assn. exec.; b. South Orange, N.J., Aug. 3, 1922; s. Karl Gottlieb and Mildred (Reid) H.; A.B., Princeton, 1943; LL.B., Yale, 1948; D.Phil. (Rhodes scholar), Oxford U., 1950; m. Patricia Stratton Adams, Oct. 11, 1947; children—Timothy Adams, Karl Gottlieb III, Catherine Anne, Amy. Admitted to N.Y. bar, 1951; asso. Sullivan & Cromwell, N.Y.C., 1950-54; spl. asst. to under-sec. state for adminstrn., staff dir. sec. state's pub. com. on personnel, 1954-55; dir. spl. project Richardson Found., 1955; dep. asst. sec. def. Nat. Security Council Affairs and Plans, alternate def. mem. Nat. Security Council Planning Bd., 1956-57; spl. asst. to Pres. of U.S., vice chmn. Operations Coordinating Bd., adviser Nat. Security Council Planning Bd., 1958-61; counsel to Rogers, Hoge, Hills, N.Y.C., 1961-63; pres. Aerospace Industries Assn. Am., Inc., Washington, 1963—; dir. Union Trust Co., Washington. Chmn. Council Def. and Space Industry Assns., 1964; chmn. internat. coordinating council Aerospace Industries Assn.; chmn. Nat. Aero. Noise Abatement Council, 1964; bd. dirs. Expt. in Internat. Living, Outward Bound. Alumni trustee Princeton U. Served with AUS, 1943-46. Mem. Am. Bar Assn., Phi Beta Kappa, Phi Delta Phi. Home: 6 W Kirke St Chevy Chase MD 20015 Office: 1725 Desales St Washington DC 20036

HARRA, CHARLES CLAYTON, edn. adminstr.; b. Greensboro, N.C., June 20, 1924; s. Charles Emmanuel and Shirley (Clayton) H.; B.A., Rollins Coll., 1949; m. Marilyn Bennett Hoffman, Sept. 23, 1952 (div. July 1964); 1 dau., Virginia Bennet. Controller Ringling Museum Art, Sarasota (Fla.) 1959-65; bus. mgr. New Coll., Sarasota, 1965—. Served with USAAF, 1943-45, 51-53. Decorated Air medal with silver cluster. Home: PO Box 1898 Sarasota FL 33579

HARRAWOOD, PAUL, univ. dean; b. Akin, Ill., Aug. 28, 1928; s. Raymond E. and Verdie Alma (Galbraith) H.; B.S., U. Mo. at Rolla, 1951, M.S., 1956; Ph.D. (NSF fellow), N.C. State U., 1967; m. June Anne Harris, Nov. 28, 1953; 1 dau., Laura Anne. Instr. civil engring. U. Mo. at Rolla, 1954-56; asst. prof. civil engring. Duke, 1956-67, asst. dean engring., 1961-62; asso. prof. civil engring. Vanderbilt U., Nashville, 1967-70, prof., 1970—, asso. dean engring., 1967—, acting dean engring., 1970-71; test engr. McDonnel Aircraft Corp., 1957; constrn. mgmt. engr. U.S. Army C.E., 1958. Served with USNR, 1951-54. Mem. Am. Soc. C.E., Soc. Am. Mil. Engrs., Am. Soc. Engring. Edn., Am. Assn. Higher Edn., A.A.A.S., Sigma Xi, Tau Beta Pi, Chi Epsilon. Home: 5314 Camelot Ct Brentwood TN 37027 Office: Vanderbilt U Box 1607 Sta B Nashville TN 37203

HARRELL, CHARLES HOPKINS, coll. adminstr.; b. Snow Hill, N.C., May 1, 1932; s. William and Fannie (Young) H.; B.S., East Carolina U., 1955; postgrad., U. Ky., 1964; m. Faye Watson, May 22, 1955; children—Kelly, Rene, Charles Jr. Auditor, N.C. Revenue Dept., 1955-59, Burlington Industries, Greensboro, N.C., 1959-63; bus. mgr., treas. Mount Olive (N.C.) Coll., 1963—. Bd. dirs. F.W.B. Childrens Home, 1968-69, pres. alumni assn., 1968-69. Commr., Mount Olive Housing Authority, 1969-74. Recipient Outstanding Young Man of Year award, 1965; Founders award A.R.C., 1967. Mem. N.C. Financial Aid Adminstrs., So. Assn. Coll. and Univ. Bus. Officers, Assn. Sch. Bus. Officers, Internat. (senator, life mem.), U.S. (nat. dir. 1968), N.C. (v.p. 1967, state project chmn. 1968-69), Mount Olive jr. chambers commerce, Mount Olive C. of C. (sec. 1972-73, pres., dir. 1973-74). Mason (32 deg., Shriner), Woodman of World. Clubs: Trojan (treas.), Wayne (N.C.) Country, Goldsboro Country (dir.). Home: 116 N Breazeale Av Mount Olive NC 28365 Office: 209 Breazeale Av Mount Olive NC 28365

HARRELL, JAMES ANDREW, dentist; b. Elkin, N.C., July 14, 1922; s. Roy Brannock and Mattie Reid (Doughton) H.; student U. N.C., 1939-42; D.D.S., Va. Commonwealth U., 1945; m. Idabel Jane Gibbs, June 19, 1945; children—James Andrew, Deborah (Mrs. Robert Lee Kirkham III), Gavin Gibbs, Stephen Westall. Pvt. practice dentistry, Elkin, N.C., 1945—; V.P. Dillon and Norman, Inc., 1969—; dir. Yadkin Valley Bank and Trust Co., United Savs. and Loan Assn. Commr., City of Elkin, 1961-67, mayor, 1967—. Bd. dirs. YMCA, pres. 1962; bd. dirs. Hugh Chatham Meml. Hosp., United Fund, pres. 1964; pres. N.C. Dental Found., 1971—. Served with AUS, 1943-45, USNR, 1945-46, 52-54. Decorated Fauchard medal; named Man of Year, Kiwanis Club, Elkin, 1968. Fellow Internat. Coll. Dentists, Am. Coll. Dentists, Royal Soc. Health; mem. Blue Ridge (pres. 1968), N.C. (pres.-elect 1972—), Second Dist. (pres. 1960-61) dental socs., Pierre Fouchard Acad., Omicron Kappa Upsilon. Democrat. Methodist (chmn. bd., lay leader). Kiwanian (pres. 1963). Home: 430 Hawthorne Rd Elkin NC 28621 Office: 128 W Main St Elkin NC 28621

HARRELL, LIMMIE LEE, JR., lawyer; b. Jackson, Tenn., Aug. 15, 1941; s. Limmie Lee and Mary Benthal (Nowell) H.; B.S., Memphis State U., 1963, J.D., 1966; m. Judy Faye Lynchard, Sept. 3, 1964; children--Limmie Lee III, Mary Kimberly. Admitted to Tenn. bar, 1966, since practiced in Trenton; partner Harrell, Nowell & Harrell, 1966-72, Harrell & Harrell, 1972—. Chmn., March of Dimes, 1967-68. Sec., Trenton Zoning Bd., 1966—. Mem. C. of C. (dir. 1967-70), Memphis State U. Alumni Assn. (pres. 1972-73), Omicron Delta Kappa, Sigma Alpha Epsilon, Delta Theta Phi. Democrat. Baptist. Elk, Moose. Club: Pinecrest Country (pres.). Home: 202 Armory St Trenton TN 38382 Office: Court SQ Trenton TN 38382

HARRELL, ROY ALVIN, JR., govt. ofcl.; b. Fort Worth, Jan. 9, 1936; s. Roy Alvin and Lucile (Ingham) H.; B.A., U. Tex., 1957, 59; M. Internat. Service, Am. U., 1960; certificate Nat. U. Mexico, 1956; licensiate Stellenbosch U., 1961, LL.B., Washington, 1973; m. Charlotte Elizabeth Purcell, Feb. 11, 1967; 1 dau., Carol Elizabeth. Translator, Library Congress, Washington, 1958-60; intelligence analyst Dept. State, Washington, 1960-62; program operations analyst Am. embassy, Conakry, Guinea, 1962-65; econ. support officer AID, Dept. State, Washington, 1965-67; attache for econ. affairs Am. embassy, Ft. Lamy, Tehad, Africa, 1967-70; chief budget dir. Office Planning for Internat. Security Affairs, Dept. State, Washington, 1970—. Recipient Outstanding Service award U.S. Govt., 1965. Mem. Pi Delta Phi, Sigma Delta Pi, Alpha Phi Omega, Phi Sigma Alpha. Methodist. Mason, Rotarian. Contbr. profl. and religious jours. Home: Drawer B Ozona TX 76943 Office: Dept State Washington DC

HARRELSON, AUSTIN BARROW, physician; b. Richmond, Va., May 28, 1936; s. Austin Isaih and Virginia Ann (Barrow) H.; B.S., Hampden Sydney Coll., 1957; M.D., Med. Coll. Va., 1962; m. Peggy Ann Gregson, June 10, 1962; children—Peter Craig, Michael Sean, Austin Barrow, John Gregson. Intern, Med. Coll. Va., Richmond, 1962-63, resident, 1963-66, asst. prof. neurology, 1966-72, asso. clin. prof., 1973—; pvt. practice specializing in neurology, Richmond, 1969—; mem. staff Med. Coll. Va., St. Mary's, Richmond Meml., Retreat, St. Luke's, Johnston-Willis, Chippenham, Stuart Circle, Grace hosps. (all Richmond). Sec.-treas. Neuro Assos., Inc., 1971—. Bd. dirs. Adult Devel. Center, 1971—. Served to capt. U.S. Army, 1966-68; Hawaii. Diplomate Am. Bd. Psychiatry and Neurology. Mem. Va. Neurol. Soc. (sec. treas. 1972—), Phi Beta Kappa, Alpha Omega Alpha. Clubs: Commonwealth, Willow Oaks Country, 2300. Home: 3625 Hastings Dr Richmond VA 23235 Office: Suite 305 1805 Monument Av Richmond VA 23220

HARRELSON, MICHAEL ASBURY, educator; b. Shelby, N.C., Apr. 22, 1931; s. Asbury Carr and Jane (Gardner) H.; B.S., Appalachian State U., 1962, M.A., 1966; Ph.D. (research fellow) U. Ga., 1969; m. Judith Means Pope, Nov. 24, 1960; children—Michael Kent, William Thomas, Robert Stephen. Instr. biology Waco (N.C.) Schs., 1958-65; mem. faculty Gardner Webb Coll., Boiling Springs, N.C., 1968—, prof., 1970—, head dept. biology, chemistry and geology, 1972—. Bd. dirs. Cleveland County League on Conservation, 1972—. Served with AUS, 1956-57. Postdoctoral fellow Bowling Green (O.) State U., 1972. Mem. A.A.A.S., Nat. Biology Tchrs. Assn., Sigma Xi. Contbr. articles on tropical ecology to profl. jours. Home: Box 831 Boiling Springs NC 28017 Office: Dept Biology Gardner Webb Coll Boiling Springs NC 28017

HARRIES, WYNFORD LEWIS, physicist, educator; b. Llanon, Carmarthenshire, Wales, June 1, 1923; s. Garfield Wynford and Jane (Jones) H.; B.Sc. with honors, U. Wales, 1949; D.Phil., U. Oxford (Eng.), 1953; m. Natalie Pamela Gratkowski, Nov. 29, 1958. Came to U.S., 1953, naturalized 1960. Research asso. Mass. Inst. Tech., Cambridge, 1953-54; asst. dir. research Clevite Transistor Products, Waltham, Mass., 1954-56; sr. project engr. Internat. Tel. & Tel. Corp., Nutley, N.J., 1956-60, cons. research labs., 1961-65; mem. research staff, plasma physics lab. Princeton, 1960-70; prof. physics Old Dominion U., Norfolk, Va., 1970—. Cons. dept. ophthalmology N.Y. Med. Coll., 1968—. Served to capt. British and Indian Armies, 1943-47. NASA grantee, 1973. Fellow Am. Phys. Soc., Inst. Physics (London), Instn. Elec. Engrs. (London); mem. I.E.E.E. (sr.), Sigma Xi. Contbr. profl. jours. Patentee in field. Home: 8545 I Tidewater Dr Norfolk VA 23503 Office: Dept Physics Old Dominion Univ Norfolk VA 23508

HARRIGAN, ANTHONY HART, editor, author; b. N.Y.C., Oct. 27, 1925; s. Anthony H. and Elise (Hutson) H.; m. Elizabeth Ravenel, Aug. 16, 1950; children—Anthony Hart III, Elliott McPherson, Elizabeth Chardon, Mary Ravenel. Asso. editor The News and Courier, Charleston, S.C., 1958—, asst. editor, 1968-70; exec. v.p. U.S. Indsl. Council, Nashville, 1970—, bd. dirs. Ednl. Found.; mem. nat. strategy com. Am. Security Council; lectr. U.S. Nat. War Coll., other mil. and acad. orgns. Chgo. Episcopalian. Author: The Editor and The Republic, 1954; Red Star Over Africa, 1964; Defense Against Total Attack, The New Republic, 1965; One Against The Mob, 1966; A Guide to the War in Vietnam, 1967; American Perspectives, 1972. Contbr. Am. and European scholarly and mil. jours. Home: 54 Legare St Charleston SC 29401 Office: Stahlman Bldg Nashville TN 37201

HARRIGAN, WILLIAM PATRICK III, educator; b. New Orleans, Aug. 2, 1934; s. William Patrick and Violet Louise (Wuest) H.; B.S. in Edn., Loyola U., New Orleans, 1957; M.F.A., in Theater, Tulane U., 1960; Ph.D. in Speech, La. State U., 1972; m. Evelyn Sue Lagattuta, May 31, 1958; children—Kelli Susan, Patti Marie, Lesli Bel. Instr., Lamar State Coll. Tech., Beaumont, Tex., 1960-62, asst. prof., 1969-71; instr. La. State U., New Orleans, 1962-66; Loyola U., New Orleans, 1967-68; St Bernard Jr. Coll., Chalmette, La., 1968-69; asst. prof. Lamar U., Beaumont, 1971—. Dir. Children's Theater and Creative Dramatics, Beaumont Parks and Recreation Dept., 1972, 73; pres. bd. Beaumont Community Players, 1971-73. Served with AUS, 1957-58. Mem. Am., Children's, Am. Community theater assns., Tex. Assn. Coll. Tchrs., Nat. Collegiate Players, S.W. Theater Conf. (dir.), Alpha Psi Omega, Phi Mu Alpha. Research on history S.W. Theater Conf., 1972—.

HARRINGTON, ALFRED DAVID, JR., accountant; b. Miami, Fla., Feb. 25, 1929; s. Alfred David and Caroline (Truluck) H.; B.S., U. Fla., 1951; m. Anne V. Sulm, Dec. 19, 1953; children—Marilyn Anne, Brian David. Partner Ring, Mahony & Arner, C.P.A.'s, Miami, 1951-52, Ft. Lauderdale, Fla., 1954-69; partner Coopers, Lybrand & Montgomery, Ft. Lauderdale, 1969—. Campaign chmn., Broward County Tb and Health Assn., Inc., 1961-62, dir., 1963-64; treas. Broward Community Coll. Found., Inc. Served from 2d lt. to 1st lt., AUS, 1952-54. Mem. Am., Fla. insts. C.P.A.'s, Estate Planning Council of Broward County, Delta Tau Delta. Democrat. Home: 1700 SE 10th St Fort Lauderdale FL 33316 Office: 1 Financial Plaza Suite 2500 Fort Lauderdale FL 33394

HARRINGTON, ARNOLD WHITMAN, elec. engr.; b. Winter Haven, Fla., Dec. 3, 1931; s. Elizur Whitman and Doris (Bartlett) H.; B.S. in E.E., Ga. Tech., 1953; m. Joyce Marie Johnson, July 30, 1954; 1 dau., Pamela Jean. Engring. mgr. Turner Electric Works, Jacksonville, Fla., 1955-71; head elec. dept. for power generation Reynolds, Smith & Hill, Jacksonville, 1971—. Served to lt. (j.g.) USNR, 1953-55. Registered profl. engr., Fla., Ga., Ala. Mem. I.E.E.E. (sr.; chmn. 1973-74), Fla. Engring. Soc. (sr.), Nat. Soc. Profl. Engrs. (sr.), Am. Guild Organists, Eta Kappa Nu, Tau Beta Pi, Phi Kappa Phi, Alpha Tau Omega. Republican. Episcopalian. Home: 6933 Dongalla Ct Jacksonville FL 32211 Office: 4019 Boulevard Center Dr Jacksonville FL 32207

HARRINGTON, CHARLES WRIGHT, librarian; b. Miami, Fla., July 29, 1923; s. Frederick H. and Ina (Hamilton) H.; B.A., U. N.C., 1944; M.A., U. N.M., 1953; postgrad. Tulane U., 1953-60; M.S. in L.S., La. State U., 1961. Librarian trainee Queens Borough Pub. Library, N.Y.C., 1961-62; dir. activities Instituto Guatemalteco Americano U.S. Binational Center, Guatemala City, Guatemala, 1947-49; adminstrv. dir. Instituto Cultural Dominico-American, Ciudad Trujillo, Dominican Republic, 1949-51; head librarian Centenary Coll., Shreveport, La., 1963—. Library cons. U. Minn.-Ford Found. Cooperative project with U. Concepcion (Chile), 1967-69. Served with USNR, 1943-46. Mem. A.L.A., La. Library Assn., Ozark Soc. Episcopalian. Home: 7441/2 Delaware St Shreveport LA 71106

HARRINGTON, EVANS, educator, author; b. Ala.; student Miss. Coll.; Ph.D., U. Miss. Prof. Am. lit. and creative writing U. Miss.; Faulkner scholar. Recipient Henry Bellaman award creative writing. Bread Loaf Writers Sch. fellow. Author: The Prisoners (novel); Faulkner's Mississippi; Land into Legend (film). Editor Per/Se mag. Contbr. short stories to mags. Address: U Miss University MS 38677*

HARRINGTON, JAMES ELMER, govt. ofcl.; b. Bethlehem, N.H., Dec. 14, 1927; s. James Elmer and Berenice (Morrill) H.; B.S., Va. Mil. Inst., 1949; m. Harriett Whitmore, June 10, 1964; children—Nancy, Mary, Alexander, David, Mollie. With Pinehurst Inc. (N.C.), 1952-72, sec.-treas., 1964-67, pres., 1967-72; exec. v.p. Sugar Mountain Co. resort devel., Banner Elk, N.C., 1972-73; sec., N.C. Dept. Natural and Econ. Resources, Raleigh, 1973—. Sec., N.C. Republican Exec. Com., 1964; del. Nat. Rep. Conv., 1964; precinct, county and congl. dist. chmn. Rep. party, 1952-68. Served to 1st lt. AUS, 1949-52. Home: 2109 St James Rd Raleigh NC 27607 Office: Box 27687 Raleigh NC 27611

HARRINGTON, JAMES LOYD, city ofcl.; b. Nederland, Tex., July 5, 1938; s. Oren Joseph and Lena Evelyn (Jefferson) H.; student Tex. Firemen's Tng. Sch. Tex. A. and M. u., 1967; m. Gloria Sue Lester, June 11, 1955; children—Samuel Pierce, Christopher Todd. Fireman, Nederland Fire Dept., 1951-58, asst. chief, 1958-65; chief Port Neches (Tex.) Fire Dept., 1965—. Instr. Ann. Tex. Firemen's Tng. Sch., Tex. A. and M. U., 1965-71, Lamar U. Firemen's Tng. Sch., 1970-71. Co-chmn. Port Neches (Tex.) Fall Festival, 1971. Served with AUS, 1961-63. Recipient Fire Chief of the Year award Sabine-Neches Chief's Assn., 1969. Mem. Tex. Fire Chief's Assn., S.E. Tex. Fire Marshal's Assn., Sabine-Neches Chief's Assn. (pres. 1972-73; Fire Chief of Year award 1969). Lion. Home: 2634 Hampton Lane Port Neches TX 77651 Office: 1209 Merriman St Port Neches TX 77651

HARRINGTON, KENNETH RAY, san. engr.; b. nr. Nashville, Aug. 10, 1925; s. Charles Edward and Nona May (Long) H.; B.E., Vanderbilt U., 1950; M.D., U. Mich., 1957; LL.B., YMCA Law Sch. at Nashville, 1962; m. Dorothy Jean Ralston, Nov. 16, 1944; children—Brenda Jean, Ronnie Oeser, Kenneth Ray. Admitted to Tenn. bar, 1962; chief san. engr. Davidson County Health Dept., Nashville, 1950-61, asst. dir. pub. works, 1961-63, dir. met. dept. water and sewerage services, 1963—. Served with USNR, 1943-46. Named Pub. Servant of Year, Nashville Real Estate Bd., 1966. Registered profl. engr., Tenn. Mem. Ky.-Tenn. Water Pollution Control Assn. (chmn. 1966). Home: 322 Pineway Dr Nashville TN 37217 Office: 802 Stahlman Bldg Nashville TN 37201

HARRINGTON, LEONARD RILEY, social worker; b. Miami, Fla., Aug. 22, 1939; s. Irving and Margaret (Allison) H.; B.A. cum laude, U. Miami, 1961; M.S.W., Tulane U., 1963. Social worker VA Hosp., New Orleans, 1964—, Protestant Home for Babies, New Orleans, 1964—; instr. field work La. State U. Sch. Social Welfare, Baton Rouge, 1968—; clin. social worker Southeastern Alcoholism Clinic, New Orleans, 1969—; caseworker Orleans Parish Dept. Pub. Welfare, 1964, Charity Hosp. of La., New Orleans, 1963. Mem. Nat. Assn. Social Workers, Council on Social Work Edn., Nat. Conf. on Social Welfare. Episcopalian. Home: 1208 Bourbon St New Orleans LA 70116 Office: 1601 Perdido St New Orleans LA 70146

HARRIS, ARTHUR HORNE, educator; b. Middleborough, Mass., May 18, 1931; s. Frank Arthur and Winifred (Deane) H.; B.A., U. N.M., 1958, M.S., 1959, Ph.D., 1965; student U. Ariz., 1961-62; m. Anita June Pennington, Nov. 21, 1962; children—Tina Melissa, Rebecca Ann, Megan Aneen. Asst. prof. Ft. Hays (Kan.) State Coll., 1963-65; asst. prof. U. Tex. at El Paso, 1965-67, asso. prof., 1967-71, prof., 1971—; research cons. Museum of N.M., 1965-67, 1970; research cons. Sch. Am. Research, 1966, 68—. Served with AUS, 1951-53. NSF Predoctoral fellow, 1959-60, 1961-62, Basic Research grant, 1967-70; Nat. Geog. Soc. grant, 1971-72. Fellow Tex. Acad. Sci. (v.p. environmental scis. sect. 1972); mem. Am. Soc. Mammalogists, Soc. Vertebrate Paleontology, Southwestern Assn. Naturalists, Am. Quaternary Assn. Author: (with others) Ecological Distribution of Some Vertebrates in the San Juan Basin, New Mexico, 1963; (with F.W. Eddy): Vertebrate Remains and Past Environmental Reconstruction in the Navajo Reservoir District, 1963. Contbr. articles to sci. jours. Home: 1231 Baltimore St El Paso TX 79902 Office: Dept Biol Scis U Tex at El Paso El Paso TX 79968

HARRIS, BILLY JACKSON, mfg. co. exec.; b. Salisbury, N.C., Feb. 20, 1941; s. William Jackson and Annie Frances (Tallant) H.; B.S., Clemson U., 1962; postgrad. U. Fla., 1965-67; M.S., U. N.C., 1971; m. Barbara Sue McSwain, Mar. 2, 1960; children—Katherine Teresa, Julia Marie, Brian Jackson. Sr. design engr. Pratt & Whitney Aircraft, West Palm Beach, Fla., 1962-67; asst. mgr. corporate research Gilbarco, Inc., subsidiary Exxon Corp., Greensboro, N.C., 1967-71; mgr. corporate finance McDaniel Lewis & Co., Greensboro, N.C., 1971-72; mgr. corporate engring. Hackney & Sons Inc., Washington, 1972—. Chmn. advancement com. Blackbeard council Boy Scouts Am. Served to 1st lt., Ordnance Corps, AUS, 1963-65. Registered profl. engr., N.C. Mem. Am. Soc. M.E., Soc. Advancement Mgmt., Soc. Automotive Engrs., Greensboro Jr. C. of C. (project chmn. 1969). Methodist (chmn. worship commn. 1966-67). Kiwanian. Club: Washington Yacht and Country. Patentee in field. Home: 106 Palmer Place Washington NC 27408 Office: 400 Hackney Av Washington NC 27889

HARRIS, BYRON LEWIS, bank exec.; b. Atlanta, Dec. 23, 1937; s. Byron Paul and Dena (Lewis) H.; B.A., Vanderbilt U., 1959; postgrad. Sch. Banking of South, 1968; m. Ann Frederick Pegram, Nov. 28, 1969; children—John B. Lyle, Martha Lyle, Jay Lyle (step-children), Byron Lewis. With First Nat. Bank Atlanta, 1959—, comml. trainee, 1959-64, asst. cashier, 1964-68, asst. v.p., 1968-69, v.p., 1969—, asst. dir. marketing, 1973, mgr. trust bus. devel., 1973—, pres., 1973—. Program chmn. Leadership Atlanta, 1969-70, chmn., 1970-71; div. chmn. United Appeal, 1970—, mem. budget com., 1971—. Bd. dirs. Met. Atlanta Council Alcohol and Drugs, 1971-73, Atlanta Florence Crittenden Services Inc., 1971-74. Mem. Atlanta C. of C. (subcom. vice chmn. 1970), Phi Delta Theta. Kiwanian (dir. 1969-71, pres., 1971-72). Club: Capital City (Atlanta). Home: 517 Arden At Argonne NW Atlanta GA 30305 Office: First Nat Bank Atlanta PO Box 4148 Atlanta GA 30302

HARRIS, CARL MATTHEW, educator; b. Bklyn., Mar. 29, 1940; s. Benjamin and Marion (Neidich) H.; B.S., Queens Coll., 1960; M.S., Poly. Inst. Bklyn., 1962, Ph.D. (N.Y. State Regents fellow, Nat. Def. Edn. Act fellow), 1966; m. Alice Ilene Follender, Nov. 2, 1969; children—Naomi Chandra, Margo Suzanne. Mem. tech. staff Western Electric Co., Inc., Princeton, N.J., 1965-67, Research Analysis Corp., McLean, Va., 1967-70; asso. prof. operations research George Washington U., Washington, 1970—. Cons. D.C. Dept. Corrections, 1973—, Resource Mgmt. Corp., 1972—, Civil Service Commn., 1971. Mem. Inst. Math. Statistics, Math. Assn. Am., Operations Research Soc. Am. (asso. editor jour. 1971—), Inst. Mgmt. Scis. (local chmn. 1970-72), Sigma Xi. Contbr. articles to profl. jours. Home: 6314 Valley Rd Bethesda MD 20034 Office: Dept Operation Research George Washington U Washington DC 20006

HARRIS, CARLETON, state justice; b. Pine Bluff, Ark., Dec. 31, 1909; s. Frank A. and Ada (Rodgers) H.; student Union U., Jackson, Tenn., 1929-31; LL.B., Cumberland U., 1932; LL.D., Ouachita Bapt. Coll., 1960; m. Marjorie Wilson, Apr. 20, 1934; 1 son, Eugene Starke. Admitted to Ark. bar, 1932; practice in Pine Bluff 1932-48; pros. atty., Pine Bluff, 1947-48; judge 4th Chancery Dist. Ark., 1949-56; chief justice Ark. Supreme Ct., 1957—. Pres. Ark. Jud. Council, 1955. Mem. Ark. Ho. of Reps., 1933-38. Mem. nat. council Boy Scouts Am.; past dir. Pine Bluff Pub. Library, Pine Bluff Community Chest; disaster relief chmn. Jefferson County A.R.C., 1943—; past v.p. Jefferson County Men of Chs.; mem. exec. com. So. Bapt. Conv., 1967—. Recipient Outstanding Lawyer award Ark. Bar Assn. and Ark. Bar Found., 1973. Mem. Am., Ark., Jefferson County (pres. 1942) bar assns., Central States Shrine Assn. (past pres.), Nat. Conf. Chief Justices (chmn. 1966-67). Democrat. Baptist. Mason (past grand lodge orator: Shriner, past potentate), Lion (pres. Pine Bluff 1936). Home: 2005 Laurel St Pine Bluff AR 71601 also Plaza Towers Apts Little Rock AR 72201 Office: Justice Bldg Little Rock AR 72201

HARRIS, CHARLES EDGAR, wholesale grocery co. exec.; b. Englewood, Tenn., Nov. 6, 1915; s. Charles Leonard and Minnie (Borin) H.; m. Dorothy Wilson, Aug. 20, 1938; children—Charles Edgar, William John. With H.T. Hackney Co., Knoxville, Tenn., also Athens and Greenville, Tenn., 1948—, treas., 1958-72, v.p., 1964-71, pres., chief adminstrn. officer, 1971-72, pres., chmn., chief exec. officer, 1972—, also dir.; pres., dir. Appalachian Realty Corp., Knoxville, Morsan Holding Co., Knoxville, Park Oil Co., Alcoa, Tenn., Knoxoil Co., Knoxville, Carolina Oil and Gas Co., Bryson City, N.C.; chmn. bd., dir. Valley Oil Co., Athens, Tenn., Hackney Carolina Co., Murphy, N.C., Hackney Harlan Co., Harlan, Ky., Haywood Wholesale Grocery Co., Waynesville, N.C., Maryville Wholesale Grocery Co. (Tenn.), Brink's, Inc., Knoxville, Testoil Co., Harlan, Ky., Central State Oil Co., Mid State Investment Corp. (both McMinnville, Tenn.). Mem. exec. bd. Great Smoky Mountain council Boy Scouts Am., 1956-57; bd. dirs. Met. YMCA, Knoxville. Mem. Knoxville Wholesale Credit Assn. (dir. 1955-58, pres. 1956-57), Knoxville C. of C. (dir. 1973—). Baptist (deacon 1957—). Rotarian. Home: 7709 Westland Dr Knoxville TN 37919 Office: Fidelity Bldg Knoxville TN 37902

HARRIS, DAVID CRERAR, elec. engr.; b. Bklyn., June 1, 1931; s. Harold Crerar and Dorthea Esther (Teachman) H.; B.Sc., London (Eng.) U., 1955. With Gen. Electric, various locations, 1956—, mgr. information systems Apollo system, Daytona Beach, Fla., 1972—. Cons. computer applications. Mem. I.E.E.E. (sr. mem., chmn. 1965-66), Daytona Dog Fanciers Assn. (pres. 1969-70). Home: Box 888 Orange City FL 32763 Office: Box 2500 Daytona Beach FL 32015

HARRIS, DAVID K., mortgage co. exec.; b. Louisville, Aug. 27, 1938; s. Abel J. and May (Kaplan) H.; student Ky. Mil. Inst., 1953-56; B.B.A., U. Miami, Coral Gables, Fla., 1960; m. Barbara Kaplan, Dec. 20, 1959; children—Julie, Edward, Lisa. With Midwest Mortgage Co., Miami, Fla., 1961—, v.p., 1964-66, exec. v.p., 1966—; pres. Diversified Realty Inc., Miami, 1968—; dir. City Bank North Miami, Investors Tax Sheltered Properties. Mem. citizens bd. U. Miami, 1972—. Served to 1st lt. AUS, 1960-61. Mem. Mortgage Bankers Assn. Clubs: Standard of Miami, Kings Bay Country, Ocean Reef. Home: 12000 SW 69th Pl Miami FL 33156 Office: 120 NE 9th St Miami FL 33132

HARRIS, DONALD PENN, electronics engr.; b. Austin, Tex., Nov. 28, 1930; s. John Stuart and Sarah (Penn) H.; B.S., U. Tex., 1953, postgrad. Law Sch., 1972—; M.S., So. Methodist U., 1958; Ph.D. (NSF fellow), Stanford, 1963; m. Barbara Elizabeth Baker, June 1, 1958; children—Carole Marie, Marilyn June, Lana Susan, Evan Joseph. Engr., Collins Radio Co., Dallas, 1955-58, sr. asso. engr., 1963-71; engr. Nat. Bur. Standards Radio Propagation Labs., Boulder, Colo., 1958-60; research scientist Lockheed Aircraft Co., Palo Alto, Cal., 1960-63; sr. engr.-scientist Tracor, Inc., Austin, 1971-72, now cons. Cons. Microwave Communications, Inc., Washington, Automation Products Corp., Austin. Bd. dirs., pres. Austin chpt. Zero Population Growth. Served to lt. (j.g.) USNR, 1953-55. Mem. Phi Sigma Kappa, Alpha Phi Omega, Phi Eta Sigma, Eta Kappa Nu, Tau Beta Pi, Phi Delta Phi. Unitarian. Clubs: Toastmasters Internat. (past pres.), Austin Organic Gardeners (v.p.). Contbr. articles profl. jours. Home: 3301 French Pl Austin TX 78722 Office: 6500 Tracor Lane Austin TX 78721

HARRIS, EDWARD GRANT, physicist, educator; b. Morristown, Tenn., Mar. 10, 1924; s. George Temple and Gladys Turley (Grant) H.; B.S., U. Tenn., 1948, M.S., 1950, Ph.D., 1953; m. Sara Ann Waldron, Feb. 3, 1962; 1 dau., Heather Ann. Physicist, Naval Research Lab., Washington, 1953-57; prof. physics U. Tenn., Knoxville, 1957—. Cons., Oak Ridge Nat. Lab., 1957—. Served with AUS, 1942-45. Decorated Air medal. Fellow Am. Phys. Soc. Author: A Pedestrian Approach to Quantum Field Theory, 1972. Home: 8205 Corteland Dr Knoxville TN 37919

HARRIS, EWING JACKSON, lawyer; b. Sylvia, Tenn., Mar. 17, 1901; s. John Clifton and Sarah Frances (Walker) H.; ed. pub. schs. Tenn. and Detroit; LL.B., Cumberland U., 1928; m. Lena Sue Hartman, Mar. 28, 1931; children—Frances Ann Harris (Mrs. Frank Avent), Marjorie Sue Harris (Mrs. Dean Lucht), Ewlene Harris. Admitted to Tenn. bar, 1928 and practiced in Bolivar, 1932—; city atty., Bolivar, 1942—; county atty. Hardeman County, 1942-70; dir. Bank of Bolivar. Pres. State Bd. of Elections, 1949-53, Tenn. Democratic Exec. Com. 1949-51, 1953-55; mem. Tenn. State Senate, 1937-39; del. Tenn. Constl. Conv., 1965. Fellow Am. Coll. Probate Counsel; mem. Am., Tenn. (bd. govs. 1959-62, mem. Ho. Dels. 1973-75, mem. spl. joint com. on ct. modernization), Hardeman County bar assns., Am. Judicature Soc., C. of C. (pres.1958), Phi Beta Gamma. Democrat. Methodist (trustee). Mason, Elk, Rotarian. Clubs: West Tenn. Executives (v.p.). Home: 332 Sycamore St Bolivar TN 38008 Office: Bank of Bolivar Bldg Box 148 Bolivar TN 38008

HARRIS, FRANK MAURICE, lawyer; b. St. Petersburg, Fla., Oct. 16, 1902; s. William B. and Mamie (McMullen) H.; J.D., U. Fla., 1925; m. Frances B. Coryell, Aug. 16, 1927; children—Frank Maurice, Richard C., Jeannine (Mrs. John L. Green, Jr.), Marilyn H. (Mrs. James F. Mills), Carolyn H. (Mrs. Richard W. Nelson). Admitted to Fla. bar, 1924; sr. mem. Harris, Clark, Green, and Piper St. Petersburg, 1963—. Chmn. bd. Union Trust Nat. Bank of St. Petersburg; dir. Landmark Banking Corp. Fla. Chmn. Fla. Bd. Control, 1949-53. Mem. Blue Key, Delta Chi, Delta Theta Phi. Presbyn. Mason (Shriner), Elk. Home: 8 Brightwaters Circle NE St Petersburg FL 33704 Office: W Coast Title Bldg 30 6th St N St Petersburg FL 33731

HARRIS, HAROLD FLOYD, judge; b. Rogers, Tex., Aug. 30, 1929; s. Claude Leo and Lois (Rawls) H.; B.S. in Elec. Engring., Tex. A. and M., 1955, M.S. in Elec. Engring., 1956; J.D., U. Tex., 1970; m. Benigna Ann Durst, Feb. 23, 1951; children—Donald Blake, Benigna Susan. Design engr. Tex. Instruments, Dallas, 1956-57, project mgr., 1957-61, tng. control dept., 1962, mgr. components optics br., 1963-68; admitted to Tex. bar, 1970; pvt. practice law, 1970-71; county judge Bell County, Tex., 1971—. Pres. Central Tex. Council Govts.; chmn. exec. com. Central Tex. Alcohol Safety Action Project. Cubmaster Boy Scouts Am., 1963-64; football coach YMCA, 1965—. Trustee Kinsolving Canyon Lodge. Served with USNR, 1950-54. Mem. Tex., Bell-Mills-Lampasas bar assns., Tex. Soc. Profl. Engrs., Internat. Platform Assn., Tex. Aggie Band Assn., Eta Kappa Nu. Mem. Ch. Christ (deacon). Home: 2210 N 9th St Temple TX 76501 Office: Bell County Courthouse Belton TX 76513

HARRIS, HARWELL HAMILTON, architect, educator; b. Redlands, Cal., July 2, 1903; s. Frederick Thomas and May Julia (Hamilton) H.; student Pomona Coll., 1921-23, Otis Art Inst., 1923-25; m. Jean Murray Bangs, Feb. 23, 1937. Sculptor, 1926-29; practice architecture with Richard Neutra, 1929-32; pvt. practice, 1933—, Los Angeles, 1933-51, Austin, Tex., 1951-56; prin. Harris & Sherwood, Ft. Worth, 1956-57; architect with office in Dallas, 1958-62; lectr. U. So. Cal., 1945, 46; vis. critic Columbia, 1943, Yale, 1950, 52; design cons. to Nat. Orange Show, 1950-56; grad. design critic Columbia, 1960-61, dir. sch. architecture U. Tex. 1951-55; prof. architecture N.C. State U., 1962-73. Prin. works include Lowe House, 1934, Fellowship Park House, 1935, Havens House, 1941, Birtcher House, 1942, Wyle House, 1947, Johnson House, 1948, English House, 1950, Chadwick Sch., 1951, Tex. State Fair House, 1954, J. Lee Johnson House, 1956. Am. Embassy, Helsinki, 1957, Havens Meml. Plaza, Berkeley, Cal., 1961, Greenwood Mausoleum, Ft. Worth, 1960, Treanor House, 1959, St. Giles Presbyn. Ch., 1969, others; prin. projects: the Segmental House for Revere Copper & Brass Co., 1942, Pottenger Hosp., 1946, Palos Verdes Coll., 1947, Homestyle Found. House for S. West, 1956. Recipient 1st prize Pitts. Glass Inst., 1937, 1938. Fellow A.I.A.; mem. Congres Internationaux d'Architecture Moderne (sec. Am. chpt. 1932, chpt. for relief and postwar planning, 1944), Tau Sigma Delta. Home: 124 Cox Av Raleigh NC 27605 Office: 122 Cox Av Raleigh NC 27605

HARRIS, HERBERT J., indsl. engr.; b. Rochester, N.Y., May 20, 1923; s. Harry Zax and Celia S. Harris; B.S. in Indsl. Engring., U. Ala., 1950; certificate bus. adminstrn., U. Buffalo, 1958; m. Mary Frances McHugh, July 9, 1955; children—Ann C., James W., Stephen J., Patricia M. Prodn. engr. Hewitt Robins Inc., Buffalo, 1950-56; quality control engr. Gen. Electric Co., Buffalo, 1956-57; plant indsl. engr. Fedders Corp., Buffalo, 1957-58; Firewell Co., Cheektowaga, N.Y., 1958-59; indsl. engr. Linde div. Union Carbide Corp., Tonawanda, N.Y., 1959-62; staff indsl. engr. P.O. Dept., Washington, 1962-68; chief indsl. engr. FDA, 1968-73; project dir. VA, 1973—; chmn. Joint Bd. Sci. Engring., 1974-75. Pres. Chevy Chase (Md.) Swimming Assn., 1970-71. Served with AUS, 1943-46. Mem. Am. Inst. Indsl. Engrs. (sec. Niagara Frontier chpt. 1960, pres. Nat. Capital chpt. 1967-68, dir. 1968-73, nat. dir. govt. liaison 1968-71, nat. dir. govt. div. 1971-73). Home: 3509 Dundee Dr Chevy Chase MD 20015 Office: VA 810 Vermont Av NW Washington DC 20420

HARRIS, HORATIO PRESTON, dentist; b. Savannah, Ga., Sept. 25, 1925; s. Horatio Preston and Faustine Althia (Williams) H.; B.S., Howard U., 1951, D.D.S., 1956; m. Barbara Elaine Monroe, Sept. 16, 1950; children—Gary Preston, Patricia Lynn, Michael Monroe, Conrad Wayne, Nancy Elaine (dec.), David Matthew, Cathy Colleen, Robert Horatio, Roxanne Denise. IBM specialist VA, Washington, 1949; intern oral surgery St. Elizabeth Hosp., 1956-57; individual practice dentistry, Washington, 1957—; dental officer Bur. Dental Health, 1963-65; instr. Howard U., 1966-67, asst. prof., 1967-71; mem. courtesy staff oral surgery Freedman's Hosp. Served with USNR, 1943-46. Mem. Am., Nat., D.C. dental assns., R.T. Freeman Soc., Omega Psi Phi. Home and office: 1400 Franklin St NE Washington DC 20018

HARRIS, HOYT CLARK, physician; b. Sparta, Tenn., May 27, 1920; s. Bob Floyd and Otie Mae (Poore) H.; student David Lipscomb Coll., 1940; LL.B., Middle Tenn. State U., 1943; M.D., U. Tenn., 1946; m. Beverly Jolet, June 20, 1946 (dec. 1967); children—Linda Ellen (Mrs. John E. Hinds), Hoyt Clark, Stephen Jolet. Rotating intern Baroness-Erlanger Hosp., Chattanooga; resident surgery Bapt. Meml. Hosp., Memphis; practice medicine specializing in gen. surgery, Lewisburg, Tenn., 1957—; chief of staff Lewisburg Community Hosp. Dir. First Nat. Bank Lewisburg. Served with M.C., AUS, World War II. Diplomate Am. Bd. Abdominal Surgery. Fellow Am. Coll. Angiology, Internat. Acad. Proctology; mem. Am. Soc. Abdominal Surgeons, Am., Tenn., Middle Tenn. med. assns., Marshall County Med. Soc., Lewisburg C. of C. Republican. Mem. Ch. of Christ (Sunday sch. tchr.), Mason (Shriner). Home: 334 Oakwood Dr Lewisburg TN 37091 Office: Med Arts Clinic 3d Av North Lewisburg TN 37091

HARRIS, HUGH PATE, ret. army officer; b. Anderson, Ala., June 15, 1909; s. Leo C. and Maude Ethel (Alsup) H.; B.S., U.S. Mil. Acad., 1931; student Inf. Sch., 1938, Armed Forces Staff Coll., 1946, Command and Staff Coll., 1948, Nat. War Coll., 1950; hon. degrees Clemson U., The Citadel; m. Jane Boyd, Aug. 24, 1934 (dec. 1958); 1 dau., Beverly Boyd (Mrs. I.E. Jenkins); m. 2d, Kathleen Burns, 1961; 1 dau. (adopted), Betsy. Commd. 2d lt. AUS, 1931, advanced through grades to gen.; unit comdr. 22d Inf., 1931-34, Hawaiian div., 1934-37, 5th Inf. div., 1940-41; assigned airborne units, Ft. Benning, Ga. and Ft. Bragg, N.C., 1942-46; instr. Army Staff Coll., 1948; chief staff U.S. 13th Airborne Div., 1944-46, 18th Airborne Corps, 1951-52, 2d Army, 1953-55; liaison with Canadian Army, Joint Chiefs Staff, 1948; regt. comdr. 224th Inf., 40th Div., Korea, 1952; dep. chief staff for operations 8th Army, Korean War, 1953; comdg. gen., Berlin, 1955; div. comdr. 11th Airborne Div., Germany, 1956; dep. chief of staff for operations, plans and tng. G3, U.S. Continental Army comdg. gen. U.S. Army Inf. Center, Ft. Benning, Ga., 1960; comdg. gen. I Corps (Group), Korea, 1961; comdg. gen. 7th Army, 1962, Continental Army Command, 1964; comdr.-in-chief Army Strike Forces, 1964; pres. The Citadel, Charleston, S.C., 1965-70. Wildlife commr., S.C.; mem. So. Interstate Nuclear Bd. Decorated D.S.M. with cluster, also Silver Star, Legion Merit with clusters (U.S.); D.S.M. with cluster (Korea). Mason (32 deg.). Club: Optimist. Assisted preparation airborne lit. for U.S. Army tng. system. Home: Box 774 Bonneau SC 29431

HARRIS, HUNTINGTON, business exec.; b. N.Y.C., May 15, 1914; s. Hayden Bertlett and Lina (Small) H.; student U. Chgo., 1931-37; B.S., Am. U., 1939; Ph.D., Columbia, 1950; m. Mary Winifred Hutchison, Oct. 9, 1944; children—Susan Valeria (Mrs. Philip E. Smith), Henry John Hayden. Expert witness Dept. Justice, 1940-41; pres. Press Intelligence, Inc., 1946-66; chmn. bd. Farrington Mfg. Co., 1959-63, Adrema, Ltd., 1961-64; now engaged in investments; dir. Quadri-Science, Inc., Harris Trust and Savs. Bank, Chgo., Peoples Nat. Bank, Leesburg, Va.; pres. Radio sta. WAGE, Leesburg. Pres. Nat. Cathedral Assn., Washington. Trustee, pres. Asheville (N.C.) Sch.; trustee Syracuse U., Brookings Instn., Washington. Served from capt. to col. OSS, 1941-46. Decorated Medal for Freedom; Ouissam Alouite (Morocco), Fellow Royal Soc. Arts London. Episcopalian. Clubs: University (Washington and N.Y.C.); Chicago; Nat. Press, Metropolitan (Washington). Home: RFD 1 Leesburg VA 22075 Office: 1028 Connecticut Av NW Washington DC 20036

HARRIS, JACK, broadcasting ofcl. Pres., gen. mgr. KPRC-TV, Houston. Address: KRPC-TV 8181 Southwest Freeway PO Box 2222 Houston TX 77027*

HARRIS, JAMES BRANTLEY, extension personnel dir.; b. Marietta, Ga., Oct. 7, 1940; s. James Robert and Floy (Spratlin) H.; B.S., U. Ga., 1962, M.S., 1964; Ed.D., Cornell U., 1970; m. Emily Anne Byrd, Jan. 18, 1964; children—Cynthia Byrd, James Brantley, Elizabeth Anne. Research asst. U. Ga., 1962-64; NSF fellow U. P.R., summer 1962; asst. county extension agt. Walker County, Ga., 1964-65; extension tng. specialist and instr. extension edn. U. Ga., Athens, 1965-71, extension personnel devel. coordinator, asst. prof., 1971—. Mem. Adult Edn. Assn. U.S.A., Ga. Adult Edn. Council, Nat. Assn. County Agrl. Extension Agts., Phi Delta Kappa, Xi Sigma Pi, Alpha Zeta, Gamma Sigma Delta. Lion. Contbr. articles in field to profl. jours. Home: Route 3 Spinks Rd Athens GA 30601 Office: Cooperative Extension Service U Ga Athens GA 30602

HARRIS, JAMES DOUGLAS, JR., lawyer; b. Tallassee, Ala., Feb. 12, 1943; s. James Douglas and Edna Marie (Flournoy) H.; A.B., U. Ala., 1960, J.D., 1964; m. Sara Jean Brooks, May 7, 1966; children—Jennifer Brooks, James Douglas III, Stewart Katherine. Admitted to Ala. bar, 1967, U.S. Supreme Ct. bar, 1971; mem. firm Harris & Harris, Montgomery, Ala., 1967—. Active United Appeal. Mem. Ala. Ho. of Reps., 1970—. Bd. dirs. YMCA Youth Legislature. Served with AUS, 1967-69. Decorated Bronze Star medal. Mem. Am. Legion, V.F.W., Jr. C. of C., Phi Alpha Delta, Sigma Chi. Democrat. Baptist. Home: 1254 Westmoreland Av Montgomery AL 36106 Office: Union Bank Bldg Montgomery AL 36104

HARRIS, JAMES GORDON, clergyman; b. Little Rock, Ark., Oct. 27, 1913; s. James Gordon and Ellen (McManaway) Ill.; B.A., La. Bapt. Coll., 1935; Th.M., M.R.E., Southwestern-Bapt. Theol. Sem., 1939; D.D., Ouachita Bapt. U., 1956; m. Tunis Johns, Jan. 10, 1939; children—Gordon, John, Jane. Ordained to ministry Bapt. Ch., 1933; pastor First Bapt. Ch., Bunkie, La., 1940-45, Calvary Bapt. Ch., Birmingham, Ala.,1945-48, Beech St. First Bapt. Ch., Texarkana, Ark., 1948-54, University Bapt. Ch., Ft. Worth, 1954—; preacher Columbia Ch. of Air, CBS Radio, 1955, Christmas Service, NBC Radio, 1963. Mem. Radio and TV Comm. So. Bapt. Conv., 1953-59, mem. Fgn. Mssion Bd., 1971—, 1st v.p., 1973-74; mem. Christian life commn. Bapt. Gen. Conv. Tex., 1959-66, 69—, v.p., 1965-66, 71-72, mem. exec. bd., 1964-72, chmn., 1969-71; moderator Tarrant Bapt. Assn., 1962-63; pres. Gen. Ministers Assn., Ft. Worth, 1963-65, Bapt. Pastor's Conf., Ft. Worth, 1967-68. Mem. Mayors Com. on Human Relations, Ft. Worth, 1965. Bd. dirs. Ft. Worth United Fund, 1960-69. Trustee Baylor U., 1964-73. Mem. Southwestern Bapt. Theol. Sem. Alumni Assn. (pres. 1974-75). Rotarian. Home: 3413 Lawndale Fort Worth TX 76133 Office: 2720 Wabash St Fort Worth TX 76133

HARRIS, JANET DOROTHEA, ret. educator; b. Boston, Feb. 13, 1915; d. Ralph and Linna (Ehrenfried) Harris; B.S. in Edn., Boston U., 1936, M.Ed., 1946. Tchr. pub. schs., Winchendon, Mass., 1937-40; tchr. remedial reading pub. schs., Farmington, Conn., 1940-43; tchr. pub. schs., West Hartford, Conn., 1943-50, Newton, Mass., 1950-72. Mem. Assn. Supervision and Curriculum Devel., Internat. Reading Assn., Newton Tchrs. Assn., Photog. Soc. Am., Internat. Platform Assn., Palm Beach Round Table, Art Inst. Palm Beaches, Lake Worth Art League. Club: Lake Worth Camera. Author articles in field. Home: Lake Clarke Gardens 2615 S Garden Dr Apt 201 Lake Worth FL 33460

HARRIS, JEAN LOUISE, physician; b. Richmond, Va., Nov. 24, 1931; d. Vernon Joseph and Jean Louise (Pace) Harris; B.S., Va. Union U., 1951; M.D., Med. Coll. Va., 1955; m. Leslie John Ellis, Jr., Sept. 25, 1955; children—Karen Denise, Pamela Diane, Cynthia Suzanne. Intern Med. Coll. Va., Richmond, 1955-56, resident internal medicine, 1956-57, fellow, 1957-58; fellow Strong Meml. Hosp.-U. Rochester (N.Y.) Sch. Medicine, 1958-60; research asso. Walter Reed Army Inst. Research, Washington, 1960-63; practice medicine specializing in internal medicine, allergy, Washington, 1964-71; instr. medicine Howard U. Coll. Medicine, Washington, 1960-68, asst. prof. dept. community health practice, 1969—; prof. family practice Med. Coll. Va., Va. Commonwealth U. dir. Center Community Health and lectr. dept. med. care and hosps. Johns Hopkins, Balt., 1971-73; asst. clin. prof. dept. community medicine Charles R. Drew Postgrad. Med. Sch., Los Angeles, 1970-73; adj. asst. prof. dept. preventive and social medicine U. Cal. at Los Angeles, 1970-72; chief bur. resources devel. D.C. Dept. Health, 1967-69; exec. dir. Nat. Med. Assn. Found., Washington, after 1970. Cons. div. health manpower intelligence Dept. Health, Edn. and Welfare, 1969—. Bd. dirs. Health Facilities Planning Council, Travelers Aid Soc. Recipient East End Civic Assn. award, 1955. Fellow Royal Soc. Health (Eng.); mem. Am. Acad. Med. Adminstrs., Am. Pub. Health Assn., Am. Assn. Hosp. Planning, Nat. Assn. for Community Devel., Dist. Med. Soc., Nat. Med. Assn., Med. Chirurgical Soc. D.C., Beta Kappa Chi, Alpha Kappa Mu, Sigma Xi. Home: 3318 Chatham Rd Richmond VA 23237 Office: Health Scis Div Virginia Commonwealth U 11th and Marshall Sts Richmond VA 23219

HARRIS, JESSE DAVID, JR., apparel mfg. co. exec.; b. Pine Bluff, Ark., Oct. 4, 1943; s. Jesse David and Dorothy (Barnes) H.; student U. Tex., 1961-64; B.B.A., E.Tex. State U., 1971; m. Lydia Joyce Oliver, Nov. 23, 1968; children—Lydia Michelle, Jessica Lee, Jesse David III. Systems analyst E-Systems, Inc., Greenville, Tex., 1970-73; mgr. lingerie div. Dotty Dan, Inc., Groveton, Tex., 1973—. Served with USAF, 1964-68. Address: Box 50 Groveton TX 75845 Office: Box 505 Groveton TX 75045

HARRIS, JESSIE G. (MRS. HUBERT LAMAR HARRIS), ednl. adminstr.; b. Athens, Ga., May 12, 1909; d. Wiley Jackson and Dora (Hilley) Ginn; B.B.A., U. Ga., 1956; A.B., Ga. State Coll., 1960; m. Hubert Lamar Harris, Nov. 25, 1930; children—Mary Ann Harris (Mrs. William Wallace Holley), Hubert Lamar, Dorothy Elizabeth (Mrs. Ronald Zazworsky), Martha Susan (Mrs. R.R. McCue, Jr.). Various secretarial positions, ins. and law offices, 1923-30; sec. div. of gen. extension U. Ga., 1930-35, asst. dir. div. gen. extension, 1935-47; asst. compilations survey Univ. System, Ga., 1949-50, adminstrv. asst. to regents, 1951-63, asst. exec. sec., 1963-67, asso. exec. sec., 1967-73, asst. vice chancellor personnel, 1973—. Asst. exec. dir. State Scholarship Commn., 1965-66. Mem. Am. Assn. U. Women (chmn. study group 1964-66, treas. 1972-74), Crimson Key Honor Soc., Mortar Board, So. Hist. Assn., Atlanta Hist. Soc., Phi Chi Theta, Delta Mu Delta, Psi Chi. Club: Atlanta Writers. Home: 765 Douglas Rd NE Atlanta GA 30342 Office: 244 Washington St NW Atlanta GA 30334

HARRIS, JOHN DEAN, tax-investment adviser; b. Tulsa, June 29, 1946; s. Fred Dean and Jerry Anne (Raney) H.; B.S., Okla. State U., 1968; J.D., U. Houston, 1971; m. Susan Valorie Burns, Feb. 14, 1970; 1 son, Scott Dean. Tax supr. Peat, Marwick, Mitchell & Co., Houston, 1968-73; tax-investment adviser, Dallas, 1973—. Pres., bd. dirs. Klienwood Municipal Water Dist.; pres. Bus. Student Council, Okla. State U., 1968. Served to 1st lt. Finance Corps, AUS. Mem. Am. Inst. C.P.A.'s, Tex. Soc. C.P.A.'s, State Bar Tex., Houston Estate and Financial Forum, Phi Kappa Phi, Beta Gamma Sigma, Sigma Nu. Home: 6826 Delmeta Dr Dallas TX 75240 Office: 1000 Firto-Lay Tower Dallas TX 75235

HARRIS, JOHN LEWIS, broadcast exec.; b. Dothan, Ala., Jan. 7, 1933; s. John Lewis and Barbara Eugenia (Simmons) H.; student U. Ala., 1951-52, 56-57, 57-58; m. Dolores Anita Rolen, June 19, 1957; children—Helen Eugenia, John Lewis III, Barbra Kay. Announcer, program dir. WDIG radio, Dothan, 1957-60; sta. mgr. WPEX-FM, Pensacola, Fla., 1960-63; mgr. operations WKRG AM/FM, Mobile, 1963-70; v.p., gen. mgr. WLPR radio, Mobile, 1970—. Vice pres., Creative Ideas, Inc., Mobile, 1973—; cons., ednl. radio sta. Springhill Coll., Mobile, 1972—. First v.p. Mims Youth Football Assn., 1973. Served with AUS, 1952-56. Recipient Nat. Sigma Delta Chi Distinguished Journalism award for editorials, 1970, Ala. Sigma Delta Chi award for editorials, 1971. Mem. Nat. Assn. FM Broadcasters (chmn. bd. 1971—), FM Radio Pioneers, Advt. Fedn. Greater Mobile (pres. 1972-73), Sigma Delta Chi (pres. 1973—). Home: 408 LaBorde Dr Mobile AL 36609 Office: PO Box 1092 Mobile AL 36601

HARRIS, JOHN WOODS, banker; b. Galveston, Tex., Sept. 23, 1893; s. John Woods and Minnie (Hutchings) H.; LL.B., U.Va., 1920; m. Eugenia Davis, June 14, 1917; children—Eugenia (Mrs. Archibald Rowland Campbell, Jr.), Anne (Mrs. Donald C. Miller), Joan (Mrs. Alvin N. Kelso), Florence (Mrs. Marshall McDonald, Jr.) (dec.).

Admitted Tex. bar, 1920; practiced as atty., mng. agt. oil, farm, ranch properties in Tex., 1922—; dir. Hutchings Sealy Nat. Bank, 1930-58; chmn. exec. com., chmn. bd. First Hutchings Sealy Nat. Bank, Galveston, 1960—; pres. Hutchings Joint Stock Assn., 1936—; dir. Galveston Corp., Cotton Concentration Co., Gulf Transfer Co., Tex. Fibreglas Products, Inc., Galveston. Vice pres., chmn. land com. The Sealy and Smith Found. for John Sealy Hosp.; pres. Galveston Found. Inc.; pres. bd. Rosenberg Library, Galveston Orphans Home. Served as aviator USN, 1918. Mem. Sons of Republic of Tex., Am. Legion, The Early and Pioneer Naval Aviators Assn., Delta Kappa Epsilon. Episcopalian. Clubs: Galveston Artillery; Farmington Country (Charlottesville, Va.). Home: 2603 Av O Galveston TX 77550 Office: US Nat Bank Bldg Galveston TX 77550

HARRIS, LEONARD CROSSLEY, physician, educator; b. South Africa, Apr. 14, 1919; s. Charles Edgar and Gladys Mary (Grose) H.; M.B. B.Ch., U. Witwatersrand, South Africa, 1944; M.D., U. Pretoria, South Africa, 1949; m. Theresa Anne Kozik, July 4, 1956; children—Lynette, Nereide, Charles, Siobhan. Came to U.S., 1960. Intern Johannesburg Gen. Hosp., 1945-46; resident Pretoria Gen. Hosp., 1946-48; practice medicine specializing in pediatric cardiology, Galveston, Tex., 1961—; dir. pediatric cardiology, prof. pediatrics U. Tex. Med. Br., 1961—. Served with South African M.C., World War II. Fellow Am. Coll. Cardiology; mem. Am. Pediatric Soc., Cardiology Club of Tex., Am. Heart Assn. (research com. Tex. affiliate). Contbr. numerous articles to profl. jours. Home: 1913 Carter Lane La Marque TX 77568 Office: U Tex Med Br Galveston TX 77568

HARRIS, LESTER JEROME, mortgage co. exec.; b. Toledo, Sept. 22, 1926; s. Abel J. and May (Kaplan) H.; student U. Ind., 1945, U. Louisville, 1946-47; m. Carol J. Bernstein, Aug. 6, 1950; children—Sinda (Mrs. Michael Tepprof), Suzanne (Mrs. Terry Biggs), Robin Patricia, Linda Diane. Gen. contractor, owner Fairlawn Builders, Miami, Fla., 1949-60; with Midwest Mortgage Co., Miami, 1959—, exec. v.p., 1963-73, pres., 1973—; v.p. Warwick Enterprises, Louisville, 1967—, Southeast Life Ins. Co., Miami, 1973—, Southeast Title Ins. Co., Miami, 1971—, Meridian Abstract & Title Co., Miami, 1969—. Mem. U. Louisville Assos., 1964—, citizens bd. U. Miami, 1971—. Served with USNR, 1943-44. Mason (Shriner); mem. B'nai B'rith. Home: 5515 Orduna Dr Coral Gables FL 33146 Office: 120 NE 9th St Miami FL 33132

HARRIS, LOUIS CECIL, lawyer; b. Roba, Ala., July 3, 1906; s. Henry Jackson and Anne Laurie (Swint) H.; LL.B., Chattanooga Coll. Law, 1929, LL.M., 1930; m. Ella M. Brown, June 10, 1932; children—Louis Cecil, Helen (Mrs. James C. Dale, III). Admitted to practice Tenn. bar, 1929, U.S. Dist. Ct. bar, 1931, U.S. Supreme Ct bar, 1956, U.S. Ct. Appeals bar, 1957, U.S. Ct. Mil. Appeals bar, 1956; practiced in Chattanooga, 1929—; sr. mem. firm Harris, Moon & Meacham (name now Harris, Moon, Bell & McCallie), 1967—. Mem. adv. commn. Tenn. Supreme Ct., 1965—. Pres. Chattanooga Council Community Forces, 1958-61, Met. Council for Community Services, Inc., 1972-74; pres. Chattanooga Travelers Aid Assn., 1957-58; v.p. region 4 Nat. Travelers Aid Assn., 1957-61. Bd. dirs. United Fund Greater Chattanooga, 1962—; vice chmn. adv. bd. Chattanooga Hamilton County Health Dept., 1971—; Served as lt. col. AUS, 1942-46. Named Outstanding Optimist Chattanooga Optimist Club, 1944. Fellow Internat. Soc. Barristers; mem. Internat. Assn. Ins. Council, Am., Tenn., Chattanooga bar assns., Am. Judicature Soc., Delta Theta Phi. Presbyn. (tchr. Louis Harris Bible class 1947—; del. commr. to Gen. Assembly Columbus, O., 1958; elder 1938—; clk ch. 1971—). Kiwanian (pres. Chattanooga 1966; lt. gov. div. 3 Ky.-Tenn. dist. internat. 1971-72). Clubs: Mountain City (sec. 1966-67, 68-69), Chattanooga Golf and Country (v.p. 1957-58). Home: 1504 Sunset Rd Chattanooga TN 37405 Office: 1217 Hamilton Nat Bank Bldg Chattanooga TN 37402

HARRIS, LOUIS PAUL, state ofcl.; b. Cin., Oct. 18, 1924; s. Morris and Bess (Libbert) H.; student U. Cin., 1946-48; m. Peggy Lou Leeper, Aug. 10, 1952; 1 dau., Michele. News editor radio sta. WCNH, Quincy, Fla., 1948-49, radio sta. WTAL, Tallahassee, 1950-56; travel editor Fla. State News Bur., Fla. Dept. Commerce, Tallahassee, 1956-63, mgr. Fla. Welcome Stas., 1963-68, asst. bur. chief marketing and tourism, 1969-71, acting bur. chief, 1971-72, adminstrv. asst. to the dir. State of Fla. Tourism, 1973—, state coordinator N.Y. World's Fair, Fla. Pavilion, 1964. Served with USAAF, 1942-46; PTO. Recipient award Midwest Travel Writers, 1960, 64. Mem. Capital Press Corps (charter). Home: 1113 Wisteria Dr Tallahassee FL 32303 Office: 107 W Gaines St Tallahassee FL 32304

HARRIS, LUTHER DELBERT, supt. schs.; b. Searcy, Ark., Sept. 1, 1918; s. James Elbert and Mary Ella (Henderson) H.; B.A., Harding Coll., 1940; M.A., Geroge Peabody Coll., 1949; Ed.S., U. Ark., 1970; m. Reedie Bridges, Mar. 3, 1940; children—Luther Delbert, Jr., Ruth (Mrs. Ronald MacDonald). Prin., coach Alpin (Ark.) Pub. Schs., 1940-41, Judsonia (Ark.) Pub. Schs., 1941-43; supt. schs., Kensett, Ark., 1943-51; prin. Paris (Ark.) High Sch., 1951-61, Blytheville (Ark.) Sch. Dist., 1961-63, dir. instrn. 1963-65, asst. supt. instrn., 1965-70, supt. schs., 1970—. Served with USNR, 1944-46. Mem. Ark. Assn. Supervision and Curriculum Devel. (pres. 1968-69), Ark. Edn. Assn. (dir. 1957-58), Ark. Dept. Edn. (chmn. adv. council 1969-71), Paris C. of C. (pres. 1960). Methodist (sec. ofcl. bd. 1954—, lay speaker 1954-72). Kiwanian (pres. 1960). Club: Key (sponsor 1951-70) (Paris, Blytheville). Home: 732 Adams St Blytheville AR 72315 Office: 614 Chickasawba St Blytheville AR 72315

HARRIS, MARGARET PARSONS (MRS. JOHN MALCOLM HARRIS), civic worker; b. Tampa, Fla.; d. William H., Jr. and Bonnie (Crews) Parsons; student Fla. State U.; B.A., U. N.C., 1945; m. John Malcolm Harris, Aug. 16, 1946; children—John Malcolm, William D., Donna M. Mem. women's com. Houston Symphony Soc. Bd. dirs. Houston Grand Opera Assn. Mem. Harris County Heritage Soc., Women's Inst. Houston, Mus. Fine Arts, Friends of Bayou Bend, Delta Delta Delta. Republican. Episcopalian. Clubs: Racquet, Briar, University, Champions Golf (Houston). Home: 2928 Del Monte Dr Houston TX 77019

HARRIS, MARGWYN SAMUEL, educator; b. Columbus, Tex., Oct. 24, 1923; s. Earl Preston and Elizabeth (Wright) H.; B.S., Prairie View State Coll., 1947; M.S., Atlanta U., 1949; postgrad. (Canadian Nat. Sci. grantee), U. Toronto, 1954-57; m. Harriet Bernice Robbins, June 7, 1944; 1 dau., Sheree Denise. Prin., Hillard High Sch., Bay City, Tex., 1948-49; asst. prof. biology Tex. So. U., 1949-66; sci. tchr. Galena Park (Tex.) Sr. High Sch., 1966—. Democratic alternate election judge, precinct 158, Harris County, Houston, 1960—. Committeeman, Boy Scouts Am., Houston, 1969—; life mem. State of Tex. P.T.A. Served to 1st lt., inf. AUS, 1943-46. Mem. N.E.A., Tex. Assn. Coll. Tchrs. (chpt. pres. 1965-66), Tex. State Tchrs. Assn. (sec. 1969), Tex. Classroom Tchrs. Assn. (pres. Galena Park dist. 1970-71), Phi Beta Sigma, Beta Kappa Chi. Home: 3305 Sunbeam St Houston TX 77051 Office: Galena Park Sr High Sch Galena Park TX 77547

HARRIS, NORMAN OLIVER, coll. ofcl.; b. Shinglehouse, Pa., May 27, 1917; s. Theodore Clifton and Amelia (Rappenecker) H.; student Bucknell U., 1935; D.D.S., Temple U., 1939; M.S. in Dentistry, Ohio State U., 1952; m. Grace Haynes, June 26, 1953; 1 son, Gary. Intern, USPHS, 1939; pvt. practice, Norristown, Pa., 1940; dental adviser UN China, 1946-47; entered USAAF, 1947, advanced through grades to lt. col. USAF, 1953, ret., 1963; assigned USAF Sch. Aviation Medicine, San Antonio, Tex., 1953-61; faculty Dental Sch. U. P.R., San Juan, 1963—, prof. gen. histology, 1966—, dir. research, 1964—. Mem. Am. Dental Assn., Internat. Assn. Dental Research, Am. Ednl. Research Assn., Am. Chem. Assn., Am. Pub. Health Assn. Author: Histologia Geral, 1973. Served with AUS, 1941-46. Home: 450 Ponce de Leon St San Juan PR 00905 Office: School Dentistry Univ Puerto Rico San Juan PR 00905

HARRIS, POLLY ADAIR ELSTEIN (MRS PAUL HARRIS), pub. relations exec.; b. Kansas City, Mo., Dec. 18, 1924; d. Mordy A. and Lyllian (Harris) Elstein; A.A., Kansas City Jr. Coll., 1943; B.S. in Psychology, U. Mo. at Kansas City, 1945; m. Paul Harris, Mar. 31, 1949. Mem. bus. staff U. Mo., Kansas City, 1945-49; radio broadcaster, writer El Paso, Tex., 1950-55; writer, accountant exec., pub. relations dir. Mithoff Advt., 1956-68; pub. relations dir. Empire Aircraft; dir. Harris & Harris Pub. Relations Fashion, hairstyle TV commentator, 1958—; publicity dir. El Paso-Southwestern Sun Carnival, 1959—; speaker on Civic Theater; dir. Press Club Gridiron Show; mus. comedy dir. El Paso Theater Downtown; dir. hist. pageants State Nat. Bank. Mem. El Paso Bd. Devel., 1972—. Recipient Feature Writing award Tex. Press Women; awards Voice of Am.; named Woman of Yr., El Paso Herald-Post, 1971-72. Mem. El Paso Advt. Club (pres. 1972—, dir., Achievement award 1959, 60, 61, Outstanding Mem. award 1964), Internat. Platform Assn. Clubs: Press (dir.), Empire (dir.), Bullfight (El Paso). Home: 6212 Papago Dr El Paso TX 79903 Office: 2810 Montana El Paso TX 79903

HARRIS, RAMON STANTON, physician; b. Nashville, Oct. 2, 1926; s. Richard Howard and Carrie (Davis) H.; student Fisk U., 1943-45; student John Carroll U., Case Western Reserve U.; M.D., Meharry Med. Coll., 1963; m. Ruthie Lois Chatmon, Apr. 25, 1947; children—Richard S., Sandra (Mrs. Michael Corrado), Frances Lynn. Intern Hubbard Hosp., Nashville, 1963-64; resident Kings County Hosp., Bklyn., 1964-67, staff anesthesiologist, 1967-68; chief of anesthesiology Meharry Med. Coll., 1968-73; practice medicine specializing in aneshtesiology, Nashville. Served with AUS, 1945-46. Mem. Tenn. Soc. Anesthesiologists, Soc. Acad. Anesthesia Chmn., Am. Soc. Anesthesiologists. Home: 4209 Drakes Branch Rd Nashville TN 37218 Office: 1005 18th Av N Nashville TN 27308

HARRIS, REUBEN EARLE, pub. service adminstr.; b. Memphis, Mar. 17, 1921; s. Reuben A. and Louise (Farmer) H.; B.S., U. Tenn., 1948, M.S., 1957; m. Mary Evelyn Caldwell, Dec. 28, 1942; children—Mary Harris (Mrs. Phillip Wayne Lynn), Elizabeth Anne (Mrs. William D. Cantrell), Phyllis Elaine, Matthew Caldwell. Design engr. Monsanto Chem. Corp., Oak Ridge, 1946-47; mech. engr. Phillips Petroleum Co., Bartlesville, Okla., 1947-51; project engr. Union Carbide Nuclear Corp., Oak Ridge, 1951-56; design engr. Boeing Airplane Co., Wichita, Kan. 1956-58; reactor engr. U.S. AEC, Washington, 1958-63; dir. Center Indsl. Services, U. Tenn., Nashville, 1963—. Vice mayor, Brentwood, Tenn., 1971. Served to 1st lt. USAAF, 1944-46. Registered profl. engr., Tenn., Kan. Mem. Brentwood C. of C. (pres. 1971), Order of Engr., Tau Beta Pi, Phi Kappa Phi, Am. Soc. Quality Control, Am. Mgmt. Assn. Home: 204 Arnold Rd Brentwood TN 37027 Office: 323 McLemore St Nashville TN 37203

HARRIS, RICHARD BURL, lawyer; b. Wister, Okla., May 1, 1926; s. Claib and Lehmon (Baldwin) H.; B.A., East Central State Coll., Ada, Okla., 1949; LL.B., U. Okla., 1955; m. Janis Willey, July 5, 1949; children—Richard Burl, Dawn Carole. Admitted to Okla. bar, 1955; practice law, Ada, Okla., 1955—. U.S. commr., 1965-67; atty. Ada City, 1967-69; atty. Stratford City, 1968-73. Chmn., Christmas Seals, drive chmn. Ada Community Chest, 1961, pres., 1962. Mem. Pontotoc County Democratic Central Com. Trustee East Central State Coll. Found., Ada; trustee First Methodist Ch. of Ada Found., sec. 1970. Served with USNR, 1944-46, 50-52; PTO. Recipient spl. service award Community Chest, 1961, 62, 64. Mem. Am., Okla., Pontotoc County (pres. 1956) bar assns., Okla. Assn. Def. Counsel (v.p. 1967), Ada C. of C., E. Central State Coll. Alumni Assn. (pres. 1970-71). Methodist. Home: 414 W Kings Rd Ada OK 74820 Office: PO Box 817 Townsend Bldg Ada OK 74820

HARRIS, RICHARD WARWICK, librarian; b. LaPorte, Ind., Jan. 22, 1919; s. Clarence Eugene and Winnie Louise (Brown) H.; B.A., North Central Coll. at Naperville, Ill., 1940; M.L.S., U. N.C., 1966; m. Carolyn Louise Simmons, Nov. 27, 1968; 1 dau., Laura Kathryn. Commd. USAAF, 1940, advanced through grades to maj. USAF, 1960; C.B.I., 1942-43; with hdqrs. Air Weather Service, 1945; instr. meteorology, 1947-51; with Far East Air Force, 1951-53, 19th Air Force, 1962-64; serials librarian Med. Center Library, Duke U., Durham, N.C., 1966-67; sci. librarian Tex. A. and M. U., College Station, 1967-69; library dir. Tex. State Tech. Inst., Waco, 1959-72; dir. Learning Resources Center, Chattanooga State Tech. Community Coll., 1972—. Cons., RocketDyne, McGregory, Tex., 1968. Decorated Air medal. Mem. A.L.A., Beta Phi Mu. Home: 824 Sutton Dr Hixson TN 37343

HARRIS, ROBERT BROMLEY, ednl. adminstr.; b. Denton, Tex., Feb. 4, 1911; s. Robert Bromley and Elizabeth (Chambers) H.; B.S., North Tex. State U., 1932; M.A., U. Mo., 1936; Ed.D., U. Tex. at Austin, 1952; m. Anna Belle Smith, June 4, 1938; 1 son, Robert Bromley III. Tchr. James Bowie Elementary Sch., Dallas, 1932-36; tchr., coach W.H. Adamson High Sch., Dallas, 1936-42, 1945-47; prin. Ben Milam Elementary Sch., Dallas, 1947-50, Rosemont Elementary Sch., 1950-53, L.V. Stockard Jr. High Sch., 1953-60, Bryan Adams High Sch., 1960-70; dir. secondary edn. Sch. Adminstrn. Bldg., Dallas, 1970—. Served with USAAF, 1942-45. Mem. Nat. Assn. Secondary Sch. Prins., Nat., Tex. assns. for suprs. and curriculum devel., Am. Assn. Sch. Adminstrn., Tex., Nat. P.T.A.'s, Dallas Sch. Adminstrs. Assn. (v.p. 1957-58). Presbyn. (deacon 1955-58, elder 1958-61, Sunday sch. tchr. 1954—). Mason (32 deg., Shriner), Kiwanian. Home: 2834 Gladiolus Lane Dallas TX 75233 Office: 3700 Ross Av Dallas TX 75204

HARRIS, ROBERT HARDING, aerospace exec.; b. Montgomery, Ala., Oct. 31, 1920; s. Augustus Jackson and Florence (Hirch) H.; B.Aero. Engring., Auburn U., 1947; postgrad., Union Coll., 1948, Emory U., 1962-63; m. Zuma Jeanette Williams, Aug. 30, 1946; children—Susan Elaine (Mrs. Franklin Mills Lindsey), Margaret Ann, Robert Harding, Nancy Jeanette. With Gen. Electric Co., 1947—, guided missile engr., Schenectady, N.Y., 1947, application engr., aviation, 1948-49, rectifier, motor specialist, Atlanta, 1950, sales engr., 1951-55, mgr. Atlanta territory, aviation and def., 1956-59, regional def. rep., 1960-61, mgr. Atlanta dist. operation, def. programs div., 1962-69, mgr. Eastern region operation, aerospace programs relations div., 1969—. Bd. dirs. Ga. chpt. Leukemia Soc. Am. Served to capt. USAAF, 1942-45. Decorated D.F.C., Air medal. Mem. Am. Inst. Aero and Astronautics, Am. Helicopter Soc., Aviation Hall of Fame, Air Force Hist. Found., Air Force Assn. (chpt. pres. 1965), Elfun Soc. (pres. 1960), Atlanta C. of C. (chmn. aviation com.), Tau Beta Pi, Pi Tau Sigma, Omicron Delta Kappa, Sigma Nu. Methodist. Rotarian (v.p.). Clubs: Aviation Executives (Miami, Fla.); Cherokee Town and Country (Atlanta). Home: 4147 Paran Pines Dr NW Atlanta GA 30327 Office: Suite 417 1800 Peachtree Rd NW Atlanta GA 30309

HARRIS, ROBERT SMITH, architect, engr.; b. Dallas, Oct. 4, 1922; s. Jesse Whitfield and Della (Smith) H.; B.S. in Civil Engring., U. Tex., 1951, B.S. in Archtl. Engring., 1951, M.S. in Archtl. Engring., 1955; m. Anna Margaret Boutwell, June 17, 1948; children—Robert Smith, Helen Ann. Draftsman Landauer & Guerrero, Dallas, 1948-49; jr. engr. Landauer, Guerrero & Shafer, 1951-52, structural designer A.J. Boynton Co., 1952-53; instr. U. Tex. at Austin, 1953-55; archtl. engr. Tex. Industries, Dallas, 1955-56; architect Stanley Brown Co., 1956-57; architect Pipeline Engring. Co., 1957-58; partner engring. and archtl. firm Barnard, Harris & Ancira, 1958; pvt. practice as architect and engr., Dallas, 1958-60; archtl. engr. Campbell-Taggart, Inc., 1960-61; architect Gen. Services Adminstrn., 1961; architect and engr. Southwest region Internal Revenue Service, 1961-66; architect, engr. Collins Radio Co., Dallas, 1966-72; architect, chief engr. Delta Bldg. Systems, Dallas, 1972—; chincilla rancher, 1969—. Served to 1st lt., AUS, 1942-46, 1st lt. to lt. col., U.S. Army Res., 1946-69. Registered profl. engr., Ia., Tex., Okla., Miss., Ga., La., Cal., Ky., Mo., Ark., Colo. Mem. A.I.A., Tex. Soc. Architects, Nat., Tex. socs. profl. engrs., Am. Concrete Inst., Am. Assn. Archtl. Engrs., Am. Wood Preserving Assn., Illuminating Engring. Soc., Prestressed Concrete Inst., Am. Inst. Econ. Research, Alpha Tau Omega. Lion, Toastmaster. Home: 1604 Marquette Dr Richardson TX 75080 Office: 10848 Luna Rd Dallas TX 75220

HARRIS, RODGER SHERMAN, librarian; b. Milw., Jan. 24, 1932; s. John Coman and Laura (Rodgers) H.; B.S., U. Wis., 1953, M.S., 1955; M.L.S., U. Okla., 1971; m. Kathryn Astrid Mygdal, Dec. 21, 1956; children—Laura Margaret, Tod Sherman. Jr. geologist Shell Oil Co., Hobbs, Las Vegas, N.M., Midland, Sweetwater, Tex., Houston, 1956-57; prodn. geologist Shell Devel. Co., Houston, 1958; geologist Shell Oil Co., Midland, Tex., 1959-70; geology and zoology librarian U. N.C. at Chapel Hill, 1970-72, personnel librarian and adminstrv. asst. to head cataloger L. R. Wilson Library, 1972, acting head catalog dept., 1973, head catalog dept., 1973—. Pres. Midland Civic Concerts Assn., 1964-67; pres. Friends of Midland County Pub. Library, 1966, treas., 1963-65, 67, mem. county library bd., 1969-70, chmn. 1970; bd. dirs. YMCA, Midland, 1969-70. Mem. West Tex. Geol. Soc. (chmn. library com. 1969-70), U. N.C. Library Staff Assn. (pres. 1972-73), N.C. Library Assn., Beta Phi Mu. Home: 316 Ridgecrest Dr Chapel Hill NC 27514

HARRIS, RUSSEL CLEMONS, JR., constrn. co. exec.; b. Waycross, Ga., Apr. 7, 1937; s. Russel Clemons and Ruth May (Joyner) H.; B.S., Ga. Inst. Tech., 1959; m. Rena Hoyt Clark, Oct. 29, 1960; children—Sally Burney, Rena Clark. Vice-pres. W. S. Clark & Sons, Tarboro, N.C., 1962—; pres. Harris Industries, Inc., Tarboro, N.C., 1964—, R & S Enterprises, Inc., Tarboro, 1968—, Tarboro Inn, 1971—. Mem. Tarboro Edgecombe Devel. Com., Coastal Plains Devel. Commn. Bd. dirs. Wesleyan Coll. Found. Served with USMCR. Mem. Nat. Fertilizer Solutions Assn. (dir.), Ind. Mfrs. Com., Merchants Assn. Episcopalian (jr. warden 1968-69). Home: St Andrews Extension Tarboro NC 27886 Office: 495 W St James St Tarboro NC 27886

HARRIS, SAMUEL WALTER, petroleum engr.; b. Maysville, Okla., June 6, 1918; s. Otis and Dora Ada (Johnson) H.; B.S., U. Okla., 1942; m. Amaree Aeolus Holloway, July 28, 1940; children—Sammy Gene, Tommy Dean, Ginger (Mrs. Jerry Lee Hickey). With Asphalt Soils Lab., Anderson Pritchard Oil Co., Cyril, Okla., 1942-45; with Halliburton Oil Well Cementing Co., Duncan, Okla., 1945-48; refinery engr., maintenance supt., refinery mgr., gen. mgr. petroleum refining Kerr McGee Corp., Oklahoma City, 1948—. Registered profl. engr., Okla. Home: 2721 NW 61st St Oklahoma City OK 73112 Office: McGee Center Tower Oklahoma City OK 73102

HARRIS, STANLEY SUTHERLAND, judge; b. Washington, Oct. 19, 1927; s. Stanley Raymond and Elizabeth (Sutherland) H.; student Va. Poly Inst., 1945; B.S., U. Va., 1951, J.D., 1953; m. Rebecca L. Ashley, Aug. 1, 1964; children—Scott Sutherland, Todd A., Mark A. Admitted to D.C. bar, 1953; asso. Hogan & Hartson, Washington, 1953-64, partner, 1964-70; judge D.C. Superior Ct., 1971-72, D.C. Ct. of Appeals, 1972—. Dir. Allen Weather Corp., 1963-68, Newfound Corp., 1969-70. Gen. counsel, dir. Landon Alumni Assn., 1962-70; trustee Landon Sch. Corp., 1965-68. Served with AUS, 1945-47. Mem. Am. (vice chmn. gas, electric and nuclear energy com. 1966-67, vice chmn. adminstrv. practice and specialization in the law com. 1968-70, vice chmn. communications com. 1969-70), FCC (sec. 1964-66, exec. com. 1966-69) bar assns., Bar Assn. D.C. (chmn. ann. conv. com. 1969-70, bd. dirs. 1970-72), Raven Soc., Phi Kappa Sigma, Phi Delta Phi, Pi Delta Epsilon. Republican. Clubs: Metropolitan, Barristers (sec. 1969-70), Chevy Chase (Washington), Home: 9621 Weathered Oak Ct Bethesda MD 20034 Office: DC Ct Appeals Washington DC 20001

HARRIS, STEVEN EARL, city ofcl., civil engr.; b. Mayking, Ky., May 30, 1933; s. Spence Edward and Sadie Elizabeth (Hoolbrook) H.; B.S. in C.E., U. Ky., 1957; m. Patricia A. Tucker, Dec. 27, 1953; children—Steven Earl, James Edward. Constrn. engr. Verville Constrn. Co., 1953-63; city engr., Maysville, Ky., 1963—. Registered profl. engr., Ky. Mason (Shriner). Lion. Mem. Christian Ch. (mem. ch. bd. 1962—). Home: Main St Tollesboro KY 41189 Office: 1008 Forest Av Maysville KY 41056

HARRIS, THOMAS JESSE, cons. aviation and transp.; b. Chgo., Mar. 16, 1915; s. Elijah George and Sarah Stewart (Wright) H.; student Northwestern U., 1934-38; m. Marilynn Lois Tenny, Mar. 14, 1942; children—Thomas Elijah, Kendra Jane (Mrs. Don C. Denman), Elizabeth Anne, Jefferson Wright. With Am. Airlines, Inc., various locations, 1938-57, European cargo mgr. Am. Overseas Airlines, London, Eng., 1947-50, system dir. cargo sales parent co., N.Y.C., 1950-57; v.p., gen. mgr. Aero Commander, Inc., Bethany, Okla., 1957-63; founder, pres. Mgmt. Enterprises, -Inc., Oklahoma City, 1963—; v.p., dir. Air Center, Inc., Bethany; chmn. Mgmt. Enterprises Internat., Ltd., Oklahoma City, London. Del., Republican Nat. Conv., 1964; Rep. candidate U.S. Senate, 1964. Chmn. trustees Nat. Right to Work Legal Def. Found., Washington, 1969—. Served to lt. comdr. USNR, 1942-46. Recipient Distinguished Service medal FAA, 1972. Mem. Am. Inst. Aeros. and Astronautics, Soc. Automotive Engrs., Am. Inst. Traffic and Transp., Alpha Kappa Psi. Conglist. Clubs: Wings, Metropolitan, Marco Polo (N.Y.C.); Army Navy, National Aviation (Washington); Petroleum (Oklahoma City). Home: 327 NW 18th St Oklahoma City OK 73103 Office: 4040 Lincoln Blvd Oklahoma City OK 73105

HARRIS, T(OM) C., editor; b. Parrott, Va., July 28, 1908; s. T.C. and Mena (Cassie) H.; student pub. schs.; m. Patricia Brock, May 19, 1929; children—Margaret and Patricia (twins), Sharon. Successively reporter, city editor, mng. editor, exec. editor, exec. v.p., gen. mgr., asso. editor St. Petersburg (Fla.) Times, 1923-68; exec. editor, El Mundo, San Juan, P.R., 1968—. Mem. Inter-Am. Press Assn. (dir. former chmn. com. freedom of press), C. of C. Club: St. Petersburg Yacht. Home: 1075 14th Av N St Petersburg FL 33705 Office: Apartado 2408 San Juan PR 00936

HARRIS, VINCENT MADELEY, bishop; b. Conroe, Tex., Oct. 14, 1913; s. George Malcolm and Margaret (Madeley) H.; student St. Mary's Sem., La Porte, Tex., 1932-34, Pontifical N.Am. Coll., Rome, Italy, 1934-39; S.T.B., Pontifical Gregorian U., Rome, 1936, J.C.B., 1939; J.C.L., Cath. U. Am., 1940. Ordained priest Roman Catholic Ch., 1938; prof. St. Mary's Sem., La Porte, Tex., 1940-51; sec.-treas. St. Mary's Sem., Houston, 1952-66; chancellor Diocese of Galveston-Houston, 1948-66, diocesan consultor, 1950-66; 1st bishop of Beaumont, Tex., 1966-71; coadjutor bishop, Austin, 1971, 2d bishop, Austin, 1971—. Made domestic prelate with title Rt. Rev. Msgr., 1956. Decorated knight grand cross Equestrian Order of Holy Sepulchre of Jerusalem. Mem. Alumni Assn. N.Am. Coll, in Rome. K.C. (Tex, chaplain 1967-69). Home: 4007 Balcones Dr Austin TX 78731 Office: 1600 N Congress Av Austin TX 78701

HARRIS, WARREN WHITMAN, chemist-physicist; b. Duluth, Minn., Oct. 14, 1918; s. Edwin Thomas and Ethel N. (McCauley) H.; A.B., Columbia, 1940; m. Tessie Koverda, Oct. 11, 1945; children—Walter H., Helen W. (Mrs. Thomas L.N. Knight). Chemist, Hat Corp. of Am., Norwalk, Conn., 1940-42; research asso. Columbia U. div. war research, N.Y.C., 1942-45; chemist gaseous diffusion plant Union Carbide Corp., Oak Ridge, 1945-68; chemist, physicist Union Carbide Nuclear Co., Oak Ridge Nat. Lab., 1968—. Participant, Internat. Union Crystallography, Madrid, Spain, 1956. Mem. Research Soc. Am., Electron Microscopy Soc. Am., A.A.A.S., U.S. Power Squadron. Contbr. articles profl. jours. Patentee method for felting fur.

HARRIS, WILEY DOWD JR., clergyman; b. Raleigh, N.C., Oct. 15, 1945; s. Wiley Dowd and Eileen Finch (Ellis) H.; A.B. with honors, Atlantic Christian Coll., 1968; M.Div., Brite Divinity Sch., Tex. Christian U., 1971; m. Billie Tankard, June 23, 1968; 1 dau., Amanda. Ordained to ministry, Christian Ch., 1971; minister, Fort Myers (Fla.) Christian Ch. (Disciples of Christ), 1971—. Mem. state com. Christian Action of Christian Ch., Fort Myers, 1972—; laison officer, Lee County Mission Board, 1973—. Vice pres. Adult Adv. Bd. for Emergency Sch. Assistance Act. Mem. Lee County Ministerial Assn. (v.p. 1973—). Democrat. Home: 1436 Rosada Way Fort Myers FL 33901 Office: 5010 McGregor Blvd Fort Myers FL 33901

HARRIS, WILLIAM H., radio personality; b. Logan, W.Va., Sept. 18, 1941; s. William and Elaine (Stollings) H.; student Davidson Coll., N.C., 1959-60; A.B., W.Va. U., 1963; m. Sandra Lowe, Apr. 11, 1969. Morning air personality, talk show host WAJR Radio, Morgantown, W.Va., 1962-70; morning air personality WFLA Radio, Tampa, Fla., 1970—. Frequent guest speaker, emcee, celebrity participant in bus., civic and charity functions. Served as 1st lt. AUS, 1964-66. Decorated Air medal, Army Commendation medal; named One of 13 Finalists for Air Personality of Year, Billboard mag., 1973. Mem. Kappa Alpha. Home: 5233 Picador Ct Tampa FL 33617 Office: WFLA Radio Box 1410 Tampa FL 33601

HARRIS, WILLIAM HAROLD, computer co. exec.; b. Durant, Okla., Aug. 23, 1929; s. William Harold and Audrie (Harper) H.; B.S., Okla. State U., 1957. Coordinator Western Co., Fort Worth, 1959-65; project mgr. service bur. Applied Indsl. Dynamics, Fort Worth, 1965-68; asst. treas. Comml. Computer Services, Fort Worth, 1968—. Served with USNR, 1951-55. Mem. Nat. Machine Accountants Assn. Home: 2206 Voyagers Arlington TX 76012 Office: 309 W 7th St Fort Worth TX 76104

HARRIS, WILLIAM HENRY, newspaper publisher; b. Laurel, Miss., May 24, 1925; s. Edgar G. and Beulah (Ligon) H.; B.S., Miss. State U., 1948; m. Wanda Marie West, Dec. 10, 1947 (dec. May 1973); children—Beulah Marie (Mrs. Harry Luke, Jr.), William Henry, Carol Elizabeth, Edgar West. With Daily Times Leader, West Point, Miss., 1945—, editor, pub., 1952—; pub. Starkville (Miss.) Daily News, 1960—; dir. Clay County Fed. Savs. & Loan Assn., West Point, Miss. Pres., Miss. Econ. Council, 1969-70. Commr., Golden Triangle Regional Airport, 1966—. Served with USAAF, 1943-45. Mem. Miss. Press Assn. (past pres.), So. Newspaper Pub. Assn., Sigma Chi. Baptist (deacon). Rotarian (past pres.). Home: 948 E Main St West Point MS 39773 Office: 227 Court St West Point MS 39773

HARRIS, WILLIAM MADISON, banker; b. Farmville, Va., Feb. 28, 1932; s. William Madison and Ann (Thackston) H.; B.S., Coll. William and Mary, 1953; m. Marian Leonie Burks, July 27, 1957; children—Ann Holladay, William Claiborne, Elizabeth Madison, John Spencer Randolph. Dist. traffic supr., traffic engr., traffic supr.-personnel Chesapeake & Potomac Telephone Co. of Va., Richmond, Norfolk, Lynchburg, 1953-63; personnel dir. Central Nat. Bank of Richmond, 1963-71; v.p. personnel Planters Nat. Bank, Rocky Mount, N.C., 1971—; lectr. U. Richmond, 1965-71. Co-chmn. United Givers Fund, 1961-68. Mem. Henrico County Republican Com., 1964-66. Mem. exec. bd. Va. Coll. Placement Assn., 1968-69; bd. dirs. Richmond Senior Center, 1970-71. Served as lt. USNR, 1953-56. Mem. Am. Soc. Personnel Adminstrn. (past pres. Richmond), S.R. (sec. Va. chpt. 1970-71), Richmond C. of C., Sigma Epsilon Pi, Kappa Alpha, Republican. Presbyn. (elder). Clubs: Cosmopolitan (pres. 1958) (Lynchburg); Fishing Bay Yacht (commodore 1970) (Deltaville, Va.); Benvenue Country (Rocky Mount). Home: 210 Gravely Dr Rocky Mount NC 27801 Office: 131 N Church St Rocky Mount NC 27801

HARRIS, WILLIAM OVERTON, JR., physician; b. Norfolk, Va., Sept. 27, 1933; s. William Overton and Thelma (Dalton) H.; A.B., Va. Mil. Inst., 1955 M.D., Med. Coll. Va., 1959; m. Sally Ann Lauck, June 7, 1958; children—Grayson Lauck, William Overton III. Intern medicine Med. Coll. Va., 1959-60, resident medicine, 1962-65; spl. fellow neurology Mayo Clinic, 1965-67; practice medicine specializing in neurology, Richmond, Va., 1967-69, Newport News, Va., also Hampton, 1969—, asst. prof. neurology Med. Coll. Va., Richmond, 1967-69, clin. asst. prof. neurology, 1969—; neurologist, Hampton Roads Neurol. Center, Newport News, Va., 1969—; neurology cons. Kecoughtan VA Hosp.; mem. staff Riverside Hosp., Newport News, Va., Dixie Hosp., Hampton, Va., Mary Immaculate Hosp., Hampton, Va. Bd. dirs. Peninsula Multiple Sclerosis Soc., Peninsula Muscular Dystrophy Soc. Served as capt. USAF, 1960-62. Recipient Henry W. Woltman award Mayo Clinic, 1968. Diplomate Am. Bd. Internal Medicine, Am. Bd. Neurology and Psychiatry. Mem. Am. Acad. Neurology, A.C.P., A.M.A., So. Med. Assn., Va. Med. Soc., Peninsula Acad. Medicine, Newport News Med. Soc. Home: 20 Beverly Hills Dr Newport News VA 23606 Office: 11 Bruton Av Newport News VA 23606

HARRISBERGER, LEE, univ. dean; b. Denver, Sept. 24, 1924; s. Ivan A. and Gail E. (Hinrichs) H.; B.S., U. Okla., 1945; M.S., U. Colo., 1950; Ph.D., Purdue U., 1963; m. Ruth B. Hauffe, Aug. 14, 1969; children—Russel Surgeson, Ronald Surgeson, Dianne, Judy, David. Instr., Murray Jr. Coll., Tishomingo, Okla., 1946-49; asst. prof. mech. engring. U. Utah, 1950-54; asso. prof. mech. engring. N.C. State Coll., Raleigh, 1955-60; instr. mech. engring. Purdue U., 1961-63; Halliburton prof., head mech. and aerospace engring. Okla. State U., Stillwater, 1963-71; dean sci. and engring. U. Tex. of Permian Basin, Odessa, 1971—. Cons. NSF, Worcester Poly. Inst. Bd. dirs. Midland-Odessa Symphony, Odessa Civic Concert Series. Served to lt. (j.g.) USNR, 1943-46. NSF Sci. Faculty fellow, 1960-62. Mem. Am. Soc. M.E., Am. Soc. Engring. Edn. (1st place winner Young Engr. Tchrs. Paper Contest 1952, v.p. 1970-73, chmn. long range planning com. 1973, editor Mech. Engring. News mag. 1966-71, editor ERM mag. 1969-71, dir. 1970—). Author: Mechanization of Motion, 1963; Engineersmanship, 1966. Contbr. articles profl. jours. Home: Route 1 Box 585 Odessa TX 79763

HARRISON, A. CLEVELAND, educator; b. McRae, Ark., Aug. 17, 1924; s. Allie and Floy (Honea) H.; A.A. with honors, Little Rock Jr. Coll., 1947; B.S. cum laude, Ohio State U., 1949, M.A., 1951; M.A., U. Ark., 1958; Ph.D. with honors, U. Kan., 1967; m. Marian Blair Gammill, June 22, 1946; children—Kathleen Louise (Mrs. John Hillman McCord), Lee Cleveland. Instr. Little Rock Jr. Coll., 1949-50; grad. teaching asst. Ohio State U., 1950-51; asst. prof. Little Rock U., 1951-59; asst. prof. U. Ark., 1959-65, asso. prof., 1965-69, prof., 1969; prof., head dept. theatre Auburn U., 1970—; asso. editor drama So. Speech Jour., 1969—; fine arts cons. Monett (Mo.) Area Fine Arts Program; fine arts cons. Bella Vista (Ark.) Fine Arts Camp, 1967-68. Bd. dirs. Little Rock (Ark.) Community Theatre, 1962-65. Served with AUS, 1943-46. Decorated Purple Heart medal. Recipient G.J. Francis Meml. award, 1947. Mem. Nat. Collegiate Players, So. Speech Communication Assn., Am. Theatre Assn., U. and Coll. Theatre Assn., Southeastern Theatre Conf., Am. Speech Assn., Am. Assn. U. Profs., Delta Psi Omega, Alpha Psi Omega, Phi Theta Kappa, Phi Delta Kappa. Author (with V. Baker, M.B. Hart and R.T. Eubanks): Principles of Effective Speaking, 1961. Contbr. essays, reviews to fine arts, speech jours. Home: 805 Cary Dr Auburn AL 36830 Office: Dept Theatre Auburn U Auburn AL 36830

HARRISON, AIX BARNARD, educator; b. Zearing, Ia., Feb. 14, 1925; s. J. Rollin and Anna (Barnard) H.; B.S., U. Ill., 1949, M.S., 1950; Ph.D., Mich. State U., 1959; m. Gwen Adair Laufer, Jan. 7, 1950; children—George Andrew, Nancy Ann. Tchr. pub. schs., Galva, Ill., 1949-50; asst. prof. phys. edn. Okla. State U., Stillwater, 1950-56, asso. prof., 1958-67, prof., 1968—. Served to 2d lt. USAAF, 1942-45. Fellow Am. Coll. Sports Medicine; mem. Okla. (pres. 1967), Am. assns. health, phys. edn. and recreation, Nat. Coll. Phys. Edn. Assn. for Men, Phi Epsilon Kappa. Mason (Shriner). Home: 1019 W Cantwell St Stillwater OK 74074 Office: Depf Phys Edn Oklahoma State Univ Stillwater OK 74074

HARRISON, BILL, gypsum co. exec.; b. Oklahoma City, Okla., Oct. 2, 1930; s. Josiah James and Rose (Cantrell) H.; B.S.A., Okla. State U., 1955; m. Betty Ann Frey, June 2, 1950; children—Charles William, Robert Theadore, David Bishop, John Josiah. Pres., Harrison Gypsum, Inc., Lindsay, Okla., Nat. Interstate Life Ins. Co., LIC Corp., First Am. Bank, Purcell, Okla. Mem. Lindsay City Council, 1959-62; chmn. McClain County Soil Conservation Bd., Okla., 1967—; mem. Okla. Gov.'s Bd. Legislative Compensation. Served to lt., USAF, 1950-52. Mem. Delta Tau Delta. Methodist. (chmn. bd. 1965-67). Rotarian, Elk. Address: Box 336 Lindsay OK 73052

HARRISON, DAMON WILSON, state ofcl.; b. Aurora, Ky., Apr. 27, 1918; s. Wilson Bryan and Edith (Morris) H.; A.B., Western Ky. U., 1939; postgrad. U. Ky., 1939-41; m. Annie Pierce Steger, Mar. 5, 1966; children—Wendolyn Winifred Harrison Helton, Bryan Louis, Damon Wilson. Research supr. U.S. Employment Service, Frankfort, Ky., Louisville, 1941-42, 46-48; research dir. Ky. Dept. Econ. Security, 1948-57; dir. research and indsl. devel. Louisville C. of C., 1957-60; research and planning dir. Ky. Dept. Commerce, Frankfort, 1960-71, acting commr. commerce, 1971-72, commr., 1972—; chmn. Ky. Energy Council. Served with USMCR, 1942-46. Decorated Purple Heart. Mem. Beta Gamma Sigma. Democrat. Presbyn. Home: 216 Briarcliff Apt 12 Frankfort KY 40601 Office: Capital Plaza Tower Frankfort KY 40601

HARRISON, EMMETT CARROLL, credit bur. exec.; b. nr. Calvary, Ga., Aug. 19, 1931; s. Hadley Thomas and Mae (Johnson) H.; B.S., Fla. State U., 1958; student Southeastern Mgmt. Inst., U. N.C., 1958-65; m. Catherine Arrington, June 3, 1956 (div.); children—Emmett C., Thomas Hadley. Asst. mgr. Midland Finance Co., Tallahassee, 1954-55; pres., treas. Credit Bur. of Tallahassee, Inc., 1955—; pres. Ha-La Corp., 1964—. Instr. financial mgmt. Southeastern Mgmt. Inst., U. N.C., 1964—, Midwest Mgmt. Inst., U. Kan., 1966—. Trustee Southeastern Mgmt. Inst., U. N.C., 1961-63. Served with AUS, 1952-54. Mem. Asso. Credit Burs. Am. (dir. 1965-66, 67—), Asso. Credit Burs. Fla. (pres. 1964-66, treas. 1966—), Asso. Credit Burs. S.E. (pres. 1965—, dir. 1962-65), State Fla. Consumers Council, Tallahassee C. of C. Methodist. Rotarian. Home: 2104 Ridgetop St Tallahassee FL 32303 Office: 1710 S Gadsden St Tallahassee FL 32301

HARRISON, GILBERT NEWTON, lawyer; b. Brownwood, Tex., Dec. 25, 1909; s. Gilbert Newton and Belle (Grinnan) H.; B.A., U. Mich., 1931, J.D., 1933; m. Joyce Manwaring, Dec. 3, 1955; children—Sarah, Penelope, Gilbert Nicholas. Admitted to Tex. bar, 1933, since practiced in Brownwood; city atty., 1948—. Dir. First Nat. Bank, Brownwood. Trustee Hall Bros. Found. Served to capt. AUS, 1942-46. Mem. Tex. Bar Assn., Sigma Chi. Episcopalian. Home: 803 Center Av Brownwood TX 76801 Office: First Nat Office Bldg Brownwood TX 76801

HARRISON, GRESHAM HUGHEL, lawyer; b. Johnson County, Ga., June 19, 1924; s. James W. and Geneva (Jordan) H.; J.D., Mercer U., 1954; m. Leslie Powell, Aug. 27, 1943; 1 son, Samuel Hughel. Admitted to Ga. bar, 1955; with State of Ga. Dept. of Law, 1954-63; asst. atty. gen. State of Ga., 1956-63; sr. partner Harrison & Garner, Lawrenceville. Sec., dir. Gwinnett Comml. Bank, Lawrenceville; judge Recorder's Ct., Gwinnett, Ga. Pres. cystic fibrosis Ga. chpt. NCFR Found., 1963-69; mem. Gwinnett County Research and Devel. Bd. Served with USNR, 1943-45; ETO; as Momm 1/c, 1951-52. Mem. Am., Ga., Gwinett County (pres. 1967-68) bar assns., Am. Legion (post comdr.), Gwinett C. of C. Presbyn. (elder). Kiwanian. Home: 331 Perry St SW Lawrenceville GA 30245 Office: 151 Pike St NE PO Box 88 Lawrenceville GA 30245

HARRISON, HUGH THOMAS, chemist; b. Lockesburg, Ark., Nov. 16, 1928; s. Emmett Edgar and Grace (Pickens) H.; B.S., State Coll. Ark., 1951; M.S., U. Okla., 1957; m. Kathryn Alberta Couch, Aug. 20, 1950; children—Kathryn Grace, Hugh Thomas, Allen Albert. Chemist Dowell div Dow Chem. Co., Tulsa, 1955-57; fluorine chemist Ozark-Mahoning Co., Tulsa, 1957-59; with Dowell div Dow Chem. Co., Tulsa, 1959—, patent and information services specialist, 1963—. Served as lt. AUS, 1946-48, 51-52. Mem. Am. Chem. Soc. (gen. chmn. SW regional meeting 1959, chmn. 1963-64), A.A.A.S. Patentee in field. Home: 3302 E Haskell St Tulsa OK 74115 Office: PO Box 50334 Tulsa OK 74150

HARRISON, JOSEPH A., sugar co. exec.; b. Phila., Sept. 13, 1925; s. William Thomas and Iola (Collins) H.; B.E.E., Drexel Inst. Tech., 1952; m. Christine Victoria Brown, July 14, 1965; children—Joseph A., Kevin, Brian, Kirk, Keith, George, GiGi. Draftsman Nat. Sugar Refinery Co., Phila., 1948-49, engr., 1949, gen. supt., 1952-55, plant mgr., 1955-59, asst. v.p., 1959-60, v.p., 1960-66; asst. v.p. J. Aron & Co., Supreme, La., 1966, gen. mgr., 1966, v.p. adminstrn., 1967, now v.p. operations; dir. Pioneer Bank, N.J.; mgr. G & H Land Co. Mem. Twp. Com., Glouschester, N.J., 1960-63; chmn. exec. com., mem. police jury, Assumption Parish, La., 1973—. Bd. dirs. Assumption Parish Gen. Hosp. Served with USNR, World War II. Mem. Sugar Inst. Tech. (dir. 1952), Cane Sugar Research (dir. 1960), Cane Sugar League, Am. Legion, V.F.W. Lion. Patentee electrical controls. Home: Supreme LA 70396 Office: 336 Magazine St New Orleans LA 70130

HARRISON, JOSEPH WELLMAN, research economist; b. Washington, Jan. 11, 1929; s. Ralph H. and Bernice (Pirkey) H.; B.A., U. Va., 1952, M.A., 1958, Ph.D., 1964; m. Virginia B. Barnes, Dec. 1, 1953; children—Leigh M., Bruce B. Research economist Va. Dept. Hwys., Charlottesvillle, 1956-59, U. Miss., University, 1959-60; economist, programmer Amerad Corp., Charlottesville, 1961-62; economist Nat. Resources Evaluation Center, Office Emergency Planning, Washington, 1962-63; economist Gen. Electric Co., Syracuse, N.Y., 1964-67, Washington, 1967-72; mem. tech. staff Gen. Research Corp., Arlington, Va., 1972-73; economist Inst. for Def. Analyses, Arlington, 1973—. Mem. Am. Econs. Assn., Am. Acad. Polit. and Social Sci., Delta Sigma Pi. Office: 400 Army-Navy Dr Arlington VA 22202

HARRISON, REESE LENWOOD, JR., lawyer, economist; b. San Antonio, Jan. 5, 1938; s. Reese Lenwood and Ruth (Fischer) H.; B.B.A., Baylor U., 1959, M.S., 1965; J.D., So. Meth. U., 1962; m. Judith Karen Scott, Oct. 9, 1964. Admitted to Tex. bar, 1962, U.S. Supreme Ct. bar, 1968; practiced in San Antonio, 1962—; mem. firm Oppenheimer, Rosenberg, Kelleher & Wheatley, 1972; chief criminal sect., asst. U.S. atty., San Antonio, 1964-72. Sec. Tex. DeMolay Found., 1961—. Served with USAF, 1963-64. Recipient Distinguished Service award San Antonio Jr. C. of C., 1973. Mem. Soc. Govt. Economists (dir. 1971-72), Am. Finance Assn., Am., So. econ. assns., Nat. Assn. Bus. Economists, Inter-Am., Fed. (pres. San Antonio chpt. 1971-72), Am., San Antonio (chmn. criminal law com. 1972-74) bar assns., State Bar Tex., Nat. Dist. Attys. Assn., Judge Advs. Assn., Am. Judicature Soc. Mason (Shriner). Club: Town (San Antonio). Home: 11630 Sandman St San Antonio TX 78216 Office: Travis Park West Bldg San Antonio TX 78205

HARRISON, RICHARD REX, dentist; b. Wewoka, Okla., Mar 27, 1922; s. Thomas Franklin and Perney Ethel (Williams) H.; B.A., U. Okla., 1944; D.D.S., Baylor U., 1946; m. Eunice Spurgin Knapp, Sept. 14, 1951. Practice gen. dentistry, Wewoka, Okla., 1946-49, Comanche, 1949-51, Oklahoma City, 1953—. Served to capt. U.S. Army. Mem. Am., Oklahoma, Oklahoma County dental assns., Okla. Gem and Mineral Soc., Okla. Ornithological Soc., Nat. Audubon Soc., Nat. Woodcarvers Assn. Baptist. Mason. Home: 4113 NW 21st Terrace Oklahoma City OK 73107 Office: 3416 NW 23d St Oklahoma City OK 73107

HARRISON, ROSALIE THORNTON (MRS. PORTER H. HARRISON), educator; b. Birmingham, Ala., Jan. 24, 1917; d. John William and Zora (Whetstone) Thornton; A.B., Samford U., 1937; M.A., U. Ala., 1945; postgrad. Tchrs. Coll., Columbia, Catholic U. Am., George Washington U., Am. U., U. Md., D.C. Tchrs. Coll.; m. Porter Harmon Harrison, Apr. 12, 1941; 1 son, Porter Harmon. Tchr., Pinson (Ala.). Sch., 1937-41; tchr., asst. prin. Avondale Estates (Ga.) Elementary Sch., 1941-45; asst. tchr. Horace Mann-Lincoln Sch. of Tchrs. Coll., Columbia, 1946; instr. English, Samford U., 1948; tchr. Lakeview Sch., Birmingham, 1948-49, Hazelwood and McFerran Sch., Louisville, 1950-53; with D.C. Pub. Schs., 1956—; tchr. Congress Heights Elementary Sch., Washington, 1956-63; guidance counselor Barnard Elementary Sch., Washington, 1963—; tchr. Children's Sch., U. Ala., summers 1939-41; adminstr. D.C. Project Head Start, summers 1966-69, coordinator parent program, summers 1968-69; prin. Congress Heights-Savoy Elementary Summer Sch., 1971, Blow-Bowen Elementary Summer Sch., 1972. Del. Congress of Baptist World Alliance, Rio de Janeiro, Brazil, 1960, Miami, Fla., 1965; dir. D.C. Bapt. Conv. Summer Mission Camp Girls Aus., 1955; dir. Bapt. Tng. Union, Riverside Bapt. Ch., Washington, 1954-65, also mem. choir, council, mem. numerous coms., officer, 1953—. Mem. N.E.A. (life), Am., Nat. Capital personnel and guidance assns., Council for Exceptional Children, D.C. Counselors Assn., Am. Assn. Sex Educators and Counselors, Columbian Women of George Washington U., Alpha Delta Kappa. Clubs: Research, Ministers Wives (Washington). Home: 3828 17th Pl NE Washington DC 20018 Office: 5th and Decatur Sts NW Washington DC 20011

HARRISON, STANLEY EARL, research firm exec.; b. Northup, O., Nov. 19, 1930; s. Stanley Mervin and Helen Mildred (Northrup) H.; B.S. in Elec. Engring., Ohio State U., 1958; M.S. in Elec. Engring., U. N.M., 1962; m. Doris Ann Powell, June 21, 1953; children—Brenda Kay, Anne Elizabeth, David Stanley, Anita Lynn. Mem. tech. staff Sandia Corp., Albuquerque, 1958-63; supr., program mgr. nuclear div. Martin-Marietta Corp., Balt., 1963-68; dir. western operations Braddock, Dunn & McDonald, Inc., Albuquerque, 1968-72, v.p. operations, Vienna, Va., 1972-74, exec. v.p., 1974—, also exec. v.p. BDM Services Co., Vienna, 1971—. Served with USAF, 1948-52. Registered profl. engr., Ohio. Mem. Assn. U.S. Army, I.E.E.E. (sr. mem.), Ohio State U. Assn. (life), Eta Kappa Nu, Pi Mu Epsilon. Methodist (past chmn. ofcl. bd.). Mason (Shriner); mem. Order Eastern Star. Clubs: Four Hills Country, Petroleum (both Albuquerque); Presidents, Admirals. Contbr. profl. jours. Home: 1417 Montague Dr Vienna VA 22180 Office: 1920 Aline Av Vienna VA 22180

HARRISON, THOMAS JAMES, elec. engr.; b. Wausau, Wis., May 13, 1935; s. Glenn M. and A. Laura (Barclay) H.; B.E.E., Carnegie Inst. Tech., 1957, M.E.E., 1958; Ph.D., Stanford, 1964; m. Marilyn Lawrance, Sept. 7, 1957; children—Nancy E., Kristine A. Design engr. IBM Corp., Poughkeepsie, N.Y., 1958-59, asso. engr., Peekskill, N.Y., 1960, staff adv. engr., San Jose, Cal., 1960-68, sr. engr., Boca Raton, Fla., 1968—. Mem. U.S. Nat. Com. for Internat. Electrotech. Commn., 1972—. Served with AUS, 1959. Mem. Instrument Soc. Am. (sr. mem.; dir. standards and practices bd. 1971—), Am. Soc. Testing and Materials, Am. Nat. Standards Inst., I.E.E.E., Sigma Xi, Tau Beta Pi, Delta Upsilon, Omicron Delta Kappa, Eta Kappa Nu, Phi Kappa Phi. Author, editor: Handbook of Industrial Control Computers, 1972; contbr. to tech. handbooks. Patentee analog-to-digital converters, sampling filter. Home: 375 E Royal Palm Rd Boca Raton FL 33432 Office: IBM Corp PO Box 1328 Boca Raton FL 33432

HARRISON, WILLIAM GROCE III, chem. co. exec.; b. Jacksonville, Fla., Jan. 19, 1934; s. William Groce and Mabel Ruth (Hopson) H.; student U. Va., 1951-53, U. Colo., 1953, Midwestern U., 1954; m. Jane Grace Napier, Jan. 20, 1953; with Dowell, Inc., Wichita Falls, Tex., 1954-57; founder Select Industries, Inc., Wichita Falls, 1957, pres., dir., 1957—; dir. Academic Funds, Inc., St. Louis, Computer Utilities, St. Louis. Christian Scientist. Mason (32 deg.). Home: 2180 Av J Wichita Falls TX 76308 Office: Box 4126 Wichita Falls TX 76308

HARRISON, WINNIE MYRTLE BROADWAY (MRS. JULIUS C. HARRISON), clubwoman; b. Madisonville, Tex.; d. Isaac Newton and Eugenia (Stafford) Broadway; student Acad. Collegiate Inst., 1910-11, Bryan Bapt. Acad., 1912-13; m. Julius C. Harrison, Dec. 30, 1914; children—Ina Eugenia (Mrs. Ferrell Keefer), Barbara Avis,

(Mrs. Samuel Franklin Hiser), Myrtle Lee, Martel Wayne, Gloria June. Pres. of women Oak Cliff Christian Ch., Dallas, 1932-33, Magnolia Christian Ch., Ft. Worth, 1935-36; supt. Vacation Bible Schs., 1946-48, Black Presbyn. Missions 1946-50 pres. Aeolian Music Club, Spartanburg, S.C., 1953-54, Woman's Club, Spartanburg, 1954, 62, Glad Gardeners Garden Club, 1962. Homemakers Garden Club, 1964, Jubal Music Club, Spartanburg, 1954-56, 61-65, 68-69. Past President's Assembly, Spartanburg, 1964-65; bd. mem. S.C. Fedn. Music Clubs, 1950—, chaplain, 1968—; mem. com. for nat. past pres. scholarship fund Nat. Fedn. Music Clubs, also life mem.; hon. mem. Philharmonic Music Club, Spartanburg; sponsor Spartanburg Little Theatre, Music Found. of Spartanburg; bd. dirs. Music Found. Spartanburg. Served with USAAF, 1944-45. Presbyn. (asst. organist 1969-70). Mem. Order Eastern Star. Home: 216 Ponce de Leon St Spartanburg SC 29302

HARSTAD, ANDREW JOHN, systems engr.; b. Hillsboro, N.D., Jan. 19, 1932; s. Henry Joseph and Ruth June (Bendickson) H.; B.A., U. N.D., 1959; m. Nola Kathleen McGuire, Nov. 3, 1962; children—Eric, Eve. Engr., Western Electric Co., Fort Lee, Va., 1959-62; systems engr. guided missile range div. Pan Am. Airways, Patrick AFB, Fla., 1962-66; systems engr. Apollo/Saturn and Skylab programs IBM, Huntsville, Ala., 1966—. Ala. state chmn. U. N.D. Devel. Fund Dr., 1973. Served with Security Service, USAF, 1950-54. Mem. I.E.E.E., Am. Legion, V.F.W. Home: 2608 Rita Lane Huntsville AL 35810 Office: 150 Sparkman Dr Huntsville AL 35803

HART, ADAM CARTWRIGHT, mgmt. cons.; b. York, S.C., Sept. 21, 1921; s. George Henry and Mary Catherine (Cartwright) H.; B.S., Hobart Coll., 1942; M.S., Hofstra Coll., 1955; postgrad. McCoy Coll., Johns Hopkins, 1955-60, U. Cal. at Los Angeles, 1967, U. S.C., 1968; m. Margaret Virginia Johnson, Aug. 11, 1944; children—Virginia Lee, Katherine (Mrs. Joseph M. Iacovelli), A. Cartwright, Kerry S. Research chemist M. Lowenstein & Sons textiles, Rock Hill, S.C., 1946-48; prin. engr. electronics Bendix Radio, Balt., 1955-59; mgr. mil. marketing NCR, Washington, 1959-62; systems engr. Bendix Radio, Balt., 1962-66; adminstr. S.C. Tech. Services Program, Columbia, 1966-68; product planning mgr. Universal Bus. Machines, Columbia, 1968-69; mgr. devel. computer service Wilbur Smith & Assos., Columbia, 1969-70; cons. design information systems Bus. and Community Devel. Services, Columbia, 1970—. Instr., Midlands Tech. Edn. U., Columbia, 1970—. Served with inf. AUS, 1942-46, with arty., 1948-55. Decorated Bronze Star. Registered profl. engr., S.C. Mem. I.E.E.E. (chmn. 1971). Episcopalian. Mason. Home: 315 N Trenholm Rd Columbia SC 29206 Office: Key Life Bldg 3101 Carlisle St 29205

HART, ALLIE CARROLL, state ofcl.; b. Madison, Ga.; d. Joseph Martin and Maud (Atkinson) Hart; A.B., Brenau Coll.; M.A., U. Ga. Former serials cataloger U. Ga. Libraries; asst. archivist Ga. Dept. Archives and History, Atlanta, 1957-64, dir., 1964—, dir. Ann. Archives Inst., 1967—. Mem. Ga. Council for Environmental Quality, 1969, Ga. Commn. for Nat. Bicentennial Celebration, 1970—, Ga. Heritage Trust: Adv. Commn., 1972—; adv. bd. Inman Park Restoration, Inc., 1971-72, Foxfire Fund, Inc., Rabun Gap, Ga., 1973—; mem. operations com. Richard B. Russell Found., 1971—; tech. adv. com. Westville Historic Handcrafts, 1973—; mem. regional adv. council Nat. Archives and Records Service, 1972—; vice chmn. commn. on archives and history United Methodist Ch., 1973—, chmn. archives com., mem. bicentennial com., 1973—. Trustee R.J. Taylor, Jr. Found. R.J. Reynolds Found. coastal research grantee. Fellow Soc. Am. Archivists (state and local records com. 1966-68, mem. council); mem. Am. Records Mgmt. Assn. (dir., sec. Atlanta chpt. 1966-70), Ga. League Hist. Socs. (v.p., pres. 1968-71), Ga. Hist. Soc. (curator 1966—), Atlanta Audubon Soc., S. Atlantic Archives and Records Conf. (co-founder), Phi Beta Kappa, Alpha Delta. Democrat. Methodist. Club: Soroptimist. Home: 18 Peachtree Circle NE Atlanta GA 30309 Office: Ga Dept of Archives and History 330 Capitol Av SE Atlanta GA 30334

HART, ARTHUR THOMAS, II, govt. ofcl.; b. nr. Chase City, Va., May 24, 1937; s. Arthur Derieux and Julia Catherine (Gordon) H.; B.S., Va. Poly. Inst. and State U., 1958; postgrad. bus. adminstrn. Va. Commonwealth U., 1968-69; m. Peggy Disselkoen, Sept. 9, 1960; children—Arthur Thomas III, Moneesa Lois. Regulatory insp. Va. Dept. Agr. and Commerce, Richmond, 1958-60, field supr., 1960-63, supr. paint, pesticide and hazardous substances sect., 1964-73; dir. rural resources services and dir. Va. Soil and Water Conservation Commn., 1973—. Mem. Assn. Am. Pesticide Control Officers (nat. sec. 1972-73). Baptist (deacon). Optimist. Home: 203 Naman Rd Richmond VA 23229 Office: 203 Governor St Richmond VA 23219

HART, CARL ORLANDO, aerospace engr.; b. Enid, Okla., Dec. 9, 1904; s. Caius O. and Anna (Musgrave) H.; student Okla. State U., 1923-26; B.S. in Aerospace Engring., Okla. U., 1961, M.S., 1965; m. Norma Putman, May 19, 1926; children—Orlando Joe, Rudy J. Field engr. MacCray Refrigeration Co., 1937-42; gen. engr. U.S. Air Force, Tinker AFB, Okla., 1943-50, supervisory gen. engr. 1950-56, chief product engring. div., 1956-61, chief propulsion engring. br., 1961-66, chief aero. tchr. indsl. and middle mgmt. U.S. Air Force, 1959-66, chief aero. systems br., 1966-68, chief value engring. br., 1968-71, chief engring. planning br., 1971-74; partner Cons. Engring. Service, Hart-Henderson, Okla., 1952—. Recipient Sustained Superior award U.S. Air Force, 1965. Registered profl. engr., Okla. Mem. Nat., Okla. socs. profl. engrs., I.E.E.E. (vice chmn. 1960). Democrat. Methodist (chmn. bd. trustees). Mason. (K.T.). Patentee in field. Home: 8113 Victoria Dr Oklahoma City OK 73159

HART, CARL RAYMOND, ret. civil engr.; b. Rio Vista, Tex., Mar. 27, 1905; s. John Chitwood and Leila (Sandusky) Hart; student John Tarlton Jr. A. and M. U., 1924-26; B.S., Tex. Tech. U., 1931; m. Ruth Smith, Aug. 6, 1930; children—Carl Raymond, Robert Franklin. With engring. dept. Santa Fe R.R., Temple, Tex., 1927-28; with Tex. Hwy. Dept,, Lubbock, 1932—, supervising resident engr., 1970-73. Registered profl. engr., Tex. Mem. Tex., Am. socs. profl. engrs., Tex. Pub. Employees Assn. Mem. Ch. of Christ. Mason. Home: 3605 47th St Lubbock TX 79413

HART, DAVID R., chemist, chem. engr., b. Denbo, Pa., July 26, 1926; s. David Moffitt and Bess (Raffle) H.; student Bucknell U. Jr. Coll., 1943-44; B.S. in Chemistry, Auburn U., 1951; M.S. in Chem. Engring., U. Ala., 1970, postgrad., 1970—; m. Carol Jo Dorrough, Dec. 17, 1950; children—John Mark, Jody Camille. Research chemist Monsanto Chem. Co., Anniston, Ala., Dayton, O., Decatur, Ala., 1951-55; area supr. Liberty Powder Def. Corp., Childersburg, Ala., 1955-56; project engr. Cramet, Inc., Chattanooga, 1956-58; chm. engr. Allied Chem. Corp., Hopewell, Va., 1958-59; with U.S. Pipe & Foundry Co., Birmingham, Ala., 1959—, research chem. engr., 1959-70, dir. chem. research, 1970—. Vis. prof. chem. engring. Auburn (Ala.) U., 1971—. Served with USNR, 1944-46. Nat. Def. Edn. Act fellow, U. Ala., 1968-70. Mem. Am. Inst. Chem. Engrs., Am. Chem. Soc., Sigma Xi, Phi Lambda Upsilon, Phi Kappa Phi, Tau Beta Pi, Omega Chi Epsilon. Club: American Contract Bridge League (life). Research in synthetic fibers. Home: 4123 Camp Horner Rd Birmingham AL 35243 Office: 3500 35th Av North Birmingham AL 35207

HART, ELMER FRANKLIN, coll. adminstr.; b. Lexington, Ky., Aug. 11, 1944; s. Elmer Bayse and Nada (Amburgey) H.; B.S. in Civil Engring., Va. Poly. Inst. and State U., 1967, M.S. in Civil Engring., 1968; postgrad. U. Mo., 1969, W. Va. U., 1971; m. Carol Sue Morgan, Dec. 22, 1966; children—Tonya Morgan, Angie Caroline. Engrs. aide TVA, Chattanooga, 1963-66; asst. prof. Bluefield (W.Va.) State Coll., 1967-72, dir. pre-engring., 1968-69, asst. dir. div. tech., 1969-72, registrar, dir. admissions, 1970-71, dir. financial aid, 1971—, pres. faculty council, 1969-70. Cons. engr. Chinquipin Devel. Corp., Mudfork Devel. Corp., Lakeview Devel. Corp., Mudfork Coal Co., Seay Constrn. Co. Mem. Bluefield Flood Control Com., 1973, W.Va. Regional Planning Task Force, 1973. Sec.-treas. Tazewell County Republican Club, 1970-73. Bd. dirs. Learning Resources Computer Network, W.Va. Ednl. Computer Network. Recipient Distinguished Service award Kiwanis Club, 1969, NSF fellowship U. Mo., 1969. Registered profl. engr., Va. Mem. Nat. Soc. Profl. Engrs. (chpt. v.p.), Am. Soc. C.E., Am. Tech. Edn. Assn., Am. Soc. Engring. Edn., W.Va. Land Surveyors Assn., W.Va. Assn. Admissions Officers, Va. Poly. Inst. and State U. Alumni Assn., Bluefield State Area Investment Club (v.p. 1972—), Tau Beta Pi, Chi Epsilon, Kappa Theta Epsilon. Kiwanian (pres. Bluefield 1972-73). Clubs: Graham Investors, Richwood Golf (Bluefield). Home: Route 3 Box 296 Bluefield VA 24605 Office: Bluefield State Coll Bluefield WV 24701

HART, FREDERICK DONALD, assn. exec.; b. N.Y.C., May 12, 1915; s. Lewis T. and Charlotte (Hyde) H.; M.E., Cornell U., 1936, M.M.E., 1937; m. Ann Wright, Apr. 18, 1942; children—Anne, Charlotte, Jane. Mgmt. engr. E.I. duPont de Nemours Co., 1937-44; exec. v.p. Temco, Inc., Nashville, 1944-57, pres., 1957-64; pres. Lear Siegler Internat., 1964-66; adminstrv. dir. Am. Gas Assn., Arlington, Va., 1966-68, mng. dir., 1968—, pres., 1971—; dir. Indusmin Ltd., Clarendon Bank and Trust Co. Past pres. Inst. Appliance Mfrs., Gas Appliance Mfrs. Assn. Mem. Am. Ordnance Assn. (v.p. 1958-63), N.A.M. (v.p. 1960-65), Nashville C. of C. (past pres.), Cornell U. Council, Am. Nat. Standards Inst. Clubs: Belle Meade Country (Nashville); Cornell, Union League, Pinnacle (N.Y.C.); Washington Golf and Country, International (Washington). Home: 1061 Wilson Blvd Arlington VA 22209 Office: 1515 Wilson Blvd Arlington VA 22209

HART, HERBERT CARLTON, psychologist; b. Ironton, O., Mar. 2, 1026; s. William Carl and Gertrude (Layne) H.; B.A., U. Fla., 1954, M.A., 1956, Ph.D., 1959; m. Frances Lee Lloyd, Jan. 2, 1947; children—Jan C., Melissa A., Julie M. Staff psychologist Bryce Hosp., Tuscaloosa, Ala., 1959-61; acting chief psychologist VA Hosp., Tuscaloosa, 1961-63, asst. chief, Marion, Ind., 1963-65; asst. prof. extension div. U. Ind., 1963-65; chief psychologist VA regional office, Columbia, S.C., 1965-68, also asst. prof. U. S.C., Columbia; sr. field assessment officer Peace Corps, Escondido, Cal,, 1968; chief psychologist VA Center, Jackson, Miss., 1968-70; clin. asst. prof. Med. Sch., U. Miss., Jackson, 1968-70; cons. U. So. Miss., Hattiesburg, 1968—, U. Hosp., Jackson, 1968-70; chief psychology service VA Hosp., Richmond, Va., 1970—; asst. prof. Med. Coll. Va., 1972—. Dir. New Stage Summer Film Festival, Jackson, 1969. Served with AUS, 1944-46, 48-52. Mem. S.C. Aero. Assn., Am., Southeastern, Miss., Va., Richmond psychol. assns. Publications in video tape, drug addiction, alcohol abuse. Home: 5526 Jamson Rd Richmond VA 23234 Office: McGuire VA Hosp Richmond VA 23249

HART, JACQUELINE SPOERER, physician; b. Balt., July 11, 1934; d. Paul M. and Lillian (Spoerer) Hart; B.S., Rice Inst., 1956; M.D., U. Tex., Galveston, 1961. Intern, John Sealy Hosp., Galveston, 1961-62, resident internal medicine, 1962-65, internal medicine fellow endocrinology and metabolism, 1965-66; internal medicine fellow oncology and hematology M.D. Anderson Hosp. and Tumor Inst., Houston, 1966-67, asst. prof. medicine, 1969—; practice medicine specializing in internal medicine, Houston, 1967—. Exec. sec. Lymphoma Task Force, Nat. Cancer Inst., Washington. Fellow Royal Soc. Health; mem. A.M.A., Am. Soc. Internal Medicine, So., Tex. med. assns., World, Harris County med. socs., Postgrad. Med. Assembly South Tex., S.W. Cancer Chemotherapy Group for Cancer Research, Leukemia Soc. Am., Am. Soc. Clin. Oncology, Am. Soc. Hematology, Am. Med. Women's Assn. N.Y. Acad. Scis., Doctors Club, Mu Delta, Alpha Epsilon Iota. Club: Mayfair University (Houston). Home: 5301 Brae Burn Dr Bellaire TX 77401 Office: MD Anderson Hospital and Tumor Institute 6723 Bertner Av Houston TX 77025

HART, KENNETH WAYNE, accountant; b. Dallas, Sept. 1, 1932; s. Claude Lester and Opal Marcy (Gaston) H.; B.B.A., N.Tex. State U., 1960; m. Mary Ella Stover, Apr. 25, 1955; children—Kenneth Wesley, Claude David, Marcie Rani. Sta. agt., Braniff Airways, Dallas, 1954-60; tax accountant Humble Oil, Houston, 1960-67; pvt. practice C.P.A., Garland, Tex., 1967—. Chmn. audit com. Circle 10 council Boy Scouts Am., 1972—; organizer, 1st pres. Arrowhead Property Owners, Montgomery County, 1965-67. C.P.A., Tex. Mem. Am. Inst. C.P.A.'s, Tex. Soc. C.P.A.'s, Dallas Estate Council. Home: Route 2 Royse City TX 75089 Office: 3632 Dividend Dr Garland TX 75042

HART, RAYMOND KENNETH, physicist; b. Newcastle, Australia, Feb. 15, 1928; s. William Kenneth and Olive (Palmer) H.; student Newcastle Tech. Coll., 1944-49; D.I.C., Imperial Coll., London, 1952; Ph.D. (research fellow), U. Cambridge (Eng.), 1955; m. Betty Joyce Bingemann, Sept. 5, 1952; children—Timothy Kenneth, Rowena Jane. Came to U.S., 1958, naturalized, 1967. Sci. research officer Dept. Supply Australia, Melbourne, 1955-58; research scientist Argonne (Ill.) Nat. Lab., 1958-69; prin. research scientist Ga. Inst. Tech., Atlanta, 1970—. Cons., United Aircraft, Elion Instruments, High Voltage Engring. Corp., Oak Ridge Nat. Lab., Jet Propulsion Lab. Com. chmn. Indian Trails dist. Boy Scouts Am., 1965-67, com. mem. Polaris dist., 1971-72. Fellow Inst. Physics (London), Royal Australian Chem. Inst.; mem. Am. Phys. Soc., Electron Microscopy Soc. Am. (dir. 1969-72, bull. editor 1971—), Midwest Soc. Electron Microscopists (pres. 1964-65), Southeast Electron Microscopy Soc., Sigma Xi. Contbr. articles to profl. jours. Home: 585 Royervista Dr Atlanta GA 30342

HART, ROBERT THEODORE, elec. engr.; b. Chickasha, Okla., Apr. 15, 1933; s. Joseph Luther and Eva Jane (Whitehurst) H.; B.S. in E.E., U. Okla., 1957; m. Alice Cordelia Pierson, May 22, 1959; 1 dau., Julie Ann. With Collins Radio Co., Richardson, Tex., 1957-67; microwave engr., 1959-61, space systems engr., 1961-64, test dir. space systems, 1964-67; mgr. devel. Omega-T-Systems, Richardson, 1967-71; mgr. receiver systems Scientific Communications, Garland, Tex., 1971—. Served with AUS, 1950-52; Korea. Registered profl. engr., Okla. Mem. I.E.E.E. Recipient Idea of Year award Electronic Design Mag., 1964. Patentee in electronic circuits. Contbr. electronic publs. Home: 517 Park Lane Richardson TX 75080 Office: 3425 Kingsley Rd Garland TX 75041

HART, WILSON REESE, chemist; b. Binghamton, N.Y., Sept. 16, 1916; s. Wilson Taylor and Erma Marie (Reese) H.; Peddie Sch., 1935; B.S., Columbia, 1939; m. Elva Elizabeth Drake, July 14, 1943. Owner, Columbia Labs. (S.C.), 1943-65, Coastal Labs., Pawleys Island, S.C., 1965—. Lectr., U. S.C., 1949-57. Chief devel. S.C. State Devel. Bd., 1949-57; dir. S.C. Regional Blood Center, Columbia, 1957-64. Served with Chem. Warfare Div., AUS, 1942-43. Mason (33 deg.). Home: PO Box 242 Pawleys Island SC 29585 Office: Coastal Labs US Hwy 17 Pawleys Island SC 29585

HARTER, BASIL THOMAS, physician; b. Oklahoma City, Mar. 3, 1925; s. Basil Douglas and Hazel Leota (Thomas) H.; student U. Okla., 1943-44, Tex. Christian U., 1944-45; M.D., Johns Hopkins, 1950; m. Myra Ellen Spinner, June 25, 1953; children—Geoffrey Thomas, Melissa Ellen. Intern, Johns Hopkins, 1950-51, Kings County Hosp., Bklyn., 1951-52; resident Malden (Mass.) Hosp., 1952, 54-55, Boston Lying-In Hosp and Free Hosp. for Women, Boston, 1955-58; practice medicine, specializing in gynecology and obstetrics Bristol, Tenn. and Bristol, Va., 1958—; mem. staff Bristol Meml. Hosp. Chmn. Com. for Bristol Arts Council, 1965-72. Bd. dirs. United Fund, Bristol Tenn-Va., 1971-73; chmn. bd. dirs. Bristol Concert Ballet Col., 1964-72. Served to lt. M.C., USNR, 1952-54. Mem. C. of C. (dir. 1973—). Republican. Episcopalian. Home: 100 Pinecrest Lane Bristol VA 24201 Office: 249 Midway St Bristol TN 37620

HARTER, NEWMAN WENDELL, dentist; b. Ulmers, S.C., Aug. 11, 1923; s. Newman and Lucy Marie (Kinard) H.; B.S., The Citadel, 1947; D.D.S., Emory U., 1947; m. Dorothy Virginia Wright, June 2, 1944; children—Newman Wendell, Mark Richard. Gen. practice dentistry, Hampton, S.C., 1947—. Served with AUS, 1943-44. Chmn. financial drive Coastal Empire council Boy Scouts Am., 1955-56; pres. P.T.A., 1964. Mem. Am. Dental Assn. Coastal Dist. Dental Soc. (sec.-treas. 1952-53, pres. 1953-54), Am. Legion (past comdr.). Mason (Shriner), Lion, Order Eastern Star (past pres.). Home: PO Box 487 Hampton SC 29924 Office: 200 Elm St E Hampton SC 29924

HARTFELDER, HERBERT EDWARD, food exec.; b. Kansas City, Kan., Jan. 8, 1914; s. George and Christine (Rollwagen) H.; ed. Kansas City Jr. Coll., Dallas Coll. of So. Meth. U.; m. Ailene Townsend; children—Jack Fryar, Patricia Anne (Mrs. Richard A. Haberman), Orra Christine (Mrs. Charles Simpson), Mary Lee (Mrs. Jack Plunkett). With Oak Farms Dairies, 1936—, sec., treas., v.p., 1936-46, pres., 1953—; dir. Southland Corp., 1956—, exec. v.p., 1961-68, pres., 1968—, vice-chmn., 1974—; pres. Midwest Dairies. Velda Dairies, Embassy Dairies, Harbison Dairies, Cabell's Dairies, Adohr Farms; dir. Oak Cliff Bank & Trust Co. Bd. dirs. Milk Industry Found. Mem. Nat. Assn. Accountants (pres. Dallas 1945), Dairy Products Inst. Tex. (pres. 1953), Internat. Assn. Ice Cream Mfrs. (dir., mem. exec. com.), So. Assn. Food Mfrs. (pres.), Newcomen Soc. Methodist. Clubs: Petroleum, Dallas Athletic, Dallas, Brookhollow Golf, Northwood Country. Home: 3525 Turtle Creek Blvd Dallas TX 75219 Office: 2828 N Haskell St Dallas TX 75204

HARTFORD, WINSLOW HOPPER, educator; b. Newton, Mass., June 1, 1910; s. James Bradley and Alice Maria (Winslow) H.; A.B., Boston U., 1928; S.B., Mass. Inst. Tech., 1930; Ph.D., 1933; m. Mary Emily Haviland, Douglas Bennett, Janet Winslow (Mrs. Paul C. Clifford, Jr.). Research chemist Mut. Chem. Co. Am., Balt., 1934-45, research supr., 1945-58; research supr. indsl. chem. div. Allied Chem. Corp., Syracuse, N.Y., 1958-63, sr. scientist, 1963-69; asso. prof. chemistry Belmont (N.C.) Abbey Coll., 1970—; cons. Syracuse, and Charlotte, N.C., 1969—. Mem. Metrolina Environmental Information Network, 1972—, Charlotte Choral Soc., 1970—, Little Theatre Charlotte, 1970—, Mint Mus. Drama Guild, 1970—. Fellow A.A.A.S., Am. Inst. Chemists; mem. Am. Chem. Soc. (Md. chmn. 1952), Am. Assn. U. Profs., Am. Wood Preservers Assn. (gen. chmn. preservatives 1959-67), Am. Forestry Assn., Sigma Xi. Presbyn. Author: (with R.F. Gould) Boy Scout Chemistry Merit Badge Handbook, 1957. Contbr. articles to profl. jours. Patentee in field. Home: 1413 Redcoat Dr Charlotte NC 28211 Office: Belmont Abbey College Belmont NC 28012

HARTGROVE, BILLY RAY, ins. co. exec.; b. Beaumont, Tex., Sept. 10, 1931; s. L.B. and Virginia (Ledenham) H.; student McNeese State Coll., Lake Charles, La., 1949-52, U. Houston, 1959-60; m. Evelyn Summers, Mar. 31, 1955; children—Billy Ray, Brian Lee. Vice pres. Great Midwest Life Ins. Co., Oklahoma City, 1962-64; v.p., sec. Security Brokers Investment Corp., Oklahoma City, 1964-66, Great Midwest Life Ins., 1967-69; v.p., sec. United Investors, Inc., 1969-73, pres., 1974—; v.p., sec. Mid-American Investors Life Ins. Co., Oklahoma City, 1969-71, pres., 1971-72 (merged into Investors Life), pres. Investors Life, 1973—. Served to lt. (j.g.) USNR, 1952-57. Club: Twin Hills Golf and Country. Home: 4813 NW 73d St Oklahoma City OK 73132 Office: 2644 NW 63d St Box 20749 Oklahoma City OK 73120

HARTLEY, MARGARET LOHLKER, editor; b. St. Paul, July 28, 1909; d. William Arnold Lohlker and Edna (Hughes) Lohlker; B.A., Pomona Coll., 1930; m. Roland English Hartley, Oct. 14, 1942 (div. Jan. 1944). Editorial asst. So. Meth. U. Press., Dallas, 1947-49, mng. editor, 1949-61, editor, 1961—, asso. dir., 1971—; asst. editor S.W. Review, Dallas, 1947-61, mng. editor, 1961-63, editor, 1965—. Adj. asso. prof. English, So. Meth. U., 1973—. Mem. Southwestern Am. Lit. Assn., Tex. Inst. Letters, Phi Beta Kappa. Home: 3500 Granada Av Dallas TX 75205 Office: So Meth U Press Dallas TX 75275

HARTLEY, VIRGIL AGAN, editor; b. Miami, Fla., Dec. 20, 1931; s. John Frederick and Thelma Naniska (Dasher) H.; B.A., Emory U., 1954; m. Nancy Elizabeth Smathers, Sept. 18, 1954 (div. Feb. 1973); children—Elisabeth Anne, John Charles; m. Margaret Hylton Jones, Sept. 1, 1973. Editor, Dade County Times, Trenton, Ga., 1954; writer Atlanta Constn., 1954-56; mng. editor Atlanta mag., 1961-62; writer Ga. Power Co., 1962-64; editor Emory Mag., Atlanta, 1964—. Served with AUS, 1956-59. Mem. Chi Phi. Home: 1778 Ponce de Leon Av NE Atlanta GA 30307 Office: Gatewood House Emory U Atlanta GA 30322

HARTMAN, FREDERICK COOPER, biochemist; b. Memphis, Aug. 17, 1939; s. Fred Francis and Raymie Constance (Cooper) H.; B.S., Memphis State U., 1960; M.S., U. Tenn. at Memphis, 1962, Ph.D., 1964; m. Patricia Jean Ballard, Sept. 7, 1961; children—Patricia Suzanne, Sheila Katherine. Research asso. U. Ill., Champaign, Ill., 1964-66; sr. research biochemist Oak Ridge Nat. Lab., 1966—. Prof. biomed. scis. U. Tenn. at Knoxville, part time, 1969—. USPHS fellow, 1962-64, 65-66. Mem. Am. Soc. Biol. Chemists, N.Y. Acad. Scis., Am. Chem. Soc., A.A.A.S. Contbr. profl. jours. Home: 123 Nebraska St Oak Ridge TN 37830 Office: Div Biology Oak Ridge Nat Lab Oak Ridge TN 37830

HARTMAN, JAMES AUSTIN, geol. engr.; b. Lanark, Ill., Jan. 29, 1928; s. Llewelyn John and Gladys May (Doyle) H.; B.S., Beloit Coll., 1951; M.S. (Union Carbide research fellow 1954-56), 1955; Ph.D., U. Wis., 1957; m. Zoe Marie Wiley, June 16, 1951; children—Victoria, Lester. Geologist, Reynolds Jamaica Mines, Jamaica, 1951-53; geologist U.S. Steel, N.Y., summer 1954, Union Carbide Ore Co., Surinam, 1956-57; with Shell Oil Co., New Orleans and Houston, 1957—, regional geol. engr., New Orleans, 1970—, sr. staff geol. engr., 1971—. Pres., Jefferson Com. for Better Schs., Metairie, La., 1961-63, Westgate P.T.A., Kenner, La., 1964. Bd. mgrs. YMCA, 1972-74. Served with AUS, 1946-47. Mem. Am. Assn. Petroleum Geologists (New Orleans del. 1973—), A.A.A.S., Soc. Petroleum Engrs., Am. Inst. Mining Engrs., New Orleans Geol. Soc., Sigma Xi. Contbr. to profl. jours. Home: 4512 Newlands St Metairie LA 70002 Office: Box 60193 New Orleans LA 70160

HARTMAN, JAMES THEODORE, educator; b. De Ridder, La., June 13, 1925; s. George Bernhardt and Mary Gertrude (Moore) H.; B.S., Ia. State U., 1949; B.S., Northwestern, 1949, M.D., 1952; m. Jean Ann Rinehart, Dec. 29, 1954; children—James Theodore, Thomas Moore, Martha Susan. Intern Charity Hosp. of La., New Orleans, 1952-53; resident U. Mich. Hosp., Ann Arbor, 1953-57; registrar Nuffield Orthopaedic Centre Oxford U., Eng., 1957-58; instr. orthopedic surgery U. Mich., Ann Arbor, 1958-61; mem. staff Cleve. Clinic, 1961-68; chmn. dept. orthopedic surgery Cook County Hosp., Chgo., 1968-71; asso. prof. Northwestern U., Chgo., 1968-71; prof., chmn. dept. orthopedic surgery Tex. Tech. U. Sch. Medicine, Lubbock, 1971—. Served as AUS, 1943-46. Diplomate Am. Coll. Surgeons. Mem. A.M.A., Am. Orthopedic Assn., Assn. Bone and Joint Surgeons, Am. Acad. Orthopedic Surgeons, Sigma Xi, Phi Delta Theta, Nu Sigma Nu. Contbr. profl. jours. Home: 2207 Slide Rd Lubbock TX 79407 Office: Dept Orthopedic Surgery Texas Tech Univ Lubbock TX 79409

HARTMAN, WALTER MICHAEL, corrosion engr.; b. McKeesport, Pa., Aug. 26, 1925; s. Arthur Henry and Hettie Carpenter (Michael) H.; B.S, U. Pitts., 1949; postgrad. U. Tex., 1956, Hahnemann Med. Coll., 1957-59 children—Cathy, Carol, Cynthia, Sandra. Corrosion engr. A.V. Smith Engring. Co., Narberth, Pa., 1960-66, mgr. so. operations, Charlotte, N.C., 1966-72, v.p. So. div., 1972—. Served with USNR, 1943-46. Registered profl. engr., Pa., Del., Va., N.C., S.C., Ga., Ala. Mem. Nat. Soc. Profl. Engrs., Am. Water Works Assn., Nat. Assn. Corrosion Engrs., Profl. Engrs. N.C., N.C. Assn. Professions, U.S. Power Squadron, Charlotte Engrs. Club. Presbyn. Club: Ski Bees (Charlotte, N.C.). Home: 3807 Frontenac Av Charlotte NC 28205 Office: PO Box 3272 Charlotte NC 28203

HARTMAN, WILLIAM ISLES, univ. adminstr.; b. Boston, June 29, 1918; s. Nicholas and Nellie (McKay) H.; B.S., Okla. State U., 1950, M.S., 1951; postgrad. Harvard, 1954, U. Okla., 1958; m. Edythe Locke, Oct. 14, 1944; children—William Warren, Holly Isles, Edwin Brian. Dir. occupational safety and health tng. project U. Okla., Norman, 1955—, dir. safety and supervisory training, 1963—. Chmn. Nat. Task Force System Safety Com., 1971; mem. coll. sect. Nat. Com. Fleet Supervisors Tng., 1965—. Vice pres. pub. affairs Okla. Safety Council. Served with USNR, 1940-45. Decorated Air medal (2). Recipient leadership award Nat. Com. Fleet Suprs., 1968. Mem. Am. Assn. Oilwell Drilling Contractors (mem. edn. com. 1970-72), Am. Soc. Safety Engrs. (pres. 1965-66), Oilwell Drilling Contractors Assn. Australia. Home: 1404 Lincoln St Norman OK 73069

HARTNETT, JAMES JOSEPH, lawyer; b. Sioux City, Ia., Sept. 5, 1929; s. Thomas Joseph and Florence Ann (Graves) H.; B.B.A., U. Tex., 1957, LL.B., 1959; m. Emily High, Oct. 1955; children—Will Ford, James, Ellen, Robert, Jay, Fred, Melinda. Admitted to Tex. bar, 1958; mem. firm Turner, Hitchins, McInerney, Webb & Hartnett, Dallas, 1958—; lectr. So. Meth. U. Law Sch. Served with USAF, 1951-53. Fellow Am. Coll. Probate Counsel; mem. Am., Dallas (chmn. probate, trusts and estates sect.) bar assns., State Bar Tex. Home: 9110 Devonshire St Dallas TX 75209 Office: Merc Bank Bldg Dallas TX 75201

HARTON, THOMAS GORDON, water resources engr.; b. Phila., Apr. 12, 1909; s. Horace Decatur and Alice Vera (Yarbrough) H.; B.S. in C.E., U. Tenn., 1933; m. Margaret Isabelle Burch, June 22, 1960; m. Eddie Ruth Horton, Apr. 25, 1942 (div. 1949); 1 son, Thomas Dean. With TVA, Knoxville, 1933-41, 46; prin. engr. U.S. Bur. Reclamation, Washington, 1946-47; commd. maj. C.E., U.S. Army, 1947, advanced through grades to col., 1958; ret., 1964; dir. planning div., office water and air resources Dept. Natural and Econ. Resources N.C., Raleigh, 1964—. Alt. mem. Ohio River Basin Commn., 1971—, S.E. Basins Inter-Agy. Com., 1967—. Registered profl. engr., Tenn. Fellow Am. Soc. C.E.; mem. Soc. Am. Mil. Engrs., Am. Soc. Photogrammetry, A.A.A.S., Phi Kappa Phi, Tau Beta Pi, Sigma Phi Epsilon. Club: Raleigh Country. Supervisory editor Wise Management of North Carolina Water Resources, 3 vols., 1966-67. Home: 625 Macon Pl Raleigh NC 27609 Office: PO Box 27687 Raleigh NC 27611

HARTRANFT, JOSEPH BECKWITH, JR., assn. exec.; b. Buffalo, May 24, 1915; s. Joseph Beckwith and Leila Cooledge (Sherman) H.; B.A., Wharton Sch. of U. Pa., 1937; m. Dorothy Mae DuQuoin, Dec. 31, 1937; m. 2d, Evelyn Lapariere Melby, July 3, 1948 (dec. Feb. 1964); 1 dau., Diane Lynn. Mem. staff Aircraft Owners and Pilots Assn., 1939—, pres., 1952—; pres. Aircraft Owners and Pilots Found., 1951—, Aircraft Owners and Pilots Service Corp., 1953—, Internat. Council Aircraft Owners and Pilots Assns., 1961—; dir. Avemco Corp. Sec. Interdeptl. Air Traffic Control Bd., War Aviation Com.; mem. bd. Aviation Devel. Adv. Com., Joint Mil.-Civilian Air Def. Com.; founder U.S. Air Guard, 1940; adv. bd. Nat. Intercollegiate Flying Assn.; mem. Radio Tech. Commn. for Aero. Trustee Bates Found. Aero. Edn. Served to lt. col. USAAF, World War II. Mem. S.R., Royal Aero Club (hon.), Washington Air Derby Assn. (hon.), Nat. Citizens Commn. Internat. Coop., Nat. Aviation Club, Aero Club Washington. Rotarian. Clubs: Pacific; U. Pa. (Washington); Nantucket (Mass.) Yacht; Executives (Chgo.); Columbia Country (Chevy Chase, Md.); Annapolis Yacht (Md.). Home: 4405 East West Hwy Bethesda MD 20014 Office: Aircraft Owners and Pilots Assn 7315 Wisconsin Av Bethesda MD 20014 also PO Box 7550 Schiphol-Central Netherlands also 44 Washington St Nantucket MA 02554

HARTSFIELD, HENRY WARREN, JR., astronaut; b. Birmingham, Ala., Nov. 21, 1933; s. Henry Warren and Alice Norma (Sorrell) H.; B.S., Auburn U., 1954; postgrad. Duke, 1954-55, Air Force Inst. Tech., 1960-61; M.S., U. Tenn., 1970; m. Judy Frances Massey, June 30, 1957; children—Judy, Keely. Commd. U.S. Air Force, 1955, advanced through grades to lt. col.; grad. Aerospace Research Pilot Sch., 1965; astronaut Dept. Def. Manned Orbiting Lab. Program, 1966-69, Lyndon B. Johnson Space Center, NASA, Houston, 1969—. Recipient Meritorious Service medal. Office: Code CB NASA-Lyndon B Johnson Space Center Houston TX 77058

HARTSON, MAURICE JOHN, JR., ins. agt.; b. New Orleans, Jan. 20, 1906; s. Maurice J. and Marguerite (Calongne) H.; grad. Loyola U. of South, 1922-26; m. Elizabeth Freret, June 6, 1929; children—Liseanne (Mrs. J. Parham Werlein), Maurice J. III, Elizabeth. In ins. bus., 1924—; pres. M.J. Hartson, Inc., New Orleans, 1937—; dir. Lafayette Ins. Co.; dir., v.p. Columbia Homestead Assn. Past chmn. New Orleans Fire Prevention Bd.; pres. New Orleans Community Chest, 1952, 73; pres. United Fund Greater New Orleans, 1962-63; pres. adv. com. Convent of Good Shepherd; pres. St. Marys Boys Orphan's Asylum; chmn. Civic Affairs Com.; pres. New Orleans Area Health Planning Council. Bd. dirs. St. Mary's Dominican Coll., New Orleans Speech and Hearing Center; mem. pres.'s council Jesuit High Sch. Recipient Weiss award Nat. Council Christians and Jews. Mem. Nat. Assn. Ins. Agts. (dir., mem. exec. com.), War of 1812 Soc., Blue Key (elected hon. mem. 1963), Sigma Alpha Epsilon. Catholic. Most loyal gander Blue Goose. Clubs: Pickwick (past pres.); Serra (pres. New Orleans; dist. gov.); Stratford, New Orleans Country, Southern Yacht. Home: 1528 Webster St New Orleans LA 70118 Office: 332 Carondelet St New Orleans LA 70130

HARTUNG, CARL ADAM, physician; b. Crawford, Tenn., Jan. 29, 1910; s. Carl F.J. and Magda Rose (Scheiterle) H.; B.S., U. Tenn., 1929; M.D., Tulane U., 1933; M.S., U. Cin., 1936; m. Virginia Deakins, Apr. 25, 1938; children—Carl Adam, James D. Intern, Cin. Gen. Hosp., 1933-34, resident, 1935-36; practice medicine specializing in internal medicine and cardiology, Chattanooga, 1938—. Cons. physician Erland, Meml., Parkridge, Newell, Tri-County, Tenn. Chest hosps. (all Chattanooga). Trustee U. Tenn. Chattanooga Found. Served to lt. col AUS, 1942-46. Fellow A.C.P., Am. Coll. Cardiology, Am. Coll. Chest Disease; mem. A.M.A., Am. Coll. Geriatrics, Am. Coll. Gerentology, Alpha Omega Alpha. Methodist. Kiwanian. Clubs: Mountain City, Chattanooga Golf and Country; Fairland (Lookout Mountain). Home: 1698 Riverview Rd Chattanooga TN 37405 Office: 744 McCallie Av Chattanooga TN 37402

HARTZOG, GEORGE BENJAMIN, JR., lawyer; b. Colleton County, S.C., Mar. 17, 1920; s. George Benjamin and Mazell (Steedly) H; student Wofford Coll., Spartanburg, S.C., 1937, LL.D., 1972; B.S. in Bus. Adminstrn., Am. U., 1953; LL.D., Washington U., 1971, U. Ariz., 1972; L.H.D., Lincoln (Ill.) Coll., 1972; m. Helen Carlson, June 28, 1947; children—George, Nancy, Edward. Admitted to S.C. bar, 1942, Mo. bar, 1963, Supreme Ct. U.S., 1949, U.S. Dist. Ct. D.C., 1970; with Bur. Land Mgmt. and Nat. Park Service, Dept. Interior, 1946-62; exec. dir. Downtown St. Louis, Inc., 1962-63; asso. dir. Nat. Park Service, 1963-64, dir., 1964-72; practice law, Washington, 1972—; prof. pub. adminstrn. Washington Pub. Affairs Center, U. So. Cal. Bd. dirs. Wolf Trap Found. for Performing Arts; trustee Nat. Recreation and Park Assn. Mem. Am., Fed., D.C. bar assns., Am. Judicature Soc., Internat. Platform Assn., Washington Nat. Monument Soc. (emeritus). Clubs: Boone and Crockett (asso.), Cosmos, Nat. Lawyers, Internat., Rotary (Washington). Home: 1643 Chain Bridge Rd McLean VA 22101 Office: 900 17th St NW Washington DC 20006

HARVEY, ALBERT CLYDE, lawyer; b. Knoxville, Tenn., June 30, 1939; s. Albert Clyde and Dorothy (Kearney) H.; B.S. in Polit. Sci., U. Tenn., 1961, J.D., 1967; m. Nancy Rutherford, Mar. 24, 1962; children—Anne Kearney, Elizabeth Moore. Admitted to Tenn. bar, 1967; law clk. Justice Larry Creson, Tenn. Supreme Ct., 1967-68; mem. firm Thomason, Crawford & Hendrix, Memphis, 1968—; asst. pub. defender Shelby County, 1969-71; lectr. med. units U. Tenn., 1972—. Treas., Goodwill Boys Club. Served to maj. USMCR, 1961-64. Mem. Tenn. Bar Assn. (pres. Young Lawyers Conf. 1972—), Young Lawyers Memphis (pres.), U. Tenn. Alumni Assn. (bd. govs. 1973—, pres. Memphis chpt. 1971-72), Marine Corps Res. Officers Assn. (chpt. v.p.), Order of Coif, Omicron Delta Kappa, Phi Kappa Phi, Phi Gamma Delta. Episcopalian. Mason. Club: Phoenix (1st v.p.). Editor: Tenn. Law Rev., 1966-67. Home: 1529 Vance Av Memphis TN 38104 Office: 100 N Main Bldg Memphis TN 38103

HARVEY, ARTHUR, oil exec.; b. Edom, Tex., Sept. 26, 1895; s. John Arthur and Mary Ann (Williams) H.; student pub. schs. Minden, Tex.; m. Sylva Vogelsong, July 9, 1929; children—Inez Elizabeth (dec.), Arthur Herbert, Sylva Ann. Postal clk., spl. agt., intelligence unit Bur. Internal Revenue, Treasury Dept., 1920-39; owner Tex-Harvey Oil Co., 1939—, now operating in Tex., crude oil producer. Discoverer of Tonti Oil Field, Marion, Ill., Angus Oil Field, Navarro County, Tex., East Long Lake Oil Field, Anderson County, Tex., Tex-Harvey Oil Field, Midland and Glasscock Counties, Tex. Mem. Ret. Officers Assn. U.S. Baptist. Club: Denver Athletic. Home: 334 Peerman Pl Corpus Christi TX 78411

HARVEY, ARTHUR EDWIN, JR., value engring. mgr.; b. Brewton, Ala., May 7, 1918; s. Arthur Edwin and Ruby M. (Britton) H.; B.S., Auburn U., 1940, M.S., 1946; m. Mae-Parish Singletary, June 7, 1942; children—Judy-Parish (Mrs. Forrest Robert Spiva), Janet-Corrine, Arthur Edwin III, James Britton, Deborah-Ann (Mrs. Rick Lynn Coates). Devel. engr. Pitts. Plate Glass, Barberton, O., 1947-50; project engr. Govt. Labs., Akron, 1950; statis. chem. engr. Thiokol Chem. Corp., Huntsville, Ala., 1951-53; chief equipment and facilities, research and engr. labs. Redstone Arsenal (Ala.), 1953-56; chief engr. services Army Ballistic Missile Agy., 1956-58, dep. chief quality assurance, 1958-59, chief value analysis, 1959-62, value engring. mgr. Army Missile Command, 1962—; pres. Harvey Enterprises, Ala. Waterways, Inc.; chem. engring. cons.; cons. Main Battle Tank for Value Engring., 1967; lectr., producer value engring. movies. Served to capt. with AUS, 1940-45. Decorated Bronze Star with oak leaf cluster, Purple Heart; recipient First Place trophy for two movie prodns. Indsl. Mgmt. Soc., 1966, 68. Fellow Soc. Am. Value Engrs. (past chpt. pres., internat. meritorious award 1966, fellow award 1967, life mem. award 1970, pres.'s spl. award 1971, spl. value engr. award Redstone chpt. 1969); mem. Army Materiel Command Value Engring. Mgrs. Council, Ala. Soc. Profl. Engrs. (value engr. year award 1969), Am. Inst. Chem. Engrs., Soc. for Advancement of Mgmt., Am. Soc. Quality Control, Assn. U.S. Army, Am. Def. Preparedness Assn., Electronic Industries Assn., Sales and Marketing Execs. Assn., Tennessee Valley Geneal. Soc., C., Ret. Officers Assn., Alpha Phi Omega (pres.), Phi Lambda Upsilon. Lutheran. Elk. Clubs: Redstone Yacht (dir.), Redstone Officers. Contbr. articles to profl. jours. Home: 12001 Rockcliff Dr NW Huntsville AL 35810 Office: US Army Missile Command Redstone Arsenal AL 35809

HARVEY, AUBREY EATON, JR., ednl. adminstr.; b. Lynchburg, Va., Sept. 28, 1911; s. Aubrey Eaton and Janie Jillette (Thornhill) H.; B.S., U. Va., 1939, Ph.D., 1946; M.S., Syracuse U., 1941; m. Jaquelin Ambler Nicholas, Aug. 26, 1939; 1 son, Aubrey Eaton III. Dir. Ark. Water Resources Research Center U. Ark., Fayetteville, 1964-71, coordinator univ. research, asso. dean Grad. Sch., 1971—, dir. grad. programs with U.S. Air Force Europe, 1971—. Mem. Am. Chem. Soc., Sigma Xi, Sigma Chi. Episcopalian (sr. warden 1963-64). Contbr. articles to profl. jours. Home: 1408 Elmwood Dr Fayetteville AR 72701

HARVEY, CLARENCE CHARLES, JR., chemist; b. Winona, Miss., June 29, 1918; s. Clarence Charles and Ezilda (Pegues) H.; B.A., U. Miss., 1939, M.S., 1941; m. Frances Byers Harris, Aug. 21, 1943; children—Douglas Pegues, George Milton. With Ethyl Corp., Baton Rouge, 1941—, comml. devel. rep., 1957-60, mgr. market research, 1960—. Sec.-treas. Launder-Mart, Inc., Baton Rouge, 1946-70. Pres. Baton Rouge Indsl. Forum, 1947-49. Vice pres. Civic Assn., 1952-53; commr. Istrouma Council Boy Scouts Am., 1957-62, chmn. troup, 1953-68. Mem. Am. Chem. Soc. (sec. 1947), Am. Inst. Chemists, Chem. Marketing Research Assn. (chmn. pub. and pub. relations com. 1973-74), Nat. Assn. Corrosion Engrs. Methodist. Author: (with others) Sur face Protection of Metals, 1953. Home: 6168 Chandler Dr Baton Rouge LA 70808 Office: 451 Florida St Baton Rouge LA 70801

HARVEY, GEORGE, JR., physician; b. Canton, Miss., Nov. 9, 1912; s. George and Patty (Person) H.; B.A., Vanderbilt U., 1935, M.D., 1938; m. Rosa Marion Fox, Apr. 2, 1941; children—Rosa Marion (Mrs. Perry Carroll), George III, Mary Lucinda. Intern and asst. resident in internal medicine Balt. City Hosps., 1938-39; fellow in internal medicine Mayo Clinic, Rochester, Minn., 1940, 41, 46, 47; pvt. practice internal medicine Jackson, Miss., 1948-54, Jackson, Tenn., 1954—; v.p. Jackson Community Antenna, Inc. Trustee Union U., 1966-72. Served from lt. to maj. Med. R.C., 1942-46. Diplomate Am. Bd. Internal Medicine. Fellow A.C.P.; mem. Am., Tenn., So. med. assns., Am. Coll. Chest Physicians, V.F.W., Am. Legion, Beta Theta Pi, Phi Chi. Baptist. Home: 36 Northwood Jackson TN 38301 Office: 700 W Forest St Jackson TN 38301

HARVEY, HATHAWAY K., physician; b. New Castle, Ind., May 15, 1939; s. Horace Eugene and June (Parker) H.; B.A., DePauw U., 1957; M.D., Ind. U., 1965; m. Nancy Elisabeth Grant, June 10, 1962; children—John, Brad. Intern, Marion County Gen. Hosp., Indpls., 1965-66; resident otolaryngology Ind. U., 1966-70; practice medicine, specializing in otolaryngology, head and neck surgery, Chattanooga, 1970—; mem. teaching staff Baroness Erlanger Hosp.; mem. active staff Meml., Parkridge hosps., Chattanooga. Bd. dirs. Preschool Vision and Hearing Screening. Mem. Hamilton County Med. Soc., A.M.A., A.C.S., Am. Council Otolaryngology, Am. Acad. Facial Plastic and Reconstructive Surgery, Y.M.C.A. Presbyn. (deacon). Clubs: Bent Tree, Chattanooga Golf and Country. Author: Selective Neurectomy Facial Nerve, 1972. Home: 57 Carriage Hill Signal Mountain TN 37377 Office: 1000 E 3d St Chattanooga TN 37413

HARVEY, ROBERT, lawyer, state senator; b. Swifton, Ark., May 22, 1914; s. W.R. and Lula (Shaver) H.; A.B., LL.B., Vanderbilt U. Former dep. pros. atty.; former mem, Ark. Ho. of Reps.; mem. Ark. Senate. Dir. Mcht.'s Planter's Bank Newport, Ark. Chmn. Ark. Legislative Council, 1965-67; mem. Ark. Constl. Study Commn., Ark. Constl. Conv.; state treas. Ark. Democratic Com. Served with AUS World War II. Mem. Jackson County Farm Bur. (pres.). Methodist. Lion. Address: Swifton AR 72471 also Legislative Bldg Little Rock AR 72201

HARVEY, WILLIAM BRANTLEY, JR., lawyer, state legislator; b. Walterboro, S.C., Aug. 14, 1930; s. William Brantley and Thelma (Lightsey) H.; A.B., in Polit. Sci. (2d honor grad.), The Citadel, 1951; J.D. magna cum laude, U. S.C., 1955; m. Helen Coggeshall, Dec. 30, 1952; children—Eileen L., William Brantley III, Helen C., Margaret D., Warren C. Admitted to S.C. bar; practiced in Beaufort, S.C., 1955—; sr. partner firm Harvey, Battey, Macloskie & Bethea; mem. S.C. Ho. of Reps. from Beaufort County, 1958—, chmn. rules com., mem. constl. revision com. Dir. Peoples Bank, Tidewater Investment & Devel. Corp. Served to lt. AUS, 1952-54. Mem. Am., S.C., Beaufort County bar assns., Phi Beta Kappa, Kappa Alpha, Phi Delta Phi. Democrat. Presbyn. (elder; tchr. Sunday sch.). Home: 501 Pinckney St Beaufort SC 29902 Office: PO Box 1107 1001 Craven St Beaufort SC 29902

HARVIN, JAMES SHAND, plastic surgeon; b. Sumter, S.C., Dec. 19, 1929; s. Harry Lewis and Gladys Alice Mary (Shand) H.; student The Citadel, 1946-48; A.B., Duke, 1951; M.D., Med. Coll. S.C., 1953; m. Abbie Leah Bradham, Sept. 1, 1951; children—Gail Stephanie, James Shand, Steven Lewis, Carol Ann. Intern, Wayne County Gen. Hosp., Eloise, Mich., 1953-54; commd. 1st lt. USAF, 1954, advanced through grades to lt. col., 1966; resident gen. surgery Barnes Hosp., St. Louis, 1956-58, fellow plastic surgery, 1959-60, resident plastic surgery, 1960-61; fellow hand surgery Passavant Meml. Hosp., Chgo., 1959; preceptor gen. surgery Wright-Patterson USAF Hosp., 1961-63, asst. chief plastic surgery service, staff surgeon gen. surgery service, 1961-62; asst. chief plastic surgery service Wilford Hall USAF Hosp., Lackland AFB, Tex., 1962-63, chief plastic surgery service, 1963-67; asso. prof., chief div. plastic and maxillofacial surgery Med. U. S.C., Charleston, 1967—; cons. VA Hosp., Charleston, 1967—; staff mem. Charleston County Hosp., 1967—; cons. staff St. Francis Hosp., Charleston; cons. Charleston Naval Hosp. Diplomate Am. Bd. Plastic Surgery, Am. Bd. Surgery. Fellow A.C.S.; mem. Am., Southeastern socs. plastic and reconstructive surgeons, Mil. Assn. Plastic Surgeons, Soc. Air Force Clin. Surgeons, Assn. Mil. Surgeons, Soc. USAF Flight Surgeons, Aerospace Med. Assn., Am. Cleft Palate Assn., Soc. Head and Neck Surgeons, S.C. Pub. Health Assn., Am., S.C., So. med. assns., Charleston County Med. Soc., Pi Kappa Alpha, Phi Chi. Contbr. articles profl. jours. Home: Route 1 Box 484 Bohicket Rd Johns Island SC 29455 Office: 80 Barre St Charleston SC 29401

HARWELL, ERVIN LUNSFORD, lawyer; b. Putnam, Tex., Aug. 24, 1888; s. Lunsford Dillard and Elizabeth (Hutchison) H.; student Poly. Coll., Ft. Worth, 1909-10, U. Colo., 1911-13; B.A., U. Tex., 1915; m. Eunice Peele, Sept. 10, 1919; 1 dau., Dorothy (Mrs. Allen D. Tarrant). Admitted to Tex. bar, 1919; practicing atty., Abilene, Tex., after 1919; former mem. firm Wagstaff, Harwell, Alvis & Pope, now ret. from active practice. Dir. Citizens Nat. Bank, Abilene. Served as 2d lt., U.S. A.C., World War I. Mem. Abilene C. of C. Methodist (ofcl. bd.). Home: 3490 Ward Dr Abilene TX 79605

HARWELL, HELON BALDWIN (MRS. JOHN EARL HARWELL), educator; b. Center, Tex., Jan. 6, 1921; d. Aaron F. and Bernice (Gibson) Baldwin; B.S., Stephen F. Austin State Coll., 1948; M.R.E., S.W. Bapt. Theol. Sem., 1949, D.R.E., 1955; M.A., N.E. Mo. State Tchrs. Coll., 1962; Ph.D., E. Tex. State U., 1967; m. John Earl Harwell, Aug. 22, 1953. Instr., Tex. Christian U., Ft. Worth, 1950-52; tchr. St. Joseph Acad., Tucson, 1953-54; asst. prof. psychology E. Tex. Bapt. Coll., Marshall, 1954-56, 62-65; asso. prof. childhood edn. New Orleans Bapt. Theol. Sem., 1956-61; prof. elementary edn. S.W. Bapt. Coll., Bolivar, Mo., 1965-67; asso. prof. edn. Nicholls State U., Thibodaux, La., 1967—, acting head spl. edn. dept., 1973—. Cons. kindergarten edn. workshops. Mem. Assn. Childhood Edn. Internat., Assn. Student Teaching, La. Tchrs. Assn., Alpha Chi. Contbr. kindergarten resource book, also articles to profl. and religious jours. Home: Route 1 Box 220 Supercharge Dr Thibodaux LA 70301

HARWELL, JACK UPCHURCH, editor; b. Mobile, Ala., Oct. 18, 1932; s. Hoyt Horace and Minnie Eleanor (Upchurch) H.; B.S., Samford U., 1953; m. Blanche Virginia Beard, Dec. 21, 1954; children—Ronald Horace, Donald Ray. Pub. relations specialist U.S. Air Force, 1956; asso. editor Christian Index newsmag. Ga. Bapt. Conv., Atlanta, 1957-66, editor, 1966—. Adviser, Americans United for Separation Ch. and State, 1966-71. Bd. dirs. Ga. Council on Alcohol Problems. Served with AUS, 1953-55. Recipient Spl. Citation for outstanding achievement in mass communications Samford U., Birmingham, Ala., 1967. Mem. Atlanta Press Club, Sigma Delta Chi. Baptist (deacon 1958—). Author: Bulldozer Revolution, 1965; (with Louie D. Newton) Fifty Golden Years, 1959; An Old Friend With New Credentials, 1972. Home: 3159 Beech Dr East Point GA 30344 Office: 2939 Flowers Rd South Atlanta GA 30341

HARWELL, KENNETH EDWIN, educator; b. Kellyton, Ala., Nov. 22, 1936; s. Kelly Edwin and Etta Antionette (Sasser) H.; B.S. (Anchor Rome Mills scholar), U. Ala., 1959; M.S. (Tau Beta Pi fellow 1959-60, Cal. Tech. scholar 1959-63), Cal. Inst. Tech., 1960, Ph.D., 1963; m. Betty Ruth Miller, June 12, 1959 (dec. Nov. 1966); 1 dau., Kathryn Ruth; m. 2d, Sharon Elizabeth Hilton, Aug. 18, 1968; children—Karen Elizabeth, Kenneth Hilton. Asso. engr. Gen. Dynamics, Ft. Worth, 1959; grad. research and teaching asst. Cal. Inst. Tech., Pasadena, 1959-63; engr. Jet Propulsion Lab., Pasadena, 1960; prof. dept. aeronautics Auburn (Ala.) U., 1963—; vis. research prof. Research and Devel. and Engring. Lab. U.S. Army Missile Command, Redstone Arsenal, Ala., 1973-74. Cons. Hayes Internat.

Corp., Birmingham, 1965-67, Ballistic Research Lab., Aberdeen, Md., 1969, U.S. Air Force, Eglin AFB, Fla., 1972-73. Recipient Ford Found. Resident fellowship Am. Soc. Engring. Edn., 1973-74. Mem. Am. Inst. Aeronautics and Astronautics, Am. Phys. Soc., Baptist Alumni Assn. U. Ala. (v.p. 1972-73, pres. 1973-74, dir. 1969-72), Capstone Engring. Soc., Sigma Xi, Tau Beta Pi, Theta Tau, Sigma Tau, Sigma Pi Sigma. Contbr. articles to profl. jours. Home: 919 Bibb St Auburn AL 36830

HARWOOD, JOHN ELLIS, state ofcl.; b. Asheville, N.C., Jan. 7, 1916; s. John Ellis and Gertrude Franklin (Clash) H.; student Coll. William and Mary, 1932-35; m. Nathalie Hubbard, June 26, 1937 (dec. May 28, 1961); children—Nathalie Dean (Mrs. Robert Colby Perkins), Gertrude Clash (Mrs. Richard C. Stevens); m. 2d, Mary Lancaster Hubbard, Nov. 3, 1965. With survey party mapping Jamestown Island, Nat. Park Service, 1935; draftsman and design engr. Va. Dept. Hwys., Richmond, 1935-54, asst. location and design engr., 1954-58, location and design engr., 1958-64, asst. chief engr., 1964, dir. programming and planning, 1964-65, dep. commr., chief engr., 1965—. Served with AUS, World War II. Mem. Am. Soc. C.E., Am. Assn. State Hwy. Ofcls., (mem. engring. policy com.), Am. Rd. Builders' Assn. (past dir.). Episcopalian. Home: 4805 Rodney Rd Richmond VA 23230 Office: 1221 E Broad St Richmond VA 23219

HARWOOD, RICHARD LEE, journalist; b. Chilton, Wis., Mar. 29, 1925; s. Luther Milton and Ruby (Heath) H.; A.B., Vanderbilt U., 1950; m. Beatrice Bottrell Mosby, Dec. 18, 1950; children—Helen, John, Richard, David. Reporter Nashville Tennessean, 1947-52, Louisville Courier-Jour. and Times, 1952-61, Washington corr., 1961-65; nat. corr. Washington Post, 1966-68, nat. editor, 1968-70, asst. mng. editor, 1970—. Served with USMCR, 1942-46; PTO. Nieman fellow Journalism Harvard, 1955-56; Carnegie fellow journalism Columbia, 1965-66. Recipient citation Nat. Edn. Writers Assn., 1957; George Polk Meml. award L.I. U., 1967, 71; Distinguished Service medal Sigma Delta Chi, 1967, 71. Mem. Soc. Nieman Fellows (dir. So. chpt. 1959-61), Am. Civil Liberties Union (dir. Ky. 1959-61), Am. Polit. Sci. Assn. (citation 1960). Democrat. Clubs: National Press, Federal City (Washington). Author: Lyndon, a Biography of L.B. Johnson. Contbr. articles to nat. mags. Home: 4521 Drummond Av Chevy Chase MD 20015 Office: 1515 L St Washington DC 20005

HARWOOD, ROBERT HEWETT, plantation exec.; b. Trenton, Tenn., Mar. 1, 1920; s. Robert Hewett and Evelyn Hope (Wade) H.; B.S., U.S. Naval Acad., 1942; M.S., U.S. Naval Post Grad. Sch., 1946; student Indsl. Coll. Armed Forces, 1964-65; M.S., George Washington U., 1965; m. Zenobia Frith Pratt, Apr. 4, 1943; children—Mary Buie, Evelyn Hope (Mrs. William R. Liebke), Robert Henry. Commd. ensign USN, 1941, advanced through grades to capt., 1961; comdg. officer submarine, 1946-54; nuclear submarine div. comdr., 1957-61; submarine attack squadron comdr., 1965-66; comdr. Naval Ordnance Plant, Chgo., 1962-64; ret., 1968; v.p. Frithland Plantation, Inc., Bunkie, La., 1966—; dir. mgmt. sci. Gulf South Research Inst., Baton Rouge, 1972—; dir. Turner Lumber Co. (LeMoyen, La.); lectr. La. Dept. Pub. Safety. Mem. tech. com. La. Criminal Justice Information System and Nat. Crime Information Center, 1970-71; active Boy Scouts Am., Cub Scouts. Decorated Silver Star, Bronze Star medal. Mem. Am. Soc. Tool and Mining Engrs., U.S. Naval Acad. Alumni Assn., Indsl. Coll. Armed Forces Assn., Tau Kappa Omega. Democrat. Episcopalian. Clubs: Avoyelles Country. Home: Frithland Plantation Box 643 Bunkie LA 71322 Office: 6271 Boone Dr Baton Rouge LA 70808

HARWOOD, THOMAS EVERETT, lawyer; b. Trenton, Tenn., Oct. 10, 1923; s. Robert Hewitt and Evelyn (Wade) H.; student Union U., 1941, 1946-47; B.S., George Peabody Coll., 1949, M.A., 1950; LL.B., Cumberland U., 1960; J.D., Samford U., 1969; student Slippery Rock State Coll., 1943, Vanderbilt U., 1949-50; m. Elizabeth Ann Auston, June 6, 1948; 1 dau., Mary Ann. Property accountant U.S. Govt., Milan (Tenn.) Arsenal, 1941-42; head internal audit Proctor and Gamble Defense Corp., Milan, Tenn., 1951-58; bus. mgr. Cumberland U., 1958-60; admitted to Tenn. bar, 1961; practice law, Trenton, Tenn., 1960—; asst. prof. bus. adminstrn. Cumberland U., 1960; city atty., Dyer, Tenn., 1964-71; county atty. Gibson County (Tenn.) 1966-68; mem. Gibson County Quar. Ct., 1968—. Trustee Florence N. Jordan Charitable Trust. Served with USAAF, 1942-46. Mem. Tenn., Gibson County bar assns., Tenn., Am. trial lawyers assns., V.F.W. (post comdr. 1946-47). Presbyn. (elder). Moose. Rotarian (v.p. 1969-70, pres. 1970-71). Home: Rt 3 Trenton TN 38382 Office: 115 W Court Sq Trenton TN 38382

HARWOOD, THOMAS PERKINS, JR., state ofcl.; b. Green Bank, W.Va., Jan. 22, 1929; s. Thomas Perkins and Mary (Moomau) H.; B.A., Va. Mil. Inst., 1950; LL.B., U. Va., 1956; m. Mary Virginia Ambrose, June 30, 1956; children—Sally Christian, Thomas Perkins III, Leland Hunter. Admitted to Va. bar, 1956; asso., partner Lane, Paul & Rudd, attys.-at-law, Richmond, Va., 1956-60; dep. commr. Indsl. Commn. of Va., Richmond, 1960-64, commr., 1964-73; commr. Va. Corp. Commn., 1973—. Served to 1st lt. inf. AUS, 1950-53. Decorated Purple Heart. Mem. Am., Va., Richmond bar assns., D.A.V., Am. Legion, Kappa Alpha, Sigma Nu Phi, Omicron Delta Kappa. Democrat. Presbyn. (elder 1962—, trustee 1963—). Home: 2736 Kenbury Rd Richmond VA 23225 Office: PO Box 1197 Richmond VA 23209

HASELDEN, DAN RUFF, telephone engr.; b. Lexington, N.C., Dec. 17, 1931; s. Willis J. and Madge (Ruff) H.; B.S., Western Carolina U., 1958; m. Jo R. David, Nov. 12, 1950; children—Cathy A. Dan R. Engr., Western Electric Co., Winston-Salem, N.C., 1958-60; asso. mem. tech. staff Bell Tel. Labs., Winston Salem, 1960-64; engr. Gen. Electric, Columbis, S.C., 1964-65; engr., facilities adminstr. So. Bell Tel. & Tel. Co., Columbia, 1964—. Served with USAF, 1952-55. Mem. I.E.E.E., Am. Chem. Soc. Lion. Home: 725 Woodland Hills Columbia SC 29210 Office: So Bell Tel and Tel Baker Bldg Columbia SC 29201

HASELWOOD, SCOTT, electronics engr.; b. Thomas, Okla., Oct. 14, 1921; s. William Earl and Ruth Elmira (Scott) H.; student U.S. Naval Acad., 1941-44; B.S., U. Okla., 1956; M.S., St. Louis U., 1966; m. Betty Jane Schneider, Dec. 9, 1944; children—Glenna Jane (Mrs. John Blackford), William Scott, Elaine Marie and Ellen Lee (twins). Electronic engr. McDonnel Aircraft Corp., St. Louis, 1956, electronic group engr., 1956-64; sr. group engr. Conductron Co., St. Charles, Mo., 1964-66; chief Guidance Devel. Center, Martin-Marietta Corp., Orlando, Fla., 1966-69, project engr. antenna tracking system NASA, 1969-71, tech. dir. electro-optical simulation system, 1971—; instr. elec. lab., research asst. U. Okla., 1954-56. Served with USNR, 1944-46. Mem. I.E.E.E., Am. Ordnance Assn., Internat. Oceanographic Inst. Democrat. Mem. Christian Ch. (trustee, elder). Mason (32 deg.). Contbr. articles profl. jours. Home: 2671 Vine St Orlando FL 32806 Office: PO Box 5837 Orlando FL 32805

HASENFUS, HAROLD JOSEPH, mech. engr.; b. N.Y.C., Apr. 9, 1921; s. Joseph Vincent and Ethel Elizabeth (Galvan) H.; B.Mech. Engring., Coll. City N.Y., 1943; m. Mary Margaret Boone, Nov. 6, 1945; children—James Joseph, Stephen Francis, Jean Marie, Edward Harold. Chief rocket br. Ballistic Research Labs., Aberdeen Proving Ground, Md., 1948-60; head space surveillance operations center Naval Weapons Lab., Dahlgren, Va., 1960-61, tech. dir. Naval Space Surveillance System, 1961—; U.S. Army del. to U.S.-U.K.-Canada Tripartite Conf. Armaments, Explosives and Propellants, Quebec, Can., 1959; U.S. Navy rep. creation high speed data link connecting large navy computers at Dahlgren with USAF computers at Eglin AFB, Fla., 1969-70; U.S. Navy del. U.S.-U.K.-Can. Tripartite Conf. Artificial Earth Satellites, Bermuda, 1971. Served to 1st lt. AUS, 1943-48. Recipient Navy award merit as leader of winning groups, 1960, 72. Mem. Am. Rocket Soc. (pres. Md. 1960), Am. Inst. Aeros. and Astronautics (dir. Balt. 1960-62), Am. Soc. M.E., Am. Math. Soc., A.A.A.S., Am. Def. Preparedness Assn., Assn. Computing Machinery, Pi Mu Epsilon. Clubs: Officers (Dahlgren). Home: Box 439 Dahlgren VA 22448 Office: Naval Space Surveillance System Dahlgren VA 22448

HASERICK, JOHN ROGER, dermatologist; b. Mpls., Sept. 23, 1915; s. Ernest and Addie (Swanson) H.; B.A., Macalester Coll., 1937; M.D., U. Minn., 1941; m. Jane Fleckenstein, May 10, 1941; children—John Roger, Jane (Mrs. Fred Furland). Intern, Ancker Hosp., St. Paul, 1940-41; resident Univ. Hosps., Mpls., 1941-42, 46-47; practice medicine specializing in dermatology, Cleve., 1948-70, Pinehurst, N.C., 1970—; head dermatology dept. Cleve. Clinic, 1948-67; prof. dermatology Case Western Res. U., Cleve., 1967-70; dermatologist Pinehurst Dermatology, 1970—; clin. prof. dermatology Duke, 1970—. Served with M.C., AUS, 1942-46. Diplomate Am. Bd. Dermatology (examiner 1967—, pres. 1973). Mem. Am. Acad. Dermatology (pres. 1973), Am. Soc. Dermatopathology (pres. 1973-74). Home: Grove Rd Southern Pines NC 28387 Office: Pinehurst Dermatology Pinehurst NC 28374

HASHIMOTO, KEN, physician, educator; b. Niigata, Japan, June 19, 1931; s. Takashi and Kiku (Matsumoto) H.; M.D., Niigata U., 1955; m. Noriko Sakai, Oct. 15, 1961; children—Naomi, Martha, Eugene, Amy. Came to U.S., 1963, naturalized, 1968. Intern U.S. Army Hosp. Tokyo, Japan, 1955-56; resident U. Md. Hosp., Balt., 1956-58, Mass. Gen. Hosp., Boston, 1958-59; asst. prof. dermatology Tufts U. Sch. Medicine, 1965; prof. medicine, asso. prof. anatomy U. Tenn. Coll. Medicine, Memphis, 1968—; chief dermatology sect. Memphis VA Hosp. Recipient Med. Investigationship award VA, 1969—. Fulbright scholar, 1956-59. Mem. Am. Acad. Dermatology, Electron Microscope Soc. Am., Soc. for Investigative Dermatology, Am. Fedn. Clin. Research, Memphis Dermatol. Soc. (pres.), Sigma Xi. Author: Appendage Tumors of the Skin, 1968. Contbr. chpts. to texts and sci. publs. Home: 4837 Aspen St Memphis TN 38128 Office: 1030 Jefferson St Memphis TN 38104

HASKELL, PRESTON HAMPTON III, constrn. co. exec.; b. Birmingham, Ala., Oct. 6, 1938; s. Preston Hampton and Mary Wyatt (Rushton) H.; B.S., Princeton, 1960; spl. student Mass. Inst. Tech., 1961-62; M.B.A., Harvard, 1962; m. Joan Elizabeth Smith, June 9, 1961; children—Elizabeth Rushton, Preston Hampton IV, Sally Milne. Vice pres. S.S. Jacobs Co., Jacksonville, Fla., 1962-65; pres. Preston H. Haskell Co., Jacksonville, 1965—; dir. Gen. Environmental Equipment Co., Inc.; trustee Barnett-Winston Investment Trust. Treas., bd. dirs. Cathedral Found. of Jacksonville, Jacksonville Council of Arts; bd. dirs. Jacksonville Symphony Assn., 1969-71, Duval unit Am. Cancer Soc., 1967-68; trustee Riverside Presbyn. Day Sch. Registered profl. engr., Fla., Ala., S.C., Va. Mem. Jacksonville Area C. of C. (bd. govs.), Princeton Alumni Assn. N.Fla. (pres. 1970-71). Republican. Episcopalian. Clubs: Timuquana Country, Florida Yacht, Meninak. Home: 5509 Fair Lane Jacksonville FL 32210 Office: 1061 Riverside Av Jacksonville FL 32204

HASKEW, NANCY STONE (MRS. BALLARD LEE HASKEW), banker; b. Johnsonville, S.C., Mar. 18, 1939; d. William Austin and Pearline (McDaniel) Stone; student Mt. Olive Coll., 1956-57, Northwestern U., 1970, U. S.C., 1972; m. Ballard Lee Haskew, Sept. 30, 1970; children (by previous marriage)—William Wallace Altman, III, Angela Nan Altman. With C & S Nat. Bank, Charleston, S.C., 1957-59; with Bankers Trust, Cola, S.C., 1962-65; with So. Bank & Trust Co., Greenville, S.C., 1961-62; with Pamplico (S.C.) Bank & Trust, 1967-68; with Rogers, Newman & Cauthen, Inc., advt., pub. relations and marketing, Columbia, S.C., 1968-70, adminstrv. asst. to pres., 1968-70; dir. marketing The Nat. Bank of S.C., Sumter, 1970—. Asst. dir. Carillon Ball, 1968-70; pub. chmn. United Fund, 1970-71. Mem. S.C. Bankers Assn., Nat. Assn. Bank Women (chmn. S.E. regional pub. relations com.), Am. Fedn. Advertisers (membership com. 1972—), Bank Marketing Assn. (chmn. membership devel. com. 1973). Clubs: Taiwan Internat.; U.S. Officers' Wives; Air Force Officers' Wives. Home: 516 N Hampton St Sumter SC 29150 also F108 Ya Ming Shan Republic of China

HASKINS, JACK LIONEL, JR., elec. engr.; b. Vredenburgh, Ala., Oct. 9, 1935; .s Jack Lionel and Myra Lee (Boothe) H.; B.E.E., U. Fla., 1959; m. Thelma Irene Smith, Apr. 9, 1961; 1 son, Jack Stephen. Comml. sales engr. Gulf Power Co., Pensacola, Fla., 1959-65, comml. sales supr., 1966-68, mgr. sales, 1969, mgr. rates and tech. services, 1970—. Mem. Bay County Com. of 100, 1964-65, City-County Drug Abuse Commn., 1972—. Served with AUS, 1957-59. Mem. Southeastern Electric Exchange (chmn. comml. sales sect. 1969-70), Edison Electric Inst. Home: 4030 Arbutus Dr Pensacola FL 32504 Office: 75 N Pace Blvd Pensacola FL 32502

HASKO, STEPHEN, weights and measures engr.; b. Racine, Wis., Jan. 29, 1922; s. Paul and Katherine (Rohacek) H.; student U. Wis. at Racine, 1940-41; B.S., U. Mo., 1948; student Mich. Coll. Mining and Tech., 1943-44, Purdue U. at Anderson, 1948; m. Mabel Lucille Thornton, May 7, 1949; children—Barbara Ann, Stephen Timothy. Asst. ceramic engr. Nat. Tile & Mfg. Co., Anderson, Ind., 1948-50; ceramic engr. Ceramic Arts Studio, Madison, Wis., 1950-52; ceramic and aerospace engr. inorganic materials div. Nat. Bur. Standards, Washington and Gaithersburg, Md., 1952-64, engr. Office Weights and Measures, Washington, 1964—. Served with AUS, 1943-46. Lucy Wortham James scholar, 1942. Mem. Am. Ceramic Soc., Keramos, Nat. Inst. Ceramic Engrs., Tau Beta Pi, Phi Kappa Phi. Lutheran (v.p. 1950). Club: Lutheran Laymen's League. Research ceramic wall and floor tile; ceramic artware; high temperature nuclear ceramics; weights and measures engring. Home: 10707 Glenhaven Dr Silver Spring MD 20902 Office: Office of Weights and Measures Nat Bur Standards Washington DC 20234

HASS, CHARLES GLEN, educator; b. Mansfield, O., Mar. 7, 1915; s. Charles William and Ethel Vernice (Newlon) H.; B.A. (Edith Boughton Denious scholar 1933-37), U. Denver, 1937; M.A., Stanford, 1946; Ed.D., Columbia, 1953; m. Margaret Mary Walters, June 12, 1940; 1 son, Rolland Glen. Tchr. pub. schs., Denver, 1937-42; elementary sch. prin., Battle Creek, Mich., 1949-50; asst. supt. schs., Arlington, Va., 1950-58; prof. edn. U. Fla., Gainesville, 1958—. Vis. prof. U. Denver, 1942, N.Y. U., 1958-61, U. Colo., 1961, U. Utah, 1961. Served to capt. AUS, 1942-46. Mem. John Dewey Soc. (nat. pres. 1967-69), Soc. Prof. Edn. (nat. pres. 1971-72), Assn. Supervision and Curriculum Devel. (nat. bd. dirs. and nat. exec. bd., 1956-62, 72-76). Club: Torch. Author: In Service Education Today, 1957. Author and editor: Readings in Curriculum, 2d edit., 1970, Readings in Secondary Teaching, 1970, Readings in Elementary Teaching, 1971; Curriculum Planning: A New Approach, 1974; editor, co-author: Leadership for Improving Instruction, 1960. Home: 1116 N W 61 Terrace Gainesville FL 32601

HASSE, WARREN LOUIS, broadcasting exec.; b. Mauston, Wis., Oct. 15, 1923; s. Louis A. and Bertha (Hasse) H.; student U. Wis., 1941; m. Romelle Helen Johnson, Jan. 31, 1944; children—John Louis, Mary Sue. Classified advt. mgr. Portage (Wis.) Daily Register, 1947-48; sports editor Pampa (Tex.) News, 1948-50, mng. editor, 1950-52; co-owner radio sta. KPDN, 1952-60, owner, gen. mgr. 1960—; dir. Pampa Community Hotel. Dir. MBS Affiliates adv. com., 1974—. Chmn. Gray County March of Dimes Campaign, 1955, United Fund Campaign, 1957; mem. Boy Scout Council; mem. Pampa (Tex.) Sch. Bd., 1968-74, sec., 1969, pres., 1971-72; treas. Top O' Tex. Rodeo Assn., 1967-72; Mr. Little League Baseball, 1973—. Bd. dirs. A.R.C., United Fund, Top O' Tex. Found., W.Tex. Univ. Found. Served from aviation cadet to 1st lt., bombardier-navigator USAAF, 1941-45; ETO. Decorated D.F.C., Air medal with 4 oak leaf clusters. Recipient Outstanding Young Man award Jaycees of Pampa, 1957; named Sportscaster of Yr., Panhandle Sports Hall of Fame, 1965; Adult Leader of Yr., 1966; West Texan of Yr., Lambda Chi Alpha, 1969. Mem. C. of C. (pres. 1958-59). Presbyn. Clubs: Kiwanis (dist. lt. gov. 1958; dist. pub. relations chmn. 1961-62), Pampa Country. Home: 1704 Christine St Pampa TX 79065 Office: Radio Sta KPDN Pampa TX 79065

HASSELL, MORRIS WILLIAM, lawyer; b. Jacksonville, Tex., Aug. 9, 1916; s. Alonzo Seldon and Cora (Rainey) H.; A.A., Lon Morris Coll., 1936; LL.B., U. Tex., 1942; m. Mauriete Watson, Sept. 3, 1944; children—Morris William, Charles Robert. Tchr. Cherokee County Pub. Schs., 1937-38; admitted to Tex. bar, 1942; pvt. practice since 1946, mem. firm Norman, Rounsaville Hassell; sec. The S.W. Title and Guaranty Co. of Tex.; dir. First State Bank of Rusk; chmn. bd. Swift Oil Co.; sec. H & I Oil Co., I, H & I, Inc. County atty. Cherokee County, Tex., 1943-46; mayor of Rusk, 1959-63. Scoutmaster, Boy Scouts Am., 1944-45; Dem. nominee for County atty., 1942 and 1944; v.p. Jr. Bar of Tex., 1944. Mem. state adv. com. Wesley Found., Austin, Tex.; bd. devel. Lon Morris Coll. Mem. C. of C. (pres.), Am., E. Tex. (dir. 1964-65) bar assns., State Bar Tex. (dir.; chmn. gen. practice sect. 1967-68, chmn. profl. ethics com. 1970—). Methodist (steward). Odd Fellow, Mason, Kiwanian (dist. lt. gov.). Office: First State Bank Bldg Rusk TX 75785

HASSKARL, ROBERT ALBERT, museum dir.; b. Brenham, Tex., July 24, 1929; s. Robert Albert and Willie (Knolle) H.; B.S., U. Tex., 1956; M.Ed., Sam Houston State Coll., 1957; D.Ed., U. Okla., 1963; m. Eula Faye Richardson, Apr. 30, 1956; children—James Robert, Leif Robert. Prof. history Blinn Coll., 1957-61; lectr. social sci. U. Okla., 1961-63; prof. edn. East Central State Coll., 1964-66, dir. Upward Bound Program, 1966—, coordinator Upward Bound and Spl. Services, 1971—, museum dir., 1964—. Served with USAF, 1948-55. Decorated Air medal. Mem. Phi Alpha Theta, Phi Delta Kappa, Kappa Delta Pi. Author: Brenham, Texas 1844-1958 Guide to Heraldry, 1959; Knolle Family of Texas, 1959. Home: Route 4 Box 268 Ada OK 74820 Office: East Central State Coll Museum Ada OK 74820

HASSKARL, WALTER FREDERICK, JR., physician; b. Brenham, Tex., July 6, 1917; s. Walter Frederick and Dora (Roberts) H; B.A., U. Tex., 1939, M.D., 1942; M.S., U. Minn., 1949; m. Carolyn Joan Boyle, Aug. 6, 1947; children—Joan, Ann, Lee, John. Intern, Phila. Gen. Hosp., 1943, M. and S. Hosp., San Antonio, 1945; resident State Sanitorium, 1944; practice medicine, specializing in gen. surgery, Brenham, Tex., 1949—; surgical fellow Mayo Clinic, Rochester, Minn., 1945-48, 1st asst., 1948-49; pres. Brenham Clinic Assn., 1965-72; chief surgery St. Jude Hosp., Brenham; mem. staffs Bohne Meml. Hosp., Brenham, Lee Meml. Hosp., Giddings, Grimes County Hosp., Navasota, Goodnight Meml. Hosp., Caldwell; dir. devel. bd. U. Tex. Med. Sch., 1970—. Dir. Farmers Nat. Bank, Brenham, Tex. Mayor, City of Brenham, Tex., 1968-72. Served with USAF, 1953-55. Mem. Am., Tex. med. assns., Tex. Surgical Soc., Brenham C. of C. (pres. 1963), Alumni Assn. U. Tex. (rep. 1961-64), U. Tex. Cowboys, Mayo Clinic Alumni, Assn. (bd. dirs. 1971—), Kappa Sigma, Alpha Kappa Kappa. Elk. Clubs: Champions Golf (Houston); Brenham (Tex.) Country. Home: 1907 Tison St Brenham TX 77833 Office: Academy and Baylor Sts Brenham TX 77833

HASSLACHER, ROBERT NEIL, govt. ofcl.; b. South Amboy, N.J., Jan. 19, 1931; s. George John and Lillian Beatrice (Brown) H.; student Hiram Coll., 1949-50; B.B.A., Baylor U., 1961; postgrad. U. Tenn., 1968-69; m. Barbara Jeannine Farmer, Jan. 1, 1955; children—Neil Ross, Eric John. Gen. mgr. Marlin (Tex.) C. of C., 1961-63; marketing rep. H.J. Heinz, Dallas, 1963-65; regional economist U.S. Army C.E., Galveston, Tex., 1965-66; regional economist Nat. Resource Analysis Center, Leesburg, Va., 1966-68; industry economist U.S. Bur. Mines, Knoxville, Tenn., 1968-70; dir. econs. U.S. Dept. Housing and Urban Devel., Birmingham, Ala., 1970—. Chmn., Falls County, Tex. Parole Bd., 1961-63; exec. officer Mil. Police Co. Tex. State Guard Res., 1961-66. Served with USAF, 1950-54. Mem. Am. Econ. Assn., Soc. Govt. Economists, Ala. Social Scis. Adv. Com. Author: Impact of Sulfur Emission Controls on Fuel Marketing Patterns, 1970; The Phosphate Industry in the Southeastern U.S. and Its Relationship to World Mineral Fertilizer Demand, 1969; course U.S. Civil Service Commn., 1971. Home: 3443 Meadow Woods Dr Birmingham AL 35216 Office: 15 S 20th St Birmingham AL 35233

HASSLINGER, THOMAS WILLIAM, systems design engr.; b. Gainesville, Fla., Feb. 9, 1937; s. William and Anna (Nolan) H.; student Central Fla. Community Coll., 1958-60; B.E.E., U. Fla., 1962, M.E., 1970; m. Dempsey Jo Nichols, June 9, 1962; children—Michael, Dawn. With Radiation div. Harris-Intertype Corp., Melbourne, Fla., 1963—, engr., 1963-64, sr. engr., 1964-67, lead engr., 1967-72, asso. prin. engr., 1972—. Chmn., St. Joseph's Parish Bd. Edn., 1971-72. Served with AUS, 1955-58. Mem. I.E.E.E., Alpha Pi Mu. Roman Catholic. Club: Collegiate Civitan (v.p. 1959). Author: Design of Functional Redundancy, 1971; (with others) co-author, editor Design of Automated Redundancy Verification, 1971. Office: PO Box 37 Melbourne FL 32901

HASTINGS, DAVID CANFIELD, r.r. exec.; b. Ashland, Va., Dec. 25, 1915; s. Edgar Morton and Carmen Estelle (Robertson) H.; B.S. in Civil Engring., Va. Mil. Inst., 1937; m. Lavinia Catherine Ingraham, Nov. 15, 1941; children—Cathy (Mrs. William R. Carmichael, Jr.), David Canfield. With Pa. R.R., 1937-46, supr. track, 1945-46; with Richmond, Fredericksburg & Potomac R.R. Co., 1946-60, supt., 1955-60; gen. supt. terminals A.C.L. R.R. Co., Jacksonville, Fla., 1960-62, asst. v.p. operations, 1964-65, v.p. operations, 1965-67; gen. mgr. Clinchfield R.R. Co., Erwin, Tenn., 1962-64; v.p. transp. and maintenance Seaboard Coast Line R.R. Co., Jacksonville, 1967-70, v.p. operations, 1970-73, exec. v.p., 1973—, also dir., mem. exec. com.; pres., dir. Seacoast Transp. Co., Jacksonville Terminal Co.; exec. v.p. Tampa So. R.R. Co.; v.p., dir. Duval Connecting R.R. Co., Norfolk & Portsmouth Belt Line R.R. Co.; exec. v.p., dir., mem. exec. com. Columbia, Newberry & Laurens R.R. Co.; dir., mem. exec. com. Fruit Growers Express Co.; dir. Haysi R.R. Co., North Charleston Terminal Co., L. & N. R.R. Co., Atlantic Nat. Bank of Jacksonville, Ft. Myers So. R.R. Co., Gainesville Midland R.R. Co., Tampa & Gulf

Coast R.R. Co., Bd. dirs. Met. YMCA, Jacksonville; adv. bd. Salvation Army. Served to brig. gen. AUS, 1943-46; ETO. Decorated Bronze Star medal with V, Army Commendation medal, Legion of Merit. Registered profl. engr., Va. Mem. Am. Assn. R.R. Supts., Am. Ry. Engring. Assn., Am. Soc. C.E. (asso.), Assn. Am. R.R.s, Assn. U.S. Army, Fla. State (dir.), Jacksonville Area (gov.) chambers commerce, Nat. Def. Transp. Assn., Navy League U.S., Roadmasters and Maintenance of Way Assn. Am., Res. Officers Assn. U.S., Soc. Am. Mil. Engrs., Transp. Assn. Am. Methodist. Mason (Shriner). Clubs: Florida Yacht, Ponte Vedra, River, Timuquana Country, Ye Mystic Revellers. Home: 4605 Argonne Lane Jacksonville FL 32210 Office: 500 Water St Jacksonville FL 32202

HASTINGS, JAMES CECIL, state ofcl.; b. Delight, N.C., Aug. 1, 1943; s. J.C. and Selma Nancy (Short) H.; B.S., Appalachian State Coll., 1966, M.A., 1968; m. Karen Blalock, July 5, 1963; children—Kimberly Michaele, James Cory. Recreation dir. City of Boone (N.C.), 1967-70; area dir. pub. relations Nat. Cystic Fibrosis Research Found., 1970-72; field dir. Com. to Re-Elect the Pres., 1972; mem. gov.'s staff State of N.C., 1972, travel and promotion dir., 1973—. Mem. Tryon Palace Commn. Travel Council, State of N.C., 1973—. Adv. bd. N.C. Community Colls.; bd. dirs. N.C. Jaycee Meml. Found., N.C. Jaycee Found. Boys Home, Girls Haven, Spl. Olympics of N.C. Recipient award Heart Fund, 1971. Mem. U.S. Travel Service, So. Travel Dirs. Council, Discover Am. Travel Orgn., Am. Soc. Travel Agts., N.C. Jaycees (pres. 1973-74). Methodist. Toastmaster (v.p. 1971). Home: 6800 Woodmere Dr Raleigh NC 27611 Office: PO Box 26674 Raleigh NC 27611

HASTINGS, RAYMOND ELLIS, coll. dean; b. Hobart, Okla., Mar. 20, 1917; s. Joel Henry and Alvaretta Marie (Haynes) H.; student U. Okla., 1934-38; B.A., Anderson Coll., 1951; M.Div. cum laude, Anderson Sch. Theology, 1958; postgrad. Perkins Sch. Theology, summers 1967, 68, (fellow) Hebrew Union Coll., Jerusalem, summer 1966; m. Elna Mae Stuart, Oct. 7, 1938; children—Colleen (Mrs. Robert L. Pyle), Walter G. and Warren D. (twins). Ordained to ministry Ch. of God, 1940; pastor, Amorita, Okla., 1939-40, Florahome, Fla., 1941-42, Homestead, Fla., 1942-44, Albuquerque, 1945-46, Anderson, Ind., 1947-50; missionary, Cayman Islands, 1951-54, Jamaica, 1958-60, Guyana, 1961-62, Mexico, 1962-65; dean students, instr. Gulf Coast Bible Coll., Houston, 1965-70; tchr. English, Am. Cultural Inst., Saltillo, Mexico, 1963-64; acad. dean, instr. Bay Ridge Christian Coll., Kendleton, Tex., 1971—. Address: Box 726 Kendleton TX 77451

HASTY, FREDERICK GRIER, orthodontist; b. Carthage, N.C., Apr. 29, 1932; s. Wade Hampton and Lora (Johnson) H.; B.S., High Point Coll., 1954; D.D.S., U. N.C., 1958, M.S., 1962; m. Josephine Tilley, Sept. 4, 1954; children—Michael Alan, David Hampton, Robert Grier. Pvt. orthodontic practice, Fayetteville, N.C., 1963—; cons. Ft. Bragg Dental Clinic, 1963-65, Pope AFB Dental Clinic, 1969—. Mem. Mayors Council Pub. Relations, 1969-70. Bd. dirs. YMCA, Fayetteville, 1966-68, Indsl. Devel. Corp., Fayetteville, 1967-69. Served with AUS, 1958-61. Diplomate Am. Bd. Orthodontics. Mem. Am. Dental Assn., Am., So. assns. orthodontists, N.C. (mem. exec. com., chmn. 1972-73), 4th Dist. (pres. 1972-73) dental socs., Orthodontic Research Study Club (charter pres.). Club: Exchange (charter pres.). Dist. editor N.C. Dental Jour., 1968-70. Home: 2836 Skye Dr Fayetteville NC 28303 Office: 3401 Melrose Rd Fayetteville NC 28304

HASTY, GERALD RICHARD, educator, ret. army officer; b. Pekin, Ill., Apr. 12, 1926; s. Leslie Parke and Bernice Arthene (Brown) H.; B.S., Bradley U., 1952; M.B.A., 1954; postgrad. Harvard, 1961; M.A., Am. U., 1962; Ph.D., Northwestern U., 1963; LL.B., Blackstone Sch. Law, 1968; postgrad. summers U. Toledo, 1958, U. Me., 1963, State U. N.Y. at Buffalo, 1963, Armed Forces Staff Coll., 1968, Air War Coll., 1965; m. Betty Anne Osmundson, June 23, 1951; children—Grant Rutledge, Mark Osmund, Deborah Anne. Commd. 2d lt. U.S. Army, 1954, advanced through grades to lt. col., 1966; chief Q.M. Supply div. 7th Logistical Command, Korea, 1961-62; comdg. officer 34th Supply and Service Bn., Vietnam, 1966, also dir. adminstrn. 58th Field Depot; exec. asst. joint logistics rev. bd. Office Sec. Def., Washington, 1969-70; comdg. officer Charleston (S.C.) Army Depot, 1970-72; joint logistics plans officer on staff comdr.-in-chief UN Command, 1972-73; logistics staff officer Joint and Strategic Forces Directorate, Army Concepts Analysis Agy., Bethesda, Md., 1973-74, ret.; asst. prof. pub. adminstrn. George Washington U., Washington, 1964-65, 67, asso. prof., 1968-69, 73; vis. prof. polit. sci. Bapt. Coll., Charleston, 1970-72, now asso. prof.; tchr., lectr., various colls., U.S. Korea, Vietnam. Counselor, Boy Scouts Am., 1968—; mem. citizen's adv. and action council to gov. Coastal Carolina Community Pre-release Center, S.C. Dept. Corrections. Bd. dirs. Charleston Safety Council. Served AUS, 1944-50. Decorated Legion of Merit with oak leaf cluster, Purple Heart with oak leaf cluster. Mem. Charleston Trident C. of C., La. Societe Francaise deBienfaisance de Charleston, Navy League, Fed. Exec. Assn. (com. on govt.-wide policy areas), Armed Forces Mgmt. Assn., S.C. Law Enforcement Officers Assn., Nat. Def. Transp. Assn., Am. Bar Assn., Pi Sigma Alpha, Tau Kappa Epsilon. Lutheran. Mason (32 deg., Shriner), Kiwanian. Home: 1282 Winchester Dr Charleston SC 29407

HATCHER, CLIFF CICERO, III, security dealer exec.; b. Atlanta, Mar. 2, 1923; s. Cliff Cicero and Elizabeth Horton (Lochridge) H.; LL.B., Emory U., 1948; m. Elizabeth Heath Coleman, Feb. 8, 1952; children—Cliff Coleman, Elizabeth Hollis. Vice-pres., dir., mgr. municipal bond dept. Furman Securities Co., Greenville, S.C., 1957—. Financial cons., City of Greenville, North Charleston Consol. Pub. Service Dist., 1966—. Mem. ad hoc com. Greenville County Planning Commn., 1964—; dir. S.C. Municipal Council, 1963-69. Served with USAAF, 1942-45, USAF, 1951-57, now lt. col. Res. ret. Decorated D.F.C., Air medal with three oak leaf clusters. Mem. Investment Bankers Assn., Greenville C. of C. (mem. finance com. 1968-71), Sigma Alpha Epsilon. Episcopalian. Clubs: Poinsett, Greenville Country. Home: 217 Rock Creek Dr Greenville SC 29605 Office: Daniel Bldg Greenville SC 29602

HATCHER, DANNY RAY, librarian; b. Murray, Ky., Sept. 16, 1947; s. William Otis and Blanche Bearnese (Vaughn) H.; B.A., Murray State U., 1970; M.L.S., George Peabody Coll., 1972; m. Anna Mae Chandler, July 16, 1966; 1 dau., Heather Victoria. Asst. dir. spl. collections div. Murray State U. Libraries, 1969-70, dir. microphotography div., 1971; grad. asst. Country Music Found. Library and Media Center, Nashville, 1971, archivist, 1972-73, dir., 1973—, asst. dir. program in Anglo-Am. music, 1972. Owner, mgr. Nat. Geneal. Pubs., Nashville, 1969—, Ky. Reprint Co. subsidiary, 1969—, Hist. Microfilms subsidiary, 1969—; owner, mgr. House of Heather, Books and Periodicals, Nashville, 1974—. Mem. Music, Southeastern, Tenn., Nashville library assns., Country Music Assn., Assn. for Recorded Sound Collections, Nat. Acad. Rec. Arts and Scis., Am. Folklore Soc., Am. Assn. State and Local History, John C. Waters Hist. Soc. Ky. (founder), Jackson Purchase Hist. Soc. Ky., West Central Ky. Family Research Assn. (charter), Beta Phi Mu, Kappa Alpha. Editor: Notebooks of John C. Waters, Kentucky Historian, 1969; Lemon's Handbook of Marshall County, Kentucky, 1894, 1971; 1880 Atlas of Graves County, Kentucky, 1880, 1971; Histories and Biographies of Ballard, Calloway, Carlisle, Fulton, Graves, Hickman, McCracken, and Marshall Counties, Kentucky, 1885, 1972; History of Calloway County, Kentucky, 1931, 1972; Tenn. Librarian, 1973—; coordinating and photog. editor Jackson Purchase Sesquicentennial Publs., 1969; regional coordinating editor Pictorial History of Kentucky, 1971; book rev. editor Jour. Country Music, 1972—; series editor rec. tech. series Country Music Found. Press, 1973—. Contbr. articles to profl. and hist. publs. Home: 2301 Elliott Av Nashville TN 37204 Office: 700 16th Av S Nashville TN 37203

HATCHER, HERSCHEL FISHER, JR., dentist; b. Moultrie, Ga., Oct. 19, 1922; s. Herschel Fisher and Annie Ruth (Seagroves) H.; student North Ga. Coll., 1939-40, Mercer U., 1946; B.S., Stetson U., 1948; D.D.S., Emory U., 1953; postgrad. U. N.C., 1956, 60; m. Martha Lois Roberts, July 29, 1945; children—Brenda Lynn, Herschel Fisher III. Individual practice dentistry, Decatur, Ga., 1953—; instr. pedodontics Emory U., Atlanta, 1953-58, asso. prof., 1957-58. Served with USAAF, 1942-46. Mem. Am., Ga. dental assns., No. Dist. (treas. 1959-60), 5th Dist. (exec. council 1964-67) dental socs., Psi Omega, Beta Beta Beta, Gamma Sigma Epsilon. Methodist. Lion (v.p. 1955). Home: 628 Park Lane Decatur GA 30033 Office: 250 E Ponce de Leon Av Decatur GA 30030

HATCHER, MARTHA OLIVIA TAYLOR (MRS. FRANK PRIDGEN HATCHER SR.), educator; b. Birmingham, Ala., Feb. 17, 1920; d. Sanford Allia and Mary (McCullough) Taylor; B.S., Howard Coll., 1936-40; M.Ed. in Sci. Edn., U. Ga., 1966, Ed.D., 1973; tchrs. certificate Brenau Coll., 1964; m. Frank Pridgen Hatcher, Sr., Nov. 7, 1941; children—Frank Pridgen, Martha Elizabeth, Nancy Louise. Chief bacteriologist vet. div. Ga. Dept. Agr., Atlanta, 1943-45; supr. surg. pathology lab. Jefferson Hillman Hosp., Med. Coll. Ala., Birmingham, 1945-46, research asst. in pathology, 1945-46; mgr. offices Fran Mar Farms, Inc., Gainesville, Ga., 1957-66; instr. biology Gainesville Jr. Coll., 1966-67, asst. prof. biology, 1967, acting chmn. div. natural scis. and maths., after 1968, now chmn. div., asso. prof. biology; accompanist music dept. Brenau Coll., Gainesville, 1959-61. Chmn. Gray Ladies Vol. Services, Gainesville chpt. A.R.C., 1957-62; sec. Yohah Council Girl Scouts Am., 1959-61. Bd. dirs. Community Concert Assn. Gainesville, 1968-70. NSF Sci. Faculty fellow in microbiology, 1970-71. Mem. Am. Assn. U. Profs., A.A.A.S., Am. Guild Organists, Am. Inst. Biol. Scis., Nat., Ga. edn. assns., Nat. Assn. Biology Tchrs., Assn. S.E. Biologists, Nat. Assn. Research Sci. Teaching, Ga. Acad. Sci. Nat. Sci. Tchrs. Assn., Am. Legion Aux. (pres. 1948-50), U.D.C. (chpt. pres. 1949-51), Nat. Faculty Assn. Community and Jr. Colls., Am. Soc. Microbiology, Am. Assn. U. Women, Kappa Delta Pi, Alpha Epsilon Delta, Delta Zeta. Clubs: Music (pres. 1950-52), Federated Music (sec. 1957-58) (Gainesville). Home: 840 Memorial Dr NE Gainesville GA 30501 Office: PO Box 1358 Gainesville Jr Coll Gainesville GA 30501

HATCHER, MILDRED (OBERA), educator; b. Murray, Ky.; d. William Thomas and Lorena (Taylor) Hatcher, Jr.; B.S. magna cum laude, Murray State U., 1927; M.A., George Peabody Coll. Tchrs., 1930, postgrad., summers 1932, 48; postgrad. Vanderbilt U., 1930, U. Wis., summer 1947, Ind. U., summer 1964; D. Litt., P.E. U., 1967. Asst. prin., head English dept. Hardin (Ky.) High Sch., 1927-29; tchr. math. city pub. schs., Paducah, Ky., 1930-34; tchr. English, Paducah Tilghman High Sch., 1934-48; critic tchr. Murray State U., summer 1946; asst. and asso. prof. English, Austin Peay State U., Clarksville, Tenn., 1948-60; asst. prof. English, Murray State U., 1960-61; asso. prof., 1961-74. Commd. Ky. col., 1966. Mem. Conf. Coll. Composition and Communication, Nat. Council Tchrs. English (del. 1958-59, spl. pub. relations rep. golden anniversary 1960, dir. 1959-72, judge ann. writing awards 1961-68, mem. spl. pub. relations com. 1963-69), Ky. Hist. Soc., Ky. (dir. 1965-68, v.p. 1968-70, pres. 1971-73), Tenn. (v.p. 1957, pres. 1958-60) folklore socs., Middle Tenn. English Assn. (v.p. 1959-62, liaison officer 1959-60), U.D.C. (pres. 1955-56), D.A.R. (chpt. regent 1953-54), Murray State U. Alumni Assn. (v.p. 1945-46), Marquis Library Soc. (adv. bd. 1969), Chi Alpha Pi, Kappa Delta Pi, Delta Kappa Gamma. Baptist. Clubs: Nat. Writers; Woman's. Contbr. articles and poems to profl. jours. Poems included in ann. Nat. Poetry Anthology, 1953-60. Home: 1305 Olive Blvd Murray KY 42071

HATCHER, WILLIAM JULIAN, JR., educator; b. Augusta, Ga., July 21, 1935; s. William Julian and Norvell (Kelley) H.; B.Ch.E. with honors Ga. Inst. Tech., 1957; M.Ch.E., La. State U., 1964, Ph.D., 1968; m. Sharon Lynn Hancock, Jan. 18, 1958; children—Jeffrey Craig, Rebecca Lynn, Michael William. Research engr. Esso Research Labs., Baton Rouge, La., 1960-66; research asso. La. State U., 1966-68; sr. research engr. Esso Research Labs., Baton Rouge, La., 1968-69; asso. prof. chem. engring. U. Ala., 1969—, dept. head, 1973—; cons. U.S. Bur. Mines, 1972—. Served to lt. USMC, 1957-60. NSF Research grantee, 1970-72. Mem. Am. Inst. Chem. Engrs., Am. Soc. Engring. Edn., Phi Kappa Phi, Tau Beta Pi, Phi Eta Sigma, Omega Chi Epsilon, Phi Lambda Upsilon. Methodist. Contbg. author: Environmental Engineering Handbook, 1973, Computer Programs for Chemical Engineering Education, Vols. II and IV, 1972. Research in petroleum processes, 1960-66; air pollution control, 1968-69; catalysis, 1970—. Home: 30 Woodland Hills Tuscaloosa AL 35401 Office: PO Box 6312 University AL 35486

HATFIELD, CECIL CURTIS, physician, banker; b. Saltville, Va., Aug. 19, 1908; s. James Abram and Sarah (Osborne) H.; B.S., Roanoke Coll., 1930; M.D., Med. Coll. Va., 1934; m. Laura Margaret Horne, Oct. 7, 1939; 1 son, James Andrew. Intern St. Vincent's Hosp., Erie, Pa., 1934-35; practice medicine, Saltville, Va., 1936; indsl. physician Olin Mathieson, Saltville, 1936-66; dir. 1st Nat. Bank, Saltville, Va., 1949—, pres., 1963—. Various positions Boy Scouts of Am., 1930—; pres., Saltville Rescue Squad, 1958-60; Pres., YMCA, 1972—, dir. So. dist., 1968-70; bd. dirs. Highland Community Coll., 1970—. Democrat. Methodist. Mason, Kiwanian (lt. gov. 1960). Address: Drawer C C Saltville VA 24370

HATFIELD, DONALD GENE, educator, artist; b. Detroit, May 23, 1932; s. Floyd L. and Helen R. (Nehmer) H.; A.A., Northwestern Mich. Coll., 1958; B.A., Mich. State U., 1960, M.A. 1961; M.F.A., U. Wis., 1962; m. Marilyn Ann Grindstuen, Sept. 10, 1960; children—Suzanne, John, Kathleen. Tchr. art, elementary art supr. Auburndale (Wis.) High Sch., 1962-64; asst. prof. art Auburn (Ala.) U., 1964-71, asso. prof., 1971—; exhibited in group shows at numerous state and nat. exhbns.; one-man shows Wis. State Coll., La Crosse, 1963, Auburn U., 1967, Columbus (Ga.) Mus. Arts and Crafts, 1968, Birmingham (Ala.) Mus. Arts and Crafts, 1968, Savannah (Ga.) Art Assn., 1962, Birmingham So. Coll., 1970, Montgomery Mus. Art, 1970, LaGrange (Ga.) Coll., 1971, others; two-man show Montgomery (Ala.) Museum Art, 1969. Served with USN, 1952-56. Recipient purchase award Annual Exhbn. of Wis. Art, Milw. Art Center, 1964, La Crosse (Wis.) State Coll., 1963; numerous others. Mem. Internat. Platform Assn., V.F.W., Ala. Art League (pres. 1970-73), Birmingham Art Assn. Presbyn. Elk. Home: 550 Forest Park Circle Auburn AL 36830

HATFIELD, GENE EDWIN, cons. engring. co. exec.; b. West Point, Ky., Dec. 29, 1928; s. Walter Ned and Ressie (Hart) H.; B.S. in Civil Engring., U. Ky., 1954; m. Mildred Ann Murphy, Aug. 22, 1952; children—Michael Edwin, Walter Harrison, William Arch. Resident engr. Ky. Dept. Hwys., 1954-57; design engr. Nichols Engring. Co., Union City, Tenn., 1957-61; v.p. Edward T. Hannan & Assos., Inc., Paducah, Ky., 1962-70, dir. 1966-70, dir., Evansville, Ind., 1967-70; pres., chmn. bd. Community Program Cons., Inc., Paducah, 1971—; dir. South/West Planning Assos., Bryan, Tex. Mem. Fulton (Ky.) Ind. Bd. Edn., 1960—, vice chmn., 1964-66, chmn., 1966—; exec. dir. Fulton Municipal Housing Commn., 1959-61; mem. Fulton Planning Commn., 1956-59; mem. Fulton Urban Renewal and Community Devel. Agy., 1969-71. Served to maj. mil. assistance and adv. group AUS, Japan, 1961-62. Registered profl. engr., Ky.; registered land surveyor. Mem. Am. Water Works Assn., Water Pollution Control Fedn., Nat., Ky. socs. profl. engrs., Ky. Hist. Soc., Ky. Sch. Bds. Assn. (regional chmn. 1973—, state dir. 1973—), Sigma Nu. Mem. Christian Ch. (ofcl. bd. 1955—, chmn. 1965-67, vice chmn. 1967-70, bd. elders 1960—). Home: 103 Henderson Dr S Fulton KY 42041 Office: 700 Jefferson St Paducah KY 42001

HATFIELD, JACK KENTON, lawyer; b. Medford, Okla., Jan. 26, 1922; s. Loate L. and Cora (Walsh) H.; B.S., Phillips U., 1947, A.B., 1953; J.D., Oklahoma City U., 1954; m. Dorothy Ann Keltner, Dec. 5, 1943; children—Susan Kathryn (Mrs. Michael F. Dean), Sally Ann (Mrs. William Frohnapfel). Admitted to Okla. bar, 1954; practice accounting and law, Enid, 1954-58; chief br. budget and finance Dept. Interior, Southwestern Power Adminstrn., Tulsa, 1958-67, dep. asst. adminstr. for adminstrn., 1967-69, chief div. mgmt. services, 1969-70, chief div. financial mgmt., 1970-71, chief div. adminstrv. mgmt., 1971-73, dir. planning staff, 1973—. Organizer, dir. Profl. Mens Assn. Kansas City, Inc., Profl. Mens Assn, Okla., Inc.; dir. Griffin Producing Co., Calumet Ranch Co. Organizer, trustee Garfield County Cerebral Palsy Clinic for Speech and Hearing. Served with AUS, 1943-46. C.P.A. Mem. Am. Inst. C.P.A.'s, Okla. Soc. C.P.A.'s Am., Okla., Tulsa County bar assns. Republican. Methodist. Home: 2976 E 75th St Tulsa OK 74136 Office: NBT Bldg Tulsa OK 74103

HATFIELD, JOHN DEMPSEY, chemist; b. Sneedville, Tenn., Aug. 18, 1919; s. George Harrison and Della Mae (Livesay) H.; A.B., U. Tenn., 1938, M.S., 1939; Ph.D., Purdue U., 1942; m. Mary Wills Hollingsworth, Oct. 14, 1943; children—Elizabeth (Mrs. Charles Edmond Baddley), Mary (Mrs. Thomas Gail LeCroy), John, Kemper. Chemist, E.I. duPont de Nemours & Co., Richmond, Va., 1939; fellow, asso. chemist Purdue U., 1940-42; research chemist TVA, Muscle Shoals, Ala., 1943—. Chmn. Gordon Research Conf., 1968. Chmn. Lauderdale County chpt. A.R.C., 1960-61. Served with USNR, 1944-46. Recipient Environmental Protection Agy. grants, 1967, 70. Mem. Am. Chem. Soc. (sect. chmn., chmn., councilor). Presbyn. (elder). Rotarian. Contbr. articles to profl. jours. Home: 1224 Sorrento Rd Florence AL 35630 Office: Div Chem Devel TVA Muscle Shoals AL 35660

HATFIELD, WILLIAM EMERSON, educator; b. Ransom, Ky., May 31, 1937; s. Emerson B. and Gardner (Hatfield) H.; B.S., Marshall U., 1958, M.S., 1959; Ph.D., U. Ariz., 1962; m. Peggy Ransom, Dec. 17, 1955, (div. Nov. 1967); children—Timothy Edward, Robert Bruce, Maryan, Julia, Ellen. Postdoctoral research asso. U. Ill., 1962-63; asst. prof. inorganic chemistry U. N.C. at Chapel Hill, 1963-67, asso. prof., 1967-72, prof., 1972—; vis. prof. N.C. Central U., 1964-65; cons. Ventron Corp., Cahn Instrument Co. Recipient Cahn Instrument Co. Applications award, 1965. Internat. Nickel Co. scholar, 1956-58; Koppers Co. fellow, 1960; NSF summer fellow, 1961; Continental Oil Co. fellow, 1961-62; Ariz. Wilson fellow, 1961. Mem. Am. Chem. Soc., The Chem. Soc. (London), Sigma Xi. Democrat. Author (with R.A. Palmer) Problems in Structural Inorganic Chemistry; (with W.E. Parker) Symmetry in Chemical Bonding and Structure, 1974. Contbr. numerous articles to sci. jours. Home: 400 Wesley Dr Chapel Hill NC 27514 Office: Dept Chemistry U NC Chapel Hill NC 27514

HATGIL, PAUL PETER, artist, educator; b. Manchester, N.H., Feb. 18, 1921; s. Peter and Katherine (Karkadou) Hatgilakos; B.S., Mass. Sch. Art; M.F.A., Columbia, 1951; m. Katherine Haritos, Feb. 22, 1948. One man shows Southwest Craft Center, Houston, Baker Gallery, Lubbock, Tex.; exhibited Tex. Fine Arts Assn., 1951-61, Delgado Mus. Art, 1953, Miami, Fla., 1956, Syracuse (N.Y.) Mus. Art, 1956, Internat. Exhbn., Washington, 1954, 56, Community Lutheran Ch., Victoria, Tex., 1957, Southwest Ceramic Exhbn., 1960, Smithsonian Instn., 1962, Munson-Williams-Proctor Inst., 1962, America House, N.Y.C., 1962, 65, Carnegie Inst., 1963, Little Rock Art Center, 1963, U.S. Senate Office Bldg., Washington, 1964, Philbrook Art Center, 1964, So. Meth. U., 1964, Hardin-Simmons U., 1964, U. Chattanooga, 1965, N.Y. World's Fair, 1965, Hemisfair Pavilion, 1968, Internat. Minerals Corp., Skokie, Ill., 1968, Southwest Tchrs. Coll., 1969, Tex. Design Craftsmen, Houston, 1969, Sol Del Rio Gallery, 1969; executed murals Huston-Tillotson Coll., Austin, Tex., 1961; executed mosaic murals St. Paul's Lutheran Ch., Austin, 1959, sta. KTBC-TV, Austin, 1960, Tex. Luth. Coll., 1961, U. Tex. Bus. Bldg., 1962, FAA, Panama Canal, 1963, Design Assos. Bldg., Dallas, 1964, Freemont Complex, Dallas, 1965, others; ceramics and sculpture in permanent collections Laguna Gloria Mus., Austin, Witte Meml. Mus., McNay Art Inst.; mem. faculty U. Tex. at Austin, 1951—, prof. art, 1964—, curator U. Mus., 1964-67; cons. in field. Served with USAAF, 1943-46. Research grantee U. Tex., 1969. Mem. Am., Southwest ceramic socs., Am. Assn. Museums, Am. Assn. U. Profs., Am. Craftsmen, Nat. Assn. Art Educators, Tex. Fine Arts Soc., Tex. Designers-Craftsmen. Mem. Greek Orthodox Ch. Contbr. articles to profl. art jours. Home: 1401 Red Bud Trail Austin TX 78746

HATHAWAY, AMOS TOWNSEND, naval officer, educator; b. Pueblo, Colo., Dec. 5, 1913; s. James Amos and Nina (North) H.; B.S., U.S. Naval Acad., 1935; postgrad. U.S. Naval War Coll., 1947-48; M.A. in Teaching, Duke, 1965-66; m. Marianne Langdon Train, June 10, 1937 (dec. Dec. 1972); children—Joan Langdon, Marianne Train, Melinda North (dec.), Barbara Spencer, Sarah Townsend; m. 2d, Joyce Brians McDaniel, May 17, 1973; 1 son, James Banks McDaniel. Commd. ensign U.S. Navy, 1935, advanced through grades to capt., 1954; exec. officer, navigator destroyer minesweeper Zane, Guadalcanal, 1942; command destroyer Heermann, Battle off Samar, 1944; mem. faculty U.S. Naval Acad., 1945-47, U.S. Naval War Coll., 1951-53; mem. war staff Gen. MacArthur, Korea, 1948-50, writer theater logistic plan Inchon Landing, 1950; exec. officer cruiser St. Paul, 1950-51; command Destroyer Div. 92, 1953-54, command attack transport Okanogan, 1958-59; command cruiser Rochester, 1959-60; mem. joint staff Joint Chiefs of Staff, 1961-63, dir. logistic plans Office Chief of Naval Operations, 1963-65, ret., 1965; asst. prof. math. The Citadel, Charleston, S.C., 1966—. Decorated Navy Cross, Legion of Merit (2), Bronze Star (2), Mem. Math. Assn. Am., U.S. Naval Acad. Alumni Assn., U.S. Naval Acad. Athletic Assn. (dir. 1945-47), U.S. Naval Inst., Kappa Delta Pi. Club: Army Navy Country (Arlington, Va.). Home: 11 Sayle Rd Charleston SC 29407

HATHAWAY, CHARLES WALTER II, optometrist; b. Columbus, Ind., Oct. 21, 1942; s. Charles Walter and Grace (White) H.; A.B., Ind. U., 1964, B.S., 1965, O.D., 1967; m. Mary Cathleen Devins, Aug. 26, 1967; 1 dau., Devin Ellen. Practice optometry, Tallahassee, 1967—. Mem. Tallahassee Civic Center Com., 1971-72, Tallahassee-Popayon Sister City Commn., 1970-72. Bd. dirs. Leon County United Way. Fellow Am. Acad. Optometry, Coll. Optometrists in Visual Devel.; mem. Am. Optometric-Assn., N.W. Fla. Optometric Soc. (pres.

1972-74), Jr. C. of C. Clubs: Optimist, Apalachee Bay Yacht (commodore 1971), Torch, Killearn Golf and Country. Home: 2304 Vinkara Dr Tallahassee FL 32303 Office: 906 Thomasville Rd Tallahassee FL 32303

HATHEWAY, JOHN LOCKWOOD, pipeline co. exec.; b. Tulsa, Sept. 23, 1930; s. Elliott Keith and Grace Edna (Lockwood) H.; B.S., Okla. State U., 1953; m. Betty Lou Wells, Nov. 18, 1956; children—Eric Wells, John Kent, Lynne Elizabeth. Resident engr., Cities Service Oil Co., Bartlesville, Okla., 1955-58; with Williams Brothers Co., Tulsa, 1958-70, sr. engr., 1963-66, mgr. engring., 1966-69, v.p., 1969-70, v.p., gen. mgr., 1970-71; pres. William Brothers Engring. Co., Tulsa, 1971—; dir. Protech Internat., B.V. Schiedam, Holland. Pres., Alaskan Resource Scis. Corp., Anchorage, 1973—. Served to 1st lt. USAF, 1953-55. Registered profl. engr., Okla. Mem. Instn. Engrs. Australia, Nat. Soc. Profl. Engrs., Okla. Soc. Profl. Engrs., Petroleum Club Tulsa, Pipeliners Club Tulsa. Home: 5221 S 68th E Av Tulsa OK 74145 Office: 321 S Boston Av Tulsa OK 74103

HATTER, FORNEY KING, ocean terminal exec.; b. Montgomery, Ala., June 13, 1913; s. James A. and Annie (King) H.; student Auburn U., 1931-32, Massey Bus. Coll., 1933; m. Blanche West, June 12, 1937; children—Melinda (Mrs. A.B. Hankins, Jr.), Eulila (Mrs. J.D. Odom), Susan (Mrs. R.L. Weekly). Bookkeeper Pace-Holland Co., Pensacola, Fla., 1937-38, Robertsdale, Ala., 1938-53; with Ala. State Docks, Mobile, 1953—, sec.-treas., comptroller, 1970—. Served with arty. AUS, 1944-46. Mem. Nat. Assn. Accountants, Port Trafficland Transportation Club. V.F.W. Mem. Disciples of Christ Ch. Club: Lake Forest Country (Spanish Fort, Ala.). Home: PO Box 414 Spanish Fort AL 36527 Office: PO Box 1588 Mobile AL 36601

HATTON, JULIAN RAY, agrl. products co. exec.; b. Brutus, Ky., Jan. 9, 1931; s. Joseph Leon and Lois (Crippen) H.; B.S., U. Fla., 1952; m. Betty Joan Barwick, Jan, 6, 1953; children—J. Ray II, Henry B., Leslie Joan, Shelley Jean. Supr. pest control U. Fla., 1951-52; field foreman Joe Hatton & Sons, Pahokee, Fla., 1952-54; pres. Hatton Bros., Inc., 1954-73; v.p. Palm Beach Sugar Corp., 1962—. Mem. Sch. Improvement Com., Pahokee, Fla., 1967-71; mem. Fla. State com. Agr. and Soil Conservation Service, U.S. Dept. Agr. Mem. Entomol. Soc. Am., Alpha Zeta, Lambda Chi Alpha. Republican. Methodist. Elk, Lion (pres. 1968-69). Home: 2927 Bacom Point Rd Pahokee FL 33476 Office: Drawer 558 Pahokee FL 33476

HATTON, THURMAN TIMBROOK, JR., horticulturist; b. Bartow, Fla., Feb. 4, 1922; s. Thurman Timbrook and Pearl Catherine (Holliday) H.; B.S., U. Fla., 1943, M.S., 1949; Ph.D., Wash. State U., 1953; m. Eileen Marie Snowber, Jan. 25, 1947; children—Mary, Nina, Alexa, Michele. Asst. prof. U. P.R., Mayaguez, 1949-50; instr. Wash. State U., Pullman, 1950-53; extension specialist N.C. State U., Raleigh, 1953-55; investigations leader charge Dept. Agr. Market Quality Research Lab., Miami, Fla., 1955-68, research leader charge market quality and transp. research, Orlando, Fla., 1968—; teaching fellow U. Fla., 1948-49, prof., 1972—. Bd. dirs. Am. Youth Exchange Program. Served to col. arty., AUS, 1943-48. Decorated Air medal; recipient Ann. Research award Fla. Fruit and Vegetable Assn., 1973. Mem. Am. Soc. Hort. Sci., Internat. Soc. for Citriculture, Fla. Mango Forum (pres. 1961), Fla. Hort. Soc. (v.p. 1965), Sigma Xi. Rotarian. Contbr. articles profl. jours. Home: 336 Elkhorn Ct Winter Park FL 32789 Office: 2120 Camden Rd Orlando FL 32803

HAUBER, EDWIN NELSON, author; b. Centerville, N.Y., Aug. 22, 1912; s. Nelson L. and Margaret M. (Owens) H.; A.A., Menatee Jr. Coll., 1966; B.A., U.S. Fla., 1968; m. Martha L. Hamilton, Sept. 6, 1940; children—Nancy C., Andrew E., Martin N. Chief lab. instr. Capitol Radio Engring. Inst., Washington, 1940-43; technician, Jansky & Bailey, cons. engrs., Washington, 1943-45; owner, Arlington Radio Labs., Arlington, Va., 1945-54, E.N. Hauber TV Service, Bradenton, Fla., 1954-64. Mem. I.E.E.E., U.S. Power Squadron (squadron comdr. 1967-68). Author: On the Plane of the Horizon, 1972. Address: 1208 28th St W Bradenton FL 33505

HAUBOLD, CLEVE ERNST, educator, playwright; b. Bartlesville, Okla., Dec. 30, 1930; s. Cleve Albert and Doraline Omalee (Bond) H.; B.F.A., U. Tex., 1951, M.F.A., 1958, Ph.D. (Sam Shubert fellow), 1968. Instr. theatre arts Tex. Christian U., Fort Worth, 1958-59; chmn. speech theatre dept. Kilgore (Tex.) Coll., 1959-63; asst. prof. U. Tex., Austin, 1965-66; asst. prof. drama San Jose State Coll., 1968—. Dir. theatre Eastfield Coll., Mesquite, Tex., 1972—; resident playwright Dominican Coll., New Orleans, 1967; author plays Big Black Box, 1965; Follow the Elephants, 1965; The Mice Have Been Drinking Again, 1970; Tattoo, 1972; others. John Golden playwright scholar, 1966; recipient 1st prize Atlanta Jr. League Playwriting Contest, 1966. Home: 2578 Interstate Blvd Apt L Mesquite TX 75149 Office: Dept Drama Eastfield Coll 3737 Motley Dr Mesquite TX 75149

HAUCK, WARREN EARL, pharm. co. exec.; b. Saugerties, N.Y., Aug. 8, 1925; s. Charles Alfred and Matilda V. (Fuchs) H.; student Knox Coll., 1943-44, Union U., 1946-50; B.S., Albany Coll. Pharmacy, 1950; m. Mary Barry, Aug. 27, 1950; children—Daniel, Steven, Barbara, Michele, Johann, Maureen, James, Gregory. Pharmacist, Utica, N.Y.., 1950-51; founder, pres. Hiss Pharmacal Co., Utica, 1951-67; regional mgr. Reid-Provident Labs, Atlanta, 1967-68, v.p., 1969-70, exec. v.p., 1970-73, sr. v.p., 1973—, also dir. Served with USAAF, 1943-46. Mem. Nat. Assn. Pharm. Mfrs. (dir. 1971-73), Drug Chem. Allied Trades, Nat. Ethical Pharm. Assn., Pharm. Advt. Club, Kappa Si. Home: Box 195A Route 4 Alpharetta GA 30201 Office: 25 5th St NW Atlanta GA 30308

HAUGAARD, WILLIAM PAUL, educator; b. Bklyn., Jan. 19, 1929; s. William Edward and Bess (Holdzkom) H.; grad. Horace Mann Sch. for Boys, N.Y.C., 1946; A.B. magna cum laude, Princeton U., 1951; S.T.B., Gen. Theol. Sem., 1954, Th.D., 1962; m. Janet McKee Butler, June 19, 1954; children—Margaret McKee, Mary Butler. Ordained to ministry Protestant Episcopal Ch. as deacon, 1954, priest, 1954; vicar St. James Ch., Brewster, Wash., and Ch. of the Transfiguration, Twisp, Wash., 1954-58; fellow, tutor Gen. Theol. Sem., N.Y.C., 1958-62; asso. prof. ch. history Seminario Episcopal del Caribe, 1962-71, prof., 1971—, acting dean, 1962-63, 68-69, dean, 1969—, vice chancellor Caribbean Center for Advanced Studies, 1973—. Staff mem. Group Life Labs. Dept. Christian Edn., Episcopal Ch., 1956-58; additional mem. Dept. Christian Edn., Nat. Council, Episcopal Ch., 1958-59. Recipient the Daily Princetonian award, Princeton U., 1949, Rockerfeller Doctoral fellowship, 1960-62, Episcopal Ch. Found. fellowship, 1966. Mem. Am. Hist. Assn., Am. Soc. Ch. History, Renaissance Soc. Am, Phi Beta Kappa. Author: Elizabeth and the English Reformation, 1968. Editorial bd. Historical Mag. of the Protestant Episcopal Ch., 1970—. Contbr. articles to religious and hist. pubs. Address: Apartado 757 Carolina PR 00630

HAUPT, FREDERICK, III, assn. exec.; b. Louisville, Sept. 12, 1921; s. Fred L. and Marguerite (McConnell) H.; A.B., U. Louisville, 1946; postgrad. Harvard, 1946-47; m. Martha A. Montague, Mar. 31, 1949; 1 child, Frederick Christian. Pub.'s rep. Appleton-Century-Croft and Alfred A. Knopf, Inc., N.Y.C., 1947-52; mem. staff N.Y. Times, N.Y.C., 1952-53; pub. relations cons., Washington, 1953-61; pub. relations dir. Opera Soc. Washington, 1957-61; press attache Am. embassy, Bonn, Germany, 1961-62; information officer, attache U.S. Mission, Berlin, Germany, 1962-65; information officer, consul AID, Karachi, Pakistan, 1965-67; news editor Voice of Am., Rhodes, Greece, 1967; dir. pub. affairs Nat. Trust Historic Preservation, Washington, 1968—. Served with Armed Forces, 1942-46. Decorated Knight's Cross, Order Merit (Germany). Democrat. Home: 3629 Fulton St NW Washington DC 20007 Office: Nat Trust Historic Preservation 740-748 Jackson Pl NW Washington DC 20006

HAUSER, GEORGE BAXTER, univ. adminstr.; b. Chickasha, Okla., Jan. 11, 1938; s. William George and Mildred Lee (Lenochan) H.; B.A., Central State U., 1960, M.A., 1968; m. Carolyn Sue Smith, Sept. 4, 1958; children—William, Brett, Susan. Tchr., Covington High Sch., 1960-62, Cherokee High Sch., 1962-63, Woodward High Sch., 1963-64, Choctaw High Sch., 1964-68; coach Bacone (Okla.) Jr. Coll., 1968-73; coach, athletic dir. Am. Christian Coll., Tulsa, 1973—. Named Okla. Coach of Year, Okla. Jour., 1967. Mem. N.E.A., Okla. Edn. Assn., Okla. High Sch. Coaches Assn., Nat. Jr. Coll. Coaches Assn. Rotarian. Home: 3017 S Norwood Av Tulsa OK 74101

HAUSER, HARRIS MILTON, physician; b. Galveston, Tex., Oct. 20, 1932; s. Abe and Florence (Paysee) H.; student U. Tex., 1949-51, U. Houston, 1950-53; M.D., Baylor U., 1955; M.S., U. Minn., 1960; m. Jaclyn Lee Reader, Feb. 12, 1953 (div. 1970); children—Terri Lynn, Karen Louise, John Bradley, Ann Katherine, Heather Joan; m. 2d, Mary Barbara Harris, Sept. 16, 1970. Intern Methodist Hosp., Houston, 1955-56; fellow neurology and psychiatry Mayo Found., Rochester, Minn., 1956-60; chief closed psychiatry Brooke Army Hosp., Ft. Sam Houston, San Antonio, 1960-61, asst. chief neurology, 1961-62; cons. neurology Kelsey-Seybold Clinic, Houston, 1962-66; practice medicine specializing in neurology and psychiatry Hauser Clinic, Houston, 1962-70; clin. asso. prof. neurology and psychiatry U. Tex. Med. Br., Galveston, 1973—; asst. prof. neurology Baylor U. Coll. Med., Houston, 1966—; dir. EEG Labs., 1963—; mem. staff Meml., Hosp. Systems, Methodist, Heights hosps., all Houston. Recipient H. V. Jones award Mayo Found., 1960; Award of Merit, Am. Legion, 1962. Mem. A.M.A., Am. Psychol. Assn., A.C.P., Am. Acad. Neurology, Central Neuropsychiat. Assn., Am., So. (pres. 1970) EEG socs., Alpha Omega Alpha. Contbr. articles in field to profl. jours. Home: 2600 Bellefontaine Houston TX 77025 Office: Shamrock Profl Bldg Houston TX 77025

HAUTZIG, LUDWIG, hotel exec.; b. Vienna, Austria, May 31, 1920; s. Joseph and Rose (Huber) H.; B.S., Lausanne, Switzerland, 1938; m. Rosina A. Lubrano, Dec. 8, 1961; 1 dau., Anna Maria. Asst. front office mgr. Grosvenor Hotel, London, Eng., 1938; kitchen apprentice Hotel Intourist, Moscow, Russia, 1939; asst. mgr. Talati House Hotel, Tientsin, China, 1939-41, Imperial Hotel, Tientsin, China, 1941-42; mgr. Hotel de Wagon Lits de Pekin, Peking, 1942-43; regional mgr. Hong Kong, Shanghai Hotels Corp., 1943-45; mgr. Royal Dutch Airlines Hotels, Singapore, Crown Colony, Jakarta, Indonesia, 1945-51; dir. Thai Tourist Govt. Project, Erawan Hotel, Bangkok, Thailand, 1951-53; cons. Oberoi Hotels, India, Great Eastern Hotel, Calcutta, Metropole Hotel, Karachi, 1953-55, Zamora Properties, Inc., Bay View Hotel, Grand Hotel, Philippines, 1955-58; adminstrv. asst. to the pres. Jack Tar Hotels, Galveston, Tex., 1958-62; adminstrv. asst. Drake Hotels, Chgo., 1962-63; v.p., gen. mgr. Sheraton-Tampa Motor Hotel, Tampa, Fla., 1963—; vice chmn., chmn. ITT Sheraton Inns Nat. Council, 1969-71. Mem. adv. bd. Hillsborough Jr. Coll., 1972; mem. St. Joseph Hosp. Devel. Council, 1972; active Boys Clubs Am. Mem. adv. bd. Salvation Army; bd. dirs. Nat. Safety Council. Recipient Mgmt. of Year award Sheraton Hotel, 1968, 69, 72. Mem. Am., Fla. (dir. 1963-71) hotel and motel assns., Sales and Marketing Execs., Fla. Com. 100, Fla. Restaurant Assn. (mem. bd. 1964—). Merchants Assn. Greater Tampa (dir. 1964—), Tampa Hotel and Motor Motels (pres. 1966-73), Greater Tampa C. of C. (bd. govs. 1964-73). Mason (Shriner), Rotarian. Club: Palma Ceia Golf and Country, Tower (Tampa, Fla.); Executive (Chgo.); Krewe of Venus. Office: 515 E Cass St Tampa FL 33602

HAVEE, JUSTIN PAUL, airline co. ofcl.; b. Stamford, Conn., Aug. 19, 1915; s. Edward and Kathryn C. (Nollett) H.; B.B.A. cum laude, U. Ill., 1938; M.B.A., U. Miami, 1970. Technician, So. Bell. Tel. & Tel., Miami, Fla., 1936-38; engr. Western Electric Co., Miami, 1939-42; engr. Pan Am. World Airways, Inc., Miami, 1946-48, purchasing agt., 1942-46, 48-73, material mgr., 1973—. Chmn. United Fund, Miami. Mem. Assn. Am. Museums, Am. Assn. State and Local History, Fla. Anthrop. Soc., Fla. Hist. Soc., Hist. Assn. So. Fla. (exec. sec. 1942-66), Everglades Natural History Assn., Air Force Assn., Purchasing Mgmt. Assn. Fla., Nat. Assn. Purchasing Mgmt. (profl. ednl. standards certification), Greater Miami C. of C., Opera Guild of Miami. Elk. Clubs: Wings, Management, Aviation Executives (Miami). Home: 8112 SW 73d Av Miami FL 33143 Office: Pan Am Bldg Miami FL 33159

HAVIRD, CYRIL OLIVER, govt. ofcl.; b. Newberry, S.C., Nov. 27, 1923; s. Henry David and Georgia Fant (Hair) H.; student Newberry Coll., 1941-42; B.A., U. S.C., 1949, M. Ed., 1950; m. Frances Ann Dent, Mar. 21, 1951; children—David Clyde, Suzanne, Cyril Oliver. Athletic dir. Springs Mills, Lancaster, S.C., 1949-53; tchr., coach North (S.C.) High Sch., 1953-55, Eau Claire High Sch., Columbia, S.C., 1955-63; prin. Wright Jr. High Sch., 1963-65; supt. schs. Richland Sch. Dist. 2, 1965-71; exec. dir. Richland County Housing Authority, 1972—. Served with AUS, 1943-46. Mem. Nat., S.C., Richland County edn. assns., Am. Assn. Sch. Adminstrs., S.C. Assn. Sch. Supts. (dir. 1970-72; exec. com. 1959-60), Greater Columbia C. of C., Am. Legion (comdr. Eau Claire 1959-60). Lion (pres. 1965). Club: Rockbridge (Columbia). Home: 4740 Arcadia Rd Columbia SC 29206 Office: PO Box J 1973 Columbia SC 29201

HAWES, FOREMAN MCCONNELL, ret. jr. coll. pres.; b. Richmond County, Ga., Sept. 18, 1899; s. John Baptist and Daisy Lane (McCord) H.; A.B., Mercer U., 1922; M.S., Emory U., 1929; postgrad. U. Wis., Columbia; m. Lilla Kennerly Mills May 29, 1936. Instr. Locust Grove Inst., 1923-28; instr. Emory U., 1928-29; instr. Ga. Inst. Tech., 1929-35; instr. Armstrong Jr. Coll., Savannah, Ga., from 1936, dean of students, 1941-42, pres. 1943-64. Fellow Ga. Acad. Sci.; mem. Sigma Alpha Epsilon, Alpha Chi Sigma. Rotarian. Club: Oglethorpe (Savannah). Home: 1134 E 49th St Savannah GA 31404

HAWES, LILLA KENNERLY MILLS (MRS. FOREMAN MCCONNELL HAWES), librarian, hist. soc. exec.; b. Camden, S.C., Feb. 1, 1908; d. Laurens Tenney and Margaret (Johnstone) Mills; A.B., Agnes Scott Coll., 1928; B.S. in L.S., George Peabody Coll. for Tchrs., 1939; certificate preservation and adminstrn. archives Am. U., 1948; m. Foreman McConnell Hawes, May 29, 1936. Sec. chemistry dept. Ga. Inst. Tech., 1930-36; gen. asst. Savannah (Ga.) Pub. Library, 1937-40, reference asst., 1941-43, br. librarian, 1943-48; dir. Ga. Hist. Soc., Savannah, 1948—. Sec. Savannah-Chatham County Historic Site and Monument Commn., 1955-66. Bd. dirs. Youth Mus. Savannah, Inc., 1954-66, rec. sec., 1954-56, corr. sec., 1962-64; bd. dirs. Historic Savannah Found., Inc., 1955-62. Recipient award of merit Lachlan McIntosh chpt. D.A.R., 1956; award of merit Historic Savannah Found., 1966. Mem. Ga., Southeastern library assns., Soc. Am. Archivists, Am. Assn. for State and Local History, So. Hist. Assn., Ga. Hist. Soc., Savannah Hist. Research Assn. (pres. 1946-48), Am. Assn. U. Women (sec. Ga. chpt. 1943-45), Telfair Acad. Arts and Scis., League Women Voters, Nat. Soc. Colonial Dames Am. in State Ga., Victorian Soc. Savannah, Pi Gamma Mu, Delta Kappa Gamma. Presbyn. Editor: Collections of the Georgia Historical Society, Vols. X-XIV, 1952-64; Lachlan McIntosh Papers in the U. Ga. Libraries, 1968. Home: 1134 E 49th St Savannah GA 31404 Office: 501 Whitaker St Savannah GA 31401

HAWES, PEYTON SAMUEL, JR., state ofcl.; b. Elberton, Ga., June 27, 1937; s. Peyton Samuel and Virginia (Smith) H; B.A., U. N.C., 1960; LL.B., U. Va., 1963; m. Mary Gregory, June 10, 1961; children—David Cooper, Gregory Battle, Elizabeth Claiborne, Peyton Samuel III (dec.). Admitted to Ga. bar, 1964; asst. atty. gen. Dept. Law, Atlanta, 1964-66; atty. Jones, Bird & Howell, Atlanta, 1966-71, Cofer, Beauchamp & Hawes, 1971—; mem. Ga. Ho. of Reps., 1969—. Mem. Ga. Gov.'s Commn. Higher Edn. Financial Assistance; mem. Blue Ribbon Minimum Found. Program Edn. Mem. reorgn. com. Ga. Democratic party, 1969; mem. exec. com. Dem. Com. Ga., 1970—. Bd. dirs. Ga. Mental Health Assn. Mem., Am., Ga., Atlanta bar assns., Nat. Soc. State Legislators (dir. 1972—), Lawyers Club of Atlanta, Sigma Alpha Epsilon, Phi Alpha Delta. Episcopalian. Home: 80 Broad St NW Atlanta GA 30303

HAWK, JOHN CHRISMAN, JR., surgeon; b. Glade Spring, Va., May 21, 1918; s. John Chrisman and Jean (Buchanan) H.; student St. Johns U., Shanghai, China, 1934-35; B.A., B.S., Emory and Henry Coll., 1938; M.D., U. Va., 1942; m. Nancy Shepard Dinwiddie, June 17, 1941; children—Margaret J., John Chrisman III, Nancy (Mrs. Lee McGlothlin), Anna Pennington, Elizabeth G., William B., Lucy D., James A. Intern Strong Meml. Hosp., Rochester, N.Y., 1942-43; resident surgery U. Va., Charlottesville, 1947-49, 50-51, fellow pathology, 1946-47; dir. Cancer Clinic, asso. prof. surgery Med. Coll. S.C., Charleston, 1951-66; asso. clin. prof. surgery Med. U. S.C., Charleston, 1966—; practice medicine specializing in surgery, Charleston, 1966—; pres. Charleston Surg. Assos., 1970—; mem. staff Roper Hosp., St. Francis Xavier Hosp., Med. U. Hosp., Charleston County Hosp., Baker Meml. Hosp., all Charleston. Mem. Sch. Bd. Dist. 20 Charleston, 1956-65. Served with AUS, 1943-46; CBI. Bd. dirs. Jr. Achievement Charleston, 1971—. Diplomate Am. Bd. Surgery. Damon Runyan fellow, Meml. Hosp. for Cancer and Allied Diseases, N.Y.C., 1949-50. Mem. Am. Cancer Soc. (pres., 1971-72, nat. del., 1973—), Charleston County Med. Soc. (pres. S.C. div. 1964-66), S.C. Med. Assn. (v.p. 1966-67), A.M.A. (del. 1971—), Congress County Med. Socs. (dir. 1965), James Ewing Soc., Southeastern Surg. Congress, A.C.S., Soc. Head and Neck Surgeons, Am. Radium Soc., So. Med. Assn. Presbyn. (elder). Home: 1 Meeting St Charleston SC 29401 Office: 30 Bee St Charleston SC 29403

HAWK, LAWRENCE SHERMAN, civil engr.; b. Akron, N.Y., Mar. 14, 1930; s. Richard Frank and Irene Langhorn (Bishop) H.; B.S., U. Tenn., 1960; m. Francis Helen McFall, Dec. 19, 1953; children—Nancy, Debra, David. Supt. constrn. C.F.W. Constrn. Co., Fayetteville, Tenn., 1954-60; project engr. Union Carbide Nuclear Corp., Oak Ridge, 1960—. Pres. Elementary P.T.A., 1962, High Sch. P.T.A., Karns, Tenn., 1969. Recipient Young Man of Yr. award Karns Community Club, 1971. Registered profl. engr., Tenn. Lion. Home: Route 17 Bluebell Lane Knoxville TN 37921 Office: PO Box Y (MS 248) Oak Ridge TN 37830

HAWK, ROBERT MARTIN, govt. ofcl.; b. Plainfield, N.J., July 11, 1938; s. Kenneth Martin and Marianne Virginia (Concilio) H.; B.A., Am. U., 1962; postgrad. Pace Coll., 1966-67; m. Verna Marie Carlson, July 25, 1964; 1 dau., Shirley Ann. Asso. editor Air Force Times, 1959-60; editorial asso. Traffic World Mag., Washington, 1960-63; pub. relations rep. Pa. R.R., N.Y.C., 1963-66; rail div. rep. Port of N.Y. Authority, N.Y.C., 1966-67; transp. com. exec., communications com. exec. U.S. C. of C., Washington, 1967-73; spl. asst. to asst. sec. transp. for policy, plans and internat. affairs Transp. Dept., Washington, 1973—. Bd. dirs. Greenbriar Civic Assn., Fairfax, Va., 1971-72. Served to 1st. lt. AUS, 1961. Mem. Pub. Relations Soc. Am. Club: Nat. Press. Home: 4213 Marble Lane Fairfax VA 22030 Office: 400 7th St SW Washington DC 20590

HAWKES, CLARENCE DOUGLAS, neurosurgeon; b. Providence, Dec. 31, 1913; s. Enos Raymond and Louella Grace (Mason) H.; A.B., Brown U., 1936; M.D., Johns Hopkins U., 1940; m. Jean Murray, June 2, 1941; children—Richard Russell, David Robert, Judith Ellen. Intern, then asst. resident Union Meml. Hosp., Balt., 1940-42; fellow neurol. surgery Lahey Clinic, Boston, 1942-44; co-founder, partner Neurosurg. Group, Memphis, 1946—; mem. staff Meth. Hosp., Memphis; cons. staffs VA Hosp., Bapt. Meml. Hosp., City Memphis Hosps. Mem. faculty U. Tenn. Med. Units, Memphis, 1946—, clin. prof. neurosurgery, 1970—; dir. neurosurg. tng. Meth. Hosp.-VA Hosp. Neurosurg. Tng. Program, 1965—. Bd. dirs., v.p. Chickasaw council Boy Scouts Am.; bd. dirs. Soc. Crippled Children and Adults, 1954-60, Project HOPE, 1964-73; trustee Memphis Blue Cross and Blue Shield, 1967. Served to lt. USNR, 1944-46. Decorated Bronze Star with combat V. Diplomate Am. Bd. Neurol. Surgery. Fellow A.C.S.; mem. Mid-South Med. Center Council (chmn. constitution and by laws, 1966-67), Memphis and Shelby County Med. Soc. (pres., 1970), Tenn. Med. Assn. (trustee 1963-66), Am. Assn. Neurol. Surgeons (trustee 1969-71), Neurosurgical Soc. Am. (pres. 1953-54), So. Electrocencephalograph Soc. (pres., 1957-58), Memphis Surg. Soc. (pres., 1961), A.M.A., So. Med. Assn., So. Neurosurg. Soc. (pres. 1959-60), InterUrban Neurosurg. Soc., Soc. Cons. Armed Forces U.S., Tenn. Neurosurg. Soc., Memphis Neurosurg. Soc., Phi Beta Kappa, Sigma Xi. Clubs: University, Chickasaw Country. Contbr. articles to profl. jours. Home: 527 E Parkway Memphis TN 38104 Office: 220 S Claybrook St Memphis TN 38104

HAWKES, TOWNSEND DEVONSHIRE, realtor; b. Boca Grande, Fla., June 1, 1911; s. John Denvonshire and Anna Catherine (Dempsey) H.; student Jacksonville Jr. Coll., 1940-42; m. Alice Virginia Abernethy, Jan. 7, 1944; children—John W., Frederic T., Helen V., Isis Diane (dec.), Thomas D., Richard M., Robert T., James P., Charles E. Founder, Townsend Hawkes Real Estate, Jacksonville, Fla., 1935-42, 46—. Pres. Townsend Hawkes Builders, Jacksonville Beach, 1952-72. Scoutmaster, Jacksonville N.E. council Boy Scouts Am., 1931-34; active USCG Aux. Served with USCGR, 1942-46; ETO, PTO. Mem. Jacksonville Beaches Bd. Realtors (pres. 1956-57, 71-72), Jacksonville Beaches Insurors Assn. (pres. 1969-70), Navy Res. Officers Assn. (v.p. 1961), Navy League, Nat. Inst. Real Estate Brokers, Nat. Inst. Farm and Land Brokers. Kiwanian, Moose. Clubs: Ponte Vedra (Ponte Vedra Beach, Fla.); Selva Marina Country (Atlantic Beach, Fla.). Home: 1771 Beach Av Atlantic Beach FL 32233 Office: 500 N 3d St Jacksonville Beach FL 32250

HAWKINS, DAVID HENRY, cattle co. exec.; b. Blanding, Utah, Apr. 26, 1921; s. Alma Henry and Cora (Bloomfield) H.; grad. high sch.; m. Vela Washburn, May 22, 1946; children—David J., John Wayne, Virginia, Kimball Don, Patricia, Kristine, Suzanne, Matthew Karl. Mgr. cattle operations Deseret Farms of Fla., Inc., Deer Park, Fla., 1954-65, dir. 1962—; v.p., gen. mgr. Ellsworth Land & Livestock Corp., DeSoto, Ga., 1965—. Mem. County Zoning and Planning Commn. Osceola County, Fla., 1963-65. Served with USMCR, 1940-46. Decorated Purple Heart medal; recipient Presdl. citation.

Mem. Brevard County (pres. 1960-61), Fla. Cattlemen's Assn. Mem. Ch. of Jesus Christ of Latter-day Saints. Home: 1429 Ken Garden Rd Albany GA 31707 Office: Land & Livestock Corp DeSoto GA 31743

HAWKINS, DAVID ROLLO, psychiatrist, educator; b. Springfield, Mass., Sept. 22, 1923; s. James Alexander and Janet (Rollo) H.; B.A., Amherst Coll., 1945; M.D., U. Rochester (N.Y.), 1946; m. Elizabeth G. Wilson, June 8, 1946; children—David Rollo, Robert Wilson, John Bruce, William Alexander. Intern Strong Meml. Hosp., Rochester, 1946-48; Commonwealth Fund fellow in psychiatry and medicine U. Rochester, 1950-52; instr. psychiatry U. N.C. Sch. Medicine, 1952-53, asst. prof., 1953-57, asso. prof. psychiatry, 1957-62, prof., 1962-67, dir. curriculum rev. and revision, 1965-67; prof., chmn. dept. psychiatry U. Va. Sch. Medicine, 1967—, asso. dean, 1969-70; psychiatrist-in-chief U. Va. Hosp., 1967—; asso. attending physician N.C. Meml. Hosp., Chapel Hill, 1952-62, attending physician, 1962-67; cons. Watts Hosp., Durham, 1952-67, VA Hosp., Fayetteville, N.C., 1956-67, Eastern State Hosp., Williamsburg, Va., 1971—; spl. research fellow Inst. Psychiatry, U. London, 1963-64; cons. VA Hosp., Salem, Va., 1969—, mem. deans com., 1971—. Mem. small grants com. Nat. Inst. Mental Health, 1958-62; mem. nursing research study sect. NIH, 1965-67; mem. Gov.'s Commn. Mental, Indigent and Geriatric Patients, 1968-72; mem. research evaluation com. Va. Dept. Mental Hygiene and Hosps., 1971-73, chmn., 1972-73; mem. behavioral sci. test com. Nat. Bd. Med. Examiners, 1970-74. Served as capt. M.C., AUS, 1948-50. Fellow Am. Coll. Psychoanalysts (charter), Am. Psychiat. Assn., mem. Am. Psychosomatic Soc. (mem. council 1959), A.M.A., Group for Advancement Psychiatry (chmn. com. med. edn.), Royal Soc. Medicine (London), Assn. Am. Med. Colls., Am. Psychoanalytic Assn., Am. Coll. Psychiatrists, Am. Acad. Psychoanalysis, A.A.A.S., Group Analytic Soc. (London), So. Profs. Psychiatry, Washington Psychoanalytic Soc., Am. Assn. U. Profs., Soc. for Neurosci., Am. Assn. Chmn. Depts. Psychiatry (sec.-treas. 1971—), Assn. Psychophysiol. Study Sleep, Phi Beta Kappa, Alpha Omega Alpha. Review editor: Psychosomatic Medicine, 1958-70, asso. editor, 1970—. Office: U Va Sch Medicine Dept Psychiatry Charlottesville VA 22901

HAWKINS, ELINOR DIXON (MRS. CARROLL WOODARD HAWKINS), librarian; b. Masontown, W.Va., Sept. 25, 1927; d. Thomas Fitchie and Susan (Reed) Dixon; A.B., Fairmont State Coll., 1949; B.S. in L.S., U. N.C., 1950; m. Carroll Woodard Hawkins, June 24, 1951; 1 son, John Carroll. Children's librarian Enoch Pratt Free Library, Balt., 1950-51; head circulation dept. Greensboro (N.C.) Pub. Library, 1951-56; librarian Craven-Pamlico Library Service, New Bern, N.C., 1958-62; dir. Craven-Pamlico-Carteret Regional Library, 1962—; storyteller children's TV program Tele-Story Time, 1952-58, 63—. Mem. New Bern-Craven County Bicentennial Commn., 1973—. Mem. N.C. Assn. Retarded Children, N.C. Library Assn. Baptist. Club: Pilot (pres. 1957-58, v.p. 1962-63). Home: PO Box 57 Cove City NC 28523 Office: 400 Johnson St New Bern NC 28560

HAWKINS, ELMER JOHN, physician; b. Jayton, Tex., July 8, 1922; s. Elmer and Arlis (Cunningham) H.; B.S., McMurry Coll., 1942; M.D., Baylor U., 1945; m. Gabie Smallwood, June 19, 1943; children—Lou Ann (Mrs. C. Richard Bullock), James Earl, Sharon Kay, Jonathan Lewis. Intern, Meth. Hosp., Madison, Wis., 1945-46. practice gen. medicine, Roby, Tex., 1948-49, Hamlin (Tex.) Hosp. & Clinic, 1949-72, Stamford (Tex.) Clinic, 1972—; mem. staffs West Tex. Hosp., Hendricks Hosp., Abilene, Tex., Stamford Meml. Hosp. Served to capt. AUS, 1946-48. Mem. Am., Tex. med. assns., Taylor-Jones County Med. Soc. Methodist. Club: Petroleum (Abilene). Home: PO Box 23 Stamford TX 79553 Office: Stamford Clinic Stamford TX 79553

HAWKINS, FRANK, mech. engr.; b. Mountain View, Okla., Aug. 24, 1916; s. Berton Frank and Dycie (Imhoff) H.; B.S., U. Okla., 1940; m. Elizabeth Snoddy, Dec. 26, 1941; children—Frank Robert, Mary Dale (Mrs. John Reginald Cook), William Thomas, Donald Haisten. With Phillips Petroleum Co., Houston, 1945-71, mech. and maintenance supt., 1945-63, asst. plant mgr., 1963-64, plant supt., 1964-71; owner Hawkins Engring., Inc., Houston, 1971—. Del., Tex. Democratic Conv., 1961, 62. Bd. dirs. Water Dist. Tex. Served from 2d lt. to lt. col. Ordnance Dept., AUS, 1940-45. Registered profl. engr., Okla., Tex. Mem. Nat. Soc. Profl. Engrs., Am. Soc. M.E. (past chmn. Panhandle sect.). Methodist. Mason (Shriner). Club: 40-Plus (founder) (Houston). Patentee in field. Home and office: 2711 Briarhurst 20 Houston TX 77027

HAWKINS, HAROLD LESLIE, educator; b. Armada, Mich., July 28, 1921; s. Clifford Loren and Grace (Cudworth) H.; B.S., Mich. State Normal Coll., 1951; M.A., U. Mich., 1953; certificate advanced study Harvard, 1957, Ed.D., 1958; m. Barbara Joan Benner, June 2, 1951; children—Kathryn Ann, David Leslie. Supt. schs. Kimball Unit, Port Huron, Mich., and Jefferson Sch., Mt. Clemens, Mich., 1948-56, Marine City, East China Twp. Sch. Dist., Mich., 1957-62, 16th Air Force Dept. Def., Spain, 1962-64, Olean, N.Y., 1964-67; profl. endl. adminstrn., head dept. Tex. A. & M. U., College Station, 1967—. Mem. joint com. Region IV Edn. Service Center, Huntsville, Tex., 1970-73. Mem. adv. bd. The School Law Newsletter, 1971-73. Mem. Tex. Assn. Secondary Sch. Prins. (university liaison com. 1970-73), Assn. Sch. Bus. Assn. U.S. and Can. (univ. contacts research com. 1971—), Nat. Assn. Secondary Sch. Prins. (nat. adv. bd. 1971-73). Author: Texas School Law and Board Authority, 1970; Appraisal Guide for School Facilities, 1973. Home: 3406 Spring Lane Bryan TX 77801 Office: Tex A & M U College Station TX 77840

HAWKINS, LAMAR TRAVIS, constrn. co. exec.; b. Oneonta, Ala., Oct. 16, 1938; s. Claude Travis and Audrey Louise (Harp) H.; B.S. in Civil Engring., Auburn U., 1963; m. Margie Elaine Thomason, Sept. 3, 1960; children—Pam, Patti, Steve. Project engr. bridge constrn. Blount County Engring. Dept., 1956-59, project engr., 1961-62; project engr. W.S. Fowler Constrn. Co., Oneonta, Ala., 1963-66; gen. supt. Pawnee Constrn. Co., Birmingham, Ala., 1966-69, v.p., 1969-72, pres., 1972—. Mem. Am. Soc. C.E. Baptist. Lion. Home: 1101 Edwards Lake Rd Birmingham AL 35215 Office: PO Box 6257 Birmingham AL 35217

HAWKINS, REGINALD ARMISTICE, dentist, clergyman; b. Beaufort, N.C., Nov. 11, 1923; s. Charles C. and Lorena (Smith) H.; B.S., Johnson C. Smith U., 1948, B.D., 1956, LL.D., 1962; D.D.S., Howard U., 1948; m. Catherine Elizabeth Richardson, Sept. 8, 1945; children—Pauletta, Reginald Armistice, Wayne, Lorena. Practice dentistry, Charlotte, N.C., 1948—; ordained to ministry Presbyn. Ch., 1956; pastor, evangelist social edn. and action. Chmn., Southeastern Regional Investment Corp., Parker Heights Ltd., Charlotte; vice chmn. Eastern N.C. Devel. Corp., 1967—. Civil rights leader, 1948—. Mem. Black Econ. Devel. Council, Small Bus. Adminstrn., 1968. Candidate for gov. N.C., 1968, 72; del. Democratic Nat. Conv., 1968; precinct chmn. N.C. Dem. Com., 1954-65; mem. Dem. Nat. Speakers Bur., 1960-64. Trustee N.C. Central U., Durham, 1961-66; mem. N.C. Good Neighbor Council, 1963-65. Served to 1st lt. Dental Corps, AUS, 1951-53. Recipient Distinguished Service award Alpha Kappa Alpha, 1969. Fellow Royal Soc. Health; mem. Am., N.C. dental assns., Old North State (citation of merit 1968), Nat. dental socs., Acad. Gen. Dentistry, Internat. Platform Assn., N.A.A.C.P., Beta Kappa Chi, Kappa Alpha Psi. Home: 1703 Madison Av Charlotte NC 28208 Office: 1218 Beatties Ford Rd Charlotte NC 28208

HAWKINS, RICHARD CLIFTON, C. of C. exec.; b. Sycamore, O., Feb. 15, 1915; s. Howard C. and Prudence (Meck) H.; D.D., Eastern Pilgrim Coll., 1958 ; m. Helen Louise Pinner, Feb. 12, 1939; children—Richard J., Judith Ann. Pastor Pilgrim Holiness Ch., Newberry, Mich., 1939-41, Pontiac, Mich., 1941-46, youth dir. Mich. dist., 1943-46, supt., 1946-54, sec. ch. extension, 1954-66; chmn. bd. Owosso Coll., 1948-54, 1960-66; chmn. Ch. Extension Loan Fund Dirs., 1954-66; chmn. Pilgrim Manor Nursing Home Dirs., 1963-66; sec.-treas. Mid-Am. Enterprises, Inc.; former Miss. rep. U.S. C. of C., dist. mgr. Louisville Dist., 1971—. Mem. Nat. Assn. Evangelicals, Nat. Holiness Assn. Club: Lantern. Address: 8902 Shelbyville Rd Louisville KY 40222

HAWKINS, ROBERT KENNETH, elec. engr.; b. Sulpher Springs, Tex., July 10, 1920; s. Willie H. and Texie (Brown) H.; B.S. in Math and Physics, Centenary Coll., 1951; m. Elizabeth Williams, Apr. 1, 1945; children—Robert Kenneth, Richard Randall, Cindy. Transmission, distbn. engr. Southwestern Electric Power Co., Shreveport, La., 1947-60, substa., engr., 1960-67; prin., owner Hengy & Hawkins, Shreveport, 1967-69; pres. Robert K. Hawkins cons. engr., Inc., Shreveport, 1969—. Served with USN, 1938-45. Registered profl. engr., La. Mem. Am. Soc. Mil. Engrs. (pres. 1967—), I.E.E.E. (pres. 1948-49), Cons. Engrs. Council (pres. 1970—), Cons. Engrs. Council La. (state dir. 1970-73), Nat. Soc. Profl. Engrs. (sr.), Am. Soc. Mil. Engrs., Am. Soc. Heating, Refrigeration and Air Conditioning Engrs. (sr.), Illuminating Engrs. Soc. (pres. 1957-58). Kiwanian (Lt. gov. 1958-59), Elk. Club: Riverside Swim. Home: 6142 Verona Lane Shreveport LA 71105 Office: 3346 Youree Dr Shreveport LA 71105

HAWKINS, WARREN GAMALIEL, judge; b. Collinsville, Ala., Jan. 23, 1920; s. John Preston and Ida (Sanders) H.; A.B., U. Ala., 1943, LL.B., 1948; m. Valoria Opaleen Sexton, Mar. 22, 1943; children—Judith (Mrs. Thomas Richard Tumlin), John R., Cynthia. Admitted to Ala. bar, 1948; practiced in Ft. Payne, Ala., 1948-54; mem. Ala. Ho. of Reps., 1950-54; county judge DeKalb County (Ala.), 1954-71; circuit judge, Ft. Payne, 1971—. Served with AUS, 1943-46, 50-51. Mem. V.F.W., Am. Legion. Rotarian. Home: 411 3d St NW Fort Payne AL 35967 Office: Courthouse Fort Payne AL 35967

HAWKINS, WILLIAM BLEDSOE, JR., lawyer, state legislator; b. Lynchburg, Va., Aug. 27, 1911; s. William Bledsoe and Nellie W. (Rangeley) H.; A.B., Davidson Coll., 1932; LL.B., U. S.C., 1936; m. Sari N. Hestle, Dec. 1, 1945; children—Diana, William, Melissa. Admitted to S.C. bar, 1935; partner firm Hawkins & Bethea, 1935-41, 46-57, Hawkins & McInnis, Dillon, S.C., 1969—; pvt. practice 1957-69; mem. S.C. Ho. of Reps., 1967—. Dir., 1st Citizens Bank & Trust Co. Mem. adv. bd. St. Eugene Hosp.; mem. area council Boy Scouts Am. Mem. Dillon County Devel. Bd., 1965-66; chmn. Dillon County Democratic Com., 1948-54, S.C. Dem. Exec. Com., 1954—; del. state conv., 1950, 52, 54, 56, 58; fed. election commr., 1938—. Trustee Dunbar Meml. Library, U. S.C. Served as 2d lt. to lt. col., USAAF, 1941-46. Mem. Am., S.C. bar assns., Dillon County Hist. Soc., Dillon County C. of C. (dir. 1963—), Am. Legion, Res. Officers Assn. (pres. 1948-49), Fish and Game Assn. (pres. 1948), Phi Delta Phi, Phi Delta Theta. Presbyn. (chmn. deacons, trustee, elder). Mason. Clubs: Dillon County Country (pres. 1967), Rotary (pres.), Lions pres. 1937-39), Modern Woodmen (comdr. 1938-39). Home: 310 Johnson Dr Dillon SC 29536 Office: 302 W Harrison St Dillon SC 29536

HAWKS, BYRON LOVEJOY, physician; b. N.Y.C., Nov. 23, 1909; s. Everett Merle and Maria (Granger) H.; B.S., Duke, 1935; M.D., N.Y. U., 1939; m. Nan Crawford Hawks, June 21, 1941; children—Everett M., Thomas Reid, Flora F. Intern Bklyn. Hosp., 1939-41; resident obstetrics and gynecology Woman's Hosp., N.Y.C., 1941-42; asso. prof. obstetrics and gynecology U. Ark. Sch. Medicine, Little Rock, 1962-70, prof., 1970—; dir. Ark. Maternity Infant Care Project, 1965—. Served to capt. USN. Diplomate Am. Bd. Obstetrics and Gynecology. Fellow Am. Coll. Obstetrics and Gynecology; mem. A.M.A. Contbr. articles to profl. jours. Home: 105 N Plaza Dr Little Rock AR 72205 Office: U Ark Med Center Little Rock AR 72201

HAWKS, DANIEL MCCRACKEN, curator; b. Petersburg, Va., Oct. 2, 1939; s. Ernest Beckwith and Edna Earle (McCracken) H.; B.A., Hampden-Sydney (Va.) Coll., 1961; m. Nanetta Frances Tyler, June 24, 1967. Staff reporter, sports editor Farmville (Va.) Herald, 1963-65; dir. news bur., editor Alumni mag. Hampden-Sydney Coll., 1965-67; asst. to pres. Stonewall Jackson Meml. Inc., Charlottesville, Va., 1967-69; curator Jamestown Found., Williamsburg, Va., 1969—. Bd. dirs. Southside Community Theatre, 1967-69, mem. founding com.; 1967, sec. 1967. Mem. Nat. Trust Historic Preservation, Am. Assn. Museums, Assn. for the Preservation of Va. Antiquities, Va. Archeol. Soc., Va. Mus. Fine Arts, Williamsburg-James City County C. of C. (dir. 1969-72, dir. 1974—), Theta Chi, Sigma Upsilon, Pi Delta Epsilon. Episcopalian. Home: 123 Stanley Dr Williamsburg VA 23185 Office: Drawer JF Williamsburg VA 23185

HAWTHORNE, JOHN DAVID, retail hardware mcht.; b. Abingdon, Va., Apr. 30, 1923; s. Arthur Hopkins and Beulah (Crenshaw) H.; student King Coll., 1940-42, Wittenberg Coll., 1943, U. Richmond, 1946-47; m. Dorothy Jane Montgomery, May 28, 1955; children—David Malcom, Mary Elizabeth, Nancy. With George E. Failing Supply Co., 1947-49; partner Mut. Warehouse Inc., Enid, Okla., 1950-57, owner, 1957-58; partner Walker Truck Lines, Enid, 1955-57, owner, 1957-60; with Montgomery Oil Co., Enid, 1959-63; owner Rude & Co. Hardware, Enid, 1963—. Mem. Met. Area Planning Commn., Enid, 1963-67; Enid rep. Okla. Soc. Crippled Children, 1954—. Served to 1st lt. USAAF, 1943-45. Decorated Air medal with five oak leaf clusters. Mem. Okla. Assn. Realtors, Nat. Assn. Real Estate Bds., Enid Bd. Realtors, Air Force Assn., Kappa Sigma. Presbyn. (elder 1966-69). Rotarian (sec.-treas. 1964-69). Home: 425 N Oakwood Rd Enid OK 73701

HAWVER, CARL FULLERTON, financial assn. exec.; b. Fredericksburg, O., Apr. 29, 1914; s. Harley H. and Carrie (Fullerton) H.; student Adrian Coll., 1930-33; B.S., Bowling Green State U., 1937, M.A., 1939; postgrad. Fresno State Coll., 1948-49; Ph.D., Am. U., 1963; m. Frances Jewell Renick, Apr. 15, 1935; children—Karl Derek, Dennis Arthur, Karen Joyce. Tchr. Lake Twp. High Sch., Walbridge, O., 1937-41, Napoleon (O.) High Sch., 1941-43, 46-48, Fresno (Cal.) High Sch., 1948-50; adminstrv. asst. to mem. U.S. Ho. of Reps., 1950-54, Nat. Republican Congl. Com., 1954-56; aide to U.S. sec. agr., Washington, 1956-57; dir. ednl. relations Nat. Consumer Finance Assn., Washington, 1957-61, exec. v.p., chief exec. officer, 1961—. Dir. Washington U.S.O., 1965—, Nat. U.S.O., 1968—; chmn. bd. govs. Marquette U. Consumer Credit Insts., 1962-64; chmn. exec. com. Nat. Consumer Credit Conf., 1962-65; founder, dir. Nat. Found. for Econ. Edn. for Clergy, 1958-64, 67—, chmn. bd., 1971—; mem. Nat. Council Trends and Perspective, 1966-69, Nat. Council on Consumer Issues, 1967—. Served with USNR, 1943-46. Mem. Pub. Relations Soc. Am. (pres. Washington chpt. 1967, mem. nat. assembly 1967-70, nat. dir. 1970—, nat. chmn. 1973-74), Am. Soc. Assn. Execs. (Washington pres. 1967-68, nat. dir. 1968-71, Key Man award 1968), U.S. C. of C. (nat. chmn. assn. sect. 1969-73), Nat. Council Family Relations, Bur. Rehab., Sigma Alpha Epsilon, Republican. Presbyn. (elder). Club: Cosmos. Author: The Congressman's Conception of His Role, 1963; (with James A. Peterson and Roy A. Burkhart) Money and Your Marriage, 1963. Contbr. articles to profl. jours. Home: 8100 Kerry Lane Chevy Chase MD 20015 Office: 1000 16th St NW Washington DC 20036

HAWVER, WALTER WILLIAM, JR., television broadcasting exec.; b. Hudson, N.Y., Feb. 13, 1922; s. Walter William and Helen Bernadette (McAree) H.; student St. Michael's Coll., 1939-40, 40-41, A.B., 1948, M.A., 1950; student Syracuse U., 1944, Rensselaer Poly. Inst., 1945; m. Concetta Mary Grandinetti, Oct. 31, 1943; children—Marilyn (Mrs. Frank Conti), Margaret (Mrs. Peter Ferrara), Walter J., Philip, Anne Marie, Mary Michele. Reporter, sports editor Hudson Daily Star, 1941, 45-46; wire editor Burlington (Vt.) Daily News, Vt. Sunday News, 1946-49, city editor, 1949-51, mng. editor, 1951-52; radio-TV critic, columnist Albany (N.Y.) Knickerbocker News, 1952-63; city editor Albany Times-Union, 1963-65; mgr. news operations television sta. WIEN, Albany, 1965-70, television sta. KTRK, Houston, 1970—. Asso. trustee St. Michael's Coll. Served with USNR, 1942-45. Profl. Pub. Relations Council fellow, 1968. Mem. Tex. (v.p. 1971-72), N.Y. State (pres. 1970) associated press broadcasters, Sigma Delta Chi. K.C. Club: Net Set Racquet (Houston). Home: 14215 Chadbourne St Houston TX 77024 Office: PO Box 13 Houston TX 77001

HAY, RICHARD CARMAN, physician; b. Queens, L.I., N.Y., June 9, 1921; s. Richard Carman and Frances (Woodbury) H.; B.S., U. Vt., 1944, M.D., 1946; m. Martha Jean Fambrough, Mar. 2, 1957; children—Richard C., William W., Anne H., Sandra L., Bradford T., Holly K. Intern Bishop De Goesbriand Hosp., Burlington, Vt., 1946-47, resident, 1947-48; resident Hitchcock Hosp., Hanover, Vt., 1950-51; practice medicine specializing in anesthesiology, Houston, 1954—; mem. staff Meml. Bapt. Hosp.; asst. anesthesiologist Worcester (Mass.) Meml. Hosp., 1953-54; asst. prof. anesthesiology U. Tex. at Houston, 1954-61. Mem. Am., Tex. State socs. anesthesiology, Harris County Med. Soc. Home: 11514 Summerhill Houston TX 77024 Office: 1412 Meml Profl Bldg Houston TX 77001

HAYDEN, JULIUS JOHN, JR., coll. pres.; b. Pass Christian, Miss., May 19, 1920; s. Julius John and Forrest (Spring) H.; A.A., Perkinston Jr. Coll., 1940; B.S., Miss. State U., 1949, M.S., 1950; Ed.D., U. So. Miss., 1966; m. Lillian R. Aschbacher, Apr. 23, 1943; children—Julius John III, Glover Richard, Susie Stafford. Tchr., coach Lee Road Sch., St. Tammany Parish, La., 1949-50; instr. history Perkinston (Miss.) Jr. Coll., 1950-52, dean, 1952-53, pres., 1953-62; pres. Miss. Gulf Coast Jr. Coll., Perkinston, 1962—. Mem. projects com. Mississippians for Ednl. TV, 1972—, sec.-treas., 1973—; mem. Miss. Jr. Coll. Commn., 1971—; cons. edn. legislation com. Miss. Econ. Council; mem. Com. for Nat. Library Week. Adv. bd. Pine Burr area council Boy Scouts Am. Served with USAF, 1940-41, USCGR, 1941-45. Mem. Am. Assn. Jr. Colls. (legislative com.), Nat. Jr. Coll. Adminstrs. Assn. (Miss. rep. com. on policies), So. Assn. Colls. and Schs. (trustee 1971—), Sons of Confederacy, Miss. Coast Power Boat Squadron, Phi Theta Kappa (dir. 1971—). Rotarian. Home: Perkinston MS 39573

HAYES, CHARLES PATTON, JR., physician; b. Schenectady, Apr. 25, 1934; s. Charles Patton and Susan Elizabeth (Hearn) H.; student Duke U., 1952-55; M.D., Duke U. Med. Sch., 1959; m. Jo Moore Smithwick, Apr. 4, 1959; children—Barrie Elizabeth, Charles Gregory. Intern, Duke U. Med. Center, Durham, N.C.; nephrology fellow, 1962-64, mem. faculty, 1964-69, asso., 1964-66, asst. prof., 1966-69; resident internal medicine U. Tex. Med. Br. at Galveston, 1960-62; pvt. practice medicine specializing in internal medicine and nephrology, Riverside Clinic, Jacksonville, Fla., 1969—; mem. staffs Riverside and Univ. hosps., Jacksonville; asso. clin. prof. U. Fla. Med. Sch., 1971—; cons. Kidney Disease Control Branch Pub. Health Service, 1965-68; chmn. Kidney Adv. Bd., Fla., 1971—; mem. Fla. Med. Found. Peer Review Com., 1971—; mem. med. adv. bd. Fla. Kidney Found. Diplomate Am. Bd. Internal Medicine. Fellow A.C.P., Am. Heart Assn.; mem. A.M.A., Am. Soc. Nephrology, Am. Soc. Artificial Internal Organs, Fla. Kidney Found., Nat. Kidney Found., S.E. Dialysis and Transplantation Assn. (council). Clubs: Timuguana Country, Ponte Vedra. Home: 4754 Long Bow St Jacksonville FL 32210 Office: 2005 Riverside Av Jacksonville FL 32204

HAYES, DEWEY N., lawyer; b. Douglas, Ga., July 27, 1923; s. John Cleve and Mary (Walsh) H.; student S. Ga. Coll., 1946; A.B., Mercer U., LL.B., 1949; m. Margaret Haley, June 16, 1951; children—Dewey N., Franklin D., Candace L. Admitted to Ga. bar, 1949, U.S. Supreme Ct. bar, 1966; pvt. practice law; dist. atty. Waycross Jud. Circuit, Douglas, 1957—. Mem. Gov.'s Crime Commn., 1973. Mem. Ga. Ho. of Reps., 1953-54. Served with AUS, 1942-46; ETO. Mem. Douglas (v.p., 1962-63), Ga. bar assns., Dist. Attys. Assn. Ga. (pres. 1972), V.F.W., Am. Legion, Delta Theta Phi, Kappa Sigma. Democrat. Methodist. Lion, Elk, Woodman of World. Club: Douglas Golf and Country. Author: You and the Law, 1970; Georgia Warrants, 1972. Home: N Chester St Douglas GA 31533 Office: 107 S Maidson St Douglas GA 31533

HAYES, DONALD MICHAEL, educator, physician; b. Kings Mountain, N.C., Nov. 6, 1928; s. Ferd Ralph and Alice Thacker (Osteen) H.; student Charlotte Coll., 1948; B.S., Wake Forest Coll., 1951; M.D., Bowman Gray Sch. Medicine, 1954; postgrad. U. N.C., 1963-64, U. Ill., 1969; m. Kathryn Barrier, Dec. 29, 1951; children—Michael Neil, Kevin Henry, Mark Patrick. Intern, Salt Lake County Gen. Hosp., 1954-55; USPHS fellow in psychiatry Louisville Gen. Hosp., 1955-56; resident medicine N.C. Bapt. Hosp., Winston-Salem, 1956-58, fellow in medicine, 1958-60, now mem. staff; practiced medicine, specializing in internal medicine and hematology, Winston-Salem, 1959—; mem. faculty, staff Bowman Gray Sch. Medicine, Wake Forest U., Winston Salem, 1956—, instr. medicine, 1959-61, asst. dean admissions, 1960-61, asst. prof. medicine, 1959-61, asso. prof., 1966—, asso. in preventive medicine, 1967-70, prof., chmn. dept. community medicine, 1970—; cons. hematology U.S. VA Hosp., Salisbury, N.C., 1962-73. Mem. Gov.'s Com. for Community Health Assistance, 1971-73; vice chmn. Piedmont Triad Regional Health Planning Council, 1973—. Bd. dirs. N.C. Found. Mental Health Research, Inc., United Cancer Council, Inc., 1968-70, Forsyth Health Planning Council; trustee, vice chmn. Forsyth Tech. Inst. Served with USMCR, 1946-48. Diplomate Am. Bd. Internal Medicine. Fellow A.C.P.; mem. Am. Soc. Hematology, Assn. Am. Med. Colls., Am. Coll. Preventive Medicine, Am. Fedn. Clin. Research, Am. Assn. Cancer Research, Am. Soc. Clin. Oncology, Am. Pub. Health Assn., N.Y. Acad. Sci., Sigma Xi, Phi Beta Kappa, Alpha Omega Alpha. Democrat. Methodist. Home: 2484 Woodberry Dr Winston-Salem NC 27106

HAYES, GEORGE ROY, JR., state ofcl.; b. Shreveport, La., July 5, 1920; s. George Roy and Florence Hazel (Row) H.; student U. Ill., 1938-39; B.S., La. Poly. Inst., 1942; M.S., U. Ark., 1951; m. Marie Lane St. John, July 10, 1943; children—Susan Leslie (Mrs. George Virgo). Commd. lt. (j.g.) USPHS, 1943, advanced through grades to capt., 1968; various assignment including State Pub. Health entomologist, Little Rock, 1947-54; tech. cons., asst. chief and chief state aids sect., Atlanta, 1951-59; project officer Aedes aegypti

Eradication Program, New Orleans, 1964-69; vector control cons., Atlanta, 1969-72; chief solid waste and vector control La. Div. Health, Maintenance and Ambulatory Patient Services, New Orleans, 1972—. Vis. lectr. Tulane U., 1964-69, La. State U., 1972—, Delgado Jr. Coll., 1973—. Mem. Entomol. Soc. Am., Am. Mosquito Control Assn., Nat. Vector Control Conf. (chmn. elect 1974-76), Lambda Chi Alpha. Home: 2411 Comet St New Orleans LA 70114 Office: PO Box 60630 New Orleans LA 70160

HAYES, ISABELLA MALLORY (MRS. WALTER HAROLD HAYES), civic worker; b. Kewanee, Ill., Mar. 27, 1908; d. George Adelbert and Ella Bowie (Swayze) Mallory; B.A., Knox Coll., 1930, B.L.S., U. Wis., 1931; postgrad. U. Md., 1953; m. Walter Harold Hayes, Nov. 9, 1935; 1 dau., Anne (Mrs. Henry George Michel). With Kewanee Pub. Library, 1926-30; head reference dept., pub. library, Roanoke, Va., 1931-43; instr., asst. reference librarian U. Md. Library, College Park, 1949-58, head Md. and rare book room, also in charge displays and pub. relations, 1958-69, editor Library News, 1952-69. Exec. dir. Nat. Library Week in Md., 1962; chmn. First Citizens Conf. on Libraries in Md., 1965. Mem. State Adv. Com. on Day Care to Md. Dept. Social Services, 1962-72; chmn. Health and Welfare Council Prince Georges County, 1965-68. Bd. dirs. Health and Welfare Council Nat. Capital Area, Washington, 1964-68, Md. Com. for Day Care of Children, Balt., 1964-69, Prince George's County Retarded Day Care Center, 1962-69. Recipient Community Service award Health and Welfare Council Nat. Capital Area, Washington, 1968. Mem. League Women Voters (county pres. 1957-58, mem. state bd. 1958-62), Am. Assn. U. Women (2d v.p. 1972-73), Mothers Club Kappa Alpha Theta, Alpha Delta Pi (patroness). Author: Ethics of Advertising: a Selected Bibliography, 1931; Financing Presidential Campaigns, A Selected Bibliography, 1953. Home: 70 Willow Dr St Augustine FL 32084

HAYES, JOHN EDWARD ROLLINS, textile co. exec.; b. Chick Springs, S.C., June 18, 1927; s. Clifford Barron and Dorothy (Lawson) H.; grad. Asheville Sch. Boys, 1954; B.S., U. Va., 1960; m. Mary Love Cates, May 12, 1962; children—John Edward Rollins II, Robert Cates, Clifford Barron, Mary Love Cates. Pres. Hayes Textiles, Inc., Spartanburg, S.C., 1959—. Served with USNR, 1954-55. Mem. Beta Theta Phi. Home: 1040 Woodburn Rd Spartanburg SC 29302 Office: 1078 Union Rd Spartanburg SC 29302

HAYES, KYLE, lawyer; b. Purlear, N.C., Oct. 4, 1905; s. Charles Clayton and Ida (Huffman) H.; LL.B., Wake Forest Coll., 1931; m. Margaret Smithey, Nov. 10, 1932. Admitted to N.C. bar, 1930; also U.S. Supreme Ct. bar; sr. mem. firm Hayes & Hayes, North Wilkesboro, 1935—. Owner retail furniture, hardware stores; pres. The Northwestern Finance Co., North Wilkesboro. Mem. bar candidate com. 23d Jud. Dist. N.C. Republican candidate for U.S. Ho. of Reps., 1936, for lt. gov. N.C., 1946, gov., 1956, U.S. Senate, 1960. Trustee Wilkes Community Coll., Wilkesboro; adv. bd. Gardner-Webb Coll., Boiling Springs, N.C. Served with USMCR, 1942-44. Mem. Am., N.C. (gov.) bar assns., Am. Judicature Soc., Jud. Conf. 4th Circuit, Am. Trial Lawyers Assn., Practising Law Inst., Def. Research Inst. Baptist (deacon). Mason (Shriner), Elk, Moose, Kiwanian, K.P. Club: Oakwoods Country (North Wilkesboro, N.C.). Home: 604 E Main St Wilkesboro NC 28697 Office: 309 9th St North Wilkesboro NC 28659

HAYES, ORRILL WILLIAM, personnel training co. exec.; b. N.Y.C., Mar. 31, 1918; s. Anthony V. and Bertha G. (Hayes) Seferovic; student, McIntosh Coll. Bus., 1937-39; m. Elizabeth Ann Goffinet, July 6, 1968; children—Christina L., Celeste L. Profl. baseball gen. mgr. Buffalo Internat. League, 1946-52; v.p. Am. Desk Mfg. Co., 1953-59, Continental Belton Mfg. Co., 1960-63; pres. Hayes Assos., Amarillo, Tex., 1959—. Lectr. Tex. State Police Acad., 1952-61, Braniff Internat. Airways Sch., 1957-61. Maj.-aide-de-camp Gov's. staff, N.H., 1940; mem. N.H. Ho. of Reps., 1940-41; Republican nominee for lt. gov. Tex., 1962, for U.S. Congress, 1964. Adv. council U. Plano, 1972—. Served to capt. USAAF, 1942-46. Recipient Profl. Baseball Exec. of Year award The Sporting News, 1951, Good Sportsmanship award U.S. Baseball Congress, 1938; decorated Sovereign Order Knight of Malta, Late King Peter II, 1967. Author: Your Memory, Speedway To Success, 1959. Home: 6108 Hanson Rd Amarillo TX 79106

HAYES, ROBERT DEMING, educator; b. Lexington, Ky., Mar. 11, 1925; s. Roy Bagley and Esther (Brigman) H.; B.S., U. Ky., 1948, M.S., 1950; M.S., Ga. Inst. Tech., 1957, Ph.D., 1964; m. Nancy Ellen Taylor, Aug. 30, 1947 (dec. Mar. 1972); children—William T., Katherine D., Carol E., Jennifer D. Grad. asst. U. Ky., 1947-50; field engr. Western Electric Co., Winston-Salem, N.C., 1950-54; asst. research engr. Ga. Inst. Tech., Atlanta, 1954-55, research engr., 1955-64, asso. head radar br., 1965-66, asst. prof. 1958-64, asso. prof. elec. engring., 1964-66, prof., 1968—; prin. engr. Radiation, Inc., Melbourne, Fla., 1966-68. Adj. prof. Fla. Inst. Tech., 1966-68; cons. engr., 1963—; cons. Lockheed Ga. Co., U.S. Army, Pure Food, Inc., Radiation, Inc. Mem. Cobb County Planning and Zoning Commn., 1964-66, chmn., 1969-73; mem. com. Boy Scouts Am., 1954-62. Served with USAAF, 1943-46. Mem. I.E.E.E. (v.p. 1960), Cobb County C. of C., Sigma Xi, Phi Kappa Tau, Sigma Pi Sigma, Eta Kappa Nu. Presbyn. Kiwanian. Clubs: Marietta Country, Indian Hills Country. Home: 605 Chestnut Hill Rd Marietta GA 30060 Office: Ga Inst Tech Atlanta GA 30332

HAYES, THOMAS JARRELL, JR., pipeline co. exec.; b. Whitehall, Tex., Sept. 28, 1939; s. Thomas Jarrell and Ruby Vida (Welch) H.; B.B.A., Tex. A. and I. U., 1962; m. Peggy Anne Carpenter, Mar. 14, 1959; children—Brian, Kelvin. Sales engring. coordinator Cameron Iron Works, Inc., Houston, 1962-67; v.p., gen. mgr. Anbeck Co., Houston, also v.p., officer Keltron Corp., 1967-71; v.p. Zapata Pipeline Tech., Inc., Houston, 1971—. Mem. Pipeliners Club. Home: 17007 Vintage Wood Lane Spring TX 77373 Office: 11500 Kilburn St Houston TX 77055

HAYET, LEONARD, elec. engr.; b. Passaic, N.J., June 10, 1932; s. Herman and Ray (Bernenbaum) H.; B.S. in E.E., Purdue U., 1953, M.S., 1954; m. Joan Braverman, Aug. 24, 1952; children—Mindy Alyce, Philip Mark. Project mgr. Gerson Electric Co., Chgo., 1958-61; project engr., Rader & Assos., Miami, 1961-63; elec. dept. head, mng. partner Smith, Korach, Hayet, Haynie Partnership, Miami, 1963—; pres., dir. Engrs. & Planners, Inc., New Investments, Inc., Miami; dir., sec. 7th St Bldg., Inc., Miami. Mem. Urban Renewal Planning Com., 1966-68; cons. Mt. Sinai Med. Center, Miami Beach, Fla., 1964—, Cedars Lebanon Health Care Center, Miami, 1964—. Bd. dirs. Papanicolaou Cancer Research Clinic. Served with USNR, 1955-58. Mem. Cons. Engrs. Council, Am. Arbitration Assn., I.E.E.E., Fla. Engring. Soc. Patentee in field. Home: 7175 SW 115th Terrace Miami FL 33156 Office: 721 NW 21st Ct Miami FL 33125

HAYMAN, LOUIS DEMARO, JR., physician; b. Weldon, N.C., Apr. 10, 1920; s. Louis DeMaro and Bess (Widenhouse) H.; B.S. in Medicine, U. N.C., 1942; M.D., C.M., McGill U., 1943; m. Carol Deane Bessent, Aug. 30, 1945; children—Richard Louis, Susan (Mrs. Mark Williams). Rotating intern Med. Coll. Va., Richmond, 1943-44, Firestone Rubber Plantation, Liberia, 1944-45; resident in medicine VA Hosp., Oteen, N.C., 1947-49, Swannanoa, N.C., 1949-51; practice medicine specializing in internal medicine, Florence, S.C., 1951-55, also subspecializing in cardiology, Jacksonville, N.C., 1955—; dir. coronary care unit Onslow Meml. Hosp., Jacksonville, 1965—. Served with M.C., AUS, 1945-47; ETO. Named Community Man of Year, Jacksonville Jr. C. of C., 1962. Diplomate Am. Bd. Internal Medicine. Fellow A.C.P., Am. Coll. Cardiology (asso.); Am. Soc. Internal Medicine, Am., So. Med. assns., N.J. State Med. Soc. Contbr. articles to med. jours. Home: 406 Carmen Av Jacksonville NC 28540 Office: Medical Plaza Western Blvd Jacksonville NC 28540

HAYNER, WILLIAM MONTAGUE, lawyer; b. Tyler, Tex., Nov. 7, 1938; s. John Montague and Elsie (Haddad) H.; B.B.A., N.Tex. State U., 1961; J.D., Baylor U., 1963; m. Linda Joy Wood, Apr. 3, 1964; children—William Montague, Joseph Scott. Admitted to Tex. bar, 1963; practiced in Waco, 1963-65, Dallas, 1965—; asso., McLaughlin, Clark, Fisher, Gorin, & McDonald, Waco, Tex., 1963-65; partner, Holley & Hayner, 1965-67, Holley, Flagg, Hayner & Miller, 1967-72, Flagg, Cooper, Hayner, Miller & Long, Dallas, 1973—; partner, L.H. & F. Real Estate Investments, 1968—. Mem. Am., Dallas bar assns., State Bar Tex., Tex. Trial Lawyers Assn., Richardson Jr. C. of C. (v.p. 1967-68). Clubs: Engineers, Cipango (both Dallas). Home: 4512 Rheims Pl Dallas TX 75205 Office: 2001 Bryan Tower Suite 2805 Dallas TX 75201

HAYNES, BOYD WITHERS, JR., surgeon; b. Brandenburg, Ky., July 5, 1917; s. Boyd Withers and Sallie Katherine (Allen) H.; A.B., U. Louisville, 1939, M.D., 1941; m. Peggy Jane Harrison, May 21, 1955. Intern, Med. Coll. Va., Richmond, 1941-42, research fellow surgery, 1944-45, asst. resident surgeon, 1946-48, resident surgeon, 1947-48, asso. in surgery, 1948-49, asst. prof., 1953-59, asso. prof., 1960-66, prof., 1966—, chmn. div. trauma surgery, 1972—, attending surgeon in charge burn service and gen. surgery service, 1954—; asso. in surgery Baylor U. Coll. Medicine, Houston, 1949-50, asst. prof., 1951-53; cons. gen. surgery McGuire VA Hosp., Richmond, Va., 1966—. Served as maj. M.C., AUS, 1953-55. Diplomate Am. Bd. Surgery. Fellow A.C.S. (Va. pres. 1969-70); mem. Am. Burn Assn. (pres. 1969-70), Soc. U. Surgeons, Med. Soc. Va., Am. Assn. Surgery of Trauma, Am., So. surg. assns., Richmond Acad. Medicine, Va. Surg. Soc. Asso. editor Yearbook Plastic and Reconstructive Surgery, 1970—. Home: 5105 Cary Street Rd Richmond VA 23226 Office: Box 816 MCV Sta Med Coll Va Richmond VA 23298

HAYNES, CALEB VANCE, educator; b. Spokane, Wash., Feb. 29, 1928; s. Caleb Vance and Margery Ann (McLeod) H.; Geol. Engr., Colo. Sch. Mines, 1956; Ph.D., U. Ariz., 1965; m. Elizabeth Hamilton, Jan. 11, 1954; 1 dau., Lisa Anne. Mining geology cons., Denver, 1956-60; sr. engr. Martin Co., Denver, 1960-62; geologist, Nev. State Mus., 1962-63; research asst. U. Ariz., 1963-64, asst. prof., 1965-68; asso. prof. geology So. Meth. U., Dallas, 1968-73, prof., 1973—. Served with USAF, 1950-54. Recipient grants NSF, 1964—, Nat. Geog. Soc., 1966-71. Fellow Geol. Soc. Am.; mem. Soc. Am. Archaeology, A.A.A.S., Sigma Xi. Home: 6477 Highgate Lane Dallas TX 75214

HAYNES, CHARLES GUTHRIE, govt. ofcl.; b. Kansas City, Mo., Feb. 24, 1920; s. Howard and Catherine (Guthrie) H.; B.C.S., Southeastern U., 1941, M.C.S., 1946; m. Jessie Irene Smith, Oct. 27, 1941; children—Judith W. Mary Catherine (Mrs. Albert M. Warfield), Margaret Ann (Mrs. Ronald Ryan), Charles Guthrie, Stephen Jay. Accountant, Spicer and Rees, C.P.A.'s, Washington, 1939-41; spl. agt. FBI, 1941-52, 53-55, 57; staff, later dir. surveys and investigations Appropriations com. U.S. Ho. of Reps., 1952-53, 55-57; dir. internal audit Dept. Health, Edn. and Welfare, 1957-60; dir. fgn. assistance investigations Dept. of State, 1960-61; dir. inspections NASA, Washington, 1961-69; dir. hdqrs. adminstrn. NASA, 1969-70; dep. auditor gen. AID, 1970-72; insp.-gen. Dept. Housing and Urban Devel., Washington, 1972—. Chmn. bd., pres. Guthrie Properties, Inc. C.P.A., D.C. Mem. Am. Inst. C.P.A.'s, Internat. Assn. Chiefs of Police, Assn. Fed. Investigators, Soc. Former Spl. Agts. FBI, Fed. Govt. Accountants Assn. Home: 10200 Brookmoor Dr Silver Spring MD 20901 Office: Dept Housing and Urban Development 7th and D Sts SW Washington DC 20410

HAYNES, CLIFFORD RUDOLPH, physician, surgeon; b. Trinidad, Tex., June 9, 1927; s. Lewis C. and Willie Mae (Stogner) H.; B.A., U. Tex., 1949, M.D., 1951. Intern, Hermann Hosp., Houston, 1951-52; pvt. practice, Malakoff, Tex., 1952—; staff Kilman Hosp., 1952-60; staff, owner, adminstr. Haynes Hosp., 1960—; staff Henderson County Meml. Hosp.; sch. and athletic physician Malakoff Ind. Sch. Dist. Mem.-at-large Circle Ten council Boy Scouts Am. Councilman, City of Malakoff, 1955-60, mayor pro-tem, 1957, 58, 59. Mem. chancellor's council U. Tex., 1966—. Served from pvt. to sgt., AUS, 1945-46. Mem. A.M.A., So. Tex., 11th Dist., Henderson County (pres. 1955) med. socs., Am., Tex. heart assns., Tex. Soc. Athletic Team Physicians, Ex-Students Assn. U. Tex. (life), Assn. Am. Physicians and Surgeons, Internat. Platform Assn., Phi Rho Sigma. Democrat. Baptist (deacon, trustee). Rotarian (pres. 1956-57, 58-59). Home: North Terry St Monticarlo Apts Malakoff TX 75148 Office: Haynes Hosp Malakoff TX 75148

HAYNES, DOUGLAS BRYANT, JR., physician; b. Finley, Tenn., Dec. 25, 1936; s. Douglas Bryant and Ethel LaVerne (McClain) H.; M.D., U. Tenn., 1961; m. Norma Alice Riggs, Dec. 23, 1960; children—Douglas Bryant III, Sean McClain, Elizabeth Gray, Leslie Allison. Intern, City Memphis Hosp., 1961-62; dir. Coahoma County Health Dept., 1962-66; resident internal medicine U. Tenn., City Memphis hosps., 1966-69; pvt. practice internal medicine, Clarksdale, Miss., 1969-70, Dyersburg, Tenn., 1970—; mem. staff Parkview Hosp., Dyersburg, sec., 1971, v.p., 1972, chief of staff, 1973. Bd. mem. Dyer County Cancer Soc., 1971-72; mem. Delta Council, 1962-66, Coahoma County Child Welfare Adv. Council, 1964-66, Coahoma County Antipoverty Commn., 1965-66. Mem. exec. com. Dyer County Republican party, 1970—. State bd. dirs. Miss. Assn. Mental Health, 1965-66; bd. dirs. Dyersburg Community Concerts Assn., 1970—, pres., 1972-73; bd. dirs. Dyer County Heart Assn., Dyer County Fair, Dyersburg Cares, Dyersburg Humanities Council. Served with USPHS, 1962-65. Named Outstanding Young Man Miss., Jr. C. of C., 1965; recipient Distinguished Service awards Clarksdale Civitans, Clarksdale Jr. C. of C., 1965. Mem. N.W. Tenn. Acad. Medicine, A.M.A., Tenn. Med. Assn., Dyer County C. of C. Mem. Ch. of Christ (trustee nat. jour. Mission). Club: Dyersburg Country. Home: 505 Sampson Av Dyersburg TN 38024 Office: 433 Parkview St Dyersburg TN 38024

HAYNES, DOUGLAS MARTIN, physician; b. N.Y.C., Jan. 25, 1922; s. Daniel Hagood and Courtenay (Collins) H.; student Allhallows Sch., Rousdon, Devon, Eng., 1935-38; B.A., B.S., So. Methodist U., 1943; M.D. Southwestern Med. Coll., 1946; m. Elizabeth Burwell Johnson, June 17, 1961; children—Douglas Marshall, Lewis Daniel. Intern in pathology Parkland Meml. Hosp., Dallas, 1946-47, resident obstetrics and gynecology, 1949-52; chief pathology 4th med. lab., Heidelberg, Germany, AUS, 1947-49; asst. prof. Southwestern Med. Sch., U. Tex., 1952-55; asso. prof. U. Louisville, 1955-57, prof., chmn. dept., 1957-69, interim dean Sch. Medicine, 1969-70, dean, 1970-72, prof., 1972—. Diplomate Am. Bd. Obstetrics and Gynecology (asso. examiner). Fellow A.C.S., Am. Assn. Obstetricians and Gynecologists; mem. A.M.A., So. Med. Assn., Central Assn. Obstetricians and Gynecologists, Am. Coll. Obstetricians and Gynecologists, Phi Beta Kappa, Alpha Omega Alpha, Phi Chi, Delta Chi. Democrat. Presbyn. Editor: Medical Complications During Pregnancy, 1969. Contbr. articles to profl. jours. Home: 5204 Tomahawk Rd Louisville KY 40207

HAYNES, GEORGE ALLEN, optometrist; b. Paragould, Ark., Apr. 18, 1941; s. Rufus D. and Walta Mildred (White) H.; B.S., Ark. State U., 1963; D.Optometry, So. Coll. Optometry, 1966; m. Caolyn Bratton, Aug. 18, 1963; 1 dau. Staci Leigh. Individual practice optometry, Paragould, 1966—. Dir. First Nat. Bank. Pres. Mentally Retarded Assn., Paragould, 1967—; mem. East Ark. Health Planning Com., Paragould, 1971—. Bd. dir. Parks and Recreation Commn., 1968—, County Welfare Bd., 1972-73, Community Meth. Hosp., 1969—. Mem. Ark. Optometric Assn. (v.p. 1972—), C. of C. (v.p. citizens adv. com. 1969-71, dir. 1967-70). Methodist (mem. ch. bd. 1971-74). Rotarian. Home: 2 Gwendine Dr Paragould AR 72450 Office: 219 W Main St Paragould AR 72450

HAYNES, GEORGE WILLIAM, judge; b. Pelahatchie, Miss., Feb. 19, 1917; s. Charles McCaslin and Alzie (Vaughn) H.; student Millsaps Coll., 1934-35; LL.B., Jackson Sch. Law, 1951; m. Dorothy Currie, Oct. 7, 1940; 1 son, George William. Admitted to Miss. bar, 1951; practiced in Utica, 1955-66; chancery judge 5th Chancery Ct. Dist. of Miss., 1966—. Served with USMC, 1935-39, to capt. USMCR, 1942-47. Decorated Silver Star medal, Purple Heart. Mem. Am., Miss., Hinds County bar assns. Methodist. Address: Utica MS 39175

HAYNES, JOE R., lawyer; b. Lewisburg, Tenn., May 9, 1921; s. Joe R. and Margaret (Drake) H.; A.B., Carson-Newman Coll., 1943; LL.B., U. Tenn., 1948, J.D., 1948; m. Reba Inklebarger, Dec. 19, 1942; children—Joe R. III, Margaret A. Admitted to Tenn. bar, 1947; practiced in Knoxville, Tenn., 1948—; mem. firm Haynes, Watson & Kressin, 1973—. Pres., Knox County Muscular Dystrophy Assn., 1955. Bd. dirs. Knox County Red Cross, 1960, Medic, Inc.; trustee, chmn. bd. Carson-Newman Coll. Served with USAAF, 1943-45. Mem. Tenn. (gov. 1963-69), Knoxville (pres. 1966) bar assns., Gen. Alumni Assn. Carson-Newman Coll. (pres. 1958-59), Omicron Delta Kappa, Phi Delta Phi. Baptist (trustee, deacon). Home: 5816 Ridgewood Dr Knoxville TN 37918 Office: 226 Greater Tenn Bldg Knoxville TN 37902

HAYNES, LEONARD L., JR., educator; b. Austin, Tex., Mar. 16, 1923; s. Leonard L. and Thelma (Watkins) H.; A.B., Huston Tillotson Coll., 1942; B.D., Gammon Theol. Sem., 1945; Th.D., Boston U., 1948; m. Leila Davenport, Nov. 21, 1945; children—Leonard L. III, Walter Lafayette, Angeline Thelma, Leila Anne. Ordained to ministry Methodist Ch., 1948; pastor Wesley United Meth. Ch., Baton Rouge, 1960—; dean students, prof. philosophy Philander Smith Coll., Little Rock, 1948-52; dir. humanities Ark. State Coll., Pine Bluff, 1952-54; dean of coll. Claflin Coll., Orangeburg, S.C., 1952-57; pres. Morristown Jr. Coll., 1957-59; prof. philosophy and edn. Wiley Coll. Marshall, Tex., 1959-60, So. U., Baton Rouge, 1963—. Mem. Human Relations Council, Baton Rouge, 1967. Recipient Distinguished Alumnus award Boston U. Sch. Theology, 1971. Mem. Ministerial Assn. Baton Rouge, Alpha Kappa Mu, Omega Psi Phi, Mason (33 deg.). Author: The Negro Community within American Protestantism, 1619-1844, 1952. Home: 1798 77th St Baton Rouge LA 70821

HAYNES, RICHARD DUVAL, lawyer; b. Oklahoma City, Mar. 2, 1931; s. Marvin Floyd and Helen (Hays) H.; A.B., U. Okla., 1953; J.D., Washington and Lee U., 1958; m. Norine Castle, Nov. 8, 1958; children—Ellen Elizabeth, Caroline Lillie. Admitted to Okla. bar, 1958, Tex. bar, 1962; practiced in Dallas, 1961—; mem. firm Rainey, Flynn & Welch, 1958-61, Ethan B. Stroud, 1962-64, Haynes & Boone, Dallas, 1964—; counsel Electro-Sci. Investors, Inc., Dallas, 1961-62. Lectr. So. Methodist U., 1966-68, 70-73. Bd. dirs. Dallas Civic Opera Co., 1966-71. Served to 1st lt. USAF, 1955-57. Mem. Am., Okla., Dallas bar assns., State Bar Tex. Republican. Contbr. articles to profl. jours. Home: 3509 Princeton Av Dallas TX 75205 Office: 2900 LTV Tower Dallas TX 75201

HAYNIE, HUGH, editorial cartoonist; b. Reedville, Va., Feb., 1927; s. Raymond Lee and Margaret Virginia (Smith) H.; A.B., Coll. William and Mary, 1950; L.H.D., U. Louisville, 1968; m. Lois Ann Cooper, Dec. 5, 1953; 1 son, Hugh Smith. Cartoonist, Richmond (Va.) Times-Dispatch, 1950-53, Greensboro (N.C.) Daily News, 1953-55, 56-58, Atlanta Jour., 1955-56; with Louisville Courier Jour., 1958—, now editorial cartoonist; syndicated by Los Angeles Times, 1964—. Dir. Haynie Products, Inc., Balt. Served to lt. USCGR, 1944-46, 51-52; PTO, Recipient Headliner award, 1966; Freedoms Found. award, 1966, Pulitzer prize; named One of 10 Outstanding Young Men, U.S. Jr. C. of C., 1962. Mem. Soc. Alumni Coll. William and Mary (dir.), Phi Beta Kappa, Omicron Delta Kappa, Pi Kappa Alpha, Democrat. Episcopalian. Club: Windmill Point Yacht (Foxwells, Va.). Home: Indian Hills Trail and Tribal Rd Louisville KY 40207 Office: Courier Jour 525 W Broadway Louisville KY 40202

HAYNIE, THOMAS POWELL, III, physician, educator; b. Hearne, Tex., Aug. 9, 1932; s. Thomas Powell and Sue (Cummings) H.; student U. of South, 1949-51, U. Tex,, 1951-52; M.D,, Baylor U., 1956; m. Bette Maxine Hutchins, Mar. 10, 1956; children—David Powell, Amy Cummings, Sue Cummings. Intern, resident U. Mich. Med. Sch., 1956-60, instr., 1960-62, asst. prof., 1962; practice medicine, specializing in nuclear and internal medicine, Houston, 1965—; mem. staff M. D. Anderson Hosp.; asst. prof. medicine U. Tex. Med. Br., 1962-65; asso. prof. medicine U. Tex.-M. D. Anderson Inst., Houston, 1965—; chief sect. nuclear medicine U. Tex.-M. D. Anderson Hosp. and Tumor Inst., Houston, 1967—; asso. grad faculty U. Tex. Grad. Sch. Biomed. Scis., Houston, 1969—; cons. Wilford Hall U.S. Air Force Hosp., Lackland AFB, Tex., 1967—; cons preventive med. div. Space Flight Biotech. Splty. Teams NASA, Manned Space Center, Houston, 1968— Tech expert IAEA Casablanca, Morocco, 1964; mem. adv. panel on radio pharmaceuticals Am. Hosp. Formulary Service, 1970—. Fellow A.C.P.; mem. A.M.A., Soc. Nuclear Medicine, Am. Thyroid Assn. Home: 18626 Barbuda Lane Houston TX 77058 Office: 6723 Bertner St Houston TX 77025

HAYS, DONALD OSBORNE, govt. ofcl.; b. New Braintree, Mass., June 5, 1907; s. Edward Christopher and Grace Theresa Osborne (Hays) Luethi; grad. Mt. Hermon Prep. Sch., 1925; student Middlebury Coll., 1925-27; B.A., U. Colo., 1929; M.A., Columbia, 1937, postgrad. 1942; postgrad. Am. U., 1951; m. Mary Katherine Jackson Oliver, Aug. 30, 1937. Tchr. English, head dept. English, pub. schs., Colo., Pa., 1929-38; head English dept., sr. master Woodmere (L.I.) Acad., 1938-42; mgmt. analyst, asst. dir., mgmt. and planning staff Spl. Services, VA, 1946-51; asst. dir. budget and mgmt. div. NPA, 1951-53; asst. dist. commr. for adminstrn. Internal Revenue Service, Balt., 1953, asst. regional commr. for adminstrn., Boston, 1953-54, Phila., 1954-57; asst. to dir. Bur. Fgn. Commerce, Dept. Commerce, Washington, 1957-61, now the Bur. Internat. Commerce, 1961-63; dir. overseas personnel div. Office Fgn. Comml. Services, Dept. Commerce, 1963-68, dir. performance evaluation div., 1968-73, asso. dir. officer assignment div., 1973—. Dept. Commerce mem. 13th and 16th Fgn. Service Officer Selection Bd., Dept. State, 1959, 62; dep.

examiner Bd. Fgn. Service Examiners, Dept. State, Washington, 1960-73. Served from lt. (j.g.) to lt. comdr., USNR, 1942-46; mem. staff Comdr. Fourth Fleet, Recife, Brazil, 1943-44 contact negotiator, electronics div. Bur. Ships, also staff Navy Manpower Survey Bd., 1944-46, Mem. Cum Laude Soc., S.A.R. (pres. D.C. soc. 1971), Alpha Sigma Phi, Kappa Phi Kappa. Episcopalian (jr. warden 1968-73). Clubs: Metropolitan, Dacor (Washington). Home: 4000 Massachusetts Av NW Washington DC 20016 Office: Dept of Commerce Washington DC 20230

HAYS, JAMES DEFORD, fedn. exec.; b. Huntsville, Ala., Aug. 20, 1909; s. James Elgie and Rena (DeFord) H.; B.S., U. Ala., 1931; m. Annie Wade Street, Sept. 8, 1928; children—Martha DeFord Hays, James R., John Wade. Mem. staff Ala. Geol. Survey, Tuscaloosa, 1931-33; mem. staff U.S. Forest Service, Black Warrior Nat. Forest, Moulton, Ala., 1933-34; project supt. TVA Forest Nursery, Muscle Shoals, Ala., 1934-37; owner, operator Haysland Farms, Huntsville, 1937—; pres. Ala. Farm Bur. Fedn., Montgomery, Ala., 1961—, AFB Mut. Casualty Ins. Co., Montgomery, 1961—; pres., chmn. bd. Federated Guaranty Life Ins. Co., Montgomery, 1972—; chmn. bd. Am. Nat. Bank, Huntsville, Ala., 1967-69; pres. Huntsville Indsl. Assos., Inc., 1967-70; dir. State Nat. Bank, Decatur, Ala., Central & State Nat. Corp., Decatur, Central Bancshares of South, Inc.; dir. Am. Farm Bur. Fedn., Chgo. Bd. dirs., vice chmn. 4-H Found., 1965—; dir. Ala. Space Sci. Exhibit Commn., 1965—; mem. adv. council Ala. Community & Tech. Services, 1966—, Ala.-Guatemala Partners of Alliance, 1967—; pres. Huntsville Real Estate Investment Trust, 1970-72; mem. Ala. Agri-Bus. Council, 1971; Ala.-U.S. Dept. Agr. Rural Devel. Council, 1971—, Com. for Increased Funding for Vocational Edn. in Ala., 1971—; mem. plant protection bd. Dept. Agr., 1971-73; chmn. Ala. Resource Devel. Com., Montgomery, 1971-72. Mem. Ala. C. of C. (agri-bus. com. 1970—), U. Ala. at Huntsville Assos., Newcomen Soc., Gamma Sigma Delta, Gamma Alpha, Pi Kappa Alpha. Mem. Ch. of Christ. Rotarian (pres. 1959). Home: 300 Haysland Rd Huntsville AL 35802 Office: PO Box 11000 Montgomery AL 36111

HAYS, KIRBY LEE, educator; b. Cullman, Ala., Aug. 11, 1928; s. Charles K.S. and Cora Nell (Marsh) H.; B.S., Auburn U., 1948, M.S., 1954; Ph.D., U. Mich., 1958; m. E. Dean Styles, Dec. 21, 1958; children—Jane E., Melanie L. With U.S. Dept. Agr., Bur. Entomology, 1948-50; asst. prof. Auburn (Ala.) U., 1957-60, asso. prof., 1960-64, prof. dept. zoology and entomology, 1964—. Served with AUS, 1950-52. Recipient grants NIH, Am. Philos. Soc. Mem. Ecol. Soc. Am. (treas., mem. finance com. 1958-63), Entomol. Soc. Am. (mem. exec. com. S.E. br. 1972-74), Sigma Xi, Phi Kappa Phi, Phi Sigma. Elk. Contbr. articles to profl. jours. Home: 1044 Terrace Acres Auburn AL 36830

HAYS, ROBERT WILLIAM, educator; b. Atlanta, Oct. 17, 1925; s. Calvin Samuel and Elizabeth (Green) H.; student Duke, 1943-44; A.B., Presbyn. Coll., 1947; M.Ed., Emory U., 1957; m. Rebecca Guy Copeland, June 15, 1950; children—Michael Stephen, David, William. Comml. mgr. Sta. WSFT, Thomaston, Ga., 1947-48, Sta. WLBG, Laurens-Clinton, S.C., 1948; co-owner Clinton Plastic Co. (S.C.), 1948-49; instr. So. Tech. Inst., 1950-51, asst. prof., 1952-57, head dept. English, 1953—, asso. prof., 1958-60, prof., 1960—; supr. tng. course devel. Lockheed Aircraft Corp., Marietta, Ga., 1951-52. Communications cons. Served from apprentice seaman to lt. (j.g.), USNR, 1943-46. Recipient 2d place nat. Arthur Williston award for contbns. to lit. of engring. tech., 1967. Mem. Soc. for Tech. Communications, Am. Bus. Communications Assn. Author: Pacific Parodies, 1947; Principles of Technical Writing, 1965; Practically Speaking in Business, Industry and Government, 1969; Guide to Technical Writing, 1970; also numerous articles pub. in profl. and trade jours. Research on tech. communication ednl. methodology. Home: 2741 Benson Dr Marietta GA 30062

HAYS, RUTH LANIER (MRS. SIDNEY BROOKS HAYS), educator; b. Cartersville, Ga., July 22, 1940; d. Walter Henry and Anna (Roper) Lanier; B.A., Berea Coll., 1962; Ph.D., Auburn U., 1966; m. Sidney Brooks Hays, Sept. 5, 1965; 1 dau., Shanon Ashley. Asst. prof. zoology Clemson (S.C.) U., after 1965, now asso. prof.; chmn. com. on improving undergrad. teaching, 1970-71, mem. faculty senate, 1970-72, sec. faculty senate, 1972, chmn. div. biol. scis. self-study, 1970-71. Asst. dir. Jr. Girls Aux., 1969-70. Nat. Def. Edn. Act fellow, 1962-65. Mem. Sigma Xi, Gamma Sigma Delta, Phi Kappa Phi, Alpha Lambda Delta (hon.). Baptist. Home: PO Box 1528 Clemson SC 29631

HAYS, SIDNEY BROOKS, educator; b. Arab, Ala., May 31, 1931; s. Charles K.S. and Cora Nell (Marsh) H.; B.S., Auburn U., 1953, M.S., 1957; Ph.D., Clemson U., 1962; m. Ruth L. Lanier, Sept. 5, 1965; 1 dau., Shanon Ashley. Research entomologist Auburn (Ala.) U., 1958-60; asst. prof., entomologist U. Ga., 1962-63; entomologist, asst. prof. Auburn U., 1963-64; asst. prof. entomology Clemson (S.C.) U., 1964-67, asso. prof., 1967-69, prof., head dept. entomology and econ. zoology, 1969—. Served with AUS, 1954-56. Mem. Entomol. Soc. Am. (pres. S.E. br. 1974), Sigma Xi, Gamma Sigma Delta, Phi Kappa Phi, Kappa Delta Pi, Alpha Zeta. Home: PO Box 1528 Clemson SC 29631

HAYWARD, OLGA LORETTA HINES (MRS. SAMUEL E. HAYWARD), librarian; b. Alexandria, La.; d. Samuel James and Lillie (George) Hines; A.B., Dillard U., 1941; B.S. in L.S., Atlanta U., 1944; M.A., U. Mich., 1959; m. Samuel E. Hayward, July 12, 1945; children—Anne Elizabeth, Olga Patricia. Tchr., Marksville (La.) High Schs., 1941-42; head librarian Grambling (La.) Coll., 1944-46; br. librarian br. nine New Orleans Pub. Library System, 1947-48; reference librarian So. U., Baton Rouge, 1948-73, social scis. librarian, 1973—. Active Girl Scouts U.S.A. Bd. dirs. La. Diocese Episcopal Community Services. Mem. Am., La. library assns., Nat. Assn. Coll. Women, Am. Assn. U. Profs. Episcopalian. Author: Graduate Theses of Southern University 1959-71; A Bibliography of Literature By and About Whitney Moore Young, Jr., 1929-71, 1972; Publication Number One, also other bibliographies. Home: 1632 Harding Blvd Baton Rouge LA 70807

HAYWOOD, MARGARET A., judge; b. Knoxville, Tenn., Oct. 8, 1912; d. Jonathan W.M. and Mayme (Fain) Austin; LL.B., Robert H. Terrell Law Sch., 1940. 1 dau., Geraldine H. (Mrs. Porter). Admitted to D.C. bar, 1942; practiced in D.C., 1942-72; mem. D.C. Council, 1967-72; judge Superior Ct. of D.C., 1972—. Real estate broker, 1950-67. Mem. D.C. Commn. on Status of Women; bd. dirs. Nat. Capital council Girl Scouts U.S., 1968-72. Bd. dirs. Council Chs. Greater Washington, 1950-70. Mem. Lambda Kappa Mu (mem. nat. exec. bd.). Republican. Mem. United Ch. of Christ (exec. council, moderator). Home: 4424 Hunt Pl NE Washington DC 20019 Office: Superior Ct DC 440 G St NW Washington DC 20001

HAYWOOD, NORCELL DAN, architect; b. Bastrop, Tex., Jan. 23, 1935; s. Roy and Amanda (Green) H.; student Prairie-View Agrl. and Mech. Coll., 1954-55; B.Arch., U. Tex., 1960; m. Joyce Marie Smith, June 4, 1960; children—Natalie Dawn, Nan Delia, David Norcell. Planning asst., planning dept. City of Austin, Tex., 1961; draftsman-designer Eugene Wukasch, architect-engr., 1961-63; architect O'Neil Ford & Assos., 1963-68, Norcell D. Haywood & Assos., 1968-72; pres. Haywood-Jordan-McCowan, Inc., San Antonio, 1972—; dir. S.E. State Bank. Mem. Alamo Area Council Govts., 1972. Bd. dirs. Met. YMCA, 1972, New Bus. Resource Center, 1973, Project F.R.E.E., Healy-Murphy Learning Center. Recipient Certificate of Appreciation, Boy's Club Am., 1969, Merit Design award San Antonio chpt. A.I.A. 1970, Fred D. Patterson Leadership award United Negro Coll. Fund, 1972. Mem. Constrn. Specifications Inst., Minority Architects, Inc. (pres. 1971-73), A.I.A., Tex. Soc. Architects, The Sphinx, Alpha Phi Alpha, San Antonio C. of C., Dellcrest Bus. and Profl. Assn. Prin. archtl. works include Second Bapt. Ch., 2 boys clubs and Wheatley High Sch., San Antonio. Home: 4352 Wildt Rd San Antonio TX 78222 Office: 1802 SW W White Rd San Antonio Tx 78220 also 4828 Caroline St Houston TX 77004

HAYWOOD, WILLIAM THOMAS, coll. exec.; b. Columbia, Tenn., May 25, 1928; s. William Thomas and Frances (Stone) H.; student Millsaps Coll., 1945-46, Bowling Green Bus. U., 1948-49; B.B.A., U. Miss., 1951; postgrad. Tulane U., 1958-60; LL.D., Atlanta Law Sch., 1969; m. Sylvia Anne Graham, Nov. 25, 1954; children—William Thomas, Sylvia Annette, Robert Alton, Susan Lynne. Bus. mgr., instr. accounting and econs. East Central Jr. Coll., 1951-58; purchasing agt. Tulane U., 1958-59, chief accountant, 1959-60; bus. mgr., instr. econs. Mercer U., Macon, Ga., 1960-67, sec. corp., 1960—, v.p. for bus. and finance, 1967—; instr. econs. Miss. State U., 1954-56. Cons. Ford Found. N.Y.C., 1963-64; sec. Walter F. George Sch. Law Found., Macon, 1963—. Trustee, v.p. Common Fund Non-Profit Instns., 1969—. Served with USNR, 1946-48. Mem. So. (pres. 1968-69), Nat. (dir., 1969—, (pres. 1972-73) assns. coll. and univ. bus. officers, Nat. Assn. Edn. Buyers (pres. 1967-68), So. Assn. Colls. and Schs. (policies and functions com.), Beta Alpha Psi, Delta Sigma Pi, Lambda Chi Alpha. Elk. Club: Idle Hour Golf and Country (Macon). Contbr. articles to profl. publs. Home: 1546 Linden Av Macon GA 31207

HAZEL, JOHN TILGHMAN, JR., lawyer; b. Arlington, Va., Oct. 29, 1930; s. John T. and Ruth D. (Douglas) H.; B.A., Harvard, 1951, LL.B., 1954; postgrad. U. Va., 1951-52; m. Virginia Engle, July 6, 1954; children—Leigh Ann, Jack, James, Richard. Admitted to Va. bar, 1954; practiced in Fairfax, 1957—; mem. firm Phillips, Kendrick, Gearhart & Aylor, 1957-61, John T. Hazel, Jr., 1961-68, Hazel, Beckhorn & Hanes, Fairfax, Va., 1968—; asso. judge Fairfax (Va.) County Ct., 1961-65; dir. First Va. Bankshares, Inc., First Advisors, Inc., Arlington Mortgage Co. Mem. Va. Legislative Adv. Council, Land Use Com., 1972—; pres. Potomac Tb and Respiratory Diseases Assn., 1965-67. Bd. dirs. No. Va. Mental Health Assn., 1964-67; vice-rector, mem. bd. visitors George Mason U.; trustee, v.p. George Mason U. Found., Inc. Served with Judge Advocate Gen. Corps, AUS, 1954-58. Fellow Am. Coll. Trial Lawyers; mem. Am., Va. State, Fairfax County (pres. 1969-70) bar assns., Va. Trial Lawyers Assn., U. Va., Harvard alumni assns. Clubs: Harvard (1st v.p. 1966-67) (Washington). Home: 5117 Brookridge Pl Fairfax VA 22030 Office: PO Box 547 Fairfax VA 22030

HAZELL, DON BLISS, educator; b. Penalosa, Kan., Nov., 5, 1934; s. Arthur Bliss and Emma Doris (Applegate) H.; B.S., Ft. Hays (Kan.) State Coll., 1956, M.S., 1960; Ph.D., Okla. State U., 1963; m. Koula Beth Scolas, Jan. 25, 1959; children—Jon, Eric, Amy. Lab. asst. Ft. Hays State Coll., 1958-60, Okla. State U., 1961; lab. asst. grassland research Phillips Petroleum Co., 1962-63; prof. biol. scis. Southeastern State Coll., Durant, Okla., 1963—. Served with Signal Corps, AUS, 1956-58. Named Tchr. of Year, Southeastern State Coll., 1966, 67, 71. Mem. Am. Soc. Range Mgmt., Ecol. Soc. Am., Okla. Acad. Sci. (mem. exec. council 1970-71, sect. chmn. 1971), Sigma Xi, Phi Kappa Phi. Mem. Christian Ch. (elder 1963—). Lion. Home: 1915 W Liveoak St Durant OK 74701

HEACOCK, GEORGE THOMAS, indsl.-govt. cons.; b. Sylacauga, Ala., June 21, 1920; s. John Warren and Mexie (McDowell) H.; student U. Ala., 1939-40; B.C.S., Benjamin Franklin U., 1963; m. Marie Terese Baltes, Oct. 23, 1948; children—Thomas Michael, Mark Alan, David Andrew. Intelligence officer, specialist CIA, various locations, 1947-69; prin. firm Heacock Govt. Marketing Agy., Falls Church, Va., 1969—. Asst. scoutmaster, mem. exec. com. Nat. Capital Area council Boy Scouts Am., 1962-72, chmn. fund drive, 1972. Served with M.I., USNR, 1942-46. Recipient letter merit Dir. CIA, 1953. Mason. Address: 6711 Rolfs Rd Falls Church VA 22042

HEAD, PHILIP WAYNE, physician; b. Fort Smith, Ark., July 6, 1937; s. Herbert Haskell and Lessie Lee (Phillips) H.; B.S., Northeastern State Coll., Okla., 1960; M.D., Okla. U., 1964; m. Aletha Irene Tucker, June 1, 1958; children—Lori Andrea, Alissa Lynnette. Intern St. Joseph's Hosp., Wichita, Kan., 1964-65; pvt. practice medicine, Carnegie, Okla., 1965-72, Miami, Okla., 1972—. Pres. Carnegie Health Service, Inc., Head's Hand Weapons. Diplomate Am. Bd. Family Practice. Fellow Am. Geriatrics Soc.; mem. A.M.A., Am. Acad. Family Practice, So., Mid South, Okla. med. assns., Okla. Acad. Gen. Practice, Royal Soc. Health (London), Tri-County Med. Soc. (pres. 1974), Am. Coll. Emergency Physicians, Miami Jr. C. of C. Mason (Shriner), Kiwanian (pres. 1965-71. Home: 1400 15th St NE Miami OK 74354 Office: 1st Nat Bank Bldg Miami OK 74354

HEAD, RONALD ALAN, educator; b. Birmingham, Ala., May 12, 1930; s. Charles Maben and Lena Snow (Smith) H.; B.S., Birmingham-So. Coll., 1952; postgrad. Emory U., 1952; M.A., U. Ala., 1957; Ph.D. (NSF fellow), U. Pacific, 1964; m. Dorothy Mae Sheppard, Aug. 5, 1955; children—Laurie Jan, Anne Merrill. Research chemist E.I. DuPont Co., Seaford, Del., 1953; faculty Pensacola (Fla.) Jr. Coll., 1957-65; prof. Okaloosa-Walton Jr. Coll., Niceville, Fla., 1965—, chmn. dept. phys. sci., 1967—. Served AUS, 1953-55. Mem. Am. Chem. Soc., A.A.A.S. Club: Bayou Sailing (sec., treas. 1973-74) (Valparaiso, Fla.). Home: 403 James Av Valparaiso FL 32580 Office: Okaloosa-Walton Jr Coll Niceville FL 32578

HEADLEY, ANNE RENOUF (MRS. JOHN MILES HEADLEY), environmental planner; b. N.Y.C., Apr. 3, 1937; d. Henry Charles and Helen (Donovan) Renouf; grad. Emma Willard Sch., 1954; A.B., Barnard Coll., 1959; M.A., Yale, 1962, Ph.D., 1966; postgrad. Duke Law Sch., 1971, Am. U., 1974; m. John Miles Headley, July 27, 1965. Asst. prof. dept. polit. sci. U. N.C., Chapel Hill, 1966-71; legal asso., 1971-72; environmental planner. Sr. faculty fellow U.S. Dept. State, 1967; sr. staff mem., vis. research scholar Carnegie Endowment for Internat. Peace, 1968-69; mem. Nat. Adv. Council on Grad. Edn., 1970-72; sr. profl. cons. Fed. Environmental Protection Agy., Washington, 1973-74, FPC, 1974—. Mem. Nat. Com. for the Sanger Meml., 1969—. Woodrow Wilson fellow, 1958. Mem. Am. Bar Assn., Am. Polit. Sci. Assn., Am. Acad. Cons., Am. Soc. Internat. Law, Internat. Studies Assn., The Innovation Group, Tech. and Communication, Phi Beta Kappa. Democrat. Home: 700 New Hampshire Av NW Washington DC 20037

HEADLEY, ELWOOD JEAN, physician; b. Atlantic City, N.J., July 22, 1939; s. Elwood Alverson and Elizabeth Louise (Glatterer) H.; student U. of South, 1957-59; A.B., Vanderbilt U., 1962, M.D., 1966. Intern internal medicine Vanderbilt U. Hosp., Nashville, 1966-67, resident internal medicine, 1967-68; resident internal medicine Ohio State U. Hosp., Columbus, 1968-69, fellow hematology, 1969-70; fellow hematology U. Fla., Gainesville, 1972—. Prin. investigator Gainesville (Fla.) Methodone Program, 1972; mem. Region III Drug Abuse Adv. Council, 1972. Served to maj. M.C., AUS, 1970-72. Episcopalian. Home: 2700 SW Archer Rd Gainesville FL 32608 Office: Div Hematology U Fla Gainesville FL 32610

HEALY, ROBERT EDWARD, advt. exec.; b. Bklyn., Aug. 15, 1904; s. Walter F. and Florence E. (Davis) H.; grad. Dwight Prep. Sch., N.Y.C., 1924; student Pace Inst., N.Y.C., 1924-26; D.S.C. (hon.), Pace Coll., 1961; m. Lille Rose, Aug. 3, 1927; children—Lilie Jane, Patricia Anne, Robert E. (dec.); m. 2d, Wayne Clark, Jan. 11, 1957; children—Edward W., James D. Salesman, T.J. Adikes, Jamaica, N.Y., 1926, Hoover Co., 1927-28; asst. to v.p. charge sales promotion Johns-Manville Co., 1929-33; mgr. prodn. sect. advt. dept. Colgate-Palmolive Co., Jersey City, 1934-36, asst. advt. mgr. 1936-39, brand advt. mgr., 1939-42, gen. advt. mgr., 1942-46, v.p. charge advt., 1946-52; v.p., treas., dir., mem. exec. com. McCann-Erickson, Inc., 1952-53, v.p., gen. mgr., dir., mem. exec. com., 1953-54, gen. mgr. N.Y. office, 1954, exec. v.p., 1955-58, vice chmn. bd., 1958-60, chmn. bd., 1960-62, mem. finance com., 1957-61; chmn. bd. McCann-Erickson Corp. (Internat.), 1956-58; pres. Interpublic, S.A., Geneva, Switzerland, 1962-65; exec. v.p. Interpublic Group Cos., Inc., 1965-67, pres., 1967-71, chief exec. officer, 1967-71, chmn. bd., 1968-73, hon. chmn. bd., 1973—, mem. finance com., 1968—. Mem. adv. council Pace Coll. Clubs: N.Y. Athletic; Key Biscayne Yacht; Ocean Reef; Confrerie de la Chaine des Rotisseurs; Paris American. Home: 1111 Crandon Blvd Key Biscayne FL 33149 Office: 1271 Av of Americas New York City NY 10020

HEARNE, DOUGLASS DODSON, lawyer; b. San Antonio, Nov. 17, 1930; s. Noble and Grace Truman (Dodson) H.; B.A., Tex. A. and M. U., 1951; LL.B., U. Tex., 1958; m. Janet Anne Baillie, Apr. 11, 1953; children—Christopher B., Kathleen Anne, Mary Ellen, Douglass Dodson. Admitted to Tex. bar, 1957; asso. Cofer & Cofer, 1958-61; partner, Cofer, Cofer & Hearne, 1961-67, Stayton, Maloney, Black, Hearne & Babb, Austin, Tex., 1968—; dir. Beachhead Condominium, Port Aransas, Tex. Served as fighter pilot USAF, 1951-55. Mem. Am. Judicature Soc., Am., Travis County bar assns., Tex. Trial Lawyers Assn., State Bar Tex. (mem. family law council 1972-73), Phi Alpha Delta. Democrat. Presbyn. (deacon 1969-71). Club: Tex. Agricultural and Mechanical Century (College Station, Tex.). Home: 2700 Mountain Laurel Dr Austin TX 78703 Office: 505 W 12th St Austin TX 78701

HEARON, SHELBY REED (MRS. ROBERT J. HEARON, JR.), writer; b. Marion, Ky., Jan. 18, 1931; d. Charles Boogher and Evelyn Shelby (Roberts) Reed; B.A. with honors, U. Tex., 1953; m. Robert J. Hearon, Jr., June 15, 1953; children—Anne Shelby, Robert Reed. Bookkeeper, Washington and Austin, Tex., 1953-59; free-lance writer, pub. in McCall's, Redbook, 1966—. Pres. Planned Parenthood Bd., Austin, 1959-61. Mem. Authors Guild, Authors League Am., Tex. Inst. Letters, Jr. League Austin (pres. 1969-70), Pi Beta Phi. Democrat. Methodist. Author: Armadillo In The Grass, 1968; The Second Dune, 1973. Home: 4601 Cat Mountain Dr Austin TX 78731

HEARST, JOSEPH FRANCIS, journalist; b. St. Joseph, Mo., Nov. 27, 1901; s. Loren Andrew and Frances (Dunn) H.; grad. high sch.; m. Susan E. Gogerty, Feb. 6, 1932. Former reporter St. Joseph News Press, Kansas City (Mo.) Star, Internat. News Service, United Press; mem. staff Chgo. Tribune, 1943—, corr. Washington bur. Chgo. Tribune Press Service, 1944—. Mem. White House Corrs. Assn. Roman Catholic. Club: Nat. Press (Washington) Home: 4301 Columbia Pike Arlington VA 22204 Office: 1750 Pennsylvania Av NW Washington DC 20006

HEARTZ, FREDERICK RICHARD, cons. civil engr.; b. Exeter, N.H., May 12, 1921; s. Harold Francis and Catherine Mary (McEnhill) H.; B.S., U. N.H., 1944; M.S., Mo. Sch. Mines and Metallurgy, 1949; m. Barbara Louise Goodrich, June 19, 1944; 1 son, William Thomas. Asso. prof. S.D. State Coll., Brookings, 1949-57; sr. v.p. Tanner, Thomsom, D'alli & Heartz, Inc., Melbourne, Fla., 1957-61; pres. Heartz Engring. & Testing Co., Inc., Palm Bay, Fla., 1961—; lead engr. Radiation, Inc., Palm Bay, 1967-70. Instr. civil engring. Mo. Sch. Mines and Metallurgy, S.D. State Coll. Registered profl. engr., Fla., S.D. Mem. Fla. Engring. Soc., Nat. Soc. Profl. Engrs., Am. Soc. C.E., Am. Soc. Mil. Engrs., Am. Concrete Inst., Palm Bay C. of C. (v.p. 1965). Rotarian. Club: Melbourne Yacht. Home: 225 Worth Ct Palm Bay FL 32905 Office: PO Box 67 Palm Bay FL 32905

HEATH, CHARLES RAYMOND, hosp. adminstr.; b. Duck Hill, Miss., Aug. 11, 1924; s. John Arthur and Zelma Irene (Greer) H.; D.V.M., Tex. A. and M. U., 1947; postgrad. U. Ala., 1969-70; m. Esther Maudine Riley, May 8, 1949; children—Susan (Mrs. James Ronald Robertson), Charles Raymond, Cynthia Irene. Pvt. practice vet. medicine, Winona, Miss., 1947-67; adminstr. Tyler Holmes Meml. Hosp., Winona, 1967—. Owner Registered Angus Ranch, 1952-72. Pres. North Delta Hosp. Council, 1970. Served with USAAF, 1942. USPHS Tng. grantee for health services adminstr. devel. program, 1969-70. Mem. Am. Vet. Med. Assn., Am., Miss. hosp. assns. Baptist (deacon 1958—). Rotarian. Home: 431 Tyler Holmes St Winona MS 38967 Office: 1 Tyler Holmes St Winona MS 38967

HEATH, FRANK BRADFORD, dentist; b. Houston, Dec. 11, 1938; s. Robert Bradford and Maudie (Sweeney) H.; B.S., Sam Houston State U., 1961; D.D.S., U. Tex., 1965; m. Heide Jutta Marianne Schmidt, Aug. 20, 1965; children—Dirk Alan, Shannon Erika, Kent Bradford. Practice gen. dentistry, Houston, 1967—. Served with AUS, 1965-67. Mem. Houston Dist. Dental Soc., Xi Psi Phi, Delta Tau Delta. Methodist. Home: 12610 Mile Dr Houston TX 77065 Office: 12315 Jones Rd Houston TX 77070

HEATH, LESLIE ARTHUR, public accountant; b. Phila., Dec. 11, 1903; s. Albanus M. and Annie (Houpt) H.; student N.C. State Coll., 1951-52, Walton Sch. Commerce, 1921-27; LL.B., Am. Extension Sch. Law, 1949; student Exec. Program U. N.C., 1954-55; m. 2d, Margaret V. Biggers, April 11, 1955; children (by previous marriage)—Betty (Mrs. E. S. Shannonhouse), Leslie (dec.), James B., Murray A. Accountant Wolf & Co., 1921-26; resident mgr. Peat, Marwick, Mitchell & Co., 1926-42; prin. auditor RFC, 1942-44; v.p. finance Queen City Coach Co., 1944-52; pvt. practice as C.P.A., Charlotte, N.C., 1952-69; pres. Leslie A. Heath Ltd., Charlotte 1969—. Sometime instr. U. N.C., Duke, Queens Coll.; past pres. N.C. State Bd. C.P.A. Examiners, Charlotte Exec. Program. C.P.A., N.C., Pa. Mem. A.I.M. (asso.), Am. Accounting Assn., N.C. (past pres.), Charlotte Area (past pres.) assns. C.P.A.'s, Am. Inst. C.P.A.'s, Rosicrucian. Episcopalian. Mason (Shriner), Home: 1333 Queens Rd Charlotte NC 28207 Office: 1229 Greenwood Cliff Charlotte NC 28204

HEATH, WILLIAM SCHLEY, bottling co. exec.; b. Cartersville, Ga., Dec. 7, 1914; s. Alfred Taylor and Ann D. (Howell) H.; B.S., Ga. Inst. Tech., 1936; m. Marian Elizabeth Bradford, May 21, 1946; children—Dorothy Caroline (Mrs. John Bristow Jackson). With Carolina Coca-Cola Bottling Co., Sumter, S.C., 1936—, dir., 1950—, sec., 1956—, treas., 1959—; adv. bd. Nat. Bank S.C. Chmn. United Fund drive, 1954, Shaw-Sumter Community Council, 1956-68,

City-County Health Dept. Bd., 1957-60, S.C. Hwy. Safety Commn., 1962, City-County Devel. Bd., 1966-68. Bd. dirs. YMCA. Served from 2d lt. to lt. col., Arty., 1940-45. Decorated Bronze Star medal. Mem. Sumter C. of C. (dir., pres. elect), Kappa Sigma. Elk, Rotarian (past dist. gov.). Club: Sunset Country. Home: 72 Paisley Park Sumter SC 29150 Office: 712 E Liberty St Sumter SC 29150

HEBERLING, RICHARD LEON, virologist; b. Reading, Pa., May 5, 1926; s. Leon George and Anna Lucetta (Shadel) H.; B.S., Albright Coll., 1949; M.S., U. Pa., 1953; Ph.D., Pa. State U., 1957; m. Mary Jane Conbere, Jan. 27, 1958; children—Linda (Mrs. Richard Thomas Branson), Lisa, Susan. Research asso. Grad. Sch. Pub. Health, U. Pitts., 1957-60; instr. Sch. Medicine, 1960-65; research microbiologist Nat. Cancer Inst., Bethesda, Md., 1965-67; asso. found. scientist S.W. Found. for Research and Edn., San Antonio, 1967—. Asso. prof. dept. microbiology U. Tex. Sch. Medicine, San Antonio, 1973—; cons. Jour. Med. Primatology, 1972—. Served with USNR, 1944-46. Recipient award Phi Sigma, 1957. Mem. Am. Soc. Microbiology, Tissue Culture Soc., A.A.A.S., Sigma Xi, Phi Kappa Phi. Home: 363 Pike Rd San Antonio TX 78209 Office: 7480 W Commerce St San Antonio TX 78284

HEBERT, ADAM OTIS, JR., state ofcl.; b. Abbeville, La., Sept. 22, 1930; s. Adam Otis and Etta (Babineaux) H.; B.A., U. Southwestern La., 1952; M.Ed., La. State U., 1958, M.A., 1959; m. Elsie Stallworth, Aug. 7, 1965; stepchildren—Richard Stallworth, Darryl Stallworth. Tchr., Erath (La.) High Sch., 1952, 54-57, Port Allen (La.) High Sch., 1963; instr. Southeastern La. Coll., Hammond, 1959; grad. asst. La. State U., Baton Rouge, 1959-63; asst. prof. history Nicholls State Coll., Thibodaux, La., 1963-66; archivist Catholic Diocese, Baton Rouge, 1964-66; dir. La. Archives and Records, Baton Rouge, 1966—. Chmn. La. Hist. Preservation and Cultural Commn., 1968-70. Served with AUS, 1952-54. Mem. Soc. Am. Archivist, Soc. S.W. Archivists (pres. 1972-74), La. (sec.-treas.), Attakapas (pres. 1973-74) hist. assns. Editor: (with Harry T. Williams) Louisiana in the Civil War: A Chronology, 1959—; Louisiana History, 1962-63. Contbr. articles to profl. jours. Home: 370 Nassau Dr Baton Rouge LA 70815 Office: PO Box 44222 Capitol Sta Baton Rouge LA 70804

HEBERT, F. EDWARD, congressman, former editor; b. New Orleans, Oct. 12, 1901; s. Felix Joseph and Lea (Naquin) H.; student Tulane U., 1920-24; m. Gladys Bofill, Aug. 1, 1934; 1 dau., Dawn Marie. Sports reporter New Orleans Times-Picayune, 1919-20, asst. sports editor, 1920-25; asst. sports editor New Orleans States, 1925-26, polit. editor and columnist, 1929-37, city editor, 1937-40, when paper broke La. Scandals, 1939, resulting in overthrow of Huey Long Political machine (paper subsequently awarded Delta Sigma Chi plaque for courage in journalism); dir. publicity, Loyola U., New Orleans, 1926-29; dir. Central Savings & Loan Assn.; mem. 77th-92d congresses from 1st La. Dist., chmn. armed services com., 1971—. Pres., Young Men's Bus. Club of New Orleans, 1932. Mem. Delta Sigma Phi (nat. v.p. 1937-49). Democrat. Roman Catholic. Author: I Went, I saw, I Heard. Home: 5367 Canal Blvd New Orleans LA 70124 Office: House Office Bldg Washington DC 20515

HECK, CARL EDWARD, JR., civil engr.; b. Houma, La., Jan. 24, 1942; s. Carl Edward and Verna Mae (Talbot) H.; B.S. in Civil Engring., La. State U., 1964, J.D., 1968; m. Amelia Margaret Clement, Sept. 4, 1965; children—Carl Edward III, Timothy Clement, Michael Braden. Admitted to La. bar, 1968; v.p. Carl Heck Engrs., Inc., civil engrs., Houma, La., 1968—; partner Heck Realty Ltd., Houma, 1971—; v.p. Waubun Devel. Co., Thibodeaux, La. Registered profl. engr., La. Mem. Am. Soc. C.E., La. Engring. Soc., La. Land Surveyors Assn., Nat. Soc. Profl. Engrs., La., Terrebonne bar assns., Houma C. of C., Sigma Tau Sigma, Phi Alpha Delta, Kappa Sigma. Club: Houma Kiwanis (dir. since 1970—). Contbr. law rev. articles. Home: 203 Malibou Blvd Houma LA 70360 Office: 511 School St Houma LA 70360

HEDERMAN, ZACH TAYLOR, publishing co. exec.; b. Jackson, Miss., Feb. 5, 1913; s. Robert M. and Jennie Belle (Taylor) H.; B.S., Miss. Coll., 1935; B.S. Indsl. Mgmt., Carnegie Mellon U., 1938; m. Margaret Love, July 3, 1943; children—Carol Love, Zach T., Margaret Ann. Partner, Hederman Bros., Jackson, 1938—; v.p. Miss. Pub. Corp., Jackson, 1938—, Hattiesburg Am. Pub. Co. (Miss.), 1961—, Madison County Herald, Canton, Miss., 1965—; dir. Magnolia Fed. Savs. & Loan Assn. Past pres. Jackson YMCA. Chmn., Jackson Redevel. Authority. Chmn. bd. Miss. Bapt. Hosp. Served to capt. AUS, 1942-45. Mem. Capitol City Petroleum Club, Printing Industry Am. (past dir.), So. Graphic Arts Assn. (past dir.), Jackson C. of C. (past pres). Baptist (deacon, past chmn.). Kiwanian (past pres. Jackson). Club: Jackson Country. Home: 1311 Riverside Dr Jackson MS 39202 Office: Pearl at Congress Sts Jackson MS 39205

HEDGEPATH, LESLIE EUGENE, physician; b. Chillicothe, O., Dec. 16, 1922; s. Leslie Oliver and Florence Elizabeth (Gamble) H.; M.D., Howard U., 1947; m. Ruth Harris, June 28, 1949; children—Leslie Eugene, Gregory. Intern Harlem Hosp., N.Y.C., 1947-48, admitting physician, 1948-49; asst. resident in medicine Freedmen's Hosp., Washington, 1953-54, chief resident in medicine, 1954-55; practice medicine specializing in internal medicine, Washington, 1959—; instr. medicine Howard U., Washington, 1955-56, 59—, instr. physiology, 1959-64; asst. chief med. service VA Hosp., Pitts., 1956-58, chief med. service, 1958-59; attending physician Freedmen's Hosp., Howard U. Med. Service-D.C. Gen. Hosp., 1959—; sr. attending physician Washington Hosp. Center, 1961—, trustee, 1974—. Served with M.C., AUS, World War II, 1949-52. Decorated Silver Star, Bronze Star with oak leaf cluster; recipient Service award Howard U., 1968. Fellow A.C.P.; mem. Am. (com. pvt. practice 1972—), Nat. med. assns., Med. Soc. D.C. (bd. credentials 1962-64; exec. bd. 1971-73), Am. Soc. Internal Medicine, Kappa Pi. Club: Pigskin (Washington). Research in hemodynamic and angiocardiographic observations in adults with persistent left superior vena cava draining into the coronary sinus, congenital cardio-vascular anomalies in adults, incidence and significance of bacteriuria in female diabetics. Home: 1432 Iris St NW Washington DC 20012 Office: 106 Irving St NW Washington DC 20010

HEDRICK, FLOYD DUDLEY, govt. ofcl.; b. Lynchburg, Va., Jan. 19, 1927; s. Silas Dudley and Alice (Stowe) H.; grad. Va. Comml. Coll., 1948; grad. Advanced Mgmt. Program, Harvard U., 1971; m. Rachel Conelia Childress, May 27, 1950; children—Susan Kaye, Alice Rae. Purchasing agt., supt. stores Trailways, Inc., 1947-65; v.p. purchasing Macke Co., Washington, 1966-72, pres. subsidiary Atlantic Supply Co., Hyattsville, Md., 1967-72; chief procurement and supply div. Library of Congress, Washington, 1973—. Pres. Lynchburg chpt. Fed. and State Credit Unions, 1956-57. Served with USNR, 1944-46, 50-52. Mem. Am. Mgmt. Assn. (mem. purchasing planning council 1969—), Nat. Assn. Purchasing Mgmt. (v.p. 1972-73, chmn. food industry group 1970-71), Purchasing Mgmt. Assn. Washington (pres. 1969-70), Izaak Walton League (v.p. Lynchburg 1957). Mason (32 deg). Author: Purchasing Management in the Smaller Company, 1971. Home: 3824 King Arthur Rd Annandale VA 22003 Office: 10 1st St SE Washington DC 20540

HEDRICK, JERALD WILLIAM, educator; b. Kingsville, Tex., Sept. 12, 1931; s. James Oscar and Alta (Hardy) H.; B.S. in Secondary Edn., Tex. A. and I. U., 1961; postgrad. in Indsl. Edn., Tex. A. and M, 1964—; m. Joanne Schmidt, Aug. 15, 1953; children——Jerald William, Joseph Charles, James Oscar III, Jennifer Joanne Amanda. Automotive parts mgr. Chrysler Corp., Corpus Christi, Tex., 1950-57; tchr. Corpus Christi Ind. Sch. Dist., 1961-62; prof. Tex. Arts and Industries U. Kingsville, 1965—; mem. Tex. Arts and Industries U. Upward Bound faculty, summers 1967—. Chmn. Indsl. Arts Resource Com., regions I, II, and XX Tex., 1968—; mem. indsl. arts curriculum study and research project Tex. Edn. Agy. Mem. Tex. Tchrs. Assn., Nat., Tex. (sponsor 1971-72, named outstanding indsl. arts tchr. from Coastal Bend) Coastal Bend indsl. arts assns., Tex. Assn. Coll. Tchrs., Am., Tex. (pres. 1973-74) councils indsl. arts tchr. edn., Nat. Assn. Indsl. Tchr. Edn., Tex. Audio-Visual Edn. Assn., Iota Lambda Sigma (past historian Chi chpt.), Alpha Chi. Methodist. Home: 730 W Av A Kingsville TX 78363

HEDRICK, ROBERT K., financial analyst; b. Stockton, Cal., Oct. 1, 1929; s. David Dennis and Mable (Hollingsworth) H.; B.B.A., Tex. A. and M. Coll., 1951; M.B.A., So. Methodist U., 1964; LL.B., LaSalle Extension U., 1965; m. Christina Marie Davie, Feb. 1, 1961; 1 dau., Christina Roberta. Accountant, Kernaghan & Harvey, C.P.A.'s, 1958-61; pub. accountant Bright, Shinn & Strange, C.P.A.'s, Dallas, 1961-63, controller M.P. Crum Co., Dallas, 1963; investment co. examiner Small Bus. Adminstrn., Dallas, 1964-67; financial analyst, asst. v.p. First Nat. Bank, Dallas, 1967-73; asst. v.p. 1st City Nat. Bank, Houston, 1973—. Served to lt. USNR, 1951-56. Recipient Silver medal S.A.R., 1946. C.P.A., Tex. Mem. Am. Inst. C.P.A.'s, Tex. Bar, Dallas Assn. Investment Analysts, Inst. Chartered Financial Analysts, Am. Legion (past post comdr.). Mason. Home: 6006 Vanderbilt St Dallas TX 75206 Office: First City Nat Bank Bldg Houston TX 77001

HEEREMA, NICKOLAS, mathematician, educator; b. Hospers, Ia., Oct. 5, 1922; s. Albert and Gerbina (Baker) H.; student Calvin Coll., 1941-42; B.S. in Chem. Engring., U. Mich., 1944; M.S., U. Tenn., 1949, Ph.D., 1951; m. Joetta Jones, Jan. 3, 1948; children—Mark Stephen, Jane Ellen, David John, Thomas Scott, Amy Elizabeth. Research engr. Carbide & Carbon Chem. Corp., Oak Ridge, 1946-48; asst. prof. math. Fla. State U., a Tallahassee, 1951-55, asso. prof., 1955-61, prof., 1961—. Served with C.E., AUS, 1944-46. NSF grantee, 1960-73. Mem. Am. Math. Soc., Am. Assn. Math., Sigma Xi. Presbyn. Contbr. articles to profl. jours. Home: 3204 Enterprise Dr Tallahassee FL 32303

HEERLEIN, BILL HAMILTON, coll. adminstr.; b. Denver, Oct. 11, 1920; s. William Gaston and Myrtle (Space) H.; B.A., Warner Pacific Coll., 1954; m. Ruth Louise Owens, May 13, 1945; children—Donald Wayne, Gary Brent. Sec. to pres., registrar Warner Pacific Coll., Portland, Ore., 1962-66; registrar Gulf-Coast Bible Coll., Houston, 1966-68, v.p. financial affairs, 1968—. Dir. Ch. of God State Youth Fellowship Western Wash., Bremerton, 1958-61. Served with AUS, 1942-45. Home: 1135 Alexander St Houston TX 77008 Office: 911 W 11th St Houston TX 77008

HEFFERLIN, RAY ALDEN, educator; b. Paris, France, May 2, 1929; s. Milo August Ruth (Streiff) H.; B.A., Pacific Union Coll., 1951; Ph.D., Cal. Inst. Tech., 1955; m. Inelda Eunice Phillips, Sept. 4, 1954; children—Lorelei, Heidi, Missie, Jennie. Research asst. Cal. Inst. Tech., 1955; prof. physics, chmn. dept. So. Missionary Coll., Collegedale, Tenn., 1955—; vis. prof. U. Chattanooga, 1967-68. Active Vol. Fire Dept., Credit Union. Recipient grants Research Corp., Tenn. Acad. Sci., NSF. Mem. Am. Astron. Soc., Am. Phys. Soc., Tenn. Acad. Sic. Contbr. articles to profl. jours. Home: Box H Collegedale TN 37315

HEFFERNAN, JOSEPH ANTHONY, JR., physician; b. Savannah, Ga., Oct. 2, 1928; s. Joseph Anthony and Louise (Jeffrey) H.; B.S., U. Ga., 1951; M.D., Med. Coll. Ga., 1955; m. Jean Ann Stalvey, July 22, 1950; children—Nancy, Joseph, Mark, John, Gregory. Intern, Mercy Hosp., Buffalo, 1955-56; gen. practice medicine, Savannah, 1956—; chief med. cons. City of Savannah, 1966—; med. dir. Savannah Narcotic Treatment Center; cons., lectr. drug abuse mgmt. Mem. Savannah Mayor's Council on Drug Abuse, 1968—. Served with USNR, 1946-48. Mem. A.M.A., Am. Acad. Family Practice, Med. Assn. Ga., Ga. Med. Soc. Clubs: Savannah Yacht, Forest City Gun. Home: 5706 Sweetbriar Circle Savannah GA 31406 Office: 20 Med Arts Center Savannah GA 31405

HEFFNER, GEORGE PAUL, physician; b. Wapakoneta, O., Feb. 10, 1909; s. Edward Frederic and Ida Orel (Collins) H.; A.B. cum laude, Harvard, 1930, M.D., 1934; m. Eileen Mae Van Giesen, Nov. 20, 1942; children—Judith Ann, Carol Sue, Mary Kay. Intern, Lankenau Hosp., Phila., 1934-36; practice medicine specializing in internal medicine, Charleston, W. Va., 1936-70, Fort Lauderdale, Fla., 1963—; attending physician dept. internal medicine Charleston (W.Va.) Gen. Hosp., 1941-63. Founder, pres. W. Va. Diabetes Assn., 1953; established free camp for diabetic children in W. Va., 1950; founded Charleston Lay Soc. for Diabetics, 1952; founder, med. adv. dir. Charles E. Conway Diabetes Teaching School, Ft. Lauderdale, 1973; clin. asso. prof. U. Miami Med. Sch., Dept Endocrinology; attending staff Holy Cross Hosp., Beach Hosp., Fort Lauderdale, Fla. Fellow Am. Coll. Physicians; mem. A.M.A., Am. (bd. dirs. 1971—), Fla. diabetes assns. Methodist. Kiwanian, Elk. Club: Harvard (Broward County, Fla.) (v.p. 1965-71). Contbr. articles to profl. jours. Home: 1220 S E 3d Terrace Pompano Beach FL 33060 Office: 4602 N Federal Hwy Fort Lauderdale FL 33308

HEFFNER, RICHARD LOUIS, banker; b. St. Louis, Apr. 9, 1933; s. Edward Louis and Esther (Herter) H.; A.B., Columbia, 1955; M.B.A. cum laude, U. Tenn., 1965; m. Charlotte Anne Maclellan, Sept. 2, 1961; children—Richard Louis, Thomas Maclellan. Asst. advt. mgr. Richardson-Merrell, Inc., N.Y.C., 1957-60; new products market mgr. Chattem Drug & Chem. Co., 1960-64; v.p. marketing, corp. planning Dorsey Corp., Chattanooga, 1964-69, v.p., asst. sec., 1970-73; dep. adminstr. Bus. and Def. Services Adminstrn., Dept. Commerce, Washington, 1969-70, mem. nat. marketing adv. com., 1971—; pres., chief exec. officer, dir. Chattanooga Glass Co., subsidiary Dorsey Corp., 1970-73; trustee Glass Container Industry Research Corp. U.S., 1971-73; exec. v.p., exec. com. Hamilton Bancshares, Inc., Chattanooga, 1973—. Mem. Nat. Def. Exec. Res., 1969—; vice chmn. Regional Export Expansion Council, 1971—. Mem. allocations com. Chattanooga United Fund, 1961-72; bd. dirs. Chattanooga Tb and Respiratory Diseases Assn., 1962—, pres., 1969-70; v.p. Chattanooga Allied Arts Fund, 1969-70; bd. dirs. Chattanooga Family Service Agy., Chattanooga Travelers Aid Soc., 1968-69, Jr. Achievement, 1971—, Chattanooga Symphony Assn., 1973—. Served to lt. USNR 1955-57. Mem. N.A.M. (marketing com. 1967-70), Nat. Alliance Businessmen (metro chmn. 1970-71), Chattanooga C. of C. (dir. 1971—), Sigma Alpha Epsilon. Presbyn. Rotarian. Clubs: Chattanooga Golf and Country, Chattanooga Tennis; Kenwood Country (Washington). Fairyland Country (Lookout Mountain). Home: 721 E Brow Rd Lookout Mountain TN 37350 Office: 701 Market St Chattanooga TN 37402

HEFLIN, HOWELL THOMAS, chief justice Supreme Ct. Ala.; b. Poulan, Ga., June 19, 1921; s. Marvin Rutledge and Louise D. (Strudwick) H.; A.B., Birmingham So. Coll., 1942; J.D., U. Ala., 1948; m. Elizabeth Ann Carmichael, Feb. 23, 1952; 1 son, Howell Thomas. Admitted to Ala. bar, 1948, practiced in Tuscumbia; now chief justice Supreme Ct. Ala. Dir. Meth. Pub. House, 1952-64; lectr. U. Ala., 1946-48; lectr. Florence State Tchrs. Coll., 1949-52. Mem. Ala. Edn. Commn., 1957-58; chmn. Colbert County A.R.C., 1950; Ala. field dir. Crusade for Children, 1948; pres. Ala. Com. Better Schs., 1958-59; chmn. Tuscumbia Bd. Edn., 1954-64; chmn. Ala. Tenure Commn., 1959-64; pres. U. Ala. Law Sch. Found., 1964-66; co-chmn. Nat. Conf. Christians and Jews, Tri-Cities area; chmn. Brotherhood Week. Served to maj. USMCR, 1942-46. Decorated Silver Star, Purple Heart; recipient Ala. Citizen of Yr. award Ala. Cable TV Assn., 1973; Outstanding Alumnus award U. Ala. and Birmingham So. Coll., 1973; Herbert Lincoln Harley award Am. Judicature Soc., 1973. Fellow Internat. Acad. of Law and Scis., Internat. Acad. Trial Lawyers, Internat. Soc. Barristers, Am. Coll. Trial Lawyers; mem. Ala. Law Inst. (v.p.), Am., Ala. (pres. 1965-66), Colbert County (past pres.) bar assns., Ala. Bar Found. (pres.), Am. Judicature Soc., Ala. Law Sch. Alumni Assn. (pres.), Ala. Plaintiff Lawyers Assn. (pres.), V.F.W., Am. Legion, 40 and 8, D.A.V., Third Marine Div. Assn., C. of C., Omicron Delta Kappa, Phi Delta Phi, Tau Kappa Alpha, Lambda Chi Alpha. Methodist. Home: 311 E 6th St Tuscumbra AL 35674 Office: Supreme Ct Bldg Montgomery AL 36101

HEFNER, JOE DENSON, ins. agy. exec.; b. Atlanta, Tex., Sept. 20, 1930; s. Byron Denson and Marcele (Johnson) H.; B.A., N. Tex. State U., 1954; m. Cecile Cariker, Apr. 30, 1954; children—Jerri Lynn, Julie Cecile, Debra Jo. Div. mgr. Continental Oil Co., Ft. Worth, 1954-63; pres. J.D. Hefner Assos., ins., Dallas, 1964—; chmn. bd. Nat. Trust Corp., financial planners, Dallas, 1971—; dir. Commonwealth Nat. Bank, Dallas. Vice pres. Tex. div. Am. Cancer Soc., 1971—. Served to capt. 49th Armored Div., AUS, 1961-63. Mem. Million Dollar Round Table (life, chmn. estate planning program), Nat., Dallas (dir. 1970—) assns. life underwriters, Assn. for Advanced Life Underwriters, Internat. Assn. Financial Counsellors, Nat. Assn. Securities Dealers, Dallas Estate Planning Council (dir.). Contbr. articles to profl. jours. Home: 7116 Stefani Dr Dallas TX 75225 Office: 4525 Lemmon Av Dallas TX 75219

HEFNER, STEPHEN FRANK, lawyer; b. Phillips, Tex., Jan. 31, 1942; s. Cooper Frank and Nina Mae (Bailey) H.; B.B.A., So. Meth. U., 1964, J.D., 1967; m. Susan Marye Pigott, Aug. 27, 1964. Admitted to Tex. bar, 1967, since practiced in Sherman; partner Nance, Caston, Hefner, Duncan, Green & Stagner, Sherman, 1968—. Sec., asst. treas. dir. Hale Mfg. Co., Inc. Sponsor, Key Club, 1970-73. Bd. dirs. Sherman Community Players, pres., 1971-72; bd. dirs. Sherman Boys Club, Sherman Mus. Arts. Mem. Am., Tex. bar assns., Am., Tex. trial lawyers assns., Beta Alpha Psi, Phi Delta Phi. Kiwanian. Home: 100 W Scott St Sherman TX 75090 Office: 421 N Crockett St Sherman TX 75090

HEFTER, LAURENCE ROY, lawyer; b. N.Y.C., Oct. 13, 1935; s. Charles S. and Rose (Postal) H.; B.M.E., Rensselaer Poly. Inst., 1957, M.S. in Mech. Engring., 1960; J.D. with honors, George Washington U., 1964; m. Jacqulyn Maureen Miller, June 13, 1957; children—Jeffrey Scott, Sue-Anne. Admitted to Va. bar, 1964, N.Y. State bar, 1967, D.C. bar, 1973; instr. Rensselaer Poly. Inst., Troy, N.Y., 1957-59; patent engr. Gen. Electric Co., Washington, 1959-63; sr. patent atty. Atlantic Research Corp., Alexandria, Va., 1963-66; asso. atty. Davis, Hoxie, Faithfull & Hapgood, N.Y.C., 1966-69; partner firm Ryder, McAulay & Hefter, N.Y.C., 1970-73; atty. firm Finnegan, Henderson, Farabow & Garrett, Washington, 1973—. Mem. Am., N.Y. State, D.C. bar assns., George Washington (founder, pres. 1963), Am. patent law assns., Order of Coif, Alpha Epsilon Pi. Home: 7405 Pinehurst Pkwy Chevy Chase MD 20015 Office: 1775 K St NW Washington DC 20006

HEGAR, EDWARD ANDREW, elec. engr.; b. Penelope, Tex., May 20, 1909; s. Frank and Anna (Turek) H.; B.S. in Elec. Engring., U. Tex., 1936; m. Bertha Carlton, May 30, 1934. Equipment engr. S.W. Bell Telephone Co., Dallas, 1941-43, 45-51, bldg. and equipment engr., Little Rock, 1951-64, equipment maintenance engr., 1964-74, ret., 1974; mem. tech. staff Bell Telephone Labs., N.Y.C., 1943-45. Registered profl. engr., Ark., Tex. Mem. I.E.E.E., Nat., Ark. socs. profl. engrs. Presbyn. Home: 207 McMillen Trail Little Rock AR 72207 Office: 1111 W Capitol Av Room 757 Little Rock AR 72203

HEGGEN, LLOYD MARLETTE, elec. contractor; b. Woodville, Wis., Mar. 22, 1916; s. Randall and Josephine (Tyerson) H.; B.S., Tex. Technol. Coll., 1938; m. Lilly Myrl Simmons, June 4, 1939; children—Bonny Carolyn (Mrs. Joseph Blake Winston, Jr.), Charlotte Anne (Mrs. Billy Gene Pemelton), Lloyd Allen, Paula Kay. With Abernathy & Plainview Southwestern Pub. Service (Tex.), 1938-41; pres. Heggen Electric Co., elec. contractors, Mercedes, Tex., 1946—. Bd. dirs. Hildago County for Mentally Retarded, 1951-58; adv. bd. Concordia Luth. Coll., Austin, 1959-67. Served with USNR, 1945. Mem. Asso. Ind. Elec. Contractors Am. (nat. dir. 1968—), I.E.E.E., Tex. Soc. Profl. Engrs. (1st v.p. 1964), Valley C. of C. Lutheran (elder 1974). Home and office: 1 1/4 E Hwy 83 PO Box 6868 Mercedes TX 78570

HEGSTROM, WILLIAM JEAN, ednl. adminstr.; b. Macomb, Ill., Oct. 21, 1923; s. Carl William and Thelma (Canavit) H.; student Western Ill. U., 1941-42; B. Sc., Rutgers U., 1949, Ed.M. 1952; M.A. Teaching, Purdue U., 1964; postgrad. U. Fla., 1961, Fla. Atlantic U., 1965-68; Ed.D., U. Miami, 1971; m. Grace Ann Paladino, May 3, 1944; children—Elizabeth Louise (Mrs. Edward Cook), William Jean II, Jean. Tchr. jr. high sch., South Plainfield, N.J., 1949-52, high sch., Bernardsville, N.J. 1952-54, Oak St. Sch., Bernard's Twp., N.J., 1954-55, high sch., Summit, N.J., 1955-58, jr. high sch., Delray Beach, Fla, 1958-65; chmn. math. dept. John I. Leonard High Sch., Lake Worth, Fla., 1965-68, dir. Palm Beach County research project, 1966-68; adj. prof. Fla. Atlantic U., 1965-69, asso. prof., 1969-70; counselor coordinator John Leonard Adult Center, Lake Worth, 1965-68; supr. research and evaluation Palm Beach County Sch. Bd., West Palm Beach, Fla., 1970—. Served with USAAF, 1942-46. Mem. Am. Assn. U. Profs., N.E.A., Nat. Council Tchrs. Math., Math. Assn. Am., Fla. Ednl. Research Assn., Fla. Assn. Suprs. Instrn., Am. Ednl. Research Assn., Assn. Supervision and Curriculum Devel., Phi Delta Kappa. Contbr. articles to profl. jours. Home: 231 Seacrest Circle Delray Beach FL 33444 Office: School Board of Palm Beach County West Palm Beach FL 33104

HEGWOOD, DONALD AUGUSTINE, educator; b. Richton, Miss., Aug. 28, 1931; s. Clinton Patrick and Mae Neil (Munn) H.; B.S., Miss. State Coll., 1954; M.S., Miss. State U., 1959; Ph.D., La. State U., 1965; m. Frances Anne Burke, Aug. 17, 1957; children—Donald Augustine, David Burke, Christopher Lee. Vegetable research Coastal Plain Expt. Sta., Tifton, Ga., 1959-62; horticulture research La. State U., Baton Rouge, 1965-67; extension horticulturist U. Ga. Coop. Extension Service, Athens, 1967-70; vegetable research Ga. Coastal Plain Expf. Sta., Tifton, 1970-72; research, tchr. dept. horticulture U. Ga., Athens, 1972—. Served with AUS, 1954-56. Recipient Grant, U.S. Dept. Agr., 1965. Mem. Am. Soc. Hort. Sci. (chmn. vegetable crops sect. So. region 1972), Assn. So. Agr. Workers, Am. Soc.

Agronomy, Soil Sci. Soc. Am., Am. Bot. Soc., Council Soil Testing and Plant Analysis, Crop Sci. Soc. Am., Internat. Soc. Hort. Sci. Mem. editorial bd. Communications in Soil Sci. and Plant Analysis, 1972—. Home: 245 Shady Grove Dr Athens GA 30601

HEIDBRINK, VIRGIL EUGENE, paper co. exec.; b. Ireton, Ia., Dec. 4, 1925; s. Edward H. and Luella (Dittmer) H.; A.B., U.S.D., 1949; B.F.T., Am. Inst. Fgn. Trade, 1950; postgrad. Hunter Coll., 1952-53, Coll. City N.Y., 1953-54, N.Y. U. Grad. Sch. Bus., 1954-56. Export asst. fgn. trade, various firms, N.Y.C., 1951-56; with Hammermill Paper Co., Erie, Pa., 1956, Chgo., 1956-57, dist. sales mgr. S.W. ty., Dallas, 1958—. Del. Tex. Republican Conv., 1964, 70, 72. Served with Med. Dept., AUS, 1944-46, 50-51. Decorated Bronze Star. Mem. Dallas Advt. League, Phi Beta Kappa. Lutheran. Club: Toastmasters (pres. 1965, dist. gov, 1968-69). Home: 2623 Hudnall St Dallas TX 75235 Office: 6434 Maple Av Suite 400 Dallas TX 75235

HEIDORN, DONALD RICHARD, ednl. adminstr.; b. South Solon, O., Feb. 24, 1933; s. William Earl and Myrtle Ruth (Frederick) H.; B.S., Florence State U., 1960; M.A., U. Ala., 1964; m. Lucy Marie Ryan, Apr. 16, 1957; 1 son, David Earl. Tchr., coach Carbon Hill (Ala.) Bd. Edn., 1960-62; tchr., coach Muscle Shoals, (Ala.) Bd. Edn., 1962-64, coach, asst. prin., 1964-67, prin. high sch., 1967-70, supt. edn., 1970—. Bd. dirs. Jr. Achievement, YMCA, Sheffield-Tuscumbia Credit Union. Served with USNR, 1952-56. Mem. Am., Ala. assns. sch. adminstrs., N.E.A., Ala., Muscle Shoals edn. assns., So. Assn. Colls. and Schs., Florence State U. (pres. 1968), U. Ala. alumni assns., Muscle Shoals Bus. and Profl. Assn. (pres. 1971), Kappa Phi Kappa. Methodist. Lion (1st v.p. 1971). Club: Sportsmans (pres. 1968) (Florence State U.). Home: 1510 Fordsway Muscle Shoals AL 35660 Office: Avalon Av Muscle Shoals AL 35660

HEILBRON, EDWARD HENRY, sch. adminstr.; b. Chgo., July 25, 1916; s. Emil Henry and Ella (Walther) H.; A.B., Bradley U., 1938; J.D., Northwestern U., 1941; m. Florence Charlotte Olson, May 25, 1946. Admitted to Ill. bar, 1942; asst. v.p. Keystone Steel & Wire Co., Peoria, Ill., 1946-51; mgr. Harbor Club, Fort Lauderdale, Fla., 1952-60; dir. admissions Upper Sch., v.p. Pine Crest Prep. Sch., Fort Lauderdale, 1960—. Sec. bd. Broward County chpt. United Fund, 1970-71. Served to col. AUS, 1942-46. Decorated Army Commendation ribbon. Mem. Assn. Ind. Schs. Fla. (pres.), Fla. Assn. Acad. Non-Pub. Schs. (dir.), Exec. Assn. Fort Lauderdale (past dir.). Rotarian. Home: 2900 NE 33d Ct Fort Lauderdale FL 33306 Office: 1501 NE 62d St Fort Lauderdale FL 33308

HEILING, FRANK JOSEPH, r.r. exec.; b. Robstown, Tex., Mar. 28, 1914; s. Martin and Anna (Heisenberger) H.; student Johnson Bible Coll., Kimberlin Heights, Tenn.; m. Margaret M. Magruder, Jan. 17, 1936. Spl. investigator Texas City disaster, 1947; with Texas City Terminal Ry. Co., 1947—, pres., gen. mgr., 1954-56, now dir.; v.p. indsl. devel. M-K-T. R.R., 1956-59, v.p. sales and service, 1959—, also supr. pub. relations and advt., 1971—; officer and/or dir. various affiliated railroads; v.p., dir. San Antonio Belt & Terminal Co., Katy Transp. Co., Donland Devel. Co.; v.p. Southwestern States Mgmt. Co.; dir. Texas City Terminal Railway Co., Galveston, Houston & Henderson R.R. Co. Security rep., orgn. UN, San Francisco, 1945. Mem. Nat. Def. Transp. Assn., Nat. Freight Traffic Assn., Transp. Assn. Am., Am. Soc. Traffic and Transp., Traffic Clubs Internat. Clubs: Dallas Traffic, St. Louis Traffic, Press, City (Dallas), Advertising, San Antonio Transp. Home: 4015 Santa Barbara Dr Dallas TX 75214 Office: 701 Commerce St Dallas TX 75202

HEILMAN, EARL BRUCE, univ. pres.; b. La Grange, Ky., July 16, 1926; s. Earl Bernard and Nellie (Sanders) H.; diploma Campbellsville Jr. Coll., 1948; B.S., Peabody Coll., 1950, M.A., 1951, Ph.D., 1961; postgrad. U. Tenn., 1951-52, U. Omaha, summers 1953, 55, U. Ky., summers 1954, 56; LL.D., Wake Forest U., 1967; H.H.D., Campbell Coll., 1971; m. Betty June Dobbins, Aug. 27, 1948; children—Bobbie Lynn, Nancy Jo, Terry Lee, Sandra June, Timothy Bruce. Instr. bus. Peabody Coll., Nashville, 1950-51, bursar, 1957-60, adminstrv. v.p., 1963-66; instr. accounting Belmont Coll., Nashville, 1951-52; auditor Albert Maloney Co., Nashville, 1951-52; asst. prof. accounting, bus. mgr. Ky. Wesleyan Coll., Owensboro, 1952-54; treas. Georgetown (Ky.) Coll., 1954-57; treas. housing project City of Louisville, 1955-57; coordinator higher edn. and spl. schs. State of Tenn., Nashville, 1960-61; v.p. dean Ky. So. Coll., Louisville, 1961-63; pres. Meredith Coll., Raleigh, N.C., 1966-71, U. Richmond (Va.), 1971—. Dir., Central Nat. Bank. Cons. instl. studies in edn. and adminstrn., 1954—; dir., cons. long range planning confs. Fund for Advancement Edn., 1960— cons. Acad. Ednl. Devel., 1966—. Mem. steering com. Baptist Ednl. Study Task. Bd. advisers Bapt. Hosp. Sch. Nursing, 1959-60, 64—; mem. adv. bd. Richmond Ballet; bd. dirs. Bill Wilkerson Speech, Hearing Center, Richmond Symphony, United Givers Fund. Served with USMCR, 1944-47. Recipient Merit award Owensboro Jr. C. of C., 1953, Service award Agrl. and Industry U. Nashville, 1961. Mem. Nat. Fedn. Bus. Officers, Nat. Fedn. Bus. Officers Cons. Service, So. Assn. Colls. for Women (pres. 1970), Tenn. Edn. Assn., Ky. Ednl. Buyers Assn., Ky. Assn. Acad. Deans, Peabody Alumni Assn. (exec. com.), Nat., So. assns. colls. and univs. bus. officers, N.C. Assn. Colls. and Univs. (pres.-elect), Internat. Platform Assn., Richmond C. of C. (dir.), Richmond Council Year 2000, Phi Beta Kappa, Pi Omega Pi, Kappa Phi Kappa, Kappa Delta Pi, Omicron Delta Kappa, Beta Gamma Sigma, Lambda Chi Alpha, Delta Pi Epsilon. Democrat. Baptist (deacon). Rotarian. Club: Downtown (Richmond). Author: (with others) Sixty College Study, 1954. Contbr. articles to profl. publs. Developer uniform financial accounting and reporting program for Tenn. instns. higher edn. Home: 7000 River Rd Richmond VA 23229

HEIMLICH, FREDERICK JUNIOR, psychologist; b. Lafayette, Ind., Sept. 29, 1921; s. Fred J. and Esther (Lewis) H.; B.S., Purdue U., 1948, M.S., 1950, Ph.D., 1952; m. Mary M. Ryan, June 21, 1947; children—Michael E., David A., Christopher P., Barbara E.; m. 2d, Margaret Ann Becker, June 22, 1968; 1 dau., Laura R. Asst. chief psychology service VA Hosp., Marion, Ind., 1952-54; chief psychologist Beatty Hosp., Westville, Ind., 1954-57; chief psychologist Orange County Guidance Clinic, Orlando, Fla., 1957-61; pvt. practice psychology, Orlando, 1958-68; dir. adult services Brevard County Mental Health Center, Rockledge, Fla., 1968—. Served with USCGR, 1942-46. Mem. Am., Fla. psychol. assns. Home: 1716 Golfview Dr Rockledge FL 32955 Office: 1770 Cedar St Rockledge FL 32955

HEIMLICH, SETH SCHAFER, ednl. adminstr.; b. Florence, S.C., Sept. 24, 1938; s. Chester S. and Bernice (Schafer) H.; A.S., Marion Inst., 1957; B.S., Clemson U., 1959, M.S., 1970; m. Doreen (Feibusch), May 24, 1966; children—Larissa Andrea, Marc Gabriel. Commd. 2d lt. Med. Service Corps, U.S. Army, 1959, advanced through ranks to maj., 1965; dir. adult edn., Pickens County Six Mile, (S.C.), 1970—. Bd. dirs. Pickens County Literacy Assn., Clemson Art Cons.; del. to S.C. White House Conf. on Aging. Mem. Alpha Kappa Chi. Address: 110 Folger St Clemson SC 29631

HEIMSATH, CHARLES HERMAN IV, educator; b. New Haven, July 19, 1928; s. Charles Herman and Star (McDaniel) H.; B.A., Yale, 1950, Ph.D., 1957; M.Internat. Affairs, Columbia, 1952; m. Surjit Mansingh, Apr. 8, 1964; children—Arjun, Kabir; children by previous marriage—Charles V., Peter R. Instr. Yale, 1956-59; mem. faculty Am. U., Washington, 1959—, prof. South Asian studies, 1968—; resident dir. Ednl. Resources Center, New Delhi, India, 1971-73. Rockefeller Found. fellow, India, 1959-60. Mem. Assn. Asian Studies. Author: Indian Nationalism and Hindu Social Reform, 1964; (with Surjit (Mansingh) A Diplomatic History of Modern India, 1971. Home: 1408 Manchester Lane NW Washington DC 20011

HEINDL, LEOPOLD ALEXANDER, assn. exec.; b. Leningrad, USSR, Oct. 10, 1916 (parents Am. citizens); s. Alexander Joseph and Olga Ilinishna (Grossman) H.; student U. Cal. at Berkeley, 1932-36, A.B., at Los Angeles, 1938; Ph.D., U. Ariz., 1958. Geologist, Standard Oil Cal., Cal., Tex., Miss., 1938-40; various mining and constrn. work, 1940-41; chief geologist Ariz. Land Dept., Phoenix, 1948-51; geologist, hydrologist U.S. Geol. Survey, Tucson, 1951-60, Washington, 1960-66; exec. sec. U.S. nat. com. for internat. hydrological decade Nat. Acad. Sci./NRC, Washington, 1966—. Served with F.A., AUS, 1941-48. Decorated Purple Heart. Fellow Geol. Soc. Am.; mem. A.A.A.S., Am. Geophys. Soc. (exec. com. hydrology 1969—), Am. Water Resources Assn. (pres. sect. 1970-71, chmn. conf. planning com. 1973-75), Internat. Water Resources Assn. (chmn. nat. coms. com. 1972—), Am. Inst. Profl. Geologists (pres. Va. sect. 1973), Sigma Xi. Author: The Water We Live By, 1971. Home: 3577 N Powhatan St Arlington VA 22213 Office: 2101 Constitution Av NW Washington DC 20418

HEINEMAN, ALBERT FREDERICK, JR., banker; b. Pitts., Sept. 25, 1911; s. Albert Frederick and Lena Martha (McCartney) H.; B.S., U. Pitts., 1939; m. Eleanor Hazlehurst, May 14, 1936; B.S., U. Pitts., 1939; m. Eleanor Hazlehurst, May 14, 1936; children—Albert Frederick III, Neil H., Robert P., Abby M. (Mrs. Edward Robert Griesmeyer). Trust investment officer Union Nat. Bank, Pitts., 1929-64; v.p., trust investment officer Bank of Commonwealth, 1965-67; v.p., trust investment officer Nat. Bank of Sarasota, Fla., 1968—; dir. Elsbeth Corp. Served to col. USAAF, 1941-46; PTO. Decorated Air Force Commendation medal. Recipient Wright Bros. award for contbn. to aviation, 1966. Mem. Financial Analysts Soc., Am. Inst. Banking, Mil. Order World Wars, Aero Club Pitts., Alpha Kappa Psi. Republican. Presbyn. Club: Field (Sarasota). Home: 2731 Riverbluff Ct Sarasota FL 33581 Office: PO Box 5427 Sarasota FL 33579

HEINEY, ELVIE PERSHING, real estate broker; b. Hartshorn, Mo., Feb. 26, 1918; s. William Horace and Rosella Josephine (Treat) H.; student pub. schs.; m. Alice Jones, Mar. 1, 1952. Asst. foreman Norris Stamping and Mfg., Los Angeles, 1940-42; served with U.S. Army, 1942-58, ret., 1958; farmer, nr. Fayetteville, Ark., 1958-60; owner Heiney Realty Co., Fayetteville, 1962—. Served with USN, 1936-40. Decorated Purple Heart. Mem. Nat. Assn. Realtors, Ark. Assn. Realtors, Fayetteville Bd. Realtors (pres. 1966, dir. 1967-69), N.W. Ark. Gem and Mineral Soc. Address: Rural Route 7 Hwy 16E Fayetteville AR 72701

HEINL, ROBERT DEBS, JR., ret. marine corps officer, writer; b. N.Y.C., Aug. 12, 1916; s. Robert Debs and Helen (Corbin) H.; grad. St. Albans Sch., Washington, 1933, A.B. with Orations (cum laude), Yale, 1937; m. Nancy Gordon Wright, Sept. 23, 1939; children—Pamela Gordon (Mrs. John R. Burdick), Michael Charles Corbin. Commd. 2d lt. USMC, 1937, advanced through grades to col.; service at Pearl Harbor during Japanese attack, 1941, Wake Island relief expn., 1941, South Pacific, 1942, Iwo Jima, 1945, occupation of Japan, 1945, North China, 1946; dir. marine corps history, 1946-49; comdr. East Coast Islands, also served with 1st Marine div., Korea, 1952-53; later chief mil. assistance adv. group and U.S. Naval Mission, Port-au-Prince, Haiti, 1958-63; ret. 1964; cons. to U.S. Navy on long-range gun systems, 1967-68; def. corr. Detroit News, Washington bur., 1968—. Mem. Inst. for Strategic Studies. Decorated Legion of Merit with combat V, Bronze Star medal with combat V; recipient Alfred Thayer Mahan award, 1968; award of merit U.S. Naval Inst., 1968. Episcopalian. Clubs: Army and Navy; Carabao; N.Y. Yacht, Yale (N.Y.C.); American (London); Mory's; Nat. Press. Author: The Defense of Wake, 1947, Marines at Midway, 1948; The Marshalls: Increasing the Tempo, 1953; The Marine Officer's Guide, 1956, 3d edit., 1967; Soldiers of the Sea, 1962; Dictionary of Military and Naval Quotations, 1966; Victory at High Tide, 1967; Handbook for Marine NCO'S, 1970. Contbr. to Ency. Brit., Dictionary Am. Biography, Nat. Geog., Am. Heritage, Atlantic Monthly, Reporter, New Republic, Washington Post, and profl. jours. Home: 2400 California St NW Washington DC 20008 Office: 511 Nat Press Bldg Washington DC 20004

HEINZIG, FLOYD EARL, air force officer; b. Prague, Okla., Aug. 10, 1930; s. F.A. and Pearle (Raley) H.; B.S. in E.E., U. Okla., 1961; postgrad. Ohio State U., 1964, Indsl. Coll. Armed Forces, 1972; m. Alyne B. Craig, Mar. 1, 1952; children—Sandra, Sharon, Keith. Commd. 2d lt. USAF, 1951, advanced through grades to col., 1971; staff devel. engr. Hdqrs., Washington, 1968-71, dir. technology and devel. plans, aerospace, space and missile systems, Los Angeles, 1972—. Decorated Silver Star (2), D.F.C. (6). Mem. Armed Forces Communications and Electronics Assn. (dir. 1973-74), Air Force Assn., Sigma Tau, Eta Kappa Nu. Registered profl. engr., Okla. Home: Box 251 Route 1 Shawnee OK 74801 Office: SAMSO/XOTA PO Box 92960 Worldway Postal Center Los Angeles CA 90009

HEISER, RONALD ARTHUR, city govt. ofcl.; b. St. Louis, Sept. 24, 1929; s. Arthur John and Velma (Spore) H.; B.S., U. Houston, 1953, B.Arch., 1954; m. Mary Ann Mullins, June 12, 1953; children—Rhonda Ann, Sharon Lee, James Arthur. With City Planning Dept., Houston, 1952—, sr. planner, 1958-62, asst. dir., 1962—, also acting dir., 1964. Served with S.C., AUS, 1954-56. Mem. Am. Pub. Works Assn., City Planners Assn. Tex. (v.p. 1967), U. Houston Alumni Assn. Methodist. Office: PO Box 1562 Houston TX 77001

HEISLER, JOSEPH PATRICK, educator; b. Decatur, Ill., Aug. 9, 1934; s. Joseph Bernard and Helen Agnes (Griffin) H.; B.S., St. Edward's U., 1956; M.S., U. Notre Dame, 1959; Ph.D., U. Mich., 1965. Instr. Trinity High Sch., Chgo., 1956-58, Curley High Sch., Miami, Fla., 1959-61, St. Edward's High Sch., Austin, Tex., 1961-62; mem. faculty St. Edwards U., Austin, 1965—, asso. prof. math., 1968-72, prof., 1972—. Recipient NSF grants. Mem. Math. Assn. Am. Home: 3001 S Congress St Austin TX 78704 Office: Dept Math St Edwards Univ Austin TX 78704

HEITMAN, LYNN BYRON, electronic engr.; b. Dallas, Nov. 19, 1945; s. Marshall Henry and Edna Earl (Keesee) H.; B.S. (Petroleum Engrs. Club scholar, Atlantic Richfield Co. scholar), U. Tex., 1969; M.S., So. Meth. U., 1973; m. Deborah Louise Sutherland, Oct. 24, 1969. Technician, Tex. Instruments, Inc., Dallas, 1965-68, engr., 1969-71, project engr., service group, 1972—. Mem. I.E.E.E., Eta Kappa Nu, Tau Beta Pi (charter). Patentee in field. Home: 13545 Willow Bend Dallas TX 75240 Office: PO Box 5621 MS 937 Dallas TX 75222

HEIZER, KENNETH WENDELL, educator; b. Iola, Tex., Nov. 21, 1923; s. Luthern Marvin and Mary Kate (McClendon) H.; student North Tex. Agr. Coll., 1947-48; student John Tarelton Agr. Coll., 1948-49; B.S., So. Meth. U., 1950, M.S., 1951; Ph.D., U. Ill., 1962; m. Carolyn Leigh Harris, Mar. 19, 1960; children—Joyce LaNell, Kathrine Leigh, Stephen Dee, Angla Kay. Engr. radio sta. KRBA, Lufkin, Tex., 1942-43; faculty So. Meth. U., Dallas, 1951—, prof. elec. engring., 1962—, chmn. system engring. dept., 1969-72. Bd. dirs. Dallas Eye Found. Served with AUS, 1943-46. Patentee. Home: 6119 Brandeis St Dallas TX 75214

HEIZER, LLOYD ORVELL, elec. engr.; b. Richards, Tex., July 27, 1922; s. Luther Marvin and Mary Katherine (McClendon) H.; B.S. in E.E., Brown U., 1946; m. Martha Lillian Haltom, Aug. 7, 1948; children—Diana Kay (Mrs. Barry Lanier), Paul David, Mary Ellen. Engr., Dallas Power & Light Co., 1946-70, div. head, 1970—. Served with USNR, 1942-45. Registered profl. engr., Tex. Mem. Tex. Soc. Profl. Engrs., Home: 525 Meade Heath Dallas TX 75232 Office: 1506 Commerce St Dallas TX 75201

HEJTMANCIK, MILTON RUDOLPH, physician, educator; b. Caldwell Tex., Sept. 27, 1919; s. Rudolph Joseph and Millie (Jurcak) H.; B.A., U. Tex., 1939, M.D., 1943;; m. Myrtle Lou Erwin, Aug. 21, 1943; children—Kelly Erwin, Milton Rudolph, Peggy Lou. Resident internal medicine U. Tex., 1946-49, instr. internal medicine 1949-51, asst. prof. internal medicine, 1951-54, asso. prof. internal medicine, 1954-65, prof. internal medicine, 1965—, dir. heart clinic, 1949—, dir. heart station, 1965—; chief staff John Sealy Hosp., 1957-58. Served from 1st lt. to capt., M.C., AUS, 1944-46, ETO. Diplomate in cardiovascular diseases Am. Bd. Internal Medicine. Fellow A.C.P., Am. College Chest Physicians, Am. Coll. Cardiology; mem. Am. (fellow council clinical cardiology), Tex. (chmn, cardiac clinics com. 1956—, v.p., 1958), Galveston Dist. (pres. 1956) heart assns., A.M.A., Am. Fedn. Clin. Research, A.A.A.S., Tex. Acad. Internal Medicine (gov. 1971-73), Tex. Club Cardiology (pres. 1972-73), Phi Beta Kappa, Sigma XI, Alpha Omega Alpha, Mu Delta. Contbr. numerous papers on cardiovascular disease to profl. jours. Home: 118 Marlin St Galveston TX 77550 Office: 816 Strand St Galveston TX 77550

HELD, EDWARD CARLISLE, JR., oil co. exec.; b. Okmulgee, Okla., Nov. 15, 1925; s. Edward Carlisle and Caroline (Mills) H.; B.S. in Chem. Engring., U. Okla., 1950; m. Latita Ann Wittmer, June 17, 1944; children—Steven Edward, John David, Jennifer (Mrs. Steven Allan Knode), Karen Louise. Refinery product blend chemist Phillips Petroleum Co., Kansas City, Kan., 1950-53, process evaluation supr. rocket fuels div., Waco, Tex., 1954-58, tech. service engr. plastics, Bartlesville, Okla., 1958-64, supr. new plastic fabrication techniques, 1964-68, mgmt. analyst exec. dept., 1969—. Vice chmn. profl. devel. and staffing Bartlesville Edn. Council, 1972. Served with AUS, 1943-46. Registered profl. engr., Okla. Mem. Soc. Plastics Engrs. Presbyn. Contbr. articles to profl. jours. Patentee in field. Home: 2200 Parkway Dr Bartlesville OK 74003 Office: Phillips Petroleum Co Bartlesville OK 74004

HELFFERICH, FRIEDRICH G.(EORG), chemist; b. Berlin, Germany, Aug. 1, 1922; s. Karl Theodor and Anna Clara Johanna (Von Siemens) H.; Vordiplom, U. Hamburg (Germany), 1949, Diploma Chemistry, 1952; Dr. Rer. Nat., U. Goettingen (Germany), 1955; m. Barbara Schlubach, July 1947 (div.); children—Christiane (Mrs. Ulrich Wiese), Cornelia; m. Hana M. Konecna, Feb. 24, 1961; 1 dau., Stefanie. Came to U.S., 1956, naturalized, 1964. Research asst. Max-Planck Inst. Physikalische Chemie, 1951-56; scholar, research asst. Mass. Inst. Tech., 1954; research asst. Cal. Inst. Tech., 1956-58; with Shell Devel. Co., Emeryville and Houston, 1958—, supr., 1965-71, sr. research asso., 1971-72, sr. staff research chemist, 1972—. Vis. scholar Max-Planck Inst. Physikalische Chemie, 1958; lectr. U. Cal. at Berkeley, 1961-62. Chmn. Gordon Research Conf. on Ion Exchange, 1967; chmn. subcom. on terminology in ion exchange NRC, 1963-67. Served with German Army, 1941-45. Fulbright scholar, 1954; recipient Certificate of Merit, Am. Chem. Soc., 1968. Fellow Am. Inst. Chemists; mem. N.Y. Acad. Scis. Club: Commonwealth (San Francisco). Author: Ionenaustauscher, 1958; Ion Exchange, 1962; (with G. Klein) Multicomponent Chromatography, 1970. Patentee in field. Home: 327 Knipp Rd Houston TX 77024 Office: Bellaire Research Center PO Box 481 Houston TX 77001

HELLAND, GEORGE ARCHIBALD, JR., valve and oil tool mfg. co. exec.; b. San Antonio, Nov. 28, 1937; s. George Archibald and Ruth (Gorman) H.; B.S., U. Tex., 1959; M.B.A. with distinction, Harvard, 1961; m. Josephine Howell, June 9, 1962; children—Jane Elizabeth, Thomas Gorman. With Cameron Iron Works, Inc., Houston, 1961—, asst. sales mgr., 1963, dist. sales mgr., 1964, dist. sales mgr., U.K., Africa, 1965, product mgr., 1966, plant mgr., Leeds, Eng., 1967, mgr. oil tool products, 1968, v.p., 1969—. Recipient Spoke award Houston Jr. C. of C., 1962, Five Outstanding Young Texans award Tex. Jr. C. of C., 1972; named Outstanding Young Houstonian, Houston Jr. C. of C., 1972. Registered profl. engr., Tex. Mem. Am. Inst. Mining, Metall. and Petroleum Engrs., Am. Soc. M.E., Am. Petroleum Inst., Inst. Gas. Engrs. (U.K.), Tex. Soc. Profl. Engrs., Am. Wellhead Equipment Assn. (pres. 1967), Houston C. of C., Tau Beta Pi, Phi Eta Sigma, Pi Tau Sigma, Sigma Nu, Friars Soc. Presbyn. Home: 5385 Sugar Hill Houston TX 77027 Office: PO Box 1212 Houston TX 77001

HELLEN, JAMES ALBERT, clergyman; b. Meridian, Miss., Dec. 22, 1926; s. G.T. and Lela Elizabeth (Pearce) H.; B.C.S., Southeastern U., 1950; student Transylvania U., 1951-53; B.A., Tex. Christian U., 1956, M.Div., 1959; m. Jean Anderson, Nov. 9, 1947; children—James Albert, Jeffrey Alan, Carye Jean. With F.B.I., Washington, 1946-50; ordained to ministry Christian Ch., 1959; minister Brookhollow Ch., Abilene, Tex., 1958-60, 1st Ch., Pasadena, Tex., 1961-68, Bethesda Ch., Chevy Chase, Md., 1968-70, 1st Ch., Deland, Fla., 1970—. Chmn. ch. devel. dept. Gulf Coast Area Christian Chs., Houston, 1963-68; chmn. local arrangements Tex. Conv., Houston, 1964-65; mem. commn. on ministry Fla. Christian Chs. Dir. Pasadena Salvation Army, 1962-68; mem. Volusia County Mental Health Assn.; dir. Volusia County A.R.C., Deland Neighborhood Center; dir. Retarded Children's Sch., Abilene, Tex., 1958-60; chmn. bd. of Medistat-Meditrix Assn. of So. Hosp. and Clinic (Pasadena). Served with USNR, 1944-46; PTO. Mem. Am. Legion, V.F.W. Democrat. Home: 2109 E New York Av Deland FL 32720 Office: 105 W Wisconsin Av Deland FL 32720

HELLER, FRANK ALBERT, JR., city ofcl.; b. Louisville, Nov. 6, 1931; s. Frank Albert and Adeline E. (Traband) H.; B.S., U. Louisville, 1953; m. Sue Ann Baker, July 18, 1953; children—Frank Albert III, Susan, Lee. Sr. accountant E.A. Bowden, C.P.A., Louisville, 1955-62; self-employed accountant, Louisville, 1962-68; gen. partner Cecil & Heller, C.P.A.'s, Louisville, 1968—; budget officer, asst. dir. finance, acting chief accountant Dept. Pub. Finance, City of Louisville, 1962-67, dir. finance, 1967—. Bd. mgrs. St. Matthews YMCA; bd. dirs. Louisville Meml. Hosp. Served with USNR, 1953-55; now lt. comdr. Res. C.P.A., Ky. Mem. Am. Inst. C.P.A.'s, Ky. Soc. C.P.A.'s (chmn. com. local govtl. accounting and auditing 1969-70), Nat. Municipal Finance Officers Assn., Municipal Finance Officers Assn. Ky. (state chmn. 1970—), Nat. League Cities (mem. com. on revenue and finance 1969-71), Nat. Assn. Accountants, Navy League U.S. (Louisville sec. 1969), Municipal Treas. Assn. U.S., Shelby County Fish and Game Protective Assn., Louisville Police Officers Assn.

(hon.), Frat. Order Police (hon.). Home: 1127 Ridge Line Dr Louisville KY 40207 Office: City Hall Annex Louisville KY 40202 also 3415 Bardstown Rd Louisville KY 40218

HELLER, GERALD, drug store exec.; b. St. Louis, Aug. 31, 1937; s. Isadore and Ida Mae (Ludmeyer) H.; B.S., Okla. U., 1959; m. Sharon Lou Bodker, Apr. 19, 1960; children—Gregg Lorn, Tracey Jo, Scott Devin. Pharmacist, asst. mgr. Katz Drug Co., Kansas City, Mo., 1959-60; v.p., gen. mgr. B, B, & B, Inc., Oertles Drug Dept., Tulsa, Okla., 1960-73, Lud, Inc., Am. Mutual Co. Drug Dept., Oklahoma City, 1961-69, May's Drug Tulsa, Okla., 1972—; pres. Med-X Corp., 1967-71; pres. May's Drug Stores, Inc., 1974—, also dir.; dir. Rosalie Realty, Heller Realty, Hungry Lion Milw. Mem. Okla. Pharm. Assn. Democrat. Jewish religion (trustee temple 1971-73). Club: Summit (Tulsa). Home: 2647 E 38th St Tulsa OK 74105 Office: 4948 E 49th St Tulsa OK 74135

HELLER, MAX MOSES, city ofcl.; b. Vienna, Austria, May 28; s. Israel and Leah (Hirschl) H.; grad. high sch.; m. Trude Schonthal, Aug. 2, 1942; children—Francie (Mrs. Richard Huruitz), Susan (Mrs. Edward Moses), Steven Neil. Came to U.S., 1938, naturalized, 1944. Gen. mgr. Piedmont Shirt Co., 1938-45; pres., Maxon Shirt Co., 1946-68; pres. Trumax, Inc., from 1952; dir. First Piedmont Bank & Trust Co.; mem. city council, Greenville, S.C., 1969-71, mayor, 1971—. Mem. adv. council Furman U.; chmn. St. Francis Hosp., chmn. Greenville Housing Found., chmn. Gov.'s Com. on Housing; mem. Gov.'s Com. on Child Care. Bd. dirs. United Fund, Cerebral Palsy, Nat. Conf. Christian and Jews, Symphony Family Services. Named Man of Year, Nat. Council Jewish Women, 1971, S.C. and N.C. B'nai B'rith, 1972; recipient Freedom award D.A.R., 1973. Jewish religion (pres. congregation). Kiwanian; mem. B'nai B'rith. Home: 36 Pinehurst Dr Greenville SC 29609 Office: 340 N Main St Greenville SC 29601

HELLER, PEARL BAILIE (MRS. RAYMOND J. HELLER), manpower cons.; b. Turtle Creek, Pa., Aug. 12, 1918; d. John Langfitt and Hannah (Boord) Bailie; B.S., Columbia, 1949, M.A., 1950; R.N., Mt. Sinai Hosp., N.Y.C., 1943; m. Raymond J. Heller, Apr. 9, 1955. Supr. surg. wards Mt. Sinai Hosp., 1946-48; rehab. counselor Queensboro (N.Y.) Tb and Health Assn., 1950-54; program dir. Hartman Area Neighborhood Centers Assn., Houston, 1954-63, asst. to city program dir., 1963-67; now pvt. practice as manpower cons., program specialist; instr. creative writing St. Luke's Sch. Continuing Edn. Bd. dirs., treas. Neighborhood Ednl. Center. Mem. Nat. Assn. U. Women (dir., chmn. pub. information com.), Nat. Assn. Social Workers, Acad. Certified Social Workers. Author: An Outreach Demonstration, 1967; (with Malcolm S. Host) Day Care Administration, 1971. Home: 310 Stratford St Houston TX 77006

HELLER, ROBERT ANDREW, educator; b. Budapest, Hungary, Feb. 12, 1928; s. Jeno and Sara (Buzasi) H.; B.S., Columbia, 1951, M.S., 1953, Ph.D., 1958; m. Agnes Sekely, Aug. 21, 1954; children—James L., Thomas G. Research asst. dept. civil engring. Columbia, 1948-58, asst. prof., 1958-63, asso. prof., 1963-66, dep. dir. Inst. Fatigue and Reliability, 1966-67; prof. dept. engring. sci. and mechanics Va. Poly. Inst. and State U., Blacksburg, 1967—. Dir. research projects Armed Services, NASA, NSF, 1967—. NSF grantee, 1966-74. Mem. Am. Soc. Testing Materials (nat. chmn. com. on statis. methods in fatigue 1965—), Am. Inst. Aeros. and Astronautics (pres. Blue Ridge sect. 1973), Soc. Exptl. Stress Analysis, Sigma Xi. Author: (with M. Salvadori) Structure in Architecture, 1963; films Mechanics of Meterials, 1969; A World of Structure, 1973; Strength of Materials Laboratory, 1974. Editor: Am. Soc. Testing Materials Handbook, 1974. Home: 412 Stonegate Dr Blacksburg VA 24060

HELLIER, THOMAS ROBERT, JR., educator; b. Fort Pierce, Fla., Dec. 24, 1928; s. Thomas Robert and Sybil (Harmon) H.; B.A. in Edn. with honors, U. Fla., 1955, M.S., 1957; Ph.D., U. Tex. at Austin, 1961; m. Evelyn Marie Farris, June 8, 1952; children—Clark Thomas, Lisa Marie, Jana Ruth. Research scientist U. Tex. Marine Sci. Inst., Port Aransas, Tex., 1957-59; mem. faculty dept. biology U. Tex. at Arlington, 1960—, asso. prof., 1966-73, prof., 1973—. Cons. aquatic ecology. Mem. parks, open space com. N.Central Tex. Council Govts., 1970—; sec. Civitan Club, Arlington, 1963-65; active Longhorn council Boy Scouts Am., 1961—. Served with USAAF, 1948-52. Recipient Silver Beaver award Boy Scouts Am., 1970; grants Indsl. Generating Co., 1971-72, Army C.E., 1971-72, Tex. Electric Service Co., 1970—. Fellow Tex. Acad. Scis.; mem. Am. Assn. U. Profs. (v.p.), Am. Soc. Limnology and Oceanography, Am. Soc. Ichthyologists and Herpetologists, Am. Fisheries Soc., Ecol. Soc. Am., Tex. Water Conservation Assn., Sigma Xi. Contbr. profl. jours. Home: 1606 W Lovers Lane Arlington TX 76013

HELLIWELL, PAUL LIONEL EDWARD, lawyer; b. Bklyn., Sept. 17, 1914; s. L. H. and Nola C. (Harless) H.; A.B., U. Fla., 1937, J.D., 1939; m. Marjoria Mueller, Aug. 8, 1942; 1 dau., Anne Elizabeth. Admitted to Fla. bar, 1939, since practiced in Miami, specializing in corp. and ins. law, sr. partner firm Helliwell, Melrose, DeWolf; sr. v.p., gen. counsel Am. Bankers Ins. Co. of Fla., 1947-70, sec., gen. counsel, 1970—; sec., gen. counsel Am. Bankers Life Assurance Co. of Fla., 1952-70, chmn. bd., gen. counsel, 1970—; pres. Helliwell, Melrose & DeWolf Chartered; dir. 1st Nat. Bank of Homestead (Fla.); chmn. bd. Bank of Cutler Ridge, 1965—, Bank of Perrine, 1962—; pres. Fla. Shares, Inc., 1959—. Co-dir. Miami study team Nat. Comm. Causes and Prevention Violence, 1968-69; mem. Fla. Council of 100, 1971—. Vice chmn. bd. trustees Miami Art Center, 1964—. State chmn. Fla. Citizens for Eisenhower, 1952, 56; del. Rep. Nat. Conv., 1952, 56. Served as col. M.I. and OSS, AUS, 1941-46, mem. Res., 1946—. Decorated Legion of Merit with oak leaf cluster; Order Cloud and Banner (Chinese); comdr. Order of White Elephant (Thailand). Mem. Am., Fla., Dade County bar assns., Bar Assn. City N.Y., Fedn. Ins. Counsel, Orange County Bar Assn., Chi Phi, Phi Alpha Delta. Clubs: Bankers, Miami; River (Jacksonville, Fla.); Kings Bay Yacht; University (Orlando). Home: 225 Leucadendra Dr Coral Gables FL 33156 Office: 1401 Brickell Av Miami FL 33131 also 100 S Orange Av Orlando FL 32801

HELLMAN, GLENN ERNEST, sch. supt.; b. Muenster, Tex., Mar. 25, 1933; s. Arthur Bernard and Pauline (Otto) H.; B.S. in Agr., East Tex. State U., 1955; M.Ed., in Adminstrn., North Tex. State U., 1961; m. Elizabeth Rose Zimmerer, Feb. 17, 1955; children—Dwayne, Glenna, Sandra, Brian, Gina, Jeffery. Vocational agr. instr. Muester (Tex.) Pub. Sch., 1955-59, prin., 1959-63; supt. Lindsay (Tex.) Ind. Sch. Dist., 1963—. Mem. Am., Tex. assns. sch. adminstrs., N.E.A., Tex. State Tchrs. Assn. K.C. Home: 102 E 1st St Lindsay TX 76250 Office: Lindsay TX 76250

HELLMANN, MAX, govt. ofcl.; b. Beroun, Czechoslovakia, Nov. 27, 1919; s. Otto and Theresa (Jerusalem) H.; came to U.S., 1939, naturalized, 1944; B.A., Coll. of Wooster, 1942; M.A., U. Buffalo, 1947, Ph.D., 1950; m. Elizabeth Robitschek, Jan. 13, 1957. Research fellow U. N.C. at Chapel Hill, 1949-51; research chemist Nat. Bur. Standards, Washington, 1951-60; internat. sci. adminstr. NSF, Washington, 1960—. NSF rep. Rio de Janeiro, 1962-64; head NSF office, New Delhi, India, 1969-71. Served with USNR, 1944-46. Contbr. articles in field to profl. jours. Home: 11 10th St SE Washington DC 20003 Office: 1800 G St NW Washington DC 20550

HELLSTROM, RICHARD BARRY, civil engr.; b. Jacksonville, Fla., Aug. 23, 1936; s. Norton Evans and Margaret (Sample) H.; student Davidson Coll., 1954-56; B.C.E., U. Fla., 1960; m. Mary Jane Davidson, June 11, 1960; children—Michael Douglas, Mark Douglas. Resident engr. Peace River Drainage Dist., Bartow, Fla., 1960-63; engr. firm Alton A. Register & Assos., Fort Pierce, Fla., 1963; adminstrv. asst. to Fla. Sec. State, Tallahassee, 1963-68; engr. firm Beindorf & Hellstrom, Fort Pierce, 1968-72; owner, prin. firm Hellstrom & Assos., Fort Pierce, 1973—. Mem. adv. com. to bd. trustees Internal Improvement Fund, 1968-71. Mem. Fort Pierce-St. Lucie County Contractor's Licensing Bd., 1969—. Registered profl. engr., Fla. Mem. Fla. Engring. Soc. (sr. mem., named young engr. of year 1965), Am. Soc. C.E., Nat. Soc. Profl. Engrs., Fort Pierce-St. Lucie County C. of C. Democrat. Episcopalian. Rotarian. Home: 1020 Grandview Blvd Fort Pierce FL 33450 Office: Suite 202 117 S 2d St Fort Pierce FL 33450

HELLUMS, JESSE DAVID, educator; b. Stamford, Tex., Aug. 19, 1929; s. John V. and Fannie May (Beauchamp) H.; B.S., U. Tex., 1950, M.S., 1957; Ph.D., U. Mich., 1960; m. Marilyn Biel, July 13, 1957; children—Mark William, Jay David, Robert James. Process engr. Mobil Oil Co., Beaumont, Tex., 1950-54; asst. prof. chem. engring. Rice U., Houston, 1960-65, asso. prof., 1965-68, prof., 1968—, dir. biomed. engring., 1968—, chmn. dept. chem. engring., 1969—; adj. prof. Baylor Coll. Medicine, Houston, 1960—. NSF sci. faculty fellow U. Cambridge (Eng.), 1967-68; vis. prof. Imperial Coll., London, Eng., 1973-74. Served to lt. USAF, 1954-56. Mem. Am. Inst. Chem. Engrs., Am. Chem. Soc., A.A.A.S., Am. Assn. U. Profs., Am. Soc. Artificial Internal Organs, Sigma Xi, Phi Lambda Upsilon, Omega Chi Epsilon. Contbr. articles to profl. jours. Home: 2202 Albans Rd Houston TX 77005

HELM, DURY LANE, oil and gas broker, evangelist; b. Clifton, Tex., Nov. 22, 1896; s. Willis Sparks and Ellen (Lane) H.; B.S., Tex. A. and M. Coll., 1916; m. Ardella Rebecca Jones, Aug. 3, 1922 Lay leader, deacon, evangelist Ch. of Christ, 1917—; psychic psychologist; dir. polit. and pub. affairs Clara Driscoll, 1938-44; active state and nat. legislation affecting conservation and devel. natural resources, 1932-58; adviser to current state and nat. govt. ofcls., officials, 1935—. Mem. Farm Debt Adjustment Com., 1933-34; exec. asst. to dir, Tex. office OPA, 1941-43. Democratic county chmn., 1934-38; del. Dem. Nat. Conv,, 1936; mem. Nat. Dem. Club Am. Trustee Elizabeth H. Gillespie Estate, 1958—; mgr., owner W. S. Helm Estate, 1960-65; adminstr. Joseph L. Helm Estate, 1960—; trustee Willie Helm Estate, 1969—. Served from 2d lt. to 1st lt., U.S. Army, World War I. Life mem. D.A.V. Perfected a device to trace oil and gas structures. Home: Bosque County Clifton TX 76634 Office: PO Box 391 Clifton TX 76634

HELM, GERALD JAY, retail exec.; b. Forney, Tex., Feb. 19, 1938; s. J.L. and Dona M. (Slayton) H.; B.B.A., Tex. Tech. U., 1961; postgrad. U. Tex. Sch. Mgmt., 1971; m. Norma J. Harvel, May 25, 1960; children—Lisa, Rodney. Div. controller Kroger Co., Washington, also Dallas, 1961-66; controller Leonards Dept. Stores, Ft. Worth, 1966-70; financial v.p. Gibson Distributing Co., Midland, 1970-71, exec. v.p., 1971—, also dir. Bd. dirs. Permian Basin Grad. Center, Central Div. Arthritis Found. Permian Basin Better Bus. Bur. Mem. Southwest Controllers Congress (dir. 1969-70), Midland C. of C. (dir. 1973). Baptist (deacon 1973—). Home: 1703 Douglas St Midland TX 79701 Office: 405 W Indiana St Midland TX 79701

HELM, HUGH BARNETT, judge; b. Bowling Green, Ky., Dec. 27, 1914; s. Hugh Barnett and Ermine (Cox) H.; B.A., Vanderbilt U., 1935, postgrad. law sch., 1936-37, 52-53, Stanford, 1953-56; m. Vivian Loreen Downing, June 5, 1943; children—Beverly, Hugh B. III, Nathaniel Henry. Admitted to Ky. bar, 1938, Tenn. bar, 1938, U.S. Supreme Ct. bar, 1942; atty. Trade Practice Conf., FTC, Washington, 1938-42; asso. counsel U.S. Internat. Prosecution Sect. G.H.Q., SCAP, Tokyo, Japan, 1946; practiced in Nashville, 1946-53; bond specialist Swett & Crawford, San Francisco, 1956-57; resident mgr. Totten & Co., San Francisco, 1958, v.p. gen. mgr., 1959-60; sr. trial atty. Bur. Restraint of Trade, FTC, Washington, 1961-66, chief div. of adv. opinions, 1966—, acting dir. Bur. Industry Guidance, 1969-70, atty. adviser FTC Bur. Consumer Claims, adminstrv. law judge Bur. Hearing and Appeals, Social Security Adminstrn., Dept. Health, Edn. and Welfare, Chattanooga, 1971-73, adminstrv. law judge charge Western Ky. and So. Ill., Paducah, Ky., 1973—. Pres. Surety Claims Assn. No. Cal., 1957-58. Mem. Tenn. Ho. of Reps., 1949-50. Served with Inf., USAAF, 1941-45; served to capt. AUS, 1950-52. Decorated Bronze Star, Combat Infantry Badge. Mem. Am., Ky., Tenn. bar assns., Am. Acad. Polit. and Social Sci., Am. Judicature Soc., Am. Acad. Polit. Sci., Pi Sigma Alpha, Tau Kappa Alpha. Club: Commonwealth (San Francisco). Presbyn. (deacon). Home: 165 Colonial Dr Paducah KY 42001 Office: Bureau Hearings and Appeals Social Security Adminstrn Dept Health Education and Welfare Paducah KY 42001

HELM, JAYE CROCKETT, supt. schs.; b. Mertzon, Tex., Nov. 21, 1916; s. John Cornelius and Cynthia Beatrice (Sanders) H.; student Tarleton State Coll., 1934; B.S., North Tex. U., Denton, 1937, M.S., 1951; postgrad. Tex. A. and M. U.; m. Ruth LaVerne Isham, Sept. 14, 1940; children—Janis Kaye, Jimmy Jaye. High sch. prin., tchr. Newburg Consol. Sch. Dist., Comanche County, Tex., 1937-39; asst. county sch. supt., Comanche County, 1939-41, supt. schs., 1945-49; tchr. Brownwood (Tex.) Schs., 1941; supt. schs., DeLeon, Tex., 1949-54; supt. schs., Stephenville, Tex., 1954—. Chmn. United Fund, Stephenville, 1960. Served with USAAF, 1942-45. Recipient Distinguished Service award Jr. C. of C., 1965. Mem. N.E.A. (life), P.T.A., (life), Am., Tex. assns. sch. adminstrs., So. Assn. Secondary Schs. (chmn. Ft. Worth Dist.), Mid-Tex. (pres.), Tex. (mem. exec. com.) tchrs. assns., Stephenville C. of C. (past pres.). Democrat. Mem. Ch. of Christ (deacon). Mason, Lion. Home: 854 W McNeil St Stephenville TX 76401 Office: Box 453 Stephenville TX 76401

HELM, SHERRELL, civil engr.; b. Livermore, Ky., Nov. 16, 1935; s. Oreste Carter and Mary Ellen (King) H.; student Ky. Wesleyan Coll., 1954-55; B.S. in C.E., U. Ky., 1961; postgrad. U. Tenn., 1964; m. Ann Marie Helm, May 18, 1956; children—David Brian, Susan Marie. Design engr. TVA, Knoxville, Tenn., 1961-64; sr. design engr. Rust Engring. Co., Calhoun, Tenn., 1964-69; chief engr. N.E. Engring., Springfield, Mass., 1969-71; chief engr. So. Prestressed Concrete, Pensacola, Fla., 1971—. Registered profl. engr., Fla., Tenn., Ga., Ala. Mem. Am. Soc. C.E., Nat. Soc. Profl. Engrs., Am. Concrete Inst., Prestressed Concrete Inst., Fla. Engring. Soc., Tau Beta Pi, Chi Epsilon. Baptist (deacon 1968-73). Home: 8140 Fordham Dr Pensacola FL 32504 Office: PO Box 2338 Pensacola FL 32503

HELME, JAMES BUCKELEW, physician; b. Port Chester, N.Y., Apr. 27, 1924; s. James Buckelew and Mary DeHave (Van Deren) H.; grad. Choate Sch., 1942; A.B., Princeton, 1947; M.D., U. Wash., 1952; m. Josephine Coleman Douglas, May 22, 1953; children—Susan Van Deren, Catherine Douglas, Martha Buckelew, John Franklin. Intern, Kings County Hosp., Bklyn., 1952-53; intern Johns Hopkins Hosp., 1953-54, resident, 1954-55; resident Vanderbilt U. Hosp., Nashville, 1955-56; practice medicine, specializing in pediatrics, Nashville, 1957-68; instr. pediatrics and community health Meharry Med. Coll., 1968-71; pediatrician Davidson County Health Dept., 1971-72; med. dir. Nashville Drug Treatment Center, 1972—; chief pediatrics service Nashville Gen. Hosp., 1956-60. Cons., Tenn. Fine Arts Commn., 1968-70. Pres. Nashville Arts Council, 1963-65; bd. dirs. Tenn. Fine Arts Mus., 1963-65, Theatre Nashville, Nashville Pro-Musica. Served to 1st lt. USMCR, 1943-45. Mem. Nashville Acad. Medicine, Tenn. Med. Assn., Tenn., Davidson County pediatric socs., Soc. Philatelic Ams., Am. Philatelic Soc. (dir. C.Z. study group), Am. Air Mail Soc., Middle Tenn. Princeton Alumni Assn. (pres. 1962-65). Clubs: Princeton, Collectors (N.Y.C.); Colonial (Princeton). Contbr. to The Yucatan Affair, 1974. Home: 604 Enquirer Av Nashville TN 37205 Office: 2312 West End Av Nashville TN 37203

HELMERS, GORDON BERT, dentist; b. Gresham, Neb., Sept. 1, 1936; s. Albert Ferdnand and Merle (Moore) H.; student Fullerton Jr. Coll., 1955-57; A.B., U. Cal. at San Francisco, 1957-61; D.D.S., U. Ala., 1965, M.S.D. in Orthodontics, 1967; m. Jo Ella Robinson, June 23, 1962; children—John Byron, Kristen Lee. Asst. prof. orthodontics U. N.C. Dental Sch., Chapel Hill, 1967-69; practice dentistry, specializing in orthodontics, Spartanburg, S.C., 1969—. Served with Dental Corps, AUS, 1962-64. NIH teaching fellow, 1965-67. Recipient 4th place award Am. Assn. Orthodontics research contest, 1969. Mem. S.C. Dental Assn., Am. Dental Assn., Am. Assn. Orthodontics, So. Soc. Orthodontics, S.C. Soc. Dentistry for Children. Inventor dental devices. Home: 132 Fernbrook Circle Spartanburg SC 29302 Office: 319 N Pine St Spartanburg SC 29302

HELMS, JESSE, U.S. senator; b. Monroe, N.C., Oct. 18, 1921; s. Jesse A. and Ethel Mae (Helms) H.; student Wingate Jr. Coll., 1936-37, Wake Forest Coll., 1937-40; m. Dorothy Jane Coble, Oct. 31, 1942; children—Jane (Mrs. Charles R. Knox), Nancy (Mrs. John C. Stuart), Charles. City editor Raleigh (N.C.) Times, 1945-46; adminstrv. asst. to N.C. senators Smith and Lennon, Washington, 1951-53; exec. dir. N.C. Bankers Assn., Raleigh, 1953-60; exec. v.p. sta. WRAL-TV and Tobacco Radio Network, Raleigh, 1960-72; U.S. senator from N.C., 1973—. Mem. Raleigh City Council, 1957-61, chmn. law and finance com., 1957-61. Bd. dirs. N.C. Cerebral Palsy Hosp., Wake County Cerebral Palsy and Rehab. Center, Raleigh; trustee Meredith Coll., John F. Kennedy Coll. Recipient Freedoms Found award, 1962, 73; So. Baptist Nat. Award, 1972; awards V.F.W., 1970, Am. Legion, 1971, Raleigh Exchange Club, 1971. Baptist (deacon, Sunday sch. tchr.). Home: 1513 Caswell St Raleigh NC 27608 Office: Dirksen Office Bldg Washington DC 20510

HELMS, ROY STEELE, town ofcl.; b. Glade Spring, Va., Sept. 20, 1931; s. Roy Bond and Pearle (Owens) H.; student Internat. Corr. Schs., 1953-54, U. Va., 1955-57; m. Anne Blevins, Aug. 14, 1954; children—Cynthia A., Roy A. With Va. Hwy. Dept., Bristol, 1950-60; town engr. Town of Marion, Va., 1960-63, town mgr. 1963—. Bd. dirs. Presidents Club of Lees McCrae Coll., 1973. Served with AUS, 1948-50. Recipient Man of Year award Jaycees and Civitan Club, 1966, 67. Mem. Internat. City Mgrs. Assn., Va. Mgrs. Assn., Va., Marion chambers of commerce. Mason (Shriner). Home: 836 Prater Lane Marion VA 24354 Office: Main St Marion VA 24354

HELT, CHESTER LEROY, architect; b. Modesto, Cal., Aug. 24, 1936; s. Henry Carper and Elizabeth Alma (Vertrees) H.; B.S., Cal. State Poly. Coll., 1961; m. Sue Carolyn King, July 13, 1958; children—Elizabeth Marie, Cameron Carper. Draftsman, Marsh & Hawkins, architects, 1961-63; designer, job capt. Jean G. Surratt, architect, 1963-65; job capt., asso. architect T.P. Hawkins & Assos., 1965-66; project architect James B. Bell, architect, 1966-69; prin. architect C.L. Helt & Assos., Inc., Charlotte, N.C., 1969—, pres., treas., chmn. bd. Served with USNR, 1956-58. Named Boss of Year, Am. Bus. Women's Assn., 1973-74. Mem. A.I.A. (treas. Charlotte chpt. 1970-71), Home Builders Assn. Baptist (deacon 1970-73). Clubs: Civitan (Charlotte pres. 1973-74), Cotswold (Charlotte). Home: 1830 Edgewater Dr Charlotte NC 28210 Office: 119 E Independence Blvd Charlotte NC 28205

HELTON, H.L., coll. adminstr.; b. Fairfax, Okla., May 18, 1924; s. H.L. and Louise (Osborne) H.; B.S., Okla. A. and M. U., 1949, M.S., 1951; Ed.D., Wayne State U., 1958; m. Inez Gibbs, Mar. 9, 1946; children—Howard Lee, Kathleen. Tchr., Denby High Sch., Detroit, 1954-55; instr. Wayne State U., 1955; profl. indsl. arts Northeastern State Coll., Tahlequah, Okla., 1950-52, 56-58, chmn. indsl. arts, 1960-61, dir. student aids, 1963-68, dir. research and devel., 1968—. Sr. adviser, tchr. trainer Rawalpindi (West Pakistan) Poly. Inst., 1961-63; tchr. trainer, adviser Karachi (West Pakistan) Poly. Inst., 1958-60. Pub. employees chmn. United Fund Dr., Tahlequah, 1968; spl. cons. financial aids U.S. Office Edn., 1968. Served with USAAF, 1943. Mem. Okla. Assn. Student Financial Aid Adminstrs. (pres. 1966-67), Rawalpindi Am. Sch. Soc. (pres. 1961-63), Okla. Council Indsl. Atts (pres. 1958), Tahlequah C. of C., Epsilon Pi Tau, Iota Lambda Sigma, Phi Delta Kappa. Kiwanian. Home: 751 Oklahoma Av Tahlequah OK 74464

HELTON, JOHN WILLIAM, dentist; b. Colorado City, Tex., Nov. 10, 1908; s. James Monroe and Lilly Mae (Childers) H.; student U. Tex., 1926-28; D.D.S., Baylor U., 1933; postgrad. U. Pa., 1948-49; m. Nancy Maxene Travis, Nov. 9, 1936; 1 son, John William. Resident oral surgery Episcopal Hosp., Phila., 1949-50; resident anesthesia Robert B. Green Hosp., San Antonio, 1954; practice dentistry specializing in oral surgery, Jacksonville, Tex., 1933-40, San Antonio, 1954—; chief oral surgery Bapt. Meml. Hosp. Systems, 1958—; mem. staff Santa Rosa, Meth. hosps. Chief oral surgery service, dir. oral tng., clin. prof. oral surgery service U. Tex., Robert B. Green Hosp., U. Tex. Med. Sch., 1954-67; cons. oral surgery VA Hosp., Kerrville, Tex., 1958—. Served to lt. col. U.S. Army, 1940-54. Decorated Legion Merit, Bronze Star medal. Diplomate Am. Bd. Oral Surgery. Fellow Am. Coll. Dentists; mem. Am. Dental Assn., Am. Soc. Oral Surgeons, Southwest Soc. Oral Surgeons (pres. 1972—). Baptist (deacon 1950—). Mason. Home: 226 W Fair Oaks Place San Antonio TX 78209 Office: 235 E Hildebrand Av San Antonio TX 78212

HELTON, THOMAS HOWARD, govt. ofcl.; b. Milton County, Ga., May 16, 1929; s. Henry A. and Lena Mae (Nunn) H.; grad. Abraham Baldwin Agrl. Coll., Tifton, Ga., 1946-48; B.S., U. Ga., 1950, M.S., 1966; m. Katie Lee Strickland Helton, July 20, 1957. Asst. county extension agt. U. Ga., Jasper County, 1950-51, Burke County, 1952-53, De Kalb County, 1953-58, asso. county agt., 1958-60, county agt.-chmn., 1960—. Active Am. Cancer Soc., A.R.C., Ga. Heart Assn. Served to capt. AUS, 1950-53. Mem. Nat. (distinguished service award), Ga. (distinguished service award) county agts. assns., Internat. Platform Assn., Ga., Nat. farm bur. fedns., U. Ga. Alumni Soc., Alpha Gamma Rho. Baptist. Rotarian. Home: 1470 N Peachtree St Norcross GA 30071 Office: 101 Old Courthouse Ct Sq Decatur GA 30030

HELVENSTON, BRANTLY WALKER, III, ins. agy. exec.; b. Live Oak, Fla., Sept. 2, 1928; s. Brantly Walker and Mary Perry (DaMon) H.; student U. Fla., 1945-46; B.S., Fla. State U., 1949; m. Laura Harriett Cantrell, Dec. 20, 1952; children—Laura Damon, Harriett Darrow, Brantly Walker IV. Mem. firm B.W. Helvenston & Sons, Live

Oak, Fla., 1949—, partner, 1962—; dir. 1st Comml. Bank, Live Oak. Tchr. ins. course Suwannee Hamilton County area Vocational Sch., 1962—. Civic mediator Tchrs. Strike, 1968; mem. Live Oak Zoning Commn., 1960, chmn., 1969-73; mem. Gov's Adv. Com., Suwannee County, 1971—; sec.-treas. Suwannee River Water Mgmt. Dist., 1973—. Chmn. Suwannee County Democratic Exec. Com., 1970—. Acad. admissions counselor Sewanee Acad., 1971—; bd. dirs. Children's Home Soc. Fla., 1965-68. Served with AUS, 1950-52. Named Outstanding Young Man Suwannee County Jr. C. of C., 1959. Mem. Suwannee County C. of C. (v.p. 1971-72), Am. Legion, Suwannee Little Theatre (pres. 1954), Suwannee Concert Assn. (v.p. 1957); Alpha Tau Omega. Democrat. Episcopalian (vestryman 1966, sr. warden 1969). Mason (Shriner), Kiwanian (pres. 1968). Club: Suwannee Country (sec. 1960-62). Home: 600 Pine St Live Oak FL 32060 Office: 109 E Howard St Box 818 Live Oak FL 32060

HEMBREE, HUGH LAWSON, III, holding co. exec.; b. Ft. Smith, Ark., Nov. 16, 1931; s. Raymond N. and Cladys (Newman) H.; B.S. in Bus. Adminstrn., U. Ark., 1953, LL.B., 1958; m. Sara Janelle Young, Sept. 1, 1956; children—Hugh Lawson IV, Raymond Scott. In middle mgmt. Ark.-Best Freight System, Inc., Ft. Smith, 1958-61, dir., 1960—, dir. finance 1961-65, v.p., 1965—; pres., dir. Ark.-Best Corp., Ft. Smith, 1966—; pres. Hembree Farms, Inc., Ft. Smith, 1962—; chmn. exec. com., dir. Nat. Bank of Commerce, Dallas, 1968-71; chmn. 1st Bankers Real Estate Trust, 1968-72: dir. Nat. Bank Commerce, Dallas, Riverside Furniture Corp., Mid-Am. Industries, S.W. Die Casting (all Ft. Smith), Robertson Distbn. Systems, Inc., Houston, Scheduled Skyways Airlines, Fayetteville, Ark.; adv. bd. Comml. Nat. Bank of Little Rock. Pres., Westark Area council Boy Scouts Am., 1966-67, mem. nat. council, mem. regional exec. bd., 1967—, chmn. regional sustaining membership com.; treas. Endowment Trust Fund, U. Ark., bd. dirs., mem. dean's adv. com. Sch. Bus., 1969-73; chmn. bd. devel. St. Edward Community Med. Center, 1972-73. Sec., Ft. Smith-Sebastian County Joint Planning Commn., 1964—; mem. Ark. Legislative Tax Study Commn., 1969; pres. Sebastian County Mental Health Assn., 1964. Justice of peace Sebastian County, 1959—; mem. Ark. Democratic Central Com., 1968—. Bd. dirs. Jr. Achievement of Ft. Smith, Coalition for Rural Am., 1971, Ark. Council on Econ. Edn., 1964—; trustee Ft. Smith Children's Mus.; chmn. bd. trustees St. Edwards Community Hosp., 1970—. Served to 1st lt. USAF, 1953-55. Recipient Silver Beaver award Boy Scouts Am., 1969, Distinguished Service award Ft. Smith Jr. C. of C., 1965, Leadership award State of Ark., 1970; named Ark. Outstanding Young Man of Year, 1965. Mem. Nat. Assn. Devel. Orgns. (chmn. adv. com.), Ark. (v.p. 1969-73, pres. 1973—), Ft. Smith (pres., dir. 1970-73) chambers commerce, Young Pres.'s Orgn., U. Ark. Alumni Assn. (dir., bldg. com.), Am. Trucking Assn. (nat. accounting and finance council), N.A.M. (nat. dir. 1971), Ark. Arts Center, Scabbard and Blade, Delta Theta Phi, Sigma Alpha Upsilon. Episcopalian (vestryman, co-chmn. ch. finance com.). Clubs: Chapperell, Lancers, Economic (Dallas); Town, Fianna Hills Country, Ft. Smith Hardscrabble Country (Ft. Smith); Capital (Little Rock); N.Y. Athletic; Presidents (dir.) (Hendrix Coll., Conway, Ark.). Home: 3220 Park Av Fort Smith AR 72901 Office: 1000 S 21st St Fort Smith AR 72901

HEMNESS, RAY LESLIE, hosp. adminstr.; b. Milltown, Wis., Oct. 28, 1926; s. Louis H. and Maria (Ruud) H.; B.C.S., Strayer Coll., 1948; m. Peggy Ann Sims, Feb. 14, 1947; 1 dau., Deborah Kay. Treas., Standard Engring. Co., Washington, 1956-61; asst. adminstr. No. Va. Doctors Hosp., Arlington, 1961-62, adminstr., dir., 1962—, sec., 1970—; sec. Va. Doctors Properties, Arlington, 1969—; dir. Seven Corners Med. Bldgs., Inc., Falls Church, Va., 1962-71. Chpt. chmn. A.R.C., Arlington, 1967-70, now bd. dirs. Bd. dirs. No. Va. Heart Assn., Instrs., Internat. Underwater Explorers Soc. Mason (32 deg.), Rotarian. Home: 3027 Hazelton St Falls Church VA 22044 Office: 601 S Carlyn Springs Rd Arlington VA 22204

HEMP, GENE WILLARD, educator; b. Mpls., Dec. 6, 1938; s. Willard H. and Ann S. (Thompson) H.; B.S. in Aero. Engring., U. Minn., 1961, B.S. in Bus., 1962, M.S., 1963, Ph.D., 1967; m. Evelyn Helen Ploetz, Mar. 19, 1960; children—Barbara Jean, Suzanne Marie. Lectr., U. Minn., 1966-67; asst. prof. Coll. Engring., U. Fla., Gainesville, 1967-71, asso. prof., dept. engring. sci., mechanics and aerospace engring., 1971—, asst. dean, 1972—. Cons. Harry Diamond Labs., 1970-71. Mem. Am. Soc. M.E., Soc. Engring. Scis., Am. Soc. Engring. Edn., Am. Inst. Aeros. and Astronautics, Sigma Xi, Tau Beta Pi, Sigma Tau, Sigma Gamma Tau. Home: 2225 NW 19th Lane Gainesville FL 32605

HEMPHILL, CALVIN RALPH, sch. adminstr.; b. Seattle, Mar. 4, 1925; s. Ralph and Jane (Skea) H.; student U. Cal. at Los Angeles, 1946-49; B.A., Claremont Mens Coll., 1951; postgrad. U. Ams. (Mex.), 1951-52; m. Lilia Fernandez, Oct. 10, 1953; children—Arturo, Vivian, Ralph II, Eric. Supr., Hemphill Schs., Mexico, D.F., Mexico, 1951-64, exec. dir. Hemphill Schs., Los Angeles, 1964—; pres. Continental-Tech. Corp., Republic of Panama, 1955—. Co-chmn. United Fund, Mexico City, 1964, Bd. dirs. Sister City Assn., Beverly Hills, Cal.; mem. adv. com. So. Cal. Inst. Internat. Edn.; bd. affiliates Claremont Men's Coll. Served with USNR, 1943-46. Mem. Nat. Home Study Council (pres.), Young Pres.'s Orgn. Mason (Shriner). Clubs: Chapultepec Golf; Los Angeles Country; White Friars; University of Mexico. Home: Privada de Tantoran 19 Lomas Hipodromo Mexico 10 DF Mexico

HEMPHILL, JAMES ARTHUR, plastic co. exec.; b. Pickens, Miss., Oct. 3, 1923; s. E.A. and Helen (Simpson) H.; student Holmes Jr. Coll., 1941-43, U. Ala., 1945-46; m. Rachel A. Roberson, July 14, 1944; children—William Lee, James Arthur, Mary Susan, Helen Catherine. Owner, Hemphill Electric Co., Kosciusko, Miss., 1947-56; prodn. mgr. Vickers, Inc., Jackson, Miss., 1956-60; pres. R & H Mfg. Co., Jackson, 1960-63; v.p., gen. mgr. Gulf Plastics Inc., Jackson, 1963-71; adviser, cons. Briarwood Products, Jackson, 1968-71; plastics cons. Piper Industries, Memphis, 1971-72, pres. plastic div., 1972—; plastic cons. Lott Enterprises, Jackson, 1971—; dir. Piper Industries. Served with AUS, 1943-44; ETO. Mem. Soc. Plastic Engrs., Jackson C. of C., Miss. Mfrs. Assn. Home: 5425 Charter Oak Jackson MS 39211 Office: 1320 Boling St Jackson MS 39206

HEMPHILL, JAMES EUGENE, radiologist; b. Willow Springs, N.C., Sept. 17, 1913; s. James E. and Nellie S. (Jackson) H.; B.S., Hampden-Sydney Coll., 1933; M.D., U. Va., 1937; m. Mary N. Ray, June 23, 1937; children—Nancy E., Mary E., Martha N. Intern U.S. Marine Hosp., Balt., 1937-38; asst. surgeon USPHS, 1938-40; resident radiology Duke Hosp., 1940-42; asso. prof. radiology Bowman Gray Med. Sch., 1944-45; owner Hemphill Radiology Clinic, Charlotte, N.C., after 1948; now pres. Sandhill Radiology Assos. P.A. Past pres. Mecklenburg County unit Am. Cancer Soc. Diplomate Am. Bd. Radiology. Mem. A.M.A., So. Med. Assn., N.C. Radiol. Soc. (past pres.), Mecklenburg County Med. Soc. (past pres.), Am. Coll. Radiology, Radiol. Soc. N.A., Soc. Nuclear Medicine. Presbyn. Kiwanian. (elder). Club: Myers Park Country (Charlotte). Home: Lake Aimer Route 2 Box 408 Rockingham NC 28379 Office: Richmond Meml Hosp Rockingham NC 28379

HEMPHILL, WILLIAM LEE, ins., exec.; b. Greensboro, N.C., Oct. 4, 1921; s. Ross and Nell (Bean) H.; B.S., Bowling Green U., 1948; postgrad. U. N.C., 1967; m. Joan Thatcher, Sept. 20, 1945; children—William Lee II, Ross Frank. Partner, Lindsay, Squires and Everett, C.P.A.'s, Greensboro, N.C., 1948-58; chief financial and adminstrn. officer United Dairies, Inc., and predecessor co., Greensboro, 1958-72, exec. v.p., 1972—; treas. First Mortgage Ins. Co., Greensboro, 1963-73; pres. FMIC Corp. and related cos., 1972—. Cons. corp. orgn. and finance, 1958-72; chmn., Gov.'s Adv. Council Vocational Edn., 1969-71; commr. N.C. Milk Commn., 1971-72. Pres. bd. Greensboro Community Council, 1966-68; v.p. Greensboro United Community Services, 1968-69. Served with USAAF, 1942-46. Mem. Financial Execs. Inst. Democrat. Episcopalian. Home: 508 Audubon Dr Greensboro NC 27410 Office: 826 N Elm Greensboro NC 27420

HENCK, FRED WILLIAM, editor; b. Latrobe, Pa., May 10, 1921; s. Fred W. and Elsie (Adam) H.; student Ohio U., 1937-39; m. Bettye M. Hinchcliff, June 23, 1944; children—Kathryn Elizabeth, Joanne Susan, William Oliver. Editor, Independent Syndicate, Washington, 1939-40, Asso. Editors, Washington, 1940-41, Army Times, Washington, 1941; asso. editor Telecommunications Reports, Washington, 1941-48, mng. editor, 1948-52, exec. editor, 1952-64, editor, 1964—; pres., dir. Telecommunications Pub. Co., Washington, 1964—; editor Washington bur. Telephone Engr. & Mgmt., 1946—; dir. Magmt. Sci. Systems, Inc., Rockville, Md. Mem. Arlington County (Va.) Pub. Utilities Commn., 1964—, Arlington County Cable TV Adv. Com., 1973—. Served with USAAF, 1942-46. Decorated Bronze Star. Mem. Ind. Newsletter Assn. (pres. 1967). Clubs: International, Nat. Press. Home: 2407 N Quebec St Arlington VA 22207 Office: Nat Press Bldg Washington DC 20004

HENDERSON, ARTHUR FLOYD, printing co. exec.; b. Atlanta, Mar. 17, 1934; s. William Dewey and Alice H.; student Ga. State Coll., 1968-69; m. Mary Ruth Porter, Nov. 26, 1954; children—Donna, Kay, Cindy, Arthur Floyd. With Darby Printing Co., Atlanta, 1955—, salesman, 1964-66, operations supr., 1966-68, v.p., gen. mgr., 1968—. Served with USAF, 1951-55. Named Most Outstanding Apprentice Printer in Atlanta, 1958. Democrat. Baptist. Club: Craftsman. Home: 2599 Kings Park Circle Decatur GA 30034 Office: 715 W Whitehall St SW Atlanta GA 30310

HENDERSON, BILLY JOE, educator; b. Texarkana, Tex., Aug. 10, 1937; B.S. in Nuclear Engring., N.C. State U., 1959, M.S. in Physics, 1962; Ph.D. in Physics (NASA traineeship 1964-67, Alumni Found. fellow 1963), U. Ga., 1967; m. Mary Ann Riederer, July 21, 1967. Engr., Gen. Elec. Corp., Evandale, O., 1959-60; asst. prof. dept. physics U. Ga., Athens, 1967-68, Fla. Tech. U., Orlando, 1968—. Mem. Sigma Xi, Sigma Pi Sigma, Tau Beta Pi, Phi Kappa Phi. Home: 905 Lakeview Dr Winter Park FL 32789 Office: PO Box 25000 Orlando FL 32816

HENDERSON, DAVID NEWTON, congressman; b. Hubert, N.C., Apr. 16, 1921; s. Isaac Newton and Virginia (Boney) H.; B.S., Davidson Coll., 1942; LL.B., U. N.C., 1949; m. Mary Wellons Knowles. Dec. 11, 1942; children—David Bruce, Wiley Bryant, Wimbric Boney. Admitted to N.C. bar, 1949; practiced in Wallace until 1960; asst. gen. counsel com. edn. and labor Ho. of Reps., 1951-52; solicitor Duplin County Gen. Ct., 1953-57, judge, 1957-59; mem. 88th-92d congresses from 3d Dist. N.C. Served to maj. USAAF, 1942-46. Mem Am. Legion, V.F.W. Democrat. Presbyn. Mason, Lion. Home: 503 E Murphy St Wallace NC 28466 Office: Cannon House Office Bldg Washington DC 20515

HENDERSON, DONALD RAY, civil engr.; b. Washington, June 12, 1936; s. Raymond DeSales and Lillian (Hall) H.; B.S. in Civil Engring. (baseball scholar), U. Md., 1959; m. Martha Anne Heller, AUg. 27, 1955; children—Steven, Susan. With J.E. Greiner Co., various locations, 1959—, project engr., 1962-65, asst. v.p., Tampa, Fla., 1972—. Active Clearwater (Fla.) Babe Ruth League, 1966—. Mem. Am. Soc. C.E., Fla. Engring. Soc., Nat. Assn. Civil Engrs., St. Petersburg C. of C. Home: 1348 Whispering Pines Dr Clearwater FL 33516 Office: 5601 Mariner St Tampa FL 33622

HENDERSON, DOUGLAS BOYD, lawyer; b. Pitts., Sept. 21, 1935; s. Arthur G. and Mildred E. (Rickenbach) H.; B.S., Pa. State U., 1957; J.D. with honors, George Washington U., 1963; m. Olivia Lauer, July 6, 1957; children—Scotland Weaver, Keith Arthur, Heather Alice. Salesman, Arthur G. Henderson, Akron, O., 1957-59; patent agt. Swift and Co., Washington, 1959-62; admitted to Va. bar, 1962, D.C. bar, 1963; law clk. U.S. Ct, of Claims, Washington, 1962-63; practiced in Washington, 1963—; atty. Irons, Birch, Swindler and McKie, 1963-65; mem. firm Finnegan and Henderson, Washington, 1965-69, Finnegan, Henderson and Farabow, 1969-72, Finnegan, Henderson, Farabow and Garrett, 1972—. Mem. Fed., Am., Va. bar assns., Bar Assn. D.C., Am. Patent Law Assn., Patent Office Soc., Am. Judicature Soc., Phi Gamma Delta, Delta Theta Phi. Methodist. Clubs: University, Touchdown (Washington); Bethesda (Md.); Rehoboth Beach (Del.) Country. Home: 6715 Wemberly Way McLean VA 22101 Office: 1775 K St NW Washington DC 20006

HENDERSON, EDMUND MCKEILL, physician; b. Bridgetown, Va., Apr. 26, 1915; s. Upshur Kerr and Bessie Trower (Roberts) H.; M.D., U. Va., 1942; m. Mary Lawton Mathews, June 18, 1945; children—Edmund M., James Lamar, Elizabeth T., Thomas L. Intern, U.S. Naval Hosp., Parris Island, S.C., 1942-43; resident U.S. Naval Hosp., Phila.; gen. practice medicine, Nassawadox, Va., 1949—; pres. staff, chief obstetrics Northampton-Accomac Meml. Hosp. Served with M.C., USN, 1942-49. Mem. Med. Soc. Va., A.M.A., Northampton County Med. Soc. (pres. 1955-56, 71-72). Episcopalian (treas. 1962-67). Address: Nassawadox VA 23413

HENDERSON, GEORGE HALL, lumber co. exec.; b. Corrigan, Tex., Mar. 10, 1897; s. Julius Leonidas and Sarah Josephine Flavilla (Neyland) H.; student pub. schs.; m. Maurine Canon, Sept. 17, 1929; children—Mildred Louise (Mrs. Fred Edward Grinstead), George Hall. Gen. mgr. Angelina Hardwood Co., Ewing, 1923-45, v.p., 1945—; pres. Angelina Hardwood Lumber Co., Lufkin, 1945—; dir. First Bank & Trust, Lufkin. Past pres., trustee sch. bd. Lufkin Ind. Sch. Dist. Trustee Meml. Hosp. Mem. Nat. Hardwood Lumber Assn. (pres. 1946-48), Hardwood Mfrs. Inst. (pres. 1931-33), Southwestern Hardwood Club (pres. 1927-31), Angelina County C. of C. (past pres.). Methodist (trustee). Club: Lufkin (past pres., mem. bd.). Home: 906 Markus St Lufkin TX 75901 Office: 1312 Wilson St Lufkin TX 75901

HENDERSON, GEORGE ROBERT, librarian; b. Ft. Worth, May 7, 1918; s. George R. and Jessie (Mitchell) H.; Mus.B. (Theodore Presser music scholar), Tex. Wesleyan Coll., 1940; Mus.M., North Tex. State U., 1949; B.L.S., Pratt Inst., 1948; m. Frances O'Neal, June 30, 1941. Tchr. music, pub. schs., Farmersville, Tex., Ft. Worth, 1941-42; music cataloger N.Y. Pub. Library, N.Y.C., 1947-48; chief music div. Pub. Library, Washington, 1948-53; fine arts librarian Tex. Christian U., Ft. Worth, 1953-54, Dallas Pub. Library, 1954—. Instr. sch. music So. Methodist U., 1966-67. Adv. bd. Opera Action Library of Dallas Civic Opera, Dallas Symphony Assn., Dallas Chamber Music Soc. Served with AUS, 1942-45. Mem. Music Library Assn. (sec. 1950-53), Dallas Print and Drawing Soc. (pres. 1965-67), Internat. Assn. Music Libraries, Internat. Fedn. Libraries Assn., Tex. (chmn. fine arts roundtable 1964-65), S.W. library assns., Dallas (hon.), Nat., Tex. fedn. music clubs, Art Libraries Soc. N.Am. Home: 4511 Livingston Av Dallas TX 75205 Office: Fine Arts Dept Dallas Pub Library Dallas TX 75201

HENDERSON, HAROLD DOUGLAS, JR., banker; b. nr. Fulton, Ky., Nov. 26, 1930; s. Harold Douglas and Evelyn (Cunningham) H.; Certificate, Bruce Bus. Inst., 1956; grad. Banking Sch. South, La. State U., 1966; m. Verna Faye Dunning, July 19, 1949; children—Randall, Harold, Pamela Jane. With Fulton Bank, 1950—, v.p., 1962, pres., 1962—, also dir.; dir. City Drug Co. Inc., Truly Pure Dairy Inc., Mayfield, Ky., Fulton Assos. Inc. Financial adviser City South Fulton, Tenn., 1957—; sec. Airport Bd., Fulton, 1969—. Chmn. Obion County Bd. Edn. 1964—. Served with USAF, 1950-52. Mem. Fulton C. of C. (past pres.), Am. Bonanza Soc., Internat. Flying Bankers Assn. Democrat. Baptist (deacon). Home: 304 Orchard Dr South Fulton TN 42041 Office: PO Box 347 Fulton KY 42041

HENDERSON, HAROLD RAINS, engring. exec.; b. Marshall, Tex., Jan. 24, 1907; s. William D. and Dora (Strickland) H.; B.S. in Civil and Irrigation Engring., Colo. State U., 1929; m. Rose Henning, Dec. 31, 1928; children—Harold William, Robert Henning. Constrn. engr. Mo. Hwy. Dept. 1929-30, Mo. Portland Cement Co., Independence, 1930-31; project engr. Tex. Hwy. Dept., 1932-34; engr. Harrison County, Tex., 1935-42; gen. supt. McKinney Constrn. Co., Marshall, 1942-47; v.p. H. R. Henderson & Co., Marshall, 1947-58; pres. Turnbull, Inc., Marshall, 1958-70, Turnbull Corp., 1965-71, also dir.; pres. Eastex Metal Fabricators, Inc., 1970-72, EnDeCo, Inc., Marshall, 1971—; pres., dir. Pure Metals, Ltd., Geneva, Switzerland, 1962-69; cons. to City of Marshall, Harrison County, Tex., Govt. Iran for aluminum prodn. Registered profl. engr., Tex. Fellow Am. Soc. C.E. Home: 2107 N Franklin St Marshall TX 75670 Office: PO Box 329 Marshall TX 75670

HENDERSON, JAMES FREEMAN, architect; b. Macon, Ga., May 30, 1927; s. Shelton LaFayette and Nora Lillian (Watson) H.; grad. Middle Ga. Coll., 1948; grad. So. Tech. Inst., 1950; m. Betty Beck, July 8, 1950; children—Julie Pamela, Betty Jill, James Freeman. Draftsman Dennis and Dennis Architects, Macon, 1949-60; prin. Henderson & Bray Architects, Macon, 1960-65; prin. Dunwody, Dunwody, Henderson and Bray Architects, Macon, 1965-68; asso. Dennis and Dennis Architects, Macon, 1968-73; prin. Dunwoody & Co., architects, Macon, 1973—. Chmn. Jones County Planning and Zoning Bd., 1969-70; chmn. Jones County Beautification Com., 1970—. Served with USNR, 1945-46. Mem. A.I.A., Constrn. Specifications Inst., Phi Delta Theta. Methodist (trustee 1968—). Home: Route 6 Henderson Rd Macon GA 31201 Office: 600 Town Pavilion 205 Broadway Macon GA 31201

HENDERSON, JAMES HENRY, dentist; b. Henderson, N.C., Jan. 29, 1925; s. James and Sarah Elizabeth (Evans) H.; B.S., Hampton Inst., 1948; D.D.S., Meharry Med. Coll., 1953; m. Mabel Joyce White, July 21, 1956; children—Eryn Janyce, Edythe Jeannelle, James Henry. Intern VA Hosp., Tuskeegee, Ala., 1955-56; dentist La. Dept. Hosps., 1956-59; individual practice dentistry, New Iberia, La., 1957—; mem. staff Iberia Parish Hosp., Dauterive Hosp., Found. Hosp., Franklin, La.; mem. vis. staff New Orleans Charity Hosp. Dir. Bacmonila, Inc., John A. Andrews Meml. Clinics, Tuskeegee. Founder Community Progress League, 1960, pres., 1960-63; chmn., parade marshall La. Sugar Cane Festival and Fair, 1962-66; chmn. Iberia Parish Tb. Assn., 1962-70; pres. br. N.A.A.C.P., 1964-70, state bd., 1965-70, state treas., 1969—; mem. La. Commn. on Human Relations, Rights and Responsibilities, 1965-70; coach Little League Baseball, 1972. Bd. dirs. Pee Wee Football League, New Iberia. Served with AUS, 1943-46; with Dental Corps, U.S. Army, 1952-55. Recipient award of achievement Omega Psi Phi, 1962, award of merit La. Beauticians Assn., 1968. Fellow Royal Soc. Health; mem. Acad. Gen. Dentistry, Am. (diplomate nat. bd.), Nat., Chgo., Pelican State dental assns., Alpha Phi Alpha, Beta Kappa Chi. Baptist (trustee). Mason (Shriner). Club: Royal Vanders Social (New Iberia). Home: 400 S Curtis St New Iberia LA 70560 Office: 403 W Pershing St New Iberia LA 70560

HENDERSON, JAMES MARVIN, advt. exec.; b. Atlanta, Mar. 28, 1921; s. Isaac Harmon and Ruth (Ashley) H.; student Furman U., 1939-40, Clemson Coll., 1940-42, also night classes N.Y. U., 1943-44; B.S., U. Denver, 1946; grad. Advanced Mgmt. Program, Harvard, 1956; m. Donna Fern Baade, Apr. 28, 1945; children—Linda Dee, James Marvin, Deborah Fanchon. Sales supr. Gen. Foods Corp., N.Y.C., 1942-44; account exec. Curt Freiberger Advt. Agy., Denver, 1944-46; pres. Henderson Advt. Agy., Inc., Greenville, S.C., 1946—; pres. Henderson, Ayer & Gillet Advt., Charlotte, N.C., 1962-69; Henderson-Saussy Advt., New Orleans, 1966-69; dir. Citizens & So. Nat. Bank. Spl. asst. to postmaster gen., 1969-70. Mem. Greenville Youth Commn., 1953-54. Chmn. Eisenhower campaign Greenville County, 1952; Republican candidate for lt. gov. S.C., 1970. Pres. Greenville Heart Assn.; pres., bd. dirs. Greenville Mental Hygiene Clinic, United Fund. Served with AUS, World War II. Named Young Man of Year, Greenville, 1954. Mem. S.C. (past dir.), Greenville (past pres.) jr. chambers commerce, Greater Greenville C. of C. (past pres.), Young President's Orgn. (chmn. S.E. chpt.), Greenville Advt. Council (past pres.), Am. Assn. Advt. Agys. (nat. dir.). Methodist. Kiwanian. Home: Route 7 Hickory Lane Greenville SC 29609 Office: 55 S Pleasantburg Dr Greenville SC 29607

HENDERSON, JERRY DON, assn. exec.; b. Brownfield, Tex., Mar. 9, 1927; s. J.D. and Ethel May (Carter) H.; B.A., Tex. Technol. U., 1950; 1 dau., Paula (Mrs. Dennis Ray Jones); m. Burnis Marie Lyles, June 8, 1964; children—Donna George, Jacqueline George, David. With KFYO Radio, Lubbock, Tex., 1950-56; copy dir. Buckner Advt. Agy., Lubbock, 1956-60; partner Henderson Buckner Pub. Relations, Lubbock, 1960-62; with Brain Radio Promotions, Lubbock, 1962-66; pub. relations dir. United Fund, Lubbock, Tex., 1966—; pres. Brain Bag, Lubbock, 1969—. Served with USNR, 1946-48. Named Hon. adm. Tex. Navy. Mem. Nat. Communications Council United Way of Am., Pub. Relations Soc. Am., Pub. Relations Student Soc. Am. (profl. sponsor Tex. Technol. U. chpt.), Lubbock Advt. Fedn. (pres. 1970-71). Episcopalian (vestryman 1968-71, lay reader 1967—). Rotarian. Clubs: Press (dir. Lubbock), Reveliers Dance (pres. 1973-74). Pub: Sales Pitches on Tape (Jerry D. Henderson), 1971. Home: 5214 17th St Lubbock TX 79416 Office: 2201 19th St Lubbock TX 79401

HENDERSON, JOHNNIE SCOTT, cattle co. exec.; b. Crossplains, Tex., July 15, 1928; s. Johnnie Ivy and Clara (Long) H.; B.S., Tex. A. and M. Coll., 1949; M.S., Tex. Technol. Coll., 1955; postgrad. U. Minn., 1955-56; m. Margaret Viola Lynch, Jan. 30, 1959; children—Johnnie Scott, Mark, Matthew. Sch. tchr., Strawn, Tex., 1949-52; asst. agrl. agt. Harris County, Houston, 1956-60; exec. sec. Am.-Internat. Charolais Assn., Houston, 1960—; rancher Coleman and Waller Counties, Tex., 1949—. Sec., treas. U.S. Beef Breeds Council, Houston, 1970—; dir. Houston Livestock Show and Rodeo, 1969—. Served to capt. AUS, 1952-54; col. Res. Recipient Outstanding Service award C. of C., 1962, Leadership award, 1963; French Order of Merit award in agr., 1969. Mem. Nat. Assn.

Livestock Records Assns., Am. Soc. Asso. Execs., Livestock Merchandising Inst. (trustee), Tex. Soc. Execs., Tex. Comml. Agrl. Council, Res. Officers Assn., Houston C. of C. Mem. Christian Ch. Mason (Shriner, 32 deg.), Rotarian. Club: Houston Farm and Ranch. Home: 14926 Chadbourne Houston TX 77024 Office: 1610 Old Spanish Trail Houston TX 77025

HENDERSON, KAYE NEIL, civil engr., bus. exec.; b. Birmingham, Ala., June 10, 1933; s. Ernest Martin and Mary (Head) H.; B.S., Va. Mil. Inst., 1954; B.A. with honors, U. South Fla., 1967; m. Betty Jane Belanus, June 26, 1954; children—David Scott, Alan Douglas, Helen Kaye. Mgmt. trainee Gen. Electric Co., Schenectady, 1954; sales engr. Fla. Prestressed Concrete, Tampa, 1956-57; field engr. Portland Cement Assn., Tampa, 1957-63; gen. mgr. residential and comml. sales Tampa Electric Co., 1963-66; v.p. Watson & Co., architects and engrs., Tampa, 1966-69; v.p. Reynolds, Smith & Hills, architects, engrs. and planners, Jacksonville, Fla., 1969—. Vice chmn. Temple Terrace Planning and Zoning Bd., 1962-67. Pres. Guidance Center Hillsborough County, 1969. Mem. Duval County Republican Exec. Com. Bd. dirs. Salvation Army Home and Hosp. Council, 1964-69. Mem. found U. South Fla. Served to 1st lt. USAF, 1954-56. Recipient Service awards Greater Tampa C. of C., 1964-66; named Outstanding Young Man of Tampa Jr. C. of C., 1965; Outstanding Young Man of Am., U.S. Jr. C. of C., 1967. Registered profl. engr., Fla. Mem. Fla. Engring. Soc., Fla. Inst. Cons. Engrs. (dir.), Phi Kappa Phi. Republican. Episcopalian. Clubs: Ye Mystic Revellers, Timuquana Country, University (Jacksonville). Home: 4606 Yacht Club Rd Jacksonville FL 32210 Office: 4019 Blvd Center Dr Jacksonville FL 32207

HENDERSON, LOUIS CLIFTON, ins. co. exec.; b. Harlan, Ky., July 21, 1937; s. Louis Clifton and Aileen (Richmond) H.; B.S., U. Ark., 1960; m. Sharon Elizabeth Ward, Jan. 24, 1959; children—Lisa Ward, Ann Richmond. Staff accountant Price Waterhouse & Co., Houston, 1959-61; treas. Investors Preferred Life Ins. Co., 1961-68; exec. v.p. adminstrn. Am. Tidelands Life Ins. Co., Birmingham, Ala., 1965-68, exec. v.p., treas. 1968—, also dir.; asst. to pres., treas. Tidelands Capital Corp., New Orleans, 1969—, also dir. Served with Finance Corps, AUS, 1960. C.P.A., Tex. Mem. Am. Inst. C.P.A.'s, Beta Gamma Sigma, Sigma Alpha Epsilon. Presbyn. Rotarian (pres. 1970-71). Club: Vestavia Country (mem. bd. govs. 1973-74) (Birmingham). Home: 3032 Westmoreland Dr Birmingham AL 35223 Office: 1900 Crestwood Blvd Birmingham AL 35210

HENDERSON, PAUL THOMAS, avionics systems engr.; b. Bay City, Mich., June 26, 1917; s. Arthur and Grace (Hartwick) H.; student Bay City Jr. Coll., 1935-37; m. Marie Lucile Hudson, July 27, 1937; children—Paula (Mrs. Warren McClure), Joyce (Mrs. Harvey Gilkison), Christine (Mrs. Earl Teede), Rose (Mrs. Larry Bornman), Stephen B., Kent D. Indsl. engr. Kuhlman Elec. Co., Bay City, Mich., 1946-53; elec. design engr. Bell Aircraft Corp., Buffalo, 1953-59; supervising engr. electronic test lab. Fairchild Aircraft Co., Hagerstown, Md., 1959-62; instr. Electronics Inst., Harrisburg, Pa., 1962-64; avionics systems engr. Navy Dept., Kingsville, Tex., 1964—. Mem. I.E.E.E. (sr. mem.), Nat. Model R.R. Assn. Mason (K.T.). Home: 204 E Fairview Dr Kingsville TX 78363 Office: AIMD-Avionics NAS Kingsville TX 78363

HENDERSON, PHILIP S., psychologist; b. N.Y.C., Oct. 3, 1910; s. Herman and Molly (Winston) H.; B.S., City Coll. N.Y., 1930; M.A., Columbia, 1932; Ph.D., U. Tenn., 1950; postgrad. Pomona Coll., 1943, N.Y. Psychoanalytic Inst., 1937, Emory U., 1947; m. Norma Jean Edsel, July 1, 1950; children—Victor Warren, Helen Kay. Psychology intern Elmira Reformatory, 1932-33; psychology externe N.Y. Child Guidance, 1934; psychologist Sing Sing Prison, 1935-38; head psychologist Woodbourne Inst. Defective Delinquents, 1934-46; chief psychologist VA Hosp., Murfreesboro, Tenn., 1946-48, Knoxville, Tenn., 1948-49, Tuscaloosa, Ala., 1949-50, Ft. Roots, Ark., 1951-58, Augusta, Ga., 1958—. Tchr. N.Y. U., 1936-37, Pasadena Coll., 1944, U. Tenn., 1948-50. Served with AUS, 1941-45. Diplomate Am. Bd. Profl. Psychology. Mem. Am., Ga. psychol. assns. Home: 1403 Habersham Dr Augusta GA 30904 Office: VA Hosp Lenwood Wrightsboro Rd Augusta GA 30904

HENDERSON, WARREN S., state senator; b. Exeter, N.H., Nov. 14, 1927; B.A., Denison U., 1951; m. Polly Ann Schurr; children—Warren C., Susan D., Wendy L. Investment, financial exec.; now mem. Fla. Senate. Mem., chmn. Sarasota County (Fla.) Planning and Zoning Commn., 1960-63; chmn. Manatee/Sarasota Airport Authority, 1961-63; chmn. West Coast Inland Nav. Dist., 1962-63; mem. Fla. Energy Com. Del. Republican nat. conv., 1968; mem. Fla. Rep. com., 1970—. Served with USNR, World War II. Recipient awards Am. Alligator Council, 1971, Water Resources Conservation, 1973, Fla. Conservation League, 1973. Mem. Am. Numis. Assn., Internat. Oceanographic Found., Nat. Wildlife Fedn., Conservation 70's, Fla. Hist. Soc. C. of C., Phi Delta Theta. Presbyn. Elk. Mason. Address: PO Box 1358 Venice FL 33595

HENDLEY, JOSEPH OWEN, II, physician; b. Chattanooga, Aug. 18, 1937; s. Flavius Josephus and Cornelia Adelaide (Smartt) H.; B.A., Vanderbilt U., 1959; M.D., U. Pa., 1963; m. Bethany Thomas, June 8, 1963; children—John, Laura. Intern pediatrics Duke, 1963-64, resident pediatrics, 1964-65, 67-68; epidemic intelligence service officer USPHS, U. Va., Charlottesville, 1965-67; research fellow pediatrics and preventive medicine, 1965-67, asst. prof. pediatrics, 1970—; research fellow infectious diseases Harvard Sch. Pub. Health, Boston, 1968-70. Recipient Marie Lebron prize in pediatrics U. Pa., 1963. Mem. Am. Soc. Microbiology, So. Soc. Pediatric Research, Infectious Disease Soc., Phi Beta Kappa, Alpha Omega Alpha. Editor: Pediatric Newsletter, 1971—. Contbr. articles to profl. jours. Home: Route 29 S Charlottesville VA 22901

HENDON, ROBERT CARAWAY, transp. and mfg. co. exec.; b. Shelbyville, Tenn., Jan. 13, 1912; s. William Oscar and Anna Bertha (Caraway) H.; B.A. in Journalism, U. Mont., 1931, J.D., 1934; m. Ruth Perham, Apr. 23, 1936; children—Robert Caraway, Elizabeth Anne (Mrs. MacDonald Dunbar, Jr.). Admitted to Mont., Tenn. bars, 1934; gen. law practice, 1934-35; spl. agt., spl. agt. in charge FBI, 1935-39; inspr., adminstrv. asst. to dir., exec. com., 1939-47; exec. rep. to pres. Ry. Express Agy. (name changed to REA Express), 1947, various exec. positions, 1947-50, v.p. personnel, 1953-55, v.p. operations, 1955-64, v.p. industry affairs, 1964-68; v.p. Consol. Freightways, Inc., 1968—; asst. to pres., dir. personnel Mathieson Chem. Corp., 1950-52; dir. REA Leasing Corp., 1961-68, pres., 1964-67, vice chmn. 1967-68; pres., dir. REA Express Seven Arts Transvision Inc., 1965-68, TOFC Leasing Corp., 1966-68; dir., chmn. exec. com. Fast Service Shipping Terminals, 1961-68; dir., mem. exec., nominating, exam. coms., chmn. audit com. Manhattan Life Ins. Co.; dir., exec. com. Manhattan Life Corp. Bd. dirs. Nat. Safety Council, chmn. nat. safety awards com., 1960-68; trustee, exec. com. U. Mont. Found., pres., 1966-68; bd. mgrs., vice chmn. Vanderbilt YMCA, 1958-68; trustee Center for Environmental and Resource Analysis. Recipient Distinguished Service award U. Mont., 1967. Mem. Transp. Assn. Am. (mem. policy implementation and facilitation coms.), Phi Sigma Kappa, Sigma Delta Chi. Episcopalian (past vestryman, warden). Clubs: University (Larchmont, N.Y.); Propeller, Circus Saints and Sinners, Congressional Country (Washington). Author: Frontiers in Labor-Management Relations, 1956; Seniority; First In, Last Out, 1958; also articles. Home: 1128 Kensington Rd McLean VA 22101 Office: McLean Office Centre 6845 Elm St McLean VA 22101

HENDON, ROBERT CARAWAY, JR., lawyer; b. Des Moines, June 10, 1937; s. Robert Caraway and Ruth Kathryn (Perham) H.; B.A. cum laude, Princeton, 1959; certificate Woodrow Wilson Sch. Pub. and Internat. Affairs, 1959; LL.B., Yale, 1964; m. Marilyn Audrey Kennedy, Dec. 4, 1965; children—Alysha, Robert Caraway III. Admitted to Tenn. bar, 1965; practiced in Nashville, 1965—, Memphis, 1973—; asso. firm Waller, Lansden, Dortch & Davis, Nashville, 1964-71, partner, 1972—. Chmn. Princeton Schs. Com. for Middle Tenn., 1969—. Served to lt. (j.g.) USNR, 1959-61. Mem. Am., Tenn., Nashville, Memphis bar assns., Princeton Alumni Assn. Middle Tenn. (pres. 1971-72), Phi Delta Phi. Republican. Presbyn. Clubs: Belle Meade Country, Cumberland (Nashville). Home: 4509 Harpeth Hills Dr Nashville TN 37215 Office: Am Trust Bldg Nashville TN 37201 also Sterick Bldg Memphis TN 38103

HENDRICK, ALFORD GANDEY, physician; b. Franklin, Ga., Feb. 14, 1902; s. Alford Gandey and Josie Lenora (Daniel) H.; M.D., Emory U., 1930; postgrad. Johns Hopkins, 1936-37; m. Mildred Deadwyler, Sept. 7, 1951. Intern Henry Grady Hosp., Atlanta, 1930; commr. health Sylvester and Worth counties Ga. Pub. Health Dept., 1937-41; gen. practice medicine, Perry, Ga., 1941—; mem. staff Perry Houston County Hosp., 1969—, chief staff, 1971-72; med. adviser Oaks Nursing Home, Marshallville, Ga., New Perry Nursing Home, Ga. Ch. Home Mem. Houston County Bd. Health, 1944—; med. adviser, examiner Houston County Coroner's Office, 1941—; med. mem. Houston County Selective Service Bd., 1942—; med. examiner local N.G. unit, 1944-69. Served with USPHS, 1931-36. Named Man of Yr., Perry Kiwanis Club, 1958, Exchange Club, Perry, 1970. Mem. Am., So., Ga., Peach med. assns., Democrat. Methodist. Mason (32 deg., Shriner), Kiwanian. Home: 1106 1st St Perry GA 31069 Office: 1100 Swift St Perry GA 31069

HENDRICK, JAMES GILLESPIE III, agrl. engr.; b. Birmingham, Ala., June 15, 1931; s. James Gillespie and Leslie Eova (Polk) H.; B.S., Auburn U., 1958, M.S., 1960; Ph.D., Mich. State U., 1962; m. Joy Elisabeth West, June 5, 1972; children by previous marriage—Kay (Mrs. Edward Lafayette Howard), Thomas James. Researcher, tchr. dept. agrl. engring. Auburn U., 1962-68; researcher U.S. Dept. Agr., Agrl. Research Service, Nat. Tillage Machinery Lab., Auburn, Ala., 1968—; asso. prof. Auburn (Ala.) U., 1965—. Cons. U.S. Army, 1962. Served with USAF, 1952-57. Registered profl. engr., Ala. Mem. Am. Soc. Agrl. Engrs. (chmn. nat. com. 1969—), Nat. Soc. Profl. Engrs. (chmn. Auburn chpt. 1968-69), Sigma Xi, Gamma Sigma Delta. Contbr. articles to profl. jours. Home: 435 Pinedale Dr Auburn AL 36830 Office: PO Box 792 Auburn AL 36830

HENDRICKS, CHARLES MARVIN, JR., physician; b. Greenville, S.C., Jan. 31, 1926; s. Charles Marvin and Elizabeth (Cochran) H.; student Furman U., 1942-44; M.D., U. S.C., 1948; m. Norma Elizabeth Rutter, Apr. 22, 1949; 1 son, Charles Marvin III. Intern, U.S. Naval Hosp., Portsmouth, Va., 1948-50; Charity Hosp., New Orleans, 1954-56; practice medicine specializing in internal medicine, Fort Lauderdale, Fla., 1956-61; chief med. service VA Center, Dublin, Ga., 1961—, head cons. teaching program in assn. with Med. Coll. Ga., 1965—. Served with M.C., USN, 1948-54. Fellow Am. Coll. Physicians; mem. A.M.A., Phi Chi. Presbyn. Rotarian. Club: Dublin (Ga.) Country. Address: VA Center Dublin GA 31021

HENDRICKSON, ELLWOOD ROBERT, engring. co. exec.; b. York, Pa., Nov. 4, 1921; s. Elwood Harkins and Myrtle (Hollinger) H.; B.S., Pa. State U., 1942; M.S., U. Wis., 1948, Ph.D., 1950; m. Cecelia Marie Berry, June 25, 1946; 1 dau., Lynda (Mrs. Garland Cox). San. engr. Oficina Tecnica Stubbins, Caracas, Venezuela, 1946-47; instr. U. Wis., 1949-50; asso. prof. U. Fla., 1950-58, prof., 1958-66, dir. research, 1964-66, now adj. prof.; v.p. Resources Research, Inc., Falls Church, Va., 1966-68; pres. Environmental Engring., Inc., Gainesville, Fla., 1968-73, chmn. bd., 1973—; dir. Reynolds, Smith and Hills, Architects-Engrs.-Planners, Inc., Jacksonville; spl. cons. USPHS, 1954—. Chmn. Fla. Air Pollution Control Commn., 1958-66; chmn. Gordon Research Conf., 1967. Served from 2d lt. to capt. C.E., AUS, 1942-46. Recipient award for distinguished service Fla. Engring. Soc., 1968. Registered profl. engr., Fla. Diplomate Am. Bd. Indsl. Hygiene, Am. Acad. Environmental Engrs. Mem. Am. Soc. C.E. (past sect. pres.), Am. Pub. Health Assn., Nat. Soc. Profl. Engr. (dir.), Fla. Engring. Soc. (past pres.), Air Pollution Control Assn. (past pres.), Am. Soc. Testing Materials, Am. Indsl. Hygiene Assn., Water Pollution Control Fedn., T.A.P.P.I. Clubs: Gainesville Golf and Country, Tampa Yacht and Country. Author: (with H.D. Townsend) Register of Air Pollution Analysis, 1958, also others. Contbr. articles to profl. jours. Home: 2044 NW 7th Pl Gainesville FL 32603 Office: PO Box 13454 Univ Sta Gainesville FL 32604

HENDRICKSON, JEROME ORLAND, assn. exec., lawyer; b. Eau Claire, Wis., July 25, 1918; s. Harold and Clara (Halvorson) H.; student Wis. State Coll., 1936-39; J.D., U. Wis., 1942; m. Helen Phoebe Harty, Dec. 27, 1948; children—Jaime Ann, Jerome Orland. Admitted to Wis. bar, 1942, U.S. Supreme Ct. bar, 1956; pvt. practice, Eau Claire, 1946; sales and advt. mgr. Coca-Cola Bottling Co., Inc., Eau Claire, 1947-48; exec. sec. Eau Claire Community Chest, 1948-49; in charge dist. office Am. Petroleum Inst., Kansas City, Mo., 1950-53, Chgo., 1953-55; exec. dir. Nat. Assn. Plumbing-Heating-Cooling Contractors, 1955-64; exec. v.p. Cast Iron Soil Pipe Inst., Washington, 1964—; sec. Joint Apprentice Text, Inc., 1955-64. Treas. Wis. Community Chest, 1948-49. Treas. All-Industry Plumbing and Heating Modernization Com., 1956-57; co-sec. Joint Industry Program Com., 1958-64; sec. Nat. Conf. Plumbing-Heating-Cooling Industry, 1962-66; chmn. nat. conf. Plumbing-Heating-Cooling Conf., 1967-69. Served from ensign to lt. USNR, 1943-46. Mem. Am., Wis. bar assns., Am. Soc. Assn. Execs., U. Wis. Alumni Assn., Wis. Law Alumni Assn. (pres. Washington chpt. 1970-73), Bldg. Ofcls. Conf. Am., Internat. Assn. Plumbing and Mech. Ofcls., Wis. State Soc. Washington (pres. 1966-68), Am. Soc. San. Engring., Gamma Eta Gamma (pres. Upsilon chpt. 1941-42). Episcopalian. Mason (32 deg., Shriner). Clubs: Washington Golf and Country; International (Washington). Home: 4621 33d St N Arlington VA 22207 Office: 2029 K St Washington DC 20006

HENDRIX, DON COLE, city ofcl.; b. Coffeyville, Kan., Aug. 15, 1934; s. L. Clark and Josephine Elizabeth (Cole) H.; B.A., Kan. U., 1956, M.P.A., 1963; m. Carol Harshbarger, June 10, 1956; children—Stephen, Scott, Mark. Adminstrv. asst. City of San Angelo, Tex., 1958-59; city mgr., Marceline, Mo., 1959-61, Gladstone, Mo., 1961-64; dir. personnel, Kansas City, Mo., 1964-67, asst. city mgr., 1967-69, exec. dir. Law Enforcement Planning Commn., 1969-71; city mgr., Charlottesville, Va., 1971—. Served with AUS, 1957-58. Named Outstanding Grad., Kan. U., 1956. Mem. Internat. City Mgmt. Assn., Internat. Assn. Chiefs of Police, Pub. Personnel Assn. Rotarian. Home: 1946 Michael Pl Charlottesville VA 22901 Office: PO Box 911 Charlottesville VA 22902

HENDRIX, FLOYD FULLER, educator; b.Columbia, N.C., Apr. 18, 1933; s. Floyd Fuller and Dorothy (Dowling) H.; B.S. in Botany with honors, N.C. State U., 1955, M.S. in Plant Pathology, 1957; Ph.D., Cal. at Berkeley, 1961; m. Frances Greene, Jan. 25, 1955; children—Kathleen Hendrix, Floyd III, P. Burton. Plant pathologist S.E. Forest Experiment Sta., U.S. Dept. Agr., 1961-64; mem. faculty dept. plant pathology U. Ga., Athens, 1965—, prof., 1963—. Vice pres., dir. Hendrix-Dail Inc., Greenville, N.C., 1964-73, pres. 1973—; dir. Specialized Research & Cons. Co., Athens. Served with AUS, 1957. Recipient Superior Service award U.S. Forestry Service, 1973. Mem. Am. Inst. Biol. Scis. (recipient Cambell award 1963), Am. Phytopathol. Soc., Am. Mycol. Soc., Gamma Sigma Delta (recipient outstanding scientist award 1973). Contbr. profl jours. Home: Red Fox Run Athens GA 30601

HENDRIX, HAROLD BRINDLEY, elec. and mech. engr.; b. Cullman, Ala., Mar. 24, 1908; s. Columbus N. and Nancy (Reid) H.; B.S. in Elec. Engring., U. Ala., 1931, B.S. in Mech. Engring., 1933; m. Willida Gossett, Dec. 31, 1938; children—Brindley B., John B. Specification engr. Standard Co., Linden, N.J., 1936-40; elec. and mech. engr. TVA, Knoxville, 1940-42, asst. dir., chief of procurement, Chattanooga, 1954-73; cons. in engring. and purchasing, 1973—; mem. faculty U. Chattanooga Evening Coll.; mem. purchasing adv. com. City of Chattanooga. Served to lt. col. C.E., AUS, 1942-46. Registered profl. engr., Tenn. Mem. I.E.E.E. (life), Tenn. Soc. Profl. Engrs. Baptist. Patentee in field. Home: 3774 Queens Rd Chattanooga TN 37416

HENDRIX, WALTER OLON, constrn. co. exec.; b. Sylacauga, Ala., Aug. 8, 1940; s. John Ellis and Ruby Maude (Wood) H.; student Ga. Inst. Tech., 1957-60; m. Sara Frances Long, Jan. 24, 1968. Vice pres., gen. mgr. Ervin Homes of Charleston, 1960-66; asst. treas. Advance Mortgage Corp., Atlanta, 1966; chief engr. Hobart Smith Constrn. Co., Charlotte, N.C., 1967; v.p. John Crosland Co., Charlotte, 1967—. Mem. Home Builders Assn. Charlotte (2d v.p., dir.). Club: Providence Civitan (Charlotte). Home: 1019 Sundown Circle Taylors SC 29687 Office: PO Box 6745 Greenville SC 29606

HENDRY, JAMES E., lawyer, automobile club exec.; b. Perry, Fla., Nov. 7, 1912; s. Wesley Alonzo and Mae (Weaver) H.; student St. Petersburg Jr. Coll., 1930-32; J.D., U. Fla., 1935; m. Frances Swope, June 25, 1948; children—James E., Jayne L., Thomas S., John W., David F. Vice pres. Hendry Lumber Co., 1935-42, sec., treas., 1946-60; partner, mgr. Hendry Bldg. Co., 1946-60; practice law as James E. Hendry, atty., 1961—; pres. Gulf Housing Corp., 1946; sec.-mgr. St. Petersburg A.A.A. Motor Club, 1962-67, exec. v.p., gen. mgr., 1967—; v.p. Club Ins. Agy., Inc., 1962—; adv. bd. Farmer's Nat. Life Ins. Co. Admitted to Supreme Ct. bar. Mem. City Planning and Zoning Bd., 1948-57, Pinellas County Sch. Bd., 1957-66; mem. Pinellas Co. Airport Com., 1952; mem. St. Petersburg Planning Commn. Mem. citizens adv. com. St. Petersburg Jr. Coll., 1948-68, bd. govs., 1938-48, chmn. dist. bd. trustees; pres. bd. dirs. YMCA, 1951; mem. Mound Park Hosp. Bd., 1951-52; mem. bd. Pinellas County chpt. Am. Cancer Soc., chmn. Cancer Drive, 1962; mem. Civil Def. Council; pres. Fla. Sch. Bd. Assn., 1964; sec.-treas. Southeastern Conf. AAA Motor Clubs, 1964, v.p., 1965, pres., 1966, treas. Eastern Conf. AAA Motor Clubs, 1970-71, vice chmn., 1972—; exec. com. Continuing Ednl. Council Fla., 1964; mem. Nat. Com. Support Pub. Schs., 1964; mem. Pinellas Com. of 100, St. Petersburg Traffic and Safety Com., State Community Coll. Council. Pres., St. Petersburg Jr. Coll. Found. Lt. comdr. USCG Res. Mem. Am., St. Petersburg bar assns., Fla. Bar, Am. Judicature Soc., Fla. C. of C., Fla. Travel Council, Nat. Assn. Home Builders (past dir.), Contractors and Builders Assn. of Pinellas County (pres. 1953), Fla. Home Builders Assn. (v.p. 1955), Phi Delta Theta, Phi Alpha Delta. Democrat. Methodist. Kiwanian (pres. St. Petersburg 1951). Clubs: St. Petersburg Yacht, Quarterback, Commerce. Home: 409 Snell Isle Blvd St Petersburg FL 33704 Office: 1211 1st Av N St Petersburg FL 33705

HENDRY, NORMAN C., judge; b. Adel, Ga., Jan. 20, 1905; s. Andrew Alexander and Hennie Lou (Hurst) H.; student So. Fla. Coll. Law, U. Miami Law Sch.; m. Elsie May Davison, Jan. 11, 1926. Admitted to Fla. bar, 1932, since practiced in Miami; judge Civil Ct. of Dade County, 1940; now judge 3d Dist. Ct. of Appeal, Miami. Mem. Am., Dade County bar assns., Fla. Bar, Am. Judicature Soc., S.A.R., Com. of 100, Phi Alpha Delta. Democrat. Methodist. Mason (Shriner), Elk. Clubs: Exchange, Century, Flamingo. Address: 1350 NW 12th Av Miami FL 33136

HENICAN, CASWELL ELLIS, lawyer; b. New Orleans, Feb. 10, 1905; s. Joseph Patrick and Alice (Boning) H.; LL.B., Tulane U., 1926; m. Elizabeth Cleveland, June 18, 1930; children—Alice (Mrs. Claude V. Perrier, Jr.), Caswell Ellis, Margaret (Mrs. F. Gordon Wilson, Jr.), Dorothy (Mrs. Charles E. Heidingsfelder), Joseph Patrick III. Admitted to La. bar, 1926, since practiced in New Orleans; asso. firm Lemle, Moreno & Lemle, 1926-33; sr. partner firm Henican, Carriere & Cleveland, 1933-40, Henican, James & Cleveland, 1940—. Chmn. La. Bd. Pub. Welfare, 1940-47; pres. New Orleans Community Chest, 1940, Council Social Agys., 1939, Asso. Catholic Charities New Orleans, 1938, Archidiocesian Vocation Devel. Commn. Chmn. adv. bd. Mercy Hosp., Retreat House of Cenacle for Women; bd. dirs., v.p. Magnolia Sch. Decorated Knight of St. Gregory, Order of St. Louis King of France; recipient medal as most outstanding young man New Orleans Jr. C. of C., 1940, F. Edward Hebert award as most outstanding alumnus of Jesuit High Sch., 1960. Mem. Am., La., New Orleans (pres. 1958) bar assns., Soc. Hosp. Attys. Club: Serra (chpt. pres. 1960). Home: 1831 Octavia St New Orleans LA 70115 Office: 4440 One Shell Sq New Orleans LA 70139

HENINGTON, DAVID MEAD, librarian; b. El Dorado, Ark., Aug. 16, 1929; s. Bud Henry and Lucile (Scranton) H.; B.A. in History, U. Houston, 1951; M.S. in L.S., Columbia, 1956; m. Barbara Gibson, June 2, 1956; children—Mark David, Gibson Mead, Paul Billins. Young adult librarian Bklyn. Pub. Library, 1956-58; head lit. and history dept. Dallas Pub. Library, 1958, asst. dir., 1962-67; dir. Waco (Tex.) Pub. Library, 1958-62, Houston Pub. Library, 1967—. Served with USAF, 1951-55. Rotarian. Home: 6225 San Felipe Rd Houston TX 77027 Office: 500 McKinney St Houston TX 77002

HENIZE, KARL GORDON, astronomer, astronaut; b. Cin., Oct. 17, 1926; s. Fred R. and Mabel (Redmon) H.; student Dennison U., 1944-45; B.A., U. Va., 1947, M.A., 1948; Ph.D., U. Mich., 1954; m. Caroline Weber, June 27, 1953; children—Kurt Gordon, Marcia Lynn, Skye Karen, Vance Karl. Observer, U. Mich. Lamont-Hussey Obs., Bloemfontein, South Africa, 1948-51; Carnegie postdoctoral fellow Mt. Wilson Obs., Pasadena, Cal., 1954-56; sr. astronomer charge Photog. Satellite Tracking Stas., Smithsonian Astrophys. Obs., Cambridge, 1956-59; asso. prof. dept. astronomy Northwestern U., 1959-64, prof., 1964-67, on leave of absence, 1967-72; scientist-astronaut NASA, 1967—, jet pilot tng. Vance AFB, Enid, Okla., 1968-69; support crew mem. Apollo 15 Mission, 1970-71; adj. prof. U. Tex., 1972—. Guest observer Mt. Stromlo Obs., Canberra, Australia, 1961-62; cons. Ency. Brit. Films, 1959-67; Mem. astronomy subcom. NASA Space Sci. Steering Com., 1965-68. Served with USNR, 1944-46; lt. comdr. Ret. Res. Mem. Am. (vis. prof. 1958-64), Royal, Pacific astron. socs., Internat. Astron. Union, A.A.A.S., Phi Beta Kappa. Home: 18630 Point Lookout Dr Houston

TX 77058 Office: Astronaut Office NASA Johnson Space Center Houston TX 77058

HENKEL, DONALD DALE, assn. exec.; b. Oak Park, Ill., June 26, 1929; s. George Fred and Gertrude (Bradshaw) H.; B.A., Ind. U., 1951; M.S., George Williams Coll., 1955; Ph.D., U. Ill., 1967; m. Marilyn Ruth Bartle, Oct. 2, 1953; children—Scott, Donna, William. Dir. recreation, Loveland, Colo., 1955-60, Villa Park, Ill., 1960-65; mgr. office edn. and profl. services Nat. Recreation and Park Assn., Arlington, Va., 1967—. Dir. educators group, Nat. Conf. Programming, Internship, Personnel Services, Accreditation, Registration and Continuing Edn.; asso. U.S. Dept. Def. Edn. for Leisure Project and Nat. Park-Farm Project. Served to 1st lt., USAF, 1951-53. Recipient spl. award, Soc. Park and Recreation Educators, 1972. Mem. Nat. Recreation and Park Assn. Home: 6912 30th St N Arlington VA 22213 Office: 1601 N Kent St Arlington VA 22209

HENKEL, JOHN HARMON, educator; b. Kentwood, La., Aug. 14, 1924; s. William Hatton and Margaret Gwendolyn (Watson) H.; student Southeastern La. Coll., 1941-43; B.S., Tulane U., 1947, M.S., 1948; Ph.D., Brown U., 1954; m. Sara Ernestine Saucier, Apr. 23, 1948; children—Wendolyn Elizabeth (Mrs. Wayne Franklin Brackett Jr.), Sally Lee (Mrs. Howard Barry Bone Jr.), Jenny Saucier, Margaret Loraine, Pamela Ann. Jr. research technologist Magnolia Petroleum Co., Dallas, 1948-51, sr. research technologist, 1954-55; research asst. Brown U., Providence, 1951-54; asst. prof. U. Ga., Athens, 1955, asso. prof., 1958-64, prof. physics, 1964—. Dir. 19th Ann. Ga. State Sci. Fair, 1967; adviser Ga. chpt. Circle K Internat., 1966-72. Co-pres. Barrow Sch. P.T.A., Athens, 1964-66; chmn. Tulane Alumni Found., 1970—. Bd. dirs. Wesley Found., Athens, Ga., 1966-72, pres. 1971-72. Served with USNR, 1943-46. NSF fellow, 1959-60; NSF grantee, 1962-69; NRC sr. research asso., 1973-74. Fellow A.A.A.S.; mem. Am. Phys. Soc., Ga. Acad. Sci. (fellow editorial bd. 1964—, council mem. 1964-67), Sigma Xi, Sigma Chi. Methodist. Elk, Kiwanian. Club: Green Hills Country (pres. bd. dirs. Athens 1967-71). Home: 395 Hampton Ct Athens GA 30601

HENLEY, JOE RAMA, dentist; b. Greeneville, Tenn., Nov. 7, 1942; s. Orval Rama and Minnie Maude (Mathes) H.; student E. Tenn. State U., 1961-62; D.D.S., U. Tenn., 1966, M.S., 1970 Linda Anne Fletcher, Mar. 14, 1964; children—Wynne Michele, Todd Fletcher, Kendall Paige. Extern Knox County Health Dept., 1966; group practice orthodontics, Greeneville, Tenn., 1970—; individual practice, Greeneville, Tenn., 1973—. Served to capt. USAF, 1966-68. Mem. Tenn. Dental Assn., Greeneville County, 1st Dist. dental socs., Am., So. assns. orthodontics, Greeneville Jr. C. of C., Sigma Phi Epsilon, Psi Omega. Republican. Mem. Christian Ch. Moose, Eagle, Elk. Club: Metropolitan Dinner (Kingsport). Home: 410 Oriole Dr Greeneville TN 37743 Office: Towne Sq Mall Greeneville TN 37743

HENLEY, WILLIAM BRANCH, JR., lawyer; b. Dallas, Jan. 3, 1920; s. William Branch and Vesta Mae (Lister) H.; B.S., So. Meth. U., 1940, LL.B., 1942; m. Mary Key, June 24, 1950; children—Constance, Mary Key, Cynthia Luisa. Admitted to Tex. bar, 1942; practiced in Dallas, 1947-50, 52—, Houston, 1950-52; mem. firm Anderson, Henley, Shields, Bradford & Pritchard. Dir. Bank of Tex., Dallas. Asst. atty. gen. State of Tex., 1947; asst. dist. atty. Dallas, 1947-50. Bd. dirs. Dallas Day Care Assn., 1954-66, pres., 1965-66; bd. dirs. Dallas Area Cystic Fibrosis, 1972—. Served with USNR, 1942-46. Decorated Bronze Star medal. Clubs: Northwood Country (gov. 1973—), Idlewild, Terpsichorean, Calyx, Lancers. Home: 3701 Crescent St Dallas TX 75205 Office: 3100 Fidelity Union Tower Dallas TX 75201

HENNAGE, JOSEPH HOWARD, publishing, printing co. exec.; b. Washington, Jan. 2, 1921; s. Joseph Howard and Helen (Cook) H.; student pub. schs., Washington; m. June Elizabeth Stedman, Sept. 29, 1947. Organizer, pres. Hennage Creative Printers, Washington, 1945—, Jonage Investment Corp., Washington, 1958—; pres., founder Highland House Pubs., Washington, 1969—; mem. adv. bd. Am. Security & Trust Co., Washington; dir. Graphic Arts Mut. Ins. Co., United Ins. Co. Ltd., Hamilton Bermuda. Mem. fine arts com. U.S. Dept. State; exec. com. Met. Washington Bd. Trade, 1972; chmn. joint industry-govt. adv. bd. Govt. Printing Office, 1972—; chmn. Americana com. Nat. Archives, 1972. Trustee Am. Cancer Soc.; exec. com. Washington Conv. and Visitors Bur.; bd. dirs. Boys Club Washington, 1949—, recipient award for distinguished service 1951, Alumni award, 1959; mem. council for Sch. Govt. and Bus. Adminstrn. George Washington U., chmn. Printing Mgmt. Edn. Trust Fund, 1971—. Served with USNR, 1942-45. Recipient Potomacland Ambassador, Washington Bd. Trade, 1963; Freedom Found. award, 1969; Distinguished Service award U.S. Pub. Printers, 1972; citation Brit. Fedn. Master Printers, 1971. Mem. Master Printers Am. (pres. 1967-69, man of yr. award 1969), Printing Industries Am. (chmn. bd. 1969-70, v.p. pub. relations 1971-72, Graphic Arts Man of Year 1971), Printing Industry Washington (pres. 1964-65, distinguished service award 1969), Creative Printers Am. (pres. 1963-64), Master Printers Washington (pres. 1960-61), Optimists Internat. (distinguished gov. 1957-58). Methodist (dir. 1966-70). Clubs: Nat. Capitol Optimist (pres. 1953-54), Metropolitan, City Tavern of Georgetown (Washington); Columbia Country (Chevy Chase, Md.); Farmington Country (Charlottesville, Va.). Home: 6211 Highland Dr Chevy Chase MD 20015 Office: 814 H St NW Washington DC 20001

HENNECY, JAMES HOWELL, govt. buyer; b. Marion, S.C., Mar. 10, 1913; s. Gabriel Marion and Annie Laurie (Boatwright) H.; student Mercer U. 1948-51; J.D., Walter F. George Sch. Law, 1953; m. Bobbie Helen Bobo, Dec. 28, 1963; 1 dau., Ardith Erin. Plant cashier Bordens Milk Co., Macon, Ga., 1953-55; contract specialist Dept. Air Force, Robins AFB, 1955-58, contract negotiator, 1964—; law librarian, instr. in law Walter F. George Sch. Law, Mercer U., Macon, 1958-63. Active Boy Scouts Am.; spokesman Macon Citizens for Better Hwy. Planning, 1959-62. Adviser, Young Democrats Club, 1960-63. Served with AUS, 1942-45; ETO, MTO. Mem. V.F.W., Young Americans for Freedom (asso.), Marion (S.C.) Jr. C. of C. (charter), Am. Ordnance Assn., Am. Legion, Internat. Platform Assn., Alpha Tau Omega, Delta Theta Phi, Alpha Psi Omega. Baptist (deacon). Lion. Club: Toastmaster (local pres. 1965, dist. edn. chmn. 1959-60). Home: 1347-B Adams St Macon GA 31201 Office: Directorate Procurement and Prodn WRALC Robins AFB GA 31093

HENNESSEY, THOMAS EDGAR, banker; b. Anadarko, Okla., Oct. 3, 1923; s. Martin Francis and Eva Nevada (Kelly) H.; student St. John's Minor Sem., 1941-42, St. John's Major Sem., San Antonio, 1942-46; J.D., St. Mary's U., San Antonio, 1950; m. Rosemary Elizabeth Mushall, Aug. 7, 1954; children—Richard Kevin, Thomas Allen, Stephen Joseph, Laura Kathleen. Head teller, gen. ledger bookkeeper Harlandale State Bank, San Antonio, 1951-55; admitted to Tex. bar, 1951; practiced in San Antonio, 1951-56; partner Hennessey & Hennessey, 1951-56; v.p., trust officer Bexar County Nat. Bank, San Antonio, 1956—. Treas. cub pact 360 Boy Scouts Am., 1967-70; sec., bd. dirs. San Antonio Estate Planners Council. Mem. Am. Bankers Assn. (past com. chmn.), San Antonio Bar Assn., Am. Inst. Banking. Roman Catholic. Club: Fathers of Central Catholic High School, (San Antonio). Home: 403 Kate Schenck Av San Antonio TX 78223 Office: 325 N St Mary's St San Antonio TX 78291

HENNESSY, JOHN J., lawyer; b. Savannah, Ga., Dec 20, 1905; s. James W. and Lucy (Downing) H.; A.B. magna cum laude, U. Ga.; postgrad. Harvard; J.D., Georgetown Law Sch., LL.M. with highest distinction. Admitted to Ga. bar, 1931, since practiced in Savannah; mem. firm Hennessy & Hennessy, 1942-65; spl. hearing officer Dept. Justice, 1948-67. Grand marshal Armed Forces Day parade. 1970, speaker Maritime Day Observance, 1973; commentator, lector Chapel Hunter AAF, 1973. Served from lt. to lt. comdr. USCGR, 1942-46; capt. Res., 1961—. Mem. Am., Ga., Savannah bar assns., Harvard Law Sch. Assn., Georgetown U., U. Ga. alumni socs., Am. Legion, Mil. Order World Wars, V.F.W. (past post comdr., dist. judge adv.), Res. Officers Assn. (past state pres.), Navy League, Southeastern Admiralty Law Inst., Hibernian Soc., Phi Beta Kappa, Phi Kappa Phi, Delta Theta Phi. Elk (hon. life, past exalted ruler), Eagle. Mem. editorial staff Georgetown U. Law Jour., 1930-31. Home: 233 E 52d St Savannah GA 31405 Office: PO Box 1114 Savannah GA 31402

HENNIGAN, HENRY WILLIAM, chem. engr.; b. Wilson, Okla., Aug. 26, 1923; s. Thomas William and Sylvia Eltine (Allen) H.; B.S., U. Okla., 1945; postgrad. Okla. State U., 1959-62; m. Edith Cavell Bean, Sept. 4, 1943; children—Camille (Mrs. Robert B. Blomeyer II), Timothy Michael, Christopher Linn, Elizabeth (Mrs. Ronney F. Sherman), Anthony William, Vincent Paul. With Phillips Petroleum Co., Bartlesville, Okla., 1946—, now dir. petroleum engring. sect., computing dept. Mem. St. John Sch. Bd. Edn., Bartlesville, 1963-69, pres., 1967-69. Served with USNR, 1942-44. Mem. Soc. Petroleum Engrs., Phi Theta Kappa, Alpha Chi Sigma. Roman Catholic. K.C. (4 deg.). Contbr. articles profl. jours. Patentee in field. Home: 1117 S Dewey Av Bartlesville OK 74003 Office: Adams Bldg Bartlesville OK 74004

HENNING, EUGENE SOMERS, ret. aerospace engr.; b. Worcester, Mass., Mar. 17, 1914; s. William Albert and Margaret (Somers) H.; B.E.E. with high distinction, Worcester Poly. Inst., 1935; m. Mary Elizabeth Hause, Oct. 7, 1939; children—Stanley Eugene, Mary Charlotte (Mrs. James S. Frazer). With Bur. Ships, U.S. Navy Dept. Washington, 1937-57, supervisory elec. engr., 1948-57; aero. research engr. U.S. Army Ballistic Missile Agy., Huntsville, Ala., 1957-60; aerospace engr. NASA Marshall Space Flight Center, Huntsville, 1960-72; ret., 1972. Registered Profl. Engr., Ala., D.C. Mem. Am. Assn. Ret. Persons, Nat. Assn. Ret. Fed. Employees, Am. Inst. Aeronautics and Astronautics, I.E.E.E., Sigma Xi. Methodist. Home: 10214 Plantation Dr SE Huntsville AL 35803

HENNING, GEORGE DURHAM, physician; b. Johnstown, Pa., Aug. 13, 1939; s. George Herman and Inez (Durham) H.; B.A., Va. Mil. Inst., 1961; M.D., U. Va., 1965; m. Edna Florence Rives, Jan. 29, 1965; children—George Thomas, Matthew William, Edward Rives, Gretchen Elizabeth. Intern, Saginaw (Mich.) Gen. Hosp., 1965-66; resident surgery Vanderbilt U. Hosp., 1968-69, resident orthopedics, 1969-71, chief resident orthopedic surgery, 1971-72; practice medicine specializing in orthopedic surgery, Roanoke (Va.) Orthopedic Clinic Assos., 1972—; mem. staff Roanoke Meml. Hosp., Community Hosp. of Roanoke Valley, Salem VA Hosp., Shenandoah Hosp., Stonewall Jackson Hosp., Lexington, Va.; clin. instr. dept. orthopedic surgery U. Va., 1972—. Served with AUS, 1966-68. Mem. Roanoke Acad. Medicine, A.M.A., Med. Soc. Va., Southwest Va. Med. Soc. Home: 2656 Southwoods Dr SW Roanoke VA 24018 Office: 1240 3d St SW Roanoke VA 24016

HENNING, RUDOLF ERNST, coll. dean; b. Hamburg, Germany, Aug. 3, 1923 (came to U.S. 1939); s. Ernest P. and Emmy (Rosenfeld) H.; B.S., Columbia, 1943, M.S., 1947, D.Eng. Sci. (Sperry Gyroscope fellow 1949-50) 1954; m. Patricia Ann Miklas, Sept. 30, 1961; 1 dau., Patricia Emerson Irwin. With Sperry Gyroscope Co., Great Neck, N.Y., 1947-58, head engring. sect., 1954-57, head engring. dept., 1957-58; with Sperry Microwave Electronics div. Sperry Rand Corp., Clearwater, Fla., 1958-70, chief engr., 1961-70; instr. elec. engring., asst. dean Coll. Engring., U. So. Fla., Tampa, 1970-71, asso. prof., asst. dean Coll. Engring. 1971—; head engring. sci. dept. Naval Electronics Lab. Center, San Diego, 1971. Mem. devel. council Morton Plant Hosp., Clearwater, Fla., 1970-71; chmn. Pinellas County Commn. on Higher Edn., 1958-63. Served with AUS, 1944-46. Fellow I.E.E.E. (chmn. nat. symposium 1965, microwave theory and techniques group, 1968); mem. Am. Soc. Engring Edn., Sigma Xi, Tau Beta Pi. Patentee in field. Home: 400 Ponce de Leon Blvd Clearwater FL 33516

HENNINGS, LEROY, JR., librarian; b. Mt. Kisco, N.Y., Aug. 17, 1936; s. LeRoy and Gretchen (Butcher) H.; A.B., U. Miami, 1960; M.S. in Library Sci., Fla. State U., 1968. Sch. librarian, tchr. geography Glades County sch. system, Moore Haven, Fla., 1961-62; librarian U. Miami Engring. and Physics Library, Coral Gables, Fla., 1962-63; librarian Miami-Dade Jr. Coll., 1964-65; librarian gen. reference and bus., sci. and tech. depts. Miami (Fla.) Pub. Library, 1966-68; librarian interlibrary loan dept. Fla. State U., Tallahassee, 1968; dir. Martin County Pub. Library, Stuart, Fla., 1968—. Mem. Am., Fla., Southeastern library assns., Kappa Alpha. Democrat. Methodist. Home: 610 Old Dixie Hwy Jensen Beach FL 33457 Office: 701 E Ocean Blvd Stuart FL 33494

HENNINGSON, ROBERT WALTER, univ. adminstr.; b. Boston, May 29, 1921; s. Peter William and Frances (Blosoom) H.; B.S., Cornell U., 1950, M.S., 1952, Ph.D., 1956; m. Frances Emily Kratky, Aug. 19, 1944; children—Karen Daye, Nancy Elaine. Teaching asst. Cornell U., Ithaca, N.Y., 1950-56; mem. faculty Clemson (S.C.) U., 1956—, asso. prof., 1961-66, prof. food sci., 1966—, also asst. dean univ. research, 1967—. Asso. referee Assn. Ofcl. Analytical Chemists, 1964—. Served with USCGR, 1942-45; now U.S. Army Res. N.Y. State Vets. fellow, 1952-56. Mem. Nat. Council Univ. Research Adminstrs., Am. Dairy Sci. Assn., Sigma Xi, Zeta Alpha Phi, Gamma Sigma Delta. Clubs: Esquires (Clemson), Boscobel Country (Pendleton, S.C.). Contbr. articles to profl. jours. Home: 6 Poplar Dr Clemson SC 29631

HENRY, AARON EDD, Democratic nat. committeeman; b. Coahoma County, Miss., July 2, 1922; s. Edd and Mattie (Logan) H.; B.S., Xavier U., 1950; m. Noelle Michael, June 10, 1950; 1 dau., Rebecca. Sec., Miss. Pharm. Soc., 1955—. Vice chmn. Ams. for Black Aged, 1972. Del. Dem. Nat. Conv., 1968; chmn. Miss. Dem. Com., 1968—; mem. Democratic Nat. Com., 1972—; chmn. Miss. Dem. Exec. Com.; state campaign mgr. Presdl. campaign, 1972. Bd. dirs. Rural Housing Alliance, Washington, Rural Am. Alliance, Ky. State Ho., Mound Bayou (Miss.) Community Hosp., Miss. Council Human Relations; nat. bd. dirs. So. Christian Leadership Conf., So. Regional Conf. Served with AUS, 1943-46; PTO. Recipient Rosa Parks award So. Christian Leadership Conf., Outstanding Citizen's award Office Econ. Opportunity. Mem. Nat. Pharm. Assn. (pres. 1963), N.A.A.C.P. (nat. dir., pres. Miss. Conf.), Coahoma County C. of C., Am. Legion, V.F.W., Omega Psi Phi. Methodist. Home: 636 Page St Clarksdale MS 38614*

HENRY, CARROLL DEWITT, feed mfg. co. exec.; b. Taylorsville, Ky., Oct. 24, 1921; s. Clinton DeWitt and Mary (Banta) H.; grad. high sch.; m. Evelyn Van Hoy, Nov. 7, 1947; children—Alice (Mrs. Charles R. LeGette), Martin DeWitt, Charles Wood II, Jean Leigh. Laborer, Crescent Roller Mills, Inc., Taylorsville, Ky., 1935-37, truckdriver, 1937-39, salesman, 1939-46, v.p., 1946-61, pres., 1961—; farm owner, Taylorsville, Ky., 1961—. Served with USAAF, 1942-45; ETO. Decorated Air medal with twelve clusters, D.F.C. Mem. Ky. Feed and Grain Assn. (dir. 1959-62, pres. 1962-63), Louisville Feed Club, Spencer County C. of C. Baptist (deacon 1947-54). Rotarian. Home: Route 3 Taylorsville KY 40071 Office: Mill St Taylorsville KY 40071

HENRY, DANIEL RAY, life ins. co. exec.; b. Waxahachie, Tex., June 30, 1944; s. Clarence McGill and Lorene Elizabeth (Kennedy) H.; B.B.A., Baylor U., 1966; m. Victoria Elizabeth Graves, June 10, 1966; 1 son, Jason Howard. Staff accountant Ernst & Ernst, Dallas, 1966-67; staff auditor Southwestern Life Ins. Co., Dallas, 1967-70, dir. internal audit, 1970-73, asst. v.p. internal audits, 1973—. Scoutmaster Circle 10 council Boy Scouts Am., 1973—, C.P.A., Tex. Fellow Life Mgmt. Inst.; mem. Am. Inst. C.P.A.'s, Tex. Soc. C.P.A.'s, Beta Alpha Psi. Lion. Home: 102 High School Dr Waxahachie TX 75165 Office: 1807 Ross Av Dallas TX 75221

HENRY, GAILE MAURICE, JR., scrap processing co. exec.; b. San Francisco, De. 7, 1944; s. Gaile Maurice and Mary Jean (Hoffman) H.; student U. Tex., 1963-65; B.B.A., Lamar U., 1967; m. Beverly Ann Tipton, June 12, 1965; children—Rodney Wade, Alicia Ashley, Gaile Maurice III. Staff accountant Haskins & Sells, C.P.A.'s, 1967-69; co-owner Beaumont Iron & Metal Co., (Tex.), 1969—; sec.-treas. Beaumont Metal Export Co., 1972—. C.P.A., Tex. Mem. Speaker's Bur. Com., Tex. Soc. C.P.A.'s, Young Men's Bus. League, Beaumont C. of C., Sigma Nu. Episcopalian. Clubs: Beaumont, Beaumont Country; Memorial Point Yacht (Livingston, Tex.). Home: 6385 Gladys St Beaumont TX 77706 Office: 3190 Hollywood St Beaumont TX 77704

HENRY, GENE PATRICK, dir. investigation Tariff Commn.; b. Dundee, Ill., Nov. 16, 1920; s. Harry DeWitte and Edith Cora (Allensworth) H.; B.A., Hamline U., 1942; postgrad. Georgetown U., 1946-47; m. Eleanor Gwenn Kufus May 28, 1943; children—Philip Michael, David Kufus. Economist, Tariff Commn., Washington, 1943-47, 48-69, dir. investigation, 1970—; economist CIA, 1947-48, House Select Com. on Fgn. Aid, 1947. Served with USNR, 1943-46. Mem. Am. Econ. Assn. Methodist. Home: 10914 New Hampshire Av Silver Spring MD 20903 Office: US Tariff Commission 8th and E St NW Washington DC 20436

HENRY, HARVEY BENART, physician; b. Waco, Tex., Aug. 27, 1899; s. Fred and Pauline (Mueller) H.; M.D., U. Tex., 1922, B.S., 1929; m. Mary Erkle Pitts, Dec. 21, 1920; children—Harvey Benart, Mary Erkle (Mrs. Dennis Frangias), Susan Elizabeth (Mrs. Robert Kealhofer). intern, John Sealy Hosp., Galveston, Tex., 1922; practice medicine, specializing in eye, ear, nose and throat, Luling, Tex., 1922-40, Austin, Tex., 1940-60, William Clinic, Woodward, Okla., 1961, Denton, Tex., 1962-64; chief eye, ear, nose and throat VA Hosp., Alexandria, La., 1964-70; pvt. practice, Pineville, La., 1970-71, 72—; dir. chronic diseases Central La. State Hosp., 1971-72. City health officer, Luling, 1922-44; chmn. Caldwell County (Tex.) Certified Med. Milk Commn., 1932-44. Active Boy Scouts Am., Nat. council rep., 20 years. Served with U.S. Army, 1918. Recipient Silver Beaver award Boy Scouts Am., 1940. Mem. Am., La., Parish med. assns., Am. Legion. Methodist (steward 1944-58). Mason (32 deg., K.T., Shriner), Kiwanian. Home: 609 Lallah St Pineville LA 71360

HENRY, JACK HOPKINS, orthopedic surgeon; b. Lubbock, Tex., Apr. 20, 1937; s. Wells Blackburn and Mattie Allene (Hopkins) H.; B.A. in Chemistry, Tex. Tech. U., 1960; M.D., U. Tex., 1964; m. Jane Hopkins Underwood, June 10, 1965; children—David Blackburn, Robert Underwood. Intern, Ben Taub Hosp., Houston, 1964-65; resident gen. surgery U. Pa. Hosp., 1965-66; resident orthopedic surgery Columbia-Presbyn. Med. Center, N.Y.C., 1966-69, sr. Annie C. Kane fellow hip surgery, 1971-72; practice, medicine, specializing in orthopedic surgery, San Antonio, Tex., 1972—; mem. staff Methodist, Baptist, Santa Rosa, Nix Meml., N.E. Bapt., Met. Gen., San Antonio Community hosps. Nat. v.p. student A.M.A., 1963-64. Served to maj. USAF, 1969-71. Carl Berg traveling fellow, 1972. Diplomate Am. Bd. Orthopedic Surgery. Mem. Am. Acad. Orthosurgeons, Phi Gamma Delta, Nu Sigma Nu. Presbyn. Address: 1303 McCullough Av San Antonio TX 78212

HENRY, JOHN JAMES, physicist; b. White Pine, Tenn., Feb. 12, 1929; s. Herbert Holloway and Clara (Spurgeon) H.; student U. Fla., 1946-48; B.S., Lincoln Meml. U., 1954; m. Audrey Duffield, Sept. 14, 1954; children—Mark Stephen, Claudia Alexandra, John James. Instrument technician Carbide & Carbon Chem. Co., Oak Ridge, 1954-56; asso. physicist Union Carbide Corp., Oak Ridge, 1956-61, physicist nuclear div., 1961—. Instr. transistor circuit theory Oak Ridge Adult Edn. Program, 1962-65. Scoutmaster, Boy Scouts Am., Oak Ridge, 1960-62; tympanist Oak Ridge Symphony Orch., 1965—, publicity chmn., 1966-67, v.p., 1968-69. Served with USMC, 1949-52. Mem. Instrument Soc. Am. (sr.), A.A.A.S., I.E.E.E. Episcopalian. Patentee in field. Home: 639 Pennsylvania Av Oak Ridge TN 37830 Office: Y12 Plant Oak Ridge TN 37830

HENRY, JOSEPH RAYMOND, physician; b. New Albany, Miss., June 3, 1913; s. George Willis and Retta (Parker) H.; B.A., Miss. Coll., 1934; M.D., U. Tenn., 1939; m. Mary Souter Winders, Sept. 11, 1949. Intern Grace Hosp., Detroit, 1939-40; resident Brooke Army Hosp., San Antonio, 1947-50; commd. 1st lt. U.S. Army, 1939, advanced through grades to col., 1956; chief surg. service Scott AFB (Ill.) Hosp., 1950-52; comdr. George AFB Hosp., Cal., 1953-56, chief surgery 1953-56; chief profl. services USAF Hosp., Tachikawa, Japan, 1956-59; comdr. USAF Hosp., Keesler AFB, Miss., 1960-64; comdr. USAF Hosp. Wiesbaden, Germany, 1964-67, Keesler AFB, Miss., 1967-69; mem. staff Union County Gen. Hosp., Tippah County Gen. Hosp. Decorated Legion of Merit with two oak leaf clusters, Soldier's Medal, Bronze Star, Air medal (Army); recipient Miss. Magnolia medal. Diplomate Am. Bd. Surgery. Fellow A.C.S.; Internat. Coll. Surgeons; mem. A.M.A., Aerospace Med. Assn., Air Force Clin. Surgeons Soc., Air Force Flight Surgeons Soc. Baptist. Home: 1089 Hwy 30 W New Albany MS 38652 Office: 110 Colter Dr New Albany MS 38652

HENRY, JOSEPH WARD, lawyer; b. Lynnville, Tenn., Sept. 20, 1916; s. Joseph Walter and Annie Louise (Ward) H.; student Middle Tenn. State U., 1935-37; LL.B., Cumberland U. Law Sch., 1937-38; postgrad. Washington Coll. Law, 1939-40; m. Marjorie Royster Clark, June 28, 1943; children—Joseph Ward, Robert Clark. Admitted to Tenn. bar, 1940; practice law, Pulaski, Tenn., 1941—. City atty., Pulaski, 1947-53; mem. Tenn. Ho. of Reps., 1949; adj. gen., Tenn., 1953-59; chmn. Democratic Exec. Com., Giles County, Tenn., 1967-71. Bd. dirs. Cumberland Heights Found., Nashville. Served with AUS, 1941-46. Decorated Bronze Star. Fellow Am. Bar Found.; mem. Am. Legion (comdr. post 1947-48; comdr. dist. 1948-49), Tenn. (pres. 1970-71), Am. (ho. dels.) bar assns., Tenn. Trial Lawyers Assn. (pres. 1964-66), Am. Judicature Soc. (dir. 1971—), Am. Trial Lawyers Assn. Methodist. Elk. Home: 313 Rose St Pulaski TN 38472 Office: 119 S 1st St Pulaski TN 38478

HENRY, MARSHALL WEBSTER, JR., trucking co. exec.; b. Rocky Mount, N.C., Jan. 20, 1946; s. M. Webster and Nancy (Powell) H.; A.B., U. N.C., 1969; m. Gayle Sims Henry, Sept. 29, 1973; 1 son, Chadwick G. Seymour. Tchr. Nash County Schs., Nashville, N.C., 1969-70; with C.S. Henry Transfer, Inc., Rocky Mount, 1969—, sec., dir., 1972—, treas. 1973—. Mem. N.C. Motor Carriers Assn. (dir. 1973—), U.S. Power Squadrons (exec. officer Rocky Mount br. 1974-75). Club: Optimist (Rocky (Mount). Home: 1621 Maple Creek Dr Rocky Mount NC 27801 Office: PO Drawer 2306 Rocky Mount NC 27801

HENRY, MATTHEW GEORGE, bishop; b. Chapel Hill, N.C., Oct., 25, 1910; s. George Kenneth Grant and Mary Elizabeth (Harding) H.; A.B., U. N.C., 1931; B.D., Va. Theol. Sem., 1935, D.D., 1949; D.D., U. of South, 1948; m. Cornelia Catharine Sprinkle, June 30, 1937; children—Anna Catharine, George K., Matthew G., Elizabeth H. Teaching fellow in chemistry U. N.C., 1931-32; ordained to ministry Protestant Episcopal Ch., 1935; temporarily in charge St. Phillip's Ch., Durham, also St. Paul's Ch., Winston-Salem, N.C., 1935; in charge Christ Ch., Walnut Cove, St. Phillip's Ch., Germanton, Messiah Ch., Mayodan, and Emmanual Ch., Stoneville, N.C., 1936; rector Calvary Parish, Tarboro, N.C., 1936-43, Christ Ch., Charlotte, N.C., 1943-48; bishop Diocese of Western N.C., Asheville, 1948—. Pres. N.C. Council Chs., 1964-67. Trustee St. Augustine's Coll., Raleigh, N.C., Patterson Sch., U. of South. Mem. Phi Beta Kappa, Alpha Chi Sigma, Delta Upsilon. Home: 9 Crowningway Dr Asheville NC 28804 Office: PO Box 368 Black Mountain NC 28711

HENRY, ROBERT FILLMORE, bus. exec.; b. Trinity, Ala.; s. W. G. and Mary (Davis) H.; B.Ph., Emory U., 1926, student, Lamar Sch. Law, 1927; LL.D., Birmingham So. Coll., 1966; m. Annie Mae Branch, Oct. 14, 1932; children—Robert Fillmore, Anne (Mrs. J. Wallace Tidmore). Formerly pres. Birmingham So. Coll.; chmn. Robert F. Henry Tile Co., Inc., Montgomery, Ala., Montgomery Bldg. Materials Co.; dir. Nat. Waterways Conf., Inc., Union Bank & Trust Co., Ala. Gas Corp., Alagasco Energy Co. Inc. Hon. consul of Thailand. Pres. Coosa, Ala. Rivers Improvement Assn. Trustee Robert F. Henry Found.; past pres. United Appeal Montgomery, Montgomery Symphony Orch. Assn. Recipient Patriotic Civilian Service award, Dept. Army, 1963. Mem. Birmingham-So. Coll. Alumni Assn. (chmn. exec. com. of bd. trustees, past pres.), English Speaking Union (past pres. Montgomery chpt.). Mem. U.S., Ala. (dir.), Montgomery (dir., past pres.) chambers commerce, So. Tile, Marble and Terrazo Contractors Assn., Tile Contractors Assn. Am. Inc., Nat. Terrazzo and Mosaic Assn., Ala. Hist. Soc., Newcomen Soc. N. Am., Pi Kappa Alpha, Phi Delta Phi, Omicron Delta Kappa. Methodist (past chmn. bd. trustees). Clubs: Montgomery Country, Beauvoir, Crescent Lake Country. Home: 3211 Le Bron Av Montgomery AL 36106 Office: 919 Bell St Montgomery AL 36104

HENRY, ROBERT WILLIAM, bank exec.; b. Conway, Ark., Aug. 22, 1928; s. J. Wendell and Amma (Reeves) H.; A.B., Hendrix Coll., 1950; J.D., U. Ark., 1953; m. Barbara Jean Blackburn, June 10, 1951; children—Frank Wendell, Robert William, Clifford Joseph, Margaret Jeanne. Admitted to Ark. bar, 1953, U.S. Dist. Cts., 1953; partner Henry & Henry, Conway, 1953-58; individual practice, Conway, 1958-71; partner Henry & Henry, Conway, 1971—; dir. 1st Nat. Bank Conway, 1961—; city atty., Conway, 1955—. Mem. Ark. Bd. Law Examiners, 1972—. Bd. dirs. Faulkner County Day Sch., Conway, 1971—. Mem. Am., Ark., Faulkner County bar assns., Delta Theta Phi. Democrat. Methodist. Home: 7 Randolph Pl Conway AR 72032 Office: 1004 Front St Conway AR 72032

HENRY, RONALD JAMES, educator; b. Belfast, North Ireland, Feb. 5, 1940; s. William James and Mary Ann (Whyte) H.; B.S., Queens U., 1961, Ph.D., 1964; m. Norah Patricia Gibson, July 17, 1965; 1 dau., Norah Lynn. Came to U.S., 1965. Asst. lectr. Queens U., Belfast, North Ireland, 1964-65; Nat. Acad. Scis.-NRC fellow Goddard Space Flight Center, Greenbelt, Md., 1965-66; asst. physicist Kitt Peak Nat. Obs., Tucson, 1966-69; asso. prof. La. State U., Baton Rouge, 1969-73, prof. physics, 1973—. Mem. Am. Phys. Soc., A.A.A.S. Contbr. articles to profl. jours. Home: 814 Seyburn Ct Baton Rouge LA 70808 Office: La State U Baton Rouge LA 70803

HENRY, WILLIAM PATRICK, handling equipment mfg. co. exec.; b. Pontotoc, Miss., Aug. 7, 1924; s. Willie Clements and Alma (Edwards) H.; B.S. in Agrl. Engring., Tex. A and M U., 1949; m. Patsy Ruth Seveyrac, Jan. 6, 1951; children—Debra Lea, Connie Ruth. Sales engr. Short & Brownlee Co., Newport, Ark., 1950-54; v.p., head constrn. dept., 1954-58; v.p., gen. mgr. Delta Steel & Constrn. Co., West Memphis, Ark., 1958-61, pres., gen. mgr., 1961—; v.p. Gen. Investments Inc., West Memphis, 1966—; pres., mgr. Mill Machinery Mfg. Corp., West Memphis, 1967—, Mill Builders, Inc., West Memphis, 1968—. Pres. Band Boosters, West Memphis, 1969. Mem. West Memphis C. of C. (dir.), Am. Soc. Agrl. Engrs., Mid-South Soybean Assn. Methodist (mem. ch. bd.). Rotarian. Club: Meadowbrook Country (West Memphis). Home: 301 Pearce St West Memphis AR 72301 Office: 406 Woods St West Memphis AR 72301

HENSEL, LEN, radio broadcasting exec.; b. Phila., Mar. 30, 1926; s. John and Jean (Cedar) H.; B.S., Auburn U., 1948; m. Patricia Ann Rhodes, Sept. 15, 1951; children—Patricia Lynn, Janie Sue. Program dir. WOWL Radio, Florence, Ala., 1949-52; account exec. WAPI-TV, Birmingham, Ala., 1952-54; account exec., regional sales mgr. ZIV-TV Programs, 1954-62; nat. sales mgr., gen. sales mgr. WSM Radio, Nashville, 1962-71, v.p., gen. mgr., 1972—. Served with USNR, 1943-45; PTO. Mem. Sales and Marketing Execs., Nashville C. of C., Pi Kappa Alpha. Presbyn. Kiwanian. Clubs: Kennel, City (Nashville). Home: 6600 Fox Hollow Rd Nashville TN 37205 Office: PO Box 100 Nashville TN 37202

HENSEL, RUDOLPH WILLIAM, aero. engr.; b. Hamburg, Germany, Oct. 12, 1919; s. Rudolf and Louise (Schroeder) H.; came to U.S., 1921, naturalized, 1928; B.S., Mass. Inst. Tech., 1941, M.S. with honors, 1942; Aero. Engr., Cal. Inst. Tech., 1944; m. Beatrice L. Hoffman, May 29, 1948; children—William, Robert, Shirley, Thomas. Engr.-in-charge Wright Field 10 Foot Wind Tunnel, Wright Patterson AFB, 1944-47; chief data analysis dept. Cal. Inst. Tech. Coop. Wind Tunnel Pasadena. 1947-53; transonic br. mgr. propulsion wind tunnel ARO, Inc., Arnold Engring. Devel. Center, Arnold Air Force Sta., Tenn., 1953-56, chief propulsion wind tunnel, 1956-69, dir. operations, 1969-73, tech. dir., 1973—. Lectr. U. Tenn. Space Inst., 1964-69. Served from 2d lt. to maj., USAAF, 1942-47. Registered profl. engr., Cal. Asso. fellow Am. Inst. Aeros. and Astronautics (mem. nat. tech. com. 1965-68); mem. Nat., Tenn. socs. profl. engrs., Sigma Xi. Club: Lakewood Golf and Country (dir. 1967-70) (Tullahoma, Tenn.). Home: 1008 Forrest Dr Tullahoma TN 37388 Office: Arnold Air Force Station TN 37389

HENSGEN, SISTER CAROLEEN, supt. schs.; b. St. Louis, Nov. 18, 1914; d. Jules Francis and Louise (Meyer) Hensgen; student Notre Dame Coll., St. Louis, 1932-36, Quincy Coll., 1933-40; A.B., St. Louis U., 1944, M.A., 1948; postgrad. Loyola U., New Orleans, 1956, Marquette U., 1956, Georgetown U., 1962, Loretto Heights Coll., 1963, N.Y. U, 1965, Tex. A. and M., 1967, U. Utah, 1968. Joined Order Sch. Sisters Notre Dame, 1932, tchr. elementary grades, St. Francis, Quincy, Ill., 1933-40, Cathedral Sch., Belleville, Ill., 1940-42, St. Alphonsus, St. Louis, 1942-44; tchr. Latin and English Rosati-Kain High Sch., St. Louis, 1944-48; prin. Notre Dame High Sch., St. Louis, 1948-50, St. Paul High Sch., Highland, Ill., 1950-51, St. John Jr. High Sch., Burlington, Ia., 1951-56, Redemptorist High Sch., New Orleans, 1956-62, Redemptorist Sr. High Sch., Baton Rouge, 1962-67; supr. 13 elementary schs. Diocese Baton Rouge, 1962-67; supt. schs. Diocese Dallas-Ft. Worth, Dallas, 1967—. Dir. Head Start for Baton Rouge, summer 1966; rep. Title IV to Title III Cultural Program to S.Am., summer 1967. Mem. Human Relations Group Baton Rouge, 1962-67; mem. planning com. United Givers, 1967; chmn. Head Start Program, 1968-71. Bd. dirs. Community Advancement, Inc., Baton Rouge, 1966-67, War on Poverty, 1968-71, Dallas Day Care Centers, 1971—, Assn. for Prevention Blindness, 1971—; bd. dirs., mem. exec. com. S.W. Ednl. Devel. Lab. for La. and Tex. Title IV, 1967. Spl. grantee for implementation civil rights under Title III, summer 1965. Mem. Nat. Assn. Secondary Sch. Prins., La. Prins. Assn., Nat. Cath. Edn. Assn. (adv. bd. 1969—), So. Assn. Colls. and Schs., So. Assn. Ind. Schs., Assn. Supervision and Curriculum Devel., Supts. Assn. U.S. Cath. Conf. Home: Route Box 4 Irving TX 75062 Office: 3915 Lemmon Av Dallas TX 75219

HENSLEY, BILLY LEWIS, real estate developer; b. Iron City, Tenn., July 11, 1927; s. Herschel W. and Eugene (Looney) H.; grad. high sch.; m. Martha Ann Morgan, Jan. 8, 1949; children—Deborah Kay, Betty Ann. Owner, Hensley Lumber Co., Inc., Florence, Ala., 1947—, Billy L. Hensley Co., Florence, 1947—; pres. Hensley Constrn. Co., Inc., Florence, 1963—, Tourway Inns Am., motel chain, 1964—. Bd. dirs. Salvation Army. Served with AUS, 1946-47. Baptist. Clubs: Exchange, Florence Golf and Country. Home: 4201 Chisholm Rd Florence AL 35630 Office: 2230 Chisholm Rd Florence AL 35630

HENSLEY, LARRY DONALD, dentist; b. Radford, Va., Oct. 6, 1941; s. Paul Grant and Vivian (Cregar) H.; B.S., Hampden-Sydney Coll., 1964; D.D.S., Med. Coll. Va., 1968; m. Emily Anne Turner, June 15, 1968; 1 dau., Mary Lynnette. Intern U.S. Naval Hosp., Portsmouth, Va., 1968-69; practice dentistry, La Crosse, Va., 1971—. Served with USNR, 1968-71. Recipient essay award Nat. Safety Council, 1960. Mem. Am. Acad. Dentistry, Am. Sch. Health Assn., Am. Soc. Dentistry for Children, Am. Analgesia Soc., Am. Dental Assn., Am. Soc. Preventive Dentistry, Va. Dental Soc., Ruritan Soc., South Hill Jr. C. of C., Phi Beta Kappa, Delta Sigma Delta, Chi Beta Phi (nat. historian 1964-68), Sigma Zeta. Republican. Baptist. Home: 506 Chaptico Rd South Hill VA 23970 Office: Box 97 La Crosse VA 23950

HENSON, BOBBY HOWELL, communications co. exec.; b. Maylene, Ala., Jan. 10, 1936; s. Walter Emmett and Flora Bell (Dixon) H.; B.S. in Aero. Engring., Auburn U., 1960; postgrad. Northwestern U., 1961, U. Ala., 1962-64; m. Phyllis Ann Rodberg, July 30, 1960; children—Mark, Mike, Ben. Jr. engr. S. Central Bell Telephone Co., Birmingham, Ala., 1960-61, traffic supr., 1962-63, traffic mgr., 1963, sales supr., 1964-65, data system specialist, 1965-66, gen. marketing supr., 1966-70, gen. sales mgr., 1971—. Pres. Camp Civitan, Inc., Dadeville, Ala., 1971—; chmn. Civitan Found., Birmingham, 1971-73. Served with USNR, 1953-58. Recipient Outstanding Jaycee award Birmingham Jr. C. of C., 1964. Mem. I.E.E.E., Am. Marketing Assn., Sales and Marketing Execs., Am. Inst. Aerospace Scis., Birmingham C. of C. (chmn. speakers bur. 1970). Club: Civitan (dist. gov. 1972-73, internat. chmn. youth activities 1973—). Home: 2656 Foothills Dr Birmingham AL 35226 Office: PO Box 2662 Birmingham AL 35201

HENSON, DEWEY BOB, city ofcl.; b. Breckenridge, Tex., May 24, 1927; s. Dewey Thomas and Artie Mesia (Rader) H.; student Stephen F. Austin U., 1944-45, 46-47, Southwestern U., 1945-46, U. Houston, 1952; m. Betty Broussard, May 1, 1948 (dec. Sept. 1968); children—Diana Beth (Mrs. Douglas Floyd), Carolyn Sue. Lab. technician Gulf Oil Corp., 1947-48; party chief GMX Co., 1948-49; field engr. United Gas Corp., 1949-50; supt. Edgewood Homes, 1950-51; field engr. Rohm & Haas Co., 1951-53; office engr. Ebasco Services, 1953-55; dir. pub. works City of Lifkin, Tex., 1955-58; city mgr. City of Nederland, Tex., 1958—. Served with USAAF, 1945-46. Mem. Municipal Finance Officers Assn., Internat., Tex. city mgmt. assns., Nederland C. of C. (dir., sec. 1960-70). Kiwanian. Home: 832 S 14 1/2 St Nederland TX 77627 Office: 1400 Boston Av Nederland TX 77627

HENSON, ELMER LEE, utility co. exec.; b. Clarksville, Tenn., July 3, 1916; s. Elmer Lee and Nell Avrilla (Daniel) H.; student Austin Peay State Coll., 1933-36; B.S., St. Louis U., 1938; m. Margaret Ann Haley, Jan. 10, 1942; children—Elmer Lee III, Willis Edgar. With Pan Am. Airways, Brownsville, Tex., 1938-40, Braniff Airways, Dallas, 1940; with Nashville Gas Co., 1946—, v.p., 1969—. Served with USAAF, 1941-46. Mem. Engring. Assn. Nashville (pres. 1961), Tenn. Soc. Profl. Engrs. (pres. 1962), Indsl. Personnel Assn. Nashville (pres. 1972), Club: Optimist (pres. 1973—) (Nashville). Home: 2132 Old Hickory Blvd Nashville TN 37215 Office: 814 Church St Nashville TN 37203

HENSON, JERRY B., curator; b. nr. Anniston, Ala., July 1, 1922; s. Court L. and Mary (Baker) H.; student Jacksonville State U., 1948; m. Mary Higginbottham, June 29, 1959; 1 son, Jerry Ray. Patrolman, Anniston Police Dept., 1947-68; with Regar Meml. Mus. Natural History, Anniston, 1956—, curator, 1968—. Served with C.E., AUS, 1943-46. Mem. Am. Radio Relay League, Am. Meteorol. Soc. Home: PO Box 1113 Anniston AL 36201 Office: 1411 Gurnie Av Anniston AL 36201

HENSON, KENNETH WAYNE, civil engr.; b. Kalamazoo, Mar. 29, 1909; s. Stanley Willard and Irene (Hopkins) H.; B.S., U. Okla., 1933; m. Geraldine Martha Pitts, Feb. 10, 1935; children—Kenneth Wayne, Patricia Carol. Rig builder oil field constrn., 1933-37, Oilwell Supply Co., 1937-42; partner contracting bus., 1945-52; self-employed contractor oil fields, Pauls Valley, Okla., 1952-63; pres., chief engr. Hold-That-River Engring. Co., Houston, 1963—. Served from lt. (j.g.) to lt. comdr., USNR, 1942-45. Registered profl. engr., Tex., Okla., Miss., La., Ore. Mem. Nat., Tex. socs. profl. engrs., Marine Tech. Soc., Houston Pipe Liners Club, Houston Engring. and Sci. Soc. Mason (K.T.), Elk. Clubs: Toastmaster, Sierra. Patentee in field. Home: 4322 Hummingbird St Houston TX 77035 Office: PO Box 45335 Houston TX 77045

HENTGES, JAMES FRANKLIN, JR., educator; b. Perry, Okla., Feb. 6, 1925; s. James Franklin and Edna Lillian (Golliver) H.; B.S., Okla. A. and M. U., 1948; M.S., U. Wis., 1950, Ph.D., 1952; m. Iris Lavaun McGill, Mar. 10, 1946; children—Douglas Eric, Eric James, Kurt William. Instr. U. Wis., 1951-52; asst. prof. animal scis. U. Fla., 1952-56, asso. prof., 1956-66, prof., 1966—; cons. to Cuban, Venezuelan and Costa Rican govts. Served with inf. AUS, also with USAAF, 1943-46. Decorated Bronze Star. Mem. Am. Inst. Nutrition, Am. Soc. Animal Sci., Am. Soc. Range Mgmt., Sigma Xi, Phi Kappa Phi, Phi Eta Sigma, Alpha Zeta. Presbyn. Contbr. articles to profl. jours., chpts. in books. Home: 550 N W 55th St Gainesville FL 32607

HENTSCHEL, ALZA J. STRATTON (MRS. WILLIAM ERNST HENTSCHEL), artist; b. Lexington, Ky., July 2, 1911; d. Jess and Alza Garland (Proctor) Stratton; A.B., U. Ky., 1934; postgrad. Art Students League, Nat. Acad., N.Y.C., Cin. Art Acad., 1939-40, 44, U. Cin., 1945; m. William Ernst Hentschel, Nov. 18, 1939. Exhibited ceramics, etchings and paintings in nat. shows, 1930-72; head art dept. La. Coll., 1935-36; designer, mural painter theatre groups, 1936-39; designer, ceramist Kenton Hills Porcelains, Sterling Glass Co., Wadsworth Watch Case Co., 1939-47; instr. Cin. Art Acad., 1944-47, spl. mus. classes for children, 1963; co-artist, with W.E. Hentschel, mural Western & So. Life Ins. Co., Cin., 1952; art tchr., head art dept. Dixie Heights High Sch., Ft. Mitchell, 1954; exhibited in one man shows at Louisville Art Center, 1934, Burdorfs Gallery, Louisville, 1967, Town Club, Cin., 1965, Lynn Kottler Gallery, N.Y.C., 1968; exhibited in group shows Am. House, N.Y.C., 1965—, numerous travelling shows throughout U.S., S.Am., Europe; represented in permanent collections U.S., France, Italy, Venezuela, others. Recipient 1st prize Womans Art Club, 1948, 1st prize Ceramic Guild Show, Cin., 1948, hon. mention Western Hemisphere Ceramic Show, 1946. Mem. D.A.R., Womans Art Club Cin. (v.p. 1948), Profl. Artists Cin. (publicity chmn. 1944), Internat. Platform Assn., Brush and Pencil Club Lexington, Am. Assn. U. Women, So. States Art League, Ceramic Guild Cin., Ky. and So. Ind. Artists. Address: April Hill Farm 248 E Bend Rd Burlington KY 41005

HEPNER, LEON WILBURNE, educator; b. Coffeyville, Kan., May 11, 1915; s. Edgar Grant and Iva Christine (Parsons) H.; A.B., U. Kan., 1938, A.M., 1939, Ph.D., 1946; m. Ada Lillian Reiter, Jan. 3, 1942; children—Larry Benedict, Paula (Mrs. J.P. Thaxton), Patricia (Mrs. G.D. Camire), Leon Wilburne. Asso. prof. Ft. Hays (Kan.) State Coll., 1946-58; prof. entomology Miss. State U., State College, Miss., 1958—. Served with AUS, 1942-45. Mem. Entomol. Soc. Am., Soc. Systematic Zoology, Fla., Ga., Miss., Kan. (pres. 1948) entomol. socs., Sigma Xi. Home: 1 Prospect Pl Starkville MS 39759 Office: Drawer EM State College MS 39762

HERALD, WILLIAM GLENWOOD, dentist; b. Canon City, Colo., May 30, 1924; s. William Vern and Louella (Ware) H.; B.S., Okla. State U., 1950; D.D.S., U. Mo. at Kansas City, 1952; m. Leona Mae Underwood, June 9, 1944. Practice dentistry, Stillwater, Okla., 1952—. Served with AUS, 1943-46. Mem. Am., Okla. dental assns., Internat. Assn. Orthodontics, Am. Soc. Dentistry for Children, Fedn. Dentaire Internationale. Mason (32 deg.), Lion. Home: P O Box 608 Stillwater OK 74074 Office: 718 S Walnut Stillwater OK 74074

HERBERT, GEORGE RICHARD, research exec.; b. Grand Rapids, Mich., Oct. 3, 1922; s. George Richard and Violet (Wilton) H.; student Mich. State U., 1940-42; B.S., U.S. Naval Acad., 1945; D.Sc., N.C. State U., 1967; m. Lois Anne Watkins, Aug. 11, 1945; children—Gordon, Patricia, Alison, Douglas, Margaret. Line officer USN, 1945-47; instr. elec. engring. Mich. State U., 1947-48; asst. to dir. Stanford Research Inst., 1948-50, mgr. bus. operations, 1950-55, exec. asso. dir., 1955-56, asst. sec., 1950-56; treas. Am. & Foreign Power Co., Inc., N.Y.C., 1956-59; pres. Research Triangle Inst., 1959—. Dir. Central Carolina Bank & Trust Co. Mem. N.C. Bd. of Space and Tech. Mem. N.C. Gov.'s Sci. Adv. Com., tech. adv. bd. U.S. Dept. Commerce, 1964-69, N.C. Atomic Energy Adv. Com. Bd. dirs. Oak Ridge Asso. Univs., 1971—. Mem. Sigma Alpha Epsilon. Home: 46 Beverly Dr Durham NC 27707 Office: Box 12194 Research Triangle Park NC 27709

HERBERT, IRA WALLACE, educator; b. Hope, Ark., June 28, 1913; s. Joseph M. and Ethyl (Tatman) H.; B.S., Ouachita Coll., 1935; M.S., La. State U., 1937; Ed.D., Okla. State U., 1955; m. Lois Maureen Allen, Aug. 6, 1940; children—Allen Joseph, Wallace (dec.), Cecile Marie. Chmn. math. dept. Shenandoah Coll., Dayton, Va., 1938-39, Ranger (Tex.) Jr. Coll., 1940-42; prof. math. La. Poly. Inst., Ruston, 1942—, chmn. astronomy com., 1962—, dir. planetarium, 1969—, Mem. Am. Assn. U. Profs. (chpt. pres. 1964, 66), Ruston Men's Camellia Soc. (sec. 1964—). Home: 623 W Alabama St Ruston LA 71270

HERBERT, LEO, govt. ofcl.; b. Douglas, Ariz., Mar. 7, 1912; s. Kumen Ohni and Urilla (Whipple) H.; B.S., Brigham Young U., 1939; M.B.A., La. State U., 1941, Ph.D., 1944; m. Ruth Parker, June 30, 1937; children—Franklin Wayne, Dahnelle Kay (Mrs. Roger Overly), Judith Ellen (Mrs. Cary Spencer). Supr. pub. funds State of La., Baton Rouge, 1952, asst. state auditor State Auditors Office, 1952-56; dir. office of staff mgmt., dep. dir. for staff devel. Office Policy and Spl. Studies, U.S. Gen. Accounting Office, Washington, 1956-68, dir. office of personnel mgmt., 1968—; prof. accounting, head dept. bus. adminstrn. La. Polytech. Inst., 1947-52; asso. prof. accounting Brigham Young U., 1946-47; asst. prof., instr., grad. asst. La. State U., 1940-46. C.P.A., La., Utah. Mem. Fed. Govt. Accountants Assn. (chmn. edn. com. 1969-70), Am. Accounting Assn. (v.p. 1964), Am., D.C. insts. C.P.A.'s, Va. Soc. C.P.A.'s, Internat. Personnel Mgmt. Assn., Am. Assembly Collegiate Schs. Bus. (sec.-treas. 1974—, dir.), Nat. Assn. State Auditors, Comptrollers and Treasurers, Am. Soc. Pub. Adminstrn., Delta Sigma Pi, Omicron Delta Kappa, Phi Kappa Phi, Beta Gamma Sigma, Beta Alpha Psi. Contbr. articles to profl. jours. Home: 5228 N 32d St Arlington VA 22207 Office: 441 G St NW Washington DC 20548

HERBICH, JOHN BRONISLAW, educator; b. Warsaw, Poland, Sept. 1, 1922 (came to U.S. 1953, naturalized 1962); s. Henry Pawel and Jadwiga Eleonora (Lopienski) H.; B.Sc., U. Edinburgh, Scotland, 1949; M.S. in C.E., U. Minn., 1957; Ph.D., Pa. State U., 1963; postgrad. U. Cal. at Berkeley, 1964, Utah State U., 1966; m. Margaret Pauline Boylan, Jan. 27, 1951; children—Ann (dec.), Barbara K., Gregory J., Patricia J. Field engr. John Laing & Son, London, Eng., 1948; research engr. U. Delft, The Netherlands, 1949-50; intermediate engr. Aluminum Co. Can., Ltd., 1950-53; research fellow U. Minn., 1953-57; asst. prof. Lehigh U., 1957-60, asso. prof., 1960-65, prof., 1965-67; prof. civil engring., head coastal hydraulic and ocean engring. group, dir. ocean engring. programs, dir. Center for Dredging Studies, Tex. A. and M. U., College Station, 1967—; on leave as UN project mgr. Central Waterpower Research Sta., Govt. of India, Khadakwasla, Poona, 1972-73; dir. Ocean Pollution Control, Inc., Dallas; pres. Cons. and Research Services, Inc., Bryan, Tex. Pres. P.T.A. Hamilton Sch., Bethlehem, Pa., 1965-66. Served with Brit. Army, 1940-45. Recipient Karl Emil Hilgard Hydraulic Prize, Am. Soc. C.E., 1965-66; NSF Faculty-Sci. fellow, 1963-64. Registered profl. engr., Tex. Mem. Internat. Assn. Hydraulic Research, World Dredging Assn., Am. Soc. Engring. Edn., Am. Soc. C.E., Am. Soc. Oceanography, Sigma Xi, Phi Kappa Phi, Chi Epsilon. Patentee in field. Home: 764 S Rosemary Dr Bryan TX 77801 Office: Civil Engring Dept Tex A and M U College Station TX 77843

HERBLOCK, cartoonist, see Block, Herbert Lawrence

HERBST, HARVEY RAYMOND, broadcasting exec.; b. Dallas, Nov. 21, 1922; s. Fred Charles and Gertrude Louise (Dorcey) H.; B.A., U. Denver, 1944; M.A., Syracuse U., 1949; Ed.D., U. Tex., Austin, 1967; postgrad. Northwestern U., 1947-48, N.Y. U., 1951-52; m. Lila Dean Finley, Aug. 5, 1955; children—Frederick, Marian. Asst. prof. speech, journalism and drama U. Tex., 1953-55; account exec. KTBC-TV, Austin, Tex., 1955-56; asso. dir. Communication

Center, U. Tex., Austin, 1956—; sta. mgr. KLRN-TV, 1962—. Served with inf. AUS, 1943-46. Decorated Combat Inf. medal. Mem. So. Ednl. Communications Assn. (dir.), Tex. Assn. for Ednl. Television, Nat. Assn. Ednl. Broadcasters, Pi Kappa Alpha, Phi Kappa Delta. Presbyn. Rotarian. Editor: The Schedule, 1962—. Contbr. articles profl. jours. Home: 5707 Bullard Dr Austin TX 78731 Office: PO Box 7158 Austin TX 78712

HERBST (LILA) DEAN FINLEY (MRS. HARVEY RAYMOND HERBST), state ofcl.; b. Houston, May 26, 1923; d. Frank Ezra and Lila (McCullar) Finley; B.J., U. Tex., 1944; m. Harvey Raymond Herbst, Aug. 5, 1955; children—Frederick Lawrence, Marian Alice. Pub. relations writer BBC, N.Y.C., 1944-45; asst. prodn. editor Tide Mag., N.Y.C., 1945-47; woman's editor Austin (Tex.) Am.-Statesman, 1947-51; pub. affairs asst. USIA, Am. embassy, Kabul, Afghanistan, 1951-53; writer, producer KTBC-TV, Austin, 1953-55; exec. dir. Theta Sigma Phi, Austin, after 1967; now asst. program dir. Coordinating Bd. Tex. Coll. and Univ. System. Active Jr. Helping Hand. Recipient Writers Roundup award, 1969. Mem. Women in Communications (pres. Xi chpt. 1943-44, Austin chpt. 1960-61), Alpha Phi (pres. Austin Alumnae 1949). Presbyn. Club: Austin Woman's. Author: Flight to Afghanistan (juvenile novel), 1969. Home: 5705 Bullard Dr Austin TX 78731 Office: Lyndon B Johnson Bldg 17th and Brazos Sts Austin TX 78711

HERCHENROEDER, JOHN, editor; b. Louisville, May 20, 1908; s. John F. and Louise J. (Ernwein) H.; student U. Louisville, 1930; m. Elsie V. Middleton, June 5, 1948 (dec. Nov. 1971). With Courier-Jour., Louisville, 1926—, city editor 1945-65, asst. to exec. editor Courier-Jour. and Louisville Times, 1965—. Active Old Ky. Home Dist. council Boy Scouts Am., 1940. Mem. Christian Ch. Home: 106 Southampton Rd Louisville KY 40223 Office: 525 W Broadway Louisville KY 40202

HERCHER, WILLIAM DELMAR, elec. engr.; b. Pine Bluff, Ark., Nov. 26, 1908; s. Edward Daniel and Louisa Elizabeth (Glass) H.; B.S. in E.E., McKinley-Roosevelt Coll., 1944; m. Luedna Elizabeth Bayliss, Sept. 22, 1934; 1 dau., Delmar Lu (Mrs. Charles William Smith). Store front designer Standard Lumber Co., Pine Bluff Ark., 1930-40; design engr. Ark. Power & Light Co., Pine Bluff, 1940—. Chmn. Bocage Hist. Found., 1966, Jefferson County History Commn., 1972-73. Mem. I.E.E.E. Methodist (mem. ofcl. bd. 1946-66). Club: Optimist (gov. Ark. dist. 1964-65) (Pine Bluff, Ark.). Patentee in field. Home: 1811 Beech St Pine Bluff AR 71601 Office: 6th and Pine Sts Pine Bluff AR 71601

HERDKLOTZ, RICHARD JAMES, educator; b. Rockford, Ill., Dec. 26, 1940; s. Richard James and Virginia Teressa (Marelli) H.; student Rockford Coll., 1958-59; B.S., Bob Jones U., 1963; Ph.D., U. Tenn., 1970; m. Sharon Kay Brough, Aug. 10, 1963; children—James, Jeffrey, Jana Lynn, Joseph. Instr., Bob Jones U., 1963-67; mech. engr. J.E. Sirrine Engrs., 1965-67; prof. Bob Jones U., Greenville, S.C., 1970—, chmn. dept. chemistry, 1971—; chem. engr. Piedmont Engrs., 1971, 73—; asst. plant engr. Trylon Chems., 1972. Research asso. Oak Ridge Asso. Univs. Collaborative Research, 1970—. Monsanto fellow, 1968, Oran Fellow, 1969-70. Mem. Am. Chem. Soc., A.A.A.S., S.C. Acad. Scis., Sigma Xi, Pi Gamma Delta, Creation Research Soc. Baptist. Home: 12 Seminar Dr Greenville SC 29609

HEREFORD, JOHN DONALD, public accountant; b. New Market, Ala., Apr. 10, 1906; s. John Donald and Texanna (Petty) H.; B.S. in Commerce and Bus. Adminstrn., U. Ala., 1929; m. Lorence Watts, May 16, 1936; children—Susan Jane (Mrs. Willmore M. Dameron, III), Pamela. (Mrs. Maurice C. Hendrick). Staff accountant Lybrand, Ross Bros. & Montgomery, N.Y.C., 1929-47; asst. treas. May McEwen Kaiser Co., Burlington, N.C., 1948; comptroller So. Pool operations Geo. H. McFadden & Bros., Memphis, 1949; asst. comptroller Robbins Mills, Inc., Clarksville, Va., 1950-53; pvt. practice C.P.A., Clarksville, 1953—. Mem. Am. Inst. C.P.A.'s, N.Y. State, Va. socs. C.P.A.'s Phi Beta Kappa, Beta Gamma Sigma. Presbyn. (elder). Lion (dep. dist. gov. 1963-64). Address: Clarksville VA 23927

HERGOTT, RAYMOND WILLIAM, air conditioning mfg. co. exec.; b. McHenry, Ill., Dec. 31, 1931; s. Ralph James and Bertha Marie (Diedrich) H.; student U. Neb., 1950-51; m. Jean Carol Baillie, Aug. 5, 1951. Sales engr. Weldun Tool & Engring., Three Oaks, Mich., 1959-61; plant mgr. Frigiking div. Cummings Engine, 1961-67; marketing mgr. Trans Temp div. Texstar Corp., Grand Prairie, Tex., 1967-69, v.p., gen. mgr., 1969—. Mem. Airconditioning Refrigeration Inst., Am. Mgmt. Assn. Elk. Club: Las Colinas Country (dir.). Patentee in field. Home: 10519 Cromwell Dr Dallas TX 75226 Office: PO Box 870 Grand Prairie TX 75050

HERHOLD, WAYNE, hosp. adminstr.; b. Mpls., Aug. 4, 1929; B.A., Cornell Coll., Mt. Vernon, Ia., 1951; M.H.A., U. Mich., 1957; m. 4 children. Adminstrv. resident Henry Ford Hosp., Detroit; asst. dir. William Beaumont Hosp., Royal Oak, Mich., 1957-61; asso. dir. Rockford (Ill.) Meml. Hosp., 1961-65; exec. dir. Hosp. Planning Council Kanawha Valley, Charleston, W. Va., 1965-67; asst. dir. U. Wis. Med. Center, Madison, 1967-69, asso. dir., 1969-70; dir. Shands Teaching Hosp. and Clinics U. Fla., Gainesville, 1970—, also asso. prof., asso. chmn. Grad. Program Health and Hosp. Adminstrn. Mem. W. Va. Gov.'s Task Force on Health, 1966-67; mem. tech. adv. com. W. Va. Commn. Aging, 1967; mem. corporate bd. Health Planning Council, Madison; chmn. med. facilities com. Fla. Health Planning Council, 1972—; mem. Fla. Kidney Disease Council, 1971—. Served with USNR, 1952-55. Mem. Am. Coll. Hosp. Adminstrn., Am., Fla. (trustee 1972—) hosp. assns., Phi Kappa Phi. Address: Shands Teaching Hosp U Fla Gainesville FL 32610

HERIN, WILLIAM ABNER, judge; b. Macon, Ga., May 14, 1908; s. William Abner and Caroline (Davenport) H.; A.B., U. Fla., 1930, J.D., 1933 ; m. Frances Elizabeth Christian, Aug. 2, 1952. Admitted to Fla. bar, 1933; asso. firm Hudson & Cason, Miami, 1933-48; sr. judge 11th Jud. Circuit, Miami, Fla., 1949—. Sec. to Congressman J. Mark Wilcox, 4th Dist., Miami, 1936-38; legislative counsel Dade County del. Fla. Legislature, 1939, 41; legal adviser U.S. Dept. State in Far East, 1947. Pres. Nat. Conf. Met. Cts., 1969-70. Mem. adv. bd. So. Fla. council Boy Scouts Am. Bd. dirs. Met. Miami YMCA; trustee Boys' Clubs Greater Miami; bd. visitors Inst. for Ct. Mgmt., 1970—. Capt. USNR Res., Ret. Mem. Am. Law Inst., Am. Judicature Soc., Am., Dade County bar assns., Fla. Bar, S.A.R., Newcomen Soc., So. Fla. Hist. Soc., Inst. Jud. Adminstrn., Phi Beta Kappa. Methodist. Author: Trial Jurors' Handbook, 1952; Standard Grand Jury Charge, 1955; Aviation Activities of the late J. Mark Wilcox, 1955; Local Court Rules, 1957; also articles in profl. revs. Home: 470 NE 51st St Miami FL 33137 Office: Dade County Courthouse Miami FL 33130

HERION, JOHN CARROLL, educator; b. Salisbury, N.C., Sept. 5, 1927; s. John H. and Helen F. (Seaford) H.; B.S., Davidson Coll., 1949; M.D., Harvard, 1953; m. Mary Wilma MacLeod, Oct. 2, 1953; children—Gary Alan, John Murdoch, Diane Elizabeth, Carol Ann, David William. Intern, N.C. Meml. Hosp., 1953-54, med. resident, 1954-56, research fellow in medicine, 1956-57; cons. physician Watts Hosp., Durham, N.C., Wake Meml. and Dorthea Dix hosps. Raleigh, N.C.; instr. U. N.C. Sch. Medicine, Chapel Hill, 1954-61, asst. prof., 1961-65, prof. internal medicine and hematology, 1970—. Coach Pony League Baseball, Chapel Hill, 1969-72. Trustee N.C. Lutheran Homes. Served with AUS, 1946-48; PTO. Recipient Father of Year award Chapel Hill-Carrboro (N.C.) Mchts. Assn., 1966, Career Research award USPHS, 1967-72. Fellow A.C.P.; mem. A.M.A., Am. Soc. Hematology, A.A.A.S., Am. Fedn. Clin. Research, So. Soc. Clin. Investigation, So., N.C., Orange County med. socs., N.Y. Acad. Scis., Sigma Xi. Lutheran (pres. ch. council 1973). Contbr. articles to profl. jours. Home: 714 Emory Dr Chapel Hill NC 27514

HERLONG, ALBERT SYDNEY, JR., lawyer; b. Manistee, Ala., Feb. 14, 1909; s. Albert Sydney and Cora Violetta (Knight) H.; LL.B., U. Fla., 1930; m. Mary Alice Youmans, Dec. 26, 1930; children—Mary Alice (Mrs. A.G. Pattillo, Jr.), Margaret (Mrs. James H. Mayfield), Dorothy (Mrs. Charles Hay), Sydney (Mrs. Jed. J. Johnson, Jr.). Admitted to Fla. bar, 1930; practiced in Lake County, Fla., 1930-49; county judge, Lake County, 1937-49; mem. 81st-89th congresses from 5th Dist. of Fla., 90th Congress from 4th Dist. of Fla.; commr. SEC, Washington, 1969-73; partner firm Smathers, Merrigan & Herlong, Washington, 1973—. Served as capt., judge adv. gen. dept., AUS, 1941. Mem. Fla. County Judges Assn., (pres. 1943-44), Alumni Assn. U. Fla. (pres. 1947-48), Fla. State Baseball League (pres., 1947-48), Pi Kappa Phi. Democrat. Methodist. Home: 1020 Shore Acres Dr Leesburg FL 32748 Office: 888 17th St NW Washington DC 20006

HERMAN, DANIEL JACQUES, educator; b. Brussels, Belgium, Oct. 22, 1931; s. Octave Simeon and Jane Lelia (Massar) H.; came to U.S., 1951, naturalized, 1954; B.A., U. R.I., 1960; B.A., U. Louvain (Belgium), 1961; M.A., Northwestern U., 1966, Ph.D., 1968; m. Anne Bohlke, Oct. 22, 1965; 1 dau., Nicole. Asst. prof. philosophy Ithaca (N.Y.) Coll., 1967-69; asst. prof. philosophy U. West Fla., Pensacola, 1969—. Served with USMC, 1952-55. Mem. Am., Fla. philos. assns., Soc. Phenemenology and Existential Philosophy, Philosophy Soc. Study Sports. Transl. various publs. from the French. Home: 7910 Le Jeune Dr Pensacola FL 32504

HERMAN, LAURENCE TRUE, newspaper exec.; b. Chgo., Feb. 25, 1913; s. Earl Leslie and Florence (Grund) H.; A.B., Dartmouth, 1934; m. Florence Thomas Dingle, Oct. 28, 1939; children—Laurence True, Deborah Anne, Florence, Katherine. Space buyer Neisser Meyerhoff Advt. Agy., 1934; space sales Herald-Examiner, Chgo., 1935; with advt. dept. Marshall Field & Co., 1935; sales promotion mgr., retail advt. mgr. Chgo. Daily News, 1936-54; exec. dir. Waxed Paper Inst., Waxed Paper Merchandising Council, Chgo., 1955-57; advt. dir. Detroit News, 1958-65; v.p. sales & marketing, dir. Times Pub. Co., St. Petersburg (Fla.) Times, Evening Ind., Congl. Quar., Editorial Research Reports, Washington, 1967—; co-owner Mr. Steak Pontiac, Inc., Pontiac, Mich., Mr. Steak BSM, Inc., Westland, Mich., 1966—; dir. Newspaper Preprint Corp. Chmn. policy com. Met. Sunday Newspapers, 1961—. Mem. Ill. District 108 Sch. Bd., 1952-58; dir. budget Highland Park Community Fund, 1946-47; vice chmn. Chgo. Community Fund, 1948-49; chmn. A.R.C., Highland Park, 1951-52, div. chmn., Chgo., 1953-55; organizer, bd. dirs. Highland Park Civic Assn., 1954-58; chmn. bd. dirs. Mich. Career Inst., Detroit, 1965—. Mem. Am. Newspaper Pubs. Assn. (plans bd., bur. advt.), Newspaper Advt. Bur., Internat. Newspaper Advt. Execs. (dir.-at-large), St. Petersburg Advt. Fedn., St. Petersburg C. of C. (gov., pres.), Delta Kappa Epsilon. Presbyn. Clubs: Pinellas County Com. of 100, Commerce of Pinella County; St. Petersburg Sales and Marketing Execs., St. Petersburg Yacht, Treasure Island Tennis and Yacht. Home: 454 First St West Tierra Verde FL 33715 Office: 490 First Av S St Petersburg FL 33701

HERMAN, LLOYD ELDRED, mus. ofcl.; b. Corvallis, Ore., Mar. 19, 1936; s. Raymond Elmer and Luella Jane (McNabb) H.; student Ore. State U., 1954-56, U. Ore., 1958-59; B.A., Am. U., Washington, 1960. Program mgr. Office Dir.-Gen. of Museums, Smithsonian Instn., Washington, 1966-70, dir. Renwick Gallery, 1971—. Adviser, Victorian Soc. in Am. Recipient William A. Jump Meml. Found. award, 1972. Mem. Am. Assn. Museums, Am. Crafts Council, Nat. Trust for Historic Preservation, Soc. Archtl. Historians. Author: Form and Fire: Natzler Ceramics 1939-1972, 1973. Home: 16 5th St SE Washington DC 20003 Office: Renwick Gallery Smithsonian Instn Washington DC 20560

HERMAN, WILLIAM ROSS, restaurant exec.; b. Taylorsville, N.C., Nov. 25, 1921; s. Lawrence E. and Effie I. (Crouch) H.; grad. high sch.; m. Eleanor Barnes Crocken (div.); children—Larry, Nathan. Mgr. Mid-Atlantic area Nat. Toddle House Corp., Greensboro, N.C., 1938-63; founder Hermies, Inc., Florence, S.C., 1963, pres., 1963—. Bd. dirs. Florence Symphony Orch., Florence County Mental Health Assn. Served with AUS, 1943-44. Lutheran. Lion, Elk. Home: 1321 Clarendon Av Florence SC 29501 Office: PO Box 832 Florence SC 29501

HERMANSON, DEAN E(DWIN), mech. engr.; b. Sioux City, Ia., Feb. 23, 1927; s. Edwin H. and Hattie (Johnson) H.; student Morningside Coll., 1947-48; B.S. in Gen. Engring., Ia. State U., 1950; m. Mary Ann Timm, Sept. 13, 1952; children—Kent Edwin, Susan Jo. Indsl. engr. Aluminum Co. Am., Vernon, Cal., 1950-51, Wincharger Corp. subsidiary Zenith Radio Corp., Sioux City, 1951-53; engring. supr. U.S. Industries, Huntington Park, Cal., also Longview, Tex., 1953-63; chief engr. Continental Emsco div. Youngtown Sheet & Tube, Garland, Tex., 1963—. Instr. metallurgy Letourneau Coll., Longview, 1961-62. Served with USAAF, 1945-46. Registered profl. entr., Tex. Mem. Am. Petroleum Inst. (citation for service 1968), Am. Soc. M.E. (chmn. petroleum br. North Central Tex. 1970-71), Am. Inst. M.E., Am. Mgmt. Assn., Nat. Assn. Corrosion Engrs., Nat. Foster Parents Assn. Patentee in field. Home: 1114 Elizabeth Lane Richardson TX 75080 Office: Box 248 Garland TX 75040

HERNANDEZ-COLON, RAFAEL, gov. P.R.; b. Ponce, P.R., Oct. 24, 1936; s. Rafael Hernandez-Matos and Dorinda (Colon-Clavell) H.; A.B., Johns Hopkins, 1956; LL.B., U. P.R., 1959; m. Lila Mayoral, Oct. 24, 1959; children—Rafael, Jose Alfredo, Dora Mercedes, Juan Eugenio. Admitted to P.R. bar, 1959; practiced in Ponce, 1959-65, 67-69; mem. firm Hernandez Colon & Bauza, 1967-69; asso. pub. service commr. P.R., 1960-62; atty. gen. P.R., 1965-67; mem., pres. P.R. Senate, 1969-73; gov. P.R., 1973—. Lectr. civil proc. Catholic U. P.R. Law Sch., 1961-65. Mem. Nat. council Boy Scouts Am., Ponce, 1967—. Mem. Democratic Nat. Com., 1968—. Bd. dirs. Colegio Ponceno de Varones, Ponce. Named one of Ten Distinguished Young Men of P.R., Jr. C. of C. Rio Piedras, 1967. Mem. Interam., P.R. bar assns., Am. Acad. Polit. Sci., Acad. Law and Sci., Am. Acad. Polit. and Social Sci., Valley Forge Mil. Acad. Alumni Assn. (dir.), Phi Beta Kappa, Phi Eta Mu. Address: La Fortaleza San Juan PR 00902

HERNANZ, HIPOLITO, JR., mgmt. cons.; b. Buenos Aires, Argentina, June 14, 1938; s. Hipolito and Agueda Luisa (Calvino) H.; came to U.S., 1957; student Boston U., 1957-58, Georgetown U., 1958-63; m. Linda Joyce Johnson, July 22, 1961; children—Eric Stetson, Sabina Joyce. Econ. research asst. Orgn. Am. States, Washington, 1963; econs. and labor analyst Voice of Am. USIA, 1964-67; v.p., gen. mgr. CSG Corp., Washington, 1964-67; bus. mgr. WETA/TV and FM, Washington, 1968-73; comptroller WETA-TV-FM and Nat. Pub. Affairs Center TV, Washington, 1973-74; financial adviser to state and local edn. assns. N.E.A., 1974—. Latin Am. cons. for CTW (N.Y.C.); dir. Representation Unltd., (Washington); composer for the piano. Mem. Nat. Acad. TV Arts and Scis. Author: Fifteen Short Poems, 1972. Home: 5205 Redwing Dr Alexandria VA 22312 Office: 1201 16th St NW Washington DC 20036

HERNDON, JOHN FRANCIS, research found. exec.; b. Macon, Ga., June 23, 1927; s. John Albert and Mary Sophie (McKay) H.; B.A., Mercer U., 1948; M.S., Auburn U., 1953, Ph.D., 1956; postgrad. Hahnemann Med. Coll., 1959-60; m. Marjorie Leona Benson, July 10, 1948 (div. Apr. 1972); children—Marie Therese (Mrs. John Fowler), Mary (Mrs. Scott Gravitt), Elizabeth (Mrs. David Janda), Cynthia (Mrs. Dennis Jones), Katherine, John Francis, Marjorie McKay, Veronica, Regina, Angela; m. June Louise Denton, Aug. 17, 1972. Grad. research asst. Bio Research and Communicable Disease Center, Auburn (Ala.) U., 1948-51, dir. sanitation, pest control, 1951-53, research asso., 1952-53; dir. research labs. Malvern (Pa.) Inst., 1953-56; sr. research scientist Smith, Kline & French Labs., Phila., 1956-59; dir. research devel. Lemmon Pharm. Co., Sellersville, Pa., 1959-62; nutritionist-biochemist Esso Research & Engring. Co., Sinden, N.J., 1962-63; nutrition program dir. Nat. Inst. Arthritis, Metabolic and Digestive Diseases, NIH, Bethesda, Md., 1964-66; med. sci. dir., v.p. med. affairs Nat. Cystic Fibrosis Research Found., Atlanta, 1966—; pres., Denton-Herndon, Inc., 1972—. Bd. dirs., mem. sci. adv. bd. clin. biochemistry and behavior Inst. Meml. Hosp. and Devereux Found., West Chester, Pa., 1960-67; trustee, sec. Internat. Cystic Fibrosis Muscoviscidosis Assn.; trustee at large Internat. Mucoviscidosis Assn. Served with USNR, World War II. Mem. Am. Nutrition Research Council, Am. Inst. Nutrition, Am. Chem. Soc., A.A.A.S., N.Y. Acad. Scis., Phila. Biochem. Club, Phila. Physiol. Soc., Sigma Xi, Phi Kappa Phi, Gamma Sigma Delta, Gamma Sigma Epsilon. Republican. Roman Catholic. Contbr. articles to profl. jours. Patentee in field. Home: 2200 Mountain Lane Stone Mountain GA 30083 Office: 3379 N Peachtree Rd Atlanta GA 30326

HERNDON, WILLIAM BANKS, lumber mfg. co. exec.; b. Atlanta, Apr. 6, 1921; s. Oma Ernest and Kate (Banks) H.; student U. Ala., 1939-40, Tex. Technol. Coll., 1941-42; m. Martha Charma Walker, Mar. 10, 1945; children—William Banks, Robert Walker, Oma Lewis, Alan Maier. With Walker-Williams Lumber Co., Hatchechubbee, Ala., 1946—, gen. mgr., 1952-63, pres., 1963—; pres. Atlanta Forest Products, Inc., Union City, Ga., 1968-71; dir. 1st Fed. Savs. & Loan Assn., Phenix City, Ala., Atlanta Forest Products, Inc. Mem. Ala. Water Improvement Commn., 1968-71, Ala. Forestry Commn., 1969-71. Trustee Brookstone Sch., Columbus, Ga., 1969—. Served to 1st lt., Signal Corps, AUS, 1942-45. Mem. C. of C. (pres. 1969, dir.), Am. Wood Preservers Inst. (pres. 1972-73), Ala. Forest Products Assn. (pres. 1967). Methodist. Rotarian. Home: PO Box 113 Hatchechubbee AL 36858 Office: PO Box 7 Hatchechubbee Al 36858

HERNLY, HAROLD GRANVILLE, lawyer; b. St. Louis, June 2, 1908; s. Homer Granville and Jennie (Lee) H.; A.B., Lake Forest Coll., 1930; LL.B., John Marshall Law Sch., 1935; m. Harriet Weeden, Dec. 27, 1930; children—Harold Granville, James W. Admitted to Ill. bar, 1936, Washington bar, 1941, Va. bar, 1971; counsel eastern traffic exec. com. Assns. Am. R.R.s Chgo., 1935-38, Washington, 1938-40; mem. firm Wrape & Hernly, Alexandria, Va., 1940—. Mem. Am., Va. Bar assns., Motor Carrier Lawyers Assn. (pres. 1950, 51). Clubs: University (Washington), Belle Haven Country, Alexandria. Home: 1001 Janneys Lane Alexandria VA 22302 Office: 118 N St Asaph St Alexandria VA 22314

HEROLD, DONALD GEORGE, museum dir.; b. Bklyn., June 8, 1927; s. Charles George and Emmy (Partheymuller) H.; B.A., State U. N.Y. at Albany, 1948; m. Elaine A. Bluhm, Jan. 25, 1964; children—Jennifer Ann, Katherine Elaine Patricia. Dir. Miami (Fla.) Jr. Mus., 1950-51; asst. dir. Museum Village, Monroe, N.Y., 1953-56; dir. exhibits and interpretation VA. 350th Anniversary, Jamestown, 1956-57; dir. Davenport (Ia.) Pub. Mus., 1958-68, Polk Pub. Mus., Lakeland, Fla., 1968-69, Mus. Arts and Scis., Daytona Beach, Fla., 1969-70, Charleston (S.C.) Mus., 1971—. Trustee Cypress Gardens of Charleston; chmn. Charleston City Art Commn. Served with USMC, 1951-53. Mem. Am. Assn. Museums, S.E., Midwest museums confs., Am. Assn. State and Local History, Sci. Museums Dirs. Assn., Assn. Systematics Collections, S.C. Fedn. Museums (v.p.). Home: 2107 Middle St Sullivan's Island SC 29482 Office: 121 Rutledge Av Charleston SC 29401

HERON, STEPHEN DUNCAN, JR., educator; b. Jackson, Miss., Sept. 18, 1926; s. Stephen Duncan and Laura Belle (Wilson) H.; student Millsaps Coll., 1944-45; B.S., U. S.C., 1948, M.S., 1950; Ph.D., U. N.C., 1958; m. Rebecca Ann Melton, Apr. 3, 1948; children—Stephani (Mrs. Arnold Morton Emmons), Stephen Duncan III. Mem. faculty Duke, Dunham, N.C., 1950—, prof. geology, 1970—, chmn. dept., 1968—. Project geologist div. geology S.C. State Devel. Bd., 1958-70. Chmn., Eno River project com. Nature Conservancy, 1972—. Served with USNR, 1944-45. Recipient Sci. grant NSF, U.S. Park Service. Fellow Geol. Soc. Am.; mem. Internat. Assn. Sedimentologists, Am. Assn. Petroleum Geologists, Carolina Geol. Soc. (permanent sec.-treas. 1965—), Sigma Xi. Editor-in-chief: Southeastern Geology, 1958—. Contbr. articles to profl. jours. Home: 4425 Kerley Rd Durham NC 27705

HEROY, WILLIAM BAYARD, JR., univ. adminstr.; b. Washington, Aug. 13, 1915; s. William Bayard and Jessie Minerva (Page) H.; A.B., Dartmouth Coll., 1937; Ph.D., Princeton, 1941; A.M.P., Harvard, 1961; m. Dorothy Marie Meincke, June 16, 1937; children—Bayard Page, David Bassett, June Catherine (Mrs. H.E. Held), Barbara Ann. Geologist, Texaco, Fort Worth, 1941-45; geologist, Geotech. Corp., Garland, Tex., 1945-47, supr., 1947-52, v.p., 1952-60, dir., 1952-65, pres., 1960-65; group exec. Teledyne, Inc., 1965-68, asst. to pres., 1968-70; prof. dept. geol. scis. So. Meth. U., Dallas, 1970—, v.p., treas., 1970—; dir. First Nat. Bank, Richardson, Tex. Trustee Hockaday Sch.; bd. dirs. Garland Meml. Hosp., Circle Ten council Boy Scouts Am., Ft. Burgwin Research Inst., Yellowstone-Bighorn Research Inst. Fellow Geol. Soc. Am. (councilor 1967-70), A.A.A.S.; mem. Soc. Econ. Geologists, Am. Assn. Petroleum Geologists (treas. 1970-72), Soc. Exploration Geophysicists, Seismol. Soc. Am., Am. Geophys. Union, Am. Inst. Profl. Geologists, Am. Geol. Inst. (pres. 1968-69), Financial Execs. Inst., Dallas Geol. Soc. (life), Dalas Geophys. Soc. (pres. 1962-63) (life), Sierra Club, Sigma Xi. Clubs: Athletic (Dallas); Cosmos (Washington). Home: 13210 Laurelwood Lane Dallas TX 75240

HERR, JOHN MERVIN, JR., educator; b. Charlottesville, Va., July 26, 1930; s. John Mervin and Mary Belva (Byrd) H.; B.A., U. Va., 1951, M.A., 1952; Ph.D. (Coker predoctoral fellow 1956-57), U. N.C., 1957; m. Sue Highfield, Aug. 30, 1952; children—Susan Rebecca, Rachel Lynn. Instr., Washington and Lee U., 1952-54; asst. prof. Pfeiffer Coll., 1958-59; prof. dept. biology U. S.C., Columbia. AEC grantee, 1960-61, NSF grantee, 1961-63; Fulbright postdoctoral fellow U. Delhi, India, 1957-58. Mem. Internat. Soc. Plant Morphologists, Bot. Soc. Am., Am. Inst. Biol. Scis., Assn. Southeastern Biologists, S.C. Acad. Sci., S.C. Biology Assn., Sigma Xi. Discover clearing technique for study ovule devel. in flowering plants, application clearing technique to animal tissues especially tumors and cancer. Home: 6532 Sandale Dr Columbia SC 29206

HERRING, DOUGLAS ASHLEY, banker; b. Morton, Miss., Aug. 19, 1936; s. William Eastman and Pauline Virginia (Murphy) H.; student East Central Jr. Coll. at Decatur (Miss.), 1956; m. Mozelle Williams, Dec. 22, 1956; children—Kimberly Leigh, Todd Ashley. Audit clk. 1st Nat. Bank, Jackson, Miss., 1956-60; sr. examiner Miss. State Banking Dept., Jackson, 1960-63; pres. Security State Bank, Starkville, Miss., 1963—, also dir.; dir. Arnold Industries, Inc. Chmn. Oktibbeha County Community Fund, 1963. Bd. dirs. Oktibbeha County Indsl. Found., 1971. Named Outstanding Young Man of Miss. Jr. C. of C., 1968. Mem. Miss. Bankers Assn. (exec. com. 1971), Oktibbeha County C. of C. (pres. 1969). Methodist. Lion. Home: Route 5 Box 11 Starkville MS 39759 Office: PO Box 131 Starkville MS 39759

HERRING, GROVER CLEVELAND, lawyer; b. Nocatee, Fla., Dec. 9, 1925; s. Joseph I. and Martha (Selph) H.; J.D., U. Fla., 1950; m. Dorothy L. Blinn, Apr. 17, 1947; children—Stanley T., Kenneth Lee. Admitted to Fla. bar, 1950; asso. firm Haskins & Bryant, Sebring, 1950-52; practiced in West Palm Beach, Fla., 1952-60, 64—, mem. firm Blakeslee, Herring & Bie, and predecessor firm, 1953-60, Warwick, Paul & Herring, 1964-70, Herring & Evans, 1970, now Herring, Evans & Fulton; atty. City of West Palm, 1960-63, City of Atlantis, 1959-61, Town of Ocean Ridge, 1953-61, 1964-66, Village of Royal Palm Beach, 1964-72, Town of South Palm Beach (Fla.), 1966-72; spl. master-in-chancery 15th Jud. Circuit in and for Palm Beach County, 1953-54; judge ad litem Municipal Ct., West Palm Beach, 1954-55. Field rep. Lawyers Title Guaranty Fund, 1955-60, 64—; dir. Lawyers Title Services, Inc., West Palm Beach. Active PTA, Family Service Agy., Palm Beach County Mental Health Assn.; chmn. profl. sect. A.R.C., 1960; mem. Charter Revision Com. West Palm Beach, 1960-65, Palm Beach County Resources Devel. Bd., 1959—; apptd. mem. Govtl. Study Commn. by Fla. Legislature. Bd. dirs. Community Chest. Mem. Democratic Exec. Com., 1965-70. Served with USNR, 1944-46. Mem. Am., Palm Beach County (treas. 1960), John Marshall bar assns., Fla. Bar, Am. Judicature Soc., Lawyer's Title Guaranty Fund, East Coast Estate Planning Council, Nat. Inst. Municipal Law Officers, Law-Sci. Acad., Am. Trial Lawyers Assn. (asso. editor 1960—), Lawyers Lit. Club, Nat. Municipal League, U. Fla. Law Center Assn., World Peace Through Law Center, Fla. Sheriff's Assn. (hon.), U. Fla. Alumni Assn., V.F.W., Am. Legion, West Palm Beach C. of C., Civic Music Assn., Palm Beach County Hist. Soc. (pres. 1969-72), New Eng. Hist. Geneal. Soc. Boston. Mason (32 deg.), Elk, Moose. Clubs: West Palm Beach Country (hon.); Airways (N.Y.C.); History Book (Stamford, Conn.). Contbr. legal articles to profl. revs. Home: 3515 Australian Av West Palm Beach FL 33407 Office: Citizens Bldg West Palm Beach FL 33401

HERRING, NEWMAN LYNN, farmer; b. Kuttawa, Ky., Aug. 13, 1916; s. O. B. and May (Waters) H.; student Valpariso Tech. Sch., 1936-37; m. Rhea Sadler, Mar. 10, 1938; children—James Michael, David N. Farm mgr., owner farm, Eddyville, Ky., 1959—. Chmn. Lyon County Housing Commn., 1957—, Lyon County Water Commn., 1968—. Named Master Conservationist of Lyon County, 1970; recipient Commendable Community Service plaque Woodmen of World Life Ins. Soc., 1971. Mem. Lyon County Farm Bur. (dir., past pres.). Democrat. Baptist (deacon). Home: Route 2 Eddyville KY 42038 Office: PO Box 278 Eddyville KY 42038

HERRING, ROYAL ELAINE HOUSE (MRS. PETER WAYNE HERRING), savs. and loan assn. exec.; b. nr. Washington, Oct. 2, 1941; d. John Royall and Elsie Gladys (Gough) House; student Carolina U., 1960-61, Ind. U., 1971—; m. Peter Wayne Herring, Sept. 27, 1961; children—Debra Marie, Denise Marie. Legal sec. James P. Davenport, Atty., Manassas, Va., 1962-67; mgr. Commonwealth Savs. & Loan Assn., Manassas, 1967-69, exec. v.p., 1969—. Mem. Am. Savs. and Loan Inst. (pres. study chpt. 1969-72), Bd. Realtors, Manassas C. of C., No. Va. Savs. and Loan League Council. Home: 13521 Carriage Ford Rd Nokesville VA 22123 Office: 9201 Church St Manassas VA 22110

HERRINGTON, CLARENCE GOODWIN, JR., anesthesiologist; b. Memphis, July 19, 1944; s. Clarence Goodwin and Ruth Evelyn (Dawler) H.; B.A., Vanderbilt U., 1966; M.D., U. Tenn., 1969; m. Elizabeth Lee Duncan, Dec. 17, 1967; children—Clarence Goodwin III, Lara Elizabeth. Intern, Charity Hosp., New Orleans, 1970-71, resident, 1971-72; practice medicine, specializing in anesthesiology Med. Anesthesia Group, Memphis, 1973—; mem. staff Methodist Hosp., Memphis. Mem. A.M.A., Am. Soc. Anesthesiologists, Tenn. Med. Assn., Tenn. Soc. Anesthesiologists, Shelby County Med. Soc. Home: 2847 Treasure Island E Memphis TN 38118 Office: Suite 919 1331 Union Av Memphis TN 38104

HERRINGTON, JACK DONALD, city ofcl.; b. Ranger, Tex., Oct. 1, 1923; s. James Monroe and Ruby (Garber) H.; B.Arch., Tex. A. and M. U., 1948; M.Arch., U. Tex., 1952; postgrad. Princeton, 1963-64; m. Patsy Ann Wheat, May 29, 1949; children—TyAnna Kay, Donna Kristen. Asst. prof. architecture Tarleton State Coll., Stephenville, Tex., 1948-51; sr. architect Dept. Agr., Baltsville, Md., 1952-54; instr., asso. coll. architect Okla. State U., 1954-56; chief rehab. and conservation staff Renewal Assistance Office, Dept. Housing and Urban Devel., Ft. Worth, 1956-61, dep. regional dir. urban renewal, 1961-66, regional dir. urban renewal, 1966-67, asst. regional adminstr. for renewal assistance, 1967-70; exec. dir. Met. Devel. and Housing Agy., Nashville, 1970—. Mem. com. on urban growth and community devel. Tenn. Municipal League; chmn. pub. employees div. United Givers Fund. Bd. dirs. Council Community Services. Served with USAAF, 1942-45. Recipient certificate of commendation for activities with Dept. Housing and Urban Devel., 1970. Mem. Nat. Assn. Housing and Redevel. Ofcls., Nat. Housing Conf. (dir.), Tex. Urban Renewal Assn. (life), Nashville C. of C. Rotarian. Patentee in field. Home: 1139 Brookwood Lane Nashville TN 37220 Office: PO Box 846 Nashville TN 37202

HERRMANN, ALOIS, wholesale trade exec.; b. Bischofstein, Germany, Feb. 6, 1914; s. Franz and Mathilde (Dombrowski) H.; B.A. and M.A., Heeresverwaltungsakademie, Munich, Germany; m. Gerda Edith Polkehn, July 7, 1951; children—Eleanor, Gabrielle B. Came to U.S., 1957, naturalized, 1964. Trainee comml. banking Bischofsburg, Germany, 1933-35; prisoner of war in Russia, 1945-49; head import control dept. Vereinsbank, Hamburg, Germany, 1950-56; with Mt. Vernon Bank, Alexandria, Va., 1957-58; with Interarms, importer, Alexandria, 1958—, asst. treas., 1964-67, sec., 1967-70, v.p., 1970—; sec. Colonial Enterprises, 1965—. Tchr. French and German, U.S. Army, C.E., Fort Belvoir, Va., 1960-70; mem. faculty George Washington U., U. Va., 1959—, lectr. German, 1963—. Mem. West Springfield Civic Assn., Nat. Symphony Assn., Washington Performing Arts Soc., Atlantic Fellowship Found., sec. bd. Colonial Hist. Found., Alexandria, 1966—. Served to capt. Germany Army, 1935-36, 39-45. Decorated Eisernes Kreuz, Kriegsverdienstkreuz 1st Class. Episcopalian. Clubs: Springfield (Va.) Golf and Country, High Knob Country (Front Royal, Va.). Home: 8425 Forrester Blvd Springfield VA 22152 Office: 10 Prince St Alexandria VA 22313

HERRMANN, KENNETH LOUIS, physician, microbiologist; b. Cin., Nov. 16, 1934; s. Louis George and Marion (Bellows) H.; A.B., Dartmouth Coll., 1956; M.D., Harvard, 1959; m. Sara Jane Evens, June 6, 1959; children—John, Alan, Elizabeth. Commd. asst. surgeon USPHS, 1962, advanced through grades to sr. surgeon, 1967—; intern Strong Meml. Hosp., Rochester, N.Y., 1959-61, resident, 1961-62; resident Buffalo Children's Hosp., 1966-67; chief perinatal virology br. Center for Disease Control, Atlanta, 1972—. Home: 460 Chelsea Circle NE Atlanta GA 30307 Office: Center for Disease Control 1600 Clifton Rd NE Atlanta GA 30333

HERRON, ROBERT ERNEST, educator; b. Belfast, North Ireland, Dec. 11, 1936; s. Richard John Ernest and Elizabeth (Coulter) H.; B.A., Queen's U., Belfast, North Ireland, 1958; certificate edn. Nottingham U., Eng., 1958-59; D.L.C., Loughborough Coll., Eng., 1959; M.S., U. Ill., 1960, Ph.D., 1964; m. Carol Ann Frank, Feb. 24, 1962; children—Timothy John, Cara Elizabeth. Came to U.S., 1959. Postdoctoral fellow dept. physiology Inst. Occupational Health, Helsinki, 1964-65; asst. prof. Children's Research Center, U. Ill., 1965-66, asso. prof., 1966-68; asso. prof. dept. anatomy, phys. medicine and rehab. Baylor Coll. Medicine, Houston, 1968-72, prof. dept. rehab., 1972—. Dir. Motor Performance Lab., Children's Research Center, U. Ill., 1966-68; dir. Ergonomics Lab., Tex. Inst. Rehab. and Research, 1968-70, dir. Biostereometrics Lab., 1969—. Mem. policy adv. com. Adler Zone Center, Ill. Dept. Mental Health, 1966-68. Recipient award English Speaking Union, 1959-60, Presidential Citation, Am. Soc. Photogrammetry, 1972, Service Citation, Soc. Photo-optical Instrument Engrs., 1972, Grants, NASA, Dept. Transp., Nat. Tb and Respiratory Disease Assn., others, 1968-73; Fulbright scholar, 1959-60, U. Ill. fellow, 1962. Mem. Am. Soc. Photogrammetry (pres. Tex.-La. region 1971-72), Internat. Soc. Photogrammetry (sec. gen. commn. V, 1972-76), Soc. Photo-Optical Inst. Engrs. (seminar chmn. 1971-73), Instrument Soc. Am., A.A.A.S., Am. Assn. Phys. Anthropologists, Human Factors Soc. Club: Wilchester Residential (Houston). Home: 13310 Kingsride Houston TX 77024

HERSH, SEYMOUR M., journalist; A.B., U. Chgo., 1958. Formerly police reporter Chgo. News Bur., U.P.I., A.P., Chgo. and Washington; now free-lance reporter. Recipient Pulitzer prize in journalism for internat. reporting, George Polk Meml. award, Sigma Delta Chi award, Worth Bingham prize, U. Chgo. Pub. Service award. Author: Chemical and Biological Warfare: America's Hidden Arsenal, 1968; My Lai 4, A Report on the Massacre and Its Aftermath. Address: 2118 Cortland Pl NW Washington DC 20008*

HERSH, SOLOMON PHILIP, educator; b. Winston-Salem, N.C., Jan. 14, 1929; s. Max and Milly Diane (Hersh) H.; B.S., N.C. State U., 1949; M.S., Inst. Textile Tech., 1951; M.A., Princeton, 1953, Ph.D., 1954; m. Rosalie Berta Peskin, Feb. 21, 1954; children—Marla Rene, Camille. Research chemist Union Carbide Corp., South Charleston, W.Va., 1954-62; sr. research chemist Chemstrand Research Center, Research Triangle Park, N.C., 1962-66; asso. prof. textile tech. N.C. State U. Sch. Textiles, Raleigh, 1966-70, prof., 1970—, Charles A. Cannon prof. textiles, 1973—. Mem. Am. Chem. Soc., Am. Assn. Textile Chemists and Colorists, Fiber Soc., Sigma Xi. Patentee in field. Home: 2314 Weymouth Ct Raleigh NC 27612

HERSKOWITZ, ALLEN PAUL, elec. engr.; b. Bklyn., Mar. 29, 1941; s. Theodore and Sylvia (Hershkowitz) H.; B.S. in E.E., U. Miami, 1963; M.S., George Washington U., 1967; m. Susan Merle Englander, Sept. 8, 1963; children—Lisa Ann, Jason Peter. Engr., USN, Washington, 1963-67; research scientist Scope Electronics, Inc., Reston, Va., 1967-71; group mgr. system design Litton Systems, Inc., Amcom div., 1971-72; mgr. advanced programs lab. Scope Electronics, Inc., Reston, Va., 1972—. Bd. dirs. Reston Players, 1968-72; bd. dirs., v.p. Reston Community Players. Recipient Tech. Publs. award Assn. Naval Weapons Engrs. and Scientists, 1967. Mem. I.E.E.E. (chmn. U. Miami student chpt. 1962-63), Assn. Old Crows. Clubs: Nat. Space, Toastmasters, Windjammers (pres. 1967-68) (Washington). Spl features editor Miami Engr., 1962-63. Home: 2502 Fauquier Lane Reston VA 22091 Office: 1860 Michael Faraday Dr Reston VA 20070

HERZ, IRWIN MAX, JR., lawyer; b. Galveston, Tex., July 22; s. Irwin M. and Florence Cecile (Levy) H.; B.A., Rice U., 1961; J.D., U. Tex., 1964; m. Barbara Jane Ravel, July 28, 1968; children—Kenneth Vincent, Melanie Margaret. Admitted to Tex. bar, 1964, since practiced in Galveston; mem. firm Phipps, Smith & Herz, Galveston, 1964—. Dir. First Nat. Life Ins. Co., First Nat. Corp., Aberdeen Petroleum Corp. Chmn., Galveston County March of Dimes, 1967, Galveston County United Jewish Appeal, 1973; 1st v.p. Galveston County Jewish Welfare Assn., 1973, pres., 1974. Trustee Three R Trust; bd. dirs. Temple Acad. Mem. Am., Galveston County (sec. 1967-68) bar assns., State Bar Tex., Zeta Beta Tau, Phi Alpha Delta. Jewish religion (1st v.p. temple). Home: 6617 Golfcrest St Galveston TX 77550 Office: 610 US Nat Bank Bldg Galveston TX 77550

HERZSTEIN, ROBERT ERWIN, lawyer; b. Denver, Feb. 26, 1931; s. Sigmund Edwards and Estelle Ruth (Borwick) H.; A.B. magna cum laude, Harvard, 1952, LL.B. magna cum laude, 1955; m. Priscilla Holmes, July 11, 1956; children—Jessica, Emily, Robert. Admitted to D.C. bar, 1959; partner Arnold & Porter, Washington, 1958—; sec.-treas., dir. Survival Tech., Inc., Bethesda, Md., 1969—; dir. Baer Securities Corp., N.Y.C. Bd. visitors Antioch Sch. Law, Washington. Served as 1st. lt. J.A.G. Corps, AUS, 1956-58. Mem. Am., Fed. bar assns., Am. Soc. Internat. Law. Democrat. Jewish religion. Clubs: Federal City, Internat. (Washington). Home: 4962 Quebec St NW Washington DC 20016 Office: 1229 19th St NW Washington DC 20036

HESKETH, JOHN DOW, plant physiologist; b. Sebec, Me., Mar. 12, 1935; s. Norman R. and Bernice Ellen (Dow) H.; B.S., U. Me., 1956, M.S., Cornell, 1958; Ph.D., Cornell, 1961; m. Susan Martha Fahr, June 23, 1963; children—Lisa Margaret, Brian John, Jennie Mae. With Conn. Agr. Expt. Sta., New Haven, 1961-62; faculty U. Ariz., Tucson, 1962-65; with Commonwealth Sci. Indsl. Research Orgn., Canberra, Australia, 1965-68; plant physiologist Boll Weevil Research Lab., U.S. Dept. Agr., State College, Miss., 1968—. Mem. Sigma Xi, Alpha Gamma Rho, Alpha Zeta, Phi Kappa Phi. Contbr. articles to profl. jours. Home: 710 Ponderosa Dr Starkville MS 39759 Office: Boll Weevil Research Lab State College MS 39762

HESS, DANIEL NICHOLAS, nuclear engr.; b. Milw., May 3, 1920; s. Harry Edwin and Eva Gertrude (Deuster) H.; B.S., U. Wis., 1944; postgrad. U. Cal. at Berkeley, 1944-46, U. Tenn., 1946-48; m. Mary Rose Bannister, May 8, 1948; children—Daniel Cary, Hans Roderick, Mark Vincent, Timothy Steven, Dennis Edmund. Product control chemist Kurth Malting & Brewing Co., Milw., 1940-42; catalytic chemistry dept. Shell Devel. Co., Emeryville, Cal., 1944-46; tech. information specialist, nuclear power research and devel. Oak Ridge Nat. Lab., 1946-73; sr. engr. Carolina Power & Light Co., Raleigh, N.C., 1973—. Mem. civic improvement com., Norris, Tenn., 1967-69; asst. dist. commr. Gt. Smoky Mountain council Boy Scouts Am., 1963-73. Fellow Am. Inst. Chemists (state treas. 1972-73); mem. Sigma Xi, Phi Lambda Upsilon. Clubs: Wasioto Range Rowing (pres., chmn. 1973) (Clinton, Tenn.); Radio Amateur (Oak Ridge). Contbr. articles to profl. jours. Home: 4705 Yadkin Dr Raleigh NC 27609 Office: 336 Fayetteville St PO Box 1551 Raleigh NC 27602

HESS, DONALD MELVIN, TV sta. exec.; b. Toledo, Feb. 25, 1939; s. Norman Charles and Elizabeth Clara (Kreger) H.; B.S., Bowling Green U., 1961; m. Barbara Jean Abbott, Oct. 7, 1967; children—Mark Andrew, Jennifer Marie. Asst. pub. relations dir. Nat. Exchange Club, Toledo, 1961-62; asst. promotion dir. WTOL-TV, Toledo, 1964-65, promotion dir., 1966-71, program-promotion dir., 1971-73; promotion mgr. WDSU-TV, New Orleans, 1973—. Served with AUS, 1962-64. Mem. Nat. Assn. TV Program Execs., TV Bur. Advt., Broadcast Promotion Assn., Alpha Tau Omega. Mason. Club: Advertising (Toledo). Home: 5751 Norland Av New Orleans LA 70114 Office: 520 Royal St New Orleans LA 70130

HESS, MELVIN, educator; b. N.Y.C., Aug. 27, 1925; s. David and Anna (Kruger) H.; student City Coll. N.Y., 1942-43, Syracuse U., 1943; B.S., U. Okla., 1948; M.A., Washington U., St. Louis, 1949; Ph.D., U. Tex., 1952; m. Anne Lou Cabrol, June 8, 1952; children—Lenora K., Valerie B. Instr. dept. anatomy Emory U., 1952-53, asst. prof., 1953-56; asst. prof. U. Pitts., 1956-59, asso. prof., 1959-65, asst. dean Med. Sch., 1964-65; prof., head dept. anatomy La. State U. Med. Center, New Orleans, 1965—. Cons. VA Hosps., Gulfport, Biloxi, Miss., 1965—. Served with AUS, 1943-46; ETO. Mem. Am. Assn. Anatomists (program sec. 1974—), Pan Am. Assn. Anatomy, Central Am. Assn. Anatomy, Mexican, Brazilian socs. anatomy, Pan Am. Congress Anatomy (sec. gen. 1972), Endocrine Soc., Am. Soc. Cell Biology, Soc. Exptl. Biology and Medicine, Internat. Assn. Dental Research, Royal Soc. Medicine. Home: 5912 Oxford Pl New Orleans LA 70114

HESTER, JOSEPH ALLEN, JR., chem. engr.; b. Clanton, Ala., Sept. 17, 1907; s. Joseph Allen and Mae Beverly (Herring) H.; B.S., Auburn U., 1930; m. Leola Beard, Mar. 25, 1934; children—Joseph Allen III, Patricia Ann (Mrs. Fred Larsen), James Lee. Chemist, Internat. Chem. Co., East Point, Ga., 1930-31, Law & Co. Chem. Co., Wilmington, N.C., 1931-33; chief survey party U.S. Coast and Survey Hdqrs., Auburn, Ala., 1933-34; chief chemist, asst. testing engr. Ala. Hwy. Dept. Testing and Research Lab., Montgomery, 1934—. Served with AUS, 1941-47. Registered profl. engr., Ala. Mem. Am. Soc. Testing Materials, Hsy. Research Bd., Sigma Pi. Home: 2318 Elsmeade Dr Montgomery AL 36111 Office: 11 S Union St Montgomery AL 36104

HESTER, JULIAN CECIL, banker; b. nr. Clarkesville, Ga., Oct. 17, 1933; s. Joe T. and Emmie C. (Cofer) H.; B.B.A., U. Ga., 1955; certificate, U. Ga. Sch. Banking, 1963; m. Lalia Bentley, June 11, 1955; children—Joy, Julian C., Jan. Various positions to v.p. and cashier Farmers & Mchts. Bank, Washington, Ga., 1955-70; pres. Habersham Bank, Clarkesville, 1970—; dir. Scenic Properties, Inc., Financial Computer Services, Inc.; owner ins. agy. Active Victory Home, Helping Hand, Inc., A.R.C., Heart Fund, Cancer Soc. Mem. Washington City Council, 1967-69. Named outstanding regional pres. Jaycees, 1963, citizen of the year Woodmen of World, 1967; hon. col. Ga. Rebel Corps. Mem. Ga. Municipal Assn., Ga. Bapt. Assn. (past treas.), Ga. Bankers Assn., Bank Adminstrv. Inst. (past pres. N.E. Ga. chpt.), Ind. Bankers Ga. (dir.). Baptist (trustee, deacon). Rotarian (pres.). Home: 13 Barron Dr Clarkesville GA 30523 Office: PO Box 5 Clarkesville GA 30523

HESTER, LAWRENCE LAMAR, JR., educator; b. Anderson, S.C., May 23, 1920; s. Lawrence Lamar and Carrie Rose (McCelvey) H.; B.S., The Citadel, 1941; M.D., Med. U. S.C., 1944; m. Bette Catling Reckord, July 12, 1947; children—Barrie (Mrs. Robert Barry Rogers), Porcher (Mrs. Thomas Richard Rauh), Lawrence Lamar, Frances Stuart. Intern, Roper Hosp., Charleston, S.C., 1944-45, resident obstetrics and gynecology, 1945-46, 48-50; instr. Med. U. S.C., Charleston, 1950-51, asso. in obstetrics and gynecology, 1951-54, asst. prof. obstetrics-gynecology, 1954-56, prof., chmn. dept. obstetrics-gynecology, 1956—; Med. Univ. Hosp., Charleston; cons. VA Hosp., Charleston, 1966—. Served with AUS, 1946-48. Diplomate Am. Bd. Obstetrics and Gynecology. Fellow Am. Assn. Obstetricians and Gynecologists, Am. Coll. Obstetricians and Gynecologists, A.C.S., Am. Gynecol. Soc. Home: 61t Pitt St Mount Pleasant SC 29464 Office: 80 Barre St Charleston SC 29401

HEVENOR, RICHARD ANDREW, elec. engr.; b. Kearny, N.J., May 11, 1940; s. Clifford Lyle and Margaret Addison (Moore) H.; B.S. in Elec. Engring., Pa. State U., 1962; M.S. in Elec. Engring., George Washington U., 1974; m. Cora Lee Shepherd, July 23, 1966. Elec. engr. Geodesy, Intelligence, Mapping, Research and Devel. Agy., U.S. Army, Ft. Belvoir, Va., 1962-66, Engring. Research and Devel. Lab., Engr. 1966-68, Topographic Labs., 1968—. Recipient Sustained Superior Performance award Engr. Topographic Labs., 1969, Spl. Act and Service award, 1970, 71. Mem. I.E.E.E., Virginia Hills Citizens Assn. Baptist (deacon 1970—). Home: 6413 Gentele Ct Alexandria VA 22310 Office: US Army Engr Topographic Labs Ft Belvoir VA 22060

HEWITT, ROBERT LEE, educator; b. Paducah, Ky., Nov. 2, 1934; s. Lee A. and Donis (Brown) H.; student U. Louisville, 1952-55; M.D., Tulane U., 1959; m. Patricia M. Stewart, May 1, 1965; children—Heather Edgeworth, Robert Stewart, Whit Butler. Intern, Charity Hosp., Tulane U., New Orleans, 1959-60, resident, 1960-65, faculty Sch. Medicine, 1960—, asst. prof. surgery, 1968-70, asso. prof., chief cardiac surgery, 1970—; mem. staff Charity, So. Bapt., Hotel Dieu hosps., Touro Infirmary, all New Orleans; cons. several hosps. Mem. leadership forum Met. Area Com. New Orleans, 1971. Served with M.C., AUS, 1966-68. Diplomate Am. Bd. Surgery, Am. Bd. Thoracic Surgery. Fellow A.C.S.; mem. Soc. Univ. Surgeons (rep. to U.S. cardiovascular surgery adv. group), Am. Assn. Thoracic Surgery, So. Surg. Assn., Oscar Creech, Alton Ochsner, New Orleans surg. socs., Southeastern Surg. Congress, Soc. Vascular Surgery, Soc. Thoracic Surgeons, Internat. Cardiovascular Soc., Assn. Acad. Surgeons, A.M.A., La., Orleans Parish med. socs., Assn. Mil. Surgeons, New Orleans Grad. Med. Assembly, Omicron Delta Kappa, Phi Kappa Tau, Phi Chi. Episcopalian. Contbr. articles to profl. jours. Home: 6044 Camp St New Orleans LA 70118 Office: 1430 Tulane Av New Orleans LA 70112

HEWLETT, JAMES LEROY, architect; b. Parsons, Kan., Jan. 18, 1939; s. Jesse Lee and Virginia (Davies) H.; B.A., Drury Coll., 1963; B.Arch., U. Kan., 1967; m. Judith Angela Miller, June 10, 1961; children—Gregory James, Susan Elizabeth, Julie Christine. With Marshall-Waters, Architects, Springfield, Mo., 1967-68, Harper & Kemp, Architects, Dallas, 1968-69; architect Envirodynamics, Inc., Dallas, 1969-72; project mgr. resort properties, corporate officer Southwestern Dynamics, Inc., Dallas, 1972—. Served with AUS, 1956. Registered architect, Tex., Mo., Colo., Ariz. Mem. A.I.A., Nat. Council Archtl. Registration Certification, Drury Coll. Alumni Assn. (pres. Dallas chpt.), Tau Sigma Delta, Tau Beta Pi. Home: 915 Warfield Way Richardson TX 75080 Office: 3635 Noble Av Dallas TX 75204

HEWSON, W(ILLIAM) NEWLIN, statistician; b. Pocono, Pa., Sept. 5, 1922; s. William and Nancy Evans (Stokes) H.; A.B. cum laude, Gettysburg Coll., 1949; diploma Air U., 1951; Ph.D., Walden

U., 1973. Mathematician, Naval Air Engring. Center, Phila, 1952-65, Naval Ship Engring. Center, 1965-67; mathematician Naval Air Devel. Center, Warminster, Pa., 1967-70; statistician HUD, Washington, 1970—. Asst. prof. U. Pa., Phila., 1950-52, St. Joseph's Coll., Phila., 1959-61. Served to maj. USAAF, 1943-46. Mem. Operations Research Soc. Am., Am. Statis. Assn., A.A.A.S., Internat. Meditation Soc., Scabbard and Blade, Phi Sigma Iota, Sigma Pi Sigma, Kappa Phi Kappa, Sigma Nu. Toastmaster. Home: 2323 Pennsylvania Av NW #3 Washington DC 20037 Office: HUD 451 7th St SW Washington DC 20411

HEYBURN, WILLIAM II, ins. co. exec.; b. Louisville, Sept. 29, 1924; s. Alexander and Nancy (Chenoweth) H.; grad. Pomfret Sch., 1943; m. Bonnie Wright Barr, June 10, 1944; children—Julia (Mrs. Joseph Bernard Schildt), William III. Mem. sales staff B.F. Avery & Sons, Louisville, 1946-50; field underwriter Mut. of N.Y., Louisville, 1950—. Tournament chmn. Derby Open, Profl. Golf Assn., 1957, 59, Ladies Profl. Golf Assn., Bluegrass, 1965-73. Pres., YMCA, Louisville, 1972-73, Vis. Nurses Assn., 1962. Precinct capt. Republican party, 1955-73. Served with USAAF, 1943-45; ETO. Decorated Air medal with cluster. Mem. Louisville Assn. Life Underwriters, Million Dollar Round Table, Ky. (pres. 1963), U.S. golf assns. Episcopalian. Clubs: Louisville Country, Wynn Stay, River Valley; Wallon Yacht (commodore 1972-73). Home: 4 Woodhill Rd Louisville KY 40207 Office: PO Box 887 Louisville KY 40201

HEYCK, GERTRUDE PAINE DALY (MRS. THEODORE R. HEYCK), club woman; b. Houston, Nov. 30, 1910; d. David and Gertrude (Paine) Daly; student Wellesley Coll., 1929, Pembroke Coll., 1931-34; B.A., Brown U., 1934; m. Theodore R. Heyck, May 1, 1935; children—Jane Peel (Mrs. Donald H. Gaucher), Theodore Daly. Dir., Union Stock Yards, San Antonio, 1961-64. Sustaining mem. Jr. League, Houston. Mem. Harris County Heritage Soc. Club: Brown-Pembroke (v.p.). Home: 1907 Bolsover St Houston TX 77005

HEYD, LOUIS ANTHONY, JR., city ofcl.; b. New Orleans, Nov. 1, 1933; s. Louis A. and Lillian (Pritchard) H.; B.A. in Polit. Sci., Tulane U., 1955, J.D., 1959; m. Joan Marie Meyer, June 25, 1955; children—Theresa Marie, Michael Louis, Julie Ann. Admitted to La. bar, 1959; practiced in New Orleans; asst. dist. atty. Orleans Parish, New Orleans, 1961-62, criminal sheriff, 1966-74; practice law, New Orleans, 1974—. Served to lt. USMCR, 1955-57. Mem. Nat. Jail Assn. (pres. 1971-72). Home: 6110 Duplessie St New Orleans LA 70122 Office: 2700 Tulane Av New Orleans LA 70119

HEYE, GUSTAVE ROBERT, architect; b. San Antonio, Feb. 8, 1939; s. Carl Stephen and Helen Woodbridge (Moses) H.; B.Arch., Tex. Tech. U., 1968. Archtl. designer Phelps & Simmons & Assos., San Antonio, 1968—. Active United Fund. Served with USNR, 1961-63. Mem. A.I.A. Episcopalian. Kiwanian. Club: German Culture (San Antonio). Prin. archtl. works include U. Tex. Sch. Nursing, San Antonio, Social Scis. and Humanities Library Bldg., U. Tex., Austin. Home: Box 16 Bulverde TX 78163 Office: Suite 600 1177 NE loop 410 San Antonio TX 78209

HEYWARD, JEANNE, lawyer; b. Chgo.; d. Harry and Jeannette (Mowen) Heyward; B.A., U. Fla., 1952; LL.B. magna cum laude, U. Miami, 1955, J.D., 1967. Admitted Fla. bar, 1955; since practiced in Miami; mem. firm Dean and Adams, 1959-66. Mem. Dade County Bar Assn., Fla. Bar, Chi Omega, Kappa Beta Pi. Home: 8225 SW 108th St Miami FL 33156 Office: Concord Bldg 66 W Flagler St Miami FL 33130

HEYWOOD, HUMPHREY BARRETT, JR., social agy. exec.; b. Chattanooga, Aug. 15, 1908; s. Humphrey Barrett and Helen Claire (Wilcox) H.; B.B.A., U. Chattanooga, 1930; m. Rosina Costa, June 15, 1932; children—Dr. Humphrey Barrett III, Anthony C., Rosina Eleanor, Nell (Mrs. David W. Bolen), Mary Margaret (Mrs. C. Richard Pace). Dir. admissions, bus. mgr. Baylor Sch., Chattanooga, 1930-71; gen. dir., exec. v.p. YMCA of Chattanooga, 1972—; v.p., dir. WAPO Broadcasting Service; ednl. cons. Pres., Chattanooga Little Theatre; v.p. Chattanooga Symphony Orch., 1961-62; organizer Allied Arts Fund, 1969; mem. Nat. Football Adv. Rules Com., 1960. Named prep football coach of year, Coach and Athlete mag., 1955, 66. Mem. Advt. Club Chattanooga (pres. 1958), U. Chattanooga Alumni (pres. 1937-38). Clubs: Rotary, Fairyland (Chattanooga). Home: 507 Spring Valley Lane Chattanooga TN 37415 Office: 301 W 6th St Chattanooga TN 37402

HIBBARD, PAUL REID, lawyer; b. Berea, Ky., Feb. 24, 1941; s. Gilbert Reid and Grace (Chasteen) H.; B.A., Wofford Coll., 1963; J.D., U. S.C., 1966; m. Patricia C. O'melia, June 12, 1971. Admitted to S.C. bar, 1966; mem. criminal law revision com. S.C. Bar Assn., Office Atty. Gen. S.C., Columbia, 1966-67; asso. mem. firm Johnson & Smith, Spartanburg, S.C., 1967-71, partner firm Johnson, Smith & Hibbard, 1971—. Instr. comml. law Spartanburg County Tech. Edn. Center, 1967—, Wofford Coll., Spartanburg, 1970-71. Recipient distinguished service, outstanding man year awards Spartanburg Jr. C. of C., 1967. Episcopalian. Home: PO Box 13 Route 6 Johnson St Inman SC 29349 Office: PO Box 5524 Spartanburg SC 29301

HIBDON, JAMES EDWARD, educator; b. McAlester, Okla., Sept. 1, 1924; s. William Wesley and Minnie Irene (McBride) H.; student Okla. Bapt. U., 1942-43, Syracuse U., 1943; B.A., U. Okla., 1948, M.A., 1949; Ph.D., U. N.C., 1957; m. Mina Mae Gilreath, Aug. 20, 1944; children—Mary Ann, Jennifer Lee. Asst. prof. econs. Ga. State U., 1954-57, asso. prof., 1957-59; asso. prof. Tex. A. and M. U., 1959-61; asso. prof. U. Okla., Norman, 1961-67, prof., 1967—, chmn. econs. dept., 1971—. Trustee annuity bd. So. Bapt. Conv. Served with AUS, 1943-46, 50-51. Mem. Am., So., Midwest econ. assns., Southwestern Social Sci. Assn., Rocky Mountain Social Sci. Assn., Beta Gamma Sigma, Omicron Delta Epsilon. Author: Price and Welfare Theory, 1969. Home: 1501 Leslie Lane Norman OK 73069

HICKEY, JOHN KING, lawyer; b. Mt. Sterling, Ky., Oct. 15, 1920; s. John Andrew and Anna Christine (King) H.; LL.B., U. Ky., 1948; M.A., George Washington U., 1964; postgrad. Air War Coll., 1964; m. Elizabeth Jane Pattavina, Nov. 23, 1944; children—Roger Dennis, Patricia Elizabeth (Mrs. William H. Corsini, Jr.), John King II. Commd. 2d lt. USAF, 1942, advanced through grades to col., 1964; bombardier, 1942-45; judge advocate, 1948-70, assignments in U.S., Japan, Spain included chmn. bd. review, 1964-66, chief Internat. Law Div. OJAG, Washington, 1966-68; admitted to Ky. bar, 1949; dir. legal and judicial adminstrn. Council State Govts., Lexington, Ky., 1971-73; dir. continuing legal edn. Coll. Law, U. Ky., Lexington, 1973—. Decorated D.F.C. with oak leaf cluster, Air medal with four oak leaf clusters, Bronze Star medal. Mem. Am., Ky. bar assns., Phi Delta Phi. K.C. Club: Spindletop (Lexington, Ky.). Home: 3340 Nantucket Rd Lexington KY 40502 Office: Coll of Law Univ of Ky Lexington KY 40506

HICKEY, THOMAS HAROLD, physician; b. London, Ark., May 14, 1924; s. Mike J. and Anna Mae (Spillers) H.; student Ark. Poly. Coll., 1942-44; B.S., M.D., U. Ark., 1951; m. Ruth Newton, Jan. 28, 1950; children—Ellen (Mrs. Charles Malone), Nancy, Treva. Intern, Ark. Bapt. Med. Center; practice medicine, specializing in gen. practice, Morrilton, Ark., 1952—; physician Hickey White Clinic, Morrilton; mem. staff St. Anthony's Hosp., Morrilton, Conway County Hosp., Morrilton. Mem. Conway County (Ark.) Hosp. Bd., 1952—, Arkansas River Valley Action Bd., 1966—. Mayor, City of Morrilton, 1962-72. Served to staff sgt. AUS, 1943-46. Mem. Am., Ark., Conway County med. assns., Morrilton C. of C. Presbyn. (bd. synod). Mason (32 deg.). Home: 100 S Cherokee St Morrilton AR 72110 Office: 1109 E Broadway Morrilton AR 72110

HICKMAN, ROY D., mfg. co. exec., assn. exec.; b. Chattanooga, Jan. 27, 1902; B.A., U. N.M., 1925; m. Dorothy Dunkerley; 1 dau., Mary Lynn. Chmn. bd. Ala. Engraving Co., Birmingham, Platemakers, Inc., Birmingham. Past dist. gov. Rotary Internat., past dir., chmn. conv., 1958, internat. pres., Evanston, Ill., 1972-73. Past pres. Ala. Tb Assn.; chmn. adv. bd. Salvation Army, 1971-72; bd. dirs. United Appeal, 1971-72. Trustee Brooke Hill Sch. Mem. Birmingham C. of C. (past pres.), Pi Kappa Alpha. Clubs: Downtown, Executives. Presbyn. Address: 3357 Hermitage Rd Birmingham AL 35223

HICKS, ARTHUR MEREDITH, educator; b. Atlanta, Nov. 29, 1917; s. Claude and Florence Viola (Meredith) H.; A.B., Emory U., 1940, M.S., 1941; postgrad. Rutgers U., 1943; Ph.D., Auburn U., 1965; m. Lucy Catherine Werner, Feb. 27, 1943; children—Claude Bernard II, Frank Sharp, Joseph Eugene, Sue Meredith. Teaching asst. Emory U., Atlanta, 1939-41, Rutgers U., 1941-43; chemist Johnson & Johnson, New Brunswick, N.J., 1943-45, Graton & Knight Co., Worcester, Mass., 1945-50; asso. prof. LaGrange (Ga.) Coll., 1950-65, prof. chemistry, 1965—. Mem. Am. Chem. Soc., Delta Phi Alpha, Pi Alpha, Phi Lambda Upsilon. Methodist (mem. ofcl. bd. 1945-50). Home: 302 Park Av LaGrange GA 30240

HICKS, CLARENCE FLIPPO, lawyer; b. Fredericksburg, Va., Feb. 24, 1929; s. Robert Allen and Nell E. (Jones) H.; B.S., U. Va., 1950, LL.B., 1952; m. Miriam Patricia DeHardit, Dec. 27, 1952; children—Robert, Patricia, John Flippo, Paula. Adjuster, Travelers Ins. Co., 1952; asst. atty. gen. Va., 1953-59; admitted to Va. bar, 1952; practiced in Richmond, Va., 1952-59, Gloucester, Va., 1959—; mem. firm Martin, Hicks & Morris, Ltd., and predecessors, Gloucester, 1959—; dir. Williamsburg Nat. Bank; dir., sec. Middle Peninsula-No. Neck Savs. & Loan Assn. Counsel, Gov's. Commn. on Edn., 1959; chmn. Com. for Better Schs. Va., 1964-66; counsel State Va. in suit against State Md., 1958-59. Pres., Episcopal Churchman, Diocese of Va., 1968-69, pres. exec. bd., 1972-73, sec. standing com., 1973—. Mem. Va. Trial Lawyers Assn. (v.p. 1973), 13th Jud. Bar Assn. (pres. 1965-67), Alpha Kappa Psi, Sigma Nu Phi, Beta Gamma Sigma, Omicron Delta Kappa. Democrat. Rotarian. Clubs: Ruritan, Ware River Yacht (dir., sec. 1972-73) (Gloucester). Home: Pinewold Gloucester VA 23061 Office: Court Circle Gloucester VA 23061

HICKS, DAVID SMITH, city ofcl.; b. Van Buren, Ark., May 6, 1930; s. Oscar and Treva (Smith) H.; A.A., West Ark. Jr. Coll., 1957; m. Glenna Fay Brooks, Mar. 21, 1954; children—Pamela, Lisa, David Brooks, With Okla. Gas & Electric Co., 1954-66; dir. Ft. Smith (Ark.) Housing Authority, 1966—. Chmn. housing sub-com. City Citizens Adv. Com., 1968—. Bd. dirs. James S. Beckman Sr. Citizen Center, Ft. Smith. Served with AUS, 1951-53. Mem. Housing and Renewal Ofcls. (state chpt. pres. 1969—), United Comml. Travelers, Assn. U.S. Army (chpt. sec.-treas. 1967—), Ft. Smith C. of C. Home: 3401 Wirsing Av Fort Smith AR 72901 Office: 2100 N 31st St Fort Smith AR 72901

HICKS, DONALD GAIL, chemist, educator; b. Quanah, Tex., Feb. 11, 1934; s. William Martin and Clara (Bailey) H.; B.S., Murray State U., 1955; M.S., U. Ky., 1958; Ph.D., U. Tenn., 1965; m. June Kennedy, Mar. 21, 1970; children—Larry Don, Teresa Dell. Asst. prof. dept. chemistry The Citadel, Charleston, S.C., 1958-59, Murray (Ky.) State U., 1959-63; spl. lectr. U. Tenn., Knoxville, 1965; asso. prof. Ga. State U., Atlanta, 1965—. Editorial cons. Houghton-Mifflin Co., 1972—. Served with AUS, 1958. Recipient instructional film award Nat. Adv. Council Coll. Chemistry, 1968, Gustav Ohaus award Nat. Sci. Tchrs. Assn., 1972; NSF fellow, 1963-65. Fellow Am. Inst. Chemists; mem. Am. Chem. Soc. (lectr. 1971, chmn. Ga. 1973), Ga. Inst. Chemists (sec. treas. 1970-71), Southeast Soc. Applied Spectroscopy (sec. 1971-72), Am. Assn. U. Profs. (pres. chpt. 1962), A.A.A.S., Ga. Acad. Sci., Nat. Sci. Tchrs. Assn. (com. coll. sci. teaching), Sigma Xi, Phi Kappa Phi, Beta Beta Beta. Methodist. Co-author of Chem. Technician Curriculum Project, 1970-72. Home: 2477 Midvale Ct Tucker GA 30084 Office: Ga State U Atlanta GA 30303

HICKS, DOUGLAS BRECKENRIDGE, broadcasting exec.; b. Dewey County, Okla., Oct. 29, 1907; s. William Absalom and Ora Naomi (Newton) H.; A.B., Baylor U., 1929; m. Evelyne Louise Johnson, Oct. 7, 1939. Reporter, then staff writer, city editor Houston Press, 1929-41; pub. relations dir. Houston C. of C. 1941-42; sr. account exec., asst. mgr. Max H. Jacobs Pub. Relations Agy., Houston, 1946-51; pub. relations rep. Tenneco, Inc., Houston, 1951-52, pub. relations mgr., 1952-63, asst. dir. pub. relations and advt., 1963-68; partner Vets. Broadcasting Co., Houston, 1948-62; v.p. Tex. Coast Broadcasters, Inc., also Tex. Coast Broadcasters of Beaumont, Inc., 1962-68, chmn. bd., 1969—. Councilman, Bunker Hill Village, 1963-69. Served from lt. to lt. comdr. USNR, 1942-46; PTO. Mem. Pub. Relations Soc. Am., Assn. Petroleum Writers, Tex. Mid-Continent Oil and Gas Assn., Houston C. of C. Baptist. Clubs: Press (Houston); Pine Forest Country, Panorama Country, Tennwood. Home: 46 Ivy Ct Conroe TX 77301 Office: 4701 Caroline St Houston TX 77002

HICKS, ELDER BARNEY, clergyman; b. Wichita, Kan., July 11, 1907; s. Daniel H. and Carrie (Smith) H.; A.B., Washburn U., 1951; Th.B., Central Baptist Sem., 1934, D.D. (hon.), 1940; D.D., Monrovia Coll. and Indsl. Inst., Monrovia, Liberia, Africa, 1961; m. Effie Mae Hayes, Mar. 9, 1927 (dec. 1960); children—Rose Marie (Mrs. Dewey Sanderson), Milton T., James Edward, E. Barney; m. 2d, Roena S. Starks, Oct. 10, 1961. Ordained to ministry Bapt. Ch., 1934, pastor in Paxico, Kan., 1934-36, Holton and Horton, Kan., 1936-37, Duluth, Minn., 1937-42; exec. sec., missionary Bapt. Conv. of Kan., 1945-56; dir. Bapt. Ednl. Centers of Am. Bapt. Home Mission Socs., 1956-63, asso. dir community witness program, div. ch. missions, 1963-67, program asso. for inner city work, 1967-69, asst. sec. dir. parish devel., 1969-71; regional exec. minister Am. Bapt. Chs. of South, Atlanta, 1971—. Served from 1st lt. to capt., as chaplain, AUS, 1942-45. Mem. N.A.A.C.P. Office: Suite 1170 Citizens Trust Bldg 75 Piedmont Av NE Atlanta GA 30303

HICKS, GORDON T., banker; b. Sycamore, Ill.; B.S.B., Miami U., Oxford, O., 1942. Formerly with Bank Am., San Francisco; then exec. v.p. U.S. Jr. C. of C.; then v.p. bus. devel. met. div. Nat. Bank Tulsa; now pres. Eastland Bank, Tulsa. Chmn. Tulsa Park and Recreation Bd., 1956-63; mem. adv. bd. Salvation Army, 1956-60; v.p. Indian Nations council Boy Scouts Am. Trustee, mem. exec. com. Gilcrease Inst., Tulsa, 1958-66, bd. dirs., 1967—, v.p. bd., 1969-71, pres., 1971-72, chmn. bd., 1973-74; chmn. bd. trustees Okla. Osteo. Hosp. Address: Eastland Bank 14444 E 21st St Tulsa OK 74134

HICKS, HAROLD NEWTON, coal mining cons.; b. Kingfisher, Okla., July 18, 1904; s. William Newton and Retta (Flora) H.; B.S., U. Kan., 1927; m. Elsie Rucker, Aug. 5, 1938; children—Harold Newton, Amy Loretta. Engr. M.-K.-T. R.R., 1927-32, Kan. State Hwy. Commn., 1932-33; county engr., Labette County, Kan., 1933-35; resident engr. in Ill. Pittsburg & Midway Coal Co., 1935-38; research mgr. coal div. Midwest Radiant Corp., 1938-40, asst. v.p., 1940-43; preparation mgr. Truax Traer Coal Co., 1943-53, supt. preparation plant, Cenedo, W.Va., 1953-56; sales engr. Oglabay Newton Co., 1956-70; chief engr. St. Louis Briquette Co., 1942-45; self-employed as cons. to coal mining cos., Catlettsburg, Ky., 1970—. Sec. Strip Mining Investigation Commn. for Ill., 1941-43. Registered profl. engr., Kan. Mem. Am. Inst. Mining, Metall. and Petroleum Engrs., Phi Delta Theta. Republican. Rotarian. Home: Route 2 Box 224 Catlettsburg KY 41129

HICKS, HENRY STACEY, engring. co. exec.; b. Comanche, Tex., Feb. 21, 1919; s. Newton Sanford and Susan Ann (Pennland) H.; m. Verdell Marshall, May 16, 1941; children—Stacia (Mrs. Jerry Cowan), Shirley (Mrs. Jack Gregory), Sandra (Mrs. Ted Rushing), Linda. Resident engr., dist. engr. H. N. Roberts & Assos., Littlefield, Tex., 1944-47; asst. chief engr., chief engr. H. N. Roberts & Assos., Lubbock, Tex., 1947-49; pres., gen. mgr. Hicks & Ragland, Lubbock, 1950—; pres. Midwest Reprodn. Co., Inc., Hicks & Ragland Engrs., Inc.; pres. Teltronics, Inc.; dir. Ionate Corp. Am., Ranching and Real Estate, Inc. Mem. Am. Inst. Aeros. and Astronautics. Democrat. Methodist. Mason (32 deg., Shriner). Home: 3216 53d St Lubbock TX 79410 Office: Hicks & Ragland 40th and Av U Lubbock TX 79410

HICKS, HOWARD JAMES, indsl. engr.; b. nr. Knoxville, Tenn., May 23, 1924; s. Basil Ernest and Grace (Lewis) H.; B.S., U. Tenn., 1951, postgrad., 1951-55; m. Daisy Lee Haynes, Oct. 10, 1942; children—Howard James Jr., Terrell Lee. With nuclear div. Union Carbide Corp., Oak Ridge, 1951—, maintenance engr., 1967, facilities engr., 1967—. Chmn. troop com. Smoky Mountain council Boy Scouts Am., 1966-71. Served with C.E., AUS, 1943-46; PTO. Registered profl. engr., Tenn. Mem. Am. Inst. Indsl. Engrs., Tenn., Nat. socs. profl. engrs. Democrat. Baptist (deacon). Home: PO Box 395A Heiskell TN 37754 Office: Y-12 Plant Oak Ridge TN 37830

HICKS, JESSE LEE, govt. ofcl.; b. Paris, Tenn., Nov. 15, 1922; s. Harry B. and Edna Bea (Nash) H.; B.S. in Engring., U. Tenn., 1949; B.S. in Bus. Adminstrn., Franklin U., 1970; M.A. in Pub. Adminstrn., N.C. State U., 1972; m. Dorothy Cowden, June 15, 1948; children—Harry, Carol, Larry. State conservationist Soil Conservation Service, U.S. Dept. Agr., Raleigh, N.C., 1949-65, state dir., 1971—. Served to lt. col. AUS, 1944-45; ETO. Decorated Bronze Star (5). Mason (32 deg.), Kiwanian. Home: 4004 Colby Dr Raleigh NC 27609 Office: Box 27307 Raleigh NC 27611

HICKS, MARK CLYDE, JR., lawyer; b. Sevierville, Tenn., Apr. 18, 1927; s. Mark Clyde and Alice (Trotter) H.; student East Tenn. State Coll., 1946-48; LL.B., Vanderbilt U., 1951; m. Lois Dillow, Aug. 26, 1953; children—Mark C., Ellen Lynn. Admitted to Tenn. bar, 1951; law clk. firm Green & Green, Johnson City, 1951-52; probate clk. Washington County Ct., Jonesboro, Tenn., 1952; sole practice law Jonesboro, 1952-71, partner firm Hicks, Arnold & Haynes, 1971—. Dir. Banking & Trust Co., Jonesboro and Johnson City. Vice-chmn. Tri-City Airport Commn., 1962—. Chmn. exec. com. Washington County Republican party, 1954-56; sec. Tenn. Rep. party, 1968—. Bd. dirs. Meml. Hosp., Johnson City; vice-chmn. bd. Johnson City Power Bd. Served with USNR, 1945-46. Mem. Am., Tenn., Washington County bar assns., Tenn., Washington County trial lawyers assns. Presbyn. (elder). Club: Johnson City Country. Home: Old Jonesboro Hwy Jonesboro TN 37659 Office: PO Box 206 Jonesboro TN 37659

HICKS, ROBERT LEE, TV sta. exec.; b. Newton, Kan., Jan. 16, 1926; s. Albert Lee and Jessie (James) H.; student Friends U., 1944, Wichita U., 1946; m. Nelda E. Stephenson, Aug. 11, 1945; children—David Conrad, Jeffrey Bryson. Announcer, KANS radio, Wichita, Kan., 1945-50, KLRA radio, Little Rock, Ark., 1950-56; announcer, program dir. KTHS radio, Little Rock, 1956-63; dir. pub. affairs KTHV-TV, Little Rock, 1963—. Bd. dirs. Ark. chpt. Goodwill Industries Inc., Contact, Cystic Fibrosis Found. Democrat. Methodist. Home: 1508 S Buchanan St Little Rock AR 72204 Office: PO Box 269 Little Rock AR 72203

HIERONYMUS, CLARA BOOTH WIGGINS (MRS. C. HIERONYMUS), newspaper writer; b. Drew, Miss., July 25, 1913; d. Bruce Charles and Maude (Watson) Wiggins; B.A. cum laude, U. Tulsa, 1932; M.S.W., U. Okla., 1936; m. Senator Cleo Hieronymus, Apr. 24, 1937; children—Bruce Lee, Jane (Mrs. David H. Piller). Employment counselor YWCA, Tulsa, 1936-37; employment interviewer, labor market analyst State and Fed. Employment Service, Tulsa, 1937-50; instr. sociology U. Tulsa, 1938-50; book reviewer radio sta. KFMJ, Tulsa, 1942; art and drama critic, home furnishings editor The Tennessean, Nashville, after 1956; freelance writer; speaker for clubs. Pres. Samaritans, 1967-69. Recipient Dorothy Dawe award Am. Furniture Mart, 1960, 63, 65, 69, Dallas Furniture Market award, 1965, Burlington award, 1969-71, 74; named Woman of Year in Communications, Bus. and Profl. Women of Nashville, 1966. Mem. Assn. du Theatre pour les Enfants et Jeunesse, Internat. Assn. Children's Theatre, Nat. Hemophilia Soc., Nat. Arthritis Found., Nashville Childrens Theater, Cheekwood Fine Arts Center, Am. Assn. Interior Designers, Nat. Soc. Interior Designers, Theta Sigma Phi. Democrat. Methodist. Club: Centennial (Nashville). Author: (with Barbara Izard) Requiem for a Nun; On Stage and Off, 1970. Home: 2200 Hemingway Dr Nashville TN 37215 Office: 1100 Broad St Nashville TN 37202

HIESTER, TRAVIS DADE, lawyer; b. Mission, Tex., Oct. 5, 1935; s. Clarence Dade and Miriam (Webb) H.; B.S., U. Tex., 1960; LL.B., St. Mary's U., 1963; m. Marie Quick, Nov. 29, 1963; children—Cheryl Lyn, Leigh Anne, Kristen Elizabeth, Karen Frances. Admitted to Tex. bar, 1963; mem. firm Kelley, Looney, Alexander & Hiester, Edinburg, Tex., 1963—; dir. Hidalgo Savs. & Loan Assn., Edinburg. Trustee Hidalgo County Mus. Served with AUS, 1957. Mem. Tex., Hidalgo County (dir. 1965-67, 69-71) bar assns., Phi Delta Phi. Home: Route 2 Box 210-D Edinburg TX 78539 Office: PO Box 237 Edinburg TX 78539

HIETT, LOUIS ALDEN, JR., paper co. exec.; b. Memphis, Oct. 2, 1925; s. Louis Alden and Mable Ruth (Nourse) H.; B.Chem. Engring., Ga. Inst. Tech., 1949; m. Virginia Scott Wingfield, Dec. 29, 1948; children—Alden Scott, Virginia Lou, Susan Shaw. Process engr. Buckeye Cellulose Corp., subsidiary Procter & Gamble Co., Memphis, 1949-55, sect. head, 1955-60, asso. dir. tech. div., 1960-61, plant mgr., 1961-64, mgr. product devel., 1964-70, mgr. spl. projects, 1970-72, mgr. tech. div., 1972—. Mem. exec. com. Chickasaw council Boy Scouts Am., 1963. Bd. dirs. Jr. Achievement, Memphis, 1961-64, pres., 1963; bd. dirs. Shelby United Neighbors, 1962-64; bd. dirs. Memphis Metropolitan YMCA, 1965—, v.p., 1972-73. Served with AUS, 1943-45. Decorated Purple Heart. Mem. Am. Inst. Chem. Engrs., T.A.P.P.I., Memphis C. of C. (mem. exec. com., indsl. council 1961-64). Presbyn. (ruling elder 1957—). Patentee in field. Home: 5700 Sycamore Grove Lane Memphis TN 38117 Office: PO Box 8407 Memphis TN 38108

HIGDON, JAMES JACKSON, elec. engr.; b. High Springs, Fla., May 1, 1900; s. Robert Wilson and Sallie (Butler) H.; B.S. in Elec. Engring., Ga. Inst. Tech., 1923; postgrad. Chgo. Central Sta. Inst., 1924; m. Ruth Mathews, Oct. 16, 1961; children—Barbara (Mrs. C.J. Blakeley Jr.), James J. Jr. Engr., City Lakeland, Fla., 1933-40, Rural Electrification Adminstrn., various locations, 1941—, elec. engr., Denton, Tex., until 1970, cons., Denton, 1970—. Mem. Elec. Code Bd., Denton, 1971—. Mem. I.E.E.E. (life). Mason. Patentee in field. Home and address: 1201 Thomas St Denton TX 76201

HIGDON, JERRY LAFONNE, chem. co. exec.; b. Shamrock, Tex., Aug. 4, 1930; s. William Emery and Ola E. (Reeves) H.; B.S., N.M. State U., 1955; postgrad. U. Mich., 1972; m. Marilyn Speir, Dec. 17, 1951; children—Jane Lynette, Charles Lafonne, Scott Patrick. Self-employed in farm supply bus., Deming, N.M., 1955-60; salesman Red Barn Chems., Inc., Tulsa, 1960-65, br. mgr., 1965-66, mgr. retail marketing, 1966-67, mgr. fertilizer div., 1968-69, v.p. fertilizer div., 1969-73, pres., 1973—, also dir. Judge, Future Farmers Am. Proficiency Award Winners, 1971-73. Bd. dirs. Okla. Council on Econ. Edn. Mem. Tex. Fertilizer Assn. (pres. 1966), S.W. Grade Hearing Assn. (vice-chmn. 1968), Tex. Plant Food Ednl. Soc. (dir. 1969). Nat. Fertilizer Solutions Assn. (dir. 1971-73), Fertilizer Inst. (dir. 1973-73), Tulsa C. of C. (air quality standards task force 1972-73), Petroleum Club Tulsa, Alpha Zeta, Theta Chi. Methodist (Sunday Sch. supt. 1958-59). Home: Rural Route 1 Jennings OK 74038 Office: PO Box 141 Tulsa OK 74102

HIGGINBOTHAM, JAMES HENDERSON, banker; b. Park City, Ky., Dec. 30, 1933; s. Willie James and Loy Ruble (Borden) H.; B.S., Western Ky. U., 1958; postgrad. U. Ky., 1969; m. Lena Carol Hardison, Feb. 26, 1972; children by previous marriage—Darrell W., Rondal; stepchildren—Debbie Monroe, Susan Monroe. Tchr. pub. schs., 1958-69; cashier Citizen's Nat. Bank, 1969-71; exec. v.p., chief exec. officer, dir. Hartford Bank & Trust Co. (Ky.), 1971—. Chmn., Logan County Joint Cities Planning Commn., 1969-70. Served with AUS, 1953-55. Democrat. Club: Ohio County Country (Hartford). Home: Route 1 Hwy 1543 Hartford KY 42347 Office: 314 Main St Hartford KY 42347 Nashville TN 37220 Office: PO Box 846 Nashville TN 37202

HIGGINBOTHAM, RALPH DANIEL, printer; b. Flatrock, Ala., July 13, 1916; s. Emory Lawrence and Josie Ella (Atkins) H.; student Anniston (Ala.) Bus. Coll., 1934; m. Dorothy Lee Burnham, Feb. 20, 1937 (dec. Jan. 1973); children—Linda Diane, Ralph Daniel, Nancy Jo; m. Miriam Cockrell Jackson, Feb. 14, 1974. Newspaper carrier Anniston Star, 1928-33, asst. circulation mgr., 1933-35, apprentice printer, 1935-41, journeyman printer, 1941-44; printer, linotype operator Strong Printing Co., Birmingham, Ala., 1944-45; printer Birmingham Post, 1945-46; owner Stephens Printing Co., Anniston, 1946—, Sawyer Printing Co., Anniston, 1950—, Moore printing Co., 1962— (all now Higginbotham, Inc.); pres. Calhoun Pub. Co., Jacksonville, Ala., 1963-74; pub. Jacksonville News, 1963-74. Vice pres. Anniston Cerebral Palsy unit, 1966-67, pres., 1967-68; mem. Anniston Bd. Edn., 1959-74, pres., 1962-63, 66-74, pres. Anniston Com. Better Schs., 1964-65; pres. Calhoun County Drys, 1962-63; mem. exec. com. Calhoun County Baptist Assn.; 1957-61; pres. Calhoun County Bapt. Brotherhood Assn., 1959-61; dir. Ala. Coalition Better Edn., Inc., 1968-70; mem. Ala. Vocational Adv. Com., 1969-71. Trustee Judson Coll., 1968—. Named Man of Year, Anniston Star, 1970. Mem. Anniston C. of C. (dir. 1957-59, 61-62, 64-65, 67-68, 70-71, 73-74, v.p. 1967), Ala. Assn. Sch. Bds. (dir., 1961-70, pres. 1966-70), Nat. Sch. Bds. Assn. (del. 1964-70), United Comml. Travelers. Democrat. Baptist (chmn. bd. deacons 1966-68). Mason, Gideon. Clubs: Exchange (pres. 1956-57), Anniston Country. Home: 336 Wildwood Rd Anniston AL 36201 Office: 1116 Moore Av Anniston AL 36201

HIGGINBOTHAM, RONALD EUGENE, elec. engr.; b. West Union, Ill., Aug. 16, 1939; s. Hershel and Dorothy (Clouse) H.; B.S. in Math. with honors, Rose Poly. Inst., 1961; M.S. in Engring. Sci., Rensselaer Poly. Inst., 1964; Ph.D. in Elec. Engring., U. Conn., 1972; m. Phyllis Ann Quick, July 10, 1960; children—Eric Bryan, Atresa Lyn. Engr. Hamilton Standard div. United Aircraft Corp., Windsor Locks, Conn., 1961-65; research asst. U. Conn., Storrs, 1965-66, instr. dept. elec. engring., 1966-68; mem. tech. staff guidance, control systems dept. TRW Systems Corp., Houston, 1968-72, mem. tech. staff undersea surviellance project office, Washington, 1972—. Active Boy Scouts Am., 1972—. Founding pres. Conn. Evangelizing Mission, Inc., Ansonia, Conn., 1964-68, now trustee. Mem. I.E.E.E., Rose Poly. Inst. Alumni Assn. (sec. treas.), Sigma Nu. Mem. Ch. Christ (deacon 1970-72). Contbr. profl. jours. Home: 4914 Wycliff Lane Fairfax VA 22030 Office: 7600 Colshire Dr McLean VA 22101

HIGGINS, EDWIN STANLEY, educator; b. L.I., N.Y., Mar. 12, 1925; s. John Thomas and Nettie Viola (Stein) H.; B.A. cum laude, Alfred U., 1952; Ph.D., Syracuse U., 1956; m. Barbara Jean Wilson, June 20, 1958; children—Elizabeth Jean, James Edwin, Glenn David. Teaching and research asst. Alfred U., 1951-52; research fellow State U. N.Y. Med. Center, Syracuse, 1952-56; asst. prof. Med. Coll. Va., Va. Commonwealth U., Richmond, 1956-62, asso. prof., 1962-68, prof. biochemistry, 1968—. Research leader div. alcohol studies and rehab. Va . Dept. Health, 1959-73; lectr. NSF Summer Inst., 1959. Served with AUS, 1943-46; PTO. Recipient grants NIH, NSF. Mem. Soc. Exptl. Biology and Medicine (mem. council 1961-68), Am. Chem. Soc., A.A.A.S., Am. Inst. Nutrition, Am. Soc. Cell Biology, Va. Acad. Scis., Sigma Xi. Presbyn. (ruling elder 1969—). Contbr. articles to profl. jours. Home: 5928 Old Orchard Rd Richmond VA 23227

HIGGINS, KENNETH DYKE, lawyer; b. Benton, Tenn., Aug. 21, 1916; s. Fredrick Dyke and Martha Cathrine (Dunn) H.; A.A., Tenn. Wesleyan Coll., 1936; A.B., Transylvania U., 1938; J.D., Tulane U., 1942; m. June Blair Webb, June 10, 1944; children—Jane Webb (Mrs. Robert Elliott), Kenneth Dyke. Admitted to Tenn. bar, 1946, since practiced in Athens; mem. firm Higgins & Biddle. Dir. First Nat. Bank McMinn County, Tenn. Served with USNR, 1942-46. Decorated Bronze Star. Methodist. Kiwanian. Home: 1200 Wood Acres Dr Athens TN 37303 Office: 20 W Washington St Athens TN 37303

HIGGINS, KENNETH RAYMOND, landscape architect; b. Holyoke, Mass., Nov. 2, 1915; s. Alfred and Lillie (Ritter) H.; student R.I. State Coll., 1934; B.S. Mass. State Coll., 1937, B.Landscape Architecture, 1939; m. Mary Douthat Smith, Sept. 5, 1942; children—Kenneth Hewlett, Ralph Barton, Janie Lyle (Mrs. Frederick C. Levering Jr.). Landscape architect, site planner Richmond (Va.) Field Office Pub. Housing Adminstrn., 1948-51; pvt. practice landscape architecture, Richmond, 1951—. Instr., Richmond Profl. Inst., evenings 1956; cons. in field. Chmn., Richmond Beautification Com., 1954-64; treas. River Rd Citizens Assn., 1956; chmn. Monument Av. Commn., 1969-73. Bd. dirs. Berkeley Thanksgiving Fest. Served to capt. USAAF, 1942-46. Mem. Am. Soc. Landscape Architects (past Va. chmn., Pres.'s award Potomac chpt. 1968), U. Mass. Landscape Archtl. Assn., Va. Hist. Soc., Soc. Archtl. Historians, Nat. Trust for Historic Preservation, Eastern Nat. Park and Monument Assn., Assn. for Preservation Va. Antiquities (life), Am. Arbitration Assn. Lambda Chi Alpha. Episcopalian (former vestryman). Club: Country of Virginia. Address: 908 S Gaskins Rd Richmond VA 23233 Office: 908 S Gaskins Rd Richmond VA 23233

HIGGINS, LAWRENCE ERNEST, social work exec.; b. New Orleans, Oct. 2, 1907; s. Lawrence Ambrose and Marie (Jaunet) H.; B.S., Tulane U., 1928; student La. U. Sch. Social Welfare, 1931, certificate social work, 1955; m. Carolyn Belle Cresap, Oct. 20, 1933; children—Kathleen, Laureen. Welfare visitor dept. pub. welfare, New Orleans, 1937-42; asst., acting commr. La. State Bd. Pub. Welfare, 1942-48, commr., 1948-50; exec. sec. La. Youth Commn., 1950-73. Mem. ten-man survey team, IRO, Geneva, Switzerland and U.S. State Dept. to work on welfare and displaced persons problems in Germany and Austria, 1950; adminstr. Interstate Crime Compact, 1948-50; mem. La. State Bd. of Parole, 1945-48; Sec.-treas. Juvenile Ct. Commn., 1948-50; mem. state com. on planning for White House Conf. on Children and Youth, also chmn. pub. welfare sect., vice chmn. La. State adv. com., 1960, del., cons. conf. staff, 1960; dir. Nat. Council State Coms. Children and Youth, 1957-62, pres. So. States Probation and Parole Conf., 1960-61; coordinator Nat. Council Juvenile Ct. Judges Spl. Tng. Project; sec.-treas. La. Displaced Persons Commn.; pres. La. P.T.A.; adv. com. Nat. Soc. Crippled Children and Adults; chmn. La. State Inter-deptl. Com.; cons. Family Ct. East Baton Rouge Parish, La. Council for Evaluation Center Exceptional Children; adv. com. on edn. exceptional children, State Dept. Edn.; spl. adviser Pres.'s Com. on Juvenile Delinquency and Youth Crime; cons. on juvenile delinquency Nat. Conf. of Govs.; mem. Nat. Conf. of Juvenile Agys.; dir. La. Conf. Social Welfare (past pres.), Family Service Society Baton Rouge; pres. La. Conf. Correctional workers with Juveniles; nat. com. to develop standards for police service in handling juveniles, U.S. Children's Bur.; mem. nat. com. apptd. by Nat. Probation and Parole Assn. for developing revised standards for juvenile cts., vice chmn. profl. council; sec. So. States Probation and Parole Assn.; dir. La. Council Handicapped Children; exec. com. La. Conf. Retarded Children; chmn. profl. council Nat. Council Crime and Delinquency; mem. state com. White House Conf. Children and Youth, 1970, Nat. Joint Commn. Correctional Manpower and Tng.; field cons. Nat. Survey Corrections for Pres.'s Crime Commn., 1967; mem. La. Commn. Law Enforcement and Adminstrn. Criminal justice. Lectr. Tulane U., La. State U. Mem. Nat. Assn. Social Workers, Internat., La. juvenile officer's assns., Am. Pub. Welfare Assn. (nat. com. protective services for children), Nat. Conf. Social Work, Am. Acad. Polit. and Social Scis., Nat. Adult Edn. Assn., Acad. Certified Social Workers, Alpha Chi Sigma, Sigma Pi. K.C. Contbr. articles to profl. jours. Home: 3410 Hyacinth Av Baton Rouge LA 70808

HIGGS, ARTHUR RONALD, dentist; b. Miami, Fla., Feb. 3, 1938; s. Arthur Ronald and Viola (Heastie) H.; B.S., Tenn. State U., 1959; D.D.S., Meharry Med. Coll., 1963; m. Julia A. Peebles, June 31, 1963; children—Kimberly Venessa, Shera Yvonne. Practice dentistry, Houston, 1965—; mem. staff Riverside Gen., Twelve Oaks, St. Elizabeth's hosps.; faculty oral surgery U. Tex. Postgrad. Sch., 1966—. Pres., Houston Investors Soc., 1968-70. Mem. Constl. Revisions Commn. Tex. Bd. dirs. Big Bros. of Houston, Houston Council on Human Relations, Manpower Adv. Com. Served to capt. AUS, 1963-65. Mem. Am., Nat., Houston Dist., Charles A. George dental assns., Am. Acad. Gen. Dentistry, Am. Soc. Preventive Dentistry, Fedn. Dentaire Internationale, Omega Psi Phi. Home: 2221 N MacGregor St Houston TX 77004 Office: 5014 Almeda St Houston TX 77004

HIGGS, CYRUS HENRY, JR., psychiatrist; b. Greenville, Miss., Apr. 25, 1927; s. Cyrus Henry and Jessie Inez (Hightower) H.; B.A., U. Miss., 1955, med. certificate, 1953; M.D., U. Tenn., 1954; m. Edna Juanita Dye, July 6, 1957; children—Emily Cheryl, Cyrus Henry, David Allen. Intern Baptist Meml. Hosp., Memphis, 1955; staff physician Miss. State Hosp., Whitfield, 1956-58; resident medicine City of Memphis Hosp., Kennedy VA Hosp., 1958-61; resident psychiatry VA Hosp., North Little Rock, Ark., 1961-64, staff psychiatrist, 1964-67; staff psychiatrist Tenn. Psychiat. Hosp. and Inst., Memphis, 1967—; instr. psychiatry U. Tenn., 1967—. Served with USNR, 1945-46. Mem. A.M.A., Am. Psychiat. Assn., Shelby County, Memphis med. socs., Alpha Kappa Kappa. Methodist. Home: 1413 Briarwood Dr Memphis TN 38111 Office: 865 Poplar Av Memphis TN 38105

HIGHLEYMAN, DALY, business exec.; b. St. Louis, May 20, 1905; s. Locke Tiffin and Katherine (Daly) H.; grad. Pomfret Sch., 1925; student Yale, 1926-27; m. Doris DeGarmo, June 4, 1954; children—Peter Thacher, Patricia Daly. Jr. exec. de Saint Phalle & Co., N.Y.C., 1928-29; sec., treas. Tamiami Trail Land Co., Miami, Fla., 1930-38; pres. Fidelity Mortgage & Guarantee Co., Miami, 1930-32, asst, supr. cost reduction sect. indsl. engring. Consol. Vultee Aircraft Corp., San Diego, 1941-46; pres. Tikada Holding Co., 1953-55; v.p. Avenger Yachts, Inc., 1965-67, pres., 1967-69; pres. Datif Investment Corp., 1969—, Tikada Mgmt. Corp., 1969—. Active Coconut Grove Civic Club. Mem. Hist. Assn. So. Fla., Marine Hist. Assn., Internat. Oceanographic Found., Council for Internat. Visitors of Greater Miami, Miami Pioneers, Internat. Platform Assn. Clubs: Coral Reef Yacht (commodore 1963-64) (Coconut Grove, Fla.); San Diego Yacht; Yale (Miami). Home: 3737 El Prado Coconut Grove FL 33133 Office: 132 Madeira Av Coral Gables FL 33134

HIGHSMITH, PHILLIP EUGENE, educator; b. Glenmary, Tenn., Dec. 2, 1925; s. Buren C. and Mary (Rowland) H.; B.S., E. Tenn. State U., 1951; M.S., U. Va., 1956; Ph.D., Ohio State U., 1965; m. Mary L. Ledford, Aug. 1, 1952; children—John, Carol, Stephen. Tchr., Greenbrier Mil. Sch., 1952-54, Fork Union Mil. Acad., 1954-60; prof. Transylvania Coll., 1960-65; prof. physics Converse Coll., Spartanburg, S.C., 1965—. Served with AUS, World War II; ETO. Author: Adventures in Physics, 1972; Adventures in Physics Laboratory Manual, 1972; Physics, Man, and His Environment, 1974. Patentee in field. Home: 388 Lake Forest Dr Spartanburg SC 29302 Office: Converse Coll Spartanburg SC 29301

HIGHTON, RICHARD TAYLOR, educator; b. Chgo., Dec. 24, 1927; s. Albert Henry and Helen Irene (Taylor) H.; A.B., N.Y. U., 1950; M.S., U. Fla., 1953, Ph.D., 1956; m. Anne Adams, June 23, 1950; children—Barbara, Kim, Scott, Caitlin Ann. Asst. prof. zoology U. Md., College Park, 1956-62, asso. prof. zoology, 1962-73, prof., 1973—. Served with AUS, 1946-48. Mem. Evolution Soc., Am. Soc. Ichthyologists and Herpetologists, Ecol. Soc. Am., Herpetologists League, Soc. for Study Amphibians and Reptiles, A.A.A.S., Soc. Systematic Zoology, Am. Soc. Naturalists, Genetics Soc. Am., Sigma Xi. Home: 3613 Van Ness St NW Washington DC 20008 Office: Dept Zoology U Md College Park MD 20742

HIGHTOWER, DANNIE BEA (MRS. FRANK JOHNSON HIGHTOWER), civic worker; b. El Dorado, Ark., Jan. 12, 1925; d. Dan William and Ruby (Gibson) James; B.A., Smith Coll., Northampton, Mass., 1947; m. Frank Johnson Hightower, Jan. 15, 1949; children—Johnson, Michael. Pres., Jr. League of Oklahoma City, 1962-63; 1st chmn. Okla. Arts and Humanities Council, 1967-69, now bd. dirs.; mem. Presdl. Adv. Com. of Kennedy Center, 1969—. Bd. dirs. Okla. Symphony, Civic Ballet, Okla. Med. Research Found., Okla. Art Center, Oklahoma County Criminal Justice Council; trustee Casady Episcopal Day Sch. Named Woman of Year in Civic Affairs, Soroptimist Internat., 1968. Elected to Okla. Hall of Fame, 1969. Mem. Phi Beta Kappa. Home: 439 NW 15th St Oklahoma City OK 73103

HIGHTOWER, DAVID PETERSON, psychoanalyst; b. York, Ala., Nov. 15, 1912; s. Council Berry and Georgie (Mellown) H.; B.S., Birmingham So. U., 1933; M.D., Tulane U., 1937. Intern Hillman Hosp., 1937-39, chief resident medicine, 1939-40; commd. lt. (j.g.) M.C., U.S. Navy, 1940, advanced through grades to capt., 1955; clin. instr. Georgetown U., 1947-60; dir. mental hygiene unit U.S. Naval Acad., 1952-60; ret., 1960; psychoanalyst Washington Psychoanalytic Inst., 1947—; practice medicine specializing in psychotherapy, York, 1960—; cons. in psychotherapy East Miss. State Hosp., 1968—; clin. asso. div. continuing med. edn. U. Ala. Sch. Medicine, 1970—. Mem. Am., Ala., Sumter County med. assns., York C. of C. (past dir.), Kappa Alpha, Theta Kappa Psi, Beta Beta Beta, Kappa Phi Kappa. Methodist. Rotarian. Home: 110 Hightower St York AL 36925 Office: 720 4th Av York AL 36925

HIGHTOWER, JESS M., mfg. co. exec.; b. Kirksville, Mo., Feb. 9, 1922; s. Jesse Moss and Grace (Renfrow) H.; B.A., U. Tulsa, 1950, postgrad., 1951-52; m. Bette Jean Blackburn, Feb. 21, 1943; children—Jere Jean, Jess Vince, Jami Jean. Pres. Herb-O-Tone Medicine Co., Tulsa, 1946-48; free lance writer, 1949-50; reporter Tulsa Daily World, 1950-51; with McDonnell Douglas Corp., Tulsa, 1951—, mgr. external relations, editor div. publs., 1957—, mgr. pub. relations Douglas Aircrft Southeastern plant, Melbourne, Ark., 1969—. Guest lectr. U. Okla., 1969, U. Tulsa, 1970-71. Mem. Okla. Air Pollution Council, 1967—, vice chmn. Gov's Link Com., 1970—, Indian Nations Area council Boy Souts Am., 1968—; vice chmn. pub. relations com. Ark. Basin Devel. Assn., 1969—; chmn. housing com. Mayor's Com. Tulsa Model Cities Program, 1966-67. Trustee Children's Med. Center, Tulsa, 1969-75; vice chmn. Tulsa Charity Horse Show, 1965—, Tulsa Met. Zoo, 1971—. Served with AUS, 1943-45. Decorated Bronze Star medal. Mem. U. Tulsa Alumni Assn. (trustee 1965—), Nat. Mgmt. Assn., Pub. Relations Soc. Am. (dir. 1964-67), UN Assn. (dir. 1969—), Met. Tulsa C. of C. (chmn. alternative edn. task force 1973-74). Episcopalian. Mason. Clubs: Oaks Country, Tulsa Press. Author (some with pseudonym Jim Grant) articles, stories in mags., 1961—. Author, producer, dir. movie Course of Action for Okla. Retarded Childrens Assn., 1957. Home: 5345 E 22d Pl Tulsa OK 74114 Office: 2000 N Memorial Dr Tulsa OK 74115

HIGHTOWER, NEIL HAMILTON, textile mill exec.; b. Atlanta, Dec. 31, 1940; s. William Harrison and Elinor (Hamilton) H.; B.S. in Textiles, Ga. Inst. Tech., 1963; m. Barbara Ann Bauer, Dec. 28, 1963; children—Neil Jr., John, Heidi. With Thomaston Cotton Mills (Ga.), 1965—, v.p., 1971-73, sr. v.p., 1973—. Mem. Thomaston Bd. Edn., 1972—. Served with AUS, 1963-65. Methodist. Kiwanian. Home: 505 Avalon Rd Thomaston GA 30286 Office: 115 E Main St Thomaston GA 30286

HIGLEY, BRUCE WADSWORTH, orthodontist; b. Iowa City, Dec. 1, 1928; s. Lester Bodine and Harriet (Wadsworth) H.; D.D.S., State U. Ia., 1952, M.S., 1953; student Grinnell Coll., 1946-48, orthodontic certificate, 1953; m. Mary Victoria Eckey, Aug. 24, 1949; m. 2d, Marta Beatriz Velasco, Sept. 23, 1966. Research, instr. Ia. U. Dental Sch., 1952-53; practice dentistry specializing in orthodontics, South Miami, Fla., 1955—. Owner, chmn. bd., M.B.H. Enterprises, Inc., Miami, Fla., 1960—. Vice chmn. dist. council Boy Scouts Am., 1959-62; mem. personnel bd., South Miami, 1959. Served as 1st lt., Dental Corps, AUS, 1953-55. Mem. Fla. Orthodontic Soc., So., Miami socs. orthodontists, Am. Assn. Orthodontists, Fla., Am. socs. dentistry for children, Fla., Fla. East Coast, Miami dental socs., Am., South Dade dental assns., English Royal Acad., U. Kansas City Seminar, Jr. C. of C. (past dir.), C. of C. (past dir., past sec., past treas.), Fedn. Dentaire Internat., Psi Omega, Omicron Kappa Upsilon. Presbyn. (deacon). Rotarian (pres. 1961-62), Elk. Clubs: Coral Reef Yacht, Coral Gables Country, Royal Palm Tennis, Bankers, Executive (Miami). Home: 625 Biltmore Way Coral Gables FL 33134 Office: 7210 Red Rd South Miami FL 33143

HILBERG, ALBERT WILLIAM, physician; b. Michigan City, Ind., Apr. 5, 1922; s. Hugo Albert and Emily (Nallenweg) H.; B.S. with high honor, Elmhurst Coll., 1944; M.D., Ind. U., 1946; postgrad. Cornell U., 1947, State U. Ia., 1949-51; D.Sc., Elmhurst Coll., 1961; m. Rosemary Helen Kross, Aug. 22, 1943; children—Jeffrey, Eric, David, Kristin, Susan. Rotating intern Evangelical Hosp. Chgo., 1946-47; resident, Cornell U., 1947, State U. Ia., 1949-51, Hosp. Joint Disease, 1950-51; chief labs. Cancer Investigation Center, Cancer Control Br., Nat. Cancer Inst., Hot Springs, Ark., 1947-49; asst. pathology dept. pathology State U. Ia. Sch. Medicine, 1949-50, instr. pathology, 1950-51; spl. fellow in pathology Hosp. Joint Diseases, N.Y.C., 1951-52; pathologist Lab. Pathology, Nat. Cancer Inst., Bethesda, Md., 1952-57; cons. pathology div. biology and medicine AEC, Agronne Nat. Lab., 1952-59; head cytodiagnosis service, pathologic anatomy dept. Clin. Center, NIH, 1953-57; pathology cons. field investigations and demonstrations br. Nat. Cancer Inst., 1957-59, acting head cytology sect., 1959-60, asst. chief research diagnostic research br., 1960-61; chief radiation biology, research br. div. radiol. health Bur. State Services, USPHS, 1961-62, chmn. editorial com. div. radiol. health, 1961-65, dep. chief research br. div. radiol. health Rockville, Md., 1965-67, exec. sec. to radiation bio-effects adv. com., 1966-68; chief radiopathology div. I, Armed Forces Inst. Pathology, Walter Reed Army Med. Center, 1962-65, mem. editorial adv. bd., 1963-65; chmn. review com. uranium miners report Fed. Radiation Council, 1966-67; chief population studies program Nat. Center Radiol. Health, 1967-68; profl. asso. div. med. scis. Nat. Acad. Scis., NRC, Washington, 1968—. Pres., Parkside P.T.A., 1954; v.p. Eastern Jr. High Sch. P.T.A., 1964-65. Served from 2d lt. to 1st lt. M.C., AUS, 1942-47. Recipient certificate of appreciation A.C.S., 1958, certificate of merit A.M.A., 1958. Fellow Coll. Am. Pathologists, Soc. Nuclear Medicine, A.A.A.S.; mem. Internat. Acad. Pathologists, Am. Assn. Pathologists and Bacteriologists, Am. Soc. Clin. Pathologists. Author: Handbook of Exfoliative Cytology for Technicians, 1948; (with others) Reduction of Radiation Exposure in Nuclear Medicine, 1968. Contbr. articles to profl. jours. Home: 12512 Davan Dr Silver Spring MD 20904 Office: 2101 Constitution Av Washington DC 20418

HILDEBRAND, FRANK, govt. ofcl.; b. Winston-Salem, N.C., Feb. 5, 1929; s. Franklin and Mildred (Brown) H.; B.A., Tulane U., 1950; m. Joyce Bruff, May 31, 1952. Editor, asso. pub. Jennings (La.) Daily News, 1952-57; bus. editor Baytown (Tex.) Sun, 1957-58; travel editor, bus. news writer Houston Post, 1958-60; feature writer Dallas Morning News, 1960-62; exec. dir. Tex. Tourist Devel. Agy., Austin, 1963—. Nat. chmn. dir. Discover Am. Travel Orgns.; state liaison officer U.S. Travel Service; trustee U.S. Travel Data Center; mem. exec. com. Travel Research Assn.; chmn. Tex. Travel Trails Com.; dir. Tex. Travel Counselors Conf.; chmn. Conquistadores Trail Com. Served with AUS, 1950-52. Named U.S. Travel Dir. of Year, 1971. Club: Lakeway Yacht (Austin). Episcopalian. Mason (32 deg.). Home: 2701 Trail of the Madrones Austin TX 78746 Office: Austin State Office Bldg Austin TX 78711

HILDEBRANDT, ALVIN FRANK, educator; b. Spring, Tex., Dec. 31, 1925; s. Ludwig Otto and Anna (Weindorff) H.; B.S. in Physics, U. Houston, 1949; Ph.D., Tex. A. and M. U., 1956; m. Cornelia Nelle Margaret Mohle, Dec. 23, 1950; children—George Flavius, William Jon Edward. Sr. research engr., then group leader quantum physics Jet. Propulsion Lab., Pasadena, Cal., 1956-65; sr. research fellow chemistry and low temperature physics Cal. Inst. Tech., 1960-64; mem. faculty U. Houston, 1965—, prof. physics, chmn. dept., 1969—. Served with USNR, 1945-46. NASA grantee, 1968—; NSF/Research Applied to Nat. Needs Solar Tower grantee, 1973—. Mem. Am. Phys. Soc., A.A.A.S., Internat. Solar Energy Soc., Houston C. of C. (future studies com.), Sigma Psi, Sigma Pi Sigma, Phi Kappa Phi. Inventor superconduction flux pumps. Office: U Houston Houston TX 77004

HILDEEN, CATHERINE ARDELLE RIGGS (MRS. ROGER GUSTAV HILDEEN), bus. exec.; b. Mpls., Jan. 14, 1921; d. Herbert Samuel and Ardelle (Wells) Riggs; B.A., U. Minn., 1942; postgrad. U. Chgo., 1944; m. Roger Gustav Hildeen, July 1, 1944. Research worker Continental Ill. Nat. Bank, Chgo., 1942-47; personnel mgr. Wieboldt Stores, Chgo., 1947-51; v.p. personnel Greenbelt Consumer Services, Silver Springs, Md., 1952—. Mem. Am. Soc. Personnel Adminstrn. (nat. sec. 1972, dir. 1974—), Supermarket Inst. (mem. personnel com. 1966), Washington Personnel Assn. (pres. 1967-68). Home: 6512 Ridgeway Dr Springfield VA 22150 Office: 8547 Piney Branch Rd Silver Springs MD 20901

HILDRETH, PHILIP ELWIN, educator, univ. dean; b. Marlboro, N.H., Jan. 14, 1923; s. Lewis George and Mary (Adams) H.; A.B., Dartmouth, 1947; M.A., U. Cal. at Berkeley, 1951, Ph.D., 1955; m. Gretchen Meredith Swanson, Apr. 19, 1952; children—Bradley Edward, Pamela Eden, Todd Randall. Research biologist Lawrence Radiation Lab., U. Cal. at Berkeley, 1951-56, 59-67; asst. prof. biology Long Beach (Cal.) State Coll., 1956-59; distinguished prof. biology, chmn. dept. U. N.C. at Charlotte, 1967-72, chmn. div. math. and natural scis., 1968-70, dean Coll. Sci. and Math., 1970—. Served with USNR, 1944-46. Mem. Genetics Soc. Am., Am. Soc. Zoologists, Assn. Southeastern Biologists, A.A.A.S., Am. Inst. Biol. Scis., Sigma Xi. Contbr. numerous articles to sci. jours. Home: 1100 Circlewood Dr Charlotte NC 28211

HILEMAN, MELVIN J., banker; b. Wheeling, W.Va., May 6, 1929; s. Bert Norman and Mary J. (Lyda) H.; grad. Am. Inst. Banking, 1956, Stonier Grad. Sch. Banking, 1965; m. Elizabeth Ann Watson, June 10, 1950; children—Victoria L., Scott W. With Washington Loan & Trust Co. (consol. with Riggs Nat. Bank 1954), 1947—, served in all banking depts., beginning as note teller, successively asst. mgr., asst. cashier, asst. mgr., asst. v.p., asst. mgr., 1962-64, asst. v.p., mgr S.E. office, 1964-66, v.p., mgr., 1966—. Active Community Chest drives 1951-54; sect. capt. Am. Cancer Soc., Washington, 1965; active Boy Scouts Am. Trustee Morris Cafritz Meml. Hosp.; bd. advisers Inst. Family and Marriage Relations, Inc. Mem. Met. Washington Bd. Trade, Nat. Capital Active Club (sec.-treas. 1951-52), U.S. Navy League (asst. treas.), Naval Sea Cadet Corps (asst. treas.). Lion (dir.). Home: 6434 Burwell St Springfield VA 22150 Office: 1750 Pennsylvania Av NW Washington DC 20006

HILER, EDWARD ALLAN, educator; b. Hamilton, O., May 14, 1939; s. Earl and Thelma Margaret (Kolb) H.; B.S., Ohio State U., 1963, M.S., 1963, Ph.D., 1966; m. Patricia Ann Burke, Jan. 30, 1960; children—Karen Dawn, Richard Burke. Asst. prof. dept. agrl. engring. Tex. A & M U., College Station, 1966-69, asso. prof., 1969-73, prof., 1973—. Bd. dirs. Bryan Day Care Center. Registered profl. engr., Tex. Fellow A.A.A.S.; mem. Am. Soc. Agrl. Engrs., Am. Soc. Engring. Edn., Nat. Soc. Profl. Engrs., Am. Geophys. Union, Sigma Xi, Tau Beta Pi, Gamma Sigma Delta, Alpha Epsilon. Home: 2005 Briar Oaks St Bryan TX 77801 Office: Dept Agrl Engring Tex A & M U College Station TX 77843

HILGERS, WILLIAM BLANKS, lawyer; b. Lockhart, Tex., Dec. 31, 1924; s. Harry Edward and Minnie Jo (Blanks) H.; B.B.A., U. Tex., 1947, LL.B., 1949; m. Sara Leonard Lamun, Dec. 23, 1945; children—David William, John Blakely, Sara Jo, Paul Edward. Admitted to Tex. bar, 1949, since practiced in Austin; mem. firm Hilgers, Daugherty, Fielder, Golden & Kuperman, Austin, 1970—. Dir., chmn. bd. Travis Bank & Trust Co.; dir., v.p. Home Entertainment Center; dir. Appliance Assos., Inc., Bryant-Curington, Inc., Sports, Inc. Bd. dirs. James Dick Found. Performing Arts, Austin Symphony Soc. Served to 1st lt. USAAF, 1943-45. Decorated D.F.C., Air medal, Purple Heart. C.P.A., Tex. Fellow Tex. Bar Found.; mem. State Bar Tex. (dir.), Am. Inst. C.P.A.'s, Am., Travis County (pres. 1973-74) bar assns. Mem. Christian Ch. (pres. Tex. 1972-74). Mason (Shriner), Kiwanian. Club: Country (Austin). Home: Route 1 Box 45 Del Valle TX 78617 Office: 711 W 7th St Austin TX 78701

HILL, A(LFRED) GARRETT, cons. chemist; b. West Point, Miss., June 21, 1906; s. Asa Edwin and Bettie Alberta (Garrett) H.; B.A., Baylor U., 1926. M.A., 1926; Ph.D., Yale, 1932; m. Lois Jenkins, Dec. 25, 1935. Head sci. dept. Burleson Coll., 1926-28; instr. Baylor U., 1928-29; with Bound Brook (N.J.) plant Am. Cyanamid Co., 1932-63, research chemist, subsequently devel. chemist, 1939-44, chief chemist intermediates dept., 1944-46, asst. mgr. control and devel. dept., 1946-47, tech. dir. intermediates and rubber chems., 1947-55, resident tech. dir., 1955-57, mgr. pharms. mfg. dept., 1957-58, asst. plant mgr., 1958-59, plant mgr., 1959-62, asst. to gen. mgr. Organic Chems. Div., 1962-63; dir. County Bank and Trust Co., Somerset 1960-63; chmn. div. natural sci. Mobile (Ala.) Coll., 1963-67, prof. chemistry, 1963-69; v.p. Gulf Coast Inst. Research and Tech., Mobile, 1967—; mem. tech. adv. com. Tex. Air Control Bd., 1972—; staff cons. Gulf States Pollution Control, Inc., Tex., Jacksonville, 1970—; ind. cons. chemist, tech. and adminstrn. Vice chmn. Com. Aid to Edn., Mobile, 1967-69. Pres. Warren Twp. Bd. Edn., 1949-50; v.p. Somerset County Vocational Bd. Edn., 1961-63; bd. dirs. Civil Def. and Disaster Control, Warren Twp., N.J., 1950-54, 57-59; active A.R.C., bd. dirs. Plainfield (N.J.) chpt., 1956-63; trustee Warren Twp. Community Fund. 1961-63; pres. Jarratt Cemetery Assn., 1971—. Fellow Am. Inst. Chemists, Ala. Acad. Sci. (v.p. 1966-67), mem. Am. Chem. Soc., (nat. councilor 1966-69), Am. Inst. Chem. Engrs. (dir. Mobile 1967-69), Warren Twp. Civic Assn. (pres. 1946-47), Sigma Xi, Alpha Chi Sigma. Republican. Baptist (v.p. Bible class 1972—). Mason (32 deg., Shriner), Rotarian (pres. Jacksonville 1972-73, dist. gov. elect 1974-75). Contbr. articles on chems. to sci. jours. Patentee in field. Home: Beaucove Route 6 Jacksonville TX 75766

HILL, BRYCE DALE, sch. adminstr.; b. Seminole, Okla., Mar. 5, 1930; s. Charles Daniel and Ollie (Nichols) H.; B.S., East Central State Coll., 1952, M.Teaching, 1957; postgrad. U. Okla. 1959-70; profl. adminstrs. certificate, 1969; m. Wilma Dean Carter, Aug. 16, 1956; children—Bryce Anthony, Brent Dale. Tchr. pub. schs., New Lima, Okla., 1952-56, supt. pub. schs., 1956—; owner New Lima Gas Co., 1958—. Chmn. bd. dirs. Seminole County chpt. A.R.C., 1969—; v.p. bd. dirs. Redland Community Action Program, 1968-71; mem. Seminole County Rural Devel. Council. Chmn. Seminole County Democratic Central Com., 1962-64, 70-72, 74—. Mem. N.E.A., Okla. Edn. Assn., Am., Okla. assns. sch. adminstrs., Seminole County Tchrs. Assn. (pres. 1964, 71-72), Seminole County Sch. Adminstrs. Assn. (chmn. 1969-70), Seminole County Schoolmasters Club (pres. 1963-69), Seminole Hist. Soc. (v.p. 1971-73). Baptist. Home: Box 97 New Lima OK 74858

HILL, CAESAR GRANT, statistician; b. Savannah, Ga., Sept. 18, 1926; s. Raymond A. and Mary (Grant) H.; A.B., Morehouse Coll., 1949; postgrad. Atlanta U., 1950-51; m. Wanda Jean Clemens, Aug. 14, 1955; children—Stephen, Gary. Instr. math. Voorhees Coll., 1949-53; pub. relations worker Citizens for Eisenhower Congress Com., Washington, 1953-54; statistician Bur. Census 1954—, chief area sample surveys br., 1965-66, chief retail programs implementation br., 1966—; dir. 1970 Decennial Census Dist. Office, Compton, Cal., 1970, chief wholesale census br., 1970-72, spl. asst. to dep. adminstr. social and econ. statistics adminstrn., 1972-73, chief cross bus. surveys br., 1973—; dir. Census Fed. Credit Union, 1962-64. Mem. auditing com. Episcopal Diocese, Washington, 1967-70; sec.-treas. com. Boy Scouts of Am., Washington, 1960-63. Served with C.E. AUS, 1944-46. Mem. Am. Statis. Assn., Am. Marketing Assn., Census Bur. Welfare and Recreation Assn. (v.p. 1957-61). Alpha Phi Alpha. Episcopalian. Home: 1766 41st Pl SE Washington DC 20020 Office: Bur of Census Washington DC 20233

HILL, CARL MCCLELLAN, coll. pres., author; b. Norfolk, Va., July 27, 1907; s. William F. and Sarah A. (Rowe) H.; B.S. Hampton Inst., 1931; M.S., Cornell U., 1935; Ph.D., 1941; student U. Pa., 1938-40; Dr. Laws, University of Kentucky, 1966; m. Helen C. Rose, 1970; 1 dau. by previous marriage, Doris (Mrs. Richard McGhee). Asst. prof. Hampton Inst., 1931-41; asso. prof. Greensboro (N.C.) Agr. and Tech. Coll., 1941-44; prof., Tenn. Agr. and Indsl. State U., Nashville, 1944-62, head dept. chemistry, 1944-51, chmn. sch. arts and scis., 1951-58, dean sch. arts and scis., dean faculty, 1958-62; pres., prof. chemistry Ky. State U., 1962—; supr. chem. research projects TVA, 1947-50, The Research Coop., 1947-50, USAF Research and Devel. Command, 1951-52, NSF, 1951-52. Mem. Gov.'s Commn. on Status of Women; mem. adv. com. accreditation and instl. eligibility U.S. Office Edn., 1969; Bd. dirs. Am. Heart Assn., Blue Cross Hosp. Plan, So. Regional Edn. Bd. Fellow A.A.A.S., Am. Inst. Chemists, Tenn. Acad. Sci.; mem. N.E.A., Am. Chem. Soc., Agora Assembly (pres.), Ky. Edn. Assn., Ky. Council on Pub. Higher Edn., Ky. C. of C. (dir.). Sigma Xi, Omega Psi Phi. Presbyn. (elder, mem. gen. exec. bd.). Mason, (33 deg.). Author General College Chemistry, 1954; Laboratory Experiments in Organic Chemistry, 1958. Contbr. chem. articles to profl. publs. Address: Ky State University Frankfort KY 40601

HILL, CAROLYN GREGG (MRS. VICTOR G. HILL, JR.), lawyer; b. Boston, June 4, 1936; d. David A., II and Virginia (Thompson) Gregg; B.A., Wellesley Coll., 1958; J.D., Oklahoma City U., 1969; m. Richard Howland Rawls, June 15, 1957 (dec.); children—Margaret Gregg, Richard Gregg; m. 2d, Victor G. Hill, Jr., May 6, 1967; 1 son, Victor Gerald III. Treas., dir. Cardast Corp., Wilton, N.H., 1958-62, gen. counsel, dir., 1973—; customers broker N.Y. Stock Exchange, 1962-64; atty. Kerr-McGee Corp., Oklahoma City, 1969—. Finance adviser Swift Water council Girl Scouts U.S.A., Manchester, N.H., 1960-62; pres. Wilton Youth Center, 1961-63. Del. to N.H. Republican Conv., 1960, 62, 64; pres. Southegan Women's Rep. Club, 1961-62. Mem. Am., Okla. County, Okla. bar assns., Colonial Dames Am. (bd. mgrs., sec. Okla.). Clubs: Old English Sheepdog of Am., Appalachian Mountain; Oklahoma City Golf and Country. Home: 1606 Camden Way Oklahoma City OK 73116 Office: Kerr-McGee Center Oklahoma City OK 73125

HILL, CECIL JAMES, lawyer; b. Asheville, N.C., Nov. 20, 1919; s. Burton H. and Vallie (Staton) H.; A.A., Mars Hill Coll., 1941; B.S., U. N.C., 1943, J.D., 1945; m. Elizabeth T. Richardson, Dec. 15, 1945; children—Elisabeth Hartsfield, James Harrison. With W. Bowen Henderson, C.P.A., Asheville, 1941-43; admitted to N.C. bar, 1945; since practiced in Brevard; mem. firm Ramsey, Hill, Smart, 1959—. Dir. First Union Nat. Bank of N.C., Brevard. Chmn. Brevard Housing Authority. Vice pres. Brevard Music Festival Assn., 1949. Bd. dirs. Moorehead Sch. for Blind, 1965—; chmn. bd. dirs. Gov. Morehead Sch. Mem. Transylvania County Bar Assn. (pres. 1950-51), Brevard C. of C. (pres. 1957), Delta Sigma Pi. Democrat. Baptist. Mason (32 deg.), Lion (pres. 1949). Home: Woodside Dr Brevard NC 28712 Office: Legal Bldg Brevard NC 28712

HILL, CLAUD JUSTIN, assn. exec.; b. Boonesville, Ark., Aug. 3, 1923; s. Carl Justin and Clara (Elkins) H.; A.A., Little Rock U., 1950; m. Dortha Lyon, Mar. 18, 1951 children—Wayne Justin, Kenneth Erwin. Mgr. Lido Cafeteria, Little Rock, 1950-59; dir. Ark. Restaurant Assn., 1960; dep. exec. v.p. Okla. Restaurant Assn., Oklahoma City, 1960—, exec. dir., 1965—; dir. Oklahoma Egg Council. Mem. Okla. Gov.'s Com. Tourism. Served with AUS, 1943-46. Mem. Internat. Soc. Restaurant Assn. Execs. (past pres.), Am., Okla. (dir.) socs. assn. execs., Am. Mgmt. Assn. Baptist. Mason (32 deg.). Home: 712 East Dr Edmond OK 73034 Office: 2207 N Broadway Oklahoma City OK 73103

HILL, DEAN EMERSON, architect; b. Flint, Mich., July 7, 1922; s. Emerson I. and Mable (Bonnell) H.; B.Arch., U. Mich., 1948; m. Mary Lee Sneed, Sept. 3, 1946; children—Linder, Patricia, Richard. Draftsman, designer firm Walk C. Jones-Walk C. Jones Jr., Memphis, 1948-55; architect Dean E. Hill & Assos., Memphis, 1955-73, Hill-Armour Assos. Architects, 1974—. Pres., Handicapped, Inc., Memphis, 1968-69; v.p. Memphis Speech and Hearing Center, 1973—. Bd. dirs. Oral Deaf Sch. Memphis, 1958-67. Served with C.E., AUS, 1942-46. Mem. Tenn. Soc. Architects (state pres. 1961-63), A.I.A. (past pres.), Methodist (mem. adminstrv. bd.). Club: Exchange (state pres., 1973-74). Home: 431 E Erwin Dr Memphis TN 38117 Office: 3181 Poplar Av Memphis TN 38111

HILL, DONALD OLIVER, educator; b. Birmingham, Ala., Oct. 20, 1938; s. James Oliver and Gertrude (Bailey) H.; B.S. in Chem. Engring., Auburn U., 1961; M.S. in Chem. Engring., U. Ala., 1971, Ph.D. in Civil Engring., 1974; m. Caroline Stakely Keller, Dec. 26, 1959; children—William Oliver, Jamie Caroline. Process engr. Minn. Mining & Mfg. Co., Decatur, Ala., 1961-67, sr. process engr., 1967-68; cons. engr. Reichhold Chems. Inc., Tuscaloosa, Ala., 1969-71; grad. research asso. U. Ala., University, 1971-73; asst. prof. dept. civil engring. Miss. State U., Missisipi State, 1973—. Publicity chmn. Tenn. Valley council Boy Scouts Am., 1963; publicity coordinator Morgan County chpt. United Fund, 1963; adviser Jr. Achievement, Decatur, Ala., 1964-66. Served with USAF, 1961-62. Recipient outstanding Community Service award Morgan County United Fund, 1963; So. Soc. Paint Tech. grantee, 1970-71, U.S. Dept. Transp. grantee, 1972, Ala. Hwy. Dept. grantee, 1972. Registered profl. engr., Ala. Mem. Am. Inst. Chem. Engrs., So. Soc. Paint Tech., Sigma Xi, Omega Chi Epsilon. Mem. Ch. Christ. Contbr. articles to profl. jours. Home: Lampkin Rd Starkville MS 39759 Office: PO Box 2211 Mississippi State MS 39762

HILL, DOUGLAS LIVINGSTON, broadcasting exec.; b. Detroit, Apr. 22, 1922; s. Peter H. and Evelyn J. (Jones) H.; B.A., U. Md., 1940; m. Margaret M. Hrabak, May 4, 1944; children—James Q., Dale R. Reporter, Washington Times-Herald, 1938-40, Denver Post, 1945-46; newsman KJFJ, Webster City, Ia.,1947-58; salesman KHOL-TV, Holdrege, Neb., 1958; news dir. KELO-TV, Sioux Falls, S.D., 1958-66; news dir. WWBT-TV, Richmond, Va., 1966-73, pub. affairs dir., 1973—. Campaign chmn. Old Dominion Cystic Fibrosis Drive, 1973. Bd. dirs. A.R.C., Richmond, Va. Served with AUS, 1940-45. Recipient Pub. Service award On Leong Assn., 1972; award for best TV editorial, 1972, 73; 3 Douglas Southall Freeman TV documentary awards Asso. Press. Mem. Nat. Broadcast Editorial Assn., Accredited Radio-TV Galleries, Fraternal Order Police Assos., Newcomen Soc. N.Am., Sigma Delta Chi. Home: 333 Brighton Dr Richmond VA 23235 Office: 5710 Midlothian Turnpike Richmond VA 23201

HILL, DOUGLASS ORVILLE, physician; b. Oaklette, Va., Oct. 4, 1922; s. Edgar Garlicke and Clarius Verlinda (Newcombe) H.; B.S., Randolph-Macon Coll., 1944; M.D., Med. Coll. Va., 1947; m. Roberta Elaine Wildman, June 21, 1952; children—Douglass Orville, Geoffrey Lee, Mark Randolph. Intern Norfolk (Va.) Gen. Hosp., 1947-48, resident, 1948-49; resident McGuire VA Hosp., Richmond, Va., 1949-51; practice medicine specializing in internal medicine, Winchester, Va., 1951—; mem. staff Winchester Meml. Hosp.; cons. staff Morgan County Meml. Hosp., Berkeley Springs, W.Va., Shenandoah Meml. Hosp., Woodstock, Va. Med. examiner Winchester-Frederick County, 1959—. Bd. dirs. Northwestern Workshop. Fellow Am. Geriatrics Assn., Am. Coll. Angiology, Am. Coll. Chest Physicians (asso.); mem. A.C.P. (life), Am., Va. (exec. com. 1970—, v.p. 1972-73), socs. internal medicine, Am. Thoracic Soc., Winchester C. of C., Izaak Walton League, Med. Assn. Valley Va. (pres. 1971-72), A.M.A., Med. Soc. Va., Med. Soc. No. Va., So. Med. Assn., Nat. Guard Assn., Res. Officers Assn., Kappa Alpha, Phi Chi, Omicron Delta Kappa. Democrat. Methodist (trustee 1972—). Lion. Club: Winchester Country. Home: 143 Hawthorne Dr Winchester VA 22601 Office: 137 W Boscawen St Winchester VA 22601

HILL, EARL EDWARD, supt. schs.; b. Kansas, Okla., June 9, 1923; s. Earl A. and Bessie Mae (Williams) H.; B.S., Okla. State U., 1948, M.S., 1955; m. Edith Jane Boyles, July 23, 1941; children—Twila (Mrs. David Ingle), Earl Edward, Donna (Mrs. Lee Sorum), Ricky Noel. With Lockheed Aircraft Co., Burbank, Cal., 1941-44; tchr., Vale, Okla., 1947-48, Lone Wolf, Okla., 1948-50, Dewey, Okla., 1950-54, Red Rock, Okla., 1954-56, Dover, Okla., 1956-59, Hennessee, Okla., 1959-60, Oaks, Okla., 1960-67; supt. schs., Salina, Okla., 1967—. Precinct Chmn. Democratic party, Salina, 1970-72. Bd. dirs. Resource Conservation and Devel., Northeastern Okla. Community Devel. Corp. Served with USNR, 1943-44. Mem. Okla. Edn. Assn. (human relations com. 1970-71). Mason, Lion (pres. 1971-72). Home: General Delivery Salina OK 74365 Office: Box 98 Salina OK 74365

HILL, EVERETT WENTWORTH, writer; b. Russell, Kan., Jan. 10, 1884; s. John Harris and Frances Emily (Wentworth) H.; student Cascadilla Prep. Sch., Ithaca, N.Y., 1903; B.S. in Econs., Wharton Sch. Finance and Commerce, U. Pa., 1907; m. Ethel Laing, June 3, 1908 (dec.); 1 dau., Ethel; m. 2d, Cleo Riley. With Standard Oil Co., 1907-08; settled at Shawnee, Okla., in ice mfg., 1908; settled at Oklahoma City, 1922; moved to Indian Bluff Farm, James River Ozarks, 1941; moved to Lakeshore Gardens, Flathead Lake, Polson, Mont., 1945; moved to Springfield, Mo., 1963; mgr. extensive farm lands. Speaker before Rotary clubs in N.Am., other countries. Mem. Nat. Boys and Girls Week com.; mem. internat. bd. dirs. Waterton-Glacier Internat. Peace Park Assn. Mem. Kan. Ind. Oil and Gas Assn., Am. Acad. Polit. and Social Sci., Nat. Econ. League, Phi Kappa Sigma. Democrat. Episcopalian. Mason (32 deg., Shriner), Rotarian (internat. pres. 1924-25). Clubs: Polson (hon.); Oklahoma City. Author: Toward the Sun; Light Across the Valley; He Who Seeks Gold; also writer verse, essays, philos. articles, short stories. Bd. counselors Sunshine mag. adv. staff. Address: 2525 NW 62d St Apt 207 Oklahoma City OK 73112

HILL, GEORGE B(ARKER), newspaperman; b. Sulphur Springs, Tex., July 9, 1915; s. John B. and Grace (Summers) H.; student Ardmore Bus. Coll., 1931-32, Ardmore Night Law Sch., 1932-33, Okla. Baptist U., 1933-34; m. Margaret Ellen Culbertson, Sept. 19, 1943; children—John Carl, Judy (dec.), Mary (dec.). Reporter Ardmore Democrat, 1935; news editor Aransas Pass (Tex.) Progress, 1936; feature writer Ard (Okla.) Ardmoreite, 1936; news editor Madill (Okla.) Record, 1937-38, 39, 45, Ada (Okla.) Bull., 1938; pub. Tishomingo Capital-Democrat, 1940-41, 46-49, Coalgate (Okla.) Record-Register, 1949—, pub. Coalgate Pub. Co.; pres. Evans Pub. Co.; adv. dir. Atkinson Enterprises; adv. bd. TUSC. Chmn. adv. com. Sch. Journalism, Okla. State U., 1960-62. Chmn. legal pub. com. OPA, 1952-54, chmn. editorial bd., 1966-67; pres. S.E. Okla. Water Rights Assn., 1967-69; sec., treas. Okla. Water, Inc., 1970—. Del. Democratic Nat. Conv., 1964; mem. Okla. Jud. Nominating Commn., 1971-73. Served from pvt. to staff sgt. AUS, 1941-45. Recipient 56 awards Okla. Press Newspaper contests, 1946—, also 2 sweepstakes; named publisher's Aux. Nat. Editor of Week, 1954. Mem. Okla. Press Assn. (dir. 1950-58, pres. 1957), C. of C. (pres. 1968). Democrat. Baptist. Mason (chmn. pub. relations grand lodge 1966-67, 70—), Odd Fellow, Redman. Home: 505 S Byrd St Coalgate OK 74538 Office: Main St Coalgate OK 74538

HILL, JAMES MARK, physician; b. Water Valley, Miss., Oct. 7, 1918; s. Martin Luther and Lillian (Addington) H.; B.A., U. Miss., 1940, M.A., 1942, B.S., 1945; M.D., Jefferson Med. Coll., 1948. Intern, then resident Bapt. Hosp., Memphis, 1949-54; prison physician Miss. State Penitentiary, Parchman, 1950; practice medicine specializing in surgery, Memphis, 1954—; mem. staff Bapt. Meml. Hosp.; instr. anatomy U. Miss., 1943-45, prof. surg. anatomy, 1950-55. Mem. adv. bd. Peoples Protective Life Ins. Co. Served with USNR, 1945, served to lt M.C., 1955-57. Fellow A.C.S.; mem. A.M.A., So. Med. Assn., Tenn., Memphis and Shelby County med. socs., Memphis Surg. Soc., Phi Chi. Mason (32 deg., K.T., Shriner). Home: 1222 Dovecrest Memphis TN 38128 Office: 899 Madison Av Memphis TN 38103

HILL, JAMES STEWART, cons. elec. engr.; b. Washington, Dec. 2, 1912; s. Hugh Stewart and Isabel (Burch) H.; B.E.E., Case Inst. Tech., 1934; postgrad. Western Res. U., 1950-53; m. Elizabeth Barbara Metzger, June 1, 1936; children—Noel Edward, Hugh Stewart, Gary William, Dawn (Mrs. Gary Donald Lerch). Engr. United Broadcasting Co., Cleve., 1934-43; chief engr. Radio Sta. WHKK, Akron, 1943-53; v.p., sec. Smith Electronics, Cleve., 1953-58; cons. engr., Hudson, Ohio, 1958; engr., project mgr. Jansky & Bailey, Washington, 1959-64; cons. engr. Genisco Tech., Inc., Washington, 1964-69; cons. engr. RCA Service Co., Springfield, Va., 1969—; cons. com. EMC Symposium, Montreux, Switzerland, 1974; mem. faculty Fenn Coll., 1941-42, Broadcast Tech. Inst., 1942-44, Western Reserve U., 1942-44; editor Electromagnetic News Report, 1973—. Dir. Lincoln Continental Owners Club, 1968-70. Recipient I.E.E.E. Group on Electromagnetic Compatibility Certificate of Appreciation, 1969. Mem. I.E.E.E. (sr.), Theta Chi. Mason. Clubs: Hudson Tennis, Springfield Golf and Country. Author: Radio Frequency Interference Handbook, 1971; Electromagnetic Compatibility Manual, 1972. Home: 6706 Deland Dr Springfield VA 22152 Office: 5260 Port Royal Rd Springfield VA 22151

HILL, JANE MARGARET, editor; b. Youngstown, O., May 25, 1919; d. Joseph Hamilton and Edith (Lowry) Hill; B.S. with distinction in Edn., Ohio State U., 1940, M.A., 1948. Tchr. Claridon Twp. Sch., Marion County, O., 1940-42, Upper Sandusky (O.) High Sch., 1942-43; tchr. Washington Pub. Schs., 1943-61, asst. dir. dept. math., 1961-64; exec. dir. Pi Lambda Theta, Washington, 1964-70; mng. editor the Arithmetic Tchr., 1970—. Content cons. ednl. TV series Sets and Systems, 1963—; content cons. TV program on Brookline (Mass.) math project, summer 1967; mem. vis. faculty

George Washington U., 1956-57, U. Va., 1956-57, Montclair (N.J.) State Coll., summer 1959, 61, Colo. State Coll. summer 1959, 61, U. Coll. U. Md., 1961—. Mem. N.E.A. (life), Nat. Council Tchrs. Math., Math. Assn. Am., Central Assn. Sci. and Math. Tchrs., A.A.A.S. (co-author math. bibliography), Am. Assn. U. Women, Pi Lambda Theta (nat. treas.), Phi Delta Gamma, Alpha Delta Kappa, Delta Kappa Gamma. Home: 3051 Harrison St NW Washington DC 20015 Office: 1906 Association Dr Reston VA 22091

HILL, JERRY GIFFORD, lawyer; b. Beaumont, Tex., Mar. 15, 1930; s. John Howard and Ruth (Gifford) H.; A.A., Lamar Jr. Coll., 1950; B.B.A., Lamar U., 1957; J.D., U. Houston, 1961; m. Mary Joe ("Dallas") Hain, June 25, 1952; children—J. Marcus, M. Filomena, J.J. Thaddaus, Christian M.G., Gifford P.L. Admitted to Tex. bar, 1961, U.S. Dist. Ct. bar, 1962, U.S. Ct. Appeals Bar, 1970, U.S. Supreme Ct. bar, 1964; practiced in Houston, 1961—; lectr. bus. law U. St. Thomas, 1963-69. Served to lt. col. USAFR, 1951—. Mem. Am., Houston, Fed. bar assns., State Bar Tex., Am. Judicature Soc., Delta Theta Phi, Omicron Delta Epsilon. Home: 960 Chimney Rock Rd Houston TX 77027 Office: 3425 One Shell Plaza Houston TX 77002

HILL, JOHN WILLIAM, food service co. exec.; b. Vivian, La., Sept. 12, 1919; s. John William and Mary Kate (Armstrong) H.; student, La. Poly. Inst., 1938-39; m. Ethel Francis Roan, Nov. 11, 1939; children—Mikall (Mrs. Paul Norris), Mary (Mrs. Dan Bryan), John William III. Agt., Life & Casualty Ins. Co., Shreveport, La., 1940-42; roofer Shreveport Roofing Co., 1942; mgr. Morrison Cafeteria Co., Mobile, Ala., 1942-52; with Morrison Food Service, Mobile, 1952—, sr. v.p., 1968—, also dir. Bd. dirs. Mobile Christian Sch., 1972—. Mem. Ch. of Christ (elder 1969—). Mason. Club: Mobile Country. Home: 111 Lauten Court Mobile AL 36606 Office: PO Box 2608 Mobile AL 36625

HILL, L. DONALD, educator; b. St. Louis, Oct. 31, 1931; s. Lester Samuel and Pearl (Long) H. ; A.B., Trevecca Coll., Nashville, 1957; M.A., (Long) H. Peabody Coll., 1958; m. Jean Allender, June 23, 1951; 1 son, Mark LeScott. Editor Free Will. Baptist Sunday Sch. Bd., Nashville, 1957-58; tchr. Nashville schs., 1958-59; prof. Bryan Coll., Dayton, Tenn., 1959-66, exec. registrar, 1971—; supt. Rhea County schs., Dayton 1966-69; dir. continuing edn. Cleveland (Tenn.) State Coll., 1969-71. Minister of music 1st Bapt. Ch., Dayton. Active March of Dimes, Boy Scouts Am.; committeeman S.E. Tenn. Exceptional Children Found. Served with AUS, 1952-54. Mem. Nat., Tenn. edn. assns., Assn. Childhood Edn. Internat., Assn. Higher Edn., Nat. Soc. Study Edn., Phi Delta Kappa. Democrat. Baptist. Home: Edgewater Estates Dayton TN 37321

HILL, MARTIN LYONS, govt. ofcl.; b. Aiken, S.C., July 15, 1919; s. Adam Primrose and Savannah (Dunbar) H.; student Gary Coll., 1940-42; A.B., Ind. U., 1949, postgrad. Law Sch., 1949-50. With various divs. fed. govt., Washington, 1954—, statistician, statistics br. Dept. Housing and Urban Devel., 1969—. Served with USAAF, 1943-46; PTO. Mem. A.A.A.S., Am. Mgmt. Assn., Am. Statis. Assn., Nat. Assn. Housing Redevel. Ofcls., Kappa Alpha Psi. Home: 430 M St SW Washington DC 20024 Office: 451 7th St SW Washington DC 20410

HILL, MAX LLOYD, JR., realtor; b. Belleville, Ill., Aug. 15, 1927; s. Max L. and Leora (Jacobs) H.; student Purdue U., 1944-47; B.S., U.S. Naval Acad., 1951; postgrad. Harvard Law Sch., 1955-56; m. Jane Olivia Evatt, June 23, 1951; children—Larkin Payne, Max Lloyd III, Naomi Evatt. Sales engr. indsl. equipment Indsl. Welding Supplies, Inc., 1957-59; real estate salesman Simmons Realty Co., Inc., Charleston, S.C., 1959-63; pres. Max L. Hill Co., Inc., realtors, Charleston, 1963—; Charleston dir. Citizens & So. Nat. Bank S.C. Lectr. S.C. Realtor's Inst., 1967—, U. S.C. Sch. Gen. Studies and Extension, 1962—. Pres. Greater Charleston YMCA, 1965-67; mem. Charleston Planning and Zoning Commn., 1969; sec. Charleston County Bd. Assessment Control, 1972. Bd. dirs. Edn. Found., S.C. Assn. Realtors. Served with AUS, 1945-46, USNR, 1946; to 1st lt. USAF, 1951-55. Mem. S.C. Assn. Realtors (dir.), Greater Charleston Bd. Realtors (pres. 1970), Phi Gamma Delta. Methodist (ofcl. bd. 1964—). Mason. Club: Carolina Yacht. Home: 96 Ashley Av Charleston SC 29401 Office: 33 Broad St Charleston SC 29401

HILL, VICTOR, dentist; b. St. George, S.C., Oct. 18, 1926; s. John Heaton and Cora Louise (Brownlee) H.; B.S., U. S.C., 1952; D.M.D., U. Ala., 1964; m. Junelle Ferguson, Jan. 20, 1949; children—Victor Lamont, Debra Junelle. Individual practice gen. dentistry, Orangeburg, S.C., 1964—; mem. staff Orangeburg Regional Hosp., chief dental staff, 1971. S.C. state chmn. for Nat. Childrens Dental Health Week, 1970. Served with USMCR, 1946-48. Mem. Am., S.C., Coastal Dist. (v.p. 1971, pres. elect 1972) dental socs. Baptist. Club: Orangeburg Country. Home: 226 Hillsboro Rd Orangeburg SC 29115 Office: 1291 Boulevard NE Orangeburg SC 29115

HILL, WILLIAM BAPTIST, museum ofcl.; b. Birmingham, Ala., Mar. 2, 1909; s. William Henderson and Lucy R. (Baptist) H.; B.S., U. Va., also LL.B. Admitted to Va. bar, practiced law, Memphis and Boydton, Va.; founder, dir. Roanoke River Mus., Clarksville, Va., 1959—. Trustee Roanoke River Mus., Prestwould Found., Boyd Family Meml. Found. Mem. Am. Soc. Ethnohistory, Am. Anthrop. Assn., Va. Hist. Soc., Assn. Preservation Va. Antiquities (past trustee), Archeol. Soc. Va. Democrat. Author: Land by the Roanoke, 1957; The Boyds of Boydton, 1967; The Indians of Axacan and the The Spanish Martyrs, The Beginnings of Virginia, 1950, 2d edit., 1970. Address: Prestwould House Clarksville VA 23927

HILL, WILLIAM CLYDE, constrn. co. exec.; b. Chgo., Jan. 26, 1920; s. Clyde William and Elizabeth Mary (Doyle) H.; B.C.E., U. Dayton, 1940; m. Gloria M. Emmanuelli, Aug. 29, 1942; children—Gloria Elizabeth, Edward, Charles. Surveyor Greeley-Howard, Norlin, Chgo., 1940; san. engr. Chgo. Pump Co., 1940-41, 45-47; civil engr. Earl K. Burton, Inc., San Juan, P.R., 1947—, v.p., 1957—, treas., 1965—. Served with AUS, 1941-46. Registered profl. engr., Ill., P.R. Mem. Am. Soc. C.E. (sect. pres. 1952), P.R. Assn. Engrs. Architects and Surveyors, Mil. Order of World Wars (chpt. comdr. 1959), Res. Officers Assn. (dept. pres. 1957, nat. v.p. 1958), Soc. Am. Mil. Engrs., Assn. U.S. Army. Roman Catholic. Club: Serra Internat. (dist. gov. 1967-69). Home: 7W Palma Sola St Garden Hills Guaynabo PR 00619 Office: Gen PO Box 1367 San Juan PR 00936

HILL, WILLIAM FARRIS, state ofcl.; b. Manatee, Fla., Jan 24, 1927; s. William Farris and Hester (Odum) H.; A.B., Emory U., 1951; M.D., U. Tenn., 1956; M.P.H., U. Cal., 1961; m. Elizabeth Colleen Howard, Aug 27, 1947; children—William Farris III, Rebecca Lynn. Intern Greenville (S.C.) Gen. Hosp., 1956-57; dir. Highlands-Glades-Hendry County Health Dept., Sebring, Fla., 1957-67, Polk County Health Dept., Winter Haven, Fla., 1967—. Served with USNR, 1944-46, 50-51. Mem. Am., Fla. (pres. 1972) pub. health assns., A.M.A., Fla. Med. Assn., Fla. Assn. County Health Officers. Home: 138 Lake Ring Dr Winter Haven FL 33880 Office: PO Box 1480 Winter Haven FL 33880

HILL, WILLIAM LEON, advt. exec.; b. Greensburg, Pa., Sept. 4, 1932; s. Leon McDonald and Hanna (Schaffer) H.; Asso. B.A., Amarillo Coll., 1952; B.F.A., Kansas City Art Inst., 1956; m. Rae Ellen Warren, Mar. 3, 1956; children—Shaun Elise, Tamara, Warren Schaffer, Christian Canady. With Mel Richman & Assos., 1958; asst. art dir. DeGarmo Advt., N.Y., 1958; with Bloom Advt., Dallas, 1956-58, 59—, creative dir., 1963—, sr. v.p., 1965-73, exec. v.p., 1973—. Exhibited in group shows including Dallas-Ft. Worth Art Dirs. Club, 1959-68, Am. Film Festival, N.Y.C., 1966-67, Internat. Film Festival N.Y.C., 1965, Dallas Ad League, 1965-68, USIA Overseas Exhibit. Judge various Southwestern advt. and coll. exhibits. Active various community drives. Served with USNR, 1950-58. Recipient various awards; named Art Dir. of Year, Dallas-Ft. Worth Soc. Visual Communications, 1968; named top 100 Creative People U.S. Advt., 1972. Mem. Dallas-Ft. Worth Art Dirs. Club (1st v.p. 1967-68, editor Push Pin). Episcopalian. Home: 300 Sutton Pl Richardson TX 75080 Office: 3000 Diamond Park Dallas TX 75222

HILLENBRAND, BERNARD FRANCIS, assn. exec.; b. Syracuse, N.Y., May 11, 1925; s. Leonard L. and Anne (Green) H.; B.A., Syracuse U., 1949; M.P.A., Maxwell Sch. Pub. Adminstrn., 1950; m. Elizabeth M. Dwyer, July 9, 1955; children—Betsy, John, Susan, Laura. Adminstrv. analyst Budget dept. State of Wis., Madison, 1951-52; dep. dir. Am. Municipal Assn. (now Nat. League Cities), Washington, 1955-57; exec. dir. Nat. Assn. of Counties, Washington, 1957—. Mem. steering com., adv. bd. Keep Am. Beautiful, 1962—; mem. adv. com. Census of Govts. U.S. Bur. Census, 1965—; mem. Pres.'s Commn. on Employment of Handicapped, 1966—: mem. Nat. Com. Uniform Traffic Laws and Ordinances. Bd. dirs. Met. Manpower Study Washington Center for Met. Studies, Nat. Assn. Regional Councils, Nat. Tng. and Devel. Service, Pub. Tech., Inc., Labor Mgmt. Relations Service, State-County-City Service Center, Nat. Acad. Code Adminstrs. Served with inf. AUS, World War II. Decorated Purple Heart. Mem. U.S. C. of C. (mem. crime com.), Nat. Safety Council. Home: 5104 Moorland Lane Bethesda MD 20014 Office: 1735 New York Av NW Washington DC 20036

HILLERY, HERBERT VINCENT, physicist; b. Lima, O., Dec. 8, 1924; s. Archie Vincent and Elva (Wilkie) H.; B.A., Oberlin Coll., 1947; postgrad. U. Tex., 1949-60; children—Vincent Edward, Nathan Herbert. Asso. editor Oberlin (O.) Times, 1948; research scientist asso. Applied Research Labs., U. Tex., Austin, 1950—, head undersea tech., 1964-71. Served to 1st lt. USAAF, 1943-46. Recipient NSF Grant, 1972. Mem. Acoustical Soc. Am., Nava. Inst., Sigma Xi. Unitarian (trustee 1973). Patentee in field. Home: 1909 Richcreek Rd Austin TX 78757 Office: PO Box 8029 Austin TX 78712

HILLIARD, JOHN ROY, JR., educator; b. Irving, Tex., Feb. 7, 1924; s. John Roy and Nora Ruth (Hendrix) H.; B.A., Trinity U., 1947; M.A., U. Colo., 1951; Ph.D., U. Tex., 1959; m. Evelyn Joyce Herzog, Dec. 25, 1951; children—James Ronald, Richard Alan. Instr. biology and sci. Tivy High Sch., Kerrville, Tex., 1944-45; instr. biology Trinity U., 1948-51; asso. prof., head dept. biology McMurry Coll., 1951-54; teaching asst. U. Tex., 1954-55; prof., head dept. biology McMurry Coll., 1957-68; asso. prof. biology Sam Houston State U., 1968-70, prof., 1970—, dir. dept., 1972—. Bd. dirs. Community Day Care Assn. of Huntsville, Inc., 1969-70; v.p. Christian Orgn. Missionary Endeavor, 1971. Served as sgt. AUS, 1945-46. Fellow Tex. Acad. Scis.; mem. A.A.A.S., Am. Inst. Biol. Scis., Entomol. Soc. Am., Entomol. Soc., Ecological soc. Am., Southwestern Assn. Naturalists, Sigma Xi. Methodist. Research on systematics, biology and ecology of orthoptera. Home: Rt 2 Box 276-2 Huntsville TX 77340

HILLIS, CHARLES LEWIS, physician; b. Vidette, Ga., Jan. 13, 1931; s. Jake Lewis and Mamie (Kelly) H.; A.B., Emory U., 1951, B.D., 1954, M.D., 1967; m. Varese Chambless, June 14, 1953; children—Charles Lewis, Kelly, Mark. Ordained to ministry Methodist Ch., 1954; pastor, Bronwood, Ga., 1951-54, Odum, Ga., 1954-56, Reynolds, Ga., 1956-60, St. Mary's, Ga., 1960-62; intern Floyd Hosp., Rome, Ga., 1967-68; practice gen. medicine, Lafayette, Ga., 1968—; mem. staff Tri-County Hosp., Ft. Oglethorpe, Ga., sec. staff, 1972-74, vice chief staff, 1974—; pres. Drs. Clinic Lafayette, Inc., 1971-72. Coroner, Walker County, Ga., 1969-73. Mem. A.M.A., Med. Assn. Ga., Tri County Med. Soc., Delta Tau Delta. Republican. Methodist. Mason, Elk, Kiwanian (pres. 1962). Optimist (Lafayette). Home: Diamond Dr Lafayette GA 30728 Office: Box 846 N Main St LaFayette GA 30728

HILTON, JAMES GORTON, educator; b. Balt., Sept. 21, 1923; s. George Edward and Ethel Alberta (Schaeffer) H.; student Loyola Coll., 1940-42; B.S., Va. Poly. Inst., 1947; M.S., U. Tenn., 1952, Ph.D., 1954; m. Elizabeth Earline Lindsay, Sept. 21, 1946; children—James Lindsay, William Edward. Research asso. U. Va., 1948-50; asst. prof. U. Miss., 1953-55, asso. prof., 1955-58; asso. prof. Marquette U., 1959-61; asso. prof. U. Tex. Med. Br., Galveston, 1961-63, prof. pharmacology, 1963—. Cons. A.M.A. Council on Drugs, 1963-67; mem. pharmacology and endocrinology fellowship rev. panel NIH, 1964-67; mem. com. on persistent pesticides Nat. Acad. Scis., 1967-69; cons. pesticide regulation div. Environmental Protection Agy., 1970-72; Fulbright lectr. U. San Agustin, Arequipa, Peru, 1959; Fulbright scholar Gulbenkian Inst. Sci., Oeiras, Portugal, 1968. Served with USNR, 1943-46. Fellow A.A.A.S., Soc. Exptl. Biology and Medicine (chmn. S.W. sect. 1973-75); mem. Am. Physiology Soc., Am. Soc. Pharmacology and Exptl. Therapeutics, Am. Heart Assn., U.S. Chess Fedn. Episcopalian Mason (32 deg.). Contbr. articles to profl. jours. Home: 2626 Gerol Ct Galveston TX 77550

HIMES, LUTHER ROBERT, JR., city ofcl.; b. Fort Worth, Oct. 26, 1924; s. Luther Robert and Carrie Belle (Lewis) H.; Asso. Sci., North Tex. Agrl. Coll., 1943, postgrad., 1945-47; m. Lajuana Wilson, Mar. 18, 1948; children—Cathey Lynn (Mrs. James L. Robertson), Luther Robert III, Terry Lee. With Fort Worth Fire Dept., 1947—, driver fire fighting div., 1955-59, lt. fire fighting, 1959-64, capt. tng. officer, 1964-68, dist. chief, asst. fire marshall, 1968-69, fire chief, 1969—. Tchr. Tex. A. and M. U., 1964-68. Pres. Meadowbrook Little League, 1969. Served with USAAF, 1943-45. Decorated Air medal with five oak leaf clusters. Mem. Petroleum Club, West Tex., Fort Worth chambers commerce. Home: 2501 McGee St Fort Worth TX 76112 Office: 1000 Throckmorton St Fort Worth TX 76102

HINDS, CHARLES FRANKLIN, state librarian Ky.; b. Henderson, Ky., Oct. 31, 1923; s. Charles Fretwell and Ruth Alice (Carson) H.; A.B., U. Ky., 1950, M.A., 1958, M.S. in L.S., 1968, postgrad., 1968; postgrad. U. Louisville, 1950-52, 54-56, Am. U., 1961; m. Doris May Rooney, June 8, 1946; 1 son, Joseph James. Account and rate clk., auditor freight accounts L & N R.R., Louisville, 1941-53; tchr. Male High Sch., Louisville, 1953-56; dir. Ky. Hist. Soc., Frankfort, 1956-59; state historian, Ky., 1956-59; field rep. U. Ky. Libraries, Lexington, 1959-60; state archivist, records adminstr. State Archives and Records Commn., Frankfort, 1960-67; head librarian Murray (Ky.) U., 1967-73; state librarian Ky., 1973—. Lectr., U. Ky., 1960-67; instr. Ky. State Coll., 1966-67, asso. prof. Murray State U., 1967-73. Sec., mgr. Ky. Hist. Markers Program, 1956-62; chmn. State Records Control Bd., 1956-58; mem. State Archives and Records Commn., 1958-60, 67—, sec., 1960-61, chmn. State Archives and Records Commn., 1973—; mem. Civil War Centennial Commn., 1958-65. Served with AUS, 1941-45. Decorated Bronze Star medal. Mem. Ky. Tennis Assn. (sec.-treas. 1958-65, pres. 1967-68), S.A.R. (pres. Ky. chpt. 1969-70), Soc. Am. Archivists (chmn. state archives com. 1965, 66), Phi Beta Kappa, Phi Alpha Theta, Beta Phi Mu. Democrat. Episcopalian (vestryman 1967-68, sr. warden 1972-73). Rotarian, Optimist (1st v.p. 1963), Toastmaster (pres. 1964-65, lt. gov. So. div. dist. 11 1968-69). Editor: Register, state hist. quar., 1956-59; Checklist of Ky. State Publs., 1963-67. Contbr. weekly news column. Home: 130 W State St Apt 6 Frankfort KY 40601

HINDS, EDWARD COPAS, surgeon; b. Park Rapids, Minn., May 10, 1917; s. Frederick W. and Sara (Holm) H.; B.A., Baylor U., 1940, D.D.S., 1940, M.D., 1945; m. Dorothy McGuire, Sept. 4, 1943; children—Suzenne (Mrs. George E. Donnelly), James Wesley, WIlliam Edward, Christina Marie. Rotating intern Parkland Hosp., Dallas, 1945-46; resident gen. surgery Jefferson Davis Hosp., Houston, 1949-51, M.D. Anderson Hosp. and Tumor Inst., Houston, 1951-52, So. Pacific Hosp., Houston, 1952-53; fellow Jesse Jones Cancer Research, M.D. Anderson Hosp. and Tumor Inst., Houston, 1951-52; gen. practice dentistry, Dallas, 1940-42; practice medicine specializing in oral and maxillofacial surgery, Houston, 1953—; instr. oral surgery Baylor U. Coll. Dentistry, 1940-42, clin. asst. surgery, Coll. Medicine, 1949-51; asso. prof. oral surgery U. Tex. Dental Br., 1948, prof., chmn. dept. surgery, 1952—; cons. oral surgery VA Hosp., Houston, 1952—, Wilford Hall USAF Hosp., Lackland AFB, Tex., 1956—, William Beaumont Army Hosp., El Paso, Tex., 1957—, Central Office, VA, Washington, 1967—, USPHS Hosp., Galveston, Tex., 1968—. Served with M.C., USNR, 1946-48. Recipient Arnold K. Maislen award N.Y. U., 1972. Diplomate Am. Bd. Oral Surgery, Am. Bd. Surgery. Fellow A.C.S., Am. Coll. Dentists. Mem. A.M.A., Am. Soc. Oral Surgeons, Am. Soc. Maxillofacial Surgeons (pres. 1964-65), Internat. Assn. Dental Research, Am. Assn. U. Profs., Am. Assn. Dental Schs., Am. Soc. Plastic and Reconstructive Surgery, Columbia Soc. Oral Surgeons, Am. (vice chmn. sci. session com. 1965-66), Tex. dental assns., Houston Dist. Dental Soc., Tex. Med. Assn., Harris County Med. Soc., Houston Surg. Soc., Houston Soc. Oral Surgeons (pres. 1960-61), Tex. Anatomical Bd. Author: (with Arthur S. Keats) Practical Dental Monographs, 1960. Mem. editorial bd. Year Book Cancer, 1956-57 Series through 1970-71 Series, Oral Surgery, Oral Medicine, Oral Pathology, 1962-64, Oral Research Abstracts, 1966-73, Jour. Oral Surgery. Contbr. articles to profl. jours. Home: 1402 Wagon Rd Simonton TX 77476 Office: 6516 John Freeman St Houston TX 77025

HINES, CARL RICHARD, city ofcl.; b. Louisville, Mar. 23, 1931; s. Fred Richard and Ruth Lory (Johnson) H.; student U. Ill., 1949-50, U. Louisville, 1954-60, 60-62; m. Teresa M. Churchill, Mar. 5, 1960; children—Carl Richard, Keith, Cheryl, Cory. Staff mgr. Mammoth Ins. Co., 1963-65, dist. mgr., 1965-70; city dir. Housing Opportunity Centers, Inc., Louisville, 1970-72, exec. dir., 1972—. Exec. sec. Louisville Community Action Commn., 1969-70; vice chmn. Louisville Chestnut St. YMCA. Mem. Louisville Bd. Edn., 1968—, vice chmn., 1970, chmn., 1971; Served with USAF, 1951-53. Decorated Air medal, D.F.C. Optimist. Club: Just Mens. Home: 635 Southwestern Pkwy Louisville KY 40211 Office: 1111 W Broadway Louisville KY 40202

HINES, CHESLEY, pecan growers assn. exec.; b. Ripley, Miss., July 30, 1903; s. William and Mattie (Spight) H.; B.S., Miss. State U., 1926; M.S., La. State U., 1949; m. Sara Virginia Hamberlin, June 9, 1935; 1 son, Chesley. Insp., Miss. State Plant Bd., Starkville, 1926-30; county agt. Extension Hort. Coop. Extension Service, Miss. State U., 1930-68; exec. sec. Southeastern Pecan Growers Assn., Starkville, 1970—; exec. sec. Miss. Pecan Growers Assn., 1968—. Chmn. so. regional adv. com. Nat. Jr. Vegetable Growers Assn., 1945-61; mem. Youth Council, Starkville, 1953-56. Recipient Certificate of Recognition Nat. jr. Vegetable Growers' Assn., 1947, Gold Service award, 1961. Distinguished Service award Nat. Assn. County Agr. Agr. Agts., 1968, Meritorious Service award Miss. Pecan Growers Assn., 1970. Mem. Miss. Farm Bur., Epsilon Sigma Phi. Presbyn. (elder 1943-73). Home: Route 5 Box 409 Starkville MS 39759 Office: PO Box 4902 Mississippi State MS 39762

HINES, GERALD DOUGLAS, investment builder; b. Gary, Ind., Aug. 15, 1925; s. Robert Gordon and Myrtle Lillian (McConnell) H.; B.S., Purdue U., 1948; m. Dorothy Schwarz, Mar. 8, 1952; children—Jeffrey, Jennifer. Organizer, 1957, since owner Gerald D. Hines Interests, Houston. Participant Developers Conf. Joint Center Urban Studies, Mass. Inst. Tech. and Harvard; dir. South Main Bank, Galleria Bank; trustee Counsins Mortgage and Equity. Bd. dirs. devel. bd. YMCA, Houston Symphony Soc.; bd. dirs. United Fund; bd. dirs. Nat. Space Hall Fame; mem. devel. council Houston Mus. Natural Sci.; mem. adv. com. U. Houston's Sch. Bus.; bd. govs. Rice U. Served with C.E., U.S. Army, 1943-45. Named Key Houstonian, Houston Bd. Realtors, 1967; Marketing Man of Yr., Am. Marketing Assn. Houston, 1968. Mem. Urban Land Inst. (exec. com.), Houston C. of C. (dir.-at-large). Prin. works include One Shell Plaza, Galleria Post Oak, 2000 Smith Office Park Bldg., Pennzoil Pl., Houston, One Shell Square, New Orleans, Galleria West, Trans World Airlines, Inc. Adminstrn. Bldg. Kansas City, Mo. Home: 146 Radney Rd Houston TX Office: 2100 Post Oak Tower 5051 Westheimer Houston TX 77027

HINES, NEAL OLDFIELD, assn. exec., author; b. Crawfordsville, Ind., Nov 22, 1908; s. Linnaeus Neal and Bertha (Wiggs) H.; B.A., Ind. U., 1930; M.S., Northwestern U., 1941; m. Martha Perry, Sept. 17, 1946; children—Melissa, Martha Anne, Nancy. With newspapers in Ind., Wis., 1930-40; mem. journalism faculty U. Cal. at Berkeley, 1946-48; dir. publs., univ. relations, asst. to pres. U. Wash., Seattle, 1948-63; dir. information services Nat. Assn. Coll. and Univ. Bus. Officers, Washington, 1963—. Mem. AEC-U. Wash. Radiobiol. Surveys, Bikini, Eniwetok, 1949, 56, Christmas Island, 1962. Served with USAAF, 1942-46. Mem. Phi Kappa Psi, Sigma Delta Chi. Republican. Methodist. Author: Proving Ground, An Account of the Radiobiological Studies in the Pacific, 1946-61, 1962; Atoms, Nature and Man, 1966. Contbr. articles, reports to profl. jours. Home: 136 Hesketh St Chevy Chase MD 20015 Office: 1 Dupont Circle Washington DC 20036

HINES, ROBERT STICKLEY, JR., physician; b. Cleveland, Tenn., June 9, 1942; s. Robert Stickley and Ada Evelyn (Pack) H.; M.D., U. Tenn., 1966; m. Claudia Gunner, May 7, 1965; children—Shannon Evelyn, Holly Elizabeth. Intern, Phila. Gen. Hosp., 1967; gen. surgery resident Kennedy VA Hosp., Memphis, 1970; neurosurg. resident Semmes-Murphey Clinic, Memphis, 1971—. Served with USPHS, 1968-69. Mem. Alpha Tau Omega, Phi Chi, Phi Eta Sigma. Home: 1443 Carr Av Memphis TN 38104 Office: Baptist Hosp 899 Madison Av Memphis TN 38104

HINES, WILLIAM CHRISTIAN, SR., judge; b. LaFayette, Ala., Oct. 31, 1914; s. James Alexander and Lily (Christian) H.; LL.B., U. Ala., 1938; m. Elizabeth Scoggins, Apr. 19, 1942; children—William Christian, Elizabeth (Mrs. James R. Jones), Edward T. Admitted to Ala. bar, 1938; since practiced in Lafayette; mem. firm Hines & Hines; dep. circuit solicitor, Chambers County, 1939-41, 46; dir. FHA in Ala., 1966-69; judge 5th Jud. Circuit of Ala., 1969—. Mem. Ala.

Senate, 1959-63. Served with USNR, 1941-46. Mem. Phi Gamma Delta, Omicron Delta Kappa. Democrat. Methodist. Mason, Rotarian. Address: PO Box 25 LaFayette AL 36862

HINES, WILLIAM WHALEY, educator; b. Tampa, Fla., Dec. 12, 1932; s. Emmett Lee and Willie Mae (Whaley) H.; student U. Tenn., 1950-53; B.S., Memphis State U., 1954; M.S., Ga. Inst. Tech., 1958, Ph.D., 1964; m. Barbara Gayle Fayssoux, Aug. 22, 1959; children—Jennifer Fayssoux, William Whaley, Matthew Lee. Instr., Ga. Inst. Tech., 1959-61, asst. prof., 1961-65, asso. prof., 1965-68, prof. indsl. and systems engring., 1968—, asso. dir. Sch. Indsl. and Systems Engring., 1969—. Prin. cons. William W. Hines and Assos., Atlanta, 1970—. Served to 1st lt. USAF, 1954-55. Registered profl. engr., Ga., Tenn. Mem. Am. Inst. Indsl. Engrs., Am. Statis. Assn., Am. Soc. Quality Control, Am. Soc. Engring. Edn., Operations Research Soc. Am., Sigma Xi, Alpha Tau Omega, Tau Beta Pi. Methodist. Author: (with Ruiz-Pala and Avila Beloso) Waiting Line Models, 1967; (with D.C. Montgomery) Probability and Statistics in Engineering and Management Science, 1972. Editor tech. notes Jour. Indsl. Engring., 1959-69. Home: 1989 Tall Tree Dr NE Atlanta GA 30324

HINGER, JEFFREY WILSON, educator; b. Carbondale, Ill., Apr. 4, 1944; s. Charles Jefferson and Lucille (Wilson) H.; B.A. in Broadcasting, La. State U., 1965, M.A. in Journalism, 1967; m. Linda Gayle Hano, Dec. 22, 1966. Announcer, WLUX Radio, Baton Rouge, 1965; mgr. WLSU Radio, Baton Rouge, 1965-66; writer, La. State U. Office Media Services, 1965-66; faculty adviser WSAC and KSYM-FM, San Antonio Coll., 1966—, instr. broadcasting, 1966-69, asst. prof. communications, 1969—, coordinator media services, 1973—. Recipient Outstanding Service awards N.E. Kiwanis Club, 1969, 70. Mem. Internat. Broadcasters Soc. (mem. adv. bd. editors global reference work project 1969-70), Speech Communication Assn., Am. Assn. U. Profs., Tex. Jr. Coll. Tchrs. Assn., San Antonio Advt. Fedn. (mem. advt. edn. com. 1973—). Kiwanian. Home: 3501 Pin Oak Dr No 1801 San Antonio TX 78229 Office: San Antonio Coll 1300 San Pedro Av San Antonio TX 78284

HINKEL, HELEN MARY RYKOWSKI (MRS. JOSEPH LOYD HINKEL), librarian; b. Dayton, O., Oct. 28, 1911; d. John and Regina (Perzanowska) Rykowski; student U. Cal., at Berkeley, 1949, Mary Hardin Baylor Coll., 1959; m. Joseph Loyd Hinkel, Dec. 1, 1934; 1 son, Vossler Sigmund. Reference asst. Fort Meade, Md., 1950-51; library asst. Ft. Lewis, Wash., 1952-53, Fort Hood, Tex., 1957-58; head librarian Killeen (Tex.) Pub. Library, 1959-70, library dir., 1970—. Mem. Bell County Council on Alcoholism. Mem. C. of C., Am., Tex. library assns., Tex. Municipal League Librarians Assn., Tex., Killeen friends of the library, Nat. Council Cath. Women, Am. Bus. Women's Assn. (program chmn. 1969-70), Civil Air Patrol, Tex. Geneal. Soc., Internat. Soc. for Heraldry and Family Trees, Bell County Hist. Soc. Clubs: Killeen Garden, Killeen Area Music (reporter, historian). Home: 3200 Lake Ann Killeen TX 76541 Office: 711 North Gray Killeen TX 76541

HINKEL, JAMES EDWARD, city mgr.; b. Mt. Vernon, N.Y., July 1, 1920; s. Emory E. and Margaret (Ambrose) H.; B.E.E., N.C. State Coll., 1951; m. Thelma Morgan, Apr. 6, 1946; children—Laura Jeanne, David Michael, John Edward, Donald Charles. Cons. engr. B.O. Vannort Engrs., Inc., 1951-55; dir. utilities City of Monroe (N.C.), 1955-58, city mgr., 1958—. Dir. Piedmont Cities Assn. Pres. Monroe Little League. Served with USAAF, 1942-45. Registered profl. engr., N.C. Mem. I.E.E.E., Am. Pub. Works Assn., Am. Gas Assn., Nat. Soc. Profl. Engrs., Profl. Engrs. N.C., Carolinian Govtl. Purchasing Assn. Rotarian (asst. sec.). Home: 305 Bay St Monroe NC 28110 Office: Box 4 Monroe NC 28110

HINKLE, ALLEN OSCAR, JR., oil co. exec.; b. Lockhart, Tex., Aug. 22, 1919; s. Allen Oscar and Rena Kate (Hearne) H.; B.B.A., U. Tex., 1941; postgrad. Northwestern U., Chgo., 1943, Harvard, 1945; m. Margaret Mae Langham, Apr. 12, 1941; children—Margaret Ann (Mrs. Thomas A. Cox, Jr.), Mary Linda (Mrs. C. Joseph Cain), Joan Ellen. Auditor, State Tex., 1941-42; with Humble Oil & Refining Co. (name now changed to Exxon Co.), Houston, 1946—, gen. auditor, 1959—. Accounting faculty adviser N.Tex. U., 1969-72. Mem. Pres. Council, Houston Bapt. Coll., 1968-73; active YMCA. Precinct committeeman, del. Democratic party, Harris County, Tex., 1950-52. Served with USNR, 1943-46. Named Distinguished Alumni, U. Tex. Coll. Bus., 1969. C.P.A., Tex. Mem. Am. Inst. C.P.A.'s, Inst. Internal Auditors (mem. research com. 1960-74), Am. Petroleum Inst., Tex. Soc. C.P.A.'s (dir. Houston chpt. 1952-55), Houston C. of C. Baptist (deacon 1957-74). Club: Racquet (Houston); Lakeway Yacht (Austin, Tex.). Home: 439 Brown Saddle Rd Houston TX 77027 Office: 4031 Exxon Bldg Houston TX 77001

HINOJOSA, EDELMIRO, accountant; b. Grulla, Tex., Feb. 26, 1932; s. Pedro and Eva (Flores) H.; B.A., Pan Am. U., 1959; m. Feliciana Alejos, Aug. 15, 1957; children—Edelmiro, Cynthia M., Roberto A., Daniel D. Accountant, Hidalgo County Auditors Office, Edinburg, Tex., 1955-59, Bracero Transp. Co., Inc., Edinburg, 1959-61; asst. dir. Urban Renewal Agy., Edinburg, 1961-72; owner, mgr., Edelmiro Hinojosa, C.P.A., Edinburg, 1973—. Cubmaster, Boy Scouts Am., 1971—; treas. Boys Clubs Am., Edinburg, 1970-72, St. Joseph's P.T.A., 1971-72. Served with AUS, 1952-54. C.P.A., Tex. Mem. Am. Inst. C.P.A.'s Tex. Soc. C.P.A.'s. Roman Catholic. K.C. Club: Golf Assn. (Edinburg). Home: 802 S 3d St Edinburg TX 78539 Office: 1317 S Closner St Edinburg TX 78539

HINSCH, WILLIAM PAUL, ins. co. exec.; b. Bklyn., July 15, 1910; s. Henry Theodore and Elinor (Kuhn) H.; grad. high sch.; m. Eva Lee Harralson, Feb. 7, 1947; children—Patricia Ann, Melissa Ann. Asst. mgr. actuarial dept. Southland Life Ins. Co., Dallas, 1930-47; actuary, asst. sec., dir. So. States Life, Houston, 1947-49; with Am. Security Life Ins. Co. (formerly Am. Hosp. & Life Ins. Co.), San Antonio, 1949—, vice chmn. bd., chmn. exec. com., 1972—, mem. exec. com., 1959—, mem. investment com., 1959—; pres., dir. Am. Mortgage & Trust Co., 1973—; pres. United Land Co.; dir. Am. Securities Co., San Antonio. Mem. Interim Senate Ins. Study Com. Tex., 1970; mem. Hosps.-Ins.-Physicians Joint Adv. Com. Tex., 1955—; mem. adv. com. policy approval guidelines for health ins. Tex. Bd. Ins., 1970—; mem. Pres.'s Com. Employment of Handicapped, 1970, Gov.'s Com. Employment Handicapped, 1970. Bd. mgrs. Bexar County Hosp. Dist., San Antonio, 1971—; trustee Bexar County Hosp. Pension Plan; bd. dirs. Research and Planning Council, San Antonio. Served with AUS, 1943-45. Mem. Tex. Life Ins. Assn. (dir. 1969-70, mem. health maintenance orgn. study com. 1973—). San Antonio C. of C. (vice chmn. med. devel. com. 1971, mem. health services task force 1972, chmn. publs. adv. com. 1974), Conf. Actuaries in Pub. Practice, Actuaries Club Southwest (exec. com. 1953-54, 57-58), Am. Acad. Actuaries, Ins. Soc. U. Tex. (hon.), Health Ins. Assn. Am., Tex. Health Ins. Assn. (bd. dirs. 1958—, pres. 1958), Health Ins. Council. Methodist. Home: 823 Fabulous St San Antonio TX 78216 Office: PO Box 2341 San Antonio TX 78298

HINSLEY, ROBERT BENJAMIN, lawyer; b. San Francisco, Feb. 1, 1938; s. B.F. and Helen M. (Collins) H.; B.A., U. Tex., 1961, J.D., 1964; m. Cathy Hinsley, June 1, 1963; children—David, Gregg. Admitted to Tex. bar, 1964; practiced in Houston, 1964-73; partner Schlumberger, Hinsley & Westmoreland, Houston, 1966—. Bd. dirs., exec. com. Am. Heart Assn., 1970-73; chmn. bequests and donations com. Houston Heart Assn., 1972-73; bd. dirs. Big Bros. Houston, Inc., Big Bros. Houston Found., Inc., Friends Houston Pub. Library, Ct. Vols. Am. Mem. Am (del. young lawyers sect. conv. 1972), Houston (chmn. youth-abuse com. 1973), Houston Jr. (dir., treas. 1970-71, chmn. juvenile delinquency com. 1970) bar assns., State Bar Tex. Club: Toastmasters (pres Houston 1970).

HINTON, C. SNOW, mcht., mayor; b. Tuscaloosa, Ala., Dec. 10, 1918; s. Clarence S. and Mae (Auxford) H.; student U. Ala., 1937-40; m. Marilyn Morgan, Oct. 26, 1946; children—Margaret (Mrs. John Gary Hogue). Pat (Mrs. Jerry Plott). Owner Diamond Sundry, Inc., Tuscaloosa, 1946—; mayor City of Tuscaloosa, 1969—; vice-chmn. bd. City Nat. Bank, Tuscaloosa. City commr., Tuscaloosa, 1967—. Served with AUS, 1941-46. Mem. C. of C. (dir.). Baptist. Mason (Shriner), Rotarian. Home: 28 The Downs Tuscaloosa AL 35401 Office: City Hall Tuscaloosa AL 35401

HINTON, CLACY REED, lumber co. exec.; b. Lewisburg, Ky., Jan. 17, 1934; s. Leo Brent and Edith (Crafton) H.; grad. pub. high sch.; m. Maxine Logsdon, Dec. 24, 1952; children—Deloris (Mrs. Jeffrey Coursey), Cindra Jeanette, Sherri Lynn. Partner Hinton Lumber Co., Inc., Lewisburg, 1957—, pres., 1965—; partner Lewisburg Pallet Co., 1965—, Chapel Lumber Co., Russellville, Ky., 1968—. Served with AUS, 1954-56. Mem. Am. Legion. Republican. Baptist. Moose. Home and office: Route 2 Lewisburg KY 42256

HINTON, PATRICIA FERN, med. technologist; b. Booneville, Miss., June 13, 1932; d. Milliard Carroll and Mattie (Peeler) Hinton; B.S., Miss. State Coll. for Women, 1954; M.S., U. Miss., 1971. Asst. chief Univ. Hosp. Clin. Bacteriology Lab., Jackson, Miss., 1955-60; blastomycosis research lab. VA Hosp., Jackson, 1960-69; med. research in respiratory diseases VA Center, Jackson, 1969—; instr. microbiology U. Miss. Med. Sch., Jackson, 1972—. Mem. Am. Assn. U. Women, Miss. Soc. Med. Technologists (pres. 1959-60, dir. 1963), Am. Soc. Microbiologists, Med. Mycol. Soc. Am., Am. Soc. Med. Tech., Central Dist. Soc. Med. Technologists (pres. 1958), Alpha Mu Tau. Mem. Christian Ch. Contbr. articles to profl. jours. Home: 4911 Old Canton Rd Jackson MS 39211 Office: VA Center Research Lab Jackson MS 39216

HIOTT, DAVID WESTON, physician; b. Walterboro, S.C., July 29, 1942; s. Henry Plant and Mary Caroline (Beach) H.; student U. S.C., 1959-60; B.S., Med. Coll. S.C., 1963, M.S., 1965, Ph.D., 1968; M.D., Med. U. S.C., 1973; m. Barbara Arlene Shealy, Feb. 2, 1963; children—David Walter, Henry Plant, Matthew Weston. Research fellow Sch. Grad. Studies, Med. Coll. S.C., Charleston, 1963-68, instr., 1968-69, asso., 1969-70; asst. prof. Coll. Medicine Med. U. S.C., 1970-71, teaching fellow, 1971-73; rotating intern Richland Meml. Hosp., Columbia, S.C., 1973-74. Recipient Nat. award Pharm. Mfrs. Assn., 1968-70. Mem. Rho Chi. Mem. Christian Ch. Office: Richland Meml. Hosp Harden St Extension Columbia SC 29202

HIPKENS, THEODORE PETTY, health care adminstr.; b. Syracuse, N.Y., Dec. 14, 1913; s. Ernest F. and Fanny (Petty) H.; B.S., N.Y. State Coll. Forestry, 1937; postgrad. Syracuse U., 1937-38; m. Norma E. Hitchings, May 26, 1939; children—Robert, Anne, Henry. Tchr. high sch., N.Y., 1939-41; civilian instr. U.S. Army Air Force, Maxwell Field, 1941-42; rehab. exec. VA, Bath, N.Y., 1946-51; rehab. adminstr. United Mineworkers Welfare and Retirement Fund, Pitts., 1954-57; exec. dir. Home for Crippled Children, Pitts., 1957-66, sr. cons., 1966—; pres. Appalachian Regional Hosps., Lexington, Ky., 1966-73, cons., 1973—. Commr. Commn. on Edn. for Health Adminstrn. Served with USMCR, 1942-46, 51-54. Decorated Bronze Star. Fellow Am. Pub. Health Assn.; mem. Internat. Assn. Rehab. Facilities. Home: 141 Elm St Versailles KY 40383 Office: Jordan Bldg Lexington KY 40503

HIPP, HOWELL EDSEL, sch. adminstr.; b. Saluda, S.C., Mar. 2, 1925; s. Wilbert Airel and Willie Mae (Fulmer) H.; A.B., Wofford Coll., 1949; M. Edn., Furman U., 1956; postgrad. U. Ga., summers 1963-66; m. June Annise Cloyd, Jan. 1, 1950; children—Rodney, Stanley. Prin., Inman (S.C.) Elementary Sch., 1950-54, prin. high sch., 1954-55; prin. Chapman High Sch., Inman, 1956-58, Inman Jr. High Sch., 1955-56; dir. instrn. Dist. One Schs., Spartanburg County, S.C., 1958-68, supt. schs., 1968—. Cons. S.C. Migrant Edn., 1970—; mem. S.C. Textbook Com., 1967-69; counselor Epworth Children's Home, 1949-50; mem. Spartanburg County White House Conf. on Children and Youth, 1970; mem. S.C. Com. for Funding under Title 6, Elementary Sch. Edn. Act, 1970—; chmn. edn. Spartanburg County United Fund, 1967; 2d v.p. Region XII PTA Council. Bd. dirs. Charles Lee Center for Handicapped Children, Spartanburg County Speech and Hearing Clinic, Spartanburg County Tech. Edn. Center. Served with USNR, 1943-46. Mem. Spartanburg County Supts. Assn. (chmn., 1971-72), S.C. Instrnl. TV Adv. Council (chmn. 1971-72, regional chmn. 1967—), Nat., S.C., Spartanburg County (pres. 1955-56) edn. assns., Am., S.C. assns. sch. adminstrs. Methodist (chmn. bd. 1971-72, lay speaker 1970—). Rotarian (pres. local club 1973-74). Home: 25 W Miller St Inman SC 29349 Office: Box 218 Campobello SC 29322

HIRSCH, ARNOLD HARRY, pub. utility cons.; b. Phila., Dec. 25, 1895; s. Julius and Fanny (Krouse) H.; C.E. with honors, U. Pa., 1918; postgrad. Temple Law Sch., 1924-26; m. Ann B. Fieldstone, Apr. 9, 1916; children—Walter, Edwin P. Admitted to Pa. bar, 1928, U.S. Supreme Ct. bar, 1944; sales engr., indsl. rep. Phila. Electric Co., 1920-30; practice engring., law as pub. utility cons. to regulatory commns., municipalities, indsl. consumers in U.S. and Can., 1930—; rate expert, chief pub. utilities OPA, Washington, 1943-47. Hon. citizen New Orleans; hon. col. gov.'s staff State of La. Mem. Am., Fed., Phila. bar assns., Am. Judicature Soc. Mason (life). Club: Nat. Lawyers (founder) (Washington). Author tech. articles on rate-making. Home: 4501 Connecticut Av Washington DC 20008 Office: Nat Press Bldg Washington DC 20004

HIRSCHFELD, GENE WOLFE, educator; b. N.Y.C., Apr. 21, 1917; s. Herman Marcus and Esther (Orange) H.; B.A., N.Y. U., 1937, D.D.S., 1940; M.S., Old Dominion Coll., 1968; m. Mary Chenman, Sept. 23, 1943; children—Esther (Mrs. Nathaniel Cohen), Richard, JoAnn. Intern oral surgery Cumberland Hosp., 1940-41; individual practice dentistry, Norfolk, Va., 1945-66; dir. schs. of dental hygiene and assisting Old Dominion U., Norfolk, 1966—, prof. dental hygiene, 1967—. Mem. dental inst. com. Greater Norfolk area, 1967—; mem. statewide com. on curriculum for dental aux. edn. Va. Bd. Higher Edn., 1967—; cons. health careers Norfolk city schs., 1971—, S.E. Va. Planning Commn., 1971—; mem. Norfolk City Health subcom., 1968—; mem. health services div. Norfolk Model City neighborhood project, 1968-69; mem. Norfolk City Citizens' Com. on Voluntarism and Urban Life Project, 1970-71. Served with AUS, 1942-45. Fellow Internat. Coll. Dentists, Va. Dental Assn. (mem. edn. com. 1967—); mem. Am. Legion, Jewish War Vets., Nat. Conf. Christians and Jews. Jewish religion (dir. temple 1946—). Mem. B'nai B'rith. Home: 7320 Glenroie Av Norfolk VA 23505 Office: Tech Bldg Old Dominion Univ Norfolk VA 23508

HIRT, AL, musician; b. New Orleans, Nov. 7, 1922; s. Alois and Linda (Guepet) H.; student Loyola U., New Orleans, also Cin. Conservatory Music; m. Mary Patureau, Aug. 13, 1942; children—Mary Lee, Gretchen, Rebecca, Bridgid, Rachel, Stephen, Jennifer, Jefferson Davis. Profl. trumpet player, 1940—; part owner Pier 600, night club, New Orleans, 1961-64; owner Al Hirt, night club, New Orleans, 1964—; part owner New Orleans Saints Football Team; appeared Basin St. East, N.Y.C., Eden Roc Hotel, Miami, Fla., Greek Theatre, Los Angeles, Carter Barron Theatre, Washington, Pres. Kennedy's Inaugural Ball, Starlight Theatre, Kansas City, Mo., Riviera Hotel, Las Vegas, Palmer House, Chgo. and others; TV appearances on own spls., also Dinah Shore, Ed Sullivan, Andy Williams, Jimmy Dean, Perry Como shows and others; appeared in movies World by Night, Lovers Must Learn; many recs. including Honey in the Horn, Java (gold record). Served with AUS, 1942-46. Office: 809 St Louis St New Orleans LA 70112 also 1027 Bourbon St New Orleans LA 70116

HISKEY, RICHARD GRANT, educator; b. Emporia, Kan., May 21, 1929; s. Clifford and Ethel Mary (Grant) H.; B.A., Kan. State Tchrs. Coll., 1951; M.S., Kan. State U., 1953; Ph.D., Wayne State U., 1955; m. Joan T. Crooke, June 13, 1953; children—Kathleen, Elizabeth, Timothy, Charles, Jonathan. Research asso. Poly. Inst. Bklyn., 1955-58; asst. prof. dept. chemistry U. N.C., Chapel Hill, 1958-61, asso. prof., 1961-65, prof., 1965—, chmn. dept. chemistry, 1970—. Served with AUS, 1955-57. John S. Guggenheim Found. fellow 1970-71; recipient award for excellence in undergrad. teaching Standard Oil Found., 1970. Mem. Am. Chem. Soc. (com. on grad. exams. 1964-70), A.A.A.S., Sigma Xi. Asso. editor Chem. Reviews, 1963-66. Home: 521 Lake Shore Lane Chapel Hill NC 27514

HITE, JAMES LESLIE, utility co. exec.; b. Henderson, Ky., Sept. 14, 1909; s. Leslie Peyton and Mary Gladys (Flaherty) H.; student U. Ky., 1928-31, 1936, U. Mich., 1957; m. Eleanor Jean Cunn, Dec. 10, 1934 (dec.); children—James Leslie, Richard Hillman; m. 2d, Marjorie Lawson Penn, Oct. 14, 1972. Elec. engr. Ky. Utilities Co., Lexington, 1936-57, adminstrv. asst. to pres., 1957-69, asst. v.p. operations 1970-71, v.p. operations 1972—. Dir. Old Dominion Power Co., Norton Va., 1972—; Ky. rep. Def. Electric Power Adminstrn., 1967—. Registered profl. engr., Ky. Mem. I.E.E.E., Ky., Lexington chambers commerce, Triangle. Democrat. Roman Catholic. Clubs: Lexington Country, Lafayette, Cotillion. Home: 425 Chinoe Rd Lexington KY 40502 Office: 120 S Limestone Lexington KY 40502

HITT, DAVID H., univ. med. center adminstr.; b. Ala.; M.S. in Commerce and Bus. Adminstrn., U. Ala., M. Hosp. Adminstrn., U. Minn. Hosp. adminstr., 1947—; with Baylor U. Med. Center, 1952—, successively various mgmt. positions, now co-chief mgmt. Pres. Dallas Hosp. Council, 1959; mem. adminstrv. bd. Council Teaching Hosps. of Assn. Am. Med. Colls.; mem. Dallas Health Panel, Dallas Commn. Children and Youth. Recipient Earl M. Collier award Distinguished Hosp. Adminstrn. Tex., 1973. Fellow Am. Coll. Hosp. Adminstrn. (past regent); mem. Am. (trustee, past chmn. Council Financing), Tex. (trustee, treas., v.p., pres., chmn. ho. dels. 1967) hosp. assns., Am. Protestant Hosp. Assn. (past trustee), Alumni Assn. U. Minn. Program Hosp. Adminstrn. (past pres.). Club: Exchange (pres. 1957) (East Dallas). Rotarian. Contbr. numerous articles to profl. jours. Home: 7231 Twin Tree Lane Dallas TX 75214 Office: Baylor U Med Center Dallas TX 75246

HITT, EDWIN EARL, physician; b. Red Springs, Tex., Aug. 6, 1939; s. Preston Edwin and Josephine (Long) H.; A.A., Tyler (Tex.) Jr. Coll., 1959; student Eastern N.M. U., 1959-61; M.D., Tulane U., 1965; m. Patty Sue Kidd, Apr. 15, 1967; 1 dau., Felicia Dawn. Intern Meth. Hosp., Dallas, 1965-66; gen. practice medicine, Dallas, 1968—; mem. staff Dallas Meth. Hosp. Served with AUS, 1966-68. Named Outstanding Intern of Year, Meth. Hosp. Dallas, 1966. Mem. Am. Acad. Family Physicians, A.M.A., Tex., Dallas County med. socs., Dallas So. Clin. Soc., Silver Key, Phi Theta Kappa, Alpha Omega Alpha. Club: Oak Cliff Country (Dallas). Home: 6430 Autumn Woods Trail Dallas TX 75232 Office: 301 Westcliff Professional Bldg Dallas TX 75224

HIXON, GEORGE COOLEY, investment exec.; b. Jacksonville, Fla., Apr. 8, 1937; s. George Cooley and Sarah George (Hall) H.; grad. Hotchkiss Sch.; student Washington and Lee U., 1955-58; B.S., Trinity U., 1964; 1 son, George Simpson. Vice-pres., dir. Midland Investment Co., 1964; pres., dir. Hixon Devel. Co., San Antonio, 1968—; dir. La. Gen. Services. Bd. govs. S.W. Found. Research and Edn.; bd. dirs., exec. v.p. Game Conservation Internat.; bd. dirs. San Antonio Zool. Soc. Served with AUS, 1959-61. Mem. Phi Gamma Delta. Republican. Episcopalian. Clubs: Country, Argyle (San Antonio); Boston (New Orleans); African Safari (N.Y.C.); Shikar Safari, Fla. Yacht (Jacksonville); Port Aransas Rod and Reel (dir. 1973) (Tex.). Home: 330 Argyle Av San Antonio TX 78209 Office: 341 Milam Bldg San Antonio TX 78205

HO, THOMAS TONG-YUN, geologist; b. Taichung, Taiwan, China, July 2, 1931; s. Chin-tui and Wan-Hsi (Hseih) H.; B.S., Nat. Taiwan U., 1955; M.A., U. Kan., 1961, Ph.D., 1964; m. Yvonne Y.C. Lai, June 1, 1963; children—Anthony C.M., Victor S.P. Came to U.S., 1958, naturalized, 1972. Research asst. U. Kan., Lawrence, 1958-62; research asso. U. Ariz., Tucson, 1964-67; vis. scientist U. Cal. at Los Angeles, 1967; sr. research geologist Esso Prodn. Research Co., Houston, 1967—. Served to 1t. Army Rep. China, 1955-56. Fellow Geol. Soc. Am.; mem. A.A.A.S., Am. Geophys. Union, Geochem. Soc., Sigma Xi. Contbr. articles to profl. jours. Home: 2618 Anniston St Houston TX 77055 Office: PO Box 2189 Houston TX 77001

HOADLEY, JAMES CARLISLE, elec. engr.; b. Washington, Nov. 22, 1916; s. James Eliphalet and Mabel (Carlisle) H.; student U. Md., 1949-50, 59-60, George Washington U., 1956-58, Am. U., 1959-60; m. Elizabeth Earle Thode, Mar. 29, 1945; children—Richard Carlisle, Caroline Elizabeth, James Frederick. Prodn. engr. Lab. for Electronics, Boston, 1947-48; radio engr. audio sect. Nav. Air Test Center, Patuxent River, Md., 1948-51; supr. electronic engring., chief instrumentation sect. Nat. Bur. Standards, Dept. Commerce, Washington, 1951-57, mem. elec. tech. panel, 1958-72; elec. engr. Harry Diamond Labs, Washington, 1957-72, supr. electronic engring. research, supr. research and devel. nuclear vulnerability br., 1957—, mem. reactor test planning com., 1958-72. Recipient Outstanding Performance certificate Harry Diamond Labs., 1963. Registered profl. engr., Md., D.C. Mem. I.E.E.E. (sr. mem.), Nat. Soc. Profl. Engrs., Pendleton Dist. Gem. and Mineral Soc. (Senneca, S.C.). Patentee in field. Contbr. articles to profl. jours., 1949-65. Home and office: 18 Lakeside Dr Walhalla SC 29691

HOAG, W(ILLIAM) GIFFORD, govt. ofcl.; b. N.Y.C., Aug. 22, 1909; s. William John and Anna Louise (Puckhafer) H.; B.S., Cornell U., 1931, M.S., 1934; m. Diane Fisler, Feb. 24, 1939; children—Peter Marshall, John Gifford. Statistician, N.Y. State Bur. Agr. and Markets, 1933-34; with Farm Credit Adminstrn., Washington, 1934—, dir. information and extension, 1950-55, chief information service research and information div., 1955-69, asst. to gov., 1969—. Pres. Potomac Coop. Fedn., 1957-59, Rochdale Coop. Va., 1956-59, Coop. Inst. Assn., 1966-67. Bd. dirs. Greenbelt Consumer Services,

1960-62, 63-71, vice chmn. bd., 1963-65, 67-71; bd. dirs. Group Health Assn., 1964-70, pres., 1966-69; bd. dirs. Community Group Health Found., 1968-71. Recipient 50th anniversary medal Fed. Land Bank, 1967; Meritorious Service award Farm Credit Adminstrn., 1956; spl. citations Advt. Council Coops., 1969, gov. Farm Credit Adminstrn., 1970. Mem. Am. Marketing Assn., Coop. Editorial Assn. (past dir.; Klinefelter award 1963), Agrl. Relations Council (past chmn. eligibility com.), Am. Agrl. Editors Assn., Am. Assn. Agrl. Coll. Editors, Advt. Council Coops. (past sec.-treas.), Alpha Zeta, Sigma Delta Chi. Club: Nat. Press (Washington). Co-author: Banks for Cooperatives-A Quarter Century of Progress, 1959. Contbr. articles to profl. jours. Editor News for Farmer Co-ops., 1944-53; mem. editorial consulting com. Am. Inst. Coops., 1972-73. Home: 1695 Beulah Rd Vienna VA 22180 Office: Farm Credit Adminstrn 490 L'Enfant Plaza SW Washington DC 20578

HOAGE, TERRELL RUDOLPH, educator; b. Fairfield, Ia., Aug. 12, 1934; s. Henry Woodrow and Hazel Alice (Williams) H.; B.S., Parsons Coll., 1957; M.S., Ia. State U., 1963, Ph.D., 1964; postgrad. U. Ia., 1967-68; m. Mary Lee Reneker, Aug. 10, 1957; children—Terrell Lee, Jay B. Research entomologist, bee mgmt. U.S. Dept. Agr., Madison, Wis., 1964-65; asst. prof. biology Parsons Coll., Fairfield, Ia., 1965-67; asso. prof. biology Sam Houston State U., Huntsville, Tex., 1968-71, prof., 1971—. Bd. dirs. Huntsville Community Day Care Assn., 1970-73. Served with AUS, 1957-59. Recipient grants NSF, Philos. Soc. Mem. Am. Genetic Assn., Entomol. Soc. Am., Am. Soc. Cell Biology, Tex. Soc. Electron Microscopy (program chmn. 1972-73, pres. 1974), Sigma Xi, Beta Beta Beta, Chi Beta Phi, Gamma Sigma Delta. Home: Route 4 Box 105 Huntsville TX 77340

HOAGLAND, JIMMIE LEE, journalist; b. Rock Hill, S.C., Jan. 22, 1940; s. Mrs. James L. Estes; A.B. cum laude (S.C. Press Assn. scholar; J. Rin McKissick journalism scholar; Beauford Watts Ball journalism scholar; Burlington Indsl. Found. scholar), 1961; postgrad. (Rotary Found. fellow) U. Aix-en-Provence (France), 1961-62; m. Gretchen Hoagland, Oct. 10, 1970. Reporter Evening Herald, Rock Hill, summers 1958-60; copy editor N.Y. Times, Paris, France, 1964-66; city reporter Washington Post, 1966-68, African corr., hdqrs. Nairobi, Kenya, 1969—. Served with USAF, 1961-64. Recipient Pulitzer prize internat. reporting, 1971. Ford Found. fellow Columbia Grad. Sch. Journalism, 1968-69. Author: The Divided House; Civilizations in Conflict, 1972. Address: care PO Box 7866 Nairobi Kenya

HOBART, THOMAS FITZHUGH, civil engr., educator; b. Birmingham, Ala., Mar. 5, 1906; s. Lewis Alonzo and Frances (Fitzhugh) H.; B.S., Auburn U., 1927, C.E., 1944; m. Marion Johnson, Aug. 25, 1934; children—Elizabeth (Mrs. Fred Goad, Jr.), Thomas Fitzhugh. Field engr. Gulf States Steel Co., 1929-32; asst. div. engr. Ala. Hwy. Dept., 1932-46; v.p., gen. mgr. So. Amiesite Asphalt Co., Inc., North Birmingham, Ala., 1946-71; lectr. civil engring. dept. Auburn (Ala.) U., 1971—; dir. Vulcan Life & Accident Ins. Co.; cons. in field. Mem. Auburn Alumni Assn. (past pres.), Am. Soc. C.E. (past pres. Ala. sect.), Asso. Gen. Contractors Am. (past pres., dir. Ala. br.), Ala. (past pres. contractors div.), Am. (past v.p. So. dist.) road builders assns. Now deceased. Home: 309 Kimberly Dr Auburn AL 36830

HOBBS, BILLY SEWELL, ednl. adminstr., mayor; b. Columbia, Tenn., Dec. 22, 1934; s. Wilburn S. and Ethel (Fox) H.; B.A., George Peabody Coll., 1956, M.A., 1957; LL.D., Burton Coll. and Sem., 1965; m. Jaska R. Moore, Sept. 5, 1953; children—Jeffrey Moore, Joseph Sewell, James Franklin. Tchr., Spring Hill (Tenn.) High Sch., 1956-58; prin. White House (Tenn.) High Sch., 1958—; mayor City of White House, 1971—. Magistrate, Sumner County Ct., 1972—. Mem. Tenn. Edn. Assn., Nat. Soc. for Study Edn., Kappa Phi Kappa, Phi Delta Kappa. Democrat. Baptist. Mason (32 deg., Shriner), Lion. Home: East Side Dr White House TN 37188

HOBBS, GEORGE KENNETT, lawyer; b. Ardmore, Okla., Jan. 11, 1929; s. Vernon Logan and Lena (Sullivan) H.; grad. Kemper Mil. Sch., 1947; B.A. in Mgmt., Tex. Technol. U., 1951, M.B.A. in Personnel Mgmt., 1952; LL.B., So. Methodist U., 1959; m. Patricia Knight, Feb. 19, 1953; children—Sharon Heather, Susan Kelly, Kennett Logan. Sales mgr. Gen. Supply Co., Pampa, Tex., 1954-57; admitted to Tex. bar, 1959; partner firm Bass & Hobbs, Lubbock, Tex., 1959—. Lectr. mgmt., labor law Tex. Technol. U., 1961-65. Bd. dirs. Lubbock Planned Parenthood Assn., 1961. Served to 1st lt. USAF, 1952-54. Mem. Lubbock C. of C. (vice chmn. goals for seventies program 1970-71), Lubbock County, Tex., Am. bar assns. Presbyn. (ruling elder). Kiwanian (dist. 7 lt. gov.). Home: 2306 59th St Lubbock TX 79412 Office: 18 Briercroft Office Park Lubbock TX 79412

HOBBS, NED PETER, optometrist; b. Worden, Ill., Dec. 26, 1921; s. Kermit Ludolph and Marie (Massa) H.; Dr. Optometry, Ill. Coll. Optometry, 1947; postgrad. U. S.C.; m. Kathryn Louise Stonecypher, Sept. 16, 1941; children—Steven Craig, Karen Susan, Michael Jeffrey. Individual practice optometry, Darlington, S.C., 1947—. Pres. S.C. Bd. Examiners Optometrists and opticians, 1958-63. Dir. All Risks Ins. Co. County commr., Darlington County, S.C., 1964—, coroner, 1969—. Mem. med. adv. bd. Darlington County chpt. Polio Found., 1960-63; internat. chmn. equivalent standards com. Internat. Assn. Bds. Examiners Optometry; pres. Pee Dee Perpetual Care Cemetery Assn. Mem. Darlington City Council, 1950-52. Served from pvt. to capt., Med. Adminstrv. Corps, AUS, World War II; PTO. Named Citizen of Yr., Kiwanis Civic Club, 1950, Optometrist of South, So. Optometrist Jour., 1952, Optometrist of Year in S.C., 1966. Fellow Am. Acad. Optometry (pres. S.C. chpt. 1959-63); mem. Am., S.C. (pres. 1953-54) optometric assns., So. Council Optometrists (pres. 1958-59), Southeastern Optometry Congress (past sec.), Pee Dee Optometric Assn. (pres., optometrist of Year 1970), V.F.W., Am. Legion, Darlington C. of C., Royal Soc. Health, Optometric Extension Program, Am. Optometric Found., S.C. (sec.), Pee Dee Cemetarian of Year 1972) cemetery assns. Baptist. Mason (Shriner), Elk, Lion (pres. 1949-50 Outstanding Lion of Year, Darlington 1950), Toastmaster (v.p. Darlington). Home: 420 James St Darlington SC 29532 Office: 161 Cashua St Darlington SC 29532

HOBBS, OLIVER KERMIT, farm equipment mfg. exec.; b. Hobbsville, N.C., Sept. 21, 1918; s. Ephriam J. and Sallie (Brown) H.; student pub. schs., Hobbsville; m. Frances Allsbrook Piland, June 14, 1941; children—Oliver Kermit, Cynthia Russell. Service rep. Sadler Music Co., Suffolk, Va., 1939-42; service mgr. A.E. Sadler Co., Suffolk, 1945-49; gen. mgr. Shotton's Farm Service, Suffolk, 1949-58; dir. research and engring. Benthall Machine Co. Inc., Suffolk, 1958-63, dir., 1959-63; organizer, partner Hobbs Engring. Co., 1963-70; pres. Hobbs-Adams Engring. Co., 1970—. Cons. agrl. mech. devices, 1956—. Served with USNR, 1942-45; ETO. Recipient Horace Hayden Meml. trophy, 1954. Mem. Va. Farm Equipment Assn., Aircraft Owners and Pilots Assn., Woodmen of World, Suffolk-Nansemond C. of C., Suffolk-Nansemond Hist. Soc., Va. Mfrs. Assn., Internat. Platform Assn. Baptist. Clubs: Ruritan (Suffolk), Kings Fork (pres. Suffolk 1959). Patentee automotive and agrl. field. Designer mech. sampling devices, peanut harvesting equipment, automatic control devices, power transmission equipment. Home: 1202 West Point Dr Suffolk VA 23434 Office: PO Box 1833 Suffolk VA 23434

HOBBS, WILLIAM DAVID, tobacco co. exec.; b. Eden, N.C., Dec. 22, 1915; s. Edward Victor and Grace B. (Stocks) H.; student Davidson Coll., 1934-36; m. Jane Farr, Mar. 1, 1943; children—William David, Jane (Mrs. Gary S. Dean). With R.J. Reynolds Tobacco Co., Winston-Salem, N.C., 1936—, pres., 1972—; dir. RJR Industries, Winston-Salem, N.C. Nat. Bank, Winston-Salem. Chmn. Forsyth County United Fund, 1956; mem. Winston-Salem Citizens Coalition, 1971-73. Adv. bd. Salvation Army, 1968-72; bd. visitors Peace Coll., Raleigh, 1972—. Served to capt. AUS, 1941-46. Episcopalian. Clubs: Forsyth Country (Winston-Salem); Bermuda Run Country (Clemmons, N.C.). Home: 908 Kenleigh Circle Winston-Salem NC 27106 Office: Corner 4th and Main Sts Winston-Salem NC 27102

HOBBY, DIANA POTEAT STALLINGS (MRS. WILLIAM PETTUS HOBBY, JR.), newspaper editor; b. N.Y.C., Apr. 22, 1931; d. Laurence and Helen (Poteat) Stallings; B.A., Radcliffe Coll., 1952; M.A. Georgetown U., 1955; m. William Pettus Hobby, Jr., Sept. 11, 1954; children—Laura, Paul, Andrew. Book editor Houston Post, 1957—. Home: 1506 South Blvd Houston TX 77006 Office: 2410 Polk Av Houston TX 77001

HOBBY, GRETCHEN CLARK (MRS. WILLIAM M. HOBBY III), civic worker; b. Washington, Apr. 22, 1939; d. Bruce Edmund and Phyllis Bryans (Wilson) Clark; B.A., Mary Baldwin Coll., 1956; m. William M. Hobby III, Oct. 12, 1962; children—Amy, William. Asst. to slide librarian, pubs. supr., asst. chief pubs. Nat. Gallery Art, summers, 1957-59, 60-65; with art dept. Orlando (Fla.) Pub. Library 1967-68; mgr. Loch Haven Art Center Shop, Orlando, Fla., 1969—, docent, 1966-67. Chmn. teenage vols. Orange Meml. Hosp. Aux., 1968-70; mem. Orlando Opera Gala Guild, 1967-72, Orlando Civic Theatre Guild, 1971-72; dir., recording sec. Loch Haven Art Center, 1970-71, mem. council of 101 commn. and corr. sec. Winter Park Sidewalk Art Festival Assn., 1970—. Mem. Orange County Bar Assn. Aux., Am. Assn. Museums, Mus. Stores Assn. (chmn. conv. 1972, v.p., exec. com. 1973—), Mary Baldwin Coll. Alumnae Assn. (dir. 1974—). Republican. Unitarian. Editor Mus. Stores Assn. Newsletter, 1973—. Home: 749 Lake Davis Dr Orlando FL 32806 Office: Art Center Shop 2416 N Mills Av Orlando FL 32803

HOBBY, OVETA CULP (MRS. WILLIAM P. HOBBY), newspaper publisher; b. Killeen, Tex., Jan. 19, 1905; d. I.W. and Emma (Hoover) Culp; student Mary Hardin Baylor Coll., H.H.D., 1956; L.H.D., Bard Coll., 1950, Lafayette Coll., 1954; LL.D., Baylor U., Sam Houston State Tchrs. Coll., U. Chattanooga, 1943, Bryant Coll., Ohio Wesleyan U., 1953, Columbia, Smith Coll., Middlebury Coll., 1954, U. Pa., Colby Coll., 1955, Fairleigh Dickinson, Western Coll., 1956; D. Litt., Colo. Women's Coll., 1947, C.W. Post Coll., 1962; m. William P. Hobby, Feb. 23, 1931; children—William, Jessica (Mrs. Henry E. Catto, Jr.). Parliamentarian Tex. Ho. of Reps., 1926-31, incomplete terms 1939, 41, joined Houston Post as research editor, 1931, successively lit. editor, asst. editor, v.p., exec. v.p., exec. v.p. and editor, 1931-52, editor and pub., 1952-53, pres., editor, 1955-65, chmn. bd., editor, 1965—; chmn. bd. sta. KPRC, KPRC-TV; dir. Gen. Foods Corp.; chief women's interest sect. War Dept. Bur. Pub. Relations, 1941-42; apptd. dir. WAAC, 1942; commd. col. AUS, dir. WAC, 1943-45; fed. security adminstr., 1953; sec. Dept. Health, Edn. and Welfare, 1953-55. Gov. A.R.C., 1950-55; nat. vice chmn. Am. Cancer Soc. campaign, 1949; pres. So. Newspaper Pubs. Assn., 1949; mem. Am. Design Awards com.; mem. nat. com. Am. Mus. Immigration, 1956; dir. nat. bd. United Cerberal Palsy. Mem. nat. adv. com. Citizens for Eisenhower, 1956; sponsor Clark Sch. for Deaf; mem. Coll. Commn. Diocese of Tex., 1956; trustee Rice U., Eisenhower Birthplace Meml. Park; mem. Pres.'s coms. on Employment Physically Handicapped, Civilian Nat. Honors; trustee Am. Assembly, 1957—, Eisenhower Exchange Fellowships; bd. dirs. Houston Symphony Soc.; mem. S.W. adv. bd Inst. Internat. Edn.; mem. Com. of 75, U. Tex., 1958 —, mem. So. regional com. Marshall Scholarships, 1957—; mem. Carnegie Commn. of Ednl. TV; mem. Rockfeller Bros. Fund Spl. Studies Project; adv. bd. George C. Marshall Research Found., 1960—; nat. council Eleanor Roosevelt Meml. Found.; bd. dirs. Com. for Econ. Devel.; mem. nat. bd. devel. Sam Rayburn Found.; mem. Crusade for Freedom, Inc., 1958—, Bus. Com. for Arts, Inc., 1967 —, Nat. Met. Opera; bd. dirs. Corp. for Pub. Broadcasting, Tex., 1968-72, Heart Assn.; vis. com. Grad. Sch., Edn., Harvard, 1961-67; trustee Soc. Rehab. Facially Disfigured, People to People; ch. mem. Acad. of Tex., 1969—. Recipient Distinguished Service Medal, 1944; Philippine Mil. Merit medal, 1947; Honor Award for Distinguished Service in Journalism, U. Mo., 1950; Pub. of Yr. award Headliners Club, 1960; Living History award Research Inst. Am., 1960, Honor award Nat. Jewish Hosp., 1962; award for advancement and diffusion of knowledge and understanding Carnegie Corp., 1967. Mem. Gamma Alpha Chi (hon. vice chmn.). Episcopalian. Clubs: Headliners; Houston, Bayou, Ramada, Junior League (Houston). Author: Mr. Chairman (parliamentary law textbook); also syndicated column same title. Home: Houston TX 77001 Office: Houston Post 4747 Southwest Freeway Houston TX 77001

HOBBY, WILLIAM PETTUS, lt. gov. Tex.; b. Houston, Jan. 19, 1932; s. William Pettus and Oveta (Culp) H.; B.A., Rice U., 1953; m. Diana Poteat Stallings, Sept. 11, 1954; children—Laura Poteat, Paul William, Andrew Purefoy, Katherine Pettus. Asst. sec.-treas. Houston Post, 1957-59, asso. editor, 1959-60, mng. editor, 1960-63, exec. editor, 1963—, exec. v.p. Houston Post Co., 1963-65, pres. 1965—; vice chmn. Channel Two TV Co., KPRC Radio Co., 1970—. Parliamentarian, Tex. Senate, 1959; lt. gov. Tex., 1973—. Bd. dirs. Child Guidance Center Houston, 1957-63, pres., 1960-62. Served to lt. (j.g.) USNR, 1953-57. Mem. Am. Soc. Newspaper Editors, Tex. Hunter and Jumper Assn. (dir. 1953—, pres. 1959-61), U.S. Equestrian Team, Inc. (v.p. 1959-60), Houston C. of C. (dir.). Home: PO Box 326 Houston TX 77001 Office: State Capitol Capitol Sta Austin TX 78711

HOBDAY, VICTOR CARR, govt. cons.; b. Covington, Ky., Sept. 2, 1914; s. Walter and Cecil (Fryer) H.; B.S., U. Ky., 1936; M.S., Syracuse U., 1941, Ph.D., 1966; m. Mabel Elizabeth Price, Mar. 31, 1945; children—Priscilla Elizabeth, Walter Price (dec.), Cynthia Lynn. Adminstrv. asst. Ky. Dept. Revenue, Frankfort, 1936-38; city mgr. Paducah, Ky., 1947-49; cons. Municipal Tech. Adv. Service, U. Tenn., 1950, exec. dir., 1952-63, 65—; city mgr., Waxahachie, Tex., 1950-52; mem. U. Tenn. Mission, U. Panama, 1963-64; sr. research asso. Bur. Pub. Adminstrn., U. Tenn., 1964-65. Mem. Mayor's Com. on Human Relations, 1966-70; gen. chmn. Knoxville roundtable Nat. Conf. Christians and Jews, 1972-73; pres. West Hills P.T.A., 1962-63. Served to lt. col. AUS, 1941-46, now col. Res. ret. Mem. Res. Officers Assn., Am. Soc. Pub. Adminstrn. Mem. Knoxville Men's Garden Club (pres. 1968-69). Mem. Christian Ch. (deacon). Author: Sparks at the Grass Roots. Home: 5416 Smoky Trail Knoxville TN 37919 Office: White Av Bldg U Tenn Knoxville TN 37916

HOBSON, JAMES HARVEY, educator; b. Anderson County, S.C., Sept. 6, 1917; s. James Maxwell and Grace (Routh) H.; B.S., U. S.C., 1939; M.A., Emory U., 1947, Ph.D., 1953; m. Martha Louise Horton, June 1, 1946; children—Martha (Mrs. George W. Johnson III), James Harvey. Tchr., Greenwood (S.C.) High Sch., 1939-40; faculty Clemson U., Clemson, S.C., 1940—, prof. chemistry, 1954—, alumni prof. chemistry, 1969. Cons. Fiberglas, Sangamo Electric. Active Boy Scouts Am. Mem. Am. Chem. Soc., Am. Iris Soc. (sr. judge), Am. Hemerocallis Soc., Phi Kappa Phi. Presbyn. (deacon 1954-59, elder 1959-64, 66-71). Home: 222 Riggs Dr Clemson SC 29631 Office: Dept Chemistry Clemson SC 29631

HOBSON, T. FRANK, JR., judge; b. St. Petersburg, Fla., Dec. 2, 1928; s. Tolbert Francis and Mabel (Miller) H.; student Wake Forest Coll., 1946-47, U.S. Naval Acad., 1947-48; A.B., John B. Stetson U., 1951, LL.B., 1952;; m. Janet Louise Funk, Oct. 29, 1949 (div. May 1959); children—Margot Kim, Melissa Catherine; m. 2d, Janet Susan Rothermel; children—Keller Frances, T. Frank III, Thomas Carroll, Susan Elizabeth. Asst. atty. gen. State of Fla., 1952; gen. counsel Haven Ins. Co., 1954-58; practiced in St. Petersburg, 1954-60; dep. commr. for Fla. Indsl. Commn., 1959-60; circuit judge, St. Petersburg, 1960-64; partner firm Meros, Hobson & Wilkinson, 1964-65; judge 2d Dist. Ct. of Appeal, 1965—, chief judge, 1969—. Dir. v.p. Haven Ins. Co. 1956-58. Trustee Julia and Dick Pope Found., Inc. Served to capt. USMCR, 1952-54. Mem. Fla. Bar, Am., St. Petersburg bar assns. Democrat. Baptist. Home: Route 3 Box 520 Dade City FL 33525 Office: Dist Ct Appeal 2d Dist Memorial Blvd Lakeland FL 33801

HOBSON, VIRGIA BROWN (MRS. WILLIAM DYSON HOBSON), educator; b. Little Plymouth, Va.; d. Sidney and Annie (Williams) Brown; B.S., Va. State Coll., Petersburg, 1934; M.A., Tchrs. Coll., Columbia, 1955; postgrad. summers N.Y. U., 1961, 63, 67, Radford Coll., 1972; m. William Dyson Hobson, July 28, 1938; children—William Dyson, Shirley Anne. Tchr. home econs. Henry County Tng. Sch., Martinsville, Va., 1934-37, Georgetown Spl. Sch. Dist., Georgetown, Del., 1937-42, Henry County Tng. Sch., Martinsville, Va., 1942-44, 45-48; extension tchr. Va. State Coll., Petersburg, Va., 1948-49; asst. prin. Albert Harris High Sch., 1949-59, guidance dir., 1959—. Sec. bd. dirs. Martinsville-Henry County Mental Health Soc., 1960-62; bd. dirs. Nat. Conf. Christians and Jews, Martinsville Human Relations Council. Mem. N.A.A.C.P., Martinsville Tchrs. Assn. (past pres.), Am. Personnel and Guidance Assn., Va. Tchrs. Assn., N.E.A., Assn. Coll. Admission Counselors, Delta Sigma Theta (past sec.). Clubs: Modernistic Bridge; Links (pres. Martinsville-Danville chpt.). Home: 1013 W Fayette St PO Box 268 Martinsville VA 24112

HOCHE, A. HENRY, real estate exec.; b. Savannah, Ga., Nov. 3, 1931; s. Philip A. and Angela G. (Hayes) H.; student U. Fla., 1955-56; B.A., N.Y. U., 1958; m. Sarah F. Hovater, Dec. 24, 1956; children—Kathryn S., Rebecca F. Broadcaster radio sta. WMBG, Richmond, Va., 1958-59; dir. television sta. WJCT-TV, Jacksonville, Fla., 1959-60; producer Fla. ednl. TV Sta. WDBO, Orlando, 1960-64; real estate salesman Jenkins Realty, Winter Park, Fla., 1965; founder, pres. Henry Hoche Realty, Inc., realtors, Orlando, 1965—; dir. Barnett Bank of West Orlando (Fla.), 1973—. Mem. Mayor's Adv. Bd. for Devel. and Rehab., Orlando, 1965-69; vice chmn. Orange County Charter Commn., 1973-74; commr. Orlando (Fla.) Housing Authority, 1973—; founder, mem. Orange County Drug Abuse Council, 1969-72. Mem. adv. bd. Valencia Community Coll., 1972—; bd. dirs. Fla. Central East Coast Ednl. TV, Inc., 1970—, v.p., 1970-72; bd. dirs. Central Fla. Heart Assn., 1969—, campaign chmn. 1970; bd. dirs. YMCA, 1974—. Served with USNR, 1951-54. Recipient Certified Property Mgr. of Year award Central Fla. chpt. Inst. Real Estate Mgmt., 1971. Mem. Fla. Assn. Realtors (dir. 1970, 72, 74), Inst. Real Estate Mgmt. (mem. nat. governing council 1973—), Friends Orlando Pub. Library (dir. 1968—, pres. 1968-70), Orlando C. of C. (mem. com. of 200, 1973—). Kiwanian. Clubs: Orlando Country, Univ. (Orlando); King Mountain (Highland, N.C.). Home: 407 Peachtree Rd Orlando FL 32804 Office: 401 W Colonial Dr Orlando FL 32804

HOCKLANDER, JOSEPH MONROE, judge; b. Tuscaloosa, Ala., Nov. 23, 1926; s. Joseph Monroe and Delma (Perry) H.; J.D., U. Ala., 1950; m. Sadie Lucille Sullivan, Aug. 14, 1954; children—Joseph M., Ashley Delma, Leann Lucille. Admitted to Ala. bar, 1950; gen. practice law, 1950-60; judge 13th Jud. Circuit Ala., Mobile, 1961—. Mem. Ala. Ho. of Reps., 1959-60. Served with 82d Airborne Div., USAAF, 1944-46. Mem. Nat. Coll. State Trial Judges (faculty adviser), Ala. Circuit Judges' Assn. (pres.), Internat. Acad. Trial Judges (regent). Home: 255 S McGregor Av Mobile AL 36608 Office: County Court House Mobile AL 36602

HOCOTT, JOE BILL, chem. engr., educator; b. nr. Big Flat, Ark., Sept. 19, 1921; s. Jeiks Edmonds and Frances Clara (Berry) H.; B.S., U. Ark., 1945; M.S., Okla. State U., 1951. Insp. Maumelle Ordnance Works, U.S. Army Ordnance Dept., Little Rock, 1942-43; head sci. dept. Joe T. Robinson High Sch., Little Rock, 1945-46; instr. chemistry U. Tulsa, 1946-47; teaching fellow Okla. A. and M. Coll., Stillwater, 1947-49; research chem. engr. Deep Rock Petroleum Corp., Cushing, Okla., 1950, Kerr-McGee Oil Corp., Stillwater, 1951; chem. engr. cons. Joe Bill Hocott, Little Rock, 1952-55, 63—; med. technician U. Ark. Med. Center, Little Rock, 1955-56, research asso., 1956-57, instr. internal medicine, 1957-62; head chemistry dept. Little Rock Central High Sch., 1963-66; head sci. dept. Met. Vocational-Tech. High Sch., Little Rock, 1967-73. Asst. scoutmaster Boy Scouts Am., 1945-46, troop committeeman, 1945-46, 57-58, neighborhood commr., 1969-70. Bd. dirs. Ark. Jr. Sci. and Humanities Symposium, 1965-72, asst. dir., 1972. Mem. Am. Inst. Chem. Engrs., Nat. Soc. Profl. Engrs., Ark., Ark. Jr. (dist. dir. 1966—) acads. sci., Sigma Xi, Phi Lambda Upsilon, Unitarian. Home: 1010 Rice St Little Rock AR 72202

HODES, RICHARD SAMUEL, physician, state legislator; b. N.Y.C., Apr. 24, 1924; s. Stanley and Rosabel H.; B.S., Tulane U., 1944, M.D., 1946; fellow U. Minn., 1947-49; m. Marjorie Cohen, May 19, 1946; 1 dau., Marilyn. Practice medicine specializing in anesthesiology, Tampa, Fla., 1951—; head dept. anesthesiology Tampa Gen. Hosp.; clin. prof. anesthesiology U. Fla.; clin. prof. surgery and anesthesiology U. South Fla., 1973. Chmn. human resources task force intergovtl. relations com. Nat. Legislative Conf.; govtl. rep., pres. bd. dirs. Human Services Inst., Washington. Mem. Fla. Ho. of Reps., 1966—, chmn. com. health and rehab. services. Recipient Good Govt. award Fla. Jaycees. Mem. Fla. Soc. Anesthesiologists (pres. 1960). Democrat. Jewish religion. Home: 116 Ladoga St Tampa FL 33606 Office: 238 E Davis Blvd Suite H Tampa FL 33606

HODGE, JAMES DWIGHT, chemist; b. Mechanicsburg, O., July 14, 1933; s. Samuel Merrill and Helen Rachel (Moore) H.; B.S., Bob Jones U., 1956; M.S., U. Mich., 1959; Ph.D., Pa. State U., 1963; m. Mildred Louise Frady, June 3, 1955; children—Sharon Rachel, Marcia Ann, James Alan. With Shell Chem. Co., Houston, 1959-61; with Dacron research lab. E.I. duPont de Nemours & Co., Inc., Kinston, N.C., 1963—, sr. research chemist, 1966—. Collegiate football ofcl. asso. with So. Conf., 1970—. Mem. Am. Chem. Soc. (chmn. Eastern N.C. sect. 1968-69). Republican. Club: Optimist (Greenville, N.C.). Home: 237 Churchill Dr Greenville NC 27834 Office: Box 800 Kinston NC 28501

HODGE, LESTER CLARK, JR., orthodontist; b. Gainesville, Fla., Aug. 3, 1936; s. L. C. and Anne (Gocek) H.; student U. Fla., 1954-57; D.D.S., Emory U., 1961, M.S., 1965; m. Betty Jo Hunter Mar. 25,

1958; children—Lester Clark III, Shannon Lee. Individual practice orthodontics, Gainesville, 1965—. Vice-chmn. United Fund campaign, Gainesville, 1968, chmn., 1970, also bd. dirs. Mem. Gainesville Plan Bd., 1967-70; mem. North Central Planning Council, 1968—. Served to capt. Dental Corps, AUS, 1961-63. Recipient Distinguished Service award Jr. C. of C., 1969. Mem. Am. Orthondontic Soc., Am. Dental Assn., Sigma Chi, Xi Psi Phi. Rotarian (pres. 1974). Home: Callison Rd Gainesville FL 32601 Office: 3500 SW 2d Av Gainesville FL 32601

HODGELL, MURLIN RAY, univ. dean; b. Mankato, Kan., Jan. 6, 1924; s. Ray Darias and Lora (Overman) H.; student Washburn U., 1943, U. Ia., 1944; B.S., Kan. State U., 1949; M.S., U. Ill., 1952; Ph.D., Cornell U., 1959; m. Bille Ro Jean Seward, July 20, 1947; children—Janet, Kristen, Kevin. Extension architect Kan. State U., 1949-50; asst. prof. agrl. engring. U. Ill., 1950-55; mem. housing research staff Cornell U., 1955-56; asso. prof. architecture Kan. State U., 1957-63; chmn. dept. city and regional planning Rutgers U., 1963-64; dir. Sch. Architecture U. Neb., 1964-69; dean Coll. Environmental design U. Okla., Norman, 1969—. Cons. Hodgell Assos. in Architecture, Planning, Engring., 1960-69, Rockefeller Found., 1967-68. City planning dir., Manhattan, Kan., 1957, planning commr., 1958-63; chmn. Riley County, Kan., Nat. Found. and March of Dimes, 1960-62. Served to lt. (j.g.) USNR, 1943-46. Named Man of Year, Manhattan Jr. C. of C., 1959, Kan. Outstanding Young Man of Year, Jr. C. of C., 1960; recipient Distinguished Community Service award Lane-Bryant Found., 1960. Registered profl. engr., Kan. Mem. Am. Inst. Planners, A.I.A., Am. Soc. C.E., Tau Sigma Delta, Sigma Tau. Author: Contemporary Farmhouses, 1956; Zoning, 1958. Home: 712 Lindsay Av Norman OK 73069

HODGENS, PAUL MORTON, SR., hosp. adminstr.; b. Albertville, Ala., Dec. 18, 1925; s. John C. and Fannie V. (Morton) H.; diploma Snead Jr. Coll., 1946-47; B.S. in Sci., Jacksonville State Coll., 1948; postgrad. Auburn U.; m. Mary Grace Wilson, July 5, 1944; children—Lisa Grace, Paul Morton, John Bart. Med. technologist Anniston (Ala.) Meml. Hosp., 1947-58; insp. Ala Bd. Health, Oneonta, 1948-50; chief lab. technologist Sand Mountain Infirmary, Albertville, 1950-56, x-ray technician, 1953-56, purchasing agt., 1954-56; administr. Boaz (Ala.)-Albertville Hosp., 1956—. Trustee Albertville Schs. Served with USNR, 1944-45. Mem. Am. Coll. Hosp. Adminstrs., Ala. Hosp. Assn. (trustee), N.E. Ala. Hosp. Council (pres. 1958-60). Home: 311 Nixon St Albertville AL 35950 Office: PO Box 338 Boaz AL 35957

HODGES, CECIL MOYE, banker; b. Oconee, Ga., Oct. 27, 1897; s. Charlie Marshall and Berta Louise (Moye) H.; student Ga.-Ala. Bus. Coll., 1917-18; m. Mattie Louise Smith, Oct. 23, 1924; children—Mary Patsy (Mrs. Thomas Aaron Hutcheson), Rosa Ann (Mrs. Donovan Dewitt Kinnett), Cecil Moye. Founder Cecil Hodges Lumber Co., Sandersville, Ga., 1919, pres., 1919-71; pres. Cecil Farms, Inc., Sandersville, 1961, Washington Land & Timber, Inc., Sandersville, 1965; dir. George D. Warthen Bank, Sandersville. Mem. Forestry Commn. Washington County, Ga., 1960—. Mem. Central Ga. council Boy Scouts Am., Macon, 1952—. Bd. dirs. Hodges Found. Recipient award Central Ga. council Boy Scouts Am., 1954, citation Ga. Forestry Commn., 1963. Mem. Christian Ch. (elder). Mason (33 deg., Shriner), Lion (past pres. Sandersville). Home: PO Box 70 Oconee GA 31067 Office: PO Drawer B Sandersville GA 31082

HODGES, EDWARD GREY, JR., broadcasting co. exec.; b. Miami, Fla., Dec. 11, 1937; s. Edward Grey and Shirley Louise (Varner) H.; B.S. in Indsl. Mgmt., Ga. Inst. Tech., 1960; certificate exec. mgmt. N.Y. U., 1969; m. Eugenia Williams Morrison, Sept. 17, 1960; children—Christopher Grey, Jeffrey Howard, Michael Patrick. Partner Diehl Assos., Inc., editorial cons. for mags., Atlanta, 1962-63; So. editor Miller Freeman Publs., Atlanta, 1963-64, mng. editor, N.Y.C., 1964-65; mgr. publs. Previews div. Reeves Telecom Corp., N.Y.C., 1965-66, marketing mgr. Prodn. Services dir., 1966-67, v.p. marketing, 1967-68, sr. v.p. Prodn. Services div., 1968-70; mng. dir. Jefferson Prodns., TV prodns., Charlotte, N.C., 1971—; v.p. Jefferson-Pilot Broadcasting Co., 1974—. Bd. dirs. N.C. State U. Edn. Found., Greater Charlotte Dance Guild. Served as 1st lt. USMCR, 1960-62. Mem. Videotape Prodn. Assn. (charter; treas. 1969—), Nat. Indsl. TV Assn. (standards com. 1970—). Presbyn. (deacon 1968—). Home: 11 Timberidge Dr Clover SC 29710 Office: Jefferson Productions 1 Julian Price Pl Charlotte NC 28208

HODGES, JOT HOLIVER, JR., lawyer; b. Archer City, Tex., Nov. 16, 1932; s. Jot Holiver and Lola Mae (Hurd) H.; B.S., Sam Houston State U., 1954, B.B.A., 1954; J.D., U. Tex., 1957; m. Virginia Pardue, June 11, 1955; children—Deborah Lee, Jot Holiver III, Darlene Dee. Admitted to Tex. bar, 1958; asst. atty. gen. State of Tex., 1958-62; partner firm Hodges & Kerr, Houston, 1963—. Chmn. bd. Brazoria County Land & Cattle Co., Presidio Devel. Corp. Served to capt. AUS, 1957-58. Mem. Am., Tex., Houston bar assns., Assn. Trial Lawyers Am., Delta Tau Delta, Delta Theta Phi. Clubs: Houston, University. Contbr. articles to profl. jours. Home: 3527 Thunderbird St Missouri City TX 77459 Office: First City Nat Bank Bldg Houston TX 77002

HODGES, LORENTZ RYAN, JR., architect, engr.; b. Charleston, W.Va., Apr. 18, 1930; s. Lorentz Ryan and Mary Lavinia (Cabell) H.; B.S., Ga. Inst. Tech., 1957, B.Arch., 1958; m. Mary Susanne Fant, June 30, 1962; children—Lorentz Ryan III, Mary Elizabeth, James Fant. With Toombs-Amisano & Wells, Atlanta, 1958-61, Irving-Bowman & Assos., Charleston, W.Va., 1961-65, Washington, 1965-67; individual practice architecture, Alexandria, Va., 1967—. Active Belle Haven Civic Assn. Bd. dirs. Alexandria Boys Club, Mt. Vernon Recreation Assn. Served with USNR, 1951. Mem. A.I.A., Constrn. Specifications Inst., Va. Profls., Soc. Archtl. Historians. Club: Alexandria Optimist (dir.). Home: 1817 Edgehill Dr Alexandria VA 22307 Office: 116 Royal St Alexandria VA 22314

HODGES, RICHARD EDWARD, advt. and pub. relations exec.; b. Pikeville, Ky., Feb. 9, 1928; s. Richard Edward and Marian (McQueen) H.; student Washington and Lee U., 1946-48; A.B., Emory U., 1950; m. Barbara Burke, Sept. 27, 1951; children—Richard Edward, Burke Vincent. Reporter, Ashland (Ky.) Daily Ind., 1944-48, Atlanta Constn., 1950-51; mem. staff pub. relations dept. Liller, Neal, Battle & Lindsey, Inc., Atlanta, 1951-54, account exec., 1951-56, pub. relations dir. 1956-67, v.p., 1960-67, exec. v.p., 1968—, also dir. Mem. men's adv. com. Atlanta Music Club, 1965-72; chmn. spl. pub. relations adv. com. Atlanta Community Chest-United Appeal, 1966-67, v.p., 1968-72; mem. Atlanta Bd. Edn., 1973. Bd. dirs. Atlanta area Camp Fire Girls, 1958-60; bd. govs. Pub. Broadcasting Service Mem. Pub. Relations Soc. Am., So. Indsl. Editors Assn. (pres. Atlanta 1953), Atlanta Advt. Club (pres. 1962-63), Am. Assn. Advt. Agys. (com. for work with students and educators 1965-68, chmn. S.E. council 1968-69), Atlanta C. of C. (dir. 1973), Inquiry Club, Assn. Indsl. Advertisers, Fulton County Grand Jurors Assn., Sigma Delta Chi. Episcopalian. Rotarian. Home: 4615 Brook Hollow Rd Atlanta GA 30327 Office: 1300 Life of Ga Tower Atlanta GA 30308

HODGIN, WILLIAM KENDRICK, county agrl. agt.; b. Santa Rita, N.M., Mar. 27, 1923; s. William DeForrest and Herrise (Kendrick) H.; B.S., Tex. A. and M. U., 1948; m. Myra Nell Anders, Apr. 28, 1951; children—Wade K. Norris W. Ranch asst. mgr. Floyd Gage ranch, Chihuahua, Mexico, 1940-41; asst. county agr. agt. Fort Bend County, Richmond, Tex., 1948-51; county agr. agt. Goliad County, Goliad, Tex., 1951-52; farm mgr. C & M Ranch Co., Artesia, N.M., 1952-53; county agrl. agt. McMullen County, Tilden, Tex., 1954—; agrl. rep. Dept. Commerce Internat. Trade Fair, Uruguay, 1965. Served with AUS, 1943-46. Mem. Nat. (Distinguished Service award 1970), Tex. (dist. dir. 1962-64) county agrl. agts. assns., Epsilon Sigma Phi (dist. dir. 1962-64). Mason, Lion (past pres.). Author: McMullen County Program; Production Guidelines for McMullen County. Home: PO Box 215 Tilden TX 78072

HODGSON, DALE LEROY, elec. engr.; b. Duluth, Minn., Mar. 16, 1925; s. Fred Basil and Isla (Worthing) Reamer; student Marquette U., 1943-44; B.S. in Elec. Engring., Purdue U., 1946; m. Sarah Leonora LaRowe, July 14, 1946; children—Elida Juana (Mrs. William Lewis Holcomb, Jr.), Irene Belle. Sr. design engr. McDonnel Aircraft Corp., St. Louis, 1946-51; supr. engring. liaison with LTV Vought Aeros., Dallas, 1951-70, chief design liaison, 1970-72, supr. installation, power plant and retrofit engring. design, 1972—. Permanent chmn. N.Tex. Caucus Young Democrats, 1958. Served to ensign USNR, 1943-46. Registered profl. engr., Mo., Tex. Mem. I.E.E.E., Nat. Geog. Soc., Acad. Polit. Sci., Dallas Civic Opera Guild, Dallas Grand Opera Assn. Democrat. Methodist. Club: LTV Supervisors (Dallas). Contbr. to tech. publs. Home: 703 McKay Dr Arlington TX 76010 Office: LTV Vought Aero Dallas TX 75222

HODGSON, PETER CRAFTS, educator; b. Oak Park, Ill., Feb. 26, 1934; s. Jack Edward and Mary (Crafts) H.; A.B. summa cum laude, Princeton, 1956; B.D., Yale, 1959, M.A., 1960, Ph.D., 1963; m. Eva Sara Fornady, June 18, 1960; children—David Andrew, Jennifer Anne. Ordained to ministry United Presbyn. Ch., 1960; asst. prof. religion Trinity U., San Antonio, 1963-65; asst. prof. theology Vanderbilt U., Nashville, 1965-69, asso. prof., 1969-73, prof., 1973—. Mem. citizens budget adv. com. Nashville Pub. Schs., 1972-73. Woodrow Wilson fellow, 1956-57; Danforth fellow, 1956-63; Am. Assn. Theol. Schs. fellow, 1968-69; Guggenheim fellow, 1974—. Mem. Soc. for Religion in Higher Edn., Am. Acad. Religion, Soc. Phenomenology and Existential Philosophy, Phi Beta Kappa. Author: The Formation of Historical Theology, 1966; Jesus—Word and Presence, 1971; Children of Freedom, 1974. Editor: The Life of Jesus Critically Examined (D.F. Strauss), 1972-73. Editor, translator: F.C. Baur on the Writing of Church History, 1968. Home: 71 Brookwood Terrace Nashville TN 37205

HODNETTE, ROBERT EDWARD, JR., judge; b. Fort Deposit, Ala., May 17, 1913; s. Robert Edward and Clara Martha (Brooks) H.; student Auburn U., 1930-32; J.D., U. Ala., 1935; LL.M., U. Chgo., 1946; grad. Nat. Coll. State Judiciary, 1971; m. Agnes Nowling, Apr. 29, 1955; 1 dau., Martha Sue. Admitted to Ala. bar, 1935; practiced in Atmore, 1935-38, Mobile, 1947-50, 59-70; atty. claim dept. Aetna Ins. Cos., Louisville, 1939-40; asst. U.S. atty. So. Dist. Ala., Mobile, 1950-52; mem. firm Holberg, Tulley & Hodnette, 1959-70; circuit judge, Mobile, 1970—. Dir. Mobile Fed. Savs. & Loan Assn., chmn. bd., 1956—. Mem. Ala. Constn. Commn., 1972—. Served with AUS, 1940-46; ETO. Decorated Purple Heart, others. Mem. Ala. Circuit Judges Assn., Mobile, Ala., Am. bar assns., Mobile C. of C., V.F.W., Pi Kappa Alpha, Phi Alpha Delta. Methodist (dir.). Kiwanian. Office: County Ct House Mobile AL 36602

HODSON, FREDERICK WEED, JR., lawyer; b. Tulsa, Nov. 10, 1925; s. Frederick Weed and Verna Ophelia (Donnell) H.; B.A. with honors, U. Tex., 1947, LL.B., 1950; m. Barbara Jean Long, May 3, 1957; children—Frederick Weed III, David Long, Andrew James. Admitted to Tex. bar, 1950; asso. Hill, Lochridge & King, Mission, 1950-52; partner Hill, Lochridge, King & Hodson, Mission, 1953-55; mem. firm Erwin, Wagner & Hodson, Houston, 1955-67; individual practice law, Houston, 1967—. Vice pres., sec., dir. Ocean Corp., Houston; v.p., sec., treas. Midland Prodn. Corp., Houston. Pres. Walnut Bend P.T.A., 1971-72; pres. Voss West Little League, 1973—. Served as lt. USNR, 1943-46. Mem. Phi Delta Phi, Phi Kappa Sigma. Presbyn. (elder 1969—). Lion (local pres. 1966-67). Home: 10226 Holly Springs Houston TX 77042 Office: 2111 Chamber of Commerce Bldg Houston TX 77002

HOEFELMEYER, ALBERT BERNARD, recreational vehicle co. exec.; b. San Antonio, Mar. 27, 1928; s. Albert H. and Anna (McMonigal) H.; B.S., St. Mary's U., San Antonio, 1949; M.A., U. Tex. at Austin, 1950; Ph.D., Tex. A and M U., 1954; m. Shirley Jean Benson, Nov. 27, 1970 (div. Mar. 1973). Sr. nuclear physicist Gen. Dynamics Corp., Fort Worth, 1957-62, sr. research scientist, 1962-71; sole practice chem. consulting, Fort Worth, 1971-72; v.p. Burkhart Mfg. Co., Fort Worth, 1972—. Fellow Am. Inst. Chemists (profl.); mem. Am. Chem. Soc., N.Y. Acad. Scis., Radiation Research Soc., Fort Worth Bowling Assn. (pres. 1971-72, dir.), Sigma Xi, Phi Lambda Upsilon. Home: 1725 Jacqueline Ct Fort Worth TX 76112 Office: 2711 S Riverside Dr Fort Worth TX 76104

HOELTKE, LOREN HENRY, bank exec.; b. Columbus, Ind., Dec. 2, 1931; s. Henry William and Clara Mary (Arnholt) H.; A.B., Franklin Coll., 1953; grad. U. Wis. Sch. for Bank Adminstrn., 1972; m. Ruth Esther Wells, July 19, 1953; children—Mark, Amy, Victoria. With Reeves Pulley Co., Columbus, 1955-57; asst. cashier Irwin Union Bank & Trust Co., Columbus, 1957-62; with Indian River Citrus Bank, Vero Beach, Fla., 1962-74, v.p., operations officer, 1970-74; exec. v.p., cashier Flagler Nat. Bank, West Palm Beach, Fla., 1974—, also dir. Served with AUS, 1953-55. Mem. Am. Inst. Banking (bd. govs. Indian River chpt. 1972—), Bank Adminstrn. Inst., Vero Beach C. of C., Phi Delta Theta. Lutheran. Kiwanian (dir.). Home: 4806 N Dixie Hwy Apt 4 West Palm Beach FL 33407 Office: 521 S Flagler Dr West Palm Beach FL 33402

HOERMANN, SIEGFRIED ARMIN, statistician; b. Highland Park, Ill., Sept. 27, 1921; s. William and Maria (Harz) H.; B.A., U. Ia., 1943; postgrad. U. Chgo., 1946-49; m. Sheila S. Boyd, Oct. 17, 1953; children—Hillary T., Siegfried Armin II. With U.S. Bur. Census, 1950-55, 63-66, asst. acting div. chief demographic operations, 1963-66; chief farm population sect. U.S. Dept. Agr., 1955-57; statis. adviser to Iranian Govt., 1957-62; div. dir. health resources statistics Nat. Center Health Statistics, Washington, 1966—. Sec. sub-com. U.S. Nat. Com. on Health and Vital Statistics, 1967—. Pres., New Alexandria Citizens Assn., 1969-73. Served to lst lt. USAAF, 1943-46. Mem. Population Assn. Am., Am. Statis. Assn., Am. Pub. Health Assn., Internat. Union Sci. Study Population, Phi Beta Kappa, Delta Phi Alpha. Author: (with Bogue, Shryock) Streams of Migration, 1957; (with Bowles, Rohrer) Population of the Northeast 1900-1950, 1960; (with others) Health Manpower, 1968, Hospital Discharge Data, 1970; Ambulatory Medical Care, 1973. Home: 6406 16th St Alexandria VA 22307 Office: 5600 Fishers Lane Rockville MD 20852

HOETINK, HARMANNUS, educator; b. Groningen, Netherlands, Jan. 7, 1931; s. Gradus Jantinus and Hendrika (Rytema) H.; B.A., U. Amsterdam, 1950, M.S., 1953; Ph.D., U. Leiden, 1958; m. Ligia Coralina Espinal, Apr. 25, 1957; 1 son, Harman Antonie. Dir., Latin Am. Studies Center, U. Amsterdam, also prof. extraordinary U. Rotterdam, 1964-68; prof. sociology U. P.R., Rio Piedras, 1969—, dir. Inst. Caribbean Studies, 1969-73; vis. prof. sociology U. Tex., 1969, Yale, 1968. Mem. Govtl. Commn. for Inquiry Disturbances Curacao, 1969. Recipient ann. prize Latin Am. conf. Am. Hist. Assn., 1970. Mem. Am. Hist. Assn. (pres. Caribbean sect. 1971-72), Institut de Recherches Africaines Université de Paris, Royal Netherlands Soc. Arts and Letters, Dominican Geog. Soc. Author: Het Patroon Van De Curacaose Samenleving, 1958; El Pueblo Dominicano, 1971; Caribbean Race Relations, 1971; Slavery and Race Relations in the Americas, 1973. Editor: Encyclopaedia Netherlands Antilles, 1969. Mem. editorial bd. various jours. Contbr. articles to profl. publs. Office: U PR Inst Caribbean Studies Rio Piedras PR 00931

HOFF, CLAYTON HENRY, educator; b. Chgo., Feb. 1, 1926; s. Henry C. and Alicia (Koke) H.; B.A., McGill U., 1950; M.A., Washington U., St. Louis, 1951; m. Evelyn Abbey; 1 son, Gregory. Instr. English, Bloomfield Coll., N.J., also Brevard Coll., N.C., 1954-58; asso. prof. English, Pembroke (N.C.) State Coll., 1958-62; asst. prof. English, Ga. So. Coll., Statesboro, also Ga. Center for Continuing Edn., Athens, 1962—. Served with USNR, 1943-46. Mem. Ogeechee Camellia Soc., Ga. Edn. Assn., South Atlantic Modern Lang. Assn. Lutheran. Contbr. articles to profl. jours. Home: 402 Marvin Av Statesboro GA 30458

HOFF, JOHN HARLAN, indsl. coatings exec.; b. Ottumwa, Ia., July 23, 1926; s. Vincent Walker and Edna Opal (Winner) H.; student Tulsa U., 1947-48; B.S. in Civil Engring., Okla. State U., 1951; m. JoAnn McArthur, Aug. 14, 1954; children—Jim H., Don B. Pipeline engr. Midwestern Constrn. Co., Tulsa, 1951-56; salesman Reilly Tar and Chem., Tulsa, 1956-64, sales mgr., 1964-69; pres. John Hoff Co., Inc., Tulsa, 1969—; dir. CFS Corp., Tulsa. Mem. engring. council Oklahoma State U., 1950-51. Served with AUS, 1944-46. Decorated Commendation medal. Mem. Am. Soc. C.E., Nat. Assn. Corrosion Engrs., Lambda Chi Alpha. Mason. Club: Pipeliners (Tulsa). Home: 6597 E 25th Place Tulsa OK 74129 Office 7027 E 40th St Tulsa OK 74145

HOFF, VICTOR JOHN, educator; b. Cin., Oct. 18, 1929; s. John and Louise Olga (Kattner) H.; B.S., U. Ky., 1953, M.S., 1958; Ph.D., Ind. U., 1961; m. Doris Emily Baldwin, Aug. 27, 1962. Ass. prof. botany and bacteriology U. Ark., Fayetteville, 1961-66; prof. biology Stephen F. Austin State U., Nacogdoches, Tex., 1966—. Served as lt. (j.g.) USNR, 1953-56. Mem. Sigma Xi. Home: 4526 E Main St Nacogdoches TX 75961

HOFF, WILLIAM, zoo adminstr.; b. Chgo., Dec. 9, 1926; s. Christopher M. and Eva (Kroppman) H.; student Ripon Coll., 1945, Northwestern U., 1948-49; B.S., Roosevelt U., Chgo., evenings 1950-60; m. Lynn Schillo, May 3, 1947; children—Christine, Kimberly. Draftsman traffic engring. Chgo. Park Dist., 1949-51; gen. curator Lincoln Park Zoo, Chgo., 1951-61; exec. dir. Cin. Zoo, 1961-67, St. Louis Zoo, 1968-73; dir. N.C. Zool. Park, Asheboro, 1973—. Trustee Wild Animal Propogation Trust. Served with AUS, 1944-46; PTO. Mem. Am. Assn. Zool. Parks and Aquariums (dir. exec. bd. 1965-69). Home: 1626 Camden Ct Asheboro NC 27203 Office: Route 4 Box 71 Asheboro NC 27203

HOFFECKER, FRANKLIN VERNON, textile co. exec.; b. Cleve., June 23, 1911; s. Franklin R. And Helena (Williams) H.; student Wyomissing Poly. Inst., 1935; m. Martha Elizabeth Deitrick, Nov. 26, 1936; children—Frank L., Charles H., Janice L. (Mrs. Joseph W. Willis). Toolmaker, Textile Machine Works, Reading, Pa., 1930-36; supr. fixer Rogers Hosier Mill, Laurens, S.C., 1936-42; with Burlington Industries, Marion, Va., 1942; supt. MKM, Laurens, S.C., 1942-44, Chadbourn Hosier Mill, Burlington, N.C., 1944-54; plant mgr. M.K.M. Knitting Mills, P.R., 1954-55, Rockdale, Mass., 1955-56; mgr. Huntley Knitting Mill, Charlotte, N.C., 1956-62; sr. v.p., sec. Huntley of York, Ltd. (S.C.), 1962—. Mem. U.S. Power Squadron. Lutheran (v.p. council 1969-73). Elk, Mason. Home: PO Box 88 York SC 29745 Office: PO Box 419 York SC 29745

HOFFELD, DONALD RAYMOND, educator; b. Balt., Sept. 12, 1933; s. Jacob and Edna Wyllie (Smith) H.; A.B. cum laude (Meyer scholar, Carr scholar), George Washington U., 1955; M.S., U. Wis., 1958, Ph.D. (NSF fellow), U. Wis., 1958; m. Sharon Patricia Lytle, May 21, 1965; children—Rachael Elizabeth, Scott Lytle. Research scientist Psychol. Research Assos., Arlington, Va., 1958; asst. prof. psychology La. State U., Baton Rouge, 1960-63, asso. prof., 1963-73, prof., 1973—. Served as 1st lt. USAF, 1958-60. Mem. A.A.A.S., Midwestern Psychol. Assn., Phi Beta Kappa, Sigma Xi, Phi Eta Sigma. Episcopalian. Author: A Student Guide to Introductory Psychology, 1969; Introductory Psychology, 1972. Contbr. articles to profl. jours. Home: 2245 Glendale Av Baton Rouge LA 70808

HOFFMAN, ELBERT LEE, ednl. adminstr.; b. Denver, May 4, 1925; s. Elbert Emmett and Eva May (Gibbons) H.; B.A., U. Okla., 1948, M.S., 1949; M.A., Princeton, 1950, Ph.D., 1953; m. Amelia Ruth Sterling, Dec. 20, 1958; 1 son, David Lee. Psychometric fellow Ednl. Testing Service, Princeton, N.J., 1949-51; asst. prof. psychology, staff asso. Urban Life Research Inst., Tulane U., New Orleans, 1951-55; asso. prof. psychology Tulane U., 1956—, dir. financial aid, 1962-69, dir. planning, 1969—. Exec. dir. Assn. Ind. Colls. and Univs. La., 1973—. Bd. dirs. Gallery Circle Theatre. Served with inf. AUS, 1943-45. Mem. Am., La. (pres. 1960-61) psychol. assns., Am. Statis. Assn., Assn. for Instnl. Research, Soc. Coll. and Univ. Planners, La. Assn. Student Financial Aid Adminstrs. (past pres.), La. Psychologists Inc., mem. bd. examiners 1958-62, pres. 1959-60), Sigma Xi, Psi Chi, Phi Eta Sigma, Pi Kappa Alpha. Baptist (deacon 1959—). Home: 5880 Marcia Av New Orleans LA 70124

HOFFMAN, FRANKLIN GORDON, physician; b. Newark, Aug. 16, 1913; s. Joseph and Sadie (Gordon) H.; B.S., Rutgers U., 1935; M.S., U. Cin., 1938, M.D., 1942; m. Gabrielle M. Danielle Delannoy, Aug. 8, 1946. Intern Cin. Gen. Hosp., 1942-43; resident in cardiology VA Hosp., Indpls., 1952-54; practice medicine specializing in cardiology, Nashville, 1955-56, Los Angeles, 1956-57, Columbia, S.C., 1957-60, Lake City, Fla., 1960-62, Louisville, 1962—; asst. chief, chief med. service, chief cardiology USAF Hosp. Sampson AFB, N.Y., 1954-55; asst. cardiology VA Hosp., Nashville, 1956; asst. chief med. service VA Hosp., Sepulveda, Cal., 1958; chief med. service VA Hosp., Sepulveda, Cal., 1958; chief med. service VA Hosp., Dayton, O., 1959-60; chief cardiology VA Hosp., Louisville, 1960—; cons. cardiology Jewish Hosp., Louisville, 1970—; instr. histology U. Cin., 1938-40; instr. medicine Vanderbilt U., 1956-57; clin. instr. medicine U. Cal. at Los Angeles, 1957-58; asst. prof. medicine Ohio State U., 1960; clin. asst. prof. medicine U. Louisville, 1962—. Cons., Ky. Home Mut. Ins. Co., Armed Forces Exam. Sta. Served to lt. col., USAF, 1942-55. Recipient S. Vander Poole prize Rutgers U., New Brunswick, N.J., 1935. Diplomate Pan Am. Med. Assn. Fellow A.C.P., Am. Coll. Cardiology; mem. N.Y. Acad. Scis., A.M.A., Am. Heart Assn., Am. Diabetes Assn., Med. Soc. U.S.A. and Mexico, Louisville Soc. Internists, Hon. Order Ky. Cols. Club: Jefferson (Louisville). Contbr. articles to profl. jours. Home: 207 Blankenbaker Lane Louisville KY 40207 Office: VA Hosp Zorn Av Louisville KY 40202

HOFFMAN, IRWIN, orch. condr.; b. N.Y.C., Nov. 26, 1924; s. Harry and Augusta (Cohen) H.; student Juilliard Sch. Music, 1942-43, 45-48; m. Esther Glazer, Feb. 21, 1946; children—Joel H., Gary, Toby, Deborah. Condr. Phila. Orch., Robin Hood Dell, summer 1942; teaching fellow Juilliard Sch. Music, 1948; condr. Bronx (N.Y.) Symphony, 1948-52, Yonkers (N.Y.) Philharmonic, 1950-52, Westchester (N.Y.) Chamber Orch., 1950-52, Martha Craham Dance Co., 1949-50; condr., mus. dir. Vancouver (B.C., Can.) Symphony Orch., 1952-64; asso. condr. Chgo. Symphony, 1964-68, acting music dir., 1968-69; prin. condr. Grant Park Symphony, 1964-68; condr. St. Louis Little Symphony, summers 1959-64; music dir. Fla. Gulf Coast Symphony, 1968—, Belgian Radio and TV Symphony Orch., 1973—; lectr. condr. U.B.C., State Coll. Wash., 1958; guest condr. Toronto, Vancouver, Chgo., Israel Philharmonic, 1960, Dallas Symphony, 1962, Brazil, 1962, St. Louis Symphony Orch., 1963, Manchester BBC Orch., 1968-69, Strasbourg Radio Orch., 1968, Brussels Radio Orch., 1969, Orchestre Nat. Paris, 1970, Orchestre Philharmonique, 1971, New Philharmonia London, 1971; protege Serge Koussevitzky, Tanglewood, Mass., 1948-50. Served with AUS, 1943-45. Composer two string quartets, violin sonata, others. Collector autograph music manuscripts, mus. memorabilia. Home: 1901 Brightwaters NE St Petersburg FL 37704 Office: Box 2131 St Petersburg FL 33704

HOFFMAN, JULIUS, physician, educator; b. Bronx, N.Y., Feb. 4, 1921; s. Samuel and Ida (Kaplan) H.; B.A., N.Y. U., 1941, M.D., 1944; M.A., Ohio State U., 1958, M.Med. Sci., 1962; M.S., So. Ill. U., 1972; m. Ray Naomi Lockoff, June 6, 1943; children—Paul Lewis, Deborah Ann, Robert Jon. Intern, then resident, fellow neurology Kings County Hosp., N.Y.C., 1944-46, 48-49; fellow psychiatry Menninger Found. Sch. Psychiatry, 1949-51; resident pediatrics Childrens Hosp., Columbus, O., 1961-62; fellow pediatric neurology Nat. Inst. Neurol. Diseases, 1961-62; asst. prof. psychiatry Ohio State U. Coll. Medicine, 1951-53, asso. prof. Sch. Social Work, 1951-63; asso. prof. neurology and pediatrics Georgetown U., Washington, 1963-65; prof. pediatrics Howard U., 1964—; lectr. dept. psychiatry George Washington U.; lectr. Found. Advancement in Edn. in Sci., NIH, 1971—; mem. staff D.C. Gen., Childrens, Freedmens, Sibley hosps., Washington Hosp. Center. Cons. spl. asst. on mental retardation to Pres., 1963, NIH div. research facilities and resources, 1964, USPHS Neurol. and Sensory Disease Service, 1965, Civil Service Commn.; chief psychiatry Group Health Assn. Washington, 1964-73. Bd. dirs. Hughlings Jackson Found. for Neurol. Research. Served to capt. M.C., AUS, 1946-48. Diplomate Nat. Bd. Med. Examiners, Am. Bd. Psychiatry and Neurology, Am. Bd. Pediatrics. Fellow Am. Acad. Neurology, Am. Psychiat. Assn., Am. Acad. Pediatrics, A.A.A.S.; mem. Internat. Coll. Pediatrics, Internat. Child Neurology Assn., Am. Assn. on Mental Deficiency, Caducean, Phi Beta Kappa, Sigma Xi, Beta Lambda Sigma, Mu Chi Sigma. Home: 7805 Green Twig Rd Bethesda MD 20034 Office: 3000 Connecticut Av NW Washington DC 20008

HOFFMAN, PHILIP (GUTHRIE), univ. pres.; b. Kobe, Japan, Aug. 6, 1915 (parents Am. citizens); s. Benjamin Philip and Florence (Guthrie) H.; student George Washington U., 1936-37; A.B., Pacific Union Coll., 1938; M.A., U. So. Cal., 1942; Ph.D., Ohio State U., 1948; H.H.D., Jacksonville U., 1962 LL.D., U. of Ams., 1965, U. Akron, 1971; H.L.D., Pikeville Coll., 1969, Marshall U.; 1972; m. Mary Elizabeth Harding, Aug. 31, 1939; children—Philip Guthrie, Mary Victoria, Ruth Ann, Jeanne. Credit mgr. Harding Sanitarium, Worthington, O., 1938-40; instr. history Ohio State U., 1946-49; asst. prof. history U. Ala., 1949-51, asso. prof., 1951-53, dir. arts and scis. extension services, 1949-53; vice dean. asso. prof. history gen. extension div. Ore. System Higher Edn., 1953-55, dean, prof., 1955-56; dean faculty, prof. history Portland State Coll., 1956-57; v.p., dean faculties, prof. history U. Houston, 1957-61, pres., 1961—. Mem. bd. S.W. World Affairs Council Houston (pres. 1964-66), Houston Grand Opera Assn., Houston Mus. Natural Sci., Houston Research Inst., Inc., Houston Symphony Soc., Assn. Urban Univs. (pres. 1965-66), Am. Council on Edn.; mem. exec. council commn. on colls. So. Assn. Colls., 1965—, Nat. Commn. on Accrediting, 1965—; mem. Houston Com. Fgn. Relations. Served from ensign to lt. (j.g.), USNR, 1943-45. Mem. Am. Hist. Assn., Am. Assn. U. Profs., Philos. Soc. Tex., Kappa Delta Pi, Phi Kappa Phi, Phi Alpha Theta (nat. pres. 1952-54) Omicron Delta Kappa. Rotarian. Clubs: Houston, University, Petroleum (Houston); River Oaks Country; Astrodome. Contbr. articles to profl. jours. Home: 427 Brown Saddle Houston TX 77027

HOFFMAN, RUTH STERLING (MRS. ELBERT LEE HOFFMAN), physician; b. Shreveport, La., Mar. 25, 1924; d. William Woodson and Hilda Eureka (Ellis) Sterling; B.A., Blue Mountain Coll., 1947; R.N., So. Baptist Hosp. Sch. Nursing, 1951; B.S. in Nursing, Tulane U., 1954, M.D., 1958, M.Med. Sci., 1965; m. Elbert Lee Hoffman, Dec. 20, 1958; 1 son, David Lee. Rotating intern So. Bapt. Hosp., New Orleans, 1958-59, resident in internal medicine, 1959-60; fellow internal medicine Tulane U. Sch. Medicine-Charity Hosp. La., 1960-62, USPHS fellow, 1962-65; dir. Hutchinson Meml. Clinic, chief medicine center student health, asso. dir. univ. health service Tulane U., 1965—, asso. prof. medicine Med. Sch., 1970—, mem. staff. So. Baptist Hosp., New Orleans. Mem. Am. Med. Women's Assn., Orleans Parish Med. Soc., Am. Assn. U. Profs., Am. Coll. Health Assn., Am. Soc. Internal Medicine, Soc. Adolescent Medicine (charter). Baptist. Author med. articles. Home: 5880 Marcia Av New Orleans LA 70124 Office: 1430 Tulane Av New Orleans LA 70112

HOFFMAN, WILLIAM, educator, author; b. Charleston, W.Va., May 16, 1925; s. Henry William and Julia (Beckley) H.; B.A., Hampden-Sydney Coll., 1949; postgrad. Washington and Lee U., 1949-50. State U. Ia., 1950-51; m. Alice Sue Richardson, Apr. 17, 1957; children—Ruth Beckley, Margaret Kay. Prof. English, Hampden-Sydney (Va.) Coll., 1952-59, 1966—; author novels, short stories; playright; pres. Patrick Henry Acad., Charlotte Court House, Va., 1966—; dir. Elk Grocery Co., Charleston, Elk Storage and Warehouse Co., Charleston, Kay Co., Charleston. Served with AUS, 1943-46; ETO. Mem. Authors Guild, Phi Beta Kappa, Omicron Delta Kappa, Pi Delta Epsilon, Sigma Chi, Sigma Upsilon. Presbyn. (deacon). Clubs: Farmington Hunt; Charlotte Country (gov., past pres.) (Charlotte, Va.). Author: The Trumpet Unblown, 1955; Days in the Yellow Leaf, 1958; A Place for My Head, 1960; The Dark Mountains, 1962; Yancey's War, 1966; A walk to the River, 1970. Playwright: The Love Touch, 1967. Home: PO Box 241 Charlotte Court House VA 23923

HOFFMANNS, FREDERIC EVERHARDT, mech. and chem. engr.; b. Marion, O., Nov. 5, 1919; s. Johann E. and Anna Rosalie (Feil) H.; B. Chem. Engring., Ohio State U., 1942, Chem. Engr., 1959; M.S., Fla. Inst. Tech., 1969; m. Catherine Elene Mason, Sept. 27, 1952; children—John F., Ann Lynn, Paul Lewis. Dir. engring. J.M. Little & Assos., cons. engrs., Maumee, O., 1956-59; owner Hoffmanns Engring., cons. engr., Tiffin, O., 1959-60, Merritt Island, Fla. 1971—; sr. mech. engr. 1st and 2d Atlas silos Gen. Dynamics-Astronautics, Vandenburg AFB, Cal., 1960-62; engr. in charge ground support equipment, Saturn Apollo program McDonnell Douglas Corp., Kennedy Space Center, Fla., 1962—. Lectr. Fla. Inst. Tech., 1969-72. Registered profl. engr., Ohio, Fla. Mem. Am. Soc. M.E. (chmn. continuing edn. com. 1970-73), Nat. Soc. Profl. Engrs., Amateur Radio Relay League. Home: 1485 Central Av Merritt Island FL 32952 Office: PO Box 21007 Kennedy Space Center FL 32815

HOFGREN, DANIEL W., investment adviser; b. Jamestown, N.Y., June 8, 1936; s. Wilford and Ethel (Johnson) H.; B.A., Colgate U., 1958; student Columbia Law Sch., 1958-59; m. Alexandra Walton Smith, Oct. 1, 1966; 1 son, Nicholas Walton. Financial devel. officer Pan-Am. Airways, N.Y.C., 1960; spl. devel. trainee Chase Manhattan Bank, N.Y.C., 1961; partner E.J. Gould & Co., 1962-70; on leave as spl. asst. to Pres. U.S., Washington, 1969-70; v.p. corporate finance Goldman, Sachs & Co., Washington, 1970—; mem. internat. adv. com. Am. Security & Trust Co. Spl. rep. U.S. with rank ambassador Inter-Oceanic Canal Negotiations, 1970; chmn. financial adv. com. AMTRAK. Club: Racquet and Tennis of N.Y. Home: 2401 Tracy Pl NW Washington DC 20008 Office: Am Security Bldg 730 15th St NW Washington DC 20005

HOFHEINZ, ROY MARK, profl. baseball exec.; b. Beaumont, Tex., Apr. 10, 1912; s. Frederick Joseph and Nonie (Planchard) H.; student Rice Inst., 1928-29, U. Houston, 1929-30; LL.B., Houston Law Sch., 1933; m. Irene Cafcalas, July 19, 1933; children—Roy Mark, James Frederick, Dene. Admitted to Tex. bar, 1932; mem. Tex. Legislature, 1934-36; judge, Harris County, 1936-44; chmn. bd. Tex. Radio Corp., sta. KTHT, Houston, Pilot Broadcasting Corp., sta. WILD, Birmingham, 1951—; partner Houston Slag Materials Co., 1946—; chmn. bd. Houston Astros Baseball Club; v.p. Houston Consol. TV Co.; chmn. bd., pres. Houston Stars Soccer Club. Past mayor of Houston. Mem. Am. Bar Assn., Am. Arbitration Assn., Sons of Hermann. Elk, Optomist, Eagle. Clubs: Pine Forest Country, Lakeside; Houston Yacht, Briar (Houston). Home: 2400 Yorktown Dr Houston TX 77027 Office: Houston Baseball Club The Astrodome Houston TX 77025

HOFMANN, KARL HEINRICH, educator; b. Heilbronn, Germany, Oct. 3, 1932; s. Wilhelm and Auguste (Rau) H.; Dr. rer. nat., U. Tübingen (Germany), 1959, habilitation, 1962; m. Isolde Rösler, May 11, 1963; children—Claudia, Georg. Math. statistician U. Tübingen, 1959, dozent, 1962; vis. asst. prof. Tulane U., 1960, asso. prof., 1963-65, prof., 1965—; vis. prof. Inst. Advanced Study, Princeton, N.J., 1967; vis. prof. U. Paris (France), 1973. Alfred P. Sloan Found. fellow, 1966-68. Recipient E. Harris Harbison award Danforth Found., 1970. Mem. Am., German, French math. socs., Sigma Xi. Author several books. Contbr. articles to profl. jours. Home: 7532 Hampson St New Orleans LA 70118

HOGAN, EDWARD LEO, med. educator; b. Arlington, Mass., July 26, 1932; s. Patrick Francis and Margaret Mary (McSweeney) H.; B.S. summa cum laude, Tufts U., 1953, M.S. magna cum laude, 1957; m. Gail R. Manning, July 1, 1961; children—Patrick Francis, Maryellen, Maura Gail, Timothy William. Intern, Barnes Hosp., St. Louis, 1957-58: resident neurology Boston City Hosp., 1959-61; fellow in neurochemistry Tufts U. Sch. Medicine, Boston. 1964-66; asst. prof. medicine U. N.C. Sch. Medicine, Chapel Hill 1966-69, asso. prof., 1969-73; prof., chmn. dept. neurology Med. U. S.C., Charleston, 1973—. Served with M.C., AUS, 1961-63. Nat. Inst. Neurol. Disease and Stroke fellow, 1963-66. Contbr. articles to profl. jours. Home: 10 Legare St Charleston SC 29401

HOGAN, ELWOOD LEON, judge; b. Mobile, Ala., July 13, 1930; s. Walter Leroy and Mary Rose (Batchelor) H.; B.S., U. Ala., 1951, LL.B., 1956; grad. Nat. Coll. State Judiciary, U. Nev., 1973; m. Patricia Jean Russell, Dec. 15, 1956 (div. Jan. 1970); children—Patricia Lauren, Elwood Leon, Russell Lindsay, Leslie Rose. Adjuster Comml. Credit Corp., Mobile, Ala., 1951; admitted to Ala. bar, 1956: law clk. Justice Stakely, Ala. Supreme Ct., 1956; asso. Sullivan & Cameron, Mobile, 1956-57; partner DuBois & Hogan, Mobile, 1957-58, Hogan & Helt, Mobile, 1959-60, Hogan, Helt & Conway, Mobile, 1964-65; judge Gen. Sessions Ct. of Mobile, 1967-70; circuit judge 18th Jud. Circuit, Mobile, 1970—. Dir., Fowl River Marina, Inc., Mobile, Economy Auto Parts, Inc., Mobile. Mem. Ala. Ho. of Reps., 1962-69. Trustee Salvation Army. Served as 1st lt. AUS, 1951-53. Mem. Am. Judicature Soc., Am., Mobile bar assns., Ala. State Bar, Mardi Gras Mystic Soc., Alpha Kappa Psi, Phi Alpha Delta. Methodist (mem. ofcl. bd. 1960—). Kiwanian. Club: Athelstan (Mobile). Democrat. Home: 2306 Dauphin St Mobile AL 36606 Office: County Court House Court Room 2 Mobile AL 36602

HOGAN, MILTON EARL, banker; b. Durham, N.C., Feb. 5, 1919; s. Milton Earl and Carrie Lee (Pickard) H.; B.S., U. N.C., 1939; m. Mary Edith Horsfield, Aug. 14, 1943; children—Alice (Mrs. Arthur J. Slayton), Richard Horsfield. Clk. Planters Nat. Bank, 1939-41; examiner for U.S. Controller of currency, 1941-48; v.p., trust officer N.C. Nat. Bank, 1948-62; v.p. B.C. Remedy Co., 1962-67; v.p., sr. trust officer Bank of N.C., N.A., Jacksonville, 1967-73; sec. Bancshares of N.C., Inc., 1967-73; v.p., trust officer First Nat. Bank Pompano Beach (Fla.), 1973—. Mem. N.C. Order Long Leaf Pine. Served to 1st lt., AUS, 1942-46; PTO. Mem. Carolina Playmakers, Alpha Tau Omega, Delta Sigma Phi. Episcopalian. Editor: Attorney's Handbook, 1971. Home: 6540 NE 21st Av Fort Lauderdale FL 33308 Office: 2400 Atlantic Av Pompano Beach FL 33060

HOGAN, RICHARD PHILLIPS, lawyer; b. Troy, O., June 21, 1931; s. George Thomas and Florence Ann (Phillips) H.; B.S., Xavier U., 1953; postgrad. Georgetown U., 1956-58; LL.B., S.Tex. Coll. Law, 1961; m. Jane Conti, June 21, 1958; children—Richard Phillips, Mary Sean, Kathleen Keally. Statistician, Hwy. Planning Commn., Washington, 1955-56; law clk. Commn. on Govt. Security, Washington, 1956-57; sales rep. Minn. Mining and Mfg. Co., St. Paul, Albuquerque, Houston, 1957-62; admitted to Tex. bar, 1962: asst. dist. atty. Harris County Dist. Atty. Office, Houston, 1962-63; partner Helm, Jones & Pletcher, Houston, 1963—. First v.p. Westchester Jr. High Sch. P.T.A., 1972-73; pres. People for Quality Edn., 1973-74; co-chmn. alumni campaign leadership S.Tex. Coll. Law, 1973—. Mem. speakers bur. Dem. Presdl. campaigns Harris County, 1964-68. Served as 1st lt., arty. AUS, 1953-55. Fellow Tex. Bar Found.; Houston Legal Found. (dir. 1972—); mem. Am. Judicature Soc., Am., Houston (1st v.p. 1971-72, dir. 1969-71) bar assns., State Bar Tex. (dir. 1972—), Tex. (dir. 1967-71), Houston (pres. 1968-69) trial lawyers assn., Nottingham Civic Assn. (dir. 1965-68), Xavier U. Alumni Assn. (Houston chpt. pres. 1969-72), Execs. Internat., Phi Alpha Delta. Roman Catholic. Clubs: Pine Forest Country, Athletic (Houston). Home: 13931 Pebblebrook Dr Houston TX 77024 Office: Suite 800 711 Fannin Bldg Savings Bldg Houston TX 77002

HOGAN, ROBERT LEO, computer leasing co. exec.; b. Johnson City, N.Y., May 27, 1935; s. Paul William and Anna (Sejan) H.; student Pensacola Jr. Coll., 1957, Coll. Great Falls, 1965-67; m. Claire McGowan, Feb. 20, 1954; children—Elaine, Mark, Gail. Sr. educator computer dept. Univac Corp., Washington, 1965-67, account mgr. NASA Manned Spacecraft Center, Houston, 1967-68; regional mgr. U. Computing Co., Washington, 1968-69, Computer Leasing Co., Arlington, Va., 1969—. Vice-pres. Young Republican Coub, Coll. Great Falls (Mont.), 1966-67; precinct capt. Fairfax County Rep. Com., Fairfax, Va., 1969. Served with USAF, 1952-65. Mem. Assn. Computer Machinery, Alpha Phi Omega. Roman Catholic. Home: 3166 Musket Ct Fairfax VA 22030 Office: 11480 Sunset Hills Rd Reston VA 22070

HOGAN, ROBERT STEADHAM, physician; b. Birmingham, Ala., Nov. 3, 1922; s. Marion Elias and Kathleen (Steadham) H.; student Ala. Poly. Inst., 1941-43; B.S., U. Ala., 1947; M.D., Med. Coll. Ala., 1951; m. Alice Katherine Hardin, June 6, 1949; children—Robert Steadham, Nelle Lindsay, Richard Hardin, James Baker. Intern Univ. Hosp., Birmingham, 1951-52, resident, 1952-54, chief resident, 1955-56; NIH trainee arthritis, Bethesda, Md., 1954-55; practice medicine specializing in internal medicine, Birmingham, 1956-70, specializing in rheumatology, Birmingham, 1970—; mem. staff Univ., Bapt., St. Vincent's hosps.; clin. asso. prof. medicine Ala. Sch. Medicine, 1964—; med. dir. Am. Educators Life Ins. Co., 1968—; cons. VA Hosp., 1960—. Mem. State Bd. Examiners Nursing Home Adminstrs., 1970—. Bd. dirs. Ala. chpt. Arthritis and Rheumatism Found. Served to 1st lt. USAAF, 1942-45; prisoner of war, Germany. Decorated Purple Heart, Air medal with oak leaf clusters. Diplomate Am. Bd. Internal Medicine. Fellow A.C.P.; mem. A.A.A.S., Am. Rheumatism Assn., A.M.A., Am., Ala., Birmingham socs. internal medicine, Ala., Jefferson County med. socs., Birmingham C. of C., Kappa Alpha, Phi Chi, Alpha Omega Alpha, Omicron Delta Kappa, Phi Chi. Unitarian-Universalist. Rotarian. Club: Country (Birmingham, Ala.). Home: 2926 Canterbury Rd Birmingham AL 35223 Office: Med Arts Bldg 1023 20th St S Birmingham AL 35205

HOGARTH, CHARLES PINCKNEY, coll. pres.; b. Brunson, S.C., Nov. 14, 1911; s. Charles Pinckney and Maude (Griner) H.; B.S. Clemson Coll., 1932; B.D., Yale, 1935, M.A., 1941; Ph.D., Peabody Coll., 1947; m. Nancy Harris, Dec. 14, 1940; children—Nancy (Mrs. Hal McClanahan), Charles. Sec. Christian Assn., student counselor Pa. State Coll., 1935-37; asst. to pres., dir. pub. relations Lander Coll., Greenwood, S.C., 1939-41; dir. publ. relations, bus. mgr., tchr. Detroit Country Day Sch., 1941-42; dean Ward-Belmont Coll., Nashville, 1942-47; registrar Fla. State U., 1947-49; v.p., prof. psychology Gulf Park Coll., Gulfport, Miss., 1949-50, pres., 1950-52; pres. Miss. U. for Women, Columbus, 1952—. Lectr., Europe, summer 1934; research asso. Am. Council Edn., Harvard, 1938. Bd. dirs. area council Boy Scouts Am., Columbus Community Chest; chmn. bd. dirs. Miss. U. for Women Found. Mem. Columbus C. of C., N.E.A., Miss. Assn. Sch. Adminstrs., So. Assn. Colls. for Women (past pres.), Miss. Assn. Colls. (past pres.), Jr.-Sr. Coll. Conf. Miss. (past pres.), So. U. Conf. (past pres.), Am. Assn. State Colls. and Univs. (state rep.), Newcomen Soc. N.A., Pub. Instns. Higher Learning in So. States (past pres.), Miss. Edn. Assn., Pres.'s Council of State Instns. of Higher Learning in Miss. (past pres., past chmn.), Am. Assn. Sch. Adminstrs., A.I.M. (past mem. pres.'s council), Inst. Internat. Edn. (nat. council, So. regional adv. bd.), Phi Theta Kappa, Pi Tau Chi (nat. trustee), Chi Psi, Pi Gamma Mu, Kappa Pi, Pi Kappa Delta, Phi Kappa Phi, Phi Delta Kappa. Methodist. Mason. Clubs: Columbus Country, Rotary (dir.). Author: Policy Making in Colleges Related to the Methodist Church, 1949; Crisis in Higher Education, 1957; also articles in ednl. publs. Home: 1217 2d Av S Columbus MS 37901

HOGARTH, FRANCES HARRIS (MRS. CHARLES P. HOGARTH), clubwoman; b. Pensacola, Fla., July 12, 1913; d. Edward Payne and Eva (Joiner) Harris; student Freemans Bus. Coll., U. Mich.; m. Charles P. Hogarth, Dec. 14, 1940; children—Nancy Eva, Charles P. Pres.'s wife, ofcl. hostess, interior decorator cons. Gulf Park Coll., Gulfport, Miss., 1950-52; Miss. State Coll. for Women, Columbus, 1952—. Mem. Hosp. Jr. League, Albany, Ga., 1934-38; sec. Music Civic Assn., 1938; social worker A.R.C., Detroit, 1941, Nashville, 1942-44; pres. Young Women's Bible Class, West End Meth. Ch., Nashville, 1945; corr. sec. Woman's Soc. Christian Service, Nashville, 1945; pres. Ward-Belmont Jr. Coll. Woman's Club, Nashville, 1945; Columbus Pilgrimage Homes, 1952—; patroness Delta Debutante Assembly, Greenville, 1966-67, Debutante Assembly N.Y., 1967-68, Internat. Debutante Ball, 1967-68. Recipient letter appreciation Miss. State Coll. Women, 1965, 69, 70, named Queen of Hearts Faculty Wives Club, 1969. Past mem. Fannie Battle Social Workers, Fla. State U. Faculty Wives Club, Tallahassee, Gulf Coast Garden Club, Gulfport, Miss., Merry Maskers Dance Club, 20th Century Study Club, Gulfport Yacht Club, Gulfport Jr. Aux., Epsilon Sigma Alpha, now mem. Met. Dinner Club, Miss. Ofcl. Women's Clubs, Jackson, Miss. State Coll. for Women Faculty Wives Club, Columbus Country Club; Queen's Cove Club, Ltd., Freeport, Grand Bahamas (charter). Home: 1217 College Av Columbus MS 39701

HOGGE, JEROME WALLACE, JR., savs. and loan exec.; b. Newport News, Va., Oct. 18, 1935; s. Jerome Wallace and Clarke Augusta (Wallace) H.; B.B.A., Coll. William and Mary, 1960; m. Martha Anne Nicholls, Mar. 16, 1957; children—Jacquelyn P., Jerome Wallace III. With Chesapeake & Potomac Telephone Co., Newport News, Va., 1953-61; with Newport News Savs. & Loan Assn. (Va.), 1961—, v.p., 1965-67, chief exec. officer, 1967—. Vice pres. Family Service-Travelers Aid, 1968-69: vice chmn. Peninsula United Fund, 1973, chmn., 1974. Bd. dirs. Boys Club, Am. Red Cross, YMCA, Proclaim Center, Big Brothers. Served to lt. comdr. USCGR, 1960-61. Mem. Am. Inst. Real Estate Appraisers. Baptist (deacon 1968-73; treas. day sch.). Rotarian (pres. 1970). Home: 70 Settlers Rd Newport News VA 23606 Office: 2600 Washington Av Newport News VA 23607

HOGUE, TRUDEAU J., JR., elec. engr.; b. Baton Rouge, July 24, 1917; s. Trudeau J. and Ethel (Hart) H.; B.S., La. State U., 1940; m. Lois Gayle Akers, June 18, 1943; one son, Trudeau J., III. Jr. engr. South Central Bell Telephone Co,, 1942-72; engring. sales exec. R.J. Tricon Co., 1972—. Mem. exec. bd. Istrouma area council Boy Scouts Am. Served from 2d lt. to maj., AUS, 1942-45. Mem. Assn. U.S. Army, I.E.E.E., La. Engring. Soc. (pres.), Nat. Soc. Profl. Engrs. Democrat. Roman Catholic. Kiwanian. Club: Sherwood Forest Country, Camelot. Home: 9833 N Parkview Dr Baton Rouge LA 70815

HOLCOMB, CHARLES EDWARD, chem. engr.; b. Colorado Springs, Colo., July 17, 1924; s. Trafford Gilbert and Mattie Lee (Shy) H.; B.S., U. Colo., 1949; M.S., U. Wis., 1951, Ph.D., 1953; m. Margaret Sarah Turnbull, May 20, 1946; children—Brett Ian, Karen Margaret. Instr., U. Wis., Madison, 1949-53; research engr. E.I. duPont, Buffalo, 1953-58, research engr., Circleville, O., 1958-60, staff engr., 1960-65, research asso., Wilmington, Del., 1967-71, Brevard, N.C., 1971—. Pres. Knollwood Village Assn., 1964-65; active Boy Scouts Am., 1959-65. Served with AUS, 1942-46. Decorated Bronze Star medal. Mem. Am. Inst. Chem. Engrs., Sigma Xi, Tau Beta Pi, Sigma Tau, Phi Lambda Upsilon, Alpha Chi Sigma. Presbyn. (deacon 1965—). Mason. Co-patentee in field. Home: Route 3 Box 68 Hendersonville NC 28739 Office: PO Box 267 Brevard NC 28712

HOLCOMB, CHARLIE CALVIN, supt. schs.; b. Leedey, Okla., Oct. 17, 1912; s. Charles Augusta and Elmer (Williams); A.B., Southwestern State Coll., 1935; M.Ed., Okla. U., 1950, Ed.D., 1963; m. Vinita Corene Ward, Mar. 12, 1937; children—Charlotte (Mrs. Jimmie Newberry), Sandra Jeanne. Tchr. schs. Custer & Roger Mills counties, Okla., 1931-33; coach, prin. Trail (Okla.) Schs., 1934-37; tchr. Rhea Sch., Okla., 1937-38; prin. supt. Putnam (Okla.) Schs., 1938-48; supt. Lone Wolf (Okla.) Schs., 1952-57, Burns Flat (Okla.) Schs., 1948-52, 57-70; supt. Western Okla. Vocational Tech. Sch., Burns Flat, 1970—. Dir. Dill State Bank, Washita County Indsl. Corp. Dist. chmn. Lions Okla. Individual Opportunity for Achievement

Boys Ranch, 1964-65; mem. Washita County Health Bd., 1966—. Sec., treas. Midwestern Okla. Indsl. Found., 1966—; bd. dirs. Okla. Lions Eye Bank. Mem. Okla. (dir. 1964-66), County Oklahoma edn. assns., County Schoolmasters (pres. 1963-64), N.E.A., Am., Okla. assns. sch. adminstrs., Comparative Edn. Soc., Phi Delta Kappa. Democrat. Baptist. Lion (pres. 1963-64, dist. gov. 1969-70), Mason (32 deg.); mem. Order Eastern Star. Club: Burns Flat Sports. Home: 202 Bryan Av Burns Flat OK 73624 Office: PO Box 149 Burns Flat OK 73624

HOLCOMB, ELAINE PARKS (MRS. LUTHER J. HOLCOMB), sociologist, writer; b. Dallas, Nov. 22, 1916; d. Joseph Floyd and Lucy (Largent) Parks; student Randolph-Macon Woman's Coll., 1934-35, B.A., Baylor U., 1938; M.A., So. Meth. U., 1956; m. Luther J. Holcomb, Sept. 6, 1938; children—Henry, Jan (Mrs. Larry W. Flowers). With new accounts dept. Riggs Nat. Bank, Washington, 1970-71. Mem. White House Conf. on Children and Youth, 1960; pres. United Ch. Women of Dallas, 1958-59, pres. United Ch. Women of Tex., 1962-65; mem. nat. nominating com. of Ch. Women United of Nat. Council Chs., 1967-71; mem. women's planning com. Japan Internat. Christian U. Found.; bd. mgrs. Nat. United Ch. Women, Nat. Council of Chs., 1962-65; mem. exec. com. United Ch. Women of Nat. Capitol Area, 1965-68, Women's div. Washington Nat. Conf. Christian and Jews, 1965-67; ofcl. rep. to Council Nat. Orgns. for Children and Youth, 1965; adminstrv. dir. Pastoral Inst., Washington, 1968-70. Mem. bd. Girl's Found. Dallas Fedn. Women's Clubs. Recipient Brotherhood medallion Nat. Conf. Christians and Jews, 1965, Mem. Am. Assn. U. Women, Kappa Alpha Theta. Baptist. Contbr. articles to profl. jours. Home: Harbour Sq 540 N St SW Apt S604 Washington DC 20024

HOLCOMB, JAMES ELDON, elec. mfg. co. exec.; b. Rogers, Ark., Aug. 11, 1912; s. Charles Wesley and Zola Olena (Proudfit) H.; B.S., Greenville Coll., 1934; M.S., U. Ill., 1936; m. Monica Winnifred Wells, Dec. 21, 1945; children—Anne (Mrs. Steven Hunter), David James, Charles Wesley, Lynn, Beth Louise. High voltage lab. engr. Gen. Electric Co., Pittsfield, Mass., 1941-45, design engr. distbn. transformers, 1945-47, devel. engr., mfg. distbn. transformers, 1947-68; v.p. engring. Howard Industries, Inc., mfrs. distbn. transformers, Laurel, Miss., 1968—. Vice chmn. Mt. Greylock Regional High Sch. Com., Williamstown, 1960-68. Registered profl. engr., N.Y., Mass.. Mem. Nat. Soc. Profl. Engrs., I.E.E.E., Am. Soc. Testing and Materials. Episcopalian. Mason. Patentee in field. Home: 815 Cherry Lane Laurel MS 39440 Office: PO Box 1588 Laurel MS 39440

HOLCOMB, LUTHER JENKINS, govt. ofcl.; b. Yazoo City, Miss., Dec. 19, 1911; s. Thomas Luther and Willie (Jenkins) H.; student U. Okla., 1931-35; So. Baptist Theol. Sem., Louisville, 1936-38; D.D., Howard Payne Coll., 1957; m. Elaine Parks, Sept. 6, 1938; children—Henry, Jan (Mrs. Larry Wayne Flowers). Ordained to ministry Bapt. Ch., 1940; leader in youth meetings in 20 states, Nashville, 1938-39; pastor 1st Ch., Durant, Okla., 1940-42, Temple and Luther Rice Meml. Chs., Washington, 1942-46, Lakewood Ch., Dallas, 1946-58; exec. dir. Greater Dallas Council Chs., 1958-65; vice chmn. Equal Employment Opportunity Com., Washington, 1965-74. Vis. instr. dept. religion So. Methodist U., 1944; spl. religious emphasis missions for Air Force in Far East, 1953, 62, Arctic, 1956, Central Am., 1958; ofcl. adviser 53d session Econ. and Social Conf. UN, Geneva, Switzerland, 1972. Commr. Dallas Housing Authority, 1955-65; chmn. Tex. Adv. Com. to U.S. Civil Rights Com., 1963-65; dir. Council on World Affairs, 1955-65, sec.-treas. 1961-63, v.p. 1963-65. Bd. dirs. Community Chest, Dallas, 1951-53, Child Guidance Clinic, 1955-62, Timberlawn Found., 1960-67, Sr. Citizens Found., 1968—. Mem. Washington Fedn. Chs. (sec. 1943-46, exec. com. 1943-46), Tex. State Soc. in Washington (pres. 1972), Delta Upsilon. Home: Harbour Sq 540 N St SW Apt S604 Washington DC 20024 Office: 1800 G St NW Washington DC 20506

HOLCOMBE, MAXINE BOGGAN (MRS. THOMPSON A. HOLCOMBE, JR.), educator; b. Memphis; d. Marvin Brooks and Josephine (Shea) Boggan; B.S., Delta State Coll., 1932; M.A., George Peabody Coll., 1933; m. Nathan House, 1937 (dec. 1947); m. 2d, Thompson A. Holcombe, Jr., Apr. 22, 1950. Mem. faculty art Delta State Coll., Cleveland, Miss., 1933-35, 60—, asso. prof., 1968—; comml. artist, advt. mgr., Memphis, 1935-39; art agt. Am. Authors and Artists, N.Y.C., 1939-43; dir. art Greenville (Miss.) City Schs., 1944-60. Designer, dir. Greenville Christmas parade, 1952-60; cons. Christmas parades Cleveland C. of C., 1966, Leland, Miss., 1967; mem. summer staff Miss. State U., 1949, state sch. systems evaluation com., 1960—; participant First Conf. on Adminstrn. Fine Arts sponsored by Ohio State U. at N.Y. U., 1967; state chmn. Youth Art Month, 1968-70; mem. Cleveland Arts Council. Exhibited one man show Miss. Art Assn., Jackson, Capitol Savs. & Loan, Jackson, 1972; exhibited Delta State Coll. Shows, McCarty Art Gallery, Monteagle, Tenn., Crasstie Art Festival, Cleveland, U. Miss. Recipient Nat. 3d pl. award for promotion Am. Art Week Miss., Am. Artists Profl. League, 1966; Outstanding Alumnus award Delta State Coll., 1969; Distinguished Service award Jr. C. of C.; named Outstanding Civic Contbr., Miss. Federated Women's Clubs, 1972. Research grantee to study art appreciation for elementary schs., 1969-70. Mem. Nat. League Am. Pen Women (br. pres. 1968-69), Nat., Miss. (pres. 1968-69) art edn. assns., Southeastern Art Assn., Twin Cities Little Theatre, Whistle Stop Theatre, Miss. Classroom Tchrs. Assn., Miss. Edn. Assn., Kappa Delta, Delta Kappa Gamma, Kappa Pi. Designer, supr. booth assembly for Miss., Miami Nat. Conv. N.E.A., 1965; illustrator (with Nathan House): Games the World Around, 1941; designer, dir. Children's Circus Studio, Miss. Arts Festival, 1972. Contbr. illustrations to Nat. Edn. Jour., Miss. Edn. Advance; contbg. author, cons. Handbook on Elementary Art for Mississippi Schools, 1961. Home: 209 S First Av Cleveland MS 38732

HOLDEN, JAMES HARTWELL, investment counselor; b. Oklahoma City, Dec. 23, 1935; s. Rex Hartwell and Agnes (Maney) H.; B.B.A., U. Okla., 1957; m. Jo Ann Hodgson, Dec. 1, 1962; children—James Hartwell, Ann Elizabeth, Margaret Monroe. Investment officer Bank of N.Y., N.Y.C., 1958-66; pres., co-founder Holden, Tolbert & Co., Oklahoma City, 1967—; partner Resource Analysis & Mgmt. Group, Oklahoma City, 1970—; dir. S.W. Factories, Inc., Oklahoma City, 1969-72. Bd. dirs. New World Sch., Oklahoma City, 1966—, Okla. chpt. A.R.C., 1968-70. Mem. Okla. Soc. Financial Analyst (exec. com. 1973, treas. 1973), Sigma Alpha Epsilon. Republican. Presbyn. Rotarian. Home: 3300 Harvey Pkwy Oklahoma City OK 73118 Office: 2500 First Nat Center Oklahoma City OK 73102

HOLDER, HOWARD RANDOLPH, broadcasting corp. exec.; b. Moline, Ill., Nov. 14, 1916; s. James William and Charlotte (Brega) H.; B.A. Augustana Coll., 1939; m. Clementi Lacey-Baker, Feb. 21, 1942; children—Janice Clementi (Mrs. Collins), Susan Charlotte (Mrs. Charles A. Rudolph), Marjory Estelle, Howard Randolph. With radio sta. WHBF, Rock Island, Ill., 1939-41, radio sta. WOC, Davenport, Ia., 1945-47, radio sta. WINN, Louisville, 1947, radio sta. WRFC, Athens, Ga., 1948-56, radio sta. WGAU-WNGC, Athens, 1956—; pres. Clarke Broadcasting Corp., Athens, 1956—, Mid-West Broadcasting Corp., Griffin, Ga., 1965—; v.p. Washington Properties, Inc., Rome, Ga., 1969—; dir. Citizens & So. Nat. Bank Athens. Mem. adv. bd. Salvation Army, chmn., 1962, 63; chmn. Athens Parks and Recreation Bd., 1952-62; mem. adv. bd. Athens-Clarke County A.R.C., 1950-70, Clarke County Juvenile Ct., 1960-72; chmn. region IV Am. Cancer Soc., 1968; chmn. Cherokee dist. Boy Scouts Am., 1966-67, mem. adv. bd. N.E. Ga. Area council; co-pres. Friends Ga. Museum Art, 1974; sec. adv. bd Henry W. Grady Sch. Journalism, U. Ga.; bd. dirs. Athens Crime Prevention Com., 1960-70, Augustana Coll. Alumni Assn.; mem. Model Cities Policy Bd., 1970-71, Georgians for Safer Hwys., 1970. Served with AUS, 1941-46; ETO. Recipient Silver Beaver award Boy Scouts Am., 1973; Outstanding Achievement award Augusta Coll. Alumni Assn., 1973, Robert Stolz medaille, 1973; named Boss of Year, Athens Jr. C. of C., 1959; Broadcaster-Citizen of Year, Ga. Assn. Broadcasters, 1962; Employer of Yr., Athens Bus. and Profl. Women, 1969; Ky. col., 1961; Athens Citizen of Year, Athens Woman's Club, 1971. Mem. Res. Officers Assn. (pres. Athens 1962), Nat., Ga. (pres. 1961) assns. broadcasters, Ga. A.P. Broadcasters Assn. (pres. 1963), Internat. Platform Assn., Athens Area C. of C. (pres. 1970), Golden Quill, Sigma Delta Chi, Alpha Delta Sigma, Alpha Psi Omega, Phi Omega Phi, Di Gamma Kappa (Ga. Pioneer Broadcaster of Year award 1971). Rotarian (pres. Athens club 1957-58, dist. gov. 1969-70 Citizen of Yr. award 1971). Clubs: Gridiron, Touchdown (pres. Athens 1963-64). Home: 383 W View Dr Athens GA 30601 Office: 850 Bobbin Mill Rd Athens GA 30604

HOLDER, WILLIAM MOODY, pub. relations exec.; b. Tenn., Sept. 16, 1919; s. Rebble Potter and Mary Ella (Miller) H.; B.S., U. Tenn., 1942; m. Frances Nelson, Sept. 23, 1945 (div. May 1974); 1 dau., Sally (Mrs. Gary Robert Kilmer). Feature writer Nashville Tennesseean, 1944-48; advt. mgr. Blevins Popcorn Co., Nashville, 1949-53; account exec. Noble-Dury & Asso., Nashville, 1955-58, v.p., 1958-65, exec. v.p., 1965-69; chmn. Holder, Kennedy & Co., Nashville, 1965—; dir. pub. affairs and information Nat. Life & Accident Ins. Co., Nashville, 1972—. Guest lectr. pub. relations and advt. at colls. and univs. Served with AUS, 1942-44. Mem. Pub. Relations Soc. Am., U. Tenn. Nashville Assos., Pi Kappa Alpha. Episcopalian. Clubs: Belle Meade Country, Cumberland (Nashville). Home: 2601 Hillsboro Rd Nashville TN 37212 Office: National Life Center Nashville TN 37250

HOLDERNESS, HAYWOOD DAIL, telephone co. exec.; b. Tarboro, N.C., July 30, 1909; s. George A. and Harriet (Howard) H.; A.B., U.N.C., 1931; M.A., Wharton Sch. Finance U. Pa., 1933; m. Nancy Burton Braswell, Mar. 19, 1938; children—Haywood Dail, James B., Zelle B. (Mrs. John C. Jester III), Nancy duVal (Mrs. Thomas S. Reams), Russell B. With Carolina Tel. & Tel. Co., Tarboro, 1933—, sec., treas., 1937-57, v.p., 1945-57, pres., 1957-73, chmn. bd., chief exec. officer, 1973-74, also dir., mem. exec. com.; dir. United Utilities, Inc., Kansas City, Mo., Rocky Mount Investment Co. (N.C.), Sero Corp., Rocky Mount. Past chmn. Tarboro United Fund. Trustee Union Theol. Sem., Richmond, St. Andrews Presbyn. Coll. Recipient Silver Beaver award Boy Scouts Am.; Distinguished Citizens award Gov. N.C., 1967. Mem. U.S. (pres. 1966-67), N.C. (past pres.) ind. telephone assns., U. N.C. Alumni Assn. (pres. 1960-61). Presbyn. (elder). Rotarian (past pres. Tarboro). Home: 805 S Howard Circle Tarboro NC 27886 Office: Carolina Tel & Tel Co Tarboro NC 27886

HOLDERNESS, HOWARD, life ins. exec.; b. Tarboro, N.C., Nov. 2, 1902; s. George Allen and Harriet (Howard) H.; A.B., U. N.C., 1923; LL.D., U. N.C. at Chapel Hill, 1966, at Greensboro, 1969; M.B.A., Harvard, 1925; m. Adelaide Fortune, Apr. 4, 1936; children—Adelaide Lucinda, Howard, Alexandra Fortune, Richard Thurston, Pamela Louisa. Chmn. bd. Jefferson Standard Life Ins. Co., Greensboro, Jefferson-Pilot Corp.; dir. Pilot Life Ins. Co., Jefferson Standard Broadcasting Co., Carolina Tel. & Tel. Co., Tarbaro, Duke Power Co., N.C. Burlington Industries; trustee Wachovia Realty Investments. Civilian aide to Sec. of Army for N.C., 1958-62. Bd. dirs. N.C. Meml. Hosp., Chapel Hill. Recipient Citation for Distinguished Citizenship, N.C. Citizens Assn., 1970. Mem. Inst. Life Ins. (dir., mem. exec. com. 1957-60, chmn. bd. 1959), Life Ins. Assn. Am. (dir. 1957-60). Home: 2000 Granville Rd Greensboro NC 27408 Office: PO Box 21008 Greensboro NC 27420

HOLLADAY, CARLTON EDWIN, judge; b. Carrollton, Va., Nov. 10, 1902; s. Walter Jackson and Bettie (Fulgham) H.; A.B., Coll. William and Mary, 1924; m. Mary Sue Davis, June 27, 1931. Admitted to Va. bar, 1925, practiced in Va., 1925-58; judge 3d Jud. Circuit Va., 1958-73, 6th Jud. Circuit, 1973—; past v.p., dir. Bank of Sussex & Surry. Past mem. adv. bd., appeal agt. SSS; Dollar a Year speaker War Finance Com., 1943-44; past mem. bd. dirs., pres. 1934 Ruritan Nat.; trustee Va. Methodist Children's Home, 1962-66. Mem. Am., Va. bar assns., Nat. Conf. State Trial Judges, William and Mary Law Sch. Assn. (past pres.), Tidewater Automobile Assn. (hon. dir.), Order White Jacket, Phi Beta Kappa, Omicron Delta Kappa, Sigma Pi. Methodist (mem. ofcl. bd., lay leader, supt. Ch. Sch.). Mason (Shriner). Club: Wakefield Sportsmen's. Home: Wakefield VA 23888

HOLLADAY, CHARLES EDWIN, supt. schs.; b. Newton, Miss., July 12, 1918; s. Clarence O. and Gladys (Bounds) H.; B.A., Miss. Coll., 1946; M.A., Peabody Coll., 1949; Ed.D., U. Miss., 1969; m. Bess Edward, May 25, 1939; children—Charles E., Stephen E. Tchr. Duncan (Miss.) Pub. Schs., 1941-43, Enochs Jr. High Sch., Jackson, Miss., 1946-49; asst. prin. Central High Sch., Jackson, 1949-53, prin., 1953-58; supt. schs., Tupelo, Miss., 1958—. Exec. sec. N.E. Miss. TV Council, 1961—; chmn. Miss. Accrediting Commn., 1963-65; ednl. auditor Fed. project; developer ednl. mgmt. tng. program for adminstrs. N.E. Miss. Trustee Blue Mountain (Miss.) Coll. Served with USAAF, 1942-46. Recipient merit award for outstanding ednl. program Miss. Econ. Council, 1966. Mem. N.E.A. (Pace Maker award for Miss. 1965), Miss. (past pres. adult edn. div.), Tupelo edn. assns., Miss. Secondary Sch. Prins. Assn. (past pres.), Am., Miss. assns. sch. adminstrs., Mental Health Assn. Baptist (deacon). Rotarian (past dir.). Home: 626 Magnolia Dr Tupelo MS 33801 Office: PO Box 557 Tupelo MS 33801

HOLLADAY, DURAND ALLEN, lawyer, mortgage firm exec.; b. Montgomery, Ala., Mar. 15, 1925; s. Will Lee and Ruby (Allen) H.; B.S. in Aero. Engring., Ga. Inst. Tech., 1945; J.D., U. Miami, 1949; m. Mary Blanche Faver, Oct. 14, 1945; children—William Marshall, Patricia Lynn. Admitted to Fla. bar, 1949; practiced in Miami, Fla., 1949-65; mem. firm Holladay, Swann & Gardner and predecessor firm; gen. counsel Mortgage Cons., Coral Gables, Fla., 1962-65, pres., 1965-72, chmn. bd., 1972—; trustee, sec. Continental Mortgage Investors, Boston, 1966—, mng. trustee, 1972—; pres. Diversified Advisers, Inc., Coral Gables, 1969-72; chmn. bd. trustees, mng. trustee Diversified Mortgage Investors, 1969-72. Trustee U. Miami, Baptist Hosp. Served with USNR, 1945-46. Mem. Am. Bar Assn., Fla. Bar, Phi Alpha Delta, Pi Kappa Alpha. Baptist (Sunday sch. bd. 1963-69). Mason. Club: Nat. Exchange (regional v.p. 1962-63, state pres. 1959-60). Home: 4430 Santa Maria Coral Gables FL 33146 Office: 5915 Ponce de Leon Coral Gables FL 33146

HOLLADAY, JAMES FRANKLIN, wire mill exec.; b. Birmingham, Ala., Apr. 5, 1922; s. Allen A. and Mary (Campbell) H.; B.S., Ga. Inst. Tech., 1950; m. Anna Wedsworth, July 17, 1948; children—James F., David Allen, Cinthia Ann. Plant engr. Erwin Mills, Inc., Stonewall, Miss., 1950-52; plant engr. Southwire Co., Carrolton, Ga., 1952-63, v.p., 1963—, dir., 1957—. Chmn. Elec. Bd., Carrollton, 1958—; pres. Carrollton Jr. High P.T.A., 1967-68; mem. exec. com. So. Bapt. Conv. Home Mission Bd. Served to 1st lt. Inf. AUS, 1942-46. Named Plant Engr. of Year S.E. U.S., 1966. Mem. Ga. Past Dist. Govs. Assn. (pres. 1966-67), I.E.E.E., Am. Inst. Plant Engrs. (internat. sec., internat. pres. 1973-74). Baptist (deacon). Lion (dist. gov. 1963-64). Clubs: Dixie Management (v.p. 1963—), West Ga. Executive (Carrollton, Ga.). Home: 305 Kramer St Carrollton GA 30117 Office: Southwire Co Fertilla St Carrollton GA 30117

HOLLADAY, JAMES WILLIAM, dentist; b. Montpelier, Ky., June 3, 1921; s. Joe Douglas and Bessie (Young) H.; student Lindsey Wilson Coll., 1946-48, U. Ky., 1948-49; D.D.S., U. Louisville, 1953; m. Claudette Imogene Marcum, Oct. 27, 1962. Individual dental practice, Russell Springs, Ky., 1953-54, Columbia, 1954—; staff Adair County Meml. Hosp. Mem. Adair County Bd. Health, 1960-64; mem. Ky. Bd. Dental Examiners, 1965—, pres. 1967-68; mem. Ky. Bd. Dentistry, 1973—. Bd. dirs., sec.-treas. Summit Manor Nursing Home, 1967-71. Served with Signal Corps, AUS, 1942-43. Mem. Am., Ky. (exec. bd. 1961-63, 68—) dental assns., South Central Ky. Dist. Dental Soc. (pres. 1963-64, sec.-treas. 1964-65). Columbia-Adair County C. of C. (pres. 1966; chmn. indsl. com. 1973), Delta Sigma Delta, Omicron Delta Kappa, Sigma Delta, Omicron Kappa Upsilon, Phi Kappa Phi, Phi Delta. Democrat. Baptist. Lion (pres. 1972). Club: Pinewood Country. Office: 209 Burkesville St Columbia KY 42728

HOLLAND, BEN HANSON, concrete products co. exec.; b. nr. Manassas, Ga., July 4, 1913; s. Walter Deal and Mary (Jackson) H.; student Ga. So. Coll., 1932-34; m. Frances Wright, July 18, 1942; children—Ben Hanson II, Rachael Ann (Mrs. Russell W. Branch, Jr.), Jerry W., Mary Rebecca (Mrs. Mark T. Strong). Clk. Hardaway Contracting Co., Columbus, Ga., 1936-41; head bookkeeper R.H. Wright & Son, 1941-42; office mgr., sec., treas. Concrete Industries, Inc., Albany, Ga., 1945—, also dir.; treas. Concrete Service and Trucking Co., Albany. Treas. Sowega Youth Home, Albany, 1967-68, pres., 1969. Served with AUS, 1942-45. Decorated Bronze Star medal. Mem. Am. Legion. Baptist (chmn. bd. deacons 1968). Elk. Home: Route 7 Box 423 Dawson Rd Albany GA 31707 Office: 110 Baldwin Dr Albany GA 31707

HOLLAND, BEN RAY, insulation co. exec.; b. Athens, Tex., July 29, 1932; s. Richard F. and Rena T. (Lewis) H.; student Sam Houston State Coll., 1951; m. Joy Ann Smith, Oct. 10, 1955 (div. Feb. 1970); children—Robin R., Rennie A. Mechanic, Armstrong Cork Co., Dallas, 1954-58; supt. Parker-Fallis Insulation Co., Inc., Dallas, 1958-68; pres. Universal Insulation Co., Inc., Ft. Worth, 1968—. Mem. Nat., S.W. (dir. 1972—) insulation contractors assns., Am. Soc. Heating Refrigerating and Air-Conditioning Engrs., Tex. La. Ark. Master Insulators Assn. (pres. 1972-73), Sportsmen Club Tex. Mason. Home: 800 Hamstad St Fort Worth TX 76115 Office: 832 Southway Circle Fort Worth TX 76115

HOLLAND, BOBBY WENDELL, dentist; b. Liberty, Tex., Apr. 6, 1935; s. William Wesley and Hazel (Martin) H.; B.A., U. Tex., 1958, D.D.S., 1964; m. Merle Stokes, June 29, 1963; children—Guy Wesley, Beth Ann, Mark Wendell. Practice dentistry, Houston, 1964-69, Ft. Worth, 1969—. Ofcl. weather watcher Channel 5, WBAP, Ft. Worth-Dallas. Bd. dirs. Ridglea Country Club Estates Homeowner's and Civic Club, Ft. Worth Westside YMCA. Mem. Am., Tex., Houston Dist., Fort Worth dental assns., Psi Omega. Baptist (deacon). Club: Briarmeadow Civic. Home: 6912 Benito Ct Fort Worth TX 76126 Office: 2120 Ridgmar Blvd Fort Worth TX 76116

HOLLAND, EDWARD MCHARG, lawyer, state senator; b. Washington, Nov. 28, 1939; s. Edwin Trammell and Elizabeth (McHarg) H.; A.B., Princeton, 1962; LL.B., U. Va., 1965; LL.M., Georgetown U., 1967; m. JoAnn Dotson, Dec. 3, 1966; children—David Ames, Allan Taylor. Admitted to Va. bar, 1965; tax law specialist Internal Revenue Service, Washington, 1965-66; asso. Tolbert, Lewis & Fitzgerald, Arlington, Va. 1966-70; partner Wilson & Holland, Arlington, 1970—; mem. Va. Senate, 1972—; mgr., dir. Tidewater Research Found., Inc., Arlington, 1972—; dir. Arlington Mortgage Co., 1st Va. Bankshares Corp.; trustee First Va. Mortgage and Real Estate Investment Trust. Mem. Va., Arlington bar assns., Va. Trial Lawyers. Clubs: Princeton (N.J.) Quadrangle; Explorers (N.Y.C.). Home: 3168 N 21st St Arlington VA 22201 Office: 1400 N Uhle St Arlington VA 22201

HOLLAND, EDWARD RICHARD, educator; b. Houston, Jan. 23, 1933; s. Rufus Marion and Elsa Catherine (Wohn) H.; B.S. summa cum laude, U. Houston, 1970; m. Sandra Beth Schneider, Aug. 21, 1971. Owner Holland Electric Co., Houston, 1954-65; tchr. Houston Ind. Sch. Dist., 1958-66, 68-70; teaching fellow U. Houston, 1967-68; instr. electronic tech. Houston Community Coll., 1971—. Served with USMCR, 1950-53. Mem. Tau Alpha Pi, Phi Kappa Phi. Methodist. Author: Design & Analysis of Electronic Circuits, 1974; Color Television: Theory and Servicing, 1974. Home: 10518 Herald Sq Houston TX 77072

HOLLAND, JAMES RICKS, govt. ofcl.; b. Savannah, Ga., Aug. 3, 1929; s. Francis Ross and Eleanor (Struck) H.; student Armstrong Jr. Coll., 1948-49; A.B. in Journalism, U. Ga., 1954; m. Paula Helene Shepard, Feb. 14, 1959; children—Kristine, Carey, Jamie. Reporter, weekly newspaper, 1953-54; with Internat. News Service, N.Y.C., Detroit, Birmingham, Ala., and Atlanta, 1954-58; with U.P.I., N.Y.C., 1958-59, J. Walter Thompson, N.Y.C., 1959-61; with John Hancock Mut. Life Ins. Co., Boston, 1961-70, 2d v.p. advt. and pub. relations, 1966-70; spl. asst. to postmaster gen. for pub. information, Washington, 1970-71, asst. postmaster for communications and pub. affairs, 1971-73; dep. asst. sec. pub. affairs Dept. Health, Edn. and Welfare, 1973—. Served with USAF, 1950-52. Mem. Pub. Relations Soc. Am., Sigma Delta Chi. Home: 105 Summerfield Rd Chevy Chase MD 20015 Office: White House Washington DC 20500

HOLLAND, LEWIS GERALD, security broker; b. Atlanta, Feb. 17, 1936; s. Julius Kurt and Carolyn W. (Weinstock) H.; B.S., U. N.C., 1958; m. Marjorie Altshool, June 7, 1961; children—Richard L., Lewis G., Lynn Paula. With E. F. Hutton, Atlanta, 1959-63; with Robinson-Humphrey, Atlanta, 1963—, v.p., 1969-71, sr. v.p., 1971—, also dir. Div. chmn. young leadership group United Jewish Appeal, 1967; mem. com. United Appeal, 1972—; mem. Leadership Atlanta, 1971—. Bd. dirs. Arbour Acad. Served with USAF, 1959-60, 61-62. Mem. Northside Jr. C. of C. (dir. 1962, v.p., 1963, pres. 1964), Izaak Walton League (pres. 1972), Ga. Securities Dealers (co-chmn. pub. relations and advt.), Zeta Beta Tau. Republican. Jewish religion (chmn. budget and finance coms., temple). Mason. Clubs: Circle R, Commerce, Standard Town & Country (Atlanta). Home: 429 Hollydale Ct NW Atlanta GA 30342 Office: 2 Peachtree St NW Atlanta GA 30303

HOLLAND, WILLIAM MEREDITH, lawyer; b. Live Oak, Fla., Feb. 6, 1922; s. Isaac and Annie E. (Williams) H.; B.A., Fla. A. and M. Coll., 1947; LL.B., Boston U., 1951; m. Mamie Smith, June 3, 1948; children—William Meredith, Maurice. Admitted to Fla. bar, 1951, since practiced in West Palm Beach; now municipal judge, Riviera Beach, Fla. Served with AUS, 1943-46. Mem. Council Human

Relations, Am. Civil Liberties Union; cooperating atty. N.A.A.C.P. Legal Def. Fund. Mem. Am., Palm Beach County bar assns., Am. Judicature Soc., Phi Beta Sigma. Episcopalian. Home: 520 17th St West Palm Beach FL 33402 Office: 605 Clematis St West Palm Beach FL 33401

HOLLANDER, ROBERT EUGENE, city mgr.; b. Chgo., Mar. 1, 1929; s. Gustav Melton and Marjorie Polk (Hill) H.; B.A., Shimer Coll., 1969; M.A., No. Ill. U., 1972; m. Julianne Stamer, May 14, 1949; children—Gail Marjorie, Laura Ann. City mgr., Palatine, Ill., 1960-66, Savanna, Ill., 1966-69, Punta Gorda, Fla., 1970—. Sec.-treas. Charlotte County Regional Planning Council, 1972—. Served with AUS, 1948-49. Rotarian. Home: 401 Retta Esplanade Punta Gorda FL 33950 Office: 326 W Marion Av Punta Gorda FL 33950

HOLLENBACH, LOUIS JACOB, III, county judge; b. Louisville, Feb. 23, 1940; s. Louis Jacob and Marie (O'Meara) H.; B.A., U. Notre Dame, 1962; LL.B., J.D., U. Louisville, 1965; m. Carroll DeHart, Oct. 17, 1959; children—Louis Jacob IV, John Phillip, Caroline DeHart. Admitted to Ky. bar, 1965, since practiced in Louisville; mem. firm Marshall, Cochran, Heyburn & Wells, 1963-67, Segal Isenberg, Sales & Stewart, 1967-68, Hendricks, Belknap & Hollenbach, 1968-70; Jefferson County judge, Louisville, 1970—; chmn. Jefferson County Legislature, also chief county exec. Mem. Am., Ky., Louisville bar assns., Ky. Trial Lawyers Assn., Nat. Assn. Counties (dir., chmn. pollution com.), Louisville Jr. C. of C. (legal counsel 1968). Home: 3303 Natchez Av Louisville KY 40206

HOLLERS, HARDY, lawyer; b. Clarendon, Tex., May 20, 1901; s. James Lemuel and Mattie (Mays) H.; student Southwestern U., 1918-19; LL.B., U. Tex., 1927, J.D., 1927; m. Mildred Bernice Calk, Apr. 18, 1921; children—Hardy Warren, Richard Van, James Carlyle. Admitted to Tex. bar, 1927, since practiced in Austin; asst. county atty., Travis County, 1928-29; asst. dist. atty., Travis County, 1933-34; spl. dist. judge, Travis County, 1935-36. Trial counsel maj. war criminals, Nuremberg, Germany, 1945. Pres. Modern Indsl. Developers, Inc. Gen. chmn. Greater Austin Assn., 1968-72. Served from maj. to col. AUS, 1941-46; ETO. Decorated Legion of Merit (U.S.); Croix de Guerre with palm (France). Fellow Tex. Bar Found. (life); mem. Nat. Res. Officers Assn. (life), Am. Legion (past post comdr.), Tex. (past dir.), Travis County bar assns. Methodist. Mason. Home: 2710 Townes Lane Austin TX 78703 Office: Am Bank Tower Austin TX 78701

HOLLEY, EDWARD GAILON, librarian; b. Pulaski, Tenn., Nov. 26, 1927; s. Abe Brown and Maxie Elizabeth (Bass) H.; B.A. magna cum laude, David Lipscomb Coll., Nashville, 1949; M.A., George Peabody Coll., 1951; Ph.D., U. Ill., 1961; m. Robbie Lee Gault, June 19, 1954; children—Gailon Boyd, Edward Jens, Amy Lin, Beth Alison, Holley. Asst. librarian David Lipscomb Coll., 1949-51; mem. staff U. Ill., 1951-62, librarian edn., philosophy and psychology library, 1957-62; dir. libraries U. Houston, 1962-71; dean Sch. L.S., U. N.C., 1972—, vis. prof. U. Wis., 1968, North Tex. State U., 1970; cons. in field. Served to lt. (s.g.) USNR, 1953-56. Mem. Am. (pres. 1974—, Scarecrow Press award 1964), Southeastern, Tex. (pres. 1971), N.C. library assns., Assn. Coll. and Research Librarians (editor Monographs 1969-72), Phi Kappa Phi, Kappa Delta Pi, Beta Phi Mu. Democrat. Mem. Ch. of Christ. Author: Charles Evans, American Bibliographer, 1963; Raking the Historical Coals, 1967; (with Don Hendricks) Resources of Texas Libraries, 1968. Contbr. articles to profl. jours. Home: 1508 Ephesus Ch Rd Chapel Hill NC 27514

HOLLEY, IVY MARLAN, mining co. exec.; b. Poolville, Tex., Jan. 1, 1933; s. Sign Declemon and Ruby Elizabeth (Lawrence) H.; grad. high sch.; m. Sannye Sue Paschall, Jan. 7, 1956; children—Susan Gay, Tracey Marlana, Jamey Lynn. With engring. test lab. Gen. Dynamics Corp., Ft. Worth, 1956-61; equipment operator Gifford Hill & Co., Bridgeport, Tex., 1961-63, foreman, Seagoville, Tex., 1963-68, plant supt., 1968-70, plant mgr., Eagle Lake, Tex., 1970—. Served with AUS, 1953-55. Mem. Colo. County Gravel Men's Assn., Grimes County, Eagle Lake chambers of commerce. Democrat. Baptist. Home: 112 Delmas Dr Wharton TX 77488 Office: Rural Route 1 Box 55A Eagle Lake TX 77434

HOLLEY, J(AMES) ANDREW, educator; b. Clay, Miss., Dec. 29, 1898; s. Andrew and Pamelia (Hale) H.; A.B., U. Colo., 1923; M.A., Columbia, 1928, Ed.D., 1947; m. Moreta Burnett, June 14, 1924 (dec. Mar. 1936); children—William Andrew, Wanda Jean (Mrs. Roy Fish), Helen Jane (Mrs. Helen LeBar); m. 2d, Edith Johnson, June 5, 1937. Tchr. rural schs., Okla., 1916-17, prin. village schs., 1919-21; supt. schs., Luther, Okla., 1923-26; asst. high sch. insp., Okla., 1926-29; chief high sch. insp. Okla. State Dept. Edn., 1929-32, 33-36, dir. curriculum, 1936-39; spl. summer lectr. and instr. Central State Coll., Edmond, Okla., 1926, Okla. A. and M. Coll., 1930, U. Okla., 1931-32, 34-36; dep. adminstr. Nat. Youth Adminstrn., 1939-40; prof., head dept. bus. edn. Okla. State U., 1940-51, became dean sch. edn., dir. summer sessions, 1951, now emeritus; asso. ednl. adminstrn. Columbia, 1946-47; asso. dir. Nat. Council Accreditation Tchr. Edn., 1964-70; ednl. cons., 1970—. Formerly chmn. child edn. sect. Nat. Safety Congress; active North Central Assn. Colls. and Secondary Schs., 1929-64, chmn. Okla. com., 1929-32, 33-39, chmn. com. on secondary schs., 1936-38, hon. mem., 1963—; chmn. Okla. Com. Tchr. Edn. and Certification, 1953-55; mem. Nat. Commn. Accrediting Bus. Schs., 1952-65. Served with USN, 1917-18; comdr. (ret.) USNR. Fellow A.A.A.S.; mem. Am. Assn. Sch. Adminstrs., N.E.A., Okla. Edn. Assn., Am. Ednl. Research Assn., Internat. Platform Assn., Tawse, Delta Sigma Rho, Phi Delta Kappa, Phi Kappa Phi, Delta Pi Epsilon, Sigma Alpha Epsilon. Democrat. Baptist. Rotarian. Co-author books and surveys. Contbr. articles to profl. jours. Address: 1718 W 4th Av Stillwater OK 74074

HOLLEY, MAX DEAN, elec. engr., govt. ofcl.; b. Altus, Okla., June 24, 1933; s. Elza Monroe and Beulah (Carter) H.; B.S., Okla. State U., 1955; postgrad. U. Ala., 1956-59, Case Inst. Tech., 1962, U. Houston, 1963-64; m. Lee McBride, July 31, 1959; children—Kandy Lee, Dawn Michele. Distbn. engr. Pub. Service Co., Duncan, Okla., 1955-56; engring. evaluation team leader Corporal Missile, Army Rocket and Guided Missile Agcy., Ft. Bliss, Tex., 1956-58; chief electronics sect. Nike Project Office, Huntsville, Ala., 1958-63; mgr. Apollo Guidance and Nav. Devel. Office, L.B. Johnson Space Center, NASA, Houston, 1963-73, mgr. program office space shuttle avonics integration div., 1973—. Served to 1st lt. Ordnance Corps, AUS, 1956-58. Recipient Superior Performance award NASA, 1967, Superior Achievement award, 1969. Registered profl. engr., Okla. Mem. Eta Kappa Nu. Unitarian. Home: 319 Cedar Lane Seabrook TX 77586 Office: NASA LB Johnson Center Rd 1 Houston TX 77058

HOLLEY, PHILIP WILEY, govt. ofcl.; b. Lake Charles, La., Feb. 26, 1932; A.A., Texarkana Coll., 1955; B.B.A., U. Tex., 1958; grad. N.Y. Inst. Finance, 1963; M.B.A., North Tex. State U., 1968; m. Lellah Onys Nix, Dec. 28, 1956; children—Candace Ann, Cynthia Kay. Quality control staff Gen. Tire & Rubber Co., Waco, Tex., 1958-59; statistician Tex. Elect. Service Co., Fort Worth, 1959-62; adminstrv. asst. City Fort Worth, 1962-67; budget dir. Dept. Housing and Urban Devel., Fort Worth, 1967—. Instr. accounting Tarrant County Jr. Coll., Fort Worth, 1968—. Served with USAF, 1951-53. Mem. Mcpl. Finance Officers Assn., Tex. Tchrs. Assn., Pi Sigma Alpha. Home: 2912 Hunter St Fort Worth TX 76112 Office: HUD 1108 Commerce St Dallas TX 76101

HOLLEY, ROBERT LEON, physician; b. Coffeeville, Miss., Sept. 26, 1915; s. Robert Leon and Clara (Aston) H.; A.B., U. Miss., 1935, B.S., 1938, med. certificate, 1938; M.D., Tulane U., 1940; m. Jeanne Lowry, June 11, 1952. Asst. univ. physician, instr. physiology U. Miss. Sch. Medicine, 1940-42; practice medicine, Macon, Miss., 1947-49, Oxford, Miss., 1949—; asso. medicine U. Miss. Sch. Medicine, 1953-55; adminstr. Oxford Hosp., Inc., 1956-63; pres. med. staff Oxford-Lafayette County Hosp., 1965, 70. Served with inf. AUS, 1942-45. Decorated Bronze Star. Fellow Am. Acad. Family Physicians (charter); mem. Am., Miss. med. assns., N. Miss. Med. Soc., Delta Kappa Epsilon. Episcopalian. Home: 201 Park Dr Oxford MS 38655 Office: 2200 S Lamar Oxford MS 38655

HOLLEY, RUDOLPH EUGENE, lawyer, state senator; b. Aiken, S.C., Feb. 15, 1926; s. Norton Hansford and Harriett (Holley) H.; B.B.A., U. Ga., 1949, LL.B. magna cum laude, 1958; m. Louise Herman Brittingham, Sept. 19, 1953; children—Robert Eugene, Phillip Gerard, Stephen Thomas, Anna Louise, Eugene Norton. Admitted to Ga. bar, 1957, practiced in Augusta, 1958—; mem. firm Congdon and Leonard, 1958, Congdon and Holley, 1959-66, Sanders, Hester and Holley, 1967—; mem. Ga. State Senate, 1965—, Democratic majority leader, 1971—; dep. asst. atty. gen., Ga., 1964-65. Dir. West Lake Devel. Co., Augusta, Medi-Center of Augusta, Met. Land & Investment Co., Augusta. Trustee Hillcrest Meml. Park Perpetual Care Trust. Served with USAAF, 1943-45, to capt. USAF, 1949-55. Decorated D.F.C. Mem. Phi Beta Kappa, Chi Psi, Phi Kappa Phi, C. of C. Democrat. Baptist. Club: Sertoma. Editor: Ga. Bar Jour., 1957-58. Home: Route 2 Box 364 Flowing Wells Rd Augusta GA 30904

HOLLIDAY, VADIM PETER, pharm. co. exec.; b. Novocherkas, USSR, Aug. 2, 1920; s. Peter John and Katherine (Kononova) H.; brought to U.S., 1927, naturalized, 1943; B.A., Columbia, 1941; M.B.A., Harvard, 1946; m. Patricia Ruth McKenzie, Jan. 20, 1964; children—Katheryn P., Alexander V. With H.W. Kinney & Sons, Columbus, Ind., 1946-49; div. mgr. Walker Lab., Mt. Vernon, N.Y., 1949-59; pres., treas. Delta Drug Corp. Jacksonville, Fla., 1959—, also dir.; pres., treas., dir. Direct Devel. Corp., Jacksonville, 1970—; pres., dir. Gen. Microfilm Corp., Jacksonville, 1971—. Mem. adv. council Small Bus. Adminstrn., 1969-70. Served with USMCR, 1942-45. Decorated Bronze Star, Purple Heart. Named Small Bus. Adminstrn. Man of Year Fla., 1967. Mason (33 deg., Shriner). Clubs: River, University (Jacksonville). Home: 301 San Juan Dr Ponte Vedra Beach FL 32082 Office: 1032 Hendricks Av Jacksonville FL 32207

HOLLIFIELD, JOHN GEORGE, bank exec.; b. Barbourville, Ky., July 31, 1935; s. Denver Dee and Ruby (Golden) H.; student Union Coll., 1952-54; m. Barbara Hart, July 3, 1964; 1 dau., Eva Jane. With Corbin Deposit Bank & Trust Co. (Ky.), 1961—, v.p., dir. 1972—. Treas. Am. Cancer Soc., Corbin, 1962—. Mem. Friends of St. George, Descs. of Knights of Garter (Windsor, Eng.). Episcopalian. Club: Tri County Golf and Country (Corbin). Home: Rural Route 3 Box 380-A Corbin KY 40701 Office: PO Box 600 Corbin KY 40701

HOLLINGS, ERNEST FREDERICK, U.S. senator; b. Charleston, S.C., Jan. 1, 1922; s. Adolph G. and Wilhelmine D. (Meyer) H.; B.A., The Citadel, 1942; LL.B., U. S.C., 1947; m. Martha Patricia Salley, Mar. 30, 1946; children—Michael Milhous, Helen Hayne, Patricia Salley, Ernest Frederick III; m. 2d, Rita Liddy, Aug. 21, 1971. Admitted to S.C. bar, 1947; mem. S.C. Ho. of Reps., 1948-54, speaker pro tem, 1950-54; lt. gov. of S.C., 1955-59; gov. of S.C., 1959-63; practiced in Charleston, 1963-66; U.S. senator State of S.C., 1966—. Mem. Hoover Comm. on Intelligence Activities, 1954-55; mem. President's Adv. Comm. on Intergovtl. Relations, 1959-63; mem. exec. council Lutheran Ch. Am. Trustee Newberry Coll. Named one of Ten Outstanding Young Men, U.S. Jr. C. of C., 1954. Mem. Assn. Citadel Men, Hibernian Soc., Phi Delta Phi. Democrat. Lutheran. Club: Sertoma (Charleston). Home: Boyce's Wharf Charleston SC 29401 Office: Room 437 Russell Office Bldg Washington DC 20510

HOLLINGS, ROBERT M., lawyer; b. Charleston, S.C., Jan. 19, 1915; s. Adolph Gevert and Wilhelmine (Meyer) H.; A.B., Coll. Charleston, 1936; LL.B., Harvard, 1939; m. Mary Fernhout, July 21, 1944; children—Peter Fernhout, Julie (Mrs. Ronald Wallace), Robert Meyer, Mary Pamela. Admitted to S.C. bar, 1939, D.C. bar, 1940; now practice law, Charleston. Dir. Bankers Trust S.C., NA, Columbia, S.C. Chmn. Charleston Planning and Zoning Com., 1950—. Alderman, Charleston, 1947-51, mayor-pro-tem, 1950, 56-72; mem. exec. com. Berkeley Charleston Dorchester Regional Planning Council, 1968—. Trustee Carolina Art Assn.; v.p., Solicitor Charleston County Library Bd., 1953—; trustee Hist. Charleston Found. Served to maj. AUS, 1941-45; PTO. Decorated Legion of Merit. Mem. Charleston, S.C., Am. bar Assns. Democrat. Lutheran. Clubs: St. Andrews Society, Charleston, German Friendly Soc. (Charleston). Address: 67 Broad St Charleston SC 29402

HOLLINGSWORTH, BOBBY J., mathematician; b. Sunset, Tex. Aug. 17, 1927; s. Ralph E. and Georgia (Davis) H.; B.S. in Civil Engring., La. Poly. Inst., 1949; M.S., Okla. A. and M. Coll., 1951; Ph.D., Kan. U., 1955; m. Bettie Rea Fox, June 8, 1953; children—Rebecca Rea, Lee Ann. With United Gas Corp., Shreveport, La., 1955-68, research mathematician, 1955-61, operations research asso., 1961-63, corporate planning asso., 1963-65, corporate devel. analyst, 1966-68, exec. asst. corporate finance, 1968-71; mgr. financial analysis Pennzoil United, Inc., Houston, 1971—. Instr. math. evening div. Centenary Coll., 1959-65, La. Poly. at Barksdale AFB, 1965-68. Served with USNR, 1945-46. Mem. Am. Gas Assn. (research com. on transient flow 1962—), Am. Math. Soc., Soc. Indsl. and Applied Math., Canadian Math. Congress, Lambda Chi Alpha, Phi Kappa Phi. Democrat. Methodist. Home: 5339 Tilbury Houston TX 77027 Office: Southwest Tower Houston TX 77002

HOLLINGSWORTH, CECIL JAMES, hosp. adminstr.; b. Chickasha, Okla., July 5, 1908; s. William Columbus and Addie (Phillips) H.; grad. high sch.; m. Clarice Keith, May 25, 1929; 1 son, William K. Asst. cashier First Nat. Bank, 1926-30, asst. receiver comptroller of currency, 1930-35; bus. mgr. West Tex. Hosp., Lubbock, 1935-36, adminstr., 1936—; pres. SPD Service, Inc., Lubbock, 1965—; dir. South Plains Drugs, Inc. Mem. State Health Adv. Com. for Comprehensive Health Planning, 1969—; commr. Hub Home Housing Authority, 1960-63; vice chmn. Community Planning council, 1963-65. Trustee Blue Cross-Blue Shield of Tex. Mem. N.W. Tex. (past pres.), Tex. (past pres.) hosp. assns. Baptist. Kiwanian (dir.). Home: 3611 46th St Lubbock TX 79413

HOLLINGSWORTH, ROBERT ALOIS, banker; b. Kenansville, N.C., Mar. 28, 1925; s. Robert Ellis and Bertha (Smith) H.; student N.C. State Coll., 1946-47; A.B. in Accounting, King Coll., Raleigh, N.C., 1948; postgrad. So. Meth. U., 1962, San Antonio Coll., 1963; m. Patricia Ann Lundgren Hensley, Mar. 25, 1960; children—Patrice, Robert Alois. Auditor, Employers Ins. Group, San Antonio, 1949-50, dist. service mgr., 1950-52, agt., 1952-66; sr. v.p., dir. pub. relations Gt. Western Loan & Trust Co., San Antonio, 1966—, affiliated Great Western group cos., 1966—; dir. Republic Bank San Antonio. Pres., Bexar County Tb Assn., 1956-58, Beautify San Antonio Assn., 1956; mem. adv. bd. Keystone Sch., San Antonio, 1967—. Precinct chmn. Democratic party, 1970—, mem. county exec. com., 1970—. Served with AUS, 1943-46; ETO. Named Outstanding Young Man San Antonio, San Antonio Jr. C. of C., 1954, One of Five Outstanding Young Texans, 1958. Presbyn. (deacon). Mason (Shriner, 32 deg.). Home: 2819 Old Moss Rd San Antonio TX 78217 Office: 1000 N Alamo St San Antonio TX 78215

HOLLINGSWORTH, ROBERT EDMUND, editor; b. Monroe, La., June 30, 1926; s. Oswald Murray and Ora (Redfearn) H.; student U. Tex. at Austin, 1946-49; m. Ann Elizabeth Prather, July 9, 1949; 1 dau., Lynn. Reporter, Dallas Times Herald, 1949-55, polit. editor, 1955-61, city editor, 1961-63, chief Washington Bur., 1963-65, mng. editor, 1965-71, corporate adminstrv. asst. to pub. and pres., 1971-73, v.p. adminstrn., 1973—. Mem. adv. bd. journalism edn. U. Tex. System; mem. scholarship selection com. St. Johns Coll., Santa Fe; adv. com. U. Tex. at Dallas. Served with USNR, 1944-46. Mem. S.W. Journalism Forum, Am. Polit. Sci. Assn., Headliners, Sigma Delta Chi. Home: 4920 Mill Creek Rd Dallas TX 75234 Office: Herald Sq Dallas TX 75202

HOLLINSHEAD, WILLIAM LAWRENCE, engring. exec.; b. Nashville, Tenn., July 2, 1935; s. John Roberson and Elizabeth (Tanksley) H.; B.S., U. Tenn., 1957, postgrad. Space Inst., 1958-63; m. Mary Alice Hodges, June 14, 1957; children—David, Mark. Instrumentation engr. ARO, Inc., Tullahoma, Tenn., 1957-69; supr. digital design Laser Systems & Electronics, Inc., Tullahoma, 1969-71; partner, v.p. engring. Precision Internat., Inc., Tullahoma, 1971—, also dir.; dir. Tenn. Precision Engring., Inc.; cons. Tullahoma City Sch. System. Pres. Tullahoma City P.T.A. Council, 1970; dir. Tullahoma Am. Little League, 1971—; pres. Tullahoma Babe Ruth Baseball Assn., 1973—. Named Young Engr. of Yr., Tullahoma chpt. Tenn. Soc. Profl. Engrs., 1968. Mem. Tenn. Soc. Profl. Engrs., U. Tenn. Alumni Assn. (pres. Coffee County chpt. 1962-63, dir. 1960-65), Lambda Chi Alpha. Methodist (ofcl. bd.). Kiwanian (lt. gov. div. Ky.-Tenn. dist. 1967). Home: 1504 Creighton Pl Tullahoma TN 37388 Office: 329 W Lincoln St Tullahoma TN 37388

HOLLIS, LOYE YVORNE, educator; b. Bonham, Tex., July 28, 1933; s. Herman Lester and Ruby (Nicewarner) H.; student Paris Jr. Coll., 1950-51, East Tex. State U., 1951-52; B.S., Tex. Tech. Inst., 1954, M.Ed., 1959, E.Ed., 1964; m. Carolyn Huggins, Sept. 14, 1957; 1 dau., Tanya Rene. Tchr. elementary sch., Gail, Tex., 1956-57; tchr., Odessa, Tex., 1957-59, prin., 1959-63; teaching fellow Tex. Tech. Inst., Lubbock, 1963-64; asst. prof. U. Houston, 1964-66, asst. prof., chmn. dept. elementary edn., 1966-67, asso. prof., 1967—, chmn. dept. curriculum and instrn., 1967-70, asso. dean Coll. Edn., 1970—. Math. cons., dir. in-service program Harris County (Tex.) schs., 1964—; condr. math. workshops Mich. State U. East Lansing, 1966-67, U. Houston, 1965—; demonstration tchr., cons. for math. films on teaching strategies South Park Ind. Sch. dist., Beaumont, Tex., 1966—. Served with AUS, 1954-56. Mem. N.E.A., Tex. State Tchrs. Assn., Tex. (dir.), Houston assns. supervision and curriculum devel., Assn. Supervision and Curriculum Devel., Am. Edn. Research Assn., Nat. Council Tchrs. Math., Sigma Alpha Epsilon, Phi Delta Kappa, Kappa Delta Phi. Methodist (lay leader). Optimist (pres. Odessa, Tex. 1962-63). Contbr. numerous articles to profl. jours. Home: 6122 Rutherglenn Houston TX 77035

HOLLIS, WALTER JESSE, physician; b. Bossier City, La., Mar. 17, 1921; s. Charles Basil and Evie (Barber) H.; M.D., La. State U., 1945; m. Hazel Loree West, Dec. 22, 1945; children—Walter Jesse, Clara Jean, Mary Evelyn. Intern Charity Hosp. La., Shreveport, 1945-46, asst. resident, 1946-47, asso. resident, 1947-48, vis. physician, 1948-51; asst. in medicine Sch. Medicine, La. State U., 1948, mem. faculty, 1953—, prof. medicine, 1965—; practice gen. medicine, Bossier City and Shreveport, 1948-51; cardiologist Charity Hosp. La., New Orleans, 1956-64, sr. vis. physician, 1963—. Med. examiner, cons. La. Dept. Pub. Welfare, New Orleans, 1960-71; cons. S.E. La. Hosp., Mandeville, 1953-59, electrocardiagram heart sta. Hotel Dieu Hosp., New Orleans, 1971—. Served to capt. M.C., USAF, 1951-53. Diplomate Am. Bd. Internal Medicine. Fellow A.C.P.; mem. La. Med. Soc., Orleans Parish, La. med. socs., Phi Chi, Alpha Omega Alpha. Baptist. Contbr. articles to profl. jours. Home: 761 Glouster Pl Gretna LA 70053 Office: 1542 Tulane Av New Orleans LA 70112

HOLLIS, WILLIAM SLATER, educator, lawyer; b. Little Rock, Feb. 11, 1930; s. William T. and Ida Sue (Johnson) H.; B.S. in Bus. Adminstrn., U. Ark., 1952, J.D., 1969; M.A. in Econs., Memphis State U., 1962; Ph.D. in Econs., U. Miss., 1972; m. Nancy Gant, Sept. 4, 1955; children—Laura Lynn, John Pete, Leslie Carol, Mark Bruce. Mem. faculty, Delta State Coll., 1958; admitted to Ark. bar, 1958, Fed. bar, 1959, Tenn. bar, 1965, U.S. Supreme Ct. bar, 1970; practiced in Memphis, Tenn., 1959, 61-73; mem. faculty The Citadel, 1960; asso. prof. law, econs. Memphis State U., 1961-73; prof., chmn. div. bus. and econs. Hardin-Simmons U., 1973—. Participant Nat. Def. Strategy Seminar, Nat. War Coll., Washington, 1967. Mem. new govt. structure commn. Shelby County (Tenn.) Govt., 1969; pres. Taxpayers, Inc., 1968—; mem. nat. exec. com. Citizens for Decent Lit., 1968. Served with USAF, 1952-55; now lt. col. U.S. Army Res. Recipient Outstanding Tchr. award Memphis State U., 1973. Fellow Found. for Econ. Edn.; mem. Am., So. econ. assns., Am. Arbitration Assn. (mem. mgmt.-labor panel), Am. Assn. U. Profs., V.F.W. Baptist. Mason. Author: On The Etiology of Criminal Homicides, 1974. Office: Hardin-Simmons U Abilene TX 79601

HOLLOMAN, HASKELL ANDREW, ret. judge, rancher; b. Frederick, Okla., Nov. 12, 1907; s. Andrew Harvey and Dora (Prophit) H.; student Okla. State U., 1926-27, U. Okla. Coll. Law., 1935-38; m. Cornelia Louise Lewis, May 23, 1940. Admitted to Okla. bar, 1938; county atty., Frederick, Okla., 1939-41; atty. for state examiner and insp., Oklahoma City, 1941-42; asst. atty. gen. Okla., 1946; county atty. Frederick, 1946-47, county judge, 1947-49, 52-69; spl. dist. judge Southwestern Okla. Dist., 1969-71. Dir. Tex.-Okla. Fair Assn., Tillman County Mental Health Assn.; dir., past pres. Tillman County Farmers Union Assn. Served from lt. (j.g.) to lt. comdr. USN, 1942-46. Mem. Okla. Assn. County Judges (past pres.), Am. Judicature Soc., Am. Legion, Okla., Caddo County, Tillman County (past pres.) bar assns., Okla. Jud. Conf., Frederick C. of C., Okla.-Texas (director), Okla. (dir.) polled hereford assns., Tex.-Okla. (dir.), Red River Valley (past pres.), Big Pasture (dir.), Shortgrass (dir.) hereford assns., Southwestern Okla. Cattlemen's Assn. (dir.), Tillman County League of Young Democrats (past pres.), V.F.W. Democrat. Methodist. Kiwanian. Club: Frederick Golf and Country. Home: 412 N 12th St Frederick OK 73542

HOLLOMAN, JEFF JOE, physician; b. Frederick, Okla., Mar. 5, 1922; s. Andrew H. and Dora (Prophit) H.; B.S., Okla. State U., 1947; M.D., Harvard, 1951; m. Wilma Hamm, June 2, 1943; children—Lucinda, Lorraine, Andrew, Joseph. Intern U.S. Navy Hosp., Oceanside, Cal., 1951-52, resident, 1952-53; practice medicine specializing in family practice, Savannah, Ga., 1953—; chief staff Candler Gen. Hosp.; mem. staff Meml. Med. Center, Ga. Infirmary, Savannah. Diplomate Am. Bd. Family Practice. Fellow Am. Acad. Family Practice; mem. 1st Dist. (pres., 1965-66), Ga. (trustee,

1971-72) med. socs., Exchange Club. Presbyn. (elder). Home: 1216 Brightwood Dr Savannah GA 31406 Office: 313 E Hall St Savannah GA 31401

HOLLOWAY, CLARKE LEE, educator; b. Atmore, Ala., May 2, 1926; s. Albert Lee and Estelle Maude (Petty) H.; D.V.M., Auburn U., 1949, M.S., 1962; Ph.D., Ia. State U., 1969; m. Peggy Hartley, Sept. 18, 1948; children—Laura, Lee, Keith. Pvt. practice vet. medicine, Mobile, Ala., 1949-60; instr. Auburn U., Auburn, Ala., 1960-65, prof., head dept. anatomy and histology Sch. Vet. Medicine, 1968—; Nat. Inst. Neurol. Diseases and Blindness spl. fellow Ia. State U., Ames, 1965-67; asso. prof. U. Ga., Athens, 1967-68. Served with USNR, 1945-46. Mem. Am., Ala. vet. med. assns., Am. Assn. Vet. Anatomists, World Assn. Vet. Anatomists. Lion. Home: 426 Blake St Auburn AL 36830

HOLLOWAY, GEORGE REECE, tobacco co. exec.; b. Tazewell, Va., Apr. 25, 1922; s. Henry Franklin and Elizabeth (Johnson) H.; B.S., U. Ky., 1949; m. Mary Jean Michler, Nov. 9, 1946; children—Leslie Elaine, Laura Lee, Roger Wayne, Patricia Jean. Plant supt. Southwestern Tobacco Co., Lexington, Ky., 1950-56; buyer Universal Leaf Tobacco Co., Richmond, Va., 1956-58, prodn. supr., 1958-59; v.p., gen. mgr. Simcoe Leaf Tobacco Co., Ltd. (Ont., Can.), 1959-62, pres., mng. dir., 1962—. Served with USAAF, 1941-46, USAF, 1951-52. Mem. Hamilton Officers Assn. Clubs: Norfolk Country (Simcoe); Commonwealth, Deep Run Hunt (Richmond); LaSalle Hunting and Fishing (St. Alexis DesMonts, Que., Can.). Home: 8901 Tresco Rd Richmond VA 23229 Office: 2d and Hunt Sts Simcoe Ontario Canada

HOLLOWAY, GORDON ARTHUR, lawyer; b. Wichita, Kan., July 27, 1938; s. George Arthur and Marguerite (Bondurant) H.; B.B.A., U. Tex., 1960; LL.B., 1963; m. Carol Halstead Criss, Sept. 1, 1960; children—Gregory Arthur, Suzanne Criss. Admitted to Tex. bar, 1963; asso. mem. firm Sewell, Junell & Riggs, Houston, 1963-70, partner, 1970—. Bd. dirs. Meml. Drive Townhouse Condominium Assn., 1968. Mem. Tex. Assn. Def. Counsel, Am., Houston bar assns., Newcomen Soc. N.Am., Phi Alpha Delta, Phi Delta Theta. Home: 10818 Meadow Lake Lane Houston TX 77042 Office: 701 Capital Nat Bank Bldg Houston TX 77002

HOLLY, HOWARD, govt. ofcl.; b. Burgaw, N.C., Oct. 24, 1922; s. David Frank and Agnes (Ward) H.; grad. Campbell Coll., 1940; m. Elizabeth Page, June 11, 1967. Bookkeeper Kramer's Dept. Store, Wallace, N.C., 1943-61; auditor Pender County, Burgaw, N.C., 1962—, county tax supr., 1962—, clk. County Bd. Commrs., 1962—. Mem. Pender County Bd. of Edn., 1955-61, chmn. bd. 1960-61; mayor pro-tem, commr., Burgaw, 1951-54. Trustee Campbell Coll., 1968-72; bd. govs. N.C. Advancement Sch., Winston-Salem, 1967-70; trustee Cape Fear Tech. Inst., Wilmington, N.C., 1963-73; past pres. Pender Fair Assn.; exec. com., v.p. gen. bd. N.C. Bapt. State Conv., moderator Wilmington Bapt. Assn., 1969-71. Mem. N.C. Assn. County Accountants (pres.), N.C. Assn. Agrl. Fairs (past pres.). Baptist (deacon). Mason, Rotarian. Home: PO Box 4 Burgaw NC 28425 Office: County Courthouse Burgaw NC 28425

HOLMAN, (CLYDE) JOE, mfg. and oil exec.; b. Omaha, Dec. 7, 1930; s. Clyde Wilson and Eunice (Springer) H.; LL.B. magna cum laude, Woodrow Wilson Coll., 1966; m. Mary Jo Langley, Jan. 7, 1960; children—Gregory Joe, Pamela Sue (Mrs. Rick Abney), Patrick Vaughn, Glede Holman. Area sales engr. Milwhite Mud Sales Co., New Orleans, 1953-55; sales mgr. Reed Engring., New Orleans, 1955-56; spl. rep. Mayronne Mud & Chem. Co., New Orleans, 1956-59; gen. mgr. Riverside Oil Co., New Orleans, Tulsa, 1956-59; dir. indsl. sales Hammons Products Co., Stockton, Mo., 1959—, also agt.; owner, operator Holman Oil Co., Okla.; dir. Oil Patch, Inc., Oklahoma City, Ridgemore Properties, Atlanta. Served with USNR. Mem. Internat. Platform Assn., Sigma Delta Kappa. Baptist. Mason (32 deg., Shriner), Elk. Home: 1508 Woodland Dr Okmulgee OK 74447 Office: PO Box 819 Okmulgee OK 74447

HOLMAN, JAMES MARVIN, lawyer; b. Dover, Ark., Jan. 17, 1929; s. William T. and Maude (Trotter) H.; B.S., Ark. Poly. Coll., 1955; J.D., U. Ark., 1959; m. Carol Joyce Barns, May 28, 1960; children—Andrea Lynn, James Michael, Kimberly Kay. Admitted to Ark. bar, 1959; practice law, Clarksville, Ark., 1959—; municipal judge, Clarksville, 1969-72. Mem. Clarksville Bd. Edn., 1966-71, pres. bd., 1970. Served with AUS, 1951-53; Korea. Mem. Am., Ark. bar assns. Rotarian (pres. 1969-70). Home: 206 Rogers St Clarksville AR 72830 Office: 205 Sevier St Clarksville AR 72830

HOLMAN, RUDOLPH PRICE, elec. engr.; b. Sivalls Bend, Tex., July 20, 1925; s. Ernest Price and Roca (Pace) H.; B.S., Ill. Inst. Tech., 1968; m. Anna Lee Greb, Mar. 3, 1951; 1 dau., Suzanne. Field sales mgr. P.F. Collier, Oklahoma City, 1946-56; telephone engr. Western Electric Co., Chgo., 1956-59; application engr. Internat. Tel.&Tel., , Chgo., 1959-63; cons., 1963-65; dist. sales mgr. Gen. Electric Co., Chgo., 1965-67; elec. engr. communications br. TVA, Chattanooga, Tenn., 1968—. Served with USNR, 1943-46. Registered profl. engr., Okla., Tenn. Mem. Western Soc. Engrs. (vice chmn. elec. engrs. sect. 1963-66), I.E.E.E., Tenn. Soc. Profl. Engrs. Home: 6713 Shallowford Rd Chattanooga TN 37421 Office: Chattanooga Bank Bldg Chattanooga TN 37421

HOLMANN, ANNE SHARPE (MRS. E. J. HOLMANN), wholesale drug exec., bottling exec., civic worker; b. Bainbridge, Ga., Nov. 7, 1900; d. John Greenleaf and Anne Elizabeth (Sharpe) Garrett; student Salem Acad. and Coll., 1916-19; A.B., Vanderbilt U., 1922; m. Joseph Lee Brown, June 13, 1923 (dec. Apr. 4, 1931); children—Anne Poindexter (Mrs. Reginald Heber Helvenston, Jr.), Joseph Lee, John Garrett, Stephen Glenmore; m. 2d, Ernest McClelland Archer, June 22, 1933 (dec. Jan. 10, 1951); m. 3d, Edward Jacob Holmann, Mar. 29, 1952 (dec. Feb. 1972). Former sec. Jonesboro (Ark.) Coca Cola Bottling Co., pres., treas. 1951—; former pres., treas. Statesboro (Ga.) Coca Cola Bottling Co., former v.p. Archer Drug Co., Little Rock, now pres., treas.; mem. bd. Davis Wholesale Drug Co., Shreveport, La. Bd. dirs. City Beautiful Commn.; spl. mem. Musical Coterie; bd. dirs. Little Rock Progress Up; mem. health subcom. Little Rock Model Cities Orgn.; bd. dirs. Little Rock Regional Jr. Coll. Chosen Little Rock Woman of Week, Jan. 1948, Jan. 1949; Little Rock Citizen of Week, Feb. 1949; Ark. Woman Year, 1948; Little Rock Mother of Year, 1971; Ark. Mother of Year, 1972. Mem. Am. Assn. U. Women (former v.p., pres. Ark. div., past legislative chmn. Little Rock br.), YWCA, Nat. Cathedral Assn. (former state chmn.), Women's, Little Rock chambers commerce, Bus. and Profl. Women's Club, Ark. Drug Travelers, Am. Pen Women (asso.), U.D.C., D.A.R., Dames Ct. of Honor (past pres.), Daus. Am. Colonists (former treas.), Daus. Colonial Wars, Ark. Soc. (treas.), Colonial Dames Am., Delta Kappa Gamma, Alpha Omicron Pi (Elizabeth Wyman Alumnae award 1951). Methodist (steward). Clubs: Fine Arts of Ark. (past pres.), Little Rock Garden (past pres.), Womans City, Altrusa, Aesthetic, Little Rock, Little Rock Country. Home: 3518 Hill Rd Little Rock AR 72205 Office: 107 E Markham St Little Rock AR 72203

HOLMBERG, ALBERT WILLIAM, JR., publishing co. exec.; b. Orange, N.J., Sept. 18, 1923; s. Albert William and Margaret (Flanagan) H.; B.S. in Bus. Adminstrn., Lehigh U., 1947; m. Dorothy McCollum, Oct. 27, 1945 (div. 1972); children—Jeanne (Mrs. Fletcher J. Johnson, Jr.), Margaret D. (Mrs. Roy D. Duckworth III), Ellen T.; m. 2d, Ruth Sulzberger Golden, 1972; stepchildren—Stephen A.O. Golden, Arthur S. Golden, Michael D. Golden, Lynn G. (Mrs. Edward I. Dolnick). With N.Y. Times, 1947-70, circulation mgr., 1964-70; pres., gen. mgr. Chattanooga Times, 1970—; pres., dir. Times Pub. Co. Mem. No. Valley Regional High Sch. Bd., Demarest, N.J., 1958-62. Trustee Huguonot Meml. Ch., Pelham, N.Y., 1967-70. Served to 1st lt. USAAF, World War II. Rotarian. Club: Mountain City (Chattanooga). Home: 919 Scenic Hwy Lookout Mountain TN 37350 Office: 117 E 10th St Chattanooga TN 37401

HOLMBERG, RUTH SULZBERGER, printing co. exec.; b. N.Y.C., Mar. 12, 1921; d. Arthur Hays and Iphigene (Ochs) Sulzberger; A.B., Smith Coll., 1943; m. Ben Hale Golden, June 1, 1946 (div. Mar. 1965); children—Stephen A.O., Michael D., Lynn Iphigene (Mrs. Edward Dolnick), Arthur Sulzberger; m. 2d, A. William Holmberg, Jr., May 26, 1972. Reporter, N.Y. Times, summers 1939-45, dir. N.Y. Times Co., 1961—; music critic Chattanooga Times, 1946-57, dir. spl. activities, 1956—; asst. sec. Times Printing Co., 1950-60, v.p., 1956-65, pres., 1965-70, chmn. bd., 1970-72, pub., 1965—; pres., pub. Chattanooga Post, 1966-70. Pres. Chattanooga Symphony, 1959-61; trustee UTC Found., Hunter Mus. Art. Served with A.R.C., 1943-45; ETO. Sustaining mem. Jr. League. Home: 919 Scenic Hwy Lookout Mountain TN 37350 Office: 117 E 10th St Chattanooga TN 37402

HOLMES, ALEXANDER BARON, III, lawyer; b. Hendersonville, N.C., Oct. 20, 1905; s. James Hill and Septima Glover (Toomer) H.; B.A., U. N.C., 1927, LL.B., 1930; m. Phoebe Dewar Gordon, July 29, 1943; children—Alexander Baron IV, Florence Dewar (Mrs. David Charles Norton). Admitted to N.C. bar, 1930, S.C. bar, 1930; U.S. Circuit Ct. Appeals bar; practiced in Columbia, S.C., 1930-34, Charleston, S.C., 1934—; mem. firm McKay & Manning, Attys., 1930-34, Hagood, Rivers & Young, Attys., 1934-65, Holmes & Thompson, Attys., 1965-72, Holmes, Thompson & Logan, 1972—. Pres. Legal Aid Soc., Charleston, 1963-66. Mem. city and county Democratic exec. coms., Charleston. Served to lt. comdr. USNR, 1941-45. Mem. Am., S.C., S.C. State, Charleston County (pres. elect 1974-75) bar assns., Am. Judicature Soc., Nat. Assn. Railroad Trial Counsel, Charleston C. of C. (v.p. 1948-49), St. Andrews Soc. (pres. 1960-62), St. George's Soc. (pres. 1960-64), S.C. Hist. Soc., Charleston Mus., New Eng. Soc., Sigma Alpha Epsilon, Phi Delta Phi. Episcopalian (past vestryman and warden). Lion (pres. Charleston br. 1967-68), Elk. Club: Carolina Yacht (commodore 1937). Home: 18 Church St Charleston SC 29402 Office: Suite 309 Peoples Bldg 18 Broad St Charleston SC 29402

HOLMES, CHARLES EVERETT, lawyer, banker; b. Wellington, Kan., Dec. 21, 1931; s. Charles Everett and Elizabeth (Bergin) H.; B.A., Wichita U., 1953; LL.B., Okla. U., 1961; m. Lynn Lacy, Jan. 2, 1954; children—Anne Lacy, Charles Everett III, Rebecca. Trainee Halliburton Oil Well Cementing Co., Great Bend, Kan., 1956-58; admitted to Okla. bar, 1961; practiced in Tulsa, 1961—; mem. firm Rogers, Bell & Robinson, 1969-71; v.p. Nat. Bank of Tulsa, 1971—; sec. Sinclair Oil & Gas Co., Sinclair Can. Oil Co., Mesa Pipeline Co., Border Pipe Line Co., Sinclair Transp. Co., Ltd. Del. Okla. Council Cath. Diocese, 1966—; chmn. Cath. Parish Governing Body, 1968—. Served with USAF, 1954-56, 61-62. Mem. Am., Okla., Tulsa County bar assns. Home: 3824 E 60th St Tulsa OK 74135 Office: Nat Bank of Tulsa Bldg Tulsa OK 74103

HOLMES, CHARLES MASON, educator; b. North Dartmouth, Mass., Aug. 25, 1923; s. Harold Denison and Margaret Laird (Macfarlane) H.; B.S. in Chem. Engring., Cornell U., 1944, A.B., 1947; M.A., Columbia, 1950, Ph.D., 1959; postgrad. New Sch. for Social Research, 1947-49, Harvard, 1950; m. Carolyn Ann Lyons, June 25, 1960; children—Anne, Elizabeth, John. Instr., Tufts Colls., Medford, Mass., 1950-52, Duke, Durham, N.C., 1953-55; instr. Washington U., St. Louis, 1956-59, asst. prof., 1959-60; asso. prof. Transylvania U., 1960-63, prof., 1963—, chmn. dept. English, 1971—. Vis. prof. Emory U., 1964; cons. Danforth Found., 1965-67. Served with USNR, 1944-45. Andrew Mellon fellow, 1967-68. Mem. Modern Lang. Assn., South Atlantic Modern Lang. Assn., Am. Assn. U. Profs., Am. Civil Liberties Union, Phi Beta Kappa, Tau Beta Pi. Democrat. Club: Spindletop Hall (Lexington, Ky.). Author: Aldous Huxley and the Way to Reality, 1970. Home: 187 Valley Rd Lexington KY 40503 Office: Dept English Transylvania U Lexington KY 40508

HOLMES, CHARLES WILMORE, health ofcl.; b. Bloomfield, N.J., Feb. 7, 1913; s. Howard H. and Florence (Canfield) H.; A.B., Elon Coll., 1936; M.P.H., U.N.C., 1958; student N.Y.U., 1938; m. Edythe E. Holmes, 1936; children—Leigh, Carolyn, Richard, Edward. Sanitarian, Collier County Health Dept., Naples, Fla., 1952-60; environmental health dir. Sarasota County (Fla.) Health Dept., 1960-66, acting engring. sect. dir., 1966-68, adminstrv. health program analyst, 1968—. Mem. Well Drilling Bd., Sarasota County, 1962-67, Plumbing Bd., 1958-62. Pres. Fla. Environmental Health Dirs. Conf., 1966. Mem. Nat. Assn. Sanitarians, Gulf Coast Health Conf. (chmn. 1971-72). Home: 740 Canal Rd Sarasota FL 33581 Office: 1938 Laurel St Sarasota FL 33577

HOLMES, CLIFFORD NEWTON, geologist; b. Escanaba, Mich., Jan. 1, 1922; s. Joseph Theodore and Gerda (Olson) H.; B.S., U. Mich., 1943; M.S., Yale, 1948; Ph.D., U. Utah, 1960; m. Edith Ruth Bradley, Aug. 4, 1945; children—Alexander B., Cameron H., Sven E., Ivar H., Kurt O., Edith M., Alison R. Geologist, U.S. Geol. Survey, U. Kan., Lawrence, 1943, at Stanford, 1944-45, La. State U., Baton Rouge, 1945-46, Colo. Plateau Project, Grand Junction, 1948-50; sr. geologist Phillips Petroleum Co., Salt Lake City, 1952, asst. dir. exploration projects, 1953, dir. strategic minerals, 1954-58, asst. mgr. mining and milling dept., Bartlesville, Okla., 1959-63, mgr. minerals div., 1963-71, v.p., dir., 1968-71, energy adviser, 1971—. Chmn. bd. dir. Phosphate Mines, Inc., Lakeland, Fla., 1968-71. Fellow N.Y. Acad. Sci., Soc. Econ. Geologists; mem. Intermountain Assn. Petroleum Geologists (v.p. 1958), A.A.A.S., Geol. Soc. Am., Am. Assn. Petroleum Geologists, Am. Inst. Mining Engrs., Geol. Soc. Washington, Colo. Mining Assn. (dir. 1958). Sigma Xi (pres. Bartlesville chpt. 1965), Phi Kappa Phi, Sigma Gamma Epsilon. Club: Hillcrest Country (Bartlesville). Home: 1431 Valley Rd Bartlesville OK 74003 Office: Frank Phillips Bldg Bartlesville OK 74003

HOLMES, DEAN LEE, physician; b. Sandersville, Ga., Jan. 12, 1936; s. Edward Alonza and Margaret (Davis) H.; A.B., Emory U., 1958; M.D., Med. Coll. Ga., 1962; m. Barbara Jean Avant, Aug. 20, 1957; children—Keith Dean, Barbara Andrea, Shannon Rene. Intern Spartanburg (S.C.) Gen. Hosp., 1962-63; practice medicine, Sandersville, 1963—; mem. staff Meml. Hosp. of Washington County, chief staff, 1970, 73. Mem. Med. Assn. of Ga., Washington County (pres. 1970), 10th Dist. (sec.-treas. 1973-74) med. socs. Baptist. Rotarian. Home: 712 Laurel Dr Sandersville GA 31082 Office: 524 Sparta Rd Sandersville GA 31082

HOLMES, JACK DAVID LAZARUS, educator; b. Long Branch, N.J., July 4, 1930; s. John Daniel Lazarus and Waltrude Helen (Hendrickson) Holmes; B.A. cum laude, Fla. State U., 1952; M.A., U. Fla., 1953; postgrad. Universidad Nacional Autonoma de Mexico, 1954; Ph.D., U. Tex. at Austin, 1959; m. Anne Elizabeth Anthony, Sept. 6, 1952 (div. Dec. 1965); children—David H., Jack Forrest, Ann M.; m. 2d, Martha Rachel Austin, Feb. 11, 1966 (div. June 1967); m. 3d, Gayle Jeanette Pannell, July, 1967 (div. 1970); 1 son, Daniel; m. 4th, Stephanie Pasneker, Apr. 10, 1971. Instr. history Memphis State U., 1956-58; asst. prof. McNeese State Coll., Lake Charles, La., 1959-61; lectr. U. Md. at Constantina, Spain, 1962; asso. prof. U. Ala. in Brimingham, 1963-68, prof., 1968—. Reading clk. Fla. Ho. of Reps., 1955; reporter-photographer Memphis Press-Scimitar, 1957-58; cons. U.S. Parks Service, 1962, Pensacola (Fla.) Hist. Commn., 1969-70, New Orleans Cabildo Museum, 1968-73, Nat. Endowment Humanities, 1972-73. Served with inf., AUS, 1951. Charles W. Hackett fellow, 1959; Am. Philos. Soc. fellow, 1961, 66; Fulbright fellow, 1961-62; Assn. State and Local History grantee, 1966; U. Ala. grantee, 1964, 66, 68, 72, 74; Mexican Govt. grantee, 1954. Mem. Tenn. Squires, Am. Soc. Ethnohistory, Orgn. Am. Historians, So. La. hist. assns., Miss, Fla. hist. socs., Ala. Acad. Sci., S.W. Social Scis. Assn., Phi Beta Kappa, Phi Kappa Phi, Sigma Delta Pi, Phi Alpha Theta, Pi Kappa Phi. Author: Documentos ineditos para la historia de la Luisiana, 1963; Gayoso, 1965; Honor and Fidelity, 1965; Jose de Evia, 1968; Francis Baily's Journal, 1969; New Orleans: Facts and Legends, 1970; Luis de Onis Memoria, 1969; Guide to Spanish Louisiana, 1970; New Orleans Drinks and How to Mix Them, 1973; History of the University of Alabama Hospitals and Clinics, 1974; The 1779 Marcha de Galvez: Louisiana's Giant Step Forward in the American Revolution, 1974. Home: 520 S 22d Av Birmingham AL 35205

HOLMES, JACK THOMAS, marketing advt. and pub. relations co. exec.; b. Fort Worth, Mar. 30, 1915; s. Thomas W. and Margaret (Morse) H.; B.J., U. Tex., 1938; m. Janice Aliwa Nicolson, Jan. 11, 1941; 1 dau., Niki Lynn. Mail order buyer/supr. Montgomery Ward, 1939-41; regional sales mgr. WBAP-R-TV, 1948-50, ZIV TV, 1950-51; v.p., co-owner Advt. Agy., 1951-52; pres., owner Jack T. Holmes & Assos. Advt., Inc., Fort Worth, 1952—; owner Research Assos., Fort Worth, 1955—, Art Assos., Fort Worth, 1955—, Put. Relations Assos., Fort Worth, 1955—. Served to 1st lt., AUS, 1942-45. Mem. Nat. Fedn. Advt. Agys. (pres. 1958). Downtown Fort Worth Assn. (dir. 1963-67), S.W. Hort. Soc. (pres. 1959), Tex. Pub. Relations Assn. (dir. 1959), Tex. Camellia Soc. (pres. 1970), Confrerie St. Etienne, Confrerie du Guillion. Clubs: Colonial Country, Shady Oaks Country, Fort Worth. Home: 2806 6th Av Fort Worth TX 76110 Office: 2800 W Lancaster St Fort Worth TX 76101

HOLMES, ROBERT CORNELIUS, process engr.; b. Woodbury, N.J., Feb. 20, 1919; s. Walter Cornelius and Florence (Safford) H.; B.S. in Chem. Engring., U. Ill., 1939; M.S., Carnegia Inst. Tech., 1940; m. Nitta Jo Johnston, June 16, 1945; children—Jennie (Mrs. John Allen Morris), David Conant. With E.I. duPont de Nemours & Co., various locations, 1939—, sr. supr. process, Camden, S.C., 1966-68, engring. asso., 1968—. Treas., City Rose Valley, Pa., 1964. Served to maj. Signal Corps, AUS, 1941-46. Decorated Bronze Star. Registered profl. engr., Del. Mem. Am. Inst. Chem. Engrs., Delta Sigma Phi. Presbyn. Home: 3734 Northshore Rd Columbia SC 29206 Office: EI duPont de Nemours Drawer A Camden SC 29020

HOLMES, THOMAS JOSEPH, clergyman; b. Sandersville, Ga., June 1, 1917; s. Emmett Lee and Kate (Averett) Holmes; A.B., Mercer U., 1939, D.D., 1965; B.D., Southeastern Baptist Theol. Sem., Wake Forest, N.C., 1956; m. Grace Bryan, June 4, 1940; children—Lila Katherine (Mrs. Edward Simmons), Thomas Joseph. Ordained to ministry Bapt. Ch., 1936; pastor First Bapt. Ch., Hogansville, Ga., 1942-43; asso. dept. evangelism Ga. Bapt. Conv., 1944; pastor First Bapt. Ch., Manchester, Ga., 1945-51, Lakewood Heights Bapt. Ch., Atlanta, 1951-52, First Bapt. Ch., Franklinton, N.C., 1952-54, First Bapt. Ch., College Park, Ga., 1954-57, Northside Drive Bapt. Ch., Atlanta, 1957-60; dir. univ. devel. and alumni relations, asst. prof. Christianity, Mercer U., 1960-65; pastor Tattnall Sq. Ch., Macon, Ga., 1965-66, asst. to pres. Mercer Univ., 1966—. Mem. exec. com. Ga. Bapt. Conv., 1946-51, mem. endowment com., 1955-58, mem. Home Mission Bd., 1956-60; Active in A.R.C., Community Chest. Dir. bldg. fund campaign Mercer U. So. Sch. Pharmacy, Atlanta. Served as 1st lt. Ga. State Guard, 1942-43. Recipient Author of Yr. award in non-fiction Dixie Council Authors and Pubs., 1970. Mem. Nat. Soc. Fund Raisers (pres. Ga. chpt. 1970), Am. Coll. Pub. Relations Assn., Chi Alpha Omega. Author: Ashes for Breakfast, 1969. Address: Route 4 Box 278-B Newnan GA 30263

HOLMES, THOMAS VINTON, JR., dentist; b. Shreveport, La., Feb. 6, 1919; s. Thomas Vinton and Minnie Ola (Cook) H.; student Baylor U., 1936-37; B.S. in Archtl. Engring., La. State U., 1940, postgrad. Sch. Med., 1955-58, Grad. Sch., 1958-59; B.S. in Natural Scis., Centenary Coll., 1955; D.D.S., McGill U., 1963; Fieldman, So. Bell Tel. & Tel. Co., New Orleans, 1940-42, jr. engr., Baton Rouge, Shreveport, 1946-50, exchange engr., New Orleans, 1950-53, Shreveport, summer 1955; extern Charity Hosp of New Orleans, 1956-58; grad. teaching asst. dept. zoology La. State U., 1959; gen. practice dentistry, Shreveport, 1963—; mem. active staff surgery dept. Doctors Hosp., Shreveport, 1969—. Served to capt. AUS, 1942-46; CBI; col. Res. Mem. Am., La., Northwest La. dental assns., Ark.-La.-Tex. Geneal. Assn. (2d v.p., treas. 1971, 1st v.p. 1972, pres. 1973-74), Shreveport Photog. Soc. (treas. 1971, pres. 1972), Res. Officers Assn. (life), Am. Legion, Sons Republic Tex., S.C.V., Order Stars and Bars, S.A.R., Omicron Delta Kappa. Baptist (dir. 1969—). Contbr. articles to geneal. publs. Home and office: 826 Gladstone Blvd Shreveport LA 71104

HOLMES, WILLIAM ANTOINE, computer co. exec.; b. Abbeville, La., Aug. 19, 1933; s. William Jefferson and Rose (Broussard) H.; student U. Cal. at Riverside, 1957; B.S., Tex. Lutheran Coll., 1959; postgrad. U. Tex., 1960, Inst. Computer Tech., 1967, S.W. Center for Advanced Study, 1969; m. Elisabeth Anne Robeson, Sept. 29, 1957; children—Mark Orrin, Lisa Anne. Cons. Math. Engring. Assos., Inc., Dallas, 1966-69; dir. data communications Dallas Rep. Nat. Bank, 1969-70; product devel. specialist Recognition Equipment Inc., Irving, Tex., 1972—. Guest lect. So. Methodist U., Dallas, 1968-69, S.W. Center for Advanced Study, 1968-69. Served with USNR, 1951-54. Mem. Data Processing Mgmt. Assn., Assn. Computing Machinery. Inventor in field Office: 2701 Grauwyler Dr Irving TX 75060

HOLMQUEST, DONALD LEE, astronaut; b. Dallas, Apr. 7, 1939; s. Sidney Browder and Lillie Mae (Waite) H.; B.S. in Elec. Engring., So. Meth. U., 1962; M.D., Baylor U., 1967, Ph.D. in Physiology, 1968; m. Ann Nixon James, Oct. 24, 1972; 1 dau. by previous marriage, Hilary Catharine. Student engr. Ling-Temco-Vought, Dallas, 1958-61; electronics engr. Tex. Instruments, Inc., Dallas, 1962; intern Methodist Hosp., Houston, 1967-68; pilot tng. USAF, Williams AFB, Ariz., 1968-69; scientist-astronaut NASA, Houston, 1967-73; research asso. Mass. Inst. Tech., 1968-70; asst. prof. radioiogy and physiology Baylor Coll. Medicine, 1970-73, vis. prof. physiology, 1974—; adj. asso. prof. physiology Baylor Coll., 1973-74; dir. nuclear medicine dept. Eisenhower Med. Center, Palm Desert, Cal., 1973-74;

asso. prof. medicine, asso. dean medicine Tex. A & M U.-Baylor Coll. Medicine Med. Program, College Station, Tex., 1974—. Diplomate Am. Bd. Nuclear Medicine. Mem. A.M.A., Soc. Nuclear Medicine, Am. Coll. Nuclear Physicians, Assn. Advancement Med. Instrumentation, Am. Fighter Pilots Assn., Sigma Xi, Alpha Omega Alpha, Sigma Tau. Contbr. med. jours. Home: 6611 Brompton Rd Houston TX 77005 Office: Texas A & M U College Station TX 77840

HOLMSTROM, FRITZ MILTON GILBERT, anesthesiologist; b. Jamestown, N.Y., Feb. 15, 1923; s. Fritz Emanuel and Hildur Maria (Johnson) H.; student Brown U., 1940-42; M.D., Harvard, 1949, M.P.H., 1955; m. Anne Marguerite Mullikin, June 24, 1948; children—Anne M. (Mrs. Morton W. Baird), Fritz R. Intern Del. Hosp., 1949-50; gen. practice medicine, Arlington, Va., 1952-54; resident dept. anesthesiology Bexar County Hosp., San Antonio, 1969—; asst. prof. anesthesiology U. Tex. Med. Sch., San Antonio, 1971—. Served with AUS, 1942-45, USAF, 1950-52, 54-69. Decorated Legion of Merit. Fellow Am. Coll. Preventive Medicine, A.C.P., Am. Coll. Anesthesiologists; mem. A.M.A. Home: 1321 Wiltshire Av San Antonio TX 78209 Office: 7703 Floyd Curl Dr San Antonio TX 78229

HOLSHOUSER, JAMES EUBERT, JR., gov. N.C.; b. Boone, N.C., Oct. 8, 1934; s. James Eubert and Virginia (Dayvault) H.; B.S., Davidson Coll., 1956; LL.B., U. N.C., 1960. Admitted to N.C. bar; practice law; gov. N.C., 1973—. Mem. N.C. Ho. of Reps., 1963-72; chmn. N.C. Republican Com., 1968-72. Mem. Phi Delta Theta, Phi Alpha Delta. Presbyn. (deacon, treas.). Address: Adminstrn Bldg Raleigh NC 27611

HOLST, HOWARD DOUGLAS, broadcasting co. exec.; b. Pierre, S.D., Aug. 6, 1929; s. John Thomas and Rose (Kramer) H.; B.F.A., U. S.D., 1951; M.A., Memphis State U., 1966; m. Noreen Leone Paulson, July 9, 1954; children—Holly, Douglas, Heather. Program specialist WOI-TV, Ames, Ia., 1952-56; prodn. mgr. WKNO-TV, Memphis, 1956-58, program dir., 1958-61; mng. dir. WKNO-TV/FM, 1961—. Bd. dirs. Pub. Broadcasting Service. Mem. Nat. Assn. Ednl. Broadcasters (exec. bd. 1971), So. Ednl. Communications Assn. (past chmn.). Rotarian. Home: 412 N Perkins St Memphis TN 38117 Office: Memphis State U Box 80000 Memphis TN 38152

HOLSTUN, GORDON ROBINSON, educator; b. Waverly, Ala., May 28, 1910; s. P. Reese and Annie L. (Robinson H.; B.S., Ala. Poly. Inst., 1931, M.S., 1940; m. Cora Louise Hooten, Oct. 14, 1932; 1 dau., Beverly Louise. Tchr. R. E. Lee Inst., 1931-38, head social sci. dept., also athletic dir., 1936-37; prin. Lee Jr. High Sch., 1939-40; supt. Upson County (Ga.) Schs., 1941-70, Thomaston (Ga.) Pub. Schs., 1948-70; asso. prof. edn. Tift Coll., Forsyth, Ga., 1970—. Trustee Tift Coll., 1954-58, vice chmn., 1958. Mem. Ga. Edn. Assn. (dir.), State Supts. and Bd. Mems. Assn. (past pres.), Ga. Assn. County Sch. Supts. (past pres.), Ga. Assn. Sch. Adminstrs. (pres. 1960, dir.), Ga. Accrediting Commn. (vice chmn. 1960), Internat. Platform Com., Nat. Soc. Study of Edn., S.A.R., Phi Delta Kappa. Baptist (deacon). Mason (Shriner), Woodman of World. Clubs: Lions (past dist. gov., counselor), National Beta (Ga. chmn. 1969— dir., nat. pres. 1974-75). Home: 411 S Green St Thomaston GA 30286 Office: Tift College Forsyth GA 31029

HOLT, ETHAN CLEDDY, educator; Brilliant, Ala., Feb. 6, 1921; s. Austin F. and Anna (Ingle) H.; B.S., Auburn U., 1943; M.S., Purdue U., 1948, Ph.D., 1950; m. Jean Jordan, June 18, 1944; children—Janet (Mrs. Randy T. Decker), Robert Austin. Mem. faculty Tex. Agrl. Expt. Sta., Tex. A. and M. U., College Station, 1948—, asso. prof. agronomy, 1954-57, prof., 1957—. Chmn., So. Pasture and Forage Crops Improvement Conf., 1958-59, mem. exec. com. 1956-61. Served to 1st lt. inf., AUS, 1943-46. Decorated Bronze Star. Recipient distinguished research award Tex. A. and M. U., 1970. Fellow Am. Soc. Agronomy (pres. So. br. 1967). A.A.A.S.; mem. Crop Sci. Soc. Am. (chmn.-elect. div. C-6), Sigma Xi, Alpha Zeta, Gamma Sigma Delta. Contbr. profl. jours. Home: 1110 Ashburn St College Station TX 77840

HOLT, PERRY CECIL, educator; b. Livingston, Tenn., June 26, 1912; s. William Perry and Lucille (Williams) H.; B.S., Tenn. Poly. Inst., 1942; M.A., U. Va., 1948, Ph.D., 1951; m. Virgie Ford, Aug. 2, 1942; 1 dau., Susan Emily (Mrs. James Lemuel Wills West III). Instr. biology U. Va., Charlottesville, 1947-48; instr. biology U. Richmond, 1948-50; asst. prof. biology E.Tenn. State U., Johnson City, 1950-51, asso. prof., 1951-56; asst. prof. biology Va. Poly. Inst. and State U., Blacksburg, 1956-60, asso. prof. zoology, 1960-65, prof., 1965—, dir. Center for Systematic Collections, 1973. Acting asso. prof. biology Moutain Lake Biol. Sta., U. Va., summer 1952; Ford Found. faculty fellow U. Chgo., 1955-56; sr. research asso. Smithsonian Instn., 1967-68. Served with AUS, 1942-46. Recipient research grants NSF, 1957-65, J. Shelton Horseley award Va. Acad. Sci., 1968. Fellow A.A.A.S.; mem. Soc. Systematic Zoology, Soc. Am. Zoologists, Assn. Southeastern Biologists (mem. exec. com. 1969-72), Va. Acad. Sci. (chmn. publs. com. 1971—), Sigma Xi. Contbr. to profl. publs. Home: 1308 Crestview Dr Blacksburg VA 24060

HOLT, WILLIAM JOSEPH, JR., corp. exec.; b. Waco, Tex., Oct. 20, 1921; s. William Joseph and Carrie Lee (Canuteson) H.; B.S., U. Tex., 1942; grad. U. Cal. Exec. Sch. Bus., 1962; m. Anita Lillian Lowrey, June 6, 1942; children—William Joseph III, David L. Mem. research lab., mgr. creative engring. program Gen. Electric Co., Schenectady, 1942-46; chief engr. VARO, Inc., Garland, Tex., 1946-56, v.p., dir., gen. mgr. research br., 1965-71, gen. mgr. transp. systems div., 1969-71; pres., dir. Gyrex Corp., Santa Monica, Cal., 1956-65; v.p., gen. mgr. Monocab, Inc., Garland, 1971—; dir. 1st Nat. Bank of Garland. Mem. Am. Astronautical Soc., Am. Mgmt. Assn., I.E.E.E. Patentee in field. Home: 3306 Country Club Rd Garland TX 75041 Office: 2700 Oakland Av Garland TX 75041

HOLTER, WILLIAM HUDSON, mathematician, actor; b. Lock Haven, Pa., Nov. 30, 1929; s. Willard Clyde and Josephine (Tibbins) H.; B.S. magna cum laude, Franklin and Marshall Coll., 1952; M.A., Am. U., 1960; m. Margaret Lawrence, Nov. 24, 1961. Mathematician, sr. scientist, head applied math. computer analysis sect. Atlantic Research Corp., Alexandria, Va., 1953-66; project scientist Booz-Allen Applied Research, Inc., Bethesda, Md., 1966-70; tech. staff Mitre Corp., McLean, Va., 1970-72; sr. analyst Gen. Research Corp., McLean, 1972—. Actor summer stock, 1953—; actor appearing in Uniquecorn Revue, Washington, 1961-62, A Political Party, N.Y.C., 1963. Treas. Waterford Players, 1967—; bd. dirs. Waterford (Va.) Found., 1966—; gov. bd. dirs. Alexandria Little Theatre, 1957; actor dinner theater circuit, Washington, 1968—. Mem. Operations Research Soc. Am., Internat. Platform Assn., Math. Assn. Am., Soc. Indsl. Applied Math., Am. Inst. Aeros. and Astronautics, Am. Ordnance Assn., Phi Beta Kappa. Home: Box 146 Waterford VA 22190 also 523 Queen St Alexandria VA 22314 Office: Gen Research Corp McLean VA 22101

HOLTON, ABNER LINWOOD, JR., former gov. Va., govt. ofcl.; b. Big Stone Gap, Va., Sept. 21, 1923; s. Abner Linwood and Edith (VanGorder) H.; B.A., Washington and Lee U., 1944, LL.D., 1971; LL.B., Harvard, 1949; grad. Sr. Res. Officers Sch. Naval War Coll., 1965; LL.D., Va. State Coll., 1971; m. Virginia Harrison Rogers, Jan. 10, 1953; children—Virginia Tayloe, Anne Bright, Abner Linwood III, Dwight Carter. Admitted to Va. bar, 1949; mem. firm Hunter, Fox & Holton, Roanoke, Va., 1949-53; founding partner Eggleston, Holton, Butler & Glenn, Roanoke, 1954-69; gov. Commonwealth of Va., Richmond, 1970-74; asst. sec. for congl. relations Dept. State, Washington, 1974—. Chmn. So. Growth Policies Bd., 1972, So. Regional Edn. Bd., 1972-73. Chmn. Roanoke City Republican Com., 1952-54; vice chmn. Va. Rep. Central Com., 1960-69; del. Rep. Nat. Conv., 1960, 68; state campaign mgr. for H. Clyde Pearson, candidate for gov., 1961; Rep. candidate for gov., 1965; regional coordinator Nixon for Pres. Com., 1967-68; chmn. policy com. Rep. Govs.' Assn., 1972, vice chmn. assn., 1971-72, chmn., 1973. Bd. dirs. Roanoke Fine Arts Center, 1965. Served with USNR, World War II; capt. Res.; mem. Nat. Naval Res. Policy Bd., 1961-63. Mem. Am., Va. (v.p. 1965-66), Roanoke (dir.) bar assns., Washington and Lee Alumni Assn. (pres. Roanoke chpt. 1964), Roanoke C. of C. (pres. Backbone Club 1964), Omicron Delta Kappa. Republican. Presbyn. (elder 1954-57, tchr. Sunday sch. 1952-69). Clubs: Country of Va., Downtown (Richmond); ·Shenandoah (Roanoke). Home: 3125 Avenham Av SW Roanoke VA 24014 Office: Dept State Washington DC 20520

HOLTON, VIRGINIA ROGERS (MRS. ABNER L. HOLTON, JR.), civic worker; b. Roanoke, Va., Oct. 21, 1925; d. Frank W. and Anne Jett (Rogers) Rogers; B.A., Wellesley Coll., 1946; student Middlebury Coll. French Sch., 1945, Latin Am. Inst. in N.Y., 1946-47; m. Abner Linwood Holton, Jr., Jan. 10, 1953; children—Virginia Tayloe, Anne Bright, Linwood Halton III, Dwight Carter. Sec. Am. embassy, Brussels, Belgium, 1947-49; intelligence analyst CIA, Washington, 1949-52. Mem. adv. council Va. Assn. for Children with Learning Disabilities, 1971-73; hon. chmn. Richmond area chpt. Multiple Sclerosis Soc., 1970-72; state chmn. Muscular Dystrophy Assn., 1970-71; hon. chmn. Va. Easter Seal Soc. for Crippled Children and Adults, 1970-72; hon. chmn. Gov.'s Conf. on Family Food Dollar, 1970; hon. chmn. Old Dominion Symphony Council Concert Tours, 1970-72. Bd. dirs. McVitty House Nursing Home, Family Service Bd., Jr. League; bd. visitors U. Va.; mem. adv. Council Nat. Center Family. Republican. Presbyn. Address: 3125 Aronham Av SW Roanoke VA 24014

HOLTZMAN, GARY YALE, mcht.; b. N.Y.C., Aug. 7, 1936; s. Abram and Pearl Bernice (Kashetski) H.; B.B.A., Coll. City N.Y., 1958; m. Alice Ann Lang, Sept. 5, 1958; children—Bruce Neil, Sheri Lynn, Michele Dawn. Buyer, operations mgr. Bloomingdale Bros., N.Y.C., 1959-67; operations staff Allied Stores Corp., N.Y.C. and Miami, Fla., 1967-68; v.p. gen. operations mgr. Jordan Marsh Co., Miami, 1968—. Subcom. chmn. United Fund Dade County, 1971; mem. Miami Beautification Com. Served to capt. AUS, 1958. Mem. Greater Miami C. of C. Jewish religion (dir. temple). Office: 1501 Biscayne Blvd Miami FL 33132

HOLWAY, JAMES COLIN, steel co. exec.; b. Youngstown, O., Nov. 14, 1927; s. Robert G. and Marie W. (Kane) H.; B.S., Ohio State U., 1950; M.B.A., Pa. State U., 1952; m. Patricia Ann Touscany, Aug. 31, 1957; children—Moira Ann, Colin, Brent Patrick, Jamison McAndrew, Jonathan Lynch. Sales trainee U.S. Steel Corp., 1951-55; salesman Republic Steel Corp., Cleve. and Detroit, 1955-58; dist. sales mgr. Tenn. Products & Chem. Corp., Detroit, 1958-60; dist. sales mgr. Nat. Steel Corp., Charlotte, N.C., 1960-72; pres. Southeastern Steel Rolling Mills, Charlotte, 1972; pres. Decker-Holway Steel Co., Charlotte, 1973—. Served with USNR, 1945-46. Mem. Am. Inst. Mining, Metall. and Petroleum Engrs. (asso.), Internat. Platform Assn. Clubs: Country of Detroit (Grosse Pointe, Mich.); University (Detroit); Charlotte Athletic, Charlotte City, Charlotte Country. Home: 2312 Pembroke Charlotte NC 28207 Office: 1310 W Morehead St Charlotte NC 28204

HOLZ, ROBERT KENNETH, educator; b. Kankakee, Ill., Nov. 3, 1930; s. Harry H. and Margaret M. (Conway) H.; B.A., So. Ill. U., 1958, M.A., 1959; Ph.D., Mich. State U., 1962; m. Joyce F. Harpin, May 19, 1951; 1 son, Eric Robert. Asst. prof. dept. geography U. Tex. at Austin, 1962-67, asso. prof., 1967-72, prof., chmn. dept., 1972—. Served with USAF, 1951-54. Fulbright-Hays fellow, 1965; NASA-Sky Lab. grant, 1973. Mem. Assn. Am. Geographers, Am. Soc. Photogrammetry, Am. Geog. Soc., Am. Assn. U. Profs. Co-author: An Atlas of Mexico, 1970. Editor: The Surveillant Science, Remote Sensing of the Environment, 1973. Home: 2610 Fiset Dr Austin TX 78731

HOLZBERG, MARYLIN TELL (MRS. MARK HOLZBERG), merchant; b. Bronx, N.Y., Mar. 7, 1932; d. Louis and Ida R. (Holzberg) Tell; B.A., Brandeis U., 1953; m. Mark Holzberg, Sept. 5, 1954; children—Harris, Randy. Owner (with husband) Tells Originals, North Miami, Fla., 1961—. Treas. chpt. Brandeis U. Nat. Women's Com. Mem. Dade County Women's Polit. Caucus, Keystone Point Homeowners Assn. (dir.). Home: 13195 Biscayne Bay Drive North Miami FL 33161 Office: 12800 Biscayne Blvd North Miami FL 33161

HOMEWOOD, GEORGE MORGAN, JR., mgmt. cons.; b. Annapolis, Md., Aug. 3, 1924; s. George Morgan and Ellen Sharpless (Marlin) H.; Chem. E., U. Del., 1949; B.S., Syracuse U., 1950; m. Katrina Margaret Stolp, Apr. 21, 1956; 1 son, George Morgan III. Market analyst Atlas Powder Co., Wilmington, Del., 1950-55; marketing research mgr. J.T. Baker Chem. Co., Phillipsburg, N.J., 1955-62, V-C Chem. Co., Richmond, Va., 1962-65; pres. Morwood Assos., Richmond, 1965—. Dist. chmn. Boy Scouts Am., Richmond, 1965-67; v.p. Huguenot Little League, Richmond, 1969-72. Served with USNR, 1943-46. Mem. Am. Marketing Assn. (chpt. v.p. 1959-61), Am. Chem. Soc., Comml. Devel. Assn. (dir. 1963-64), Chem. Marketing Research Assn. Mason (Shriner). Club: University (Richmond). Office: 9613 Northridge Ct Richmond VA 23235

HONEYCUTT, CHARLES MILFORD, chem. co. exec.; b. Rienzi, Miss., Jan. 13, 1929; B.B.A. in Accounting, Memphis Coll. Accountancy, 1958; B.A. in Accounting, Memphis State U., 1967; 1 son, Charles Michael; 1 dau. by previous marriage, Mary Susan (Mrs. Franklin Earl Mann). Accounting mgr. Armour & Co., Memphis, 1954-62, Cherokee, Ala., 1962-63; controller W.R. Grace & Co., Memphis, 1963-67; controller Carrier Corp., Collierville, Tenn., 1967-70; treas., asst. sec. Hunter Fan & Ventillating Co., Memphis, 1970-73; controller Gen. Tire & Rubber Co., Columbus, Miss., 1973—. Sr. co. mem. Jr. Achievement Adv. Team, Memphis, 1972-73. C.P.A., Tenn. Mem. Am. Inst. C.P.A.'s, Tenn. Soc. C.P.A.'s. Home: 823 Fallwood Dr Columbus MS 39701 Office: Yorkville Rd Columbus MS 39701

HONEYCUTT, LEX EDWARD, city ofcl.; b. Gold Hill, N.C., Nov. 26, 1924; s. Charles Edward and Mary Kathleen (Hahn) H.; B.S. in Civil Engring., Duke, 1950; m. Katherine Elizabeth Barringer, June 4, 1947; children—Len Edward, Lex Edward II. Asst. dir. pub. works, City of Salisbury, N.C., 1950-55; dir. pub. works, city engr., City of Thomasville, N.C., 1955-60, City of Wilson, N.C., 1960-70, City of Lenoir, N.C., 1970—. Mem. bd. aldermen, Town of Rockwell, N.C., 1953-55; mem. N.C. Air Control Adv. Council, 1967—; mem. Solid Waste Commn., 1970—. Served with AUS, 1944-46; ETO. Registered profl. engr., N.C. Mem. Am. Pub. Works Assn. (dir. N.C. sect. 1964-65, pres. 1967), Am. Water Works Assn. (trustee N.C. sect. 1969-70), N.C. Soc. Engrs., Profl. Engrs. N.C. Presbyn. Home: 1001 Olive Av SW Lenoir NC 28645 Office: 108 Main St SW Lenoir NC 28645 28645

HONHOLT, EDITH, newspaper editor; b. Charlotte, Mich., Mar. 3, 1928; d. Herman J. and Lillian klebe (Bradley) Honholt; B.A., Cornell Coll., Mount Vernon, Ia., 1951. Sec., researcher, editorial asst. New Yorker Mag., N.Y.C., 1953-57; TV editor, TV mag. editor, editoral asst., women's reporter, women's editor Houston Post, 1957-70, asso. editor Tempo, Sunday rotogrovure Mag., 1970-71, spl. makeup editor Houston Post, 1957—, asst. day news editor, 1972-73, days news editor, 1973—. Mem. Women in Communication. Episcopalian. Home: 5529 Beverly Hill Houston TX 77027 Office: 4747 Southwest Freeway Houston TX 77001

HOOD, BILL JIM, supt. schs.; b. Brownwood, Tex., July 25, 1925; s. W. A. and Margaret (Johnson) H.; B.A., Hardin-Simmons U., 1949, M.Ed., 1952; postgrad. Sul Ross State Coll., summers 1958-61, Abilene Christian Coll., summer 1954, Tex. Tech U., 1969; m. Mary Carolyn Clark, Jan. 29, 1950; children—William Leslie, James Bruce, Steven Clark. Tchr. English high sch., Sterling City, Tex. 1951-53; tchr. English high sch. Rankin, Tex., 1953-57, jr. high prin., 1957-58, high sch. prin., 1958-63, supt., 1963-67; supt. schs., Snyder, Tex., 1967—; guest lectr. Sul Ross State U., summer 1973. Dist. com. chmn. Boy Scouts Am., 1965-67, dist. chmn., 1968-71. Served with USNR, 1943-46. Mem. Tex. Tchrs. Assn. (pres. Rankin local unit 1956-57, dist. IV 1967-68), N.E.A., Tex. Assn. Sch. Adminstrs., Am. Assn. Sch. Adminstrs., Snyder C. of C. (treas.). Baptist (mem. Christian edn. commn. Bapt. Gen. Conv. Tex.). Mason, Lion (pres. local chpt. 1963, 64, 72). Home: 3001 34th St Snyder TX 79549

HOOD, EVANS CARROL, supt. schs.; b. Sweetwater, Tex., Mar. 10, 1929; s. Marvin and Mary (Gentry) H.; B.S., North State U., 1950; M.A., Hardin-Simmons U., 1952; postgrad. Colo. State Coll., summers 1961-62; Ph.D., East Tex. State U., 1965; m. Bettie Horn, July 21, 1950; children—Marc C., Kathryne Ann. Jr. high sch. tchr., Olden, Tex., 1950-52; jr. high sch. prin., Spur, Tex., 1952-53; elementary sch. tchr., Odessa, Tex., 1953-56, elementary sch. prin., 1956-65; instr. Evening Coll., Odessa, 1958-65; dir. personnel, Odessa, 1965-66; supt. schs., Palestine, Tex., 1966—. Served with USMCR, 1946-48. Mem. Tex. Tchrs. Assn., Am., Tex. assns. sch. adminstrs., Palestine C. of C., Phi Delta Kappa. Rotarian. Home: Box 248 Palestine TX 75801 Office: Box 440 Palestine TX 75801

HOOD, GRAHAM S., found. exec.; b. Stratford-on-Avon, Eng., Nov. 6, 1936; s. Stanley G. and Lillian F. Hood; M.A. in Modern History, Keble Coll., Oxford (Eng.) U.; postgrad. Courtauld Inst. Art, London U.; m. Gale Frackelton, Aug. 5, 1961; children—Sarah, Jorin. Came to U.S., 1961. Curator European decorative arts Wadsworth Atheneum, 1961-64; asso. curator Garvan collection Yale Art Gallery, 1964-68; curator Am. art Detroit Inst. Art, 1968-71; v.p., dir. collections Colonial Williamsburg (Va.) Found., 1971—; adj. prof. history of art Wayne State U., Detroit, 1968-71; lectr. history of art U. Mich. at Ann Arbor, 1970-71. Am. Philos. Soc. grantee, 1966. Mem. Am., English ceramic circles. Cons. editor Am. Decorative Arts Series. Mem. editorial bd. Art Quar.; editorial cons. Am. Art Jour. Home: Benjamin Waller House Williamsburg VA 23185 Office: Colonial Williamsburg Found Williamsburg VA 23185

HOOD, JOHN THOMAS, JR., judge; b. Hazelhurst, Miss., Aug. 16, 1909; s. John Thomas and Minnie (Stewart) H.; B.A., La. State U., 1931, J.D., 1933; m. Alvina Ruth Good, Sept. 10, 1938; children—Susan Janet, John Stewart. Admitted to La. bar, 1933; practiced in Jennings, La., 1933-46; dist. judge La. 14th Jud. Dist., Lake Charles, 1946-60; judge Ct. Appeal, La. 3d Circuit, Lake Charles, 1960—; vis. prof. La. State U. Law Sch., 1973; vice chmn. La. Conf. Ct. of Appeal Judges. Past pres. YMCA, Lake Charles. Served to maj. AUS, 1942-46. Decorated Legion of Merit. Mem. Am., La., S.W. La. bar assns., Am. Judicature Soc., Inst. Jud. Adminstrn., La. Law Inst., La. Dist. Judges Assn. (past pres.), Appellate Judges Conf., Greater Lake Charles C. of C., Am. Legion, V.F.W., Lake Charles Power Squadron, La. Outdoor Drama Assn., La. State U. Alumni Fedn. (past pres.), La. State U. Law Sch. Alumni Assn. (past pres.), Order of Coif, Scribes, Lambda Chi Alpha, Gamma Eta Gamma (past chancellor), Omicron Delta Kappa. Presbyn. (elder). Mason, Kiwanian (past lt. gov.). Club: Lake Charles Country. Contbr. articles to profl. jours. Home: 1008 8th St Lake Charles LA 70601 Office: PO Box 3000 Lake Charles LA 70601

HOOD, WILLIS TED, dentist; b. Mt. Hermon, Ky., Apr. 25, 1934; s. Prentise and Anna (Brown) H.; student Western Ky. State U., 1952-54, 58-60; D.M.D., U. Louisville, 1964; m. Aileen Clay, Aug. 20, 1960; children—Melody, Maria, Edward Mitchell. Practice dentistry, Mt. Sterling, Ky., 1964—. Cons. Area Comprehensive Health Planning Council; mem. Montgomery County Bd. Health. Served with USNR, 1954-58. Mem. Am., Ky., Blue Grass dental assns., Am. Acad. Gen. Dentistry, Am. Analgesia Soc. Republican. Rotarian (dir. 1968—). Baptist (deacon). Home: PO Box 443 Mount Sterling KY 40353 Office: 30 W Main St Mount Sterling KY 40353

HOOKER, NATHAN HARVEY, assn. exec.; b. Leachville, Ark., Mar. 29, 1939; s. Vann and Opal (Harvey) H.; student U. Alaska, 1959-60; B.A., Hendrix Coll., 1964; postgrad. Charlotte (N.C.) Community Coll., 1969-70; m. Alice Anne Henderson, Aug. 10, 1962; children—John Mark, Patrick Ed. Mng. editor Daily Press newspaper, Paragould, Ark., 1963-66; with A.R.C., various locations, 1966—, dir. pub. relations, Charlotte, 1969-70, dir. pub. relations, fund raising Tex. Gulf Coast div., Houston, 1970-74, asst. mgr. Nat. Capital div., Washington, 1974—. Co-dir. Internat. Center Developing Nations, Houston, 1973—. chmn. troop com. Osage council Boy Scouts Am., 1965; mem. social planning council United Fund, Charlotte, 1969-70; mem. disaster task force Pres.'s Office Emergency Preparedness, 1972; mem. communications com. Houston Livestock Show and Rodeo, 1972—; co-founder, organizer Sheltered Workshop, Paragould, 1963-66. Pres. Greene County chpt. Young Democrats Assn., 1965-66. Served with AUS, 1958-61. Named Best Daily Columnist, Ark. Press Assn., 1964. Mem. Pub. Relations Soc. Am. (chmn. membership com.), Houston Area Hosp. Pub. Relations Soc. (v.p.), Nat. Conf. Social Welfare, U.S. Jr. C. of C. Club: Press (Houston). Home: 14602 Moss Creek St Cypress TX 77429 Office: 2025 E St NW Washington DC 20006

HOOKS, G. EUGENE, educator; b. Goldsboro, N.C., May 15, 1927; s. Louis Gaylor and Selma (Pittman) H.; B.S., Wake Forest U., 1950; M.Ed., U. N.C., 1952; Ed.D., Peabody Coll., 1956; m. Jean Knott, Apr. 9, 1951; children—David Eugene, Dennis Jesse, Michael Louis. Asso. prof. phys. edn. Wake Forest U., N.C., 1956-64, athletic dir., 1964—. Served with USNR, 1945-46. Rotarian. Author: Application of Weight Training to Athletics. Home: 2005 Faculty Dr Winston-Salem NC 27109

HOOKS, LANCE GILBERT, govt. ofcl.; b. Mt. Vernon, Ark., Sept. 16, 1906; s. Edward Charles and Nancy (Thompson) H.; student Washington U., 1925-27, U. Chgo., 1930-32, Northwestern U., 1933; m. Altha Floreetha Hazlewood, Sept. 6, 1932; 1 son, Daryl Lance. Marketing and information specialist U.S. Dept. Agr., St. Louis,

1925-28, Chgo., 1928-35, 40-45, San Antonio, 1935-40, Washington, 1945-64; marketinc cons. U.S. State Dept., Ministries Agr. in Brazil, Peru, Colombia, Republic of Panama, Guyana, Barbados, Vietnam, 1964-72. Cons. FAO, UN, Peru, 1969. Internat. Devel. Service Barbados, 1970. Served with AUS, 1943. Recipient Merit awards U.S. Dept. Agr., 1963, 68, 69; Superior Service award U.S. Dept. Agr. and Alpha Kappa Psi, 1968. Mem. Am. Assn. Agrl. Coll. Editors, Pub. Relations Soc. Am., Nat. Press Club. Mason (32 deg., Shriner). Home: 408 S George Mason Dr Arlington VA 22204

HOOPER, JAMES WILLIAM, mathematician; b. Tuscumbia, Ala., June 13, 1937; s. John Albert and Stella Ross (Tompkins) H.; B.S. with highest honors, Florence State Coll., 1959; M.S. in Math. (Woodrow Wilson fellow), Auburn U., 1960; M.S. in Computer Sci., U. Mo., 1971; m. Mona Elaine Nading, Dec. 27, 1959; children—Bruce, Stacey, Blaine. Grad. asst. math. Auburn (Ala.) U., 1960; instr. math. Florence (Ala.) State Coll., 1960-62; with G.C. Marshall Space Flight Center, NASA, Huntsville, 1962—, project leader, computer lang. systems, 1966—. Lectr. NSF Summer Insts., 1965-68. Mem. Phi Kappa Phi, Kappa Mu Epsilon. Mem. Ch. of Christ (deacon 1965-71). Home: 522 Delaney Rd NW Huntsville AL 35806 Office: S&E-COMP-DS Marshall Space Flight Center AL 35812

HOOPER, RUSSELL EVANS, city ofcl.; b. Grand Rapids, Mich., June 8, 1930; s. Raymond Charles and Bertha Margaret (Edwards) H.; B.S., Mich. State U., 1959; M.Pub. Works, U. Pitts., 1968; m. Marilyn Ruth Cole, Apr. 3, 1953; children—Sue M., Sandra K., Sharon A., Pat D. With Mich. State Hwy. Dept., Lansing, 1951-64, Alaska Dept. Hwys., Anchorage, 1964-67; city engr. City of Anchorage, 1967-71; dir. pub. works City of Daytona Beach, Fla., 1971—. Served with USNR, 1948-51. Am. Pub. Works Assn. fellow, 1967-68. Mem. Nat. Soc. Profl. Engrs., Am. Soc. C.E., Am. Pub. Works Assn. (sec. central region 1973-74), Inst. Municipal Engrs., Am. Water Works Assn., Fed. Pollution Control Assn., Fla. Engrs. Soc. Home: 3040 S Peninsula Dr Daytona Beach FL 32018 Office: PO Box 551 Daytona Beach FL 32015

HOOPER, WILFORD CLYDE, JR., dentist, educator; b. Houston, July 15, 1927; s. Wilford Clyde and Hilda (Gallia) H.; B.S., U. Houston, 1949; D.D.S., U. Tex., 1954; m. Mary Louise Jones, June 9, 1950; children—Donald Paul, David Clyde. Mem. faculty dental br. U. Tex., Houston, 1954—, now asso. prof. endodontics; practice dentistry specializing in endodontics, Houston, 1964—. Cons. M.D. Anderson Hosp., Houston, 1972—. Served with USNR, 1945-47. Mem. Houston Dist., Tex., Am. dental socs., Southwest Soc. Endodontists (pres.), Omicron Kappa Upsilon, Xi Psi Phi. Methodist (steward). Home: 6706 Redding St Houston TX 77036 Office: 135 Hermann Profl Bldg 6440 Fannin Houston TX 77025

HOOPER, WILLIAM THOMAS FRANCIS, educator, architect; b. Chgo., Jan. 21, 1915; s. William T.F. and Eva Mae (Murphy) H.; B.S., Purdue U., 1937; M.S., U. Pitts., 1941; postgrad. Northwestern U., 1946-50; m. Lycke Graham, Oct. 3, 1959; children—Robert, Thomas, Margaret (Mrs. Timothy J. Shields). Pvt. practice architecture, 1950-61; adviser to Royal Govt. of Afghanistan on housing and town planning for UN, 1964-67; instr. civil engring. U. Pitts., 1939-41; asst. prof. civil engring. Northwestern U., 1946-50, prof., also vis. prof. architecture U. Khartoum (Sudan), 1961-64; prof. architecture Tuskegee Inst., 1970—. Tech. adviser to Tuskegee Planning Commn., 1971—. Mem. planning com. Victory Meml. Hosp., Waukegan, Ill., 1954-59. Served to capt. C.E., AUS, 1942-46; ETO, PTO. Fellow Am. Soc. C.E.; mem. Sigma Psi, Theta Chi. Contbr. articles to profl. jours. Founder Nat. Bldg. Research Sta. of Sudan. Home: PO Box 447 Tuskegee AL 36083

HOOPER-SPEAR, EMILY FRANCIS, interior designer; b. Hamilton, Ont., Can., Sept. 3, 1891; d. Francis William and Mary Evelyn (Twizell) Hooper; B.A., Columbia, 1920; m. Alexander Spear, July 26, 1920. Advt. rep. Furniture World, N.Y.C., 1920-23; account exec. Blumenthal Bros., N.Y.C., 1923-35, Hyman & Co., N.Y.C., 1935-39, Fellows Davis, N.Y.C., 1939-42, all mems. N.Y. Stock Exchange; pvt. practice as interior designer, Miami, Fla. Mem. Nat. Soc. Interior Designers, Designers and Decorators Guild Miami, Miami Shores C. of C., Internat. Platform Assn. Clubs: Da La Casserole (Paris, France); La Gorce Country (Miami Beach, Fla.); Miami Shores Country, Jockey (Miami). Home: 10659 NE 10th Pl Miami FL 33138

HOOVER, JIMMIE HARTMAN, librarian; b. Board Camp, Ark., Nov. 5, 1930; s. James Thomas and Alice Victoria (Peters) H.; student Coll. Ozarks, 1948-49; B.A., Ark. Poly. Coll., 1952; M.S., La. State U., 1958; m. Lillian Elaine Fitzgerald, Jan. 2, 1959. With La. State U. Library, Baton Rouge and New Orleans, 1958—, head order dept., Baton Rouge, 1965-67, head govt. documents dept., 1968—, mem. faculty Sch. Library Sci., 1972-73. Served with Security Service, USAF, 1952-56. Mem. La. (bus. mgr. bull. 1964-65), Am., Southwestern library assns., Spl. Libraries Assn. (nat. govt. information service com., 1969-71), Am. Legion. Author: (with J. Norman Heard) Bookman's Guide to Americana, 6th ed., 1970. Editor Spl. Libraries Assn. Ark., Miss. and La. chpt. Bull., 1970, La. Library Assn. Coll. Sect. Bull., 1968—. Home: 1815 Myrtledale Av Baton Rouge LA 70808

HOOVER, LINN, geologist, assn. exec.; b. Balt., Apr. 13, 1923; s. Z. Linn and Harriet (Beall) H.; A.B., U. N.C., 1948; M.A., U. Mich., 1951; Ph.D., U. Cal. at Berkeley, 1959; m. Joan Patricia Williams, Jan. 31, 1953; children—Peter Linn, Hilary Joan. Geologist U.S. Geol. Survey, 1948-60; exec. sec. div. earth scis. Nat. Acad. Sci., Washington, 1960-63; exec. dir. Am. Geol. Inst., Washington, 1963—. Served with AUS, 1943-45. Fellow Geol. Soc. Am.; mem. Am. Assn. Petroleum Geologists, Am. Geophys. Union. Republican. Episcopalian. Club: Cosmos (Washington). Home: 6902 Oakridge Av Chevy Chase MD 20015 Office: 2201 M St NW Washington DC 20037

HOOVER, ROBERT MAXWELL, JR., oil co. exec.; b. Ardmore, Okla., July 26, 1932; s. Robert Maxwell and Opal Irene (Peyton) H.; B.B.A., U. Okla., 1954; m. Elizabeth Field Lane, Aug. 6, 1955; children—Robert Maxwell III, Virginia Lynn. Landman, Pan Am. Petroleum, Oklahoma City, 1957-61; land mgr. Hadson Oil & Gas Co., Oklahoma City, 1961-67; v.p., gen. mgr. Hall Jones Oil Co., Oklahoma City, 1967-70; pres. Hoover & Bracken Oil Properties, Inc., Oklahoma City, 1970—. Bd. dir. Oklahoma City Council of Camp Fire Girls, 1972-74. Served to 1st lt. USAF, 1955-57. Mem. Am., Oklahoma City assns. of petroleum landmen, Oklahoma City Geol. Soc., Sigma Alpha Epsilon. Republican. Methodist (ofcl. bd. 1966-70). Clubs: Oklahoma City Golf and Country, Petroleum, Whitehall (Oklahoma City). Home: 7209 Waverly Oklahoma City OK 73120 Office: 3232 Liberty Tower Oklahoma City OK 73102

HOOVER, THOMAS BURDETT, chemist; b. Wellsville, Pa., Jan. 17, 1920; s. Walter Wells and Ada (Burdett) H.; student Dickinson Coll., 1936-37; B.S., Pa. State U., 1942, M.S., 1946, Ph.D., 1960; m. Mamie Ruth Heald, Feb. 24, 1945; children—Carol Ann, Morris Everett. Chemist, Carbide Nuclear Co., Oak Ridge, Tenn., 1948-53; sr. scientist Applied Sci. Labs., State College, Pa., 1953-60; chemist Nat. Bur. Standards, Washington, 1960-70; research chemist S.E. Environmental Research Lab., Environmental Protection Agency, Athens, Ga., 1970—. Fellow A.A.A.S., Am. Inst. Chemists (accredited); mem. Am. Chem. Soc., Electrochem. Soc., Ga. Inst. Chemists, Sigma Xi, Phi Lambda Upsilon, Pi Mu Epsilon. Contbr. articles to profl. jours, Patentee in field. Home: 110 Richard Way Athens GA 30601 Office: SERL College Station Rd Athens GA 30601

HOOVER, WENDAL EUGENE, supt. schs.; b. Coyville, Kan., Apr. 12, 1928; s. Kermit William and Jennie Lee (Callahan) H.; student Pittsburgh (Kan.) State Tchrs. Coll., 1948-50; B.S., Tex. Christian U., 1952, M.E., 1955; m. Glenda Kay Barton, Aug. 23, 1952; children—Lana Kay, Keith Wendal, Lisa Ann. Tchr. high sch., Springtown, Tex., 1952-53; prin. elementary sch., Azle, Tex., 1953-61, supt. schs., 1961—. Served with USMC, 1946-48. Mem. Tex. Tchrs. Assn., C. of C., Tex. Am. assns. sch. adminstrs., Phi Delta Kappa. Lion. Home: 1017 Lakeview St Azle TX 76020 Office: 300 Roe St Azle TX 76020

HOPE, JOHN, govt. ofcl.; b. Atlanta, Dec. 25, 1909; s. John and Lugenia (Burns) H.; A.B., Morehouse Coll., 1930; M.A., Brown U. (Soc. Sci. Research Council jr. fellow), 1932; postgrad. (Gen. Edn. Bd. fellow), U. Chgo., 1937, 38, (Rosenwald fellow), 1940-42; m. Elise Oliver, July 19, 1933; children—John, Richard Oliver, Linda Elise (Mrs. Calvin B. Lee). Instr. econs. Morehouse Coll., Atlanta, 1932-33; chmn. dept. econs. Spelman Coll., Atlanta, 1933-45; mgr. Atlanta U. Book Shop, 1933-45; dir. indsl. relations dept. Fisk U., Nashville, 1945-61; asst. exec. dir. Pres.'s Com. Equal Employment Opportunity, Washington, 1961-65; regional dir. Equal Edn. Opportunity, Dept. Health, Edn. and Welfare, Washington, 1965-67, dir. program planning, devel. Office for Civil Rights, 1965-67, asst. dir. planning, 1967-71, dep. spl. asst. to sec. civil rights, 1971—. Cons. Allegheny County Race Relations Com., 1946-47, Trenton Council on Human Relations, 1953-55, Md. Commn. Interracial Problems and Relations, also Balt. Commn. Human Relations, 1954-55, N.J. Div. Against Discrimination, United Packinghouse Workers Am., 1948-53, Mayor's Council on Human Relations, Mpls., 1946-48, So. Regional Council, Atlanta, 1955-61. Bd. dirs. Neighborhood House, Washington, 1968—. Fed. Exec. fellow, Brookings Instn., 1971-72. Mem. Nat. Assn. Human Rights Workers (pres. 1965), Am. Econs. Assn., Am. Soc. Pub. Adminstrn., Soc. Applied Anthropology. Author: Equality of Opportunity, A Union Approach to Fair Employment, 1956; Three Southern Plants of International Harvester Company, 1953. Home: 360 N St SW Washington DC 20024 Office: Dept Health Edn and Welfare Independence Av SW Washington DC 20291

HOPE, WILLIAM DUANE, mus. curator; b. nr. Fort Collins, Colo., June 7, 1935; s. William Earl and Lois (Burnett) H.; B.S., Colo. State U., 1957, M.S., 1959; Ph.D., U. Cal. at Davis, 1964; m. Colleen Bryan, Dec. 22, 1956; children—Pamella Kay, Karen Gail, Linda Michelle. NRC of Can. postdoctoral fellow U. Toronto (Ont., Can.), 1967-68; asso. curator dept. invertebrate zoology Nat. Mus. Natural History, Smithsonian Instn., Washington, 1964—. Mem. Internat. Assn. Meiobenthologists (chmn.; editor newsletter 1968-69), Helminthological Soc. Washington, Am. Microscopical Soc. (mem. bd. reviewers jour.), Soc. Nematologists (asso. editor Jour. Nematology 1970—), Biol. Soc. Washington, Sigma Xi. Contbr. profl. jours. Home: 2620 Lake Ridge Ct Oakton VA 22124 Office: 10th and Constitution Avs Washington DC 20560

HOPKINS, AMY LONGCOPE (MRS. EDWIN BUTCHER HOPKINS), civic worker; b. Lampasas, Tex., Sept. 5, 1887; d. Edmund McLeod and Madeleine (Beall) Longcope; m. Edwin Butcher Hopkins, June 20, 1913; children—Amy (Mrs. Duke Selig), Jane (Mrs. Jack Munger), Louise (Mrs. Harris Underwood), Madeleine (Mrs. James K. Wade), Edwin Butcher. Past trustee Dallas Mus. Fine Arts, Dallas Symphony Soc.; bd. dirs. Dallas Civic Opera Assn., Found. for Humanities and Scis. of So. Methodist U., Dallas Civic Opera; mem. Pres.'s council Tex. Tech U. Found. Mem. Colonial Dames Am., Daus. Barons of Runnemede, Daus. of 1812, Daus. Republic of Tex., Dau. Founders Patriots Am., Order Crown, Dallas Council on World Affairs, Magna Charta Dames, Plantagenet Soc. Episcopalian. Clubs: Brook Hollow Golf, Dallas Petroleum, Public Affairs Luncheon (Dallas). Home: Park Towers 3310 Fairmount Dallas TX 75201

HOPKINS, BILLY GREENE, lawyer; b. Carlisle, Ky., Apr. 5, 1942; s. Charles Leslie and Catherine Francis (Greene) H.; A.B., Centre Coll. of Ky., 1964; J.D., U. Louisville, 1967; m. Barbara Louise Griffin, Sept. 11, 1971. Admitted to Ky. bar, 1967; practice of law, Carlisle, 1970—; atty. Nicholas County Bd. Edn., 1971—. Mem. exec. bd., bd. dirs. Blue Grass Area Devel. Dist. Inc. Served with USNR, 1968-70. Mem. Am. Bar Assn., Carlisle-Nicholas County C. of C. (pres. 1971-72), Carlisle Jr. C. of C. (sec. 1971-72, treas. 1973-74). Democrat. Mem. Christian Ch. (deacon 1971-74). Home: Chestnut St Carlisle KY 40311 Office: Main St Carlisle KY 40311

HOPKINS, BURTRAM COLLVER, II, architect; b. Indpls., Aug. 19, 1936; s. Burtram Wilcox and Anita Letitia (Heyland) H.; student Ia. State U., 1954-57; B.Arch., U. Okla., 1960; M.S., Columbia, 1963; m. Susan Jane Key, Apr. 2, 1960; children—Mark Collver, Julie Ann. Architect, Woodward, Cape & Assos., 1963-69; partner Woodward, Cape & Partners, 1969-70; officer Envirodynamics, Inc., Dallas, 1970, pres., 1970—; dir. Southwestern Dynamics, Inc. Mem. Urban Design Task Force, advisers Dallas Dept. Urban Devel., 1969-71; chmn. archtl. adv. com. Skyline Career Devel. Center, 1973—. Mem. A.I.A. (nat. urban planning and design com. 1974—), Tex. Soc. Architects (urban planning and design com. 1974—). Am. Soc. Planning Ofcls., Urban Land Inst., Phi Delta Theta. Home: 7214 Wild Valley Dallas TX 75231 Office: 1 Lemmon Park N McKinney Av at Blackburn Dallas TX 75204

HOPKINS, ERNEST LOYD, physician; b. Birmingham, Ala., Aug. 14, 1930; s. Clay and Ada (Fields) H.; B.S., Morehouse Coll., 1952; M.D., Howard U., 1957; L.H.D., Monrovia Coll., 1962; m. Lillie B. Blanks, Apr. 24, 1959; children—Ernest C., Loyd Byron, William E. Intern Freedmen's Hosp., Washington, 1957-58, resident, 1958-62; resident Western Res. U., Cleve., 1961-62, asst. prof. obstetrics, gynecology and physiology Howard U. Coll. Medicine, 1965-69, asso. prof. obstetrics and gynecology, 1969-73, prof., 1973—; dir. audio visual aids sect., 1967—. Attending physician Providence Hosp., Cafritz Meml. Hosp., Washington Hosp. Center, Hadley Meml. Hosp., Columbia Hosp. for Women, Freedmen's Hosp. Patron, Met. Police Boys' Clubs, 1965—, Mt. Pleasant Civic Assn. Decorated knight Humane Order of Star of African Redemption Republic of Liberia, 1962. USPHS spl. fellow, Western Res. U., Universidad de la Republica, Uruguay, 1963-65. Diplomate Am. Bd. Obstetrics and Gynecology. Mem. A.M.A., Nat. Med. Assn., Am. Coll. Obstetricians and Gynecologists, Am. Fertility Soc., Am. Heart Assn., A.A.A.S., Med. Soc. D.C. (exec. com. obstetrics and gynecology sect. 1966—). Home: 9351 Mellenbrook Rd Columbia MD 21043 Office: 1413 K St NW Washington DC 20005

HOPKINS, GEORGE MATHEWS MARKS, patent lawyer; b. Houston, June 9, 1923; s. C. Allen and Agnes Cary (Marks) H.; B.S. in Chem. Engring., Ala. Poly. Inst., 1944; student Ga. Sch. Tech., 1943-44; J.D., U. Ala., 1949; postgrad. George Washington U., 1949-50; m. Betty Miller McLean, Aug. 21, 1954; children—Laura McLean, Edith Cary. Admitted to Ala. bar, 1949, Ga. bar, 1954; asso. atty. A. Yates Dowell, 1949-50, Edward T. Newton, 1950-62; asst. dir. research, legal counsel Auburn Research Found., 1954-55; partner firm Newton, Hopkins, Jones & Ormsby, 1962-67, Newton, Hopkins & Ormsby, 1967—. Sec.-treas. Tufted Patterns, Inc., 1959-62; exec. v.p., sec., treas. Fabulous Fabrics, Inc., 1960-62; chmn. bd. Southeastern Carpet Mills, Inc., 1961—; pres. Entertainment Investors, Inc., 1967-70, GNG Corp.; dir. Drawer Systems, Inc., Xepel Inc. Served as lt., submarine service, 1944-46, 50-51. Registered profl. engr., Ga., U.S., Can. Mem. Am., Ga., Atlanta bar assns., Nat. Soc. Profl. Engrs., Am. Judicature Soc., Phi Delta Phi, Sigma Alpha Epsilon. Episcopalian. Clubs: Cherokee Town and Country, Atlanta City. Home: 765 Old Post Rd NW Atlanta GA 30328 Office: Equitable Bldg 100 Peachtree St NW Atlanta GA 30303

HOPKINS, GUY EDWARD, lawyer; b. nr. Conroe, Tex, Jan. 16, 1937; s. Guy Willis and Lilly (Morgan) H.; B.B.A., Sam Houston State U., 1960; J.D., S. Tex. Coll. Law, 1971; m. Ann Marie Etheridge, Oct. 31, 1959; children—John Paul, Mary Carol, Guy, Hilda. Admitted to Tex. bar, 1963: asso. firm Coker & Coker, Conroe Tex., 1963-64; partner firm Hopkins & Alworth, Conroe, Tex. 1965—. Mem. Montgomery County (v.p.), Houston bar assns., Tex. Trial Lawyers Assn. (dir.), Law Sci. Acad. Am., S. Tex. Coll. Law Alumni Assn., Sam Houston State U. Alumni Assn., Tex. Consumers Assn. Mason. Home: 1514 N San Jacinto St Conroe TX 77301 Office: 501 First Nat Bank Bldg Conroe TX 77301

HOPKINS, JANET E. HINES, civic worker; b. Cin.; d. Harry Hayes and Luella (Kaufmann) Hines; student Wellesley Coll., 1943-45; m. Edwin B. Hopkins, Jr., Mar. 1, 1946 (div. Aug. 1962); children—Andrew Delmar II, Christopher Brent. Mem. Jr. League Abilene, Tex., 1956—; vol. worker West Tex. Rehab. Center, 1953-60; mem. Abilene Community Theater; sponsor Abilene Philharmonic Orch., 1960—; patroness Children's Theater; dir. Abilene Philharmonic Assn., 1961-62; co-founder, chmn. Golden Horse Shoe Club for Crippled Children, 1970; chmn. Royal Lipizzan Stallion benefit for West Tex. Rehab. Center, 1970; mem. Abilene Fine Arts Mus., co-chmn. antique show, 1971; mem. Abilene Philharmonic Guild. Republican. Episcopalian. Clubs: Abilene Country, Allegro, Overture, First Nighters, Westwood, Los Aficionados. Home: 1441 Sylvan Dr Abilene TX 79605

HOPKINS, JESSE HOWARD, real estate co. exec.; b. Tamassee, S.C., Sept. 27, 1909; s. James Martin and Mattie (Lay) H.; B.S., Clemson U., 1936; postgrad., Cornell U., 1953; m. Janie Long, June 9, 1936; children—Jesse Howard, Linda (Mrs. Guy Stanley Hill), Joan (Mrs. Joe Kenneth Hill), Martin Long. Tchr. agr. high sch. Jefferson, S.C., 1936-39; tchr. State Dept. Edn., Columbia, S.C., 1936-39; county agr. agt. Anderson County (S.C.), 1941-58; real estate appraiser Pendleton Realty, 1958—, owner, Pendleton Realty, 1968-74. Trustee dist. 4 Pendleton Sch. Bd., 1945—. Recipient numerous awards. Mem. Am. Right of Way Assn., Am. Dairy Assn. (pres. S.C. chpt.), S.C. Dairy Commn. (dir. 1960-70), Tri-County Bd. Realtors (pres. 1972, dir. 1972—), Nat., S.C. bds. realtors. Mason, Lion, Rotarian. Home: The Retreat Queen St Extension Pendleton SC 29670 Office: East Queen Extension Pendleton SC 29670

HOPKINS, ROBERT HOWELL, JR., mortgage banker; b. Dallas, June 29, 1931; s. Robert H. and Pauline (Richardson) H.; B.B.A., Tex. Christian U., 1952; postgrad. Harvard Grad. Sch. Bus., 1952-53; m. Joanne Schneider, Aug. 16, 1952; children—Robert Howell III, Matthew William, Paula. Pres. Nat. Mortgage Corp. Am., Dallas, 1967—. Past pres. Christian Chs. N.M. Mem. Dallas Mortgage Bankers Assn., Tex. Christian U. Letterman's Assn. Mason. Home: 6310 Joyce Way Dallas TX 75225 Office: Box 8046 Dallas TX 75205

HOPKINS, ROBERT LEE, investment co. exec.; b. Kansas City, Kan., Oct. 23, 1924; s. John Lee and Elma Ina (Van Brunt) H.; B.S., Kan. U., 1950; m. Doris Jeanne Barackman, June 9, 1951; children—Gregory K., Robert B., Leslie Ann. Credit reporter Dunn & Bradstreet, Kansas City, Mo., 1950-54; staff accountant Martin Gladman & Co., C.P.A.'s, Kansas City, Kan., 1954-58; v.p., treas. Winfield & Co., Inc., Wichita and N.Y.C., 1958-64; v.p. accounting and data processing Security Benefit Life Ins. Co., Topeka, 1964-69; v.p., treas. Funds, Inc., Houston, 1969—; treas. Commerce Fund, Inc., Industries Trend Fund, Inc., Pilot Fund, Inc., Impact Fund, Inc., Systematic Plans, Inc., Funds Adv. Co.; dir. Systematic Plans, Inc., Funds Adv. Co. Served with USNR, 1943-46. C.P.A., Tex. Mem. Am. Inst. C.P.A.'s, Tex., N.Y. socs. C.P.A.'s. Methodist. Home: 14730 Cindywood St Houston TX 77024 Office: 711 Polk St Houston TX 77002

HOPKINS, ROBERT MERRILL, city ofcl.; b. Springfield, Mass., Aug. 13, 1938; s. Paul Reynolds and Elsie (Steinberg) H.; B.A., N. Tex. State U., 1964, M.A., 1968; m. Donna Dean Stevens, June 23, 1961; children—Kevin Reynolds, Kristi Lin. Various staff positions City of Dallas, 1960-68; asst. city mgr. City of Cocoa Beach (Fla.), 1968-71; city mgr. City of Clermont (Fla.), 1971—. Served with USCGR, 1958-60. Recipient Distinguished Pub. Servant award Clermont Jr. C. of C., 1972. Mem. Internat. City Mgmt. Assn., Alpha Chi. Kiwanian (pres. 1973-74). Home: 562 Minneola Av Clermont FL 32711 Office: 1 Westgate Plaza Clermont FL 32711

HOPKINS, ROGER ARTHUR, recording exec.; b. Charleston, S.C., Apr. 16, 1938; s. George Arthur and Adeline (Breihahn) H.; student pub. schs.; m. Margaret Faye Stanley, Dec. 31, 1960; children—Lisa Carole, Beth Dianne, Gina Gayle. Singer, rec. artist, song writer Talos Record Corp., Augusta, Ga., 1960-62; staff writer Marty Robbins Enterprise, Nashville, 1963—; pres. Little Nashville Enterprises, Inc., Charleston, S.C., 1963—, Creative Prodns., Inc., 1964—, Look Recording Corp., 1964—, also Am. Records, Hopkins & Assos. Internat., owner, pres. Hopkins Ext. Co., Inc., Vista Vending Service; v.p. CBS Security Systems Inc., RCA Leasing Corp. Baptist. Author: Common Objections Encountered in Selling. Address: 828 W Madison Av Charleston SC 29412

HOPKINS, TERRY WAYNE, dentist; b. Wewoka, Okla., Feb. 4, 1940; s. Hubert Wayne and Edra Mable (Franklin) H.; B.A., Okla. Bapt. U., 1963; D.D.S., U. Mo., 1967; m. Margaret Helen Bryan, Dec. 19, 1959; children—Gregory Wayne, Jon Eric, David Mathew, Amy Nichole. Practice dentistry, Prague, Okla., 1967-69, Shawnee, Okla., 1969—. Vice pres. BCJ Corp., Shawnee, 1970—; owner Moccasin Trail Farms, Shawnee. Cons. Redlands Community Action, Chandler, Okla., 1968—. Coach, Little League, Shawnee, 1971-72. Mem. Central Dist. Dental Soc. (sec.-treas. 1971-72, pres.-elect 1973), Okla. (ho. of dels. 1970—; chmn. council continuing edn.), Am. dental assns. Baptist (deacon). Rotarian, Elk. Home: 1901 Dougherty Dr Shawnee OK 74801 Office: 1414 N Kennedy St Shawnee OK 74801

HOPKINS, WALTER GARRISON III, educator; b. Fort Sam Houston, Tex., Mar. 31, 1942; s. Walter Garrison and Doris (Carter) H.; B.S. in Elec. Engring., U. Ala., 1964, M.S., 1969; Ph.D., Auburn U., 1970; m. Rosemary Bishop, Aug. 27, 1966; children—Melissa, Cassandra. Sci. asso. research Lockheed Missiles & Space Co., Huntsville, Ala., 1969-71; asso. prof. dept. engring. tech. Ala. A. and

M. U., Normal, 1971—, chmn. dept., 1972—. Nat. Def. Edn. Act fellow, 1964-67. Mem. I.E.E.E., Am. Soc. - Engring. Edn., A.A.A.S., Phi Kappa Psi. Home: 3805 Jamestown Dr Huntsville AL 35810 Office: Dept Engring Tech Ala A and M Univ Normal AL 35762

HOPPE, ELLSWORTH WILLIAM, city ofcl.; b. Marilla, N.Y., Nov. 22, 1917; s. Edward William and Clara (Richter) H.; student U. Buffalo, 1938-40; m. Gwen Sahli, June 17, 1939; children—William, Cheryl (Mrs. Andrew R. Haslett), Toby Sue. Teller, Citizens Nat. Bank, Lancaster, N.Y., 1937-42; property accountant, dir., purchasing agt. Curtiss Wright Corp., Camp Curtissaire, Cheektowaga, N.Y., 1942-47; sales rep. Lily Tulip Cup Corp., N.Y.C., 1947-50; owner Cayuga Supply Co., 1950-56; purchasing agt. City of Pompano Beach, Fla., 1956-63, personnel dir., 1960-61, city mgr., 1963-70; city mgr., Eustice, Fla., 1970—. Exec. dir. Teen Club, Lancaster, N.Y., 1942-44; pres. Lancaster P.T.A., 1954-55; chmn. Eustice Cancer Crusade, 1971; gov's. del. Nat. Rivers and Harbors Congress, 1969. Bd. govs. Broward County (Fla.) United Fund. Recipient Outstanding Service award Kiwanis Club, 1963-65; named Pompano Beach Boss of the Year, Nat. Secretarial Assn. Internat., 1965. Mem. Assn. Basketball Ofcls., Internat., Fla. (dir. 1969) city mgrs. assns., Fla. Police Chiefs' Assn., Lake County League of Municipalities (sec.-treas. 1972), Pompano Beach Navy League (dir. 1967-68), Pompano Beach Men's Golf Assn. Presbyn. Kiwanian. Home: 1421 Tedford Av Eustis FL 32726 Office: 10 N Gtove St Eustis FL 32726

HOPPENSTEIN, JOEL MANUEL, lawyer; b. Waco, Tex., Mar. 17, 1910; s. Zorach and Ronie (Dalkowitz) H.; student U. Tex., 1928-31; B.A., Baylor U., 1931, J.D., 1933; m. Stella Mosesman, July 7, 1935; children—Jay Marshall, Linda Carol. Admitted to Tex. bar, 1933; with W.H. Flippin Law Offices, Dallas, 1933-35; asst. city atty. City of Dallas, 1935-39; pvt. practice law, Dallas, 1939—; pres. S.W. Film Lab., Inc., Dallas, 1960—. Bd. dirs. Jewish Welfare Fedn., 1935—, v.p. 1955. Mem. Am., Dallas bar assns., State Bar Tex. Mason (Shriner). Jewish religion. Clubs: Columbian, Variety (Dallas). Home: 5762 Berkshire Lane Dallas TX 75209 Office: Republic Bank Tower Dallas TX 75201

HOPPERSTEAD, FREDRICK ALLAN, computer co. exec.; b. Princeton, Minn., Feb. 17, 1939; s. Ingvauld John and Rose Emilla (Hilken) H.; B.S. in Math., N. Tex. State U., 1965; m. Sue Carol Rowley, June 29, 1963; children—Deanna Lyn, Julie Ann. With Tex. Instruments Corp., Dallas, 1962-65; programmer, analyst Wolf Research & Devel. Corp., West Concord, Mass., 1965-66; computer project leader Univac subsidiary Sperry Rand, Chgo., 1966-69; programming mgr. Harris Communications Systems, Inc., Dallas, 1969—. Mem. Math. Assn. Am., Univac Sci. Exchange, Univac User's Assn. Home: 3809 Flamingo Dr Irving TX 75062 Office: Harris Communications Systems Inc 11262 Indian Trail Dallas TX 75229

HOPPING, WADE LEE, lawyer; b. Dayton, O., Aug. 12, 1931; s. Paul W. and Mildred L. (Flints) H.; B.A., LL.B., Ohio State U., 1953, 55; m. Mary Monroe, June 6, 1971; children—Steve Wade, Kiff, Jud, Mary Elizabeth Mendoza, Hank. Admitted to Ohio bar, 1955, Fla. bar, 1958; partner firm Adams and Hopping, Columbus, 1957-58; Fla. Supreme Ct. research asst., 1958-60, 62-64; asso. M.F. Baugher, Palm Beach, Fla., 1960-61; dir. continuing legal edn. Fla. Bar, 1964-67; legislative asst. to Fla. Gov., 1966-68; justice Supreme Ct. Fla., 1968-69; partner firm Mahoney, Hadlow, Chambers and Adams, Jacksonville and Tallahassee, Fla., 1969—. Chmn., Fla. Law Revision Council. Mem. Fla. Bar Environmental Law Com. Served to 2d lt. AUS, 1955-57. Mem. Fla. Bar, Am. Bar Assn. (chmn. elect sect. bar activities). Republican. Methodist. Kiwanian. Author: Re Attorney Client Relationship, 1963, 70; Environmental Threshold Considerations, 1974. Office: Barnett Bank Bldg Tallahassee FL 32301

HOPPS, HOWARD BERTRAM, lawyer, lectr.; b. nr. Caney, Kan., Feb. 18, 1887; s. John Jacob and Laura J. (Garrett) H.; B.O., Epworth U. (now Oklahoma City U.), 1909; m. Freda C. Andreen, Aug. 12, 1917; children—Dorothy Jeanne Millard, Howard Bertram. With transp. dept. Panama Canal, 1905-07; admitted to Okla. bar 1909; asst. county atty., Oklahoma County, 1916-17; pres. Am. Assn. Ret. Persons, 1967—, also contbr. column to local chpt. monthly; lectr. on leisure, retirement. Chmn. 5th dist. Okla. Republican party. Served with 5th div., U.S. Army, World War I; AEF. Recipient Teddy Roosevelt medal for service on Panama Canal, 1907. Mem. Okla., Ark., Mo. archeol. socs., C. of C., Am. Legion (post comdr. 1919-20, chmn. nat. finance com. 1920). Mason (32 deg.). Club: Oklahoma City Golf and Country. Author: Friend, 1967. Home: 7321 Waverly St Oklahoma City OK 73120 Office: First Nat Bldg Oklahoma City OK 73102

HOPSON, ROBERT SALMON, city ofcl.; b. Girard, Ill., Dec. 19, 1914; s. Albartus and Cora Crystal (Cramp) H.; B.S., U. Ill., 1937; M.S., Loyola U., Chgo., 1943; m. Viola Irene Allen, Oct. 9, 1937; children—Barbara Dian (Mrs. Alan Witter), Robert Craig. Sanitary engr. North Shore Municipalities, Winnetka, Ill., 1937-43, USPHS, 1943-46; chief street sanitation, chief bur. operations, dept. pub. works City of Richmond (Va.), 1946-54, dir. pub. works, 1954-70; dir. pub. works City of Charlotte (N.C.), 1970—. Mem. Am. Pub. Works Assn. (chmn. bd. trustees of edn. found. 1974—, mem. adv. council 1966—, nat. pres. 1965-66, dir. 1956-64), Blackburn Coll. Alumni Assn. (pres. 1968-69), Charlotte-Mecklenburg Environmental Quality Council. Home: 3526 Fielding Av Charlotte NC 28211 Office: 301 S McDowell St Charlotte NC 28202

HORKAN, GEORGE ARTHUR, judge; b. Moultrie, Ga., Mar. 9, 1926; s. George Arthur and Martha (Olliff) H.; A.B., Mercer U., 1950; J.D., U. Ga., 1952; m. Virginia Davis, Aug. 25, 1951; children—George Arthur III, Franklin D., Martha Virginia. Admitted to Ga. bar, 1952; mem. firm Horkan & Peters, Moultrie, 1952-69; municipal ct. judge, Moultrie, 1957-69; dist. atty. So. Circuit of Ga., Moultrie, 1969-72, superior ct. judge, 1972—. Adult adviser Moultrie Youth Center. Served with USNR, 1944-46. Mem. Moultrie Bar Assn. (pres. 1960), Am. Legion, V.F.W., Phi Kappa Phi, Phi Delta Phi. Presbyn. (elder 1969—). Elk, Kiwanian (pres. 1963). Asso. editor: Ga. Bar Jour., 1952. Home: 20 17th Av SE Moultrie GA 31768 Office: Courthouse Moultrie GA 31768

HORN, LOUIS JOHN, research editor; b. Hammond, Ind., Jan. 25, 1915; s. Louis Frank and Mary (Robl) H.; student Pittsburg Tchrs. Coll., 1935-36; B.S., Kan. State U., 1939, postgrad., 1940; m. Bonita Graham, Nov. 8, 1942; children—Toni Katherine (Mrs. Ronald L. Barnes), Louis Graham. Tool planner and designer Beech Aircraft Corp., 1940-45; engr. project Boeing Aircraft Co., 1945-46; tech. writer R. Buckminster Fuller and Fuller Houses, Inc., 1946; asst. research engr., editor Fla. Engring. and Indsl. Expt. Sta., U. Fla., 1947-48; supr. publs. Tex. Engring. Expt. Sta., Tex. A. and M. U., 1948-64; research editor Tex. Transp. Inst., College Station, 1964—. Mem. Tex. adv. com. Jr. Engring. Tech. Soc., 1963—. Chmn. orgn., extension, publicity coms. Arrow-moon dist. Houston council Boy Scouts Am., 1953-59. Bd. dirs., sec. bd. A. and M. Wesley Found. Mem. Am. Soc. Tool Engrs., Am. Coll. Pub. Relations Assn., So. Council Indsl. Devel., Sigma Delta Chi. Democrat. Methodist. Mason (32 deg., Shriner). Home: 820 S Rosemary St Bryan TX 77801 Office: Information Services Bldg College Station TX 77843

HORNAK, ANN, librarian; b. College Station, Tex., June 3, 1922; d. Josef and Anna (Drozd) Hornak; B.A., U. Tex., 1944; B.S. in L.S., U. Ill., 1945; M.Ed., U. Houston, 1956. Children's librarian Schenectady Pub. Library, 1945-47, Pasadena (Cal.) Pub. Library, 1947-49; supr. juvenile div. Houston Pub. Library, 1949-57, asst. dir., 1957—. Mem. Tex. Library Assn. (chmn. pub library div. 1963-64, rep.-at-large 1967—), Houston Library Club (pres. 1967-68), Kappa Delta Pi. Home: 1831 W Main St Houston TX 77006 Office: 500 McKinney Av Houston TX 77002

HORNBACK, RAYMOND RICE, univ. adminstr.; b. Greenville, Ky., July 19, 1934; s. Raymond C. and Daisy N. (Rice) H.; A.B., U. Ky., 1956, M.A., 1962; Ed.D., Ind. U., 1968; m. Betty J. Collins, July 28, 1966; children—Katherine Jeanelle, Raymond Rice. Staff writer A.P., 1955; dir. publicity and publs. Morehead (Ky.) State U., 1956-59, dir. pub. relations, 1959-62, asst. to pres., 1962-68, v.p. for univ. affairs, 1968-73, v.p. univ. relations, 1973—, asso. prof. higher edn., 1968-73. Served with AUS, 1963. Mem. Am. Coll. Pub. Relations Assn. (program chmn. S.E. dist. 1973, pub. affairs com. 1972—, exec. com. 1973-74), Phi Kappa Tau (long range planning com. 1971—), Phi Delta Kappa, Sigma Delta Chi. Democrat. Methodist. Clubs: Optimist (pres. 1965, dist. lt. gov.). Author: Policy Boards of Public State-Supported Institutions of Higher Education, 1968. Home: 3629 Cayman Lane Lexington KY 40505

HORNE, ALEXANDER, newspaper editor; b. Warsaw, Poland, Nov. 9, 1932; B.A., Williams Coll., 1954; married; 6 children. With Berkshire Eagle, Pittsfield, Mass., 1955-56; asst. city editor Washington Post, 1958-60, local reporter, 1960, asst. editor Potomac, 1960-62, asst. world editor, 1962-65, day nat. editor, 1965-69, nat. reporter, 1969-70, dep. nat. editor, 1970-71, editor Outlook, 1971—. Served with AUS, 1956-58. Home: 7214 Rebecca Dr Alexandria VA 22307 Office: Washington Post 1150 15th St NW Washington DC 20005

HORNE, CONRAD PHYLL, govt. ofcl.; b. Tremonton, Utah, Jan. 6, 1921; s. William Roy and Phyllis (Halladay) H.; student Utah State U., 1939-40; B.S., U. Utah, 1943; certificate meteorology U. Chgo., 1943; certificate electronics Harvard, 1944; certificate in radar principles Mass. Inst. Tech., 1944; m. Leila Rae Welling, Sept. 8, 1943; children—Judith (Mrs. Paul B. Hansen), Michael, Bryant, Kathleen, Deborah, Rebecca, David. Cons. engr. McNary & Wrathall, Washington, 1946-49; electronic engr. Office Chief Signal Officer, Washington, 1949-51; electronic engr. Fed. Civil Def. Adminstrn., Washington, 1951-53; cons. engr. J.C. McNary, Washington, 1953-61; engring. asst. to commr. FCC, Washington, 1961-66, engring. asst. to chmn., 1966-71, chief Frequency Allocation and Treaty Div., 1971-73, dep. chief engr., 1973, chief field operations bur., 1973—. Served with AUS, 1943-46. Registered profl. engr., D.C. Mem. I.E.E.E. Mem. Ch. of Jesus Christ of Latter-day Saints (local bishop 1957-64). Home: 5841 Glen Forest Dr Falls Church VA 22041 Office: 1919 M St Washington DC 20554

HORNE, JOHN E., mortgage ins. co. exec., former govt. ofcl.; b. Clayton, Ala., Mar. 4, 1908; s. John Eli and Cornelia (Thomas) H.; Normal certificate Troy State U., 1928; A.B. with honors, U. Ala. 1933, M.A. (fellow in history 1933-35), 1941, LL.D., 1970; m. Ruth F. Kleinman, July 27, 1938; children—Linda (Mrs. Richard Clark), Susan (Mrs. James K. Ewart). Tchr., Pike County, Ala., 1925-26, Columbiana, Ala., 1928-31; rep. Macmillan Pub. Co., 1935-39, Row, Peterson Pub. Co., 1939-42, 46; adminstrv. asst. to Senator John J. Sparkman of Ala., 1947-51, 54-61; adminstr. Small Def. Plants Adminstrn., 1951-53; staff dir. Democratic Senatorial Campaign Com., 1954; asst. campaign mgr. to Adlai E. Stevenson, 1956; exec. dir. Nat. Citizens Com. Kennedy-Johnson, 1960; adminstr. Small Bus. Adminstrn., 1961-63; mem. Fed. Home Loan Bank Bd., 1963-68 chmn., 1965-68; pres. Investors Mortgage Ins. Co., 1969-70, chmn., 1970—; sec. Mortgage Ins. Assos. Am., 1974—; dir. Continental Investment Corp., Boston. Pres. Pi Kappa Alpha Meml. Found., 1967-69. Served from lt. (j.g.) to lt. (s.g.) USNR, 1943-45, capt. Res. Recipient Letter of Commendation for meritorious Navy service, Outstanding D.C. Alumnus award U. Ala., 1965, Outstanding Alumnus award Troy State U., 1968. Mem. Fla. Jr. C. of C., Am. Legion, Sons Confederate Vets., V.F.W., Newcomen Soc., Ala. Hist. Soc., Phi Beta Kappa, Omicron Delta Kappa, Phi Delta Kappa, Kappa Delta Pi, Pi Kappa Alpha (chmn. nat. conv. 1958; chmn. distinguished achievement award com. 1961-62; distinguished achievement award 1966; nat. treas. 1966-68). Elk. Clubs: Nat. Press, Nat. Capital Democratic (dir.), Post Mortem, Burro, Internat., Metropolitan (Washington). Home: 415 Crown View Dr Alexandria VA 22314

HORNE, MALLORY ELI, state senator, community devel. exec.; b. Tavares, Fla., Apr. 17, 1925; s. Cleveland Reid and Clifford (Parnell) H.; student Fla. State U., 1948; LL.B., U. Fla., 1950; m. Anne Veronica Livingston, Mar. 15, 1945; children—Mallory Eli, David Albert. Admitted to Fla. bar, 1950; chmn. bd. chief exec. officer Killearn Properties, Inc., Tallahassee, 1964—; dir. Tallahassee Bank and Trust Co., Tallahassee Bank North; mem. Fla. Senate, 1966—, pres., 1972-74. Mem. Fla. Ho. of Reps., 1954-65, speaker 1962-64. Bd. dirs. pres. Tallahassee Meml. Hosp. 1965-67. Served to capt. USAAF, 1942-45. Recipient Good Govt. award Fla. Jr. C. of C., 1961; named Most Outstanding House Mem. St. Petersburg Times, 1963, Most Outstanding Senator, 1972. Mem. Fla. Bar (pres. jr. sect. 1954-55), Fla. State U. Alumni Assn., (pres. 1967). Mason, Elk. Club: Tallahassee Exchange (pres.). Home: Route 1 Box 190 Tallahassee FL 32303 Office: Suite 200 Tallahassee Bank Bldg Tallahassee FL 23201

HORNER, CHARLES EDWARD, surgeon; b. Pekin, Ill., Aug. 31, 1912; s. Robert C. and Clara (Bird) H.; B.S., Antioch Coll., 1934; M.D., Georgetown Med. Sch., 1942; m. Katherine Howe Farrington, Dec. 31, 1951. Mech. engr. Superior Engine Div., Nat. Supply Corp., Springfield, O., 1934-37; clin. instr. surgery Georgetown Med. Sch., 1950-51; practice medicine specializing in surgery, Washington, 1950-59; sr. surgeon USPHS, 1959-62, med. dir., 1962—; asso. chief surg. services USPHS Hosp., S.I., 1960-62; chief surg. service USPHS Hosp., Savannah, Ga., 1962-66; chief surgery USPHS out-patient clinic, Washington, 1966-71; dep. med. dir. Bur. Employees Compensation, U.S. Dept. Labor, Washington, 1971—. Served from 1st lt. to maj. M.C., AUS, 1943-46, ETO. Diplomate Am. Bd. Surgery. Fellow A.C.S.; mem. A.M.A., Assn. Mil. Surgeons U.S. Club: Army and Navy. Home: 4000 Massachusetts Av NW Washington DC 20016 Office: Bur Employees Compensation US Dept Labor 711 14th St Washington DC 20201

HORNER, FENTRESS THOMPSON, judge; b. Troy, N.C., Sept. 16, 1902; s. Kenneth C. and Luola (Arnette) H.; student Campbell Coll., 1923, Wake Forest Coll., 1924-25; m. Mary Frances Sawyer, June 15, 1929. Admitted to N.C. bar, 1925; practice law Elizabeth City, 1925—; mem. firm Worth & Horner; judge Pastuotank County (N.C.) Recorder's Ct., Elizabeth City, 1938-42, 46-66; chief judge Dist. Ct., 1966—. Mem. adv. bd. Albemarle Mental Health Clinic, Elizabeth City, 1958, Salvation Army, 1942; pres. Elizabeth City Boys Club, 1969. Alternate del. Democratic Nat. Conv., 1956. Served to lt. comdr. USNR, 1942-46. Mem. Am. Legion, V.F.W. Episcopalian. Elk, Improved Order of Red Men, Kiwanian. Home: 1116 E Williams Circle Elizabeth City NC 27909 Office: Elizabeth City Courthouse Elizabeth City NC 27909

HORRINGTON, EMILY MAE, research scientist; b. Statesville, N.C., Aug. 18, 1924; d. Moses H. and Myrtle (Campbell) Horrington; B.S., N.C. Coll., 1945, M.S., 1950; Ph.D., Cornell U., 1958. Health tchr. Happy Plains Sch., Taylorsville, N.C., 1945-46; instr. chemistry Paine Coll., Augusta, Ga., 1947-48; head, biology dept. Storer Coll., Harper's Ferry, W.Va., 1954-55; asso. prof. So. U., Baton Rouge, La., 1958-62; head dept. biology Elizabeth City (N.C.) State Coll., 1962-65; research scientist Bronx biol. div. Foster D. Snell, Inc., N.Y.C., 1965-69; program coordinator exptl. gerontology Orentreich Found., N.Y.C., 1969-71; chmn. div. natural scis. Livingstone Coll., Salisbury, N.C., 1971—. Cons. nutrition, lab. animal care, 1955—. Recipient Ciba Found. award, 1959. Fellow A.A.A.S.; mem. Am. Assn. Lab. Animal Sci., N.Y. Acad. Scis., Gerontol. Soc., Sci. Research Soc. Am., Sigma Xi, Beta Beta Beta, Sigma Delta Epsilon, Alpha Kappa Alpha. Home: 216 Johnson St Salisbury NC 28144 Office: Livingstone College Salisbury NC 28144

HORSLEY, THOMAS MARTIN, physician; b. Lovingston, Va., May 15, 1921; s. Thomas Martin and Ruby Temple (Harris) H.; B.S. summa cum laude, Hampden-Sydney Coll., 1942; M.D., Johns Hopkins, 1945; m. Kathleen Brady Keith, Mar. 20, 1948; children—Brian Douglas, Anne Elizabeth. Intern Ch. Home Hosp., Balt., 1945-46; resident McGuire Vets. Hosp., Richmond, Va., 1948-51; practice medicine specializing in internal medicine, Elizabeth City, N.C., 1951—; chief internal medicine Albemarle Hosp., Elizabeth City, 1956-57, 62, 65, 68, 71, pres. med. staff, 1959-60. Pres. Albemarle Med. Corp., 1971-72, Colonial Village Inc., 1971-72. Served to capt. M.C., AUS, 1946-48. Mem. A.C.P., Pasquotank, Camden, Currituck, Dare Counties Med. Soc. (pres. 1957-58), 1st Dist. N.C. Med. Soc., Med. Soc. N.C., A.M.A., Am., N.C. socs. internal medicine, Elizabeth City C. of C. Methodist (trustee). Kiwanian. Home: 2000 Rivershore Rd Elizabeth City NC 27909 Office: 1142 N Road St Elizabeth City NC 27909

HORSTMYER, KENNETH LEROY, restaurant co. exec.; b. Scotia, N.Y., Nov. 13, 1921; s. Albert William and Elizabeth May (Buhrmaster) H.; B.S. in Bus. Adminstrn., Miami U., Oxford, O., 1947; grad. bus. program Columbia, 1958; m. Madeleine Slaughter, Apr. 14, 1950; children—Kendra Sally, Linda Cheryl, Jeffrey Lee, Andrew William. Dir. new market devel. Union Carbide Corp., N.Y.C., 1960-63; exec. v.p. Quality Cts. Motels, Inc., Daytona Beach, Fla., 1963-66; pvt. bus. cons., 1966-67; pres. frozen foods div. W.R. Grace & Co., N.Y.C., 1967-70; group v.p. operations Burger King Corp., Miami, Fla., 1970—. Served with USNR, 1943-47. Mem. Am. Mgmt. Assn., Am. Marketing Assn. Home: 613 Ocean Dr Key Biscayne FL 33149 Office: 7360 N Kendall Rd Miami FL 33156

HORTON, FINAS WADE, supt. schs.; b. Fairfield, Tex., Feb. 8, 1921; s. Issac Fred and Velma Estelle (Lambert) H.; student Tex. Christian U., 1944-45; B.A., U. Tex., 1948, M.A., 1950, postgrad. 1953-56; m. Ferdel Speilman, June 23, 1946; children—Marcia (Mrs. Darryl Smith), Velma (Mrs. Karl Rivers), Rosemary. Classroom tchr. Odessa Pub. Schs., 1948-51, Austin Pub. Schs., 1952-53; asst. county supt. schs. Travis County Schs., Austin, Tex., 1953-62, county sch. supt., 1963—. Bd. dirs. Neighborhood Youth Corps, Travis County. Served with USNR, 1941-46, 51-52. Kellogg Edn. Adminstrn. scholar, 1952. Democrat. Baptist (deacon 1960—). Kiwanian. Club: Civitan (treas. 1961-63) (Austin). Home: Route #1 Box 186 Del Valle TX 78617 Office: PO Box 1748 Austin TX 78767

HORTON, GRANVILLE EUGENE, physician; b. Jean, Tex., July 2, 1927; s. James Granville and Etna (Boyle) H.; B.A., Tex. Technol. Coll., 1950; M.D., U. Tex., 1954; m. Mildred Helen Veale, June 13, 1953; children—Robert Herman Newlin, Linda Kay, Kevin Bruce, Carson Scott. Intern Detroit Receiving Hosp., 1954-55; tng. in radioactive isotope techniques Oak Ridge Inst. Nuclear Studies, 1958; practice medicine Weslaco, Tex., 1955-56, Outlar-Blair Clinic, Wharton, 1956-72; dir. dept. nuclear medicine Nightingale Hosp., El Campo, Tex., 1973—; mem. staff Horton Med. Clinic, El Campo, 1972—; part-time research asso. radioisotope dept. Methodist Hosp., Houston, 1961-66; mem. med. adv. com. and sec. med. staff Caney Valley Meml. Hosp., Wharton, Tex., 1956-72; clin. dir. Wharton County Tb Assn., 1957-67. Bd. dirs. Wharton County div. Am. Cancer Soc., pres., 1960-61; dist. dir. 8th dist. Tex., Citizens com. for Hoover Report, 1957-58. Served with USN, 1946-47. Diplomate Am. Bd. Nuclear Medicine. Fellow Am. Coll. Angiology; mem. Wharton C. of C. (dir., v.p. 1960-61), Am., Tex. (ho. of dels. 1959-61) med. assns., Soc. Nuclear Medicine, Tex. Assn. Physicians Nuclear Medicine, A.A.A.S., Law Enforcement Officers Tex., (asso.), Am. Nuclear Soc., El Campo C. of C., Phi Chi. Republican. Episcopalian. Elk. Contbr. articles to med. publs. Home: 1233 Wallace St El Campo TX 77437 Office: El Campo Profl Center Suite 104 El Campo TX 77437

HORTON, HAMILTON COWLES, JR., lawyer, state senator; b. Winston-Salem, N.C., Aug. 6, 1931; s. Hamilton Cowles and Virginia Lee (Wiggins) H.; summer student U. Grenoble (France), 1950, U. Salzburg (Austria), 1952; A.B., U. N.C., 1953, LL.B., 1956; m. Evelyn Hanes Moore, Feb. 16, 1963; 1 dau., Rosalie Hanes. Admitted to N.C. bar, 1956; asso. Craige, Brawley, Lucas & Hendrix, Winston-Salem, 1960-62, partner Craige, Brawley (formerly Craige, Brawley, Lucas & Horton), 1963—. Mem. N.C. Ho. of Reps., 1969-71, N.C. Senate, 1971—, now joint caucus leader. Mem. Gov.'s Commn. to Study Uniform Consumer Credit Code, Legislative Com. on Environmental Problems, Criminal Code Commn., Council State Goals and Policies. Former bd. dirs. Friends of Salem College Library, Ft. Defiance Restoration; trustee Salem Acad. and Coll. N.C. Symphony Soc. Served to lt. (j.g.) USNR, 1956-60; lt. Res. Mem. Am., N.C., Forsyth County bar assns., N.C. Lit. and Hist. Soc. (dir. 1971-72), Phi Beta Kappa, Phi Delta Phi, Beta Theta Pi. Republican. Mem. Moravian Ch. (central bd. trustees). Rotarian. Clubs: Torch, Old Town. Home: 10 Stump Tree Lane Winston-Salem NC 27106 Office: 210 W 4th St Winston-Salem NC 27102

HORTON, JAMES ALPHONZO, govt. ofcl.; b. Morehead City, N.C., Apr. 1, 1924; s. Curtis Henry and Ada (Becton) H.; B.S., Lincoln U., 1949; postgrad. U. Minn., 1950; m. Dorothy Monson, Jan. 6, 1954; children—Bartt, Mitchell, Stuart, Curtis. Writer, editor U.S. Dept. Agr., Washington, 1962-64, editor agrl. marketing mag., 1964-69; information chief Nat. Inst. Mental Health, Dept. Health, Edn. and Welfare, 1969-70; spl. asst. to dir. Office of Minority Bus. Enterprise, U.S. Dept. Commerce, 1970-72; dep. dir. information Agrl. Marketing Service, Dept. Agr., Washington, 1972—. Named profl. agrl. worker Profl. Agr. Workers Assn., 1966. Home: 8817 Lanier Dr Silver Spring MD 20910 Office: Agrl Marketing Service Washington DC 20250

HORTON, JAMES WRIGHT, lawyer; b. Belton, S.C., Dec. 24, 1919; s. John Aiken and Emmae (Tate) H.; B.A., Furman U., 1942; J.D., Harvard, 1948; m. Eunice Todd Rice, Nov. 20, 1948; children—James Wright, Max, Rex. Admitted to S.C. bar, 1948; mem. firm Nettle & Horton Greenville, S.C., 1948-52; partner Rainey, Fant & Horton, Greenville, 1952-70; pres. Horton, Drawdy, Dillard, Marchbanks, Chapman & Brown, Greenville, 1970—. Pres. United Fund Greenville County, 1959. Trustee Greenville County Sch. Dist., 1964-70; vice chmn. Greenville County Sch. Bd., 1969. Bd. dirs. Greenville Family and Childrens service, 1953-56, pres., 1954-55, 68-70; bd. dirs., v.p. Greenville Mental Health Clinic, 1956-59; bd.

dirs. Carolinas United, Salvation Army. 1970—. Served with USMCR, 1942-45. Decorated Silver Star. Mem. Am., S.C. bar assns., Furman Alumni Assn. Baptist. Kiwanian. Home: 2 Osceola Dr Greenville SC 29605 Office: 307 Pettigru St Greenville SC 29602

HORTON, JEAROLD POWELL, hosp. adminstr.; b. Albertville, Ala., June 30, 1930; s. William Jesse and Sally (McLendon) H.; B.S., Jacksonville (Ala.) State U., 1958; m. Bobbie June Carter, Oct. 26, 1953; children—Steven Jeffrey, Tracy Dianne. Intern med. tech. Holy Name of Jesus Hosp., Gadsden, Ala., 1957-58; chief med. technologist City Hosp., Guntersville, Ala., 1958-63, Guntersville Hosp., 1963-64; adminstr. Guntersville Hosp., 1964—. Served with USAF, 1948-52. Mem. Am., Ala. hosp. assns., Am. Coll. Hosp. Adminstrs., Am. Soc. Clin. Pathologists. Republican. Methodist. Home: Auxiliary Route 4 Guntersville AL 35976 Office: 2067 Dunlap Av Guntersville AL 35976

HORTON, J(OSEPH) REX, broadcasting engr.; b. Greeneville, Tenn., Dec. 20, 1908; s. Adolphus Bryan and Rebecca (Marshall) H.; grad. Am. Sch., 1936, Nat. Radio Inst., 1940; m. Mary Charlotte Felix, July 28, 1933; children—Joseph Rex, Robert Earl, Charlotte Anne. With A. B. Horton, bldg. constrn., Knoxville, Tenn., 1928-32; retail service sta. mgr., 1933; retail salesman Pure Oil Co., 1934-35; sta. mgr. Retail Service Orgn., Phoenix, 1936-37; route salesman Radio Sales & Service, Knoxville, 1938-42; chief engr. WBIR-AM-FM-TV, Knoxville, 1943-74. Home: 1715 North Hills Blvd Knoxville TN 37917 Office: 1513 Hutchison Av Knoxville TN 37917

HORTON, MALCOLM ALLAN, steel co. exec.; b. Littlefield, Tex., Nov. 1, 1926; s. Malcolm Foster and Berah Willie (Kennedy) H.; B.S., Tex. A. and M. U., 1947; m. Mariquette Coats, Jan. 20, 1951; children—Nan (Mrs. Jeffry Roy Ellis), Jan, Cynthia Kay. With Central Tex. Iron Works, Waco, 1947—, v.p. prodn., 1966—, also dir. Mem. Woodway City Charter Commn., 1973—. Trustee Cherokee Home for Children. Registered profl. engr., Tex. Mem. Am. Soc. M.E., Nat. Soc. Profl. Engrs., Tau Beta Pi. Republican. Mem. Ch. of Christ (elder). Rotarian. Club: Ridgewood Country. Home: 609 Topeka St Waco TX 76710 Office: 2500 Webster St Waco TX 76703

HORTON, ROBERT HENRY, civil engr.; b. Athens, Tenn., July 5, 1907; s. William Ryder and Willie (McKeldin) H.; student Maryville (Tenn.) Coll., 1926-27; B.S. in Civil Engring., U. Tenn., 1933; m. JoAnna Stubley, Oct. 11, 1957; children—Leslie M., William Stubley, Elizabeth Ann, Robert Michael, George Henry. Engr. various depts. State Rd. Dept. Fla., 1939-72, final estimate engr., 1951-72, computer engr., 1963-72; civil engr. Volusia County Pub. Works Dept., Deland, Fla., 1973—. Served to maj. AUS, 1941-46; PTO. Decorated -Bronze Star. Registered profl. engr., Fla. Mem. Am. Soc. C.E., Nat. Soc. Profl. Engrs., Fla. Engring. Soc. Home: 1011 W Howry Av DeLand FL 32720 Office: 145 W Indiana Av DeLand FL

HORTON, THEODORE LYONELL, architect; b. Stillwater, Okla., Dec. 28, 1925; s. Ollie Elmer and Odelia May (Thomas) H.; B.Archtl. Engring., Okla. A. and M. Coll., 1950; m. Martha Anne Cook, June 4, 1950; children—Gregory Lyonell, Jane Anne. Draftsmen, E. Chester Nelson, A.I.A., Ft. Smith, Ark., 1950-53, Haralson & Mott, A.I.A., Ft. Smith, 1953-56, Hortsman & Mott, A.I.A., Muskogee, Okla., 1956-60; chief draftsman James Marshall, A.I.A., Lawton, Okla., 1960-64; pvt. practice as Ted Horton, A.I.A., Lawton, 1964—. Mem. long range planning com. Lawton council Camp Fire Girls, 1970—, mem. Lawton Philharmonic Orch., 1962—. Adv. bd. Salvation Army, 1972—, A.R.C., 1973—. Served with USNR, 1944-45. Mem. A.I.A., Nat. Fedn. Ind. Bus., U.S., Lawton chambers commerce. Baptist (deacon 1953—). Club: Executive (pres. 1974) (Lawton). Home: 1517 N 33d St Lawton OK 73501 Office: 2507 N Sheridan Rd Lawton OK 73501

HORTON, THOMAS EDWARD, JR., educator; b. Houston, Jan. 12, 1935; s. Thomas Edward and Minnie Tolula (Sloan) H.; B.S., U. Tex., 1957, Ph.D., 1964; M.S. (Caterpillar research fellow), Stanford, 1958; m. Bobbie Jean Newcomb, June 8, 1963; children—Holly Anne, Thomas Edward III. Jr. mech. engr. Shell Devel. Co., Houston, 1957-58; teaching asst., research asst., research scientist U. Tex., Austin, 1959-62; research engr. Jet Propulsion Lab. Cal. Inst. Tech., Pasadena, 1962, sr. research engr., 1963-66; asso. prof. mech. engring., research engr. U. Miss., 1966-71, prof., research engr., 1971—. Cons. Army Research Office, Durham, N.C., Jet Propulsion Lab. Asso. fellow Am. Inst. Aeros. and Astronautics; mem. Am. Soc. M.E., Am. Phys. Soc., Am. Soc. for Engring. Edn. (Research award Southeastern sect. 1971), Sigma Xi, Tau Beta Pi, Pi Tau Sigma, Phi Eta Sigma. Republican. Methodist. Contbr. articles to profl. jours. Patentee in field. Home: 209 St Andrews Circle Oxford MS 38655 Office: U Miss University MS 38677

HORTON, THOMAS MANNING, orthodontist; b. Pendleton, S.C., Aug. 12, 1922; s. Childs Clinton and Frances Grace (Hughes) H.; B.S., Clemson U., 1942; D.D.S., Emory U., 1946; m. Dorothy Jeanette Sterne, Apr. 26, 1944; children—Thomas Manning, Amanda Caron. Practice orthodontics, Spartenburg, S.C., 1948-49; practice dentistry specializing in orthodontics, Columbus, Ga., 1950—; pres. Profl. Assn., Columbus, 1969—; pres. Dental Support Services, Inc., 1970—. Trustee Brookstone Sch., Columbus Coll. Found.; bd. dirs. United Givers, YMCA. Served to capt., Dental Corps, USAF, 1946-48. Fellow Am. Coll. Dentists, Ga. Dental Assn. (hon.); mem. Am., Ga. dental assns., So., Begg socs. orthodontics, Am. Assn. Orthodontics, Psi Omega. Episcopalian. Mason, Rotarian. Clubs: Big Eddy, Green Island (Columbus); Piedmont (Spartanburg). Home: 6698 Waterford Court Columbus GA 31904 Office: 1200 Wynnton Rd Columbus GA 31906

HORTON, WILLIAM LAMAR, educator; b. Rock Hill, S.C., Aug. 26, 1935; s. Luther Burns and Ruth (Stogner) H.; Mus.B., Furman U., 1956; M.Sacred Music, So. Bapt. Theol. Sem., 1958, D.Mus. Arts, 1970; postdoctoral study U. Mich., 1968; m. Peggy Ann Small, June 16, 1956; children—Richard Lamar, Ronald William, Randall Alan, Julie Anne. Minister music First Bapt. Ch., Taylors, S.C., 1954-56, Broadway Bapt. Ch., Louisville, 1956-58, First Bapt. Ch., Douglas, Ga., 1958-59; instr. music U. Ga., 1958-59, So. Bapt. Theol. Sem., Louisville, 1959-62; prof. music, chmn. dept. ch. music Ouachita Bapt. U., Arkadelphia, Ark., 1963-68; prof. music Okla. Bapt. U., Shawnee, 1968—; minister music Univ. Bapt. Ch., Shawnee, 1968—. Clinician, adjudicator music festivals throughout South and S.W.; baritone soloist various musicals, oratorios, other prodns. Trustee B.B. McKinney Music Research Found., 1972—. Mem. Music Tchrs. Nat. Assn. (exec. com. S.W. dist. 1968-74), Nat. Assn. Tchrs. of Singing (pres. Okla. chpt. 1973-75), Okla. Music Tchrs. Assn. (3d v.p. 1970—), A.S.C.A.P., So. Bapt. Ch. Mus. Conf., Phi Mu Alpha Sinfonia (Okla. province gov. 1968-73). Mason, Rotarian. Author: Introduction to Singing, 1968. Contbr. critiques, revs. to profl. jours. Composer: Song of the Lamb, 1958, Salvation to Our God, 1962, How Excellent is Thy Name, 1962, Praise Ye The Lord, 1963. Home: 18 Mojave Dr Shawnee OK 74801

HORVATH, GEORGE JOSEPH, state ofcl.; b. Komarom, Hungary, Mar. 19, 1944; s. Carl and Maria (Molidor) H.; came to U.S., 1960; B.S., Coll. City N.Y., 1966; M.S. (Creole Found. scholar 1967-72), Fla. State U., 1968, Ph.D., 1973; m. Carol Lani Hill, Mar. 29, 1969. Chief marine geologist U.S. Naval Ship Eltanin, Antarctica, 1968-69; sedimentologist Glomar Challenger, deep sea drilling project NSF, 1972; environmental specialist, dept. pollution control State of Fla., Tallahassee, 1973—. Instr. geology Tallahassee Community Coll., 1970. Leader, Boy Scouts, Caracas, Venezuela, 1959-66. Mem. A.A.A.S., Am. Soc. Limnology and Oceanography, Internat. Oceanographic Found., Smithsonian Inst., Asociacion Venezolana de Geologia Mineria y Petroleo. Contbr. articles in field to profl. jours. Office: State of Florida Dept of Pollution Control 2562 Executive Center Circle E Tallahassee FL 32301

HORWARD, DONALD DAVID, educator; b. Pitts., Jan. 9, 1933; s. Frank J. and Selena U. (Hartman) H.; B.A., Waynesburg Coll., 1955; M.A., Ohio U., 1956; Ph.D. (Wilson Found. fellow, Tozar Found. fellow, Univ. grantee), U. Minn., 1962; m. Annabel Lee Vanscyoc, July 19, 1958. Faculty adviser U. Minn., Mpls., 1958-61; instr. history Fla. State U., Tallahassee, 1961-63, asst. prof., 1963-66, asso. prof., 1966-70, prof., 1970—, asst. to chmn. dept. history, 1964-67, asso. chmn., 1967-69, acting chmn., 1969-70, chmn., 1972—. Dir. Consortium on Revolutionary Europe. Research grantee The Calouste Gulbenkian Found., Lisbon, Portugal, 1967, 72; Mem. Am. Hist. Assn., French Hist. Soc., Soc. for Army Hist. Research, Institut Napoleon, Societe Belge d'Etudes Napoleonienne, Societe d'Histoire Moderne, Societe du Chateau Imperial de Pont-de-Briques (Am. rep. com. of honor 1966—), Royal Arty. Inst., Royal Arty. Hist. Soc. (hon. mem.). Author: The Battle of Bussaco: Massena vs. Wellington, 1965; The French Revolution and Napoleon Collection at Florida State University: A Bibliographical Guide, 1973; The French Campaign in Portugal: An Account by Jean Jacques Pelet, 1973. Home: 2101 Great Oak Dr Tallahassee FL 32303

HOSEA, ADDISON, clergyman; b. Pikeville, N.C., Sept. 11, 1914; s. Addison and Alma Eugenia (Bowden) H.; student U. N.C. at Chapel Hill, 1930-31; A.B., Atlantic Christian Coll., 1938; M.Div., U. of South, 1949, D.D., 1970; postgrad. Union Theol. Sem., 1948, Duke, 1950-53; D.D., Episcopal Theol. Sem. Ky., 1968; m. Jane Eubank Marston, June 28, 1944; children—Nancy Jane, Addison III, Anne Cameron. Tchr. N.C. schs., 1932-34, 38-41; ordained deacon Episcopal Ch., 1948, priest, 1949; priest-in-charge St. Gabriel's Ch., Faison, N.C., 1949-51; rector St. Paul's Ch., Clinton, N.C., 1949-54, St. John's Ch., Versailles, Ky., 1954-70; bishop-coadjutor Diocese Lexington (Ky.), 1970, bishop, 1971—; mem. exec. council Diocese East Carolina, 1951-54; prof. N.T. lang. and lit. Episcopal Theol. Sem. Ky., 1954-59, 65-70; hon. canon Cathedral St. George the Martyr, 1964-70. Trustee U. of South, 1949-54, 70—. Served to capt. AUS, 1941-46. Mem. Soc. Bibl. Lit. and Exegesis. Home: 536 Sayre Av Lexington KY 40508 Office: 530 Sayre Av Lexington KY 40508

HOSKINS, GODFREY CURTIS, pathologist; b. Reading, Pa., Feb. 8, 1930; s. Godfrey Walter George and Elizabeth Heloise (Curtis) H.; M.D., U. Tex., 1960; m. Betty L. Bruening, June 28, 1957 (div. 1969); children—Betty Kathryn, Kent Eric Courtland; m. 2d, Rosalyn L. Hathaway, Aug. 28, 1971. Intern, Meth. Hosp., Houston, 1960-61; fellow Kings Coll., London, 1961-62, Karolinska Inst., Stockholm, 1962-64; practice medicine specializing in pathology, Dallas, 1971—; mem. staff East Dallas Hosp., Oak Cliff Med. and Surg. Hosp., Presbyn. Hosp., Dallas, Permian Gen. Hosp., Andrews, Tex.; asst. prof. anatomy Southwestern Med. Sch., Dallas, 1964-69, clin. asst. prof. pathology, 1972—, clin. asso. prof. anatomy, 1969—; instr. pathology Baylor Dental Sch., Dallas, 1969-71; vis. asst. prof. biology So. Meth. U., Dallas, 1965-66. Served with AUS, 1953-55. Diplomate Am. Bd. Pathology. Fellow Am. Soc. Clin. Pathologists, Coll. Am. Pathologists; mem. Am., Tex. med. assns., A.A.A S., Am. Soc. Microbiologists, Am. Soc. Cell Biologists, N. Tex. Soc. Pathologists, Dallas Acad. Pathologists, Dallas So. Clin. Soc., Mensa, Sigma Xi. Home: 2531 Winsted Dallas TX 75214 Office: Presbyterian Hospital 8200 Walnut Hill Lane Dallas TX 75231

HOSKINS, ROBERT NATHAN, r.r. co. exec.; b. Keota, Ia., Feb. 23, 1917; s. Frank A. and Ora E. (Wayman) H.; student U. Mo., 1934-37; B.S., Ia. State U., 1939; m. Julia L. Jones, July 19, 1946; children—Nancy Carol, Mary Susan, Julia Ann, Robert Nathan. Towerman, Sam A. Baker State Forest, Mo. Conservation Commn., 1939, sr. forester, 1940-41; extension forester Fla. Forest Service, 1941-45; indsl. forester Seaboard Air Line R.R. Co. (name changed to Seaboard Coast Line R.R. Co. 1967), Richmond, Va., 1945-46, gen. forestry agt., 1956-64, gen. indsl. and forestry agt., 1964-65, gen. mgr. indsl. devel., 1965-68, asst. v.p. containerization and spl. projects, 1968-69, asst. v.p. forestry and spl. projects, 1969—. Mem. core com. Keep Fla. Green, 1946-50, Keep N.C. Green, 1947-49; mem. Gov.'s Adv. Com. on Forestry Va. Economy, 1950-53; mem. adv. com. on forestry program in agrl. edn. Va., N.C., S.C., Ga., Fla., Ala., 1950-65; mem. adv. com. vocational edn. Va. State Bd. Edn., 1950-60; mem. profl. adv. group indsl. devel. Commonwealth Va., 1967-68; mem. staff of resources Future, 1949-50; adviser on forestry edn. So. Regional Edn. Bd., 1957-58; southeastern regional chmn. sponsoring com. Nat. Future Farmers Am. Found., 1969-73; mem. nat. adv. com. to sec. agr. on state and pvt. forestry, 1970-73; mem. Va. Agri-Bus. Council. Named Norfolk's Outstanding Young Man, Norfolk Jr. C. of C., 1951, recipient certificate of merit, 1952; recipient Distinguished Service award S.C. Agrl. Tchrs., 1953, Alumni Merit award Chgo. Alumni Assn., Ia. State U., 1954, Key to City, Mayor of Cin., 1960, Mayor of Phila., 1961, Merit award Fla. Vocational Agrl. Assn., 1965, Appreciation award Va. Agrl. Tchrs. Assn., 1967, Distinguished Service award S.C. Future Farmers Am. Assn., 1968, Spl. award for distinguished service to sponsoring com. Nat. Future Farmers Am., 1971; Order Palmetto, 1973. Mem. Am. (Merit award 1954, awards chmn. 1949-54), Ga. (liaison and coordinating com. 1955-56), N.C. (reforestation com. 1951-52), Ala., Fla. forestry assns., Va. Forests, Fla. Forest and Park Assn., Soc. Am. Foresters, Ry. Tie Assn. (chmn. conservation com. 1956-58), Forest Farmers Assn. (ednl. com. 1957-58), Am. Vocational Assn. (award merit 1958), U.S. (mem. agribus. and rural affairs com. 1972-74), Fla. State (forestry com. 1952-53), Va. State (indsl. devel. com. 1965-68), Richmond chambers commerce. Methodist (finance com. 1962-63). Elk. Clubs: Va. Press (Richmond), Soc. of Va., Hermitage Country. Author: (with M.D. Mobley) Forestry in the South, 1956. Editor SCL Forestry Bull., 1945-65. Contbr. articles to profl. jours. Home: 7605 Cornwall Rd Richmond VA 23229 Office: 3600 W Broad St Richmond VA 23230 also PO Box 27581 Richmond VA 23261

HOSNY, AHMED NABIL, educator; b. Alexandria, Egypt, July 12, 1928; s. Hassan and Naima (Mehrez) H.; B.S., Cairo U., 1952; M.S., U. Tex., 1957, Ph.D., 1963; m. Mildred Reese Barnett, Sept. 2, 1959; 1 son, Brandon Patrick. Came to U.S., 1955. Engr., Pullman Ry. Co., Cairo, Egypt, 1952-54; asst. prof. U. Houston, 1959-61; faculty U. S.C., Columbia, 1962—, asso. prof. engring., 1964—. Cons. Struthers Research & Devel. Corp., 1967—. NSF grantee, 1965-66. Mem. Am. Inst. Aeros. and Astronautics. Author: Propulsion Systems, 1966, rev. edit., 1973. Home: 230 Windsor Point Rd Columbia SC 29206

HOTCHKISS, AUBREY LEE, optometrist; b. Ft. Worth, Nov. 11, 1921; s. Robert Verlie and Eva Lee (Cross) H.; student, Tex. Wesleyan Coll., 1946-48; D.Optometry, Pa. State Coll., 1952; m. Ruth Jane Schrader, June 29, 1940. Pvt. practice optometry, Ft. Worth, 1952—. Served with USNR, 1943-45. Mem. Am., Tex. optometric assns., Am. Optometric Found., North Tex. Optometric Soc. (dist. pres. 1956-57). Mason (Shriner), Kiwanian. Home: 6072 Wimbleton Way Fort Worth TX 76133 Office: 1507 NW 25th St Fort Worth TX 76106

HOTCHKISS, WILLIAM S., physician; b. Waco, Tex., 1915; M.D., U. Tex., 1939. Intern Henry Ford Hosp., Detroit, 1940-41, surg. resident, 1947-49, resident thoracic surgery, 1949-51; sr. asst. surgeon U.S. Marine Hosp., Norfolk, Va., 1942-45, U.S. Marine Hosp., Boston, 1945-47; resident thoracic surgery McKinney (Tex.) VA Hosp., 1951; now practice medicine specializing in thoracic surgery. Served with USPHS, 1941-46. Diplomate Am. Bd. Surgery, Am. Bd. Thoracic Surgery. Fellow Am. Coll. Chest Physicians; mem. A.M.A., Med. Soc. Va. (past pres.). Address: 702 Med Tower 400 Gresham Dr Norfolk VA 23507*

HOTES, ROBERT WILLIAM, educator; b. Cleve., Jan. 29, 1942; s. Norbert William and Florence Lou (White) H.; B.A., St. Paul Coll., 1965; postgrad. St. Paul Theologate, 1966, Cath. U. Am., 1966; M.A. (Braniff Meml. scholar), U. Dallas, 1970; postgrad. Fla. State U., 1970-71; m. Lynn E. Waibel, Dec. 20, 1969; 1 dau., Joellynn Lynn. Instr., St. Marks Sch., Dallas, 1969; asst. prof. N. Fla. Jr. Coll., Madison, 1970-72; information services specialist Okaloosa-Walton Jr. Coll., Niceville, Fla., 1972—. Mem. N.E.A., Fla. Edn. Assn., Nat. Council Coll. Publs. Advisers, Fla. Assn. Community Colls., Fla. Jr. Coll. Conf. Lutheran. Lion. Prodn. chief Pastoral Life mag., 1964-65; editorial asst. Catholic Home mag., 1965-66; asso. editor Pauline View mag., 1966. Home: 511 22d St Niceville FL 32578

HOUGHTON, JAMES AUBREY, city mgr.; b. Portsmouth, Va., Aug. 28, 1925; s. Carl Clifford and Viola (Deans) H.; Chem.E., Va. Poly. Inst., 1946; m. Jean Warren, June 5, 1948; children—Nancy Rhea, Betty Jean. City purchasing agt., Portsmouth, 1951-52, adminstrv. asst. to city mgr., 1952-56; city mgr., South Boston, Va., 1956—. Bd. dirs. Halifax Community Hosp., Halifax County Community Action Agy.; bd. dirs., pres. Halifax County-South Boston YMCA. Mem. Internat. City Mgrs. Assn., Am. Soc. Pub. Adminstrn., Halifax County C. of C. (past pres.). Presbyn. (elder). Lion (past pres. South Boston). Home: 2100 Westmoreland St South Boston VA 24592 Office: City Hall 436 Main St South Boston VA 24592

HOUK, RICHARD DUNCAN, educator; b. Hobart, Okla., June 13, 1933; s. Robert Devereaux and Alline Carey (Shelton) H.; student So. Meth. U., 1956; B.S., S.W. Mo. State Coll., 1959; postgrad. U. Tenn., 1959; Ph.D., Fla. State U., 1966; m. Janice Ann Chastain, July 16, 1955; children—Jay Duncan, Scott Thomas. Instr. biology S.W. Mo. State Coll., 1959-60, Fla. State U., summer 1964; asst. prof. biology Winthrop Coll., Rock Hill, S.C., 1964-69, asso. prof., 1969-73, prof. biology, asst. to v.p. for acad. affairs, 1973—; asst. prof. biology Va. Poly. Inst., summer 1966; cons. S.C. Land Resources Commn. Pres. Citizens Concerned for Pub. Edn., Rock Hill, 1969; mem. spl. com. to study ward system York County Dist. 3, S.C., 1972. Served with USN, 1952-56; ETO. Fla. State U. nuclear sci. fellow, 1960; NSF grad. fellow, 1962, 63; recipient Phi Kappa Phi excellence in teaching award, Winthrop Coll., 1972. Mem. Internat. Assn. Plant Taxonomy, Internat. Orgn. Plant Biosystematists, Bot. Soc. Am., Am. Soc. Plant Taxonomists, Am. Inst. Biol. Scis., Nat. Assn. Biology Tchrs., Assn. Southeastern Biologists, S.C. Acad. Scis., S.C. Assn. Biology Tchrs., S.C. Biologists Assn., Mass. Hort. Soc., Sigma Xi. Home: 629 University Dr Rock Hill SC 29730

HOUSE, GEORGE ROBERT, JR., city ofcl.; b. Durham, N.C., Aug. 6, 1928; s. George Robert and Beatrice (Deahl) H.; B.A., U. N.C., 1954, certificate municipal adminstrn., 1956; m. Myra Virginia Bland, June 24, 1951; children—George Robert III, Bettye Jo. Asst. city mgr. Durham, 1954-56; city mgr., Emporia, Va., 1956-60; city mgr., Bedord, Va., 1960-61, county mgr., Forsyth County, N.C., Winston-Salem, 1961-69; city mgr., Chesapeake, Va., 1969-71, Norfolk, Va., 1971—. Served to 1st lt. USAF, 1951-53. Mem. Nat. Assn. County Adminstrs. (pres. 1969-70; dir. 1969-70), Nat. Assn. County Ofcls. (dir. 1970-71), Internat. City Mgmt. Assn., Nat. Municipal League. Home: 5740 Shendoah Av Norfolk VA 23509 Office: City Hall Norfolk VA 23501

HOUSE, RODNEY DALE, indsl. engr.; b. Huttig, Ark., Sept. 10, 1938; s. William Dale and Eunice (Evatt) H.; B.S., Ga. Inst. Tech., 1960; M.Pub. Adminstrn., Harvard, 1968; m. Jean Perry; children—Ramey, Andrea. Indsl. engr. Warner Robins Air Material Area, Robins AFB, Ga., 1960-68, supervisory indsl. engr., after 1968, now chief operations br. Fellow in Mid Career Ednl. Program in Systematic Analysis, 1967-68. Mem. Am. Inst. Indsl. Engrs. (past chpt. v.p.), Soc. Logistics Engrs. Baptist. Home: 727 Indigo Dr San Antonio TX 78216 Office: SAAMA/MMRO Kelly AFB TX

HOUSER, JOHN EDWARD, lawyer; b. Richmond, Va., Dec. 24, 1928; s. Aubrey Alphin and Winnifred (Savage) H.; B.S., U. Va., 1959, LL.B., 1959; m. Rives Pollard; children—Allen Rives Cabell Lybrook, Andrew Murray Lybrook II. Admitted to Fla. bar, Fed. bar, 1959, U.S. Supreme Ct. bar, 1970; practiced in Jacksonville, Fla., 1959—; dir. Wm. P. Poythress & Co., Richmond, Neal F. Tyler & Sons, Jacksonville. Served with AUS, 1953-57. Mem. Internat. Assn. Indsl. Accident Bds. and Commns., Maritime Law Assn. U.S., Jacksonville, Atlanta claimsmen assns., Am., Jacksonville bar assns., Fla. Bar, Fla. Def. Counsel Assn., Am. Judicature Assn., Am. Arbitration Assn., Nat. Trust for Historic Preservation, Fla. Inst. Pub. Affairs, Navy League, Jacksonville Assn. Def. Counsel, Def. Research Inst., Jacksonville U. Council, Jacksonville Symphony Assn., Fla., Jacksonville hist. socs., Cummer Gallery of Art, Jacksonville C. of C., English-Speaking Union (dir. 1970—, pres. 1974—, nat. regional chmn. 1973), Theta Delta Chi, Sigma Nu Phi. Clubs: River, Fla. Yacht; Deerwood, Ponte Vedra River, Exchange, German, Ye Mystic Revellers, University. Home: 4741 Algonquin Jacksonville FL 32210 Office: Fla Nat Bank Bldg Jacksonville FL 32202

HOUSER, JOHN WESLEY, JR., dentist; b. Orangeburg, S.C., July 10, 1918; s. John Wesley and Eva (Hollins) H.; B.S., Claflin Coll., 1940; postgrad. Atlanta U., 1941-43; D.D.S., Meharry Med. Coll., 1946; m. Louise Kelley, Sept. 18, 1943; children—John Wesley III, George. Practice dentistry, Rome, Ga., 1946—; mem. staff Floyd Hosp.; asso. dentist Battey State Hosp., Floyd County Health Services, 1950-71. Owner, pres. Brentwood Med.-Care Nursing Home, Inc., 1964—. Ga. bd. dirs. Am. Cancer Soc., 1950-58; bd. dirs. Girls Club, 1967—. Mem. City Planning Commn., 1968—. Served with AUS. Named Ga. Dentist of Year, Omega Psi Phi, 1960, Pres's award Nat. Dental Assn., 1961, Dentist of Year, 1963; recipient Service Plaque Am. Cancer Soc., 1964. Fellow Coll. Nursing Home Adminstrs; mem. Ga. Dental Soc. (pres. 1954), John A. Andrew Clin. Soc. (pres. 1963), Nat. Dental Assn. (zone v.p. 1959-64), C. of C., Phi Beta Sigma. Baptist (deacon). Mason. Home: 121 Jackson St Rome GA 30161 Office: 1006 E 1st St Rome GA 30161

HOUSEWRIGHT, JAMES TALBERTT, labor union ofcl.; b. Wesco, Mo., Nov. 23, 1921; s. Thomas Austin and Nora E. (Asher) H.; ed. Hadlay Vocational Sch., St. Louis, 1937; m. Mildred Jessie Shults, Dec. 19, 1941; children—Lana (Mrs. Lee McBeath), Linda (Mrs. Daniel Nostheide), Kathryn (Mrs. Charles Lowthers), James Talbertt. Sec.-treas. Retail Clks. Union local 725, Indpls., 1947-53;

organizing dir. Retail Clks. Internat. Assn., 1953-65, internat. dir., 1965-66, exec. asst. to pres., 1966-68, internat. pres., Washington, 1968—; v.p. AFL-CIO; mem. exec. com. Internat. Fedn. Comml., Clerical and Tech. Employees, exec. bd. Maritime Trades dept.; mem. exec. bd. Council AFL-CIO Unions Sci., Profl. and Cultural Employees. Dir. First Nat. Bank Washington. Mem. Pres.'s Com. Employment Handicapped; mem. nat. adv. com. Jobs for Vets.; mem. exec. com. Nat. Health Ins.; mem. Leadership Conf. Civil Rights. Corporate mem. Muscular Dystrophy Assns. Am., Inc.; bd. dirs. A. Philip Randolph Inst. Served with USAAF, 1942-45. Mason. Home: 1318 Gatewood Dr Alexandria VA 22307 Office: 1775 K St NW Washington DC 20006

HOUSTON, ARTHUR RICHARD, JR., civil, mech. engr.; b. Birmingham, Ala., Aug. 24, 1911; s. Arthur Richard and Irene Mary Elizabeth (Vogt) H.; student U. Ala., 1936, 37; m. Cordelia Hamby, Oct. 5, 1940; children—Cordelia (Mrs. Donald Leroy Grigsby), Janice (Mrs. Robert Tillman Alford). Clk., Birmingham Water Works Co., 1933-40, asst. engr., 1940-45; draftsman designer Ala. Power Co., Birmingham, 1945-47, engr. supr., 1947-71, staff engr., 1971—. Cons. design and safety of dams, chs. and schs., 1948—. Civil engr. Shades Mountain Civic Club, Birmingham, 1952-66. Registered profl. engr., Ala. Mem. Nat. Soc. Profl. Engrs., A.A.A.S., Birmingham Astronomy Club. Home: 1044 Shades Crest Rd Birmingham AL 35226 Office: PO Box 2641 Birmingham AL 35291

HOUSTON, DANIEL COLLIER, architect; b. Montgomery, Ala., May 21, 1923; s. Walter Howell and Caroline (Ramer) H.; B.Arch., Auburn U., 1951; m. Dorothy Lamar Smith, May 11, 1945; children—Daniel Collier, Walter Lamar. Owner Houston Assos., Architects, Albany, Ga., 1953—. Mem. State Art Commn., 1954-59. Served with Canadian Army, 1940-41, Brit. Army, 1941-42, AUS, 1942-45. Certified Nat. Council Archtl. Registration Bds. Mem. A.I.A. (dir.), Am. Legion. Elk, Lion. Address: Route 2 Box 646-A Blue Springs Rd Albany GA 31701

HOUSTON, DAVID LIPSCOMB, city ofcl.; b. Wichita Falls, Tex., June 4, 1921; s. David Lipscomb and Katherine (Blackburn) H.; B.S. in Mech. Engring., U. Tex., 1950, M.S. in Community and Regional Planning, 1970; m. Maude Cardwell, July 18, 1945 (div. Jan. 1956); children—Franklin C., Ronald D. Electric designer elec. dept. City of Austin (Tex.), 1950-52, design engr. water dept., 1953-54, planning engr. planning dept., 1955-66; city planner cons. Tex. State Dept. Health, 1966-69, chief environmental devel. program, 1970—. Served with AUS, 1942-45; ETO; lt. col. Res. Registered profl. engr., Tex. Mem. Nat., Tex. socs. profl. engrs., Am. Inst. Planners, City Planners Assn. Tex., Am. Soc. Pub. Adminstrn., Internat. Folk Dance Assn., Am. Soc. Planning Ofcls. Episcopalian. Mason (Shriner). Home: 1306 Arcadia St Austin TX 78757 Office: 1100 W 49th St Austin TX 78756

HOUSTON, JAMES GORMAN, JR., lawyer; b. Eufaula, Ala., Mar. 11, 1933; s. James Gorman and Mildred (Vance) H.; B.S., Auburn U., 1954; LL.B., J.D., U. Ala., 1956; m. Marthur Martin, Dec. 3, 1955; children—Mildred Vance, James Gorman III. Admitted to Ala. bar; law clk. Chief Justice Ala. Supreme Ct., Montgomery, 1956-57; gen. practice law, Eufaula, 1960—; atty., dir. Central Bank Eufaula. Atty., Indsl. Devel. Bd. Eufaula, Barbour County Hosp. Assn., 1961-69, dir., 72—. Chmn. Barbour County chpt. A.R.C., 1960-64; mem. Waterworks and Sewer Bd. Eufaula, 1968—. Alderman, mayor pro tem City of Eufaula, 1964—; county atty., Barbour County. Bd. dirs. Carnegie Library. Served to 1st lt., Judge Adv. Gen. Dept., USAF, 1957-60. Mem. Am., Barbour County (pres.) bar assns., Eufaula C. of C. (dir. 1961-66, past pres.), Farrah Order Jurisprudence, Omicron Delta Kappa, Phi Delta Phi. Rotarian (pres.), Kiwanian (pres.). Club: Eufaula Country (pres.). Bd. editors Ala. Law Rev. Home: Barbour Lane Eufaula AL 36027 Office: 201 E Broad St Eufaula AL 36027

HOUSTON, WALTER RAY, banker; b. Andalusia, Ala., June 13, 1911; s. Walter Howell and Callie (Ramer) H.; student pub. schs.; m. Clara Ruth Alexander, June 15, 1930; children—Warner Ray, Carol Ruth (Mrs. Kenneth L. Makant, Jr.), Beverly Clair (Mrs. James R. Eddens). Night mgr. Postal Telegraph & Cable Co., Montgomery, Ala., 1930-35; office mgr. Universal Credit Co., 1935-36; sales mgmt. trainee Sears, Roebuck & Co., Montgomery and Albany, Ga., 1936-42; with Bank of Albany, 1942-59, successively asst. cashier, cashier, v.p., exec. v.p., dir.; exec. v.p. Bank of Fulton County (merger; name now First Ga. Bank), East Point, Ga., 1959-60, pres., chmn. bd. after 1960, now vice-chmn. First Ga. Bank; appraiser for various companies, 1946-59. Mem. gov.'s staff and financial com. Commr. Housing Authority, City of Albany, 1947-58. Bd. dirs. Atlanta Girls Club, Atlanta area council Boy Scouts Am.; trustee, chmn. finance com. Fulton-DeKalb Hosp. Authority; governing bd. Woodward Acad., College Park; trustee Wesley Homes, Inc., Epworth Towers. Served with USNR, 1943-45. Mem. Ga., South Fulton, East Point (past pres.) chambers commerce, 40 and 8, Am. Legion (past comdr., past Ga. vice comdr.), Am., Ind., Ga. (pres. 1968-69) bankers assns., Ga. Hosp. Assn. Methodist (trustee Atlanta S.W. dist.). Mason (Shriner), Elk, Kiwanian (past pres.). Clubs: Atlanta Athletic, Atlanta Tarpon; Lakeside Country (dir., past pres.). Home: 2998 Pineywood Dr East Point GA 30344 Office: Bank of Fulton County East Point GA 30344

HOUTMANN, JACQUES, condr.; b. Mirecourt, France, Mar. 27, 1935; s. Georges and Paule (Saal) H.; concert license Ecole Normale de Musique, Paris, France; diploma Santa Caecilia, Rome, Italy; m. Yolaine Gerard, July 6, 1967; children—Helene, Marie-Virginie. Came to U.S., 1971. Asst. condr. N.Y. Philharmonic, 1965-66: condr. Philharmonic, Lyon, France, 1967-71; music dir. Richmond (Va.) Symphony and Richmond Sinfonia, 1971—; guest condr., Europe, U.S., S.Am. Recipient 1st prize Dimitri Mitropoulos competition, 1964. Club: 2300 (Richmond). Office: 112 E Franklin St Richmond VA 23219

HOUTS, PAUL LOUIS, editor; b. Albany, N.Y., Aug. 5, 1937; s. Louis and Ethel Margaret (Kielty) H.; B.A., Trinity Coll., Hartford, Conn., 1959. Editor Prentice-Hall, Inc., Englewood Cliffs, N.J., 1961-65; asso. editor Am. Council Edn., Washington, 1965-67; asst. dir. publns. Nat. Assn. Elementary Sch. Prins., Washington, 1967-70, dir. publns., editor, 1970—. Mem. Ednl. Press Assn. Am. (regional dir. 1973—; awards 1970, 71, 72). Editor Nat. Elementary Prin., 1970—; asso. editor Am. Jr. Colls., 1967. Home: 1026 31st St NW Washington DC 20007 Office: 1801 N Moore St Arlington VA 22209

HOUTS, RONALD CARL, educator; b. Chgo., Sept. 22, 1937; s. Wesley Montgomery and Evelyn Margaret (Kittelson) H.; B.S., U. Fla., 1959, M.S., 1960, Ph.D. (Nat. Def. Edn. Act fellow), 1963; m. Marilyn Leggett, Aug. 11, 1960; children—Ronald Scott, Katherine Leslie. Instr. U. Fla., Gainesville, 1961-63; faculty U. Ala., University, 1966—, prof. elec. engring., 1973—, project dir. NASA contract on digital telemetry, 1969-74. Adj. prof. Cochise Jr. Coll., Douglas, Ariz., 1964-65, U. Ariz., Tucson, 1965; lectr. U. Ala., Huntsville, 1973. Served to capt. Signal Corp, AUS, 1963-66. Mem. Am. Soc. Engring. Edn., I.E.E.E., Sigma Xi, Phi Kappa Phi, Sigma Tau, Phi Eta Sigma, Eta Kappa Nu, Tau Beta Pi. Author: (with Richard S. Simpson) Fundamentals of Analog and Digital Communication Systems, 1971. Home: 139 Woodland Hills Tuscaloosa AL 35401 Office: PO Box 6169 University Alabama University AL 35486

HOUTZ, DUANE TALBOTT, hosp. adminstr.; b. Kansas City, Mo., Apr. 28, 1933; B.S., U. Kan., 1955; M.H.A., Washington U., St. Louis, 1960; m. Margaret McNiel; children—Jamie Denice, Erik Siegfried. Adminstrv. resident Orange Meml. Hosp., Orlando, Fla., 1959-60, adminstrv. asst., 1960; asst. dir. teaching hosp. and clinics J. Hillis Miller Health Center U Fla., Gainesville, 1961-65, asst. prof. Center Health and Hosp. Adminstrn., 1964-65; adminstr. Highland Av. Bapt. Hosp., Birmingham, Ala., from 1965; now exec. v.p. Baptist Med. Center-Montclair, Birmingham. Pres. Birmingham Regional Hosp. Council, 1972. Vice pres. Community Service Council. Served with USAF, 1955-58. Fellow Am. Coll. Hosp. Adminstrs.; mem. Ala. Hosp. Assn. (chmn. research and edn. found. liaison com., com. emergency med. service), Nat. League Nursing (dir. health careers council). Ala. Assn. Hosp. Exec., Ala. Pub. Health Assn., Phi Delta Theta. Kiwanian (past pres., dir.). Contbr. articles to profl. jours. Address: Bapt Med Center-Montclair 800 Montclair Rd Birmingham AL 35213

HOVELAND, CARL SOREN, educator; b. Sand Creek, Wis., Oct. 25, 1927; s. Herman and Ada (Caspara) H.; B.S., U. Wis., 1950, M.S., 1952; Ph.D., U. Fla., 1959; m. Dorothy Helene Anderson, Jan. 27, 1951. Asst. agronomist Tex. Agrl. Expt. Sta., Crystal City, 1952-55; asst. in agronomy U. Fla., Gainesville, 1955-58, teaching asst. botany, 1958-59; asso. prof. Auburn (Ala.) U., 1959-68, prof. dept. agronomy and soils, 1968—. Cons. scientist Grasslands div. Dept. Sci. and Indsl. Research, Palmerston N., New Zealand, 1970. Served with USMC, 1946-48. Fellow Am. Soc. Agronomy; mem. Crop Sci. Soc. Am. (br. v.p. 1973-74), Sigma Xi, Alpha Zeta, Phi Sigma, Gamma Sigma Delta. Contbr. articles to profl. jours. Home: 561 Forestdale Dr Auburn AL 36830 Office: Agronomy and Soils Dept Auburn University Auburn AL 36830

HOVEY, LESTER EUGENE, accountant; b. La Porte, Tex., May 16, 1933; s. John Williard and Clara (Sharp) H.; student Southwestern U., 1951-52; B.B.A. cum laude, U. Tex., 1957, M.Profl. Accounting, 1961; m. Claudia Janet Meiners, June 20, 1954; children—Sheryl Susan, Sandra Kay, Richard Eugene. Audit and tax accountant Arthur Andersen & Co., Houston, 1958-60; in practice as Eugene Hovey, C.P.A., La Porte, 1961—; tchr. accountant San Jacinto Coll., part-time 1961-63. Dir. La Porte Neighborhood Center, 1961-62. Served with AUS, 1954-56. C.P.A., Tex., Mem. Am. Inst. C.P.A.'s, C. of C. (past treas.), Tex. Hosp. Assn., Tex. Assn. Hosp. Accountants, Tex. Municipal League. Mem. Community Ch. (past pres.; treas.). Home: 606 S 1st St La Porte TX 77571 Office: 902 W Main St La Porte TX 77571

HOVLAND, CARL WALLACE, data processor; b. Albert Lee, Minn., Feb. 14, 1937; s. Helmer O. and Marjorie C. (Reynolds) H.; student Luther Coll., 1955-56, Baylor U., 1968-69; m. Karen E. Robinson, Oct. 20, 1956; children—Michael, Kari, Patrick, Daniel, Amy. With RCA Co., Washington, 1963-64; sr. systems rep. Honeywell, Inc., Denver, 1964-68; dir. data processing Word, Inc., Waco, Tex., 1968—. Instr. data processing McLennan Jr. Coll., Waco, 1973. Served with USAF, 1956-60. Mem. Data Processing Mgmt. Assn. (pres. 1970). Home: 416 Wooded Crest Waco TX 76710 Office: Box 1790 Waco TX 76703

HOWALD, JOEL CARTER, architect; b. Quincy, Ill., Sept. 19, 1941; s. Herbert Hadley and Dorothy (Mustain) H.; A.A., Del Mar Coll., 1962; B.Arch., Tex. Technol. U., 1966; m. Zoe E. Tipton, Aug. 8, 1968; children—James Brandon, Shelley Leigh. Asst. prof., chmn. dept. architecture Del Mar Coll., Corpus Christi, Tex., 1966-72; project architect firm Christian, Bright, Pennington & Assoc., Corpus Christi, 1972—. Pres., P.T.A., Corpus Christi, 1973—. Mem. Am. Inst. Architects (program chmn.), Tex. Soc. Architects, Constn. Specifications Inst. (v.p. 1973—). Author: Architectural Technology, 1972. Home: 4705 Cobblestone St Corpus Christi TX 78411 Office: 902 Kinney St Corpus Christi TX 78401

HOWARD, BERNARD EUFINGER, mathematician, educator; b. Ludlow, Vt., Sept. 22, 1920; s. Charles Rawson and Ethel (Kearney) H.; student Middlebury Coll., 1938-40; B.S., Mass. Inst. Tech., 1944; M.S., U. Ill., 1947, Ph.D., 1951; m. Ruth Belknap, Mar. 29, 1942. Mem. staff Radiation Lab., Mass. Inst. Tech., 1942-45; asst. math. dept. U. Ill., 1945-50; sr. mathematician Inst. for Air Weapons Research, U. Chgo., 1951, asst. to dir., 1951-54, asst. to dir. Inst. for Systems Research, 1954-56, asso. dir., 1956-60, asso. dir. Labs. for Applied Scis., 1958-60; prof. math. U. Miami, Coral Gables, Fla., 1960—, dir. sci. computing center, 1961-64. Exec. sec. Air Force Adv. Bd. on Simulation, 1951-54; cons. Systems Research Labs., Inc., Dayton, O., 1963—, acting dir. math. scis. div., 1965; cons. Variety Childrens Research Found., 1964-66, Fla. Power & Light Co., 1968—, Shaw & Assos., 1969—. Vice pres. Pine Ridge Civic Assn., 1968—. Bd. dirs. Blue Lake Assn., 1969—. Mem. Am. Math. Soc., Soc. for Indsl. and Applied Math. (treas. S.E. sect. 1964), Am. Pys. Soc., Am. Assn. U. Profs., A.A.A.S., Assn. for Computing Machinery (chpt. chmn. 1969-70), I.E.E.E., Soc. for Computer Simulation, Sigma Xi, Phi Kappa Phi, Pi Mu Epsilon, Alpha Sigma Phi. Home: 7320 Miller Dr Miami FL 33155 Office: U Miami Coral Gables FL 33124

HOWARD, CECIL BYRON, pediatrician; b. Wallins, Ky., Apr. 16, 1927; s. William Knott and Maggie (Cawood) H.; B.A., Vanderbilt U., 1949, M.D., 1953; m. Rebekah Ann Buckley, Oct. 21, 1953; children—Mark Byron, Sally Ann, Maggie Elizabeth. Intern, U. Va. Hosp., Charlottesville, 1953-54; resident pediatrics U. Tex. Med. Br. Hosps., Galveston, 1954-56; practice medicine, specializing in pediatrics, Maryville, Tenn., 1956—; mem. staff, U. Tenn. Hosp., Knoxville; mem. staff Blount Meml. Hosp., Maryville, sec., 1959-64, chief pediatrics, 1973—. Chmn., Tuckaleechee dist. Boy Scouts Am., Maryville, 1973—. Served with AUS, 1945-47. Fellow Am., Acad. Pediatrics; mem. Blount County Med. Soc. (pres. 1966). Mem. Christian Ch. (chmn. bd. 1972-73). Club: Optimist (pres. 1973—) (Maryville). Home: 1220 S Dogwood Dr Maryville TN 37801 Office: Doctors Bldg Maryville TN 37801

HOWARD, CHARLES, educator; b. Evanston, Ill., Apr. 2, 1919; s. Marion Boyd and Mary Ruth (McLafferty) H.; B.S., U. Wis., 1940, Ph.D., 1943; m. Dorothy Mary Thompson, June 16, 1945; children—John, Robert, Margaret. Chemist, Oscar Mayer & Co., Madison, Wis., 1941-46, acting chief chemist, 1946-50; dir. product control Arbogast & Bastian, Allentown, Pa., 1951-54; asst. plant supt. Valleydale Packers, Inc., Salem, Va., 1955-60; faculty San Antonio Coll., 1960-73, prof., chmn. dept. chemistry, 1967-73; prof. chemistry U. Tex., San Antonio, 1973—. Adj. prof. chemistry St. Mary's U., San Antonio. Served with USNR, 1944-45. Mem. Am. Chem. Soc. (sect. chmn. 1974—), Sci. Research Soc. Am., Sigma Xi. Home: 211 Gramercy Pl W San Antonio TX 78212

HOWARD, C(LARENCE) EDWARD, educator; b. Roseboro, N.C., May 31, 1929; s. Hubert Royster and Irene (Britt) H.; student Campbell Coll., 1948-49; B.S., Duke U., 1953; M.S., N.C. State U., 1955; Ph.D., La. State U., 1963; m. Evelyn Kline Baker, Oct. 22, 1955; 1 dau., Wendy Gail. Teaching asst. N.C. State U., Raleigh, 1953-55; mining and geol. engr. Tungsten Mining Corp., Henderson, N.C., 1955-57; teaching asst. La. State U., Baton Rouge, 1959-63; asst. prof. geology Campbell Coll., Buies Creek, N.C., 1963-64, asso. prof., 1964-66, chmn. dept. geology, 1964—, prof., 1966—. Fellow Geol. Soc. Am.; mem. A.A.A.S., Nat. Assn. Geology Tchrs., Am. Inst. Mining Engrs., Carolina Geol. Soc., N.C. Acad. Sci., Sigma Xi. Contbr. articles in field to profl. jours. Home: PO Box 11386 Lillington NC 27546 Office: PO Box 386 Buies Creek NC 27506

HOWARD, DALE EUGENE, hosp. adminstr.; b. Grand Junction, Ia., Jan. 24, 1922; s. Virgil R. and Celene (Williams) H.; certificate in hosp. adminstrn. Ga. State Coll., 1959; m. Fabian Lee Lavender, Dec. 27, 1959; children—Celene Renee, Shannon Lee. Lab. technologist Bethesda Hosp., Ft. Dodge, Ia., 1946-52; chief x-ray lab. technologist Immanuel-St. Joseph Hosp., Mankato, Minn., 1952-54, Pipestone (Minn.) Meml. Hosp., 1955-56, Hancock Meml. Hosp., Britt, Ia., 1956-58; adminstrv. asst. Macon (Ga.) Hosp., 1959-60; asst. adminstr. Polk Gen. Hosp., Bartow, Fla., 1961-63; adminstr. Citrus County Hosp., Inverness, Fla., 1963-65, Tarpon Springs (Fla.) Gen. Hosp., 1965—. Mem. Am. Coll. Hosp. Adminstrs., Phi Epsilon Rho. Episcopalian. Home: 621 Bayshore St Tarpon Springs FL 33589 Office: 1395 S Pinellas St Tarpon Springs FL 33589

HOWARD, JAMES ARTHUR, lawyer; b. Norfolk, Va., Mar. 8, 1918; s. Harry Elmore and Grace Lee (Taylor) H.; A.B., U. N.C., 1941; LL.B., Duke, 1949; m. Ellen Roberta Logan, Mar. 5, 1945; children—James Arthur II, Martha Ellen, Susan Logan. Admitted to Va. bar, 1950; mem. firm Breeden, Howard & MacMillan, Norfolk, 1950—. Mem. bd. visitors Old Dominion U., Norfolk, 1962-69. Served to lt. comdr. USNR, 1942-45. Fellow Am. Coll. Trial Lawyers; mem. Va. State Bar (pres. 1973), Norfolk and Portsmouth (pres. 1968-69) bar assns. Mason (Shriner). Clubs: Princess Anne Country (Virginia Beach, Va.); Norfolk Yacht and Country. Home: 1301 Harmott Av Norfolk VA 23509 Office: Va Nat Bank Bldg Norfolk VA 23510

HOWARD, JOHN GARFIELD, savs. and loan exec.; b. Pineville, Ky., Nov. 11, 1935; s. Durham W. and Katherine (Morgan) H.; student U. Louisville, 1953-54, Lincoln Meml. U., 1954-55; m. Janice R. Haws, Nov. 29, 1958; children—John David, Jasper Alan. Salesman, Howard Ins. Agy., Pineville, 1958-60; teller 1st Fed. Savs. & Loan Assn., Pineville, 1961, cashier, 1962-63, asst. sec., 1964, sec., asst. mgr., 1965—, also dir.; chmn. Bell County Library Constrn. Corp.; dir. Pineville Municipal Properties Corp.; past dir. Ky. Bldg. Savs. and Loan League. City councilman, Pineville, 1970-72. Pres., Pineville Indsl. Found., 1969—; bd. dirs., adv. bd. Ky. Mountain Laurel Festival, 1968—; bd. dirs. Middlesboro-Bell County Airport Bd., 1966-73, Middlesboro-Bell County chpt. A.R.C., 1969-70; past bd. dirs. Cumberland Valley Area Devel. Dist., Upper Cumberland Council Alcohol and Drug Abuse. Served with AUS, 1955-58. Recipient Man of Yr. award City of Pineville, 1970. Mem. C. of C. (dir., pres. 1969). Presbyn. Kiwanian (pres. 1969-70). Home: PO Box 111 Paula Dr Pineville KY 40977 Office: Virginia Av at Oak St Pineville KY 40977

HOWARD, LARRY BRUCE, state ofcl.; b. Seattle, Apr. 1, 1928; s. Walter Joseph and Anita (Schnitzlein) H.; B.S., U. Mont., 1950; Ph.D., U. Minn., 1956; postgrad. Emory U., 1956-58; m. Elaine Annette Ungherini, Sept. 20, 1952; children—Randy, Rick, Laure, Lisa. Asst. dir. Ga. Crime Lab., Atlanta, 1956-59, dir., 1969—. Mem. faculty criminology Ga. State U., 1967, mem. faculty anatomy Emory U., 1971—, Ga. Police Acad., 1966—. Mem. Ga. Sci. and Tech. Commn., 1969-72; mem. Atlanta YMCA Athletic Council, 1958-59. Served with AUS, 1945-46. Mem. Am. Acad. Forensic Scis., A.A.A.S., So. Assn. Forensic Scientists, Atlanta Instrument Soc., Sigma Phi Epsilon. Home: 3106 Lanier Dr NE Atlanta GA 30319 Office: PO Box 1456 Atlanta GA 30301

HOWARD, LEWIS SPILMAN, lawyer; b. Knoxville, Tenn., Oct. 10, 1930; s. Frank Catlett and Lillian Saunders (Spilman) H.; B.S., U. Tenn., 1953, J.D., 1953; m. Louise Anne Robinson, Dec. 26, 1953. Admitted to Tenn. bar, 1953; mem. firm Kennerly, Montgomery, Howard & Finley, Knoxville, 1959—; pres., gen. counsel, dir. Coal Creek Mining & Mfg. Co., Knoxville, 1969—, Poplar Creek Coal & Iron Co., Knoxville, 1973—, Winters Gapland Co., Knoxville, 1972—. First vice pres. Knoxville Bd. of Edn., 1967-71. Served to 1st lt. AUS, 1952-56. Mem. Sigma Chi, Omicron Delta Kappa. Republican. Presbyn. Clubs: Cherokee Country, City (Knoxville). Home: 1604 Kenesaw Av Knoxville TN 37919 Office: 12th Floor Bank of Knoxville Bldg Knoxville TN 37901

HOWARD, MOSES WILKERSON, physician; b. Harlan, Ky., Aug. 25, 1909; s. George Turner and Nancy (Smith) H.; A.B., U. Ky., 1931; M.D., U. Louisville, 1933; m. Dorris Cole, Mar. 30, 1940; children—Nancy Ellen (Mrs. Charles Manis), Perry Cole, Mary Pamelia (Mrs. Fred Uhle), Jo-Anna. Intern, Bellevue Hosp., N.Y.C., 1935-36; resident Boston City Hosp., 1936-37; physician TVA, Knoxville, Tenn., 1937-38; ship physician S.S. Delvale, 1938; practice medicine specializing in urology, Knoxville, 1946-66, Naples, Fla., 1966—; mem. staff Naples Community Hosp. Served to lt. col. M.C., AUS, 1941-46. Diplomate Am. Bd. Urology. Fellow A.C.S.; mem. A.M.A., S.E. Surg. Congress, Phi Chi, Delta Tau Delta. Home: 561 Palm Circle E Naples FL 33940 Office: 837 4th Av N Naples FL 33940

HOWARD, PATRICK MCCOLLOUGH, mining engr.; b. Welch, W.Va., Nov. 8, 1938; s. Clifford Peter and Harriet (Hoge) H.; student Pikeville Coll., 1956-57; U. Ky., 1957-59; m. Mary Elizabeth Cooke, Apr. 8, 1960; children—Marjorie Marie, Patrick McCollough. Jr. designer Electric Elevator div. Dover Corp., Cin., 1959-61; chief engr. Kentland-Elkhorn Coal Corp., Pikeville, Ky., 1961-70, Feds Creek Coal Co., 1967-70; dir. engring. Ky. div. Pittston Co., 1970-71, gen. mgr. Buchanan County Mines Rapoca Resources, 1970-72; owner Mine Tech. Service, Phyllis, Ky., 1965—, Howard Homes Co., Phyllis, 1967—, Howard Enterprises, Pikeville, 1972—. Scoutmaster Boy Scouts Am. Served with inf. AUS, 1955. Mem. Nat., Ky. (chpt. pres.) socs. profl. engrs., Am. Inst. Mining, Metall. and Petroleum Engrs., Big Sandy Elkhorn Mining Inst. Republican. Presbyn. Club: Willow Brook Country. Home: PO Box 228 Grundy VA 24614 Office: Box 2774 Pikeville KY 41501

HOWARD, RHEA, newspaper pub.; b. Wichita Falls, Tex., July 25, 1892; s. Ed and Jettie Lee (Malony) H.; student Trinity U., Waxahachie, Tex., 1910-11, Eastman Coll., Poughkeepsie, N.Y., 1912; m. Kathleen Benson, Oct. 22, 1913; 1 dau., Anna Katherine (Mrs. James B. Barnett). With The Times Publishing Co. (Wichita Daily Times and Wichita Falls Record News) 1913—, pres., 1948—; v.p. and dir. Indsl. Devel., Inc., Wichita Water Irrigation Dist; dir., Burlington Ry. Past pres. Wichita Falls Sch. Bd.; mem. nat. adv. council Airline Passengers Assn.; mem. YMCA adv. bd.; active A.R.C., Wichita Falls Art Museum. Area Health Facility Planning Com. Bd. dirs. Wichita County Child Welfare and Youth Devel., Midwestern U. Found., Red River Valley Assn., Wichita Falls United Fund, Wichita Falls Symphony, Wichita Falls Bd. Commerce and Industry Texas Law Enforcement Found. Mem. Texas State Democratic Exec. Com.; past chmn. senatorial dist.; past del. Nat. Democratic Conv. Served to 1st lt. N.G. U.S. Army, World War I. Named Pub. of Yr. by Headliners Club, 1960; named Salesman of Year Wichita Falls, 1970. Mem. Am. Soc. Newspaper Editors, N. Tex. Oil and Gas Assn. (dir.), Am., So. (dir.) newspaper pubs. assns., Tex. Daily Newspaper Assn. C. of C. (dir.), Asso. Press, Tex. Council

Higher Edn. (charter; exec. com.), Sigma Delta Chi. Presbyn. Mason (Shriner, K.T., 33 deg.). Club: President's, Wichita Falls County, Wichita, Nat. Press Home: 2105 Berkley Dr Wichita Falls TX 76308 Office: Times Publishing Co PO Box 120 1301 Lamar Wichita Falls TX 76307

HOWARD, RICHARD RALSTON, physician; b. Arkansas City, Kan., May 19, 1918; s. Harry D. and Dorothy (Ralston) H.; B.S., Northwestern U., 1940, B.M., 1943, M.D., 1943; postgrad. sch. medicine U. Pa., 1948; fellowship internal medicine, cardiology, Mass. Gen. Hosp., 1950; m. Ione Zulma Mayer, Sept. 14, 1946; 1 son, Richard Ralston II. Physician, cons. Snyder-Jones Clinic, Winfield, Kan., 1946-53; pvt. practice internal medicine Slidell, La., 1953—; pres. med. staff Slidell Meml. Hosp., 1963. Served from lt. (j.g.) to lt. USNR, 1944-46. Fellow Seminars on Hypnosis Found.; mem. A.M.A., St. Tammany Parish Med. Soc. (pres. 1962), N.Y. Acad. Sci., Am. Soc. Clin. Hypnosis, C. of C. (v.p. 1962, mem. bd.), Am. Soc. Internal Medicine, Assn. Am. Physicians and Surgeons, Nu Sigma Nu, Phi Delta Theta. Mason (32 deg.). Club: Pinewood Country (bd.). Author articles in field. Home: Chateau Beaux Chenes Bonfouca LA 70458 Office: Howard Clinic 1544 Front St Slidell LA 70458

HOWARD, ROBERT JAMES, discount store exec.; b. Hot Springs, Ark., Apr. 20, 1945; s. William L. and LaRue E. (Jones) H.; grad. high sch.; m. Linda S. Crowell, Aug. 14, 1966; children—Stacy E., Robert Chad. Accountant, Garelick, Bradley & Heller, C.P.A.'s, 1967-68; accountant, Howard Bros. Discount Stores, Inc., Monroe, La., 1968, sec.-treas., 1969—; pres. J. Howard, Ltd., Monroe, 1970—. Mem. devel. council Harding Coll., Searcy, Ark., 1970. Mem. Ch. of Christ. Kiwanian. Home: 2113 Maywood St Monroe LA 71201 Office: 3030 Aurora St Monroe LA 71201

HOWARD, ROBERT LYNWOOD, physician; b. Prattville, Ala., Oct. 3, 1919; s. John Fletcher and Delila (McDonald) H.; student U. Hawaii, 1944; U. Ala., 1944-47; M.D., George Washington U., 1951; m. Shirley Sue Martin, Nov. 24, 1956; 1 dau., Susan Lynn. Intern, resident in cardiology and internal medicine Henry Ford Hosp., 1952-55; clin. instr. dept. medicine George Washington U. Med. Sch., 1955—; attending staff D.C. Gen., George Washington U., Arlington, Fairfax hosps.; cons. in cardiology and electrocardiography Arlington, No. Va. Doctors, Fairfax hosps. Served with USNR, 1942-45. Mem. Am., Va., No. Va. (past pres.) heart assns., Arlington County, D.C., Va. med. socs., A.M.A., Am. Soc. Internal Medicine, D.C. Soc. Internal Medicine, Phi Chi. Episcopalian. Mason. Club: Optimist. Home: 2745 N Radford St Arlington VA 22207 Office: 6319 Castle Pl Falls Church VA 22044

HOWARD, ROBERT PALMER, med. educator; b. Iowa City, Nov. 4, 1912; s. Campbell Palmer and Ottilie F. (Wright) H.; B.A., McGill U., 1932, M.D., C.M., 1937, M.Sc., 1947; m. Muriel Isabel Hearn, June 18, 1943; children—Campbell P., Caroline (Mrs. Charles E. Mast). Intern, fellow, asst. resident Johns Hopkins and Johns Hopkins Hosp., Balt., 1937-40; fellow Royal Victoria Hosp., Montreal, Que., Can., 1945-46; research fellow Mass. Gen. Hosp., Boston, 1947; asst. medicine and metabolism depts. Montreal Gen. Hosp., 1947-51; mem. faculty U. Okla., 1951—, prof. history of medicine, 1966—, prof. medicine, 1972—, adj. prof. history, 1970-72, adj. prof. history of sci., 1972—. Mem., then head endocrinology sect. Okla. Med. Research Found., Oklahoma City, 1951-58, asso. head cardiovascular sect., 1958-66. Served with M.C., Canadian Army, 1940-45. Josiah Macy Jr. Found. fellow, Tulane, 1967-68; USPHS fellow, 1968-69. Fellow A.C.P.; mem. Royal Coll. Physicians, Endocrine Soc., Am. Fedn. Clin. Research, Central Soc. Clin. Research, Arteriosclerosis Council, Am. Heart Assn., A.M.A., Am., Western, Okla., Oral hist. assns., Midwest Junto, Okla. Westerners, Sigma Xi, Alpha Omega Alpha. Episcopalian. Contbr. articles to profl. jours. Home: 2524 Somerset Pl Oklahoma City OK 73116

HOWARD, WILLIE ABBAY, state ofcl.; b. Tunica, Miss., June 5, 1891; d. William G. and George Anne Elizabeth (Irwin) Abbay; student U. Miss., summer 1933; m. Thomas Percy Howard, Oct. 12, 1920 (dec.); children—Thomas Percy (dec.), GeorgeAnne Irwin (Mrs. Robert Peel Sayle), Elizabeth Irwin (Mrs. Cooper Yerger Robinson). Partner, Howard Plantation, Lake Cormorant, Miss., 1922-55, owner, operator, 1955—, Commr. Yazoo-Miss. Delta Levee Bd., 1955—, Welfare dir. DeSoto County, Miss., 1932-36, DeSoto and Tate counties, 1933-34; organizer, instr. Gulf div. A.R.C., 1917-18; co-organizer, trustee DeSoto County Library Bd., 1946—; co-organizer Citizens Library Movement, DeSoto County, Miss., 1947, first Regional Library Miss., 1950, trustee, 1950-63; pres. Miss. Citizen's Library Movement, 1950-52; del. nat. conv. Nat. Rivers and Harbors Congress, Washington, 1964. Trustee Northwest Jr. Coll., Senatobia, Miss., 1943—. Mem. Miss. Fedn. Women's Clubs (state rec. sec. 1920-22), English-Speaking Union, Memphis Execs., Lower Miss. Valley Flood Control Assn. (v.p. 1961, 71) D.A.R., Colonial Dames 17th Century. Presbyn. Clubs: Memphis Country, Memphis Woman's (pres. 1968-69), Tunica County woman's (founder 1914, pres. 1916, 1921, 28-29, trustee 1915—). Editor: DeSoto County C.L.M. Handbook, 1946. Address: Howard Plantation Lake Cormorant MS 38641

HOWE, HENRY BRANCH, JR., educator; b. Atlanta, Aug. 5, 1924; s. Henry Branch and Grace Lee (Mann) H.; A.B., Emory U., 1948, M.A., 1950; Ph.D., U. Wis., 1955; m. Margaret Anne Haden, Sept. 1, 1951; children—Stephen Jeffrey, Barbara Lynn, Alan Haden. Asst. prof. Union Coll., Barbourville, Ky., 1954-57, Wake Forest Coll., Winston-Salem, N.C., 1957-59; asst. prof. microbiology U. Ga., Athens, 1959-64, asso. prof., 1964-70, prof., 1970—. Cons. McGraw-Hill Information Systems, 1966-69. Served with AUS, 1944-46. Decorated Purple Heart. Recipient M.G. Michael award U. Ga., 1965, Sigma Xi Research award, 1965; Research prize Assn. Southeastern Biologists, 1967, 71. Mem. Am. Soc. Microbiology, Mycological Soc. Am., Genetics Soc. Am., Sigma Xi, Phi Beta Kappa. Methodist. Editor: Ga. Acad. Sci. Jour., 1963—. Home: 130 Bishop Dr Athens GA 30601

HOWELL, CHARLES MAITLAND, educator; b. Thomasville, N.C., Apr. 14, 1914; s. Cyrus Maitland and Lilly Mae (Ammons) H.; B.S., Wake Forest U., 1935; M.D., U. Pa., 1937; m. Betty Jane Myers, Feb. 12, 1949; children—Elizabeth Myers, Pamela Jane. Intern, Charity Hosp., New Orleans, 1937-38; resident medicine Burlington County Hosp., Mt. Holley, N.J., 1938-39; sch. physician Lawrenceville (N.J) Sch., 1939-42; resident pathology N.C. Baptist Hosp., Winston-Salem, 1947-48; resident dermatology Columbia Presbyn. Med. Center, N.Y.C., 1948-50; resident allergy Roosevelt Hosp., N.Y.C., 1950-51; practice medicine specializing in dermatology, Winston-Salem, N.C., 1951—; mem. staff N.C. Bapt. Hosp., Forsyth Meml. Hosp.; faculty Bowman Gray Sch. Medicine, Wake Forest U., Winston-Salem, 1951—, prof., head sect. on dermatology, 1961—. Served with M.C., AUS, 1942-46. Fellow Am. Acad. Dermatology, Am. Acad. Allergy; mem. N.Am. Clin. Dermatologic Soc. Democrat. Baptist. Clubs: Old Town (Winston-Salem); Bermuda Run Country (Clemmons, N.C.). Home: 1100 Kent Rd E Winston-Salem NC 27104

HOWELL, CLINTON TALMAGE, pub. co. exec.; b. Skinnerton, Ala., July 28, 1913; s. William Horace and Narcissa (Brooks) H.; A.B., U. Ala., 1935; children by previous marriage—William B., Gloria (Mrs. Richard Walters); m. 2d, Peggy Huffman, Sept. 17, 1964; children—Gregory, Clyde, Delilah, Joey, Brooke, Clinton Talmage. Founder, pres. Howell Pubs., Nashville, 1967—. Mem. Meth. Press Assn. (pres. 1952-56). Methodist (nat. bd. pub. 1948-60). Mason. Author: Lines to Live By, 1968: Design for Living, 1969; Better Than Gold, 1970: Seasons of Inspiration, 1973: You Can, 1973: Spirit of 76, 1974. Address: 576 Annex Court Nashville TN 37209

HOWELL, EVAN PARK, physician; b. New Orleans, Nov. 5, 1936; s. Evan Park and Thelma (Marvin) H.; B.S., Tulane U., 1969, M.D., 1972; m. Suzanne C. Noland, June 3, 1961; children—Evan, Elizabeth, Ellen. Intern, Ochsner Found. Hosp., New Orleans, 1962-63; resident Charity Hosp., New Orleans, 1963-65; practice medicine, specializing in neurology, New Orleans, 1967—; mem. staff East Jefferson Hosp.; fellow in neurology Med. Sch., Tulane U., New Orleans, 1965-66, asst. prof. dept. neurology, 1969—. Diplomate Am. Bd. Psychiatry and Neurology. Home: 127 N Livingston Pl Metairie LA 70005 Office: 3333 Kingman St Metairie LA 70002

HOWELL, GORDON CONWAY, JR., educator; b. Greer, S.C., Oct. 27, 1937; s. Gordon Conway and Lula (Scott) H.; B.S., Wofford Coll., 1960; M.A., U. Ga., 1962; M.B.A., Ga. State U., 1970, Ph.D., 1974; m. Katherine Satterfield, July 28, 1956; children—Russell Gordon, Regina Katrice. Teaching asst. U. Ga., Athens, 1960-62; systems engr. IBM Corp., Atlanta, 1962-66; faculty Ga. State U., Atlanta, 1966—, prof. information systems, 1968—. Dir. Hypersystems, Inc., 1971-74. Mem. Assn. for Computing Machinery, Soc. for Mgmt. Information Systems, Pi Mu Epsilon. Home: 3939 Granger Dr Atlanta GA 30341

HOWELL, HENRY EVANS, JR., lt. gov. Va.; b. Norfolk, Va., Sept. 5, 1920; student Coll. William and Mary; LL.B., U. Va.; m. Elizabeth McCarty; children—Mary, Henry, Susan. Admitted to Va. bar; lt. gov., Va., 1971—. Mem. Va. Ho. of Dels., 1960-66, Va. Senate, 1966-71; Democratic candidate gov. Va., 1969, 73. Mem. Va. Trial Lawyers Assn., Nofolk C. of C., Izaak Walton League, Hampton Roads Fgn. Commerce Club, Hampton Rds. Maritime Assn. Episcopalian. Clubs: Mace, Propeller. Address: State Capitol Capitol Sq Richmond VA 23219

HOWELL, HUGH HAWKINS, JR., lawyer; b. Atlanta, Aug. 18, 1920; s. Hugh and Ethleen (Horne) H.; student Riverside Mil. Acad., Boys High Sch., Atlanta, Emory U.; A.B., U. Ga., 1942; LL.B., John Marshall Law Sch., 1947, LL.M., 1958, J.D., 1959, LL.D., 1960; m. Dorris Callahan; children—Hugh Howell III, James Finn. Admitted to Ga. bar. Dir. Spring Lakes Apts., Inc., Bolton Apts., High Point Apts. Mem. Ga. Vets. Service Bd., chmn., 1963-71. Served as to rear adm. USNR. Mem. Judge Advs. Assn. (nat. pres. 1968), Am. Judicature Soc., Fed. (v.p. 5th U.S. Circuit), Am., Ga., Atlanta bar assns., Atlanta Hist. Soc., Am. Legion, Navy League (nat. dir.), Naval Res. Assn. (nat. v.p.), S.A.R., S.C.V. (comdr.), Naval Hist. Found., Old Guard of Gate City Guard (comdt.), Phi Delta Theta, Sigma Delta Kappa. Mason (32 deg., Shriner). Clubs: Athletic, Ansley Golf, Old War Horse Lawyers. Veteran Luncheon, Lawyers. Home: 2811 Ridgewood Rd NW Atlanta GA 30327 Office: 1505 Rock Springs Circle NE Atlanta GA 30306

HOWELL, IRVIN NAPOLEAN, telephone co. exec.; b. Chickasaw, Ala., Jan. 3, 1922; s. Irvin N. and Effie (Pierce) H.; B.S. in Elec. Engring., The Citadel, 1951; m. Betty Lou Hinson, July 6, 1943; children—Dorothy Jean, Robert Wayne, Connie. With So. Bell Tel. & Tel., various locations. 1951-53, 55-67, div. staff engr., Memphis, 1963-64, transmission staff engr., Atlanta, 1964-67; with South Central Bell Telephone Co., Birmingham, 1967—, engring. mgr. investment and costs div., 1972-73, engring. mgr. plant extension and costs div., 1973—. Served with USCGR, 1940-46. Registered profl. egr., Tenn. Mem. Am. Inst. Elec. Engrs. (past chmn.), I.E.E.E. (sr. mem., past pres., chmn. policy and planning 1973), Nat. Assn. Corrosion Engrs. (past sec.). Home: 2529 Comanche Dr Birmingham AL 35244 Office: PO Box 771 600 N 19th St Birmingham AL 35201

HOWELL, JAMES ERNEST, JR., antenna engr.; b. Fairfax, Ala., Dec. 17, 1920; s. James Ernest and Addie Mae (Bradshaw) H.; B.E.E., Auburn U., 1947; postgrad Ga. Inst. Tech., 1948; m. M. Elizabeth Lambeth, Aug. 25, 1946; children—James Ernest III, Mary Virginia. Chief engr. Ben Hill Broadcasting Co., Fitzgerald, Ga., 1950-51; antenna engr. Redstone Arsenal, Ala., 1951—. Systems mgmt. engr. S.E. Civic Assn., 1970—. Served with USAAF, 1942-45. Decorated D.F.C., Air medal with 3 oak leaf clusters, Bronze Star; recipient Certificate Achievement, U.S. Dept. Def., 1960. Mem. I.E.E.E., Am. Ordnance Soc., Assn. U.S. Army. Baptist. Patentee in field. Home: 8117 Warden Dr Huntsville AL 35802 Office: Bldg 4488 AMSMI-UH Redstone Arsenal AL 35802

HOWELL, JAMES GOFF, assn. exec.; b. Delavan, Wis., Feb. 4, 1916; s. Dorsey G. and Rispah (Goff) H.; student Yankton (S.D.) Coll., 1932-34; J,D., U. Neb., 1938; m. Anna Louise Van Horn, Oct. 10, 1946; children—Patricia Louise (Mrs. Jon H. Knickerbocker), Deborah Lynne (Mrs. James D. Wilkinson). Constance Diane. Admitted to Neb. bar, 1938; practiced in Albion, 1938-40; spl. agt. FBI, Richmond, N.Y.C., Detroit, Omaha, 1940-46; v.p. Mountain States Employers Council, Denver, 1946-67; pres. New Orleans S.S. Assn., 1967—; dir. Internat. Trade Mart. Mem. Nat. Def. Exec. Res.; chmn. indsl. relations group Nat. Indsl. Council. Mem. Beta Theta Pi, Phi Delta Phi. Republican. Conglist. Clubs: University (Denver); Metairie (La.) Country; Plimsoll, Pickwick (New Orleans). Home: 4821 Cleveland Pl Metairie LA 70003 Office: 219 Carondelet St New Orleans LA 70130

HOWELL, JOHN B., JR., librarian; b. Greer, S.C., Oct. 25, 1925; s. John B. and Alleyne (Richbourg) H.; B.A., Furman U., 1945; B.A. in L.S., Emory U., 1946; M.S., U. Ill., 1954. Acquisitions librarian Emory U., Atlanta, 1946-51; asst. librarian Furman U., Greenville, S.C., 1951-52, Clemson (S.C.) U., 1954-58; circulation librarian U. Ga., Athens, 1958-60; librarian Miss. Coll., Clinton, 1960—. State reporter The Southeastern Librarian, 1967—. Mem. Miss. (treas. 1966-67, pres. 1970), Southeastern (treas. 1972—) library assns., A.L.A. Baptist. Editor: The S.C. Librarian, 1956-58, Miss. Library News, 1972—. Home: 118 Fairmont St Clinton MS 39056 Office: Box 47 Clinton MS 39056

HOWELL, JOHN OWEN, JR., retail mcht.; b. Nashville, Feb. 7, 1925; s. John Owen and Margaret Lee (Bowden) H.; student Middle Tenn. State Coll., 1946-47; m. Margaret Sue Stephens, Apr. 4, 1946; children—Frances Lee, Stephen Owen, Susan Lynn. With Genesco, Inc., Nashville, 1947—, successively purchasing agt. mfg. plants, style and cost engr. retail div., style dir., mdse. mgr., 1947-58, pres. Flagg Bros. div., 1958—, pres. Holiday-Wise div., 1961—, also dir., mem. exec. com., bd. govs. Genesco, Inc., exec. v.p., 1968-69, pres., chmn. finance com., 1969—; dir. 3d Nat. Bank of Nashville, Am. Security Real Estate Investment Trust. Pres., Youth, Inc. Bd. dirs., v.p. United Givers Fund of Nashville; pres. bd. trustees Bethel Coll. Served with USNR, 1943-46. Mem. Volume Footwear Retailers Assn. (pres., dir.), Nashville Area C. of C. (gov.). Presbyn. (elder). Clubs: Bluegrass Yacht and Country (Hendersonville, Tenn.); Belle Meade Country (Nashville). Home: 4006 Brush Hill Rd Nashville TN 37216 Office: 111 7th Av N Nashville TN 37206

HOWELL, MABLE GREY, lawyer; b. Hillsboro, Tex., Feb. 10, 1910; d. Robert Edward and Josephine (Glover) H.; B.A., U. Tex., 1930; LL.B. with honor, Baylor U., 1933. Admitted to Tex. bar, 1933, practiced in Waco, 1933-38, 41-46; asst. city atty., City of Waco, 1938-41; asso. atty. Pioneer Savs. Assn., Waco, 1946-51; asso. Helm, Jones, McDermott & Pletcher, Houston, 1951-61; individual practice, 1961—; substitute judge Corp. Ct. City Houston; spl. justice Ct. of Civil Appeals for 10th Supreme Ct. of Tex.; lectr. law U. Houston Coll. Law, 1963. Pres. United Cerebral Palsy Assn., Inc., 1959, rep. dir. nat. and southwestern region, 1959-61, v.p. United Cerebral Palsy Tex. Inc., 1961. Mem. State Bar Tex., Am., Houston (chmn. women's sect. 1959) bar assns., Bus. Women's Assn., Soroptimist Fedn. of Americas, Am. Assn. U. Women. Episcopalian. Club: Soroptimist (pres. 1958-59, dir. 1960). Home: 38 Bash Pl Houston TX 77027 Office: Tex Profl Tower 608 Fannin St Houston TX 77002

HOWELL, MABLE SMITH (MRS. BRUCE INMAN HOWELL), coll. librarian; b. Beaufort County, N.C., Sept. 21, 1942; d. Hyman L. and Thelma (Evans) Smith; B.S., East Carolina U., 1964, M.Ed. in L.S., 1967; postgrad. Duke, 1970; m. Bruce Inman Howell, Aug. 22, 1965; 1 son, Bruce Inman. Librarian, Lenoir Community Coll., Kinston, N.C., 1964—, dir. Learning Center, 1968—, now asso. dean Learning Resources, also instr., library tech. asst. for curriculum 1970—. Mem. N.C. State accreditation teams, 1969, 72, N.C. Com. for Edn. Librarianship, 1971. Mem. Ednl. Media Assn. (treas. dept. community colls. N.C. 1968-69, pres. 1969-71; dir. Eastern region N.C. 1967-68), N.C. Library Assn. scholarship com. 1971-75, chmn. 1974-75), Librarians Lenoir County (pres. 1974-75), Am. Assn. U. Women (rec. sec. Kinston br. 1969-71), Lenoir County Hist. Assn. Home: 3012 Englewood Dr Kinston NC 28501 Office: PO Box 188 Kinston NC 28501

HOWELL, MACK RUSSELL, forester, surveyor; b. Whittier, N.C., Apr. 28, 1931; s. William Harley and Myrtle (Varner) H.; grad. Nat. Sch. Forestry and Conservation, 1960; m. Willa Dean Teague, Oct. 26, 1951; children—William Russell, Mildred Dean, Harriet Evelyn. With U.S. Forest Service, 1951-53; area supr. land acquisition-surveys, forestry dept. Champion Papers, Inc., Murphy, N.C., 1953-62; cons. in forestry and surveying, boundary and topog. surveys, site locations, ct. surveys, Bryson City, N.C., 1962—. Mem. Am. Congress Surveying and Mapping, Soc. Am. Foresters, N.C. Forestry Assn. Presbyn. Mason. Home: PO Box 228 Bryson City NC 28713 Office: Depot St Bryson City NC 28713

HOWELL, MARK FRANKLIN, lawyer; b. El Paso, Tex., Nov. 19, 1934; s. Benjamin Randolph and Romaine (Safford) H.; B.A., Stanford U., 1956; LL.B., U. Tex., 1961; m. Linda O'Reilly, Jan. 5, 1973; children by previous marriage—Madeline, Celia. Admitted to Tex. bar, 1961; since practiced in El Paso; mem. firms Fryer, Milstead & Luscombe, 1961-62, Peticolas, Luscombe & Stephens, 1963-68, pvt. practice, 1969—. Founder, vice chmn., dir. El Paso (Tex.) Legal Assistance Soc., 1969-72; vice chmn. bd. commrs. El Paso (Tex.) Housing Authority, 1970-72; chmn. Mayor's Com. on Housing, 1969; chmn. legal com. Am. Civil Liberties Union. Bd. dir. El Paso Boys Club, 1973—. Served with AUS, 1956-58. Mem. Am., Inter-Am., El Paso bar assns., State Bar Tex., Tex. (dir. 1973—), El Paso (dir., v.p. 1972—) trial lawyers assns., Sigma Chi, Phi Delta Phi. Democrat. Episcopalian. Contbr. articles in field to profl. jours. Home: 1008 Park Rd El Paso TX 79902 Office: 1011 N Mesa St El Paso TX 79902

HOWELL, PATRICIA MARGARET, business exec.; b. Denver, Oct. 14, 1926; d. George W. and Daisy (Lawton) Howell; student Little Rock Jr. Coll., 1944, George Washington U., 1944-46, Am. Inst. Banking, 1946-47; certificate award Bur. Bus. Practice, New London, Conn., 1957. Sec., F.E.A., Washington, 1944-46; sec. to exec. v.p. Nat. Bank Commerce, Houston, 1946-47; sr. sec. Hughes Tool Co., Houston, 1947-62; pres., owner Exec. Secs., Inc., Chattanooga, 1962—. Chmn. Tex. State Conv., 1959. Mem. Sales and Marketing Execs. Assn. (exec. sec. 1964-73), Houston C. of C. (life), Houston Assn. Legal Secs. (pres. 1958), Bus. Editors Assn. (pres. 1963), Dayton Blvd. Bus. Assn. (pres. 1973-74), Chattanooga Advt. Fedn., Nat. Assn. Female Execs. Editor: The Nals Docket, 1959-62. Home: 5359 Hunter Trail Hixson TN 37343 Office: 2629 Dayton Blvd Chattanooga TN 37415

HOWELL, RALPH RODNEY, pediatrician; b. Concord, N.C., June 10, 1931; s. Fred Lee and Grace Mary (Blackwelder) H.; B.S., Davidson Coll., 1957; M.D., Duke U., 1957; m. Sarah Vosburgh Esselstyn, Nov. 19, 1960; children—Grace Meyer, Elizabeth Eriksson, John Esselstyn. Intern, Duke, 1957-58, resident pediatrics, 1958-59, research fellow in pediatrics and medicine, 1959-60; clin. asso. and staff NIH, Bethesda, Md., 1960-64; asso. prof. pediatrics Johns Hopkins, Balt., 1964-72; pediatrician-in-chief Hermann Hosp., Houston, 1972—, chmn. med. bd. 1973; prof., chmn. dept. pediatrics U. Tex. Med. Sch., Houston, 1972—; cons. pediatrics M.D. Anderson Hosp. and Tumor Inst. Mem. metabolism study sect. NIH, 1973—; mem. nat. clin. adv. com. Nat. Found. March of Dimes, 1973—. Served to sr. surgeon USPHS, 1960-64. Fellow Am. Acad. Pediatrics; mem. Am. Pediatric Soc., Soc. for Pediatric Research, Houston Pediatric Soc., Tex. Med. Assn., Pi Kappa Alpha. Club: Meml. Forest (Houston). Author: (with G.H. Thomas) Selected Screening Tests for Genetic Metabolic Diseases, 1973. Contbr. articles to profl. jours. Home: 12118 Tara Dr Houston TX 77024 Office: Program in Pediatrics University of Texas Medical School at Houston 6400 W Cullen St Houston TX 77025

HOWELL, THOMAS LEE, elec. engr.; b. Hodgenville, Ky., Nov. 23, 1943; s. George Anthony and Gertrude (Coakley) H.; B.S., U. Ky., 1966; m. Joyce Ann Wathen, May 27, 1966; 1 son, Kelly Thomas. With facilities engring. dept. IBM Corp., Lexington, Ky., 1967—, jr. engr., 1967-68, asso. engr., 1968-72, sr. asso. engr., 1972—. Named Ky. Col., 1970. Registered profl. engr., Ky. Mem. I.E.E.E., Consolidated Investment Club (pres.), Ky. Soc. Profl. Engrs. Baptist (deacon). Home: 103 Loch Lomond Dr Lexington KY 40503 Office: 740 New Circle Rd Lexington KY 40507

HOWER, DONOVAN EARL, landscape architect; b. Mifflintown, Pa., June 20, 1926; s. Earl Francis and Pauline Katherin (Gibbons) H.; B.S., Pa. State U., 1950; m. Gloria May Kruppenbach, Jan. 31, 1948; children—Donovan Earl, Lee Ann. Gen. foreman, designer W.A. Morton Jr., Coraopolis, Pa., 1950-53; landscape architect VA, Washington, 1953—, dir. land mgmt. service, 1971—. Instr. landscaping the small estate Fairfax County Recreation Dept., 1965-71; mem. Fairfax County Archtl. Review Bd., 1969—, vice chmn. 1973—. Mem. Fairfax County Hist. Preservation Commn., Fairfax, Va., 1962-69. Served with USNR, 1944-46. Mem. Am. Soc. Landscape Architects. Presbyn. (trustee 1954-58). Mason. Home: 2910 Beau Lane Fairfax VA 22030 Office: 810 Vermont Av Washington DC 20420

HOWERTON, JAMES ROBERT, physician; b. Knoxville, Tenn., Oct. 29, 1927; s. Perry Doddridge and Elizabeth (Colyer) H.; M.D., U. Tenn., 1955; m. Gretchen Mars, Dec. 27, 1955; children—Russell Mars, Todd Leah. Intern Charlotte (N.C.) Meml. Hosp., 1956-57;

family practice, Columbia, N.C., 1957-65; resident medicine Norfolk (Va.) Gen. Hosp., 1965-66; resident psychiatry Med. Coll. Va., Richmond, 1966-69; practice medicine specializing in psychiatry, Newport News, Va., 1969—; mem. staffs Riverside Hosp., Newport News, Hampton (Va.) Gen. Hosp., Mary Immaculate Hosp., Newport News; faculty Eastern Va. Med. Sch., Norfolk, 1973; clin. instr. Va. Commonwealth U., Richmond, 1970; lectr. George Washington U., 1972. Served with AUS, 1945-47. Career Psychiatry grantee Nat. Inst. Mental Health, 1970. Mem. Internat. Soc. for Study of Symbols, Am., So. med. assns., Am. Psychiat. Assn., Med. Soc. Va. (dir. 1972—), Newport News Med. Soc., Peninsula Acad. Medicine, VA Diabetes Assn. Clubs: Warwick Country, Huntington (Newport News). Home: 111 Museum Parkway Newport News VA 23606 Office: 314 Main St Newport News VA 23601

HOWERTON, JOEL DOAN, assn. exec.; b. Iuka, Miss., Nov. 11, 1892; s. George Taylor and Lula (Doan) H.; student E. Central State Coll., Okla., 1910-12; diploma Memphis State U., 1913; B.S. with honors, Miss. State U., 1915; postgrad.; m. Peggy Jackman, Sept. 6, 1918. Tchr., Lamar County (Miss.) Agrl. High Sch., Purvis, 1915-16; county agrl. agt. U.S. Dept. Agr., Adams County, Natchez, 1916-19, Lauderdale County, Meridian, Miss., 1919-61; pub. relations and spl. assignments officer E. Miss. Electric Power Assn., Meridian, 1962—. Mem. Lauderdale County 4-H Adv. Council, 1930—; chmn. rural area devel. com. 1962—, Lauderdale County Coordinating Council, 1935—, mem. tech. action panel, 1965—. Recipient awards including Distinguished Service award Nat. Assn. County Agrl. Agts., 1955. Mem. Miss. State U. Alumni Assn. (county pres. 1961, dist. pres. 1962, chpt. chmn. scholarship com. 1963—), County Farm Bur. (organizer), Meridian C. of C. Episcopalian. Mason (Shriner), Lion. Clubs: Meridian Downtown, Northwood Country. Home: 1839 Country Club Blvd Meridian MS 39301 Office: E Miss Electric Power Assn Meridian MS 39301

HOWERTON, PAUL WILLIAM, coll. adminstr.; b. Valparaiso, Ind., July 25, 1916; s. William Columbus and Kathryn Inez (Coutchure) H.; Ph.B., Northwestern U., 1949; m. Ernestine Loehrke, Mar. 26, 1938 (dec.); children—Charles Paul, Terrance Joseph; 2d. m. Helen DeFrancesco, Nov. 22, 1969. Chemist, Carbide & Carbon Chems. Corp., Whiting, Ind., 1935-42, 45-49; chemist Julius Hyman & Co., Denver, 1949-51; dep. asst. dir. CIA, Washington, 1951-62; self employed cons. in mgmt., Washington, also Rome, Italy, 1962-64, 67-70; with Am. U., Washington, 1964-67, 70-74, dir. undergrad. and grad. programs, 1964-74; resident scholar Nat. Center for Alcohol Edn., 1974—. Dir. Nat. Distbrs. Corp., 1967-68, Information for Industry, 1962-64, Internat. Data Systems Corp., 1967—, Toltec Corp., 1967-70. Bd. dirs. Soc. for Indsl. Edn., Bangalore, India, 1968—; sec., trustee Claudia Gips Found., 1971—. Served with USAAC, 1942-45. Recipient Intelligence Medal of Merit, CIA, 1962; Chester Morrill Meml. award Assn. for Systems Mgmt, 1973. Fellow A.A.A.S. Author: Russian-English Geossary of Metallurgy and Metal Terms, 1956; Information Handling: First Principles, 1963; Augmentation of Man's Intellect by Machine, 1963; (with Ralph I. Cole) Information Systems Compatibility, 1966; Data/Information Availability, 1966; Cybernetics: The Multi-Science, 1968; Management of Information Handling Systems, 1974. Contbr. articles to profl. jours. Home: 7800 Green Twig Rd Bethesda MD 20034 Office: 1901 N Moore St Arlington VA 22209

HOWIE, HENRY SANFORD, JR., children's agy. exec.; b. Abbeville, S.C., Oct. 10, 1927; s. Sanford and Anna (Biggers) H.; B.A., Presbyn. Coll., 1950; postgrad. U. Ark., 1953, Furman U., 1954, Winthrop Coll., 1955-56; M.S.W., U. N.C., 1965; m. Betty Jane Shirley, Dec. 20, 1949; children—Lynda Elizabeth, Anna Shirley, Genevieve Sharpe, Henry Sanford III, Robert Marcus. Coach, prin., Norway, S.C., 1949-50; trainee Deering Milliken, 1951-52; sch. prin., Rock Hill (S.C.) Pub. schs., 1952-57; exec. dir. Episcopal Ch. Home for Children, York, S.C., 1957—. Del., White House Conf. on Children, 1970. Bd. mem. S.C. Social Welfare Forum, 1967—, S.C. Com. on Children and Youth, 1966—; chmn. S.C. Com. on Childhood Mental Illness, 1971—; v.p. York County Council on Alcoholism, 1971-72; del. dir. S.C. Mental Health Assn.; chmn. regional adv. com. S.C. Dept. Pub. Welfare. Bd. dirs. Tri-County Mental Health Center; pres. bd. govs. Group Child Care Cons. Services. Served with USNR, 1945-46. Mem. Nat. Assn. Social Workers, Acad. Certified Social Workers, Southeastern Child Care Assn. (pres. 1966-67), York County Mental Health Assn. (pres. 1968), Pi Kappa Phi (pres. Beta chpt. 1948). Episcopalian (sr. warden 1965-67, vestryman 1955-58). Rotarian (pres. York 1964). Clubs: Springlake Country (York), Crustbreakers (pres. 1966-67). Address: Episcopal Ch Home for Children York SC 29745

HOWLETT, MAEME MARLENE DAVIS (MRS. JOHN E. HOWLETT, JR.), constrn. co. exec.; b. Louisville, Oct. 31, 1932; d. Robert and Mattie (Woods) Davis; student Howard U., 1949-50, Fisk U., 1951; B.A., Lane Coll., 1957; M.A., Tenn. State U., 1967; m. John E. Howlett, Jr., Aug. 18, 1967. Tchr., Crockett County Bd. Edn., 1957-65; grad. asst., dean Sch. Edn., Tenn. State U., 1966-67; supt. Tenn. Vocational Sch. for Girls, Nashville, 1968-71; v.p. J.E. Howlett, Jr. Enterprises, Inc., 1971—; sec.-treas. United Assn. Econ. Devel., Inc. Sec.-treas., dir. John E. Howlett, Jr. Constrn. Co. Vice pres. Tenn. Employees Credit Union, 1969-71; bd. dirs. Sons and Daughters of Charity Corp. Mem. Am. Soc. Pub. Adminstrn., Nat. Congress Parents and Tchrs., Urban League, N.A.A.C.P., Alpha Kappa Alpha. Democrat. Baptist (tchr. Sunday sch.). Elk. Address: PO Box 5705 Nashville TN 37208

HOY, DOUGLAS STUART, dentist; b. Urbana, Ill., Mar. 28, 1939; s. Harry Eugene and Eldora Christina (Larsen) H.; student U. Okla., 1957-60; D.D.S., U. Neb., 1964; m. Laurelyn Sue Buller, June 15, 1964. Resident oral surgery U. Okla. Med. Center, 1964-67; individual practice oral surgery, Norman, Okla., 1967—; mem. staff Norman Municipal Hosp., Valley View Hosp., Ada, Okla.; clin. asst. prof. oral surgery U. Okla. Health Center; cons. Griffith State Meml. Hosp., Norman. Mem. Am., Okla. dental assns., Cleveland County Dental Soc. (past pres.), Am. (del.), Okla. (pres.) socs. oral surgeons. Lion. Home: 2215 W Iowa St Norman OK 73069 Office: 500 E Robinson St Norman OK 73069

HOYT, LEON LESLIE, accountant; b. Custer City, Okla., Dec. 25, 1908; s. Leon Lothian and Nona Iris (Harman) H.; student A and M Coll., 1926-27; m. Margaret Hazel Moody, Nov. 26, 1931 (dec. May 1971); 1 dau., Catherine (Mrs. Jack Ernest Wardlow Jr.). Ledger clk. Internat. Harvester Co., Amarillo, Tex., 1927-35; statistician Soil Conservation Service, Amarillo, 1936-38; c.p.a. L.E. Cahill & Co., Amarillo, 1939-41; owner Leon L. Hoyt & Co., c.p.a.'s Amarillo, 1939—; auditor USAAF, 1941-42. Mem. bd. regents Amarillo Coll., 1959-69, chmn., 1961-62; chmn. Amarillo Coll. Found., 1964—, bd. dirs. Don and Sybil Harrington Found. 1960—, v.p., treas. 1970—; bd. dirs. Marsh Found., 1965—, v.p., sec. 1965—; trustee Wagner Found., 1965—. C.P.A. Tex., Okla. Mem. Am. Inst. C.P.A.'s, Tex. Soc. C.P.A.'s. Mason, Elk. Club: One Hundred (pres. 1972—, dir 1964—) (Amarillo). Home: 3609 Line Av Amarillo TX 79106 Office: PO Box 2211 Amarillo TX 79105

HREN, JOHN JOSEPH, educator; b. Milw., Dec. 3, 1933; s. John Stephen and Mary (Bistan) H.; B.S., U. Wis., 1957; M.S., U. Ill., 1960; Ph.D., Stanford, 1962; m. Joyce Alden Dickson, June 27, 1957; children—Karl F., Philip D., Christina M., Jonathan D. Research physicist Lawrence Radiation Lab. Berkeley, Cal., 1961-62; asst. prof. U. Fla., Gainesville, 1964-67, asso. prof., 1967-72, prof. materials sci. and engring., 1972—. Vis. scientist CSIRO, Melbourne, Australia, 1970-71; v.p. Materials Cons., Inc., Gainesville, Fla., 1971—. Served with AUS, 1953-55. NSF Postdoctoral fellow, 1962-64. Mem. A.A.A.S., Am. Inst. Metall. Engrs., Am. Inst. Physics, Sierra Club, Sigma Xi. Roman Catholic. Co-author: Field-Ion Microscopy, 1968; Elements of Physical Metallurgy, 3d edit., 1974. Mem. editorial bd. Current Contents: Phys. Scis., 1970—. Contbr. articles to profl. jours. Home: 2844 NW 4th Lane Gainesville FL 32607

HRUBECKY, HENRY FRANCIS, educator; b. Chgo., May 12, 1922; s. Charles Albert and Julia (Sperl) H.; B.S. magna cum laude, U. Ill., 1944, M.S., 1949; Ph.D., Ia. State U., 1953; m. Jean Marie Wise, June 12, 1950; children—Jennifer Lee, Valerie Jean, Christopher Paul. Mech. engr. Office Sci. Research and Devel., Washington, 1944-45; asst. prof. Ia. State U., 1949-55; asso. prof. U. Fla., 1955-61; prof. mech. engring. Tulane U., 1961—; cons. to industry, Army Missile Command, NASA. Sci. adviser U.S. Army Research Sect., Durham, N.C. NSF grantee, 1973. Mem. Am. Soc. M.E., Am. Soc. Engring. Edn., A.A.A.S., Sigma Xi, Tau Beta Pi, Sigma Tau, Pi Tau Sigma. Contbr. articles to profl. jours. Research on fluidics, boundary layer theory, fluid mechanics, interface between engring. and society; inventor in field. Home: 76 OK Av New Orleans LA 70123

HSU, TING CHEN, economist; b. Shanghai, China, Dec. 2, 1921; s. Tse Chien and Lan Ying (Tsong) H.; B.S., U. Mo., 1950, M.A., 1953; postgrad. U. Mich., 1954-56; m. Sylvia Martin, Nov. 29, 1953. Came to U.S., 1945, naturalized, 1960. Research asst. Alfred Politz, Inc., N.Y.C., 1957-58; econ. cons. P.R. Planning Bd., Santurce, P.R., 1958-59; research supr. W.R. Simmons & Assos. Research Inc., N.Y.C., 1959-60; sr. research analyst Girl Scouts U.S.A., N.Y.C., 1960-63; cons. P.R. Treasury Dept., San Juan, 1963-69, exec. dir., 1970, chief economist, 1971—. Lectr. Inter Am. U. P.R., Hato Rey, 1967—. Mem. men's adv. com. Caribe Girl Scout Council, 1967—, chmn., 1971—. Served to capt. Chinese Nationalist Army, 1943-46. Mem. Am. Econ. Assn., Tax with Representation, Financial Mgmt. Assn., Internat. Studies Assn., Alpha Pi Zeta. Club: Cosmopolitan (pres. 1951-52) (Columbia, Mo.). Home: 710 Fernandez Juncos Av Santurce PR 00907 Office: PR Treasury Dept San Juan PR 00905

HUANG, JINN-HUIE, chem. engr.; b. Djawa, Indonesia, Sept. 8, 1933; s. Khing Hun and Bie Nio (Tio) H.; B.S., Taipei Inst. Tech., 1955; M.S., U. Tokyo, 1961, Ph.D., 1964; postgrad. U. Cal., 1961-63; D.Sc., London Inst. Tech., 1973; m. Shiu-Chien Lin, July 17, 1961; children—Jen-Wei, Juliana Tjiu. Research engr. Cities Service Oil Co., Tulsa, 1967-71; sr. engr. Crest Engring., Tulsa, 1971—. Research asso. U. Va., 1964-67. Mem. Am. Inst. Mining, Metall., Petroleum Engrs., Am. Geophys. Union, N.Y. Acad. Scis., Sigma Xi. Home: 4812 S 71st East Av Tulsa OK 74145 Office: PO Box 1859 Tulsa OK 74101

HUBARD, HARRISON, utility exec.; b. Richmond, Va., Apr. 9, 1917; s. Nathaniel Walter and Helen (Harrison) H.; B.S. in Elec. Engring., Va. Mil. Inst., 1938; m. Mary Madison Knox, Sept. 7, 1940; children—Harrison, Conway Knox, Mary Knox. With Va. Electric & Power Co., 1939—, dist. mgr., Fredericksburg, 1965-67, v.p. Eastern div., Norfolk, 1967—; dir. First & Mchts. Nat. Bank of Tidewater, Norfolk. Vice pres. Jr. Achievement, Norfolk, 1972—, Norfolk Symphony, 1972—; mem. pres.'s adv. council Va. Wesleyan Coll., 1972—. Bd. dirs. Med. Center Hosps., Norfolk, United Communities Fund, Norfolk, Old Dominion Univ. Research Found., Va. Coll. Fund, Bus. Sch. Sponsors of William and Mary Coll.; trustee Tidewater Devel. Council. Served to lt. col. AUS, 1941-46. Mem. Kappa Alpha. Clubs: Princess Anne Country (Virginia Beach, Va.); Norfolk Yacht and Country, Country of Va. (Norfolk). Office: PO Box 329 Norfolk VA 23501

HUBBARD, CARROLL, JR., lawyer; b. Murray, Ky., July 7, 1937; s. Carroll and Beth (Shelton) H.; grad. Georgetown Coll., 1959, U. Louisville Law Sch., 1962; m. Joyce Lynn Hall, Aug. 20, 1966. Admitted to Ky. bar, 1962; partner Hubbard, Null & West, Mayfield, Ky., 1969—. Mem. Ky. Senate from 1st Dist. of Ky., 1967—. Home: 410 Macedonia Rd Mayfield KY 42066 Office: 118 W Broadway Mayfield KY 42066

HUBBARD, DOUGLASS HOPWOOD, mus. ofcl.; b. Oakland, Cal., May 22, 1918; s. Ocheltree Sewell and Margaret Bradfield (Hopwood) H.; student Fresno State Coll., 1936-37; A.B., U. Cal. at Berkeley, 1940; M.S., Tex. A. and M. U., 1942; m. Frances Jean Christianson, Oct. 17, 1942; children—Douglass Hopwood, Janet (Mrs. John Mott), Joan, David. Patrol insp. U.S. Border Patrol, Mexican border, Calexico, Cal., 1941-43; with Nat. Park Service, Hawaii, Yosemite Nat. Park, also Harpers Ferry, 1945-70, asst. dir. service, 1965-70; exec. dir. Admiral Nimitz Center, Fredericksburg, Tex., 1970—. Served to lt. (j.g.) USNR, 1943-45. Home: Rural Route 2 Box 130AAA Fredericksburg TX 78624 Office: PO Box 777 Fredericksburg TX 78624

HUBBARD, GEORGE WENDELL, supt. schs.; b. Albany, Okla., Feb. 19, 1927; s. Monterey R. and Helen Nancy (Capshaw) H.; B.S., Southeastern State Coll., 1947; M.S., Okla. State U., 1950; Ed.D., U. Okla., 1958; m. Marjorie Del Stewart, Aug. 6, 1950; 1 son, George Wendell. Prin., tchr. Albany (Okla.) High Sch., 1945-46; tchr., McAlester (Okla.) High Sch., 1947-50, Capitol Hill High Sch., Oklahoma City, 1950-55; asst. prin. Harding High Sch., Oklahoma City, 1955-59; supt. schs. Washington dist., Kansas City, Kan., 1959-67; supt. schs., Sherman, Tex., 1967—. Rotarian. Home: 1702 Shields St Sherman TX 75090 Office: PO Box 1156 Sherman TX 75090

HUBBARD, LAFAYETTE RONALD, author, explorer; b. Tilden, Neb., Mar. 13, 1911; s. H.R. and Ledora May (Waterbury) H.; student Swavely Prep. Sch., 1929, Woodward Prep. Sch., 1930; B.S. in Civil Engring., George Washington U., 1934; postgrad. Princeton Sch. Govt., 1945; Ph.D., Sequoia U., 1950; m. Mary Sue Whipp; children—Lafayette Ronald, Catherine May (Mrs. Gillespie), Diana Meredith deWolf, Quentin Geoffrey Macauley, Mary Suzette Rochelle, Arthur Ronald Conway. Writer aviation and travel articles, 1930—; writer of novels, 1936—; explorer, 1934—; comdr. Caribbean Motion Picture Expdn. and W.I. Minerals Expdn., 1935, Alaskan Radio-Exptl. Expdn., 1940; writer for 90 nat. mags., Hollywood studios and radio; licensed comml. glider pilot, master of motor vessels, master of sailing vessels (all oceans), radio operator. Mem. 163d Inf., Mont. N.G., 1927-28, 20th Marines, Marine Corps Res., 1930-31; served as lt. USNR, 1941-46; comdg. escort vessels and navigator in all theaters. Fellow Oceanographic Found., Am. Geog. Soc.; mem. Internat. Oceanographic Found. (life), Royal Photographic Soc. Gt. Britain (life), Cruising Assn., Writers' Guild. Founder of Scientology. Clubs: Explorers' (New York City); Capital Yacht (Washington); Port Orchard (Wash.) Yacht. Author: Buckskin Brigade, Final Blackout. Rebellion; Dianetics: Modern Science of Mental Health; and 21 other volumes on Dianetics and Scientology; also motion pictures, mag. fiction, two texts on psychology. Home: Washington DC Office: 1827 19th St NW Washington DC 20009

HUBBARD, ROBERT ALBERT, cons. transp. engr.; b. Rice, Va., Sept. 11, 1932; s. Harvey Johnson and Louise (Bradshaw) H.; B.S., Va. Mil. Inst., 1954; certificate Bur. Hwy. Traffic, Yale, 1955; m. Ann Glenn, Sept. 4, 1951; children—Robert Albert, Harvey Bradshaw, Susan Glenn. Hwy. engr. Va. Dept. Hwys., Richmond, 1954-57, dist. traffic engr., Bristol, 1957-59, asso. traffic engr., Richmond, 1959-60; prin. asso., asso. engr. Wilbur Smith & Assos., Columbia, S.C., 1960-65, prin. asso., office mgr., 1965-67, dir. computation research and devel., 1968-70, v.p., dir. internat. operations, 1970-73, exec. v.p., 1973—, also dir., 1966—; dir. Freeman, Fox, Wilbur Smith & Assos., London, Eng., 1968-70, Computation Research and Devel., London, 1968-70. Dir. program tech. confs. and lectures Ministry Pub. Works, Madrid, Spain, 1964; mem. Regional Export Expansion Council, 1971-73; mem. engring. adv. bd. Clemson U., 1972. Served to 1st lt. U.S. Army, 1955-57. Named Outstanding Young Man Am., 1966. Registered profl. engr., S.C., Ky., La., Va. Mem. Am. Soc. C.E., Nat. Soc. Profl. Engrs., Am. Cons. Engrs. Council (mem. internat. engring. com. 1971—), Inst. Traffic Engrs., Am. Rd. Builders Assn., Instn. Civil Engrs. (London), Internat. Bridge, Tunnel and Turnpike Assn. (internat. crossings com.), Engrs. Club Richmond. Baptist. Clubs: Va. Military Institute Alumni, Sportsmens (Lexington); Richland Sertoma, Summit (Columbia). Home: 3735 Oakleaf Rd Columbia SC 29206 Office: 4500 Jackson Blvd Columbia SC 29209

HUBBARD, SAMUEL FRED, supt. schs.; b. Eoline, Ala., Sept. 8, 1930; s. Harper Albert and Veda Elizabeth (Hubbard) H.; B.S., U. Ala., 1958, M.A., 1960; m. Sallie Daniel Edwards, Sept. 26, 1958; children—Freda Evelyn, Kenneth Fred. With Bibb County Bd. Edn., Centreville, Ala., 1958-63; prin. Perry County Bd. Edn., Marion, Ala., 1963-65; supt., Marion (Ala.) City Bd. Edn., 1965—. Chpt. chmn. A.R.C., 1970-72. Coll., mil. staff Gov. George C. Wallace, Ala., 1964—. Served with USN, 1951-55. Recipient Distinguished Service award Marion Jr. C. of C., 1966. Mem. Am. Assn. Sch. Adminstrs., Ala. Dept. Elementary Sch. Prins. (state membership chmn. 1970-72), Ala. Edn. Assn. Methodist (ch. sch. supt. 1968-71). Club: Civitan (gov. Ala. central dist. 1966-67, sec.-treas. 1971-72, honor key, Past Gov.'s award 1964; Marion Civitan of Year 1969). Home: School Dr Marion AL 36756 Office: Box 960 Monroe St Marion AL 36756

HUBBELL, FLOYD EUGENE, retail clothier; b. Galveston, Tex., Feb. 10, 1923; s. Francis E. and Garna (Ward) H.; student S.W. Tex. State Tchrs. Coll., 1946-47, Sam Houston State Tchrs. Coll., 1947; B.B.A., Baylor U., 1950; m. Margaret Fraser, Sept. 1, 1946; children—Allan, David, Richard, John, Ruth, Steven, Shiles. Dept. mgr., asst. mgr., mgr. J.C. Penney Co., Waco, Tex., 1950-54, Odessa, Tex., 1954-57, Midland, Tex., 1957-59, Lubbock, Tex., 1959-62, Abilene, Tex., 1962-65; owner, mgr. Hubbell's Men's Shop, Rosenberg, Tex., 1965—. Chmn. Youth Com., 1969; chmn. Easter Seals, 1969. City councilman, Rosenberg, 1968—. Served with AUS, 1943-46; PTO. Recipient Distinguished Service award Rosenberg Rotary, 1969. Mem. Rosenberg C. of C. (dir.). Baptist (deacon). Rotarian, Kiwanian. Home: 1310 Rice St Rosenberg TX 77471 Office: 5028 Av H Rosenberg TX 77471

HUBBERT, FORD WILLIAM, JR., profl. assn. editor; b. Madill, Okla., Aug. 8, 1942; s. Ford William and Jeanette Lorena (Smith) H.; B.A., Okla. City U., 1965; M.L.A., So. Meth. U., 1972; m. Ernestine Cantu, Sept. 4, 1965; children—Anne Marie, Julie Anne. Writer, office pub. information Oklahoma City U., 1965; editor, promotion writer, reporter Okla. Pub. Co., 1965-67; editor The Skeet Shooting Review, Nat. Skeet Shooting Assn., Dallas, 1967—. Nat. Skeet Shooting Assn. grantee, 1970-72. Mem. Nat. Skeeting Shooting Assn. (com. promotion and devel. collegiate shooting 1970—, mem. Hall of Fame selection com. 1970—), Outdoor Writers Assn. Am. Republican. Mem. Ch. of the Nazarene (bd. dirs. ch. 1967-73). Clubs: Dallas Gun; Nat. Gun (San Antonio). Home: 6310 Dove Hill Dr San Antonio TX 78238 Office: PO Box 28188 San Antonio TX 78228

HUBER, PAUL SPEER, JR., newspaper pub.; b. Norfolk, Va., Mar. 14, 1921; s. Paul Speer and Elizabeth (Lingamfelter) H.; grad. Woodberry Forest Sch.; student U. N.C.; m. Sarah Jane Booth, Sept. 17, 1948; children—Paul Speer III, Peter McPherson. With Landmark Communications, Inc., 1947—, now pres. and dir.; pres. Virginian-Pilot; dir. WTAR Radio Corp., Seaboard Citizens Nat. Bank. Bd. dirs. Med. Center Hosps.; v.p. United Communities Fund. Home: 1415 Daniel Av Norfolk VA 23505 Office: 150 W Brambleton Av Norfolk VA 23510

HUBER, WOLFGANG KARL, physician, educator; b. Freiburg/Breisgau, Germany, June 10, 1927; s. Richard J. and Kaete (Goetz) H.; student U. Heidelberg, 1946; M.D., U. Frankfurt/Main, 1957; m. Gudrun Lydia Beeck, June 28, 1958; 1 son, Christian Michael. Came to U.S., 1957, naturalized, 1962. Rotating intern St. Vincent Charity Hosp., Cleve., 1957-58; neuropsychiat. tng. U. Hosps., Frankfurt/Main, 1956-57, Central State Griffin Meml. Hosp., Norman, Okla., 1958-59, VA Hosp., Oklahoma City, 1959, Mental Health Clinic, Oklahoma City, 1960-61; asst. clin. dir., chief dept. neuropsychiatry Central State Griffin Meml. Hosp., Norman, Okla., 1962-67; dir. Mental Health Center, Norman, 1967—; instr., clin. cons. U. Okla. Sch. Medicine, 1963-68, asst. prof. research medicine, 1968—, research asso. exptl. therapeutics unit, dept. medicine, 1964—; clin. cons. 2792d USAF Hosp., Tinker AFB, Okla., Okla. State Penitentiary Hosp. asst. clin. prof. psychiatry and behavioral scis. U. Okla., 1971—, research psychiatrist div. clin. pharmacology, dept. medicine. Fellow Am. Psychiat. Assn. (v.p. Okla.); mem. World Fedn. Mental Health (U.S. com.), Acad. Religion and Mental Health, A.A.A.S., A.M.A., Okla. Med. Soc., Mil-Continent Psychiat. Assn., World Psychiat. Assn., N.Y. Acad. Scis. Contbr. articles to profl. jours. Home: PO Box 992 Norman OK 73069 Office: PO Box 151 Norman OK 73069

HUBERT, JOSEPH ARTHUR, lawyer; b. Northport, N.Y., Mar. 22, 1930; s. Joseph F. and Adelyn (Condon) H.; A.B., Centre Coll., 1951; LL.D., U. Miami, Coral Gables, Fla., 1956; m. Theresa Ailene Mackey, Sept. 5, 1953; children—Nancy, Lisa, James, Robert, Jean Marie. Admitted to Fla. bar, 1956; partner firm Watson, Hubert & Davis, Fort Lauderdale, Fla., 1956—; dir. Lauderdale Abstract and Title Co., 1972—, Southeast Bank of Galt Ocean Mile, 1973—. Pres., Community Service Council, 1965, Econ. Opportunity Coordinating Group Broward County, 1965; pres. United Fund of Broward County, 1967. Served with CIC, AUS, Korea, Japan, 1951-53. Mem. Am., Broward County (pres. 1969) bar assns., Fla. Bar, Execs. Assn. Ft. Lauderdale. Kiwanian. Home: 1759 SE 10th St Fort Lauderdale FL 33316 Office: 3600 N Federal Hwy Fort Lauderdale FL 33308

HUCKABEE, HARLOW MAXWELL, lawyer, govt. ofcl.; b. Wichita Falls, Tex., Jan. 22, 1918; s. Edwin Cleveland and Gladys Idella (Bonney) H.; A.B., Harvard, 1948; J.D., Georgetown U., 1951; m. Gloria Charlotte Comstock, Jan. 10, 1942; children—Bonney M., David C., Stephen M. Br. office cashier Columbian Nat. Life Ins. Co., Boston, 1935-40; admitted to D.C. bar, 1952; atty. FH, Washington, 1955-56; trial atty. Criminal sect. tax div. U.S. Dept. Justice, Washington, 1956-63, trial atty., organized crime and racketeering sect., criminal div. 1967-68, trial atty., criminal sect., tax div., 1968—; atty. Office Chief Counsel, Internal Revenue Service, Treasury Dept., Washington, 1963-67; Justice Dept. rep. on internal revenue commr.'s com. on psychiat. defenses in tax fraud cases, 1970-72. Mem. standing com. problems connected with mental exam. of accused in criminal cases before trial Jud. Conf. D.C. Circuit 1960-65. Served from pvt. to maj., AUS, 1940-45, 48-55; lt. col. Res. Decorated Bronze Star with oak leaf cluster. Mem. Nat. Council on Crime and Delinquency, Am. Correctional Service Fedn., Fed. Bar Assn. Methodist. Home: 3648 N Monroe St Arlington VA 22207 Office: US Dept Justice Washington DC 20530

HUCKABEE, MARTHA CAROLYN, pharmacist; b. Uniontown, Ala., Oct. 13, 1926; d. Thomas Fendley and Carolyn (Blakeney) Huckabee; B.S., Ala. Poly. Inst., 1947. Pharmacist, Jones Drug Co., Anniston, Ala., 1948-49, Bradford Drug Co., 1949-65; owner, pharmacist Huckabee Drugs. Uniontown, 1965—. Instr. first aid A.R.C., 1960—; dir. med. services Civil Def., Perry County, 1961—; hon. dep. sheriff Perry County, 1962—. Bd. dirs. Uniontown Community Chest. Mem. Uniontown Mchts. Assn., Nat. Assn. Retail Druggists, Am., Ala. (Perry county dir., Outstanding Pharmacy Grad. award 1947), Perry County (pres.) pharm. assns., Nat. C. of C., D.A.R. (regent Canebrake chpt.), U. D.C., Central Ala., Ala. geneal. socs., Perry County Historic Preservation Soc (dir.), Auburn, Auburn Pharmacy alumni assns., Phi Kappa Phi. Republican. Baptist. Mem. Order Eastern Star. Home: 101 Front St Uniontown AL 36786 Office: 300 N Water St Uniontown AL 36786

HUCKABEE, TOMMIE JACK, architect; b. Bonham, Tex., Apr. 8, 1936; s. Clyde Martin and Pauline Nina (Chaffin) H.; student Tex. Tech. U., 1954-56; diploma architecture Canadian Inst. Sci. and Tech., 1960; m. Sylvia Wingo, Dec. 30, 1960; children—Timothy Michael, Phyllis, Christopher Martin. Draftsman, Butler-Kimmel, architects, Lubbock, Tex., 1956-58; designer-draftsman Hermann Riherd & Assos., architects, Lubbock, Tex., 1960-68; prin., Riherd & Huckabee, architects, Lubbock, Andrews, Tex., 1968—. Archtl. cons. Andrews Indsl. Found., 1968-71. Chmn. indsl. constrn. com. Andrews Indsl. Devel. Team, 1970-71. Served with USMCR, 1958-59. Registered architect Nat. Council Archtl. Registration Bd., Tex., Okla., N.M., La. Mem. A.I.A., Tex. Soc. Architects, Andrews County C. of C. (dir. 1964-67). Democrat. Methodist (mem. bd. trustees 1963-67). Prin. archtl. works include Ward County Library, Wentworth Mfg. Co., W. Tex. Telephone Co., Monahan Jr. High Sch., Main Post Office, Commerce Tex., Greenwood High Sch., Denver City Jr. High Sch., Stanton Jr. High Sch., Andrews Middle Sch., Crane Elementary Sch., Colo. High Sch., Colorado City, Tex., Rankin Independent Sch. Dist. Athletic Bldg., Glasscock Sch. Auditorium and Classroom Bldg. Home: 203 Mesquite Lane Andrews TX 79714 Office: PO Box 1451 Andrews TX 79714

HUCKABY, DONALD HOWARD, computer, data systems exec.; b. Brownwood, Tex., July 22, 1934; s. Verie Howard and Velma Marie (Moore) H.; B.S. with highest honors, Howard Payne Coll., 1955; M.S., Tex. Christian U., 1958; m. Esther L. Crawford, Nov. 26, 1954; children—Lee Ann, Carol Elizabeth. Bookkeeper, Tex. Power & Light Co., Brownwood, 1951-55; with Gen. Dynamics, Ft. Worth, Tex., 1955—, engr., 1955-67, chief sci. computing, 1967-73, dir. central data systems center, 1973—. Instr. Tex. Christian U., Ft. Worth 1961—. Home: 3605 Wosley St Fort Worth TX 76133 Office: PO Box 748 Fort Worth TX 76101

HUDDLESTON, ELLIS WRIGHT, educator; b. Knapp, Tex., Sept. 10, 1935; s. Wright A. and Kathleen (Ellis) H.; B.S. in Agronomy, Tex. Tech. U., 1956; M.S. in Entomology, Cornell U., 1958, Ph.D. in Entomology, 1960; m. Billie Inez Alford, Aug. 12, 1958; children—Jim Bob, Kimberly Ann. Asst. prof. entomology Tex. Tech. U., Lubbock, 1960-65, asso. prof. entomology, 1965-71, prof. entomology, 1971—; asso. entomologist U. Hawaii, Honolulu, 1966-67. Cons. Utah State AID, Bolovia, 1971. Bd. dirs. Recration Villages, Inc., Ruidoso, N.M., 1970—, Tex. Tech. Fed. Credit Union, 1967—. Served to 2d lt. AUS, 1960. Recipient Spencer A. Wells award Tex. Tech. U., 1967-68. Mem. Entomol. Soc. Am. (mem. com.), Am. Soc. Range Mgmt. (mem. com. 1970), Alpha Zeta, Phi Kappa Phi. Contbr. articles to profl. jours. Home: 4604 11th St Lubbock TX 79416 Office: Entomology Sect Tex Tech Univ Lubbock TX 79409

HUDDLESTON, JOSEPH RUSSELL, lawyer; b. Glasgow, Ky., Feb. 5, 1937; s. Paul Russell and Frances (Martin) H.; A.B., Princeton, 1959; LL.B., U. Va., 1962; m. Heidi Lynn Wood, Sept. 12, 1959; children—Johanna Lynn, Lisa Diane, Kristina Lee. Admitted to Ky. bar, 1962; practiced in Bowling Green, Ky., 1962—; mem. firm Huddleston Bros.; dir. Nehi-Royal Crown Bottling and Distbg. Co., Houk Ins., Inc. Mem. Ky. Crime Commn., 1972—; mem. Adv. Com. Criminal Law Revision, 1969-71. Bd. dirs. Princeton U. Fund, 1958-59. Mem. Am., Ky. (ho. dels.), Bowling Green (pres.) bar assns., Am. Assn. Trial Attys. (dir. Ky. chpt.), Phi Alpha Delta. Clubs: Cap and Gown (Princeton); Bowling Green Country. Home: 2626 Smallhouse Rd Bowling Green KY 42101 Office: 1032 College St Bowling Green KY 42101

HUDDLESTON, WALTER DARLINGTON, U.S. senator; b. nr. Burkesville, Ky., Apr. 15, 1926; s. Walter Franklin and Lottie (Russell) H.; A.B., U. Ky., 1949; m. Martha Jean Pearce, Dec. 20, 1947; children—Stephen Pearce, Philip Dee. Program-sports dir. WKCT, Bowling Green, Ky., 1949-52; gen. mgr. WIEL, Elizabethtown, Ky., 1952-72; mem. U.S. Senate, 1972—; dir. 1st Fed. Savings & Loan Assn., Elizabethtown, Ky., Radio Sta. WLBN, Lebanon, Ky. Mem. Ky. State Senate, 1966-72, majority leader, 1970, 72; chmn. Democratic Caucus, 1968; Served with AUS, 1944-46. Mem. C. of C. (pres. 1959), Ky. Broadcasters Assn. (pres. 1958). Methodist. Club: Pendennis (Louisville). Home: 4139 N 27th St Arlington VA 22207 Office: 3327 New Senate Office Bldg Washington DC 20510

HUDDLESTON, WILLIAM ENNIS, physician; b. Batesville, Ark., Aug. 25, 1928; s. William McKinley and Edna Cecil (Ennis) H.; student Ark. Coll., 1946-48, Ark. State Tchrs. Coll., 1948-49; B.S. in Medicine, M.D., U. Ark., 1953; m. Pauline Maxine Coffman, Sept. 7, 1953; children—Thomas Kevin, Linda Marchand, Kelly Ennis. Intern, Mo. Meth. Hosp., St. Joseph, 1953-54; practice medicine, specializing in family practice, Iowa Park, Tex., 1956-57, Bridgeport, Tex., 1957—; mem. staff Bridgeport Hosp. Mem. Bridgeport City Council, 1960-72. Served with USAF, 1953-56. Diplomate Am. Bd. Family Practice. Fellow Am. Acad. Family Practice (charter), Am. Acad. Family Physicians (charter); mem. Am., Tex. med. assns., So. Med. Soc. Mason. Methodist (trustee 1962-74). Home: 26 Robinhood Lane Bridgeport TX 76026 Office: 1301 Halsell St Bridgeport TX 76026

HUDGENS, EDWARD BOONE, JR., elec. engr.; b. Nashville, Feb. 19, 1944; s. Edward Boone and Janie Hammet (Leake) H.; B.S. in E.E., Christian Brothers Coll., 1966; postgrad. Memphis State U., 1966-69; m. Abigail Carpenter Sadler, Aug. 28, 1965; children—John Elgin, Lisa Gail. Elec. engr. Office Griffith C. Burr, Cons. Engr., Memphis, 1966-67; elec. engr. Allen & Hoshall, Cons. Engrs., Memphis, 1967—. Instr. Herff Sch. Engring. Memphis State U., 1967-69. Registered profl. engr., Tenn. Mem. I.E.E.E., Instrument Soc. Am., Illuminating Engring. Soc. (sect. v.p. 1970-71), Nat., Tenn. Socs. profl. engrs. Episcopalian (mem. vestry 1971—). Contbg. editor Elec. Cons. Mag., 1973—. Home: 214 Ridgefield Rd Memphis TN 38111 Office: 2430 Poplar St Memphis TN 38112

HUDGINS, CARL THOMAS, lawyer; b. DeKalb Co., Ga., June 18, 1891; s. John H. and Mattie Mobley (Kittredge) H.; LL.B., Atlanta Law Sch., 1915;; m. Edna McDaniel, Sept. 21, 1921. Practice of law, 1915—; attorney for City of Chamblee, Ga., 1926-64. Mem. lower house Ga. Gen. Assembly, 1933-35. Mem. Georgia, Stone Mountain Circuit (past pres.), Decatur (past pres.) bar assns., Atlanta, DeKalb County (past pres.) hist. socs., Sons and Daus. of Pilgrims, Sons Confederate Vets., Old War Horse Lawyers Club, Atlanta Lawyers Club. Methodist. Mason. Club: Fort Barrington (v.p.). Home: 118 Erie Av Decatur GA 30031 Office: PO Box 1403 Decatur GA 30031

HUDGINS, CATHERINE HARDING (MRS. ROBERT SCOTT HUDGINS, IV), business exec.; b. Raleigh, N.C., June 25, 1913; d. William Thomas and Mary Alice (Timberlake) Harding; B.S., N.C. State Coll., 1929-33; grad. tchr. N.C. Sch. for Deaf, 1933-34; m. Robert Scott Hudgins, IV, Aug. 20, 1938; children—Catherine Harding, Deborah Ghiselin, Robert Scott V. Tchr., N.C. Sch. for Deaf, Morganton, 1934-36; sec. Dr. A. S. Oliver, Raleigh, 1937; tchr. N.J. Sch. for Deaf, Trenton, 1937-39; sec. Robert S. Hudgins Co., Charlotte, N.C., 1949-60, v.p., sec., treas., 1960—, also dir. Mem. Jr. Service League, Easton, Pa., 1939; project chmn. ladies aux. Profl. Engrs. N.C., 1954-55, pres., 1956-57; pres. Christian High Sch. P.T.A., 1963; program chmn. Charlotte Opera Assn., 1959-61, sec., 1961-63; sec. bd. Hezekiah Alexander House Restoration, 1949-52. Mem. N.C. Hist. Assn., English Speaking Union, Mint Museum Arts (pres. drama guild 1967-69), Daus. of Am. Colonists (state chmn. nat. def. 1973—), D.A.R. (chpt. regent 1957-59, N.C. program chmn. 1961-63, state chmn. nat. def. 1973), Children Am. Revolution (N.C. sr. pres. 1963-66, nat. bd. mgmt. 1963—, hon. sr. nat. pres. 1972—, nat. vice chmn. Southeastern region, 1965-68, sr. nat. corr. sec. 1966-68, sr. nat. 1st v.p. 1968-70, sr. nat. pres., 1970-72, nat. chmn. for D.A.R., 1970-72), Internat. Platform Assn. Presbyn. (past chmn. home missions, annuities and relief Women of Ch., past pres. Sunday Sch. class). Club: Carmel Country (Charlotte). Home: 1514 Wendover Rd Charlotte NC 28211 Office: PO Box 17217 Charlotte NC 28211

HUDGINS, MARY DENGLER, writer; b. Hot Springs Nat. Park, Ark., Nov. 24, 1901; d. Jackson Wharton and Ida (Dengler) Hudgins; B.A., U. Ark., 1924, student Rice Sch. of Spoken Word, 1925, U. Chgo., 1940, U. Wis., 1941, Emory U., 1952. Tchr., Waldo (Ark.) High Sch., 1924-25; free-lance writer, 1925-39, 60—; librarian Hot Springs Pub. Library, 1939-43; med. and gen. librarian Army and Navy Gen. Hosp., Hot Springs, 1943-59; writer articles (specializing in Ark. topics) pub. in ency., hist., lit., profl. and popular publs. Dir., Hot Springs Writer's Workshop, 1960-61; incorporator, dir. Fine Arts Council, Hot Springs, 1960—; local historian YWCA, Hot Springs; active Hot Springs Little Theater, 1928-34. Mem. Ark. Hist. Assn. (mem. bd. 1963-71, v.p. 1972—), Garland County Hist. Soc. (pres. 1962-63), Ark. (sec. spl. libraries div. 1959-60, reporter to S.W. div. A.L.A. 1955), Med. library assns., Ark. Folklore Assn. (1st v.p. 1958-59), Am. Assn. U. Women (Ark. 1st v.p. 1929-30, pres. Hot Springs br. 1927, Ark. fellowship chmn. 1959-61), Ark. Geneal. Soc. (mem. bd.), D.A.R., Altrusa Internat. Presbyn. (historian). Clubs: Hot Springs Music, Fortnightly, Sabina (pres. 1935), Current Book (pres. Hot Springs 1952, 64). Address: 1030 Park Av Hot Springs National Park AR 71901

HUDGINS, TOM MALONE, C.P.A., b. Sherman, Tex., June 12, 1925; s. Harry Middleton and Josephine (Malone) H.; grad. Kemper Mil. Sch., 1943; B.S., Austin Coll., 1948; postgrad. U. Tex., 1948-49; m. Ruth Wilder, Mar. 5, 1944; children—Josephine Jordan, Kathleen Beale, Tom M. Jr., Harry M. II, Bruce W. Ruth Ann. Sr. accountant firm Sproles & Woodard, Midland, Tex., 1950-54; prin. firm Tom M. Hudgins & Co., Sherman, Tex., 1955—. Chmn. Sherman Council Drug Edn., 1971—, Am. Heart Fund, Sherman, 1970-72, Salvation Army, Sherman, 1960-63, U.S.O., Sherman, 1964; pres. Sherman chpt. United Fund, 1955-56; mem. Devel. Bd. div. council Austin Coll., 1956—. Served with 4th Armored Div., AUS, 1944-45; ETO. C.P.A., Tex. Mem. Tex. Soc. C.P.A.'s (dir., v.p.), Am. Mgmt. Assn, Am. Inst. Mgmt., Accounting Principles Bd., Accounting Standards Assn., Am. Accounting Assn., Am. Inst. C.P.A.S. Club: Woodlawn Country (Sherman, Tex.), Tanglewood Country (Pottsboro, Tex.). Home: 1400 W Washington Av Sherman TX 75090 Office: 302 M & P Bank Bldg Sherman TX 75090

HUDGINS, WILLIAM DAVID, satellite communications co. exec.; b. Melrose, N.M., Sept. 9, 1909; s. Thomas Edward and Belle (Boyce) H.; B.S. in Elec. Engring., U. Cal. at Berkeley, 1933; postgrad. U. Pitts, 1950. Drexel U., 1960; m. Leona Clare Kennedy, June 19, 1936; children—William Boyce, Douglas Baker. Commd. ensign USN, 1933, advanced through grade to comdr., 1945; electronics officer Boston Navy Shipyard; mem. Sec. of Def. Staff Munitions Bd.; comdg. officer Shipbldg. Scheduling Acitivity, Phila.; ret., 1960; with RCA Corp., Moorestown, N.J., 1960-68; project engr. Communication Satellite Corp., Washington, 1968—. Recipient commendation letter Sec. Def., 1950, Sec. State, 1973. Registered profl. engr., Cal., Pa., D.C. Mem. I.E.E.E., Nat. Soc. Profl. Engrs., Am. Radio Relay League, Quarter Century Wireless Assn. Home: 501 G St SW Washington DC 20024 Office: 950 L'Enfant Plaza SW Washington DC 20024

HUDGINS, WILLIAM HENRY, lawyer; b. Chase City, Va., Nov. 19, 1915; s. Edward Wren and Lucy (Morton) H.; B.A. in Journalism, Washington & Lee U., 1938; J.D., U. Va., 1941; postgrad. Fgn. Service Inst., Washington, 1947. Admitted to Va. bar, 1953; vice consul Am. embassy, Santiago, Chile, 1947-48; atty. Office Judge Adv. Gen. of Navy and White House aide, 1949-50; aide flag lt. to Comdr.-in-Chief Eastern Atlantic & Mediterranean, London, Eng., 1950-51; sr. aide to comdr.-in-chief S. Europe, NATO, Naples, Italy, 1951-53; apptd. to spl. assignments as aide to supreme NATO comdr. (Gen. Eisenhower) and to King Paul of Greece, 1952-53; mil. aide de camp to Va. govs. Tuck, Battle, Stanley and Almond; atty., Chase City, Va., 1953-70; co-owner, partner Marine Transport Assos., Inc., N.Y.C., 1971—; world traveller and lectr. on fgn. affairs. Commd. midshipman USNR, 1940, advanced through grades to comdr., 1953. Decorated Commendatore de Italia (Italy). Commandeur de l'Ordre du Ouissam Alaouite Cherifien (France). Mem. Assn. Preservation Va. Antiquities, Nat. Trust for Historic Preservation, Soc. Colonial Wars, S.A.R., Soc. Descs. of Original Knights of the Garter, Magna Carta Barons, Roanoke River Art Assn., Phi Alpha Delta, Sigma Delta Chi, Omicron Delta Kappa, Beta Theta Pi. Episcopalian (vestryman 1964-65, gen. chmn. bicentennial commemoration 1966). Club: University (Washington). Home: MacCallum More 500 Walker St Chase City VA 23924

HUDLICKY, MILOS, educator; b. Prelouc, Czechoslovakia, May 12, 1919; s. Jaroslav and Marie (Babáckova) H.; Ph.D., Tech. U., Prague, Czechoslovakia, 1946; m. Alena Vyskocilova, July 2, 1946; children—Tomás, Eva. Came to U.S., 1968, naturalized, 1971. With Chem. Research Inst. Bata, Zlín, Czechoslovakia, 1940-45; asst. prof. Tech. U., Prague, 1946-54, asso. prof., 1954-58; research chemist Inst. Pharmacy and Biochemistry, Prague, 1958-68; mem. faculty Va. Poly. Inst., Blacksburg, 1968—, prof. organic chemistry, 1971—. UNESCO Postdoctoral fellow Ohio State U., Columbus, 1948. Served with Czechoslovak Army, 1946-47. Mem. Am., Czechoslovak chem. socs., Chem. Soc. (London). Club: Toastmaster. Author: Chemistry of Organic Fluorine Compounds, 1961; Organic Fluorine Chemistry, 1971; others pub. in Czech. Contbr. articles to chem. jours. Patentee in field. Home: 1005 Highland Circle Blacksburg VA 24060

HUDSON, CHARLES DAUGHERTY, ins. agy. exec.; b. LaGrange, Ga., Mar. 17, 1927; s. J.D. and Janie (Hill) H.; student Auburn U., 1945-48; m. Ida Cason Callaway, May 1, 1955; children—Jane Alice, Ellen Pinson, Charles Daugherty, Ida Callaway. Partner, Hudson Hardware Co., LaGrange, 1950-57; partner Hammond-Hudson Ins. Agy., LaGrange, 1957-58, owner, 1958—; dir., mem. exec. com. Citizens & So. Bank West Ga., La Grange, 1963—; dir., v.p. LaGrange Industries, Inc., 1956—. Mem. exec. com. Camp Viola, Lagrange, 1956—; v.p., trustee Callaway Found., Inc., 1957—, Fuller E. Callaway Found., 1965—; chmn. LaGrange chpt. United Fund, 1964—. Chmn. bd. trustees LaGrange Coll., Ga. Baptist Hosp., Atlanta. Recipient pres.'s award Colonial Life Ins. Co., 1966, 69, 70, Distinguished Alumni award Ga. Mil. Acad., 1971, Respect Law award Optimists Assn., 1967. Mem. Ga. Assn. Independent Ins. Agts., Ga. Sch. Bd. Assn. (area dir.), S.A.R., Chattahoochee Valley Art Assn. , Sigma Alpha Epsilon. Baptist (deacon 1953—). Mason, (Shriner), Elk, Rotarian (pres. club 1964-65). Clubs: Highland Country (La Grange); Commerce (Atlanta). Home: Country Club Rd LaGrange GA 30240 Office: 100 Greenville St LaGrange GA 30240

HUDSON, DICK D., utility engr.; b. Clanton, Ala., Mar. 29, 1928; s. Richard Allison and Eula Mae (Thomason) H.; B.S., Auburn U., 1949; m. Juddy Ann Routon, Feb. 9, 1952; children—Steven Mark, Cristy Ellen. Student engr. Ala. Power Co., 1948-49; engr. So. Bell Tel. & Tel. Co., Birmingham, Ala., 1949-59, marketing, Atlanta, 1959-67; design engr. So. Central Bell Telephone Co., Birmingham, 1968—. Mem. council Boy Scouts Am. Served to 1st lt. Signal Corps, AUS, 1951-52. Registered profl. engr., Ala., Ga. Mem. I.E.E.E. (sr.), Communications Soc. (chmn. 1971). Eta Kappa Nu, Tau Beta Pi, Sigma Phi Epsilon. Baptist (deacon). Lion (past pres. 1967), Toastmaster (pres. 1965). Designer automatic call distbr., 1962, small tower package for F.A.A., 1971. Home: 3416 Collingwood Rd Birmingham AL 35226 Office: 600 N 19th St Birmingham AL 35203

HUDSON, DONALD CHARLES, educator; b. Des Moines, Nov. 7, 1910; s. Charles Ross and Jessie D. O'Daniels H.; student Creighton U., 1928-29, U. Ia., 1929-30; D.D.S., State U. Ia., 1934; m. Elizabeth Evelyn Evans, Sept. 15, 1950; 1 son, Jerome Alan. Intern, Fresno (Cal.) County Hosp., 1934-35; gen. practice dentistry, Grinnell, Ia., 1935-37, San Antonio, 1963-65; commd. 1st lt. U.S. Army, 1938, advanced through grades lt. col., 1943; commd. lt. col. USAF, 1949, advanced through grades to col., 1951; ret., 1963; prof. biomaterials U. Tex., Houston, 1965-70; mem. faculty U. Tex. Dental Sch., San Antonio, 1970—, prof., chmn. dept. biomaterials, 1970—. Cons. to dental industry, 1968—. Decorated Legion of Merit. Fellow Am. Coll. Dentists; mem. Am. Dental Assn., Internat. Assn. Dental Research (pres. dental materials group 1959-60), Am. Acad. Dental Radiology, Omicron Kappa Upsilon. Lutheran. Club: Doctors (Houston). Patentee in field. Home: 502 Fenwick Dr San Antonio TX 78239 Office: 7703 Floyd Curl Dr San Antonio TX 78284

HUDSON, EDWARD RANDALL, JR., lawyer, oil producer; b. Ft. Worth, July 24, 1934; s. Edward R. and Josephine (Smith) H.; B.A., U. Tex., 1955; LL.B., Harvard, 1958; m. Ann Frasher, Sept. 19, 1959; children—Randall, Frasher. Admitted to Tex. bar, 1958, since practiced in Ft. Worth. Pres. Ft. Worth Art Assn., 1965-73, chmn. bd., 1973—; chmn. Tex. Commn. Arts and Humanities, 1973—. Trustee Mary Couts Burnett Trust; bd. dirs. Ft. Worth Opera Assn., Northwood Inst. Contemporary Arts Council, Ft. Worth Zool. Assn., William E. Scott Theater, Ft. Worth. Mem. Phi Beta Kappa. Roman Catholic. Home: 55 Westover Terrace Fort Worth TX 76107 Office: First Nat Bank Bldg Fort Worth TX 76102

HUDSON, FRANK ALDEN, educator; b. Gallup, N.M., Dec. 15, 1923; s. Arthur J. and Marcelle (Fachrig) H.; B.S., Ariz. State U., 1952; M.S., N.M. State U., 1953; Ph.D., Ore. State U., 1957; m. Elizabeth A. Townsend, Mar. 18, 1960; children—David T., Kathleen A. Animal husbandman Agr. Research Service, U.S. Dept. Agr., Bettsville, Md., 1957-60; mem. faculty Tex. Tech. U., Lubbock, 1960—, prof. animal sci., 1970—. Served with AUS, 1943-46. Decorated Bronze Star, Purple Heart. Mem. Am. Soc. Animal Sci., Am. Soc. Range Mgmt., Sigma Xi. Home: 3824 52d St Lubbock TX 79413

HUDSON, FRANK M., educator; b. Clarksville, Ark., Sept. 8, 1935; s. Robert Ellis and Florence Myrtle (Bishop) H.; B.S., State Coll. Ark., 1957; M.A., U. Tex. 1959, Ph.D., 1965; postgrad. Harvard, 1961-62; m. Sandra Lou Foster, May 19, 1957; children—Amanda Sue, Cindy Lee. Instr. math. Western State Coll. Colo., Gunnison, 1959-61; prof., chmn. math. McMurry Coll., Abilene, Tex., 1964-67; mem. faculty State Coll. Ark., Conway, 1967—, prof., chmn. math. dept., 1967—. Mem. Math. Assn. Am. Author: (with Donald W. Adlong) Introduction to Mathematics, 1970. Home: 3 Deerwood Dr Conway AR 72032

HUDSON, HUBERT R., lawyer; b. Oklahoma City, July 31, 1928; s. Hubert R. and Dorothy (Hoffman) H.; grad. Culver Mil. Acad., 1945; B.A. with highest honors, Williams Coll., 1949; LL.B., U. Tex., 1952; m. Sarah Gibbs Pell, June 25, 1949 (div. Sept. 1955); children—William Parke Custis, Sarah Gibbs; m. Nancy Paxton Moody, Dec. 4, 1959 (div. Mar. 1968). Admitted to Tex. bar, 1952; pvt. practice law Brownsville, Tex. Mem. Tex. Senate, 1956-63; chmn. State of Tex. Investments Com. Chmn. bd. S. Tex. Lumber Co., Cicero-Smith Lumber Cos., Deco-Unicel, Mex., Aspern J. Theatrical Prodns. Broadway, Automatic Insect Control Corp., Brownsville; dir. Beaver Creek Industries, Inc., Atlanta, Dalto Electronics, Norwood, N.J., El Centro Supermarkets, Brownsville, Boca Chica Leasing Co., also Brownsville Savs. & Loan, Seaport Service & Supply, High Plains Natural Gas Dallas, Southwestern Group Investors, Inc., Houston; dir., mem. exec. com., mem. trust com. First Nat. Bank, Brownsville. Part time prof. history and constnl. law Tex. S.M. Coll.; mem. Com. of 75 for reevaluation U. Tex. Dir. Texas Citizens Com., 1955-59; trustee United Fund, Brownsville, 1954-56; chmn. founding of Good Neighbor Settlement House, 1953—; dir. Valley council Boy Scouts Am., 1954-58; pres. Charro Days, Brownsville, 1954-55, chmn. Rio Grande Valley Festival of Music. Commr. City of Brownsville Water Bd., 1956—; trustee Greater Brownsville Commn. (pres. 1969—). Chmn. finance com. Tex. Southmost Coll., 1956-58; sr. trustee Hudson Found., 1956-59; dir. U. Tex. Found. Sch. Business, Grand Opera Com. Rio Grande Valley; trustee Camille Playhouse, U. Tex. Sch. Architecture, Episcopal Day School, Texas Mil. Inst.; chmn. Day Sch. Found.; bd. dirs. San Antonio Symphony Soc.; patron, trustee, co-chmn. finance com. Rio Grande Valley Zool. Soc. Recipient Outstanding Community Award Service medal Nat. Jr. C. of C., 1954, 56. Mem. Am. Bar Assn., Bar Assn. Tex., S. Tex. Heritage Soc. (trustee), Rio Grande Valley C. of C. (pres. 1960), Phi Beta Kappa, Phi Alpha Delta. Democrat. Episcopalian (vestry; dir. diocese evaluation com.). Clubs: Austin (Austin, Tex.); Piping Rock (N.Y.C.).

Author: The Roosevelt Corollary, 1949. Home: Casa Poinciana Brownsville TX 78520 Office: First Nat Bank Bldg Brownsville TX 78520

HUDSON, JAMES PAUL, museum dir.; b. Canon City, Colo.; s. James Spencer and Julia Darce (Lopez) H.; B.A., Stanford, 1931, M.A., 1933; m. Ethel Sandys Jackson, May 4, 1936; 1 son, David Spencer. Mus. curator Nat. Park Service, Yosemite Nat. Park, 1934, Muir Woods Nat. Monument, 1935, Washington, 1936, George Washington Birthplace Nat. Monument, 1937, U.S. Dept. Interior Mus., 1938-40, Morristown (N.J.) Nat. Hist. Park, 1940-43, 45-47, regional office, Richmond, Va., 1947-54, Jamestown (Va.) Mus., 1954—; head curator Colonial Nat. Hist. Park; tchr. historic site archaeology Coll. William and Mary; lectr. in field. Fellow Corning (N.Y.) Mus. of Glass, 1959; dir. tng. course for hostesses and guides Stratford Hall, Va., 1959—. Mem. No. Neck of Va. Hist. Soc., Am. Assn. Museums, Assn. for Preservation Va. Antiquities (dir. Williamsburg br. 1960-63; exec. sec. Jamestown com., Williamsburg Archeol. Soc. (past dir.), S.A.R. (chaplain Williamsburg chpt.), Archeol. Soc. Va. (dir.). Episcopalian (vestryman). Author: A Pictorial History of Jamestown, 1957; Early Jamestown Commodities and Industries, 1957; (with John L. Cotter) New Discoveries at Jamestown, 1957; Early Jamestown House and Buildings, 1964; This Was Green Spring, 1969. Contbr. articles on colonial period cultural objects to profl. publs. Research on 17th century glass, Eng., 1964. Home: 708 Powell St Williamsburg VA 23185 Office: Jamestown Museum Jamestown VA 23081

HUDSON, JOSEPH WILLIS, business exec.; b. Woodruff, S.C., Feb. 3, 1934; s. Joseph Taylor and Martha Jane (Willis) H.; student U. N.C., 1952-55; m. Elsa Garrow Perlitz, Sept. 1, 1955; children—Elsa Garrow, Joseph Willis. Sales staff Hudson & Co., Inc., Spartanburg, S.C., 1955-59, pres., 1959-73, dir., 1959-73; founder, pres. Willis Brinkman, Ins., Spartanburg, 1960-67; founder Nat. Bank Commerce, Spartanburg, S.C., 1968, chmn. bd., 1968-70 (merged First Citizens Bank & Trust Co. 1970), now dir. First Citizens Bank & Trust Co., Columbia, S.C.; owner Travel Unltd., Spartanburg, 1972—. Mem. Small Bus. Adminstrn. Adv. Council for S.C., 1969-70; chmn. S.C. Wildlife and Marine Resources Commn., 1972—; internat. adviser Game Conversation Internat., 1972—. Trustee, v.p., mem. exec. com. Ducks Unlimited. Served with AUS, 1957-59. Mem. East African Profl. Hunters Assn., Sigma Chi. Clubs: Springdale Hall (Camden, S.C.); Explorers, African Safari of New York (N.Y.C.). Home: 30 Lake Forest Dr Spartanburg SC 29302 Office: 450 E Henry St Spartanburg SC 29302

HUDSON, LARRY GILBERT, supt. schs.; b. Emerson, Ark., Feb. 27, 1933; s. John Ward and Eva Lee (McMahen) H.; B.S., So. State Coll., 1958; M.Ed., U. Ark., 1964; m. Marjorie Ann Wilbanks, July 11, 1955; children—Jody Lynn, Gina Ann. Coach, supt. Garland (Ark.) Pub. Schs., 1958-66; supt. schs. Lewisville (Ark.) Pub. Schs., 1966—. Served with AUS, 1953-55. Mem. Am. Legion, Am. Assn. Sch. Adminstrs., Ark. Edn. Assn. Baptist. Rotarian. Home: PO Box 1 Lewisville AR 71845 Office: PO Box 400 Lewisville AR 71845

HUDSON, MORLEY ALVIN, mfg. exec.; b. San Antonio, Mar. 31, 1917; s. Oscar Alvin and Ruth (Morley) H.; B.S. in Mech. Engring., Ga. Inst. Tech., 1938; m. Lucy North, Nov. 11, 1944; children—Nancy Lucile, Lucy N., Courtney Morley. Advt. engr. Allis-Chalmers Mfg. Co., West Allis, Wis., 1938-40; safety engr. Am. Surety Co., Dallas, 1940-41; chief corrosion engr. Mobil Oil Co., Beaumont, Tex., 1942-45; dist. mgr. Eggelhof Engrs., Inc., Shreveport, La., 1946-52; pres., gen. mgr. Hudson-Rush Co., Inc., Shreveport, 1952—; v.p. McElroy Metal Mill, Inc., Bossier City, La., 1962—. Pres. Community Council, Shreveport, 1965; Vice chmn. La. Gov.'s Com. on Employment of Handicapped, 1964-69. Mem. La. Ho. of Reps., 1964-68, minority leader, 1964-68; La. vice chmn. Republican party, 1969; Rep. candidate for lt. gov., 1971-72. Served with AUS, 1941-42. Named Handicapped Louisianan of Yr. Gov.'s Commn. on Employment of Handicapped, 1964. Mem. Shreveport C. of C. (dir. 1969-72), Am. Soc. M.E.'s, Omicron Delta Kappa, Tau Beta Pi, Sigma Nu, Phi Kappa Phi. Presbyn. (elder). Home: 4609 Gilbert Dr Shreveport LA 71106 Office: 819 Kings Hwy Shreveport LA 71104

HUEBNER, GEORGE LEE, JR., educator; b. Bay City, Tex., May 22, 1918; s. George Lee and Leta Belle (Taylor) H.: B.S., Tex. A. & M. U., 1946, M.S., 1951, Ph.D., 1953; m. Patricia Penelope Todd, Dec. 27, 1941; children—George, Margaret, Nancy, Anne. Monitoring officer Fed. Communications Commn., Ft. Lee, N.J., 1941-43; research engr. Ind. Exploration Co., Houston, 1946-50; sr. research scientist Tex. A. & M. Research Found., College Station, 1953-59; asso. prof. Tex. A. & M. U., College Station, 1959-60, prof. meteorology, 1962—; sect. head Tex. Instruments, Inc., Dallas, 1960-61. Cons. Tex. Instruments, Inc., Dallas, 1962-71, TRW Space Systems, Redondo Beach, Cal., 1968-70, Envicon, Inc., Clifton, N.J., 1970-73. Civil def. dir. City College Station, Tex., 1967—. Served with USNR, 1944-45. Mem. I.E.E.E., Am. Meteorol. Soc., Eta Kappa Nu, Sigma Xi, Phi Kappa Phi. Contbr. articles to profl. jours. Home: 1010 Walton Dr College Station TX 77840

HUEBNER, JOHN STEPHEN, geologist; b. Bryn Mawr, Pa., Sept. 9, 1940; s. John M. and Elizabeth (Converse) H.; A.B., Princeton, 1962; Ph.D., Johns Hopkins, 1967; m. Emily M. Zug, June 16, 1962; children—Christopher Converse, Jeffrey Worrell. Geologist, U.S. Geol. Survey, Washington, 1967—. Professorial lectr. George Washington U., Washington, 1971. Fellow Mineral. Soc. Am.; mem. A.A.A.S., Am. Geophys. Union, Am. Geol. Inst. (governing bd. 1972—, sec.-treas. 1974), Geochem. Soc. (treas. 1972—), Geol. Soc. Washington (sec. 1971-72), Sigma Xi. Home: 6102 Cromwell Dr Bethesda MD 20016 Office: US Geological Survey Reston VA 22092

HUERKAMP, FREDLRICK JOHN, orgn. exec.; b. Cin., Aug. 9, 1929; s. Frederick James and Clair S. (Schmidt) H.; student Miami U., 1947-49; B.S., Xavier U., 1951, M.B.A., 1964; m. Elizabeth Ann Brewer, July 3, 1965; 1 dau., Natalie Ann. Securities portfolio analyst First Nat. Bank, Cin., 1955-56; sales rep. Hill-Rom Co., Batesville, Ind., 1956-63; adminstrv. resident Duval Med. Center, Jacksonville, Fla., 1964; exec. sec. Health Planning Council Jacksonville Area, Inc., 1964—. Bd. dirs. Jacksonville Hosp. Council, 1964—; v.p. Jacksonville Area Research Assn., 1967. Mem. adv. com. bd. CAMPS, 1967-68; mem. adv. com. Office Econ. Opportunity, 1967—. Bd. dirs. Jacksonville Hosp. Ednl. Program, Jacksonville U. Sch. Nursing Tech. Adv. Com. Served with USAF, 1951-55. Mem. Am. Hosp. Assn., Am. Pub. Health Assn., Hosp. Information Council, Sigma Alpha. Presbyn. Home: 1590 Geraldine Dr Jacksonville FL 32205 Office: Suite 260 1045 Riverside Av PO Box 629 Jacksonville FL 32204

HUEY, GEORGE PHILIP, JR., city ofcl.; b. Graham, Tex., Apr. 4, 1931; s. George Philip and Homerette (Whatley) R.; B.S. in Floriculture, Tex. A. and M. U., 1953. With Gen. Dynamics Corp., Ft. Worth, 1956-57; floriculturist Dallas Park Dept., 1957-60, supr. park dept., 1960-62, gen. supr., 1962-66, supt. of parks, 1966-72, asst. dir. parks and recreation, 1972—. Served to 1st lt. AUS, 1953-56. Mem. Nat. Recreation and Parks Assn., S.A.R. (sec.-treas. 1961-63, v.p. 1963-64), Former Students Assn. Tex. A. and M. U., Tex. Turfgrass Assn. (pres. 1968-69), S.W. Park and Recreation Tng. Inst. (pres. 1971). Presbyn. Home: 6330 E University St Dallas TX 75214 Office: 406 City Hall Dallas TX 75201

HUEY, MARY EVELYN BLAGG (MRS. GRIFFIN BURNS HUEY), univ. dean; b. Wills Point, Tex., Jan. 19, 1922; d. Henry Hurst and Evelyn (Manning) Blagg; B.S., Tex. Woman's U., 1942, M.A., 1943; M.A., U. Ky., 1947; Ph.D., Duke, 1954; m. Dr. Griffin B. Huey, Aug. 21, 1954; 1 son, Henry Griffin. Instr. English, Tex. Woman's U., 1943-45; asst. dir. Bur. Pub. Administrn., U. Miss., 1946-47; instr. govt. North Tex. State U., 1947-51, asst. prof., 1954-63, asso. prof., 1963-66, prof., 1966-71; prof. govt., dean Grad. Sch., Tex. Woman's U., Denton, 1971—; dir. Joint U. Center for Community Services, 1966-67. Conferee, Oak Ridge Inst. Nuclear Studies Conf., summer 1965; mem. regional council Nat. Archives U.S., 1971—. Mem. bd. adjustment Planning and Zoning Commn. Denton, chmn., 1963-68; regional citizen mem. North Central Texas Council of Govts., 1968-71, bd. dirs., 1970-71; sec. Denton County Health Planning Council, 1969-73, pres., 1974; bd. dirs. North Central Tex. Health Planning Council, 1969-74. Vice chmn. Denton County Republican Com., 1960-63; mem. state steering com. Women for Nixon, 1968. Mem. Am. Assn. U. Women (local exec. bd. 1955-56, 61-62, 64-68, 73-74, pres. Denton br. 1962-63, corporate rep. 1971—), Am. Polit. Sci. Assn., Am. Soc. Pub. Administrn. (mem. council North Tex. chpt. 1966-71, pres. 1969-70, mem. nat. conf. com. 1972), Southwestern Social Sci. Assn., Tex. Assn. Coll. Tchrs. (sec.-treas. local chpt. 1958-59), Women's Aux. to Tex. Dental Assn. (dist. pres., mem. state exec. bd. 1956-61, state parliamentarian, 1958-59, state revisions chmn. 1960-61), Council Grad. Schs. U.S. (summer conf. grad. deans 1972, com. for non-degree programs 1972-73, spl. com. assessment quality in doctoral programs 1973-74, com. internal program evaluation 1973-74), Am. Assn. U. Profs., So. Polit. Sci. Assn., Southwestern Polit. Sci. Assn., League Women Voters, D.A.R. (rec. sec. Benjamin Lyon chpt. 1967-68, regent 1970-73, sr. pres. Children Am. Revolution 1968-70), Colonial Dames XVIII Century, Daus. Republic Tex., Nat. Geneal. Soc., Denton C. of C. (accreditation com. 1973), Council So. Grad. Schs., Council Tex. Grad. Schs., Nat. Trust for Historic Preservation, Pi Sigma Alpha, Delta Kappa Gamma. Presbyn. (ruling elder). Clubs: Denton County Republican Women's (charter pres. 1955-56), Ariel (parliamentarian 1956-59, chmn. lit. dept. 1971-72). Author: The Legislative Process: A Handbook for Mississippi Legislators, 1947; Texas Constitutional Revision: The Legislative Branch, 1962. Contbr. book revs. and articles to profl. Jours. Home: 2801 Longfellow Lane Denton TX 76201

HUFF, CHARLES FRANKLIN, banker; b. Atlanta, Nov. 6, 1932; s. James Franklin and Essie (Hardy) H.; B.S., Ga. Inst. Tech., 1956; diploma Stonier Grad. Sch. Banking Rutgers, 1965; grad. certificate Am. Inst. Banking, 1962; m. Geraldine Childress, Mar. 18, 1955; children—Laurie Susan, Charles Barnett. With 1st Nat. Bank Atlanta, 1956—, v.p., 1969-73, group v.p., 1973—. Chmn. Dekalb County Pension Bd., 1973, Am. Nat. Red Cross, Dekalb unit, 1972-73; treas. Am. Cancer Soc., Dekalb unit, 1970-73; chmn. Decatur-Dekalb YMCA, 1971, 72. Bd. dirs. Campfire Girls, Inc., 1968—. Served with Signal Corps, AUS, 1956-58. Mem. C. of C. (dir. 1972—). Baptist (deacon). Rotarian. Club: Druid Hills Golf. Home: 763 Park Lane Decatur GA 30033 Office: PO Drawer 219 Decatur GA 30031

HUFF, HENRY BLAIR, lawyer; b. Louisville, Aug. 30, 1924; s. Joseph B. and Mattie (Ireland) H.; B.S., LL.B., Wake Forest Coll., 1949; M.A., U. Louisville, 1958; m. Mary Anderson May 24, 1969. Admitted to N.C. bar, 1949, Ky. bar, 1954; law practice, Lenoir, N.C., 1949-54, Louisville, 1954—. OLCO, Inc. Chmn. bd. trustees City of Brownsboro Village, 1958-65; trustee Cleark Creek Bapt. Sch., 1967; exec. bd. Louisville area Council Chs., 1962—, pres., 1967—; mem. exec. bd. Ky. Bapt. Conv., chmn. finance com., 1971, 1st v.p., 1972-73, chmn. adminstrv. com. 1972-73). Served with C.E., AUS, 1943-46. Mem. Am., Ky., Louisville bar assns., Am. Judicature Soc. Home: 170 West Wind Rd Louisville KY 40202 Office: 310 W Liberty St Louisville KY 40202

HUFF, HOWARD FARMER, educator; b. Scottsbluff, Neb., Mar. 19, 1923; s. Walton Clarence and Stella Alice (Farmer) H.; B.A., Johnson Bible Coll., 1946; B.D., Vanderbilt U., 1949, M.Div., 1972; postgrad. Union Theol. Sem., 1949-51, 55-57, 62-63; scholar in residence Perkins Sch. Theology, So. Meth. U., 1970-71; m. Rosemary Bowers, June 10, 1951; children—Craig Walton, Carole Celeste, Angela Kay, Gloria Ann, Craig Kenton. Ordained to ministry Christian Ch., 1946; minister Central Christian Ch., Columbia, Tenn., 1946-49; dir. Christian edn. Victoria Congl. Ch., Jamaica, N.Y., 1949-51; with United Christian Missionary Soc., Indpls., 1951-53, Tokyo, Japan, 1951-63; prof. religion Grad. Theol. Sem., since 1963. Phillips U., Enid, Okla., 1963—. Democratic precinct chmn., 1966-70. Mem. Am. Acad. Religion, Am. Assn. U. Profs., Am. Soc. Missiology, Assn. Profs. of Missions, Okla. Edn. Assn., Theta Phi. Editor: Japan Christian Yearbook, 1953-54, Hakone Communique, 1958. Home: 1801 E Elm St Enid OK 73701

HUFF, JOHN SEATON, advt. agy. exec.; b. Louisville, Feb. 28, 1903; s. John Andrew and Ophelia (Seaton) H.; student Centre Coll., 1920; B.S., U. Pa., 1924; H.H.D., Lincoln Meml. U., 1973; m. Margaret Aline Phillips, Sept. 27, 1928; children—Nancy Elizabeth (Mrs. Gordon Lee Hathaway), Margaret Montague (Mrs. Jesse Malin Matlack). Vice pres. Thomas E. Basham Co., Louisville, 1924-31, Gardner Advt. Co., Louisville, 1931-35; founder, pres. Farson & Huff Advt., Louisville, 1935—; pres. Braitling Engraving Co., Louisville, 1942—. Mem. Civil War Centennial Commn., 1965—. Bd. dirs. Derby Festival Assn., 1954—, Salvation Army; trustee Lincoln Meml. U., Harrogate, Tenn., 1969—; founder, pres. Jr. Achievement Kentuckiana, 1963—. Mem. Nat. Athletic Inst., Rural Library Assn., Ky. Hist. Soc., Ky., Louisville chambers commerce, Asso. Industries Ky., Sigma Phi Epsilon. Republican. Christian Scientist. Mason, Optimist. Club: Pendennis. Home: 5737 Watterson Trail Louisville KY 40291

HUFF, JOHN WESLEY, educator; b. Weston, Tex., Feb. 23, 1927; s. James German Monroe and Loice (Culwell) H.; student Arlington State Coll., 1952-54; D.V.M., Tex. A. and M. U., 1958, M.S., 1962; m. Mariam Jean Davis, Sept. 23, 1950; children—Julia Ann, John Scott, Janet Lynn. Office dept. mgr. Dun & Bradstreet, Dallas, 1947-52; pvt. practice vet. medicine, Dallas, 1958; mem. staff Tex. A. and M. U., College Station, 1958—, asso. prof. vet. microbiology, 1966-74, prof., 1974—. Served with USNR, 1946. Recipient Norden Distinguished Tchr. award, 1969; Students Faculty Distinguished award, 1970. Mem. Am., Tex., Brazos County med. assns., Council of Educators of Assn. Am. Vet. Med. Colls., Phi Zeta. Methodist. Mason, Lion. Home: 3514 Spring Lane Bryan TX 77801 Office: Dept Vet Microbiology Coll Vet Medicine Tex A and M U College Station TX 77840

HUFF, MAXWELL ERNEST, physician; b. nr. Covington, Ky., Nov. 22, 1935; s. Ernest and Edrie (Sexton) H.; M.D., U. Tenn., 1959; m. Beatrice Kesterson, Jan. 17, 1959; children—Maxwell Ernest II, Warren Keith, Avery Carlton, Alison Christine. Intern and resident Erlanger Hosp., Chattanooga, 1960; family practice Oneida, Tenn., 1961—; med. examiner, Scott County, 1962—; mem. Scott County Bd. of Health, 1964—; chief-of-staff Scott County Hosp., 1965, bd. dirs. Mem. Democratic Exec. Com., 1967-68. Recipient Physician's Recognition award A.M.A., 1970. Diplomate Am. Bd. Family Practice. Fellow Am. Acad. Family Practice (charter); mem. Scott County Med. Soc. (past pres.), C. of C. Baptist. Mason, Kiwanian. Home: Hwy US 27 Oneida TN 37841 Office: 157 Cross St Oneida TN 37841

HUFF, VEARL NATHAN, elec. engr.; b. Rosedale, Wash., Jan. 21, 1917; s. Earl Rice and Hattie Dollie (Allison) H.; B.S., Kan. State U., 1939; postgrad. Stanford, 1940; m. Dorothea Frona Leland, June 1, 1941; children—Mary (Mrs. Gary L. McCartney), David L., Donald N., Edward J. With Nat. Adv. Com. for Aeros. of NASA, 1940—, head rocket engine thermodynamics, Cleve., 1946-58, head rocket trajectory analysis, Cleve., 1959-62, chief mission analysis Gemini project, Washington, 1963-68, analyst advanced missions, Washington, 1968—. Recipient Sustained Superior Performance award NASA, 1962, Superior Achievement award, 1966. Registered profl. engr., Ohio. Mem. I.E.E.E., Assn. Computing Machinery (chmn. Cleve. sect. 1962), Am. Inst. Aeros. and Astronautics, Eta Kappa Nu, Pi Mu Epsilon, Phi Kappa Phi. Mem. Christian Ch. (elder). Inventor method for testing rocket engines at simulated altitude. Home: 6513 Lone Oak Dr Bethesda MD 20034 Office: 600 Independence Av Washington DC 20013

HUFF, WILLIAM JENNINGS, educator; b. Summerland, Miss., Mar. 3, 1919; s. William Yancey and Hattie Lenora (Robinson) H.; B.S., Miss. State U., 1956; M.A. (asst. fellow 1956-59), Rice U., 1957, Ph.D. (Tex. Gulf Producing Co. fellow 1960), 1960; LL.B., U. Miss., 1947, J.D., 1969; m. Frances Ellen Rossman, Feb. 26, 1944; 1 son, John Rossman. Admitted to Miss. bar, 1947, Tenn. bar, 1948; closing atty. Commerce Title Guaranty Co., Memphis, 1947-49; atty., adviser FCC, Washington, 1953-54; asso. prof. geology U. So. Miss., Hattiesburg, 1960-65; asst. prof. natural scis. Mich. State U., East Lansing, 1966-68; asso. prof. geology U. South Ala., Mobile, 1968—. Served with USAAF, 1941-45, judge adv., 1949-52. Decorated Air medal with ten oak leaf clusters. Named Outstanding Grad. Student Rice U., 1959-60. Mem. Miss., Tenn. bars, Am. Assn. Petroleum Geologists, Soc. Econ. Mineralogists and Paleontologists, Paleontol. Research Soc., N.Y. Acad. Scis., Ala. Geol. Soc., Am. Assn. U. Profs. Mason (Shriner). Contbr. articles to various publs. Home: 5917 Montfort Rd S Mobile AL 36608

HUFFINE, WAYNE WINFIELD, educator; b. Greenville, N.M., July 21, 1919; s. Ed. D. and Della (Oldham) H.; B.S., Okla. State U., 1946, M.S., 1947; Ph.D., Purdue U., 1953; m. Jean Edwards, Oct. 22, 1943. Instr. Okla. State U., Stillwater, 1946-67, asst. prof., 1947-50, 1953-55, asso. prof., 1955-60, prof. agronomy, 1960—; research asst. Purdue U., Lafayette, Ind., 1950-53. Cons. agronomy Imperial Ethiopian Coll. Agr. and Mech. Arts, 1960. Served with AUS, 1943-44. Fellow Am. Soc. Agronomy (div. chmn. 1957-58, dir. 1958-59, 72—), A.A.A.S. Asso. editor Crop Sci., 1960-62, 66-68. Home: 1502 N Washington St Stillwater OK 74074

HUFFINES, HILMAN HOWARD, county agrl. agt.; b. Hilham, Tenn., Oct. 16, 1919; s. Theodore Thurston and Maudie (Flatt) H.; B.S., U. Tenn., 1949, M.S., 1972; div.; children—Gwenell (Mrs. Delane Streeter), Beryl (Mrs. Richard Grandon), Dwaine Howard. Asst. county agrl. agt., Morgan County, Tenn., 1949-51; county agrl. agt., Lewis County, 1951-53, Scott County, 1953—. Served with U.S. Army AC, 1942-46. Decorated D.F.C., Air Medal. Named Am. Tree Farmer. Mem. Am. Farm Bur., County Agts. Assn., Block and Bridle, Internat. Platform Assn., Epsilon Sigma Phi. Kiwanian (local pres. 1961). Author: The Making of a Man and Other Poems, 1970. Home: PO Drawer H Oneida TN 37841 Office: Fed Office Bldg Oneida TN 37841

HUFFINES, VERNAL LEON, accountant; b. Wichita Falls, Tex., Nov. 2, 1938; s. Leon Noble and Dorothy Mae (Hoffman) H.; B.B.A., Midwestern U., 1964; m. Janeth Marie Cook, June 26, 1964; children—John Edwin, Jan Cherise, Lori Lynn, Wendell Leon. Staff accountant Stewart, Davis, Mathis & West, Wichita Falls, 1963-71, partner, 1971-73; partner, accountant Mathis, West, Huffines & Co., Wichita Falls, 1973—. Chmn., Young Life in N. Central Tex. Area, 1972—. Bd. dirs., finance chmn. A.R.C., 1970-71. Mem. Am. Inst. C.P.A.'s, Tex. Soc. C.P.A.'s (chpt. dir. 1973—, pres. 1972-73, state dir.), Fellowship Christian Athletes (dir.), N. Tex. Estate Planning Council (dir.). Methodist (treas. 1972-74). Clubs: Sertoma (pres. 1971-72, chmn. bd. dirs. Wichita Falls 1972-73); Wichita Falls Country. Home: 2304 Brookhollow St Wichita Falls TX 76308 Office: Oil and Gas Bldg Wichita Falls TX 76301

HUFFINGTON, ROY MICHAEL, oil co. exec.; b. Tomball, Tex., Oct. 4, 1917; s. Roy Mackey and Bertha (Michel) H.; B.S., So. Meth. U., 1938; M.A., Harvard, 1941, Ph.D., 1942; m. Phyllis Gough, Oct. 26, 1945; children—Roy Michael, Terry Lynn. Field geologist Humble Oil & Refining Co., N.M., 1946-51, sr. geologist, Houston, 1951-53, div. exploration geologist, 1953-56; with Roy M. Huffington, Inc., Houston, 1956—, pres., 1967—. Chmn. bd., dir. Huffington Ocean Trawlers, Inc., Brownsville, Tex., 1972—; dir. Met. Nat. Bank, Houston. Sponsor Pin Oak Charity Horse Show, Houston, 1966—. Adv. dir. Meml. Hosp. Assos., Houston, 1966—. Served to lt. comdr. USNR, 1942-45. Decorated Bronze Star, Presdl. Unit Citation. Fellow Geol. Soc. Am., A.A.A.S. (life), Am. Assn. Petroleum Geologists; mem. Houston C. of C., Houston Livestock Show and Rodeo (life), Tex. Research League, Navy League U.S. (life), C. of C. of U.S., Ind. Petroleum Assn. Am. (dir. 1966—), Tex. Ind. Producers and Royalty Owners, Tex. Mid-Continent Oil and Gas Assn., Am. Inst. Profl. Geologists, Geochem. Soc., Am. Soc. Oceanography, Natural Gas Men Houston, S.A.R., Alpha Tau Omega. Presbyn. (trustee 1965—). Clubs: Houston, Petroleum, Country (Houston); Petroleum (New Orleans). Contbr. articles to various publs. Home: 6123 Longmont Dr Houston TX 77027 Office: 2210 Tenneco Bldg Houston TX 77002

HUFFMAN, JERRY WAYNE, assn. ofcl.; b. Arkadelphia, Ark., Aug. 25, 1944; s. Charlie E. and Eldie Mae (Wetherington) H.; A.A. San Jacinto Coll., 1965; B.A. in Journalism, U. Houston, 1970; m. Deborah Ann Hessley, Oct. 4, 1969. Asst. mgr. Pasadena (Tex.) C. of C., 1966-68, 70; mgr. La Porte-Bayshore C. of C., La Porte, Tex., 1971—. Served with AUS, 1968-70. Named Outstanding student San Jacinto Coll., 1965. Mem. La Porte Bayshore Jaycees (dir. 1971, v.p. 1972, pres. 1973), Gulf Coast, East Tex., Tex. chambers commerce mgrs. assns., Phi Theta Kappa. Baptist. Mason (32 deg., Shriner), Rotarian (com. chmn. 1971—, sec. 1973). Home: 429 Shadylawn La Porte TX 77571 Office: PO Box 996 La Porte TX 77571

HUFFMAN, JOSEPH GRANT, state ofcl.; b. Petersburg, W.Va., June 5, 1933; s. Richard A. and Carmen (Hiser) H.; B.A. in Secondary Edn., Shepherd Coll., 1957; M.S. in Rehab. Counseling, W.Va. U., 1965; m. Elaine Sheppard, Dec. 27, 1958; children—Jalane Adaire, Jayma Lynn. Tchr., coach pub. high schs., W.Va., 1957-59, Fla., 1959-61; social case worker W.Va. Dept. Welfare, Petersburg, 1961-62; counselor field office Div. Vocational Rehab., Martinsburg, W.Va., 1962-63, Weston (W.Va.) State Hosp., 1965, sr. counselor, 1966, unit supr., 1966-67; program supr. Va. Dept. Vocational Rehab., Western State Hosp., Staunton, 1967—. Served with Signal Corps,

AUS, 1953-55. Mem. Nat. Rehab. Assn., Nat. Rehab. Counseling Assn. Mem. United Brethern Ch. Mason. Home: 910 Selma Blvd Staunton VA 24401 Office: Rehab Unit Western State Hosp New Site Staunton VA 24401

HUFFMAN, LOUIE CLARENCE, educator; b. Dundee, Tex., Dec. 29, 1926; s. James S. and Elizabeth D. (Williams) H.; student Tex. Tech. U., 1947-50; B.S., Midwestern U., 1952, M.Ed., 1954; M.A., U. Tex., 1963, Ph.D. (NSF Sci. faculty fellow 1965-66), 1967; m. Dorothy Marie Moser, Apr. 16, 1954; children—Debra, Kent, Brenda. Tchr. pub. schs., Wichita Falls, Tex., 1952-55; mem. faculty Midwestern U., Wichita Falls, 1955—, prof. math., 1969—, chmn. dept., 1968—. Served with AUS, 1945-47. Mem. Tex. Assn. Coll. Tchrs. (sec., treas. 1970—), Math. Assn. Am. (sect. chmn. 1971-72), Alpha Chi, Phi Kappa Phi. Home: 3203 Milby St Wichita Falls TX 76308 Office: Dept Math Midwestern U Wichita Falls TX 76308

HUFFMAN, RUFUS CHARLES, educator; b. Bullock County, Ala., Feb. 5, 1927; s. Nathan Luther and Mary Liza (Gambles) H.; B.S., Ala. State U., 1952, Ed.M., 1966; postgrad. N.Y.U., 1968; m. Callie Iola Harris, July 28, 1948; children—Rufus Charles, Henry Nathaniel. Tchr., prin. Russel County Bd. Edn., 1947-49, Autauga County Bd. Edn., Prattville, Ala., 1951-53, Bullock County Bd. Edn., Union Springs, Ala., 1953-56, 1963-67, Randolph County Bd. Edn., Cuthbert, Ga., 1956-63; coordinator, treas., mgr. Seasha Fed. Credit Union, Tuskegee Institute, Ala., 1968-70; edn. field dir. spl. contribution fund N.A.A.C.P., Tuskegee Institute, 1970—. Tchr., coach, prin., cons. Neighborhood Health Centers. Vice pres. Bullock County Improvement Orgn.; chmn. Bullock County Coordinating Com.; pres. Union Springs br. N.A.A.C.P.; v.p. Bullock County adv. council Office Ecn. Opportunity; founder Leadership U., Florence, S.C.; organizer S.E. Ala. Self-Help Assn. Fed. Credit Union; chmn., mem. selection com. Ala. Leadership Devel. Program Fellows Assn. Named Tchr. of the Year, Bullock County, 1963-64; Ford Found. Leadership Devel. fellow. Mem. N.E.A., Bullock County Tchrs. Assn. (pres.), Bullock County Athletic Assn. (pres.). Baptist (deacon). Elk, Mason. Home: 223 Underwood Av Union Springs AL 36089 Office: Scott and Calloway Sts Tuskegee Institute AL 36088

HUFFSTUTLER, RONALD GENE, educator; b. McAlester, Okla., Feb. 10, 1936; s. Riley and Ellie (Carver) H.; B.S., West Tex. State U., 1960; M.S., Colo. State U., 1961, PH.D., 1967; m. Sharon Kay Daniel, Jan. 8, 1958; children—Steven Michael, David Wayne. Instr. math. West Tex. State U., Canyon, 1961-64; instr. math. Colo. State U., Ft. Collins, 1964-67; asso. prof. math. West Tex. State U., Canyon, 1967-71, prof. math., 1971—. Recipient Faculty Excellence award W. Tex. State U., 1973. NSF Sci. Faculty fellow, 1966-67, NSF grad. fellow, 1964-65. Mem. Nat. Council Tchrs. Math. (chpt. v.p. 1973-74), Math. Assn. Am., Tex. Assn. Coll. Tchrs., Sigma Xi. Mem. Ch. of Christ (deacon 1960—). Home: 2411 15th Av Canyon TX 79015

HUGE, ROBERT RUSSELL, indsl. editor; b. Cleve., Sept. 23, 1938; s. Russell Martin and Jeannette Elizabeth (Warner) H.; B.A., Ohio U., 1961; m. Patricia Lehr Hall, Nov. 24, 1961; children—Margery Elizabeth, Elizabeth Hall. Editorial asst. Newspaper Enterprise Assn., Cleve., 1961-62, editor, 1962-65; writer Ashland Oil, Inc. (Ky.), 1965-66, editor Ashland Dealer, 1966-70, editor Ashland News, 1966—, editor Valvoline World, 1970, editor publs., 1971—. Recipient award of merit Internat. Assn. Bus. Communicators, 1965, award of excellence, 1966. Episcopalian (sec. vestry 1971-74). Contbr. poems and stories to profl. pubs. Home: 824 Edgwood Av Ashland KY 41101 Office: PO Box 391 Ashland KY 41101

HUGER, KILLIAN LOEW, JR., diversified industry exec.; b. New Orleans, Sept. 7, 1928; s. Killian Loew and Miriam Deare (Hopkins) H.; B. Comml. Sci., Tulane U., 1953; m. Eugenie Penick Jones, Oct. 24, 1953; children—Sally Polk, Eugenie Elizabeth, Deborah Hopkins, Caroline Merrick, Miriam Hopkins, James Middleton. With Celotex Corp., New Orleans, 1952-54, New Orleans Pub. Service, 1949-52, Avondale Shipyard, 1954—, Beer & Co., 1954—; pres. Huger Constrn. Co., Inc., 1954—; pres. Charlotte Devel. Co., Inc., 1955—; pres. Central Marine Service, Inc., 1962—; v.p. Canal Barge Co., 1964—; pres., dir. Interstate Fed. Savings and Loan Assn., 1971— (all New Orleans). Mem. Tulane U. Annual Giving Com., 1965-68; active United Fund, 1968-69, Heart Fund, 1968. Trustee Metairie Park Country Day Sch.; v.p. Joseph M. and Eugenie P. Jones Found., 1968. Served with USNR, 1946-48. Mem. New Orleans C. of C., Internat. House, Clubs: Petroleum, Plimsoll, Boston, Southern Yacht (New Orleans). Home: 1112 State St New Orleans LA 70118 Office: 1200 Hibernia Bank Bldg New Orleans LA 70112

HUGGETT, RICHARD WILLIAM, JR., physicist, educator; b. Frazee, Minn., July 2, 1930; s. Richard William and Alice (Hammer) H.; B.A., Concordia Coll., 1951; M.S., Ind. U., 1953, Ph.D., 1957; m. Ethel Caroline Furbay, Aug. 16, 1952; children—Laurie, James, Heather, Ariana. Asst. prof. physics La. State U., 1957-61, asso. prof., 1961-65, prof., 1965—; vis. physicist Max Planck Inst. for Extraterrestrial Physics, Garching nr. Munich, West Germany, 1969-70. Research grants, NSF, NASA, Research Corp., AEC. Fellow Am. Phys. Soc., A.A.A.S.; mem. Am. Assn. U. Profs., Am. Civil Liberties Union, Common Cause, Sigma Xi. Contbr. articles to physics jours. Home: 955 Verdun Dr Baton Rouge LA 70810 Office: Dept Physics and Astronomy La State U Baton Rouge LA 70803

HUGGINS, LAWRENCE CHANDLER, civil engr.; b. Istachatta, Fla., Feb. 22, 1913; s. Ira Francis and Effie Lee (Langford) H.; B.S., U. Fla., 1934; m. Helen Summers, Dec. 24, 1935; children—Loretta Coleen (Mrs. John T. Smith), Frank Augustus, Jr. Civil engr. U.S. Forest Service, 1934-38; design engr. Smith & Gillespie, engrs., Jacksonville, Fla., 1938-45; staff engr. Burlington Industries, Greensboro, N.C., 1947-62; design engr. Eastern Engring. Corp., Atlanta, 1962-65; v.p. Patterson & Dewar, engrs., Decatur, 1965-67; individual practice profl. civil engring., Decatur, Ga., 1967-69; prin. engr. Catalytic, Inc., engrs., Charlotte, N.C., 1969—, head civil dept. Enwright Asso., Inc., Greenville, S.C., 1972—. Served with USNR, 1943-46. Registered profl. engr. Ga., N.C. Mem. Nat., Ga. socs. profl. engrs., Am. Water Works Assn., Water Pollution Control Fedn. Baptist. Home: 15 Beaufort St Greenville SC 29607 Office: Haywood Rd Greenville SC 29606

HUGH, RUDOLPH, educator; b. Muskegon, Mich., Mar. 3, 1923; s. Walter and Maria (Miliniewycz) Mezynski; H.; B.S., Mich. State U., 1948; Ph.D., Loyola U. Sch. Medicine, 1954; m. Violet Ella Bowen, Sept. 27, 1963. Dir. labs. Evanston (Ill.) Health Dept., 1953-54; asst. research prof. bacteriology George Washington U. Sch. Medicine, 1954-57, asst. prof. bacteriology, 1957-60, asso. prof. microbiology, 1960-68, prof., 1968—. Lectr. Naval Grad. Dental Sch., Nat. Naval Med. Center, 1972—; cons. Nat. Insts. Health Clin. Center, 1962—; mem. faculty Am. Soc. Clin. Pathology Ednl. Center, Chgo., 1972—. Vice pres. Harbour Square Owners' Inc., 1973—. Diplomate Am. Bd. Microbiology. Fellow Washington Acad. Scis., Am. Acad. Microbiology; mem. A.A.A.S., Am. Pub. Health Assn., Am. Soc. Microbiology, Soc. Gen. Microbiology (U.K.), South Central Assn. for Clin. Microbiology, Sigma Xi. Office: The George Washington U Med Center Dept Microbiology 2300 Eye St NW Washington DC 20037

HUGHES, BENNY HARRY, lawyer; b. Beaumont, Tex., Sept. 8, 1934; s. Benny Henry and Lillian (Richards) H.; B.B.A. with highest honors, U. Tex., 1956, M. Pub. Accounting, 1959, LL.B. with honors, 1960; m. Allison Holmgreen, June 23, 1956; children—Seth Edward, Eugene Holmgreen, John Charles. Admitted to Tex. bar, 1960; mem. firm Orgain, Bell & Tucker, Beaumont, 1960—. Pres. sch. bd. South Park Ind. Sch. Dist., 1973—. Bd. dirs. YMCA, Beaumont, 1966-73; trustee Beaumont Econ. Devel. Found., 1972—. C.P.A., Tex. Mem. Am., Jefferson County bar assns., State Bar Tex., Tex. Soc. C.P.A.'s, Tex. Utility Lawyers Assn., Beaumont C. of C. (dir. 1973—), Beta Gamma Sigma, Beta Alpha Psi, Phi Delta Phi, Phi Gamma Delta. Episcopalian (trustee found. 1965—). Rotarian (dir. 1970-73). Club: Beaumont Country. Home: 1340 Thomas Rd Beaumont TX 77706 Office: Beaumont Savs Bldg Beaumont TX 77701

HUGHES, BILLY RAY, coll. adminstr.: b. El Dorado, Ark., Feb. 14, 1932; s. Jesse Gordon and Bonnie Vay (Middlebrooks) H.; B.S.E., Henderson State Coll., 1954. M.S.E., 1957; m. Carolyn Ann Lee, Nov. 30, 1957; children—Barry Ray, Lee Ann. Tchr., Huttig (Ark.) Pub. Schs., 1955-56. McNeil (Ark.) Pub. Schs., 1957-59; tchr., coach Marvell (Ark.) Pub. Schs., 1959-60; dir. spl. edn., Crossett, Ark., 1960-65; news dir. Texarkana Coll. (Tex.), 1965-68, dean students, 1968—. Editorial dir. Wonder State Publs., 1965. Pres., Texarkana (Tex.) Baseball Assn., 1971. bd. dirs., 1972-73. Mem. Nat. Rifle Assn. (life). Outdoor Writers Assn. Am., Am., S.W., Tex. assns. student personnel adminstrs., Theta Alpha Phi. Republican. Presbyn. (deacon 1968-70). Rotarian. Author: American Handmade Knives of Today. 1972; (with others) Gun Digest Book of Knives, 1973. Contbr. articles to profl. jours. Home: 110 Royale Dr Texarkana TX 75501

HUGHES, CHARLES ERVIN, govt. ofcl.; b. Sherman, Tex., Apr. 30, 1927; s. Roy Ervin and Mary Estelle (Fowler) H.; B.A., U. Tex., 1949, J.D., 1951; m. Wilma Dean Haralson, Dec. 25, 1954. Admitted to Tex. bar, 1951; pvt. practice law, Sherman, 1951—; U.S. magistrate, 1971—. Mem. Tex. Ho. of Reps., 1950-62; chmn. Grayson County Democratic Com., 1966-72. Served with U.S. Mcht. Marine, 1944-45. Mem. Grayson, North Tex. bar assns., State Bar of Tex., Phi Delta Phi. Democrat. Baptist. Elk. Home: Route 2 Box 64-J Denison TX 75020 Office: 104 S Crockett St Sherman TX 75090

HUGHES, CHARLES WILLIAM, banker; b. Danville, Ky., Mar. 31, 1910; s. Charles W. and Edith (Galloway) H.; B.A., Vanderbilt U.; LL.D., Bethel Coll., 1969; m. Emily Ann Thomas, Aug. 31, 1934; children—Thomas, Robert, William. Tchr., Columbia Mil. Acad., 1935-40; with Hermitage Securities Co., Nashville, 1945-49; exec. sec. bd. finance Cumberland Presbyn. Ch., Memphis, 1949-50; with Valley Fidelity Bank and Trust Co., Knoxville, Tenn., 1951—, sr. v.p., 1960-69, pres., 1969-71, vice chmn., 1971—; lectr. Sch. Consumer Banking, U. Va., 1962-71. Bd. dirs. United Fund, 1956-62. Served to lt. comdr. USNR, 1941-45. Recipient Presdl. Commendation. Mem. Knoxville C. of C. (dir. 1959-63). Home: 303 Mayflower Rd Knoxville TN 37920 Office: Clinch and Market Sts Knoxville TN 37901

HUGHES, DAVID JAMES, physician; b. Charleston, S.C., Jan. 15, 1924; s. John W. and Blanche (Houser) H.; B.S., The Citadel, 1943; M.D., Emory U., 1947; m. Ann C. McCurdy, Dec. 21, 1945; children—Judy L., Janice L., Jay. Intern Grady Meml. Hosp. Atlanta, 1947-48, resident 1948-50; pvt. practice internal medicine, Atlanta, 1953—; mem. staff Emory U., Ga. Baptist, Grady Meml. Hosps., St. Joseph's Infirmary; asst. prof. clin. medicine Emory U. Sch. Medicine, 1957-65, clin. asso. prof. medicine, 1965—. Served to capt., M.C., AUS, 1950-53. Mem. Am., Ga., Fulton County med. assns., So. Med. Soc., Am., Ga. heart assns., Emory U. Alumni Assn. (pres. 1967-68). Home: 918 Oakdale Rd NE Atlanta GA 30307 Office: Decatur North Profl Bldg Decatur GA 30030

HUGHES, EDWIN RENE, judge; b. St. Louis, Apr. 4, 1936; s. Thomas W. and Renee Marie (Blancg) H.; B.S., Ind. U., 1960; J.D., Tulane U., 1963; m. Ann C. Williams, May 27, 1961; children—Priscilla Renee, Jean Clinton, Nancy Elaine, John E. Admitted to La. bar, 1963; asso. firm Davenport, Farr & Kelly, Monroe, La., 1963-66; town atty. Jena, La., 1966-71; asst. dist. atty., Jena, 1971; dist. judge, Jena, 1972. Trustee LaSalle Gen. Hosp., 1971-72. Served with AUS, 1954-57. Democrat. Methodist. Mason, Kiwanian (Jena pres. 1971-72, internat. lt. gov. 1973-74). Home: 217 Roberts St Jena LA 71342 Office: PO Drawer D Jena LA 71342

HUGHES, FELIX AUSTIN, JR., physician; b. Okolona, Ark., Oct. 29, 1907; s. Felix Austin and Francis (Orsburn) H.; A.B., Henderson-Brown Coll., 1927; M.D., Vanderbilt U., 1932; M.Sc., U.P., 1936; m. Francis Elizabeth Warren, Mar. 2, 1938; children—Felix Austin III, Michael, David. Intern, Davidson County Tb Hosp., Nashville, 1930-32, resident, 1932-33; resident U. Pa., 1933-34; fellow in surgery Robert Packer Hosp., Sayre, Pa., 1934-37; pvt. practice medicine, Prescott, Ark., 1937-40; indsl. practice, Nashville, 1937-38; tb clinician Tenn Health Dept., 1940-41, Memphis and Shelby County, 1941-42; chief thoracic surgery sect. Memphia VA Hosp., 1946-71; asso. prof. surgery U. Tenn. Med. Sch., 1961—; dir. tb div. Memphis and Shelby Health Dept., 1971—; mem. staff Baptist Meml. Hosp., Memphis, 1971—. Served with USAAf, 1942-46. Diplomate Am. Bd. Surgery. Mem. Nevada and Clark County Med. Soc. (pres. 1937), Memphis Thoracic Soc., Thoracic Surgery Group (founder), Am. Assn. Thoracic Surgeons, Soc. Thoracic Surgeons, A.M.A., Tenn., Memphis med. socs. Roman Catholic. Club: Chickasaw Country. Contbr. numerous articles to surg. jours. Home: 263 N Rose Rd Memphis TN 38117 Office: Memphis and Shelby County Health Dept 714 Jefferson Av Memphis TN 38105

HUGHES, FRANKLIN FLETCHER, govt. ofcl.; b. Meridian, Miss., May 24, 1921; s. Fletcher Franklin and Florrie Leona (Pogue) H.; student Meridian Jr. Coll., 1939-41; B.S., Miss. State U., 1948, M.S., 1970; m. Mary Frances Ford, June 2, 1950; children—Benford F., Maretta A. On-farm tng. instr. County Dept. Edn., Meridian, 1948-50; asst. county agt., 4-H leader Miss. Agrl. Extension, State College and Pascagoula, Miss., 1950-54, asso. county agt., Covington County, 1954-58; county leader Jefferson Davis County, Prentiss, Miss., 1959-64, 65—. Pres. Jefferson Davis Council on Aging, 1971—; instl. rep. Comalada dist., Pine Burr council Boy Scouts Am., 1963-70. Pres. Co-ordinating Council Jefferson Davis County, 1965; mem. inter-alumni council State Instns. Higher Learning, 1965—. Served to sgt. AUS, 1942-46. Mem. Jefferson Davis County Livestock Assn. (sec.-treas. 1959—), Miss. County Agts. Assn. (dir.), Miss. Assn. County Agrl. Agts., Nat. Assn. County Agts. (Distinguished Service award 1973), Am. Forestry Assn., Nat. Rifle Assn., Nat. Geog. Soc., Epsilon Sigma Phi. Baptist (deacon 1952—, Sunday sch. supt. 1961-64, 66-68). Mason, Rotarian (pres. 1968-69). Home: Box 687 Prentiss MS 39476 Office: PO Box H Prentiss MS 39476

HUGHES, GEORGE FARANT, JR., safety engr.; b. Roanoke, Va., June 22, 1923; s. George Farant and Pattie (Shafer) H.; B.S., Va. Mil. Inst., 1948; m. Frances Miriam Perdue, July 1, 1950. With roadway maintenance dept. N. & W. Ry. Co., Roanoke, Va., 1948, with Liberty Mut. Ins. Co., Roanoke, Balt., 1949-61, asst. div. mgr., Pitts., 1962-63; safety supr. Westinghouse Electric Corp., Balt., 1963-64; supr. safety and accident prevention, Buffalo, 1965-67; safety dir. U.S. Naval Weapons Sta., Yorktown, Va., 1967-73; head indsl. safety U.S. Naval Safety Center, Norfolk, Va., 1973—. Served with AUS, 1943-46, 50-52. Decorated Bronze Star with oak leaf cluster, Purple Heart. Registered profl. engr., Va.; certified safety profl. Mem. Am. Soc. Safety Engrs. (profl. mem.), Western N.Y. Safety Conf. (dir. 1966-67), Nat. Soc. Profl. Engr. Home: 520 Randolph St Williamsburg VA 23185 Office: Naval Safety Center Norfolk VA 23511

HUGHES, HANSEL LEIGH, chemist; b. Kirksey, Ky., Mar. 17, 1917; s. Alford Leigh and Tellie Valarah (Ezell) H.; B.S., Murray State U., 1937; M.S. (fellow), U. Ill., 1946; m. Edith Kathleen Vaden, Mar. 11, 1943; children—Kaye Vaden, David Leigh. Instr. pub. sch., Trenton, Tenn., 1937-38, Sikeston, Mo., 1938-40, Pensacola, Fla., 1940-41; instr. chemistry Murray (Ky.) State U., 1941-42; lab. supr. Hercules Powder Co., 1942-45; instr. chemistry U. Ill., 1945-46; prof. chemistry, chmn. dept. Carthage (Ill.) Coll., 1946-49; asso. prof. chemistry Catawba Coll., Salisbury, N.C., 1949-56. Norfolk (Va.) div. William and Mary Coll., 1956-62; organic chemist Norfolk Naval Shipyard, Portsmouth, 1962—. Fellow Am. Inst. Chemists: mem. A.A.A.S., Am. Chem. Soc., Soc. Am. Mil. Engrs., Nat., Cape Henry Audubon socs., Va. Acad. Sci. Home: 5103 Powhatan Av Norfolk VA 23508 Office: Norfolk Naval Shipyard Bldg 184 Portsmouth VA 23709

HUGHES, HAROLD E., assn. exec.; ed. U. Ia.; m. Eva Mercer, 1941; 3 daus. Engaged in trucking bus.; mem., formerly chmn. Ia. Commerce Commn.; organizer, mgr., Ia. Better Trucking Bur.; gov. Ia., 1963-69; mem. U.S. Senate from Ia., 1969-72; pres. Internat. Congress on Alcoholism and Addictions, 1972—. Mem. Democratic Commn. on Party Structure and Del. Selection, 1969-72. Served with AUS, World War II; ETO. Mem. Am. Legion. Democrat. Methodist. Mason (Shriner) K.P. Home: 813 Carrie Ct McLean VA 22101

HUGHES, ISRAEL HARDING, JR., city ofcl.; b. Greensboro, N.C., June 5, 1923; s. Israel Harding Sr. and Josephine (Bowen) H.; A.B., U. N.C., 1944; M.Pub. Adminstrn., U. Mich., 1948; m. Dorothy Jean Curtis, Aug. 1, 1953; children—Jean, Thomas Harding, David, Jo Lynn. City planning asst., Flint, Mich., 1948-49; adminstrv. asst. to city mgr., Winston-Salem, N.C., 1949-51, budget dir., 1951-58; city mgr., Aiken, S.C., 1958-63, Durham, N.C., 1963—. Served with USNR, 1943-46, lt. comdr. Res. (ret.). Mem. Internat. City Mgmt. Assn. Episcopalian. Rotarian. Office: City Hall Durham NC 27702

HUGHES, JOHN DAVID, lawyer; b. Lubbock, Tex., Apr. 24, 1935; s. John Alvin and Pauline Goode (Noble) H.; student Kemper Mil. Sch. and Coll., 1953-54; B.B.A., U. Tex., 1958; J.D., Am. U., 1961; m. Karin Lofgren, Apr. 17, 1965; children—John Erik, Stefan David. Admitted to Tex. bar. 1964: practiced in Lubbock, 1964-74; asst. county atty., Lubbock County. Tex., 1964; jr. partner Pharr. Trout & Jonex, 1964-73; asst. chief div. transp. atty. gen.'s Office of Tex., 1974—. Instr. comml. law Am. Inst. Banking, Lubbock, 1966-67; lectr. Tex. Tech. Sch. Law, Lubbock, 1970-73. Mem. exec. bd. South Plains council Boy Scouts Am., 1969-73. Bd. dirs. Lubbock Symphony Orch. Served with AUS, 1961-63. Mem. Am., Lubbock County (dir. 1968-71) bar assns., State Bar Tex., Delta Theta Phi. Methodist (conf. chmn. Ch. and Soc. N.W. Tex. Jurisdictional Conf. 1972-73). Kiwanian. Home: 4702 Timberline Austin TX 78746 Office: Atty Gen's Office State of Texas PO Box 12548 Austin TX 78711

HUGHES, JOHN THOMAS, educator; b. Selma, N.C., July 5, 1919; s. John Thomas and Anne (Hood) H.; B.S., Wake Forest Coll., 1940; D.D.S., U. Md., 1947; M.P.H., U. N.C., 1958, D.P.H., 1963; m. Elizabeth Smith Disney, Nov. 1, 1947; children—John Thomas, Robert Fred. Tchr., Wilson County Sch., N.C., 1940-42; individual practice dentistry, Pittsboro, N.C., 1947-55; pub. health dentist N.C. State Bd. Health, 1955-57, asst. dir., 1960-66, research coordinator, 1963-66; asso. prof. dept. health adminstrn. Sch. Pub. Health, U. N.C. at Chapel Hill, 1966-71, prof., 1971—, dir. dept. continuing edn., 1973—, prof. dept. dental ecology Sch. Dentistry, 1967—. Supr. residents N.C. Bd. Health, 1966-74; dist. com. Occoneechee council Boy Scouts Am., 1960-72; mem. Chatham County (N.C.) Morehead Scholarship Selection Com., 1959-72, chmn., 1960-74; sec.-treas. Pittsboro (N.C.) Swimming Assn., 1960-63; pres. Pittsboro PTA, 1958-62. Chmn. Pittsboro Planning Bd., 1970-72. Exec. bd. N.C. Council on Food and Nutrition. Served with AUS, 1942-44. Diplomate Am. Bd. Dental Pub. Health (sec.-treas. 1974). Fellow Am. Coll. Dentists, Am. Pub. Health Assn.; mem. Am. Dental Assn., N.C. (com. chmn. 1960-65), 3d Dist. dental socs., Am. Pub. Health Assn., N.C. Pub. Health Assn. (chmn. 1958-72). Author: Family Patterns of Dental Disease, 1963, (with John T. Fulton) Life Cycle of Human Teeth, 1964, Natural History of Dental Disease (with John T. Fulton), 1965. Editorial bd. The Health Bulletin, 1962-65. Home: PO Box 237 Pittsboro NC 27312 Office: Room 260 School of Public Health Dept of Health Adminstrn UNC Chapel Hill NC 27514

HUGHES, KENNETH JAMES, govt. ofcl.; b. Glencoe, Okla., May 18, 1921; s. James Andrew and Winnie (Wilkerson) H.; B.Ch.E., Okla. State U., 1943; m. Doris Elizabeth Fortson, Oct. 12, 1946; children—Marilyn (Mrs. Corry B. Peacock), Janet Susan. Petroleum pilot plant engr. Bur. Mines, Bartlesville, Okla., 1946-49, sr. combustion engr., 1949-55, chem. engr. Air Pollution studies, 1955-59, supt. Bartlesville Energy Research Center, 1959-62, exec. asst. to research dir., 1962—. City comr., Bartlesville, 1971-74, vice-mayor, 1971-72; mem. Bartlesville Utility Com., 1972-73. Served with USNR, 1944-46. Recipient Meritorious award Dept. Interior, named Outstanding Engr., Bartlesville, 1970. Mem. Nat. Soc. Profl. Engrs. (chmn. constitution and bylaws com. 1971-73), C. of C. (water and edn. subcom. 1959-73), Am. Legion (vice-comdr. 1969-70), Okla. Soc. Profl. Engrs. (pres. 1970-71), Am. Chem. Soc. (pres. 1957-58). Democrat. Presbyn. (elder 1967-69). Elk, Kiwanian (pres. 1973-74). Contbr. articles to profl. jours. Home: 305 SE Rockwood St Bartlesville OK 74003 Office: Cudahy and Virginia Sts Bartlesville OK 74003

HUGHES, LARRY WAYNE, educator; b. Corning, Ohio, Mar. 12, 1931; s. Arthur Kenneth and Helen Marie (Turner) H.; B.A., U. Toledo, 1956, M.A., 1958; Ph.D., Ohio State U., 1965; m. Phyllis J. Selter, Mar. 28, 1953; children—Kevin, Douglas, David. Cost accountant Doehler-Jarvis Co., Toledo, O., 1951-53; teacher Hudson (Mich.) High Sch., 1956-58; prin. Waldron (Mich.) High Sch., 1958-60; supr. schs. Hardin County, O., 1960-62; supt. schs., Crestline, O., 1964-67; prof. ednl. adminstrn. U. Tenn., 1967—; pvt. ednl. cons. sch. dists. throughout nation. Nat. Def. Grad. fellow, 1962-64; I.D.E.A. Kettering Found. fellowship, 1966; recipient E.E. Lewis award, 1963-64. Mem. Tenn. Elem. Prins. Assn. (exec. sec. 1971-73), Nat. Soc. for Study of Edn., Am. Edn. Research Assn., Am. Assn. U. Profs., Phi Delta Kappa, Alpha Sigma Phi. Author: Education and the Law, 1971; contbg. author Social Foundations of Education, 1974; Performance Objectives for Principals, 1973; Handbook of Contemporary Education, 1974. Writer, dir. 2 tng. films in decision making. Contbr. numerous articles to periodicals. Home: 4046 Towanda Trail Knoxville TN 37919 Office: 220 Henson Hall U Tenn Knoxville TN 37916

HUGHES, NATHANIEL CHEAIRS, JR., ednl. adminstr.; b. Chattanooga, Dec. 21, 1930; s. Nathaniel Cheairs and Celeste (Jacoway) H.; B.A., Yale U., 1953; M.A., U. N.C., 1956, Ph.D. (Waddell fellow 1957-59), 1959; m. Buckner Latimore, Nov. 26, 1954; children—Nathaniel Francis Cheairs, David Latimore, Samuel

Buckner. Tchr. Webb Sch., Bell Buckle, Tenn., 1959-62; headmaster St. Mary's Episcopal Sch., Memphis, 1962-73; instr. Memphis State U., 1963-66; headmaster Girls' Prep. Sch., Chattanooga, 1973—. Mem. Shelby County Hist. Commn., 1972-73. Trustee Memphis and Shelby County Mental Health Center, 1966-72, chmn. 1970-71; trustee St. George's Sch., 1967-70. Served to capt. USMC, 1953-63. Mem. Tenn., So. hist. assns., Poetry Soc. Tenn., Tenn. Geneal. Soc. Episcopalian (vestryman 1963-71, lay reader 1959-73). Author: General William J. Hardee, 1965; Instruction Manual Prohibits Painting Over Portholes (poetry), 1973. Home: 1610 Carroll Lane Chattanooga TN 37405 Office: PO Box 4045 Chattanooga TN 37405

HUGHES, ROBERT RULE, physician; b. Jacksonville, Fla., Aug. 6, 1929; s. William and Isabella (Craig) H.; student Southwestern U. at Memphis, 1947-49; M.D., U. Tenn. Coll. Medicine, 1952; m. Willie Ann Burkes, Dec. 7, 1957; children—Craig Ian, Leslie Burkes. Intern Jefferson Davis Hosp., Houston, 1953-54; resdient, Baylor U. Affiliated Hosps., Houston, 1959-61; practice medicine, specializing in obstetrics and gynecology, 1961—; asso. prof. dept. obstetrics and gynecology U. Tenn. Coll. Medicine, 1967-73, prof., 1973—, dir. div. Gynecologic Oncology, 1967—. Com. chmn. Memphis area Uterine Cancer Task Force, Am. Cancer Soc., 1973. Served with USAF, 1954-56. Mem. Central Assn. Obstetricians and Gynecologists, Am., So. med. assns., Soc. Gynecologic Oncologists, Felix Rutlege Soc. (pres. 1973-74), Tenn. State, Memphis obstet. and gynecol. socs., Memphis, Shelby County med. socs., N.Y. Acad. Sci., Assn. Profs. Gynecology and Obstetrics. Home: 5751 Woodbriar Cove Memphis TN 38117 Office: 800 Madison Av Memphis TN 38163

HUGHES, VESTER THOMAS, JR., lawyer; b. San Angelo, Tex., May 24, 1928; s. Vester Thomas and Mary Ellen (Tisdale) H.; student Baylor U., 1945-46; B.A. with distinction, Rice U., 1949; LL.B. cum laude, Harvard, 1952. Admitted to Tex. State bar, 1952; law clk. U.S. Supreme Ct., 1952; asso. firm Robertson, Jackson, Payne, Lancaster & Walker (name later changed to Jackson, Walker, Winstead, Cantwell & Miller), Dallas, 1955—, partner, 1958—; dir. Exell Cattle Co. LX Cattle Co., Post Co., Post Am. Corp., Stewart Engring. Co., Murphy Oil Corp., First Nat. Bank Mertzon (Tex.), Austin Industries, Inc. Vis. prof. law So. Methodist U. Grad. Sch. Tax counsel Dallas Community Chest Trust Fund. Bd. dirs. Byrd Found., Larry and Jane Harlan Found., Troy Post Found., Found. for Christian Cummunication, Goodwill Industries Dallas; trustee Dallas Bapt. Coll.; trustee, exec. com. Tex. Scottish Rite Hosp. for Crippled Children; bd. overseers vis. com. Harvard Law Sch., 1969—. Served to lt. AUS, 1952-55. Mem. Am. Bar Assn. (mem. council sect. taxation 1969—), Am. Law Inst. (mem. council 1966—), Phi Beta Kappa, Sigma Xi. Baptist. Mason (33 deg.); mem. Order Eastern Star. Home: 1222 Commerce St Dallas TX 75202 Office: First Nat Bank Bldg Dallas TX 75202

HUGHES, WALTER THOMPSON, JR., physician; b. Cleveland, Tenn., May 16, 1930; s. Walter Thompson and Millie (Collett) H.; student Tenn. Polytechnic Inst., 1948-51; M.D., U. Tenn., 1953; m. Frances Jeanette Skinner, Nov. 24, 1957; children—Carla, Gregory, Christopher. Intern Knoxville Gen. Hosp., 1954-55; resident U. Tenn. Coll. Medicine, 1955-57; practice medicine, specializing in Pediatrics, Cleveland, Tenn., 1959-60; instr. U. Louisville, 1961-62, asst. prof., 1962-64, asso. prof., 1964-67, prof., 1968-69, acting chmn. dept. pediatrics, 1968-69; chief infectious deseases service St. Jude Children's Research Hosp., Memphis, 1969—; prof. pediatrics and microbiology U. Tenn., 1969—; mem. staff St. Jude Children's Research Hosp. Served with AUS, 1957-59. Diplomate Am. Bd. Pediatrics. Fellow Am. Acad. Pediatrics; mem. Infectious Disease Soc. Am., Soc. Pediatric Research, Am. Soc. Microbiology, Internat. Soc. Animal and Human Mycology, Med. Mycol. Soc. Am. Author: Pediatric Procedures, 1964. Contbr. numerous articles to profl., med. jours. Home: 578 Center Dr Memphis TN 38112 Office: 332 N Lauderdale St Memphis TN 38101

HUGHES, WILLIAM CASWELL, physician; b. Evington, Va., Apr. 23, 1918; s. Earl Byrd and Loulie Gaither (Porter) H.; B.A., Lynchburg Coll., 1939; postgrad. U. Louisville, 1945-47; M.D., U. Cin., 1951; m. Florence Elizabeth Holtman, Feb. 14, 1946; children—William Caswell (dec.), Mary Katherine. Sch. prin., tchr., Pittsylvania County, Va., 1939-41; intern Med. Coll. Va., 1951-52; practice gen. medicine, Franklin County, Boones Mill, Va., 1952—; mem. staff Franklin Meml. Hosp., pres. med. staff, 1971—; mem. staff Roanoke Meml. Hosp. Served to maj. USAF, 1941-45. Decorated D.F.C., Air medal, Purple Heart. Mem. Soc. Gen. Practice, Am. Assn. Family Practice, Roanoke Acad. Medicine, Va. Med. Soc., A.M.A., Alpha Omega Alpha. Methodist. Club: Willow Creek Country. Home: Route 5 Box 34 Rocky Mount VA 24151 Office: Boones Mill VA 24065

HUGIN, ADOLPH CHARLES, lawyer, engr., inventor; b. Washington, Mar. 28, 1907; s. Charles and Eugenie (Vigny) H.; B.S. in Elec. Engring., George Washington U., 1928; M.S. in Elec. Engring., Mass. Inst. Tech., 1930; postgrad. Union Coll., 1944; J.D., Georgetown U., 1934; LL.M., Harvard, 1947; S.J.D., Catholic U. Am., 1949. Admitted to Mass. bar, D.C. bar, U.S. Supreme Ct. bar, U.S. Ct. Customs and Patent Appeals bar, Va., U.S. Ct. Claims bar; examiner U.S. Patent Office, 1928; engr. Gen. Electric Co., Lynn, Mass., 1928-30, patent investigator, Washington, 1930-33, patent atty., Washington and Schenectady, 1933-46, engr., Schenectady, 1942-45, organizer, instr. patent practice course, 1945-46; practiced in Cambridge, Mass., 1946-47; vis. prof. law Catholic U. Am., 1949-55; practice law, cons. engr. Washington, 1947—. Bd. dirs. St. Margaret's Fed. Credit Union, 1963-67, 1st v.p., 1965-67. Mem. Schenectady com. Boy Scouts Am., 1940-42; charter mem., 1st bd. mgrs. Schenectady Catholic Youth League, 1935-38, hon. life mem. 1946; chmn. St. Margaret's Bldg. Fund, 1954; lector St. Margaret's (Md.) Parish, 1966-68, lector-commentator St. Michael's (Va.) Parish, 1969—; mem. St. Margaret's Parish Council, 1969-71. Registered profl. elec. and mech. engr., D.C.; registered patent atty. U.S. Patent Office. Mem. Holy Name Soc. (parish pres. 1950-52, pres. Prince Georges County sect. 1953, pres. Washington archdiocesan union 1953-55), St. Vincent de Paul Soc. (parish conf. pres. 1965—, pres. county particular council 1959-61, rep. Prince George County on Washington Archdiocesan Central Council Soc. 1961-62), St. Margaret's Parish Con-fraternity of Christian Doctrine (pres. 1960-61), Council of Catholic Men (pres. so. county deanery 1956-58, 65-68), Men's Retreat League (exec. bd. Washington, 1954-58, St. Margaret's Retreat Group capt. 1965-68), Nocturnal Adoration Soc., John Carroll Soc., Elfun Soc., Nat., D.C. socs. profl. engrs., Am. Bar Assn., Am. Patent Law Assn., Delta Theta Phi. Club: Catholic Men's First Friday. Author: Trade Regulatory Arrangements and the Antitrust Laws, 1949. Editor-in-chief Bull. Am. Patent Law Ann., 1949-54; editor notes and decisions Georgetown Law Jour., 1933-34. Contbr. articles in fields patents, copyrights, antitrust, radio and air law to profl. jours. Patentee in field dynamoelectric machines, dynamometers, insulation micrometers, ecology and pollution control, mus. instruments, others. Home: 7602 Boulder St North Springfield VA 22151 Office: Nat Press Bldg Washington DC 20004

HUH, OSCAR KARL, JR., geologist, oceanographer; b. Hackensack, N.J., Nov. 29, 1935; s. Oscar Karl and Gloria M. (Quinones) H.; B.A., Rutgers U., 1957; M.S., Pa. State U., 1959, Ph.D., 1968; m. Wanda Pauline Kuhn, July 9, 1966; 1 dau., Melanie Ramona. Field geologist regional geol. studies Pa. State U., East Central Ida., 1957-59; research geologist, instr. Pa. State U., University Park, 1962-67; oceanographer Naval Oceanographic Office, Washington, 1967—. Served from ensign to lt., USNR, 1959-62. Mem. Am. Assn. Petroleum Geologists, Soc. Econ. Paleontologists and Mineralogists, Am. Geophys. Union, A.A.A.S. Research on Upper Mississippian Stratigraph, Ida., bottom currents So. Cal., coastal waters South Korea, Korean Strait, Sea of Japan; discovered oceanographic use Def. Meteorol. Satellite program, 1971-73. Home: 112 Williamsburg Dr Silver Spring MD 20901 Office: Ocean Sci Dept Naval Oceanographic Office Washington DC 20373

HUISMAN, GARY BRANT, librarian; b. Grand Haven, Mich., Apr. 8, 1940; s. Henry J. and Jennie (Hoebeke) H.; A.B., Calvin Coll., 1963; postgrad. U. Mich., summer 1964, M.S.L., Western Mich. U., 1966. Librarian, Covenant Coll., Lookout Mountain, Tenn., 1966—. Mem. A.L.A., Assn. Coll. and Research Libraries, Assn. for Advancement Christian Scholarship. Home: 404 Carter Dr Lookout Mountain TN 37350

HULA, JAMES ALBERT, mfg. co. exec.; b. DeValls Bluff, Ark., July 7, 1939; s. Emil V. and Nellie (Lawman) H.; grad. high sch.; m. Linda L. Clark, July 16, 1973; children by previous marriage—Vicky, Mary, Phyllis. Farmer, nr. Rose Bud, Ark., 1959-62; heavy equipment operator Amis Constrn. Co., Oklahoma City, 1962-65; constrn. foreman Bituminous, Inc., Pine Bluff, Ark., 1968-71; salesman Improved Constrn. Methods, Inc., Jacksonville, Ark., 1971—, dist. mgr., Clinton, Tenn., 1973—. Mason. Address: Route 1 Box 117-A Clinton TN 37716

HULEN, ALFRED CLAYTON, research inst. exec.; b. Mexico, Mo., Jan. 25, 1904; s. Edward Kennan and Blanche (Gillespie) H.; student U. Mo., 1921-23; m. Margaret Worner, Sept. 30, 1931; children—Kennan, Margaret (Mrs. Bobby Ray Huggins), Clayton, Martha (Mrs. Kevin H. McKenna). Mem. accounting staff Mo. Power & Light Co., Jefferson City, Mo., 1923-40, sr. accounting and fiscal officer, 1941-46; comptroller Slick Airways, Inc., 1946-48; accountant, bus. mgr. Earl F. Slick, 1948-50; controller, asst. treas. Southwest Research Inst., San Antonio, 1950-55, treas., asst. sec., 1955-61, sec.-treas., 1961-69, v.p. finance, sec., 1970-72, sec., cons. to pres., 1973—; sec.-treas. Southwest Patents, Inc., San Antonio; dir., asst. sec.-treas. Sci. Indsl. Park, San Antonio. Mem. Am. Mgmt. Assn., Nat. Assn. Accountants, Tex. Good Roads Assn., San Antonio C. of C., Baptist. Optimist (life), Modern Woodman of Am. Home: 8401 N New Braunfels St San Antonio TX 78209 Office: 8500 Culebra Rd San Antonio TX 78284

HULKA, JAROSLAV FABIAN, physician; b. N.Y.C., Sept. 29, 1930; s. Jaroslav Hugo and Milada (Touskova) H.; B.A., Harvard, 1952; M.D., Columbia, 1956; m. Barbara E. Sorenson, Nov. 13, 1954; children—Carol Ann, Gregory Fabian, Bryan Herbert. Intern Roosevelt Hosp., N.Y.C., 1956-57; resident Sloane Hosp. for Women, Columbia-Presbyn. Med. Center, N.Y.C., 1957-60; Josiah Macy, Jr. fellow Columbia-Presbyn. Med. Center, 1960-61; practice medicine specializing in obstetrics and gynecology, 1961—; asst. prof. obstetrics and gynecology U. Pitts. Sch. Med., 1961-66, asso. mem. grad. faculty, 1962-66, acting chmn. dept. obstetrics and gynecology, 1963-64; asso. prof. dept. obstetrics and gynecology Sch. Medicine, U. N.C. at Chapel Hill, 1967—, asso. prof. dept. maternal and child health, 1967—, asso. dir. Carolina Population Center, 1967—. Diplomate Am. Bd. Obstetrics and Gynecology. Fellow Am. Coll. Obstetricians and Gynecologists; mem. Soc. for Gynecol. Investigation, Am. Assn. Gynecol. Laparoscopists (trustee), Assn. Profs. Obstetrics and Gynecology, Am. Fertility Soc., A.A.A.S., A.M.A. Home: 2317 Honeysuckle Rd Chapel Hill NC 27514 Office: Obstet and Gynecol Dept Meml Hosp Chapel Hill NC 27514

HULL, BEN LEROY, physician; b. New Florence, Pa., Nov. 20, 1895; s. Ben Covode and Sadie (Decker) H.; A.B., U. Pa., 1921, M.D., 1925, M.Med.Sci., 1940; postgrad. Mass. Gen. Hosp., Boston, Reconstrn. Hosp., N.Y.C., 1933-34; m. Helen Hauk Stevens, June 27, 1926; children—Suzanne E., Jess Stevens. Intern, Ancon (C.Z.) Hosp., 1925-26; practice medicine, specializing in orthopaedic surgery, Altoona, Pa., 1926-58; chief orthopaedic surgery Gorgas Hosp., C.Z., 1958-63; orthopedist dept. medicine and surgery VA Regional Office, St. Petersburg, Fla., 1963—. Med. adviser Polio Found., Blair County, Pa., 1941-58. Served with U.S. Army, 1917-19. Diplomate Am. Bd. Orthopaedic Surgery. Fellow Am. Acad. Orthopaedic Surgery, A.C.S., Internat. Coll. Surgeons; mem. A.M.A., Pa. Med. Soc., Am. Assn. Ry. Surgeons. Home: 3704 El Centro St St Petersburg Beach FL 33706 Office: VA Regional Office St Petersburg FL 33706

HULL, DOYLE EDWIN, banker; b. Hawthorne, Cal., May 18, 1933; s. James Everett and Sadie Ellen (Lucas) H.; B.S. in Bus. Adminstrn. cum laude, N.E. Mo. State Tchrs. Coll., 1957; postgrad. Rutugers U. Stonier Grad. Sch. Banking, 1967-69; m. Camilla Suzanne Oestreich, June 9, 1962; children—Patricia Lynn, Doyle Edwin, David Brian. With Va. Nat. Bank and predecessor, Norfolk, 1957—, sr. v.p., mgr. mortgage loan operations, 1964-73, corporate exec. officer asset mgmt., 1973—; pres. VNB Equity Corp., 1973—; dir. Mortgage Investment Corp., Richmond, Va., exec. v.p., 1969—. Vice chmn. Norfolk Model City Commn., 1971—. Bd. dirs. Tidewater Assn. Home Builders Scholarship Found., Tidewater Assn. Credit Mgmt., Tidewater Community Colls. Served with USMCR, 1951-54. Mem. Norfolk C. of C. Methodist. Mason. Club: Harbor (Norfolk). Home: 7615 Nancy Dr Norfolk VA 23518 Office: Virginia National Bank 1 Commercial Pl Norfolk VA 23510

HULL, JOHN L., JR., oil field equipment mfg. co. exec.; b. Houston, Sept. 25, 1924; John L. and Emma (Thigpen) H.; student Rice U., 1941-43, U. Minn., 1943; B.A. cum laude U. Tex., 1948; m. LaVerne Lillian Tieman, June l, 1948; children—John, James, Robert, Richard. With Gray Tool Co., Houston, 1948—, mgr. services div., 1953-60, v.p. services, 1960-71, sr. v.p. in charge operations, 1971—, also dir.; dir. Equipos Petroleous Nacionales, Gray Tool Co., Europe, Gray Tool Co. de Venezuela; Rector Well Equipment Co. Served with USAAF, 1943-46. Decorated Air medal. Mem. Assn. Well Head Equipment Mfrs. (pres. 1972). Home: 10214 Cliffwood St Houston TX 77035 Office: 7135 Ardmore St Houston TX 77001

HULL, WAYLAND ELROY, physiologist; b. Milton, Wis., Nov. 13, 1918; s. Lester Willard and Helen (Cottrell) H.; A.B., Milton Coll., 1941; Ph.D., Duke U., 1949; D.Sc., Milton Coll., 1967; m. Helen Virginia LaFond, June 19, 1943; children—Jeffrey, Nancy J., Brian. Aviation physiologist Wright-Patterson AFB, O., 1942-47, 1949-53; asst. prof. physiology Sch. Medicine, Duke, 1953-58, asso. prof., 1958-64; chief space medicine br. crew Systems div. NASA, Houston, 1964-66, tech. asst. to dir. life scis. Johnson Space Center, Houston, 1966—. Markle scholar in med. scis., 1954-59. Mem. Am. Physiol. Soc. Club: NASA Amateur Radio. Contbr. articles to sci. jours. Home: 410 Biscayne St Seabrook TX 77586 Office: Directorate of Life Scis Johnson Space Center NASA Houston TX 77058

HULLENDER, HOWARD CLIFTON, JR., restaurant chain exec.; b. Coral Gables, Fla., Aug. 25, 1936; s. Howard Clifton and Vivie Blanche (Halsell) H.; student U. Miami at Coral Galbes, 1956-58, Fla. State U., 1960-61; m. Anne Williams, Jan. 5, 1962; children—Howard Clifton III, Melissa, Lee, Michael. Store mgr., McDonalds, Tallahassee, 1961; with McDonalds Corp., Atlanta, 1962—, regional mgr., 1968, v.p., 1969—. Mem. Jr. C. of C. (dir. 1963-65). Home: 789 Winsor Pkwy NE Atlanta GA 30342 Office: 1975 Century Blvd Atlanta GA 30345

HULLETT, JAMES CALVIN, banker; b. Bowling Green, Ky., Mar. 17, 1910; s. James Calvin and Stella (Neal) H.; student Northwestern U., 1929-30; m. Patricia Anne O'Sullivan, Nov. 25, 1936; children—James Neal, Joseph Walter. Clk. Hartford (Conn.) Ins. Group, 1929-32, spl. agt., 1933-40, asst. mgr. Western dept., Chgo., 1940-44, v.p., 1944-53, chmn. bd., pres., chmn. finance com., 1953-64, ret., 1964; dir. Conn. Bank & Trust Co., Hartford, Conn., 1953-69; Dime Sav. Bank, Hartford, Conn., 1953-64; Phoenix Mutual Life Ins. Co., Hartford, 1953-59; Hartford Elec. Light Co., 1953-64; Emhart Mfg. Co., 1953-64; chmn. bd. dirs. First Nat. Bank & Trust Co., Naples, Fla., 1971—. Pres., chmn. bd. dirs. Naples (Fla.) Community Hosp. Mem. Nat. Bd. Fire Underwriters (pres. 1956-58). Clubs: Naples Yacht (vice commodore 1972-73), Port Royal Beach, Royal Poincinana Golf. Home: 4160 Cutlass Lane Naples FL 33940 Office: First Nat Bank & Trust Co Naples FL 33940

HULSEY, PAUL DOUGLAS, police chief; b. Beeville, Tex., Sept. 22, 1934; s. Paul Salis and Nancy Pauline (Wisenbaker) H.; A.A., Tex. Southmost Coll., 1959; postgrad. Tex. A. and I. U., 1966, Sam Houston State U., 1971; m. Mary Jo Alsobrook, May 25, 1957; children—Douglas, Steve, Daniel, Tamara. Patrolman, Police Dept., Harlingen, Tex., 1955-56, Plainview, Tex., 1960-63, Hale County Sheriff's Dept., 1963-64; with Kingsville (Tex.) Police Dept., 1965—, police chief, 1968-72; chief police, Amarillo, Tex., 1972—. Team capt. United Fund, Kingsville, 1969. Bd. dirs. Big Bros. Amarillo, Amarillo Community Center. Served with AUS, 1952-55. Decorated Purple Heart; recipient distinguished service and outstanding citizen award Jr. C. of C., 1960. Mem. F.B.I. Acad. Assos. Tex., Tex. Police Chief's Assn. (exec. bd. 1970-72), Tex. Police Assn. (v.p. 1973). Office: Chief Police Police Dept Amarillo TX 79101

HULTMAN, CHARLES WILLIAM, educator; b. Oelwein, Ia., Apr. 6, 1930; s. John William and Alma (Loeb) H.; B.A., Upper Ia. U., 1952; M.A., Drake U., 1957; Ph.D., U. Ia., 1960; m. Irene Oliver, June 7, 1957; children—Susan, Gregory. Asst. prof. U. Ky., Lexington, 1960-64, prof. econs., 1967—, chmn. dept. econs., 1969-71, asso. dir. Center for Developmental Change, 1971-73; vis. asso. prof. U. Cal., 1964-65. Served with AUS, 1952-55. Fulbright lectr. Ireland, 1967-68. Mem. Am., So., Midwest econ. assns. Lutheran. Author: International Finance, 1963; American Business and the Common Market, 1964; Problems of Economic Development, 1967; Ireland in the World Economy, 1969; (with M. Wasserman, R. Ware) International Economics, 2d edit., 1969; Financing Unemployment Compensation in Kentucky, 1972; An Analysis of Kentucky Unemployment Insurance Costs, 1973. Home: 3341 Crown Crest Lexington KY 40502

HUMBER, LUCIE BERTHIER (MRS. ROBERT LEE HUMBER), civic worker; b. Paris, France, Feb. 24, 1895; d. Louis Adolphe and Honorine (Rouxel) Berthier; Brevet Superieur, U. Paris, 1913, Certificate d' Aptitude Pedagogique, 1918, Diplome d'Etudes Superieures, 1927; m. Robert Lee Humber, Oct. 16, 1929; children—Marcel Berthier, John Leslie. Came to U.S., 1940, naturalized, 1944. Tchr. French, pub. schs., Herblay, 1915-19; tchr. pvt. sch., Hinckley, Eng., 1919-22; exec. sec. Am. Univ. Union, Paris, 1922-29. Pres., Greenville (N.C.) Woman's Club, 1945-47; mem. N.C. Gov.'s Com. Rd. and Sch. Program, 1949-50, Gov.'s Adv. Com. Hwy. Safety, 1950-51, N.C. Edenton Hist. Commn.; v.p. N.C. Legislative Council, 1952-54, 68—; mem. adv. council N.C. Art Soc.; chmn. UN Week, Greenville; adv. com. Who's Who. Bd. dirs. N.C. Women's Council, N.C. Mental Health Assn., 1951-57. Recipient James Wesley White silver cup for landscape painting N.C. Fedn. Women's Club, 1960. Mem. Am. Assn. U. Women (N.C. pres. 1947-51, mem. exec. com. 1947-63, chmn. civil def. 1951-54, chmn. bldg. fund 1957-62, state bd. mem. 1968—, area chmn. for study world problems 1972—), Nat. Trust for Historic Preservation, Pitt County Democratic Women (mem. state bd. 1968-69), UN Assn., Am. Legion Aux. North Carolina Soc. Preservation of Antiquities, Pitt County Mental Health Assn., Asso. Artists N.C., East Carolina Art Assn., United World Federalists, N.C. Symphony Soc., Pitt County Hist. Assn. Democrat. Mem. French Reformed Ch. Research on history secondary edn. in U.S. Home: 117 W 5th St Greenville NC 27834

HUMBER, ROBERT LEE, lawyer; b. Greenville, N.C., May 30, 1898; s. Robert Lee and Lena Clyde (Davis) H.; A.B., Wake Forest Coll., 1918, LL.B., 1921, LL.D., 1949; M.A., Harvard, 1926; B. Litt., Oxford (Eng.) U.; Rhodes scholar from N.C., 1923; Am. field service fellow U. Paris, 1926-28; LL.D., U. N.C., 1958; H.H.D., Duke U., 1967; m. Lucie Berthier, Oct. 16, 1929; children—Marcel Berthier, John Leslie. Admitted to N.C. bar, 1920; tutor dept. govt. history and econs. Harvard, 1919-20; lawyer and bus. exec., Paris, France, 1930-40. Founded at Davis Island, N.C., Dec. 1940, Movement for World Fedn. whose prins. and objectives were embodied in a resolution, approving World Fedn., that has been passed by 16 State Legislatures of U.S. Rep. So Council on Internat. Relations, San Francisco Conf., 1945, Vice pres. United World Federalists, 1947-50, mem. Nat. Exec. Council, 1947-49, pres. N.C. br., 1961-64, co-founder, 1947; v.p. N.C. Baptist Conv. 1947. Trustee Meredith Coll., 1947-50, Wake Forest Coll., 1951-54, 59-60, pres. bd., chmn. exec. com., 1960, life trustee, 1970—. Chmn., N.C. Art Commn., 1951-61; mem. N.C. State Arts Council, chmn., 1964-67; mem. Edenton Hist. Commn., pres., 1962—, bd. dirs. Coastal Plains Planning and Devel. Commn., 1962—, chmn. 1962-64; chmn. bd. trustees N.C. Mus. Art, 1961—; mem. N.C. Conservatory Commn., 1962-63, N.C. Capital Planning and Heritage Sq. Commn., 1962-65, Gov.'s Study Com. in Vocational Rehab. 1967—, N.C. Mus. of Art Bldg. Commn., 1967—, Pitt County Devel. Commn., 1959—; bd. dirs. Pitt County chpt. A.R.C., 1957—; mem. N.C. Mus. Art Found., 1963—. Alternate del. Democratic Nat. Conv., 1956; mem. N.C. Senate, 1959, 61, 63. Bd. dirs., mem. exec. com. N.C. State Symphony; mem. Tryon Palace Commn.; trustee Pitt Indsl. Edn. Center (chmn. 1961-64), Pitt Tech. Inst. (chmn. 1964—). Served as 2d lt., F.A., U.S. Army, 1918. Awarded World Govt. News medal for most outstanding service by an individual to World Fedn., 1948, Am. War Dads Prize for greatest single contbr. toward World Peace, 1948; Salmagundi medal for enduring service to art on state and nat. level, 1966; Peace award Am. Freedom Assn., 1967. Mem. N.C. Art Soc. (dir. 1945—, chmn. exec. com. 1949-61, pres. 1955-61), N.C. Lit. and Hist. Assn. (pres. 1950), Roanoke Island Hist. Assn. (chmn. 1955-59), Pitt County Hist. Soc. (pres. 1964-68), Community Coll. Trustees Assn. (pres. 1968—), Am. Legion, Epsilon Pi Tau, Omicron Delta Kappa, Sigma Phi Epsilon, Phi Beta Kappa, Phi Delta Phi. Democrat. Baptist. Rotarian. Clubs: Watauga (Raleigh); Salmagundi, Harvard, Century (N.Y.C.). Author of resolution: The Declaration of the Federation of the World. Home: 117 W 5th St Greenville NC 27834

HUMBLE, DONALD GARFIELD, lawyer; b. Taft, Tex., Feb. 26, 1927; s. Garfield Lafayette and Minnie May (Foster) H.; A.A., Temple Jr. Coll., 1948; J.D., Baylor U., 1950; m. Betty Sue Maedgen, Aug. 30, 1947; children—Mark Maedgen, Monty Garfield. Admitted to Tex. bar, 1950; mem. firm Camp & Camp, 1951-59, Humble & Magre, 1966-74; county judge, Milam County, Tex., 1959-66. Dir. Citizens Nat. Bank of Cameron (Tex.). Served with USNR, 1944-46. Fellow Tex. Bar Found.; mem. Cameron C. of C. (pres. 1972, McCullin award). Methodist. Mason. Home: 902 E 7th St Cameron TX 76520 Office: 105 E Main St Cameron TX 76520

HUME, HUBERT MARION, city ofcl.; b. Taylorsville, Ky., Apr. 4, 1903; s. John Francis and Amanda (Snider) H.; student Western Ky. U., 1923-28; B.S., U. Ky., 1929; m. Mary Evelyn Chester, July 17, 1929; children—Betty Carolyn (Mrs. Roy L. Watts), Judith Evelyn (Mrs. Ronald Barker), Hubert Gregory. Tchr. Spencer County (Ky.) Elementary Schs., 1922-23, 1924-25, 1927-28; prin. Brewers (Ky.) High Sch., 1928-31; supt. Spencer County Schs., Taylorsville, Ky., 1932-42; prin. Orangeburg High Sch., Maysville, Ky., 1942-44; supt. Mason County Schs., Maysville, 1955-68; farm service supr. Carnation Milk Co., Southeastern U.S., 1944-55; city mgr., Maysville, 1969-74, ret., 1974. Mem. Maysville C. of C., Am. Rose Soc. Baptist (Sunday sch. tchr. 1932—). Mason, Lion. Home: 3 Bryant Circle Maysville KY 41056 Office: 3d and Bridge Sts Maysville KY 41056

HUME, MARGARET MAE WILLIAMS (MRS. DAVID HUME), hosp. cons.; b. San Antonio, Feb. 2, 1921; d. Homer Talmage and Mae (Sumner) Williams; B.A., Tex. State Coll. for Women, 1942; Med. Technologist, Scott and White Sch. Tech., 1943; postgrad. Our Lady of the Lake, 1939, U. Okla., 1946, Tex. Agrl. and Indsl. U., 1961-62; m. David Hume, June 19, 1966; 1 dau., Margeann Hume. Dept. dir. bacteriology, serology Scott and White Hosp., Oklahoma City, 1945-47; hosp. adminstr. Meml. Hosp., Goliad, Tex., 1950-55, Meml. Hosp., Eagle Pass, Tex., 1965-67, hosp. cons., 1967—. Tech. cons., 1956-62; hosp. adminstrn. cons., 1963-65. Pres. P.T.A., Freer, Tex., 1963; dir. Tri-County P.T.A., 1964; leader Gulf Coast council Girl Scouts Am., 1957-62; sec., variety show dir. Band Booster, 1959-65. Mem. Am. Assn. U. Women, Am. Soc. Med. Technologists, Pan-Am. Round Table (sec. 1941), Tex. Hosp. Assn., Alumni Assn. (v.p. 1950), Delian, Beta Beta Beta. Presbyn. Mem. Order Eastern Star. Home: Margarita Ranch Box 1212 Eagle Pass TX 78852 Office: 503 Quarry St Eagle Pass TX 78852

HUME, MARIAN RUBY, educator; b. nr. Marshall, Mo., Oct. 19, 1924; d. James Patterson and Clara (Leimkuehler) Hume; Asso. Edn., S.W. Bapt. Coll., 1944; B.A. cum laude, Baylor U., 1949; M.R.E., New Orleans Bapt. Theol. Sem., 1951, D.R.E., 1964; postgrad. U. Mo., 1945, 57, 69, 71. Tchr. rural schs., Saline County, Mo., 1942-48; minister edn. Grey Stone Bapt. Ch., Durham, N.C., 1951-53; minister edn., music Bapt. Temple Ch., Reidsville, N.C., 1953-54; worker Good Will Center, New Orleans and Columbia, S.C., 1954-56; tchr. math., music, English, Pilot Grove (Mo.) High Sch., 1956-58; supr. Presch. Lab. Sch., New Orleans Bapt. Theol. Sem., 1962-64; prof. math. and religious edn. Wingate Coll., N.C., 1964-70; tchr. Union County (N.C.) Schs., 1970—. Mem. Am. Assn. U. Women (fellowship chmn. 1965-1972), Math. Assn. Am., Nat. Council Tchrs. Math., A.A.A.S., N.E.A., N.C. Assn. Educators, Religious Edn. Assn., D.A.R., Woman's Missionary Union. Baptist. Club: Wingate Womans (dept. chmn. 1968-1974). Home: 410 N Main St Wingate NC 28174

HUMENIK, FRANK JAMES, educator; b. Bklyn., May 26, 1937; s. Frank Joseph and Pauline (Sepsi) H.; B.S. in Civil Engring., Ohio State U., 1963, M.S. (fellow 1964-65), 1966, Ph.D., 1969; m. Sue Anne Chaney, July 2, 1960; children—Kerry Lynne, James David Francis. Draftsman H.K. Ferguson Co., Cleve., 1956-58; instr. Ohio State U., Columbus, 1967-68; asst. prof. biol. and agrl. engring. dept. N.C. State U. at Raleigh, 1969-72, asso. prof., 1973—, asso. head dept., head Biol. and Agrl. Engring. extension, 1973—. Cons. on agrl. waste mgmt. and treatment systems for animal, domestic and indsl. waste, 1970—. Registered profl. engr., Ohio, N.C. USPHS grantee, 1965-67. Mem. Am. Soc. C.E. (mem. com. 1972—), Am. Soc. Agrl. Engring., Sigma Xi, Chi Epsilon. Contbr. articles to research publs. Home: 6000 Clare Ct Raleigh NC 27609

HUMPHREY, DONALD GRAY, mus. ofcl.; b. Hutchinson, Kan., May 3, 1920; s. Earl and Elizabeth (Nesbitt) Gray; B.F.A., U. Kan., 1948; M.F.A., U. Ia., 1950, Ph.D., 1958; m. Laverne I. Welk, Aug. 25, 1944; children—Marsha L., Mark N. Instr. art U. Ia., Iowa City, 1950-51; asst. prof. art U. Okla., Norman, 1952-58; dir. Philbrook Art Center, Tulsa, 1959—. Adj. prof. art U. Tulsa, 1967-72. Mem. Tulsa Arts Council, 1960—; visual arts chmn. Okla. Arts and Humanities Council, 1964-70; mem. State Art Collection Com., Tulsa, 1970-72; mem. Arts Commn., City of Tulsa, 1974—. Served with AUS, 1942-46. Mem. Am. Assn. Museums, Am. Fedn. of Arts, Okla. Museums Assn., Assn. Art Mus. Dirs., Southwestern Art Assn. (pres. 1972—). Lutheran. Club: Tulsa. Home: 4621 S Quaker St Tulsa OK 74105 Office: 2727 S Rockford Rd Tulsa OK 74114

HUMPHREYS, GRUNDY WEST, leather goods co. exec.; b. Huntsville, Ark., June 1, 1889; s. John Patterson and Clementine (Bradshaw) H.; student N. Tex. State U.; m. Ruth Abrams, July 20, 1920; 1 dau., Elaine (Mrs. J.R. Floyd). Tchr. pub. schs., Tex., 1908-18; organizer Justin Leather Goods Co., Nocona, Tex., 1919, pres., gen. mgr., chmn. bd., 1955—. Mem. City Council, Nocona, 1931-37. Recipient Distinguished Citizen award, 1965. Mem. Nocona C. of C. (pres.). Home: 410 Sherman St Nocona TX 76255 Office: 105 Clay St Nocona TX 76255

HUMPHREYS, HOMER ALEXANDER, educator; b. nr. Waynesboro, Va., Feb. 7, 1902; s. Lewis Greenberry and Annie (Sampson) H.; B.A., Bridgewater Coll., 1928; M.A., U. Va., 1941, research fellow, 1943-44; m. Ruth Elizabeth Gilbert, Sept. 1, 1926; children—Faye (Mrs. Hezekiah Sadler), Joye (Mrs. James Malcolm Hart Harris, Jr.), Anne (Mrs. Richard Edward Talman), Homer Alexander, Jane (dec.), Kaye (Mrs. Ralph Franklin Jones, Jr.). Instr. Moyock (N.C.) High Sch., 1928-29; prin. Darlington Heights (Va.) High Sch., 1929-33, Green Bay (Va.) High Sch., 1934-44; supervising prin. West Point (Va.) High Sch., 1944-65; gen. supr. instrn. Williamsburg-James City County Schools, 1965-67; dir. aviation edn. Mont. State U., Missoula, also Eastern Coll. Edn., Billings, Mont., summers 1954, 55, U. Va., Charlottesville, summers 1956-71; instr. Coll. William and Mary Extension, 1963-68. Coordinator, Civil Def., King William County and Town of West Point, 1950-61. Served from 2d lt. to lt. col. USAF, Civil Air Patrol, 1945—; dir. aviation edn. Va. Wing, Civil Air Patrol, 1956-65. Mem. N.E.A. (past 1st zone v.p. dept. audio-visual instrn.), Va. High Sch. League (chmn. 1955-57), King William-King and Queen Edn. Assn. (pres. 1956-58), Phi Delta Kappa. Kiwanian (pres. West Point 1949, lt. gov. capital dist. div. four 1956). Author: A History of Education in Prince Edward County, Va., 1941; column Wings Over Va., 1956-62; also numerous articles, reports and surveys. Home: 110 Oxford Circle Williamsburg VA 23185

HUMPHREYS, HORACE STEELMAN, food co. exec.; b. Memphis, Oct. 3, 1908; s. Arther Maurice and Lotti (McAllister) H.; student tech. high sch.; m. Lourene Lemons, Apr. 20, 1930; 1 son, Horace Steelman. Meat market mgr. Kroger Co., Memphis, 1926-33, meat supr., 1933-38; pres., gen. mgr. Atlanta Sea Food Co., 1938-40; mgr. rail stock div., trainer salesmen Armour & Co., Atlanta, 1940-42; br. mgr. Booth Fisheries Corp., Chgo. and Louisville, 1942-44; meat buyer Louisville div. Great A & P Co., 1944-46, divisional mgr. fish and poultry sales, 1946-47, meat sales mgr., 1947-48, asst. sales mgr., 1948-50, sales mgr., 1950-53; owner, operator H.S. "Bud" Humphreys Co., Inc., food brokers, Memphis and Jackson, Miss., 1953—; dir. Humphreys-Clower Co., Inc., Jackson. Mem. Memphis, Nat. food brokers assns. Methodist. Mason. Club: Chickasaw Country (Memphis). Office: 3798 Premier Av Memphis TN 38118

HUMPHREYS, JERRY K., physician; b. Murray, Ky., July 23, 1938; s. Thomas Ather and Zula Aileen (Walker) H.; B.A., Vanderbilt U., 1959, M.D., 1962; m. Martha Lee Smith, June 12, 1959; children—Martha Aileen, Jerry K., Thomas Smith. Intern Vanderbilt U., Nashville, 1962-63, resident pathology, 1963-66; practice medicine specializing in pathology, Nashville, 1966—; mem. staffs Baptist Hosp., Nashville, Donelson (Tenn.) Hosp., Nashville Gen. Hosp.; asst. clin. prof. pathology Vanderbilt U., Nashville, 1968—. Fellow Am. Soc. Clin. Pathologists, Coll. of Am. Pathologists; mem. Am., Tenn. med. assns., Nashville Acad. Medicine, Tenn. Soc. Pathologists. Methodist (mem. adminstrv. bd. 1974—). Home: 5200 Stanford Dr N Nashville TN 37215 Office: 2010 Church St Nashville TN 37203

HUMPHREYS, LIONEL NELSON, JR., supermarket exec.; b. Greeneville, Tenn., Oct. 1, 1940; s. Lionel Nelson and Blanche (Mitchell) H.; B.S., U. Tenn., 1961; m. Dorothy M. Humphreys, June 25, 1957; children—Lionel Nelson III, Sharon Dianne. Personnel mgr. Super Dollar Markets, Greeneville, 1961-62, store mgr., 1963-64, v.p., 1965-69, pres., 1969—; dir. Quality Foods, Inc., Humphreys & Co., Inc., First Nat. Bank, Greeneville. Mem. bd. Regional Planning Commn., 1972—. Mem. Christian Ch. Elk, Kiwanian. Home: 702 Franklin St Greeneville TN 37743 Office: 1000 W Irish St Greeneville TN 37743

HUMPHREYS, MICHAEL MCAULIFFE, clergyman; b. Llandaff, Wales, Sept. 29, 1923; s. Curtis Adolphus and Gerda Wilhelmina Maria (Bachman) H.; A.B., Llandaff U., 1950; M. Sacred Theology, Julian Sem., 1953; Ph.D., McGill U., 1961. Came to U.S., 1938, naturalized, 1942. Ordained to Western Rite Orthodox Ch., 1959; parish priest, various parishes, 1960-65; co-pastor Community of Christ Our Bro., Atlanta, 1966-67, superior gen. Soc. of St. John Chrysostom, Atlanta, 1965—, exec. dir. Atlanta Audio Project, 1968—, asso. therapist Atlanta Alternative Therapy Project, 1972—. Cons. therapist Human Potential Inst., Atlanta, 1972-74. Chmn., Good Music Citizen's Com., Atlanta, 1969-74; mem. adv. bd. Radio Free Ga., 1973-74. Mem. I.E.E.E., Soc. Audio Consultants. Home: 4715 Wieuca Rd Atlanta GA 30342 Office: 2126 Faulkner Rd Atlanta GA 30324

HUMPHREYS, RAYMOND V., orgn. exec.; b. Huntington, W.Va., May 3, 1911; s. Edward and Zelda (Henson) H. Editor, pub. The Chronicle, Huntington, 1930-35; exec. sec. to mayor, Huntington, 1935-36; exec. sec. W. Va. Republican Finance Com., 1937-38; pres. Asso. Underwriters, 1938-42, Raymond V. Humphreys Assos., 1946-51; mem. W.Va. Ho. Dels., 1951-52; cons. to Congressman Will E. Neal, Washington, 1953; v.p. Trail-Craft Corp., 1955-57; exec. v.p. Nat. Sales Corp., 1955-57; field rep. Nat. Republican Congl. Com., Washington, 1957-60, dir. edn. and tng., 1960-63; dir. edn. and tng. Rep. Nat. Com., 1963-69; owner Raymond V. Humphreys Assos., polit. mgmt. consultants, 1969—; author, developer Moblzn. Rep. Enterprise program. Rep. candidate for Ho. of Reps. for 4th Dist. W. Va., 1936-38. Served from pvt. to maj., AUS, 1942-46, maj. AUS, 1951-52. Mem. Nat. (dir. 1950-51). W. Va. (pres. 1948-49) mut. ins. agts. assns. Baptist. Author: Republican Mobilization Training School Handbook, 1960. Contbr. articles to profl. publs. Home: Bull Run Battlefield Haymarket VA 22069 also Lonesome Cedar Farm Hurricane WV Office: 325 Pennsylvania Av SE Washington DC 20003

HUMPHREYS, THOMAS GREEN, JR., gas utility co. exec.; b. Birmingham, Ala., Oct. 7, 1913; s. Thomas Green and Martha Juliet (Freeman) H.; grad. pub. high sch., 1931; m. Lydia Elizabeth McBain, Oct. 5, 1940; children—Thomas Green III, Patricia E. (Mrs. Stephen Richard Troy). With Ala. Gas Corp., Birmingham, 1941—, chief radio engr., 1948-55, project engr., 1955-57, asst. chief engr., 1957-61, chief engr., 1961-64, mgr. tech. services, 1964—. Cons. Utility Tool Co., Birmingham, 1965—, Samford U., 1947-71, Jefferson County Personnel Bd., 1948-65. Mem. Nat. Industry Adv. Com. FCC, 1965—. Bd. dirs. Jefferson County (Ala.) Anti-TB Assn., 1967; trustee Internat. Endowment Found., 1973-74. Mem. Am. Ordnance Assn., I.E.E.E., Nat. Assn. Corrosion Engrs., Am. Gas. Assn. (award merit 1967), So. Gas Assn., Nat. Gas Assn. (dir. Ala. chpt. 1971—, v.p. 1972—), Utilities Telecommunications Council (nat. chmn. 1956-57), Birmingham Amateur Radio Club, Relay House Birmingham. Republican. Presbyn. Rotarian (gov. internat. dist. 686 1973-74, pres. local chpt.). Patentee U.S. and foreign of electronic pipe and cable locator. Home: 2245 Pine Crest Dr Birmingham AL 35216 Office: 1918 1st Av N Birmingham AL 35295

HUMPHREYS, WALTER JAMES, educator; b. Magnolia, Ark., July 5, 1922; s. James Taylor and Mary (Cornish) H.; A.B., U. Cal. at Berkeley, 1950, M.A., 1955, Ph.D., 1961; m. Gladys Euryl Kiely, Sept. 4, 1953; children—Jeffrey, Gail, Catherine. Research zoologist U. Cal. at Berkeley, 1961-67; asso. prof. cell biology Ia. State U., Ames, 1967-68; prof. zoology, dir. electron microscopy lab. U. Ga., Athens, 1968—. Served with AUS, 1942-46. Mem. S.E. Electron Microscopy Soc. (chmn.), Electron Microscopy Soc. Am. (mem. exec. council), A.A.A.S., Am. Soc. Cell Biology, Soc. Devel. Biology. Contbr. profl. jours. Home: 170 Cedar Creek Dr Athens GA 30602 Office: Electron Microscopy Lab Barrow Hall Univ Ga Athens GA 30602

HUMRICKHOUSE, GEORGE RANDOLPH, lawyer; b. Boydton, Va., Dec. 27, 1909; s. John Johnson and Mary Elizabeth (Pleasants) H.; B.S., U. Va., 1933, LL.B., 1933; m. Margaret Page Thompson, Apr. 3, 1941; children—Mary Frances, George Randolph. Admitted to Va. bar, 1933; asso. Hutcheson and Hutcheson, Boydton, 1933-42; asst. U.S. atty. Eastern dist. Va., 1942-47, U.S. atty., 1947-51; partner Williams, Mullen, and Christian and predecessor firms, Richmond, Va., 1951—. Chancellor, Episcopal Diocese Va., 1958—, dep. to Gen. Conv. Diocese Va. and So. Va., 1946—. Bd. dirs. Friends of Library, Richmond. Mem. Am., Va., Richmond bar assns. Democrat. Mason. Home: 4504 Seminary Av Richmond VA 23227 Office: United Va Bank Bldg Richmond VA 23219

HUNDLEY, LOUIS REAMS, educator; b. Greenwood, Va., May 22, 1926; s. Elijah Dupuy and Louise Agnes (Reams) H.; B.S., Va. Mil. Inst., 1950; postgrad. U. Va., 1947-49; M.S., Va. Poly. Inst., 1953, Ph.D., 1956; m. Katheryne Leigh Tindall, July 18, 1953; 1 dau., Mary Louise. Asst. Instr. Va. Mil. Inst., Lexington, 1950-51, asst. prof., 1956-60, asso. prof., 1960-65, prof. biology, 1965—, acting head dept. biology, 1965-67; instr. Radford (Va.) Coll., part-time, 1954; instr. Va. Poly. Inst., Blacksburg, 1956. Served with AUS, 1944-46. Mem. Am. Physiol. Soc., Va. Acad. Sci., Assn. Southeastern Biologists, A.A.A.S., Sigma Xi, Phi Beta Pi, Kappa Alpha. Contbr. articles to profl. jours. Home: 309 Letcher Av Lexington VA 24450

HUNGATE, JOSEPH IRVIN, JR., educator; b. Killarney, W.Va., Apr. 30, 1921; s. Joseph Irvin and Nellie (Lickliter) H.; A.B. cum laude, Concord Coll., 1948; M.A., U. Chgo., 1950; Ph.D., U. Tex., 1963; postgrad. St. Louis U., 1948-49; m. Betty Lou Hatzenbuehler, Sept. 11, 1948; children—Ann Elisabeth, Joseph Irvin III, Sue Carol. Disaster rep. Chgo. chpt. A.R.C., 1950; chief psychiat. social work service Valley Forge Army Hosp., Phoenixville, Pa., 1951; psychiat. caseworker Fitzsimons Army Hosp., Denver, 1952-53; chief med. social work service Ft. Jackson, S.C., 1953-55; class dir., social work specialist program Army Med. Sch., San Antonio, 1955-58; asso. prof. social work U. Tex., 1959-68; dean and prof. social work Grad. Sch. Social Work, U. S.C., Columbia, 1968—, dean Coll. Allied Health Professions, 1973—. Teaching cons. Austin State Hosp., 1963-68, William S. Hall Psychiat. Inst., 1972; spl. cons. Tech. Tng. div. Bur. Family Services, Dept. Health Edn. and Welfare, Washington, 1962-65; mem. profl. adv. com. S.C. Mental Health Assn.; chmn. S.C. Gov.'s Com. on Criminal Justice, Crime and Delinquency, 1968—; mem. S.C. Gov.'s Health and Welfare Council, 1969-71. Served to 1st lt. USAAF, 1942-45, capt. M.S.C., AUS, 1950-58. Decorated Air medal with 3 oak leaf clusters, Purple Heart. Mem. Nat. Assn. Social Workers, Acad. Certified Social Workers, Council on Social Work Edn., Am. Assn. U. Profs., S.C. Welfare Forum. Author: A Guide for Training Public Welfare Administrators, 1965; articles in profl. jours. Home: 3433 Willow Ridge Rd Columbia SC 29206

HUNNICUTT, WARREN, JR., real estate broker; b. Columbus, Ga., May 15, 1924; s. Warren P. and Louise S. (Scarbrough) H.; student U. Fla., 1946-48; m. Dorothy M. Barber, Sept. 6, 1947; children—Warren IV, Robert B. With Hunnicutt & Assos., Inc., St. Petersburg, Fla., 1946—, pres., dir. 1964—. Served with USAAF, 1943-46. Mem. Am. Inst. Real Estate Appraisers (chpt. pres. 1972), Soc. Real Estate Appraisers (chpt. pres. 1968), Am. Soc. Real Estate Counselors, St. Petersburg Bd. Realtors (dir.). Home: 7946 9th Av S St Petersburg FL 33707 Office: 3160 5th Av N St Petersburg FL 33731

HUNT, DAVID FORD, lawyer; b. Fort Worth, Apr. 7, 1931; s. John Greffery and John Bernice (Ford) H.; B.S., N. Tex. State U., 1954; LL.B., Vanderbilt U., 1960, J.D., 1960. Admitted to Tex. bar, 1961, law clk. U.S. Dist. Judge, Amarillo, 1960-62; asso. Baker, Jordan, Shaw & Foreman, Atty., Dallas, 1962-63, Thompson, Knight, Simmons & Bullion, Attys., 1963-67; partner Holloway & Hunt, Attys., Dallas, 1967-70; partner David Ford Hunt, Dallas, 1970—. Pres. N. Tex. State U. Lambda Chi House Corp., 1965-68; sec., dir. Bootstrap Boys Ranch, Roanoke, Tex., 1971—; pres. So. Meth. U. Lambda Chi Found., 1972—, Vanderbilt U. Law Alumni, Dallas, 1972—. Served with AUS, 1954-56. Mem. Fed., Am., Tex. (mem. com. 1972—), Dallas bar assns., Am. Judicature Soc., Am. Bd. Trial Advocates, Lambda Chi (nat. chancellor 1966-68), Phi Delta Phi. Clubs: Chaparral, Engineers (Dallas). Home: Route 3 Roanoke TX 76262 Office: 2001 Bryan Tower Dallas TX 75201

HUNT, EARL GLADSTONE, JR., bishop, coll. pres.; b. Johnson City, Tenn., Sept. 14, 1918; s. Earl Gladstone and Tommie Mae (DeVault) H.; B.S., E. Tenn. State U., 1941; M.Div., Emory U., 1946; D.D., Tusculum Coll., 1956, Duke, 1969; LL.D., U. Chattanooga, 1957; D.C.L. (hon.), Emory and Henry Coll., 1965; m. Mary Ann Kyker, June 15, 1943; 1 son, Earl Stephen. Ordained to ministry Methodist Ch., 1944; pastor Sardis Meth. Ch., Atlanta, 1942-44; asso. pastor Broad Street Meth. Ch., Kingsport, Tenn., 1944-45; pastor Wesley Meml. Meth. Ch., Chattanooga, 1945-50, First Meth. Ch., Morristown, Tenn., 1950-56; pres. Emory and Henry Coll., 1956-64; resident bishop The Charlotte Area, Meth. Ch., 1964—. Pres. Inst. Homiletical Studies, 1966—. Pres. Southeastern Jurisdiction Coll. Bishops, 1973. Participant Meth. series Protestant Hour, nationwide broadcast, 1956; mem. Meth. Gen. Bd. Edn., 1956-68; del. Meth. Gen. Conf., 1956, 60, 64; del. S.E. Jurisdictional Conf., 1952, 56, 60, 64, pres., 1973. Bd. fellows Interpreters' House, Inc. Trustee Brevard Coll., Emory U., Greensboro Coll., High Point Coll., Pfeiffer Coll., Lake Junaluska Meth. Assembly, Bennett Coll.; bd. mgrs. Charlotte Meth. Home; chmn. gen. commn. on family life United Meth. Ch., 1968-72, mem. gen. council ministries, 1972—; bd. visitors Duke Div. Sch.; mem. Com. One Hundred, Emory U. Named young man of Year, Morristown Jr. C. of C., 1952. Mem. Newcomen Soc., Pi Kappa Delta. Home: 3912 Beresford Rd Charlotte NC 28211 Office: Cole Bldg 207 Hawthorne Lane Charlotte NC 28204

HUNT, FRANCIS LEONARD, mfg. co. exec.; b. Newark, Apr. 1, 1932; s. John Franklin and Regina Bernadette (Schilling) H.; B.S. in Civil Engring., Rutgers U., 1953; M.B.A., Clemson Furman U., 1974; m. Lois Ann Brand, Sept. 29, 1956; children—Michael Kevin, Rachel Ann. Structural engr. Austin Co., Cleve., 1956-58, Constrn. Specialties, Inc., Cranford, N.J., 1958-60; with The DM Co. div. Baldt Corp., Simpsonville, S.C., 1960—, sales mgr., 1968-70, pres., 1970—. Pres., Kendall Park (N.J.) First Aid and Rescue Squad, 1960-64; mem. Indsl. Devel. Commn., South Brunswick, N.J., 1964-66. Served with USAF, 1953-56. Registered profl. engr., N.J. Mem. Nat. Soc. Profl. Engrs., Rutgers Engring. Soc. (pres. 1963-64), Am. Mgmt. Assn., C. of C. Club: Greenville VIP. Patentee in field. Office: PO Box 308 Simpsonville SC 29681

HUNT, JACOB TATE, educator; b. Sweetwater, Tenn., Aug. 22, 1916; s. Samuel Lon and Grace (Beals) H.; A.B., Maryville Coll., 1938; M.S., U. Tenn., 1941; Ph.D., U. Cal. at Berkeley, 1950; postgrad. U. Ill., 1956-57; m. Harriet Elizabeth Durnell, June 17, 1944; 1 son, Steven Craig. Tchr. pub. schs., Tenn., 1938-40, Wash., 1940-42; instr. U. Cal. at Berkeley, 1946-48; vis. prof., 1963; asst. prof. Western Res. U., Cleve., 1948-51; asst. prof. ednl. psychology U. N.C., 1951-56, asso. prof., 1956-57; asso. prof. spl. edn. U. Ariz., 1957-60, prof., chmn. dept. spl. edn., 1960-64; prof., chmn. spl. edn. U. Wash., 1964-68; prof., chmn. spl. edn. U. Ga., 1968—; vis. prof. U. Colo., 1960, 62, U. Ill., 1957—. Bd. dirs. Pima County (Ariz.) Assn. Mental Health, 1958-63; adviser Cerebral Palsy Assn., Am., 1958-60. Served with USNR, 1942-45. Ford Found. fellow, 1956-57. Mem. Am. Ednl. Research Assn., Am. Psychol. Assn., Am. Assn. Mental Deficiency, Council Exceptional Children, Internat. Reading Assn. Editor: High Sch. jour. 1952-56, Am. Ednl. Research Assn. Newsletter, 1959-64. Rev. of Ednl. Research, 1964-69; asso. editor Exceptional Children, 1966—; editorial bd. Internat. Jour. Edn., 1967—, Jour. Spl. Edn., 1968—, Scientia Paedagogica Experimentalis, 1966—. Home: 105 Chinquapin Way Athens GA 30601

HUNT, JAMES MATHEWS, architect; b. Elberton, Ga., Aug. 2, 1915; s. Looney H. and Annie Lee (Gaines) Hunt; student Ala. Poly. Inst., 1937; B.S., Clemson U., 1938; m. Mary Elizabeth Jenkins, Sept. 13, 1947; children—James Mathews, Annie Elizabeth, Howard Jenkins. Jr. architect Housing Authority Architects City of Charleston, S.C., 1938-39; archtl. aide to Housing Authority City of Charleston, S.C., 1939-42, 46-47; archtl. cons. Liberty Granite Co., Elberton, Ga., 1947-48; self-employed as architect, Elberton, Ga., 1948-72; chmn. bd. Hunt, Enloe, West, McLean & Assos., Inc., Elberton, Ga., and Atlanta, 1972—; dir. Elberton Devel. Co., Inc. Chmn. Gov's Commn. on State Bldg. Constrn. and Financing, 1971;

mem. State Bd. Examination, Qualification and Registration Architects, 1971-76; alternate bd. examiners Nat. Council Archtl. Registration Bds. Lt. col. Aide de Camp Gov. Marvin Griffin, 1955-59, Gov. S. Ernest Vandiver, 1959-62; admiral Ga. Navy, 1971-74. Mem. Democratic Exec. Com. Ga., 1971-73. Served to 1st lt., C.E., AUS, 1942-46; PTO. Recipient Appreciation awards Producer's Council, Atlanta chpt., 1967, Ga. Assn. A.I.A., 1968, Atlanta chpt. A.I.A., 1969; mem. Family of Year Ga. Federated Women's Club, 1970. Mem. A.I.A. (pres. Ga. 1968, pres. North Ga. 1969, mem. nat. housing com. 1971, 72, 73, regional rep. 1974), V.F.W., Am. Legion, Soc. Am. Mil. Engrs. Baptist (deacon 1948—). Rotarian. Clubs: Country (Elberton, Ga.); Carolina Yacht (Charleston, S.C.). Prin. archtl. works include Marriott Motor Hotel, Atlanta, 100 pub. housing projects, S.C., Ga. Home: 136 Parkwood Dr Elberton GA 30635 Office: PO Drawer 808 16 Chestnut St Elberton GA 30635

HUNT, JOE BYRON, state ofcl.; b. Mammoth Spring, Ark., Jan. 23, 1907; s. John Fisher and Iuka (Woodall) H.; student Okla. U., 1927-28; m. Anna Maude Dial, Oct. 8, 1935; 1 dau., Jo Ann. Ins. agt., Edna, Tex. until 1942; mgr. rating dept. Okla. Ins. Bd., 1942-54, pres., 1955—; commr. Okla. Ins. Dept., Oklahoma City, 1955—. Chief ins. man Chickasaw Nation of Indians, 1960—. Mem. Okla. Burial Bd., 1955—; state dir. Firemens Relief and Pension Fund, Policeman's Pension and Retirement System, Motor Vehicle Assigned Risk Plan, 1955—; mem. Okla. Hwy. Safety Coordinating Com.; hon. lt. gov., Okla., 1960—. Dist. vice chmn. Last Frontier council Boy Scouts Am., asst. on exec. com. Oklahoma City United Fund, 1959. Mem. Seminole (Okla.) City Council, 1935. Bd. dirs. Jane Brooks Sch. for Deaf; trustee Okla. Fire Fighter Museum. Recipient Oscar, Iota Nu Sigma, 1957; Citation for Meritorious Service, Employment for Physically Handicapped, 1957; Distinguished Service award Gov.'s Com. on Employment of Handicapped, 1970; Distinguished Service award Okla. Rehab. Assn., 1970; named Boss of Yr., Galatea chpt. Am. Bus. Women's Assn., 1971-72. Mem. Nat. Assn. Ins. Commrs. (fed. liaison com., zone 5 chmn. 1960-73), Profl. Fire Ins. Soc., Internat. Assn. Fire Chiefs, Okla. Retired Firemen's Assn. (hon. life), Fedn. Ins. Council, Am. Assn. U. Tchrs. Ins., Oklahoma City C. of C. Presbyn. (past pres., trustee). Lion (charter). Home: 4309 NW June St Oklahoma City OK 73112 Office: Will Rogers Meml Bldg State Capital Complex Oklahoma City OK 73105

HUNT, JOSEPH THOMAS, dentist; b. nr. Louisburg, N.C., June 21, 1923; s. Joseph Baldy and Annie Aileen (Edwards) H.; student Louisburg Jr. Coll., 1940-41, Wake Forest U., 1941-43; D.D.S., Med. Coll. Va., 1946; m. Dora Perrle Webster, Jan. 24, 1945; children—Joseph Thomas, Garry D., Timothy W., Debby G., Stephanie M. Practice dentistry, Henderson, N.C., 1947-50, 53—; pres. Pentose Devel. Corp., Henderson, N.C., 1971—; dir. People's Bank and Trust Co. Bd. dirs. N.C. Dental Found., 1951. Served with AUS, 1943-44, USAF, 1951-53. Mem. Am. Dental Assn., N.C., 4th Dist. dental socs., N.C. Soc. Anesthesiology, Pierre Fauchard Acad., Psi Omega. Elk. Home: 1835 Summit Rd Henderson NC 27536 Office: 519 S Chestnut St Henderson NC 27536

HUNT, JOSEPH VICTOR, cons. pub. adminstrn.; b. Phila., July 21, 1905; s. James Francis and Alice (Malone) H.; B.S., St. Joseph's Coll., 1932, LL.D., 1969; A.M., U. Pa., 1941; LL.D., Gallaudet Coll., 1969; m. Dolores Consilia Hede, Oct. 19, 1935; children—Rosemary Dolores, Joseph Michael, Dolores, Cecilia. Asst. dir. Anthracite Industries research in operations of local govt., Schuykill and Northumberland counties, Pa., 1932-36; chmn. dept. bus. adminstrn. St. Joseph's Coll., Phila., 1936-41; sr. bus. economist OPA, Washington, 1941-42; chief div. adminstrv. mgmt. Bur. Old-Age and Survivors Ins., Social Security Bd. (now Social Security Adminstrn., Dept. of Health, Edn. and Welfare), Washington, 1942-43; asso. commr. Vocational Rehab. Adminstrn., Dept. Health, Edn. and Welfare, 1943-67, commr. Rehab. Services Adminstrn., 1967-69, dep. commr. Community Services Adminstrn., 1970-72; cons. pub. adminstrn., 1972—. Recipient Christophers Nat. award, 1953; Superior Service award, Dept. Health, Edn. and Welfare, 1958, Distinguished Service award, 1961; Pres.'s award Nat. Rehab. Assn., 1966, Nat. award Goodwill Industries Am., 1968; named Washington Alumnus of Year, St. Joseph's Coll., 1962. Mem. Am. Assn. Workers for Blind, Internat. Soc. Rehab. of Disabled, Nat. Rehab. Assn., Am. Pub. Welfare Assn., John Carroll Soc., Nat. Soc. Sci. Honor Soc., Pi Gamma Mu. Roman Catholic. Club: Nat. Press (Washington). Home and office: 109 N George Mason Dr Arlington VA 22203

HUNT, J(ULIAN) COURTENAY, artist; b. Jacksonville, Fla., Sept. 17, 1917; s. Julian Schley and Ruth Rosalind (Loftin) H.; student Ringling Sch. Art, 1946-47, Farnsworth Sch. Art, 1948-52. Artist, 1950—; tchr. pvt. classes painting, 1950—; exhibited in one-man shows at Cummer Gallery of Art, Jacksonville, 1963—, Flair Gallery, Palm Beach, Fla., 1970-71; exhibited in group shows at Palm Beach Art Gallery, Soc. Fine Arts, Palm Beach, 1968-69, Audubon Artists of Am., N.Y.C., Allied Artists Am., N.Y.C., 1952-56, Atlanta High Mus., 1950-54, St. Augustine (Fla.) Art Assn., 1970-73, Sarasota (Fla.) Art Assn., 1952-56; portraits in permanent collections U. Fla., Gainesville, Jacksonville U., City Hall of Jacksonville, Duval County Circuit Ct., Jacksonville. Served with USAAF, 1942-46; ETO. Address: PO Box 247 Orange Park FL 32073

HUNT, RUSSELL FRANK, lawyer, banker; b. Wagoner, Okla., Apr. 27, 1909; s. W.T. and Martha (Rose) H.; student U. Okla., 1928-29; LL.B., Cumberland U., 1931; m. Margaret Kerr, Mar. 30, 1932; 1 son, Russell Kerr. Admitted to Okla. bar, 1931, since practiced in Tulsa; v.p. First Nat. Bank & Trust Co. of Tulsa, 1950-55, exec. v.p., 1955-66, vice chmn., 1966—; dir. Am. Gen. Life Ins. Co. Okla. Chmn. Okla. Ordnance Works Authority; mem. Tulsa Urban Renewal Authority. Bd. Dirs. Tulsa Community Chest. Mem. Tulsa C. of C. (past pres., dir.), Res. City Bankers Assn., Am., Okla. bar assns. Mason (32 deg., Shriner). Clubs: Southern Hills (past pres., dir.), Tulsa (past dir.) (Tulsa). Home: 2916 S Yorktown St Tulsa OK 74114 Office: Box 1 Tulsa OK 74102

HUNT, THOMAS WEBB, music educator; b. Mammoth Spring, Ark., Sept. 28, 1929; s. Thomas Hubert and Ethel (Webb) H.; B.Mus., Ouachita Bapt. U., 1950; student Julliard Sch. Music, 1946, Memphis State U., 1950; M. Mus., N. Tex. State U., 1957, Ph.D., 1967; m. Martha Laverne Hill, July 22, 1951; 1 dau., Melana Claire. Tchr., Osceola (Ark.) High Sch., 1950-52, 54-56; choral dir. First Bapt. Ch., 1954-56; fellow N. Tex. State U., 1957-60; organist First Bapt. Ch., Denton, Tex., 1957-61; mem. faculty Okla. Coll. for Women, 1961-63; organist First Bapt. Ch., Chickasha, Okla., 1962-63; faculty Southwestern Bapt. Theol. Sem., 1963—; faculty Spanish Bapt. Sem., Barcelona, Spain, 1969-70; organist Gambrell St. Bapt. Ch., 1963-67; dir. Ft. Worth Euterpean Piano Quartets, 1966-68; concerts and lectures, U.S., Europe, Orient, S.Am. Dir. Orient-wide Conf. on Music Missions, 1973. Served with AUS, 1952-54. Mem. Nat. Guild of Piano Tchrs., Am. Coll. Musicians, Soc. for Ethnomusicology, Hymn Soc. Am., Ft. Worth League Composers, So. Bapt. Ch. Music Conf., Phi Mu Alpha, Pi Kappa Lambda, Alpha Chi. Author music: Gentle Guide, 1961; Voluntary on Old Hundredth, 1963; Tonal Materials in the Organ Works of Messiaen, 1957; The Dictionaire de musique of Jean-Jacques Rousseau, 1967; A Canticle of God's Love, 1973; Salvationist, 1973; Communicative Method in Musical Evangelism, 1973; also articles in field. Home: 3617 Walton St Fort Worth TX 76133

HUNT, WILLIAM FREDERICK, JR., statistician; b. Montclair, N.J., Aug. 22, 1943; s. William Frederick and Elizabeth Catherine (Bridge) H.; B.A. cum laude (N.J. State scholar), Rutgers U., 1966, M.S., 1968; postgrad. Pa. State U., 1972; m. Janice E. Warsley, May 27, 1967; children—William Frederick III. Teaching asst. Rutgers U., New Brunswick, N.J., 1966-67; supervisory math. statistician Environmental Protection Agy., Research Triangle Park, N.C., 1970—. Co-dir. H&R Assos., Research Triangle Park, 1973—. Bd. dirs. Bluestone Homeowners Assn., 1973—. Served to lt. USPHS, 1968-70. Me. Am. Statis. Assn., Air Pollution Control Assn., Phi Beta Kappa, Sigma Xi. Home: 5832 Sandstone Dr Durham NC 27707 Office: EPA/OAQPS Research Triangle Park NC 27711

HUNTER, ARVEL HATCH, ednl. adminstr.; b. Rigby, Ida., Dec. 19, 1921; s. Franklin Walker and Hannah (Hatch) H.; B.S., Brigham Young U., 1954; M.S., Ohio State U., 1955; Ph.D., N.C. State U., 1959; m. Genevieve Webb, July 21, 1950; children—Alen, Lynda (Mrs. C. Leslie Smith), Marsha (Mrs. Douglas Palessas), Carl. Asst. prof. N.C. State U. at Raleigh, 1958-60, dir. Control Lab., 1967—; research asso. Wash. State U. at Prosser, 1960-61; regional agronomist Cal. Chem. Co., Portland, 1961-64. Owner Custom Lab. Equipment Co., Raleigh, 1969—; bd. dirs. Agrl. Environmental Systems, Inc., Raleigh, 1973—. Served with AUS, 1943-46. Mem. Am. Soc. Agronomy, Am. Hort. Soc. Home: 5000 Northglen Dr Raleigh NC 27609

HUNTER, CHARLES EDWIN, mfrs. rep.; b. Oklahoma City, Nov. 8, 1910; s. Charles Edwin and Gertrude (Buchanan) H.; diploma Christian Bros. Coll., 1931; student Memphis State U., 1932-33; m. Marguerite Catledge, May 29, 1954; children—Charles Edwin, Timothy, Kipling, Holly. Salesman Standard Coffee Co., New Orleans, 1933-35, stock clk. Orgill Bros., Memphis, 1935-36; athletic dir. Memphis Park Commn., 1936-37; adjustor Gen. Contract Purchase Corp., 1938-39, unit mgr., 1940-41; salesman Tommy Tucker Co., 1946-47; pvt. bus. as mfrs. rep., Conyers, Ga., 1947—. Served from pvt. to pfc., USMCR, 1942-45. Home: RFD 3 Box 30 McCalla Rd Conyers GA 30207 Office: PO Box 250 Conyers GA 30207

HUNTER, DEAN DWIGHT, JR., city ofcl.; b. Ft. Worth, Sept. 5, 1926; s. Dean D. and Ollie (Sears) H.; B.S., Ohio State U., 1950; M. Govtl. Adminstrn., U. Pa., 1959; m. Pauline Lane, June 15, 1957; children—Jane Ellen, Jan Caroline, Jill Marie, Dean Jon. Asst. to city mgr., Corpus Christi, Tex., 1958-59; mgr. City of Mountlake Terrace, Wash., 1959-66; city mgr., Frankfort, Ky., 1966-68; asst. chief adminstrv. officer, New Orleans, 1968—. Commr., Snohomish County Airport, 1961-66. Served to maj. USAF, 1945, 50-53; mem. Res. Presbyn. Home: 2139 Valentine Ct New Orleans LA 70114 Office: City Hall New Orleans LA 70112

HUNTER, EDWARD, editor, author, analyst; b. N.Y.C., July 2, 1902; s. Edward and Rose (Weiss) H.; self ed.; m. Tatiana Pestrikoff, June 30, 1932 (div. May 1961); children—Robert, Tate Ann. Reporter, news editor various newspapers, including New Orleans Item, N.Y. Post, N.Y. American, Phila. Bull., San Francisco Bull.; reporter Paris edit. Chgo. Tribune, 1924-25; news editor Japan Advertiser, Tokyo, 1927, editor Hankow (China) Herald, 1928-29, Peking Leader, 1929-30; covered Japanese conquest of Manchuria, Spanish Civil War, Italian conquest of Ethiopia, Internat. News Service, 1931-36; pioneered in revealing brainwashing, putting word into written language; staff cons. various govt. agys. including Senate Internal Security Subcom.; editor monthly publication Tactics, 1964—. Cons. psychol. warfare USAF, 1953-54. Served as propoganda warfare specialist AUS, with morale operations sect., OSS, Asia, World War II. Author: Brain-Washing in Red China, 1951, rev. edit., 1971; Brainwashing: The Story of Men Who Defied It, 1956, rev., retitled: Brainwashing: From Pavlov to Powers, 1960; The Story of Mary Liu, 1957; The Black Book on Red China, 1958; The Past Present: A Year in Afghanistan, 1959; In Many Voices: Our Fabulous Foreign-Language Press, 1960; Attack by Mail: A Textbook on Communist Tactics, 1964; Tactics for 1964; Tactics for 1965; Tactics for 1966; Tactics for 1967; Tactics for 1968; Tactics for 1969; Tactics for 1970; Tactics for 1971; Tactics for 1972. Contbr. articles on psychol. warfare, polit. extremism numerous mags. Clubs: Overseas Press, Silurians. Address: 4114 N 4th St Arlington VA 22203

HUNTER, GORDON COBLE, banker; b. nr. Greensboro, N.C., July 29, 1894; s. Samuel G. and Lalah Vance (Coble) H.; student U. N.C., 1915-17; m. Ethel Gray Wilson, Jan. 26, 1918; children—Rebecca Vance (Mrs. V. Paul Vittur), Rachel Gray (Mrs. George J. Cushwa). With Am. Exchange Nat. Bank, Greensboro, 1919-31; bank examiner FDIC, 1933; exec. v.p. Peoples Bank, Roxboro, N.C., 1933-57, pres., 1957—, chmn. bd., 1960—; chmn. bd. First Union Nat Bank, Roxboro; dir. Radio Sta. WRXO, Morris Telephone Co., Reinforced Plastic Container Corp., Roxboro Devel. Corp. Treas. Town Bd. of Roxboro, 1934-60. Person County chmn. A.R.C., 1937-38, U.S.O Drive, 1943-44; N.C. chmn. Nat. Found. 4-H Club, 1955-57; an organizer, bd. dirs. Person County Meml. Hosp.; mem. N.C. Correction and Tng. Bd., 1943-47, N.C. Merit System Bd., 1948-51, N.C. Bd. Conservation and Devel., N.C. Forestry Adv. Com. Served to 2d lt. inf. U.S. Army, 1917-18. Named Citizen of Year, Person County, 1956; recipient citation for 25 yr. devoted service Nat. Found.; Certificate of Appreciation in recognition 25 yrs. leadership for sales U.S. Savs. Bonds, U.S. Dept. Treasury. Mem. Am. (nat. research council 1955-57, exec. com. 1946-49, regional v.p. 1958-60, N.C. legislation com. 1960-62), N.C. (pres. 1945-46) bankers assns., Roxboro C. of C. (1st pres. 1935), Am. Legion (past comdr. Lester Blackwell post), 40 and 8, Order Long Leaf Pine. Methodist (steward). Rotarian (past pres. Roxboro). Home: 115 Academy St Roxboro NC 27573 Office: 203 N Main St Roxboro NC 27573

HUNTER, JAMES ALSTON, physician; b. Ross, Tex., Nov. 20, 1915; s. James Alston and Ellanor (Kirkpatrick) H.; A.B., Baylor U., 1936; M.D., U. Tex., 1940; m. Lucy Elizabeth Eaton, July 23, 1939; children—Andrea Alston (Mrs. Ronald D. Strong), Kirk Patrick, James Eaton, Lucy Ann; m. 2d, Margaret Elizabeth Ziegert, May 20, 1966; children—Mary Margaret, William Allen. Rotating intern John Sealy Hosp., Galveston, Tex. 1940-41; surg. resident USPHS Hosp., Detroit, Wayne State U., 1947-49; med. officer Coast Guard Icebreaker Northwind, Byrd-Navy Antarctic Expdn., 1946-47; adminstr. USPHS Hosps. Vineyard Haven, Mass., Balt., Detroit, Springfield, Mo., Alaska Native Hosp., Anchorage, 1950-62; sr. med. officer Coast Guard Tng. Center, Cape May, N.J., 1962-67; ret., 1967; staff psychiatrist Rusk (Tex.) State Hosp., 1967—, also dir. maximum security unit. Mem. devel. council Baylor U. Fellow Royal Soc. Health (Eng.); mem. Am. Coll. Hosp. Adminstrs. A.A.A.S., Assn. Mil. Surgeons, A.M.A., Tex. Med. Assn., Cherokee County Med. Soc. (pres. 1972), Alpha Epsilon Delta, Nu Sigma Nu. Democrat. Disciple of Christ. Rotarian, Mason. Home: 108 S Main St Rusk TX 75785 Office: Rusk State Hosp Rusk TX 75785

HUNTER, JAMES CHARLES, oil co. exec.; b. Kansas City, Mo., Jan. 28, 1931; s. James Madison and Zelma Allene (Jefferson) H.; B.A., William Jewell Coll., 1952; postgrad. U. Mo., 1957-61 Region advt. rep. Cities Service Oil Co., Kansas City, Mo., 1955-61, div. advt. and promotion mgr., 1962-64, marketing pub. relations mgr., Tulsa, 1964-67, asst. mgr. pub. relations, 1967-69, program mgr. pub. relations, 1969-72; mgr. pub. relations Southeast, Cities Service Co., Atlanta, 1972—. Lectr., Am. Mgmt. Assn., N.Y.C., 1970, Chgo., 1971; mem. pub. relations adv. com. Fla. Phosphate Council, 1972; mem. communications com. Fertilizer Inst., 1972, Am. Mining Congress. Mem. exec. com., bd. dirs. Goodwill Industries Atlanta. Bd. govs. William Jewell Coll. Alumni Assn. Served with AUS, 1952-54. Mem. Kansas City (Mo.) Advt. Roundtable, Assn. Petroleum Writers, Pub. Relations Soc. Am., Am. Petroleum Inst. (So. region adv. com. on pub. relations), Atlanta C. of C., Lambda Chi Alpha, Pi Kappa Delta. Methodist. Club: Atlanta Press. Home: 111 Adrian Pl Cross Creek Pkwy NW Atlanta GA 30327 Office: 3445 Peachtree Rd NE Atlanta GA 30327

HUNTER, JEHU CALLIS, biologist; b. Washington, Mar. 11, 1922; s. Jehu Louis and Alice (Callis) H.; B.S. cum laude, Howard U., 1943; m. Frances Henrietta Simons, Aug. 16, 1966; children—Joyce Alessandra (Mrs. Harry Stanton, Jr.), Maria Alice, Roberto Jehu (by previous marriage). Grad. asst. zoology Howard U., 1947-48; research technician Nat. Cancer Inst., NIH, Bethesda, Md., 1949-51, biologist, 1953-62, research biologist, 1962-65, sci. adminstr. Nat. Inst. Child Health and Human Devel., 1965-69, asst. dir. for planning, 1969—. Served with AUS, 1943-47, 51-52. Decorated Bronze Star. Travel grantee to Attend 8th Internat. Cancer Congress, 1962. Mem. Am. Soc. for Cell Biology, A.A.A.S., Royal Soc. Medicine, Soc. Developmental Biology. Contbr. articles to profl. jours. Research in cell physiology. Home: 7822 16th St NW Washington DC 20012 Office: NIH Bethesda MD 20014

HUNTER, JOHNNIE PEARL DE BRUCE (MRS. NATHAN HUNTER), librarian; b. Enterprise, Miss., Jan. 30, 1910; d. John Henry and Susie (Thomas) DeBruce; B.S. in Elementary Edn., Jackson State Coll., 1958; postgrad. (Nat. Def. Edn. Act advanced librarianship scholar) U. Ariz., 1966, U. So. Miss., 1968-69; m. Nathan Hunter, Apr. 9, 1939; children—Nathan, Martha (Mrs. Alfred Ross), Mary E., Carrie P. Tchr., Enterprise pub. schs., 1937-39, 49-60; librarian Central High Sch., Enterprise, 1960-70; elementary librarian Enterprise West Campus, 1970-71; jr. high librarian Enterprise East Campus, 1971-74. Cub pack den mother Choctaw Area council Boy Scouts Am., 1970-71, troop leader Girl Scouts Am., 1969-74. Democratic primary election clk. Enterprise precinct, 1971. Named Mother of Year Jackson State Coll. Alumni Assn., 1972. Mem. Miss., Southeastern library assns., N.E.A., Miss. Tchrs. Assn., Clarke County Tchrs. Assn. (sec. 1974). Baptist (ch. financial sec. 1962-74, Sunday sch. tchr. 1960-74). Home: PO Box 97 Enterprise MS 39330 Office: Enterprise East Campus Library Enterprise MS 39330

HUNTER, MARJORIE ROSE, newspaper corr.; b. Bethany, W.Va., June 2, 1922; d. Joshua Allen and Minnie (Gilliland) Hunter; A.B., Elon Coll., 1942. Reporter News and Observer, Raleigh, N.C. 1942-48, Houston Press, 1949; reporter, polit. corr. Winston-Salem (N.C.) Jour., 1950-61; mem. Washington bur. N.Y. Times, 1961—. Mem. N.C. Soc., Washington Press Club, White House Corrs. Assn. Corcoran Gallery Art, Episcopalian. Home: 3517 R St NW Washington DC 20007 Office: 1920 L St Washington DC 20036

HUNTER, MARY JANE BURNS (MRS. JOSEPH LAWTON HUNTER), journalist; b. Atlanta, Oct. 31, 1919; d. Cecil Olney and Mary (Cheves) Burns; student U. Ga., 1935-36, High Mus. Sch. Art, Atlanta, 1937; m. Joseph Lawton Hunter, Oct. 8, 1944; children—Mollie, Ellen. Landscape designer, horticulturist, Fort Lauderdale, Fla., 1960-65, Freeport, Grand Bahama I., 1965-66; writer, garden columns Freeport News, 1966-68, mem. editorial staff, 1968-70, editor weekly entertainment supplement, 1968-70; women's editor Cape Coral (Fla.) Breeze, 1970—. Corr. various travel publs., Bahamas, 1969—. Recipient 2d Pl. Feature Writing award Weekly div. Better Newspaper Contest, Fla. Press Assn., 1970, 2d Pl. Womens News award, 1972, State Media award community service Fla. Easter Seal Soc., 1972. Mem. Internat. Platform Assn., Ft. Myers Soc. Symphony Women. Contbr. articles to publs. Office: The Breeze PO Box 846 Cape Coral FL 33904

HUNTER, ORA ANDERSON (MRS. STILL HUNTER), educator; b. Bay Springs, Miss., Aug. 4, 1905; d. Sidney Hugh and Sue (Daniel) Anderson; B.A., U. Ala., 1925, M.A., 1957, advanced profl. diploma, 1961; postgrad. Columbia, 1926; m. Still Hunter, Aug. 25, 1929 (dec. 1952); children—Mary Elizabeth (Mrs. Thomas Hartley Murray), Still. Chmn. English dept. Carbon Hill (Ala.) High Sch., 1927-30; chmn. social studies dept. Walker County High Sch., Jasper, Ala., 1945—, guidance counselor, 1951—; instr. English lit. and composition Walker Jr. Coll. Counselor freshmen, U. Ala., Tuscaloosa, summer 1959. Pres., P.T.A., Jasper, 1943-45, Thursday Study Club, Jasper, 1937-38; chmn. family finance Ala. Fedn. Women's Clubs, 1938. Named Woman of Month, Mountain Eagle, 1953, Tchr. of Year of Walker County. Mem. Nat., Ala. edn. assns., Assn. Classroom Tchrs., Am. Personnel and Guidance Assn. (asso.), Nat. Vocational Guidance Assn. (asso.), U. Ala. Guidance Inst., Walker County Tchrs. Assn. (pres. 1964-65), D.A.R. (regent chpt. 1954-58), Phi Beta Kappa, Kappa Delta Pi, Delta Kappa Gamma (treas. Jasper 1957-58). Democrat. Baptist. Mem. Order Eastern Star (worthy matron Jasper 1944). Home: 1403 3d Av Jasper AL 35501 Office: Walker County High Sch Highland Av Jasper AL 35501

HUNTER, RICHARD EDMUND, plant pathologist; b. Jersey City, Jan. 26, 1923; s. Frederick William and Margaret (Dahlgren) H.; B.S., Rutgers, 1949; M.S., Okla. State U., 1951, Ph.D., 1968; m. Edith Earline Clark, June 2, 1946; children—Catherine (Mrs. John Bennett Hays), Margaret Ann (Mrs. Frank Quintana), Richard Clark. Asst. in biology N.M. State U., State College, 1951-55; instr., research plant pathologist Okla. State U., Stillwater, 1958-68, asst. prof., 1968-71, asso. prof., 1971-72; research plant pathologist Nat. Cotton Pathology Research Lab., College Station, Tex., 1972—. Chmn. photography com. Cotton Disease Council, 1965—. Served to capt. USAAF, 1943-46. Mem. Am. Phytopath. Soc., Alpha Zeta, Phi Sigma, Sigma Xi. Presbyn. (deacon 1951-54, 66-69). Contbr. articles to various jours. Home: 3410 Spring Lane Bryan TX 77801 Office: Nat Cotton Pathology Research Lab PO Drawer JF College Station TX 77840

HUNTER, RUBY SUE (MRS. CHARLES FORCE HUNTER), cons.; b. Hico, Tex., Aug. 21, 1921; d. David Henry and Beulah (Boatwright) Persons; B.A., U. Tex., 1942; m. Charles Force Hunter; children—Shelley (Mrs. Roy Rudolph Richardson), Mary (Mrs. Jack McMasters Stone), Margaret. Air traffic controller CAA (now FAA), San Antonio and Houston, 1942-52; writer Bissonet Plaza News, 1969-72; coordinator Goals for La., 1971-74; adminstrv. dir. Jeff Publs., Inc., 1974—. Pres. United Ch. Women East Jefferson (La.), 1958-59, League Women Voters Jefferson Parish, La., 1961-64; pres. League Women Voters La., 1967-71, also bd. dirs., 1962-67; mem. probation services com. Community Services Council, Jefferson, 1966-73, v.p., 1970-72; mem. Library Devel. Com. La., 1967-71, Nat. Com. for Support of Pub. Schs., 1967-72; mem. Goals Found. Council Met. New Orleans, 1969—, sec. 1970, 72; mem. Goals La. Task Force State and Local Govt., 1969-70; pres. MMM Investment Club, 1969-72; bd. mem. New Orleans Area Health Planning Council,

1969—; adv. council La. State Health Planning, 1971—, La. Commn. Status of Women, 1971-72, La. Consumer Council, 1971-72; mem. La. Citizens Ednl. Found. Criminal Justice, 1973—, Council Internat. Visitors, 1972—; title I adv. council La. State Dept. Edn., 1970-72. Recipient Outstanding Citizens award Rotary Club, Metairie, La., 1962. Mem. New Orleans Panhellenic (pres. 1956-57), Lamar Soc., La. Civil Service League, Alpha Xi Delta. Presbyn. (elder). Home: 210 Stewart Av River Ridge LA 70123

HUNTON, RICHARD EDWIN, physician; b. Boonville, Ind., Dec. 23, 1924; s. Edwin Chandler and Nellie Celicia (Wright) H.; A.A., George Washington U., 1947, A.B., 1949, M.D., 1952; m. Agnes Katherine Setser, Aug. 22, 1953; children—Jennifer Leigh, Richard Edwin. Instrument maker U.S. Naval Obs., Washington, 1942-44; intern Gallinger Municipal Hosp., Washington, 1952-53; resident Spartanburg (S.C.) Gen. Hosp., 1953-54; practice gen. medicine ltd. to women, Scurry Clinic, Greenwood, S.C., 1954—; mem. staff Self Meml. Hosp., Greenwood. Mem. allied health adv. com. Piedmont Tech. Coll. Bd. dirs. Greenwood County Mental Health Assn., Greenwood County chpt. A.R.C., Greenwood County Tb Assn.; trustee Faith Home Alcoholic Rehab. Center. Served with AUS, 1944-45. Decorated Purple Heart. Fellow Am. Acad. Family Practice; mem. Am., S.C. med. assns., Nat. Rehab. Assn., D.A.V., 95th Inf. Div. Assn., Nat. Rifle Assn., Phi Beta Kappa, Phi Eta Sigma. Baptist. Club: Christian Business Men's Committee. Author: Formula for Fitness, 1966. Home: 112 Wendover Rd Greenwood SC 29646 Office: Scurry Clinic Greenwood SC 29646

HUPP, EUGENE WESLEY, educator; b. Bloomfield, Neb., Feb. 23, 1933; s. William S. and Alice (Josiassen) H.; student Norfolk Jr. Coll., 1950-51; B.S., U. Neb., 1954, M.S. 1956; Ph.D., Mich. State U., 1958; m. Phyllis Glover, June 22, 1957; children—Stephen, Michael, Alice. NSF predoctoral fellow Mich. State U., East Lansing, 1956-57, grad. research asst., 1957-58; asst. scientist Agrl. Research Lab., Oak Ridge, Tenn., 1958-60, asso. scientist, 1960-62; asso. prof. Tex. A. and M. U., College Station, 1962-65; asso. prof. biology Tex. Woman's U., Denton, 1965-69; prof., 1969—. Served with USNR, 1953-55. Fellow Tex. Acad. Sci.; mem. Radiation Research Soc., Soc. for Study Reprodn., Am. Soc. Animal Sci., Am. Soc. for Lab. Animal Sci. Home: 909 Edgewood PL Denton TX 76201

HURD, PAUL D(AVID), JR., museum curator; b. Chgo., Apr. 2, 1921; s. Paul David and Ruth Dorathea (Bick) H.; B.S., U. Cal. at Berkeley, 1947, M.S., 1948, Ph.D., 1950; m. Grace Isabelle Beak, May 10, 1953; children—Kathryn Lee, Rodney Wayne, Philip James. With U. Cal. at Berkeley, 1948-70, lectr. entomology, 1954-65, prof., 1965-70, entomologist, 1965-70; curator dept. entomology Smithsonian Instn., Washington, 1970—, chmn., 1971—. Asso. program dir. NSF, 1967-68, cons., 1968-73. Served with USNR, 1942-45. John Simon Guggenheim Meml. fellow, 1959-60, Fulbright research scholar, 1959-60; Arctic Inst. N.Am. grantee, 1956-58, NSF grantee, 1960—. Fellow Cal. Acad. Scis.; mem. A.A.A.S., Am. Entomol. Soc., Am. Soc. Zoologists, Arctic Inst. N. Am., Assn. Tropical Biology (pres. 1969-70), Bee Research Assn., Biol. Soc. Washington, Biosystematists (sec. 1960-67), Cooper Ornithol. Soc., Entomol. Soc. Am. (mem. governing bd. 1972—), Entomol. Soc. Washington, Kan. Entomol. Soc., Internat. Assn. Plant Taxonomists, Pacific Coast Entomol. Soc. (editor 1952-63), Soc. Systematic Zoology, Washington Biologists Field Club, Western Soc. Naturalists, Sigma Xi. Club: Cosmos (Washington). Author: A Classification of the Large Carpenter Bees, 1963. Editor Pan-Pacific Entomologist, 1950-63. Home: 3410 Stoneybrae Dr Falls Church VA 22044 Office: Dept Entomology Smithsonian Institution Washington DC 20560

HURLBERT, RAYMOND DONALD, ednl. television exec.; b. Pitts., Mar. 21, 1902; s. Ernest Sanford and Alice Lillian (Jenkins) H.; A.B., Birmingham So. Coll., 1924, M.A., 1936; m. Rachel Bell, Apr. 1, 1925 (dec. Mar. 1939); m. 2d, Wynelle Una Reeves, Aug. 20, 1941; children—Raymond Donald, Marion Patricia, Ramona Wynelle. High sch. tchr., Birmingham, Ala., 1924-30; elementary sch. prin., Birmingham, 1930-55; gen. mgr. Ala. Ednl. TV Commn., Birmingham, 1953-73; cons. R.P.I. Cons. Services, 1973—. Pres. Birmingham area council Boy Scouts Am., 1948-49. Mem. Nat. Assn. Ednl. TV (pres. 1968), Nat. Assn. Ednl. Broadcasters TV (chmn. bd. 1962-63), Ala. Edn. Assn. (pres. 1948), Ala. Battleship Commn. (exec. com. 1963-70), Ala. Ednl. TV Commn. (pres. 1953-55), Birmingham Area Crepe Myrtle Assn. (pres. 1960), Kappa Phi Kappa, Alpha Tau Omega, Omicron Delta Kappa. Rotarian (dist. gov. 1962). Contbr. articles to profl. jours. Home: 1853 Southwood Rd Birmingham AL 35216 Office: 110 Office Park Dr Birmingham AL 35223

HURLBURT, HARVEY ZEH, chem. engr.; b. Kellogg, Ida., Sept. 2, 1921; s. Harvey Seymour and Vera (Zeh) H.; B.A., U. Tex., 1942, B.S., 1943, M.S. (Standard Oil Cal.) 1948; Sc.D., Mass. Inst. Tech., 1950; m. Gertrude Mildred Lepick, May 7, 1943; children—Geoffrey, Victoria (Mrs. Sidney H. Stevens), Veronica, Susan (Mrs. James R. Bruton, Jr.), Barbara, Claudia, Tobias, Octavia. Process engr. U.S. Rubber Co., Institute, W.Va., 1943-47; research engr. Consol. Chem. Industries, 1950-55; mgr. Peisar Research Labs. Stauffer Chem. Co., Houston, 1955—. Registered profl. engr., Tex. Patentee processes for mfg. heavy inorganic chems. Home: 7814 Santa Elena Dr Houston TX 77017 Office: 8410 Manchester St Houston TX 77012

HURLEY, CLAY BOHANNAN, hosp. adminstr; b. Birmingham, Ala., July 25, 1931; s. John L. and Bettie (Clay) H.; B.S., Florence State Coll., 1962; m. Marion Louise Black, July 10, 1958. Adminstrv. asst. Colbert County Hosp., Sheffield, Ala., 1960-62; adminstr. Cullman (Ala.) Hosp., 1962-67; cons. Applied Mgmt. Controls Co., 1967-69; adminstr. George H. Lanier Meml. Hosp., Langdale, Ala., 1969—. Served with USNR, 1950-54. Mem. Am. Coll. Hosp. Adminstrs., Ala. Hosp. Assn., N. Ala. Hosp. Council, Beta Beta Beta, Phi Kappa Alpha. Episcopalian (trustee). Home: 1406 N 8th Av Lanett AL 36863 Office: 4800 48th St Langdale AL 36864

HURLEY, ELIZABETH ANN, educator; b. Ft. Worth, Nov. 20, 1912; d. Frank Evans and Lillie B. (Bailey) Hurley; B.S., Tex. Woman's U., 1934, M.A., 1952; postgrad. Columbia, summer 1938, U. Minn., summer 1967, (Newspaper Fund fellow) Tex. Tech. U., summer 1969. Mem. staffs Lufkin (Tex.) Daily News, 1934-41, A.P., Austin, Tex., 1941; mng. editor Marshall (Tex.) News-Messenger, 1941-45, Denton (Tex.) Record-Chronicle, 1945-49; instr. journalism Tex. Woman's U., 1951-53; tchr. journalism, adviser weekly sch. newspaper and yearbook Pampa (Tex.) High Sch., 1953—. Vice pres. Denton Record-Chronicle, 1945-49; participant, speaker various confs., publs. workshops. Recipient Gold Key award Columbia Scholastic Press Assn., 1964; named Outstanding High Sch. Journalism Tchr. Tex. Interscholastic League Press Conf., U., Tex., 1964. Edith Fox King award ILPC, 1970; Pioneer award Nat. Scholastic Press Assn., 1970. Mem. Tex. Assn. Journalism Dirs. (pres. 1963, state dir., rep. nat. assns. 1964-65), Tex. (faculty chmn. 1963, 1968, Trail blazer award 1973), West Tex. (faculty pres. 1959) high sch. press assns., Journalism Edn. Assn. (medal of merit 1969), S.W. Council Student Publs. (pres. 1970), N.E.A., Tex. State Tchrs. Assn., Tex. Classroom Tchrs. Assn., Women in Communications, Delta Kappa Gamma. Presbyn. Contbr. articles to newspapers, mags. Home: 319 N Somerville St Pampa TX 79065 Office: Pampa High School 111 E Harvester St Pampa TX 79065

HURLEY, FRANK THOMAS, JR., realtor; b. Washington, Oct. 18, 1924; s. Frank Thomas and Lucille (Trent) H.; A.A., St. Petersburg Jr. Coll., 1948; B.A., U. Fla., 1950. Reporter St. Petersburg (Fla.) Evening Independent, 1948-53; editor Arcadia (Cal.) Tribune, 1956-57; reporter Los angeles Herald Express, 1957; v.p. Frank T. Hurley Assos., Inc. Realtors, 1958-64, pres., 1964—. Mem. St. Petersburg Beach Bd. Commrs., 1965-69; candidate Fla. Ho. of Reps., 1966; chmn. Pinellas County Traffic Safety Council, 1968-69. Pres. Pass-A-Grille Community Assn., 1963, Gulf Beach Bd. Realtors, 1969; mem. St. Petersburg Museum Fine Arts. Served with USAAF, 1943-46. Mem. Fla. Assn. Realtors (dist. v.p. 1971), Vina del Mar Island Assn., Am. Legion, Sigma Delta Chi, Sigma Tau Delta. Home: 2808 Sunset Way St Petersburg Beach FL 33706 Office: 2506 Pass-A-Grille Way St Petersburg Beach FL 33706

HURLEY, JAMES FRANKLIN, III, newspaper editor, publisher; b. Salisbury, N.C., July 22, 1931; B.A. in Journalism, U. N.C., 1953; postgrad. Am. Press Inst., Columbia U., 1962, 66; m. Frances Geraldine Trammell, June 11, 1958. Reporter, Salisbury (N.C.) Post, 1955-62, editor, 1962—; pub. Cooleemee Jour.; pres. Davie County Pub. Co., Holmes Investment Co., Salisbury, Post Pub. Co., Salisbury; dir. Western N.C. Pub. Co., Lincolnton, Wachovia Bank & Trust Co., Salisbury. Bd. dirs. United Fund, YMCA; chmn. Lincoln Park Swimming Pool Drive, 1963, Rowan County Morehead Scholarship Selection Com., 1966—. Served with 3d Inf. Div., AUS, 1953-55. Named Young Man of Year, Jr. C. of C., 1962; editorial writing 1st prize N.C. Press Assn. newswriting competition, 1960-62, 67, Sports 1st prize, 1962. Mem. N.C. Assn. Afternoon Newspapers (pres. 1966), Salisbury-Rowan C. of C. (pres. 1962), Am. Legion, Salisbury-Rowan Mchts. Assn. (bd. dirs.), Phi Beta Kappa, Zeta Psi. Democrat. Presbyn. (chmn. bd. deacons). Elk. Club: Salisbury Country (dir.). Home: 219 W Corriher Av Salisbury NC 28144 Office: Salisbury Evening Post W Innes St Salisbury NC 28144

HURLEY, ROY SAMUEL, oil field service co. exec; b. Minden, La., Feb. 5, 1924; s. Louis Samuel and Eula (Petrey) H.; B.S., La. Tech. U., 1949; student U. Tex. at Austin, 1949; m. Dean English, Dec. 21, 1947; children—Rebecca, Nancy, C.P.A., partner acctg. firm Herring & Hurley, Shreveport, La. 1949-57; v.p. Tri-State Oil Tool Industries, Inc., Bossier City, La., 1957-62, pres., 1962—, dir., 1962—; dir. Bossier Bank & Trust Co., Bossier City, La. Served with AUS, 1943-46. Mem. Shreveport C. of C., Shreveport Petroleum club, La. Tech. Alumni Found. (pres. 1971-72), Bossier City C. of C. (dir. 1970-72), Petroleum Equipment Suppliers Assn. (dir. 1969—), La. Soc. C.P.A.'s. Methodist. Clubs: Rotary, East Ridge Country (pres. 1964, Shreveport, La.). Home: 341 Corinne Circle Shreveport LA 71106 Office: PO Box 5757 Bossier City LA 71010

HURLOCK, CHARLES HAYNES, JR., realtor; b. Houston, Dec. 4, 1911; s. Charles Haynes and Lillie Otis (McGaffey) H.; student U. Tex., 1929-31, U. Houston, 1931-32; m. Bettie Mae Herring, Mar. 11, 1939; 1 dau., Bettie Driscoll (Mrs. Gordon Conger Hale). Mgr. rental dept. Union Central Life Ins. Co., Houston, 1933; fee appraiser HOLC, Houston, 1933-35; staff valuator FHA, Houston, 1935-37; pres. Hurlock Realty Corp., Houston, 1937-63; owner Hurlock Co., Realtors, Houston, 1963—; founding dir. Spring Branch Bank, Houston, 1953. Co-founder Houston Housing Devel. Corp., 1968, treas., 1969; co-founder Charles Hurlock, Sr. Ednl. Found., 1963. Mem. Houston Zoning Commn., 1962. Bd. dirs. Houston Lighthouse for Blind, 1954-68, 73—. Named Realtor of Yr., Houston Bd. Realtors, 1964. Mem. Soc. Real Estate Appraisers (chpt. pres. 1959), Nat. Assn. Realtors (mem. realtors Washington com. 1964-69), Tex. Assn. Realtors (dir. 1962-66). Home: 1003 S Ripple Creek Dr Houston TX 77027 Office: Appraisers Bldg 3633 Allen Pkwy Houston TX 77019

HURSEY, RUDOLPH JULIAN, dentist; b. Lakeland, Fla., July 31, 1927; s. Rudolph Julian and Margaret Francis (Griggs) H.; B.S., Wofford Coll., 1950; D.D.S., Georgetown U., 1954; m. Jean Moore, June 24, 1948; children—Mary (Mrs. James Edwin Stanton), Susan Melinda, Laura Jean. Dental intern Childrens Hosp., Washington, 1954-55; practice dentistry specializing in pedodontics, Spartanburg, S.C., 1955—. Mem. Mayor's Adv. Council, Spartanburg, S.C., 1968—; mem. Broad River Tb. Assn., 1967—. Served with USNR, 1945-47. Mem. Am. Dental Assn., S.C., Piedmont Dist., Spartanburg County (pres. 1958) dental socs., Southeastern Soc. Pedodontics (sec. 1971, pres. elect 1973), S.C. Soc. Dentistry for Children (pres. 1963), S.C. Assn. Pedodontists (pres. 1969-71), Sertoma Club, Delta Sigma Delta. Methodist (financial sec. adminstrv. bd. 1967). Club: Spartanburg Country. Home: 1310 Pinecrest Rd Spartanburg SC 29302 Office: 444 Kennedy St Spartanburg SC 29302

HURST, FANNIE MAE FANT (MRS. JOHN H. HURST), biologist, educator; b. Waco, Tex.; d. Bennett B. and Fannie (Green) Fant; B.A. cum laude, Baylor U., 1948, M.A. with honors, 1950; Ph.D., Purdue U., 1955; postgrad. (NSF fellow) U. Okla. History Sci. Inst., 1961; m. John H. Hurst, June 8, 1932; 1 dau., Pauline Carol (Mrs. Allen Clark Cullens). Instr. biology Baylor U., Waco, Tex., 1948-49, 52-53, asst. prof., 1953-59, asso. prof., 1959-68, prof., 1968—, dir. herbarium, 1973—; instr. Purdue U., Lafayette, Ind., 1949-52. Vis. scientist Tex. Acad. Sci., 1963—; counselor Tex. Jr. Acad. Sci., 1964—. Past dir., past mem. edn. com. McLennan County chpt. Am. Cancer Soc. Fellow Tex. Acad. Sci.; mem. A.A.A.S., Bot. Soc. Am., Internat. Assn. Plant Taxonomists, Internat. Soc. Plant Morphologists, Nat. Assn. Biology Tchrs. (coll. membership chmn. for Tex.), North Tex. Biol. Soc. (v.p. 1959-60, pres. 1968-69), Southwestern Assn. Naturalists, Am. Assn. U. Profs., Am. Inst. Biol. Scis., Am. Assn. U. Women (higher edn. com. Waco br. 1960-63), Ft. House Soc. Historic Preservation, Sigma Xi (sec. Baylor club), Alpha Chi, Beta Beta Beta, Sigma Delta Epsilon. Democrat. book revs. to Bios. Research on endodermis of smilax, nutritional studies of aspergillus, phylogeny of liliales. Home: 400 Rice Av Waco TX 76708

HURST, THOMAS CHARLES III, transp. co. exec.; b. Norfolk, Va., June 17, 1920; s. Thomas Charles and Eliza (Toler) H.; B.E.E., U.S. Naval Acad., 1942; summer student Oxford U., 1964; Am. U., 1968-69; m. Nancy Gifford Owen, Dec. 25, 1947; children—Terry Lee (Mrs. Homer Howard Haisten III), Leigh Gifford. Commd. ensign, U.S. Navy, 1942, advanced through grade to capt., 1962, submarine comdr., 1952-55, internat. relations, 1962-65, adv. U.S. State Dept. in Nuclear Warfare, 1966-69; ret., 1970; sr. v.p., dir. Norfolk Baltimore & Carolina Lines, Norfolk, Va., 1970—; cons. engr. Active Boy Scouts Am. Asso. fellow Am. Inst. Aeronautics and Astronautics, Traffic Club. Club: Propeller. Home: 2840 N Kings Rd Virginia Beach VA 23452 Office: 937 Water St Norfolk VA 23510

HURT, FRANK BENJAMIN, educator; b. Ferrum, Va., Oct. 22, 1899; s. John Kempleton and Lelia (Angle) H.; A.B., Washington and Lee U., 1923; M.A., U. Va., 1925; A.M. Princeton, 1926; grad. study Johns Hopkins, 1929-30; additional study Harvard, summers 1938-40; m. Mary Ann Wescott, June 3, 1943. Teaching fellow, University N.C., 1926-27; Instr., Ferrum Jr. Coll., 1927-29; asso. prof. polit. sci., Western Md. Coll., 1930-65, prof. emeritus, 1965—, head div. polit. sci., 1949; head div. social sci. Ferrum (Va.) Jr. Coll., 1965—, prof. emeritus, 1970—; lectr. sch. spl. and continuation studies U. Md., 1950-65; instr. summers Hun Sch., Princeton, 1927-32. Dir. First Nat. Bank. Mem. Am. Polit. Sci. Assn., Am. Hist. Assn., Am. Acad. Polit. and Social Sci., Nat. Collegiate Fgn. Lang. Soc., Franklin County Hist. Soc. (pres. 1969-70), Am. Assn. U. Profs., Pi Gamma Mu. Democrat. Methodist. Lion (pres. Ferrum 1968). Address: Ferrum Jr Coll Ferrum VA 24088

HURT, HARRY, oil co. exec.; b. Dallas, Feb. 20, 1899; s. Harry Aldenhoff and Margaret (Sweet) H.; B.S., Va. Mil. Inst., 1919; postgrad. Columbia, 1920; m. Margaret Regina Bitting, June 12, 1950; children—Harry III, Margaret Dorothy, William Richard, Dorothy Margaret. Began career as trainee, The Tex. Co.; partner Callery & Hurt Co., Houston; gen. partner Hurt Oil Co., Ltd., Houston, 1952—; dir. Capital Nat. Bank of Houston. Served with USNR, World War II. Mem. Am. Petroleum Inst., Mid-Continent Oil and Gas Assn., Am. Wildcatters (charter mem.), Houston C. of C (mem. steering com. Aviation com.). Clubs: Houston Country, River Oaks, Ramada (Houston); Racquet and Tennis (N.Y.C.); Seminole (Palm Beach, Fla.) Home: 2198 Troon Rd Houston TX 77019 Office: 1510 First City Nat Bank Bldg Houston TX 77002

HURT, PAUL VICTOR, govt. ofcl.; b. Cotapaxi, Colo., Aug. 8, 1927; s. Frank Nelson and Ruth Ione (Johnson) H.; B.S., Colo. State U., 1951; M.S., N.M. State U., 1957; m. Marion Jean Williams, June 13, 1959; children—Carla, Jennifer, Peter. With Wis. Crop and Livestock Reporting Service, Madison, 1959-60; with U.S. Dept. Agr., 1960—, with Fla. Crop and Livestock Reporting Service, Orlando, Fla. 1970—. Served with USNR, 1945-46, 52-53. Mem. A.A.A.S., Biometric Soc., Orgn. Profl. Employees Dept. Agr., Alpha Zeta, Alpha Gamma Rho. Home: 3541 Baxter Dr Winter Park FL 32789 Office: 1222 Woodward Av Orlando FL 32803

HURTT, OSCAR LEE, JR., chemist; b. Cedar Bluff, Ala., Mar. 29, 1920; s. Oscar Lee and Aouda (Goodson) H.; B.S., Samford U., 1944; M.S., Birmingham-So. Coll., 1960; m. Florrie E. Thompson, Sept. 14, 1943; children—Oscar Lee III, Claude David, Betty (Mrs. Martin Locklear). Chemist, Am. Cast Iron Pipe Co., Birmingham, 1943-45; chief chemist Prodn. Foundry div. Jackson Industries, Birmingham, 1945-50, Connors Steel div. H.K. Porter Co., Inc., Birmingham, 1950—. Mem. Am. Chem. Soc. (past chmn. Ala. sect.), Am. Inst. Chemists (past chmn. Ala. chpt.), Am. Soc. Metals. Baptist. Rotarian. Club: Birmingham Coin (pres. 1950-51). Home: 405 S 85th St Birmingham AL 35206 Office: PO Box 577 Birmingham AL 35201

HUSBAND, CHARLES WILLIAM, state ofcl.; b. Reidsville, N.C., Apr. 23, 1924; s. Charles Howard and Lottie Myria (Julian) H.; grad. high sch.; m. Swanny Lillian Moody, Aug. 14, 1946; 1 son, Charles William. Clk. U.S.P.O., Franklinville, N.C., 1946-47; with Burlington Mills, Inc., Randleman, N.C., 1947-49, Cornelison Hosiery Mill, Asheboro, N.C., 1949-51, Burke Hosiery Mill, Asheboro, 1951-54; Salesman Western & So. Ins. Co., Asheboro, 1954-61; with N.C. Dept. Correction, Asheboro, 1961—, capt., 1971-72, supt. Randolph County subsidiary, 1972—. Served with USMCR, 1942-45; PTO. Home: Route 2 Box 280 Asheboro NC 27203 Office: PO Box 848 Asheboro NC 27203

HUSKETH, ALMA ORMOND (MRS. EDWARD THOMAS HUSKETH, JR.), librarian; b. Dover, N.C., Aug. 17, 1918; d. William Henry and Ella Carrie (White) Ormond; B.A. in English, Woman's Coll. U. N.C., 1939; M.S. in L.S., U. N.C. at Chapel Hill, 1966; m. Edward Thomas Husketh, Jr., June 12, 1943; children—Edward Thomas III, William Ormond, Craig Moss. Tchr., Wilton (N.C.) High Sch., 1939-44, 46-51, 57-61; tchr. Lenoir County (N.C.) Schs., 1944-46; librarian South Granville High Sch., Creedmoor, N.C., 1962—. Cons. rev. panel N.C. Emergency Sch. Assistance Program, 1971, Emergency Sch. Aid Act, 1973, 74. Mem. scholarship com. U. N.C. at Greensboro, 1969-73; Granville county dir. N.C.P.T.A., 1970-72. Bd. dirs. Richard H. Thornton Pub. Library, Oxford, N.C. Mem. N.C. Edn. Assn. (sec. East Central dist. 1965), N.C. Classroom Tchrs. Assn. (pres. Granville County unit 1951-52), N.C. High Sch. Library Assn. (dir. East Central dist. 1969—), Nat. Grange, Alpha Delta Kappa (pres. chpt. 1972-74). Methodist (Sunday sch. tchr. 1940—; dir. youth activities 1962-73; active Women's Soc. Christian Service). Home: Box 198 Brassfield Rd Creedmoor NC 27522 Office: PO Box 395 South Granville High School Creedmoor NC 27522

HUSSAIN, A.K.M. FAZLE, educator; b. Dacca, Bangladesh, Jan. 20, 1943; s. Md. Tarik and Begum (Farhat-un-Nessa) Ullah; B.Sc. Engr. (Mech.), Bangladesh U., 1963; M.S. (Fulbright fellow), Stanford, 1966, Ph.D. (August Berner Honors fellow), 1969; m. Rehana Ahmed, Nov. 10, 1968. Came to U.S., 1965, naturalized, 1971. Design engr. Nganj Dock Ltd., Bangladesh, 1960-63; lectr. dept. mech. engring. Bangladesh U., 1963-65; research asst. dept. mech. engring. Stanford, 1965-69; vis. asst. prof. dept. mechanics Johns Hopkins, 1969-71; asst. prof. mech. engring. U. Houston, 1971-73, asso. prof., 1973—, dir. Aerodynamics and Turbulence Lab., 1972—. Reviewer jours., cons. various engring. firms. Recipient Eckert prize Stanford, 1971. Research grantee NSF, 1971—, Office Naval Research, 1972—, U. Houston, 1971-72. Mem. Am. Phys. Soc., Am. Soc. M.E., Am. Soc. for Engring. Edn., Houston Engring. and Sci. Soc. Club: Woodshire Civic (Houston). Editor: Pakistan Engr., 1963-65; Procs. Inst. of Engrs., 1963-65; Bangladesh U. Ann. Jour., 1963. Contbr. articles to profl. jours. Home: 4119 Mischire St Houston TX 77025

HUSSEY, ROBERT JONES, cotton co. exec.; b. Memphis, Sept. 25, 1904; s. Clarence Wellington and Neva (Jones) H.; student Columbia Mil. Acad., 1922; LL.B., U. Ala., 1926; m. Kathleen Conant, Nov. 10, 1931; children—Robert Jones, Richard W., Edwin C. Pres., owner C.W. Hussey & Co., Memphis, 1935—; v.p. Growers Equipment Co. Pres. Memphis Cotton Exchange. Chmn. bd. trustees Presbyn. Day Sch.; trustee Memphis U. Sch., Hussey Found. Mem. Alpha Tau Omega. Presbyn. (elder). Home: 4185 Gwynne Rd Memphis TN 38103 Office: 110 S Front St Memphis TN 38103

HUSSEY, WILLIAM DAVIS, trade assn. exec.; b. Boston, July 20, 1933; s. Simeon A. and Marjorie (Rice) H.; B.S., Fla. So. Coll., 1958; student U. Fla., 1951-53; m. Elizabeth Ann Hatton, Sept. 10, 1960; children—William Davis, Jeffrey Rice. With Fla. Savs. & Loan League, Orlando, 1958—, sec., 1961—, exec. v.p., 1962—; dir. Fla. Informanagement Services, Inc., Orlando. Served with AUS, 1953-55. Mem. Fla. Soc. Assn. Execs. (pres., dir.), Savs. Assn. Trade Execs., Am. Soc. Assn. Execs., U. Fla. Alumni, Fla. State, Orlando chambers commerce, Sigma Alpha Epsilon, Pi Delta Epsilon. Clubs: University, Citrus, Tallahassee Country, Country (Orlando); Capitol Hill (Washington). Home: 1200 W Audubon Pl Orlando FL 32804 Office: 109 E Church St Orlando FL 32802 also PO Box 2246 Orlando FL 32802

HUSSMAN, WALTER E., newspaper publisher, broadcaster; b. Bland, Mo., July 20, 1906; s. Walter J. and Anna (Vaughn) H.; student U. Mo., 1929-32; m. Betty M. Palmer, Dec. 24, 1931; children—Gayle (Mrs. Richard S. Arnold), Marilyn (Mrs. James M. Augur), Walter E. With Palmer Newspapers, Camden, Ark., 1933—, mgr. bus., advt., 1947-57, asst. pub., 1947—, pres., owner 1970—;

pres. Marigayle Realty Co., Camden, 1970—; pres., controlling owner Wehco, Inc., cable TV, radio and TV stas. Mem. Ark. Judiciary Commn., 1965-67; chmn. Ark. Citizens Judicial Council, 1967-68. Served to maj. AUS, 1942-45. Recipient Gavel award, Certificate Merit, Am. Bar Assn., 1969. Mem. Ark., Camden (past pres.) chambers commerce Ark., So., Tex. Daily (past pres.) newspaper assns., Nat. Overseas press clubs, Inter-Am. Press Assn., Am., Soc. Newspaper Editors, Nat. Broadcasters Club, Am. Judicature Soc., Sigma Delta Chi, Pi Kappa Alpha. Presbyn. (trustee). Clubs: Camden Country, The Shreveport (La.), Shreveport Country. Home: 1890 Marigayle Lane Camden AR 71701 Office: 113 Madison St Camden AR 71701

HUSTED, JOHN EDWIN, educator; b. Lucasville, Ohio, Oct. 12, 1915; s. Edward Winthrop and Mary (Cary) H.; B.S., Hampden-Sydney Coll., 1939; student Va. Poly. Inst., summers 1938-40; M.A., U. Va., 1942; Ph.D., Fla. State U., 1970; m. Kathryn Fay Stewart, June 18, 1942; children—Stewart Winthrop, Mary (Mrs. Terry Michael Hewett). Teacher sci. Crewe (Va.) High Sch., 1938-40; chemist, geologist U.S. Geol. Survey, Washington, 1942-45; plant chemist Consol. Feldspar Corp., Erwin, Tenn., 1945-46; instr. geology and chemistry Washington and Lee U., 1946-48; geologist Humble Oil & Refining Co., Midland, Tex., 1948-49; chmn. geology dept. Trinity U., 1949-51; resident geologist Va. Iron, Coal & Coke Co., Roanoke, Va., 1951-55; prin. geologist Battelle Meml. Inst., 1955-57; research scientist Ga. Inst. Tech., 1958-63, head mineral engring. group, 1960-66, asso. prof. geology, 1963-67, head mineral engring. br., 1966-72, research prof. geology, 1967-71, prof. geology, 1971—; mem. Ad Hoc List of Visitors, Accreditation, Engring. Council for Profl. Devel., 1968—; dep. dir., designate Minerals Civil Def. Exec. Reserve U.S. Dept. Interior, Emergency Minerals Adminstrn., Southeastern U.S., 1969-72, dir. designate Miscellaneous Non-Metals div., 1972—. NSF Sci. Faculty fellowship, 1966-67. Fellow Geol. Soc. Am.; mem. Am. Assn. Petroleum Geologists, Am. Geophys. Union, Am. Inst. Mining, Metall. and Petroleum Engrs. (mem. nat. council dels. 1966-67), Soc. Mining Engrs. (mem. edn. com. 1965-68, 1970—), Ga. Geol. Soc. (mem. council 1961-62), Sigma Xi. Mem. editorial adv. bd., author indsl. minerals sect. Mining Engineering Handbook, 1973; mem. editorial bd. 4th edn. Industrial Minerals and Rocks. Home: 252 Mt Vernon Dr Decatur GA 30030 Office: Engring Expt Sta Ga Inst Tech Atlanta GA 30332

HUSTON, BEATRICE FAE (MRS. JOHNNIE W. HUSTON), educator; b. Granbury, Tex., Oct. 7, 1926; d. Charles Wolfton and Clara (Hembright) Moore; A.A., Weatherford Jr. Coll., 1945; B.B.A., North Tex. State U., 1947; M.A., Stephen F. Austin State U., 1952, D.Ed., Baylor U., 1967; m. Johnnie Weldon Huston, June 5, 1948; 1 son, Schulyn Medzell. Tchr. bus. Granbury (Tex.) High Sch., 1947-48, Canton (Tex.) High Sch., 1948-51; tchr. bus. and lang. arts Nacogdoches (Tex.) Jr. High Sch., 1951-52; tchr. bus. Nacogdoches (Tex.) High Sch., 1952; instr. Stephen F. Austin State U., 1952; tchr. English Belton (Tex.) Jr. High Sch., 1955; tchr. bus. and edn. Mary Hardin-Baylor Coll., 1956-72, instr., 1956-60, asst. prof., 1960-63, asso. prof., 1963-67, prof., 1967—, now chmn. dept. bus. adminstrn. and econs., distinguished prof. Treas. Belton P.T.A., 1965-66; mem. citizens adv. bd. Mary Hardin-Baylor Coll. Mem. Belton Bus. and Profl. Women's Club (rec. sec. 1958-60), Am. Assn. U. Women (v.p. 1958-60, pres. Wesleyan Service Guild 1949), Nat., Tex. bus. edn. assns., Internat. Platform Assn., Tex. Soc. Coll. Tchrs. Edn., Delta Kappa Gamma (charter pres. Eta Theta chpt. 1963-65). Mem. Order Eastern Star (worthy matron 1958). Home: 203 E 23d Av Belton TX 76513 Office: Box 414 MH-B Sta Belton TX 76513

HUSTVEDT, ERLING HALVOR, investment counselor; b. Washington, Dec. 11, 1919; s. Olaf Mandt and Irene (Cooper) H.; B.S., Mass. Inst. Tech., 1941; M.A. Tufts U., 1947; student George Washington U., 1959-64; m. Jane Elizabeth Parker, July 16, 1960; children—Eric, Elin (Mrs. Thomas Edward Bull), Scott, Dana, Nancy, Kent. Cons. indsl. engr., Portland, 1947-53, San Francisco, 1953-57; tchr. Menlo Sch., Menlo Park, Cal., 1957, St. Albans Sch., Washington, 1957-59; teaching fellow George Washington U., Washington, 1959-61; operations research analyst Nat. Bur. Standards, Washington, 1966-71; dep. dir. Federalism Seventy-Six, 1971-73; investment counselor, Washington, 1973—. Trustee Alfred D. Cooper Fund, 1966—. Served as capt. Office Chief of Naval Operations, USNR, 1942-45. Mem. Naval Res. Assn. (nat. v.p. 1965, nat. historian 1970—), Aircraft Owners and Pilots Assn., Mil. Order of Carabao, Phi Beta Epsilon. Club: Massachusetts Institute Technology (Washington). Home: 5105 Philip Rd Annandale VA 22003 Office: 824 Connecticut Av NW Washington DC 20006

HUTCHENS, JIMMIE ROGER, community agy. dir.; b. Winston-Salem, N.C., Nov. 14, 1941; s. Paul and Ruby Elizabeth (Shore) H.; A.A., Mitchell Jr. Coll., 1963; B.A., U. N.C., 1965; certificate, Johns Hopkins U. (fellow), 1969. Tchr. Iredell County Bd. Edn., Statesville, N.C., 1965-68; exec. dir. Yadkin Valley Econ. Devel. Dist., Boonville, N.C., 1969—. Pres., Yadkin Hist. Soc., 1965-72; chmn. Historic Richmond Hill Law Sch. Commn., 1970—; mem. Yadkin County Bicentennial Commn., 1972—, N.C. Vocational Edn. Council, 1973—. Precinct officer Republican party, 1965-70. Mem. Yadkin County Bd. Edn., 1971—. R.J. Reynolds econ. fellow, 1966; Found. for Econ. Edn. fellow, 1968. Mem. N.C. Community Action Assn., N.C. Folklore Soc., N.C. Lit. and Hist. Assn., N.C. Soc. Local Historians, U. N.C. at Chapel Hill Alumni Assn., Mitchell Coll. Alumni Assn. Rep. Home: Route 4 Box 269 Yadkinville NC 27055 Office: PO Box 328 River Rd Boonville NC 27011

HUTCHESON, EDWARD CHAPPELL, lawyer; b. Houston, Mar. 11, 1920; s. William Palmer and Eleanor Lee (Thomson) H.; A.B., Princeton, 1942; LL.B., S. Tex. Coll. of Law, 1949; m. Beatrice Hale Chew, July 22, 1944; children—Edward Chappell, Beatrice (Mrs. Robert J. Seymour), Joseph C. II. Admitted to Tex. bar, 1949; partner Hutcheson, Taliaferro & Hutcheson, Houston, 1949-69; individual practice law, Houston, 1969—. Pres., Julia C. Hester House, Houston, 1958-60; chmn. Houston chpt. World Neighbors, Inc., 1963; pres. Tex. Bill of Rights Found., 1964-65. Chmn. bd. dirs. Amigos de las Americas, 1973; trustee S. Tex. Coll. of Law, Houston. Served to lt. USNR, 1942-45. Mem. State Bar Tex., Am., Houston bar assns., Am. Judicature Soc., Houston Philos. Soc., Phi Delta Phi. Episcopalian. Clubs: Forest (Houston); Conanicut Yacht (Jamestown, R.I.). Author: The Freedom Tree, 1970. Home: 2521 Stanmore Dr Houston TX 77019 Office: Suite 407 2727 Kirby Dr Houston TX 77006

HUTCHESON, JAMES BYRON, physician; b. Roanoke, Va., July 17, 1922; s. James Byron and Kathleen (Marmon) H.; A.B., Emory and Henry Coll., 1943; M.D., U. Va., 1946; m. Judith Anne Baldwin, Dec. 27, 1950; children—Mary Lee, Nancy Reed, Jill Marmon, James Byron IV (dec.), Holly. Intern Med. Coll. Va., Richmond, 1946-47; resident pathologist N.Y. Hosp., 1949-52; pathologist, dir. labs. Lewis-Gale Hosp., Roanoke, 1952-55; pathologist, chief anat. pathology Baylor U. Med. Center, 1955-59; instr. pathology Cornell Med. Sch., N.Y.C., 1952-53; asso. prof. Baylor U. Grad. Research Inst., Dallas, 1955-59; asso. prof. Baylor U. Sch. Dentistry, Dallas, 1955-59; clin. asst. prof. U. Tex., Southwestern Med. Sch., Dallas, 1955-59; pathologist, chief anat. pathology Tampa Gen. Hosp., 1959—, dir. pathology, 1962—, vice chief of staff, 1968-69; dir. pathology U. Community Hosp., 1962-69; pres. Drs. Hutcheson, Ruffolo, Hooper & Assos., Tampa, 1961—, Pathol. Assos., Tampa, 1969—; clin. prof. pathology U. South Fla., 1971—. Dir. N.J. Life Ins. Co., Davis Blvd. Corp., 1st Nat. Bank, Plant City, Fla., 1963-69. Bd. dirs. Am. Cancer Soc., 1959—, pres. Hillsborough County unit, 1968-69, bd. dirs., mem. exec. com. Fla. div., 1972—. Served as lt. (j.g.) USNR, 1947-49. Research grantee Am. Cancer Soc., 1951-53, Mead Johnson Research grantee, 1962, USPHS research grantee, 1962, 67-70. Diplomate Am. Bd. Pathology. Fellow A.C.P., Coll. Am. Pathologists; mem. Am., So. med. assns., Fla., Hillsborough County med. socs., Am. Soc. Clin. Pathologists, Am. Assn. Blood Banks, Soc. Exptl. Biology and Medicine, Fla. Soc. Pathologists, Intersoc. Cytology Council, Am. Assn. Pathologists and Bacteriologists, Am. Soc. Cytology, Fla. West Coast Pathology Assn. (pres. 1968-73). Rotarian. Clubs: Torch, University, Tampa Yacht and Country, Palma Ceia Golf and Country. Contbr. articles to med. jours. Home: 3609 Beach Dr Tampa FL 33609 Office: Tampa Gen Hosp Davis Island Tampa FL 33606 also 1 Davis Blvd Davis Islands Tampa FL 33606

HUTCHESON, JOHN YOUNG, lawyer; b. Mecklenburg, Va., July 7, 1896; s. Herbert Farrar and Mary H. (Young) H.; legal edn. U. of Va., 1927; student William and Mary Coll. Admitted to Va. bar 1928, since practiced at Boydton. Mem. Am., Va. bar assns., Kappa Sigma. Address: Boydton VA 23917

HUTCHESON, THOMAS BARKSDALE, r.r. exec.; b. Gloucester, Va., Nov. 3, 1913; s. Henry Edmunds and Evelyn Byrd (Lee) H.; B.S., Va. Poly. Inst., 1935; grad. Advanced Mgmt. Program, Harvard, 1953; m. Virginia Henderson Chisolm, June 4, 1938; children—Katurah H., Virginia (Mrs. John Ritchie, Jr.). Various engring. assignments Seaboard Air Line R.R. Co., Norfolk and Richmond, Va., 1935-48, asst. chief engr., 1948-58, v.p., chief engr., 1958-67; asst. v.p. engring. and maintenance of way, chief engr. Seaboard Coast Line R.R., Jacksonville, Fla., 1967—. Served from 2d lt. to maj. AUS, 1942-45; PTO. Registered profl. engr., Va., N.C., S.C., Ga., Ala., Fla. Fellow Am. Soc. C.E. (Norfolk pres. 1956-57); mem. Am. Ry. Engring. Assn. (dir. 1962-65, pres. 1967-68), Am. Soc. Testing and Materials, Am. Wood Preserving Soc. Clubs: Commonwealth (Richmond); Ponte Vedra (Jacksonville). Home: 1825 Elizabeth Pl Jacksonville FL 32205 Office: 500 Water St Jacksonville FL 32202

HUTCHINS, CHARLES ANTHONY, social worker; b. Forrest City, N.C., Aug. 7, 1931; s. John Samuel and Carolyn (McKenzie) H.; B.A., Furman U., 1957; M.S.W., Fla. State U., 1959; post-grad. work, U. of Wash., 1968-69, Certificate community Mental Health; m. Eva Grey Martin, June 27, 1953; children—Anna Camille, Ralph Edwin, John Paul. Ednl. asst. Northside Meth. Ch., Greeneville, S.C., 1955-57; caseworker Family Service Assn., Greenville, 1957-58; caseworker Holston Methodist Children's Home, Greeneville, Tenn., 1959-61, dir. social service dept., 1961-69, dir. children's services, 1969-72, asso. exec. dir., 1972-73; acting exec. dir. Nolachuckey-Holston Area Community Mental Health Center, Greeneville, 1972-73; asst. to exec. dir. Epworth Children's Home, Columbia, S.C., 1973—; v.p. Tenn. Conf. of Social Workers, 1963—; cons. social work. Chmn. personnel com. Cherokee Guidance Center; chmn. edn. com. S.C. Mental Health Assn.; del. gen. conf. United Meth. Ch., 1968, 70, 72, del. Southeast jurisdiction conf., 1964, 68, 72, lay work S.C. conf. Alderman, City of Greenville, Tenn., 1964-66; Election commr. Greene County, 1968-73. Served with AUS, 1949-52. Decorated Purple Heart, Bronze Star, Combat Infantryman's badge. Named Social Worker of Yr., Knox area chpt. Nat. Assn. Social Workers, 1970; Mem. Nat. Assn. Social Workers, Acad. Certified Social Workers, Am. Group Psychotherapy Assn., V.F.W., D.A.V., Am. Legion. Methodist. Mason (32 deg., Shriner). Home: 106 Cardiff St Columbia SC 29209

HUTCHINS, DERRELE CAMDEN, agriculturist; b. Greenville, S.C., Aug. 12, 1926; s. J. Sam and Carolyn (McKenzie) H.; B.S., Clemson U., 1951, postgrad., 1952, 53, 56, 57, 59; m. Betty Lucille Sloan, Aug. 12, 1949; children—Derrele Camden, David Michael, Barbara Gale, Daniel Sloan. Vets. farm tng. instr. Oconee pub. schs., 1947-48; tchr. vocational agr. Oconee County pub. schs., 1951-54; asst. county agt. Clemson U. Extension Service, Spartanburg, S.C., 1954-57, extension marketing specialist, Columbia, S.C., 1957-65, marketing information specialist, 1965-68, dir. information filter center, 1965-70, asso. extension specialist marketing, 1968-70; agr. specialist marketing S.C. Dept. Agr., Columbia, 1970-72, internat. marketing specialist, 1972—. Adviser, cons., exec. sec., dir. pub. relations S.C. Fresh Fruit and Vegetable Assn., 1959—, coordinator scholarship fund, 1963—; marketing cons. S.C. Peach Council and Promotion Bd., 1970—; chmn. marketing com. Nat. Peach Council, 1973—; exec. sec. Agr. Survival Assn., 1973—. Master Cleveland Grange, 1952-54, Green Pond Grange, 1955-56; organizer Springdale (S.C.) Community Scouters, 1964, pres., 1964-70, 73—; mem. Richland-Lexington County Coordinating Council, 1965-66. Served with USNR, 1944-46. Mem. Atlantic Internat. Marketing Assn. (pres. 1974—), Tamassee Alumni Assn. (sec.-treas. 1958-68), Epsilon Sigma Phi. Methodist (chmn. ecumenical affairs 1969-72, supt. ch. sch. 1959-70). Mason. Home: 2201 Platt Springs Rd West Columbia SC 29169 Office: PO Box 11280 Columbia SC 29211

HUTCHINS, MARY IMOJEANE KEYS ALLEN (MRS. P.O. HUTCHINS), bus. exec. b. Lockney, Tex., Aug. 12, 1911; d. Arthur Russell and Ruth Francis (Simpson) Keys; high sch. grad.; m. Ira Russell Allen, 1932 (dec. 1957); 1 son, Arthur Lewis; m. 2d, P.O. Hutchins, June 10, 1959 (dec. 1966). Nurse tng. Lubbock (Tex.) San., 1928-31; owner salons, W.Va., Va., 1932-62; organizer, sec., pres. Schs. Cosmetology, Inc., Richmond and Hampton, Va., 1961—, also dir. pres. Va. Sch. Hair Design, Inc. Mem. Registered Profl. Hairdressers Bd. Examiners, 1962—, chmn., 1965-66, ind. examiner, 1974; regional v.p. Nat. Interstate Council of State Bds., 1969-71; mem. visitation teams Nat. Accrediting Cosmetology Commn.; mem. Indsl. Vocational Adv. Bd. Mem. Va. Hairdressers and Cosmetologists Assn. (v.p.), Peninsula Bus. and Profl. Club, Va. Allied Council Cosmetology (pres. 1969-70), Va. Hair Fashion Com. (charter mem., treas.), Va. Beauty Sch. Assn. (treas.). Baptist. Home: Box 14 Hampton VA 23669 Office: 9903 Warwick Blvd Newport News VA 23601

HUTCHINS, THOMAS HARWARD, architect; b. Raleigh, N.C., Apr. 2, 1920; s. John Henry and Ella (Harward) H.; student N.C. State U., 1937-39, 46-47; student Stanford U., 1943-44; m. Virginia Catherine Clemens, Nov. 3, 1941; children—Shirley Stevens, Jennie Louise, Rebecca Ann, Carl Stanley, Catherine Lee. Practicing architect, Statesville, N.C.. 1949—. Served with AUS, 1943-46. Recipient Dumont Design award fpr Church Architecture, 1965, 69. Home: 1101 Lakeside Dr Statesville NC 28677 Office: 1525 Davie Av PO Box 549 Statesville NC 28677

HUTCHINSON, FLAVOUS LEO, educator; b. Guntown, Miss., Aug. 5, 1923; s. Lawrence Elmer and Rennie (Bates) H.; LL.B., U. Miss., 1950, M.Ed., 1957, J.D., 1968; m. Mamia Ruth Sullivan, Sept. 16, 1945; children—Richard Sullivan, Flavia Ruth, Lawrence Patrick, Charles Christopher. Admitted to Miss. bar, 1950; practiced in Tupelo, Miss., 1950—; tchr. Saltillo (Miss.) High Sch., 1950-51; credit mgr. Wm. R. Moore Dry Goods Co., Memphis, 1951; tchr. New Harmony Sch., Blue Springs, Miss., 1952-53, supt., 1953-54; tchr. Walnut Sch., Lambert, Miss., 1954-55; lectr. So. Ill. U., 1956-57; asst. prof. law Valparaiso U., 1957-58; asso. prof. bus. law Miss. State U., 1958-65; prof. bus. law, 1965—. Chmn. action com. Oktibbeha County Democrats for L.B. Johnson, 1964; parliamentarian Miss. Dem. Conf., 1965. Served with USNR, 1943-45. Kellogg Research Fellow, 1955. Mem. Am., Miss. bar assns., Am. Trial Lawyers Assn., Am. (del. nat. conv. 1967-68), S. Central Regional (pres. 1966-67) bus. law assns., Am. Assn. U. Profs. (chpt. pres. 1965—), Internat. Platform Assn. Contbr. articles to profl. jours. Home: 1300 Fillmore St Tupelo MS 38801 Office: 813 Varsity Dr Tupelo MS 38801

HUTCHINSON, LEONARD HUGH, educator; b. Richwood, W.Va., July 5, 1917; s. Leonard Anthony and Elverta (Groves) H.; B.S.M.E., Purdue U., 1939; Cert. Meteorology U. Chgo., 1943; M.Ed., Ga. State U., 1971; m. Sophia Farbach, Mar. 14, 1942; 1 dau., Tevis. Commd. 2d lt., U.S. Air Force, 1941, advanced through grades to lt. col., 1968, staff meteorologist, 1943-68, comdr. 21st Weather Squadron, Torrejon Air Base, Spain, 1956-59, comdr. 32d Weather Squadron, Dobbins AFB, Ga., 1959-61, dir. Joint Typhoon Warning Center, Guam, 1961-63, staff weather officer USAF Command Post, & Air Force One, 1963-65, staff weather officer Joint Task Force Eight AEC, 1965-68, ret., 1968; tchr. sci. math. College Park High Sch., Atlanta, 1968-70; asst. to dean Sch. Urban Life, Ga. State U., 1970—. Mem. Am. Meteorol. Soc., Am. geophys. Union, Am. Legion, Delta Tau Delta. Patentee control of tropical cyclone formation. Home: 7312 Cardigan Circle NW Atlanta GA 30328 Office: Sch Urban Life Ga State U University Plaza Atlanta GA 30303

HUTCHINSON, RICHARD CHARLES, mgmt. cons.; b. Franklin, Mass., Dec. 9, 1916; s. Charles Bassett and Helen Adeline (MacCarthy) H.; B.S., Mass. Inst. Tech., 1937; M.Engring. Adminstrn., U. South Fla., 1968; m. Mary Ellen Johnston, Oct. 19, 1940; 1 dau., Judith (Mrs. Joseph W. Hodges III). Various positions in diversified industries, 1937-70; sr. indsl. engr. Internat. Minerals & Chem. Corp., Bartow, Fla., 1958-70; mgr. indsl. engring. Systems Devel., Inc., Bartow, Fla., 1970-74; mgmt. cons., 1974—; dir. Sayre (Pa.) Printing Co., 1951-74. Registered profl. engr., Fla. Named Outstanding Indsl. Engr. Southeastern U.S., Am. Inst. Indsl. Engrs., 1963-64. Mem. Nat. Soc. Profl. Engrs., Am. Inst. Industrial Engrs. (chpt. pres. 1961-62, nat. dir. community services 1963-65), Fla. Engring. Soc. Mason (Shriner). Home: 716 Shady Lane Lakeland FL 33803 Office: PO Box 1516 Bartow FL 33830

HUTCHINSON, RICHARD GLENN, physician; b. LaGrange, Ga., Aug. 18, 1933; s. Richard and Margaret Ann (Jordan) H.; B.A., Emory U., 1951-55; M.D., Med. Coll. Ga., 1959; m. Celeste Clanton, June 20, 1959; children—Richard Glenn, Wendell Clanton. Intern, Bapt. Hosp., Nashville, 1959-60; resident internal medicine Med. Coll. Ga. Hosps., Augusta, 1960-63; Ga. Heart Assn. cardiology fellow, 1963-64; staff physician VA Hosp., Jackson, Miss., 1966-67; instr. medicine U. Miss. Med. Sch., Jackson, 1967-69, asst. prof., attending physician, 1969—, also dir. univ. coronary drug research clinic. Mem. EKG com. Nat. Hypertension Study. Served to capt. USAF, 1964-66. James Bruce Traveling scholar A.C.P., 1970; Miss. Heart Assn. Research grantee, 1971-72. Fellow Am. Coll. Angiology, Internat. Coll. Angiology; mem. A.C.P., Am. Fedn. Clin. Research, Am. Heart Assn., Am. Coll. Chest Physicians, Hinds County (mem. hypertensive screening com.), Miss. heart assns., Jackson Acad. Medicine (sec.-treas.), Sigma Xi, Eta Sigma Psi. Methodist. Contbr. articles to prof. pubs. Home: 1840 Springridge Dr Jackson MS 39211 Office: 2500 N State St Jackson MS 39216

HUTCHINSON, WILLIAM SEELY, JR., chem. engr.; b. Washington, D.C., Oct. 30, 1914; s. William Seely and Susan Eleanora (Buckler) H.; B.S. in Chem. Engring., Lehigh U., 1936; S.M., Mass. Inst. Tech., 1949; student Nat. War Coll., 1960-61; m. Sara Elizabeth Stauffer, Nov. 24, 1937; children—William Seely III, Ann Darby. Salesman, Gen. Chem. Co., N.Y.C., 1936-39; product sales mgr. Mallinckrodt Chem. Works, St. Louis, 1939-41; commd. 1st lt. U.S. Army, 1941, advanced through grades to col., 1952; chief declassification and publ. Manhattan Engr. Dist., 1945-47; armorer George Shot, Operation Greenhouse, Los Alamos Sci. Lab., Eniwetok, 1951; chief weapons effects test div. Def. Atomic Support Agy., 1957-60; chief staff for nuclear testing Joint Task Force Eight, Washington, 1964-66; ret., 1966; chem. engr. Cornell Lab., Thailand, 1964-69, Buffalo, 1970-71; dep. dir. pub. works City of Jacksonville, Fla., 1971—. Republican candidate U.S. Congress 15th Dist. Pa., 1966. Decorated Silver Star, Legion Merit with oak leaf cluster, Purple Heart (U.S.); Italian Mil. Valor Cross. Registered profl. engr., D.C., Pa. Mem. Nat. Assn. Counties (solid waste task force, 1972-73), Am. Chem. Soc., Am. Pub. Works Assn., Nat. Soc. Profl. Engrs., Chemists Club N.Y., S.A.R., Psi Upsilon. Republican. Episcopalian. Clubs: Army Navy (Washington); Royal Bangkok Sports; Ponte Vedra (Fla.); Army Navy Country (Arlington, Va.); Royal Varuna Yacht (Thailand); Jacksonville Naval Yacht. Home: Jacksonville FL Office: 220 E Bay St Jacksonville FL 23302

HUTCHISON, WILLIAM FORREST, educator; b. Lakeland, Fla., Oct. 7, 1925; s. Chester Boyer and Verna Louise (Warren) H.: B.A., Emory U., 1949, M.S., 1952; Ph.D., Tulane U., 1958; m. Nellie Niles Booth, June 5, 1951; children—Florence Niles, David Forrest, Martha Ellen, Rebecca Warren, Robert Chester. Instr. parasitology Tulane U. Sch. Medicine, New Orleans, 1954-55: asst. prof. preventive medicine and clin. lab. sci. U. Miss. Sch. Medicine, Jackson, 1955-59, asso. prof., 1959-71., prof., 1971—. Cons. Jackson VA Hosp., 1955—; parasitologist. U. Hosp., Jackson, Miss., 1955-72. Served with AUS. 1943-46. La. State U. Sch. Medicine fellow in tropical medicine, 1959. Mem. A.A.A.S., Am. Soc. Parasitologists, Am. Soc. Tropical Medicine and Hygiene, Internat. Filariasis Assn., S.E. Assn. Parasitologists, Miss. Acad. Sci. (pres. 1972-73), Sigma Xi, Phi Sigma, Kappa Alpha. Club: Yacht (commordore 1973) (Jackson). Home: 1910 Bellewood Rd Jackson MS 39211

HUTSELL, JAMES KENDALL, newspaper editor; b. Columbia, Mo., Dec. 3, 1907; s. John Hedges and Eulah (Keene) H.; B.J., U. Mo., 1929, postgrad., 1930-32. News desk Des Moines Tribune, 1929-30; editor Columbia (Mo.) Herald-Statesman, 1935-37; columnist Mo. Press Assn., Columbia, Mo., 1937-39; news editor Hattiesburg (Miss.) Am., 1942-43; news desk New Orleans States, 1943-45; telegraph editor Asheville (N.C.) Times, 1945-48, Pensacola (Fla.) Journ., 1948-54; editor Ala. Courier, Athens, Ala., 1956-57; telegraph editor Huntsville (Ala.) Times, 1957-61, asso. editor, 1961—, editor editorial page, 1966—. Dir. publicity Mo. State Fair, Sedalia, Mo., 1939-41. Served as civilian in pub. relations with AUS, 1941-42. Mem. Huntsville Lit. Assn., Huntsville Hist. Soc., U. Mo. Alumni Assn., Appalachian Wildflowers (dir.), Sigma Delta Chi, Kappa Tau Alpha. Club: The Press (Huntsville Alabama). Author: History of the Missouri Press Association, 1931; A Stylebook for Newspaper Editors and the Law of the Press, 1951; The Harvest Years (ann. brochure), 1964—; also, articles in profl., lit., gardening, hist. mags. Home: Harvest Hill RFD 1 Box 311 Harvest AL 35749 Office: 2317 Memorial Pkwy SW Huntsville AL 35805

HUTTON, JAMES LAWRENCE, lawyer; b. Marion, Va., June 29, 1932; s. Joseph Hugh and Mary Creola (Hall) H.; B.A., Emory and Henry Coll., 1957; LL.B., U. Richmond, 1965; m. Phyllis Juanita Meade, Sept. 19, 1958; children—Christopher Todd, Vicki Leigh. Admitted to Va. bar, 1965; mem. firm Gilmer, Sadler, Ingram,

Sutherland & Hutton, Blacksburg, Va., 1965—; judge Blacksburg (Va.) Municipal Ct., 1968-73; substitute judge Montgomery County and Blacksburg Dist. Ct., 1969—. Pres. Smyth County Young Dem. Club, 1959-60; 9th dist. chmn. Young Dem. Clubs Va., 1961-62. Served with AUS, 1952-54. Mem. Am., Va. Pulaski County, Montgomery County bar assns., Blacksburg C. of C. (pres. 1970), Phi Delta Phi. Baptist. Kiwanian (pres. 1969-70). Home: PO Box 908 Blacksburg VA 24060 also 305 Hemlock Dr Blacksburg VA 24060 Office: 209 N Main St Blacksburg VA 24060

HUTTON, JOHN JAMES, physician; b. Ashland, Ky., July 24, 1936; s. John James and Alice (Virgin) H.; A.B., Harvard, 1958, M.D., 1964; m. Mary Ellyn LaBach, June 13, 1964; children—Mary Rebecca, John Stafford. Intern Mass. Gen. Hosp., Boston, 1964-65; med. resident U. Ky. Med. Center, Lexington, 1967-68; chief mammalian genetics Roche Inst. of Molecular Biology, Nutley, N.J., 1968-71; asso. prof. medicine, hematology-oncology U. Ky. Sch. Medicine, Lexington, 1971—; chief, med. services Lexington VA Hosp., 1973—. Adj. asst. prof. human genetics and devel. Columbia, 1969-71; cons. Nat. Inst. Environmental Health Services, 1973—. Served with USPHS, 1965-67. Recipient Research Career Devel. award NIH, 1972-73. Mem. Am. Soc. Biol. Chemists, Am. Soc. for Clin. Investigation. Contbr. articles in field to profl. jours. Home: 409 Lakeshore Dr Lexington KY 40502 Office: VA Hospital Medical Service Lexington KY 40507

HUXTABLE, DEANE LAMONT, state ofcl.; b. Mason City, Ia., Jan. 16, 1918; s. Frank A. and Golda L. (Douglas) H.; student Mason City Jr. Coll., 1938, Am. U., 1946; children—Douglas, Stephen, Denice. Social sci. analyst Nat. Office Vital Statistics, Washington, 1946-50; state registrar Ore. Bd. Health, Portland, 1950-59; dir. health records and statistics Va. Dept. Health, Richmond, 1959—. Tech. cons. for UN, Kenya, East Africa, 1962-63; cons. for U.S. Dept. State, Korea, 1971; cons. for Pan Am. Health Orgn., Brazil, 1973. Served with USAF, 1940-46; lt. col. Res. ret. Mem. Pub. Health Conf. on Records and Statistics (nat. chmn. 1957-58), Am. Assn. Vital Records and Pub. Health Statistics (pres. 1967-68). Home: 808 Brook Hill Rd Richmond VA 23227 Office: PO Box 1000 Richmond VA 23208

HYATT, FRANCIS MARION, city ofcl.; b. Marietta, Okla., Feb. 21, 1905; s. Frank W. and Gertrude (Sholly) H.; student Ia. Wesleyan Coll., 1924-25; m. Alice Louise Waterman, June 17, 1934; children—Philip W., James Robert. Owner, operator radio sales and service co., Ottumwa, Ia., 1926-40; announcer, mgr. sta. WJHO, Opelika, Ala., 1940-51; announcer sta. WAUD, Auburn, Ala., 1951-60; exec. dir. Opelika Housing Authority, 1951—. Dir. Founder's Investment Corp. Instr. shelter mgmt. Opelika Civil Def., 1963—. Chmn. Opelika Park and Recreation Bd., 1947-52, Lee County chpt. A.R.C., 1961-64, Opelika Library Bd., 1942-46; chmn. Lee County Welfare Bd., 1958—, Ala. pres., 1963-64; chmn. Birmingham Regional Blood Bank, A.R.C., 1967-71; mem. adv. com. Region 6 Combined Service Territory, Birmingham Area A.R.C., 1965-71; chmn. Ala. div. adv. com. A.R.C., 1971—. Recipient Outstanding Citizen award Opelika Jr. C. of C., 1962. Mem. Ala. Assn. Housing Authorities (pres.), C. of C. (v.p. 1952), Sigma Phi Epsilon. Methodist (chmn. ofcl. bd. 1961-63). Rotarian (pres. Opelika 1945-46). Home: 1004 Fitzpatrick Av Opelika AL 36801 Office: 316 Pleasant Dr Opelika AL 36801

HYCHE, JAMES KELLY, retail lumber co. exec.; b. Jasper, Ala., Jan. 22, 1915; s. James M. and Cannie Bell (Narramore) H.; grad. U. Ala., 1942; m. Elizabeth B. Brunner; children—Mary K., Sharon J. Salesman North Ala. Lumber Co., Jasper, 1935-39, mgr., 1939-58; owner Delta Bus Lines, Black and Gold Safety Cabs, Delta Transfer, Jasper, 1940-52; salesman Grayson Lumber Co., Birmingham, Ala., 1958-59, v.p., 1959—. Former dir. Black Warrior council Boy Scouts Am.; chmn. War Fund campaign, Walker County, 1944; chmn. Walker-Winston County Boy Scout Fund Drive, 1946; fund chmn. A.R.C., 1948. Recognized Library of Congress for Home Housing System, 1956. Mem. Birmingham Assn. Home Bldrs., Retail Dealers Assn. Democrat. Methodist. Mason (Shriner). Clubs: Kiwanis of Jasper (dir. 1943-48, pres. 1948), Birmingham Kiwanis, Vestavia Country. Home: 2613 Kingswood Rd Vestavia Birmingham AL 35226 Office: 715 N 39th St Birmingham AL 35222

HYDE, EDD HOWELL, aluminum co. exec.; b. Fayette, Ala., Apr. 15, 1912; s. Charles Banks and Daisy Pearl (Propst) H.; B.S., U. Ala., 1933; m. Marguerite Riley, Aug. 22, 1942; children—John Banks, Edd Howell. Aide on staff Rep. William H. Bankhead, Jasper, Ala., 1936-40; exec. sec. Senator John J. Sparkman, Huntsville, Ala., 1946-56; with Reynolds Metals Co., Washington, 1956—, v.p., 1970—. Served to maj. AUS, 1942-46. Mem. Bus.-Govt. Relations Council, Clubs: University, Internat., Washington Golf and Country, Carlton (Washington); Burning Tree (Bethesda, Md.). Home: 3815 N Nelson St Arlington VA 22207 Office: 1620 I St NW Washington DC 20006

HYDE, JAMES SYLVESTER, JR., lawyer; b. Chattanooga, June 17, 1926; s. James Sylvester and Althea (Baker) H.; student North Ga. Mil. Coll., 1944; B.A., U. Chattanooga, 1950; LL.B., U. Tenn., 1951, J.D., 1968; m. Opal M. England, Nov. 14, 1947; children—Delisa, Lieda, Nada, Eldon. Lab. foreman E. I. Dupont, 1951-54; claim rep. State Farm Mut. 1955-59; ins. adjuster Pritchett Co., 1959-61; admitted to Tenn. and Fed. bar, 1962; gen. practice, Chattanooga, 1962—. Lectr. anthropology. Served with AUS, 1944-46. Mem. Soil Conservation Soc. Am. (sec.-treas.), Phi Delta Phi. Baptist. Club: Chattanooga Geology. Author: Wildwood Wonder, 1973; December's Poems, 1973. Home: 8440 Chambers Chattanooga TN 37421 Office: Profl Bldg Chattanooga TN 37402

HYDE, PAUL MARTIN, educator; b. San Francisco., Jan. 27, 1923; s. Wilfrid Raymond and Aurelia (Feider) H.; B.S., U. San Francisco, 1947; M.S., U. Cal. at Berkeley, 1950; Ph.D., St. Louis U., 1953; m. Mary Jane Oldenburg, Aug. 18, 1956; children—Laurie, Amy, Patrick. Instr. dept. medicine U. Wash., 1953-57; asst. prof. dept. biochemistry La. State U. Med. Sch., 1957-63, asso. prof., 1963-69, prof. biochemistry, 1969—; cons. Pathology Assos. of New Orleans, 1972—. Vice pres. New Orleans Archdiocesan Sch. Bd., 1968-70. Served with AUS, 1943-46. NIH grantee, 1961—. Mem. Am. Chem. Soc., Am. Soc. Biol. Chemists, Endocrine Soc., Soc. Exptl. Biology and Medicine, Sigma Xi. Contbr. numerous articles to sci. jours. Home: 4528 Neyrey Dr Metairie LA 70002 Office: 1542 Tulane Ave New Orleans LA 70112

HYDE, RICHARD MOOREHEAD, educator; b. Pierre, S.D., Feb. 11, 1933; s. Charles Lee and Florence Lucille (Moorehead) H.; B.A., U.S.D., 1955, M.A., 1956; Ph.D., U. Minn., 1962; m. Ruth Marie Curry, Aug. 21, 1953; children—Roderick, Scott, Dawn. Asst. prof. San Francisco State Coll., 1960-62; asst. prof. U. Mo., 1962-65; prof. U. Okla., 1965—; pres. Custom Immization Service, Oklahoma City, 1972—; cons. Mercy, South Community hosps., both Oklahoma City. NSF predoctoral fellow, 1955-56; USPHS predoctoral fellow, 1959-60, spl. fellow, 1968-69. Mem. Am. Soc. Microbiology, Am. Assn. Immunologists, Am. Acad. Microbiology, Sigma Xi. Mason (32 deg.). Contbr. articles to sci. jours. Home: 1217 W Hefner St Oklahoma City OK 73114 Office: PO Box 26901 Oklahoma City OK 73190

HYDER, CHARLES MONROE, ednl. adminstr.; b. Hickory, N.C., Jan. 3, 1926; s. Adrian Alvin and Violet Irene (Cline) H.; B.S. magna cum laude, Appalachian State U., 1951, M.A., 1955; Ed.D., Duke U., 1968; m. Ruth Wilene Kiser, Feb. 24, 1950; 1 son, Charles Michael. Tchr., adminstr. Charlotte-Mecklenburg Schs., Charlotte, N.C., 1952-66; grad. asst. Duke U., Durham, N.C., 1966-68; asso. prof. edn., dir. elementary edn. U. Tenn., Chattanooga, 1968-71, dir. human services program, 1971—, prof. edn., 1972—, dean Coll. Profl. Studies, 1973—. Vis. prof. U. Ga., West Ga. State U., 1969. Dir. Model Cities Bd. Tng. Program, Chattanooga, 1969; dir. U. Tenn. Parent-Child Center Evaluation Team, 1970—; cons. sch. systems, Tenn., Ga. Served with USNR, 1943-47, 51-52. Recipient Ivy award U. Tenn., 1971, Gen. Alumni Pub. Service award, 1973; U. Chattanooga Found. grantee, 1970. Mem. Kappa Delta Pi, Phi Delta Kappa, Pi Gamma Mu. Methodist. Democrat. Home: 4200 Rogers Rd Chattanooga TN 37411

HYDRICK, ANDREW JACKSON, JR., judge; b. Orangeburg, S.C., Oct. 23, 1919; s. Andrew Jackson and Maude (Riley) H.; A.B., Wofford Coll., 1940; LL.B., U. S.C., 1947; m. Christa Mae Seim, Mar. 6, 1943; children—Christa Ann (Mrs. James Chesley Hunter, Jr.), Carol Seim (Mrs. Tilden Frederick Riley, III). Admitted to S.C. bar, 1947; practiced in Orangeburg, 1947-73; mem. firm Hydrick & Hydrick, 1947-60, A.J. Hydrick, Jr., 1960-73; county atty. Orangeburg County, S.C., 1951-71; judge Family Ct., Orangeburg County, 1971-73; county judge, Orangeburg County, 1973—. Chmn. Orangeburg County chpt. Nat. Found.-March of Dimes, 1951-73. Served with inf. AUS, 1942-46. Mem. Am., S.C. bar assns. Democrat. Methodist. Kiwanian (pres. 1965). Home: 2110 Woodland Dr NE Orangeburg SC 29115 Office: County Court House Orangeburg SC 29115

HYMAN, ALBERT LEWIS, physician; b. New Orleans, Nov. 10, 1923; s. David and Mary (Newstadt) H.; B.S., La. State U., 1943; M.D., 1945; postgrad. U. Cin., U. Paris (France), U. London (Eng.); m. Neil Steiner, March 27, 1964; 1 son, Albert Arthur. Intern, Charity Hosp., 1945-46, resident, 1947-49, sr. vis. physician, 1959-63; resident Cin. Gen. Hosp., 1946-47; instr. medicine La. State U., 1950-56, asst. prof. medicine, 1956-57; asst. prof. medicine Tulane U., 1957-59, asso. prof., 1959-63; asso. prof. surgery Tulane Med. Sch., 1963-70, prof. research surgery in cardiology, 1970—; dir. Cardiac Catheterization Lab., 1957—; sr. vis. physician Touro Hosp., Touro Infirmary, Hotel Dieu; chief cardiology Sara Mayo Hosp.; cons. in cardiology USPHS, New Orleans Crippled Children's Hosp., St. Tammany Parish Hosp., Covington, La. area VA; electrocardiographer Metairie Hosp., 1959-64, Sara Mayo Hosp., Touro Infirmary, St. Tammany Hosp.; cons. cardiovascular disease New Orleans VA Hosp.; cons. cardiology Baton Rouge Gen. Hosp. Diplomate Am. Bd. Internal Medicine. Fellow A.C.P., Am. Coll. Chest Physicians, Am. Coll. Cardiology, Am. Fedn. Clin. Research; mem. Am. (fellow and regional rep. council clin. cardiology), La. (v.p. 1974) heart assns., Am. Soc. Pharmacology and Exptl. Therapeutics, So. Soc. Clin. Investigation, So. Med. Soc., Am. Physiol. Soc., N.Y. Acad. Scis. Home: 5550 Jacquelyn Ct New Orleans LA 70124 Office: 3629 Prythania St New Orleans LA 70115

HYMAN, PETER DEWITT, lawyer; b. Florence, S.C., July 11, 1927; s. Cannie E. and Ethel (Harrell) H.; J.D. U. S.C., 1954; LL.M., Harvard U., 1970; m. Vera Jane Church, Sept. 18, 1954; children—Helen Sheffield, Martha Elizabeth, Peter DeWitt. Admitted to S.C. bar, 1953; sr. partner, trial counsel law firm Hyman, Morgan and Brown, Florence, S.C., 1955. Dir. Peoples Bank of S.C., Florence. Magistrate Florence County, S.C., 1955-59; mem. S.C. Ho. of Reps., 1960-70, chmn. subcom. on higher edn., 1968-70. Served to col. AUS, 1943-73. Decorated D.F.C., Air medal with two stars. Mason, Elk. Home: 420 Brettwood St Florence SC 29501 Office: 120 Courthouse Sq Florence SC 29501

HYSON, CHARLES DAVID, economist; b. Hampstead, Md., Dec. 29, 1915; s. Harry Perry and Rose (Miller) H.; A.B., St. John's Coll., Annapolis, 1937; M.S., U. Md., 1939; M.A., Harvard, 1942, Ph.D., 1943; m. Winifred Chandler Prince, Sept. 7, 1946; children—David Prince, Pamela Chandler, Christopher Perry. Agri. economist FCA, 1939-40; staff Surplus Marketing Adminstrn., Washington, 1940-41; resident tutor, then sr. tutor Harvard, 1942-49, research asso., 1943-44, resident cons. Grad. Sch. Pub. Adminstrn., 1943-49, instr. econs., 1946-48, asso. dir. marketing research program, 1948-49; regional economist, then chief prices and cost of living br. U.S. Bur. Labor Statistics, 1944-46; indsl. economist Fed. Res. Bank Boston, 1946-48; asst. econ. commr. ECA Mission to Norway, Oslo, 1949-50; trade specialist, staff spl. rep. in Europe, Paris, 1950, spl. asst. to chief of mission ECA, Mut. Security Agy., Lisbon, Portugal, 1950-52; dep. dir. U.S. Operations Mission to Portugal, Mut. Security Agy., FOA, ICA, 1952-55; spl. rep. to Portugal, ICA, 1955-57, chief Western Europe div., Washington 1957-59, chief European div., 1959-60; Nat. War Coll., 1960-61; counselor of embassy for econ. affairs Am. Embassy, Lisbon, 1955-57; dep. asst. dir. for exec. staffing AID, Washington, ,1961-62; adviser for econ. affairs Office Material Resources, AID, 1962-63, spl. asst. for econs. and trade, 1963—. Dep. nat. export expansion coordinator, dep. exec. dir. Cabinet Com. Export Expansion, 1964. Mem. internat. secretariat and econ. adv. conf. on Human Skills in Decade Devel., San Juan, P.R., 1962; mem. trade com. for White House Conf. on Internat. Cooperation, 1965. Decorated Order of Merit (Portugal); recipient Spl. Commendation and Meritorious Service award, Superior Honor award U.S. Govt. Mem. Am. Fgn. Service Assn., Royal Econ. Soc., Am. Acad. Polit. and Social Sci., Am. Econ. Assn., Am. Agrl. Econs. Assn., Sigma Alpha Epsilon. Clubs: Harvard (Washington); Keene Valley (N.Y.) Country; Internat. (Washington); Edgemoor (Bethesda). Contbr. articles econ. jours. Home: 7407 Honeywell Lane Bethesda MD 20014 Office: Dept of State Washington DC 20523

IACOBUCCI, GUILLERMO ARTURO, chemist; b. Buenos Aires, Argentina, May 11, 1927; s. Guillermo Cesar and Blanca Nieves (Brana) I.; M.Sc., U. Buenos Aires, 1949, Ph.D. in Organic Chemistry, 1952; m. Constantina Maria Gullich, Mar. 28, 1952; children—Eduardo Ernesto, William George. Came to U.S., 1962, naturalized, 1972. Research chemist E.R. Squibb Research Labs., Buenos Aires, 1952-57; research fellow in chemistry Harvard, Cambridge, Mass., 1958-59, prof. psytochemistry U. Buenos Aires, 1960-61; sr. research chemist Squibb Inst. Med. Research, New Brunswick, N.J., 1962-66; head bio-organic chemistry labs. Coca-Cola Co., Atlanta, 1967—. John Simon Guggenheim Meml. Found. fellow, 1958. Mem. A.A.A.S., Assn. Harvard Chemists, Am. Chem. Soc., N.Y. Acad. Scis., Am. Soc. Pharmacognosy, Assn. Quimica Argentina. Contbr. articles on organic chemistry to sci. jours. Patentee in field. Home: 160 North Mill Rd NW Atlanta GA 30328 Office: Coca Cola Co PO Drawer 1734 Atlanta GA 30301

IANNICELLI, JOSEPH, chem. exec.; b. N.Y.C., Aug. 5, 1929; s. Peter and Catherine (Gulotti) I.; S.B., Mass. Inst. Tech., 1951, Ph.D., 1955; m. Alma Joyce Head, 1958 (div.); children—Mark, Rex, Regina. With E.I. duPont de Nemours & Co., 1955-60; tech. dir. J.M. Huber Corp., Huber, Ga., 1960-70; pres., chmn. bd. Aquafine Corp., Brunswick, Ga., 1970—. Fellow Am. Inst. Chemists; mem. T.A.P.P.I., Am. Chem. Soc., Clay Minerals Soc., N.Y. Acad. Scis. Contbr. articles to profl. jours. Patentee in field. Home: 796 S Beachview Dr Jekyll Island GA 31520 Office: 157 Darien Hwy Brunswick GA 31520

IBACH, DOUGLAS THEODORE, clergyman; b. Pottstown, Pa., July 23, 1925; s. Hiram Christian and Esther (Fry) I.; B.S. in Edn., Temple U. (Phila.), 1950, postgrad. Sch. Theology, 1950-52; M.Divinity, Louisville Presbyn. Theol. Sem., 1954; m. Marion Elizabeth Torok, Sept. 2, 1950; children—Susan (Mrs. William Lunstrum), Marilyn Lee, Dougals Theodore, Grace Louise. Ordained to ministry Presbyn. Ch., 1953; Pastor, Pewee Valley, Ky., 1952-55, West Nottingham Presbyn. Ch., Colora, Md., 1955-61, Irwin, Pa., 1961-67, Knox Presbyn. Ch., Falls Church, Va., 1967-72, United Christian Parish Reston (Va.), 1972—. Youth Ministry cons. Nat. Capital Union Presbytery, 1967—. Mem. Am. Civil Liberties Union. Served with USNR, 1943-44. Mem. Council Chs. Greater Washington (pres.), Piedmont Synod U.P. Ch. (dir. youth, camping), Acad. Parish Clergy (dir.), Fairfax County Council Chs. (pres.). Club: American Field Service (Vienna, Va.). Home: 11709 Riders Lane Reston VA 22091 Office: 2329 Hunters Woods Plaza Reston VA 22091

IBRAHIM, IBRAHIM MOAYYAD, educator; b. Haifa, Israel, June 23, 1941; s. Moayyad and Raifeh (Sudki) I.; came to U.S. 1960, naturalized 1969; B.A., Shorter Coll., 1964; M.S., Clemson U., 1966, Ph.D., 1970; m. Iris Brann, July 14, 1966; 1 son, Darian. Head soccer coach Clemson (S.C.) U., 1967—, asst. prof. food sci. 1970—. Named Coach of the Year, Atlantic Coast Conf., 1973, regional, 1973. Mem. Intercollegiate Soccer Football Assn. Am. (so. regional chmn. 1970). Home: 111 Ashley Clemson SC 29631

ICHINOSE, HERBERT, physician; b. Koloa, Kauai, Hawaii, July 25, 1931; s. Samuro and Katsue (Yamamoto) I.; student U. Hawaii, 1949-51; B.S., Tulane U., 1953, M.D., 1957; m. Elaine Okimoto, Dec. 19, 1955; children—Linda, Lorna, John, Eugene. Intern Charity Hosp. New Orleans, 1957-58, resident, 1958-62; practice medicine, specializing in pathology, New Orleans, 1958—; vis. pathologist Charity Hosp., 1964—; cons. pathologist Methodist Hosp., New Orleans, 1972—; mem. faculty dept. pathology Med. Sch., Tulane U., New Orleans, 1958—, asso. prof., 1967-71, prof., 1971—. Service Club scholar, 1949, USPHS grantee, 1954; recipient John Herr Musser Meml. award Tulane Med. Sch., 1957, Undergrad. Research award Borden Co., 1957. Diplomate Am. Bd. Pathology. Mem. New Orleans Acad. Pathology (pres.), Thoracophilus Soc., Orleans Parish, La. med. socs., A.M.A., N.Y. Acad. Scis., Am. Soc. Clin. Pathologists. Contbr. articles to profl. jours. Home: 2813 Calhoun St New Orleans LA 70118 Office: 1430 Tulane St New Orleans LA 70112

ICHIYE, TAKASHI, educator; b. Kobe, Japan, Oct. 1, 1921; s. Mankichi and Toyo (Yumoto) I.; student First Coll. (Tokyo, Japan), 1939-42; B.S., U. Tokyo, 1944, D.Sc., 1953; m. Chiyoko Nagao, Oct. 6, 1952; children—Toshiko, Keiko. Came to U.S., 1957, naturalized, 1972. Oceanographer, Kobe (Japan) Marine Obs., 1946-55; asso. chief oceanographic sect. Japan Meteorol. Agy., Tokyo, 1955-57; vis. scientist Woods Hole (Mass.) Oceanographic Inst., 1957-58; asst. prof. Fla. State U., Tallahassee, 1958-63; sr. research asso. Columbia, 1963-68; prof. Tex. A. and M. U., College Station, 1968—. Served to lt. (j.g.) Japanese Navy, 1944-45. Recipient Dir.'s award Central Meteorol. Obs. (Japan), 1950. Mem. Am. Geophys. Union, Am. Meteorol. Soc., Sigma Xi. Author: Oceanography (in Japanese), 1955. Editor: Diffusion in Ocean and Fresh Waters, 1964. Home: 1205 Westover St College Station TX 77840

IDDINS, MILDRED, librarian; b. Fountain City, Tenn., Sept. 14, 1915; d. Joseph Franklin and Lucy Ann (Chandler) Iddins; A.B., Carson-Newman Coll., 1936; B.S., Peabody Coll., 1941. Tchr., Bell House, Knoxville, Tenn., 1936-37; tchr.-librarian Roane County High Sch., Kingston, Tenn., 1937-41; librarian Dandridge (Tenn.) High Sch., 1941-43; army librarian Ft. Oglethorpe, Ga., 1943-44; librarian Carson-Newman Coll., Jefferson City, Tenn., 1944—. Mem. Am., Southeastern, Tenn. library assns., Assn. Univ. Women. Clubs: Monday Literary, Modern Book. Home: 403 Russell St Jefferson City TN 37760 Office: Library Carson-Newman Coll Jefferson City TN 37760

IDE, ROY WILLIAM, III, lawyer; b. Geneva, Ill., Apr. 23, 1940; s. Roy William and Jenny Logan (Coleman) I.; B.A. cum laude, Washington and Lee U., 1962; LL.B., U. Va., 1965; M.B.A., Ga. State U., 1972; m. Gayle Marie Oliver, Jan. 27, 1967; children—Oliver Logan, Jennifer Nava. Law clk. U.S. 5th Circuit Ct. Appeals, Atlanta, 1965-66; admitted to Ga. bar, 1966; asso. firm King & Spalding, Atlanta, 1966-71; partner firm Huie, Brown & Ide, Atlanta, 1971—. Pres. Ga. Indigents Legal Services, Inc., 1970-72; bd. dirs., mem. exec. com. Nat. Legal Aid and Defender Assn.; bd. dirs. Atlanta Legal Aid Soc., Ga. Legal Services Program, Youngmen's Roundtable. Mem. Am. Bar Assn. (sec. young lawyers sect. 1973), State Bar Ga. (exec. council younger lawyers sect. 1970-72, sec. 1972, pres.-elect 1973). Club: Lawyers (Atlanta). Home: 1215 W Wesley Rd NW Atlanta GA 30327 Office: 822 Fulton Fed Bldg Atlanta GA 30303

IDELSON, GEORGE, advt. agy. exec.; b. Annapolis, Md., Feb. 13, 1925; s. Michael Norman and Amanda Leah (Milwitzky) I.; B.S. cum laude, N.Y. U., 1947; m. Evelyn Joy Merson, Feb. 14, 1960; children—Adam Merson, Holly Amanda. Advt. prodn., writer R.H. Macy's, N.Y.C., 1947-50; divisional advt. mgr. The Hecht Co., Washington, 1950-58; advt. account supr. Henry J. Kaufman & Assos., Inc., Washington, 1958—; dir. Jet Rent A Car, Ile de France Corp.; instr. George Washington U., 1960-70. Trustee, Georgetown Day Sch. Served with AUS, 1943-45. Decorated Purple Heart, Bronze Star medal with oak leaf cluster; recipient numerous creative advt. awards. Mem. Am. Marketing Assn. (pres. Washington chpt. 1967-68), Beta Gamma Sigma Home: 3035 Newark St NW Washington DC 20008 Office: 1050 31st St NW Washington DC 20007

IEYOUB, KALIL PHILLIP, educator; b. Lake Charles, La., Aug. 21, 1935; s. Phillip Assad and Virginia (Khoury) I.; B.S. in Chemistry, McNeese State Coll., 1958; M.S., La. State U., 1965, Ph.D. (NSF grantee, Cities Service Corp. grantee, Dr. Charles E. Leates Meml. Fund grantee), 1967; m. Julie Ann Christ, Dec. 26, 1959; children—Christopher Paul, Laura Ann, Allison Claire, John Kalil. Mem. faculty dept. chemistry McNeese State U., Lake Charles, 1967—, now prof. chemistry. Served to 2d lt. inf. AUS, 1958-59. Mem. McNeese Alumni Assn. (dir. 1969-72), Blue Key, Phi Lambda Upsilon. Home: 2020 Charvais Dr Lake Charles LA 70601

IFFT, EDWARD MILTON, govt. ofcl.; b. Grove City, Pa., July 19, 1937; s. John Thomas and Edith Marie (Patterson) I.; B.S. in Physics Antioch Coll., 1960; U.S./USSR Cultural Exchange student Moscow State U., 1964-65; Ph.D. in Physics (NSF fellow 1960-63), Ohio State U., 1967; m. Ardith Jeanne Felts, Aug. 12, 1967; 1 son, John Raymond. Research physicist U.S. Naval Research Lab., Washington, 1956-57, Argonne (Ill.) Nat. Lab., 1958; phys. sci. officer Arms Control and Disarmament Agy., Washington, 1967-73; polit.-mil. officer Bur. Politico-Mil. Affairs Dept. State, Washington, 1973—; mem. U.S. delegation to Strategic Arms Limitation Talks, Helsinki, Finland and Vienna, Austria, 1969-72, Geneva, Switzerland, 1972—. Mem. Am. Phys. Soc. Contbr. articles to profl. jours. Home: 6825

Wheatley Ct Falls Church VA 22042 Office: Dept State PM/DCA Washington DC 20520

IKARD, FRANK NEVILLE, petroleum assn. exec.; b. Henrietta, Tex., Jan. 30, 1913; s. Lewis and Ena (Neville) I.; A.B., U. Tex., 1936, LL.B., 1936; m. Jean Hunter, Oct. 15, 1940 (dec. Apr. 1970); children—Frank Neville, William Forsyth; m. 2d, Jayne Brumley, July 22, 1972. Admitted to Tex. bar, 1936; mem. firm Bullington, Humphrey & Humphrey, Wichita Falls, 1937-47; judge 30th Jud. Dist. Ct., Wichita Falls, 1947-52; mem. 81st to 86th congresses from 13th Tex. dist.; exec. v.p. Am. Petroleum Inst., Washington, 1963, pres., N.Y.C., 1963-70, pres., Washington, 1970—; dir. VLN Corp., N.Y.C., Union Trust Co., Washington. Mem. natural gas adv. council Fed. Power Commn., 1964-70; mem. adv. bd. Center for Strategic Studies, Washington, 1966-69; mem. Nat. Petroleum Council, 1964-60; mem. Pres.'s Nat. Adv. Com. on Hwy. Beautification, 1966-68, Pres.'s Nat. Citizens Commn. on Internat. Cooperation, 1965-68; mem. Pres.'s Industry-Govt. Spl. Task Force on Travel, 1966-68; mem. U.S. nat. conf. World Energy Congress, 1967-69, World Petroleum Congresses, 1963-70. Trustee John F. Kennedy Center for Performing Arts, Washington; vice chmn. bd. regents U. Tex. at Austin. Served with AUS, 1942-45. Mem. Am. Bar Assn., State Bar of Tex., Ind. Petroleum Assn. Am., Japan-Am. Soc. Episcopalian. Mason. Clubs: Burning Tree (Chevy Chase, Md.); City (Dallas); Carleton, City Tavern Assn., Internat., Metropolitan (Washington); Hemisphere, 28, University (N.Y.C.). Home: Shoreham West 2500 Calvert St NW Washington DC 20008 Office: 1801 K St NW Washington DC 20006

IKENBERRY, HENRY CEPHAS, JR., lawyer; b. Cloverdale, Va., Mar. 23, 1920; s. Henry Cephas and Bessie (Peters) I.; B.A., Bridgewater Coll., 1947; J.D., U. Va., 1947; m. Margaret Sangster Henry, July 3, 1943; children—Anna Catherine (Mrs. Fawell), Mary Margaret. Admitted to Va. bar, 1947, W.Va. and D.C. bars, 1948; asso. Steptoe & Johnson, Washington, 1947-49, 50-53, partner, 1953—; asst. counsel Gen. Aniline & Film Co., N.Y.C., 1949-50. Mem. com. on unauthorized practice D.C. Ct. Appeals, 1972—. Served ensign to lt. comdr. USNR, 1941-46, commanded anti-submarine vessels, participated Atlantic, Philippine, Okinawa campaigns. Mem. Am., Va. bar assns., Bar Assn. D.C. (chmn. comml. and bus. law com. 1969-72), Raven Soc., Am. Legion, Newcomen Soc. in N.Am., Order of Coif, Phi Delta Phi, Tau Kappa Alpha. Presbyn. (ruling elder 1970-72). Clubs: Metropolitan (Washington); Chevy Chase (Md.); Farmington Country. Home: 3725 Cardiff Rd Chevy Chase MD 20015 Office: 1250 Connecticut Av Washington DC 20036

ILER, ARTHUR TRIPLETT, judge; b. Rockport, Ky., Mar. 3, 1900; s. William Perry and Nellie (Young) I.; student Western Ky. State Coll., 1917-19; LL.B., Columbus U., 1934; m. Kathryn Wallace, June 19, 1927; children—Richard W., William Perry II. With Washington Herald, Washington News, 1930-33; with FHA, D.C., Ky., 1934-40; admitted to Ky. bar, 1935; practiced in Louisville, 1940-41; asst. atty. gen. Ky., 1941-43; atty. Muhlenberg County, 1954-56; circuit judge 45th Jud. Dist. Ky., Greenville, 1956—; farmer, horse raiser, 1950—. Pres., Muhlenberg County Fair Bd., 1948-58. Bd. dirs. Travelers Protective Assn. Served with inf. U.S. Army, 1918. Named Man of Year, Central City C. of C., 1958. Mem. Am. Legion (post comdr.), 40 and 8, Ky. Thoroughbred Assn., Sigma Delta Kappa. Presbyn. (elder). Clubs: All States Society (past pres. Washington); Rotary (past pres. Central City, Ky.). Home: 1004 Broad St Central City KY 42330 Office: Court House Greenville KY 42345

ILLE, BERNARD GLENN, ins. co. exec.; b. Ponca City, Okla., Feb. 8, 1927; s. Frank L. and Marie (Cornwell) I.; B.S., Okla. U.; m. Mary Lou Allen, Aug. 23, 1952; children—Meredith, Leslie, Frank. Agt. Phoenix Mut. Life Ins. Co., Oklahoma City, 1953-55; gen. agt. Farmers & Bankers Life Ins. Co., Oklahoma City, 1955-56; various positions United Founders LIfe Ins. Co., Oklahoma City, 1956-66, pres., 1966-70, chmn. bd., pres., 1970—, also dir.; pres., chmn. bd., dir. Reis Corp., Oklahoma City; dir. Founders Bank & Trust, Oklahoma City; chmn. bd., dir. United Founders Life Ins. Co. Ill., Chgo.; dir. Modern Security Life, Springfield, Mo., LSB Industries, Inc., Landmark Land, Inc. (both Oklahoma City). Trustee John Galvin Meml. Scholarship Fund. Served with USCGR, 1945-46. C.L.U. Mem. Nat. Football Found. Hall of Fame (chpt. pres. 1966—), Young Presidents Orgn., Kappa Alpha Alumni Assn. (past pres.). Club: Quail Creek Golf and Country. Home: 3117 Elmwood St Oklahoma City OK 73116 Office: 5900 Mosteller Dr Oklahoma City OK 73112

ILLICH, IVAN, philosopher; b. Vienna, Austria, Sept. 4, 1926; s. Petar and Ellen (Regenstreif) I.; Lic.U. Philos., Gregorian U., Rome, 1945, Lic.U. Theology, 1950; Dr. Fac. Phil., U. Salzburg, 1951. Vice pres. U. Santa Maria, Ponce, P.R., 1956-60; ind. author, 1960—; researcher Center for Intercultural Documentation, Cuernavaca, Mexico, 1961—, pres. bd., 1963-68. Mem. Council Higher Edn., Commonwealth P.R., 1959-61. Author: Celebration of Awareness, 1970; Deschooling Society, 1971; Tools for Conviviality, 1973; Energy and Equity, 1974. Contbr. to various jours. and mags. Home: Casa Blanca Rancho Tetela APDO 479 Cuernavaca Mexico

ILLIG, KENNETH WILLIAM, mfg. co. exec.; b. Cambridge, Mass., Oct. 13, 1922; s. William Ernest and Clara Ida (Reidel) I.; student Tufts U., 1940-44; M.B.A., U. Chgo., 1965; m. Henrietta Tosel Morford, Nov. 16, 1968; children—Bruce K., Gerry K. With Gen. Electric Co., Bridgeport, Conn., 1946-47; br. mgr. RCA Service Co., New Haven, 1947-49, Chgo., 1950-52; sales engr. Chgo. Standard Transformer Co., 1952-55; pres., gen. mgr. Countryside Electronics Corp., Palatine, 1955-59; with Automatic Switch Co., 1959—, mgr. dist. office, Dallas, 1968—; dir. D A F C Inc., Addison, Tex. Served with USNR, 1942-46. Mem. I.E.E.E., Am. Econ. Assn., Am. Marketing Assn., Sales and Marketing Execs. Internat., Am. Statis. Assn., Aircraft Owners and Pilots Assn., Dallas C. of C., Zeta Psi. Methodist. Mason (Shriner). Home: 13118 Brushcreek St Dallas TX 75240 Office: 8609 NW Plaza Dr Dallas TX 75225

IMBURG, IRVING JEROME, dentist; b. Richmond, Va., July 7, 1924; s. Samuel and Nettie (Meyers) I.; student Med. Coll. Va., 1942-43, Washington U. at St. Louis, 1943-44; D.D.S., Med. Coll. Va., 1948; m. Clare Cardozo, Dec. 21, 1948; children—Catherine (Mrs. Richard M. Kaplan), Susan, Nancy Elizabeth. Gen. practice dentistry, Richmond, Va., 1948-50, Falls Church, Va., 1952— founder William Byrd Free Dental Clinic, Richmond, 1948; mem. courtesy staff Alexandria (Va.) Hosp.; pres. Drs. Imburg, Rudin & Coleman & Rock, Ltd., Falls Church, 1971—. Pres. MacArthur Sch. P.T.A., Alexandria, 1965, Howard Middle Sch. P.T.A., Alexandria, 1966; v.p. T.C. Williams High Sch. P.T.A., Alexandria, 1968-69. Served with AUS, 1943-44, to capt. USAF, 1950-52. Fellow Internat. Coll. Dentists; mem. No. Va. (pres.), Fairfax (past pres.) dental assns., Commonwealth Dental Study Club (co-founder 1963, past pres.), Va. Dental Assn. (continuing edn. com. 1970—, ho. of dels. 1972-74), D.C. Dental Soc., Am. Dental Assn., Alpha Sigma Chi. Jewish religion (pres.-elect congregation). Editor No. Va. Dental Newsletter, 1966-67. Home: 1230 Kingston Pl Alexandria VA 22302 Office: 6319 Castle Pl Falls Church VA 22044

IMEL, ARTHUR BLAINE, architect; b. Blackwell, Okla., Dec. 30, 1921; student Okla. Mil. Acad., 1939-41; B.Arch. (A.I.A. award student), U. Okla., 1950. Draftsman, U. Okla. and Wichita, Kan., 1949-50; past mem. firm Buchner & Imel; pvt. practice A. Blaine Imel, architect; now mem. firm Stanfield, Imel & Walton, Tulsa; prin. works include Tradewinds Motor Hotel and Restaurant (award Am. Restaurant Soc., 1960), Tulsa, Key Club and Banquet Hall, Tulsa, 1961, Perkins High Sch., 1955, Admiral State Bank, 1961, Robert Fulton Elementary Sch., 1960, fellowship hall and classes Yale Av. Presbyn. Ch., 1960. Tech. adviser, mem. design bd. Civic Center, Tulsa; mem. Mayor's Street Light Com. Served to maj. USMCR, 1942-45. Mem. A.I.A. (chpt. dir. 1957-60), Tulsa C. of C. (planning com. 1955). Author: Esempi, 1952. Asst. editor Perspective Mag. Address: 3816 S Erie St Tulsa OK 74135

IMLER, ALLISON E(LLWOOD), radiologist, oncologist; b. Altoona, Pa., Nov. 15, 1910; s. Thomas H. and Lydia E. I.; B.S., U. Pitts., 1933, M.D., Hahnemann Med. Coll. Phila., 1937; m. Elwys Fawl, Feb. 19, 1946; children—Teresa Carol, Thomas Allison, Stephen, Daniel. Intern, Hahnemann Hosp., Phila., 1937-38; resident in cancer Jeanes Hosp. of Phila., 1938-41; pvt. practice medicine, specializing in radiology and oncology, Birmingham, Ala., 1947—; group practice Lloyd Noland Hosp. and Clinic, Fairfield, Ala.; asso. prof. radiology, dir. univ. tumor clinic Med. Coll. Ala., 1946-47, asso. prof. oncology, 1949-50; cons. staff Brookwood Hosp., Homewood, Birmingham. Served as maj. M.C., AUS, Walter Reed Gen. Hosp., Washington, 1941-42, Torney Gen. Hosp., Palm Springs, Cal., 1942-44, Letterman Gen. Hosp., San Francisco, 1944-46. Diplomate Am. Bd. Radiology, therapeutic radiology, 1941, radiology, 1944. Fellow Am. Coll. Radiology, Am., Internat. colls. surgeons, Southeastern Surg. Congress; mem. Radio. Soc. N.A., Jefferson County Med. Soc., So., Ala. med. assns., Ala., Pa. radiol. socs., A.M.A., Am. Roentgen. Ray Soc. Contbr. med. jours. Home: 1912 Shades Crest Rd Birmingham AL 35216 Office: Lloyd Noland Hosp Fairfield AL 35064

IMM, VAL DELLA, writer; b. Mankato, Minn., Mar. 11, 1930; d. Val M. and Gertrude (Fehlandt) I.; student Bethany Lutheran Coll., Mankato State Coll. Fashion editor Tex. Fashion Mfg. Assn., 1959-60; soc. editor, columnist Dallas Times Herald, 1960—. Bd. dirs. Soc. for Abandoned and Neglected Children, Spl. Care Sch. Handicapped Children. Recipient Southwestern Journalism Found. award, 1968; Tex. U.P.I. award, 1968; award in field Interpretive Writing, 1968. Mem. Dallas Council on World Affairs. Clubs: Dallas Gun, Lakewood (Dallas). Lutheran. Home: Maple Terrace 3005 Maple Av Dallas TX 75201 Office: Dallas Times Herald Dallas TX 75202

IMMASCHE, FRANCIS WILLIAM, econ. adviser, farmer; b. Saffordville, Kan., Oct. 21, 1907; s. William George and Margaret (Lyles) ImM.; B.S., Kan. State U., 1929; M.A., U. Chgo., 1933. Livestock economist Armour & Co., Chgo., 1930-31, Fed. Farm Bd., Washington, 1931-33; asst. chief, econ. and credit research div., FCA, Washington, 1933-42; dep. dir. livestock and dairy div. U.S. Dept. Agr., Washington, 1947-65, adviser on livestock and wool situation, including Australia and New Zealand, 1971—; pres. Goldpoint Mining Co. (Nev.), 1941—; farmer, Chase County, Kan. Pres. Meml. Lawn Cemeteries Assn., Emporia, Kan., 1959-70. Served from 1st lt. to col. USAF, 1942-47; now col. USAF ret. Mem. Sigma Alpha Epsilon, Alpha Zeta, Alpha Kappa Psi. Clubs: Congressional Country (Washington); Saddle and Sirloin (Chgo.); Indian Wells (Cal.) Country. Home: 3133 Connecticut Av Washington DC 20008 also Strong City KS 66869

INGE, MILTON THOMAS, educator; b. Newport News, Va., Mar. 18, 1936; s. Clyde Elmo and Bernice Lucille (Jackson) I.; B.A., Randolph-Macon Coll., 1959; M.A., Vanderbilt U., 1960, Ph.D., 1964; m. Betty Jean Meredith, Dec. 27, 1958; 1 son, Scott Thomas. Instr. English, Vanderbilt U., 1962-64, vis. prof. English, summer 1969; asst. prof., asso. prof. Am. thought and lang. Mich. State U., 1964-69; asso. prof. English, Va. Commonwealth U., Richmond, 1969-73, prof., 1973—, chmn. dept. English, 1974—. Gen. editor Research Guides in English, Am. Critical Tradition series (David Lewis Pub.); editorial cons. several pubs.; reader English Composition Test, Coll. Entrance Exam. Bd., 1967, 69; book reviewer Nashville Tenneseean, Richmond Times-Dispatch, Menomonee Falls Gazette. Bd. dirs. Friends of Richmond Pub. Library, Nat. Newspaper Archive and Acad. Comic Art, San Francisco. Fulbright-Hays grantee to teach Am. lit. Spain, 1967-68, Argentina, 1971, research grantee Am. Philos. Soc., 1970, Mich. State U., 1965, 66, 68. Coll. Teaching Career fellow So. Fellowships Fund, 1959-62. Mem. Modern Lang. Assn., Am. Studies Assn., Popular Culture Assn., Soc. Study So. Lit. (exec. council 1971-73), Melville Soc., Thoreau Fellowship, Am. Assn. Tchrs. Spanish and Portuguese, Phi Beta Kappa, Omicron Delta Kappa, Pi Delta Epsilon, Lambda Chi Alpha. Club: Virginia Writers. Author: (with T.D. Young) Donald Davidson: Essay and Bibliography, 1965, Donald Davidson, 1971. Editor: Sut Lovingood's Yarns, 1966; High Times and Hard Times, 1967; Agrarianism in American Literature, 1969; A.B. Longstreet, 1969; Faulkner: A Rose for Emily, 1970; Wm. Byrd of Westover, 1970; Studies in Light in August, 1971; Bartleby the Inscrutable, 1975; Ellen Glasgow: Centenary Essays, 1975; also Resources for American Literary Study, 1971—. Office: Dept English Va Commonwealth U Richmond VA 23284

INGE, VERNON EUGENE, lawyer; b. Newport News, Va., Nov. 28, 1938; s. Clyde Elmo and Bernice Lucile (Jackson) I.; B.A., Randolph-Macon Coll., 1962; J.D., U. Richmond, 1965; m. Catherine Lee King, Aug. 6, 1960; children—Vernone Eugene Jr., William Richard. Admitted to Va. bar, 1965; atty. Richmond, Va., 1965-67, 1969—; asst. city atty. Richmond, 1967-69; pres. Marlboro Constrn. Co., Richmond, T.W. Moore Furniture Co., Richmond; partner Staple 3, 1968. Pres., dir. Grace House. Mem. Va. Trial Lawyers Assn., Va. State Bar. Home: 7117 Riverside Dr Richmond VA 23225 Office: 2922 Hathaway Rd Richmond VA 23225

INGER, GEORGE ROE, educator; b. Detroit, Jan. 27, 1933; s. Hartwell C. and Madeleine S. (Roe) I.; B.S., Wayne State U., 1954, M.S., 1956; Ph.D., U. Mich., 1960. Aerodynamicist Douglas Missile Systems, Santa Monica, Cal., 1960-62; research scientist Aerospace Corp., El Segundo, Cal., 1962-66; chief fluid physics br. McDonnell-Douglas Astronautics, Huntington Beach, Cal., 1966-70; vis. prof. Von Karman Inst., Brussels, Belgium, 1966-70; prof. aero. engring. Va. Poly. Inst., 1971—; cons. NATO-AGARD, Cal. Tech. Jet Propulsion Lab., industry. Detroit Bd. Edn. fellow, 1954-55; Douglas Aircraft, Bendix and Lear Corp. fellow, 1956-60. Asso. fellow Am. Inst. Aeros. and Astronautics; mem. Am. Soc. M.E., Am. Physics Soc., Am. Astronautical Soc., Am. Aviation Hist. Soc., Sigma Xi, Phi Kappa Phi, Sigma Gamma Tau. Research on basic theory of high temperature reacting gas flows, aerodynamics. Office: Virginia Polytechnic Institute Blacksburg VA 24061

INGERSOLL, PHILIP FRANK, elec. engr.; b. Richmond, Va., Sept. 28, 1937; s. Everett Harold and Marie (Rush) I.; B.S., Johns Hopkins, 1960; postgrad. Kan. State U., 1960-62; M.S. (Harry Diamond Labs. fellow), George Washington U., 1968; m. Solveig Maren Hegre, June 26, 1965; 1 son, Evan Bjorn. Physicist, Harry Diamond Labs., Washington, 1962-65, elec. engr., 1965-73, research and devel. supr., 1973—, also mem. computer steering com. Mem. I.E.E.E., A.A.A.S., Am. Def. Preparedness Assn. Patentee in field. Office: Harry Diamond Labs Br 430 Washington DC 20438

INGERSON, FRED EARL, geologist, educator; b. Barstow, Tex., Oct. 28, 1906; s. Fred Percy and Mamie (Carson) I.; A.B., Simmons U., 1928, M.A., 1931, Sc.D. (hon.), 1942; Ph.D., Yale, 1934; postgrad. U. Innsbruck, 1934-35; m. Martha Anna Duncan, June 5, 1930; children—Mary (dec.), Fred Earl. Instr., Yale, 1932-34; asst. phys. chemist, geophys. lab. Carnegie Instn. of Washington, 1935-39, phys. chemist, 1939-43, petrologist, 1943-47; ofcl. investigator contracts Office Sci. Research and Devel., 1942-45; geologist, chief geochemistry and petrology br. U.S. Geol. Survey, Washington, 1947-57, geologist, 1957-58; prof. geology U. Tex., 1958, asso. dean grad. sch., 1961-65, prof., 1965—; mem. Yale expdn. to Nfld., 1933; survey quartz, Brazil, 1945; mem. adv. bd. Geologisch Rundschau, 1948-54; mem. div. geol. and geog. and div. chemistry and chem. tech. NRC, 1951-54; Lab. Tech. Petrofabric Analysis; spl. lectr. geology U. Mich., 1938. Recipient Day medal Geol. Soc. Am., 1955; Distinguished Service medal U.S. Dept. Interior, 1959. Fellow Am. Geophys. Union (charter), Geochem. Soc. India (hon.), Commn. One Forming Fluids (hon.), Mineral. Soc. Am. (treas. 1941-58, translation editor 1959-67), Geol. Soc. Am. (council 1946, 47-50); mem. Internat. Commn. on Geochemistry (sec. 1960-63, v.p. 1963-65), Internat. Assn. Geochemistry and Cosmochemistry (pres. 1965-72), Assn. Earth Sci. Editors (charter), Internat. Assn. Volcanology and Chemistry of Earth's Interior (exec. com. 1967-71), Mineral. Soc. London, Soc. Française de Mineralogie, Deutsche Mineralogische Gesellschaft, Soc. Geol. Mexicana, Am. Geol. Inst. (vis. scientist 1961, translation com. 1958, chmn. 1958-61; Internat. field Inst. to Brazil 1966), Soc. Econ. Geologists, Geochem. Soc. (pres. 1955-57, translation com. 1958, translation editor 1958-70), Geochem. Soc. Japan, Geol. Soc. Brazil, Mineral. Assn. Can., Sigma Xi, Sigma Delta Pi, Kappa Delta Pi, Phi Kappa Phi. Club: Foreign Policy. Exec. editor Geochelmica et Cosmochimica Acta, 1950-61, editorial adv. bd., 1961-66; editor-in-chief Internat. Series of Monographs on Earth Science, 1955; chmn. bd. editors Internat. Geology Rev., 1959-62; editorial bd. Minerallus Deposita. Author sci. articles. Home: 3402 Mount Connell Dr Austin TX 76731

INGHAM, MERTON CHARLES, oceanographer; b. Stockton, Cal., Jan. 9, 1930; s. Merton Lewis and Hazel May (DeLegh) I.; B.S., Ore. State Coll., 1953; M.S. (NSF fellow), Ore. State U., 1959, Ph.D. (U.S. Fish and Wildlife Service fellow), 1965; m. Nancy Marguerite Davies, June 25, 1955; children—Steven Charles, Janice Marguerite, Donna Elizabeth. Research ocenaographer U.S. Dept. Interior, Bur. Comml. Fisheries, Miami, Fla., 1965-69; tech. dir. U.S. Coast Guard Oceanographic Unit, Washington, 1969-71; research oceanographer Nat. Oceanic and Atmospheric Adminstrn., Washington, 1972—. Served with AUS, 1953-55. Mem. Am. Soc. Limnology and Oceanography. Home: 7120 Hadlow Ct Springfield VA 22152 Office: National Oceanic and Atmospheric Adminstrn Washington DC 20235

INGLE, GEORGE WILLIAM, chem. co. exec.; b. Lynbrook, N.Y., May 11, 1917; s. William Thomas and Emma Amelia (Johnston) I.; A.B., Colgate U., 1938; M.S., Inst. Paper Chemistry, 1940; m. Jeannette Donaldson, Sept. 14, 1946; children—Grant M., William T., Susan M., Jeanne B. With Monsanto Co., 1940—, beginning as control chemist, successively color physicist, supt. color and control labs., research group leader, research sect. leader, research mgr. analytical and phys. testing, 1940-68, tech. liaison mgr., Washington, 1968—. Dir. Mass. Moderators Assn., 1966-68. Town moderator, Hampden, Mass., 1950-69. Mem. Soc. Plastics Industry, Am. Chem. Soc., Am. Soc. Testing and Materials, Internat. Orgn. for Standards. Presbyn. Club: Cosmos (Washington). Contbr. articles profl. jours. Home: 6827 Wemberly Way McLean VA 22101 Office: 1101 17th St Washington DC 20036

INGLE, ROBERT MAURICE, biologist; b. Danville, Ill., July 1, 1917; s. Charles Frank and Nellie May (Lyon) I.; B.S., U. Ill., 1939; M.S., U. Miami, 1951; m. Anne Elizabeth Lorber, Jan. 19, 1947; children—Robert Maurice, Charles F., Allison John. Sr. biologist, dir. research Fla. Dept. Natural Resources, Tallahassee, 1949-72; pres., dir. research Conservation Consultants, Inc., Tallahassee, 1972—. Cons. govts. of Venezuela, Cuba, Bahamas. Mem. Am. Commn. to Administer Cuban Fisheries Treaty, 1961, numerous coms. Atlantic States Fishery Commn., Gulf States Fishery Commn. Served with USNR, 1941-45. Recipient Achievement award U.P.I., Fla., 1969, Achievement award Fla. State Govt., 1972, Meritorious Accomplishment award Southeastern Fisheries Assn., 1971. Mem. Alpha Tau Omega. Author: Sea Turtles, 1949. Contbr. articles to profl. jours. Home: 2306 Mission Rd Tallahassee FL 32304 Office: Barnett Bank Bldg Tallahassee FL 32301

INGRAM, ANNE G., educator; b. Carrollton, Ga., April 24, 1926; d. Irvine Sullivan and Martha (Munro) Ingram; student W. Ga. Coll., 1941-43; A.B., U. N.C., 1944; M.A., U. Ga., 1948; Ed.D., Columbia, 1962; postgrad. U. Oslo (Norway), 1965. Instr., La. Poly. Inst., Ruston, 1950-51; asst. prof., U. Miss., Oxford, 1951-54, Western Ill. U., Macomb, 1960-61, George Washington U., 1961-62; asso. prof. U. Md., College Park, 1962—. Mem. Am. Assn. U. Profs., A.A.H.P.E.R., Nat. Assn. Women Deans and Counselors, Internat. Assn. Sport Psychology, Am. Sociol. Assn., Alpha Delta Pi. Author: (with James H. Humphrey) Introduction to Pnysical Education for College Students, 1969; Moving with Music—A Syllabus for Teaching Dance and Rythms, 1969. Contbr. articles to profl. jours. Home: 114 Hillcrest Dr Carrollton GA 30117 Office: Cole Bldg U Md College Park MD 20740

INGRAM, CHARLES CLARK, JR., utility exec.; b. Henryetta, Okla., Dec. 10, 1916; s. Charles Clark and Winnie (Edwards) I.; B.S., U. Okla., 1940; m. Maxine Waterbury, Jan. 29, 1939; children—James C., Jack R. With Okla. Natural Gas Co., Tulsa, 1940—, beginning as laborer, successively engr., asst. chief engr., supt. gas purchase and reserves, operating supt., v.p. land and geol. dept., exec. v.p., pres., 1940-71, chmn. bd., 1966—, chief exec. officer, 1971—; dir. Nat. Bank of Tulsa, Sooner Fed. Savs. & Loan Assn. Mem. Okla. Pub. Expenditures Council, Thomas Gilcrease Inst. Am. History and Art; gov. Am. Citizenship Center; v.p. at large Ark. Basin Devel. Assn.; mem. adv. bd. Downtown Tulsa, Unltd.; chmn. bd. trustees Frontiers of Sci. Found. Okla.; mem. adv. bd. Internat. Oil and Gas Ednl. Center of Southwestern Legal Found.; mem. pres.'s bd. visitors, Research Inst. alumni council and univ. acad. fellows, trustee U. Okla. Bd. dirs. Tulsa Philharmonic Soc.; trustee Okla. Safety Council. Served to maj., ordnance AUS, 1941-46. Registered profl. engr., Okla. Mem. Am. Assn. Petroleum Geologists (asso.), Am. Inst. Mining, Metall. and Petroleum Engrs., A.I.M. (pres.'s council), Am. Mgmt. Assn., Am. Petroleum Inst., Engrs. Soc. Tulsa, Ind. Petroleum Assn. Am. (dir.), Okla. Ind. Petroleum Assn., Oklahoma City, Okla. State, Tulsa chambers commerce, Okla. Press Assn., Propeller Club U.S., Tulsa Geol. Soc., Am. (dir.), So. (past pres.) gas assns., Asso. Industries Okla. (dir.) Interstate Natural Gas Assn. Am. (dir.), Inst. Gas Tech. (trustee), Mid-Continent Oil and Gas Assn. (dir., exec. com. Kan.-Okla. div.), Nat. Alliance of Businessmen (chmn. Eastern Okla. and Tulsa 1973-74), N.Am. (dir.), Okla. Petroleum Council (dir.),

Sigma Tau, Sigma Gamma Epsilon. Mason. Clubs: Southern Hills Country (gov., past pres.), Summit, Tulsa, Tulsa Press, Cedar Ridge Country (Tulsa). Home: 3707 S Delaware Pl Tulsa OK 74105 Office: PO Box 871 Tulsa OK 74102

INGRAM, EDITH JACQUELINE, judge; b. nr. Sparta, Ga., Jan. 16, 1942; d. Robert T. and Katherine (Hunt) Ingram; B.S. in Edn., Fort Valley (Ga.) State Coll., 1963. Store mgr. High's Dairy Products, Washington, summers 1956-63; tchr. Moore Elementary Sch., Griffin, Ga., 1963-67; tchr. Hancock Central Elementary Sch., Sparta, Ga., 1967-68; judge Ct. of Ordinary, Sparta, 1969—. Pres., Ogeechee-Lake View Mgmt. Co., Inc., 1972—. Mem. state and local govt. adv. com. Office Econ. Opportunity; mem. Hancock County Concerned Citizens Orgn. Mem. Hancock County Democratic Club, 1967—; mem. Ga. Dem. Exec. Com. Treas. Hancock County chpt. Ga. Council on Human Relations, Sheriff's Retirement Assn. Ga., Ordinaries Retirement Ga.; sec. Hancock County Com. for Social and Econ. Devel.; mem. Oconee Area Minority Adv. Com., Labor Dept., East Central Com. for Opportunity. Mem. Sheriff's Assn. Ga., County Officers Assn. Ga., N.A.A.C.P., Fort Valley State Coll. Alumni Assn., Nat., Internat. assns. probate judges, Bus. Devel. Instn., Ordinaries Assn. Ga., Delta Sigma Theta. Baptist. Club: Hancock Womens. Home: 718 New St Sparta GA 31087 Office: PO Box 151 Sparta GA 31087

INGRAM, ERSKINE BRONSON, II, business exec.; b. St. Paul, Nov. 27, 1931; s. Orrin Henry and Hortense (Bigelow) I.; student Vanderbilt U., 1950; A.B., Princeton, 1953; m. Martha Robinson Rivers, Oct. 4, 1958; children—Orrin Henry II, John Rivers, David Bronson, Robin Bigelow. With Ingram Oil & Refining Co., 1955-61, v.p., treas., 1958-61; v.p., treas. Ingram Corp., Nashville, 1962, pres., dir., 1963—; dir. subsidiaries; dir. Weyerhaeuser Co., 1st Trust Co. St. Paul, Synercon Corp.; chmn. bd. Capitol Chevrolet Co. Vice chmn. Tenn. Indsl. and Agrl. Devel. Commn. Trustee, Vanderbilt U.; mem. bd. trust Montgomery Bell Acad.; bd. dirs. Ingram Found., Nashville Boys Club. Served to lt. (j.g.), USNR, 1953-55. Mem. Nashville Area C. of C. (dir.). Clubs: Belle Meade Country (Nashville); Augusta (Ga.) Nat. Golf; Seminole Golf (Palm Beach, Fla.). Home: 120 Hillwood Dr Nashville TN 37205 Office: 4304 Harding Rd Nashville TN 37205

INGRAM, GLYNN EDWYNN, utility exec.; b. Montgomery, Ala., May 12, 1926; s. Van Buren and Bessie (Furlong) I.; grad. pub. high sch.; m. Mary Ella Cox, June 3, 1946; children—Mary (Mrs. William Johnson), Joy (Mrs. Edward Nelson), Dwayne Edwynn. With Atlanta Gas Light Co., 1952—, supr. machine accounting, 1956-60, head data processing dept., 1960—. Instr. data processing Massey Jr. Coll., Atlanta, 1961-62, DeKalb County Tech. Sch., Decatur, 1963-64. Mem. Data Processing Mgmt. Assn. (past pres., recipient individual performance award 1966), Atlanta Jr. C. of C. Mem. Ch. of Christ (elder). Home: 1698 Glen Haven Circle Decatur GA 30032 Office: PO Box 4569 Atlanta GA 30302

INGRAM, HUGH BEDIEL, state ofcl.; b. Jacksonville, Fla., Dec. 29, 1922; s. Hugh Bediel and Carrie A. (Mills) I.; B.A., U. Fla., 1950, M.Ed., 1953; m. Elizabeth Caroline Koch, July 29, 1944; children—David Hugh, Jonathan Edward. English and math. tchr. Bradford High Sch., Starke, Fla., 1950-52; prin. Lawtey Jr. High Sch., Lawtey, Fla., 1952-59; supervising prin. Bradford High Sch., Starke, 1959-62; dir. profl. rights and responsibilities Fla. Edn. Assn., Tallahassee, 1962-68, exec. sec.-treas. dept. second sch. prins., 1966-67; exec. dir. Fla. Profl. Practices Commn., Tallahassee, 1968—. Served to 1st lt. AUS, 1943-46. Mem. Nat., Fla. edn. assns., Fla. Dept. Secondary Sch. Prins., Nat. Assn. Secondary Sch. Prins., Nat. Assn. Ednl. Standards and Profl. Practices (pres. 1974—), Fla. N.G. Officers Assn., N.G. Officers Assn. Am., Phi Delta Kappa. Home: 1724 Dora Dr Tallahassee FL 32303 Office: Tallahassee Bank & Trust Bldg Tallahassee FL 32301

INGRAM, JOHN WILSON, corp. exec.; b. Varadam, Miss., Nov. 13, 1919; s. William Russell and Ruby Corrine (McMurray) I.; grad. Peabody High Sch., Trenton, Tenn., 1937; m. Helen Clara Yoakum, Jan. 20, 1951. With Great Atlantic & Pacific Tea Co., 1938-48; with Fischer Lime and Cement Co., North Little Rock, Ark., 1948—, v.p., mgr., 1964-72, sr. v.p., 1972—; mem. nat. adv. council Armstrong Cork Co., 1962, 70. Pres. City Chain Store Council, 1941-42. Recipient Distinguished Sales award Memphis Sales Mgrs. Club, 1950. Mem. Assn. Bldg. Distbrs. Ark. (past pres.), Ark. Home Builders Assn. (life mem. Spike Club), Ark., Little Rock, North Little Rock chambers commerce, Nat. Bldg. Material Distbrs. Assn., Ark. Lumbermans Assn., S.W. Lumber Assn. Baptist. Mason (Shriner). Club: North Hills Country (Sylvan Hills, North Little Rock). Home: 4809 Hickory St Apt 5 North Little Rock AR 72116 Office: 1650 E Washington St North Little Rock AR 72114

INGRAM, LEROY, archtl. engr.; b. Houston, Oct. 8, 1937; s. Jack Ulyses and Mattie Lee (Bolden) I.; B.S., Prairie View A. and M. Coll., 1967; m. Quency Pearl Lipscomb, June 23, 1962; children—Leroy, Rochele Denise, Darrel Wayne. Aerospace equipment draftsman Lockheed Aircraft Corp., Houston, 1963-66; design engr. Lane & Price, Inc., cons. engrs., Baytown, Tex., 1966-68; structural design engr. Bernard Johnson Engrs., Inc., Houston, 1968-70; design engr. Kentron-Hawaii, Ltd. div. LTV Aerospace Corp., Houston, 1970—; treas. Alpha Engring. Corp., Houston, 1972—. Chmn. adv. com. Inter-Am. Forum, Tex. and Mexico, 1973-74. Bd. dirs. Health Care, Inc., Houston, 1972-75. Named Most Outstanding Houston Jaycee, 1971; Senator, Jr. Chamber Internat., 1973. Mem. Am. Concrete Inst., Soc. Am. Mil. Engrs. (chpt. v.p. 1969), Am. Rifle Assn., Gulf Coast Soc. Prairie View Engrs. (v.p. 1973, parliamentarian 1974). Baptist (deacon 1968—). Home: 1505 Patterson St Houston TX 77007 Office: 1720 NASA Rd-1 Houston TX 77058

INGRAM, ROBERT A., physician; b. Dallas, June 6, 1922; s. Henry Lee and Bernice (Benedict) I.; B.A., Rice Inst., 1947; M.D., U. Tex., 1951; m. Dorace McGill, Sept. 7, 1946; 1 dau., Ruth Elizabeth. Intern, Baptist Meml. Hosp., San Antonio, 1951-52; practice gen. medicine, Orange, Tex., 1952—; mem. staff Orange Meml. Hosp. Served with USNR, 1944-46. Diplomate Am. Bd. Family Practice. Mem. Am. Acad. Family Practice, Am., Tex. med. assns., Internat. Platform Assn., Mensa. Home: 1906 Link Orange TX 77630 Office: 908 12th St Orange TX 77630

INGRAM, SAM HARRIS, coll. pres.; b. Acton, Tenn., Jan. 31, 1928; s. John Q. and Lois (Abernathy) I.; B.S., Bethel Coll., 1951; M.A., Memphis State U., 1953, Ed.D., U. Tenn., 1959; m. Betty Ann White, July 14, 1950; children—Sam W., Glenn D. Elementary tchr., elementary prin., secondary prin. McNairy County Schs., Selmer, Tenn., 1949-57; asso. dir. curriculum Tenn. Dept. Edn., Nashville, 1959, 61; asso. prof. edn. Memphis State U., 1961, 62; chmn. edn. dept. Middle Tenn. State U., Murfreesboro, 1962-67, dean sch. edn., 1967-69; pres. Motlow State Community Coll., 1969—. Served with USMCR, 1946-47. Home: 205 Lake Circle Dr Tullahoma TN 37388

INLOW, ROBERT FRANCIS, investment co. exec.; b. Oklahoma City, Okla., Nov. 19, 1936; s. Robert Frost and Evelyn (Milburn) I.; B.B.A., North Tex. State U., 1959; postgrad. So. Meth. U., 1965-68; M.B.A., Pepperdine U., 1974; m. Julie Scott Barnes, June 13, 1964; 1 son, Robert Julian. Investment banker First Nat. Bank in Dallas, 1962-64; sr. v.p., mgr. income property financing and devel. Hinton Mortgage & Investment Co., Dallas, Houston also Albuquerque, 1969-73; pres. Jones & Inlow, Inc., mortgage bankers, Dallas, 1974—. Served to capt. USAF, 1959-68. Mem. Dallas Mortgage Bankers Young Mens Assn. (pres. 1967), Delta Sigma Pi. Baptist. Home: 9628 Dartridge Dr Dallas TX 75238 Office: Suite 512 One Turtle Creek Village Dallas TX 75219

INMAN, DENNIS HISEY, lawyer; b. Lebanon, Tenn., May 4, 1947; s. William Howell and Billie (Hisey) I.; B.S., U. Tenn., 1969, J.D., 1970; m. Jacqueline Wright, Mar. 13, 1971; 1 dau., Sharon Elizabeth. Admitted to Tenn. bar, 1971; mem. firm Taylor, Inman & Tilson, Morristown Tenn., 1970—. Dir. Hasson-Bryan Hardware Co., JCL Clin. Research Corp., Knoxville, Tenn. Mem. Am., Tenn. bar assns. Morristown Jaycees, Order of Coif, Phi Kappa Phi, Sigma Nu, Omicron Delta Kappa. Home: 436B W 1st St N Morristown TN 37814 Office: PO Box 1799 Morristown TN 37814

INMAN, HARRY A., lawyer; b. Rochester, N.Y., Aug. 2, 1924; A.B., Harvard, 1948; LL.B., U. Va., 1951. Admitted to N.Y. bar, 1952, D.C. bar, 1953; partner firm Patton, Boggs & Blow, Washington, Ortiz, Ramos & Inman, Mexico City, Mexico. Mem. Am. (chmn. sect. internat. and comparative law 1971—), Fed. (mem. conf. com. Inst. on Legal aspects of European Community), Inter-Am. (mem. council) bar assns., Bar. Assn. D.C., Am. Soc. Internat. Law. Author: Legal and Economic Aspects of Incorporation in Mexico, 1966. Office: Ortiz Ramos & Inman Morelos 98-103 Mexico City Mexico also 1200 17th St NW Washington DC 20036

INMAN, ROY LESTER, city ofcl.; b. Pueblo, Colo., June 21, 1917; s. Harry K. and Mae B. (Rosenberg) I.; B.S., U. Md., 1952; M.A., George Washington U., 1963; m. Eva Greer, Mar. 9, 1941; 1 son, Johnny K. Commd. 2d lt. U.S. Army, 1940, advanced through grades to col., 1955, ret., 1970; city mgr. Griffin, Ga., 1970—. Served with AUS, 1936-37. Decorated Silver Star medal, Legion of Merit, Bronze Star medal, Purple Heart, Commendation medal (U.S.); Order of Sacred Treasure (Japan), Order of Orange Nassau (Netherlands), Fouregier (Belgian). Elk. Rotarian. Home: 649 Laura Dr Griffin GA 30223 Office: PO Box 95 Griffin GA 30223

INNIS, JOHN JAMES, surgeon; b. Hillsboro, Tex. Mar. 6, 1920;; s. John Edward and Eula Vita (Renshaw) I.; B.S. Southwestern La. Inst., 1943; M.D., Baylor U., 1949; postgrad. Tulane U., 1955-58; m. Gladys Lucille Griffin, June 27, 1949; children—John James, Sharion Denise, m. 2d, Macye Ruth Steele children—William Eric, Grace Elaine. Chemist Down Chem. Co., Freeport, Tex., 1942-45; intern Charity Hosp., New Orleans, 1949-50; gen. practice medicine, Fairfield, Tex., 1952-55; asst. in orthopedic surgery Tulane U., 1955-58; practice medicine, specializing in orthopedic surgery. Fort Worth, 1958—; mem. staff All Saints, Harris, St. Joseph, Peter Smith hosps. (all Ft. Worth); ednl. dir. chief orthopedics Fort Worth Childrens Hosp. Served as officer M.C., AUS, 1950-52. Decorated Bronze Star. Diplomate Am. Bd. Orthopedic Surgeons. Mem. Tex. Med. Assn., Tarrant County Med. Soc., A.M.A., Internat. Coll. Surgeons. Author films, articles orthopedic field. Home: 4401 Inwood St Fort Worth TX 76109 Office: 1401 8th Av Fort Worth TX 76104

INNIS, PAULINE, author; b. Torquay, Devon, Eng.; student U. Manchester, U. London; m. Bernard B. Coleman, Sept. 30, 1946 (dec. 1954); m. Walter Deane Innis, Aug. 1, 1959. Came to U.S., 1954. Author: Hurricane Fighters, 1962; Ernestine or the Pig in the Potting Shed, 1963; The Wild Swans Fly, 1964; The Ice Bird, 1965; Wind of the Pampas, 1967; Fire from the Fountains, 1968; Astronumerology, 1971; Gold in the Blue Ridge, 1973. Mem. Criminal Justice com. D.C. Commn. Status Women; membership chmn. Welcome to Washington Club, 1961-64; co-chmn. Internat. Workshop Capital Speakers' Club, 1961-64; pres. Children's Book Guild, 1967-68; dir. Ednl. Communications. Bd. dirs. Washington Goodwill Industries Guild, 1962-66. Named Hoosier Woman of Yr., 1966. Mem. Soc. Woman Geographers, English-Speaking Union (mem. bd.), Spanish-Portuguese Group of D.C. (pres. 1965-66), Opera Soc. Nat. Ballet Soc. (v.p. women's bd.), Friends Kennedy Center (charter). Episcopalian. Clubs: Am. Newspaper Women's (pres. 1971-73), Gibson Island (Md.), Nat. Press. Home: Skipper's Row Gibson Island MD also Watergate West Washington DC

INNIS, WALTER DEANE, ret. naval officer, govt. ofcl.; B.S., U.S. Naval Acad., 1932; grad. Naval War Coll., 1948; m. Pauline B. Coleman, Aug. 1, 1959. Commd. ensign USN, 1932, advanced through grades to rear adm.; designated naval aviator, 1936; served in Atlantic Neutrality Patrol, 1941, Mediterranean area, 1942, Aleutians, 1942-43, S.W. Pacific, Saipan, 1944, Iwo Jima, Okinawa, Japan, 1945, Korea and Formosa Strait, 1950-51; exec. officer Naval Air Sta., Dutch Harbor, Alaska, 1943; comdg. officer U.S.S. Bering Strait, 1944-45, exec. officer U.S.S. Philippine Sea, 1950-51; comdg. officer Naval Air Sta., Corpus Christi, Tex., 1946; attended Naval War Coll., 1947-48; faculty Naval War Coll., 1948-50; mem. staff sec. def., Washington, 1954-56, mem. U.S. delegation Austrian state treaty, Vienna, 1955, mem. staff U.S. ambassador to NATO, Paris, France, 1956-57; mem. spl. mission from Pres. Eisenhower to Marshall Tito, Yugoslavia, 1955, mem. operations coordinating bd., Washington, 1954-56; spl. asst. to chief Bur. Aeros., Navy Dept., Washington, 1957-59; mem. staff Sec. of Navy, 1959; cons. Argentine Govt., Buenos Aires, 1959-60; Washington cons. The MITRE Corp., Bedford, Mass., 1962-64; systems analyst Navy Dept., 1964—. Decorated Legion of Merit, Bronze Star. Mem. Operations Research Soc. Am., Naval Hist. Found., Navy League U.S., Naval Acad. Found., Netherlands-Am. Found., Nat. Hist. Found., Nat. Trust for Hist. Preservation, Halcyon Found., Nat. Ballet Soc., Friends of Kennedy Center, Armed Forces Mgmt. Assn., English-Speaking Union, Naval Acad. Alumni Assn., Ind. Soc., Nat. Audubon Soc., Ret. Officers Assn. Republican. Presbyn. Clubs: Gibson Island (Md.); Gibson Island Yacht Squadron; Army-Navy (Washington); Explorers. Co-author: Gold in the Blue Ridge, 1973. Author spl. studies for Navy Dept. and Naval War Coll., MITRE Corp. Home: Watergate West 2700 Virginia Av NW Washington DC 20037 also Skippers Row Gibson Island MD 21056 Office: Bldg 196 Washington Navy Yard Washington DC 20390

INSKEEP, GEORGE ESLER, chemist; b. Wilmington, Del., Dec. 25, 1918; s. Mark McKinley and Helen Janet (Esler) I.; B.S. in Chem. Engring., Pa. State Coll., 1940; M.S., U. Ill., 1941, Ph.D., 1943; m. Kathryn Hadley, Feb. 5, 1955. Research chemist Office of Rubber Research, Urbana, Ill., 1942-45, Firestone Tire & Rubber Co., Pottstown, Pa., 1945-49, E.I. duPont, Wilmington, Del., 1949-61; research chemist Philip Morris, Inc., Richmond, Va., 1961—, also asst. patent officer, 1966—. Dist. committeeman Robert E. Lee council Boy Scouts Am., 1972—. Mem. Am. Chem. Soc., Am. Inst. Chemists, Sigma Xi. Episcopalian. Club: Willow Oaks Country. Patentee in field. Home: 6812 Westcott Dr Richmond VA 23225 Office: Box 26583 Richmond VA 23261

INZANA, JOHN THOMAS, statistician; b. Cleve., Apr. 20, 1938; s. Marion and Caroline (Mazza) I.; A.B., Western Res. U., 1960; A.M., Ind. U., 1963; m. Barbara Ann Raynor, June 19, 1965; children—Carolyn Marie, JoAnn Marion. Dir. statistics dept. Ind. Div. Labor, Indpls., 1965-67; statistician survey Bur. Labor Statistics, Office Occupational Safety and Health Statistics, U.S. Dept. Labor, Washington, 1967—. Vice pres. Citizens for Better City, 1971-73, mem. exec. bd., 1970—. Recipient distinguished achievement award U.S. Dept. Labor, 1972. Mem. Washington Statis. Soc. (exec. bd., sec.-treas.), Am. Statis. Assn. (mem. nat. membership com.), Lambda Chi Alpha, Alpha Kappa Delta. K.C. Office: NALC Bldg 100 Indiana Av NW Room 418 Washington DC 20212

IPSEN, KENT FORREST, artist, glassworking; b. Milw., Jan. 4, 1933; s. Victor August and Muriel (White) I.; B.S., U. Wis., 1961, M.S., 1964, M.F.A., 1965; m. Shyla Mae Fischer, Nov. 7, 1957; children—Vicki Lynn, Steven Jay, Lisa Ann, Laura Kay, Nina Beth. Exhibited in group shows Toledo Mus., Mus. Contemporary Crafts, N.Y.C., Smithsonian Instn., Washington, Chicago Art Inst., Scripp's Coll., Ball State U.; represented in permanent collections Milw. Art Center, LaCrosse (Wis.) U., Bergstrom (Wis.) Art Center, Kohler (Wis.) Art Center, Johnson Wax Co. Craft Collection, Western Mich. State U., Corning Glass Center, Toledo Mus. Art, Chgo. Art Inst. Asst. prof. glassworking Mankato (Minn.) State Coll., 1965-68; asso. prof. glassworking Chgo. Art Inst., 1969-73; asso. prof., chmn. dept. crafts Va. Commonwealth U., Richmond, 1973—. Artist-in-residence Prairie Sch., Racine, Wis., 1971—, No. Ariz. U., 1972. Served with AUS, 1954-56. Mem. Am. Craftsmen's Council, Wis. Designer-Craftsmen, Ill. Craft Council (pres. 1970-72), Nat. Council for Edn. in Ceramic Arts, Phi Sigma Epsilon, Presbyn. Home: 11761 Bollingbrook Dr Richmond VA 23235 Office: Va Commonwealth U Richmond VA 23220

IRBY, BOBBY NEWELL, educator; b. Meridian, Miss., Mar. 17, 1932; s. William Ezra and Ada (Smith) I.; A.A., E. Miss. Jr. Coll., 1955; B.A., U. Wash., 1957; M.S., U. Miss., 1962, Ed.D. (Nat. Def. Edn. Act fellow), 1967; m. Lois Pettit, Mar. 15, 1953; 1 dau., Karen Ruth. Tchr. sci. Chamberlain-Hunt Acad., Port Gibson, Miss., 1957-58; tchr., head dept. sci. pub. schs., Clarksdale, Miss., 1959-61, 63-64; instr. chemistry N.E. La. U., Monroe, 1964-65, asst. prof., 1967-69; asso. prof., chmn. dept. sci. edn. U. So. Miss., Hattiesburg, 1969—. Pres., Irby, Pettit, Gonnet, Inc. Served with USAF, 1950-53. Fellow Am. Inst. Chemists; mem. Am. Chem. Soc., Nat., Miss. sci. tchrs. assns., A.A.A.S., Miss. Acad. Sci., Phi Delta Kappa. Contbr. articles profl. jours. Home: 108 Saratoga Circle Hattiesburg MS 39401

IRBY, CLAUD JAMES, JR., educator; b. Meridian, Miss., Dec. 9, 1931; s. Claud James and Mary (McCharen) I.; B.S. in Elec. Engring., La. Tech. U., 1958, M.S., 1961; Ph.D., U. Ala., 1969; m. Dorothy Ann Willard, July 28, 1952; children—Dana, Paul, Leland, Rachel, Mary. Instr. La. Tech. U., Ruston, 1959-62; asst. prof. dept. elec. engring. Miss. State U., Starkville, 1962-69; asso. prof. engring. Ark. State U., Jonesboro, 1969—. Vice pres. Bldg. Cons., Inc., Jonesboro, 1973—. Served with USNR, 1951-55. NSF fellow, 1966-67. Registered profl. engr., Ark., La. Mem. Am. Soc. Prof. Engrs., Alpha Gamma Rho, Tau Beta Pi, Eta Kappa Nu, Phi Kappa Phi. Home: 101 University Dr Jonesboro AR 72401 Office: Dept Engring Ark State U State University AR 72467

IRBY, DANIEL WALLACE, elec. engr.; b. Dumas, Ark., Mar. 6, 1929; s. Stephen Warren and Roberta (Mattmiller) I.; B.S. in Elec. Engring., U. Ark., 1953; m. Agnes Marie Lyon, June 15, 1952; children—Dana Robin, Robert Douglas. With Memphis Light, Gas & Water Co., 1955—, design and records engr., 1968-70, chief elec. engr., 1970—. Served to 1st lt. USAF, 1953-55. Mem. I.E.E.E., Engrs. Club. Memphis. Methodist (mem. ofcl. bd.). Home: 4108 Tutwiler Av Memphis TN 38122 Office: 220 S Main St Box 388 Memphis TN 38145

IRBY, WILSON, ry. exec.; b. El Dorado, Ark., Sept. 5, 1914; s. Arlie Jerry and Sallie (Mason) I.; B.S., Ouachita Baptist U., 1937; m. Ruth Eloise Garrett, Feb. 21, 1947; children—Dennis Wilson, John Arleigh. Clk. El Dorado & Wesson Ry., El Dorado, 1937-47, agt., 1947-72, traffic mgr., 1951-72, gen. auditor, sec.-treas., 1953—, also dir. Mem. El Dorado City Council, 1966-74. Served with AUS, 1942-46. Decorated Royal Order Scotland; hon. Legion of Honor, Order De Molay, DeMolay Cross of Honor. Mem. Ark. Passenger and Freight Assn., El Dorado C. of C., Ark. Municipal League. Democrat. Methodist. Mason (32 deg., Shriner), K.T. (grand comdr. 1971-72). Home: 508 E Block St El Dorado AR 71730 Office: PO Box 46 El Dorado AR 71730

IRLINGER, FRANK SERAPH, engr.; b. N.Y.C., Dec. 11, 1929; s. Franz and Josephine (Knott) I.; Asso. in Applied Sci., Pratt Inst., 1960; B.S. in Engring., Cooper Union Sch. Engring and Sci., 1967; M.B.A. magna cum laude, Middle Tenn. State U., 1972; m. Elsie Munster, Dec. 28, 1951; children—Frank Ernest, Ronald Walter. Machine devel. engr. Automotive Products div. Scovill-Schrader, N.Y.C., 1957-67, machine devel. mgr., Dickson, Tenn., 1967-68, engring. mgr. research and devel., 1968—. Mem. adv. com. mech. engring. tech. Nashville State Tech. Inst. Served with AUS, 1951-53. Registered profl. engr., Tenn.; certified mfg. engr. Mem. Pi Tau Sigma, Delta Mu Delta, Soc. Automotive Engrs., Nat. Soc. Profl. Engrs., Am. Soc. M.E. (chmn. Nashville sect. 1972-73), Nat. Mgmt. Assn. (pres. Schrader chpt. 1972, Outstanding Service award 1972). Home: 6805 Alto Vista Dr Nashville TN 37205 Office: PO Box 586 Dickson TN 37055

IRONS, CARY FREDERICK, physician; b. Pickaway, W.Va., Feb. 3, 1913; s. Cary F. and Sallie (Gibson) I.; A.B., Washington and Lee U., 1933; M.D., Med. Coll. Va., 1941; m. Malene Grant, June 10, 1939; children—Thomas Grant, Ben Gibson, Cary Frederick. Pvt. practice medicine, Greenville, 1945—; coll. physician East Carolina Coll., 1947—, dir. student health service, 1967—; sec. Med. Arts Clinic, 1950-61, v.p., 1961—. Pres. med. staff Pitt County Meml. Hosp., 1959-60; mem. N.C. Bd. Nurse Registration and Nursing Edn. Served from lt. to capt. M.C., AUS, 1942-45. Decorated Bronze Star. Diplomate Am. Bd. Family Practice. Fellow Am. Geriatrics Soc.; mem. N.C., Pitt County med. socs., A.M.A., Am. Acad. Gen. Practice. Democrat. Methodist. Rotarian (pres. elect). Home: 1104 W Rock Spring Rd Greenville NC 27834 Office: Infirmary East Carolina U Greenville NC 27834

IRVIN, J(OHN) LEA, ret. engr.; b. Victoria, Tex., Oct. 6, 1897; s. Thomas S. and Leila (Ragland) I.; student pub. schs., Internat. Corr. Schs., Advanced Mgmt. program Harvard; m. Dorothy Vivyan Walker, Jan. 17, 1926; 1 dau., Pat C. (Mrs. E. L. Raulston). Design and constrn. West Texas Gulf Pipe Line Co., 1917-20, machine shop foreman, 1920-22, machine shop supt., 1922-24, asst. chief engr., 1924-29, asst. gen. supt., 1929-47, supt. pipe lines, 1947-49, mgr., 1949-52, became gen. mgr. all pipe lines, U.S. and Can., 1952, now pres. and dir.; pres., dir. Gulf Refining Co.; v.p., dir. Four Corners Pipe Line Co.; dir. Lurel Pipe Line Co. Registered profl. engr. Tex., La. Mason (32 deg., Shriner). Clubs: Engineers, Petroleum. Home: 6418 Auden Houston TX 77005

IRVIN, JOHN PATTESON, TV mgmt. firm exec.; b. N.Y.C., May 9, 1943; s. James Kee and Jane (Patteson) I.; B.S., Stetson U., 1968; M.S. in Radio and TV, Syracuse U., 1969; m. Carol Patricia Lazzo, Dec. 30, 1968. With Gulf TV Corp., Houston, 1969—, program producer, 1971-72, gen. mgr., asst. to v.p., 1972-73, gen. mgr., asst. to pres., 1973—. Chmn. Houston Area Broadcasters Com. for Joint

Community Leader Ascertainment, 1973-74. Chmn. pub. relations com. San Jacinto Lung Assn., Houston, 1970—; mem. adult services budget com. United Fund, Houston, Harris County, 1971—; mem. Steering Com. for Creation of Voluntary Action Center, 1973—; explorer adviser Sam Houston council Boy Scouts Am., 1972—. Bd. dirs. San Jacinto Lung Assn., Center for Multihandicapped Children. Served with USNR, 1964-66; Vietnam. Recipient Vol. of Year award San Jacinto Lung Assn., 1972. Home: 10390 Hammerly Blvd Houston TX 77043 Office: 1945 Allen Pkwy Houston TX 77019

IRVIN, THOMAS T., state ofcl.; b. Hall County, Ga., July 14, 1929; s. C.T. and Gladys (Hogan) I.; ed. pub. schs., White County, Ga; m. Edna Bernice Frady, June 1, 1947; children—James Thomas, Johnny Mark, David Lewis, Londa Lynn, Lisa Ann. Engaged in lumber bus., 1946—, real estate bus., 1950—; mem. Ga. Ho. of Reps. from Habersham County, 1967, asst. adminstrv. floor leader, 1967; exec. sec. to gov. Ga., 1967-68; commr. agr. State of Ga., 1969—. Past bd. dirs., v.p., pres. Ga. Sch. Bds. Assn.; past bd. dirs. Ga. Jr. C. of C. Baptist (deacon). Mason (Shriner). Home Route 1 Mount Airy GA 30563 Office: 19 Hunter St SW Atlanta GA 30334

IRVINE, JAMES BOSWORTH, chem. co. exec.; b. Lexington, Ky., Apr. 15, 1914; s. James Parsons and Marie Haskell (Bosworth) I.; B.S. in Indsl. Chemistry, U. Ky., 1937; m. Martha Ellen Campbell, July 27, 1937; children—James Campbell, Lewis Bosworth. Analytical chemist Hercules Powder Co., Wilmington, Del., 1937; devel. chemist Quaker City Chem. Co., Phila., 1938-40; gen. textile chemist Collis & Aiken Corp., Phila., 1940-45; dir. product devel. Quaker Chem. Corp. (formerly Quaker Chem. Products Co.), Conshohocken, Pa., 1945-60, process engr., 1960—. Active Boy Scouts Am.; pres. local P.T.A., 1947-48. Mem. Skippack Twp. Zoning Bd., 1959-60. Mem. Assn. Textile Technologists, Am. Assn. Textile Chemists and Colorists (nat. councillor 1973—, tech. judge North Piedmont sect. 1965-72), Am. Chem. Soc., Textured Yarn Assn. Am., Piedmont Mineral. Soc., Sigma Alpha Epsilon. Episcopalian. Clubs: Chatmoss Country (Martinsville, Va.); Piedmont Mineral (past pres.), Starmount Country (Greensboro, N.C.); Meadow Greens Country (Eden, N.C.); N.C. Wolfpack (Raleigh, N.C.). Contbr. articles to profl. jours. Home: 3508 Starmount Dr Greensboro NC 27403 Office: Quaker Chem Corp Conshohocken PA 19428

IRVINE, REED JOHN, economist; b. Salt Lake City, Sept. 29, 1922; s. William J. and Edna Jessup (May) I.; B.A., U. Utah, 1942; postgrad. U. Colo., 1943-44, U. Wash., 1949; B.Litt. (Fulbright scholar), Oxford U., 1951; m. Kay Araki, Aug. 14, 1947; 1 son, Donald. With War Dept., Tokyo, Japan, 1946-48; economist. Bd. Govs. Fed. Res. System, Washington, 1951—. Chmn. bd. dirs. Accuracy in Media, Inc., Washington, 1971—. Served with USNR, 1942-43, USMCR, 1943-46. Mem. Phi Beta Kappa. Mem. Ch. of Jesus Christ of Latter-day Saints. Club: Internat. Economists (chmn. 1968) (Washington). Home: 11120 Nicholas Dr Silver Spring MD 20902 Office: Federal Reserve Bd Washington DC 20551

IRWIN, IVAN, JR., lawyer; b. Dallas, Dec. 10, 1933; s. Ivan and Charlotte Halliday (Shoupe) I.; B.A., So. Meth. U., 1954, LL.B., 1957; m. Carol Jane Eklund, Jan. 30, 1970; children—Catherine Ann, Ivan III, Margaret Lynn. Admitted to Tex. bar, 1957; partner firm Shank, Irwin, Conant, Williamson & Grevelle, Dallas, 1960—. Dir. Giffin Industries, Inc., Chilton Corp., First Realty Bank & Trust Co., Dallas. Vice pres. Dallas County Assn. Blind, 1972—, bd. dirs., 1968—; trustee Dallas County Assn. for Blind Trust Fund. Recipient Distinguished Service award Dallas Jr. Bar Assn., 1963. Mem. Am., Dallas (chmn. unauthorized practice law com. 1972—) bar assns., State Bar Tex., Trial Attys. Assn. Am., Phi Delta Theta, Phi Alpha Delta. Republican. Episcopalian. Contbr. articles legal jours. Home: 4703 Cherokee Trail Dallas TX 75209 Office: 2827 First Nat Bank Bldg Dallas TX 75202

IRWIN, PAT, justice; b. Leedey, Okla., June 12, 1921; s. Marvin J. and Ollie D. (Newton) I.; student Southwestern State Coll., 1939-41; LL.B., U. Okla., 1949; m. Margaret Boggs, Aug. 18, 1950; children—William, Margaret. Admitted to Okla. bar, 1949; county atty., Dewey County, 1949-50; pvt. practice law, 1950-58; sec. to commrs. land office State Sch. Land Commn., State Okla., 1955-58; justice State Supreme Ct. Okla., 1959—, chief justice, 1969-70. Mem. Okla. State Senate, 1950-54. Served as capt. USMC, 1942-46; PTO. Mem. Am. Legion, Delta Theta Phi. Democrat. Mason. Home: 1325 Andover Ct Oklahoma City OK 73120 Office: State Capitol Bldg Oklahoma City OK 73102

IRWIN, WILLIAM CLYDE, elec. engr.; b. Chattanooga, Nov. 2, 1935; s. David Clyde and Winona Lillian (Wilson) I.; B.S., U. Tenn., Knoxville, 1958; postgrad. U. Tenn. Space Inst., Tullahoma, 1967-70, U. Tenn. at Chattanooga, 1971-73; m. Tevania K.Z. Gilbreath, Sept. 6, 1973; children—Joy Marie, Winona Kay, William Clyde II. Student engr., engr. Electric Power Bd., Chattanooga, 1954-60; engr. Martin-Marietta, Inc., Orlando, Fla., 1960-62; engr., quality assurance staff adviser Aro, Inc., Arnold Engring. and Devel. Center, Tullahoma, 1967-70; system projects engr., office supr. elec. engring. div. Hensley-Schmidt, Inc., Chattanooga, 1970—. Mem. Vols. for Internat. Tech. Assistance, 1968—. Active, Arthritis Found., Muscular Dystrophy Assn., Easter Seals Birth Defects Funds; counselor YMCA Boys Club, 1952-53. Recipient Presdl. Commendation award Aro, Inc., 1964. Registered profl. engr., Tenn. Mem. Nat., Tenn. socs. profl. engrs., Order of Engrs., Chattanooga Engrs. Club. Mem. Ch. of Nazarene (past trustee). Contbr. articles profl. jours. Home: Office: Am Nat Bank Bldg Chattanooga TN 37402

IRZYK, ALBIN FELIX, ret. army officer; b. Salem, Mass., Jan. 2, 1917; s. Felix and Sophia (Mroczka) I.; A.B., U. Mass., 1940; M.A., Am. U., 1966; grad. Armor Sch., 1949, Command and Gen. Staff Coll., 1950, Nat. War Coll., 1958; m. Laura Evelyn Abbott, May 14, 1946; children—Elizabeth Jane, Albin Felix, Laura Evelyn. Commd. 2d lt. U.S. Army, 1940, advanced through grades to brig. gen., 1963; assigned 3d U.S. Cav., 1940-42; tank battalion comdr., chief staff 4th Armored Div., Europe, 1942-45; mem. staff, faculty Armor Sch., Ft. Knox, Ky., 1947-49, 51-54; staff officer to comdr.-in-chief Pacific, Hawaii, 1954-57; chief Office Internat. Affairs, Dept. Army Gen. Staff, 1958-61; regtl. comdr. 14th Armored Cav., Fulda, Germany, 1961-62; asst. chief staff plans, operations and tng. Hdqrs., 7th U.S. Army, Stuttgart, Germany, also Allied Land Forces, Central Europe, Fontainebleau, France, 1962-65; asst. comdt. U.S. Army Armor Sch., Ft. Knox, 1965-67; comdg. gen. U.S. Army Hdqrs. Area Command, Saigon, Vietnam, 1967-68; asst. div. comdr. 4th Inf. Div., Vietnam, 1968-69; comdg. gen., Ft. Devens, Mass., 1970-71; ret., 1971; gen. mgr. Palm Beach (Fla.) Acad., 1971—. Active Boy Scouts Am., Girl Scouts. Decorated D.S.C., D.S.M., Silver Star with oak leaf cluster, Legion of Merit, Purple Heart with oak leaf cluster, Air medal with 10 oak leaf clusters; Croix de Guerre (France); Czech War Cross; Chuong My medal (Korea); recipient silver anniversary All American award Sports Illus. mag., 1964, Sir Thomas More award Nat. Council Cath. Men, 1965. Mem. 4th Armored Div. Assn. (pres. 1964-65), Legion of Valor, Hon. Order Ky. Cols. Contbr. articles profl. jours. Home: 2527 S Flagler Dr West Palm Beach FL 33401 Office: 690 N County Rd Palm Beach FL 33480

ISAAC, EUGENE LEONARD, educator; b. Natchez, Miss., Aug. 15, 1915; s. Samuel and Isabelle (Armstrong) I.; B.S., Alcorn A. and M. Coll., 1940; M.S., Ia. State Coll., 1950; Edn. Specialist, Kan. State Tchrs. Coll., 1965; m. Ardelma G. Brown, June 19, 1943; children—Genette Leonardo, Doris Gene. Tchr. vocational tng. Oak Park High Sch., Laurel, Miss., 1940-43, 46-49; counselor Utica (Miss.) Inst., 1950-51; head carpentry and woodworking dept. Savannah (Ga.) State Coll., 1951-58; chmn. tech. edn. div. Mississippi Valley State Coll., Itta Bena, 1958—. Cons. tech. edn. Served with AUS, 1943-45. Recipient Service to Youth award YMCA, Savannah, 1958; Meritorious Service award Mississippi Valley State Coll. YMCA, 1967; Meritorious Service award Utica field chpt. Phi Delta Kappa, 1965. Mem. Indsl. Arts in Elementary Sch. Miss. Tchrs. Assn., Am., Magnolia State (pres. 1963-64) vocational assns., Am. Council on Indsl. Arts Tchr. Edn., Internat. Platform Assn., Am. Legion, Phi Delta Kappa. Methodist (chmn. finance com. 1968—, steward 1968—). Home: PO Box 40 Mississippi Valley State Coll Itta Bena MS 38941

ISAACKS, RUSSELL ERNEST, biochemist; b. Humble, Tex., July 25, 1935; s. Archie Brockman and Esther Estelle (Pylate) I.; student Northwestern State U., Natchitoches, 1953-54; B.S., McNeese State U., 1956; M.S., Tex. A. and M. U., 1959, Ph.D., 1961; m. Henrietta Jeanette Bevil, June 12, 1954; children—Sally Ann and Scott Russell (twins). Chemist, VA Hosp., Dallas, 1964-65, Miami, 1965—. Research asst. prof. medicine U. Miami, 1970—. Served with USPHS, 1961-64. Recipient Superior Service unit citation USPHS, 1964. Mem. Poultry Sci. Assn., Am. Chem. Soc., Soc. Protozoology, Fla. Acad. Sci., A.A.A.S., Sigma Xi. Mason. Contbr. articles to profl. jours. Home: 8965 SW 115th Terrace Miami FL 33156 Office: 1201 NW 16th St Miami FL 33125

ISAACS, WILLIAM RAYMOND, mfg. co. exec.; b. Louisville, Nov. 1, 1931; s. William Thomas and Ruth Annie (James) I.; B.E.E., U. Louisville, 1954; postgrad. U. N.H., 1961-66; m. Barbara Ann Brewer, May 21, 1954; children—Teresa (Mrs. William M. Clark), Sandra, Stephen. Project engr. Gen. Electric Co., Somersworth, N.H., 1955-67, project engr. Arrow Hart Murray div., Earlysville, Va., 1967-69, mgr. quality control Arrow Hart Murray div., Earlysville, 1969—. Chmn. sch. bldg. com., Dover, N.H., 1965-67. Mem. Sch. Bd., Dover, 1964-67. Mem. I.E.E.E., Am. Electroplating Soc., Nat. Elec. Mfrs. Assn. (chmn. gen. engring. com. meter mounting equipment 1964-67). Patentee in field. Home: 713 Park St Charlottesville VA 22901 Office: Route 660 Earlysville VA 22936

ISBELL, ARTHUR FURMAN, educator; b. Lubbock, Tex., Feb. 12, 1917; s. Arthur Hill and Sarah Edna (Clark) I.; B.A., Baylor U., 1937; M.A., U. Tex. at Austin, 1941, Ph.D. (Univ. fellow), 1943; m. Edith Lola Roberts, Apr. 2, 1942; children—Arthur Furman, Linda Ann (Mrs. John Gurasich), James Lemoyne. Chemist, Gen. Mills Research Labs., Mpls., 1934-50; Monstanto Chem. Co., Anniston, Ala., 1951-53, Buckman Labs., Memphis, 1950-51; mem. faculty Tex. A and M U., College Station, 1953—, asso. prof. chemistry, 1953-56, prof., 1961—. Mem. A and M Consol. Sch. Bd., 1961-66. Recipient Tex. A and M Faculty Distinguished Achievement award for research, 1964; USPHS grantee, 1958-65. Mem. Am. Chem. Soc. (nat. council 1960-66), Am. Inst. Chemists, Phi Kappa Phi. Mason. Contbr. articles to profl. jours. Patentee in field. Home: 800 Delma St Bryan TX 77801 Office: Dept Chemistry Texas A and M Univ College Station TX 77843

ISBELL, RAYMOND EUGENE, educator; b. nr. Tuscumbia, Ala., Jan. 13, 1932; s. Travis H. and Alice (Kiser) I.; B.S. in Chemistry and Math., Florence State U., 1953; M.S. in Organic Chemistry, U. Ala., 1957, Ph.D. in Phys. Chemistry, 1958; m. Shirley Anne James, June 5, 1953; children—Michael Travis, Joni Dianne. Research chemist Rhom & Haas, Huntsville, Ala., 1956-60; chemist TVA, Wilson Dam, Ala., 1960-64, project leader, 1964-65; asso. prof. Florence (Ala.) State U., 1965-68, prof., 1968—, also chmn. dept. chemistry, 1973—. Cons. in field. Served with Chem. Corps, AUS, 1953-55; Korea. Decorated Army Commendation medal. AEC grantee, 1957-58. Mem. Am. Chem. Soc. (past pres. local sect.), Ala. Acad. Sci. (state v.p.), Sigma Xi, Phi Kappa Phi (past pres.), Kappa Mu Epsilon, Gamma Sigma Epsilon, Alpha Chi Sigma. Contbr. articles to profl. jours. Home: 101 Hiram St Sheffield AL 35660 Office: PO Box 659 Florence State U Florence AL 35360

ISLEY, MAX, architect; b. Yanceyville, N.C., June 8, 1929; s. Charles Henry and Media (Ward) I.; student U. Okla., 1947-49; B.Arch., N.C. State U., 1957; M.Arch., Harvard, 1959; m. Elizabeth Jane Skinner, Jan. 16, 1955; children—Alexander Max, Malcolm Ward, Nathan Charles, Duncan Walter. Faculty, Sch. Architecture, Mont. State Coll., 1957-58; with O. Berg & Assos., Architects, Bozeman, Mont., 1959-60; architect John D. Latimer & Assos., Architects, Durham, N.C., 1960-69; partner in charge Durham office Smart/Woodall/Isley & Herring Inc., architects and planners, Durham, Raleigh, Greenville, 1969—. Served with CIC, AUS, 1952-54. Mem. A.I.A., Durham Council Architects (pres.). Home: 5327 Yardley Terrace Durham NC 27707 Office: 602 W Chapel Hill St Durham NC 27702

ISPHORDING, WAYNE CARTER, educator; b. Willow Grove, Pa., Sept. 26, 1937; s. William and Anna (Suplee) I.; A.A., U. Fla., 1960, B.S. with honors, 1962, M.S., 1963; Ph.D., Rutgers U., 1966; m. Geneva Christene Spencer, Oct. 31, 1959; children—Gregory, Brian, Gary. Teaching asst. Rutgers U., New Brunswick, N.J., 1963-65, research asst., 1965-66; mem. faculty dept. geology U. South Ala., Mobile, 1966—, asso. prof., 1969-72, prof., 1973—. Dept. Interior grantee, 1965-66, Army Research Office grantee, 1973—. Mem. Geol. Soc. Am., Am. Assn. Petroleum Geologists, Soc. Econ. Paleontologists and Mineralogists, Ala. Geol. Soc., Sigma Xi, Sigma Gamma Epsilon, Sigma Tau Sigma. Contbr. articles to profl. jours. Home: 5506 Richmond Rd Mobile AL 36608

ISRAEL, FIROOZ, engring. co. exec.; b. Tehran, Iran, Sept. 13, 1941; s. Hay and Helen (Sadga) I.; B.S. with honors, Am. Coll. (Iran), 1963; M.S. in structural engring., Ga. Inst. Tech., 1964; m. Gisele Cohen, Mar. 21, 1965; 1 son, Daniel F. Came to U.S., 1963, naturalized, 1968. Research engr. Ga. Tech. Engring. Expt. Sta., Atlanta, 1964; structural engr. Vogt-Ivers & Assos., Atlanta, 1964-69; prin., head structural dept. Lockwood Greene, Inc., Atlanta, 1969—. Chmn. Young Engrs. Com. Ga., 1972-73. Registered profl. engr., Ga., Ohio, N.C., Va., Tex., Ky., Ala. Mem. Am. Soc. C.E., Nat., Ga. (dir. Atlanta chpt., state dir., charter pres. North Atlanta chpt. 1974—) socs. profl. engrs., Am. Concrete Inst., Profl. Soc. for Nuclear Def., Met. Assn. Urban Designers and Environmental Planners, Ga. Engring. Found. (dir.), Nat. Ga. Inst. Tech. Alumni Assn., Internat. Soc. Soil Mechanics and Found. Engring. (U.S. nat. com.). Jewish religion. Editor Ga. Profl. Engr. mag., 1969-70. Home: 2718 Parkview Dr NE Atlanta GA 30345 Office: 1776 Peachtree St NW Atlanta GA 30309

ITO, TAKERU, biochemist, educator; b. Tokyo, Japan, May 10, 1928; s. Kiyoshi and Kimi (Tsukada) I.; came to U.S., 1951, naturalized, 1965; B.S., Trinity U., San Antonio, 1954; M.S. Okla. State U., 1956; Ph.D., U. Cal. at Berkeley, 1958; m. Lois Colleen Johnson, Aug. 5, 1959; children—Miki Ann, Elizabeth Leigh. Asst. prof. physiol. chemistry Ohio State U., Columbus, 1962-67; prof. biology East Carolina U., Greenville, N.C., 1967—. U. Pa. Postdoctoral fellow, 1958-60, USPHS fellow, 1961-62; USPHS grantee, 1965-68. Mem. A.A.A.S., Am. Soc. Microbiology, Sigma Xi. Contbr. articles on biochemistry to profl. jours. Home: 2008 Pinecrest Dr Greenville NC 27834 Office: Box 2577 Greenville NC 27834

IUELE, JOHN, condr.; b. Italy; came to U.S., 1928; grad. Mich. State U., 1941, Julliard Sch. Music, 1944. Tchr. instrumental music pub. schs., camps, colls.; trumpet player Detroit Symphony, N.Y. Symphony, Boston Symphony, City Center Opera Orch., Radio City Music Hall Orch., Atlanta Symphony, N.Y. Philharmonic; asst. condr. N.Y.C. Symphony, Atlanta Symphony; organizer, condr. Atlanta Civic Orch., Atlanta Civic Ballet Co.; guest condr. Lansing (Mich.) Symphony, Brevard Music Center Orch., N.C.; condr. Winston-Salem (N.C.) Symphony, 1952—. Home: 2211 Buena Vista Rd Winston-Salem NC 27104 Office: 610 Coliseum Dr Winston-Salem NC 27104

IVER, WILLIAM HENRY, dentist; b. Port Chester, N.Y., June 22, 1917; s. Alex R. and Beulah (Levy) E.; student U. Wis., 1936-38; D.D.S. cum laude, Georgetown U., 1942; m. Raye Bennett, Mar. 23, 1967; children—Robert Drew, Randolph, Carole. Pvt. practice dentistry, Miami Beach, Fla., 1945—. Dir. Lincoln Small Bus. Investment Corp., Ka-Line Mfg. div. Sun Engring. Corp. Served to lt. comdr. USNR, 1942-45. Mem. Am., Fla., East Coast, Miami Beach dental assns. Clubs: Cricket, Jockey, Carriage. Home: Cricket Club Miami FL Office: 605 Lincoln Rd Miami Beach FL 33139

IVERSON, JOHN WILLIE, educator, clergyman; b. Jacksonville, Fla., Dec. 9, 1942; s. John Willie and Gertrude (Moton) I.; A.A., Southwestern Christian Jr. Coll., 1966; B.S., Abilene Christian Coll., 1968; postgrad. Southwestern Bapt. Theol. Sem., 1968-75; m. Patricia M. Spencer, Mar. 2, 1948; children—John Willie, Spencer Warren. Ordained to ministry Ch. of Christ, 1968; minister of edn. Univ. Ch. of Christ, Cleve., 1968-69; athletic dir., instr. phys. edn. Southwestern Christian Jr. Coll., Terrell, Tex., 1969—; minister Latimer St. Ch. of Christ, Ennis, Tex., 1972-73, Easterview Ch. of Christ, Dallas, 1973-74. Address: PO Box 10 Terrell TX 75160

IVESTER, ZOE ANN, social worker; b. Sayre, Okla., Jan. 8, 1927; d. William Lando and Golda (Hodgson) I.; B.S. Okla. State U., 1948; M.S.W., U. Denver, 1956; student Okla. Coll. Women, 1944-45. Caseworker Okla. State Welfare Dept., child welfare supr., field rep., 1948-51, 1963—; caseworker Am. Red. Cross, Kan., 1951-54; caseworker Kan. Childrens Service League, 1955-59; child welfare supr. Nev. State Welfare Dept., 1959-62, also dist. dir. Mem. Nat. Assn. Social Workers, Assn. Certified Social Workers, Am. Pub. Welfare Assn., D.A.R. Methodist. Mem. Order Eastern Star. Home: Box 57 Sayre OK 73662 Office: Beckham County Dept Welfare Sayre OK 73662

IVEY, CLAUDE ALLEN, mech. engr.; b. Atlanta, Oct. 8, 1934; s. Claude Wary and Kathleen (May) I.; B.Mech. Engring., Ga. Inst. Tech., 1956, postgrad., 1958-62; m. Peggy Carolyn Tankersley, Nov. 24, 1954; children—Mike, Kathleen, Belinda, Susan. Research engr., instr. Ga. Inst. Tech., Atlanta, 1955-63; chief engr. Gen. Adjustment Bur., Atlanta, 1963-66; pres., firm Cerny & Ivey Assos. Inc., Atlanta, 1967—, also chmn. bd. Coordinator fund dr. Am. Heart Assn., 1972-73; mem. Gov.'s Adv. Com. Housing, 1973—; coach Youth Football League, 1965-70. Served with AUS, 1955-63. Registered profl. engr., Ga. Mem. Ga. Soc. Profl. Engrs. (chmn. state ethics com.), Nat. Fire Protection Assn. Baptist. Clubs: Milton High Athletic (Alpharetta, Ga.), Ga. Tech. Alumni Assn. (Atlanta). Home: Rte 2 Box 431 Alphoretta GA 30201 Office: 652 Angier Av NE Atlanta GA 30308

IVEY, DON LOUIS, transp. research engr., educator; b. Ft. Worth, Nov. 17, 1935; s. Alvis Durwald and Edythe Mae (Hart) I.; student Rice Inst., 1954-57; B.S. in Civil Engring., Lamar State Coll. of Tech., 1960; M.Engring., Tex. A. and M., 1963, Ph.D. (Nat. Def. Edn. Act fellow), 1964; m. Mary Lou Keele, Nov. 5, 1966; children—Donna Stewart, John Raymond, Rachel Annette. Asst. research engr. Tex. Transp. Inst., College Station, Tex., 1963-66, asso. research engr., 1967-71, research engr. 1971—; asso. prof., Tex. A. and M. U., College Station, 1967-71; prof. 1971—, head Hwy. Safety Research Center, 1971—. Cons. structural engring., hwy. safety. Named Outstanding Young Engr. of the Year, Tex. Soc. Profl. Engrs., 1970. Registered prof. engr., Tex. Mem. Am. Soc. Testing Material (com. E-17 1971—), Am. Soc. C.E., Am. Concrete Inst. (com. 526 Low Cost Housing), Hwy. Research Bd. (com. A2B04 since 1971—). Contbr. articles on hwy. safety to profl. jours. Research in areas of forgiving roadside and vehicle-roadway interaction. Home: 3710 Sweetbriar St Bryan TX 77801 Office: Tex Transp Inst Tex A and M U College Station TX 77843

IVEY, MARVIN, educator; b. Orlando, Fla., Jan. 17, 1932; s. Elbert Marion and Martha Douglass (Somerville) I., B.S. in Sci. Edn., U. Fla., 1953, M.Ed., 1957, D.Ed., 1961; m. Bette Ra Perry, June 11, 1953; children—Marvin Lee, Susan Rebecca. Tchr. Cherokee Jr. High Sch., Orlando, 1953-54; grad. asst., fellow U. Fla., 1956-59; mem. faculty St. Petersburg (Fla.) Jr. Coll., 1959—, prof. geology, 1970—, chmn. dept. natural sci., 1964—; tchr. on TV, 1962-64. Mem. sci. adv. com. St. Petersburg Sci. Center. Served with AUS, 1954-56. Life fellow A.A.A.S., Internat. Oceanographic Found.; mem. Geol. Soc. Am., Nat. Assn. Geology Tchrs. (sec.-treas. S.E. sect. 1962-67), Am. Assn. U. Profs., Com. to Save Our Bays, Fla. Acad. Scis., Nat. Audubon Soc., Nat. Wildlife Fedn., Common Cause, Phi Delta Kappa. Author study guides, lab. manuals. Home: 14452 Hillview Dr Largo FL 33540 Office: 6605 5th Av N St Petersburg FL 33710

IVEY, ROBERT GENE, librarian; b. DeQuincy, La., Aug. 27, 1940; s. Evans Oslyn and Vicy Yvonne (Young) I.; B.A., McNeese State U., Lake Charles, La., 1963; postgrad. Southwestern Baptist Theol. Sem., 1964-65.; m. Tchr., Westlake (La.) High Sch., 1963-64; librarian, tchr. Deweyville (Tex.) Ind. Sch. Dist., 1965-69; librarian La. Correctional and Indsl. Sch., DeQuincy, 1969—. Mem. Calcasieu Parish Bicentennial Com., 1973—. Mem. exec. bd. S.W. La. Library Regional Planning System, 1971—. Mem. So., La. (chmn. adult edn. com. 1971-72), Calcasieu (pres. 1972-73) library assns., Lake Charles Community Concert Assn. Democrat. Baptist (organist 1971—, chmn. nominations com. 1972-73). Woodman of World (v.p. 1972-73). Club: DeQuincy Optimist (chmn. nominating and inter club coms. 1971-72). Author article. Home: 317 Yoakum Av DeQuincy LA 70633 Office: PO Box 1056 DeQuincy LA 70633

IVIE, JOHN MARK, psychiatrist; b. Memphis, Feb. 17, 1933; s. James M. and Gladys (Brooks) I.; M.D., Memphis State U., 1955-59; M.D., U. Tenn., 1962; m. Shirley Marie Gilliland, Dec. 30, 1955 (div. Feb. 1966); 1 dau., Marianne. Intern, St. Joseph Hosp., Memphis, 1962-63; resident U. Tenn. dept. psychiatry, Memphis, 1963-66; staff psychiatrist Tenn. Psychiat. Hosp. and Inst., Memphis, 1966-67; pvt. practice psychiatry, 1967—; cons. Ark. Div. Vocational Rehab. Served with USAF, 1950-55. Mem. A.M.A., Tenn., Memphis, Shelby County med. assns., Am. Psychiat. Assn., Lambda Chi Alpha, Phi Rho Sigma, Chi Beta Phi. Home: 881 S Perkins Av Memphis TN 38117 Office: 5050 Poplar Av White Station Tower Memphis TN 38117

IZYDORE, ROBERT ANDREW, chemist; b. McKeesport, Pa., July 13, 1943; s. Rudolph S. and Cecilia E. (Skruch) I.; B.S. in Chemistry, Pa. State U., 1965; Ph.D. in Organic Chemistry, Duquesne U., 1969; m. Madeline Bonacci, Dec. 10, 1964 (div. Jan. 1970); children—Robert R., Kenneth M. Instr. Pa. State U. at McKeesport, 1968-69; research asso. Duke, 1969-71; asso. prof. chemistry N.C. Central U. at Durham, 1971—. Mem. Am. Chem. Soc. Research in nitrogen heterocyclics. Home: 1010A Burch Av Durham NC 27701

JABBOUR, J.T., physician; b. Tiptonville, Tenn., Aug. 5, 1927; s. T.J. and Freda (Hamra) J.; B.S., U. Tenn., 1948, M.D., 1951; m. Helen Block, Feb. 16, 1957; children—Ben, Magda, Kenny, Monica, Elena. Intern. Baylor Hosp., Dallas, 1952-53; resident pediatric Neurology U. Minn., 1958-61; practice medicine, specializing in pediatrics, Memphis, 1965—; asst. prof. pediatric neurology U. Okla., 1961-65; chief sect. on pediatric neurology, asso. prof. pediatric neurology U. Tenn., 1967-73, prof. pediatrics, 1973—, also dir. pediatric neurology tng. program. Bd. dirs. Central Garden Area Assn., Memphis. Served with USNR, 1945-46. Author: Pediatric Neurology Handbook, 1973. Home: 267 S Belvedere Blvd Memphis TN 38104 Office: 848 Adams St Memphis TN 38103

JABLONOWSKI, DONALD ROBERT, diversified industry exec.; b. Waco, Tex., Nov. 1, 1934; s. Richard William and Elizabeth Louise (McKinney) J.; student Tex. Technol. Coll., 1953-54; B.B.A., Baylor U., 1957; m. Rosemary Ames, June 21, 1958; children—Donald Robert, Elizabeth, Suzanne. Controller Anderson, Clayton & Co. S.A., Switzerland, 1961-62, treas., controller, 1962-65; treas. Anderson, Clayton S.A., Brazil, 1965-69; internal auditor Anderson, Clayton & Co., Houston, 1959-61, asst. treas., 1969—. Served with AUS, 1957-59. Mem. Financial Execs. Inst. (chmn. financial mgmt. com. 1971, chmn. archives com. Houston 1972, chmn. edn. com. 1973-74), Houston C. of C., Nat. Assn. Accountants, Am. C. of C. for Brazil, Am. Soc. of Sao Paulo (1st v.p., gov. 1966-68, recipient award of merit 1968), Am. Mgmt. Assn. Presbyn. (elder 1971, deacon 1973, treas. ch. 1974). Rotarian. Clubs: Wall STreet (N.Y.C.); Houston, Brae-Burn (Houston). Home: 8 W Shady Lane Houston TX 77042 Office: 1010 Milam St Houston TX 77002

JABLONSKI, T. HENRY, ednl. adminstr.; b. Wilmington, Del., Jan. 9, 1915; s. Frank W. and Wladysawa (Wilchinska) J.; B.S., Trenton State Coll., 1938; m. Laura Marian Depue, Nov. 7, 1936; children—Thaddeus Henry, Alice (Mrs. Thayer Smith), Frank, Alfred, Jon, Kathryn, Laura, Richard. Indsl. arts instr. Merchantville (N.J.) High Sch., 1939-43; Radnor High Sch., Pa., 1943-45; asst. exec. dir. Pa. Soc. for Crippled Children, 1945-52; pres. Washington Coll. Acad., Washington College, Tenn., 1952—. Pres., Washington County Soc. for Crippled Children, 1958-60. Active Boy Scouts Am. Presbyn. Mason, Rotarian. Home: Washington College TN 37681

JACHIMCZYK, JOSEPH ALEXANDER, physician, lawyer; b. Bridgeport, Conn., Sept. 15, 1923; s. Michael A. and Mary M. (Wozny) J.; M.D., U. Tenn., 1948; LL.B., Boston Coll. Law Sch., 1958; m. Loretta T. Slomski, June 17, 1950; children—Jane, Michael, Peggy, Mary. Intern, Queen's Hosp., Honolulu, 1948-49; resident pathology Hamot Hosp., Erie, Pa., 1949, Norwalk (Conn.) Hosp., 1949-50, City Hosp., Cleve., 1950-53; asst. med. examiner State of Md., Balt., 1953; teaching fellow Harvard Dept. Legal Medicine, Boston, 1954-57; sr. surgeon USPHS, Boston, 1954-56; forensic pathologist, chief med. examiner Harris County, Houston, 1957—; admitted to Tex. bar, 1959. Served with AUS, 1943-45. Fellow Coll. Am. Pathologists, Am. Soc. Clin. Pathologists; mem. Am. Acad. Forensic Scis., Internat. Acad. Pathology, U.S. Mil. Surgeons Assn., Am., Houston bar assns., Tex., Harris County med. socs. Home: 3403 Bradford Pl Houston TX 77025 Office: County Courthouse Houston TX 77002

JACK, WILLIAM HARRY, lawyer; b. Kaufman, Tex., Dec. 13, 1899; s. William Harry and Kosci (Snow) J.; LL.B., U. Tex., 1922, A.B., 1923; m. Marian Price, Nov. 27; 1928 (dec.); children—Robert W., Patricia Allen (Mrs. J.W. Porter, Jr.), Marian E. Jenkins; m. 2d, Josephine Hunley Dillon, Aug. 16, 1969. Admitted to Tex. bar, 1922; partner Jack & Jack, attorneys, Corsicana, Texas, 1923-26; mem. Saner, Jack, Sallinger & Nichols, Dallas, 1926—. Dir. Booth, Inc. Pres., dir. Blanche Mary Taxis Found.; dir. past pres. Child's Guidance Clinic; vice chmn. bd. trustees Southwestern Legal Found. Served as pvt. U.S. Army, 1918, maj. USAAF, 1942-44; lt. col. U.S. Army Res. Fellow Am. Bar Found., Southwestern Legal Found, Am. Coll. Probate Counsel (pres. 1963-64); mem. State Bar Tex. (past dir., v.p.), Dallas (pres. 1951), Am. (ho. of dels.) bar assns., Phi Beta Kappa, Phi Delta Phi, Sigma Delta Chi. Democrat. Presbyn. (elder; bd. Christian edn. Presbyn. Ch. U.S.). Mason (Shriner). Clubs: National Exchange (past v.p.; pres.), Dallas Country, Dallas, Chaparral. Home: Terrace House 3131 Maple Av Dallas TX 75201 Office: Republic Nat Bank Bldg Dallas TX 75201

JACKSON, ALTO LOFTIN, lawyer; b. Clio, Ala., June 6, 1914; s. William Alto and Lula Jane (Loftin) J.; B.S., U. Ala., 1935, J.D., 1937; m. Emma Pearl Norton, Mar. 28, 1941; children—Caroline Jane, Pearl (Mrs. Ronald H. Strawbridge), Alto Loftin, Robert Olon. Admitted to Ala. bar, 1937; practiced in Clio, 1937-39, 56—; mem. firm Jackson & Jackson, Clayton and Clio, Ala., 1939-41, 45-56. Asst. prof. Troy (Ala.) State U., 1967—. Mem. Town Council, Clio, 1948-52; chmn. Barbour County Bd. of Edn., Clio, 1954—. Served with AUS, 1942-45. Mem. Farrah Law Soc., Wiregrass Hist. Soc., Alpha Kappa Psi. Democrat. Methodist (lay leader 1960—). Author: So Mourns the Dove, 1965. Home: 146 Brundidge St Clio AL 36017 Office: PO Box 146 Clio AL 36017

JACKSON, ALVY CONRAD, civil engr.; b. Newcastle, Tex., Apr. 27, 1940; s. Alvy Murphy and Inez Fannie (Ozmer) J.; B.S., U. N.M., 1962, M.S. (Ideal Cement Co. fellow), 1963; m. Mary Ann Compton, June 23, 1963; children—Eric Conrad, Kenneth Harold. Engr., Rocketdyne div. Rockwell Internat., Bethany, Okla., 1963-66, sr. engr. Aero Comdr., 1966—. Registered profl. engr., Okla. Mem. Gen. Aircraft Mfrs. Assn. Lion. Home: 728 Nancy Lynn St Norman OK 73069 Office: 5001 N Rockwell St Bethany OK 73008

JACKSON, BETTY RUTH, architect, structural engr.; b. Pawhuska, Okla., Jan. 5, 1927; d. Fred Hildreth and Ruth (Daniels) Jackson; B.S. in Archtl. Engring., U. Okla., 1949, M.C.E., 1950 With Hudgins, Thompson, Ball & Assos., Inc., architects, engrs., planners, Oklahoma City, 1948—, draftsman, 1948, 49, jr. engr., 1950-54, jr. architect, 1950-57, structural engr., project architect, 1957—. Adj. prof. architecture U. Okla. Registered profl. engr., Okla.; licensed architect, Okla. Mem. A.I.A., Nat. Okla. socs. profl. engrs. Episcopalian. Club: Altrusa (past pres. Norman club). Prin. archtl. works include Will Rogers World Airport Terminal, 1966, FAA Aero. Center, 1957 (both Oklahoma City), Amarillo (Tex.) Airport Terminal, 1970. Home: 643 Okmulgee St Norman OK 73069 Office: Hudgins Thompson Ball & Assos 1411 Classen Blvd Oklahoma City OK 73106

JACKSON, BLYDEN, educator; b. Paducah, Ky., Oct. 12, 1910; s. George Washington and Julia Estelle (Reid) J.; A.B., Wilberforce U., 1930; A.M., U. Mich., 1938, Ph.D. (Rosenwald fellow 1947-49), 1952; m. Roberta Bowles, Aug. 2, 1958. Tchr. English, Louisville pub. schs., 1934-45; asst., then asso. prof. English, Fisk U., 1945-54; prof. English, head dept. So. U., 1954-62, dean Grad. Sch., 1962-69; prof. English, U. N.C., Chapel Hill, 1969—, asso. dean Grad. Sch., 1973—; spl. research criticism Negro lit. Mem. Coll. Lang. Assn. (pres. 1957-59), Modern Lang. Assn., Nat. Council Tchrs. English (Distinguished lectr. 1970-71, chmn. coll. sect. 1971—), Coll. English Assn., Speech Assn. Am., La. Edn. Assn., Alpha Phi Alpha. Contbr. articles to profl. jours. Asso. editor CLA Bull., 1959—; mem. editorial adv. bd. So. Lit. Jour. Home: 102 Laurel Hill Rd Chapel Hill NC 27514

JACKSON, BURL THURSTON, accountant, lawyer; b. Waldo, Ark., May 19, 1907; s. John Andrew and Ethel (Thrailkill) J.; H.A., LaSalle Extension U., Chgo., 1932; LL.B., Ark. Law Sch., 1941; student N.Y.U. Inst. on Fed. Taxation, 1951, 58; m. Lelia Gordon, Aug. 6, 1930. Bookkeeper Am. Grocer Co., Little Rock, 1928-31; bookkeeper, mgr., asst. to pres., legal and tax counsel Comml. Warehouse Co., Inc., 1931-51, now sec.-treas., dir., legal counsel; sec.-treas., dir. legal counsel Merchants Transfer Warehouse Co., Inc.; sec.-treas. Porter Foods, Inc.; admitted to Ark. bar, 1941; practice accounting and tax law, 1951—. Ark. chmn. Membership Com. Tax Inst. Trustee Little Rock Boys Club Athletic Field. C.P.A., Ark., La. Mem. S.W. Warehouse and Transfermen's Assn. (v.p. Ark. 1951-52), Ark. Soc. C.P.A.'s Am. Inst. Accountants, Am., Ark. bar assns., Am. Assn. Atty.-C.P.A.'s, Am. Arbitration Assn. (nat. panel arbitrators). Baptist (chmn. bd. deacons). Kiwanian. Home: 1312 S Tyler St Little Rock AR 72204 Office: 1800 E Roosevelt Rd Little Rock AR 72206

JACKSON, CARL DEAN, bank exec.; b. Dallas, Aug. 14, 1935; s. Carl Casca and Denith Beatrice (Stewart) J.; B.B.A., So. Meth. U., 1956; m. Priscilla Alden Walker, June 1, 1962; 1 son, Carl Edward. With Nat. Bank of Commerce, Dallas, 1963-70, v.p., 1965-70; pres. Colonial Nat. Bank, Garland, Tex., 1970—. Instr. Southwestern Grad. Sch. of Banking, Dallas, 1972-74. Mem. adv. com. United Way, Garland, Tex., 1973-74; bd. mgmt. YMCA, Garland, 1971-73; mem. community adv. com. for mid-mgmt. program Eastfield Coll., Dallas County Jr. Coll. System, 1972-74. Served to capt. USAF, 1956-60. Mem. Am. Inst. Banking, Robert Morris Assos., Alpha Kappa Psi. Lion (sec., treas. 1967-69). Home: 4022 Stonebridge Dallas TX 75206 Office: PO Box 1568 Garland TX 75040

JACKSON, CARL LOWIS, JR., state ofcl.; b. Little Rock, Apr. 23, 1938; s. Carl Lowis and Alpha Gertrude (Wood) J.; grad. high sch.; m. Janice Carol Blackwood, Apr. 4, 1958; children—Julie Ann, Kipling Anthony. With Ark. Mil. Dept., North Little Rock, 1956—, adminstrv. technician, 1956—. Mem. Police Community Relations Task Force, 1972—, Hillcraft Corp. vets, rehab., 1973—. Mem. North Little Rock Planning Commn. Bd. Adjustment, 1972-73. Bd. dirs. Adult Handicapped Center, 1973—. Recipient Ark. Citizens Merit certificate, 1973, Outstanding Jr. C. of C. award Ark., 1968-79, North Little Rock, 1967-68, 68-69, Mem. Nat. Fedn. Fed. Employees, Non-commissioned Assn. Ark. (editor 1973-74), Ark. (state v.p. 1969-70, chmn. bd. 1972-73), North Little Rock (state chmn. govt. affairs 1973-74) jr. chambers commerce. Editor: Ark. Jaycee mag., 1969, 70-71. Home: 4408 Arlington St North Little Rock AR 72116 Office: 2600 Poplar St North Little Rock AR 72114

JACKSON, CHARLES WAYNE, coll. adminstr.; b. Carlisle, Ark., June 23, 1929; s. Terrell and Margaret (Sanders) J.; A.B., Hendrix Coll., 1952; M.Ed., U. Ark., 1958, Ed.D., 1966; grad. Inst. Ednl. Mgmt., Harvard, 1972; m. Marette McCauley, July 1, 1950; children—Charles Wayne, Retta Cauley, Shelia Lucyle. Tchr., pub. schs., Wright, Ark., 1950-54; prin. pub. schs., Augusta, Ark., 1954-59; supt. pub. schs., Swifton, Ark., 1959-63; asso. editor Ark. Sch. Bds. Assn. publs. U. Ark., Fayetteville, 1964-65; v.p. adminstrn. S. State Coll., Magnolia, Ark., 1965—. Chmn. A.R.C., Augusta, 1955. Bd. dirs. Magnolia Boys Club. Mem. Am. Assn. Higher Edn., Ark. Edn. Assn. (v.p. higher edn. 1972-73, pres. 1973-74), N.E. Ark. Schoolmasters Club (pres. 1960), Phi Delta Kappa (historian 1964), Kappa Delta Pi. Methodist (chmn. ofcl. bd. 1961). Rotarian. Home: 201 Reeves Terrace Magnolia AR 71753 Office: So State Coll Magnolia AR 71753

JACKSON, CLAYTON LEROY, ins. exec.; b. Owen Sound, Ont., Can., Aug. 25, 1917; s. Chester C. and Edna (Green) J.; B.A., U. Toronto, 1949; m. Eula E. Gardner, Aug. 20, 1946; children—Heather, Alan. Came to U.S., 1955. Asst. actuary Mut. Life of Can., Waterloo, Ont., 1953-55; asst. actuary United Life and Accident Ins. Co., Concord, N.H., 1955, actuary, 1955-69, v.p., 1958-65, sr. v.p., 1965-69, also dir.; v.p., actuary Am. Nat. Ins. Co., Galveston, Tex., 1969-70, sr. v.p., actuary, 1970—. Served with Canadian Army, 1943-46. Fellow Canadian Inst. Actuaries, Soc. Actuaries, Life Office Mgmt. Assn.; mem. Actuaries Club S.W., Am. Acad. Actuaries, Internat. Actuarial Assn., Am. Risk and Ins. Assn. Conglist. Office: 1 Moody Plaza Galveston TX 77550

JACKSON, CRAYTON TROY, educator; b. Frenchburg, Ky., Dec. 9, 1916; s. John Boyd and Emma (Jackson) J.; M.A., U. Ky., 1948; Ed.D. (Anna B. Constock Nature Study fellow), Cornell U., 1958; m. Bernice Hogsed, Sept. 2, 1939; 1 son, Benjamin Crayton. Rural elementary tchr., Montgomery County, Ky., 1937-41; sci. supr. E. Tenn. State U., Johnson City, 1948-52; prof. sci. edn. Morehead (Ky.) State U., 1958-72; fgn. service officer, Brazil, 1962-63; clin. prof. Pikeville (Ky.) Coll., 1973—. Sci. edn. cons. Xerox Corp., 1967—; cons. Follette Book Co., 1971-72. Councilman, Morehead, 1967-71. Served with USNR, 1943-45. Recipient Presdl. citation Assn. Am. Sanitarians, 1970. Named Ky. col. Mem. Am. Nature Study Soc. (pres. 1971), N.E.A., A.A.A.S., Common Cause, Nat. Sci. Tchrs. Assn., Phi Delta Kappa. Mason (Shriner), Kiwanian. Address: Pikeville Coll Pikeville KY 41501

JACKSON, DELLA ROSETTA HAYDEN, civic worker, educator; b. Mill Spring, N.C., Mar. 2, 1905; d. Robert Twitty and Amanda (Petty) Hayden; B.A., Johnson C. Smith U., 1948; M.A., N.C. Coll., 1956; m. G. Franklin Davenport, Sept. 28, 1930 (dec. Jan. 1936); children—Evelyn Frances (Mrs. Alonzo David Petty), Amanda Elizabeth (Mrs. Lourn Clinton Gray), Robert Franklin; m. 2d, Clarence Eugene Jackson, Oct. 30, 1943 (dec. Mar. 1951); children—Mae Carolyn (Mrs. Joseph Williams, Jr.), Clarence Stinson. Tchr., Stony Knoll Sch., Polk County, N.C., 1927-30, Tryon Sch., 1930-31, Pea Ridge Sch., 1932-39, Union Grove Sch., 1939-48, Edmund Embury Sch., 1949-51, Cobb Elementary Sch., Tryon, N.C., 1951-65; tchr. adult edn. Isothermal Community Coll., Mill Spring, N.C., 1971-74; organizer, librarian Stony Knoll Community Library, 1937—, pres., 1972—, also chmn. bd. trustees; spl. edn. tchr. Polk Central High Sch., Mill Spring, 1966-69. Mem. Central Highlands Health Council, 1968-70; 2d v.p. Polk County Homemakers Council; pres. Polk County Extension Homemakers, 1974-75; sec.-treas. Polk County Community Devel. Council; mem. Ancillary Manpower Planning Bd., Region C, 1972—; leader, 4-H Club; v.p. Polk County Child Devel. Council, 1971—, Eastern Appalachian Children's Council, 1971-73; chmn. Polk County Child Care Com., 1971—; mem. Polk County Emergency Med. Service Adv. Com., 1973—. Bd. dirs. Isothermal Health Council, sec., 1972—; bd. dirs. Polk County Mental Health Council, 1972-73, St. Luke Hosp. Aux., 1970, Regional Health Council Eastern Appalachia, 1970—, Named Mother of Year, Afro, 1948, Mother of Year, Homemakers Council Polk County and Western Dist. N.C., 1971; recipient certificate service N.C. Recreation Soc., 1962, certificate leadership for service Western N.C. Community Devel. Program Asheville Agrl. Devel. Council, 1962. Mem. League Women Voters (dir. 1970—), Stony Knoll Recreation Soc. Club: Stony Knoll Community (pres. 1959-62). Home: Box 95 Mill Spring NC 28756

JACKSON, DOROTHY LOUISA GREENLEE (MRS. FRED KNOX JACKSON), ct. reporter; b. Hamburg, Ia., Feb. 19, 1911; d. Henry Oliver and Mattie (Landreth) Greenlee; student pub. schs.; m. Fred Knox Jackson, Oct. 3, 1944. Asst. county ct. reporter, Auburn, Neb., 1927-29; sec. local atty., 1927-29; sec. Berksons, Kansas City, Mo., 1929-33; corr. A.A.A., Washington, 1933-36; sec. Intelligence Unit, Kansas City, St. Louis, 1936-40; free-lance ct., conv. reporter, St. Louis, 1940-44; free-lance ct. reporter, Prattville, Ala., 1948—; contract reporter Ala. Pub. Service Commn., Montgomery. Co-owner, operator Prattville Quick Freeze, 1948-63; owner Quiet Acre, Cottonwood, Ala., 1968-73. Chmn., Autauga County Operation Santa Claus, State Christmas Card, Bryce Mental Hosp., Tuscaloosa, Ala., 1963-70. Mem. Nat. League Am. Pen Women (br. pres. 1964-68, state v.p. 1970-71, state pres. 1972-74), Birmingham Opera Guild, Ala. Writers Conclave, Montgomery Press and Authors Club (pres. 1971-72), Ala. Shorthand Reporters Assn., Montgomery Assn. Legal Secs., Nat. Shorthand Reporters Assn., Internat. Platform Assn., Ala. Poetry Soc. Club: Autauga County Bus. and Profl. Women's (named County Woman of Achievement 1971). Author: Fallen Leaves, 1968; Poody, Story of a Cat-Nothing But a Cat, 1970. Home: 856 Gillespie St Prattville AL 36067 Office: 132 Adams Av Montgomery AL 36104

JACKSON, ELMO LOUIS, economist, price analyst, b. 1913; B.S., Fla. U., 1935; A.M., Harvard, 1937, Ph.D., 1942; m. Corinne Reginna Klemm, Jan. 31, 1948. Econ. cons., def. counsel, U.S. vs. Am. Tobacco Co. et al, 1940-41; engaged research and writing on consumption of tobacco products from 1900-40; tobacco tax cons. U.S. Treasury, 1942; tobacco price economist OPA, 1942; economist U.S. Dept. Agr., 1938-40; instr. econs. Harvard, 1945-46; asso. prof. econs. and statistics U. Fla., 1946-56, prof. econs., 1956—; leader study research group at Vanderbilt U. to examine econ. problems in marketing prin. types of tobacco leaf, 1950-51; vis. prof. Old Dominion Coll., 1967-68. Served as 2d lt. to maj. F.A., AUS, 1942-46; overseas. Mem. Am., So. econ. assns. Author: The Pricing of Cigarette Tobaccos, 1955. Home: 1515 NW 14th Av Gainesville FL 32601

JACKSON, EUGENE, JR., govt. ofcl.; b. Alligator, Miss., Feb. 16, 1931; s. Eugene and Josephine (Robinson) J.; B.S. in Civil Engring., Howard U., 1959; m. Amelia Yvonne Savage, Aug. 25, 1956. Civil engr. U.S. Bur. Reclamation, Denver, 1960-66; equal opportunity specialist Urban Mass Transp. Adminstrn., Dept. Transp., Washington, 1966-69, chief div. external programs, 1969—. Served to maj. USAF, 1951-55. Registered profl. engr., Colo., Tex. Mem. Am. Soc. C.E. (mem. com. passenger terminals), Nat., Colo. socs. profl. engrs. Home: 13107 Cabinwood Dr Silver Spring MD 20904 Office: 2100 2d St SW Washington DC 20590

JACKSON, FRED CAMERON, lawyer; b. Clarks, La., Sept. 6, 1929; s. Leonard L. and Mabel (Allen) J.; B.A., La. State U., 1950, J.D., 1956; m. Anne Purnell Smith, Sept. 10, 1955; children—Nanette Davis, Jefferson Purnell, Martie Anne, Fred Cameron, James Alexander. Admitted to La. bar, 1956; practiced in St. Francisville, La.; mem. firm Kilbourne, Dart & Jackson, St. Francisville, 1960; asst. dist. atty. 20th Jud. Dist. La., 1964-72. Served with AUS, 1950-53. Mem. Am., La. bar assns., Nat. Dist. Attys. Assn., Am. Legion, V.F.W., Scabbard and Blade, Kappa Sigma. Mason (Shriner). Club: West Feliciana Civic (past pres. St. Francisville). Home: PO Box 267 St Francisville LA 70775

JACKSON, GEORGE LINTON, judge; b. Gray, Ga., Oct. 31, 1923; s. Joseph Benjamin and Lillie P. (Mobley) J.; student Middle Ga. Coll., 1943; A.B., Mercer U., 1945, LL.B., 1948; m. Helen Edna Durrett Childs, May 10, 1974; children—Dauphin, Vess, Durrett, George Linton. Admitted to Ga. bar, 1947; practiced in Gray, Ga., 1948-68; mem. Ga. Ho. of Reps., 1951-57; mem. Ga. Senate, 1957-59; county atty. Jones County, 1955-59, 65-68; judge Superior Ct. Ocmulgee Circuit, 1968—. Lion Home: PO Box 276 Gray GA 31032

JACKSON, GILFORD LEROY, educator, b. Healdton, Okla., May 26, 1919; s. William Martin and Nancy Luellen (Wolfe) J.; student Coll. William and Mary, 1957-58, Centenary Coll. La., 1962-63; B.A., U. Okla., 1964, M.A., 1965, Ph.D., 1969; m. Peggy Merle Bigby, June 17, 1947. Enlisted U.S. Navy, 1940, advanced through grades to sr. chief petty officer, 1958; ret., 1962; asst. prof. govt. Northwestern State U. La., 1965-67; asso. prof. govt. N.E. La. U., Monroe, 1968—, chmn. dept., 1969—. Mem. Southwestern Social Scis. Assn., La. Polit. Sci. Assn., Pi Sigma Alpha, Phi Alpha Theta. Home: 1625 Park Av Monroe LA 71201 Office: 700 University Av Monore LA 71201

JACKSON, JAMES ROBERT, neurosurgeon; b. Fayetteville, N.C., Sept. 4, 1931; s. William Samson and Rebecca A. (Johnson) J.; student Wake Forest Coll., 1949-52; M.D., Duke, 1956; m. Dial Gray Boyle, Dec. 15, 1956; children—James Robert, R. Gray, Dial Boyle, Lloyd F.B. Intern, Duke Hosp., Durham, N.C., 1956-57, resident neurol. surgery 1957-62; practice medicine, specializing in neurol. surgery, Lakeland, Fla., 1965—; attending staff Univ., VA hosps., Jackson, Miss., 1964-65; neurol. surgeon Watson Clinic, Lakeland, 1965—; asst. prof. neurol. surgery U. Miss., Jackson, 1964-65. Dir. Fla. Midland Corp., Lakeland. Pres. Cleveland Ct. P.T.A., Lakeland, 1970-71. Served to capt. USAF, 1962-64. Fellow A.C.S.; mem. A.M.A., Am. Assn. Neurol. Surgeons, Congress Neurol. Surgeons, So., Fla. med. assns. Presbyn. (deacon 1972—). Contbr. articles to profl. jours. Home: 2301 Hawthorne Trail Lakeland FL 33803 Office: Watson Clinic Lakeland Fl 33802

JACKSON, JERRY LEE, rubber co. exec.; b. Nashville, Aug. 9, 1939; s. Robert Lee and Pauline (Jones) J.; B.S., U. Tenn., 1962; m. Crilla Aleece Wolfe, Dec. 30, 1967; children—Jerry Lee, Angela Michelle. Coop. student Colonial Rubber Works, Inc., Dyersburg, Tenn., 1959-62, chief chemist, 1962-68, v.p., tech. service dir., 1968—. Chmn. Dyer County (Tenn.) Republican Com., 1969-71; state chmn. Tenn. Young Rep. Fedn., 1971-73; Presdl. elector, 1972. Recipient Outstanding Local Young Rep. Chmn. award Tenn. Young Rep. Fedn., 1967. Mem. Am. Chem. Soc. (chmn. local arrangement com. rubber div. 1971, dir. rubber div. 1973—), So. Rubber Group (chmn. 1969-70, Man of Year 1972), U. Tenn. Alumni Assn. (pres. Dyer County chpt. 1968-69). Moose, Kiwanian. Home: 1836 William Cody St Dyersburg TN 38024 Office: 150 S Connell Av Dyersburg TN 38024

JACKSON, JOHN WINGFIELD, lawyer; b. Washington, Dec. 30, 1905; s. E. Hilton and Ann (Wingfield) J.; B.S. in Econs., U. Pa., 1928; J.D. with highest honors, George Washington U. Law Sch., 1932; m. Eleanor Murdoch Lind, Jan. 14, 1935; children—John Wingfield, Margaret (Mrs. Jerry R. Russom), Beverley Anne L. (Mrs. James J. Johnston, Jr.). Admitted to D.C. bar, 1931, Va. bar, 1941; individual practice law, Washington, 1933, 41-61, Va., 1941—; investigator Dept. Interior, PWA, 1933-36; asst. U.S. Atty., D.C., 1936-41; sometime spl. asst. to atty. gen. U.S., 1952-54. Cons., OSS, 1945; adj. prof. law George Washington U. Law Sch., 1947—; substitute judge Juvenile and Domestic Relations Ct. Arlington County, Va., 1966—.

Former mem. bd. dirs. Washington Criminal Justice Assn., Arlington chpt. A.R.C. Mem. No. Va. Estate Planning Council (pres. 1966-67), Nat. Assn. Estate Planning Councils (dir. 1966-70, 72—), Order of Coif, Phi Delta Phi. Club: Metropolitan. Home: 4844 N Rock Spring Rd Arlington VA 22207 Office: 1400 N Uhle St Arlington VA 22201

JACKSON, LILA MONTEZ (MRS. ALONZO C. JACKSON), bank dir.; b. nr. Paris, Tenn., Nov. 23, 1908; d. Charles Mother and Olive Vera (Barton) Brockwell; student pub. schs. Henry County, Tenn.; m. Thomas Albert McDaniel, Mar. 8, 1925; 1 dau., Carol (Mrs. Ancil Ray McDuffee); m. 2d, Alonzo Costello Jackson, Oct. 28, 1967. Co-owner, asst. mgr. McDaniels Dept. Stores, various locations, Tenn., 1930-54; co-owner, office mgr. R.E.A. Jackson Bldg., Apts. and Offices, Paris, 1955-61; co-owner, mgr. comml. and residential properties, Paris, 1961—; co-owner, operator Greystone Hotel, Paris, 1965—; dir. 1st Trust & Sav. Bank, Paris, 1965—. Host radio program Happenings in Our Community, WTRR, Paris, 1970—. Bd. dirs. Sr. Citizens Assn., Tenn. TB and Respiratory Disease Assn. Mem. Retail Mcht. Assn., C.of C. (co-chmn. tourist and recreation com. 1969-70), Quota Internat., Inc. (named Paris Woman of Yr. 1970), Bus. and Profl. Women's Assn. (bd. dirs., 1970), Internat. Platform Assn. Baptist. Club: Blossomway Garden. Home: Jackson Manor Paris TN 38242 Office: 301 W Washington St Paris TN 38242

JACKSON, LUKE, dentist; b. Recovery, Ga., Sept. 17, 1919; s. John Barnabus and Malissie (Jones) J.; B.S., Ga. State Coll., 1942; student Atlanta U., 1945-46; D.D.S., Meharry Med. Coll., 1951; m. Lillian L. Henderson, June, 1953 (div. Nov. 1957); children—Charles L., Wayne D.; m. 2d, Shirley Ann Head, Aug. 21, 1959; children—Shirlee Barnetta and Shirlene Elizabeth (twins). Instr. prosthetic dentistry Meharry Med. Coll., 1951-53; pvt. practice dentistry, Chattanooga, Tenn., 1953—. Chmn. bus. div. Chattanooga Council for Community Action, 1963-68; mem. Bi-racial Mayors Com., 1963; mem. bd. mgmt. Henry br. YMCA, 1965-70. Served with USNR, World War II. Diplomate Nat. Bd. Dental Examiners (pres. Pan-Tenn. 1957-59), Tenn. Dental Assn., George W. Hubbard Dental Soc. (pres. 1951—). Baptist (trustee 1955—, coordinator bldg. council 1970-71). Home: 5124 Lantana Lane Chattanooga TN 37416 Office: 752 E 9th St Chattanooga TN 37403

JACKSON, MAYNARD HOLBROOK, JR., lawyer, mayor of Atlanta; b. Mar. 23, 1938; A.B. Morehouse Coll.; J.D., N.C. Central U. Admitted to bar, 1965; founder, former sr. partner firm Jackson, Patterson & Parks; vice mayor, pres. bd. aldermen Atlanta 1970-73, mayor, 1974—. Address: 68 Mitchell St NW Atlanta GA 30303

JACKSON, PRINCE ALBERT, JR., coll. pres.; b. Savannah, Ga., Mar. 17, 1925; s. Prince Albert and Julia (Robinson) J.; B.S., Savannah State Coll., 1949; M.S., N.Y. U., 1950; postgrad. U. Kan., 1961-62, NSF fellow Harvard, 1962-63; Ph.D., Boston Coll., 1966; m. Marilyn Striggles, Dec. 22, 1950; children—Prince Albert III, Rodney Mark, Julia Lucia, Anthony Brian, Philip Andrew. Tchr. sci., math. William James High Sch., Statesboro, Ga., 1950-55; faculty Savannah State Coll., 1955—, asso. prof. math., physics, 1966-71, chmn. natural sci. div., dir. instl. self study, 1969-71, pres., 1971—. Athletic dir. St. Pius X High Sch., Savannah, 1955-64; teaching fellow, vis. instr. Boston Coll., 1964-66; cons. sci., math. Vice pres. Bd. Pub. Edn. Savannah and Chatham County, 1971—; mem. edn. com. U.S. Cath. Conf., 1971—; mem. So. Regional Edn. Bd., 1971—; mem. Chatham-Savannah Charter Study Com. Bd. mgrs. W. Broad St. YMCA, Savannah, 1962; vice chmn. St. Pius X Ednl. Council, Savannah, 1967—; mem. exec. com. So. Regional Edn. Bd., 1973-74, N.A.A.C.P., Savannah, 1968—; adviser Community Devel. Corp., Savannah, 1969; bd. dirs. Ga. Heart Assn., Goodwill Industries, A.R.C., Boy Scouts Am.; trustee Ga. Econ. Council; adv. bd. Savannah Area Minority Contractors Assn. Served with USNR, 1942-46. Recipient Outstanding leadership and Service award Savannah State Coll. Nat. Alumni Assn., 1967, Liberty Bell award Savannah Bar Assn., 1973, Benedictine medal of excellence, 1974, others. Mem. A.A.A.S., Am. Assn. U. Profs., N.E.A., Ga. Tchrs. Edn. Assn., Nat. Sci. Tchrs. Assn., Nat. Council Tchrs. Math., Am. Edn. Research Assn., Nat. Council on Measurement in Edn. Nat. Inst. Sci., Savannah Area C. of C. (dir.), Alpha Phi Alpha (Man of Year 1960, 67, So. Region Man of Year 1967), The Frogs, Inc., Phi Delta Kappa, Alpha Phi Omega, Beta Kappa Chi, Alpha Kappa Mu, Kappa Delta Pi. Roman Catholic (pres. Holy Name soc. 1969—, mem. pastoral council 1967—). K.C. Home: 1215 E Duffy St Savannah GA 31404

JACKSON, RANDALL C(ALVIN), lawyer; b. Baird, Tex., Mar. 21, 1919; s. Rupert and Anna (Faust) J.; J.D., U. Tex., 1946; B.B.A., 1941; m. Betty S. Johnson, June 18, 1955; 1 son, Randall Calvin. Admitted to Tex. bar, 1946, practiced in Baird, 1946-62, Abilene, 1962—; sr. partner firm Jackson & Jackson, 1949—. Vice pres., dir. 1st Nat. Bank, Baird; dir. T. S. Lankford & Sons Co.; dir., gen. counsel Bank of Commerce, Abilene. Mem. Tex. Securities Bd., 1966-69; chmn. Abilene Spl. Housing Study Com. Former pres. bd. dirs. Boys Ranch, Abilene; former chmn. bd. regents Tex. Woman's U., 1961-66; past finance chmn. Chisolm Trail council Boy Scouts Am. Del., Dem. Nat. Conv., 1960, 64; mem. Tex. Dem. Exec. Com., 1960-64. Enlisted USAC, 1942, disch. capt., 1946, assigned Exec. Office Statis. Control Unit, Guam. Fellow Am. Coll. Probate Counsel; mem. Southwestern Legal Found., Tex. Bar Found. (charter mem.), State Bar Tex. Am., Callahan-Taylor County (dir.) bar assns., Am. Judicature Soc., Am. Hereford Assn., Tex. Hereford Assn., Nat. Cattlemen's Assn., Am. Legion (past comdr.), Abilene C. of C. Methodist (chmn., dist. trustee). Mason (32 deg., Shriner). Clubs: Headliners (Austin, Tex.); Abilene Country (Abilene). Home: Route 2 Box 703 Abilene TX 79601 Office: Bank of Commerce Bldg Abilene TX 79602

JACKSON, RAYMOND CARL, educator; b. Medora, Ind., May 7, 1928; s. Thornton Comodore and Flossie Oliva (Booker) J.; A.B., Ind. U., 1952, A.M., 1953; Ph.D., Purdue U., 1955; m. T. June Snyder, Oct. 24, 1947; children—Jeffrey Wayne, Rebecca June. Instr. in biology U. N.M., Albuquerque, 1955-57, asst. prof. biology, 1957-58; asst. prof. botany U. Kan., Lawrence, 1958-60, asso. prof., 1961-64, prof., 1964-71, chmn. dept. 1969-71; prof., chmn. dept. biol. scis. Tex. Tech. U., Lubbock, 1971—. Served with USAF, 1946-49. NSF grantee, 1958-71. Mem. Am. Soc. Naturalists, Soc. for Study Evolution, Bot. Soc. Am., A.A.A.S., Internat. Assn. Plant Taxonomy, Am. Soc. Plant Taxonomists, Am. Inst. Biol. Scis., Internat. Orgn. Plant Biosystematists. Editor: U. Kan. Sci. Bull., 1965-68. Contbr. articles to profl. jours. Home: 3726 64th Dr Lubbock TX 79413 Office: Biological Sciences Dept Texas Tech Univ Lubbock TX 79409

JACKSON, RICHARD ELLIS, chem. co. exec.; b. Humnle, Tex., Dec. 5, 1923; s. Walter Scott and Emma Rose (Ellis) J.; B.S. in Mech. Engring., Tex. A. and M. Coll., 1948; m. Katherine Ann Middleton, Nov. 28, 1946; 1 son, Richard Ellis. With E.I. duPont de Nemours & Co., Inc., 1948—, asst. works mgr. Sabine River works, Orange, Tex., 1967-69, works mgr., 1969—. Mem. Citizens Coordinating Com. Orange, 1969—, Citizens Action Com. and Com. One Hundred, Orange, 1973-74. Bd. dirs. Orange County Meml. Hosp.; mem. devel. found. Lamar U. Served to capt. USMCR, 1943-46. Mem. Tex. Research League (dir.), Orange C. of C., Orange Mental Health Assn. (pres.), Tex. Chem. Council, Tex. Mfrs. Assn. Methodist (ofcl. bd. 1968—). Club: Sunset Grove Country (dir. 1974—). Lion, Rotarian. Home: 2609 Country Club Dr Orange TX 77630 Office: PO Box 1089 Orange TX 77630

JACKSON, ROBERT BRUCE, JR., educator; b. Drakes Branch, Va., June 5, 1929; s. Robert Bruce and Ruby Aurelia (Broocks) J.; B.S. cum laude, Davidson Coll., 1950; Ph.D., Duke, 1957; m. Jean Ann Edwards, July 1, 1961; children—Julia Estelle, Elizabeth Broocks. High sch. tchr. Battle Ground Acad., Franklin, Tenn., 1950-51; teaching asst. Duke, 1953-56; prof. math. Davidson (N.C.) Coll., 1956—. Cons., U. N.C. operations analysis standby unit, 1955-62. Served with AUS, 1951-53. Mem. Math. Assn. Am. Presbyn. (deacon, elder). Home: 207 Crescent Dr Davidson NC 28036 Office: Dept Math Davidson NC 28036

JACKSON, ROBERT DAVIS, plastics exec.; b. Louisville, Jan. 1, 1928; s. George Lewis and Oma Colleen (Davis) J.; student U. Louisville, 1947-50; m. Elizabeth Jean Glisson, Nov. 5, 1945; children—Cecilia Lynn (Mrs. Patrick R. Callahan), Robert Davis. Engr. to mgr. Liberty Engring. & Mfg. Co., Louisville, 1949-59; pres. Plastic Engring. of Hawaii, Honolulu, 1959-62; mgr. Liberty Engring. & Mfg. Co., 1962-66; pres. Liberty Plastics & Metals Co., Louisville, 1966—. Served with USMC, 1944-47, 50-52. Mem. Soc. Plastic Engrs., Am. Platers Soc., Nat. Assn. Corrosion Engrs. (dir. 1961-62). Mason (Shriner). Home: Rt 3 Box 330G LaGrange KY 40031 Office: PO Box 743 Louisville KY 40201

JACKSON, RUTH BERTHA LAVENDER (MRS. HOWARD JAMES JACKSON), civic worker; b. Seney, Mich., Oct. 19, 1914; d. Edward John and Bertha (Knuth) Lavender; A.B., U. Mich., 1937, postgrad., 1958-63; postgrad. U. Ga., Va. Poly. Inst.; m. Howard James Jackson, June 29, 1939; 1 son, James Howard. Tchr., Newberry (Mich.) High Sch., 1937-39, Rutland (O.) High Sch., 1942-43; exec. sec. Valley Day Sch., Charleston, W. Va., 1950-52; tchr. courses landscape design W. Va. State Coll., 1967—. Sec., Kanawha County Planning and Zoning Commn., 1959-70; pres. League Women Voters W. Va., 1963-70; mem. Gov.'s Commn. on Status Women, 1963-70; Nat. Com. for Support Pub. Schs., 1963-70, Citizens Air Pollution Control Council, 1965-70; chmn. Vol. Service Bur., 1965-66; mem. Gov.'s Task Force on Surface Mining, 1966, Citizens Adv. Commn. W. Va. Legislature, 1967-70, State Adv. Com. on Mental Health, 1966-70; co-chmn. State Citizens for Constl. Conv., 1967-70; adv. mem. Charleston Municipal Planning Commn., 1967-70; mem. recreation planning com. Action for Appalachian Youth-Community Devel., 1967; mem. womans com. Charleston Symphony Orch.; mem. W. Va. Planning Assn. Bd. dirs. Sunrise Found., Community Council Kanawha Valley; trustee United Fund Kanawha Valley; incorporator W. Va. Cleanup, Inc. Recipient citation for Lane-Bryant Community Achievement Awards, 1967; named Top Clubwoman of Year Charleston Gazette-Mail, 1961. Mem. U.S. Figure Skating Assn. (nat. chmn. program devel.), Charleston Rose Soc., Nat. Council State Garden Clubs, Phi Beta Kappa, Phi Kappa Phi, Pi Lambda Theta. Clubs: Greensboro Figure Skating, W.Va. Garden (chmn., sec.-treas. judges council); Essex Skating (N.J.). Contbr. articles to profl. publs. Home: 701 Leawood Dr Greensboro NC 27410

JACKSON, THEODORE KING, lawyer; b. Mobile, Ala., Dec. 27, 1910; s. Theodore King and Lollie Belle (Gould) J.; student Lawrenceville Sch., 1926-30; J.D., U. Ala., 1935; m. Louise Mason Hempstead, Aug. 2, 1937; children—Theodore King III, Robert Hempstead. Admitted to Ala. bar, 1935; partner Armbrecht, Jackson & DeMouy and predecessor firms, Mobile, 1935—. Pres., Jacksoco Oil Co., 1965—; dir. Ala. Dry Dock & Shipbldg. Co. Chmn. bd. Sr. Bowl Assn., 1969—. Bd. dirs. Boys Clubs Mobile; pres., chmn. bd. Mobile Arts and Sports Assn., 1969—; trustee Mobile Opera Guild, Univ. Mil. Sch. Served as comdr. USNR, 1941-46. Mem. Am., Ala., Mobile bar assns., Am. Judicature Soc., Am. Soc. Internat. Law, Maritime Law Assn. U.S. (1st v.p. 1958-60), Ind. Petroleum Assn. (v.p., dir. 1959—), Mid-Continent Oil and Gas Assn. (v.p., dir. 1965—), Comite Maritime International (titulary mem.). Episcopalian (vestryman 1960). Rotarian. Clubs: Propeller, Country (Mobile). Home: 2205 Springhill Av Mobile AL 36607 Office: Mchts Nat Bank Bldg Mobile AL 36602

JACKSON, TIMOTHY EDWARD, utilities exec.; b. Hutchinson, Kan., July 6, 1941; s. Samuel Lee and Jessie Virginia (Morgan) J.; B.A., Northwestern U., 1963; M.B.A., U. Chgo., 1968; m. Carol June Ruddy, Aug. 13, 1966; 1 dau., Jennifer Morgan. Plant service chemist E.I. duPont de Nemours & Co., Chgo., 1965-67; systems engr. IBM Corp., Chgo., 1967-68; systems analyst Lone Star Gas Co., Dallas, 1968-70, treas., 1970-72, v.p., treas., 1972-74; cons. Foster Assos. Inc., Washington, 1974—. Treas., bd. dirs., Dallas Civic Ballet. Bd. dirs. Jr. Achievement. Served with USNR, 1963-65. Mem. Am. Gas Assn., Am. Petroleum Inst. Home: 502 Virginia Av Alexandria VA 22302 Office: 1101 17th St NW Washington DC 20036

JACKSON, WALTER DUNAWAY, dentist; b. El Dorado Springs, Mo., Aug. 22, 1917; s. Walter John and Ferol (Dunaway) J.; B.S., S.W. Mo. State Coll., 1940; D.D.S., Kansas City U., 1950; m. Norma Louise Lovan, Nov. 18, 1942; children—Alan Scott, Thomas Farrell, Jay Norman. Practice dentistry, Miami, Okla., 1950—; mem. staff Miami Bapt. Hosp. Served with USNR, 1942-46. Mem. Pierre Fauchard Acad., Am., Okla., Dist. dental assns., Am. Legion, V.F.W. Mason, Rotarian. Home: 420 Bay St Miami OK 74354 Office: Robinson Bldg Miami OK 74354

JACOB, CAROL G., physician; b. Hamburg, Germany, Mar. 27, 1921; d. Leo and Claire (Lewisohn) Jacob; R.N., Johns Hopkins Hosp. Sch. Nursing, 1946; B.S., Johns Hopkins, 1950; M.A., U. Chgo., 1951; postgrad. Roosevelt U., 1955-57; M.D. cum laude Woman's Med. Coll. Pa., 1961. Came to U.S., 1940, naturalized, 1945. Head nurse surg. pediatrics Johns Hopkins Hosp., Balt., 1946-48; head nurse med. pediatrics State U. Ia. Clinics, Iowa City, 1948-50, U. Chgo. Clinics, 1951-53; head nurse psychiat. nursing Psychosomatic and Psychiat. Inst. Research and Tng., Michael Reese Hosp., Chgo., 1953-55; supr. psychiat. nursing St. Luke's Hosp., Chgo., 1955-57; rotating intern Montefiore Hosp., Pitts., 1961-62; resident teaching fellow psychiatry U. Pitts. Sch. Medicine and Western Psychiat. Inst. and Clinic, Pitts., 1962-63; staff psychiatrist VA Hosp., Pitts., 1963-64; resident psychiatry Sheppard and Enoch Pratt Hosp., Towson, Md., 1964-65, St. Elizabeth's Hosp., Washington, 1965-67; practice of medicine, specializing in psychiatry, Washington, 1967—; candidate Washington Psychoanalytic Inst., 1968—. Cons. psychiatrist Group Health Assn., Washington, 1968-73. Mem. A.M.A., Am. Psychiat. Assn., Am. Psychoanalytic Assn., Washington Psychiat. Soc., Med. Soc. D.C., Mortar Bd. Alpha Omega Alpha. Jewish religion. Address: 309 N St SW Washington DC 20024

JACOB, GEORGE RICHARD, lawyer; b. Norfolk, Va., Oct. 1, 1900; s. George R. and Sarah Wilkins (Dalby) J.; student Tex. A. and M. Coll., 1916; B.A., U. Va., 1919, LL.B., 1921; m. Cornelia Frances Jordan, Jan. 29, 1931; children—Arlene (Mrs. James William Singleton), George Richard. Admitted to Va. bar, 1921, Ga. bar, 1921; practiced in Talbotton, Ga., 1933—. Dir. The Utelwico, Inc., Talbotton. Sec., Ga. bar, 1963—; mem. Ga. Jud. Selection Commn., 1972—. Chmn. Talbot County chpt. A.R.C., 1942—. Mem. Am., Ga. (sec. 1961—), Chattahoochee Jud. Circuit (past pres.) bar assns., Am. Judicature Soc., Old War Horse Lawyers Club, Lawyers Club (past pres. Columbus, Ga.), English-Speaking Union, Phi Gamma Delta. Episcopalian (jr. warden). Address: Talbotton GA 31827

JACOB, WILLIS HARVEY, army officer, physiologist; b. Lake Charles, La., June 4, 1943; s. Alzetta (Guillory) J.; B.S., So. U., 1965; Ph.D., U. Kan., 1971. Asst. instr. physiology U. Kan., 1966; asst. prof. biology So. U., 1970-71; commd. 2d lt. U.S. Army, 1965, advanced through grades to capt., 1971—, chief basic sci. br. Medicine and Surgery div. Acad. Health Scis., Ft. Sam Houston, Tex., 1971—. Nat. Def. Edn. Act Title IV fellow, 1970. Mem. Am. Inst. Biol. Sci., A.A.A.S., N.Y. Acad. Sci., Sigma Xi, Phi Lambda Upsilon, Alpha Phi Alpha (treas. 1963-64, pledge master 1964-65, undergrad. chpt. adviser 1966-70). Baptist. Research on hormonal regulation of metabolic processes. Contbr. articles to sci. jours. Home: 1216 Opelousas St Lake Charles LA 70601 Office: Med and Surg div AHSUSA Ft Sam Houston TX 78234

JACOBS, ALBERT JERRY, supt. schs.; b. Beaver County, Okla., Dec. 24, 1924; s. Albert Leroy and Viola (Adams) J.; B.S., W. Tex. State Coll., 1948, M. Adminstrv. Edn., 1951; m. Wilma Jean Miller, Sept. 7, 1948; children—Sharlette Jean, Edward Leroy. Tchr., coach Canyon (Tex.) Ind. Sch. Dist., 1948; prin. Texline (Tex.) Ind. Sch. Dist., 1949-52; supt. schs. Channing (Tex.) Ind. Sch. Dist., 1952-56; supt. schs. Lefors (Tex.) Ind. Sch. Dist., 1956-62, Edna (Tex.) Ind. School Dist., 1962-67, Canyon (Tex.) Ind. Sch. Dist., 1967—. Dir. Lefors Community Credit Union; dir., past pres. Gulf Bend Center for Handicapped Children. Served with AUS, 1943-46. Mem. N.E.A. (life), Tex. Adminstrs. Assn., Tex. (life), Dallam-Hartley (past pres.), Gray-Roberts (past pres.) tchrs. assns., Panhandle Assn. Sch. Supts. (past pres.), Am. Assn. Sch. Adminstrs., Lower Guadalope Supts. Assn. (pres.), Canyon C. of C., Red Red Rose, Phi Delta Kappa. Methodist. Mason. Lion (pres. Lefors 1959-60, dist. zone chmn.), Rotarian. Home: 6 Country Club Dr Canyon TX 79015 Office: 910 11th St Canyon TX 79015

JACOBS, ARTHUR HOWARD, dentist; b. Bklyn., June 6, 1941; s. Milton and Ruth (Freilich) J.; A.B. in Chemistry, Lafayette Coll., 1962; D.M.D., U. Pa., 1966; m. Joyce Linda Belgene, Nov. 23, 1963; children—Jodi Lynn, Jamie Lee. Asso., George S. Pankey, dentist, St. Cloud, Fla., 1968; pvt. practice dentistry, Orlando, Fla., 1968—. Tchr., cons. dental asst. program Fla. So. Coll. 1967—. Served to capt. Dental Corps, USAF, 1966-68. Mem. Am., Fla., Orange County dental assns., Am. Soc. Preventive Dentistry, Internat. Inst. Hypnosis, Am. Analgesia Soc., Am. Profl. Practice Assn. Jewish religion (bd. dirs. temple 1970-71, v.p. temple men's club 1970-71). Home: 8929 Crichton Woods Ct Orlando FL 32811 Office: 4853 S Orange Av Orlando FL 32806

JACOBS, BOBBY ROWE, cons. structural engr.; b. Cullman, Ala., July 7, 1931; s. Thomas Jefferson and Irma (Brock) J.; student St. Bernard Coll., 1953-54; B.C.E. with honors U. Fla., 1957; m. Barbara Gwendolyn Yost, Mar. 21, 1959; children—Kelli Gwendolyn, Joy Lee, Jennifer Renee, Kara Elizabeth. Sr. design engr. Brockway, Weber & Brockway, Engrs. Inc., West Palm Beach, Fla., 1957-63; test supr. Saturn I and IB launch vechicle dynamics Space div. Chrysler Corp., Huntsville, Ala., 1963-66; sr. research engr. Northrop Space Labs., Huntsville, Ala., 1966-68; pres. B. R. Jacobs Consulting Engrs. Inc., Decatur, Ala., 1968—. Served with USAF, 1949-52. Mem. Nat. Soc. Profl. Engrs., Cons. Engrs. Council, Decatur C. of C. Baptist (Sunday sch. tchr. 1971-73). Club: Burningtree Country. Home: PO Box 1422 Decatur AL 35601 Office: 500 14th St SE Decatur AL 35601

JACOBS, EUGENE ROBERT, physician; b. N.Y.C., Sept. 22, 1929; s. Kalman Monroe and Sylvia (Hurwitz) J.; B.A. cum laude, Syracuse U., 1951; M.D., State U. N.Y. at Syracuse, 1955; m. Carol Ruth Levine, July 1, 1951; children—Lori Ellen, Susan Robin. Intern Temple U. Hosp., 1955-56, resident radiology, 1956-59; chief radiology U.S. Army Hosp., Ft. Jay, N.Y., 1959-61; dir. radiology Nat. Orthopaedic and Rehab. Hosp., Arlington, Va., 1961—; mem. No. Va. Orthopaedic and Allied Specialties Clinic, Alexandria, 1965—. Mem. Alexandria Sanitation Authority, 1967—. Served to capt. AUS, 1959-61. Diplomate Am. Bd. Radiology. Mem. Alexandria Med. Soc., Med. Soc. Va., Am., So. med. assns., Am. Coll. Radiology, A.C.P., Va. Water Pollution Control Assn., Phi Delta Epsilon. Home: 1307 Kingston Av Alexandria VA 22302 Office: 2500 N Van Dorn St Alexandria VA 22302

JACOBS, FREDERIC WEIL, foundry exec.; b. Indpls., Oct. 25, 1917; s. Frederic Burnham and Mina (Price) J.; B.S., Case Inst. Tech., 1939; m. Honora Mary Masters, Jan. 17, 1942; children—Frederic C., Gary N., Philip J. Metallurgist, Lake City Malleable Co., Cleve., 1939-41, chief metallurgist, Ashtabula, O., 1944-48, asst. plant mgr., 1948-50; prodn. mgr. Columbus Malleable Iron Co., 1941-44; chief metallurgist Tex. Foundries, Inc., Lufkin, Tex., 1950-57, tech. dir., 1957—. Chmn. tech. com. Malleable Research and Devel. Found., 1973. Bd. dirs. Angelina County Tb Soc.; bd. dirs. Salvation Army, Lufkin, chmn. bd., 1972-73. Mem. Am. Foundrymen's Soc. (exec. com. 1961—), Malleable Founders Soc. (chmn. research and tech. com. 1968-70), Tex. Soc. Profl. Engrs. (state dir. 1962-65, chpt. chmn. 1961), Alpha Delta, Phi Kappa Tau. Methodist (chmn. commn. on edn. 1969-71, chmn. council on ministries 1971-73). Kiwanian (dir. 1971-73, 1st v.p. 1973-74). Club: Exchange (v.p. 1968). Home: 1112 Wildbriar Dr Lufkin TX 75901 Office: PO Box 1608 Lufkin TX 75901

JACOBS, GEORGE, govt. ofcl., electronics engr.; b. N.Y.C., July 16, 1924; s. Benjamin W. and Henrietta (Myerson) J.; B.E.E., Pratt Inst., 1949; M.S., U. Md., 1960; grad. Fed. Exec. Inst., 1969; m. Beatrice Gregerman, May 27, 1947; children—Michele (Mrs. Robert Gordon), Joy Pamela. Dir. telecommunications, chief frequency div. USIA, Washington, 1949—; mem. Interdept. Radio Adv. Com.; cons.; participant internat. telecommunications confs.; mem. U.S. commn. Internat. Union Radio Sci. Served to 2d lt., USAAF, 1943-45. Decorated Air medal. Fellow I.E.E.E.; mem. Am. Radio Relay League (life). Club: Nat. Broadcasters (Washington). Contbr. articles to tech. jours. Home: 11307 Clara St Silver Spring MD 20902 Office: USIA Washington DC 20547

JACOBS, HAROLD WEINBERG, lawyer; b. Kingstree, S.C., June 5, 1923; s. Theodore C. and Edith (Weinberg) J.; student Clemson Coll., 1940-42; B.S., U.S. Naval Acad., 1945; LL.B., U. S.C., 1960; m. Jacqueline Everington, May 11, 1947; children—Patricia (Mrs. John C. Torri), Janet C., James C. Admitted to S.C. bar, 1960; partner law firm Nexsen, Pruet, Jacobs & Pollard, Columbia, S.C., 1960—. Served with USN, 1945-57. Mem. S.C. (pres. 1973—, chmn. exec. com. 1971-72), Richland County (chmn. grievance com. 1965-68) bar assns., S.C. Def. attys. Assn. (pres. 1970-71), S.C. Jud. Council (chmn. jud. reform com. 1971—), S.C. Supreme Ct. (chmn. character and fitness com. 1972—). Episcopalian. Clubs: Palmetto, Spring Valley Country (both Columbia, S.C.). Home: 5 Northlake Rd Columbia SC 29204 Office: 1231 Washington St Columbia SC 29201

JACOBS, KENNETH CHARLES, educator; b. McAllen, Tex., Sept. 17, 1942; s. Kenneth Clarence and Esther Charlene (Kusener) J.; B.S., Mass. Inst. Tech., 1964; Ph.D., Cal. Inst. Tech., 1969; m. Frances Elinor Allred, June 1, 1968. Asst. prof. astronomy U. Va., Charlottesville, 1970—. Cons. astronomy, Augusta (Ga.) Coll., 1972;

vis. scientist Max-Planck Inst., Munich, Germany, summer 1972. Mem. Charlottesville Zero Population Growth, 1970—, Citizens for Albermarle (County), 1972—. Nat. Merit scholar, 1960-64; Center for Theoretical Physics fellow, U. Md., 1968-70; NSF grantee, 1970-71; sesquicentennial asso. U. Va., 1974-75. Mem. Am. Astron. Soc., Am. Phys. Soc., A.A.A.S., Sigma Xi, Tau Beta Pi, Phi Sigma Kappa, Eta Kappa Nu. Author: (with E.V.P. Smith) Introductory Astronomy and Astrophysics, 1973. Editor: (with W.C. Saslaw) The Emerging Universe, 1972. Home: 21 Westover Hills Route 2 Charlottesville VA 22901

JACOBS, MYLON CECIL, JR., oilfield co. exec.; b. Tulsa, Apr. 25, 1936; s. Mylon Cecil and Freda (Davis) J.; student Okla. U., 1955-59; m. Karen Joyce Seacat, Sept. 12, 1968; children—Mark, Michael Douglas, Mylon Cecil III, Melissa. Salesman, Western Supply Co., Tulsa, 1959-63; pres., dir. Mylon C. Jacobs Supply Co., Tulsa, 1963—; pres., dir. Southeastern Kan. Gas Co. Trustee Jacobs Industries. Mem. So. Gas Assn. Republican. Methodist. Club: Southern Hills Country. Home: 7203 E 47th St Tulsa OK 74145 Office: 4252 S 74 E Av Tulsa OK 74101

JACOBS, WALLACE JEROME, food processing co. exec.; b. Knapp, Wis., Jan. 13, 1933; s. Keith August and Vida (Rightman) J.; student Wis. State U., Eau Claire, 1953-55, Mich. State U., 1965-66; m. Karen Ann Hotchkiss, Mar. 26, 1955; children—Jody Ann, James Wallace. With Philip Morris Inc., N.Y.C., 1957-69; v.p. sales Golden Shore Seafoods Inc., Brunswick, Ga., 1971—; dir. Food Shippers Assn., Kansas City, Mo. Served with USMCR, 1950-52. Mem. Pi Sigma Epsilon. Mason. Club: V.F.W. (Eau Claire). Home: 914 Blue Heron Dr Brunswick GA 31520 Office: 1415 Bay St Brunswick GA 31520

JACOBS, WILLIAM DONALD, educator; b. Birmingham, Ala., Apr. 18, 1928; s. Albert Rowdy and Thelma (Petty) J.; B.S., Coll. Charleston, 1951; M.S., Clemson U., 1954; Ph.D., U. Va., 1958; m. Dorothy Nell Kidd, Apr. 5, 1963. Instr., Clemson U., 1952-54; instr. Gordon Mil. Inst., 1954-55; asst. prof. analyt. chemistry U. Ga., 1958-65; asso. prof. U. West Ga., 1965-69; prof. analyt. chemistry Stillman Coll., 1969—. Mem. Am. Chem. Soc., Sigma Xi. Home: 834 Clinton Dr Tuscaloosa AL 35401 Office: Stillman Coll Tuscaloosa AL 35401

JACOBSON, ANTONE GARDNER, educator; b. nr. Salt Lake City, May 22, 1929; s. Rufus Ingman and Marvell (Gardner) J.; A.B., Harvard, 1951; Ph.D., Stanford U., 1955; m. Jacqueline James, July 26, 1962; children—Lauren, Eric. Mem. faculty dept. zoology U. Tex. at Austin, 1957—, asso. prof., 1961-68, prof., 1968—, dir. Devel. and Reprodn. Research Center; instr. Marine Biol. Lab., Woods Hole, Mass., 1969-70. Cons. NIH, 1972—. Harvard Nat. scholar, 1947-51, Henry Newell Honors scholar, 1951-55; NIH grantee, 1958—. Mem. Internat. Soc. Developmental Biologist, Soc. Developmental Biology, Am. Soc. Zologist, A.A.A.S., Sigma Xi. Contbr. profl. jours. Home: 201 Skyline Dr Austin TX 78746 Office: Dept Zoology Univ Tex Austin Tx 78712

JACOBSON, BERNARD, lawyer, investment co. exec.; b. Hartford, Conn., Feb. 27, 1930; s. Samuel Barnard and Lillian (Canter) J.; A.B., Amherst Coll., 1951; LL.B., Columbia, 1954; m. Florence Ellen Greenberg, Oct. 7, 1956; children—Daniel, Alice, Nancy. Admitted to Conn. bar, 1955, Fla. bar, 1957; practiced in Miami, 1957—; mem. firm Fine, Jacobson, Block & Semet, Miami, 1968—; pres. Mortgage Investment Services, Inc., 1973—, dir., 1973—; trustee Republic Mortgage Investors, 1968—, sec., 1969—. Chmn. Dade County Citizens Adv. Com. on Community Improvement, 1969-70. Lectr. law U. Miami, 1965-66. Served with CIC, AUS, 1955-57. Mem. Am., Fla., Dade County bar assns., Phi Delta Phi. Home: 90 N Prospect Dr Coral Gables FL 33133 Office: 2401 Douglas Rd Miami FL 33145

JACOBSON, DAVID, rabbi; b. Cin., Dec. 2, 1909; s. Abraham and Rebecca (Sereinsky) J.; A.B., U. Cin., 1931; rabbi, Hebrew Union Coll., 1934, D.D. (hon.), 1959; Ph.D., St. Catherine's Coll., U. Cambridge (Eng.), 1936; LL.D., Our Lady of Lake Coll., 1964; m. Helen Gugenheim, Nov. 6, 1938; children—Elizabeth Ann, Dorothy Jean (Mrs. Sam Miller). Instr., Hebrew Union Coll., 1933-34; rabbi W. Central Liberal Congregation, London, Eng., 1934-36, Indpls. Hebrew Congregation, 1936-38, Temple Beth-El, San Antonio, 1938—. Pres., Kallah of Tex. Rabbis, 1950-51; mem. rabbinical tenure and security com. Central Conf. Am. Rabbis, pres. S.W. region 1969-70, chmn. health com., 1967-73; chmn. Rabbinical Placement Commn., Tex. Ethics Com.; mem. com. on welfare reform Tex. Senate, 1970; arbitrator San Antonio Typographical Union 172; founder U. Ind. Hillel Found., 1938; pres. San Antonio Soc. Crippled Children and Adults, 1963-66; pres. Goodwill Industries San Antonio, 1956-60, also mem. bd.; mem. bd. Goodwill Industries Am., 1965—; pres. Bexar County chpt. Nat. Tb Assn., 1955-57; founder Community Welfare Council San Antonio, 1944, pres., 1951-53; pres. Tex. Social Welfare Assn., 1967-69; life mem., exec. com. Tex. United Community Services, Inc., 1970—, U.S.O. Nat. Council, 1968—; commr. Housing Authority San Antonio, 1954-58; v.p. S.W. region Am. Jewish Com. Bd. dirs. Our Lady of Lake Coll., Nat. Jewish Welfare Bd., 1964-72, Nat. Council Crime and Delinquency; bd. govs., overseer Hebrew Union Coll. Jewish Inst. Religion, 1966-69; bd. dirs. S.W. Texas Meth. Hosp., San Antonio Med. Found., Alamo council Boy Scouts Am., Children's Hosp. Found., Keystone Sch., San Antonio, Am. Social Health Assn., Nat. Assn. State-wide Health and Welfare, Cath. Youth Orgn.; pres. San Antonio Area Found., 1965-73, San Antonio Manpower Devel. Council, 1968—. Served as chaplain USNR, 1944-46. Recipient Silver Beaver award Boy Scouts Am., 1958, Aristotle-Aquinas award Cath. Coll. Found. S.A., 1959, Golden Deeds award Exchange Club San Antonio, 1959; Keystone award Boys Clubs Am., 1962; Edgar J. Helms award Goodwill Industries Am., 1972; named outstanding Jew, Nat. Conf. Christians and Jews, 1961, Outstanding Citizen of Year, Sembradores de Amistad, 1971. Mem. Tex. P.T.A. (hon. life), Soc. Bibl. Lit., San Antonio Ministers Assn., Nat. Conf. Social Welfare (bd. 1967-69), Sigma Alpha Mu, Pi Tau Pi. Rotarian. Clubs: Torch (past pres.), Argyle (San Antonio). Author: Social Background of the Old Testament, 1942; The Synagogue Through the Ages, 1958; also articles. Home: 207 Beechwood Lane San Antonio TX 78216 Office: 211 Belknap Pl San Antonio TX 78212

JACOBSON, DONALD RICHARD, educator; b. Everest, Kan., July 27, 1927; s. Andrew and Elizabeth (Torkelson) J.; B.S., Kan. State U., 1951, M.S., 1952; Ph.D., U. Md., 1955; m. Marie M. Mullane, Oct. 18, 1952; children—James J., Dean R., Ross E., Mark A. Asst. prof. animal nutrition U. Ky., Lexington, 1956-58, asso. prof., 1958-63, prof., 1963—. Served to capt. USAF, 1946-60. Fulbright fellow, New Zealand, 1970; Moorman Mfg. Co. travel fellow, 1974; Soybean Council lectr. tour, Belgium, Luxembourg, Holland, Germany, 1963; recipient Am. Inst. Nutrition travel grant, 1963, 66, Nutrition Research award Am. Feed Mfrs. Assn., 1964. Fellow Am. Inst. Chemists, A.A.A.S., Am. Inst. Biol. Scis., N.Y. Acad. Sci. (chmn. feeding and mgmt. com. 1966), Am. Dairy Sci. Assn., Tau Kappa Epsilon, Alpha Zeta, Sigma Xi. Lion. Editorial bd. Jour. Dairy Sci., 1970-73. Contbr. profl. jours. Home: Route 3 Huffman Mill Rd Lexington KY 40505 Office: Dept Animal Science Univ KY Lexington KY 40506

JACOBSON, HELEN G. (MRS. DAVID JACOBSON), civic worker; b. San Antonio; d. Jac Elton and Rosetta (Dreyfus) Gugenheim; B.A., Hollins Coll.; m. David Jacobson, Nov. 6, 1938; children—Elizabeth Ann, Dorothy Jean (Mrs. Sam Miller). News, spl. events staff NBC, N.Y.C., 1933-38. First v.p. San Antonio, Bexar County council Girl Scouts U.S.A., 1957-63; Tex. state rep. UNICEF, 1964-69, bd. dirs. U.S. Com. UNICEF; chmn. Mayor's Commn. on Status of Women. Bd. dirs. Nat. Fedn. Temple Sisterhoods, Temple Beth-El Sisterhood; bd. dirs. Community Guidance Center, chmn. bd., 1960-63; bd. dirs. Sunshine Cottage Sch. for Deaf Children, chmn. bd., 1952-54; pres. bd. trustees San Antonio Pub. Library, 1957-61; nat. trustee Nat. Council on Crime and Delinquency, 1964-70, now bd. mem. Tex. council; trustee San Antonio Mus. Assn., 1964-73; trustee Nat. Assembly Social Policy and Devel., sec., 1969—; bd. dirs. Community Welfare Council, pres., 1968-70; bd. dirs. Tex. United Community Services; bd. dirs. Foster Grandparents Bexar County, pres., 1968-69, v.p., 1970-73; bd. dirs. San Antonio Urban Coalition; mem. gov.'s steering com., del. 1970 White House Conf. on Children and Youth. Recipient Headliner award for civic work San Antonio chpt. Theta Sigma Phi, 1958; named Vol. Woman of Year, Express-News, 1959; honored San Antonio chpt. Nat. Conf. Christians and Jews, 1970. Mem. San Antonio Women's Fedn., Tex. Fedn. Women's Clubs (past bd. mem. Alamo dist.), Nat. Council Jewish Women, Symphony Soc. (women's com.). Club: Argyle. Home: 207 Beechwood Lane San Antonio TX 78216

JACOBSON, LEONARD I., educator, psychologist; b. Bklyn., Aug. 9, 1940; s. Harry L. and Violet (Natkin) J.; A.B. cum laude (N.Y. State Regents scholar), City U. N.Y., 1961; Ph.D., State U. N.Y., Buffalo, 1966. Research psychologist Children's Hosp., Buffalo, 1965-66; asst. prof. psychology U. Miami, Coral Gables, Fla., 1966-71, asso. prof. psychology, 1971—, adj. asst. prof. Guidance Center, 1969-70; cons. Sunland Tng. Center at Miami, Opa-Locka, 1969-72; clin. psychology cons. Community Mental Health Services Clinic, Miami, 1968—; cons. BKR exptl. project Sunland Tng. Center, Miami, 1970, Camarillo (Cal.) State Hosp., 1970; cons. clin. psychology Mailman Center for Child Devel., U. Miami Sh. Medicine, 1972—. USPHS clin. fellow, 1962-63, research grantee NSF, 1966-68, Nat. Inst. Mental Health, 1967-68, NIH, 1968, Soc. for Psychol. Study Social Issues, 1969, NASA, 1969-71. Mem. Am., Southeastern, Western, Fla. psychol. assns., Am. Assn. U. Profs., Fla. Conf. U. Profs., A.A.A.S., Assn. for Advancement of Behavior Therapy, Am. Assn. on Mental Deficiency, Soc. for Research in Child Devel., Am. Ednl. Research Assn., Psychonomic Soc., Soc. Life Scis., Soc. for Psychotherapy Research, Southeastern Assn. for Behavior Therapy, Am. Acad. Polit. and Social Scis., Acad. Polit. Sci., Soc. Pediatric Psychology, Sigma Xi, Psi Chi. Republican. Contbr. articles to profl. publs. Home: 6273 Sunset Dr South Miami FL 33143 Office: Dept Psychology U Miami Coral Gables FL 33124

JACOBSON, RALPH WILLIAM, dentist; b. Bronx, N.Y., May 21, 1939; s. Irving and Jean (Linial) J.; student Emory U., 1957-59; D.D.S., U. Md., 1963; m. Phyllis Kay Weiner, Feb. 28, 1960; children—Michael Scott, Laurie Ann. Pvt. practice dentistry, Miami, Fla., 1965—; mem. staff Variety Children's Hosp., Miami, 1965—. Served to capt. Dental Corps, USAF, 1963-65. Fellow Gorgas Odontological Soc.; mem. Am. Dental Assn., E. Coast Dist., S. Dade County dental socs., Alpha Omega. Contbr. articles to Dental Students Mag. Home: 7345 SW 123d Terrace Miami FL 33156 Office: 9230 Bird Rd Miami FL 33165

JACQUES, WILFRED JAMES, JR., lawyer, financial cons. co. exec.; b. Chatham, Ont., Can., May 5, 1932; s. Wilfred James and Almeda (Buie) J.; student U. Ga., 1950-51; B.A., U. Western Ont., 1956; LL.B., U. Ga., 1956; LL.M., N.Y. U., 1964; student Advanced Mgmt. Program, Harvard, 1970; m. Mary Aleece Strickland, Mar. 7, 1958; 1 son, Wilfred James III. Admitted to Ga. bar, 1957; with Deen and Jacques attys. at law, Alma, Ga., 1957-63; with Straus Duparquet Inc., House Counsel, N.Y.C., 1964-65; with Harrell Internat. Inc. & Subsidiaries, Jacksonville, Fla., 1965-71, sr. v.p., dir., until 1971; chmn. Jacques Co., Financial Cons., 1971—. Home: Route 1 Waycross GA 31501 Office: 701 Carswell Av Waycross GA 31501

JAEGER, KURT SCOTT, petroleum engr.; b. East Orange, N.J., Sept. 26, 1920; s. Kurt Hammond and Dorothy Scott (Scott) J.; B.S., U. Tulsa, 1950; m. Jewell Helen Bennett, Nov. 24, 1945; children—Susan Rae (Mrs. Donald Frederick), Gina Elizabeth (Mrs. K.E. Ingram). Draftsman, Webster Engring. Co., Tulsa, 1947-48, jr. engr., 1948-50, asst. chief engr., 1950-60. chief engr., 1960-65; supr. burner engring. Forney Engring. Co., Dallas, 1966—. Served with USNR, 1942-44. Registered profl. engr., Okla. Baptist (deacon 1950—). Patentee in field. Home: 216 Brookview Dr Hurst TX 76053 Office: 3405 Wiley Post Rd Addison TX 75001

JAEGER, RICHARD MORROW, educator; b. Neponset, N.Y., Dec. 5, 1938; s. Harold and Bessie (Galpen) J.; B.A., Pepperdine Coll., 1962; M.S., Stanford, 1964, Ph.D. (Dept. Health, Edn. and Welfare research trainee), 1970; m. Judy Sharon McKenzie, Nov. 16, 1960. With Space Tech. Labs., Aerospace Corp., Los Angeles, 1958-62; statistician Western Devel. Labs., Philco Corp., 1962-64; sr. research engr. Gen. Motors Research Labs., Santa Barbara, Cal., 1964-65; math. statistician Stanford Research Inst., Menlo Park, Cal., 1965-67; chief of evaluation methodology, dir. fed./state staff U.S. Office Edn., Washington, 1967-71; asso. prof. U. South Fla., Tampa, 1971—; vis. lectr. Howard U., 1968-69; asst. prof. Va. Poly. Inst., 1970-71. Cons., Nat. Inst. Edn., U.S. Office Edn., Fla. Dept. Edn., 1971—, Ednl. Testing Service, 1971-72, Ohio Dept. Edn., 1972, Cal. Dept. Edn., Ohio State U., 1972-73, Va. Poly. Inst., 1972—, Hillsborough Community Coll., 1973. Mem. Am. Statis. Assn., Psychometric Soc., Am. Ednl. Research Assn., Nat. Council on Measurement in Edn. Asso. editor Jour. of Educational Measurement. Contbr. articles to profl. jours. Home: 617 Sunset Lane Lutz FL 33549 Office: U South Fla FAO 292 Tampa FL 33620

JAGGERS, CHARLES STANLEY, supt. schs.; b. Mt. Pleasant, Tex., Oct. 29, 1932; s. Worth and Loretta (Redfern) J.; B.S., East Tex. State U., 1956, M.Ed., 1961; m. Kay Louwayne Branum, Jan. 1955; children—Patricia Lou, Chuck Bradley, Janna Ruth. Football coach, Anna, Tex., 1956, Frisco High Sch., 1957-63; athletic dir. Bridgeport (Tex.) High Sch., 1963-66; prin. high sch., Bridgeport, 1966-68; supt. schs., Wheeler, Tex., 1968-70; supt. schs., Quanah, Tex., 1971—. Served with USNR, 1951-53. Lion. Home: PO Box 65 Quanah TX 79252 Office: PO Box 150 Quanah TX 79252

JAGIELLO, WALTER EDWARD, mus. pub.; b. Chgo., Aug. 1, 1930; s. John Joseph and Katharine (Mirek) J.; ed. Holy Innocents Sch., Chgo., 1937-45; m. Jeanette Kozak, Mar. 17, 1972; children by previous marriage—Edward, Julieann, James. Founder Jay-Jay Record Co., Chgo., 1952, pres., 1971—; entertainer as Lil Wally, 1945—; pres. Jay Jay Pub. Co., 1955—, Walters Music Co., 1966—, Lil Wally Music Prodns., 1960—, Splty. Distbn. Co., Inc., 1969—; drummer, vocalist, band leader. Bd. dirs. Panair. Named to Polka Hall of Fame, Songwriters Hall of Fame. Mem. Internat. Polka Assn., Nat. Acad. Rec. Arts and Scis. Composer over 1500 mus. compositions; rec. 120 albums and 310 singles. Address: 910 Bay Dr Miami Beach FL 33141 Office: 316 NE 80th Terrace Miami Beach FL 33138

JAMES, ADVERGUS DELL, JR., coll. adminstr.; b. Garden City, Kan., Sept. 24, 1944; s. Advergus Dell and Helen Gertrude (Lee) J.; B.S., Langston (Okla.) U., 1966; M.S., Okla. State U., 1969; m. Anna Glenn, Dec. 25, 1971. Asst. registrar Langston U., 1966-68, instr. bus. dept., dir. admissions and records, 1969-70; grad. asst. Okla. State U., 1968-69; asst. prof. bus. dept., dir. student financial aid Prairie View (Tex.) A. and M. U., 1970—. Regional instr. data mgmt. and systems for 2-year colls. Mem. Am., Okla. assns. collegiate registrars and admissions officers, Nat. Bus. Edn. Assn., Am. Vocational Assn., Nat. Assn. for Financial Assistance to Minority Students, So. Coll. Personnel Assn., Higher Edn. Alumni Council, Langston U., Okla. State U. alumni assns., N.A.A.C.P., Nat., Southwestern assns. student financial aid adminstrs., Phi Beta Lambda, Alpha Phi, Phi Delta Kappa, Kappa Delta Pi. Mason (32 deg.), Optomist (charter Prairie View chpt.); mem. Order Rising Star. Home: 7815 Water Park Lane Houston TX 77038 Office: Drawer C Prairie View TX 77445

JAMES, ALBERT LAW III, lawyer; b. Florence, S.C., Aug. 10, 1943; s. Albert Law and Marion (Graham) J.; B.A., Davidson Coll., 1965; J.D., U. S.C., 1969; m. Finley Ann Stith, Apr. 12, 1969; 1 dau., Finley Lucas. Admitted to S.C. bar, 1968; asso. law firm Paulling & James, Darlington, S.C., 1971—, partner, 1971—. Dir., Citizens & So. Nat. Bank S.C., Darlington. Bd. dirs. Darlington, United Fund. Served with AUS, 1969-71. Decorated Bronze Star. Mem. S.C., Am. bar assns., Phi Beta Kappa, Beta Theta Pi, Phi Delta Phi. Presbyn. (chmn. bd. deacons 1971—). Kiwanian (dir. 1971-73). Club: Darlington Country (dir. 1971—). Home: 138 North St Darlington SC 29532 Office: 112 Cashua St Darlington SC 29532

JAMES, BENJAMIN ESCOTT, accountant; b. Edwardsville, Pa., Aug. 18, 1895; s. Benjamin Reese and Catherine (Escott) J.; B.S. in Econ., U. Pa., 1921; m. Lola M. White, Apr. 29, 1923; children—Patricia Jane (Mrs. R.G. Bullock Jr.), Benjamin Escott Jr. Accountant, John W. Gunby, Jacksonville, Fla., 1922-26; owner, operator firm Benjamin E. James, C.P.A., Jacksonville, 1926-46; sr. partner firm James & Harris, Jacksonville, 1946—; dir. Petroleum Carrier Corp., Jones Bros. Co., Jacksonville. Mem. Fla. Bd. Accountancy, 1965-69, chmn. 1968-69. Mem. adv. bd. Boys Home Assn., Jacksonville, 1935-45, Big Bros, Assn., 1935-40. Served with U.S. Army, 1917-19; ETO. C.P.A., Fla. Mem. So. States Accountants Conf. (pres. 1945), Fla. (pres. 1931), Am. insts. C.P.A.'s, Nat. Assn. State Bds. Accountancy, Am. Accountants Assn., Am. Legion, Sigma Nu, Beta Alpha Psi (hon.). Episcopalian (vestryman). Clubs: Meninak (pres. 1940), Timuquana Country, Seminole, Fla. Yacht, St. John's Dinner, Ye Mystic Revelers (all Jacksonville). Home: 1560 Lancaster Terrace Jacksonville FL 32204 Office: Fla Nat Bank Bldg Jacksonville FL 32202

JAMES, CHARLES GRIFFIN, banker; b. Chireno, Tex., June 4, 1933; s. Earnest Marlin and Edna Myrtle (Little) J.; B.S., Stephen F. Austin State U., 1952; M.R.E., Southwestern Bapt. Sem., 1958; m. Betty Jean Powell, Feb. 12, 1955; 1 dau., Ruth Ann. With City Pub. Service Bd., San Antonio, 1959-66; asst. v.p. Groos Nat. Bank, San Antonio, 1968-72, v.p. charge Computer Center, 1972—; instr. data processing San Antonio Coll., 1966—. Mem. Bexar County Hist. Survey Com., 1973—. Served with USAF, 1953-55. Mem. Data Processing Mgmt. Assn. (past v.p., dir. San Antonio chpt.), Assn. Computing Machinery, Sons Republic Tex., Sons Confederate Vets., Order Stars and Bars, Stephen F. Austin State U. Alumni Assn., State Assn. Tex. Pioneers, S.A.R. Baptist. Home: 239 Tophill Rd San Antonio TX 78209 Office: 246 E Commerce St San Antonio TX 78295

JAMES, ERICH WILLIAM, lawyer; b. Memphis, Mar. 25, 1931; s. Jesse Arvin and Alma Louise (Meyer) J.; B.A., Vanderbilt U., 1953, J.D., 1960; m. Edith Brooks Proctor, Jan. 16, 1965; children—Letitia Vance, Erich William. Admitted to Tenn. bar, 1960, since practiced in Memphis; asso. atty. Tual, Allan, Keltner & Lee, 1960-61; partner Lee, James & Hall, 1961-63; asso. atty. Waring, Walker, Cox & Lewis, 1963-65, partner, 1965-72; partner Waring, Cox, James, Sklar & Allen, 1972—. Served to 1st lt. USMC, 1953-57. Mem. Am., Tenn., Memphis, Shelby County bar assns., Tenn. Def. Lawyers Assn., Def. Research Inst., Assn. Trial Lawyers Am., Am. Judicature Soc., Phi Kappa Sigma, Phi Delta Phi. Mason. Club: Farmington Country. Asso. editor: Vanderbilt Law Rev., 1959-60. Home: 2343 Woodbridge Cove Memphis TN 38138 Office: Sterick Bldg Memphis TN 38103

JAMES, GEORGE EDWARD, JR., ins. co. exec.; b. Richmond, Va., Jan. 27, 1921; s. George Edward and Ruthe Mae (Brightwell) J.; jr. accounting degree Va. So. Coll., 1947; m. Patricia Ann Howery, Nov. 29, 1969; children—Edward Derekson, Brenda Leigh, Amy Page. Financial clk. mortgage loans Jefferson Standard Life Ins. Co., Greensboro, N.C., 1947-49; successively salesman, asst. field mgr., supt. agys., tng. dir. Shenandoah Life Ins. Co., Roanoke, Va., 1949-62, asso. mgr. field, 1962-63, regional supt. agys., 1966-67, dir. manpower devel., 1967-68, asst. v.p. agys., 1968, 2d v.p. marketing, 1968—; v.p. agys. Estate Life Ins. Co., Roanoke, 1963-65; pres. Am. Standard Life Ins. Co., Poplar Bluff, Mo., 1966; v.p. Shenandoah Equity Services, Roanoke, 1971—, prin., tng. cons., 1969—. Asst. dist. commr. Blue Ridge council Boy Scouts Am., 1964-65. Served to 3d class petty officer USNR, World War II; PTO. C.L.U. Mem. Roanoke C. of C., Am. Soc. Life Underwriters, Nat. Assn. Life Underwriters. Baptist (deacon 1960—, supt. Sunday sch. 1960-68). Club: Raleigh Court Lions (pres. 1965). Home: 4054 Southwick Circle Roanoke VA 24018 Office: 2301 Brambleton Av Roanoke VA 24015

JAMES, GRACE MARILLYN, physician; b. Charleston, W.Va., Aug. 12, 1923; d. Edward Lawrence and Stella Grace (Shaw) J.; B.A., W.Va. State Coll., 1944; M.D., Meharry Med. Coll., Nashville, 1950; div.; 1 son, David Marshall. Gen. rotating intern Harlem Hosp., N.Y.C., 1950-51, resident pediatrics, 1951-52; resident pediatrics Vanderbilt Clinic, Babies Hosp., Columbia Presbyn. Med. Center, N.Y.C., 1952-53; traineeship in child psychiatry Nat. Inst. Mental Health, Creedmoor State Hosp., Queens Village, N.Y., 1964-65; tng. fellow Care of Handicapped Children, Childrens Evaluation and Rehab. Clinic, Albert Einstein Coll. Medicine, Yeshiva U. at Jacobi Hosp., 1966; camp physician Camp Woodlands, Phoencia, N.Y., 1952; practice medicine, specializing in pediatrics, Louisville, 1953-64, 67—; child health physician Louisville and Jefferson County Dept. Health, 1953-55, pub. sch. physician, 1962-63; mem. staff West End Day Care Center; mem. attending staff Childrens Hosp., Louisville; asst. vis. psychiatrist, full-time staff child psychiatry Kings County Hosp. Center, Bklyn., 1965-66; dir. diagnostic and evaluation div. Frankfort (Ky.) State Hosp., 1966; dir. Diagnostic and Evaluation Service, div. mental retardation Dept. Mental Health, Frankfort, 1966-67; instr. child health U. Louisville Sch. Medicine, Louisville Gen. Hosp., 1953-62, asst. clin. prof. pediatrics, 1962—; asst. clin. vis. prof. pediatrics Meharry Med. Coll., Nashville, 1970; clin. pediatrician Kosair Crippled Childrens Hosp., Ky. Commn. for Handicapped Children, 1968—; pres. West Louisville Med. Center, 1972—; mem. active staff Red Cross Hosp., Childrens Hosp., Louisville; mem. courtesy staff Jewish Hosp., St. Josephs Hosp., St. Anthonys Hosp., Meth. Evang. Hosp., Nortons Hosp., Louisville, Geo. W. Hubbard Hosp., Nashville; pres. med. staff Red Cross Hosp., 1963; mem. Action Research team, U. Louisville. Chmn. instns. and agys. com. Louisville Human Relations Com., 1961-64; chmn. com. on sch. dropouts Louisville Urban League, 1963; Community Council mem. Family Service Orgn., 1958-62; mem. housing adv. com. Dept. Housing Inspection, City of Louisville, 1970—; mem. health and welfare council United Way, Louisville, 1971—; mem. steering liaison com. Health Maintenance Orgn., Louisville, 1971—. Bd. dirs. Louisville br. N.A.A.C.P., 1953-55, West End Day Care Center, 1960-63. Diplomate Am. Bd. Pediatrics. Fellow Am. Acad. Pediatrics (mem. community health com. 1971—), Am. Assn. Mental Deficiency; mem. A.M.A., Nat. (vice chmn. sect. on pediatrics 1962-66), Ky. med. assns., Jefferson County (alternate del. 1959-60), Falls City (sec. 1960-64, 72-73, pres. 1974—, chmn. community health services 1971—) med. socs., Ky., Louisville pediatrics socs., Delta Sigma Theta. Home: 684 S 44th St Louisville KY 40211 Office: 4221 W Broadway Louisville KY 40211

JAMES, G(UY) M(ASTEN), mfg. co. exec.; b. Winston-Salem, N.C., May 3, 1914; s. Maloy Cowan and Della May (Pierce) J.; B.A., U. Tenn., 1934. Sec., gen. mgr. James Hosiery Mills, Inc., Greeneville, Tenn., 1936—. Mem. Civic Music Club, Greeneville, 1958—. Served from 2d lt. to col. AUS, 1934-36, 40-46. Decorated Bronze Star. Mem. Pi Kappa Alpha. Presbyn. Clubs: Cherokee Country, City (Knoxville, Tenn.); Twin City (Winston-Salem); Link Hills Country (Greenville); New Orleans Country; Lake Placid (N.Y.); Army and Navy (Washington). Home: 501 W Main St Greenville TN 37743 Office: 110 Elm St Greenville TN 37743

JAMES, HIBBARD GARRETT, communications exec.; b. Cin., Dec. 16, 1922; s. Edward M. and Elizabeth Cheyney (Garrett) J.; S.B., Harvard, 1945; postgrad. Columbia Tchrs. Coll., 1954, Springfield Coll., 1955-56; m. Betty Miles, March 30, 1963. Faculty, New Eng. Conservatory Music, 1945-46, Tilton Acad,, 1946-47; pub. relations dir. Wichita Community Chest, 1948-51, Indpls. Community Chest, 1951-53, YMCA of Greater N.Y., 1953-58, nat. capital area United Givers Fund, 1958-69; communications dir. Washington Cathedral (D.C.), 1969—; producer Overview, WRC-TV, 1970—. Vis. lectr. pub. relations N. Va. Community Coll., 1966—. Mem. pub. relations Councils Am., 1952-66; mem. broadcast and film commn. Nat. Council Chs., 1969—. Chmn. bd. trustees Cheyney (Pa.) Burying Ground, 1963—. Mem. Pub. Relations Soc. Am. (accredited), Washington Shakespeare Soc. (dir.). Mem. Soc. of Friends. Clubs: Players (N.Y.C.); Nat. Broadcasters, Nat. Press (Washington). Author: Poesie, 1943; German Opera in Boston, 1945. Music critic various publs., 1954-60; book reviewer Washington Evening Star, 1963—; archtl. critic Washington Daily News, 1967-72. Home: 521 5th St Washington DC 20003 Office: Washington Cathedral Mount St Alban Washington DC 20016

JAMES, JOHN V., corp. exec.; b. Plains Twp., Pa., July 24, 1918; s. Stanley S. and Catherine M. (Jones) J.; B.S. in Econs., U. Pa., 1941, certificate in mgmt., 1948; m. Helen L. James, June 25, 1949; 1 dau., Barbara Ann. Office mgr., controller Carr Consol. Biscuit Co., Wilkes Barre, Pa., 1941-42; div. controller Corning Glass Works, 1948-56, mgr. budgets and procs., 1956-57; asst. controller Dresser Industries, Inc., Dallas, 1957-58, v.p. finance subsidiary Clark Bros. Co., Olean, N.Y., 1958-60, controller parent co., 1960-65, v.p., 1962-65, group v.p. machinery, 1965-68, exec. v.p., 1968-69, pres., chief exec. officer, 1970—, also dir. Served to capt. AUS, 1943-46. Mem. Financial Execs. Inst., Nat. Assn. Accountants (dir. 1960-62), Beta Gamma Sigma. Conglist. Mason, Rotarian (pres. Corning 1957). Home: 7222 Azalea Lane Dallas TX 75230 Office: Republic National Bank Bldg PO Box 718 Dallas TX 75221

JAMES, JOSEPH B., educator; b. Clearwater, Fla., July 17, 1912; s. L. P. and Ilah J. (Miles) J.; A.B.E., U. Fla., 1934, A.M., 1935; Ph.D., U. Ill., 1939; m. Jacquelyn McWhite, June 8, 1937; children—Glenn Joseph, William Bruce. Instr. gen. extension div. U. Fla., 1935-36; asst. and fellow U. Ill., 1936-39; head dept. history and polit. sci. Williamsport Dickinson Jr. Coll., 1939-40; Union Coll., Ky., 1940-43; dean of faculty William Woods Coll., 1943-45; head dept. social studies Miss. State Coll. for Women, 1945-58; dean of coll. Wesleyan Coll., Macon, Ga., 1958-71, Callaway prof. polit. sci., 1971—; vis. prof. summer sessions U. Fla., U. Miss., Florence (Ala.) State Tchrs. Coll., Middle Tenn. State Coll. Mem. So. Polit. Sci. Assn., So. Hist. Assn., Assn. Coll. Honor Socs. (council mem.), Phi Beta Kappa (past pres. Middle Ga. Grad. Assn.), Phi Kappa Phi, Kappa Delta Pi, Kappa Phi Kappa, Pi Gamma Mu (nat. pres. emeritus). Methodist (adminstrv. bd.). Rotarian. Author: The Framing of the Fourteenth Amendment, 1956, rev. edit., 1965. Contbr. to scholarly Jours. and reference publs. Home: 3450 Osborne Pl Macon GA 31204

JAMES, JOSEPH SHEPPARD, state ofcl.; b. Gum Spring, Va., May 25, 1902; s. Richard Gregory and Lillie (Sale) J.; student Va. Mechanics Inst.; m. Virginia Lambeth, June 27, 1925; children—Joseph Sheppard, Beverly (Mrs. Willard Travell Weeks). Asst. auditor pub. accounts State of Va., Richmond, 1944-67, auditor pub. accounts, 1967—. Instr. accounting Va. Mechanics Inst., 1934-51. C.P.A., Va. Home: 3850 Brook Rd Richmond VA 23227 Office: 302 State Office Bldg Richmond VA 23219

JAMES, M(ALOY) C(OWAN), mfg. co. exec.; b. Star, N.C., Jan. 4, 1886; s. William Henry and Annie Florence (Usher) J.; student Mars Hill Coll., 1902-07; m. Della May Pierce, June 29, 1911; children—Guy Masten, Maloy Cowan. Various positions, 1909-36; founder pres. The James Hosiery Mills, Inc., Greeneville, Tenn., 1936—. Presbyn. Mason (32 deg., Shriner). Club: Cherokee Country (Knoxville, Tenn.). Home: 501 W Main St Greeneville TN 37743 Office: 110 Elm St Greeneville TN 37743

JAMES, MALOY COWAN, JR., textile co. exec.; b. Winston-Salem, N.C., May 14, 1922; s. Maloy Cowan and Della May (Pierce) J.; student U. Tenn., 1938-40;; m. Anna Lou Witt, Oct. 25, 1949. Treas., James Hosiery Mills, Greeneville, Tenn., 1934-62; owner, pres. James Knitting Co., Inc., Greeneville, 1962—. Served with AUS, 1943. Mem. U.S. (sectional affairs com. 1969—), Tenn. (v.p. 1958, 67-68, pres. 1959, 69) golf assns., Am. Legion, Pi Kappa Alpha. Presbyn. Elk, Moose. Clubs: Link Hills (pres. 1954-58; dir. 1954-65) (Greeneville); Cherokee (Knoxville, Tenn.); Ponte Vedra (Fla.). Home: 101 Monument Av Greeneville TN 37743 Office: 1000 W Irish St Greeneville TN 37743

JAMES, MARSHALL ORR, ednl. adminstr., clergyman; b. Anderson, S.C., Feb. 25, 1929; s. Jesse Alvin and Flora Louise (Shore) J.; B.S., Furman U., 1949; M.S., La. State U., 1951; B.A., Oxford U., Eng., 1956, M.A., 1959; S.T.B., Gen. Theol. Sem., 1957, Millsaps Coll., 1965; m. Winifred Griffith Wills, Nov. 17, 1957; children—Frederick Martin St. John, David Marshall, Jonathon Andrew. Ordained to ministry Protestant Episcopal Ch. as deacon, 1956, priest, 1958; pastor chs., Greer, S.C., 1957-59, Clemson, S.C., 1959-63; chaplain Clemson Coll., 1959-63, prof. philosophy, 1960-63; headmaster St. Andrew's Episcopal Sch., Jackson, Miss., 1965-71; canon St. Andrews Cathedral, Jackson; dir. religion dept. St. Martin's Protestant Episcopal Sch., Metairie, La., 1971—. Active various community drives. Served with AUS, 1951-54. Mem. Phi Kappa Phi. Rotarian. Home: 401 Haring Rd Metairie LA 70003 Office: 5309 Airline Hwy Metairie LA 70003

JAMES, NORMA WHITENER (MRS. JOHN WARREN JAMES), civic worker; b. Lincolnton, N.C., Feb. 14, 1903; d. John Roadman and Hattie (Hull) Whitener; student U. Fla., 1925; m. John Warren James, Sept. 13, 1937 (dec. Dec. 1943). Mem. Broward Hosp. Auxiliary, 1950-55, Opera Guild, 1952-59, Civic Music Assn., 1956-58; chmn. Broward County unit Am. Cancer Soc., 1950-51, hon. life mem. bd. dirs. Mem. Internat. Platform Assn., Nova U. Assn. (charter mem. Ft. Lauderdale). Club: Golden Hills Turf and Country. Home: PO Box 38 Fort McCoy FL 32637

JAMES, OPAL RUTH, petroleum co. exec., rancher; b. Burkburnett, Tex., Feb. 11, 1922; d. Paul John and Velma Ada (Sessums) James: B.S. in Chem. Engring., Tex. Tech. U., 1949. B.S. in Indsl. Engring., 1949. Process engr. Hudson Engring. Corp., Houston, 1951-56, mgr. data processing, 1956—. Registered profl. engr., Tex. Mem. Tex. Soc. Profl. Engrs., Assn. of Computing Machinery. Home; 102 Capri St Sugar Land TX 77478 also Route 2 Whitney TX 76692 Office: 5900 Hillcroft Houston TX 77036

JAMES, PHILIP WAYNE, assn. exec.; b. Dallas, Sept. 11, 1934; s. Dalton L. and Minnie R. (Caldwell) J.; B.S., Tex. Tech. U., 1957, M.S., 1964; m. Peggy J. Welling, May 31, 1971. Field sec. Tex. Tech. Ex-Students Assn., 1957-60, exec. dir., 1960—; sec.-treas. Tex. Tech Loyalty Fund, 1960—; pres. Tex. Tech Spltys., Inc., 1974—. Instr. mass communications dept. Tex. Tech U., 1971. Bd. dirs. Tex. Tech U. Found. Recipient Regional and nat. awards in alumni activities Am. Alumni Council. Mem. Am. Alumni Council (dir. 1969-74), Internat. Platform Assn., Sigma Delta Chi, Phi Delta Kappa, Alpha Phi Omega. Mason (Shriner), Rotarian. Clubs: Tex. Tech Century, Red Raider (Lubbock); Dallas Press. Editor Tex. Techsan, 1960-72. Home: 3002 60th St Lubbock TX 79413 Office: Tex Tech U Lubbock TX 79409

JAMES, ROBERT EDGAR, religious instn. exec.; b. Dallas County, Ala., Mar. 15, 1940; s. Thedford James and Lillian Beatrice (Simmons) J.; student U. Alaska, 1964; B.S., Ala. State U., 1967; m. Annie Walton, Sept. 15, 1965. With YMCA, Montgomery, Ala., 1959-62, exec. dir., 1967—. Communications specialist Blue Ridge Found, N.C., 1971—; co-ordinator Joint Action in Community Service, Montgomery, Ala., 1970; chmn. human rights com. Montgomery Community Action, 1972-73; vice chmn. group III, United Appeal campaign, 1973; mem. Montgomery Improvement Assn. Served with USAF, 1962-66. Named Vol. of Year, Joint Action in Community Service S.E. Region, 1974, nat. honoree, 1974. Mem. N.A.A.C.P., Ala. State U. Alumni Assn. (pres. 1973-74), U.S. Assn. YMCA Dirs. Elk. Home: PO Box 1582 Montgomery AL 36103 Office: 1201 Cleveland Av Montgomery AL 36108

JAMES, ROBERT LEIGH, author, banker, lawyer; b. Worthington, O., July 29, 1918; s. Frank and Jessie (Brummitt) J.; student Ind. U., 1937-39, U. Cal., Los Angeles, 1938; A.B., U. Chgo., 1941, J.D., 1947; m. Genevieve Palmer Capouch, Oct. 4, 1943; 1 dau., Alexandra Mary. U.S. Fgn. Service officer, 1947-50; admitted to Ill. bar, 1947, also D.C., Cal. bars; atty. Bank of Am., 1951-52; land and legal rep. Western hemisphere Cal. Exploration Co., 1952-58; v.p. Moa Bay Mining Co., Nicaro Nickel Co., Island Exploration Co., 1958-60; v.p., Washington rep. Bank of Am. N.T. and S.A., San Francisco, 1960—. Served to lt. comdr. USNR, 1941-46. Mem. Wash. Inst. Fgn. Affairs, U.S. C. of C. (mem. internat. com.), Theta Chi. Clubs: The Nineteen Twenty-five F Street, City Tavern Assn., Chevy Chase, Metropolitan. Internat. (Washington); University (N.Y.C.). Author: The Chameleon File, 1967; The Capitol Hill Affair, 1968; The Push-Button Spy, 1970; Penelope's Zoo, 1971; Janus, 1973; Triple Mirror, 1973. Home: 4301 Bradley Lane Chevy Chase MD 20015 Office: 1800 K St NW Washington DC 20005

JAMES, WILLIAM GAIL, dentist; b. Boyce, La., Aug. 4, 1921; s. John Fielding and Edna Earle (LaCaze) J.; D.D.S., Loyola U., New Orleans, 1945; m. Mary Francis Lohman, June 9, 1951; children—Jennifer, William, Richard, Melissa. Practice dentistry, Alexandria, La., 1947-48, 52—; asso. with Dr. William G. Vernon, Alexandria, 1948-52; mem. staff Rapides Gen. Hosp., St. Francis Cabrini Hosp. Served with USNR, 1945-47. Fellow Internat. Coll. Dentists, Pierre Fauchard Acad., Acad. Internat. Dentistry; mem. Am. (ho. dels. 1966-68), La. (pres. 1965), 8th Dist. (pres. 1950) dental assns., Delta Sigma Delta. Democrat. Methodist (ofcl. bd.). Clubs: Alexandria Golf and Country, Alexandria Optimist (charter). Contbr. articles to dental jours. Address: 3912 Parliament Dr Alexandria LA 71301

JAMES, WILLIAM WESLEY, JR., utility exec.; b. Gulfport, Miss., Feb. 24, 1936; s. William Wesley and Mamie (Swanner) J.; B.E.E., Miss. State U., 1958; m. Beverly Elaine Banderet, Oct. 28, 1952; children—William Wesley III, Cheryl Elaine, Carl Byron, Troy Lee. With Fla. Power & Light Co., Miami, 1957—, system operations engr., 1969-72, supr. distbn., 1972-73, mgr. apprentice tng., 1973—. Chmn. elec. tech. craft com. Manatee Vocational & Tech. Center, Bradenton, Fla., 1959-69; coach basketball and football Boys' Club, Bradenton, 1961-64; football coach Pop Warner League, 1970-73; mem. gen. adv. bd. tech. edn. Manatee Jr. Coll., 1959-69, Manatee Profl. Guidance Bd., Pub. Schs., 1961-68, council Manatee County P.T.A., 1964-67. Registered profl. engr., Fla. Mem. Fla., Nat. socs. profl. engrs., I.E.E.E., Fla. Engring. Soc. Methodist (mem. ofcl. bd.). Home: 11800 SW 68th Ct Miami FL 33156 Office: PO Box 3100 Miami FL 33101

JAMIESON, ADDIE MAE, civic worker; b. Ripley, Miss., May 9, 1919; d. Jesse Darnel and Frances Ardena (Moore) Jamieson; A.B., Blue Mountain Coll., 1943; M.A., Scarritt Coll., 1949; postgrad. Emory U., summers, 1953, 58. Tchr. Dry Creek Elementary Sch., Booneville, Miss., 1939-43, Slate Spring (Miss.) High Sch., 1944, Wilkinson County, 1945, Ripley High Sch., 1945-47; rural worker Fla. Conf., Tallahassee Dist., 1949-55; coordinator Ga. Coop. Rural Work, North and South Ga. Confs. Methodist Ch., Macon, 1955-60; dir. Christian edn. Mulberry St. Meth. Ch., Macon, Ga., 1960-65, coordinator Holston Meth. Conf., Johnson City, Tenn., 1965-72. County dir. Cancer Drive, Liberty County, Fla., 1951; charter mem. Ga. Meth. Federal Credit Union, 1969—, v.p. bd. dirs., 1963-65; mem. exec. com. North Miss. Town and Country Commn., 1972—. Bd. dirs. Wesley Found., Ga. So. Coll., Statesboro, 1963-64. Mem. South Ga. Conf. Meth. Ch. (exec. com. 1955-60, Holston conf. 1965-72, bd. edn. 1955-63, exec. com. 1960-63, pres. deaconess bd., 1957-59, interconf. com. Meth. student work 1960-64, fellowship Christian edn. com. 1962-63), United Meth. Deaconess Home Missionary Service (com. 1964-72, Juris rep., chmn. by-laws, 1964-72) Louisville Bus. and Profl. Women's Club. Home: PO Box 127 Louisville MS 39339

JAMISON, JIMMIE HERSHEL, elec. engr.; b. Galveston, Tex., Aug. 4, 1925; s. Hershel Connell and Ersie Cornel (Keeling) J.; B.S., Tex. A. and M. U., 1950; m. Betty Jane Shillott, Jan. 28, 1948; children—Cynthia Ann, Karen Louise. Distbn. engr. Dallas Power & Light Co., 1950-55; engr. elec. sales Joslyn Mfg. & Supply Co., Abilene, Tex., 1955—. Precinct chmn. Republican Party, 1968-73. Served with USMCR, 1941-45. Decorated Bronze Star, Purple Heart. Mem. I.E.E.E., Tex. Bd. Profl. Engrs. K.C. Club: Abilene Exchange. Home: 2909 Salinas Dr Abilene TX 79605 Office: PO Box 2734 Abilene TX 79604

JAMISON, JOHN AMBLER, circuit judge; b. Florence, S.C., May 14, 1916; s. John Wilson and Elizabeth Ambler (Fleming) J.; LL.B., Cumberland U., 1941; postgrad. George Washington U., 1943-44; grad. Indsl. Coll. Armed Forces, 1962; J.D., Samford U., 1969; m. Mildred Holley, Sept. 22, 1945. Admitted to S.C. bar, 1941, Va. bar 1942, U.S. Supreme Ct. bar, 1945; atty. Va. Div. Motor Vehicles, Richmond, 1947-54; practice law, Fredericksburg, 1954-72; asso. judge County Cts. Stafford and King George Counties, Va., Municipal Ct., Fredericksburg, 1956-72; judge 15th Va. Jud. Circuit, 1972—. Dir., counsel Nat. Bank of Fredericksburg, 1968-72. Mem. adv. com. Gov.'s Hwy. Safety Commn., 1956-58; pres. Fredericksburg Rescue Squad, 1960-62, now hon. life mem. Chmn. bd. Fredericksburg Area Mental Hygiene Clinic, 1962-63; bd. dirs. Rappahannock Area Devel. Commn., 1960-66. Served from ensign to comdr. USNR, 1941-46; comdg. officer Richmond Naval Res. Div., 1948-54; naval aide to gov. of Va., 1954-72. Recipient award S.C. Confederate War Centennial Commn., 1965. Mem. Am., S.C., Va., 15th Va. Jud. Circuit (pres. 1959-60, 69-70) bar assns., Va. Trial Lawyers Assn., Am. Judicature Soc., Cumberland Order Jurisprudence, Res. Officers Assn. U.S., Am. Legion (post comdr. 1951-52), Blue Key, Sigma Delta Kappa. Episcopalian (past vestryman, lay reader). Mason (32 deg., Shriner, Jester), Kiwanian (dir.). Address: PO Drawer 29 Fredericksburg VA 22401

JAMISON, KING WELLS, JR., educator; b. Meridian, Miss., Aug. 8, 1931; s. King Wells and Edna (May) J.; B.S., Union U., 1952; M.A., George Peabody Coll. Tchrs., 1953, Ph.D., 1962; m. Mary Catherine Ramsey, Nov. 15, 1953; children—Benjamin King, Julie Audrey, Jeffery Ramsey, Kendall Axley. Tchr. Fernandina Beach (Fla.) High Sch., 1956-58, West Memphis (Ark.) High Sch., 1958-59; lectr. dept. applied math. Vanderbilt U., 1961-62; chmn. dept. math., dir. tchr. edn. Ky. So. Coll., 1962-66; prof. math. Middle Tenn. State U., Murfreesboro, 1966—. Active Boy Scouts Am. Served with USNR, 1953-56. Mem. Nat. Council Tchrs. Math., Tenn. Math. Tchrs. Assn., Middle Tenn. Edn. Assn., Phi Delta Kappa. Baptist (deacon 1970-73). Contbr. articles to math. jours. Home: 520 E Main St Murfreesboro TN 37130

JAMISON, RICHARD MELVIN, virologist; b. Rayne, La., Oct. 28, 1938; s. Melvin Linwood and Lina Katharine (Muller) J.; M.S. (USPHS fellow), Baylor U. Coll. Medicine, 1962, Ph.D., 1966; m. Diane E. Cella, Oct. 24, 1964; children—Richard Wilhelm, Diane Elizabeth, Bonny Alyssa. Research asso. Oak Ridge Nat. Lab., 1966-67; asst. prof. U. Colo. Med. Center, Denver, 1967-70; virologist La. State U. Med. Center Shreveport, 1970—. Mem. A.A.A.S., Electron Microscopy Soc. Am., Am. Soc. for Microbiology. Research in tumor viruses, host-virus interactions and picornaviruses. Home: 2034 Audubon Place Shreveport LA 71105 Office: PO Box 3932 Shreveport LA 71130

JANDA, ROBERT JAMES, mfg. co. pres.; b. Cedar Rapids, Ia., Oct. 9, 1937; s. Joseph Frank and Florence Ann (Indra) J.; B.A. in Physics, Coe Coll., 1960, B.A. in Bus. Adminstrn., 1960; m. Frances Kay Ward, Apr. 28, 1962; children—Diane Elizabeth, David Alan. Research asst. cosmic ray lab. State U. Ia., Iowa City, 1960-63; staff scientist NASA, Goddard Space Center, 1963-66; pres. Gammaflux, Inc., Reston, Va., 1966—. Patentee microwave dryer for plastics, laser modulator cell, triaxial oscilloscope. Author: Space Solar Cell Power Systems, 1963—. Home: RFD 2 Richland Acres Sterling VA 22170 Office: 1821 Micheal Faraday Dr Reston VA 22090

JANEWAY, RICHARD, coll. dean; b. Los Angeles, Feb. 12, 1933; s. VanZandt and Grace Eleanor (Bell) J.; A.B., Colgate U., 1954; M.D., U. Pa., 1958; m. Katherine Esmond Pillsbury, Dec. 23, 1955; children—Susan Kent, David VanZandt, Elizabeth Anne. Intern Hosp. U. Pa., 1958-59; resident N.C. Bapt. Hosp., Winston-Salem, 1963-66; practice medicine specializing in neurology, Winston-Salem, 1966—; mem. faculty Bowman Gray Sch. Medicine, Wake Forest U., Winston-Salem, 1966—, prof. neurology, 1971—, dir. cerebral vascular research center, 1969-71, dean sch., 1971—. Cons. neurology VA Hosp., Salisbury, N.C., 1969; mem. spl. task force on arteriosclerosis Nat. Heart and Lung Inst., 1971—; joint com. for stroke facilities, 1969-72; chmn. policy com. Winston-Salem/Forsyth County Bd. Edn., 1970—. Served to capt. USAF, 1959-63. USPHS fellow, 1956; Markle scholar, 1968—. Fellow A.C.P.; mem. Am. Neurol. Assn., N.Y. Acad. Sci., Am. Heart Assn., Assn. Am. Med. Colls., Phi Beta Kappa, Alpha Omega Alpha. Rotarian. Home: 2815 Country Club Rd Winston-Salem NC 27104

JANN, WILLIAM KENNETH, SR., ordnance engr.; b. Bklyn., Sept. 1, 1925; s. Gustav Albert and Mary Louise (Gerhart) J.; B.S. in Mech. Engring., U. Colo., 1949; grad. Command and Gen. Staff Coll., 1969; M.A. in Pub. Adminstrn., U. Okla., 1970; postgrad. Indsl. Coll. Armed Forces, 1968-71; m. Clara Louise Dellva, Apr. 23, 1949; children—William Kenneth, Donald Charles, Patricia Marie. Research engr. Bur. Mines Oil Shale Demonstration Plant Rifle, Colo., 1949-50, Bur. Reclamation, Denver, 1950-51; mech. engr. Stearns Rogers Engring. Co., Denver, 1951-52, U.S.N. Pub. Works and Utilities Office, Great Lakes, Ill., 1952-54; ordnance engr. U.S. Army Ordnance Ammunition Command, Joliet, Ill., 1954-56; various key engring. mgmt. positions, currently dep. project mgr. Pershing weapon system Army Ballistic Missile Agy. (name changed to U.S. Army Missile Command), Redstone Arsenal, Ala., 1956—; instr. nat. security mgmt. course Indsl. Coll. Armed Forces, U.S. Army Reserve, Huntsville, Ala., 1971—. Served to staff sgt. USAAF, 1944-45; now lt. col. U.S. Army Res. C.E. Decorated Air medal with four oak leaf clusters. Registered profl. engr., Ala. Mem. Am. Ordnance Assn., Res. Officers Assn. U.S., Assn. U.S. Army, Delta Sigma Phi. Elk. Home: 1406 Elmwood Dr SE Huntsville AL 35801 Office: USAMICOM Redston Arsenal AL 35809

JANSEN, WILLIAM HUGH, educator; b. Stamford, Conn., Mar. 2, 1914; s. William Henry and Caroline (Dunlop) J.; A.B., Wesleyan U., Middletown, Conn., 1935; Ph.D., Ind. U., 1948; m. Violet E. Schraft, Sept. 7, 1937; children—Mary (Mrs. H.K. Kuehner), William Hugh II. Tchr., Williston Acad., Easthampton, Mass., 1935-37; tutor Ind. U., Bloomington, 1937-41, lectr., 1941-42, instr., 1942-49; faculty U. Ky., Lexington, 1949—, prof. English and folklore, 1973—, coordinator overseas programs, 1961-65; vis. prof. U. Ankara (Turkey), 1951-53, Bandung Inst. Tech., Indonesia, 1958-61. Del., Am. Council Learned Socs., 1973—. Fulbright lectr., 1951-52; Ford Found. Faculty fellow, 1955-56; sr. fellow Nat. Endowment for Humanities, 1972-73. Mem. Am. Folklore Soc., Internat. Soc. for Folk-Narrative Research, Folklore Soc. (Gt. Britain), Ky. Folklore Soc. Democrat. Episcopalian. Gen. editor Memoirs of Am. Folklore Soc., 1968-73, Bibliog. and Spl. series Am. Folklore Soc., 1968-73. Contbr. articles to profl. jours. Home: 602 Pasadena Dr Lexington KY 40503

JANSSEN, JAMES HAJO, metallurgist; b. Pekin, Ill., Sept. 21, 1909; s. Gerhardt U. and Alpha (Norris) J.; B.S., U. Ill., 1931; D.Sc. in Metallurgy, McKinly Roosevelt U., 1934; m. Beatrice R. Atteberry, Aug. 18, 1962; children—Shirley Ann (Mrs. Robert A. McDonald). Wire mill metallurgist Keystone Steel & Wire Co., Peoria, Ill., 1934-40; ferrous metallurgist Western Cartridge Co., East Alton, Ill., 1940-43; chief metallurgist Colo. Fuel & Iron Co., Buffalo, 1945-47, asst. chief metallurgist Eastern div., Buffalo, 1947-50; chief metallurgist Pratt & Letchworth Foundry, Buffalo, 1950-55, Ft. Pitt

Steel Foundry, McKeesport, Pa., 1955-56, Keokuk Steel Castings (Ia), 1956-59; corp. cons., chief metallurgist Halliburton Services, Duncan, Okla., 1959—; pres. Janssen Metall. Cons. Services, Duncan. Served with AUS, 1943-45. Registered profl. engr., Okla. Mem. Am. Soc. for Metals, Nat. Soc. Corrosion Engrs. Mason (Shriner). Office: 2206 Chisholm Dr Duncan OK 73533

JANSSEN, MELVIN RUSSEL, economist; b. Minonk, Ill., Oct. 12, 1921; s. John Evers and Greta Johanna (Cassens) J.; B.S., U. Ill., 1943, M.S., 1948; M.P.A. (Ferguson fellow), Harvard, 1948, A.M. (Ferguson fellow), 1949, Ph.D., 1953; m. Marianna Kilian, Aug. 4, 1943; children—Elaine (Mrs. Frederick C. Cue), Paul M., Joanne F., Lee K. Research asst. U. Ill., 1946-47; agrl. economist U.S. Dept. Agr., Lafayette, Ind., 1949-64, leader No. and Western Area, Washington, 1964-65, asst. dir. field coordination Econ. Research Service, Washington, 1965-73, asst. dir., 1973—. Asst. prof. agrl. econs. Purdue U., 1961-64. Chmn. Sch. Reorgn. Adv. Com., Lafayette, 1959-64. Served with AUS, 1943-46. Decorated Air medal with oak leaf cluster. Mem. Am. Econ. Assn., Am., Western, So. agrl. econ. assns. Mem. United Ch. of Christ. Home: 6063 N 6th St Arlington VA 22203 Office: Research Div Rural Development Service Dept Agr Washington DC 20250

JANUS, MURRAY JOSEPH, lawyer; b. Richmond, Va., July 8, 1938; s. Marvin and Sylvia F. (Brown) J.; A.B., Dartmouth, 1960; LL.B., U. Va., 1963; m. Ellen C. Lieberg, Mar. 8, 1964; children—Laurie Lynn, Beth Anne. Admitted to Va. bar, 1963; partner Bremner, Byrne & Baber, Richmond, 1963—; guest lectr. U. Va. Law Sch., U. Richmond Law Sch., 1970—. Mem. Mayor's Com. on Crime, 1972-73. Bd. dirs. Jewish Community Center, Richmond. Served with USAF, 1963. Recipient Am. Spirit Honor medal, 1963. Mem. Am., Va. (pres. criminal bar sect.), Richmond (past pres. jr. bar sect.), Richmond Criminal (pres.) bar assns. Jewish religion. Clubs: Bull and Bear, Jefferson Lakeside. Contbr. articles to profl. jours. Home: 300 Tarrytown Dr Richmond VA 23229 Office: 7th and Franklin Bldg Richmond VA 23219

JANZEN, JERRY LEE, engring. exec.; b. Enid, Okla., Oct, 28, 1936; s. Abe H. and Vivian (Bradley) J.; student Phillips U., 1954-56; B.S., Okla. State U., 1960, M.S., 1963; m. Mary Ann Johnson, Dec. 3, 1960; children—Sherry Lynn, Terry Kay. Lead engr. Western Electric Co., 1960-64; project engr. FAA, 1964-67; prin. Arthur Young & Co., Oklahoma City, 1967—. Vis. asst. prof. Okla. State U., 1964. Registered profl. engr., Okla. Mem. Am, Inst. Indsl. Engrs. (chpt. pres. 1969—), Nat., Okla. Socs. profl. engrs., Am. Prodn. and Inventory Control Soc., Bank Adminstrn. Inst. Club: Engineers. Contbr. articles to profl. publs. Home: 3713 NW 68th St Oklahoma City OK 73116 Office: Liberty Tower Oklahoma City OK 73102

JARBOE, CHARLES HARRY, educator; b. Louisville, Oct. 3, 1928; s. Charles Henry and Mary Elizabeth (O'Daniel) J.; B.Sc., U. Louisville, 1951, Ph.D., 1956; children—Jamisene L., Charles H., Richard J., Herman H., Nancy H., Elizabeth A. Chief scientist Brown and Williamson Tobacco Corp., Louisville, 1958-62, cons., 1962-64; asso. prof. pharmacology Sch. Medicine U. Louisville, 1962-72, prof., 1972—, dir. toxicology and drug abuse, 1972—. Cons. Am. Tobacco Corp., 1971-72, Abbott Labs., 1971-72; mem. equine vet. sci. adv. com. Ky. Racing Commn., 1973—, Ky. Trotting Commn., 1973—. Chmn. water safety com. A.R.C., Ky., 1965-70. Served with USMC, 1945-48. AEC postdoctoral fellow, 1956; Nat. Heart Inst. spl. fellow, 1961; named Outstanding Preclin. prof. Sch. Medicine U. Louisville, 1967-68; grantee USPHS, NSF and drug industry. Mem. Am. Chem. Soc., Chem. Soc. (London), Am. Soc. Pharmacology and Exptl. Therapeutics, Sigma Xi, Phi Kappa Phi, Phi Lambda Upsilon, Alpha Kappa Kappa. Contbr. profl. jours. Patentee in field. Home: 1040 Cherokee Rd Louisville KY 40204

JARMAN, FRANKLIN MAXEY, apparel co. exec.; b. Nashville, Nov. 10, 1931; s. Walton Maxey and Sarah (Anderson) M.; B.S., Mass. Inst. Tech., 1953. With Third Nat. Bank, Nashville, 1953; with Genesco Inc., 1957—, treas., 1962-64, financial v.p., 1963-65, exec. v.p., 1965-68, pres., 1969—, also dir.; dir. First Am. Nat. Bank, 721 Corp.; pres. Beacon Aircraft Inc., 1963—; v.p. S.H. Kress Co., 1963—. Trustee Christian Mission Found. Served to lt. (s.g.) USNR, 1953-58; capt. USAF, Res. Mem. Sigma Alpha Epsilon. Club: Belle Meade Country (Nashville). Home: 4524 Beacon Dr Nashville TN 37215 Office: 111 7th Av N Nashville TN 37202

JARMAN, JOHN, congressman; b. Sallisaw, Okla., July 17, 1915; s. John H. and Lou Neal (Jones) J.; student Westminster Presbyn. Coll., Fulton, Mo., 1932-34; A.B., Yale, 1937; LL.B., Harvard, 1941; m. Ruth Virginia Bewley, Feb. 25, 1942 (dec. 1964); children—Jay, Susan, Stephen; m. 2d, Marylin Grant, Feb. 10, 1968. Admitted to Okla. bar, 1941, since practiced Oklahoma City. Mem. ho. of reps. Okla. State Legislature, 1947; mem. state senate, 1949; mem. 82d-93d Congresses, 5th Okla. Dist. Served with AUS, 1942-45. Home: 1805 Huntington Oklahoma City OK 73116 Office: Rayburn House Office Bldg Washington DC 20515

JARMAN, JULIAN A., physician; b. Eatonton, Ga., 1909; M.D., Med. Coll. Ga., 1934. Intern, Trinity Hosp., Bklyn., 1934-35; sr. intern Queens Gen. Hosp., Jamaica, N.Y., 1935-36, asst. resident in surgery, 1936-37; resident in surgery Mt. Sinai Hosp., N.Y.C., 1937-38, asst. pathologist, 1938-39, asst. and research fellow, 1939-40, asst. surg. pathologist, 1939-40, clin. asst. surgeon, 1940-41; commd. in U.S. Army, 1941, advanced through grades to col.; ret., 1962; med. adviser Fulton-DeKalb Hosp. Authority, 1962-65; chief staff VA Hosp. Atlanta, 1965-69, dir., 1969—. Decorated Bronze Star medal, Army Commendation medal, Air Force Commendation medal. Diplomate Am. Bd. Surgery. Fellow A.C.S. Office: VA Hosp 1670 Clairmont Rd NE Box 29457 Atlanta GA 30329

JARMAN, THOMAS RODES, JR., banker; b. Charlottesville, Va., Nov. 19, 1929; s. Thomas Rodes and Augusta (Firth) J.; student U. Va., 1948-51; B.B.A., U. Richmond, 1957; m. Paula Knickerbocker, June 19, 1955 (div. Oct. 30, 1966); children—James Cardwell, Kenneth Mills. Salesman, Addressograph-Multigraph Corp., Richmond, Va., 1957-59; with United Va. Bank State Planters (later transferred to United Va. Bankshares Inc.), Richmond, 1959—, comml. marketing services officer, 1967—. Served with AUS, 1952-54. Mem. Pub. Relations Soc. Am., Richmond Pub. Relations Assn. (membership chmn. 1970-71). Clubs: Country Club of Virginia, Deep Run Hunt, Farmington Country. Home: 7 Country Squire Lane Richmond VA 23229 Office: 900 E Main St Richmond VA 23219

JARRELL, JAMES EARL, JR., lawyer; b. Bremerton, Wash., May 4, 1940; s. James Earl and Esther (Gravell) J.; B.S., U. Richmond, 1962; student N.C. State U., 1965-66; J.D., T.C. Williams Law Sch., 1968; m. Anne L. Coleman, Aug. 6, 1960; 1 son, James E. Asso. chemist Philip Morris, Inc., Richmond, Va., 1960-65; admitted to Va. bar, 1968; mem. firm Coleman & Jarrell, attys., Fredericksburg, 1968—; Commonwealth atty. Spotsylvania County, Va., 1970-72. Dir. Universal Land Corp., Rappahannock Savs. & Loan Assn., Rappahannock Devel. Corp., Pitts Theatres, Inc. Bd. dirs. Ben. T. Pitts Found. Mem. Democratic Com., 1969—. N.C. State Research grantee, 1966. Mem. Va. State Bar, Am., Va. trial lawyers assns. Contbr. articles on analytical chemistry to sci. jours. Patentee in processing of tobacco byproducts. Home: 1305 Sophia St Fredericksburg VA 22501 Office: Box 112 Spotsylvania C H VA 22553

JARVIS, CHARLES WALTON, dentist; b. Waxahachie, Tex., Feb. 17, 1923; s. John Pelham and Betty (Douglass) J.; student U. Houston, 1948-49, Tex. A. and M. U., 1940; B.S., U.S. Naval Acad., 1944; D.D.S., U. Tex., 1953; m. Maxine Spiller, Jan. 26, 1946; 1 dau., Pam (Mrs. John Chester Foster). Pvt. practice dentistry, San Marcos, Tex., 1953—; pub. speaker, 1960—; pub., human relations lectr. Dentral br. U. Tex., 1961—. Served with USN, 1941-44, 1946-48. Mem. Omicron Kappa Upsilon. Mem. Christian Ch. Kiwanian (pres. 1960). Recorded speeches: Prescription for the Happy Life, 1970; This Won't Hurt—Much!, 1971. Home: 107 Rogers Ridge San Marcos TX 78666 Office: PO Box 1094 San Marcos TX 78666

JARVIS, HAROLD SIMS, banker; b. Chattanooga, Nov. 21, 1930; s. Storm Harold and Evelyn Leftwich (Sims) J.; B.A., U. Ala., 1952; LL.B., Woodrow Wilson Coll. Law, 1958; postgrad. Grad. Sch. Banking, Rutgers U., 1959; m. Joan Church, Aug. 28, 1954 (div. Mar. 1969); 1 son, Harold Sims. Mem. trust dept. Birmingham Trust Nat. Bank (Ala.), 1952-54; comptroller currency, nat. bank examiner U.S. Treasury Dept., Atlanta, 1954-55; mem. trust dept. 1st Nat. Bank, Atlanta, 1955-59; admitted to Ga. bar, 1958; sr. trust officer Citizen & So. Nat. Bank S.C., Greenville, 1959-67, v.p., head urban affairs devel. dept., Columbia, 1967—. Instr. estate planning Furman U., Greenville, 1963-64. Mem. finance com. Greenville County Found., 1965-66; mem. legacy com. S.C. chpt. Am. Cancer Soc., 1967; treas. Hosp. Bldg. Fund-Raising Compaign, Greenville, 1968-69; mem. adv. com. local commemorative events S.C. Tricentennial Commn., 1970—; mem. adv. council comprehensive health planning State Bd. Health, 1970—. Bd. dirs. Tamassee (S.C.) D.A.R. Schs., 1963-69, Community Council, Greenville, 1968-69, S.C. Wildlife Fedn., 1968—; mem. adv. bd. Juvenile-Domestic Relations Ct., Richland County, 1970—; trustee Columbia Indsl. Edn. Center, 1970—; adv. trustee Action Found., 1969—. Mem. Am., Ga. bar assns., Ala. Alumni Assn. (pres. 1967—). Home: 1757 Tall Pines Circle Columbia SC 29205 Office: 1801 Main St Columbia SC 29204

JARVIS, JAMES HOWARD II, judge; b. Knoxville, Tenn., Feb. 28, 1937; s. Howard F. and Eleanor (Bidwell) J.; J.D., U. Tenn., 1960; m. Pamela K. Duncan, Aug. 23, 1964; children—James Howard, Eleanor Leslie, Ann Duncan, Kathryn Blane, Louise Ereckson. Admitted to Tenn. bar, 1960, asso. firm O'Neil, Jarvis, Parker and Williamson, Knoxville, 1960-68; mem. firm O'Neil, Parker, Williamson and Jarvis, Knoxville, 1968-70; mem. firm Meares, Dungan and Jarvis, Maryville, Tenn., 1970-72; judge Law and Equity Ct., Blount County, Maryville, 1972—. Bd. dirs. Montvale YMCA camp, St. Andrews Episcopal Ch. Sch.; chmn. bd. Peninsula Psychiatric Hosp. Mem. Am., Tenn., Blount County, Knox County bar assns., Am. Judicature Soc., Sigma Chi, Phi Delta Phi. Home: Route 1 Blackberry y Farm Walland TN 37886 Office: Law and Equity Court Blount County Courthouse Maryville TN 37801

JARVIS, ROBERT GLENN, lawyer; b. San Benito, Tex., Jan. 20, 1938; s. Robert Harral and Helen Aline (Cruse) J.; B.A., Rice U., 1960; J.D., U. Tex. at Austin, 1963; m. Patricia Joyce Morgan, June 11, 1960; children—Jeffery Glenn, Robert Todd, Tate Morgan. Admitted to Tex. bar, 1963, U.S. Supreme Ct., 1973; mem. firm Ewers, Toothaker, Ewers, Abbott, Talbot, Hamilton & Jarvis, McAllen, Tex., 1963—. Chmn. city March Dimes, 1964-65, county vice chmn., 1965-66, adviser to bd. dirs., 1966-67. Mem. McAllen Traffic Commn., 1969-71, McAllen Ind. Sch. Dist. Bd. Trustees, 1973—, sec., 1973-74. Bd. dirs. McAllen United Fund, 1972—, McAllen Citizens' League, 1973-74; bd. dirs. Boys' Club, 1965—, pres., 1973; Mem. C. of C. (chmn. civic affairs com. 1971-72), Am. Bar Assn., State Bar Tex., Tex. Bar Found. (state dir. 1969-70), State Jr. Bar Tex. (pres. 1969-70), Hidalgo County Bar Assn. (sec.-treas. 1964-65, dir. 1969-70, 73-74). Methodist. Rotarian. Home: Route 2 Box 2025 McAllen TX 78501 Office: PO Box 3670 McAllen TX 78501

JARVIS, ROY JOE, physician; b. Sneedville, Tenn., Mar. 19, 1928; s. Roy Fisher and Lena (Moles) J.; student E. Tenn. State U., 1946-48, Lincoln Meml. U., 1948-49; M.D., U. Tenn., 1952; m. Emily Jane Jurney, Sept. 28, 1953; children—Janice Lynn, Roy Joe, Alice Kay. Intern Bapt. Hosp., Memphis, 1952-53; gen. practice medicine, Sneedville, 1953-55; resident pediatrics Med. Coll. Ga., Augusta, 1957-58, Grady Hosp., Atlanta, 1958-59; pvt. practice ltd. to pediatrics, Kingsport, Tenn., 1959-70, 72—; with Tenn. Dept. Pub. Health, 1970-72. Served with M.C., AUS, 1955-57. Diplomate Am. Bd. Pediatrics. Fellow Am. Acad. Pediatrics; mem. A.M.A., Tenn. Med. Soc. Mason, Moose. Home: Route 9 King Valley Rd Kingsport TN 37663 Office: Professional Bldg Colonial Heights Kingsport TN 37663

JARY, LLOYD WALKER, architect; b. Ft. Worth, Nov. 12, 1933; s. Lloyd Walker and Mary (Roderus) J.; B.Arch., U. Tex. at Austin, 1960; student Tex. A. and M. U., 1951-53; m. Mary V. Canales, Apr. 18, 1958; children—Lloyd Walker III, Elisa Ruth, Mary Bettina, Pamela Ann. With Bartlett Cocke & Assos., 1960-61, Reginal Roberts & Assos., 1961-62; pvt. archtl. practice, San Antonio, 1962—; sec. br. Montel, Inc. Mem. bd. review San Antonio Hist. Dist., 1970—; chmn. Madonna Neighborhood Center; dir. Town N. YMCA; chmn. State Vols. Council Mental Health Mental Retardation, 1969-70, Vols. at San Antonio State Hosp., 1968-70. Bid. dirs. San Antonio Bldrs. Assn. Named outstanding young man of San Antonio, Jr. C. Of C., 1965. Mem. A.I.A., Tex. Soc. Architects, Constr. Specifications Inst. (past chpt. pres.). K.C. Home: 16175 Jones Maltsberger Rd San Antonio TX 78216 Office: 3211 Nacogooches Rd San Antonio TX 78217

JASPER, JOSEPH JAMES, judge; b. Wheeling, W.Va., July 16, 1927; s. James M. and Adele (George) J.; A.B., U. Ala., 1953, LL.B., 1954; m. Beatrice Imogene Lancaster, Sept. 2, 1954 (dec. Apr. 1972); children—Mary Ann, Debra Faye, Joseph Norman, Lisa Elizabeth. Admitted to Ala. bar, 1954; gen. practice law, 1954-65; elected judge Trussville (Ala.) Recorders Ct., 1958-63; judge Birmingham (Ala.) Recorders Ct., 1963-65, presiding judge, 1965-69; circuit judge 10th Jud. Circuit Ala., 1969—. Mem. Inner Club Safety Com., Mayor's Traffic Safety Coordinating Com. Served with USNR, 1945-46, 50-52. Recipient Erskine Ramsay Civic award, 1970. Mem. Am., Ala., Birmingham bar assns., Ala. circuit judges assn., Amvets, V.F.W., Fraternal Order Police, Sigma Delta Kappa. Roman Catholic. Eagle, K.P., Knight of Khorrassan. Home: 315 Lawson Rd Birmingham AL 35215 Office: Jefferson County Court House Birmingham AL 35203

JASPER, MARTIN THEOPHILUS, educator; b. Hazlehurst, Miss., Mar. 19, 1934; s. Thomas Theophilus and Alice Maie (Norton) J.; B.S., Miss. State U., 1955, M.S., 1962; postgrad. Stevens Inst. Tech., 1963; Ph.D., U. Ala., 1967; m. Mary Altha Ledbetter, Nov. 2, 1963; children—Nellie Rebecca, Alice Hesta, Martin Theophilus, Mary Margaret, William Richard. Engr., Am. Cast Iron Pipe Co., Birmingham, Ala., 1955-56; plant metallurgist Vickers, Inc., Jackson, Miss., 1957-59; sr. design engr. missile div. Chrysler Corp., Huntsville, Ala., 1959-60; instr. mech. engring. Miss. State U., 1960-63, asst. prof., 1966-68, asso. prof., 1968—. Served to 2d lt. M.S.C., AUS, 1956-57. NSF fellow, 1963; NASA fellow, 1963-66. Registered profl. engr., Miss. Mem. Am. Soc. M.E. (chmn. Miss. sect. 1971-72), Soc. Mfg. Engrs. (chpt. chmn. 1969-70), Am. Soc. Engring. Edn., Miss. Acad. Sci., Sigma Xi, Pi Mu Epsilon, Tau Beta Pi, Pi Tau Sigma. Democrat. Baptist. Mason (K.T., Shriner), Kiwanian. Contbr. articles to profl. jours. Research on fluid dynamics, combustion and incineration, systems design and analysis. Home: PO Box 155 Mississippi State MS 39762

JAVELLAS, INA JUNE, social worker; b. Pawhuska, Okla., June 15, 1934; d. Tom D. and Grace E. (Hyde) Javellas; B.A., U. Okla., 1956, M.S.W., 1958. Social work asst. Central State Griffin Meml. Hosp., Norman, Okla., 1957-58, psychiat. social worker, 1958-62; social work supr. Enid State Sch., 1962-63; social work supr. Eastern State Hosp., Vinita, Okla., 1963; psychiat. social worker Community Services Project, Tulsa, 1963-65; coordinator community mental health div. Dept. Mental Health, Oklahoma City, 1965—. Participant teaching program for student nurses Central State Griffin Meml. Hosp., Norman, Okla., 1960-62, psychiat. residency teaching program, 1961-62; cons. tng. headstart program trainees Okla. State U., 1966, Vista workers tng. program, 1966; mem. Gov.'s Adv. Com. for Planning Vocational Rehab. Services and Sheltered Workshops and Facilities, chmn. task force on sheltered workshops and rehab. services, 1966-68; cons. tng. seminar Urban League, U.S. Dept. Labor, Neighborhood Program Trainees, 1968; mem. health edn. com. Interagy. Tech. Panel for Study of Health Edn. of Children and Youth in Okla., 1969-70; mem. Gov.'s Adv. Com. on Employment of Handicapped, 1969-70; participant Project Hope, Internat. Social Service Project, 1964-69; cons. Nat. Inst. Mental Health, 1972—; mem. Okla. Bd. Registration Social Workers, 1961—. Bd. dirs. Okla. Health and Welfare Assn., 1972—. Grad. Counselor scholar Phi Mu, Memphis 1956-57. Recipient citation Tulsa County Mental Health Assn., 1966; named Outstanding Young Woman in Am., 1965. Mem. Nat. Assn. Social Workers (sec. ad hoc com. on grad. edn. Western Okla. chpt. 1969-71, named social worker of year 1970), Conf. Social Workers in State and Territorial Mental Health Programs (editor Newsletter 1967—, chmn. elect 1973-75), Am. Assn. U. Women, Acad. Certified Social Workers, Phi Mu. Republican. Episcopalian. Home: 3447 SE 44th St Apt 231 Del 74th St Oklahoma City OK 73135 Office: PO Box 53277 State Capitol Station Oklahoma City OK 73105

JAWA, MANJIT SINGH, educator; b. Patiala, India, Aug. 5, 1934; s. Sardar Hari Singh J and Sardarni Kartar Kaur, J.; M.A., Panjab U., 1955; diploma Indian Inst. Tech. (Kharagpur), 1964; Ph.D., Indian Inst. Tech. (New Delhi), 1967; m. Swaran Kaur Manchanda, Sept. 12, 1964; children—Gurpreet, Amandeep. Came to U.S., 1967. Statis. investigator Panjab Govt., 1956-58; lectr. Panjab U., 1958-62; revenue collector Panjab Govt., 1962-63; asst. prof. U. Mo., 1967-70; asso. prof. Hartwick Coll., 1970-71; prof. math. Fayetteville unit. U. N.C., 1971—, registrar of exams., 1958-60, chmn. dept., 1960-62. Contbr. articles to profl. jours. Home: 2704 Larry St Fayetteville NC 28301 Office: U NC Fayetteville NC 28301

JAY, CHARLES ALLEN, savs. and loan exec.; b. Fitzgerald, Ga., May 15, 1938; s. Harvey Lamar and Lydia (Coney) J.; A.B., Mercer U., 1960; postgrad. Sch. Exec. Devel., U. Ga., 1960-64; m. Kerry Jean Finlayson, Dec. 2, 1967; children—Kristy Lyn, Kelly Allyn. Vice pres. Security Fed. Savs. & Loan Assn., Perry, Ga., 1961-66; v.p., Home Fed. Savs. & Loan Assn., Macon, Ga., 1966-69, exec. v.p., mng. officer, 1969—. Chmn. bd. dirs. Macon chpt. Am. Cancer Soc.; bd. dirs., past pres. United Cerebral Palsy; bd. dirs. A.R.C., 1969-71; trustee Mercer U., mem. exec. com., finance com.; trustee Tift Coll., Forsyth, Ga., 1967-70; past mem. exec. com. Central Ga. council Boy Scouts Am. Named One of Five Outstanding Young Men of Ga., 1968, Outstanding Civic Leader of Am., 1969. Mem. Macon C. of C. (hon. life, dir.), Sigma Alpha Epsilon. Baptist (deacon, supt. Sunday sch.). Elk. Club: Idle Hour Country, Houston Lake Country. Home: 4268 Old Club Rd E Macon GA 31204 Office: 691 Cherry St Macon GA 31201

JAY, JAMES ALBERT, ins. co. exec.; b. Superior, Wis., Aug. 24, 1916; s. Clarence William and Louie (Davies) J.; student pub. schs., Mpls.; m. Margie Hoffpauir, Dec. 23, 1941; 1 son, James A. Franchise with The Stauffer System of Cal., 1946-49; Ala. dist. mgr. Guaranty Savs. Life Ins. Co., Montgomery, Ala., 1949-51, state mgr. La., 1951—, dir., 1952—, La. gen. agent, 1964—; La. gen agt. Gen. United Life Ins. Co. of Des Moines, 1969—. Com. chmn. Attakapas council Boy Scouts Am., Alexandria, La., 1955, council commr., 1961-62, commr. Manchac dist., 1967—. Served as cpl. USMC, 1942-45, PTO. Decorated Purple Heart. Mem. Baton Rouge Life Underwriters Assn., C. of C., Internat. Platform Assn. Methodist. Elk. Home: 5919 Clematis Dr Baton Rouge LA 70808 Office: 3404 Convention St Baton Rouge LA 70806

JAYCOX, WARREN CECIL, lawyer; b. East Fishkill, N.Y., Aug. 26, 1899; s. Charles Wilbur and Mabel (Horton) J.; LL.B. magna cum laude, Boston U., 1919. Admitted to Mass. bar, 1921; asso. with law firm Ropes, Gray, Best, Coolidge and Rugg, Boston, 1925-42; legislative atty. CAB, Washington, 1946-65; mem. law firm Schleit & Jaycox, 1966—. Served as pvt. U.S. Army, 1918; served from capt. to lt. col. USAAF, 1942-46; col. Res. Mem. Am., Fed. bar assns., Judge Adv. Gens. Assn., S.A.R. Presbyn. Mason. Club: University (Washington). Home: 3133 Connecticut Av NW Washington DC 20008 Office: 1028 Connecticut Av NW Washington DC 20036 also 214 West St Duxbury MA 02332

JEAN, FLOYD HAROLD, communications and data processing co. exec.; b. Akron, O., Nov. 28, 1928; s. Ansleum Floyd and Jennifer (Bogle) J.; B.E.E. cum laude, U. Akron, 1955; M.E.E., U. N.M., 1959, postgrad. 1959-61; m. Phyllis Ann Bellamy, Apr. 4, 1953; children—Mark William, Jennifer. Engr., Sandia Lab., Albuquerque, 1955-59, Dikewood Corp., Albuquerque, 1959-63, ITT, Falls Church, Va., 1963-66, Jet Propulsion Lab., Pasadena, Cal., 1966-68; dir. system evaluation Computer Scis. Corp., Falls Church, 1968-72, v.p. communications, electronics engring., 1972—. Pres., N.M. Council on Human Relations, 1962. Served with USAF, 1946-49. Mem. I.E.E.E. (sec. Albuquerque chpt. 1962, v.p. 1963), Air Force Assn., Nat. Security Indsl. Orgn., Assn. U.S. Army, Sigma Xi, Sigma Tau, Omicron Delta Kappa. Home: 3824 Acosta Rd Fairfax VA 22030 Office: 6565 Arlington Blvd Falls Church VA 22046

JECKO, PERRY TIMOTHY, theatre producer, educator; b. Washington, Jan. 24, 1938; s. Perry Joseph and Cora Elizabeth (Timothy) J.; B.A., Yale, 1959, M.F.A., 1967; m. Mary Louise Long, Oct. 20, 1962; children—Christopher Brendan, Nicholas Benjamin. Producer, dir. performing arts Smithsonian Inst., Washington, 1967-70; tchr. Back Alley Theatre, Washington, 1970-73; dir., 1970—; tchr. Washington Theatre Club, 1971—; tchr. pub. schs. Arlington County, Va., 1970—; dir. Internat. Children's Day, Wolf Trap Farm Park, Vienna, Va., 1973; actor films Dept. Health, Edn. and Welfare, Dept. Navy, also TV commls., 1967—. Bd. dirs. Arlington Theatre Assos. Served to lt. USNR, 1959-63. Mem. U.S. Olympic Swimming team, 1956; Nat. and World Record Holder 110 yard butterfly, 400 yards free style relay, 400 yard individual medlay, 1952-59. Mem. Am. Theatre Assn., Am. Fedn. TV and Radio Artists, Screen Actors Guild. Home: 21 W Walnut St Alexandria VA 22301

JEFFARES, DONALD JACKSON, cons.; b. McDonough, Ga., Mar. 16, 1936; s. Arthur and Ruby (Jackson) T.; B.Ceramic Engring., Ga., Inst. Tech., 1959; m. Susan Hull, Aug. 7, 1956; children—Lori Susan, Donna Allyson, Donald Jackson. With Ferro Corp., Tyler, Tex., 1959-66; with Fla. Tile Industries, Lakeland, Fla,, 1966-70, v.p. mfg., 1967-69, v.p., gen. mgr. tile div., 1969-70; cons., 1970—; pres. Jefco Inc.; real estate broker, 1973—. Bd. dirs. Fla. Midland Corp., Lakeland. Mem. Am. Ceramic Soc., Methodist (mem. adminstrv. bd., chmn. finance com.). Rotarian. Home: Rt 1 Box 336 Lakeland FL 33803 Office: 1526 Commercial Park Dr Lakeland FL 33802

JEFFERIES, RICHARD MANNING, JR., lawyer; b. Walterboro, S.C., Oct. 30, 1919; s. Richard Manning and Annie S. (Savage) J.; A.B., U. S.C., 1942, LL.B., 1947; m. Emily Brown, Aug. 22, 1942, children—Richard Allan, Emily McBurney. Admitted to S.C. bar, 1947; partner Brown, Jeffries & Mazursky, Barnwell, S.C., 1947-70, Brown, Jeffries & Boulware, 1970—. Pres., Barnwell Industries, Inc., 1958—. Chmn. S.C. Ednl. TV Commn., 1957—. County chmn. A.R.C., Barnwell, 1955-57; bd. visitors Presbyn. Coll., Clinton, S.C. Sec., treas. Barnwell County Democratic Exec. Com., 1948—. Served to lt. USNR, 1942-45. Mem. Am. Legion (past comdr.). Presbyn. (deacon). Lion (past pres.). Home: 1906 Main St Barnwell SC 29812 Office: State Bank & Trust Co Bldg Barnwell SC 29812

JEFFERS, LEROY, lawyer; b. Ferris, Tex., Oct. 15, 1909; LL.B., U. Tex., 1932. Admitted to Tex. bar, 1932; mem. firm Vinson, Elkins, Searls, Connally & Smith, Houston. Chmn. bd. regents U. Tex., 1957-59. Mem. Tex. Constl. Revision Commn., 1973-74; chmn. Tex. Gov.'s Study Project on Criminal Justice Standards and Goals; pres. Houston Legal Found.; bd. regents S. Tex. Sch. Law; trustee Episcopal Theol. Sem. S.W.; past chmn. bd. dirs. Tex. Bill of Rights Found. Fellow Am. Coll. Trial Lawyers; mem. State Bar Tex. (pres. 1973-74), Am. (chmn. sect. of antitrust 1970-71), Houston (pres. 1968-69) bar assns. Office: First City Nat Bank Bldg Houston TX 77002

JEFFERSON, BEN ROBERT, oil investments exec.; b. Stamford, Tex., Nov. 7, 1933; s. Ephriam Dent and Ethel (Owens) J.; B.S., Tex. Technol. U., 1956; J.D., Baylor U., 1968; m. Imogene Hays, May 16, 1951; 1 son, Edward Du Wayne. Geophysicist, So. Geophys. Co,, Ft., Worth, 1952-53; geologist Pan Am. Petroleum Corp. (now Amoco Prodn. Co.), Ft. Worth, 1957-65; admitted to Tex. bar, 1968; trust officer Frost Nat. Bank, San Antonio, 1968-69; asst. v.p., fund mgr. Prudential Funds, Inc., Dallas, 1969-72; pres., dir. Barrons Resources, Inc., Dallas, 1972-73; ind. oil operator, Dallas, 1973—. Mem. Am. Bar Assn., Tex. State Bar, Am. Assn. Petroleum Geologists, Dallas Geol. Soc., Dallas Assn. Petroleum Land Men, Sigma Gamma Epsilon, Delta Theta Phi. Home: 3322 High Vista Dr Dallas TX 75234 Office: 211 N Ervay St Suite 510 Dallas TX 75201

JEFFORDS, JOE SAM, state ofcl.; b. Lamar, S.C., Sept. 2, 1912; s. Samuel Joseph and Bessie Irene (Boykin) J.; B.S. in Civil Engring., Clemson U., 1936; m. Mary Emma Colclough, June 18, 1938; children—Samuel Joseph II, Ben Colough. With S.C. Hwy. Dept., 1936-42, W.C. Olsen Cons. Engrs., Raleigh, N.C., 1942-43, McClean Contracting Co., Balt., 1943-45; with S.C. Hwy. Dept., 1945—, dist. engr., 1967—. Mem. design and drafting adv. com. Orangeburg-Calhoun Tech. Ednl. Center, 1968—. Mem. S.C. Soc. Engrs. Methodist (ofcl. bd. 1960-66; trustee 1969—). Lion (v.p. 1st Orangeburg 1969). Home: 337 Pinehill St Orangeburg SC 29115 Office: PO Box 1086 Orangeburg SC 29115

JEFFREYS, ALVIS WALDO, JR., psychologist; b. South Hill, Va., Mar. 13, 1923; s. Alvis Waldo and Connie (Dodson) J.; student Hampden-Sydney Coll., 1941-43; B.A., U. Va., 1948; M.A., Mich. State U., 1950; Ph.D., U. Houston, 1953; m. Virginia Ogilvie, June 28, 1948; children—Jay C., Jan S. Instr. U. Tex. Med. Sch., 1950-52; asst. prof. Commonwealth U., Richmond, Va., 1953-54; chief psychologist Western State Hosp., Staunton, 1954—, dir. alcoholic unit, 1954—. Pres. Appalachian Dulcimer Corp., Staunton, 1962—. Served with USNR, 1943-45. Home: 232 W Frederick St Staunton VA 24401 Office: Western State Hosp Staunton VA 24401

JEFFRIES, ALEXANDER HARDIE, JR., architect; b. Richmond, Va., Dec. 28, 1937; s. Alexander Hardie and Georgia Bryan (Grinnan) J.; grad. Hill Sch., Pottstown, Pa., 1956; student Hampden-Sydney Coll., 1956-57; B.Arch., U. Pa., 1961; m. Roberta Fleming Rust, Nov. 15, 1969; 1 son, Alexander Hardie, III. With Weihe, Black, Jeffries & Strassman, Architects (and predecessors), Washington, 1961—, partner, 1968—. Mem. A.I.A. (corporate mem.). Contbr. design of office bldgs. and apts. in Washington area, including Crystal City, Arlington, Va., Skyline Center, Fairfax County, Va. Home: 1722 Hoban Rd NW Washington DC 20007 Office: 1101 17th St NW Washington DC 20036

JEFFRIES, CHARLES RAY, assn. exec.; b. Cleburne, Tex., Nov. 13, 1938; s. Joe Norris and Lillie Mae (Foster) J.; B.F.A., Tex. Christian U., 1961; M.A., Trinity U., 1972; postgrad. Colo. State Coll. at Greeley, 1965; m. Sharon Calverley, Sept. 1, 1962; 1 son, Charles Brett. Tchr. high sch. drama, Hobbs, N.M., 1961-62, MacArthur High Sch., San Antonio, Tex., 1964-67, Highlands High Sch., San Antonio, 1968—; state dir. Internat. Thespian Soc., 1969-70, regional dir., 1970-71, bd. dirs., 1972—; founder, 1st pres. Youtheatre, Fort Worth, 1956-58; asst. adminstrv. staff Casa Manana Musicals, Fort Worth, 1958-59; artistic dir. Hobbs Community Theatre, 1961-63; actor Little Theatre of Rockies, Greeley, Colo., 1963; dir. entertainment Fort Sam Houston Theatre, U.S. Army, 1964; lighting designer Peninsula Playhouse, New Braunfels, Tex., 1965; asst. mgr. Hemisfair Theatre & Arena, San Antonio, 1967-68; bd. dirs. Billboard Theatre, San Antonio, 1966-70, pres., 1969-70; instr., tech. dir. Incarnate Word Coll., San Antonio, 1970-71; chmn. drama instrs. San Antonio Ind. Sch. Dist., 1970-74. Recipient Tex. Star award KBAT radio, 1970, Citizen of the Day award KEEZ radio, 1971. Mem. Secondary Schs. Theater Assn. (regional dir. 1971—, nat. bd. dirs. 1972—, membership sec. 1973—, editor newsletter 1973—), Tex. Secondary Sch. Theatre Assn. (bd. dirs. 1967-72), S.W. Theatre Assn. (chmn. secondary schs. div. 1969-73), Alpha Psi Omega. Home: 1027 Sumner St San Antonio TX 78218 Office: 3118 Elgin St San Antonio TX 78210

JEKO, LESLIE JEWEL, accountant; b. Port Arthur, Tex., Mar. 1, 1930; s. Jewel Edward and Hazel (Heard) J.; B.B.S., Trinity U., 1954; B.B.A., U. Tex., 1957; m. 2d, Parr Davidson, Dec. 24, 1950; children—Catherine Parr, Cynthia Lea. Auditor, Ernst & Ernst, Houston, 1957-60; asst. controller David C. Bintliff Interests, Houston, 1961-62; div. auditor Pure Oil Co., Houston, 1962-64; pvt. practice accounting, Houston, 1964—; sec., dir. W.W. Properties, Inc., Houston, 1970—. Served with USAF, 1950-54. Mem. Am. Inst. C.P.A.'s, Tex., Houston socs. C.P.A.'s, Petroleum Accountants Soc. Houston. Baptist. Mason. Home: 7718 Bellaire Blvd Houston TX 77036 Office: 3813 Buffalo Speedway Suite 104 Houston TX 77006

JELKS, FREEMAN NAPIER, securities co. exec.; b. Hawkinsville, Ga., Mar. 15, 1903; s. Nathaniel Augustus and Lila Jeanette (Napier) J.; student U. Va., 1920-21; LL.B., U. Ga., 1925; m. Retta Fannin Coney, Oct. 30, 1928; children—Freeman Napler, Jr., Retta (Mrs. Allen I. Vance). Salesman Citizens & So. Co., Savannah, Ga., 1926-33; with Johnson, Lane, Space, Smith & Co., Inc., Savannah, 1933-73, v.p., 1933-73. Mem. Phi Delta Theta, Phi Delta Phi. Baptist (deacon 1927-73). Clubs: Chatham, Oglethorpe, Golf (pres. 1944-45) (Savannah). Home: 28 E 56th St Savannah GA 31405 Office: 101 E Bay St Savannah GA 31401

JELKS, LOUIS ROLLWAGE, physician, surgeon; b. Memphis, Nov. 16, 1906; s. Dr. John Lemuel and Minnie (Rollwage) J.; M.D., U. Tenn. Coll. Medicine, 1933; m. Ruth Goddard, May 4, 1929; children—Leigh (Mrs. Wade Hughes Threlkeld), Louis Rollwage. Intern, Knoxville (Tenn.) Gen. Hosp., 1933-34; asso. with father, Dr. J.L. Jelks for postgrad. work in surgery, Memphis, 1934-35; practice medicine, specializing in surgery, Reidsville, Ga., 1935—; adminstr., owner Jelks Hosp., 1938—; examining physician SSS, 1940—, N.G. (both Tatt Co.), 1948—. Mem. Tattnall County Sch. Bd. Dir. FHA, Reidsville, Ga., mem. Civil Def. Bd. Mem. Am., So. med. assns., Ga., S.E. Ga. (pres. 1969), 1st Dist. Ga. med. socs., Am. Soc. Abdominal Surgeons. Methodist. Club: Vidalia Country. Home: 416 Brazell St N Reidsville GA 30453 Office: Jelks Clinic 203-7 Main St Reidsville GA 30453

JELSMA, EDWARD RICHARD, transp. cons.; b. Enid, Okla., Mar. 15, 1915; s. Edward Darwin and Orilla (Hackathorn) J.; B.S., Okla. State U., 1937, M.S., 1938; postgrad. Stanford, 1939-40; m. Marjorie Marie Crain, Feb. 12, 1948; children—Schuyler, Richard, Lisa. Asst. to tax counsel Standard Oil Co. Cal., San Francisco, 1940-41; dep. fiscal dir. Bur. Ordnance, U.S. Navy Dept., Washington, 1946-48, asst. fiscal dir. dept., 1948-49; profl. mem. Interstate and Fgn. Commerce Com., U.S. Senate, 1949-55; dir. bur. transport econs. and statistics ICC, 1955-58; pres. E.R. Jelsma & Assos., transp. cons., 1958—; grad. asst. Okla. State U., 1937-38; instr. Northwestern State Coll., 1938-39, Am. U., 1946-49; guest lectr. U. Louisville, 1942-43. Served from ensign to lt. comdr. USNR, 1941-46. Mason. Author: Minimum Wage Legislation, 1938. Address: 1811 Morningside Dr Mount Dora FL 32757

JEMISON, FRANK ZIMMERMAN, financial, motor hotel, real estate exec.; b. Memphis, July 10, 1920; s. William Dearing and Blanche (Zimmerman) J.; B.S., Miss. State U., 1941; m. Peggy Boyce, Apr. 10, 1947; children—Frank Zimmerman, Marguerite Bailey, David Marshall. Exec. v.p. W.D. Jemison & Sons, Inc. subsidiary AMCON Internat., Inc., Memphis, 1945-55, pres., 1955—; chmn. bd., treas., dir. AMCON Internat., Inc., 1968—; chmn. bd., dir. Modern Diversified Industries, Valdosta, Ga.; exec. v.p., dir. Winter Garden Freezer Co.; dir. Tenn. Foods, Inc., United Foods, Inc. Bd. dirs. Edn. For Freedom, Atlanta; mem. pres.'s council Southwestern U. Memphis; trustee, treas. Memphis U. Sch. Mem. Chief Execs. Forum. Presbyn. (elder). Rotarian. Clubs: University, Memphis Country. Home: 1054 Aubudon Dr Memphis TN 38117 Office: AMCON International Inc 2731 Nonconnah Blvd S PO Box 30303 Memphis TN 38130

JEMISON, RICHARD ALLEN, printing co. exec.; b. Birmingham, Ala., July 5, 1936; s. Richard Allen and Lois (Brooks) J., Jr.; B.S. in Civil Engring., U. Fla., 1959; m. Sandra Joan Hollins, Aug. 16, 1957; children—Maurice, Leslie, Kell, Bryce, Susannah. With St. Petersburg Printing Co. Inc. (Fla.), 1961—, exec. v.p., 1965—; pres. Graphics Media, Inc., St. Petersburg, 1970—, Graphic House, Inc., Orlando, Fla., 1969—; dir. First State Charter Bank. Chmn. indsl. com. Com. of 100, 1971—; mem. St. Petersburg Zoning Bd., 1967—. Served to 1st lt. C.E. U.S. Army, 1959-61. Clubs: Dragon (St. Petersburg), University (Gainesville, Fla.). Home: 441 Villa Grande Av S St Petersburg FL 33707 Office: 118 18th St S St Petersburg FL 33712

JEMISON, THEODORE JUDSON, religious ofcl.; b. Selma, Ala., Aug. 1, 1918; s. David Vivian and Henrietta (Phillips) J.; B.S., Ala. State Coll., 1940; D.M., Va. Union U., 1945, D.D., 1971; D.D., Natchez Coll., 1953; m. Aug. 4, 1945; children—Bettye Jane, Dianne Frances, Theodore Judson. Ordained to ministry Baptist Ch.; pastor Mt. Zion Bapt. Ch., Staunton, Va., 1945-49; pastor Mt. Zion First Bapt. Ch., Baton Rouge, 1949—; gen. sec. Nat. Bapt. Conv., USA, Inc., 1953—; mem. bd. control Nat. Council Chs. in U.S. Mem. La. Rights Commn.; mem. Baton Rouge Community Relations Com. Named Citizen of the Year for outstanding contbns. in civics, recreation, edn., religion City of Baton Rouge; named Minister of the Year, Nat. Beta Club, 1973; recipient Distinguished Service award to Edn., East Rouge Edn. Assn., 1973. Mem. N.A.A.C.P., Frontiers Internat. (pres. Baton Rouge chpt.), Alpha Phi Alpha. Baptist. Mason (Shriner). Home: 915 Spain St Baton Rouge LA 70802 Office: 356 East Blvd Baton Rouge LA 70802

JEMISON, WILLIAM DEARING, JR., hotel chain exec; b. Memphis, July 3, 1918; s. William D. and Blanche (Zimmerman) J.; student Southwestern U., 1937-38; B.S. in Bus. Adminstrn., Miss. State U., 1940; postgrad. U. Tenn., 1947; m. Eva Lee Williams, Nov. 12, 1947; children—Blanche Lee, William Dearing, Ethel Gay. With W.D. Jemison & Sons, 1953-56, exec. v.p., 1956-63; pres. Mid-Continent Corp., 1963; pres. AMCON Internat., Inc. and predecessor cos., Memphis, until 1973, vice chmn. bd., 1973—. Mem. exec. com. Future Memphis, 1963—; pres. Porter Leath Children's Center, 1960—. Served to maj. USAAF, 1942-46. Mem. Home Builders Assn. (past pres.), Nat. Assn. Home Builders (dir. 1953-60), Memphis C. of C. (dir.), Kappa Alpha. Clubs: University, Chickasaw Country (Memphis). Home: 47 Avon St Memphis TN 38117 Office: 2731 Nonconnah Blvd PO Box 30303 Memphis TN 38130

JENKINS, ADAM, JR., coll. bus. mgr.; b. North Carrollton, Miss., Sept. 9, 1942; s. Adam and Annie (Hill) J.; B.S., Alcorn A. and M. Coll., 1967; student U. Omaha, summer 1968; Miss. State U., 1968-69; m. Margaraee Gordon, June 10, 1962; children—Vernon, Randolph, Darryl. Cashier Utica (Miss) Jr. Coll., 1967-68, bus. mgr., 1969—; cons. Natchez Jr. Coll. Mem. Miss. Jr. Coll. Bus. Mgrs. Assn., Nat. Assn. Colls. and U. Bus. Officers, N.E.A., Miss. Teachers Assn., N.A.A.C.P., Phi Beta Sigma (sec.-treas. 1971-72). Home: North Carrollton MS 38947 Office: Utica Jr Coll Utica MS 39175

JENKINS, ANDREW HAILE, research engr.; b. Florence, S.C., Nov. 23, 1925; s. Walter Eugene and Cullie (Weber) J.; B.M.E., U. S.C., 1950; M.S., U. Ala., 1965; m. Melblynn Allison McCants, July 6, 1947; children—Drew Weber, Brent Allison. Design engr. Chrysler Corp., Dayton, Ohio, 1950-51; field engr. DuPont Co., Camden, S.C. and Pensacola, Fla., 1951-53; design engr. U.S. Navy, Charleston, S.C., 1953-55; chief mech. engr. J. Gordon Turnbull, Cons. Engr., Cleve., 1955-56; research engr. U.S. Army, Huntsville, Ala., 1958—; owner, opr. Mill Hollow Angus Farm, Union Grove, Ala., 1962—; instr. re-entry physics U. Ala. at Huntsville, 1967. Served with USNR, 1943-46. Mem. Nat. Soc. Profl. Engrs., Am. Angus Assn., Assn. U.S. Army, Am. Soc. Mech. Engrs., Nat. Geographic Soc., Aircraft Owners and Pilots Assn., Cattleman's Assn. Baptist. Contbr. articles hypersonic, supersonic flow; compressible flow; high energy laser advanced research to sci. jours. Home: 8004 Camille Dr SE Huntsville AL 35802 Office: US Army Missile Command AMSMI-RRP Huntsville AL 35809

JENKINS, CHARLES RODERICK, physician; b. Ellisville, Miss., Nov. 20, 1912; A.B., U. Ala., 1932; M.D., Tulane U., 1936. Intern, Highland Sanitarium, Shreveport, La., 1936-37; resident Lutheran Hosp., Balt., 1937-38, Akins (S.C.) Hosp., 1939-40, Brooks Gen. Hosp., San Antonio, 1945; pvt. practice medicine, specializing in family practice, Ellisville, 1939-40, Laurel, Miss., 1945—. Served to lt. col. M.C., AUS, 1940-45. Diplomate Am. Bd. Family Practice. Fellow Am. Acad. Family Practice; mem. A.M.A., Miss. Med. Assn. (pres. 1972-73), Jones County, South Miss. med. socs., Miss. Acad. Family Practice (pres. 1968-69), Southeastern Surg. Congress. Office: The Medical Center 535 5th Av Laurel MS 39440

JENKINS, CLARA BARNES, educator; b. Franklinton, N.C.; d. Walter and Stella (Griffin) Barnes; B.S., Winston-Salem State U., 1939; M.A., N.C. Central U., 1947; Ed.D., U. Pitts., 1965; postgrad. N.Y. U., 1947-48, U. N.C., N.C. Agrl. and Tech. State U.; m. Hugh Morris Jenkins, Dec. 24, 1949 (div. Feb. 1955). Faculty Fayetteville State U., 1945-53, Rust Coll., Holly Spring, Miss., 1953-58; asst. prof. Shaw U., 1958-64; now prof. edn. and psychology St. Paul's Coll., Lawrenceville, Va.; vis. prof. edn. Friendship Jr. Coll., Rock Hill, S.C., summer 1947, N.C. Agr. and Tech. State U., summers 1966-73. United Negro Coll. Fund Faculty fellow, 1963-64; grant recipient Am. Bapt. Conv., Valley Forge, Pa., 1963-64. Mem. Am. Assn. U. Profs., Nat. Soc. for Study Edn., N.E.A., Am. Assn. U. Women, Am. Hist. Assn., Va. Edn. Assn., Am. Acad. Polit. and Social Sci., A.A.A.S., Internat. Platform Assn., Doctoral Assn. Educators, Assn. Tchr. Educators, Marquis Biog. Library Soc., Am. Assn. for Higher Edn., Acad. Polit. Sci., Am. Psychol. Assn., History of Edn. Soc., Phi Eta Kappa, Zeta Phi Beta. Episcopalian. Home: 920 Bridges St Henderson NC 27536 Office: St Pauls Coll Lawrenceville VA 23868

JENKINS, DEE SAMUEL, freight co. exec.; b. Ava, Mo., Feb. 10, 1910; s. Robert Fulton and Louetta Harris (Campbell) J.; grad. high sch.; m. Oma B. Thompson, Apr. 15, 1933; 1 dau., Donna Dee (Mrs. Gerald Robert Wade). With Ford Motor Co., Detroit, 1925-29; farmer, nr. Ava, 1929-57; v.p. in charge of fleet maintenance Rocket Freight Lines Co., Tulsa, 1957—; fleet dir. Tuloma, Inc., 1963—. Baptist. Home: 5342 E 4th St Tulsa OK 74112 Office: 2921 Dawson Rd Tulsa OK 74110

JENKINS, DONALD, banker; b. Milw., Jan. 22, 1919; s. Lee C. and Mathilda (Thielecke) J.; student Columbia, 1940-41; m. Gloria J. Killans, Apr. 15, 1945; children—Victoria G. (Mrs. Guy Bowers), Michael S., Roseanna L., Roberta M. Asst. to treas. Bank of Commerce, N.Y.C,, 1945-46; v.p., treas. Community State Bank, Albany, N.Y., 1947-62; (also dir.); v.p., sec. Financial Gen. Bankshares Inc., Washington, 1962—; dir. Bank of Buffalo, Chesapeake Nat. Bank (Towson, Md.), Peoples Nat. Bank (Leesburg, Va.), Valley Nat. Bank (Harrisonburg, Va.), Financial Gen. Bankshares Inc. (Washington), Morris Plan Corp. (N.Y.C.). Mem. Va., Consumer bankers assns. Lion. Club: Farmington Country (Va.). Home: 9022 Hamilton Dr Fairfax VA 22030 Office: Financial General Bankshares Inc 1701 Pennsylvania Av NW Washington DC 20006

JENKINS, HAYDEN ISRAEL, veterinarian; b. Quanah, Tex., Jan. 27, 1919; s. Israel Benjamin and Onie (Williams) J.; D.V.M., Tex. A. and M. Coll., 1948-53; m. Katherine Virginia Wright, Oct. 14, 1943; children—Gloria Kay, Judy May, Kathy Gail; m. 2d, Olga Van Loh, Jan. 19, 1974. D.V.M. animal disease eradication U.S. Dept. Agr., Albuquerque, 1953-54; owner Quanah Animal Clinic, 1954—; asst. instr. parasitology Tex. A. and M. Coll., 1948-51, zoology asst., 1948-49, surgery instr., 1951-53. Veterinarian, Hardeman County, 1955—; chmn. animal health Farm Bur., 1957—. Bd. dirs. 4H and Future Farmers Am. Ann. Show and Bldg. Com. Served with USAAF, 1941-45. Named hon. chpt. Farmer Future Farmers Am., 1960; recipient 4H Achievement Plaque, 1960. Mem. Tex. Vet. Med. Assn., Am. Legion. Baptist. Clubs: Lions, Toastmaster. Research in injectible parasitology, exptl. surgery, cancer, virus x in horses. Home: 4305 Rhea Rd Wichita Falls TX 76803 Office: 4305 Rhea Rd Wichita Falls TX 76803

JENKINS, HERBERT NEFF, contractor; b. Elizabethtown, Ky., Oct. 14, 1936; s. James Ray and Helen Dorothy (Nusz) J.; B.S., Ga. Inst. Tech., 1958; m. Wilhelmina Bond Milton, July 12, 1958; children—Robert Gregory, Kirk Christopher. With Jenkins-Essex Co., Inc., Elizabethtown, 1958—, v.p.-treas., 1970—, v.p. constrn. div., 1970—, corp. treas., 1964—; instr. engring. Elizabethtown Community Coll., U. Ky. Image builder Charlotte Region, Butler Mfg. Co., 1971, career builder, 1972. Mem. Hardin County Ednl. Council, 1970—. Served with AUS, 1958-60. Mem. Asso. Builders and Contractors, Ky. Homebuilders Assn., Ky. Retail Bldg. Materials Dealers, Am. Inst. Mgmt., Sigma Alpha Epsilon. Democrat. Roman Catholic. K.C., Rotarian. Club: Elizabethtown Country (dir. 1968-71, pres. 1970). Home: 903 Dogwood Circle Elizabethtown KY 42701 Office: 142 E Dixie Av Elizabethtown KY 42701

JENKINS, HERNDON HERALD, JR., electronics engr.; b. Atlanta, Aug. 25, 1931; s. Herndon Herald and Mary Virginia (Duke) J.; B.S. in Elec. Engring., Ga. Inst. Tech., 1956, M.S., 1960; m. Dorothy M. Adams, Apr. 24, 1954; children—Richard Steve, Deborah Ann. Teaching asso. Elec. Engring. Sch., Ga. Inst. Tech., Atlanta, 1954-56, research engr. Engring. Expt. Sta., 1957-60, 64—; research engr. Johns Hopkins Applied Physics Lab., Silver Spring, Md., 1956-57, Radiation, Inc., Melbourne, Fla., 1960-64. Served with AUS, 1951-53. Mem. I.E.E.E. (group chmn. Atlanta group 1971-72). Home: 1268 Blueberry Trail Decatur GA 30033 Office: 225 North Av NW Atlanta GA 30332

JENKINS, JOHN HOLMES, III, publisher; b. Beaumont, Tex., Mar. 22, 1940; s. J. Holmes and Sue (Chalmers) J.; grad. U. Tex., 1963; m. Maureen Vera Mooney, June 5, 1962; 1 son, John Holmes IV. Pub., The Pemberton Press, Austin, 1962—, Southwestern Art Jour., 1965—, Jenkins Book Pub. Co., Inc., 1968—; pres. Country Store Gallery, Inc., 1963—, The Jenkins Co., 1962—, Fine Arts Corp., 1969—, India, Inc., 1969—. Bd. dirs. Collectors Inst. Served with AUS, 1966. Fellow Tex. State Hist. Assn.; charter mem. Western History Assn.; mem. Appraisers Assn. Am., Delta Tau Delta. Author: Recollections of Early Texas, 1958; Neither The Fanatics Nor the Fainthearted, 1963; Honest Bob and the Texas Congress, 1964; Jenkins Land Guide to the City of Austin, 1964; Cracker Barrel Chronicles, 1965; Patriotic Songs and Poems of Early Texas, 1966; Aubudon's Southwest, 1967; The Texas Navy, 1967; The Life of Frank Hamer, 1968; Papers of the Texas Revolution, 1973. Home: Cromwell Hill Austin TX 78703 Office: Box 2085 Austin TX 78767

JENKINS, R. LEE, diversified co. exec.; b. Beggs, Okla., 1929; A.B., U. Okla., 1952, LL.B., 1956; LL.M., N.Y. U., 1959. Admitted to Okla. bar, 1956; asso. firm Allende & Brea, 1959-60; exec. v.p., gen. counsel White Eagle Internat., Inc., 1960-65; v.p. corporate devel. Plough, Inc., Memphis, 1965-72, sr. v.p., 1972-73, exec. v.p., 1973—, also dir.; dir. Schering-Plough Corp. Served to capt. USMCR, 1952-54. Home: 10830 E Shelby Dr Collierville TN 38017 Office: 3030 Jackson Av Memphis TN 38151

JENKINS, RICHARD COLEMAN, lawyer; b. Little Rock, Nov. 10, 1937; s. Clarence Richard and Virginia (Coleman) J.; student U. Ark., 1955-58; B.A., So. Methodist U., 1959, LL.B., 1962, postgrad., 1970; m. Marian Jack, Oct. 7, 1961 (div. Sept. 1972); 1 son, Jack Coleman; m. 2d, Shelly Lawrence, Feb. 19, 1974. Admitted to Tex. bar, 1962; asst. city atty., Dallas, 1962-63; practice law, Dallas, 1963—; asso. mem. firm Richard D. Haynes, 1965-68; partner firm McClung & Jenkins, 1968-70, firm Muse, Currie & Kohen, 1970-73, firm Jenkins

& Ederer, 1974—. Sec., treas. Tex. Rotary Clubs Chorus, Inc., 1972—. Bd. dirs. Dallas Legal Services Found., Inc., 1967-71. Mem. Am., Dallas, Dallas Jr. (pres. 1966) bar assns., State Bar Tex., Phi Alpha Delta, Sigma Alpha Epsilon. Republican. Methodist (mem. adminstrv. bd. 1969-72). Clubs: Rotary, Dallas Country (both Dallas). Home: 5641 Monticello St Dallas TX 75206 Office: 1717 Adolphus Tower Main and Akard Dallas TX 75202

JENKINS, ROBERT DARRELL, state ofcl.; b. Potecasi, N.C., July 11, 1929; s. Arthur Thomas and Martha (Draper) J.; B.S., N.C. State U., 1951; m. Anne Hodge Beale, June 1, 1952; children—Robert Darrell, David Thomas. Vocational agr. tchr. Hobbsville, N.C., 1953-54, Jackson, N.C., 1954-61; marketing specialist N.C. Dept. Agr., 1961-64; food industries specialist and regional rep. N.C. Dept Conservation and Devel., 1964-66, asso. exec., 1966—; exec. sec. N.C. Yam Commn., Inc. Served with AUS, 1951-53. Decorated Bronze Star. Mem. Kappa Phi Kappa, Alpha Gamma Rho. Democrat. Baptist. Mason. Home: 528 Cooper Rd Raleigh NC 27610 Office: 505 Oberlin Rd Raleigh NC 27605

JENKINS, ROBERT WARLS, JR., chemist; b. Richmond, Va., June 12, 1936; s. Robert Warls and Catherine Mary (Leaker) J.; B.S., Va. Mil. Inst., 1958; M.S., Purdue U., 1961; grad. U.S. Army Advanced Officer Course, 1972; m. Alma Francis Rowe, Aug. 2, 1958; children—Mark Collins, Robert Brent, Hunter Rowe. Instr. chemistry Va. Mil. Inst., 1960-61; asst. prof. chemistry U. Va. Summer Sch., 1961; research chemist radiation effects br. U.S. Naval Research Lab., Washington, 1963-65; project leader, sr. research scientist Philip Morris Research Center, Richmond, 1965—; pres. R.W. Jenkins, Inc., Richmond, 1965—. Mem. tech. adv. com. Va. Air Pollution Control Bd. Served to maj. AUS, 1961-63. Mem. Am. Chem. Soc., Nat. Blue Ridge rifle assns., Res. Officers Assn., Va. Antique Arms Collectors (dir.). Episcopalian. Contbr. articles to profl. jours. Home: 105 Gun Club Rd Richmond VA 23221 Office: PO Box 26583 Richmond VA 23261

JENKINS, THOMAS EVERTS, ofcl. NSF; b. Scranton, Pa., Apr. 21, 1924; s. William Arthur and Thelma Marie (Archer) J.; student Lincoln U., 1940-43; A.B. in Pub. Adminstrn., U. Cal. at Berkeley, 1947, postgrad., 1947-48; postgrad. Am. U., 1950-52; m. Carrie L. Moore, Nov. 27, 1963; children—Maria, Thomas, Carolyn, Jacqueline, Brent. Analyst, budget officer Naval Research Lab., Washington, 1951-55, dep. comtroller, bus. mgr. Project Vanguard, 1955-58; adminstrv. officer Goddard Flight Center NASA, Greenbelt, Md., 1958-59. program mgmt. officer space flight programs, Washington, 1959-61, asst. dir. mgmt. reports, 1961-63, dir. program reports div., 1963-68, asst. dir. Apollo Project, 1968-69; dep. asst. dir. adminstrn. NSF, 1969-72, asst. dir. for adminstrn., 1972—. Served with USNR, 1943-46. Recipient Superior Civilian Service award Dept. Navy, 1960, Exceptional Service medal NASA, 1969. Mem. Am. Mgmt. Assn., Soc. Advancement Mgmt., Am. Soc. Pub. Adminstrn., A.A.A.S. Home: 2847 Hillcrest Dr SE Washington DC 20020 Office: NSF 1800 G St NW Washington DC 20550

JENKINS, WILLIAM LEWIS, lawyer, govt. ofcl.; b. Detroit, Nov. 29, 1936; s. Lewis C. and Maud (Wilson) J.; B.S., Tenn. Tech. Inst.; J.D., U. Tenn.; m. Mary Kathryn Myers, June 12, 1959; children—Rebecca, Georgeanne, Lewis, Douglas. Admitted to Tenn. bar, 1962; practice law, Rogersville 1962-70; partner firm Hyder, Jenkins & Boyd, 1962-70; mem. Tenn. Ho. of Reps. from Hancock County, 1962-70, speaker, 1969-70; commr. conservation State of Tenn., 1971—. Bd. dirs. TVA, 1972—. Served with AUS, 1959-60. Home: Colonial Rd Rogersville TN 37857

JENKINS, WILLIAM ODELL, broadcaster; b. Carthage, Tenn., Sept. 3, 1940; s. Odell Pickering and Sara Elizabeth (Stone) J.; B.S., Middle Tenn. State U., Murfreesboro, 1970; grad. U.S. Army Information Sch., Ft. Slocum, N.Y., 1960; m. Marion Elizabeth Eades, June 26, 1964; children—Geoffrey Marc, William Christopher. Staff announcer/AM, WCOR, Lebanon, Tenn., 1957-58, WMAK, Nashville, 1958-60; staff announcer, sports dir. AFRS, Anchorage, 1961-63; staff announcer KENI, Anchorage, 1961; booth KENI-TV, Anchorage, 1961-62, KTVA-TV, Anchorage, 1962-63; staff announcer KFQD, Anchorage, 1962-63; staff announcer news WENO, Madison/Nashville, 1963; staff announcer/AM news WABD, Ft. Campbell, Ky., 1963-64; staff announcer, news dir. WLVN, Nashville, 1964; program dir. WABD, Ft. Campbell, 1965-66; staff announcer WLAC-FM, Nashville, 1967, WSIX-FM, Nashville; staff announcer/AM, WBIR, Knoxville, Tenn., 1967-68; staff announcer WSIX, Nashville, 1968—; dir weather services, on-air weatherman WSIX-TV, Nashville, 1970—, also adviser, dir. Exploring program WSIX-AM-FM-TV. Appeared with Circle Players, Vanderbilt U. Theatre, Peabody Players, Nashville, Actors Workshop, Persidio Players, San Francisco, Theatre Anchorage, Ft. Campbell Players. Served with AUS, 1960-63. Home: 3204 Jonesboro St Nashville TN 37214 Office: 441 Murfreesboro Rd Nashville TN 37210

JENNEMANN, VINCENT FRANCIS, geophysicist; b. St. Louis, Nov. 27, 1921; s. Leo F.X. and Agnes (Robbe) J.; B.S., St. Louis U., 1947, M.S., 1949; postgrad. Columbia, 1951-53; Ph.D., U. Tulsa, 1972; m. Frances Louise Robinson, Apr. 27, 1946; children—Frances (Mrs. Jeffrey Bullock), Catherine (Mrs. Derek Audley), Martha, Charles, Mark, Joseph, Mary. Instr. math. St. Louis U., 1946-48; research geophysicist Sun Oil Co., Beaumont, Tex., 1948-51; research scientist Standard Oil Co. (Ind.), Tulsa, 1954-67, computer analyst, 1967-73, staff programmer analyst. 1973—. Served to 1st lt. USAAF, 1943-45. Decorated D.F.C., Purple Heart, Air medal. Mem. Soc. Exploration Geophysicists, Am. Geophys. Union, European Assn. Exploration Geophysicists, Seismol. Soc. Am., Sigma Xi. Democrat. Roman Catholic. Home: 203 Sunset Dr Tulsa OK 74114 Office: PO Box 591 Tulsa OK 74102

JENNINGS, AMY REBECCA, librarian; b. Murfreesboro, Tenn., May 17, 1907; d. E. Bertram and Lillian Lee (Jordan) Jennings; student Middle Tenn. State Tchrs. Coll., 1929-33; A.B., Cumberland U., 1940; B.S. in L.S., George Peabody Coll. Tchrs., 1942. Tchr., prin. pub. schs. Wilson County, Tenn., 1927-39; librarian city sch. systems, Tenn., Miss., 1939-42; reference librarian Law Library, Social Security Bd., Washington, 1943, Law Library, U.S. Dept. Agr., Washington, 1943-44; chief librarian NLRB, Washington, 1944-47; chief librarian FTC, Washington, 1947-72, librarian, adviser to exec. dir. for adminstrn., 1972-73. Trustee Falls Church (Va.) Pub. Library. Mem. Law Librarians' Soc. D.C. (sec. 1946-48), Spl. Libraries Assn. (Washington chpt. chmn. legislative reference sect. 1946-48), D.A.R., Nat. Trust Historic Preservation, Va. Hist. Soc., Va. Library Assn. (trustee sect.). Episcopalian. Contbr. articles to profl. jours. Home: 417 Poplar Dr Falls Church VA 22046

JENNINGS, ARTHUR HOWARD, agrl. exec.; b. Tulia, Tex., May 14, 1909; s. Richard Otto and Nora (Johnson) J.; B.S., West Tex. State U., 1933; m. Anna Myrtle Duke, Nov. 30, 1933; children—Linda (Mrs. James Brent Joy), Eldon Ray. Tchr. Y-L Sch., Muleshoe, Tex., 1933-34; tchr. Salem Sch., Tulia, 1934-35; tchr. Stone Sch., Canyon, Tex., 1935-39; farmer nr. Tulia, 1941—; dir. Houston Elevator, 1959—, Tulia Feed Lot, 1963—, Houston Fertilizer Supply 1959—; owner farm Yuma, Ariz. and Tulia, 1962—. Bd. dirs. Lubbock Christian Coll. Democrat. Mem. Central Ch. Christ (elder 1958—). Home and office: Route 1 Tulla TX 79088

JENNINGS, FEENAN DEE, ofcl. NSF; b. Los Angeles, Aug. 11, 1923; s. John Thomas and Rhesa Lorrain (Owens) J.; A.A. Compton Jr. Coll., 1948; B.S. in Chem. Engring., N.M. A. and M.U., 1950; postgrad. Scripps Instn. Oceanography, U. Cal., 1950-51, 53-55, U. Cal. at Los Angeles, 1951-52; m. Marylou Foreman, Dec. 26, 1965; children—David, Lorraine. Sr. engr. Scripps Instn. Oceanography, 1955-58; oceanographer Geophysics br. Office Naval Research, 1958-66. dir. ocean sci. and tech. div., 1966-70; head office internat. decade ocean exploration NSF, Washington, 1970—. Served with USNR, 1942-46. Recipient Meritorious Civilian award Dept. Navy, 1960; Superior Ser. award, 1966; Mil. Oceanography award, 1970. Home: 1918 Taylor Av Oxon Hill MD 20022 Office: 1800 G St NW Washington DC 20550

JENNINGS, FRANK CLAY, author, publisher, printing co. exec.; b. Garrard County, Ky., June 30, 1913; s. Hamlet Manford and Jane (Reynolds) J.; student pub., pvt. schs. Ky.; m. Helen Maurine Music, Aug. 24, 1940. Area finance officer Fed. Works Agy., Ky., 1935-41; chief wage adminstr. War Dept., Ft. Knox, 1942-46; free lance writer, 1947-49; asso. editor Thoroughbred Record, 1950-51, mng. editor, 1952-54, exec. dir. Thoroughbred Record, Inc., gen. mgr. Thoroughbred Press, Inc., 1955—, treas., 1957—; dir. v.p., treas. Record Pub. Co., Inc., 1963—. Mem. Lexington Kennel Club, Throughbred Club Am., Thoroughbred Farm Mgrs. Club: Blue Grass Sportsmens' League. Home: 1715 Courtney Av Lexington KY 40502 Office: PO Box 580 Lexington KY 40501

JENNINGS, GORDON LANIER, petroleum co. exec.; b. Shreveport, La., Mar. 18, 1930; s. Gordon and Dimple (Pace) J.; B.S. in Chem. Engring., La. State U., 1953; m. Carla Marie Mahan, Aug. 4, 1962; children—Alan Christopher, Susan Lynn, Karin Elizabeth, Liane Marie. Jr. engr., engring. dept. Tex. Eastern Transmission Corp., Shreveport, 1953-58, supr. plans and research gas div., 1958-61, supr. gas div. staff, Houston, 1961-67, mgr. corporate planning and devel., 1967-69, v.p., 1969—. Pres. Houston Center Corp. subsidiary Tex. Eastern Transmission Corp., 1971—. Councilman City of Hedwig Village, Tex., 1964-70; mem. mayor's com. on Overhead Structures, Houston, 1973—. Served to capt. AUS, 1950-52. Registered profl. engr., La. Mem. Houston C. of C. (chmn. downtown com. 1973—), Sigma Nu. Clubs: Houston, Lakeside Country. Home: 726 Magdalene Dr Houston TX 77024 Office: 921 Main St Houston TX 77001

JENNINGS, HENRY SMITH, JR., physician; b. Cordele, Ga., May 22, 1922; s. Henry Smith and Lillian (Cannon) J.; B.S., Emory U., 1942, M.D., 1945; m. Elizabeth Pruett Martin, Sept. 28, 1943; children—Elizabeth M., Henry Smith III. Intern Grady Meml. Hosp., Atlanta, 1945-46; resident Lawson VA Hosp., 1948-50, Emory U. Hosp., 1950-51; mem. staff Emory U. Clinic, 1951-53; partner Jennings, Stribling, Poole and Butts, Gainesville, Ga., 1953-71; partner Northeast Ga. Diagnostic Clinic, Gainesville, 1971—; instr. medicine Emory U. Sch. Medicine; dist. med. cons. Vocational Rehab. div. State Dept. Edn. Dir. Gainesville Nat. Bank. Commr. Gainesville Housing Authority, 1965; mem. Chattahoochee Dist. com. Boy Scouts Am., 1957-59. Bd. dirs. Ga. Med. Care Found.; trustee Hall County Hosp. Authority. Served to capt. M.C., AUS, 1946-48. Diplomate Am. Bd. Internal Med. Mem. Ga. Heart Assn. (pres. 1966-67), Ga. Soc. Internal Medicine (pres. 1961-62), Med. Assn. Ga. (v.p. 1964-66), A.M.A., Hall County Med. Soc. (pres. 1961-62), A.C.P., So. Med. Assn., Sigma Alpha Epsilon, Phi Chi. Methodist (chmn. adminstrv. bd. 1968-70). Clubs: Chattahoochee Country, Kingwood Country; Atlanta City. Home: 1304 Springdale Rd NE Gainesville GA 30501 Office: 710 Broad St NE Gainesville GA 30501

JENNINGS, HOWARD WILLIAM, II, optometrist; b. Rochester, N.Y., Oct. 30, 1925; s. Howard W. and Nellie (Smith) J.; A.B., U. Rochester, 1949; B.S. in Optometry, Ohio State U., 1952; m. Rita Mary Thomas, Dec. 30, 1954; 1 son, Howard William III. Pvt. practice optometry, Boynton Beach, Fla., 1955—; naval architect. Founder, pres. Fla. Vision Found., Inc., 1961. Served with AUS, 1944-46. Decorated Purple Heart. Recipient Editors award Optometric Weekly, 1966. Diplomate Nat. Bd. Optometry. Mem. Am., Fla. (exec. com.), Fla. East Coast (pres. 1965-66) optometric assns., U.S. Naval Inst., Alpha Kappa Kappa, Sigma Chi. Episcopalian. Lion (past v.p. Boynton Beach), Rotarian. Designer, builder replica 17th century colonial vessel Peregrine, 1974. Office: 435 NW 2d St Boynton Beach FL 33435

JENNINGS, JOHN MELVILLE, assn. exec.; b. Toano, Va., Oct. 22, 1918; s. John Melville and Grace Armistead (Davis) J.; B.A., Coll. William and Mary, 1938, LL.D., 1968; M.A., Am. U., 1948. Curator manuscripts and rare books Coll. William and Mary, 1939-43, 46-47; librarian Va. Hist. Soc., Richmond, 1948-51, dir., 1953—. Vice chmn. Va. Historic Landmarks Commn.; adv. bd. Assn. Preservation Va. Antiquities, The Papers of John Marshall, The Papers of James Madison; cons. Robert E. Lee Meml. Found.; Served with USNR, 1944-46, 51-53. Fellow Soc. Am. Archivists; mem. Bibliog. Soc. Am., Am. Hist. Assn., Mass. Hist. Soc., Am. Antiquarian Soc. Home: 204 N Granby St Richmond VA 23220 Office: PO Box 7311 Richmond VA 23221

JENNINGS, PAUL, labor union ofcl.; b. Bklyn., Mar. 19, 1918; ed. RCA Inst., Crown Heights Labor Sch.; m. Dorothy; children—Paul, Eileen. Electronic technician Sperry-Gyro, Bklyn.; successively mem. union organizing com., shop steward, grievance and shop chmn., acting pres. local union Internat. Union Elec. Radio and Machine Workers, AFL-CIO, later mem. exec. bd., treas., local pres., from 1948, exec. sec. Dist. 4, from 1949, later exec. sec. Dist. 3, now internat. pres., also v.p. AFL-CIO. Vice pres. non-proliferation, nuclear reactor safety. Mem. adv. com. AEC, 1956-62, mem. adv. com. reactor safeguards, N.Y.C. CIO Council, also chmn. merger com.; v.p. N.Y. State CIO Council, also co-chmn. merger com.; mem. exec. bd. N.Y. Central Labor Council; chmn. Internat. Fedn. Elec. and Electronics Co. Council Com.; chmn. Elec. and Electronics Industry Co. Council, Internat. Metalworkers Fedn., 1968. Mem. N.Y.C. Mayor's Com. on Exploitation; labor del. OECD; mem. council Hofstra U.; mem. AFL-CIO Civil Rights Com. Trustee State U., N.Y., Urban League. Address: 1126 16th St NW Washington DC 20036

JENNINGS, RICHARD LOUIS, civil engr., educator; b. Newark, N.J., July 28, 1933; s. Louis Alpheus and Florence Eva (Warnecke) J.; student Marietta Coll., 1951-54; B.S. in Math., Ohio U., 1956, B.S. in Civil Engring., 1957; M.S. in Civil Engring., U. Ill., 1958, Ph.D. (NASA-ASEE fellow), 1964; m. Jan Hayden Bush, Sept. 2, 1956; children—Sheryll, Gregory. Constrn. supt. Am. Tel. & Tel. Co., White Plains, N.Y., 1955-56; prof. civil engring. U. Va., Charlottesville, 1963—. Cons. in structural analysis and aerospace tech. Pres. Charlottesville P.T.A. Council, 1969-73; chmn. joint bd. Charlottesville-Albemarle Tech. Edn. Center, 1973-74. Bd. dirs. Planned Parenthood of Central Va., 1969-74, Piedmont Dist. Va. Congress of Parents and Tchrs., 1970-72. Mem. Charlottesville City Sch. Bd., 1972—. Mem. Am. Soc. C.E., Sigma Xi, Tau Beta Pi, Alpha Tau Omega. Democrat. Episcopalian. Clubs: Torch, Colonnade. Contbr. articles on defections of radio telescopes, cable, overloaded hwy. pavements and earthquakes to profl. publs. Home: 1607 Jamestown Dr Charlottesville VA 22901

JENNINGS, RUFUS EDWARD, sch. prin.; b. Saluda, S.C., Jan. 8, 1909; s. John D. and Martha (Chapman) J.; B.A., Newberry Coll., 1933; M.Ed., U. S.C., 1948; m. Virginia Timmerman, Dec. 22, 1936. Jr. high sch. prin., athletic coach Edgefield (S.C.) High Sch., 1933-41; asst. prin., coach Tarpon Springs (Fla.) High Sch., 1941-44, prin., 1949-51; athletic dir., coach Plant City (Fla.) High Sch., 1945-49; supervising prin. Arcadia City (Fla.) Sch., 1951-57; asst. prin. Boone High Sch., Orlando, Fla., 1957-58; prin. Colonial High Sch., Orlando, 1958-71, Parker Elementary Sch., Edgefield, S.C., 1971-72, Wardlaw Acad., Johnston, S.C., 1972—. Served with U.S. Mcht. Marine, 1944-45. Mem. Orange County Secondary Principals Organization (pres. 1963), Metro Conf. (pres. 1964-65), Fla. High Sch. (dist. dir. Dist. VII 1966-67) athletic assns., P.T.A. Fla. Clubs: Lions, Kiwanis (dir. 1953). Home: Martintown Rd Clarks Hill SC 29821 Office: Wardlaw Acad Johnston SC

JENNINGS, RUTHERFORD CRAIG, lawyer; b. Phila., Oct. 17, 1939; s. Robert Jenks and Mary Elizabeth (Craig) J.; B.A., Northwestern U., 1961; LL.B., George Washington U., 1965; m. Joan Ellen Dolfin, June 6, 1959; children—Steven Craig, David Alan. Supply specialist Navy Dept., U.S. Govt., Washington, 1961-66; admitted to Va. bar, 1966; partner Slenker, Brandt & Jennings, Arlington, 1966—. Mem. sports and recreation com. Arlington County Bd., 1972—. Dean, No. Va. Alumni chpt. Delta Theta Phi, 1971—. Mem. Am., Va., Arlington County bar assns., Va. Trial Lawyers Assn., Am. Judicature Soc. Club: Arlington Cubs Youth (v.p. 1970—). Home: 3100 N Nottingham St Arlington VA 22207 Office: 1012 N Utah St Arlington VA 22201

JENNINGS, WALTER STANLEY, physician; b. nr. Norfolk, Va., Apr. 22, 1926; s. Walter Edward and Edna (Davis) J.; A.A., Coll. William and Mary, Norfolk div., 1946; student U. Va., 1946-47; M.D., Med. Coll. Va., 1951; m. Emily Estelle Doughty, July 27, 1947; children—Stanley, Jennifer, Elizabeth Helon. Intern, Norfolk Gen. Hosp., 1951-52; practice medicine, Hickory, Va., 1952, South Norfolk, Chesapeake, 1952—; mem. staff Leigh Meml., Norfolk Gen., Kings Daus. hosps. Pres. Harstan Corp. Chmn. Chesapeake Hosp. Authority. Served with USAAF, 1944-45. Mem. A.M.A., Norfolk County, So. med. socs., Theta Kappa Psi. Home: 1160 Virginia Av Chesapeake VA 22046 Office: 1446 Chesapeake Av South Norfolk Chesapeake VA 22324

JENSEN, ALVIN CARL, ednl. adminstr.; b. North Lake, Wis., Apr. 15, 1921; s. Frank Roy and Amelia (Nelson) J.; B.Ed., Wis. State U., 1958; M.A., George Washington U., 1960, Ed.D., 1967; m. Marilyn Ann Sorenson, Oct. 6, 1954; children—Allyn Mary, Peter Stuart. Commd. 2d lt. U.S. Army, 1942, advanced through grades to col.; mem. staff Joint Chiefs of Staff, 1963-67, office asst. Sec. Def., 1967-70; ret., 1970; asso. dean, dir. credit programs Coll. Gen. Studies, George Washington U., 1970—, faculty adviser to Alpha Alpha chpt. Alpha Sigma Lambda, 1971—. Committeeman Arlington County troop council Boy Scouts Am., 1970—. Mem. Am. Assn. Sch. Adminstrs., Am. Assn. U. Profs., Am. Assn. Higher Edn., Phi Delta Kappa (editor chpt. newsletter 1960-70, pres. 1973-74). Presbyn. (ruling elder session 1967-69, 71—). Clubs: University, Ft. Meyer Officers. Home: 3188 Key Blvd Arlington VA 22201 Office: 2003 G NW Washington DC 20006

JENSEN, GILBERT WALTER, pump co. exec.; b. Rockford, Ill., Mar. 19, 1926; s. Jens C. and Anna Belle (Crowe) J.; B.S. in Mech. Engring., Ill. Inst. Tech., 1951; m. Ruby Eileene Jones, Sept. 22, 1945; children—Arnold Eric, Steven Craig, Karen Kristine. Asso., Am. Gas Assn. Research Lab., Cleve., 1951-52; research engr. George D. Roper Corp., Rockford, 1952-57; chief engr. Avon Mfg. Co., Rockford, 1957-59; with Roper Pump Co., Commerce, Ga., 1959—, pres., 1968—. Instr. tank truck sch. Purdue U., 1962-63. Pres. P.T.A., Loves Park, Ill., 1958-59, 70—. Bd. dirs. Petroleum Equipment Inst. Served with USMCR, 1942-46. Mem. Assn. Indsl. Advertisers (dir. 1969-70), Hydraulic Inst. (chmn. rotary sect. 1969-70, pres. 1974-75), Commerce C. of C. (bd. dirs. 1970—), Am. Legion, Pres. Assn. N.Y.C. Presbyn. Kiwanian. Clubs: Athens (Ga.) Country; Kingwood Country, Sky Valley Ski (Clayton, Ga.); Ponte Vedra Country (Jacksonville, Fla.). Patentee in field. Home: 265 Lakeland Dr Athens GA 30601 Office: Box 269 Commerce GA 30529

JENSEN, RANDOLPH AUGUST, chem. engr.; b. Cottonwood, Minn., May 25, 1919; s. Ole and Olga (Gollnick) J.; B.S. in Chem. Engring., U. Minn., 1940; M.S., State U. Ia., 1946; m. Mary Elizabeth Jacobs, Apr. 11, 1942; children—Marilee (Mrs. Leonard Heydt), Randi Jean, Scott Daniel. Process engr. Cliffs Dow Chem. Co., 1940-42; instr. Engring. Expt. Sta., Pa. State U., 1942-43; research asso. Inst. Hydraulic Research, State U. Ia., 1943-46; project engr. U.S. Synthetic Rubber Labs., U. Akron, 1946-47; research engr. Battelle Meml. Inst., 1947-51; group leader chem. engring. dept. Houston plant Rohm & Haas Co., 1951-62, chief chem. engr. Louisville plant, 1962-71; pollution control engr. Rohm & Haas Ky., Inc., Louisville, 1971—. Chmn. bd. trustees City of Blue Ridge Manor, 1967-70. Recipient Meritorious Service award Div. 10, NDRC, 1946. Registered profl. engr., Ky. Mem. Am. Inst. Chem. Engrs. (chmn. Louisville sect. 1969-70). Christian Scientist. Club: Swingin' Y Square Dance (pres.). Home: 11108 Kilrenny Ct Louisville KY 40243 Office: PO Box 1559 Louisville KY 40201

JENSEN, TOM, state legislator, business exec.; b. Knoxville, Tenn., Oct. 28, 1934; s. Irving Oscal and Christine (Scarbrough) J.; B.S. U. Tenn., 1952-59; m. Carolyn Frances Carter, June 17, 1960; children—Lucinda Anne, Thomas Carter. Pres., chmn. bd. Jensen Industries, Knoxville, which includes Delta Devel. Corp., Knoxville Casket Co., So. Automatic Sprinkler Corp., Precision Electric Co., Inc., Vacationland Industries, Inc.; mem. Tenn. Ho. of Reps., 1967—, majority whip, 1969-70, minority leader, 1971—. Mem. Nat. Com. on Uniform Traffic Laws; chmn. Edn. Commn. of States Task Force on Post secondary Ednl. Instns.; commr. Edn. Commn. of States; chmn. intergovt. relations com. Nat. Legislative Conf.; del. Nat. Conf. Criminal Justice, White House Conf. on Aging, 1971; co-chmn. Nat. Symposium on Environmental Legislation; bd. advisers Carson Newman Coll., Knoxville YWCA. Bd. dirs. United Cerebral Palsy; trustee Children's Mus. Knoxville. Recipient Outstanding Community Service, Knoxville Jr. C. of C., 1963, Nat. Govtl. Affairs Award, 1965; named Outstanding Young Man Knoxville, 1970. Mem. Am. Bottled Water Assn., Nat. Assn. Ind. Businessmen, Nat. Soc. State Legislators (pres.), Nat. Conf. State Legislative Leaders, Tenn. Jr. C. of C. (v.p. 1966, sec. treas. 1967), Knoxville C. of C. Republican (mem. Knox County Exec. com.). Home: 2323 Juniper Dr Knoxville TN 37912 Office: War Memorial Bldg Nashville TN 37219

JENSEN, WALLACE NORUP, physician, educator; b. Moroni, Utah, Aug. 31, 1921; s. Edward Norup and Agnethe (Christensen) J.; B.S., U. Utah, 1943, M.D., 1945; m. Phoebe B. Carlson, May 16, 1947; children—Christopher, Johanna, Jonathan. Intern, Med. Service Johns Hopkins Hosp., 1945-46; asst. resident, resident U. Utah Hosps., 1948-50; Sr. Damon Runyon fellow in medicine, 1952-53; asst. prof. medicine Duke Sch. Medicine, chief hematology sect. Durham VA Hosp., asst. dir. radioisotope lab., 1953-55; head div.

hematology U. Pitts. Sch. Medicine, 1958-63, prof. medicine, 1963-67; spl. fellow NIH, 1963-64; Commonwealth Found. Fund fellow, 1963-64; prof. medicine, vice chmn. dept. medicine Ohio State U. Coll. Medicine, 1967-69, Bruce K. Wiseman lectr., 1973; prof., chmn. dept. medicine George Washington U. Med. Center, Washington, 1969—. Cons., FDA, 1966—, VA Hosps., 1960—, Leukemia Soc., Inc., 1957-64, Office Surgeon Gen., 1970—, Center for Sickle Cell Anemia, Howard U., 1972; cons., bd. dirs. NIH Clin. Center, 1972; mem. space medicine med. adv. council NASA, 1967—. Trustee Mt. Ida Jr. Coll., Newton, Mass. Served as capt. M.C., AUS, 1946-48. Malcolm C. Grow lectr. Soc. Air Force Physicians, 1973. Diplomate Am. Bd. Internal Medicine (bd. examiners 1950—, exec. com.). Fellow A.C.P.; mem. A.M.A., Internat., Am. (adv. bd.) socs. hematology, Am. Soc. Clin. Investigation, Am. Soc. Genetics, Am. Soc. Internal Medicine, Assn. Am. Physicians, Central Soc. Clin. Research, Nat. Blood Club (v.p. 1962-63). Club: Cosmos (Washington). Contbr. articles to profl. jours. Home: 4940 Western St Chevy Chase MD 20016 Office: 2150 Pennsylvania St Washington DC 20037

JENTZ, GAYLORD ADAIR, educator, author; b. Beloit, Wis., Aug 7, 1931; s. Merlyn Adair and Delva (Mullen) J.; B.A., U. Wis., 1953, J.D., 1957, M.B.A., 1958; m. JoAnn Mary Hornung, Aug. 6, 1955; children—Katherine Ann, Gary Adair, Loretta Ann, Rory Adair. Admitted to Wis. bar, 1957; pvt. practice law, Madison, 1957-58; from instr. to asso. prof. bus. law U. Okla., 1958-65; vis. instr. to vis. prof. U. Wis. Law Sch. summers 1957-65; asso. prof. to prof. U. Tex., 1965-68, prof., 1968—, chmn. gen. bus. dept., 1968-74. Served with AUS, 1953-55. Recipient Outstanding Tchr.'s award, Tex. U. Coll. Bus., 1967. Mem. Am. Arbitration Assn. (nat. panel 1966—), Am. (pres. 1971-72), So. (pres. 1967) bus. law assns., Tex. Assn. Coll. Tchrs. (pres. Austin chpt. 1967-68, exec. com. 1969-70, state pres. 1971-72, Jack G. Taylor Teaching Excellence award 1971), Wis. Bar Assn. Author: (with others) Business Law Text and Cases, 2d edit., 1968; Tex. Uniform Comml. Code, 1967, rev. edit., 1972. Contbr. articles to profl. jours. Dep. editor Social Sci. Quarterly, 1966—; editorial staff Am. Bus. Law Jour., 1967-69, editor-in-chief, 1969-74. Home: 4106 North Hills Dr Austin TX 78731

JENTZSCH, RICHARD ALVIN, orthodontist; b. Chgo., Dec. 4, 1892; s. Richard and Ella (Zuerkel) J.; D.D.S., U. Ill., 1926, M.S., 1931; m. Adeline M. Hayek, Nov. 8, 1934 (dec. 1958); m. 2d, Pauline R. Jones, Mar. 9, 1964. Faculty, U. Ill., 1926-36; practice dentistry specializing in orthodontics, 1926—, now ret. Mayor, Village of Wood Dale, Ill., 1943-47. Served with U.S. Army, 1918-19. Mem. Ill., Chgo. (past v.p.) dental socs., Am. Dental Assn., Chgo. Assn. Orthodontists, USCG Aux., Navy League U.S., Omicron Kappa Upsilon, Tau Kappa Epsilon. Home: 909 Shell Point Village Fort Myers FL 33901

JEREMIAS, CHARLES GEORGE, educator; b. Marlboro, Mass., July 8, 1920; s. Charles Nicolas and Ruth May (Mather) J.; B.S., U. Ga., 1942; postgrad. R.I. State U., 1943; Ph.D., Tulane U., 1949; m. Mary Ruth Palmer, Nov. 26, 1942; children—Donna Ruth (Mrs. Terence Wayne Brummett), Charles Palmer. Research chemist U.S. Rubber Co., Providence, 1942-45; research chemist Tenn. Eastman Co., Kingsport, 1948-60; research group leader So. Dyestuff Co., Charlotte, N.C., 1960-62; acting head dept. chemistry Newberry (S.C.) Coll., 1962-64, head dept. chemistry, 1964—. Cons., J.P. J.P. Stevens Co. Fellow Am. Inst. Chemists (dist. dir.); mem. Am. Chem. Soc., Soc. Dyers and Colourists, Am. Assn. U. Profs. (pres. Newberry chpt. 1964-65), S.C. Inst. Chemists (state councilor 1970-72, pres. 1972-73), Am. (dir. Carolina Dist. 1968—), Newberry County (councilor 1967-68, v.p. 1972—) rose socs., Nat. Ry. Hist. Soc. (pres. E.Tenn. chpt. 1959-60), Am. Biographic Inst. (hon. bd. advisers 1971). Democrat. Presbyn. Club: Mid-Carolina Country. Contbr. articles to profl. jours. Home: Route 2 Box 143-K Newberry SC 29108

JERMANN, WILLIAM HOWARD, educator; b. Cleve., June 29, 1935; s. Edmund Leo and Dorothy (Roob) J.; B.E.E., U. Detroit, 1958, M.A., 1962; Ph.D., U. Conn., 1967; m. Elaine Tiihonen, June 22, 1963; children—William, Mary Cay, Robin Lynn. Instr. in elect engring. U. Detoit, 1961-62; asst. prof. elec. engring. U.S. Coast Guard Acad., New London, Conn., 1962-67; asso. prof. Memphis State U., 1967-73, prof. elec. engring., 1973—; adj. asst. prof. elec. engring. Rensselaer Poly. Inst., Hartford (Conn.) Grad. Center, 1966-67; electronics engr. U.S. Navy Underwater Sound Lab., New London, Conn., summer 1967, 71. Mem. adv. com. Tenn. Tech. Inst., Memphis 1971—. Served to lt. AUS, 1958-60. Recipient Featured Engr. award Memphis State U., 1970; NSF grants. Mem. Computers in Edn. Soc. (dir. zone 2 1973-74), Am. Soc. Engring. Edn. (Memphis State U. coordinator), I.E.E.E. (Memphis State adv. 1962—), Sigma Xi, Phi Kappa Phi. K.C. Contbr. articles to profl. publs. Home: 4903 Greenway St Memphis TN 38117 Office: Dept of Electrical Engring Memphis State University Memphis TN 38152

JERMSTAD, GLEN LYNCH, mfg. co. exec.; b. St. Louis, July 10, 1935; s. Robert J. and Lorene (Lynch) J.; B.S., U.S. Naval Acad., 1958; grad. U.S. Naval Sch. Justice, 1959, U. Naval Sch. Flight Tng., 1958; m. Merle Warner Katterjohn, June 8, 1957; children—Glen Lynch, George K., Curtis W. Commd. ensign U.S Navy, 1957, advanced to lt., 1960, ret., 1962; v.p. Katterjohn Concrete Products, Inc., North Little Rock, 1962—, gen. mgr., 1962-67. Ark. dir. Office Econ. Opportunity, Little Rock, 1967-68; spl. cons. rural and urban affairs to gov. Ark., 1968-69, spl. asst. for fed. and state relations, 1969-71, chmn. So. Gov.'s Exec. Staff Adv. Com., 1970-71, spl. cons. bus. devel. in aviation field, 1971-72; exec. dir., sec. Coalition for Rural Am., Washington, 1972; sec. Rural Resources Inst., Washington and Little Rock, 1972—. Dir. Ark. Nixon/Agnew Campaign, 1968; mem. Pulaski County Election Commn., 1965-66; chmn., commr. North Little Rock Planning Commn., 1964-68. Bd. dirs., v.p. N. Little Rock Boys Club, 1964-67. Recipient Outstanding Young Man award N. Little Rock, 1965. Mem. Ark. Sales and Marketing Execs. Club (dir. 1967-68), North Little Rock C. of C. (dir. 1966-68). Episcopalian. Rotarian, Elk. Club: North Hills Country. Home: 6900 Flintrock North Little Rock AR 72116 Office: PO Box 5269 North Little Rock AR 72119

JERNIGAN, JESS EARL, oil and gas co. exec.; b. Paris, Tex., Jan. 14, 1913; s. Frank W. and Maude H. (Harry) J.; B.S. in C.E., Okla. State U., 1937; m. Rose Marie Wells, Sept. 7, 1937; children—Robert Mark, Janet Kay (Mrs. John D. Bradley), Stephen Alan, James Bradford. Petroleum engr. Pan Am. Petroleum, Oklahoma City, 1937-46; cons. engr. petroleum Oklahoma City, 1947-50; partner Jernigan & Morgan Oil Co., Oklahoma City, 1950-70, pres. Jernigan-Morgan Transmission Co., Oklahoma City, 1950-70, Pacific Oil & Gas Co., Oklahoma City, 1970—. Mason. Club: Oklahoma City Golf and Country. Home: 1903 Bedford Dr Oklahoma City OK 73116 Office: Colcord Bldg Oklahoma City OK 73102

JEROME, JUDSON BLAIR, author; b. Tulsa, Feb. 8, 1927; s. Ralph and Gwendolyn (Stewart) J.; M.A., U. Chgo., 1950; Ph.D., Ohio State U., 1955; m. Martha-Jane Pierce, June 20, 1948; children—Michelle, Elizabeth, Penelope, Jennifer, Christopher. Prof. lit. Antioch Coll., 1953-73; author: Light in the West, 1962; The Poet and the Poem, 1963; The Ocean's Warning to the Skin Diver and Other Love Poems, 1964; The Fell of Dark, 1966; Serenade, 1968; Poetry: Premeditated Art, 1968; Culture Out of Anarchy: The Reconstruction of American Higher Education, 1969; Families of Eden: Communes and the New Anarchism, 1974; contbr. short stories to lit. jours.; contbr. to anthologies, also collections containing poems and prose to lit. jours.; columnist Writer's Digest, 1961—; contbr. numerous poems to lit. periodicals, jours., mags., 1954—; poetry editor Antioch Review, 1955-69. Served with USAAF, 1943-45. Recipient Amy Lowell Travelling Poetry scholarship, 1960-61; Huntington Hartford Found. fellow, 1959; recipient William Carlos Williams award in Fiction, 1963. Home: Downhill Farm Hancock MD 21750 Office: Downhill Farm Hancock MD 21750

JESSUP, JOE LEE, mgmt. cons., educator; b. Cordele, Ga., June 23, 1913; s. Horace Andrew and Elizabeth (Wilson) J.; B.S., U. Ala., 1936; M.B.A., Harvard Grad. Sch. Bus. Administrn., 1941; LL.D., Chung-Ang U., Seoul, Korea, 1964; m. Genevieve Quirk Galloway, Aug. 29, 1946; 1 dau., Gail Elizabeth. Sales rep. Proctor & Gamble, 1937-40; liaison officer bur. pub. relations U.S. War Dept., 1941; spl. asst. and exec. asst. Far Eastern div. and office exports Bd. Econ. Welfare, 1942-43; exec. officer office deptl. adminstrn. Dept. State, 1946; exec. sec. adminstr.'s adv. council War Assets Adminstrn., 1946-48; v.p. sales Airkem Capitol & Service Co., 1948-49; pres. Jessup & Co., 1957—; dir. Hunter Assos. Labs., Inc., Fairfax, Va., 1965-69; asso. prof. bus. administrn. George Washington U., 1949, prof., 1952, asst. dean Sch. Gov., 1951-60. Dir. Giant Food, Inc., Washington, 1971—, Internat. Careers Inst., Inc., Los Angeles, 1972—. Coordinator resources mgmt. program U.S. Air Force, 1951-60; regional chmn. Harvard Bus. Sch. Fund, 1960—. Del. 10th Internat. Mgmt. Conf., Sao Paulo, Brazil, 1954, 11th, Paris, France, 1957, 12th, Sydney and Melbourne, Australia, 1960, 13th, N.Y.C., 1963, 14th, Rotterdam, Holland, 1966, 15th, Tokyo, Japan, 1970, 16th, Munich, Germany, 1973; mem. Md. Econ. Devel. Adv. Commn., 1973. Served from 2d lt. to lt. col. AUS, 1941-46. Decorated Bronze Star; recipient certificate of appreciation Sec. of Air Force, 1957. Mem. Acad. Mgmt., Am. Mgmt. Assn., Soc. Advancement Mgmt., Alpha Kappa Psi. Clubs: Harvard (N.Y.C.); Harvard Business School (v.p. programs 1960—), Congressional Country, International (Washington). Home: 8539 W Howell Rd Bethesda MD 20034 Office: 5454 Wisconsin Av Chery Chase MD 20015

JESSUP, PERCY WELLS, JR., dentist; b. Lumberton, N.C., Sept. 12, 1941; s. Percy Wells and Merle (Savage) H.; B.S. in Chemistry, U. N.C., 1963, D.D.S., 1967; m. Martha C. Phillips, July 19, 1970; children—Lance Wells, Caroline Kelly. Practice dentistry, Fayetteville, N.C., 1969—. Served to capt. Dental Corps, AUS, 1967-69. Mem. Am. Dental Assn., Am. Acad. Gen. Dentistry, Am. Assn. Dentists, Am. Soc. Preventive Dentistry, Am. Soc. Dentistry for Children, Greater Fayetteville Dental Soc. (treas. 1973-74). Presbyn. Club: Toastmasters (pres. Cape Fear club 1971—; gov. area 10 since 1971). Home: 566 Rayconda St Fayetteville NC 28304 Office: 1647 Owen Dr Fayetteville NC 28304

JETER, ROBERT MCKENZIE, physician; b. Bradford, Tenn., June 29, 1906; s. Joshua Edgar and Wynona (Bandy) J.; certificate Max Morris Sch. Pharmacy, Macon, Ga., 1927; B.A., Vanderbilt U., 1934, M.D., 1937; m. Frances Imogene Cooper, June 23, 1927; children—Mary Ellen (Mrs. William S. Sullivan). Intern, Vanderbilt Hosp., Nashville, 1938-39, Bellevue Hosp., N.Y.C., 1938, St. Thomas Hosp., Nashville, 1938-39; gen. practice medicine, Gleason, Tenn., 1939; municipal health officer. Chmn. bd. Bank Gleason. Named Man Year, P.T.A., 1956. Fellow Commonwealth Fund. Mem. Phi Beta Kappa, Alpha Omega, Alpha, Pi Kappa Alpha. Rotarian. Home: 305B College St Gleason TN 38229 Office: 305A College St Gleason TN 38229

JETT, HORACE WILBUR BABE, city adminstr., b. Ft. Worth, July 21, 1931; s. James Madison and Bessie Opal (Morgan) J.; student Midwestern U., 1949-50, North Tex. State U., 1950-51; B.S. in Commerce, Tex. Christian U., 1957; m. Peggy Jane Lewis, Dec. 19, 1958; children—Gayla Ann, John Brady. Sales and real estate rep. Continental Oil Co., Plainview, Tex., 1957-61, Amarillo, Tex., 1961-62; v.p. sales Cooks Oil Co., Ft. Worth, 1967-69; real estate rep. Ward Food Inc., Dallas, 1969-70; adminstr. City of Benbrook, Tex., 1970—. Dir. Benbrook State Bank. Served to capt. AUS, 1953-60; Korea. Recipient Student Achievement award Wallstreet Jour., 1956. Mem. Tex. City Mgrs. Assn., Tex. Christian Univ. C. of C. (treas. 1956, pres. 1957). Mem. Christian Ch. (chmn. bd. 1962-63). Mason. Club: Ft. Worth Gun. Home: 4632 Williams Rd Fort Worth TX 76116 Office: 101 Del Rio St Benbrook TX 76126

JETT, JAMES PHILLIP, banker; b. Salem, Ill., Nov. 6, 1943; s. Garnet Hollingsworth and Martha (McNanama) J.; B.S., U. Ark., 1965; postgrad. Northwestern U., 1970; m. Angela Gay Godsey, June 21, 1964; children—Angela Michelle, James Phillip, Mary Katherine. Asst. v.p. Worthen Bank & Trust Co., Little Rock, 1965-71; div. mgr. First Nat. Bank, Hot Springs, Ark., 1971—; asst. sec. First Ark. Bankstock Corp. Commr., Garland County Cultural Commn., 1973—. Pres., Central Ark. Sigma Chi Alumni; bd. dirs. Hot Springs Conv. Bd., Boy Scouts Am.; trustee Salvation Army. Served to capt. AUS, 1965-67. Mem. Bank Marketing Assn., Am. Mgmt. Assn., Sigma Chi. Rotarian. Home: 201 Markwood St Hot Springs AR 71901 Office: PO Box 1000 Hot Springs AR 71901

JETT, JOHN LYNDELL, city ofcl.; b. Sparta, Tenn., Dec. 12, 1936; s. Charles O. and Charlie Mae (Jarvis) J.; B.S., Tenn. Tech. U., 1958; m. Annelle Bockman, Aug. 17, 1958; 1 son, John Lyndell. Mgmt. trainee, then asst. br. plant mgr. Davis Cabinet Co., Nashville, 1958-59; with Sparta Monumental Works, Inc., 1959-73, v.p., mgr., 1965-73; pres., dir. Sparta Electric System, Sparta Water & Sewer Highland Cemtery Corp., Sparta, 1966-73; mem. bd. aldermen City of Sparta, 1969-73, city judge and recorder, 1973—, city adminstr., 1973—. Bd. dirs. Sparta Airport Authority, 1973—, Sparta Little League, A.R.C. Presbyn. (deacon). Mason (Shriner). Club: Civitan (v.p. Sparta 1966-67) Home: Route 10 Sparta TN 38583 Office: 114 E Bockmam Way Sparta TN 38583

JETTON, ALLEN CARPENTER, banker; b. Union Grove, Ala., Dec. 31, 1908; s. David Mitchell and Alice Elmira (Carpenter) J.; B.S., Jacksonville (Ala.) State Tchrs. Coll., 1930; m. Rosalie Black, Dec. 11, 1931. Tchr. schs., Marshall County (Ala.) 1926-30, prin., 1931-43; agt. Liberty Nat. Life Ins. Co., Albertville, Ala., 1943-48; bookkeeper Forrester & Dickerson Furniture Co., Guntersville, Ala., 1948-52; with Citizens Bank of Guntersville 1952—, pres., 1966-68, chmn. bd., 1968—; dir. Val Monte Shores, Inc., 1966—; v.p. Citizens Realty Co., 1965— (both Guntersville). Dir. Guntersville Electric Bd., 1970—. Mem. Ala. Bankers Assn. Baptist. Clubs: Civitan (sec.-treas. 1967), Val Monte Country (Guntersville). Home: 13 Ringold St Gundersville AL 35976 Office: 370 Broad St Guntersville AL 35976

JEWELL, FRANK RANDALL, lawyer; b. Middletown, N.Y., Aug. 8, 1930; s. Frank Harris and Theodosia Hall (Randall) J.; B.A., Hamilton Coll., 1952; LL.B., U. Tex. at Austin, 1955; m. Margaret Clark, Dec. 29, 1955; children—Frank Harris III, Laurie K., Walter S., Michael John. Admitted to Tex. bar, 1973, U.S. Supreme Ct., 1970; asst. dist. atty. Dallas, 1955-56; mem. firm Hultgren, Jewell & Kolb, Dallas, 1956—. Mem. Dallas Assn. Trial Lawyers, Am. Assn. Trial Lawyers, Am. Bd. Trial Advocated, Tex. Assn. Trial Lawyers. Episcopalian. Home: 4338 Shirley Dr Dallas TX 75229 Office: 614 Adolphus Tower Dallas TX 75202

JEWELL, ROBERT BURNETT, engring. exec.; b. Binghampton, N.Y., Mar. 20, 1906; s. Howard Clinton and Anne (Burnett) J.; B.S. in Civil Engring., Lehigh U., 1928; m. Helen Louise Pflug, May 18, 1935; children—Robert William, Linda Louise. Asst. engr. Friestedt Found. Co., N.Y., 1928-30; asst. engr. Port of N.Y. Authority, 1930-39; with Mason & Hanger Co., 1939-43, field engr. Rays Hill Tunnel, 1939-40; chief draftsman Radford Ordnance Works, 1940-41; asst. chief engr. design Badger Ordnance Works, 1942; resident engr. constrn. Bklyn.-Battery Tunnel, 1942-43; job mgr. hemp mill constrn., Polo, Ill., 1943; with Silas Mason Co., 1943-55; asst. prodn. supt. operation La. Ordnance Plant, 1943-46, chief engr. design of facilities U.S. AEC, Ia. Ordnance Plant, 1947-48; project mgr. constrn. Fort Randall Dam Outlet Works Tunnels, 1948-50, AEC Pantex Ordnance Plant, 1951-52; project mgr. engring. services AEC Nev. Test Site, 1951-53; chief engr., co. rep. Harvey Canal Tunnel, 1953-55; v.p. Mason & Hanger-Silas Mason Co., Inc., 1955—, v.p., chief engr., 1959-64, v.p. for operations, 1964—, also dir. Registered profl. engr., N.Y., Ky. Fellow Am. Soc. C.E.; mem. Am. Concrete Inst., Am. Inst. Aeros. and Astronautics, Nat. Soc. Profl. Engrs., Am. Ordnance Assn., The Moles, The Beavers, Tau Beta Pi. Presbyn. Rotarian. Clubs: Engineers (N.Y.), Lexington Country. Home: 1036 The Lane Lexington KY 40504 Office: 200 W Vine St Lexington KY 40507

JEWETT, ROBERT ELWIN, educator; b. Jackson, Mich., Feb. 3, 1934; s. Elwin S. and Pearl Marie (Hull) J.; M.D., U. Mich., 1958. Intern Toledo Gen. Hosp., 1958-59; asst. resident Univ. Hosp., Ann Arbor, Mich., 1959-60; clin. investigator Ciba Pharm. Co., Summit, N.J., 1960-62; postdoctoral fellow Med. Center U. Kan., Kansas City, 1962-65; mem. faculty Sch. Medicine Emory U., Atlanta, 1965—, asso. prof. pharmacology, 1969—, program dir. physicians asso. program, 1972—. Nat. Inst. Neurol. Disease and Blindness spl. fellow, 1963-65. Mem. Assn. Physicians Asst. Programs, Am. Soc. Pharmacology and Exptl. Therapeutics, A.A.A.S., Sigma Xi, Alpha Omega Alpha. Contbr. profl. jours. Edit. adv. bd. Psychopharmacologia, 1973—. Office: Dept Pharmacology Emory U Atlanta GA 30322

JEWETT, WILLIAM AMORY, coll. adminstr.; b. Gardner, Mass., Oct. 1, 1919; s. Everett Porter and Mae Virginia (Crowley) J.; grad. Mt. Hermon Sch., 1937; A.B., Brown U., 1941, postgrad., 1946-47; m. Alva Althea Pearson, June 14, 1942; 1 dau., Linda (Mrs. Harry M. Wales). Placement officer, asst. to pres., registrar Brown U., 1945-51; civilian adminstrv. officer U.S. Army, Washington, Munich, Germany and Taipei, Taiwan, 1952-65; v.p. mgmt. Melmar Corp., Perrine, Fla., 1966-69; v.p. financial affairs Mt. Vernon Coll., Washington, 1969—. Trustee, v.p. Nat. Soc. Prevention Blindness. Served to lt. comdr. USNR, 1945. Mem. Nat. Assn. Coll. and Univ. Officers, Assn. Financial Aid Adminstrs., So. Assn. Coll. Bus. Officers. Home: 1911 Kenbar Ct McLean VA 22101 Office: 2100 Foxhall Rd Washington DC 20007

JILES, CHARLES WILLIAM, educator; b. Vienna, La., Aug. 11, 1927; s. Robert Algin and Selma (Willis) J.; B.S. in Elec. Engring., La. Poly. Inst., 1949, B.A. in Math., 1949; M.S. in Elec. Engring., Okla. State U., 1950, Ph.D., 1955; m. Opal Earl Baber, Aug. 27, 1950; children—David Lee, Linda Sue, Ruth Ann, Darrell Wayne. Instr. elec. engring. Okla. State U., 1949-55; specialist design Gen. Dynamics Corp., Ft. Worth, 1955-60; prof. elec. engring., nat. cons. automatic controls U. Tex. at Arlington, 1960—; pres., Arlington Engring. Asso., Inc., 1960-66. City councilman Benbrook, Tex., 1957-60; pres. Tarrant County Joint Bds. Christian Chs., 1962-64. Registered Profl. Engr., Tex., Okla. Mem. Am. Astroautics Soc., I.E.E.E., Am. Soc. Engring. Edn., Sigma Xi, Tau Beta Pi, Phi Kappa Phi, Eta Kappa Nu, Sigma Pi Sigma. Kiwanian (past chmn. support of chs. com. chmn. internat. relations). Author: (with S.F. Crumb) Transients in Linear Systems. Home: 620 Westview Terrace Arlington TX 76013

JIMENEZ, MIGUEL AMGEL, chemist; b. Matanzas, Cuba, Oct. 2, 1912; s. Miguel Andres and Maria (Soledad) J.; B.S., U. Havana (Cuba), 1941; M.S. (chemistry fellow), U. Cal. at Berkeley, 1945; Ph.D., U. Mass., 1959; m. Olga de la Torre, Nov. 21, 1948; children—Olga Marie, Michael Allen. Came to U.S., 1943, naturalized, 1952. Sch. tchr., Cuba, 1935-37; with Agrl. Expt. Sta., Havana, 1945-46, H.J. Heinz Co., Berkeley, Cal., 1946, Minute Maid Co., Plymouth, Fla., 1947-60, Coca-Cola Co., Orlando, Fla., 1960-62; with Reynolds Metals Co., Richmond, Va., 1962—, sr. research scientist, 1973—. Chmn. new bldg. and fund campaign Marymount High Sch., Richmond, 1970. Travelling scholar U. Havana, 1943-45. Fellow A.A.A.S., Am. Inst. Chemists (nat. chmn. state insts.); mem. Am. Chem. Soc., N.Y. Acad. Scis., Am. Soc. Microbiology, Inst. Food Technologists, Va. Acad. Sci., Packaging Inst. U.S.A., Am. Soc. Brewing Chemists, Scientific Manpower Commn., Sigma Xi, Phi Tau Sigma. Clubs: Engineers (Richmond); University (Winter Park, Fla.). Contbr. articles to profl. jours. Editor: Chem. Abstracts, 1963-70. Home: 1604 Treboy Av Richmond VA 23226 Office: Reynolds Metals Co 10th and Byrd Sts Richmond VA 23219

JIMENEZ-TORRES, CARLOS FEDERICO, physician; b. Aquada, P.R., Oct. 19, 1921; s. Carlos and Pura (Torres) Jimenez; student U. P.R., 1936-39; M.D., George Washington U., 1943; postgrad. radiology U. Pa., 1948-49; m. Domitila Ferrer, June 18, 1949; children—Lorraine, Carlos Federico, Luis Javier, Pura Elaine, Janet Arlene. Intern Fajardo Dist. Hosp., 1943-44; resident Presbyn. Hosp., Phila., 1949-51; physician VA Center and Hosp., San Juan, P.R., 1946-48; practice medicine specializing in radiology, Ponce, P.R., 1952—; instr. radiology U. Pa. Sch. Medicine, 1950-51; lectr. radiology U. P.R. Sch. Medicine, 1952—; cons. in radiology Ponce Med. Center. Bd. dirs., past treas. Liceo Ponceno. Served with AUS, 1944-46. Diplomate Am. Bd. Radiology. Mem. Am., Pan Am., P.R. med. assns., Am. Coll. Radiology, P.R., Inter-Am. radiol. socs., Am. Legion, USCG Aux., U.S. Power Squadron. Roman Catholic. K.C., Lion (past dist. zone chmn., past pres. Ponce). Club: Ponce Yacht (dir.). Home: 16 Universidad St Ponce PR 00731 Office: Lorraine Bldg Ponce PR 00731

JOANOS, JAMES EMANUEL, judge; b. Tallahassee, June 28, 1934; s. Emanuel George and Theologia (Patragas) J.; B.S., Fla. State U., 1956; LL.B., Yale, 1962; m. Betty Lou Whittle, May 25, 1957; children—Julia Lee, Janet Theologia, James Emanuel. Admitted to Fla. bar, 1962; research asst. Fla. 1st Dist. Ct. Appeals, Tallahassee, 1962-63; mem. firm Dye & Joanos, 1963-68, Joanos, Parsons & Hayes, 1969-71; judge Leon County Felony Ct. Record, 1971-72; circuit judge 2d Jud. Circuit, Fla., 1973—; v.p. Capital Sq. Bldgs., Inc., Tallahassee, 1968—. Served with USAF, 1956-59. Recipient Distinguished Service award Tallahassee Jr. C. of C., 1967; Fla. State U. Gold Key outstanding alumnus award, 1967. Mem. Fla., Tallahassee bar assns., Tallahassee (pres. 1964-65), Fla. (v.p. 1965-66) jr. chambers commerce, Fla. State U. Alumni Assn. (pres.), Gold Key, Omicron Delta Kappa, Phi Delta Phi, Sigma Chi, Pi Sigma Alpha. Episcopalian. Mason (Shriner), Elk. Home: 2001 Seminole Dr Tallahassee FL 32301 Office: Leon County Courthouse Tallahassee FL 32302

JOBSIS, FRANS FREDERIK, educator; b. Jakarta, Indonesia, Apr. 1, 1929; s. Gerrit Jozef and Maria (van der Vliet) J.; came to U.S., 1948, naturalized, 1955; B.S., U. Md., 1951; M.S. in Zoology, U. Mich., 1953, Ph.D., 1958; m. Sarah Perkins Long, Dec. 28, 1951 (div. Dec. 1973); children—Catherine Theresa, Gerrit Jozef, William Thorne, Maria Margaretha, Paul Dugald. Fellow, U. Amsterdam (Netherlands), 1959, Nobel Inst., Stockholm, Sweden, 1960; asst. prof. biophysics, physiology U. Pa., Phila., 1961-64; asst. prof. dept. physiology Duke U., Durham, N.C., 1964-66, asso. prof., 1966-68, prof., 1968—. Guggenheim Found. fellow, 1971-72. Mem. A.A.A.S., Am. Physiol. Soc. Home: 1542 Hermitage Ct Durham NC 27707 Office: Dept Physiology and Pharmacology Duke Univ Durham NC 27710

JOERNS, JACK CHASE, aerospace engr., govt. ofcl.; b. Chgo., July 9, 1917; s. Arnold and Estelle (Chase) J.; student Northwestern Mil. and Naval Acad., 1933-35, Ill. Inst. Tech., 1935-36; B.S. in Aero. Engring, St. Louis U., 1940; postgrad. Tex. Christian U., 1955-57; m. Rita Mary Phipps, Oct. 21, 1944; m. 2d, Susan Jones Clements, Feb. 14, 1967; 1 son, Dana Beowulf Christian. Sr. engr. Gen. Dynamics Corp., Ft. Worth, 1948-56; engr. Puget Sound Naval Shipyard, Bremerton, Wash., 1957-58, Bell Helicopter Co., Ft. Worth, 1958-62; sci. specialist Edgerton, Germeshausen & Grier, Las Vegas, Nev., 1962-63; aerospace engr. NASA Manned Spacecraft Center, Houston, 1964—. Bd. dirs. U.S. Parachute Assn., Monterey, Cal. Served to flight lt. RAF, 1941-45. Mem. Am. Inst. Aeros. and Astronautics, Soc. Automotive Engrs., Am. Ordnance Assn., Nat. Geog. Soc. (mem. Vilcabamba Expdn. 1963), Exptl. Aircraft Assn. Republican. Presbyn. Elk. Clubs: OX-5 (Pitts.). Home: 18410 King's Lynn Houston TX 77058 Office: NASA Manned Spacecraft Center Houston TX 77001

JOFTES, SAUL EUGENE, assn. exec.; b. N.Y.C., Nov. 1, 1914; s. Yoineh and Manya (Rodier) J.; Adj in Arts, Harvard, 1941; M.A., Boston U., 1941; J.D., Northeastern U., 1936, LL.M., 1938; postgrad. Harvard Law Sch., 1939; m. Miriam Minna Uretsky, Feb. 22, 1938. Lectr. Boston U., 1940-44, Law Sch., 1944-46; instr. U.S. Army specialized Tng. Program, 1942-44; lectr. govt. Harvard, 1946-47; edn. dir. Anti-Defamation League B'Nai B'rith, Boston, 1947-48, dir. European office, Paris, France, 1948-52, dir. Latin Am. office, Santiago, Chile, 1953, dir. internat. affairs, Washington, 1953-67, sec.-gen. internat. council, 1959-67, research dir., 1967-68; dir. gen. World Confedn. Nat. Jewish Orgns., Washington, 1969—. Non-govtl. rep. at UN, Coordinating Bd. Jewish Orgns., 1949-67; observer for B'nai B'rith at Nurenberg Trials, Germany, 1949. Mem. nat. bd. sponsors Inst. Am. Strategy; nat. voter adv. bd. Am. Security Council. Mem. Am. Soc. Internat. Law, Harvard Law Sch. Assn., Harvard Club N.Y.C. Mem. B'nai B'rith. Home: 6410 Cross Woods Dr Falls Church VA 22044

JOHAM, HOWARD ERNEST, educator; b. Los Angeles, Oct. 12, 1919; s. James Joseph and Ada (Richardson) J.; B.A. in Biology, U. Cal. at Santa Barbara, 1941; M.S. in Plant Physiology, Tex. A. and M. U., 1943; Ph.D. in Botany (Anderson-Clayton fellow), Ia. State U., 1950; m. Myrtle Ruth Franze, Aug. 23, 1942; children—Suzanne Margaret, James Reinhold. Asst. plant physiologist Tex. Agrl. Expt. Sta., Tex. A. and M. U., College Station, 1946-50; mem. faculty dept. plant scis., Tex. A. and M. U., College Station, 1950, asso. prof., 1955-59, prof., 1959—. Pres. Chem-Phyto Consulting Service, Inc., College Station, 1965—. Mem. U.S. Dept. Agr. Task Force Cotton Research, 1967-69. Served with AUS, 1944-46; ETO. Fellow Tex. Acad. Sci.; mem. Am. Soc. Plant Physiologist (pres. So. sect. 1961, mem. nat. exec. bd. 1962-65), Scandinavian Soc. Plant Physiology, Am. Soc. Agronomy, Sigma Xi, Phi Kappa Phi, Gamma Sigma Delta. Shriner (32 deg.). Home: Route 2 Box 146 Bryan TX 77801 Office: Plant Scis Dept College Station TX 77843

JOHANSON, LAMAR, educator; b. Kyle, Tex., Oct. 31, 1935; s. M. Clyde and Bonnie Jane (Battle) J.; B.S., S.W. State U., 1957, M.A., 1958; Ph.D., Tex. A. and M. U., 1967; m. Marilynn Frances Timberlake, July 2, 1960. Asso. prof. biology Tarleton State U., Stephenville, Tex., 1967-71, prof., 1971-73, head dept. biol. scis., 1973—. Dir. 1st Nat. Bank of Hico (Tex.). Dir. Stephenville C. of C. Served to capt., USAF, 1958-61. NASA predoctoral fellow, 1965-67. Fellow Tex. Acad. Sci.; mem. A.A.A.S., Am. Inst. Biol. Scis., Am. Soc. Plant Physiologists, Am. Peanut Research and Edn. Assn., Tex. Assn. Coll. Tchrs., Tex. Assn. Future Homemakers of Am. (hon.), Sigma Xi. Mason. Club: Stephenville Optimist (lt. gov. internat. 1971-72). Contbr. articles to sci. jours. Home: PO Box 57 Stephenville TX 76401 Office: Tarleton State U Stephenville TX 76402

JOHN, DAVID RUSSELL, JR., financial cons.; b. N.Y.C., Sept. 8, 1937; s. David Russell and Elizabeth (Dumbris) J.; B.S., U. Pa., 1959; m. Carolyn Beer, Nov. 24, 1962; children—Jennifer Lynn, David Russell III, Jessica Elaine. Exec. trainee Mfrs. Trust Co., N.Y.C., 1959-60; v.p. Fla. Capital Corp., Palm Beach, 1960-68; v.p. finance, dir. Cinecom Corp., N.Y.C., 1968-69; chmn. bd. Indsl. Electronics Assos., Inc., Palm Beach, 1969-71; chmn. bd., pres. Beefy King Internat., Inc., 1970-71; chmn. bd., pres. Southeastern Consultants, Inc., Palm Beach. Dir. Mcht. Police of Palm Beaches, Inc. Mem. Fla. N.G., 1960-66. Mem. Sigma Nu. Home: 242 List Rd Palm Beach FL 33480 Office: P B Towers 44 Cocoanut Row Palm Beach FL 33480

JOHN, LEWIS GEORGE, coll. dean; b. Waco, Tex., Nov. 25, 1936; s. Lewis Hervin and Margaret Elizabeth (Reese) J.; B.A., Washington and Lee U., 1958; postgrad. (Fulbright scholar) U. Edinburgh (Scotland), 1958-59; M.P.A. (Woodrow Wilson fellow), Princeton, 1961; Ph.D. (H. Lehman fellow), Syracuse U., 1973; m. Annette Louise Church, June 3, 1961; children—Andrew, Christopher. Exec. trainee Office Sec. Def., Washington, summers 1960, 61; dir. student financial aid and placement Washington and Lee U., Lexington, Va., 1963-66, 68-69, dean students, asst. prof. politics, 1969—. Chmn. Rockbridge Area Drug Council, 1973—. Served to lt. AUS, 1961-63. Mem. Am. Soc. Pub. Adminstrn., Am. Polit. Sci. Assn., Am. Econ. Assn., Nat. Assn. Student Personnel Adminstrs., Va. Assn. Student Personnel Adminstrs. (sec.-treas. 1973), So. Coll. Personnel Assn., Phi Beta Kappa, Omicron Delta Kappa, Omicron Delta Epsilon. Home: 8 Edmondson Av Lexington VA 24450

JOHN, PETER WILLIAM MEREDITH, educator; b. Porthcawl, Wales, Aug. 20, 1923; s. Mervyn Edward and Dorothy (Meredith) J.; B.A., Oxford (Eng.) U., 1944, M.A., 1948, Dip. Statistics, 1949; Ph.D., U. Okla., 1955; m. Elizabeth Ann Harper, Mar. 19, 1954; children—Christopher D.H., Ann Meredith. Came to U.S., 1949, naturalized, 1955. Instr. dept. math. U. Okla., 1953-55; asst. prof. U. N.M., Albuquerque, 1955-57; research statistician Chevron Research Co., Richmond, Cal., 1957-61; asst. prof. U. Cal. at Berkeley, 1958-61; mem. faculty U. Cal. at Davis, 1961-67, asso. prof., 1961-66, prof., 1966-67; prof. dept. math. U. Tex. at Austin, 1967—. Served with RAF, 1943-46. Author: Statistical Design and Analysis of Experiments, 1971. Home: 3702 Gilbert St Austin TX 78703 Office: Dept Math Univ Tex Austin TX 78712

JOHNS, BENJAMIN RILEY, JR., architect; b. Richmond, Va., July 14, 1921; s. Benjamin Riley and Marie Blanche (Williams) J.; B.S. in Archtl. Engring., N.C. State Coll., 1948; m. Geraldine Charlotte Price, Sept. 10, 1945; children—Benjamin Riley III, Pamela P. Draftsman, E. Tucker Carlton, architect, Richmond, 1940, 41, 46-48, architect, 1948-54; draftsman Dept. Conservation and Devel., N.C. Dept. State Parks, summer 1942; propr. Ben R. Johns, Jr., architect, Richmond, 1954—. Pres. West Grace Corp., Richmond, Va., 1970-71. Mem. Richmond Bd. Zoning Appeals, 1955-60, 62—, chmn. 1967-69, 74; mem. Richmond City Council, 1960-62, Richmond Planning Commn., 1960-62. Bd. dirs. Children, Inc. Served with AUS, 1942-45; lt. col. Res. ret. Mem. A.I.A. (corporate mem.; pres. Richmond sect. Va. chpt. 1959-60), Va. Citizens Planning Assn., Constrn. Specifications Inst. (corporate mem.), Va. Assn. Professions, Richmond C. of C., Richmond First Club (pres. 1959-60), N.C. State Alumni Assn. (pres. Richmond 1958, 59), Central Richmond Assn. (dir. 1960-62), USCG Aux. (flotilla comdr. 1971), Am. Arbitration Assn. (panel arbitrators), Am. Legion, Navy League. Methodist. Mason (K.T., Shriner). Clubs: Windmill Point Yacht (Foxwells, Va.); Downtown of Richmond (pres. 1963-64). Home: 4530 W Seminary Av Richmond VA 23227 Office: 5 W Grace St Richmond VA 23220

JOHNS, HORACE E., JR., polit. worker; b. Murfreesboro, Tenn., Mar. 26, 1945; s. Horace E. and Dorothy (Ezell) J.; B.A., Vanderbilt U., 1967, J.D., 1970. Admitted to Tenn. bar, 1970; asso. firm Haynes, Hull & Ray, Tullahoma, 1971-72; adminstrv. asst., legal counsel to Tenn. State Treas., Nashville, 1972-74; asst. campaign Wiseman for Gov., Tenn., 1974. Mem. Davidson County Young Democrats, 1972—. Served with AUS, 1970-71. Mem. Am. Legion. Club: YMCA (Nashville). Home: Murfreesboro Rd Eagleville TN 37060

JOHNS, JAY JOSE, physician; b. Round Rock, Tex., Oct. 30, 1900; s. George Washington and Claudia Genoma (Nelson) J.; B.S., U. Tex., 1924, M.D., 1924; m. Catherine Hildegarde Davison, Sept. 17, 1924; children—Mary Victor (Mrs. John J. Kane), Hildegarde (Mrs. J.H. Stjepcevich). Intern Taylor (Tex.) Sanitorium, 1924-25; practice medicine specializing in gen. practice and surgery, Taylor, 1924—; founder The Johns Clinic, 1946—; founder The Johns Hosp., 1948, chief staff, 1955—; dir. City Nat. Bank. Trustee Johns Community Hosp., chmn. fund drive, 1971—. Named Taylor Citizen of the Year, C. of C., 1968. Fellow A.C.S.; mem. Am., Tex. (v.p. 1968) med. assns., Southwestern Surg. Congress (founding mem.), Seventh Dist. Med. Soc. (councilor 1959-68). Home: 717 Huff St Taylor TX 76574 Office: 720 W 6th St Taylor TX 76574

JOHNS, RICHARD ALTON, JR., pub. co. exec.; b. Tyler, Tex., July 17, 1929; s. Richard Alton and Annie Sarah (Hill) J.; A.A., Tyler Jr. Coll., 1948; B.A., North Tex. State U., 1950; m. Joan Turner, Nov. 8, 1958; children—Richard Andrew, Janis. Fashion artist Kline's Dept. Store, Tyler, 1950; engring. illustrations editor Gen. Dynamics Corp., Fort Worth, 1951-61; artist, writer, editor Tyler Star Pub. Co., 1961—. Fashion art advt. cons., stores, Tyler. Served with F.A., AUS, 1950-51. Presbyn. Author: Thirteenth Apostle, 1966; Garden of the Okapi, 1968; Return to Heroism, 1969; (play) The Legacy, prod. on TV, 1965. Home: 912 W Camellia St Tyler TX 75701 Office: PO Box 1073 Tyler TX 75701

JOHNS, STANLEY ARMITAGE, aerospace systems engr.; b. Youngstown, O., Aug. 15, 1930; s. Russell Armitage and Gertrude (Stanley) J.; B.Aero. Engring., Ohio State U., 1954; m. Patricia C. Crow, May 6, 1961; children—Jeannette, Keating, Juliette. Aero. engr. Army Ballistic Missile Agy., Huntsville, Ala., 1956-60; aero. engr. Marshall Space Flight Center, Huntsville, 1960—, now systems engr. Spacelab Program Office. Served with AUS, 1954-56. Registered profl. engr., Ala. Mem. Human Factors Soc. (pres. chpt.). Home: 5703 Tannahill Circle Huntsville AL 35802 Office Marshall Space Flight Center AL 35812

JOHNSON, ALCEE LABRANCHE, educator; b. Fernwood, Miss., July 22, 1905; s. Jonas Edward and Bertha (LaBranche) J.; student Alcorn Coll., 1925; A.B., Fisk U., 1927; M.A., Columbia, 1956; postgrad. U. So. Cal., 1962; D. Humanities (hon.), Miss. Bapt. Sem., 1972; m. Thelma M. Wethers, Dec. 25, 1931; children—Joyce (Mrs. James L. Bolden), Al Wethers. Instr. Prentiss (Miss.) Inst. Jr. Coll., 1927-30, dir. instrn., 1931-36, 37-71, pres., 1971—; Miss. state supr. Survey Vocational Edn. and Guidance, Office Edn., Dept. Interior, Washington, 1936-37; chmn. bd. dirs. State Mut. Fed. Savs. & Loan Assn.; inst. rep. Heifer Project, Inc. Mem. Miss. Regional Med. Program, Merit Commn. Miss. Econ. Council, Phelps-Stokes Fund Conf. Edn. Leaders. Former chmn. Western div. Boy Scouts Am., com. mem. JDC Mut. Fed. Credit Union, 1960—; del. White House Conf. on Aging, 1971; mem. Miss. Probation and Parole Bd., 1972—. Mem. Voters League, 1964—, now pres. elect. Bd. dirs. So. Miss. Econ. Devel. Dist. So. Interracial Commn. grantee, 1930; recipient Silver Beaver award Boy Scouts Am., 1960. Mem. Am., Miss. (past pres.), 6th Dist. (past pres.) tchrs. assns., N.E.A. (life), N.A.A.C.P. (local coordinator), Jefferson Davis County, Miss. chambers commerce, Alpha Phi Alpha, Phi Delta Kappa. Mem. Ch. of Christ (trustee). Mason (33 deg.). Home: PO Box 112 Prentiss MS 39474 Office: Drawer C Prentiss MS 39474

JOHNSON, ALFRED MASSEY FISHER, hydrologist, engr.; b. Belding, Mich., Jan. 7, 1912; s. Charles and Marie (Belliss) J.; B.C. in Civil Engring., Mich. State U., 1935; m. Ruth Marian Arnold, June 8, 1938; children—Charles Ernest, William Alfred. Sr. engring. aide TVA, Chattanooga, 1935-36; jr. engr. Miss. River Commn., Vicksburg, 1937-41; hydraulic engr. U.S. Geol. Survey, Chattanooga, 1948-70, hydrologist, Atlanta, 1970—. Served to lt. col. Arty., AUS, 1941-47. Decorated Bronze Star medal. Recipient Silver Beaver award Boy Scouts Am., 1964. Registered profl. engr., Tenn. Mem. Am. Soc. C.E. (v.p. 1967-68), Nat. Soc. Profl. Engrs. (v.p. 1967-68), Nat. Ry. Hist. Soc., Tenn. Valley R.R. Mus. Author: (with W.J. Randolph) Floods on Chattanooga Creek, 1962; (with George Wood) Characteristics of Tennessee Streams, 1962; (with John Wilson) Water Use in Tennessee, 1968-70; (with R. Fred Carter) Water Use in Georgia, 1974. Home: 710 Peachtree St NE Apt 1208 Atlanta GA 30308 Office: 6481 Peachtree Industrial Blvd Suite B Doraville GA 30340

JOHNSON, ANDREW EMERSON, III, sch. adminstr.; b. Monterey, Va., July 26, 1931; s. Andrew Emerson and Virginia (Miller) J.; B.S., Hampden-Sydney Coll., 1952, Litt.D., 1969; M.Ed., U. N.C. at Chapel Hill, 1959; Nat. Def. Edn. Act fellow Williams Coll., 1967; m. Rophelia Simpson, Aug. 6, 1955; children—Rebecca, Andrew Emerson IV. Instr. math. Norfolk (Va.) Acad., 1952-56, head math. dept., instr. Bible, 1957-59, asst. headmaster, 1959-61; headmaster North Cross Sch., Roanoke, Va., 1961-69; headmaster Charlotte (N.C.) Country Day Sch., 1969-73; pres. Westminster Sch., Atlanta, 1973—. Chmn. edn. govt. div. United Fund, 1967; mem. adv. com. Roanoke City Chaplain, 1967-69. Bd. dirs. Community Concert Series, Charlotte, 1971—; trustee Roanoke Fine Arts Center, 1967-69. Mem. Nat. Assn. Prin. Schs. for Girls, Country Day Sch. Headmasters Assn., Omicron Delta Kappa. Presbyn. Mason, Rotarian. Clubs: Charlotte City, Olde Providence Racquet and Swim. Address 1424 W Paces Ferry Rd NW Atlanta GA 30327

JOHNSON, ANDREW JAY, coll. adminstr.; b. Beaumont, Tex., Sept. 27, 1933; s. Andrew Jay and Lois C. (Harper) J.; B.A., U. Tex., 1954; M.A., U. Ind., 1955, Ph.D., 1964; M.A. in L.S., U. Chgo., 1966; m. Betty Holmes, Jan. 30, 1955; children—Laura Kathleen, Letitia. Instr. Schreiner Inst., Kerrville, Tex., 1955-56, admissions counselor, 1956-57; mem. faculty Lamar U., Beaumont, 1958—, prof. history, 1968—, dir. library services, 1967-69, v.p. acad. affairs, 1969-73, v.p. adminstrn., 1973—. Lectr. Grad. Sch. Library Sci., U. Tex. at Austin, 1967-68; cons. S.W. Ednl. Devel. Lab., Dallas, 1966. Mem. Beaumont Library Commn., 1966-69; pres. Am. Heart Assn., Beaumont, 1971-72; mem. budget com. United Appeals, 1970-73. Trustee All Saints Episcopal Sch., 1966—. So. Fellowships Found. fellow, 1956, 60-61. Mem. S.E. Tex. Social Studies Confs. (dir. 1963-65), Beta Phi Mu, Phi Alpha Theta. Episcopalian. Rotarian. Home: 2093 Central Dr Beaumont TX 77706

JOHNSON, ARTHUR ALBIN, educator; b. Chgo., Feb. 24, 1925; s. Claus Martin and Esther (Youngberg) J.; B.A., U. Minn., 1950; M.S., U. Ill. at Urbana, 1952, Ph.D., 1955; m. Martha Kathryn Himmel, Sept. 1, 1951; children—David, Kathryn, Kristen, Paul, Julie. Mem. faculty Hendrix Coll., Conway, Ark., 1955—, asso. prof. natural sci., 1957-59, prof. dept. biology, 1959—; vis. lectr. U. Ill. at Urbana, summers 1964, 65. Served with inf. AUS, 1943-46. Fellow A.A.A.S.; mem. Am. Soc. Parasitologists, Nat. Audubon Soc., Am. Micros. Soc., Am. Wildlife Fedn., Sigma Xi. Contbr. profl. jours. Home: 53 Meadowbrook Dr Conway AR 72032

JOHNSON, BEN BUTLER, physician; b. Bklyn., May 23, 1920; s. Louis Collins and Jeanne Farrell (Payne) J.; grad. Choate Sch., 1937; A.B., Harvard, 1942, M.D., 1944; m. Barbara Ann Maltby, Dec. 22, 1962; children—Louis Collins III, Charles Martin, Michael David, Mary Jeanne, Margaret Ann. Intern N.Y. Hosp., 1944-45; resident Bellevue Hosp., N.Y.C., 1947-49; research fellow medicine Bassett Hosp. and Stanford, 1949-53; instr., asst. prof. medicine Stanford, 1955-59; practice medicine specializing in internal medicine and nephrology, Jackson, Miss., 1959—; mem. staff Univ. Hosp.; chief renal and electrolyte div. dept. medicine U. Miss. Med. Center, 1959—; asst. prof. U. Miss., 1959-62. asso. prof. medicine, 1962—; dir. Diabetes Clinic, Stanford Hosps., 1956-59. Mem. Miss. Nutrition Council, 1961—, chmn., 1962-64. Bd. dirs. Kidney Found. of Miss., 1964-71, sec.-treas., 1965-71, chmn. med. adv. bd., 1971-73; mem. nat. med. adv. council Nat. Kidney Found., 1970—, sec., 1971-73. Served to lt. (j.g.) M.C., USNR, 1945-46; served to lt. USNR, 1953-55. Diplomate Am. Bd. Internal Medicine, Nat. Bd. Med. Examiners. Fellow A.C.P.; mem. Am., Internat. socs. nephrology, Endocrine Soc., Am. Diabetes Assn., Am. Soc. Internal Medicine, Am. Fedn. for Clin. Research, Western Soc. for Clin. Research, Am., Miss. heart assns., Soc. Mayflower Descs. (surgeon-gen. Miss. soc. 1971—), Am. Assn. U. Profs. (pres. Miss. conf. 1968-69), Sigma Xi. Contbr. articles to profl. jours. Home: 1540 Kimwood Circle Jackson MS 39211 Office: Univ of Miss Medical Center 2500 N State St Jackson MS 39216

JOHNSON, BENJAMIN FRANKLIN, mining co. exec.; b. Virgie, Ky., June 21, 1931; s. Fon Mayo and Nora (Newsom) J.; B.S., Bowling Green Coll. at Commerce, 1953; m. Betty G. Maynard, July 24, 1950; children—Charles Franklin, Mark Douglas, Paul Sheldon. Jr. accountant Albert B. Maloney & Co., C.P.A.'s, Hopkinville, Ky., 1953-55; pres. Ideal Elkhorn Coal Co., Inc., Pikeville, Ky., 1964-71; treas. Famous Elkhorn Coal Sale, Inc., Pikeville, 1955-69; pres. Bull Creek Mining Corp., Hazard, Ky., 1969-73; v.p. Gaynell Coal Co., Inc., Hazard, Ky., 1973—; pres. Betty Jean Coal Co., Inc., Hazard, 1974—. C.P.A., Tenn. Address: PO Box 125 Jeff KY 41751

JOHNSON, BILLY JOE, environmental affairs exec.; b. Wetumka, Okla., Sept. 22, 1929; s. Joe Willie and Lutie Elizabeth (Roberts) J.; B.S., Okla. A. and M. Coll., 1956; M.E., Okla. U., 1966; C.E., U. Houston, 1971; m. Mona Jean Hays, Apr. 1, 1951; children—Vicki Linn, Joe Kent. Asphalt chemist Kan. State Hwy. Commn., El Dorado, 1953-54; chemist Halliburton Co., 1956-60, sr. chemist, 1960-66, div. chemist, service sales engr., 1966-72, coordinator environmental services, 1968-72, dir. environmental affairs, 1972—; cons. engr. Served with USN, 1948-52; PTO. Registered profl. engr., Okla., Ark., La., Tex. Mem. Tex. Safety Assn., Nat. Safety Council, S.E. Ia. Safety Assn., Soc. Petroleum Engrs. of Am. Inst. Mining Engrs., Petroleum Equipment Suppliers Assn., Nat. Ocean Industries Assn., Tex. Mfg. Assn., Rubber Mfg. Assn. Patentee in field. Home: 5418 Braeburn Dr Bellaire TX 77401 Office: PO Box 27526 Houston TX 77027

JOHNSON, BRUCE KING, physician, educator; b. Harriman, Tenn., Oct. 24, 1918; s. Samuel King and Laura Monro (Jones) J.; B.S., Birmingham-So. Coll., 1940; M.D., U. Tenn., 1944; m. Leila Newman Wright, Apr. 4, 1942 (dec. Nov. 1957); children—Bruce King, Samuel Paul, Thomas Sterling, Leila Anne; m. 2d, Iris Dudley Thomas, Mar. 14, 1959. Intern Hillman Hosp. and Norwood Hosp., Birmingham, Ala., 1944-45; resident N.C. Bapt. Hosp.-Bowman Gray Med. Sch., Winston-Salem, 1949-51; sr. resident U. Ala. Hosps., Birmingham, 1951; gen. practice medicine, Flat Creek, Ala., 1945-49, specializing in internal medicine, Birmingham, 1952—; med. dir. Birmingham Med. Group Clinic, 1959-68; mem. staff, bd. dirs. Simon-Williamson Clinic and Norwood Properties, Inc.; mem. active staff U. Ala. Hosps.; mem. active and teaching staff Bapt. Med. Center, Princeton; mem. courtesy staff Bapt. Med. Center, Montclair, St. Vincents Hosp., South Highlands Infirmary; clin. instr. U. Ala., 1952-63, clin. asst. prof. dept. internal medicine, 1963—. Bd. dirs. Vis. Nurse Assn., 1962-69, chmn. med. adv. bd., 1970—. Fellow A.C.P.; mem. Birmingham Soc. Internists, Birmingham Acad. Medicine, Am., Ala. socs. internal medicine, A.M.A., Am. Heart Assn., So., Ala., Jefferson County med. assns., Lambda Chi Alpha, Omicron Delta Kappa (hon.), Alpha Kappa Kappa, Alpha Omega Alpha. Methodist (mem. adminstrv. bd.). Home: 3016 Warrington Rd Birmingham AL 35223 Office: 801 Princeton Av SW Birmingham AL 35211

JOHNSON, BUDDY (BOB) CHARLES, TV newscaster; b. Overton, Tex., Apr. 21, 1933; s. Harry J. and Marie (Westfall) J.; student Lamar State Coll., 1951-52; m. Audrey Barras, Nov. 7, 1953; children—Charles L., Matthew H., Leah M., Lori Ann, Marcus A. Announcer, KBMT-TV, Beaumont, Tex., 1956-57, KTBC-TV, Austin, 1957, KPAC-TV, Port Arthur, Tex., 1957-61; news dir. KRGV-TV, Weslaco, Tex., 1961-62, KATC-TV, Lafayette, La., 1962-64; newscaster, reporter WBRZ-TV, Baton Rouge, La., 1964—. Mem. Press Club Baton Rouge. Home: 9382 El Cajon St Baton Rouge LA 70815 Office: 1650 Highland Rd Baton Rouge LA 70821

JOHNSON, CAROLYN BAKER (MRS. WILLIAM ROY JOHNSON), civic worker; b. Frankfort, Ind.; d. Earl Quincy and Maud (Johnson) Baker; student pub. schs., Detroit; m. William Roy Johnson, May 19, 1930; children—Jacqueline (Mrs. Edward James Twiford), Doris Johnson. Sec., Pere Marquette R.R., Detroit, 1922-24; sec. U.S. Customs, Fort St., Detroit, 1925-30. Pan Am. Liaison Com. Womens Orgns., Washington, 1958—, 3d v.p., 1966-68, 68-70, rec. sec. 1960-66; rec. sec. Salvation Army Aux., Washington, 1968-69; mem. Woman's Guild Swartzell Meth. Home for Children, pres., 1956-60. Bd. dirs. Barkers Home, Falls Church, Va., 1966-68. Mem. Womans Soc. Christian Service (life). Methodist. Clubs: Capital Speakers (governing bd. 1969-70), Metropolitan Womens Bridge (pres. 1968-70). Home: 4234 42d St NW Washington DC 20016

JOHNSON, CECIL C., ins. exec.; b. Mexico, Mo., Oct. 13, 1903; B.S. in Elec. Engring., U. Mo., 1928; M.B.A., U. Denver, 1941; grad. Advanced Mgmt. Program, Harvard, 1956; m. Ola B. Bently, June 15,

1927; 1 son, C. Bryce. Chmn. finance com., dir. Phila. Life Ins. Co., 1968—; dir. Tenn. Life Ins. Co., Houston Nat. Bank. Mem. Tau Beta Pi, Eta Kappa Nu. Presbyn. Clubs: Wall Street (N.Y.C.); River Oaks Country, Ramada, Houston. Home: 3726 Inwood Dr Houston TX 77019 Office: PO Box 2511 Houston TX 77001

JOHNSON, CHARLES A., JR., assn. exec.; b. Amory, Miss., Nov. 17, 1911; B.S., Miss. State U., 1932, M.S., 1945. Tchr. sci. Amory High Sch., 1937-41, prin., 1941-45; supt. Canton Pub. Schs., 1945-52, Starkville Pub. Schs., 1952-65; exec. sec., editor jour. Miss. Edn. Assn., 1965—, v.p., 1964. Mem. N.E.A., Am. Assn. Sch. Adminstrs., Phi Delta Kappa. Office: Miss Edn Assn 219 N President St Box 22529 Jackson MS 39205*

JOHNSON, CHARLES OWEN, lawyer; b. Monroe, La., Aug. 18, 1926; s. Clifford U. and Laura (Owen) J.; B.A., Tulane U., 1946, J.D., 1969; LL.B., Harvard, 1948; LL.M., Columbia, 1955. Admitted to La. bar, 1949, practiced in Monroe, 1949-50; mem. law editorial staff West Pub. Co., St. Paul, 1953; atty. Office of Chief Counsel, Internal Revenue Service, Washington, 1955—, chief Ct. Appeals br. Tax Ct. Div., 1968—. Served with AUS, 1950-52. Mem. Fed., La. bar assns., Nat. Lawyers Club, Soc. Colonial Wars (dep. sec. D.C. chpt.), S.A.R. (nat. trustee, pres. D.C. soc.), Soc. War of 1812 (past pres. D.C. soc.), S.C.V., Sons Union Vets., S.R., St. Andrew's Soc. Washington, Royal Soc. St. George, Sons and Daus. of Pilgrims, Huguenot Soc. S.C., Soc. Descs. Jersey Settlers, La. Colonials, Jamestowne Soc., Soc. Descs. Old Plymouth Colony, Order Ams. of Armorial Ancestry, Soc. Descs. Colonial Clergy, Hereditary Order Descs. Colonial Govs. (2d dep. gov. gen.), Order Founders and Patriots of Am. (past gov.), Order First Families Miss. 1699-1817 (gov. gen. 1967-69), Soc. Cin., Nat., Va. geneal. socs., Miss., Va. hist. socs., Phi Beta Kappa. Mason (Shriner, K.T., 32 deg.); mem. Order Eastern Star. Clubs: Pendennis of New Orleans (charter mem.); Arts of Washington. Author: The Geneology of Several Allied Families, 1961. Home: 2111 Jefferson Davis Hwy Apt 109 Arlington VA 22202 Office: Office of Chief Counsel Internal Revenue Service Washington DC 20224

JOHNSON, CHARLTON GRAHAM, agrl. engr.; b. Columbus, Ga., Mar. 21, 1920; s. Charlton Graham and Mattie Elba (Waters) J.; student Ga. Sch. Tech., 1938-39, 46-47, U. Ala., 1965-68; m. Mary Frances Saffold, Jan. 7, 1939; children—Charlton Graham, John Lamar, Mary Martha, Thomas Carson. Sales engr. Centennial Cotton Gin Co., Columbus, Ga., 1948-57; chief engr., 1957-60; engr., Moss Gordin Lint Cleaner Co., Memphis, 1960-61; chief engr. Gordin Unit System, Amite, La., 1961-63, Moss-Gordin Co., Amite, La., 1963-64; design engr. Continental-Moss-Gordin, Prattville, Ala., 1964-68; asst. supt. refinery Riverside Oil Mill, Marks, Miss., 1968-69; chief engr. Pacific Bldgs., Inc., Marks, Miss., 1969—. Chmn. Weracoba council Cub Scouts Am., 1960. Commr. elections, Quitman County, Miss. Registered profl. engr., Ala., Miss. Served with USNR, 1944-45. Mem. Nat. Soc. Profl. Engrs., Am. Soc. Agrl. Engrs., Miss. Engring. Soc. Republican. Home: 251 Lamar St Marks MS 38646 Office: Pacific Bldgs Inc Covington Rd Marks MS 38646

JOHNSON, CLEMENT OLE, profl. engr.; b. Savannah, Ga., Aug. 21, 1901; s. Peter Ole and Minnie (Clement) J.; B.S., Ga. Inst. Tech., 1926; m. Mary Allender, July 30, 1955. Coop. student Central of Ga. Ry. Co., Savannah, 1922-26, chemist, chief chemist, 1926-41, asst. mech. engr., 1946; research and test engr. Seaboard Airline R.R., Jacksonville, Fla., 1946-59; mgr. chem. dept., field engr. R. W. Hunt Co., Chgo., 1959-67; profl. engr. C.O. Johnson, Savannah, 1967—. Served to maj. AUS, 1941-44; maj. Res. ret. Mem. Am. Soc. Testing and Materials, Am. Soc. M.E., Nat. Assn. Ry. Engrs. of Tests, Am. Ry. Engring. Assn. Episcopalian. Elk. Home: 10 E Jones St Savannah GA 31401 Office: 10 E Jones St Savannah GA 31401.

JOHNSON, CLIFFORD LEE, JR., hosp. adminstr.; b. Hattiesburg, Miss., May 15, 1928; s. Clifford Lee and Velma (Grimsley) J.; B.S. in Bus. Adminstrn., U. So. Miss., 1952; m. Margaret Moseley, Mar. 8, 1952; children—Clifford Lee III, Beverley Victoria, Margaret Amelia, Kendall Moseley. Asst. adminstr. Forrest County Gen. Hosp., Hattiesburg, 1954-58; adminstr. Jefferson Davis County Hosp., Prentiss, Miss., 1958-67; exec. dir. Grenada County (Miss.) Hosp., Grenada, 1967—. Mem. Miss. Medicaid Tech. Adv. Com., 1970—, Health Planning Adv. Council div. Miss. Comprehensive Health Planning, 1973—; mem. liaison com. Miss. State Bd. Health. Pres. Grenada County chpt. Am. Cancer Soc., 1972-73, dir., 1973-74; pres. Dixie Youth Baseball, Prentiss, 1965-67; chmn. United Givers Fund; charter mem., past pres. Grenada Fine Arts Playhouse. Bd. dirs. Miss. div. Am. Cancer Soc. Served with USMCR, 1946-48, with AUS, 1952-53. Mem. Am. Coll. Hosp. Adminstrs. (award of merit 1969), Am., Miss. (bd. govs. 1966-69) hosp. assns., Southeastern Hosp. Conf., Delta Hosp. Council (pres. 1969), U. So. Miss. Alumni Assn. (Distinguished Service award 1966, chpt. pres. 1969-70, exec. com. 1969—), Grenada County, Jefferson-Davis County (Man of Year 1967, pres. 1966, chmn., mem. doctor's com.) chambers commerce, Kappa Alpha. Democrat. Presbyn. (deacon). Rotarian (editor Rotary Radiation, pres. 1973-74). Club: Grenada Country, Home: 133 Union St Grenada MS 38901 Office: 960 Avent Dr Grenada MS 38901

JOHNSON, CLIFTON HERMAN, historian-archivist; b. Griffin, Ga., Sept. 13, 1921; s. John and Pearl (Parrish) J.; student U. Conn., 1943-44; B.A., U. N.C., 1948, Ph.D. 1959; M.A. U. Chgo., 1949; postgrad. U. Wis., 1951; m. Rosemary Brunst, Aug. 2, 1960; children—Charles, Robert, Virginia. Tutor, LeMoyne Coll., Memphis, 1950-53, asst. prof., 1953-56, prof., 1960-61, 63-66; asst. prof. East Carolina Coll., 1958-59; asst. librarian and archivist Fisk U., 1961-63; dir., Amistad Research Center, New Orleans, 1966—. Dir., Nat. Com. Against Discrimination in Housing, 1967—. Served with AUS, 1940-45. Mem. So. Hist. Assn., Soc. Am. Archivists, Assn. for Study Negro Life and History, Orgn. Am. Historians, Nat. Assn. Human Rights Workers, Nat. Cath. Conf. for Inter-racial Justice. Author: (with Carroll Barber) The American Negro: A Selected and Annotated Bibliography for High Schools and Junior Colleges, 1968. Editor: God Struck Me Dead: Religious Conversions and Experiences and Autobiographies of Ex-Slaves, 1969. Home: 6910 Manchester St New Orleans LA 70126 Office: Dillard New Orleans LA 70122

JOHNSON, CLINTON CHARLES, dentist; b. Hector, Minn., Aug. 15, 1927; s. Oscar Theodore and Mayme (Burris) J.; B.A. in Chemistry, Macalester Coll., 1953; B.S. in Dentistry, U. Minn., 1957, D.D.S., 1957, M.S. in Dentistry, 1965; m. Irene Julia Gross, July 19, 1952; children—Deborah, Kent, Constance, Cynthia, Mark. Staff dentist VA Hosp., Mpls., 1960-65; oral pathologist Armed Forces Inst. Pathology, Washington, 1965-67; chief dental service VA Hosp., Buffalo, 1967-72, VA Hosp., Dallas, 1972—. Instr., U. Minn. at Mpls., 1962-65; asso. prof. State U. N.Y. at Buffalo, 1967-72, Coll. Dentistry, Baylor U., Dallas, 1972—, S.W. Med. Sch., Dallas, 1972—. Served with AUS and USAF, 1946-47, 50-51, 58-60. Diplomate Am. Bd. Oral Pathology. Fellow Am. Coll. Dentists, Am. Acad. Oral Pathology; mem. Am., Tex. dental assns., Dallas County Dental Soc. Contbr. profl. jours. Home: 1910 Delta Dr Arlington TX 76012 Office: VA Hosp 4500 S Lancaster Rd Dallas TX 75216

JOHNSON, CONE, physician, educator; b. Eastland, Tex., Nov. 20, 1926; s. Earle Clay and Eloise (Trigg) J.; B.S., North Tex. State U., 1949; M.D., U. Tex., Galveston, 1954; m. Patricia Zeller, Oct. 20, 1956; children—Deborah Lynn, Cynthia Kay, Barbara Anne. Intern John Sealy Hosp., Galveston, 1954-55; resident medicine U. Tex. Med. Br. Hosps., 1955-58; commd. 1st lt. M.C., U.S. Air Force, 1956, advanced through grades to maj., 1962; ret., 1963; mem. sr. staff Scott-White Clinic, 1963-68; practice medicine specializing in respiratory therapy and environmental diseases, Abilene, Tex., 1968-69, 70; asso. Cardiopulmonary Inst., Meth. Hosp., Dallas, 1969-70; clin. asst. prof. medicine U. Tex. Southwestern Med. Sch., Dallas, 1969—; clin. asso. prof. medicine Tex. Tech U. Sch. Medicine, 1974—; med. dir. respiratory therapy service and pulmonary physiology labs. West Tex. Med. Center Hosp., Abilene, 1970—, Abilene State Sch., Tex. Dept. Mental Health and Retardation, 1971-73, Simmons Meml. Hosp., Sweetwater, Tex., 1970—, Cox Meml. Hosp., Abilene, 1970—, Med. Center Meml. Hosp., Big Spring, Tex., 1973—; cons. in pulmonary physiology VA Hosp., Big Spring, 1968—. Dir. Respiratory Therapy Assos., Abilene. Bd. dirs. West Tex. Med. Center Research Found., 1968. Served with USNR, 1943-46. Diplomate Am. Bd. Internal Medicine with subsplty. pulmonary diseases. Fellow A.C.P., Am. Coll. Chest Physicians (pres. Tex. chpt.); mem. A.A.A.S., Research Engring Soc. Am., Am. Coll. Sports Medicine, A.M.A., Am. Fedn. Clin. Research, Am. Thoracic Soc., Am. Heart Assn. (dir.), Aero Medics of Tex., Central Tex. Research Soc., N.Y. Acad. Scis., Mu Delta (award for outstanding intern 1955). Contbr. articles to profl. jours. Home: 770 Sayles Dr Abilene TX 79605 Office: 1026 N 21st St Abilene TX 79601

JOHNSON, DAVE TOBIN, ins. co. exec.; b. Pensacola, Fla., May 2, 1909; s. Joseph I. and Annie (Tobin) J.; grad. parochial schs.; m. Mary Catherine Comforter, Dec. 16, 1937; children—Mary Catherine (Mrs. James R. Thompson), Patricia Ann (Mrs. Gregory Deal), David Tobin Jr. With Fisher-Brown, Inc., Pensacola, 1923—, asst. sec., 1932-39, v.p., 1939-50, exec. v.p., 1950-55, pres., 1955—; pres. Friendly Finance Co.; dir. Citizens & Peoples Nat. Bank. Chmn. U. West Fla. Found., Inc.; mem. adv. bd. Bapt. Hosp. Served with USMCR, 1943-45. Named Boss of Year, Bus. Man of Year, 1963; recipient Kiwanis Cup for Outstanding Civic Achievement, 1963. Mem. Pensacola Fire and Casualty Agts. (past pres.), Nat. (past chmn. nat. advt. com., fidelity, surety com., v.p., mem. exec. com., past pres.), Fla. (past pres.) assns. ins. agts. Democrat. Roman Catholic. Rotarian, Elk, K.C. (4 deg.). Clubs: Pensacola Country, Senio Hills Country, Yacht. Home: 1517 N 19th Av Pensacola FL 32503 Office: Box 711 Pensacola FL 32593

JOHNSON, DAVID FREEMAN, biochemist; b. Nashville, Jan. 28, 1925; s. David Freeman and Coma Mae (Davidson) J.; B.S., Allegheny Coll., 1947, D. Sc., 1972; M.S., Howard U., 1949; Ph.D., Georgetown U., 1957; m. Gloria D. Tapscott, Oct. 24, 1947; children—Toni Y., David G. Instr. Howard U., Washington, 1949-50; research chemist Freedmens Hosp., Washington, 1950-51; research biochemist NIH, Bethesda, Md., 1952—, instr. Grad. Sch., 1960—. Mem. Am. Governing Bd. Univs. and Colls., 1972—. Trustee Prince George's Community Coll., Largo, Md., 1969—, Allegheny Coll., Meadville, Pa. Fellow Am. Soc. Exptl. Biology; mem. Am. Chem. Soc., A.A.A.S., Endocrine Soc., Kappa Alpha Psi. Contbr. to profl. jours. Home: 1011 Carrington Av Washington DC 20027 Office: National Institute Health Bethesda MD 20014

JOHNSON, DAVID L(IVINGSTONE), engring. ednl. adminstr.; b. Gustavus, O., Feb. 17, 1915; s. David Charles and Margaret (Delaney) J.; A.B., Berea Coll., 1936; M.A., State U. Ia., 1938, B.S. in Elec. Engring., 1942; M.S., Okla. State U., 1950, Ph.D., 1957; m. Eugenia Gibson McQuarie, Jan. 23, 1954. Instr. U.S. Naval Tng. Sch., Okla. State U., 1942-44; field engr. Airborne Coordinating Group, 1944-45; instr. Spartan Sch. Aeros., Tulsa, 1945-48; asst. prof. Okla. State U., 1948-55; prof., head dept. elec. engring. La. Tech U., Ruston, 1955—. Cons. automatic controls. Registered profl. engr., La., Okla. Mem. A.A.A.S., I.E.E.E., Am. Soc. Engring. Edn., Assn. Computing Machinery, Nat. Soc. Profl. Engrs., Soc. Indsl. and Applied Math., Am. Assn. U. Profs., Am. Soc. Information Sci., Instrument Soc. Am., Sigma Xi, Eta Kappa Nu, Phi Kappa Phi, Pi Mu Epsilon, Sigma Tau, Tau Beta Pi. Home: 1610 Valley St Ruston LA 71270

JOHNSON, DELWIN PHELPS, tobacco co. exec.; b. Rocky Mount, N.C., Mar. 24, 1926; s. Clyde McLaurin and Beulah Lee (Rooks) J.; B.S., N.C. State U., 1948; m. Yvonne Montague Finch, Nov. 27, 1954; children—Diana Lynn, Kathy Louise. Insecticide chemist N.C. Dept. Agr., 1948-57; research chemist Union Carbide Chems. Co., 1957-64; group leader R.J. Reynolds Tobacco Co., Winston-Salem, N.C., 1964-70, sect. head, 1970—. Mem. Am. Chem. Soc., Sigma Xi. Democrat. Baptist. Moose. Contbr. articles to profl. jours. Home: 3021 St Claire Rd Winston-Salem NC 27106 Office: RJ Reynolds Tobacco Co 401 N Main St Winston-Salem NC 27102

JOHNSON, DEWEY E(DWARD), dentist; b. Charleston, S.C., Mar. 19, 1935; s. Dewey Edward and Mabel (Momeier) J.; A.B. in Geology, U. N.C., 1957, D.D.S., 1961. Practice dentistry, Charleston, S.C., 1964—, asso. to Stanley H. Karesh, D.D.S., 1970—. Served to lt. USNR, 1961-63. Mem. Royal Soc. Health, Charleston C. of C. (mem. cruise ship com. 1969), Am. Dental Assn., Charleston Dental Soc., Hibernian Soc., Charleston Museum, Internat. Platform Assn., Phi Kappa Sigma, Sigma Gamma Epsilon, Psi Omega. Conglist. Optimist. Home: 142 S Battery Charleston SC 29401 Office: 112 1/2 Ashley Av Charleston SC 29402

JOHNSON, DEWEY MACON, judge; b. Fla., Apr. 6, 1907; s. Alexander Love and Annie Lou (Bassett) J.; LL.B., U. Fla., 1930; m. Margie Kimbrough, May 5, 1945; 1 dau., Sandra (Mrs. Allen Campbell). Admitted to Fla. bar; practiced law, 1930-65; judge 1st Dist. Ct. of Appeal, Quincy, Fla., now Tallahassee. Past mem. Fla. Ho. of Reps., Fla. Senate. Office: First Appellate Dist Ct Tallahassee FL 32351

JOHNSON, DICK LANSDEN, lawyer; b. Nashville, Sept. 17, 1922; s. Hollis and Florence (Lansden) J.; student Murray State Coll., 1940-41; B.S. cum laude, Presbyn. Coll., 1943; J.D., Northwestern U., 1948; m. Nancy Alcott Kaiser, Sept. 7, 1946; children—Sandra (Mrs. Frank M. Eggers), Dick L. Jr., Fredric K. Admitted to Tenn. bar, 1948, Ill. bar, 1949; asst. U.S. atty., Nashville, 1949-52, U.S. atty., 1952-53; with firm Osborn, Johnson & Davies, Nashville, 1953-54, Shull & Johnson, 1954-55; individual practice, Elizabethtown, Tenn., 1955-63; partner firm Simmonds, Herndon, Johnson, Coleman, Johnson City, Tenn., 1963—. Served with USNR, 1943-46; PTO. Mem. Washington County, Tenn., Am. bar assns. Presbyn. (elder deacon). Kiwanian, Elk, Mason (32 deg.). Home: 910 Woodland Ave Johnson City TN 37601 Office: 409 E Watauga St Johnson City TN 37601

JOHNSON, DONALD ROSS, govt. ofcl.; b. Chgo., Feb. 9, 1920; s. George William and Grace (Roos) F.; B.Sc., U. Ill., 1943; M.Sc., U. Minn., 1951; m. Beryl Lucille Edman, June 15, 1947; children—Gary Ross, Lynn Kay, Lee Ross, Laura Kay. Research asst. entomology U. Minn., St. Paul, 1946-48; asst. entomologist State of Minn., St. Paul, 1948-51; dep. chief malaria eradication program AID, Washington, 1957-64; med. entomologist USPHS, Djakarta, Indonesia, 1951-53, office of internat. health, Washington, 1953-57, chief spl. services Aedes aegypti eradication program, Atlanta, 1964-66; sanitarian dir. malaria program Center For Disease Control, USPHS, Atlanta, 1966-73; malaria cons. AID, 1974—. Served to lt. (j.g.) USNR, 1943-46. Mem. A.A.A.S., Am. Mosquito Control Assn. (chmn. Worldwide com.), Entomol. Soc. Am. (chmn. sect. 1958), Indian Soc. Malaria and Other Communicable Diseases. Lutheran. Contbr. articles to publs. Home: 1362 N Decatur Rd NE Atlanta GA 30306 Office: 1600 Clifton Rd Atlanta GA 30333

JOHNSON, EDD WILSON, hosp. adminstr.; b. New Middleton, Tenn., Sept. 23, 1911; s. James Frank and Lydia (Clark) J.; student Air U., 1946, LaSalle Law Sch., 1951; m. Ruby West, July 25, 1941; children—James David, Martha (Mrs. Martha Stephens), John Daniel. Commd. 2d lt., U.S. Air Force, 1930, advanced through grades to lt. col., 1959; personnel officer, 1945-50, air insp. mgmt. analysis, 1952-56; ret., 1959; adminstr. Miller County Hosp., Calquitt, Ga., 1967-69; adminstr. Worth County Hosp., Sylvester, Ga., 1969-73, Mitchell County Hosp., Camilla, Ga., 1973—. Chmn. bd. U.S. Civil Service Examiners in Northeast Air Procurement Dist., Boston, 1951. Mem. Am. Legion. V.F.W. Lion, Kiwanian. Home: Route 1 Box 168 Colquitt GA 31737

JOHNSON, EDNA FAY, (MRS. LANDON CARTER JOHNSON, JR.), data processor; b. Tennyson, Tex., Aug. 23, 1923; d. Eddie H. and Mary Elizabeth (Hodges) Hogan; student San Angelo Coll., 1940-41; B.A., Howard Payne Coll., 1944; M.A., U. Tex., 1948; m. Landon Carter Johnson, Jr., Aug. 23, 1945; children—Robert Eugene, William Luke, John Michael. Principal Tennyson Pub. Schs., 1942-43; instr. in math. Ranger (Tex.) Jr. Coll., 1943-44; tchr. math. Brownwood (Tex.) High Sch., 1944-45; asst. prof. math. Howard Payne Coll., Brownwood, 1945-54; data processing analyst Continental Oil Co., Ponca City, Okla., 1955-63, sr. analyst operations research, 1965—; instr. data processing No. Okla. Coll., Tonkawa, 1963-65. Mem. SHARE, Inc. (math. programming mixed integer com. 1969—). Pres. Mother's Club Ponco City Future Farmers of Am., 1968-69. Mem. Math. Assn. Am., Am. Assn. U. Women, Assn. Computing Machinery, Alpha Chi. Democrat. Baptist. Home: 8 Woodlands Ponca City OK 74601 Office: Drawer 1267 Ponca City OK 74601

JOHNSON, EDWARD WAYNE, real estate exec.; b. Danville, Va., Feb. 20, 1941; s. Hedrick Kessley and Dorothy May (Yeatts) J.; B.S., Va. Poly. Inst., 1963; m. Margie Buettner, Apr. 11, 1964; children—Gina Marline, Angela Dawn, Anne Wayne. Vice pres. Riverdan Investment Corp., Danville, 1964-66; pres. Hedrick Johnson Devel. Corp., Danville, 1966—. Served with USCGR, 1963-64. Mem. Home Builders Assn. Danville (pres. 1972-74), Va. Homebuilders Assn. (dir., 1969—), Alpha Kappa Psi, Omicron Delta Kappa. Lutheran. Lion, Toastmaster, Optimist. Club: Danville Golf. Home: 2057 Woodlake Dr Danville VA 24541 Office: 2321 Riverside Dr Danville VA 24541

JOHNSON, EDWARD WILLIAM, mech. engr.; b. Chgo., May 3, 1909; s. Axel Edward and Hilda (Johansson) J.; B.S., Ill. Inst. Tech., 1934, B.S. in Mech. Engring., 1935; postgrad. Carnegie Inst. Tech., 1936-40, Mass. Inst. Tech., 1943, McGill U., 1950, George Washington, U., 1953-57; m. Irmgard Marie Zeisberg, Mar. 15, 1957; 1 son, Robert David. Jr. mech. engr. Internat. Harvester Co., Chgo., 1934-39; asst. insp. naval material U.S. Navy Dept., Pitts., 1939-40; asso. mech. engr. U.S. Army Ordnance, Balt., 1940-42; mech. engr., asst. chief vehicle devel. U.S. Army C.E., Ft. Belvoir, Va., 1946-47, chief engring. sect. climatic research, 1947-48; environmental engr. Bur. Yards and Docks, Washington, 1948-52, head research programming, 1953-57; mech. engr. U.S. Naval Weapons Lab., Dahlgren, Va. 1957-59; head engring. specifications U.S. Naval Weapons Plant, Washington, 1959-60; sr. engr., asst. chief procurement U.S. Bur. Pub. Rds., 1960-62; asst. chief postal lab., office research engring. U.S. Post Office Dept., Washington, 1962-71; v.p. Basic Testing Labs., Inc., Centreville, Va., 1971-72; program mgr. design and devel. Value Engring. Co., Alexandria, Va., 1972—. Served with USNR, 1943-46. Registered profl. engr., D.C. Mem. Am. Soc. M.E., Am. Inst. Aeros. and Astronautics, Nat., D.C., Va. socs. profl. engrs., Am. Ordnance Assn., Am. Polar Soc., Explorers Club, Swedish Hist. Soc. Mason (32 deg., Shriner). Contbr. articles to profl. jours. Home: 6944 Essex Av Springfield VA 22150 Office: Alexandria VA 22303

JOHNSON, ELMO MARSENE, lawyer; b. Houston, Apr. 20, 1937; s. Elmo and Jacqueline Lois (Carothers) J.; B.A., Rice Inst., 1958; LL.D., U. Tex., 1961; m. Carol M. Mitchell, June 23, 1966; children—Elmo M., Jacqueline C. Admitted to Tex. bar, 1961, practiced in Galveston, 1962—; asso. firm Markwell, Stubbs, Decker, Dalehite, & Youngblood, 1962-71; mem. firm Decker & Johnson, 1971-73. Instr. Tex. Maritime Acad., Galveston, 1966-68, Galveston Coll., 1968-70. Trustee Galveston Ind. Sch. Dist.; bd. dirs. St. Mary's Hosp., Galveston, 1971—. Served with AUS, 1961. Named Outstanding Young Man of Year, Galveston Jr. C. of C., 1965. Mem. Am. Hosp. Assn., Soc. Hosp. Attys. Mason (Shriner). Kiwanian (pres. 1967). Home: 310 Church Galveston TX 77550 Office: 2200 Market Suite 504 Galveston TX 77550

JOHNSON, EMILY WINIFRED, club woman, educator; b. Hamilton, N.C., July 28, 1890; d. George Thomas and Catherine Ann Elizabeth (Powell) Johnson; student Longwood Coll., 1909-11; A.B., George Washington U., 1924; M.A., Tchrs. Coll., Columbia, 1932. Tchr. elementary and high sch., Va., Md., Fla., 1911-17, 20-21, 24-27; clk. Govt. Service War Trade Bd., Treasury Dept., 1917-20, War Dept., 1940-44; coll. tchr., demonstration tchr., supr. Va. and N.C. Tng. Sch., Mary Washington Coll., 1928. Tchr. Tng. Dept. Greene and Ashe Counties, N.C., 1928-32, Western Carolina Tchrs. Coll., Cullowhee, N.C., 1932-35; supr. elementary schs., Spring Hope and Penderlea, N.C., Russell County, Va., 1939-40; information specialist, pub. health analyst, editor staff pub. health reports, Pub. Health Service, U.S. Dept. Health, Edn. and Welfare, 1944-60; coordinator Civil War Centennial Lectures, U. Va. No. Center, Arlington, 1960-62; mem. Pan Am. Liaison Com. of Women's Orgn. staff mem. Golden Anniversary White House Conf. Children and Youth. Mem. assn. and women's com. Nat., Arlington symphonies. Mem. Acad. Polit. Sci., Am. Acad. Polit. and Social Sci., Va. Mus. Fine Arts, U.O.C. (charter, historian, chaplain George Washington Custis Lee chpt.), Civil War Hist. Assn., Va. (life), Arlington hist. socs., George Washington U. Alumnae Assn., Armed Forces Writers League, Longwood Coll. Alumni Assn. (pres. Wash. chpt., dir.), Gen., Va. (historian no. dist. 1951-55), Arlington (officer-at-large) fedns. women's clubs, Internat. Platform Assn., Nat. Trust for Hist. Preservation. Mem. Ch. of Resurrection. Clubs: Washington, Columbia University (past pres., past trustee); Women's (pres. 1949-53) (Cherrydale). Home: Goodwin House 4800 Fillmore Av Alexandria VA 22311

JOHNSON, EMMETT JOHN, educator; b. New Orleans, Apr. 17, 1929; s. Francis Lawrence and Emily (Sahuc) J.; B.S. magna cum laude, Loyola U. of South, 1952; M.S., La. State U., 1954, Ph.D., 1957; m. Mary Evangeline Knettles, Sept. 4, 1955; children—Michele Emily, Denise Marie. With U. Miss. Med. Sch., 1958-65, Ames Research Center of NASA, Moffett Field, Cal., 1965-67, Stanford Med. Sch., 1957-58, 65-67; lectr., research asso. Tulane U. Sch. Medicine, 1967—. Research participant Oak Ridge Nat. Labs., summers 1962, 63, Service de Biochemie Cellulaire of Institut Pasteur,

1974—. Dir. summer theatre youth program Jackson Little Theatre, 1961; mem. LePetit Theatre du Vieux Carre, 1973. Served with AUS, 1946-47. Recipient Lederle med. faculty award, 1962-65, sustained superior performance award NASA, 1965-66, predoctoral research award Sigma Xi, 1957; NRC postdoctoral fellow, 1957-58; So. Assn. Fellowship Fund predoctoral fellow, 1955-57. Fellow Am. Acad. Microbiology; mem. Am. Soc. Microbiology (councilor South Central br. 1970-72), A.A.A.S., Am. Chem. Soc., Genetics Soc. Am., Soc. Gen. Physiologists, Soc. Exptl. Biology and Medicine, Soc. Biol. Chemistry, Sigma Xi. Research on physiology of autotrophic bacteria, regulatory phenomena in bacteria, electron transport and oxidative phosphorylation in chemolithotrophic bacteria, molecular genetics. Home: 1631 Killdeer St New Orleans LA 70122

JOHNSON, FRANCIS RUSS MARION, banker; b. Durant, Miss., Sept. 11, 1909; s. Edwin Rembert and Margaret Lauda (Comfort) J.; student Millsaps Coll., 1926-27, Rutgers U. Grad. Sch., 1937-41; grad. Am. Inst. Banking; m. Rosalind Gwin Hutton, Apr. 14, 1943; 1 dau., Martha Ryburn (Mrs. Robert Lafayette Stainton). With Mchts. Bank & Trust Co., Jackson, Miss., 1927-33; with Deposit Guaranty Nat. Bank, Jackson, Miss., 1933—, v.p. investments, 1946-53, exec. v.p., dir., from 1953, chmn. exec. com., 1958-69, chmn. bd., chief exec. officer, 1969—, also dir.; with Deposit Guaranty Corp., Jackson, 1968—, chmn. bd., chief exec. officer, 1969—, also dir.; dir. Miss. Power and Light Co., Jackson, Carthage Bank (Miss.). Staff mem. gov. of Miss., 1964-68, 72—. Past pres. Andrew Jackson council Boy Scouts Am., now mem. exec. com. Region V, mem. exec. bd. Andrew Jackson council, mem.-at-large Nat. council; active fund raising for United Givers, various civic, religious and cultural orgns., hosps., ch.-related schs., liberal arts colls.; mem. Miss. Agrl. and Indsl. Bd.; former mem. Miss. Gov.'s Emergency Council; commr. Gen. Assembly, Presbyn. Ch. U.S.A., mem. Bd. Annuities and Relief, chmn. finance com.; pres. Bd. dirs. Miss. Econ. Council; 1958. Served from pvt. to capt., AUS, 1942-46; ETO. Mem. Am. (past Miss. rep. exec. council, past mem. exec. com. state bank div., mem. govt. borrowing com.), Miss., Ind. (past dir.) bankers assns., Jackson Clearinghouse Assn. (past pres.), Com. for Econ. Devel. (trustee), Miss. C. of C. (past pres.), Newcomen Soc., Am. Legion, Chi Psi. Presbyn. (elder). Lion. Clubs: Jackson Country; Summit (Memphis); Boston (New Orleans). Home: 4323 Brook Dr Jackson MS 39206 Office: 200 E Capitol St Jackson MS 39205

JOHNSON, F(RANK) SAM, JR., govt. petroleum engr.; b. Dallas, Aug. 24, 1932; s. Frank Sam and Mary Ellen (Swinney) J.; B.S., Tex. A. and M. U., 1955; postgrad. Tulsa U., 1959-67, Okla. State U., 1963-68; m. Margaret Ann Bluethman, Aug. 17, 1956; children—Christopher Lee, Mary Elizabeth, Keith Stuart. Trainee, Western Co., Healdton, Okla., 1955; jr. engr. Sun Oil Co., Odessa, Tex., 1957-58; petroleum engr. U.S. Bur. of Mines, Bartlesville, Okla., 1958—; treas., dir. Sixth & Osage, Inc., Bartlesville, 1969-72. Pres. Hover P.T.A., Bartlesville, 1969-70; tribe chief YMCA Indian Guides, 1970; chmn. Bartlesville Tech. Career Adv. Com., 1963-68, also dir. Bd. dirs. Osage Christian Camp. Served with AUS, 1955-57. Registered profl. engr., Okla. Mem. Am. Inst. M.E. (pres. Bartlesville, sec. Petroleum Engrs. sect. 1968-69, dir. 1965-68), Jaycees (chmn. project com. 1959-64). Mem. Ch. of Christ (deacon, dir. Lost Sheep program 1969—). Contbr. articles to profl. publs. Home: 811 Sooner Park Dr Bartlesville OK 74003 Office: PO Box 1398 Bartlesville OK 74003

JOHNSON, FREDERICK DEAN, food co. exec.; b. Shreve, O., Feb. 27, 1911; s. Harry H. and Grace Marcella (Cammarn) J.; A.B., Coll. Wooster (O.), 1935; m. Haulwen Elizabeth Richey, June 19, 1937; children—Frederick Dean II, Mary Haulwen, Grace Elizabeth. Dir. research Bama Co. (now Bama Products Borden Foods div. Borden Inc., Birmingham, Ala., 1961-65, dir. research, Houston, 1965—. U.S. del. FAO/WHO Codex Alimentarius Commn. Processed Fruits and Vegetables, 1973. Bd. dirs. Afton Oaks Civic Club, 1967-70. Mem. Nat. Preservers Assn. (chmn. quality control adv. com. 1969-73, chmn. standards com. 1973—), Inst. Food Technologtists (charter), Am. Chem. Soc. (past sec., chmn. Wooster sect.), A.A.A.S. Republican. Presbyn. (ruling elder). Home: 4546 Shetland Lane Houston TX 77027 Office: 5501 Clinton Dr Houston TX 77020

JOHNSON, GARY REID, univ. adminstr.; b. Ingram Branch, W.Va., Feb. 23, 1934; s. Ernest Reid and Sophrona Edyth (Tredway) J.; Mus.B., U. Mich., 1954, M.B.A., 1956, M.A., 1958. Sponsored research asst. bus. mgr. U. Mich., 1958-65; spl. asst. to dean U. Cal. at Davis, 1965-69; asst. to vice chancellor for health scis. U. Cal. at San Diego, 1969-74; dir. budget and finance Health Scis. Center Tex. Tech. U., 1974—. Cons. Hawaii Legislative Coms. on Higher Edn., 1968-72. Mem. Assn. Am. Med. Colls. (bus. officers sect. So. region group on bus. affairs), Tau Kappa Epsilon, Alpha Kappa Psi, Phi Mu Alpha, Kappa Kappa Psi. Contbr. articles to profl. jours. Home: PO Box 5430 Lubbock TX 79417

JOHNSON, GARY WAYNE, elec. engr.; b. Covington, Okla., Oct. 17, 1940; s. John D. and Geraldine Bernice (Johnson) J.; B.S. in Elec. Engring., Okla. State U., 1964; m. Coe Ann Swift, Aug. 24, 1963; children—Jeffrey Wayne, Gregory Scott. With NASA, Houston, 1964—, former group leader power control and lighting, now head equipment and installation sect., subsystem mgr. Skylab Command and Service Modules, 1972, mem. Apollo-Soyuz test project working group, 1972—. Mem. Apollo 204 fire investigation; leader Apollo 13 investigation elec. team; mem. lunar landing test accident bd.; mem. wire investigation team. Recipient Hamilton Watch award, 1964; Sustained Superior Performance award NASA, 1965, Superior Achievement award, 1970; certificate of commendation, 1971, NASA Exceptional Service medal, 1974. Mem. I.E.E.E., Tex. Soc. Profl. Engrs., Eta Kappa Nu, Sigma Tau, Phi Kappa Phi, Lambda Chi Alpha. Lutheran (bd. stewardship 1970-71, chmn. stewards 1971-73, mem. ch. council 1971-73). Contbr. reports, articles, revs. to profl. lit. Home: 2005 Williamsburg Ct S League City TX 77573 Office: Nasa Rd 1 Houston TX 77058

JOHNSON, GEORGE, JR., physician, educator; b. Wilmington N.C., Apr. 6, 1926; s. George W. and Evelyn (Hill) J.; B.S., U. N.C., 1948, certificate medicine, 1950; M.D., Cornell U., 1952; m. Marian Patterson Ritchie, July 1, 1950; children—Sally Hope, George William, David Ritchie, Robert Hill. Intern, resident surgery N.Y. Hosp., 1952-59; pvt. surg. practice, 1959-62; asst. prof. to prof., chief div. vascular surgery U. N.C., 1962—, Roscoe B.G. Cowper distinguished professorship in surgery, 1973—. Mem. adv. com. N.C. Emergency Med. Services. Served to 1st lt. inf., AUS, 1944-46. Mem. Univ. Assn. Emergency Med. Services (pres.), A.C.S. (pres. N.C. chpt.), Durham-Orange County Med. Soc. (pres. 1971). Club: Rotary (Chapel Hill). Home: 410 Westwood Dr Chapel Hill NC 27514

JOHNSON, GEORGE TERRY, dentist; b. Elkin, N.C., Apr. 17, 1939; s. Walter Presley and Carolyn (Maxwell) J.; student Wake Forest U., 1957-60; D.D.S., U. N.C., 1964. Individual practice dentistry, Sparta, N.C., 1964—; mem. dental adv. com. Blue Ridge Dental Health Commn., 1972—. Chmn. Am. Flag Display Project, 1970-71; dir. Alleghany County Rescue Squad, 1969-71; mem. Morehead Scholarship Com. Alleghany County. Mem. Blue Ridge Dental Soc. (v.p. 1968-69, sec.-treas. 1972-74), N.C. Dental Soc., Am. Dental Assn., Delta Sigma Delta. Republican. Baptist (young people's Sunday sch. supt. 1965-67). Lion (program chmn. 1966-69, pres. 1969-70). Home: PO Box 98 Sparta NC 28675 Office: 617 Doctor's St Sparta NC 28675

JOHNSON, GERALD RICHARD, lawyer; b. Johnson City, Tenn., Mar. 15, 1943; s. Charles Robert and Edna (McCorkle) J.; B.S. in Econ. and History, East Tenn. State U., 1966; J.D., U. Tenn., 1969; m. Helen Bundrun, Sept. 2, 1968; children—Monica Irene, and Tiffany Jean (twins). Admitted to Tenn. bar, 1969; asso. mem. firm Guinn, Carter, Myers & Saylor, Johnson City, Tenn., 1969-71, partner, 1971—. Capt., United Fund, Johnson City, 1971; mem. adv. bd. Dawn of Hope sch. mentally retarded, 1972—, Appalachian Christian Student Fellowship, 1972—. Vice chmn. Washington County Democratic party, 1972—. Mem. Tenn., Am. trial lawyers assns., Am., Tenn., Washington County bar assns., Johnson City Jr. C. of C. (past pres.; recipient outstanding young man year award 1972), Phi Alpha Delta. Home: 900 Crocus St Johnson City TN 37601 Office: 500 Profl Bldg Johnson City TN 37601

JOHNSON, GILMER BROOKS, physician; b. Jackson, Miss., Sept. 12, 1916; s. Gilmer Brooks and Lena Leoti (Brown) J.; student Sul Ross State U., 1934-35, 46-47; B.S., Northwestern U., 1948, M.D., 1950; m. Avis Elizabeth Palmer, Oct. 9, 1942; children—Carolyn (Mrs. Samuel Neal Braudt), Gilmer Brooks III, David Wallace. Intern Baylor U. Med. Center, Dallas, 1951; practice family medicine, Plainview, Tex., 1952—; mem. staff Central Plains Gen. Hosp., E. O. Nichols Meml. Hosp., Plainview; asso. clin. prof. Tex. Tech U. Med. Sch. Served with AUS, 1943-46. Decorated Bronze Star. Diplomate Am. Bd. Family Practice. Fellow Am. Acad. Family Practice; mem. A.M.A. (Physician's Recognition award 1970), Hale-Briscoe-Swisher-Floyd County Med. Soc. (pres. 1962-63). Baptist (deacon). Home: 205 Yucca Terrace Plainview TX 79072 Office: 814 W 8th St Plainview TX 79072

JOHNSON, GORDON OTIS FRASER, mfg. co. exec.; b. Boston, May 1, 1926; s. Richard Newhall and Margaret L. (Paisley) J.; student Mass. Inst. Tech., 1944-45, Tufts Coll., 1945-46; B.A., Stanford, 1948; M.B.A., Harvard, 1950; m. Frances Brigham, Dec. 29, 1951; children—Gordon F.B., Susan Chapman, Brigham Newhall, Christian Paisley Ball. With ECA, 1950-52; dir. marketing LogEtronics Inc., Springfield, Va., 1955-67, pres., 1967—, chief exec. officer, 1968—, also dir., 1957—; dir. LogEtronics A.G., Zurich, Switzerland. Served with USNR, 1944-46, 52-54. Mem. Stanford, Mass. Inst. Tech., Harvard alumni clubs, Soc. Photog. Scientists and Engrs. (Service award 1965; pres. Wash. chpt. 1965-66; program and conf. chmn. Symposia on Unconventional Photographic Systems 1964-67, sr. mem. 1972), Research and Engring. Council Graphic Arts Industry, Tech. Assn. Graphic Arts. Home: 3512 Saylor Pl Alexandria VA 22304 Office: 7001 Loisdale Rd Springfield VA 22150

JOHNSON, HAROLD KENNETH, coll. adminstr.; b. Washington County, Tenn., Jan. 18, 1926; s. Charles C. and Frances B. (Leonard) J.; B.S., East Tenn. State U., 1949, M.A., 1954; m. Mary Emma Carter, May 22, 1953; children—Harold Kenneth II, Jeff Carter, Jana Beth. Tchr. of bus. Sulphur Springs High Sch., Jonesboro, Tenn., 1949-52; prin. Boones Creek Elementary Sch., Jonesboro, 1952-54, Boones Creek High Sch., 1954-56; with East Tenn. State U., Johnson City, 1956—, asst. bus. mgr., 1956—. Vice pres. Johnson City-Washington County chpt. A.R.C., 1973-74. Methodist (mem. adminstrv. bd. 1942-74). Clubs: Boones Creek Community (pres. 1949-52), Boones Creek Ruritan (pres. 1966-67) (Jonesboro). Home: Rural Route 4 Johnson City TN 37601

JOHNSON, HERMAN BLUITT, savs. and loan assn. exec.; b. Canton, Miss., July 28, 1925; s. Clark Albert and Gertrude (Shivers) J.; B.S. in Bus. Adminstrn., Anderson (Ind.) Coll., 1948; m. Harriett Lucille Joiner, July 5, 1948; children—Judy Diane (Mrs. John D. Worrel), Nancy Carol, Barbara Lynn. Owner, operator H&H Grocery and Market, Meridian, Miss., 1949-54; mgr. Godwin Radio and TV Co., Birmingham, Ala., 1954-58; v.p., treas. First Fed. Savs. and Loan Assn., Sylacauga, Ala., 1958—; dir. Investors Fidelity Life Ins. Co. Treas. Sylacauga Salvation Army, 1966-68; campaign chmn. Sylacauga United Givers Fund, 1969, pres., 1973. Bd. dirs., v.p. Talladega Acad., 1970-73; trustee Warne So. Call., Lake Wales, Fla., 1965-73; bd. dirs. local Boy Scouts Am., 1971—, Sylacauga Beautification Council, 1972—. Mem. Sylacauga C. of C. (dir., v.p. 1970-73). Mem. Ch. of God (trustee 1952—, vice chmn. 1972—). Kiwanian (pres. Sylacauga 1963, lt. gov. 1965). Home: 2404 Lake Terrace Sylacauga AL 35150 Office: Norton Av Sylacauga AL 35150

JOHNSON, HOBART CLAY, lawyer; b. Virgie, Ky., Apr. 23, 1931; s. George Franklin and Vesta (Roberts) J.; A.B., Eastern Ky. U., 1952; LL.B., U. Louisville, 1958; m. Jean Howard, Aug. 14, 1959; children—Benjamin Clay, Amy Ann. Admitted to Ky. bar, 1958; practiced in Pikeville, 1958—; mem. firm Stratton, Johnson & May, 1967—; pres. Gov. Elkhorn Coal Co., Inc., 1967—, also dir.; pres. Mountain Cable Systems, Inc., 1967—; also dir.; sec.-treas. Mormar Mining Co., Inc., 1969—; dir. Citizens Bank of Pikeville, Eastern Ky. Broadcasting Corp., Greater Ky. Broadcasting Corp., Lawrence County Broadcasting Corp., Jellico Broadcasting Corp., Mormar Mining Co., Inc., Blue Grass Augers, Inc., U.S. commr., 1960-62; asst. county atty., Pike County, Ky., 1965-71. Served with USAF, 1952-56. Mem. Am., Ky., Pike County (pres. 1965) bar assns., Delta Theta Phi. Home: Box 295 Virgie KY 41572 Office: Ward Bldg Second St Pikeville KY 41501

JOHNSON, HOWARD ARTHUR, SR., research exec.; b. London, Ind., Dec. 16, 1923; s. Arthur and Ihez (Smiley) J.; A.B., Franklin Coll. Ind., 1949; M.A., Wesleyan U., Conn., 1950; m. Joy Anne Nelson, July 19, 1947; children—Howard A., Kraig N. Physicist U.S. Naval Ordnance Plant, Indpls., 1950-54; operations research analyst Air Proving Ground Command, Eglin AFB, Fla., 1954-58; chief operations analysis 3d Air Force in Eng., 1958; dep. chief operations analysis USAF Europe, Wiesbaden, Germany, 1958-61; dir. operations model evaluation group air force (OMEGA), also sr. mgmt. staff Washington Research Center Tech. Operations, Inc., Washington, 1961-63; sr. staff scientist Spindletop Research, Inc., Lexington, Ky., 1963-66, mgr. comparative effectiveness research div., 1966-67; research dir. Vitro Services div. Vitro Corp. Am., Ft. Walton Beach, Fla., 1967-68; sci. asst. to dir. of test Armament Devel. and Test Center, Eglin AFB, Fla., 1968-73, sr. operations research scientist Tactical Air Warfare Center, 1973—. Cons. Supreme Hdgrs. Allied Powers, Europe, 1960-61, USAF, 1964-65, U. Ky. Med. Center, 1967, Gulf South Research Inst., 1968—. Served with USAAF, 1943-45; mem. USAF Res. Decorated Air medal. Mem. Operations Research Soc. Am., Inst. Mgmt. Scis., Am. Statis. Assn., Mil. Operations Research Soc., A.A.A.S., N.Y. Acad. Scis., Washington Operations Research Council, Sigma Xi, Phi Delta Theta. Mason (32 deg., Shriner). Home: 309 Yacht Club Dr NE Fort Walton Beach FL 32548 Office: USAFTAWC (OA) Eglin AFB FL 32542

JOHNSON, IRA OTIS, JR., precision instrument co. exec.; b. Spencer, Tenn., Mar. 14, 1917; s. Ira Otis and Sallie (Mohon) J.; B.S., U. Tenn., 1940; m. Laurine C. Crawley, Apr. 2, 1938 (div. Feb. 1946); children—Ira Otis III, Melvin C.; m. 2d, Darless L. Lane, Feb. 5, 1947; children—Mike Joe, Luke Martin. Tracer, State Hwy. Dept., Nashville, 1936; lab. asst. bridge sect. Am. Lava, Chattanooga, 1938-40: draftsman Fulton Syphon div. Robertshaw Controls Co., Knoxville, Tenn., from 1940, now v.p., gen. mgr., also dir. Bd. dirs. United Fund, Knoxville, Tenn., 1970-71, Smoky Mountain council Boy Scouts Am., Jr. Achievement, Knoxville, Smoky Mountain div. A.R.C. Mem. Am. Soc. M.E., Instrument Soc. Am., Fulton Mgmt. Club, Soc. Mfg. Engrs., Tech. Soc. Knoxville, Greater Knoxville C. of C. (dir.). Mem. Ch. of Christ. Rotarian. Home: 7101 Cheshire Dr Knoxville TN 37919 Office: Box 400 KnoxvilleTN 37901

JOHNSON, JAMES MCDADE, lawyer; b. Shreveport, La., Dec. 5, 1939; s. Leslie Neill and Nell (McDade) J.; student La. Tech. U., 1957-59; B.A., La. State U., 1961, J.D., 1964; m. Glenda Gail Roth, Jan. 27, 1962; children—Danielle Denise, Kimberly Dawn. Admitted to La. bar, 1964, since practiced in Minden; partner Campbell, Campbell, Marvin & Johnson, 1964—. Sec.-treas. Highland Homes, Inc.; sec. Profl. Cosmetics, Inc.; dir. Johnson Ford, Inc., Winwood Utilities Co., Inc.; partner Sibley Rd. Devel. Co. Asso. legal counsel U.S. Jr. C. of C., 1970-71, gen. legal counsel, 1971-72. Chmn. Minden Democratic Exec. Com., 1964—. Recipient Distinguished Service award as outstanding young man of year, Minden, 1970. Mem. Am., La., Webster Parish bar assns., Am. Trial Lawyers Assn., Am. Judicature Soc. Episcopalian. Home: 814 Nella St Minden LA 71055 Office: PO Box 834 Minden LA 71055

JOHNSON, JAMES PAUL, congressman, lawyer; b. Yankton, S.D., June 2, 1930; s. Fred J. and Evelyn (Shoenberger) J.; B.A., Northwestern U., 1952, LL.B., 1959; m. Nancy Brown, June 16, 1952; children—Dea Lyn, Julie Conner, Drake Bartel. Admitted to Colo. bar, 1959, practiced in Ault and Ft. Collins, Colo.; mem. firm Johnson, Anderson & Dressel, 1970—; pros. atty. 8th Jud. Dist. Colo., 1959-66; municipal judge Ault, 1962-65. Instr. bus. law Colo. State U., Ft. Collins, 1959-64. Congressman 4th Dist. Colo., 1973—. Mem. Poudre R-1 Sch. Bd., 1969-71. Trustee San Francisco Theol. Sem., 1968—. Served with USMCR, 1952-56. Mem. Am., Colo., Larimer County (pres. 1971-72) bar assns., C. of C., Dean's Law Club. Presbyn. (elder 1964—). Elk. Home: 8003 Greentree Rd Bethesda MD 20034 also 922 Gregory Rd Ft Collins CO 80521 Office: Cannon Bldg Washington DC 20515

JOHNSON, JAMES SYLVESTER, printing co. exec.; b. Andalusia, Ala., Dec. 25, 1939; s. Chester Sylvester and Mary Ethel (Spivey) J.; B.S., Fla. State U., 1963; m. Heather Dianne Hancock, Dec. 29, 1962; children—Olivia, Eric. With Rose Printing Co., Inc., Tallahassee, 1961-63, asst. controller, 1963-67, controller, 1967-71, treas., after 1971, now gen. mgr. Home: 1813 Sharon Rd Tallahassee FL 32303 Office: 2503 Jackson Bluff Tallahassee FL 32304

JOHNSON, JEROME DOYLE, banker; b. Bee Branch, Ark., May 18, 1919; s. John H. and Cora S. (Odom) J.; student State Coll. Conway (Ark.), 1967-68; m. Nevalynn Aldridge, June 7, 1941; 1 son, Ricky L. With Cleburne County Bank, Heber Springs, Ark., 1939—, exec. v.p., until 1962, pres., 1962—. Mem. Cleburne County Adv. Com. Extension Com., 1965—. Bd. dirs. Cleburne County Soil Conservation Com., 1950—; sec., 1958—. Served with USAAF, 1943-45; ETO. Mem. Heber Springs C. of C. Democrat. Methodist. Mason (32 deg.), Rotarian. Home: Route 2 Box 103 Herber Springs AR 72543 Office: 300 Main St Heber Springs AR

JOHNSON, JEROME WALTER, lawyer; b. Port Arthur, Tex., Dec. 26, 1925; s. Sam W. and Edith (Upton) J.; B.A., U. Tex., 1949, LL.B., 1951; m. Madelyn A. Sinclair, Aug. 28, 1949; children—Julia Sinclair (Mrs. Evans), Mary Haise, Sara Madeline, Shannon Elizabeth, Ellen Grey, Amy Ballard, Polly Hall. Admitted to Tex. bar, 1950, practiced in Amarillo; partner firm Underwood, Wilson, Sutton, Barry, Stein & Johnson, Amarillo, 1956—; chmn. bd. Amarex, Inc., Oklahoma City, 1969-72, now dir.; dir. Maywood, Inc., Amarillo. Active in govtl. affairs. Bd. regents State Sr. Colls. Tex., pres., 1972-74. Served to 1st lt. USAF, 1944-46. Mem. Am. Bar. Assn., State Bar Tex. Democrat. Episcopalian. Home: 2802 Harmony St Amarillo TX 79106 Office: PO Box 9158 Amarillo TX 79105

JOHNSON, JESSIE LARUE, librarian, musician; b. Sedalia, Mo. Dec. 3, 1908; d. Thomas Henry and Jessie Lee (Harris) Johnson; pupil Elizabeth Estle Rucker, Basil D. Gauntlett, Paul Van Katwijk; Asso. Music, Stephens Coll., 1928; Mus.B., So. Meth. U., 1931; B. Pub. Sch. Music, 1933, Mus.M., 1948; certificate library service Columbia, 1947. Instr. piano So. Meth. U., 1931-37; librarian Dallas Ind. Sch. Dist., 1936—. Asst. librarian Children's Library Pretoria Pub. Library, Republic South Africa, 1966-67; program annotator chamber mus. series Dallas Museum Fine Arts, 1956-62. Recipient Mu Phi Epsilon award So. Meth. U., 1931. Served as lt. USNRWR, 1943-46. Mem. Pro Musica (chmn. 1962-64, program chmn. 1950-53, 69-70), Dallas Chamber Music Soc. (dir. 1954—) Am. Assn. U. Women, Am., Tex. library assns., Dallas Assn. Sch. Librarians, Stephens Coll. Alumnae Assn., Mu Phi Epsilon (life). Methodist. Contbr. articles to profl. jours.; concert revs. to newspapers. Home: 4524 Belclaire Av Dallas TX 75205 Office: Thomas J Rusk Sch 2929 Inwood Rd Dallas TX 75235

JOHNSON, JOHN A., communications co. exec.; b. Milw., 1915; A.B., DePauw U., 1937; J.D., U. Chgo., 1940; LL.M,, Harvard, 1946. Admitted to Ill. bar, 1946; atty. Office Gen. Counsel, Burlington & Quincy R.R., 1940-41; with firm Wilson & McIlvaine, 1941-43; asst. Office UN Affairs, Dept. State, Washington, 1946-48; atty. gen. counsel Office Sec. Air Force, 1948-52, gen. counsel Office Air Force, 1952-58; gen. counsel NASA, 1958-63; dir. internat. arrangements Communications Satellite Corp. (COMSAT), Washington, 1963-64, v.p. internat., 1964-73, sr. v.p., 1973—; pres. COMSAT Gen. Corp., also dir.; dir. CML Satellite Corp., Nicaraguan Telecommunications Satellite Co. U.S. rep. Interim Communications Satellite Com., chmn., 1964-67, 68-69; U.S. gov. INTELSAT, 1973-74. Mem. Am. Bar Assn., Am. Soc. Internat. Law, Inter-am Bar Assn. Contbr. articles to profl. jours., also to Ency. Brit. Home: 3643 N Nelson St Arlington VA 22207 Office: 950 L'Enfant Plaza S SW Washington DC 20024

JOHNSON, JOHN ARTHUR, charitable orgn. exec.; b. Chgo., Sept. 29, 1911; s. Andrew John and Clara E. (Dow) J.; B.A., Gustavus Adolphus Coll., St. Peter, Minn., 1936; postgrad. U. Minn., summer 1938, Northwestern U., summer 1939, Purdue U., 1945; m. Audrey England Nelson, Sept. 28, 1940; children—Susan Andrea (Mrs. Paul Harvey Daniel), Scott Bradley. Tchr., Bd. Edn., Duluth, Minn., 1937-42; youth counselor U.S. Employment Service, Duluth, 1942; dir. rehab. for blind Minn. Div. Welfare, 1942-43; personnel adminstr. Honeywell, Inc., Mpls., 1944-54; exec. dir. Columbia Lighthouse for the Blind, Washington, 1954—. Pres. Gen. Council Workshops for Blind; bd. dirs. Nat. Industries for Blind, N.Y.C.; trustee, chmn. standards com., vice chmn. exec. com. Commn. on Accreditation of Rehab. Facilities; mem. adv. bd. Mpls. Soc. for Blind, 1942-54. Recipient Distinguished Alumni award Gustavus Adolphus Coll., 1968. Club: Fairfax (Va.) Country. Home: 619 S Woodstock St Arlington VA 22204 Office: 2021 14th St NW Washington DC 20009

JOHNSON, JOHN EDWARD, JR., physician; b. Galveston, Tex. May 7, 1925; s. John Edward and Mary (Blasdel) J.; B.A., U. Tex., 1944, M.D., 1948; m. Mary Shirley Jimerson, Feb. 23, 1946; children—Meredith, Anna, Jeb, Susan, Michael, Jamie. Instr. dept.

Internal Medicine Med. Sch., U. Tex., Galveston, 1954-56, asst. prof., 1956-63; asso. dir. med. research, dir. clin. pharmacology WMS Merrell Co., Cin., 1963-69; med. dir. Alcon Labs., Fort Worth, Tex., 1969-72; intern U. Tex. Med. Center hosps., Galveston, 1948-49, resident, 1949-51, 53-54; practice medicine, specializing in internal medicine, endocrinology, Fort Worth, 1972—; mem. staff Harris, St. Joseph, All Saints, Cook Children's hosps. (all Ft. Worth). Vice chmn. Galveston Citizen Charter Commn., 1962-63. Founding mem. bd. dirs. Med. Research Fedn. Tex., 1956-63. Mem. Theta Kappa Psi. Democrat. Unitarian. Contbr. profl. jours. Home: 2340 Mistletoe Av Fort Worth TX 76110 Office: 1221 W Lancaster Av Fort Worth TX 76102

JOHNSON, J(OHN) R(ALPH), agronomist; b. Hull, Ga., Apr. 9, 1912; s. William A. and Dora Ann (Brown) J.; B.S.A., U. Ga., 1933, postgrad., 1950-52; children—Patricia Ann, Martha Carolyn, Rebecca Sue. Agronomist, U.S. Forestry Service, Rolla, Mo., 1934-37; tchr. pub. schs., Ringgold, Ga., 1938-41; agronomist, U. Ga., Athens, 1941-53, head extension agronomy dept., 1954-73, prof., 1963-73, prof., head dept. emeritus, 1973—. Recipient Superior Service award U.S. Dept. Agr., 1962; Distinguished Faculty award U. Ga. Coll. of Agr., 1966; Service to Agr. award Gamma Sigma Delta, 1968. Fellow Am. Soc. Agronomy; mem. Crop Sci. Soc. Am., Soil Sci. Soc. Am., Ga. Plant Food Ednl. Soc. (life mem.; exec. sec.; Decennial award 1963, Twenty Year award 1973), Ga. Soybean Assn., Ga. Weed Control Soc. Author numerous ednl. bulls. on forage crops, cereals, soil fertility, fertilizers. Contbr. articles to profl. jours. Initiated soil fertility and forage programs in Ga. Home: PO Box 5128 Athens GA 30604

JOHNSON, JOHN WILLIAM, JR., lawyer; b. Langdale, Ala., July 19, 1920; s. John William and Cordelia (Harrell) J.; B.S., U. Ala., 1942, LL.B., 1947; m. Elsie Brinson, June 24, 1950; children—John William III, Robert Lee, Curti Morrell. Admitted to Ala. bar, 1947; pres., dir. First Fed. Savs. & Loan Assn., West Point, Ga., Citizens Nat. Bank, Shawmut, Ala. Mem. Ala. Senate, 1951-55. Served to 1st lt. AUS, 1943-46. Home: 6105 26th Av Langdale AL 36864 Office: 201 Johnson Blvd Lanett AL 36863

JOHNSON, JOHNNY RAY, educator; b. Chatham, La., Dec. 19, 1929; s. Dave Ernest and Bessie (Morris) J.; B.S., La. Tech. U., 1951; M.S., Auburn U., 1953, Ph.D., 1959; m. Betty Ann Moore, Oct. 21, 1960; children—Todd Michael, John Fitzgerald, Shauna Renee. Asst. prof. math. La. Tech. U., 1958-62; asso. prof. math. Appalachian State U., 1962-63; prof. elec. engring. La. State U., Baton Rouge, 1963—; mem. staff Combat Operations Research Group, Ft. Monroe, Va., summer, 1957; mathematician Boeing Co., New Orleans, summer 1965. Pres. Wildwood PTA, 1973-74. Served with AUS, 1954-56. Mem. I.E.E.E., Sigma Xi, Tau Beta Pi, Phi Kappa Phi, Eta Kappa Nu, Pi Mu Epsilon. Author (with David E. Johnson) Mathematical Methods in Engineering and Physics, 1965, Graph Theory with Engineering Applications, 1972. Home: 953 W Lakeview Dr Baton Rouge LA 70810

JOHNSON, JOSEPH BELTON, dentist; b. Osaka, Va., Feb. 12, 1928; s. George Washington and Roxie Ann (Richmond) J.; B.S. in Civil Engring., Va. Poly. Inst. and State U., 1951; postgrad. Emory and Henry Coll., 1956-57; D.D.S., Va. Commonwealth U., 1962; m. Geraldine Tate, June 2, 1956; 1 dau., Ann Mary. Civil engr. hydraulic engring. div. TVA, Knoxville, Tenn., 1954-56; gen. children's dentist Va. State Health Dept., Richmond, Nelson County and Henrico County, 1962-63; individual practice dentistry, Bon Air, Va., 1963—; pres. Dr. Joseph B. Johnson, Inc. Chmn. Chesterfield County Republican Com., 1969. Served to 1st lt. C.E., AUS, 1951-53; lt. col. Res. Mem. Am., Va. dental Assns., Richmond Dental Soc., Southside Dental Study Club, Navy League. Mason (Shriner). Club: Salisbury Country (Richmond). Home: 3830 Wainfleet Dr Richmond VA 23235 Office: 8710 Choctaw Rd Bon Air VA 23235

JOHNSON, JOSEPH E., ednl. adminstr.; b. Vernon, Ala., July 9, 1933; B.A., Birmingham-So. Coll., 1955; M.A., U. Tenn., 1960, Ed.D., 1968; m. Patricia Carole Johnson children—Kent, Kelly. Research asso., instr. polit. sci. U. Tenn., 1958; dir. budget div., dep. commr. finance and adminstrn., exec. asst. to gov. State of Tenn., 1960-63; exec. asst. to pres. U. Tenn., 1963-68, exec. asst. to pres., v.p. instl. research, 1968-70, v.p. devel. and adminstrn., 1970, chancellor med. units, 1970-71, v.p. health affairs, chancellor med. units, 1971-73; exec. v.p., v.p. devel. U. Tenn. System, Knoxville, 1973—. Served with AUS, 1956-58. Mem. N.E.A., Tenn. Edn. Assn., Am. Coll. Pub. Relations Assn., Assn. Instl. Research, Am. Ednl. Research Assn., Phi Beta Kappa, Omicron Delta Kappa, Phi Kappa Phi. Kiwanian. Mem. Ch. of Christ. Address: U Tenn System Office Exec VP Knoxville TN 37916

JOHNSON, JOSEPH EGGLESTON, III, educator, physician; b. Elberton, Ga., Sept. 17, 1930; s. Joseph E. and Marie (Williams) J.; B.A. cum laude, Vanderbilt U., 1951, M.D., 1954; m. Judith Haynes Kemp, Jan. 21, 1956; children—Joseph Eggleston IV, Judith Ann, Julie Marie. Intern Johns Hopkins Hosp., Balt., 1954-55, resident 1957-61, mem. faculty and staff, 1961-66; mem. faculty and staff U. Fla. Teaching Hosp. (J. Hillis Miller Health Center), 1966-72; instr. medicine Johns Hopkins, 1961-62, asst. prof. medicine, 1962-66, asst. dean for student affairs, 1963-66; asso. prof. medicine U. Fla., 1966-68, prof., 1968-72, chief div. infectious diseases, 1966-72, asso. dean, 1970-72; prof., chmn. dept. medicine Bowman Gray Sch. Medicine, Wake Forest U., 1972—; cons. U.S. Army Biol. Labs., 1966—. Served to lt. USNR, 1956-57. John and Mary R. Markle scholar, 1962; Royal Soc. Medicine travelling fellow, 1970-71. Diplomate Am. Bd. Internal Medicine. Fellow A.C.P. (postgrad. Mead Johnson scholar 1960-61), Royal Soc. Medicine; mem. soc. Exptl. Biology and Medicine, Am. Assn. Immunologists, Am. Acad. Allergy, Am. Clin. and Climatological Assn., So. Soc. Clin. Investigation, Am. Soc. Microbiology, N.Y. Acad. Sci., Am. Fedn. Clin. Research, Infectious Diseases Soc. Am., Phi Beta Kappa, Sigma Alpha Epsilon (chpt. pres. 1950), Phi Chi (chpt. pres. 1953-54), Omicron Delta Kappa, Alpha Omega Alpha. Contbr. to sci. jours. and texts. Home: 3500 Quarterstaff Pl Winston-Salem NC 27104 Office: Bowman Gray Sch Medicine Wake Forest U Wake Forest NC 27103

JOHNSON, JOSEPHINE ANN (MRS. NORMAN L. JOHNSON), librarian; b. Chgo., July 29, 1912; d. William Garrett and Gertrude (Shepler) Roach; A.B., St. Mary's Coll., 1935; M.L.S., Nazareth Coll. (now Spalding Coll.), 1958; m. Norman Lyle Johnson, Aug. 26, 1940. Br. library asst. South Bend (Ind.) Pub. Library, 1938-40; asst. reference dept. Louisville Free Pub. Library, 1944-57, head reference dept., 1957-63; chief librarian Courier-Jour. and Louisville Times Library, 1963—. Discussion leader Am. Press Inst. Seminar, 1967, So. Newspaper Pubs. Assn. Workshop, 1971. Mem. Ky. (pres. 1961-62), Spl. (chmn. newspaper div. 1967-68) library assns., Louisville Library Club. Contbr. articles to profl. jours. Home: 2612 Landor Av Louisville KY 40205 Office: 525 W Broadway Louisville KY 40202

JOHNSON, KENNETH OWEN, audiologist, assn. exec.; b. St. Paul, Jan. 26, 1920; s. Ernest Wilbert and Anna Mae (Little) J.; B.A., Macalester Coll., St. Paul, 1946; M.A., U. Minn., 1948; Ph.D., Stanford, 1952; m. Dorothy Schlesselman, Sept. 5, 1949. Chief, audiology and speech correction program VA, Washington, 1954-56, past. cons. acoustical audiology; dir. San Francisco Hearing and Speech Center, 1956-57; asst. clin. prof. dept. surgery Stanford Med. Sch., 1957; exec. sec. Am. Speech and Hearing Assn., Washington, 1957—, dir. Deafness, Speech and Hearing Publs., 1959—, past pres.; chmn. Coalition Ind. Health Professions, 1970-71; cons. for speech, hearing and lang. to Head Start program, 1968-72; mem. research fellowship bd. U.S. Vocational Rehab. Adminstrn., 1964-71. Bd. dirs. Com. Handicapped People to People Program; trustee Am. Speech and Hearing Found. Certified in speech pathology and audiology Am. Speech and Hearing Assn. Fellow Am. Speech and Hearing Assn. (editor jour.); mem. A.A.A.S., Am. Phychol. Assn., Speech Assn. Am., Internat. Assn. Logopedics and Phoniatrics. Home: 7303 Broxburn Ct Bethesda MD 20034 Office: 9030 Old Georgetown Rd Washington DC 20014

JOHNSON, KERMIT ALONZO, univ. pres.; b. Boaz, Ala., Dec. 16, 1911; s. John Arree and Eunice (Pruett) J.; B.S., U. Ala., 1938, M.A., 1944; Ed.D., Columbia U., 1949; m. Golda Watson, Mar. 21, 1932; 1 dau., Judith Kay. Tchr., Cullman County (Ala.) Schs., 1929-36; prin. Garden City (Ala.) Jr. High Sch., 1936-43; prin. Kate Duncan Smith DAR High Sch., Grant, Ala., 1943-45; supt. Tuscaloosa County (Ala.) Schs., 1945-59; asso. supt. Jefferson County Schs., Birmingham, Ala., 1959-61, supt., 1961-68; pres. U. Montevallo (Ala.), 1968—; instr. U. Ala., Tuscaloosa, 1949-59, Birmingham So. Coll., 1960. Participant Fulbright Act, Italy, Netherlands. Mem. Commn. of the States Compact. Bd. dirs. Birmingham Civic Symphony Assn., Boy Scouts Am., Community Chest; chmn. Shelby County March of Dimes. Mem. Ala. Assn. Sch. Adminstrs. (pres. 1951-53), So. Assn. Colls. and Schs. (com. on admission to membership for sr. colls.), Ala. Edn. Assn. (pres. 1963-64), Ala. Congress Parents and Tchrs. (2d v.p. 1958-61), N.E.A. (life), Am. Assn. Sch. Adminstrs. (life). Rotarian (past pres. Tuscaloosa chpt.). Club: Birmingham Executives. Home: Flowerhill Montevallo AL 35115

JOHNSON, L. BARNEY, hosp. exec.; b. Winter Haven, Fla., Sept, 9, 1940; s. Ewel Willard and Elizabeth Mary (Baugh) J.; B.A., U. South Fla., 1965; M.H.A., U. Minn., 1967; m. Janice Marie Gunderson, Mar. 4, 1967; children—Leslie Brent, Timothy Willard, Jason Scott. X-ray technologist Baptist Hosp., Plant City, Fla., 1962-65, Watson Clinic, Lakeland, Fla., 1965; asst. adminstr. Winter Haven Hosp.; 1967-68, adminstr., 1968-73, chief exec., 1973—. Pres. Central Fla. Comprehensive Health Planning Council; regional sec. Regional Drug Abuse Council; mem. Winter Haven Drug Abuse Council. Mem. Grievance Bd. City of Winter Haven. Mem. Am., Fla. hosp. assns., Am. Acad. Med. Adminstrs., Am. Mgmt. Assn., West Central Fla. Hosp. Council (sec.-treas.), Am. Pub. Health Assn., Nat. League Nursing. Rotarian. Home: 2101 9th St SE Winter Haven FL 33880 Office: 200 Av F NE Winter Haven FL 33880

JOHNSON, LADY BIRD, CLAUDIA ALTA TAYLOR (MRS. LYNDON BAINES JOHNSON); b. Karnack, Tex., Dec. 22, 1912; d. Thomas Jefferson Taylor; B.A., U. Tex., 1933, B. Journalism, 1934; LL.D., Tex. Woman's U., 1964; Litt.D., U. Tex., 1964, Middlebury (Vt.) Coll., 1967; L.H.D., Williams Coll., 1967; H.H.D., Southwestern U., 1967; m. Lyndon Baines Johnson (36th Pres. U.S.), Nov. 17, 1934 (dec. 1973); children—Lynda Bird (Mrs. Charles S. Robb), Luci Baines (Mrs. Patrick J. Nugent). Mgr. husband's congl. office, Washington, 1941-42; owner, operator radio-TV sta. KTBC, Austin, Citation 1942—, cattle ranches, Tex., 1943—, also cotton and timberlands, Ala. Hon. chmn. numerous civic and charitable orgns., drives; founder Com. for more Beautiful Capital, 1965; mem. Adv. Bd. Nat. Parks, Historic Sites, Bldgs. and Monuments; co-chmn. Nat. Cultural Center; mem. nat. com. Helen Keller World Crusade for Blind; active environmental, nat. beautification projects. Hon. trustee Washington Gallery Modern Art; regent U. Tex. Recipient Togetherness award McCall's Mag., 1958, Crystal citation Fashion Group Phila., 1961, Distinguished Achievement award Washington Heart Assn., 1962, citation Nat. Assn. Colored Women's Clubs, 1962, Humanitarian award Ararat chpt. B'nai B'rith, Industry citation Am. Women in Radio and TV, 1963, Humanitarian citation Vols. Am., 1963; numerous others. Mem. Federated Bus. and Profl. Women's Club, (Business woman's award 1961), Am. Assn. U. Women (life Tex. div.), Internat. Club II, Women in Communications (citation 1961), others. Episcopalian. Author: A White House Diary, 1970. Narrator TV prodn. A Visit to Washington with Mrs. Lyndon B. Johnson, 1965. Address: LBJ Ranch Stonewall TX 78671

JOHNSON, LARRY WILSON, club exec.; b. Raleigh, N.C., Jan. 24, 1938; s. Lewis Marvin and Della (Wilson) J.; A.A., Campbell Coll., 1957; A.B., U. N.C., 1960, M.Ed., 1965; children—Elizabeth, Anne, John. Tchr. indsl. edn. pub. schs., Cary, N.C., 1960-63; asst. state supr. State Bd. Edn., Raleigh, 1963-65; founder, nat. exec. dir. Vocational Indsl. Clubs of Am., Falls Church, Va., 1965—. Mem. Loudoun County Adv. Com. on Vocational Edn., Leesburg, Va., 1974—; U.S.A. del. Internat. Skill Olympics Organizing Council, Madrid, Spain, 1973—; chmn. Nat. Coordinating Council for Vocational Student Orgn., Washington, 1972; chmn. bus. edn. adv. com. Fairfax County Bd. Edn., 1972, mem. adult edn. adv. com., 1972-73. Mem. Nat. Assn. for Trade and Indsl. Edn., Am. Vocational Assn., Vocational Indsl. Clubs of Am. Office: 105 N Virginia Av Falls Church VA 22046

JOHNSON, LAWRENCE DAVID, civil engr.; b. Tacoma, Jan. 26, 1937; s. Franklin Ernest and Frances Gloria (Martin) J.; B.S., U. Wash., 1959; M.S., U. Cal., Berkeley, 1961, Ph.D., 1962; m. Nancy Lou Mallory, Aug. 7, 1971. Research engr. Hanford Labs., Richland, Wash., 1962-66; civil engr. U.S. Army Engrs. Waterways Expt. Sta., Vicksburg, Miss., 1969—. Served as 1st lt. C.E., AUS, 1967-69. Registered profl engr., Miss. Mem. Am. Soc. Testing Materials, Am. Soc. C.E., Am. Soc. Mil. Engrs., Phi Beta Kappa, Sigma Xi, Tau Beta Pi. Home: 510 Melrose Vicksburg MS 39180 Office: PO Box 631 Vicksburg MS 39180

JOHNSON, LECTOY TARLINGTON, physician; b. Tyler, Tex., Nov. 28, 1931; s. Lectoy Tarlington and Adele (Delley) J.; B.S., Tex. Coll., 1952; M.D., Howard U., 1956; postgrad. Washington U. Sch. Medicine, 1958-60; m. Helen Collier, Sept. 14, 1958; children—Lectoy Tarlington III, Lynelle Teresa. Intern Homer G. Phillips Hosp., St. Louis, 1956-57, resident surgeon, 1957-58; resident anesthesiologist Washington U. Sch. Medicine, 1958-59, asst. in anesthesiology, 1959-60; practice medicine specializing in anesthesiology, Houston, 1960—; chmn. dept. anesthesiology St. Joseph's Hosp., Houston, 1969—, acad. chief, chmn. dept., 1970—; lectr. anesthesiology U. Tex. Dept. Continuing Edn.; clin. instr. U. Tex. Med. Sch., Houston, 1972—; asst. prof. biology Tex. So. U., Houston, 1972—. Mem. Am. Bd. Anesthesiology, Am. Coll. Anesthesiology, Internat. Anesthesia Research Soc., Undersea Med. Soc., Kappa Alpha Psi, Chi Delta Mu. Clubs: Houston Diving Assn., Bronze Eagles Flying. Home: 3612 Parkwood St Houston TX 77021 Office: 2000 Crawford St Houston TX 77002

JOHNSON, LEE ENSIGN, JR., univ. adminstr.; b. New River, Tenn., May 26, 1931; s. Lee Ensign and Sadie (Duffey) J.; B.Engring., Vanderbilt U., 1953, B.D., 1959; M.S. in Elec. Engring. (Ford fellow), Case Inst. Tech., 1962, Ph.D. (Ford fellow), 1963; m. Dona Simpson, Dec. 23, 1955; children—Lee, Michael, Steven, Susan. Engr., Aladdin Electronics Co., Nashville, 1955-59; mem. faculty dept. elec. engring., Vanderbilt U., Nashville, 1959—, asso. prof., 1966-71, prof., 1971—, also asso. provost, 1970—. Served to lt. (j.g.) USNR, 1953-55. Mem. I.E.E.E., Sigma Xi, Tau Beta Pi. Methodist. Home: 4612 Skymont Dr Nashville TN 37215

JOHNSON, LEON DIBRELL, III, utility co. exec.; b. Richmond, Va., May 1, 1917; s. Leon D. and Alice (Faulkner) J., Jr.; B.S. in Elec. Engring., Va. Poly. Inst., 1939; m. Frances Palmore, Oct. 28, 1939; children—Gail (Mrs. John F. Heil), Leon Dibrell IV. Engr., Va. Elec. and Power Co., Richmond, 1939, 45-50, systems planning engrs., 1950-57, chief design engr., 1957-60, dist. mgr., Alexandria, 1960-65, mgr. power supply, 1965-67, mgr. engring. and constrn., 1967-68, v.p., 1968—. Served from ensign to lt. USNR, 1942-45. Decorated Bronze Star medal. Registered profl. engr., Va. Mem. I.E.E.E., Va., Richmond chambers commerce. Presbyn. Mason. Club: Meadowbrook Country (Richmond). Home: 6411 St George Rd Richmond VA 23234 Office: 700 E Franklin St Richmond VA 23219

JOHNSON, LEONARD ROY, educator; b. Chgo., Jan. 31, 1942; s. Leonard W. and Pearl C. (Anderson) J.; A.B., Wabash Coll., 1963; Ph.D., U. Mich., 1967; m. Jeanne Stewart, Dec. 26, 1964; children—Melinda, Ashley, Matthew. Instr. physiology U. Cal. at Los Angeles Sch. Medicine, 1967-69; asst. prof. U. Okla. Sch. Medicine, Oklahoma City, 1969-70, asso. prof., 1971-72; prof. physiology U. Tex. Med. Sch. Houston, 1972—. Recipient NIH career devel. award, 1972—. Mem. Am. Physiol. Soc., Endocrine Soc. mem. editorial bds. Am. jours. Physiology and Gastroenterology, 1973—. Home: 1210 Pear Tree Lane Houston TX 77090

JOHNSON, LYNWOOD ALBERT, educator; b. Macon, Ga., Oct. 4, 1933; s. Benjamin Albert and Dorothy (Mallard) J.; B.I.E., Ga. Inst. Tech., 1955, M.S. in Indsl. Engring., 1959, Ph.D., 1965; postgrad. Ia. State U., 1961. Indsl. engr. E.I. duPont de Nemours & Co., Inc., Aiken, S.C., 1955-57; faculty Ga. Inst. Tech., Atlanta, 1958-64, 66—, prof. indsl. and systems engring., 1968—; supr. Kurt Salmon Assos., Inc., 1964-66. Mgmt. cons. Mem. Coll.-Industry Com. for Material Handling Edn., 1967-69. Callaway fellow, 1957-58. Registered profl. engr., Ga. Mem. Am. Inst. Indsl. Engrs. (sr.), Operations Research Soc., Inst. Mgmt. Scis., Sigma Xi, Kappa Alpha, Tau Beta Pi, Phi Kappa Phi, Phi Beta Sigma. Author: An Introduction to Linear Programming with Application, 1966; Operation Research in Production Planning, Scheduling and Inventory Control, 1974. Mem. editorial bd. Jour. Indsl. Engring., 1964-68. Home: 55 Pharr Rd NW Atlanta GA 30305 Office: Sch Indsl and Systems Engring Ga Inst Tech Atlanta GA 30332

JOHNSON, MARTIN WOLFE, lawyer; b. Benton, Ky., July 25, 1941; s. Jack William and Mary Irene (Wolfe) J.; B.S., Lambuth Coll., 1967; J.D., Memphis State U., 1970; m. Sandra F. Edwards, Dec. 28, 1972. Admitted to Ky. bar, 1970, Fed. bar, 1971; mem. firm Lovett & Lewis, Benton, 1970-72, partner, 1973—. Atty., City Benton, 1973. Served with AUS, 1962-64. Recipient Am. Jurisprudence award 1967, Bur. Nat. Affairs award, 1970. Mem. Marshall County C. of C., Benton Indsl. Found., Am., Ky., Marshall County bar assns., Kappa Sigma, Phi Alpha Delta. Methodist (trustee). Lion (pres. 1971-72). Home: 405 W 8th St Benton KY 42025 Office: 1114 Main St Benton KY 42025

JOHNSON, MARVIN GERALD, govt. ofcl.; b. Meridian, Tex., Dec. 6, 1915; s. Martin Robert and Olga (Erickson) J.; A.B., Bethany Nazarene Coll., 1938; postgrad. Okla. Central State Coll., 1939, Tulsa U., 1942; m. Geneva Vondell Ingle, Oct. 27, 1939; children—Gerald Dennis, Larry Eugene, Richard Alan. Civil engr. C.E., U.S. Army, Tulsa, 1939—, chief relocations br., 1965—; dir. Tulsa Fed. Employees Credit Union, 1963—, pres., 1966-67. Committeeman Boy Scouts Am., Tulsa, 1950-56; dir. Burroughs Civic Assn., 1954-56; dir. Lombard Youth Recreation Assn., 1962-66, pres., 1965. Served with USMCR, 1943-46. Decorated Air medal; recipient Superior Performance award U.S. Army, 1959, 66. Registered profl. engr., Okla. Mem. Nat., Okla. socs. profl. engrs. Home: 3721 S Darlington St Tulsa OK 74135 Office: US Corps Engrs 420 S Boulder St Tulsa OK 74101

JOHNSON, MARYALYCE, psychiat. social worker; b. Youngstown, O., Sept. 20, 1933; d. Arthur Wherry and Elizabeth (Campbell) Johnson; A.B., Birmingham-So. Coll., 1956; M.S.S.W., U. Tenn., 1959; m. Robert J. Bartelt, Nov. 9, 1967 (div. 1970). Clin. social worker VA Regional Office, Nashville, 1959-62; instr. U. Tenn. Coll. Medicine, Memphis, 1962-64; adminstrv. asst. Mental Health Center, Morristown, Tenn., 1964-65; supr. Fla. State Hosp., Chattahoochie, 1965-66; community placement social worker VA Hosp., Downey, Ill, 1966-68; cons. Dade County Criminal Ct., Miami, Fla., 1969-70; pvt. practice psychiat. social work, Miami and Largo, Fla., 1968-70; social work cons. in med. aging and mental health, St. Petersburg, 1970—; field instr. Fla. State U. Sch. Social Work, 1974—. Mem. Nat. Assn. Social Workers, Acad. Certified Social Workers, Gerontol. Soc. Episcopalian. Address: 7875 2d Av S St Petersburg FL 33707

JOHNSON, MEBANE WALKER, JR., elec. engr.; b. Burlington, N.C., July 3, 1947; s. Mebane Walker and Lena (Russell) J.; B.S. in Elec. Engring., N.C. State U., 1969; m. Lucinda Kay Allison, July 1, 1967; 1 son, Brian Scott. Group leader Harris Controls Co., Melbourne, Fla., 1969—. Mem. I.E.E.E. Presbyn. Home: 1113 SE Dade Circle Palm Bay FL 32905 Office: PO Box 430 Melbourne FL 32901

JOHNSON, MILTON RAYMOND, JR., elec. engr., educator; b. Shreveport, La., Nov. 5, 1919; s. Milton Raymond and Mattie Jewell (Batchelor) J.; B.S., La. Tech. U., 1940; postgrad. Tulane U., 1940-41; M.S., Okla. State U., 1951; Ph.D., Tex. A. and M. U., 1963; m. Grace Evelyn Hogan, Mar. 4, 1942; children—Rebecca (Mrs. Donny Ray Walker), Nancy Raye, Frank Milton. Plant engr. Gen. Electric Co., Ft. Wayne, Ind., 1941-42, design engr. D.C. and A.C. motors, 1942-47; mem. faculty dept. elec. engring. La. Tech. U., Ruston, 1947—, prof., 1954—. Cons. engr. Delta Research & Devel. Corp., Ruston, 1952-57; 70-71; teaching cons. La. Power & Light Co., 1971-72. Mem. Ruston Planning and Zoning Commn., 1962—, vice chmn., 1965-67, chmn., 1967—. NSF sci. faculty fellow, 1959-60. Registered profl. engr., La., Ark. Mem. I.E.E.E., Am. Soc. for Engring. Edn., La. Engring. Soc., Tau Beta Pi, Eta Kappa Nu. Democrat. Baptist. Club: Optimist (Ruston). Home: 810 Robert St Ruston LA 71270 Office: Box 4967 Tech St Ruston LA 71270

JOHNSON, NORMA HOLLOWAY, judge; b. Lake Charles, La.; grad. D.C. Tchrs. Coll.; J.D., Georgetown U.; m. Julius A. Johnson. Tchr., Taft Jr. High Sch., 1955-63; trial atty. civil div. Dept; Justice, 1963-67; asst. corp. counsel Govt. D.C., Washington, 1967-70; judge Superior Ct. D.C. Democrat. Office: Superior Ct DC Washington DC

JOHNSON, NORMAN AARON, JR., pub. service commr.; b. Philadelphia, Miss., June 8, 1921; s. Norman Aaron and Bobbie (Jasper) J.; B.S., Miss. State U., 1942; m. Mary Grace Stringer, May 16, 1946; children—Norman Aaron III, Amanda. Mcht., farmer; state comdr. Miss. Am. Legion, 1951-52; mayor, Philadelphia, 1953-55; chmn. Miss. Pub. Service Commn., Philadelphia, 1955—. Pres. Neshoba County Fair Assn., Inc.; chmn. bd. dirs. Miss. chpt. Arthritis

Found. Served with USMCR, 1941; with AUS, 1943-45. Mem. Nat. (exec. com.), Southeastern (pres. 1971-72) assns. regulatory utility commrs., Am. Legion, 40 and 8, V.F.W., C. of C., Farm Bur., Sigma Phi Epsilon. Mason (Shriner). Home: 506 Peebles St Philadelphia MS 39350 Office: Walter Sillers State Office Bldg Jackson MS 39201

JOHNSON, PAUL BURKE, radio exec.; b. Washington, Aug. 11, 1935; s. Paul and Gladys (Hobbs) J.; student Morris Brown Coll., 1953-57; m. Barbara Ann Fisher, May 29, 1960; children—Toie, Paul, Keemeit, India. With WAOK radio, Atlanta, 1957—, former announcer, program dir., 1968—. Served with AUS, 1958-60. Named Young Man Year, Y's Men's Club Internat., 1972. Mem. Omega Psi Phi. Baptist (trustee). Home: 20 E Lake Dr SE Atlanta GA 30317 Office: 75 Piedmont Av NE Atlanta GA 30303

JOHNSON, PERRY ELLIOTT, real estate broker; b. Dover, Fla., Oct. 31, 1933; s. John A. and Beulah A. (Claville) J.; B.S.A., U. Fla., 1955; m. Jean Woodard, Dec. 21, 1952; children—Deborah Jean, Gregory Elliott, Sean Dale. Vocational agrl. tchr. Fort Meade (Fla.) High Sch., 1955-57; real estate salesman and broker Perry E. Johnson, Realtor-Appraiser, Plant City, Fla., 1958—. Pres. Joe Nyberg Realty, Inc., Plant City, 1971—; adj. prof. U. Fla., Plant City, 1970-74. Pres. Plant City Bd. Realtors, 1972—. Mem. horseman's com. Fla. Downs, Tampa, 1973-74. Named Realtor of the Year, Plant City Bd. Realtors, 1972. Mem. Nat. Assn. Ind. Fee Appraisers, Fla. Thoroughbred Breeders Assn. Elk. Home: Rural Route 7 Box 371 Plant City FL 33566 Office: PO Box 1411 Plant City FL 33566

JOHNSON, PHAY BATSON, accountant; b. Argyle, Tex., Dec. 9, 1899; s. Lewis and Rachel (Austin) J.; student Met. Bus. Coll., 1924, YMCA Sch. Commerce, 1929; B.S., Jefferson U., 1933; m. Lillie Mae Hamm, Sept. 12, 1936; 1 dau., Hazel Marie (Mrs. Bobby Denman Wilson). With IRS, Dallas, 1924-62, sr. agt., 1946-53, sr. reviewing officer, 1954-62; accountant, prin. firm Phay B. Johnson, Dallas, 1962—. Instr., YMCA Sch. Commerce, Dallas, 1933-34. C.P.A., Tex. Mem. Alpha Psi Lambda. Methodist. Mason (32 deg., K.T. Shriner). Club: Golf (Dallas). Address: 739 W 12th St Dallas TX 75208

JOHNSON, PHILIP CARL, JR., physician; b. White Plains, N.Y., Nov. 12, 1924; s. Philip Carl and Josephine (Losee) J.; B.S., U. Mich., 1948, M.D., 1949; m. Virginia Ford Snyder, June 1, 1960; children—Philip Carl III, Christopher Carl. Intern internal medicine U. Hosp., U. Mich., 1949-50, resident, 1951-54, asst. dir. radioisotope unit, 1954; chief radioisotope service, asst. dir. profl. services for research VA Hosp., Oklahoma City, 1955-60; dir. radioisotope lab. Meth. Hosp., Houston, 1960—, mem. attending service internal medicine, 1960—; instr. dept. medicine U. Mich., 1954; asst. prof. medicine U. Okla. Med. Sch., 1955-58, asso. prof., 1958-60; asso. prof. medicine Baylor Coll. Medicine, 1960-67, prof., 1967—. Mem. State Radiol. Adv. Bd., 1967—. Served to 1st lt. USAF, 1952-54. Fellow A.C.P., Am. Coll. Angiology; mem. A.M.A., A.A.A.S., Am. Soc. Clin. Pharms. and Therapeutics, Am. Fedn. Clin. Research, Soc. Nuclear Medicine, Central Soc. Clin. Research, Am. Thyroid Assn., So. Soc. Clin. Investigation. Home: 12122 Rip Van Winkle St Houston TX 77024 Office: 1200 Moursund Av Houston TX 77025

JOHNSON, PHILLIP EUGENE, educator; b. Bostic, N.C., Feb. 25, 1937; s. Lin Joe and Gertrude (Pitman) J.; B.S., Appalachian State U., 1959; M.A., Am. U., 1966; M.A., George Peabody Coll., 1963, Ph.D., 1968; postgrad. N.C. State U., 1971, Cambridge U., 1973; m. Carolyn Roberta Long, Dec 23, 1959; 1 son, Philip Marc. Tchr. math., Fredericksburg, Va., 1960-61, Fairfax County, Va., 1961-63; faculty U. Richmond, 1963-65, Vanderbilt U., 1966-71; prof. math. U. N.C., Charlotte, 1971—. Served with USMCR, 1960. Grantee, NSF, 1960-63, summers 1961-63, Ga. U., summer 1965. Mem. Math. Assn. Am., Nat., N.C. councils tchrs. math., Am. Assn. U. Profs., Pi Mu Epsilon. Author: A History of Set Theory, 1972. Contbr. articles to profl. jours. Home: 6717 Pencade Lane Charlotte NC 28215

JOHNSON, RALPH ALLEN, elec. products co. exec.; b. Reading, Pa., Oct. 10, 1925; s. Ralph Schultz and Sarah Elizabeth (Reider) J.; B.S., U. Fla., 1951; M.B.A., Harvard, 1959; m. Dorothy Anita Spearman, Mar. 24, 1951; children—Mark, Jeffrey, Ann. Exec. v.p., gen. mgr. Real Eight Co., Inc., Melbourne, Fla., 1973—; pres. Fla. Leasing Corp., 1960-62. Pres. Indian River Players, 1952-53; vice chmn. Brevard chpt. A.R.C., 1966-70; chmn. Brevard Econ. Devel. Council, 1968; active Brevard Hosp. Assn. Served with AUS, 1943-46. Decorated Bronze Star medal. Mem. Nat. Council Tech. Services Industries (dir. 1970—), Am. Mgmt. Assn., I.E.E.E., Phi Kappa Phi. Mem. Reformed Ch. Mason. Club: Eau Gallie Yacht (comdr. 1972) (Indian Harbour Beach, Fla.). Home: 980 Whitmire Dr Melbourne FL 32935 Office: Box 460 Melbourne FL 32901

JOHNSON, RICHARD ALVIN, research center exec.; b. Edwardsville, Ill., July 8, 1934; s. William and Elma Marie (Blixen) J.; B.S., George Washington U., 1960; m. Waltraud Adam, Jan. 24, 1959; children—Richard Alan, Teresa Lynn. Electronic field engr. Gen. Dynamics/Electronics, 1960-65; systems engr. ITT Fed. Labs., 1965-66; program analyst Gen. Elec. Co., 1966-71; dir. Miss. State U. Research Center, 1971—; bd. dirs. Advanced Devels., Inc., Bay St. Louis, Miss. Environmental Protection Systems Co., Jackson, Miss. Served with Signal Corps, AUS, 1955-58. Recipient tech. award in environmental sci. Am. Astronautical Soc., 1970. Mem. I.E.E.E., Am. Mgmt. Assn. Author: (with others) Operations Management, 1972. Contbr. tech. articles to profl. jours. Home: 2207 O'Donnell Blvd Gulfport MS 39501 Office: Bldg T-221 NASA/MTF Bay St Louis MS 39520

JOHNSON, RICHARD BARRY, educator, accountant; b. Quanah, Tex., July 28, 1946; s. William J. and Betty Earle (McBay) J.; B.B.A., U. Tex., 1968, M.B.A., 1969; m. Jane Ellen Green, Oct. 18, 1969. Staff accountant Price Waterhouse & Co., Dallas, 1969-71; asst. prof. Tarrant County Jr. Coll., Hurst, Tex., 1971—; owner C.P.A. practice, Arlington, Tex., 1972—. Trustee Lay Ministries Pubs., Inc., Arlington. C.P.A., Tex. Mem. Am. Inst. C.P.A.'s, Tex. State Soc. C.P.A.'s, Phi Gamma Delta. Kiwanian. Club: Six Flays-Sunrise (sec. Arlington 1972—). Home: 2109 Twin Elms St Arlington TX 76012 Office: 2401 W Park Row Arlington TX 76013

JOHNSON, RICHARD CAMPBELL, banker; b. Winter Garden, Fla., Oct. 11, 1928; s. Jesse Wilder and Marjorie (Campbell) J.; B. Landscape Architecture, U. Fla., 1950; m. Betty Jean Kelley, Aug. 10, 1949; 1 son, Richard Kelley. Exec. v.p. Seminole Nurseries (Fla.), 1950—; dir. Sylvan Abbey Meml. Park, Clearwater, Fla., 1958—; vice chmn. bd. Bank of Seminole, 1960—; chmn. bd., pres. First Comml. Bank, St. Petersburg, Fla., 1964—; vice chmn. First Community Bank, Largo, Fla., 1969—; chmn. bd. Northside Community Bank, 1972—, First Community Bank West Pasco; chmn., chief exec. officer Community Banks Fla.; chmn., pres. Countryside Community Bank, Clearwater, Fla., 1973—; chmn. Redington Community Bank, Redington Shores, Fla., 1973—; dir. Clearwater Mall Community Bank, Fla. Power Corp., St. Petersburg. Past chmn. St. Petersburg Zoning Bd. Bd. dirs. local Goodwill Assn., Salvation Army, Boy Scouts Am., Pinellas County United Fund. Served to maj. USAF, 1952-54. Mem. Fla. Nurserymen and Growers Assn. (pres. 1966), Fla. Bankers Assn., St. Petersburg Area C. of C. (pres. 1969), Pinellas County Com. 100, Kappa Sigma. Methodist. Kiwanian (pres. 1964). Clubs: Pinellas Country Commerce; St. Petersburg Yacht. Home: 801 65th St N St Petersburg FL 33710 Office: PO Box 3367 Seminole FL 33540

JOHNSON, RICHARD CARL, educator; b. Chgo., Sept. 2, 1933; s. Carl Helmer and Anne Katherine (Johnson) J.; B.A. in Liberal Arts, U. Chgo., 1954; postgrad. U. So. Cal., 1956-57; B.A. in Philosophy, U. Cal. at Los Angeles, 1958; M.A., U. Colo., 1962; m. Ann Elizabeth Faust, July 3, 1958; children—Eric Richard, Tawny Elizabeth. Asst. to acad. dean U. Colo., Boulder, 1963-65; dean students Tougaloo (Miss.) Coll., 1965-67, asst. prof. philosophy, 1967—, chmn. dept. philosophy and religion, 1969—. Cons. adult basic edn. research project Boston U., 1970. Pres., Jackson Area Council on Human Relations, 1969-71; treas. Am. Civil Liberties Union of Miss., 1971—, mem. exec. com., 1970—; founding bd. mem. Community Coalition for Pub. Schs., 1970-73. County and state del. Democratic party, 1963-64. Served with AUS, 1954-56. Mem. Am., Miss. (pres. 1972-73) philos. assns., Southwestern Philos. Soc., Urban League, Am. Assn. U. Profs., Beta Theta Pi. Mem. Ecumenical Ch. Reconciliation. Home: 735 Lawrence Rd Jackson MS 39206 Office: Tougaloo Coll Tougaloo MS 39174

JOHNSON, ROBERT BRUCE, chemist; b. Birmingham, Ala., June 15, 1922; s. Walter Newhall and Sara (Hamilton) J.; B.S., Birmingham-So. Coll., 1946; postgrad. Ohio State U., 1949; M.S., U. Ala., 1953; m. Elizabeth Lay, Aug. 11, 1962. Research asso. biochem. Spies' Nutrition Clinic, Hillman Hosp., Birmingham, Havana, Cuba, 1944-46; research asso. Med. Coll. Ala., 1946-55; chemist dept. toxicology and criminal investigation State of Ala., 1955-58, toxicologist in charge Birmingham div., 1958—; instr. in forensic sci. Mem. Jefferson County Citizens Com. of the Study of Juvenile Delinquency; adv. bd. Jefferson State Jr. Coll., Birmingham. Fellow Am. Inst. Chemists; mem. Am. Chem. Soc., A.A.A.S., Ala. Peace Officers Assn., Ala. Acad. Sci., Sigma Xi. Presbyn. Mason (32 deg., Shriner). Home: 1508 S 13th St Birmingham AL 35205 Office: Public Health Bldg 1912-8th Av S Birmingham AL 35233

JOHNSON, ROBERT DECKER, mortgage banking co. exec.; b. Altus, Okla., May 12, 1917; s. S.H. and Carrie Mae (Brown) J.; B.A., So. Meth. U., 1937, M.A., 1938; m. Kathleen Leeds, Dec. 23, 1940; children—Judy, Sally, Kathy. Vice pres. Dallas Fed. Savs. & Loan, 1946-49; v.p. Murray Investment Co., 1949-61, vice chmn., 1973—; pres. Home Mortgage & Investment Co., Dallas, 1961-73; dir. Citizens Nat. Bank, Dallas, Great Am. Res. Ins. Co., Dallas. Served to comdr. USNR, 1944-46. Mem. Tex. (dir.), Dallas mortgage bankers assns., Pi Kappa Alpha. Home: 4432 N Versailles St Dallas TX 75221 Office: 1818 N Akard St Dallas TX 75201

JOHNSON, ROBERT MARTELL, newspaper pub. co. exec.; b. El Paso, Tex., Dec. 22, 1927; s. Frank Denton and Cora (Smith) J.; student San Antonio Jr. Coll., 1946-48; B.J., U. Tex., 1950; m. Jackie Eladean Hale, Jan. 16, 1953; children—Robert Hale, Mark Denton. Reporter Winnsboro (Tex.) News, 1950; advt. salesman Galveston (Tex.) News-Tribune, 1952-53; advt. salesman Dallas Morning News, 1953-64; asst. to pres. News-Texan, Inc., 1964-65, pres., 1965—, dir., 1972—. Served with inf. AUS, 1950-52. Home: 10110 Mapleridge Dr Dallas TX 75238 Office: 4880 Alpha Rd Farmers Branch TX 75234

JOHNSON, ROBERT MILTON, drainage engr., city ofcl.; b. Putnam, Ala., Jan. 5, 1894; s. Robert Blakely and Elizabeth Anne (Bates) J.; student George Washington U., 1924-25; B.S. in Civil Engring., U. Fla., 1929, M.S. in Engring., 1937, C.E. (hon.), 1931; m. Alda Twilley Elzey, June 28, 1919; children—Robert Milton, James Harrison, William Elzey. Hydraulic research U. Fla., Gainesville, 1934-37; engr. City of Augustine (Fla.), 1937-40; water treatment supr. City of Tampa (Fla.), 1940-45, asst. city engr., 1945—, drainage engr., 1945-72. Served to capt. USMC, 1915-21; head ordnance dept., Guam, 1920-21. Registered profl. engr., Fla. Democrat. Baptist. Mason, Woodman of World. Home: 714 S Orleans Av Tampa FL 33606 Office: 404 E Jackson St Tampa FL 33602

JOHNSON, ROBERT PETER, physician; b. Springfield Gardens, N.Y., Sept. 10, 1930; s. Stanley Frances and Viola Josephine (Verinsky) J.; student Palm Beach Jr. Coll., 1948-50; B.S., U. Fla., 1952; M.D., Tulane, 1956; m. Barbara Louise Skipper, Dec. 26, 1965; children—Gordon Raymond, Robert Peter. Intern Jackson Meml. Hosp., Miami, Fla., 1956-57; univ. physician U. Miami (Fla.), 1960-62 physician, team physician Fla. State U. at Tallahassee, 1962-66, 71—; practice medicine, Tallahassee, 1966—; mem. staff Tallahassee Meml. Hosp., chmn. exec. com., 1971—. Served with M.C., USNR, 1957-60. Fellow Am. Acad. Sports Medicine; mem. Fla. Acad. Family Practice (v.p. 1973-74), Am. Acad. Family Practice, A.M.A., Assn. Mil. Surgeons U.S., So. Med. Assn., Fla. Med. Assn. (mem. ad hoc com. drug abuse), Big Bend TB and Respiratory Disease Assn. (chmn. med. adv. com.), Capital Med. Soc. (pres. 1974), Springtime Tallahassee. Kiwanian (v.p. Tallahassee club 1971). Home: 1006 Lothian Dr Tallahassee FL 32303 Office: 1330 Miccosukee Rd Tallahassee FL 32303

JOHNSON, ROGER EDWIN, govt. ofcl.; b. Glendale, Cal., Nov. 22, 1906; s, Jonathan Edwin and Jennie (Smith) J.; A.B., U. So. Cal., 1928, LL.B., 1930; m. Louise Thompson, Apr. 18, 1930; children—Jonathan Edwin, Amelia (Mrs. F. Lynn Alexander), Willa Ann. Admitted to Cal. bar; practice law, Whittier, Cal., 1930-43; chief litigation atty, regional office OPA, Los Angeles, 1943-44; asst. v.p. Superior Oil Co., Washington, 1944-61; v.p. Superior Oil Internat., Tripoli, Libya, 1961-63, exec. v.p., gen. counsel, London, Eng., 1963-70; spl. asst. to Pres., Exec. Office Pres., Washington, 1970-74; spl. asst. to chief protocol Dept. State, Washington, 1974—. Mem. Cal. State Bar, Pi Kappa Alpha, Phi Alpha Delta. Republican. Mem. Christian Ch. Mason (Shriner). Clubs: Congressional Country, Washington. Home: Apt 1405-E 4201 Cathedral Av NW Washington DC 20016 Office: The White House Washington DC 20500

JOHNSON, RONALD CARL, educator; b. Milw., Sept. 5, 1935; s. Carl Walter and Valeska Ella (Schulz) J.; B.S., Lawrence Coll., 1957; Ph.D., Northwestern U., 1961; m. Susan Nancy Anderson, Aug. 27, 1960; children—Erica Susan, Laura Karen. Faculty, Emory U., Atlanta, 1961—, prof. chemistry, 1973—. Mem. Ga. Acad. Sci. (chmn. chemistry sect. 1965-66, chmn. tech. programs 1972—), Am. Chem. Soc., A.A.A.S., Am. Assn. U. Profs. (sec.-treas. 1967-69), Phi Beta Kappa. Author: (with F. Basolo) Coordination Chemistry, 1964; Introductory Descriptive Chemistry, 1966; (with R.A. Day Jr.) General Chemistry, 1974. Contbr. articles to profl. jours. Home: 702 Luckie Lane Atlanta GA 30329

JOHNSON, RONALD ROY, educator; b. De Smet, S.D., Dec. 8, 1928; s. Roy Leonard and Edna Florence (Harrison) J.; B.S., S.D. State Coll., 1950, M.S., 1952; Ph.D., Ohio State U., 1954; m. Sally Jeanne Shamel, Oct. 9, 1955; children—Denetia, Jennifer, Melissa, John Scott. Asst. prof. Ohio Agrl. Research and Devel. Center, Wooster, and Ohio State U., 1955-60, asso. prof., 1960-65, prof., 1965-69; prof. animal nutrition and biochemistry Okla. State U., Stillwater, 1969-74; prof., head dept. animal sci. U. Tenn., Knoxville, 1974—. Nutrition cons. USPHS, 1958, 60. Lt. col. Army Res. Sr. postdoctoral fellow USPHS, 1965-66. Mem. Am. Soc. Animal Sci., Am. Dairy Sci. Assn., Am. Inst. Nutrition, Sigma Xi, Phi Kappa Phi. Mem. editorial bd. Jour. Animal Sci., 1963-68. Home: 2901 Fox Ledge Lane Stillwater OK 74074

JOHNSON, ROOSEVELT, JR., orgn. exec.; b. Conroe, Tex., Feb. 22, 1924; s. Roosevelt and Lossie Dee (Mitchell) J.; B.S., Central State Coll., 1949; postgrad. U. N.M., 1950-51, George Williams Coll, 1953-56; m. Juanita Brooks, Oct. 15, 1951; 1 dau., Melonee Danette. Clk. U.S. P.O., Dallas, 1950; sec. YMCA, Dallas, 1951-55, exec. sec., Wichita Falls, Tex., 1955-61, exec. dir., Dallas, 1961-69; exec. dir. Dallas Urban League, 1969—. Jurist All-Am. City award Nat. Municipal League, 1973. Past chmn. jr. bd. dirs. Gt. Liberty Life Ins. Co., Dallas. Chmn. Alpha Merit Group Com., Inc., Dallas; mem. Dallas Safety Commn., 1966—; mem. adv. bd. Youth Opportunity Center, 1967—; mem. Dallas Park and Recreation Bd. Bd. dirs. State Fair Tex. Served with USAAF, 1942-45. Mem. Nat. Assn. Inter-group Relations (treas. chpt. 1969—), Assn. YMCA Secs., Alpha Phi Alpha. Methodist. Mason (32 deg.), K.P. Home: 2521 South Blvd Dallas TX 75215 Office: 2606 Forest Av Dallas TX 75215

JOHNSON, ROY DOZIER, data processor; b. Tallahassee, Fla., Dec. 11, 1936; s. James Dennis and Mary Lou (Stein) J.; B.S., Fla. State U., 1961; m. Joy Blalock, June 3, 1961; children—Brian D., Alan T., Kristi M. Programmer, Pratt & Whitney Aircraft Co., West Palm Beach, Fla., 1961-62; sci. programmer Gen. Electric Co., Marshall Space Flight Center, Huntsville, Ala., 1962-65; systems analyst, programmer Systems Engring. Labs., Ft. Lauderdale, Fla., 1965-66; asst. dir. mgmt. systems div. Office Auditor Gen., State of Fla., Tallahassee, 1966-73, dir. legislative systems and data processing, 1973—. Served with USAF, 1959-60. Mem. Assn. Computing Machinery, Data Processing Mgmt. Assn. Baptist. Home: 2314 San Pedro Av Tallahassee FL 32304 Office: Holland Bldg Tallahassee FL 32304

JOHNSON, ROY EDWARD, educator, musician; b. Kansas City, Mo., May 28, 1923; s. Edward and Mabel (Bloom) J.; B.Music Edn., U. Neb., 1945; M.Music Edn., So. Methodist U., 1958, D.F.A. (hon.), 1973; m. Emma Sue Depwe, June 26, 1948; 1 dau., Susan. Voice tchr. Baylor U., Waco, Tex., 1946-51; minister of music First Meth. Ch., Pampa, Tex., 1951-57, Methodist Ch., Dallas, 1958-67; choral dir. Pearce High Sch., Richardson, Tex., 1967-68, Hillcrest High Sch., Dallas, 1968—; dir. music Ridgewood Park Methodist Ch., Dallas, 1968—. Mus. dir. charity shows, 1958—. Mem. Nat. Fellowship Methodist Musicians (pres. 1965-67), U. Neb. Alumni Assn. (life), Phi Mu Alpha Sinfonia (life). Kiwanian (dir. 1958—). Writer texts anthems: O God of All, Above, Below, 1967; Loud Roar of the Rocket, 1970; O Church of God, Reach Up, Reach Out, 1970; O God, Our Strength and Refuge Sure, 1968; O Men of God, Arise, 1968; Sing Hosanna, 1967; Jesus, Savior, Holy Child, 1970; Rejoice, O Christian Folk, Rejoice, 1970; Jesus, Joy of Every Soul, 1969; Darkness, 1969; A Child's Journey through the Christian Year, 1967; Sing to Our God, 1973. Home: 2255 Springhill Dr Dallas TX 75228 Office: 9924 Hillcrest Av Dallas TX 75230

JOHNSON, RUFUS CLIFTON, JR., city ofcl.; b. Atmore, Ala., Oct. 15, 1923; s. Rufus C. and Annie (Thomas) J.; B.S., Auburn U., 1944; M.S., U. Ala., 1948; m. Jean Roberts, June 25, 1950; children—Emily Elyse, Rufus C. III. Office engr. Polglaze & Basenberg, Engrs., Birmingham, Ala., 1946-47; project engr. Sullivan, Long & Haggerty, Gen. Contractors, Birmingham, Ala., 1948-49, McGowan Constrn. Co., Opelika, Ala., 1949-50; propr. own firm, Douglas, Ga., 1950-60; city mgr., Douglas, 1960—. Served with AUS, 1944-46. Mason (Shriner). Home: 702 E Jefferson St Douglas GA 31533 Office: E Bryan St Douglas GA 31533

JOHNSON, RUFUS SLAYDEN, JR., architect; b. Clarksville, Tenn., Nov. 2, 1925; s. Rufus S. and Audrey (Shelby) J.; student U. Tenn., 1946-47; B.S., Ga. Inst. Tech., 1950, B.Arch., 1951; m. Nancy Rebecca Holloman, July 28, 1945; children—Nancy Rue, Linda Sue, Rufus Slaydon, Carol Ann. Designer, Speight & Hibbs, Architects, Clarksville, 1950-53, asso., 1953-59; partner firm Speight, Hibbs & Johnson, Architects, Clarksville, 1959-60; partner Hibbs & Johnson, Architects, Clarksville, 1960—, v.p., 1963-72, pres., 1972—; pres. Rufus Johnson & Assos., Architects, Planners and Constrn. Mgrs., 1973—. Chmn., Clarksville-Montgomery County Regional Planning Commn., 1953-68; pres. Tenn. Citizens Planning Assn., 1965-66; chmn. Montgomery County chpt. A.R.C., 1963-64; pres. Ky.-Tenn. Vol. Council, Ft. Campbell, Ky., 1956; dir., exec. com. United Givers Fund, 1965-66; mem. Clarksville Montgomery County Bd. Appeals, 1953-68; chmn. Harriett Cohn Mental Health Center, 1972-73. Chmn. bd. dirs. Ed Norman Scholarship Trust. Served with USMCR, 1943-46. Mem. A.I.A. (chpt. treas. 1962), Am. Soc. Planning Ofcls., Clarksville-Montgomery County C. of C. (dirs., exec. com. 1973). Methodist (chmn. council ministers 1969-72, chmn. adminstrv. bd. 1973-74). Mason. Club: Clarksville Golf and Country. Home: 725 Kleeman Dr Clarksville TN 37040 Office: 634 Franklin St Clarksville TN 37040

JOHNSON, SAMUEL LAWRENCE, clergyman; b. Tyne Dock, Eng., Aug. 16, 1909 came to U.S., 1910, naturalized, 1930; s. Samuel and Florence Ann (Woody) J.; B.A., Carleton U., 1930; B.D., Andover Newton Theol. Sch., 1933; D.D., Piedmont Coll., 1954; m. Alice Martha Duncan, Nov. 9, 1935; children—S. Thomas, Denine Ann, Lawrice Kay. Ordained to ministry Conglist. Ch., 1933; minister Crombie St. Congl. Ch., Salem, Mass., 1933-41, Park Manor Ch., Chgo., 1941-51, Boulevard Congl. Ch., Detroit, 1951-60, 1st Congl. Ch., Kokomo, Ind., 1960-65, Pilgrim Congl. Ch., Birmingham, Ala., 1965—. Bd. dirs. Ministry to U. Ala., Birmingham. Mem. Soc. Bibl. Lit., Nat. Assn. Profs. Hebrew, So. Assn. Marriage Councilors. Mason, Moose, Rotarian. Author: Pig's Brother; The Squirrel's Bank Account. Home: 20 Gaywood Birmingham AL 35213 Office: 1430 John Wesley Circle Birmingham AL 35210

JOHNSON, SHELBY, state ofcl.; b. South, Ky., Nov. 11, 1923; s. James Henderson and Bertha (Hayes) J.; B.S., Western Ky. State Coll. 1950; M.P.H., U. N.C., 1957; m. Doris Zetta Tomes, Dec. 28, 1945; 1 dau., Shelby Sue (Mrs. Jan Carroll Burleson). Tchr. vocational agr. Sunfish (Ky.) High Sch., 1950-54; with Ky. State Dept. Health, Frankfort, 1954—; dir. environmental br. Bur. for Health Services, Ky. Dept. Human Resources, 1974—. Mem. exec. bd. Interstate Milk Shipments Conf., 1965—, chmn., 1967-71, dir. environmental services program, 1967—. Served with AUS, 1941-45. Recipient Nat. Sanitarians award, 1971. Mem. Ky. Assn. Milk, Food, and Environmental Sanitarians (pres. 1963-64), Central States Assn. Food and Drug Ofcls. (pres. 1959-60, 65-66), Nat. Labeling Com. on Milk and Dairy Products (vice chmn. 1963-69), Assn. Food and Drug Ofcls. So. States (pres. 1970-71), Assn. Food and Drug Ofcls. U.S. (exec. bd. 1972—). Mason (32 deg., Shriner). Home: 179 Sunset Dr Frankfort KY 40601 Office: 275 E Main St Frankfort KY 40601

JOHNSON, THOMAS, economist; b. Halletsville, Tex., Feb. 12, 1936; s. Louis C. and Gladys (Gilmore) J.; A.A. with high honors, Navarro Jr. Coll., 1955; B.A. with honors, U. Tex., 1957; M.A., Tex. Christian U., 1962; M. Exptl. Statistics, N.C. State U., 1967, Ph.D., 1969; m. Cleta Joy Anderson, Sept. 8, 1956; children—David Eugene, Michael Joseph, Mark Alan. Engr. Gen. Dynamics, Fort Worth, 1957-61; engr. Ling Temco Vought Aeros., 1961-64; analyst Research

Triangle Inst., 1964-69; research asso. N.C. State U., 1969; dir. manpower research So. Meth. U., 1970—, chmn. econs., 1971-72. Cons. Research Triangle Inst., 1969-71, Southland Corp., 1969-72, ABT Assos., 1970-71. Recipient Nat. Def. Edn. Act fellowship N.C. State U., 1968-69; NSF grantee N.C. State U., 1969. Mem. Operations Research Soc. Am., Am. Statis. Assn., Econometric Soc., Am., So. econ. assns., Phi Kappa Phi, Phi Theta Kappa, Pi Mu Epsilon. Baptist. Home: 508 S Lois Lane Richardson TX 75080 Office: Dept Econs and Statistics So Meth U Dallas TX 75275

JOHNSON, THOMAS FRANK, economist; b. Lynchburg, Va., Sept. 27, 1920; s. Thomas Frank and Inez (McDaniel) J.; student Lynchburg Coll., 1939-41; B.A., U. Va., 1943, M.A., 1947, Ph.D., 1949; m. Margaret Ann Emhardt, Dec. 29, 1951; children—Thomas Emhardt, Sarah Lee, William Harrison Johnson. Economist U.S. Dept. Agr., Washington, 1949-51, U.S. C. of C., 1951-54; asst. commr. FHA, 1954-58; dir. legislative analysis Am. Enterprise Inst. for Pub. Policy Research, Washington, 1958-59, dir. research, 1960—. Sec.-treas. Inst. Social Sci. Research, Washington. Trustee Alexandria Hosp. Served to lt. USNR, 1943-45, PTO; lt. comdr. Res. Mem. Am., So., Royal econ. assns., Nat. Tax Assn., Am. Finance Assn., Nat. Assn. Bus. Economists (chpt. pres. 1971). Episcopalian. Club: Cosmos. Contbr. articles to profl. jours. Home: 1113 N Gaillard St Alexandria VA 22304 Office: 1150 17th St NW Washington DC 20036

JOHNSON, THOMAS NELSON PAGE, JR., investment banker; b. Farmville, Va., Mar. 2, 1918; s. Thomas Page and Elizabeth Rebecca (Robertson) J.; grad. Woodberry Forest Sch., 1937; B.A., U. Va., 1946; postgrad. bus. law U. Richmond; m. Helen Elizabeth Smith, July 7, 1942; children—Mary Parke, Thomas Nelson Page III, Elizabeth Anne, Helen, James. Asst. supt. leaf dept. Export Leaf Tobacco, Richmond, Va., 1944-47; mgr. Eastern Bldg. Supply Co., Norfolk, Va., 1947-50; pres. North Linkhorn Devel. Corp., 1950-58; account exec. Anderson & Strudwick, Virginia Beach, Va., 1958-60; sales mgr. Scott and Stringfellow, Richmond, Va., 1960-62; br. mgr. Anderson & Strudwick, Virginia Beach, 1962-63; v.p. Investment Corp. Va., Norfolk, 1963—; gen. partner Coriva Assos., dir. CRV Inc., Carmatic Systems Inc., Automotive Exchange, Va. Ventures, Inc., Wythe Corp. Former trustee, mem. exec. com. Student Aid Found. U. Va., now chmn. athletic adv. com. Served as pilot, 1st lt. USAAF, 1941-43. Mem. Raven Soc., Financial Analyst Soc., Soc. Descs. of Signers Declaration of Independence, Bond Club Va. (mem. exec. com), Phi Gamma Delta. Clubs: Princess Anne Country (Virginia Beach, Va.); Country of Va. (Richmond); Farmington Country (Charlottesville); Harbor, Virginia (Norfolk). Home: 221 63d St Virginia Beach VA 23451 Office: United Va Bank Bldg Norfolk VA 23510

JOHNSON, WALLACE HAROLD, govt. ofcl.; b. Cleve., Oct. 7, 1939; s. Wallace Harold and Esther Emma (Miller) J.; B.A., Ohio U., 1961; postgrad. Rutgers Sch. Law, 1961-62; J.D., U. Toledo, 1965; m. Donna Mae Simpson, June 9, 1962; children—Kimberley, Todd, Victoria, Eric. Joined Justice Dept., 1965; chief Organized Crime and Racketeering Strike Force, Miami, Fla., 1968-69; minority counsel Criminal Laws subcom. Senate Jud. Com., Washington, 1969-70; asso. dep. atty. gen. U.S., 1970-72; spl. asst. to the Pres., 1972-73; asst. atty. gen. land and resources div. Dept. Justice, 1973—. Mem. Am. Bar Assn., Bar Assn. D.C. Republican. Home: 1858 Foxstone Dr Vienna VA 22180 Office: Land and Natural Resources Div Dept Justice Washington DC 20530

JOHNSON, WAYNE RAYMOND, physician; b. Duluth, Minn., Nov. 2, 1934; s. Ray Carl and Hildur Elizabeth (Nelson) J.; B.A., Gustavus Adolphus Coll., 1956; B.D., Augustana Theol. Luth. Sem., 1960; M.D., U. Miami, 1968; m. Darlene Marian Cross, Sept. 12, 1959; children—Gwynne, Matthew. Mission developer Luth. Ch. Am., 1960-64; intern Jackson Meml. Hosp., Miami, Fla., 1968; resident physician U. Miami, Jackson Meml. Hosp., 1969-70; practice medicine, Hollywood, Fla., 1971—; mem. edn. com. Hollywood Meml. Hosp., 1971—; dir. med. edn., dept. family medicine U. Miami Sch. Medicine, 1971, asst. prof., 1971—. Diplomate Am. Bd. Family Practice. Fellow Am. Acad. Family Practice (pres.-elect Broward County chpt.); mem. A.M.A., Am., Fla. acads. family physicians, Broward County Med. Assn., Phi Chi. Lutheran (mem. exec. bd. Fla. synod 1970—). Home: 1501 NW 74th Terrace Hollywood FL 33024 Office: 3939 Hollywood Blvd Hollywood FL 33021

JOHNSON, WILEY, lawyer; b. Corsicana, Tex., Mar. 17, 1908; LL.B., So. Meth. U., 1932. Admitted to Tex. bar, 1932; now mem. firm Johnson, Bromberg, Leeds & Riggs, Dallas. Mem. Dallas, Am. bar assns. Address: 1500-211 North Ervay Bldg Dallas TX 75201

JOHNSON, WILLIAM ALEXANDER, educator; b. Ennis, Tex., June 22, 1922; s. William Frederick and Lillian (Wilson) J.; student U. S.W. La., 1938-40; B.S., La. State U., 1943, M.S., 1949; Ph.D., U. Minn., 1952; m. Joy Maxine Marchand, Apr. 2, 1946; 1 dau. Mary Judith (Mrs. Robert M. Coleman), David William. Faculty dept. poultry sci. La. State U., Baton Rouge, 1948—, asso. prof., 1962-65, prof., 1965—. Vis. prof. Ia. State U., Ames. 1959-60. Mem. Istrouma Area council Boy Scouts Am., 1960-70. Chmn. bd. Internat. Hospitality Found. Served with USNR, 1943-46. Mem. Poultry Sci. Assn., World Poultry Sci. Assn., Poultry Industries La., Sigma Xi, Gamma Sigma Delta. Home: 5757 Chandler Dr Baton Rouge LA 70808 Office: Dept Poultry Sci La State U Baton Rouge LA 70803

JOHNSON, WILLIAM E. III, lawyer; b. Dallas, Dec. 5, 1943; s. William E. Jr. and Gloria Jane (Warner) J.; A.B., Princeton, 1966; J.D., U. Tex., 1969; LL.M., So. Meth. U., 1970; m. Lindé Lee Roy, Jan. 19, 1974. Admitted to Tex. bar, 1969; atty. Howell, Johnson, Mizell, Taylor, Price & Corrigan, Dallas, 1969—. Lectr. seminars Tex. Assn. C.P.A.'s, , Tex. Assn. Pub. Accountants, others. Group leader atty.'s unit United Way, 1973; exec. mem. 500, Inc.; mem. adv. council Dallas Community Chest Trust Fund; mem. devel. council Baylor Coll. Dentistry. Mem. Am., Tex., Dallas (chmn. bar candidates com. 1973) bar assns., Order of Coif, Phi Delta Phi. Clubs: Northwood, Cipango, Calyx, Chimeras. Home: 4615 N Versailles Dallas TX 75209 Office: 2700 Republic Nat Bank Tower Dallas TX 75201

JOHNSON, WILLIAM GARNETT, state ofcl.; b. Providence, Ky., Sept. 30, 1911; s. John Riley and Zita Marguerite (Lucas) J.; student Western Ky. State Coll., 1930-32, U. Ky., 1940-41, George Washington U., 1944-45; m. Elizabeth Hagan Mudd, May 23, 1942; children—William Garnett, Sarah Marguerite (Mrs. John W. Lowery, Jr.). Supr. research and statistics Ky. Unemployment Compensation Commn., Frankfort, 1942-44; chief activities reports unit Bur. Employment Security, Washington, 1944-47; exec. asst. to Ky. commr. econ. security, Frankfort, 1948-55, 55-69, exec. dir. Bur. Employment Security, Dept. Econ. Security, 1969-71; commr. Ky. Dept. Econ. Security, 1955, acting commr., 1971-72, chmn. econ. security task force on mgmt. and orgn., 1972—. Project dir. Asian manpower seminar AID-Internat. Assn. Personnel in Employment Security, Manila, Philippines, 1970-71, project dir. Latin Am. manpower seminar, Panama City, Panama 1971-72; project dir. African Manpower Seminar, Nairobi, Kenya, 1973. Mem. Internat. Assn. Personnel in Employment Security (internat. pres. 1956-57), Interstate Conf. Employment Security Agys. (regional v.p. 1971-72, adminstrv. finance com. 1973), Internat. Council for Personnel Devel. in Employment Security (chmn. 1956), Am. Pub. Welfare Assn., Ky. Welfare Assn., Council for Profl. Advancement, Ky. Hist. Soc. Methodist. Optimist (v.p. East Frankfort 1967-68). Contbr. articles to profl. jours. Home: 401 Hiawatha Trail Frankfort KY 40601 Office: Capitol Annex Office Bldg Frankfort KY 40601

JOHNSON, WILLIAM KIRK, JR., architect; b. Kansas City, Mo., Jan. 24, 1936; s. William Kirk and Ella (Howard) J.; B. Arch., U. Tex. at Austin, 1961; m. Evangeline Sue Grun, June 5, 1956; children—Kim, Lori, Lisa, Pam. Designer Philip Carrington, architect, San Antonio, 1961-67, Ayres & Ayres, San Antonio, 1968-69, Harrell & Hamilton, architects, Dallas, 1969; project architect The Oglesby Group, Inc., Oglesby, Wiley, Halford, Dallas, 1970-72; prin. Oglesby Group, Oglesby, Wiley, Halford, Johnson, 1973—. Named hon. citizen Tex., 1966. Mem. A.I.A. (dir. San Antonio chpt. 1967-68), Tex. Soc. Architects. Presbyn. (deacon 1965-68). Home: 3134 Darvany St Dallas TX 75220 Office: 710 N Saint Paul Dallas TX 75201

JOHNSON, WILLIAM MARTIN, govt. ofcl.; b. Alexander, N.D., Mar. 11, 1916; s. Martin Bernard and Jessie Beatrice (Hanson) J.; B.S., N.D. State U., 1936; M.S., U. Wis., 1938; Cal. Inst. Tech., 1944; m. Carol R. Ladwig, May 28, 1939; children—Lynne (Mrs. Thomas S. Manaugh), Larissa (Mrs. E. Joseph Schneider). With Dept. Agr., soil correlator, then prin. soil correlator Dept. Agr., Lincoln, Neb., 1946-47, 49-53, various positions, 1954-71, dep. adminstr. Soil Conservation Service, Washington, 1971—; prof. charge soils N.D. State U., 1938-43; prof. soils Facultad Nacional de Agronomia, Medellin, Colombia, 1948. Chmn. Exchange Mission to Soviet Union, 1964. Served with lt. comdr. USNR, 1943-46. Decorated Bronze Star, Air medal with gold star. Fellow Wis. Alumni Research Found. Fellow Am. Soc. Agronomy; mem. Internat. Soil Sci. Soc., Soil Sci. Soc. Am. (asso. editor proc. 1961-63), Brit., Belgian socs. soil sci., Sigma Xi, Alpha Gamma Rho, Alpha Zeta, Gamma Alpha. Club: Cosmos (Washington). Home: 1111 DeVere Dr Silver Spring MD 20903 Office: Soil Conservation Service Dept Agr Washington DC 20250

JOHNSON, WILLIAM ROYSTER, architect; b. Raleigh, N.C., Aug. 18, 1901; s. Charles Cousins and Maude Eleanor (Harris) J.; student Hampden-Sydney Coll., 1918-21; student U. Va., 1921-25, Art Students League, 1926-27; m. Elizabeth Terry Niedringhaus, Oct. 9, 1959; 1 son, William Royster. Designer, M.S. Wyeth, architect, 1925-26, chief designer, 1927; designer Wyeth & King, architects, 1926, partner, 1932; partner Wyeth, King & Johnson, architects, Palm Beach, Fla., 1944-73; individual practice William R. Johnson, Architect, Palm Beach, 1973—. Mem. archtl. rev. commn., Town of Palm Beach. 1971—. Bd. dirs. Palm Beach Art League, 1948-55, pres., 1954-55. Recipient Hon. Mention, Archtl. League N.Y., 1938. Mem. A.I.A., Soc. Four Arts, Palm Beach Art League, Kappa Sigma. Democrat. Episcopalian. Clubs: Bath and Tennis, Everglades (gov. 1970—) (Palm Beach); St. Louis Country. Prin. archtl. works include Vietor Residence, Palm Beach, Norton Gallery and Sch. of Art, West Palm Beach, Fla., Dining Hall, Mercersburg Acad., Gerard Lambert residence, Manalapan, Fla. Home: 214 Plantation Rd Palm Beach FL 33480 Office: 207 Royal Palm Way Palm Beach FL 33480

JOHNSON, WILLIAM STANLEY, educator; b. Camden, Tenn., Dec. 9, 1939; s. William Curtis and Virginia (Harned) J.; B.S., U. Tenn., 1961; M.S., Clemson U., 1965, Ph.D., 1967; m. Jacquelyn Eve Smith, Aug. 23, 1963; children—William Steven, Kathryn Eve. Design engr. Pratt & Whitney Aircraft Corp., 1961-63; prof. mech. engring. U. Tenn., Knoxville, 1967—. Cons. TVA Mem. Am. Soc. M.E. (dir.), Am. Inst. Aeros. and Astronautics, Am. Soc. Engring. Edn., Sigma Xi, Tau Beta Pi, Phi Kappa Phi, Sigma Alpha Epsilon, Pi Tau Sigma. Contbr. articles to profl. jours. Home: 9121 Carlton Circle Concord TN 37720 Office: U Tenn Knoxville TN 37916

JOHNSON, WILLIAM THEODORE KIM, physicist; b. Keijo, Chosen, Japan, Aug. 8, 1938 (parents Am. citizens); s. Ural Alexis and Patricia Ann (Tillman) J.; B.S. (NSF fellow), U. N.C., 1962; M.S., Am. U., 1966, Ph.D., 1970; m. Maria Antonia Cavanagh, June 23, 1973; 1 stepson, Matthew Noel Murray. Physicist, Harry Diamond Labs., Dept. of Army, Washington, 1960-63; AEC fellow Nat. Bur. Standards, Gaithersburg, Md., 1967-70; staff researcher Rand Corp., Santa Monica, Cal., 1970-72; mem. tech. staff Gen. Research Corp., Arlington, Va., 1972—. Cons. Sci. Applications Inc., La Jolla, Cal., 1970-71; Rand Corp., Santa Monica, Cal., 1972-73. Mem. Am. Phys. Soc. Home: 6516 Ridge St McLean VA 22101 Office: 7655 Old Springhouse Rd McLean VA 22101

JOHNSON, WILLIS WITHERSPOON, JR., food brokerage exec.; b. Fort Smith, Ark., Sept. 30, 1913; s. Willis Witherspoon and Jennie (Eberle) J.; student Princeton, 1931-32; B.S., U. Va., 1935; m. Eugenia Branch Peek, May 17, 1939; children—Genie (Mrs. William B. Sigler), Elizabeth (Mrs. John D. Bridgforth). Partner Willis Johnson Co. (name changed to Willis Johnson Co. Inc. 1961), Little Rock, 1937-61, pres., 1961—. Trustee Ark. Childrens Hosp., Little Rock., 1953—, pres., 1958-60. Served to lt. comdr. USNR, 1942-45. Mem. Nat. Food Brokers Assn. (nat. chmn. 1954), Sigma Alpha Epsilon. Presbyn. (elder). Rotarian (pres. local club 1971-72). Clubs: Little Rock, Country (Little Rock). Home: 129 Normandy Rd Little Rock AR 72207 Office: 520 E Markham St Little Rock AR 72203

JOHNSON, WYATT THOMAS, JR., newspaper editor; b. Macon, Ga., Sept. 30, 1941; s. Wyatt Thomas and Josephine Victoria (Brown) J.; A.B., U. Ga., 1963; M.B.A., Harvard, 1965; m. Edwina Mac Chastain, Dec. 29, 1963; children—Wyatt Thomas III, Crista Farie. Reporter, mgmt. trainee Macon (Ga.) Telegraph and News, 1958-65; White House fellow, 1965; asst. press sec. to Pres. of U.S., 1966, dep. press sec., 1967, spl. asst. to the Pres., 1968-69; exec. asst. to Lyndon B. Johnson, 1969-70; exec. v.p. Tex. Broadcasting Corp., Austin, 1970-73; editor Dallas Times Herald, 1973—; mem. exec. com. City Nat. Bank. Chmn. Nat. Found. for Central Tex., 1972; nat. chmn. Lyndon Baines Johnson Commerative Stamp Com. Bd. dirs. Lyndon B. Johnson Found.; adv. bd. Sch. Journalism, U. Ga., Sch. Communications and Sch. Bus., U. Tex. Named Outstanding Young Man Ga. Jr. C. of C., 1967, one of five outstanding Young Texans, 1973, one of 10 outstanding Young Men of Am. U.S. Jr. C. of C., 1974, Man of Year, Sigma Nu, 1962. Mem. Headliners, Sigma Delta Chi, Omicron Delta Kappa, Phi Kappa Phi, Phi Eta Sigma. Club: Rotary (Austin). Author: (with Lee Moore) Automating Newspaper Composition, 1965. Home: 4811 Hallmark Dallas TX 75229 Office: Dallas Times Herald 1101 Pacific Dallas TX 75202

JOHNSTAD, ERROL, labor union exec.; b. Wis.; student Marquette U., U. Ill., U. Md., U. Tenn.; grad. with honors in math. Washington U., St. Louis; postgrad. propulsion and space engring. U. Mo.; m. Jean Winninger; children—Kristin, Kara, Kurt. Formerly flight test engr., test pilot McDonnell Douglas Co.; then flight engr. Pan Am. World Airways; formerly chmn., contract negogiator Flight Engrs. Internat. Assn., then v.p. chpt., v.p. for internat. affairs, now pres.; mem. gen. bd. AFL-CIO. Served with USAF. Named Airman of Year Gov. Wis. Mem. Alpha Epsilon Delta. Address: Flight Engrs Internat Assn 905 16th St NW Washington DC 20006*

JOHNSTON, CHARLES ERNEST, optometrist; b. Winchester, Va., Mar. 29, 1928; s. Wilbur Russell and Vergie Pauline (Carpenter) J.; student Shepherd Coll., 1951-54; B.S., So. Coll. Optometry, 1959, D.Optometry, 1959; m. Amelia Irene Rockwell, Nov. 11, 1950; children—Erica Lynn, Benjamin Luther. Technician, Bausch & Lomb, Winchester, 1945-47, Brondstater Opticians, Winchester, 1947-48; with Winchester P.O., 1949-50, 51-52; individual practice optometry, Winchester, 1959—. Organizer, Va. Optometric Polit. Action Com., 1974; treas. Northwestern Mental Health Assn., 1967-69; chmn. troop com. Boy Scouts Am., 1969-74. Served with U.S. Army, 1948-49, 50-51. Fellow Am. Sch. Health Assn.; mem. Am. Optometric Assn., So. Council Optometrists (trustee 1972-74), Va. (pres. 1973-74), Shenandoah Valley (pres. 1964-68) optometric socs., Tau Kappa Epsilon, Phi Theta Upsilon. Methodist (steward 1969—). Home: 327 Ridge Av Winchester VA 22601 Office: 27 W Boscawen St PO Box 1026 Winchester VA 22601

JOHNSTON, CHARLES LOUIS, JR., hematologist, educator; b. Danville, Pa., Nov. 4, 1923; s. Charles Louis and Lilian Taylor (Kerns) J.; A.B., U. N.C., 1947, M.S., 1949; M.D., U. Pa., 1953; m. Marjorie Sarah Hohenstein, Dec. 22, 1951; children—John Clinton, Sarah Annette, Bruce Fredrick, Charles Leif. Intern, Phila. Gen. Hosp., 1953-54; resident Hosp. U. Pa., Phila., 1954-56; research asst. U. N.C., Chapel Hill, 1956-59, asst. prof., 1960-65; prof. Med. Coll. Va., Richmond, 1965—. Served with AUS, 1943-46. Recipient USPHS Research Career Devel. award, 1960-65. Fulbright research fellow, Oslo, Norway, 1959-60. Diplomate Am. Bd. Pathology in Hematology. Mem. Am. Soc. Clin. Pathology, Am. Soc. Hematology, Am. Soc. Exptl. Pathology, Am. Soc. Physiology, Soc. Exptl. Biology and Medicine, Med. Soc. Va., Richmond Acad. Medicine, Acad. Clin. Lab. Physicians and Scientists, Assn. Clin. Scientists, Sigma Xi, Mason. Clubs: Briarwood Swim and Racquet, Willow Oaks Country. Contbr. sci. articles to med. jours. Home: 3509 Hastings Dr Richmond VA 23235 Office: 1200 E Broad St Richmond VA 23298

JOHNSTON, DONALD NEWHALL, county ofcl.; b. Sidney, O., Dec. 26, 1918; s. Chester L. and Elizabeth (Newhall) J.; student Miami U., Oxford, O., 1936-40; B.S., Fla. State U., 1952, M.S. in Govt.-Pub. Adminstrn., 1964; m. Isola Nelson, Jan. 17, 1942; children—Kristin Jean, Scott Anthony, Joel Bruce, Erin Beth. With Gen. Machinery Corp., Hamilton, O., 1941-42, Met. Life Ins. Co., Janesville, Wis., 1947-48; entered USAAF as pvt., commd. 2d lt. USAAF, 1942, trans. to USAF, 1947, advanced through grades to lt. col., 1954; asst. prof. air sci., tactics Fla. State U., 1949-53; chief base procurement div. and asst. dir. procurement and prodn. Hdqrs. Air Tng. Command, Randolph AFB, 1959-63, ret., 1963; village mgr. Village Granville (O.), 1965-66; exec. sec. Washington County (Va.), Abingdon, 1966-72; County adminstr. Franklin County, Va., 1973, Campbell Co., Va., 1973—. Mem. Internat. City Mgrs. Assn., Nat. Assn. County Adminstrs., Va. Assn. Counties (exec. bd.), Va. Assn. County Adminstrs. (past pres.), Nat. Municipal League, Am. Legion, V.F.W., Sigma Chi. Methodist. Mason. Home: 143 Stonewall Heights Abingdon VA 24210 Office: County Courthouse Rustburg VA 24588

JOHNSTON, FREDERICK SWAIN, JR., food brokerage exec.; b. Plant City, Fla., May 14, 1924; s. Frederick Swain and Rosemary (Lee) J.; student Emory U., 1942-43, U. N.C., 1945-46; m. Brucie Nelson Humphery, June 17, 1953; children—Frederick III, Jenifer Lee, Mary Bruce. With Fla. Citrus Exchange (now Seald-Sweet Sales), Tampa, 1946-48, MacDonald div. (now Coca-Cola Foods div.) Clinton Foods Co., Auburndale, Fla., 1948-50; now pres. Columbia Brokerage Co., Inc., Tampa. Served with inf. AUS, 1944-45. Mem. Food Brokers Assn., Tampa, Nat., Washington food brokers assns., Kappa Alpha. Episcopalian. Clubs: University, Tampa Yacht and Country, Ye Mystic Krewe of Gasparilla (all Tampa). Author: Logic of Relationship, 1968; Fundamental Relationships and their Logical Formulation, 1974. Home: 1005 Bayshore Blvd Tampa FL 33606 Office: Suite 316 1211 N West Shore Blvd Tampa FL 33607

JOHNSTON, GARVIN H., state ofcl.; b. Marion County, Miss.; grad. Pearl River Jr. Coll.; B.S., Ed.D., U. So. Miss.; M.A., U. Ala.; m. Willene Bullock; 1 dau., Judy Beth (Mrs. Thomas Walley). Successively tchr., prin. and supt. elementary and high sch., supr. high sch. Miss. Dept. Edn.; pres. Pearl River Jr. Coll., Poplarville, Miss., 1953-68; supt. edn. State of Miss., Jackson, 1968—. Chmn. Miss. Bd. Edn., Miss. Jr. Coll. Commn.; mem. Council Chief State Sch. Officers, also rep. other boards; mem. state adv. com. for vocational and tech. edn. Bd. dirs. Miss. Econ. Council, former mem. edn. com. Served with AUS, World War II. Named Citizen of Year, Poplarville, 1967. Mem. Am. Legion, Poplarville Club (past pres.), Miss. Edn. Assn. (past pres.), Miss. Jr. Coll. Assn., Miss. Assn. Colls., Miss. Hist. Soc. Baptist (deacon). Mason, Rotarian. Office: Box 771 501 Sillers SE State Office Bldg Jackson MS 39205

JOHNSTON, HARRY RAYMOND, electric co. exec.; b. Pitts., Dec. 17, 1922; s. Harry Wright and Myrtle Estelle (Bryant) J. With Westinghouse Co., Pitts., also Raleigh, N.C., 1940-43, 45—, traffic mgr., Raleigh, 1956—. Pres., chmn. bd. Wake County Soc. for Prevention of Cruelty to Animals, Raligh, 1968—; pres. N.C. Humane Fedn., 1972—. Served with AUS, 1943-45. Mem. Triangle Traffic Assn. (dir.). Home: 919 Brookside Dr Raleigh NC 27604 Office: Box 9533 Raleigh NC 27603

JOHNSTON, HUGH BUCKNER, educator, historian; b. Wilson County, N.C., Apr. 11, 1913; s. Hugh Bolden and Ruth (Thomas) J.; A.B., Davidson Coll., 1933; A.M., George Washington U., 1946; m. Elizabeth Aldrich Briggs, Nov. 8, 1941 (div. 1953); children—Hugh Bolden III, Thomas Owen Drakeford; m. 2d, Edna Elizabeth Long, Oct. 23, 1953; 1 son, Hugh Bolden IV. Adminstrv. asst. Am. Nat. Red Cross, Washington, 1941-46; instr. Instituto Chileno-Norteamericano de Cultura, Santiago, Chile, 1947-50; prof. langs. and history Atlantic Christian Coll., Wilson, N.C., 1955—. Historian, Wilson County, 1938—. Mem. Modern Lang. Assn., Soc. War 1812, Am. Assn. Tchrs. Spanish, S.A.R., N.C. State Lit. and Hist. Assn., Carolina Charter Corp., S.C.V., Order First Families of Va., N.C. Soc. Preservation Antiquities, Jamestowne Soc., Order Stars and Bars, Am. Assn. U. Profs., Sigma Phi Epsilon. Conservative. Presbyn. Moose. Home: Thomas Farms Wilson NC 27893

JOHNSTON, IRA JUDSON, accountant; b. Willard, Mo., Mar. 11, 1924; s. Jesse Walter and Martha (Crutcher) J.; student Bryant and Stratton Bus. Coll., Louisville, 1947; m. Ann Laura Allen, May 28, 1949; children—Mary Jane, Joel Allen. Insp., Retail Credit Co., Madisonville, Ky., 1947-55, Daytona Beach, Fla., 1955-56; jr. accountant J.W. Johnston Jr., Brinkley, Ark., 1956-60; accountant Ligon Specialized Hauler, Inc., Madisonville, 1960-64; partner Amick & Helm C.P.A.'s, Madisonville, 1964—; dir. North City Ford, Inc., Madisonville, West Ky. Poultry, Inc., Central City, A&G Farm Fresh Eggs, Inc., Central City. Served with AUS, 1943-45. Decorated Combat Infantrymen Badge. Baptist (deacon). Lion (dist. gov. 1970-71). Home: 1707 Hillcrest St Madisonville KY 42431 Office: 173 W Lake St Madisonville KY 42431

JOHNSTON, JAMES ROBERT, elec. engr.; b. Cookeville, Tenn., Feb. 10, 1931; B.S., Tenn. Tech. U., 1954; m. Mattie F. Rodgers, Sept. 18, 1949 (dec. Oct. 1968); children—James E., Mark R.; m. 2d, Dorothy R. Miller, June 26, 1970; step-children—Lee O., Janey A.,

Peggy Sue Miller. Elec. maintenance dept. head Union Carbide Nuclear div. Oak Ridge Nat. Lab., 1954-66; supt. electric shop Dow Chem. Co., Freeport, Tex., 1966-69, supt. magnesium prodn. plant, 1969-73, project mgr., 1973—. Registered profl. engr. Tenn., Tex. Mem. Nat., Tex. socs. profl. engrs., I.E.E.E. (sr. mem., sec. subcom. on measurements of dielectrics), Am. Soc. for Testing and Materials. Home: 129 Red Bud St Lake Jackson TX 77566 Office: Dow Chem Co Freeport TX 77541

JOHNSTON, JERRY LYNN, oil field equipment exec.; b. Hampton, Ark., Apr. 26, 1933; s. Clarence and Zula (Blann) J.; B.S., Okla. U., 1955, M.S., 1956; m. Gayle Ann Toland, July 16, 1955; children—Karen L., Susan G., Robert Mark. Pres., Universal Oilfield Supply, Inc., Oklahoma City; v.p. Toland & Johnston, Inc.; partner Toland & Johnston; pres. Johnston Supply, Inc. Registered profl. engr., Okla., La. Episcopalian. Club: Quail Creek Golf and Country (Oklahoma City). Home: 11700 N Bryant St Oklahoma City OK 73111 Office: 3409 SE 74th St Oklahoma City OK 73109

JOHNSTON, J(OHN) BENNETT, U.S. senator; b. Shreveport, La., June 10, 1932; s. J. Bennett and Wilma (Lyon) J.; student Washington and Lee U., 1950-51, 52-53, U.S. Mil. Acad., 1951-52; LL.B., La. State U., 1956; m. Mary Gunn, 1956; children—J. Bennett III, Norman Hunter, Mary Lyon, Sarah Lee. Admitted to La. bar, 1956; mem. firm Johnston, Thornton & Pringle, Shreveport; U.S. senator from La., 1972—. Mem. Shreveport United Fund drive. Mem. La. Ho. of Reps., 1964-68, La. Senate, 1968-72. Former bd. dirs. Goodwill Industries. Served with U.S. Army, 1956-59. Named Outstanding Young Man of Year Shreveport Jr. C. of C., 1966. Mem. Am., La. Shreveport bar assns., Phi Delta Theta. Democrat. Baptist. Mason (Shriner). Office: 432 Russell Office Bldg Washington DC 20510

JOHNSTON, JULIAN ST. CLAIR, elec. engr.; b. Hattiesburg, Miss., July 3, 1924; s. Julian S. and Mabel (Potter) J.; B.E.E., La. State U., 1947; m. Katherine Ann Trowbridge, Feb. 19, 1955; children—Paul Andrew, Lynne Elizabeth, Cynthia Claire, Kathy Ann, Nancy Jean. Office adminstr. C.E., Memphis, 1945; test engr. Gen. Electric Co., Schenectady, 1947, plant engr., Jackson, Miss., 1948-51; sr. elec. engr. Lockheed Aircraft Corp., Marietta, Ga., 1951-66; individual practice cons. engr., Smyrna and Atlanta, 1966—. Republican committeeman Cobb County, Ga., 1962—. Served with AUS, 1943-45. Mem. I.E.E.E., Illumination Engring. Soc., Am. Legion, Soc. Am. Mil. Engrs., Tau Beta Pi. Republican. Methodist. Home: 142 Cumberland Dr Smyrna GA 30080

JOHNSTON, KENNETH JOHN, radio astronomer; b. N.Y.C., Oct. 9, 1941; s. John James and Marian (Nugent) J.; B.E.E., Manhattan Coll., 1964; Ph.D., Georgetown U., 1969; m. Therese Clasen, June 25, 1966. Postdoctoral research asso. Nat. Acad. Sci.-NRC, Naval Research Lab., Washington, 1969-71; lab. radio astronomer, 1971—. Instr., U. Va. No. Va. Regional Center, Falls Church, 1970—. Mem. Am. Astron. Soc., Internat. Union Radio Sci., Internat. Astron. Union, Sigma Xi. Home: 7305 Wickford Dr Alexandria VA 22310 Office: Naval Research Lab Code 7132 Washington DC 20390

JOHNSTON, LEWIS DUPUY, JR., dentist; b. South Boston, Va., June 23, 1920; s. Lewis Dupuy and Mary Easley (Craddock) J.; B.S., Hampden-Sydney Coll., 1942; D.D.S., Med. Coll. Va., 1950; m. Anne Washington Lee, Jan. 12, 1952; children—Lee, Lewis, Betty. Gen. practice dentistry, South Boston, 1950—. Mem. South Side Regional Planning Commn., 1968—. Mem. City Council, 1958—. Vice pres. Martinsville Convalescent Home. Served to capt. USMCR, 1942-46. Mem. Am. Dental Assn., Piedmont Dental Soc., Am. Acad. Gen. Practice, Acad. Dental Analgesia, Am. Soc. Preventive Dentistry, Kappa Sigma, Delta Sigma Delta. Presbyn. (elder). Home: 1316 South St South Boston VA 24592 Office: 526 Main St South Boston VA 24592

JOHNSTON, MARGUERITE (MRS. CHARLES WYNN BARNES), journalist; b. Birmingham, Ala., Aug. 7, 1917; d. Robert C. and Marguerite (Spradling) Johnston; A.B., Birmingham-So. Coll., 1938; m. Charles Wynn Barnes, Aug. 31, 1946; children—Susan, Patricia, Steven, Polly. Reporter, Birmingham News, 1939-44; Washington corr. Birmingham News, Birmingham Age-Herald and London Daily Mirror, 1945-46; columnist Houston Post, 1947-69, mem. editorial bd., asso. editor, 1969—. Lectr., 1947—; spl. lectr. U. Houston, 1965-66; del. Asian-Am. Women Journalists Conf., Honolulu, 1965; del. 1st World Conf. Women Journalists, Mexico City, 1969. Bd. dirs. Tex. Bill of Rights Found., 1962-64; adv. bd. Houston Council on Alcoholism. Recipient Theta Sigma Phi Headliner award, 1954; certificate of merit Gulf Coast chpt. Am. Soc. Safety Engrs., 1960; Agnese Carter Neims award Planned Parenthood, 1968. Mem. Houston Press Club, Mortar Bd., Phi Beta Kappa. Author: Public Manners, 1957; A Happy Worldly Abode, 1964. Home: 5319 Cherokee St Houston TX 77005 Office: Houston Post Houston TX 77001

JOHNSTON, RICHARD MILLER, ins. agt.; b. Orange, N.J., Dec. 16, 1933; s. Ralph M., Jr. and Virginia (Miller) J.; B.S. in Aero. Engring., U. Md., 1961; m. Lynda Adelle Myers, June 16, 1960; children—Kathryn, Julia, Richard, Meridith. Asso. Lawrence W. Myers Ins. Agy., Lake Worth, Fla., 1961—; sec.-treas. C & J Life, Inc., 1966—. Chmn. United Fund Palm Beach County, 1969—. Served with USAF, 1952-56. Mem. Lake Worth C. of C. (pres.), Phi Sigma Kappa. Conglist. (trustee). Rotarian (pres. 1968—). Home: 1528 N Lakeside Dr Lake Worth FL 33460 Office: 803 Lake Av Lake Worth FL 33460

JOHNSTON, RUPERT BERNARD, economist; b. Shannon, Miss., Jan. 13, 1919; s. John Riley and Lydia (Sanderson) J.; B.S., Miss. State U., 1950, M.S., 1951; Ed.D., Cornell U., 1960; m. Bertie Mae Stevens, Dec. 20, 1940; children—William Riley, Richard Allen, Robert Arthur, Mary Jean. Research asst., acting instr. agrl. econ. dept. Miss. State U., Mississippi State, 1951-52, asst. extension economist & Co., Coop. Extension Service, 1952-55, asso. extension economist, 1955-57, leader extension econs. dept., 1957-73, leader rural devel. Miss., 1973—. Bd. dirs. Wesley Found., Miss. State U. Served with USMC, 1944-46. Mem. Am. Farm Econs. Assn., Nat. Assn. County Agrl. Agts., Miss. Farm Mgrs. and Rural Appraisers Assn., Civitan (dist. gov. 1963), Epsilon Sigma Phi, Alpha Zeta, Gamma Sigma Delta. Home: PO Box 772 Mississippi State MS 39762

JOHNSTON, STANLEY DAVID, accountant; b. Birmingham, Ala., Sept. 9, 1935; s. William Farris and Edith (Shepard) J.; B.S., U. Ala., 1957; student U. Md., 1953-54; m. Joan Propst, June 2, 1956; children—Diana Jean, Gregory David. Staff accountant Arthur Andersen & Co., Atlanta, 1957-59; mgr. Downs & Box, Birmingham, Ala., 1960-63; partner Johnston & Raburn, Huntsville, 1963-70, Johnston, Brown & Co., Huntsville, 1970—. Mem. Huntsville Indsl. Expansion Com., 1968—. Mem. Am. Inst. C.P.A.'s, Ala. Soc. C.P.A.'s, Huntsville C. of C., U. Ala. Alumni Assn. (past v.p.), Beta Gamma Sigma, Kappa Sigma. Presbyn. Home: 2905 Barcody Rd Huntsville AL 35802 Office: 444 State Nat Bank Bldg Hunstville AL 35801

JOHNSTON, STEVE RENWICK, physician; b. Valdosta, Ga., Mar. 5, 1913; s. Sydney Kitrell and Kathryn (Stump) Smith; student U. Fla., 1930-33; M.D., Emory U., 1937; m. Christine P. Johnston; children (by previous marriage)—Venetia (Mrs. William M. Darby), Kathleen. Tchr. biology dept. U. Fla., 1931-33; intern Grady Hosp., Atlanta, 1936-37, Ga. Bapt. Hosp., Atlanta, 1937-38; practice gen. medicine, Okeechobee, Fla., 1938-40, Ft. Pierce, Fla., 1940-54; practice medicine specializing in abdominal surgery, obstetrics, gynecology, Clewiston, Fla., 1954-59, Okeechobee, 1959—; mem. staff and officer Hendry Gen. Hosp.; chief of staff Okeechobee Gen. Hosp.; pres. elect Okeechobee County Hosp.; chief of staff Ft. Pierce Meml. Hosp. Chmn. cub pack com. Cub Scouts Am., Okeechobee; mem. nat. voter adv. bd. Am. Security Council. Cons. USN Amphibious Tng. Base, Ft. Pierce, 1941-46. Recipient Certificate of Appreciation, Pres. of U.S. for service with SSS; award and scroll as one of South's Outstanding Personalities, 1971. Diplomate Am. Bd. Abdominal Surgery. Fellow Am. Geriatric Soc., Pan Am. Cancer Cytology Soc., Internat. Corr. Soc. Obstetrics-Gynecology, Am. Soc. Abdominal Surgeons, Am., Internat. colls. angiology, Internat. Acad. Law and Sci., Royal Soc. Health; mem. A.M.A., So. Fla. (better govt. com.) med. assns., Okeechobee, St. Lucie, Martin County (v.p. 1948-49, pres. 1951-52) med. socs., Nat., Fla. rehab. assns., Am. Brahaman Breeders Assn., Am. Quarter Horse Assn., Am. Palomino Horse Breeders Assn., Fla. Palomino Exhibitors Assn. (1st. v.p., dir.), Internat. Platform Assn., Delta Tau Delta, Phi Chi, Gamma Sigma Epsilon, Alpha Epilson Delta, Phi Eta Sigma. Home: 1009 SW 14th St Okeechobee FL 33472 Office: 209 NW 7th St PO Box 1227 Okeechobee FL 33472

JOHNSTON, WILLIAM FRANK, dentist; b. Copperhill, Tenn., May 27, 1922; s. Leon and Sarah Helen (Dickens) J.; B.S., Union Coll., 1948; D.D.S., U. Tenn., 1954; m. Elizabeth Norman, Nov. 20, 1943; children—Betsy, Patsy. Individual practice dentistry, Madisonville, Tenn., 1954—. Chmn. Monroe County Health Dept., Madisonville Housing Authority, sec. Madisonville Regional Planning Commn. Bd. dirs. Houston Park, Madisonville Indsl. Commn. Served with AUS, 1943-46. Mem. Am., Tenn. dental assns., Delta Sigma Delta. Presbyn. (trustee, elder). Mason. Home: Philpott St Madisonville TN 37354 Office: Carson St Madisonville TN 37354

JOINER, CHARLES LEE, ednl. adminstr.; b. Birmingham, Oct. 16, 1939; s. Kenneth Alexander and Florice (Johnson) J.; A.B., Central Wesleyan Coll., 1962; M.A., U. Ala., 1967, Ph.D., 1968; m. Gloria Melyndia Holt, June 23, 1962; children—Amy Melissa, Rebecca Malyndia. Asso. dir. Bur. Research, Community Service, U. Ala., Birmingham, 1968-69, dir., 1969—. Cons. in health planning field. Trustee Central Wesleyan Coll., Central, S.C. Mem. So. Econ. Assn., Ala. Acad. Sci., Birmingham C. of C. (chmn. manpower, vocational edn. com. 1970-72). Mem. Wesleyan Ch. (adminstrv. bd.) Home: 2113 Ridgeview Dr Birmingham AL 35216

JOLLY, ALAN GORDON, advt. exec.; b. Franklin, Ky., Sept. 8, 1930; s. James W. and Rebecca (Henson) J.; A.B., Colgate U., 1950; postgrad. U. Louisville, 1963-66; m. Martha Beverly Logan, Aug. 20, 1950; children—Brent Alan, Beverlee Anne. Radio announcer Bowling Green (Ky.) Broadcasting Co., 1947-50; advt. specialist Gen. Electric Co., Schenectady, Syracuse, N.Y., Bridgeport, Conn., Louisville, 1950-63; v.p., treas., dir. Zimmer-McClaskey-Lewis, Advt., Louisville, 1963—. Served from pvt. to 2d lt. USAF, 1950-53. Mem. Am. Marketing Assn. (chpt. dir. 1968-69), Louisville Advt. Club. Baptist (pub. relations cons.). Home: 8608 Holston Rd Lousville KY 40222 Office: 1469 S 4th St Louisville KY 40201

JOLLY, EDWARD MARTIN, engring. cons. co. exec.; b. Plain Dealing, La., Dec. 24, 1924; s. Herbert Martin and Myrtice Lillian (Hamiter) J.; B.S. Mech. Engring., La. Tech. U., 1949; m. Juanita Marie Biggs, Nov. 28, 1947; children—Donna (Mrs. William Wayne Wilson), Kaye (Mrs. Kenneth Alfred Cochran), Celeste, Lisa, Jennifer. With E.M. Freeman & Assos., Cons. Engrs., Shreveport, La., 1949-60; pres. Aillet, Fenner, Jolly & McClelland, Inc., Cons. Engrs., Shreveport, 1960—. Chmn., Engring. and Sci. Council, Shreveport, 1970-71. Served with AUS, 1943-45. Decorated Purple Heart, Bronze Star. Mem. Nat. Soc. Profl. Engrs., La. Engring. Soc. (chpt. pres. 1968-69), Am. Soc. C.E., Soc. Am. Mil. Engrs. (past chmn. 1964-65). Methodist (chmn. bd. dirs. 1970-72). Mason (Shriner). Clubs: S. Lakeshore Community (pres. 1958-60), Shreveport Swim (pres. 1970-73). Home: 3052 Gorton Rd Shreveport LA 71109 Office: 1055 Louisiana Av Shreveport LA 71101

JOLLY, RALPH MERRELL, accountant; b. Corning, Ark., June 28, 1940; s. Harles Leon and Alma Lee (Merrell) J.; B.A., Quachita U., 1962; 1 son, F. Vincent. Staff accountant Chatham, Brady, Lafferty & Cox, 1969-70; supr. spl. cost accounting Blue Cross-Blue Shield, Dallas, 1970-73; pvt. accounting practice, Dallas, 1971-73; staff accountant Hospitality Mgmt. Corp., Dallas, 1973—. Served with USNR, 1963-65. Mem. Tex. Soc. C.P.A.'s, Am. Inst. C.P.A.'s, Dallas Estate Planning Council. Home: 3701 Turtle Creek Apt 7D Dallas TX 75219 Office: 2 Tutle Creek Suite 1800 Dallas TX

JOLLY-FRITZ, ROLETTA OLGA (MRS. RALPH A. FRITZ), psychiat. cons.; b. Pleasantville, Ia., Sept. 17, 1896; d. Francis M. and Ida E. (Smith) Jolly; B.S., U. Ia., 1919, M.D., 1923; m. Ralph A. Fritz, July 9, 1925; children—Lolita (Mrs. Jesse S. Binford, Jr.), Jolee, Marcia (Mrs. Edwin S. Hartman). Intern, Psychopathic Hosp., Iowa City, Ia., 1923-24, psychiatrist, 1925-31; practice medicine specializing in psychiatry Pittsburg, Kan., 1928-42, 43-45; sr. psychiatrist Central State Hosp., Nashville, 1942-43; psychiatrist in-unit for children Allentown (Pa.) State Hosp., instr. Sch. Affiliated Nurses, 1946-56; chief out-patient clinic Osawatomie (Kan.) State Hosp., 1956-59; dir. Central Neb. Mental Hygiene Clinic, 1959-65; clin. psychiatrist Guilford County (N.C.) Mental Health Clinic, Greensboro, 1966-73; psychiat. cons. Guilford County Children and Youth Clinic, 1973—. Lecturing prof. Vanderbilt Med. Sch., Meharry Med. Coll., Nashville, 1942-43. Fellow Am. Psychiat. Assn. (life); mem. A.M.A., World Med. Assn., World, Midcontinent psychiat. assns., N.C., Guilford County med. socs., Am. Med. Women's Assn., World Fedn. for Mental Health, N.C. Mental Health Assn., N.C. Psychiat. Soc. Methodist. Home: 708 Plummer Dr PO Box 8003 Greensboro NC 27410 Office: 300 E Northwood St Greensboro NC 27401

JONAS, JOHN CHARLES, personnel exec.; b. Warsaw, Ind., Aug. 24, 1926; s. John Charles and Margarete Irene (Underwood) J.; B.S., Ill. Inst. Tech., 1952; m. Mary Elizabeth Rice, Nov. 5, 1948 (div. May 1970); children—Robert D., Nancy Lynn. Specialist electronic equipment, tech. writer Electronic Supply Office U.S. Navy, Great Lakes, 1947-52; head specifications dept., components engring. div. Raytheon TV & Radio Corp., Chgo., 1952; with Lear Siegler Inc., Grand Rapids, Mich., 1952-64, tech. writer, 1962-63, staff engr., 1963-64; freelance tech. writer, Grand Rapids, 1964-65; personnel mgr., sales engr. Techniques, Inc., Grand Rapids, 1965-68; personnel mgr. Advanced R & D Inc., engrs., Orlando, Fla., 1968—. Served with USNR, World War II; PTO. Mem. I.E.E.E. Home: 638-4 N Semoran Blvd Winter Park FL 32789 Office: 3100 Clay Av Orlando FL 32804

JONES, ALAN IVEY, investment co. exec.; b. Shreveport, La., Oct. 20, 1938; s. Joseph Reid and Ruby (Ivey) J.; student Kilgore Jr. Coll., 1957-59; B.S., Tex. Christian U., 1962; postgrad. So. Meth. U., 1967-69; m. Camilla Ann Patrick, Nov. 22, 1972; children by previous marriage—Juliana, Kathleen Elizabeth. Owner, Alan I. Jones Ins., Dallas, 1962-66; asso. Henry S. Miller Co., Dallas, 1966-69; v.p. M.L. Godwin Investments, Inc., Dallas, 1968-71; chmn. Alan I. Jones Investments, Inc., Dallas, 1971—; chmn. Alan I. Jones Devel. Co., Resource Energy Corp. Served with USNR, 1962, 68. Mem. Sales and Marketing Execs. Dallas, Dallas C. of C., Dallas Better Bus. Bur., Internat. Platform Assn. Presbyn. (deacon 1967-68). Rotarian (pres. chpt. 1967-68, dist. sec. 1970-71). Home: 3912 University Blvd Dallas TX 75205 Office: 3128 Lemmon Av East Dallas TX 75204

JONES, ALBERT CECIL, JR., civil engr.; b. Montevallo, Ala., July 29, 1938; s. Albert Cecil and Thelma Evelyn (Hearn) J.; B.C.E., Auburn U., 1959; m. Elizabeth Virginia Olive, Nov. 28, 1959; 1 son, Albert Cecil III. Bridge and bldg. supr. So. Ry., 1962-65; process engr. So. Ry., Atlanta, 1965-69; sr. design engr. Rust Engring., Birmingham, Ala., 1969-72; mgr., Harland Bartholomew & Assos., Birmingham, Ala., 1972—, asso. partner, 1974—. Mem. faculty U. Ala., Birmingham, 1971-72. Served to 1st lt. C.E. AUS, 1960-62. Registered profl. engr., Ala., Ark., Ky., Miss. Mem. Am. Soc. C.E., Inst. Traffic Engrs. (affiliate mem.). Mason (Shriner). Clubs: The Club, Relay House (Birmingham). Home: 2122 Vestridge Ct Birmingham AL 35216 Office: 6 Office Park Circle Suite 112 Birmingham AL 35223

JONES, ALBERT PEARSON, lawyer; b. Dallas, Tex., July 19, 1907; s. Dr. Bush and Ethel (Hatton) J.; student So. Meth. U., 1924; A.B., U. Tex., 1927, A.M., 1927, LL.B., 1930; m. Annette Lewis, Oct. 3, 1936; children—Dan Pearson, Lewis Avery. Admitted to Tex. bar, 1930, to U.S. Dist. Ct. So. and Eastern Jud. Dists. Tex., U.S. Ct. Appeals 5th Circuit, U.S. Supreme Ct.; asso. Baker, Botts, Andrews & Wharton, Houston, 1930-43; mem. firm Helm & Jones, Houston 1943-62; prof. law U. Tex. at Austin, 1962—; 1st asst. to atty. gen. State of Tex., 1963-64 (on leave). Trustee St. Lukes Hosp., 1949-62, Lulu Bryan Rambaud Charitable Trust, 1947-62. Fellow Am. Coll. Trial Lawyers; mem. State Bar Tex. (pres. 1950-51, dir. 8th congl. dist. 1948-50), Houston, Am. bar assns., Am. Law Inst., Order of Coif, Phi Beta Kappa, Phi Delta Phi. Episcopalian. Clubs: Houston Country; Country (Austin). Home: 4 Niles Rd Austin TX 78703 Office: 2500 Red River St Austin TX 78705

JONES, ALFRED IRVIN, JR., utility engr.; b. Richmond, Va., Apr. 29, 1929; s. Alfred Irvin and Indie (Phillips) J.; B.S.E.E., Va. Poly. Inst., 1956; postgrad. U. Richmond, 1956-62. Planning engr. Potomac dist. Va. Elec. & Power Co., Alexandria, 1962-68, dist. engr. Southside Dist., South Boston, Va., 1968-70, staff engr. System Planning, Richmond, 1970—. Served with USN, 1947-52. Mem. I.E.E.E. Home: 2311 Halifax Av Richmond VA 23224 Office: 7th and Franklin Sts Richmond VA 23220

JONES, ANDREW PAT, elec. engr.; b. Hereford, Tex., July 6, 1913; s. Andrew M. and Mina (Dameron) J.; B.S. in Elec. Engring., Tex. A. and M. U.; teaching certificate W. Tex. State U.; m. Helen Barber, Nov. 16, 1947; children—Robert Lee, Martha Lynn (Mrs. John C. Gocio). Chief planning engr. Central Power & Light Co., Corpus Christi, Tex., 1953-64; mgr., exec. engr. S. Central Electric Cos., Little Rock, 1964—. Pres., Yule Toy Bd., Corpus Christi, 1964. Bd. dirs. Christian Campsite Assn., Little Rock. Served with USNR, 1942-46, 51-53; PTO, ETO. Registered profl. engr., Tex., Ark. Mem. I.E.E.E. (sr.), Tex. Soc. Profl. Engrs., Nat. Rifle Assn., Tau Beta Phi. Home: 211 McMillen St Little Rock AR 72207 Office: 238 Tanglewood St Little Rock AR 72207

JONES, B. CORINE, bank exec.; b. Statesboro, Ga., Jan. 28, 1925; d. Mallie C. and Maude (Gay) Jones; grad. high sch. Clk. Western Auto Supply Co., Savannah, Ga., 1943-46; teller Carolina Nat. Bank, Anderson, S.C., 1950-51; with Liberty Nat. Bank & Trust Co., Savannah, 1946-50, 59—, clk., 1959-69, asst. cashier, 1969-72, banking officer, 1972—. Active United Community Services, March of Dimes, Cancer Soc. Mem. Inter City Credit Council (Named outstanding credit women 1965, 71), Savannah Credit Womens Club (pres. 1959-60), Ga. Assn. Credit Women (pres. 1970-71), Credit Women Internat., Nat. Assn. Bank Women, Am. Inst. Banking, Soc. Certified Consumer Credit Execs. Home: 3605 E Gate Dr Savannah GA 31404 Office: PO Box 8668 Savannah GA 31402

JONES, BEN WILLIS, former coll. pres.; b. Washington, Ga., Apr. 27, 1917; s. Willis Rayden and Ruth (Hinton) J.; B.S., Ga. So. Coll., 1940; M.A., George Peabody Coll. for Tchrs., 1946; Ed.D., U. Tex., 1950; m. Winna Weeks, Dec. 21, 1946; children—Christopher Dan, Kevin Weeks. Prin. Cedar Springs (Ga.) Jr. High Sch., 1939-40, Prospect Jr. High Sch., Montecello, Ga., 1940-42, Rogers & Albert Pike Sch., Ft. Smith, Ark., 1946-47; asst. dir. extension, asso. prof. edn. U. Miss., 1949-52; pres. N.E. Miss. Jr. Coll., 1952-56; pres. Navarro Coll., Corsicana, Tex., 1956-73. Mem. steering com. Tex. Program of Nursing Edn. under Kellogg Program; mem. Tex. Gov.'s Com. on Edn. Beyond High Sch.; mem. Bapt. Edn. Study Task, 1966-68. Trustee East Tex. Bapt. Coll. Served from cadet to maj. USAF, 1942-45. Decorated D.F.C., Air Medal with eight oak leaf clusters. Mem. Am. Assn. Jr. Colls. (adminstrn. commn. 1959-62, legislation com. 1965-68), Miss. Jr. Coll. Assn. (v.p. 1955-56), Tex. Jr. Coll. Athletic Conf. (pres. 1957, v.p. 1962-63), C. of C., Tex. Jr. Coll. Assn. (pres., finance com. 1963-69), Tex. Jr. Coll. Football Fedn. (pres. 1963-66), Phi Theta Kappa (hon.), Phi Delta Kappa, Kappa Delta Pi, Pi Gamma Mu. Baptist (deacon, vice chmn. deacons 1959-60, 68, chmn. long range planning com. 1970, mem. bldg. com. 1972-73). Rotarian. Home: 1007 Bryn Mawr St Corsicana TX 75110

JONES, BILLY RUAL, physician; b. Amarillo, Tex., June 11, 1926; s. Rual and Bess (Crutchfield) J.; B.S., Tufts U., 1946; M.D., Columbia, 1950; m. Elizabeth Anne Corbey, May 3, 1952; children—Deborah Anne, Kevin Timothy, Sharon Elizabeth, Julia Marie, Anne Claire. Intern Roosevelt Hosp., N.Y.C., 1950-51, resident, 1951-53; resident VA Hosp., Nashville, 1956-57; practice medicine specializing in internal medicine, Amarillo, 1957—; past pres. staff High Plains Bapt. Hosp.; past chief staff N.W. Tex. Hosp.; past chief med. service Bapt. Hosp., N.W. Tex. Hosp., St. Anthony's Hosp.; asso. prof. medicine Tex. Tech U. Sch. Medicine. Pres. Potter-Randall County Heart Assn., 1959, 63. Bd. dirs. Potter-Randall County Blood Bank, 1962-66; trustee Dad's Assn., Tex. Tech U. Served with USNR, 1944-45, 54-56. Mem. A.M.A., Am. Soc. Internal Medicine, A.C.P., Tex. Med. Assn., Tex. Acad. Internal Medicine, Tex. Soc. Internal Medicine, Potter-Randall County Med. Soc. Baptist. Rotarian. Clubs: Amarillo, Tascosa Country (Amarillo); Palo Duro (Canyon, Tex.). Home: 2808 Teckla St Amarillo TX 79106 Office: 5211 W 9th St Amarillo TX 79106

JONES, BOBBY LEE, city ofcl.; b. Lundale, W.Va.. Apr. 20, 1933; s. Sherman R. and Sylvia (Lanbert) J.; student St. Johns River Jr. Coll., 1965; m. Barbara Jean Usina, Dec. 15, 1955; children—Theresa Ann, Thomas Lambert. Bobby Lee. Slate picker Logan County Coal Co., Lundale, W.Va., 1950-52; dir. pub. works City of St. Augustine, Fla., 1967—. Regional chmn., sec. Fla. Water and Pollution Control Operators Assn., 1969. Served with USNR, 1952-56. Mem. Am.

Water Works Assn., Fla. Pollution Control Assn. Mason (Shriner). Home: 4 Milton St St Augustine FL 32084 Office: PO Drawer 210 St Augustine FL 32084

JONES, BUDDY CALVIN, museum curator; b. Gladewater, Tex., Oct. 31, 1938; s. James Lafayette and Wavie Estelle (Dorsett) J.; B.A., U. Okla., 1961, M.A., 1968; m. Patsy Ann Olive, Apr. 18, 1965. Established Caddo Indian Museum, Longview, Tex., 1958, dir., 1958-61, curator, 1961—; archaeologist Archives, History and Records Mgmt. div. Office of Sec. of State of Fla., Tallahasssee, 1968—. Dir. field activities East Tex. Archaeol. Soc., Tyler, Tex., 1956. Served with AUS, 1963. Mem. Am., Tex. archaeol. socs., Soc. for Hist. Archaeol. Soc., Fla. Anthrop. Soc. Home: 2912 Jim Lee Rd Tallahassee FL 32301 Office: Office Sec of State State Capitol Tallahassee FL 32304

JONES, CECIL DERWENT, ret. publisher, civic leader; b. Thompson Station, Tenn., July 9, 1905; s. James Allen and Cammye Sowell (Evans) J.; student Battle Ground Acad., Franklin, Tenn., Emory U., 1924-26; m. Allie Tucker Yarbrough, July 27, 1929; children—Cecil Derwent, David Sterling. With Methodist Pub. House, Nashville, 1926-70, clk., 1926-27, asst. credit mgr., 1927-30, v.p., 1956-64, v.p. charge publs. div. 1963-64, exec. v.p., 1964-70, ret., 1970; with Abingdon Press 1930-64, salesman, 1930-40, asst. mgr., 1940-56, mgr., 1956-63. Mem. Nat. Council Chs., C. of C., Protestant Ch. Owned Pubs. Assn. (v.p.), Sigma Sigma Chi. Rotarian. Home: 2020 Stonehurst Dr Nashville TN 37215

JONES, CECIL HELLNER, ins. exec.; b. Birmingham, Ala., Feb. 14, 1906; s. Herman and Lilliam (Oldham) J.; A.B., George Washington U., 1931; student Hampden Sydney Coll., 1925-29; m. Virginia Shippey, May 5, 1933; children—Lilliam Oldham (Mrs. Charles D. Joyner); m. 2d, Eileen Barrows, Mar. 25, 1972. Various positions U.S. Govt., 1932-39; legislative rep. marble industry, Washington, 1939-40, Knoxville (Tenn.) C. of C. Ind. Devel., Washington, 1940-41; merchandising analyst Coca Cola Co., 1941-45; group rep. John Hancock, Atlanta, 1946-49; regional mgr. Home Life of N.Y., Atlanta, 1949-57, v.p., 1957—, also dir.; dir. Am. Heritage Life Ins. Co., Jacksonville, Fla. Vice-chmn. Duval County Bd. Edn., 1969-71. Served with AUS, 1945-46. Mem. Newcomen Soc. N. Am., Kappa Sigma. Presbyn. Clubs: University, Touchdown, International (Washington); Touchdown, Capital City (Atlanta); Hidden Hills Country; River. Home: Deerwood 10124 Leisure Lane Jacksonville FL 32207 Office: 11 E Forsyth St Jacksonville FL 32218

JONES, CHARLES ALVIS, clergyman, librarian; b. Alexander City, Ala., Aug 7, 1926; s. Ulio I. and Bertha (Smith) J.; A.B., Samford U., 1951; B.D., Southwestern Bapt. Theol. Sem., 1964; M. in Librarianship, Emory U., 1965; postgrad. Troy (Ala.) State Coll., 1955, New Orleans Bapt. Theol. Sem., 1955, North Tex. State U., 1962, U. Ga., 1971—; m. Hazel Smith, May 23, 1948; children—Margaret Elizabeth, Hazel Rebecca. Ordained to ministry Baptist Ch., 1950; pastor Bapt. chs. Covington County, Ala., 1950-52, 55-61, Conecuh County, Ala., 1952-55, 58-60, Sunny South, Ala., 1954-55, Cobb, Tex., 1961-62, Connerville, Okla., 1964, Tate, Ga., 1967-69, Hiawassee, Ga., 1971-72, Villa Rica, Ga., 1972-73, Commerce, Ga., 1974—; prin. elementary sch. Covington County (Ala.), 1955-57, 58-59, tchr. jr. high sch., 1959-60; tchr. Hawaii Bapt. Acad., Honolulu, 1962-63; librarian, part-time instr. speech and Bible, Reinhardt Coll., Waleska., Ga., 1965-69; librarian Truett McConnell Coll., Cleveland, Ga., 1969-71; instr. div. librarianship Emory U., Atlanta, 1966: instr. library edn. extension center U. Ga., Canton, 1967; instr. library edn. U. Ga., summer 1969, full time, 1971—. Mem. Am., Southeastern, Ga. (chmn. coll. and univ. library sect. 1969-71) library assns., Ga. Edn. Assn., Trident, Beta Phi Mu, Phi Kappa Phi. Optimist. Home: 183 Sunset Dr Athens GA 30601 also Route 3 Jefferson GA 30549

JONES, CHARLES EDWARD, educator; b. Oklahoma City, June 10, 1928; s. Edward Elmo and Stella (Rogers) J.; B.S., U. Ark., 1952, M.S., 1956; Ph.D., Tex. A. and M. U., 1962; m. Elaine Marian Scheele, Sept. 8, 1929; children—Kenneth, David, Douglas, Roger, Scott. Jr. engr. Convair Aircraft, San Diego, 1952-53; engr. McDonnell Aircraft, St. Louis, 1953; instr. physics Mo. Sch. Mines, 1953-54; instr. physics Tex. A. and M. U., 1958-62; asso. prof. physics U. Ark., 1962-70; prof. physics, head dept. East Tex. State U., 1970—; cons. NSF Summer Inst. Program in India, 1970. Served with AUS, 1948-49. Danforth fellow, 1961. Mem. Am. Assn. Physics Tchrs. Am. Phys. Soc. Lutheran. Lion. Home: Rural Route 1 Campbell TX 75422 Office: Physics Dept East Tex State U Commerce TX 75428

JONES, CHARLIE CROWELL, investment co. exec.; b. Samson, Ala., Oct. 13, 1927; s. Moses Prett and Minnie Mae (Powell) J.; B.A., Baylor U., 1954; m. Helen E. Hollingshead, Sept. 4, 1954; children—Helen Denise, Charles Mark, Andrew Crowell. Adminstrv. v.p. United Services Planning Assn., Ft. Worth, 1965—; sec. United Diversified Corp., 1970—; asso., gen. agt. Ind. Research Agy. for Life Ins. Served to lt. USNR, 1954-65; comdr. Res. Mem. Naval Res. Assn., Res. Officers Assn., Navy League Baptist. Kiwanian. Club: Ridglea Country (Ft. Worth). Office: 6000 Camp Bowie Blvd Fort Worth TX 76116

JONES, CLARENCE ROLLINS, mech. engr.; b. Ashton, S.C., Nov. 7, 1923; s. Clarence Rollins and Susan (Black) J.; B.S. in Mech. Engring., Clemson A. and M. Coll., 1947, M.S., 1949; m. Eunice Varn Polk, July 26, 1944; children—Susan Varn, Mary Deborah. Instr., Clemson (S.C.) Coll., 1947-49; project engr. Patchen & Zimmerman Engrs., Augusta, Ga., 1950-51; owner, cons. engr., architect Jones Engring. Co., engring., archtl. firm, Augusta, Jones & Assos., architects and engrs., 1951—; founder, sr. partner Jones & Fellers, architects and engrs., Augusta, Columbia, S.C., now pres.; chmn. bd. Mid-South Corp., Augusta; v.p. So. Industries Investment Co., Augusta; dir. Rhodes-Murphy Co., Safety Shelter Corp., Citizens & So. Nat. Bank, Augusta. Vice chmn. Citizens Adv. Com. City of Augusta; mem. emergency resources planning com. State of Ga., 1961—. Served from pvt. to 1st lt. AUS, 1942-47; PTO. Registered profl. engr., 18 states. Mem. Cons. States Engrs. Assn. Ga., Am. Soc. Heating Refrigerating and Air Conditioning Engrs., Am. Soc. M.E., Am. Inst. Cons. Engrs., Soc. Am. Mil. Engrs., Nat. Council State Bds. Engring. Examiners, Nat. (nat. dir., v.p., chmn. liaison com.), Ga. (dir.) socs. profl. engrs., Profl. Engrs. in Pvt. Practice, Augusta C. of C., Instn. Engrs.-Jamaica. Methodist (bd. stewards). Mason, Lion (dir. Augusta 1960—). Club: Augusta Country, Augusta Sailing; Pinnacle; President's, Elks, Ale, Quail and Tale, Ducks Unlimited. Prin. works include design of various comml., indsl. and instnl. facilities throughout U.S., Central Am., S.A. Home: 3445 Walton Way Augusta GA 30904 Office: Mid-South Bldg Augusta GA 30903

JONES, CLIFFORD EDWARD, accountant; b. Darby, Pa., May 13, 1943; s. Clifford Enoch and Lou Allie (Broome) J.; B.B.A., U. Houston, 1967; m. Sandra Suzanne Spain, Dec. 17, 1965; 1 son, Clifford Evan. Auditor, Peat, Marwick, Mitchell & Co., Houston, 1967-69; asst. controller Gulf Resources & Chem. Corp., Houston, 1969-71; mgr. internal auditing Riviana Foods, Inc., Houston, 1971-73, mgr. control and adminstrn. Riviana Foods, Inc., U.S.A. subsidiary, 1973—; instr. Becker CPA Review Course, Tex. Hunter Safety Tng. Program. Served with AUS, 1961. Mem. Inst. Internal Auditors, Am. Inst. C.P.A.'s, Tex. Soc. C.P.A.'s. Clubs: Internat. Sportsmans, Fred Bear Archery (Graylong, Mich.). Home: 10503 Dunbrook St Houston TX 77070 Office: PO Box 2636 Houston TX 77001

JONES, CONSTANCE JAUCHLER, mathematician; b. Jefferson City, Mo., Jan. 24, 1922; d. Thomas Griffith and Miriam Maude (Jauchler) Jones; B.A., Incarnate Word Coll., 1943; M.A., U. Tex., 1950; postgrad. Harvard, 1943-44, Mass. Inst. Tech., 1944, Clark U., summer 1959, Rutgers State U., summer 1960, U. Tex. at Austin, part time, 1962-68. Instr. sci. Incarnate Word Coll., San Antonio, 1946-47; analytical chemist Tex. Pharmacal Co., San Antonio, 1951-57; asst. prof. math. San Antonio Coll., 1957-62; teaching asst. U. Tex., Austin, 1962-66; asst. prof. math. Trinity U. San Antonio, 1966-69; cons. mathematician, San Antonio, 1969-71; mathematician Office Mgmt. Analysis, Lackland AFB, Tex., 1971-72; asst. prof. math. Incarnate Word Coll., 1972-73. Mem. League Women Voters, 1955—, San Antonio Conservation Soc., 1955—; judge Alamo Dist. Sci. Fair, 1957-59, 67, 72, Navy award Internat. Sci. Fair, Dallas, 1966, Fort Worth, 1969. Served with USNR, 1944-46. Named Hon. adm. Tex. Navy. Mem. Am. Chem. Soc. (treas. 1960), Res. Officer Assn, A.A.A.S., Tex. Acad. Sci., Math. Assn. Am., Am. Math. Soc., U.S. Naval Inst., Daus. Republic Tex. (v.p. 1957-59, 71-73), Incarnate Word Coll. Alumnae Assn. (pres. 1952-54), Sigma Xi. Home: 148 E Elsmere St San Antonio TX 78212

JONES, CRAIG SCOTT, physician; b. Baldwin, Kan., Aug. 7, 1918; s. Pearl West and Elizabeth (Scott) J.; A.B., Baker U., 1939; M.D., U. Kan., 1944; m. Mary Louise Rundell, Mar. 14, 1942; children—Craig Michael, Beth Kathleen (Mrs. Charles Kruchek), Kerry Bruce, Gordon Scott. Intern Ancker Hosp., St. Paul, 1944; resident internal medicine U. Kan., Kansas City, 1946-49; practice medicine specializing in internal medicine, Fayetteville, Ark., 1949-50, Tulsa, 1950—; mem. staff Hillcrest Med. Clinic, St. John's Hosp., St. Francis Hosp., Doctor's Hosp. Tulsa; asst. clin. prof. medicine U. Okla., Tulsa, 1971; clin. cardiology fellow St. Joseph's Hosp., Ann Arbor, Mich., 1967. Served with USNR, 1944-46. Fellow A.C.P., Am. Coll. Cardiology; mem. Tulsa County Med. Soc., Okla. Med. Assn., A.M.A., Sigma Phi Epsilon, Phi Beta Pi. Mason. Home: 2813 E 47th Pl Tulsa OK 74105 Office: 1145 S Utica St Suite 202 Tulsa OK 74104

JONES, DALE PASCHAL, oil field service co. exec.; b. Gillham, Ark., Oct. 19, 1936; s. Ray Elgin and Alma Lee (Wheeler) J.; B.S., U. Ark., 1958; postgrad. U. Md., 1959-60, So. Meth. U., 1966, U. Okla., 1970; m. Anita Ruth Collier, Dec. 28, 1963; children—Lee Anna, Leisa Raye. Auditor, Arthur Andersen & Co., St. Louis, 1958-59, sr. auditor, Dallas, 1962-65; auditor Halliburton Co., Dallas, 1965-67; financial coordinator Eastern Hemisphere, Halliburton Services, London, Eng., 1967-70, asst. to controller, Duncan, Okla., 1970-71, v.p. finance, 1971—, also dir. County chmn. Stephens County Republican Party, 1973—. Bd. dirs. YMCA, Okla. Polit. Action Com. Served to 1st lt. USAF, 1959-62. Mem. Am. Inst. C.P.A.'s, Okla. Soc. C.P.A.'s (dir.), U. Ark. Alumni Assn., Financial Execs. Inst., Am. Mgmt. Assn., Am. Petroleum Inst., Duncan C. of C. Baptist (chmn. bd. deacons). Elk, Rotarian. Home: 2721 Stagestand Rd Duncan OK 73533 Office: 1015 Bois D'Arc Duncan OK 73533

JONES, DANIEL BURR, psychologist; b. Omaha, Aug. 20, 1922; s. Daniel Burr and Flora (Tichnor) J.; B.A., U. Fla., 1943; M.S., Tulane U., 1950; Ph.D., U. Mo. at Kansas City, 1965; m. Bettie Garrison, Dec. 9, 1946; children—Daniel T. and Jeffrey B. (twins). Commd. 2d lt. U.S. Army, 1943, advanced through grades to lt. col., 1963; various assignments including South Pacific, Korea, Pentagon, Army Command and Staff Coll.; sr. scientist Operations Research, Inc., Silver Spring, Md., 1963-66; chief human factors engring. Western div. McDonnell Douglas Astronautics Co., Culver City, Cal., 1966-69; chief human engring. Martin Marietta Corp., Orlando, 1969—; lectr. grad. div. Inst. Aerospace Safety and Mgmt., U. So. Cal., Los Angeles, 1967-72, adj. prof. indsl. engring. Fla. Tech. U., 1971-72. Decorated Bronze Star medal. Mem. Am. Acad. Polit. and Social Sci., Human Factors Soc., Assn. Engring. Psychologists, Tulane U. Alumni Assn. (dir.). Home: Rt 3 Box 936 Orlando FL 32811 Office: Martin Marietta Corp PO Box 5837 Orlando FL 32805

JONES, DON HOWARD, civil engr., educator; b. Isabella, Tenn., Feb. 17, 1933; s. William Howard and Cosbie (Brooks) J.; B.S., U. Tenn., 1959, M.S., 1969; m. Martha Ann Burkhart, May 28, 1954; children—Donna Lucy, Rebecca Fay. Clerk, Kaighan & Hughes & Rust Engring. Co's., Oak Ridge, 1953-55; swimming instr., camp counselor YMCA, Knoxville, Tenn., 1951-53; rodman, engring. aid Tenn. Hwy. Dept., Knoxville, 1951-59, resident engr., 1959-63, sr. resident engr., 1963-64, utility relocation engr., 1964-65, regional right-of-way engr., 1965-72; asst. prof. civil engring., asst. dir. Transp. Research Center, U. Tenn., Knoxville, 1972—. Mem. Am. Soc. C.E. (v.p. 1969), Tenn. Soc. Profl. Engrs. (chpt. pres. 1971-72), Am. Soc. Photogrammetry, Chi Epsilon. Home: Sterwart's Ferry Pike Hermitage TN 37076

JONES, DONALD HARL, geologist; b. Crowley, La., Nov. 4, 1926; s. Lara J. and Mary Edwina (Harl) J.; B.A., U. Tenn., 1950; m. Florence G. Sanders, Sept. 1, 1951; children—Kyle D., Greg A. Ind. oil invester, Crowley, 1950—; dir. First Nat. Bank, Crowley. Active Civil Service Commn., Crowley; chmn. La. State Sci. Found. Served with AUS, 1952. Mem. Ind. Petroleum Assn. Am., Lafayette Geol. Soc., Crowley C. of C. (dir. 1964-66), Am. Legion, Theta Xi. Democrat. Methodist (chmn. bd. 1969-70). Mason (Shriner), Lion. Club: Bayou Bend Country (pres. 1961) (Crowley). Home: 304 W 14th St Crowley LA 70526 Office: PO Box 27 Crowley LA 70526

JONES, DYCHE, food chain exec.; b. Tyner, Ky., May 2, 1915; s. Frank Woodson and Bess (Flinchum) J.; student U. Tenn., 1932-33, Union Coll., 1933-34; m. Pauline Chesnut, Jan 22. 1935; 1 son, William Frank. Pres., Dyche Jones Food Stores, London, Ky., 1935—. Pres. London-Laurel County Devel. Assn., 1969-71; treas. Laurel County Homecoming, 1944—, d.c. chmn., 1953-54. Sec. Clearcreek Mountain Preachers Sch., Pineville, 1949-53. Baptist (deacon). Kiwanian (dir., pres. 1953, lt. gov. dist. 1973-74). Home: 607 N Main St London KY 40741 Office: 208 S Broad St London KY 40741

JONES, EARL, coll. pres.; b. Canton, Okla., Aug. 4, 1925; s. Hercel C. and Florence (Hill) J.; B.S., Ore. State U., 1949; M.S., Inter-Am. Inst. of OAS (Turrialba, Costa Rica), 1958; Ed.D., Mont. State U., 1962; m. Eleanor Harriett Vance, July 15, 1952; children—Beverly Anne, Mark Earl, James Richard, Cindy Kay. Tchr. pub. schs., Ontario, Ore., 1949-55; dir. rural programs KSRV, Ontario, 1955-56, KSLM, Salem, Ore., 1956; vocational dir. Arcata (Cal.) Pub. Schs., 1956-57; instr. Inter-Am. Inst., 1957-58, asst. prof., 1960-62; asso. prof. sociology U. Cal. Los Angeles, 1963-66; prof. sociology, edn., asso. dean. Tex. A. and M. U. Coll. Edn., College Station, 1967-71; pres. Incarnate Word Coll., San Antonio, 1971—. Dir. research Caribbean Inst. Sociology, Anthropology, Caracas, Venezuela, 1963-65; chair prof. U. Chile Sch. Law, Santiago, Valparaiso, 1965-66; vis. prof. Royal Danish Acad., Copenhagen; 1955, U. P.R., Mayaguez, 1960, Cath. U., Caracas, 1963-65, U. Pacific, 1966, Cal. State Coll. Los Angeles, Cal. State Coll. San Francisco, 1968; prof. Juarez Lincoln Center Univ. Without Walls program Antioch Coll., 1973—; cons. Mexican-Am. Cultural Center, San Antonio, 1973—. Mem. Gov.'s Coms. on Confluence Tex. Cultures, 1969—, to Reconstruct Tchr. Edn., 1969—; cons. Cabinet Com. on Spanish Speaking Peoples, 1972—. Served with USMCR, 1943-46. Recipient Presdl. citation Republic Guatemala, 1969; Standard Oil Distinguished Teaching award, 1970. Mem. Am. Sociol. Assn., Rural Sociol. Soc., Soc. Comparative Edn., N.E.A., Alpha Zeta, Phi Delta Kappa. Democrat. Roman Catholic. Lion. Author: Rural Youth in the Americas, 1960; Lideracao, 1961; A Study of the Costa Rican Extension Service, 1962; The Cooperative Extension Services of Jamaica, 1962; Supervision en Extension Agricola, 1963; Latin American Literature for Youth, 1968; Some Perspectives on the Americas, 1968; Self-Identification and the Americas, 1970. Home: 320 Park Dr San Antonio TX 78212

JONES, EARL IRVEN, mfg. co. pres.; b. Vernon, Wilbarger, Tex., Aug. 16, 1928; s. Roy J. and Rockie (Oglesby) J.; B.B.A., So. Meth. U., 1956, M.B.A. (Univ. Trustee scholar), 1958; m. Avis June Koontz, Oct. 18, 1947; children—Lindy, Layne, Shelley, Lance. Sr. engr. Chance Vought Aircraft, Dallas, 1957-60; indsl. engr. mgr. Tyler Pipe Industries (Tex.), 1960-67; indsl. engr. mgr. Texstar Corp., Grand Prairie, Tex., 1967-68, v.p., 1970—; pres. Texstar Plastics, Grand Prairie, 1969—. Served with USAF and AUS, 1951-54, Korea. Decorated Am. Spirit Honor medal. Mem. Am. Inst. Indsl. Engrs. (pres. E. Tex. chpt. 1965-66), Tex. Safety Council (regional v.p. 1964-65), Am. Soc. Safety Engrs., Dallas Sales and Marketing Execs., Sigma Iota Epsilon. Home: 2628 Avenida Loop Irving TX 75062 Office: PO Box 1530 Grand Prairie TX 75050

JONES, ED, congressman; b. Yorkville, Tenn., Apr. 20, 1912; s. Will Frank and Hortense (Pipkin) J.; B.S. U. Tenn., 1934; postgrad. U. Wis., U. Mo.; D.Litt., Bethel Coll.; m. Llewellyn Wyatt, June 9, 1938; children—Mary Liew (Mrs. Robert S. McGuire), Jennifer Wilson. Insp., Tenn. Dept. Agr., 1934-36; supr. Tenn. Dairy Products Assn., 1936-41; agrl. agt. Ill. Central R.R., West Tenn., 1941-48, Yorkville, 1953-69; commr. agr. State Tenn., 1949-52; asso. farm dir. Radio Sta. WMC, Memphis, Tenn., 1952-69. Pres., bd. dirs. Yorkville (Tenn.) Telephone Coop., 1950—; elected to U.S. Ho. Reps. in spl. election 8th Congl. Dist. Tenn., 1970; reelected mem. 92d Congress. State chmn. Farmers for Kennedy-Johnson, 1961. Pres. bd. trustees Bethel Coll., 1950-67. Named Man of Year, Progressive Farmer mag., 1952, Man of Year, Memphis Agrl. Club. Mem. 4-H (state farmer). Cumberland Presbyn. (elder 1940—). Mason (Shriner), Moose, Elk. Home: Yorkville TN 38389 Office: House Office Bldg Washington DC 20515

JONES, EDSEL TENSLEY, lawyer; b. Cunard, W.Va., Sept. 24, 1925; s. Ernest Lee and Elsie Christine (Burford) J.; student Concord Coll., Athens, W.Va., 1947-49; B.S., U. Tenn., 1953; M.B.A., U. Ky., 1968, J.D., 1968; m. Robin Hunt Adair, July 13, 1947; children—Mark Henson, Tensley Adair. Indsl. engr. Sylvania Electric Products, Inc., Huntington, W.Va., 1953-57, sr. indsl. engr., Winchester, Ky., 1958-59, supr. indsl. engring., 1959-65; admitted to Ky. bar, 1968; practice law, Winchester, 1968—. Counsel, Winchester Mcpl. Utilities Commn., 1970—. Mayor, Winchester, 1966-70; city atty., Winchester 1972—. Bd. dirs. Clark County Hosp., Winchester, 1966-70. Served with USNR, 1943-45. Registered profl. engr., Ky. Mem. Am., Ky., Clark County (pres. 1973-74) bar assns., Blue Key, Tau Beta Pi, Phi Kappa Phi, Chi Beta Phi, Kappa Delta Pi, Phi Delta Pi. Mem. Christian Ch. (deacon). Rotarian. Home: 127 Hampton Av Winchester KY 40391 Office: 68 S Main St Winchester KY 40391

JONES, EGBERT MALONE, elec. engr.; b. Memphis, Dec. 16, 1928; s. Egbert Adlai and Willie Wise (Swepston) J.; B.S. in Math., U. of South, Sewanee, Tenn., 1950; E.E., U. Cin., 1955. Process engr. nuclear div. Union Carbide Corp., Paducah, Ky., 1955-65; profl. engr. E.T. Hannan & Assos., cons. engrs., Paducah, Evansville, Ind., 1965-69; profl. engr. Erhart, Eichenbaum, Rauch & Blass, architects and E.K. Riddick, engr., Little Rock, 1969—; elec. cons. Committeeman, Quapaw council Boy Scouts Am., 1971—. Mem. I.E.E.E., Instrument Soc. Am., Nat. Rifle Assn., Nat. Soc. Profl. Engrs. Methodist. Kiwanian. Patentee in field. Home: 10 Nottingham Rd Little Rock AR 72205 Office: Continental Bldg Little Rock AR 72201

JONES, ELISE JESSIE, physician; b. Coldwater, Miss., June 2, 1922; d. Elmer and Mary (McKinnon) J.; B.A., B.S., U. Miss., 1944; M.D., U. Tenn., 1947. Intern, Bapt. Hosp., Little Rock, 1947-48; resident Meth. Hosp., Memphis, VA, U. Tenn. hosps., 1948-55; practice medicine specializing in pathology, Memphis, 1957—; mem. staff, pathologist Oakville Hosp., Memphis; mem. staff City Memphis Hosps., 1957—; instr. pathology U. Tenn. Sch. Medicine, Memphis, 1953-57, asst. prof., 1957—. Diplomate Am. Bd. Pathology. Mem. Am., Tenn., Memphis and Shelby County med. assns., Am. Soc. Clin. Pathologists, Am. Assn. U. Profs., Am. Assn. U. Women, Coll. Pathologists. Home: 57 N Somerville St Memphis TN 38104 Office: 858 Madison St Memphis TN 38103

JONES, ELIZABETH RIEKE (MRS. WAYNE VAN LEER JONES), club woman; b. Chgo., Oct. 15, 1903; d. Henry Edward and Vina Genevieve (Coulter) Rieke; A.B., Northwestern U., 1925; m. Wayne Van Leer Jones, Jan. 14, 1926; 1 son, Wayne Van Leer, II. Dir. Houston Grand Opera Assn. Mem. Nat. Assistance League (mem. nat. finance com. 1970-72), U. Women's Alliance (pres. 1951-53, scholarship chmn. 1963—), Houston Geol. Aux. (parliamentarian 1950-51, 60-61, 63-64), Kappa Kappa Gamma, Theta Sigma Phi. Republican. Presbyn. Home: 5672 Longmont Dr Houston TX 77027

JONES, ENOS TRUELL, lawyer; b. Avery, Tex., July 17, 1920; s. Enos E. and Lula K. (Peacock) J.; grad. Paris (Tex.) Jr. Coll., 1939; student So. Meth. U., 1941; LL.B., Baylor U., 1948, J.D., 1969; m. Mamie Terry, Feb. 4, 1971; children—John Enos, Philip, Cindy. Admitted to Tex. bar, 1948; county atty. Floyd County, Floydada, Tex., 1949-52; asst. atty. gen., Austin, 1953-54; atty. Dept. Interior, Amarillo, 1957-63; pvt. practice, Amarillo, 1963—. Served with USAAF, 1941-45. Mem. Am. Legion (past post comdr.). Lion. Home: 3604 Nebraska St Amarillo TX 79106 Office: Fisk Bldg Amarillo TX 79101

JONES, ERIC WYNN, univ. adminstr.; b. St. Martins, Shropshire, Eng., Sept. 24, 1924; s. Albert Wynn and Ida (Wynn) J.; mem. Royal Coll. Vet. Surgeons (Aleen Cust scholar), London (Eng.) U., 1946; Ph.D., Cornell U., 1949; postdoctorate Oak Ridge Inst. Nuclear Studies, 1958; m. Florence Marie Wynn, July 3, 1948; 1 dau., Sarah Elizabeth. Came to U.S., 1947, naturalized, 1962. House surgeon Royal Vet. Coll., U. London, 1946-47, asst. dept. anatomy, 1947; grad. fellow Cornell U., Ithaca, N.Y., 1947-49; practice vet. medicine, Maidenhead, Eng., 1950-51; lectr. vet. surgery U. Bristol (Eng.), 1951-54; mem. faculty, adminstrv. staff Okla. State U., Stillwater, 1954—, asso. prof., 1956-59, prof., 1959—, also dir. clin. research vet. med. research program, 1956—, research, grad. edn., 1969—. Recipient outstanding engring. award Okla. Soc. Profl. Engrs., engring. wonder award, both 1973. Fellow Harvard Sch. Medicine, 1973-74. Fellow Am. Coll. Vet. Surgeons (founding fellow); mem. Am. Vet. Med. Assn., British, Okla. vet. assns., Research Workers Animal Disease Assn., Brit. Assn. Vet. Anesthetists, Reticuloendothelial Soc., Am. Assn. Vet. Clinicians, Am. Assn. Equine Practitioners, Okla., Am. (pres. 1973-74) socs. vet. anesthesiology, Okla. Zool. Soc., Nat. Council Univ. Research

Adminstrs. Author: Veterinary Anesthesia, 1973. Inventor in field. Home: 924 Osage Dr Stillwater OK 74074

JONES, EVERETT RILEY, JR., oil co. exec.; b. Leitchfield, Ky., July 28, 1918; s. Everett Riley and Margie (Hatfield) J.; student Spencerian Comml. Coll., 1936-37, U. Louisville, 1946-47; m. Lois Gibbins, July 15, 1950; children—Stacey Rae, Rande Leigh. Sec.-treas., dir. Lafitte Oil Corp., Louisville, 1947-49; partner Fryer & Hanson Drilling Co., Dallas, 1950-58; pres., dir. Bengal Producing Co., Dallas, 1959—; dir. Dallas County Small Bus. Devel. Center, Inc. Trustee S.W. Engring. Found. Served to capt. USAAF, 1942-45. Decorated D.F.C., Air medal with 4 oak leaf clusters. Episcopalian. Club: Engineers (past pres.) (Dallas). Home: 6231 Desco Dr Dallas TX 75225 Office: Meadows Bldg Dallas TX 75206

JONES, FABER BENJAMIN, chemist; b. Rochester, Minn., Dec. 4, 1932; s. William H. and Ethel (Smith) J.; B.S., Ohio State U., 1954; m. Barbara E. Stevens, Feb. 11, 1966; children—Lee Diane, Christopher Kent, Lisa Karen, Timothy Aaron. Asst. chief polymer research Battelle Meml. Inst., Columbus, O., 1953-63; tech. dir. Evans Adhesives Co., Columbus, 1963-64; mgr. chem. applications br. Phillips Petroleum Co., Bartlesville, Okla., 1964—. Mem. Am. Chem. Soc., Am. Hereford Assn. Contbr. articles to tech. jours. Patentee adhesives, sealants, synthetic polymers, specialty chems. Home: Box 42 Nowata OK 74048 Office: Phillips Research Center Bartlesville OK 74003

JONES, FRANCIS DUNN, JR., veterinarian; b. Alexandria, La., July 27, 1943; s. Francis Dunn and Evelyn Ray (Coats) J.; B.S., U. Mo., Columbia, 1965, D.V.M., 1967; m. Mary Arrington, Sept. 7, 1966; children—Francis Dunn III, Mary Evelyn. Fed. veterinarian, Opelousas, La., 1967; pvt. practice with Mason Animal Hosp., Little Rock, 1970, Hart & Jones Vet. Clinic, Conway, Ark., 1970—. Served to capt. Vet. Corps, U.S. Army, 1968-70. Pfizer Sr. Vet. Student scholar, 1966. Mem. Am., Mo., Ark., vet. med. assns., Am. Assn. Feline Practitioners, Phi Zeta, Alpha Zeta, Gamma Sigma Delta. Baptist. Home: Route 4 Conway AR 72032 Office: Hart & Jones Vet Clinic Route 4 Conway AR 72032

JONES, FRANK EMERSON, physician; b. Memphis, June 10, 1934; s. Frank Emerson and Madeline (Jackson) J.; M.D., U. Tenn., 1958; M.S. in Orthopedic Surgery, U. Minn., 1967; m. Audrey Jeanne Wojcik, May 15, 1960; children—Catherine Ann, Ann Elizabeth, Daniel Fuller, Patricia Barry. Intern, D.C. Gen. Hosp., Washington, 1958-59; resident gen. surgery U. Vt. Hosp., 1959-60, orthopedics Mayo Clinic, 1960; practice medicine specializing in orthopedic surgery, Nashville, 1967—; mem. staffs Vanderbilt, Hubbard, Bapt., St. Thomas hosps.; asst. clin. prof. orthopedic surgery Vanderbilt U., Nashville; asso. prof. Meharry Med. Coll., Nashville, 1973—. Bd. dirs. social action com. Conf. Christians and Jews, Easter Seal Camp for Crippled Children. Served to capt. M.C., AUS, 1961-62. Mem. Am. Acad. Orthopedic Surgeons, A.C.S., Am. Soc. Surgery of Hand. Home: 724 Summerly Dr Nashville TN 37209 Office: 1919 Hayes St Nashville TN 37203

JONES, FRANKLIN CLINTON, oil co. exec.; b. Oklahoma City, Mar. 30, 1934; s. S.J. and Mildred (Autry) J.; B.S., Okla. U., 1956; m. Berdenia June Wheeler, Jan. 23, 1954 (div. Oct. 4, 1971); children—Deana Kathleen, Jeffery Steven, Gregory Clinton, Jennifer Rene; m. 2d, Julia Del Rogers, Aug. 10, 1972. Geologist, Lone Star Producing Co., San Antonio, 1956-58, Corpus Christi, Tex., 1958-61, dist. geologist, San Antonio, 1961-66, dist. exploration mgr., Oklahoma City, 1966-72, dir. exploration, Dallas, 1972-73, Gulf coast exploration mgr., Houston, 1973—. Served with AUS, 1950-52. Mem. Am. Assn. Petroleum Geologists, Houston Geol. Soc., Houston Petroleum Club. Republican. Methodist. Mason. Home: 12985 Trail Hollow Houston TX 77024 Office: 4151 SW Freeway Houston TX 77027

JONES, GEORGE HILES, JR., assn. exec.; b. St. Louis, Mar. 17, 1932; s. George H. and Florence (Harris) J; B.A., Birmingham So. Coll., 1954; 1 son, Robert Wolford. Divisional sales mgr. Ebosco Industries, 1954-57; sect. mgr. Ala. Assn. Credit Execs., Birmingham, 1957-63; exec. v.p. Deep South Tire Dealers and Retreaders Assn., Birmingham, 1964—; pres. Assn. Mgmt. Services, Inc. 1969—. Mem. Ala. Gov.'s. Safety Coordinating Com., 1967—. Recipient top award Credit Assn. for Membership, 1958, 59, 60; award Nat. Tire Dealers and Retreaders Assn., 1967, 69. Mem. Nat. Assn. Credit Mgmt. (chmn. secretarial council 1963), Am. Soc. Assn. Execs., Ga. Safety Council, Ala., Ga. hwy. users confs., Ala.-La., Miss., Ind. Auto Dealers Assn. (exec. v.p.), Miss. Gasoline Dealers Assn. (exec. v.p.), Ala. Ind. Bus. Assn. (pres.), Ga. Auto and Truck Wreckers Assn. (exec. v.p.), Ala. Council Assn. Execs., Miss. (exec. dir.), Ala. (exec. dir.) auto salvage assns., Alpha Tau Omega. Episcopalian (vestryman 1967-68). Club: West Homewood Civic (pres. 1962) (Homewood, Ala.). Home: 4630 Old Looney Mill Rd Birmingham AL 35212 Office: 5116 1st Av N Birmingham AL 35222

JONES, GERRE LYLE, marketing and pub. relations cons.; b. Kansas City, Mo., June 22, 1926; s. Eugene Riley and Carolyn (Newell) J.; B.J., U. Mo., 1948, postgrad., 1953-54; m. Charlotte Mae Reinhold, Oct. 30, 1948; children—Beverly Anne, Wendy Sue. Exec. sec. C. of C., Ill., 1948-50; field rep. Nat. Found. for Infantile Paralysis, N.Y., 1950-57; dir. pub. relations Inst., Logopedics, Wichita, Kan., 1957-58; owner Gerre Jones & Assos., Pub. Relations, Kansas City, Mo., 1958-63; information officer Radio Free Europe Fund, Munich, Germany, 1963-65, named spl. asst. to dir. pub. relations, 1965; exec. asst. pub. affairs Edward Durell Stone, architect, 1967-68; dir. communications Vincent C. Kling & Partners, Phila., 1969-71; marketing cons. Ellerbe Architects, Washington, 1972; v.p. Gaio Assos., Ltd., Washington, 1972-73, exec. v.p., 1973—. Served with USAAF, 1944-45; maj. Res. Mem. Internat. Radio and Television Soc., Nat. Assn. Sci. Writers, Pub. Relations Soc. Am., Internat. Assn. Chiefs Police, Sigma Delta Chi, Alpha Delta Sigma, Phi Delta Phi. Republican. Mason. Clubs: Kansas City Press; Overseas Press; Deadline (N.Y.C.); Philadelphia Press. Author: How to Market Professional Design Services, 1973. Contbr. articles to profl. jours. Home: 2123 Tunlaw Rd NW Washington DC 20007 Office: 1301 20th St NW Washington DC 20036

JONES, GORDON ERVIN, educator; b. Greenwood, Miss., July 23, 1936; s. Gordon Ervin and Julia Marie (Mounger) J.; B.S., Miss. State U., 1958; Ph.D., Duke, 1964; m. Linda Dry, Nov. 11, 1961; children—Gordon Scott, Chad Myrick. Faculty physics Miss. State U., 1964—, prof., 1972—. Mem. Am. Assn. Physics Tchrs., Am. Phys. Soc., Miss. Assn. Physicists, Sigma Xi, Phi Kappa Phi, Omicron Delta Kappa, Pi Kappa Alpha. Presbyn. Contbr. articles to profl. jours. Home: 105 Edgewood Dr Starkville MS 39759 Office: PO Box 5167 Mississippi State MS 39762

JONES, GRIER PATTERSON, lawyer; b. Ft. Worth, June 26, 1942; s. Kenneth Hugh and Nancy (Culver) J.; B.A., U. of South, 1964; LL.B., U. Tex., 1967. Admitted to Tex. bar, 1967; asso. Shannon, Gracey, Ratliff & Miller, Ft. Worth, 1967-69; atty. Southland Life Ins. Co., Dallas, 1969-74, Mobil Oil Corp., Dallas, 1974—. Tchr. ins. law Life Office Mgmt. Assn. Mem. Am., Tex., Dallas bar assns., Phi Alpha Delta, Phi Gamma Delta. Republican. Episcopalian. Clubs: Colonial Country, Steeplechase (Ft. Worth); Dallas Athletic. Home: 4625 Cedar Springs Rd Dallas TX 75219 Office: 2303A Mobil Bldg 108 S Akard Dallas TX 75201

JONES, GUY LANGSTON, educator; b. Kinston, N.C., June 7, 1923; s. Jay Carl and Lanie (Tyson) J.; B.S., N.C. State U., 1947, M.S., 1950; Ph.D., U. Minn., 1952; m. Margaret Brickle Weldon, Oct. 2, 1948; children—Margaret Elizabeth (Mrs. George Howard Harvey), Guy Langston. Mgr., Lower Coastal Plains Tobacco Research Sta., Greenville, N.C., 1947-49; research fellow dept. agronomy N.C. State U., 1949-50, in charge variety evaluation dept. crop sci., 1952-65, prof. in charge agronomy extension, 1965—; research asst. U. Minn., 1950-52. With A.I.D., Guatemala, 1964-65, The Philippines, 1964-65, Inst. Tobacco, Dominican Repub., 1963, Ministry Agr. Venezuela, 1959. Served with inf. AUS, 1943-46. Recipient Outstanding Leader award N.C. Agrl. Extension Service, 1973, Outstanding Extension Service award N.C. State U., 1973. Mem. Am. Soc. Agronomy, Crop Sci. Soc. Am., N.C. Soil Sci. Soc., Pesticide Assn. N.C., Plant Food Assn. N.C., Sigma Xi, Gamma Alpha, Gamma Sigma Delta, Epsilon Sigma Phi, Alpha Zeta. Asso. editor Agronomy Jour., 1969—. Home: 3435 Blue Ridge Rd Raleigh NC 27612

JONES, GWENDOLA MITCHELL (MRS. JIM ARTHUR JONES), social worker; b. Jacksonville, Fla., Jan. 21, 1936; d. David A. and Merca (Judge) Mitchell; student Hampton Inst., 1952-53; B.S., Tuskegee Inst., 1957; M.A., U. Chgo., 1965; m. Jim Arthur Jones, Apr. 9, 1959; children—Gwendola Evon, Murray Charles. Tchr., Duval County Bd. Pub. Instrn., Jacksonville, 1957-58; social worker Fla. Dept. Pub. Welfare, Jacksonville, 1958-63, state welfare cons., 1965-66, family and childrens supr., 1966-67, orientation tng. supr., 1967-68, casework supr., 1968-70, supr. welfare program, 1970-72; dir. clin. social services div. health Fla. Dept. Health and Rehab. Service, 1972—. Mem. Fair Housing Council, Jacksonville, 1969—; mem. policy adv. bd. Parent Child Center, 1969-70, Summer Head Start, 1969-70; mem. policy adv. bd. Jacksonville Urban Missions, United Meth. Ch., 1967—; mem. agy. adv. com. social work edn. project Univ. Systems Fla., 1972—; mem. Statewide Family Planning Task Force, 1970-71. Mem. Nat. Assn. Social Workers (chpt. sec. 1967-69), Fla. Fedn. Social Workers (v.p. 1968—), Am. Assn. U. Women, Nat. Assn. Black Social Workers, Nat. Council Negro Women, Womens Soc. Christian Service, Delta Sigma Theta. Democrat. Methodist. Home: 6526 Manhattan Dr Jacksonville FL 32208 Office: PO Box 210 Jacksonville FL 32201

JONES, HARRY CALVERT, indsl. power engr.; b. Clark, Mo., Feb. 24, 1925; s. Harry Lee and Elizabeth Mae (Harmer) J.; B.S., Tex. A. and I. U., 1950; m. Elizabeth Barbara Erchinger, Nov. 21, 1951; children—James C., Dale A. Asst. constrn. engr. Magic Valley Elec. Co., Mercedes, Tex., 1950-51; indsl. engr. Central Power & Light Co., Corpus Christi, Tex., 1951-53, Alice, Tex., 1953—. Mem. Alice Planning and Zoning Commn., 1971-73. Served with USAAF, 1943-45. Registered profl. engr., Tex. Mem. I.E.E.E., Tex. Soc. Profl. Engrs., Petroleum Elec. Power Assn. Home: 1912 Alta Vista St Alice TX 78332 Office: Drawer 52 Alice TX 78332

JONES, HARRY MCCOY, cons. engr., investor; b. Stillwater, N.Y., Oct. 19, 1896; s. Louis Benson and Isabelle (Gray McCoy) J.; B.S., U.S. Naval Acad., 1918; grad. work finance, N.Y. U., 1927-28; m. Caroline A. Murray-Browne, May 10, 1969. Financial work Wall St. firms, N.Y.C., 1927-28; engring. work Walker Signal Equipment Co., 1928-30; dist. mgr. Dry-Ice Corp. of Am., 1930-34; pvt. practice cons. engring., 1934-37; partner Weaver Asso., 1937-39; sr. partner Dunn & Jones, engrs., 1940-48, sole partner, 1949-65; dir. Malmstrom Chem. Co., Linden, N.J.; pres. dir. H-H Inc., real estate and investments, 1940—. U.S. Naval Acad. Found., 1946—, chmn., 1946-64; pres. trustee H. McCoy Jones Found.; trustee Textile Museum, Washington, 1967-72. Served as midshipman USN, 1915-18, ensign to lt., 1918-26, lt. to lt. comdr., USNR, 1926-43. Recipient Meritorious Pub. Service citation Dept. Navy; Scroll of Honor, Navy League U.S.; Ann. award U.S. Naval Acad. Alumni Assn. N.Y., 1961; named Hon. Adm., Brigade of Midshipmen, U.S. Naval Acad. Mem. Mil. Order of World Wars, Soc. Am. Mil. Engrs., Am. Def. Preparedness Assn., Am. Soc. Naval Engrs., Soc. Naval Architects and Marine Engrs., Assn. Interstate Commerce Practitioners, U.S. Naval Acad. Athletic Assn., U.S. Naval Acad. Alumni Assn., Navy League U.S. (life), U.S. Naval Inst. (life), Rug Soc. Washington (pres.), Internat. Hajji Baba Soc. (pres.). Episcopalian. Clubs: Army and Navy, Army and Navy Country, Cosmos (Washington); Hajji Baba, Army and Navy (N.Y.); Family, Marines' Memorial (San Francisco); Prospectors (Reno); Oriental Rug (Toronto, Ont., Can.); Las Cruces (Baja California, Mexico); Royal Hero (London, Eng.). Lectr., writer, collector Oriental rugs. Contbr. numerous articles to antique and collectors' mags. Home: 2280 Idlewild Dr Reno NV 89502 Also: 6122 Massachusetts Av NW Washington DC 20016

JONES, HOMER WALTER, JR., math. statistician; b. N.Y.C., Sept. 3, 1925; s. Homer Walter and Margaret (Campbell) J.; M.E., Stevens Inst. Tech., 1947, M.S., 1950; M.B.A., Am. U., 1959; M.S., George Washington U., 1965, postgrad. in math. statistics, 1965-70; m. Shirley Jean Dabbs, June 15, 1957; children—Laura Gwen, Linda Margaret. Cost estimator Standard Oil Devel. Co., Linden, N.J., 1947-51; product devel. engr. Wallace & Tiernan, Inc., Belleville, N.J., 1957-58; math. statistician U.S. Treasury Dept., Internal Revenue Service, Washington, 1959—. Pres., team capt. IRS Chess Club, 1970—; certified intermediate tournament dir., 1973—. Pres. D.C. Chess League, 1967-69, exec. dir., 1969-73, now bd. dirs. Served with USNR, 1944-45. Mem. Am. Statis. Assn., Inst. Math. Statistics, Nat. Treasury Employees Union (exec. v.p. 1974), U.S. Chess Fedn. (regional v.p. 1973—, S.W. Ga. champion 1973). Republican. Presbyn. (chmn. budget com. 1971, treas. 1971-72, deacon 1970-72, elder 1973—, pres. adult Bible class 1973-74). Editor: Kings File mag., 1974—. Home: 2503 Taylor Av Alexandria VA 22302 Office: 12th and Constitution Av NW Washington DC 20224

JONES, HORACE CHARLES, textile co. exec.; b. Benton, Ky., Nov. 12, 1910; s. Horace Cleveland and Evalena (Darnall) J.; diploma commerce Northwestern U., 1935; m. Loretta Louise Schille, June 12, 1937; children—Charles D., Margaret L. Investment analyst City Nat. Bank & Trust Co., Chgo., 1930-38; treas. Fed. Home Loan Bank of Chgo., 1938-43; with Hickman, Williams & Co., Cin., after 1947—, v.p., 1959-64, pres., after 1964; now pres. Burlington Industries, Greensboro, N.C. Treas. YMCA of No. Ky., after 1965; exec. allocation bd. Community Chest of Cin., 1969; mem. adv. council William Booth Meml. Hosp., Covington, Ky., after 1967. Served to lt. USNR, 1943-46. C.P.A., Ohio. Mem. Am. Iron and Steel Inst., Am. Inst. C.P.A.'s. Baptist. Clubs: Fort Mitchell (Ky.) Country; Cincinnati. Office: Burlington Industries 301 N Eugene St Greensboro NC 27401

JONES, HOUSTON GWYNNE, historian; b. Yanceyville, N.C., Jan. 7, 1924; s. Paul Hosier and Lemma (Fowlkes) J.; B.S., Appalachian State Coll., 1949; M.A., Peabody Coll., 1950; postgrad. summers N.Y. U., 1951-52, Am. U., 1957; Ph.D., Duke, 1965. Prof. history Oak Ridge (N.C.) Mil. Inst., 1950-53; vis. prof. history Western Carolina Coll., summer 1955; chmn. div. social scis. W. Ga. Coll., 1955-56; state archivist N.C. Dept. Archives and History, Raleigh, 1956-68, dir. dept., 1968-72; state historian, adminstr. Office Archives and History, Dept. Art, Culture and History, 1972-73; state historian, dir. div. archives and history Dept. Cultural Resources, 1973-74; curator N.C. Collection, U. N.C. Library, Chapel Hill, 1974—. Adj. prof. history N.C. State U., 1966-74. Chmn. policy group Nat. Conf. State Historic Preservation Officers, 1972-74. Served with USNR, 1942-46. Recipient Cannon Cup for Historic Preservation, 1971; Distinguished Alumni award Appalachian State U., 1971. Fellow Soc. Am. Archivists (pres. 1968-69); mem. Am., So. hist. assns., Am. Assn. for State and Local History (mem. council 1972—), Nat. Trust for Historic Preservation, Orgn. Am. Historians, N.C. Lit. and Hist. Assn. (sec.-treas. 1969—), Inst. Early Am. History and Culture (mem. council 1970-73). Author: Bedford Brown: State Rights Unionist, 1956 (winner R.D.W. Connor award); For History's Sake, 1966 (Waldo Gifford Leland prize); The Records of a Nation, 1969. Editor-in-chief N.C. Hist. Rev., 1968-74; mem. editorial bd. William and Mary Quar., 1970-73. Address: NC Collection University of NC Library Chapel Hill NC 27514

JONES, HOWARD LEON, educator; b. Phoenixville, Pa., Oct. 20, 1940; s. Walter R. and Marie (McCann) J.; B.S., Millersville (Pa.) State Coll., 1962; M.A., U. Tex., 1964, Ph.D., 1966; m. Renda M. Nowell, Dec. 28, 1963. Project asso., research asso., instr. U. Tex., 1964-66; vis. prof. Okla. State U. summer, 1965; asst. prof. sci. edn. Syracuse U., 1966-68; asso. prof. edn. U. Houston, 1968-73, prof. edn., 1973—, asso. dir. competency-based tchr. edn. program, 1971-73, dir., 1973—; sci. cons. Eastern Regional Inst. for Edn., 1967-69; cons. Exploratory Com. for Assessment of Edn. Progress, Cons. Edn. Testing Service. Fellow A.A.A.S.; mem. Am. Ednl. Research Assn., Nat. Sci. Tchrs. Assn., Nat. Assn. Research in Sci. Teaching, Assn. Supervision and Curriculum Devel. Contbr. articles to profl. jours. Home: 1503 Ashford Pwy Houston TX 77077

JONES, J. BENTON, JR., educator; b. Tyrone, Pa., Apr. 4, 1930; s. J. Benton and Ethel May (Reynolds) J.; B.S. in Agrl. Sci., U. Ill., 1952; M.S. in Agronomy, Pa. State U., 1956, Ph.D., 1959; m. Marilyn Ann Schroer, June 11, 1955; children—J. Benton III, Karin, Kristin. Asst. prof. Ohio Agrl. Research and Devel. Center, Wooster, 1959-63, asso. prof., 1963-66, prof., 1966-68; extension agronomist, prof. agronomy U. Ga., Athens, 1968—. Served with USNR, 1952-54. Fellow A.A.A.S.; mem. Am. Soc. Agronomy, Soil Sci. Soc. Am., Soc. Hort. Sci., Internat. Soc. Soil Sci., Council Soil Testing and Plant Analysis (chmn. 1970-72, sec.-treas. 1972—), Applied Spectroscopy Soc., Am. Chem. Soc., Sigma Xi. Christion Scientist (chmn. bd. dirs. Athens 1969-70, treas. 1970-72). Editor: Com. Soil Sci. and Plant Analysis, 1970—. Home: 115 Sweet Gum Dr Athens GA 30601 Office: 2400 College Station Rd Athens GA 30601

JONES, J. MACK, civil engr.; b. Temple, Tex., Oct. 25, 1913; s. Jesse Oliver and Ruby (McCulloch) J.; student Temple Jr. Coll., 1931-32, U. Ark., 1936; children—Exa Virginia, Janice. Field engr. Brazos River Dist., Temple, 1936-37; field engr. U.S. Dept. Agr., College Station, Tex., 1937-38; asst. city engr., Corsicana, Tex., 1939-40, city engr., 1940-42; engring. mgr. Limestone County, Grosbeck, Tex., 1947-49; pvt. cons. engr., 1949-62; civil engr. C.E., U.S. Army, Ft. Chaffee, Ark., 1962-64, Laughlin AFB, Tex., 1964-67, airfield pavement engr. Hdqrs. ATC, USAF, 1967—. Speaker water, sewage short course Tex. A. and M. U., College Station, 1939—. Served to capt. USMCR, 1942-47. Recipient Outstanding Performance award U.S. Army, 1963. Registered profl. engr., Tex. Mem. Tex., Nat. socs. profl. engrs., Soc. Am. Mil. Engrs., Tex. Water Utilities Assn., Sigma Phi Epsilon, Theta Tau. Home: PO Box 8572 San Antonio TX 78208 Office: Hq ATC DEMM Randolph AFB TX 78148

JONES, JACK DOYLE, ednl. adminstr.; b. Madison, S.C., Feb. 10, 1936; s. Ramsay Doyle and Peggy (Jarrett) J.; student Emory U., 1954-55; B.S. in Edn., U. Ga., 1958; M.A. (NSF fellow), Peabody Coll., 1962; m. Sarah Ellen Shropshire, July 29, 1962; children—Hope, Brian. Tchr. Stephens County High Sch., Toccoa, Ga., 1958-65; instr. Central Piedmont Coll., Charlotte, N.C., 1965-66; asst. prof. biology, dir. student activity Gainesville Jr. Coll. (Ga.), 1966—. Mem. N.E.A., Am. Inst. Biol. Scis. Baptist. Home: Route 6 Edgewater Terr Gainesville GA 30501 Office: Gainesville Coll Gainesville GA 30501

JONES, JACK EARL, educator; b. nr. Elberton, Ga., July 30, 1925; s. William Amos and Katherine Ivy (McCall) J.; B.S., U. Ga., 1948, M.S., 1950; Ph.D., La. State U., 1961; m. Georgia Henrietta Weathers, Sept. 1, 1946; 1 dau., Lynda Dianne. Grad. asst. U. Ga., 1948-49; instr. Elbert County Bd. Edn., 1949-50; faculty agronomy La. State U., Baton Rouge, 1950—, prof., 1968—. Served with USAAF, 1943-45. Decorated Air medal with 3 oak leaf clusters. Mem. Am. Soc. Agronomy, Crop Sci. Soc. Am., La. Assn. Agronomists, Sigma Xi, Alpha Zeta, Gamma Sigma Delta. Mason. Home: 246 Maxine Dr Baton Rouge LA 70808

JONES, JACK RADFORD, architect; b. Bradenton, Fla., Jan. 31, 1929; s. Berry Smith and Mary Ritchie (Whitehead) J.; A.A., U. Fla., 1948, B.Arch., 1954; postgrad. Fla. State U., 1948; m. June Johns, May 8, 1960; children—Cathye, Charles C., Cheryl, Robin, Adrianne. Foreman, Paul A. Miller-Miller Constrn. Co., Inc., Leesburg, Fla., 1957-59; sec.-treas. Miller Constrn. Co., Inc., Leesburg, 1959-63; self-employed as architect, Leesburg, 1959—. Mem. Leesburg Planning and Zoning Bd., 1961-71, chmn., 1969-70; mem. Lake County Bd. Examiners, 1968—, chmn., 1968-69. Served to lt. USNR, 1954-57. Recipient Home Design award A.I.A., 1967, Mem. A.I.A. (dir. Mid-Fla. chpt. 1970, pres. Mid-Fla. chpt. 1973), Leesburg Area C. of C. (pres. 1970), Gargoyle. Episcopalian (lay reader 1968—, warden 1973, mem. diocesan liturgical commn. 1970, diocesan planning commn. 1973). Elk, Rotarian. Club: Boat (Leesburg, Fla.). Home: 712 Boylston St Leesburg FL 32748 Office: 613 W Dixie Av Leesburg FL 32748

JONES, JAMES GRADY, physician; b. Pembroke, N.C., Dec. 19, 1933; s. Alton Bruce and Nora (Revels) J.; A.A., Mars Hill Coll., 1953; B.S., Wake Forest Coll., 1955; M.D., Bowman Gray Sch. Medicine, 1959; m. Jerre Roper, June 6, 1959; children—James Grady, Robert Glenn. Intern Grady Meml. Hosp., Atlanta, 1959-60; pvt. practice gen. medicine, Jacksonville, N.C., 1963-65, Jones-Kitchen Clinic, P.A., Jacksonville, 1965—; mem. staff Onswlow Meml. Hosp., chief staff, 1964-65; asso. clin. prof. family medicine U. N.C., East Carolina Med. Sch. Commr. edn. com. Regional Med. Program N.C., 1965—; med. examiner Selective Service System, 1962—; chmn. Housing Authority, Jacksonville, 1969—. Trustee Coastal Carolina Community Coll., Jacksonville. Served to lt. USNR, 1960-62. Mem. Am. (com. on edn.), N.C. (pres. 1972-73) acads. gen. practice, N.C. Med. Soc. (v.p.). Baptist. Contbr. articles to jours. Home: 610 Little John Av Jacksonville NC 28540 Office: 510 College St Jacksonville NC 28540

JONES, JAMES IRVIN, state govt. ofcl.; b. Sparta, Wis., Aug. 22, 1929; s. Irvin Scott and Veda Lee (Stone) J.; B.S., U. Wis., 1956, M.S., 1960, Ph.D., 1964; m. Alice Jean Smedbron, June 29, 1951; children—Judith, Sandra, Patricia, Glen. Forest fire fighter Wis. Conservation Commn., 1946-48; teaching asst. U. Wis., 1955-57; exploration geologist Surinam Mining Co., 1955; research asst. Wis. Alumni Research Found., 1957-61; research instr. U. Miami, 1961-64; cons. marine geologist ARCO, 1964-70; asst. prof. marine geology U.

Miami, 1964-67, asso. prof., 1967; asso. prof. oceanography Fla. State U., 1967-73; research coordinator Fla. Coastal Coordinating Council, Tallahassee, 1973-74; sr. planner Fla. div. State Planning, 1974—. Cons. Fla. Bd. Regents, 1972. Mayor, City of Monroe Park (Wis.), 1955-56. Served with USNR, 1948-52. Grantee NSF, Office Naval Research, Wis. Alumni Research Found. Mem. Am. Geophys. Union, Paleontol. Soc. Am., Miami (hon. life), Southeastern geol. socs., Sigma Xi. Democrat. Editor: A Symposium of Recent South Florida Foraminifera, 1971; Proc. Internat. Conf. on Tropical Oceanography, 1967; A Summary of Knowledge of the Eastern Gulf of Mexico, 1973. Home: Route 2 Box 618 Tallahassee FL 32301 Office: 309 Magnolia Office Plaza Tallahassee FL 32301

JONES, JAMES RAPHAEL, social planning adminstr.; b. Mobile, Ala., Oct. 9, 1942; s. Carl Hubert, Jr. and Willie Frankie (Cathey) J.; B.S., U. Ala., 1964, postgrad., 1965-68; postgrad. Human Devel. Inst., Atlanta, 1969-70, Americana Coll., 1970-71; m. Joan Irene Miles, Aug. 4; children—James Raphael, Brian Alexander, Tabitha Mia. Salesman, Office Supply Co., Mobile, 1961-62, Druid Supply Co., Tuscaloosa, Ala., 1962-64, Gulf Am. Land Corp., Huntsville, Ala., 1964-65; electronic engr. U.S. Army, Huntsville, 1965-66; sec.-mgr. Affiliated Achievement Enterprises, Inc., Huntsville, 1966; elec. engr., human relation coordinator, space support div. Sperry Rand Corp., Huntsville, 1966-71; tng. coordinator Personal Awareness Inst., 1969—; project dir. Model Project on Aging, S. Ala. Regional Planning Commn., Mobile, 1972—. Organizer, chmn. Huntsville/Madison Clean Air Com., 1969-71; organizer-at-large Chicasaw Dist., Boy Scouts Am., 1968-70, councilman Cub Scout Troop 369, 1969-70; chmn. Madison County Crusade, Cancer Soc., 1969; mem. Sesquicentennial Celebration Com., 1969; pres. Monday Club, 1973—. Bd. dirs. Community Action Com.; nat. dir. Inner Peace Movement; founding dir. Christian Dynamics. Recipient Orbit award Sperry Rand Corp., 1967, 69, Walt Weisman award Huntsville Jr. C. of C., 1970, Ryan DeGrafenried award Ala. Jr. C. of C., 1971; named One of Five Outstanding Jaycees in Nation, U.S. Jr. C. of C., 1970, One of Four Outstanding Men of Ala., Ala. Jr. C. of C., 1971. Mem. Ala. (program dir., v.p. Dist. IV), Mobile (chmn. various coms.) jr. chmabers commerce. Lutheran. Club: Toastmasters (Mobile). Home: PO Box 754 Mobile AL 36601 Office: PO Box 1665 Mobile AL 36601

JONES, JAMES ROBERT, elec. engr.; b. Conway, Ark., Aug. 22, 1937; s. Thomas D. and Mabel (Sikes) J.; B.E.E., Tex. A. and M. U., 1960, M.E.E., 1968, postgrad., 1968-69; m. Nelda Faun Miller, Nov. 24, 1960; children—Janis Rae, James Robert, John Richard, Julie Rose, Fred Briggs. Elec. engr. Southwestern Pub. Service Co., Amarillo, Tex., 1960-65; instr. dept. elec. engring., engr. Tex. A. and M. U., Elec. Power Inst., 1965-69; chief elec. engr. Tippetts-Abbett-McCarthy-Stratton, Engrs., Architects, Arlington, Tex., 1969—. Cons. Dow Chem. Co., Freeport, Tex., Tex. Instruments, Dallas; Power Engrs., Inc., College Station, Tex. Scoutmaster, Llano Estacada council Boy Scouts Am., 1964, asst. cubmaster, 1970-72, cubmaster Longhorn council, 1972-73. Eldon Durrett scholar, Woffard Cain scholar, 1955; Rowan Drilling Co. scholar, 1956. Mem. I.E.E.E., Power Engring. Soc., Indsl. and Gen. Applications Soc., Illumination Engring. Soc., Phi Eta Sigma, Eta Kappa Nu. Pioneer infrared inspection for elec. utility systems, 1965-69; developer fiberoptic billboard type taxiway signs, 1970; devels. in airfield lighting, 1969—. Office: 604 Av H E Arlington TX 76011

JONES, JOHN EARLE, electro-mech. engr.; b. Union, S.C., Nov. 23, 1931; s. John Earle and Eleanor (Thomas) J.; B.S., U. S.C., 1953; M.S., Mass. Inst. Tech., 1957; m. Phyllis Ann Hobson, Dec. 11, 1954; children—Margaret Royce, Eleanor Thomas, Elizabeth Anne. Project engr. Gen. Electric Co., Waynesboro, Va., 1957-61; engring. mgr. IBM, 1961-73; dir. engring. Disston Corp., Danville, Va., 1973—. Served from ensign to lt. USN, 1953-56; comdr. Res. Registered profl. engr., Va. Mem. Am. Soc. M.E., Tau Beta Pi, Sigma Alpha Epsilon. Republican. Episcopalian (vestryman). Patentee in field. Home: 318 Linden Dr Danville VA 24541 Office: Disston Inc Danville VA 24541

JONES, JOHN GRAHAM, printing corp. exec.; b. Hubbard, Tex., Feb. 3, 1918; s. Prince Rupert and Alice (Graham) J.; student Baylor U., 1935-40; m. Wilma Marie Richter, Apr. 13, 1941; children—Ronald Graham, Judith Gay (Mrs. David Gary Evans). Salesman, Curry Office Supply, Waco, Tex., 1940-42, mgr., Austin, Tex., 1946-50; mgr., Whitley Co., Austin, 1950—, pres., 1961—. Mem. Better Bus. Bur. Served with AUS, 1942-46. Mem. Printing Industry of Am., Printing Industry Austin (past pres.), Austin C. of C. Baptist (deacon). Club: Craftsmans (past pres.). Home: 1512 Forest Trail Austin TX 78703 Office: 301 Brazos St Austin TX 78701

JONES, JOHN LEWIS, music pub.; b. N.Y.C., Jan. 3, 1922; s. George and Caldonia M. (Batts) J.; B.S., N.C. State Tchrs. Coll., 1915; m. Louise F. Faison, July 26, 1948; children—John Lewis, George W., Paula M. Pres., Elvitrue Rec. Music Pub. Co., Wilmington, N.C. and N.Y.C., 1952—; founder Music Makers Network Am.-Prodns., N.Y.C.; concert pianist; affiliated pub. Broadcast Music, Inc. Active N.C. Soc. Civil Liberties. Mem. Am. Fedn. Musicians, Music Pubs. Assn., N.C. Homebuyers Assn., AFTRA. Baptist. Elk. Home: Creekwood N 2603 McClammy St Wilmington NC 28401 Office: 1306 Castle St PO Box 3022 Wilmington NC 28401

JONES, JOHN MARTIN, III, publisher; b. Sweetwater, Tenn., Dec. 11, 1914; s. Oliver King and Byrd (Browder) J.; grad. Washington and Lee U., 1937; m. Martha Arnold Susong, June 29, 1940; children—John Martin, IV, Alexander Susong, Gregg King, Edith Susong, Sarah Ingles. Advt. mgr. Gilman Paint & Varnish Co., Chattanooga, 1938-42; gen. mgr. Greeneville (Tenn.) Daily Sun, 1946—, editor, pub., 1950—; pres. Greeneville Pub. Co., Newport Pub. Co., Post Athenian Co.; pub. Athens (Tenn.) Daily Post Athenian, Marengo Pub. Co., Monroe Pub. Co.; v.p., dir. Tenn. Electro Minerals Corp., Agrl. Lime Co.; dir. First Nat. Bank, Greeneville, Sweetwater Hosiery Mills, Hamilton Nat. Bank Knoxville, Tenn. Mem. Gt. Smoky Mountain Nat. Park Commn., 1960—, State Armories Commn., Nashville, 1959—, Tenn. Higher Edn. Commn.; chmn. Govs. Emergency Traffic Safety Com., 1963; v.p. Sequoyah council Boy Scouts Am., 1958—; pres. Greene County Indsl. Found., 1950-52. Del., Democratic Nat. Conv., 1956, 60, 64, 68. Alumni bd. Washington and Lee U.; bd. dirs. Greeneville Emergency and Rescue Squad, A.R.C., Greene County Library; trustee Mental Hosp. Bd. Tenn., Tenn. Tb Hosps., Tenn.-Wesleyan Coll., Am. Newspaper Pubs. Assn. Found. Served from 2d lt. to lt. col. AUS, 1942-45. Recipient Pres.'s Cup for outstanding service in field journalism Tenn. Press Assn., 1952. Mem. Tenn. Press Assn. (pres. 1962-63), Alumni Assn. Washington and Lee U. (dir.), Greeneville C. of C. (past pres., Man of Yr. 1950), Nat. Press Club, Am. (dir.), So. (dir., trustee) newspaper pubs. assns. Kappa Sigma. Episcopalian. Elk. Clubs: Gatlinburg (Tenn.) Ski; Link Hills Country, Exchange (Greeneville); City (Knoxville); Cumberland (Nashville). Home: Hilltop Greeneville TN 37743 Office: 200 S Main St Greeneville TN 37743

JONES, JOHN ORVILLE, lawyer; b. Duncan, Okla., Apr. 3, 1936; s. William Charles and Lela Irene (McDowell) J.; B.B.A., U. Okla., 1960, LL.B., 1963; m. Sara Trotti Hurtig, May 26, 1973. Admitted to D.C. bar, 1963, Tex. bar, 1969; trial atty. tax div., U.S. Dept. Justice, Washington, 1963-65, Ft. Worth, 1965-67, atty. in charge, 1967-69; mem. firm Sands, Tyler, Trimble and Jones, Dallas, 1969-70; mem. firm Turner, Hitchins, McInerney, Webb & Hartnett, 1970-73, mem. firm Atwell, Cain, Davenport & Jones, 1973—. Dir. Cathey Office Furniture & Supplies, Inc., Dallas. Served with USMCR, 1958-60. Mem. Okla., Tex., Fed., Dallas bar assns., C. of C., Phi Delta Phi, Delta Tau Delta. Methodist. Club: N. Dallas Racquet. Home: 1613 Tree House Lane Plano TX 75074 Office: 2605 Republic Bank Tower Dallas TX 75201

JONES, JOHN WALTER, JR., engineer; b. Miami, Fla., Nov. 23, 1913; s. John Walter and Elinor Burwell (Hickson) J.; student Colo. Sch. Mines, 1933-35; m. Mildred Vivian Puckett, July 20, 1940; children—Elinor Burwell (Mrs. Ralph T. Pyles), Melanie Vivian (Mrs. Byron K. Brown), Ann Spotswood (Mrs. Udy C. Wood, Jr.), Walter Martin, Pamela Sue. Office engr. Biscayne Engring. Co., Miami, 1935-41; asst. airport engr. Pan Am. Airways, 1941-50; propr. J. Walter Jones, Jr. and Assos., South Boston, Va., 1950—; pres. South Boston Devel. Corp., 1967—. Mem. Va. Bd. Exam. and Certification Architects, Profl. Engrs. and Land Surveyors, 1964—, pres., 1968. Fellow Am. Soc. C.E.; mem. Am. Congress Surveying and Mapping, Danville Soc. Engring. and Sci. (pres. 1967), N.C. Soc. Surveyors, Va. Assn. Surveyors (pres. 1962), Kappa Sigma. Mason, Lion. Home: 8 Maplewood Dr PO Box 773 South Boston VA 24592 Office: Security Bldg 554 N Main St South Boston VA 24592

JONES, JULIUS VICTOR, wholesale trade co. exec.; b. Atoka, Okla., Apr. 28, 1926; s. Jacob Jasper and Eva Lena (Garrett) J.; student McMurray Coll., 1943-44, Chillicothe Coll., 1946-47; m. Jocie Belle Ellyson, Oct. 1, 1948; 1 son, David Gregory. Clk., Am. Smelting & Refining Co., Amarillo, Tex., 1947-49; asso. Ind. O. & G. Lease Brokerage, Amarillo, 1949-58; sec.-treas. Ponca Wholesale Mercantile Co., Amarillo, 1958—. Served to sgt. AUS, 1944-46. Mem. Amarillo C. of C., Amarillo Wholesale Credit Assn. Republican. Episcopalian. Mason; mem. Order Eastern Star. Composer: Keynotes March, 1970. Editor: Ponca-Standard, 1966—. Home: 3400 Rusk St Amarillo TX 79109 Office: 4146 Georgia St Amarillo TX 79110

JONES, L. HALL, mortgage banker, realtor; b. Collierville, Tenn., Mar. 25, 1901; s. Samuel Anderson and Loretta (Hall) J.; m. Louise W. Green, June 20, 1923; children—Mary Louise (Mrs. Thomas Prewitt), L. Hall. Pres., dir. Joyner-Heard Co., Memphis, 1952, Joyner, Heard and Jones, Inc., Memphis, 1952—; sr. partner Joyner, Heard & Jones, realtors, Memphis; pres., dir. Poplar-Highland Plaza, Inc., Memphis, 1953—, Laurelwood Shopping Center, Inc., Memphis, 1961—. Episcopalian. Clubs: Memphis Country, Tenn. Home: 78 E Galloway St Memphis TN 38111 Office: 54 S Prescott St Memphis TN 38111

JONES, LEAH ALBERTA, ret. educator; b. Ridgeland, S.C., Oct. 4, 1903; d. Paul Wesley and Fannie (Malphrus) Jones; B.S., U. Ga., 1947; M.A., George Peabody Coll. for Tchrs., 1951. Tchr. elementary sch. Ridgeland, 1928-51, prin., 1951-69, elementary supr. Jasper County Schs., 1969-71. Sec., S.C. Tchr. Edn. and Profl. Standards Commn., 1966-69. Asso. chmn. Jasper County Centennial Commn., 1961-62; mem. civil def. teaching staff; chmn. Jasper County Tricentennial Schs. Participation Program. Chmn. bd. trustees Frederic R. Pratt Meml. Library, Ridgeland. Named Jasper County Woman Year, 1962-63, 69-70, S.C. Career Woman of Year, 1970. Mem. Jasper County Edn. Assn. (past pres.), Dist. I Elementary Prins. Assn. (past pres.), Ridgeland Bus. and Profl. Women's Club (past pres.), N.E.A. (life), Sr. Citizens Am. (life), Delta Kappa Gamma (life). Mem. Order Eastern Star. Address: Great Swamp Rd Ridgeland SC 29936

JONES, LEE WENDELL, cons. structural engr.; b. Kansas City, May 12, 1929; s. Roy E. and Rachel (Matson) J.; B.S., U. Ill., 1950; m. Iris Ruth Barbier, Mar. 14, 1954; children—Casey Alan, Nancy Lee, Kirk Steven, Clifford Scott, Karl Stewart. Structural engr. Frank A. Busse, Cons. Engr., Memphis, 1950, Walter P. Moore, Cons. Engr., Houston, 1953-66; v.p., dir. Walter P. Moore & Assos., Cons. Engrs., Houston, 1967-74, sr. v.p., 1974—. Mem. bd. mgmt. Westland br. YMCA, Houston, 1968-69, chmn. bd., 1969—. Served to 1st lt. C.E., AUS, 1950-52. Profl. engr. La., Tex. Mem. Am. Soc. C.E., Am. Concrete Inst., Cons. Engrs. Council, Soc. Am. Value Engrs. Methodist. Kiwanian (dir. S.W. Houston 1971—). Club: Civic. Home: 11630 Ashcroft St Houston TX 77035 Office: 2905 Sackett St Houston TX 77006

JONES, LEONARD BONHAM, physician; b. Gregory, Tex., Jan. 18, 1911; s. Charles Von and Ethel Jean (Butler) J.; B.S., Tex. A. and M. Coll., 1932; M.D., U. Tex., 1938; m. Velma Irene Zwilling, June 28, 1941; children—Bonnie (Mrs. David Lee Northcutt), Leana Irene (Mrs. John B. Turbeville, Jr.), Glenda (Mrs. Ronald Lee Detling), Justin Bonham. Intern, resident, Cleve., 1938-41; gen. practice medicine, San Antonio, 1946—; pres. profl. staff S.W. Tex. Meth. Hosp. Served to lt. col., M.C., AUS, 1941-46. Mem. Tex. Acad. Gen. Practice (pres.), Internat. Med. Assembly S.W. Tex. (pres.), Bexar County Med. Soc. (pres.) San Antonio C. of C. (dir.). Presbyn. Mason, Kiwanian. Home: 3213 Castledale St San Antonio TX 78230 Office: 929 Manor Dr San Antonio TX 78228

JONES, LEONARD LEE, accountant; b. Mulberry, Kan., Aug. 27, 1938; s. Lloyd Keith and Beulah Isadore (Hunsaker) J.; B.S., Kan. State Coll., 1960; postgrad. Kan. State Coll., Tex. Christian U., Kan. U., U. Tex. at Arlington; m. Marilyn Ann Gammaitoni, May 27, 1961; children—Kerri Lynnette, Brett Ashley. Bank examiner F.D.I.C., Kansas City, Mo., 1961; cost accountant Didde-Glaser, Inc., Emporia, Kan., 1961-63; audit mgr. Arthur Young & Co., Ft. Worth, 1963-70; partner Larue, Lawrence, Wood & Kelley, Ft. Worth, 1970-72; controller, treas. Crest Container Corp., Ft. Worth, 1972-73; partner Lee Jones C.P.A., Fort Worth, 1973—; dir. Bondurant Corp., Profl. Pharm. Co., Thermo Envases, S.A. (Mexico City); financial cons. Treas., dir. Rolling Downs, Inc., 1970—; adviser Jr. Achievement of Tarrant County, 1965-67. Del. Tarrant County (Tex.) Rep. Conv., 1968. Trustee Bondurant Corp. Employees Pension Trust. C.P.A., Tex., Okla. Mem. Am. Inst. C.P.A.'s, Tex. Soc. C.P.A.'s, Nat. Assn. Accountants, Hosp. Financial Mgmt. Assn., N.Am. Mensa, Ltd., N. Tex. Mensa (v.p. 1968). Republican. Methodist. Club: Ft. Worth Cosmopolitan (judge adv. S.W. Fedn. 1972-73). Home: 3013 Elsinor Dr Fort Worth TX 76116 Office: 6300 Ridglea Pl Fort Worth TX 76116

JONES, LEWIS EARLE, JR., physician; b. Ware Shoals, S.C., Mar. 17, 1932; s. Lewis Earle and Alpha Belle (Cox) J.; B.S., Furman U., 1954; M.D., Med. U. S.C., 1957; m. Dolores Page, Nov. 24, 1955; children—Jimmie, Belle, Kathy, Lewis. Intern, Greenville (S.C.) Gen. Hosp., 1958-59; practice medicine, specializing in family medicine, Greenville, 1961—; mem. staff Greenville Gen. Hosp., St. Francis Hosp., Greenville. Served with USAF, 1959-61. Mem. A.M.A. Am. Acad. Family Practice, S.C. Med. Assn. Baptist (deacon 1966—). Home: 8 Andrea Lane Greenville SC 29607 Office: 1635 E North St Greenville SC 29607

JONES, LEWIS POSEY, govt. ofcl.; b. Sheridan, Ind., Jan. 23, 1921; s. James Ira and Bertha (Masden) J.; student Ohio Wesleyan U., 1938-41, Ohio State U., 1941-42; B.S., Purdue U., 1943; m. Ellen Chloupek, Aug. 29, 1942; children—Donald L., Nancy E. (Mrs. W.L. Hawkins), J. Lawrence. Sr. engr. Aeroproducts div. Gen. Motors Corp., 1944; chief engr. Thompson Trailer Corp., Alexandria, Va., 1949-50; sr. project engr. U.S. Navy Dept., 1950-54; asst. to comdr. U.S. Naval Aviation Safety Center, Norfolk, Va., 1954-60; sr. analyst NASA, 1960-65, dep. dir. program and spl. reports div., 1965-70; program review officer NSF, Washington, 1970—. Served to lt. (j.g.), USNR, 1944-46. Recipient Apollo achievement award NASA, 1969, Rear Adm. L.D. Coates award Bur. Naval Weapons, 1965. Mem. Am. Inst. Aeros. and Astronautics, A.A.A.S. Home: 404 E Jefferson St Falls Church VA 22046 Office: 1800 G St N W Washington DC 20550

JONES, LLOYD GEORGE, educator; b. Hobart, La., Aug. 6, 1919; s. Henry Clinton and Carrie Virginia (Underwood) J.; B.S., La. State U., 1949, M.S., 1950; Ph.D., Purdue U., 1953. Faculty horticulture La. State U., Baton Rouge, 1953—, prof., 1961—. Served with USNR, 1942-45. Mem. A.A.A.S., Soil Sci. Soc. Am., Am. Soc. Plant Physiology, Am., Internat. socs. hort. sci., Sigma Xi, Phi Kappa Phi, Gamma Sigma Delta. Democrat. Baptist. Home: PO Box 55 Watson LA 70786 Office: La State U Baton Rouge LA 70803

JONES, MARION CLARK, petroleum co. exec.; b. Pine Bluff, Ark., Dec. 5, 1921; s. Stephen Herbert and Ethel (Stevens) J.; student So. State Coll., Magnolia, Ark., 1939-41; m. Bonnie A. Anton, Dec. 10, 1943; children—Steve, Marian (Mrs. Randy Pharr). With McAlester Fuel Co., Magnolia, 1941—, exploration mgr., 1966-69, v.p., mgr. oil dept., 1969—. Alderman, Magnolia City Council, 1962—. Served with USNR, 1942-45; ETO, PTO. Mem. Midcontinent Oil and Gas Assn. (v.p.), Ark. Petroleum Council (v.p.), Am. Landman's Assn. (charter mem.), Magnolia C. of C. (past pres.). Methodist. Rotarian. Home: 1028 Honeysuckle St Magnolia AR 71753 Office: McAlester Bldg Magnolia AR 71753

JONES, MAX KESLER, univ. adminstr.; b. Hereford, Tex., May 9, 1938; s. Harold Kesler and Maudetha (Miller) J.; B.A., Tex. Christian U., 1960; M.Div., Yale, 1964; m. Suzanne Smith, Sept. 8, 1962; children—Kinley Nan, Kyle Weldon, Lacey Suzanne. Ordained to ministry Christian Ch., 1964; minister Christian Ch., Roswell, N.M., 1964-67; regional dir. Joint Action in Community Service, Austin, Tex., 1967-69; asst. dean Sch. Law, So. Meth. U., Dallas, 1967-69; dir. regional campaigns Tex. Christian U., Ft. Worth, 1971-74; pres. Ark. Council Ind. Colls. and Univs., Little Rock, 1974—. Cons. planning and devel. United Meth. Ch., 1969-71. Mem. Am. Pub. Relations Assn., Am. Alumni Council, Ft. Worth C. of C. (mem. membership com. 1972-73), Ft. Worth Area Council Chs. (dir. 1972-74). Democrat. Rotarian. Office: 309 Center St Room 110 Little Rock AR 72201

JONES, MERRIAM ARTHUR, educator; b. Hankinson, N.D., Jan. 4, 1913; s. Arthur Phineus and Abramina (Gunderson) J.; B.A., U. N.D., 1933; postgrad. U. Minn., 1933-36; Ph.D., George Washington U., 1950; m. Alvilda Grace Bangs, June 6, 1933; children—Marilyn (Mrs. Daniel Feldkamp). With U.S. Treasury, 1936, Bur. Standards, 1936-37, War Dept., 1937-39; cryptanalyst Fed. Expt. Sta., Mayaguez, P.R., 1939-46; chemist U.S. Dept. Agr., Washington, 1946-51; chemist, research mgmt. adviser AID, State Dept., Guatemala, Haiti, Iraq, Iran, Lebanon and Turkey, 1951-68; asst. div. chmn. phys. scis., prof. chemistry No. Va. Community Coll., Annandale, 1968—. Served with AUS, 1935-36. Mem. Am. Chem. Soc., Sigma Xi, Alpha Chi Sigma. Contbr. to profl. jours. Home: 5936 N 3d St Arlington VA 22203 Office: Dept Chemistry Northern Virginia Community College Annandale VA 22003

JONES, MILNOR, surgeon; b. Athens, Tenn., Mar. 14, 1925; s. Cyril William and Billie (Dodson) J.; B.A., Vanderbilt U., 1945, M.D., 1948; m. Miriam Conner, Aug. 29, 1953; children—Cyril William III, Miriam Conner, Jonathan Milnor, Camille Chambers. Intern, Grady Meml. Hosp., Emory U., Atlanta, 1948, resident surgery, 1949-52, chief resident surgery, 1952-53, instr. surgery, 1952-53; practice medicine, specializing in surgery, Athens, Tenn., 1953—. Dir., mem. exec. com. First Nat. Bank of McMinn County. Vice chmn. Athens Bd. Edn., 1967—. Chmn. bd. trustees Epperson Hosp., Athens, 1970—; trustee Tenn. Mil. Inst., 1973—. Diplomate Am. Bd. Surgery. Fellow A.C.S., Southeastern Surg. Soc.; mem. Chattanooga Acad. Surgeons, A.M.A., So. Med. Assn. Democrat. Episcopalian. Home: 127 Highland Av NE Athens TN 37303 Office: 7 Grove St Athens TN 37303

JONES, MORTON EDWARD, chemist; b. Alhambra, Cal., Apr. 12, 1928; s. Edward P. and Bonnibel S. (Sanford) J.; B.S., U. Cal. at Berkeley, 1949; Ph.D. in Chemistry, Cal. Inst. Tech., 1953; m. Patricia L. Walker, Mar. 18, 1951; children—Shelley, Steven, Kent, Jay. With Tex. Instruments, Inc., Dallas, 1953—, sr. scientist, 1961-65, dir. Phys. Scis. Research Lab., 1965—. Mem. materials sci. vis. com. U. So. Cal., 1967—; chmn. Solid State Device Research Conf., 1968; vice chmn. Gordon Research Conf. on Chemistry and Metallurgy of Semicondrs., 1971. Mem. Richardson Park and Recreation Commn., 1966-71; chmn. judging Internat. Sci. Fair, 1966; chmn. judging Dallas Regional Sci. Fair, 1966-69, dir., 1972. Precinct vice chmn. Dallas Republican Com., 1954-62; del. Tex. Rep. Conv., 1964, 68; alternate del. Nat. Rep. Conv., 1968; mem. exec. com. Tex. Rep. Com., 1968—; chmn. Tex. Patronage com. Exec. Office Pres. and Sci. Agys., 1969—. Mem. I.E.E.E. (sr.), Electrochem. Soc. (past vice chmn. semicondrs.), Tex. Acad. Sci., Sigma Xi. Episcopalian. Contbr. articles to tech. jours., chpts. to books. Patentee in field. Home: 619 Northill St Richardson TX 75080 Office: PO Box 5936 MS 145 Dallas TX 75222

JONES, MYRTIS IDELLE (MRS. C.W. JONES), librarian; b. Prescott, Ark., May 16, 1908; d. Andrew Brice and Ethel (Hardwick) Barham; A.A., Little Rock Jr. Coll., 1952; B.Ed., Ark. State Tchrs. Coll., 1958; M.L.S., George Peabody Coll. Tchrs., 1965; m. B.H. Harrison, Oct. 31, 1925, (div. Mar. 1933); children—Jack Barham, Charles Ray, Mary Anna (Mrs. Paul O. Scheie); m. 2d, J.W.E. Moore, Mar. 16, 1933 (dec. June 1950); children—William Robert, Jonathan Edward, Ethel Rachel (Mrs. Robert Hubka), Paul David; m. 3d. C.W. Jones, June 2, 1952. Library asst. Little Rock Jr. Coll., 1950-52; librarian Holly Grove (Ark.) High Sch., 1955; librarian Vanndale (Ark.) High Sch., 1955-56; librarian Stuttgart (Ark.) Sr. High Sch., 1956-59; supr. sch. libraries Stuttgart Pub. Schs., 1956-59; librarian Ark. Sch. for the Blind, Little Rock, 1959—; mem. Library Com. of the Commn. on Standards and Accreditation of Services of the Blind; mem. awards com. Joseph Campbell Citation. Mem. Ark. Student Librarians Assn. (sponsor exec. councils 1957—), Assn. Am. Librarians, A.L.A., Library Service to the Blind, Ark. Library Assn. (v.p. 1966-67), Southwest Library Assn., Council Exceptional Children, Assn. Educators of the Visually Handicapped (chmn. library sci. workshop 1964-68), Ark. Edn. Assn., Ark. Assn. Classroom Teachers, N.E.A., Internat. Platform Assn., Alpha Beta Alpha. Mem. Ch. Nazarene. Mem. Order Eastern Star. Home: 5608 Geyer Springs Little Rock AR 72209 Office: 2600 W Markham St Little Rock AR 72203

JONES, NELSON EARL, savs. & loan assn. exec.; b. Coffeyville, Kan., Mar. 1, 1909; s. Robert R. and Margaret Mae (Latham) J.; B.S., Ga. Inst. Tech., 1932; LL.B., U. Mich., 1938; m. Mary Elizabeth Heffernan, Aug. 10, 1939; children—Elizabeth Ann, Dennis Kamrad. Admitted to Mo. bar, 1938; practice law, Joplin, Mo., 1942-46; prof. law Ohio No. U., 1946-48; asst. prof. bus. law Mich. State U., 1948-50; admitted to Fla. bar, 1950, practice in Titusville, 1950-57; pres. First Fed. Savs. & Loan Assn. of Titusville, 1957—; v.p., dir. Brevard Nat. Bank; dir. Brevard Underwriters Inc.; dir. Mut. Ins. Service. Mem. East Central Fla. Regional Planning Council, 1967-70; mem. Brevard County Community Services Council, 1968-71; mem. investment com. Jess Parrish Meml. Hosp., Titusville. Bd. dirs. Brevard County Rehab. Center; bd. dirs. Brevard County Mental Health; trustee Brevard Community Coll. Mem. Indian River C. of C. (pres. 1952-53), Delta Theta Phi, Delta Sigma Pi. Mason. Rotarian (pres. 1958-61). Home: 3129 S Washington Av Titusville FL 32780 Office: 300 S Washington Av Titusville FL 32780

JONES, OLIVER HASTINGS, assn. exec.; b. Altoona, Pa., Dec. 9, 1922; s. Oliver Hastings and Mary (Herman) J.; B.A., St. Francis Coll., Loretto, Pa., 1948; M.A., Pa. State U., 1949, Ph.D., 1961; m. Margaret Ann Vogel, July 4, 1942; children—Thomas, William, David, Robert, Richard. Analyst, div. bank operations, bd. govs. Fed. Res. System, 1951-55; sr. economist, research dept. Fed. Res. Bank Cleve., 1955-59; asso. research economist, real estate research program Grad. Sch. Bus. Adminstrn., U. Cal. at Los Angeles, 1959-61; economist Stanford Research Inst., 1961-62; dir. research Mortgage Bankers Assn. Am., Washington, 1962-67, exec. v.p., 1968—; cons. economist Oliver Jones & Assos., Washington, 1967-68; professorial lectr. Am. U., 1967—. Served with AUS, 1942-45. Mem. Am. Statis. Assn., Am. Econ. Assn., Am. Finance Assn., Nat. Assn. Bus. Economists, Lambda Alpha. Club: Cosmos (Washington). Author: (with Leo Grebler) The Secondary Mortgage Market, 1961. Home: 743 Delaware Av SW Washington DC 20024 Office: 1125 15th St NW Washington DC 20005

JONES, OSCAR FREER, JR., lawyer; b. Oglesby, Tex., Oct. 15, 1909; s. Oscar Freer and Margaret G. (Greenwood) J.; student U. Tex., 1926-31, U. Ky., 1929; m. Laila E. Wallace, June 7, 1930 (div.); children—Oscar Freer III, James W., Betsy (Mrs. Wm. K. Kirkgard); m. 2d, Louise Bailey, Feb. 10, 1972. Admitted to Tex. bar, 1933, U.S. Supreme Ct. bar, 1949; practiced in Waco, Tex., 1933-71, Austin, Tex., 1972—; partner firm Sheehy, Jones, Cureton, Westbrook & Lovelace and predecessors, 1936-70; v.p., gen. counsel, dir. Am.-Amicable Life Ins. Co., Waco, 1938-69; asst. dist. atty., Waco, 1970-71; atty. for Tex., Gen. Land Office, Vets. Land Bd., 1971. Past mem., trustee Waco Sch. Bd. Mem. Assn. Life Ins. Counsel. Methodist. Home: 2004 Elton Lane Austin TX 78703 Office: 2116 Hancock Dr Austin TX 78756

JONES, OSCAR FREER III, lawyer; b. Cuero, Tex., Mar. 26, 1932; s. O.F. and Laila (Wallace) J.; student Baylor U., 1950-52; B.B.A., U. Tex., 1954, LL.B., 1956; m. Saxche Nanne O'Keefe, June 23, 1956; children—Christopher Wallace, James Brittain, Patrick O'Keefe. Admitted to Tex. bar, 1956; with firm Jones, Boyd, Westbrook & Lovelace, Waco, Tex., 1956-64, Guittard, Henderson, Jones & Lewis, Victoria, Tex., 1964-72; pvt. practice law, Victoria, 1972—. Bd. dirs. Victoria YMCA, Victoria chpt. United Fund, Victoria chpt. Am. Cancer Soc., Victoria chpt. A.R.C. Mem. Victoria Bar. Assn. (pres.), Tex. Assn. Def. Counsel, Fedn. Ins. Counsel, Am. Judicature Soc., Trial Attys. Am., T Assn. U. Tex., Phi Delta Theta. Episcopalian (vestryman). Rotarian. Home: 306 Birchwood St Victoria TX 77901 Office: PO Drawer E Victoria TX 77901

JONES, PAUL EDWARD, clergyman; b. New Boston, O., Jan. 26, 1916; s. Thurman Talmage and Stella (Ivers) J.; A.B., Butler U., 1937, postgrad. 1941; D.D., Milligan Coll., 1955. Ordained to ministry Christian Ch., 1937; minister 1st Christian Ch., Hillsboro, O., 1942-45, 47-53; minister, Pitts., 1945-47; minister 1st Christian Ch., Newnan, Ga., 1953—. Speaker to religious, fraternal, civic and ednl. groups, 1942—. Trustee, Christian's Hour nat. religious broadcast, 1950—; selected Overseas Preaching Mission, USAF, 1965. Mem. Nu Sigma Nu. Democrat. Mason (33 deg., Shriner), Optimist; mem. Order DeMolay (chaplain Ohio exec. council). Author articles religious publs. Home: 8 Elm St Newnan GA 30263 Office: First Christian Ch Jackson and Elm Sts Newnan GA 30263

JONES, PAUL ISAIAH, supt. schs.; b. Sidney, Tex., June 19, 1913; s. William I. and Lena L. (Hellums) J.; student Tarleton Coll., 1933-35; B.S., Howard Payne Coll., 1947; M.A., W. Tex. U., 1950; postgrad. Tex. Tech. U., 1971; m. Addie Lee Cotten, June 10, 1939; 1 son, William Paul. Bookkeeper shipping Walker-Smith Wholesale, Brownwood, Hobbs, N.M., 1935-37; salesman Tex. News Co., Dallas, 1937-39; tchr. pub. schs., Hasse, Tex., 1940-41; electrician, numerous locations, 1941-45; tchr. pub. schs., Sidney, 1945-48, supt., 1946-48; tchr. math. high sch., Littlefield, Tex., 1948-49, prin., 1949-65, asst. supt., 1965-67, supt., 1967-74. Chmn. P.T.A., 1957; chmn. Dist. Athletic Conf., 1967-68. Democratic precinct chmn. 1956-62; del. State Dem. Conv., 1960. Mem. County Sch. Adminstrs. (chmn. 1954, 62), Elementary Prins. Assn. (dist. chmn., mem. state exec. bd. 1958), Am., Tex. assns. sch. adminstrs. Rotarian. Home: 224 E 23d St Littlefield TX 79339 Office: 105 N Lake St Littlefield TX 79339

JONES, PAUL R., govt. ofcl.; b. Bessemer, Ala., June 1, 1928; s. William J.; student Ala. State Coll. at Montgomery; M.A., Howard U., postgrad. Queens Coll., Fisk U., Yale, U. Chgo., U. Cal. at Berkeley; m. Bess Hackett; 1 son, Paul R. Pub. relations field rep. Johnson Publs., Chgo., exec. sec. interracial com. Jefferson County Coordination Council Social Forces, Ala., probation officer, Birmingham, Ala.; propr. pub. relations agy., restaurant, Birmingham; fed. probation officer; mem. com. Conciliation Services, Washington; citizen participation adviser Model Cities program Dept. Housing and Urban Devel., Washington; exec. dir. Model Neighborhood Com., Charlotte, N.C.; staff asst. Exec. Office Pres., Washington; dir. Office Civil Rights Nat. Hwy. Safety Bur., Washington; dep. dir. Peace Corps, Thailand; spl. asst. to asso. dir. domestic and antipoverty operations ACTION, Washington, now regional dir. ACTION programs, Atlanta. Mem. adv. bd. Housing Authority; mem. Council Alcoholism. Bd. dirs. Community Action Agy., Nat. Assembly Social Policy and Devel. Recipient citation U.S. Atty. Gen. sustained superior performance, 1966; honors conciliation efforts City of Tuskegee (Ala.); ciation Watts Com. Alert Patrol, Los Angeles; named Outstanding Citizen in Community Services Los Amigas, Inc., Charlotte. Mem. Nat. Model Cities Dirs. Assn. (chmn.), Am. Soc. Planning Ofcls., Mental Health Assn., Am. Soc. Pub. Adminstrn., Assn. Intergroup Relations Ofcls., Fed. Probation and Parole Officers Assn. Contbr. articles to profl. jours. Office: ACTION Region IV 730 Peachtree St NE Atlanta GA 30308

JONES, RAGON ENTRENKEN, cons. engr.; b. Georgianna, Ala., Oct. 28, 1922; s. James Daniel and Ola Mae (McLain) J.; B.S. in Mech. Engring., U. Ala., 1949; student Alexander Hamilton Bus. Mgmt., 1957; m. Nellie Ruth Simpson, Mar. 15, 1948; children—Lynda Nell, Barry Lee, Daniel Ragon. Engr., draftsman J.B. Converse & Co., Mobile, Ala., A.C. Parker, 1946; city engr. Tuscaloosa, Ala., 1947-49; grad. tng. course Allis-Chalmers Mfg. Co., Milw., 1949-50; eng. Standard Brass & Mfg. Co., New Orleans, 1951; gen. practice mech. contracting. engring., research, cons., Mobile, 1952-64; cons. engr., 1952—; faculty Tex. A. and M. U., 1971-72. Mgr., coach Dixie Little League, Gulfport, Miss., 1967, 68, 69, Dixie Sr. League, 1969, sr. all-star mgr., 1971. Served with USNR, 1942-45. Recipient Gen. Electric award for heat pump devel., 1955. Registered profl. engr., Ala., La., Miss., Tex. Baptist. Patentee in field. Home: 518 Arrowhead Dr Richardson TX 75080 Office: One North Park Suite 121 8950 N Central Expressway Dallas TX 75231

JONES, RAY CLARK, agribus. exec.; b. Flowery Branch, Ga., Apr. 11, 1929; s. Clark T. and Effie (Barker) J.; student Abraham Baldwin Agrl. Coll., 1946-48; B.S., U. Ga., 1950; m. Evelyn Allen, Apr. 23, 1949; children—Carol (Mrs. Larry R. Pinson), David, Regina. Teacher Fannin County Bd. Edn., 1950-51; dairy farmer, Hall County, Ga., 1951-54; tchr. Gwinnett County Bd. Edn., 1954-55; with Crystal Farms, Inc., Chestnut Mountain, Ga., 1955—, pres., 1971—. Mem. Ga. Poultry Producers Assn. (dir. 1958-63, sec., 1961-63, Ga. Poultry Fedn. (chmn. edn. com. 1973-74), Nat. Egg Assn. (dir. 1967-70, sec. 1967-68), Ga. Egg Assn. (dir. 1970-74). Presbyn. Kiwanian (pres. 1972-73). Home: Box 85 Chestnut Mountain GA 30502 Office: Box 101 Chestnut Mountain GA 30502

JONES, RICHARD LLOYD, JR., newspaper exec.; b. Nyack, N.Y., Feb., 22, 1909; s. Richard Lloyd and Georgia (Hayden) J.; student Culver Mil. Acad., 1925, Tome Sch., Port Deposit, Md., 1926; Ph.B., U. Wis., 1932; m. Martha Meredeth Corder, Mar. 4, 1933; children—Richard, Dana. Apprentice mech. depts. Tulsa Tribune, 1933-34, with telegraph desk, 1935, display advt. dept., 1935-38, became v.p., bus. mgr., 1938, now pres.; v.p., bus. mgr. Newspaper Printing Corp., 1941-51, pres., 1951; v.p., treas. Hennepin Paper Co., Little Falls, Minn., 1953-56; dir. Brookside State Bank, Tulsa, N.Y. World's Fair 1964-65, Douglas Aircraft Co., A.P. Chmn. Tulsa Airport Authority; dir. state fair, livestock expn., Tulsa. Served as lt. USNR, World War II, comdg. officer gun crew U.S.S. Sharon Victory, U.S.S. Dickinson Victory. Mem. Tulsa C. of C. (dir. 1954—, pres. 1960-61), So. Newspaper Pubs. Assn. (chmn. labor com. 1948-52, pres. 1953-54, chmn. bd. 1954-55), Am. Newspaper Pubs. Assn. (chmn. bd. bur. advt. 1956-58), Aviation Writers' Assn., Phi Gamma Delta. Unitarian. Club: Southern Hills Country (Tulsa). Home: 1754 E 30th St Tulsa OK 74114 Office: Tulsa Tribune 315 S Boulder St Tulsa OK 74110

JONES, ROBERT BRINKLEY, JR., elec. engr.; b. Richmond, Va., June 12, 1910; s. Robert Brinkley and Rose (Morris) J.; B.S. in Engring., U. Va., 1932, Elec. Engr., 1933; m. Valerie LeMasurier, June 22, 1940; children—Robert B. III, Rosemary (Mrs. Delchi Serfilippi Jr.), Valerie (Mrs. Frank Turner Rea), Michael Harrison (dec.). With Chesapeake & Potomac Telephone Co. Va., Richmond, 1935—, engring. asst. 1941-46, engr., 1946—. Asst. dist. commiteeman Robert E. Lee council Boy Scouts Am., 1967-68. Served to lt. comdr. USNR, 1943-46. Registered profl. engr., Va. Mem. I.E.E.E. (sr.), Nat. Soc. Profl. Engrs. Episcopalian. Home: 3433 Grove Av Richmond VA 23221 Office: 703 E Grace St Richmond VA 23219

JONES, ROBERT CUBA, cultural center exec.; b. Gilbara, Oriente, Cuba, May 12, 1902; s. Sylvester and May (Mather) J.; A.B., Earlham Coll., 1923; postgrad. George Williams Coll., 1923-24, U. Chgo., 1923-40; LL.D., Earlham Coll., 1969; m. Ingeborg Hecht, Sept. 15, 1946; 1 dau., Diana May. Dir., Pan Am. Council, Chgo., 1940-42; asso. chief div. labor and social affairs Pan Am. Union, 1942-46, chief, 1946-49; sr. social affairs officer UN, 1949-53; dir. Internat. Cultural Center, Mexico, 1953-71, chmn. bd., 1971—. Mem. Staff Pres.' Commn. on Migratory Labor, 1950-51. Recipient Distinguished Alumni award George Williams Coll. Distinguished Service certificate Western Ill. U. Fellow A.A.A.S., Am. Sociol. Assn.; mem. Am. Polit. Sci. Assn., Am. Econ. Assn., Am. Anthrop. Assn., Soc. for Study Social Problems, Mexican Anthrop. Soc., Mexican Sociol. Assn., Societe des Americanistes de Paris. Author books and articles in field. Home: Antillas 13 Mexico 13 DF Mexico

JONES, ROBERT DALE, lawyer; b. Fort Worth, Oct. 16, 1934; s. Algernon S. and Florence Marie (Kimbell) J.; B.A., U. Tex. at Austin, 1960, J.D., 1964; m. Beverly Jones, Dec. 24, 1965; children—Jennifer Susan, Michael Clay, Steven Jerome. Admitted to Tex. bar, 1964, U.S. Ct. Mil. Appeals, 1968, U.S. Supreme Ct. bar, 1970; asso. mem. Procter, Maloney & Fullerton, Austin, 1964-65, Les Procter, 1965-66; partner Procter & Jones, 1966—. Partner, Jones Trust real estate investment, Austin, 1968—. Campaign mgr. Travis County Atty., 1968-72. Bd. dirs. Hope House mentally retarded children, Austin Assn. Retarded Children. Served with USMCR, 1953. Mem. Austin Jr. (pres. 1969-70), Tex., Travis County bar assns., V.F.W., Am. Legion. Democrat. Home: 1607 Sharon Lane Austin TX 78703 Office: Capital Nat Bank Bldg Austin TX 78701

JONES, ROBERT E., JR., congressman, lawyer; b. Scottsboro, Ala., June 12, 1912; s. Robert E. and Augusta (Smith) J.; LL.B., U. Ala., 1937; m. Christina Francis, Apr. 9, 1938; 1 son, Robert E. Admitted to Ala. bar, 1937; established law practice with firm, Brewton and Jones, Scottsboro, Ala.; elected judge, Jackson County Ct., 1940, reelected in absentia, 1945; elected to 80th Congress in spl. election to fill vacancy created by John J. Sparkman's election to U.S. Senate; mem. 81st-93d congresses from Ala. 5th Dist. Served as gunnery officer USN, 1942-46, Atlanta, PTO. Mem. V.F.W., Am. Legion, Kappa Alpha. Home: Scottsboro AL 35768 Office: House Office Bldg Washington DC 20515

JONES, R(OBERT) EUGENE, educator, author; b. Emporia, Kan., July 21, 1924; s. Carl Shem and Edna Elizabeth (Ratcliff) J.; B.S., Kan. State Tchrs. Coll., 1949; M.A., U. Cal. at Berkeley, 1954, postgrad., 1958-59; m. Alice Rose Landham, Aug. 7, 1960; 1 son, Carlin Eugene, 1 stepdau., Elizabeth Ruth Edwards. Coordinator distributive edn. Victoria (Tex.) Pub. Schs., 1949-52; dormitory supr., ednl. counselor Nurnberg (Germany) Am. Dependents Schs., 1954-55; western states mgr. Lang. Master Dept., McGraw-Hill Book Co., San Francisco, 1956-57; research asst., cons. on field service projects, sch. edn. U. Cal., Berkeley, 1957-58; asst. prof. edn., supr. student tchrs. Jacksonville (Ala.) State U., 1959-73, dir. acad. ednl. advisement Sch. Edn., 1973—. Cons. in curriculum and instrn. Pres., Anniston (Ala.) PTA, 1966, Jacksonville Elementary P.T.A., 1971-72; active Boy Scouts Am. Served with USAAF, 1943-45; CBI. Mem. N.E.A., Ala. Edn. Assn., Phi Delta Kappa, Kappa Delta Pi. Kiwanian. Author: Acme Plan of Instruction, 1966. Contbr. articles to profl. jours. Home: 706 7th Av Jacksonville AL 36265

JONES, ROBERT HUBBARD, real estate exec.; b. Charlotte, N.C., May 29, 1928; s. Raymond Allen and Lucille Seymour (Hubbard) J.; B.C.E., Ga. Inst. Tech., 1951; m. Louise McLendon, June 18, 1964; children—Stephen Alan, Darrel Scot; stepchildren—John E. Bailey, Jr., Ralph M. Bailey. Pres., Old S. Investment Co., Atlanta, 1963—; pres. RHJ, Inc., Atlanta, 1961—; pres. All Pro Enterprises, Inc., Atlanta, 1971—. Chmn. United Appeal, 1959, Ocean View Meml. Hosp. Fund Drive, 1958. Mem. Ocean Hwy. Assn. (dir., v.p. 1958-59), Myrtle Beach C. of C. (pres. 1958-59). Rotarian. Club: Georgia Tech. 1000 (Atlanta). Home: 3873 Dumbarton Rd NW Atlanta GA 30327 Office: 331 Cleveland Av SW Atlanta GA 30315

JONES, ROBERT L., JR., lawyer; b. Apr. 5, 1922; A.B., Hendrix Coll., 1942; LL.B. with honors, U. Ark., 1948. Admitted to Ark. bar, 1948, since practiced in Fort Smith; spl. asst. U.S. Atty.'s Office, 1950; U.S. commr., 1949-50. Served as 1st lt. AUS, 1950-52. Fellow Am. Coll. Trial Lawyers; mem. Am., Ark. (pres. 1969-70), Sebastian County bar assns., Internat. Assn. Ins. Counsel, Phi Alpha Delta. Address: Merchants National Bank Bldg Fort Smith AR 72902

JONES, ROBERT LEE, elec. engr.; b. Hilham, Tenn., Sept. 10, 1922; s. Taylor Lee and Mary Florence (Dale) J.; B.S. in E.E., Tenn. Tech. U., 1950; m. Martha Opaline Owens, Mar. 18, 1950; children—Deborah (Mrs. William C. Barbee Jr.), Rodney L., Sharon K. With IBM, Triangle Park, N.C., 1950—, devel. engr., 1960-73, mgr. product devel. orgn., 1973—. Senator, Jr. Chamber of Commerce Internat., 1959. Served with AUS, 1942-47. Mem. Am. Inst. E.E., I.E.E.E. Mason (Shriner), Optimist (past pres.). Home: 5018 Shamrock Dr Raleigh NC 27612 Office: PO Box 12275 Research Triangle Park NC 27709

JONES, ROBERT RUSSELL, cons. engr.; b. Kearney, Neb., Feb. 26, 1922; s. Russell H. and Emma (Braksiek) J.; cadet USCG Acad., 1940-42; B.S. in Engring., U. Mich., 1943; m. Mary Ruth Martin, June 30, 1944; children—Mary Elizabeth, John Russell. Jr. naval architect Md. Drydock Co., Balt., 1943-46; mech. engr. Pub. Bldgs. Adminstrn., Washington, 1946-53, chief mech. estimator, 1958-61, chief mech.-elec. engr., 1961-67; partner Syska & Hennessy cons. engrs., 1967—; asso. Gen. Engring. Assos., Washington, 1953-58. Pres., Tulip Hill Citizens Assn., 1962-63. Registered profl. engr., D.C., Md., Va., N.C., Pa., Cal., Mich. Mem. Nat. Soc. Profl. Engrs., Am. Soc. Heating, Air Conditioning and Refrigeration Engrs., Am. Soc. Plumbing Engrs., Washington Bldg. Congress, Bldg. Mgrs. Assn., Tau Beta Pi. Methodist. Mech. engr. designer 3 U.S. embassies. Home: 1 Bay Tree Lane Washington DC 20016 Office: 1720 Eye St NW Washington DC 20006

JONES, ROGER HODGES, educator; b. Quicksand, Ky., May 14, 1929; s. Roger Walter and Mattie M. (Hodges) J.; A.B., Georgetown Coll., 1951, M.A., U. Ky., 1959; Ed.D., Ind. U., 1973. Tchr. English, Estill County High Sch., 1951-52; tchr. art, journalism and Spanish, Breathitt County High Sch., 1953-65; prof. art edn. Morehead State U., 1965—, chmn. university senate. Del. World Confedn. Orgns. of Teaching Profession, Addis Ababa, Ethiopia, 1965—. Ky. Col.; recipient distinguished alumni award, Georgetown Coll., 1965. Mem. Upper Ky. Schoolmasters Club (pres.), Upper Ky. River (pres.), Ky. pres. dept. classroom tchrs.), Morehead State U. (pres.) edn. assns., Nat. Assn. State Edn. Assn. Pres.'s (v.p.), Phi Delta Kappa, Kappa Delta Pi, Kappa Pi, Sigma Tau Delta. Home: 216 Bell Ct E Lexington KY 40508 Office: Morehead State University Morehead KY 40351

JONES, RONALD, mech. engr.; b. Evansville, Ind., Aug. 25, 1924; s. Sylvester H. and Elton (Ashworth) J.; B.S., Purdue U., 1949; m. Betty Jeanne Albright, Feb. 23, 1946; children—Donald Michael, Paula Janeen, Keith Allen, Kevin Bryce. With Phillips Petroleum Co., 1950—, engr., Bartlesville, Okla., 1950-57, materials engr., Odessa, Tex., 1957-64, cons. engr., 1964—. Served with USNR, 1943-46. Registered profl. engr., Okla. Mem. Nat. Assn., Corrosion Engrs. Democrat. Home: 3420 Boulder St Odessa TX 79760 Office: 4th and Washington St Odessa TX 79760

JONES, ROSCOE HENRY, city ofcl.; b. Vinita, Okla., Dec. 25, 1925; s. Henry Ezekiel and Zella (Arvin) J.; B.S., Okla. A. and M. U., 1947; M. City Planning, Harvard, 1950; m. Ruth Evelyn James, June 4, 1954; children—Curtis Albert, Linda Thea, Cynthia Lynn. Dir. planning Met. Dade County, Miami, Fla., 1959-64; with City of Houston, 1964—, dir. city planning, 1964—. Asso. prof. Coll. Architecture, U. Houston, 1964-68. Served to lt. C.E., AUS, 1951-53. Mem. Am. Inst. Planners. Rotarian. Home: 2008 Milford St Houston TX 77006 Office: 4100 City Hall Annex Houston TX 77002

JONES, ROY JUNIOS, educator; b. Longview, Tex., Nov. 15, 1925; s. Sam and Evangeline (Fury) J.; B.S. in Psychology, Morgan State U., 1951; M.S., Howard U., 1954; Ph.D. in Social Psychology, Am. Univ., 1961; m. Pauline Carol Finley, Sept. 16, 1947; children—Roderick, Arlyss, Valerie. Chief psychol. services, dir. research Crownsville (Md.) State Hosp., 1961-62; dir. tng. Washington Action for Youth, 1963-64; mem. faculty, adminstrn. Howard U., Washington, 1964—, asst. clin. prof. psychiatry, 1967-69, prof. urban studies, 1969—, also dir. Center Community Studies, 1967-72, Urban Studies Program, 1969-72, asst. dean Grad. Sch., 1967-71. Pres. Social Systems Intervention, Inc., Washington, 1967—; cons. govt., pub. and pvt. agys. Mem. D.C. adv. com. U.S. Commn. Civil Rights, 1968, govt. rev. bd. Mayor's Youth Opportunity Service, 1969, bd. overseers Dag Hammarskjold Coll., Columbia, Md., 1967-71; chmn. Bd. Examiners Psychologists, Washington, 1972—. Bd. dirs. Washington Heart Assn., 1969—; chmn. gov. bd. Council Univ. Insts. Urban Affairs, 1970—. Served with AUS, 1944-46. Decorated Bronze Star medal. Mem. Am. Soc. Tng., Devel. (nat. chmn. profl. standards, ethics com. 1969), Am., Eastern, D.C., Md. psychol. assns., A.A.A.S., Soc. Psychol. Study Social Issues, Nat. Assn. Minority Group Urbanologists (dir.), Psi Chi, Alpha Kappa Mu. Cons. editor: Jour. of Profl. Psychology, 1969—. Home: 1342 Kalmia Rd NW Washington DC 20012 Office: 3603 14th St NW Washington DC 20010

JONES, RYMAN CHARLIE, city ofcl.; b. Buford, Ga., Apr. 23, 1944; s. Carson Edward and Mozelle (Little) J.; A.S., So. Tech. Inst., 1965; m. Alecia Carol Gardner, Aug. 15, 1965; 1 son, Ryman Charlie. Bldg. ofcl. City of Decatur, Ga., 1965-69, supt. sanitation, 1969-74; chief Bur. Solid Waste Mgmt., City of Richmond (Va.), 1974—. Mem. Fleet Supt. Assn., Am. Pub. Works Assn. (pres. Ga. chpt. 1973-74, dir. 1970-73). Home: 1560 Newell Rd Richmond VA 23225 Office: 900 E Broad St Richmond VA 23219

JONES, SANFORD LOGAN, endocrinologist, educator; b. Hazard, Ky., Sept. 22, 1925; s. David and Grace Elizabeth (Terry) J.; B.S., Eastern Ky. State Coll., 1950; M.S., U. Ky., 1956; Ph.D., U. Tenn., 1960; m. June Elizabeth Daugherty, Aug. 18, 1956; children—Sanford Logan, Henry Mason, Catherine Elizabeth. High sch. sci. tchr. Perry County (Ky.) Schs., 1950-55; instr., research asso. U. Tenn., 1960-61; asst. prof. biology Eastern Ky. State Coll., 1961-62, asso. prof. biology, 1963-65; prof. biology Eastern Ky. U., Richmond, 1965—. Dir. Summer Inst. for Secondary Tchrs.-NSF grant, 1970; mem. Coll. Research Program-U. Ill., 1969; attended Workshop in Molecular Techniques in Developmental Biology, U. Cal., San Diego, 1973. Served with USAAF, 1943-45. Decorated Air medal. Mem. Am. Soc. Zoology, Sigma Xi. Home: 204 Bristol Dr Richmond KY 40475

JONES, SCRANTON, lawyer, educator; b. Ft. Worth, July 29, 1921; s. Harper and Elizabeth (Boulware) J.; student Tex. Christian U., 1938-40; B.A., U. Tex., 1942, LL.B., 1947; m. Joyce Pegram, Sept. 6, 1947; children—Allison, Julieanne. Admitted to Tex. bar, 1947; since practiced in Ft. Worth; partner Jones & Morris, Attys. Ft. Worth, 1952-68; spl. asst. atty. gen. Tex., Austin, 1962-63; asst. prof. bus. law Tex. Christian U., 1968—; v.p., dir. S. Tex. Water Co., Rosharon; city councilman, mayor pro-tem Ft. Worth, 1963-67. Bd. dirs. Tarrant County Hist. Soc., Council on Alcoholism (pres. Tarrant County Area 1968-69). Served with USNR, 1942-46. Mem. Am., Ft. Worth bar assns., State Bar Tex., Am. Legion. Episcopalian. Mason, Rotarian (dist. gov. 1967-68). Home: 4309 Inwood Rd Fort Worth TX 76110 Office: Tex Christian U Fort Worth TX 76129

JONES, THOMAS FRANKLIN, JR., univ. pres., elec. engr.; b. Henderson, Tenn., July 9, 1916; s. Thomas Franklin and Adye Mae (Moore) J.; B.S., Miss. State Coll., 1939; M.S., Mass. Inst. Tech., 1940, ScD., 1952; LL.D., The Citadel, 1968; D.Eng., Purdue U., 1971; m. Mary Katherine Butterworth, Mar. 9, 1942; children—Thomas, James, Jonathan, Katherine, Andrew. Physicist underwater sound, harbor def. Naval Research Lab., 1941-47; instr. Mass. Inst. Tech., 1947, research asso. guided missiles, analog computation and analysis, 1948-49, asst. prof., 1949-54, asso. prof. charge circuits, electronics and measurement lab., 1954-58; head Purdue U. Sch. Elec. Engring., 1958-62; pres. U. S.C., 1962—. Spl. adviser NSF, 1961-66; mem. Nat. Acad. Scis. Adv. Commn. on Post-Doctoral Study, 1966-69; exec. com. Hwy. Research Bd., 1967-70; mem. Nat. Sci. Bd., 1966-72; mem. adv. bd. on ednl. requirements to sec. navy, 1963-66; dir. Engrs. Council Profl. Devel., 1964; chmn. tech. adv. bd. Western Union Telegraph Co., 1966-69; mem. study com., regents commn. on doctoral edn. State Edn. Dept., State U. N.Y., 1972-73. Pres. So. Assn. Land Grant Colls. and State Univs., 1970. Recipient Meritorious Civilian Service award U.S. Navy; named South Carolinian of Year, 1966, Columbia (S.C.) Salesman of Yr., 1969. Fellow A.A.A.S., I.E.E.E. (v.p. profl. group on edn.; bd. dirs. 1962, 64-67, mem. exec. com. 1962; editor 1962, mem. editorial bd. 1963-64); mem. Am. Soc. Engring. Edn., Nat. Acad. Engring., Newcomen Soc., Sigma Xi, Phi Eta Sigma, Kappa Mu Epsilon, Tau Beta Pi, Eta Kappa Nu, Theta Xi, Phi Beta Kappa, Phi Mu Alpha. Home: President's Home U South Carolina Columbia SC 29208

JONES, THOMAS L., educator; b. Breckinridge County, Ky., Apr. 10, 1931; s. V.A. and Elizabeth (Lambirth) J.; B.S., U. Ky., 1959, LL.B., 1961; LL.M., U. Mich., 1965; m. Shelley Edwards, July 15, 1961. Asst. prof. law U. Ala., Tuscaloosa, 1962-65, asso. prof., 1965-68, prof., 1968—, acting dean Sch. Law, 1970-71; acting dir. Ala. Law Inst., 1972—. Vis. prof. U. Ky., Lexington, 1965, U. Ill. Coll. Law, 1971-72; Ala. commr. to Nat. Conf. Commrs. on Uniform State Laws, 1967—. Served with USAF, 1951-55. Editor Ala. Will Manual Service, 1965—. Home: 907 Indian Hills Dr Tuscaloosa AL 35401

JONES, THOMAS OSWELL, ofcl. NSF; b. Oshkosh, Wis., May 13, 1908; s. Hugh Edwards and Jane (Davies) J.; B.S., Wis. State U., 1930; Ph.M., U. Wis., 1934, Ph.D., 1937; m. Phyllis Elizabeth Jackson, Aug. 19, 1950; children—Elizabeth Carol, Phyllis Jane. Faculty, Haverford Coll., 1937-56, prof. chemistry, 1954-56; with NSF, Washington, 1956—, div. dir. environmental scis,, 1965-69, dep. asst, dir. for nat. and internat. programs, 1969—; asst. to sect. chief Metall. Lab., Chgo., 1944-45, sect. chief info. div., 1945-46; vis. prof. chemistry U. Wis., 1954-55. Decorated Order Al Merito (Chile); recipient Meritorious Ser. medal NSF, 1970. Mem. Am. Chem. Soc., Am. Geophy. Union, A.A.A.S., Phi Beta Kappa, Sigma Xi. Contbr. articles on nuclear scis., isotopes, atomic weights, tracer techniques profl. jours. Home: 7504 Holiday Terrace Bethesda MD 20034 Office: 1800 G St Washington DC 20550

JONES, VARNAKALE LORENZO, geophysicist, physicist; b. Carthage, Mo., Aug. 8, 1902; s. Harry Lorenzo and Lenore (White) J.; B.A., U. Okla., 1925, M.S., 1927; postgrad. U. Colo., 1927-28, U. Okla., 1931-32. Asst. physics dept. U. Okla., 1925-27, instr. physics, 1931-32; geophysicist Amerade Petroleum Corp., summer 1927; instr. physics, U. Colo., 1927-28; research and devel. cons., Chelsea, Okla., 1928-31; cons. physics and geophysics, Tulsa, exploration control geophysicist Barnsdal Oil Co. (Tulsa), 1936; cons. geophysics, instr. physics, U. Tulsa, 1943-44, head dept. geophysics, 1946-51; geophysicist Standard Oil & Gas, Tulsa, 1944-45; research geophysicist Geophys. Devel. Corp., also geophys. interpreter Frost Geophys. Corp., both Tulsa, 1945-46; chief geophysicist Terrametric Exploration Co., Tulsa, 1951—. Collaborator, Okla. Geol. Survey, sr. author Vertical Magnetic Intensity Map of Okla., 1963-64. Mem. Tulsa Astron. Soc. (pres. 1942-43), Am. Geophys. Union, Seismol. Soc. Am., European Assn. Exploration Geophysics, Soc. Exploration Geophysics (editorial asst. 1959-60), Am. Inst. Physics, Am. Assn. Physics Tchrs., Tulsa, (v.p. 1948-49, editor proc. 1956-57), Oklahoma City geophys. socs., Tulsa, Oklahoma City geol. socs., Sigma Xi, Sigma Pi Sigma, Alpha Sigma Delta, Phi Gamma Kappa. Presbyn. Mason (32 deg., K.T., Shriner). Club: High Twelve (Tulsa). Research and publs. in profl. jours. Home: 1335 E 18th St Tulsa OK 74120 Office: PO Box 3731 Tulsa OK 74152

JONES, WALTER BEAMAN, congressman; b. Fayetteville, N.C., Aug. 19, 1913; s. Walter George and Fannie (Anderson) J.; B.S., N.C. State U., 1934; m. Doris Long, Apr. 26, 1934; children—Dot Dee Moye, Walter Beamon II. Mem. N.C. Gen. Assembly, 1955-59; mem. N.C. Senate, 1965; mem. 89th-93d congresses 1st Dist. N.C. Dir. Security Savs. & Loan Assn., Farmville, N.C. Mayor, Farmville, 1949-53. Former trustee Campbell Coll., U. N.C. Recipient Watchdog of Treasury award Nat. Assn. Businessmen, 1966; named Farmville Man of Year, 1955. Democrat. Baptist (deacon). Mason (32 deg., Shriner), Elk, Rotarian, Moose. Home: May Blvd Farmville NC 27828 Office: Cannon House Office Bldg Washington DC 20515

JONES, WALTER THOMAS, airport mgr.; b. Atlanta, Jan. 12, 1938; s. Walter F. and Katharine (Henning) J.; B.B.A., Ga. State U., 1963; m. Helen Hazelrigs, July 15, 1958; children—Michael, Daryl, Katherine. Statistician, Atlanta Bd. Edn., 1960-62; airport economist, chief accountant City Atlanta, 1962-64, asst. airport mgr. Atlanta Airport, 1964-68; airport mgr. City El Paso Internat. Airport and Indsl. Park, 1968—. Mem. Airport Operators Council Internat. (internat. bd. dirs. 1972-74), Am. Assn. Airport Execs., Tex. Transp. Needs Adv. Council, Tex. Airport Needs Council. Methodist. Home: 3101 Copper St El Paso TX 79930 Office: El Paso International Airport El Paso TX 79925

JONES, WELDON MAXEY, banker; b. Ardmore, Okla., Dec. 8, 1911; s. Fred Buckner and Ella (Burrow) J.; student Phoenix Jr. Coll., 1933-34, U. Ariz., 1931-32; m. Janet Day, Mar. 10, 1940; children—Diana Day (Mrs. Robert L. Wynne), Donald B. Vice pres. Valley Nat. Bank, Phoenix, 1934-55; pres., dir. San Angelo Nat. Bank (Tex.), 1955-74, chmn. bd., 1974—. Served to maj. USAAF, 1942-46. Clubs: San Angelo Country, River (San Angelo); Kiva (Phoenix). Home: 1201 Algeria Dr San Angelo TX 76901 Office: San Angelow Natl Bank San Angelo TX 76901

JONES, WESLEY FLETCHER, JR., surgeon; b. Jackson, Tenn., Aug. 13, 1925; s. Wesley F. and Rachel (Jones) J.; B.A., Vanderbilt U., 1949, M.D., 1952; m. Helen Rebecca White, June 28, 1948; children—Rebecca Jane, David Alan, Laura Lynn. Intern, John Gaston Hosp., Memphis, 1953; resident gen. and thoracic surgery, Kennedy VA Hosp., Memphis, 1954-59; practice medicine specializing in surgery, Jasper, Ala., 1959-61, Lexington, Tenn., 1961—. Served with AUS, 1944-46. Fellow A.C.S., Southeastern Surg. Congress. Home: 473 Colonial Dr Lexington TN 38351 Office: 157 W Church St Lexington TN 38351

JONES, WILLIAM CLIFTON III, lawyer; b. Elk City, Okla., Aug. 3, 1939; s. William Clifton, Jr. and Mildred Etna (Reed) J.; B.S., Tex. Christian U., 1961; J.D., U. Tulsa, 1967; m. Delores Rae Carter, Dec. 23, 1965; 1 son, David Lynn. With Gus J. Karey, C.P.A., Oklahoma City, 1963-65; accountant Pan Am. Petroleum Corp., Tulsa, 1965-67; tax atty. Sunray DX Oil Co., Tulsa, 1967-68, Cities Service Oil Co., Tulsa, 1968-69; v.p. corporate planning White Shield Oil & Gas Corp., Tulsa, 1969-73; admitted to Okla. bar, 1968; practice law, Tulsa, 1968—. Served to 1st lt. U.S. Army, 1961-63. Mem. Am., Okla. bar assns., Kappa Sigma, Phi Alpha Delta. Club: Tulsa. Home: 6843 E 56th St Tulsa OK 74145 Office: 16 E 16th St Tulsa OK 74119

JONES, WILLIAM DENVER, educator; b. Jenkinjones, W.Va., Apr. 14, 1935; s. William Clyde and Verda Lucille (Shrewsbury) J.; B.A., Berea Coll., 1958; M.A., Vanderbilt U., 1961, Ph.D., 1963; m. Melba Revonda Mayberry, Sept. 13, 1958; children—Mark Allen, Lisa Gayle. Research asso. thermonuclear div. Oak Ridge Nat. Lab., 1963-70; asso. prof. physics U. S. Fla., Tampa, 1970-72, prof., asst. chmn. physics dept., 1972—. AEC Health Physics fellow, 1958-60; NSF fellow, 1961-62; Oak Ridge Asso. Univs. grantee, 1970-72; U.S. AEC grantee, 1970-72, 72—; Air Force Cambridge Research Lab. grantee, 1971—. Mem. Am. Phys. Soc., Am. Assn. Physics Tchrs., A.A.A.S., Fla. Acad. Sci., Research Engring. Soc. Am., Sigma Xi. Reviewer: Phys. Rev. Letters, Physics of Fluids, Rev. Sci. Instruments, AEC, NSF. Contbr. articles to profl. jours. Home: 13504 Shady Shores Dr Tampa FL 33612

JONES, WILLIAM FRANCIS, educator; b. Sanford, N.C., Sept. 5, 1927; s. Allen and Clara Fawell (Robertson) J.; student Hampden Sydney Coll., 1947-50, Davis and Elkins Coll., 1950-51, Potomac State Coll., 1951; B.A., Davis and Elkins Coll., 1951; postgrad. Va. Poly. Inst. and State U., 1958, Va. Inst. Marine Sci., 1960; M.S., Madison Coll., 1958; Ed.D., U. Va., 1968; m. Frances Howard Pancake, Aug. 18, 1951; 1 dau., Sarah Parsons. Chmn. sci. dept. Lousia County High Sch., 1951-52; biology tchr. Handley High Sch., Winchester, Va., 1952-58, chmn. sci. dept., 1956-58; mem. biology dept. faculty Madison Coll., Harrisonburg, Va., 1958—, asso. prof. biology, 1968—. Mem. Va. Resource-Use Edn. Council, 1968—. NIH grantee, 1961. NSF grantee, 1965. Mem. Assn. for Edn. of Tchrs. in Sci., Nat. Sci. Tchrs. Assn., Ecol. Soc. Am., Am. Assn. U. Profs., Va. Sci. Tchrs. Assn., Va. Ind. Sci. Tchrs. Assn., Va. Acad. Sci., Va. Ednl. Assn., Va. Sci. Suprs. Assn., Kappa Delta Pi, Phi Delta Kappa. Home: 725 S Main St Harrisonburg VA 22801

JONES, WILLIAM LEON, SR., mfg. co. exec.; b. Coffeeville, Ala., May 27, 1912; s. William Sam and Minnie (Clanton) J.; grad. high sch.; m. Sara Frances Price, Nov. 16, 1941; children—William Leon, John Larry, Judy (Mrs. Robert Mathew Free). Parts man Parts Service Corp., Montgomery, Ala., 1933-45; owner Selma Parts Service Co., Inc. (Ala.), 1945-51; chief exec. officer Bush Hog, fabricated metal products co., Selma, 1952—; dir. Citizens Bank & Trust Co., Selma, 1960—. Mem. Ala. C. of C. (bd. dirs. 1968—), Selma C. of C. (bd. dirs. 1966—). Mason (Shriner). Clubs: Selma Country, Civitan (pres. 1957) (Selma). Home: 206 Hooper Dr Selma AL 36701 Office: Box 1039 Selma AL 36701

JONSON, WILLIAM CRAWFORD, JR., ednl. research adminstr.; b. Greenville, Ky., Jan. 22, 1910; s. William Crawford and Elizabeth (Martin) J.; B.S., U.S. Naval Acad., 1932; m. Frances Wier, Dec. 26, 1937; children—Frances Ann (Mrs. James R. Lloyd), Robert Crawford, Thomas Alexander. Commd. ensign USN, 1932, advanced through grades to rear adm., 1959; ret., 1959; comdg. officer U.S.S. Avocet in Pearl Harbor during Japanese attack, 1941, prof. naval sci. Auburn (Ala.) U., 1956-59; dir. Auburn Research Found., 1959-67; asst. dir. engring. expt. sta. Auburn U., 1967—. Decorated Bronze Star medal. Mem. Ret. Officers Assn., U.S. Naval Acad. Alumni Assn. Rotarian (treas. 1968-69). Home: PO Box 483 1403 E Glenn Av Auburn AL 36830 Office: Ramsay Hall Auburn U Auburn AL 36830

JONSSON, JOHN ERIK, instrument mfg. co. exec.; b. N.Y.C., Sept. 6, 1901; s. John Peter and Ellen Charlotte (Palmquist) J.; M.E., Rensselaer Poly. Inst., 1922, D.Eng. (hon.), 1959; D.Sc., Hobart and William Smith Coll., 1961, Austin Coll., 1963; LL.D., So. Meth U., 1964, Carnegie-Mellon U., 1972, Skidmore Coll., 1972; D.C.L., U. Dallas, 1968; D.H.L., Okla. Christian Coll., 1973; m. Margaret Elizabeth Fonde, Feb. 8, 1923; children—Philip R., Kenneth A., Margaret Ellen. Engring., mfg. and sales Aluminum Co. Am., 1922-27; pres. Automobile Distbr. Co., 1927-29; with Tex. Instruments, Inc., Dallas, 1930—, successively supt. lab., asst. sec., sec.-treas., v.p., treas., 1930-51, pres., 1951-58, chmn. bd., 1958-66, hon. chmn. bd., 1967—; dir. Equitable Life Assurance Soc. U.S., Republic Nat. Bank of Dallas; asso. dir. Citizens State Bank, Richardson, Tex., Mem. Am. Revolution Bicentennial Commn., Urban Transp. Adv. Council. Chmn. bd. Dallas-Ft. Worth Regional Airport; mayor, Dallas, 1964-71. Pres. bd. dirs. Excellence in Edn. Found., Dallas; chmn. bd. Lamplighter Sch., Inc., Dallas; trustee Callier Hearing and Speech Center, Austin Coll., Sherman, Tex., U. Dallas, Irving, Tex., Rensselaer Poly Inst., Troy, N.Y., Skidmore Coll.; chmn. bd. dirs., Ednl. Facilities Lab.; bd. visitors Tulane U. Recipient Advancement Research medal Am. Soc. Metals, 1964; Industrialist award Soc. Indsl. Realtors, 1965—; Bene Merenti medal, 1966; Gantt medal, 1968; Horatio Alger award, 1969; Hoover medal, 1970; Schmidt medal, 1972; Chauncey Rose medal Rose-Hulman Inst., 1972; named Industrialist of Year Soc. Indsl. Realtors, 1965. Mem. Soc. Exploration Geophysicists, Newcomen Soc., Nat. Planning Assn. (nat. planning council), Conf. Bd. (mem. sr. adv. council), Nat. Acad. Engring., Am. Mgmt. Assn. (life), A.I.A. (hon.), Petroleum Club (past pres.); Phi Beta Kappa (hon.), Tau Beta Pi (hon.). Clubs: Dallas Country, Dallas Petroleum (Dallas); Chaparral; Brook Hollow Golf. Home: 4831 Shadywood Lane Dallas TX 75222 Office: Republic Bank Tower Dallas TX 75201

JONSSON, MARGARET ELIZABETH FONDE (MRS. JOHN ERIK JONSSON), civic worker, club woman; b. Mobile, Ala., Sept. 22, 1902; d. Hiram Cornelius and Carrie (Watkins) Fonde; diploma Maryville Poly. Sch. Bus., 1919; M.Litt., Skidmore Coll., 1964; m. John Erik Jonsson, Feb. 8, 1923; children—Philip Raymond, Kenneth Alan, Margaret Ellen. Accounting dept. asst. Aluminum Co. Am., Alcoa, Tenn., 1919-23. Mem. Dallas Woman's Club, 1935—, bd. govs., 1958-63, pres., 1961-62, chmn. adv. bd., 1963-65; mem. Dallas Garden Center, 1959—, pres., 1964-65; bd. dirs. KERA; adv. bd. Dallas Civic Opera, Red Cross Office of Vols.; former mem. women's com. State Fair Tex. Trustee Dallas Mus. Fine Arts, Women's div. State Fair Tex., Marianne Scruggs Garden Club, Standard Study Club. Mem. Woman's Council Dallas County, Woman's Aux. Dallas County Hosp. Dist. (life), Dallas Health and Sci. Mus. (life), Woman's Aux. Nat. Jewish Hosp., Dallas Theater Center, League Women Voters, Dallas Symphony League, Dallas Geol. and Geophys. Aux. Republican. Presbyn. Clubs: Brook Hollow Golf, Country, Chaparral, City, Dallas Press (Dallas); Corinthian Yacht. Home: 4831 Shadywood Lane Dallas TX 75209

JOOR, RUTH HOUSTON (MRS. WILLIAM E. JOOR), civic worker; b. N.Y.C.; d. Hough and Belle (McIntyre) Houston; B.A., Ohio Wesleyan U., M.A., Columbia; m. William E. Joor, Oct. 8, 1938; children—William E. III, Nancy Ruth. Asst. editor Good Housekeeping Mag., 1931-38. Bd. dirs. League Women Voters, Ridgewood, N.J., 1949-52, Houston, 1956-62, pres;, 1959-61; bd. dirs. League Women Voters Tex., 1962-70, pres., 1966-70; pres. bd. dirs. Ridgewood P.T.A., 1951-52; participant Tex. Assembly, 1967, 70; Gov.'s Commn. on Tex. Urban Devel., 1970-72; mem. citizens adv. com. Tex. Constl. Revision, 1973—. Mem. Alpha Gamma Delta. Methodist. Author: Bermuda Vacation, 1940. Home: 1306 Ben Hur Dr Houston TX 77055

JOPLIN, GEORGE ADAMS III, newspaper publisher; b. Lexington, Ky., May 18, 1928; s. George Adams and Barthenia Cynthia (Sallee) J.; A.B., Centre Coll., Danville, Ky., 1950; M.S. in Journalism, Columbia, 1951; student Sch. Internat. Relations, Georgetown U., 1952; m. Alice Jean Summers, May 30, 1952; children—Jane, George Adams IV, John. Editor, pub. daily and weekly newspapers, 1954—; pres. Commonwealth-Jour., Inc., Somerset, Ky., 1964—; dir. First & Farmers Nat. Bank, Somerset. Pres. Pulaski County Indsl. Found., 1964-66. Publicity chmn. Pulaski County Republican Party, 1954—. Bd. dirs. Pulaski County chpt. Ky. Soc. Crippled Children. Served with USAF, 1951-54. Named Outstanding Young Man, Somerset Jaycees, 1963. Mem. Nat. Newspaper Assn. (dir.), Ky. Press Assn. (pres. 1964, Man of Yr. award 1965), Somerset-Pulaski C. of C. (dir. 1955-70, 72—), Centre Coll. Alumni Assn. (dir. 1962-68, 72—), Beta Theta Pi, Sigma Delta Xi. Presbyn. (elder). Rotarian (pres. Somerset 1962). Home: 515 Harvey's Hill Somerset KY 42501 Office: 102 N Maple St Somerset KY 42501

JORDAN, ANNE KNIGHT (MRS. CARL R. JORDAN), civic worker; b. Tampa, Fla., July 8, 1918; d. William Mitchell and Pearl Louise (Brown) Knight; grad. Cortez Peters Bus. Sch., Washington, 1941; B.A., Howard U., 1949, postgrad. 1955; postgrad. Savannah State Coll., 1957, Catholic U. Am., 1958, U. Ga. for Continuing Edn., 1967-68, Armstrong State Coll., 1970-72; m. Carl Rankin Jordan, Jan. 15, 1949; children—Carmen Antoinette, Karen Terez, Harold Kevin. With Social Security Agy., Balt., 1941-42; staff Foster Care Services, Dept. Children's Welfare, govt. of D.C., Washington, 1943; tchr. spl. edn., Savannah, Ga., 1957. Del. Nat. Council Catholic Women, Washington, 1964, Nat. Council Negro Women, Washington, 1969, White House Conf. on Food, Nutrition and Health, Washington, 1969; pub. relations dir. Women in Community Service, Savannah, 1965; chmn. family and parent edn. com. Savannah Deanery Council Cath. Women, 1965; organizer Savannah chpt. Nat. Tots and Teens Inc., 1965, Adopt-A-Family Project for Miss. Delta Poverty Area, 1970; sponsor Ga. Council on Human Relations, 1973—. Mem. exec. bd. Savannah chpt. Nat. Found.-March of Dimes, chmn. Mother's March, 1969, del. Leadership Conf., San Diego, 1969; adv. bd. Savannah Speech and Hearing Center, vol. screening program, 1965—. Served with WAC, 1943-46. Mem. Woman's Aux. Nat. Med. Assn. (adminstrv. sec. 1965-68, pres. 1969-70, chmn. exec. bd. 1970-71, organizer Jr. Nat. Med. Assn. 1970), N.A.A.C.P. (life, membership chmn. Savannah br, 1959-60, del. conv. 1959, 60), Woman's Aux. Ga. State Med. Assn. (pres. 1961-62, organizer Future Doctors of Ga. Clubs 1961), Woman's Aux. South Atlantic Med. Soc. (pres. 1956), League of Women Voters, Sigma Gamma Rho (Sigma of Year 1962). Roman Catholic (pres. guild 1954-56, moderator forum Diocesan Council Cath. Women 1965). Editor: Happy Homemaker Health Book. 1970; mem. adv. bd. New Lady Mag., 1970—. Home: 1627 Mills B Lane Av Savannah GA 31405

JORDAN, ARCHIBALD CURRIE, educator; b. Caldwell, N.C.; s. Archibald Currie and Octavia Graham (Stroud) J.; A.B. Duke U., A.M., Columbia U.; postgrad. Duke U. Law Sch; m. Jane Myers, Sept. 2, 1941; children—Ann Myers, Patsy Jane, Sally Rida, Julie Anna. Gen. Edn. Bd. fellow Columbia U.; admitted to N.C. bar; adviser N.C. Textbook Commn.; asst. prof. English, Duke U. Past pres., chmn. research com. N.C. English Teachers Council; v.p. Coll. English Assn. of N.C., Va. and W.Va. Mem. A.A.A.S., So. Atlantic Modern Lang. Assn., Am. Assn. U. Profs., Am. Dialect Soc., N.C. English Tchrs. Assn., Am., N.C. bar assns., Council for Basic Edn., Phi Delta Kappa, Kappa Delta Pi. Democrat. Presbyn. Author: Essentials of English Composition; College English Tests (forms Aand B); College Handbook of Composition; Fundamentals of College Composition; How to Write Correctly; Everyday Grammar; A Comprehensive Examination in the Fundamentals of Correct English Usage, 1960; The Writer's Manual, 1963, rev. edit., 1967. Asst. to editors So. Jour. Orthopaedic Surgery. Address: Box 6006 Duke U Durham NC 27708

JORDAN, BARBARA C., congresswoman; b. Houston, Feb. 21, 1936; d. Arlyne Jordan; B.A., Tex. So. U.; J.D., Boston U., 1959, then LL.D. Admitted to Tex. bar; adminstrv. asst. to county judge, Harris County; mem. Tex. Senate, 1966-72, pres. pro tem, chmn. Labor and Mgmt. Relations Com. and Urban Affairs Study Com.; mem. 93d Congress from 18th Dist. Tex. Mem. Pres.'s Commn. on Income Maintenance Programs; chmn. adv. com. Tex. Pub. Service Careers Program; mem. environmental health com. Council State Govts., So. Conf. Mem. exec. com. Nat. Democratic Policy Council. Bd. dirs. Nat. Urban League. Named One of 10 Most Influential Women in Tex., One of 100 Women in Touch With Our Time, Harpers Bazaar mag. Mem. Am., Tex., Mass. bar assns., Tex. Trial Lawyers Assn., N.A.A.C.P., So. Regional Council, Julia C. Hester House Found. Baptist. Office: 1725 Longworth House Office Bldg Washington DC 20575

JORDAN, BYRON GLEN, banker; b. Placid, Tex., Sept. 7, 1925; s. John Edward and Margaret (Squires) J.; student U. Houston, 1950, 55; m. Arvis Hammons, Aug. 10, 1945; children—Ronald, Glen. Vice pres., Bank of Southwest Houston, 1950-61; partner Peat Marwick Mitchell, N.Y.C., 1961-70; pres. State Nat. Bank El Paso, 1970—. Chmn. Excellence Fund U. Tex. at El Paso, 1970. Chmn. Project GAIN, 1971-72. Mem. Mayors Adv. Council, 1973-74. Bd. dirs. Jr. Achievement, 1970-73, Boys Club Am., 1970-73, Yucca council Boy Scouts Am., 1970-73, United Way El Paso, 1973—, El Paso Cancer and Radiation Center, 1972-73, YMCA, 1973-74, El Paso Mus. Art, 1970-73. Served with USAAC, 1943-45. Mem. C. of C. (dir. 1973—), Assn. U.S. Army, Bankers Club N.Y. Clubs: El Paso Country, Coronado Internat. (El Paso). Home: 905 Thunderbird St El Paso TX 79912 Office: PO Box 1072 El Paso TX 79958

JORDAN, CEDRIC ROY, educator, entomologist; b. Marion, S.C., Nov. 6, 1922; s. Cedric Roy and Sara (Foxworth) J.; B.S., Clemson Coll., 1947; M.S., Tex. A. and M. U., 1950, Ph.D., 1952; m. Dorris Jane Opt, Aug. 29, 1948; children—William Roy, Judith Elaine. Extension entomologist U. Ga., Athens, 1952—, asso. prof. entomology, 1952-57, prof., 1957—, head extension dept. entomology, 1958—, chmn. div. entomology, 1968—. Served to 2d lt. USAAF, 1943-45. Mem. Ga. Entomol. Soc. (pres. 1955-56), Entomol. Soc. Am. (pres. S.E. br. 1970-72), Nat. Assn. County Agr. Agts. (Dist. Service award 1969), U. Ga. Flying Club, Sigma Xi, Alpha Zeta, Epsilon Sigma Phi, Gamma Sigma Delta. Found new genus and species Strepsiptera, Membracixinos Jordani Pierce. Home: 759 Riverhill Dr Athens GA 30601

JORDAN, CHARLES DANIEL, physician; b. Greenville, N.C., Apr. 4, 1914; s. William Daniel and Rosa Ella (Randolph) J.; A.B., East Carolina Tchrs. Coll., 1935; M.A., George Peabody Coll., 1938; postgrad. Duke, 1940-42; M.D., Med. Coll. Va., 1948. Tchr. sci. Elm City (N.C.) High Sch., 1935-38; faculty Ga. State Coll. for Women,

Milledge, 1938-40; intern Johnston-Willis Hosp., Richmond, Va., 1948-49; resident obstetrics and gynecology Docts Hosp., Cleve., 1949-50; practice gen. medicine, Bethel, N.C., 1950-69; asst. dir. student health East Carolina U., Greenville, 1969—, also asst. prof. medicine, mem. admissions com. Dir. Home Savs. and Loan Assn., Bethel. Bd. dirs. county and state chpts. Am. Cancer Soc., Pitt County chpt. Eastern Tb and Respiratory Disease Assn. Served with AUS, 1942-44. Mem. Am. Heart Assn., A.M.A., N.C., Pitt County med. socs., Am. Acad. Gen. Practice, So., Seaboard, Tristate med. socs., Am., N.C. Camellia socs., Assn. Am. Physicians and Surgeons. Rotarian. Home: Hammond St Bethel NC 27812 Office: Infirmary East Carolina U Greenville NC 27834

JORDAN, CHARLES LEMUEL, educator; b. Ash Grove, Mo., May 28, 1922; s. Lemuel and Nellie (Woods) J.; Ph.B., U. Chgo., 1948, B.S. in Math., 1949, M.S. in Meterology, 1951, Ph.D., 1956; m. Ruth U. Cameron, July 14, 1942 (div. Apr. 1946); 1 son, Lewis E.; m. 2d, Elizabeth L. Sawyer, Sept. 8, 1951 (dec. July 1962); children—Karen L., Kathleen L.; m. 3d, Patricia J. Dagg, Apr. 23, 1964; children—Kimberly S., Kyle D., Keith C. Cons., Air Weather Service, Andrews AFB, Md., 1954-56; research meteorologist Nat. Hurricane Research Project, U.S. Weather Bur., West Palm Beach, Fla., 1956-57; asso. prof. dept. meteorology Fla. State U., Tallahassee, 1957-63, prof., 1963—, also chmn. dept., 1963-70. Served with USAAF, 1942-46. Fellow Am. Meteorol. Soc. (rep. to NRC 1970-72); mem. Am. Geophys. Union, A.A.A.S., Royal Meteorol. Soc. (Eng., fgn. mem.), Sigma Xi. Contbr. articles to profl. jours. Home: 2913 Lasswade Dr Tallahassee FL 32303 Office: Dept Meteorology Fla State U Tallahassee FL 32306

JORDAN, DIXON, real estate developer, grain broker; b. Cherry Valley, Ark., Apr. 13, 1908; s. Robert Maurice and May (Curtner) J.; student John Marshall Sch. Law, 1931; m. Mamie Cotter, Apr. 30, 1948; children—Julie, Jennifer. Accountant, John F. Clark & Co., brokers, Chgo., 1929-32; salesman Julius Matthews Spl. Agy., advertisers, Chgo., 1932-36; customer's broker Lamson Bros. & Co., Chgo., 1936-41, Thomson & McKinnon, brokers, Chgo., 1941-42; pres. Standard Commn. Co., Memphis, 1947—; pres. Valley Forge Apts., Inc., Memphis, 1966—; owner, mgr. 40 S. Morrison Apts., Memphis, 1966—. Served to capt. USAAF, 1942-46; PTO. Mem. Memphis Bd. Trade (pres. 1955, dir.), Memphis Grain and Hay Assn. Presbyn. Clubs: Chickasaw Country; Tennessee, Cesac (Memphis). Home: 2282 Madison Av Memphis TN 38104 Office: 176 Hillview Av Memphis TN 38109

JORDAN, DUPREE, JR., publisher, pub. relations exec., educator, cons.; b. Decatur, Ga., May 14, 1929; s. DuPree and Roslyn (Moncrief) J.; A.B., Mercer U., 1947; postgrad. Crozer Theol. Sem., 1948; M.Ed., Emory U., 1954; LL.B., Atlanta Law Sch., 1951, LL.D., 1963; Litt.D., Evang. Bible Coll. and Sem., 1970; m. Margaret Virginia Malone, Dec. 28, 1948; children—Margaret, DuPree III, Roslyn, Terri Lee. Ordained to ministry Bapt. Ch., 1945; reporter Macon (Ga.) Telegraph, 1945-47, Chester (Pa.) Times, 1948-49; news dir. WVCH, Chester, 1948-49; asso. dir. Radio-TV Commn., So. Bapt. Conv., 1949-52, acting dir., 1952-53; tchr. Westminister Schs. and Atlanta div. U. Ga., 1953-55; pastor Duluth (Ga.) Bapt. Ch., 1953-54; editor, pub., owner West End Star, Atlanta weekly newspaper, 1955-67; owner, pub. Piedmont Satellite, 1967-68, North DeKalb Record, Chamblee, 1956-64, Tri County Graphic, 1962-64; pres. Jordan Enterprises, Success Publs., Inc., Jordan & Jordan, advt. and pub. relations; dir. Successful Selling Seminars; pres. Ga. Coll. for Leadership Devel.; dir. numerous corps. Mem. Gov.'s Com. for a World's Fair in Atlanta; mem. Rapid Transit Com. of 100; dir. pub. affairs for S. States Office Econ. Opportunity, 1965-69, spl. asst. to regional dir., 1967-69, nat. religious liaison dir., 1968-69; exec. dir. Assn. Pvt. Colls. and Univs. in Ga., 1970—; mem. cons. staff Gov. Ga., 1962-66, 70-74, Bd. dirs. Atlanta Girls Club, Boy Scouts Am., YMCA. Recipient numerous awards from various orgns., including Ga. Press Assn., Nat. Editorial Assn., Sigma Delta Chi, Jr. C. of C.; Distinguished Service award Office Econ. Opportunity, 1967; DuPree Jordan, Jr., Day proclaimed Dec. 18, 1973. Mem. Pub. Relations Soc. Am., Nat. Editorial Assn., Ga. Press Assn. (bd. mgrs.), Adminstrv. Mgmt. Soc. (dir. Atlanta chpt.), Am. Mgmt. Assn., Am. Soc. Pub. Adminstrn., Soc. Advancement Mgmt., Am. Soc. Tng. Dirs.; Sales and Marketing Execs. Internat., Sales and Marketing Execs. Atlanta, Assn. Mgmt. Cons., Inc., Internat. Mgmt. Council, Mgmt. Assn. Atlanta, Am. Marketing Assn., Ga., Internat. assns. bus. communicators West End (pres. 1962), Chamblee-Doreville (pres. 1963) businessmen's assns., Ga., DeKalb County, Atlanta chambers commerce, Am., Ga. socs. assn. execs., Soc. Assn. Mgrs., Christian Council Met. Atlanta (pres. 1973), Sigma Delta Chi (dir. Atlanta chpt. 1963). Club: Nat. Press. Home: 1204 Warren Hall Lane NE Atlanta GA 30319 Office: 3330 Peachtree Rd NE Atlanta GA 30326

JORDAN, HOWARD, JR., univ. adminstr.; b. Beaufort, S.C., Dec. 28, 1916; s. Howard and Julia (Glover) J.; A.B., S.C. State Coll., 1938; spl. student Howard U., 1938-39; Ed.D., N.Y. U., 1956; m. Ruth Menafee, Feb. 14, 1943; 1 dau., Judith Louise. Mem. Faculty, S.C. State Coll., Orangeburg, 1941-63, prof. edn. and psychology, chmn. dept. edn., dean Sch. Edn., 1950-60, dean faculty, 1960-63; pres. Savannah (Ga.) State Coll., 1963-71; vice chancellor-services U. System Ga., Atlanta, 1971—. Mem. Savannah-Chatham County Area Econ. Opportunity Authority; chmn. Orangeburg County Cancer dr., 1948-49, Orangeburg County Crippled Childrens Soc. dr., 1950. Trustee Mather Sch. and Jr. Coll. Served with AUS, 1942-46; ETO. Mem. Am., S.C. psychol. assns., Nat. Soc. Study Edn. Nat. (dept. higher edn.), Palmetto edn. assns., Alpha Phi Alpha, Sigma Pi Phi. Episcopalian (vestryman, sec.). Mason. Address: 2640 Laurens Circle SW Atlanta GA 30311

JORDAN, JOHN WILLIAM, tech. dir.; b. Pitts., Apr. 25, 1912; s. Frank Craig and Harriet Sophia (Caywood) J.; A.B., Marietta Coll., 1934, Sc.D., 1959; Ph.D., Columbia, 1938; m. Marian Emily Spies, June 1, 1936; children—Emily (Mrs. Robert Q. Oaks), Frank, John, Edward, Andrew. Asst. food analysis and colloids Columbia, 1935-38; with Mellon Inst., Pitts., 1938-39; plant chemist Pitts. Corning Corp., Port Allegany, Pa., 1939-41; sr. fellow Mellon Inst., 1941-51; tech. dir. Baroid div. NL Industries, Houston, 1951—; dir. Enenco, Inc. Mem. Am. Chem. Soc., Am. Ceramic Soc., Clay Minerals Soc. (pres. 1973-74), Horseless Carriage Club Am., Phi Beta Kappa, Sigma Xi. Contbr. articles to tech. jours. Patentee in field. Home: 1801 Sherwood Forest Houston TX 77043 Office: PO Box 1675 Houston TX 77001

JORDAN, LEMUEL RUSSELL, hosp. exec., educator; b. Smithfield, N.C., Oct. 21, 1924; s. Thomas and Sophronia Lee (Creech) J.; A.A., Mars Hill Coll., 1943; A.B., Amherst Coll., 1947; M.A., Columbia, 1949; postgrad. (Ernest H. Abernathy fellow for research in so. industry 1952-53, Inst. for Research in Social Sci. research fellow 1953-54) U. N.C., 1949-50, 52-54; m. Jean Hildebrand Marrow, Dec. 15, 1951; children—Jean H., Rebecca and Judy. Faculty mem. Sch. Bus. Adminstrn., U. N.C., 1954-55, bus. mgr. Med. Outpatient Clinics, 1955-56; dir. outpatient dept. Duke, 1957-59, asst. prof. hosp. adminstrn., 1957-59; asst. supt. Duke Hosp., 1957-59; dir. teaching hosp. and clinics J. Hillis Miller Health Center at U. Fla., Gainesville, also asso. prof. mgmt. Coll. Bus. Adminstrn., 1959-65, asso. prof. health and hosp. adminstrn. Coll. Health Related Services, 1963-65; pres. Birmingham Baptist Med. Centers, 1965—; prof. health services adminstrn. U. Ala., 1969-72, adj. prof., preceptor, 1973-74; guest lectr. George Washington U., 1969—; adj. faculty hosp. adminstrn. Washington U., 1971—. Pres. Birmingham Area Manpower Resource Devel. Planning Bd., 1967-70, vice chmn., 1971-73; pres. Festival of Arts, 1972; mem. exec. com. Ala. Regional Med. Program Adv. Group, 1968—, pres., 1968, sec., 1971-74; mem. Ala. Adv. Council on Vocational Edn., 1973—; mem. protocol com. for primary care Robert Wood Johnson Found., 1973-74; mem. exec. com. Downtown Action Com., 1972—. Served with AUS, 1943-46; from sgt. to 2d lt. USAF, 1950-51; maj. Res. ret. Fellow Am. Coll. Hosp. Adminstrs. (mem. bd. govs.' task force rev. com. 1971-73; rep. to accrediting commn. grad. edn. hosp. adminstrn. 1972—; testimonials com. 1968-70; del. to Nat. Health Forum 1970); mem. Am. Hosp. Assn. (mem. long-range planning manual devel. com. 1970-72, pub. relations rev. com. 1970-72), Am. Protestant Hosp. Assn. (trustee, chmn. church, health and welfare relations 1970-71, chmn. council govtl. relations 1971-73), Birmingham Area C. of C. (chmn. operation native sons and daus., indsl. ambassador, edn. com., v.p. edn. and manpower 1970-72), Ala. Hosp. Assn. (dir., sec.-treas. 1970-71, pres. 1973, chmn. bd. trustees 1974), Birmingham Regional Hosp. Council (dir.), Community Service Council Birmingham and Jefferson County (dir., pres. 1974—), Better Bus. Bur. Birmingham (dir. 1967-68, 2d v.p. 1969-70, pres. 1970-72), Duke Hosp. Alumni Assn. (hon.), Theta Xi, Alpha Kappa Psi (div. and dist. councilor Mideast dist. 1953-56, nat. v.p. 1956-59, nat. pres. 1959-61). Baptist. Kiwanian. Mem. editorial bd. Modern Health Care, 1974. Home: 4161 Kennesaw Dr Birmingham AL 35213 Office: 3201 4th Av S Birmingham AL 35222

JORDAN, LYNDON KIRKMAN, JR., physician; b. Mount Olive, N.C., Jan. 6, 1935; s. Lyndon Kirkman and Rachael Loucille (Hazelton) J.; B.A., Duke, 1957, M.D., 1961; m. Beverly Hayes Brooks, Aug. 19, 1961; children—Lyndon Kirkman III, Christopher Page, Patrick Brooks. Intern, Watts Hosp., Durham, N.C., 1961-62; staff physician Dorothea Dix Hosp., Raleigh, N.C., 1962; practice gen. medicine, Smithfield, N.C., 1964—; mem. staff Johnston Meml. Hosp., Smithfield, chief staff, 1971; asst. prof. community health scis. Duke Med. Sch., 1972—, dir. family practice residency, 1972-73. Sponsor, presenter Jordan Citizenship award Mt. Olive Coll., 1959-71. Bd. dirs. Johnson County United Fund, 1966-69. Served with USAF, 1962-64. Named Rotarian of Year, 1969-70. Diplomate Am. Bd. Family Practice (charter). Mem. A.M.A. (Physician Recognition award 1971), 4th Dist. Med. Soc. N.C. (v.p. 1970, pres. 1971), N.C. (del. 1971), Johnson County (sec. 1968) med. socs., Am. Acad. Family Physicians, Smithfield-Selma C. of C. (dir. 1971-72). Rotarian (pres. Smithfield 1971-72). Home: 205 W Holding St Smithfield NC 27577 Office: 415 N 7th St Smithfield NC 27577

JORDAN, PAUL HOWARD, JR., surgeon; b. Bigelow, Ark., Nov. 22, 1919; s. Paul Howard and Marie Theresa (Lewis) J.; B.S. (Univ. scholar), U. Chgo., 1941, M.D., 1944; M.S. (Univ. fellow), U. Ill., 1950; m. Lois Regnell, Apr. 6, 1944; children—Kristine (Mrs. Frank Henyey), Craig T., Patricia L. Intern, St. Lukes Hosp., Chgo., 1944-45, resident, 1945-46; resident Hines VA Hosp., 1950-53; clin. asst. prof. surgery U. Cal. at Los Angeles, 1953-58; asso. prof. U. Fla. Med. Sch., Gainesville, 1959-64; chief surgery Houston VA Hosp., 1964—; also prof. surgery Baylor Coll. Medicine, Houston. Served with M.C., AUS, 1946-48. NIH fellow, 1949-50, 58-59. Diplomate Bd. Surgery. Mem. Am. Surg. Assn., Soc. U. Surgeons, Am. Physiol. Soc., Soc. Exptl. Biology and Medicine, Am. Gastroent. Soc., Tex. Surg. Soc. Home: 2123 MacArthur Houston TX 77025 Office: 1200 Moursund Av Houston TX 77025

JORDAN, ROBERT PAUL, editor, author; b. Omaha, July 6, 1921; s. Paul Hyde and Lillian Ada (Walters) J.; B.A., George Washington U., 1947; postgrad. Am. U., 1953-54; m. Jane Carol Taylor, Sept. 8, 1956; children—Robert Paul, Meredith, Julia. Asst. Sunday editor Washington Post, 1946-61; writer, editor Nat. Geog. Mag., Washington, 1962—. Served with AUS, 1942-46, USAF, 1951-53. Recipient Recognition award Higher Edn. Alumni Council Okla., 1971. Mem. White House Corrs. Assn., Overseas Writers, Nat. Geneal. Soc., Washington Press Club, Sigma Delta Chi. Presbyn. Author: The Civil War, 1969. Cons. editor: The Mighty Mississippi (Bern Keating), 1971; As We Live and Breathe (various authors), 1971; American Cowboy (Bart McDowell), 1972; Great American Deserts (Rowe Findley), 1972; The Alps (various authors), 1973. Home: 9717 Brimfield Ct Potomac MD 20854 Office: 17th and M Sts NW Washington DC 20036

JORDAN, VERNON E., assn. exec.; b. Atlanta, Aug. 15, 1935; grad. DePauw U., 1957; LL.B., Howard U., 1960; m. Shirley M. Yarbrough; 1 dau., Vickee. Law clk. to Donald Hollowell, 1960; field sec. Ga. br. N.A.A.C.P., 1962; then dir. So. Regional Council's voter edn. project; now exec. dir. Nat. Urban League; also exec. dir. United Negro Coll. Fund. Mem. Nat. Adv. Commn. Selective Service, White House Conf. to Fulfill These Rights. Office: 136 Marietta St NW Atlanta GA 30318

JORDAN, WILLIS POPE, JR., physician, educator; b. Rossville, Ga., Oct. 7, 1918; s. Willis Pope and Mary Sue (Cook) J.; B.S., Emory U., 1939, M.D., 1943; m. Jewelle Turner, June 26, 1952; children—Willis Pope III, Jennifer Sue, Julianne, Jerri Lucille. Intern Emory U. Hosp., Atlanta, 1943-44; resident Columbus Med. Center, Ga., 1944; chief resident, 1944-45; preceptorship in urology, Columbus, Ga., 1947-52; asst. resident in surgery, VA Hosp., Atlanta, 1952-53; asst. resident in urology VA Hosp., New Orleans, 1953-54, sr. resident, 1954-55; sect. chief in urology VA Hosp., Lake City, Fla., 1955-68; clin. asso. in surgery U. Fla. Coll. Medicine, Gainesville, 1964-65, asst. prof. surgery, 1965-68; sect. chief in urology VA Hosp., Memphis, 1968—; asso. prof. surgery, asso. prof. urology U. Tenn. Coll. Medicine, 1968—, dep. chmn. dept. urology, 1972—; chmn. Combined U. Tenn.-VA Urology Teaching Conf., 1968-73. Mem. hormone com. Urological Research Group, 1968; sec. Nat. Cyrosurgery Prostate Study Group, 1968; mem. Senate Faculty U. Tenn. Coll. Medicine, 1971—. Served to capt. M.C. AUS, 1945-47. Diplomate Am. Bd. Urology. Fellow A.C.S.; Amem. Am. (mem. Southeastern sect. sci. awards com. 1959, reception com. 1962), VA (treas. 1964-66, exec. com. 1964, pres. 1968-69) urological assns., A.M.A., So. Med. Assn., Assn. VA Urologists, Soc. for Cyrobiology, Soc. for Cyrosurgery, Bowers Surical Soc., Societe de Urologie Internale, Soc. Univ. Urologists, Assn. Am. Med. Schs., Soc. Govt. Service Urologists, Royal Soc. Medicine. Contbr. numerous articles to profl. pubs. Home: 1910 Ridgeway Rd Memphis TN 38117 Office: VA Hospital Jefferson Av Memphis TN 38104

JORDIN, MARCUS WAYNE, educator; b. Idaho Falls, Ida., May 23, 1927; s. Clair and Mary Ellen (Kyler) J.; B.S. in Pharmacy, Ida. State U., 1949; M.S. (Am. Found. Pharm. Edn. fellow), Purdue U., 1952, Ph.D., 1954; m. Ruth Joan Christensen, July 28, 1956; children—Robert, John. Faculty dept. pharmacology U. Ark., Little Rock, 1954—, prof., 1964—, chmn. dept., 1954—, dir. outpatient pharmacy, 1967—. Served with USNR, 1945-46. Mem. Am. Pharm. Assn., Sigma Xi, Rho Chi, Phi Lambda Upsilon. Presbyn. Home: 309 Brookside Dr Little Rock AR 72205 Office: 4301 W Markham St Little Rock AR 72201

JORDON, JAMES ALONZO, edn. co. exec.; b. Pitts., Oct. 13, 1923; s. James and Adelaide (Graves) J.; B.S., U. Pitts., 1947, M.Litt., 1948; LL.B., Duquesne U., 1961; m. Marion O. Bond, Sept. 10, 1950. Bus. mgr. Carter & Jordon Co., Pitts., 1948-50; pres. Jordon Supply Co., Pitts., 1950-55; with Koppers Co., Inc., Pitts., 1955-66, mgr. transp. research and devel., 1957-63, legal counsel, 1963-66; dir. ednl. systems Westinghouse Electric Corp., 1966-67, gen. mgr. comml. and indsl. div. Westinghouse Learning Corp., 1967-68, v.p. Urban Systems Devel. Corp., subsidiary, 1968-69; pres. Career Acad. Learning Systems, Inc., 1969-71, Community Learning Corp., 1971—; admitted to Pa. bar, 1964; pres. Minority Investments, Inc. Mem. Pitts. City Council, 1960-66; mem. Mayor's Com. on Econ. Devel., Washington. Bd. dirs. Action Housing, Pitts., Pitts. Health and Welfare Assn., Pitts. World Affairs Council, Pitts. Family and Childrens Service, Urban League Pitts., Pitts. br. N.A.A.C.P.; trustee Carnegie Inst., Carnegie Library, Robert Morris Jr. Coll.; chmn. bd. Bus. and Job Devel. Corp.; bd. dirs. Pitts. Pub. Parking Authority, Community Services Pa.; bd. visitors U. Pitts., Del. Democratic Nat. Conv., 1960, 64. Served with AUS, 1943-46. Named one of 100 most promising young men under 40 in Pitts., Time mag. and Pitts. C. of C., 1953; one of 3 most outstanding men in Pa., Pa. Jr. C. of C., 1957. Mem. Pa., Allegheny County bar assns., Greater Pitts. C. of C. Home: 3005 Doeg Indian Ct Alexandria VA 22309 Office: 1026 6th St NW Washington DC 20001

JORDRE, WILLIAM STARLING, ret. mech. engr.; b. Mantorville, Minn., June 1, 1906; s. John I. and Anna (Andrist) J.; student Antioch Coll., 1924-28; B.M.E., U. Minn., 1931; m. Hazel E. Olson, Nov. 21, 1931; children—Starling Ann (Mrs. F.W. Kephart, Jr.), Sue H. (Mrs. Laurence J. James), Diane (Mrs. George C. Meyerratken), J. William, JoAnn. Erector, Babcock & Wilcox Co., Barberton, O., 1931-38, dist. erection supt. Cin. office, 1938-43, Chgo. office, 1943-45; exec. v.p., dir. Oberle-Jordre Co., Inc., 1945-74; dir. Crestview Lands, Inc. Bd. dirs. Boilermakers Nat. Health and Welfare Fund. Mem. Engring. Soc. Cin., Nat., Ohio, socs. profl. engrs., Am. Soc. M.E. Episcopalian. Mason (32 deg.). Clubs: Bonne Aire Country, Summit Hills Country, Bankers. Home: 1360 East Bend Rd Burlington KY 41005

JORGENSEN, MATT LAWRENCE, architect; b. San Francisco, Apr. 10, 1905; s. Mathias and Anne (Seeberg) J.; A.B., U. Cal. at Berkeley, 1927; M.Arch., Harvard, 1929; m. Lois Carolyn McDonald, June 22, 1940; children—Carolyn (Mrs. Robert M. Bush), Maren (Mrs. Alan T. Hicks), Anna Lauren. Faculty dept. architecture Ga. Inst. Tech., Atlanta, 1929-42, prof., 1938-42; sole practice, Atlanta, 1936-42; mem. firm Abreu & Robeson, Inc., Atlanta, 1942—, chief designer, 1944-48, sr. officer, 1946—, sr. v.p., sec., also dir. Mem. High Mus. Art, Atlanta. Registered profl. engr., Ga. Fellow A.I.A. (past sec. Ga.), Am. Hosp. Assn., Am. Assn. Hosp. Planning, Internat. Hosp. Fedn., Nat. Soc. Profl. Engrs. Clubs: Cherokee Town and Country, Harvard, Atlanta City (Atlanta). Home: 3162 Lenox Rd NE Atlanta GA 30324 Office: 135 Walton St NW Atlanta GA 30303

JORGENSON, WALLACE JAMES, broadcasting co. exec.; b. Mpls., Oct. 31, 1923; s. Peter and Adelia (Bong) J.; student St. Olaf Coll., 1942-43; A.B., Bowling Green State U., 1944; L.H.D., Lenoir-Rhyne Coll., 1971; m. Solveig Elizabeth Tvedt, Feb. 24, 1945; children—Kristin, Peter, Mark, Lisa, Philip. Staff announcer WCAL, Northfield, Minn., 1941-43; officer in charge Armed Forces Radio Network, Kyushu, Japan, 1945-46; mgr. KTRF, Thief River Falls, Minn., 1946-48; with Jefferson-Pilot Broadcasting Co., Charlotte, N.C., 1948—, v.p., 1966-68, exec. v.p., 1968—; dir. TV Advt. Reps., N.Y.C. Chpt. chmn. A.R.C., 1969-70, bd. dirs., 1970—, vice chmn. resolutions com. Bd. dirs. Charlotte Symphony; chmn. bd. dirs. Lenoir Rhyne Coll., 1971—; bd. dirs., trustee United Community Services. Served to 2d lt. USMCR, 1942-46. Recipient Distinguished Service award Lenoir Rhyne Coll., 1969. Mem. Charlotte C. of C. (dir. 1973—). Clubs: Charlotte City, Quail Hollow Country (Charlotte). Home: 3210 Eastburn Rd Charlotte NC 28210 Office: 1 Julian Price Pl Charlotte NC 28208

JORGESON, CHARLES MILTON, JR., textile co. exec.; b. Park Ridge, Ill., Apr. 17, 1914; s. Charles Milton and Marjorie Althea (Allen) J.; B.S., Purdue U., 1938; grad. Exec. Program, Carnegie Inst. Tech., 1955; grad. Sch. Indsl. Adminstrn. Cornell U., 1967; m. Sylvia Strickland, Jan. 20, 1971; children—Craig Marshall, Brent Wilson. Indsl. engr. B.F. Goodrich Co., Akron, O., 1941-45; indsl. engr. B.F. Goodrich Co., Miami, Okla., 1945; staff supt. B.F. Goodrich Textile Products, Thomaston, Ga., 1945-67, prodn. supt. 1967-68, gen. mgr., 1968—. Mem.-at-large Nat. council Boy Scouts Am., 1960—, mem. exec. bd. Flint River council 1950—. Chmn. Thomaston Bd. Edn., 1969-70. Bd. dirs. Textile Edn. Found., Inc., 1969—, So. Indsl. Relations Conf. Mem. Ga. Textile Mfrs. Assn. (dir. 1969-73), Phi Kappa Psi. Baptist. Contbr. to textbooks for textile industry. Home: 306 Johnston Dr Thomaston GA 30286 Office: 325 Goodrich Av Thomaston GA 30286

JOSEFIAK, EUGENE JOSEPH, physician; b. Buffalo, Mar. 1, 1926; s. John Nicholas and Sophia (Lewandowski) J.; B.A., U. Buffalo, 1948, M.A., 1950; Ph.D., Duke, 1952, M.D., 1956; m. Theodora Kubik, June 28, 1950; children—John, Eugene, Paul, Ann, James. Biology asst. U. Buffalo, 1948-50; fellow bacteriology and immunology Buffalo Gen. Hosp., 1956, intern, 1956-57; resident pathology Bowman Gray Med. Sch., 1957-60, also instr. pathology, 1957-62; instr. biology Roanoke Coll., 1965; pathologist Macon (Ga.) Hosp., 1962, Roanoke Meml. Hosp., 1963—. Trustee Roanoke Meml. Hosp. Found., Roanoke Meml. Hosp. Med. Tech. Scholarship. Served with AUS, 1944-46. Grantee, Office Naval Research, NIH. Mem. Coll. Am. Pathologists, A.M.A., Mycol. Soc. Am., Va. Med. Soc., Roanoke Acad. Medicine, Am. Assn. Blood Banks, Am. Soc. Cytology, Va. Acad. Sci., Va. Soc. Pathology. Club: Roanoke Country. Home: 1901 Grandin Rd SW Roanoke VA 24015 Office: Profl Bldg Roanoke VA 24014

JOSEPH, DORRIS GEORGE, coll. dean; b. Palmetto, La., May 9, 1922; s. Charles and Katherine (Jabour) J.; B.S., U. Southwestern La., 1951; M.Ed., La. State U., 1953, Ed.D., 1963; m. Myrtle Spears, Dec. 14, 1941; children—Dennis George, Donna Therese (Mrs. Day), Jeri Lynn (Mrs. Landry). Dir., Vets. Trade Sch., Sunset, La., 1949-51; tchr. Palmetto High Sch., 1951-53; instr. U. Southwestern La., Lafayette, 1953-63; dir. student teaching Nicholls State U., Thibodaux, La., 1963-66, dean Coll. Edn., 1966—. Served with USAAF, 1942-45. Mem. La. Tchrs. Assn., Assn. for Tchr. Edn., Confraternity Christian Doctrine, Delta Sigma Phi, Phi Delta Kappa, Kappa Delta Pi. Lion. Author: A Student's Guide to Louisiana History, 1962; A Teacher's Guide to Louisana History, 1962. Home: 103 Creole Lane Thibodaux LA 70301

JOSEPH, ELEANOR COHEN (MRS. PERCY T. JOSEPH), librarian; b. Waco, Tex., July 10, 1919; d. Lawrence B. and Sadie (Weinberger) Cohen; B.A., Newcomb Coll., 1940; B.L.S., La. State U., 1941; m. Percy T. Joseph, Jan. 6, 1944; children—Edward L., David B. Librarian, New Orleans Pub. Library, 1941-43; sec. Howell, Soskin Pub. Co., N.Y.C., 1944; asst. librarian Rapides Parish Library, 1946-48; head reference dept. East Baton Rouge Parish Library, 1954-74, head reference services, 1974—. Mem. pres. United Cerebral Palsy Assn. Greater Baton Rouge, 1954—. Recipient Baton Rouge Jr. C. of C. Outstanding Pub. Servant award, 1962. Mem.

Baton Rouge Library Club (pres. 1962), La. Library Assn. (chmn. La. Lit. award com. 1963, chmn. Essae M. Culver award com. 1966, chmn. pub. library sect. 1965-66), A.L.A. (reference and subscription books rev. com. 1971). Home: 1816 Chopin Dr Baton Rouge LA 70806 Office: 700 Laurel St Baton Rouge LA 70802

JOSEPH, KENNETH EDWARD, educator; b. LaJunta, Colo., Aug. 17, 1927; s. John Henry and Veda Viola (Wilson) J.; B.A., Adams State Coll., 1951; M.S., Mich. State U., 1968, Ph.D., 1970; m. GeorgeAnna Morgan, Sept. 24, 1949; children—Kenneth G., Keith M. Investigator FBI, 1951-70, supr. tng. div., Washington, 1970-72; head dept. edn. and communication arts FBI Acad., Quantico, Va., 1972—. Dir. Muskegon (Mich.) Jr. Hockey Assn., 1960-65, Greater Lansing (Mich.) Jr. Hockey Assn., 1965-70. Served with USNR, 1945-47. Mem. Am. Assn. Higher Edn., Assn. Supervision and Curriculum Devel., Am. Assn. Community and Jr. Colls., Nat. Soc. Study of Edn., Am. Legion, Phi Delta Kappa. Mason, Elk. Office: FBI Academy Quantico VA 22135

JOSEPHSON, LEONARD M(ELVIN), educator; b. Ashland, Wis., Dec. 4, 1913; s. Axel Erland and Bertha Louise (Mattson) J.; B.S., U. Wis., 1936, Ph.D., 1941; m. E. JoAnn O'Dell, June 22, 1940; children—Louise, Jon Baard. Agt. U.S. Dept. Agr., Madison, Wis., 1933-37; asst. U. Wis., 1937-39; sec. Malt Research Inst., Madison, 1939-43; agronomist U. Ky., 1943-51; corn breeder, Union of S. Africa, 1951-54; research agronomist U.S. Dept. Agr., prof. agronomy U. Tenn., 1954-70; prof. plant and soil sci. U. Tenn., 1970—. Recipient plant breeding citation, Northrup, King & Co., 1970, award of merit, Gamma Sigma Delta, 1970. Fellow Am. Soc. Agronomy; mem. Am. Genetics Assn., Genetics Soc. Am., Sigma Xi, Phi Eta Sigma, Alpha Zeta, Gamma Alpha, Gamma Sigma Delta, Delta Theta Sigma. Presbyn. (elder). Club: Torch (internat. pres. 1969). Home: 7025 Kinzalow Dr Knoxville TN 37919

JOSLIN, EVERETTE EARL, mobile home moving and repair co. exec.; b. Amsterdam, N.Y., Nov. 24, 1919; s. Clarence Ansel and Ida (Mosher) J.; grad. Amsterdam Sch. Commerce, 1938; m. Elizabeth D. Ruback, Sept. 15, 1940; children—Dale, Larry, Roger. Petroleum service man GLF Exchange, Batavia, N.Y., 1938-41; bookkeeper War Dept., Washington, 1941-43; mgr. So. States Petroleum Co-Op, Leesburg, Va., 1943-45; dairy farmer, Amsterdam, N.Y., 1945-56; driver P.S. Dubrey Trucking, Fultonville, N.Y., 1956-66; with Lee County Mobile Home Service, Ft. Myers, Fla., 1967—, partner, 1967-69, pres. corp., 1969—. Mem. Lee County Mobile Home Adv. Bd., 1972—. Mem. Southwest Mobile Home Assn., Lee County C. of C. Home: Route 2 Box 343 North Fort Myers FL 33903 Office: 464 Pine Island Rd North Fort Meyers FL 33903

JOUFFRAY, VICTOR MANUEL, farm machinery co. exec.; b. San Antonio, Mar. 27, 1925; s. Alexander Octavious and Amelia F. (Funoll) J.; B.A., St. Mary's U. Tex., 1949; m. Evelyn Marie Rubendoll, Nov. 29, 1946; children—Kathryn (Mrs. Edwin Borque), Victor Manuel, Christine Marie, Debra Ann. Zone mgr. Internat. Harvester co., South Tex., 1949-56; asst. store mgr. Goodyear Tire & Rubber Co., Corpus Christi, Tex., 1956-57; sales mgr. Hill Hardware & Implement Co., Robstown, Tex., 1957-58; co-owner, sales mgr. Mathis Equipment Co. (Tex.), 1958-63; with John Bean Co., FMC Corp., San Antonio, 1964—, S.W. area sales mgr. agrl. machinery div., 1971—. Pres., Mathis Little League, 1959-62; dir. Civil Def., Mathis, 1959-62. Served with USNR, 1942-46. Mem. Tex., N.M., La., Okla. pecan growers, Tex. Indsl. Weed Control Conf. (steering com. 1973-75), Ark. Horticulture Assn., Tex. Peach and Plum Growers, Tex. Pest Control Assn., Tex. Turf Grass Assn., Tex. Hardware and Implement Assn., Houston Livestock Show Assn. Lion, Moose. Address: 6834 Crown Ridge Dr San Antonio TX 78239

JOURARD, SIDNEY MARSHALL, educator; b. Toronto, Ont., Can., Jan. 21, 1926; s. Albert Louis and Anna (Rubinoff) J.; B.A., U. Toronto, 1947, M.A., 1948; Ph.D., U. Buffalo, 1953; m. Antoinette Ruth Hertz, June 20, 1948; children—Jeffrey, Martin, Leonard. Faculty dept. psychology U. Fla., Gainesville, 1958—, prof., 1964—; practice psychotherapy, Gainesville, 1958—. Author: Personal Adjustment, 1958, 63; Transparent Self, 1964, rev. edit., 1971; Self-Disclosure, 1971, Disclosing Man to Himself, 1968, Healthy Personality, 1974. Home: 1506 SW 35th Pl Gainesville FL 32608

JOURNEAY, GLEN EUGENE, physician, educator; b. Orange, Tex., June 14, 1925; s. Fred Young and Gertrude Lillian (Martin) J.; B.A., Rice U., 1945, B.S. in Chem. Engring., 1947; Ph.D., U. Tex., 1952; M.D., U. Tex. at Galveston, 1960; m. Betty Jo Cooper, Sept. 4, 1948; children—Carol (Mrs. Robert Kaler), David Glen, Stephen Dunson, Nancy Catherine, Janet Elizabeth. Research chemist Dow Chem. Co., Freeport, Tex., 1948-49; research chemist Monsanto Chem. Co., Texas City, Tex., 1951-54, group leader, 1954-56; intern U. Tex. Teaching Hosps., Galveston, 1960-61; practice medicine, Texas City, 1961-63, Austin, 1963—; faculty biomed. engring. and environmental health engring. U. Tex., Austin, 1964—; mem. staffs Brackenridge, Seton, St. Davids hosps., Austin, 1963—; instr. St. Mary's Sch. Nursing, Galveston, 1957-61; physician Beeler-Manske Clin. Indsl. Medicine, Texas City, 1961-63. Mem. Captial Area Health Planning Commn., Austin, 1970-72; mem. exec. bd. Capital area council Boy Scouts Am., 1968—. Served with USNR, 1943-46. Recipient Silver Beaver award Boy Scouts Am., 1972. Mem. Am., Tex. med. assns., Am. Acad. Family Practice, A.A.A.S., Am. Acad. Clin. Toxicology, Alpha Omega Alpha, Sigma Xi Epsilon, Phi Lambda Upsilon. Home: 3908 Sierra Dr Austin TX 78731 Office: 7101 Woodrow St Austin TX 78757

JOWDY, ALBERT WILLOUGHBY, educator; b. New Bern, N.C., Mar. 31, 1922; s. Albert Willoughby and Genevieve (Fysal) J.; B.S., U. N.C., 1943, M.S., 1949, Ph.D., 1954; m. Florence Millicent McKendry, Feb. 1, 1955; children—Albert Willoughby III, Jeffrey W. Instr. U. N.C., Chapel Hill, 1949-54, asst. prof., 1955-60, asso. prof., 1962-66; asso. prof. U. Ga., Athens, 1966-70, prof., head dept. pharmacy adminstrn. and pharm. services, 1970—. Served with USNR, 1944-46. Mem. Am., Ga., N.C. pharm. assns., Am., Ga. pub. health assns., Acad. Pharm. Scis. Home: 350 Rivermont Rd Athens GA 30601

JOY, EDWIN DOUGLAS, JR., oral surgeon; b. Bridgeport, Conn., June 15, 1933; s. Edwin Douglas and Bernadette (Fagan) J.; B.A., Yale, 1954; D.D.S., U. Pa., 1958; m. Beverly Edwards, Aug. 29, 1953; children—Edwin Douglas III, David Michael. Intern, Phila. Naval Hosp., 1958-59; resident Med. Coll. Va., 1962-65; practice dentistry specializing in oral surgery, Richmond, Va., 1965-71; mem. staff Norfolk Gen., DePaul hosps., Gen. Hosp. Virginia Beach; asso. prof. oral surgery Med. Coll. Va., Richmond, 1965—; dir. dept. dentistry DePaul Hosp., 1967-71. Served to lt. comdr. USNR, 1958-62. Diplomate Am. Bd. Oral Surgery. Mem. Am. Dental Assn., Am. Soc. Oral Surgeons, Va. Soc. Oral Surgeons, Tidewater Dental Study Club, Norfolk C. of C., Omicron Kappa Upsilon, Delta Sigma Delta. Roman Catholic. Lion. Home: 7525 Marilea Rd Richmond VA 23225 Office: Dept of Oral Surgery Medical College of Va Richmond VA 23298

JOY, ROBERT JOHN THOMAS, physician, army officer; b. South Kingstown, R.I., Apr. 5, 1929; s. Angelo Francois and Mary Frances (Egan) J.; B.S., U. R.I., 1950; M.D., Yale, 1954; M.A., Harvard, 1965; m. Beverly June Boxser, July 5, 1952; children—Robert L.F., Lisa. Commd. 1st lt. M.C., U.S. Army, 1954, advanced through grades to col., 1970; intern, resident Walter Reed Gen. Hosp., 1954-58; basic sci. fellow Walter Reed Army Inst. Research, 1958-59; dir. environmental physiology Army Med. Research Lab., Ft. Knox, Ky., 1960-61; comdg. officer Army Research Inst. Environmental Medicine, Natick, Mass., 1961-62; chief U.S. Army Med. Research Team, Vietnam, 1965-66; chief med. research div. Med. Research and Devel. Command, Washington, 1968-69; dep. for med. and life scis. Office Dir. Def. Research and Engring., Washington, 1970-71; dep. dir., dep. comdt. Walter Reed Army Inst. Research, Washington, 1971—. Dir. staff White House Conf. on Food, Nutrition and Health, 1969. Decorated Legion of Merit with 2 oak leaf clusters. Recipient Osler medal, 1954; Hoff medal, 1959; John Shaw Billings award, 1966. Fellow A.C.P.; mem. Am. Physiol. Soc., Soc. Exptl. Biology and Medicine, Assn. Mil. Surgeons U.S., Am. Fedn. Clin. Research, Am. Assn. History Medicine, A.A.A.S., Am. Mil. Inst. Editor monographs in tropical medicine and med. history. Contbr. articles to profl. jours. Home: 5821 Highland Dr Chevy Chase MD 20015 Office: 6825 16th St Washington DC 20012

JOYCE, EUGENE LAWRENCE, lawyer; b. Kingston, N.Y., Dec. 22, 1917; s. James H. and Pauline (O'Neill) J.; student U. Ala., 1941; J.D., U. Tenn., 1951; m. Mary Margaret Williams, Sept. 17, 1941; children—Lisa, Lori. Admitted to Tenn. bar, 1951; sr. partner Joyce, Anderson, Wood & Meredith, Oak Ridge, 1951—; chmn. bd. Bank Oak Ridge. Anderson County atty., 1954-60. Pres., Oak Ridge Indsl. Devel. Bd., 1965. Bd. dirs. U. Tenn. Research Corp. Served with AUS, 1942-44. Named Oak Ridge Man of Year, C. of C., 1951; recipient Columbus award for pub. service K.C., 1964. Mem. Anderson County Bar Assn. (pres. 1962). Home: 103 W Overlook Dr Oak Ridge TN 37830 Office: Town Hall Kentucky Av Oak Ridge TN 37830

JOYCE, EVELYN ELIZABETH NORDSTROM (MRS. JOHN THOMAS JOYCE III), granite co. exec.; b. Texarkana, Tex., Mar. 22, 1920; d. Erick Sven and Signe (Johnson) Nordstrom; student U. Okla., 1936-40; m. John Thomas Joyce III, Dec. 27, 1946; children—Gigi Evelyn, John Michael. With Roosevelt Granite Co., Inc., Snyder, Okla., 1940—, v.p., 1945-60; pres., 1960—; pres. Southwestern Granite Supply Co., Snyder, 1957—. Del. dist. and state Republican convs., 1968, 70, 71, 72. Mem. Delta Gamma Alumae. Home: Route 1 Box 112 Snyder OK 73566 Office: Box 307 Snyder OK 73566

JOYCE, FRANK, farmer; b. Olive Hill, Tenn., Feb. 24, 1909; s. T.F. and Beulah (Porter) J.; B.S.A., U. Tenn., 1930; m. Anna Louise Beachboard, May 24, 1934; children—Nancy Elizabeth, Alice Ruth, Jean Ann. Asst. farm mgmt. specialist U. Tenn. Agrl. Extension Service, Knoxville, 1930-44; farmer, Winchester, Tenn., 1944—; dir. Tenn. Farmers Mut. Ins. Co., 1948-63; mem. stockholders com. 1st Nat. Bank of Franklin County. Agrl. rep. Tenn. Indsl. and Agrl. Devel. Commn., 1953-59; citizens adv. com. Tenn. Legislative Council Edn. Study, 1956-57; planning com. Tenn. Conf. Edn. Beyond High Sch., 1958. Mem. Middle Tenn. Farmers Inst. (pres. 1951), Tenn. Farm Bur. Fedn. (dir. 1946-62), Franklin County Farm Bur. (pres. 1946-54, dir. 1945-73), Franklin Farmers Coop. (dir. 1948-51, 52-54, sec.-treas. 1957-63, pres. 1964-70), Tenn. Rural Health Improvement Assn. (past dir.), Murfreesboro Prodn. Credit Assn. (dir. 1948-54), Franklin County C. of C. (dir. 1958-59), U. Tenn. Alumni Assn. (council 1954-55). Am. Hereford Assn., Alpha Zeta, Phi Kappa Phi. Mem. Church of Christ (former elder). Club: University of Tenn. Block and Bridie (hon.). Monthly contbr. The Progressive Farmer, 1946-61. Address: RFD 1 Winchester TN 37398

JOYNER, C(AREY) DAN, real estate broker; b. Greenville, S.C., Aug. 6, 1937; s. Carl Cox and Frances (Hatcher) J.; B.A., Furman U., 1959; m. Katherine Poole, Dec. 28, 1958; children—Beth, Lynn, Carey Dan. Salesman real estate firm, Greenville, 1962-64; pres. C. Dan Joyner & Co., real estate and ins., Greenville, 1964—; dir. Community Bank of Greenville, Fidelity Fed. Savs. and Loan Assn. of Greenville. Pres. Greenville Multiple Listing Service, 1969-70; state dir. Nat. Multi-List Service, 1971-72. Co-chmn. United Fund Drive, Greenville County, 1973, gen. chmn., 1974; co-chmn. Greenville County Cancer Drive, 1973; chmn. Furman U. Loyalty Fund, 1973-74. Trustee Greenville Auditorium, 1973-74; chmn. marketing adv. bd. Greenville Tech., 1973-74; bd. dirs. Greenville Blood Assurance Plan, 1973-74, Furman U. Athletic Assn., 1973-74. Served to 2d lt. AUS, 1959-62. Recipient Distinguished Service award Greenville Jr. C. of C., 1967, S.C. Realtor of Yr. award, 1973, Greenville Realtor of Yr. award, 1973. Mem. Greenville Bd. Realtors (pres. 1971-72), S.C. Real Estate Assn. (dir.), Home Builders Assn. (dir.), Furman U. Alumni Assn. (nat. pres. 1974). Clubs: Greenville Touchdown, Greater Greenville Basketball (v.p. 1973-74), Paladin (dir. 1973-74); Greenville Country (past gov.). Home: 2015 Cleveland St Greenville SC 29607 Office: 745 N Pleasantburg Dr PO Box 5757 Greenville SC 29606

JOYNER, JUDITH REBECCA, educator; b. Meggetts, S.C., Aug. 14, 1920; d. Ernest Luther and Rebecca (Butler) Joyner; student Martha Berry Coll., 1938-40; B.S., Appalachian State U., 1942, M.A., 1957; postgrad. U. N.C., Temple U.; Ph.D., U. S.C., 1960. Tchr., High Sch., Tabor City, N.C., 1942-43; dir. clubs and programs Am. Nat. Red Cross; Holland and Germany, 1945-47; coll. instr. Heidelberg and Berlin, 1947-48; employee relations chief, Berlin, 1948-50; employee utilization chief, Munich, 1950-52; mgmt. analyst Frankford Arsenal, Phila., 1952-54; tchr. High Sch., Loris, S.C., 1957-58; grad. instr. U. S.C., 1958-60, asst. prof., 1960-64, asso. prof., 1964-71, prof., 1971—, chmn. ednl. founds. Coll. Edn. Mem. state bd. League Women Voters S.C., 1966-67. Mem. South Atlantic Philosophy Edn. Soc. (pres. 1968-70), S.C. Edn. Assn., History Edn. Soc., Am. Assn. U. Profs., Nat. Soc. Study Edn., Nat. Soc. Am. Archivists, Delta Kappa Gamma. Contbr. articles to profl. jours. Home: 57 Churchill Circle Columbia SC 29206

JUBERG, RICHARD CALDWELL, physician, educator; b. Bismarck, N.D., Sept. 26, 1930; s. Oscar Leroy and Dora Eleanor (Caldwell) J.; B.A., Carleton Coll., 1952; M.D., U. Mich., 1956, M.S., 1963, Ph.D., 1966; m. Betty Lou Eisemann, Aug. 24, 1957; children—Cathlin Patrice, Daland Richard, Breton Chester, Gretchen Elissa, Saren Camille, Madren Lenore. Intern, Charity Hosp. La., New Orleans, 1956-57; asst. prof. pediatrics W.Va. U., 1966-69; asso. prof. med. genetics, pediatrics Crippled Children's div. U. Ore., 1969-70; asso. prof. pediatrics La. State U. Sch. Medicine, Shreveport, 1970-73, prof., 1973—; mem. cons. staff Shriners Hosp. for Crippled Children. Pres., Creswell Athletic Assn., 1973-74. Mem. Am. Soc. Human Genetics, Am. Genetics Assn., Soc. for Study Social Biology, A.A.A.S., Am. Assn. Mental Deficiency, So. Soc. Pediatric Research, La. Acad. Sci., Soc. Pediatric Research, Sigma Xi. Contbr. articles to profl. jours. Home: 241 Gladstone Blvd Shreveport LA 71104

JUDGE, ELMER FRANKLIN, data processing exec.; b. Perkins, Okla., May 30, 1915; s. William Homer and Eva May (Barnes) J.; student Okla. A. and M. U., 1933-36, Wichita State U., 1954-56; m. Wanda Morris Eggen, Jan. 17, 1969; stepchildren—Carla, Marlene, Stanley, Cherylee, Curtis; 1 son, William. Tabulating machine operator Okla. Employment Security Commn., 1938-41; supr. data processing Cessna Aircraft Co., Wichita, Kan., 1941-43; tabulating machine operator Okla. A. and M. Coll., 1946-52; mgr. data processing Cessna Aircraft Co., 1952-69; mgr. systems and data processing Okla. Pub. Co., Oklahoma City, 1969—; guest lectr. Wichita State U. Bus. mgr. Jr. Achievement; loaned exec. United Fund; chmn. adv. com. data processing Wichita Pub. Schs., Wichita State U., 1961-69; mem. data processing adv. com. Okla. State U. Tech. Sch. Served with AUS, 1943-46. Mem. Data Processing Mgmt. Assn. (life, past internat. pres.), Assn. Systems Mgmt., Nat. Accountants Assn. Democrat. Baptist. Moose, Lion (pres. 1969). Contbr. articles to profl. jours. Home: 5821 NW 71st St Oklahoma City OK 73132 Office: 500 N Broadway Oklahoma City OK 73125

JUDICE, C(HARLES) RAYMOND, judge; b. Lafayette, La., July 3, 1929; s. Rene and Letie (Bertrand) J.; student Southwestern La. U., 1946-47; B.B.A. U. Houston, 1956; J.D., S. Tex. Coll. Law, 1961. Admitted to Tex. bar, 1961; mem. firm Judice, Ogg & Merrill, Houston, 1961-63; Judge Municipal Ct., Houston, 1963-74, Ct. of Domestic Relations, Houston, 1973-74; exec. dir. Tex. Civil Jud. Council, 1974—. Mem. Tex. Constl. Revision Commn., 1972. Bd. dirs. Houston Cancer Soc., Houston Council on Alcoholism. Served with USAF, 1948-49, 50-51. Recipient gavel award for jud. leadership, 1966, award for best rehab. program N. Am. Judges Assn., 1966, Amicus Curiae award, 1968, Outstanding Jud. Service award for Constn. devel., 1973. Mem. Houston Bar Assn., State Bar Tex. (vice chmn. spl. commn. on cts. of spl. jurisdiction 1969-70, chmn. com. on cts. spl. jurisdiction 1967-68), N. Am. Judges Assn. (chmn. sect. alcoholism and drugs 1967-68, bd. govs. 1969-74, chmn. by-laws com. 1969-74), Tex. Assn. Municipal Judges (pres. 1966-67, dir. 1967—), S. Tex. Coll. Law Alumni Assn. (pres. 1966-67, dir. 1967—), Phi Alpha Delta (dist. justice 1964-66, supreme historian 1966-68, supreme sec. 1968-70, supreme adv. 1970-72, supreme vice justice 1972-74, justice Houston alumni chpt. 1968-69). Author: Phi Alpha Delta Law Fraternity: A History, 1969; Contbr. articles to profl. jours. Office: 308 W 15th St Suite 312 Austin TX 78701

JUDKINS, JOSEPH FAULCON, JR., educator; b. Richmond, Va., May 12, 1938; s. Joseph Faulcon and Annie (Gwaltney) J.; B.S. in Civil Engring., Va. Poly. Inst., 1960, M.S., 1965, Ph.D., 1967; m. Elizabeth Anne Smith, June 24, 1961; children—Catherine, Kimberly, Amy. Asst. prof. civil engring. Auburn (Ala.) U., 1967-71, Gottlieb asso. prof., 1971—. Cons. civil, environmental engr. Served with USAF, 1960-63. Mem. Am. Soc. C.E., Am. Water Works Assn., Water Pollution Control Fedn., Chi Epsilon, Phi Kappa Phi, Theta Chi. Club: Saugahatchee Country. Contbr. articles to tech. jours. Home: 202 Redwood Ct Auburn AL 36830

JUERGENSEN, HANS, educator, poet; b. Upper Silesia, Germany, Dec. 17, 1919; s. (foster) Hermann A. and Dora (Grossmann) J.; B.A., Upsala Coll., 1942; Ph.D., Johns Hopkins, 1951; Hon. Dr., Boswell Inst., Loyola U. of South, 1970; m. Ilse D. Lobenberg, Oct. 27, 1945; 1 dau., Claudia Jeanne. Came to U.S., 1934, naturalized 1943. Instr. German, U. Kan., 1951-53, Johns Hopkins, summers 1949-53; asst. prof., asso. prof. English, chmn. dept. Quinnipiac Coll., 1953-61; prof. humanities U.S. Fla., 1961—; art critic Tampa Times, 1961-67; one man shows at Studio Gallery, N.Y., Tampa (Fla.) Art Inst. Served with AUS, 1942-45. Fellow Conn. Acad. Arts and Scis., Poetry Soc. Am.; mem. Nat. Fedn. State Poetry Socs. (pres. 1968-70), C. of C., Delta Phi Alpha (hon.), Omicron Delta Kappa. Democrat. Jewish religion. Author: I Feed You From My Cup, 1958; In Need for Names, 1961; Existential Canon, 1965; Florida Montage, 1966; Sermons From The Ammunition Hatch of The Ships of Fools, 1968; From The Divide, 1970; Hebraic Modes, 1972; Points of Departure, 1974. Home: 7815 Pine Hill Dr Tampa FL 33617

JUHL, ROLF, govt. fisheries adminstr.; b. Santurce, P.R., Nov. 8, 1919; s. Theodor Cristian and Lili Eleonor (Moessen) J.; student Milw. State Tchrs. Coll., 1946-48; B.S., U. Wash., 1950; postgrad. U. Miami, 1951, Scripps Inst. Oceanography, 1953; m. Eleanor Lorraine Skladanek, Feb. 24, 1948; children—Dana Lynn, Vanessa Gail, Melani Ann, Cory Francis. Fishery biologist Inter-Am. Tropical Tuna Commn., San Diego, 1951-53; mgr. tuna cannery Nat. Packing Co., Ponce, P.R., 1953-59, Cal. Packing Corp., Mayaguez, P.R., 1960-64; fishery biologist U.S. Bur. Comml. Fisheries, 1959-60, Pascagoula, Miss., 1964-67; coordinator Puerto Rican Dept. Agrl., San Juan, 1967-73; fish program mgr. U.S. Dept. Commerce, Pascagoula, 1973—; pres. Marine Foods Corp., Ponce, 1971-73; cons. fishery devel., P.R., 1967-73. Served with AUS, 1940-45. Decorated Bronze Star (3). Recipient U.S. Govt. Service awards, 1966, 67. Mem. Marine Tech. Soc., Gulf & Caribbean Fish Inst., Assn. Marine Labs. of the Caribbean, A.A.A.S. Contbr. articles on fishery devel. and oceanography to profl. jours. Home: 3 Celeste Dr Moss Point MS 39563 Office: PO Box 1207 Pascagoula MS 39567

JUMPER, CHARLES FREDERICK, chemist, educator; b. Prosperity, S.C., Nov. 4, 1934; s. Keister O'Neal and Mattie Lee (Hendrix) J.; B.S., U. S.C., 1956, M.S., 1957; Ph.D., (NSF fellow), Fla. State U., 1961; m. Peggy June Harris, Mar. 19, 1967; 1 son, Frederick Harris. Research asso. Oak Ridge Nat. Labs., 1956-57; instr. Univ. S.C., Columbia, 1960-61; research chemist Bell Telephone Labs., Murray Hill, N.J., 1961-62; faculty chemistry The Citadel, Charleston, S.C., 1962—, prof., 1969—. NSF grantee, 1959. Mem. Am. Chem. Soc. (chmn. S.C. sect. 1970), S.C. Acad. Sci., S.C. Hist. Soc., Am. Assn. U. Profs., Sigma Xi, Phi Beta Kappa. Republican. Lutheran. Contbr. articles to sci. jours. Address: The Citadel Charleston SC 29409

JUMPER, KENNETH MARTIN, banker; b. Waco, Tex., Mar. 30, 1929; s. Cecil D. and Jewell D. (Posey) J.; student Central City Coll., Waco, Tex., 1947; m. Nita Lee Webb, Dec. 26, 1969; children—Ronnie, Rickey, Kenneth Ray, Jeff, Ginger. Teller, Citizens Nat. Bank, Waco, 1947-51; asst. v.p. 1st Nat. Bank, Odessa, Tex., 1951-58; pres. Nat. Bank Odessa, 1959—; also dir.; dir. Am. Energy Co., Odessa. Bd. dirs. Salvation Army, 1965—, Odessa Indsl. Found., 1970—. Mem. C. of C. (bd. dirs. 1970-71), Am., Tex. bankers assns. Lutheran. Mason (Shriner), Rotarian. Home: 4218 Kirkwood St Odessa TX 79760 Office: PO Box 634 Odessa TX 79760

JUNG, CLARENCE ROBERT, JR., educator; b. Walnut Ridge, Ark., Aug. 23, 1924; s. Clarence R. and Virginia (Cravens) J.; B.A., DePauw U., 1947; M.A., Ohio State U., 1949, Ph.D., 1953; m. Jeanne Sparks, Dec. 28, 1947; children—David, Dinah, Andrew. Instr. Ohio State U., 1947-53; asst. prof. econ. Coe Coll., 1953-55, asso. prof., chmn. dept., 1955-56; economist Standard Oil Co., Ind., 1956-65; asso. prof. managerial econ. Boston U., 1965-66; prof. econs. U. Richmond (Va.), 1966—, chmn., 1967—; cons. Va. Electric and Power Co., 1966—, Va. Hwy. Users Assn., 1968-69. Served with USAAF, 1943-46. Mem. Am. Econ. Assn., Am. Assn. U. Profs. Club: Torch. Home: 1612 Princeton Rd Richmond VA 23227

JUNG, DEXTER ADOLPH, JR., dentist; b. Galveston, Tex., Aug. 8, 1921; s. Dexter Adolph and Lucile Elizabeth (Housinger) J.; B.A., Rice U., 1942; D.D.S., U. Tex., 1945; m. Thana Ruth Roberts, June 16, 1946; children—Dexter Adolph III, Robert Loyd. Practice dentistry in McAllen, Tex., 1947—; chief dental staff, McAllen Gen. Hosp., 1971—. Bd. dirs. McAllen chpt. Salvation Army. Served with USNR, 1945-47. Mem. Rio Grande Dental Soc. (pres.), Omicron Kappa Upsilon, Psi Omega. Mem. Seventh Day Adventist Ch. (elder)

Home: 1613 Esperanza St McAllen TX 78501 Office: 312 N 10th McAllen TX 78501

JUNG, JAMES MOSER, educator; b. Kannapolis, N.C., May 25, 1928; s. Daniel and Lelan (Lee) J.; B.S., Davidson Coll., 1949; certificate secondary edn. in math. and scis. Catawba Coll., 1955; M.Ed., U. N.C., 1956, Ph.D., 1962; m. Patty June Ludwig, Apr. 4, 1958; children—Daryn Anita, Dayna Adrien, Deanne Alisa, David Kendall, Krystal DeEtte. Prof., chmn. dept. chemistry Campbell Coll., Buies Creek, N.C., 1962—. Served with inf. AUS, 1951-53. E.I. DuPont de Nemours & Co. sci. tchr. fellow, 1955; Petroleum Research Found. fellow 1960. Tenn. Eastman Co. fellow, 1961, Danforth asso., 1971. Home: PO Box 248 Buies Creek NC 27506

JUNG, RODNEY C., physician; b. New Orleans, Oct. 9, 1920; s. Frederick Charles and Clara (Cuevas) J.; B.S. in zoology with honors, Tulane U., 1941, M.D., 1945, M.S. in parasitology, 1950, Ph.D., 1953. Intern Charity Hosp. La., New Orleans 1945-46; dir. Hutchinson Meml. Clinic, 1948; asst. parasitology Tulane U., 1948-50, instr. tropical medicine, 1950-53, asst. prof., 1953-57, asso. prof. tropical medicine 1951-63, prof. tropical medicine, 1963—, head div. tropical medicine, 1960-63; health dir. City of New Orleans, 1963-70; internist-in-charge Ill. Central Hosp., New Orleans, 1956-70; sr. vis. physician Charity Hosp., 1959—; sr. asso. in gastroenterology Touro Infirmary; John and Mary Markie Scholar in med. sci.; area cons. tropical medicine VA, 1959; cons. in tropical medicine USPHS Hosp., 1958; mem. com. on parasitic diseases Armed Forces Epidemiological Bd. Mem. bd. New Orleans Health Planning Council. Served as lt. (j.g.) M.C., USNR, 1946-48. Diplomate Am. Bd. Internal Medicine. Fellow A.C.P.; mem. Internat. Society Tropical Dermatology, Am. Royal socs. tropical medicine and hygiene, Am. Soc. Parasitologists, La. State, Orleans Parish med. socs., Nat. Rifle Assn., La. Mosquito Control Assn., La. Pub. Health Assn., Am., La. socs. internal medicine, Am. Def. Preparedness Assn., Phi Beta Kappa, Sigma Xi, Alpha Omega Alpha. Presbyn. Home: 6126 Clara St New Orleans LA 70118 Office: 3600 Chestnut New Orleans LA 70115

JUNGEMANN, EDWARD FREDERICK, airlines exec.; b. Savannah, Ga., Aug. 26, 1918; s. Edward F. and Sara (Masters) J.; grad. Dallas Aviation Sch. and Air Coll., 1938; m. Helen Annette Brown, Aug. 17, 1941; children—Susan Claire, Mary Bothwell, Ann Louise. Flight instr. Strachan Skyways, Savannah, 1939-41; v.p., gen. mgr. Airflight, Inc., Savannah, 1945-57; pres. Savannah Air Service, Inc., 1958—. Trustee Gen. Aviation Mgmt. Found., Va. Tech. U. Served with USAAC, 1941-45. Mem. Antique Aircraft Assn. Presbyn. Clubs: LaVida Country (Savannah, Ga.), Exchange (Savannah, Ga.). Home: 606 Windsor Rd Savannah GA 31406 Office: Travis Field PO Box 6692 Savannah GA 31405

JUNKIN, MARION MONTAGUE, artist, educator; b. Chunju, Korea, Aug. 23, 1905 (parents Am. citizens); s. William McCleery and Mary (Leyburn) J.; A.B., Washington and Lee U., 1927, Arts D., 1949; student Art Students League N.Y., 1927-30; studied with Luks, Locke & McCartan, 1930-32; m. Marguerite Eddy, Sept. 16, 1933; children—Michael Eddy, Margo Patricia. Prof. fine arts, asso. dir. Richmond Sch. Arts, Coll. William and Mary, 1933-42; asso. prof., head dept. fine arts Vanderbilt U., 1941-49; prof., head dept. fine arts Washington and Lee U., Lexington, Va., 1949—, now emeritus; exhibited in one man shows at Joseph Luyber Gallery, N.Y.C., 1946, 47, Va. Mus. Fine Arts, 1948; exhibited in group shows at Whitney Mus., 1936, Corcoran Gallery, 1933, Art Inst. Chgo., 1933, N.Y. Worlds Fair, 1939, Pa. Acad. Fine Arts, 1933, Butler Art Inst., 1943, Carnegie Inst., 1949; fresco paintings in Memphis, Richmond, Roanoke, Va. Mem. Va. Fine Arts Commn., 1939-42. Recipient awards from Va. Mus. Fine Arts, Richmond Acad. Fine Arts, Butler Art Inst., IBM Corp., Brooks Meml. Gallery. Mem. Am. Assn. U. Profs., Omicron Delta Kappa. Episcopalian. Home: 801 Stonewall St Lexington VA 24450

JUNKINS, JOHN LEE, educator; b. Carters, Ga., May 23, 1943; s. George M. and Alice L. (Searcy) J.; B.S., Auburn U., 1965; M.S., U. Cal. at Los Angeles, 1967, Ph.D. with distinction, 1969; m. Nancy Elouise Click, Dec. 26, 1965; children—John Stephen, Kathryn Lynn. With NASA, Huntsville, Ala., 1961-65; engring. scientist McDonnell Douglas Astronautics Co., Santa Monica, Cal., 1965-70; prof. engring. U. Va., Charlottesville, 1970—. Cons. Naval Weapons Lab., Dahlgren, Va., Def. Mapping Agy., Washington. Named Outstanding Engring. Grad., Auburn U., 1965. Mem. Am. Inst. Aeros. and Astronautics, Am. Soc. Photogrammetry, Sigma Xi, Sigma Gamma Tau. Contbr. articles to profl. jours. Home: Box 80 Broomley Charlottesville VA 22901

JURGENSMEYER, HAROLD JACOB, pub. co. exec.; b. Kansas City, Kan., Dec. 15, 1931; s. Frank Steven and Johanna (Weidinger) J.; B.S., U. Mo., 1958; m. Dorothy Marie Cahoon, Aug. 20, 1951; children—Donna, Kenneth, Steven, Jean. Computer salesman, Birmingham, Ala., N.Y.C., Miami, Fla., 1958-63; marketing sales mgr. IBM Corp., Atlanta, 1963-64; subsidiary newspaper operations mgr. Miami Herald Pub. Co., 1965-66, dir. subsidiaries and spl. projects, 1967, bus. mgr., treas., dir., 1968, v.p., gen. mgr., dir., 1969—; v.p. operations Knight Newspapers, Inc., Miami, 1973—; dir. Channel 4 Co. Unit chmn. United Fund, 1968. Vice pres., bd. dirs. Greater Miami Coalition; v.p., mem. exec. com. So. Fla. council Boy Scouts Am.; mem. adv. bd. U. Miami Sch. Bus. Served with USAF, 1952-56. Recipient Student Achievement award Wall St. Jour., 1958. Mem. Fla. C. of C. (dir.), Fla. Press Assn. (dir.), Beta Gamma Sigma. Republican. Roman Catholic. Clubs: Bath, Bankers, Standard, Riviera Country. . Home: 11730 SW 67th Ct Miami FL 33156 Office: 1 Herald Plaza Miami FL 33101

JURTSHUK, PETER, JR., educator; b. N.Y.C., July 28, 1929; s. Peter and Mary (Ferens) J.; A.B., N.Y. U., 1951, M.S., Creighton U., 1953; Ph.D., U. Md., 1957; postdoctoral fellow enzyme chemistry U. Wis., 1959-63; m. Rebecca J. Jones, Jan. 2, 1971; 1 son, Peter III. Asst. prof. pharmacology L.I. U., Bklyn, Coll. Pharmacy, 1957-59; asst. prof. enzyme chemistry U. Wis., 1962-63; asst. prof. microbiology U. Tex. at Austin, 1963-69; asso. prof. biology U. Houston, 1970—; mem. vis. biologists program Am. Inst. Biol. Scis., 1969-72. NIH grantee, 1964—. Fellow Am. Inst. Chemists; mem. Am. Soc. Microbiology (pres. Tex. br.), Am. Soc. Biol. Chemists, Am. Soc. Cell Biology, N.Y. Acad. Scis., A.A.A.S., Am. Assn. Univ. Profs., Am. Chem. Soc., Sigma Xi, Contbr. articles to profl. jours. Home: 3107 Norris Dr Houston TX 77025

JUST, CAROLYN ROYALL, lawyer; b. Shanghai, China, Sept. 15, 1907; d. Francis Martin and Mary Dunklin (Sullivan) Royall; Ph.B., U. Chgo., 1934; J.D., De Paul U., 1938; LL.M., George Washington U., 1940; grad. Inter-Am. Acad. Comparative Internat. Law. Havana, Cuba, 4th Session, 1949, 5th Session, 1950; 7th Session, 1955, 9th Session, 1957; Certificate, Hague Acad. Internat. Law, 31st Session, 1960; m. Robert Just, Dec. 17, 1925 (dec. Nov. 1943). Violin tchr., 1925-30; chief of staff Concessions Dept., Century of Progress Chgo. Exposition, 1933; editorial asst., sec. to Dr. Forest Ray Moulton, permanent sec. A.A.A.S., 1930-38; admitted to D.C. bar, 1938, practiced in Washington, 1938; admitted to Ill. bar, 1940; admitted U.S. Supreme Ct. bar, 1941; with U.S. Dept. of Justice, atty. Lands Div., 1938-43; atty. Antitrust Div., 1943-50; atty. Tax Div., 1950—. Mem. D.C. Citizenship (formerly I Am An American) Day Com. (chmn. com. citizenship recognition, 1946, gen. sec., 1947-50); mem. Atty. Gen.'s Adv. Com. on Citizenship and del. representing Dept. of Justice to nat. confs. on citizenship at Phila., 1946. Washington, 1947, 48, and 1950-55, N.Y.C., 1949. Mem. Am. Bar Assn. (sects. of taxation, antitrust internat. law, past chmn. com. on relations with internat. bar orgns.; adv. com. on pub. relations 1962-65; mem. com. facilities Law Library Congress 1952-59), Fed. Bar Assn. (formerly asst. editor Fed. Bar Jour.), Nat. Assn. Woman Lawyers, Bar Assn. of D.C., Women's Bar Assn. D.C., Internat. Bar Assn. (charter parton, del. to confs. N.Y.C., 1947, London, Eng., 1951, Madrid, 1952, Salzburg, 1960, Mexico City, Mexico, 1964; chmn. credentials com. Madrid 1952), Inter-Am. Bar Assn. (Gold medal 1972); del. confs. Havana, Cuba, 1941, Mexico City, 1944, Santiago, Chile, 1945, Lima, Peru, 1947, Detroit, 1949, Sao Paulo, Brazil, 1954, Dallas, 1956, Buenos Aires, 1957, Miami 1959, Bogota, Colombia, 1961, San Jose, Costa Rica 1967, Quito, Ecuador, 1972, Rio de Janeiro, Brazil, 1973; reporter gen.; council 1945-72), Am. Law Inst., Am. Soc. Internat. Law, George Washington U. Alumni Assn., U. Chgo. Alumni Assn., Am. Judicature Soc., Am. Assn. U. Women, Club de las Americas (pres. 1964-65), D.A.R., Internat. Law Assn. (Am. br.), Internat. Fiscal Assn., Pi Gamma Mu, Kappa Beta Pi, Phi Delta Gamma. Mem. George Washington U. Symphony Orch., Gault Chamber Music Players, Amateur Chamber Music Players, Friday Morning Music Club. Home: Harbour Sq 520 N St SW Washington DC 20024 Office: U S Dept of Justice Washington DC 20530

JUSTICE, CORNELIA WINBORNE (MRS. HORACE ALTON JUSTICE), artist, critic; b. Norfolk, Va.; d. Littleton Augustus and Edna (Wade) Winborne; student Coll. William and Mary; m. Horace Alton Justice, Dec. 10, 1943. Exhibited in one man shows Norfolk Mus. Arts, 1959, Cofer's Galleries, Norfolk and Virginia Beach, 1962-64; exhibited in museums Eng. and Scotland, 1964, Cannes, France, 1966, Cognac, France, 1969, Can., 1969; exhibited in numerous group shows throughout country, 1957—, two traveling exhbns., museums and colls. U.S., 1971-72, 75 Am. Women Artists, Florence, also Naples, Italy, 1972; represented in permanent collections La Musee de La Napoule, Cannes, Norfolk Art Mus., Le Musee de la Napoule, Cannes, Alfred Khouri Meml. Instr. advanced painting Norfolk Mus. Arts, 1960-61, Jewish Community Center, Norfolk, 1961-62; art critic Norfolk Virginian-Pilot and Portsmouth Star, 1959-60, Ledger-Dispatch, Norfolk and Beacon, Virginia Beach, 1966-68. Del. Arts Council Tidewater, Va., 1960—; mem. Norfolk Mus. Arts Council, 1959—. Recipient Best in Show awards Internat. Azalea Festival, Norfolk, 1959, Confederacy Competition Outdoor Amphitheater, Virginia Beach, 1959, Internat. Azalea Festival, 1969; 1st hon. mention award Les Semaines Internationales de la Femme, Cannes, 1969. Mem. Tidewater Artists Assn. (past pres.), Nat. Assn. Women Artists, Am. Craftsmens Council, Virginia Beach Art Assn., Norfolk Hist. Soc., Mus. Modern Art, Va. Mus. Fine Arts, Hermitage Found. Mus., Norfolk Mus. Arts, Norfolk Soc. Arts, Internat. Platform Assn., Va. Press Women's Assn., Art Council Tidewater. Art critic Ledger-Star, 1966—. Address: 619 Stockley Gardens Norfolk VA 23507

JUSTICE, JOHN KEITH, educator; b. Martinsville, Tex., Aug. 26, 1920; s. John Joseph and Martha Rebecca (Hanna) J.; B.S., Stephen F. Austin State U., 1942; B.S., Tex. A. and M. U., 1948, M.S., 1949; Ph.D., Utah State U., 1961; m. Vera Nina Brough, May 31, 1943; children—John Keith, James Brough, Irion David, Dale Kittrell. Prin., Black Jack Jr. High Sch., Attoyac, Tex., 1942-43; instr. Tex. A. and U., College Station, 1949-50; faculty Abilene (Tex.) Christian Coll., 1950—, prof. agronomy, 1962—, head dept. agr., 1961—. Pub. service soil testing service, 1951-61; cons. soil, 1950—. Cubmaster, Chisholm Trail council Boy Scouts Am., 1960-61; pres. P.T.A. Abilene Christian High Sch., 1964-66; chmn. conservation com. Middle Clear Fork Soil Conservation Dist., 1969-71. Served to lt. (j.g.) USNR, 1943-46. Named Tchr. of Year, Abilene Christian Coll., 1961; Piper prof., 1963. NSF fellow, 1962. Mem. C. of C., W. Tex. C. of C., Nat. Assn. Colls. and Tchrs. Agr. (pres. 1966-67), Am. Soc. Agronomy, Soil Sci. Soc. Am., Soil Conservation Soc. Am., Sigma Xi. Home: Route 1 Box 55 Abilene TX 79601

JUSTICE, WILLIAM S., physician, photographer; b. Lincoln, N.C., May 21, 1900; s. Butler Alexander and Eliza Shipp (Bynum) J.; A.B., U. N.C., 1920, postgrad., 1921-22; M.D., Harvard, 1926. Intern pathology Mass. Gen. Hosp.; intern surgery, then resident surgery Boston City Hosp.; practice medicine specializing in surgery, Asheville, N.C., 1931-69; mem. surg. staff Meml. Mission Hosp., Asheville, 1931-69, chief staff, 1955, 56, emergency room physician, 1969—; mem. staff Biltmore Hosp., Asheville, 1931-51, chief staff, 1951; mem. staff Aston Park Hosp. 1931-69. St. Joseph's Hosp., 1931—. Noted photographer wild flowers N.C. Mem. Sigma Alpha Epsilon, Phi Chi. Co-author: Wild Flowers of North Carolina. Address: 14 White Oak Rd Asheville NC 28803

JUSTIS, ELVIS JEFF, JR., physician; b. Memphis, Jan. 15, 1933; s. Elvis Jeff and Catherine (McKay) J.; B.S. Southwestern U., Memphis, 1953; M.D., U. Tenn., 1956; m. Sally Vandervort, Sept. 21, 1970; children—Catherine, Jeff R., Louisa, Steve, Kim. Intern, U. Tenn. Research Center, 1957-48; resident Campbell Clinic, Memphis, 1961-64; practice medicine specializing in orthopaedic surgery, Wiesbaden, Germany, 1965-67, Memphis, 1968—; mem. staff Campbell Clinic; asso. staff mem. Bapt. Meml. Hosp., Memphis; cons. in orthopaedics Arlington Hosp. and Sch., Memphis, civilian cons. in orthopaedics USAF Hosp., Keesler AFB, Biloxi, Miss., 1968—; chief orthopaedics USAF Hosp., Wiesbaden, 1965-67; clin. instr. in orthopaedics U. Tenn., Memphis, 1968—. Served with USAF, 1959-67. Fellow A.C.S., mem. Am., Tenn., Mid-South med. assns., Memphis, Shelby County med. socs., Am. Acad. Orthopaedic Surgeons, Tenn. Orthopaedic Soc., Flying Physicians Assn. (charter), Sigma Alpha Epsilon, Phi Chi. Republican. Presbyn. Contbr. articles to profl. jours. Home: 4209 Walnut Grove Rd Memphis TN 38117 Office: 869 Madison Av Memphis TN 38104

JUSTUS, KARL BENNET, assn. exec.; b. Clinton, Ia., June 3, 1912; s. Raymond George and Mae (Switzer) J.; B.A., Asbury Coll., 1933; B.D., Asbury Theol. Sem., 1935; LL.D., Pacific U., 1957; m. Eileen N. Becker, Mar. 4, 1947; children—John R. Ordained to ministry Methodist Ch., 1940; minister St. Paul's Meth. Ch., Sykesville, Md., 1937-42; regional dir. Nat. Conf. Christians and Jews, San Francisco, 1946-61, nat. v.p., 1961-62; exec. dir. Mil. Chaplains Assn., Washington, 1962—. Served as chaplain, USNR, 1942-45. Recipient Pub. Service award NBC, 1957; George Washington Honor medals editorial, Freedoms Found., 1970, 71, 72, 73, 74. Mem. Mil. Order World Wars (comdr.). Republican. Clubs: Commonwealth, Marines Memorial (San Francisco). Editor: The Military Chaplain, 1962—. Home: 5613 Southwick St Bethesda MD 20034 Office: 7758 Wisconsin Av Washington DC 20014

JYDSTRUP, RONALD ALBERT, assn. exec.; b. Mpls., Feb. 13, 1923; s. Albert E. and Ellen V. (Brandelius) J.; B.B.A., U. Minn., 1948, M.H.A., 1950; m. Lyla Lauraine Johnson, June 24, 1972; children by previous marriage—Karen, Jan, Nan, Kathleen, Mary Ellen. Instr. hosp. adminstrn. course U. Minn. also hosp. cons. James A. Hamilton & Asso., Mpls., 1950-53; sec., accounting specialist Am. Hosp. Assn., also spl. lectr. St. Louis U. and U. Minn., 1953-56; dir. N.D. Blue Cross also spl. lectr. U. Minn., 1956-61; sec. Dist. 10 Blue Cross Plans, 1958-61; exec. dir. N.Y. Regional Hosp. Council, Rochester, 1961-67; sec. Hosp. Reviewing and Planning Council, 1961-67; asst. sec. Rochester Hosp. Fund, 1961-67; v.p. Block, McGibony & Assos., health and hosp. consultants, Silver Spring, Md., 1967-70; dir. planning and devel. Group Health Assn., Washington, 1970—. Cons., Dept. Health, Edn. and Welfare, 1970—; vis. lectr. George Washington U. Mem. Fargo United Fund Planning Com., 1959-61; mem. Montgomery County (Md.) Health Planning Adv. Council, 1973—; chmn., mem. bd. dirs. Fargo Community Council of Social Agys., 1958-61; pres., dir. Red River Valley council Camp Fire Girls, 1957-61; bd. dirs. Home Care Rochester, Monroe County; mem. N.Y. State Hosp. Rev. and Planning Council's Com.; mem. steering com. health div. Council Social Agys. Rochester, Monroe County; mem. adv. com. on study prepayment plans Columbia U. Hosps.; chmn. council mgrs. com. Hosp. Purchasing Bur., N.Y.C. Bd. dirs. Mpls. War Meml. Blood Bank, 1953, Mental Health Council Rochester and Monroe County. Recipient Silver Key, Mpls. Jr. C. of C., 1953; Sabre Hamilton award U. Minn., 1950. Fellow Royal Soc. for Health; mem. U. Minn. Alumni Assn. (pres., dir. Red River Valley chpt.), Am. Assn. Hosp. Accountants, Am. Hosp. Assn., N.Y. State Hosp. Assn., Beta Alpha Psi. Lutheran. Home: 10607 Weymouth St Bethesda MD 20014 Office: 2121 Pennsylvania Av NW Washington DC 20037

KAATZ, LAWRENCE EARL, architect; b. nr. Lubbock, Tex., Mar. 5, 1935; s. Edgar B. and Helen (Nolte) K.; student Arlington State Coll., 1953-55; B. Architecture, Tulane U., 1960; m. LaWanna Lawrence, July 7, 1962; 1 dau., Vonda Michele. Architect L.M. Gernsbachen, 1955-56, various firms, 1956-66, Grogam & Scoggins, 1966, College Inns, 1966, Kirk & Voich, 1967-68; archtl. specification writer Harwood K. Smith, Dallas, 1968-72; Architectonics, Inc., Dallas, 1972—. Served with AUS, 1960-62. Mem. Constrn. Specifications Inst. Lutheran. Home: 2907 Duff Dr Arlington TX 76010 Office: 2902 Southland Center Dallas TX 75201

KAATZ, TORREY ALEXANDER, JR., TV announcer; b. Toledo, Dec. 14, 1936; s. Torrey Alexander and Esther Ann (Bueche) K.; B.A., North Central Coll., Naperville, Ill., 1958; m. Marlene Avis Benninga, Oct. 11, 1959; children—Torrey III, Peter Scott. Sports announcer, play by play sta. WAGN, Menominee, Mich., 1958, WTUB, Coldwater, Mich., 1958, sta. WKMF, Flint, Mich., 1959-61, sta. WMOA, Marietta, O., 1961-66, sta. WTNT, Tallahassee, Fla., 1966-68, sta. WCVU, Portsmouth, Va., 1969-70, WAVY-TV, Portsmouth, 1970—. Sports dir. United Way-United Fund, Norfolk, 1972. Presbyn. (deacon). Club: Norfolk Sports. Home: 4243 Redfern Lane Chesapeake VA 23321 Office: 801 Middle St Portsmouth VA 23704

KACHEL, HAROLD STANLEY, educator, mus. ofcl.; b. Elmwood, Okla., Jan. 25, 1928; s. Samuel W. and Mary (Bukowski) K.; B.S., Panhandle A. and M. Coll., 1952; M.S., Okla. State U., 1955; Ed.D., Colo. State Coll., 1967; m. Barbara Joan Overton, Aug. 9, 1955; children—Connie Lynn, Stanley Duane, Lea Ann. Tchr. Yarbrough Sch., Eva, Okla., 1952-56, prin., 1956-57; instr. Panhandle State Coll., Goodwell, Okla., 1957-60, asst. prof., 1960-65, asso. prof., acting head dept. indsl. arts, 1965-67, prof. applied art, head dept. indsl. arts, 1967—, chmn. div. applied art, 1972—; mus. curator No Man's Land Hist. Mus., Goodwell, Okla., 1967—. Served with USAAF, 1946-48. Mem. Am. Assn. U. Profs. (pres. 1963-64), Am., Okla. indsl. arts assns., Am. Council on Indsl. Arts Tchr. Edn., Okla. Edn. Assn., Okla. Anthrop. Soc., N.W. Ark. Archeol. Soc., Kappa Delta Pi, Phi Kappa Phi. Lion. Home: Box 307 Goodwell OK 73939

KACIR, STANLEY, lawyer; b. Temple, Tex., July 10, 1927; s. August and Bettie Marie (Lesikar) K.; B.B.A., U. Tex., 1951, LL.B., 1951; m. Nelta Josephine Collier, Dec. 23, 1950; children—Karl, Kyle, Katherine, Karen, Kent. Admitted to Tex. bar, 1950; pvt. practice with father, Temple, 1951-53; partner firm Kacir, Lesiker, Kacir & Everton, Temple, 1953—; judge Corp. Ct., City of Temple, 1953-56; county atty. Bell County, Belton, Tex., 1957-60; dist. atty. 27th Judicial Dist., Belton, 1960-72. Served with USNR, 1945-46. Mem. State Bar Tex., Bell, Lampasas, Mills Counties Bar Assn. (past pres.), Central Tex. Police Officers, Am. Judicature Soc., Dist. and County Attys. Assn. Tex. (asso.), Tex. Criminal Def. Lawyers Assn., Temple C. of C., V.F.W., Am. Legion. Mason (Shriner); mem. Order Eastern Star. Home: 3209 Pin Oak Dr Temple TX 76501 Office: Temple Nat Bank Bldg Suite 206 Temple TX 76501

KADLECEK, EDWARD JOHN, JR., mgmt. engr.; b. Houston, July 31, 1934; s. Edward John and Louise (Jakubec) K.; B.S. in Mech. Engring., U. Houston, 1958, B.S. in Indsl. Engring., 1961; m. Marilyn Martha Holtman, Nov. 3, 1962; children—Edward John III, Karen Ann, Nancy Lynn. Chief engr. Fed. Steel Corp., Houston, 1964-65; chief maintenance indsl. engring. dept. Structural Metals, Inc., Sequin, Tex., 1965-67; chief programs devel. 12th C.E. squadron USAF, Randolph AFB, Tex., 1967—. Ambassador, Tex. Folklife Festival; chmn. Czechfest, New Braunfels; mgr. Little League; committeeman Cub Scouts. Recipient Sustained Superior Performance award Def. Dept., 1968, Outstanding Performance award, 1972. Registered profl. engr., Tex. Mem. Nat. Soc. Profl. Engrs., Am. Inst. Indsl. Engrs., Tex. Profl. Engrs. Soc., Wurst Assn. New Braunfels, Phi Kappa Theta. Eagle. Home: 367 Oakcrest St New Braunfels TX 78130 Office: 12 CES Randolph AFB TX 78148

KAESER, CLIFFORD RICHARD, leisure products mfg. co. exec.; b. Boise, Ida., Feb. 17, 1936; s. Clifford M. and Bertha (Minton) K.; B.A., Coll. of Ida., 1959; J.D., Yale, 1962; m. Judith Rae Frisk, Feb. 23, 1973; children from previous marriage—Richard Lynn, Cindy Marie. Admitted to Cal. bar, 1962; asso. firm Lawler, Felix & Hall, Los Angeles, 1962; asst. div. counsel Lockheed Missile & Space Div., Sunnyvale, Cal., 1963; group counsel, then acquisition counsel Litton Industries, Beverly Hills, Cal., 1963-68; adminstrv. v.p., gen. counsel Hitco, Los Angeles, 1968-70; pres. Chaparral Industries, Inc., 1970-72; pres. Red Dale Coach Cos. subsidiaries Armco Steel Corp., to 1972; v.p., gen. counsel Conroy, Inc., San Antonio, 1972—. Mem. Am. Bar Assn., State Bar Cal., Am. Mgmt. Assn., Mchts. and Mfrs. Assn. Home: 3802 Lomita St San Antonio TX 78230 Office: Conroy Sq 3355 Cherry Ridge Dr San Antonio TX 78213

KAHLER, MARY ELLIS, librarian; b. Santiago, Chile, Aug. 2, 1919; d. John William and Edna (Doan) Ellis; A.B., Swarthmore Coll., 1940; B.L.S., Drexel Inst. Tech., 1949; M.A., George Washington U., 1953; Ph.D. in History, Am. U., 1968; m. Joseph W. Darlington, Aug. 17, 1940 (dec. 1948); m. 2d, George W. Kahler, Feb. 11, 1950. Library asst. Post Library, Fort Dix, N.J., 1944-48; with Library of Congress, 1949—, asst. chief serial record div., 1953-56, chief, 1957-66, asst. chief of union catalog div., 1966-70, asst. dir. Hispanic Found., 1971-73, chief Latin Am., Portuguese and Spanish div., 1973—. Mem. A.L.A. (chmn. serials sect. resources and tech. services div. 1959-60, mem. coms., dir. at large 1967-70), Latin Am. Studies Assn. (chmn. com. on scholarly resources 1971—), Spl. Libraries Assn. (local chpt. corr. sec. 1963-64, state rep. A.L.A., Recruitment Network 1966-1968, A.L.A. councilor 1969-72), D.C. Library Assn. (sec. 1964-65), Soc. Am. Archivists, Am. Hist. Assn., Am. Assn. U. Women, Phi Beta Kappa, Phi Alpha Theta. Home: 6395 Lakeview Dr Falls Church VA 22041 Office: Library of Congress Washington DC 20540

KAHLON, PREM SINGH, educator; b. India, June 16, 1936; s. Bahadur Singh and Harnam Kaur (Bajwa) K.; B.S., Punjab U., 1956; M.S., La. State U., 1962, Ph.D., 1964; m. Darshan Bhatti, Aug. 27, 1967; children—Paul, Jay. Came to U.S., 1961, naturalized, 1973. Asst. prof. biology Talladega Coll., 1964-65; prof. biology Alcorn Coll., 1965-66; prof. biology Tenn. State U., Nashville, 1966—. Vis. prof. Tech. Aqua Biol. Consortium; research participant Oak Ridge Asso. Univs. Pres., India Assn. Nashville, 1967-68, 70-71. Bd. dirs. Nashville chpt. March of Dimes. Research fellow Rockefeller Found., 1962-64; Research grantee NSF, 1973, Dept. Agr., 1973. Recipient Key to City Baton Rouge, 1964. Mem. Tenn. Acad. Sci., India Soc. Genetics and Plant Breeding (life), A.A.A.S., Gamma Sigma Delta. Home: 605 Harpeth Knoll Rd Nashville TN 37221

KAHN, ALAN BRUCE, realty exec.; b. Columbia, S.C., Apr. 15, 1940; s. Irwin and Katie (Bogen) K.; A.B., Duke, 1962; M.B.A., George Washington U., 1965; m. Charlotte Segelbaum, Feb. 28, 1965; children—Kevin Alexander, Monique Beth, Charles Benjamin. Dir. research Kahn-So. Corp., Columbia, 1965-68, real estate, finance exec., 1968-72; pres. Kahn Devel. Co., Columbia, 1972—; mem. adv. bd. Columbia office Bankers Trust of S.C., 1970—. Mem. adv. bd. Providence Hosp., Columbia, 1973—; chmn. dr. Bonds Israel, Columbia, 1972-73. Bd. dirs. Columbia Area Mental Health Center, 1968—, chmn., 1972; bd. dirs. Columbia Phil. Orch. Served with AUS, 1961. Jewish religion. Home: 6338 Golbranch Rd Columbia SC 29202 Office: PO Box 1608 Columbia SC 29202

KAHN, ELLIS IRVIN, lawyer; b. Charleston, S.C., Jan. 18, 1936; s. Robert and Estelle (Kaminski) K.; A.B., The Citadel, 1958; LL.B., U. S.C., 1961; postgrad. So. Meth. U., 1962-63; m. Janice Weinstein, Aug. 11, 1963; children—Justin, David, Cynthia Anne. Admitted to S.C. bar, 1961; law clk. U.S. Dist. Judge Robert W. Hemphill, Columbia, 1964-66; with firm Solomon, Solomon, Kahn & Roberts, Charleston, 1966—. Served to capt. USAF, 1961-64. Mem. Am., S.C. bar assns., Am. (state committeeman), S.C. trial lawyers assns., Phi Delta Phi (chpt. pres. 1960). Democrat. Jewish religion. Mem. B'nai B'rith (pres. 1968-71). Editor: The Brigadier, 1957-58. Home: 316 Confederate Circle Charleston SC 29407 Office: 39 Broad St Charleston SC 29402

KAHN, HANNAH, poet; b. N.Y.C., June 30, 1911; d. David and Sarah (Seigelbaum) Abrahams; m. Frank M. Kahn, Mar. 5, 1941; children—Melvin A., Daniel Lyon, Vivian Dale. Poet, poems pub. in nat. mags., 1938—; song, Stranger, 1956; (poems) Eve's Daughter, 1963; poetry rev. editor Miami (Fla.) Herald, 1958—. Tchr. creative writing Miami Dade Jr. Coll., 1971. Recipient Ralph Chency poetry award, 1946, Jessie Rittenhouse award, 1947, Jane Judge award, 1951, 71, Norfolk prize, 1954, John David Leitch award, 1954, 70, Poetry Soc. of Great Britain and Am. Parsons Sonnent award, 1957; George Washington honor medal Freedoms Found., 1962; 2d prize for ann. award Poetry Soc. Am., 1970. Mem. poetry socs. Am., Va., Ga., Laramore Radar Poetry Group, Theta Sigma Phi, Phi Lambda Phi (hon.). Co-editor: Wind Song (poems), 1969. Home: 40 NE 69th St Miami FL 33138

KAHN, ROBERT IRVING, rabbi; b. Des Moines, Dec. 12, 1910; s. Morris and Sadie F. (Finkelstein) K.; B.A., U. Cin., 1932; D.H.L., Hebrew Union Coll.-Jewish Inst. Religion, 1950, D.D., 1960; m. Roxelle Rosenthal, Dec. 29, 1940; children—Alfred J., Edward B., Sharon F. Rabbi, 1935; rabbi, Congregation Emanu El, Houston, 1944—. Served with AUS, World War II. Recipient Silver Beaver award Boy Scouts Am., George Washington Honor medal Freedoms Found. Mem. Central Conf. Am. Rabbis (pres. 1973-74), Houston Rabbinical Assn. (pres. 1961-62), Kallah Tex. Rabbis (pres. 1939-40), Union Am. Hebrew Congregations (mem. bd. 1972-74). Mason (33 deg., Shriner). Rotarian. Home: 3609 S Braeswood Blvd Houston TX 77025 Office: 1500 Sunset Blvd Houston TX 77005

KAHN, WALTER KURT, elec. engr., educator; b. Germany, Mar. 24, 1929; s. Simon and Hilde Betty (Ullmann) K.; B.E.E., Cooper Union, 1951; M.E.E., Poly. Inst. Bklyn., 1954, D.E.E., 1960; m. Barbara Fairberg, Mar. 25, 1962; children—Hilde Elisabeth, Jonathan Daniel. Engr., Wheeler Labs., Inc., 1951-54; research asso. Microwave Research Inst., Poly. Inst. Bklyn., 1954-60, asst. prof. elec. engring., asst. to dir. Microwave Research Inst., 1960-62, asso. prof. electrophysics, 1962-68, prof. electrophysics, 1968-69; liaison scientist U.S. Office Naval Research, London br., 1967-68; prof. engring. and applied sci., dept. elec. engring. and computer sci. George Washington U., Washington, 1969—, chmn. dept., 1970—. Mem. tech. staff Bell Telephone Labs., Murray Hill, N.J., summer 1963, IBM Thomas J. Watson Research Center, summer 1969; cons. RCA, Sperry Rand, Maxson Electronics Corp., Inst. for Def. Analyses. NATO sr. fellow in sci., spring 1973. Fellow I.E.E.E.; mem. A.A.A.S., Optical Soc. Am., Internat. Sci. Radio Union (Commn. VI), Philos. Soc. Washington, Sigma Xi, Eta Kappa Nu, Tau Beta Pi. Asso. editor: Transactions on Microwave Theory and Techniques, 1964. Contbr. articles to profl. jours. Patentee in field. Home: 7709 Hamilton Spring Rd Bethesda MD 20034 Office: George Washington U Washington DC 20006

KAIN, FRANCIS THOMAS, city mgr.; b. Boston, May 17, 1923; s. Francis Thomas and Marguerite (Moore) K.; A.B., U. Fla., 1951; M.A., Rollins Coll., 1971; m. Mary Jane Sherman, Oct. 1, 1948; children—Adrienne (Mrs. Michael G. Malinowski), Julia, Rosemary, Nancy. Asst. city mgr., Vero Beach, Fla., 1959-61, Ft. Lauderdale, Fla., 1961-64; city mgr., Boynton Beach, Fla., 1964-67; asst. city mgr., Daytona Beach, Fla., 1967-71; mgr., Hollywood, Fla., 1971—. Served with USNR, 1942-46. Mem. Internat. City Mgmt. Assn. Home: 218 S 56th Terrace Hollywood FL 33023 Office: 2600 Hollywood Blvd Hollywood FL 33022

KAISER, GEORGE, farm bur. exec.; b. Elberta, Ala., Nov 27, 1911; s. Paul and Anna (Hollich) K.; student pub. schs.; m. Gertrude Steigerwald, Jan. 26, 1939; children—George P., Gertrude (Mrs. S.D. Denney), Lynda (Mrs. R.P. Krulis), Sidney, Norman. Farmer, Foley, Ala., 1943—; dir. S. Baldwin Bank, Foley. Pres., Baldwin County Farm Bur., 1958—; dir. Ala. Farmer's Market Authority, 1966—, Pesticide Inst. Ala., 1966-69, Ala. Farm Bur., 1971—. Bd. dirs. S. Baldwin Hosp., 1954—, pres., 1956-62; trustee St. Benedict Sch., 1964-68. Mem. S.W. Ala. Pecon Assn. (dir. 1961—), Baldwin County Cattlemens Assn. (dir. 1963-67), Foley C. of C. (dir. 1950-58). Rotarian (pres. 1965-66). Roman Catholic. Address: Rt 2 Box 23 Foley AL 36535

KAISER, GERARD ALAN, surgeon; b. Bklyn., Dec. 9, 1932; s. Harry and Lois (Friedman) K.; A.B., Princeton, 1954; M.D., Columbia, 1958; m. Joyce Ellen Kosh, June 5, 1955; children—Beth, Jordan, Charles. Intern, Presbyn. Hosp., N.Y.C., 1958-59, resident gen. surgery, 1964-65, cardiac surgery, 1967-68; practice medicine specializing in thoracic and cardiovascular surgery, N.Y.C., 1968-71, Miami, Fla., 1971—; asst. prof. surgery Mt. Sinai Sch. Medicine, 1968-69; asso. prof. Columbia U. Coll. Phys. and Surgs., N.Y.C., 1969-71; prof. U. Miami, 1971—, also chief thoracic and cardiovascular surgery Sch. Medicine and Jackson Meml. Hosp. Bd. dirs. Miami Heart Assn. Otto G. Storm investigator Am. Heart Assn., 1970. Served to lt. comdr. USPHS, 1962-64. Diplomate Am. Bd. Surgery, Bd. Thoracic Surgery. Mem. Am. Assn. Thoracic Surgery, Soc. U. Surgeons, Assn. Acad. Surgery, A.C.S., Soc. Thoracic Surgeons, Am. Coll. Cardiology. Office: Sch Medicine U Miami Miami FL 33152

KAISER, KURT FREDERIC, recording exec.; b. Chgo., Dec. 17, 1934; s. Otto and Elisabeth (Suemper) K.; student Am. Conservatory Music, 1954-56; B.M., Northwestern U., 1958, M.M., 1959; D. Sacred Music (hon.), Trinity Coll., 1973; m. Patricia Jane Anderson, Aug. 14, 1956; children—Kristine, Kent, Craig, Timothy. Vice pres., dir. music, dir. Word, Inc., Waco, Tex., 1959—; dir. Baylor Religious Hour Choir. Mem. A.S.C.A.P. Baptist (deacon). Composer: (folk musicals) Tell It Like It Is, 1969; Natural High, 1969; I'm Here, God Is Here, Now We Can Start, 1973; (songs) Pass It On, 1969; Bring Back the Springtime, 1970; Master Designer, 1969; It's Our World, 1970; God's People, 1974; Sunday Mornin, 1974; Sunshine Thoughts, 1974. Home: 4910 Brooks Dr Waco TX 76710 Office: 4800 W Waco Dr Waco TX 76710

KAISER, LEO URBAN, printing and pub. cos. exec.; b. Elyria, O., July 29, 1902; s. Joseph and Agnes (Hauck) K.; student Spencerian Bus. Coll., 1920, Ohio Bus. Coll., 1921; m. Lorene Peine, Apr. 9, 1927; children—Martha (Mrs. William D. Justice), Betsy (Mrs. Robert J. Garlington). Trainee, Am. Multigraph Co., Cleve., 1919-21, factory rep., Houston, 1921-25; founder, owner Premier Printing and Letter Service, Houston, 1925-29, (inc. 1959), pres., 1959-73, chmn. bd., 1973—; v.p. Texantics, Unlimited, Houston, 1952—; pres. Premier Advt. Co., Inc. Mem. Navy League, Mail Advt. Service Assn., Direct Mail Advt. Assn., Houston Advt. Club, Printing Industry Assn., S.W. Mail Producers Guild, Soc. Am. Magicians, Internat. Brotherhood Magicians, Internat. Wine and Food Soc., Les Amis du Vin. Clubs: Warwick, Old Capitol, April 7th, University, Astrodome. Home: 5001 Doliver Dr Houston TX 77027 Office: 2120 McKinney Av Houston TX 77003

KAISER, ROBERT LEE, engr.; b. Louisville, June 28, 1935; s. Harlan K. and LaVerne (Peterson) K.; student U. Louisville, 1953-54, U. Ky., 1958-61; m. Carol L. Grimm, July 5, 1956; children—Robin Lee, Robert Jr. Draftsman, deisgner E.R. Ronald & Assos., Louisville, 1953-54, Thompson-Kissell Co., 1954-56; estimator, engr. George Pridemore & Son, Lexington, Ky., 1956-58; designer, engr., supr. Frankel & Curtis, Lexington, 1958-61; engr. Hugh Dillehay & Assos., 1961-65; owner, engr., operator K-Service, Inc., 1965—; cons. Frantz, Inc., mech. contractors. Mem. charter commn. merger Lexington-Fayette County govts. Registered profl. engr. Mem. Nat., Ky. socs. profl. engrs., Lexington C. of C., Am. Soc. Heating Ventilating and Air Conditioning Engrs. Episcopalian. Lion (v.p. local club). Home: 3172 Roxburg Dr Lexington KY 40503 Office: 741 Westland Dr Lexington KY 40504

KAITZ, HYMAN BENJAMIN, statistician; b. Chelsea, Mass., May 17, 1916; s. Morris and Rebecca (Aptaker) K.; B.A., George Washington U., 1942; M.A., 1950; postgrad. Stanford, 1943; m. Naoni Savan, Dec. 26, 1949; children—Emily, Edward. Statistician, nat. income div. Dept. Commerce, 1946-54; v.p. WCFM Recording Corp., 1952-55; acting chief div. financial and actuarial services U.S. Dept. Labor, 1954-58; asst. chief statistics div. Internat. Bank for Reconstruction and Devel., Washington, 1958; statis. cons., div. manpower and employment statistics Bur. of Labor Statistics, 1959-62, asst. chief, offic econ. growth studies, 1962-63; dir. indsl. growth staff Bus. and Def. Services Asminstrn., U.S. Dept. Commerce, 1963-66; chief div. statis. standards Bur. Labor Statistics, U.S. Dept. Labor, 1966-71, asst. commr. for current employment analysis, 1971-73; pres. CSR Assos., 1973—; cons. com. on nat. statistics Nat. Acad. Scis., 1973—. Served from pvt. to staff sgt. USAAF, 1942-46. Mem. Am. Statis. Assn., Am. Econ. Assn., Royal Statis. Soc., Inst. Math. Statistics, Econometric Soc., Phi Beta Kappa. Author articles in field. Home: 7216 Beechwood Rd Hollin Hills Alexandria VA 22307 Office: GAO Bldg Washington DC 20212

KALE, HERBERT WILLIAM, II, zoologist, ecologist; b. Trenton, N.J., Dec. 24, 1931; s. Samuel Stewart and Julia (Steward) K.; B.S., Rutgers U., 1954; M.S., U. Ga., 1961, Ph.D., 1964; m. Charlotte Ross Jones, July 29, 1961; children—Kathleen Elizabeth, Thomas, John. Teaching and research asst. U. Ga., Athens, 1957-64; ornithologist Encephalitis Research Center, Fla. Bd. Health, Tampa, 1964-66; now vertebrate ecologist Fla. Med. Entomology Lab., Vero Beach, Fla. Served with AUS, 1954-56. Mem. Ecol. Soc. Am., Am. Ornithologists' Union, Wilson, Cooper, Ga., Fla. ornithol socs., Nat., Fla. Audubon socs., Carolina Bird Club, Am. Soc. Mammalogists, British Ornithologists' Union, A.A.A.S., Sigma Xi, Theta Chi, Phi Sigma. Republican. Home: 35 1st Ct SW Vero Beach FL 32960 Office: Fla Medical Entomology Lab PO Box 502 Vero Beach FL 32960

KALLUS, FRANK THEODORE, physician, educator; b. La Grange, Tex., Aug. 19, 1936; s. Frank Theodore and Rita Edith (Parma) K.; B.S., Tex. A. and M. U., 1966; M.D., U. Tex. Southwestern Med. Sch., 1961, Ph.D. (USPHS fellow 1966-70), 1970; m. Mary Joyce Manry, Feb. 12, 1963; children—Jennifer Ann, Angela Marie. Intern, Meth. Hosp., Dallas, 1961-62; research fellow anesthesiology Southwestern Med. Sch., Dallas, 1965-66, instr. physiology, 1970, asst. prof. anesthesiology, 1972—; asst. prof. physiology and biophysics La. State U. Sch. Medicine, Shreveport, 1970-72. Served as capt. USAF, 1962-64. Mem. Am. Physiol. Soc., A.M.A., Tex. Med. Assn., Dallas County Med. Soc., Am., Tex., Dallas County socs. anesthesiology, Sigma Xi, Phi Eta Sigma, Phi Kappa Phi. Home: 4117 Shenandoah St Dallas TX 75205 Office: 5323 Harry Hines St Dallas TX 75235

KALMAN, JACK RICHMOND, civil engr.; b. Chelsea, Mass., June 6, 1910; s. Max Manuel and Bessie (Richmond) K.; B.S., Mass. Inst. Tech., 1932; M.S., Okla. U., 1957; m. Mabel Dorthy Cottrell, Aug. 30, 1937; children—Jacqueline J. (Mrs. Robert C. Poe), Teresa Ann (Mrs. Douglas B. Brown), Joan Richmond (Mrs. Thomas A. Player), Julie (Mrs. Julie Loughran Cottrell). Commd. 2d lt. C.E., U.S. Army, 1940, advanced through grades to lt. col., 1954, planning officer No. area ETO, 1952-54, ret., 1954; engr. city Norman (Okla.), 1954-56; pvt. practice cons. engr., Norman, 1954—; pres. Kalman and Assos., Inc., Precision Testing Labs., Inc. Mem. Nat., Okla. socs. profl. engrs., Soc. Am. Mil. Engrs. Mason (Shriner), Lion. Home: 239 Crestmont St Norman OK 73069 Office: 925 N Flood St Norman OK 73069

KALMANOFF, GEORGE, economist; b. N.Y.C., Sept. 17, 1917; s. Peter and Rebecca (Wassilkowski) K.; B.A. magna cum laude, Coll. City N.Y., 1936, M.S. in Edn., 1938; postgrad. Am. U., 1944-53; m. Jean Paulive, July 4, 1940; children—Barbara (Mrs. Charles Folick), Ellen. Tchr. Spanish, N.Y.C. and Washington, 1936-42; economist OPA, Washington, 1942-44; economist Fgn. Econ. Adminstrn., Dept. of Commerce, Washington, 1944-50; economist UN Econ. Commn. for Latin Am., Washington, 1950-53; econ. adviser Nat. Planning Office, Govt. of Colombia, Bogota, 1953-54, econ. cons., Bogota, 1954-58; asso. dir. Internat. Research Projects, Columbia U. Law Sch., N.Y.C., 1958-65; Econ. cons. City N.Y., 1958-65; group chief econs. dept. World Bank, Washington, 1965-69, dep. dir. indsl. projects dept., 1969—. Mem. Am. Econ. Assn., Soc. for Internat. Devel., Phi Beta Kappa, Sigma Delta Pi. Author: (with A. O. Hirschman) Investment in Central America, 1956; (with W. G. Friedman) Joint International Business Ventures, 1961; (with W. G. Friedmann and R. Meagher) International Financial Aid, 1966. Home: 5402 Wehawken Rd Washington DC 20016 Office: World Bank 1818 H St NW Washington DC 20433

KALNINS, ZELMA-ALVINE GRINFELDS (MRS. PETERIS KALNINS), cytopathologist; b. Riga, Latvia, Sept. 3, 1908; d. Roberts Andrejs and Katrine (Lode) Grinsfelds; M.D., U. Latvia, Riga, 1932, postgrad., 1938; m. Peteris Kalnins, Dec. 24, 1949. Came to U.S., 1951, naturalized, 1957. Intern, Univ. Hosp., Riga., 1932-33; resident, 1933-36; resident City Hosp., Liepaja, Latvia, 1936-38, doctor-ordinator dept. obstetrics and gynecology, 1938-44; practice medicine, specializing in obstetrics and gynecology, Liepaja, 1938-44; secundarius County Hosp. dept. gynecology and obstetrics County Hosp., Leoben, Austria, 1944-46; health supr., physician Displaced Persons' Camp, Camp Ohmstede, Oldenburg, Germany, 1947-51; fellow in cytology dept. pathology Bowman Gray Sch. Medicine, Wake Forest U., Winston-Salem, N.C., 1952-55; instr. pathology, 1955-62, asst. prof. clin. cytology, 1962-69, asso. prof., 1969—, dir. lab. exfoliative cytology, 1956-58, asso. dir. cytopathology lab., also Sch. Cytotech., 1962-69, dir. clin. cytology labs., also Sch. Cytotech., 1969—. Fellow Royal Soc. Health (London), Internat. Acad. Cytology; mem. Assn. Am. Med. Coll., Am. Med. Women's Assn., Am. Soc. Cytology, Latvian Med. and Dental Assn. in U.S. Contbr. articles to med. jours. Home: 184 N Hawthorne Rd Winston-Salem NC 27104 Office: 300 Hawthorne Rd SW Winston-Salem NC 27103

KAMENITSA, MAXINE ANNA ELLIOTT, ednl. specialist; b. Neodesha, Kan.; d. William Thomas and Beulah (Morrow) Elliott; B.S., N. Tex. State U., 1950; M.A., Tex. Woman's U., 1958; m. William Thomas Kamenitsa, Sept. 28, 1943; children—Dennis Elliott, Laura Katherine, Cindy Ann. Grad. asst. Tex. Women's U., Denton, 1951-53, dir. pre-sch. demonstration sch., summer 1956; supt.-tchr. pre-sch. classes Ft. Worth Children's Mus., 1954-60; instr. child devel. Tex. Christian U., Ft. Worth, 1958-60; tchr. kindergarten, 2d grade Ft. Worth Ind. Sch. Dist., 1960-68; early childhood specialist S.W. Ednl. Devel. Lab., Austin, 1968-70; cons. early childhood and elementary edn. Edn. Service Center, Region XI, Ft. Worth, 1970—. Mem. N.E.A., Assn. Childhood Edn., Tex. Tchrs. Assn., Nat. Assn. Edn. Young Children Elementary-Kindergarten-Nursery Educators, Am. Assn. U. Women, Women in Communications, (chpt. pres. 1945-47, dir. 1966-68), Tex. Assn. Supervision and Curriculum Devel., Nat. Assn. Tchrs. Math., Internat. Reading Assn., Alpha Delta Kappa. Presbyn. Club: Fort Worth Ski. Author: Parents' Handbook, 1958, 59, 60. Officer Bob Drawing Book, 1958. Co-author: Preschool-Kindergarten Handbook for Teachers, 1967. Contbr. early childhood curriculum central cities project Ft. Worth Ind. Sch. Dist., 1970. Home: 2017 David Dr Fort Worth TX 76111 Office: 2821 Cullen St Fort Worth TX 76107

KAMENSKE, GLORIA LEE CHEEK, psychologist; b. Battle Creek, Mich., Oct. 26, 1931; d. George W. and Edith (Olds) Cheek; A.B., U. Mich., 1953; M.A., Mich. State U., 1955, Ph.D., 1965; m. Bernard H. Kamenske, Dec. 19, 1960. Counselor women's dormitories Mich. State U., East Lansing, 1953-54, statis. teaching asst. psychology dept., 1954-56, research asst. Labor and Indsl. Relations Center, 1956-58; social psychology intern VA Hosp., Ann Arbor, Mich., 1958-59; research psychologist personnel research br. Adj. Gen's Office, Dept. Def., Washington, 1959-60; research asso. tng. methods div. Human Resources Research Office, Washington, 1960-62; manpower research analyst Office of Manpower, Automation and Tng. Dept. Labor, Washington, 1962-63; research asso. Bur. Social Sci. Research, Washington, 1963-65; supervisory research psychologist Social Analysis Nat. Center Health Services Research and Devel., USPHS, 1965-70; social sci. adviser Office of Sec. Health, Edn. and Welfare, 1970-73, psychologist Center for Population Research, NIH, Bethesda, Md., 1973—. Cons. Dept. Labor, 1962-63, Union Theol. Sem., 1963-65. Recipient award for service Psi Chi, 1957. Fellow Am. Pub. Health Assn.; mem. D.A.R., Am., Midwestern, Eastern, D.C. psychol. assns., Interamer. Soc. of Psychol., Internat. Council of Psychologists, Internat. Union Sci. Psychology, Population Assn. Am., Am., Internat. sociol. assns., Psi Chi. Contbr. numerous articles in field to profl. and trade jours. Home: One Buttonwood Lane Washington DC 20016 Office: Center for Population Research Landow Bldg Nat Inst Child and Human Devel NIH Dept Health Edn and Welfare Bethesda MD 20014

KAMEROW, MARTIN LAURENCE, accountant; b. Washington, Aug. 25, 1931; s. Jacob A. and Anne (Adler) K.; B.C.S., Benjamin Franklin U., 1951, M.C.S., 1952; m. Corinne Perlmeter, Mar. 24, 1951; children—Deborah, Jacqueline, Haskell. Staff accountant various C.P.A. firms, Washington, 1949-52; individual practice accounting, Washington, 1952-59; partner firm Kamerow & Serber, Washington, 1959-63; sr. partner firm Harab, Kamerow & Serber, Washington, 1963—; lectr. Am. U., 1956—; lectr. tax seminars and insts. cons. to editor book div. U.S. News & World Report. Mem. nat. council United Synagogue of Am., 1969—, regional treas., 1969—; mem. exec. com. United Jewish Appeal; mem. Zionist Youth Commn.; pres. L.D. Brandeis dist. Zionist Orgn. Am., also mem. nat. bd. dirs. Bd. dirs. World Council Synagogues: v.p., bd. dirs. Jewish Nat. Fund. Served with inf. AUS, 1951-53. Recipient Nat. Kidney Found. Service award, 1969. C.P.A., Washington. Mem. Am. Inst. C.P.A.'s, Assn. Practicing C.P.A.'s (pres. 1972—), Inst. C.P.A.'s in Israel, Sigma Alpha Rho. Jewish religion (v.p. temple). Clubs: Nat. Press (Washington), Touchdown (Washington). Author: (with S.A. Kaufman) Consolidated Financial Statements, 1958; (with S. Green) U.S. News and World Reports Book on Income Taxes, 1st edit., 1971, 2d edit., 1972; contbg. author: (with Margaret Daly) Teach Your Wife to be a Widow. Home: 405 E Indian Spring Dr Silver Spring MD 20901 Office: 805 15th St NW Washington DC 20005

KAMIENSKI, CONRAD WILLIAM, chem. co. exec.; b. N.Y.C., Dec. 23, 1929; s. Bronislaus and Anastasia (Wichniarek) K.; B.S., Coll. City N.Y., 1950; M.S., Rensselaer Poly. Inst., 1957; Ph.D., U. Tenn., 1967; m. Diane A. Buschke, Sept. 6, 1952; children—Annette, Julia, Paula. Chemist Gen. Elec. Co. Research Labs., Schenectady, N.Y., 1952-57; chemist Lithium Corp. Am., Bessemer City, N.C., 1957-61, dir. organic research div., 1961-70, dir. chem. div., 1970—; tchr. organic chemistry Belmont Abbey Coll., 1963-64, 69-70. Dir. Catawba Valley Lung Assn.; mem. respiratory com. N.C. Lung Assn. Accredited profl. chemist. Mem. Am. Chem. Soc., Am. Inst. Chemists, Research Soc. Am., Sigma Xi, Phi Lambda Upsilon. Contbr. articles profl. jours. and encys. Patentee in field. Home: 516 Eastwood Dr Gastonia NC 28052 Office: Box 795 Bessemer City NC 28016

KAMINSKY, BERNARD SHAW, dentist; b. Johnstown, Pa., Dec. 25, 1922; s. Oscar and Rebecca (Nathan) K.; student U. Wis., 1943, Otterbein U., 1948-50; D.D.S, Temple U., 1954; m. Ruby Rosalind Pomerantz, Mar. 21, 1951; 1 dau., Kala Sue. Individual practice gen. dentistry, Fredericksburg, Va., 1954—. Served with 96th Inf. Div., AUS, 1943-45. Decorated Bronze Star medal. Mem. Acad. Gen. Dentistry, John A Kolmer Hon. Med. Soc. Temple U., Am. Dental Assn., Am. Endodontic Soc., V.F.W. (vice comdr. 1956), Alpha Omega, Alpha Epsilon Delta. Jewish religion. Mem. B'nai B'rith. Club: Beth El Men's (Richmond, Va.). Home: 1001 Lomas Ct Richmond VA 23229 Office: 1101 Caroline St Fredericksburg VA 22401

KAMM, ROBERT B., univ. pres.; b. West Union, Ia., Jan. 22, 1919; s. Balthasar and Amelia (Etter) K.; B.A., U. No. Ia., 1940; M.A., U. of Minn., 1946, Ph.D., 1948; m. Maxine Moen, July 10, 1943; children—Susan, Steven. Tchr. Belle Plaine (Ia.) High Sch., 1940-42; research asst., counselor Gen. Coll., U. Minn., 1946-48; dean of students Drake U., 1948-55; dean student personnel services Tex. A. and M. U., 1955-56, dean basic div. and student personnel services, 1956-58; dean coll. arts and scis. Okla. State U., 1958-65, v.p. acad. affairs, 1965-66, pres., 1966—. Mem. regional com. Student Personnel Work for South, 1956; mem. commn. coll. student Am. Council Edn., 1957-60; chmn. Nat. Conf. Acad. Deans, Stillwater, 1961-62; chmn. Mid-Am. State Univs. Assn., 1968-69; pres. Bi-State Mental Health Assn., 1968-70; mem. nat. vocational rehab. and edn. adv. com. VA, 1970—; mem. Pres.'s Commn. on Observance of 25th Anniversary of UN. Bd. visitors Air U., 1967-70. Civilian radio instr. USAAF, 1942-44, coordinator on staff, 1944; naval aviation radar technician USNR, 1944-46. Elected to Okla. Hall of Fame, 1972; recipient Outstanding Achievement award U. Minn., 1971; Alumni Achievement award U. No. Ia., 1970. Fellow Am. Psychol. Assn.; mem. Am. Coll. Personnel Assn. (mem. exec. council 1954-56, pres. 1957), Am. Personnel and Guidance Assn., Nat. Vocational Guidance Assn., So. Coll. Personnel Assn., Nat. Assn. Student Personnel Adminstrn., Assn. Higher Edn., N.E.A. (nat. com. gen. edn. 1961-64), Assn. State Univ. and Land Grant Colls. (chmn. div. arts and scis. 1963-64, co-chmn. home econs. div. 1968-70), Stillwater C. of C. (v.p. 1965-67), Phi Kappa Phi, Omicron Delta Kappa (mem. nat. council 1970—), Kappa Kappa Psi, Phi Delta Kappa, Psi Chi, Kappa Delta Pi, Blue Key, Theta Alpha Phi, Kappa Mu Epsilon, Alpha Phi Omega, Phi Mu Alpha Sinfonia. Methodist. Rotarian (pres. 1962-63). Contbr. edn. profl. jours. Address: 1600 N Monroe St Stillwater OK 74074

KAMMERER, WILLIAM JOHN, educator; b. Rochester, N.Y., Oct. 8, 1931; s. Rudolph William and Margaret (Weinhold) K.; B.A., U. Rochester, 1954; M.S., U. Wis., 1955, Ph.D., 1959; m. Jean E. Zinn, Aug. 24, 1957; children—Karen Sue, Karl Scott. Asst. prof. operations research Case Inst. Tech., 1959-60; faculty math. Ga. Inst. Tech., Atlanta, 1960—, prof., 1971—. Wis. Alumni research fellow. Mem. Am. Math. Soc., Soc. Indsl. and Applied Math., Sigma Xi, Phi Beta Kappa, Phi Kappa Phi. Home: 3430 Pin Oak Circle Atlanta GA 30340

KAMPRATH, EUGENE JOHN, educator; b. Seward, Neb., Jan. 9, 1926; s. John Fred and Meta (Meyer) K.; B.S., U. Neb., 1950, M.S., 1952; Ph.D., N.C. State U., 1955; m. Katharine Arnold, Aug. 18, 1956; children—Sara, John. Faculty dept. soil sci. N.C. State U., Raleigh, 1955—, asso. prof., dir. soil testing div. N.C. Dept. Agr., 1958-63, prof., 1963—. Recipient Research award Soil Sci. Soc. N.C., 1969. Fellow Am. Soc. Agronomy; mem. Soil Sci. Soc. Am. (editor-in-chief proc. 1969—), Soil Conservation Soc. Am. (Commendation award 1968, Profl. Service award N.C. chpt. 1966), Sigma Xi, Gamma Sigma Delta, Alpha Zeta. Home: 101 Merwin Rd Raleigh NC 27606

KANATZAR, HOBART DOUGLAS, indsl. engr.; b. San Antonio, Sept. 21, 1919; s. Floyd J. and Mary (Ritchie) K.; B.S. in Indsl. Engring., Okla. State U., 1959; m. Gloria Brunson, Nov. 4, 1944; children—Douglas W., Holliann (Mrs. Ronald M. Dawson), Deelyn. Enlisted USAF, 1940, advanced through grades to maj., 1958, test pilot, Tinker AFB, Okla., 1953, Dobbins AFB, Ga., squadron engring. officer, Elmendorf, Alaska, 1947-49, ret., 1960; engr. mgmt. engring. Kelly AFB, Tex., 1960—. Decorated D.F.C., Air medal. Mem. Nat., Tex. socs. profl. engrs. Pioneer in devel. of estimating equation to forecast manning requirement with projected workload changes. Home: 834 Firefly Dr San Antonio TX 78216 Office: Kelly AFB TX 78241

KANE, HOWARD L., educator; b. Pitts., Dec. 11, 1911; s. Benjamin Hertz and Rose (Julius) K.; B.S., U. Pitts., 1932, Ph.D., 1936; m. Belle Friedman, Aug. 20, 1932; children—Benita (Mrs. Matthew Jaro), Harriet (Mrs. Lawrence Lihs). Chief research chemist Nat. Starch Products, N.Y.C., 1936-46; v.p. Polymer Industries, Inc., Stamford, Conn., 1946-64; chmn. div. mathematics and sci. Edison Community Coll., Ft. Myers, Fla., 1964—; instr. chemistry U. Conn., 1954-58. Dir. S.W. Fla. Opera Assn., 1972. Fellow A.A.A.S.; mem. Am. Chem. Soc., Fla. Assn. Community Colls., Sigma Xi, Pi Tau Phi, Phi Delta Kappa. Rotarian (pres. Stamford 1964). Patentee adhesive compositions of matter. Home: 1264 Cleburne Dr Fort Myers FL 33901

KANE, JAMES FRANCIS, educator; b. Phila., Nov. 22, 1942; s. John Aloysius and Margaret Mary (Burke) K.; B.S., St. Joseph's Coll., Phila., 1964; postgrad. St. Louis U., 1964-65; Ph.D., State U. N.Y. at Buffalo, 1969; m. Roselyn Marie Passmore, June 25, 1966; children—Mary Ellen, James Robert. Asst. prof. microbiology, med. units U. Tenn., Memphis, 1970—. USPHS postdoctoral fellow Baylor Coll. Medinine, Houston, 1968-70; recipient grants Research Corp., 1973-74, NSF, 1973—. Mem. Am. Soc. Microbiology, Sigma Xi. Office: Dept Microbiology Univ Tenn Memphis TN 38103

KANE, JOHN EWING, economist, accountant; b. Quitman, Ark., Apr. 2, 1914; s. Robert Lee and Beulah (Jenkins) K.; B.S., U. Ark., 1936, M.S., 1939; postgrad. U. Minn., 1940; Ph.D., Am. U., 1950; m. Katherine Edna Miller, Sept. 10, 1939; children—Carolyn, Phyllis Anne. Accountant, Lion Oil Co., El Dorado, Ark., 1937-39; instr. U. Ark., Fayetteville, 1939-41, asst. prof., asso. prof., prof., 1946—, asso. dir. Bur. Bus. and Econ. Research, 1949-50, chmn. dept. gen. bus., 1950-55, chmn. dept. econs., 1966—, chmn. athletic council, 1966—, acting v.p. finance, 1967-68; economist U.S. Dept. Commerce, 1942-43; exec. v.p. McIlroy Bank, Fayetteville, 1956-58, bus. and econ. cons., dir. Bd. dirs., faculty Southwestern Grad. Sch. Banking, Dallas; faculty Sch. Banking of South, Baton Rouge, faculty Nat. Assemblies for Bank Dirs. Sec.-treas. N.W. Ark. Regional Airport Authority. Served to lt. comdr. Supply Corps. USNR, 1943-46. Mem. Southwestern Social Sci. Assn. (past pres.), Am. Inst. C.P.A.'s, Ark. Soc. C.P.A.'s, Am. Econ. Assn., Am. Finance Assn., Am. Accounting Assn., So., Midwest econ. assns., Fayetteville C. of C. (past treas.), Alpha Kappa Psi. Methodist (bd. dirs.). Contbr. to Financial Accounting Theory, 1965. Home: 1245 Columbus Blvd Fayetteville AR 72701

KANE, MANUEL EDWARD, textile mfg. co. exec.; b. Boston, July 19, 1920; s. Samuel Lawrence and Sonia Frances (Shore) K.; grad. Moses Brown Sch., 1939; A.B., Harvard, 1943; m. Muriel Helma Stewart, June 20, 1948; children—Steven M., Michael R. With N.Am. Mills, Inc., Gastonia, N.C., 1945—, sec.-treas., 1973—. With Kane Industries, patent licensing, Gastonia, 1971—; dir. Carolina State Bank, Gastonia. Bd. dirs. Gaston County Cancer Soc., 1968—. Served with AUS, 1942-43. Home: 4409 Simsbury Rd Charlotte NC 28211 Office: PO Box 1698 Gastonia NC 28052

KANE, MATTHEW J(OHN), lawyer; b. Guthrie, Okla., July 15, 1910; s. Matthew J. and Kathleen (Reagan) K.; LL.B., U. Okla., 1932; m. Marjorie Kennedy, Sept. 15, 1934; 1 son, Matthew John III. Admitted to Okla. bar. 1932, since practiced in Pawhuska; dir. Nat. Bank Commerce, Pawhuska, Exchange Bank, Skiatook, Okla., Barnsdall State Bank. Mem. Okla. Bd. Bar Examiners, 1938-43; mem. Commn. on Uniform State Laws, 1949-53. Bd. dirs. Loy Found. Served to lt. comdr. USNR, 1943-45. Mem. Am., Okla. bar assns., Sigma Chi, Phi Delta Phi. Democrat. Roman Catholic. Rotarian. Home: 1515 Prudom St Pawhuska OK 74056 Office: Commerce Bldg Pawhuska OK 74056

KANE, PHILIP FRANCIS, electronics co. exec.; b. London, Eng., Dec. 1, 1920 (came to U.S. 1957, naturalized 1970); s. Cornelius and Frances Rose (Witney) K.; B.Sc., London U., 1948; m. Sybil Dorothy Silk, Oct. 17, 1942; children—Michael, Moira (Mrs. Ronald Edward Gillum). Technician Standard Telephones & Cables, Ltd., London, 1938-48; research chemist Laporte Chems., Ltd., Luton, Eng., 1949-52, chief analyst, 1952-57; supr. research Chemagro Corp., Kansas City, Mo., 1957-59; dir. lab. Tex. Instruments, Inc., Dallas, 1959—. Fellow Royal Inst. Chemistry (London); mem. Soc. Analytical Chemists (London), Soc. Applied Spectroscopy (pres. North Tex. sect. 1972—, gen. chmn. nat. meeting 1972—), Dallas Soc. Analytical Chemists (past chief analyst; award 1967). Author: (with Graydon B. Larrabee) Characterization of Semiconductor Materials, 1970. Editor: (with Graydon B. Larrabee) Characterization of Solid Surfaces, 1973. Home: 1919 Lake Forest Rd Grapevine TX 76051 Office: Tex Instruments Inc PO Box 5936 M/S 147 Dallas TX 75222

KANE, ROBERT EDWARD, JR., lawyer; b. Melrose Park, Ill., Mar. 2, 1942; s. Robert Edward and Mildred Ida (Danuser) K.; A.A., Mars Hill Coll., 1961; B.A., Coll. William and Mary, 1963, B.C.L., 1966; m. Harriett Anne Wade, Aug. 3, 1968; 1 son, Franklin Wade. Admitted to Va. bar, 1966, since practiced in Richmond; asso. Parker & Sullivan, 1966-67, partner, 1967-69; partner Parker, Sullivan & Kane, 1969-71, Sullivan & Kane, 1972—. Mem. Am., Va., Richmond bar assns., Am., Va., Richmond trial lawyers assns., Am. Judicature Soc., Sigma Alpha Epsilon, Phi Alpha Delta. Home: 1007 Foxcroft Rd Richmond VA 23239 Office: 1508 Willow Lawn Dr Richmond VA 23230

KANE, SAM, meat co. exec.; b. Spisske Podhradie, Czechoslovakia, June 23, 1919; s. Leopold and Bertha (Narcisenfeld) Kannengiesser; grad. Rabbinical Coll. Galanta, 1939; m. Aranka Feldbrand, Jan. 15, 1946; children—Jerry, Harold Ira, Esther Barbara. Came to U.S., 1948, naturalized, 1953. Pres. Sam Kane Wholesale Meat, Inc., Corpus Christi, Tex., 1956—, Sam Kane Meat, Inc., Corpus Christi, 1956—, Sam Kane Packing Co., Corpus Christi, 1962—, Kane Enterprises, Inc., Corpus Christi, 1956—. Pres., Jewish Welfare Appeal, 1962—; v.p. Combined Jewish Appeal, 1968, chmn. bd., 1962-64. Recipient award chmn. bd. edn. B'nai Israel Synagogue, 1965; Israel Service award, 1966. Jewish religion (pres. synagogue 1964-65). Mem. B'nai B'rith. Home: 27 Hewit Dr Corpus Christi TX 78404 Office: 9001 Leopard St Corpus Christi TX 78410

KANES, WILLIAM HENRY, educator, geologist; b. N.Y.C., Oct. 15, 1934; s. George and Helen (Scott) K.; B.S. in Geol. Engring., City Coll. N.Y., 1956; M.S. in Geology, W.Va. U., 1958, Ph.D., 1965; m. Patricia Joan Smith, Aug. 9, 1959; children—Katherine Joan, Karen Lynn, Kenneth Andrew, Matthew George. With Esso Prodn. Research Co., 1960-67, sr. exploration geologist, Libya, 1966-67; sr. exploration geologist Esso Standard Libya, 1968-69; asst. prof. W.Va. U., 1970; asso. prof. geology U. S.C., Columbia, 1971—; cons. in field. Served to 1st lt. C.E., AUS, 1958. Grantee NSF, 1971, 73, Dept. Interior, 1971, Columbia Gas Co., 1971-72, Union Oil Co., 1971-72, U. S.C., 1971, U.S. Senate, 1970. Mem. A.A.A.S., Am. Assn. Petroleum Geologists, Soc. Econ. Paleontologists and Mineralogists, Sigma Xi, Sigma Gamma Epsilon, Phi Kappa Sigma. Methodist (committeeman). Editor: Geology, Archaeology and Prehistory of the Southwest Fezzan, Libya, 1968. Home: 237 White Falls Dr Columbia SC 29210

KANSAS, ROBERT ELLIS, elec. engr.; b. N.Y.C., Mar. 4, 1926; s. Morris and Betty (Kaplan) K.; B.E.E., Coll. City N.Y., 1945; M.E.E., Poly. Inst. Bklyn., 1947; postgrad. Harvard, 1949-52; m. Helene Felner, May 28, 1949; children—Susan, Geoffrey, Tina. With Philco Corp., Phila., 1953-58; with missile and surface radar div. RCA Corp., Moorestown, N.J., 1958-64; with RCA Service Co., Patrick AFB, Fla., 1964—, mgr. re-entry tech. staff, missile test project, 1973—. Mem. Brevard County Democratic Exec. Com., 1970, Satellite Beach Charter Revision Commn., 1973. Mem. I.E.E.E., Fla. Engring. Soc. (v.p. 1973-74), Sigma Xi, Tau Beta Pi, Eta Kappa Nu, Epsilon Nu Gamma. Democrat. Jewish religion. Office: M U 290 Bldg 423 Patrick AFB FL 32925

KANTER, JACK CECIL, dentist; b. Norfolk, Va., Nov. 29, 1916; s. Samuel and Rose (Berman) K.; student Coll. William and Mary, Norfolk Div., 1934-35; D.D.S., Med. Coll. Va., 1939; postgrad. Temple U., 1962; m. Henrietta Salsbury, Jan. 16, 1946. Individual practice dentistry, Norfolk, 1939—; instr. dental assts. Coll. William and Mary, 1952, 54, 57; chief of dentistry DePaul Hosp., 1959-62; mem. staff Norfolk Gen. Hosp.; mem. med. adv. bd. Norfolk Area Med. Authority. Dir. Unico Corp. Mem. adv. bd. Speech and Hearing Center of Old Dominion. Served to lt. comdr., Dental Corps, USNR, 1942-46; ETO. Mem. Am., Va., Va.-Tidewater (past pres.) dental assns., Am. Cleft Palate Assn., Am. Assn. Maxillofacial Prosthetics, Southeastern Acad. Prosthodontics, Fraternal Order Police Assos. (past dir.), Jewish War Vets., Norfolk Firemens Assn., Alpha Omega, Omicron Kappa Upsilon, Sigma Zeta, Sigma Epsilon Pi. Jewish religion (dir. temple). Mason; mem. B'nai B'rith. Contbr. articles to profl. jours. Patentee in field. Home: 7812 Michael Dr Norfolk VA 23505 Office: 200 Military Circle East Bldg Norfolk VA 23502

KANTOR, DAVID, librarian; b. Atlanta, Ga., Nov. 2, 1915; s. Sam and Celia (Shafran) K.; B.S., U. Fla., 1938; Licentiate in microbiology Universite Libre de Bruxelles, 1939; B.L.S., Drexel U., 1941; m. Lee Finberg, Nov. 26, 1942. Cataloger U. Fla., 1941-42, chem.-pharmacy librarian, 1942-43; tech. librarian U. S. Army Signal Corps, Ft. Monmouth, N.J., 1943-44; librarian Wash. State Reformatory, 1944-46, 47-49; librarian Farragut Coll., 1946-47; librarian Cal. Dept. Corrections, Folsom Prison, 1949-62; dir. ext. Volusia County Pub. Libraries, Daytona Beach, Fla., 1962-63, dir. libraries Volusia County, 1964—; cons. instn. libraries Fla. State Library, State Bur. Blind Services, Fla. Mem. Cal. (pres. Golden Empire dist. 1958, dir. 1958), Am. (regional membership com. 1955, hosp. and instns. com. 1956), Fla. (chmn. pub. library sect. 1970-71, v.p., pres. 1972-73) library assns. Author: Survey of Public Library Service in Volusia County, 1964; Survey of Libraries and Library Services in the State Institutions of Florida, 1967. Office: Volusia County Public Libraries City Island Daytona Beach FL 32014

KAO, TIMOTHY WU, educator; b. Shanghai, China, July 20, 1937; s. Chun Hsian and Sing Fong (King) K.; B.Sc. with honors, U. Hong Kong, 1959; M.S., U. Mich., 1960, Ph.D., 1963; m. May Y.M. Lee, July 24, 1965; children—Michelle, Erika. Came to U.S., 1959, naturalized, 1972. Research engr. Cities Service Research & Devel. Co., Tulsa, 1961; research fellow Cal. Inst. Tech., 1963-64; faculty Cath. U. Am., Washington, 1964—, prof. aerospace and atmospheric scis., 1970—. NSF grantee. Mem. Am. Meteorol. Soc., Sigma Xi. Contbr. articles to profl. jours. Home: 702 Buccaneer Ct Silver Spring MD 20904 Office: Cath U Am Washington DC 20017

KAPLAN, EDWARD STEVEN, neurosurgeon; b. Memphis, Nov. 16, 1933; s. Jack and Violet Katherine (Needleman) K.; B.A., Yale, 1955; M.D., Columbia, 1959; M.S., U. Minn., 1964; m. Linda Cecile Stone, July 1, 1958; children—Andrew Stone, Jeffery Stone. Intern, Columbia Presbyn. Hosp., N.Y.C., 1960; resident Mayo Clinic, Rochester, Minn., 1960-64, Kennedy VA Hosp., Memphis, 1964; practice neurosurgery Memphis Neurosurg. Clinic, 1964—; mem. staff Bapt., LeBonheur, City, St. Joseph, Meth. hosps., Memphis. Instr. neurology U. Tenn., Memphis, 1965—. Diplomate Am. Bd. Neurol. Surgery. Mem. Congress Neurol. Surgeons, Am. Assn. Neurol. Surgeons, A.M.A., Phi Beta Kappa, Beta Theta Pi. Jewish religion. Home: 424 Sweetbriar St Memphis TN 38138 Office: 910 Madison St Memphis TN 38103

KAPLAN, HARRIET JANE (MRS. STANLEY N. KAPLAN), broadcasting exec.; b. Chgo., Sept. 26, 1933; d. Leslie H. and Harriet (Marks) Atlass; B.A., Rollins Coll., 1955; m. Stanley N. Kaplan, Mar. 15, 1964; 1 dau., Leslie. Asst. producer CBS radio-TV, Chgo., 1955-56, producer, 1955-57, dir. pub. affairs programming, 1957-60; radio, TV dir. Cushman, Veeck & Samuel Agy., Chgo., 1960-64; owner, operator radio sta. WAYS, Charlotte, N.C., 1964—, WAPE radio sta., 1971—. Mem. A.R.C. Pub. Information, Charlotte, 1969—. Bd. dirs. Nat. Conf. Christians and Jews, Human Relations Council. Mem. N.C. Women's Polit. Caucus, Women in Communications, Gamma Phi Beta. Home: 714 Edgehill Charlotte NC 28207 Office: 400 Radio St Charlotte NC 28214

KAPLAN, HARRY LIONEL, printing co. exec.; b. Bklyn., May 13, 1910; s. Bernard J. and Gussie (Harris) K.; grad. high sch.; m. Bess Donsky, Aug. 14, 1934; children—Barbara Jean, Nancy Jane (Mrs. Charles G. Lubar), Leon Jay. Pres. Am. Poster & Printing Co. (name changed to Am. Printing and Lithographing Co.), 1935-69, now chmn. bd.; pres. Am. Graphics, Dallas, 1969—; pres. Abco, Inc., Am. Legal Printing Co., Inc., Irrigation Age, Inc., Am-Equity Press, Inc.; sec.-treas. Tradetype Dallas, Inc. Pres. Dallas Big Bros., 1948-49, Citizens' Traffic Commn., 1961-63; chmn. Juvenile Driver License Com., 1959-60; mem. Dallas Com. for Good Schs.; active Community Chest, A.R.C., Am. Med. Center, United Jewish Appeal, Nat. Conf. Christians and Jews. Bd. dirs., chmn. juvenile com. Dallas Crime Commn. Mem. Printing Industry Am. (v.p. Dallas chpt. 1965), C. of C. Jewish religion. Mason (33 deg., Shriner), Lion. Home: 6042 Prestonshire Lane Dallas TX 75225 Office: 1600 S Akard St Dallas TX 75215

KAPLAN, HERBERT LARRY, real estate pres.; b. Lancaster, Pa., July 29, 1936; s. Edward Charles and Elinor Dorothy (Miller) K.; B.A., U. Pa., 1958, LL.B., 1961; m. Louise Krogstad, May 5, 1962; children—Anthony D., Elisabeth Anne. Admitted Fla. bar, 1961, U.S. Supreme Ct., 1968; asso. mem. firm Orr & Lazar, Miami, 1961-63; partner Orr, Triester & Kaplan, Miami 1963-64, Kaplan & Shapiro, Miami Beach, 1964-69; pres. Royal Palm Beach Colony, Inc. devel., Miami, 1969—; dir. Miami Nat. Bank, Investors Tax Sheltered Real Estate Ltd. Mem. Dade County Drug Abuse Task Force. Mem. Dade County, Fla. bar assns., Am. Inst. Mgmt. (pres.'s council, 1971—). Home: 7000 SW 146th St Miami FL 33158 Office: 8101 Biscayne Blvd Miami FL 33138

KAPLAN, JERRY, surgeon; b. Memphis, July 28, 1932; s. Rubin and Celia (Rofman) K.; M.D., U. Tenn., 1956; m. Annabelle Beyer, Aug. 31, 1956; children—Mark, Valerie, Hugh, Susan. Intern, John Gaston Hosp., 1956-57; resident Kennedy VA Hosp., Memphis, 1959-63, Good Samaritan Hosp., Los Angeles, 1963-64; practice medicine specializing in gen. surgery, Memphis, 1964—; mem. staff Bapt. Meml., St. Joseph hosps. Home: 5944 Brierdale Cove Memphis TN 38137 Office: 22 N Pauline St Memphis TN 38105

KAPLAN, MARSHALL ALLEN, economist; b. Chgo., May 21, 1929; s. Benjamin and Rose (Altman) K.; B.S., Ill. Inst. Tech., 1950; M.A., U. Chgo., 1952, Ph.D., 1960; m. Carol M. Green, May 23, 1968; children—Robert, Elizabeth. Research asso. U. Chgo. Center for Agrl. Econs., 1953-54; instr. Williams Coll., Williamstown, Mass., 1954-56; sr. economist Pres.'s Council Econ. Advisers, Washington, 1956-64; economist Fed. Home Loan Bank Bd., Washington, 1964—. Lectr., Georgetown U., 1962-66. Mem. Am. Econ. Assn. Author: Demand for Food, 1954. Contbr. articles on housing markets and econ. outlook, savs. and loan market structure to profl. jours. Home: 3044 Davenport St NW Washington DC 20008 Office: Federal Home Loan Bank Board 101 Indiana Av NW Washington DC 20552

KAPLAN, MARVIN IRWIN, dentist; b. Bklyn., Feb. 8, 1937; s. Solomon and Lillian (Warm) K.; B.A., Bklyn. Coll., 1957; D.D.S. (N.Y. Regents medicine and dentistry scholar), N.Y. U., 1961, certificate in orthodontics, 1967; m. Victoria Spring, July 30, 1961; children—Lisa, Robert. Asso., Dr. Angelo Rocco Lombardi, orthodontist, Jersey City, 1967-69; practice dentistry specializing in orthodontics, Newport News, Va., 1969—. Served as capt. AUS, 1961-63. Mem. Am., Tidewater assns. orthodontists, So., Va. socs. orthodontists, Peninsula Dental Soc., James River Jr. C. of C. (dir. 1971—), Alpha Omega. Club: Toastmasters (v.p. 1971-72) (Hampton, Va.). Home: 11 Meeting Rd Newport News VA 23606 Office: 13193 Warwick Blvd Newport News VA 23602

KAPLAN, NORMAN MAYER, physician, educator; b. Dallas, Jan. 2, 1931; s. Isadore Joseph and Sarah Rebecca (Bernstein) K.; B.S., U. Tex., 1950, M.D., 1954; m. Eva Schnitzer, Dec. 17, 1950 (div. Mar. 1974); children—Marcia, Cynthia, Carolyn, Diane. Intern, resident Parkland Hosp., Dallas, 1954-58; research fellow NIH, Bethesda, Md., 1960-61; faculty U. Tex. Health Sci. Center, Dallas, 1961—, prof. medicine, 1970—; dir. endocrine clinic Parkland Hosp.; cons. U.S. Army, USAF, VA Hosp. Pres., League Ednl. Advancement, Dallas, 1965-68, Jewish Vocational Counseling Service, 1970-73; mem. exec. com. Jewish Welfare Fedn., 1968—. Served with USAF, 1958-60. Research grantee USPHS, 1961—. Fellow A.C.P.; mem. Am. Soc. Clin. Investigation, Dallas Diabetes Assn. (pres. 1972-73). Author: Clinical Hypertension, 1973. Home: 6906 Northaven St Dallas TX 75230 Office: 5323 Harry Hines Blvd Dallas TX 75235

KAPLAN, ROBERT, labor union ofcl.; b. Chgo., June 27, 1910; s. Abraham Louis and Sarah (Weitzman) K.; B.S. in Econs., Northwestern U., 1937; m. Grace Liebenson, July 27, 1934. Marketing and research staff Sachs Advt. Agy., Chgo., 1932-34; economist Lord & Thomas, Chgo., 1935-40; research dir. United Mine Workers Am., Washington, 1942-47, statistician, 1968-71, actuary, 1972-74, cons. actuary, 1974—; on loan U.S. Dept. Labor study reducing indsl. accidents, 1942-44. Mem. Conf. Actuaries in Pub. Practice, 1966—. Served with USN, World War II. Mem. Am. Acad. Actuaries, Am. Econ. Assn. Home: Apt 702 3601 Wisconsin Av NW Washington DC 20016

KAPLAN, STANLEY BARUCH, educator, physician; b. Memphis, Jan. 6, 1931; s. Leon Labe and Henrietta (Schaffer) K.; student Vanderbilt U., 1948-51; M.D., U. Tenn., 1954. Intern, Jefferson Med. Coll. Hosp. Phila., 1955; resident U. Tenn.-City Memphis Hosp., 1958-61; practice medicine specializing in internal medicine and rheumatology, Memphis, 1961—; faculty medicine U. Tenn., Memphis, 1961—, prof., 1973—; attending physician City of Memphis, Bapt. Meml. hosps.; cons. VA Hosp., 1965—, Meth. Hosp., 1962—, U.S. Naval Hosp., 1974, B'nai B'rith Home and Hosp. for Aged, 1962—. Program dir. U. Tenn. Arthritis Clin. Research Center, 1968—. Bd. dirs. Les Passees Rehab. Center, W. Tenn. chpt. Arthritis

Found. Served to capt. AUS, 1956-58. Diplomate Am. Bd. Internal Medicine. Mem. A.M.A., Tenn., So. med. assns., Memphis and Shelby County Med. Soc., Memphis Acad. Internal Medicine, Alpha Omega Alpha. Home: 232 S Highland St Memphis TN 38111

KAPLAN, STANLEY NORRIS, broadcasting exec.; b. Cleve., Apr. 23, 1926; s. Joseph S. and Tylie (Menitoff) K.; B.A., N.Y. U., 1950, M.A., 1951; M.A., Harvard Bus. Sch., 1952; m. Harriet Atlass, Mar. 15, 1964; children—Susan, Leslie Ann. Vice pres. sales Balaban Stas., St. Louis, 1958-60; pres. Mars Broadcasting Co., Stamford, Conn., 1960-63; gen. mgr. WMEX-Radio, Boston, 1963-65; pres., chief exec. officer SIS Radio, Inc., Charlotte, N.C., 1965—. Mem. N.C. Council on Crime and Delinquency, 1969—, N.C. Zool. Authority, 1969—. Mem. research com. Radio Advt. Bur., N.Y.C., 1969—. Chmn. steering com. Mecklenburg (N.C.) Democratic Com., 1968; campaign mgr. lt. gov. N.C., 1968; del. Dem. Nat. Conv., Chgo., 1968; dir. nat. media McGovern for Pres. Com., 1972. Bd. dirs. Charlotte Area Fund, Boys Town, Opportunities Industrialization Center, Medgar Evers Found. Served with inf. AUS, 1943-45; ETO. Decorated Purple Heart with 2 oak leaf clusters, Bronze star, Silver Star. Clubs: University, Beauclere Country, Chgo. Yacht. Home: 714 Edgehill Rd Charlotte NC 28207 Office: 400 Radio Rd Charlotte NC 28214

KAPLAN, WILLIAM, textile mill exec.; b. Newark, Dec. 7, 1934; s. Sam and Betty (Franklin) K.; B.S., Lowell Technol. Inst., 1956; m. Barbara Esther Weiss, Dec. 31, 1964; children—Deborah Renee, David Joshua. Founder, Wyndmoor Knitting Mills, Inc., Elizabeth, N.J., 1956, pres., 1956—; founder McGowen Mfg. Co., Inc., Elizabeth, 1958, pres., 1958—; founder N.C. Spinning Mills, Inc., Lincolnton, N.C., 1963, pres. 1963—; pres. Houser Spinning Mills, Inc., Cherryville, N.C., 1967—. Mem. Am. Assn. Chemists and Colorists. Home: 4524 Belknap Rd Charlotte NC 28211 Office: PO Box 818 Lincolnton NC 28092

KAPLOW, HERBERT ELIAS, news corr.; b. N.Y.C., Feb. 2, 1927; s. Solomon and Belle (Bernstein) K.; B.A., Queens Coll., 1948; M.S.J., Northwestern U., 1951; m. Betty Rae Koplow, Aug. 10, 1952; children—Steven E., Robert G., Lawrence M. News corr. NBC News, Washington, 1951-72, ABC News, Washington, 1972—; lectr. Served with AUS, 1945-46. Recipient alumni award Northwestern U., 1959, Queens Coll., 1963. Mem. Sigma Delta Chi. Home: 211 Van Buren St Falls Church VA 22046 Office: 1124 Connecticut Av NW Washington DC 20036

KAPNER, LEWIS, judge; b. West Palm Beach, Fla., May 21, 1937; s. Irving Michael and Mildred (Pikelny) K.; B.A., U. Fla., 1958; student Harvard, summer 1956, George Washington U., summer 1961; J.D., Stetson U., 1962; postgrad. Fla. Atlantic U., 1970—, Nat. Coll. State Judiciary, 1973; m. Dawn Beth Grossman, Aug. 30, 1964; children—Steven Marshall, Kimberly Anne, Michael Scott, Allison Lori. Admitted to Fla. bar, 1962; asst. county solicitor Palm Beach County, 1962-65; city prosecutor West Palm Beach, 1965-66; partner Kapner & Kapner, 1965-67; legal counsel Palm Beach County Legislative Delegation, 1967; judge Juvenile and Domestic Relations Ct., Palm Beach County, 1967-73, judge Circuit Ct., 1973—; del. White House Conf. on children, 1970; regional chmn. Gov.'s Task Force on Delinquency, 1969-71; mem. Gov.'s Task Force on Drug and Alcohol Abuse, 1969-71. Charter pres. Palm Beach County Young Republicans, 1965; gen. counsel Fla. Young Republicans, 1966-67; candidate Fla. Senate, 1967. Pres. Community Services Council, 1969; pres. Internat. Found. for Gifted Children; v.p. Palm Beach County chpt., mem. nat. exec. com. Am. Jewish Com.; pres. Palm Beach County Assn. for Gifted. Served with USMCR, 1958-65. Recipient Distinguished Service award West Palm Beach Jaycees, 1971; named one of five outstanding young men in Fla., Fla. Jaycees, 1971. Mem. Fla. (chmn. jour. editorial bd.), Palm Beach County (past com. chmn.) bar assns., Mensa, Blue Key, Phi Delta Phi, Phi Alpha Theta, Tau Epsilon Phi. Republican. Jewish religion. Contbr. articles to profl. jours., newspapers. Home: 258 Country Club Rd Palm Beach FL 33480 Office: County Courthouse West Palm Beach FL 33401

KAPPES, CHARLES R., journalist; b. Evanston, Ill., Mar. 17, 1942; s. J. Henry and Lyla Ethel (Jensen) K.; student Broward Community Coll., 1961-62. News dir. WMJR-FM, Ft. Lauderdale, Fla., 1963-64; newsman WINZ, Miami, Fla., 1965-66; newsman WGBS, Miami, 1966-67, editorial dir., 1967—. Free-lance reporter, TV producer. Recipient 6 Editorial awards A.P., 1968, 69, 70, 71, 72, 73, various awards Fla. Edn. Assn., Radio TV News Dirs., Freedoms Found. Mem. Sigma Delta Chi. Home: 301 Kansas Av Fort Lauderdale FL 33312 Office: 710 Brickell Av Miami FL 33131

KAPPLER, ROBERT PAUL, elec. engr.; b. Moberly, Mo., Nov. 4, 1938; s. Edward Louis and Margaret (Sump) K.; gen. edn., certificate Moberly Jr. Coll., 1956-58; B.S. in Elec. Engring., U. Mo., 1961, M.B.A., 1970; m. Marilyn Sue Lankford, June 20, 1964; 1 dau., Christiana Susanne. Elec. engr. Army Test and Evaluation Command, White Sands Missile Range, N.M., 1961-71, Office Asst. Chief Staff for Force Devel., Pentagon, Washington, 1971—. Vice pres. adminstrn., control procedures Profl. Investment Co. N.M., Alamogordo, 1971-73. Mem. I.E.E.E., Nat. Soc. Profl. Engrs., Am. Inst. Aero. and Astronautics (pres. Inland Missile Range chpt. 1967), Beta Gamma Sigma. Roman Catholic. Home: 3708 Persimmon Circle Fairfax VA 22030 Office: Hdqrs Dept Army ATTN DAFD-ZBG Pentagon Washington DC 20310

KAPPUS, KARL DANIEL, biologist; b. Cleve., July 2, 1938; s. Robert D. and Dolores (Zwerman) K.; B.S., Ohio State U., 1960, M.S., 1962, Ph.D., 1964. NRC postdoctoral asso. Army Biol. Labs., Frederick, Md., 1964-66; research asso. Ohio State U., 1967; research entomologist Nat. Communicable Disease Center, Atlanta, 1967-68, research ecologist, 1968—. Mem. Wildlife Disease Assn., Entomol. Soc. Am., A.A.A.S., Sigma Xi. Home: 454 Superior Av Decatur GA 30030 Office: 1600 Clifton Rd Atlanta GA 30333

KAREM, MARY JANE (MRS. FRED J. KAREM), lawyer; b. Louisville, Oct. 27, 1908; d. Edmund Gibbs and Virginia (Allen) Mansfield; B.A., Catherine Spalding Coll. (formerly Nazareth Coll.), 1931; J.D. magna cum laude, U. Louisville, 1948; m. Fred J. Karem (dec.); children—Virginia C., James F., Edmund Peter, David Kevin, Jane Catherine. Admitted to Ky. bar, 1949; gen. practice Karem & Karem, attys., Louisville, 1949—. Committeewoman Dem. Party, 1952—. Bd. counselors, sec. Catherine Spalding Coll.; mem. Louisville and Jefferson County Human Relations Commn. Named Ky. col., Bus. Woman of Year, Louisville Bus. and Profl. Women's Club, 1967; recipient Caritas medal Spalding Coll., 1968. Mem. Nat. Assn. Women Lawyers, Nat. Cath. Theatre Conf., Cath. Theatre Guild of Louisville, Am. Ky., Louisville bar assns., Bellarmine Coll. Athletic Assn., Bellarmine Coll. Parents Assn., Jefferson County (Ky.) Women Lawyers (pres.), Internat. Platform Assn., Catherine Spalding Coll. Alumnae Assn. (pres.), Bellarmine's Womens Council (exec. bd.), English Speaking Union. Clubs: Highland Woman's, Catherine Spalding Coll. Luncheon. Home: 1857 Alfresco Pl Louisville KY 40205 Office: Lincoln Fed Bldg Louisville KY 40202

KARICKHOFF, SAMUEL WOODFORD, chemist; b. Buckhannon, W.Va., Oct. 22, 1943; s. Myrle F. and Mildred Geneivie (Bailey) K.; B.S. cum laude, W.Va. Wesleyan Coll., 1965; Ph.D., Fla. State U., 1971; m. Marilyn Marie Lundell, 1964; children—Samuel Brent, Lisa Ann. Postdoctoral chemist U.S. Environmental Protection Agy.-S.E. Water Lab., Athens, Ga., 1971-72, research chemist S.E. Environmental Research Lab., Athens, 1972—. NASA trainee, 1965-68. Recipient Bronze medal for commendable service U.S. Environmental Protection Agy., 1972. Mem. Am. Chem. Soc., Omicron Delta Kappa, Sigma Eta Sigma. Contbr. articles to profl. jours. Home: 348 Cherokee Ridge Rd Athens GA 30601 Office: College Station Rd Athens GA 30601

KARKALITS, OLIN CARROLL, JR., univ. dean; b. Pauls Valley, Okla., May 31, 1916; s. Olin Carroll and Mabel Claire (Patterson) K.; B.S. in Chem. Engring., Rice U., 1938; M.S., U. Mich., 1941, Ph.D. (Ethyl Corp. fellow), 1950; m. Barbara Sue Robinson, Aug. 19, 1961; children—Kay Ann, Karen Sue. Group leader Am. Cyanamid Co., Boundbrook, N.J., 1948-56; mgr. research Petro-Tex Chem. Corp., Houston, 1956-66, asst. dir. engring., 1966-72; dean engring. and tech. McNeese State U., Lake Charles, La., 1972—. Spl. cons. Levingston Engrs., Inc. Vol. staff worker United Fund. Trustee, Evang. Christian Edn. Found. Registered profl. engr., La., Tex. Mem. Am. Inst. Chem. Engrs., A.A.A.S., Am. Assn. Cost Engrs., Am. Soc. Engring. Edn., Sigma Xi, Tau Beta Pi, Phi Lambda Upsilon. Patentee in field. Home: 1161 Bayouwood Dr Lake Charles LA 70601

KARLIN, SAMUEL, surgeon; b. Portland, Me., Sept. 7, 1908; s. Myer and Gussie (Rosoff) K.; A.B., Harvard, 1928, M.D., 1932; m. Alece J. Geisenberger, June 27, 1938 (dec. Mar. 1973); children—Robert A., Richard M.; m. 2d, Janet Elsas, Jan. 1, 1974. Intern, Touro Infirmary, New Orleans, 1933-34, resident, 1934-36, chief surgery, 1959-63; clin. prof. surgery La. State U., New Orleans, 1950—. Vice chmn. profl. div. New Orleans United Fund, 1963. Trustee Newman Sch., New Orleans. Served to maj. AUS, 1942-46. Decorated Bronze Star. Diplomate Am. Bd. Surgery. Fellow A.C.S., Southeastern Surg. Congress, Surg. Soc. La.; mem. New Orleans Surg. Soc. (pres. 1965). Club: Harvard of La. (pres. 1964-67). Home: 3185 Octavia St New Orleans LA 70125 Office: 3600 Prytania St New Orleans LA 70115

KARMIN, MONROE W., journalist; b. Mineola, N.Y., Sept. 2, 1929; s. Stanley and Phyllis (Appelbaum) K.; m. Mayanne Sherman, Oct. 30, 1955; children—Paul, Betsy. Spl. writer Wall Street Journal, Washington. Recipient Pulitzer prize for nat. reporting, 1967, Sigma Delta award for gen. reporting, 1967. Home: 7011 Beechwood Dr Chevy Chase MD 20015 Office: Nat Press Bldg Washington DC 20004

KARNS, CHARLES WESLEY, govt. ofcl.; b. Waynesboro, Pa., July 15, 1920; s. Charles Donald and Mary Caroline (Bobb) K.; B.A., Dickinson Coll., 1941; M.A., Northwestern U., 1948; m. Thelma Margaret Sprow, Dec. 26, 1946; children—Katherine Mary, Charles Wesley III, Dorothy Margaret. Staff mem. Center Naval Analyses, Operations Evaluation Group, Arlington, Va., 1951-71; operations research analyst Office Sec. Def., The Pentagon, Washington, 1971—. Served with USNR, 1942-46. Tutorial fellow Northwestern U., 1941-42. Mem. Math. Assn. Am., Operations Research Soc. Am., Phi Beta Kappa, Beta Theta Pi. Methodist. Home: 8629 Redwood Dr Vienna VA 22180 Office: Office Dir Defense Research and Engring The Pentagon Washington DC 20301

KARRAKER, JOHN RICHARD, banker; b. DeSota, Mo., Nov. 14, 1928; s. John Wilson and Mary Olga (Van Hecke) K.; student Brown Bus. Coll., 1947, Northwestern U., 1962, 66, 68; m. Frances Walker Flowers, Dec. 20, 1950; children—Marlo, Wayne, Renee. Trust officer Ga. R.R. Bank & Trust Co., 1952-65; sr. v.p., gen. trust officer Nat. Bank Ga., Atlanta, 1965-72, sr. v.p. br. adminstrn., 1972—. Instr. trusts Ga. Bankers Assn., U. Ga., Athens, 1968—. Citizen mem. Fulton County Employees Pension Fund, 1966-70; crusade chmn. Fulton County Cancer Soc., Inc., 1972, v.p., 1973-74. Bd. dirs., mem. finance com. Met. Atlanta Boys' Clubs, Inc.; trustee Frank & William Bone Found., Milledgeville, Ga., Met. Found. Atlanta. Served with AUS, 1948-52. Mem. Am. Inst. Banking, Ga. Bankers Assn. (mem. exec. com. trust div. 1968-72), Atlanta Life Underwriters Assn., Estate Planning Council Atlanta. Roman Catholic. Clubs: Cherokee Town and Country, Commerce (Atlanta). Home: 496 Manor Ridge Dr NW Atlanta GA 30305 Office: 34 Peachtree St Atlanta GA 30301

KARST, CHARLES EDWARD, lawyer, mayor; b. New Orleans, Sept. 18, 1931; s. Charles and Ethel Marie (Drouin) K.; B.A., Tulane U., 1952; J.D., Loyola U., 1965; m. Judith Ward Steinman, Dec. 27, 1965; children—Alexander Regard, Alicia Barrows. Indsl. engr. Boeing Co., New Orleans, 1963-66; admitted to La. bar, 1965; atty. Ward-Steinman & Karst, New Orleans, 1965-67, Alexandria, La., 1966—. Dir. Maderas Conglomeradas S.A. Mayor, City of Alexandria, La., 1969-73; v.p. Cenla Mayor's Council, 1971, pres., 1972. Bd. dirs. Rapides Parish Planning Commn. Served with USAF, 1952-54. Mem. Am. Trial Lawyers Assn., Am., La., Alexandria bar assns., La. Municipal Assn. (v.p. 1972-73), Alexandria C. of C. (dir.), V.F.W., Am. Legion. Roman Catholic. Lion. Home: 2236 Jackson St Alexandria LA 71301 Office: 1128 5th St Alexandria LA 71301

KARTUS, JACK LEE, dept. store exec.; b. Bessemer, Ala., Dec. 1, 1918; s. Harry and Esther (Kaufman) K.; student, U. Ala., 1938-42; m. Miriam Bresler, Jan. 23, 1943; children—Margaret, Lisa, Sallie, Harry. With Outlet Co., Bessemer, 1950—, pres., 1954—. Bd. dirs. United Appeal, Bessemer. Served to 1st lt. USAAF, 1941-46, USAF, 1950. Mem. C. of C. (v.p. retail div. 1969—). Home: 3139 Pine Ridge Rd Birmingham AL 35213 Office: PO Box 398 Bessemer AL 35020

KARZON, ALLAIRE URBAN (MRS. DAVID T. KARZON), lawyer; b. Newark, July 18, 1925; d. Paul J. and Aurelia (Hemmen) Urban; B.A., Wellesley Coll., 1945; LL.B., Yale, 1947; m. David T. Karzon, May 18, 1946; children—David T., Elizabeth Urban. Admitted to Md. bar, 1948, N.Y. bar, 1952, Tenn. bar, 1969; atty. Office Alien Property Dept. Justice, 1948-49; atty. law dept. RCA, N.Y.C., 1950-52; asso. Hodgson, Russ, Andrews, Woods & Goodyear, Buffalo, 1952-55, partner, 1955-68; v.p., gen. counsel, dir. Performance Systems, Inc., Nashville, 1969-70; partner Neal, Karzon & Harwell, Nashville, 1971-72; dir. law Aladdin Industries, Inc., Nashville, 1972-73, v.p. law, 1973—; v.p. law Aladdin Synergetics, Inc., 1973—; dir. Aladdin Exco, Inc., Aladdin Western Export Corp., Temp-Rite Internat., Inc., 1972—. Lectr. law Vanderbilt U., 1971—. Pres. bd. mgrs. Vis. Nursing Assn. Buffalo; mem. exec. com. Council Vis. Nurse Assns. N.Y. State; sec., trustee Western N.Y. Ednl. TV, Inc.; bd. dirs., sec. Sr. Citizens Inc., Nashville; bd. dirs. Planned Parenthood Assn. Nashville, 1973—. Recipient award trust div. N.Y. State Bankers Assn. 1966. Mem. Am., Tenn., Nashville bar assns., Phi Beta Kappa. Presbyn. Club: Nashville Wellsley (v.p. 1973—). Home: 1049 Overton Lea Rd Nashville TN 37220 Office: 703 Murfreesboro Rd Nashville TN 37204

KASE, FRANCIS JOSEPH, govt. ofcl.; b. Most, Austria, Sept. 21, 1910; s. Francis and Alberta (Retovska) K.; came to U.S., 1949, naturalized, 1954; Dr. jur., Charles U., Prague, Czechoslovakia, 1934; D.P.S., Acad. Polit. Sci., Prague, 1934; Ph.D., George Washington U., 1963. Practiced law, Czechoslovakia, 1933-35; govt. ofcl. Land Govt. Bohemia, 1935-45; counsel, div. chief Ministry Fgn. Trade, Czechoslovakia, 1945-48; sec.-treas., research analyst Internat. Peasant Union, Washington, 1951-54; librarian, mem. legal staff U.S. Copyright Office, Library of Congress, Washington, 1956-66; librarian Patent Office Search Center, U.S. Dept. Commerce, 1966-71; law librarian Price Commn., 1971-72; librarian Patent Office, Dept. Commerce, 1972—. Mem. Am. Polit. Sci. Assn., Am. Acad. Polit. and Social Sci., Copyright Office Lawyers' Assn., Pi Gamma Mu. Author: Handbook of Czechoslovak Foreign Trade, 1948; Soviet Theory of People's Democracy, 1963; Copyright in Continental Europe, 1967; Copyright in Czechoslovakia, 1967; People's Democracy, 1968; Foreign Patents, 1972. Contbr. to profl. jours. Research polit. theory, comparative govt. and law, law of intellectual property, library sci. Home: 5206 Little Falls Dr Bethesda MD 20016 Office: Patent Office Dept Commerce Washington DC 20231

KASH, ROSCOE CONKLING, physician; b. Muskogee, Okla., Dec. 11, 1906; s. S. Perkins and Alice (Bowman) K.; A.B., U. Ky., 1925; M.D., Vanderbilt U., 1929; M.P.H. (Commonwealth Fund fellow), Johns Hopkins, 1939; m. Ladye Ruth Stephens, Sept. 6, 1932; children—Graham Stephens, Lewis LeSueur. With hosp. div. USPHS, 1929-33; intern U.S. Marine Hosp., Ellis Island, N.Y., 1929-30; resident Marine hosps., New Orleans, Pitts.; 1930-33; asst. surgeon Tenn. Health Dept., 1933-44; pvt. practice medicine, Lebanon, Tenn., 1945—. Dir. First Nat. Bank of Lebanon. Mem. Ch. of Christ. Mason, Odd Fellow. Author: Medical Essays, 1958. Home: 619 W Spring St Lebanon TN 37087 Office: 202 S College St Lebanon TN 37087

KASMAN, FRANKLIN GERALD, dentist; b. Bay City, Tex., Feb. 3, 1941; s. Jake and Helen (Greenberg) K.; D.D.S., U. Tex., 1966; certificate in endodontics, Tufts U., 1970; m. Golda Sue Golub, June 19, 1966; children—Jonathan Alan, Beverly Michelle. Individual practice endodontics, Worcester, Mass., 1968-70, Austin, Tex., 1970—; cons. endodontics USAF; faculty U. Tex. Dental Br.; dental cons. Nat. Conf. Bilingual Edn. Cons., chmn. edn. com. Austin Sch. Dist.; founder Project Care. Served with USAF, 1966-68. Decorated Hosp. Commendation medal. Mem. Am. Soc. Dentistry for Children (Achievement award 1966), Zionist Orgn. Am., Tex. Dental Soc., Am. Assn. Endodontics. Jewish religion (pres. temple brotherhood). Home: 6404 Sumac St Austin TX 78731 Office: 311 Med Park Tower Austin TX 78705

KASS, BENNY LEE, lawyer; b. Chgo., Aug 20, 1936; s. Herman and Ethel (Lome) K.; B.S., Northwestern U., 1957; LL.B., U. Mich., 1960; LL.M., George Washington U., 1967; m. Salme Lundstrom, Aug. 30, 1963; children—Gale, Brian. Admitted to D.C. bar, 1960; atty. Maritime Adminstrn., 1960-61; counsel House Information Subcommittee, 1962-65; asst. counsel Senate Adminstrv. Practice Subcom., Washington, 1965-69; pvt. practice law, Washington, 1969—; mem. firm Boasberg Hewes Klores & Kass; prof. communication law Am. U.; pub. mem. Nat. Advt. Rev. Bd., 1971—; commr. D.C. Conf. on Uniform State Laws. Chmn. consumer affairs subcom., Mayors Econ. Devel. Com., 1968-70; chmn. Ad Hoc Com. on Consumer Protection, 1965—. Served with USAF, 1961-62. Am. Polit. Sci. Assn. Congl. fellow, 1966. Mem. Am., Fed. bar assns., Am. Polit. Sci. Assn., Sigma Delta Chi. Contbr. articles profl. jours. Home: 3642 Jocelyn St NW Washington DC 20015 Office: Boasberg Hewes Klores & Kass 1225 19th St NW Washington DC 20036

KASSIN, HAROLD HOWARD, lawyer; b. Bklyn., Dec. 2, 1927; s. Louis and Anna (Gorelick) K.; student Columbia, 1948; J.D., U. Miami, 1951; m. Delores Jean Robey, Nov. 27, 1971. Admitted to Fla. bar, 1951, U.S. Supreme Ct. bar, 1955, also other U.S. bars; pvt. practice law, Miami, Fla. Sec., Kassin Investment Corp., Miami, Flagler-Ponce Realty Corp., Miami. Served with AUS, 1946-47. Mem. Am., Fla., Dade County bar assns., Fla. Real Estate Broker, Nu Beta Epsilon (So. regional chancellor). Democrat. Home: 1921 NE 188th St Sky Lake North Miami Beach FL 33162 Office: Biscayne Bldg 19 W Flagler St Miami FL 33130

KASSIRA, EDWARD NAIM, educator; b. Mosul, Iraq, Sept. 15, 1932; s. Naim Elias and Madliene M. (Safar) K.; M.B., Ch.B., Baghdad U., 1959; M.P.H., Johns Hopkins, 1965; M.Sc., Harvard, 1967; Ph.D., George Washington U., 1970; m. Nadira Al-Naaman, Mar. 15, 1963; children—Firas, Zainab, Gassan. Came to U.S., 1964. Asst. dean Mosul Sch. Medicine, 1962-64; research fellow Harvard Sch. Pub. Health, 1966-67; research asso. George Washington U., 1968; guest scientist dept. microbiology Naval Med. Research Inst., Nat. Naval Med. Center, 1968-69; asst. prof. epidemiology George Washington U. Med. Center, Washington, 1968—, Koulbinkian Found., 1964-68. Mem. Am. Pub. Health Assn., Am. Soc. Microbiology, Am. Assn. Tchrs. Preventive Medicine, Sigma Xi. Home: 6805 Columbia Pike Annandale VA 22003 Office: 2300 Eye St Washington DC 20037

KASSIS, RAYMOND, dentist; b. Zahley, Lebanon, Dec. 23, 1937; came to U.S., 1952, naturalized 1961; s. Aziz Habib and Zakia (Shahid) K.; B.S. in Chemistry, Coll. Charleston, 1961; D.D.S., Georgetown U., 1968; m. Becky Jones, Dec. 9, 1973. Research chemist Charleston Rubber Co. (S.C.), 1962-64; individual practice dentistry, Charleston, 1969—. Recipient S. Keith Johnson Sci. award Pre-med. Club Coll. Charleston, 1961; NSF research grantee, 1960. Mem. Am. Dental Assn., Charleston, Coastal Dist. dental socs., Charleston C. of C., Charleston (Dental) Study Club (pres.). Home: 1296 Hwy 171 Charleston SC 29403 Office: 1247 Savannah Hwy Charleston SC 29407

KASTEN, FREDERICK H., anatomist, educator; b. N.Y.C., Mar. 7, 1927; s. Isaac and Anna (Goldblum) K.; B.A., U. Houston, 1950; M.A. (Rosalie B. Hite fellow), U. Tex., Austin, 1951, Ph.D. (AEC fellow, NSF fellow), 1954; postgrad. Oak Ridge Inst. Nuclear Study, summer 1952, Alton B. Jones Cell Sci. Center, Lake Placid, N.Y., summer 1971; m. Agnes Marie Garrison, Feb. 2, 1949; children—Fred L., Stephen D.I., Donald J., Glenn T. Cancer research scientist Roswell Park Meml. Inst., 1954-56; instr. biology Tex. A. and M. Coll., 1956, asst. prof., 1957-61; research coordinator, dir. dept. ultrastructural cytochemistry Pasadena Found. for Med. Research, 1963-70; adj. asst. prof. anatomy U. So. Cal., 1963-67, adj. asso. prof., 1968-70; asst. clin. prof. pathology Loma Linda (Cal.) U. Sch. Medicine, 1965-67, asso. clin. prof., 1968-70; prof. anatomy La. State U. Med. Center, New Orleans, 1970—, course dir. med. histology, 1971—, cell biology, 1970—, anatomy curriculum com., 1971—, grad. council, 1972—. Cons. Nat. Heart and Lung Inst., 1971—, Nat. Cancer Inst., 1973—; First Feulgen Meml. lectr. Justus-Liebig U., Germany, 1962; guest lectr. Tulane U. Med. Sch., 1964, 73, Acads. of Sci. in Eastern Europe, 1968, S.W. div. Am. Assn. Cancer Research, Galveston, Tex., 1972. Served with USNR, 1945-46. NSF fellow Justus-Liebig U., 1961-62; NSF fellow Institut de Recherches Scientifique sur le Cancer, Villejuif, France, 1962; NIH-Nat. Cancer Inst. Spl. Research fellow, 1962-63. Mem. Am. Assn. Anatomists, Tissue Culture Assn. (chmn. Honor B. Fell div. 1973—), Am. Assn. Cancer Research, Am. Soc. Cell Biology (chmn. local com. nat. meeting New Orleans 1971), Am. Soc. Zoologists, Biol. Stain Commn. (trustee), Am. (chmn. local com. nat. meeting San Diego 1970, New Orleans 1971), German histochem. socs., A.A.A.S., La. Electron Microscope Soc., Sigma Xi. Contbr. articles to profl. jours. Home: 5718 Chatham Dr New Orleans LA 70122 Office: 1100 Florida Av New Orleans LA 70119

KASTL, FRANK JOHN, elec. engr.; b. Yukon, Okla., Apr. 11, 1918; s. John J. and Fannie (Policky) K.; B.S., Okla. State U., 1941; m. Helen L. Vrana, June 28, 1946; children—David Gene, John F., Steven Lynn, Kathy Sue, Ann Marie. With Southwestern Pub. Service Co., 1946-60; with U.S. Corp. Engrs., 1961; elec. engr. Bechtel Corp., 1962; lead engr. Boeing Aircraft, 1963; sr. facilities engr. Bur. Reclamation, Dept. Interior, 1963-64; project specialist U.S. Air Force, 1965-66, electronic engr., 1967-68; elec. engr. Bur. Indian Affairs, Dept. Interior, Anadarko, Okla., 1969-70; asst. chief engr. engr. VA Hosp., Oklahoma City, 1971—. Served to maj. AUS, 1941-46; ETO. Decorated six Bronze Star medals. Registered profl. engr., Tex., Okla. Home: 1512 Homeland St Norman OK 73069 Office: 921 NE 13th St Oklahoma City OK 73104

KASTNER, HAROLD HENRY, JR., state ofcl.; b. Paola, Fla., Jan. 4, 1928; s. Harold Henry and Essye (Sutton) K.; B.S. in Econs., Fla. State U., 1955, M.S. in Econs., 1958; Ed.D. in Jr. Coll. Adminstrn., U. Fla., 1962; m. Cecilia Ann Franklin, July 30, 1955; children—Kathryn Diane, Susan Claire, Harold Lawrence. Tchr., West Palm Beach (Fla.) High Sch., 1955-57; head social sci. div. St. John's River Jr. Coll., Palatka, Fla., 1958-60; cons. social studies, econs., resource-use edn. Fla. State Dept. Edn., Tallahassee, 1962-65; dean coll. Polk Jr. Coll., Winter Haven, 1965-69, v.p., 1967-69: asst. dir. div. community colls. Fla. Dept. Edn., Tallahassee, 1969—, mem. regulations com., 1971—; project dir. In-Service Tng. Workshops for Community Div. Chmn., Title V Elementary and Secondary Edn. Act, 1972-73; co-dir. Social Work Planning Research Project, Social and Rehab. Services div. Dept. Health, Edn. and Welfare, 1970-72. Adv. com. Southeastern Ednl. Lab., 1966-70, Fla. adv. com. Nat. Def. Edn. Act, Title III, 1965-68; cons. on disadvantaged So. Regional Edn. Bd., 1969-70, Community Coll.-Univ. Articulation Com., 1971-73; pres. Instructional Enterprize, Inc., 1969—. Exec. dir., dir. Fla. Council Econ. Edn., 1963-65; cons. Nat. Family Finance Workshop, Madison, Wis., 1964; chmn. social studies com. So. States Work Conf., Daytona Beach, Fla., 1965. Bd. dirs. Fla. State Dept. Edn. Credit Union, 1965. Served with AUS, 1950-53. U.S. Office Edn. research grantee, Kellogg fellow; Am. Legion Merit award and medal. Mem. Am. Econs. Assn., Fla. Council Social Studies, Fla. Tech. Edn. Assn., Nat. Council on Community Services, Am. Assn. Jr. Colls., Fla. Assn. Community Colls., Fla. Soc. Assn. Execs. (chmn. edn. com. 1965), Phi Kappa Phi, Phi Delta Kappa, Alpha Tau Omega. Contbr. numerous articles and dissertations to ednl. jours. Mem. editorial bd. Higher Edn. Collaborative Planning in Higher Edn. for Professions Monograph Series. Home: 1103 Sandhurst Dr Tallahassee FL 32303 Office: Fla Dept Edn Tallahassee FL 32301

KATHAN, WILLIAM KEITH, editor; b. Galveston, Tex., July 2, 1931; s. Kenneth Herbert and Anna Mae Reynolds (Thornton) K.; B.S. in Journalism, So. Methodist U., 1956; m. Sarah Marcella McBryde, June 20, 1958; 1 son, Kenneth James. Corr., United Press, New Orleans, 1956-57; courthouse reporter, gen. assignments Dallas Times Herald, 1957-60; film editor, writer WBAP-TV Tex. News, Fort Worth, 1960-62. editor Life Lines, Life Line Found., Washington, Dallas, 1962—. Served with USAF, 1948-52. Independent. Baptist. Office: 4330 N Central Expressway Dallas TX 75206

KATTAWAR, GEORGE WILLIFORD, educator; b. Beaumont, Tex., Aug. 10, 1937; s. Williford John and Lilly (Angelo) K.; B.S., Lamar U., 1959; M.S., Tex. A. and M. U., 1961, Ph.D., 1964; m. Euginia Louise Lee, Oct. 21, 1962; children—George Jeffrey, Gregory Williford, Karen Lee. Theoretical physicist Los Alamos Sci. Lab., 1963-64; research physicist Esso Prodn. Research Co., Houston. 1964-66; asst. prof. physics N. Tex. State U., 1966-68; asso. prof. physics Tex. A. and M. U., 1968-73, prof., 1973—. Vis. scientist S.W. Center Advanced Study, summers 1966-68; cons. Gen. Dynamics Corp., Naval Ammunition Depot. Grantee, NASA, Office Naval Research. Mem. Optical Soc. Am., Am. Astron. Soc., Sigma Xi. Mason. Contbr. articles to profl. jours. Home: Route 4 Box 829 Bryan TX 77801 Office: Tex A and M U College Station TX 77843

KATTERHENRY, ARNOLD ALLEN, civil engr.; b. New Knoxville, O., June 10, 1906; B.C.E., Ohio State U., 1928; M.S., U. Fla., 1956; m. Ann Sue Derrick, Dec. 22, 1934; children—Arnold Allen, John G. Civil engr. TVA, 1933-46; self-employed as engr., Chattanooga, 1946-48; asst. prof. civil engring. U. Fla., 1948-61; hwy. engr. Fed. Hwy. Adminstrn., Atlanta, 1961—. Registered profl. engr., Ga. Fellow Am. Soc. C.E. (chmn. nat. com. on engring. surveys 1962-66). Elk. Club: Puroga Investment (Atlanta). Home: 4536 E Brookhaven Dr NE Atlanta GA 30319 Office: 900 Peachtree St Atlanta GA 30309

KATTERJOHN, GEORGE WILLIAM, concrete products co. exec.; b. Paducah, Ky., Apr. 15, 1899; s. George William and Maude (Kelly) K.; student U. Ill., 1917-19; m. Merle Warner, Jan. 4, 1929; children—Ann (Mrs. William Jere Longshore), Merle (Mrs. Glen Jermstad), Georgia N. Owner, mgr. Katterjohn Bldg. Co., Paducah, Ky., 1957—, Katterjohn Concrete Co., Owensboro, Ky., 1946—, Katterjohn Concrete Products, Little Rock, 1952—. Mem. Paducah-McCracken County Airport Commn., 1946-73. Bd. dirs. U. Ill. Found. Served with Armed Forces, World War I. Mem. Beta Theta Pi. Mason. Clubs: Elks, Paducah Country. Home: 40th and Pines Rd Paducah KY 42001 Office: Katterjohn Bldg 1500 Broadway Paducah KY 42001

KATTUS, JAMES ROBERT, metallurgist; b. Cin., Aug. 25, 1922; s. Albert A. and Matilda (Gerling) K.; B.S., Purdue U., 1944; m. Josephine Bremer, Mar. 2, 1946; children—Josephine, Robert, Sandra, Laura, Patricia. Research metallurgist Naval Reserach Lab., Washington, 1944-46; chief metallurgist Anderson Electric Corp., Birmingham, Ala., 1947-52; dir. metall. research So. Research Inst., 1952-66; gen. mgr. Bethea Co., Inc., Birmingham, 1966-68; consulting metallurgist, Birmingham, 1968—. Bd. dirs. St. Vincent Sch. of Nursing, Birmingham. Served with USNR, 1943-46. Mem. Am. Soc. for Metals, Am. Soc. for Testing and Materials, Am. Inst. Mining and Metall. Engrs. Contbr. articles to profl. jours. Patentee in field. Home and office: 112 Azalea Rd Birmingham AL 35213

KATZ, CATHERINE MONNIER MINOCK WILFERT (MRS. SAMUEL LAWRENCE KATZ), physician, educator; b. Inglewood, Cal., July 26, 1936; d. Daniel Francis and Betty (Cronemiller) Minock; B.A. cum laude, Stanford, 1958; M.D. cum laude, Harvard, 1962; m. James Norris Wilfert, Dec. 29, 1962 (div. Nov. 1969); children—Rachel Ann, Catherine Claiborne; m. 2d, Samuel Lawrence Katz, July 23, 1971. Intern medicine Boston City Hosp., 1962-63; resident in pediatrics Bowman Gray Sch. Medicine, N.C. Bapt. Hosp., Winston-Salem, 1963-64; resident in pediatrics Children's Hosp., Boston, 1964-65, post-doctoral fellow infectious diseases, 1965-67; practice medicine specializing in pediatrics Boston, 1965-69, Durham, N.C., 1969-72; clin. asso. Beth Israel Hosp., Boston, instr. pediatrics Harvard Med. Sch., 1967-69; asst. prof. pediatrics Duke, 1969—, asst. prof. microbiology, 1971—; cons. Watts Hosp., Durham, 1969—. Mem. Am. Acad. Pediatrics, N.C. Pediatric Soc. Home: Rt2 Piney Mountain Rd Chapel Hill NC 27514

KATZ, ELI GERALD, hosp. engr.; b. Newark, Jan. 6, 1935; s. Solomon and Zelda (Girion) K.; B.S. in Civil Engring., Newark Coll. Engring., 1956; m. Phyllis Harriet Steiner, Feb. 28, 1960; children—Heidi, Linda, Daniel. Asst. chief engr. VA Hosp., Phila., 1962; owner, operator Anesthetizing Location Inspection Service, Inc., Summit, N.J., 1962—; dir. engring. N.Y. Med. Coll., N.Y.C., 1965-67; resident engr. Kennedy Community Hosp., Edison, N.J., 1967; adminstrv. engr. Mt. Sinai Med. Center, Miami Beach, Fla., 1967—. Sec. com. on safe use of electricity in hosps. Nat. Fire Protection Assn., 1971—; mem. Dade County (Fla.) Bd. Rules and Appeals for Safety and Fire Prevention, 1969—. Served to lt. (j.g.) USNR, 1956-59. Registered profl. engr., Fla. N.J. Mem. Am. Soc. Hosp. Engrs., Nat. Soc. Profl. Engrs. Fla. Engring. Soc., Pi Delta Epsilon, Chi Epsilon. Jewish religion. Home: 2160 NE 207th St North Miami Beach FL 33162 Office: 4300 Alton Rd Miami Beach FL 33140

KATZ, HERBERT MARVIN, educator; b. Bklyn., Apr. 4, 1926; s. Abraham and Edna (Goldstein) K.; B.Ch.E., Coll., City N.Y., 1949; M.S., U. Cin., 1949, Ph.D., 1953; m. Evelyn Greene, July 1, 1954; children—Susan, Joel. Asst. chem. engr. Argonne (Ill.) Nat. Lab., 1954-56; chem. engr. Brookhaven Nat. Lab., Upton, N.Y., 1957-66; prof., chmn. chem. engring. Howard U., Washington 1968—. Treas., Human Relations Com. Eastern Suffolk County, N.Y., 1964-65, Alliance for Democratic Reform, Montgomery County, Md., 1969-70. Served with AUS, 1944-46. Mem. Am. Inst. Chem. Engrs., Am. Chem. Soc., Sigma Xi. Patentee in field. Home: 1602 Sherwood Rd Silver Spring MD 20902 Office: Dept Chem Engring Howard U Washington DC 20001

KATZ, MICHAEL, garment mfr.; b. Kolki, Poland, Nov. 23, 1923; s. Moshe and Chasie (Upstein) K.; B.S., Warsaw (Poland) Poly. U., 1952, M.S., 1960; m. Jan. 20, 1959 (div.); 1 son, Mitchel. Came to U.S., 1966, naturalized, 1973. Structural designer, architect, engr., cons. engr., 1952-66; with Farkas & Barron Cons. Co., N.Y.C., 1966-67; designer, v.p., gen. mgr. Marlene, Inc., Nashville, 1967—. Ky. col.; named hon. citizen Russell Springs, Ky., 1970. Home: 6001 Old Hickory Blvd Hermitage TN 37076 Office: Marlene Inc Hartsville TN 37074

KATZ, MORT, psychiat. social worker; b. Bklyn., May 27, 1925; s. Morris and Sophie (Guttman) K.; B.A., Sarah Lawrence Coll., June, 1949; M.S.S.W. Columbia, 1951; m. Ellen Loeb, July 18, 1964. Psychiat. social worker Hillside (N.Y.) Hosp., 1951-53; import agt. B. Sessler Co., N.Y.C., 1953-57; founder Consol. Helicopters, 1959-62; psychiat. social worker Dallas State Mental Health Clinic, 1962-69; pvt. practice family therapy, Dallas, 1969—. Cons. Center Hosp. Alcoholism, 1972-74. Served with AUS, 1943-46; PTO. Fellow Am. Orthopsychiat. Assn.; mem. Family Therapy Assn. of Tex. (pres. 1969-70), Dallas Group Therapy Soc., Acad. Certified Social Workers, Leukemia Soc. Dallas (sec. 1968-69). Author: Marriage Survival Kit, 1972. Home: 4318 Briar Creek Lane Dallas TX 75214 Office: 2930 Turtle Creek Pl Dallas TX 75219

KATZ, SAMUEL LAWRENCE, educator, physician; b. Manchester, N.H., May 29, 1927; s. Morris and Ethel (Lawrence) K.; A.B. magna cum laude, Dartmouth, 1948; M.D. cum laude, Harvard, 1952; m. Betsy Jane Cohan, June 27, 1950; children—Samuel Lawrence, John L., David L., Deborah Susan, William L., Susan Johanna, Penelope Jennifer; m. 2d, Catherine Minock Wilfert, July 23, 1971. Intern, Beth Israel Hosp., Boston, 1952-53, resident, 1952-53; resident Children's Hosp. Boston, 1953-54, 55-56, Mass. Gen. Hosp., 1954-55; research fellow to asst. prof. Harvard Med. Sch., 1958-68; prof., chmn. dept. Duke Med. Sch., 1968—, Wilburt C. Davison prof., 1972—; research virology, virus vaccines, immunization NIH, Am. Acad. Pediatrics, FDA, Macy Found., Nat Jewish Hosp. (Denver), Multiple Sclerosis Soc., Harvard Med. Alumni Council. Served with USNR, 1945-46. Nat. Found. fellow, 1956-58. Mem. Am. Soc. Clin. Investigation, Soc. Pediatric Research, Am., New Eng. pediatric socs., Infectious Diseases Soc. Am., Am. Assn. Immunologists, Am. Acad. Pediatrics. Contbr. to books, articles to profl. jours. Developer (with John F. Enders) attenuated live measles-virus vaccine. Home: Route 2 Piney Mountain Rd Chapel Hill NC 27514 Office: Duke Med Center Durham NC 27710

KATZ, STANLEY IVAN, retail trade exec.; b. Detroit, Aug. 2, 1931; s. Harry Leo and Netta (Petchon) K.; student Duke, 1949-51; B.A., Franklin and Marshall Coll., 1953; m. Barbara Haworth, Aug. 12, 1959 (div. Sept. 1966); children—Kathy Rachael, Elizabeth Sarah. With Hartley's Inc., Miami, Fla., 1956—, buyer sportswear, 1958-68, v.p., 1969—. Served with M.I., AUS, 1953-56. Mem. South Fla. Franklin and Marshall Coll. Alumni Assn. (pres. 1973), Pi Lambda Phi. Club: Miami Downtown Optimists (pres. 1960-61). Home: Dinner Key Marina Miami FL 33100 Office: 205 Northside Plaza Miami FL 33147

KATZEN, SALLY, lawyer; b. Pitts., Nov. 22, 1942; d. Nathan and Hilda (Schwartz) Katzen; B.A. magna cum laude, Smith Coll., 1964; J.D. magna cum laude, U. Mich., 1967. Congl. intern Senat Subcom. on Constl. Rights, Washington, summer 1963; legal research asst. civil rights div. Dept. Justice, Washington, summer 1965; law clk. U.S. Ct. Appeals, Washington, 1967-68; admitted to D.C. bar, 1968, U.S. Supreme Ct. bar, 1971; asso. firm Wilmer, Cutler & Pickering, Washington, 1968—. Mem. Bar Assn. D.C., Washington Council Lawyers, Women's Legal Def. Fund, Am. Civil Liberties Union, Order of Coif. Editor-in-chief U. Mich. Law Rev., 1966-67. Home: 1246 27th St NW Washington DC 20007 Office: 900 17th St NW Washington DC 20006

KATZENTINE, UCOLA COLLIER (MRS. ARTHUR F. KATZENTINE), radio sta. exec.; b. Tonkawa, Okla., Aug 2, 1905; d. Clyde and Lula (Wills) Collier; student Central Mo. State Coll., 1923-25.; m. Arthur Frank Katzentine, June 11, 1928. Vice pres., dir. womens program Sta. WKAT. Miami Beach, Fla., 1937-42, v.p., mng. dir., 1942-46, pres., owner, 1960—. Mem. Sigma Sigma Sigma. Democrat. Roman Catholic. Clubs: Surf (Miami Beach); Palm Bay (Miami, Fla.); Army and Navy (Washington). Home: 4745 Pine Tree Dr Miami Beach FL 33140 Office: 1759 Bay Rd Miami Beach FL 33139

KATZIN, MORDICAI, optometrist; b. Winston-Salem, N.C., Dec. 22, 1923; s. Samuel Leazer and Hettie (Vosk) K.; D.Optometry, Pa. Coll. Optometry, 1944; m. June Rubenstein, Dec. 28, 1947; children—Marcy, David. Pvt. practice optometry, Winston-Salem, 1945-47, Jacksonville, N.C., 1948—. Lectr. So. Council Optometry, Middle Atlantic Optometric Conf., N.C. Optometric Soc. Mem. exec. council Jacksonville U.S.O., 1953—; pres. Onslow County Tb Assn., 1955-64; mem. profl. adv. com. State Commn. for Blind, 1969-70; mem. N.C. Commn. for Blind, 1970—. Chmn. Jacksonville Planning and Zoning Bd., 1967; dir. Civil Def., Jacksonville and Onslow County, 1960-65. Mem. Am. Optometric Assn., Am. Acad. Optometry, So. Council Optometry, N.C. Optometric Soc. (pres. 1963-64), Beta Sigma Kappa. Kiwanian (pres. 1966); mem. B'nai B'rith. Research soft contact lenses. Home: 4 Park Pl Jacksonville NC 28540 Office: 200 Doctors Dr Suite K Jacksonville NC 28540

KAUDER, EMIL LEOPOLD FERDINAND CHRISTOPHER, economist; b. Berlin, Germany, June 23, 1901 (came to U.S., 1938, naturalized 1945); s. Hugo and Ernestine (Freifräulein von Feilen) K.; Ph.D., U. Berlin, 1924; m. Helene I. Riegner, July 11, 1943; children—Eunice, Henry Hugh. Expert on custom duties German textile industry, 1928-38; fgn. lang. tchr. Am. prep. schs., 1938-46; prof. econs. various Am. univs. and colls., 1947-68; research worker Hitotsubachi U., Kunitachi, Japan, 1960-61; prof. emeritus, distinguished lectr. U. South Fla., Tampa, 1968—. Served with German Army, 1921. Invited as speaker at centenary of Menger's Principles of Economics, 1971 by U. Vienna and Austrian Republic. Republican. Episcopalian. Author: History of Marginal Utility, 1966. Contbr. articles to profl. jours. Home: 6761 22d Way S St Petersburg FL 33712

KAUFMAN, HARRY, mfg. co. exec.; b. Zhitomir, Russia, May 31, 1918; s. Benjamin and Sarah (Zanon) K.; came to U.S., 1923, naturalized, 1928; student Cooper Union High Sch. Engring., 1938-40; m. Ida Solotar, Jan. 23, 1945; children—Susan Lynn, Lawrence Gordon. Tool and gage maker N.Y. Thread Grinding Co., N.Y.C., 1938-41; prodn. design engr. Paragon Design & Devel. Co., N.Y.C., 1941-44; chief tool engr. J.A. Maurer Co., N.Y.C., 1944-46; founder, chmn. OK Machine & Tool Corp., Bronx, 1946—; dir. Quadri Corp., Pheonix. Bd. dirs. Bayberry Community Assn., New Rochelle, N.Y., 1964-67. Mem. Am. Soc. Tool and Mfrs. Engrs. (sr.). Patentee in telecommunication and electronic tools and devices. Home: 5709 White Hickory Circle Tamarac FL 33313 Office: 3455 Conner St New York City NY 10475

KAUFMAN, HERBERT E., physician, ophthalmologist; b. N.Y.C., Sept. 28, 1931; s. Benjamin and Claire (Krinsky) K.; grad. Peddie Sch., Heightstown, N.J., 1948; A.B., Princeton, 1952; M.D. magna cum laude, Harvard, 1956; m. Eleanor Rosenblum, June 30, 1957; children—Stephen, Joshua, Claire. Intern, 1956-57; clin. asso. in both clin. ophthalmology and research NIH, 1957-59; trainee Mass. Eye and Ear Infirmary, Boston, 1959-62, also head Uveitis Lab.; asso. prof., chief ophthalmology U. Fla., Gainesville, 1962-64, prof., chmn. dept. ophthalmology, prof. pharmacology, 1964—, acting dean Coll. Medicine, 1972—. Bd. dirs. N. Fla. Eye Bank; trustee Assn. for Research in Ophthalmology. Named one of the Ten Outstanding Young Men in Am., Jaycees, 1968; recipient Humanitarian award Lions Internat., 1968. Editor, Jour. Investigative Ophthalmology. Contbr. med. research papers to profl. jours. Office: Dept Ophthalmology Univ Fla Coll Medicine Gainesville FL 32610

KAUFMAN, JACK HAMMER, lawyer; b. San Antonio, Dec. 15, 1925; s. Leon Brown and Karleen Wilma (Hammer) K.; B.B.A., U. Tex., 1950, J.D., 1951; m. Estelle Lieberman, June 18, 1950; children—William Thomas, Karleen Pearl, Nancy Ann. Admitted to Tex. bar, 1951, U.S. Supreme Ct. bar, 1965; asst. dist. atty. Bexar County, San Antonio, 1951-55; practice law, San Antonio, 1955—. Dir., Northside Bank, San Antonio. Councilman, City of San Antonio, 1961-65; trustee San Antonio Waterworks Bd., 1966-73, chmn., 1972-73. Served with USAAF, 1944-45. Mem. San Antonio, Tex., Am. bar assns., Zeta Beta Tau. Jewish religion (trustee temple 1955—, pres. 1967-69). Kiwanian. Home: 8104 Countryside Dr San Antonio TX 78209 Office: 900 Alamo National Bldg San Antonio TX 78205

KAUFMAN, STANFORD MORTON, lawyer; b. Dallas, Jan. 5, 1945; s. Harold M. and Wanda G. (Young) K.; B.B.A., So. Meth. U., 1967 J.D., 1970; m. Martha Sue Kershenbaum, Aug. 21. 1971. Tax staff Touche Ross & Co., Dallas, 1967-71; admitted to Tex. bar, 1971; practiced in El Paso, 1971—; asso. firm Goodman, Hallmark & Akerd, 1971—. C.P.A., Tex. Mem. Am., Tex., El Paso bar assns., El Paso Tax Inst. (mem. com. 1973), Tex. Soc. C.P.A.'s. Mem. B'nai B'rith (sec. 1973—). Home: 6241 Twilight El Paso TX 79912 Office: E Mo Bldg TX 79901

KAUFMAN, WILLIAM HENRY, physician; b. Balt., Jan. 6, 1913; s. Henry and Helen (Boucher) K.; B.A., Johns Hopkins, 1934; M.D., Duke 1937; M.S., U. Va., 1947; m. Beth Pearse, May 27, 1939; children—John Pearse, Elizabeth, Richard Boucher. Intern. asst. resident in medicine Duke U. Hosp., 1937-39; asst. resident in dermatology U. Va. Hosp., 1939-41, resident, fellow in dermatology, 1945-47; pvt. practice dermatology, Roanoke, Va., 1947—; dermatologist community and regional hosps.; vis. dermatologist out-patient dept., clin. asso. prof. dermatology U. Va., 1965—; cons. U.S. Vets. Hosp. Served from 1st lt. to maj. M.C., USAAF, 1941-45, ETO, Panama Canal Zone. Fellow A.C.P., Am. Acad. Dermatology; mem. A.M.A., Med. Soc. Va., So. Med. Assn., Va. (pres. 1965-67), Washington dermatol. socs., Roanoke Acad. Medicine (pres. 1959-60), Sigma Xi. Episcopalian. Clubs: Roanoke Country (Roanoke). Editorial bd. Va. Med. Monthly. Home: 2511 Cornwallis Av Roanoke VA 24014 Office: 127 McClanahan St Roanoke VA 24014

KAUFMANN, FRANK SALOMON, paper box co. exec.; b. Mannheim, Germany, Mar. 26, 1911; s. David and Sofie (Hausmann) K.; B.B.A., U. Heidelberg (Germany), 1931, M.B.A., 1932, Dr.Ec., 1933; m. Liese B. Herzog, Dec. 23, 1935; 1 dau., Rita Jane. Came to U.S., 1939, naturalized, 1945. Trained in papermaking and carton mfr. in Germany; mgr., partner Kartonagen Fabrik Kaufmann & Co., Germany, 1935-38; in def. work in U.S., 1939-45; prodn. mgr. Spear Box Co., N.Y.C., 1945-50; sales service and scheduling mgr. Mead Corp. div. Mead Packaging, Inc., Atlanta, 1950-52, dir. purchases and central planning, 1952-59, dir. fgn. market devel., 1960-61; dir. internat. markets Mead S.A. subsidiary Mead Corp., Zug, Switzerland, 1961-63; dir. marketing services Mead Packaging Internat., Inc., 1964-68, asst. v.p. marketing, 1968—; dir. information center Mead Packaging Div., 1969—; asso. prof. Internat. Inst., Ga. State U., 1970—. Mem. Ga. Internat. Trade Assn. (pres.), Zionist Orgn. Am. (dir.), Delta Sigma Pi. Jewish religion. Mem. B'nai B'rith; Mason. Home: 1270 W Peachtree St NW Atlanta GA 30309 Office: Mead Packaging PO Box 4417 Atlanta GA 30302

KAUFMANN, JAMES ARON, physician; b. Detroit, Dec. 15, 1923; s. Adolph and Dena (Lieberman) K.; student Vanderbilt U., 1942-44; M.D., U. Tenn., 1947; m. Jane Monness Lippman, Dec. 27, 1951; children—Nancy Hope, Robert Scott. Intern, Emory U., Grady Meml. Hosp., 1947-48; resident Pratt Diagnostic Hosp., Boston, 1949-50, Louisville Gen. Hosp., 1950-51; practice medicine, specializing in internal medicine, Atlanta, 1952—; mem. staff Grady Meml. Hosp., Crawford W. Long Hosp., St. Joseph Infirmary; clin. research fellow in pharmacology Emory U. Sch. Medicine, 1948-49, instr. medicine, 1952-57, asso. in medicine, 1958—. Mem. gov. bd. Fulton County Heart Council, 1958-64; mem. med. adv. bd. Atlanta Tb Assn., 1953, bd. dirs., 1966—; cons. in medicine South Fulton Hosp., 1963—; U.S. rep. Internat. Com. on Clin. Cardiovascular Disease, Vienna, Austria, 1960; co-dir. med. program Ga. State Legislature, 1970—; bd. dirs. Civic Theater, 1970—; regent Anti-Defamation League, 1968—; patron's soc. Crawford W. Long Meml. Hosp., Atlanta, 1970—; chmn. State Com. on Quackery, 1970—. Exec. com. governing bd., steering com. Fulton County Democratic Party, 1966—. Chmn. bd. trustees Kaufmann Found. Diplomate Am. Bd. Internal Medicine. Fellow A.C.P.; mem. A.M.A., Ga., So., Fulton County (chmn. standing com. on pub. policy and legislative com. 1966—, chmn. council govtl. affairs 1970—) med. assns., Am. Coll. Chest Physicians, Am., Ga. trudeau socs., Am. Ga. heart assns., Am., Ga. diabetes assns., Am. Geriatrics Soc., Am. Coll. Cardiology, Am. Gerontol. Soc., Am. Coll. Angiology, Am. Soc. Internal Medicine, Am. Thoracic Soc. Mem. B'nai B'rith (pres.

1964-65). Contbr. articles to profl. jours. Home: 3635N Stratford Rd NE Atlanta GA 30305 Office: 950 W Peachtree St NW Atlanta GA 30309

KAVANAGH, ROGER PIERCE, JR., constrn. co. exec.; b. Greenwich, Conn., Aug. 27, 1917; s. Roger Pierce and Eleanor (Geffem) K.; student Princeton, 1936-38; m. Jeanette Rusovich, June 5, 1943; children—Basil John, Roger Pierce III. Mgr., N.M. Timber Co., 1938-40; salesman Am. Houses, Inc., N.Y.C., 1945-53; pres. Kavanagh, Smith & Co., Greensboro, N.C., 1953-66; pres. Westminster Co., Greensboro, 1967—; dir. N.C. Nat. Bank. Mem. N.C. Conservation and Devel. Bd., 1960-64; state chmn. Radio Free Europe, 1966. Served with Ordnance Dept., AUS, 1941-45. Decorated Bronze Star. Mem. Nat. Assn. Home Builders, Greensboro C. of C. (past dir.). Home: 605 Sunset Dr Greensboro NC 27408 Office: 200 W Wendover St Greensboro NC 27405

KAY, DAVID CYRIL, psychiatrist; b. Sault Ste. Marie, Mich., Sept. 5, 1932; s. James Martin and Helen Elizabeth (Dixon) K.; B.S., Wheaton (Ill.) Coll., 1954; M.D., U. Ill., Chgo., 1958; m. Carla Kay Kunkel, Dec. 27, 1961; children—David Carl, James Andrew, Rachel Elizabeth, Thomas Milton. Intern, Presbyn.-St. Lukes Hosp., Chgo., 1958-59; resident psychiatrist Ill. State Psychiat. Inst., Chgo., 1961-64; staff physician USPHS Hosp., Ft. Worth, 1959-61; staff psychiatrist Nat. Inst. Mental Health Clin. Research Center, Lexington, Ky., 1964-66, staff physician Addiction Research Center, 1964-66, chief exptl. psychiatry unit, 1966-69, chief exptl. psychiatry sect., 1969—; clin. asso. prof. dept. psychiatry U. Ky. Med. Sch. Pres., Valley Civic Assn., Lexington, 1972-73; mem. Citizens Adv. Commn. on Planning and Zoning, 1972-73. Nat. Inst. Mental Health Career Devel. Program fellow, 1961-66. Diplomate Am. Bd. Psychiatry and Neurology. Mem. Internat. Brain Research Orgn., Soc. for Neurosci., Am. Soc. Pharmacology and Exptl. Therapeutics, Am. Psychiat. Assn., Am. Soc. Clin. Pharmacology and Therapeutics, A.M.A., N.Y. Acad. Sci., A.A.A.S., Christian Med. Soc., Assn. for Psychophysiol. Study Sleep. Republican. Home: 136 Westgate Dr Lexington KY 40504 Office: Nat Inst Drug Abuse Addiction Research Center Lexington KY 40507

KAY, MICHAEL BOYCE, lawyer; b. Memphis, Jan. 27, 1944; s. William Albert and Mary Josephine (Ray) K.; B.S., Memphis State U., 1966, J.D., 1968; m. Sharon Lee Doughty, Sept. 3, 1966 (div. Nov. 1972); 1 dau., Priscilla Anne. Admitted to Tenn. bar, 1968; mem. firm Ratner, Sugarmon & Lucas, Memphis, 1968—. Pres., Spring Creek Devel. Co., Inc., Memphis, 1969—. Mem. Am. Judicature Soc., Tenn., Am. bar assns., Delta Theta Phi. Club: Summit. Asso. editor Memphis State U. Law Rev., 1967-68. Home: 1768 Trezevant St Memphis TN 38114 Office: 525 Commerce Title Bldg Memphis TN 38103

KAY, SAUL, pathologist; b. N.Y.C., Feb. 13, 1914; s. Wolf and Rose (Savitzky) Kossovsky; B.A., N.Y. U., 1936; M.D., N.Y. Med. Coll., 1939; m. Grace Calef, Aug. 31, 1940; 1 dau., Deborah. Intern, Harlem Hosp., N.Y.C., 1939-41; resident Fordham Hosp., 1941-42, N.Y. Postgrad. Med. Sch. and Hosp., 1946-48, Columbia Presbyn. Med. Center, 1948-50; practice medicine specializing in pathology, Richmond, Va., 1950—; prof., chmn. dept. surg. pathology Med. Coll. Va., 1952—. Served to maj. AUS, 1942-45. Decorated Bronze Star medal. Mem. Coll. Am. Pathology, Va. Acad. Sci., Richmond Acad. Medicine, Am. Soc. Clin. Pathology, Internat. Acad. Pathology, Am. Assn. Pathology and Bacteriology, Am. Soc. Cytology, A.M.A. Va. Path. Soc. Home: 322 Charmian Rd Richmond VA 23226 Office: Med Coll Va Richmond VA 23298

KAYE, CARMEN JIMENEZ (MRS. SIDNEY KAYE), physician; b. Loiza, P.R., Apr. 18, 1918; d. Julio and Elvira (Calzada) Jimenez; B.S., U. P.R., 1938; M.P.H., U. Mich., 1945; M.D., Med. Coll. Va., 1952; m. Sidney Kaye, June 7, 1951; children—Cynthia Susan, Frederic Joseph. Intern, Med. Coll. Va. Hosp., Richmond, 1952-53; resident VA Hosp., Richmond, 1953-54; physician outpatient dept. Med. Coll. Va., 1956-59; clin. investigator A.H. Robins Co., Richmond, 1959-62; dir. geriatrics program Mental Health Program P.R., Rio Piedras, 1964—. Instr. gerontology U. P.R. Sch. Pub. Health 1969—. Pres. bd. dirs. Junta de Servicios a Ciudadanos de Mayor Edad, Inc., 1972—. Fellow Am. Geriatrics Soc.; mem. Am. Gerontological Assn., Alpha Omega Alpha. Home: 116 Lilas Urb Santa Maria Rio Piedras PR 00927 Office: Psychiat Hosp Rio Piedras PR 00927

KAYE, HOWARD, cons. polymer chemist; b. N.Y.C., Dec. 9, 1938; s. Louis and Beatrice (Schwarz) K.; B.S., Poly. Inst. Bklyn., 1960, Ph.D., 1965; m. Lilian Gausboel, Dec. 27, 1966; children—Elizabeth Helen, Richard John. Research chemist Franklin Inst., Phila., summer 1960; NIH postdoctoral fellow U. Cambridge (Eng.), 1965-67; prof. chemistry Tex. A. and M. U., 1967-73; pres. Howard Kaye & Assos., Houston, 1973—. NSF grantee, 1970-72, Robert Welch grantee, 1970, petroleum research grantee Am. Chem. Soc., 1967-69. Mem. Am. Chem. Soc. (chmn. Southeastern Tex. polymer group 1972), Chem. Soc. London, Biophys. Soc., A.A.A.S., Am. Assn. Univ. Profs., Sigma Xi, Phi Lambda Upsilon. Contbr. articles to profl. jours. Patentee in field; inventor polyvinyl purines and pyrimidines. Home and office: PO Box 39086 Houston TX 77034

KAYE, JOHN, educator; b. Fort Herkimer, N.Y., July 1, 1915; s. Stephen and Eva (Plesnik) K.; B.S. in Mech. Engring., Cal. Inst. Tech., 1939, M.S., 1948; m. Isabelle Gonzales, Aug. 13, 1949; 1 dau., Lynne. Research engr. Cal. Inst. Tech., Pasadena, 1945-50; faculty dept. mech. engring. George Washington U., Washington, 1950—, asso. prof., 1953-68, prof. engring., applied sci., 1968—. Expert engring. economy UNESCO, Lima, Peru, 1966-68. Registered profl. engr., Cal. Fellow A.A.A.S.; mem. Am. Soc. M.E., Am. Soc. Engring. Edn., Operations Research Soc. Am., Inst. Mgmt. Scis., Am. Assn. U. Profs. Clubs: George Washington University (Washington), Lake of Woods (Va.) Country. Office: George Washington U Washington DC 20006

KAYE, KENNETH CHARLES, lawyer; b. Houston, Sept. 15, 1942; s. Walter R. and Margaret (Schoning) K.; B.A., Ohio Wesleyan U., 1964; LL.B., U. Tex., 1968; m. Patsy Jane Hays, Aug. 7, 1971. Admitted to Tex. bar, 1968, since practiced in Dickinson and League City, Tex.; asso. Hancock, Bellard & Gay, 1968-70; partner Hancock, Bellard, Gay & Kaye, 1971-73; pvt. practice law, League City, 1973—. Mem. Am., Tex., Galveston, Mainland, Galveston Jr. (treas., v.p.) bar assns., Alpha Tau Omega. Home: 4115 Manorfield Dr Seabrook TX 77586 Office: 913 W Main League City TX 77573

KAYE, ROBERT ADOLPH, govt. ofcl.; b. La Moure, N.D., Aug. 30, 1921; student N.D. Agrl. Coll., 1940-41; A.A., George Washington U., 1947, A.B., 1948, A.M., 1950, D.B.A., 1961; m. Margaret Eck Myklebust, July 22, 1945; children—Robert Michael, Margaret Lynne. Engring. aid Pub. Roads Administrn., Alaska Hwy., 1942-44, Inter-Am. Hwy., Nicaragua, 1944-45; transp. specialist Bur. Pub. Roads, Washington, 1945-57; chief traffic mgmt. br. U.S. AEC, Washington, 1957-70; dir. Bur. Motor Carrier Safety, Fed. Hwy. Adminstrn., Dept. Transp., 1970—. Professorial lectr. bus. adminstrn. George Washington U., 1953—; nat. co-chmn. Nat. Transp. Week, 1967. Active Bel-Air Civic Assn. Chmn. bd. dirs. Bur. Pub. Roads Fed. Credit Union, 1954; dir. Asso. Traffic Clubs Am., 1967—. Recipient William A. Jump Meml. Found. award, 1956, superior performance award, AEC, 1959. Mem. Gen. Alumni Assn. George Washington (governing bd. 1968-70), Nat. Def. Transp. Assn., Alpha Kappa Psi, Artus, Delta Nu Alpha. Club: Traffic (pres. 1967-68, dir. 1968-69) (Washington). Contbr. articles to profl. jours. Home: 4420 Stark Pl Annandale VA 22003 Office: DOT Hdqrs Bldg Washington DC 20591

KAYE, SAMUEL HARVEY, architect; b. Columbia, S.C., Sept. 27, 1940; s. James B. and Mary Louise (Harvey) K.; B.Arch., Auburn U., 1963; m. Patsy Cummings, June 27, 1964; children—Kimbellee Cummings, Elizabeth Harvey, Mary Catherine. With Yeates & Gaskill, Architects, Memphis, 1965-68; architect Walk Jones & Francis Mah, Inc., Memphis, 1968-73, Samuel H. Kaye, Architect, Columbus, Miss., 1974—; sec.-treas. Kaye Coca-Cola Bottling Co. Bd. dirs. Community Design Center of Memphis. Served with AUS, 1963-65. Mem. A.I.A. (dir. Memphis chpt.). Rotarian. Constrn. Specifications Inst. Important works include St. Jude Children's Research Hosp. Addition, First Nat. Bank Operations Center. Home: 424 7th St S Columbus MS 39701 Office: 201 McGahey Bldg Columbus MS 39701

KAYLER, EDWIN MORELAND, indsl. relations exec.; b. Copperhill, Tenn., June 18, 1907; s. Samuel J. and Lorena (Moreland) K.; student U. Tenn., 1926-29, U. Chattanooga, 1941; m. Lora Helen Jones, July 3, 1934; children—James Edwin, Julia Ann (Mrs. Robert Calvin Haynes), Lora Elizabeth. Prodn. mgr., corp. sec. Am. Mfg. Co., Chattanooga, 1936-47; personnel dir. Chattanooga Box & Lumber Co., 1947-68, Gilman Paint & Varnish Co., 1968—. Dir., coordinator Mgmt. Devel. Inst., U. Tenn. at Chattanooga, 1960—; tchr. self improvement subjects McKenzie Sch. and Chattanooga Pub. Schs., 1956—. Mem. Chattanooga Indsl. Personnel Club (chpt. dir. 1967, pres. 1959), Soc. for Advancement Mgmt. (v.p. 1971). Baptist. Mason, Lion (pres. Red Bank, Tenn. 1944-45, dist. gov. 1946-47). Home: 4703 Florida Av Chattanooga TN 37409 Office: 216 W 8th St Chattanooga TN 37401

KAYLOR, HOYT MCCOY, educator; b. Alexander City, Ala., Aug. 17, 1923; s. Jesse Daniel and Elsie (Hanson) K.; B.S., Birmingham So. Coll., 1943; M.S., U. Tenn., 1949, Ph.D., 1953; m. Frances McKinnon, July 21, 1957; 1 dau., Leigh Ann. Faculty dept. physics and astronomy Birmingham (Ala.) So. Coll., 1952—, asso. prof., 1958—, chmn. dept., 1952—. Research asso. U. Fla., summer 1965. Served with USNR, 1944-46. Mem. Ala. Acad. Sci. (treas.), Am. Phys. Soc., Optical Soc. Am., Sigma Xi, Alpha Tau Omega. Methodist. Home: 939 9th Court W Birmingham AL 35204

KAYS, KEITH SEVIER, architect; b. Memphis, Nov. 5, 1941; s. Harold and Helen (Holtzschue) K.; B.Arch., Auburn U., 1966; m. Jacqueline Lee Wood, July 8, 1967; children—Jennifer Lee, Theodore Wood. Designer William W. Bond Jr. & Assos., Architects, Memphis, 1962-67; instr. Memphis State U., 1966-68; partner-in charge design Walk Jones & Francis Mah, Inc., Memphis, 1967-71; owner, prin. architect Keith S. Kays, Architecture/Planning, Memphis, 1971-74, Keith Kays & Assos., 1974—. Mem. project area com. tech. adv. Kansas Street Urban Renewal, 1968-73; chmn. Service and Social Conditions Com., Memphis, 1970. Bd. dirs. Family Service of Memphis, Runaway House. Recipient Alabam Gas Corp. scholarship, 1965. Mem. A.I.A. (mem. publs. com. 1967-70, chmn. Memphis Community design center, 1968-72), Tenn. Soc. Architects, Constrn. Specifications Inst., Sigma Alpha Epsilon. Clubs: University, Summit, Tennessee, Wolf River Soc. Home: 1437 Carr Av Memphis TN 38104 Office: Upper 83 Madison Av Memphis TN 38103

KAYSER, EDGAR WILLIAM, JR., ins. exec., civic leader; b. El Paso, Tex., Apr. 30, 1913; s. Edgar William and Gladys (Dyer) K.; grad. Wharton Sch. U. Pa.; m. Patricia Patterson, Feb. 5, 1972; children—Edgar William III, John Douglas. Ins. exec.; past chmn. El Paso Estate Planning Council. Pres. Southwestern Sun Carnival Assn., 1969; chmn. fund com. Hotel Dieu, YWCA; chmn. finance com. El Paso Symphony Orch. Assn. Alderman, El Paso City Council, 1947-51; campaign mgr. mayoral campaigns. Bd. dirs. A.R.C., 1951—, Child Welfare Bd., 1953-61, United Fund, 1960-61. Served with USNR, 1941-45; PTO. Mem. El Paso Assn. Life Underwriters (pres. 1960, Man of Year 1967), Gen. Agts. and Mgrs. Assn. (pres. chpt.), Navy League U.S. (pres. 1965-66), El Paso C. of C. (past dir., chmn. Armed Forces com.), Sigma Chi. Episcopalian (vestryman). Kiwanian (pres. 1962-63, dir. 1964). Clubs: International (pres. 1964); Los Caballeros; El Paso Country. Home: 920 Blanchard St El Paso TX 79902 Office: 1212 State Nat Plaza El Paso TX 79901

KAZEN, ABRAHAM, JR., congressman; b. Laredo, Tex., Jan. 17, 1919; student U. Tex., 1937-40, Cumberland Law Sch., Lebanon, Tenn., 1941; m. Consuelo Raymond; children—Abraham III, Mrs. E. C. Dillman, Jr., Christina (Mrs. Ronald K. Attal), Catherine, Jo-Betsy. Admitted to Tex. bar, 1942; mem. firm Raymond, Alvarado & Kazen, Laredo, 1946-55; mem. Tex. Ho. of Reps., 1947-52; mem. Tex. Senate, 1952-66, pres. pro tempore, 1959; acting gov. State of Tex., 1959; mem. 90th-93d congresses from 23d Dist. Tex. Served to capt. USAAF, World War II; NATOUSA; MTO; CBI. Named Man of Year, also Father of Year, Laredo. Mem. Tex., Laredo bar assns., Laredo Internat. Fair and Exposition, Washington's Birthday Celebration Assn., Am. Legion, V.F.W., U. Tex. Ex-Students Assn. Democrat. K.C. Home: Laredo TX 78040 also 2408 Lakevale Dr Vienna VA 22180 Office: 1514 Longworth House Office Bldg Washington DC 20515

KEADY, JACK LELAND, newspaper editor; b. Joplin, Mo., Nov. 27, 1914; s. Matthew Norris and Myrtle (Wallace) K.; student La Salle U., 1958-59; m. Alice Louise Mattox, Oct. 4, 1940; 1 son, John Leland. Reporter, Arkansas Democrat Co., Little Rock, 1934-38, sports editor, 1938—. Bd. dirs. Ark. Hall of Fame. Served with AUS, 1942-46 Mem. Nat. Sportscasters-Sportswriters Assn. (Ark. Sportswriter of the Year award, 1966), Nat. Assn. Baseball Writers, Football Writers Assn. Am. Home: 1114 N Harrison St Little Rock AR 72205 Office: Capital Avand Scott St Little Rock AR 72201

KEAHEY, JAMES HOWARD, lawyer; b. Dallas, Apr. 15, 1934; s. Howard Pugh and Mary (Maloney) K.; B.J., U. Tex., 1955, LL.B., 1958; m. Barbara Lucille Wilson, July 4, 1969; children—Margaret, James, John Patrick. Admitted to Tex. bar, 1958; asso. mem. firm Clark, Thomas, Harris, Denius & Winters, Austin, 1958-61, partner, 1962-65; sole practice, Austin, 1966-68; partner firm Hart, Keahey & Hart, Austin, 1969—. Judge, City West Lake Hills, Tex., 1971—. Chmn. ballot security com. Travis County Republican party, 1970, 72. Mem. Phi Beta Kappa, Sigma Delta Chi, Phi Delta Phi, Order Coif. Episcopalian. Home: 414 Brady Lane Austin TX 78746 Office: Brown Bldg Austin TX 78701

KEANE, MARK EDWARD, assn. exec.; b. Chgo., Sept. 10, 1919; s. Fred J. and Mary E. (Sullivan) K.; B.S. in Pub. Service Engring., Purdue U., 1941; m. Carolyn Mims, Sept. 12, 1942; children—Mark Edward, Daniel, Dennis, Brian, Paul, Mary, Peter, Barry. Intern pub. adminstrn. Nat. Inst. Pub. Affairs, Washington, 1941-42; staff cons. Pub. Adminstrn. Service, Chgo., 1945-48; asst. to city mgr., Wichita, Kansas; 1948-49; city mgr., Shorewood, Wis., 1950-53, Oak Park, Ill., 1953-62, Tucson, 1962-66; dir. land and facilities devel. adminstrn. Dept. Housing and Urban Devel., Washington, 1966-67; exec. dir. Internat. City Mgmt. Assn., Washington, 1967—. Served to maj. AUS, 1942-45. Mem. Nat. Acad. Pub. Adminstrn. Home: 3522 Rittenhouse St Washington DC 20015 Office: 1140 Connecticut Av NW Washington DC 20036

KEARLEY, ARTHUR JAMES, lawyer; b. Mobile, Ala., Sept. 29, 1900; s. Joseph Dennis and Lula Ann (Bradley) K.; L.L.B., U. Ala., 1923; m. Dorothy Lucille Williams, Oct. 13, 1951. Admitted to Ala. bar, 1923; since practiced in Mobile, Ala.; mem. firm Kearley & McConnell, 1958—. Served with AUS, 1942-43. Hon. fellow Mobile Coll. Mem. Am., Ala., Mobile (pres. 1969—) bar assns., Farrah Law Soc., Phi Delta Phi. Baptist. Mason, Lion (pres. 1944-45). Home: 264 Levert St Mobile AL 36607 Office: Van Antwerp Bldg Mobile AL 36602

KEARLEY, FRANCIS JOSEPH, JR., educator; b. Mobile, Ala., July 7, 1921; s. Frank Joseph and Josephine (Nelson) K.; B.S., Spring Hill Coll., 1942; M.S., Vanderbilt U., 1944, Ph.D., 1950; m. Jeanne Burtu, Jan. 23, 1954; children—Douglas Burtu, Theodore Francis, Carmen Elizabeth. Faculty dept. chemistry Spring Hill Coll., Mobile, 1953—, prof., chmn. dept., 1966—. Served with USNR, 1944-46. Mem. Am. Chem. Soc., Ala. Acad. Sci., Sigma Xi. Episcopalian. Home: 4121 Ursuline Dr Mobile AL 36608 Office: Dept Chemistry Spring Hill Coll Mobile AL 36608

KEARNEY, RUSSELL FRANKLIN, JR., dentist; b. Greenwood, Miss., Nov. 6, 1939; s. Russell Franklin and Mary Henrietta (Humphries) K.; B.A., U. Miss., 1961; D.D.S., U. Tenn., 1965; m. Vivia Nell Best, Aug. 19, 1961 (div. Mar. 1974); children—Karon Elizabeth, Robert Humphries, Mary Lucene. Individual practice dentistry, Memphis, 1966-67, Yazoo City, Miss., 1967—. Mem. Yazoo County Jr. C. of C. (dir. 1968, v.p. 1969), Psi Omega, Sigma Nu. Rotarian. Home: Clubview Apts Yazoo City MS 39194 Office: PO Box 958 Yazoo City MS 39194

KEAY, JAMES WILLIAM, banker; b. Manley, Ia., Nov. 16, 1921; s. William J. and Valborg (Biorn) K.; B.A. in Econs., U. Colo., 1947; M.B.A., Northwestern U., 1948; grad. Rutgers U. Grad. Sch. Banking, 1956, Advanced Mgmt. Program, Harvard, 1964; m. Frances Lee Oglesby, Mar. 20, 1954; children—Martha Evelyn, James William, Stuart Enslie. With Republic Nat. Bank, Dallas, 1949—, asst. cashier, 1953, asst. v.p., 1953-56, v.p., 1956-61, sr. v.p., 1961-63, mem. exec. com., 1962—, exec. v.p. loans, 1963-65, exec. v.p. adminstrn., 1965, pres., dir., 1965-74, chmn. bd., chief exec. officer, 1974—; dir. United Fidelity Life Ins. Co., Howard Corp., Gen. Automotive Parts Corp., Dallas Power & Light Co., Austin Industries. Bd. dirs. State Fair of Tex., United Way Met. Dallas County. Served with AUS, World War II; ETO, MTO. Mem. Assn. Res. City Bankers, Am. Bankers Assn., Pi Gamma Mu. Lutheran (elder). Clubs: Idlewild, Brook Hollow Golf, Dallas, Dallas Petroleum, Dallas Country, Terpsichorean, Preston Trail Golf (Dallas). Home: 3920 Gillon Av Dallas TX 75205 Office: Republic Nat Bank PO Box 5961 Dallas TX 75222

KECK, J(ULIAN) WYLLY, engr.; b. Savannah, Ga., Oct. 23, 1899; s. Thomas Peter and Henrietta (Altman) K.; student Baylor U., 1921-24; m. Kathleen Russell, Oct. 15, 1924; children—Julian Wylly, Kathleen (Mrs. Roland T. Ross). Plant engr. Tex. Power & Light Co., Waco, 1920-24, East Tex. Pub. Service Co., Marshall, 1924-25; supt. power plants Fla. Power & Light Co., Miami, 1925-58, v.p., 1958-71, cons., 1971—; cons. engr. J. Wylly Keck & Assos., Atlanta, 1950—, Diamond Power Splty. Corp., Lancaster, O., 1958—. Mem. Fla. Bd. Engring. Examiners, 1940-67, pres., 1942-44, 55-56, 59-63. Recipient Engr. of Year citation S.E. Fla. Engrs., 1955, Distinguished certificate Nat. Council State Bd. Engr. Examiners, 1960. Registered profl. engr., Fla., N.Y. State. Fellow Fla. Engring. Soc. (past pres.), Am. Soc. M.E.; mem. Nat., Fla. socs. profl. engrs., Newcomen Soc. N.Am. Presbyn. Mason (K.T.). Clubs: Biscayne Bay Yacht (Miami); Coral Gables Country. Contbr. numerous engring. articles. Patentee in field. Home: 2520 San Domingo St Coral Gables FL 33134 Office: 4200 W Flagler St Miami FL 33101

KEE, DONALD REX, lawyer, banker; b. DeLeon, Tex., Aug. 23, 1926; s. Rex D. and Lela J. (Ross) K.; LL.B. cum laude, Baylor U., 1950, J.D. cum laude, 1969; m. Bettye Joyce Millhollon, Nov. 7, 1946; children—Richard Dow, Bonnie Kim. Admitted to Tex. bar, 1950; practiced in Wichita Falls, 1950-54, 55-57; atty. Clint Murchison Interests, Dallas, 1955-57; pres., dir. Gulf Coast Leaseholds, Houston, 1958-61; v.p., dir. Talon Petroleum C.A., Caracas, Venezuela, 1965-69; exec. v.p., trust officer Am. Nat. Bank, Amarillo, Tex., 1972—. Served with USNR, 1944-46; PTO. Mem. Tex. Bar Assn. Democrat. Baptist. Lion. Home: 1554 S Alabama St Amarillo TX 79102

KEE, LELAND BARRON, lawyer; b. Groveton, Tex., June 18, 1917; s. James Taylor and Mary (Wheat) K.; B.S., North Tex. U., Denton, 1939; LL.B., U. Tex., 1948; m. Marie Harkins, July 16, 1938; children—Susan Miranda, Nancy, Leland Barron. Admitted to Tex. bar, 1948, since practiced in Angleton; partner firm Davis & Kee, 1963—. Dir. First Nat. Bank Angleton. Mem. Tex. Bd. Corrections, 1961-67; chmn. Brazoria County Transp. Commn., 1972-73; pres. Brazoria County Community Chest, 1955. Sec. bd. trustees Angleton Ind. Sch. Dist., 1952-61; bd. dirs. Brazoria County United Fund, 1971—. Served to comdr. USNR, 1941-46. Mem. State Bar Tex., Brazoria County Bar Assn. (pres. 1969), Brazoria County (pres. 1956), Angleton (pres. 1970, Outstanding Service award 1973) chambers commerce. Rotarian (charter, pres. Angleton 1953). Home: 2 Pecan Pl Angleton TX 77515 Office: 912 N Velasco St Angleton TX 77515

KEE, WALTER ANDREW, librarian; b. Phila., July 12, 1914; s. Walter Leslie and Regina (Corcoran) K.; B.S., Purdue U., 1949; M.S., Columbia, 1951; m. Genevieve Nolan O'Hair, Dec. 2, 1943; children—Kathleen Leslie (Mrs. F. Edwin Johns), Sheila Nolan. Instrument maker Brown Instrument div. Mpls.-Honeywell, Phila., 1936-42; engring., phys. scis. librarian N.Y. U., 1950-51; librarian E. I. Dupont de Nemours, Savannah River Lab., Aiken, S.C., 1951-55; head library, documents sect. Martin Co., Balt., 1955-59; librarian U.S. AEC, Washington, 1959-66, tech. utilization officer, 1966-69, chief library br. Hdqrs. Services div., 1969—. Served with USNR, 1942-45. Mem. Spl. Libraries Assn. (chmn. documentation div. 1957-58, chmn. engring. div. 1964-65, chmn. nuclear sci. div. 1969-70), Am. Soc. Information Sci. Episcopalian. Home: 5832 Conway Rd Bethesda MD 20034 Office: USAEC Div Hdqrs Services Washington DC 20545

KEEBLE, SYDNEY FRAZER, JR., life ins. co. exec.; b. Nashville, Sept. 30, 1928; s. Sydney Frazer and Martha (Estes) Lawrence; B.A., Vanderbilt U., 1949, J.D., 1951; m. Sheila Anne Broderick, Aug. 29, 1959; children—Grace Barrett, Patrick Estes, Anne Gray McLaughlin. Admitted to Tenn. bar, Fed. bar, 1951; with Life & Casualty Ins. Co. of Tenn., Nashville, 1951—, atty., 1951-55, ordinary agt., 1955-57, agt., 1958, staff mgr., 1959, dist. mgr., 1960-61, dir. marketing research, 1961-63, asst. v.p., 1963-64, v.p., 1964-70, sr. v.p., 1970—, also dir., mem. exec., finance and sr. mgmt. coms.; dir. First Am. Nat. Bank. Bd. dirs. Nashville Boys' Club; pres. St. Mary's Villa; pres. Nashville YMCA, Tenn. Bot. Gardens and Fine Arts Center; trustee Harpeth Hall Sch., Nashville YMCA Found. Served to 1st lt. AUS, 1952-54. Decorated Bronze Star medal. Mem. Am., Tenn., Nashville bar assns., Nashville Assn. Life Underwriters, Phi Delta Theta, Phi Delta Phi, Omicron Delta Kappa. Clubs: Exchange (past pres.), Belle Meade Country (pres.); Cumberland of Nashville (past dir.), Nashville City; Leland (Mich.) Country. Home: Truxton Pl Nashville TN 37205 Office: Life & Casualty Tower Nashville TN 37219

KEECH, RICHMOND B., judge; b. Washington, Nov. 28, 1896; s. Leigh R. and Anne L. (Contee) K.; LL.B., Georgetown U., 1922, LL.M., 1923; m. Alice Cashell Berry, Sept. 24, 1957. Engaged in pvt. practice of law, Washington, 1922-25; asst. corp. counsel D.C., 1925-30, people's counsel, 1930-34; law mem. and vice chmn. Pub. Utilities Commn., 1934-40; corp. counsel and as such also served as gen. counsel Pub. Utilities Commn., 1940-45; an adminstrv. asst. Pres. of U.S., 1945-46; judge, U.S. Dist. Ct. for D.C., 1946-66, chief judge, 1966, active sr. judge, 1966—. Served in transport service with U.S. Navy, World War I. Mem. Bar Assn. of D.C., Phi Alpha Delta, Am. Legion. Episcopalian (jr. warden). Clubs: The Barristers, Potomac Hunt, Masters of Foxhounds Assn. Am., Rotary, Lawyers, Metropolitan, Chevy Chase, Am. Foxhound, Va. Foxhound. Home: 12930 Travilah Rd Potomac MD 20854 Office: US Dist Ct for DC Washington DC 20001

KEEFE, JOHN RICHARD, JR., anatomist, educator; b. Sandusky, O., Jan. 31, 1935; s. John Richard and Ethel Jessamine (Summers) K.; B.S., John Carroll U., 1960, M.S., 1965; Ph.D., Case Western Res. U., 1969; m. Nancy Esther Pekoc, Aug. 8, 1959; children—Terence Matthew, Kristen Ann. Research asso. Cleve. Psychiat. Research Found., 1960-65; research asso., electron microscopist Case Western Res. U., 1965-69, USPHS research fellow, dept. anatomy, 1965-69; instr. anatomy U. Va. Med. Sch., Charlottesville, 1969-71, asst. prof. anatomy, 1971—. USPHS research grant Nat. Eye Inst., 1971—. Mem. Am. Assn. Anatomists, So. Soc. Anatomists, Am. Soc. Cell Biology, Soc. for Developmental Biology, Am. Assn. Zoologists, Assn. for Research in Vision and Ophthalmology. Contbr. articles to profl. jours. Home: 203 Woodbrook Dr Charlottesville VA 22901

KEEFE, LEONARD RAWLINGS, newspaper exec.; b. Norfolk, Va., Jan. 17, 1914; s. George Edward and Fannie (White) K.; student Syracuse U. Grad. Sch. Sales Mgmt. and Marketing, summers 1958-59; advanced mgmt. course Grad. Sch. Bus. Adminstrn., U. Va., 1963; m. Dorothy Evans Branch, May 19, 1952. Copy boy advt. Ledger-Star, Norfolk, 1933-36, salesman retail advt. staff, 1936-51; asst. mgr. gen. advt. Virginian Pilot and Ledger-Star, Norfolk, 1951-60, mgr. gen. advt., 1960-71, dir. spl. projects, 1971—. Served to capt., inf., AUS, 1942-46. Decorated Bronze Star, Combat Infantryman's Badge. Democrat. Methodist. Lion (bd. dirs. 1956-61, 70-71, pres. 1961-62). Club: Norfolk Sports (bd. dirs. 1954-55, 65-66, pres. 1958, scholarship found. chmn. 1958). Home: 211 E 42d St Norfolk VA 23504 Office: 150 W Brambleton Av Norfolk VA 23501

KEEFE, WILLIAM EDWARD, educator; b. Norfolk. Va., Feb. 23, 1923; s. John Wesley and Esther (Hogshire) K.; B.S., Va. Poly. Inst. and State U., 1959, M.S., 1964; Ph.D., Med. Coll. Va., 1966; m. Mary Elizabeth Barrett, Dec. 7, 1946; children—Catherine (Mrs. Michael James Wright), William E. Exec. v.p. Norfolk Brass & Copper Corp., 1946-58; asst. prof. dept. biophysics Med. Coll. Va., Richmond, 1966—. Prin., pres. William E. Keefe Constrn. Co., Norfolk, 1954-56; pres. Nat. Compound Corp., Norfolk, 1955-58. Mem. troop com. Robert E. Lee council Boy Scouts Am., 1964—. Served with AUS, 1943-46. PTO. NIH fellow, 1961-66; A.D. Williams grantee, 1967. Mem. Internat. Solar Energy Soc., Am. Nuclear Soc., Washington, Am. crystallographic socs., Richmond Physics Club, Am. Inst. Physics, Am. Phys. Soc., Sigma Epsilon Pi. Mason. Contbr. articles to profl. jours. Home: 1104 West Av Richmond VA 23220 Office: 11th & Marshall Richmond VA 23298

KEEGAN, JOSEPH ROGER, statistician; b. N.Y.C., Jan. 20, 1927; s. Roger Joseph and Beatrice (Reape) K.; B.S., L.I. U., 1954; M.Pub. Adminstrn., N.Y.U., 1956, postgrad., 1956-58; postgrad. Am. U., 1963, George Washington U., 1964; m. Patricia Ellen Ford, Dec. 15, 1962; 1 son, Michael Roger. Statistician, N.Y.C. Dept. Health, 1956-59, N.Y. State Div. Employment, N.Y.C., 1959-60, Albany, N.Y., 1960-62; statistician Internal Revenue Service, Washington, 1963—. Served with AUS, 1945-46. Mem. Am. Statis. Assn., Am. Vets. Com., English Speaking Union, Intercollegiate Assn. (v.p. 1959-60). Office: Internal Revenue Service 1114 Constitution Av Washington DC 20224

KEEN, JOHN PAUL, utility co. engr.; b. Washington, Dec. 8, 1936; s. Paul Elmore and Sarah Anne (Howell) K.; B.S. Engring., George Washington U., 1959, M. Engring. Adminstrn., 1965; m. Audrey Patricia Silcox, June 25, 1960; children—John Michael, Karen Howell. With Potomac Electric Power Co., Washington, 1960—, engr. system planning elec. engring. div., 1972—. Mem. I.E.E.E., George Washington U. Alumni Assn., Gate and Key Frat., Pi Kappa Alpha. Episcopalian. Club: Kilowatt (Falls Church, Va). Home: 3445 Upside Court Falls Church VA 22042 Office: 1900 Pennsylvania Av NW Washington DC 20006

KEEN, PAUL, govt. ofcl.; b. Trammel, Ky., Sept. 27, 1900; s. Edward Jackson and Lou Etta (Holland) K.; A.A., Bethel Coll., 1921; A.B., Union U., 1922; J.D., U. Ky.; m. Sarah Anne Howell, June 12, 1933; children—Edward Shain, John Paul. Prin. Ozark (Ala.) City High Sch., 1922-23. Dale County High Sch., Ozark, Ala., 1923-24; admitted to Ky. bar, 1926, D.C. bar, 1932; with D.C. Govt., Washington, 1928-69, chief property insp., 1928-42, bus. mgr., Glenn Dale Sanatorium, 1942-50, deputy supt. Dist. Gen. Hosp., 1950-57, exec. asst. Dept. Pub. Health, 1957-64, regulations devel. officer, 1964-69, ret., 1969. Bd. dirs. Found. Mentally Retarded Children of Chesapeake dist. Civitan Internat., Inc., 1959-73. Recipient Distinguished Service award U. Ky., 1971; Honor Key award Civitan Internat. Mem. D.C. (life), Fed. (chmn. admissions com. 1970-73) bar assns., D.C. Bar, Am. Judicature Soc., Met. Washington Bd. Trade, Ky. Soc. of Washington (past pres.), Phi Alpha Delta. Baptist. Clubs: Civitan, University Ky. Alumni, Nat. Lawyers, Capitol Hill (life) (Washington); Internat. Town and Country (Fairfax, Va.). Home: 209 W Greenway Blvd Falls Church VA 20046

KEENAN, ARTHUR GEORGE, educator; b. Finland, June 12, 1920; s. Aaro and Rosa (Friman) K.; came to U.S., 1923, naturalized, 1928; B.S. (James Harris scholar, Edward Blake scholar, A.A.A.S. scholar), U. Toronto, 1941, M.S. (Reuben Wells Leonard fellow), 1942, Ph.D. (Canadian Industries Ltd. fellow), 1944; m. Margaret Krenz, May 8, 1947. Research chemist Canadian Industries Ltd., McMasterville, Que., 1944-47; research chemist NRC, Ottawa, Ont., 1947-49; research asso. Cornell U., 1949-50; asst. prof. Champlain Coll., State U. N.Y., Plattsburg, 1950-52; asso. prof. Ill. Inst. Tech., Chgo., 1952-57; prof. chemistry U. Miami, Coral Gables, Fla., 1957—. Mem. Am. Chem. Soc. (chmn. Miami sub-sect. 1960). Contbr. articles to profl. jours. Patentee in field. Home: 4220 Santa Maria Coral Gables FL 33146

KEENAN, CHARLES WILLIAM, educator; b. Fort Worth, Apr. 10, 1922; s. Charles and Mary (Markey) K.; B.S., Centenary Coll. La., 1943; Ph.D., U. Tex., 1949; m. Elizabeth Alden Pabody, Feb. 3, 1945; children—John Markey. Faculty dept. chemistry U. Tenn., Knoxville, 1949—, prof., 1958—, asso. dean Liberal Arts, 1973—. NSF fellow Cambridge (Eng.) U., 1957-58, 64-65. Served with USNR, 1945-46. Recipient Outstanding Tchr. award U. Tenn., 1972. Mem. Am. Chem. Soc., Am. Assn. U. Profs., Brit. Soc. Philosophy Sci., History Sci. Soc., Sigma Xi. Author: (with J.H. Wood) General College Chemistry, 1957, 61, 66, 67; (with W.E. Bull, J.H. Wood) Fundamentals of College Chemistry, 1963, 68, 72. Home: 4501 Appleby Ridge Knoxville TN 37920 Office: Liberal Arts U Tenn Knoxville TN 37916

KEES, CLIFTON HOMER, corp. exec.; b. Brookhaven, Miss., Oct. 14, 1910; s. I. Clifton and Etta (Moore) K.; B.B.A., Tulane U., 1933; m. Beall Barnes, Oct. 12, 1936; children—Clifton Homer, Martha (Mrs. William P. Orrick). Bond dept. Whitney Nat. Bank, New Orleans, 1937-39; v.p. Brookhaven Bank and Trust Co., Miss., 1940-43; statistician White, Hattier and Sanford, New Orleans, 1946-50; partner Ducournau and Kees, investment bankers, New Orleans, 1950—; v.p., dir. New Orleans Land Co., 1961—. Served from lt. (j.g.) to lt., USNR, 1944-46. Mem. Investment Bankers Assn. Am., La. Bankers Assn., Financial Analysts Soc. New Orleans, New Orleans Bond Club, New Orleans Opera Club. Methodist. Home: Tchefuncta Club Estates Covington LA 70433 Office: St Charles and Gravier Sts New Orleans LA 70130

KEFFER, WALTER FRANCIS, chem. co. exec.; b. Los Angeles, Dec. 3, 1913; s. Walter Griffith and Florence Maybelle (Kidder) K.; B.S. in Chem. Engring., Ia. State U., 1935; m. Barbara Apple, June 7, 1936; children—Eleanor (Mrs. Charles F. Bode), Judith (Mrs. Charles F. Gosser), Lawrence Thomas. Engr. Johns-Mansville, Waukegan, Ill., 1935, Raymond Pulverizer div., 1935-36; with Internat. Filter Co., Chgo., 1936-37; with Tenn. Corp., Copperhill, 1937-70, gen. mgr. 1968-70; v.p. Indsl. Chem. div. Cities Service, Atlanta, 1970—. Served with USAAF, 1941-46. Mem. Am. Inst. Chem. Engrs., Am. Inst. M.E., Alpha Chi Sigma. Republican. Episcopalian. Kiwanian. Club: Cherokee Town and Country (Atlanta). Home: 3364 Chatham Rd NW Atlanta GA 30305 Office: 3445 Peachtree Rd NE Atlanta GA 30326

KEGLEY, GEORGE ANDREW, newspaper editor; b. Wytheville, Va., May 15, 1928; s. Estel Stephen and Ruth (Brown) K.; B.A., Roanoke Coll., 1949; m. Louise Fishburn Fowlkes, May 31, 1958; children—George Andrew, Mary Louise, Robert Parker, Richard Fowlkes. Reporter, Roanoke (Va.) Times, 1949—, bus. writer, 1959-66, bus. editor, 1966—; editor Va. Luth., Roanoke, 1961—. Mem. Va. State Library Bd., 1972—; mem. adv. bd. Roanoke Bicentennial Commn. Bd. dirs. Roanoke City Rescue Mission. Served as pfc. AUS, 1951-53. Mem. Roanoke Hist. Soc. (dir., editor soc. jour.), Va. History Fedn. (dir. 1968-72), Kappa Alpha. Lutheran. Club: Roanoke German. Home: Tinker Creek Lane Roanoke VA 24019 Office: 201 Campbell Av SW Roanoke VA 24010

KEHL, WILLIAM WADDINGHAM, lawyer; b. Watertown, N.Y., Apr. 12, 1937; s. George William and Laura (Waddingham) K.; grad. Phillips Exeter Acad., 1955; B.A., Harvard, 1959; LL.B., U. Va., 1965; m. Elizabeth Lyles Adams, May 6, 1961; children—William Waddingham, John Lyles Boyd. Admitted to S.C. bar; partner firm Wyche Burgess Freeman & Parham, Greenville, S.C., 1966—. Dir. several cos., Greenville. Pres., Civic Chorale Assn., 1972-74, Greenville Rehab. Workshop, 1971-73; v.p. Greenville Housing Found., 1973—. Served with USNR, 1959-62. Mem. Am., S.C. (exec. com. young lawyers sect.) bar assns., Order Coif, Phi Alpha Delta. Episcopalian. Rotarian. Home: 7 Seven Oaks Dr Greenville SC 29605 Office: 44 E Camperdown Way Greenville SC 29603

KEHLER, BERNAD CLAUD, dentist; b. Shamokin, Pa., Nov. 15, 1916; s. John Garfield and Lucy Rebecca (Reed) K.; student St. Petersburg Jr. Coll., 1934-35; D.D.S., Emory U., 1939; m. Dorothy Mildred MacLawhon, Aug. 21, 1941; children—Bernard Claud, Keith G. Dentist-in-charge Kiwannis Childrens Dental Clinic, West Palm Beach, Fla., 1939-40, Ellory, S.C., 1940; practice dentistry, St. Petersburg, Fla., 1940-42, 46—. Served to maj. USAF, 1942-46. Fellow Am. Coll. Dentists (hon.), Royal Soc. Health (hon.); mem. Fla. (historian 1960-66), West Coast (pres. 1961-62), Pinellas County (pres. 1951; editor Pinellas County News 1957-59) dental socs. Methodist (supt. sch. 1958; treas. 1956-71, chmn. finance com. 1956-58, vice chmn. bd. trustees 1970-71, chmn. bd. trustees 1972-73). Clubs: Exchange (pres. St. Petersburg 1963-64; Outstanding Exchangite award 1955), St. Petersburg Yacht. Home: 401 Coffee Pot Riviera St Petersburg FL 33704 Office: 285 8th St N St Petersburg FL 33701

KEHOE, CATHARINE ELLEN, pvt. sch. owner, educator; b. New Orleans, Feb. 3, 1929; d. Charles Vincent and Catharine Ann (Roth) Kehoe; B.A., Ursuline Coll., 1949; M.A. with honors, U. So. Miss., 1951. Head dept. health, phys. edn. Ursuline Coll., New Orleans, 1951-53; chmn. dept. health, phys. edn. St. Mary's Dominican Coll., New Orleans, 1953-64; pres. Kehoe Day Camp and Swimming Sch., New Orleans, 1957—; pres., prin., prof. Kehoe Acad., New Orleans, 1962—. Vol. water safety, first aid instr. A.R.C., 1945-70; chmn. New Orleans bd. Nat. Ofcls. Rating Com., 1957-58. Fellow A.A.H.P.E.R.; mem. Am. Assn. U. Profs., Nat., La. assns. secondary sch. prins., Nat., So. assns. phys. edn. coll. women, Internat. Platform Assn., Phi Epsilon Kappa. Home: 265 Midway Dr New Orleans LA 70123 Office: Kehoe Acad 10931 Jefferson Hwy New Orleans LA 70123

KEIG, EUGENE RAY, physician; b. nr. West Union, Ia., Sept. 8, 1903; s. Harry and Laura (Ray) K.; D.O., Des Moines Still Coll., 1933; L.M., Rotunda Hosp., Dublin, Ireland, 1953; studied U. Vienna, 1959; m. Alice Johnston, Dec. 15, 1926; 1 son, Harry. Resident Rotunda Hosp., Dublin, Ireland, 1938, 53, Geneva (Switzerland) U. Hosp., 1953; pvt. practice obstetrics and gynecology, Mason, W.Va., 1933-50, St. Petersburg, Fla., 1950—; pres. Doctor's Hosp., Inc., St. Petersburg, Fla., 1953—. Mayor of Mason, W.Va., 1938-48. Mem. Sigma Sigma Phi. Mason. Home: 384 15th St N St Petersburg FL 33705 Office: 401 15th St N St Petersburg FL 33705

KEIGER, ROBERT KASON, lawyer; b. Winston-Salem, N.C., June 28, 1934; s. Joseph Lee and Mamie Alberta (Spainhour) K.; B.S. in Accounting, U. N.C., 1956; J.D., Wake Forest Coll., 1960; m. Ann Hayden Williams, Aug. 9, 1969; children—Karol Kimberly, Christopher Kason, Dee Dee Thornton. Salesman, Indera Mills Co., Winston-Salem, 1956-57, dir., 1957—; clk. Oldtown Telephone System, Inc., Winston-Salem, 1957-60, dir., 1957—; admitted to N.C. bar, 1960, since practiced in Winston-Salem. Solicitor, Kernersville (N.C.) Recorders Ct., 1961-68; judge Kernersville Ct., 1968-69; atty. Town of Kernersville, 1961—. Mem. Am., Forsyth County bar assns., Forsyth County Jr. Bar, Phi Alpha Delta. Democrat. Presbyn. Home: 2500 Lullington Dr Winston-Salem NC 27101 Office: Pepper Bldg Winston-Salem NC 27101

KEILEN, JOHN JACOB, rubber co. exec.; b. Pitts., Oct. 24, 1915; s. John Jacob and Mary Jane (Hare) K.; B.S., Carnegie Inst. Tech., 1936, M.S., 1937; Dr. Chem. Engring., Poly. Inst. Bklyn., 1949; m. Eleanor Yunker, Aug. 3, 1940. Research engr. W.Va. Pulp & Paper Co., N.Y.C., 1937-41; project leader W.Va. Pulp and Paper, Charleston, S.C., 1941-47, project dir., 1947-53, dir. new product devel., 1953-58; dir. research and devel. Charleston Rubber Co., 1958-66, v.p. research and devel. 1965—, dir., 1969—; pres., dir. Domex Internat., Inc. Fellow Am. Inst. Chemists; mem. Am. Chem. Soc., A.A.A.S., Am. Inst. Chem. Engrs., Am. Nuclear Soc., Am. Soc. Testing Materials, Soc. Plastics Engrs. Club: Charleston Chemical Engineers. Contbr. articles to profl. jours. Patentee in field. Home: 152 Gordon St Charleston SC 29403 Office: 3370 Rivers Av Charleston SC 29405

KEILLER, JAMES BRUCE, coll. dean, clergyman; b. Racine, Wis., Nov. 21, 1938; s. James Allen and Grace (Modder) K.; diploma Beulah Heights Bible Coll., 1957; B.A., William Carter Coll., 1963, Ed.D. (hon.), 1973; LL.B., Blackstone Sch. Law, 1964; M.A., Evang. Theol. Sem., 1965, B.D., 1966, Th.D., 1968; m. Darsel Lee Bundy, Feb. 8, 1959; 1 dau., Susanne Elizabeth. Ordained to ministry internat. Pentecostal Assemblies, 1957; pastor Maranatha Temple, Boston, 1957-58, Midland (Mich.) Full Gospel Ch., 1958-64; dean of coll. Beulah Heights Bible Coll., Atlanta, 1964—, trustee, 1964—; nat. dir. youth and Sunday sch. dept. Internatl. Pentecostal Assemblies, 1958-64, dir. world missions, Atlanta, 1964—, youth commn., 1958-64, missions com., 1964—, exec. bd., 1964—, missionary editor Bridegroom's Messenger, 1964—. Named Alumnus of Year, William Carter Coll., 1965. Mem. Woodmen of World, So. Accrediting Assn. Bible Insts., Bible Colls. and Bible Sems. (exec. sec.), Am. Security Council, Soc. for Pentecostal Studies, Ind. Order Foresters, Am. Acad. Religion, Evang. Theol. Soc. Kiwanian. Home: 892 Berne St SE Atlanta GA 30316 Office: 906 Berne St SE Atlanta GA 30316

KEILLER, THOMAS MITCHELL, elec. engr.; b. Galveston, Tex., Mar. 2, 1898; s. William and Jane Julia (McLaughlin) K.; B.A., Rice U., 1920; B.S., Mass. Inst. Tech., 1922; m. Catherine Marie Roeller, June 20, 1925 (dec.). With Houston Electric Co., 1922-24; engr. Stone & Webster, Inc., Houston, 1924-25, Gulf State Utilities Co., Beaumont, Tex., Lake Charles, La., 1925-34, 35-42; engr. El Paso Electric Co., 1934-35; chief elec. engr. Dickson Gun Plant, Houston, 1942-44; planning engr., asst. supt. engring., cons. Houston Lighting & Power Co., 1945-65; cons. elec. engr., Houston, 1965—. Past engring. chmn. Joint Archtl. and Engring. Council Tex. Served with U.S. Army, 1917-19; to lt. comdr. USNR, 1944-46. Decorated Silver Star medal, Army Commendation medal. Registered profl. engr., Tex. Fellow I.E.E.E.; mem. Nat., Tex. socs. profl. engrs., Houston Engring. and Sci. Soc., Theta Xi. Address: 2 Crestwood Dr Houston TX 77007

KEIM, SHEWELL DEBENNEVILLE, elec. engr.; b. Takoma Park, Md., Nov. 5, 1918; s. Thomas Daniel and Zaida (Westerlund) K.; B.S. in Elec. Engring., U. Md., 1949; grad. Fed. Exec. Inst., 1973; m. Lelia G. Bateman, Dec. 6, 1952; 1 son, John S. With Navy Dept., 1949—, chief engr. Marine Corps br. Naval Ships Engring. Center, Washington, 1959-67, tech. dir. Marine Corps div. Naval Electronics Systems Command, 1967—; mem. engring. com., tech. dept. Dept. Agr. Grad. Sch., 1959—. Served with AUS, 1941-45. Recipient Superior Performance award Bur. Ships Dept. Navy, 1962, letter of appreciation, 1963; Superior Achievement award Naval Electronics Systems Command, 1973. Mem. I.E.E.E., Philos. Soc. Washington, Moysone Assn. Contbr. articles to profl. jour. Home: Box 560 Route 1 Accokeek MD 20607 Office: Naval Electronic Systems Command Washington DC 20360

KEIRNS, WENDELL JEFF, trade assn. exec.; b. Bloomville, O., Mar. 3, 1942; s. Edward Jefferson and Lois (Rhoad) K.; student Ohio State U., 1960-62; B.C.S., Tiffin (O.) U., 1966; postgrad. Mich. State U., 1967-68, 71-73; m. Sandra Lee Powers, June 5, 1965; 1 son, Jeffrey Scott. Field sec. Ohio Pharm. Assn., Columbus, 1966-68; exec. dir., adminstr. Fla. Pharm. Assn., Tallahassee, 1968-69; exec. dir. Nat. Glass Dealers Assn., Washington, 1969—. Organizer first homecoming, Young Republicans and Young Democrats clubs at Tiffin U., 1965. Bd. regents Mich. State U. Inst. Orgn. Mgmt. Recipient Outstanding Student of Year award, 1965, Jaycee Spoke award, 1968; named Outstanding Young Man of Year, 1968, Community Leader of Am., 1969. Mem. Am., Washington socs. assn. execs., Nat. Execs. Club, U.S. (bd. regents Insts. Orgn. Mgmt. 1973—, chmn. consumer safety glazing com. 1971-72), Nat. Jr. chambers commerce, Phi Theta Pi. Home: 107 N Columbus St Arlington VA 22203 Office: 1000 Connecticut Av NW Washington DC 20036

KEISER, DAVID PAUL, elec. co. exec.; b. Dover, O., Jan. 12, 1926; s. Henry Patrick and Edith Anne (Herzig) K.; B.E.E., Marquette U., 1946; M.A., Western Mich. U., 1959, M.B.A., 1963; m. Mary Elizabeth Pate, June 30, 1951; children—David Paul, Lisa Anne. Sales engr. Westinghouse Electric Corp., Detroit, 1947-51, Kalamazoo, 1953-65, supr. personnel devel. programs, Pitts., 1965-66, mgr. marketing personnel devel., 1966-68, marketing mgr. small power transformer, South Boston, Va., 1968—. Served with USNR, 1946, 51-53. Mem. Am. Marketing Assn., Sales and Marketing Execs. Internat., Res. Officers Assn. K.C., Elk, Kiwanian. Club: Danville (Va.) Golf. Home: 324 River Oak Dr Danville VA 24541 Office: Box 920 Hwy 58W South Boston VA 24592

KEISER, FREDERICK CHARLES, banker; b. Sharon, Pa., Mar. 23, 1923; s. Frederick Claire and Myrtle Mae (Hurst) K.; B.A., Centre Coll., Danville, Ky., 1948; m. Betty Ann Noe, Feb. 10, 1948; children—Charles Hurst, Nancy Noe, Robert Walker. With Internat. Harvester, 1948-53, asst. dist. credit mgr., 1950-53; with Farmers Deposit Bank, Eminence, Ky., 1954—, pres., 1967—; partner Keiser Ins. Agy., Eminence, 1954—. Served with AUS, 1943-46. Mem. Ky. (dir. 1971-74), Eminence (pres. 1973) chambers commerce. Presbyn. (clk. of session 1968-70). Home: 207 S Main St Eminence KY 40019 Office: 103 S Main St Eminence Ky 40019

KEISER, HENRY BRUCE, lawyer, pub.; b. N.Y.C., Oct. 26, 1927; s. Leo and Jessie (Liebeskind) K.; B.A. with honors, U. Mich., 1947; LL.B. cum laude, Harvard, 1950; m. Jessie E. Weeks, July 12, 1953; children—Betsy Cordelia, Matthew Roderick. Admitted to N.Y. bar, 1950, D.C. bar, 1955, Fla. bar, 1956, U.S. Supreme Ct. bar, 1954; trial atty. CAB, Washington, 1950-51; head counsel alcoholic beverages sect. OPS, 1951-52; legal asst. to Judge Eugene Black, Tax Ct. U.S., 1953-56; practiced in Washington, 1956—; pres., chmn. bd. Fed. Pubs., Inc., 1959—; chmn. bd. Gene Galasso Assos., Inc., Washington, 1963—. Adv. cabinet Southeastern U., 1965—; cons., AEC, 1965—; professorial lectr. Dept. Agr., 1960—, George Washington U., 1961—, U. San Francisco, 1965-66, Coll. William and Mary, 1966—, Cal. Inst. Tech., 1967-72, U. So. Cal., 1973—. Served to 1st lt. Judge Adv. Gen. Corps, USAF, 1951-52; maj. Res. Fellow Nat. Contract Mgmt. Assn.; mem. Fed. (nat. council 1966—), Am. (mem. council pub. contracts sect.) bar assns., Fla. Bar, Bar Assn. D.C. (dir. 1965-66, chmn. adminstrv. law sect. 1964-65). Jewish religion. Home: 6009 Plainview Rd Bethesda MD 20034 Office: 1725 K St NW Washington DC 20006

KEISLER, JAMES EDWIN, educator; b. Spartanburg, S.C., Aug. 20, 1929; s. Efird Bryan and Eunice Mabel (Sease) K.; B.S., Midland Coll., 1949; M.A., U. Mich., 1954, Ph.D., 1959; m. Patience Catherine Weidt, Dec. 28, 1950; children—James Edwin, William Bryan, Paul Timothy. Faculty, La. State U., Baton Rouge, 1959—, prof. math., 1973—, asso. chmn. dept., 1970—. Served with AUS, 1951-53. Lutheran. Home: 215 Stanford Av Baton Rouge LA 70808

KEISTER, THOMAS CLINTON, dentist; b. Tannersville, Va., Mar. 14, 1897; s. Charles Tate and Lilly Gordon (Spraker) K.; D.D.S., Vanderbilt U., 1925; m. Doris L. Hutcherson, Apr. 18, 1936; children—Thomas Clinton, Larry Charles. Mem. staff dental clinics Va. Health Dept., U.S. Pub. Health, 1925-29; gen. practice dentistry, Charlottesville, Va., 1929—; Pres. Component no. 7 of Va., Shenandoah Valley, 1950-51. Mem. Am. Dental Assn., Charlottesville Dental Soc. (pres. 1944-45), English-Speaking Union, Delta Sigma Delta. Elk, Lion (v.p. Charlottesville 1935-36). Clubs: Redland, Farmington Country (Charlottesville). Home: 1803 Blue Ridge Rd Charlottesville VA 22903 Office: 206 E Market St Charlottesville VA 22901

KEITH, DONALD WAYNE, broadcast exec.; b. Springville, Ala., Dec. 12, 1947; s. Clyde Euel and Doris Jean (Griffin) K.; B.A., U. Ala., 1970; m. Charlene Higdon, Sept. 12, 1967; 1 son, Michael Andrew. Chief announcer U. Ala., Tuscaloosa, 1966-70; music dir., sports dir. WNPT Radio, Tuscaloosa, 1967-70; news dir. WVOK Radio, Birmingham, Ala., 1972—. Counselor, Columbia Sch. Broadcasting; speaker U. Ala. Radio-TV Workshop, Assn. Women in Radio and TV Meeting. Recipient certificate Billboard mag. air personality competition, 1971. Mem. U. Ala. Nat., Jefferson County alumni assns., Alpha Epsilon Rho. Club: Birmingham Amateur Radio. Home: 462 Ridgewood Av Fairfield AL 35064 Office: Box 1926 Birmingham AL 35201

KEITH, DWIGHT TAYLOR, publisher, coach; b. Argo, Ala., Oct. 19, 1900; s. Jefferson Davis and Vianna (Taylor) K.; A.B., U. Ala.; m. Randa Rasco, Aug. 19, 1925; children—Carole Lita (Mrs. Richard Harvin), Dwight Leo. Founder, pub. mag. Coach & Athlete, Atlanta, 1938—; coach high schs., Ala., Miss., Ga., 1923-42; asst. football coach Ga. Inst. Tech., Atlanta, 1942-52, varsity basketball coach, 1943-47, sports publicity dir., 1942-47. Founder, Ga. Prep. Sports Hall of Fame; sec.-treas. Ga. Athletic Hall of Fame. Mem. Ga. Athletic Coaches Assn. (sec., dir. ann. coaching clinic), Am. Football Coaches Assn. (mgr. Coach of the Year clinic Dist. 4), Nat. High Sch. Athletic Coaches Assn. (organizer, exec. sec.), Nat. Football Writers Assn., U.S. Basketball Writers Assn., Atlanta Press Club, Sigma Delta Chi. Presbyn. Mason (Shriner), Kiwanian. Home: 2644 W Wesley Rd NW Atlanta GA 30327 Office: 1421 Mayson St NE Atlanta GA 30324

KEITH, EUGENE VANCE, supt. schs.; b. Afton, Okla., Dec. 30, 1929; s. Lon Frank and Hazel (Mustain) K.; student Northeastern A. and M. Coll., Miami, Okla., 1948-50; B.S., U. Wichita, 1955; M.S., Kan. State Coll., 1961; postgrad. Okla. State U.; m. Mildred Jeannine Laramore, Jan. 6, 1951; children—Sheryl Lynne, Cynthia Maureen, Karen Kay. Tchr., coach Kiowa (Kan.) High Sch., 1955-58, Medicine Lodge (Kan.) High Sch., 1958-60; asst. high sch. prin. Miami (Okla.) High Sch., 1960-63; supt. schs. Medford (Okla.) Pub. Schs., 1963-69; asst. supt. Guymon (Okla.) Pub. Schs., 1969-70, supt., 1970—. Served with AUS, 1951-53. Mem. N.E.A., Am., Okla. assns. sch. adminstrs. Baptist. Rotarian, Lion. Home: 6049 Sunset Dr Guymon OK 73942

KEITH, HOWARD BARTON, thoracic surgeon; b. Enid, Okla., Aug. 23, 1932; s. John Austin and Dorothy Olive (Murphy) K.; M.D., U. Okla., 1957; m. Joanne Norman Keith, Mar. 12, 1954; children—Preston J., Kimberly Ann, Shaun Howard, Spencer Norman. Intern surgery U. Okla. Med. Center, Oklahoma City, 1957-58, resident 1958-63; practice medicine specializing in surgery, Oklahoma City, 1958-63, specializing in thoracic-cardiovascular and gen. surgery, Shattuck, Okla., 1963—; mem. staff Newman Med. Center, Newman Meml. Hosp. Mem. adv. com. Physicians Asso. Program, 1973—, Adv. Com. on Med. Care for Pub. Assistance Recipients, 1971—; cons. region 6 utilization and peer rev. Dept. Health, Edn. and Welfare, 1973—; med. adviser N.W. Okla., Okla. Tb Assn., 1964—. Mem. Bd. edn. Shattuck Pub. Sch. System, 1964-71. Bd. dirs. Convalescent Center Mf Shattuck, 1964—; exec. bd. dirs. Great Salt Plains council Boy Scouts Am., 1969—, mem. finance com., 1970—; bd. dirs. Western Rural Health Services Orgn., 1974—. Mem. Am., Okla. (chmn. state peer rev. com. 1965—) med. assns., A.C.S., Am. Coll. Chest Physicians, Soc. Thoracic Surgeons, So. Thoracic Surg. Assn., Southwestern Surg. Congress, Okla. Surg. Assn., Okla. Thoracic Soc. Lion (pres. 1967-68). Home: 822 E 8th St Shattuck OK 73858 Office: Newman Med Center Inc 905 S Main St Shattuck OK 73858

KEITH, JOHN WILLIAM, furniture mfg. co. exec.; b. Millen, Ga., Apr. 15, 1926; s. Harley H. and Ethel Fay (Watson) K.; student Ind. U., 1944-46; m. Margaret Ellen Showalter, Nov. 30, 1946; children—Alan, John William, Julia. Partner, mgr. Keith Furniture Co., West Palm Beach, Fla., 1949-60; mfr. rep. Flex Steel Industries, Le Brun Bros. Mfg. Co., West Palm Beach, 1960-62; sales mgr. Le Brun Bros., Inc., Greensboro, N.C., 1962-65; sales mgr. Rhyne Co., Marianna, Fla., 1965-68, pres., 1969-72; v.p. Furniture div. Lehigh Portland Cement Co., Marianna, 1973—. Recipient Design awards Furniture U.S.A., 1969-73. Mem. Furniture Club Am., So. Furniture Club, C. of C. (dir. 1970-72), Phi Kappa Psi. Republican. Methodist. Rotarian (dir. 1971-73). Club: Marianna Country (dir. 1970—). Home: 2504 Caverns Rd Marianna FL 32446 Office: E Lafayette St Marianna FL 32446

KEITH, LAWRENCE HAROLD, chemist; b. Morris, Ill., Apr. 5, 1938; s. Harold Melbourne and Shirley Ione (Cooper) K.; B.S., Stetson U., 1960; postgrad. U. S.C., 1960-61; M.S., Clemson U., 1963; Ph.D., U. Ga., 1966; m. Virginia Margaret Hunt, Nov. 1, 1969. Environmental pollutant research chemist U.S. Environmental Protection Agy., S.E. Environmental Research Lab., Athens, Ga., 1966—. Founder, pres. KCP, Inc., 1973—; spl. cons. joint U.S.-Polish grant, 1973. Mem. Am. Chem. Soc. (sec. N.E. Ga. sect. 1967-69, councilor 1970—, mem. nat. com. meetings and expns. 1972—, exec. bd. div. environmental chemistry 1972-73, asst. sec. div. 1973—, Ga. Acad. Sci., Sigma Xi, Gamma Sigma Epsilon, Kappa Kappa Psi. Elk. Contbr. chpts. to The Alkaloids-Chemistry and Physiology, 1970; Chemistry of the Alkaloids, 1970; Fate of Organic Pesticides in the Aquatic Environment, 1972. Contbr. articles profl. jours. Home: 515 Cedar Creek Dr Athens GA 30601 Office: EPA-SERL College Sta Rd Athens GA 30601

KEITH, THOMAS JOSEPH, realtor; b. Lumberton, N.C., May 31, 1941; s. Fred Rulfs and Grace (Butler) K.; student N.C. State U., 1959-61; B.S., Campbell Coll., 1964. Asst. mgr. Keith Farm Co., St. Pauls, N.C., 1964—; sec.-treas. Keith Realty Co., St. Pauls, N.C. 1965—; dir. Robeson County Farm Bur., Lumberton, N.C., Town and Country Bank. Mem. Robeson County Republican Exec. Com. 1964—, chmn., 1968—; sec.-treas. 7th Congl. Dist. Republican Com., 1966—. Mem. New River Grape Growers Assn. (past dir.), Campbell Coll. Alumni Assn. (sec.-treas. 1968), Jr. C. of C. (v.p. 1967), Lumberton Bd. Realtors (pres. 1968), Am. Inst. Real Estate Appraisers, St. Pauls C. of C. Baptist. Club: Pine Crest Country. Home: 2100 N Elni St Lumberton NC 28358 Office: 209 W Broad St St Pauls NC 28384

KELLAM, LUCIUS JAMES, JR., oil distbg. co. exec.; b. Belle Haven, Va., Sept. 25, 1911; s. Lucius James and Carrie (Polk) K.; student Trinity Coll., Hartford, Conn., 1931-35, D.Sc. (hon.), 1972; m. Dorothy Douglass, Sept. 12, 1936; children—Dorothy Douglass (Mrs. Hugh L. Patterson), Lucius James, III. Treas., Sturgis Oil Co., Inc., Belle Haven, 1935-38, pres., 1938-46; pres., dir. Kellam Distbg. Co., Inc., Belle Haven, 1946—; pres. Shore Savs. & Loan Corp., Accomac, Va., 1961-70, chmn. bd., 1970—; pres. Kellam Propane Gas Co., Inc., Belle Haven, 1956—; dir. Va. Nat. Bank, Va. Indsl. & Devel. Corp., Peoples Trust Bank; dir. Smith-Douglass Co., Inc., 1954-65. Chmn., Chesapeake Bay Ferry Commn., 1954-60, Chesapeake Bay Bridge & Tunnel Commn., 1960—; mem. Va. Safety Council, Accomack County, 1951—; mem. Delmarva Adv. Council, Salisbury, Md., 1964-70, pres., 1970—. Mem. Accomack County Democratic Central Com., 1947—, State Dem. Finance Com., 1965; del. Dem. Nat. Conv., 1960. Trustee Old Dominion Coll. Ednl. Found., Norfolk, Va., St. James Sch., Hagerstown, Md., Eastern Va. Med. Sch. Found., Broadwater Acad., Exmore, Va., Va. Mus. Fine Arts; trustee, exec. com. Northampton Accomack Meml. Hosp., treas. 1964—, pres., 1967, 68; bd. dirs. Tidewater Automobile Assn., 1941—, v.p., 1964—; bd. dirs. Internat. Bridge, Tunnel and Turnpike Assn., 1962-66, Tidewater Regional Health Planning Council, 1968—; bd. dirs., v.p., Ocean Hwy. Assn., 1954—; bd. dirs., 1st v.p. Va. Travel Council, 1953-66; bd. dirs. Va. Travel Devel. Council, 1967—. Served to lt. USNR, 1943-46. Mem. Delta Psi. Episcopalian. Rotarian (pres. 1939). Clubs: Eastern Shore Yacht and Country (Melfa, Va.); Princess Anne Country (Virginia Beach, Va.); Commonwealth, Downtown (Richmond, Va.); Harbor (Norfolk, Va.); St. Anthony (N.Y.C.). Home: Mt Pleasant Belle Haven VA 23306 Office: Kellam Distbg Co Belle Haven VA 23306

KELLEHER, HERBERT DAVID, lawyer; b. Camden, N.J., Mar. 12, 1931; s. Harry and Ruth (Moore) K.; B.A. with honors (Olin scholar), Wesleyan U., 1953; LL.B. with honors (Root Tilden scholar) N.Y. U., 1956; m. Joan Negley, Sept. 9, 1955; children—Julie, Michael, Ruth, David. Admitted to N.J. bar, 1957, Tex. bar, 1962; clk. N.J. Supreme Ct., 1956-59; asso. mem. firm Lum, Biunno & Tompkins, Newark, 1959-61; partner firm Matthews, Nowlin, Macfarlane & Barrett, San Antonio, 1961-69; sr. partner Oppenheimer, Rosenberg, Kelleher & Wheatley, Inc., San Antonio, 1969—. Founder., gen. counsel, dir. S.W. Airlines Co., Dallas, 1967—. Campaign coordinator Connally for Gov., 1961, 63, 65, Bexar County dir. Bentsen for Senator, 1970; chmn. Senate Dist. 19 Democratic Com., 1968-70; del. Dem. Nat. Conv., 1964, 68. Pres., Travelers Aid Soc. San Antonio. Pres. bd. trustees St. Mary's Hall, San Antonio. Mem. Am., San Antonio, N.J. bar assns., State Bar Tex., Order Alamo, Tex. Cavaliers. Home: 144 Thelma Dr San Antonio TX 78212 Office: 711 Navarro St San Antonio TX 78205

KELLER, BERNARD GERARD, JR., educator; b. New Orleans, Dec. 18, 1936; s. Bernard Gerard and Gertrude Esther (Stiles) K.; B.S., Loyola U. at New Orleans, 1959; M.S., U. Miss., 1964, Ph.D., 1966. Asst. prof. Mercer U. So. Sch. Pharmacy, Atlanta, 1966, asso. prof., 1967, prof., 1968-69; prof. Southwestern State Coll. Sch. Pharmacy, Weatherford, Okla., 1969—, asst. dean, 1972—. Vis. prof. U. Miss. Sch. Pharmacy, summers 1967, 68. Fellow Am. Found. for Pharm. Edn., Am. Coll. Apothecaries (asso.); mem. Am. Pharm. Assn., Nat. Assn. Retail Druggists, Omicron Delta Kappa, Alpha Sigma Nu. Author: Pharmaceutical Marketing an Anthology and Bibliography, 1969; Introduction to Clinical Pharmacy lab. manual, 1973. Home: PO Box 60304 Oklahoma City OK 73106 Office: Sch Pharmacy Southwestern State Coll Weatherford OK 73096

KELLER, CHARLES, JR., constrn. co. exec.; b. Detroit, Oct. 20, 1908; s. Charles and Frances (Rosenfield) K.; B.S., U.S. Mil. Acad., 1930; B.S. in Mech. Engring., Mass. Inst. Tech., 1933; m. Rosa Freeman, Dec. 28, 1932; children—Charles III, Mary (Mrs. Luis M. Zervigon), Caroline (Mrs. Philip H. Loughlin III). Commd. 2d lt. C.E., U.S. Army, 1930, advanced through grades to col., 1944; resigned, 1945; with Nat. Am. Bank, New Orleans, 1939-41; pres. Keller Constrn. Corp., New Orleans, 1946—. Pres. Pub. Affairs Research Council La., 1960-61, United Fund Greater New Orleans Area, 1955; chmn. Central Area Com., New Orleans, 1959-61; trustee Com. Econ. Devel., 1964—. Decorated Bronze Star medal with 2 oak leaf clusters, Legion of Merit with oak leaf cluster; Legion of Honor, Croix de Guerre with palm (France). Registered profl. engr., La. Mem. Asso. Gen. Contractors Am. (pres. 1963), Am. Soc. C.E., Soc. Am. Mil. Engrs., Nat. Soc. Profl. Engrs. Home: 1701 Arabella St New Orleans LA 70115 Office: PO Box 50039 New Orleans LA 70150

KELLER, CHARLES, III, civil engr.; b. Ancon, Panama Canal Zone, Apr. 6, 1935; s. Charles and Rosa (Freeman) K.; B.S., Stanford, 1957; M.B.A., Harvard, 1961; m. (div.); children—Charlotte, Charles Wade. Resident engr. City and County of San Francisco, 1958-59; data processing analyst New Orleans Public Service, Inc., 1961-63; v.p. Keller Constrn. Corp., New Orleans, 1963-71; asso. corporate finance dept. Kohlmeyer & Co., New Orleans, 1971-73; project mgr. Heevy Assos., New Orleans, 1973—; pres. Gen. Enterprises, Inc., New Orleans, 1962—. Bd. dirs. New Orleans Philharmonic Symphony, 1962—, v.p., 1969-72; bd. dirs. New Orleans Speech and Hearing Center, 1963-69, pres., 1969; bd. dirs. Isidore Newman Sch., 1970—, United Way Greater New Orleans, 1972—, Vols. of Am., New Orleans, 1971—. Served with AUS, 1958. Registered profl. engr. Mem. Bur. Govtl. Research, C. of C. of New Orleans, Am. Soc. C.E., Am. Soc. Military Engrs., Nat. Soc. Profl. Engrs., La. Engring. Soc., Am. Arbitration Assn. (panel mem.), Internat. House, Phi Beta Kappa, Tau Beta Phi. Democrat. Clubs: New Orleans Country, New Orleans Lawn Tennis. Home: 1510 State St New Orleans LA 70118 Office: 1516 Jefferson Hwy New Orleans LA 70121

KELLER, CHRISTOPH, JR., clergyman; b. Bay City, Mich., Dec. 22, 1915; s. Christoph and Margaret Ely (Walter) K.; grad. Lake Forest (Ill.) Acad., 1934; B.A., Washington and Lee U., 1939; student Grad. Sch. Theology, U. South, 1954; certificate spl. work, Gen. Theol. Sem., N.Y.C., 1957; S.T.D. (hon.), Gen. Theol. Sem.; D.D. U. South; m. Caroline P. Murphy, June 22, 1940; children—Caroline, Cornelia, Cynthia, Kathryn, Christoph, Elizabeth. Planter, Alexandria, La., 1940—; pres. Deltic Farm & Timber Co., El Dorado, Ark., 1948-51; exec. v.p. Murphy Corp., El Dorado, 1951-54, dir., 1948—; ordained priest P.E. Ch., 1957; rector, Harrison, Ark., also charge missions in Eureka Springs and Mountain Home, Ark., 1957-61; rector St. Andrews Episcopal Ch., Jackson, Miss., 1962-67; dean St. Andrews Cathedral, Jackson, until 1967; bishop coadjutor Diocese of Ark., 1967-70, diocesan bishop 1970—. Dir. Tallalah State Bank (La.), 1950-51. Bd. trustees Gen. Theol. Sem., P.E. Diocese Ark., 1957-62, mem. exec. council, 1958-60, chmn. dept. promotion, 1958-60, Gen. Theol. Sem., N.Y.; exec., com. P.E. Diocese Miss., 1963-65; dept. Gen. Conv. P.E. Ch., 1958, 61, 64, 67. Pres. La. Aberdeen Angus Breeders Assn., 1947, La. Delta Council, 1950; chmn. United Fund El Dorado, 1952; Mem. Madison Parish (La.) Sch. Bd., 1952-53. Trustee All Saints Jr. Coll., Vicksburg, Miss., 1949-51, Kent Sch., Conn., U. South, Sewanee, Tenn. Served as officer USMCR, World War II. Mem. Pi Kappa Alpha (pres. 1939). Home: 1809 Beechwood Rd Little Rock AR 72207 Office: 300 W 17th St Little Rock AR 72206

KELLER, DOUGLAS DOYLE, dentist; b. Bastrop, La., Apr. 5, 1932; s. Douglas Jewel and Annie L. (Anderson) K.; student La. State U., 1950-52, N.E. La. State Coll., 1953; D.D.S., Loyola U. of New Orleans, 1957; postgrad. U. So. Cal., 1958; m. Martha Florence Brown, May 31, 1953; children—Ann, Nancy, Douglas. Individual practice dentistry, Bastrop, 1959—; mem. staff Morehouse Gen. Hosp., Bastrop, 1959—. Mem. La. State Bd. Dentistry, 1970—. Mem. Morehouse Parish aux. police force, 1967—; organizer, planner Prairie View Acad., Bastrop, 1969-72. Bd. dirs. No. La. Health Planning Council, Council for Dental Care Corp. Served with USNR, 1957-59. Mem. Am., Internat. coll. dentists, Am., La. (dir., also trustee Dental Relief Fund 1967-70), 5th Dist. (pres. 1964) dental assns., Am. Dental Soc. Dentistry for Children, Am. Assn. Dental Examiners, La. Farm Bur., Bastrop C. of C. Baptist (deacon, tchr. 1959-69). Lion. Clubs: Morehouse Country (Bastrop). Home: 1602 Parson Dr Bastrop LA 71220 Office: 312 Durham St Bastrop LA 71220

KELLER, GERALD CHRISTIAN, physician; b. New Orleans, Apr. 24, 1934; s. Dewey Cronelius and Aurelie Mary (Weber) K.; B.S. cum laude in Biology, Loyola U. of South, New Orleans, 1956; M.D., La. State U., 1959; m. Joan Mary Arnold, Dec. 28, 1957; children—Sharon, Chris, John, Jennifer, Jody, Dan, Scott, Roger. Intern, Madigan Army Hosp., Tacoma, Wash., 1959-60; practice gen. medicine, Mandeville, La., 1963—; staff St. Tammany Parish Hosp., 1963—, sec.-treas., 1970—, v.p., 1971-72, chief of staff, 1971-73. Clin. instr. dept. gen. practice La. State U. Med. Sch., New Orleans, 1970—. Pres., Our Lady of the Lake Sch. Bd., 1967-69, v.p., 1969-71, chmn. fund drive, 1966—; mem. Olympia Carnival Orgn., 1966—. Alderman, Mandeville, La., 1968—, mayor pro tem, 1968-72. Served to capt. AUS, 1958-63. Diplomate Am. Bd. Family Practice (charter). Mem. St. Tammany Parish Med. Soc. (pres. 1971—), Mandeville C. of C. K.C. Clubs: Covington (La.) Country; Ponchatrain Yacht, King's of Juno (Mandeville). Home: 2733 North St Mandeville LA 70448 Office: 2810 Florida St Mandeville LA 70448

KELLER, JAMES ALAN, realtor; b. Cin., Apr. 24, 1927; s. Nathan Hale and Dorothy Elaine (Feld) K.; B.B.A., U. Tex., 1949; m. Madelyn Kaufman, June 4, 1950; children—Susan, Patricia, Lynn, Nancy. Salesman, William J. Elliott Co., El Paso, Tex., 1949-51; pres. James A. Keller, Realtors, El Paso, 1951—; sec., dir. Holiday Parks Am., Inc., 1971—. Mem. El Paso County Planning Commn., 1955-56; v.p. El Paso Jr. C. of C., 1952-58. Served with USNR, 1945-46. Mem. El Paso Bd. Realtors (pres. 1962), Soc. Indsl. Realtors (pres. Ariz., N.M., Tex. chpt. 1972-73), Nat. Assn. Realtors, Tex. Realtors Assn. Clubs: Del Norte (v.p. 1973-74), Coronado Country (sec., dir. 1971-74). Home: 908 Cherry Hill Lane El Paso TX 79912 Office: 510 N Mesa St El Paso TX 79901

KELLER, OSWALD LEWIN, JR., chemist; b. N.Y.C., May 24, 1930; s. Oswald Lewin and Katherine Doris (Leiding) K.; B.S., U. of South, 1951; Ph.D. (Rockefeller fellow, Visking Corp. fellow), Mass. Inst. Tech., 1959; m. Dona Claire Guild, Oct. 9, 1953; children—Christopher Guild, Claire, Elaine, Elizabeth. Chemist, Oak Ridge Nat. Lab., 1960-66, dir. transuranium research lab., 1966—. Mem. transplutonium program com. AEC, 1966—, panel on nuclear physics Nat. Acad. Scis., 1971-73. Served with AUS, 1954-56. USPHS fellow, Mass. Inst. Tech., 1959-60. Mem. A.A.A.S., Am. Chem. Soc., Am. Phys. Soc., Phi Beta Kappa. Home: 101 Morgan Rd Oak Ridge TN 37830 Office: PO Box X Oak Ridge TN 37830

KELLER, RICHARD LAURENCE, labor economist; b. Deering, N.D., Mar. 21, 1922; s. Herman and Alice (Keane) K.; B.B.A., U. Portland, 1960, M.B.A., 1961; m. Sarah Jane Hurst, Mar. 1, 1968. Research asst. U. Portland, 1960-61; accountant Fed. Housing Administrn., Washington, 1962-66; economist Dept. Labor, Washington, 1966—. Mem. Am. Statis. Assn., Alpha Kappa Psi. Independent. Roman Catholic. Home: 1200 S Court House Rd Arlington VA 22204 Office: 4077 F 441 G St NW Washington DC 20212

KELLERMAN, ROBERT EUGENE, petroleum co. exec.; b. Beggs, Okla., Dec. 20, 1927; s. John Austin and Mary (Bungard) K.; B.S. in Petroleum Engring., U. Tex., 1949; m. Shirley Pulley, Sept. 3, 1949; children—Robert Scott, Shelby Kay. Dist. engr. Republic Natural Gas Co., 1949-52; dist. engr., chief engr., gen. mgr. Tex. Crude Oil Co., Ft. Worth, 1952-71; pres. N.Am. Internat., Inc., 1965-71, Petroleum Leaseholds, Inc., 1965-71, Tex. Crude Oil Co., Inc., 1965-71; v.p. Pipeline Transp. Inc. 1965-71; pres. Oppenheimer Oil & Gas, Inc., Ft. Worth, 1971—; dir. Am. Quasar Petroleum, Gateway Nat. Bank. Mem. Ft. Worth City Art Commn. Central area chmn. Oil Information Com., 1958-60, recipient silver certificate for service, 1958. Registered profl. engr. Mem. Tex. Mid-Continent Oil and Gas Assn., Am. Petroleum Inst., Am. Inst. Mining, Metall. and Petroleum Engrs., Ind. Petroleum Assn. Am. (dir.), Tarrant County Tex. Ex-Students Assn. (pres. 1967), Friars, Ft. Worth Wildcatters (dir.), Tau Beta Pi, Sigma Gamma Epsilon. Democrat. Mem. Disciples of Christ (deacon, elder). Home: 1517 Hillcrest St Fort Worth TX 76107 Office: 3309 Winthrop St Suite 207 Fort Worth TX 76116

KELLETT, WILLIAM HIRAM, JR., educator, designer; b. Bryan, Tex., Oct. 15, 1930; s. William Hiram and Elizabeth (Minsky) K.; A.A., Victoria Coll., 1954; B.Arch., Tex. A. and M. U., 1960, M.Arch., 1967; m. Christiana Maria Binsch, Feb. 2, 1962 (div.); children—Elizabeth Julia, Rene Janine, Kira Lorraine; m. 2d, Ann Robertson Wilkins, Dec. 11, 1971; children—Robert, Patricia. Elec. technician W.E. Kutzschbach Co., Bryan, Tex., 1950-51; engring. technologist Johnston & Davis, Victoria, Tex., 1952-54; mech., elec. systems designer Hall Engring. Co., Bryan, 1955-62; prof. environmental design Tex. A. and M. U., College Station, 1962—; mech. and elec. systems designer Environments, Inc., Bryan, 1962—. Vice chmn. City Charter Com., Bryan, 1969; chmn. Bd. Equalization, 1969-70. Mem. Illuminating Engr. Soc., Am. Assn. U. Profs., Am. Soc. Heating, Refrigeration and Air Conditioning Engrs., Refrigeration Engrs. and Tech. Assn., Phi Theta Kappa, Tau Beta Pi, Tau Sigma Delta. Home: 1000 Esther Blvd Bryan TX 77801 Office: Coll Architecture and Design Tex A and M U College Station TX 77840

KELLEY, BROWN WILSON, dentist; b. Irvine, Ky., Jan. 2, 1899; s. James S. and Annie (Wilson) K.; student U. Ky., 1917-18; D.D.S., U. Louisville, 1925; m. Lellyn Phillips Durrett, Feb. 16, 1927 (dec.); children—Brown Wilson, James D. Gen. practice dentistry, Louisville, 1925—. Instr. U. Louisville Sch. Dentistry, 1925-37. Served with USN, 1918. Mem. Am., Ky. dental assns., Louisville Dist. Dental Soc., League Ky. Sportsmen (pres. 1934, dir. 1934—), Southend Civic League, Psi Omega, Omicron Kappa Epsilon. Mem. Christian Ch. Clubs: University (sec. 1927), Mercator (Louisville). Home: 100 Ash Av Pewee Valley KY 40056 Office: Fincastle Bldg 325 Broadway Louisville KY 40202

KELLEY, CARLTON WILLIAM, jr. coll. pres.; b. Cullman, Ala., Mar. 19, 1906; s. Monroe Morgan and Louisa Anna (Livingston) K.; B.A., Birmingham So. Coll., 1927; M.A., U. Ala., 1945; L.H.D., Athens Coll.; m. Louella Masterson, Nov. 26, 1937; 1 dau., Ellen Frances. Accountant, Lone Star Cement Co., Birmingham, Ala., 1929-31; tchr. Decatur (Ala.) High Sch., 1931-42; supr. war prodn., also tng. dir. John C. Calhoun Tech. Sch., Decatur, 1942-47; pres. Calhoun Jr. Coll., Decatur, 1947—. Mem. Nat., Ala. edn. assns., Am., Ala. vocational assns., Ala. Assn. Sch. Adminstrs., Am. Assn. Schs., Nat. Assn. Jr. Colls., So. Assn. Secondary Schs., Am. Tech. Edn. Assn., Ala. Commn. for Better Schs., Huntsville, Decatur and Athens chambers commerce, Iota Lambda Sigma, Delta Sigma Phi. Methodist. Lion. Address: Box 427 Decatur AL 35601

KELLEY, CHAPMAN, artist; b. San Antonio, Aug. 26, 1932; s. Ralph Payne and Ruby (Sloane) K.; spl. art student Trinity U., 1948-50; student Pa. Acad. Fine Arts, 1951-55; m. Joan Catherine Wisner, Jan. 8, 1953; children—Cole Chapman II, Kevin Carson. Exhibited numerous one man shows, Dallas, Houston, Austin, Corpus Christi, San Antonio, Longview (all Tex.), Tulsa, N.Y.C., Memphis, New Orleans, San Francisco; exhibited group shows including Ringling Nat. Exhibit, Sarasota, Fla., 1959, Southwestern Print and Drawing Exhibit, 1959, Southwestern Art Invitational, Dallas Mus. Fine Art, 1960, 157th Pa. Acad. Ann., 1962, Former Students Exhibit at Pa. Acad. Fine Arts, 1962, Butler Inst., Youngstown, O., Corcoran Gallery, Washington, 1963, Cummer Gallery Art, 1964, Abilene (Tex.) Fine Arts Mus., 1964, Okla. Art Center, Okla. City, 1964-67; represented in permanent collections Dallas Mus. Fine Arts, Tex. Instruments, Inc., Colorado Springs Fine Arts Center, Mulvane Art Center, Topeka, Okla. Art Center, Witte Meml. Mus., San Antonio, 1st Nat. Bank of Dallas, Tex., numerous other pub. and pvt. collections. Owner, operator Atelier Chapman Kelley, art sch., gallery, frame shop, Dallas; panelist Matrix for Arts Symposium, Center Advanced Studies, U. Ill., 1967; also lectr. Recipient awards including State Fair Tex. Purchase prize 22d Ann. Tex. Painting and Sculpture Exhibit, 1960; S.J. Wallace Truman prize N.A.D.; 1963, Childe Hassam Purchase award Am. Acad. Arts and Letters. William Emlen Cresson European traveling scholar, 1954-55, 1st prize Tex. Painting and Sculpture Exhbn., 1964, 8 State Ann. Painting and Sculpture Exhibit, Okla. Art Center, 1965, Purchase award Nat. Sun Carnival show, El Paso Mus. Home: 5511 Fairfield Dallas TX 75205 Office: 2526 Fairmount St Dallas TX 75201

KELLEY, DRENAN, sociologist, educator; b. Irasburg, Vt., Oct. 4, 1917; s. Charles Wesley and Grace (Collins) K.; student Concord (N.H.) Coll. Bus., 1935-37; A.B. magna cum laude, Harvard, 1950; M.A., U. Minn., 1957; Ph.D., La. State U., 1961; m. Delores Myrtle Ritter, July 2, 1956. Instr., Laconia (N.H.) Bus. Coll., 1938-40; instr. U. Minn., 1952-53; social sci. analyst USAF, MacDill AFB, Fla., 1956; instr. La. State U., 1959-60; asst. prof. San Fernando Valley State Coll., Northridge, Cal., 1961-63; asso. prof. U. Ga., Athens, 1963—, asso. dept. head, 1965-69; vis. lectr. Fla. State U., 1970; sec. S-61 So. regional research project USDA, 1964-66, chmn., 1966-67, vice chmn., 1967-68; sec. so. rural sociology research com. Farm Found., 1969-71, vice chmn., 1971-73, chmn., 1973-74. Active Ga. Easter Seal Soc., Athens-Clarke County Mental Health Soc., Univ. Centers for Rational Alternatives. Mem. Democratic nat. com. 1968—, Ga. Dem. party Forum, 1968—. Served with AUS, 1940-46. Recipient award of merit Fort Dix, N.J., 1945, Metzger award Am. Inst. Cooperation, 1957. Mem. Am. Sociol. Assn., Rural Sociol. Soc. (past com. chmn., mem. exec. council), So. Sociol. Soc., Am. Assn. U. Profs., Ga. Sociol. and Anthrop. Assn. (pres. 1973-74), Am. Civil Liberties Union, Menninger Found., Ga. Sheriffs Assn., Smithsonian Assos., Internat. Platform Assn., Alpha Kappa Delta. Contbr. articles to profl. jours. Home: 381 Beechwood Dr Athens GA 30601

KELLEY, EOGHAN NEWMAN, architect; b. Sanford, Fla., Oct. 12, 1932; s. Harold H. and Viola (Hage) Kastner; student Marquette U., 1951, U. Fla., 1951-52, 56-58; m. Jennifer Castello, June 28, 1958; children—Christopher, Maureen, Kevin, Monica. Practice architecture, Sanford, 1964—. Served with USMCR, 1952-55. Important works include Idyllwilde Elementary Sch., 1970, Teague Middle Sch., Forest City Elementary Sch., Brantley High Sch. Office: 500 W Seminole Blvd Sanford FL 32771 also PO Drawer 1898 Sanford FL 32771

KELLEY, GRACE WINIFRED COOKNEY (MRS. TRUMAN LEE KELLEY), civic worker; b. London, Eng.; d. William and Annie (Howe) Cookney; student pub. and pvt. schs., Eng.; m. Francis Dufty Madge, June 9, 1921 (div. July 1936); 1 dau., Joyce Winifred (Mrs. Duane Callahan); m. 2d, Truman Lee Kelley, Aug. 4, 1936 (dec.); children—Kalon Lee, Kenneth Truman. Came to U.S., 1922, naturalized, 1937. Sec. Assistance League of Santa Barbara, 1950, projects chmn., 1953—; pres. Fla. Atlantic Music Guild, 1968; 1st v.p. Boca Raton Music Study Club, 1971-72. Mem. Nat. Soc. Arts and Letters (ways and means chmn. 1963, treas. 1965-66, mem. nat. bd.; pres. Santa Barbara 1967-68), Internat. Platform Assn. English Speaking Union (dir.). Republican. Episcopalian. Clubs: Birnam Wood Golf, Boca Raton Golf, Montecito Country, Garden (conservation chmn. 1952). Home: 700 S Ocean Blvd Boca Raton FL 33432

KELLEY, HERBERT DAVID, JR., civil engr.; b. Akron, O., Dec. 4, 1937; s. Herbert David and Marie (Bonebrake) K.; B.S. in Civil Engring., U. Akron, 1960; m. Pauline Emmanuel, Dec. 23, 1967; children—Kathryn Marie (Mrs. Jay Willis), Kimberly Ann (Mrs. Randell Kerr), Dana Lyn, Bryan David. Engr. sewer engring. div. Bur. Engring., Akron, O., 1963-69; chief design engr. firm Adair & Brady, Inc., Lake Worth, Fla., 1969-73; pres. Kelley Engring. Assos., Inc., West Palm Beach, Fla., 1973—. Served with USAF, 1960-61. Registered profl. engr., Ohio, Fla. Mem. Am. Soc. C.E., Am. Soc. Mil. Engrs., Nat., Ohio socs. profl. engrs., Fla. Engring. Soc. Club: Sons of Herman (Akron). Prin. author: Geodetic Control Network - City of Akron, Ohio, 1965. Home: 7310 W Lake Dr West Palm Beach FL 33406 Office: 1744 N Military Trail West Palm Beach FL 33406

KELLEY, JOHN TOWNSEND, dentist; b. Waco, Tex., Apr. 28, 1915; s. John Townsend and Edna Earle (Ewing) K.; student Baylor U., 1931-34; D.D.S., U. Mo., 1938; m. Margaret A. Stone, Dec. 29, 1936; children—John Townsend III, James E., Margaret (Mrs. Gary Tipton). Gen. practice dentistry, Taylor, Tex., 1938-41, practice ltd. to orthodontics, El Paso, Tex., 1945—; preceptorship in orthodontics Dr. W. T. Chapman, El Paso, 1945-46. Bd. dirs. Southwestern Children's Home, El Paso. Served with AUS, 1941-45. Decorated Bronze Star, Silver Star. Diplomate Am. Bd. Orthodontics. Mem. Am. Dental Assn., Am. Soc. Orthodontists, El Paso Dental Soc. (pres. 1952-53). Episcopalian. Clubs: El Paso Skeet, Coronado Country (El Paso). Home: 4015 Las Vegas St El Paso TX 79902 Office: El Paso Med Center El Paso TX 79902

KELLEY, JOHN WYNNE, JR., lawyer; b. Nashville, Sept. 23, 1931; s. John Wynne and Myrtle Josephine (Hawkins) K.; B.A., Vanderbilt U., 1955, J.D., 1959; m. Lynn Page Edgerton, June 14, 1958; children—John Wynne III, Howard E., Page W., Virginia H. Admitted to Tenn. bar, 1959, since practiced in Nashville; asso. Hooker, Keeble, Dodson & Harris, 1959-71; partner Ortale, Kelley, Herbert & Crawford, 1971—. Mem. Tenn. Ho. of Reps., 1963-65. Served with USAF, 1952-53. Mem. Am., Tenn., Nashville (sec.-treas. 1971, dir. 1972—) bar assns., Am. Judicature Soc., Barristers Club (pres. 1967), Kappa Sigma, Phi Delta Phi. Roman Catholic. Club: Serra. Home: 416 Hunt Club Rd Nashville TN 37221 Office: Third Nat Bank Bldg Nashville TN 37219

KELLEY, MELVIN WILLARD, polystyrene container co. exec.; b. Clinton, Ind., Nov. 3, 1933; s. Raymond Willard and Evelyn (Hestella) C.; A.B. in Chemistry, Ind. U., 1961, M.B.A. in Mgmt., 1962; m. Erma Kaywin Kuhns, May 17, 1953; children—Kathryn Elaine, Deborah Lynne. Indsl. engr. prodn. incentives Eli Lilly & Co., Indpls., 1962-65, prodn. coordinator Elanco div., 1965-66, purchasing agt., 1966-68, mgr. purchasing Creative Packaging div., 1968-70, mgr. distbn. services, Roanoke, Va., 1970-73, mgr. material planning cosmetic prodn., 1974—. Faculty, Ind. Central Coll., 1963-65, Ind. U., Indpls., 1965-70. Served with AUS, 1954-56; ETO. Mason. Home: 118 Sawyer Dr Salem VA 24153 Office: 4411 Hollins Rd Roanoke VA 24003

KELLEY, OMER JOSEPH, govt. ofcl.; b. Akron, Colo., May 30, 1914; s. John A. and Cecilia (Heitman) K.; B.S., Colo. State U., 1939, M.S., 1940; Ph.D., Ohio State U., 1942; m. Frances E. Wilson, Dec. 24, 1940; children—Michael, Kevin, Dianne (Mrs. Duncan Baird), Kerry Kim, Shannon. With U.S. Dept. Agr., various locations, 1943-61, chief soil, water mgmt. research Western div., Fort Collins, 1947-53, agrl. adminstr. western soil, water mgmt. research br. Agrl. Research Service, Beltsville, Md., 1953-61; mgr. Agrl. Research Center, Stanford Research Inst., Menlo Park, Cal., 1961-66; dir. office agr. Bur. Tech. Assistance, AID, State Dept., Washington, 1966—. Pres. Ravenwood Citizens Assn., Falls Church, Va., 1968-69. Recipient Rockefeller Pub. Service award Woodrow Wilson Sch. Pub. Adminstrn., Princeton, 1954, Distinguished Alumni award Ohio State U., 1972. Fellow Am. Soc. Agronomy, A.A.A.S.; mem. Sigma Xi, Gamma Sigma Delta, Phi Lambda Upsilon. Elk. Contbr. articles to profl. jours. Home: 3259 Juniper Lane Falls Church VA 22044 Office: AID Washington DC 20523

KELLEY, WILLIAM NIMMONS, physician; b. Atlanta, June 23, 1939; s. Oscar Lee and Will (Nimmons) K.; M.D., Emory U., 1963; m. Lois Ann Faville, Aug. 1, 1959; children—Margaret Paige, Virginia Lynn, Lori Ann, William Mark. Intern, Parkland Meml. Hosp., Dallas, 1963-64, resident medicine, 1964-65; sr. resident medicine Mass. Gen. Hosp., Boston, 1967-68; staff asso. Lab. Biochemistry and Metabolism, NIAMD, NIH, Bethesda, Md., 1965-66, clin. asso. sect. on human biochem. genetics Arthritis and Rheumatism br., 1966-67; teaching fellow medicine Harvard, 1967-68; asst. prof. medicine Duke Med. Center, Durham, N.C., 1968-69, asst. prof. medicine, asst. prof. biochemistry, 1969-70, chief div. rheumatic and genetic diseases, dept. medicine, asst. prof. medicine and biochemistry, 1970-71, chief div. rheumatic and genetic diseases, asso. prof. medicine, asst. prof. biochemistry, 1971—. Cons. Womack Army Hosp., Ft. Bragg, N.C. Chmn., Young Mens Com. for Health Affairs, 1971-72. Recipient C.V. Mosby award, 1963; John D. Lane award USPHS, 1969; Geigy Internat. prize of Rheumatology, 1969; Research Career Devel. award USPHS, 1972—. Mead Johnson scholar, 1967; Clin. scholar Am. Rheumatism Assn., 1969-72. Diplamate Am. Bd. Internal Medicine. Fellow A.C.P.; mem. Am. Soc. Clin. Investigation, Am. Soc. Biol. Chemists, Am. Fedn. Clin. Research (nat. council, sec.-treas. So. sect.), Am. Rheumatism Assn. Episcopalian. Asso. editor: Metabolism, 1972—; cons. editor Life Scis., 1973—; editorial bd. Arthritis and Rheumatism, 1972—; mem. editorial adv. bd. Research in Exptl. Medicine, 1971—. Contbr. articles to profl. jours. Home: 3500 Donnigale Av Durham NC 27705

KELLOGG, ANGEL IVEY (MRS. KARL BRITTAN KELLOGG), club woman; b. Seattle, Nov. 30, 1922; d. Joseph Nettles and Margaret (Armstrong) Ivey; B.S., U. Wash., 1948; m. Karl Brittan Kellogg, Aug. 12, 1955. Dietetic intern N.Y. Hosp., 1949; dietitian Providence Hosp., Seattle, 1953-55. Chmn. local affairs Baton Rouge chpt. League Women Voters, 1955-56, chmn. state affairs, 1956-57, chmn. finance, 1956-57, 1st v.p., 1958-59, bd. dirs. La., 1957-60; bd. dirs. Baton Rouge YWCA, 1957-60, sec. bd. dirs., 1958-59, chmn. pub. relations, 1957-59, chmn. nominating com., 1959-60; capt. United Givers, Baton Rouge, 1962-63, vice chmn., 1964; editor newsletter Baton Rouge Civic Symphony Women's Auxiliary, 1958-59, 1st v.p., 1958-59, pres., 1959-60; bd. dirs. Baton Rouge Civic Symphony Assn., 1957-60; family investigator Goodfellows, 1962-63; vol. Am. Cancer Soc., Baton Rouge, 1963-64, sect. leader; mem. edn. com. La. Commn. Status of Women, 1965-68; chmn. Equal Rights Amendments Com. of Baton Rouge, 1970-71. Precinct committeewoman 45th dist. Seattle Dem. Party, 1954-55. Mem. Baton Rouge Chamber Music Soc., La. Ornithol. Soc., Internat. Platform Assn., La. State Women's Polit. Caucus, Nat. Orgn. Women. Democrat. Methodist. Clubs: Bocage Racquet, Baton Rouge Country (Baton Rouge). Contbr. story mag. Home: 2360 Fairway Dr Baton Rouge LA 70809

KELLOGG, GLEN T., san. engr., state ofcl.; b. Geraldine, Mont., May 15, 1915; s. Roecoe J. and Pearl (Yeamans) K.; B.S. in Chemistry, Jamestown Coll., 1937; B.S. in Civil Engring., U. Ia., 1940; M.S. in San. Engring., U. N.C., 1949; m. Martha H. Hoss, Nov. 25, 1942; 1 son, Glen T. Pub. health engr. Miss. Health Dept., Jackson, 1940-41; san. engr. Ft. Belvoir (Va.) Engrs. Bd., 1941-42; with Ark. Health Dept., Little Rock, 1947—, prin. san. engr., 1949-51, asst. dir., 1951-55, chief san. engr., dir. bur. san. engring., 1955-71, dir., chief engr. Bur. Constrn. Pvt. Services, 1971—. Mem. Ark. Well Drilling License Com., 1969, Ark. Mobile Home Standards Commn., 1973. Served with AUS, 1942-46. Recipient Henry B. Davis award Am. Soc. San. Engring., 1968; award Ark. Plumbing Contractors, 1968. Registered profl. engr., Ark. Mem. Water Pollution Control Fedn., Nat., Ark. socs. profl. engrs., Am. Water Works Assn. (past chmn. S.W. sec., recipient Fuller award 1963, sec.-treas. 1966-73), Ark. Pub. Health Assn., Fed. Sewage and Indsl. Wastes Assn. (Ark. dir.), Theta Tau. Methodist. Home: 15 Sun Valley Rd Little Rock AR 72205 Office: Ark Health Dept Little Rock AR 72201

KELLY, CATHERINE BURTON, judge; b. Washington, Dec. 12, 1917; d. William Francis and Catherine (Burton) Kelly; B.A., Smith Coll., 1939; J.D., George Washington U., 1951. Admitted to D.C. bar, 1951; practiced in Washington; with firm Kelly & Nicolaides, 1951-53; asst. U.S. atty., 1953-57; asso. judge D.C. Ct. Gen. Sessions, 1957-67; asso. judge D.C. Ct. Appeals, 1967—. Recipient George Washington U. Alumni Achievement award, 1965. Mem. Am., D.C., D.C. Unified, D.C. Womens, Fed. bar assns., Nat. Assn. Women Lawyers, Am. Judicature Soc., Nat. Lawyers Club, Nat. Fedn. Bus. and Profl. Womens Clubs. Kappa Beta Pi. Club: Washington. Home: 4501 Connecticut Av NW Washington DC 20008 Office: 400 F St NW Washington DC 20001

KELLY, CLARENCE MARION, govt. ofcl.; b. Kansas City, Mo., Oct. 24, 1911; s. Clarence Bond and Minnie (Brown) K.; A.B., U. Kan., 1936; LL.B., U. Mo. at Kansas City, 1940; m. Ruby Dyeantha Pickett, Aug. 28, 1937; children—Mary Ruth (Mrs. Edward Ragland Dobbins, Jr.), Kent Clarence. With FBI, 1940-61, spl. agt. in charge, Birmingham, Ala., 1957-60, Memphis, 1960-61; chief of police, Kansas City, Mo., 1961-73; dir. FBI, Washington, 1973—. Mem. Mo. Law Enforcement Assistance Council, Jefferson City. Bd. dirs. Boys' Club, United Fund, Starlight Theatre Assn. Served with USNR, 1944-46. Recipient J. Edgar Hoover gold medal award, 1970, Reverence for Law award Eagles, 1971, award for contbns. to law enforcement Dictograph Co., 1971. Mem. Internat. Assn. Chiefs of Police (mem. organized crime com., mem. narcotics and dangerous drugs com., dir.), Mo. Police Chiefs, Tenn.-Miss. Peace Officers, Mo. Peace Officers (dir.), Phi Delta Phi, Sigma Nu. Mem. Christian Ch. (elder). Office: Hdqrs FBI 9th St and Pennsylvania Av NW Washington DC 20535

KELLY, DEE J., lawyer; b. Bonham, Tex., Mar. 7, 1929; s. Dee Cleveland and Era Lee (Jones) K.; A.B., Tex. Christian U., 1950; LL.B., George Washington U., 1954; m. Janice LeBlanc, Dec. 30, 1954; children—Cynthia L., Dee J., Craig LeBlanc. Admitted to Tex. bar, 1954, U.S. Supreme Ct. bar, 1960; asst. to Ho. of Reps. speaker Sam Rayburn, Washington, 1949-51, 53-54; legal examiner oil and gas div. R.R. Commn. Tex., Austin, 1955-56; gen. counsel Moncrief Oil Interests, Ft. Worth, 1958-63; pvt. practice law, Ft. Worth, 1963—. Bd. dirs. Tex. Turnpike Authority, 1967—, chmn., 1969; mem. Interstate Oil Compact Commn., 1968—. Bd. Regents Tax. Sr. Coll. System, 1969—. Mem. Fort Worth, Tarrant County, Am. bar assns., State Bar Tex., Tex. Bar Found., Fort Worth C. of C. Democrat. Clubs: River Crest Country, Fort Worth, Shady Oaks Country. Home: 1315 Hillcrest St Fort Worth TX 76107 Office: 727 Fort Worth Nat Bank Bldg Fort Worth TX 76102

KELLY, EDWARD ARTHUR, lawyer; b. Houston, Mar. 16, 1903; s. Michael and Annie (Althaus) K.; B.A., Rice U., 1926; J.D., U. Tex., 1929; m. Hermena Hancock, Dec. 30, 1937. Admitted to Tex. bar, 1929; asso. firm Franklin & Blankenbecker, Houston, 1929-37; partner firm Franklin, Kelly, Graham & Laughter, Houston, 1937—. Dir. Greater Houston Bank, H.H. Null Contractors & Engrs., Manchester Terminal Corp., Houston Cotton Exchange and Bd. Trade, all Houston. Mem. Am., Houston bar assns., State Bar Tex., Am. Judicature Soc. Clubs: Houston World Trade, Old Capitol, Association Rice Alumni. (all Houston). Home: 20 Crestwood St Houston TX 77007 Office: 1300 Prairie Av Houston TX 77002

KELLY, FRANK ALLAN, lawyer; b. Kingsport, Tenn., Mar. 22, 1940; s. Frank H. and Lovie (Baker) K.; B.A. in History, Tenn. Technol. U., 1962; J.D. (Cooper D. Schmidt fellow), U. Va., 1965; m. Mary Alice Boyd, Aug. 3, 1963; children—Alice Jones, Tricia Ann. Admitted to N.Y. bar, 1965, Va. bar, 1965, Tenn. bar, 1966; asso. firm Everett, Johnson & Breckenridge, N.Y.C., 1965-66; partner firm Hunter, Smith, Davis, Norris & Treadway, Kingsport, Tenn., 1966—. Dir. Oakwood Markets Inc., Kingsport. Adviser Boys Club, Kingsport, 1967—; mem. Kingsport Citizens Adv. Com., 1966—, Tri-Cities Planning Council, 1967—, Kingsport Mental Health Assn., 1966—. Mgr. Sullivan County div. Baker for Senate U.S., 1972. Bd. dirs. Kingsport chpt. A.R.C. Mem. Kingsport (v.p.), Tenn., N.Y. State, Va. bar assns., Nat. Life Underwriters Assn. Elk, Moose. Clubs: Ridgefields Country, Kingsport Racquet Inc. Editor: Va. Jour. Internat. Law, 1964-65. Home: 621 Ridgefields Rd Kingsport TN 37660 Office: 1101 Eastman Rd Kingsport TN 37664

KELLY, HAROLD CLAYTON, supt. schs.; b. Burns, Miss., Sept. 4, 1923; s. E.G. and Eula Mae (Winstead) K.; B.S.E., U. Miss., 1948, M.S. in Sch. Adminstrn. and Supervision, 1951, postgrad. 1960-65, advanced adminstr's. certificate, 1966; postgrad. Peabody Coll. Tchrs., summer 1958; m. Hannah Beeks Pitts, Oct. 27, 1951. Coach, sci. tchr., Batesville, Miss., 1948-49; sci. tchr., high sch. coach Yazoo City (Miss.) Schs., 1949-52, athletic dir., coach, 1952-54, jr. high sch. prin., 1953-54, high sch. prin., 1954-65, asst. supt., 1963-65, supt., 1965—. Mem. sch. evalution com. Miss. Accrediting Com., 1969—. Chmn. govt. and schs. div. United Givers Fund, 1958-62. Served with 5th Army Inf., AUS, 1942-45; ETO. Decorated Purple Heart; named Outstanding Citizen Civitan Club, 1970. Mem. Nat., Miss. (resolutions com. 1969—), Yazoo County edn. assns., Miss. Assn. Sch. Supts., Am. Assn. Sch. Adminstrs., Council Ednl. Facility Planners, Council Pub. Schs. (sec.-treas. 1969—), Yazoo County C. of C., Phi Delta Kappa. Methodist (trustee 1969—, mem. adminstrv. bd. 1961—). Home: 2051 Wildwood Terrace Yazoo City MS 39194 Office: 1133 Calhoun Av Yazoo City MS 39194

KELLY, HENRY JERVEY, state ofcl.; b. D'Lo, Miss., Nov. 16, 1906; s. Thaddeus Madison and Mabel (Robertson) K.; B.S. in Civil Engring., Ga. Tech. U., 1927; m. Claire Bennett, Mar. 1, 1947; children—Thomas J., Peter B., Nancy C. Engr. firm Stone & Webster, Houston, 1928-29, Humble Oil & Refining Co., Houston, 1930-31, TVA, Knoxville, Tenn., 1932-42; commd. 1st lt. C.E., U.S. Army, 1942, advanced through grades to col., 1945; mem. staff Gen. Eisenhower, ETO, World War II; comdg. officer 2d Engring. Constrn. Group, Korea, 1952-53; logistics staff officer Far Eastern Command Hdqrs., 1953-55; comdg. officer Schenectady Gen. Depot, 1956-58; engr. 12th U.S. Army Corps, Atlanta, 1959-60; dep. engr. South Atlantic div., Atlanta, 1960-62; ret., 1962; asst. dir. Fla. Bd. Conservation, Tallahassee, 1962-69, adminstrv. asst. Fla. Dept. Natural Resources, 1970—. Decorated Bronze Star, Legion Merit; Croix de Guerre with palm (Belgium). Registered profl. engr., Ga. Fellow Am. Soc. C.E.; mem. Pi Kappa Alpha. Methodist. Rotarian. Home: 3203 Enterprise Dr Tallahassee FL 32303 Office: 200 E Gaines St Tallahassee FL 32304

KELLY, HERBERT VALENTINE, lawyer; b. nr. Lawrenceville, Va., Feb. 14, 1920; s. William Herbert and Mary (Lundy) K.; B.A., William and Mary Coll., 1940, B.C.L., 1942; m. Beverly Elizabeth Peebles, Apr. 17, 1948; children—Herbert Valentine, Priscilla Lee. Admitted to Va. bar, 1941; mem. firm Jones, Blechman, Woltz & Kelly, Newport News, Va., 1941—, partner, 1949—. Chmn., Nat. Conf. Christians and Jews Brotherhood Week, 1952; mem. Gov.'s Adv. Com. on Redistricting State Va., 1960; mem. Va. Adv. Com. for Salvation Army, 1970—; chmn. Capital Fund campaign Peninsula council Boy Scouts Am., 1958, pres. council, 1963-65; chmn. Peninsula chpt. A.R.C., 1953; nat. bd. United Funds and Councils Am., 1958-60; campaign chmn. Peninsula chpt. United Fund., 1955, pres., 1956-57. Bd. dirs. Fort Eustis Transp. Mus.; trustee William and Mary Ednl. Found. Served to capt. USAAF, 1941-43. Recipient Silver Beaver award Boy Scouts Am., 1969; named Outstanding Young Man of Year, Jr. C. of C. Peninsula, 1954. Mem. Newport News Bar Assn. (pres. 1965), Va. State Bar (council 1968-71). Rotarian. Clubs: James River Country, Peninsula Sports. Home: 28 Jacobs Lane Newport News VA 23606 Office: 2600 Washington Av Newport News VA 23607

KELLY, JOHN PAUL, elec. engr.; b. Louisville, Oct. 1, 1931; s. Joseph Francis and LaDoska (DeJarnett) K.; B.S. in Elec. Engring., U. Ky., 1953; M.S. in Engring. Sci., N.C. State U., 1968; postgrad. Ohio State U., 1966-67, Wake Forest Coll., 1960; m. Edythe Mae Crady, Jan. 21, 1932; children—Byron David, Barry Douglas, Paul Michael, Karla Marshalle. With Western Electric Co., 1958—, contract rep. U.S. Army, 1958-60, staff grad. engr. tng., 1960-64, instr., planning engr. data processing system design Bell Tel. Labs., 1964-67, devel. engr. information systems devel., Greensboro, N.C., 1967-68, system engr., 1968—. Republican candidate County Commrs., N.C., 1962; vice chmn. Young Reps. N.J., 1966-67. Bd. dirs. So. Pilgrim Coll., Kernersville, N.C., sec., 1969—; bd. dirs. United Wesleyan Coll., Allentown, Pa. Served as staff sgt. USAF, 1951-55. Recipient Commendations U.S. Army, 1960, 64. Registered profl. engr., N.C. Presbyn. (pres. N.C. Wesleyan men 1969—). Author: Community Development Survey, 1960. Home: 2012 Medhurst Dr Greensboro NC 27410 Office: Dept 5214 Western Electric Co Greensboro NC 27400

KELLY, MARY CLAIRE COLEMAN (MRS. OTIS B. KELLY), coal corp. exec.; b. Lohrville, Ia., Sept. 16, 1916; d. Melvin M. and Virginia (Skeens) Coleman; B.A., Berea Coll., 1962; M.A., U. Ky., 1968, M.S. in L.S., 1967, postgrad., 1973; m. Otis B. Kelly, Apr. 10,

1935 (dec. July 1958); children—Floyd M., Lila Sue (Mrs. Kermit Bentley), Otis B., Lona Gail (Mrs. Franklin Casebolt), Verva Anne (Mrs. Morris Galitz). Pres., Greasy Creek Coal Co., Shelbiana, Ky., 1946-50; v.p. Sutton By-Products Coal Corp., Pikeville, Ky., 1956-58, pres., 1958—; pres. Sutton-Coleman Corp., 1968-73; propr. Claire's Book and Gift Shop, 1969-73; research asst. Council of So. Mountains, Berea, Ky.; 1959-60; child welfare worker Wise County Welfare Dept., Wise, Va., 1965; librarian Pikeville Free Pub. Library, 1966, Rowan County Pub. Library, Morehead, Ky., 1967, Louisville Free Pub. Library, 1968. Bd. dirs. Ky. Research Fedn., 1962-64, 72-73. Mem. Am. Assn. U. Women (pres. Pike County br. 1971-72), Pike County (pres. 1970-71), Ky. hist. socs. Republican. Baptist. Club: Graduate Education U. Ky. Editor: Pike County Sesquicentennial History, 1972. Home: PO Box 7027 Lexington KY 40502

KELLY, PAUL DEWILL, JR., lawyer; b. Jasper, Tenn., Sept. 16, 1927; s. Paul DeWitt and Ida (Miller) K.; J.D., Vanderbilt U., 1952; m. Mary Jane Ferris, Oct. 1, 1960; children—Ann Ferris, Elizabeth Neal, Paul DeWitt III. Admitted to Tenn. bar, 1952; since practice in Jasper; sr. partner firm Kelly & Leiderman; county atty. Marion County, Tenn. 1954—. Dir. Tenn. Consol. Coal Co., Marion Trust & Banking Co., Jasper. Served with AUS, 1946-47. Mem. Am., Tenn. (past v.p. jr. bar sect., bd. govs.), Marion County (past pres.) bar assns. Democrat. Episcopalian. Address: Betsy Pack Dr PO Box 488 Jasper TN 37347

KELLY, RICHARD, judge, b. 1924; A.B., Colo. State Coll. Edn.; J.D., U. Fla. Admitted to bar, 1952; judge 6th Circuit Ct., Fla., 1960—. Mem. Am., Fed. bar assns. Address: County Bldg Port Richey FL 33552

KELLY, ROBERT EMMETT, educator; b. Cape Girardeau, Mo., Nov. 26, 1929; s. Robert Emmett and Gladys (Admas) K.; B.S., S.E. Mo. State U., 1950; M.S., U. Mo., 1952; Ph.D., U. Conn., 1959; m. Sarah Grace Combs, June 6, 1962; children—Katelyn, Frank, Tara. Physicist, E.I. DuPont de Nemours & Co., Inc., Aiken, S.C., 1957-59; faculty dept. physics U. Miss., University, 1959—, prof., 1966—. Sci. research with Los Alamos, Boeing, Gen. Electric, Am. Optical, Lawrence Radiation Lab., Woods Hole Oceanographic. Served with Signal Corps, AUS, 1954-56. AEC fellow, 1965; NASA fellow, 1970-71. Mem. Am. Radio Relay League, Am. Geophys. Union, Am. Fedn. Musicians, Sigma Xi, Sigma Pi Sigma. Methodist. Clubs: Amateur Radio (U. Miss.). Woodwind performer various civic symphonies, concert bands. Contbr. articles to profl. jours. Home: PO Box 493 University MS 38677

KELLY, ROBERT FRANK, biochemist; b. Fond du Lac, Wis., May 21, 1919; s. William and Marie Ida (Ruechel) K.; student Oshkosh (Wis.) State Tchrs. Coll., 1940-42; B.S., U. Wis., 1948, M.S., 1953, Ph.D., 1955; m. Olive Ann Bloedow, July 31, 1944; children—Paul R., Kathryn (Mrs. Allen Atkins), Patricia, Jean, Daniel, Michael. Farmer, 1938-43; tchr. vocational agr. Waukesha High Sch., 1948-51; prof. meat and animal sci. Va. Poly. Inst. and State U., Blacksburg, 1955—. Cons., Williams-Waterman Fund, N.Y.C., Ohio Dept. Agr., Pa. Dept. Agr.; judge Nat. Ham-Bacon-Sausage Show. Sec., Diocesan Council Catholic Men, 1972-73. Served with USAAF, 1944-46. Mem. A.A.A.S., Am. Meat Sci. Assn. (dir. 1967-68, recipient Distinguished Tchr. award 1973), Inst. Food Technologists, Am. Soc. Animal Sci., Res. Officers Assn. (pres. Montgomery chpt.), Meat Judging Coaches Assn. (pres. elect), Sigma Xi, Gamma Sigma Delta, Alpha Zeta. Editor: Meat Evaluation Handbook, 1968. Contbr. articles profl. jours. Home: 2801 Shadow Lake Rd Blacksburg VA 24060

KELLY, ROBERT PERRY, lawyer; b. Hockerville, Okla., Nov. 21, 1926; s. Harry Boon and Verna (Hires) K.; A.B., U. Mo., 1950, LL.B., 1952, J.D., 1969; m. Ella Borden Craig, Aug. 6, 1950; children—Edna Sue, Verna Kay, Henry Boon. Admitted to Okla. bar, 1952, U.S. Supreme Ct. bar, 1971; practiced in Pawhuska; sr. partner Kelly & Gambill, 1965—. Mem. Bd. Edn. Ind. Dist. 2, 1964—. Served with USAAF, 1945-47. Mem. Am., Okla., Osage County bar assns., Pawhuska C. of C. (dir. 1959-62). Republican. Presbyn. Kiwanian (lt. gov. Div. 15, chmn. laws, regulations and resolution Tex.-Okla. Dist.). Bd. editors Mo. Law Rev., 1950-52. Home: 315 E 16th St Pawhuska OK 74056 Office: 6th and Kihekah Sts Pawhuska OK 74056

KELLY, ROBERT WITHERS, educator; b. Stanford, Ky., Oct. 20, 1926; s. Ernest and Alpha (Lile) K.; A.B., Centre Coll. of Ky., 1949; M.S., U. Ore., 1950; postgrad. U. Ky., 1950-51; Ph.D., U. Mo., 1956; m. Elizabeth Linnette Bright, Aug. 16, 1948; children—James Robert, William Burdette. Instr., Campbellsville (Ky.) Coll., 1951-53; asso. prof. Southeastern La. Coll., Hammond, 1956-63, Ariz. State Coll., Flagstaff, 1963-64; faculty Furman U., Greensville, S.C., 1964—, prof. zoology 1964—. Served with AUS, 1944-46. Mem. Am. Soc. Zoologists, Southeastern Biologists, S.C. Acad. Sci., Sigma Chi, Phi Kappa Phi. Home: PO Box 247 Travelers Rest SC 29690 Office: Biology Dept. Furman U Greenville SC 29613

KELLY, THOMAS ALEXANDER, economist; b. Nashville, Nov. 6, 1912; s. Timothy Aloysius and Alice Inez (Scruggs) K.; B.A., Vanderbilt U., 1933, M.A., 1940, Ph.D., 1950; m. Elizabeth Douglass Levine, Feb. 14, 1942; children—Mary E., Sarah J., Timothy A., Ellen D. Instr. econs. Vanderbilt U., 1946-47; asst. prof. bus. adminstrn. Miss. State Coll., 1947-51, asso. prof., 1951-55; chmn. econs. and bus. adminstrn. Roanoke Coll., 1955-59; prof. bus. adminstrn. Lynchburg Coll., 1959-65; economist Va. Div. Indsl. Devel., Richmond, 1965—. Mem. Soc. Advancement Mgmt. (v.p. membership Richmond chpt. 1966-67, v.p. research and devel. 1972-73), So. Econ. Assn. Author: Impact of World War II on the Southeastern U.S., 1951; (with Ben M. Wofford) Mississippi Workers, 1955. Contbr. articles to profl. jours. Home: 8830 Chippenham Rd Richmond VA 23235 Office: State Office Bldg Richmond VA 23219

KELLY, THOMAS LAWRENCE, JR., utility exec.; b. Mobile, Ala., Nov 1, 1921; s. Thomas Lawrence and Alma (Zimlich) K.; grad. pub. high sch.; m. Margaret Ecc Leston, Jan. 20, 1946 (dec. Mar. 1969); children—Thomas L. III, Robert T., William T., Michael T., Daniel T.; m. 2d, Margaret Carol McCue, Dec. 4, 1971. With Mobile Gas Service Corp., 1940—, asst. storekeeper, 1953-60, purchasing agt., supr. stores, 1960—. Served with AUS, 1943-46. Mem. Nat. Assn. Purchasing Mgmt. (2d v.p.), Mobile Assn. Purchasing Mgmt. (1st v.p. 1974—). Home: 2756 Dauphin St Mobile AL 36606 Office: 2828 Dauphin St Mobile AL 36606

KELLY, WILLIAM FREDERICK, constrn. co. exec.; b. New Orleans, Nov. 20, 1912; s. William Frederick and Ada (de Trunillon) K.; student pub. and parochial schs.; m. Eloise Mary Generes, Feb. 15, 1939; children—Carmen Mary (Mrs. Jean-Paul Vandenabeele), Pamela Ann (Mrs. Kenneth Francis Sills), Elizabeth Mary, Micaela Margaret, Allen William, Amelie Eloise. Foreman, Globe Constrn. Co., New Orleans, 1930-35; with W. Horace Williams Co., contractors, New Orleans, 1935-38; owner William F. Kelly Constrn. Co., New Orleans, 1939-50; exec. v.p. Kelly Generes Co., Inc., New Orleans, 1950-60; owner Ebilco, Inc., Avondale, La., 1960—, Kelly Systems, 1965—; pres. Kelven, Inc., 1962—. Mem. Civil Air Patrol. Mem. Asso. Gen. Contractors, Home Builders Assn. Greater New Orleans (pres. 1970), Prestress Concrete Inst., New Orleans C. of C. Democrat. Roman Catholic. Clubs: New Orleans Country, New Orleans Athletic, Covington Country, Lamplighter. Home: 100 Bellaire Dr New Orleans LA 70124 Office: 245 S Jamie Blvd Avondale LA 70094

KELSO, ROBERT EARL, army officer; b. Bristow, Okla., Sept. 23, 1930; s. Fred Earl and Edna Mae (Mitchell) K.; B.A., U. Tulsa, 1954; grad. Command and Gen. Staff Coll., 1970; m. Gloria Marie Groesbeeck, July 5, 1957; children—Gloria Marie, Barbara Ann. Joined U.S. Army as pvt., 1944, advanced through grades to lt. col., 1973; information officer 25th Inf. Div., 1970; sec.-treas. U.S. Armor Assn., editor Armor mag., 1971-73; chief community relations Hdqrs. 5th U.S. Army, Ft. Sam Houston, Tex., 1973—. Decorated Bronze Star with 2 oak leaf clusters, Meritorious Service medal, Air medal, Purple Heart, Joint Service Commendation medal. Home: 485 Wheaton Rd Fort Sam Houston TX 78234 Office: Hdqrs 5th Army Fort Sam Houston TX 78234

KELSON, KEITH R., govt. ofcl.; b. Wales, Utah, Aug. 11, 1918; B.A. in Zoology, U. Utah, 1939, M.A., 1941, Ph.D., 1949; m. Elaine Kelson; children—James, Carolyn. Teaching asst. U. Utah, 1936-41, instr. zoology, 1946-49; teaching asst. Tex. A. and M. Coll., 1941; postdoctoral research U. Kan., 1949-54; with NSF, Washington, 1954—, dep. asst. dir., then dep. div. dir. div. sci. personnel and edn., 1954-65, dir. div. pre-coll. edn., 1965-66, now acting dep. asst. dir. for edn. Fellow A.A.A.S. (mem. council); mem. Am. Soc. Mammalogists, Wildlife Soc., Soc. Study Evolution, Soc. Systematic Zoologists, Sigma Xi, Phi Sigma. Author: (with E. Raymond Hall) The Mammals of North America (2 Vols.). Contbr. articles to profl. jours. Home: 5311 Baltimore Av Chevy Chase MD 20015 Office: NSF 1800 G St NW Washington DC 20550*

KELTON, ELMER STEPHEN, writer, editor; b. Andrews, Tex., Apr. 29, 1926; s. Robert William and Neta Beatrice (Parker) K.; B.A., U. Tex., 1947; m. Anna Lipp, July 3, 1947; children—Gary, Stephen Lee, Kathryn. Agrl. editor San Angelo (Tex.) Standard-Times, 1948-63; editor Sheep and Goat Raiser Mag., San Angelo, 1963-68; asso. editor West Tex. Livestock Weekly, San Angelo, 1968—. Served with AUS, 1944-46. Recipient Spur award Western Writers Am., 1957, 72. Mem. Western Writers Am. (pres. 1962-63), Sigma Delta Chi. Methodist. Elk. Author: The Day the Cowboys Quit, 1971; The Time It Never Rained, 1973; others. Home: 2460 Oxford San Angelo TX 76901 Office: 2601 Sherwood Way, San Angelo TX 76901

KEMMERER, HAROLD RICHARD, ret. oil co. exec.; b. Ashley, Pa., Sept. 27, 1913; s. Abraham and Anna Elizabeth (Richards) K.; B.S., Pa. State U., 1935; m. Alice Crinetta Meyers, June 10, 1935; children—Paul Richard, Barbara Ellen, Stephen Allen (dec.). With Shell Oil Co., Houston, 1935-73, gen. mgr. petrochems. div., 1965-70, gen. mgr. pub. affairs, 1970-73; aircraft power plant cons., World War II. Mem. Bd. Pub. Affairs Council, Washington, 1970-73. Fellow Am. Inst. Chemists; mem. Am. Soc. Lubrication Engrs., Soc. Automotive Engrs., Am. Chem. Soc. Phi Lambda Upsilon. Home: 111-A Buckingham Dr Lakehurst NJ 08733

KEMP, LAMAR ELLIOTT, lawyer; b. Atlanta, Dec. 5, 1912; s. Thomas Ardell and Rosalie (Elliott) K.; A.B.J., U. Ga., 1936; LL.B., Atlanta Law Sch., 1946; M.A., U. Md., 1960; m. Willise Carter, Oct. 5, 1940 (dec. Oct. 1961); children—Carolyn Clyde, Barbara Lamar. With advt. dept. Atlanta Constn., 1936-40, 49-50; with pub. relations dept. Atlantic Steel Co., 1940-43; in personnel and pub. relations U.S. Civil Service Commn., Atlanta, 1943-46; admitted to Ga. bar, 1946, U.S. Supreme Ct. bar, 1953, D.C. bar, 1955; information specialist Hdqrs. 7th Army, Atlanta, 1946-47; cons. So. Pub. Relations Inst., Atlanta, 1947-48; atty. Nat. Labor Relations Bd., Atlanta, 1948-49; editor Ga. Petroleum Retailer, Atlanta, 1950; information specialist, historian Hdqrs., Air Force Armament Center, Eglin, AFB, Fla., 1951-52; personnel-pub. relations PRNC Bd. Civil Service Examiners, Washington, 1952-56; adminstrv. and personnel-pub. relations Hdqrs. AFSC also 459th TCW, Balt. and Washington, 1956-62; information officer Bur. Fed. Credit Unions, U.S. Dept. Health Edn. and Welfare, Washington, 1962-65; lawyer, pub. relations counsel, manpower utilization cons., 1965—; tax counsel, 1972—. Faculty communications law Am. U., 1960-61. Pres., Murray Hill Citizens Assn., 1963-64; v.p. Indian Head Hwy. Area Action Council, 1964-65; co-founder, treas. So. Prince Georges County Congress Civic Assns., 1963-64, v.p., 1973—; founder, pres. Oxon Hill (Md.) Recreation and Cultural Council, 1964-71, v.p., 1971—. Trustee Forest Heights (Md.) Elementary Sch., 1953-56; bd. dirs. Prince Georges Citizens Planning Assn., 1965—. Mem. Am., Fed., Inter-Am. bar assns., Am. Soc. for Internat. Law, Prince Georges County Citizens Polit. Action Assn., Fed. Profl. Assn., Soc. Personnel Adminstrn., Ga. State Soc. Washington (dir. pub. relations 1965—), Internat. Platform Assn., Nat. Assn. Ret. Fed. Employees (pres. chpt. 1972-73), Delta Theta Phi. Democrat. Methodist. Club: Oxon Hill (Md.) Methodist Men's (pres. 1954-56). Home: 8000 Carey Branch Pl Oxon Hill MD 20022

KEMP, LYSANDER SCHAFFER, editor; b. Randolph, Vt., Nov. 13, 1920; s. Lysander Schaffer and Dorothy Burnton (Schontag) K.; B.A., Bates Coll., 1942; M.A., Boston U., 1946. Instr. English, U. Buffalo, 1946-50, asst. prof., 1950-53; writer, Spanish translator, Jocotepec, Mexico, 1953-59, Guadalajara, Mexico, 1959-65; editor, U. Tex. Press, Austin, 1966—. Served with AUS, 1942-45. Rockefeller Found. grantee, 1960-61. Democrat. Author: The Northern Stranger, 1946; The Conquest, 1971. Translator 8 books. Home: 814 E 30th St Austin TX 78705

KEMP, PATRICK SAMUEL, educator; b. Galveston, Tex., Aug. 2, 1932; s. Samuel Herbert and Florence (Moor) K.; B.A., Rice U., 1953; M.P.A., U. Tex., 1956; Ph.D. in Accounting, U. Ill., 1959; m. Carol Margaret Boren, Aug. 22, 1959; children—Robert Wade, Cathleen Anne. Asst. prof. Emory U., Atlanta, 1959-61, asso. prof., 1961-62; asso. prof., chmn. dept. accounting U. Richmond, 1962-65, prof., chmn. dept., 1965-68; prof. Va. Poly. Inst. and State U., Blacksburg, 1968—. Vis. prof. Northeastern U., 1967. C.P.A., Tex., Ill. Mem. Am. Accounting Assn., Am. Inst. C.P.A.'s, Nat. Assn. Accountants, Va. Soc. C.P.A.'s, Alpha Kappa Psi, Beta Alpha Psi, Beta Gamma Sigma, Omicron Delta Kappa. Author: Accounting for the Manager, 1970; French transl., 1971. Contbr. articles to profl. jours. Home: 25 Laurel Dr Blacksburg VA 24060

KEMP, THOMAS DUPREE, III, sch. adminstr.; b. Charlotte, N.C., Apr. 12, 1934; s. Thomas Dupre and Edith J. K.; A.B., U. N.C., 1956; M.A., Columbia, 1964; m. Joan E. Klecan, Oct. 6, 1956 (div. Aug. 1971); children—Barbara Joan, Thomas Brendan; m. 2d, Patricia G. Thames, Apr. 27, 1974. Asst. headmaster Windward Sch., White Plains, N.Y., 1960-66; bd. dirs., 1962-66; headmaster, bd. dirs. Southside Country Day Sch., Jacksonville, Fla., 1966—. North Fla. area liaison officer coordinator USAF Acad., 1967—. Bd. dirs. Jacksonville Pub. Library, 1970—, v.p., 1973—. Served to maj. USAF, 1957-62. Mem. Fla. Council Ind. Schs. (dir., sec. 1971—), Phi Delta Kappa. Clubs: Deerwood Country, University (Jacksonville); Ponte Vedra Country (Ponte Vedra Beach, Fla.). Home: 7929 Los Robles Ct Jacksonville FL 32216 Office: 8161 Southside Blvd Jacksonville FL 32216

KEMPER, ROBERT MITCHELL, JR., cost estimating engr.; b. Hapeville, Ga., Mar. 20, 1926; s. Robert Mitchell and Joelma (Gibson) K.; student N.C. State Coll., 1943-44, Ohio State U., 1944-45; B.S. in Civil Engring., U. Tenn., 1949; m. Janette Jackson, June 5, 1948; children—Kathy Jo, Barbara Ann, Linda Susan. Design engr. nuclear div. Union Carbide Corp., Oak Ridge, 1953-55, constrn. engr., 1955-61, cost estimating engr., 1961—; partner R.M. Kemper & Son, Oak Ridge, 1954-60. Chmn. UN Com. Oak Ridge, 1957-58; campaign dir. Oak Ridge chpt. March of Dimes, 1958; pres. Savoyards, Light Opera Co., Oak Ridge, 1958-59; merit badge counselor Pellissippi dist. Smoky Mountain council Boy Scouts Am., 1959—; active Girl Scouts U.S., 1958-69. Served with S.C., AUS, 1943-46, C.E., 1950-51. Registered profl. engr., Tenn. Mem. Dixie Round Dance Council (chmn. 1972-73), Tenn. Soc. Profl. Engrs., Sons Confederate Vets., Order Star and Bars (aide to comdr.-in-chief), Germanna Found., V.F.W., Am. Legion. Square, round dance choreographer, lectr., instr. Home: 102 Case Lane Oak Ridge TN 37830 Office: Nuclear Div Union Carbide Corp Oak Ridge TN 37830

KEMPFER, HELEN FRIEND (MRS. HOMER H. KEMPFER), state ofcl.; b. nr. Troy, O.; d. W.R. and Lena O. (Shook) Friend; B.S., Bowling Green State U., 1945; M.A., Columbia, 1955; student Am. U., 1950-52, Purdue U., 1953-54; m. Homer H. Kempfer, Dec. 31, 1955. Tchr. Champaign County (O.) Schs., 1940-42; research asst. N.E.A., Washington, 1952; asst. dir. Nat. Home Study Council, 1955-59, exec. sec. Accrediting Commn., 1958-59; editor Indian Jour. Adult Edn., New Delhi, 1960-63; dir. research Indian Adult Edn. Assn., 1962-63; head, corr. program Grad. Sch., U.S. Dept. Agr., Washington, 1963-66; pres. Inst. Ind. Study, Inc., 1968; research analyst Wis. Dept. Health and Social Services, Madison, 1968-70; asso dir. Cosmetology Accrediting Commn., 1970-71, Nat. Study Accreditation Vocational Tech. Edn., 1970-72; supr. research Va. State Dept. Corrections, 1973—. Mem. Am. Personnel and Guidance Assn., Indian Adult Edn. Assn., Adult Edn. Assn. U.S.A., Am. Vocational Assn., Internat. Council on Corr. Edn., Nat. Soc. Programmed Instrn., Am. Soc. Assn. Execs. Author numerous books, pamphlets, articles. Home: 11336 Orchard Lane Reston VA 22090 Office: 22 E Cary St Richmond VA 23219

KEMPTER, RUDOLPH HARBISON, JR., govt. ofcl.; b. St. Albans, Vt., Sept. 5, 1922; s. Rudolph Harbison and Marjorie (Prentiss) K.; B.S. in Engring., U. Notre Dame, 1948; postgrad. in bus. adminstrn. U. Cal. at Berkeley, 1949; m. Margaret Ann Gilkinson, Oct. 15, 1950; children—Carlton J., Bryan C., Paul C. Apprentice engr. Grumman Aircraft Engring. Corp., Bethpage, N.Y., 1942-43; test engr. U.S. Navy Indsl. Plant, Pomona, Cal., 1958-62; rocket devel. engr. Aero-jet Gen. Corp., Azusa, Cal., 1954-57; missile system program mgr. Navy Dept., Washington, 1962-66; dep. dir. value engring. Office Sec. Def., Washington, 1966-70, staff engr. prodn. engring., 1971—. Partner, Kempter-Rossman Internat., Washington, 1973—. Staff lectr. Schs. Engring., George Washington U., 1968—, Va. Poly. Inst., 1969—, Va. Mil. Inst., 1969—; doctoral adviser George Washington U. Grad. Sch. Bus. Adminstrn., 1970—. Served with USNR, 1943-46; PTO; 1950-54, Korea. Recipient certificate commendation Asst. Sec. of Def., 1969; certificate of merit for cost reduction achievement U.S. Navy, 1966. Mem. Soc. Am. Value Engrs. (officer), Soc. for Performance Improvement, Sigma Phi. Presbyn. Contbr. numerous articles on tech. mgmt. and value engring. to tech. jours. Home: 1616 Chain Bridge Rd McLean VA 22101 Office: Pentagon Washington DC 20301

KEMPTHORNE, RICHARD LEWIS, constrn. industry exec.; b. Orange, N.J., Jan. 7, 1927; s. James Lewis and Eleanor (McKelvey) K.; Asso. Bus. Adminstrn., Nichols Coll., 1949; B.S., Syracuse U., 1951; m. Alice Clair Prost, Feb. 26, 1949; children—James Lewis III, Ann. Vice pres. Sprayed Insulation Inc., Newark, 1951-53; head Columbia Acoustics & Fireproofing Co., Stanhope, N.J., 1954-56; chief exec., sec.-treas. Fla. Insulation & Fireproofing Co., Miami, 1957-65; pres., dir. Sprayed Fibers, Inc., Miami, 1963-71, Spraydon Overseas Corp., Miami, 1966-71; v.p. Tex. Fireproofing Co., Houston, 1960-63; pres., dir. Sprayon Research Corp., Ft. Lauderdale, Fla., 1964—; pres., dir. Midwest Sprayon Corp., Miami, 1966-71, Sprayon Internat. Inc., N.Y.C., 1971-73. acoustical cons. Mem. bd. elections Young Republicans of Miami, 1958—. Pres. Miami Shores Prep. Sch., 1968-72. Served with USNR, 1944-46. Mem. Am. Soc. Testing Materials, Nat. Fireprotection Assn., Internat. Assn. Walls and Ceilings Contractors, Amateur Athletic Union. Clubs: Miami Shores Country (pres. swimming assn. 1964-67); Palm-Aire Country. Patentee in field. Address: 5701 Bayview Dr Fort Lauderdale FL 33308

KENDALL, HENRY ELI, ret. state ofcl; b. Shelby, N.C., Aug. 24, 1905; s. Henry E. and Mary (Wiseman) K.; B.S. in Civil Engring., N.C. State Coll., 1926; m. Katharine Kerr, June 21, 1947. Engr., Plumer & Wiseman Co., Danville, Va., 1926-30; asst. office mgr. Dibrell Bros., Shanghai, China, 1930-36; chief operation plants N.C. Sch. Commn., Raleigh, 1937-42; chmn. N.C. Employment Security Commn., Raleigh, 1946-73; ret., 1973. Mem. Gov.'s Com. Employment Handicapped, 1962—, Com. Aging, 1956—, Com. Refugee Relief, 1957-67, Pres.'s Com. Employment Handicapped, 1957—, Bur. Vet. Re-employment Rights, 1950-66; spl. cons. European manpower conditions U.S. Dept. Labor, 1963; bd. dirs. N.C. Manpower Devel. Corp., State Employees Credit Union; adv. council N.C. Com. Children and Youth; adv. com. State Tech. Services; exec. com. Gov.'s Council Econ. Devel. Served from 1st lt. to lt. col. C.E., AUS, 1942-46. Recipient Outstanding Service commendation Pres.'s Com. Employment Handicapped, 1965, also certificate of appreciation, 1967; Outstanding Service award V.F.W., 1966; citation Distinguished Pub. Service N.C. Citizens' Assn., 1973; Pub. Service award Gov.'s Com. Employment Handicapped. Mem. Internat. Assn. Personnel in Employment Securities (merit award 1968), Interstate Conf. Employment Security Agys. (pres. 1953, 62, mem. legislative com. 1969-70, mem. com. conf. constn. and code 1969-70), Raleigh Engrs. Club, N.C. Soc. Engrs., Am. Legion (chmn. N.C. resolutions com. 1956—), V.F.W., N.C. State U. Gen. Alumni Assn. (v.p. 1948, pres. 1949), Am. Legion (chmn. legislative com. 1973-74), Phi Kappa Phi, Pi Kappa Alpha, Tau Beta Pi, Theta Tau. Presbyn. Mason, Lion. Home: 2814 Exeter Circle Raleigh NC 27608

KENDERDINE, JAMES MARSHALL, educator; b. Washington, May 12, 1941; s. John Marshall and Su Anne (Carroll) K.; student Duke, 1959-64; B.S., Ind. U., 1965, M.B.A., 1967, D.B.A. (Am. Marketing Assn. fellow, Gen. Electric Research fellow), 1970; m. Nancy Sloan Ingram, Aug. 25, 1964; 1 son, James Adams. Teaching asso. Ind. U. at Bloomington, 1966-69; asst. prof. marketing U. Okla. at Norman, 1969—. Cons. econs. Oklahoma City Urban League, 1970—. Chmn. United Fund, Okla. U., 1970, 71; commr. Norman Human Rights Commn., 1972—, vice-chmn., sec., 1973—. Mem. Am. Marketing Assn., Am. Mgmt. Assn., Am. Mensa Soc. (pres. central Okla. chpt. 1969-71), U.S. Naval Inst., World Future Soc., Theta Chi, Beta Gamma Sigma, Omicron Delta Kappa. Lion. Home: 814 Jona Kay Terrace Norman OK 73069

KENDERDINE, JOHN MARSHALL, mfg. co. exec.; b. Ft. Worth, Dec. 6, 1912; s. Robert Leonard and Caroline (Raab) K.; B.S. in Petroleum Engring., Tex. A. and M. Coll., 1934; grad. Army War Coll., 1953, Advanced Mgmt. Program, Harvard, 1959, Exec.

Decision Inst., 1962; m. Su Anne Carroll, Feb. 26, 1937; children—James Marshall, Su Carroll (Mrs. Henry F. Hain III). Petroleum engr. Gulf Oil Corp., 1934-37; br. mgr. Norvell-Wilder Supply Co., Midland, Tex., 1938-41; commd. 1st lt. U.S. Army, 1941, advanced through grades to brig. gen., 1962; mil. logistician in France, Germany and U.S., World War II; spl. asst. to adminstr. War Assets Adminstrn., 1946; mil. staff and command assignments, 1947-60; joint petroleum officer Europe, 1961; exec. dir. supply operations Def. Supply Agy., 1962-65; comdr. Def. Indsl. Supply Center, Phila., 1965-66, Def. Personnel Support Center, Phila., 1966-67; ret., 1967; v.p. spl. tech. Scott Paper Co., Phila., 1967-70; pres. C.F. Adams, Inc., Fort Worth, 1970—. Mem. Phila. Edn. Council. Decorated D.S.M., Legion of Merit, Joint Service Commendation medal, Commendation ribbon with 3 oak leaf clusters. Registered profl. engr., Tex. Mem. Soc. Logistics Engrs., Def. Supply Assn., Assn. U.S. Army, Airline Passengers Assn. (adv. bd.), Phila. C. of C. (dir. 1966). Club: Airways. Contbr. articles on handling and safety of aviation fuels, especially turbine fuels to profl. jours. Home: 3212 Chapparal Lane Fort Worth TX 76109 Office: Box 253 Fort Worth TX 76101

KENDRICK, AUBREY EARL, JR., furniture mfg. co. exec.; b. Tampa, Fla., June 6, 1934; s. Aubrey Earl and Avis (Bernard) K.; student U.N.C., 1951-53; m. Susan C. Forgette, Sept. 15, 1956; children—Aubrey Earl III, Tracy T., Susan A. Salesman, Sumter Cabinet Co. (S.C.), 1956—; v.p., dir. Newton Mfrs. Co., Hickory, N.C., 1963-65; sec.-treas., dir. Lincoln Hall, Hickory, 1966—; pres., dir. Wood Products Internat. Inc., Charlotte, N.C., 1968—; v.p. D. & J. Maintenance & Supply Inc., Atlanta; dir. Reliable Frame Co., Hickory, 1963-68. Served with AUS, 1953-56. Address: 2701 Pencoyd Lane Charlotte NC 28210

KENDRICK, HERBERT SPENCER, JR., lawyer; b. Brownfield, Tex., Nov. 16, 1934; s. Herbert Spencer and Elsie (Woosley) K.; B.B.A., So. Methodist U., 1957, LL.B., 1960; LL.M., Harvard, 1961; m. Carol Ann Puckett, Sept. 6, 1958; children—Herbert Spencer III, Kathryn Gene. Admitted to Tex. bar, 1960; trial atty. tax div. U.S. Justice Dept., Washington and Ft. Worth, Tex., 1961-65; practiced in Dallas, 1965—; partner Kendrick & Kendrick, 1965-69, Turner, Rodgers, Winn, Scurlock & Sailers, 1969-71, Kendrick & Kendrick, 1971—. Lectr. taxation Law Sch., So. Methodist U., Dallas, 1966—. Mem. Am., Tex., Dallas bar assns., Phi Alpha Delta, Sigma Alpha Epsilon. Presbyn. Mason (32 deg., Shriner). Club: Dallas. Author: (with John J. Kendrick, Jr.) Texas Transaction Guide, 10 vols., 1972, 73. Home: 4421 Larchmont Av Dallas TX 75205 Office: Republic Nat Bank Tower Dallas TX 75201

KENEFAKE, EDWIN WILLIAM, marketing exec.; b. Robinson, Ill., Sept. 7, 1911; s. Thomas J. and Mary Ann (Byrne) K.; B.S., U. Notre Dame, 1934, M.S., 1936; m. Anna Marie Harran, Sept. 4, 1937; children—George, Thomas, Robert, Vincent, Mary Pat. With Gen. Electric Co., 1936—, mgr. marketing power line carrier, telecommunications products dept., Lynchburg, Va., 1940—. Mem. I.E.E.E. (chmn. tech. com. 1959-61, sr. mem.). K.C. Club: Oakwood Country. Patentee in field. Home: 1433 Trents Ferry Rd Lynchburg VA 24503 Office: Mount View Rd Lynchburg VA 24502

KENKNIGHT, GLENN ELLIS, plant pathologist; b. Canby, Oreg., Nov. 26, 1910; d. Charles Eber and Carrie (Calusen) KenK.; B.S., Carleton Coll., 1934; M.S., Mich. State U., 1937; Ph.D., 1939; m. Velma Campbell, Apr. 13, 1940; children—Robert C., Glenndolyn (Mrs. Donnie Hallman). Plant pathologist Tex. A. and M. U., 1940-42, U. Ida., 1942-45, Cal. Dept. Agr., 1945-48, U.S. Dept. Agr., 1948-73; cons. plant pathologist, Shreveport, 1973—. Scoutmaster, Boy Scouts Am., 1952-59. Mem. Am. Phytopath. Soc. Selected Spantex peanut variety; co-inventor hot water seed treater; inventor Exacta game. Address: 9517 Palmetto Lane Shreveport LA 71108

KENNAMER, HAL JACOB, govt. ofcl.; b. Greenbrier, Ark., May 19, 1910; s. Zachary T. and Nancy Adaline (Jordan) K.; B.S., State Coll. Ark., 1941; M.S., U. Ark., 1949; m. Lucille Love, Aug. 25, 1930; children—Joan (Mrs. Charles Lee Dean), William Earl. Tchr. rural schs., Faulkner County, Ark., 1930-38; rural sch. prin. Cross County, Ark., 1938-40; prin. high sch., Pulaski County, 1943-44, Crossett, Ark., 1944-46; supt. schs., Hamburg, Ark., 1946-48, Paris, Ark., 1948-68; program specialist, region 7, U.S. Office Edn., Dallas, 1968—. Mem. Nat., Ark. edn. assns., Am. Assn. Sch. Adminstrs., Phi Delta Kappa, Kappa Delta Pi, Phi Alpha Theta. Democrat. Baptist. Kiwanian. Home: 2612 Monticello Dr Mesquite TX 75149 Office: US Office Edn 1114 Commerce St Dallas TX 75202

KENNAMER, KENNETH ROBERT, newspaper editor; b. Royse City, Tex., Aug. 25, 1931; s. Ovid Arlee and Mary (Shook) K.; student Kilgore Coll., 1948-50; B.A., North Tex. State U., 1956; m. Joycelyne Hendry, May 4, 1957; children—Alison Diane, Kimberly Ann. Sports writer Longview Jour., 1947-48; athletic publicity dir. Kilgore Coll., 1948-50; reporter Texarkana Gazette, 1950-51, Lubbock Avalanche, 1956-57; reporter San Antonio Express, 1957-59, city editor, 1959-68, asst. mng. editor, 1968-69, mng. editor, 1969—. Instr. journalism St. Mary's U., San Antonio, 1960-62. Served with CIC, AUS, 1952-54. Home: 204 Wisteria St San Antonio TX 78213 Office: San Antonio Express Av E and 3d St San Antonio TX 78206

KENNEDY, ALBERT THORNTON, mfr.; b. Greenville, S.C., Nov. 4, 1918; s. Alfred Doby and Jane Swann (Thornton) K.; student Ga. Inst. Tech., 1940, U. Ga., 1941; m. Gayle England, June 24, 1971; stepchildren—Charles, Cynthia Gayle, Martha Hurt Bickerstaf. With Davidson-Kennedy Co., Atlanta, pres., 1950—, also dir.; dir. So. Cross Industries, D-K Pneumatics, N. Pryor St. Corp., Whitewater Corp.; co-owner Kennedy Properties. State finance chmn. Rep. candidate Gov. of Ga., 1966; campaign chmn. Congressman Fletcher Thompson, 1972; mem. Rep. Nat. Finance Com. of Ga. Trustee Lovett Sch. Served with USAAF, 1942-44. Mem. Atlanta C. of C., N.A.M. (past dir.), Ga. Bus. and Industry Assn. (past dir.). Clubs: Rotary, Commerce, Capital City, Piedmont Driving (past dir.), Honasassa Fishing (pres.), Atlanta City (dir.), Peachtree Golf (Atlanta). Home: 2868 Andrews Dr NW Atlanta GA 30305 Office: 1090 Jefferson St NW Atlanta GA 30318

KENNEDY, CORNELIUS BRYANT, lawyer; b. Evanston, Ill., Apr. 13, 1921; s. Millard Bryant and Myrna (Anderson) K.; A.B., Yale, 1943; J.D., Harvard, 1948; m. Anne Martha Reynolds, June 20, 1959; children—Anne Talbot, Lauren Asher. Admitted to Ill. bar, 1949, D.C. bar, 1965; practiced in Chgo., 1949-54, 55-59, Washington, 1965—; sr. mem. firm Kennedy & Webster, Washington, 1965—; asst. U.S. atty., Chgo., 1954-55; counsel to minority leader U.S. Senate, Washington, 1959-65. Pub. mem. Adminstrv. Conf. U.S., chmn. com. rule making and pub. information. Past trustee St. Johns Child Devel. Center, Washington. Served with USAAF, 1943-46. Mem. Am. (chmn. adminstrv. conf. com.), Fed., Chgo. bar assns. Clubs: Gibson Island (Md.); F Street, Metropolitan, Capitol Hill (Washington); Adventurers (Chgo.). Contbr. articles in field to profl. jours. Home: 7720 Old Georgetown Pike McLean VA 22101 Office: 888 17th St NW Washington DC 20006

KENNEDY, EDWARD JAMES, civil engr.; b. Akron, O., May 22, 1918; s. John Francis and Mary (Appelget) K.; student Balt. Poly Inst., 1931-35; B.S., U. Md., 1938; m. Alice Anne Noon, Jan. 12, 1942; children—Patricia, John F., Joan, Edward James, Bairbre, Robert H. Engr. water resources div. U.S. Geol. Survey, 1938—, dist. engr., Topeka, 1961-67, asst. dist. chief, Lawrence, Kan., 1967, dist. chief, Nashville, 1967-71, floor plain mgmt. hydrologist, Washington, 1971—; water resources cons. Kan. C. of C., 1964-67. Recipient Outstanding award U.S. Geol. Survey, 1959. Registered profl. engr., Kan. Fellow Am. Soc. C.E.; mem. Nat., Tenn. socs. profl. engrs., Engrs. Assn. Nashville, Middle Tenn. Fed. Execs. Assn. (past pres.). Roman Catholic. Home: 11506 Running Cedar Rd Reston VA 22091 Office: Geol Survey Nat Center Reston VA 22092

KENNEDY, EUGENE RICHARD, univ. dean; b. Scranton, Pa., July 3, 1919; s. Thomas Aloysius and Margaret (Culkin) K.; B.S., U. Scranton, 1941; M.S., Cath., 1943; Ph.D., Brown U., 1949; m. Marjorie Anne Giblin, July 24, 1945; children—Anne, Michael, Christine. Instr., Brown U., 1946-48; instr. Cath. U., Washington, 1949-51, asst. prof., 1951-55, asso. prof., 1956-66, prof. microbiology, 1966—, dean Grad. Sch. Arts and Scis., 1973—. Cons., microbiologist Providence Hosp., Washington, 1953—; cons. Warner-Lambert Research Inst., 1971-73. Served to capt. M.C., AUS, World War II. Diplomate Am. Acad. Microbiology. Mem. Am. Soc. Microbiology, A.A.A.S., Washington Acad. Sci., Sigma Xi. Home: 11804 Saddlerock Rd Silver Spring MD 20902 Office: Grad Sch Arts and Scis Cath U Washington DC 20017

KENNEDY, FRANCIS JOSEPH, educator; b. Scranton, Pa., Mar. 15, 1910; s. Michael Martin and Delia (McManmon) K.; A.B., Catholic U., 1933; M.A., U. Pa., 1936, postgrad., 1937-38, Columbia, 1938, Yale, 1948, Boston U., 1948, Tulane U., 1951-52, La. State U., 1949, 51, 62-63; m. Lorena Frances Fort, Apr. 20, 1963. Tchr., West Phila. Cath. Boys High Sch., 1930-34; asst. prof. econs. and social scis. LaSalle Coll., Phila., 1934-38; asso. prof. econs. and social scis. U. Scranton (Pa.), 1938-40; credit and operating mgr. B.F. Goodrich Tire & Rubber Co., Washington, 1941-42; supervising mineral economist U.S. Bur. Mines, Washington, 1942-46; instr. econs. U. Conn., New London, 1946-47; asso. prof. econs. and internat. trade Loyola U. Coll. Bus. Adminstrn., New Orleans, 1947-55; chief statistician U.S. Army Port Embarkation, New Orleans, 1955-56; tchr. DeLaSalle High Sch., New Orleans, 1956-57, Orleans Parish Pub. Schs., 1958-61; tchr. econs., English and sociology, coordinator distributive edn. Thibodaux (La.) High Sch., 1961—. Adviser, Propeller Club, 1947-55, founder, 1947; pub. relations, liaison officer various bus. firms., 1947-55; mem. com. econ. edn. La. Dept. Edn., 1964—; dir. LaFourche Parish Manpower Survey; mem. Thibodaux Area Econ. Found. Bd. dirs. Thibodaux Youth Council, 1963—, Playhouse, 1965—. Recipient Outstanding Service awards Nat. Distributive Edn. Club Am., 1965, La. Distributive Edn. Club Am., 1965. Mem. Distributive Edn. Assn. La. (Outstanding Tchr. 1965, pres. 1964-66), Am., Cath., So. econ. assns., N.E.A., La. Tchrs. Assn., Am. Vocational Assn., So. Finance Assn., Nat. Cath. Edn. Assn., Nat. Assn. Distributive Edn. Tchrs. (nat. legislative chmn., v.p. So. region), Thibodaux C. of C. (v.p.), Distributive Edn. Clubs Am., Council Distributive Tchr. Edn., Phi Delta Kappa. Roman Catholic. Rotarian (pres. 1971-72). Author: Vocational Education in LaFourche Parish, 1969-74; Vocational-Technical Skill Needs in LaFourche Parish, 1973. Home: 306 Dunboyne Pl Thibodaux LA 70301

KENNEDY, FRANK THOMAS, investment banker; b. Florence, Ala., Sept. 11, 1938; s. William Charles and Frances Jane (Foxworthy) K.; B.S., Stetson U., 1960; m. Waldo Lynn Frierson, Aug. 25, 1961; children—Frank Thomas, Waldo Deborah, Kathryn Lynn. Exec. tng. program Exchange Security Bank Birmingham (Ala.), 1961-63; asst. v.p. Hendrix & Mayes, Birmingham, 1963; v.p. Hendrix, Mohr & Head, Inc., Birmingham, 1963-69; v.p., dir. Hendrix, Mohr & Yardley, Inc., Birmingham, 1969—. Bd. dirs. Shades Valley YMCA, 1969—; mem. YMCA Bus. Mens Club, 1964—. Served to 2d lt. inf. AUS, 1960-61; capt. res. Mem. Birmingham Numismatic Soc., Investment Bankers Assn., Ala. Security Dealers Assn., Izaak Walton League, Pi Kappa Alpha Alumni Assn., Pi Kappa Alpha. Episcopalian. Clubs: Alpha, Birmingham Country, Birmingham Coin (pres. 1968-70), Downtown (dir. 1966-68) (Birmingham); Turtle Point Country (Florence). Home: 4349 Kennesaw Dr Birmingham AL 35213 Office: 2020 First Nat-So Nat Bldg Birmingham AL 35203

KENNEDY, G. HAL, pub. relations firm exec.; b. Grand Saline, Tex., Mar. 26, 1933; s. Hal Sevier and Myra Euphrosene (Germany) K.; B.A., Southwestern U., 1954; m. Connie Lee Johnson, Oct. 10, 1953; children—Lisa Lee, Jack Scot. Editor, The Williamson County Sun, Georgetown, Tex., 1953-54, The Alice News (Tex.), 1954-57; plant pub. relations dir. Lone Star Steel Co. (Tex.), 1957-62; asst. mgr. pub. relations div. Marathon Oil Co., Findlay, O., 1962-64; pub. relations dir. Edward Lamb Enterprises, Toledo, O., 1964-66; pres. Holder, Kennedy & Co., Inc., Nashville, 1966—. Mem. Spl. Police Commn., City of Nashville, 1971—. Recipient Spl. Bus. Achievement award Southwestern U., 1972. Mem. Pub. Relations Soc. Am. Mason (32 degree, Shriner). Club: City (Nashville). Home: 376 Elmington Av Nashville TN 37205 Office: 2020 21st St Nashville TN 37214

KENNEDY, HARVEY JOHN, JR., lawyer; b. Barnesville, Ga., Apr. 9, 1924; s. Harvey John and Marisu (Reeves) K.; grad. Gordon Mil. Coll., 1942; J.D., U. Ga., 1949; diplomate psychology Colo. Christian Coll., 1973; m. Jean McRitchie King, Apr. 8, 1950; children—Marisu, Jean Gay. Admitted to Ga. bar, 1948; county atty., Lamar County, 1950-52; city atty., Barnesville, Ga., 1953-65; atty. Lamar Elec. Membership Corp.; atty. Lamar County, 1958-60, 65-68; atty. Town of Milner (Ga.), 1963-68; govt. appeal agt. local bd. 89, 1958—. Trustee Gordon Mil. Coll., 1953-63. Served as 2d lt. to capt., 86th Inf. Div., ETO, PTO, AUS, 1942-46; capt. U.S. Army Judge Adv. Gen. Corps. Res., 1949-52. Decorated Bronze Star medal. Mem. Am. Judicature Soc., Am., Ga. (bd. govs. 1957-58), Flint Circuit (pres. 1961, 64-65) bar assns., Am. Trial Lawyers Assn., Internat. Platform Assn., State Bar Ga., Peace Officers Assn. Ga. (asso.), Am. Acad. Polit. and Social Sci., Ga. Assn. Plaintiffs Trial Attys. (v.p. 1968-72), Ga. Trial Lawyers Assn. (v.p. 1972—), Am. Legion, V.F.W., Chi Phi, Delta Theta Phi. Democrat. Baptist. Mason (32 deg., Shriner), Moose, Rotarian (pres. 1959-60). Home: 392 Spencer St Barnesville GA 30204 Office: 217 Zebulon St Barnesville GA 30204

KENNEDY, JAMES DRAKE, warehouse exec.; b. Chilton, Tex., Aug. 10, 1893; s. David and Eliza Jane (Drake) K.; LL.B., Chattanooga Coll. Law, 1920; postgrad. LaSalle Extension U., 1921; m. Jessie Isabel McKensie, Aug. 26, 1917; children—Mary Kathryn (Mrs. Paul McQuiddy), James Drake. Tchr., Normal Sch., Chillicothe, Mo., 1914-15, Alta. (Can.) Coll., Edmonton, 1915-16, Ramona (Okla.) High Sch., 1916-18; auditor, credit mgr. Chattanooga Roofing & Foundry Co., 1919-22; admitted to Tenn. bar, 1920; practiced in Chattanooga, 1922-24; accountant, Chattanooga, 1922-24; v.p. Cahill Co., Chattanooga, 1925-31, pres., 1931-42; mgr. pvt. properties, Tenn., Tex., 1942-50; pres. Cherokee Warehouses, Inc., Chattanooga, 1950—. Mem. Tenn. Bd. Accountancy, 1923-24. C.P.A., Tenn. Author: They Were Right, 1957. Home: 600 E Brow Rd Lookout Mountain TN 37350 Office: 521 W 31 St Chattanooga TN 37410 also PO Box 1607 Chattanooga TN 37401

KENNEDY, JAMES ROBERT, cons. data processing; b. Birmingham, Ala., Jan. 4, 1933; s. William Herschel and Irene Josephine (Stege) K.; B.S., Ga. Inst. Tech., 1961; postgrad. U. Mich., 1963, 68; m. Elizabeth Withers, Apr. 6, 1963; children—James Robert, William Caldwell. Sr. sci. programmer Lockheed Ga. Co., Marietta, 1961-67; with Computer Scis. Corp., Huntsville, Ala., 1967-71, asst. operations mgr., 1968-70, project mgr., 1970-71; mem. tech. staff MITRE Corp., Huntsville, 1971-73; software devel. mgr. SCI Systems Inc., 1973—. Prin. investigator data processing cost and schedule analysis devel. for light area def. systems, 1972; instr. data processing and related subjects; guest research asst. Mass. Inst. Tech., Cambridge, 1963-64; mem. ballistic missile def. research and devel. software standards com. U.S. Army Source Selection and Evaluation Bd., 1973. Pres., YMCA, Ga. Tech., 1954-55. Served with USN, 1955-59. Mem. Assn. Aeros. and Astronautics, Assn. Computing Machinery, Assn. Computer Programmers and Analysis (sr.), Soc. Information Display (co-founder, v.p. 1970-71). Delta Tau Delta. Home: 737 Mira Vista Dr Huntsville AL 35802 Office: 8620 S Memorial Pky Huntsville AL 35802

KENNEDY, JERRY LEDFORD, surgeon; b. Knoxville, Tenn., Jan. 11, 1942; s. Ausbie Ledford and Helen Louise (Cosby) K.; M.D., U. Tenn., 1966; m. Mary Elizabeth Solomon, Jan. 17, 1969; children—Karen Alison, Steven Clark. Intern, Baroness Erlanger Hosp., Chattanooga, 1966-67; resident, 1967-71; practice medicine, Tullahoma, Tenn., 1973—; mem. staff John Harton Meml. Hosp., Tullohoma, Coffee County Hosp., Chgo. Served with USAF, 1971-73. Diplomate Am. Bd. Surgery. Home: 102 Davonshire Pl Tullahoma TN 37388 Office: 106 Westside Dr Tullahoma TN 37388

KENNEDY, JOHN HINES, physician; b. Washington, Nov. 1, 1925; s. John A. and Viera Miriam (Hines) K.; student Princeton, 1943-45; M.D., Harvard, 1949; m. Barbara Field, Dec. 22, 1947 (dec. Jan. 1971); children—Virginia (Mrs. H.L. Serra), Anne (Mrs. Al F. Ehrbar), John, Sarah Boudinot, Mark Montgomery, Joan Loomis; m. 2d, Ann White Stockton, Jan. 2, 1972; stepchildren—Christine Heron Stockton, Sarah Boudinot Stockton, Mary Evelyn Stockton. Intern Mass. Gen. Hosp., 1949-50, asst. resident, 1950-51, 63-64, resident, 1954-55; sr. registrar thoracic unit Frenchay Hosp., Bristol, Eng., 1959-60; clin. asst. in surgery U. Bristol-Bristol Royal Infirmary, 1959-60; dir. div. thoracic surgery Cleve. Met. Gen. Hosp., 1962-69; research asso. Engring. Design Center Case Inst. Tech., 1966-69; asst. prof. thoracic surgery Case Western Res. U., 1962-69; dir. circulatory assist project group NIH, Case Western Res. U., 1967-69, Baylor Coll. Medicine, Houston, 1969—; dir. Taub Labs. for Mech. Circulatory Support on NIH grant, Baylor Coll. Medicine, 1970—, mem. admissions com., 1971—, prof. surgery Cora and Webb Mading Dept. Surgery, 1969—; adj. prof. biomed. engring. Rice U., Houston, 1969—, mem. com. grad. students Biomed. Engring. Lab., 1970—. Cons. site visitor Program Project grants Nat. Heart and Lung Inst., NIH, 1970. Served to lt. (s.g.) M.C., USNR, 1951-53. Decorated Bronze Star award with Combat V. Diplomate Am. Bd. Surgery, Am. Bd. Thoracic Surgery. Fellow Am. Coll. Cardiology, A.C.S.; mem. Am. Assn. Thoracic Surgery, Am. Assn. U. Profs., Am. Coll. Chest Physicians (mem. com. pulmonary surgery 1961—), Am. Heart Assn. (mem. council cardiovascular surgery 1968—; mem. exec. com. 1970—), Am. Soc. Artificial Internal Organs, Am. Thoracic Soc., Houston Heart Assn. (v.p. 1971), Internat. Cardiovascular Soc., Soc. Thoracic Surgeons, Soc. Cryobiology, Sigma Xi. Author: Support of the Failing Circulation: The Use of the Heart Lung Machine in Clinical Cardiac Failure, 1967; Outline of Thoracic Surgery for Medical Students, 1968. Contbr. articles to profl. jours. Producer, author numerous films in field. Designer suture-holding ring for valvular prosthesis. Home: 2215 Albans Rd Houston TX 77005 Office: Baylor Coll Medicine 1200-Moursand Av Houston TX 77025

KENNEDY, JOHN LEONIDAS, elec. engr.; b. Nashville, Feb. 4, 1924; s. John Leonidas and Sara Elizabeth (Thomas) K.; B.S. cum laude, Vanderbilt U., 1949; postgrad. Syracuse U., 1949-50, Kan. U., 1957, So. Meth. U., 1968-70; m. Alice Cornelia Turney, Aug. 25, 1946; children—Rebecca Ann, Jennifer Elizabeth. Engr., Capehart Farnsworth Co., Ft. Wayne, Ind., 1950-52; engring. group head Wilcox Electric Co., Kansas City, Mo., 1952-60; systems engr. Collins, Dallas, 1960—. Served with USNR, 1942-46. Registered profl. engr., Tex. Mem. Tau Beta Pi. Home: 5739 Lindenshire Lane Dallas TX 75230 Office: 1200 N Alma Rd Richardson TX 75080

KENNEDY, JOHN PAYSON, recreation center exec.; b. Atlanta, Jan. 16, 1933; s. John Payson and Frances Jeannette (Law) K.; student Erskine Coll., 1950-52; B.A., Emory U., 1954, M.A. (Univ. fellow), 1959; M.S., U. Ill., 1961; m. Aurelia Turpin, Sept. 14, 1954; children—Catherine Aurelia, Frances Winifred, John Payson, Stewart McRae. Instr. Longwood Coll., Farmville, Va., 1957-59; instr. Hampden-Sydney (Va.) Coll., 1957-59, reference librarian, 1959-60; commerce and sociology librarian U. Ill. Library, Urbana, 1961-63, research asso., 1963-65; data processing librarian Ga. Inst. Tech. Library, Atlanta, 1965-73; pres. Nantahala Outdoor Center, Inc., Bryson City, N.C., 1973—. Vis. lectr. Atlanta U. Library Sch., 1969, Emory U. Div. Librarianship, 1970. Scoutmaster Atlanta area council Boy Scouts Am., 1963—. Served as spl. agt., CIC, AUS, 1954-56. Mem. Ga. Canoeing Assn. (pres. 1968), Phi Beta Kappa. Home: Nantahala Outdoor Center Bryson City NC 28713

KENNEDY, JOSEPH HOWARD, banker; b. Terra Ceia, Fla., Jan. 17, 1929; s. Joseph Howard and Mildred (Perry) K.; B.S. in Bus. Adminstrn., The Citadel, 1952; m. Joyce Ann Hamilton, June 21, 1952; children—Karen, Joseph Howard. With Palmetto Bank and Trust Co. (Fla.), 1956—, pres., 1968—, also dir.; founding dir., vice chmn. bd. 1st Comml. Bank of Manatee County, 1973—. Served to 1st lt. USAF, 1951-56. Mem. Am., Fla. bankers assns., Palmetto Jr. C. of C. (pres. 1963—, dir. 1960-63), Manatee County C. of C. (treas. 1965, pres. 1971-72). Kiwanian. Club: Bradenton Country. Home: 2201 7th St Palmetto FL 33561 Office: 700 8th Av Palmetto FL 33561

KENNEDY, K. DOYLE, constrn. co. exec.; b. Clintwood, Va., June 1, 1932; s. Kermit DeWitt and Tessie Parkis (Colley) K.; B.S. in Civil Engring., Duke, 1953; postgrad. Northwestern U., 1956-57, Alexander Hamilton Inst., 1963; m. Mary Margaret Loos, July 30, 1971; children (by previous marriage)—Beverly, Shirley, Peggy. Engr., U.S. Bur. Reclamation, Sacramento, 1951-52; self employed as surveyor, Durham, N.C., 1952-53; civil engr. Shell Oil Co., Indpls., 1955-57; self employed as cons. engr., Indpls., 1956-57; pres., gen. mgr., chmn. bd. Kennedy Constrn. Co. of New Smyrna Beach, Fla., 1957—, chmn. bd. Profit Sharing Trust, 1962—; cons. engr., New Smyrna Beach, 1960—. Served with C.E., AUS, 1953-55. Recipient Distinguished Service award, Kiwanis, 1963, Kiwanian of Year award, 1973. Mem. Am. Soc. C.E., New Smyrna Beach C. of C., Daytona Beach, Fla. skin divers assns., Underwater Soc. Am. Baptist (deacon 1959—, mem. ch. council 1959-70). Kiwanian (pres. 1961, 1973-74, dist. chmn. agr. and conservation 1971—). Clubs: Halifax Sport Fishing (v.p. 1968—) (Daytona Beach), New Smyrna Beach Flying (pres. 1968—). Home: 909 Faulkner St New Smyrna Beach FL 32069 Office: PO Box K New Smyrna Beach FL 32069

KENNEDY, ORVILLE ANDERSON, dentist; b. Louisville, Jan. 4, 1898; s. Thomas Worsley and Madge Pet (Willard) K.; Pharm.G., U. Ky., 1921; D.D.S., U. Louisville, 1925; m. Hazel Irene Tutt, Oct. 29, 1936; 1 dau., Georgia (Mrs. William Lynn Higginbotham, Jr.). Individual practice dentistry, Louisville, 1925-42, Cairo, Ga., 1946—; mem. staff Grady County Hosp., Cairo, Ga. Mem. faculty U.

Louisville, 1925-27. Served to maj. Dental Corps, AUS, 1942-46. Mem. Am. Legion, Kappa Psi, Delta Sigma Delta, Theta Nu Epsilon, Sigma Pi Upsilon. Home: 1401 7th St NW Cairo GA 31728 Office: 200 1st St SE Cairo GA 31728

KENNEDY, PHILIP DALTON, JR., lawyer; b. Statesville, N.C., Mar. 9, 1919; s. Philip Dalton and Elise (Weedon) K.; A.B., Atlantic Christian Coll., 1938; LL.B., U. N.C., 1942. Admitted to N.C. bar, 1944, Fla. bar 1958; practiced Charlotte, N.C., 1945-57, West Hollywood, Fla., 1958—; city atty. City of Miramar, 1958-59, councilman, 1959-65; municipal judge, 1963—. Served from ensign to lt., USNR, 1942-45. Mem. Fla. Bar, N.C., Broward County bar assns. Presbyn. Asso. editor N.C. Law Rev., 1940-42. Address: PO Box 4215 Hollywood FL 33023

KENNEDY, WALLACE ALBERT, educator, psychologist; b. Monteverde, Fla., Apr. 2, 1929; s. George Leslie and Lucy Elizabeth (Bible) K.; A.B., Fla. State U., 1951, M.A., 1952, Ph.D., 1956; m. Patricia Burghard, June 30, 1950; children—Lois, Wally B., Lucy, Lora. Postdoctoral fellow Harvard, 1956-57; from asst. prof. to prof. psychology Fla. State U., 1957—, dir. clin. tng., 1968—; pvt. practice psychology, Tallahassee, 1959—. Mem. perinatal research com. Nat. Inst. Mental Health. Served with AUS, 1947-48. Diplomate Am. Bd. Examiners Profl. Psychology. Mem. Fla. State Bd. Examiners Psychology (chmn. 1965-67), Am., Southeastern (pres. 1968), Fla. (pres. 1967) psychol. assns., Soc. Research in Child Devel. Research in normative data on Negro intelligence and achievement in Southeastern U.S., motivation of sch. children, psychotherapy of phobias. Home: Route 5 Box 363 K Tallahassee FL 32301

KENNEDY, WILLIAM CHARLES, educator; b. St. Paul, Sept. 7, 1935; s. Fred Clarence and Beatrice Evelyn (Munson) K.; B.S., U. Minn., 1962; M.F.A., U. Wis., 1967; m. Patricia Rae Ringer, July 21, 1962; children—William Charles, Derek Thomas. Tchr. art Beloit (Wis.) Pub. Schs., 1962-64, Madison (Wis.) Pub. Schs., 1965-66; research asst. U. Wis., 1966-67, teaching asst., 1967; freelance graphic designer, Madison, 1967-68; publs. designer Wis. State U. at Whitewater, 1968; asst. prof. art U. Tenn., 1968—, adviser Coll. Liberal Arts, 1971—, curriculum chmn. dept. art, 1972—; design cons. to industry; artist, works exhibited in one and two-man shows, pub. collections. Bd. dirs. Knoxville Montessori Assn., 1968-71, v.p., 1969-70. Served with USAF, 1955-58. Mem. Am. Assn. Univ. Profs., Coll. Art Assn., Southeastern Coll. Art Conf., Southeastern Graphics Council. Home: 7018 Shady Land Dr Knoxville TN 37919

KENNEDY, WILLIAM RICHARD, spectroscopist; b. St. Louis, Aug. 9, 1922; s. William Herschel and Irene (Stege) K.; student Auburn U., 1942-43; B.S., Birmingham So. Coll., 1944; m. Anita Corinne Burns, Mar. 13, 1948; children—Cheryl Lynn, Gwendolyn Marie. Spectroscopist, Am. Cast Iron Pipe Co., Birmingham, Ala., 1944-45, chief spectroscopist, 1945—. Mem. Am. Soc. Testing Materials (com. sec. 1963-67, vice chmn. 1968-72, chmn. 1972—, E-2 Steel Ingot award, 1972. Soc. for Applied Spectroscopy (sect. pres. 1950-54), So. Assn. Spectrographers. Presbyn. (elder). Home: 341 Orchid Rd Birmingham AL 35215 Office: PO Box 2727 Birmingham AL 35202

KENNELLY, MICHAEL FRANCIS, univ. pres.; b. Moyvane, Ireland, May 22, 1914; s. Timothy J. and Mary Jane (Hanrahan) K.; came to U.S., 1930; B.A., Spring Hill Coll., 1939; B.Ed. with honors, Univ. Coll., Dublin, Ireland, 1948; M.A.Ed. with honors, Nat. U. Ireland, 1949. Joined Soc. of Jesus, 1933, ordained priest Roman Cath. Ch., 1946; prin. St. John's High Sch., Shreveport, La., 1949-53; rector, prin. Jesuit High Sch., Tampla, Fla., 1953-59; founder, pres. Strake Jesuit Coll. Prep. Sch., Houston, 1959-70; pres. Loyola U., New Orleans, 1970—, chmn. bd. dirs., 1968-71, bd. dirs., 1968-74. Dir. sta. WWL-TV-AM, New Orleans. Cons. to superior New Orleans Province Jesuits, 1962-68; mem. Bd. Jesuit Univ. Presidents, 1970-74. Mem. New Orleans Met. Area Commn., Information Council Americas, Council for Better La., Internat. House, Goals Found. Met. New Orleans. Bd. dirs. Internat. Mart, New Orleans. Mem. Presidents of Pvt. Higher Edn. in La., K.C. Home: 6363 St Charles Av New Orleans LA 70118

KENNER, CHARLES THOMAS, educator; b. Waxahachie, Tex., Oct. 20, 1910; s. Francis Buckner and Rozetta (Morse) K.; B.S. magna cum laude, Trinity U., Waxahachie, 1932; M.S. (teaching fellow), U. Tenn., 1935; Ph.D., U. Tex. at Austin, 1939; m. Bessie Will Harrison, Mar. 21, 1942; 1 dau., Elizabeth Anne (Mrs. Walter Ross Purkey). Instr. chemistry U. Tex. at Austin, 1935-38; asst. prof. The Citadel, Charleston, S.C., 1938-42; chief chemist Hurley div. Thor Corp., Chgo., 1946; dir. research Central Testing, Inc., Chgo., 1947; mem. faculty So. Meth. U., Dallas, 1948—, asso. prof. chemistry, 1951-54, prof., 1954—. Owner, Kenner Labs., Dallas, 1955—; sci. adviser Dallas Dist. FDA, 1967—. Mem. advanced sci. cluster adv. com. Dallas Ind. Sch. Dist., 1971—. Bd. dirs. Dallas Regional Sci. Fair, 1963—. Served with AUS, 1942-46. Recipient Phi Eta Sigma Outstanding Tchr. award, 1960, Favorite Doctor award Meth. Hosp. Sch. Nursing, 1970. Mem. Am. Chem. Soc., A.A.A.S., Am. Assn. Bioanalysts, Soc. Applied Spectroscopy, Met. Philos. Soc., Dallas Soc. Analytical Chemists (Analyst of Yr. award 1968), Sigma Xi, Phi Lambda Upsilon. Author: Analytical Separations and Determinations, A Textbook in Quantitative Analysis, 1971; Laboratory Directions for Analytical Separation and Determinations, 1971; Instrumental and Separation Analysis, 1973. Contbr. articles to profl. jours. Home: 7210 Clemson Dr Dallas TX 75214

KENNER, JOANNE (MRS. JOHN CATLETT ALLENSWORTH), physician; b. Abilene, Tex., Apr. 26, 1924; d. Claude William and Elizabeth (Kirby) Kenner; B.A., Hardin-Simmons U., 1947; M.D., Southwestern Med. Sch., 1947; m. John Catlett Allensworth, Oct. 15, 1955. Intern St. Joseph's Hosp., Ft. Worth, 1947-48, rotating resident in gen. surgery, 1948-49; resident physician in obstetrics and gynecology, Harris Hosp., Ft. Worth, 1949-50, Doctor's Hosp., N.Y.C., 1950-51, Woman's Hosp., N.Y.C., 1951-54; practice medicine, specializing in obstetrics and gynecology, Ft. Worth, 1954-55, Mineral Wells, Tex., 1955—; mem. staff Palo Pinto Gen. Hosp., Mineral Wells. Civilian cons. Beach Army Hosp., Ft. Welters, Tex., 1956—; dir., physician Community Family Planning Center, Mineral Wells, 1967—. Diplomate Am. Bd. Obstetrics and Gynecology. Fellow A.C.S., Am. Coll. Obstretrics and Gynecology; mem. Am., Tex. med. assns., Tri-County Med. Soc.; Tex. Soc. Obstetricians and Gynecologists. Office: 208 NW 2d St Mineral Wells TX 76067

KENNEY, RICHARD ALEC, educator; b. Coventry, Eng., Oct. 4, 1924; s. Alec and Dorothy Ada (Cooke) K.; B.Sc. with honors, U. Birmingham, Eng., 1945, Ph.D., 1947; m. Bette Gladys Green, Aug. 8, 1959; 1 son by previous marriage—Michael Alec. Came to U.S., 1967. Lectr. physiology U. Leeds, Eng., 1947-51; with Colonial Research Service, Nigeria, 1951-54; staff mem. W.H.O., S.E. Asia Region, 1955-60; chmn. physiology U. Singapore, 1960-65; reader physiology U. Melbourne, Australia, 1965-67; prof. physiology George Washington U. Med. Center, 1968—, chmn. dept., 1970—. Tutor physiology Royal Australian Coll. Surgeons, 1965-67. Mem. Physiol. Soc. (London), Am., Australian physiol. socs., Renal Assn. (London), Internat. Nephrological Soc. Contbr. articles to profl. jours. Home: 4424 Reservoir Rd NW Washington DC 20007 Office: 2300 Eye St NW Washington DC 20037

KENNINGTON, DAVID HILTON, electronics mfr.; b. New Boston, Tex., Mar. 1, 1927; s. Joseph Temple and Murtie Almeta (Atchley) K.; B.B.A., So. Meth. U., 1947; m. Dorothy Frances Bayer, July 29, 1961; children—Craig Hilton, Clark Bayer, Clayton Atchley. Materials mgr. Varo, Inc., Garland, Tex., 1953-57; product marketing mgr. Tex. Instruments, Dallas, 1957-62; pres., founder Thermalloy, Inc., Dallas, 1962—; dir. Plastronics, Inc., Thermo-Jet, Inc., Match Point Industries, Am. Pennant Co. Cons. Area dir. Democratic Party. Bd. dirs. CCA Found. Served with USNR, 1944-46. Mem. Garland C. of C. (dir.), Lambda Chi Alpha. Methodist (chmn. bd.). Home: 4405 McFarlin St Dallas TX 75205 Office: 2021 W Valley View St Dallas TX 75234

KENNY, ROBERT LEWIS, real estate devel. exec.; b. Spencer, Ia., May 4, 1926; s. James Roy and Grace M. (Lewis) K.; student Baylor U., 1948-50; children by previous marriage—Colleen Ann, Robin Faye, James Carleton, Dwight Lewis. Vice pres. Travel-Eze Mfg. Co., Spencer, Ia., 1945-47; asst. plant mgr. Stoddard Mfg. Co., Mason City, Ia., 1947-49; civilian flight instr. USAF, Hondo (Tex.) AFB, 1951-58; dir. mem. services Medina Electric Coop., Hondo, 1958-60, Magic Valley Electric Coop., Mercedes, Tex., 1960-71; v.p. Paradise Isle Devel. Corp., 1972—. Mem. Tex. Indsl. Devel. Council., 1968-71; pres. South Tex. Indsl. Devel. Com., 1970-71; v.p. Medina County Sheriffs Possee, 1955-57; county campaign dir. March of Dimes, 1964; county chmn. Nat. Found., 1965. Adv. bd. Tex. A. and M. U., 1970. Served with USAAF, 1943-45, with USAF, 1950-51. Mem. Tex. Assn. Assessing Officers (asso.), Optomist (v.p. 1957, 71). Rotarian (v.p. Mercedes club). Home: Boca Chica Branch Brownsville TX 78520

KENSHALO, DANIEL RALPH, educator, psychologist; b. West Frankfort, Ill., July 27, 1922; s. Daniel Ralph and Edith (Schroeder) K.; A.B., Washington U., 1947, Ph.D., 1953; children—Daniel Ralph, Rebecca Carolyn, Mark Hoyt, Janice Machelle; m. Mary Janice Gordon, Aug. 28, 1970. Faculty physiol. psychology Fla. State U., 1950—, prof., 1959—. Vis. prof. physiology U. Marburg, Germany, 1969, U. Claude Bernard, Lyon, France, 1973. Served as officer USNR, World War II. NSF grantee, 1955-57, 1964-71; NASA grantee, 1961-64; NIH grantee, 1967-68. Fellow Am. Psychol. Assn., A.A.A.S., N.Y. Acad. Scis., Internat. Neuropsychology Soc., Soc. Neurosci.; mem. So. Soc. Philosophy and Psychology (sec. 1959-62, pres. 1963), Am., Eastern physiol. socs., Psychonomic Soc., Sigma Xi, Psi Chi. Cons. editor: Handbook of Perception, vol. 3, 1974; Perception and Psychophysics, 1973. Contbr. numerous articles to sci., profl. jours. Home: 2414 Delgado Dr Tallahassee FL 32304

KENT, BARTIS MILTON, physician; b. Terrell, Tex., June 23, 1925; s. Bartis William and Annie (Smalley) K.; student So. Meth. U., 1942-44; M.D., Baylor U., 1948; m. Ann L. Kiel, July 6, 1954; children—Susan Ruth, Martha Lucille, Bartis Michael. Intern Jefferson Davis Hosp., Houston, 1948-49; resident pathology Mass. Meml. Hosps., Boston, 1951; resident in internal medicine Baylor U., 1953-56; indsl. physician Humble Oil Co., Houston, 1949-51; instr. dept. medicine U. Ia., 1956-58; staff physician Ia. City VA Hosp., 1956-58; practice medicine specializing in internal medicine, Muskogee, Okla., 1958—; dir. radiosotope service Muskogee Gen. Hosp. Cons. Muskogee VA Hosp. Chmn., Muskogee County chpt. Am. Nat. Red Cross, 1963-65. Served with USAF, 1951-53. Decorated Air medal. Diplomate Am. Bd. Internal Medicine. Mem. A.C.P., Indsl. Med. Assn., Soc. Nuclear Medicine, Am. Fedn. Clin. Research, Am. Heart Assn., Aero Med. Assn., Am., Okla. socs. internal medicine, Muskogee C. of C. Methodist. Mason (Shriner). Home: 800 N 45th St Muskogee OK 74401 Office: 211 S 36th St Muskogee OK 74401

KENT, BRUCE MARTIN, ednl. adminstr.; b. nr. Rocky Mount, Va., Mar. 13, 1915; s. Robert Lee and Rose (Martin) K.; B.S., Coll. William and Mary, 1935, M.Ed., 1952; postgrad. U. Va., 1935-36; m. Clara May Bousman, June 8, 1938; children—Nancy (Mrs. W. H. Young, Jr.), Mary (Mrs. R. Gaines Steer). Prin., Henry Elementary Sch., 1948-51; guidance dir. Franklin County High Sch., 1951-56, asst. prin., 1956-59, prin., 1959-69; gen. supr. Franklin County Pub. Schs., Rocky Mount, 1969-73; adminstrv. asst. to supt. schs., Franklin County, 1973—. Dir. Bankers Trust Co., Rocky Mount, 1957—, chmn. bd., 1972—. Mem. Ruritan Nat. (dist. gov. 1951), Va. High Sch. League (group bd. chmn., mem. exec. com. 1966-68), Va. Edn. Assn., Nat. Assn. Secondary Sch. Prins. Methodist. Lion. Home: Route 1 Rocky Mount VA 24151

KENT, JERARD ALLEN, engring. and constrn. co. exec.; b. New Orleans, Mar. 4, 1933; s. John Alva and Hilda (McGovern) K.; Indsl. Engr., Tulane U., 1956; grad. La. State U., 1958; m. Shirley Watson, Apr. 27, 1954; children—Jerard Allen, Paul S., Hope M., Judey A., Deborah A., Jeffrey J., Gregory J. Sr. adminstrv. engr. Kaiser Aluminum & Chem. Corp., Gramercy, La., 1958-59; v.p. finance Wellman-Lord Inc., Lakeland, Fla., 1959-68, v.p. Planning and diversification, 1969-73, also dir.; pres. Constrn.-Engr. Cons., Inc., 1973—; pres. G-M Indsl. Enterprises, Inc., G-M Properties, Inc., Indsl. Park Utilities, Inc., Eaton Park, Fla.; dir. N.Am. Steel Corp., Lakeland, Hatteras Indsl. Corp., New Bern, N.C., Delta Fabricators Inc., Baton Rouge. Bd. dirs. United Fund, Lakeland, A.R.C., Cath. Charities, Orlando, Fla.; treas. St. Leo (Fla.) Coll., 1969—, also bd. dirs. Served to capt. AUS, 1952-54. Mem. Financial Exec. Inst. (dir.), Nat. Assn. Accountants (dir.). Republican. Roman Catholic (mem. parish council, 1967—). Home: Route 5 Box 201 Clarendon Av Lakeland FL 33801 Office: PO Box 2211 Lakeland FL 33803

KENT, JOEL GILBERT, indsl. engr., govt ofcl.; b. Bklyn., Mar. 13, 1933; s. Sidney Louis and Rose (Levin) K.; B.S., U. Miami, 1958; m. Sandra Snyder, Sept. 3, 1956; children—Daniel Howard, Neil Victor. Broadcast engr. sta. WVCG, Coral Gables, Fla., 1955-56; planning engr., proposal coordinator Dynatronics, Inc., Orlando, Fla., 1958-63; mgr. proposals and advt. Systems Engr. Labs., Ft. Lauderdale, Fla., 1963; sr. engr. writer RCA Service Co., Cocoa Beach, Fla., 1963-64; sr. indsl. engr. Brown Engr. Co., Cocoa Beach, 1964; Apollo data mgr., installation data/reports mgr. NASA, John F. Kennedy Space Center, Fla., 1964—. Bunker scholar, 1969; recipient Pres.'s certificate merit, 1972. Internat. Graphoanalysis Soc., Mem. Am. Inst. Indsl. Engrs. (dir. Cocoa Beach chpt. 1964-67), Internat. Graphoanalysis Soc. (faculty, congress and inst.), Internat. Platform Assn., Am. Def. Preparedness Assn. (NASA rep. for engring. data mgmt. 1967—), Fla. Graphoanalysts (v.p. 1972—), Inner Circle. Home: 601 Robert Way Satellite Beach FL 32937

KENT, JOHN BRADFORD, lawyer; b. Jacksonville, Fla., Sept. 5, 1939; s. Frederick Heber and Norma (Futch) K.; grad. Phillips Exeter Acad., 1957; B.A., Yale, 1961; J.D., U. Fla., 1964; LL.M. in Taxation, N.Y. Grad. Sch. Law, 1965; m. Monett Powers, Dec. 18, 1969; children—Katherine Lane, Monett Bradford, Susan Whitfield Powers. Admitted to Fla. bar, 1964; asso. atty. firm Ulmer, Murchison, Kent, Ashby & Ball, Jacksonville, Fla., 1965-67; partner firm Kent, Sears, Durden & Kent and predecessor firms, Jacksonville, 1967—; pres. Kent Theatres, Inc., Jacksonville, 1967-70, v.p., gen. counsel, 1970—, also dir.; dir. Kent Enterprises, Inc., Kent Properties, Inc., Melbourne Theatres, Inc., Blanding Theatres, Inc. Mem. exec. com., chmn. finance com., treas., trustee St. Mark's Episcopal Day Sch., Jacksonville; mem. state pub. relations, fund raising com. Children's Home Soc. Fla., 1970-71, 1st v.p., N.E. div., 1972—, dir., asst. counselor, 1974—. Bd. dirs. Jacksonville Legal Aid Soc.; bd. govs. Fla. Jr. Coll. at Jacksonville Found. Mem. Am., Fla. bar assns., Am. Judicature Soc., Nat. Assn. Theatre Owners (dir. 1972), Nat. Assn. Theatre Owners Fla. (v.p. 1968-72), Delta Kappa Epsilon, Phi Delta Phi, Manuscript Sr. Hon. Soc. (Yale). Rotarian. Episcopalian (vestryman). Clubs: Ponte Vedra (Ponte Vedra Beach, Fla.); Friars, Ye Mystic Revellers, Timuquana, University, YMCA, Fellowship of Christian Athletes (Jacksonville); Highlands (N.C.) Country; Mory's Assn. (New Haven). Home: 4815 Arapaho Av Jacksonville FL 32210 Office: 870 Florida Bank Bldg Jacksonville FL 32202

KENT, ROSEMARY MAY (MRS. DONALD EAST KENT), pub. health educator; b. Bartlesville, Okla., Jan. 26, 1913; d. William Ernest and Christine (Ruble) May; A.B., Agnes Scott Coll., 1933, M.A., Emory U., 1934; postgrad. (Mary Pemberton Nourse fellow) Vassar Coll.; M.P.H., U. N.C., 1946, Ph.D., 1949; m. Donald East Kent, Dec. 25, 1937. Tchr. high sch., Hamilton County, Tenn., 1934-40; health edn. coordinator Norris Area, TVA, 1940-43; health cons. City Pub. Schs., Winston-Salem, N.C., 1943-45; ednl. dir. N.C. div. Am. Cancer Soc., 1947-51; asso. prof. pub. health edn. U. N.C. Sch. Pub. Health, Chapel Hill, 1951-72, prof. emeritus, 1972—; prof. health edn. U. Tenn., Knoxville, 1970—. With Nat. Tng. Lab., Bethel, Me., 1967; cons. Headstart Evaluation and Research Center, U. Hawaii, 1968; curriculum cons. USPHS, Indian Health Service, 1969—, WHO Faculty Travel fellow Western Pacific and S.E. Asia, 1956. Fellow Am. Pub. Health Assn., Soc. Pub. Health Educators (charter); mem. N.C. Pub. Health Assn., N.C. Assn. Health Educators, Assn. Supervision and Curriculum Devel., A.A.A.S., Delta Kappa Gamma, Delta Omega. Contbr. articles to profl. jours. Office: U Tenn 1914 Andy Holt Av Knoxville TN 37916

KENWARD, FRANKLIN MONROE, dentist; b. Gary, Ind., Dec. 7, 1919; s. Charles Franklin and Mabel Clair (Monroe) K.; B.S., Ind. U., 1947; D.D.S. cum laude, Loyola U., Chgo., 1952; m. Marcia Hoover, Sept. 4, 1948; children—Scott Franklin, Christopher Floyd. Practice dentistry, Miami, Fla., 1952—; dir. Omega Ins. Agy., Phila. Served with USNR, 1942-45. Fellow Internat. Coll. Dentists (sec.-gen., registrar U.S. sect.); mem. Am., Fla., dental assns., Miami Dental Soc. (pres. 1963-64), Coconut Grove C. of C. (pres. 1965-66), Am. Dental Interfrat. Council (pres. 1968), Blue Key, Omicron Kappa Upsilon, Psi Omega (nat. pres. 1963-64, editor Frater 1965-74). Club: Exchange (pres. 1956) (Miami). Editor: Fla. Dental Jour., 1969-74. Home: 6090 Killian Dr Miami FL 33156 Office: 3138 Commodore Plaza Miami FL 33133

KENYON, RALPH CLIFFORD, state ofcl.; b. Columbus, Mont. Nov. 14, 1930; s. Vernon P. and Ethel (Weppler) K.; B.Arch., Mont. State Coll., 1953; m. Dalcie Mae Langston, May 1, 1955; children—Jana Sue, Karla Jean. Architect, Drake and Gustafson, Billings, Mont., 1955-63, div. architecture and engring. Dept. Adminstrn., State of Mont., Helena, 1963-65; state controller, Montana, 1965-69; with office of State Planning, Fla., 1969-72, state budget office, 1972—. Served with AUS, 1953-55. Mem. Meth. Youth Fellowship Mont. (pres. 1949-50). Republican. Methodist. Home: 2103 Evergreen Dr Tallahassee FL 32303 Office: Dept Adminstrn Capitol Bldg Tallahassee FL 32303

KENYON, RICHARD LEE, assn. exec.; b. Athens, Ill., Dec. 11, 1917; s. Thomas W. and Elizabeth (Kincaid) K.; A.B., U. Ill., 1938; Ph.D., U. N.C., 1942; m. Carol Ann Elward, July 5, 1951; children—Colleen, Stephanie, Jan, Christopher. DuPont postdoctoral fellow U. Ill., 1942-43; research chemist central research dept. E.I. du Pont de Nemours & Co., Wilmington, Del., 1943-46; asso. editor Chem. and Engring. News, Chgo., 1946-50, editor, 1956-62; asso. editor Indsl. and Engring. Chemistry, Chgo., 1946-50; European editor Chem. and Engring. News, Indsl. Engring. Chemistry, London, Eng., 1950-53; mng. editor Jour. Agrl. and Food Chemistry, Washington, 1953-56; editorial dir. Applied Jours., Am. Chem. Soc., Washington, 1959-62, dir. applied publs., 1962-64, dir. publs. Am. Chem. Soc., 1965-71, dir. pub. affairs and communication, 1971—, dir. planning and information systems, 1967-69. Mem. patent adv. com. U.S. Patent Office, 1968-72; mem. sci. information council NSF, 1960-64, chmn., 1964; mem. publs. com. Internat. Union Pure and Applied Chemistry, 1969—. Mem. Am. Chem. Soc., A.A.A.S., Soc. Chem. Industry (Gt. Britain), Chem. Soc. (London). Clubs: Federal City, Cosmos (Washington). Office: 1155 16th St NW Washington DC 20036

KENYON, THOMAS GENE, judge; b. Okmulgee, Okla., Feb. 7, 1927; s. William A. and Beulah Mae (Hopper) K.; student U. Okla., 1944-45; LL.B., So. Meth. U., 1951; m. Velta Colleen Moore, Aug. 6, 1949; children—Karen Lynne (Mrs. Don Hickman), Terry Frazier. Admitted to Tex. bar, 1951, since practiced in Freeport; asso. Kenyon Mobile Home Sales, 1955-56; criminal dist. atty., 1963-66; judge City of Freeport; judge Ct. Domestic Relations Brazoria County, Tex., 1973—. Dir. Brazosport Abstract Co., K & K Mobile Home Ranch, Inc., Velasco Properties, Inc., Coastal Broadcasting, Inc. Bd. dirs. Brazeria County United Fund; chmn. bd. Brazoria County Youth Homes. Regent Brazosport Coll. Served with AUS, 1945-46, with USAF, 1951-53; comdr. USCG Aux. Mem. Tex., Brazoria County bar assns., Tex. Trial Lawyers Assn., Am. Legion (past comdr.). Home: Route 2 Box 415 Freeport TX 77541

KEOGH, JOSEPH LLOYD, educator; b. South St. Paul, Minn., Apr. 24, 1923; s. Joseph Harry and Elizabeth (Roth) K.; B.S., St. Thomas Coll., St. Paul, 1948; M.S., U. Minn., 1951, Ph.D., 1954; m. Mary Catherine Koch, Dec. 27, 1946; children—Mary (Mrs. R.R. Carman), Susan (Mrs. Daniel Rensing), Jean, John, Patrick, Ruth. Soil chemistry La. State U., Homer, 1954-57; faculty dept. agronomy U. Ark. at Marianna, 1957—, prof. soil fertility, 19—. Chmn. bd. dirs. Lee County Library. Served with AUS, 1943-46. Mem. Soil Sci. Soc. Am., Internat. Soil Sci. Soc., Am. Soc. Agronomy. K.C., Lion. Contbr. articles to profl. jours. Home: Route 4 Box 5 Marianna AR 72360 Office: Drawer 767 Marianna AR 72360

KEPLEY, THOMAS HOWARD, securities co. exec.; b. Salisbury, N.C., Jan. 31, 1933; s. Thomas Oscar and Helen Gould (Gantt) K.; B.S., U. N.C., 1955; certificate honor investment banking Northwestern U., 1959; certificate achievement N.Y. Inst. Finance, 1969; m. Elizabeth Ann Doscher, Nov. 25, 1961; children—Thomas Howard, Elizabeth Anne Gilmore. With McCarley & Co., Inc., mems. N.Y. Stock Exchange, Am. Stock Exchange, Asheville, N.C., 1956-58, Columbia, S.C., 1958—, mgr. S.C. bond dept., 1958-64, v.p., 1964-72, exec. v.p., 1972—, also dir.; chmn. bd. dirs., pres. H.W. Bischoff Transp. Co., Columbia and Charleston, S.C., 1968—; dir. Computerecords, Inc., Columbia. Chmn. Sports-A-Rama, 1969; mem. U. N.C. Edn. Found., Columbia Com. 100, 1965—. Trustee Incarnation Devel. Found., Columbia, 1973—; adv. bd. Lutheran Theol. So. Sem., Columbia, 1973—. Served with AUS, 1956-58. Recipient George Washington Honor medal Freedom Found., Valley Forge, Pa., 1969, Key to City Seoul (Korea), 1958. Mem. N.Y. Stock Exchange (allied), Am. Stock Exchange (allied), Nat. Security Traders Assn. (conduct and ethics com. 1973—), Securities Dealers

Carolinas (sec. 1965, v.p. 1971-72, pres. 1972-73, chmn. bd. 1974—), Columbia C. of C., Hibernian Soc., Smithsonian Assos., Kappa Alpha. Lutheran (chmn. worship and music com. 1971-72, vice chmn. finance com. 1972, chmn. ch. council 1973—, pulpit com. 1973—). Mason. Clubs: Forest Lake, Sertoma (Columbia); Walnut Hill Hunt (Wateree, S.C.). U. S.C. Gamecock Century. Home: 4765 Heath Hill Rd Columbia SC 29206 Office: 1 Hotel Wade Hampton Columbia SC 29202 also PO Box 1730 Columbia SC 29202

KEPNER, WOODY, public relations exec.; b. Millersburg, Pa., June 30, 1920; s. E. Elwood and Charlotte (Dressler) K.; student pub. schs.; m. Palma M. Brown, Feb. 10, 1943; children—Linda Louise (Mrs. Peter G. Henke), Dawn Annette (Mrs. Glenn Kendrick), Tana Lee (Mrs. J. Wayne Tracy). Free lance reporter Williamsport Grit, Harrisburg Telegraph, Harrisburg Patriot-News, Harrisburg Sunday Courier, 1935-41; reporter, feature and spl. events writer, photo editor, news editor, news bur. mgr. Miami (Fla.) Publicity Dept., 1945-53, dir., 1953-57; pres., owner Woody Kepner Assos. Inc., Miami, 1957—. Vice pres. United Fund Dade County, 1963—. Served with USNR, 1942-45. Mem. Pub. Relations Soc. Am., Fla. Pub. Relations Assn., Dade County C. of C. Home: 6901 SW 120th St Miami FL 33156 Office: 3361 SW 3d Av Miami FL 33145 also 919 3d Av New York City NY 10022 also Lima Peru

KEPPEL, DAVID HEARNE, ret. govt. ofcl.; b. Cazenovia, N.Y., Mar. 16, 1909; s. Frederick Dudley and Mary (Hearne) K.; A.B., Syracuse U., 1932; diploma N.Y. Sch. Social Work, Columbia, 1937; m. Ruth Paige, Apr. 23, 1938; children—Judith K. (Mrs. Leonard Greenwald), Paige K. (Mrs. Dale E. Bellowich). Dep. commr. Me. Dept. Health and Welfare, 1944-48; dir. welfare city Hartford (Conn.), 1948-64; cons. on vol. agys. Dept. Health, Edn. and Welfare, Washington, 1964-66, program planning specialist Bur. Social Welfare, 1966-68; social work program specialist Med. Services Adminstrn., 1968-72; ret., 1972; tchr. pub. welfare adminstrn. N.Y. State Pub. Welfare Inst., Cornell U., Ithaca, N.Y., summers 1951-53, Springfield (Mass.) Coll., 1956; mem. Gov's Com. on Unemployment Compensation, 1951. Bd. dirs. Social Adjustment Commn., Hartford. Mem. Am Pub. Welfare Assn. (past dir.), Nat. Assn. Social Workers, Nat. Assn. on Mental Deficiency, Conn. Assn. Local Pub. Welfare Adminstrs. (past pres.). Conglist. Home: 7308 Brookcrest Pl Annandale VA 22003

KEPPLER, CHARLES BRIEL, physician; b. Richmond, Va., Feb. 13, 1917; s. Philip and Addie (Huffman) K.; B.S., U. Richmond, 1937; M.D., Med. Coll. Va., 1941; m. Myrtis Myrick Elliott, Dec. 1, 1942; children—Charles B., Kristina E., Melinda E. Intern Norfolk (Va.) Gen. Hosp., 1941-42, resident, 1946; practice medicine specializing in internal medicine, Sewanee, Tenn., 1948-69; mem. staff Emerald Hodgson, Harton Meml., Coffee County hosps.; clin. dir. Multicounty Mental Health Center, Tullahoma, Tenn., 1969—. City councilman, Sewanee, 1965-68. Bd. dirs. Emeral Hodgson Hosp., Learning Disability Center, Sewanee. Served with AUS, 1942-46. Decorated Bronze Star medal with oak leaf cluster. Mem. A.M.A., Tenn., Franklin County med. socs., Phi Beta Pi, Theta Chi. Home: Box 277 Sewanee TN 37375 Office: 1803 N Jackson St Tullahoma TN 37388

KERBY, ANNIE MARGUERITE BEASLEY (MRS. JAMES KENNETH KERBY), nurse, club woman; b. nr. Pontotoc, Miss., Jan. 23, 1927; d. William Cecil and Mary (Lyon) Beasley; student Miss. State Coll. for Women, 1945-47; grad. Bapt. Meml. Hosp. Nursing, Memphis, 1950; student Memphis State U., 1947-48, 58-59, U. Tenn., 1965-66; m. James Kenneth Kerby, Jan. 9, 1954; children—Rebecca Zane, Kenneth Waterman Hewett, Lyon Galloway, Ritchey King. Staff nurse Le Bonheur Hosp., Memphis, 1954-57; nurse Memphis VA Hosp., 1960—. Com. chmn. Maternal Welfare League, 1962-63; vol. 1st aide work A.R.C.; active Memphis Symphony League, 1962—; chmn. spl. features com. Greater Memphis Christian Women's Club, 1968; D.A.R. rep. to Memphis City Beautiful Commn., 1966; organizer, sponsor local chpt. Children Am. Revolution, 1966, sr. pres., 1966-68, state promoter, 1969-70. Mem. D.A.R. (chpt. chmn. hist. markers 1966), Daus. Am. Colonists, Memphis Geneal. Soc., Tenn. League Nursing, So. Dames Am. (sec. 1971—), Nat. League Nursing, Tenn. Fedn. Women's Clubs. Club: Luncheon Forum (Memphis). Home: 1849 Central Av Memphis TN 38104 Office: 1030 Jefferson Av Memphis TN 38115

KERBY, LESLIE GLEN, bank exec.; b. Sweetwater, Tex., May 10, 1938; s. Leslie George and Fannie Lorene (Price) K.; student Cisco Jr. Coll., 1956-60; B.B.A., Tex. Tech. Coll., 1962; postgrad. So. Meth. U., 1967-70; m. Ethel Lavonia Weldon, Oct. 5, 1956; children—Carie Lynn, Sandra Denise, Paul Glen. Bookkeeper, 1st Nat. Bank, Baird, Tex., 1956-60; with First Nat. Bank, Lubbock, Tex., 1960-62; asst. nat. bank examiner U.S. Dept. Treasury, Dallas and Abilene, Tex., 1962-65, nat. bank examiner, 1965-67; examiner-in-charge of Abilene, Tex. sub-region, 1967-68; with Central Nat. Bank, San Angelo, Tex., 1968—, exec. v.p., mem. adv. bd., 1973—. Bd. dirs. Tom Green County Library, 1970—, chmn., 1973-74; bd. dirs. W. Tex. Lighthouse for Blind, 1972—; bd. dirs. San Angelo United Fund, 1972—, treas. 1973—, vice chmn., 1974; bd. dirs. San Angelo Indsl. Fund, 1971—; bd. dirs. Mental Health-Mental Retardation Center, San Angelo, 1971—, chmn., 1973-74; bd. dirs. Salvation Army, 1972—. Mem. Am. Inst. Banking (dir. San Angelo chpt. 1968-71), Robert Morris Assos. (bank rep. 1967-71), Phi Alpha Kappa. Methodist (dir. finance commn. 1972—). Odd Fellow. Clubs: River (dir. 1971—, sec.-treas. 1974), San Angelo Country. (San Angelo). Home: 3349 Tanglewood Dr San Angelo TX 76901 Office: 18 W Beauregard San Angelo TX 76901

KERN, CLIFFORD DALTON, meteorologist; b. Oakland, Cal., Jan. 6, 1928; s. Arthur William and Blanche Naomi (Brown) K.; A.B., U. Cal. at Berkeley, 1952; certificate in Meterology U. Cal. at Los Angeles, 1953, M.A., 1958; Ph.D., U. Wash., 1965; m. C. Joyce Durant, Feb. 21, 1951; children—Michael Richard, Janice Rae, Michelle Ann. Commd. 2d lt. USAF, 1952, advanced through grades to lt. col., 1972; staff meteorologist Air Force Systems Command, McClelland AFB, Cal., 1953-55, Hanscom Field, Mass., 1955-56, 58-61, Vietnam, 1964-65, Air Force Satellite Control Facility, Sunnyvale, Cal., 1965-67, Air Force Global Weather Central Offutt AFB, 1969-71, Los Angeles Air Force Sta., 1971-72; ret., 1972; asst. prof. St. Louis U., 1972; vis. scientist Nat. Center Atmospheric Research, Boulder, Colo., 1972-73; with Atomic Energy div. E.I. duPont de Nemours & Co., Savannah River Lab., Aiken, S.C., 1973—. Served with AUS, 1946-48. Decorated Bronze Star medal, Air medal with one oak leaf cluster. Mem. Am. Meteorol. Soc., Am. Geophys. Union, Sigma Xi. Mason. Home: 1449 Moultrie Dr Aiken SC 29801 Office: Savannah River Lab EI duPont de Nemours & Co Aiken SC 29801

KERN, WILLIAM JAMES, elec. engr.; b. Newark, Jan. 28, 1924; s. William Francis and Frances Gertrude (Jowitt) K.; B.S., Rutgers U., 1957; m. Elina Maria Govin, Nov. 2, 1951; children—William Michael, Francis Joseph. Jr. engr. devel. lab. Diehl Mfg. Co., Finderne, N.J., 1955-56; engr. test and calibration Electronics div. Curtiss-Wright Corp., Carlstadt, N.J., 1957-58; elec. engr., dept. adminstr. State of N.C., Raleigh, 1958-60; test facilities engr. Electronics div. Westinghouse Corp., Balt., 1961-62; test engr. Electronics Communications, Inc., St. Petersburg, Fla., 1962-63; elec. engr. Olin Mathison Corp., Macintosh, Ala., 1963; elec. engr. C.E. Squadron, MacDill AFB, Fla., 1963—. Served with USAAF, 1942-48, USAF, 1951-52. Mem. I.E.E.E. Home: 3908 Leila Av Tampa FL 33616 Office: 1 Civil Engring Squadron Engring Div MacDill AFB Fla 33608

KERNAN, MARTIN HEALY, JR., elec. engr.; b. Balt., June 9, 1938; s. Martin Healy and Dorothra Anita (Krug) K.; B.S. in Elec. Engring., Christian Bros. Coll., Memphis, 1962. Network engr. light, gas and water div. City of Memphis, 1965-74, supr. underground transmission and network engr., 1974—. Served with USNR, 1962-64. Mem. I.E.E.E., Am. Bowling Congress (hospitality chmn. 1966, audit chmn. 1972, chmn. transfer and membership 1973-74), Dixie Motor Club. Moose. Home: 3919 Allison Av Memphis TN 38122 Office: 220 S Main St Memphis TN 38103

KERR, BEN J., III, lawyer; b. Seattle, Jan. 28, 1943; s. Ben J., Jr., and Marrian Grace (Hardie) K.; B.B.A., So. Meth. U., 1965, LL.B., 1967; m. Dianna C. Rea, Aug. 28, 1964; children—Kevan Lynn, Kelley Rea. Admitted to Tex. bar, 1967; pvt. practice law, Dallas, 1967—. Mem. Tex., Tex. Jr. bar assns., Sigma Alpha Epsilon, Pi Eta Sigma. Clubs: Cypress Springs Country (Winnsboro, Tex.); Mineola (Tex.) Country. Contbr. articles to profl. jours. Home: PO Box 251D Quitman TX 75783 Office: PO Box 509 Quitman TX 75783

KERR, BEN JONES, JR., banker; b. Denison, Tex., June 14, 1918; s. Ben Jones and Ethyl (Caldwell) K.; B.A., U. Okla., 1940; M.B.A., Harvard, 1941; m. Marrian Grace Hardie, Sept. 16, 1941; children—Ben Jones III, Janet Lynn (Mrs. Norman W. Smith), Guy Hardie. Joined USN, 1941, served to lt. comdr., ret., 1948; exec. sec. Richard Gill Co., San Antonio, 1950-51; wholesale rep., Nat. Security & Research Corp., N.Y.C., 1951-53; with Merc. Nat. Bank at Dallas, 1953—, asst. trust officer, 1954-55, trust officer, 1955-56, asst. v.p., 1959-66, v.p., exec. trust officer, 1966-70, sr. v.p., exec. trust officer, 1970—; dir. Horn Blueprint Co., King Ranch Oil & Lignite Co. Adviser Southwestern Grad. Sch. Banking So. Meth. U. 1966—; mem. exec. com. Dallas County Heart Assn., 1967—; pres. Dallas Estate Council, 1961-62. Mem. Am. Soc. Corporate Secs. (pres. Dallas regional group 1966-67), Dallas Assn. Security Dealers. Presbyn. Mason (Shriner). Club: Oklahoma University (past pres.) (Dallas). Home: 4444 Larchmont Dallas TX 75205 Office: Mercantile Nat Bank at Dallas PO Box 5415 Dallas TX 75222

KERR, CHARLES MACDONALD, III, inst. exec.; b. New Orleans, July 3, 1912; s. Charles Macdonald, II and Helen M. (Coppee) K.; B.B.A., Tulane U., 1935; postgrad. Seminars Bard Coll., Rhinebeck, N.Y., 1957-58; m. Eleanor Carol Morris, July 8, 1961; children—Charles M. IV, Theresa Helen. Cost accountant Nfld. (Can.) Constructors, Marquise, 1941-42; treas. Cuban Mining Co., El Cristo, Oriente, Cuba, 1943-44; supr. field accounting Pendleton Shipyards, New Orleans, 1944; mem. nat. staff A.R.C., cons. amputee rehab. to Surgeons Gen., U.S. Army, USN, Washington, 1944-47; co-organizer, dir. patient tng. Kessler Inst. Rehab., West Orange, N.J., 1948-50; dir. amputee tng. Hasbrouck Heights (N.J.) Hosp., 1950; office mng. North Atlantic Constructors, N.Y.C., 1951-52; dir. Nat. Inst. for Amputee Rehab., Montclair, N.J., 1952—; cons. phys. rehab. Ochsner Found. Hosp., New Orleans; cons. phys. edn. dept. Tulane U.; dir. Inst. Devel. Human Performance, 1972—. Tchr. seminars, Phila., N.Y.C., West Orange, Montclair, 1958-63; lectr. Internat. Congress Surgeons, U. Madrid, USPHS, Inst. Gen. Semantics, Lakeville, Conn., N.Y. Soc. Gen. Semantics; past pres. Bell-Kerr Realty Co., Bell-Kerr Corp.; past dir. Dizzy Dean Corp., Jackson, Miss.; master clinician Lifetime Sports Found.; cons., lectr. George Washington U. Recipient War Dept. commendation for service to injured servicemen World War II, 1945; named Man of Year, Goodwill Industries New Orleans, 1959. Mem. Am. Badminton Assn. Clubs (chmn. nat. rules com., chmn. Nat. Umpires Assn.). Clubs: Tulane (dir. N.Y.C.), Montclair Tennis (pres., dir.). Author: (with Dr. H. H. Kessler) Civilian Amputees in action, 1948; (with Signe Brunnstrom) The Leg Amputee: Pre-Prosthetic Training, 1951; Training of the Lower Extremity Amputee, 1956. Home: Box 4033 New Orleans LA 70118

KERR, JAMES WILSON, stamp and coin co. exec.; b. Balt., May 21, 1921; s. James W. and Laura Virgia (Wright) K.; B.S. with honors, Davidson Coll., 1942; M.S., N.Y.U., 1948; postgrad. Freiburg U., 1957-60, Brookings Inst., 1970; m. Mary Thomas Montgomery, Feb. 25, 1945; children—April (Mrs. Rodney H. Miller), Catherine (Mrs. Charles M. Wood III) (dec.), Wilson, Andrew. Commd. 2d lt. U.S. Army, 1942, advanced through grades to lt. col., 1964; with inf., World War II, Korea; electronic staff, Ft. Bragg, N.C., 1948-51; weapons research, N.M., 1953-57; adviser French Army, 1957-60; staff electronics, Ft. Monroe, Va., 1960-62; research mgr., div. dir. Civil Def., Pentagon, 1962-64, as civilian, 1964—; v.p. Latherow & Co., Arlington, Va., 1965—. Advanced English instr. French Army, 1957-60; cons. Am. Nat. Red Cross Mus., 1968—, Smithsonian Instn. Dept. Postal History, 1966—. Vol. fireman N.Y. State, 1946-48, Fairfax County, Va., 1969—, leader Kit Carson council Boy Scouts Am., 1938—; chmn. library bd., Orangeburg, N.Y., 1946-48. Decorated Bronze Star medals (4), Purple Heart; recipient Silver Beaver award Boy Scouts Am., 1956. Fellow Explorers Club; mem. Nat. Acad. Scis. (mem. com. on fire research 1970—), Internat. Assn. Fire Chiefs (chmn. fire research com. 1969—), Fed. Fire Council, Nat. Fire Protection Assn. (chmn. hosp. disaster com. 1973), A.A.A.S., S.A.R., Black Forest Mardi Gras (Germany), Nat. Broadcasters Club, Pentagon Officers Athletic Club, Phi Beta Kappa, Gamma Sigma Epsilon, Delta Phi Alpha. Presbyn. (elder 1963—). Author: Korean-English Phrase Book, 1951; 19th Century Korea Postal Handbook, 1965. Editor Korean Philately mag., 1971—. Contbr. articles to profl. jours. Office: Def Civil Preparedness Research Pentagon Washington DC 20301

KERR, JOHN THOMAS, chem. co. exec.; b. South Bend, Ind., Mar. 17, 1924; s. Thomas Herbert and Faye (Mulinex) K.; B.S. in Mech. Engring., U. Ala., 1949; m. Anne Babbitt, May 2, 1950; children—Beverly, Barbara, Thomas, Lorraine. Design engr. Rust Engring. Co., Birmingham, Ala., 1951-55; with Thiokol Chem. Corp., Marshall, Tex., 1955—, prodn. mgr., 1965-70, dir. operations, 1970—. Bd. dirs. Camp Fire Girls, Harrison County. Served with USNR, 1942-45. Registered profl. engr., Tex., Ala. Mem. Am. Soc. M.E. Mason. Home: 4404 Bridle Path Marshall TX 75670 Office: PO Box 1149 Marshall TX 75670

KERR, JOHN WARD, JR., accountant; b. Fort Monroe, Va., July 30, 1937; s. John Ward and Florence (Bricker) K.; B.B.A., Old Dominion U., 1960; J.D., George Washington U., 1965; m. Carole Anne Alexander, Jan. 18, 1958; children—Katherine Lynne, John Ward III, Elizabeth Carole. Appellate conferee and agt. Internal Revenue Service, Washington, 1960-65; tax dir. Leach, Calkins & Scott, Richmond, 1965-67; tax mgr. Coopers & Lybrand, Richmond, 1967-69; tax mgr. Peat, Marwick, Mitchell & Co., Richmond, 1969-72; tax coordinator J.K. Lasser & Co., Jacksonville, Fla., 1972-73; partner Goodman & Co., Norfolk, Va., 1973—. Instr. taxation U. Richmond, Jacksonville U., Old Dominion U., Norfolk. C.P.A. Mem. Am. Inst. C.P.A.'s, Va. Soc. C.P.A.'s (tax com. chmn.), Richmond Chpt. C.P.A.'s (tax com. chmn.), Nat. Assn. Accountants, Fed. Govt. Accountants Assn., Alpha Kappa Psi, Pi Kappa Alpha, Phi Alpha Delta. Presbyterian. Kiwanian. Club: Harbor (Norfolk). Home: 1160 Revere Point Rd Virginia Beach VA 23455 Office: Bank of Virginia Bldg Norfolk VA 23455

KERR, RALPH WALDO, chemist; b. Mongaup Valley, N.Y., May 19, 1899; s. Marvin Orrin and Minnie (Ballard) K.; A.B., Columbia, 1921, M.A., 1924, Ph.D., 1924; m. Anne E. Mabbett, Nov. 24, 1949; children—Robert, Barbara, Charlotte. Asst. in chemistry Columbia, 1922-24, instr. biochemistry, research asso., 1924-29; research chemist Corn Products Co., Argo, Ill., 1929-60, cons., 1960—. Served with USN, 1918. Mem. Am. Chem. Soc., N.Y. Acad. Scis., A.A.A.S., Fla. Gulf Coast Art Center, Archives Fla. Art, Sigma Xi. Author, editor: Chemistry and Industry of Starch, 1944. Contbr. articles on starch products and chem. derivatives, enzyme chemistry to sci. jours. Patentee starch products, chem. derivatives, prodn. dextrose by enzymatic hydrolysis. Address: 1858 Venetian Point Dr Clearwater FL 33515

KERR, RAYMOND LAWRENCE, cons. indsl. engr., govt. ofl.; b. Plainview, Tex., May 18, 1911; s. Lawrence Almon and Dovie (Chumbley) K.; B.S. in Archtl. Engring., Tex. A. and M. Coll., 1935; M.S. in Indsl. Engring., U. Houston, 1954; postgrad. psychology, 1954-65; m. Myrtle Lucile Pine, July 17, 1937; children—Sandra Lucille, Douglas Raymond. Asst. plant engr. Texaco, Inc., 1935-42, asst. mgr., 1946-54, mgr. packaging div., 1954-59; cons. indsl. engring., mgmt., Tex., La., 1959-65; tech. supr. trade, indsl. edn. La. Dept. Edn., Baton Rouge, 1965-68; exec. asst., div. vocational edn. La. Dept. Edn., 1968-73; cons. engr. devel. new state police facilities La. Dept. Pub. Safety, 1973—. Chmn. community drive United Fund, Port Arthur, Tex., 1957. Served to lt. col., C.E., AUS, 1942-46. Registered profl. engr., La., Tex. Fellow Royal Soc. Arts (London, Eng.); mem. La. Engring. Soc., Nat. Soc. Profl. Engrs., Am. Inst. Indsl. Engrs., Kappa Pi, Psi Chi. Home: Route 5 Box 449 Denham Springs LA 70726 Office: La Dept Pub Safety Foster Dr Baton Rouge LA 70821

KERR, WILLIAM GRAYCEN, lawyer; b. Oklahoma City, Oct. 18, 1937; s. Robert Samuel and Grayce (Breene) K.; B.A., U. Okla., 1959, LL.B., 1962; m. Joffa Gemar, Aug. 4, 1956; children—Joffa, Kavar, Mara. Admitted to Okla. bar, 1962, since practiced in Oklahoma City; v.p. Citizens Finance Co., Oklahoma City, 1963-65; chmn. Citizens Bank Ada (Okla.), 1966-72; dir. Farmers and Mchts. Bank Tulsa; chmn. Bristol, Inc., Downey, Cal., 1970-72, Pub. Leasing Corp., Oklahoma City, 1969-70. Chmn. Okla. Democratic Central Com., 1967-69. trustee Kerr Found., Nat. Cowboy Hall of Fame. Mem. Phi Delta Theta, Phi Alpha Delta. Home: 2414 Smoking Oak Norman OK 73069 Office: Fidelity Plaza Oklahoma City OK 73102

KERRICK, LOUIS ALLEN, personnel exec.; b. Elizabethtown, Ky., July 11, 1942; s. Merritt Allen and Thelma Pauline (Hunt) K.; B.S., U. Ky., 1964, M.B.A., 1966; m. Margaret Jo Patterson, June 4, 1966; 1 son, Patrick Allen. Personnel mgr. Corning Glass Works, Harrodsburg, Ky., 1966—. Dir., Shaker Investments, Tempo Investments. Bd. dirs. Mercer County Youth Council, Legend of Daniel Boone Drama. Served with AUS, 1966-67. Named Rotarian of the Year, 1970, Outstanding Young Man of Mercer County, Harrodsburg C. of C., 1970, Jaycee of the Year, 1969. Mer. Harrodsburg Jr. C. of C. (pres. 1971). Baptist (supt. Sunday Sch. dept. 1969—). Rotarian. Home: 375 College Manor Harrodsburg KY 40330 Office: Corning Glass Works Houghton Dr Harrodsburg KY 40330

KERRIDGE, ISAAC CURTIS, JR., economist; b. Corpus Christi, June 22, 1924; s. Isaac Curtis and Hertha Emma (Koepke) K.; student Del Mar Coll., 1941-43; B.A., U. Tex., 1948, M.A., 1952; m. Ruth Stewart, May 10, 1958; children—Elizabeth, Ronald. Research analyst Prudential Ins. Co., Houston, 1953-55; operations research analyst Hughes Tool Co., Houston, 1956-61, staff asst., 1962-63, staff economist, 1963-73, asst. sec.-treas., economist, 1973—. Served with AUS, 1943-46, 50-51. Mem. Ind. Petroleum Assn. Am., Am. Econ. Assn., Nat. Assn. Bus. Economists, Houston Soc. Financial Analysts, Phi Sigma Kappa. Republican. Club: Warwick (Houston). Research on oil and gas well drilling costs. Home: 2440 Inwood Dr Houston TX 77019 Office: PO Box 2539 Houston TX 77001

KERRIGAN, ROBERT EMMETT, lawyer; b. New Iberia, La., Sept. 30, 1902; s. John Esmond and Alice (Fourcade) K.; A.B., Tulane U., 1923, LL.B., 1925; m. Catherine Wiggin Gomila, Sept. 21, 1939; children—Catherine Torrey, Robert Emmett. Admitted to La. bar, 1925, practiced New Orleans, 1925—, mem. firm Deutsch, Kerrigan & Stiles, 1926—. Past pres. Assn. Cath. Charities. Mem. Am. Law Inst., Am. Coll. Trial Attys., Internat. Acad. Trial Lawyers, Internat. Assn. Ins. Counsel, Fedn. Ins. Counsel, Am., La. bar assns., Am. Judicature Soc., Assn. of Commerce, Bur. Govtl. Research. Clubs: Louisiana, New Orleans Country (past pres.), Pickwick. Home: 1630 Valmont St New Orleans LA 70115 Office: Ohe Shell Sq New Orleans LA 70139

KERSEY, ROBERT LEE, JR., tobacco products co. exec.; b. Richmond, Va., Nov. 6, 1922; s. Robert Lee and Emma Edith (Kersey) K.; B.S. in Chemistry, U. Richmond, 1948; m. Katherine Ann Crowder, Sept. 6, 1943. Project chemist Standard Oil Co., Whiting, Ind., 1948-53; chemist Liggett & Myers, Inc., Durham, N.C., 1953-60, supr. flavor research, 1960-66, spl. asst. to dir. research, 1966-72, mgr. product devel. div., research dept., 1972—. Served with USNR, 1942-45. Decorated Air medal. Mem. Am. Chem. Soc., Inst. Food Technologists. Home: 2520 Ross Rd Durham NC 27703 Office: W Main St Durham NC 27702

KERSEY, WILLIAM HEWELL, educator; b. Shellman, Ga., Aug. 4, 1912; s. Jeffrie Randolph and Annie Wayne (Hewell) K.; B.A., Pasadena Coll., 1954; M.S., Baylor U., 1959; Ph.D., Loma Linda U., 1969; m. Hazel Grace Monteith, Nov. 23, 1940. Mem. faculty Pasadena Coll., 1954-62, Cal. Bapt. Coll., 1962-70; mem. faculty E. Tex. Bapt. Coll., Marshall, 1970—, now prof. chemistry. Teaching fellow Baylor U., 1957-59. Served with USMCR, 1935-39. Mem. Am. Chem. Soc., A.A.A.S., Tex. Acad. Sci. Home: 700 Rainey St Marshall TX 75670

KERSTEN, ROBERT DONAVON, univ. dean; b. Carlinville, Ill., Jan. 30, 1927; s. Fred William and Beulah (Surber) K.; student Westminster Coll., Fulton, Mo., 1945, Yale, 1945-46, Northwestern U., 1946; B.S., Okla. State U., 1949, M.S., 1956; Ph.D. (Standard Oil Found. fellow 1959-60, Royal E. Cabell fellow 1960), Northwestern U., 1961; m. Bonita Sue McCool, May 13, 1950; children—Susan, John. Mem. faculty dept. civil engring. Ariz. State U., Tempe, 1957-68, asso. prof., 1958-60, prof., chmn. dept., 1960-68; dean Coll. Engring., Fla. Technol. U., Orlando, 1968—, dir. univ. research, 1968-69; vis. scholar Stanford (Cal.) U., 1966. Cons. Flight Safety Found., 1961-62. Trustee Scottsdale Baptist Hosp. (Ariz.), 1967-68. Served with USNR, 1945-47. Registered profl. engr., Ariz., Fla., Okla. Mem. Am. Soc. Engring. Edn. (mem. awards com.), Nat. Soc. Profl. Engrs. (state pres. 1967-68; trustee Inst. Certification Engring. Technicians), Am. Soc. C.E., Fla. Engring. Soc., Sigma Xi, Chi Epsilon, Tau Beta Pi, Sigma Tau, Phi Delta Theta, Pi Gamma Mu. Author: Engineering Differential Systems, 1969. Contbr. profl. jours. Home: 590 Dommerich Dr Maitland FL 32751 Office: PO Box 25000 Orlando FL 32816

KERSTETTER, REX EUGENE, educator; b. Ashland, Kan., Nov. 22, 1938; s. Roy Everett and Blanche Elizabeth (Sailor) K.; B.S., Fort Hays Kan. State Coll., 1960, M.S., 1963; Ph.D. (NASA traineeship), Fla. State U., 1967; m. Elizabeth Sue Edwards, June 5, 1960; children—Kelvin Tod, Derek Edward. Asst. prof. biology Furman U., Greenville, S.C., 1967—. Pres., Greater Greenville Environmental Council, 1972-73. NSF summer research fellow, Purdue U., 1969. Mem. A.A.A.S., Bot. Soc. Am., Am. Soc. Plant Physiologists, Kan., S.C. acads. sci., Sigma Xi. Author: The Ecosphere: Organisms, Habitats and Disturbances, 1974. Home: 25 Zelma Dr Greenville SC 29609

KERSTING, ALBERT FREDERICK, mgmt. cons.; b. Mobile, Ala., Jan. 2, 1914; s. Albert Frederick and Aileen (Austill) K.; grad. Marion Inst., 1934; student George Washington U., 1947-49, Tex. Christian U., 1957-60; m. Elizabeth L. George, Nov. 23, 1940; children—Albert Frederick, Elizabeth (Mrs. Milton Drummond Brown), Katherine Austill. Joined USN, 1935, advanced through grades to comdr., 1945, ret., 1957; asst. to dir. prodn. Chance Vought Aircraft Corp., 1957-60; in charge improvement mgmt. LTV Aerospace, Inc., 1960-63; established Kersting & Assos., Dallas, 1959, pres., 1963—. Active Boy Scouts Am.; mem. S.W. area planning com. YMCA, 1963-69. Ky. Col. Recipient achievement award, sec. navy, 1945; 1st pl. award, movie contest in work simplification application in industry Indsl. Mgmt. Soc., 1959-62. Mem. Am. Inst. Indsl. Engrs. (adv. bd. aerospace div. 1966, dir. 1960-65), Soc. for Advancement Mgmt. (Dallas pres. 1961-62, v.p., treas. internat. 1970-71), Indsl. Mgmt. Clubs (nat. exec. council 1963-69), Indsl. Mgmt. Soc., Indsl. Mgmt. Club (Dallas pres. 1960-61, exec. bd. 1959-62), Tex. Mgmt. Cons. Assn. (pres. 1964-65), Tex. Mfrs. Assn., Dallas C. of C., Internat. Work Simplification Inst. (founding mem., exec. v.p. 1970-71, pres. 1971-72, trustee 1967), S.W. Work Simplification Council (founding mem., adv. bd. 1959-67). Episcopalian (licensed lay reader, chmn. laymans work Diocese of Dallas 1963, 70, exec. council). Rotarian. Home: 4447 Alta Vista Lane Dallas TX 75229 Office: 4159 Buena Vista St Dallas TX 75204

KERTZ, HAROLD ALLAN, lawyer; b. Allentown, Pa., Dec. 2, 1906; s. Christian J. and Elizabeth (Rudy) K.; J.D., Georgetown U., 1928; LL.M., Catholic U., 1932; m. Genevieve Hastings, May 1, 1944; 1 son, Robert Allan. Admitted to D.C. bar, 1929; practiced law, Washington, 1928-31; trust officer Nat. Met. Bank, Washington, 1931-40; partner Roberts & McInnis, 1940-54, Mercier, Kertz & Sanders, 1954-57; vice chmn. Pub. Utilities Commn. D.C., 1957-62; prof. of wills and estates, Georgetown U., Washington, 1955-65; dir. Harlowe Typography, Inc., Sho-Tel, Inc., Chesapeake Graphics, Inc., The Chemmet Co., O'Donnell's Sea Grill, Inc., R.E. Darling Co., Basic Boats, Inc., James R. Dunlop, Inc. Mem. ICC Practitioners Assn., FCC Bar, Am., D.C. bar assns., Sigma Nu Phi. Episcopalian. Clubs: Columbia Country, University, Nat. Press, Farmington Country, The Counsellors. Legal contbg. editor to Trusts and Estates. Home: 2500 Virginia Av NW Washington DC 20037 Office: 1906 Sunderland Pl NW Washington DC 20036

KERWIN, JOSEPH P., physician, astronaut; b. Oak Park, Ill., Feb. 19, 1932; B.A., Coll. Holy Cross, 1953; M.D., Northwestern U., 1957; m. Shirley Ann Good; 1 dau., Sharon. Intern D.C. Gen. Hosp., 1957-58; commd. lt. comdr. U.S. Navy, 1958; flight surgeon Marine Air Group 14, Cherry Point, N.C., Fighter Squadron 101, Oceana Naval Air Sta., Virginia Beach, Fla.; staff flight surgeon Air Wing 4, Cecil Field, Fla.; now astronaut Manned Spacecraft Center, Houston; mem. Skylab crew, 1973. Address: Manned Spacecraft Center Houston TX 77058*

KESNER, DOUGLAS FLOYD, hosp. adminstr.; b. Cleveland, Okla., Aug. 11, 1932; s. Floyd and Jenave H. (Rubert) K.; B.B.A., So. Meth. U., 1960; M.H.A., Trinity U., 1970; m. Miss Cochran, May 23, 1957; children—Denise Kay, Mary Michelle. Adminstr., Parkland Hosp., Dallas, 1960-62, Meth. Hosp., Dallas, 1962-64, Garland (Tex.) Med. Center, 1965-66, Logan (W.Va.) Med. Found., 1967-68, Colonial Convalescent Center, St. Clairsville, O., 1967-68, Nicholas County Hosp. Dist., Lexington, Ky., 1969—; lectr. Trinity U., Ky. U.; Past bd. dirs. KNHA, Hunt Med. Found.; bd. dirs., v.p. Mediplex Mental Health Services, Inc., Houston; v.p. Deer Park Mediplex, Inc. Served with AUS, 1953-55. Named Health Adminstr. of Year, West Tex., 1965. Fellow Am. Coll. Nursing Home Adminstrs.; mem. Am. Coll. Hosp. Adminstrs., Am., Tex. hosp. assns., Ky. Nursing Home Assn. (past pres.), Dallas chambers commerce. Home: 3502 McFarlin Blvd Dallas TX 75205 Office: PO Box 12633 Dallas TX 75225

KESSINGER, JOHN ROY, banker; b. Dhahran, Saudi Arabia, Aug. 8, 1940 (parents Am. citizens); s. Arthur Gan and Beatrice Mae (Fullerton) K.; student U. Pitts., 1958-59, St. Petersburg Jr. Coll., 1960-61; B.B.A., U. Houston, 1963; m. Sara Relfe Smith, June 5, 1965; children—Arthur Gan, Rebecca Relfe, James Bland. Adminstrv. asst. First Nat. Bank Clearwater (Fla.), 1966-68, asst. trust officer, 1968-70, trust investment officer, 1970, v.p., trust investment officer, 1971, sr. investment officer Trust dept., 1970—. Served to sgt. AUS, 1964-66. Mem. Central Fla. Financial Analyst Soc., Fla. Bankers Assn. (mem. trust investment com. 1973-74), Dunedin Nat. Little League (dir. 1969-73, treas. 1972, pres. 1973). Episcopalian (vestry 1970-72, lay reader 1968—, chmn. finance com. 1972—). Home: 2051 Brendla Rd Clearwater FL 33515 Office: Box 179 First National Bank Clearwater FL 33517

KESSINGER, RICHARD CLAUDE, cons. engr.; b. Atlanta, Nov. 14, 1935; s. Richard Sheridan and Mary Jane (Thompson) K.; student Cumberland Jr. Coll., 1958-60; B.S., U. Tenn., 1963; m. Phyllis Marie Parrott, Dec. 1, 1958; children—Brian Keith, Joseph Sheridan, James Lewis. Design engr. Rust Engring. Co., Birmingham, Ala., 1963-65, J.E. Sirrine Co., Greenville, S.C., 1965-66, Lockwood Greene Engrs., Inc., Spartanburg, S.C., 1966-68; head structural dept. Delta Engring., Inc., Spartanburg, 1968-69; cons. structural engr., Spartanburg, 1969-70; chief engr. Tindall Concrete Products, Inc., Spartanburg, 1970-73; pvt. practice as Gerald M. Sullivan, Inc., cons. engr., Springfield, Tenn., 1973—. Served with USN, 1954-58. Registered profl. engr., S.C., N.C., Ky., Tenn. Mem. Am. Soc. C.E., Nat. Soc. Profl. Engrs., Chi Epsilon. Home: Route 1 Box 140 Cedar Hill TN 37032 Office: 802 S Main St Springfield TN 37172

KESSLER, EDNA ANNE LEVENTHAL (MRS. MURRAY ARTHUR KESSLER), artist, educator, interior designer; b. Kingston, N.Y., Mar. 13, 1910; d. Max and Dora (Cohen) Leventhal; grad. Parsons Sch. Design, 1929; postgrad. Columbia, N.Y.U., Queens Coll., Instituto San Miguel de Allende (Mexico); m. Murray Arthur Kessler, June 17, 1937; children—Robert Sheldon, Kenneth Charles. Faculty Parsons Sch. Design, 1928-30; head counselor Camp Co-Ma-Ha, Rock Hill, N.Y., summers 1932-37; pres. Edna Leventhal Millinery Shop, 1935-37, Edna Thal Millinery Shop, N.Y.C., 1937, Edna L. Kessler, Interiors, Jamaica, N.Y., 1941-69, Miami Beach, Fla., 1970—; art instr. Temple Sholom, Floral Park, N.Y., 1960-67; pvt. instr., Jamaica, 1967-70, Miami, Fla., 1970—; one-man shows Frederick Thompson Found., Hollis, N.Y., 1962, Little Gallery, N.Y.C., 1964, Manhasset (N.Y.) Art Gallery, 1964, Temple Sholom, Glen Oaks, N.Y., 1965, Hollywood (Fla.) Playhouse Gallery, 1972, 74, Mayfair Gallery, 1973, Flagler Fed. Savs. and Loan, 1974, others; exhibited in group shows at Witte Meml. Mus., San Antonio, Smithsonian Instn., Washington, Parrish Mus., Southampton, N.Y., IBM Gallery, Poughkeepsie, N.Y., Nat. Acad., many others. Active Cub Scouts. Dir. Jamaica Estates Hebrew Center. Recipient best in show Nat. Art League, Art League Nassau County, 1961, Grand Prix D'Aquarelle, La Biennale Internationale, Vichy, France, 1966, Hollywood Seven Arts Festival, 1971; 1st prize Island Art Guild, 1964, L.I. Fair, 1965, Parrish Art Mus., 1965, 67, Art League of Nassau County, 1967, Herrick art Show, 1967; award Met. Miami Art Flower Show, 1969, 70, 71, award Miami Boat Show, 1969, 70, 71, 72, 73, Internat. Boat Show, 1971, 74, award Allied Arts, 1970, 71, 72, 74, Miami Art League, 1971, 72, many others. Mem. Nat. Art League L.I. (Gold medal 1961, past dir.), Am. Artist Profl. League, Hudson Valley Art Assn., Island Art Guild, Art League Nassau County (Best in Show award 1962), Malverne Art Assn., Allied Arts N. Miami (dir. 1971—), Miami Art Center, Miami, Nat., Broward art guilds, Catherine Lorillard Wolfe Art Club. Art work and articles published in fifteen books, U.S., France, Italy. Home: 1050 93d St Bay Harbor Islands FL 33154

KESTNER, NEIL RICHARD, educator; b. Milw., Dec. 11, 1937; s. Louis George and Erna (Sander) K.; B.S., U. Wis., 1960; M.S., Yale, 1962, Ph.D., 1964; m. Arlene Katherine Schweigerdt, June 10, 1967. Postdoctoral fellow U. Chgo., 1963-64; asst. prof. dept. chemistry Stanford, 1964-66; asso. prof. La. State U., Baton Rouge, 1966-71, prof., 1971—, also dir. freshman chemistry, 1973—. Alfred P. Sloan Found fellow, 1967-71; NSF grantee, 1965-72. Mem. Am. Chem. Soc., Am. Phys. Soc., Sigma Xi. Clubs: Pelican Yacht (New Roads, La.), U.S. Power Squadron (Baton Rouge). Author: (with H. Margenau) Theory of Intermolecular Forces, 1969, 71; (with J. Jortner) Electrons in Fluids, 1973. Home: 345 Baird Dr Baton Rouge LA 70808 Office: Dept Chemistry La State U Baton Rouge LA 70803

KETCHAM, ORMAN WESTON, judge; b. Bklyn., Oct. 1, 1918; s. Walter Seymour and Arline (Weston) K.; A.B., Princeton, 1940; LL.B., Yale, 1947; m. Anne Phelps Stokes, Dec. 22, 1947; children—Anne Weston, Helen Louisa Phelps, Elizabeth Miner, Susan Stokes. Admitted to D.C. bar, 1948; practiced in Washington, 1948-52; Washington rep. Fund for the Republic, 1953; asst. gen. counsel U.S. Fgn. Operations Agy., 1953-55; trial atty. Antitrust div. U.S. Dept. Justice, Washington, 1955-57; Judge Juvenile Ct. D.C., Washington, 1957-71; asso. judge Superior Ct. D.C., 1971—. Adj. prof. law Georgetown U. Law Center, 1963-67, U. Va. Law Sch., 1971—. Bd. dirs. Nat. Council Crime and Delinquency, 1973—. Served as lt. comdr., USNR, 1941-46. Recipient Princeton Club award Distinguished Community Service, 1972. Mem. Am. Bar Assn., Bar Assn. D.C., Nat. Council Juvenile Ct. Judges (pres. 1965-66), Internat. Assn. Youth Magistrates (v.p. 1966—), Am. Law Inst. Conglist. Clubs: Cosmos (Washington); Chevy Chase. Author: (with Monrad G. Paulsen) Cases and Materials Relating to Juvenile Courts, 1967. Home: 2 E Melrose St Chevy Chase MD 20015 Office: 410 E St NW Washington DC 20001

KETCHEL, MELVIN M., physiologist; b. Pontiac, Mich., June 1, 1922; s. John S. and Sarah (Musicante) K.; student Purdue U., 1943-44; A.B., Olivet Coll., 1948; M.S., Western Res. U., 1949; Ph.D., Harvard, 1954; m. Elisabeth Boessenkool, Oct. 25, 1958; children—Charles, Jean, John. Instr. biology Fenn Coll., 1948-49; teaching fellow biology Harvard, 1950-51, research asst. biophys. chemistry, 1954-55; research asso. cytology Protein Found. Labs., 1955-56; research asso. surgery Harvard Med. Sch., asst. surgery Peter Bent Brigham Hosp., Boston, 1956-59; scientist Worcester Found. Exptl. Biology, Shrewsbury, Mass., 1959-63, sr. scientist, 1963-65; asso. prof. Tufts U., 1965-68, prof., 1968-72; sr. postdoctoral fellow NSF, Eng., 1971; dir. Oak Ridge Population Research Inst., 1972—. Bd. dirs. Planned Parenthood Assn. So. Mountains. Mem. Northboro (Mass.) Sch. Com., 1962-65. Served with AUS, 1943-46. Mem. A.A.A.S., Am. Physiol. Soc., Soc. for Study Reprodn., Soc. for Study Fertility, Transplantation Soc. Contbr. articles to profl. jours. Home: 138 Morningside Dr Oak Ridge TN 37830 Office: PO Box 117 Oak Ridge TN 37830

KETNER, RALPH WRIGHT, supermarket exec.; b. nr. Salisbury, N.C., Sept. 20, 1920; s. George Robert and Effie (Yost) K.; student Tri-State Coll., 1937-39; m. Ruth Jones, Aug. 1, 1947; children—Linda, Robert. Gen. mgr. Excel Grocery, Salisbury, 1950-56; head grocery buyer Winn-Dixie Stores, Raleigh, N.C., 1956-57; pres., treas., dir. Food Town Stores, Inc., Salisbury, 1957—; sec.-treas., dir. Food Town Investment Co.; pres., treas., dir. Save-Rite, Inc.; dir. Security Bank & Trust Co. Dir. Rowan County Vocational Rehab. Workshop; mem. adv. bd. Salvation Army. Served with AUS, 1942-46. Named N.C. grocer of year, 1972-73. Mem. N.C. Food Dealers Assn. (dir., past pres.), Sales Exec. and Mgmt. Club (v.p., dir.), Salisbury Rowan C. of C. (past dir.), Mchts. Assn. (pres.). Presbyn. (elder). Rotarian (past dir.). Patentee inventory form. Home: 1031 Mocksville Av Salisbury NC 28144 Office: Julian Rd Salisbury NC 28144

KETTER, PAUL STEPHEN, city ofcl.; b. Chgo., Dec. 6, 1932; s. Paul Leroy and Dorothy (Taylor) K.; student Northwestern U., 1959, Washington and Jefferson Coll., 1960, Marshall U., 1961-64, Tex. Christian U., 1965-68; m. Dorthy Jean Million, July 15, 1965; children—Marie, Therese, Paula Jean, Leslie Elizabeth. Asst. football coach Marshall U., Huntington, W.Va., 1961-63; adminstr. asst. City of Ft. Worth, 1965-72; asst. supt. Dept. Sanitation, City of Dallas, 1972—; editor, pub. Coaches Clearing House, Fort Worth, 1971-72; owner Big State Music Pub. Co., Dallas, 1973—, Dove Records, Dallas, 1973—, Star Talent Mgmt., Dallas, 1973—, Pineapple Music Pub. Co., Dallas, 1973—. Coach, publicity dir. Haltom City Pee-Wee Football Assn., 1966-72; adviser on athletics Texian chpt. DeMolay, 1970-72. Served with AUS, 1953-55. Mem. Broadcast Music, Inc., Am. Pub. Works Assn., Inst. for Solid Waste, Tex. Pub. Works Assn., Nat. Music Pubs. Assn., Country Music Assn., A.S.C.A.P. Mason. Composer: The Things I Left Behind, 1973. Home: 1311 Candlelight Av Duncanville TX 75116 Office: 2721 Municipal St Dallas TX 75215

KETTLES, ROBERT CAREW, city ofcl.; b. Ypsilanti, Mich., Jan. 9, 1925; s. Albert Grant and Cora (Stobie) K.; B.A., Mich. State Coll., 1946-52; m. Joanne Attwood, Oct. 25, 1952; children—Brooke Elizabeth, Craig Carew. Mem. Mich. Senate, 1953-54; with Ford Motor Co., Lansing, Mich., 1954-60; pres. Bob Kettles Ford Sales, Caro, 1960-65; v.p. sales Gen. Aviation, Inc., Lansing, 1965-67; adminstr. housing rehab. and neighborhood improvement Orlando, Fla., 1967—; sales mgr. Stone Island Properties, Enterprise, Fla. Active various community drives. Chmn. finance com. Republican Party, Tuscola County, Fla. Served with AUS, 1943-46, 51-52. Home: 102 Timber Trail Stork Island Enterprise FL 32763 Office: PO Box 6 Enterprise FL 32763

KEUPER, JEROME PENN, univ. pres.; b. Fort Thomas, Ky., Jan. 12, 1921; s. Clarence J. and Aileen (Miller) K.; B.S., Mass. Inst. Tech, 1948; M.S., Stanford U., 1949; Ph.D., U. Va., 1952; m. Natalie Packard Snow, Apr. 17, 1948; children—Melanie, Philip. Sr. physicist Remington Arms Co., Bridgeport, Conn., 1952-58; sr. scientist, mgr. systems analysis RCA, Cape Kennedy, Fla., 1954-58; pres., founder Fla. Inst. Tech., Melbourne, 1958—. Mem. Fla. Bd. Independent Colls., Univs., 1963—; pres. The Palm Soc. Internat., 1970-72; mem. Fla. Council 100, 1970—; charter mem. Missile, Space and Range Pioneers, Inc., 1966—; mem. Fla. Bd. Ind. Colls. and Univs.; mem. commn. on colls. So. Assn. Colls. and Schs.; chmn. council of presidents Ind. Colls. and Univs. Fla., 1972-73. Served to 1st lt. Office Strategic Services, AUS, 1941-45. Recipient Silver Knight Mgmt. award Nat. Mgmt. Assn.; Jerome P. Keuper Sch., Bogota, Colombia, named in honor, 1971. Mem. Am. Phys. Soc., Am. Soc. Computing Machinery, Brit. Interplanetary Soc., Marine Tech. Soc., Operations Research Soc. Am., and Omega Phi Delta. Mason (Shriner). Home: 404 Banyan Way Melbourne Beach FL 32951 Office: PO Box 1150 Melbourne FL 32901

KEVER, JUSTIN A., lawyer; b. Wolf Bayou, Ark., June 1, 1924; s. Larkin Dixon and Mary (Foust) K.; B.BA., U. Tex., 1947, LL.D., 1949; m. Charlice Morris, Aug. 24, 1947; children—Justin Andrew, Jean Elizabeth, Scott Dixon, Leigh Ann. Admitted to Tex. bar, 1949; since practiced in San Angelo, with partner firm Hardeman, Smith & Kever and predecessor firms, 1963-73; partner firm Hardeman, Kever, Ratliff & Fohn, 1973—; asst. dist. atty., San Angelo, 1954-56, dist. atty. 51st Judicial Dist. Tex., 1953, 57-63. Trsutee San Angelo Ind. Sch. Dist. Served with USNR, 1943-46. Mem. Tom Green County, Tex., Am. bar assns. Lion. Home: 2814 Oak Forest St San Angelo TX 76901 Office: 129 S Irving St San Angelo TX 76901

KEY, CLYDE WINSTON, lawyer; b. Bethpage, Tenn., July 19, 1904; s. Charles D. and Eula (Harrell) K.; J.D., U. Tenn., 1925; m. Frances Stuart, Nov. 3, 1928 (div. June 1948); children 1 dau., Charlotte (Mrs. Charles Taylor Marrow); m. 2d, Louise Derrington, Dec. 24, 1948. Admitted to Tenn. bar, 1925, U.S. Supreme Ct. bar, 1935; practiced in Knoxville, 1925—; partner firm Kennerly & Key, 1925-44; sole practice, 1944-53; partner firm Key, Lee & Layman and predecessor firm, 1953—. Dir., sec. several corps., Knoxville; counsel Tenn. div. So. Ry. Co., 1953—. Fellow Am. Coll. Trial Lawyers; mem. Am., Tenn. (past pres.), Knoxville (past pres.) bar assns., Tenn. Soc. S.R. (past pres.), Nat. Assn. R.R. Trial Lawyers, Am. Judicature Soc., Phi Kappa Phi, Order Coif, Phi Alpha Delta. Elk. Clubs: Civitan, Senators, City, Fort Loudon Yacht (Knoxville). Home: 458 Cherokee Blvd Knoxville TN 37919 Office: 623 Market St Knoxville TN 37902

KEY, FLOYD MARTIN, county ofcl.; b. Megargel, Tex., Sept. 14, 1926; s. George Andrew and Margaret Estell (Campbell) K.; B.S., Tex. A and M. U., 1948, postgrad., 1967-70; postgrad. Colo. State U., 1969; M.S.T., Tarleton State Coll., 1973; m. Sarah Beth Mayes, Dec. 30, 1948; children—John Martin, Sally Ann, Spencer Andrew. Farmer, Olney, Tex., 1948-56; asst. county agrl. agt., Brownwood, Tex., 1956-61; county agrl. agt., Meridian, Tex., 1961-65, Comanche, Tex., 1965—. Trustee Comanche Child Care Center. Served with AUS, 1945-46. Mem. Comanche C. of C. (dir. 1969-70), Epsilon Sigma Phi. Baptist. Lion. Address: Box 705 Comanche TX 76442 Mailing Address: Box 705 Comanche TX 76442

KEY, FRANKLIN PASCHALL, mfr.; b. Puryer, Tenn., Jan. 26, 1917; s. Grover Lee and Gertie Wilson (Fuller) K.; grad. Tolers Bus. Coll., 1938; spl. courses U. Tenn.; m. Esther Naomi Morsch, Oct. 2, 1949; children—Richard, Frank, Robert, Donna. Sec. to pres. Golden Peacock, Inc., Paris, Tenn., 1938-40; adminstrv. officer TVA, 1941-54; controller W.L. Jackson Mfg. Co., Chattanooga, 1954-69, v.p. finance and corporate devel., 1969—; sec.-treas., dir. Jackson Properties Co. Mem. Am. Guild Organists. Democrat. Home: 5705 Garrett Dr Hixson TN 37343 Office: 1205 E 40th St Chattanooga TN 37401

KEY, GRIFFIN THEOBALD, III, elec. engr.; b. Eufaula, Ala., Dec. 26, 1924; s. Griffin Theobald and Virginia (Corbitt) K.; B.E.E., Auburn U., 1948; m. Betty Ann Lee, July 28, 1945; children—Deborah Ann (Mrs. Joe Petranka), Judith Corbitt. Mgr. outside constrn. G. T. Key Co., 1948-56, gen. mgr., 1956-65, owner, gen. mgr., 1965—. Served to 2d lt. USAF, 1943-45. Registered profl. engr., Ala. Mem. Phi Delta Theta. Kiwanian (pres. Capital City club 1971). Home: 1554 Gilmer Av Montgomery AL 36104 Office: 931 N McDonough St Montgomery AL 36104

KEY, JOHN MORRIS, elec. co. exec.; b. Summitville, Ind., Mar. 5, 1922; s. Elmer F. and Margieree (Weaver) K.; student Gen. Motors Inst., 1940-43, U. Wis., 1943-44, U.S. Naval Acad., 1944; m. Alice Fuselier, Sept. 2, 1949; children—Scott, Peggy, Gary. Tool maker Delco Remy, 1940-43; process engr. A.B. Dick Co., 1946-48; pres., mgr. Marine Elec. Repairs, 1948-54; pres., gen. mgr. Owesen & Co., Inc., New Orleans, 1948-69; pres., gen. mgr. Anixter New Orleans, Inc., 1969—; pres. YEK, Inc., H. & K. Equipment Co., Inc. Mem. adv. bd. Salvation Army New Orleans. Served with USNR, 1943-46. Named Man of Year, Salvation Army, 1965. Mason (Shriner). Clubs: Plimsoll, New Orleans Country (New Orleans). Home: 5645 Evelyn Ct New Orleans LA 70124 Office: 315 Notre Dame St New Orleans LA 70130

KEYES, ROGER GENE, mech. engr.; b. Portsmouth, O., Dec. 12, 1939; s. Ulric Carven and Grace (Watts) K.; student So. Meth. U., 1957-58, 59-60; B. Mech. Engring., U. Fla., 1964; m. Lula Bertha Crosby, Apr. 18, 1964; children—Vinson Paul, William Eugene. Engr., Martin Marietta Aerospace Co., Orlando, Fla., 1960—. Sec.-treas., dir. High Meadow Devel. Corp., Orlando, 1972—; asst. to pres. Land of Growth Investment Corp., Orlando, 1971—. Charter mem. Citizens Com. for Better Edn., 1967; com. mem. Orlando Boy Scouts Am., 1973—. Registered profl. engr., Fla. Mem. Am. Soc. Mech. Engrs. (Fla. sect. chmn. 1972-73, alt. nat. agenda com. 1973), Nat. Soc. Profl. Engrs., Fla. Engring. Soc. Republican. Methodist. Home: Route 5 Box 138A Orlando FL 32807 Office: PO Box 5837 Orlando FL 32805

KEYS, CHARLES EVEREL, educator; b. Richland Center, Wis., May 10, 1921; s. Everel Evender and Ruth Naomi (Siggelkow) K.; A.B., Greenville Coll., 1943; Ph.D., U. Kan., 1952; m. Lavena Juanita Stevens, Sept. 4, 1944; children—Charlene (Mrs. Richard Elmore), Steven, Dalen. Prof. biology Asbury Coll., Wilmore, Ky., 1951-56, 60-64; prof., chmn. sci. div. Roberts Wesleyan Coll., North Chili, N.Y., 1956-60; prof. biology Florence (Ala.) State U., 1964-68, 71—; prof., chmn. biology dept. Seattle Pacific Coll., 1968-71. Vis. prof. Malone Coll., Canton, O. summer 1962; cons. Seattle Urban Acad., 1970; researcher Oak Ridge Inst. Nuclear Studies, 1954. Mem. Ky. Merit Council for Local Bds. of Health, 1960-64. Served with AUS, 1943-46; PTO. Mem. Ala. Acad. Sci., Am. Assn. Zoologists, Am. Inst. Biol. Scis., Nat. Assn. Biology Tchrs., Sigma Xi. Republican. Home: Route 9 Box 56 Florence AL 35630 Office: Dept Biology Florence State Univ Florence AL 35630

KEYWORTH, DONALD ARTHUR, chem. co. exec.; b. Flint, Mich., Apr. 21, 1930; s. Vern and Lillian May (Holcomb) K.; B.S., U. Mich., 1951; M.S., Mich. State U., 1954; Ph.D., Wayne State U., 1958. Head quality controls Lapaco Paint and Varnish Co., Lansing, Mich., 1951-52; research chemist Wyandotte Chems. (Mich.), 1957-61; asso. research dir. Universal Oil Products, Des Plaines, Ill., 1961-67; tech. dir. Sci. and Ednl. Services, Houston, 1967-68; dir. research and devel. Tenneco Hydrocarbon Chems. div., Pasadena, Tex., 1968—. Indsl. adv. bd. curriculum devel. Tex. State Tech. Inst., 1971—. Served with AUS, 1954-56. Mem. Sci. and Ednl. Services (dir. 1967), Am. Inst. Chemists, Am. Chem. Soc. (prof. in charge 1968-69, indsl. cons. to ChemTeC project, 1971), Am. Inst. Physics, Soc. Applied Spectroscopy, Am. Soc. Testing Materials, Anachems,

Sigma Xi, Phi Lambda Upsilon. Author: Chemistry of the Elements, 1971; Chemistry for Technicians, 1969; Flame Emission and Atomic Absorption Spectroscopy, 1968. Contbr. articles to profl. publs. Home: 5324 Dora St Houston TX 77005 Office: Tenneco Hydrocarbon Chemicals Div PO Box 849 Pasadena TX 77501

KHAIROLLAHI, VALI, physician; b. Iran, Sept. 15, 1932; s. Ali and Zahra (Akkas) K.; M.D., Tehran (Iran) Med. Sch., 1958; m. Debrah Reagan, Mar. 21, 1973. Came to U.S., 1958, naturalized, 1970. Intern, So. Bapt. Hosp., New Orleans; resident Bapt., Charity hosps., New Orleans; asso. prof. surgery, mem. hosp. staff U. Tenn., 1967—. Fellow A.C.S. Home: 12200 Oakland Hill Concord TN 37720 Office: 1928 Alcoa Hwy Knoxville TN 37920

KHARE, SNATOSH KUMAR, physician; b. Lucknow, India, May 8, 1939; s. Chandrakant Prasad and Savitri (Devi) K.; M.B., B.S., King George Med. Coll., Lucknow, 1962; m. Pratibha, May 24, 1963; children—Geeta, Sanjaya. Came to U.S., 1966, naturalized, 1972. Intern, Pines County Hosp., Paramus, N.J.; resident State U. Kings County Med. Center, Bklyn.; asst. prof. pediatrics Meharry Med. Coll., Nashville, 1970-73; chmn. dept. pediatrics Mercy Hosp., Birmingham, Ala., 1972—; dir. Jefferson Clinic, Birmingham. Diplomate Am. Bd. Pediatrics. Fellow Royal Coll. Physicians Can. Am. Acad. Pediatrics (corr.). Home: 2122 Montreat Way Birmingham AL 35216 Office: 1515 6th Av S Birmingham AL 35233

KIBLER, ROBERT JOSEPH, educator; b. Dayton, O., Oct. 6, 1934; s. Robert Joseph and Pauline (McFann) K.; B.S., Ohio State U., 1957, M.A., 1959, Ph.D., 1962; m. Sharon Colleen McCollum, June 27, 1954; children—Valerie Deanne, Vance Aric, Lora Megan. Instr., research asso. Ohio State U., 1959-62; asst. prof. ednl. psychology So. Ill. U., 1962-65, dir. Ednl. Research Bur., 1964-67, asso. prof., 1966-67; asso. prof. communication Purdue U., 1967-69; prof. communication Fla. State U., Tallahassee, 1969—. Served to lt. AUS, 1957-58. Recipient Central States Speech Assn. Outstanding Young Tchr. award, 1964. Mem. Internat. Communication Assn. (dir. 1974—), Am. Psychol. Assn., Am. Ednl. Research Assn., Speech Communication Assn. (adminstrv. com. 1969-73), Nat. Council on Ednl. Measurement. Author: Behavioral Objectives and Instruction, 1970; Speech Communication Behavior, 1971; Objectives for Instruction and Evaluation, 1974. Asso. editor: So. Speech Communication Jour. 1969-71; series editor: Prentice Hall, 1969—. Contbr. chpts. to books, numerous articles to profl. jours. Home: 2936 Brandemere Dr Tallahassee FL 32303

KIDD, BARRON, oil co. exec.; b. Brownwood, Tex., Nov. 12, 1901; s. George W. and Annie (Barron) K.; student Howard Payne Coll., 1918-21; B.A., U. Tex., 1925, B.B.A., 1925; m. Ann Hughes, Apr. 25, 1958; 1 son, Barron Ulmer. With Stark Lumber Co., Orange, Tex., 1925-27; ind. oil operator, Dallas, 1927—; chmn. bd. Cardinal Chem., Inc., Oil Patch Equipment Sales and Rentals Ltd. Mem. Petroleum Club, Phi Gamma Delta. Republican. Presbyn. Clubs: Non Resident Links and River (N.Y.C.); Dallas Country, Brookhollow, Preston Trails Golf (Dallas); Jupiter Island (Hobe Sound, Fla.). Home: 8726 Douglas St Dallas TX 75225 Office: Oak Plaza Bldg 3707 Rawlins St Dallas TX 75219

KIDD, JUANITA A. HOPKINS (MRS. CLYDE E. KIDD), educator; b. Guntown, Miss., Aug. 12, 1918; d. Holbert Thomas and Pearl (Coleman) Hopkins; B.S., East Central State Coll., Ada, Okla., 1939; M. Teaching, Central State U., Edmond, Okla., 1959; m. Clyde E. Kidd, Nov. 24, 1937; children—Kenton E., Mary Kathryn. Tchr., Ada High Sch., 1939-40, Asher (Okla.) High Sch., 1945-46, Putnam City Jr. High Sch., Oklahoma City, 1953-58; guidance counselor, dean of girls Putnam City High Sch., Oklahoma City, 1958-69; dir. coll. and high sch. relations Central State U., 1970—. Mem. Tchr. Edn. and Profl. Standards Commn., 1963-66, state chmn., 1966-67; state chmn. P.T.A. Exceptional Child Com.; mem. Ednl. Policies Com. State of Okla., 1962-63; mem. Gov.'s Mental Health Com., 1963-64; sec. sub-com. on juvenile problems, 1963-64; mem. Gov.'s Com. Ednl. Problems, 1964; del. Nat. Conf. on Rural Edn., 1964; mem. Council for Human Relations, 1968, Okla. Human Relations Com., 1970—; chmn. Okla. Ednl. TV Authority, 1972—. Mem. Jefferson-Bryan State Democratic Women's Club. Mem. Okla. (pres. 1963-64) Putnam City (sec.-treas. 1958-61) edn. assns. Central Dist. Dept. Classroom Tchrs. (pres. 1962-63), Am., Okla. personnel and guidance assns., Okla. Assn. Women Deans and Counselors, Central Dist. Guidance Assn. (pres. 1961), N.E.A. (mem. legislative commn. 1966-70, dir. Okla. 1967—, life), Am. Assn. U. Women (legislative chmn, 1962-64), Delta Kappa Gamma (v.p. 1972-73, pres. 1974-76), Kappa Delta Pi, Kappa Kappa Iota. Democrat. Mem. Ch. of Christ. Home: Route 1 Box 215 Wagoner OK 74467 Office: Adminstrn Bldg Central State U Edmond OK 73034

KIDWELL, DICKEN EVANS, lawyer; b. Louisville, Nov. 17, 1931; s. Carson Trigg and Nellie Blanche (Evans) K.; B.S., U. Tenn., 1953, LL.B., 1959; m. Barbara Carolyn Cargile, Sept. 3, 1961; children—Laura, Julia. Spl. agt. FBI, Albany, N.Y., 1959-61; admitted to Tenn. bar, 1959; pvt. practice law, Knoxville, Tenn., 1961-65, Murfreesboro, Tenn., 1965—. Pres., dir. Rutherford County Guidance Center, 1969—. Served to 1st lt. USAF, 1953-56. Mem. Am., Tenn., Rutherford County (pres. 1974) bar assns., Am. Judicature Soc., Assn. Trial Lawyers Am. Presbyn. (elder). Home: 1310 Halifax Ct Murfreesboro TN 37130 Office: 300 E Main St Murfreesboro TN 37130

KIDWELL, ROLLO EUGENE, lawyer; b. Dallas, June 4,, 1908; s. Charles Weems and Lessie Louise (Graber) K.; student So. Methodist U., 1926-28; LL.B., U. Tex., 1933; m. Alice Gertrude Thatcher, July 9, 1945; children—Sue, Molly (Mrs. Foster Jerome Sanders, Jr.). Admitted to Tex. bar, 1933; mem. firm Callaway, Reed, Kidwell & Brooks, Attys., Dallas, 1933-62; v.p., gen. counsel ETMF Freight System, Dallas, 1962—. Mem. Am., Dallas bar assns., State Bar Tex., Motor Carrier Lawyers Assn. Clubs: Tejas (Austin, Tex.); Brookhaven Country (Dallas). Home: 5518 Winston Ct Dallas TX 75220 Office: 2355 Stemmons Freeway Dallas TX 75207

KIEFFER, MARVIN LEWIS, lawyer; b. Weiner, Ark., Mar. 11, 1923; s. Jake and Matilda (Ziegenhorn) K.; B.S. in Pub. Adminstrn., U. Ark., 1950, LL.B., 1951; m. Julia Elizabeth Barker, Aug. 31, 1947. Admitted to Ark. bar, 1951; examining agt. U.S. Bur. Internal Revenue, Little Rock and Jonesboro, Ark., 1951-59; individual practice law, Jonesboro, 1959—. Bd. dirs. Jonesboro YMCA, 1960-70, pres., 1965. Served with AUS, 1943-46. Mem. Craighead County (pres. 1971-72), Ark. (chmn. audit com. 1965-70), Am. bar assns. Baptist. Mason, Kiwanian (lt. gov. Mo.-Ark. div. XVI 1970-71). Club: Jonesboro (pres. 1965). Home: 706 Melton Dr Jonesboro AR 72401 Office: McAdams Trust Bldg Jonesboro AR 72401

KIEL, GEORGE RALPH, ret. pub. relations exec.; b. Hackensack, N.J., Sept. 24, 1911; s. Frederick William and Olga Madeline (Thoma) K.; B.S., U. Va., 1933; m. Elsie Andrews Lee, May 19, 1945; 1 dau., Carol Anne (Mrs. Thomas O. Otto III). Reporter, Bergen Evening Record, Hackensack, N.J., 1933-37; pub. relations account exec. Arthur L. Green & Assos., N.Y.C., 1937-41; v.p. Hal Leyshon & Assos., Miami, 1941-46; pres. G. Ralph Kiel & Assos., Miami, 1946-50; v.p. Leyshon & Assos., Miami, 1955-60; gen. mgr., dir. publicity Bahamas Devel. Bd., Nassau, 1950-54; v.p. pub. relations Wackenhut Corp., Coral Gables, Fla., 1960-73. Bd. dirs. Miami Lighthouse for Blind, 1955-68. Mem. Pub. Relations Soc. Am., Greater Miami Pub. Relations Assn. (pres. 1949-50), U. Va. Alumni Assn., Delta Upsilon. Democrat. Episcopalian. Clubs: Coconut Grove Sailing (Miami); Country (Coral Gables, Fla.); Coconut Grove Civic (v.p. 1960-61) (Miami, Fla.). Contbr. articles to profl. jours. Home: 3911 Battersea Rd Coconut Grove Miami FL 33133 Office: 3280 Ponce de Leon Blvd Coral Gables FL 33134

KIEPPER, ALAN FREDERICK, city ofcl.; b. Syracuse, N.Y., July 3, 1928; s. John Carl and Sarah (McFadden) K.; A.B. cum laude, U. N.H., 1950; M.P.A., Wayne State U., 1960; m. Edith Harper, June 28, 1953; children—Patricia Ellen, Jane Elizabeth, Paul Frederick, Nancy Diana (dec.). Adminstrv. intern City of Richmond, Va., 1953, budget and mgmt. officer, 1953-59; asst. to county mgr. Montgomery County, Rockville, Md., 1959-63; county mgr. Fulton County, Atlanta, 1963-67; asst. city mgr., Richmond, 1967, city mgr., 1967-72; gen. mgr. Met. Atlanta Rapid Transit Authority, 1972—. Bd. dirs Nat. Assn. County Adminstrs., 1965-67, Inst. for Rapid Transit, 1972—; mem. pub. ofcls. adv. council office Econ. Opportunity; mem. Va. Gov.'s Adv. Com. on State-Local Cooperation, 1970-72; chmn. Va. Twin-Trailer Study Commn., 1969, mem. Twentieth Century Fund Task Force on Democratic Devel. of New Towns, 1970. Bd. dirs. Richmond chpt. Nat. Conf. Christians and Jews, 1967-72, Atlanta Assn. Retarded Children, 1964-67; bd. dirs. Richmond area Assn. Retarded Children, 1967-71, pres., 1969. Served to 1st lt. AUS, 1951-53. Mem. Internat. City Mgmt. Assn., Am. Transit Assn., Am. Soc. Pub. Adminstrn. (pres. Va. chpt. 1970), Municipal Finance Officers Assn., Alpha Tau Omega, Tau Kappa Alpha, Phi Kappa Phi, Pi Gamma Mu. Episcopalian. Home: 5614 Queensborough Dr NE Atlanta GA 30328 Office: 100 Peachtree St NW Atlanta GA 30303

KIERNAN, OWEN BURNS, ednl. adminstr.; b. Randolph, Mass., Mar. 9, 1914; s. Thomas Francis and Elizabeth (Burns) K.; B.S., Bridgewater (Mass.) State Tchrs. Coll., 1935; M.Ed., Boston U., 1940; Ed.D., Harvard, 1950, L.H.D. (honoris causa), Lesley Coll., 1956; LL.D. (honoris causa), Northeastern U., 1961; Litt.D. (honoris causa), Stonehill Coll., 1965; Ped.D. (honoris causa), R.I. Coll., 1966; Sc.D. (honoris causa), Boston U., 1968; m. Esther Harriet Thorley, July 13, 1940; children—Joan Ann, Nancy Elizabeth, John Albert. Prin. Henry T. Wing High Sch., Sandwich, Mass., 1938-44; supt. schs., Wayland and Sudbury, Mass., 1944-51, Milton, 1951-57; commr. edn. State of Mass., 1957-68; exec. sec. Nat. Assn. Secondary Sch. Prins., Washington, 1969—. Past chmn. Mass. Bd. Edn., Mass. Bd. Vocational Edn.; corp. mem. Mass. Inst. Tech.; trustee U. Mass., Lowell Tech. Inst., Mus. Fine Arts, Mus. Sci. Boston, Boston U. Mem. Am. Assn. Sch. Adminstrs., New Eng., Mass. supt. assns., Council Chief State Sch. Officers (pres. 1967), Phi Delta Kappa. Home: 12301 Delevan Dr Herndon VA 22070 Office: 1904 Association Dr Reston VA 22091

KIESEWETTER, EVELYN VAUGHT CUNDIFF (MRS. FRANK HOWARD KIESEWETTER), educator; b. Meridian, Miss.; d. William E. and Neatie (Vaught) Cundiff; student Meridian (Miss.) Sch. Music, 1920-27, Cin. Conservatory Music, 1931; A.B., U. Ky., 1938, M.A., 1953, postgrad., 1953—; m. Frank Kiesewetter. Tchr. elementary sch., Lexington, Ky., 1930-57; ednl. cons. Houghton Mifflin Co., Boston, 1957-59; part time mem. faculty U. Ky., Lexington, 1954-60, Morehead State U., 1959; with Zaner-Bloser Co., Columbus, O., summers 1962-69; program dir. Lexington Recreation Dept., 1937. Mem. adv. com. Juvenile Ct., Lexington, 1955-57; mem. Henry Clay Meml. Found., 1955—, Blue Grass Trust For Historic Preservation, 1960—. Bd. dirs. Central Ky. Concert and Lecture Series. Mem. Ky. Edn. Assn., Nat., Buckley Hills Audubon socs., Phi Beta, Kappa Delta Pi. Club: Spindletop Hall. Address: Apt 408 Merrick Place 3516 Milam Lane Lexington KY 40502

KIESEWETTER, FRANK HOWARD, ret. design engr.; b. Covington, Ky.; s. Frank John and Lynda (Pursifull) K.; student U. Cin.; B.S. in Engring., U. Ky.; m. Evelyn Vaught Cundiff; 1 son by previous marriage, Frank Reid. Ret. sr. design engr. Emery Industries, Cin. Past pres. Green Twp. Sch. Bd.; past v.p. Oak Hill Bd. Edn., active Boy Scouts Am.; mem. dist. com. Henry Clay Meml. Found. Served to maj. USAF, World War II. Recipient Scouter award Registered profl. engr., Ohio. Mem. U. Ky. Alumni Assn. (life), Blue Grass Trust Hist. Preservation, Nat. Buckley Hills Audubon socs., Demolay Legion of Honor, Cin. Opera Guild, Ky. Admirals, Ky. Civil War Round Table, Res. Officers Assn., Boat Owners Council Am. (charter). Presbyn. (deacon, trustee). Mason. Club: Spindletop Hall Country. Home: Apt 409 Merrick Pl 3520 Milam Lane Lexington KY 40502

KIEVMAN, MICHAEL S., broadcasting co. exec.; b. Naugatuck, Conn., Apr. 9, 1923; s. Samuel Joseph and Anna (Savage) K.; grad. bus. adminstrn. Columbia, 1943; m. Christine Elizabeth Lyles, June 24, 1948; children—Christopher, Carson, Michele, Corin. With Columbia Pictures, Hollywood, Cal., 1946-50; program and prodn. mgr. KOPO-TV, Tucson, 1950-57; sales mgr. ZIV-TV, Los Angeles, 1957-63, Warner Bros.-TV, N.Y.C., 1963-64; gen. sales mgr. sta. WLWD, Dayton, O., 1964-65; v.p. programming Avco Broadcasting, Cin., 1965-68; v.p. programming Cox Broadcasting, Atlanta, 1968—. Guest lectr. U. Ga., Athens, 1968—. Mem. Ohio State Fair Com., 1965-68; mem. steering com. A.R.C., 1963-65. Served with AUS, 1943-46. Decorated Purple Heart, Silver Star. Named Broadcaster of Year, Tucson Broadcasters, 1956. Mem. Nat. Assn. TV Execs. (mem. all industry music com. 1970—), Broadcast Pioneers, Country-Western Assn., Broadcast Exec. Forum, Nat. Acad. Arts and Scis. Clubs: Atlanta Athletic (Atlanta); Cincinnati Athletic, Summit Hills Country (Cin.). Home: 282 Tara Trail Atlanta GA 30327 Office: 1601 W Peachtree St NW Atlanta GA 30309

KIGER, ROBERT GARY, physician; b. Nashville, Feb. 4, 1934; s. William Odell and Ruby (Munn) K.; B.S., U. S.C., 1954; M.D., Vanderbilt U., 1958; m. Shirley Coker, Sept. 3, 1955; children—Robert Christopher, Mark Ryan. Intern, Vanderbilt Univ. Hosp., Nashville, 1958-59; resident medicine and cardiology Med. Coll. Ga., 1959-63; practice medicine specializing in cardiology, Columbia, S.C., 1963-66, Nashville, 1967-71; co-dir. cardiac lab. Med. Center NASA, George C. Marshall Spaceflight Center, Huntsville, Ala., 1966-67; dir. cardiovascular services Providence Hosp., Columbia, S.C., 1972—; cardiology cons. Human Performance Lab. Dept. Phys. Edn. U.S.C. Vice-chmn. S.C. Gov.'s Adv. Council Phys. Fitness Diplomate Am. Bd. Internal Medicine, Am. Bd. Cardiovasular Disease. Fellow A.C.P., Am. Coll. Cardiology, Clin. Council Cardiology; mem. S.C. Heart Assn. Author: Surgical Forum, 1959. Home: 53 Northlake Rd Columbia SC 29204 Office: Providence Hosp Columbia SC 29204

KILBURN, ROBERT WILLIAM, dir. research; b. Great Falls, Mont., Mar. 26, 1914; s. Percy Gordon and Myrtle (Ritz) K.; B.A., U. Cal. at Los Angeles, 1938; m. Thelma Taylor, Dec. 20, 1969; children by previous marriage—Robert G., Sherry Rae. Chemist Treesweet Corp., Santa Ana, Cal., 1937-45; research chemist FMC, Santa Jose, Cal., 1945-50; dir. research Citrus World, Inc., Lake Wales, Fla., 1950—; pres. Aqua Klear Corp. Chmn. A.R.C., 1970; active Boy Scouts Am., 1951-69. Fellow A.A.A.S.; mem. Inst. Food Technologists (chmn. Fla. chpt. 1956), Am. Chem. Soc., Pollution Control Fedn., Assn. Food Drug Ofcls. U.S., Lake Wales C. of C. (dir. 1957). Presbyn. (deacon). Club: Lake Wales Rotary (pres. 1955). Contbr. articles profl. jours. Patentee in field. Home: 920 Carton Av Lake Wales FL 33853 Office: Citrus World Inc Box 1111 Lake Wales FL 33853

KILGORE, SAMUEL GORDON, civil engr.; b. Fort Mede, Fla., Oct. 4, 1914; s. John Lewis and Edna Rose (Wood) K.; Chem. E., Ga. Sch. Tech., 1935; m. Joetta Lovelace, Oct. 11, 1952; children—Gordon, Andrew, John Lewis II, William Stewart. Photographer, Atlanta, Miami, Pitts., 1936-42; realtor, West Palm Beach and Tallahassee, Fla., 1946-48; abstractor, right of way agt., civil engr. Fla. Rd. Dept., Tallahassee, 1948—; owner, operator Kilgore's Sales & Service. Served with USAAF, 1943-45. Registered profl. engr., Fla. Home: 515 Short St Tallahassee FL 32303 Office: Haydon Burns Bldg Tallahassee FL 32304

KILLEBREW, JAMES ROBERT, architect, engr.; b. Okmulgee, Okla., Dec. 10, 1918; s. Robert Herman and Edith (Tyler) K.; B.S. in Archtl. Engring., U. Tex., 1948; m. Prebel Lee Thompson, Nov. 14, 1966; children—Debra Lee, Tod Nenian; 1 dau. (by previous marriage), Laura Janice. Sr. partner Killebrew-Rucker and Assos., architects and engrs., Wichita Falls, Tex., 1954—, works include elementary schs., one selected by Tex. Edn. Agv., as one of 25 outstanding since 1950, Bethania Hosp., Parker Sq. State Bank, Texas Hwy. Dept. Bldgs., 1st State Bank, Archer City Hosp., Muenster Meml. Hosp., Gen. Hosp., Plainview, Tex., Vernon (Tex.) Hosp., Vernon Geriatrics Psychiat. Hosp., Wichita Gen. Hosp., Gen. Hosp., Nocona, Tex., addition to Crippled Childrens Hosp., Wichita Falls, Tex., Sci. Bldg., Phys. Edn. Bldg. of Midwestern U., Teenage Drug Addiction Center, Vernon, Tex., hosps. at Eastland, Tex., other pub. bldgs. Asst. instr. Midwestern U. Served from ensign to lt. comdr. USNR, 1940-45, PTO, capt. Res. Archtl. License. Mem. Nat., Tex. (pres. North Tex. chpt. 1960-61, sec.-treas. 1958-59) socs. profl. engrs., Am. Soc. Archtl. Engrs. (charter mem.), A.I.A. (pres. Wichita Falls chpt. 1966-67), Am. Soc. Heating, Ventilating and Air Conditioning Engrs., C. of C. (chmn. beautification com. 1958-59, bldg. code com. 1955-56, aviation com. 1958-59; dir.), Navy League, U.S. (pres. 1967-68); Fine Art Soc. Tex. (bd. dirs., pres. 1970, chmn. bd. 1973). Mem. Christian Ch. (deacon). Home: 1559 Hanover St Wichita Falls TX 76302 Office: 202 Central Plaza Wichita Falls TX 76302

KILLEBREW, STEVE LEE, accountant; b. Richmond, Va., Jan. 19, 1926; s. O. Steve and Elizabeth H. (Wagner) K.; B.B.A., U. Tex., 1951; m. Gloria M. Mire, May 4, 1947; children—Stephanie (Mrs. L. Wesley Crippen), Kathryne (Mrs. James K. Girouard), Kent M., Beth Ann. Staff accountant O. Steve Killebrew & Co., 1951-59, office mgr., 1959-66, gen. partner, 1966—; pres. Live Oak Cemetery, 1972—; treas. B.C.D., Inc., C.K.D., Inc., Dandy Doole, Inc.; dir. First State Bank of Groves (Tex.). Treas., Assn. of Retarded, 1969—. Served with USMCR, 1944-47; PTO. Decorated Purple Heart. C.P.A., Tex., La. Mem. Am. Inst. C.P.A.'s, Sertoma Internat. (past pres. Port Arthur, dist. gov. E. Tex. 1971-73, state dir. 1973-74). Club: Port Arthur Country. Home: 2042 Ray Av Groves TX 77619 Office: 2348 Procter St Port Arthur TX 77640

KILLEN, CLARENCE AVERY, JR., comptroller; b. Reids, La., June 6, 1930; s. Clarence Avery and Bertha Mae (Martin) K.; B.B.A., Sam Houston U., 1962; m. Bobbie Ann Pullen, Apr. 30, 1949; children—Barbra Lynn (Mrs. William H. Humble, Jr.), Brenda Leigh, Edgar Avery. Asst. state auditor Office of Tex. State Auditor, 1959-66; comptroller Pan Am. U., 1966—, prof. accounting, 1968-74; partner Automated Mgmt. Services Co.; practicing accountant. Dir. Amazing Grace Hour, Inc. Served with USMC, 1946-52. C.P.A., Tex. Mem. Am. Inst. C.P.A.'s. Home: 607 Highland Av McAllen TX 78501 Office: Pan American University Edinburg TX 78539

KILLGORE, CHARLES ALDEN, chem. engr., univ. dean; b. Lisbon, La., Aug. 19, 1934; s. Millard B. and Alice D. (Monk) K.; B.S., La. Tech. U., 1956, M.S., 1963; postgrad. Ia. State U., summer 1961, Kan. State U., summer 1965, Okla. State U., 1968-71; m. Patti Jean Nicholas, June 1, 1954; children—Michael D., Byron Neill, Chris Alan. Instr. chem. engring., La. Tech. U., Ruston, 1959-62, asst. prof. chem. engring., 1962-69, also dir. nuclear center, asso. prof., 1969-73, also dir. nuclear center, asso. dean engring., also dir. Engring. Research, 1973—. Cons. mgmt. and radiation. Sec. Lincoln Parish Coordinating Com. Bd. dirs. Cedar Creek Sch., chmn., 1972—; bd. dirs. Wesley Found., treas., 1972—; bd. dirs. Ouachita Valley Council Boy Scouts Am. Served to capt., USAF, 1956-59. Recipient Silver Beaver award Boy Scouts Am., 1969. NSF fellow, 1968, 69, 71. Mem. Am. Inst. Chem. Engrs., La. Engring. Soc., Health Physics Soc., Am. Soc. Engring. Edn., (named outstanding faculty mem. 1970), Am. Nuclear Soc., Tau Beta Pi, Omicron Delta Kappa. Methodist. Lion (pres. 1972-73). Author: Evaluation of Potential Uses for Radiation Processing in Louisiana Industries, 1966; Lecture Notes on CPM, 1964. Address: Box 4875 T S Louisiana Tech Univ Nuclear Center Ruston LA 72170

KILLIAN, ROBERT EDWARD, pub. relations exec.; b. Ft. Worth, Sept. 1, 1934; s. Cecil Coy and Alma Nora (Adair) K.; B.A., Tex. Tech U., 1956; m. Gwen Gracey, Aug. 6, 1955; 1 son, Kirk Alexander. Pub. relations dir. Community Pub. Service Co., Ft. Worth, 1960-66; cons. Towers, Perrin, Forster & Crosby, Phila., 1966-67; pub. relations adviser Mobil Oil Corp., Dallas, 1967-68; pub. relations dir. Recognition Equipment, Inc., Dallas, 1968-70; v.p. Tracy-Locke Pub. Relations, Dallas, 1970—. Served to maj. inf., AUS, 1956-57. Mem. Pub. Relations Soc. Am., Nat. Investor Relations Inst., Advt. Club Dallas, Phi Gamma Delta. Republican. Home: 2402 E Prairie Creek St Richardson TX 75080 Office: 1407 Main St Dallas TX 75202

KILLMER, HUGH DOUGLAS, dentist; b. Duluth, Minn., May 24, 1910; s. Raleigh Edward and Pearl Ida (Heath) K.; D.D.S., Washington U., 1936; postgrad. Northwestern U., 1937, U. Tex., Houston, 1955-65; m. Grace E. Perry, Aug. 16, 1952; children—David, Paul, Jonathon, Carey, Robert, Charles, Gwenda, Bill. Individual practice dentistry, St. Louis, 1936-41, 47-49; staff dentist VA Hosp., Alexandria, La., 1944-49; staff dentist VA Hosp., Houston, 1949-57, chief dental service, 1957-66; dental field supr. VA Central Office, Washington, 1966-71; chief dental service VA Hosp., Waco, Tex., 1971—. Adj. prof. Tex. State Tech. Inst. James Connally Campus, Waco, Bd. dirs. D.C. Bapt. Conf. Served with AUS, 1941-47. Decorated Legion of Merit. Fellow Am. Coll. Dentists; mem. Am. Prosthodontic Soc., Am. Assn. Hosp. Dentists, Am. Equilibration Soc. (chmn. constn. by-laws com. 1974, mem. credential com. 1974), Internat. Assn. Dental Research, Am. Dental Assn. Baptist (chmn. finance com. 1970-71). Club: Optimist (v.p. 1960-61) (Houston). Home: 7217 Brentwood Circle Waco TX 76710 Office: VA Hospital Memorial Dr Waco TX 76703

KILLOUGH, WALTER WILLIAM, ret. business exec.; b. Hobart, Okla., Aug. 29, 1904; s. James Payton and Lessie (Gentry) K.; student Okla. State U., 1923-25; m. Allie Nell Watson, Aug. 28, 1927; children—Mickey June (Mrs. Emerson Ellwood Lynn), Walter William. With Internat. Harvester Co., 1935-68, blockman, Oklahoma City, 1935-39, asst. br. mgr. Des Moines, 1939-43, war materials div.,

Chgo., 1943-44, mng. dir., chmn. IHC Australia Pty. Ltd., Melbourne, Victoria, 1950-62, pres. IHC of Can. Ltd., Hamilton, Ont., Can., 1961-62, v.p., Chgo., 1963-68. Decorated Order Brit. Empire. Mem. Soc. Automotive Engrs. Methodist. Home: 1215 Canterbury Ct Arlington TX 76013

KILPATRICK, EARL BUDDY, biologist, educator; b. Burkburnett, Tex., June 21, 1920; s. Earl Kennedy and Margaret May (Chitwood) K.; B.S., U. Okla., 1942, M.S., 1949, Ph.D. (NSF fellow), 1959; m. Jack Ann Nichols, Apr. 20, 1956; children—Cheryl, Janet (Mrs. John Thomas), Toni (Mrs. Charles Stiefer), John, Alan, Rebecca. Asst. prof. biology Southeastern State Coll., Durant, Okla., 1949-60, asso. prof., 1960-62, prof., 1962—, also head dept. biology, 1961—. Mgr., treas. Southeastern Tchrs. Credit Union, 1973—. State chmn. Long Range Planning Com., 1971-72. Bd. dirs. Okla. Lions Eye Bank, 1969—, treas., 1973—. Served to capt. AUS, 1942-46; ETO; col. Res. Fellow Okla. Acad. Sci. (cons. speakers bur. 1966—); mem. A.A.A.S., Southwestern Assn. Naturalists, Res. Officers Assn., Gideon's, Sigma Xi, Sigma Tau Gamma (faculty adv. 1956—). Lion (zone chmn. 1968-69, dist. gov. 1969-70, pres. 1970-71). Home: 1223 N 5th St Durant OK 74701

KILPATRICK, JAMES LOWE, oilwell drilling contractor; b. Haynesville, La., Feb. 8, 1931; s. Dayton Barnett and Illa (Lowe) K.; B.S., La. Poly. Inst., 1953; m. Carolyn Earlene Hargrove, Dec. 27, 1953; children—Barney, Kim, Mark, Pam. Petroleum engr. Monsanto Chem. Co., El Dorado, Ark., 1955-57; petroleum engr. Murphy Corp., El Dorado, 1957-60; petroleum engr., asst. to v.p., gen. mgr. drilling, sr. v.p. Ocean Drilling & Exploration Co., New Orleans, 1960—; dir. Rimrock (U.K.), Rimrock Drilling, Canam Offshore, Odeco Nehon, Odeco (U.K.). Served with USNR, 1953-55. Mem. Am. Inst. Mining, Metall. and Petroleum Engrs., Am. Assn. Oilwell Drilling Contractors (dir.). Home: 2423 Hudson Pl New Orleans LA 70114 Office: 1600 Canal St New Orleans LA 70112

KILPATRICK, KERRY EDWARDS, educator; b. Balt., Mar. 17, 1939; s. Stanley Alexander and Elsa Clare (Kalwa) K.; B.S.E., U. Mich., 1961; M.B.A., Harvard, 1963; M.S., U. Mich., 1967, Ph.D., 1970; m. Ellen Louise Vandernaald, Feb. 27, 1965; children—Andrew Kerry, Jeffrey Bart. Engr. Chevrolet Motor div. Gen. Motors Corp., 1957-62; Buick Motor div., 1963-65; research asst. U. Mich., 1966-70; prof., dir. health systems research U. Fla., 1970—; cons. Bur. Health Resources Devel. of Human Resources Adminstrn. Dept. Health, Edn. and Welfare. Alfred P. Sloan scholar, 1958-61; NSF trainee, 1965-66. Mem. Operations Research Soc. Am., Inst. Mgmt. Sci., Am. Inst. Indsl. Engrs., I.E.E.E., Human Factors Soc., Sigma Xi, Tau Beta Pi, Pi Tau Sigma, Phi Kappa Phi, Alpha Pi Mu, Phi Eta Sigma. Contbr. articles to profl. jours. Home: 1340 NW 25th Terrace Gainesville FL 32601

KIMBALL, AUBREY PIERCE, educator; b. Lufkin, Tex., Oct. 20, 1926; s. Aubrey Joseph and Eula Bernice (Pixley) K.; B.S., U. Houston, 1958, Ph.D., 1961; postdoctoral Stanford Research Inst., 1961-62; m. Celia Cruz, Dec. 26, 1953 (div.); children—Kathleen, Erin, Lisa. Research biochemist Stanford Research Inst., 1962-67; asso. prof. biochemistry U. Houston, 1967-72, prof., 1972—. Served with USNR, 1944-46, 50-52. Roche fellow, 1952-54. Grantee Robert A. Welch, 1968-76, NIH, 1971-74. Fellow Am. Inst. Chemists; mem. Am. Chem. Soc. (dir. Southeastern sect.), N.Y. Acad. Sci., Am. Assn. Cancer Research Soc. Exptl. Biology and Medicine, A.A.A.S., Sons Rep. of Tex. Editor: (with J. Oro') Prebiotic and Biochemical Evolution, 1972. Contbr. articles to sci. jours. Home: 3811 Link Valley Houston TX 77025

KIMBALL, DANIEL P., judge; b. Springfield, La., Oct. 10, 1915; s. Louis R. and Harriet Elizabeth (Sibley) K.; B.A., La. State U., 1938, LL.B., 1947; m. Katherine C. Kleinpeter, Apr. 12, 1941; children—Carolyn Kay (Mrs. Sidney J. Babin), Marilyn Sue, Madelyn Ann. Admitted to La. bar, 1947; practiced in West Baton Rouge, La., 1947-61; city atty. Brusly, La., 1953-61, Rosedale, La., 1960-61, Port Allen, 1953-61, Grosse Tete, La., 1952-61, judge 18th Jud. Dist. Ct., Port Allen, La., 1961—. Dir. Bank of West Baton Rouge, Port Allen. Dist. advancement chmn., vice chmn. dist. exec. com. Boy Scouts Am., 1952-54; sec. Bd. Commrs., Atchafalaya Basin Levee Dist., 1940-42, 46-48; v.p., program chmn. Blue Ridge Inst. for So. Juvenile Ct. Judges, 1966-67, pres., 1967-68; mem. Jud. Council La., 1967—; adv. com. for preparation new juvenile code La., 1970—. Dir. Baton Rouge Port Devel. Assn., 1951-55, Donaldonville Mental Health Center, 1965—, West Baton Rouge Retarded Persons Assn., 1966—. Served with AUS, 1942-45. Mem. La. Bar Assn. (mem. ho. dels. 1955-56), La. Council Juvenile Ct. Judges (sec. 1964-65, v.p. 1965-66, pres. 1966-67), Am. Legion (post comdr., dist. judge adv., vice comdr., dept. judge adv.). Lion (past sec. Port Allen). Office: Port Allen LA 70767

KIMBALL, VERA F., editor, writer; b. Seward, Alaska, Feb. 8, 1903; d. Irving L. and Della (Carpenter) Kimball; A.B., Columbia, 1929; m. William T. Castles, Jr., Dec. 2, 1942. On clerical staff Legislature of Ty. of Alaska, 1923; with Alaska R.R., Anchorage, 1923-24, N.A. Newspaper Alliance, Met. Mus. Art, Gen. Foods Corp., Todd-Robertson & Todd (all N.Y. City), part time 1924-29; asst. to sec. Am. Inst. Chemists, 1929-35; editor The Chemist, N.Y.C., 1935-68, asso. editor, 1968-70. Mem. N.Y. Acad. Scis., Am. Inst. Chemists (hon. life, sec. S.C. chpt.), A.A.A.S., Cook Inlet Hist. Soc., Alaska (charter mem.), Chester County (S.C.) Hist. Soc. Club: Barnard College (N.Y. City). Author: Firearms and Their Use (with W. T. Castles), 1942; Your Future in Chemistry (with M. R. Bhagwat), 1943. Contbr. to World Scope Ency., The Ency. of Chemistry, year books, profl. and popular mags. Home: Magnolia Apts B-4 Chester SC 29706 Office: Route 2 Chester SC 29706

KIMBEL, WILLIAM ANTHONY, govt. cons., corp. exec.; b. N.Y.C., Jan. 5, 1888; s. Anthony and Eleanor (Haubner) K.; B.S., Columbia, 1909; m. L. Maud Windeler, Jan. 17, 1920; children—Joyce (Mrs. Kimbel Gunnels), Richard Anthony. Asst. mil. attache U.S., Embassy, London, 1916; pres. A. Kimbel & Son, archtl. and decorative contractors and mfrs., N.Y.C., 1922-41; asst. to dir. OSS. 1941-45; owner, pub. Myrtle Beach (S.C.) News, 1946-48; adminstrv. dir. Anglo-Am. Council on Productivity, 1948-50; pres. Midcoast Investment, Myrtle Beach, 1950-51, also dir. pub. relations Hi-Q div. Aerovox Corp., Quality Courts United. U.S. rep. Econ. Commn. for Europe, 1954, 55; adviser delegation UNESCO, 1954; cons. Dept. of State, 1953—. Pres. Am. Inst. Decorators, 1938-40, Coastal Ednl. Found. of S.C., 1965; mem. S.C. Adv. Commn. on Edn., 1965—. Served with U.S. Army, World War I, AEF. Recipient Medal of Merit, Columbia. Mem. Pilgrims Soc. Am., Am. Camellia Soc., U.S. Seniors Golf Assn., S.C. Hist. Soc., Winyah Indigo Soc. Clubs: Metropolitan, Chevy Chase (Washington) University, Racquet and Tennis. Ardsley Curling (founder, past pres.), Ardsley (N.Y.); Dunes Golf and Beach (founder, dir.) (Myrtle Beach). Home: Wachesaw Plantation Murrells Inlet SC 29576 Office: Box 1526 Myrtle Beach SC 29577

KIMBERLIN, SAM OWEN, JR., assn. exec.; b. Wichita Falls, Tex., Feb. 4, 1928; s. Sam Owen and Ruth (Crowell) K.; B.B.A., U. Tex., 1951, LL.B., 1953; postgrad. Rutgers U., 1972; m. Alison Gray, Dec. 20, 1955; children—Samuel Scott, David Winston. First asst. dist. atty. Travis County, Tex., 1953-54; asst. atty. gen. Tex., 1955-56; gen. counsel Tex. Dept. Banking, 1956-62; exec. dir. Assn. State Chartered Banks in Tex., 1962-64; exec. v.p. Tex. Bankers Assn., 1964—. Pres., Conf. So. Bankers Assn. Execs., 1967-68; mem. Banking Laws Com., Tex. Bar Assn. Bd. dirs. Sch. of Banking of the South, Baton Rouge. Served with USMCR, 1946-48. Mem. Tex. Bar Assn., Am., Tex. socs. assn. execs., Phi Alpha Delta, Phi Delta Theta. Contbr. articles to banking jours. Home: 3503 Scenic Hills Dr Austin TX 78703 Office: Vaughn Bldg Austin TX 78701

KIMBERLING, CARROLL FRANKLIN, JR., supermarket exec.; b. Oklahoma City, Aug. 31, 1947; s. Carroll Franklin and June Marie (Joyce) K.; B.B.A., Tex. Christian U., 1969; m. Nancy Farrell Felton, Jan. 2, 1970. Corporate v.p. Kimberlings Supermarkets, Oklahoma City, 1965—; dir. Oklahoma City Profl. Football Club, Inc. Bd. dirs., chmn. Oklahoma City chpt. March of Dimes; bd. dirs. Oklahoma City Skyline Urban Ministry, Oklahoma City Partners for Progress. Mem. Nat. Assn. Retail Grocers U.S., Okla. (dir.), Oklahoma City retail grocers assns., Oklahoma City C. of C., Oklahoma City All Sports Assn. (dir. 1970—), Delta Tau Delta. Republican. Methodist (mem. bd.). Clubs: Young Men's Dinner, Quail Creek Golf and Country. Home: 12513 Springwood St Oklahoma City OK 73120 Office: 4545 Windsor Mall Oklahoma City OK 73127

KIMBERLY, GEORGE DOUGLAS, physician; b. Hot Springs, N.C., Nov. 26, 1932; s. David and Willeene Garrison (Glenn) K.; A.A., Mars Hill Coll., 1952; B.S., Wake Forest Coll., 1954; M.D., Bowman Gray Sch. Medicine, 1958; m. Sybil Hope Davis, Sept. 7, 1957; children—Joanna Bess, George Douglas, John Davis. Intern N.C. Bapt. Hosp., Winston-Salem, 1958-60; gen. practice medicine, Bakersville, N.C., 1960-68; partner practice medicine, Mocksville, N.C., 1969—; mem. staff Davie County Hosp., Mocksville, trustee, 1970—. Mem. Am. Cancer Soc. Davie County, 1971-72; mem. Gov.'s Adv. Council Comprehensive Health Planning, 1971—. Mem. Davie-Rowan County Med. Soc., Med. Soc. N.C., A.M.A., Am., N.C. acads. family practice. Home: 713 Magnolia Av Mocksville NC 27028 Office: 717 Hospital St Mocksville NC 27028

KIMBROUGH, HARRIS MCDONALD, JR., dentist; b. Amarillo, Tex., Apr. 24, 1932; s. Harris McDonald and Jewel Evelyn (Scales) K.; student Yale, 1950-52, Tex. U., 1952-53; D.D.S., Baylor U., 1957; postgrad. Amarillo Coll., 1971; B.A. in Psychology, West Tex. State U., 1974; children—Katrina, Robin, Ned, Risa, Mike, Cinamon. Individual practice dentistry, Amarillo, 1960—, Pampa, Tex., 1962-67; instr. dental assts. course Amarillo Coll., 1969, cons. Alcoholic Recovery Center, 1969—. Dental coordinator Civil Def., 1963-65. Pres., trustee Ceta Glen Conf. on Alcoholism; bd. dirs. Amarillo Mentally Retarded Center, Alcoholic Recovery Center, Unity Ch. Montessori Sch. Served to lt. Dental Corps, USN, 1956-60. Fellow Am. Acad. Pedodontics; mem. Am., Tex. dental assns., Panhandle Dist. Dental Soc. (editor), v.p.), Am. Acad. Gen. Practice, Am. Soc. Dentistry for Children, Omicron Kappa Upsilon. Club: Amarillo County. Home: 7 Tascociata Circle Amarillo TX 79106 Office: 2312 Georgia St Amarillo TX 79109

KIMBROUGH, WILLIAM HORACE, state ofcl.; b. Springville, Ala., Aug. 8, 1913; s. James R. and Bertie (Newman) K.; B.S., U. Ala., 1934, M.A., 1940; LL.D., Jacksonville State U., 1972; m. Thelma Fagan, June 8, 1938; children—Gay Nell, William Edwin. Tchr., Piedmont (Ala.) High Sch., 1934-37, Sylacauga (Ala.) High Sch., 1937-42; supt. Piedmont City Schs., 1942-67; dir. div. adminstrn. and finance State Dept. Edn., 1967—. Sec., Piedmont Community Chest. Mem. Ala. High Sch. Athletic Assn. (pres. 1949-51), Ala. Edn. Assn. (pres. 1959-60), Ala. Assn. Sch. Adminstrs. (pres. 1963-65). Methodist (dir. choir 1943-67). Lion (pres. 1944-46). Home: 2508 Oxford Dr Montgomery AL 36111 Office: State Office Bldg Montgomery AL 36104

KIMERER, NEIL BANARD, SR., psychiatrist, educator; b. Wauseon, O., Jan. 13, 1918; s. William and Ruby (Upp) K.; B.S., U. Toledo, 1941; M.D., U. Chgo., 1944; postgrad. (fellow) Menninger Sch., 1947-50; m. Ellen Jane Scott, May 23, 1943; children—Susan Leigh, Neil Banard, Brian Scott, Sandra Lynn. Intern, Emanuel Hosp., Portland, Ore., 1944; resident psychiatry Winter VA Hosp., Topeka, 1947-50; asst. physician Central State Hosp., Norman, Okla., 1950, cons., 1955—; chief out-patient psychiat. clinic U. Okla. Sch. Medicine, Oklahoma City, 1951-53, instr. dept. psychiatry, 1951-52, asso. prof., 1952-53, asst. prof. dept. psychiatry, neurology and behavioral scis., 1955-61, asso. prof., 1961-69, clin. prof., 1969—; practice medicine specializing in psychiatry, Oklahoma City, 1953—; med. dir. Oklahoma City Mental Health Clinic, 1953-68; cons., spl. lectr. dept. psychology U. Okla., Norman, 1951-58. Mem. Comprehensive Health Survey Com., Oklahoma City, 1961—; mem. exec. com. Okla. Family Life Assn., 1958-60; bd. dirs. Oklahoma City Jr. Symphony Soc., 1959. Served as pfc, ASTP, 1943-44; to capt. M.C., AUS, 1945-47, Diplomate Am. Bd. Psychiatry. Fellow Am. Psychiat. Assn.; mem. Am., Okla. State med. assns., Oklahoma County Med. Soc., Oklahoma City Clin. Soc., Okla. Psychiat. Soc., Okla. (pres. 1956, 60-62), Mid-Continent psychiat. socs., A.A.A.S., Okla. Health and Welfare Assn., Alpha Kappa Kappa (pres. Nu chpt. 1943). Rotarian. Author: To Get and Begot, 1971. Contbr. article in field to profl. jour. Home: 2800 NW 25th St Oklahoma City OK 73107 Office: 2600 NW Hwy Oklahoma City OK 73112

KIMES, THOMAS FREDRIC, educator; b. Phoenixville, Pa., July 24, 1928; s. Wilmer Grey and Mary (Clymer) K.; B.S., Ursinus Coll., 1949; M.A., U. Tex., 1956; Ph.D., Carnegie-Mellon U., 1962; m. Marion Massengill, Oct. 17, 1952 (div. 1974); children—Christine Elizabeth, Thornton Grey. Instr., Carnegie Inst. Tech., part-time 1956-59; sr. mathematician Bettis Atomic Power Lab., Pitts., 1959-62; prof. math. Austin Coll., Sherman, Tex., 1962—, chmn. dept., 1962-73, dir. Interactive Computing Services, 1972—. Mathematician, reliability analyst Tex. Instruments, summer 1965; NSF lectr., summers 1969-70; vis. prof. U. Lancaster (U.K.), 1970; chmn. North Tex. APL Users' Group, 1973—. Dir. Sherman Tutorial and Edn. Program, 1964-73, pres., 1969; campaign worker United Fund, 1963-68; group leader Uganda Operation Crossroads Africa, 1966. Served with USAF, 1950-54. NSF Faculty fellow, summer 1969. Mem. Prehistoric Soc. (U.K.), Am. Math. Soc., Math. Assn. Am., Sigma Xi, Phi Kappa Phi, Pi Mu Epsilon, Sigma Pi Sigma. Democrat. Presbyn. (elder gen. assembly 1973). Home: 1419 N Travis St Sherman TX 75090

KIMPLE, WILLIAM CARLISLE, packaging co. exec.; b. Dallas, Dec. 13, 1928; s. Louis C. and Gladys (Halsell) K.; student N. Tex. U., 1945-47; B.S., So. Meth. U., 1954; m. Patsy C. Brazil, Feb. 16, 1952; children—Cheryl, Lisa, Robin. With Dixico, Dallas, 1954—, successively salesman, sales mgr., 1954-61, promotion and advt., 1958-61, sec., 1958—, dir., 1958—, v.p., regional mgr., 1965-69, sr. v.p. indsl. relations, 1969—, exec. v.p. operations, 1973—; dir. Am. Savings & Loan Assn. Served with AUS, 1951-53. Home: 1344 Bar Harbor Dallas TX 75232 Office: 1415 S Vernon St Dallas TX 75224

KINARD, FRANK EFIRD, state ofcl.; b. Newberry, S.C., Jan. 15, 1924; s. James C. and Katherine (Efird) K.; B.S., Newberry Coll., 1946, A.B., 1947; M.S., U. N.C., 1950, Ph.D. in Physics, 1953; m. Mary Angelyn McNease, June 25, 1952; children—Sally Garner, Anne Dreher, James McNease (dec.). Instr. U. N.C., 1948-52; physicist E.I. DuPont de Nemours and Co., Aiken, S.C., 1953-63, dir. univ. relations office, Aiken, 1963-67; exec. dir. S.C. Commn. Higher Edn., Columbia, 1967; asst. dir., 1968—. Mem. Oak Ridge Engring. Edn. Adv. Com., 1965-67; chmn. S.C. Adv. Com. Sci. and Tech., 1974—. Served with USAAF, 1943-46. Mem. Am. Nuclear Soc. (edn. com. 1964-66), Am. Phys. Soc., A.A.A.S., S.C. Acad. Sci., Sigma Xi. Episcopalian. Home: 801 Albion Rd Columbia SC 29205 Office: 1429 Senate St Columbia SC 29201

KINARD, JOHN ERNEST, JR., lawyer; b. Newberry, S.C., Oct. 18, 1939; s. John Ernest and Blanche Ruth (Lominick) K.; student Clemson U., 1957-60; B.A., U. S.C., 1961, LL.B., 1964; m. Kay Livingston Davis, July 21, 1963; children—Kay Marie, Audrey, John. Admitted to S.C. bar, 1964, since practiced in Camden; mem. firm Savage, Royall, Kinard & Sheheen, 1964—. Mem. Camden Alcoholics Commn., 1971-72, Kershaw County Commn. on Alcohol and Drug Abuse, 1973; sec. Camden Charity Horse Show, 1967—; drive chmn. United Fund, Kershaw County, 1965; vice chmn. Wateree Community Actions, 1971-72; adviser to registrants SSS, 1970-73. Mem. S.C. Bar, Am., Kershaw County (pres. 1968), S.C. bar assns., Sertoma Club (pres. 1968). Mason. Home: 1704 Lakeview St Camden SC 29020 Office: 1111 Church St Camden SC 29020

KINCHELOE, MORRIS CLIFFORD, graphic arts co. exec.; b. Louisville, Oct. 28, 1907; s. Willard Xavier and Lillian David (Davis) K.; student Internat. Corr. Schs., U. Louisville extension, also YMCA courses; m. Vera Iola Morr, Sept. 2, 1938; children—Donna (Mrs. D. Calvert Brand), Joan Ellen, Thomas M. Office boy Commonwealth Life Ins. Co., Louisville, 1923-24; instr., auto driver Browder Hoskins, Louisville, 1924-29; from shop mechanic to methods engr. Am. Air Filter Co., Louisville, 1929-50; pres. Fine Arts Reprodn. Co., Inc., Louisville, 1950—. Mem. Ky. Militia, 1941-42. Mem. Sales Execs. Club Louisville, Advt. Club Louisville, Printing Industry Ky., Screen Printing Assn. Internat., Better Bus. Bur. Greater Louisville, Louisville Area C. of C. Mason (Shriner), Rotarian. Club: Owl Creek Country (Anchorage, Ky.). Home: 11805 Cedardale Rd Anchorage KY 40223 Office: 1500 Arlington Av Louisville KY 40206

KINCHELOE, WARREN ARTHUR, cons. engr.; b. Waco, Tex., Nov. 2, 1908; s. Charles Hamilton and Maude Mora (Eason) K.; student U. Va., 1927-28; B.S., U. Tex., 1933; m. Marilyn DeFoe Miller, July 18, 1937; 1 dau., Nedralyn Ann (Mrs. Richard Eric Finlan). Supr. Bell Telephone Co., Dallas, 1934-42; chief engr. S.W. Marshall, Dallas, 1946-48; with Forrest & Cotton, Inc., cons. engrs., Dallas, 1956—, staff specialist elec. and mech., 1972—. Pres. Employees Credit Union, Dallas, 1968-70. Served to lt. comdr. USNR, 1942-45. Decorated D.F.C. Registered profl. engr., Tex. Mem. Nat., Tex. socs. profl. engrs., I.E.E.E., Dallas Elec. League (dir. 1969-71). Methodist. Clubs: Dallas Automobile; Toastmasters (pres. 1965) (Dallas). Home: 3640 Southwestern Dallas TX 75225 Office: 8700 Stemmons Freeway Dallas TX 75247

KINDER, JACK DARROW, dentist; b. Andrews, S.C, Dec. 7, 1931; s. Lucian Percy and Sallie Elizabeth (Fitzgerald) K.; student Newberry (S.C.) Coll., 1957-59; D.D.S., Emory U., 1963, M.S.D., 1970; m. Sylvia Talu Oxner, June 4, 1952; children—Stephen Darrow, Lucian Scott. Gen. practice dentistry, Hartsville, S.C., 1963-68; spl. practice orthodontics, Sumter, S.C., 1970—. Pres. Darlington County Assn. Retarded Children, 1966-68. Mem. Am., S.C. dental assns., Am. Assn. Orthodontists, So. Soc. Orthodontists, Pee Dee Dental Soc. Mason, Kiwanian, Elk. Home: 528 Benton Ct Sumter SC 29150 Office: 541 Oxford St Sumter SC 29150

KINDLEY, LEE MURRAY, govt. ofcl.; b. Mt. Airy, Md., June 28, 1921; s. Oscar Murray and Edith Augusta (Peddicord) K.; B.A., Western Md. Coll., 1942; M.S., Stevens Inst. Tech., 1957; Ph.D., George Washington U., 1970; m. Mary C. Mack, Aug. 23, 1948; children—Catherine, George. Chemist U.S. Indsl. Chems., 1945-52; polymer chemist Melpar, Inc., 1952-55; food technologist Gen. Foods Corp., Tarrytown, N.Y., 1955-57; engr. Melpar, Inc., 1958-66; chemist Air Reduction, Inc., 1957-58; polymer chemist Naval Ordnance Lab., 1966-67; research chemist Office of Saline Water of U.S. Dept. Interior, Washington, 1967—. Served with AUS, 1942-46; col. Res. Mem. Am. Chem. Soc. K.C., Elk. Contbr. articles to profl. jours. Patentee in field. Home: 7406 Ellwood Pl Springfield VA 22150 Office: Dept Interior Washington DC 20204

KINDRED, ALTON RICHARD, educator; b. Clermont, Fla., Jan. 8, 1922; s. Carl Landow and Eva Frances (Isaac) K.; B.S., Fla. So. Coll., 1943, M.A., 1949; m. Lucia Claire Morris, Aug. 23, 1942; children—Marsha Louise (Mrs. David F. Lovelace), Alton Richard, John Morris. Clk.-gen. Watson Labs., Leesburg, Fla., 1946; bursar Fla. So. Coll., 1946-62; prof., chmn. data processing Manatee Jr. Coll., Bradenton, Fla., 1962—. Served with USMCR, 1943-46, 50. Mem. Data Processing Mgmt. Assn. (pres. Sarasota-Manatee chpt. 1962-64), Fla. Assn. Ednl. Data Systems (pres. 1971-72). Methodist (treas. Fla. conf. 1961-62). Author: Data Systems and Management, 1973. Home: 2707 Rutgers Av Bradenton FL 33507

KING, BOYD FRANKLIN, economist; b. Knoxville, Tenn., Mar. 6, 1937; s. Boyd Edwin and Amy Leeta (Brewer) K.; B.S., U. Tenn., 1959; postgrad. Vanderbilt U., 1961-64; m. Robbie June Whaley, Jan. 28, 1967. Asst. bank examiner Fed. Deposit Ins. Corp., St. Louis, 1959-61; instr. econs. Georgetown U., 1964-69; sr. economist Fed. Res. Bank, Atlanta, 1969—. Mem. Am., So. econ. assns. Baptist. Home: 1283 Oakdale Rd NE Atlanta GA 30307 Office: Fed Res Bank of Atlanta Fed Res Sta Atlanta GA 30303

KING, CALVIN ELIJAH, mathematician, educator; b. Chgo., June 5, 1928; s. David Aaron and Barbara Josephine (Smith) K.; A.B. Morehouse Coll., 1949; M.A in Math., Atlanta U., 1950; Ph.D., Ohio State U., 1959. Instr. math. Jackson (Miss.) State Coll., 1953-55; faculty Tenn. State U., Nashville, 1958-62, prof. math, 1964—; prof. math. Fed. Advanced Tchrs. Coll., Lagos, Nigeria, 1962-64. Served with CIC, AUS, 1951-53. Mem. Nat. Council Tchrs. Math., Math. Assn. Am., Beta Kappa Chi, Omega Psi Phi. Home: 626 N 5th St Nashville TN 37207

KING, CHARLES JAMES, lawyer; b. Atlanta, Feb. 3, 1925; s. Lewis Reed and Mary (Green) K.; J.D., U. Miami, 1955; m. Lydia V. Schuster, May 27, 1950; children—Janet H. (Mrs. Glenn Hargrave), Annette L., James R., Elaine H. Trust officer Broward Nat. Bank, Ft. Lauderdale, Fla., 1955-57; admitted to Fla. bar, 1955; practiced in Ft. Lauderdale, 1957—; mem. Fla. Ho. of Reps., 1967-70; municipal judge, 1966-67; atty. Broward County Transp. Authority. Mem. Fla., Broward County bar assns., Am. Arbitration Assn., Delta Theta Phi. Home: 213 NE 40th St Oakland Park FL 33308 Office: 1750 E Commercial Blvd Fort Lauderdale FL 33308

KING, CHARLES OSSIE, air conditioning contractor; b. nr. Franklin, Ind., Nov. 17, 1919; s. Ossie Lloyd and Lily Mae (Ervin) K.; grad. high sch.; m. Ruth Isabel LePage, July 12, 1944; children—Charles E., Carolyn R., Michael J. Mech. supt. Gen. Am. Transp. Corp., Orlando, Fla., 1946-51; salesman Boys Roofing & S/M Works, Inc., West Palm Beach, Fla., 1951-58; pres. Air Conditioning Designers, Inc., West Palm Beach, 1958—. Served with USN,

1937-45. Mem. Am. Soc. Heating, Refrigerating and Air Conditioning Engrs. (pres. Gold Coast chpt.), Palm Beach County Roofing and Sheet Metal Contractors Assn. (past pres.), Palm Beach Country Air Conditioning Contractors Assn. (past pres.), Am. Subcontractors Assn. (pres. Gold Coast chpt.), Nat. Assn. Sheet Metal and Air Conditioning Contractors, Refrigeration Service Engrs. Soc., Fla. Roofing, Sheet Metal and Air Conditioning Contractors Assn. (past pres.). Rotarian (past pres.). Contbr. articles to jours. Home: 17 Harbor Dr Lake Worth FL 33460 Office: 1601 N Military Trail West Palm Beach FL 33406

KING, CHARLES WILLIS, power system analysis cons.; b. nr. Clarion, Pa., Nov. 17, 1935; s. James Byers and Dorothy Louise (Lusher) K.; B.S. cum laude, Washington Coll., 1957; M.S., U. Pitts., 1961; m. Audrie Ann Demchisin, Sept. 16, 1962; children—Elizabeth Ann, Charles Byers. Engr. Westinghouse Electric Co., Pitts., 1957-62; dir. elec. utility applications C-E-I-R, Inc., Arlington, Va., 1962-67; pres. Computing and Utility Services, Los Angeles, 1967-69; gen. mgr. Univ. Computing Co., Dallas, 1969—; tchr. Inst. Advanced Tech., 1963-67. Mem. I.E.E.E. Contbr. articles to profl. jours. Research on application of digital computers to power system problems for elec. utilities. Home: 15750 Daleport Circle Dallas TX 75240 Office: 7200 N Stemmons Pkwy Dallas TX 75247

KING, CORETTA SCOTT (MRS. MARTIN LUTHER KING, JR.), lectr., writer, civic worker; b. Marion, Ala., Apr. 27, 1927; d. Obidiah and Bernice (McMurray) Scott; A.B., Antioch Coll., 1951; Mus.B., New Eng. Conservatory Music, 1954; L.H.D., Boston U., 1969; m. Martin Luther King, Jr., June 18, 1953 (dec. Apr. 1968); children—Yolanda Denise, Martin Luther III, Dexter Scott, Bernice Albertine. Concert debut, Springfield, O., 1948, numerous concerts throughout U.S.; concerts India, 1959; performances Freedom Concert; voice instr. Morris Brown Coll., Atlanta, 1962; lectr., writer. Del. White House Conf. Children and Youth, 1960; sponsor Sane Nuclear Policy, Com. on Responsibility, Mobilization To End War in Viet Nam, 1966, 67, Margaret Sanger Meml. Found.; pres. Martin Luther King, Jr. Meml. Center; active YWCA. Bd. dirs. So. Christian Leadership Conf., Martin Luther King, Jr. Found. Gt. Britain; trustee Robert F. Kennedy Meml. Recipient Outstanding Citizenship award Montgomery (Ala.) Improvement Assn., 1959, Merit award St. Louis Argus, 1960, Distinguished Achievement award Nat. Orgn. Colored Women's Clubs, 1962, Louise Waterman Wise award Am. Jewish Congress Women's Aux., 1963, Myrtle Wreath award Cleve. Hadassah, 1965, Wateler Peace prize, 1968, numerous others; named Woman of Year, Utility Club N.Y.C., 1962, Woman of Year, Nat. Assn. Radio and TV Announcers, 1968. Mem. Nat. Council Negro Women (Ann. Brotherhood award, 1957), Women Strike for Peace (del. disarmanent conf. Geneva, Switzerland 1962, citation for work in peace and freedom 1963), Women's Orgn. Internat. League for Peace and Freedom, United Church Women (bd. mgrs.), Alpha Kappa Alpha (hon.). Baptist (mem. choir, guild adviser). Club: Links (Human Dignity and Human Rights award Norfolk chpt. 1964). Author: My Life With Martin Luther King, Jr., 1969. Home: 234 Sunset Av NW Atlanta GA 30314

KING, DAN MADISON, librarian; b. Muncie, Ind., Nov. 7, 1914; s. Arthur Daniel and Grace Hamilton (Campbell) K.; A.B., Hanover Coll., 1938; B.S. in L.S., Syracuse U., 1940; postgrad. McGill U., Ball State U., N.Y. U. Asst., Muncie (Ind.) Pub. Library, 1938-39; asst. reference dept. N.Y. Pub. Library, 1940; dist. supr. WPA Library Service Project, Indpls., 1940-42; asst. librarian in charge art sch. library Cooper Union, N.Y.C., 1942-43, librarian in charge, 1943-46; chief reference dept. Grand Rapids (Mich.) Pub. Library, 1946-48; asst. reference dept. N.Y. Pub. Library, 1948-49; librarian Minn. Hist. Soc., St. Paul, 1949-54; head librarian Ky. Wesleyan Coll., Owensboro, 1954—, now prof. library sci. Library cons. Tex. Gas Transmission Corp., Owensboro, Ky., 1960-61; mem. spl. coms. for coll. visitations So. Assn. Colls. and Schs., Atlanta, 1963—. Mem. Am., Spl. (chmn. nat. museum div. 1953-54), Southeastern, Ky. (pres. 1964-65) library assns., Phi Delta Theta. Presbyn. Club: Filson (Louisville). Contbr. articles to profl. jours. Home: 2313 S York St Owensboro KY 42301 Office: 3000 Frederica St Owensboro KY 42301

KING, DONALD ROY, govt. ofcl.; b. Lakewood, O., Jan. 22, 1927; s. Frank McKinley and Clare Karen (Peterson) K.; B.Sc., Baldwin Wallace Coll., 1949; M.Sc., Ohio State U., 1951, Ph.D., 1952; m. Virginia Hope Shauck, Dec. 20, 1947; children—Bruce D., Douglas M. Mem. faculty Tex. A. and M. U., College Station, 1953-63; research mgmt. specialist Dept. Agr., Washington, 1963-67; tech. asst. Office Sci. and Tech., Exec. Office Pres., Washington, 1967-70; sci. adviser State Dept., 1970—. Served with AUS, 1945-46. Recipient Meritorious Service award Dept. Agr., 1965. Mem. A.A.A.S., Entomol. Soc. Am., Profl. Entomologists Assn., Sigma Xi. Home: 8108 Kane Ct Alexandria VA 22308 Office: Environmental Affairs Dept State Washington DC 20520

KING, EDWARD DUNCAN, real estate co. exec.; b. Ga., Feb. 12, 1896; s. Alfred Fawcett and Leila (Sweat) K.; grad. Savannah High Sch.; m. Ruth Holmer, July 12, 1922; 1 son, Carl Duncan. Clk., Nat. Bank of Savannah, 1916-17, Furse & Lawton, cotton brokers, Savannah, 1917; asst. cashier Exchange Bank Savannah, 1919-22; with A.F. King & Son, realtors, Savannah, 1922—, pres., 1941—. Pres., Tax Payers Assn. Chatham County, Savannah, 1959—; treas. Pure Water Council, Savannah, 1962—; mem. Bd. Policy Liberty Lobby, Washington, Nat. Com. Against Fluoridation, Washington. Bd. dirs. Savannah Vol. Guards. Served with CAC, U.S. Army, 1917-19; AEF in France. Mem. Savannah Real Estate Bd., Ga. Assn. Real Estate Bds., Am. Legion, Vets. World War I U.S.A., Sons Confederate Vets., Conservatives. Baptist. Home: 321 E 52d St Savannah GA 31405 Office: 112 Congress St W Savannah GA 31401

KING, EDWIN WALLACE, educator; b. Melrose, Mass., Oct. 15, 1918; s. Edwin Wallace and Alice Pauline (Anderson) K.; B.S., U. Mass., 1941; M.S., Va. Poly. Inst., 1947; Ph.D., U. Ill., 1951; m. Flora Prussia Day, Dec. 22, 1951; children—Edwin Wallace, Philip Day. Instr., Va. Poly. Inst., Blacksburg, 1947-48; research asso. U. Wis., Madison, 1951-53; asst. prof. entomology Cornell Coll., Mt. Vernon, Ia., 1953-57; faculty Clemson (S.C.) U., 1957—, prof., 1966—. Served with San. Corps, AUS, 1942-46. Home: 105 Poole Lane Clemson SC 29631

KING, ELBERT AUBREY, JR., educator; b. Austin, Tex., Nov. 12, 1935; s. Elbert Aubrey and Vera (Barber) K.; B.S., U. Tex., 1957, M.A., 1961; Ph.D., Harvard, 1965; m. Peggy Jean Smothers, June 3, 1957; children—Lisa Marie, Cynthia Dawn. Geologist, NASA Manned Spacecraft Center, 1963-67, curator lunar samples, 1967-69; prof. geology, chmn. dept. U. Houston, 1969—. Lectr.; cons. space programs, geology, mineralogy; NASA lunar sample prin. investigator mineralogy and petrology for all Apollo sample missions; mem. Apollo 11 sample preliminary exam. team. Trustee Univs. Space Research Assos., 1973-74. NASA grantee, 1969—. Fellow Meteoritical Soc.; mem. Mineral. Soc. Am., Geol. Soc. Am. (Spl. commendation 1972), Am. Geophys. Union, Nat. Rifle Assn. Editor: Proc. Third Lunar Sci. Conf., vol. 1, 1972; asso. editor: Proc. Fourth Lunar Sci. Conf., 1973. Contbr. articles to tech. jours. Home: 602 Cedar Lane Seabrook TX 77586 Office: U Houston Houston TX 77004

KING, FRANK HENRY, mgmt. cons.; b. Washington, Aug. 31, 1918; s. Charles Henry and Julia (Fiorini) K.; B.S., Va. Poly. Inst., 1951; M.S., Okla. State U., 1958; M.B.A., Cal. Western U., 1964; m. Dorothy Elizabeth Earles, June 20, 1951; children—Vicki Faye, Donna Gale, Frank Gregory, Rodney Steven, David Patton, Robin Annice, Raymond Michael. Sr. staff devel. engr. USAF contract mgmt. div., Los Angeles, 1964-65; sr. staff reliability engr. U.S. Army Material Command, Gravelly Point, Va., 1965-66; tech. dir. value engring. Hdqrs. USAF Systems Command. Andrews AFB, Md., 1966-70; mgmt. cons., 1970—; lectr. in field. Served with AUS, 1943-46, USAF, 1953-62. Registered profl. engr., Okla. Mem. Soc. Am. Value Engrs. (dir.), Am. Def. Preparedness Assn., Omicron Delta Kappa, Sigma Tau. Pi Tau Sigma. Address: 4725 Pebble Bay Circle Vero Beach FL 32960

KING, FRANK PICKETT, state agrl. mus. dir.; b. Preston, Ga., Feb. 15, 1910; s. John Amos and Elizabeth Louise (Stevens) K.; B.S.A., U. Ga., 1932, M.S., 1935; Ph.D., Cornell, 1948; m. Eva Frances Rees, June 27, 1937; children—Janice (Mrs. Hansel Wilson Allen), Frances (Mrs. Joseph Asbury Haley). Field rep., farm loan div. Met. Life Ins. Co., Americus and Cordele Ga., Columbia, S.C., 1935-38; asso. prof. agrl. econs. U. Ga., Athens, 1938-48, prof., acting head dept., 1948-50; dir. Coastal Plain Expt. Sta., Tifton, Ga., 1950-73; dir. Ga. Agrirama living hist. farm and village and agrl. mus., Tifton, 1973—; dir. C&S Bank Tifton. Am. Cyanamid fellow, 1934-35; Gen. Edn. Bd. fellow, 1945-46; Found. for Econ. Edn. fellow, 1949. Mem. Am. Farm Econ. Assn., Soc. Agrl. Workers, Tift County C. of C. (past dir.), Alpha Zeta, Phi Kappa Phi, Gamma Sigma Delta. Baptist (deacon). Rotarian (past pres., dir.). Author: (with Paul W. Chapman) Efficient Farm Management, 1948; Better Farm Management, 1956. Home: 805 Wilson Av Tifton GA 31794 Office: Ga Agrirama Authority Tifton GA 31794

KING, G. JOSEPH, lawyer; b. S.I., N.Y., Sept. 4, 1940; s. Michael Joseph and Bertha E. (Plancon) K.; B.A., Manhattan Coll., 1963; A.M. in Econs., U. Notre Dame, 1964; J.D., Georgetown U., 1968; m. Elizabeth Watkins Wiefling, Mar. 22, 1969; 1 son, Michael Welden. Teaching asst. U. Notre Dame, 1963-64; internat. economist U.S. Tariff Commn., 1964-66; legislative asst. U.S. Dept. Interior, Washington, 1967; economist, bd. govs. Fed. Res. System, Washington, 1967-68; admitted to D.C. bar, 1970; law clk. to chief judge U.S. Dist. Ct. for N.J., 1968-69; law clk. to sr. judge U.S. Ct. Appeals for 3d Circuit, 1969-70; asso. Howrey, Simon, Baker & Murchison, Washington, 1970—. Lectr. econs. and internat. trade Wagner Coll., 1969-70. Mem. Am. Bar Assn., Bar Assn. D.C., Am. Econ. Assn., Phi Delta Phi. Home: 6666 32d St NW Washington DC 20015 Office: 1730 Pennsylvania Av NW Washington DC 20006

KING, GERALD LAMAR, investment co. exec.; b. Anniston, Ala., Apr. 12, 1922; s. Thomas Cobb and Sadie (Cox) K.; B.A., U. Ala., 1943, postgrad. in law, 1941-43; m. Martha Morrow Patton, July 29, 1943; children—Gerald Lamar, Thomas Patton, Martha Cox. With T.C. King Pipe & Foundry Co., Anniston, Ala., 1946-61, v.p., 1946-61, sec., 1946-61; partner T.C. King Co., Anniston, Ala., 1945-61; plant mgr. Anniston Soil Pipe div. U.S. Pipe & Fory Co., 1961—; pres. King Factors, Inc., Anniston, 1961—; dir. Anniston Nat. Bank. Commr. Anniston Airport Bd., 1955—. Trustee Stringfellow Meml. Hosp., Anniston. Served to capt. AUS, 1943-46; PTO. Mem. Nat. Planning Council, Alpha Tau Omega. Club: Anniston Country. Home: 8 Sunset Dr Anniston AL 36201 Office: Box 1148 Anniston AL 36201

KING, HARRY ROBERTSON, savs. and loan exec.; b. Louisville, Apr. 13, 1922; s. Harry Robertson and Grace Elizabeth (Ruter) K.; student Hanover Coll., 1942; certificate in credit mgmt. U. Louisville, 1953; m. Frances Lawton, Feb. 12, 1947; children—Harry Robertson III, Joseph L. Sec., Colonial Fed. Savs. & Loan Assn., Louisville, 1948-55, exec. v.p., 1955-57, pres., 1957-68, pres., chmn. bd., 1968—; dir. Dean Tire & Rubber Co. Campaign treas. Louisville and Jefferson County Republican Party, 1964-66. Pres., Louisville Theatrical Assn., 1964-65; v.p. Better Bus. Bur., 1958-60; bd. dirs. Ky. chpt. Arthritis Found., 1963-68; mem. pres.'s civic council Bellarmine Coll., 1970—. Served with USAAF, 1942-45; ETO. Mem. Ky. Savs. and Loan League (pres. 1965), Louisville Urban League, English Speaking Union. Episcopalian. Clubs: Louisville Boat, Pendennis. Home: 431 Country Lane Louisville KY 40207 Office: 3808 Lexington Rd Louisville KY 40207

KING, HERBERT I-TURN, hosp. exec.; b. Shanghai, China, May 27, 1936; s. Yu-I and Shee-Cheng (Chen) K.; B.A., Nat. Taiwan U., 1957; B.C.S., Seattle U., 1964; M.B.A., U. Wash., 1966; m. Peggy Young, July 4, 1964; children—Henry C., Patricia C. Came to U.S., 1959, naturalized, 1973. Accountant, Quinn & Calahan, Moses Lake, Wash., 1966-68; mgmt. systems programmer Lockheed Electronic Corp., Houston, 1968; mng. accountant Ernst & Ernst, Houston, 1968-69; dir. budget and analysis CCVI Hosp. Services, 14 hosps., Houston, 1969—. C.P.A., Tex. Mem. Am. Inst. C.P.A.'s, Tex. Soc. C.P.A.'s, Am. Mgmt. Assn., Hosp. Financial Mgmt. Assn. (dir. 1973-74). Club: Newport Country. Home: 18715 Martinique St Houston TX 77058 Office: 6400 Lawndale St Houston TX 77023

KING, HOWARD PICKETT, lawyer; b. Greenville, S.C., Apr. 13, 1939; s. William George and Maude Carrier (Pickett) K.; B.S. (Presdl. scholar), The Citadel, 1961; J.D., U. Tenn. and U. S.C., 1966; m. Nancy Leslie Ariail, Mar. 3, 1962; children—Nancy Leslie, Ariail Elizabeth. Admitted to S.C. bar, 1966, U.S. Supreme Ct. bar, 1973; mem. firm Bryan, Bahnmuller, King & Goldman and predecessor firms, Sumter, S.C., 1966—, partner, 1969—. Instr., U. S.C. extension at Shaw AFB, 1966-67, Sumter Area Tech. Edn. Center, 1968. Served as lt. AUS, 1961-63. Mem. Am., S.C. bar assns., S.C. State Bar, Assn. Am. Trial Lawyers, C. of C., Order Wig and Robe, Phi Delta Phi. Lion (dir.). Club: Sunset Country. Home: 7 Glendale Ct Sumter SC 29150 Office: 17 E Calhoun St Sumter SC 29150

KING, IRA JOE, dentist; b. Belgreen, Ala., May 7, 1905; s. William Robert and Mollie Jo (Hester) K.; student Auburn U., 1924, Birmingham So. Coll., 1929-30, Howard Coll., 1931; D.D.S., U. Louisville, 1937; m. Evelyn Lydia Smith, Nov. 2, 1937; children—Jo Ann (Mrs. Ronald Ray Simmons), Mollie (Mrs. Lewis McCoy Martin). Co. dentist West Blocton Coal Mines (Ala.), part time, 1937-41, McWane Cast Iron Pipe Co., Birmingham, Ala., part time 1939-56; individual practice dentistry, Birmingham, 1937—; mem. staff Children's Hosp., Birmingham, 1938-39. Vice pres., finance chmn. West End Little League, Birmingham, 1962-66. Mem. Jefferson County Sportsman's Assn. (v.p. 1960-61). Mason (Shriner). Home: 1549 Bay Av Birmingham AL 35211 Office: 1925 29th Av S Homewood AL 35209

KING, IRVIN RAY, physician; b. Gibson City, Tenn., Sept. 14, 1939; s. Lowell Russell and Vera Myrle (Hall) K.; student U. Tenn., Knoxville, 1957-61, M.D., Memphis, 1965; m. Jane Elizabeth Peters, Dec. 28, 1959; children—Steven Anthony, Lisa Gayle. Intern, U.Tenn., 1965-66; resident obstetrics and gynecology, 1968-71; pvt. practice ltd. to obstetrics and gynecology, Knoxville, 1971—. Served with USNR, 1966-68. Mem. E. Tenn. Obstet. and Gynecol. Soc., Knoxville Acad. Medicine, Tenn. Med. Assn., A.M.A. Home: 1810 Merchants Rd Knoxville TN 37912 Office: 4741 Broadway NE Knoxville TN 37918

KING, IVAN DEWITT, JR., engr., land surveyor; b. Enoree, S.C., Dec. 9, 1925; s. Ivan DeWitt and Clara (Montjoy) K.; B.S., Clemson U., 1949; m. Peggy Anne Eskew, July 6, 1946; children—Richard Kenneth, Bryan Theodore. Tng. program Va. Hwy. Dept. 1949-50, mem. research dept., 1950-51; partner Aldridge, Moon and King, cons. engring., Columbus, Ga., 1951-62; owner King Engring. Service, Winter Haven, Fla., 1962—. Served with USNR, 1942-46. Family named All-American Family from Ga., 1960. Mem. Winter Haven C. of C., Nat., Ga. (past pres. Columbus chpt.) socs. profl. engrs., Fla. Engring. Soc. (past pres. Ridge chpt.), Am. Soc. C.E., Ridge Chpt. Profl. Land Surveyors, Tau Beta Pi, Phi Kappa Phi. Baptist (deacon). Home: 558 E Lake Elbert Dr NE Winter Haven FL 33880 Office: 427 E Central Av Winter Haven FL 33880

KING, JAMES ALLEN, dentist; b. Dallas, Mar. 4, 1936; s. William Marion and Lillie Belle (Garrett) K.; B.A., North Tex. State Coll., 1958; D.D.S., Baylor U., 1962; m. Sally Ann Latlippe, Dec. 26, 1959; children—James Allen, John Andrew, Peter Daniel, Timothy Vincent. Individual practice dentistry, Irving, Tex., 1964—. Gen. dentist Dental Pub. Health, City of Dallas, 1968—. Bd. dirs. YMCA, 1972-74. Served with AUS, 1962-64. Mem. Am., Tex. dental assns., Dallas County Dental Soc., Irving Dental Study Club (sec.-treas. 1971-72, pres. 1972-73). Democrat. Methodist (mem. ofcl. bd. 1971-72). Rotarian. Home: 1944 Valley Oaks St Irving TX 75061 Office: 812 O'Connor St Irving TX 75061

KING, JAMES BILLY, computer services exec.; b. Jonesboro, Ark., June 5, 1924; s. George Edward and Lera Geneva (Jackson) K.; B.A. in Bus. Adminstrn., U. Miss., 1949; m. Dorothy Shively, Dec. 27, 1947; children—David William, Suzanne. Operations staff service bur. IBM, Memphis, 1949-53, marketing rep. data processing div., Omaha, 1954-58, account mgr. fed. systems div., Washington, 1959-62, account mgr. data processing div., Winston-Salem, N.C., 1962-68; v.p., dir. information services Integon Corp., Winston-Salem, 1969—; dir. Integon Computer Corp. Served with AUS, 1943-46. Mem. Am. Mgmt. Assn., Winston-Salem C. of C. Home: 819 Chester Rd Winston-Salem NC 27104 Office: 420 N Spruce St Winston-Salem NC 27102

KING, JAMES LAWRENCE, dist. judge; b. Miami, Fla., Dec. 20, 1927; s. James Lawrence and Viola (Clodfelter) K.; B.A. in Edn., U. Fla., 1949, LL.B., 1953; m. Mary F. Kapa, June 1, 1961; children—Lawrence Daniel, Kathryn Ann, Karen Ann, Mary Virginia. Admitted to Fla. bar, 1953; asso. firm Sibley & Davis, Miami, 1953, 55-57, partner Sibley, Giblin, King & Levenson, 1957-64; judge 11th Jud. Circuit, Miami, 1964-70; U.S. dist. judge, 1970—; asso. justice Supreme Ct. Fla., 1965; asso. judge Ct. Appeal, 3d Dist. 1965-66, 2d Dist., 1967, 4th Dist., 1968. Adv. com. jud. activities Jud. Conf. U.S., 1973—. Mem. state exec. council U. Fla., 1956-59; mem. Bd. Control Fla. Governing State Univs. and Colls., 1964. Served to 1st lt. USAF, 1953-55. Recipient Service award Presidents State Univs., 1965. Mem. Fla. Bar (pres. jr. bar sect. 1963-64, bd. govs. 1958-63, award of merit young lawyers sect. 1967), Am., Fla., Dade County, Miami Beach bar assns., Univ. Fla. Hall of Fame, Fla. Blue Key, Pi Kappa Tau, Phi Delta Phi. Democrat. Methodist. Club: University. Home: 11950 SW 67th Ct Miami FL 33138 Office: US Court House 300 NE 1st Av Miami Fl 33101

KING, LLOYD ELIJAH, JR., physician; b. Mayfield, Ky., Sept. 10, 1939; s. Lloyd Elijah and Mary Frances (Lowe) K.; B.A., Vanderbilt U., 1961; M.D., U. Tenn., 1967, Ph.D., 1970; m. Wanda Gail Waller, Dec. 28, 1968. Postdoctoral fellow U. Tenn., 1968-69; intern, City of Memphis hosps., 1969-70, resident in internal medicine, 1970-71; resident in dermatology U. Tenn. Grad. Sch. Med. Sci., Memphis, 1971-72, instr. anatomy dept., 1971-74, instr. dermatology, 1973—; postdoctoral fellow dermatology VA Hosp., Memphis, 1972-74. Served with USNR, 1961-63. Mem. Sigma Xi, Phi Chi, Sigma Alpha Epsilon. Democrat. Episcopalian. Home: 1667 Hapano Germantown TN 38138 Office: VA Hosp 1030 Jefferson Av Memphis TN 38103

KING, NAT BOZEMAN, lawyer; b. St. Louis, Nov. 9, 1907; s. Nat Kennard and Marie (Heisner) K.; B.S., Tex. Tech. U., 1929. Admitted to Tex. bar, 1932; gen. practice law Neel & King, Laredo, Tex., 1934-42; pvt. practice law, Laredo, 1963—; fgn. service officer, 1942-63; spl. asst. Guayaquil, Buenos Aires, Montevido, and London, 1942-46; attache, 1st sec., consul, Bern, 1947-48; 1st sec., consul, Paris, 1951-52; counselor, Praha, 1952-54; counselor econ. affairs, Baghdad, 1955-56; consul gen., Dacca, 1957-61; with Office Insp. Gen. Fgn. Assistance, U.S. Dept. State, 1962-63. U.S. del. Inter-Allied Reparation Agy., U.S. dep. commr. Tripartite Commn. for Restitution Monetary Gold, Brussels, 1949-50. Mason. Club: University (Washington). Home: Hamilton Hotel Laredo TX 78040 Office: Sames Moore Bldg Laredo TX 78040

KING, RALPH BUXTON, JR., dentist; b. Greenwood, Miss., Apr. 24, 1933; s. Ralph Buxton and Eunice Francis (Jones) K.; student La. Poly. Inst., 1951-52, La. State U., 1952-53; D.D.S., U. Tenn., 1956; m. Mary Lee Banner, Nov. 24, 1956; children—Anne Jones, Mary Winston. Dentist Va. Health Dept., 1956-57; individual practice dentistry, Monroe, La., 1959—. Served with AUS, 1957-59, 61-62. Fellow Am. Coll. Dentists; mem. Am., La. dental assns., Am. Assn. Endodontists, So. Endodontic Study Group, Fifth Dist. Dental Soc. (pres. 1959), Kappa Alpha, Psi Omega. Presbyn. (elder, deacon 1961—). Club: Bayou DeSiard Country (dir. 1971—) (Monroe). Home: 2202 Island Dr Monroe LA 71201 Office: 1101 Royal Av Monroe LA 71201

KING, ROBERT THOMAS, editor; b. Hillside, N.J., Oct. 29, 1930; s. Philip Arthur and Lucy (Davis) K.; ed. Emmanuel Coll. at Cambridge, Eng., 1948-50; B.A., Birmingham (Eng.) U., 1954; postgrad. Shakespeare Inst., Stratford-Upon-Avon, Eng., 1954-55. Trainee Oxford U. Press., N.Y.C., 1957-59; chief copy editor N.Y. U. Press, N.Y.C., 1959-61, editor 1961-63, mng. editor, 1963-66; dir. U. S.C. Press, Columbia, 1966—. Club: Grolier. Home: 1520 Senate St Columbia SC 29201 Office: University Press Columbia SC 29208

KING, ROLLIN WHITE, airline co. exec.; b. Cleve., Apr. 10, 1931; s. Warren Griffin and Elizabeth (White) K.; student Choate Sch., 1946-48; student Cornell U., Ithaca, N.Y., 1950-54; B.A., Western Res. U., 1955; M.B.A., Harvard, 1962; m. Marcia Gygli, May 10, 1956 (div.); children—Rollin White, Edward Prescott. Mem. mgmt. staff NSA, Washington, 1955-60; v.p. King, Pitman Co., investment counsel, San Antonio, 1962-63; pres. Southwest Airlines, Inc., San Antonio, 1963-68; exec. v.p. operation, dir. Southwest Airlines Co., Dallas, 1967—. Cons. air transp. Dept. Communication Royal Thai Govt., Bangkok, 1969. Served with AUS; 1956-58. Mem. San Antonio Livestock Exposition (bd. dirs.). Clubs: Harvard Club N.Y.C.; Harvard of Dallas, The St. Anthony (San Antonio). Address: Apt 1137 15301 Preston Rd Dallas TX 75240

KING, RUFUS, lawyer; b. Seattle, Mar. 25, 1917; s. Rufus Gunn and Marian (Towle) K.; A.B., Princeton, 1938; post. Stanford, 1940-41; LL.B., Yale, 1943; m. Janice L. Chase, June 15, 1941 (div. June 1951); children—Rufus, Agnes S.; m. 2d, Elvine R. Rankine. Instr. Princeton, 1938-39; admitted to N.Y. bar, 1944, D.C. bar, 1948, Md. bar, 1953; partner Rice and King, Washington, 1953-63; pvt. practice in Washington, 1965—; counsel Senate Crime Com., 1951, also other congl. coms.; cons. Pres.'s Commn. Law Enforcement and Adminstrn. Justice, 1966-67. Chmn. joint com. narcotic drugs Am. Bar Assn. and A.M.A., 1956—; chmn. disaster protection com. Washington Bd. Trade, 1956-58; chmn. D.C. Com. on Pub. Schs., 1956-57; pres. Montgomery County Community Psychiat. Clin., 1963-65. Mem. Am. (chmn. criminal law sect. 1957-60, sec. 1954-57, mem. ho. dels. 1960—, spl. com. minimum standards adminstrn. justice 1965—), N.Y., Md. bar assns., Bar Assn. D.C., Am. Law Inst., Scribes (pres. 1968—). Clubs: Princeton (N.Y.), Nassau, Colonial (Princeton); Metropolitan, Lawyers (Washington); American (Miami, Fla.). Author: Gambling and Organized Crime, 1969; The Drug Hang-Up, 1972. Contbr. articles profl. jours. Home: 3524 Williamsburg Lane NW Washington DC 20008 Office: Woodward Bldg Washington DC 20005

KING, STEVEN CLARENCE, govt. ofcl.; b. Plainfield, N.H., Dec. 12, 1921; s. Clarence W. and Flora Belle (Rogers) K.; B.S., U. N.H., 1947; M.S., Cornell U., 1951, Ph.D., 1953; m. Dorothy C. Fentress, Feb. 14, 1967; children (by previous marriage)—Gordon S., Nancy E. Foreman Ken-La Farms, Claremont, N.H., 1947-48; geneticist Fuzzydele Farms, Elverson, Pa., 1948-49; asst. prof. Cornell U., 1953-55, asso. prof. 1955-56; animal geneticist U.S. Dept. Agr., Lafayette, Ind., 1956-59; geneticist Mt. Hope Farm, Batavia, N.Y., 1959-60; br. chief poultry U.S. Dept. Agr., 1960-63, asst. dir. animal husbandry div., 1963-64, staff scientist, 1964-66, asst. dir. animal husbandry div., 1966-68, asst. dir. research devel. and evaluation staff, 1968-70, dep. adminstr. Agrl. Research Service, 1970—. Served to capt. USAAF, 1943-46. Decorated Air medal with oak leaf cluster. Fellow A.A.A.S.; mem. Poultry Sci. Soc., World's Poultry Sci. Soc., Am. Inst. Biol. Sci. Contbr. articles to profl. jours. Home: 12601 Meadowood Dr Silver Spring MD 20904 Office: Beltsville Agrl Research Center Beltsville MD 20705

KING, VORIS, wholesale grocery co. exec.; b. Lake Charles, La., Jan. 20, 1917; s. Alvin Olin and Willie Lee (Voris) K.; student U. South, 1934-36; m. Frances Thompson, Dec. 19, 1935; children—Charles Stirling, Virginia Lee (Mrs. Sanford Ayres), William Voris, Alvin Bardine. Sec. King Corp., Lake Charles 1958-68; v.p. Little Lake Misere Corp., Lake Charles, 1958—; pres., gen. mgr. Kelly, Weber & Co., Inc., Lake Charles, 1961—; pres. Lake Charles Grain & Grocer Co., Inc., 1961—; dir. Am. Bank Commerce. Chmn. 7th dist. La. U.S.O., 1953—, nat. dir., 1969—; pres. Calcasieu-Cameron chpt. A.R.C., 1957, Calcasieu Area Safety Council, 1960, Lake Charles Marina Bd., 1964; pres. Orange Grove-Graceland Cemetery Assn., 1968—; mem. adv. bd. Salvation Army, 1964-70, adv. bd. laymen Lake Charles Seamen's Center, Inc., 1964—, adv. council area 3 Civil Def., 1953—, Lake Charles Sr. Civilian Adv. Council, 1953—. Bd. dirs. S.S.S., S.W. dist. Fat Stock Show and Rodeo, Inc., Lake Charles Civic Symphony, Calcasieu Area council Boy Scouts Am., Lake Charles chpt. Nat. Conf. Christians and Jews, La. Heart Assn., Calcasieu Parish Heart Fund Assn., McNeese State U. Found.; trustee Centenary Coll. La., 1972—. Served with USNR, 1943-45. Recipient Outstanding Citizen award Lake Charles Salvation Army, 1964, Brotherhood award Nat. Conf. Christians and Jews, 1972. Mem. U.S. (v.p. 1962—), La. (pres. 1952) wholesale grocers assns., Lake Charles Assn. Commerce (civic award 1960, pres. 1964), Better Bus. Bur. (pres. 1958), La. Tourist Assn., Blue Key. Methodist (chmn. bd. trustees 1965—). Mason (32 deg., Shriner), Odd Fellow, Rotarian, Elk. Clubs: Lake Charles Golf and Country; Pioneer, Contraband Citizens' Band (pres. 1962), Coastal (dir.). Home: PO Box 28 Lake Charles LA 70601 Office: Box 1120 Lake Charles LA 70601

KING, WILLIAM C., accountant; b. Stockdale, Tex., Oct. 9, 1911; s. William H. and Neppie (Ware) K.; B.B.A., Baylor U., 1936; postgrad. St. Mary's Law Sch., 1938-39; m. Mayme Johnson, Sept. 15, 1945; children—Kathleen (Mrs. Ronald Koehler), William E. Office mgr. A.B. Frank Co., 1936-42; supr. Ernst & Ernst, San Antonio, 1945-51; pvt. practice pub. accounting, San Antonio, 1951—. Served with USNR, 1942-45; ETO. C.P.A., Tex. Mem. Am. Inst. C.P.A.'s, Tex. Soc. C.P.A.'s. Presbyn. (elder, trustee). Odd Fellow (grand noble 1954, trustee 1971). Home: 443 Oak Glen Dr San Antonio TX 78209 Office: 1802 NE Loop 410 San Antonio TX 78217

KING, WILLIAM HAMPTON, accountant, state ofcl.; b. Heidelberg, Miss., Oct. 1, 1909; s. William E. and Sarah E. (Covington) K.; student Hinds Jr. Coll., 1925-28; B.A., U. Miss., 1930; postgrad. YMCA Grad. Sch., Nashville, 1930-33; m. Eldridge Douglas Banks, July 6, 1934; children—Carolyn Douglas (Mrs. E.J. Andrew), Sarah Kathryn (Mrs. Joe Miklas). Social worker Tenn. Transient Bur. and Resettlement Adminstrn., Nashville, Crossville, 1934-35; cannery mgr. Homesteads Co-op Assn., Crossville, 1935-39; instr. social studies Clarke Jr. Coll., Newton, Miss., 1940; transp. supr. U.S. War Dept., Flora, Miss., 1941-44; accountant Woods Bldg. Supply Co., Jackson, Miss., 1945-47, Scott Bldg. Supply & Allied Corps., Cleveland, Miss., 1947-53; staff auditor Miss. Dept. Audit, Jackson, 1953-55, asst. dir., 1956-61, dir., 1962-63; auditor pub. accounts State of Miss., Jackson, 1964—. C.P.A., Miss. Mem. Am. Inst. C.P.A.'s, Miss. Soc. C.P.A.'s (pres. Jackson chpt. 1959), Nat. Assn. State Auditors, Controllers and Treasurers (treas. 1969, pres. 1973), Municipal Finance Officers Assn., Little Theatre of Jackson, Jackson Music Assn., Jackson Symphony League. Democrat. Methodist (ofcl. bd.). Mason. Clubs: Knife and Fork (dir. 1969-72), Optimist (pres. 1969-70, lt. gov. 1970-71) (Jackson, Miss.). Home: 404 Colonial Circle Jackson MS 39211 Office: PO Box 1060 Sillers State Office Bldg Jackson MS 39205

KING, WILLIAM RILEY, banker; b. Pineville, La., Dec. 15, 1934; s. William R. and Gertrude (Dillon) K.; student La. State U., 1953-54; B.B.A., La. Coll., 1960; m. Lynn Louise Bagley, Mar. 28, 1959; children—Robert, Donald. Mgmt. trainee Rapides Bank, Alexandria, La., 1958-60; asst. credit mgr. Sears Roebuck & Co., Dallas, 1960-63; asst. credit mgr. Titche-Goettinger, Dallas, 1963-65; v.p., exec. officer retail credit div. Preston State Bank of Dallas, 1965-72, v.p., dir. marketing, 1972—. Instr., Dallas Inst. Retailing, 1963—, adult div. Dallas Jr. Coll., 1964—. Dir. Nat. Credit Card Sch. for Bankers. Served with USMCR, 1953-57. Fellow Soc. Certified Consumer Credit Execs.; mem. Internat. Consumer Credit Assn. (dir. 1967-71), Charge Account Bankers Assn. (dir. 1971-72), Consumer Credit Assn. Dallas (pres. 1970), Tex. Consumer Credit Assn. (v.p. 1970), Bank Marketing Assn. (v.p. chpt. 1973-74), Dallas, S.W. football ofcls. assns., Sales and Marketing Execs. Dallas. Kiwanian. Office: PO Box 12000 Dallas TX 75225 Home: 11320 Buchanan Dr Dallas TX 75228

KING, WILLIS, ret. govt. ofcl.; b. Fayette County, O., May 24, 1908; s. Harry J. and Alma F. (Dobbins) K.; B.Sc. in Edn., Wilmington Coll., 1929; M.A., Haverford Coll., 1930; Ph.D., U. Cin., 1939; D.Sc., N.C. State U., 1968; m. Frances Hall, June 8, 1935; children—Stephen H., Susan F. (Mrs. Jerry C. Tash), Christopher W. Wildlife technician Great Smoky Mountains Nat. Park, Gatlinburg, Tenn., 1934-40; chief fishery biologist N.C. Wildlife Resources Commn., Raleigh, 1940-49; with Tenn. Game and Fish Commn., Nashville, 1949-51; with U.S. Fish and Wildlife Service, 1951-57, asst. regional dir., Atlanta, 1955-57; chief div. fishery services Bur. Sport Fisheries and Wildlife, U.S. Dept. Interior, Washington, 1957-71, asst. dir., 1971-73. Served to lt. USNR, 1944-45. Mem. Am. Fisheries Soc. (hon.), Am. Inst. Biol. Scis., Sigma Xi. Contbr. articles to publs. Home: 5336 Wapakoneta Rd Washington DC 20016

KING, WILLIS ALONZO, JR., dentist; b. Sussex, N.J., Aug. 19, 1941; s. Willis Alonzo and Louise (Collins) K.; student Clemson U., 1958-61; D.D.S., Emory U., 1965, M.S.D., 1969; m. Emily Florilla Willis, Aug. 25, 1961; children—Angela Renee, Michael Willis, Christine Lynn. Individual practice children's dentistry, Greenville, S.C., 1969—. Cons. child care groups, 1969—. Served to capt. Dental Corps, AUS, 1965-67. Recipient award Am. Soc. Dentistry for Children, 1965. Mem. Am. Soc. Preventive Dentistry, Am. Soc. Dentistry for Children, Am. Acad. Pedodontics, Am., S.C. dental assns., Southeastern Soc. Pedodontics, Greenville County (sec.-treas. 1970, v.p. 1973, pres. 1974), Piedmont Dist. dental socs., Omicron Kappa Upsilon. Presbyn. Home: 5 Donington Dr Greenville SC 29607 Office: 25 Sweetbriar Rd Greenville SC 29607

KING, WOODROW WILSON, forester; b. Bethlehem, Pa., Sept. 27, 1914; s. Robert Charles and Sara Josephine (Levering) K.; B.S., Pa. State U., 1942; M.F., Duke, 1948; m. Minnie Elizabeth Talley, Dec. 21, 1947; children—Robert Dwight, Pamela Janette. Jr. asst. forester TVA, Asheville, N.C. and Chattanooga, Tenn., 1944-47, staff forester, 1955-62, supr. timber harvesting and processing, Norris, Tenn., 1963—; dist. forester Ky. Div. Forestry, Mayfield, 1948; wood utilization technologist Tex. Forest Service, Lufkin, 1949-52, acting head forest products lab., 1953-54. Mem. Norris Vol. Fire Dept., 1955-60. Served to lt. inf., AUS, 1942-44. Decorated Bronze Star Citation (France). Mem. Soc. Am. Foresters (sec.-treas. Deep South sect. 1950), Forest Products Research Soc. (chmn. Mid-South sect. 1966), Soc. Wood Sci. and Tech., Xi Sigma Pi. Co-author: Manual of Southern Forestry, 1954. Home: 10 Dairypond Rd Norris TN 37828 Office: TVA Forestry Bldg Norris TN 37828

KINGERY, JIMMIE LYNN, statistician; b. Enid, Okla., Nov. 2, 1939; s. Elwood Perry and Vera (Nelson) K.; B.S. in Edn., East Central State Coll., 1964; M.S., U. Okla., 1968; m. Judy Kay Thomas, Jan. 23, 1965; children—Melinda, Deborah. Data processing operations mgr. U. Okla. Med. Center, 1967-68; math. statistician, dir. computer operations Robert S. Kerr Environmental Research Lab., Ada, Okla., 1968—; mayor, Ada, 1973-74; adj. prof. computer sci. East Central State Coll. City councilman, Ada, 1972-74. Served with USMCR, 1958-60. Mem. Am. Statis. Assn. Kiwanian. Home: 505 Webb St Ada OK 74820 Office: Box 1198 Ada OK 74820

KINGMAN, EDWARD ROCKWELL, banker; b. Somerville, Mass., Jan. 2, 1917; s. Stanley Russell and Grace (Rockwell) K.; A.S.A. with honors, Bentley Coll. Accounting and Finance, 1936; B.B.A. with high honors, Northeastern U., 1951, M.B.A. with high honors, 1955; M.A. with honors, George Washington U., 1955; m. Margaret Hooker, Aug. 9, 1946; children—Edward R., Nancy Margaret. Dir., pres. Security Small Bus. Investment Co., Arlington, Va., 1963-69; exec. v.p., dir. Anderson-Stokes Inc., Rehoboth Beach, Del., 1971-73; pres., chief exec. officer Atlantic Nat. Bank, Ocean City, Md., 1974—; treas., dir. Second Nat. Bldg. & Loan, Ocean City, 1972-74; prin. Kingman Assos. Financial Cons. and Real Estate Brokers, Arlington, 1965—; guest lectr. Navy Financial Mgmt. Program George Washington U., 1955-62. Chmn., Arlington Bd. Edn., 1967; dir., treas. Nat. Assn. Partners of Alliance, 1967-69; v.p., treas. The Nature Conservancy, Washington, 1968-71. Bd. dirs. Navy Supply Corps Found.; trustee Civil Service Retirement Fund, Arlington, 1967-70, U.S. Navy Supply Corps Found., 1972—; adv. council Conservation Trust of P.R., 1971—. Served to capt. USN, 1941-63; ret., 1963. Mem. Govs. Trade Commn. Brazil, Am. Inst. Banking (Va. legislative adv. com. 1965-66), Va. Edn. Assn., Nat. Sch. Bds. Assn., Nat. Assn. Mil. Comptrollers (nat. v.p. 1962-63). Home: 4851 35th Rd N Arlington VA 22207 Office: 48 Rehoboth Av Rehoboth Beach DE 19971

KINGREA, CHARLES LEO, petrochem. supt.; b. Barren Springs, Va., Aug. 17, 1923; s. Shirley Leonard and Lena Rose (Williams) K.; B.S., Va. Poly. Inst., 1943, M.S., 1951, Ph.D., 1953; m. Lola Margaret McCreary, Mar. 15, 1946; children—Richard Owen, David Leonard, Kay Ann. Owner, mgr. Kingrea Milling Co., Narrows, Va., 1946-53; process devel. engr., mgr. Ethyl Corp., Baton Rouge, 1953-68, gen. supt. operations, Pasadena, Tex., 1968—; tchr., research fellow Va. Poly. Inst., 1951-53. Served from 2d lt. to capt., AUS, 1943-46. Tenn. Eastman research fellow, 1952-53. Mem. Sigma Xi, Tau Beta Pi, Phi Lambda Upsilon. Club: Clear Lake Home: 4022 Laurel Grove St Seabrook TX 77586 Office: Box 472 Pasadena TX 77501

KINLAW, DENNIS FRANKLIN, coll. pres.; b. Lumberton, N.C., June 26, 1922; s. Wade Hampton and Sally (Burney) K.; A.B., Ashbury Coll., Wilmore, Ky., 1943; B.D., Asbury Theol. Sem., 1946; grad. student Princeton Theol. Sem., 1953-55, New Coll., U. Edinburgh (Scotland), 1955; M.A., Brandeis U., 1961, Ph.D. in Mediterranean Studies, 1967; LL.D., Houghton (Mich.) Coll., 1971; m. Elsie Katherine Blake, Dec. 31, 1943; children—Elizabeth Ann (Mrs. Alan Coppedge), Dennis Franklin, Katherine. Ordained to ministry Methodist Ch., 1951; pastor N.C. Conf., 1949-53, Loudonville, N.Y., 1955-61; vis. prof. Seoul (Korea) Theol. Coll., 1959; asso. prof., then prof. O.T. langs. and lit. Asbury Theol. Sem., 1963-68; pres. Asbury Coll., 1968—. Mem. Ky. ann. conf. United Meth. Ch. Recipient Distinguished Alumnus award Asbury Theol. Sem., 1961. Mem. Soc. Bibl. Lit., Evang. Theol. Soc., Am. Acad. Religion, Nat., Ky. edn. assns., Am. Assn. Higher Edn., Am. Sch. Oriental Research, Commmn. Higher Edn. Ky. Author: Ecclesiastes and Song of Solomon, Wesley Biblical Commentary, Vol. II, 1968. Editor: (Kenneth Geiger) Word and Doctrine, 1966, Further Holiness Insights, 1964; One Divine Moment, 1970. Home: 404 Akers Av Wilmore KY 40390

KINLAW, MURRAY CARLYLE, JR., banker; b. Lumberton, N.C., Jan. 11, 1941; s. Murray C. and Jackie (Worsley) K.; B.S., Wake Forest Coll., 1963; M.B.A., U. N.C., 1965; m. May Olivia Boney, June 5, 1965; children—Murray Carlyle III. Financial analyst, trust account portfolio mgr. Wachovia Bank & Trust Co., Winston-Salem, N.C., 1965—, asst. v.p., 1971-74, v.p., 1974—. Chmn. small bus. Forsyth County Heart Assn., 1973—; active United Fund, Forsyth County, N.C. Served with AUS, 1967-68. Mem. Am. Inst. Bankers, N.C. (treas. 1973—), Atlanta socs. financial analysts. Democrat. Presbyn. Home: 2639 Forest Dr Winston Salem NC 27104 Office: PO Box 3099 Winston-Salem NC 27102

KINNAIRD, JOHN MORROW, lawyer; b. Lancaster, Ky., Apr. 11, 1921; s. John Gill and Margaret (Morrow) K.; LL.B., U. Ky., 1948; m. Sarah Anne Denny, Aug. 9, 1942; children—Ann Margaret, Patsy McKee, Jula Jordan. Admitted to Ky. bar, 1948; pvt. practice firm Denny & Kinnaird, Nicholasville, Ky., 1948-55; asst. atty gen., Ky., 1948-49; gen. counsel Ky. State Police, 1949-50; asst. commr. Dept. Motor Transp., Ky., 1950-51, commr. motor transp., 1951-55; asst. to v.p. Consol. Freightways, Inc., Arlington, Va., 1956-58, v.p., 1958-61; admitted to D.C. bar, 1961; practiced law, D.C., 1961—; counsel Galland, Kharasch, Calkins & Lippman, Washington, 1961-65; partner firm Rea, Cross, Knebel & Kinnaird, Washington, 1965-67; exec. sec. Com. Transp. Practices of Nat. Motor Freight Traffic Assn., 1962-67; spl. counsel Am. Trucking Assn., Inc., 1967-69, asst. chief counsel pub. affairs, 1969—, v.p. govt. relations div., 1971—. Served as officer USAAF, World War II. Decorated D.F.C. with oak leaf cluster, Air medal. Mem. Am., Ky. bar assns., Motor Carrier Lawyers Assn., ICC Practitioners Assn., Am. Soc. Traffic and Transp., Transp. Assn. Am. (dir.), Phi Delta Phi, Sigma Alpha Epsilon. Presbyn. (elder). Mason. Clubs: Nat. Lawyers, Belle Haven Country; Litchfield Country (Pawleys Island, S.C.). Home: 7108 Park Terrace Dr Alexandria VA 22307 Office: 1616 P St NW Washington DC 20036

KINNAMON, KENNETH ELLIS, biologist; b. Denison, Tex., May 28, 1934; s. William Ellis and Mary (McGill) K.; B.S., Okla. State U., 1955; D.V.M., Tex. A. and M. U., 1959; M.S., U. Rochester, 1961; Ph.D., U. Tenn., 1971; m. Carolyn Anne Cline, June 7, 1957; children—Jon Kenneth, Keith B., Clark D. Lab. officer radiochemistry Walter Reed Army Inst. Research, Washington, 1959-60; chief radioisotope lab. U.S. Army Med. Research and Nutrition Lab., Denver, 1961-65; chief dept. surveillance inspection U.S. Army Med. Dept. Vet. Sch., Chgo., 1965-68, chief vet. tech. liaison team, 1968; chief dept. biology Walter Reed Army Inst. Research, Washington, 1972—; cons. U.S. Army Surgeon Gen., 1972—. Served with AUS, 1959—. Mem. Radiation Research Soc., Internat. Soc. Exptl. Hematology, A.A.A.S., Am. Vet. Med. Assn., Am. Sci. Assn. Home: 12613 Montclair Dr Silver Spring MD 20904 Office: Dept Biology Walter Reed Army Inst Research Washington DC 20412

KINNAN, ROY FRANK, sales exec.; b. Tulsa, Nov. 9, 1915; s. Ralph P. and Dessie J. (Wilson) K.; student U. Tex., 1935-37; m. Mary Emma Paternostro, Mar. 8, 1938; children—Ann Carol (Mrs. John R. Helton), Pamela Kay. Engr., salesman Oil Well Supply Co., Dallas, 1938-41; sales engr. Gates Rubber Co,, Tulsa, 1941-55, sales mgr., Okla. and Ark., 1956-61, southwest sales mgr., Dallas, 1962—. Named Outstanding Nat. Dist. Mgr., 1966. Mem. Dallas C. of C. Methodist. Mason (32 deg.), Toastmaster (award 1963). Royal Oaks Country. Home: 4718 Forest Bend Rd Dallas TX 75234 Office: 1030 Dragon St Dallas TX 75207

KINNEBREW, JACKSON ALLENDER, pub. accountant; b. Pauls Valley, Okla., Aug. 14, 1915; s. Jackson Alvin and Dorella (Allender) K.; A.B., U. Okla., 1935; m. Mary Lucille Metcalfe, Feb. 27, 1940; children—Jackson Metcalfe, James Alvin, Mary Louise. Vice pres. Kinnebrew Motor Co., Oklahoma City, 1935-41, Denison Motor Co., 1946-51; farmer, Pauls Valley, 1951-64; pub. accountant Jack Kinnebrew, 1961-72; partner Kinnebrew & Readnour, Pauls Valley, 1972—. Served with AUS, 1941-46. Mem. Am. Inst. C.P.A.'s, Okla. Soc. C.P.A.'s, C. of C. (dir., treas. 1963—), Phi Beta Kappa, Beta Theta Pi. Presbyn. Mason (32 deg., Shriner), Elk. Home: 200 Rennie Rd Pauls Valley OK 73075 Office: 110 W Paul St Pauls Valley OK 73075

KINNEY, ABBOTT FORD, radio broadcasting exec.; b. Los Angeles, Nov. 11, 1909; s. Gilbert Earl and Mabel (Ford) K.; student Ark. Coll., 1923, 26, 27; m. Dorothy Lucille Jeffers, Sept. 19, 1943; children—Colleen, Joyce, Rosemary. Editor Dermott News, 1934-39; partner Delta Drug Co., 1940-49; pres., gen. mgr. S.E. Ark. Broadcasters, Inc., Dermott and McGhee, 1951—; corr. Comml. Appeal, Memphis, Ark. Gazette, Little Rock, 1935-53; research early aeronautics Inst. Aero. Scis., 1941, castor bean prodn., 1941-42; mem. bd. McGhee-Dermott Indsl. Devel. Corp. Mem. Ark. Geol. and Conservation Commn., 1959-63, Ark. State Planning Commn. 1963—; mem. Miss. River Parkway Commn.; exec. bd. DeSoto Area Council Boy Scouts Am.; past pres. Hosp. Adv. Bd.; mem. Chicot Fair Assn. Bd., Park Commn.; chmn. Chicot County Library Bd. Recipient Silver Beaver award Boy Scouts Am. Mem. Nat. Assn. Radio and TV Broadcasters, Ark. Broadcasters Assn. Ark. (charter mem. Ark. Econ. Council), S.E. Ark. (charter) chambers commerce, Ark. Hist. Assn. (charter), Am. Numis. Assn., A.I.M., Chicot County Hist. Soc. (charter). Rotarian (past pres., sec.). Adv. editorial bd. Internat. Broadcasters Soc. Home: Dermott AR 61738 Office: Dermott AR 61738 also McGhee AR 71654

KINNEY, BURTON CHESTER, motor carrier exec.; b. Worcester, Mass., Sept. 15, 1917; s. Alfred R. and Edith (Creamer) K.; student Biltmore Jr. Coll., 1937; LaSalle Extension U., 1944; m. Mary Elizabeth Jennings, Sept. 3, 1948; children—Caroline (Mrs. William Michael McConochie), Betty (Mrs. Robert Dempsey), Anita Jeanne (Mrs. Dan Thornton). With Ga. Hwy. Express, Inc., Atlanta, 1943-58, successively rate clk., chief rate clk., overcharge claim agt., asst. traffic mgr., 1948-53, gen. traffic mgr., 1953-58; gen. traffic mgr. Terminal Transport Co., Inc., Atlanta, 1958, v.p. traffic, 1958—. Mem. Central and So. Motor Freight Tariff Assn. (dir. 1965-73), Transp. Club Atlanta (pres. 1955), Nat. Classification Com., I.C.C. Practitioners Assn. (chpt. chmn. 1956), Traffic Clubs Internat. (dir. 1957-66, regional v.p. 1966-70), Am. Soc. Traffic and Transp. (pres. Atlanta chpt. 1973, certified), Fla. Trucking Assn., So. Shipper and Motor Carrier Council (pres. 1969-70), Nat. Assn. Shipper-Motor Carrier Confs. (v.p. 1972), Delta Nu Alpha (chpt. pres. 1955, regional nat. v.p. 1957-61). Home: 406 Homestead Rd Rex GA 30273 Office: 248 Chester Av SE Atlanta GA 30316

KINNEY, DOUGLAS MERRILL, geologist; b. Los Angeles, Feb. 24, 1917; s. Douglas Mudge and Elisabeth Brier (Stratton) K.; B.A., Occidental Coll., 1937; M.S., Yale, 1942, Ph.D., 1951; m. Jeanette Elizabeth Dawless, Mar. 21, 1942; children—Douglas Merrill, Frederick D., Deborah J. Geologist Union Oil Co., Cal. and Rocky Mountain states, 1937-40; geologist U.S. Geol. Survey, Ark., Mo., Utah, Cal. and Colo., 1942-73, geologic map editor, 1956—. Vice pres. for N.Am. of Commn. Geol. Map of the World. Fellow Geol. Soc. Am.; mem. Geol. Soc. Washington (pres. 1973), Am. Assn. Petroleum Geologists, Phi Beta Kappa, Sigma Xi. Home: 5221 Baltimore Av Washington DC 20016 Office: U S Geological Survey Sunrise Dr Reston VA 22092

KINNEY, ROBERT LEROY, real estate exec.; b. Everett, Wash., Apr. 21, 1938; s. Audrey Ralph and Vera (Davis) K.; student Purdue U., 1956-57; B.B.A. with honors, U. Hawaii, 1960; m. Carol Elizabeth Webster, Aug. 5, 1961; children—Daniel Bryan, Andre Renard. Asst. to pres. Mt. Vernon Sand & Gravel Co. (Wash.), 1960-61; asst. to v.p. commr. and indsl. real estate div. Del E. Webb Corp., Phoenix, 1962-64; v.p. Lomas & Nettleton Financial Corp., Dallas, 1965-69; pres. subsidiary cos. Lomas & Nettleton Properties, Inc., 9900 Meml. Inc., Imperial Interiors, Inc., Dallas, 1967-68, pres. subsidiary Vistamar, Inc., San Juan, P.R., 1968; pres., dir., chief exec. Caribbean Equities Corp., St. Croix, V.I., 1969—. Mem. Photog. Soc. Am., Am. Mus. Natural History, Nat. Audubon Soc., U. Hawaii Found., Phi Kappa Phi. Home: Estate La Grande Princess Christiansted St Croix VI 00820 Office: PO Box 871 Christiansted St Croix VI 00820

KINNISON, PAUL, JR., architect; b. San Antonio, June 3, 1938; s. Paul and Margaret Virginia (Saunders) K.; B.Arch., Tex. A. and M. U., 1961; m. Trudy Jo Chance, Dec. 15, 1967. Mem. firm, O'Neil Ford & Assos., San Antonio, 1966-68, pvt. practice Paul Kinnison Jr., San Antonio, 1968—. Bd. dirs. San Antonio Community Housing Devel. Corp. Served with AUS, 1961-63. Mem. A.I.A. (pres. San Antonio chpt. 1974), Tex. Soc. Architects. Methodist. Address: 418 W French Pl San Antonio TX 78212

KINNON, BOBBY RAY, banker; b. Kountze, Tex., Aug. 29, 1939; s. Ray and Dorothy Lee (Thompson) K.; prestandard certificate, Am. Inst. Banking, 1968, gen. certificate, 1973; m. Kathryn Jeannette Broussard, Aug. 1, 1968; children—Dena, Donna, Deanna, Danita, Dana. Carpenter, Kountze, Tex., 1958-60; then engaged in communications Tex. Dept. Pub. Safety, Beaumont; with Peoples State Bank, Kountze, Tex., 1960-64; with Citizens State Bank, Woodville, Tex., 1965—, cashier, security officer, 1969-74, v.p., cashier, 1974—. Active various coms. Western Weekend and Dogwood Festival, Woodville, 1966—; scoutmaster Boy Scouts Am., Woodville, 1967—; recipient Scouters award, 1970. Named Boss of Year Tyler County Am. Bus. Women Assn., 1970; recipient Dist. award of merit Boy Scouts Am., 1973. Mem. Tyler County C. of C. Democrat. Methodist. Kiwanian (pres. club 1973). Home: Livingston Hwy Woodville TX 75979 Office: 102 W Bluff Woodville TX 75979

KINSBOURNE, MARCEL, neurologist, pediatrician, educator; b. Vienna, Austria, Nov. 3, 1931; s. David and Mathilde (Gaster) Kinsbrunner; B.A., Oxford U., Eng., 1952, M.A., 1956; M.D., Guy's Hosp., London, 1955; m. Paula Joan Caplan, Nov. 10, 1972; children—David Stanley, Daniel Kevin, Jeremy Benjamin. Came to U.S., 1967, naturalized, 1972. Intern, Lewishom Hosp., London, Eng., 1955-56; resident Hosp. for Sick Children, London, 1957-58; practice medicine specializing in neurology and pediatrics, Durham, N.C., 1967—; mem. staff Duke Hosp.; asso. prof. pediatrics, neurology Duke, 1967—. Diplomate Am. Bd. Pediatrics. Fellow Am. Neurol. Assn., Am. Psychol. Assn. Contbr. articles to profl. jours. Home: 2528 Wrightwood St Durham NC 27705 Office: Box 2948 Duke Hosp Durham NC 27710

KINTZLEY, RUSS, newspaper editor; married; 2 children. Asso. editor editorials The Times-Picayune, New Orleans. Mem. Am. Soc. Newspaper Editors, Phi Gamma Delta. Club: Plimsoll. Home: 1239 Eleonore St New Orleans LA 70115 Office: 3800 Howard Av New Orleans LA 70140

KINZBACH, ROBERT BENTON, mech. engring. cons.; b. Houston, Mar. 8, 1908; s. Frank and Anna (McGuire) K.; student U. Tex., 1926-31; m. Mary Chandler Lyman, Aug. 25, 1931; children—Mary Ellen (Mrs. Richard O. Wilson), Harriett Ann (Mrs. J. DeWitt Morrow, Jr.). Vice pres. Kinzbach Tool Co., Inc., 1931-60; pres. Kinzbach Engring. Co., Houston, 1961-69. gen. mgr., 1969-70; engring. cons., Houston, 1970—. Mem. Am. Soc. M.E. (sect. chmn.), Am. Soc. Tool and Mfg. Engrs., Am. Soc. Metals, Am. Ordnance Assn., Am, Petroleum Inst., Nomads, Houston Engring. and Sci. Soc. (past pres.), Sigma Phi Epsilon, Tau Beta Pi. Presbyn. (elder). Mason, Kiwanian. Club: Houston. Patentee in field. Home: 6203 Valley Forge Dr Houston TX 77027 Office: PO Box 36289 Houston TX 77036

KIPER, RALPH ORIAN, architect; b. Gilbert, La., Dec. 4, 1919; s. Ernest Richard and Luella (Huggins) K.; B.Arch., Auburn U., 1942; m. Kittye Leah Buford, Mar. 18, 1944; children—Ralph Orian, Kittye Leah, Keith Lloyd. Pvt. practice architecture, Shreveport, La., 1949—. Served to 1st lt., arty. AUS, 1942-46. Mem. A.I.A. Mason (Shriner). Club: Shreveport, Petroleum, East Ridge Country. Home: 957 Audubon St Shreveport LA 71105 Office: Petroleum Tower Shreveport LA 71101

KIRBO, CHARLES HUGHES, Democratic nat. committeeman; b. Bainbridge, Ga., Mar. 5, 1917; s. Ben and Ethel (West) K.; LL.B., U. Ga.; m. Margaret LeGette, May 20, 1951; children—Charles Hughes, Susan Ray, Betsy Anne, Katherine. Partner law firm King & Spalding, Atlanta. Chmn. Ga. Dem. party; mem. nat. Dem. com; chief of staff Ga. Gov. Jimmy Carter. Served to maj. Armed Forces, World War II. Home: 10705 Stroup Rd Roswell GA 30075 Office: 2500 Trust Co Ga Bldg Atlanta GA 30303

KIRBY, BRIAN GABRIEL, hotel exec.; b. Budapest, Hungary, Aug. 1, 1936 (came to U.S. 1962); s. Ronald G. and Agnes Caroline (Balog) K.; grad. liberal arts Kent Coll., Canterbury, Eng., 1954; degree with honors hotel mgmt. Ecole Hoteliere, Lausanne, Switzerland, 1956-59; m. Virginia Joyce Nixon, Feb. 10, 1962; children—Brian Alan, Patria Christine, Andrea Agnes. Food and beverage mgr. Pontchartrain Hotel, New Orleans, 1962-64; resident mgr. Gran Hotel Bolivar, Lima, Peru, 1964-66; gen. mgr. Pick Nationwide Inn, Columbus, O., 1966-68; asst. gen. mgr. Pick Congress Hotel, Chgo., 1969, v.p., gen. mgr. Exec. House, Washington, 1969—. Mem. Washington Conv. Bur., 1969—, Washington Bd. of Trade, 1969—. Served with Brit. Army, 1954-56. Recipient English Lit. award Kent Coll., 1954; Prix des anciences eleves Swiss Hotel Mgmt. Sch., 1959; decorated Officer Confrerie de la Chaine des Rotisseurs. Mem. Confrerie de la Chaine des Rotisseurs (vice archiviste Washington chpt. 1969—, pres. Washington chpt. 1972—), Washington Hotel Assn. (1st v.p. 1973—), Hotel Sales Mgmt. Assn., Mem. Ch. of Eng. Lion, Optimist. Club: Skal. Home: 1515 Rhode Island Av NW Washington DC 20005 Office: Executive House Washington DC 20005

KIRBY, HENRY VANCE, physician; b. Harrison, Ark., Apr. 3, 1908; s. Leander Bender and Virgie May (Vance) K.; B.S., U. Ark., 1931; M.D., Washington U., St. Louis 1933; m. Elva C. Hudson, June 21, 1936; children—Henry Hudson, Carol Anne (Mrs. Ross Lander Fordyce), Helen Vance (Mrs. W. Peyton Daniel, Jr.). Rotating Intern DePaul Hosp., St. Louis, 1933-34; gen. practice medicine, Harrison, Ark., 1934—; mem. staff Boone County Hosp., Harrison, 1st chief of staff, 1950, dir. N.W. Ark. Tumor Clinic and Registry, 1973—; dir. Hudson Packing Co., Harrison, 1946-49. Local examiner Selective Service System, 1940-42; mem. Boone County adv. com. to N.W. Ark. Econ. Devel. Dist., 1969—; active Boy Scouts Am. Mem. bd. Harrison Sch. Dist., 1947-58, pres., 1952-53; 56-58; coroner, Boone County, Ark., 1963—. Served to capt. M.C., AUS, 1942-45. Decorated Bronze Star medal. Fellow Am. Acad. Family Practice; mem. Am. Legion, A.M.A., Ark. Acad. Gen. Practice (state dir. 1957-58), Ark. (Councilor 9th Dist. Med. Soc. 1970—), Boone County (pres. 1940-41) med. socs., N.W. Ark. Wildlife Assn. (dir. 1972-73), Lambda Chi Alpha, Phi Beta Pi. Democrat. Presbyn. (elder 1959-62, 71—). Rotarian. Clubs: Bridge, Supper (Harrison). Home: 1001 W Nicholson St Harrison AR 72601 Office: Boone County Med Center 651 N Spring St Harrison AR 72601

KIRBY, LOWRY DALE, physician; b. Lafayette, Tenn., Nov. 29, 1926; s. Floyd McPherson and Lou Audra (Knight) K.; student David Lipscomb Coll., 1945-46; B.A., Vanderbilt U., 1949; M.D., U. Tenn., 1953. Intern, St. Thomas Hosp., Nashville, 1954; resident Bapt. Hosp., Nashville, 1957-59; practice medicine specializing in pediatrics, Nashville, 1959—. Mem. adv. com. Tenn. Commn. on Children's Service. Chmn. bd. dirs. AGAPE; bd. dirs. Cheekwood Fine Arts Center, Historic Sites Fedn. Served with M.C., AUS, 1955-57. Mem. A.M.A., Tenn., So. med. assns., Nashville Acad. Medicine, Tenn., Nashville pediatric socs. Club: Nashville City. Home: 628 Timber Lane Nashville TN 37215 Office: 3725 Nolensville Rd Nashville TN 37211

KIRBY, MARJORIE TARLETON, educator; b. Marianao, Cuba, June 6, 1927 (parents Am. citizens); d. Carroll Scott and Willelah (Neal) Kirby; B.A., Birmingham So. Coll., 1949; postgrad. U. Havana, 1950; M.A., U. N.C., 1956, Ph.D., 1971. Tchr., Phillips Sch., Candler Coll., Marianao, 1949-52, 55-58, Coffee High Sch., Florence Ala., 1952-55, 58-62; asso. prof. Spanish, dir. Latin Am. studies Queens Coll., Charlotte, N.C., 1962—. Mem. Am. Assn. Tchrs. Spanish and Portuguese (v.p. N.C. chpt. 1974), Latin Am. Studies Assn., South Atlantic Modern Lang. Assn., Am. Assn. U. Profs, Am. Folklore Soc. Methodist. Contbr. poems to lit. mags. Home: 2201 Sarah Marks Av Charlotte NC 28203

KIRCHHEIMER, WALDEMAR F(RANZ), physician, microbiologist; b. Schneidemuhl, Germany, Jan. 11, 1913; M.D., U. Giessen (Germany), 1947; Ph.D., U. Wash., 1949; m. 1945. Research physician King County Tb Hosp., Seattle, 1942-46; Tb research asso. U. Wash., 1946-47, instr. microbiology, 1948-49; asst. prof. bacteriology Northwestern U. Med. Sch., 1949-53, asso. prof., 1953-56; dep. safety dir., med. bacteriologist, Ft. Detrick, Md., 1956-61; mem. research staff U.S. Inst. Allergy and Infectious Diseases, 1961-62; chief microbiology sect. USPHS Hosp., Carville, La., 1962-64, chief lab. br., 1965-71, chief lab. research br., 1971—; clin. prof. microbiology, tropical medicine and med. parasitology La. State U., New Orleans, 1973—. Mem. leprosy panel U.S.-Japan Joint Med. Sci. Program, 1965-72; project officer for research in India on transmission of leprosy U.S. Govt., 1972—. Med. dir. USPHS, 1965—. Recipient Superior Service medal Dept. Health, Edn. and Welfare, 1971. Mem. Am. Soc. Microbiology. Research leprosy treatment, immunology, biology of the leprosy bacillus, host-parasite interaction, exptl. leprosy. Address: USPHS Hosp Carville LA 70721

KIRCHNER, JOHN WAYNE, elec. engr.; b. Louisville, May 16, 1947; s. George Adam and Eva Myrtle (Tomes) K.; B.E.E., U. Louisville, 1969, M. Engring., 1973; m. Mary Lois Norris, July 14, 1973; 1 dau., Shannon. Elec. engr. Naval Ordnance Sta., Louisville, 1969-72, weapons systems mgmt. trainee, 1972-74, project engr. Naval Ordnance Systems Command, Washington, 1974—. Instr. electronics lab. U. Louisville, 1968-69. Mem. Nat. Soc. Profl. Engrs., I.E.E.E. Home: 1709 Trent Av Louisville KY 40216 Office: Code 50C Southside Dr Louisville KY 40214 also ORD 5532 Nat Center 2 Washington DC 20362

KIRILL, PETER, metals co. exec.; b. N.Y.C., June 29, 1912; s. Kirill Victor and Tatiana (Prudnick) Bobrowsky; B.C.S., N.Y.U., 1935; m. Beverly Langhorne, June 2, 1944; children—Peter, Langhorne, William D. Dist. sales mgr. Liberty Mut. Ins. Co., N.Y.C., 1946-48; regional mgr. Stewart Warner Corp., Chgo., 1948-57; pres. Alemite Co. Fla., Inc., Jacksonville, 1957—; dir. Fla. Dealer and Growers Bank, Jacksonville. Bd. dirs. Boys Home, YMCA. Served with USNR, 1942-45. Decorated Silver Star medal; recipient citation sec. Navy, 1962-70. Mem. Navy League (nat. v.p.), Gator Bowl Assn. (v.p. 1969—), Jacksonville (gov. 1969-70), Westside Council Area (past chmn.) Chambers Commerce, Phi Gamma Delta. Rotarian. Clubs: University, River, Timuquana, Jacksonville Quarterback (past capt.), Fla. Yacht, Reveliers (Jacksonville). Home: 2532 Holly Point Rd Orange Park FL Office: 5281 Edgewood Ct Jacksonville FL 32205

KIRILLA, GEORGE MAJER, mgmt. cons.; b. Carthage, Mo., June 14, 1910; s. George and Julianna deCaudroi (Majer) K.; student Rochester U., 1930-31, Northwestern U., 1943-45; B.S., Pacific States U., 1947, LL.D., 1968; postgrad. Harvard, 1957, U. San Francisco, 1962; m. Charmaline Opal Kaufmann, June 23, 1940; children—Charmla Georgine (Mrs. Hermann Novak, Jr.), Dollyna Dee (Mrs. McNair Worrell Perry). Exec., Douglas Aircraft Co., Santa Monica, Cal. and Park Ridge, Ill., 1937-45, Moore Corp., 1945-46, Climax Industries, 1946-47, Cannon Electric Devel. Co., 1948-50; asso., dir. bus. planning pub. relations Booz, Allen & Hamilton, internat. mgmt. consultants, 1950-52; internat. mgmt. cons., adviser U.S. Navy Dept., 1952-54, U.S. Small Bus. Adminstrn., 1954-56, 58-65, U.S. Dept. State/Govt. of Republic of China and Taiwan Provincial Govt., 1956-58, U.S. Dept. Def., 1965-71; v.p. Broadmoor Corp., 1973—. Cons., adviser U.S. Legislators and House Select Com. on Small Bus., 1966-71, U.S. Small Bus. Adminstrn. Council for Small Bus., 1971—; chmn. United Cursade, 1960, 61; adviser World Bus. and Internat. Trade Techniques, U. San Francisco, 1962, A.R.C., 1973; co-adminstr. Julianna Kirilla Estate, 1968. Trustee Frank Kirilla Trust. Recipient Presdl. Distinguished Civilian Service medal, 1942; also other citations and awards of merit. Mem. World Affairs Council, Am. Assn. for UN, Dept. Def. Small Bus. and Econ. Utilzn. Council, Nat. Rifle Assn., Psi Sigma Iota (life). Clubs: Peninsula Golf and Country; Grand Hotel Recreation. Author: Incentive System, 1944; Small Business--Its Importance to the American Way of Life, 1969. Address: 3601 Connecticut Av NW Washington DC 20008

KIRK, DAVID CLARK, JR., chemist; b. Newark, May 19, 1924; s. David Clark and Florence May (Kilgour) K.; B.Ch.E., Lehigh U., 1944; M.S., Bklyn. Poly. Inst., 1951; Ph.D., U. Ia., 1953; m. Frances W. Sutherland, May 2, 1953; children—Winifred, Linda, Andrew. Chem. engr. Am. Dyewood Co., Bellville, N.J., 1946-48; chemist Merck & Co., Rahway, N.J., 1948-50; research chemist Hercules Inc., Wilmington, Del., 1953-59; dir. fundamental research Ecusta Paper div. Olin Corp., Pisgah Forest, N.C., 1959-69, dir. research and devel., 1969—. Mem. Transylvania County Planning and Zoning Bd., 1967-72; mem. Transylvania County Bd. Social Services, 1972—, chmn., 1973. Mem. Am. Chem. Soc. (chmn. Western Carolinas sect. 1970), Am. Inst. Chemists, T.A.P.P.I., (chmn. coll. relations subcom. 1971—), Sci. Research Soc. Am., Tech. Assn. Graphic Arts, Tau Beta Pi, Phi Lambda Upsilon. Home: River Ridge Route 3 Brevard NC 28712 Office: PO Box 200 Pisgah Forest NC 28768

KIRK, DONALD WILLIAM, architect, engr.; b. W. Concord, Minn., Feb. 6, 1921; s. Donald William and Manila (Nordman) K.; B.S. in Archtl. Engring., U. Tex. at Austin, 1943; m. Wanda Goodwin, Sept. 9, 1961; children—Kathy, Don, Mike, Andrew, Kira. Structural engr. Gen. Dynamics Corp., 1943-45, Wyatt C. Hedrick, architect, Ft. Worth, 1946, Preston M. Geren, architect, Ft. Worth, 1947-56; propr. Don W. Kirk, architect-engr., Ft. Worth, 1956-65; partner architecture and engring. firm Kirk & Gist, Dallas, 1964—, Kirk & Voich, Ft. Worth, 1967—; v.p. Metroplex Architects, Irving, Tex.; dir. Kibah Corp., Ft. Worth; prin. works include erection tower for Moscow Dome, 1959, Leonard's M&O Subway, Ft. Worth, 1962-63, skywalk between Continental Nat. Bank and garage, Ft. Worth, 1972, Bell Helicopter plant, Ft. Worth, 1957-74. Chmn. Ft. Worth Bldg. Code Rev. Com., 1968-70. Mem. A.I.A., Nat. Council Archtl. Registration Bds., Cons. Engrs. Council (pres. Tex. 1958), Am. Soc. C.E. (mem. task com. for Bibliography on Bolted and Riveted Joints 1959). Mason, Rotarian. Clubs: Colonial Country, River Crest Country, Ft. Worth, Ridotto, Steeplechase (Ft. Worth). Contbr. articles to profl. publs. Office: PO Box 572 Fort Worth TX 76101

KIRK, JAMES CURTIS, oil co. exec.; b. Hubbard, Tex., May 10, 1921; s. James Floyd and Edna Pearl (Windham) K.; B.S., Baylor U., 1944; Ph.D., Ohio State U., 1949; m. Esta Mae Thomas, Aug. 11, 1944; children—James Lee, Carol Lyn, Steven Thomas, Gilbert Paul. Analytical chemist Pan Am. Refining Corp., Texas City, Tex., 1944-46; with Continental Oil Co., Ponca City, Okla., 1949-57, 60—, research chemist, supervising research chemist, 1949-57, gen. mgr. research and devel., 1967—; mgr. research Petroleum Chems., Inc., Lake Charles, La., 1957-60. Vice chmn. Okla. Air Pollution Adv. Council, 1967-71; mem. Sch. Bd. for Kay County Vo-Tech. Sch., 1971—. Mem. Am. Chem. Soc. (past sect. chmn.), Soap and Detergent Assn. (past com. chmn.). Republican. Mem. Christian Ch. Kiwanian. Address: Drawer 1267 Ponca City OK 74601

KIRK, JOHN ALAN, correctional supt.; b. Vincennes, Ind., Mar. 16, 1941; s. Melvin McLung and Mary Elizabeth (Glezen) K.; B.A., Evansville Coll., 1963; M. Div., Duke, 1966; postgrad. Correctional Inst., E.C.U., 1971; m. Judith Guden, Aug. 28, 1965; children—John Alan, Jeffery Guden. Ordained to ministry Meth. Ch., 1967; chaplain N.C. Dept. of Correction, Raleigh, 1965-69; chaplain intern Duke Med. Center, Durham, N.C., 1966-67; mem. staff clin. tng. Central Prison, Raleigh, N.C., 1969; inner city dir. YMCA, Nashville, 1969-71; supt. N.C. Dept. Correction, McCain, 1971—. Instr. Sandhills Community Coll., Southern Pines, N.C., 1971. Chmn. Mayors Council on Youth Opportunities, Nashville, 1970-71. Bd. dir. Met. Action and Tng. Service, Nashville, 1970-71. Mem. Assn. for Clin. Pastoral Edn., Acacia, Kappa Chi (nat. pres. 1962-63). Methodist. Mason, Kiwanian. Home: 500 Fairway Dr Southern Pines NC 28387 Office: PO Box 58 McCain NC 28361

KIRK, JOHN MICHAEL, landscape architect; b. El Paso, Tex., Oct. 12, 1942; s. Robert Pugh and Francis Newberry (McClure) K.; A.A., N.M. Mil. Inst., 1963; B. Landscape Architecture, U. Ga., 1967; m. Joyce Elizabeth Pruet, Oct. 29, 1964 (div. Feb. 1972); 1 dau., Joyce Michelle. Pvt. practice as landscape architect, Birmingham, Ala., 1965; landscape architect, contractor Landscape Services, Birmingham, Ala., 1966-67, 69-72; landscape architect, pres. Environmental Design Collaborative, Birmingham, Ala., 1972—. Cons. to various archtl. offices; cons. Beautification Bd., City of Homewood, Ala., 1971—. Served to 1st lt. C.E., AUS, 1967-69. Mem. Am. Soc. Landscape Architects (sec., treas. Ala. sect. 1969-72). Republican. Presbyn. Home: 3140 Napoleon Ct Birmingham AL 35243 Office: PO Box 43346 Birmingham AL 35243

KIRK, ROBERT LANGFORD, lawyer; b. Waco, Tex., May 8, 1915; s. James Drake and Betty Maude (Boyd) K.; LL.B., Baylor U., Waco, 1938, J.D., 1969; m. Oma Frances Dickerson, July 18, 1971; 1 dau., Roberta Jean (Mrs. Patrick McMillan). Admitted to Tex. bar, 1938; pvt. practice, Olton, 1939-42; county atty., Lamb County, Tex., 1947-50, county judge, 1953-57; asst. gen. atty., treas., sec., dir. Woodmen of World Life Ins. Soc., Omaha, 1957-61; pvt. practice law, Littlefield, Tex., 1961—. Pres., W.Tex. Judges and Commrs. Assn., 1957-58. Served with Air Transport Command, 1942-46. Mem. Tex., Neb. bar assns., Littlefield C. of C. (dir.), Am. Legion (post comdr., dist. comdr.). Mason (Shriner), Lion. Home: PO Box 388 Littlefield TX 79339 Office: 334 Phelps Av Littlefield TX 79339

KIRK, VIRGINIA, clin. psychologist; b. Kirksville, Mo., Dec. 22, 1895; d. Sherman and Harriet Rose (White) Kirk; A.B., Drake U., 1917; B. Nursing, Yale, 1927, M.S., 1930; Ph.D., U. Chgo., 1949. Research asst. Yale Psycho-Clinic, 1930-31; dir. nursing Emma Pendleton Bradley Home, Riverside, R.I., 1931-35; research asso. Williamson County Child Guidance Study, Franklin, Tenn., 1935-42; instr. clin. psychology sch. medicine Vanderbilt U., 1943-47, asst. prof., 1947-53, asso. prof., 1953-60, asso. clin. prof., 1960-61, emerita, 1961—; pvt. practice cons. clin. psychologist, 1961—; cons. clin psychologist Family and Children's Service, 1953-73, SCOR, Vanderbilt U. Hosp., 1963—; lectr. U. Tenn. Sch. Social Work, 1951-60. Recipient Distinguished Service award Drake U., Drake U. Nat. Alumni Assn., 1965. Fellow Am. Psychol. Assn., Inc.; mem. A.A.A.S., Tenn. Acad. Sci., Southeastern, Midwestern, Tenn. psychol. assns., Am. Assn. Mental Deficiency, Am. Speech and Hearing Assn., Orton Soc. Author articles in field. Home: 666 Timber Lane Regency Park Nashville TN 37215

KIRK, WILBER WOLFE, marine corrosion lab. exec.; b. Brownsville, Pa., Sept. 21, 1932; s. Wilber Kenneth and Alice (Wolfe) K.; B.S., Otterbein Coll., 1954; M.S. (U.S. Navy Ednl. fellow 1957-59), Ohio State U., 1959; m. Dolores Ruth Tomer, Nov. 13, 1954; children—Kenneth Andrew, Karen Sue, Kelly Lynn, Kevin Thomas. Engr., Bettis Atomic Power Lab., Pitts., 1958-62; engr., Internat. Nickel Co., Inc., Wrightsville Beach, N.C., 1962-67, supr., 1967-68, mgr. Francis L. Laque Corrosion Lab., 1968—. Mem. marine tech. adv. com. Cape Fear Tech. Inst., 1970-72. Served with AUS, 1954-56. Mem. Am. Soc. Metals (chpt. chmn. 1971-72), Nat. Assn. Corrosion Engrs., Am. Soc. Testing and Materials, C. of C. (mem. marine resources com. 1968-71), Am. Inst. Mining, Metall. and Petroleum Engrs., Offshore Tech. Conf. (program com. 1974—), Sigma Xi. Methodist (trustee 1971-72). Rotarian. Clubs: Port Propeller (edn. chmn. 1971), Cape Fear Country, Executives (Wilmington, N.C.). Home: 5105 Clear Run Dr Wilmington NC 28401 Office: PO Box 656 Wrightsville Beach NC 28480

KIRK, WILLIAM SMITH, dentist; b. Salisbury, N.C., Apr. 22, 1928; s. Frank Walter and Suzanne Sovereign (Smith) K.; student U. N.C., 1944-45, postgrad., 1957-58; D.D.S., Northwestern U., 1949; m. Lois Jean Smith, Feb. 5, 1951; children—William Smith, Margaret Suzanne, Timothy Davis. Individual practice dentistry, Salisbury, 1952-57; practice orthodontics, Salisbury, 1958—. Bd. dirs. North Hills Christian Sch., 1966-73. Served with USAF, 1949-52; ETO. Mem. Am. Dental Assn., Am. Assn. Orthodontists, So. Soc. Orthodontists, N.C. Orthodontic Soc. (pres. 1973—), N.C. Dental Soc., Flying Dentists Assn., World Radio Missionary Fellowship, Inc. (spl. rep. 1964), Second Dist. Dental Soc. N.C. (pres. 1969). Presbyn. (elder 1954). Rotarian. Home: 318 Camelot Dr Salisbury NC 28144 Office: 1819 Brenner St Salisbury NC 28144

KIRKBY, DAVID RANDALL, engring. mgr.; b. Grand Rapids, Mich., Aug. 6, 1930; s. William Walter and Ethelyn Susan (Pellow) K.; B.Ch.E., U. Del., 1952; postgrad. Drexel Inst. Tech., 1955, U. Toledo and U. Pa., 1958-60, Wayne State U., 1963-64; m. Virginia E. Myers, Aug. 4, 1956; children—Leslie Ann, Kenneth William. Chem. engr. Atlantic Refining Co., Phila., 1953; process engr. Gulf Oil Corp., Phila., 1953-60, Hydrocarbon Research, Inc., N.Y.C., 1960-61, Foster Wheeler Corp., Livingston, N.J., 1961-63; sr. prodn. engr., utility shift supt. Pennsalt Chems. Corp., Wyandotte, Mich., 1963-65; with Davy Powergas, Inc., and predecessor firms, Lakeland, Fla., 1965-69, 70—, mgr. process engring., 1970—; mgr. proposals Allied Chem. Corp., Morristown, N.J., 1969. Served with USNR, 1963-65. Registered profl. engr., Fla. Mem. Am. Inst. Chem. Engrs. Republican. Presbyn. Home: 4922 W White Oak Dr Lakeland FL 33803 Office: PO Box 2436 Lakeland FL 33803

KIRKENDALL, WALTER MURRAY, physician, educator; b. Louisville, Mar. 31, 1917; s. Charles Allen and Margaret C. (Caplinger) K.; M.D., U. Louisville, 1941; m. Margaret Jane Allen, Mar. 31, 1948; children—William Charles, James Allen, Matthew John, Thomas Murray, David Edward, Nancy Jane, Mary Margaret, Kathryn Ann, Joseph Howard, Michael Bruce. Intern, Univ. Hosps., Iowa City, 1941-42, resident internal medicine, 1946-49; jr. asst. resident internal medicine Gen. Hosp., Louisville, 1945-46; research asst. anatomy U. Louisville Coll. Medicine, 1938-39; staff mem. State U. Ia. Hosps., 1949-72; asst. dept. internal medicine U. Ia. Coll. Medicine, 1949-50, asso., 1950-51, asst. prof., 1951-52, clin. asso.

prof., 1952-58, asso. prof., 1958-59, prof., 1959-72, dir. cardiovascular research labs., 1958-70, dir. renal-hypertension-electrolyte div., 1970-72; chief med. service VA Hosp., Iowa City, 1952-58, cons. in medicine, 1958-72; prof. medicine U. Tex. Med. Sch., Houston, 1972—, dir. Program in Internal Medicine, 1972—; dir. med. service Hermann Hosp., 1972—. Cons., VA Nat. Programs for Research in Therapy of Hypertension, 1958—, USPHS Coop. Study on Treatment Hypertension, 1967—; mem. med. adv. bd. Council High Blood Pressure Research, Am. Heart Assn.; mem. exec. com. Undergrad. Cardiology Tng. Programs, Nat. Heart Inst., 1969-72. Served from 1st lt. to maj., M.C., AUS, 1942-46. Decorated Army Commendation medal; recipient Bierring award Ia. Tb. and Health Assn., 1966; named Internist of Year, Ia. Soc. Internal Medicine, 1971. Louis Mark lectr. Am. Coll. Chest Physicians, 1963. Diplomate Am. Bd. Internal Medicine. Fellow A.C.P., Am. Coll. Cardiology; mem. A.M.A., Am. Assn. U. Profs., A.A.A.S., Central Clin. Research Club, Am. Fedn. Clin. Research (counselor Midwestern sect. 1955-57), Central Soc. Clin. Research, Am. Coll. Chest Physicians (bd. govs. Ia. 1964), Internat., Am. socs. nephrology, Internat. Soc. Cardiology, Am. Clin. and Climatol. Assn., Soc. Exptl. Biology and Medicine, So. Soc. Clin. Investigation, N.Y. Acad. Scis., Assn. Profs. Medicine, Am., Houston socs. internal medicine, Nat. Kidney Found., Am. Coll. Pharmacology and Chemotherapy, Am. Thoracic Soc., Am. Soc. Pharmacology and Exptl. Therapeutics, Tex. Med. Assn., Harris County Med. Soc., Sigma Xi, Phi Chi, Alpha Omega Alpha. Contbr. articles profl. jours. Home: 5203 Del Monte Dr Houston TX 77027 Office: 6400 W Cullen St Houston TX 77025

KIRKHAM, ED SHELTON, city ofcl.; b. Lamar County, Tex., Jan. 4, 1928; s. John F. and Lela Mae (Wood) K.; ed. jr. coll.; m. Oleta Norris, July 3, 1948; children—Daryl Shelton, Joe Mack, Cheryl Beth. With San Angelo (Tex.) Fire Service, 1949-68, chief dept., 1963-68; chief Austin (Tex.) Fire Dept., 1968—. Trustee Austin Boys' Club. Mem. Internat., Tex. fire chiefs' assns., Nat. Fire Protection Assn. Home: 4602 Kiowa Pass Austin TX 78745 Office: 401 E 5th St Austin TX 78701

KIRKLAND, EDGAR LEROY, govt. ofcl.; b. Ft. Davis, Ala., May 2, 1913; s. James Jackson and Mamie (Johnson) K.; grad. high sch.; m. Flora Margaret Law, Aug. 23, 1941. Engr. asst. Macon County (Ala.) Hwy. Dept., 1938-40; equipment insp. U.S. Army Corps Engrs., Mobile, Ala., 1940-43; vet. coordinator, charge vet. tng. program Macon County Bd. Edn., 1947-54; postmaster, Ft. Davis, 1954—. Served with USAAF, 1943-47. Mem. Nat. Assn. Postmasters U.S. Mason. Address: Fort Davis AL 36031

KIRKLAND, EDWIN CAPERS, educator; b. Charleston, S.C., Sept. 14, 1902; s. William Clark and Lalla (Stokes) K.; A.B., Wofford Coll., 1922; M.A., Vanderbilt U., 1924; Ph.D., Northwestern U., 1934; m. Mary L. Neal, Sept. 14, 1930. Various teaching positions, 1922-31; instr. U. Tenn., 1931-37, asst. prof., 1937-41, asso. prof., 1941-46; asso. prof. English, U. Fla., Gainesville, 1946-51, prof., 1951—. Am. consul, cultural officer Am. Consul Gen., Bombay, India, 1954-56. Fulbright Research grantee, Calcutta, India, 1962-63; Am. Philos. Soc., Research grantee Brit. Mus., summer 1963, 66. Mem. Modern Lang. Assn., Am., Asian (exec. bd. 1963—), Indian folklore socs., S. Atlantic Modern Lang. Societe Internationale d'Ethnologie et de Folklore, Southeastern Folklore Soc. (pres. 1939), Phi Beta Kappa. Editor So. Folklore Quar., 1969—. Home: 629 SW 27th Ct Gainesville FL 32601

KIRKLAND, JOHN DAVID, oil co. exec.; b. McAllen, Tex., June 6, 1933; s. O.D. and Daisy (Donohoe) K.; B.A., Yale, 1955, LL.B., 1958; m. Ann Wales, June 15, 1957; children—David, Solace, Robert. Admitted to Tex. bar, 1958; atty. Baker, Botts, Shepherd & Coates, Houston, 1958-67; v.p. in charge finance Pennzoil Co., Houston, 1967-73, exec. v.p., dir., 1973—. Mem. Am., Tex. bar assns. Home: 3620 Inverness Houston TX 77019 Office: Southwest Tower Houston TX 77002

KIRKLAND, RICHARD HORACE, physician, educator; b. Richmond, Va., Mar. 22, 1924; s. John Roy and Mary Frances (Ford) K.; student Med. Coll. Va. Sch. Pharmacy, 1941-43, M.D., Med. Coll. Va., 1948; m. Ninette P. Purviance, Oct. 12, 1946; children—Diane Sharon, Lisa Lee. Intern, resident internal medicine Med. Coll. Va., 1948-52, asst. prof. medicine, 1953-69, prof., 1969—; resident exptl. radiology U. Cal., San Francisco, 1952-53; practice medicine specializing in internal medicine, Richmond, 1953—. Served with AUS, 1943. Fellow Nat. Cancer Inst., 1952-54. Fellow A.C.P.; mem. Med. Soc. Va., Richmond Acad. Medicine. Home: 8002 University Dr Richmond VA 23229 Office: Med Coll Va Richmond VA 23219

KIRKLAND, WALLACE TALMAGE, real estate appraiser, cons.; b. Guntersville, Ala., July 15, 1931; s. Grover and Ona (McClendon) K.; B.S., Auburn U., 1953; postgrad. U. Fla., 1955-56; m. Martha Alma Cotter, June 2, 1962; children—Lorraine Phyllis, Dawn Ellen. Pres., Kirkland Builders, Guntersville, 1958-59; asso. regional appraiser Gen. Services Adminstrn., Atlanta, 1959-65; pres. Kirkland & Co., Atlanta, 1965—. Served with USAF, 1953-55. Mem. Am. Inst. Real Estate Appraisers, Soc. Real Estate Appraisers, Pi Kappa Phi, Delta Sigma Pi. Home: 1656 Merton Rd NE Atlanta GA 30306 Office: 400 Colony Square Tower Atlanta GA 30361

KIRKMAN, LOWELL DOUGLAS, architect; b. Winston Salem, N.C., Jan. 9, 1943; s. Everett Lee and Mattie Lillian (Moon) K.; B.S., Davidson Coll., 1969; B.Arch., Ga. Inst. Tech., 1968; m. Karen Lee Lightbody, Feb. 20, 1965; children—Douglas, Nathan. Job capt. Surratt, Smith & Abernathy, asso. architects, Charlotte, N.C., 1967-69; architect James Franklin, architects, planners, Chattanooga, 1969-71; prin., Asso. Architects & Engrs., Inc., Chattanooga, 1971—. Bd. dirs. Dalton-Whitfield Group Home. Mem. A.I.A., Am. Soc. Planning Ofcls., Tenn. Soc. Architects, Dalton-Whitfield C. of C. (dir.), Alpha Tau Omega, Tau Sigma Delta. Methodist (trustee, mem. adminstrv. bd. 1971-73). Elk, Rotarian. Home: PO Box 1033 Dalton GA 30720 Office: 514 Lookout St Chattanooga TN 37403

KIRKPATRICK, EDITH KILLGORE (MRS. CLAUDE KIRKPATRICK), club worker, educator; b. Lisbon, La., Nov. 14, 1918; d. Thomas Morton and Bessie (Melton) Killgore; B.A. summa cum laude, La. Coll., 1938; Mus.M., La. State U., 1965; student Juillard Sch. Music, 1938; m. Claude Kirkpatrick, Aug. 21, 1938; children—Claude Kent (dec.), Thomas Killgore, Edith Kay, Charles Kris. Tchr. voice, Sulphur, Lake Charles, Jennings, La., 1940-60; instr. voice and music McNeese State Coll., Lake Charles, La., 1956-58; vis. asst. prof. La. State U., 1967-68; choir dir. 1st Bapt. Ch., Sulphur, Jennings, 1938-55, Baton Rouge 1967-68. Vice pres. Burgess Lumber Co., Jennings, 1955-66. Capt. drive A.R.C., 1958, Boy Scouts Am., 1952-56, United Giver 1964; womens' state chmn. La. Coll. Bldg. Fund Crusade, 1967; Bd. dirs. Baton Rouge Symphony, 1969—, pres. aux., 1968-69. Recipient La. Coll. Distinguished Alumni award, 1961. Mem. Nat. Fedn. Music Clubs, (state pres. 1966-69, dist. pres. 1972-74), Nat Fedn. Womens Clubs, La. Bapt. Womans Union (state pres. 1960-63), Nat. Assn. Tchrs. Singing, Nat. Music Tchrs. Assn., Nat. Music Educators Assn., Mortar Bd. Alpha Chi, Beta Pi Theta, Sigma Alpha Iota, Phi Kappa Phi, Pi Kappa Lambda, P.E.O., Baton Rouge Opera Guild (pres. 1970-72). Democrat. Baptist (1st woman mem. La. exec. bd. (1970—). Co-author: Star Ideals, 1963; also articles in profl. jours. Address: 128 S Lakeshore Dr Baton Rouge LA 70808

KIRKPATRICK, JERALD LEE, clergyman; b. McAllen, Tex., Dec. 28, 1944; s. Joseph Rayner and Elnora Marian (Anderson) K.; B.A. summa cum laude, Tex. Christian U., 1967; B.D., Yale U., 1970. Dir. ch. sch. Church of Christ, Yale U., New Haven, Conn., 1969-70; ordained to ministry Christian Ch., 1970; asso. minister First Christian Ch., El Paso, 1970-73; minister of edn. First Christian Ch., Amarillo, Tex., 1973—. Mem. gen. bd. Christian Ch. (Disciples of Christ) in U.S. and Can., 1969-71, mem. program and arrangements com. of gen. assembly, 1969-71. Mem. El Paso County Conf. of Chs. (chmn. com. on religious edn. 1972-73), Tex. Assn. of Christian Ch. Educators (pres. 1972-73), Religious Edn. Assn., Council on Christian Unity, Phi Alpha Theta. Democrat. Club: Am. Bus. (Amarillo). Home: 2800 SW 16th St Amarillo TX 79102 Office: 3001 Wolflin Av Amarillo TX 79109

KIRKPATRICK, KENNETH LOUIE, constrn. co. exec.; b. Bonham, Tex., Mar. 1, 1920; s. U. and Josephine (Thomas) K.; grad. high sch.; m. Dorothy Estelle Gunn, Sept. 17, 1949; children—Gary Phillips (stepson), Kenneth Louie, Jackie Lynn. With F.W. Woolworth, 1939; mgr. M.E. Moses Co., 1941-47; with Clark Loyd 5 and 10 cent Store, 1948-50; pres. Kirk's Variety Store, Inc., Killeen, Tex., 1951-59; pres. Beauty Homes, Inc., Killeen, 1969—, Jackie Lynn, Inc., Killeen, 1964—, Cove Lanes, Inc., Copperas Cove, Tex., 1952—; owner Kirk's Real Estate, Killeen, 1960—. Pres., Ft. Hood Bd. Realtors, 1969—; dir. Killeen Community Cowhouse Motor Hotel. Mem. Hardin Baylor Citizens Adv. Com., 1970—. Bd. dirs. Killeen Indsl. Found., A.R.C. Served with AUS, 1942. Kirk's Hall, Killeen Girl Scouts Friendship House, named in his honor, 1962. Mem. Homebuilders Assn. (pres. 1971—), Tex. Assn. Realtors (state dir. 1969—), Killeen C. of C. (dir. 1969—), Assn. U.S. Army (dir. 1971—, 1st v.p. 1972-73). Home: 3210 Lake Ann St Killeen TX 76541 Office: 1006 N 38th St Killeen TX 76541

KIRKPATRICK, SAMUEL ALEXANDER, educator; b. Harrisburg, Pa., Oct. 24, 1943; s. Samuel Alexander and Dorothy Elizabeth (Macfarlane) K.; B.S., Shippensburg State Coll., 1964; M.A. (Pa. Congress Parents and Tchrs. fellow, J.A. Finnegan fellow), Pa. State U., 1966, Ph.D. (NSF fellow), 1968; m. Pamela Ann Richter, June 13, 1965; children—Shaun Alexander, Neal William. Asst. prof. polit. sci. U. Okla., Norman, 1968-71, asso. prof., 1971—, also dir. Bur. Govt. Research. Vis. asst. prof. U. Mich., Ann Arbor, 1970; state supr. NBC election forecasts, 1969—; research cons. State Office Community Affairs and Planning, 1972. Charter mem. Oklahomans for a Modern Constn., 1969—. Am. Polit. Sci. Assn. state legis. service fellow, 1971—; Pa. State U. Grad. Sch. fellow, 1967-68. Mem. Southwestern (exec. council, v.p. 1972—), Midwestern, Am., So. polit. sci. assns., Am. Assn. Pub. Opinion Research, Am. Sociol.. Assn., Southwestern Social Sci. Assn., Phi Kappa Phi, Pi Sigma Alpha, Phi Sigma Pi, Kappa Delta Pi. Author: (with David R. Morgan) Urban Political Analysis, 1972: Quantitative Analysis of Political Data, 1973. Editor (with Lawrence K. Pettit) Social Psychology of Political Life, 1972. Editorial bd. Am. Jour. Polit. Sci., 1971—; mem. editorial policies com. Social Sci. Quar., 1969—. Home: 1017 Whispering Pines Dr Norman OK 73069

KIRKPATRICK, WILLIAM KIRNEY, physician; b. Beaumont, Tex., Sept. 22, 1929; s. Jewel Bryant and Vera Gladys (Alexander) K.; B.S., S.W. Tex. U., 1952; M.D., U. Tex. at Galveston, 1957; m. Eugenia Maxine Sanders, June 23, 1954; children—Stephen Sanders, Ross Alexander, Sara Katherine. Intern St. Joseph's Hosp., Ft. Worth, 1958; gen. practice, San Antonio, 1962—; mem. staff Santa Rosa, Baptist Meml., St. Benedicts's and Grace Lutheran hosps. Served with M.C., USAF, 1958-61. Biology teaching fellow S.W. Tex. U., 1952; USAF fellow U. Tex. 1956-57. Fellow Am. Acad. Family Physicians (charter); mem. Tex. Acad. Family Physicians, A.M.A. (Recognition award 1970), Internat. Med. Assembly S.W., Tex., Bexar County med. socs., Alpha Kappa Kappa. Democrat. Episcopalian. Lion. Contbr. articles to profl. jours. Home: 318 Glad Dr San Antonio TX 78223 Office: 2915 S Presa St San Antonio TX 78210

KIRSCHKE, WILLIAM, condr., musical dir.; b. Tex.; ed. Tex. Christian U., Ind. U.; pupil Walter Ducloux U. So. Cal.; postgrad. Univ. Conservatorium, Australia; pupil Henri Touzeau Melbourne (Australia) Philharmonic. Formerly condr. Roswell (N.M.) Symphony Orch.; formerly asst. condr. N.C. Symphony; now music dir., condr. El Paso (Tex.) Symphony; numerous guest condr. appearances; participating condr. Am. Symphony League East Coast Inst. Condrs. Recipient Kenan Found. award Young Artist Musicians, A.S.C.A.P. award for performance of Am. Music, Sigma Alpha Iota award. Address: 7371 Franklin Rd El Paso TX 79915

KIRSCHNER, EDWIN J., business exec.; b. N.Y.C., Dec. 26, 1919; s. M. Betty (Kenner) K.; student U. Florence (Italy), 1945-46, Coll. of William and Mary, Va. Poly. Inst., 1942; B.S., Am. U., 1950, M.A., 1951, postgrad., 1951-54; m. Eleanor Maxwell, Aug. 15, 1956; children—John Erik, Richard Scott, Caroline Lee, Jacqueline Jean. Transp. and aviation officer AID, U.S. Dept. of State, 1957-63; mil. planner USAF, 1952-56; mgr. transp. systems and aerospace mgmt., applied sci. and tech. divs. Litton Systems, Inc., Bethesda, Md., 1967-68; transp. adviser Peat, Marwick, Livingston & Co., Washington, 1968-69; pres. E.J. Kirschner & Assos., 1969—; pvt. transp. cons. to govt. and industry, Washington, 1963-67, 68—; cons. to under sec. Transp., 1970-73. Mem. faculty Am. U., 1963-64; adj. prof. Niagara U., 1969-70. Nominating com. mem. Aerospace Hall of Fame, 1964—. Mem. transp. adv. bd. to Montgomery County (Md.) Council, 1968—. Served to capt. AUS, 1943-47; now col. Res. Mem. Am. Airship Assn. (chmn. bd. trustees 1958—), Nat. Def. Transp. Assn. (chmn. edn. com.). Author: The Zeppelin in the Atomic Age, 1957; Civil Aviation, 1958. Contbr. to encys., also articles transp. and aerospace to publs. Home: 5300 Westbard Av Washington DC 20016

KIRSHBAUM, JOSEPH, musician; b. San Diego, Dec. 12, 1911; s. Louis and Sophia (Friedman) K.; Mus.B., Yale, 1934, Mus.M., 1935; Postgrad. Cornell U., 1935-37; m. Gertrude Morris, Sept. 25, 1935 (dec. Jan. 1973); children—Howard Morris, Daniel Robert, Ralph Henry, Shirley Ann. Asst. in music Cornell U., Ithaca, N.Y., 1935-37; instr. music Oberlin (O.) Coll., 1937-40; prof. music Bethany Coll., Lindsburg, Kan., 1940-44; asso. prof. music North Tex. State U., Denton, Tex., 1944-50; chmn. music dept. Tyler Jr. Coll., 1950—; condr., mus. dir. East Tex. Symphony Orch., 1950—; concert violinist. Ditson fellow for grad. study Yale, 1934; vis. prof. music Sterling (Kan.) Coll., 1942-43, McPherson (Kan.) Coll., 1943-44; concertmaster San Diego Symphony Orch., summers 1958-59. Recipient certificate merit for distinguished service to art and profession music, Yale U. Sch. Music Alumni Assn. Mem. Tyler (pres. 1956-57, 68-69, 69-70), Tex. (pres. 1960-62) music tchrs. assns., Tex. Assn. Music Schs. (mem. articulation com. 1968-69), Music Tchrs. Nat. Assn. (exec. com. unit, 1947-48, regional chmn. 1968-69, Yale Sch. Music Alumni Assn. (pres. 1973-74), Phi Mu Alpha Sinfonia (hon.). Jewish religion (pres. temple 1964-66). Rotarian. Home: 1004 W Rusk St Tyler TX 75701

KIRTLAND, CLIFFORD M., JR., broadcasting exec.; b. Buffalo, Jan. 15, 1924; s. Clifford M. and Honor (Fowler) K.; B.A., Mich. State U., 1945; M.B.A., Harvard, 1947; m. Jane McCullough, Aug. 31, 1951; children—Kim, Jimmy, Tommy, John. Sr. accountant Price Waterhouse & Co., 1947-51; v.p., treas., controller Abstract & Title Corp., 1951-54, Transcontinent TV Corp., 1955-63; exec. v.p., sec., treas. Cox Broadcasting Corp., Atlanta, 1963—; dir. Sci. Atlanta, Inc., Hawick Fund, Inc. Mem. bd. mgmt. Northside br. Atlanta YMCA; bd. dirs. Met. Atlanta A.R.C.; trustee Lovett Sch.; mem. bd. visitors Emory U. Served with USNR, World War II; PTO. Mem. N.Y. Ga. socs. C.P.A.'s, Financial Execs. Inst., Nat. Assn. Broadcasters, Inst. Broadcasting Financial Mgmt. (dir.), Harvard Bus. Sch. Atlanta (1st v.p.). Presbyn. Rotarian (dir.). Clubs: Harvard (Atlanta and N.Y.C.); Peachtree Golf (Atlanta). Home: 988 Dumbarton Ct NW Atlanta GA 30327 Office: 1601 W Peachtree St NE Atlanta GA 30309

KIRTLEY, STEPHEN EDWIN, clergyman; b. Oklahoma City, Nov. 20, 1939; s. Edwin Lankford and Edna Mae (Curtis) K.; B.A., Central State Coll., 1962; B.D. (Sem. scholar), Lexington Theol. Sem., 1965, D. Min., 1974; m. Kay Lu Pierce, July 29, 1962; 1 dau., Sarena Beth. Ordained to ministry Christian Ch., 1965; minister Colemansville Christian Ch., Berry, Ky., 1962-63, Pine Knot (Ky.) Christian Ch., 1963-65; minister youth Nicholasville (Ky.) Christian Ch., 1963; minister Mt. Vernon Christian Ch., Monroe, Ga., 1965-66, Christian Ch., Plainview, Tex., 1972—. Mem. Commn. Plains Christian Ch. in Tex., 1974—. Bd. dir. A.R.C., 1973—, Christian Manor Apts., Plainview, Tex., 1973—. Served to capt. AUS, 1966-72. Mem. Plainview Ministerial Assn. (v.p. 1974-75). Lion. Home: 1302 Garland Plainview TX 79072 Office: 910 Kokomo Plainview TX 79072

KISE, MEARL ALTON, chem. co. exec.; b. Allentown, Pa., Feb. 14, 1908; s. John H. and Emma C. (Wertman) K.; B.S., Lehigh U., 1930; Ph.D., Yale, 1933; m. Julia Bacsics, Sept. 20, 1930; children—John A., Peter E. Instr. chemistry Yale, 1930-32; sr. Textile Found. fellow Yale, 1933-35; research chemist, project leader nitrogen sect., solvay process div. Allied Chem. & Dye Corp., 1935-47, asst. to chief of research, Hopewell, Va., 1948-49; dir. research and devel. Va. Chems. Inc., Portsmouth, Va., 1949-71, v.p. research and devel., 1972—; v.p. VirChem of Can., Ltd., Cornwall, Ont. and Pointe Claire, Que., 1970—. Chmn. Portsmouth Sch. Bd., 1960-72. Pres. Portsmouth Humane Soc., 1970—; treas., trustee Old Dominion U. Research Found., Norfolk, Va.; chmn. bd. trustees Hampton Rds. Ednl. TV Assn., 1966-72. Fellow A.A.A.S.; mem. Am. Chem. Soc. (past chmn. Hampton Rds. sect.), T.A.P.P.I., Am. Soc. Heating, Refrigerating and Air-Conditioning Engrs., Am. Assn. Textile Chemists and Colorists, N.Y., Va. (editor chemistry sect. 1958-63, sec. 1958-59, chmn. 1959-60) acads. sci., Soc. Plastics Engrs., Phi Beta Kappa, Sigma Xi. Lutheran. Contbr. articles to profl. jours. Patentee in field. Home: 112 Monitor Rd Portsmouth VA 23707 Office: 3340 W Norfolk Rd Portsmouth VA 23703

KISER, WILLIAM RUSSELL, lawyer; b. Wise, Va., Apr. 16, 1921; s. Henry Jefferson and Vivian Russell (McLemore) K.; A.B., Washington and Lee U., 1942, LL.B., 1943; m. Keta Virginia Still, Oct. 11, 1939; children—Jennifer (Mrs. David R. Khaliel), Billie (Mrs. Gregory A. Picklesimer). Admitted to Va. bar, 1943; partner Kiser & Kiser, Wise, 1943—. Commr. accounts Circuit Ct. Wise County, 1970-73. Named Ky. col. Mem. Va. State Bar, Wise County Bar Assn. (pres. 1956-57), Pi Kappa Alpha, Phi Delta Phi. Republican. Baptist. Kiwanian. Home: Spring St Wise VA 24293 Office: Main St Wise VA 24293

KISPERT, WAYNE EARL, constrn. co. exec.; b. Clinton, Ind., Sept. 26, 1925; s. Ortie Curtis and Euphemia Broatch (Thorburn) K.; student Ind. State Tchrs. Coll., 1943-44; B.S. in C.E., Purdue U., 1950; m. Patricia Mason, June 20, 1948; children—Kenneth Allen, Philip Neil, David Wayne. Hydraulic engr. U.S. Geol. Survey, Indpls., 1948-51; control engr. constrn. E.I. duPont DeNemours, Wilmington, Del., 1951-55; gen. supt. Anning Johnson Co., Indpls., 1955-60, v.p. constrn., Melrose Park, Ill., 1960-71, sr. v.p., Orlando, Fla., 1971—; dir. Anning Johnson Supply & Mfg. Co., Orlando. Pres., Medinah (Ill.) Civic Assn., 1964-65, bd. dirs., 1965-68. Exec. bd. DuPage Area council Boy Scouts Am., 1968-70; bd. dirs. Spring Valley Lake Assn., Medinah, Ill., 1963-65. Served with USNR, 1943-45. Mem. Am. Soc. C.E., Am. Soc. Testing Materials, Nat. Acoutical Contractors Assn. (com. chmn. 1965-67), Cellular Concrete Assn. (pres. 1973), Am. Legion. Presbyn. Mason. Club: Bay Hill. Home: 6118 Cheshire Lane Bay Hill Orlando FL 32811 Office: 7001 Lake Ellenor Dr Orlando FL 32809

KISSINGER, HENRY ALFRED, govt. ofcl; b. Fuerth, Germany, May 27, 1923; s. Louis and Paula (Stern) K.; A.B. summa cum laude, Harvard, 1950, M.A., 1952, Ph.D., 1954;; m. Ann Fleischer, Feb. 6, 1949 (div. 1964); children—Elizabeth, David; m. 2d, Nancy Maginnes, Mar. 31, 1974. Came to U.S. in 1938, naturalized, 1943. Exec. dir. Harvard internat. 1951-69, lectr. dept. govt., 1957-59, dir. def. studies program, 1958-69, asso. prof. govt., 1959-62, prof., 1962-71, faculty Center Internat. Affairs, Harvard; asst. to the Pres. for nat. security affairs, 1969-73; Sec. of State, 1973—; dir. nuclear fgn. policy Council Fgn. Relations, 1955-56; dir. spl. studies project Rockefeller Bros. Fund, Inc., 1956-58. Cons. operations research office, 1950, cons. to dir. Strategy Bd., 1952, cons. Operations Coordinating Bd., 1955-56, cons. weapons systems evaluation group, 1956-60; cons. NSC, 1961-62, U.S. Arms Control and Disarmament Agy., 1961-67; cons. Dept. of State, 1965-69. Served with AUS, 1943-46. Recipient citation Woodrow Wilson prize for best book in fields of govt., politics, internat. affairs, 1958. Mem. Am. Polit. Sci. Assn. Council Fgn. Relations, Am. Acad. Arts and Scis., Phi Beta Kappa. Clubs: Cosmos, Federal City (Washington); St. Botolph (Boston); Century (N.Y.C.). Author: Nuclear Weapons and Foreign Policy, 1957; A World Restored; Castlereagh, Metternich and the Restoration of Peace 1821-22, 1957; The Necessity for Choice: The Prospects of American Foreign Policy, 1961; The Troubled Partnership; A Reappraisal of the Atlantic, Alliance, 1965. Editor: Problems of National Stretegy; Confluence, An Internat. Forum, 1951-58. Contbr. articles to profl. jours. Office: Sec of State Dept of State 2201 C St Washington DC 20520

KISSLING, FRED RALPH, JR., ins. agy. exec.; b. Nashville, Feb. 10, 1930; s. Fred Ralph and Sarah Elizabeth (FitzGerald) K.; B.A., Vanderbilt U., 1952, M.A., 1958; m. Jane Kirkpatrick, Sept. 12, 1959; children—Sarah FitzGerald, Jane Kirkpatrick. Spl. agt. Northwestern Mut. Life Ins. Co., Nashville, 1953-62, gen. agt., Lexington, Ky., 1962—; pres. Employee Benefit Cons., Inc., Lexington, 1961—; partner Kennington Assos., 1967—; pub. leader's mag., 1972—; dir. Bank of Lexington. Adv. bd. Salvation Army, Lexington, 1971—. C.L.U. Mem. Am. Soc. Chartered Life Underwriters (chpt. pres. 1969-70, regional v.p. 1972-73), Ky. Gen. Agts. and Mgrs. Assn. (pres. 1965-66), Nat. Assn. Life Underwriters (life mem. Million Dollar Round Table), Am. Soc. Pension Actuaries (dir. 1971—, pres. 1974), Sigma Chi. Mason (Shriner). Clubs: Cincinnati; Nashville City; Lexington, Lexington Polo; Lafayette. Author: Sell and Grow Rich, 1966. Editor: Questionaire in Pension Planning, 1971, Questionnaire in Estate Planning, 1971. Home: 728 Old Dobbin Circle Lexington KY 40502 Office: 98 Dennis Dr Lexington KY 40503

KISSNER, JACOB, mfg. co. exec.; b. Frankfurt on Main, Germany; s. Josef and Lina (Sann) K.; ed. business coll.; m. Johanna Ditt, Aug. 27, 1931; 1 dau., Olivia. Founder, owner Folbot Works, London, 1932-35; founder, 1935, since pres. Folbot Corp., L.I.; developer Folbot paddle and cruising excursions, White Water Sport, 1937; lectr. Mem. Am. Canoe Assn., Jamaica Estates Assn., Pack and Paddle Soc. Roman Catholic. Clubs: Kiwanis (pres.), Touring Kayak. Author: Foldboat Holidays, 1941; Fabulous Folbot Holidays, 1972; contbr. articles, picture stores to profl., sport publs. Holder Nat. White Water championship, 1941—. Office: Stark Indsl Park Charleston SC 29405

KITABCHI, ABBAS EQBAL, physician, educator; b. Tehran, Iran, Aug. 28, 1933; s. Hossein E. and Khanom (Moheet) K.; B.A., Cornell Coll., 1954; M.S., U. Okla., 1956, Ph.D., 1958, postgrad. fellow, 1958-60, M.D., 1965; m. Gloria Crocker, Feb. 22, 1957; children—Karen, Kathryn, Kelly. Came to U.S., 1950, naturalized, 1964. Intern, U. Okla., VA hosps., 1965-66; practice medicine specializing in endocrinology and metabolism, 1966—; sr. fellow endocrinology U. Wash., 1966-68, instr. medicine, 1966-67, attending staff U. Wash. Hosp., 1967-68; asst. prof. medicine U. Tenn., 1968-71, asso. prof. biochemistry, 1968-72; asso. chief of staff, chief labs. endocrinology and metabolism VA Hosp., Memphis, 1968-73; prof. biochemistry, asso. prof. medicine U. Tenn., 1971-73, program dir. Clin. Research Center, 1973—, prof. medicine, biochemistry, sect. chief endocrinology and metabolism dept. medicine, 1973—. Pres., Scenic Hills PTA, 1970. Okla. Med. Research Inst. fellow, 1958-60; NIH spl. fellow, 1966-68; NIH grantee, 1962—. Diplomate Am. Bd. Internal Medicine. Mem. Am. Chem. Soc., Am. Inst. Nutrition, Am. Fedn. Clin. Research, Endocrine Soc., Central Soc. Clin Research, Am., So. socs. clin. investigations, Memphis Acad. Internal Medicine, Am. Soc. Biol. Chemists, Am., Tenn. (pres. 1973) diabetes assns. Contbr. numerous articles to profl. jours. Home: 5527 Pecan Grove Lane Memphis TN 38117 Office: 951 Court Av Memphis TN 38163

KITCHEN, JACK S., savs. and loan pres.; b. Glasgow, Mo., May 6, 1916; s. William Barnes and Margaret Armine (Meyer) K.; student U. Mo., 1935-36, 36-37; m. Hulda Gordon Rhodes, Feb. 16, 1942; children—Jack S., Helen (Mrs. Peter T. Ready), Margaret (Mrs. Dennis N. Eggemeyer). Teller, Glasgow Savs. Bank, 1935, Commerce Trust Co., Kansas City, Mo., 1938-39; with Community State Bank, Kansas City, Mo., 1939-40; corr., bank dept., City Nat. Bank & Trust Co., Kansas City, Mo., 1945-49; v.p. SW Nat. Bank, El Paso, Tex., 1949-57; pres. 1st Savs. & Loan Assn., El Paso, 1957—. Treas., Salvation Army Bd., 1959-72; pres. Southwestern Athletics, 1967-71; pres. Southwestern Sun Carnival Assn., 1971. Served with USNR, 1941-66. Decorated Air medals (8), D.F.C. Mem. Phi Delta Theta. Presbyn. (elder, deacon, trustee). Mason (Shriner), Kiwanian (pres. 1964). Club: El Paso. Home: 1800 N Stanton St #1008 El Paso TX 79902 Office: 506 N Mesa St El Paso TX 79901

KITTREDGE, WILLOUGHBY EATON, physician; b. Napoleonville, La., Oct. 28, 1909; s. Willoughby Eaton and Mamie (Foucher) K.; B.S., Tulane U., 1929, M.D., 1933; m. Ruth Sullivan, June 26, 1936; children—Susan (Mrs. Jerome Hoskins), Sally (Mrs. Hugh Evans). Intern, Touro Infirmary, New Orleans, 1933-34, resident urology, 1934-35; fellow urology Tulane U., New Orleans Charity Hosp., 1935-57; instr. urology Tulane U., 1937-39, asst. prof., 1939-49, asso. prof., 1949-58, clin. prof., 1958—; mem. staff Ochsner Found. Hosp.; sr. vis. staff New Orleans Charity Hosp.; pvt. practice medicine, specializing in urology, New Orleans, 1937-41; partner Ochsner Clinic, 1957—, bd. mgrs., 1965—, past chmn. personnel and staff exec. coms.; chief dept. urology Ochsner Clinic and Ochsner Found. Hosp., 1961-70, pres. hosp. staff, 1955-56. Dir. Fidelity Bldg. & Loan Assn.; chmn. adv. bd. Orleans Service Corp., 1958-65. Pres., New Orleans Area Health Planning Council, 1970. Diplomate Am. Bd. Urology (pres. 1969, cons. 1970—). Fellow A.C.S. (com. chmn., bd. govs.); mem. A.M.A. (chmn. urol. sect. 1964-65), So., Pan Am. med assns., La., Orleans Parish (pres. 1967-68) med socs., Am. Urol. Assn. (pres. 1972, com. chmn., pres. 1964, past com. chmn. Southeastern sect.), La. Urol. Soc. (pres. 1961), Clin. Soc. Genitourinary Surgeons, Am. Assn. Genitourinary Surgeons, Internationale Societe d'Urologie (exec. com.), Soc. U. Urologists, New Orleans Grad. Med. Assembly (pres. 1964), Council Med. Splty. Socs. (v.p. 1970), Am. Assn. Clin. Urologists (chmn. finance com. 1969), Soc. Colonial Wars, S.R., Phi Chi, Delta Tau Delta. Contbr. articles to profl. jours. Home: 5801 St Charles Av New Orleans LA 70115 Office: 1514 Jefferson Hwy New Orleans LA 70121

KITTRELL, FLEMMIE PANSY, ret. educator; b. Henderson, N.C., Dec. 25, 1904; d. James Lee and Alice (Mills) Kittrell; grad. Acad. Hampton Inst., 1924; B.S., Coll. Hampton Inst., 1928; Ph.D. (Rosenwald scholar 1929; Gen. Edn. Bd. scholar 1933), Cornell U., 1936. Dean students Bennett Coll., Greensboro, N.C., 1930-40; dean of women Hampton Inst., 1940-44; prof., head dept. home econs. Howard U., Washington, after 1944, now prof. emerita; spl. assignment U.S. State Dept. to Liberia, West Africa, 1947-48; Fulbright prof. Baroda U., India, 1950, mem. bd. studies for faculty of home sci., 1956. Home econ. cons. ICA in Baroda, India under U.S. Dept. State, 1953-55; cons. edn. program Leopoldville, Congo Republic, 1961—, leader 22 Ind. women to Japan, U.S. State Dept. project, 1955; lecture tour East and West Africa for U.S. Dept. State, 1958. Del. Internat. Congress of Home Econs., Stockholm, Sweden, 1949; del. Meth. Ch. to Internat. Missionary Council in Willingen, Germany, 1952; del. UN Conf., Geneva, 1959; mem. nat. bd. YWCA, 1959; FAO nutrition assignment to India, 1960; State Dept. cultural exchange tour, West Africa, 1961; mem. group Airlift of Understanding to Bangladesh, 1972; U.S. observer Conf. on New Horizons for Women of Africa, Morocco, 1971; AID sponsored observer Zaire, 1972; convener Ph.D. nutrition exam. U. Madras (India), 1972. Trustee Sibly Hosp., Hampton Inst.; mem. home econ. council Cornell U., 1964; bd. dirs. Washington chpt. UN. Recipient Liberian (West Africa) award for outstanding service to country, 1948; Hampton Alumni award, 1955; Gold Key Award, Am. Tchrs. Assn., 1962; Internat. award Century Club Bus. and Profl. Women, 1965; Cornell U. Alumni award for contbn. to human devel., 1968; Hampton Inst. Centennial medal, 1968. Fellow A.A.A.S.; mem. Soc. Prodigal Son, N.C., Am. Assn. U. Women, Am. Dietetics Assn., Am. Home Econs. Assn., Women's Internat. League for Peace and Freedom, Sigma Xi, Sigma Delta Epsilon, Phi Kappa Phi, Pi Lambda Theta, Omicron Nu, Beta Kappa Chi. Home: 3200 Warder St Washington DC 20010

KIVETT, CHARLES THOMAS, judge; b. Carthage, N.C., Jan. 1, 1927; s. Charles Anderson and Sally (Russell) K.; A.B., Catawba Coll., 1950; LL.B., U. N.C., 1955; m. Hilda Lee Kern, Aug. 21, 1951; children—Charles Thomas, Teresa Lee. With Blue Bell, Inc., Greensboro, N.C., 1951-52; trust officer, Security Nat. Bank (now N.C. Nat. Bank), Greensboro, 1955-61, asst. v.p. comml. dept., 1962-63; admitted to N.C. bar 1955, practiced in Greensboro, 1963—, solicitor (pros. atty.), City Ct. Greensboro, 1964-65; dist. solicitor, 12th Dist., State N.C., 1967-69; resident judge Superior Ct., 18th Jud. Dist., Greensboro, 1969—. Mem. N.C. Criminal Code Commn., 1972—. Mem. N.C. Adv. Council, Small Bus. Adminstrn., 1963-64, N.C. Employment Security Commn., 1964. Mem. nat. com. N.C. Young Democrats, 1959-60, spl. asst. to pres. 1963-64, pres. Guilford County, 1956-57; Dem. nominee N.C. Ho. of Reps., 1964; del. to Atlantic Assn. Young Pol Leaders, Oxford, Eng., 1965. Served with USNR, 1944-46; PTO. Named Outstanding Young Dem. N.C., 1965. Mem. N.C., Greensboro bar assns. Methodist. Mason (Shriner). Home: 923 Winterlochen Dr Greensboro NC 27410 Office: Guilford County Courthouse Greensboro NC 27402

KIZER, JOHN FUQUA, lawyer; b. Milan, Tenn., Dec. 22, 1916; s. John William and Martha Jane (Fuqua) K.; LL.B., U. Va., 1940; m. Virginia Martin Meacham, Aug. 14, 1943; children—John Fuqua, Walter Morris. Admitted to Tenn. bar, 1940, practiced in Milan, 1946-51; 63—; commr. finance and taxation Nashville, 1951-52; circuit judge 13th Jud. Circuit Tenn., Milan, 1952-63; mem. firm Drake & Kizer, 1947-51; pvt. practice law, 1963—. Dir. Milan Banking Co., Milan, 1969—. Served to capt. Judge Adv. Gen. Corps, AUS, 1942-46; ETO. Mem. Am., Tenn., Gibson County bar assns. Rotarian. Home: 315 Park Av Milan TN 38358 Office: 110 W Front St Milan TN 38358

KIZZIA, COOPER, ins. agt.; b. Murfreesboro, Ark., June 8, 1938; s. Hurley Fred and Clarice (Hare) K.; student Texarkana Coll., 1957-58; B.B.A., So. State Coll., 1961; m. Helen Martin, Dec. 18, 1960; children—James Cooper, Julie Lynn. Concrete technician Midway Constrn. Co., Conway, Ark., 1961-62; with contract dept. Ark. La. Gas Co., Little Rock, 1962-63; mgr. Pike County Ins. Agy., Murfreesboro, 1963—; dir. Pike County Bank. Chmn. Pike County Housing Authority, 1965—; vice-chmn. Pike County Devel. Council, 1966—; mem. Murfreesboro Water and Sewer Commn., 1968—. City recorder, Murfreesboro, 1969—. Bd. dirs. Pike County Fair Assn. Mem. Ark. Assn. Ins. Agts., Murfreesboro C. of C. (dir.). Methodist. Lion. Home: Box 232 Murfreesboro AR 71958 Office: 101 N Washington St Murfreesboro AR 71958

KLAPMAN, WILLIAM TURNER, lawyer; b. Greenwood, S.C., Apr. 17, 1927; s. Rodney Kyle and Nora Elizabeth (Turner) K.; student Clemson U., 1944-45; LL.B., U. S.C., 1951; m. Betty Lou Campbell, Dec. 21, 1951; children—Mellie Elizabeth, Julia Victoria. Admitted to S.C. bar, 1951; with legal dept. OPS, Columbia, S.C., 1951-52; staff adjuster Farm Bur. Ins. Cos., Orangeburg, S.C., 1952-60; pvt. practice, Orangeburg, 1960—. Atty. Orangeburg County, 1970. Served with USNR, 1945-46. Mem. S.C. Trial Lawyers Assn., S.C. County Attys. Assn., Am. Legion (past post comdr.). Democrat. Baptist. Rotarian. Home: 871 Ellis St Orangeburg SC 29115 Office: 370 S Paul St NE Orangeburg NC 29115

KLASS, PHILIP JULIAN, journalist; b. Des Moines, Nov. 8, 1919; s. Raymond N. and Ann (Traxler) K.; B.S., Ia. State U., 1941. Elec. engr. Gen. Electric Co., Schenectady, 1941-52; sr. avionics editor Aviation Week and Space Tech. mag., Washington, 1952—. Fellow I.E.E.E.; mem. A.A.A.S., Aviation/Space Writers Assn., Nat. Press Club. Author: UFOs-Identified, 1968; Secret Sentries in Space, 1971. Home: 560 N St SW Washington DC 20024 Office: Nat Press Bldg Washington DC 20004

KLAUS, KENNETH BLANCHARD, musician, educator; b. Earlville, Ia., Nov. 11, 1923; s. Kenneth R. and Iris (Blanchard) K.; B.A., U. Ia., 1947, M.A., 1948, M.F.A., 1949, Ph.D., 1950; m. Marian Ida Fyler, June 8, 1947; children—Kenneth Sheldon, Karl Sherman. Prof., La. State U., Baton Rouge, 1950—, Alumni prof., 1966—; asso. condr. Baton Rouge Symphony, 1965—; prin. viola, 1950—. Served with USAAF, 1942-45; ETO. Mem. Am. Soc. Univ. Composers, Am. Musicol. Soc., Internat. Webern Soc., Berg Soc., Schoenberg Soc., Am. Mus. Library Assn., Am. Fedn. Musicians, Am. String Tchrs. Assn. (state pres.), Phi Mu Alpha, Omicron Delta Kappa, Pi Kappa Lambda, Phi Kappa Phi, Delta Phi Alpha. Author: The Romantic Period in Music. Composer over 60 compositions, 1940—. Home: 823 Kenilworth Pkwy Baton Rouge LA 70808

KLECHAK, THOMAS LEWIS, dentist; b. Washington, Sept. 19, 1940; s. Thomas and Margaret Bell (Lewis) K.; B.S., Wake Forest U., 1966; D.D.S., U. Md., 1965; M. Sc., U. N.C., 1971; m. Diane Lorraine Donald, Aug. 15, 1964; children—Thomas Lewis, James Donald. Practicing orthodontist, Jacksonville, Fla., 1971—; mem. faculty Fla. Jr. Coll. Mem. Young Republicans. Served as capt. Dental Corps, USAF, 1965-69. Mem. Am., Fla. dental assns., N.E. Dist., Jacksonville dental socs., Am. Assn. Orthodontists, So. Soc. Orthodontists, Soc. Dentistry for Children, Acad. Dentistry, Jacksonville C. of C. (exec. council), Omicron Kappa Upsilon. Clubs: Rotary (v.p.), Ponte Vedra, Century (Jacksonville). Home: 7249 Trails End Jacksonville FL 32211 Office: 819 Townsend Blvd Jacksonville FL 32211

KLECK, DAVID MILBURN, pub. relations exec.; b. Alexandria, La., Sept. 10, 1921; s. William Rheinhardt and Sidney (Milburn) K.; B.A., Tulane U., 1948; m. Dorothy Cynthia Williams, June 10, 1950; children—John Milburn, Nancy Milburn, Susan Lee. Reporter, sub-editor Times-Picayune, New Orleans, 1948-52; v.p. Gulfside, Inc., New Orleans, 1952-55; New Orleans mgr. Godwin Advt. Agy., 1955-62; owner David M. Kleck & Assos., New Orleans, 1962—. Adviser Jr. League New Orleans, 1965-67. Bd. dirs. Family Service Soc., 1953-54, Travelers Aid Soc., 1960-65, Adv. Com. to Juvenile Cts., 1960-62, La. Soc. Mental Health, 1964-66. Served to lt. USNR, 1943-46. Mem. Pub. Relations Soc. Am., Internat. House New Orleans, Kappa Sigma, Navy League (v.p. 1965-67). Democrat. Club: Lawn Tennis. Home: 5353 Marcia Av New Orleans LA 70124 Office: 520 John Hancock Bldg New Orleans LA 70130

KLEEMAN, FRANCIS SIDNEY, cons. environmental and chem. engr.; b. Springfield, Mo., Jan. 17, 1916; s. Walter E. and Louise S. (Thieme) K.; B.S., Washington U., 1937; M.S., U. Mich., 1940; postgrad. U. Pitts., 1940-43, U. Miami, 1969-70; m. Virginia Ellen Frisinger, Sept. 6, 1941; children—David F., Robert E., Janice E. (Mrs. Gerald E. Kardas). Partner New Castle Foundry Co. (Pa.), 1947-49; pres. Kleeman Alloy & Chem. Co., Havertown, Pa., 1960-67; v.p. engring. Applied Research Labs, Hialeah, Fla., 1968-69; pres. Kleeman Engring., Inc., Ft. Lauderdale, Fla., also v.p. engring. Nalews, Inc., Ft. Lauderdale, 1973—; environmental seminar cons. Broward Community Coll. Civic rep. Mainlands sect., Tamarac, Fla., 1968-69. Fellow Am. Inst. Chemists; mem. Nat. Soc. Profl. Engrs., Fla. Engring. Soc., Am. Soc. Metals, Water Pollution Control Fedn., Air Pollution Control Assn., Am. Foundrymens Soc., Iota Alpha. Contbr. articles profl. jours. Patentee in field. Home: 4300 NW 44th St Fort Lauderdale FL 33313 Office: 1507 NW 47th Av Fort Lauderdale FL 33313

KLEEMAN, RICHARD PENTLARGE, assn. exec.; b. N.Y.C., June 24, 1923; s. Arthur S. and Alice (Pentlarge) K.; grad. Choate Sch., 1940; A.B., Harvard, 1946; m. Rosslyn A. Shore, Jan. 1, 1950; children—Nancy, Alice, Katherine, David. Joined Mpls. Star and Tribune, 1946, reporter, copyreader, 1946-51, asst. city editor, 1951-53, asst. news editor, 1953-54, Sunday news editor, 1954-55, named news editor (edn.), 1955; Washington corr. Mpls. Tribune, 1966-72; asst. dir. Washington office Assn. Am. Pubs., Inc., 1972-73, dir., 1973—. Served to 1st lt. AUS, 1942-46. Recipient Nat. Sch. Bell award, 1961. Mem. Am. Newspaper Guild, Planned Parenthood Fedn. Am. (dir. 1958-61), Planned Parenthood Mpls. (past pres.), Phi Beta Kappa, Sigma Delta Chi (past pres. Minn., past regional dir. SDX Found. bd.) Club: Nat. Press. Home: 3642 Upton St NW Washington DC 20008 Office: 1920 L St NW Washington DC 20036

KLEILER, FRANK MUNRO, govt. ofcl.; b. Green Bay, Wis., Apr. 17, 1914; s. Frank Andrew and Addie (Munro) K.; A.B., Antioch Coll., Yellow Springs, O., 1938; student Am. U., Washington, 1937-38; m. Frances Pauline Brezon, Apr. 10, 1939; children—David Allen, James Robert. Reporter, Evening Star, Washington, 1935-36, Boston Herald, 1936-37; clk. to bd. mem. Nat. Mediation Bd., 1937-39; asst. to bd. mem. Nat. Labor Relations Bd., 1939-41, field examiner, Cleve., 1941-42, Indpls., 1942-43, Chgo., 1943-44, regional dir., Pitts., 1944-47, exec. sec., Washington, 1947-51, 53-60; disputes dir. WSB, 1951-52, pub. mem. review and appeals com. 1952-53; dep. commr. Bur. Labor-Mgmt. Reports, Dept. Labor, 1960-62, dir. Office Welfare and Pension Plans, 1962-63, dir. Office Labor-Mgmt. and Welfare Pension Reports, 1963-70, dep. asst. sec. for planning and evaluation, 1970-74; Washington corr., asso. editor Employee Benefit Plan Rev., also EBPR Research Reports, 1974—. Mem. Acad. Polit. Sci., Indsl. Relations Research Assn. Home: 9100 Warren St Silver Spring MD 20910

KLEIMAN, ARIEL, educator; b. Cordoba, Argentina, Oct. 27, 1939; s. Marcos and Sofia (Blank) K.; diploma on econ. and social statistics Interam. Statis. Inst., Santiago, Chile, 1963; diploma on transport planning Latin Am. Inst. Econ. and Social Planning of UNO, Santiago, 1964; C.P.A., Economist, Cordoba Nat. U., 1965; M.S., Mexican Nat. U. Electronic Computing Center, 1966, M.Engring., 1974; diploma Internat. Center for Advancement Mgmt. Edn., Stanford, 1970; m. Elena Kovalsky, Jan. 21, 1966. Faculty schs. of econs. and social and polit. scis. Mexican Nat. U., Mexico City, 1967-68, Grad. Sch. Engring., 1967—, Grad. Sch. Bus., 1968-71, head statistics dept., 1967-69, head math. and statistics sect. Sch. Mgmt., 1970-72, head operations research sect. Grad. Sch. Engring., 1971—, acad. sec. Grad. Sch. Engring., 1973-74, head social and human scis. dept. Sch. Engring., 1974—. Cons. operations research and econs. Mgmt. Cons., Inc., Mexico City, 1967-70, Modern Engring. Techniques, Inc., Mexico City, 1972-73. OAS fellow, 1963; UN Econ. and Social Council fellow, 1964; UNESCO fellow, 1966; Ford Found. fellow, 1969-70. Mem. Mexican Inst. Planning and Operation of Systems, Am. Statis. Assn., Econometric Soc., Researchers and Tchrs. Soc. Mexican Nat. U. Author: Sets: Mathematical Applications to Management, 1972; Matrices: Mathematical Applications to Economics and Management, 1973. Home: 25 Minerva St Apt 501 Mexico 19 DF Mexico Office: Grad Sch Engring Mexican Nat U University City Mexico 20 DF Mexico

KLEIN, BARNEY ISADORE, JR., physician; b. Kerrville, Tex., Apr. 6, 1929; s. Barney Isadore and Zelpha Catherine (Green) K.; student Tex. Western U., 1955-56, Stephen F. Austin State Coll., 1956-58; M.D., U. Tex., 1962; m. Patsy Virginia Johnson, Dec. 21, 1954; children—Howard Felix, Julia Catherine, Cynthia Ann. Intern St. Joseph's Hosp., Ft. Worth, 1962-63; gen. practice Littlefield (Tex.) Hosp. and Clinic, 1963—; health officer Lamb County, 1965-66; med. adviser to A.R.C. chpt., 1967—. Served with AUS, 1954-56. Mem. Tex. Acad. Gen. Practice (v.p. South Plains chpt. 1967), Lamb County Med. Soc. (sec.-treas. 1965, v.p. 1966, pres. 1967), Theta Kappa Psi, Alpha Chi. Methodist (chmn. bd. missions 1966-69, chmn. council on ministries 1969-71). Home: 1414 Cherry Blossom Littlefield TX 79339 Office: 401 W 6th St Littlefield TX 79339

KLEIN, EDWARD LAWRENCE, govt. ofcl.; b. Roscoe, Pa., Feb. 17, 1936; s. Julius Herman and Grace Regina (Carroll) K.; B.S., Pa. State U., 1958, M.S., 1961; M.B.A., Baylor U., 1963; Ph.D., La. State U., 1968; m. Linda Anne Copeland, Aug. 24, 1963; children—Paul, John, Erin, Stephanie. Asst. dist. forester Md. Dept. Forests and Parks, Oakland, 1958-60; teaching and research aide Pa. State U., 1960-61; instr. forestry La. State U., 1963-68; market analyst Northeastern Forest Expt. Sta. of U.S. Forest Service, Princeton, W.Va., 1968-69; supr. econs. and marketing sect. div. forestry, fisheries and wildlife T.V.A., Norris, Tenn., 1969—; cons.; producer television program on La. plywood industry, 1965. Mem. Soc. Am. Foresters, Forest Products Research Soc. (nat. div. chmn. 1971-72), Xi Sigma Pi. Roman Catholic. K.C. Home: 3841 Montevista Rd Cleveland OH 44121 Office: TVA Forestry Bldg Norris TN 37828

KLEIN, ELIAS, scientist; b. Leipzig, Germany, Oct. 26, 1924 (came to U.S., 1934, naturalized 1943); B.S., Tulane U., 1951, M.S., 1952, Ph.D., 1954; m. Beverly J. Aronowitz, May 9, 1948; children—Jerrold, Jon, Meryl. Head investigation U.S. Dept. Agr. lab., New Orleans, 1954-58; with Courtaulds, Inc., Mobile, Ala., 1958-67, dir. research and devel., 1965-67; sci. dir. Gulf South Research Inst., New Orleans, 1967—. Adj. prof. Loyola U., 1970—; cons. VA Hosp., 1970—. Served with AUS, 1943-45. Fellow Am. Inst. Chemists; mem. Am. Chem. Soc., Sci. Research Soc. Am. Contbr. articles to profl. jours. Patentee in field. Home: 4430 St Bernard Av New Orleans LA 70122 Office: PO Box 26500 New Orleans LA 70126

KLEIN, LOUIS SAMUEL, accountant; b. Chgo., Sept. 13, 1908; s. Joseph and Lena (Groveman) K.; C.P.A., U. N.Y., 1946; m. Syd Bass, June 2, 1934; children—Letty Sandra, Adele Phylis, Walter Jay. Acct., auditor Federated Purchaser, Inc., N.Y.C., 1932-35; comptroller, acct. Ala. Braid & Ribbon Co., C. M. Offray & Son, Gadsden, 1935-37; practicing C.P.A., 1937—; partner Bloomberg, Max, Louis S. Klein & Co., Gadsden, Klein, Harwood & Lambert, now partner Cherry, Bekaert & Holland; pres., dir. Comml. & Financial Corp. Auditor Gadsden Concert Assn., 1961-72; mem. Jewish Welfare Bd. Etowah County. Mem. C. of C., N.Y., Ala. (past v.p., chmn. Gadsden-Anniston chpt.) socs. C.P.A.'s, Am. Inst. C.P.A.'s, Am., So. insts. mgmt., Am. Accounting Assn., B'nai B'rith, Coosa Lodge (past pres.). Mem. Beth Israel Temple (past pres.). Club: Civitan Internat. (past pres., lt. gov.). Home: 102 Cleveland Ct Gadsden AL 35901 Office: 752 Chestnut St Gadsden AL 35901

KLEIN, MILTON, govt. ofcl.; b. St. Louis, Jan. 13, 1924; s. Isador and Ilona (Tichler) K.; B.S. in Chem. Engring., Washington U., St. Louis, 1944; M.B.A., Harvard, 1950; m. Frances Motto, Dec. 28, 1947; children—Richard, Barbara, Janet. Chem. engr. Argonne Nat. Lab., Chgo., 1946-48; with AEC, Chgo., 1950-60, asst. mgr., 1958-60; with NASA/AEC, Washington, 1960-71, mgr., dir. Space Nuclear Systems Office, 1967-71; asso. adminstr. for research, devel., demonstrations Fed. Railroad Adminstrn., Washington, 1971-74; asst. gen. mgr. for energy devel. programs AEC, 1974—. Mem. staff dirs. group Pres.'s Space Task Group, 1969. Mem. adv. com. sci. and tech. manpower Ill. Selective Service System, 1957-60. Served with USNR, 1944-46. Mem. Am. Inst. Aeros. and Astronautics, A.A.A.S., Am. Nuclear Soc., Sigma Xi, Tau Beta Pi. Club: Torch (Washington, dir.). Home: 6404 Tulsa Lane Bethesda MD 20034 Office: Atomic Energy Commn Washington DC 20545

KLEIN, NORMAN LESTER, chem. engr.; b. Balt., Feb. 27, 1912; s. George W. and Anna (Willerhausen) K.; student Johns Hopkins, 1930-32; B.S. in Chem. Engring., Ga. Inst. Tech., 1937; m. Mary Leonard, Nov. 25, 1937; children—Roy Alan, Mary Lee. Research engr. Rohm & Haas Co., Phila., 1937-38; lubrication engr. Shell Oil Co., Inc., Balt., 1938-42; chief fuel, lubricants sect. Office Chief Ordnance, Dept. Army, Washington, 1946-59, dep. chief research br.,

1959-60, sci. adviser to chief, 1960-62, asst. dep. for labs., 1962—; dir. chemistry and materials research Materiel Command, U.S. Army, 1962—. Mem. sub. com. aircraft fuels NACA, Washington, 1955-60; adv. research com. chem. energy systems NASA, Washington, 1961—. Served as lt. col., AUS, 1942-46. Fellow Am. Inst. Chemists; mem. A.A.A.S., Soc. Automotive Engrs. Contbr. numerous articles in field to jours. Home: 9118 Cherrytree Dr Alexandria VA 22309 Office: care Office Dep for Labs US Army Materiel Command Washington DC 20025

KLEIN, PHILIPP HILLEL, chemist; govt. ofcl.; b. N.Y.C., Sept. 14, 1926; s. Raphael and Lillian Rae (Wald) K.; student Bard Coll., 1942-43, 44-45, Columbia Sch. Engring., 1943-44; B.S. in Chemistry Syracuse U., 1948, M.S. (office of Naval Research fellow) in Phys. Chemistry, 1951, Ph.D. (AEC fellow), 1953; m. Charlotte Feuerstein, June 21, 1953; children—Joshua David, Daniel William, Jonathan Henry. Research asso. Knolls Atomic Power Lab., Gen. Electric Co., Schenectady, 1952-56; phys. chemist Gen. Electronics Lab., Syracuse, N.Y., 1956-61; research staff Sperry Rand Research Center, Sudbury, Mass., 1961-66; physicist NASA, Cambridge, Mass., 1966-70; sect. head U.S. Naval Research Lab., Washington, 1970—. Mem. Orthodox Jewish Council of Syracuse, 1957-61. Bd. dirs. Hebrew Acad. Greater Washington, 1970-73, Silver Spring Jewish Center, 1970—. Served with USNR, 1945-46. Fellow Am. Inst. Chemists; mem. I.E.E.E. (chmn. com. on solid state devices 1962-63), Am. Ceramic Soc., Am. Phys. Soc., Am. Assn. for Crystal Growth, Electrochem. Soc. Contbr. articles on radiation effects, crystal growth and energy conversion to sci. jours. Home: 11704 Stonington Place Silver Spring MD 20902

KLEIN, ROBERT M., govt. ofcl.; b. McKeesport, Pa., Jan. 12, 1926; s. Milton E. and Hilda (Lichtenstein) K.; student U. Ky., 1943-44; A.B., George Washington U., 1949, M.A., 1955; grad. Nat. War Coll., 1973; m. Jan Lloyd Lawson, Mar. 18, 1950; children—Leslie Jan, Malcolm Lawson, Randal Todd. Asst. Japan desk officer U.S. Dept. Commerce, Washington, 1950-54, sr. Philippine desk officer 1954-60, commerce dept. mem. U.S. Investment Survey Mission to Thailand, 1959, chief Japan-Korea sect., Dept. Commerce, 1962-64, dep. dir. Far East div., 1964-72, dir. gen. comml. policy div., 1973—; comml. attache, U.S. Embassy, Seoul, Korea, 1960-62. Lectr. Fgn. Service Inst., 1969-72. Mem. U.S. Civil Service Commn. Bd. of Examiners for Economists, 1965-66; head U.S. delegation to ann. meeting trade com. UN Econ. Commn. for Asia and Far East, 1968. Served with AUS, 1944-46, ETO. Recipient Bronze medal for superior service U.S. Dept. Commerce, 1967. Mem. Am. Econ. Assn. Unitarian. Home: 1608 Sherwood Hall Lane Alexandria VA 22306 Office: US Dept Commerce Washington DC 20230

KLEIN, STEPHEN BARRY, physiol. psychologist, educator; b. Portsmouth, Va., Sept. 15, 1946; s. Clarence I. and Beverly (Golden) K.; B.S., Va. Poly. Inst., 1968; M.S., Rutgers U., 1969, Ph.D. (USPHS fellow), 1971; m. Janet Kay Linkous, Feb. 25, 1966; children—Dora, David, Jason. NSF trainee, 1968; asst. prof. psychology Old Dominion U., Norfolk, Va., 1971—. USPHS grantee, 1972. Mem. Psychonomic Soc. Contbr. articles to sci. jours. Home: 3345 Lakecrest Dr Virginia Beach VA 23452 Office: Old Dominion Univ Hampton Blvd Norfolk VA 23508

KLEIN, THOMAS MARTIN, economist; b. Detroit, Aug. 9, 1928; s. Maurice and Ruth (Fink) K.; B.A., U. Mich., 1949, M.A., 1951, Ph.D., 1958; m. Judith Veit Simon, June 20, 1958; children—Michael, Margaret, David, Richard, Edward. Asst. prof. econs. Hamilton Coll., 1957-59; economist balance of payments div. Internat. Monetary Fund, 1959-62; economist div. internat. finance, bd. govs. Fed. Res. System, 1962-67; chief commerce industry and banking div. U.S. Civil Adminstrn., Ryukyu Islands, 1967-69; economist Internat. Bank for Reconstrn. and Devel., Washington, 1969—. Served with AUS, 1950-52. Mem. Am. Econ. Assn., Royal Econ. Soc. Home: 4008 Ingersol Dr Silver Spring MD 20902 Office: 1818 H St NW Washington DC 20433

KLEINERMAN, MORRIS, psychiatrist; b. Spring Valley, N.Y., May 18, 1907; s. David and Rose (Pilinis) K.; B.S., Coll. City N.Y., 1929; M.D., U. St. Andrews, 1933; m. Gertrude Janet Cohen, June 6, 1945; children—Ruth Anne, Martha Joan, Deena Adrian. Intern Manhattan Gen. Hosp., N.Y.C., 1933-34; resident St. Elizabeth's Hosp., Washington, 1934-35, staff psychiatrist, 1935-47; medicine specializing in psychiatry, Washington, 1947—; clin. prof. psychiatry George Washington U. Med. Sch., 1965—. Served to maj. AUS, 1942-46. Fellow Am. Psychiat. Assn. (life); mem. A.M.A., Assn. Am. Med. Colls., Washington Psychiat. Soc. (pres. 1963-64), Phi Delta Epsilon. Home: 7207 Rollingwood Dr Chevy Chase MD 20015 Office: 2520 L St NW Washington DC 20037

KLEINERT, ERWIN JOHN, JR., educator; b. Lansing, Mich., Mar. 14, 1931; s. Erwin John and Inez Mae (Stanton) K.; A.B. in English, U. Mich., 1952, M.A. in Edn., 1959, Ph.D. in Edn., 1964; m. Jeanne M. Anderson, June 18, 1955; children—Christopher, Scott, Braddock. Tchr. pub. schs., Ann Arbor, Mich., 1956-64; prin. Glenbrook North High Sch., Northbrook, Ill., 1964-67; dir. Fla. Migratory Child Research Center, U. Miami, 1967-69; prof. edn., U. Miami, Coral Gables, Fla., 1967—. Cons. to Fla. Sch. Desegregation Center, Ala. Center for Intercultural Edn., Miccosukee Indians Environmental Edn. Served with USNR, 1952-56. Recipient James B. Edmondson award U. Mich., 1963-64. Mem. Am. Assn. for Supervision and Curriculum Devel., Phi Delta Kappa. Author: Migrant Child in Florida, 1970. Contbr. articles to profl. publs. Home: 7260 SW 109 Terrace Miami FL 33156

KLEINKNECHT, CHRISTIAN FREDERICK, fraternal orgn. exec.; b. Washington, Feb. 14, 1924; s. Christian Frederick and Nell May (Barr) K.; B.C.S., Benjamin Franklin U., 1954; m. Gene E. Kamm, Jan. 21, 1949; children—Gene Ellen (Mrs. Richard Loope), Henry, Scott, Joan. Concessionaire, Washington Baseball Washington Club, 1943-46; grand sec. gen. Supreme Council of 33 deg. Masons, Washington, 1946—. Sec., Scottish Rite Found. Served with USNR, World War II. Mem Anglo Am. Tourist Assn. (treas., dir.), Nat. Sojourners (hon.). Republican. Mem. Ch. of Christ. Clubs: Columbia Country (Chevy Chase, Md.); University (Washington). Home: 505 Harding Dr Silver Spring MD 20901 Office: 1733 16th St NW Washington DC 20009

KLEINKNECHT, KENNETH SAMUEL, govt. ofcl.; b. Washington, July 24, 1919; s. Christian Frederick and Nell May (Barr) K.; B.S. in Mech. Engring., Purdue U., 1942; m. Patricia Jean Todd, May 24, 1947; children—Linda May, Patricia Ann, Frederick William. With NASA, 1942-51, project engr. Lewis Research Center, Cleve., 1951-59; successively aero. research scientist, head operations engring., advanced projects mgmt. officer, Edwards AFB, Cal., 1959-62; tech asst. to dir., Johnson Space Center, NASA, Houston, 1962-63, mgr. Mercury Project, 1963-67, dep. mgr. Gemini Program, 1967-70, mgr. Apollo Command and Service Modules, mgr. Skylab Program, 1970-74, dir. flight operations, 1974—. Mem. exec. bd. Sam Houston Area council Boy Scouts Am., Houston, 1972-73. Trustee Vol. Fire Dept., Seabrook, Tex., 1970-72. Recipient Group achievement awards NASA, 1962, 64, 66, medal for outstanding Leadership NASA, 1963, Exceptional Service medal, NASA, 1960, Distinguished Service medal, 1969, 73; John J. Montgomery award San Diego chpt. Nat. Soc. Aerospace Profls., 1963. Fellow Am. Astronautical Soc., Am. Inst. Aeros. and Astronautics (asso). Mason (33 deg.). Home: 219 Whispering Oaks Dr Seabrook TX 77586 Office: NASA Johnson Space Center Houston TX 77058

KLEINMANN, JACK HENRY, assn. exec.; b. Bronx, N.Y., Sept. 1, 1932; s. Max and Helen (Weinstein) K.; B.A., Bklyn. Coll., 1953, M.A., 1955; Ed.D., Columbia, 1960; m. Ellen Kalberman, June 30, 1954 (div.); children—Laurie, Deborah; m. 2d, Joi Hase Winegar, Sept. 16, 1972. Tchr. pub. schs., N.Y.C., 1953-58; adminstrv. asst. to head of dept. ednl. adminstrn. Tchrs. Coll., Columbia, 1958-59; adminstrv. asst. to supt. schs., White Plains, N.Y., 1959-62; salary cons. and specialist in urban problems N.E.A., Washington, 1962-65, asst. dir. research div., 1965-66, dir. spl. services div., 1966-67, exec. sec., asso. exec. sec. Commn. on Profl. Rights and Responsibilities, 1967-68, dir. planning and organizational devel., 1968—. Served with AUS, 1954-56. Mem. Baroque Arts Soc. Washington (sec.). Author: (with others) Principles of Staff Personnel Administration in Public Schools, 1959; Fringe Benefits for Public School Personnel, 1962; Guidelines for Professional Negotiation, 1963, rev., 1965; Employer Cooperation in Group Insurance Coverage of Public School Personnel, 1964-65, 1966; (with T.M. Stinnett and M. Ware) Professional Negotiation in Public Education, 1966; Profiles of Excellence: Recommended Criteria for Evaluating the Quality of a Local School System, 1966. Contbr. articles to profl. jours. Home: 6315 Utah Av NW Washington DC 20015 Office: 1201 16th St NW Washington DC 20036

KLEPCZYNSKI, WILLIAM JOHN, astronomer; b. Phila., Apr. 16, 1939; s. William and Theresa (Drzalowski) K.; B.A., U. Pa., 1961; M.A., Georgetown U., 1964; Ph.D., Yale U., 1969; m. Gloria Shell, Oct. 14, 1961. Astronomer U.S. Naval Obs., Washington, 1961—. Mem. Am. Astron. Soc., Internat. Astron. Union, A.A.A.S., Inst. Navigation. Home: 2327 King Pl NW Washington DC 20007 Office: US Naval Obs Washington DC 20390

KLEPPER, ROBERT CLARENCE, county ofcl.; b. Luray, Va., July 25, 1928; s. Clarence D. and Jane (Steele) K.; A.B., Carson-Newman Coll., 1951; postgrad. George Washington U., 1964; m. Jo Dolores Peters, Apr. 12, 1946; children—Robert Clarence, Michael Tyree. City mgr. Altavista (Va.), 1956-60; spl. asst. Norfolk (Va.) Redevel. and Housing Authority, 1960-62; asst. city mgr. Chesapeake (Va.), 1962-66; adminstr. Prince George (Va.) County, 1966-72, New Kent (Va.) County, 1972—. Served with AUS, 1946-48. Recipient Meritorious Service award A.R.C., 1955. Mem. Internat. City Mgmt. Assn., Nat. Assn. Counties. Baptist. Mason (Shriner). Club: Prince George (Va.) Ruritan. Home: 19 Martha Washington Rd New Kent VA 23124 Office: New Kent Courthouse New Kent VA 23124

KLIBANOFF, MORRIS, retail trade co. exec.; b. Jackson, Tenn., Jan. 29, 1917; s. Hyman and Lillie (Aizenshtat) K.; student Vanderbilt U., 1934-36; B.S., Northwestern U., 1938; m. Roslyn Miriam Bookholtz, Mar. 3, 1940; children—Judith (Mrs. Ronald R. Ingle), Ruth (Mrs. Ronald H. Berg), Hank, Deborah, Daniel. Owner The Bootery, Florence, Ala., 1938—, Kaye's, Florence, Ala., 1938—. Chmn. Tenn. Valley Boy Scouts Am., 70-71, Jewish Federated Charities, 1971—; pres. Temple B'nai Israel, 1965-66. Chmn. Lauderdale County Draft Bd., 1953-73, Florence Planning Commn., 1953—. Bd. dirs. Salvation Army, Downtown Florence Unlimited. Served to 2nd. lt. AUS, 1943-46. Recipient Silver Beaver award Boy Scouts Am. Mem. C. of C., Nat. Shoe Retailers Assn. Exchange Club (pres. 1956-57). Mem. B'nai B'rith. Home: 733 Pleasant Dr Florence AL 35630 Office: 111 N Court St Florence AL 35630

KLIER, ALTON WILLIAM, ins. agy. owner; b. Fredericksburg, Tex., Jan. 23, 1928; s. William and Hilda (Wehmeyer) K.; student Tex. Luth. Coll., 1946-47; m. Joanne Howe, Sept. 16, 1951; children—Kaye, Kandis, Kari. Mortgage loan officer, v.p. Community Savings & Loan Assn., 1968-72; owner, mgr. Eckhardt & Klier, Fredericksburg, 1948-68, 72—. Trustee Hill Country Meml. Hosp. Recipient Distinguished Service award Jr. C. of C., 1963. Mem. Nat., Tex. assns. ins. agts., Fredericksburg C. of C. (dir. 1969). Lutheran (trustee 1959-63). Lion. Home: Mason Rd Fredericksburg TX 78624 Office: 300 W Main St Fredericksburg TX 78624

KLINE, DAVID GELLINGER, educator; b. Phila., Oct. 13, 1934; s. David Francis and Lois Ann (Gellinger) K.; A.B. in Chemistry, U. Pa., 1956, M.D., 1960; m. Carol Anne Loewen, Mar. 1, 1958; children—Susan, Robert, Nancy. Intern, U. Mich., Ann Arbor, 1960-61, resident in gen. surgery, 1961-62, teaching asso. in neurosurgery, 1964-67; research investigator Walter Reed Army Inst. Research and Walter Reed Gen. Hosp., 1962-64; instr. La. State U. Med. Sch., New Orleans, 1967-68, asst. prof., 1968-70, asso. prof., 1970-73, chmn. neurosurgery, 1971—, prof., 1973—. Cons., USPHS Health Center Hosp., Keesler Air Force Base Hosp.-Lederle Labs.; vis. investigator Delta Regional Primate Center, Covington, La. Bd. mem. Dana G. How Social Service Fund. Served with M.C. AUS, 1962-64. Recipient Frederick Coller Surg. prize, 1967; numerous grants. Mem. Am. Acad. Neurol. Surgery, Am. Assn. Neurol. Surgeons, Soc. U. Neurosurgeons, Assn. Acad. Surgery, A.C.S., Phi Beta Kappa, Kappa Sigma, Phi Chi, others. Contbr. articles to sci. jours. Home: 46 Thrasher St New Orleans LA 70124

KLINE, HARRY BYRD, pub. speaker agy. exec.; b. Nevada, Mo., July 30, 1897; s. George W. and Bonnie M. (Garrett) K.; B.A., Phillips U., 1920, B. Speech Arts, 1922; m. Marian K. Shimeall, Aug. 15, 1923 (dec. Feb. 1968); children—Jerome W., Madelyn Weldon; m. 2d, Dorothy Champlin May, Nov. 26, 1968. Owner, dir. So. Sch. Assemblies, Dallas, 1930-57, Harry Byrd Kline Celebrity Service, Dallas, 1957—; owner-developer Flamingo Bay retirement village, Pine Island, 1960-67. Pres., Tex. Laymen's League, 1948-51. Mem. Internat. Platform Assn. (pres. 1971-72, gov. 1970—), Greater Pine Island (Fla.) C. of C. (pres. 1962-63), S.A.R., Nat. Entertainment Conf., Tex. Farm Bur. Mem. Christian Ch. Home: 5516 Williamstown Rd Dallas TX 75230 Office: Harry Byrd Kline Celebrity Service PO Drawer 87 Dallas TX 75221

KLINE, IRVING BERTHOLD, automobile sales exec.; b. Balt., May 20, 1894; s. Jacob D. and Amelia (Schoolherr) K.; ed. Friends Quaker Sch., Balt. City Coll.; m. Isabelle Hofflin, Oct. 8, 1925; children—Richard Hofflin, James Martin. Owner, propr. Kline Motor Co., Balt., 1916-17, Kline Chevrolet Sales Corp., Norfolk, Va., 1925—; dir. Hewett Chevrolet, Myrtle Beach, S.C., 1971—; past pres. Consolvo Tent Co. Mem. Gen. Motors Dealer Planning Com. Mem. OPA Bd., 1941-45; capt. Norfolk Aux. Fire Dept., 1941-45; organizer, past pres. Norfolk Safety Council, Norfolk Traffic Ct., Tidewater Better Bus. Bur., Norfolk Citizens Emergency Com.; mem. Nat. Safety Council, Pres.' Hwy Safety Com., Va. Traffic Safety Study Commn., Gov.'s Hwy. Safety Com. Bd. dirs. DePaul Hosp., Easter Seal Soc., Am. Humane Soc., Soc. for Prevention Cruelty to Animals, Tidewater Multiple Sclerosis Assn. Served with USNR, 1918-20. Recipient Time Mag. Quality Dealer award, 1971; Distinguished Service citation Nat. Auto Dealers, 1966. Mem. Tidewater Automobile Assn. (1st pres., dir.), Va., Norfolk Retail Mchts. Assn. (dir.), Norfolk-Portsmouth Auto Dealers Assn. (past pres.), Va. Dealers Assn. Friends of Myer House, Chrysler Mus., Am. Legion, Fraternal Order Police Assn. (Outstanding Citizen award 1953), Norfolk Dog Tng. Club, Saints and Sinners (past pres.). Mason, Kiwanian (camp dir.). Clubs: Greenbrier Saddle (founder, past pres.) (Chesapeake, Va.); Commodore Country (Virginia Beach, Va.). Home: 1440 Kline Dr Virginia Beach VA 23452 Office: 1301 Monticello Av Norfolk VA 23510

KLINE, JACOB, educator; b. Boston, Aug. 3, 1917; s. Joseph and Jennie (Goldman) K.; B.S., Mass. Inst. Tech., 1942, M.S., 1951; Ph.D. (NSF fellow), Ia. State U., 1962; m. Barbara Fine, Dec. 22, 1957; children—David, Jonathan, Pamela. Electronics engr. Internat. Tel. & Tel. Co., Newark, 1942-46; chief viedeo sect., optical research lab. Boston U., 1946-48; research asst. Mass. Inst. Tech., Cambridge, 1948-51, research engr., 1951-52; mem. faculty U. R.I., Kingston, 1952-66, asso. prof. engring. elec., 1956-60, dir. biomed. engring. program, 1962-66; prof., dir. biomed. engring. program U. Miami, Coral Gables, Fla., 1966—. Cons., Boston Psychiat. Hosp., Tufts Coll. Dental Sch., Boston, Mass. Mental Health Center, Boston, Cable Electric Corp., Providence, South Miami Hosp., Venice (Fla.) Hosp., St. Francis Hosp., Miami Beach, Leviton Mfg. Co., Bklyn., others. NASA/Am. Soc. Engring. Edn. fellow, summers 1965, 66. Mem. I.E.E.E. (dir. 1943—), Am. Soc. Artificial Organs, Am. Assn. Advancement Med. Instrumentation. Contbr. to profl. jours. Patentee myocardial prosthetic device. Home: 1445 Trillo Av Coral Gables FL 33146 Office: Dept Biomedical Engineering Univ Miami Coral Gables FL 33124

KLING, ROBERT EDWARD, JR., graphics cons.; b. York, Pa., May 29, 1920; s. Robert Edward and Gladys (Kinneman) K.; m. Doris M. Gilroy, June 11, 1943 (dec.); children—Robert Edward, III, Stephen Campbell; m. 2d, Mary Apostolou, May 29, 1969; children—Jonathan Bradford, Susan Meridith. Apprentice Govt. Printing Office, Washington, 1938, various positions, 1938-61, asst. supt. platemaking div., 1961-62, spl. asst. to 14th pub. printer U.S., 1962-70, supt. documents, 1970-73; graphic communications cons., 1973—. Pres. City Council, Hyattsville, Md., 1960-69. Served to lt. col. C.E. USNR, 1941-45, 50-52. Author: The Government Printing Office, 1970. Home: 701 Notley Rd Silver Spring MD 20904

KLING, SIMCHA, clergyman, author; b. Dayton, Ky., Jan. 27, 1922; s. Eli and Anna (Niman) K.; B.A., U. Cin., 1943; M.A., Columbia, 1947; M.Hebrew Lit., Jewish Theol. Sem., 1948, D.H.L., 1958; m. Edith Leeman, June 15, 1947; children—Elana, Adina, Reena. Rabbi, 1948, Congregation B'nai Amoona, St. Louis, 1948-51, Beth David, Greensboro, N.C., 1951-65, Adath Jeshurun, Louisville, 1965—. Instr. sociology U. Louisville, 1968-71. Sec., Religion and Race Com., 1968-72; mem. Louisville Bd. Rabbis (pres. 1970-71). Mem. Jefferson County Welfare Commn., 1969-72. Bd. dirs. Nat. Acad. Adult Jewish Studies, Israel Pub. Affairs Com., Histadrut Ivrit. Mem. Rabbinical Assembly Am., Am. Jewish Hist. Soc., Am. Jewish Congress. Author: Servant of His People, 1960; Man of Iron, 1965; A Sense of Duty, 1968; Joseph Klausner, 1970. Home: 2240 Millvale Rd Louisville KY 40205 Office: 2401 Woodbourne Av Louisville KY 40205

KLINGEN, THEODORE JAMES, chemist, educator; b. St. Louis, Oct. 7, 1931; s. Leonard Joseph and Margaret Mary (Ehlenz) K.; B.S. in Chemistry, St. Louis U., 1953, M.S., 1955; Ph.D. (Nuclear Sci. Found. fellow), Fla. State U., 1962; m. Maura E. Downey, Sept. 1, 1958; children—Joseph Leonard, Ann Margaret. Research sci. McDonnell-Douglas Corp., St. Louis, 1962-64; faculty chemistry U. Miss., 1964—, prof., 1970—, dir. Radiation Research Center, 1972—. Chmn., Oxford council Boy Scouts Am. Served to capt. USAF, 1955-57. Mem. Am. Chem. Soc., Am. Phys. Soc., Am. Nuclear Soc., Sigma Xi, Pi Mu Epsilon. Contbr. articles to research jours. Patentee in field. Home: 117 Pine Crest Dr Oxford MS 38655

KLINGENBERG, JOSEPH JOHN, educator; b. Bellevue, Ky., Nov. 16, 1919; s. Joseph Gerhardt and Freda Mae (Deye) K.; B.S., Xavier U., 1941; M.S., U. Cin., 1947, Ph.D. (Law fellow), 1949; m. Evelyn Morwessel, Feb. 14, 1942 (dec. Apr. 1954); children—M. Jean (Mrs. Thomas Wash), Rosemary (Mrs. Harlan Schmidt), Mary Evelyn, Joseph, Evelyn; m. 2d, Ruth Fedders, Aug. 11, 1962 (dec. July 1965). Faculty chemistry Xavier U., Cin., 1949—, prof., 1960—. Vis. lectr. U. Cin., 1966, 69; sci. adviser Cin. dist. FDA, 1967-72; dir. NSF Summer Inst., 1959. Served to lt. USAAF, 1942-45. Decorated Air medal. Mem. Ohio Acad. Sci. (vis. lectr. 1963-71), Am. Chem. Soc. (2nd. vice chmn. Cin. sect. 1964-65), Soc. Applied Spectroscopy (pres. Cin. sect. 1970-71), Sigma Xi, Phi Lambda Upsilon. Author: (with Kenneth Reed) Introduction to Quantitative Chemistry, 1965. Home: 51 Pleasant Ridge Fort Mitchell KY 41017 Office: Dana and Parkway Cincinnati OH 45207

KLINTWORTH, GORDON KENNETH, pathologist, educator; b. Fort Victoria, Rhodesia, Aug. 4, 1932; s. John George and Iveagh Irene (Gordon) K.; came to U.S., 1962, naturalized, 1967; B.Sc., U. Witwatersrand, South Africa, 1954, M.B., B.Ch., 1957, B.Sc. (hon.), 1961, Ph.D., 1966; m. Felicity Helen Tait, Dec. 14, 1957; children—Susan, John, Sandra. Intern, resident Johannesburg (S. Africa) Gen. Hosp.; faculty Duke, 1964—, prof. pathology, 1973—. Vis. prof. U. London Inst. Ophthalmology, 1970. Victor Kark scholar, 1961-62; USPHS fellow, 1962-64; Louis B. Mayer scholar, 1972-73. Recipient Research Career Devel. award Nat. Eye Inst., 1971—. Diplomate Am. Bd. Pathology. Mem. Am. Soc. Exptl. Pathology, Am. Assn. Pathologists and Bacteriologists, N.Y. Acad. Sci., Internat. Acad. Pathology, Am. Assn. Neuropathologists, A.A.A.S., Am. Acad. Neurology, Assn. for Research in Vision and Ophthalmology, Eastern Ophthalmic Pathology Soc., Nat. Geog. Soc., Sigma Xi. Author: (with B.F. Fetter, W.S. Hendry) Mycoses of the Central Nervous System, 1967. Contbr. articles to med. jours. Home: 2718 Spencer St Durham NC 27706

KLOCK, BENNY LEROY, astronomer; b. Washington, Oct. 29, 1934; s. LeRoy and Ertie (Crouse) K.; B.A., Cornell U., 1956, M.S., 1960; Ph.D., Georgetown U., 1964; m. Margaret Ann Sherman, June 1, 1957; children—Mark Steven, Lorri Ann, Brian Lee. Dir. No. Transit Circle div. U.S. Naval Obs., Washington, 1960—. Com. chmn. Boy Scout troop, Rockville, Md., 1969-72. Served to capt. USAAF, 1957-59. Mem. Internat. Astron. Union, Am. Astron. Soc., A.A.A.S., Sigma Xi. Republican. Contbr. articles in field to profl. jours. Home: 13907 Arctic Av Rockville MD 20853 Office: US Naval Obs Washington DC 20390

KLOCK, DAVID JULIAN, govt. ofcl.; b. Schenectady, May 19, 1938; s. Edwin J. and Eleanor (Taft) K.; B.A., Middlebury Coll., 1960; Ph.D., Columbia, 1969. Internat. economist U.S. Treasury, Washington, 1968—, now dep. dir. Office Internat. Financial Analysis. Served with AUS, 1960-62. Fulbright Student grantee, Philippines, 1966-67. Mem. Am. Econ. Assn. Home: 405 Queen St Alexandria VA 22314 Office: 15th and Pennsylvania Av NW Washington DC 20220

KLOEPFER, HENRY WARNER, educator; b. Roseville, O., Feb. 25, 1913; s. John Alexander and Mayme Grace (Ivett) K.; B.A., Ohio State U., 1934, M.A., 1938, Ph.D., 1942; B.S., Muskingum Coll., 1935; m. Ruth Elizabeth McCoy, May 26, 1936; children—Jean (Mrs. John Baringer), Karol, Ruth Ann (Mrs. Milton E. Burglass), John. Faculty biology Dakota Wesleyan U., Mitchell, S.D., 1942-46; dean

Coll. Emporia (Kan.), 1946-47, Coll. Ozarks, Clarksville, Ark., 1947-52; prof. human med. genetics Tulane U. Med. Sch., New Orleans, 1952—. Danforth lectr. numerous colls., univs., 1960-65. Mem. bd. Community Relations Council, New Orleans, 1960-73, v.p., 1969-70, treas., 1972-73; mem. bd. Am. Friends Service Com., Phila., 1961-67, mem. regional exec. com., 1961-73. Recipient numerous NIH grants. Mem. Am. Soc. Human Genetics (treas. 1957-60; mem. bd. 1961-63), Problem Commn. on Neurogenetics World Fedn. Neurology (founding mem. 1961, sec. 1961-64), Internat. Dermatoglyphics Assn. (founding mem. 1971, sec. 1971-73). Contbr. articles to various publs. Home: 3033 Louisiana Av Pkwy New Orleans LA 70125

KLOEPFER, WILLIAM JOHN, JR., public relations exec.; b. Evanston, Ill., June 14, 1923; s. William John and Alma (Koch) K.; B.S., Northwestern U., 1949; m. Nancy Lee Henninger, Nov. 26, 1958; children—Joan Helen, Elizabeth Koch. Gen. assignment reporter Athens (Tex.) Daily Rev., 1949-50; Capitol Hill reporter Washington Times-Herald, 1950-51; news editor NBC and Liberty Networks, Washington, 1951-52; asst. to dir. pub. relations Republican Nat. Com., Washington, 1952-55; adminstrv. asst. U.S. Rep. Laurence Curtis (Mass.), Washington, 1955-56; chief Office of Information, CAB, Washington, 1956-59; dir. pub. information Pharm. Mfrs. Assn., Washington, 1959-67; v.p. pub. relations Tobacco Inst., Washington, 1967-71, sr. v.p., 1971—. Served with AUS, 1943-46. Mem. Nat. Press Club, Pub. Relations Soc. Am., Nat. Assn. Sci Writers. Club: Bethesda Country (Md.). Home: 7429 Haddington Pl Bethesda MD 20034 Office: 1776 K St NW Washington DC 20006

KLONTZ, HAROLD EMERSON, educator; b. Lombard, Ill., May 17, 1914; s. Emerson Carlyle and Augusta (Williams) K.; B.A., Berea Coll., 1935; Ph.D., U. N.C., 1948; m. Mary Ross Paysinger, June 10, 1944; 1 dau., Anne. Tchr. pub. schs., N.C., 1935-40; grad. asst. U. N.C., 1940-42, instr. econs. and statistics, 1942-46; prof. Auburn (Ala.) U., 1946—; Smith-Mundt exchange prof. U. Khartoum, Sudan, 1961-62; cons. statistician Anniston Ordnance Depot, Red River Arsenal. Trustee, treas. Alice Carr Trust Fund. Mem. Am. Statis. Assn., Am., So. econ. assns., Ala. Acad. Sci., Am. Inst. for Decision Scis. (charter mem.), Delta Sigma Pi, Omicron Delta Epsilon. Democrat. Methodist (pres. Men's Club 1965-66). Rotarian (pres. 1965-66). Home: 839 Moores Mill Rd Auburn AL 36830

KLONTZ, MARY PAYSINGER (MRS. HAROLD E. KLONTZ), educator, librarian; b. Rock Hill, S.C., Apr. 4, 1918; d. John Benjamin and Annie (Caldwell) Paysinger; B.A., Columbia Coll., 1938; B.S. in L.S., U. N.C., 1943; M.Ed., Auburn U., 1968; m. Harold Emerson Klontz, June 10, 1944; 1 dau., Florence Anne. Librarian, tchr. pub. schs. of S.C., 1938-44; librarian instr. Sch. Library Sci., U. N.C., 1944-46; librarian Auburn (Ala.) Pub. Library, 1947-49, Horseshoe Bend Regional Library, Dadeville, Ala., 1957-63; library supr. Auburn City Schs., 1963-68; with Learning Resources Center, Sch. Edn., Auburn (Ala.) U., 1969-70, asst. prof. Sch. Edn., 1970—, also instr., summers 1965-68. Cons. Khartoum, Sudan, Jan.-Mar. 1962. Trustee Auburn Pub. Library, 1956-63; mem. bd. zoning adjustment, Auburn, 1956-62. Mem. Am., Ala., Southeastern library assns., Am. Assn. U. Women (local pres. 1950-53), Fedn. Women's Clubs (nominating del. 5th dist. 1956-58). Woman's Soc. Christian Service, League Women Voters (chmn. local organizing com. 1956-57, pres. 1959-61), Nat., Ala. edn. assns., Delta Kappa Gamma (pres. 1974—). Home: 839 Moore's Mill Rd Auburn AL 36830

KLOPFENSTEIN, PHILIP ARTHUR, art center exec.; b. Lake Odessa, Mich., Apr. 28, 1937; s. Glendull Carl and Bernice E. (Shumway) K.; B.A., Mich. State U., 1961; M.A., Western Mich. U., 1964; certificate art adminstrn., Harvard U., 1970; m. Anna Jo Davis, Aug. 27, 1960. Tchr. pub. schs., Hopkins, Mich., 1961-63, Paw Paw (Mich.) pub. schs., 1963-65; faculty Little Rock U., 1965-68; sales rep. Prentice-Hall, Englewood Cliffs, N.J., 1968-69; TV writer and tchr. Ark. Ednl. TV, Conway, 1969-70; dir. Southeast Ark. Arts and Sci. Center, Pine Bluff, 1970—; exhibited in one-man shows at Simmons First Nat. Bank (Ark.), 1971, Ark. Dept. Edn., Little Rock, 1973, El Dorado (Ark.) Art Center, 1974; condr., participant various profl. workshops. Commn. mem. Ark. State Dept. of Edn., Elementary Secondary Edn. Act Title III, Fed. Programs, Pine Bluff, 1973—; pres. elect Ark. Mus. Conf., Pine Bluff, 1975—. Served with AUS, 1957-59. Grantee in fine arts, 1970-73. Mem. Am. Assn. of Museums, Ark. Edn. Assn., Mid-So. Watercolorists. Trustee Jefferson County History Commn., 1971. Rotarian. Home: 2203 W 38th St Pine Bluff AR 71601 Office: Civic Center Pine Bluff AR 71601

KLOPFER, PETER HUBERT, zoologist, ednl. adminstr.; b. Berlin, Germany, Aug. 9, 1930; s. Hubert R. and Edith (Brauer) K.; B.A. with honors, U. Cal. at Los Angeles, 1952; Ph.D., Yale, 1957; m. Martha Smith, 1955; children—Erika, Lisa, Margrete. Instr. sci. Windsor Mountain Sch., Lenox, Mass., 1952-53, head dept. sci., 1955-56; asst. prof. dept. zoology Duke, 1958-63, asso. prof., 1963-67, prof., 1967—, dir. Field Sta. Animal Behavior Studies, 1968-73, also asso. dir. Primate Facility, 1970—. Vis. prof. dept. zoology Tel-Aviv (Israel) U., 1970. editorial adviser Springer Verlag, 1970—. Mem. Am. Friends Service Com., 1967—; mem. animal care com., 1966-68, 72—. Bd. dirs. Carolina Friends Sch., chmn., 1973—. Research fellow Nat. Inst. Mental Health U. Cambridge (Eng.), 1957-58, Nat. Inst. Mental Health spl. postdoctoral fellow, 1964; recipient Career Devel. award Nat. Inst. Mental Health, 1965-70, Outstanding Prof. award, Duke, 1968, Research Scientist award Nat. Inst. Mental Health, 1970. Fellow A.A.A.S., Animal Behavior Soc. Mem. Soc. of Friends. Author: Behavioral Aspects of Ecology, 1962; (with J.P. Hailman) Introduction to Animal Behavior, 1967; Habitats and Territories, 1969; Instinct is a Cheshire Cat: A Primer on Animal Behavior, 1973. Editor: Perspectives in Ethology, 1973; asso. editor Jour. Exptl. Zoology, 1970—. Home: Route 1 Box 184 Tierreich Farm Durham NC 27705

KLOS, WILLIAM ANTON, elec. engr., educator; b. Houston, Aug. 14, 1936; s. Andrew Anton and Ruth Irene (Walters) K.; B.S. in Mech. Engring. cum laude, U. Houston, 1963, Ph.D. in Elec. Engring. (NASA fellow), 1969; m. Rose Lee O'Bryan, Feb. 3, 1962; 1 son, Vaughn Bryan. Grad. research asst. U. Houston, 1966-69; principal engr. Lockheed Electronic Co., Houston, 1969-70; asso. prof. elec. engring. U. Southwestern La., Lafayette, 1970—, head dept., 1970—. Pres. P.T.A., Broussard, La., 1971-72. Served with USAF, 1954-58. Registered profl. engr., La., Tex. Mem. I.E.E.E. (sec.-treas. Lafayette sect. 1972-73), La. Engring. Soc. (sec. Lafayette chpt. 1972-73, 1st v.p. Lafayette chpt. 1973-74, pres. 1974-75), Sigma Xi (sec. U. Southwestern La. club 1971-73), Eta Kappa Nu (nat. dir. 1971-73, v.p. 1973-74, pres. 1974-75), Tau Beta Pi, Phi Kappa Phi. Home: Route 3 Box 357 Arnaudville LA 70512 Office: U Southwestern Louisiana Box 3890 Lafayette LA 70501

KLOTZ, HERBERT WERNER, corp. exec.; b. Berlin, Germany, Feb. 24, 1917; s. Herbert and Gertrude (Koppel) Klotz; B.A., Zuoz (Switzerland) Coll., 1935; student U. Zurich (Switzerland), 1935-36; m. Patricia Radford Hopkins, Apr. 3, 1954; children—Radford Werner, Leslie Ritchie, James Taylor. Came to U.S., 1937, naturalized, 1944. With Smith, Barney & Co., and predecessor, N.Y.C., 1937-42, W.E. Hutton & Co., N.Y.C., 1946-48; engaged in mgmt. personal investments, 1949-52; with Winslow, Douglas & McEvoy, N.Y.C., 1953-54; pres., treas. Tex. Securities Corp., N.Y.C., 1954-57, Southwest Adv. Services, Inc. N.Y.C., 1954-57; with Alex Brown & Sons, Washington, 1957-60; spl. asst. to sec. commerce, 1961, dep. to sec. commerce, 1961-62, asst. sec. commerce for adminstrn., 1962-65; exec. v.p. Am. Growth Investment Co., 1966-67; dir. Govt. Systems Center, Kurt Salmon Assos., Inc.; mgmt. cons., 1968-69; pres. Quest Research Corp., 1970—. Dir. Nat. Com. Bus. and Profl. Men and Women for Kennedy-Johnson, 1960. Served to 1st lt. AUS, 1942-45; maj. Res. ret. Democrat. Episcopalian. Clubs: Nat. Press, 1925 F Street, Metropolitan, Federal City (Washington); Warrenton Hunt, Fauquier (Warrenton, Va.). Home: 1401 Langley Pl McLean VA 22101 Office: 6845 Elm St McLean VA 22101

KLUD, LEON WILLIAM, economist, govt. ofcl.; b. Mena, Ark., Sept. 19, 1941; s. Leo Glenn and Hilta Abilene (Cogburn) K.; student U. Ore., 1959-61; B.A. cum laude, Seattle Pacific Coll., 1963; M. Govtl. Adminstrn. with honors (Pub. Finance Grad. fellow 1963-67), U. Pa., 1965, M.A., 1969, postgrad., 1965-70; m. Patricia Ann Nelson, Dec. 31, 1965. Economist, Joint Com. on Internal Revenue Taxation, U.S. Congress, Washington, 1967—. Mem. Am. Econ. Assn., Nat. Tax Assn., Soc. Govt. Economists, Am. Acad. Polit. and Social Sci., Alpha Kappa Sigma, Beta Gamma Sigma. Mem. Open Bible Standard Ch. (trustee 1968-70, 71—, treas. 1971-72). Clubs: Wharton Graduate School, Capitol Hill Tennis (dir. 1971-72) (Washington). Home: 8431 Forrester Blvd Springfield VA 22152 Office: 5210 Dirksen Senate Bldg Washington DC 20510

KLUTTS, WILLIAM ALONZO, newspaper editor; b. Ripley, Tenn., June 26, 1928; s. Alonzo and Helen (Given) K.; A.B., U. Chgo., 1947, grad. student, 1947-49. With Chgo. bur. Asso. Press, 1945-49; editor, co-publisher The Lauderdale Co. Enterprise, Ripley, Tenn., 1949-65, editor, pub., 1966—, gen. mgr. Enterprise Comml. & Indsl. Supplies, Ripley, 1961—; v.p., dir. Ripley Devel. Corp. Vice chmn. Ripley Housing Authority, 1962-66, chmn., 1966-69, exec. dir., 1970—. Mem. nat. council Boy Scouts Am., 1955—, mem. W. Tenn. council, 1955-67; pres., 1958; pres. Consol. Charities, Inc., 1955—. Trustee Union U., Jackson, Tenn. 1960-65; adv. council Tenn. Civil War Centennial Commn., 1960-65. Served with AUS, 1950-52, capt. Res.; transferred to lt. USNR, 1966, now lt. comdr. Res. Coroner Lauderdale County, 1956—; exec. sec. West Tenn. Mayors Conf., 1961—. Winner 21 U. Tenn. press awards. Mem. Am. (life), W. Tenn. (life; v.p.) hist. socs., Tenn. Press Assn., Tenn. Future Farmers (hon.), C. of C. (pres. 1954). Baptist (deacon, trustee). Clubs: 30 (Memphis); Rotary (pres. 1957). Contbr. hist. articles profl. jours. Home: 157 Lake Dr Ripley TN 38063 Office: 145 E Jackson St Ripley TN 38063

KNAPE, CLIFFORD STANLEY, psychologist; b. Austin, Tex., Dec. 7, 1916; s. Carl Johann and Edla (Widerstrom) K.; B.A., U. Tex., 1941, M.A., 1941; M.A., Baylor U., 1951; Ph.D., U. Tex., 1958; m. Anne Sabra Ramsey, May 30, 1942; children—Mildred Anne, Sabra Jane, Carl Guinn. Clk-psychometrist Rehab. div. Tex. Dept. Edn., Austin, 1935-37, parttime, 1937-41; psychologist U.S. VA, Waco, Tex., 1945-51, 53—, now chief psychology service; adj. prof. Baylor U., 1953—. Trustee, Waco Ind. Sch. Dist., 1964—, pres., 1969—; bd. mem. Tex. Rehab. Commn., 1969—. Served with USAAF, 1941-45, to maj. USAF, 1951-53. Mem. Am., Tex. psychol. assns., Nat., Tex. (pres. 1962-63) rehab. assns., McLennan Mental Health Assn. (pres. 1962-63), Tex. Assn. for Mental Health (v.p. for program 1964), Tex. Congress Parents and Tchrs. (state mental health chmn. 1962-65), Phi Beta Kappa. Democrat. Presbyn. Home: 1024 N 18-A St Waco TX 76707 Office: VA Hosp Waco TX 76703

KNAPE, GERALD BEARNDT, newspaper editor, pub.; b. Austin, Tex., Mar. 6, 1912; s. Otto and Hulda (Swenson) K.; student U. Tex., 1929-31; corr. student Nixon Clay Coll., 1932; 1 dau., Frances (Mrs. Robert Wimberley). With Tex. Posten, Austin, 1933—, editor, pub., 1961—. Mem. cav. Tex. N.G., 1931-34, 1st lt., 1973—. Decorated Order Conferred Vasa, Sweden; recipient 50th award Tex. Press Assn., 1965; named hon. commodore Tex. Tidelands Guard, 1953. Mem. Am. Legion Drum and Bugle Corps (drum maj. 1962—). Democrat. Methodist. Mason (32 deg., Shriner). Clubs: Austin Advertising (sec. 1935), Austin Optimist, Austin Scandinavian (pres. 1960). Composer: In the Mist and Fog I See a Light, 1959; Just Let Me Forget, 1963; Honky Tonk Gals from Wilbarger Creek, 1963. Home: 607 Theresa St Austin TX 78703 Office: 900 W Koenig Lane Austin TX 78765

KNAPP, GEORGE HAWARD, communications supr.; b. Charleston, W.Va., July 31, 1920; s. Arthur O. and Leona (Wilson) K.; student pub. schs.; m. Juanita May Board, Mar. 22, 1956; children—Shirley (Mrs. Roy W. Gossett), Barry, David (by previous marriage). Technician Western Electric Co., Charleston, W.Va., 1941-42; engrs. aide Signal Corps Gen. Devel. Labs., Ft. Monmouth, N.J., 1942; transmitter engr. WTMA, Charleston, S.C., 1946-47; electronics specialist CAA, Charleston, 1947-55; supr. communications div. City of St. Petersburg, 1955—. Served with AUS, 1942-46. Mem. I.E.E.E., Internat. Platform Assn., Asso. Pub.-Safety Communications Officers. Home: 3990 20th St N St Petersburg FL 33714 Office: PO Box 2842 St Petersburg FL 33731

KNAPP, JOHN LAURENCE, social scientist; b. Washington, Sept. 30, 1935; s. Joseph Grant and Carol (West) K.; B.A., U. Colo., 1957; M.A., Duke, 1960; Ph.D., U. Va., 1970; m. Trilbie Lee Ferrell, Oct. 6, 1962; children—Laurence Freston, Paget Ferrell. Budget analyst U.S. Dept. Agr., 1960; asst. economist Fed. Res. Bank, Richmond, 1960-62; economist A. State of Va. Div. Indsl. Devel. and Planning, Richmond, 1962-66, economist B. Div. State Planning and Community Affairs, 1966, chief research sect., 1967-71, dep. dir., 1971-73; research dir. Tayloe Murphy Inst., U. Va., Charlottesville, 1973—. instr. Univ. Coll. U. Richmond, 1962-64, 68-72. Served with AUS, 1959-65. Mem. Am., So. econ. assns., Phi Beta Kappa. Home: 2242 Brandywine Dr Charlottesville VA 22901 Office: Tayloe Murphy Inst Box 3430 Charlottesville VA 22903

KNAUR, JOHN SHERMAN, JR., aero. engr.; b. Dallas, Mar. 7, 1924; s. John Sherman and Lillian (Summer) K.; student N. Tex. Agrl. Coll., 1941, So. Meth. U., 1947; B.S. in Aero. Engring., U. Colo., 1949, postgrad., 1949-50; m. Jean Davey, Sept. 13, 1947; children—John D., James A., Sandra Lee, Nancy Jean. Aero. structures design upper atmosphere research U. Colo., Boulder, 1948-50; preliminary design engr. Gen. Dynamics, Fort Worth, 1950-60; research specialist Boeing Co., Wichita, Kan., 1960-63, sr. group engr., Huntsville, Ala., 1963-70; mgr. corp. engring. Brougham Industries Inc., Sanger, Tex., 1970—. Mgr. Apollo landing system rev. and certification NASA, 1967-68. Block capt. Republican party, 1966-68, phone com. capt., 1967-68. Served with USAAF, 1942-45; ETO. Decorated Air medal with clusters, Bronze Star. Recipient New Tech. award NASA, 1969. Registered profl. engr., Tex., Ala. Fellow Am. Inst. Aeros. and Astronautics (tech. chmn. local sect. 1954-63). Mason (Shriner). Home: 7211 Briley Dr Fort Worth TX 76188 Office: 101 Bolivar St Sanger TX 76266

KNEE, RUTH IRELAN (MRS. JUNIOR K. KNEE), health care cons.; b. Sapulpa, Okla., Mar. 21, 1920; d. Oren M. and Daisy (Daubin) Irelan; B.A., U. Okla., 1941, certificate social work, 1942; M.A., U. Chgo., 1945; m. Junior K. Knee, May 29, 1943. Psychiat. social worker, asst. supr. Ill. Psychiat. Inst., U. Ill. at Chgo., 1943-44; psychiat. social worker USPHS Employee Health Unit, Washington, 1944-46, chief psychiat. social worker, 1946-49; psychiat. social work asso. Army Med. Center, Walter Reed Army Hosp., Washington, 1949-54; psychiat. social work cons. Dept. Health, Edn. Welfare, Region III, Washington, 1955-56; with Nat. Inst. Mental Health, Chevy Chase, Md., 1956-73, chief spl. grants support sect., 1966-67, chief mental health care adminstrn. br., 1967-72, asso. dep. adminstr. health services and mental health adminstrn., 1972-73; dep. dir. Office Nursing Home Affairs Dept. Health, Edn., and Welfare, 1973-74; cons. in field, 1974—. Fellow Am. Pub. Health Assn. (sec. mental health sect. 1968-70, chmn. 1971-72), Am. Orthopsychiat. Assn.; mem. Am. Assn. Psychiat. Social Workers (pres. 1951-53), Nat. Conf. Social Welfare (nat. bd. 1968—, 2d v.p. 1973-74), Council on Social Work Edn., Nat. Assn. Social Workers (chmn. competence study com., practice and knowledge com. 1963-71), Am. Pub. Welfare Assn., D.A.R., Phi Beta Kappa, Psi Chi. Home: 8809 Arlington Blvd Fairfax VA 22030

KNEEBONE, ROBERT W., banker; b. Ishpeming, Mich., Apr. 19, 1899; s. Thomas J. and Eliza (Rutter) K.; B.A., U. Mich., 1921, M.S., 1922; LL.D., Howard Payne Coll., 1962; m. Ruth Burdette Black, Oct. 1, 1925. Assistantship, U. Mich., dept. polit. sci., 1921-22; Grad. Sch. Banking, Rutgers U., 1944-45; mem. staff. Detroit Bur. Govtl. Research, Detroit, 1922; exec. sec. Community Welfare Fedn. and Community Chest, Charleston, W. Va., 1922-24; mem. staff. Am. City Bur., Chgo., 1924-26; advt. sales staff Curtis Pub. Co., Chgo., 1926-32; Western advt. mgr. Banking (jour. Am. Bankers Assn.), 1932-44; dep. mgr. Am. Bankers Assn., in charge Chgo. office and western mgr. Banking, 1944-48; mng. dir. Nat. Auto. Dealers Assn., Washington, 1948-49; v.p., mem. adv. com. Tex. Nat. Bank Commerce, Houston, 1950-57, sr. v.p., 1957-67, cons. v.p., 1967—. Dean, So. Meth. U. Southwestern Grad. Sch. Banking, 1963-67. Mem. Boy Scout Council, 1952—; dir. United Fund Houston and Harris County, 1954, campaign chmn., 1955, pres., 1957; bd. dirs. United Community Funds and Councils of Am., Inc.; state treas. Radio Free Europe; pres. bd. dirs. U.S.O., Houston, 1967-68, mem. nat. bd. govs., 1966-72, nat. council, 1967—; bd. dirs. YMCA, 1960-72; chmn. Tex. Youth Council, 1957-73; pres., exec. com. Greater Houston Conv. and Visitors Council, 1962—; pres. Tex. Tourist Council, 1957-73; Grad. Sch. Banking Found.; bd. dirs. U. Houston Found., Research and Devel. Found. Howard Payne U. Served in World War I. Recipient Distinguished Alumnus Service award U. Mich., 1972, Non-alumnus award U. Houston, 1972; Perpetual Volunteerism award United Fund Houston; U.S.O. Nat. Council Service award, 1974. Mem. Am., Tex. bankers assns., Community Welfare Planning Assn., Houston Zool. Soc. Houston Symphony Soc. Clubs: Presidents (U. Mich.); Houston, Houston County. Home: 1400 Hermann Dr Houston TX 77004 Office: Tex Commerce Bank Houston TX 77002

KNEECE, ROBERT EDWARD, lawyer; b. Columbia, S.C., Dec. 20, 1933; s. Otis Salter and Elise (Blackmon) K.; LL.B., U. S.C., 1958; m. Margaret Ann Medders, June 1, 1957; children—Melanie Carol, Robert Edward, Richard Otis, Milinda Kyle, Rexford Patrick, Margaret Ann. Admitted to S.C. bar, 1958; practiced in Columbia, 1958—; mem. firm Kneece, Kneece & Brown; mem. S.C. Gen. Assembly, 1966—. Dir. Raco Investments, 1st Palmetto State Bank & Trust. Chmn. House Judiciary, 1969; vice chmn. Crime Study Com., 1968, Ins. Study Com., 1969. Mem. Am., S.C., Richland County bar assns., Am., S.C. trial lawyers assns., Columbia C. of C. Mason (Shriner). Club: Palmetto Sertoma, Columbia, S.C. Home: 4110 Parkman Dr Columbia SC 29205 Office: 1338 Pickens St Columbia SC 29201

KNEEDLER, WILLIAM HARDING, physician; b. Phila., Aug. 13, 1900; s. Henry Martyn and Alice (Harding) K.; A.B., Princeton, 1922; M.D., U. Pa., 1926; postgrad. London Sch. Tropical Medicine and Hygiene, 1929-30; m. Christina Butler Harris, Apr. 30, 1930; children—Alice Harding (Mrs. J.J. Crate), Cornelia Harris (Mrs. I.B. Hudson Jr.), William Howard. Intern, Pa. Hosp., 1927-29; Presbyn. med. missionary, Thailand, 1930-41, 49-51; cons. tropical medicine Jefferson Hosp., Phila., 1942-47; practice internal medicine, Concord, N.C., 1951—; mem. staff Cabarrus Meml. Hosp., Concord, 1951—; asso. in medicine Jefferson Med. Sch., 1942-47. Diplomate Am. Bd. Internal. Medicine. Fellow A.C.P.; mem. A.M.A., Am. Soc. Internal Medicine. Home: 234 Scenic Dr NE Concord NC 28025 Office: 865 N Church St Concord NC 28025

KNEESE, VICTOR SCOTT, lawyer; b. Dallas, Nov. 7, 1939; s. Victor Carl and Katherine (Dunne) K.; B.B.A., U. Tex., 1961, LL.B., 1964; m. Carolyn Beatrice Calvin, Dec. 27, 1962; 1 son, Kyle Calvin. Admitted to Tex. bar, 1964, U.S. Dist. Ct. Eastern Dist. Tex. bar, 1971, No. Dist. Tex. bar, 1964, So. Dist. Tex. bar, 1968, U.S. Ct. Appeals 5th Circuit bar, 1967, U.S. Supreme Ct. bar, 1972; practiced in Dallas, 1964-67, Houston, 1967—; asso. firm Cervin and Stanford, 1964-67, Childs, Fortenbach, Beck and Guyton, 1967—. Mem. State Bar Tex. (chmn. com. on coordination with other groups 1971—), State Jr. Bar Tex., Am. (mem. com. on practice and procedure under Nat. Labor Relations Act, Houston, Houston Jr. bar assns., Alpha Tau Omega. Clubs: Houston Racquet, Am. Sportsmens. Home: 3109 Avalon Place Houston TX 77019 Office: 402 Pierce St Houston TX 77002

KNEZ, EUGENE IRVING, anthropologist; b. Clinton, Ind., May 12, 1916; s. Edward and Ida (Bosonetto) Pearson; A.B., U. N.M., 1941; postgrad. Ind. U., 1941, Yale 1948, U. Wash., 1949; Ph.D., Syracuse U., 1959; m. Jiae Chol. Mar. 15, 1952; children—Pamela, Alan. Chief, Nat. Bur. Culture, Am. Mil. Govt. in Korea, 1945-46; mus. positions with grad. work Yale Peabody Mus., Wash. State Mus., 1948-49; cultural affairs officer, regional pub. affairs officer Am. embassies, Korea and Japan, 1949-53; instr., lectr. Hunter Coll. and Syracuse U., 1954-59; anthropologist, curator Asian anthropology Smithsonian Instn., Washington, 1959—. Served to capt. AUS, World War II, now col. Res. Decorated Bronze Star medal; recipient Smithsonian Instn. Spl. award, 1965. Republic of Korea commendation, 1962, Asia Found. fellow, 1958. Fellow Am. Anthrop. Assn.; mem. Anthrop. Soc. Washington (former treas.). Smithsonian Senate of Scientists (former councilor), Am.-Korea Soc. Washington (chmn.), Japan-Am. Soc. Washington, A.A.A.S. Author: Korean Mutual Aid Groups: Persistence and Change: A South Korean Village: Sam Jong Dong; sr. author: A Selected and Annotated Bibliography of Korean Anthropology, 1968. Organizer numerous mus. exhbns., latest being Bhutan: The Land of Dragons, 1973. Home: 5060 Linnean Av NW Washington DC 20008 Office: Smithsonian Instn Washington DC 20560

KNEZEVICH, VLADIMIR JOHN, cons. engr.; b. Newcomerstown, O., July 20, 1937; s. Joe Vladimir and Ann (Shirila) K.; B. Indsl. Engring., Ga. Inst. Tech., 1960; postgrad. U. Miami, 1963; m. Wilmeth Gail Austin, Dec. 26, 1958 (div. Jan. 1967); children—Kim, John William; m. 2d, Geraldine Ann Palacino, Apr. 24, 1970; 1 dau., Nicole Marie. Plant engr. Aerodex, Inc., Miami, Fla., 1960-63, chief engr., 1964-68; project field engr. Aerojet Gen., Homestead, Fla., 1963-64; cons. engr. Howard Needles, Tammen & Bergendoff, Miami, 1968—; chmn. bd. Designs Internat., Miami, 1967—; sec. Endyke Constrn. Co., Inc., Miami, 1974—. Cons. engring. pvt. practice, Miami, 1968—; pres. Dovla Corp., Miami Shores, 1972—. Registered profl. engr., Fla., Ohio. Mem. Nat. Soc.

Profl. Engrs., Fla. Engring. Soc. Home: 711 NE 93d St Miami Shores FL 33138 Office: PO Box 2098 AMF Miami FL 33159

KNIBB, JOHN HADDON, clergyman; b. South Norfolk, Va., Aug. 16, 1926; s. John Haddon and Mina Henrietta (Hall) K.; student Randolph-Macon Coll., 1943-44; B.S., Worcester Poly. Inst., 1946; postgrad. Lynchburg Coll., 1947-48; M.Div., Yale, 1951; m. Evelyn Maxine Williams, June 24, 1950; children—Teresa (Mrs. John Edward Evans III), Anita Marie, John Mark Allen. Ordained to ministry Christian Ch., 1951; pastor Rocky Mount (Va.) Christian Ch., 1951-56, Mackinaw (Ill.) Christian Ch., 1956-61, Calvary Christian Ch., Covington, Va., 1961-67, Hampton (Va.) Christian Ch., 1967—. Pres. S. Piedmont dist. Christian Chs. Va., 1953-54, pres. New River dist., 1962-63, state chmn. dept. evangelism, 1970-72; mem. com. on recommendations Internat. Conv. Christian Chs., Indpls., 1964-65; mem. state bd. Va. Conv. Christian Chs., Richmond, 1970-72. Chmn. Community Chest, Mackinaw, Ill., 1958-61. Bd. dirs. Downtown Hampton Day Care Council, 1970—, pres. bd. 1973—. Served to lt. (j.g.) USNR, 1944-51. Mem. Peninsula Clergy Assn., Lynchburg Coll. Alumni Assn. (mem. com. on admissions 1965-66). Home: 8 Hillcrest Circle Hampton VA 23666 Office: PO Box 399 151 E Mercury Blvd Hampton VA 23669

KNIGHT, ALLEN MARVIN, machinery co. exec.; b. Los Angeles, Oct. 6, 1931; s. Fredick Allen and Louise (Marvin) K.; B.S. in E.E., U. Tex., 1951; m. Edrie Bradley, May 16, 1959; children—Cheryl Dane, Tracy Allen. Staff engr. Western Electric Co., Chgo., 1955-56; field engr. L. E. Wooten Cons. Engrs., Raleigh, N.C., 1956-57; v.p. Carolina Communications Engrs., Statesville, N.C., 1957-63; v.p. Garrison Machinery Co., Statesville, 1963-72, also dir.; exec. v.p., dir. Garrison Equipment Corp., Statesville, 1972—; dir. Electromec, Statesville. Served with USN, 1951-54. Mem. Am. Mgmt. Assn., Numerical Control Soc., Plastic Packaging Distbr. Assn. (pres.). Mason, Elk. Patentee in field. Home: 603 Georgia Av Statesville NC 28677 Office: PO Drawer 391 Statesville NC 28677

KNIGHT, CHARLES RICHARD, gas co. exec.; b. Cleve., Feb. 10, 1920; s. Claude M. and Margarite (Weimer) K.; B.A., Miami U., 1941; M.S. (Alfred P. Sloan fellow), U. Denver, 1942; m. Doris Jane Lamp, Sept. 9, 1941; children—Elizabeth Jane, Charles Richard. Asst. dir. Ala. Legislative Reference Service, Montgomery, 1946-50; dir. research Ala. C. of C., Montgomery, 1950-53; market analyst T.C.I. div. U.S. Steel Corp., Birmingham, Ala., 1953-57, mgr. comml. research, 1957-64; asst. to pres. Ala. Gas Corp., Birmingham, 1964-69, v.p., asst. sec., 1969—. Chmn. Ala. Bus. Research Council, 1965-67. Bd. dirs. Operation New Birmingham. Served to lt. comdr. Supply Corps, USNR, 1942-46. Mem. Am. Marketing Assn., U.S. C. of C., Sigma Nu. Methodist. Club: Exchange Mount Brook, Ala. Home: 94 Crestview Dr Mount Brook AL 35213 Office: 1918 First Av N Birmingham AL 35203

KNIGHT, CLIFFORD L., oil field equipment, indsl. valves mfg. co. exec.; b. Beaver, Okla., Feb. 11, 1920; s. George L. and Goldie (Burk) K.; student Hill's Bus. U., 1946-47; m. Sybil C. Rachal, Dec. 8, 1945; children—Jennifer (Mrs. Bill Robertson), Sherry (Mrs. Bill Jacobs), Vickie L. Gen. mgr. DEMCO, Inc., Oklahoma City, Okla., 1950-66, pres., 1966—, dir., 1948—; dir. Oklahoma Nat. Bank. Mem. adv. council Southwestern Coll., 1972; v.p., dir., mem. exec. com. United Appeal of Greater Oklahoma City, 1970. Mem. adv. bd. Salvation Army; bd. dirs. U. Okla. Research Inst.; chmn., bd. dirs. Jr. Achievement of Greater Oklahoma City. Served with AUS, 1941-45. Decorated Bronze Star medal. Mem. Soc. Advancement of Mgmt. (pres. Oklahoma City chpt. 1969-70). Home: 13040 Twisted Oak Rd Oklahoma City OK 73120 Office: PO Box 94700 829-845 SE 29th St Oklahoma City OK 73109

KNIGHT, DAVID WINSTON, educator; b. South Pittsburg, Tenn., Sept. 15, 1933; s. Charles Oscar and Alma Ruth (Hood) K.; B.S.A., U. Fla., 1958; M.Ed., Miss. Coll., 1961; Ph.D., Fla. State U., 1966; m. Carol Ann Southerland, Aug. 26, 1961; children—Anne, Allison, Shelley. Asst. prof. spl. edn. N.E. La. State U., Monroe, 1965; dir. Reading Center, U. So. Miss., Hattiesburg, 1966-71; vis. lectr. U. Ill. at Urbana, 1971-72; Calloway prof. edn. Oglethorpe U., Atlanta, 1972—. Cons. to pub. schs. on reading, instrn., in-service programs. Recipient numerous grants. Mem. Internat. Reading Assn., Nat. Reading Conf., Phi Delta Kappa. Baptist. Contbr. profl. jours. Home: 3126 Frontenac Ct Atlanta GA 30319 Office: 4400 Peachtree Rd NE Atlanta GA 30319

KNIGHT, DELOS LAVERN, JR., pub. relations exec.; b. Bogalusa, La., July 3, 1931; s. Delos Lavern and Ruth (Vineyard) K.; B.A., La. State U., 1952; m. Margaret Frances Rucker, Apr. 10, 1955; children—Delos Lavern III, Kevin T., Anne Ruth, Timothy O. Program dir. radio sta. WIKC, Bogalusa, 1954-59; pub. relations rep. Crown Zellerbach Corp., Bogalusa and Baton Rouge, 1959-61, pub. relations mgr., 1961-64, mgr. corp. communications, 1964-71, mgr. pub. affairs, 1972—. Served to 1st lt. AUS, 1952-54. Recipient Distinguished Service award Bogalusa Jr. C. of C., 1956. Mem. Pub. Relations Soc. Am. (pres. Baton Rouge 1970), So. Forest Inst. (chmn. pub. relations com. 1968-70), Sigma Delta Chi. Methodist. Rotarian. Club: Camelot (Baton Rouge). Home: 881 Sinclair Dr Baton Rouge LA 70815 Office: PO Box 3375 Baton Rouge LA 70821

KNIGHT, EDWARD HENRY, psychoanalyst; b. New Orleans, June 14, 1922; s. Edward Henry and Mamie (Lawrence) K.; B.S., La. State U., 1943, M.D., 1945; New Orleans Psychoanalytic Inst., 1960; m. Mary Knox, Aug. 14, 1951; children—Victoria, Alan Henry, Cynthia, Carolyn, Jennifer, Jeremy. Intern Aultman Gen. Hosp., Canton, O., 1945; resident, fellow Menninger Sch. Psychiatry, Topeka, 1948-51; clin. prof. psychiatry La. State U. Sch. Medicine, New Orleans, 1951—; tng. analyst New Orleans Psychoanalytic Inst., 1965—; chief div. psychiatry Truro Infirmary, New Orleans, 1966-67. Mem. assembly's com. on the minister and his work Prsbyn. Ch., Atlanta, 1959—. Mem. Orleans Parish Sch. Bd., 1971—. Served to capt. AUS, 1946-48. Recipient Mental Health award La. Mental Health Assn., 1964. Diplomate in psychiatry Am. Bd. Neurology and Psychiatry. Fellow Am. Psychiat. Assn.; mem. La. Psychiat. Assn. (pres. 1961-62). Home: 7325 Hampson St New Orleans LA 70118 Office: 1303 Antonine St New Orleans LA 70115

KNIGHT, EUGENE STEPHEN, pub. relations dir.; b. Wilmington, N.C., Sept. 21, 1913; s. Eugene Bridgers and Jessie Maude (Frink) K.; B.B.A., N.C. State U., 1935; m. Margaret Hodges Smith, June 14, 1941; children—Eugene Stephen, James Smith. Extension radio specialist N.C. State U., Raleigh, 1935-43; ednl. dir. Central Carolina Farmers, Inc., Durham, N.C., 1946-47; editor Patriot-Farmer Greensboro, N.C. News-Rec., 1947-50; dir. pub. relations and advt. FCX, Inc., Raleigh, N.C., 1950—. Served with AUS, 1943-46. Democrat. Episcopalian (vestryman 1962-65, sec. 1964-65). Home: 2761 Toxey Dr Raleigh NC 27609 Office: PO Box 2419 Raleigh NC 27602

KNIGHT, H. STUART, govt. ofcl.; b. Sault Ste. Marie, Ont., Can., Jan. 6, 1921; grad. police adminstrn. Mich. State U., 1948; postgrad. Indsl. Coll. Armed Forces, 1962, Princeton, 1965-66; m. Betty L. Cooley; 5 children. Formerly police officer Detroit and Berkeley, Cal.; with U.S. Secret Service, 1950—, spl. officer Detroit office, then with Presdl. Protective Detail, Washington, until 1961; spl. agt. in charge Vice Presdl. Protective Detail, 1961-63, spl. agt. in charge spl. investigations, 1963-65, asst. spl. agt. in charge Los Angeles office, 1966-70, spl. agt. in charge, Washington, 1970-71, asst. dir. for adminstrn., 1971-73, dir., 1973—. Served with U.S. Army, 1942-46; PTO. Decorated Silver Star, Bronze Star, Purple Heart; recipient certificate exceptional civilian service Dept. Treasury, 1958. Fellow Nat. Inst. Pub. Affairs; mem. Am. Soc. Pub. Adminstrn., Internat. Assn. Chiefs Police, Alpha Phi Sigma. Home: Falls Church VA Office: Secret Service Dept Treasury Washington DC 20220*

KNIGHT, JAMES L., newspaper exec.; b. Akron, O., 1909. Chmn. exec. com. Knight Newspapers, Inc.; pres. Knight Pub. Co., Charlotte, N.C.; pub. Charlotte Observer, Charlotte News; chmn. bd. Miami (Fla.) Herald Pub. Co. dir. keynoter Pub. Co., Gables Pub. Co., Asso. Press, So. Prodn. Program, Inc., Boca Raton News; pres., dir. Tallahassee Democrat. Mem. Am. (dir.), So. (pres. 1957, chmn. bd. 1958) newspaper pubs. assns. Clubs: Portage Country (Akron, O.); Bath, LaGorce, Indian Creek, Surf (Miami, Fla.); Detroit; Chicago; Key Largo Angelers, Hatteras Marlin, Nat. Press; Lyford Cay (New Providence, Bahamas). Home: The Surf House 8995 Collins Av Surfside FL 33154 Office: care Miami Herald 1 Herald Plaza Miami FL 33101

KNIGHT, JAMES PERRY, JR., wholesale and retail tire chain exec.; b. Columbus, Miss., Dec. 19, 1929; s. James Perry and Eloise (Copeland) K.; student Miss. State U., 1947-49; m. Janice Dell Jackson, Aug. 23, 1953; children—Geoffrey, Jay, James Perry III. With White Stores, Fort Worth, 1949-59, store mgr., 1951, dist. mgr., 1955-59; owner Hercules Western Tire, Babcock Stores, Jack & Harry's Stores, others; chmn. bd. dirs. Babcock's Auto Stores, Arlington, Tex., 1969—; with Hercules Western Tire Co., Arlington, 1964—, now chmn. bd., chief exec. officer; owner, chmn. bd. Morton Foods, Inc., Dallas; chmn. bd. dirs. Hercules Aviation Corp., J-K Ranches, J.P. Knight & Sons, K-C Investments; K-D Investments, Gt. South West Nat. Bank, First State Bank. Served with USAF, 1946-47. Rotarian (pres. Ft. Worth chpt. 1969-70). Home: 1201 Greenbriar St Arlington TX 76013 Office: 3200 E Randol Mill Rd Arlington TX 76011

KNIGHT, JAMES ROLAND, judge; b. Quitman, Ga., Apr. 5, 1911; s. William Roland and Gussie (Jarvis) K.; student South Ga. State Coll., 1931; m. Mary F. Kimble Knight, Dec. 2, 1934; children—Betty Frances (Mrs. John Horton), James R. Profl. baseball player, 1931-34; cafe bus., 1934-39; engr. C.E., 1939-50; investigator U.S. Dept. Labor, 1950-53; sales rep. Ford Motor Co., 1953-64; judge Ct. Ordinary, Brooks County, Ga., 1965—. Chmn., Quitman City Commn., 1959. Mem. Brooks County Live Stock Assn., Brooks County Farm Bur. Baptist. Lion. Home: 203 E Lake Dr Quitman GA 31643 Office: Brooks County Ct House Quitman GA 31643

KNIGHT, JEANNE ENID (MRS. REGINALD CAYWOOD KNIGHT), educator; b. Moretown, Vt., Dec. 6, 1923; d. Fred Moore and Jean Baird (Clark) Sellars: A.B., Hunter Coll., 1946; M.A., Columbia, 1948: m. Reginald Caywood Knight, Nov. 9, 1951: children—Jeanne Enid, Houghton Caywood, Eliot Holladay. Lectr. Wagner Coll., 1946-47, critic, 1940-42, instr. English lit., lit. criticism, creative writing, 1947-51; dramatics coach Wagner Players, 1946, Dutch Reformed Players, S.I., N.Y., 1948-49, Island Players Exptl. Theater, S.I., 1950-51; charge nursery sch. Holy Trinity Parish Day Sch., Collington, Md., after 1967: staff St. Peter and Paul, Miami, after 1968. Mem. Longboat Key (Fla.) Art Center, Sarasota, Manatee art assns., Women's League for Peace and Freedom, Sigma Tau Delta. Episcopalian. Home: Box 15 Vicksburg MS 39180

KNIGHT, JOHN SHIVELY, newspaper publisher; b. Bluefield, W.Va., Oct. 26, 1894; s. Charles Landon and Clara Irene (Scheifly) K.; student Tome Sch., Md., 1911-14, Cornell U., 1914-17, LL.D., U. Akron, 1945, Northwestern U., 1947, Kent State U., 1958, Ohio State U., 1961, U. Mich., 1969, Oberlin Coll., 1969, Colby Coll., 1969; medal for achievement in journalism, Syracuse U., 1946; m. Katharine McLain, Nov. 21, 1921 (dec. 1929); children—John Shively (killed in Germany, Mar. 29, 1945), Charles Landon, Frank McLain; m. 2d, Beryl Zoller Comstock, Jan. 24, 1932; 1 dau., Mrs. Kenneth Hewitt. Newspaper reporter and exec., 1920-25; mng. editor Akron (O.) Beacon Journal, 1925-33, editor 1933—; editorial dir. Springfield (O.) Sun. 1925-27, Massillon (O.) Independent, 1927-33, pres., 1933-37; chmn. bd., pub. Miami (Fla.) Herald, 1937-61, now editorial chmn., pres. Beacon Journal Pub. Co., Knight Newspapers, Inc., to 1966, now editorial chmn.; purchased and discontinued Miami (Fla.) Tribune, 1937; purchased Detroit Free Press, 1940, pres. and editor, 1940-67, now editorial chmn.; owner, editor and pub. Chgo. Daily News, 1944-59, v.p. Charlotte (N.C.) News, 1959—, also Talahassee Democrat. Chief liaison officer between U.S. and Brit. censorship, London, Eng., 1943-44. Trustee Cornell U., U. Miami, Nat. Jewish Hosp.; bd. dirs. N.Y. World's Fair. Served in Motor Transport Corps, 113th Inf., in AAC, AEF, 1917-19. Awarded Frank M. Hawks Meml. Trophy, 1947; Citation of Merit from Poor Richard Club, 1946; honor award, distinguished service journalism, U. Mo., 1949; recipient Brotherhood of Children award, 1946, La Prensa award, 1954, Am.'s Found. award, 1959, John Peter Zenger award, 1967, Pulitzer prize for distinguished editorial writing, 1968. Carr Van Anda award Ohio U., 1970; others; cited outstanding Chicagoan in Inter-Am. relations by U.S.-Uruguay alliance, 1952. Established Knight Meml. Fund commemorating his father; La Prensa Scholarship furthering Inter-Am. understanding. Mem. Am. Soc. Newspaper Editors (past pres.), V.F.W., Am. Legion, A.P. (past dir., chmn. finance com., mem. exec. com.), 40 and 8, Phi Sigma Kappa, Sigma Delta Chi. Episcopalian. Clubs: Portage Country (Akron); Tin Whistles (Pinehurst, N.C.); Bath, Indian Creek (Miami); Union (Cleve.); Detroit, Detroit Athletic, Detroit Economic, Grosse Pointe Country (Detroit); Burning Tree Golf (Washington); Racquet, Chicago, Tavern, Casino, Commercial, Saddle and Cycle (Chgo.); Old Elm (Ft. Sheridan, Ill.); Glenview (Golf, Ill.). Home: 255 N Portage Path Akron OH 44309 Office: 44 E Exchange St Akron OH 44309 also Miami Herald 1 Herald Plaza Miami FL 33101 also Free Press Detroit MI 48226

KNIGHT, KENNETH LEE, educator; b. Saunemin, Ill., Mar. 16, 1915; s. Scott Lee and Mariette Edwards (Jewett) K.; B.Ed., Ill. State U., 1937; M.S., U. Ill., 1939, Ph.D., 1941; m. Ruth Marie Hines, Apr. 8, 1944; children—Kimbell Lee, Richard Lee, Robert Lee, Karen (Mrs. William Auld), Alan Lee. Commd. ensign USN, 1941, advanced through grades to capt., 1957, ret., 1962; prof. Ia. State U., Ames, 1962-66, U. Ga., 1966-68; prof. entomology, head dept. N.C. State U., Raleigh, 1968—. Mem. tropical medicine and parasitology study sect NIH 1965-68. Mem. Am. Mosquito Control Assn. (pres. 1973-74), Entomol. Soc. Am. (pres. 1974—). Home: 2126 Buckingham Rd Raleigh NC 27607

KNIGHT, LUTHER AUGUSTUS, JR., educator; b. Clarendon, Ark., Dec. 19, 1930; s. Luther Augustus and Emma Mae (Henderson) K.; B.S.E., Ark. State Coll., 1957; M. Combined Scis., U. Miss., 1961, Ph.D., 1969; m. Janis Marguerite King, Aug. 21, 1955; children—Scott Stephen, Charles Luther. Tchr. sci. Jonesboro (Ark.) High Sch., 1956-57, Fisk (Mo.) High Sch., 1957-60, Clarkton (Mo.) High Sch., 1961-64; asso. prof., asso. research prof. biology U. Miss., 1972—; instr. biology Univs. Center, Jackson, Miss., 1972. Served with USAF, 1950-54. NSF Summer Inst. grantee, 1958-61. Mem. Am. Micros. Soc., Am. Soc. Limnology and Oceanography, Am. Fisheries Soc., Assn. Southeastern Biologists, A.A.A.S., Miss. Acad. Scis., Sigma Xi. Contbr. articles to profl. jours. Home: 5837 Kinder Dr Jackson MS 39211

KNIGHT, ROBERT CARROLL, pulp mill engr., constrn. mgr.; b. Lancaster, S.C., May 14, 1933; s. John Monroe and Mattie (Belk) K.; B.C.E., U. S.C., 1956; m. Donna Lynne Rhodes, June 28, 1952; children—Barbara (Mrs. William Michael Bumgardner), Robert Carroll, Nancy Pauline, Douglas Monroe, Wendy Suzanne, John Donald; m. 2d, Elizabeth Anne English Newton, May 19, 1974. Tech. trainee Internat. Paper Co., Mobile, Ala., 1956, asso. engr., project engr., 1956-57, project engr., Natchez, Miss., 1958-59, 1959-60, Mobile, Ala., 1960-61, Moss Point, Miss., 1961-62, Bastrop, La., 1962-63, dept. chief, Mobile, Ala., 1963-64, asst. constrn. engr., Springhill, La., 1964, dept. chief pulp, Bastrop, 1964-66, dept. chief large pulp, Bastrop, 1966-67, pulp mill design engr., Vancouver, B.C., Can., 1967-68, plant engr., Panama City, Fla., 1968-70; pres. Indsl. Processes Inc., Birmingham, Ala., 1970-71; mgr. pulp mill design Continental Can Co., Greenville, S.C., 1971, mgr. pulp mill design, Hodge, La., 1971-73, Augusta, Ga., 1973—, project mgr. Hodge Stretch Program, Hodge, 1973—, project mgr. 12 MM Capital Expansion at Paper Mill, Hodge, 1973—; project mgr. B.E. & K., Birmingham, Ala., 1974—. Served with AUS, 1950-52. Registered profl. engr., S.C., Ga., Me., Ala., Miss., La. Ark., Tex.; Registered Nuclear Fallout Shelter Analyst U.S. Dept. Def. Mem. Am. Mgmt. Assn., Am. Welding Soc., T.A.P.P.I., Am. Soc. M.E. Home: 129 Hillcrest Lancaster SC 29720 Office: 1900 28th Av S Birmingham AL 35209

KNIGHT, WOODSON, r.r. exec.; b. Sharpsburg, Ky., Mar. 18, 1913; s. William Rufus and Mary (Cracraft) K.; A.B., U. Ky., 1934; m. Winston Byron, Sept. 28, 1935; children—Robin Woodson, William Robert. With newspapers and A.P., 1935-43; editor Atlantic Richfield Co., Phila., 1945-65; pub. relations dir. Louisville & Nashville R.R., 1965-73; asst. v.p. pub. relations and advt. Seaboard Coast Line Industries, 1973—. Co-chmn. Louisville area chpt. A.R.C., 1970—. Served with USNR, 1943-45. Mem. R.R. Pub. Relations Assn., Pub. Relations Soc. Am., Am. Assn. Indsl. Editors (pres. 1959-60), Delaware Valley Assn. Editors (pres. 1954-55). Rotarian. Home: 3305 Springcrest Dr Louisville KY 40222 Office: 908 W Broadway Louisville KY 40201

KNIPPERS, OTTIS JEWELL, judge; b. Florien, La., Oct. 30, 1913; s. Christopher Columbus and Dona (Lockwood) K.; student Vaughan Sch. Music, 1929-30, U. Minn.; m. Opal Inez Moody, Jan. 28, 1938; children—Jan Carolyn, Ottis Jewell, Nancy Gayle. Profl. singer, 1929-38; operated retail stores, 1938-67; judge Lawrence County Ct., 1966—. Dir. Tenn. River and Tributaries Assn., 1960-64, Duck River Devel. Assn., 1960-64, Tenn. Elk River Devel. Agy., 1963—. Mem. So. Regional Edn. Bd., 1959-61, Mid South Regional Health Program, 1969—, Tenn. Assn. Advancement Child Care, 1969—, S. Central Tenn. Med. Services Council, 1969—, Tenn. Intergovtl. Com., 1966—, State Tenn. Adv. Council Mental Retardation, 1968—, State Tenn. Adv. Com. Services to Children and Their Families, 1969—; chmn. Lawrence County Gen. Hosp., 1966—; vice chmn. Columbia Area Mental Health Center, 1969—. Mem. Tenn. Ho. of Reps., 1941-44, 49-51, Tenn. Senate, 1956-60. Served from pvt. to sgt. AUS, 1944-46, ETO. Mem. Am. Legion, V.F.W., C. of C., Tenn. Council Juvenile Ct. Judges (pres. 1973—). Democrat. Methodist (asso. dist. lay leader). Club: Lions (Lawrenceburg). Author, composer, poet. Office: Court House Lawrenceburg TN 38464

KNOOP, WERNER CALDWELL, city ofcl., business exec.; b. Hancock County, Ia., Mar. 30, 1902; s. Charles Werner and Jessie (Olmstead) K.; B.S. in Civil Engring., Ia. State U., 1924; m. Faith Yingling, Sept. 4, 1926; 1 dau., Athalia May (Mrs. Karl Robert Kullander). Engr. Truscon Steel Co., Youngstown, O., Chgo., Omaha, 1924-29; owner Capitol Steel Co., Little Rock, 1929-40; cons. engr., 1940-46; exec. v.p. Baldwin Co., contractors, Little Rock, 1946-64, pres., 1964—; pres. Eureka Brick & Tile Co., Clarksville, 1949—; v.p. Clarkeville Machine Works, Inc. Exec. com. bd. dirs. Nat. Safety Council. Pres. sch. bd., Little Rock, 1947, mayor, 1957-62; chmn. Little Rock Parking Authority, 1966—; mem. Gov.'s Traffic Safety Adv. Commn. Pres. bd. dirs. Little Rock Jr. Coll., 1947; bd. dirs. Johnson-Knoop Found.; mem. internat. com. YMCA World Service; mem. 50 for the Future; past pres. Little Rock AFB Community Relations Council; mem. Little Rock Com. Fgn. Relations. Registered profl. engr. Fellow Am. Soc. C.E. (past dir. Mid-South sect.); mem. Nat. Soc. Profl. Engrs., Asso. Contractors Am. (mem. nat. safety com., pres. Ark. chpt.), Little Rock C. of C. (pres. 1970). Presbyn. (elder). Clubs: Rotary, Little Rock, Country of Little Rock. Home: 6 Ozark Point Little Rock AR 72205 Office: 322 Gaines St Little Rock AR 72201

KNOPP, PAUL JOSEPH, mathematician, educator; b. San Antonio, Jan. 3, 1934; s. Claude Clifford and Pauline Alice (Hasselmeier) K.; B.S., Spring Hill Coll., 1957; A.M. (NSF fellow), Harvard, 1958; Ph.D., U. Tex., 1962; m. Margaret Mary Belluomini, June 8, 1963, children—Cynthia, Elizabeth, John. Asst. prof. math. U. Mo., Columbia, 1962-64; asst. prof. math. U. Houston, 1964-67, asso. prof., 1967—. Recipient Teaching Excellence award U. Houston, 1970. Mem. Math. Assn. Am. (asso. dir. Com. Undergrad. Program Math. 1971-72, exec. dir. 1972-73), Am. Math. Soc. Author: Linear Algebra: An Introduction, 1973. Home: 9726 Braesmont St Houston TX 77035

KNOTT, ROBERT REAVES, radio co. exec.; b. Rotan, Tex., June 21, 1933; s. Proctor B. and Lula Maud (Holderness) K.; B.S., So. Meth. U., 1956. Asst. writer Girard Life Ins. Co., Dallas, 1956-58; asst. advt. and pub. relations mgr., 1959-62, advt. and pub. relations mgr., 1962-64; account exec., pub. relations Kontrak Corp., 1964-67, Workman Advt. Agy., 1967-68; pub. relations mgr. Collins Radio Co., 1968—. Mem. Pub. Relations Soc. Am., Sigma Delta Chi. Home: 4040 Travis St Dallas TX 75204 Office: Collins Radio Co Dallas TX 75207

KNOTTS, BURTON RAY, elec. engr.; b. Pocahontas, Ark., Oct. 24, 1930; s. Burton Dee and Lily (Sago) K.; B.S., U. Ark., 1957; m. Mary Catherine DeClerk, June 9, 1955; children—David Ray, Anna Catherine, Joan Marie. Chief specifications unit C.E., U.S. Army, Little Rock dist., 1957—. Mem. U.S. Com. on Large Dams. Served with USAF, 1949-52. Recipient Commendation award for elec. designs U.S. Army, 1966. Registered profl. engr., Ark. Mem. I.E.E.E., Nat. Soc. Profl. Engrs., Soc. Mil. Engrs., Constrn. Specifications Inst. Toastmaster, K.C. Home: 7316 Dahlia Dr Little Rock AR 72209 Office: 700 W Capitol St Little Rock AR 72203

KNOWLES, CHARLES ULMER, elec. engr.; b. Lynn, Mass., Jan. 8, 1927; s. Lester Douglas and Janet (Tripp) K.; B.S., Northeastern U., 1955; m. Jean Margaret Mondor, Sept. 1, 1951; children—Paul Douglas, Stephen Edward. With Western Electric Co., Inc., 1955—, sr. engr. Arlington, Va., 1964—. Cons. C & P Telephone Co's., Washington, 1964—. Bd. dirs., v.p. Greater Springfield (Va.) Vol. Fire Dept., 1973—. Active Boy Scouts Am., 1966—. Served with USNR, 1944-46. Recipient A.R.C. Service award, 1973. Mem. I.E.E.E.

Home: 5942 Thomas Dr Springfield VA 22150 Office: 1201 S Hayes St Arlington VA 22202

KNOWLES, DAVID JOHN, elec. engr.; b. San Francisco, Nov. 30, 1918; s. James Henry and Theodosia (Harris) K.; B.S.E.E., Rice U., 1942; M.S.E.E., U. Tenn., 1958; m. Marjorie Thompson Hastings, July 20, 1945; children—John Keith, Nancye Eileen (Mrs. Thomas A. Van Brunt), Martha Elizabeth. Design and devel. engr. Sylvania Electric Co., Emporium, Pa., 1942-48; devel. engr. Oak Ridge Nat. Lab., 1948-63, group leader, 1963-71, asst. sect. head, 1971—, Mem. I.E.E.E., Tau Beta Pi. Home: 114 Carnegie Dr Oak Ridge TN 37830 Office: PO Box X Oak Ridge TN 37830

KNOWLES, DOYLE BLEWER, hydrologist; b. Tulia, Tex., July 6, 1924; s. James Hamilton and Sydney (Blewer) K.; B.S., Tex. Technol. Coll., 1944; m. Joe Ann Watkins, Dec. 17, 1955; children—Bobbie Louise, Teresa Ann, William Doyle, Cheryl Lynne, Patricia Elaine. Hydraulic engr. Tex. Bd. Water Engrs., Austin, Tex., 1946-47, U.S. Geol. Survey, various locations, 1947-61; chief water resources div., Geol. Survey Ala., University, 1961-69, sr. hydrologist, publs. officer, 1969—; partner P. E. La-Moreaux Assos., cons. groundwater hydraulogists, Tuscaloosa, Ala., 1961-71, sr. hydrologist, treas., dir., 1971-74; pres., chief hydrologist Doyle Knowles Assos., Inc., 1974—. Served with USNR, 1944-45. Registered profl. engr., Tex., Ala. Mem. Am. Soc. C.E., Am. Geophys. Union, Am. Water Works Assn., Nat. Water Well Assn., Am. Chem. Soc., Am. Acad. Sci., Am. Forestry Assn. Contbr. articles to sci. jours. Home: 28 Brookhaven Dr Tuscaloosa AL 35401 Office: Box 2321 Tuscaloosa AL 35401

KNOWLES, THOMAS GEORGE, architect; b. Ft. Worth, Feb. 17, 1928; s. George Lucian and Mary Inez (Eddins) K.; student Tex. A. and M. U., 1945-46, 48-49, U. Houston, 1949-50; grad. Internat. Corr. Schs., 1954; m. Dorothy Genell Peacock, Dec. 22, 1951; children—Mark, Warren, Steven Lloyd, Glenn Russell. Asso. architect B.M. Smith, G. Marble, S. Brown, Roper, Vance, Harper and Kemp, architects, Dallas, 1952-60; prin. T.G. Knowles, architect, Dallas, 1960-65; asso. architect Simons, Tyler, Tex., 1965-73; prin. T.G. Knowles, architect, Tyler, 1973—. Active Boy Scouts Am., 1967—. Bd. dirs. Tyler Civic Choral, treas. Served with USNR, 1946-48. Mem. A.I.A. (dir. N.E. chpt. 1973), Tex. Soc. Architects, Constrn. Specification Inst., Tyler C. of C. Republican. Baptist. Kiwanian. Prin. works: Salem Ch., Dallas, 1962; Garland (Tex.) Bible Coll. Dormitory, 1963; Big Town Nursing Home, Mesquite, 1964; Med. Center Hosp., Tyler, 1968; Jr. Coll. Library, Tyler, 1967. Home: 2407 Hunter St Tyler TX 75701 Office: 530 S Beckham St Tyler TX 75701

KNOWLES, WARREN ELLIOTT, city mgr.; b. Gloucester, Mass., Mar. 27, 1923; s. Elliott Perry and Louise Gertrude (Crichet) K.; B.S., U. Me., 1948, postgrad., 1949; m. Ava Melissa Bryan, Nov. 3, 1972; children—Tracy Lee Marie, Sinda Gay. Town mgr. Town of Berwick, Me., 1949-52, Town of Derry, N.H., 1952-53; city engr. City of Sanford, Fla., 1953-54, city mgr., 1954—; adj. instr. polit. sci. Fla. Tech. U.; municipal mgmt. cons. Dake & Assos. Mem. Sanford-Semonole Art Assn.; trustee Gen. Sanford Meml. Library; bd. dirs. United Fund. Served with C.E., AUS, 1943-46. Recipient good govt. award, Jr. C. of C., 1962, distinguished service award, 1957. Mem. Fla. City and County Mgmt. Assn. (pres. 1965-66), Internat. City Mgmt. Assn., Nat. Municipal League, Kappa Sigma. Democrat. Methodist. Home: 2015 Lily Ct Sanford FL 32771 Office: PO Box 1778 Sanford FL 32771

KNOWLTON, CHARLES W., lawyer; b. Columbia, S.C., 1923; A.B., U. S.C., 1943; LL.B., Harvard, 1949. Admitted to S.C. bar, 1949; now mem. firm, Boyd, Knowlton, Tate & Finlay, Columbia. Mem. Am. Coll. Probate Counsel, Am. Judicature Soc., Richland County (pres. 1968-69), S.C. (chmn. exec. com. 1969), Am. bar assns., Phi Beta Kappa, Omicron Delta Kappa. Address: Boyd Knowlton Tate & Finlay 1250 SCN Center Columbia SC 29201

KNOX, SAMUEL ROSCOE, mathematician, educator; b. Water Valley, Miss., Jan. 4, 1926; s. Roscoe Cragin and Mattie Lee (Johnson) K.; B.A., U. Miss., 1948, M.A., 1949; Ph.D. (So. Faculty fellow), Va. Poly. Inst., 1962; m. Dorothy Jo Walker, June 5, 1949; children—Samuel Cragin, Amy Ruth. Faculty Millsaps Coll., Jackson, Miss., 1949—, B.E. Mitchell prof. math., 1962—, chmn. dept., 1960—. Served with USMCR, 1943-46. Mem. Am. Statis. Assn., Math. Assn. Am. (vice chmn. 1961-62, chmn. 1965-66, gov. 1970-71). Home: 1600 Linden Pl Jackson MS 39202

KNOX, WILLIAM T., govt. ofcl.; B.A., Mercer U.; M.S., Va. Poly. Inst. With Esso Research and Engring. Co., 1938-64; with Office Sci. and Tech. Exec. Office Pres., Washington, 1964-66; v.p. McGraw-Hill, Inc., from 1966; now dir. Nat. Tech. Information Service, Dept. Commerce. Chmn. Council Communication Smithsonian Instn. Mem. Information Industry Assn. (founder; pres.). Address: 3563 Hamlet Pl Chevy Chase MD 20015

KNUCKLES, JOSEPH LEWIS, educator; b. Lumberton, N.C., Mar. 17, 1924; s. Dr. William H. and Sadie M. (Lewis) K.; B.S., N.C. Central U., 1948, M.S., 1950; Ph.D., U. Conn., 1959. Asst. prof., dean men Bishop Coll., 1950-51, chmn. sci. dept., 1951-52; instr. biology, math. Fayetteville State U., 1956-59, prof., biology coordinator, 1959-67, prof., chmn. dept. biol. and phys. scis., 1967—, acting chmn. div. sci. and math., 1973—. Dir. Consortium for Promotion Acad. Excellence in Biology, 1972-74. Served with AUS, 1942-46, ETO; to lt. USPHS, 1959—. Mem. Am. Inst. Biol. Scis., Nat. Geog. Soc., Am. Soc. Parasitologists, A.A.A.S., Am. Entomol. Soc., Am. Assn. U. Profs., Assn. Res. Officers, Sigma Xi, Phi Beta Sigma. Mason. Contbr. articles to profl. jours. Home: PO Box 970 Lumberton NC 28358 Office: PO Box 965 Fayetteville NC 28301

KNUDSEN, KNUD JOHANNES, elec. engr.; b. Sonderho, Denmark, Mar. 15, 1899; s. Henrik and Carolina (Johanson) K.; Examin Artium in Math. and Phys. Sci., State Sch. of Randers, 1919; E.E., Internat. Corr. Schs., 1931; m. Else Lange, Aug. 14, 1928. Came to U.S., 1937, naturalized, 1942. Chief engr. Hickok Elec. Instrument Co., 1937-42; chief instrument engr. Halsey Taylor Co., 1942-43; research engr. U.S. Time Corp., Waterbury, Conn., 1943-44; chief electronics engr. Lewis Engring. Co., Naugatuck, Conn., 1944-48, chief engr., 1948-63, dir. engring., 1963-64, hon. dir. engring., 1964-69; cons. profl. engr., Daytona Beach, Fla., 1969—. Mem. Radio Amateur Civil Emergency Service, Civil Def., 1953-58. Served to 2d lt., F.A., Denmark, 1920-24, army A.C., 1926. Recipient Best Paper prize, Initial Paper prize, McCutcheon award, Am. Inst. Elec. Engrs., 1942; Distinguished Achievement award USAF, 1956. Registered profl. engr., Conn., Fla., Ohio. Fellow I.E.E.E. (life); mem. Cleve. Engrs. Soc. (life), Fla. Engring. Soc. (respect mem.), Nat. (life), Conn. socs. profl. engrs. Mason (32 deg., Shriner). Patentee in field. Address: 102 Venetian Way Daytona Beach FL 32019

KNUDSON, ALFRED GEORGE, JR., geneticist, educator, univ. dean; b. Los Angeles, Aug. 9, 1922; s. Alfred George and Mary Gladys (Galvin) K.; B.S., Cal. Inst. Tech., 1944, Ph.D. (John Simon Guggenheim Found. fellow, Nat. Found. fellow), 1956; M.D., Columbia, 1947; m. Paula Louise Schaie, June 14, 1947; children—Linda Louise, Nancy Sue, Dorene Joyce. Intern, Huntington Meml. Hosp., Pasadena, Cal., 1947-48; resident N.Y. Hosp., 1948-49, Los Angeles Children's Hosp., 1949-50; chmn. dept. pediatrics City of Hope Med. Center, Duarte, Cal., 1956-62, chmn. dept. biology, 1962-66; prof. pediatrics State U. N.Y., Stony Brook, 1966-69, also asso. dean; asso. dir. edn. M.D. Anderson Hosp. and Tumor Inst., 1969-70; prof. med. genetics, dean U. Tex. Grad. Sch. Biomed. Scis., Houston, 1970—. Cons. NIH, 1964—, NRC, 1971—. Served to lt. M.C., AUS, 1951-53. Diplomate Am. Bd. Pediatrics. Mem. Am. Soc. Human Genetics. Author: Genetics and Disease, 1965. Home: 3514 Glen Arbor Houston TX 77025 Office: Texas Medical Center Houston TX 77025

KNUTSON, GERALD LOYD, univ. adminstr.; b. McLean, Tex., June 8, 1929; s. Youel A. and Margaret J. (Malone) K.; A.A., Graceland Jr. Coll., 1949; student West Tex. State U., 1949-50; B.S., Central Mo. State Coll., 1955, M.S. in Edn., 1956; Ph.D., U. Okla., 1968; m. Norma Audette Smoot, June 7, 1953; children—Linda Kaye, Gary Lynn. Pub. sch. tchr., adminstr., 1955-58; agt. Southwestern Life Ins. Co., Tulsa, 1958-67; instr. U. Okla., Norman, 1967-68, dir. research in gerontology, Extension, Tulsa, 1968-69; dir. ednl. services Okla. State U., 1969—. Cons., Okla. White House Conf. on Aging, 1970—. Bd. advisers Okla. State U. Student Union. Served with USN, 1950-54. Grantee in gerontology Dept. Health, Edn. and Welfare, 1958-59. Mem. Adult Edn. Assn., Nat. Univ. Extension Assn. Mem. Reorganized Ch. of Jesus Christ of Latter-day Saints. Rotarian. Home: 1102 N Lincoln St Stillwater OK 74074

KOBB, ALEX, dentist; b. N.Y.C., May 28, 1938; s. Louis and Gladys (Landsman) Kobrinetz; B.A., Harpur Coll., 1959; D.D.S., Temple U., 1964; m. Marcia Lynn Goldberg, June 9, 1962; children—Amy Jo, Wendy Lee. Leukemia research asst. Downstate Med. Center, Bklyn., 1959-60; practice dentistry, Hollywood, Fla., 1966—; mem. staff Hollywood (Fla.) Meml. Hosp. Mem. Dade County Dental Research Inst., Miami, 1969—. Campaign worker Jewish Welfare Fedn., Hollywood, Fla., 1967-71; v.p. Young Leaders Council, 1971-72. Bd. dirs. Fla. region Anti-Defamation League. Served with USNR, 1964-66. Recipient Alumni award Temple U. Sch. Dentistry, 1964. Mem. Am. Dental Assn., Acad. Gen. Dentistry, East Coast Dist. Dental Soc., Fla. Dental Assn., Am. Soc. Preventive Dentistry, Greater Hollywood Dental Soc. (treas. 1972-73, sec. 1973-74), Jewish War Vets. Jewish religion. Home: 622 N Rainbow Dr Hollywood FL 33021 Office: 3816 Hollywood Blvd Hollywood FL 33021

KOBERLEIN, JAMES HERSCHEL, elec. engr.; b. Vandalia, Ill., Apr. 17, 1941; s. James Sylvanis and Beulah Naomi (Summerlott) K.; student Eastern Ill. U., 1961; B.S., U. Ill., 1966; m. Kay Dianne Evans, Aug. 25, 1963; children—David, Susan. With Tex. Instruments, Inc., Dallas, 1967—, sr. engr. microwave landing systems, 1973—. Com. Chmn. Boy Scouts Am., Dallas, 1970—. Mem. I.E.E.E., Nat. Soc. Profl. Engrs. Home: 3626 Edgewood Dr Garland TX 75042 Office: 13500 N Central Dallas TX 75222

KOBLAS, JAMES A., TV broadcasting co. exec.; b. Huron, S.D., Apr. 5, 1943; s. Archie William and Irene E. (Roberts) K.; student U. Omaha, 1962-64; m. Donna M. Lange, Nov. 15, 1964; children—James Scott, Jamee Joel. Floor mgr. KMTV, Omaha, 1963; announcer, engr. radio sta. KNCY, Nebreska City, 1963-65; announcer, salesman WPCF Radio Panama City, Fla., 1966; sports dir. WALA-TV, Mobile, Ala., 1966—. Named Elector for Ala. Sports Hall of Fame 1972. Mem. Nat. Assn. Sports Broadcasters and Sports Writers. Home: 66 Burtonwood Dr Mobile AL 36608 Office: PO Box Mobile AL 36601

KOBREN, SAM RUDOLPH, TV broadcasting co. exec.; b. El Paso, Tex., Jan. 24, 1929; s. Jake and Etta (Alfman) K.; B.B.A., U. Tex., El Paso, 1951; m. Lenore Plaut, Nov. 9, 1958; children—Scott, Barry. Account exec. Mott & Reid Pub. Relations, El Paso, Tex., 1949-51, 53-55; pres. McMath Printing, Inc., El Paso, 1958-61; gen. sales mgr. station KDBC-TV, El Paso, 1961—. Mem. selection com. El Paso Athletic Hall of Fame, 1971—. Mem. El Paso Bd. Devel., 1972—. Served to 1st lt. USAF, 1951-53. Mem. El Paso C. of C. Clubs: Touchdown (sec. 1972—), Advertising. Home: 536 Stonebluff St El Paso TX 79912 Office: 2201 Wyoming St El Paso TX 79999

KOCH, JOHN SUMNER, lawyer; b. Chgo., Dec. 10, 1931; s. Summer Leibnitz and Lucille (Baumann) K.; grad. Phillips Acad., Andover, 1949; A.B., Yale, 1953; J.D., Northwestern U., 1959; m. Constance Chadwell, Oct. 1, 1955; children—Anne Elizabeth, John Sumner, Sarah Grace, Peter Chadwell. Editor, Conn. Shore; 1951; reporter City News Bur. Chgo., Chgo. Daily News, 1955-56; admitted to Ill. bar, 1959, D.C. bar, 1960; asso. Covington & Burling, Washington, 1959-68, partner, 1968—. Mem. Am. Bar Assn., Bar Assn. D.C., Am. Judicature Soc., Aurelian Honor Soc., Scroll and Key. Clubs: University (Chgo.); Yale (N.Y.C.); National Lawyers, City Tavern; Fence; Elizabethan. Home: 2952 Macomb St NW Washington DC 20008 Office: 888 16th St NW Washington DC 20006

KOCH, RONNEY RAY, petroleum engr.; b. Cape Girardeau, Mo., Mar. 29, 1933; s. Calvin John and Mamie (Margraf) K.; B.S. in Chemistry, S.E. Mo. State Coll., 1954; B.S. in Petroleum Engring., U. Okla., 1960; m. Patricia Ione Woody, Feb. 11, 1961; children—Sally Lynn, Carolyn Kay. Chemist, Reynolds Metals Co., Richmond, Va., 1957; engr. Cal. Co., Barataria, La., 1960; engr., devel. engr., group leader Halliburton Services, Duncan, Okla., 1960—. Served with AUS, 1955-57. Registered profl. engr., Okla. Mem. Soc. Petroleum Engrs., Am. Inst. Mining, Metall. and Petroleum Engrs., Tau Beta Pi, Pi Epsilon Tau. Republican. Lutheran (elder). Patentee in field. Home: Route 1 Box 255 Duncan OK 73533 Office: PO Drawer 1431 Duncan OK 73533

KOCHER, JOEL OWEN, city ofcl.; b. Galena, Kan., Sept. 21, 1902; s. Daniel Shanor and Cora (Cullifer) K.; grad. high sch.; m. Anna Margaret Rutherford, Feb. 11, 1940; 1 son, John J. Traffic officer, mgr. Brand Dunwoody Milling Co., Joplin, Mo., 1922-29; mgr. grain dept. Gen. Mills, Incs., Wichita Falls, Tex., 1930-34, Houston, 1935, Wichita, Kan., 1936-56, Enid, Okla., 1957-62; exec. sec., treas. Enid Bd. Trade, 1963—. Recipient Meritorious Service award Okla. 4-H Club, 1966. Mem. Nat. grain Trade Council, Okla. Grain and Feed Dealer Assn. (treas., exec. sec. 1971—), Grain and Feed Dealers Nat. Assn., Nat. Indsl. Traffic League. Republican. Presbyn. (elder). Kiwanian. Club: Oakwood Country. Home: 110 S Coolidge St Enid OK 73701 Office: 1st Nat Bank Bldg Enid OK 73701

KOCIAN, CHARLES JOSEPH, statistician; b. Lansford, Penn., Mar. 31, 1921; s. Emerich S. and Mary (Pavlacka) K.; B.S., Lycoming Coll., 1950; postgrad. Am. U., intermittently 1950—; m. Jean M. Costenbader, Nov. 11, 1950. Statistician welfare, retirement fund United Mine Workers Am., Washington, 1950-61, dental pub. health and research Dept. Health, Edn. and Welfare, 1961, Mil. Sea Transp. Service, USN, 1961-63; supervisory statistician Rural Electrification Adminstrn. U.S. Dept. Agr., 1963-65, Office Surgeon Gen., U.S. Army, 1965—. Dir. Capitol Investment Corp., 1959-60. Served with AUS, 1942-45. Mem. Am. Econ. Assn., Am. Statis. Assn., Nat. Assn. Accountants, Fed. Profl. Assn. Methodist. Mason (32 degree); mem. Order Eastern Star. Patentee steering controlled automobile headlights. Home: 2000 F St NW Washington DC 20006 Office: Forrestal Bldg 10th and Independence Av Washington DC 20315

KOEBBEMAN, SKIP, educator, sculptor; b. Cleve., Nov. 11, 1943; s. Ralph Frank and Rose Marion (Dinse) K.; student No. Ill. U., 1961-63; B.F.A., U. Ill., 1967, M.F.A., 1971; m. Marcia Ann Schunk, Oct. 16, 1970. Indsl. designer Nat. Lock Co., Rockford, Ill., 1967-68; tool designer Sundstrand Aviation, Rockford, 1968-69; mem. faculty Louisville Sch. of Art, 1971—, chmn. dept. sculpture since 1971—; exhibited in one-man shows at Barras Gallery, Louisville, 1973, U. Ill., Krannert Art Mus., Champaign, 1973, Billy Son Gallery, Iowa City, Ia., 1973; exhibited in group shows at Ill. State Fair Profl. Artists Exhibition, Springfield, 1972, Louisville Salute to the Arts Exhibition, Citizens Bank Art Gallery, 1972, Mid States Exhibition, Evansville (Ind.) Art Mus., 1973. Home: 1405 Elm Rd Anchorage KY 40223 Office: Louisville School of Art 100 Park Rd Anchorage KY 40223

KOEHLER, ROBERT EARL, writer, editorial cons.; b. Oconomowoc, Wis., July 6, 1924; s. George John and Ida Mae (Watterson) K.; B.A., U. Wis., 1948. Asst. editor The Feed Bag, Milw., 1948-49; publicity dir. Spencerian Coll., Milw., 1949-52; asso. editor The Confectioner, Milw., 1952-53; editorial asst. Pacific Builder & Engr., Seattle, 1953-54; editor Architecture/West, Seattle, 1954-62; asso. editor, mng. editor A.I.A. Jour., Washington, 1962-65, editor, 1965-73; writer, editorial cons., 1973—. Recipient Outstanding Publ. award for artwork, layout and makeup Western Soc. Bus. Publs., 1959. Mem. A.I.A. (hon.), Wis. Alumni Assn., Sigma Delta Chi. Editor: 50th Anniversary Annual of The Mountaineers, 1956. Contbg. author to Parents Mag. Yearbook, 1966-70. Home: 1748 Corcoran St NW Washington DC 20009

KOEHLER, WARD LEE, lawyer; b. Akron, O., Apr. 14, 1926; s. Orlo Oscar and Bernice Novelle (Sweet) K.; A.B. with honors, Ill. Coll., 1950; J.D., U. Mich., 1953; m. Kathryn Sara Ponsford, Nov. 4, 1927; children—Paul Edward, Thomas Orlo, Christine Bernice, Bruce Allen. Admitted to Ill. bar, 1953, Mich. bar, 1954, Tex. bar, 1954: practiced in Dallas, 1956-59, El Paso, 1959—; mem. Long & Koehler, 1961—. Republican county chmn., El Paso County, Tex., 1968-69; 29th Senatorial Dist. Committeeman, Tex. Rep. State Exec. Com., 1972—. Mem. Am., Tex., El Paso bar assns., State Bar Tex., Phi Beta Kappa. Home: 3831 O'Keefe Dr El Paso TX 79902 Office: 12A El Paso Nat Bank Bldg El Paso TX 79901

KOEHN, ROBERT CECIL, JR., physician; b. Los Angeles, Mar. 7, 1928; s. Robert Cecil and Lucille Marie (Farwell) K.; B.S., U. Tenn., 1950, M.D., 1951; m. Myrtle Lottie Inman, Nov. 18, 1950; children—Larry W., Robert Cecil III, Lisa (Mrs. Dennis Jarrell). Intern, Bapt. Meml. Hosp., Memphis, 1952; resident obstetrics and gynecology Fitzsimons Army Hosp., Denver, 1953-57; commd. 1st lt. USAF, 1952, advanced through grades to maj., 1962; chief obstetrics and gynecology 7505th USAF Hosp., Eng., 1957-60, Sheppard AFB, Tex., 1960-62; ret., 1962; pvt. practice obstetrics and gynecology, Clarkesville, Tenn., 1962—; mem. staff Meml. Hosp., Clarksville, chief of staff, 1972. Bd. dirs. Vocational Rehab. Center, Clarkesville. Diplomate Am. Bd. Obstetricians and Gynecologists. Fellow Am. Coll. Obstetrics and Gynecology; mem. C. of C. (chmn. recreation com.), A.M.A., Tenn. Med. Assn., Tenn., Nashville obstetrics and gynecology socs., Am. Fertility Soc. Kiwanian. Home: 1751 Cedarcroft St Clarksville TN 37040 Office: 1637 Madison St Clarksville TN 37040

KOEN, BILLY VAUGHN, educator; b. Graham, Tex., May 2, 1938; s. Ottis Vaughn and Margaret May (Branch) K.; B.A. in Chemistry, U. Tex., 1960, B.S. in Chem. Engring., 1961; S.M. in Nuclear Engring., Mass. Inst. Tech., 1962, Sc.D., 1968; Diplome d'ingenieur in Genie Atomique (Rotary Internat. fellow), L'institut Nat. des Scis. et Techniques Nucleaires, Saclay, France, 1963; m. Deanne Rollins, June 3, 1967; children—Kent Vaughn, Douglas Branch. Research asst. Los Alamos Sci. Lab., summers 1961, 65, Cadarache, French AEC Lab., summer 1963, Argonne (Ill.) Nat. Lab., summer 1964, Mass. Inst. Tech., Cambridge, 1963-66; asst. prof. U. Tex. at Austin, 1968-71, asso. prof. nuclear engring., 1971—, dir. Bur. Engring. Teaching. Vis. cons. Los Alamos Sci. Lab., 1969; cons. French AEC, Saclay, 1971-72; lectr. on engring. edn. and self-paced instruction, profl. meetings. Recipient Outstanding Teaching award Standard Oil Ind. Found., 1969, Distinguished Adviser award Coll. Engring., U. Tex. at Austin, 1970; Oak Ridge nat. fellow, 1961-63; NSF grantee, 1969-70; Fulbright travel grantee, France, 1971; Univ. Research Inst. grantee, 1971. Registered profl. engr., Tex. Mem. Am. Nuclear Soc., Am. Soc. Engring. Edn., N.Y. Acad. Scis., A.A.A.S., Assn. des Ingenieurs en Genie Atomique, Sigma Xi, Phi Beta Kappa, Tau Beta Pi, Alpha Chi Sigma, Pi Lambda Upsilon, Omega Chi Epsilon, Phi Eta Sigma, Pi Tau Sigma. Contbr. articles on engring. edn. and tech. articles to sci. jours. U.S. and France. Home: 3500 Greystone St Austin TX 78731 Office: Dept of Mechanical Engineering University of Texas Austin TX 78712

KOENIG, NATHAN, econ. cons.; b. N.Y.C., Mar. 20, 1907; s. Samuel and Lena (Penner) K.; B.S., U. Conn., 1930; m. Rose Edith Rosenblum, Nov. 24, 1929; children—Judith Barbara (Mrs. Alvin P. Wolfman), Susan Ruth (Mrs. Fredric J. Freed), Martha Jean (Mrs. Stuart L. Bindeman). Agrl. pub., writing, 1930-33; pub. information work U.S. Dept. Agr., Washington, 1933-43; agrl. editor U.S. News and World Report, Washington, 1943-45; exec. asst. to U.S. Sec. Agr., Washington, 1945-48, asst. to sec., confidential asst. to asst. sec. Marketing and Fgn. Agr., Washington, 1948-54; spl. asst. to adminstr. Consumer and Marketing Service, U.S. Dept. Agr., Washington, 1954-65; econ. cons., 1965—. Mem. U.S. Food and Agr. Survey Mission, Japan, Korea, 1947; mem. U.S. delegation spl. cereals conf. Internat. Emergency Food Council, Paris, 1947; rep. U.S. Govt. numerous internat. confs. on internat. food standards. Recipient U.S. Dept. Agr. Superior Service award, 1955, Distinguished Alumni award U. Conn., 1965. Mem. Am. Agr. Econ. Assn., Soc. Internat. Devel., Am. Acad. Polit. and Social Sci., Acad. Polit. Sci., N.J. Agrl. Soc., Pi Kappa Delta, Phi Epsilon Pi. Clubs: National Press, International of Washington. Writer numerous articles, reports in field. Home: 4501 Connecticut Av Washington DC 20008

KOENIG, PAUL EDWARD, chemist, educator; b. Gallup, N.M., May 30, 1929; s. Leo Henry and Marie Barbara (Kolar) K.; B.S., U. Ariz., 1950, M.S., 1952; Ph.D., U. Ia., 1955; m. Norma Adelaide Putnam, Dec. 26, 1950; children—Michael, Lawrence, Karen, Thomas, Paula, Thecla, Gretchen, Monica. Chemist, Ethyl Corp., Baton Rouge, La., 1955-58; asst. prof. chemistry La. State U., Baton Rouge, 1958-63, asso. prof., 1963-67, also asst. head dept. chemistry, 1963-67, asso. dean Grad. Sch., 1967-70, prof., asst. vice chancellor acad. affairs., 1970—. Mem. Am. Chem. Soc. (Charles E. Coates meml. award 1972), Am. Inst. Chemists, Sigma Xi, Phi Beta Kappa, Phi Kappa Phi, Omicron Delta Kappa, Phi Kappa Theta. Club: Serra. Contbr. articles to sci. jours. Patentee in field. Home: 2006 Cherrydale St Baton Rouge LA 70808 Office: Office of Academic Affairs Louisiana State Univ Baton Rouge LA 70803

KOERNER, UDA HENRY, architect; b. Chgo., Dec. 4, 1902; s. Henry and Nellie (Klipp) K.; B.Ed., Colo. State U., 1939; m. Hattie May Morgan, Sept. 29, 1927; children—Judith, Henry, John. Instr. architecture Chgo. Pub. Schs., 1932-62; prin. U.H. Koerner, architect,

Nashville, 1930—; architect Equitable Ch. Builders, Inc., Nashville, 1965—. Registered profl. engr. Ill. Mem. A.I.A. (Chgo. chpt. 1955—), Guild for Religious Architecture. Principal works: St. Anthony Ch., Chgo., 1960; Ch. of Christ, Kingsville, Tex., 1965; 1st Bapt. Chs., Dayton, Tenn., 1966; Etowah, Tenn., 1973; Univ. Bapt. Ch., Baton Rouge, 1973. Home: 4303 Gray Oaks Dr Nashville TN 37204 Office: 2702 Nolensville Rd Nashville TN 37211

KOESTER, ENGELBERT LEO, r.r. exec.; b. Cin., Apr. 19, 1913; s. Henry Bernard and Amelia Florence (Klaine) K.; B.A., Xavier U., 1934; m. Helen G. Keefe, Dec. 26, 1942; children—Leacarol (Mrs. Dennis Larkin), Thomas L., Stephen K., David K. Newspaper reporter Cin. Times Star, 1935-46; pub. relations dir. Cin. C. of C., 1946-54; pub. relations dir. Crosley div. Avco Mfg., 1954-60; indsl. devel. mgr. State of Ky., Louisville & Nashville R.R. Co., 1968-74; mgr. pub. communications Seaboard Coast Line Industries, Inc., 1974—. Mem. pub. relations com. Hoover Commn. for Govt. Reorgn., 1956-58; vice-chmn. Ky. Indsl. Devel. Council, 1966-67. Mem. R.R. Pub. Relations Assn. (v.p.), Pub. Relations Soc. Am. (v.p. Bluegrass chpt. 1970-71), Xavier U. Alumni Assn. (pres. 1954). Democrat. Roman Catholic. Contbr. articles to profl. jours. Home: 710 Wicklow Rd Louisville KY 40207 Office: 908 W Broadway Louisville KY 40201

KOEVENIG, JAMES LOUIS, educator; b. Postville, Ia., Mar. 18, 1931; s. Louis Otto and Mildred B. (Harrington) K.; student Cumming Sch. Art, 1948-51, Med. Coll. Ga., 1952-53; B.A. (Noyes scholar), U. Ia., 1955, Ph.D. (Univ. scholar Univ. fellow) 1961; M.A., State Coll. Ia., 1957; postgrad. summer U. Ala., U. N.H., 1972; m. Kathleen D. Ohloff, Aug. 15, 1954; children—Kimberly Kay, Kurt Louis. Tchr. elementary sch. State Center, Ia., 1955-56; asst. prof. zoology San Diego State Coll., 1961-62; resident cons. biol. scis. curriculum study U. Colo., Boulder, 1962-64, vis. lectr. biology 1963-64; asso. prof. botany U. Kan., Lawrence, 1964-71, prof., 1971-72; prof. biology Fla. Tech. U., Orlando, 1972—. Cons. Ednl. Testing Service, 1965-68, Commn. on Undergrad. Edn. in Biol. Scis., 1965-68; participant Am. Sci. Film Forum, India, 1965, UNESCO panel on short films, 1964. NSF Sci. Faculty fellow Princeton, 1967-68; recipient H. Bernerd Fink award for teaching excellence, 1970; Hope award, 1971; CINE golden eagles; others. Mem. A.A.A.S., Am. Assn. U. Profs., Am. Sci. Film Assn. (regional v.p. 1965-67), Bot. Soc. Am., Internat. Wildlife Fedn., Mycol. Soc. Am., Nat. Assn. Biology Tchrs. (exec. council 1963-64), Am. Inst. Biol. Scis., Nat. Wildlife Fedn., Scientist Inst. Pub. Information, Phi Beta Kappa, Sigma Xi, Phi Eta Sigma, Beta Beta Beta, Author, dir. ecology films. Home: 373 Mead Dr Oviedo FL 32765 Office: Dept Biol Scis Fla Tech U Orlando FL 32816

KOH, KWANGIL, mathematician, educator; b. Seoul, Korea, July 8, 1931; s. Moon Young and On Soon (Kim) K.; came to U.S., 1956, naturalized, 1970; student Seoul U., 1950-51; B.S., Auburn U., 1959, M.S., 1960; Ph.D., U. N.C., 1964; m. Toni Lee, Mar. 15, 1958; children—Debra, James, Patricia. Teaching fellow U. N.C., Chapel Hill, 1960-64; asst. prof. math. N.C. State U., Raleigh, 1964-66, asso. prof., 1966-68, prof., 1968—. Served to capt. Republic of Korea Army, 1951-55. Mem. Am. Math. Soc., Am. Math. Assn., Sigma Xi (Research award 1968), Phi Kappa Phi, Pi Mu Epsilon. Contbr. articles on math. to sci. jours. Home: 4812 Metcalf Dr Raleigh NC 27612

KOHL, JOHN PRESTON, clergyman, chaplain; b. Allentown, Pa., Dec. 26, 1942; s. Claude Evan and Edna Lenoir (Woodland) K.; B.A. in English, Moravian Coll., 1964; M.Div., Yale, 1967; postgrad. U. Colo., 1967-68; m. Nancy Ann Christensen, Mar. 11, 1966; children—John Preston, Mark Christian. Ordained to ministry Congregational Ch., 1967; pastor Christ Congl. Ch., New Smyrna Beach, Fla., 1968-71, First Congl.-United Ch. Christ, Hutchinson, Minn., 1971-73; capt., chaplain U.S. Army, Fort Hood, Tex., 1973—. Mem. Volusia County (Fla.) study commn. White House Conf. on Children and Youth, 1969-70; mem. bi-racial com. Emergency Sch. Act Program, Volusia County, 1970-71; mem. governing bd. Volusia County Chaplaincy Assn., 1969-71; instl. rep. Boy Scouts Am., New Smyrna Beach, 1970-71. Bd. dirs. Smyrna Child Devel. Center, 1969-71; v.p. bd. dirs. Hutchison Pre-Sch. Center, 1971—, v.p., 1971-72, pres., 1972-73. Mem. Phi Sigma Tau. Club: Optimists (Hutchinson). Home: 1508 Camilla Ct Killeen TX 76541 Office: 2d Armored Div Meml Chapel Fort Hood TX 76544

KOHLAND, WILLIAM FRANCIS, educator; b. Chester, Pa., May 13, 1925; s. Francis William and Martha Marie (Pittman) K.; A.A., Rutgers, 1949; A.B., Bucknell U., 1951; M.S., Ph.D., U. Tenn., 1969; postdoctoral study Western Mich. U., 1971; m. Sylvia R. Hurlock, Jan. 5, 1957; 1 son, Louis. Deck officer marine div. United Fruit Co., 1946-48; operations agt. United Air Lines, 1954-59; asst. prof. Edinboro State Coll., 1959-67; asso. prof. Middle Tenn. State U., Murfreesboro, 1967—. Served with USNR, 1943-46. Danforth grantee, 1961-62. Mem. Nat. Assn. Geology Tchrs., Geol. Soc. Am., Soil Sci. Soc. Am., Am. Soc. Agronomy, Internat. Soil Sci. Soc., Assn. Am. Geographers, Delta Sigma Phi, Theta Alpha Phi. Republican. Methodist. Home: Route 8 Murfreesboro TN 37130

KOHLER, ANNE TRIMBLE, state ofcl.; b. Ft. Worth, Sept. 4, 1925; d. Terrell Marshall and Elizabeth (Llewellyn) Trimble; B.S., U. Tex., 1948, M.A., 1952; m. William R. Kohler, Aug. 10, 1950 (dec. Feb. 1961); children—Robert Daniel, Raymond Llewellyn. Dir., Pease Elementary Child Care Center, Austin, Tex., 1948-55; psychiat. social worker Austin State Hosp., 1959-61, vocational rehab. counselor for mentally ill., 1961-69; research utilization specialist Tex. Rehab. Commn. and Region VI Dept. Health, Edn. and Welfare, Austin, 1969-72; program adminstr. research utilization project Tex. Gov.'s Com. Aging, Austin, 1972—. Mem. Am., Tex. personnel and guidance assns., Austin Social Welfare Assn. (pres. 1969), Tex. United Community Services, Nat., Tex. rehab. counseling assns., Tex. Psychol. Assn., Mental Health Assn. Austin-Travis County, Austin Personnel Assn., Internat. Soc. Rehab. of Disabled, Internat. Assn. Scholar and Profl. Guidance. Contbr. articles to profl. jours. Home: 3902 Idlewild St Austin TX 78731 Office: 1212 Guadalupe PO Box 12786 Capitol Sta Austin TX 78711

KOHLER, CHARLOTTE, editor; b. Richmond, Va., Sept. 16, 1908; d. Edwin Charles and Augusta F. (Bromm) K.; B.A., Vassar Coll., 1929; M.A., U. Va., 1933, Ph.D., 1936; Litt.D., Smith Coll., 1971. Instr. English, Woman's Coll., U. N.C., 1936-41, asst. prof., 1941-42; mng. editor Va. Quar. Rev., 1942-46, editor, 1946—; asso. prof. English, U. Va., 1965-71, prof., 1971—. Mem. Am. Assn. U. Women, Phi Beta Kappa. Home: 1900 Edgewood Lane Charlottesville VA 22903 Office: One W Range Charlottesville VA 22903

KOHLHAAS, ROBERT FRANK, lawyer; b. Algona, Ia., Dec. 12, 1923; s. Philip Joseph and Adelaide (Harig) K.; student Loras Coll., 1940-42; B.A., Ia. U., 1947, LL.B., 1950; m. Charlotte Maxine Zirkle, June 14, 1956; children—Kim Michell, Kathy Ann, Gregory Michael, Christopher Mark. Asso. firm Adams, Porter & Radigan, Arlington, Va., 1952-56; mem. firm Tramonte, Kohlhaas & Garnier, Falls Church, Va., 1956—; admitted to Va. bar, 1956, practiced law, Arlington, 1956-70, Falls Ch., 1970—. Pres., Poplar Heights Recreation Assn., 1971. Served with USNR, 1942-46. Mem. Ia., Va., Am. bar assns., Phi Kappa Theta, Delta Theta Phi. Democrat. Roman Catholic. Club: Internat. Town and Country. Home: 7501 Venice Court Falls Church VA 22043 Office: 210 E Broad St Falls Church VA 22046

KOHLMEIER, LOUIS MARTIN, JR., newspaper reporter; b. St. Louis, Feb. 17, 1926; s. Louis Martin and Anita (Werling) K.; B.J., U. Mo., 1950; m. Barbara Anne Wilson, Nov. 15, 1958; children—Daniel Kimbrell, Ann Werling. Staff writer Wall Street Jour., St. Louis and Chgo., 1952-57, Washington, 1960—; staff writer St. Louis Globe-Democrat, 1958-59. Served with AUS, 1950-52. Recipient Nat. Headliners Club award nat. reporting, 1959, Sigma Delta Chi award Washington corr., 1964, Pulitzer prize nat. reporting, 1964. Author: The Regulators— Watchdog Agencies and the Public Interest, 1969. Home: 5902 Madawaska Rd Washington DC 20016 Office: 1015 14th St NW Washington DC 20005

KOHN, ANTHONY, physician; b. Gyor, Austria-Hungary, Dec. 24, 1906; s. Sigmond and Bertha (Kronfeld) K.; B.S., Coll. City N.Y., 1927; M.D., Tufts U., 1931; m. Vera Emanuel, Mar. 6, 1956; step children—Flour L. (Mrs. Curt Strand), Frank Emanuel. Asst. in surgery L.I. Coll. Hosp., 1931-32; intern Worcester (Mass.) City Hosp., 1932-34; resident surgeon Mt. Sinai Hosp., N.Y.C., 1934-35; practice medicine, 1935—; attending endocrinologist Suffolk Psychiat. Hosp., 1960-72; endocrinologist Southside, Bay Shore, N.Y., 1956-72; asst. vis. endocrinologist Fordham hosps., N.Y.C.; cons. endocrinologist, chief radioisotope service Central Isllp (N.Y.) State Hosp., 1956-72; radioisotope staff Jewish Meml. Hosp., N.Y.C., 1954-70; cons. atomic medicine Huntington (N.Y.) Hosp.; cons. internal medicine Pilgrim State Hosp., 1956-72. Del. Internat. Goitre Conf., London, 1960, Internat. Endocrine Congress, Copenhagen, Denmark, 1960; clin. cons. N.Y. State Dept. Health; cons. endocrinologist Suffolk State Sch., Melville, N.Y., 1962-72. Served to capt. M.C., U.S. Army, 1941-45; ETO. Diplomate Nat. Bd. Med. Examiners. Fellow Clin. Soc. N.Y., Diabetes Assn.; mem. Amateur Radio Med. Soc., Soc. Nuclear Medicine, Psycho-Endocrine Assn., Am. Diabetes Assn., A.M.A., American Fertility Soc., Am. Soc. Internal Medicine, N.Y. State, Suffolk County (chmn. grad. edn. com.; chmn. atomic medicine com.; pres. 1960-61), Fla. med. socs., Dade County Med. Assn., Southside Clin. Soc. (sec. 1948-72), Am. Nuclear Soc., N.Y. Acad. Scis., A.A.A.S., Soc. for Sci. Study Sex (editor news bull.), Gemmological Assn. Gt. Britain, Biol. Engring. Soc. of Gt. Britain (corr. mem.), I.E.E.E. (profl. tech. group on bio-med. electronics), N.Y. State Assn. Professions, Suffolk County Community Council, Lapidary and Gem Soc. N.Y. (pres. 1967-68), Tropical Audubon Soc., Miami Mineral. and Lapidary Guild, Fla. Marine Aquarium Soc., Fla. Craftsmen, Gt. South Bay Power Squadron, Am. Radio Relay League, Alpha Omega Alpha. Mason (Shriner). Contbr. articles to profl. jours. Home: 1111 Crandon Blvd Apt A-301 Key Biscayne FL 33149

KOHN, VERA GROSS, physician; b. Kimberley, S. Africa, June 7, 1906; d. Frank and Lilian (Jacobs) Gross; B.A., Grey Coll., Union of S. Africa, 1923; M.B., Ch.B., U. Witwatersrand (S. Africa), 1941; m. Stanley Victor Emanuel, Apr. 14, 1927 (div.); children—Fleur (Mrs. Curt Strand), Frank Victor; m. 2d, Dr. Anthony Kohn, Mar. 6, 1956. Came to U.S., 1949, naturalized, 1955. Pvt. practice, Johannesburg, S. Africa, until 1949; cons. cerebral palsy N.Y. State Health Dept., 1949-50; pvt. practice, L.I., 1950—; mem. med. staff Southside Hosp., Bay Shore, Good Samaritan Hosp., West Islip, attending pediatrician Suffolk Psychiatric Hosp.; cons. pediatrician Central Islip State Hosp. Clin. cons. pediatrics N.Y. Dept. Health. Diplomate of Child Health, Royal Coll. Phys. and Surgs., Eng.; mem. Royal Coll. Physicians Edinburgh, 1946; diplomate Am. Bd. Pediatrics. Fellow Am. Acad. Pediatrics; mem. N.Y. State Suffolk County med. socs., Fla., Dade County, Am. Women's med. assns., Brit., S. Africa med. assns., Am. Assn. Univ. Women, Alumni Assn. Babies Hosp. Columbia-Presbyn. Med. Center, Southside Clin. Soc., Women's Med. Soc. N.Y. State, Miami Mineral. and Lapidary Guild, Fla. Audubon Soc., Fal. Craftsmen, Fla. Marine Aquarium Soc. Home: 1111 Crandon Blvd Apt A 301 Key Biscayne FL 33149

KOIKE, THOMAS ISAO, physiologist, educator; b. Watsonville, Cal., July 27, 1927; s. Rokuzo and Toshi (Koika) K.; student U. Ill., 1945-46, San Jose State Coll., 1947-48; A.B., U. Cal. at Berkeley, 1951, Ph.D., 1958; m. Kay Yamada, Sept. 11, 1955; children—Paul I., Maya. Research physiologist U. Cal., Berkeley, 1958-61; research physiologist U. Cal., Davis, 1963-65; asst. prof. physiology U. Ark. Sch. Medicine, Little Rock, 1965-69, asso. prof., 1969—. Served with AUS, 1946-47. NIH postdoctoral fellow U. Cal., Davis, 1961-63. Mem. A.A.A.S., Am. Assn. U. Profs., Am. Physiol. Soc., N.Y. Acad. Sci., Soc. Exptl. Biol. Medicine, Sigma Xi, Phi Beta Kappa. Club: Ark. Fly Fisherman's. Home: 100 Winnwood Rd Little Rock AR 72207

KOLAR, RONALD EDWARD, constrn. co. exec.; b. Englewood, N.J., Nov. 2, 1936; s. Edward A. and Sara Jane (Emerick) K.; B.S. in Civil Engring., Northwestern U., 1959; m. Janet Sue Harrell, Aug. 15, 1964; children—Eric Scott, Alan Edward. Project engr. B.B. McCormick & Sons, Contractors, Jacksonville Beach, Fla., 1963-65, contract adminstr., 1965-68, v.p., 1968-73; v.p. devel. and planning Amelia Island Co., Fernandina Beach, Fla., 1973—. Served to lt., C.E., USNR, 1959-63. Registered profl. engr., Fla., Vt. Mem. Am. Soc. C.E., Soc. Am. Mil. Engrs., Alpha Delta Phi. Presbyn. Home: 36 Sea Marsh Rd Fernandina Beach FL 32034 Office: PO Box 1160 Fernandina Beach FL 32034

KOLB, ALEXANDER KARL, dairy products mfr.; b. Moline, Ill., Oct. 18, 1921; s. Karl and Sarah Elizabeth (Genung) K.; ed. pub. schs., bus. and accounting courses; m. Amy LeeRhodes, Nov. 14, 1946; children—Pattie Elizabeth, Michael Alexander. Stockroom clk. F.W. Woolworth, 1940-41; advt. dept. John Deere Plow Co., 1941-42; purchasing dept. Rock Island Arsenal, 1942; sr. accountant Frank C. Sproul, Moline, 1946-51; office mgr., v.p., controller, dir. Maola Milk & Ice Cream Co., New Bern, N.C., 1951—; dir. New Bern Savs. & Loan Assn.; sec.-treas., dir. Zip Marts, Inc., House of Treats, Inc., Maola Properties, Inc. Bd. dirs. New Bern United Fund; sec. New Bern Urban Renewal Com., 1962-63; chmn. adv. bd. Salvation Army, 1972-73. Served with USMC, 1942-46. Chmn. accounting com. Milk Industry Found. C.P.A., N.C. Mem. Internat. Assn. Ice Cream Mfrs. (chmn. accounting com.), Am. Inst. C.P.A.'s, N.C. Assn. C.P.A.'s, Nat. Assn. Accountants. Republican. Presbyn. (deacon, elder). Home: 2302 Grace Av New Bern NC 28560 Office: Drawer S New Bern NC 28560

KOLB, AVERY EGGER, govt. ofcl., author; b. Hattiesburg, Miss., May 14, 1921; s. Avery Egger and Mattie (Giles) K.; student U. So. Miss., 1939-40, Cite U., Paris, 1945, Northwestern U., 1954, Indsl. Coll. Armed Forces, 1967-68, George Washington U., 1968-69; m. Joan Richards, Sept. 19, 1946; children—Avery E. III, Elaine (Mrs. Clifton J. Achee), Jean (Mrs. Lawrence E. Grunewald), June (Mrs. Robert M. Young), Evan Richards, Joyce. Artist-author New Orleans, 1945; agt. Eastern Airlines, New Orleans, 1946-48; plans ofcl. Dept. Army, Washington, 1948-56; moblzn. staff ICC, 1956-59; nat. resources planning officer OCDM, 1959-61; economist Office of Emergency Planning, 1962-69; chief guidance and review div. and interagy. coordination div. Office Emergency Preparedness, 1969—; free-lance writer, pub., 1959—. U.S. rep. to NATO Indsl. Planning Com., 1969-73; operations chief Phase I Econ. Stablzn. Program, 1971; staff dir. Pres.'s Joint Bd. on Fuel Supply and Transport, 1971-73. Dir. Musart, allied arts instrn., Fairfax, Va. Served to lt. col. AUS, 1940-45. Decorated Croix de Guerre with palm, 1945. Author: Jigger Whitchet's War, 1959; Kolb Family Genealogies, 1970. Contbr. articles in field to profl. jours. Home: 6417 Julian St Springfield VA 22150 Office: Office of Preparedness GSA Washington DC 20504

KOLB, CHARLES RUDOLPH, govt. ofcl.; b. Vicksburg, Miss., Apr. 14, 1920; s. Karl and Theresa (Thiel) K.; B.S. in Geology, La. State U., 1947, M.S. in Geology, 1949, Ph.D. in Geology, 1959;; m. Bertha Ragsdale, Oct. 9, 1951; 1 son, Charles H. Geologist, Fredrick Snare Engring. Corp., Santiago, Chile, 1949-50; geologist U.S. Army Engr. Waterways Expt. Sta., Vicksburg, 1950-53, asst. chief geology br., 1953-56, chief geology br., 1956-62, chief geology br. Waterways Expt. Sta., 1965—; research scientist, chief environmental scis. div. Research and Devel. Office, Alaska, 1963-64. Lectr. various univs.; instr. Vicksburg Grad. Center, Miss. State U., 1967—; cons. engring geology, 1956—; cons., expert witness engring. geology and litigation Mississippi River Delta and Flood plain, 1965—. Served with USAAF, 1943-45. Decorated Air medal with four oak leaf clusters, D.F.C. with two oak leaf clusters; recipient superior sustained performance award Dept. Army, 1958, Outstanding Performance award, 1963 award for best paper Jour. Sediment Petrology, 1954, best paper award Gulf Coast Geol. Socs., 1965. Fellow Geol. Soc. Am. (chmn. river engring. panel, mem. publs. com.), A.A.A.S.; mem. Am. Inst. Profl. Geologists, Am. Assn. Petroleum Geologists, Miss. Geol. Soc., Internat. Soc. Sedimentation, C. of C., Sigma Xi. Lion. Club: Engineers (pres.) (Vicksburg). Contbr. numerous articles to profl. jours. Home: 3314 Highland Dr Vicksburg MS 39180 Office: Geology Waterways Expt Sta Vicksburg MS 39180

KOLB, JOHN GEORGE, savs. and loan exec.; b. Washington, Nov. 25, 1904; s. John J. and Marie Salome (Jung) K.; B.S., Wharton Sch. Finance and Commerce, U. Pa., 1927; m. Madaline Victoria Showalter, Oct. 6, 1934; children—John George, Ronald Victor (dec.). Treas. Oriental Bldg. Assn., 1938-61, pres., 1961-73, chmn., 1973—. Mem. Theta Xi. Mason. Home: 1909 Upshur St NW Washington DC 20011 Office: 600 F St NW Washington DC 20004

KOLB, NATHANIEL KEY, JR., architect; b. Sherman, Tex., Aug. 17, 1933; s. Nathaniel Key and Nelcine (Dial) K.; B.Arch., Tex. A. and M. U., 1957; M.Arch., U. Pa., 1960; m. Catherine Conner, Nov. 1958; children—Nathaniel Key III, Mary Catherine, Amy Monica, Peter Paul, John Conner, Elizabeth Dial. Designer, Caudill, Rowlett & Scott, Architects, Houston, 1955-58; instr., dir. program for basic studies in architecture Tex. A. and M. U., 1958-59; designer Vincent G. Kling, Phila., 1959-61; adj. asst. prof. Columbia, 1961-62; designer William B. Tabler, N.Y.C., 1962-63; partner Harrell & Hamilton, Architects and Planners, Dallas, 1963—. Lectr., vis. critic U. Tex., mem. Spl. Com. to Evaluate Archtl. Edn. in Tex. Mem. A.I.A., Tex. Soc. Architects. Home: 4402 Rawlins St Dallas TX 75219 Office: Republic Bank Tower Dallas TX 75201

KOLE, JOHN WILLIAM, journalist; b. Zeeland, Mich., Jan. 27, 1934; s. John Henry and Una (Messer) K.; B.A., Mich. State U., 1955; M.S., Northwestern U., 1956; Nieman fellow, Harvard, 1962-63; m. Betty Lou Zuege, Sept. 15, 1956; children—Linda Sue, Leslie Ann, James David, Sara Louise, Susan Margaret. Reporter, Milw. Jour., 1956-64, reporter, Washington Bur., 1964-70, chief Washington Bur., 1970—. Recipient awards Am. Polit. Sci. Assn., 1961, Milw. Press Club, 1960-63, 72. Mem. White House Corrs. Assn., Sigma Delta Chi. Clubs: Gridiron, Nat. Press (Washington). Home: 2542 N 23d Rd Arlington VA 22207 Office: Nat Press Bldg Washington DC 20004

KOLLER, HERBERT R., information scientist, cons.; b. Cleve., 1921; B.S. in Chemistry, Western Res. U., 1942; J.D., Am. U., 1952; m. Shirley Leavitt; children—Donald, Laura, Mrs. Willard C. Van Horne. Chemist, Indsl. Rayon Co.; research worker information systems U.S. Patent Office; dir. client services EBS Mgmt. Consultants, Washington; prin. information scientist Leasco Systems and Research Corp., Bethesda, Md.; exec. dir. Am. Soc. for Information Sci., Washington; now prin. asso. Moshman Assos., Inc., Bethesda; tchr., lectr. information sci. and tech. Mem. Assn. for Computing Machinery, Am. Chem. Soc., Am. Fedn. Information Processing Socs., Nat. Acad. Scis.-Nat. Research Council, Internat. Fedn. for Documentation. Editor several profl. jours. Office: 6400 Goldsboro Rd Bethesda MD 20034

KOLLMORGEN, GERALD MARK, immunologist, educator; b. Bancroft, Neb., June 23, 1932; s. Arthur Frederick and Dorathea (Lase) K.; B.A., U. Ia., 1957, M.A., 1960, Ph.D. (USPHS fellow), 1963; m. Jeanne E. Buenz, Dec. 19, 1954; children—Steven, Linda, Nancy, Terry. Instr. radiation research lab. U. Ia., 1962-63; asst. biologist div. biol. and med. research Argonne (Ill.) Nat. Lab., 1965-66; asso. mem. cancer sect. Okla. Med. Research Found., Oklahoma City, 1966—. Asso. prof. dept. radiol. scis. U. Okla., Oklahoma City, 1966—; cons. St. Anthony Hosp., 1972—, VA Hosp., Oklahoma City, 1966—. Baseball coach YMCA, 1973—. Served with inf. AUS, 1953-55. Postdoctoral fellow Argonne Nat. Lab., 1963-65. Mem. A.A.A.S., Tissue Culture Assn., Radiation Research Soc., Am. Soc. for Cell Biology, Am. Assn. for Cancer Research, Am. Inst. Biol. Scis., Am. Pub. Health Assn., Assn. Am. Med. Colls., Greater Oklahoma City Radiol. Soc., Am. Assn. U. Profs., Soc. for Exptl. Biology and Medicine, Am. Inst. Aeros. and Astronautics, Fedn. Am. Scientists, Smithsonian Assos., Okla., N.Y. acads. Sci., Sigma Xi. Lutheran (pres. ch. 1973—). Editor: Medical Radiation Biology 1973. Contbr. articles to sci. jours. Home: 4988 NW 30th Pl Oklahoma City OK 73122 Office: 825 NE 13th St Oklahoma City OK 73104

KOLMEN, SAMUEL NORMAN, educator, physiologist; b. Brownsville, Tex., Mar. 20, 1930; s. F. Joseph and Cyla (Gerson) K.; student Tex. Southmost Coll., 1947-48, Baylor U. Coll. Medicine, 1950-53; B.A., U. Tex., 1954, Ph.D., 1957; m. Barbara Kass, June 13, 1954; children—Benita, Jeannette. Asst. prof. physiology U. Tex. Med. Br., 1958-63, asso. prof., 1963-68, prof., 1968—, head div. physiology, Shriners Burns Inst., 1968-73, research coordinator, 1970—, mem. grad. faculty U. Tex. Med. Br., 1963—. J.W. McLaughlin fellow, 1955-57; Jeane B. Kempner fellow, 1957-58. Mem. A.A.A.S., Am. Burns Assn., Am. Inst. Biol. Scis., Am. Physiol. Soc., Biochem. Soc. (Eng.), Internat. Soc. Lymphology, Soc. Exptl. Biology and Medicine, Microcirculatory Soc., Pan Am. Med. Assn., Am. Heart Assn. (mem. council on thrombosis 1970—), Sigma Xi. Jewish religion (pres. 1970-73). Editor: Tex. Reports on Biology and Medicine, 1964-68. Developer blood flow through probe for pH, pO2, PCO2; chronic thoracic duct-esophageal fistula preparation. Home: 7766 Beaudelaire St Galveston TX 77550 Office: N 610 Texas Av Shriners Burns Inst Galveston TX 77550

KOLP, ROBERT JASPER, civil engr.; b. Scranton, Pa., Dec. 5, 1927; s. Peter William and Edna Anna (Black) K.; B.S., Case Inst. Tech., 1950; postgrad. Indsl. Electronics Sch., Detroit, 1962-64; m. Patricia Jean Haley, June 10, 1950; children—Gregory O., Roberta L., David P., Daniel J., Mark A. Engr., Baldwin Bros. Paving Co., Girard, Pa., 1950-51; civil engr. Courtney Engring. Co., Cleve., 1951-52; hwy. engr. George M. Brewster, contractor, Kingston, N.Y., 1953-54; group supt. Houdaille Constrn. Materials, Inc., Portland, Pa., 1954-61; area mgr. E.C. Levy Slag Co., Detroit, 1961-64; v.p. Wyoming Sand

& Stone Co., Falls, Pa., 1964-67; chief engr. Rinker Materials Corp., West Palm Beach, Fla., 1967—. Scout master Boy Scouts Am., 1959-61. Served with AUS, 1946-47. Registered profl. engr., N.J., Pa., Ohio, Mich., Fla. Mem. Am. Concrete Inst., Am. Soc. for Testing Materials, Fla. Engring. Soc., Nat. Soc. Profl. Engrs., Am. Soc. Hwy. Engrs. Presbyn. Home: 624 Inlet Rd North Palm Beach FL 33408 Office: PO Drawer K West Palm Beach FL 33402

KOMAREK, EDWIN VACLAV, agrl. researcher; Chgo., June 4, 1909; s. Fredrick Albert and Stella (Hlavka) K.; student U. Chgo., 1927-31; D.Sc., Fla. State U., 1971; m. Elizabeth Hester Barker, July 19, 1935; children—Edwin, Elizabeth B. Mammalogist, Chgo. Acad. Sci., 1928-34; asst. dir. Co-op. Quail Study Assn., 1934-43; agrl. dir. Greenwood Plantation, supt., mgr. Greenwood Seed Co., Thomasville, Ga., 1945—; exec. sec. Tall Timbers Research Sta., Tallahassee, 1958—; hon. research asso. in zoology Smithsonian Instn., 1965—. Mem. gov. bd. Agrl. Research Inst., 1965-69. Dir. Tall Timbers Research, Inc. Chmn. Ann. Fire Ecology Conf., Ann. Conf. Ecol. Control Animals by Habitat Mgmt. Mem. Chgo. Acad. Scis., Am. Soc. Mammalogists. Contbr. articles to profl. jours. Home: Birdsong Plantation Thomasville GA 31792 Office: Greenwood Seed Co Thomasville also Tall Timbers Research Sta Tallahassee FL 32301

KOMINSKI, JOHN JOSEPH, staff Library of Congress; b. Springfield, Mass., Oct. 8, 1937; s. Joseph Henry and Jenny Marie (Jarosz) K.; B.A. in Journalism, U. Mass., 1959; LL.B., Georgetown U., 1962, J.D., 1967; m. Frances Janet Saladigo, Sept. 29, 1962; children—Mark, Eric, Therese, Kathryn, Marla, Russell, Ruth. Admitted to Md. bar, 1965; legal specialist Am.-Brit. law Library of Congress, Washington, 1962-67, asst. gen. counsel, 1967-69, gen. counsel, 1970—. Served with AUS, 1963-65. Mem. Am., Md., Fed. (v.p. Capitol Hill chpt. 1969-71, pres. 1971—), Internat. Inst. Space Law. Home: 2601 Bluhaven Ct Silver Spring MD 20906 Office: Library of Congress 10 1st St SE Washington DC 20540

KONDO, YOJI, astronomer; b. Hitachi, Japan, May 26, 1933; s. Tsuneo and Hama (Yamada) K.; B.A., Tokyo U. Fgn. Studies 1958; M.S., U. Pa., 1963, Ph.D., 1965; m. Ursula Tuetermann, Sept. 10, 1965; children—Beatrice, Cynthia. Came to U.S., 1960; naturalized, 1968. Asst. prof. U. Pa., Phila., summer 1965; Nat. Acad. Scis.-NRC research asso. NASA Goddard Space Flight Center, Greenbelt, Md., 1965-68; staff astronomer NASA Johnson Space Center, Houston, 1968-69, chief astrophysics sect., 1969—; adj. grad. faculty U. Houston, 1968—; adj. asso. prof. U. Okla., 1971-72, adj. prof., 1972—. Fellow A.A.A.S.; mem. Internat. Astron. Union (chmn. com. for astron. observations outside earth's atmosphere 1970—), Am. Aston. Soc. Contbr. articles to profl. jours. Home: 18307 Hereford Lane Houston TX 77058 Office: NASA Johnson Space Center Houston TX 77058

KONDONASSIS, ALEXANDER JOHN, educator; b. Kozani, Greece, Feb. 8, 1928; s. John I. and Eve (Hatzistylianou) K.; came to U.S., 1948, naturalized, 1960; A.B. (Edward Rector scholar), Depauw U., 1952; M.A., Ind. U., 1953, Ph.D., 1961; Patricia Mundorf, Feb. 2, 1956; children—John, Yolanda. Lectr., Ind. U., Ft. Wayne, 1956-58; faculty dept. econs. U. Okla., Norman, 1958—, asso. prof., 1962-64, prof., 1964—, chmn. dept., 1961-71, David Ross Boyd prof., 1970—, dir. advanced program in econs., 1971—. Fulbright prof. Athens (Greece) Sch. Econs. and Bus. Sci., 1965-66; guest lectr. various groups, 1963—. Mem. Gov.'s Adv. Council on Export Expansion, 1964-65, adv. council Inst. Mediterranean Affairs, N.Y.C., 1967—. Bd. dirs. Okla. Council Econ. Edn., Am. Friends Wilton Park, N.Y.C. Recipient Okla. U. Regent award for superior teaching, 1964. Mem. Am., So., Midwest, S.W. econ. assns., Am. Assn. U. Profs., (chpt. pres.), Econ. History Assn., Beta Gamma Sigma, Omicron Delta Epsilon. Contbr. articles to profl. jours. Home: 512 Manor Dr Norman OK 73069

KONDUROS, JAMES SAMUEL, lawyer; b. Anderson, S.C., Aug. 18, 1931; s. Samuel William and Georgia (Antonakos) K.; J.D., U. S.C., 1954; m. Conalee Malek, Mar. 22, 1961; children—Gregory James, Samuel James, Gia Terese. Admitted to S.C. bar, 1954; legislative asst. U.S. Senator Olin D. Johnston, Washington, 1961-64; rep., IBM Corp., Washington, 1964-66; exec. dir. S.C. Appalachian Commn., Greenville, 1966-67; exec. asst. to Gov. Robert E. McNair, Columbia, S.C., 1967-71; partner, McNair, Konduros, Corley, Singletary & Dibble, Columbia, S.C., 1971—. Mem. Pres.'s Exec. Res., 1965. Mem. inaugural com. staff Pres. Lyndon B. Johnson, 1965; mem. platform study com. Democratic Nat. Com., 1972; S.C. rep. Appalachian Regional Commn., 1967-70, adviser, 1971-72. Served to capt. USAF, 1954-56. Mem. Am., S.C. bar assns., Ex-U.S. Senate Employees Assn., Phi Delta Phi, Lambda Chi Alpha. Home: Route 7 Box 297E Lexington SC 29072 Office: Suite 1 9th Floor Jefferson Square Columbia SC 29201

KONIG, RONALD HOWARD, educator; b. Albany, N.Y., Aug. 12, 1932; s. Howard and Mildred C. (Manning) K.; B.S., St. Lawrence U., 1954; M.S., Cornell U., 1956, Ph.D., 1959. Mem. faculty U. Ark., Fayetteville, 1959—, asso. prof. geology, 1966-71, prof., chmn. dept., 1971—. Cons. geologist, 1963—. Mem. Geol. Soc. Am., Am. Inst. Mining, Metall, Petroleum Engrs., Soc. Econ. Geologists, Sigma Xi. Home: 280 S Hill St Fayetteville AR 72701

KONIKOFF, BENJAMIN SAMUEL, dentist; b. Chgo., July 16, 1912; s. Samuel and Manya Konikoff; D.D.S., Loyola U., 1945; M.S., La. State U., 1959; student So. State U., 1934-35; m. Gloria V. Stanley, Feb. 3, 1945; children—Benjamin S., Susan Lynn, Charles Edward, Constance, Robert. Practice dentistry, Baton Rouge, 1948—; mem. staff Our Lady of Lake Hosp., Baton Rouge Gen. Hosp.; dental cons. to industry; cons. prof. dept. food sci. La. State U.; clin. asst. prof. Sch. Dentistry. Trustee Borrow Dental Milk Found. Served as lt. Dental Corps, USNR, 1945-47. Fellow Royal Soc. Health (Gt. Britain); mem. La. Dental Soc., Am., La. 6th Dist. dental assns., East Baton Rouge Parish Dental Soc. (pres. 1965-66), Internat. Assn. Dental Research, A.A.A.S., Inst. Food Tech., Pierre Fauchard Acad., Sigma Xi, Delta Sigma Delta, Theta Beta, Gamma Sigma Delta. Democrat. Roman Catholic. Research: milk as a vehicle for fluorides to prevent dental cavities in children. Home: 4457 Broussard St Baton Rouge LA 70808 Office: 4731 North Blvd Baton Rouge LA 70806

KONIKOWSKI, TAD, chemist; b. Pomorze, Poland, Nov. 22, 1911; s. Paul Joachim and Thekla (Czaja) K.; B.A., U. Poznan, 1933, M.A., 1934; m. Wanda Dulemba, Jan. 1, 1939; children—Janusz Andrew, Roman Paul, George Jerzy, Les Leszek. Came to U.S., 1947, naturalized, 1953. Exec. mgr. Gdynia Pharm. Co. (Poland), 1935-37; research chemist cancer research lab. Chem. Hormone Corp., N.Y.C., 1947-55; sci. asst. med. dept. Brookhaven Nat. Lab., Upton, N.Y., 1956-62; research scientist U. Tex. M.D. Anderson Hosp. and Tumor Inst., Houston, 1962—. Sci. adviser Inst. fur Medizin, Kernforschungsanlage, Julich, W. Germany, 1965-66. Served with Polish Navy, 1938-39. Mem. N.Y. Acad. Sci., Soc. Nuclear Medicine, Am. Chem. Soc., Am. Inst. Biol. Scis., Univ. Faculty Club. Contbr. profl. jours. Research in neutron capture therapy, radioactive isotopes in medicine, use of med. atomic reactors, diagnostic nuclear medicine. Home: 2818 Fairhope St Houston TX 77025 Office: 6723 Bertner Av Houston TX 77025

KONKEL, RONALD MARION, economist; b. Winona, Minn., Feb. 16, 1939; s. Hubert John and Dorothy Margaret (Ries) K.; A.B., Wichita State U., 1961; M.A., Tulane U., 1968; m. Dorothy M. Terry, June 21, 1958; children—Karen, Christopher, Julie. Tchr., S.E. High Sch., Wichita, Kan., 1961-62; cost analyst NASA Manned Spacecraft Center, Houston, 1964-66; economist NASA Hdqrs., Washington, 1966-72; budget examiner Office Mgmt. and Budget, Washington, 1972—. Mem. Am. Econ. Assn. Home: 709 Smallwood Rd Rockville MD 20850 Office: New Exec Office Bldg Washington DC 20503

KONKLE, WARD WHITNEY, editor, educator; b. Altoona, Pa., Oct. 29, 1908; s. Edson Charles and Mary Catherine (Adams) K.; student Carnegie Inst. Tech., 1927; B.A., U. Pitts., 1930; m. Dorothy Jane Callender, July 18, 1931; children—Patricia L. (Mrs. John Wade), Ronald W., Alan R. Instr. English and radio speech Wooster (O.) High Sch., 1945-52; editor Ohio Agr. Experiment Sta., Wooster, 1952-57; supr. editor Agr. Research Service, USDA, Washington, 1957-58; head tech. pub. sect., supr. tech. writing tech. program ARS, 1958-62; asst. chief publs. br., 1962-63, editor Agrl. Sci. Rev., 1963—, also asst. chief div. information Office Mgmt. Services, 1963—, instr. spl. lectr. Grad. Sch., 1960—. Recipient awards for outstanding performance in teaching tech. writing USDA, 1962, 67. Mem. Am. Assn. Agrl. Coll. Editors, Am. Med. Writers Assn., Am. Radio Relay League. Lutheran. Author: Technical Writing, 1967. Home: 617 Greenbrier Dr Silver Spring MD 20910 Office: US Dept Agr OMS-DI Washington DC 20250

KONRAD, HERMANN, cons. pollution control engr.; b. Berlin, Germany, Dec. 6, 1926; s. Erich and Ida (Frank) K.; C.E., U. Cauca, Popayan, Colombia, 1955; postgrad. in hydraulics U. Andes, Mérida, Venezuela, 195 19, 1953; children—Marianela, Ann Astrid. Came to U.S., 1966, naturalized, 1972. R.R. constrn. work in Colombia, Madigan-Hyland Cons. Engrs., N.Y.C., 1955-57; asst. prof. hydraulics U. Andes, 1958-62, head hydraulics lab., 1960; cons. engr. irrigation projects in Colombia, Bogota, 1962-66; with environmental dept. Gilbert Assos., Reading, Pa., 1966-68; asso., also sr. design engr. for water and pollution control facilities Post, Buckley, Schuh & Jernigan, Inc., Miami, Fla., 1968—. Registered profl. engr., Fla. Mem. Am. Soc. C.E., Fla. Engring. Soc., Nat. Soc. Profl. Engrs. Home: 1420 S Bayshore Dr Miami FL 33131 Office: PO Box 764 Miami Springs FL 33166

KONYNDYK, GORDON WILLIAM, elec. engr.; b. nr. Grand Rapids, Mich., Oct. 3, 1941; s. Corneil William and Gertrude (Faber) K.; Asso. Sci., Grand Rapids Jr. Coll., 1961; B.S. in Elec. Engring., U. Mich., 1965; postgrad. U. Tenn., 1965-70; m. Wanda Lois Sharon Honea, Dec. 17, 1965; children—Launa Jade, Lainie Kellie. Elec. engr. Aro, Inc., Arnold Air Force Sta., 1965—. Referee, State of Tenn. Secondary Schs., Nashville, 1973—. Registered profl. engr., Tenn. Mem. Tullahoma Jr. C. of C. (v.p. 1972—). Home: Route 4 Box 133 Tullahoma TN 37388 Office: Aro Inc ETF TI Arnold AF Station TN 37388

KOO, ROBERT CHUNG JEN, horticulturist, educator; b. Shanghai, China, Mar. 20, 1921; s. Tse Zung and Ge Tsung (Tse) K.; came to U.S., 1940, naturalized, 1961; B.S., Cornell U., 1944; M.S., U. Fla., 1950, Ph.D., 1953; m. Margaret Wei Shan Chung, Mar. 19, 1949; children—Robert, Kenneth, Dennis. Lang. specialist civil service U.S. Dept. Navy, 1945-47; faculty horticulture U. Fla., Lake Alfred, 1953—, prof., 1969—. Cons. horticulture to citrus growers, various cos. U.S. Dept. Interior Water Resources research grantee, 1970-73. Mem. Am. Soc. Hort. Sci., Fla. Hort. Soc. (Presdl. gold medal award 1965), Sprinkler Irrigation Soc., Am. Agronomy Soc., Crop and Soil Sci. Soc. Fla. Episcopalian. Rotarian (sec. 1972-73, v.p. 1973—). Author: (with others), The Role of Potassium in Agriculture, 1968. Home: 2223 12th St NW Winter Haven FL 33880 Office: PO Box 1088 Lake Alfred FL 33850

KOON, CLYDE HURLSTON, supt. schs.; b. Sheridan, Ark., Feb. 10, 1911; s. Jacob Eddie and Lula (Johnson) K.; B.S., Coll. Ozarks, 1935; M.S., U. Ark., 1947; m. Thelm Beatrice McDougal, July 11, 1937; children—Norman Carrol, Lou L. (Mrs. James Ferguson), Eddie Mac. Sci. tchr., coach Malvern Sch. Dist., 1935-41; sci. tchr., coach, prin. Hughes (Ark.) Sch. Dist., 1941-44; supt. schs. McCrory (Ark.) Sch. Dist., 1944-54, Harrisburg (Ark.) Sch. Dist., 1954-62, Sheridan Sch. Dist., 1962—. Recipient Outstanding Alumni award Coll. Ozarks, 1953. Chmn. Grant County Econ. Opportunity Council, 1966-72; chmn. Grant County Health Adv. Com., 1969-71. Democrat. Baptist (deacon 1942—). Rotarian. Club: Country (Sheridan). Home: Rural Route 2 Box 521 Sheridan AR 72150 Office: 400 N Rock St Sheridan AR 72150

KOON, WARREN HENRY, newspaper editor; b. Spartanburg, S.C., Dec. 6, 1923; s. Henry Smith and Una B. (Finger) K.; B.A., Wofford, Coll., 1948; m. Laura Frances Hudgens, Feb. 14, 1947; 1 son, Kerry Warren; m. 2d, Martha Hamilton Carson, May 30, 1970; stepchildren—Kim, Kevin, Kelly. Pub. relations dir. Wofford Coll., 1948; reporter Spartanburg Herald, 1948; reporter Louisville Times, 1948-51; telegraph editor Asheville (N.C.) Times, 1952-55; exec. sports editor Charleston (S.C.) Post and News-Courier, 1955-65; columnist Charleston Post, 1965-68; mng. editor Rock Hill (S.C.) Evening Herald, 1968-69; mng. editor Tuscaloosa (Ala.) News, 1969-70; editor-pub. Natchez (Miss.) Democrat, 1970—. Served with USMCR, 1942-46. Recipient A.P. S.C. State Writing awards, 1955, 56, 60, 61, 66, 68, U.S. Osteo. Assn. Nat. award for writing, 1968. Mem. So. Conf. Sportswriters (pres.), S.C. Assn. Sportswriters (pres.), Nat. Assn. Writers/Broadcasters (writer of year 1963-64). Author: View From Up Here, 1964. Home: 800 N Union St Natchez MS 39120 Office: 501 N Canal St Natchez MS 39120

KOONTZ, WARREN WOODSON, JR., physician, educator; b. Lynchburg, Va., June 10, 1932; s. Warren Womack and Mary Winston (Woodson) K.; B.A., Va. Mil. Inst., 1953; M.D., U. Va., 1957; m. Edwin Coburn Sykes, June 16, 1957; children—Warren S., Mary Edwina. Intern, N.Y. Hosp., 1957-59, resident surgery, 1958-59, 62-66; asst. prof. surgery Harvard Med. Sch., Boston, 1969-70; practice medicine, specializing in urology, Richmond; prof. chmn. div. urology Med. Coll. Va., Commonwealth U., Richmond, 1970—. Cons. urology Portsmouth Naval Hosp., Crippled Childrens Hosp., McGuire VA Hosp. Diplomate Am. Bd. Urology. Fellow A.C.S.; mem. A.M.A., Am. Urol. Assn., Soc. Pediatric Urology, Soc. Internat. Urologic, Alpha Omega Alpha. Club: Westwood Racquet. Contbr. articles to profl. publs. Home: 204 N Moreland Rd Richmond VA 23298 Office: Box 176 Medical College Virginia Richmond VA 23298

KOPALD, S.L., JR., chem. co. exec.; b. Memphis, Sept. 4, 1921; s. S.L. and Ethel (Goodman) K.; B.S., Washington and Lee U., 1943; Indsl. Adminstr., Harvard Grad. Sch. Bus. Adminstrn., 1943; m. Amelia Daves, Aug. 5, 1946; children—Nancy, Stephen L., Jack D., David R. With Humko Products, Memphis, 1946—, successively purchasing mgr., asst. to pres., 1948-50, v.p., 1950-54, exec. v.p., 1954-73; pres. Humko Sheffield Chem. Co., 1973—; dir. Union Planters Nat. Bank, Bus. Music Corp., Memphis. Chmn. campaign Memphis Community Chest, 1957; mem. Memphis and Shelby County (Tenn.) Planning Commn., 1958-60. Vice chmn. Shelby County Rep. com.; chmn. Tenn. Rep. com. 1971—. Bd. govs., chmn. Hebrew Union Coll.-Jewish Inst. Religion, Cin. Served with AUS, 1943-46; ETO. Mem. Fatty Acid Producers Council (chmn. steering com. 1968-73), Omicron Delta Kappa. Republican. Jewish religion. Home: 4880 Lake Dr Memphis TN 38117 Office: 5050 Poplar St Memphis TN 38117

KOPLIN, ALLEN NORMAN, physician; b. Hartford, Conn., May 15, 1919; s. Samuel and Belle (Black) K.; B.A., N.Y.U., 1939; M.D., Middlesex U., 1943; M.P.H., U. Minn., 1947; m. Pauline Ipsen, July 1, 1946; children—Michael Dean, Kathie Lynn. Intern Knickerbocker Hosp., N.Y.C., 1943-44; with fgn. quarantine div. USPHS, Miami, Fla., 1944, war food adminstrn., Yakima, Wash., 1944-46; chief field demonstration unit Nat. Cancer Inst., 1947-48; area med. adminstr. United Mine Workers of Am. Welfare and Retirement Fund. Birmingham, Ala., 1948-71, area med. adminstr., Knoxville, Tenn., 1963-71, dep. exec. med. officer, Washington, 1971—; lectr. U. Tenn. Sch. Pub. Health Edn., 1969; vis. prof. Meharry Med. Coll., Nashville, 1965—. Chmn. profl. adv. com. Helen McNabb Mental Health Center, Knoxville, 1969. Diplomate Am. Bd. Preventive Medicine. Fellow Am. Coll. Preventive Medicine, Am. Pub. Health Assn. (chmn. com. equal health opportunity 1970—). Home: 1509 Gordon Cove Dr Annapolis MD 21403 Office: 907 15th St NW Washington DC 20005

KOPP, EDGAR WILLIAM, univ. dean, educator; b. Louisville, Jan. 28, 1926; s. Edgar W. and Eve (Higbee) K.; B.S., Ga. Tech., 1945, B.S.E. 1947, M.S.E., 1948; m. Carolyn Chesser, June 13, 1948; 1 son, Edgar, III. Tech. staff Ford Motor Co., 1948-55; asst. dean engring., prof. U. Fla., 1955-63, asst. dean faculty, prof., 1963-64; dean, prof. engring. U. So. Fla., Tampa, 1964—. Vice pres., mem. bd. dirs. UNIVINC, Inc., 1967-71; bd. dirs. Seminole Bank of Tampa. Mem. council Boy Scouts Am., Tampa, Fla., 1969-71; mem. Com. of 100, Tampa, 1965-70; mem. Gov.'s Com. on Fee Negotiation; chmn. Cons. Engrs. of Dept. of Transp.; mem. exec. com. Tampa Arts Council, 1967-70. Bd. dirs. Safety Council Tampa, 1967—; chmn. bd. dirs. Berkely Preparatory Sch., Tampa, Fla., 1968-70; trustee USF Found., 1964-67, 71—. Served to lt. comdr. USNR. Registered profl. engr., Fla. Tau Beta Pi, Omicron Delta Kappa. Rotarian, Mason (Shriner). Home: 811 Grove Park Av Tampa FL 33609

KOPP, OTTO CHARLES, geologist, educator; b. Bklyn., July 22, 1929; s. Frank Henry and Hattie Margaret (Gruhn) K.; B.S., U. Notre Dame, 1951, M.A., Columbia, 1955, Ph.D., 1958; m. Helen E. Shotkowski, Sept. 4, 1954; children—Michael, Patricia, Mary Beth, Paul. Asst. prof. geology U. Tenn., Knoxville, 1958-63, asso. prof., 1963-68, prof., 1968—. Cons. Oak Ridge Nat. Lab., 1959—. Served with AUS, 1951-54. Recipient Centennial of Sci. award Notre Dame U., 1965. Fellow Geol. Soc. Am., Mineral. Soc. Am.; mem. Nat. Assn. Geology Tchrs., Sigma Xi. Home: 5808 Meadow Glen Dr Knoxville TN 37919

KOPPEIN, RICHARD ARTHUR, oilseed processing co. exec.; b. Elkhorn, Wis., Feb. 10, 1937; s. Donald Albert and Betty Jane (Meadows) K.; student U. Wis., Madison, 1960; m. Carolyn Joy Pinnow, Oct. 29, 1960; children—Thomas Karl. Mgmt. trainee to head soy feeds dept. A.E. Staley Mfg. Co., Decatur, Ill., 1960-68; asst. to pres. Hartsville Oil Mill (S.C.), 1968-69, v.p. commodities, 1969—, also dir. Bd. dirs. Hartsville Community Players, 1973—. Served with AUS, 1956. Mem. S.C. Soybean Assn. (dir. 1970—), Carolina Feed Mfrs. (dir. 1970-72), Am. Soybean Assn. (supporting mem.), Carolinas-Va. Grain Dealers, Theta Delta Chi. Methodist. Clubs: Hartsville Golf and Country; Country of S.C. Home: Route 2 Forest Hills Hartsville SC 29550 Office: 1501 5th St Hartsville SC 29550

KOPPLIN, JULIUS OTTO, educator; b. Appleton, Wis., Feb. 6, 1925; s. Julius A. and Renata (Peters) K.; B.E.E., U. Wis., 1949; M.E.E., Purdue U., 1954, Ph.D., 1959; m. Lola Mae Boldt, Sept. 16, 1950; children—William J., John D., Mary Susan, James R. Corrosion engr. No. Ind. Pub. Service Corp., Hammond, Ind., 1949-53; instr. elec. engring. Purdue U., 1954-58; asst. prof. elec. engring. U. Ill., 1958-61, asso. prof., 1961-68; prof., chmn. elec. engring. dept. U. Tex., El Paso, 1968—. Vis. prof. Mass. Inst. Tech., 1961, U. Colo., 1967. Served with USAAF, World War II. Decorated Purple Heart medal, Air medal. Recipient U. Ill. Teaching award, 1965. NASA-ASEE Faculty fellow, 1966. Mem. I.E.E.E., Am. Soc. Engring. Edn., A.A.A.S., Sigma Xi, Eta Kappa Nu, Sigma Pi Sigma. Contbr. articles to sci. jours. Home: 724 Rinconada Lane El Paso TX 79922

KORDA, MARION AMELIA, musician, librarian; b. Portland, Me., June 14, 1922; d. Joseph and Anna (Miller) Korda; B.A., U. Me., 1943; M.S. in L.S., Columbia, 1953. Music therapist Camp Edwards, Mass., 1945; Y-teen program dir. YWCA, New Bedford, 1946-47; mem. Louisville Orch. as violinist and violist, 1947—; music librarian, asso. prof. bibliography (music research) U. Louisville Sch. Music, 1947—. Mem. Music (bd. dirs., mem.-at-large), Ky library assns., Am. Assn. U. Profs., Sigma Alpha Iota (patroness). Club: Louisville Library. Home: 3111 Talisman Rd Louisville KY 40220

KORENBLIT, JACK IZAAK, realtor; b. Lublin, Poland, June 7, 1916; s. Samuel Mayer and Bella (Wekstein) K.; student U. Reims (France), 1934-35; chemist degree U. Caen, Calvados, France, 1938, Engr. Chemistry, 1939; m. Paula Geliebter, Oct. 17, 1937; children—Gloria Fay (Mrs. Alan Steckler), Gilbert Martin. Came to U.S., 1946, naturalized, 1952. Owner, chemist Velvet Cosmetics, Manila, Philippines, 1939-41; prisoner of war, Santo Thomas, Manila, P.I., 1942-45; self-employed in export bus., 1946-55; asso. Leo Aranoff, Miami Beach, Fla., 1956-58; owner Allsun Realty, Miami Beach, 1958—; pres. Trend Realty, Inc., Cocoa Beach, 1964—. Pres., Multiple Listing Service Cape Kennedy Area Bd. Realtors, 1968-69. Chmn. realtors and developers div. United Way, 1973. Mem. Fla. Assn. Realtors (Creative Bus. Ability in Real Estate award 1971, v.p. 1971, life dir.), Cape Kennedy Area Bd. Realtors (Realtor of Year 1969; 71, pres. 1973), Cape Kennedy Area C. of C. (Citizen of Year 1971, pres. 1972, life dir.), Melbourne Area Bd. Realtors (hon. life). Democrat. Jewish religion. K.P. Home: 133 Bimini Rd Cocoa Beach FL 32931 Office: 142 Minutemen Causeway Cocoa Beach FL 32931

KORGEN, BENJAMIN JEFFRY, phys. oceanographer; b. Duluth, Minn., Jan. 6, 1931; s. Benne Hansen and Helen Louise (Slattum) K.; B.S., U. Minn. at Duluth, 1956; M.A., U. Mich., 1958; Ph.D., Ore. State U., 1969; m. Judith Kay Waggoner, Aug. 15, 1959; children—Susan Kay, Jeffry David, James Matthew. Phys. oceanographer U. N.C., 1969—; visual cons. Harper & Row (N.Y.C.); textbook writer for Allyn & Bacon, Inc., Boston; mem. TeVega Expdn., 1965. Served with USN, 1951-54. Grantee, NSF, 1971, Naval Oceanographic Office, 1972, N.C. Bd. Sci. and Tech., 1972. Mem. Am. Geophys. Union, Am. Soc. Limnology and Oceanography, Am. Assn. Univ. Profs., Geol. Soc. Am., A.A.A.S., Internat. Oceanographic Found., Smithsonian Instn. (nat. asso.), Internat. Platform Assn. Contbr. articles to sci. jours. Research on circulation of continental shelf waters, modelling the Aves swell on Caribbean Sea floor. Home: 1923 Fountain Ridge Rd Chapel Hill NC 27514

KORGEN, REINHARD LUNDE, scientist; b. Newfolden, Minn., Dec. 31, 1906; s. Hans Iverson and Anna Maria (Lunde) K.; A.B., Carleton Coll., 1930; M.A., Harvard, 1931, Ph.D., 1945; m. Dorothy Merriman, Dec. 24, 1942; children—Kristi, Anders. Prof. math. Bowdoin Coll., 1931-65; exec. dir. Northeastern Research Found.,

Inc., 1959-62; program dir. Coll. Tchr. Programs NSF, Washington, 1963—. Lectr. operations research Tech. U. Denmark, 1958. Fellow A.A.A.S.; mem. Am. Math. Soc., Phi Beta Kappa. Conglist. Clubs: Harvard, Abracadhbra (Washington). Home: 4402 Elm St Chevy Chase MD 20015 Office: Edn Directorate NSF Washington DC 20550

KORIN, BASIL PETER, educator; b. Oxford, Conn., Sept. 15, 1932; s. Peter and Mary (Malvisio) K.; B.A., U. Conn., 1957; M.S., Stanford, 1960; Ph.D., George Washington U., 1967; m. Marlyn Waggener, Mar. 21, 1959; 1 dau., Hope W. Math. analyst Lockheed Missiles and Space Div., 1957-60; math. statistician Bur. Census, 1960-61; faculty math. and statistics Am. U., Washington, 1961—, prof., chmn. dept., 1973—. Vis. prof. math. Am. U. Beirut, 1969-70. Served with AUS, 1952-54. NSF sci. faculty fellow, 1966-67. Mem. Inst. Math. Statistics, Am. Statis. Assn., Am. Assn. U. Profs., Phi Beta Kappa, Sigma Xi, Phi Kappa Phi. Contbr. articles to profl. jours. Home: 4304 Yuma St NW Washington DC 20016

KORJUS, VERONICA MARIA ELISABETH, portrait artist; b. Estonia, Feb. 2; d. Voldemar L. and Mary E. (Krusenberg) Korjus; student Higher State Acad. Art, Estonia, 1940-42, Stockholm U., 1943-45, Phoenix Sch. Art, 1953-56, Nat. Acad. N.Y., 1960-61; M.A., Columbia, 1952; pvt. studies Louvre, Paris, 1961, Nat. Mus., Stockholm, 1945-47, Stuttgart Staats Mus. (Germany), 1961, Acad. La Grande Chaumiere, Paris, France, 1961, Riiks Mus., Amsterdam, 1969. Came to U.S., 1949, naturalized, 1954. One-man shows including Poughkeepsie IBM Art Gallery, 1964, Center Art Gallery, N.Y.C., 1964, 65, Lucian Art Gallery, N.Y.C., 1965, 66, Hotel Loudres, Nice, France, 1966, Hotel Victoria, Maiorca, Spain, 1966, other hotels Italy, 1966, N.Y.C. Chem. Bank, 1967, Barbizon Hotel, N.Y.C., 1969; exhibited in group shows including Barnard Coll. Art Assn., N.Y.C., 1969, hotels Lisbon, Portugal, Tangier, Morocco, Paris, France, 1966; represented in permanent collections at World Council Chs., N.Y.C.; portrait commns. include Countess Maria Therese Perez de Cavanillas, Ambassador to UN Dr. Jan Papanek, Ingrid Bergman, Dr. Robert J. McCracken. Lectr. IBM Country Club, 1964-65, Riverside Arts, N.Y.C., 1965-67, Deer Hill Conf., Wappingers Falls, N.Y., 1968, Paris, 1970, Cape Coral (Fla.) Yacht Club, 1972; radio talks on painting, 1964; travel to Europe, Middle East and Far East, Africa, Exec. gen. sec. Council European Women in Exile, 1956-60. Mem. Am. Artists Profl. League, Fraternitas Artis, Internat. Platform Assn. Mem. Order of Eastern Star. Address: 5350 Del Monte Ct Cape Coral FL 33904

KORNBLUE, EDWIN BENJAMIN, dentist; b. N.Y.C., Apr. 17, 1932; s. Harry and Tania (Bressler) K.; A.B., U. Mich., 1952; D.D.S., N.Y. U., 1956; m. Norma Jean Short, Dec. 23, 1960 (div.). Individual practice dentistry, Boca Raton, Fla., 1960—; instr. Atlantic Coast Dental Research Clinic, 1966—, dir., 1972-73, co-chmn. implantology sect., 1971—; mem. staff Boca Raton Community Hosp. Mem. Exec. bd. Boca Raton Sch. Action Assn., 1968—; chmn. Dental Edn. in Pub. Schs., Boca Raton, 1966-68. Served with Dental Corps, USNR, 1956-69; capt. Res. Mem. Naval Res. Assn., Am. Acad. Periodontology, Am., Fla. dental assns., Palm Beach County, Atlantic Coast Dist. dental socs., Am. Acad. Implantology, Southeastern Acad. Prosthetic Dentistry, U.S. Dental Tennis Assn. Boca Raton C. of C. (chmn. health and welfare com. 1968-69). Democrat. Unitarian. Clubs: Boca Raton (Fla.) Hotel and Delray Beach Tennis, Player's (founder, dir.) (Delray Beach, Fla.); Underwater Explorers (Freeport, Bahamas). Home: 720 NE 5th Av Boca Raton FL 33432 Office: Weir Plaza 855 S Federal Hwy Boca Raton FL 33432

KORNEGAY, HOBERT, dentist; b. Meridian, Miss., Aug. 28, 1923; s. Hobert and Mary Louise (Gaines) K.; B.S., Morehouse Coll., 1945; D.D.S., Meharry Med. Coll., 1948; postgrad. Med. Field Service Sch., 1953, Walter Reed Inst. Dental Research, 1968-71; m. Ernestine Price, June 10, 1948; children—Carmen Kateena, Patricia Louise, James Price, Donna Michele. Individual practice dentistry, Meridian, 1948-53, 1955—; mem. staffs Riley's Hosp., Meridian, Matty Hersee Hosp., Meridian. Cons. preventive dentistry Miss. Head Start, U. P.R. Dental Sch., 1970-71; cons. Miss V.I. Program, 1970-71, USPHS, 1971-72; clinician Jackson Comprehensive Health Clinic, Utica, Miss., 1970-72; dental surgeon Volt Tech. Corp., Atlanta, 1971-72, Westinghouse Learning Corp., Washington and Silver Spring, Md., 1971-72. Mem. Govs. com. Health Needs Children Miss., 1971-72; mem. task force Miss. Council Child Devel., 1971; chmn. Chetaw Area Council Boy Scouts Am., 1955-65; chmn. Lauderdale Econ. Opportunity Program, 1971-72; dir. Meridian Redevel. Authority Urban Renewal, 1971-72. Bd. dirs. St. Francis Homes, 1971—. Served as capt. AUS, 1953-55. Mem. Acad. Gen. Dentistry, Nat., Am. dental assns., Am. Pub. Health Assn., Pierre Fauchard Acad., N.A.A.C.P. (life), Meridian C. of C., Omega Psi Phi. Republican. Baptist (trustee 1950-72, treas., 1970-72). Mason (Shriner), Elk, Toastmaster (pres. 1969-72). Contbr. articles to newspaper. Home: 1420 39th Av Meridian MS 39301 Office: 2416 5th St Meridian MS 39301

KORNEGAY, HORACE ROBINSON, assn. exec., lawyer; b. Asheville, N.C., Mar. 12, 1924; s. Marvin Earl and Blanche Person (Robinson) K.; student Ga. Sch. Tech., 1943-44; B.S., Wake Forest U., 1947, J.D., 1949; m. Annie Ben Beale, Mar. 25, 1950; children—Horace Robinson, Kathryn Elder, Martha Beale. Admitted to N.C. bar, 1949, practiced in Greensboro, 1949-60; mem. firm Stanley & Kornegay, 1949-50; asst. pros. atty. superior ct. Guilford County, N.C., Greensboro, 1951-53; pros. atty. 12th Solicitorial dist. N.C., Guilford and Davidson Counties, mem. U.S. Ho. of Reps., 1954-60; 6th Dist. N.C., 1961-69; v.p., counsel Tobacco Inst., Washington, 1969-70, pres., exec. dir., 1970—. Dir. Tobacco History Corp., Inc., Durham, N.C. Mem. N.C. Democrat Club, past pres. N.C. Young Democrat Clubs. Bd. dirs. Sir Walter Raleigh Meml. Commn.; bd. visitors Wake Forest U. Sch. Law. Served with AUS, 1943-46. Decorated Purple Heart, Bronze Star medal, Combat Infantryman's Badge. Mem. Greensboro, N.C., Am., Fed. bar assns., Carolina Charter Assn., Alpha Sigma Phi, Phi Delta Phi, Omicron Delta Kappa. Methodist. Rotarian. Clubs: National Lawyers, International of Washington, Geroge Town, Congl. Country. Home: 7709 Charleston Dr Bethesda MD 20034 also 1201 Grayland St Greensboro NC 27400 Office: 1776 K St NW Washington DC 20006

KOROLOGOS, TOM CHRIS, govt. ofcl.; b. Salt Lake City, Apr. 6, 1933; s. Chris T. and Irene (Kolendrianos) K.; B.A., U. Utah, 1955; M.S. (Grantland Rice Meml. fellow 1957; Pulitzer traveling fellow 1958), 1958; m. Carolyn Joy Goff; children—Ann, Philip Chris, Paula. Reporter Salt Lake Tribune, 1950-60, N.Y. Herald Tribune, 1958; account exec. David W. Evans & Assos., Salt Lake City, 1960-62; pres. sec. to Senator Wallace Bennett of Utah, Washington, 1962-65, administrv. asst., 1965-71; spl. asst. to Pres. Nixon, 1971-72, dep. asst., 1972—. Served with USAF, 1956-57. Mem. Ahepa. Greek Orthodox. Home: 8222 Smithfield Av Springfield VA 22152 Office: White House Washington DC 22150

KOSANOVICH, MICHAEL, physician; b. Gary, Ind., June 21, 1934; s. Nicholas and Sara (Todorovich) K.; A.B., Ind. U., 1956, M.D., 1959; m. Pauline Anne Nielsen, Mar. 4, 1960; children—Michael, Wendy Lynn. Intern, Cook County Hosp., Chgo., 1960; pub. health officer City of Milw., 1961; resident in pathology Ind. U. Med. Center Indpls., 1961-65; practice medicine specializing in pathology, Ft. Benning, Ga., 1965-67; pathologist Baroness Erlanger Hosp., Chattanooga, 1967—, dir. cytogenetics lab., 1965—. Precinct chmn. Republican party, Chattanooga, 1968—. Served with AUS, 1965-67. Mem. Coll. Am. Pathologists, Am. Soc. Clin. Pathology, Internat. Acad. Pathologists, Am. Soc. Microbiology. Episcopalian. Home: 64 Carriage Hill Dr Signal Mountain TN 37377 Office: Baroness Erlanger Hosp Chattanooga TN 37403

KOSCHNY, WILLIAM SIMON, chem. engr.; b. Newport, R.I., Aug. 21, 1921; s. William and Theresa Marie (Czforeck) K.; B.S., Northeastern U., 1949; M.S., McKinley-Roosevelt, Inc., 1952; M.E.A., George Washington U., 1958; postgrad. Am. U., 1958-66; m. Bertha Margaret Clarkin, Jan. 1953 (div. Apr. 1958); children—Theresa Mary and Laura Louise (twins); m. 2d, Mae Margarette McVay Leader, June 20, 1962. Asst. to gen. supt. Lewiston Gas Light Co. (Me.), 1949-50; cadet chem. engr. Lynn Gas & Electric Co. (Mass.), 1950-51; ordnance engr. Bur. Ordnance, USN, Newport, 1951-53, Washington, 1953-54, mech. engr., Bur. Aeros., 1954-56, aero. research engr., 1956-58; mil. intelligence specialist, chief staff intelligence U.S. Army, Washington, 1958-62; supervisory gen. engr. U.S. P.O. Dept., 1962-69, head planning and systems analysis research div., bur. research and engring., Washington, 1962-66, chief design assurance and value engring. div., bur. research and engring., Bethesda, Md., 1966-67, personal staff asst. to asst. dir. engring., Washington, temporary detail as tech. adviser to U.S. Postal Service Inst., Bethesda, Md., 1967-69; tech. adviser/gen. engr. tech. proposal evaluation staff, Bur. Research and Engring., Washington, 1969-71, gen. engr. program mgr. Area Mail Systems div. Bulk Mail Dept. Operations Group, U.S. Postal Service, Washington, 1971—. Served with USAAC, 1943. Registered profl. engr., D.C., R.I. Mem. Am. Chem. Soc. (sr. mem.), Am. Inst. Indsl. Engrs. (sr. mem., rec. sec. 1964-65), Fed. Profl. Assn. Washington (sr.), Soc. Am. Value Engrs., R.I. Honor Soc., Pi Sigma Alpha. Contbr. articles to various publs. Home: 5704 Robinwood Lane Falls Church VA 22041 Office: Bulk Mail Dept-Operations Group US Postal Service Washington DC 20260

KOSKI, ONNIE RUDOLPH, dentist; b. Excatawpa, Miss., June 7, 1929; s. Onnie Severi and Clara Louise (Cropp) K.; B.A., U. Miss., 1953; D.D.S., U. Tenn., 1956; m. Peggy Ann Green, Dec. 30, 1951; children—Laura Leigh, Peggy Suzanna, Arnall Rudolph, John Erick, Zilah Jane. Dentist, Okla. State Pub. Health, Oklahoma City, 1956-57; individual practice dentistry, Petal, Miss., 1957-64, Memphis, 1964-65; asst. chief dental service VA Center, Bonham, Tex., 1965-69; chief dental service VA Hosp., Huntington, W.Va., 1969-71; chief dental service VA Center, Wichita, Kan., 1971-73; chief dental service VA Hosp., Houston, 1973—. Adj. asst. prof. dental hygiene Wichita State U., 1971—; resource cons. Dental Asst. Sch., Wichita, 1971; clin. asso. prof. dept. medicine (periodontics) U. Tex. Dental Br., Houston, 1973—. Bd. dirs. VA Wichita Employee's Credit Union. Served with USN, 1947-50, now maj. Army Res. Recipient meritorious service award State of W.Va., 1971, Dir.'s commendation VA Center, Wichita, 1973. Mem. Wichita Dental Hygiene Assn. (adv. bd. 1971-74), Wichita Dental Asst. Sch. (adv. com. 1971-74). Kiwanian, Rotarian. Clubs: Shocker's (Wichita State U.); McConnel USAF Officer's. Home: 11015 Albury St Houston TX 77035 Office: 2002 Holcombe Av Houston TX 77031

KOSSACK, CARL FREDERICK, educator; b. Chgo., May 30, 1915; s. Walter Edward and Elizabeth Marie (Jost) K.; B.A., U. Cal. at Los Angeles, 1935, M.A., 1936; Ph.D., U. Mich., 1939; m. Elizabeth Pride Ayres, June 24, 1940; children—Barbara (Mrs. Eggleston), Charles A., Edgar W., Howard W., Kenneth A., William S. Asst. prof. math. U. Ore., 1939-47; scientist OSRD, Washington, 1944-45; air. intelligence specialist USAF, Washington, 1946-47; prof., head dept. math. and statistics Purdue U., 1947-59; research staff mem. IBM Corp., Yorktown Heights, N.Y., 1959-63; dir. Lab. for Computer Sci., Grad. Research Center, Dallas, 1963-65; prof., head dept. statistics and computer sci. U. Ga., Athens, 1965—. Cons. USPHS, USAF, Office of Pres., Am. Tel. & Tel. Mem. Am. Math. Soc., Inst. Math. Statistics, Operations Research Soc., Biometrics Soc., Am. Statis. Assn., Sigma Xi, Phi Kappa Phi. Contbr. articles to profl. jours. Home: 100 Gatewood Circle Athens GA 30601

KOSSMANN, CHARLES EDWARD, educator, cardiologist; b. Bklyn., Apr. 20, 1909; s. Edward and Anna (Seidel) K.; B.S., N.Y. U., 1928, M.D., 1931, Med. Sc.D., 1938; postgrad. U. Mich., 1934; m. Margaret Musgrave, Dec. 28, 1946; children—Michael Musgrave, Margaret Olive. Intern, Bellevue Hosp., N.Y.C., 1931, house physician, 1932-33, mem. staff, 1934-67, chief adult cardiac clinic, 1940-56, cons., 1968—; asst. in medicine U. Mich. Med. Sch., 1934; practice medicine, N.Y.C., 1935-67; instr. N.Y. U. Sch. Medicine, 1938-42, asst. prof., 1942-49, asso. prof., 1949-64, prof. medicine, 1964-67; prof. medicine, chmn. div. circulatory diseases U. Tenn. Coll. Medicine, Memphis, 1967—; mem. staff Lenox Hill Hosp., N.Y.C., 1937-64, chief adult cardiac clinic, 1949-56, cons. cardiologist, 1964-67; mem. staff Univ. Hosp., N.Y.C., 1949-67, City of Memphis Hosps., 1968—; cons. physician Norwalk (Conn.) Hosp., 1962-67, N.Y. VA Hosp., 1964-67, Memphis VA Hosp., Bapt. Meml. Hosp., Memphis. Mem. com. aviation medicine NRC, 1947-50; cons. to surgeon gen. USAF, 1948-53, George Washington U. Computer Facility, 1966; chief cons. in cardiology Central Office, VA, 1951-56; mem. sci. adv. bd. to chief of staff USAF, 1952-56; med. insp. N.Y.C. Bd. Edn., 1958-67; mem. med. bd. Irvington House, 1954-67; chmn. tng. grants and awards com. Nat. Heart Inst., 1960-64; cons. div. regional med. programs USPHS, 1966-73; mem. central com. Memphis Regional Med. Program, 1968-73. Served with M.C., USAF, 1941-45; col. Res. (ret.). Decorated Legion of Merit. Diplomate Am. Bd. Internal Medicine (mem. exam. bd. cardiovascular disease 1950-55). Fellow A.A.A.S., A.C.P., N.Y. Acad. Scis., N.Y. Acad. Medicine; mem. Am. (chmn. So. regional research rev. adn adv. com. 1968-70), N.Y. (pres. 1961-63), Tenn. (research com. 1968-71), Memphis (bd. dirs. 1968—) heart assns., N.Y. U. Sch. Medicine Alumni Assn. (pres. 1961-62), Am., Tenn., Memphis, Shelby County med. socs., Harvey Soc., Soc. Alumni Bellevue Hosp., Am. Soc. Clin. Investigation (emeritus), Sociedad Mexicana de Cardiologia, Soc. Exptl. Biology and Medicine, Assn. Am. Physicians, Assn. Univ. Cardiologists, Memphis Acad. Internal Medicine, Memphis Med. Seminar (pres. 1971-72), Sigma Xi, Alpha Omega Alpha. Clubs: University (N.Y.C.); Silver Spring Country (Ridgefield, Conn.); Memphis Athletic. Editor: Advances in Electrocardiography, 1958; Diseases of the Heart and Blood Vessels, Nomenclature and Criteria for Diagnosis, 6th edit., 1964; asso. editor Advances in Internal Medicine, 1969—; mem. editorial bd. Am. Heart Jour., 1948-49, Circulation, 1950-51, 58-63, 64-68; Cardiologia, 1949-70, Circulation Research, 1952-57, Am. Jour. Cardiology, 1972-77; mem. editorial bd. Bull. N.Y. Acad. Medicine, 1959-68, chmn., 1962-68. Contbr. articles on circulation and electrophysiology to med. jours. Home: 6365 Wood Bridge Rd Memphis TN 38138 Office: 800 Madison Av Memphis TN 38163

KOSSOFF, STANLEY MORTON, retail trade co. exec.; b. N.Y.C., Apr. 6, 1925; s. Leon and Augusta (Adler) K.; B.S. in Bus. Mgmt., N.Y. U., 1948; m. Georgette Roslyn Rubin, Nov. 25, 1948; 1 dau., Lynn Candice. Asst. sales mgr. Barclay Mfg. Co., N.Y.C., 1946-50; pres. Lillie Rubin Affiliates, Inc., Miami Beach, Fla., 1950—. Served to 2d lt. USAF, 1943-45. Republican. Jewish religion. Clubs: Westview Country, Friars. Home: 126 W San Marino Dr Miami Beach FL 33139 Office: 1037 Lincoln Rd Miami Beach FL 33139

KOTT, JOSEPH, architect; b. June 12, 1924; s. John and Michalena (Lyznicki) K.; B.S., U. Kan., 1949; m. Jane Marie Sweeney, June 25, 1945; children—Joy Elva (Mrs. Ralph Emery), Jann Marie, John, Joellyn, Jennifer. Chief draftsman Edward M. Fuller, Architect, North Kansas City, Mo., 1949-51; asso. mem. Perkins & Will, Architects, Chgo., 1951-59; exec. v.p. Swenson & Kott, Architects, Nashville, 1959-65; prin. Joe Kott & Assos., 1968—. Served with USNR, 1943-46. Mem. A.I.A., Constrn. Specifications Inst. (chpt. v.p. 1968). Home: 5620 S Hillview Dr Route 2 Brentwood TN Office: 1600 Hayes St Nashville TN 37203

KOTTKE, EMMETT WILLIAM, accountant; b. Louisville, Feb. 15, 1918; s. Hugo C. and Elsie (Horn) K.; A.A., U. Louisville, 1937, B.A., 1942; m. Mildred Virginia Parker, Oct. 10, 1942; children—Charles Douglas, Barbara Lynne. Mem. inventory control staff, Western Electric Co., Louisville, 1937-40; mgr. inventory control Goodyear Engring. Corp., Charlestown, Ind., 1940-43; sr. accountant C.B. Compton Co., Louisville, 1946-49; partner, Compton, Kottke & Bown, Louisville, 1949—. Pres., dir. Indiana Mat & Mop Rentals, Inc., Indpls., 1967—; sec., dir. Community Towell Service, Louisville, 1956—, Nashville, 1956—; sec., dir. Community Shop Towel Service, Inc., Louisville, 1956—, Crittenden Corp., Louisville, 1965—; treas. State Bd. Accountancy, 1964, pres., 1967. Dist. commdr. Cherokee Dist. council Boy Scouts Am., 1960; mem. exec. bd. Old Ky. Home council, 1962-64. Mem. Jefferson County Budget Com., 1953-64; pres. Estate Planning Council, Louisville, 1969. Served with AUS, 1943-46. Mem. C. of C., Am. Inst. C.P.A.'s (council), Ky. Soc. C.P.A.'s (state pres. 1956-57), U. Louisville Alumni Assn. Methodist. Mason (Shriner), Kiwanian. Clubs: Pendennis, Jefferson. Home: 1001 Alta Circle Louisville KY 40205 Office: 310 W Liberty St Louisville KY 40202

KOTWAL, KEKI RUSI, dentist; b. Bombay, India, Jan. 5, 1939 (came to U.S. 1961, naturalized, 1966); s. Rusl T. and Arnavaz R. (Shroff) ; B.D.S., U. Bombay, 1960; M.S. in Prosthodontics, U. Ala., 1963, D.M.D., 1965; m. Marie Catherine Cox Graham, Aug. 31, 1962; children—Nevil Eric, Rusty Warren. Individual practice dentistry, Bombay, 1960-61; clin. asst. prosthodontic dept. Sir C.E.M. Dental Sch., 1960-61; commd. capt. U.S. Army, 1965, advanced through grades to lt. col., 1973; prosthodontist Hosp. Dental Clinic, Ft. Jackson, S.C., 1965-66; comdg. officer Mobile Prosthodontic Team, Korea, 1966-67, prosthodontist Pentagon Dispensary Dental Clinic, Washington, 1967-70; chief prosthodontics Center Dental Clinic, William Beaumont Army Med. Center. Dental Clinic, El Paso, 1970—. Cons. prosthodontics Whitesands Missile Range Dental Clinic, 1971—, Pub. Health Clinic, Gallup, N.M., 1971—. Social worker Municipalty Social Center, Bombay, intermittently 1958-59. Diplomate Am. Bd. Prosthodontics. Fellow Am. Coll. Prosthodontics; mem. Am. Dental Assn., William Beaumont Gen. Hosp. Prosthodontic Study Club. Home: 579 Hase St El Paso TX 79906 Office: William Beaumont Gen Hosp Box 70001 El Paso TX 79920

KOURI, JOSEPHINE (MRS. RENE PELLEYA), physician; b. Havana, Cuba, Oct. 9, 1919; d. J.B. and Josefina (Barreto) Kouri; M.D., Havana U., 1943; m. Rene Pelleya, Aug. 15, 1945; children—Rene J. Josefina (Mrs. G. Pino), Maria, Roberto. Intern, Univ. Hosp., Havana, 1943-44, Kendall Hosp., Miami, Fla., 1961-62; asst. prof. U. Havana, 1943-46; resident in psychiatry Jackson Meml. Hosp., Miami, 1963-66; practice medicine specializing in psychiatry, Miami, 1966—; mem. staff South Fla. State Hosp., Hollywood, 1966—; cons. div. rehab. and vocation South Fla. Mental Hosp. Mem. South Fla. Psychiat. Soc., Dade County Med. Assn., Am. Psychiat. Assn. Clubs: Cuban Women's, Big Five (Miami). Author: (with Pedro Kouri) Lecciones de Parasito logia. Home: 400 Como St Coral Gables FL 33146 Office: 420 S Dixie Hwy Suite 4C Coral Gables FL 33146

KOUW, WILLY ALEXANDER, psychologist, educator; b. Leiden, Netherlands, Dec. 20, 1932; student U. Leiden, 1956-58; B.A., McMaster U. (Can.), 1961; Ph.D., U. Tex., 1965; m. Petronella C. Schnelle, Sept. 9, 1957; children—Brigitte S., Ingrid L., Astrid L. Edith R., Victor S. Social sci. research asso. U. Tex., 1964-65 fellow clin. child psychology med. br., Galveston, 1965-66, asst. prof. psychology, 1966-67, clin. asst. prof. dept. psychiatry U. Tex. Med. Sch. at San Antonio, 1967—; pvt. practice psychology, 1967—. Field psychologist U.S. Dept. Health, Edn. and Welfare, summer 1963; field assessment officer Peace Corps, 1965-66; cons. San Antonio State Hosp., Tex. Dept. Mental Health and Mental Retardation; mem. profl. adv. com. Bexar County, bd. trustees for mental health and mental retardation, 1968-73; pres. San Antonio Research Found., 1969-73. Served with Royal Dutch Army, 1952-54. Mem. Am., Tex., Bexar County (pres.) psychol. assns., Tex. Assn. Children with Learning Disabilities, N.Y. Acad. Scis. Address: 6601 Blanco Rd San Antonio TX 78216

KOWALIK, VIRGIL CECIL, educator; b. Sinton, Tex., Feb. 8, 1932; s. Cecil Henry and Rose Mary (Jendrusch) K.; B.S., St. Mary's U., Tex., 1953; postgrad. Fla. State U., 1953-54; M.A., U. Tex. at Austin, 1961, Ph.D., 1966; m. Marilyn Yvonne LeClerc, Aug. 8, 1959; Spl. instr. meteorology U. Tex., 1959-61; instr. physics and math. St. Edward's U., Austin, 1961-63; faculty math. Tex. A. and I. U., Kingsville, 1965—, prof., 1968—, chmn. dept., 1966—. Spl. instr. U. Tex. at Austin, summers 1961-65; research meteorologist Balcones Research Center, Austin, 1960-61, 63-64. Served to 1st lt. USAF, 1953-59. Mem. Am. Math. Soc., Math. Assn. Am., Am. Meteorol. Soc. K.C. Home: 839 W Av G Kingsville TX 78363

KOWALSKE, RICHARD MACKEY, banker; b. Melbourne, Fla., Jan. 18, 1925; s. Fred Detrick and Eva (Mackey) K.; B.S. in Bus. Adminstrn., U. Fla., 1949, M.B.A., 1950; m. Margaret Elizabeth Maybury, June 23, 1957; children—Richard John, Darren Andrew. Asst. v.p. First Nat. Bank Miami, 1950-59; v.p. William E. Pollock & Co., Miami, 1959-64; sr. v.p. First Nat. Bank, Ft. Lauderdale, Fla., 1965—; v.p., treas. Landmark Banking Corp., Ft. Lauderdale, 1970—; dir. 1st Nat. Bank Eau Gallie, Melbourne, Fla., Indialantic Beach Bank. Treas. Opera Guild Ft. Lauderdale, 1970—. Bd. dirs., chmn. Downtown Devel. Authority; bd. dirs. Broward County Traffic Council, Ft. Lauderdale Mus. Arts; bd. dirs., exec. v.p. Boys Club Broward County. Served with C.E., AUS, 1943-46. Mem. Exec. Assn. Ft. Lauderdale (dir. 1969-71), Fla. C. of C., Phi Gamma Delta, Phi Etta Sigma. Clubs: Coral Ridge Country, Tower (Ft. Lauderdale). Home: 2748 NE 34th St Fort Lauderdale FL 33306 Office: PO Box 8009 Fort Lauderdale FL 33310

KOWALSKI, CARL LEON, broadcasting co. exec.; b. New Haven, Oct. 20, 1920; s. Leon Marion and Helena Francis (Rubazewicz) K.; student U. Conn., 1939-42, Capital Radio Engring. Inst., 1946-48; m. Sara Oma Gable, Apr. 21, 1944; children—John Stanley, Keith Leon. With Silliman, Moffet & Kowalski, 1949—, cons. radio engr., Atlanta, 1968—. Served with USAAF, 1942-46. Home: 3986 Powers Ferry Rd NW Atlanta GA 30342 Office: Same

KOWERT, ARTHUR HERMAN, newspaper editor; b. Staunton, Ill., July 4, 1911; s. H.G.T. and Mathilde (Schuricht) K.; B.B.A., U. Tex., 1934; m. Elise Weber, Nov. 11, 1937; children—Bruce A.,

Nancy L. With Fredericksburg Pub. Co. (Tex.), 1935—, sec.-treas., 1941—; pres. Johnson City (Tex) Record-Courier, Inc., 1967—; pres. Hill County Community Press Inc., Fredericksburg, 1969—. Mem. Bd. Edn., Fredericksburg Ind. Sch. Dist., 1951-63. Mem. Tex. (pres. 1953-54), S. Tex. (pres. 1944-45) press assns., Fredericksburg C of C. Lutheran. Lion. Home: 107 E Schubert St Fredericksburg TX 78624 Office: 108 E Main St Fredericksburg TX 78624

KRAFT, JOSEPH, journalist; b. S. Orange, N.J., Sept. 4, 1924; s. David Harry and Sophie (Surasky) K.; A.B., Columbia, 1947; student Princeton, 1948-49, Inst. Advanced Study, 1950-51; LL.D., Claremont Grad. Sch., 1973; m. Polly Winton, Jan. 6, 1960. Editorial writer Washington Post, 1951-52; staff writer N.Y. Times, 1953-57; Washington corr. Harper's mag., 1962-65; syndicated columnist Washington Post, Chgo. Daily News, others, 1963—. Served with AUS, 1943-46. Mem. Council Fgn. Relations, Phi Beta Kappa. Club: Century (N.Y.C.). Author: The Struggle for Algeria, 1961; The Grand Design, 1962; Profiles in Power, 1966; The Chinese Difference, 1973; regular contbr. to New Yorker mag. Home: 3021 N St NW Washington DC 20007

KRAFT, LELAND MILO, JR., soil engr.; b. Gloversville, N.Y., Feb. 27, 1942; s. Leland Milo and Doris E. (Snyder) K.; B.C.E., Ohio State U., 1965, M.S., 1965, Ph.D., 1968; m. Rita Anne Lawyer, Sept. 2, 1967; children—Lisa Anne, Michelle Leigh. With Ohio State U., 1964-68, research asso. civil engring. dept., 1967-68; soil engr. Columbus (O.) Testing Lab., 1968-69; asst. prof. civil engring. Auburn U., 1969-72. Cons., Scott Constrn. Co., Opelika, Ala., 1971-72, City of Auburn, 1971-72, Harman, White and Assos., Inc., Opelika, 1970-72; project engr. McClelland Engr., Inc., Houston, 1972—. Am. Soc. C.E. (chmn. soil mechanics found. div. tech. activities com. Ala. sect. 1970-72), Am. Soc. Testing and Materials, Hwy. Research Bd., Sigma Xi, Chi Epsilon, Tau Beta Pi. Contbr. articles to tech. jours. Home: 2020 Briargreen Dr Houston TX 77077 Office: McClelland Engr Inc 6100 Hillcroft St Houston TX 77036

KRAHN, ROBERT ARNO, elec. engr.; b. Neudorf, Sask., Can., Jan. 27, 1929; s. Walter Frederick and Matilda (Obenauer) K.; student U. Md., 1951; B.S., U. Mo., 1961; m. Stella M. Darnofall, Jan. 19, 1957; children—Judith Ellen, Robêrt Arno. Came to U.S., 1932. Transmission design engr. Bur. of Reclamation, Denver, 1961-68; transmission and substa. design engr. Southwestern Power Adminstrn., Tulsa, 1968-69, area engr., mgr. fed. electric power system, Muskogee, Okla., 1969—. Agy. chmn. Combined Fed. United Appeal, Muskogee, 1971-73. Served with AUS, 1947-56. Mem. I.E.E.E. Lutheran (v.p. Laymen's league 1967-68). Home: Rural Route 1 Box 93C Muskogee OK 74401 Office: 1409 WE Shawnee PO Box 1569 Muskogee OK 74401

KRAKEL, DEAN, mus. adminstr.; b. Ault, Colo., July 3, 1923; s. Elden A. and Gretta (Cross) K.; B.A., Colo. State Coll., 1950; M.A., U. Denver, 1951; postgrad. U. Colo. Extension Center, 1959; m. Iris Moneta Lesh, June 27, 1947; children—Ira Dean, Susan E. (dec.), Jennie Lynn, Jack Remington. Exhibits preparator Colo. Hist. Soc., Denver, 1951-52; cataloguer, 1951; archivist, asst. prof. in library U. Wyo., 1952-56; Curator, dept. dir., dir. USAF Acad. Mus., Col., 1956-61; dir. Thomas Gilcrease Inst. Am. History and Art. Tulsa, 1961-64; mng. dir. Nat. Cowboy Hall Fame and Western Heritage Center, Oklahoma City, 1964—, trustee, asst. sec. exec. com., 1969—. Served with AC, USNR, 1943-46. Mem. Am. Assn. Museums, Western Historians, Cowboy Artists of Am. (hon. mem.), Oklahoma City C. of C., Okla. Zool. Soc. (dir.), Okla. Westerners. Author: South Platte Country, History North Colorado, 1954; The Saga of Tom Horn, 1954; James Boren, Study in Discipline, 1968; Tom Ryan, Painter in Four Sixes Country; End of the Trail, Odyssey of A Statue, 1973. Home: 2500 E 122d St Oklahoma City OK 73111 Office: 1700 NE 63d St Oklahoma City OK 73111

KRAMER, BRUCE STEPHEN, lawyer; b. Many, La., May 24, 1944; s. Sol and Sylvia (Wolder) K.; B.A. cum laude, Washington and Lee Coll., 1966; J.D. with honors, George Washington U., 1969; m. Barbara Alice Levi, May 29, 1967; children—Scott, Melissa. Admitted to Tenn. bar, 1969, U.S. Supreme Ct. bar, 1973; law clk. Fulbright, Crooker, Freeman, Bates & Jaworski, Washington, 1968-69, Judge Robert McRae, Memphis, 1969-70; mem. firm Rosenfield, Borod, Bogatin & Kremer, Memphis, 1970—. Vice pres., chmn. legal com. Tenn. Am. Civil Liberties Union, 1972-73; cons. Memphis Runaway House, 1971, Memphis Alcohol and Drug Council, 1972, Memphis Mental Health Center, 1973. Mem. Am., Tenn., Shelby County, Memphis bar assns., Young Lawyers (dir.). Home: 2401 Eastover Dr Memphis TN 38117 Office: UP Bank Bldg Memphis TN 38103

KRAMER, JOHN KENNETH, mfg. co. exec.; b. Toledo, O., Jan. 19, 1931; s. Norman J. and Loretta (Lehmkuhle) K.; B.S. in M.E., U. Toledo, 1954; m. Violet Marie St. Laurent, May 30, 1959; children—John E., David N., Jennifer M. Sr. indsl. engr. Rubbermaid Inc., Wooster, O., 1961-63, chief indsl. engr., 1963-65, corporate chief indsl. engr., 1965-67; dir. mfg. Rubbermaid Comml. Products, Inc., Winchester, Va., 1967-70; v.p. mfg., 1970—. Exec. bd. Shenandoah Council Boy Scouts Am., 1971—. Bd. dirs. United Fund, 1968-72, treas., 1969. Mem. Soc. Plastics Engrs., Shendadoah Valley Mfrs. Assn. (bd. dirs. 1972—), Winchester C. of C. Home: Route 6 Box 325 Winchester VA 22601 Office: 3124 Valley Av Winchester VA 22601

KRAMER, RICHARD JOHN, cons. ecologist; b. Fairmont, Minn., May 27, 1938; s. John Nilus and Genevieve Mary (Devine) K.; B.A., St. John's U., Minn., 1960; M.S., Ariz. State U., 1962; Ph.D., Rugers U., 1968; m. Patricia Ann Cahill, Aug. 3, 1968; children—Therese Ann, Devin Patrick. Park mgr., interpretative naturalist Mercer County Park Commn., Trenton, N.J., 1965-67; asst. prof. biology Mary Baldwin Coll., Staunton, Va., 1967-72, also interpretive naturalist George Washington Nat. Forest (Va.) U.S. Forest Service, 1969; mgr. ecol. scis. br., dept. environmental quality and conservation HNTB Cons. Engrs., Alexandria, Va., 1972—; grad. sch. faculty U.S. Dept. Agriculture, Washington, 1973—. Served to capt. AUS, 1962-64. Johnson and Johnson fellow, 1966-67. Mem. Ecol. Soc. Am., Am. Inst. Biol. Scis., A.A.A.S., Torrey Bot Club, Nature Conservancy, Nat. Wildlife Assn., Nat. Audubon Soc., Am. Forestry Assn. Roman Catholic. Home: 12304 Cedarwood Ct Woodbridge VA 22191 Office: 201 N Washington St Alexandria VA 22314

KRAMER, ROBERT IVAN, pediatrician; b. Providence, July 31, 1933; s. Louis Irving and Jessica Priscilla (Shore) K.; A.B., Brown U., 1954; M.D., Tufts U., 1958; m. Joan Thalheimer, Apr. 27, 1963; children—Lisa Ann, Robin Louise, Jessica Florette, Megan Leigh. Intern, Yale-New Haven Med. Center, 1958-59, resident in pediatrics, 1959-60; chief resident Children's Med. Center, Dallas, 1960-61; fellow in chest diseases, mem. faculty Southwestern Med. Sch., Dallas, 1963-65, asso. prof., 1971—; practice medicine specializing in pediatrics, Dallas, 1965—; dir. Nat. Cystic Fibrosis Research Center, Dallas, 1963—; mem. staffs Baylor U., St. Paul, Presbyn., Children's hosps., all Dallas; chest cons. Scottish Rite Hosp. for Crippled Children, Dallas. Served with USNR, 1961-63. Nat. Cystic Fibrosis Research Found. grantee, 1963—. Clubs: Royal Oaks Country, Willow Bend Polo and Hunt, Cipango (Dallas). Home: 5838 Colhurst St Dallas TX 75230 Office: 8226 Douglas St Dallas TX 75225

KRAMISH, ARVIN MORRIS, govt. ofcl.; b. Denver, July 1, 1924; s. Max and Anne (Kaufman) K.; B.A., U. Denver, 1947, M.A., 1949; J.D., George Washington U., 1956, Ph.D., Am. U., 1970; m. Shirley Kastein, July 1, 1950; children—Marci Jane, Gary Robert. Admitted to Md. bar, 1956; trainee Dept. of State, Washington, 1949-50, U.S. resident officer, Germany, 1950-52, intelligence officer, 1952-55; fgn. affairs officer Office of Civil Affairs, Dept. of Army, Washington, 1955-61; assigned to Nat. War Coll., 1961-62; staff asst. to dir. arms control Office Sec. Def., 1963-65; sr. dir. ins. Overseas Pvt. Investment Corp., State Dept., 1965—. Served with AUS, 1943-46; lt. col. Res. Home: 8214 Larry Pl Chevy Chase MD 20015 Office: OPIC Washington DC 20527

KRANTZ, SANFORD BURTON, physician; b. Chgo., Feb. 6, 1934; s. Max and Fannie (Orenstein) K.; A.B., U. Chgo., 1954, B.S., 1955, M.D., 1959; m. Sandra R. Goldstein, Dec. 28, 1958; children—Michael David, Marcy Sharon, Alan Thomas, Sarah Ann. Intern, U. Chgo. Hosps., 1959-60, asst. resident medicine, 1960-63; NATO postdoctoral fellow biochemistry U. Glasgow, 1964-65; asst. chief hematology service clin. center NIH, Bethesda, Md., 1966-70; chief hematology unit VA Hosp., Nashville, 1970—; asst. prof. medicine U. Chgo. Hosps. and Argonne Cancer Research Hosp., Chgo., 1965-68; asso. prof. medicine Vanderbilt U., 1970—. Recipient Joseph A. Capps prize for med. research, 1964. USPHS postdoctoral fellow, 1962-64; NATO postdoctoral fellow, 1964; Leukemia Soc. scholar, 1965-68; NIH grantee, 1971—. Mem. Am. Fedn. Clin. Research, A.A.A.S., Am. Soc. Hematology, Central Soc. Clin. Research, Am. Soc. Clin. Investigation, Am. Soc. Exptl. Pathology, Sigma Xi. Author: (with L.O. Jacobson) Erythopoietin and the Regulation of Erythropoiesis, 1970. Home: 838 Rodney Dr Nashville TN 37203

KRANZ, MARTIN EMILE, lawyer; b. New Orleans, Mar. 3, 1900; s. John Martin and Carolyn (Von Behren) K.; B.A., Loyola U., New Orleans, 1920, J.D., 1921, LL.M., 1922; m. Ysabelita Hamilton, Apr. 15, 1926; children—Fritzi (Mrs. Jack L. Martin), Mitzi. Admitted to La. bar, 1921; since practiced law specializing in civil law in New Orleans. Sec., legal adviser bd. assessors La. Assessors Assn., 1938—, La. Assessors Retirement fund, 1950—; lectr. ad valorem taxation. Atty., Salvation Army, 1948—, pres. adv. bd. 1955; exec. bd., New Orleans area Boy Scouts Am., 1947—, atty., 1961—. Fellow Internat. Acad. Law and Sci.; mem. Am., La., New Orleans bar assns., Friends Pub. Schs. La. (pres. 1936). Mason (33 deg.). Contbr. articles ad valorem taxation to profl. jours. Home: 1407 Poland Av New Orleans LA 70117 Office: Maison Blanche Bldg New Orleans LA 70112

KRASHEVSKI, STEFAN HAROLD, govt. ofcl.; b. Borzymih, Poland, Sept. 11, 1918; s. Leon and Jozefa (Klosinski) K.; diploma engring. agronomy Swiss Fed. Poly. U., Zurich, 1944; diploma Swiss Tropical Inst., Basel, 1945; Ph.D., State Coll. Wash. 1952; m. Annemarie Kurz, Sept. 20, 1947; children—Richard S., Steven D. Sci. co-worker Brown Swiss Cattle Assn., Zug, Switzerland, 1945-47; teaching asst. State Coll. Washington, 1948, exptl. aide, 1949-52, jr. soil scientist, 1953, research asso., 1953-55, asst. soil scientist, 1955-57, 58-59; soil fertility expert FAO, UN, Rome, Italy, also Baghdad, Iraq, 1957-58; soil research adviser Internat. Coop. Adminstrn., Ankara, Turkey, 1959-63; soil adviser, Salinity AID, U.S. Dept. State, Lahore, Pakistan, 1964-70, sr. research and grants adviser, program analyst, Washington, 1970—. Served with Polish Army, 1939, French Army, 1940. Mem. Am. Fgn. Service Assn., A.A.A.S., Combatant Volontaire de la France, Scientist Polish Origin, Southwood Civic Assn., Dept. State Recreation Assn. Contbr. articles to profl. jours. Home: 9008 Nomini Lane Alexandria VA 22309 Office: AID Dept State Washington DC 20523

KRATOCHVIL, L(OUIS) GLEN, lawyer; b. Highland, Wis., Oct. 11, 1922; s. John A. and Emma (Pusch) K.; LL.B., J.D., U. Wis., 1951; m. Evelyn Gregory, Sept. 12, 1946; 1 son, Louis Glen. Admitted to Wis. bar, 1951, Tex. bar, 1952, U.S. Supreme Ct., 1956; landman Shell Oil Co., Houston, 1951-52; mem. firm Murphy & Crystal, Houston, 1953-55; asst. U.S. atty. So. Dist. Tex., 1955-57; partner firm Schirmeyer & Kratochvil, Houston, 1957—. Pres., Young Republican Club U. Wis., 1950; pres. McGregor Terrace Civic Club, Houston, 1954. Served as pilot USNR, World War II; PTO. Mem. Am., Tex., Wis., Fed., Houston bar assns., Maritime Law Assn., Wis. Alumni Assn. Houston (pres. 1972—). Phi Alpha Delta. Lion (pres. 1955). Club: Brazos River (treas. 1970—). Home: 302 Kickerillo Dr Houston TX 77024 Office: 3460 One Shell Plaza Houston TX 77002

KRAUS, ERIC (BRADSHAW), educator; b. Liberec, Czechoslovakia, Mar. 22, 1913; s. Paul and Bertha (Frank-Mandello) K.; Dr. rer. nat., Charles U., Prague, 1946; m. Heather Bradshaw Johnson, Jan. 6, 1942; children—Nigel James, Sibella, Deborah Alison. Came to U.S., 1960. With Commonwealth Sci. and Indsl. Research Orgn., Australia, 1946-49, Snowy Mountains Hydro-Elec. Authority, Australia, 1951-60, Woods Hole (Mass.) Oceanographic Inst., 1961-66; prof., chmn. dept. atmospheric sci. and phys. oceanography U. Miami, 1967—. Spl. lectr. Sydney U., 1948-52; head UN Tech. Assistance Mission to Brit. E. Africa, 1955-56; adj. prof. Yale, 1961-63. Served with RAF, 1940-46. Rossby fellow, 1960-61. Fellow Am., Royal meteorol. socs.; mem. Am. Geophys. Union, Sigma Xi. Author: Ocean-Atmosphere Interaction, 1972. Asso. editor Jour. Phys. Oceanography, 1970—. Contbr. articles to profl. jours. Home: 3575 St Gaudens St Coconut Grove FL 33133 Office: Box 9115 Coral Gables FL 33124

KRAUSE, LAWRENCE BERLE, economist; b. Detroit, Dec. 8, 1929; s. Paul Henry and Lena Blair (Blair) K.; B.A., U. Mich., 1951, M.A., 1952; Ph.D. (Alumni fellow 1952-54); Harvard, 1958; m. Sallye Kirstein, Dec. 20, 1953; children—Leonard Blair, Jason Andrew. Asst. prof. Yale, New Haven, 1958-63; sr. fellow Brookings Inst., Washington, 1963-67, 69—; sr. staff Council Econ. Advisers, Washington, 1967-69. Lectr. internat. econs. Johns Hopkins U., 1968—; bd. editors Internat. Orgn., 1969—; mem. editorial adv. bd. Orbis, 1968—. Mem. research council Fgn. Policy Research Inst., 1971—. Served to 1st lt. USMCR, 1954-56. Recipient Osterweil Prize U. Mich., 1951, Sims Prize, 1950. Mem. Am. Econ. Assn. Phi Beta Kappa, Phi Kappa Phi, Phi Eta Sigma. Author: Federal Tax Treatment of Foreign Income, 1964; European Economic Integration and the United States, 1968; Sequel to Bretton Woods, 1971. Home: 3361 Stephenson Pl NW Washington DC 20015 Office: 1775 Massachusetts Av NW Washington DC 20036

KRAUSE, MANFRED OTTO, physicist; b. Stuttgart, Germany, Mar. 11, 1931; s. Friedrich Bernhard and Fridel Ernstine (Mann) K.; B.S., Technische Universität Stuttgart, 1954, diploma in physics, 1957, Ph.D., 1960; m. Josephine Winifred Cammer, Dec. 26, 1963. Came to U.S., 1960, naturalized, 1970. Sr. physicist Wm. H. Johnston Labs., Inc., Balt., 1960-63; sr. scientist Oak Ridge Nat. Lab., 1963—. Fellow Am. Phys. Soc.; mem. A.A.A.S., Smithsonian Instn., Natural History Soc., Audubon Soc. Author: Electron Spectrometry in Atomic Innershell Processes, 1974. Contbr. articles on electron-, charge-, and x-ray spectrometry to sci. publs. Discoverer X-ray spectrometry based on photoelectric effect, 1971. Home: 137 Scenic Dr Oak Ridge TN 37830 Office: Oak Ridge National Laboratory PO Box X Oak Ridge TN 37830

KRAUSHAAR, DAVID I., govt. ofcl.; b. N.Y.C., Mar. 27, 1918; s. Meyer and Rosalind (Baruth) K.; B.A., Cornell U., 1939; J.D., Columbia, 1942; m. Ruth Gertrude Lasker, Jan. 5, 1947; children—Jonathan M., Rosalind E., Judah S. Admitted to N.Y. bar, 1942; gen. practice law Kraushaar & Kraushaar, N.Y.C., 1946-51; atty.-adviser N.P.A., 1951-52; atty.-adviser Broadcast Bur., FCC, Washington, 1952-59, trial examiner, adminstrv. law judge, 1959—. Served to capt., USAAF, 1942-46; MTO; lt. col. Res. (ret.). Mem. Am. Bar Assn. Jewish religion. Home: 3810 Howard St Annandale VA 22003 Office: 1919 M St NW Washington DC 20554

KRAUSS, HERBERT LEE, educator; b. Topeka, Aug. 24, 1916; s. S.J. Leopold and Emma (Strickrott) K.; B.S., U. Kan., 1939; M.Eng., Yale, 1941, D.Eng., 1964; m. Anne McClenny, May 8, 1971; children—Ray Herbert, Terry John. Instr. elec. engring. New Haven Coll., 1940-45; faculty elec. engring. Yale, 1941-66, asso. prof. engring. and applied sci., 1961-66; prof. elec. engring. Va. Poly. Inst. and State U., 1966—. Vis. prof. elec. engring. Duke, 1965, Va. Poly. Inst. and State U., 1965-66. Fellow I.E.E.E.; mem. Sigma Xi, Tau Beta Pi, Sigma Tau. Lion. Author: (with Reich, Ordung, Skalnik) Microwave Theory and Techniques, 1953, Microwave Principles, 1957; (with Reich, Skalnik) Theory and Applications of Active Devices, 1966. Home: 1014 Highland Circle Blacksburg VA 24060

KRAUSS, WILLIAM EDWARD, mech. engr.; b. Cleve., May 12, 1928; s. Jacob and Helen (Fuchs) K.; B.M.E., O. State U., 1950, M.Sc., 1953; Ph.D., U. Fla., 1970; m. Barbara Allen Marlin, Aug. 3, 1957; children—Vicki Ellen, Lori Anne. Process engr. U.S. Steel Corp., Clairton, Pa., 1950-51; asso. engr. N.Am. Aviation, Columbus, O., 1951-52; research asso. Ohio State U. Research Found., Columbus, 1953-54; sr. propulsion engr. Gen. Dynamics Corp., Fort Worth, 1954-59; sr. staff engr. Martin Marietta Corp., Orlando, 1959—. Mem. adj. faculty Fla. Technol. U., Orlando, 1972-73, U. So. Cal., Los Angeles, 1973, Valencia Community Coll., Orlando, 1973. Recipient Research grantee Martin Marietta, 1968-69. Registered profl. engr., Ohio, Fla., Tex. Asso. fellow Am. Inst. Aeros. and Astronautics (asso., Service award); mem. Am. Soc. M.E. (treas. 1973-74), Fla. Engring. Soc. (sr.), Nat. Soc. Profl. Engrs. (sr.), Sigma Xi, Phi Kappa Phi, Theta Xi. Mem. Christian Ch. (elder). Mason (Shriner). Home: 2900 Clemwood St Orlando FL 32803 Office: PO Box 5837 Orlando FL 32805

KRAVIS, GEORGE ROBERTS, II, broadcasting exec.; b. Tulsa, Sept. 11, 1938; s. Raymond Field and Bessie (Roberts) K.; grad. U. Okla., 1960. Mem. prodn. dept. stas. KOKH FM/TV, KETA/TV, Oklahoma City, 1959-60, sta. KOED/TV, Tulsa, 1959-60; founder, owner radio sta. KRAV, Tulsa, 1962; owner radio sta. KFMJ, Tulsa, 1966—; mem. ABC/FM Radio Bd., 1968. Mem. Okla. Art Collection Com., Tulsa Arts Commn., 1969-73; vice chmn. Tulsa Civic Ballet Bd. Bd. dirs. Arts Council of Tulsa, Philbrook Art Center, Cystic Fibrosis, Multiple Sclerosis, Tulsa Philharmonic. Mem. Okla. Broadcasters Assn., Nat. Assn. FM Broadcasters (dir.), Nat. Assn. Broadcasters (mem. FM Radio com. 1964). Clubs: Tulsa, Tulsa Press, Tulsa Country, Summit, University. Address: KRAV/KFMJ PO Box 746 Tulsa OK 74101

KREAGER, DAVID JAY, JR., lawyer; b. Tulsa, Apr. 28, 1929; s. David Jay and Ethel Mae (Martin) K.; B.A. with honors, Tex. A. and M. U., 1950; J.D. with honors, U. Tex., 1953; m. Ann Fleetwood, Mar. 22, 1949; children—David, Michael, Cameron, Heather, Gretchen, Paige. Admitted to Tex. bar, 1953, since practiced in Beaumont; partner firm Orgain, Bell and Tucker. Mem. Beaumont Civil Service Commn., 1961-70. Mem. State Bar Tex. (dir. 1973—), Am., Jefferson County (pres. 1960-61) bar assns., Tex. Assn. Def. Counsel (v.p. 1970), Am. Judicature Soc., Fedn. Ins. Counsel, Internat. Assn. Ins. Counsel, Order of Coif. Presbyn. Rotarian. Home: 1245 Nottingham Lane Beaumont TX 77706 Office: PO Box 1751 Beaumont TX 77704

KREBS, PETER JOACHIM, pharm. co. exec.; b. Gleiwitz, Germany, Dec. 15, 1925; s. Willi and Edith Marlene (Pindus) K.; Abitur, Schlesische Friedrich's Wilhelm Universitët, Breslau, 1944; J.D. magna cum laude, Woodrow Wilson Coll. Law, 1973, LL.M., 1974; m. Rose Maria Guerrero Vasquez Godoy, Feb. 12, 1965; children—Patricia-Johanna, Glenda. Came to U.S., 1947, naturalized, 1952. Div. mgr. E.S. Miller Labs., Los Angeles, 1950-55; with Medics Pharm. Corp., Decatur, Ga., 1955—, pres., chmn. bd., 1959—; dir. U.S. Chem. Corp., Decatur, U.S. Chem. Drug Products Div., Inc. Mem. State Bar Ga., Am. Bar Assn., Nat. Ethical Pharm. Assn., Am. Soc. Legal History, Parenteral Drug Mfg. Assn., Alpha Tau, Sigma Delta Kappa. Home: 3643 Winbrooke Lane Tucker GA 30084 Office: 203 Rio Circle Decatur GA 30030

KREBS, ROCKNE, sculptor; b. Kansas City, Mo., Dec. 24, 1938; s. Arthur Sandford and Lorine (Fisher) K.; B.F.A., Kan. U., 1961; m. Denise De Agostino, Apr. 16, 1966 (div. 1973); 1 dau., Heather. Exhibited in group shows at Ann. Exhibition of Contemporary Am. Sculpture, Whitney Mus., N.Y.C., 1966, 68, 69th. Am. Exhibition Chgo. Art Instr., Walker Art Center, Mpls., 1971, Los Angeles County Mus. of Art, Los Angeles, 1971; exhibited at U.S. Pavilion of World's Fair, Osaka, Japan, 1970. Served to lt. USNR, 1962-65. Recipient Cassandra Found. award, 1969, Nat. Endowment for Arts fellow, 1970, Guggenheim Found. fellow, 1972. Artist fellow Washington Gallery of Modern Art, 1968; fellow Mass. Inst. Center for Advanced Visual Studies, 1974. Major works include Light is the City at Night, New Orleans, 1970, Rite de Passage, 1971, Sky Bridge Green. Patentee in light-reflection apparatus for Laser light structures. Home: 2009 Belmont Rd NW Washington DC 20009 Office: 1737 Johnson Av NW Washington DC 20009

KREIMER, HERBERT FREDERICK, JR., mathematician, educator; b. Cin., Feb. 19, 1936; s. Herbert Frederick and Virginia Ann (Newstedt) K.; B.S., Yale, 1958, Ph.D. (hon. Woodrow Wilson fellow, NSF fellow), 1962; m. Sarah Jane Klein, June 10, 1961; children—Caroline Louise, Herbert Frederick III. Asst. prof. math. Fla. State U., Tallahassee, 1962-65; vis. asso. prof. Northwestern U., Evanston, Ill., 1965-66; asso. prof. Fla. State U., 1966—. Mem. Math. Assn. Am., Am. Math. Soc., Sigma Xi, Phi Beta Kappa. Contbr. research articles to math. jours. Home: 605 Live Oak Plantation Rd Tallahassee FL 32303

KREIPKE, MERRILL VINCENT, govt. ofcl.; b. Evansville, Ind., Feb. 14, 1916; s. Charles Edwin and Ida (Hufnagel) K.; student Evansville Coll., 1931-33; B.S. in Civil Engring., Purdue U. 1936; postgrad. George Washington U., 1960-62;; m. Dorothy Louise Neu, July 17, 1937; children—Karen Jean, Jane Ann. Engr., Office of City Engr., Evansville, 1936-39; engr. soil mechanics and materials Army Engrs. Dist., Louisville, 1939-51, chief, found. and materials br., Louisville, 1951, engr. research and devel. Office Chief Engrs., U.S. Army, Washington, 1956-61, engr. Office Chief Research and Devel., Washington, 1961—, chief terrestrial scis. br. Environmental Scis. div. Office Chief of Research and Devel. Dept. of Army, Washington, 1971-73, chief Environmental Scis. Office, 1973—, chief geophys. scis., 1970-71. Individual practice cons. engr. soils and founds., 1951-56. Permanent sec. Quadripartite Standing Working Group on Ground Mobility (Armies of U.S., U.K., Can., Australia), 1957—; project officer U.S., NATO Long Term Sci. Study Land Based Mobility, 1966—; exec. mem. subgroup T (ground mobility) Tech.

Coop. Program, U.S. Nat. Leader, 1967—; project leader U.S., NATO Long Term Sci. Study Complementary Mobility, 1968—; acting chief Geophys. Scis. Br., Office Chief Research and Devel., Washington, 1969-70, acting chief Terrestrial Scis. Br., 1970—. Mem. camp site devel. com. N.Va. council Girl Scouts U.S.A., 1957-60. Served from ensign to lt. (j.g.) USNR. 1944-46. Recipient Meritorious Civilian Service medal Dept. Army, 1966. Registered profl. engr., Ky., Ind. Va. Fellow Am. Soc. C.E.; mem. Soc. Am. Mil. Engrs., Internat. Soc. Terrain-Vehicle Systems (charter). Presbyn. (deacon, elder). Home: 3060 Hazelton St Falls Church VA 22044 Office: 3045 Columbia Pike Arlington VA 22204

KREITZER, WILLIAM HENRY, oil co. exec.; b. Knightstown, Ind., Sept. 27, 1923; s. Lawrence Edward and Elsie (Jordan) K.; student Ind. U., 1941-42; B.S., Purdue U., 1948; m. Mary Louise Hole, Oct. 26, 1946; children—Crystal Louise, Lawrence William, Karen Lee; m. 2d, Jean Alma Morris, Nov. 8, 1959. Various engring. and supervisory positions Mobil Oil Corp., St. Louis, Indpls., N.Y.C., 1948-60, operating mgr. S.W. div., 1960-63, wholesale plant mgr., 1963-64, market devel. mgr., 1964, marketing planning mgr., 1964-65, v.p. gas liquids, Houston, 1965—; pres., chmn. bd. Petrolane Gas Co., Inc., Natchitoches, La. Served as 2d lt. USAAF, 1943-45. Decorated Purple Heart, Air medal with 2 oak leaf clusters; named Distinguished Engring. Alumnus Purdue U., 1970. Mem. Mo. Soc. Profl. Engrs., Am. Mgmt. Assn., Am. Petroleum Inst., Sigma Alpha Epsilon. Republican. Methodist. Home: 14427 Twisted Oak Lane Houston TX 77024 Office: Houston Natural Gas Bldg 1200 Travis St Houston TX 77002

KRELL, BENNIE WILLIAM, electronic co. exec.; b. Columbia, S.C., Aug. 21, 1904; s. Luther Arthur and Bessie (Brickle) K.; student U.S.C., 1924-26; m. Julia Crosland, July 15, 1928; 1 dau., Jacquelyn (Mrs. Williams). Owner, operation Dixie Radio Supply Co., Columbia, 1929-46; pres., gen. mgr. Dixie Radio Supply Co., Inc., Columbia, 1946—. Mason (Shriner), Elk. Home: Route 1 Box 261 Eastover SC 29044 Office: 1900 Barnwell St Columbia SC 29202

KREMER, LOWELL JEROME, wholesale trade exec.; b. Pitts., Feb. 22, 1931; s. Jerome Boris and Betty (Friedman) K.; B.A. in Econs., U. Mich., 1952; m. Lois Ann Steinberg, Dec. 21, 1952; children—Lyn R., Lori Lee, Jeffrey B. Sales mgr. Magnolia Liquor Co., Inc., New Orleans, 1956-59; gen. mgr. United Beverage Co., Oklahoma City, 1959-65; v.p., gen. mgr. Duval Spirits, Inc., Jacksonville, Fla., 1965—. Served with USNR, 1953-56. Mem. Sales and marketing Execs., Sigma Alpha Mu. Office: PO Box 4670 Jacksonville FL 32201

KRENTZMAN, BEN, U.S. dist judge; b. Milton, Fla., Mar. 21, 1914; s. Isaac B. and Juanita (Rogers) K.; B.S., LL.B., U. Fla., 1938; m. Wilma McMullen, Nov. 30, 1946; children—John Arthur, Mary Louise, Elizabeth Rogers. Admitted to Fla. bar, 1938; practiced in Clearwater, Fla., 1938-41; 46-67; U.S. judge Tampa Div., Middle Dist. Fla., 1967—. Served to lt. col. AUS, 1941-46. Decorated Bronze Star. Home: 1541 Walnut St Clearwater FL 33515 Office: PO Box 3209 Tampa FL 33601

KREPS, CLIFTON H., educator; m. Juanita M. Kreps; 3 children. Wachovia prof. banking U. N.C. at Chapel Hill. Address: U North Carolina Sch Bus Chapel Hill NC 27514*

KREPS, JUANITA M. (MRS. CLIFTON H. KREPS), economist, univ. adminstr.; m. Clifton H. Kreps.; 3 children. James B. Duke prof. econs., v.p. Duke U., also dean Woman's Coll., asst. univ. provost; dir. N.Y. Stock Exchange. Author books including Sex in the Marketplace: American Women at Work; Lifetime Allocation of Work and Income. Address: 115 E Duke Bldg Duke U Durham NC 27708*

KRIEGMAN, GEORGE, psychoanalyst, psychiatrist; b. Chgo., Sept. 14, 1917; s. Peter Isaac and Bertha (Share) K.; A.B., U. Ill., 1939, M.S., 1942, M.D., 1943; m. Lois Harriet Smason, Jan. 31, 1941; children—Lesley, Diane, Mitchell, Bruce. Candidate, Washington Sch. Psychiatry, 1944-51, Washington Psychoanalytic Inst., 1944-50; intern St. Elizabeths Hosp., Washington, 1943-44, resident, 1944-45; practice medicine, specializing in psychiatry, Richmond, Va., 1947—; asst. prof. Sch. Nursing, Med. Coll. Va., 1950-58; lectr. psychiatry Richmond Profl. Inst., 1951-58, U. Va., 1958-62; instr. Washington Psychoanalytic Inst., 1958-61; asst. clin. prof. psychiatry Med. Coll. Va., 1959-64, asso. clin. prof., 1964-68, clin. prof. psychiatry, 1968—; cons. Family and Childrens Service Soc., 1947-73, Va. State Dept. Pub. Welfare, Child Care Bur., 1947-52, VA Hosp., Roanoke, Va., 1652-57; profl. adv. bd. Va. Mental Health and Mental Retardation, 1971—. Served to capt. AUS, 1945-47. Fellow Am. Psychiatry Assn., Am. Acad. Psychoanalysts; mem. Am. Psychoanalyst Assn., Neuropsychiat. Soc. Va., Richmond Acad. Medicine, Acad. Religion and Mental Health. Clubs: Torch, Bull and Bear. Home: 26 Malvern Av Richmond VA 23221

KRISCH, JOEL, motel exec.; b. Roanoke, Va., June 23, 1924; s. Samuel J. and Miriam (Weinstein) K.; student Va. Poly. Inst., 1941-43; m. Nancy Jane Scher, Jan. 2, 1950; children—Kathryn Jane (Mrs. Jack Loeb), Linda Scher, Samuel J. II. Partner bus. firm, Roanoke, 1946-57; exec. officer motel corps., Roanoke, 1957-62; pres. Am. Motor Inns, Inc., Roanoke, 1962—; dir. Providers Benefit Co., Phila. Bd. dirs. Va. Poly. Inst., State U. Ednl. Found. Served with AUS, 1943-45. Mem. Roanoke Valley C. of C. (dir.). Jewish religion. Mason (Shriner). Home: 5208 Archer Dr SW Roanoke VA 24014 Office: 1917 Franklin Rd SW Roanoke VA 24014

KRISHNAMURTI, PULLABHOTLA VENKATA, educator; b. Gudivada, India, Mar. 1, 1923; s. Gagadharao Pullabhotla and Ramartnam Pullabhotla K.; G V M.C., Madras Vet. Coll., 1948; B.V.Sc., U. Madras, 1949, D.V.P., 1958; M.S., U. Wis., 1961; Ph.D., Tex. A. and M. U., 1967; m. Tejovati Chada, July 6, 1949; children—Swarna Bala, Madhu Bala, Suresh, Kiran Bala, Sridhar. Came to U.S., 1959, naturalized, 1973. Asst. prof. U. Andhra, Tirupati, India, 1954-58; research asst. U. Wis., 1959-63; research microbiologist Hy-Line Poultry Farms, Des Moines, 1964-65; research asst. Tex. A. and M. U., 1965-66; asso. prof. Tuskegee Inst., 1966-68; asso. prof. to prof. microbiology Savannah State Coll., 1969—; state veterinarian, India, 1948-57. Mem. Am. Soc. Microbiology, World Poultry Sci. Assn., Indian Vet. Assn., Sigma Xi, Phi Zeta. Contbr. articles to profl. jours. Home: 6002 Fairview Av Savannah GA 31406

KRISTIANSEN, MAGNE, elec. engr., educator; b. Elverum, Norway, Apr. 14, 1932; s. Martin and Ella (Sobye) K.; came to U.S., 1958, naturalized, 1967; B.S. in Elec. Engring., U. Tex. at Austin, 1961, Ph.D. (Ford Found. fellow), 1967; m. Aud Bohn, July 6, 1957; children—Sonja Bohn, Eric Bohn. Research engr. U. Tex., Austin, 1964-66; faculty Tex. Technol. U., Lubbock, 1966—, prof., 1971—, dir. plasma lab., 1966—. Cons. def. products div. Varo, Inc., Garland, Tex., 1970-71. Served with Royal Norwegian Air Force, 1950-58. Recipient Hamilton award U. Tex., 1961; Spencer A. Wells award Tex. Technol. U., 1972. NSF grantee, 1967—; AEC grantee, 1968-71; Air Force Office Sci. Research grantee, 1968—; State of Tex. grantee, 1966—. Mem. A.A.A.S., I.E.E.E., Am. Phys. Soc., Am. Nuclear Soc., Sigma Xi, Tau Beta Pi, Eta Kappa Nu, Phi Kappa Phi. Contbr. articles to profl. jours. Home: 3514 66th Dr Lubbock TX 79413

KRIVOY, WILLIAM AARON, pharmacologist; b. Newark, Jan. 2, 1928; s. Samuel and Rose (Hirschenhorn) K.; B.S., Georgetown U., 1948; M.S., George Washington U., 1949, Ph.D., 1953. Pharmacologist, Chem. Corps Med. Labs., Army Chem. Center, Md., 1950-54; postdoctoral research fellow U. Pa., 1954-55, dept. pharmacology U. Edinburgh (Scotland), 1955-57; instr. dept. pharmacology Tulane U., 1957-59; asst. prof. dept. pharmacology Baylor U., 1959-63, asso. prof., 1963-68; with Nat. Inst. Mental Health, Addiction Research Center, Lexington, Ky., 1968—, now pharmacologist. Mem. Am. Soc. Pharmacology and Exptl. Therapeutics, Brit. Pharm. Soc., Soc. Exptl. Biology and Medicine N.Y. Acad. Scis., Am. Coll. Neuropsychopharmacology, Biophys. Soc., Tex. Acad. Sci., Western Pharmacology Soc., Sociedade Brasileira de Farmacologia e de Terapeutica Experimental, Sigma Xi. Contbr. numerous articles to profl. jours. Home: 1565 Alexandria Dr Lexington KY 40504 Office: Nat Inst Mental Health Addiction Research Center Lexington KY 40507

KRIZ, GEORGE JAMES, educator; b. Brainard, Neb., Sept. 20, 1936; s. George Jacob and Rose Agnes (Havlovic) K.; B.S., Ia. State U., 1960, M.S., 1962; Ph.D., U. Cal. at Davis, 1965; m. Patricia Elizabeth Kelly, June 18, 1960; children—Rosalie Sue, Richard Patrick, Thomas George. Faculty agrl. engring. N.C. State U., 1965—, prof., 1973—, asso. head dept., 1969-73, asst. dir. for research N.C. Agrl. Expt. Sta., 1973—. Cons. Nat. Def. Edn. Act fellow, 1962-65. Mem. Sigma Xi, Phi Kappa Phi, Gamma Sigma Delta, Alpha Zeta. Rotarian. Contbr. articles to tech. jours. Home: 302 Oak Ridge Rd Cary NC 27511 Office: PO Box 5847 Raleigh NC 27607

KROES, ROGER LEE, solid state physicist; b. Racine, Wis., Dec. 3, 1935; s. Stephen A. and Ann W. (Dolata) K.; B.S., Marquette U., 1957, M.S., 1960; Ph.D., U. Mo., 1968; m. Margaret E. Roach, June 20, 1964; children—Katherine M., Steven R. Engr., AC Spark Plug Co., Oak Creek, Wis., 1959-64; physicist Marshall Space Flight Center, NASA, Huntsville, Ala., 1968—. Recipient Sustained Superior Performance award Marshall Space Flight Center, 1970, Outstanding Performace Rating award, 1971. Mem. Am. Phys. Soc., Sigma Xi. Home: 902 Coronado Av Huntsville AL 35802 Office: S&E-SSL-TR Marshall Space Flight Center Huntsville AL 35812

KROGDAHL, WASLEY SWEN, educator; b. Springfield, Ill., Jan. 17, 1919; s. Swen Julius and Grace Blight (Wasley) K.; B.S., U. Chgo., 1939, Ph.D., 1942; m. Margaret Kiess, July 25, 1942; children—Matthew, John, Marthine. With Naval Ordnance Lab., Washington, 1942-43; faculty U. S.C., 1943-45; astronomer Yerkes Obs., Williams Bay, Wis., 1945-46; faculty Northwestern U., 1946-58; prof. astronomy U. Ky., Lexington, 1958—. Vis. lectr. Am. Astron. Soc. Chmn., State Central Com., Am. Party of Ky., 1973. Mem. Am., Royal astron. socs. Author: Astronomical Universe, 1952. Home: 3493 Castleton Way N Lexington KY 40502

KROGSTAD, ROBERT WELLINGTON, mfg. co. pres.; b. Muskegon, Mich., Sept. 9, 1919; s. Johan Eddre and Ella (Olsen) K.; B.S. in Mech. Engring., Mich. State U., 1941; m. Barbara Pelouze Cutler, Jan. 12, 1946 (div. Nov. 1969); children—John Gifford, Jane Cutler, Barbara Ann; m. 2d, Anne Marie Rockefeller, June 5, 1971 (separated 1972). Vice pres. engring. Thomas Industries, Fort Atkinson, Wis., 1950-57; exec. v.p., gen. mgr. Carnes Corp., Verona, Wis., 1957-69; pres., co-owner Leer Mdg. Co., New Lisbon, Wis., 1969-73; pres., owner Nat. Irrigation Co., Fort Lauderdale, Fla., 1973—. Finance chmn. 2d Dist. Wis. Republican party, 1963-65, chmn. candidates com. Dane County, Wis., 1962-63; chmn. Knowles for Gov. campaign Dane County, 1966. Served with USNR, 1943-46. Mason. Clubs: Valley (Madison); Tennis (Ft. Lauderdale), Naples Bath and Tennis (Fla.). Home: 3951 Gulfshore Blvd North Apt 501 Naples FL 33940 Office: 5048 S State Rd #7 Fort Lauderdale FL 33314

KROL, JOSEPH, engr., educator; b. Warsaw, Poland, Jan. 14, 1911; s. Kazimierz and Feliksa (Tokarzewski) K.; M.S., Warsaw (Poland) Inst. Tech., 1937; Ph.D. U. London (Eng.), 1947; m. Evelyn Swingland, Apr. 15, 1952. Came, to U.S., 1956, naturalized, 1962. Tech. officer with directorate ammunition prodn. Brit. Ministry of Supply, London, Eng., 1941-45; research scientist U. London, 1946-47; cons. engr., Montreal, Que., Can., 1948-51; asso. prof. mech. engring. U. Manitoba (Can.), 1951-56; prof. indsl. engring. Ga. Inst. Tech., 1956—. Recipient George Stephenson prize, 1951. Registered profl. engr., Ga. Fellow Instn. Mech. Engrs.; mem. Am. Inst. Indsl. Engrs., Engring. Inst. Can., Corp. Profl. Engrs. Que., Am. Econ. Assn., Am. Soc. Mech. Engrs., Instrument Soc., Am., A.A.A.S., Am. Statis. Assn., Econometric Soc., Inst., Mgmt. Scis., Sigma Xi. Author articles on engring. and mgmt. subjects. Home: 210 North Av NW Atlanta GA 30313

KROLL, MILTON P., lawyer; b. Paterson, N.J., 1914; A.B., U. W. Va., 1934; LL.B., Harvard, 1937. Admitted to N.J. bar, 1938, D.C. bar, 1949; atty. SEC, 1940-48, asst. gen. counsel, 1948-52, asso. gen. counsel, 1952-53; now mem. firm Freedman, Levy, Kroll & Simonds, Washington; lectr. law George Washington U., 1952-59. Mem. Bar Assn. D.C., Am. Law Inst., Fed., Am. bar assns., Phi Beta Kappa. Address: Freedman Levy Kroll & Simonds 1730 K St NW Washington DC 20006

KRONICK, DAVID ABRAHAM, librarian; b. Connelsville, Pa., Oct. 5, 1917; s. Barnet L. and Rose L. (Miller) K.; B.A., Western Res. U., 1940, B.S. in L.S., 1941; Ph.D., U. Chgo., 1956; m. Marilyn Abramson, Oct. 25, 1959; children—Steven Leonard, Beryl Leah. Librarian, Western Res. U. Sch. Medicine, Cleve., 1946-49, U. Mich. Med. Sch., Ann Arbor, 1955-59; dir. Cleve. Med. Library, 1959-64; chief reference div. Nat. Library Medicine, Washington, 1964-65; librarian U. Tex. Med. Sch., San Antonio, 1965—. Pres. Friends San Antonio Pub. Library, 1967-68, Tex. Council Health Scis. Libraries, 1969. Served to capt. M.C., AUS, 1941-46. Council Library Resources fellow, 1971. Mem. Med. Library Assn., Am. Assn. History Medicine, Am. Soc. Information Sci. Mem. B'nai B'rith. Contbr. articles to profl. jours. Home: 1223 Mount Riga Dr San Antonio TX 78213 Office: U Tex Health Sci Cntr 7703 Floyd Curl Dr San Antonio TX 78284

KRONSBERG, AVRAM, retail store exec.; b. Charleston, S.C., Aug. 27, 1936; s. Edward and Hattie (Barshay) K.; student Tulane U., 1956-59; m. Marlene Alfred, Apr. 23, 1959; children—Avram, Edward III. With Edward's, Inc., Charleston, 1959—, pres., 1973—; dir. S.C. Nat. Bank. Pres. S.C. Coastal Environmental Coalition, 1973. Bd. dirs. Boy Scouts Am., Charleston Bicentennial Commn., Jr. Achievement, 1970-72, Charleston Mini Parks, Jewish Community Center, Charleston Day Sch., 1969-71. Served with AUS, 1959-65. Mem. Carolina Art Assn. (pres.), Charleston Trident C. of C. (pres. 1974). Jewish religion. Club: Charleston Country. Home: 46 King St Charleston SC 29401 Office: 5000 LaCross Rd Charleston SC 29405

KROP, STEPHEN, pharmacologist; b. N.Y.C., Sept. 24, 1911; s. James D. and Mary (Badeker) K.; B.S., George Washington U., 1939; M.S., Georgetown U., 1940; Ph.D., Cornell U., 1942; m. Mary Lulick, July 28, 1934; children—Elaine Stephanie (Mrs. Max P. Wallenburg), Marianne Elizabeth, Paul Nicholas, Thomas Monroe. Faculty Cornell U. Med. Coll., 1939-44, Yale Med. Sch., 1944-46; dir. pharmacological research U.S. Army Chem. Corps Med. Research Labs., 1946-48; exptl. pharmacologist Squibb Inst., New Brunswick, N.Y., 1948-49; dir. pharmacological research Warner Inst., N.Y.C., 1949-51; research asst., dir. Chem. Biol. Coordination Center NRC, 1951-52, mil. chem. research coordinator, 1952-57; dir. pharmacological research Ethicon, Somerville, N.J., 1957-63; chief drug pharmacology br. Bur. Drugs U.S. FDA, Washington, 1963—. Professorial lectr. Georgetown U. 1963—. Pres. Ethicon Research Found., 1958-63. Fellow N.Y. Acad. Scis., A.A.A.S.; mem. Am. Soc. Pharmacology and Exptl. Therapy, Am. Physiol. Soc., Exptl. Biology and Medicine, Am. Indsl. Hygiene Assn., Soc. Toxicology, Harvey Soc., Sigma Xi. Democrat. Roman Catholic. Club: Cosmos. Contbr. articles to profl. jours. Home: 7908 Birnam Wood Dr McLean VA 22101 Office: 200 C St SW Washington DC 20204

KROPP, PAUL JOSEPH, educator; b. Springfield, O., June 29, 1935; s. Paul John and Loretta Ann (Turner) K.; B.S. summa cum laude, U. Notre Dame, 1957; Ph.D., U. Wis., 1962; m. Patricia Marie Morrissey, July 28, 1962; children—David Edward, Sonia Marie. Research chemist Proctor & Gamble Co., Cin., 1961-65, head organic photochemistry group, 1965-69, coordinator univ. relations, 1969-70; prof. chemistry U. N.C., Chapel Hill, 1970—. Chief judge, mem. exec. com. Cin. Golden Gloves, 1966-70. Sloan fellow, 1972-74. Recipient Merck award, 1973. Mem. Am. Chem. Soc., Chem. Soc. London, Phi Lambda Upsilon, Alpha Chi Sigma. Contbr. articles to profl. jours. Home: 606 Concordia Ct Chapel Hill NC 27514 Office: Dept Chemistry U NC Chapel Hill NC 27514

KRUEGER, GEORGE EDWARD, dentist, prosthodontist; b. Chgo., Mar. 10, 1921; s. Alonzo and Elizabeth Olive (Matthews) K.; Student U. Ill. at Champaign, 1938-40, D.D.S., Northwestern U., 1943, postgrad. 1964-65; M.S. in Clin. Dentistry, Prosthodontics, Marquette U., 1967; m. Joan Eileen Fellows, Aug. 6, 1949; children—Leila Joan (Mrs. Julius J. Zschau) and George Edward (twins), Leslie Joyce, Lydia June and Laura Jean (twins), Gerard Edmund, Gregory Eric, Gordon Elliott. Practice dentistry, Waukegan, Ill., 1946-65, practice limited to prosthodontics, Waukegan, 1965-72, St. Petersburg, Fla., 1972—; asst. clin. prof. Marquette U., Milw., 1967-72, asso. clin. prof., 1972; prosthetic cons. U.S. Navy Hosp., Great Lakes, Ill., 1968-72. Served with USNR, 1943-46, ret. Res., 1956. Diplomate Am. Bd. Prosthodontics. Fellow Am. Coll. Prosthodontists, Am. Coll. Dentists; mem. Am., Fla. dental assns., Am. Prosthodontic Soc., Am. Equilibration Soc. (dir. 1968-70, 73—, sec. 1970-73), West Coast Dist. Dental Soc., Carl O. Boucher Prosthodontic Conf. (charter), Pierre Fauchard Acad., Federation Dentaire Internationale, Am. Philatelic Soc., Soc. Philatelic Ams., Bur. Issues Assn., Delta Chi. Roman Catholic. K.C. (4 deg.). Home: 125 Park St S St Petersburg FL 33707

KRUM, ALVIN ANDREW, physiologist; b. Fresno, Cal., May 14, 1928; s. Andrew and Margret (Walter) K.; A.B., U. Cal., 1950, Ph.D., 1957; m. Joyce Carter, June 26, 1954; children—Jeffrey, Judith. Research physiologist U. Cal. at San Francisco, 1957-58; postdoctoral fellow U. Utah, 1958-59; research physiologist U. Cal. at San Francisco, 1959-61, U. Ark., 1961—. Served with Chem. Corps, AUS, 1950-52. Lederle fellow, 1964-67; research grantee, NIH, 1962-73. Mem. Am. Physiol. Soc., Soc. Exptl. Biology and Medicine, Endocrine Soc., A.A.A.S., Am. Assn. U. Profs. Contbr. articles to profl. jours. Home: 11516 Happy Valley St Little Rock AR 72207 Office: 4301 W Markham St Little Rock AR 72201

KRUMBEIN, NATHANIEL, furniture co. exec.; b. Alliance, O., June 5, 1914; s. Leo and Esther (Simowitz) K.; B.S., U. Ga., 1937; Ph.G., U. S.C., 1938; m. Amy Meyers, Feb. 15, 1944; children—Charles H., Joyce T., Michael M., Lee B. Asst. mgr. Converse Pharmacy, Spartansburg, S.C., 1938, Armstrong Pharmacy, Greenville, S.C., 1938-39; mgr. Lane Drug Store, Anniston, Ala., 1939-40; pres. Kay Drug Co., Charlotte, N.C., 1946-49; salesman, Heilig-Meyers Furniture Co., Richmond, Va., 1950-51, credit mgr., 1952, store mgr., 1952-58, dist. supr., 1958-66, dir. operations, 1966-68, v.p., 1968-71, mem. exec. com., 1965—, also dir. vice pres., bd. dirs. Jewish Community Center, 1958-60; chmn. exec. com., chmn. regional adv. bd. Va.-N.C. Anti-Defamation League, 1963-71. Bd. dirs. Richmond Jewish Community Council, Nat. Joint Distbn. Com. Served to maj. AUS, 1940-46. Recipient Man of Year award Va.-N.C. Anti-Defamation League, 1973. Mem. U. Ga. Alumni Assn. (v.p. bd. mgrs. 1963-69; Distinguished Service award 1970), Alpha Epsilon Pi (nat. pres. 1971). Mason. Club: Lakeside Country (Richmond). Home: 17 Oak Lane Richmond VA 23221 Office: 3228 W Cary St Richmond VA 23221

KRUMNOW, WILLIAM EARL, dentist; b. Otto, Tex., Apr. 5, 1929; s. Robert Lee and Anne (Sonntag) K.; student Baylor U., 1946-48; D.D.S., U. Tex. Sch. Dentistry, 1952; m. Georgia Dee Dralle, June 11, 1950; children—Michael, Lana, Dina, Jacob. Individual practice dentistry, Waco, Tex., 1952-53, Taft, Tex., 1955—. City councilman, Taft, 1961-72, mayor, 1972—. Served with AUS, 1953-55. Mem. Am., Tex. dental assns., Nueces Valley Dist. Dental Soc., V.F.W., Psi Omega. Roman Catholic. Rotarian (pres. 1964-65). Home: 727 Field St Taft TX 78390 Office: 231 McIntyre St Taft TX 78390

KRUSE, EDWARD DONALD, sch. adminstr.; b. Pitts., Oct. 23, 1912; s. Henry J. and Marie (Grinner) K.; B.S., Slippery Rock State Coll., 1935; M.S., U. Pitts., 1941, D.Ed., 1963; m. Lorna M. Kruse; children—Edward Warren, Karl F. Vicki L. Tchr. physics, chemistry, biology, psychology, driver and safety edn. West View (Pa.) High Sch., 1935-50; prin. secondary schs. North Hills Joint Schs., Ross Twp., Pa., 1950-54, asst. supervisory prin. for curriculum, 1954-58, supt. schs., 1958-72; survey staff Nat. Assn. Trade and Tech. Schs., Nat. Schs. Cosmotology, So. Assn. Schs. and Colls., 1972—. Adminstrv. cons. library services Pa. Dept. Pub. Instrn., 1963-72; mem. staff Comprehensive Sch. Survey, U. Pitts., 1962-72; co-sponsor Sch. Medicine-High Sch. Cancer Research, 1960-72; also Teaching Internship Program, 1959-72; mem. exec. bd. Allegheny County Audio-Visual & Film Library, 1960-72; Elementary and Secondary Edn. Act, Title III, Western Region, Pa., 1965-72; chmn. profl. services adv. com. No. Area Vocational-Tech. Sch., Pitts., 1964-72; dir. Asso. Ednl. Cons., Pitts., 1967-72. Chmn. Allgheny County Schs. div. United Fund, 1960-72. Chmn. Joint Community Recreation Bd., Pitts., 1964-72; bd. mgmt. Pitts. YMCA, Passavant Hosp., Pitts. Served with USAAF, 1942-46; CBI. Recipient awards in devel. libraries in pub. schs. Pa. Dept. Pub. Instrn., 1962, leadership in curriculum devel. 1962, contbn. to essential field instrnl. materials, 1963, Distinguished Library Service award for sch. adminstrs., 1970; award Am. Assn. Sch. Libraries, 1970, 71; Gov.'s award Commonwealth of Pa., for outstanding leadership in ednl. adminstrn. Pa. Ho. of Reps. citation ednl. leadership and adminstrv. practices, 1972. Mem. Tri-State Sch. Study Council (sec. 1963-70, pres. 1970, v.p. 1971), Phi Delta Kappa. Presbyn. (chmn.). Author: Preferred Classroom Practices and the Extent of Their Use in Selected Junior High Schools, 1964. Address: 9771 NW 37th St Coral Springs FL 33065

KRUSE, OLAN ERNEST, educator; b. Coupland, Tex., Sept. 6, 1921; s. Max Edward and Irma Pauline (Miller) K.; B.S., Tex. A. and I. U., 1942; M.A., U. Tex., 1949, Ph.D., 1951; m. Lucille Thomas, Sept. 4, 1942; children—John E., James L. Radar engr. Signal Corps Radar Labs., Belmar, N.J., 1942-43; prof., chmn. dept. physics Stephen F. Austin State Coll., 1953-56, Tex. A. and I. U., 1956—. Mem. Kingsville Zoning and Planning Commn., 1963-71. Served to lt. USNR, World War II. Author: Tech. Physics Lab. Manual, 1957; Gen. Physics Demonstration Manual, 1959, rev., 1973. Contbr. articles to profl. jours. Patentee in field. Home: 325 Seale St Kingsville TX 78363

KRUSE, PAUL ROBERT, librarian, educator; b. What Cheer, Ia., Feb. 26, 1912; s. Carl Fred and Phoebe (Mumby) K.; A.B., John Fletcher Coll., 1933; B.S. in L.S., U. Ill., 1940; Ph.D., U. Chgo., 1958; m. Esther Moe, June 3, 1939; 1 son, Robert Leroy. Librarian, John Fletcher Coll., Oskaloosa, Ia., 1932-33; librarian Bolles Sch., Jacksonville, Fla., 1934-38; reference librarian Jacksonville Pub. Library, 1938-42; reference asst. in charge reference collections Library of Congress, Washington, 1942-45; established library for UN Conf., San Francisco, 1945; instr. library sch. Cath. U., Washington 1943-48; bibliographer Ency. Brit., 1946-47; editor A. N. Marquis Co., 1949; vis. asst. prof. library sch. U. So. Cal., 1950, George Peabody Coll., 1950-51; reorganized library for Rollins Coll., Winter Park, Fla., 1951-52; vis. asso. prof. library sch. U. Ill., 1952-53; asso. prof. library sch. U. Denver, 1954-55; librarian Golden Gate Coll., San Francisco, 1955-65; asso. prof. sch. Library and Information Scis. North Tex. State U., Denton, 1965—. Fulbright lectr., library adviser U. Teheran, 1962-64, U. Ceylon, 1964-65. Library cons. U.S. AID, Universidad Santa Maria la Antigua, Panama, 1968. Active Community and profl. theatre groups. Mem. Am., Tex. library assns., Spl. Libraries Assn. (conf. chmn. 1961). Republican. Methodist. Mason (32 deg., Shriner). Author: The Story of the Encyclopedia Britannica, 1763-1943. Editor Index for Lend Lease Weapon for Victory, 1944; bibliographies for Ten Eventful Years, 1947. Contbr. articles to profl. jours. Home: 2207 Jacqueline St Denton TX 76201

KRUSER, ROSS WELLS, govt. ofcl.; b. Hampton, Ia., Oct. 1, 1906; s. Ross Wells and Alvena Frances (Denison) K.; B.S., Ia. State U., 1931; m. Esther Valetta Siberts, Dec. 26, 1931 (dec. Feb. 1968); children—Patricia (Mrs. Ronald E. Schultz), Betty (Mrs. Frank Bartolett). Surveyman C.E. and TVA, Rock Island, Ill., and LaFollette, Tenn., 1931-34; with Bur. of Pub. Roads and Fed. Hwy. Adminstrn., Washington, 1934—, dir. Office Hwy. Operations, 1970—. Recipient Quality Increase award Bur. Pub. Roads, 1963; Meritorious Service award Dept. Commerce, 1951. Fellow Am. Soc. C.E., Am. Assn. of State Hwy. Ofcls.; mem. Am. Road Builders Assn., Hwy. Research Bd., Am. Pub. Works Assn. Home: 4919 25th Rd N Arlington VA 22207 Office: 400 7th St SW Washington DC 20590

KRUTCHKOFF, RICHARD GERALD, educator; b. N.Y.C., Dec. 23, 1933; s. Irving and Minnia (Michalinsky) K.; A.B., Columbia, 1956, M.A., 1958, Ph.D., 1964; m. Marion Belle Demme, June 12, 1960; children—Barbara, Robyn, Daniel. Instr. physics Wilkes Coll., Wilkes-Barre, Pa., 1958-60; lectr. physics Queens Coll., City U. N.Y., 1960-64; asst. prof. statistics Va. Poly. Inst., Blacksburg, 1964-65, asso. prof., 1965-68, prof., 1968—. Tech. adviser Water Resrouces Research Center Va., 1965—; adviser, Va. Center Environmental Studies, 1970—; pres., Stochastics, Inc., 1969—. Mem. exec. bd. Gilbert Linkous Elementary Sch. P.T.A. Fellow Am. Statis. Assn. (chmn. Va. chpt. 1972—); mem. A.A.A.S. (life), Biometric Soc., Inst. Math. Statistics, Internat. Statis. Inst., Water Pollution Control Fedn., Am. Inst. Physics, Am. Phys. Soc., Am. Math. Soc., Va. Acad. Sci. (chmn. statistics sect. 1972—). Author: Probability and Statistical Inference, 1970. Asso. editor Am. Statistician, 1969-72; editor in chief Jour. Statis. Computation and Simulation, 1971—. Contbr. articles to profl. jours. Home: 1302 Westover Dr Blacksburg VA 24060

KU, TIMOTHY TAO, educator; b. Chaochow, China, Mar. 26, 1926; s. Chu-Tung and Chao-Yuen (Yang) K.; B.S., U. Nanking (China), 1948; M.F., Mich. State U., 1950; Ph.D., 1954; m. Victoria Feng, June 17, 1950; children—Lawrence A., Albert J. Came to U.S., 1948, naturalized, 1962. Cons. forester T.S. Coile Inc., Durham, N.C., 1955-58; asso. prof. forestry U. Ark. at Monticello, 1959-63, prof., 1963—. Mem. Soc. Am. Foresters, Xi Sigma Pi. Lion. Home: PO Box 3067 U Ark Monticello AR 71655 Office: Dept Forestry U Ark Monticello AR 71655

KUBE, HAROLD DEMING, business cons.; b. Buffalo, Wyo., June 16, 1910; s. Carl C. and Inez (Mather) K.; B.S., U. Neb., 1932; M.B.A., Harvard, 1934; m. Shirley Smith, Aug. 25, 1934; children—Robert Ford, Thomas Smith. Statistician, Internal Revenue Dept., Washington, 1934-35; financial analyst Farm Credit Adminstrn., Washington, 1935-36; indsl. economist Dept. Commerce, 1936-41, economist, 1946-48 economist WPB, 1941-43; dir. planning and research div. Smaller War Plants Corp., 1943-44; with Cambridge Group Study, 1948-50; head econs. and statis. dept. Nat. Found. for Infantile Paralysis, 1950-51; cons. materials policy commn. Pres. of U.S., 1951-52; bus. mgr., treas., asst. sec. Jansky and Bailey div. Atlantic Research Corp., Alexandria, Va., 1952-63; prof. engring. adminstrn. George Washington U., 1963-64; mgnt. cons., asso. Resources Devel. Assos., Washington, 1964—. Dir. Washington Indsl. Investments, Fauquier Savs. & Loan Assn. Mem. Fauquier County Econ. Devel. Com., 1962-68, Fauquier County Planning Commn., 1968-72. Served with USNR, 1944-46. Mem. Am. Econ. Assn., I.E.E.E., Beta Gamma Sigma, Beta Theta Pi. Episcopalian. Co-author: Industry Action to Combat Pollution, 1966. Home: RFD 1 Broad Run VA 22014

KUCERA, LOUIS STEPHEN, educator, virologist; b. New Prague, Minn., June 23, 1935; s. Stanley Thomas and Helen Ann (Janda) K.; B.A., St. John's U., 1957; M.S., Creighton U., 1959; Ph.D., U. Mo., 1964; m. JoAnn Dorothy Martinson, Aug. 22, 1959; children—Gregory, Gary, Stephen, Scott. Postdoctoral fellow (applied virology) sect. microbiology Mayo Clinic, Rochester, Minn., 1964-66; postdoctoral fellow (basic virology) labs. virology and Immunology St. Jude Children's Research Hosp., Memphis, 1966-68; asst. prof. labs. virology and immunology St. Jude Children's Research Hosp., U. Tenn. Med. Units, Memphis, 1968-70; asst. prof. dept. microbiology Bowman Gray Sch. Medicine Wake Forest U., Winston-Salem, N.C., 1970—. Vice pres. Home and Sch. Assn. Our Lady Mercy Cath. Sch., Winston-Salem, 1973-74. Served with AUS, 1959-60. NIH research project grantee. Mem. A.A.A.S., Am. Soc. for Microbiology, Sigma Xi. Author: (with others) Fundamentals of Medical Virology, 1974. Home: 2951 N Bridge Rd Winston-Salem NC 27103

KUCHMAK, MYRON, chemist; b. Jaworiv, Ukraine, Mar. 26, 1915; s. Paul and Catherine (Fedun) K.; M.S., Lwiv Poly. Inst., 1939; Ph.D., Mich. State U., 1961; m. Luba Golenko, Nov. 1, 1943; 1 son, George. Came to U.S., 1950, naturalized, 1961. Instr. Lwiv Poly. Inst., Ukraine, 1939-41; research asst. Lwiv Chamber of Agr., 1941-44; lab., technician Mich. State U., East Lansing, 1956-58, research asst., 1958-61, NIH fellow, 1961-63; supervisory research chemist Center for Disease Control, Atlanta, 1963-70, chief Lipid Standardization Lab., 1970—; sci. dir. Internat. Reference Center for Lipid Determination in Cardiovascular Research, WHO, 1970—. Recipient Superior Service award Dept. Health, Edn. and Welfare 1965. Mem. Am. Chem. Soc., Am. Oil Chem. Soc., Am. Plant Physiol. Soc. A.A.A.S., in field to profl. jours. Home: 3288 Raymond Dr Doraville GA 30340 Office: 1600 Clifton Rd Atlanta GA 30333

KUDIESY, NORMA MARTHA, librarian; b. Burlington, Vt., Nov. 21, 1931; d. Jacob J. and Margaret M. (Alafat) Kudiesy; B.S., U. Vt., 1954; M.L.S., Tex. Woman's U., 1969. Br. Librarian Spl. Services Libraries, Ft. Bliss, Tex., 1967-69, reference librarian, 1969—. Mem. Altar Soc., Cath. Daus. Am., Tex., Border Regional (exec. bd. 1970-71) library assns., Am. Legion Aux. (sec. 1953-55), Northeast Bus. and Profl. Assn., Ninety Nines. Roman Catholic. Home: 5401 Raymond Telles El Paso TX 79924 Office: Spl Service Libraries Fort Bliss TX 79916

KUEBLER, GEORGE FREDERICK, mus. ofcl.; b. Rochester, Ind., Dec. 1, 1928; s. Frederick George and Loretta (Leyh) K.; B.S., Manchester Coll., 1950; M.A. for Tchrs., Ind. U., 1956; postgrad. Purdue U., 1960-62; m. Marilyn Joan Fidler, Aug. 19, 1950; children—Stephen, Michael, Susan, Richard, Jonathan. Art instr. Angola, Ind., 1950-55; elementary art cons., Elkart, Ind., 1955-58; asst. prof. art dept. Purdue U., Lafayette, Ind., 1958-65; curator extension service Nat. Gallery Art, Washington, 1965-70; dir. Hathorn Gallery, Skidmore Coll., Saratoga Springs, N.Y., 1970-72; dir. Oklahoma Art Center, Oklahoma City, 1972—. Cons. U.S. Office Edn., 1967-69, Pa. State Dept. Edn., 1965-66; asst. prof. George Washington U., 1966-67. Bd. dir. Art Edn. Workshops, 1960-65. Mem. Nat. Art Edn. Assn., Western Arts Assn. (sec., treas. 1962-65), Western Assn. Art Museums, Am. Assn. Museums. Home: 3024 Carlton Way Oklahoma City OK 73120 Office: 3113 Pershing Blvd Oklahoma City OK 73107

KUEHNE, HUGO FRANZ, JR., architect; b. Austin, Tex., Oct. 8, 1924; s. Hugo Franz and Sybil (Glass) K.; B.Arch., U. Tex., 1952; m. Marjorie Marie Willard, Oct. 29, 1971; children—Marja (Mrs. George Michael Douglas), Ruose Ryan Williams, Darius Meyers Williams. Draftsman, Kuehne, Brooks & Barr, Austin, 1952-57; asso. Keuhne, Brooks & Barr, 1957-60; bldg. insp. City of Westlake Hills, Tex., 1960, Westlake Hills Planning Commn., 1960-61; with Kuehne, Kuehne & Milburn, Austin, 1960-63; partner Kuehne & Turley, Austin, 1963—. Dir. Austin Civic Ballet Soc. Sec., City of Westlake Hills City Council, 1960-63, mayor pro-tem, 1962-68. Served with USNR, 1942-46. Mem. A.I.A., Tex. Soc. Architects, Sigma Chi, Sphinx. Conglist. Home: 3617 Westlake Dr Austin TX 78746 Office: Internat Life Bldg Austin TX 78701

KUEKES, EDWARD GRAYSON, psychologist; b. Berea, O., Aug. 12,, 1924; s. Edward Daniel and Clara (Gray) K.; B.A., Baldwin Wallace Coll., 1949; Ph.D., U. Tex., 1955; student Case-Western Reserve U., 1947-48; m. Roberta Jean Edmonds, June 3, 1950; children—Sherrill Jane, Edward David. Psychology trainee VA Hosp., Temple, Tex., 1951-52, Waco, Tex., 1952-54, VA Mental Hygiene Clinic, San Antonio, 1954-55; staff psychologist San Antonio Mental Hygiene Clinic, 1955-68; chief psychology service VA Hosp., Oklahoma City, 1968—, dir. Human Interaction Lab., 1973—; asso. prof. med. psychology U. Okla., 1968—, asso. dir. Internship Tng., 1968-73. Cons. State Alcohol Program, 1955-67, Alpha House, San Antonio, 1967-68. Panel moderator Tex. Employment Commn., 1968. Served with AUS, 1943-46. Decorated Purple Heart. Mem. Am., Okla. psychol. assns., Soc. for Preservation and Encouragement of Barbershop Quartet Singing, Singing Sooners, Lambda Chi Alpha. Home: Route 13 Box 110AA 6300 Commodore Lane Oklahoma City OK 73132 Office: 921 NE 13th St Oklahoma City OK 73104

KUFFREY, CLYDE EUGENE, dentist; b. Atlanta, July 17, 1929; s. Charles George and Mary Helen (Andrews) K.; student Coll. Arts and Scis. Emory U., 1948-50; D.D.S., Emory U., 1954; m. Valiere Jane Smith, Aug. 30, 1969; children—Lisa Carol, Robert Alton. Individual practice gen. dentistry, Atlanta, 1958—. Pres. Kuffrey Devel. Corp., Atlanta, 1969-70. Served with USNR, 1954-58. Mem. Am., Ga., No. Dist. dental assns., Fifth Dist. Dental Soc., Xi Psi Phi. Republican. Baptist. Mason (Shriner). Home: 4805 Cherrywood Lane Atlanta GA 30342 Office: 702 Medical Arts Bldg Atlanta GA 30308

KUHLER, RENALDO GILLET, mus. ofcl.; b. Teaneck, N.J., Nov. 21, 1931; s. Otto August and Simonne L. (Gillet) K.; B.A., U. Colo., 1961. Curator of history Eastern Wash. State Hist. Soc. Mus., Spokane, 1962-67; museum artist-illustrator N.C. State Mus. of Natural History, Raleigh, 1969—. Designer, executor of art work for awards, brochures, pamphlets and periodicals Dept. of Agr. in N.C., 1972-74; designer, executor of emblem N.C. Student Acad. of Sci., 1973. Mem. Nat. Trust for Historic Preservation, Am. Assn. Museums, Friends of Earth, Common Cause, N.C. Student Acad. Sci. (hon.). Democrat. Office: Box 27647 Raleigh NC 27611

KUHN, ANNE NAOMI WICKER (MRS. HAROLD B. KUHN), educator; b. Lynchburg, Va.; d. George Barney and Annie (Hicks) Wicker; diploma Malone Coll., 1933, Trinity Coll. Music, London, 1937; A.B., John Fletcher Coll., 1939; M.A., Boston U., 1942; postgrad. (fellow) Harvard, 1942-44, Boston U.; m. Harold B. Kuhn. Instr., Emmanuel Bible Coll., Birkenhead, Eng., 1936-37; asst. in history John Fletcher Coll., University Park, Ia., 1938-39; librarian Harvard, 1939-44; tchr. adult edn. program U.S. Armed Forces, Fuerstenfeldbruck Air Base, Germany, 1951-52; prof. Union Bibl. Sem., Yeotmal, India, 1957-58; lectr. Armenian Bible Inst., Beirut, Lebanon, 1958; prof. German, Asbury Coll., Wilmore, Ky., 1962—. Del. Youth for Christ World Conf., 1948, 50, London Yearly Meeting of Friends, Edinburgh, Scotland, 1948, World Council Chs., Amsterdam, 1948, World Friends Conf., Oxford, Eng., 1952, World Methodist Conf., Oslo, Norway, 1961, Deutscher Kirchentag, Dortmund, Germany, 1963, Internat. Conf. World Evangelization Lausanne, Switzerland, 1974. Recipient German Consular award, Boston, 1965, Thomas Mann award Boston U., 1967. Fellow Goethe-Institut fur Germanisten, Munich, 1966-68, 70-71. Mem. Am. Assn. U. Women, Am. Assn. Tchrs. German (del. conf. 1974), N.E.A., Ky. Ednl. Assn., Lincoln Lit. Soc., Delta Phi Alpha (award 1963, 65). Mem. Soc. of Friends. Club: Cosmopolitan (Lexington, Ky.). Author: (pamphlet) The Impact of the Transition to Modern Education Upon Religious Education, 1950; The Influence of Paul Gerhardt upon Wesleyan Hymnody, 1960. Home: 406 Kenyon Av Wilmore KY 40390

KUHN, CEDRIC W., educator; b. Milroy, Ind., Dec. 23, 1930; s. Paul Jacob and Effie (Eubank) K.; B.S., Purdue U., 1956, M.S., 1958, Ph.D., 1960; m. Barbara Jo Buhler, Sept. 9, 1956; children—Mark Alyn, Kathy Jo. Asst. plant pathologist Ga. Expt. Sta., 1960-65, asso. plant pathologist, 1965-68, dept. head, 1966-68, asso. prof. U. Ga., Athens, 1968-70, prof., 1970—. Scoutmaster, Flint River council Boy Scouts Am., 1963-65; mem. Council on Human Relations, 1963-67. Served with USMCR, 1952-54. NIH grantee, 1965-67; U.S. Dept. Agr. Co-op. State Research Service grantee, 1973—. Mem. Am. Phytopath. Soc. Am., A.A.A.S., Ga. Acad. Sci., Sigma Xi. Asso. editor: Phytopathology, 1972—. Contbr. articles to sci. jours. Home: 220 Davis Estates Rd Athens GA 30601

KUHN, CHARLES, indsl. exec.; b. Cin., Nov. 29, 1919; s. Leo and Vivian (Van Hallenger) K.; m. Elma Jane Smith, Nov. 19, 1943; children—James Roland, Karen Jo Ann. Vice pres. Fansteel Metall. Corp., 1950-55, Hills McCanna Co., 1955-58; v.p. Dresser Mfg. div. Dresser Industries, Inc., 1958-60, pres., 1960-64, group v.p., dir. parent co., 1964-65; exec. v.p., 1965-68, pres., 1968-70, also chief operations officer, dir. subsidiary cos.; pres., dir. Weil-McLain Co., Inc., Dallas, now chmn. bd., chief exec. officer; dir. Gen. Portland Corp., Dallas, Valley View State Bank, Dallas. Served with USNR, 1940-42. Mem. Am. Gas Assn., Newcomen Soc. N.Am., Am. Water Works Assn., Pa. Soc., Canadian Gas Assn., Tex. Mid-Continent Oil & Gas Assn., Home: 5015 Tanbark Rd Dallas TX 75229 Office: 10400 N Central Expressway Dallas TX 75231

KUHN, CHARLES HENRY, civil engr., city ofcl.; b. Cin., Feb. 25, 1902; s. Josiah N. and Clara (Mudersbach) K.; C.E., U. Cin., 1925; m. Florence Mildred Johnson, Aug. 19, 1925; children—C. Richard, Marilyn Ellen (Mrs. Wm. E. Harvey). Civil engr. Pa. R.R. M. of W., 1925; asst. city engr., Ft. Thomas, Ky., 1926-29, city engr., 1930-67, city cons., 1968—. Chmn. Hwy. Commn., 1956—. Vice pres. Campbell County Promotion Council, 1962—; bd. Campbell County YMCA. Named Ky. Outstanding Community Leader, 1952. Mem. Internat. City Mgrs. Assn., Am. Soc. Planning Ofcls., Ky. Soc. Profl. Engrs. Methodist. Mason Home: 32 Crown Point Fort Thomas KY 41075 Office: 130 N Fort Thomas KY 41075

KUHN, HAROLD BARNES, educator; b. Belleville, Kan., Aug. 21, 1911; s. John William and Ida Alice (Morey) K.; diploma Malone Coll., 1934; A.B. magna cum laude, John Fletcher Coll., 1939; S.T.B., Harvard, 1942, S.T.M., 1943; Ph.D. (Hopkins fellow), 1944, postgrad., 1965-67, 70; postgrad. study U. Munich (Germany), 1951-52; D.D., Houghton Coll., 1970; m. Anne Naomi Wicker, June 11, 1934. Ordained to ministry Soc. of Friends, 1935; pastor Rescue (Va.) Friends Ch., 1934-36, Dartmouth (Mass.) Friends Ch., 1939-41, Waldo Congl. Ch., Brockton, Mass., 1941-44; lectr. theology Emmanuel Bible Coll., Birkenhead, Eng., 1936-47; asst., dept. history Harvard, 1942-44; research fellow in philosophy U. Ky., 1944-45; prof. philosophy religion Asbury Theol. Sem., Wilmore, Ky., 1944—, chmn. div. theology, philosophy religion, 1959—; interim minister West Medway (Mass.) Congl. Ch., 1966-67; research scholar univs. Mainz, Erlangen, London, Free U. Berlin, 1960; lectr. World Congress Evangelism, Berlin, 1966: vis. prof. philosophy of religion Eastern Nazarene Coll., 1965-67. Observer, World Council Chs., Amsterdam, Netherlands, 1948; fellow Goethe Inst., Munich, Germany, summer 1967; lectr., retreat leader Ft. Campbell, Ky., U.S. Army, 1968; retreatmaster U.S. Army Europe, summers 1957, 60, 65, 68, 69-74, Chaplain div. Fort Polk, 1974; del. World Conf. Methodism, Oslo, Norway, 1961, Evangelischer Kirchentag, Munich, Germany, 1961, Dortmund, Germany, 1963; chaplains supply, missioner AUS, USAF, Europe, 1953-74; dir., lectr. Flying Seminar to Bible Lands, 1954; ednl. cons. USAF, Europe, 1951-52; prof. Union Theol. Sem., Yeotmal, India, 1957; lectr. U.S. Army War Coll., 1962. Inst. Social Change, Norman, Okla., 1965, 190th Anniversary U.S. Chaplains Corps, Berlin, 1965; protestant del. Notre Dame Conf. on Vatican II, 1966; lectr. Nat. Conf. Adult Christian Edn., Notre Dame, 1972; participant Internat. Congress World Evangelization, Lausanne, Switzerland, 1974. First aid instr. A.R.C., 1942; active refugee relief and rehab., Germany, 1945—. Trustee Melone Coll., Canton, D.; bd. dirs. Christian Freedom Found. Named Alumnus of Year, Malone Coll., 1968. Mem. Soc. Bibl. Lit., Am. Assn. U. Profs., Evang. Theol. Soc., Acad. Polit. Sci., Am. Assn. Christian Social Ethics, Am. Philos. Assn., Am. Assn. Tchrs. German (del. conf. Germany 1974), Delta Phi Alpha, Theta Phi. Club: Harvard Faculty. Author: Colossians and Philemon (Aldersgate Bibl. series); An Examination of Liberal Theology, 1943. Editor Asbury Seminarian, 1946—; cons. editor Zondervan Pub. Co. 1964—; editorial bd. Christianity Today, 1956—, contbr., editor-at-large, 1970—. Contbr. articles to religious jours. Home: 406 Kenyon Av Wilmore KY 40390

KUHN, RAYMOND EUGENE, educator, biologist; b. Biloxi, Miss., Sept. 6, 1942; s. Elmer George and Elma Jane (Cummings) K.; B.S. in Biology, Carson-Newman Coll., 1965; Ph.D. in Zoology, U. Tenn., Knoxville, 1968; m. Judith Ann Davis, Dec. 21, 1964; 1 dau., Rachel Elizabeth. Asst. prof. biology Wake Forest U., Winston-Salem, N.C., 1968—. Research participant Oak Ridge Asso. U., 1971. Mem. A.A.A.S., Am. Soc. Zoologists, N.C. Acad. Scis. (chmn. membership com. 1971-74, exec. com. 1972-75), Sigma Xi, Blue Key. Home: 501 Commonwealth Dr Winston-Salem NC 27104

KUIPER, JOHN BENNETT, govt. ofcl.; b. Ann Arbor, Mich., June 22, 1928; s. John and Elizabeth (Bennett) K.; A.B., U. Ky., 1950; postgrad. Ill. Inst. Tech., 1950-51; M.A., U. Ia., 1957, Ph.D. 1960; m. Ellen Tredway, June 27, 1953; children—Anne E., Paul B., John R., Mark T. Cinematographer dir. Reela Films, Inc., Miami, Fla., 1953-55; sound camerman NBC-TV, Africa, summer 1955; asso. prof. TV-Radio Film U. Ia., Iowa City, 1963-67; head motion picture sect. Library Congress, Washington 1965—; adj. prof. N.Y. U., 1973—; lectr. U. Minn., U. Cal., Yale, N.Y. U., Washington, others. Served with Signal Corps, AUS, 1951-53. Recipient Amsterdam Student Union Prize, 1960. Mem. Washington Film Council (pres.), Soc. for Film Study (pres.), Univ. Film Assn. Contbr. profl. jours. Home: 3801 Underwood St Chevy Chase MD 20015 Office: Library Congress Washington DC 20540

KULLEN, ALLAN SAMUEL, pub. co. exec.; b. Washington, Feb. 20, 1942; s. Sol and Eunice E. (Statland) K.; B.S. in Printing Mgmt., Carnegie Inst. Tech., 1963; postgrad. U. Cal. at Berkeley, 1964, Am. U., 1965; m. Diane Klein, Nov. 24, 1968; children—Allison Sondra, Todd Philip. Editorial dir. Books, Inc., Washington, 1965—, v.p., 1968—; dir. United Pub. Corp. Guest instr. for adult edn. program Cath. U., Washington, 1971. Created Internat. Library Negro Life and History. Home: 7723 Groton Rd Bethesda MD 20034 Office: 1213 K St NW Washington DC 20015

KUNIYOSHI, SEIJI, editor; b. Naha, Okinawa, Japan, Aug. 30, 1931; s. Yukei and Fumi (Toyama) K.; B.S., Jumamoto U., 1954; M.S., Northwestern U., 1960; m. Evelyn P. Eugenio, May 23, 1970; children—Narito, Lisa. Came to U.S., 1958, naturalized, 1973. Microwave engr. Ferrotec, Inc., Newton, Mass., 1963-64; with Scripta Publishing, Inc., Washington, 1964—, technical editor, translator, since 1964—. Mem. I.E.E.E. Home: 6230 30th St Arlington VA 22207 Office: 1511 K St NW Washington DC 20005

KUNKEL, JOSEPH EARL, bldg. constrn. exec.; b. Newport, Ark., Jan. 16, 1937; s. Karl Frederick and Ida Elnora (Johnson) K.; B.S., U. Ark., 1959; m. Terrell Jean Davis, Sept. 20, 1942; children—Kimberly Kay, Joseph Glynn. Sales engr. Armco Steel, 1959-65; mgr. bldg. constrn. Fraser Constrn. Co., Ft. Smith, Ark., 1965-68; pres. Kunco, Inc., Ft. Smith, 1968—. Active Boy Scouts Am. Lutheran. Home: 3825 Free Ferry Rd Fort Smith AR 72901 Office: PO Box 758 Fort Smith AR 72901

KUPPERS, JAMES RICHARD, educator, phys. chemist; b. Newland, Ind., Aug. 4, 1920; s. Herman Jacob and Gladys Caroline (Harlow) K.; B.S., U. Fla., 1943, Ph.D., 1957; M.S., La. State U., 1947; m. Faith Channell Farnham, Mar. 13, 1944; children—James F., Theresa H., Kathryn C., Mary (Mrs. Roy S. Smart). With United Fruit

Co., Panama, Costa Rica and Honduras, 1947-54; with E.I. duPont de Nemours & Co., Inc., Kinston, N.C., 1957-60; faculty Pfeiffer Coll., Meisenheimer, N.C., 1960-64; faculty U. N.C., Charlotte, 1965—, prof. chemistry, 1968—. Served to lt. (j.g.) USNR, 1943-46. Fellow A.A.A.S., Am. Inst. Chemists; mem. Am. Chem. Soc. (chmn. Carolina-Piedmont sect. 1971), Sigma Xi (pres. U. N.C. at Charlotte 1969). Patentee in field. Home: 3207 Connecticut Av Charlotte NC 28205

KURKE, MARTIN I., psychologist; b. Bklyn., Jan. 9, 1924; s. Jacob William and Miriam (Vexler) K.; B.A., N.Y. U., 1949; M.A., U. Buffalo, 1953; LL.B., LaSalle U., 1973; Ph.D., Am. U., 1963; m. Joy B. Edinger, Aug. 26, 1951 (div. Dec. 1971); children—Kathy A., David S.; m. 2d, Patricia Lee Crutchfield, Dec. 27, 1971; adopted children—Harold T., Kathleen J., Leslie B. Hedges. Engring. psychologist, operations research analyst Bell Aircraft Corp., Buffalo, 1952-54; research psychologist U.S. Army Human Engring. Lab., Aberdeen Proving Ground, Md., 1954-57; sr. human factors analyst Dunlap & Assos., Washington, 1957-61; sr. operations research analyst, prin. staff scientist Tech. Operations, Inc., various locations Va., 1961-68; program mgr., sr. research asso. Human Scis. Research Inc., McLean, Va., 1968-69; dir. research Aires Corp., McLean, 1969-70; chief drug control div., chief information devel. and analysis div., chief psychologist Bur. Narcotics and Dangerous Drugs, Dept. Justice, Washington, 1970-73, chief psychologist and chief spl. studies Drug Enforcement Adminstrn., Dept. Justice, 1973—. Pvt. practice psychology, Va., 1964-70; tech. cons. Psychotech. Lab., Bihar, India, 1967—. Mem. Democratic Com. Fairfax County Va., 1966-70. Bd. dirs. Koinonia Found., Springfield, Va., 1967-68. Served with AUS, 1943-46. Decorated Bronze Star, Purple Heart, Combat Med. Badge. Recipient Grand prize Aero Digest Design Forum, 1955. Fellow A.A.A.S.; mem. Am. Acad. Polit. and Social Sci., Am. Psychol. Assn., Am. Psychology Law Assn., Ergonomics Research Soc., Human Factors Soc., Law and Soc. Assn., Operations Research Soc., Sigma Xi. Contbr. profl. jours. Home: 4519 Arendale Sq Alexandria VA 22309 Office: Drug Enforcement Administration US Dept Justice 1405 I St NW Washington 20537

KURODA, PAUL KAZUO, educator; b. Fukuoka, Japan, Apr. 1, 1917; s. Kanjiro and Shigeko (Tanaka) K.; B.S., Tokyo Imperial U., 1939, Sc.D., 1944; m. Louise Morren, Sept. 16, 1953; children—Paul, Annette, Mitzi. Came to U.S., 1949, naturalized, 1955. Asst. prof. Tokyo Imperial U., 1944-49; asst. prof. chemistry U. Ark., 1952-55, asso. prof., 1955-61, prof., 1961—. Recipient Japan Chem. Soc. award, 1949, Am. Chem. Soc. Southwest award, 1970, So. Chemist award, 1973—. Mem. Am. Chem. Soc., Am. Geophys. Union, A.A.A.S., Am. Inst. Chemists, Geochem. Soc. Home: 908 Eva St Fayetteville AR 72701

KURRAS, HERBERT LEWIS, banker; b. Patchogue, N.Y., Dec. 15, 1932; s. Charles A. and Anna E. (Reuther) K.; B.S., Fla. State U., 1954; LL.B., Stetson Coll. Law, 1959; m. Diane Fisher, Aug. 11, 1956; children—Kevin, Sherylyn, Lisa, Heather. Admitted to Fla. bar, 1960; trust officer First Nat. Bank of Hollywood (Fla.), sr. v.p. Sun Bank of Bal Harbour, N.A. (formerly Community Nat. Bank & Trust Co.), Bal Harbour, Fla., 1964—, also dir. Mem. endowment com. U. Miami, 1967—. Mem. Corporate Fiduciaries Assn. S.E. Fla. (pres. 1972-73), Am., Fla. bar assns., Delta Sigma Pi, Delta Theta Phi. Home: 2100 N 51st Av Hollywood FL 33021 Office: 9600 Collins Av Bal Harbour FL 33154

KURTH, WALTER RICHARD, assn. exec.; b. Normal, Ill., Jan. 21, 1932; s. Walter H. and Irene (Freitag) K.; B.S., U. Ill., 1954; m. Mary Elisabeth Taylor, Aug. 23, 1958; children—Mary Helen, Sarah Jane, Elisabeth Irene. Publ. dir. Asso. Credit Burs. of Am., Inc., St. Louis, 1954-57, marketing dir., 1957-62, asst. gen. mgr., 1962-66, asst. gen. mgr., treas., Houston, 1966-68, adminstrv. v.p., treas., 1968-69, exec. v.p., treas., 1969—; vice chmn. bd. ACB Services, Inc., 1974—; sec.-treas. Credit Bur. Automation, Inc., Houston, 1966—; vice chmn. bd. Credit Services Internat., 1974—. Bd. mgrs. Thompson Retreat Center, St. Louis, 1963-64. Mem. Houston Dist. Small Bus. Adminstrn., 1971—. Republican precinct chmn., 1969—, chmn. dist. 15 fund drive, 1970—. Mem. Am. Mgmt. Assn., Am., Tex., Houston (pres. 1974) socs. assn. execs., Star and Scroll (pres. 1953), C. of C., Alpha Kappa Lambda. Presbyn. (elder). Mason (32 deg., Shriner). Home: 13422 Butterfly Lane Houston TX 77024 Office: 6767 Southwest Freeway Houston TX 77036

KURTZ, SAMUEL MORDECAI, architect, b. Russia, Feb. 21, 1904; s. Louis and Nadia (Form) K.; came to U.S., 1904, naturalized, 1919; grad. diploma in architecture Cooper Union Inst., 1925; certificate archtl./engring. design Columbia, 1927; certificate Coll. City N.Y., 1928-29, N.Y. U., 1942; m. Mary G. Weisthal, Sept. 3, 1928; children—Gerald Norman, Elliot Robert. With Architects, York & Sawyer, N.Y.C., 1926-27, Samuel M. Kurtz, architect, N.Y.C., 1947-54, Kiff, Voss & Franklin, architects, N.Y.C., 1954-71; pvt. practice as cons. architect, North Miami Beach, Fla., 1971—. Mem. N.Y.C. Mayor's Panel of Architects, 1950-70; mem. archtl./engring. selection bd. Bd. Higher Edn. N.Y.C., 1968-69. Fellow A.I.A. (Rutkins award N.Y. chpt. 1966); mem. N.Y. Soc. Architects (pres. 1967-68), N.Y. State Assn. Architects (award 1968), Am. Arbitration Assn. (nat. panel arbitrators 1950-70). Mason. Home: 3849 NE 169th St North Miami Beach FL 33160 Office: 16499 NE 19th Av North Miami Beach FL 33160

KURTZKE, JOHN FRANCIS, neurologist, educator; b. Bklyn., Sept. 14, 1926; s. John Ambrose and Teresa Rose (Knipper) K.; B.S. summa cum laude, St. John's U., 1948; M.D., Cornell U., 1952; m. Margaret Mary Nevin, June 30, 1950; children—John Francis, Catherine, Elizabeth, Joan, Robert, James, Christine. Intern, Kings County Hosp., Bklyn., 1952-53; resident in neurology VA Hosp., Bronx, N.Y., 1953-56; chief neurology service VA Hosp., Coatesville, Pa., 1956-63, VA Hosp., Washington, 1963—; instr. Jefferson Med. Coll., Phila. 1958-61, asso., 1961-63, asst. prof. clin. neurology, 1963; clin. asso. prof. Georgetown Med. Coll., 1963-65, asso. prof., 1965-68, prof. neurology, 1968—, prof. community medicine, 1970—. Cons. in neurology U.S. Naval Hosp., Bethesda, Md., 1966—, to Surgeon Gen. Navy, 1970—. Mem. task force on neurol. services Joint Commn. on Neurology, 1971—; mem. working group on epidemiology Nat. Adv. Commn. on Multiple Sclerosis, 1973—; mem. med. adv. bd. Nat. Multiple Sclerosis Soc., 1966—; mem. internat. med. adv. bd. Internat. Fedn. Multiple Sclerosis Socs., 1972—. Served with USNR, 1944-46; capt. M.C. Res. Recipient Certificate of Merit Surgeon Gen. Navy, 1969. Diplomate Am. Bd. Neurology. Fellow A.C.P., Am. Acad. Neurology (chmn. sect. on neuroepidemiology 1971—), A.A.A.S.; mem. Pan Am. Med. Assn., Assn. Mil. Surgeons, A.M.A., Am. Assn. U. Profs., Assn. for Research in Nervous and Mental Disease, Am. Pub. Health Assn., Soc. Epidemiology Research, Am. Epilepsy Soc., N.Y. Acad. Sci., So. Med. Assn. Author, co-author Epidemiology of Multiple Sclerosis, 1968; Epidemiology of Cerebrovascular Disease, 1969; Epidemiology of Neurologic and Sense Organ Disorders, 1973. Contbr. chpts. to textbooks. Home: 7509 Salem Rd Falls Church VA 22043 Office: VA Hosp Washington DC 20422

KURYLO, LYDIA MARGARET CARTER (MRS. WALTER KURYLO), librarian; b. Cawood, Ky.; d. Milton Russell and Alice (Browning) Carter; student Cumberland Coll., 1939-40; B.S., Union Coll., 1946; postgrad. U. Va., 1962-64, 68, Madison Coll., 1962, 67; m. Walter Kurylo, Mar. 2, 1946; children—Carter, Wally. Tchr. pub. sch. Harlan County, Ky., 1941-43; clk, D.C. Govt., 1943-45; Kindergarten tchr. Childrens' Workshop, Falls Church, Va., 1958; pub. sch. tchr., Fairfax County, 1959-61; librarian Annandale (Va.) High Sch. 1961—. Mem. N.E.A., Fairfax Edn. Assn., Va., Fairfax library assns., Beta Chi Alpha. Episcopalian (exec. bd. women's aux. 1960-61). Home: 3250 Peace Valley Lane Falls Church VA 22044 Office: 4700 Medford Dr Annandale VA 22044

KURYLO, WALTER, lawyer; b. Chgo., Oct. 17, 1914; s. William and Mary (Skrzat) K.; J.D., Washington Coll. Law (now Am. U.), 1938; student George Washington U., 1938-43, 46-47; B.S., Am. U., 1949, M.A., 1954, Ph.D., 1960; m. Lydia Margaret Carter, Mar. 2, 1946; children—H. Carter, Wally Clark (dau.). Spl. programs coordinator Bur. Pub. Rds., Dept. Commerce. Washington, 1935-59; mem. hearing bds. on Pollution of Interstate Waters of Mo. River by Sioux City (Ia.) and St. Joseph (Mo.), 1959; profl. staff mem. Senate Com. on Commerce, Transp. Study Group, 1959-61; transp. policy planning officer Bur. Pub. Rds., Dept. Commerce, 1961, exec. sec. Organizing Com. for 9th Pan-Am. Hwy. Congress, 1961-63, sec.-gen., 1963, chief studies and application staff Office Right-of-way and Location, 1964-65; transp. program planning officer Office Planning, 1966-68; chief state programs div. Office Pieline Safety, Dept. Transp., 1968-73; sec., dep. asst. gen. council Nat. Assn. Regulatory Utility Commrs., 1973—, part-time faculty mem. Sch. Govt. and Pub. Adminstrn., Am. U., 1957-69. Mem. staff Pres.'s Hwy. Safety Conf., 1946-47, Pres.'s Water Resources Policy Commn., 1950. Interagy. Water Policy Rev. Com., 1951, Subcom. on Benefits and Costs, Fed. Inter-agy. River Basin Com., 1951-53, Presdl. Adv. Com. on Water Resources Policy, 1954-55, Interagy. Com. on Water Resources, 1954-59; chmn. Fairfax County Citizen's Com. Sch. Bonds, 1965; mem. Fairfax County School Bd., 1967-70; chmn. Fairfax County Citizens for Superior Environment and Edn. Bonds, 1970. Served from pvt. to s/sgt. USAAF, 1943-46. Recipient silver service medal Dept. of Commerce; merit award Am. Assn. State Hwy. Ofcls.; Distinguished Service award as sec. gen. 9th Pan Am. Hwy. Congress; Exceptional Service award Dept. Transp., 1973; named Citizen of Yr. Fairfax County, 1966. Mem. Am. U. Honor Soc., Pi Sigma Alpha, Sigma Nu Phl. Episcopalian. Prin. author: Navigational Clearance Requirements for Highway and Railroad Bridges, 1955; also author tech. papers in profl. and trade jours. Directed nationwide study of navigational clearances in bridges across navigable waterways, 1952-55. Home: 2607 Midway St Falls Church VA 22046 Office: Nat Assn Regulatory Utility Commrs PO Box 684 Washington DC 20044

KURZHALS, PETER RALPH, aero. engr.; b. Berlin, Germany, Aug. 20, 1937; s. Rudolf and Ruth Elfriede (Steinhaus) K.; B.S. (with honors), Va. Poly. Inst., 1960, M.S., 1962, Ph.D., 1966; m. Dorothea Maria Frijters, Nov. 20, 1965; 1 son, Eric Peter. Aerospace engr. NASA Langley Research Center, 1960-66, head stability and control sect., 1966-70, head stability and control br., Hampton, Va., 1970-71; chief guidance and control Office Aero. and Space Tech. NASA Hdqrs., 1971-73, dir. guidance control and information systems, 1974—. Instr. undergrad. aerodynamics courses Va. Poly. Inst., 1961. Recipient Langley Inventions and Contbns. awards, 1965, 67; Langley Research Center Spl. Service award, 1967. Harvard Program for Mgmt. Devel. fellow, 1973. Registered profl. engr., Va. Mem. Am. Inst. Aeros. and Astronautics, Soc. Aero. Engrs. (chmn. missiles and space vehicle subcom. aerospace control and guidance systems com. 1963—), Sigma Xi, Tau Beta Pi, Phi Kappa Phi, Sigma Gamma Tau, Kappa Theta Epsilon. Club: Langley Yacht (Hampton, Va.). Home: 8411 Conover Pl Alexandria VA 22308 Office: 600 Independence Av Washington DC 20546

KURZWEG, FRANK TURNER, physician; b. Plaquemine, La., Aug. 7, 1917; s. Victor Julius and Willie Gertrude (Turner) K.; S.B., Harvard, 1938, M.D., 1942; M.S., U. Minn., 1947; m. Harriet Britt, Dec. 3, 1956; children—Frank Turner, Gretchen Elaine. Intern, Charity Hosp. La., New Orleans, 1942-43; fellow, 1st asst. surgery Mayo Clinic, Rochester, Minn., 1943-47; practice medicine specializing in gen. and thoracic surgery, New Orleans, 1948-56, Miami, Fla., 1956-68, Shreveport, La., 1968—; chief surg. staff Confederate Meml. Med. Center, Shreveport, 1970—; chief surgery VA Hosp., Shreveport, 1968—; instr. surgery Tulane Med. Sch., New Orleans, 1949-56; asso. prof. U. Miami Sch. Medicine, Coral Gables, Fla., 1956-59, prof., 1959-1968; prof., head dept. surgery, head div. surgery La. State U. Sch. Medicine, Shreveport, 1968—. Chmn. bd. dirs. Consol. Cos., Inc., New Orleans, 1951—. Served to 1st lt. AUS, 1942-43. Diplomate Am. Bd. Surgery, Am. Bd. Thoracic Surgery. Fellow A.C.S.; mem. A.M.A., La., Shreveport med. socs., New Orleans Surg. Soc., Southeastern Surg. Congress, Alumni Assn. Mayor Found., Soc. Thoracic Surgeons, Soc. Surgery Alimentary Tract, Alpha Omega Alpha, Nu Sigma Nu. Contbr. articles to profl. jours. Home: 6043 Gilbert Dr Shreveport LA 71106 Office: PO Box 3932 La State U Med Center Shreveport LA 71130

KURZWEG, ULRICH HERMANN, educator; b. Jena, Germany, Sept. 16, 1936; came to U.S., 1947, naturalized, 1952; s. Hermann Herbert and Erna Herta (Michaelis) K.; B.S., U. Md., 1958; M.A. (Woodrow Wilson fellow), Princeton, 1959, Ph.D. in Physics, 1961; m. Sophia Speth, Dec. 21, 1963; 1 dau., Tina. Sr. theoretical physicist United Aircraft Research Labs., East Hartford, Conn., 1962-68; prof. engring. sci. and mechanics U. Fla., Gainesville, 1968—; adj. asst. prof. Rensselaer Polytech. Inst. Hartford Gra. Center, 1964-67, adj. asso. prof., 1967-68. Fulbright grantee, 1961-62; recipient Sigma Tau-Beta Pi award for excellence in undergrad. engring. teaching, 1970, 73. Mem. Am. Phys. Soc., N.Y. Acad. Scis., A.A.A.S., Sigma Xi, Sigma Tau. Contbr. articles to sci. jours. and revs. Home: 3755 SW 6th Pl Gainesville FL 32601

KURZYNSKE, FRANK, mech. engr.; b. Fond du Lac, Wis., Nov. 6, 1925; s. Frank A. and Viola A. (Miller) K.; student Tex. A. and M. U., 1943; B.S., Tenn. Tech. U., 1959; M.S., Kan. State U., 1950; m. Edna B. Trent, May 24, 1946; children—Robert C., F. Richard, J. Kevin, Mark T., E. Todd. Design engr. Nashville Bridge Co., 1950-51; prin. house designer, plant engring. dept. AVCO Corp., 1951-55; cons. engr. E.C. Horn, 1955-57; owner F. Kurzynske & Assos., cons. engr., Nashville, 1957—, Knoxville, Tenn., 1972—. Bd. dirs. Family Life Services; trustee Madison Hosp. Served with USAAF, 1942-46. Mem. Constrn. Specifications Inst. (past pres. Nashville), Am. Soc. Heating, Ventilating and Refrigeration Engrs. Kiwanian. Clubs: Torch (Nashville); Nashville City. Home: 1105 Graycroft Rd Madison TN 37115 Office: 2020 21st Av S Nashville TN 37212 also 601 Concord St Knoxville TN 37919

KUYKENDALL, DAN H., congressman; b. Cherokee, Tex., July 9, 1924; s. Tom G. and Sarah J. Kuykendall; B.S., Tex. A. and M. U., 1947; m. Jacqueline Meyer, July 6, 1951; children—Dan H. Jr., John Meyer, Kathleen Virginia, Jacqueline Kay. Various managerial positions with Proctor & Gamble, Tex., Ky., 1947-55, mgr. 5 mid-south states, Memphis, 1955; with Equitable Life Assurance Soc. U.S., N.Y., 1965-66; mem. 90th-93d congresses from 8th dist. Tenn., mem. interstate and fgn. commerce com., transp. and aeros. com. Past chmn. Presdl. Task Force on Revenue Sharing and Govt. Reorgn.; mem. exec. com. Rep. Congl. Com. Served to lt. USAAF, 1942-45. Methodist. Home: 7902 Greentree Rd Bethesda MD 20034 Office: Longworth Bldg Washington DC 20515

KUYKENDALL, JOHN M., JR., lawyer; b. Charleston, Miss., Sept. 14, 1915; B.A., U. Miss., 1938, LL.B., 1940. Admitted to Miss. bar, 1940, U.S. Supreme Ct. bar, 1956; spl. agt. FBI, 1940-43; asst. atty. gen. State Miss., 1947-51; atty. Miss. Bldg. Commn., 1951-55; now mem. firm Overstreet & Kuykendall, Jackson, Miss. Served to lt. USNR, 1943-46. Mem. Hinds County, Fed., Am. bar assns. Club: Nat. Lawyers. Address: Overstreet & Kuykendall 829 Deposit Guaranty Bank Bldg Jackson MS 39201

KUYKENDALL, WILLIAM DEAN, banker; b. Henrietta, N.C., Nov. 9, 1936; s. John and Lorena (Banks) K.; bank mgmt. certificate U. Va., 1968; m. Faye Blankenship, Nov. 16, 1957; children—Debra Faye, Deana Louise. Br. mgr. First Nat. Bank of Danville (Va.), 1953-65; v.p. Schoolfield Bank & Trust Co., Danville, 1965-73; exec. v.p., cashier Bank of Hartwell (Ga.), 1973—. Treas. William T. Sutherlin Acad., 1969, trustee, chmn. finance com., 1969—. Club: Sertoma (past treas., dir.) (Danville). Home: 216 Athens St Hartwell GA 30643 Office: Corner W Howell and Webb Sts Hartwell GA 30643

KUYRKENDALL, ROY CLAYTON JR., architect, engr.; b. McComb, Miss., Mar. 16, 1923; s. Roy Clayton and Mattie Jane (Lang) K.; student U. Ala., 1946-48; LL.B., U. Miss., 1950, B.S. in Civil Engring. and B.S.E.A., 1952, J.D., 1965; m. Dorothy Mae Taylor, July 28, 1946; children—Karl T., Lisa Joann, Robert C. Prin., Kuyrkendall Assos., Hedrick, Harte & Kuyrkendall and Kuyrkendall & Proffer, Architects and Engrs., 1955-65; dir. constrn. East Baton Rouge, (La.) Sch. Bd., 1965—; works include Tara, Central, Belaire sr. high schs. Served with USAAF, 1943-46. Decorated Air medal. Mem. La. Engring. Soc., Nat. Soc. Profl. Engrs., Council Ednl. Facility Planners. Methodist. Mason (Shriner, 32 deg.). Home: 10887 Sandringham Dr Baton Rouge LA 70815 Office: 1050 S Foster St Baton Rouge LA 70821

KUZMICKI, FELIX DAVIS, city ofcl.; b. Wylam, Ala., June 30, 1912; s. William W. and Felicia A. (Thomas) K.; B.A., U. Ala., 1948; m. Alice Elizabeth Tamplin, Aug. 9, 1941. Pres., mgr. S.E. Engring. Service, Monroeville and Birmingham, Ala., 1948-51; engr.-designer John W. Galbreath, Birmingham, Phila., and Twin Harbors, Minn., 1951-54; cons., appraiser, 1954-56; pub. works adminstr., city engr. Office City Engr., Bessemer, Ala., 1956—. Mem. tech. com. Regional Planning Commn., Birmingham, 1967. Served to maj. USMCR, 1942-45. Mem. Am. Pub. Works Assn., Am. Rd. Builders Assn., Inst. Municipal Engring., 3d Marine Div. Assn. (regional v.p. 1967), Kiwanian. Home: 348 Park Av Birmingham AL 35226 Office: 1800 3d St Bessemer AL 35020

KWIE, WILLIAM WIE LIAM, environmental health specialist; b. Jakarta, Indonesia, Mar. 7, 1931; s. Teck and Nocs (Tan) K.; B.S., Bandung Inst. Tech., 1955; M.A., U. Tex. at Austin, 1958, Ph.D., 1962. Came to U.S. 1956, naturalized, 1971. Tech. dir. Columbia Organic (S.C.), 1966; research asso. U. Tex. at Austin, 1967-69; asst. prof. Cameron Coll., 1969-72; environmental health specialist Tex. Health Dept., Austin, 1973—; asso. prof. Huston Tillotson Coll., Austin, 1968-69. Mem. Am. Chem. Soc. (sec. Wichita Falls-Duncan sect. 1971), Am. Assn. U. Profs., Phi Lambda Upsilon. Editor: Current Abstracts of Chemistry and Index Chemicus, 1972-73. Home: 308 El Paso St Austin TX 78704 Office: 8520 Shoal Creek St Austin TX 78758

KWON, TAI HYUNG, educator; b. Yechon, Korea, Sept. 15, 1932; came to U.S., 1960; s. Myung Jin and Ki Young Kwon; B.S., U. Ga., 1963, M.S., 1965, Ph.D., 1967; m. Young Ju Choi, July 25, 1969; 1 son, Wade. Postdoctoral research fellow Ga. Inst. Tech., Atlanta, 1967-69; asst. prof. physics U. Montevallo (Ala.), 1969—. Served to capt. arty. Republic Korea Army, 1953-60. Recipient Wheatley Physics award, 1963; Frederick Gardner Cottreel Grantee, 1971. Mem. Am. Phys. Soc., Am. Assn. Physics Tchrs., Phi Beta Kappa, Sigma Xi, Phi Kappa Phi. Contbr. articles to sci. jours. Home: 1877 Tall Timbers Dr Birmingham AL 35226 Office: Dept Physics University Montevallo Montevallo AL 35115

KYLE, FRANK KENNETH, city ofcl.; b. Carthage, Mo., Oct. 3, 1919; s. Frank Luther and Iva Victoria (Fadler) K.; B.C.E., Mo. U. at Rolla, 1941; LL.B., U. Mo. at Kansas City, 1953; m. Freda Soulis, Mar. 1, 1953; children—Victoria Ann, Theodore Kenneth, Kathryn Nell, John Charles Phillip. Adminstrv. research asst. City Kansas City, Mo., 1953-54; city mgr., Chadron, Neb., 1954-57, Ashland, Ky., 1957-62, Independence, Mo., 1962-66; municipal mgmt. specialist for State N.Y., 1966-69; city mgr., Goldsboro, N.C., 1969—. Served as 1st lt. C.E. AUS, 1941-44. Mem. Internat. City Mgmt. Assn. (city mil. base relations com. 1973), N.C. City and County Mgmt. Assn. (dir. 1974). Kiwanian (dir. Goldsboro Club 1971-73). Home: 904 S Taylor St Goldsboro NC 27530 Office: PO Drawer A City Goldsboro NC 27530

KYLE, HENRY CARPER, III, lawyer; b. San Antonio, Dec. 19, 1937; s. Henry Carper and Marian Morris (Camp) K.; B.A., Rice U., 1959; J.D., U. Tex., 1964; m. Brenda Joyce Gary, Sept. 6, 1965. Admitted to Tex. bar, 1964; partner firm Kyle, Walker & Kyle, San Marcos, Tex., 1964—. Dist. chmn. Twin Valleys dist. Boy Scouts Am., 1966-67; pres. San Marcos Jaycees, 1967-68. Mem. bd. San Marcos Indsl. Found. Served to lt. (j.g.) USNR, 1959-61. Mem. State Bar Tex. (dist. grievance com. 1970—), San Marcos C. of C., Delta Theta Phi. Methodist. Rotarian. Home: 200 Ridgeway San Marcos TX 78666 Office: East Side Courthouse Sq San Marcos TX 78666

KYLE, JAMES WELDON, elec. engr.; b. Arden, N.C., May 14, 1909; s. Charles Wilburn and Dessie Haseltine (Lance) K.; student Nat. Radio Inst., 1928-32, Capitol Radio Engring. Inst., 1932-34, RCA Radio and TV Inst., 1946-47; m. Ethel Harris Owen, Apr. 6, 1957; children—William Charles, James Edward. Apprentice technician WWNC, Asheville, N.C., 1928-32; operating engr. WOS, Jefferson City, Mo., 1932-34; chief engr., v.p. Havens & Martin, Inc., Richmond, Va., 1934-65; chief engr. Roy H. Park Broadcasting of Va., Richmond, 1965-74; sales engr. video products div. AVEC Electronics Corp., Richmond, 1974—. Mem. adv. bd. Salvation Army, 1954-56, mem. social service center com. 1954—. Mem. I.E.E.E., Richmond Broadcast Engring. Assn. Baptist (life deacon 1953—). Mason (32 degree). Home 5811 S Crestwood Av Richmond VA 23226 Office: 2002 Staples Mill Rd Richmond VA 23230

KYLE, WILLIAM LOCKHART, JR., ins. co. exec.; b. Naysville, Ky., May 12, 1927; s. William Lockhart and Rebecca (Winter) K.; B.S. in Bus. Adminstrn., U. N.C., 1949; m. Jane Carol Tagge, Jan. 20, 1957; children—Celia William Lockhart III, Jane. Pres., Carolina Home Life Ins. Co., Jacksonville, Fla., 1958-65; sr. v.p., treas. Voyager Life Ins. Co., Jacksonville, 1965—; v.p. acquisitions Nat. Life of Fla. Corp., Jacksonville, 1968—; dir. Jacksonville Nat. Bank. Served with USNR, 1945-46. Mem. Financial Analysts Soc. Jacksonville, Jacksonville C. of C. Clubs: Timuquana Country, River, University (Jacksonville).

Home: 4637 Wadham Lane Jacksonville FL 32210 Office: PO Box 2918 Jacksonville FL 32203

LA BARRE, WESTON, anthropologist; b. Uniontown, Pa., Dec. 13, 1911; s. Isaac Weston and Artemisia van Meter (Hannah) La B.; A.B. summa cum laude, Princeton, 1933; Ph.D., Yale, 1937; m. Maurine Boie, July 9, 1939; children—John Boie Keasbey, David Quinton Lefebvre, Louise Anne Stephens. Research intern, Menninger Clinic, 1938-39; instr. Rutgers U., 1939-43; with war Relocation Authority, Topaz, Utah, 1943; asst. prof. Duke, 1946-48, asso. prof., 1948-58, prof., 1958—, James B. Duke prof., 1970—; tchr. summer schs. N.Y.U., 1942, U. Wis., 1947, Northwestern U., 1949, U. N.C., 1951, U. Minn., 1955; vis. clin. prof. U. N.C. Med. Sch., 1955—. Editor-in-chief Landmarks in Anthropology, 1965—; cons. Com. on Adolescence, Group for Advancement Psychiatry. Sponsor Durham Friends Sch. Served with USNR, 1943-46. Recipient Geza Roheim Meml. award, 1958. Sterling fellow Yale, 1937, Guggenheim fellow, 1946. Fellow Am. Anthrop. Assn., Current Anthropology; mem. Phi Beta Kappa, Sigma Xi. Author: The Peyote Cult. 1938; The Aymara Indians of the Lake Titcaca Plateau, Bolivia, 1948; The Human Animal, 1954; Materia Medica of the Aymara, 1960; They Shall Take Up Serpents: Psychology of the Southern Snakehandling Cult, 1962; (with others) Normal Adolescence: Its Dynamics and Impact, 1968; The Ghost Dance: Origins of Religion, 1970. Home: Mt Sinai Rd Route 1 Durham NC 27705

LABODA, GERALD, oral surgeon; b. Phila., Aug. 15, 1936; s. Lewis and Rose (Waldman) L.; student Temple U., 1954-56; D.D.S., Temple U., 1960; postgrad. U. Pa., 1960-61 ; m. Sheila Lois Plasky, Aug. 2, 1956; children—Amy Sue, Michele Beth, Alane Cheryl, Bruce Herbert. Intern oral surgery Jefferson Med Coll. Hosp., Phila., 1961-62, resident, 1962-63; practice dentistry specializing in oral surgery. Fort Myers, Fla., 1965—; mem. staffs Ft. Myers Community Hosp., Lee Meml. Hosp., Fort Myers, Lehigh Acres (Fla.) Gen. Hosp. Pres. Caloosa Aircraft Leasing, Inc.; pres., dir. Lamanda, Inc., Ft. Myers. Dir. Flordeco Inc. Bd. dirs. YMCA. Served as capt. Dental Corps, AUS, 1963-65. Diplomate Am. Bd. Oral Surgery, Pan Am. Med. Soc. Fellow Am. Dental Soc. Anesthesiology, Internat. Assn. Oral Surgeons, Internat. Assn. Maxillo Facial Surgeons; mem. Am., Southeastern Fla. socs. oral surgeons, Fla. Dental Soc. Anesthesiology (past pres.), Am. Dental Assn., Fla., S.W. Fla., W. Coast Dist. dental socs. Home: 5089 Northampton Dr Fort Myers FL 33901 Office: 3900 S Broadway Fort Myers FL 33901

LABOON, ROBERT BRUCE, lawyer; b. St. Louis, June 14, 1941; s. Joseph Warren and Ruth Evelyn (Aab) LaB.; B.S., Tex. Christian U., 1963; J.D. cum laude (Robert Storey, Jr. scholar), So. Methodist U., 1965; m. Ramona Ann Hudgins, Aug. 24, 1963; children—John Andrew, Robert Steven. Admitted to Tex. bar, 1965; asso. atty. Liddell, Sapp, Zivley & Brown, Houston, 1965-70, gen. partner, 1970—; dir. Westwood Commerce Bank. Sec., dir. Houston Estate and Financial Forum. Bd. dirs., mem. exec. com. Houston Epilepsy Assn.; bd. dirs. Found. for Children; dir., officer several pvt. charitable founds. Mem. Am., Houston bar assns., State Bar Tex., Houston Bus. and Estate Planning Council, Beta Gamma Sigma, Phi Kappa Sigma. Presbyn. Mason. Clubs: Houston, Plaza (Houston). Editor: Southwestern Law Jour., 1964-65. Home: 807 Hedwig Way Houston TX 77024 Office: 510 Gulf Bldg Houston TX 77022

LABORDE, ADRAS PAUL, editor; b. Bordelonville, La., Dec. 5, 1912; s. Enos J. and Lillie (Bordelon) L.; student Tyler Comml. Coll., 1929; m. Blanche Bordelon, Sept. 30, 1932; children—Joyce L., Adras P. (dec.), Michael A. Radio operator U.S. Mcht. Marine, 1929-32; bi-lingual newscaster radio sta. WWL, New Orleans, 1932-33; owner wholesale drug firm, Marksville, La., 1933-41; telegraph editor Alexandria (La.) Daily Town Talk 1945-50, editor, 1950—. Served with USAAF, 1941-45. Recipient 1st place ann. editorial contest U.P.I., 1962, 63, 64, 66, 68; Meehan conservation award Scripps-Howard Founds., 1966; decorated Knight of St. Gregory, 1972. Mem. Am. Soc. Newspaper Editors, Rapides Wildlife Assn., Young Men's Bus. Club (past pres.). Author: Roger Wilco, 1944; Ransdell of Louisiana: A National Southerner, 1951. Contbr. articles profl. jours. Home: 2107 Texas Av Alexandria LA 71301 Office: 128 Washington St Alexandria LA 71301

LABORDE, MARY PURCELL (MRS. JOSEPH GASTON LABORDE), club woman, ret. educator; b. Pelican, La., May 19, 1905; d. George Dowell and Ela Lee (Browne) Purcell; Christian culture diploma M.E. Ch. S., 1922; licensed instr., Mansfield (LI.) Female Coll., 1923; postgrad. La. State U., 1924, 45, Centenary, 1925-26; certificate N.Y. Sch. Interior Decorating, 1931; B.A., Nicholls State Coll.; m. Joseph Gaston LaBorde, Apr. 14, 1926; 1 son, Joseph Newton. Tchr. Caldwell Parish, La., 1923-25; tchr. S. Highlands Sch., Shreveport, La., 1925-26; tchr. Lady of Mercy Sch., Baton Rouge, 1958-60, St. Theresa's Sch., Sheveport, 1960-61, Trinity Elementary Sch., Baton Rouge, 1969-70. Recipient awards (2) Nat. Soc. So. Dames Am., 1966. 2d v.p. U.D.C., Henry W. Allen chpt., Baton Rouge, 1960-61, 3d v.p. Martha Ried chpt., 1954-57; bd. dirs. Children of Confederacy, Emma Gayle McFadden chpt., Jacksonville, Fla., 1955-57, dir. John McGrath chpt., Baton Rouge, 1958-60; mem. and del. Katherine Livingston chpt. D.A.R., Jacksonville, 1949-52, del. nat. congress, 1950, 63, treas., Kan Yuk Sa, 1955-57, del. state conf., 1964; organized Jr. Nat. Soc. Sons and Daus. of Pilgrims; active Gray Ladies A.R.C.; mem. Confederate Mus., Richmond, Va., 1971-72; hostess Found. for Hist. La., 1965-71. Mem. Descs. Knights of Garter, Plantagenet Soc., Ams. Royal Descent, Nat. Trust Historic Preservation, Magna Charta Dames (v.p. La. Soc. 1967-69, rec. sec. 1974—), Nat. Soc. Sons and Daus. of Pilgrims (gov. La. br. 1962-64, nat. rec. sec. 1965-66, del. nat. congress 1963, del. Gen. Ct., state registrar 1968-70), Nat. Soc. So. Dames, Am. (award 1966, charter; La. eye bank chmn. 1964-65, v.p. La. 1964-65, award of merit 1967), U.D.C. (nat. com. preservation hist. sites and records 1967-68, nat. and state geneal. records 1967-69, rec. sec. H.W. Allen chpt. 1966-67, chmn. music 1967-68), W.S.C.S., Tchrs. Assn., La. Parliamentarians, Nat. Assn. Parliamentarians, Huguenot Soc. La. (compiled handbook), Marquis Biog. Library Soc. (adv.), Washington Family Descs., Tex. Geneal. Soc. Methodist (youth dir.). Clubs: Music, Baton Rouge Women's; Baton Rouge Music. Home: 11645 Archery Dr Baton Rouge LA 70815

LABRY, DAN SMITHSON CLARK, food co. exec.; b. Jacksonville, Fla., Oct. 7, 1919; s. Walter Lee and Anna Mildred (Oliver) Clark; B.S., U. Fla., 1941; m. Helen Louise Seaton, Jan 28, 1944 (div.); children—Dan Smithson Clark, Robert, Lisa, Diane. With Labry, Snyder & Brodeur, Jacksonville, Fla., 1946—, pres., 1960—. Served with AUS, 1941-46. Decorated Legion of Merit. Mem. Pi Kappa Alpha. Democrat. Episcopalian. Rotarian. Club: Fla. Yacht (commodore 1970-71) (Jacksonville). Home: 1915 Larco Rd Jacksonville FL 32207 Office: PO Box 2728 Jacksonville FL 32203

LACAFF, TED BUNCE, JR., oil co. exec.; b. Emporia, Kan., Mar. 9, 1928; s. Ted B. and Doris (Broussard) L.; A.A., Lamar Tech. Inst., 1947; B.S., U. Tex., 1950; m. Mary Conley Jones, Oct. 7, 1951; children—Sally, Becky, Ted, David, Mary Ann. Geol. scout Gulf Oil Corp., Midland, Tex., 1950-52; petroleum geologist Argo Oil Corp., Midland, 1952-59; gen. supt. Tex. Am. Oil Corp., Midland, 1959-61, gen. mgr., 1961-63, v.p., 1963-68, exec. v.p., 1968-69, pres., chief exec. officer, 1969-70, dir., 1966-70; v.p., dir., Australian Oil Corp., Midland, 1963-68; v.p. Western Oil Shale Corp., Midland, 1965-68, pres. 1968-70, dir., 1965-70; v.p. Tex. Am. Sulphur Co., Midland, 1967-69, pres., 1969-70, dir. 1967-70; pres., dir. Pacific Union Gas Co., Midland, 1963-67; sr. v.p., dir. Internat. Energy Co., 1968-69, pres., chmn. bd., dir., 1969-70; pres., dir. Tex. Am. Oil Mgmt. Co., 1969-70; div. mgr. domestic oil and gas Am. Trading & Prodn. Corp., 1970—. Pres. Young Republicans, 1952. Bd. dirs. Am. Cancer Soc., 1966-67. Mem. Am. Assn. Petroleum Geologists, West Tex. Geol. Soc., Geol. Soc. Australia, Permian Basin Petroleum Assn., N.M. Oil and Gas Assn., Permian Basin Landmen's Assn., Sigma Nu. Roman Catholic. K.C., Elk. Clubs: Racquet, Midland Country. Home: 2100 Seaboard St Midland TX 79701 Office: 300 W Texas St Midland TX 79701

LACATSKI, ALBERT THOMAS, telephone co. exec.; b. Minersville, Pa., Mar. 10, 1926; s. Thomas M. and Anna (Kushlick) L.; B.S., Ind. Inst. Tech., 1951; m. Margaret Jane Mahoney, July 16, 1949; children—James Thomas, Carol Ann. Engr., So. Bell Tel. & Tel. Co., West Palm Beach, Fla., 1951-59, supervising engr., Delray Beach, Fla., 1959-66, dist. engr., Daytona Beach, Fla., 1966—. Served with USAAF, 1944-49. Registered profl. engr., Fla. Mem. Fla. Engring. Soc., Nat. Soc. Profl. Engrs., I.E.E.E. (past sec., vice chmn.). Home: 330 Emory Dr Daytona Beach FL 32018 Office: 711 Volusia Av Daytona Beach FL 32015

LACK, FREDELL, concert violinist; b. Tulsa, Feb. 19, 1922; d. Abram I. and Sarah (Stillman) L.; grad. Juilliard Grad. Sch. Music, 1943; m. Ralph David Eichhorn, July 10, 1947; children—Ardis, Eric Joel. Made debut as soloist with St. Louis Symphony, 1939; Town Hall debut recital, 1943; numerous recitals subsequently, at Town Hall, Carnegie Hall, Philharmonic Hall, Tully Hall (all N.Y.C.); tours in U.S., Can., Central Am., Hawaii, 1943—; featured soloist coast-to-coast Mut. Network radio program, 1946-47; concertmistress Little Orch. Soc., N.Y.C., 1947-49; founder, 1st violin Lyric Art String Quartet, Houston, 1956; rec. for Allegro, Mus. Appreciations: artist in residence, prof. U. Houston, 1961—, mem. Virtuoso Piano Quartet; ann. concert tour, Europe, 1959—; has appeared with orchs. including Pitts., Portland, Salt Lake City, Houston, San Antonio, Albuquerque, Tulsa, Baton Rouge, also BBC, Royal Philharmonic (London, Eng.), Rias (Berlin, Germany), Oslo, Stockholm Philharmonics, Concertgebouw (Amsterdam). Bd. dirs. Houston Humane Soc.; founder Young Audiences Chamber Music concerts, Houston. Recipient MacDowell Club Young Artists' award, 1942, Nat. Fed. Mus. Clubs Young Artists' award, 1943, Bklyn. Acad. Mus. Young Artists' award, 1945; one of 12 laureates of Queen Elizabeth of Belgium Internat. Competition, 1951. Home: 4202 S MacGregor St Houston TX 77004

LACK, LEON, educator; b. Bklyn., Jan. 7, 1922; s. Jacob and Yetta (Wolf) L.; A.B., Bklyn. Coll., 1943; M.S., Mich. State Coll., 1948; Ph.D., Columbia, 1952; m. Pauline Kaplan, Feb. 11, 1948; children—Elias, Joshua, Johanna, Adina, Evonne. Asst. prof. Johns Hopkins Sch. Medicine, 1955-65; prof. pharmacology Duke Med. Center, Durham, N.C., 1965—. Mem. Am. Soc. Biol. Chemists, Am. Pharmacology. Home: 2936 Welcome Dr Durham NC 27705

LACKEY, FRED THOMAS, JR., indsl. engr., govt. ofcl.; b. Tuscaloosa, Ala., Aug. 28, 1931; s. Fred Thomas and Ruby L. (Essary) L.; Asso. in Sci. Engring., Marion Mil. Inst., 1951; B.S. in Indsl. Engring., U. Ala., 1959; m. Nancy Zoe Greene, June 5, 1955; children—Thomas Ogden, Charmion Zoe, Lana Frances. Asst. civil engr. Ala. Hwy. Dept., Tuscaloosa, 1956-59; jr. indsl. engr. Directorate Supply and Transp., Mobile (Ala.) Air Materiel Area, Dept. Air Force, 1959-60, indsl. engr., 1960-61, project indsl. engr., team leader, 1961-64, staff indsl. engr. mgmt. engring., 1964-66; project gen. engr. NIKE-X Project Office System Integration Dept. Army, Redstone Arsenal, Ala., 1966-68, gen. engr., group leader for system requirements U.S. Army Safeguard System Command, Huntsville, Ala., 1968-73, gen. engr., group leader for Ground Support hardware containers, 1973—. Football coach Little League, Huntsville, 1966-67; mem. troop com. Boy Scouts Am., Huntsville, 1970—. Served with AUS, 1953-56. Recipient Sustained Superior Performance award U.S. Army, 1967, Outstanding Performance awards, 1972, 74. Registered profl. engr., Ala. Mem. Am. Inst. Indsl. Engrs. (sr.; sec., treas. 1962-63, pres., chmn. bd. 1964-65), Assn. U.S. Army, Greater Huntsville Round and Square Dance Assn., Tennessee Valley Square Dance Assn. (pres., chmn. bd. dirs. 1973), Lambda Chi Alpha. Episcopalian (house and grounds commn. 1972-73, chmn. stewardship commn. 1973). Clubs: Officer's (Redstone Arsenal); Mountain Squares Square Dance (pres., chmn. bd. 1971-72) (Huntsville).

LACKEY, GEORGE FINLEY, engr. exec.; b. Boaz, Ala., Apr. 11, 1927; s. Jesse James and Mae (Bruce) L.; B.S., Auburn U., 1952; m. Lois Jean Garland, Feb. 5, 1955; children—Heather Jean, George Finley. Engr. in tng. Elliott Co., Jeannette, Pa., 1952-53, application engr., 1953-56, field engr. Div. Carrier Corp., Atlanta, 1956-59; mech. engr. Gen. U.S. Army Missile Command, Redstone Arsenal, Ala., 1959-64, chief Aero-GSE Engring. Br., Nike Hercules Project Office, 1964-69, configuration mgr., 1969-71, configuration mgr. Air Def. Spl. Items Mgmt. Office, 1971-72, configuration mgr., chief Product Assurance and Test div., 1972-73, systems engr., spl. systems mgmt. office Nike Hercules div., 1973—. Served with USNR, 1945-46. Mem. Am. Soc. M.E., Am. Legion, V.F.W., Assn. U.S. Army, Nat. Rifle Assn., Sigma Phi Epsilon. Episcopalian. Club: Civitan (hon.). Home: 206 Lackey St Boaz AL 35957 Office: Special Systems Management Office Redstone Arsenal AL 35809

LACKEY, GUY ANNANDALE, educator; b. Sharon, Tenn., July 23, 1891; s. Benjamin F. and Mary E. (Harwell) L.; A.B., U. Okla., 1918; A.M., U. Chicago, 1924, 4 year grad. work; m. Florence Woodard, Apr. 7, 1917; children—Virginia (Mrs. C. C. Mathews), Woodard; m. 2d Wylma Black, Dec. 24, 1944; 1 son, Guy Annadale, Jr. Teacher and supt. pub. schs., Okla., 1910-21; head dept. edn. Chicora (S.C.) Coll., 1921-24, Huron Coll., S.D., 1924-25; summer instr. Central Coll., Okla., 1920, U. S.C., 1923, with Army A.C. Tech. Tng. Sch., 1942-43; collaborator and fellow U. Chgo. human devel. dept., 1943-44; prof. edn. and psychology Okla. State U., 1925-61, prof. emeritus, lectr. edn. and psychology, 1961—; vis. prof. edn. Southwestern Coll., Winfield, Kan., 1964-65; prof. psychology State U. Geneseo, N.Y., 1965-66; participant numerous work-shops, now cons. Mem. A.A.A.S., N.E.A., Nat. Soc. Study Edn., Pi Gamma Mu. Kappa Delta Pi, Phi Delta Kappa, Phi Kappa Phi, Psi Chi, Phi Beta Kappa Democrat. Unitarian. Author books, bulls., numerous articles. Home: 326 S Stallard Av Stillwater OK 74074

LACKEY, MONTGOMERY ISAIAH, educator; b. nr. Moulton, Ala., Sept. 20, 1934; s. Robert Isaiah and Luelen (Fergerson) L.; student Tech. Sch. USAF, 1955, U. South Fla., Nat. Aviation Acad., 1967-68; m. Maria Elza Cavalcanti, July 1, 1961; children—John Allan, Maria Lue. Jr. engr. Hamner Electronics Corp., Princeton, N.J., 1961-63; field engr., customer service engr. tech. rep. and computer div. Philco Corp., Phila. and Willow Grove, Pa., 1963; field engr. digital systems specialist Bendix Field Engring. Corp., Santiago, Chile, 1963-67; technician Geospace Systems Inc., St. Petersburg, Fla., 1968; instr. electronics and tech. Tech. Edn. Center (name changed to Pinellas Vocational Tech. Inst. 1970), Clearwater, Fla., 1968—. Rep., Nat. Assn. Securities Dealers, 1969—; free-lance flight instr. Mem. Civil Air Patrol, St. Petersburg-Clearwater Suncoast Squadron, 1969—; mem. com. Cub Scout pack com. Boy Scouts Am., 1972. Served with USAF, 1954-58. Mem. I.E.E.E., Am., Fla. vocational assns., Pinellas Classroom Tchrs. Assn., Pilots Internat. Assn. Home: 7073 Darien Way Clearwater FL 33516 Office: 6100 154th Av N Clearwater FL 33516

LACKEY, RICHARD STEPHEN, bus. exec.; b. Hinds County, Miss., Oct. 4, 1941; s. Claud Johnson and Jewel Margaret (Biggs) L.; B.S., Miss. State U., 1963; m. Saralyn Dickerson, Nov. 26, 1965; 1 dau., Ellen. With Lackey Lumber & Bldg. Material, Inc., Forest, Miss., 1965—, v.p., 1965—; pres. Deep South Oil & Gas, Inc., Forest, 1971—, Geneal. Reference Co., Inc., Forest, 1970—; with Lackey Charolais Farms, Forest, 1968—, pres., 1970—. Publisher, co-editor Miss. Geneal. Exchange Quar., 1970—; lectr. Nat. Archives Inst. Geneal. Research, Washington, 1972—. Mem. exec. com. Scott County Dem. party, 1966-70. Bd. dirs. Scott County A.R.C., 1965-68, chmn. bd., 1968-69. Mem. Miss. Cattlemens Assn., Miss. Charolais Assn., S.A.R., S.C.V., Order of Stars and Bars, Miss. (dir. 1974-76), Scott County (pres. 1965-67) hist. socs., Miss. Geneal. Soc. Baptist. Lion. Contbr. articles in field to profl. jours. Home: 438 E 1st St Forest MS 39074 Office: 100 1st Av Forest MS 39074

LACKEY, WALTER JACKSON, ceramic engr.; b. Shelby, N.C., Feb. 6, 1940; s. Walter Jackson and Ruth Hendrich (Dixon) L.; B.S. in Metall. Engring. N.C. State U., 1961, B.S. in Ceramic Engring., 1961, M.S., 1963, Ph.D. (Ford Found. fellow), 1969; m. Betty Waneta Peek, July 11, 1961; children—Amy Ruth, Laura Waneta. Ceramic engr. Batelle Northwest Lab., Richland, Wash., 1963-65; engr. Douglas Aircraft Co., Charlotte, N.C., 1965-66; research asst. N.C. State U., Raleigh, 1966-69; ceramic engr. Oak Ridge (Tenn.) Nat. Lab., 1969—. Instr. N.C. State U., Raleigh, 1961-63. Mem. Am. Soc. for Metals, Am. Ceramic Soc., Keramos, Sigma Xi, Phi Kappa Phi, Tau Beta Pi. Home: 103 Newcrest Lane Oak Ridge TN 37830 Office: PO Box X Oak Ridge National Lab Oak Ridge TN 37830

LACKEY, WILLIAM LEE, lawyer; b. Pensacola, Fla., Aug. 21, 1942; s. William Washington and Martha Ann (Williams) L.; B.A., Vanderbilt U., 1964, J.D., 1967; m. Linda Jane Smith, July 23, 1967; children—William Benjamin, Ann Elizabeth. Admitted to Tenn. bar, 1967, U.S. Supreme Ct., 1973; partner firm Lackey & Lackey, Savannah, 1970—; pres., dir. KLC Corp., 1973—; partner Tenn. Valley Title Co., 1972—. Bd. dirs. Lad and Lass Day Care Center, Inc., 1971—, pres., 1971-73. Served to 1st lt. AUS, 1967-70. Mem. Tenn. Bar Assn., Am., Tenn. (dir. 1972—) trial lawyers assns., Savannah Hardin County C. of C. (sec. 1973-74). Methodist. Lion. Author: (with Edward A. Kizer) Summary of Tennessee Law and Practice, 1969. Home: 1320 Morning Side Circle Savannah TN 38372 Office: PO Box 268 507 Water St Savannah TN 38372

LACKEY, WILLIAM W., lawyer; b. Nashville, Feb. 21, 1917; B.A., Vanderbilt U., 1938, J.D., 1940. Admitted to Tenn. bar, 1940; asst. dist. atty. Davidson County, 1945-48; mem. firm Lackey & Lackey, Savannah, Tenn.; U.S. magistrate, 1965—. Mem. Am., Hardin County, 22d Jud. Dist. (pres. 1969-70) bar assns., Bar Assn. Tenn. (legal aid and referral service com. 1958-59, chmn. domestic relations com. 1962-63, gov. 1968-71), Phi Delta Phi. Office: Lackey & Lackey 507 Water St Savannah TN 38372

LACY, DONALD MICHAEL, tv. exec.; b. Terrell, Tex., Sept. 22, 1938; s. Rex Edward and Gertrude (Hogan) L.; B.F.A., Tex. Christian U., 1957-61. With KTVT TV, Fort Worth, Tex., 1961—, asst. promotion mgr., 1964, sr. taping dir., Dallas 1965-68, prodn. supr., 1968—; operations mgr. KSTW-TV, Tacoma, Wash., 1974—. Cons., So. Methodist U., various advt. agys. in Dallas. Mem. Nat. Rifle Assn. (life). Home: 219 Elm Dr Terrell TX 75160 Office: 10111 N Central Expressway Dallas TX 75231 also 6111 N 15th St Tacoma WA 98406

LACY, J(OSEPH) TOLBERTTE, coll. dean; b. Augusta, Ga., July 18, 1915; s. James and Sarah (Tolbert) L.; A.B., Paine Coll., 1937; M.A., Atlanta U., 1955, 6th year specialist certificate, 1964; LL.D., Zion Coll., 1970; m. Ruth Yvonne Jefferson, Sept. 21, 1940; children—LaRonce (Mrs. Johnny Grissom), Reta Jo. Supervising prin. Central High Sch., Sylvania, Ga., 1940-71; dean student affairs Paine Coll., Augusta, 1971—; prof. Sch. Edn., Atlanta U., summer sch. Explorer Post adviser Boy Scouts Am., 1940-73; chmn. exec. council Screven County Citizens Betterment Council, 1966. Mem. local bd Selective Service System, Ga. Recipient Silver Beaver award Boy Scouts Am., 1960. Mem. Nat. Assn. Student Personnel Adminstrs., Ga. Tchrs. and Edn. Assn. (dir. 1963-65), Ga. Tchr. Edn. Council, Ga. Assn. Educators (chmn. profl. rights and responsibilities commn.). Baptist. Mason. Club: Schoolmasters. Home: 119 Clark Av Sylvania GA 30467

LACY, STERLING SMITH, JR., petroleum engr.; b. El Dorado, Ark., Dec. 5, 1924; s. Sterling Smith and Ruby Lee (Bailey) L.; student Ore. State Coll., 1944-45; B.S., Tex. A. and M. Coll., 1947; m. Emma Lee Morgan, Nov. 29, 1947; children—MaryEllen, Carolyn. With McAlester Fuel Co., Magnolia Ark., 1947—, dist. engr., 1952-54, chief engr., 1954-66, asst. supt., 1967—. Chmn. Magnolia Municipal Water Commn., 1956—. Mem. steering com. U.S. Regional Synod Ark., Okla., La., Tex. Presbyn. Ch., 1972, chmn. task force legal matters, trustees and founds., 1972, chmn. bd. trustees Synod Red River, 1973-74, rep. Gen. Assembly, 1974. Served with AUS, 1944-46; to 1st lt., C.E., AUS, 1951-52. Named Magnolia Young Man of Year, 1959. Registered profl. engr., Tex. Mem. Mid-Continent Oil and Gas Assn. (com. chmn. La. Ark. div. 1962-64), Am. Petroleum Inst. (chpt. chmn. 1950), Soc. Petroleum Engrs., Am. Inst. Mining Engrs., Am. Water Works Assn. Ark. Audubon Soc. (pres. 1967-69). Presbyn. (elder; moderator). Home: 203 Troy St Magnolia AR 71753 Office: PO Box 10 McAlester Bldg Magnolia AR 71753

LADD, JAMES WALLACE, retail co. exec.; b. Knoxville, Tenn., Mar. 23, 1929; s. James Franklin and Rosalie (Wallace) L.; student U. Tenn., 1951; m. Barbara McDonald, June 2, 1951 (div. June 1973); children—James Alan, Kathryn Diane, Cynthia Ann, Hugh McDonald. With White Stores, Inc., Knoxville, 1951—, v.p., 1970—. Dir. Bank of Knoxville, 1972—. Chmn. planning council United Community Services, Knoxville, 1968-70; v.p. Community Improvement Found., Knoxville, 1972—. Bd. dirs. YMCA, 1961-67, Travelers Aid, 1966—, Jr. Achievement, 1969—. Served to 1st lt. inf. AUS, 1952-54. Presbyn. (deacon 1954-67, elder 1967-70). Club: Cherokee Country (Knoxville). Home: 3624 Maloney Rd Knoxville TN 37920 Office: 133 N Broadway Knoxville TN 37901

LAFEVERS, ANCIL TILFORD, telephone co. exec.; b. Bexar, Ark., Jan. 26, 1922; s. Robert E. and Ora (Ross) L.; student Ark. Poly. Coll., 1940-42; B.S., U. Ill., 1948, M.Ed., 1956; m. Betty Mae Stice, Nov. 23, 1943; children—Nancy Ann, Becky Jean. Sci. instr. Birmarck (Ill.) High Sch., 1948-50, Altamont (Ill.) High Sch., 1948-50; exec. v.p. Nat. Trail Telephone Co., Altamont, 1952-62; pres., gen. mgr. Ill. State Telephone Co., Mascoutah, 1963-67; pres. Gopher State Telephone Co., St. Paul, Lake State Telephone Co., St. Paul, Minn. Telephone Co., St. Paul, N.D. Telephone Co., Devils Lake, divs. Continental Telephone Service Corp., 1967-68, v.p., gen. mgr.,

1968-71, mgr. Upper Midwest div., St. Paul, 1968-71, v.p., gen. mgr. S.W. div., Dallas, 1971—; pres. Continental Telephone Co. Tex.; v.p., gen. mgr. Bison State Telephone Co., Custer, S.D., Cornhusker State Telephone Co., Wisner, Neb., Haxtun Telephone Co. (Colo.), Mona Short Line Telephone Co., Sundance, Wyo., Hawkeye State Telephone Co., Knoxville, Ia. Telephone Co., Knoxville, all 1968-71; v.p. Bald Knob Telephone Co., Russellville, Ark., Central La. Telephone Co., Jena, Nassau Bay Telephone Co., Fairfield, Tex., Okla. State Telepone Co., Russellville, Ark., Tex. Tel. & Tel. Co., Fairfield, West Tex. Telephone Co., Andrews, Western Ark. Telephone Co., Russellville, all 1971—. Served with AUS, 1942-45. Mem. Ind. Telephone Pioneer Assn., Tex. Telephone Assn. (dir. 1971—, treas. 1972), Tex.-Okla. Telephone Assn. (treas. 1973), St. Paul C. of C. Democrat. Methodist. Mason. Home: 6641 Ridgeview Circle Dallas TX 75240 Office: 10300 N Central Expressway Dallas TX 75231

LA FLEUR, ROBERT ALEX, state ofcl.; b. Washington, La., Jan. 26, 1922; s. Alex Golden and Lima (Brignac) LaF.; B.S., La. State U., 1947, M.S., 1956; m. Cora Lee Babin, Nov. 25, 1950. Biologist Tex. A. and M. Research Found., Bryan, 1948-49; La. Wildlife and Fish Commn., New Orleans, 1950-62; exec. sec. La. Stream Control Commn., Baton Rouge, 1962—. Served with USNR, 1943-46. Named La. Conservationist of Year, 1969. Mem. Water Pollution Control Fedn., Am. Water Works Assn., Am. Inst. Biol. Scis., La. Biologists Assn. (chmn. 1961—, sec.-treas. 1962—), State and Interstate Water Pollution Control Adminstrs. (pres. 1970-71). Home: 1859 Shawn Dr Baton Rouge LA 70806 Office: PO Drawer FC La State U Baton Rouge LA 70803

LAFON, JOHN WALTER, san. engr.; b. Norman, Okla., Feb. 11, 1937; s. James Earl and Galdys Martha (Quigg) LaF.; B.S. in Civil Engring., U. Okla., 1959, M.S. in San. Engring. (USPHS trainee award 1962), 1963; m. Sandra Gaven Durden, Dec. 28, 1966; children—Pamela Louise, John Walter. Sanitary engr. Fed. Water Pollution Control Adminstrn., Jackson, Miss., 1964-66, Atlanta, 1966-67, Chattanooga, 1967-70; san. engr. Environmental Protection Agy., Chattanooga, 1970-71, Nashville, 1971—. Served to lt. AUS, 1959-63; sr. asst., san. engr. USPHS, 1964-66. Registered profl. engr., Okla. Mem. Water Pollution Control Assn., Commd. Officers Assn. Home: Route 3 Williamsburg Pl Franklin TN 37064 Office: Environmental Protection Agency 4004 Hillsboro Rd Nashville TN 37215

LAFON, WALDO SHOWALTER, utility co. exec.; b. Union, W.Va., Jan. 3, 1917; s. William M. and Jessamine (Showalter) L.; B.S., Va. Poly. Inst., 1939; B.S. in Elec. Engring., Mass. Inst. Tech., 1963; m. Elizabeth Stayton, July 6, 1973; children by previous marriage—Martha English (Mrs. Robert Stephenson), Rebecca English (Mrs. James Layne), Kathryn Steinmetz. With Appalachian Power Co., 1939-57, div. mgr., Beckley, W.Va., 1952-57; asst. gen. mgr. Ky. Power Co., Ashland, 1957-68, exec. v.p., 1968—, dir., 1966—. Dir. Am. Electric Power Service Corp., 1965—. Served to capt. Signal Corps, AUS, 1942-45. Mem. Ky. C. of C. (chmn. legislative com. 1970). Democrat. Mem. Christian Ch. (deacon 1960-70). Elk, Rotarian. Home: 3122 Calvin St Ashland KY 41101 Office: PO Box 1428 Ashland KY 41101

LAFONT, HAROLD MATHEW, lawyer; b. Conran, Mo., July 1, 1907; s. Lafayette and Clara (Vaughn) L.; LL.B., George Washington U., 1929; m. Jane Powell, Nov. 11, 1937; children—Bill, Gail (Mrs. Billy Huie). Admitted to Tex. bar, 1929; practiced in Plainview, Tex., 1929—; mem. firms LaFont, Tunnell Formby LaFont and Hamilton, 1929—; county judge Hale County, Tex., 1932-39; dist. atty., Plainview, 1942-49; dist. judge, Plainview, Tex., 1957-63. Dir. First Nat. Bank, 1963—, chmn. bd., 1974—. Mem. Tex. Ho. of Reps., 1949-53. Mem. State Bar Tex., Hale County Bar Assn. Mason (Shriner, 32 deg.). Kiwanian. Home: PO Box 1173 Plainview TX 79072 Office: PO Box 1510 Plainview TX 79072

LAFONTAINE, HARRY, motion picture co. exec.; b. Copenhagen, Denmark, May 23, 1913 (came to U.S. 1951, naturalized 1956); s. Henri and Johanne (Jensen) LaF.; B.M.E., Danish Inst. Tech., 1934; M.E.E., Aarhus Tech. U., 1938; m. Edith M. Harris, Oct. 24, 1960. Roving news reel camerman, 1934-39; produced War in Finland full length documentary feature, several major releases, 1945-50, including Red Menace, 1950; motion picture instr. U. Houston, 1951-53; pres., chmn. Nationwide Sch. Cinematography, Miami, Fla., 1954—; owner LaFontaine Prodns. Served as capt., 1939-40, group comdr. Danish Underground, 1940-45. Decorated Mannerheim War medal, Suomi Vinter War medal. Clubs: Royal Danish Yacht (Copenhagen); International Adventure (London); Racquet and Yacht (Maimi and France). Home: 7930 East Dr Miami Beach FL 33141 Office: Parkley House PO Box 551 Miami FL 33138

LAGAN, HENRY DUANE, physician; b. Enid, Okla., Nov. 30, 1932; s. James Henry and Thelma Estelle (Lyday) L.; B.S., Phillips U., 1954; M.D., U. Okla., 1964; m. Lota Dee Bouher, May 14, 1955; children—Duana Dee, Lynn Alison, Tim Duane, Lee Andrew. Intern Wesley Med. Center, Wichita, Kan., 1964-65; practice family medicine, Okeene, Okla., 1965-70, 71—; dir. student health service Oral Roberts U., Tulsa, 1970-71; asso. preceptor U. Okla. Sch. Medicine, 1965—; team physician Okeene High Sch., 1965—. Served with USAF, 1954-57. Mem. Am. Coll. Sports Medicine, A.M.A., Okla. State Med. Assn., Am. Acad. Family Practice. Republican. Methodist (mem. ofcl. bd. 1970—, lay del. 1971-74). Home: PO Box 395 Okeene OK 73763 Office: PO Box 389 Okeene OK 73763

LAGATTUTA, VINCENT LOUIS, JR., oral surgeon, educator; b. New Orleans, Mar. 25, 1931; s. Vincent Louis and Evelyn Marie (Bel) L.; B.S., U. Southwestern La., 1953; D.D.S., Loyola U. of South, 1956; certificate U. Pa., 1960; m. Mary Margaret Ehrensing, June 27, 1955; children—Margaret, Vincent H., Mark, Paul, Anne, Louis. Intern in oral surgery Charity Hosp., New Orleans, 1956-57, sr. resident in oral surgery, 1960-61; instr. oral pathology, Loyola U., 1960-61; pvt. practice oral surgery, Baton Rouge, La., 1961—; asso. clin. prof. oral surgery La. State U., Baton Rouge, 1969—; chief oral surgery div. Earl K. Long Hosp., Baton Rouge, 1969—; chief dental staff Our Lady of the Lake Hosp., 1966-67, Baton Rouge Gen. Hosp., 1965-66. Served with USAF, 1957-59. Diplomate Am. Bd. Oral Surgery. Fellow Internat. Assn. Oral Surgeons; mem. Am., Southeastern socs. oral surgeons, Pan Am. Med. Assn., La. Soc. Oral Surgeons, A.A.A.S., Am., La., 6th Dist. dental assns., Pierre Fauchard Acad., Blue Key, Xi Psi Phi. K.C. Club: Serra (Baton Rouge). Home: 1659 S Tamarix St Baton Rouge LA 70808 Office: 3850 Convention St Baton Rouge LA 70806

LAHR, NIELS LONGFIELD, elec. engr.; b. Babson Park, Fla., Apr. 18, 1933; s. Ralph Oliver and Muriel (Longfield-Smith) L.; B.S. in Elec. Engring., U. Fla., 1957; m. Mary Ann Newman, May 5, 1957; children—Sharon Denise, Susan Longfield, Kelly Anna, Shanna Lynn. Space test vehicle engr. Boeing Co., Kennedy Space Center, Cape Kennedy, Fla., 1957—. Named to Apollo/Saturn V Roll of Honor, 1972. Methodist (mem. adminstrv. bd.), Collaborator NASA tech. disclosure, 1970. Home: 27 Valencia Rd Rockledge FL 32955

LAI, VINCENT CHINTU, hydraulic engr.; b. Changhua, Formosa, Aug. 5, 1930; s. Huosheng and Kao Luan (Kao) L.; B.S., Nat. Taiwan U., 1953; M.S., U. Ia., 1957; Ph.D. (Univ. fellow), U. Mich., 1962; m. Sue Shu-Chen Yang, Aug. 24, 1963; children—Albert H., Emily H. Came to U.S., 1955, naturalized, 1969. Civil engr. pub. works div. Dept. Constrn., Taiwan Provincial Govt., 1954-55; research hydraulic engr. water resources div. U.S. Geol. Survey, Washington, 1961-63, Portland, Ore., 1963-65, Arlington, Va., 1965-73, Reston, Va., 1973—. Asso. prof. civil engring. Howard U., Washington, 1972—. Mem. Am. Soc. C.E., Assn. Computing Machinery, Am. Geophys. Union, Internat. Assn. Hydraulic Research, Sigma Xi. Home: 6814 Glenmont St Falls Church VA 22042 Office: Water Resources Div US Geol Survey Reston VA 22092

LAIER, JAMES EMIL, civil engr.; b. Allentown, Pa., May 15, 1941; s. Emil Albert and Hildegard (Nussbaumer) L.; B.S., Citadel, 1964; M.S., W.Va. U., 1965; Ph.D., U. Fla., 1973; m. Diana Lynn Kahler, June 27, 1964; children—Constance Lynn, Debra Ann. Soils engr. McClelland Engrs., Houston, 1972-73; soils engr., Law Engring. Testing Co., Tampa, Fla., 1973—. Served to capt. C.E., AUS, 1965-69. Decorated Bronze Star, Commendation medal, Air medal. Recipient Student award Am. Soc. C.E., 1965. Mem. Am. Soc. C.E. (sec., treas. soils and structural group 1973—), Nat. Soc. Profl. Engrs., Assn. of Citadel Men, Internat. Soc. Soil Mechanics and Found. Engrs., Sigma Chi. Home: 6915 Williams Dr Tampa FL 33614 Office: PO Box 15697 Tampa FL 33614

LAIL, EUGENE FRANKLIN, ednl. adminstr.; b. Shelby, N.C., Feb. 8, 1922; s. Tinsley Peter and Hettie Pearl (Parker) L.; B.A., Furman U., 1949, M.A., 1957; Edn. Specialist, U. Ga., 1962; m. Carolyn Elizabeth Brooks, Mar. 21, 1951; 1 dau., Eugenia Elizabeth. Student dir. Furman U. Bands, 1946-49; band dir. pub. schs., Greer, S.C., 1950-53; dir. music, pub. schs., Williamston, 1953-57, coordinator music Crisp County Schs., Cordele, Ga., 1957-62; prin. elementary sch., Vienna, 1962-65; supervising prin. Harlem Pub. Schs., 1965-68; asst. prof. edn. Ga. Coll., Milledgeville, 1968-70; prin. Putnam County High Sch., Eatonton, Ga., 1970—; musical arranger, condr. Lail Merritt Orch., 1951-57; trombonist Greenville (S.C.) Symphony Orch., 1951-57. Cons., Baldwin County Schs., Ga., 1970-72, Ga. Coll. at Milledgeville, 1970-71; dir. vocational edn. Putnam County Schs., Eatonton, 1971-72. Musical arranger, dir. S.C. Am. Legion Drum and Bugle Corps, 1955-56; columnist Eatonton Messenger. Served with AUS, 1942-45. Named Star Tchr., Ga. State C. of C., 1959. Mem. Nat., Ga. edn. assns., Nat. Assn. Secondary Sch. Prins., Am. Assn. U. Profs., Woodmen of the World, Phi Delta Kappa. Mason, Kiwanian. Composer: Brazilica, 1957, Street Scenes for Band, 1962. Author: Functional Factors in Native Musical Ability that Relate to School Achievement, 1957. Home: 113 Westminister Dr Eatonton GA 31024 Office: 305 N Madison Av Eatonton GA 31024

LAINE, WILLIAM JOHN, textile co. exec.; b. N.Y.C., June 23, 1922; s. John Joseph and Alice (Merlinjones) L.; student Princeton, 1944; m. Laurie Caulway, Dec. 3, 1949; children—William John, Peter Bradford. Field service engr. Pratt & Whitney Aircraft, East Hartford, Conn., 1942-44; selling agt. textiles, 1947-55; v.p. Mass. Mohair Plush Co., N.Y.C., 1956-60, 65-68; pres. Rockingham Mills, (N.C.), 1960-61; pres. Carpet Industries, Inc., Kings Mountain, N.C., 1968—; v.p. Neisco Industries, Inc., 1973—. Served with USAAF, 1944-46. Home: 2647 Hampton Av Charlotte NC 28207 Office: Carpet Industries Inc Kings Mountain NC 28086 also Neisco Industries Inc Kings Mountain NC 28086

LAING, WILLIAM GAVIN, physician; b. Atlanta, Feb. 5, 1932; s. John Gavin and Leora (Pollock) L.; B.S., U. Tenn., 1951; M.D., U. Tenn., 1955; m. June Ann McBee, June 16, 1959; children—Leslie Ann, Lance Gavin, Grant Gavin, Katherine Ann, Cynthia Ann. Intern, St. Thomas Hosp., Nashville, 1955-56; resident internal medicine Cooke County Hosp., Chgo., 1959-61; resident gastroenterology Hines (Ill.) VA Hosp., 1961-62, chief resident, 1962; practice medicine specializing in gastroenterology, Knoxville, Tenn., 1962—; mem. teaching staff U. Tenn. Meml. Research Center and Hosp., Knoxville, 1962—; chief medicine Ft. Sanders Presbyn. Hosp., 1965, 66, 73, mem. exec. com. 1965-67, 73; treas. Academic Enterprises, Knoxville, 1971-73; mem. liaison com. East Tenn. Nursing Assn., 1973—. Served with USN, 1957-59. Mem. Knoxville Acad. Medicine (treas. 1973-74, Knoxville Acad. Medicine (mem. exec. council 1973-74, chmn. diet manual com. 1972). Club: Century. Home: 303 Weisgarber St Knoxville TN 37919 Office: 1928 Alcoa Hwy Physicians Office Bldg Knoxville TN 37920

LAIR, HARRY REDMON, lawyer; b. Cynthiana, Ky., Apr. 28, 1910; s. Redmon Eugene and Bessie Clay (Dedman) L.; student Ga. Mil. Acad., 1927-29; B.S., U. Ky., 1933; LL.B., Jefferson Sch. Law, 1936; LL.B., U. Louisville, 1951; m. Margaret Jabine Newsom., Dec. 21, 1940; children—Jennie Scott, Harry Redmon. Admitted to Ky. bar, 1936; master commr. Harrison Circuit Ct., 1937—; gen. counsel Harrison Rural Electric Coop. Corp., 1939—; Cynthiana City atty., 1942-54, 58-66; spl. circuit judge Harrison Circuit Ct., 1951, 53, 55; atty. Farmers Nat. Bank, 1957—. Mem. Am., Ky., Harrison County (past pres.) bar assns., Phi Delta Theta, Omicron Delta, Kappa, Delta Sigma Phi. Presbyn. Home: 550 E Pike Cynthiana KY 41031 Office: 11 E Pike St Cynthiana KY 41031

LAIR, NARD, physician; b. Amarillo, Tex., June 7, 1916; s. Albert H. and May (Lair) Jett; B.S., Tex. Tech. U., 1939, M.S., 1940; M.D., U. Tenn., 1947; m. Clara Lee Hethcoat, Feb. 14, 1948; children—Dana, Marcy, Kevin. Intern Baylor U. Hosp., Dallas, 1947-48; resident in surgery Norfolk Gen. Hosp. (Va.), 1948-49; pvt. practice medicine specializing in surgery and aerospace medicine, Dallas, 1952—; mem. staffs Baylor Med. Center, Dallas, St. Paul Hosp., Dallas, NASA, Houston. Cons. FAA, 1958—, med. div. FBI, 1959—, CIA, 1959—; med. monitor, observer Apollo 11-Apollo 16, also Skylab I, II, III. Served with AUS, 1943-46. Named Hon. Med. Cons. to Queen Eng., 1971. Fellow Am. Acad. Family Practice, Dallas So. Clin. Soc., Royal Soc. Health (London), Am. Acad. Air Controllers; mem. Civil Air Med. Assn., Air Medics Med. Aviation Assn., Pan Am., Tex. med. assns., Tex. Aeros. Commn., Am. Soc. X-Ray Technicians, Mensa, Flying Physicians Assn., Am. Guild Organists, Phi Beta Pi. Home: 9331 Lake Highlands Dr Dallas TX 75218

LAIRD, ANGUS MCKENZIE, found. exec.; b. Opp, Ala., Oct. 9, 1903; s. John Henry and Ada (Zorn) L.; A.B., U. Fla., 1927, M.A., 1928; postgrad. Syracuse U., 1928-29, U. Chgo., 1930-31; m. Myra Adelia Doyle, June 8, 1938; children—Victoria Mell (Mrs. Henry Ackerman), Nan McKenzie (Mrs. Samuel Hughes). Teaching fellow Syracuse U., 1928-29; prof. history and polit. sci. U. Fla., Gainesville, 1929-30, 37-46, U. Denver, 1931-37; dir. Fla. Merit System, Tallahassee, 1946-60; v.p., dir. Municipal Code Corp., Inc., Old St. Augustine Road Estates, Inc.; pres. Huesack Enterprises, Inc.; editor Wakulla News, 1967-71, editor emeritus, 1971—; pres. Fla. Heritage Found., 1973—. Recipient citation Fla. Cabinet, 1961. Mem. Fla. Pub. Health Assn. (pres. 1955), Fla. Pub. Personnel Assn. (pres. 1953), Pub. Personnel Assn. U.S. and Can. (hon., exec. council 1958-60), Fla. Heritage Found. (pres. 1973—), Kappa Sigma (historian). Author: City Manager Government in Florida, 1929; (with Wilson K. Doyle) Government and Administration in Florida, 1955; Centennial History of Kappa Sigma, 1969. Home: 507 Plantation Rd Tallahassee FL 32303

LAIRD, LESBIA REESE (MRS. DENNIS ELVIN LAIRD), librarian; b. Winfield, Ala., Oct. 24, 1918; d. John Houston and Callie (Gilpin) Reese; student Tex. Coll. Arts and Industries, 1936-37; B.A., Tex. Womens U., 1941; student N. Tex. State U., summer 1942; m. Dennis Elvin Laird, Nov. 24, 1956. Librarian high sch., Mercedes, Tex., 1941-44, U.S. Naval Air Tng. Sta., Corpus Christi, Tex., 1944-46, U.S. Army, Camp Lee, Va., 1946-47, Germany, 1947-52, USAF, Wolters AFB, Mineral Wells, Tex., 1952-55, Brooks AFB, Tex., 1955—. Mem. Tex., Bexar County, Southwestern library assns., Beta Sigma Phi. Democrat. Home: Route 14 Box 345 San Antonio TX 78221 Office: Base Library Brooks AFB TX 78235

LAIRD, WILSON MORROW, petroleum assn. exec.; b. Erie, Pa., Mar. 4, 1915; s. Charles William and Elizabeth (Morrow) L.; B.A. cum laude, Muskingum Coll., 1936, D. Sc., 1964; M.A., U. N.C., 1938; Ph.D., U. Cin., 1942; m. Reba Allene Latimer, Aug. 8, 1938; children—Douglas, David, Donald, Dorothy (Mrs. Dennis Kaatz). Geologist Pa. Geol. Survey, summers 1936, 37, 40; prof. geology, head dept. U. N.D., 1940-69; dir. Office Oil and Gas, Dept. Interior, Washington, 1969-71; dir. exploration Am. Petroleum Inst., Washington, 1971—; N.D. state geologist, 1941-69; geologist U.S. Geol. Survey, summers 1944, 45. Fellow Geol. Soc. Am.; Mem. Am. Assn. Petroleum Geologists (Pres.'s award 1947), N.D. Acad. Sci., Washington Geol. Soc., Assn. Geology Tchrs., Sigma Xi, Sigma Gamma Epsilon. Club: Touchdown (Washington). Contbr. articles to profl. jours. Home: 1807 Wainwright Dr Reston VA 22090 Office: Am Petroleum Inst 1801 K St NW Washington DC 20006

LAIRSON, EARL CHARLES, accountant; b. McComb, Okla., Feb. 12, 1928; s. William Henry and Mattie Lea (Pierce) L.; B.S., U. Okla., 1950; m. Virginia Lou Cagle, Dec. 22, 1951; children—Karen, Mark Earl, Eric Charles, Dawn. Mgr., Ernst & Ernst, C.P.A.'s, Houston, 1952-68; partner, Main Lafrentz & Co., C.P.A.'s, Houston, 1968-70; owner, partner Earl Lairson & Co., C.P.A.'s, Houston, 1970—. Served with AUS, 1946-47. C.P.A., Tex., Okla., La. Mem. Am. Inst. C.P.A.'s, Nat. Assn. Accountants, Am. Accounting Assn. Mason (Shriner). Club: Houston. Home: 5010 Park Gate Houston TX 77002 Office: 1512 Bank Southwest Bldg Houston TX 77002

LAIT, ROBERT MORRIS, wholesale trade co. exec.; b. El Paso, Tex., Sept. 1, 1928; s. Jack and Josephine (Saner) L.; grad. N.M. Mil. Inst., 1947; B.S. in Civil Engring., U. Tex. at El Paso, 1951; m. Miriam Feinberg, Jan. 30, 1955; children—Linda Sue, Jan Ellen, Amy Jo, Russell M. Constrn. engr. Robert E. McKee, gen. contractor, El Paso, 1950-55; v.p. El Paso Pipe and Supply Co., 1955-71; founder Symcon, Inc., El Paso. Mem. exec. bd. Yucca council Boy Scouts Am., 1969-71; cabinet mem. Jewish Community Center. Served to 1st lt. AUS, 1951. Mem. A.I.M. (mem. pres.'s council 1970-71), Am. Waterworks Assn., N.M. Mining Assn., Nat. Microfilm Assn. Jewish religion (trustee temple). Mason (Shriner). Home: 420 Borealls Lane El Paso TX 79912 Office: Suite 9A El Paso Nat Bank Bldg El Paso TX 79901

LAKE, I. BEVERLY, N.C. Supreme Ct. justice; b. Wake Forest, N.C., Aug. 29, 1906; B.S., Wake Forest Coll., 1925; LL.B., Harvard, 1929; LL.M., Columbia, 1940, S.J.D., 1947; m. Gertrude Bell; 1 son, I. Beverly. Admitted to N.C. bar, 1928; prof. law Wake Forest Coll., 1932-51; asst. atty. gen. of N.C., 1952-55; mem. firm Lake, Boyce and Lake, Raleigh, N.C.; now justice N.C. Supreme Ct., Raleigh. Am., N.C., Wake County bar assns., N.C. State Bar, Phi Alpha Delta. Author: Discrimination by Railroads and Other Public Utilities, 1947; North Carolina Practice Methods, 1952. Home: 403 N Main St Wake Forest NC 27587 Office: Justice Bldg Raleigh NC 27601

LAKE, JOHN BYRON, publisher; b. Follansbee, W.Va., Nov. 30, 1920; s. William Henry and Helen Alberta (Sanders) L.; student Ohio State U., 1939-40; m. Katharine Ann Kerr, June 28, 1947; children—Charlotte, Cynthia, Diane. With Lancaster (O.) Eagle-Gazette, 1947-56, advt. mgr., 1950-56; advt. dir. Elizabeth (N.J.) Daily Jour., 1956-60; advt. dir. St. Petersburg (Fla.) Times, 1960-66, gen. mgr., 1966-69, exec. v.p., 1969-71, pub., 1971—; pres. Semit Corp., St. Petersburg; v.p. Congl. Quar., Inc., Washington. Mem. Fla. Council of 100. Bd. dirs. U. South Fla. Found.; trustee Poynter Fund. Served with USNR, 1941-45; with USAF, 1951-53. Named Outstanding Man of Year Lancaster Jr. C. of C., 1949. Mem. Fla. Press Assn. (dir., pres. 1974), Fla. (dir., exec. bd.), St. Petersburg Area (past pres.) chambers commerce. Presbyn. Home: 1105 Brightwaters Blvd NE St Petersburg FL 33704 Office: 490 First Av S St Petersburg FL 33701

LAKE, MICHAEL KENNEDY, aerospace engr.; b. Whittier, Cal., Oct. 17, 1925; s. Francis Wilbur and Geraldine Kennedy (Mack) L.; B.S., U.S. Naval Acad., 1949; B.S. in Aero. Engring., U. Tex., Austin, 1958. Engr., Convair, Fort Worth, 1958-59, AEDC, Tullahoma, Tenn., 1959-62, FAA, Oklahoma City, 1962-64, NASA, Houston, 1964—. Comml. pilot. Active YMCA, Houston, 1964—. Served with USN, 1943-55. Decorated Air medal with oak leaf cluster; recipient Sustained Superior Performance award NASA, 1965. Home: 414 Stratford St #10 Houston TX 77006 Office: NASA JSC Houston TX 77058

LAMAR, CARL FLETCHER, state ofcl.; b. Hancock, County, Ky., Oct. 7, 1914; s. Edmund Newman and Hallie Fletcher (Winkler) L.; B.S., Western Ky. U., 1937; M.S., U. Ky., 1949, Ph.D., 1957; m. Ruby Miller, Nov. 10, 1939; children—Don Miller, Carla Jean. Tchr. agrl. edn. Meade County (Ky.) High Sch., 1937-42; supr. agrl. edn. Ky. State Dept. Edn., Frankfort, 1945-46, state dir. vocational edn., 1967—; tchr. agrl. edn. U. Ky., Lexington, 1954-65, dir. research vocational edn., 1965-67. Served with USMC, 1942-45. Recipient award Ky. Future Farmers, Ky. Future Homemakers, certificate of merit VA; 1973. Mem. Am. Assn. Sch. Adminstrs., Am. Vocational Assn. (Ky. panel for reorgn. 1972-73), N.E.A., Nat. Assn. State Dirs. Vocational Edn., So. Assn. Colls. and Schs. (exec. com. of com. on occupational ednl. insts. 1967-74), United Comml. Travelers, Gamma Sigma Delta, Phi Delta Kappa (pres. Alpha Nu chpt. 1959). Democrat. Baptist. Mason, Rotarian (charter mem.), Lion. Author: Vocational Teaching, 1958; Teaching Vocations, 1968, Spanish edit., 1971. Home: 357 Glendover Rd Lexington KY 40503 Office: 20th Floor Capital Plaza Tower Frankfort KY 40601

LAMAR, CLEVELAND JAMES, assn. exec.; b. Atmore, Ala., Apr. 21, 1924; s. Grover Cleveland and Fanny Bell (Washington) L.; B.S., Ala. State U., 1949, M.Edn., 1954; YMCA certificate, Springfield Coll., 1965; m. Annie Ruth Wilkerson, Aug. 28, 1949; children—Cleveland James, Mona Lisa (Mrs. Richard Carroll Butler), Torlorf Pinza, Ave Maria, Arturo Laertes, Alvino Degage, Caruso Noel. Instr., Eutaw, Ala., 1949-58; boys work sec. G.W. Carver br. YMCA, Shreveport, La., 1959; exec. dir. Samuel F. Harris br. YMCA, Athens, Ga., 1962-63; exec. dir. Dearborn St. YMCA, Mobile, Ala., 1964—. Vice pres., bd. dirs. Mobile Area Com. for Tng. and Devel., 1965-70; bd. dirs. N.A.A.C.P., Manna House, YMCA Blue Ridge Assembly. Served with AUS, 1943-46. Recipient certificate of achievement in phys. edn. Southeast Region YMCA, 1960, certificate of achievement Nat. Bd. YMCA's, 1965. Mem. Ala. Tchrs. Assn.

(life), Assn. Profl. Dirs., Phi Beta Sigma. Baptist. Club: Century (Mobile). Home: 455 Summerville St Mobile AL 36617 Office: 309 Washington Av Mobile AL 36603

LAMB, ARTHUR JEFFERSON, JR., lawyer; b. Amarillo, Tex., Nov. 18, 1929; s. Arthur Jefferson and Mildred Lee (Rambo) L.; B.B.A., West Tex. State U., 1954; J.D., U. Tex., 1957; m. Pearlene Jenkins, Aug. 1, 1959; children—Teri, Kim, Jeff, Slater. Admitted to Tex. bar, 1957; mem. firms Cutrer & Lamb, Houston, 1957-58, Franks & Lamb, Houston, 1958-59; practiced in Amarillo, 1959—; dir. Miller Nat. Corp. Prof. law South Tex. Law Sch., Houston, 1957-59. Trustee J.T. Cronin Trust. Served with USAF, 1950-54. Home: 6303 Jameson St Amarillo TX 79106 Office: 301 E 7th St Amarillo TX 79101

LAMB, BOYD DAWSON, mfg. co. exec.; b. Glenville, W.Va., Mar. 18, 1919; s. William C. and Francis (Radcliff) L.; B.A., Glenville State Coll., 1941; m. Bobbie Dee Campbell, June 2, 1948; children—Wonda (Mrs. Edward Heil), Dianne, Boyd D. Asst. to sales mgr. S.K. Wellman Co., Cleve., 1941-43; sales engr. Bunting Brass & Bronze Co., Toledo, 1947-49; with Behring's Bearing Service Co., Houston, 1950—, v.p., gen. mgr., 1969—; v.p. Motion Industries, Birmingham, Ala. Pres. Sales Marketing Execs. Internat., Beaumont, Tex., 1964-65. Served to lt. (j.g.) USNR, 1944-46. Mem. Assn. Iron and Steel Engrs. Presbyn. (chmn. bd. deacons 1953-64). Mason (Shriner), Rotarian. Club: Champion Golf (Houston). Home: 1510 Corral Route 16 Houston TX 77090 Office: 1412 Clay St Houston TX 77052

LAMB, GILBERT PAYTON, broadcasting co. exec.; b. Hazel, Ky., June 10, 1907; s. Thomas Melvin and Sarah Ann (Lannom) L.; grad. high sch.; m. Olabelle Singleton, Nov. 21, 1939 (dec. Jan. 1964); 1 dau., Magann (Mrs. Jack Regnald Rennels); m. 2d, Marie Sones, Mar. 14, 1972. Actor-musician Guy Bert Davis, 1924, Brunks Comedians, 1926, Harley Sadler and His Own Co., 1930, Hazel Hurd Players, 1931, Toby Young, 1932; owner Gilbert Lamb Co., Clayton, N.M., 1948-50; salesman, announcer radio sta. KICA, Clovis, N.M., 1954-56; with radio sta. KMUL, Muleshoe, Tex., 1956—, partner, mgr., 1956—. Mem. Tex. Gov's. Adv. Com. on Alcoholism, 1957-59; pres. Nat. Mule Meml. Assn., 1960—; chmn. United Fund Campaign, 1965; vice chmn. alcoholism adv. com. Tex. South Plains Assn. of Govts., 1972. Bd. dirs. Am. Lung TB Assn., West Tex. area. Named Outstanding Mcht. Muleshoe Jaycees, 1966; Outstanding Radio Exec., Federated Womens Club, 1967; Zeus award ESA Sorority, 1966-67. Mem. Tex. Panhandle Heritage Found. (life mem., dir. 1968), C. of C. (dir. 1957-60; Outstanding Citizen award 1956), Sigma Delta Chi. Methodist (mem. ofcl. bd. 1958-61). Rotarian (v.p. 1973—). Home: 723 W Av E Muleshoe TX 79347 Office: PO Box 486 Muleshoe TX 79347

LAMB, JAMIE PARKER, JR., engring. educator; b. Boligee, Ala., Sept. 21, 1933; s. Jamie Parker and Cletus (Hixson) L.; B.S., Auburn U., 1954; M.S., U. Ill., 1958, Ph.D., 1961; m. Nancy Catherine Flaherty, June 11, 1955; children—David Parker, Stephen Patrick. Asst. prof. engring. mechanics N.C. State U., Raleigh, 1961-63; asst. prof. mech. engring. U. Tex., Austin, 1963-67, asso. prof. 1967-70, prof., 1970—, chmn. mech. engring. dept., 1970—. Cons. LTV Aerospace Corp., Dallas, Marshall Space Flight Center, Huntsville, Ala., Tracor, Inc., Austin, Rocketdyne, McGregor, Tex., ARO, Inc., Tullahoma, Tenn. Served to 1st lt. USAF, 1955-57. Mem. Am. Soc. M.E., Am. Inst. Aeros. and Astronautics, Am. Soc. for Engring. Edn., Sigma Xi, Pi Tau Sigma, Tau Beta Pi. Baptist. Contr. articles to profl. jours. Home: 2605 Pinewood Terrace Austin TX 78757

LAMB, JOHN WILLIAM, orthopedic surgeon; b. Greensboro, N.C., July 15, 1937; s. Benjamin Clayton and Margaret Belle (Kelly) L.; B.S., U. Chgo., 1959, M.D., 1964; m. Linda Helena Kinnicutt, June 13, 1970; children—John William, Helena Adeline. Intern Kings County Hosp., Bklyn., 1964-65; resident Albany (N.Y.) Med. Center Hosp., 1967-71; staff Albany Med. Coll., 1971-72, U.S. VA Hosp., Albany, 1971-72; cons. surgeon Children's Clinic, N.Y., 1971-72; practice medicine specializing in orthopedic surgery, Nashville, 1972—. Served to capt. M.C., AUS, 1965-67. Diplomate Am. Bd. Orthopedic Surgery. Mem. A.M.A., Tenn. Med. Assn., Davidson County Med. Soc. Home: 6534 Cornwall Dr Nashville TN 37205 Office: 2010 Church St Nashville TN 37203

LAMBERT, ARTHUR GORMAN, lawyer; b. Washington, Feb. 10, 1899; s. Wilton J. and Elizabeth (Gorman) L.; grad. The Hill Sch., 1918; A.B., Princeton, 1922; LL.B., Harvard, 1925; m. Mary Lemon Sipple, Sept. 4, 1926; children—William S., Arthur Gorman. Admitted to D.C. bar, 1926; partner firm Lambert & Hart, Washington, 1930; asst. U.S. dist. atty., Washington, 1929-33; partner firm Lambert, Furlow, Elmore & Heidenberger and predecessor firms, Washington and Rockville, Md., 1933—; v.p., dir., mem. exec. com. Madison Nat. Bank, Washington. Chmn. bd. mgrs. Village of Chevy Chase (Md.), 1955-64, atty., 1964—. Atty., trustee Suburban Hosp. Assn., Inc., Bethesda, Md.; chmn. bd. trustees Landon Sch. Served with U.S. Army, World War II. Clubs: Metropolitan (Washington); Chevy Chase; Hillsboro (Pompano Beach, Fla.); Wianno (Cape Cod, Mass.). Home: 17 Grafton St Chevy Chase MD 20015 Office: 1629 K St NW Washington DC 20006 also 22 W Jefferson St Rockville MD 20850

LAMBERT, CHARLES LEROY, textile products co. exec.; b. Frisco City, Ala., Oct. 4, 1932; s. Benjamin Franklin and Eula Lee (Bryan) L.; grad. pub. high sch.; m. Louise R., Jan. 19, 1957; children—Charles Leroy, James Michael, Steven Eugene. With Vanity Fair Mills, Inc., Monroeville, Ala., 1956—, operations mgr., 1957-58, programmer, 1958-60, systems analyst, 1960-62, supr. IBM, 1962, data processing mgr., 1967—. Cons. to H.D. Lee Co., Kansas City, Mo., 1971. Bd. dirs. Monroe Acad., Monroeville, 1972—. Served with USAF, 1951-55; Korea. Baptist. Lion (pres. 1965). Home: 505 Todd St Monroeville AL 36460 Office: 111 Alabama Av Monroeville AL 36460

LAMBERT, EALON M., state ofcl.; b. Red Level Ala., Dec. 11, 1919; s. Thomas Madison and Estella (Kilpatrick) L.; student Auburn U., 1936-38, 39-40; m. Mary Louise Herndon, May 27, 1967; children—(by previous marriage) Brenda Joyce (Mrs. Joseph Levert Jordan). Marcia Ann; step-children Teresa, Jannie, Suellen Powers. Mem. Opelika (Ala.) City Commn., 1950-63; mayor, Opelika, 1952-58; mem. Lee County Democratic Exec. Com., 1958—; chmn. Pardon and Parole Bd., Montgomery, Ala., 1963—. Operator Superior Glass Co., Opelika, 1947-67. Del. 3d Congl. Dist. to Nat. Dem. Conv., 1956. Served with USAAF. World War II. Baptist. Home: 45 W Edgemont Av Montgomery AL 36104 Office: State Adminstrv Bldg Montgomery AL 36104

LAMBERT, JAMES WELLS, ret. editor, pub. co. exec.; b. Natchez, Miss., Nov. 23, 1904; s. James K. and Grace (Wells) L.; B.A., Jefferson Coll., 1925; m. Mary Beane, Nov. 17, 1935; children—James Wells, Gay (Mrs. Ellis Lord), Will B. Reporter, Natchez Democrat, 1925-33, city editor, 1933-40, mng. editor, 1940-48, editor and pub., 1948-70. Bd. dirs. Marion Taylor Fund. Mem. Natchez-Adams County C. of C. (dir.), Miss. Press Assn. (pres. 1968-69), La.-Miss. A.P. Assn. (pres. 1968-69). Rotarian, Elk. Home: 208 S Union St Natchez MS 39120 Office: 503 N Canal St Natchez MS 39120

LAMBERT, JERRY ROY, agrl. engr., educator; b. Benton, Ill., Sept. 16, 1936; s. William Roy and Nancy Pauline (Sample) L.; B.Agrl.Engring., U. Fla., 1958, M.S.E., 1962; Ph.D. (NSF fellow 1960-64), N.C. State U., 1964; m. A. Jean Connell, June 10, 1955; children—W. Roy, Jerry Alan, C. Renea. Design engr. trainee Soil Conservation Service, U.S. Dept. Agr., Gainesville, Fla., 1958-60; asst. prof. agrl. engring. Clemson (S.C.) U., 1964-68, asso. prof., 1968-72, prof., 1972—. Mem. Am. Soc. Agrl. Engrs., Am. Soc. for Engring. Edn., Sigma Xi, Phi Kappa Phi, Sigma Tau, Tau Beta Pi, Gamma Sigma Delta. Mem. Ch. of God. Home: Route 3 Box 414 Anderson SC 29621 Office: Clemson Univ Clemson SC 29631

LAMBERT, JOHN ROBERT, JR., constrn. co. exec.; b. Lake Village, Ark., Mar. 2, 1914; s. John Robert and Elizabeth Ruth (Humphreys) L.; student pub. schs.; m. Grace Lillian Levee, Feb. 12, 1934; children—Donald Gordon, John Robert III, Charles Sterling, William Stephen, Lawrence Lucius, Lillian Elizabeth (Mrs. Ernesto Marten), Robert James, Ruth Humphreys (Mrs. Thomas Frank Harmon), Richard Christian, Patricia Anne, Randolph Jay. With various constrn. cos., 1930-39; policeman State of La., 1939-42; with Delta Ship Yard, New Orleans, 1942-46; founder, owner, mgr. John R. Lambert, Jr., contractor, Kenner, La., 1946—; owner cattle ranch, Point Coupee Parish, La. Mem. Greater New Orleans Expressway Commn., 1960-62, chmn., 1962—. Trustee St. Martins Episcopal Sch. Served with U.S. Army, 1930-31. Named hon. citizen of Miami, Fla., Niagara Falls, N.Y., New Orleans. Mem. La. Motor Transport Assn. Episcopalian (vestryman). Home: 518 Green Acres Rd Metairie LA 70003 Office: 921 Duncan St Kenner LA 70062

LAMBERT, PHILLIP E., judge; b. Shawnee, Okla., Dec. 11, 1932; B.A., U. Okla.; J.D., Oklahoma City U.; m.; 4 children. Admitted to Okla. bar; former legal asst. to U.S. Dist. Judge Fred Daughtery; chief judge City of Oklahoma City, also judge Oklahoma City Municipal Criminal Ct., 1965—. Mem. council judges Nat. Council on Crime and Delinquency; commr., cts. chmn. Okla. Crime Commn.; mem. gov.'s com. Prisoner Pre-Release Center; instr. Oklahoma City Police Dept. Police Acad.; mem. adv. bd. Alcohol Safety Countermeasures Program; mem. police-community relations com. Community Relations Commn.; mem. Oklahoma City Traffic Safety Coordinating Com., Criminal Justice Planning Council, Oklahoma City, Mayor's Youth Adv. Com. Bd. dirs. Oklahoma City Council Alcoholism, Oklahoma County Mental Health Assn., Okla. Halfway House; founder, dir. Young Offenders Ct.-Probation Project, Alcohol Rehab. Ct. Class Project. Mem. Am. (adv. com. traffic ct. program), Okla., County bar assns., N. Am. Judges Assn., Am. Judicature Soc., Nat. Council Judges, Nat. Conf. Spl. Ct. Judges, Am. Acad. for Jud. Edn. (charter bd. mem.). Address: 700 Couch Dr Oklahoma City OK 73102

LAMBERT, RAYMOND SAMUEL, architect; b. Dallas, June 14, 1934; s. Irving W. and Gladys (Bernbaum) L.; B.Arch., Tex. Agrl. and Mechanical Coll., 1958; m. Hanna Rebecca Goldman, June 9, 1957; children—Craig Neil, Debra Jean. Urban planner, city plan dept. City of Dallas, 1958-59; planner Springer & Foeller, Dallas, 1961-63; architect Joe Gordon & Assos., Dallas, 1963-65; architect, planner Bentley-Gordon & Assos., Dallas, 1965-67; architect Raymond S. Lambert & Assos., Dallas, 1967—. Bd. dir. Akiba Acad. Day Sch., Dallas, 1970—. Served with Ordnance Corps, AUS, 1959-61. Mem. Nat. Council Archtl. Registration Bds., Nat. Assn. Housing Redevel. Orgn., N. Central Tex. Council Govts. (mem. codes com. 1971), A.I.A., Tex. Soc. Architects. Jewish religion. Mason; mem. B'nai B'rith (pres. 1970-71). Home: 3240 Townsend Dr Dallas TX 75229 Office: 11346 Emerald St Dallas TX 75229

LAMBERT, ROY KENNETH, constrn. co. exec.; b. Bloomburg, Tex., Oct. 3, 1939; s. Francis Roy and Dora (Berry) L.; B.S. in Civil Engring., Arlington State U., 1962; m. Mollie Jean McDaniel, Sept. 2, 1960; children—Susan Janelle, Cary Gene and Gary Dean (twins). Civil engr. Forrest & Cotton, Inc., cons. engrs., Dallas, 1962-66; civil engr. City of Grand Prairie, Tex., 1967; city mgr., Plano, Tex., 1968-71; now pres. Lambert & Waddell, Inc. Mem. N.Central Tex. Council of Govts. Water Utility Profl. Devel. Tech. Adv. Com., 1969-71, Urban Devel. Manpower Adv. Com., 1969-71. Trustee U. Plano, Plano Ind. Sch. Dist. Served with USMCR, 1962. Registered profl. engr., Tex. Mem. E.Tex., Plano (dir. 1969) chambers commerce, Tex. Soc. Profl. Engrs. Presbyn. (deacon). Rotarian (past pres.). Home: 1909 Midcrest Dr Plano TX 75074

LAMBERT, SAM M., ednl. cons.; b. Canebrake, W.Va., Mar. 10, 1913; s. Sam M. and Callie (Patton) L.; A.B., W.Va. U., 1935, M.A., 1938; Ed.D., George Washington U., 1955; m. Juanita R. Bates, Apr. 1938; children—Sylvia, Rebecca. Tchr., W.Va. pub. schs., 1935-39; supr. sch. transp. W.Va. Dept. Edn., 1939-41, supr. research and sch. plants, 1943-45; dir. research and pub. relations W.Va. Edn. Assn., 1945-50; asst. dir. research div. N.E.A., 1950-55, asso. dir. research div., 1955-56, dir. div., 1956-65, asst. exec. sec. information services, 1965-67, exec. sec. assn., 1967-73. Cons., Nat. Assn. Elementary Sch. Prins. Bd. dirs. Ednl. Research Service, Inc. Author: The Other Side of Teaching; Reducing the Drop-Out Rate in Education. Editor books in edn. Contbr. articles to profl. jours. Home: 3144 Oliver St NW Washington DC 20015 Office: 1801 N Moore St Arlington VA 22209

LAMBERTH, EDWIN GRADY, dentist; b. Alexander City, Ala., Jan. 27, 1929; s. Manuel Grady and Mary Lewis (McIntosh) L.; D.M.D., U. Ala., 1958; m. Elizabeth Ellis, Sept. 5, 1953; children—Lisa, Grady, Kathryn, Brooks. Gen. practice dentistry, Alexander City, 1958—. Replace missionary in Africa, 1967. Served with AUS, 1950-52. Decorated Purple Heart, Korean Service medal with 3 bronze service stars. Mem. Am. Dental Assn., 2d Dist. Dental Soc., Sigma Nu. Baptist (deacon). Club: Alexander City Country (past pres.). Home: 409 N Central Av Alexander City AL 35010 Office: 207 Franklin St Alexander City AL 35010

LAMBIS, JOHN MARTIN, broadcasting co. exec.; b. Newport, R.I., Oct. 9, 1949; s. James Apostolos and Josephine (Biresch) L.; student Elkin's Inst. Electronics, 1968; diploma R.I. Sch. Broadcasting, 1968; m. Patricia Ann Ledford, Feb. 26, 1967; 1 son, John James. Announcer, elec. engr. Knight Broadcasting Co., WSAR Radio, Boston, 1968-71; prodn. mgr., creative dir. Jefferson Pilot Broadcasting Co., WBT Radio, Charlotte, N.C., 1971—. Exec. producer/creator History of West Coast Sound, 1973—; radio broadcast lectr., instr. Garringer High Sch., 1972-73; pub. service adviser on recruiting campaigns Army and Air Nat. Guard, 1971-73. Active various community drives. Recipient Meritorious award Army and Air Nat. Guard, 1972; Gabriel award, 1974. Republican. Greek Orthodox. Home: 2017 Greenway Av Charlotte NC 28208 Office: 1 Julian Price Pl Charlotte NC 28205

LAMBOU, VICTOR WILLIAM, govt. ofcl.; b. New Orleans, Apr. 28, 1929; s. Victor T. and Regina (Byrnes) L.; B.S., La. State U., 1952, M.S., 1953; m. Lorraine Granier, Jan 31, 1953; children—Denita, Geralyn, Roger, Vickie. Fishery research biologist La. Wildlife and Fisheries Commn., 1953-64; dir. fishery research lab., U. Okla., Norman, 1964-66; Fed. Water Pollution Control Adminstrn., U.S. Dept. Interior, 1966—, chief pesticide program. Washington, 1969—. Mem. Biometric Soc., Am. Fisheries Soc., Am. Soc. Ichthyologists and Herpetologists, Am. Soc. Limnology and Oceanography, Wildlife Soc., Ecol. Soc. Am., Fed. Water Quality Assn., Am. Inst. Biol. Sci., A.A.A.S., Gulf and Caribbean Fisheries Inst. Contbr. articles to profl. pubis. Home: 7527 June St Springfield VA 22150 Office: Water Program Environmental Protection Agency Washington DC 20242

LAMICA, LOUISE WILSON, journalist; b. Supply, N.C., Sept. 21, 1927; d. Frank and Rosa Dewey (Clemmons) Holden; student U. N.C., 1953; m. George Edward Lamica, Feb. 22, 1951; children—Darlene Gail (Mrs. Dale Buck), George Edward, Cathy (Mrs. David Kendrick). With Star-News Newspapers, Inc., Wilmington, N.C., 1947-54, 57—, edn. editor, 1970—; operator with Washington Post-Times Herald, 1955-56. Recipient awards N.C. County and Local Historians, 1959, Newspaper Inst. Am., 1962, N.C. Council Chs., 1964, N.C. Assn. Educators, 1970, 73. Mem. Edn. Writers Assn., N.C. Press Assn. (award 1961), N.C. Press Women's Assn. (award 1964). Contbr. articles to various publs. including Wildlife of N.C., State mag., Guideposts, Ladies Circle. Home: 1513 Parmele Dr Wilmington NC 28401 Office: PO Box 840 Wilmington NC 28401

LAMKIN, WILLIAM PIERCE, religious assn. exec.; b. Ansley, La., Oct. 17, 1919; s. John Mays and Carrie Ellen (Posey) L.; student La. Coll., 1941-43; A.B., U. N.C., 1947; m. Irma Hazel Page, Dec. 30, 1948; children—John Page, Mary Jean, Carol Ellen; m. 2d, Jane Eagar Mills, Mar. 17, 1973; 1 stepdau., Jennifer. Copyreader, religious editor, asst. city editor, night city editor, city editor Charlotte (N.C.) Observer, 1948-61; news dir. Presbyn. Ch. in the U.S., Atlanta, 1961—. Mem. gen. communications and interpretation com. Nat. Council Chs., 1961—; mem. interpretation com. Cons. on Ch. Union; bd. dirs. Presbyn. Survey, TRAV. Served with USAAF, 1943-45. Decorated D.F.C. with 3 oak leaf clusters, Air medal with 4 oak leaf clusters. Mem. Pub. Relations Soc. Am. Democrat. Home: 4890 High Point Rd NE Atlanta GA 30342 Office: 341 Ponce de Leon Av NE Atlanta GA 30308

LAMON, HARRY VINCENT, JR., lawyer; b. Macon, Ga., Sept. 29, 1932; s. Harry Vincent and Helen (Bewley) L.; B.S. cum laude, Davidson Coll., 1954; LL.B. magna cum laude, Emory U., 1958; m. Ada Healey Morris, June 17, 1954; children—Hollis Morris, Helen Kathryn. Admitted to Ga. bar, 1958; D.C. bar, 1965; practiced in Atlanta, 1958—; mem. firm Hansell, Post, Brandon, Dorsey, 1958-73, Henkel & Lamon, 1973—. Lectr. law Emory U., 1960—; pres. So. Fed. Tax Inst., Inc., 1967—; dir. Sockwell Enterprises, Inc., Baier Corp., Fulton Bros. Electric Co., Leaselite, Inc., Meidinger & Assos., Inc. Mem. adv. bd. Salvation Army, 1963—; mem. Met. Atlanta Boys Clubs, Inc., 1964—; mem. exec. com. Atlanta Area council Boy Scouts Am., 1974—. Served to 1st lt. AUS, 1954-56. Fellow Am. Coll. Probate Counsel, Atlanta Estate Planning Council, Am. Law Inst.; mem. Am., Ga., D.C., Atlanta, Fed. bar assns., Lawyers Club Atlanta, Atlanta Execs. Assn., Nat. Emory U. Law Sch. Alumni Assn. (past pres.), Phi Beta Kappa, Omicron Delta Kappa, Phi Delta Phi, Phi Delta Theta (province pres. 1964-68). Episcopalian. Mason (Shriner), Kiwanian (pres. Downtown Atlanta). Clubs: Breakfast, Commerce, Capital City, Cherokee Town and Country Contbr. articles prof. jours. Home: 3375 Valley Rd NW Atlanta GA 30305 Office: 2500 Peachtree Center Cain Tower 229 Peachtree St NE Atlanta GA 30303

LAMONICA, CARL JOSEPH, sci. adminstr.; b. Colver, Pa., Aug. 17, 1920; s. Joseph and Josephine (LaBianca) LaM.; B.S. in Physics, U. Pitts., 1948, M.A. in Physics, 1950; postgrad. U. Okla., 1967-68, Grad. Sch. Dept. Agr., 1968, 70, Control Data Inst. Advanced Tech., 1973; m. Helen Louise Bednar, Dec. 27, 1947; children—Carole Joan (Mrs. Doulgas R. Manley), Thomas Carl, Anita Marie, Michael Joseph. With Nav. Weapons Lab., various locations, 1953—, head aeroballistics and weapon control div., Dahlgren, Va., 1968-71, dir. Computer Facilities Center, 1972—, also mem. several coms., bds. Chmn. Nav. Weapons Lab. Swimming Club, 1959-63; active Capital and Rappahannick (Va.) councils Boy Scouts Am., 1959—; mem. Nav. Weapons Lab. P.T.A., 1957—. Chmn. Nav. Weapons Lab. Sch. Bd., 1963—. Served to maj. USAAF, ETO. Fellow Am. Inst. Chemists; mem. A.M.A., N.Y. Acad. Sci., Fed. Profl. Assn. (v.p.), Am. Inst. Aeros and Astronautics, Res. Officer Assn., V.F.W. Roman Catholic. Lion. Club: Dahlgren Golf (pres., chmn. bd. dirs.). Contbr. to profl. jours. Home: PO Box 123 Dahlgren VA 22448 Office: US Naval Weapons Lab Dahlgren VA 22448

LAMOTHE, GEORGE OSCAR, pub. relations and advt. co. exec.; b. Newport, Vt., Apr. 21, 1941; s. George Oscar and Rose (Gilbert) LaM.; B.A., New Eng. Coll., 1964; m. Millie Bumgarner, Aug. 8, 1964. Journalist and columnist Statesville (N.C.) Record and Landmark, 1964-69; pres. LaMothe, Inc., pub. relations and advt., Statesville, 1969—; sec. Allen Grady Advt. Agy., Statesville, 1974—. Cons. Hettrick Mfg. Co., 1970-73. Tchr. photography South Iredell High Sch., 1967-68. Dir. pub. relations Nat. Drug Abuse Found., 1973. Mem. Pub. Relations Soc. Am., N.C Pub. Relations Soc. Lion (dir. 1966-67), Elk. Club: Statesville City. Home: 853 Wendover St Statesville NC 28677 Office: PO Box 5414 Statesville NC 28677

LAMOTTE, STEWART FICKES, JR., circuit judge; b. Red Lion, Pa., May 28, 1921; s. Stewart Fickes and Lottie (Reichard) LaM.; B.B.A., U., Miami, 1943; J.D., 1948; m. Jane Elizabeth Love. Dec. 25, 1950; children—Stewart Fickes, III, Susan Lucille, Sandra Catherine. Admitted to Fla. bar. 1948; practice law, Ft. Lauderdale, Fla., 1948-63; judge indsl. claims Fla. Indsl. Commn., 1961-63; judge County, Ft. Lauderdale, 1963-68; circuit judge, 1968—. Pres., Am. Cancer Soc., Broward County, 1961-63. Served to 1st lt. USMCR, 1943-46. Decorated Purple Heart. Mem. Am. Legion, Phi Delta Phi. Methodist. Mason (Shriner), Elk. Clubs: High Hampton Country. Lauderdale Yacht (gov.). Home: 103 Fiesta Way Fort Lauderdale FL 33301 Office: Broward County Ct House Fort Lauderdale FL 33301

LAMPARTER, WILLIAM SMITH, furniture mfr.; b. Metuchen N.J., July 1, 1926; s. William George and Irma Lanyon (Smith) L.; student Bowdoin Coll., 1943-45; A.B., Duke, 1947, A.M., 1948. Furniture buyer R.H. Macy & Co., N.Y.C., 1958-66; furniture and contract merchandiser Asso. Merchandising Corp., N.Y.C., 1966-68; v.p. Century Furniture Co., Hickory, N.C., 1968, dir., 1968—; v.p., gen. sales mgr., 1969—. Chmn. exec. com. Friends of Duke U. Library, 1971—; gifts chmn. class of 1947, Duke U. Loyalty Fund; pres.'s asso. Duke, 1973—. Trustee Jiranek Sch. Furniture Design, N.Y.C., 1964—; pres. Fort Defiance, Inc. (N.C.), 1971—. Mem. Royal Instn. Cornwall (Eng.), Newcomen Soc., Delta Sigma Phi. Republican. Presbyn. Club: Lake Hickory (N.C.) Country. Home: 831 12th Av NW Hickory NC 28601 Office: 401 11th St NW Hickory NC 28601

LAMPKIN, ANDREW JACKSON, chem. engr.; b. Baldwin, Miss., Sept. 11, 1923; s. Andrew J. and Etna (Harrelson) L.; B.S., Miss. State Coll., 1950; m. Betty Anne Dent, July 1, 1948; children—Joanne, Deborah Jane, Andrew Jackson, III. Chem. engr. Miss. State Hwy. Dept., Tupelo, 1950; chem. engr. TVA, New Johnsonville, Tenn., 1951-62, mech. engr., Drakesboro, Ky. 1962-68, power plant results supr. Shawnee Plant, Paducah, Kentucky, 1968—. Alderman for New Johnsonville, 1956-60. Served with Signal Corps, AUS, 1944-46. Registered profl. engr. Tenn., Miss. Mem. Internat. Platform Assn., Paducah Art Guild, Alpha Tau Omega, Alpha Phi Omega. Democrat.

Baptist (deacon). Home: 452 Cardinal Lane Paducah KY 42001 Office: PO Box 2000 Paducah KY 42001

LAMSON, BYRON SAMUEL, clergyman, author; b. Boone, Ia., June 4, 1901; s. Danforth C. and Nora (Cussins) L.; student Los Angeles Pacific Coll., 1919-21, Litt.D., 1962; A.B., Greenville Coll., 1923; M.A., U. So. Cal., 1928; postgrad. U. Rochester, 1928, Northwestern U., 1940-42; D.D., Seattle Pacific Coll., 1948; m. Freda Burritt, Sept. 8, 1925 (dec. Aug. 1964); children—Mary Virginia, Lillian Burritt (Mrs. Bradley Sarvis); m. 2d, Betty E. Kline, July 30, 1965. Ordained to ministry Methodist Ch., 1925; pastor Free Meth. Chs., Cal., 1923-27, Ill., 1940-44; dean Los Angeles Pacific Coll., 1927-30, pres., 1930-39; v.p. Greenville (Ill.) Coll., 1939; gen. missionary sec. Free Meth. Ch., 1944-64, dir. research for ch. growth, 1964-71; editor Free Methodist, Free Methodist Pub. House, Winona Lake, Ind., 1964-71; asso. pastor Free Meth. Ch., St. Petersburg, Fla., 1970—. Chmn. Cooperating Home Bds. for Union Bibl. Sem., Yeotmal, India, 1951-64. Mem. Psi. Chi. Author: To Catch the Tide, 1963; Modern Prayer Miracles, 1935; Holiness Teachings of New Testament Literature, 1935; Lights in the World, 1951; Venture, 1960. Address: 2660 52d St N St Petersburg FL 33710

LAMSON-SCRIBNER, DENIS, securities co. exec.; b. Annapolis, Md., June 10, 1934; s. Frank Hamilton and Mercy Dees (Foster) L.S.; B.Chem. Engring., Rensselaer Poly. Inst., 1956; postgrad. Morris Harvey Coll., 1956-61; postgrad. W.Va. U., 1961-63; m. Julia Augusta Moseley, Mar. 31, 1956; children—Julia A., Frank H. III, William F. Prodn. engr. Union Carbide Corp., Charleston, W.Va., 1956-63, financial analyst, N.Y.C., 1963-65, bus. analyst, 1965-66, mgr. reports and analysis, 1966-68; account exec. Frost, Johnson, Read & Smith, Inc., Charleston, S.C., 1968—, v.p., dir., 1969-71, sec., dir., 1971—; treas., dir. FJRS Financial Services Inc., 1973—. Allied mem. N.Y. Stock Exchange, Inc., 1969—. Served to capt. Chem. Corps., AUS, 1957-64. Mem. S.C. Amateur Athletic Union (v.p. 1973—), Internat. Assn. Financial Planners, Fouragere Soc., Charleston Swim Assn. (treas. 1973), Sigma Xi. Republican. Episcopalian. Rotarian. Club: Country of Charleston. Home: 1576 Fairway Dr Charleston SC 29412 Office: 49 Broad St Charleston SC 29402

LANCASTER, ALICE CUNNINGHAM (MRS. OWEN EDWIN LANCASTER, JR.), psychiat. social worker; b. Galveston, Tex.; d. Henry Eugene and Leona (Murray) Cunningham; B.A., Southeastern La. Coll., 1949; M.S.W., Our Lady of Lake Coll., 1960; m. Owen Edwin Lancaster, Jr., June 3, 1955; stepchildren—Owen Edwin III, Blake. Tchr., Ponchatoula (La.) High Sch., 1932-45, Marion High Sch., Lake Charles, La., 1952-55; recreation worker, program dir. A.R.C., Washington, Manila, Kyoto, Japan, 1945-47, social worker, Houston, 1947-48, Maxwell AFB, Ala., Camp Polk, La., Ft. Bragg, N.C., 1950-52; social worker Tex. Cradle Soc., San Antonio, 1955-60; med. social worker Bexar County Hosp. Dist. Robert B. Green Hosp., San Antonio, 1960-61; psychiat. social worker San Antonio State Hosp., 1961—, acting dir. social service dept., 1964-65, asst. dir., 1965-68, chief social worker, 1968—, adminstrv. coordinator social service dept., 1971—, chief social work services, 1974—; lectr. in field. Vol., A.R.C., San Antonio, 1961. Mem. Nat. Assn. Social Workers, Acad. Certified Social Workers, Mental Health Assn., Worden Sch. Social Service Alumni Assn. (pres. 1967). Episcopalian. Contbr. articles to profl. jours. Home: 425 S Vandiver Rd San Antonio TX 78209 Office: PO Box 23310 San Antonio TX 78223

LANCASTER, CARROLL TOWNES, JR., assn. exec.; b. Waco, Tex., Mar. 14, 1929; s. Carroll T. and Beatrice (Hollaman) L.; student U. Tex., 1948-51, 52-53; m. Catherine Virginia Frommel, May 29, 1954; children—Loren Thomas, Barbara, Beverly, John Tracy. Sales coordinator Union Tank div. Butler Mfg. Co., Houston, 1954-56, sales rep., New Orleans, 1956-57, br. mgr., 1957-60; asst. to exec. v.p. Maloney-Crawford Mfg. Co., Tulsa, 1960-62; marketing cons., sr. asso. Market/Product Facts, Tulsa, 1962-63; market devel. asst. Norriseal Controls div. Dover Corp., Houston, 1963-66; area dir. Arthritis Found., Houston, 1966-69, dir. S.W. div., 1969-70; exec. dir. United Cerebral Palsy Tex. Gulf Coast, 1971—. Christian edn. tchr., 1966-70, supr., 1971, asst. youth football coach, Bellaire, 1967-68, 70-71. Mem. Houston-Galveston Area Health Commn. Study Group. Bd. dirs. Council Chs. of Greater Houston, 1966-68, v.p., 1968. Served with USNR, 1946-48, 51-52. Recipient award for securing free blood for indigent Harris County Hosp. Dist., 1968. Mem. Am. Marketing Assn., Tex. Soc. Fund Raisers, Delta Sigma Phi. Episcopalian. Home: 4711 Fleetwood St Bellaire TX 77401 Office: 4189 Bellaire Blvd Houston TX 77025

LANCASTER, EDGAR HUNTER, JR., lawyer; b. Brookhaven, Miss., June 13, 1918; s. Edgar Hunter and Willie (Butler) L.; B.S., La. Poly. Inst., 1939; LL.B., La. State U., 1948, J.D., 1968; m. Beverly Marie Vedros, Apr. 1, 1944; children—Michael Eugene, Patricia Ann, Edgar Hunter III. Performance supr. U.S. Dept. Agr., 1939-41; admitted to La. bar, 1948; gen. practice law, Tallulah, La., 1948—. Dir. So. Nat. Bank of Tallulah. Rep. La. State Legislature, 1952-68. Mem. council La. Law Inst., 1964—. Trustee, mem. exec. com. Pub. Affairs Research Council La. Served as sgt. AUS, 1942-45. Mem. Madison Parish C. of C. (dir., past pres.). Clubs: Tallulah Rotary, Tallulah Country. Home: 311 Cleveland St Tallulah LA 71282 Office: 510 E Asnew St Tallulah LA 71282

LANCASTER, JAMES ROYDON, data systems engr.; b. Tiffin, O., Aug. 13, 1929; s. John Herrold and Florence Lura (Stinchcomb) L.; B.E. in Elec. Engring., Vanderbilt U., 1951; M.S. in Elec. Engring., U. Tenn. Space Inst., 1967; m. Aulean Moore, Dec. 22, 1949; children—James Roydon, Tim Martin. Instrumentation engr. ARO, Inc., Arnold Air Force Sta., Tenn., 1954-56, group supr. digital equipment, 1956-57, sect. supr. data systems engring., 1957-72, staff engr., 1972—. Instr. U. Tenn. Space Inst., part time, 1972—. Treas. Duck River Area Council on Alcohol and Drug Dependence, 1971-72. Served with USNR, 1951-54; ETO. Mem. I.E.E.E. (chmn. data processing subcom. 1964-68). Home: 103 Stratford Ct Tullahoma TN 37388 Office: Arnold AF Station TN 37389

LANCASTER, JAMES WILLARD, utility exec., indsl. engr.; b. Sheridan, Ark., Apr. 29, 1937; s. Joe D. and Lillian Pauline (Speck) L.; B.S. in Indsl. Edn., 1959; m. Betty Jean Cartwright, Dec. 3, 1960; 1 dau., Sandra Jean. Design engr. Arkla Industries, Russellville, Ark., 1959-63; engr. Rockwell Mfg. Co. (name changed to Rockwell Internat.), Sheridan, 1963-65, plant supt., 1965-68, materials mgr., 1968-73; mgr. gas meter repair plant Ark. La. Gas Co., Sheridan, 1973—. Tchr. adult edn. courses Sheridan High Sch.; tchr. mgmt. and supervision courses Pine Vocational Sch., Pine Bluff, Ark. Chmn. troop com. Boy Scouts Am. Alderman, City of Sheridan, 1966—, mem. City Planning Commn., 1965—. Named One of Outstanding Young Men, Ark. Jaycees, 1971. Mem. Grant County C. of C. Methodist (trustee 1972—, finance chmn. 1967, chmn. com. for future planning 1972—, Sunday sch. tchr. 1968—). Rotarian (pres. 1971). Club: Sheridan Country. Home: Route 2 Box 520 Sheridan AR 72150 Office: Box 416 Sheridan AR 72150

LANCASTER, JOSEPHAS JACKSON, educator; b. Gainesville, Ga., Apr. 16, 1924; s. James Walter and Lena (Braselton) L.; student Piedmont Coll., 1941-42, Syracuse U., 1942, U. Ill., 1943-44; B.S. in agr., U. Ga., 1949, M.S., 1952; Ed.D., Cornell U., 1959; m. Sarah Frances Waters, July 17, 1954; children—Lynn, Charles, Martha Jane, Joseph. Mem. faculty U. Ga. Coll. Agr., Athens, 1949—, agrl. economist, 1955-59, prof., head dept. extension edn., 1959—. Mem. sub.-com. on staff tng. and devel. Extension Com. on Orgn. and Policy, 1969—, chmn., 1972. Bd. dirs. S.G. Chandler Meml. Scholarship Fund. Served with AUS, 1942-45; ETO. Mem. Ga. Adult Edn. Council (pres.), Adult Edn. Assn. U.S.A. (conf. chmn. 1970, exec. com. 1970-72), Nat. Geog. Soc., A.A.A.S., Phi Kappa Phi, Gamma Sigma Delta. Baptist. Kiwanian. Author: (with others) The Cooperative Extension Service, 1966. Home: Route 3 Box 239 Gainesville GA 30501 Office: Extension Bldg Lumpkin St U Ga Athens GA 30601

LANCASTER, PURVIS TALMADGE, sch. adminstr.; b. Fayettesville, N.C., Aug. 28, 1924; s. James Robert and Mary Elizabeth (Deaton) L.; A.A., Louisburg Coll., 1945; A.B., High Point Coll., 1947; M.A., East Carolina U., 1951; Ed.D., Duke, 1965; m. Earlene Lois Jewett, July 26, 1952; children—Holly, John Talmadge. Supt. schs. Dept. Def. Schs., Central Germany, 1960-61; supt. schs. Dept. Def. Schs., France, 1962-66; supt. Camp Lejeune (N.C.) Dependent Schs., also faculty mem. East Carolina U., 1966—. Served with USNR, 1942. Recipient Letter of Commendation Comdt. USMC, 1968, Commendation for meritorious service Dept. Navy, USMC, 1971; named Boss of Year, Jacksonville (N.C.) chpt. Am. Bus. Women Assn., 1971. Mem. Am. Assn. Sch. Adminstrs., N.C. Supts. Assn., N.E.A., N.C. Assn. Educators, Nat. Sojourners (hon.). Methodist. Rotarian. Home: 407 Carmen Av Jacksonville NC 28540 Office: Office of Supt Bldg 855 Marine Corps Base Camp Lejeune NC 28542

LANCASTER, RALPH DOUGLAS, banker, journalist; b. Greenville, N.C., Jan. 17, 1939; s. Heber Daniel and Rosa Lee (Smith) L.; student Coll. of The Albemarle, 1961, Am. Press Inst. Columbia, 1967, Mgmt. Sch., Wake Forest U., 1968; m. Sandra Anne Jones, Apr. 2, 1961; children—Ralph Douglas, Julie Dianne, Jeffrey Alan. Reporter Greensboro (N.C.) Record, 1962-63, city editor, 1968—; mem. staff pub. relations dept. Pilot Life Ins. Co., 1965-68; mgr. pub. relations Wachovia Bank & Trust Co., Winston Salem, N.C., 1973—. Served with USCGR, 1958-62. Recipient Nat. Headliner award Nat. Headliners Assn., 1967, Roy M. Howard award, 1968. Mem. Pub. Relations Soc. Am., Nat. Investor Relations Inst. Home: 4050 Dresden Rd Winston-Salem NC 27104 Office: Wachovia Bldg Winston-Salem NC 27106

LANCE, THOMAS BERTRAM, banker, state ofcl.; b. Gainesville, Ga., June 3, 1931; s. Thomas Jackson and Annie Rose (Erwin) L.; student Emory U., 1948-50, U. Ga., 1951; Grad. Sch. Banking of South, La. State U., 1956; grad. Grad. Sch. Banking Rutgers U., 1963; m. Lethia Belle David, Sept. 9, 1950; children—Thomas Bertram, David Jackson, Stuart Austin, Claude Beverly. Exec. v.p. Calhoun (Ga.) Nat. Bank, 1958-63, pres., 1963-74, chmn. bd., 1974—, dir., 1958—; pres. CNB Investments, Inc., Calhoun, 1958—; state hwy. dir. Ga., Atlanta, 1970-73; dir. Astro Dye Works, Inc., Calhoun Chem. & Coating Co. Crown Crafts, Modern Fibers, Shaheen Carpet Mills, Multi-Developers, Inc., Edward LaceyMills, Inc. Chmn. 7th Dist. Savs. Bond Drive; chmn. Ga. Hwy. Authority; mem. Ga. Bd. Pub. Safety; mem. pres.'s adv. council Agnes Scott Coll.; chmn. Chair of Pvt. Enterprise, Ga. State U.; active various community drives. Bd. dirs. Ga. div. Am. Cancer Soc., Ethel Harpst Children's Home; trustee Ga. Found. Ind. Colls., Reinhardt Coll., Cherokee, Boy's Estate, Dalton, Ga.; mem. adv. council Ga. State Coll. Mem. A.I.M. (pres. council 1965), Ga. Bankers Assn. (2d v.p.), U. Ga. Alumni Soc. (v.p. 7th dist.), Young Presidents Orgn. Methodist (dist. lay leader). Rotarian. Home: 409 E Line St Calhoun GA 30701 Office: 115 Wall St Calhoun GA 30701

LAND, ELLIOTT LEE, coll. adminstr.; b. Virginia Beach, Va., Oct. 20, 1926; s. Cecil Peter and Berite Aileen (Lee) L.; student Bob Jones U., 1951-53; B.A., Columbia Bible Coll., 1955; M.Ed., U. Va., 1960, D.Ed., 1969; m. Judith Ann Roberts, May 5, 1962; children—Mark Todd, Eric Garth. Tchr., Linkhorn Park Elementary Sch., 1955-56; asst. prin. Kempsville Elementary Sch., 1956-57; prin. Aragona Elementary Sch., 1957-62, Pembroke Elementary Sch., 1962-64, Hermitage Elementary Sch., 1964-66; asst. dir. student teaching U. Va., Charlottesville, 1966-67, asst. cons. to Va. Pub. Sch. Systems, 1966-67, instr. Sch. Gen. Studies, 1967-69; dir. Head Start Program, Fluvanna (Va.) County Sch. Bd., 1967-69; asst. prof. philosophy of edn. Longwood Coll., Farmville, Va., 1967-69, dir. J.P. Wynne Campus Sch., 1969—. Founder, Virginia Beach Tchrs. Bowling League, 1959-64, Aragona Bowling League for Youth, 1960-62; adviser Honors Program, Longwood Coll., 1968—; coordinator Tchr. Aide Program, Prince Edward County Pub. Schs., 1968-69; co-chmn. Sub Region II, White House Conf. on Youth, 1970. Served with USNR, 1944-46. Mem. Nat., South Atlantic philosophy of edn. socs., Am. Assn. U. Profs., Lab. Sch. Adminstrs. Assn., Am. Assn. Sch. Adminstrs., Kappa Delta Pi. Lion. Home: 1001 6th Av Farmville VA 23901

LAND, EUGENE STUART, cons.; b. Beaumont, Tex., Nov. 18, 1918; s. Amos W. and Mary Marie (Cooper) L.; B.B.A., U. Tex., 1947; m. Mary Jane Dear, May 2, 1943; children—Eugene Cooper, Betty Jane, Donald Stuart. Pres., Inter-Am. Devel. Corp., Houston, 1955-59; pres. Land & Co., Inc., Houston, 1959-66; corporate devel. asso. Dempsey-Tegeler & Co., Inc., Houston, 1966-69; v.p. corporate devel. dept. Rowles, Winston & Co., Inc. Houston, 1969-72; cons. corporate finance, merger and acquisitions Stuart Land & Assos., Houston, 1972—. Mem. Houston Bd. Realtors, Nat. Assn. Merger and Acquisition Consultants (dir.). Home: 1712 Hollister Dr Houston TX 77055 Office: 1530 West Belt N Houston TX 77043

LAND, FREDERIC HERMAN, mfg. co. exec.; b. Batesville, Miss., July 11, 1908; s. Herman Harris and Margaret (Seaton) L.; B.S.C., U. Miss., 1931; m. Johnnie Christine Murphy, Dec. 22, 1934; children—Betty Ann (Mrs. James Carlisle Scott), Nancy Seaton (Mrs. James J. Baldwin III). Asst. store mgr. A & P Tea Co., Columbus, Miss., 1931-35; dist. mgr. So. Oil. Co., Columbus, 1935-37; field supr. USES, Jackson, Miss., 1937-43; field rep. War Manpower Commn., Atlanta, 1943-46; pres. Marshall & Williams So. Corp., Greenville, S. C., 1946-64; exec. v.p. Marshall & Williams Co., Greenville and Providence, 1964-68, sr. v.p., 1968—; dir. Piedmont Food Processing Co., Greenville. Served with USNR, 1944-46. Mem. Greenville C. of C., Am. Textile Mfrs. Assn. (asso.), Kappa Sigma. Republican. Presbyn. Mason (Shriner). Clubs: Greenville Country, Poinsett (Greenville). Home: 709 Byrd Blvd Greenville SC 29605 Office: 620 S Pleasantburg Dr Greenville SC 29606

LAND, MARY ELIZABETH, author; b. Benton, La., Sept., 1908; d. Thomas Taylor and Elizabeth (Langford) Land; student Gulf Park (Miss.) Coll., 1924-25; grad. Cheyney-Trent Sch. Poetry, Cal., 1937; children—Patricia (Mrs. Phineas Stevens), George Thomas Land. Staff writer La. Conservation Rev. div. edn. La. Dept. Conservation, 1940-41; editor weekly syndicated column Outdoors South, 1947-48; staff writer So. Outdoors Mag., 1959-61, West Bank Guide, New Orleans, 1962-63; commentator for own conservation, outdoor program Miss. Soundings, WGCH, Gulfport, Miss. Chmn., New Orleans Spring Fiesta, 1947; chmn. spring fiesta La. Poetry Soc., 1948. Recipient certificate of merit Nash Motors, 1953; 1st pl. award for books, short stories and poetry La. Press Women, 1969. Mem. D.A.R. (past program chmn. Metairie Ridge chpt.), Nat. League Am. Pen Women (Blue Ribbon award So. Region Gulf Coast br. 1948, pres. Miss.), Nat. Fedn. Am. Press Women (1st pl. award 1960, 2d pl. award 1969), Colonial Dames XVII Century (certificate of recognition 1971), Nat. Soc. Arts and Letters (co-founder New Orleans chpt., mem. exec. bd.), Outdoor Writers Assn. Am., La. Outdoor Writers Assn. (past dir.), Internat. Womens Fishing Assn., Fedn. Musicians Jackson. Author: (poetry) Shadows of the Swamp, 1940; Mary Land's Louisiana Cookery (co-winner So. Books of Year in ann. So. Books Competition), 1955; New Orleans Cuisine, 1969; (poetry) Abode, 1972. Home: 1314 Williams Av Natchitoches LA 71457

LAND, OTTIS CLARK, constrn. co. exec.; b. Ben Wheeler, Tex., Jan. 16, 1924; s. Ottis Autley and Vera Safara (Clark) L.; student, Kilgore Jr. Coll., 1941-43; B.S. in Civil Engring., So. Meth. U., 1947; m. Colesta Deloris Hatchel, Mar. 6, 1945; children—Dana T., Michael C., Debra D. Designer hwys. and bridges Tex. Hwy. Dept., Dallas, 1947-48; designer expressways and bridges City of Dallas, 1948-51; asst. to gen. supr. Austin Road Co., Dallas, 1951-55; with Reynolds Land, Inc., Tyler, Tex., 1955—, pres., gen. mgr., 1962—; dir. First Soinest Savs. & Loan. Served to lt. (j.g.), USNR, 1944-47. Mem. Tex. Soc. Profl. Engrs., Assn. Gen. Contractors (dir. 1973—), C. of C. (chmn. new industries com. 1972-74, mem. hwy. com. 1973—). Republican. Rotarian (chmn. new membership com. 1972-73, mem. edn. com. 1972—, co-chmn. exchange students com. 1974—). Home: Cumberland Rd Tyler TX 75701 Office: 2700 S Sowest Loop 323 Tyler TX 75701

LAND, SAMUEL BUCHANAN, ins. agt.; b. Baskerville, Va., Dec. 15, 1916; s. Samuel Wesley and Mary Beatrice (Buchanan) L.; B.S., Va. Poly. Inst., 1938, M.S., 1939; m. Eunice Gray Caroon, July 6, 1941; children—Samuel Buchanan, Eunice (Mrs. John F. Carroll, Jr.). County agt. Va. Extension Service, 1939-41; marketing specialist Va. Dept. Agr., 1946-47; mgr. coop. Farm Supply Store, South Hill, Va., 1948-53; owner Land Ins. Agy., South Hill, 1953—; dir. Citizens Bank, Inc. Mem. Mecklenburg County Sch. Bd., 1959—, now chmn. Served from 1st lt. to capt. AUS, 1941-45. Methodist (supt. Sunday sch. 1964-72). Mason, Lion (pres. 1964-65). Home: Route 1 South Hill VA 23970 Office: Box 488 South Hill VA 23970

LAND, WALTER KELLY, county ofcl.; b. Lodi, Miss., Sept. 30, 1917; s. Walter Benjamin and Willie Belle (Emerson) L.; B.A., 1946, M.A., 1948; m. Rosabelle Jordan, June 20, 1944; 1 son, Guy Paul. High sch. prin., Cumberland, Miss., 1942-44, Ingomar, Miss., 1944-46, Abbeville, Miss., 1946-48, Macon, Miss., 1948-53, Big Black, Miss., 1960-62, also guidance counselor, 1948-62; county welfare agt. Webster County, Miss., 1962—. Sec. Webster County Fair Assn., 1955; pres. Eupora Band Boosters, 1965, 68. Named Rotarian of the year, 1964. Mem. Miss. Edn. Assn., Am. Personnel and Guidance Assn., N.E.A., Montgomery County Tchrs. Assn. (pres.), Miss. Conf. Social Welfare, Miss. Assn. County Welfare Agts. (pres. 1969). Rotarian (pres. 1969, treas. 1974). Home: Box 291 Route 1 Eupora MS 39744 Office: Drawer B Eupora MS 39744

LANDA, ALFONS, lawyer, bus. exec.; b. Chgo., Dec. 14, 1897; s. Alfonso and Frances (Claes) L.; student Georgetown U., 1922; LL.B., George Washington U., 1925; student Oxford (Eng.) U., 1925; m. Alexandra Francesca; 1 son, Alfonso. Began with law firm of Joseph E. Davies, 1926, partner firm, 1935; now sr. mem. Davies, Richberg, Tydings, Landa & Duff. Pres. Detroit & Cleve. Navigation Co., 1954, Colonial Airlines, N.Y.C., 1951; dir., chmn. exec. com. Fairbanks Whitney Corp., 1959-62; chmn. bd. Fairbanks, Morse & Co., Chgo., 1958-62, Baruch-Foster Corp., 1955-62; pres., dir. Marquis Who's Who, Inc., 1969; v.p., dir. Walker & Dunlop, Inc. Enlisted with 132d Ill. Inf., 1917; served World War I. Decorated chevalier de l'Ordre du Saint Sepulchre. Mem. A.I.M. (dir.). Clubs: Racquet and Tennis, Brook (N.Y.C.); Travellers (Paris); Everglades, Bath and Tennis, Seminole (Palm Beach). Home: 150 El Vedado Rd Palm Beach FL 33480 Office: 1125 15th St NW Washington DC 20005

LANDAU, SOL, clergyman; b. Berlin, Germany, June 21, 1920; s. Ezekiel and Helene (Grynberg) L.; B.A., Bklyn. Coll., 1949; M.Hebrew Lit., Jewish Theol. Sem., 1951; M.A., N.Y. U., 1958; postgrad. Fla. State U., 1969-74; m. Gabriela Mayer, Jan. 14, 1951; children—Ezra M., Tamara A. Rabbi, 1951; rabbi Whitestone (N.Y.) Hebrew Center, 1952-56; co-rabbi Park Synagogue, Cleve., 1956-60, 63-65; rabbi Beth Hillel Congregation, Wilmette, Ill., 1960-63, Beth David Congregation, Miami, Fla., 1965—. Pres., Dade County Mental Health Assn., 1973—; pres. Dade County Youth Adv. Bd. Bd. overseers Dropsie U., Phila. Served with AUS, 1942-45. Recipient Jerusalem award, citation City Miami, award Dade County Mental Health Assn. Mem. Rabbinical Assembly (pres. S.E. Region), Am. Assn. U. Profs., Adult Edn. Assn., Jewish War Vets., Sr. Centers Dade County. Author: Christian-Jewish Relations; Length of Our Days; Bridging Two Worlds. Home: 519 SW 25th Rd Miami FL 33129 Office: 2625 SW 3d Av Miami FL 33129

LANDAUER, JERRY GERD, journalist; b. Stuttgart, Germany, Jan. 16, 1932; s. Adolph and Meta (Marx) L. brought to U.S., 1938, naturalized 1944; A.B., Columbia, 1953; postgrad. U. Bonn (Germany), 1953-54; m. Susan Lois Ecker, June 23, 1963. Local news reporter Washington Post, 1956-60; Capitol Hill reporter U.P.I., 1960-62; reporter Washington bur. Wall St. Jour., 1962—. Recipient Raymond Clapper Meml. award, 1964; Sigma Delta Chi Distinguished Serviced award for Washington corr., 1964; prize for investigative reporting Drew Pearson Found., 1973. Mem. Assn. Alumni Columbia Coll., Tau Epsilon Phi. Club: Nat. Press (Washington). Home: 3 Riggs Ct NW Washington DC 20036 Office: Nat. Press Bldg Washington DC 20005

LANDAUER, LEO L., engr.; b. Dallas, Oct. 5, 1907; s. Leo L. and Mabel Cahn (Levy) L.; C.E., Cornell U., 1927; m. Blonda E. Bostick, Aug. 1953. Engr. various offices, 1927-29; cons. engr. C. L. Kribs, Jr., Dallas, 1929-34, partner Kribs & Landauer, Dallas and Houston, 1934-41, pres. Landauer & Shafer, Dallas, Houston, El Paso and Little Rock, 1945-56, Leo L. Landauer & Assos., Inc., cons. engrs., Dallas, Tex., Little Rock, Baton Rouge, Washington, 1956—. Served as comdr. USNR, 1941-45. Registered profl. engr., Tex., Okla., Ark., N.M., La., Miss., D.C., Ariz. Mem. Am. Soc. C.E., Nat., Tex. socs. profl. engrs., Am. Soc. Heating, Ventilating and Air Conditioning Engrs., Am. Soc. Mil. Engrs., U.S., Tex. cons. engrs. council. Clubs: Engineers, Cipango (Dallas). Home: 9345 Sunnybrook Lane Dallas TX 75220 Office: 3811 Rawlins St Dallas TX 75219

LANDERS, CHARLES THOMAS, television exec.; b. Harrodsburg, Ky., May 13, 1927; s. Grant and Viola Elizabeth (Sharp) L.; student United Electronics Lab., Louisville, 1947-49, Tri State Coll., Angola, Ind., 1953; m. Anna Louise Phillips, Sept. 6, 1952; children—Teresa (Mrs. Benjamin O. Upton), Sandra. With test dept. Cape Hart Farnsworth, Ft. Wayne, Ind., 1949-50, 52; repairman electronic equipment, Lexington, Ky., 1953-56; equipment engr. Western Electric Co., Chgo., 1956-57; communications engr. United Electronics, Louisville, 1957-60; chief engr. WKPC-TV Channel 15, Louisville, 1957-61, dir. engring., 1962—; chief engr. WFPL and WFPK-FM, 1962-68. Cons. sta. WIPB, Muncie, Ind., audio visual dept. Louisville Free Pub. Library. Served with USMCR, World War

II, Korean War. Mem. Soc. Motion Picture and TV Engrs., Nat. Assn. Ednl. Broadcasters, Internat. Broadcast Soc. Mason, Moose, Hon. Order Ky. Cols. Home: 425 Wood Rd Louisville KY 40222 Office: PO Box 1515 Louisville KY 40201

LANDERS, ROBERT LELAND, agency exec., condr.; b. Durant, Okla., July 31, 1919; s. Charles G. and Sheila (Bratton) L.; student Southeastern State Coll., 1938-40, U. Md; m. Eunice Hassinger, Sept. 4, 1943; children—Robert L., Carol Elaine, Joan, Cynthia, Mary Lynne. Head music dept. McAlester (Okla.) Pub. Schs., 1947-48; dir. bands U. Md., 1950-54; asst. condr. San Carlo Opera Co., 1942-45; commd. warrant officer USAAF, 1940, advanced through grades to capt., 1955, ret., 1965; condr. 529th Air Force Band, Atlantic City and Buckley Field, Colo., 1942-45, Singing Sgts., ofcl. chorus, 1948-65; asso. condr. USAF Band and Symphony Orch., 1963-65; pres. Robert Landers Agy.; former condr. Capital Hill Symphony Orch., Robert Landers Chorale; now exec. v.p., gen. mgr. Fla. Symphony Orch.; minister of music Eldbrooke Meth. Ch., Washington 1949-67; condr. Tampa Oratorio Soc., dir. music Manhattan Av. Meth. Ch., Tampa, Fla., 1967; now minister music First Congl. Ch., Winter Park, Fla. Bd. mgrs. Tampa Boys Club. Mem. Am. Bandmasters Assn., Phi Beta Mu, Kappa Psi. Club: Civitan. Home: 4222 Stonewall Dr Orlando FL 32806 Office: PO Box 782 Orlando FL 32808

LANDIS, FRED STANLEY, constrn. co. exec.; b. Pitts., Feb. 6, 1920; s. Harry and Rebecca (Freedel) L.; B.S. in Civil Engring., Carnegie Mellon U., 1940; m. Ida Evelyn Baty, Jan. 8, 1944; children—James Charles, Carol Thomas Dunne, John Michael. Insp. constrn. Albright & Friel, Aberdeen, Md., 1940-41; v.p., chief engr. Keller Constrn. Corp., New Orleans, 1945-55; pres. Landis Constrn. Co., Inc., New Orleans, 1955—. Mem. New Orleans Bd. Standards and Appeals, 1967-72. Pres. Jr. Achievement of New Orleans, 1972, bd. dirs., 1964—. Served to lt. col. C.E., AUS, 1941-45; ETO. Decorated Legion of Merit, Silver Star, Bronze Star, Purple Heart (U.S.); Croix de Guerre (France). Mem. Am. Soc. C.E. (treas. 1972—), Asso. Gen. Contractors Am. (chpt. dir. 1968—), Am. Arbitration Assn. Home: 1473 Nashville Av New Orleans LA 70115 Office: 241 Industrial Av New Orleans LA 70121

LANDISS, CARL WILSON, educator; b. Clarksville, Tenn., May 6, 1914; s. Clarence W. and Ollie (Dunaway) L.; B.S., Abilene Christian Coll., 1935; M. Ed., Tex. A and M U., 1947; D. Ed., Pa. State U., 1951; m. Georgia Belle Fleeman, Feb. 8, 1936; children—Carolyn Rhea (Mrs. James Byron Graves), William Coleman. Tchr., Sylvester pub. schs., 1935-36; Kansas City pub. schs., 1936-43; prof. Tex. A and M U., College Station, 1943-67, prof., head dept. health and phys. edn., 1967—. Referee Bluebonnet Bowl, 1963, 68, Cotton Bowl, 1965, 67, 72; mem. College Station Recreational Council, 1967—, Planning and Zoning Commn., College Station, 1969—; councilman, College Station, 1958-64. Bd. dirs. College Station United Chest. Served as lt. USNR, 1944-46. Recipient State Honor award Tex. Assn. for Health, Phys. Edn. and Recreation, 1964. Mem. Tex. Assn. for Health, Phys. Edn. and Recreation (past pres.), A.A.H.P.E.R., Internat. Soc. for Psychology of Sport and Phys. Activity, A.A.A.S., S.W. Football Ofcls. Assn., Phi Kappa Phi, Phi Epsilon Kappa, Phi Delta Kappa. Mem. Ch. of Christ. Mason, Kiwanian. Author: (with C.B. Corbin and L.J. Dowell) Concepts and Experiments in Physical Education, 1968. Contbr. articles profl. jours. Home: 803 Dexter Dr College Station TX 77840

LANDREAU, ANTHONY NORMAN, museum exec.; b. Washington, Apr. 2, 1930; s. Norman Bayle and Caroline Hill (Griffin) L.; student Catholic U., 1951-52; B.A., Black Mountain Coll. (N.C.), 1956; m. Anita May Jester, Oct. 15, 1965; children—John Celestin, Christopher Anselm, Geoffrey Olson. Cons. textiles, Bolivia, 1965-66; asso. curator Textile Mus., Washington, 1967-70, acting dir., 1971-72, exec. dir., 1972—. Trustee, Greater Washington Ednl. Telecommunications Assn., Kindler Found., Washington. Served with USNR, 1948-50. Nat. Endowment Arts study fellow, 1973. Mem. Washington, N.Y. rug socs., Am. Assn. Museums, Am. Archaeol. Soc. Club: N.Y. Hajji Baba. Author: (with W.R. Pickering) From the Bosphorus to Samarkand: Flat-Woven Rugs, 1969. Contbr. articles on oriental rugs to profl. jours. Home: 507 Greenbrier Dr Silver Spring MD 20910 Office: Textile Museum 2320 S St NW Washington DC 20008

LANDRENEAU, RODNEY EDMUND, JR., physician; b. Mamou, La., Jan. 17, 1929; s. Rodney Edmund and Blanche (Savoy) L.; M.D., La. State U., 1951; m. Colleen Fraser, June 4, 1952; children—Rodney Jerome, Michael Douglas, Denise Margaret, Melany Patricia, Fraser, Edythe Blanche. Intern Charity Hosp., New Orleans, 1951-52, resident, 1952-54, 56-58; practice medicine specializing in surgery, Eunice, La., 1958—; pres., dir. Eunice Med. Center, Inc., 1960—; mem. staff Moosa Meml. Hosp. Eunice, 1958—; vis. staff Opelousas Gen. Hosp., 1958—; cons., staff Lafayette (La.) Charity Hosp. cons. staff surgery Savoy Meml. Hosp., Mamon, La. Dir. Acadiana Bank & Trust Co. Mem. La. State Hosp. Bd., 1972—. Served M.C. AUS, 1954-56. Diplomate Am. Bd. Surgery. Fellow Internat. Coll. Surgeons, A.C.S., (local chmn. com. trauma), Southeastern Surg. Congress, Pan Pacific Surg. Congress; mem. Am. Bd. Abdominal Surgeons, Am. Geriatrics Soc., St. Edmunds Athletic Assn., St. Landry Parish Med. Soc. (pres. 1969-71). Rotarian (dir. Eunice). Home: 1113 Williams St Eunice LA 70535 Office: Eunice Medical Center Eunice LA 70535

LANDRIEU, MOON, mayor; b. New Orleans, July 23, 1930; s. Joseph and Loretta L.; B.B.A., Loyola U., 1952, LL.B., 1954; m. Verna Satterlee, Sept. 25, 1954; children—Mary, Mark, Melanie, Michelle, Mitchell, Madeleine, Martin, Melinda, Maurice. Atty. firm Landrieu, Calogero & Kronlage, 1957-70, mayor City of New Orleans, 1970—. Mem. La. Ho. of Reps., 1960-66; councilman, New Orleans, 1966-70. Served with AUS, 1954-57. Democrat. Roman Catholic. Home: 4301 S Prieur St New Orleans LA 70125 Office: 1300 Perdido St New Orleans LA 70112

LANDRITH, GEORGE CLAY, business exec.; b. Los Angeles, Nov. 29, 1915; s. William George and Mary (Wickersham) L.; student pub. schs.; m. Frances Jordan, Oct. 28, 1935; children—Nicholas J., George Clay. Vice pres. Thomas L. Dawson, gen. contracting, Kansas City, Mo., 1934-39; owner, operator Landrith Constrn. Co., Alexandria, Va., 1939-45; owner Belle View Apts., Alexandria, 1947—; dir. 1st Va. Bankshares Corp., Arlington, Va., 1st Commonwealth Ins. Co., Richmond, Va. Mem. Va. Hwy. Commn., 1962-70; mem. Fairfax County Planning Commn., 1948-60, Bd. Fairfax County Suprs., 1960, Richmond Met. Authority, 1966-70, Va. Met. Areas. Transp. Study Commn.; bd. dirs. Alexandria Community Health Center, 1953-54, Alexandria Boys Club, 1958-62; mem. dist. council Salvation Army, 1958-62; sponsor Alexandria Little League, 1953—; dir. trustees Fairfax County Hosp., 1957-59. Treas., Fairfax County Democratic Com., 1948-49. Trustee George Mason Coll., Fairfax, Va. Mem. Fairfax County C. of C. (dir. 1953, 71). Clubs: Belle Haven Country (Alexandria, Va.); Commonwealth (Richmond, Va.); Farmington Country (Charlottesville, Va.). Home: 6319 Olmi-Landrith Dr Alexandria VA 22307 Office: 1605 Belle View Blvd Alexandria VA 22307

LANDRUM, CARROL FRAZIER, physician; b. nr. Taylorsville, Miss., Apr. 3, 1926; s. Joseph David and Emma Elizabeth (Meadows) L.; student Perkinston Jr. Coll., 1946-47; B.S., Millsaps Coll., 1948; M.D., Tulane U., 1952; postgrad. in pediatrics Harvard, 1969-70. Intern, Brooke Gen. Hosp., Ft. Sam Houston, Tex., 1952-53; practice medicine, Biloxi, Miss., 1954-58, Smith County, Miss., 1958-59, Edwards, Miss., 1959—. Served to capt. USAF, 1952-54. Mem. Internat. Platform Assn. Baptist. Mason, Rotarian. Research in causes of malignant diseases. Home: PO Box 198 Edwards MS 39066

LANDRUM, JOHN HINTON, librarian; b. Greenwood, S.C., Nov. 25, 1944; s. Julius Parson and Mary Louise (Hinton) L.; student Clemson U., 1962-64; A.B., Erskine Coll., 1966; M.S. in L.S., U. N.C., 1967. Reference librarian S.C. Library, Columbia, 1967-70, dir. reader services, 1970—. Served with AUS, 1968. Mem. S.C., Southeastern library assns., A.L.A., South Caroliniana Soc., S.C. Hist. Assn., Beta Phi Mu. Home: 5526 Lakeshore Dr Columbia SC 29206 Office: 1500 Senate St Columbia SC 29201

LANDRUM, PHILIP MITCHELL, congressman; b. Martin, Ga., Sept. 10, 1907; s. Philip Davis and Blanche (Mitchell) L.; A.B., Piedmont Coll., Demorest, Ga., 1939; student Mercer U., La. State U.; LL.B., Atlanta Law Sch., 1941;; m. Laura Brown, July 30, 1933; children—Phillip Mitchell, Susan. High sch. athletic dir., coach, Bowman, Ga., 1932-35, Nelson Ga., 1935-37; supt. pub. schs. Nelson, 1937-41; admitted to Ga. bar 1941; asst. atty. gen. State Ga., 1946-47; exec. sec. Gov. Ga., 1947-48; practice of law, Jasper, 1949—; mem. 83rd-93rd Congresses, 9th Dist. Ga. Served USAAF, 1942-45. Mem. Ga. Bar Assn., Am. Legion, V.F.W. Democrat. Baptist. Mason, Elk. Home: Jasper GA 30143 Office: House Office Bldg Washington DC 20515

LANDRY, FRANCES LEGGIO (MRS. JULES F. LANDRY), lawyer; b. Baton Rouge, Aug. 11, 1908; d. George and Josephine (Loicano) Leggio; B.A., La. State U., 1926, J.D. (valedictorian), 1934; m. Jules F. Landry, Aug. 9, 1934; 1 dau., Frances Harriet. Admitted to La. bar, 1934, since practiced law with husband as Landry & Landry, Baton Rouge; lectr. La. State U. Law Sch., 1942-43; atty. for parish tax collector, 1940-46; spl. asst. atty. gen. La., 1968-70; sec.-treas. Wooddale Comml. Properties, Inc.; dir., owner Lafayette Gallery; v.p., dir. Bank of Commerce & Trust Co., St. Francisville, La. Former vice chmn. Beautification Commn. for City Baton Rouge; pres. E. Baton Rouge Parish Library Bd. Control. Formerly active Girl Scouts, Salvation Army. Mem. Internat., Inter-Am., Am., La., Baton Rouge bar assns., Am., La. (past vice chmn. trustees sect.) library assns., La. State U. Law Sch. Alumni Assn. (pres. 1968-70), Order of Coif, Pi Sigma Alpha, Phi Delta Delta, Phi Kappa Phi, Mu Sigma Rho. Clubs: Woman's, Inc. (bd. mgrs.); Quota (internat. pres. 1942-44). Home: 2036 Lake Hills Pkwy Baton Rouge LA 70801 Office: 348 Lafayette St Baton Rouge LA 70801

LANDRY, GEORGE ALLEN, city ofcl.; b. Lafayette, La., Apr. 30, 1934; s. George and Bertha (Richard) L.; B.S., U. Southwestern La., 1956, Geol. Engr., 1969; m. Geraldine Foco, May 30, 1954; children—Gary, Cynthia. Engr. trainee Lane Wells Oil Service, Lafayette, La., 1956-57; safety engr. La. Dept. Hwys., Baton Rouge, 1960-64, traffic engr., 1964-68; city traffic engr. City of Lafayette, La., 1968-71, dir. pub. works, 1971—. Bd. dir. Lafayette Coordinating Com., 1969-73. Served to capt. USAF, 1957-60. Mem. Am. Pub. Works Assn. (dir. 1971—), Inst. for Transp., Lafayette C. of C. Kiwanian (pres. elect 1974). Home: 236 River Rd Lafayette LA 70501 Office: 733 Jefferson St Lafayette LA 70501

LANDRY, JULES FRANCIS, lawyer, banker, industrialist; b. St. Francisville, La., Nov. 9, 1906; s. Jules F. and Elizabeth (Desposito) L.; LL.B., La. State U., 1932; m. Frances C. Leggio, Aug. 9, 1934; 1 dau., Frances Harriet. Admitted to La. bar, 1932; with firm Landry & Landry, Baton Rouge, 1932—, now chmn. emeritus; chmn. bd. Capital Bank & Trust Co., Baton Rouge, 1955-73, acting pres., 1962; pres., chmn. bd. Bank of Commerce & Trust Co., St. Francisville, La.; pres. Rue Lafayette Mortgage Corp., 1952—, Bellingrath Hills, Inc., 1955-68, Goodwood Homesites, Inc., 1958-66, Wooddale Comml. Properties, Inc., 1962. Pres. Baton Rouge Symphony Assn., 1962-65; area chmn. U.S. Savs. Bond Com. Mem. La. State U. Found.; trustee Gulf S. Research Inst. Mem. Internat., Inter-Am., La., Am., Baton Rouge bar assns., La. State U. Law Sch. Alumni Assn. Roman Catholic. Elk, K.C. Clubs: Internat. House, Baton Rouge Country, City (Baton Rouge).Home: 2036 Lake Hills Pkwy Baton Rouge LA 70801 Office: 348 Lafayette St Baton Rouge LA 70801

LANDRY, MATTHEW ANDREW, JR., accountant; b. Denver, Dec. 23, 1942; s. Matthew A. and Sara Jane (Carter) L.; B.B.A. with highest honors U. Tex., 1964, M.B.A., 1965; m. Alice Faye Heitkamp, Aug. 10, 1963; children—Thomas and Terry (twins). With Peat, Marwick, Mitchell & Co., C.P.A.'s, Houston, 1965—, partner, 1972—. Frequent speaker on banking topics; faculty mem. Sch. Banking of South, La. State U., Baton Rouge, 1969—. Adviser, Jr. Achievement, 1966—. Arthur Young & Co. scholar, 1964. Mem. Houston Livestock Show and Rodeo Assn., Tex. Soc. C.P.A.s (dir. 1973—), Nat. Assn. Accountants, Am. Inst. C.P.A.'s, Phi Kappa Phi, Beta Gamma Sigma, Beta Alpha Psi. Club: Plaza. Home: 4914 Alba St Houston TX 77018 Office: 4300 1 Shell Plaza Houston TX 77002

LANDRY, RICHARD ANDREW, JR., elec. engr.; b. Orange, Tex., Aug. 31, 1927; s. Richard Andrew and Kassie Eloise (Mitchell) L.; B.S., La. State U., 1949; m. Barbara Alice Houser, June 22, 1957; children—Dianna Faith, Kyle Mitchell. Lighting engr. Gulf States Utilities Co., Port Arthur, Tex., 1949-55; lighting engr. Gulf States Utilities Co., Beaumont and Port Arthur divs., 1955-57, supr. lighting sales promotion, 1957-68, system sales application engr., 1968-70, indsl. engr. Western div., Conroe, Tex., 1970—. Vice chmn. Am. Cancer Soc. Crusade, Montgomery County, Tex., 1972—. Republican precinct chmn., Beaumont, 1968-70. Bd. dirs. Montgomery County chpt. Am. Cancer Soc. Served with USNR, 1945-46. Registered profl. engr., Tex. Mem. I.E.E.E., Illuminating Engring. Soc. (dir. San Jacinto chpt. 1966), Lambda Chi Alpha. Methodist (mem. adminstrv. bd.). Home: 13 Woody Creek Dr Conroe TX 77301 Office: PO Box 158 Conroe TX 77301

LANDRY, RUDOLPH MATAS, physician; b. New Orleans, Feb. 17, 1919; s. Lucian H. and Lowell (Sedgwick) L.; B.S., Tulane U., 1939, M.D., 1942; M.S., U. Minn., 1949; m. Jane E. Willius, Feb. 27, 1943; children—Rudolph Matas, Jane Elizabeth, Fredrick Willius Lucian. Intern, Touro Infirmary, New Orleans, 1942-43; fellow Mayo Clinic, Rochester, Minn., 1946-50; mem. staff Ochsner Clinic, instr. surgery Tulane U., New Orleans, 1950-52; practice medicine specializing in surgery, Chattanooga, 1952-72; mem. staffs Newell Hosp., Meml. Hosp., Erlanger Hosp., 1952-72; asst. med. dir. Interstate Life Ins. Co., Chattanooga, 1973—. Chmn., Tenn. Valley Med. Assembly, 1964. Served with USNR, 1943-46. Mem. Alpha Omega Alpha, Delta Kappa Epsilon, Nu Sigma Nu. Clubs: Fairyland, Lookout Mountain Golf (Lookout Mountain, Tenn.). Contbr. to profl. publs. in field. Home: 207 Watauga Lane Lookout Mountain TN 37350 Office: 540 McCallie Av Chattanooga TN 37402

LANDRY, TOM, profl. football coach; b. Mission, Tex., Sept. 11, 1924; ed. U. Tex.; m.; children—Tom, Kitty, Lisa. With N.Y. Yankees, All-Am. Conf., 1949-50; with N.Y. Giants, Nat. Football League, 1950-60, def. halfback, 1950-53, player-coach, 1954, 55, asst. coach, 1956-60; head coach Dallas Cowboys, Nat. Football League, 1960—. Served with Armed Forces, World War II. Coach Eastern Conf. champions, 1966, 67. Home: Dallas TX 75221 Office: Dallas Cowboys 6166 N Central Expressway Dallas TX 75206*

LANDRY, WALTER JOSEPH, engring. co. exec.; b. Jeanerette, La., Mar. 14, 1934; s. Walter E. and Dorothy (Rodriguez) L.; student U. Southwestern La., 1952-55; m. Faye Marie Webre, Sept. 17, 1955; children—Susan, Jennifer, Sandra, Michael, Walter, Christine, Julie, Stephen, Rebecca, Robert, Timothy. Material foreman Dupont Fabricators, 1955-57; sugar cane harvesting contractor, Jeanerette, 1957-59; with J. & L. Engring. Co., Inc., Jeanerette, 1959—, v.p. operations, 1969-71, exec. v.p., gen. mgr., 1971-73, pres., 1973—; dir. Sugarland State Bank, Jeanerette, Maquinaria Azucarera, Mexico; pres. Manufacturera 3-M Mexico, 1972—. Mem. Jeanerette Civil Service Bd., 1970—. Mem. Jeanerette C. of C. (dir. 1967—). Democrat. Roman Catholic. Contbr. articles to sugarcane internat. trade mags. Home: 689 Janice St Jeanerette LA 70544 Office: PO Box 620 Jeaneretta LA 70544

LANDSMAN, HENRY, elec. engr.; b. Detroit, Nov. 14, 1914; s. Benjamin and Elsie (Streit) L.; B.S. in Elec. Engring., U. Ill., 1934; m. Leah Jeanette Weisberger, May 24, 1936; 1 son, Bennett Albert. Elec. engring. supr. U.S. Navy Dept., 1941-46; elec. engr. Frank H. McEnney, 1946-49; chief engr. U.S. Hoffman Machinery Corp., 1949-57; elec. engr. Lord Electric Co. Inc., Los Angeles, 1957-70, v.p., mgr., 1970—, contract adminstr., 1961—, cons. mgmt. adviser, 1954—. Registered profl. engr., Pa., Conn., Ohio, Del., Ky. Mem. Am. Soc. M.E., I.E.E.E., Am. Ordnance Assn., Am. Soc. Metals, Nat. Soc. Profl. Engrs., U.S. Army Roster of Ammunition. Contbr. articles to profl. jours. Patentee in mech. field. Home: East Town House Apt 306 4590 Beechnut St Houston TX 77035 Office: 5543 Armour Dr Houston TX 77020

LANDY, BURTON AARON, lawyer; b. Chgo., Aug. 16, 1929; s. Louis J. and Clara (Ernstein) L.; B.S., Northwestern U., 1950; J.D., U. Miami, 1952; student Nat. U. Mexico, 1948; scholar U. Havana, 1951; fellow Inter-Am. Acad. Comparative Law, Havana, Cuba, 1955-56; m. Eleonora M. Simmel, Aug. 4, 1957; children—Michael Simmel, Alisa Anne. Admitted to Fla. bar, 1952; gen. practice law in Latin Am. field, Miami, 1955—; partner law firm Ammerman & Landy, 1957-63, Paul, Landy and Beiley, 1964-69; lectr. Latin Am. bus. law U. Miami, 1972—, also Internat. Law Confs. Mem. Nat. Conf. on Fgn. Aspects of U.S. Nat. Security, Washington, 1958; mem. organizing com. Miami regional conf. Com. for Internat. Econ. Growth, 1958; mem. U.S. Dept. Commerce Regional Export Expansion Council, 1969—. Dir. Inter-Am. Bar Legal Found. Served with USAF Judge Adv. Gen. Dept., 1952-54, in Korea, 1953-54; maj. USAF Res. Hon. mem. Bar of Republic of South Korea, 1954. Mem. Inter-Am. (asst. sec.-gen. 1957-59, treas. 11th conf. 1959, co-chmn. jr. bar sect. 1963-65, mem. organizing com. I-VI, Inter-Am. aviation law confs.; mem. council 1969—), Am. (chmn. com. arrangements internat. and comparative law sect. 1964-65), Spanish-Am., Fla. (vice chmn. administrv. law com. 1965, vice chmn. internat. and comparative law com. 1967-68, chmn. aero. law com. 1968-69), Dade County (chmn. fgn. laws and langs. com. 1964-65) bar assns., Am. Fgn. Law Assn. (pres. Miami 1958), Miami Jr. C. of C., Phi Alpha Delta. Contbr. articles to legal jours. Home: 6255 Old Cutler Rd Miami FL 33131 Office: Pan Am Bank Bldg Miami FL 33131

LANE, DANIEL MCNEEL, physician; b. Ft. Sam Houston, Tex., Jan. 25, 1936; s. Samuel Hartman and Mary Maverick (McNeel) L.; student U. Tex., 1953-57; M.D., Southwestern Med. Sch., Dallas, 1961; M.S., U. Tenn., 1967; Ph.D., U. Okla., 1973; m. Carolyn Ann Spruiell, Nov. 28, 1958; children—Linda Ann, Daniel McNeel, Maury Spruiell, Oleta Katherine. Intern, Children's Med. Center, Dallas, 1961-62, resident pediatrics, 1962-63; chief pediatric resident U. Miss., Jackson, 1962-64; fellow hematology U. Tenn., Memphis, 1964-66; asst. prof. pediatrics U. Okla., Oklahoma City, 1966-72; asso. prof. pediatrics Tulane Med. Sch., New Orleans, 1972-73; head hematology-oncology dept., mem. pediatrics dept. Oklahoma City Clinic, 1973—; treas., Across The Street, Inc., Norman, Okla., 1969—; pres. Crosstimbers, Inc., Norman, 1971—; sec. Poplar Pike, Inc., Realtors, Memphis, 1972—. Nat. trustee Nat. Hemophilia Found., 1966-68, Okla. pres., 1966-67. USPHS fellow pediatric hematology, 1965-66; Nat. Heart and Lung Inst. spl. research fellow, 1969-72. Diplomate Am. Bd. Pediatrics. Fellow Am. Acad. Pediatrics; mem. Am., Okla. med. assns., Oklahoma County Med. Soc., N.Y. Acad. Scis., A.A.A.S., Am. Fedn. Clin. Research, Soc. Pediatric Research, Am. Assn. Cancer Edn. Club: Oklahoma City Tennis (pres. 1969-72). Contbr. articles to profl. jours. Home: 1504 Guilford Lane Oklahoma City OK 73120 Office: 301 NW 12th St Oklahoma City OK 73103

LANE, DAVID LAWRENCE, mfg. co. exec.; b. Houston, May 2, 1942; s. Jack and Rhea (Cohen) L.; B.S. in Econs., U. Pa., 1963; M.B.A., Harvard, 1965; m. Helaine L. Wayne, May 18, 1969; children—Robert Lawrence, Rachel Anne. Cons., Farb Miller & Beerman, Houston, 1965-66; European financial dir. Cameron Iron Works Inc., Edinburgh, Scotland, 1966-70; v.p. finance Fluidic Industries, Inc., Houston, 1970-72; controller Internat. Systems & Controls Corp., Houston, 1972-73, v.p., 1973—. C.P.A., Tex. Mem. Am. Inst. C.P.A.'s, Tex. Soc. C.P.A.'s, Financial Execs. Inst., Wharton Alumni Club of Houston (v.p. 1973—). Home: 5468 Holly Springs St Houston TX 77027 Office: 2727 Allen Pkwy Houston TX 77019

LANE, DONALD EDWARD, judge; b. Chevy Chase, Md., June 10, 1909; s. John Albert and Virginia Louise (Payson) L.; B.S., Yale, 1931; ed. George Washington U. Law Sch.; m. Virginia Plugge, Sept. 1, 1938; children—Diana Randall (Mrs. Louis A. Ebersold), Adair Payson. Admitted to D.C. bar, 1935; pvt. practice law, Washington, 1935-41, 45-54; commr. U.S. Ct. Claims, 1954-69; judge U.S. Ct. Custom and Patent Appeals, 1969—. Patent adviser Manhattan Project, 1943. Served to comdr, USNR, 1941-45. Mem. Am. Bar Assn., Am. Patent Law Assn. (past sec., bd. mgrs.), Bar Assn. D.C., Am. Judicature Soc., Washington Patent Lawyers Club (past pres.). Clubs: Columbia Country (Chevy Chase, Md.); University, Cosmos (Washington). Home: 5040 Loughboro Rd NW Washington DC 20016 Office: US Ct Custom and Patent Appeals Washington DC 20439

LANE, EDWARD EMERSON, state legislator; b. Richmond, Va., Jan. 28, 1924; s. Edward Thorp and Karen (Vick) L.; student Va. Poly. Inst., 1942-43; LL.B., U. Richmond, 1948; m. Jean Wiltshire, July 4, 1944; children—Edward Emerson, Gregory. Admitted to Va. bar, 1949; practice in Richmond, 1949—; propr. Edward E. Lane & Assos., Inc., 1970—; mem. Va. Ho. Dels. from Richmond, 1954—, Dist., vice chmn. appropriations com., chmn. com. corps., ins. and banking. Co-chmn. Va. Adv. Council Endl. TV; mem. Gov. Va. Adv. Budget Com.; mem. Va. Adv. Legislative Council, also mem. various coms.; mem. Potomac River Commn., Commn. to Study Sources of Revenue for Va. Pres. Va. Assn. Workers for Blind, 1967, Robert E. Lee council

Boy Scouts Am., 1968, Central Richmond Assn., 1967; v.p. Richmond Jaycees, 1951, Va. Jaycees, 1952; mem. bd. Central Va. Ednl. TV, Jr. League Speech Center, Richmond Pub. Forum; chmn. Richmond Muscular Dystrophy campaign, 1968, Richmond Beautification Com., 1951, ann. Christmas Nativity at Carillon, 1952. Chmn. Jefferson-Jackson Day Dinner, 1957. Named Outstanding Young Man in Richmond, 1952, in Va., 1952. Served as pilot USAAF, World War II. Recipient Silver Beaver award Boy Scouts Am. Mem. Va. Assn. Professions (past pres.), Richmond Trial Lawyers Assn. (past pres.), West Richmond Businessmen's Assn. Democrat. Episcopalian (Sunday sch. tchr., dept. supt.). Moose. Home: 6301 Ridgeway Rd Richmond VA 23226 Office: 700 Building Suite 1604 Richmond VA 23219

LANE, EDWARD WOOD, JR., banker; b. Jacksonville, Fla., Apr. 4, 1911; s. Edward Wood and Anna Virginia (Tallaferro) L.; A.B., Princeton, 1933; LL.B., Harvard, 1936; m. Helen Spratt Murchison, Oct. 16, 1948; children—Edward Wood III, Helen Palmer, Anna Tallaferro, Charles Murchison. Admitted to Fla. bar, 1936; partner firm McCarthy, Lane & Adams, and predecessors, Jacksonville, 1941-60; vice-chmn., dir. Atlantic Nat. Bank, Jacksonville, 1966—; pres., chief exec. officer Atlantic Bancorp, also dir.; dir. Fla. Pub. Co. Trustee Cummer Museum Found.; bd. dirs. Jacksonville Community Chest-United Fund. Served to lt. comdr. USNR, World War II. Mem. Jacksonville Area C. of C. (com. 100), Phi Beta Kappa. Clubs: Florida Yacht, Timuguana Country, River, University (Jacksonville); Ponte Vedre (Fla.). Home: 3790 Ortega Blvd Jacksonville FL 32210 Office: Atlantic Nat Bank West Bay Station Jacksonville FL 32203

LANE, HELEN S. MURCHISON (MRS. EDWARD W. LANE, JR.), civic worker; b. Boston, June 1, 1924; d. Charles H. and Helen (Spratt) Murchison; A.B., Sweet Briar Coll., 1946; m. Edward W. Lane, Jr., Oct. 16, 1948; children—Edward W. III, Helen Palmer, Anna Taliaferro, Charles Murchison. Mem. Jacksonville Cultural and Historic Preservation Commn., 1971-73. Bd. dirs. Jr. League Jacksonville, Fla., 1954-60, pres., 1959-60; chmn. Symphony Ball, Jacksonville, 1960; restorer 1893 Victorian home; mem. fine arts com. Jacksonville C. of C., 1972-73; mem. Arts Assembly of Jacksonville. Regional dir. exec. com. Alumni Council Sweet Briar Coll., 1968-70; trustee Bartram Sch., 1971-74. Bd. dirs. Jacksonville Symphony Orch., 1973-74. Mem. Colonial Dames. Clubs: Jacksonville Garden (life); Acacia Garden. Pub.: The Best of Lucifer, 1969; The Queen Victoria Cooks, 1971. Home: 3790 Ortega Blvd Jacksonville FL 32210

LANE, JAMES WILLIAM, elec. engr.; b. Jackson, Miss., Sept. 2, 1938; s. Fred Conn and Essie Lee (Tierce) L.; A.A., Miss. Delta Jr. Coll., 1958-60; B.S. in Elec. Engring., Miss. State U., 1965; m. Joyce Ann Rains, May 27, 1959; children—Jim, Jeffrey Alan. Engr. North, Beasley and Swayze, cons. engrs., Jackson, 1966-71; design engr. Leigh Watkins III & Assos., cons. engrs., Jackson, 1971—. Active Boy Scouts Am. Recipient Eagle Scout and Silver Explorer award Boy Scouts Am., 1954, God and Country award Sumner (Miss.) Bapt. Ch., 1953. Registered profl. engr., Ala., Miss., Tex. Mem. Nat. Soc. Profl. Engrs., Miss. Engring. Soc. Baptist. Home: 939 Autumn Dr Jackson MS 39212 Office: 4523 Office Park Dr Jackson MS 39203

LANE, SISTER M. CLAUDE, archivist-librarian; b. Dobbin, Tex., Feb. 7, 1915; d. Michael W. and Mary Lou (Pace) Lane; student U. Tex., 1934-47, U. Houston, 1936-39; B.A., Our Lady of Lake Coll., 1953; M.L.S., U. Tex., 1961. Tchr., choral dir. elementary and high schs. Dominican Sisters Houston, 1934-60; tchr.-librarian elementary and high schs., Tex., Cal., 1953-64; prin. St. Marys Elementary Sch., Orange, Tex., 1958-60; archivist Cath. Archives of Tex., Austin, 1960-61, summers 1961-64, full time 1964-67, 71—, in absentia, 1967-71; tchr. high schs., Tex., Cal., 1961-64; librarian St. Pius X High Sch., Houston, 1967-71. Library cons. Office of Edn., Diocese of Austin, 1964-69, 71—. Shelter mgr. Austin-Travis County Dept. Civil Def., 1965-67. Mem. Am., Cath., Tex. (sec.-treas. Archives Round Table 1967-68, chmn. 1970-71) library assns., Am. Sch. Librarians Assn., Am., Tex. hist. assns., Soc. Am. Archivists, Am. Assn. State and Local History, Am. Cath. Hist. Assn., Tex. Hist. Found. and Survey Commn., Soc. Southwest Archivists. Author: Catholic Archives of Texas: History and Preliminary Inventory, 1961. Contbr. profl. jours. Home: Newman Hall Austin TX 78705 Office: 16th and N Congress Sts PO Box 13327 Capitol Sta Austin TX 78711

LANE, MARGARET BEYNON TAYLOR (MRS. HORACE C. LANE), librarian; b. St. Louis, Feb. 6, 1919; d. Archer and Alice (Jones) Taylor; B.A., La. State U., 1939, J.D., 1942; B.A. in L.S., Columbia, 1941; m. Horace C. Lane, Jan. 6, 1945; children—Margaret Elizabeth, Thomas Archer. Reference and circulation asst. Columbia Law Library, N.Y.C., 1942-44; law librarian, asst. prof. U. Conn. Sch. Law, Hartford, 1944-46; law librarian La. State U. Law Sch. Baton Rouge, 1946-48; recorder documents Sec. of State's Office, Baton Rouge, 1949—. Mem. U.S. Adv. Council to Pub. Printer on Depository Libraries, 1972—. Treas. Delta Iota House Bd. of Kappa Kappa Gamma Frat., 1965-68. Mem. Am. (chmn. interdiv. com. on pub. documents 1967-70), La. library assns., La., Baton Rouge bar assns., Phi Delta Delta, Kappa Kappa Gamma. Club: Baton Rouge Library. Home: 7545 Richards Dr Baton Rouge LA 70809 Office: 1515A Choctaw Dr Baton Rouge LA 70804

LANE, MARION POTTER, JR., clergyman; b. Waco, Tex., June 20, 1921; s. Marion Potter and Hattie (Richter) L.; student Peabody Coll., 1939-41; A.B., Wittenberg U., 1943, B.D., 1945, M.Div., 1972; postgrad. Cornell U., 1945-46; M.A., Vanderbilt U., 1959; postgrad. Luth. Theol. So. Sem., 1969; m. Mable Sue Stirewalt, June 23, 1946; 1 son, William Marion. Ordained to ministry Luth. Ch., 1945; missionary Andhra Evang. Luth. Ch., United Luth. Ch. Am., India, 1946-52; mission developer, pastor in Hampton, Va., 1953-56; pastor in Parrottsville, Tenn., 1956-62, St. Paul's Luth. Ch., Shenandoah, Va., 1962—. Sec. central dist. Va. synod Luth. Ch. Am., 1965-72, dean Blue Ridge area, 1972—, chmn. com. on publs., 1967-72, valley regional coordinator on ministry. 1971-72. Mem. men's com. Japan Internat. Christian U. Found.; adv. bd. Massanutten Mental Health Center (pres. 1967-69). Trustee Luth. Children's Home of South, 1972—. Mem. Va., Page County (pres. 1965-66) councils chs., Page County Ministerial Assn. (pres. 1963-65, 72-74, treas. 1965-66), Luth. Soc. Worship, Music and Arts, Page County Heritage Assn., Page County Farm Bur. Club: Ruritan. Contbr. to devotional quar., also weekly newspaper column. Address: RFD 1 Box 130 Shenandoah VA 22849

LANE, MILLS B., JR., banker; b. Savannah, Ga., 1912; m. Anne Waring; children—Mills B. IV, Anita. Entered banking bus. with Citizens & So. Nat. Bank of Savannah, now vice-chmn., chief exec. officer, Atlanta; dir. Bibb Mfg. Co., Coca Cola Bottling Co. Miami, Ga. Power Co., Winn Dixie Stores. Mem. Young Pres. Orgn. (dir.). Home: 2 W Muscogee Av NW Atlanta GA 30305 Office: Citizens & So Nat Bank 35 Broad St PO Box 4899 Atlanta GA 30301

LANE, MONTAGUE, educator, physician; b. N.Y.C., Aug. 28, 1929; s. George and Ida (Korn) L.; B.A., N.Y. U., 1947; M.B., Chgo. Med. Sch., 1952, M.D., 1953; M.S., Georgetown U., 1957; m. Carol Higelman, June 30, 1957; children—Laura Diane, Adam Reuben. Clin. asso. Nat. Cancer Inst., NIH, 1954-56, sr. investigator Clin. Pharmacology and Exptl. Therapeutics Service, attending physician gen. med. br. Nat. Cancer Inst., 1957-60; asso. in medicine George Washington U. Med. Sch., 1957-60; asst. prof.-asso. prof. depts. pharmacology and medicine Baylor U. Coll. Medicine, Houston, 1960-67; prof. depts. pharm. and medicine Baylor Coll. of Medicine, 1967—, head div. clin. oncology dept. pharmacology, 1969—. Mem. study sect. Nat. Cancer Inst., 1966-69, mem. cancer clin. investigations rev. com., 1972—; chmn. new agts. com. S.W. Cancer Chemotherapy study group. Diplomate Am. Bd. Internal Medicine (mem. subcom. on med. oncology 1974—). Mem. A.C.P., Am. Inst. for Nutrition, Am. Soc. for Clin. Oncology (program chmn. 1970), Am. Soc. for Pharmacology and Exptl. Therapeutics (exec. bd. clin. div. 1969—), Am. Soc. Clin. Pharmacology and Therapeutics (pres. 1971-72), Am. Soc. for Hematology, Houston Soc. Internal Medicine (v.p. 1973-74), Am. Assn. for Cancer Research, Harris County Med. Soc. Asso. editor Cancer Research, 1970—. Home: 6401 Brompton Rd Houston TX 77005 Office: 1200 Moursund Houston TX 77025

LANE, PERRY VIRGIL, television tng. tape co. exec.; b. Humboldt, Tenn., May 10, 1921; s. Lyle Luther and Nell (Warmath) L.; B.S. in Mech. Engring., U. Tenn., 1945; m. Catherine Prince; children—Jean (Mrs. James Troutner), Thomas Perry, Jill (Mrs. David T. Jackson). Gen. foreman Combustion Engring., Chattanooga, 1947-56; mgr. Nat. Contractors, Inc., Chattanooga, 1956-61; mgr., v.p. TEC Supply Co., Inc., Chattanooga, 1961—; pres., Tel-A-Train, Chattanooga, 1973—. Registered profl. engr., Tenn. Mem. Soc. Advancement Mgmt. (pres. 1966). Tenn. Soc. Profl. Engrs. (pres. Chattanooga chpt. 1972), Chattanooga Engrs. Club (pres. 1960). Home: 140 Palisades Dr Signal Mountain TN 37377 Office: PO Box 950 Chattanooga TN 37401

LANE, THOMAS ALPHONSUS, journalist, author; b. Revere, Mass., Nov. 19, 1906; s. Thomas Andrew and Julia (Fitzpatrick) L.; B.S., U.S. Mil. Acad., 1928; B.S. in C.E., Mass. Inst. Tech., 1932; grad. Nat. War Coll., 1953; m. Jean Margaret Gee, June 3, 1933; children—Jean, Michael Stuart, Julia Ann (Mrs. Donald Rasmussen), Thomas C. Commd. 2d lt. U.S. Army, 1928, advanced through grades to maj. gen., 1957; exec. officer to Air Engr., Hdqrs., USAAF, 1942; exec. officer, operations officer Engr. sect. Gen. Hdqrs., S.W. Pacific area, 1943-45; joint operations Rev. Bd., 1946; dist. engr., Little Rock, 1948-50; dist. engr. Okinawa, 1950-52; engr. commr. D.C., 1954-57; comdg. gen. Ft. Leonard Wood, Mo., 1957-60; pres. Mississippi River Commn., 1960-62; ret., 1962; syndicated columnist, author, lectr., editor, 1962—. Instr. civil engring. and mil. history U.S. Mil. Acad., 1935-39; engring. instr. and chief logistics div. Air Command and Staff Sch., 1946-48; exec. dir. Inst. for Human Progress, 1962-63. Pres. Ams. for Constitutional Action, 1965-69. Decorated D.S.M. with oak leaf cluster. Fellow Am. Soc. C.E.; mem. Wash. Soc. Engrs. (hon.). Clubs: Army-Navy (Washington); Army Navy Country (Arlington, Va.); National Press (Washington). Author: The Leadership of President Kennedy, 1964; The War for the World, 1968; Cry Peace: The Kennedy Years, 1969; American on Trial: The War for Vietnam, 1971. Editor-in-chief Strategic Rev., 1972—. Home: 6157 Kellogg Dr McLean VA 22101

LANE, WALTER WISHART, JR., physician; b. Kansas City, Mo., Apr. 4, 1934; s. Walter Wishart and Geraldine (Faley) L.; student The Citadel, 1952-54; B.S., U. Tampa, 1961; M.D., U. Fla., 1965; m. Nancie June Hoopingarner, Nov. 24, 1956; children—Pamela Ann, Sharon Jane, Melissa Ellen, Stacie Lee. Intern, Lloyd Noland Hosp., Birmingham, Ala., 1965-66; pvt. practice medicine, Temple Terrace, Fla., 1966—. Mem. nat. adv. council Council on Econ. Opportunity. Served with USNR, 1955-59. Recipient A.M.A. Gold medal, 1966; named one of Am.'s 10 Outstanding Young Men, U.S. Jr. C. of C., 1966; Alumnus of Year, U. Tampa Alumni Assn. Mem. A.M.A., Am., Fla. (mem. pub. relations com. 1967-68) acads. gen. practice. Columnist, Patient Care mag. Editorial bd. Parent Care, Mgmt. Concepts. Home: 612 Downs Temple Terrace FL 33617 Office: 5202 Busch Blvd Tampa FL 33617

LANEY, WILLIAM ROLAND, architect; b. Denton, Tex., Mar. 27, 1918; s. William Roland and Dovie Elizabeth (Parker) L.; B.Arch., Tex. A. and M. U., 1947; m. Vera Davidson, Oct. 10, 1941; children—William R., Robert Davidson, Georgia Elizabeth. Asso. firm Wyatt C. Hedrick, Ft. Worth, 1950-55; prin. Roland Laney, architect, Denton, 1955-66; architect John R. Thompson & Assos., Dallas, 1966-70, Oglesby Group, Inc., 1971-73, Harwood K. Smith & Partners, Inc., 1973—. Mem. Denton County Hist. Survey Com., 1960—, Denton Bldg. Code Bd., 1960-66. Served with USAAF, 1943-46. Mem. A.I.A., Tex. Soc. Architects, Denton C. of C., Downtown Bus. and Profl. Assn. Presbyn. (deacon 1953—, elder 1960—). Kiwanian. Prin. works include Johnie Christian residence, 1950, I.W. Janssen residence, 1966, Master Plan and Terminal Municipal Airport, Denton, 1964, Library and Swimming Pool for Civic Center, Denton, 1966, Municipal and Community bldgs., Denton, 1966. Home: 2508 Robinwood St Denton TX 76201 Office: 2902 Southland Center Dallas TX 75201

LANFORD, CARL CLINTON, municipal utilities cons.; b. Woodruff, S.C., Apr. 16, 1904; s. Benjiman Martin and Mary Irene (Ezell) L.; B.S. in Elec. Engring., Ga. Inst. Tech., 1926; m. Mary Sue Bobo, June 6, 1926; children—Mary Suzanne, Sylvia Irene, Carlene Maxwell, Carl Clinton. Lab. asst. Ga. Inst. Tech., 1927; instr. Brown Jr. High Sch., Atlanta, 1928; with Ga. Power Co., Atlanta, 1929-32; engr. Bd. Pub. Works, Gaffney, S.C., 1933-38; supt. utilities, Newton, N.C., 1938-42; engr., mgr. utilities Bd. Pub. Works, Greer, S.C., 1942-69; mgr. municipal devel. Lockwood Green Engring., Spartanburg, S.C., after 1969. Observer, spl. group to Western Europe on water and waste water, 1963, 72. Treas., Grear Relief Agy., 1943-69. Recipient award U.S. Dept. Commerce, 1965, Fuller award, Man of Year Am. Water Works Assn. sect., 1969, Municipal award S.C. Municipal Assn., 1969. Registered profl. engr., S.C., Ga. Mem. I.E.E.E., Am. Water Works Assn. (chmn. S.E. sect. 1961-62), Fed., S.C. (chmn.) water pollution control assns. Mason (Shriner), Kiwanian (treas., sec. 1945-67). Home: 500 Taylor Rd Greer SC 29651

LANG, JOHN ALBERT, JR., govt. ofcl., educator; b. Carthage, N.C., Nov. 15, 1910; s. John Albert and Laura (Kelly) L.; B.A., U. N.C., 1930, M.A., 1931; grad. student Mercer U., 1931-32; m. Catherine Gibson, Nov. 20, 1947; children—John Albert III, Richard Gibson, Laura Catherine, Martha Elizabeth. Head English dept. Ga. Mil. Acad., 1931-33; pres. Nat. Student Govt. Fedn., N.Y.C., 1933-35; asst. to dir., edn. program Civilian Conservation Corps, 1935-38; adminstr. for N.C., NYA, 1938-42; staff asst. Better Health Assn., N.C., 1946-47; adminstrv. asst. to Congressman C.B. Deane, 1947-56; staff specialist govt. operations com. Ho. of Reps., 1956-57; adminstrv. asst. to Congressman R. E. Jones, 1957-61; dep. for Res. and ROTC affairs Office Sec. Air Force, 1961-64; acting spl. asst. to sec. air force for manpower, personnel and res. forces, 1965-66; adminstrv. asst. to sec. air force, 1964-71; professorial lectr. George Washington U., 1969-71; v.p. for external affairs East Carolina U., Greenville, N.C., 1971-72, vice chmn. for external affairs, 1973—; sec. N.C. Dept. Mil. and Vets. Affairs, 1972-73; lectr. profl. civic and ednl. groups, 1933—. Vice chmn. N.C. Democratic Conv., 1946. Bd. dirs. Washington Community Chest. Served from pvt. to maj. USAAF, 1942-46; ETO, PTO; maj. gen. USAF Res. Decorated Legion of Merit, Meritorious Service medal, Air Force Commendation medal, Army Commendation medal; recipient Algernon Sullivan award, 1931; Mangum Oratorial award U. N.C., 1931; citation NYA, 1938-42; scroll appreciation N.C. State Bd. Health, 1946; service citation Congl. Secretaries Club, 1956; Exceptional Civilian Service award Dept. Air Force, 1964, 66; citation N.C. Bur., 1944, Air Force Assn., 1964, 71, Am. Legion, 1962; certificate of recognition Md. Jr. C. of C., 1961; Distinguished Service citation Res. Officers Assn., 1963. Mem. Am. Acad. Polit. and Social Sci., Acad. Mgmt., Am. Soc. Pub. Adminstrn., Res. Officers Assn., Air Force Assn. (Civilian Personnel Council), Am. Legion, V.F.W., U. N.C. Alumni Assn., Nat. Vocational Guidance Assn., Air Force Assn., Phi Beta Kappa. Elk. Author articles, bulls., studies, surveys, reports in field. Home: 114 King George Rd Greenville NC 27834

LANG, LAWRENCE COPLEY, judge; b. Laredo, Tex., Nov. 14, 1919; s. Arthur Wilton and Katherine (Devine) L.; B.J., U. Tex., 1948, M.J., 1949; LL.B., St. Mary's U., San Antonio, 1956; m. Jeannette Lusk Brickell, Aug. 28, 1949. Tchr., Tex. Southmost Coll., San Antonio Ind. Sch. Dist., 1952-56; admitted to Tex. Bar, 1956; city prosecutor, San Antonio, 1956-58; judge, San Antonio, 1959—. Served as warrant officer, AUS, 1942-46; ETO. Recipient award Nat. Council on Alcoholism, 1967. Mem. Sigma Delta Chi, Delta Theta Phi. Elk. Home: 9910 Titan Dr San Antonio TX 78217 Office: 302 S Laredo St San Antonio TX 78204

LANG, SYLVAN STEPHEN, lawyer; b. San Antonio, Sept. 18, 1935; s. Sylvan and Mary (Reinhardt) L.; grad. Tex. Mil. Inst., 1953, B.S., U. Pa., 1957; LL.B., U. Tex., 1961; m. Dorothy Dreeben, June 11, 1960; children—Sylvan Stephen, Ellen E., Nathan S. Admitted to Tex. bar, 1961; mem. firm Lang, Cross, Ladon, Boldrick & Green, San Antonio, 1961—, partner, 1966—; sec. Live Oak Realty Co., 1973—; sec. Mid-Loop, Inc., 1973—; dir. Tex. State Bank. Chmn., Selective Service Bd., Bexar County, Tex., 1967-73. Bd. dirs. Bexar County chpt. A.R.C., Jewish Social Service Fedn. San Antonio, 1969-73, United Jewish Appeal. Served to capt. AUS, 1957-58. Recipient leadership award San Antonio Jewish Social Service Fedn., 1971. Mem. Am., San Antonio, San Antonio Jr. (sec.-treas. 1964) bar assns., State Bar Tex. (mem. various coms.), Phi Epsilon, Phi Delta Phi. Jewish religion (trustee temple 1967-71). Home: 218 Oakhurst St San Antonio TX 78209 Office: 1565 Frost Bank Tower San Antonio TX 78205

LANGDON, JAMES LLOYD, food co. exec.; b. Smithfield, N.C., Oct. 6, 1918; s. James Uriah and Ruth (Dunn) L.; B.S., N.C. State U., 1940; postgrad. Asheville (N.C.) Law Sch., 1948, Northwestern U., 1953, Yale, 1955, Syracuse U., 1965; m. Madelyn Earl Pope, July 10, 1943; children—Madelyn Carol (Mrs. Ben Whitely Baker), Sheila Jeanne (Mrs. Clayton Pierce). Agrl. devel. agt. Carolina Power & Light Co., 1946-49; gen. mgr. Farmer Supply Co., 1949-50; exec. v.p. N.C. Dairy Products Assn., Raleigh, 1950-59; dir. marketing dairy div. Pet, Inc., Johnson City, Tenn., 1959-69, v.p. marketing, 1969, v.p. operations, 1969, exec. v.p., gen. mgr., 1969-70, pres., 1970—; dir. First Peoples Bank. Bd. dirs. So. States Indsl. Council, Milk Industry Found. Served to lt. col. USAAF, 1941-45. Mem. Pub. Relations Soc. Am., Tenn. Dairy Products Assn. (dir.), Internat. Assn. Ice Cream Mfrs. (v.p., dir.), So. Assn. Dairy Food Mfrs., Am. Legion, Phi Kappa Phi. Mem. Christian Ch. Club: Johnson City Country. Home: Route 4 Knoll Vue Farm Johnson City TN 37601 Office: PO Box O CRS Johnson City TN 37601

LANGE, CARL JAMES, ednl. adminstr.; b. Seneca, Pa., June 1, 1925; s. Otto Carl and Rose Marie (Jetter) L.; B.S., Duke, 1945; M.S., U. Pitts., 1948, Ph.D., 1951; m. Veronica Judith Turocy, Jan. 15, 1950; children—David Carl, Veronica Jean. Task leader Humrro, George Washington U., 1953-60, dir. research, 1960-64, asst. dir. planning, 1964-69, asst. v.p. research univ., 1969—. Cons. NSF. Bd. dirs. Nat. Lab. for Higher Edn., chmn., 1973—; bd. dirs. Sch. for Contemporary Edn., 1972—. Served with USNR, 1943-45. Fellow Am. Psychol. Assn.; mem. Sigma Xi. Home: 8520 Raleigh Av Annandale VA 22003 Office: 2121 I St Washington DC 20006

LANGE, GLEN EVERETT, educator; b. Ft. Madison, Ia., Jan. 22, 1923; s. Clarence Edwin and Mary (Duff) L.; B.C.S, Drake U., 1950; M.A., Hardin-Simmons U., 1960; Ph.D., U. Mo., 1969; m. Thalen Redfern Ogg, Oct. 12, 1947 (div.); children—John Redfern, Andrew Charles, Megan Ruth. With Bill Curphy Co., Des Moines, 1950-55; chief accountant Zelrich Co., Dallas, 1955-58; instr. Hardin-Simmons U., Abilene, Tex., 1958-60, U. Mo., Columbia, 1960-62; prof. accounting Western Ky. U., Bowling Green, 1962—, dept. head, 1964—. Commr., City of Bowling Green, 1969—. Served with USAAF, 1943-46. Mem. Delta Sigma Pi. Episcopalian. Home: D-101 Royal Arms Apt Bowling Green KY 42101

LANGE, JEAN RUTHVEN WILSHIRE, writer; b. Eastbourne, Sussex, Eng., Jan. 28, 1902; d. Ruthven Matcham and Millicent Ida (Thomson) Wilshire; student Northfield Pvt. Coll., Watford, Eng., 1919-20; m. Hans Albrecht F. Lange, Apr. 4, 1931 (dec. Aug. 1965); children—Anneliese Johanna, Jack H.; 1 stepdau., Ingeborg Edith. Appeared in Brit. theatre prodns. Rose Marie, 1925-27, The Barretts of Wimpole Street, 1932, Payment Deferred, 1931; appeared in Spanish theatres, Madrid, Barcelona, Valencia, 1924; appeared with Dame May Whitty's Repertory Co., London, 1928-29; news corr. Radio Free Europe, Frankfurt am Main, Germany, 1952-55; dir. pub. relations Montclair (N.J.) Art Mus., 1956-61; writer, producer KLRN-TV, ednl. TV, San Antonio/Austin, 1962—. Mem. U.S. Com. for Refugees, 1960—, Assn. for UN, 1958-61. Recipient citation for services to refugee cause U.S. Com. for Refugees, 1961. Mem. Am. Women in Radio and TV, Women in Communications, Rho Tau Sigma. Contbg. editor San Antonio Mag., 1967-68. Contbr. articles to mags. Home: 8035 Fredericksburg Rd 15 San Antonio TX 78229

LANGE, ROBERT DALE, physician; b. Redwood Falls, Minn., Jan. 24, 1920; s. John Christian and Bertha Semelia (Eggen) L.; B.A., Macalester Coll., 1941; M.D., Washington U., St. Louis, 1944; m. Mary Jane Adams, Sept. 16, 1944; children— Ruth (Mrs. Walter Rehm), John Carl. Intern, Barnes Hosp., St. Louis, 1944-45; resident U. Minn. Hosp., Mpls., 1945-46; dir. St. Louis Regional Blood Center, 1948-51; scientist Atomic Bomb Casualty Commn., Hiroshima, Japan, 1951-53, Nicollet Clinic, Mpls., 1953-54; asst. prof. medicine Washington U., St. Louis, 1956-61; asso. prof. medicine Med. Coll. Ga., Augusta, 1962-64; research prof., asst. dir. Meml. Research Center, U. Tenn., Knoxville, 1965—; practice medicine, specializing in internal medicine, Knoxville, Tenn., 1965—; Chmn., Erythropoietin Subcom. Nat. Heart and Lung Inst., 1973—. Served as maj. M.C., U.S. Army, 1954-56. Mem. Sigma Xi, Alpha Omega Alpha, Pi Phi Epsilon, Phi Beta Pi. Methodist. Contbr. articles profl. jours. Home: 8116 Bennington St Knoxville TN 37919 Office: 1924 Alcoa Hwy Knoxville TN 37920

LANGER, MARSHALL JAY, lawyer, banker; b. N.Y.C., May 30, 1928; s. Samuel and Edna (Klein) L.; B.S. in Econs., U. Pa., 1948; J.D. summa cum laude, U. Miami, 1951; m. Sally Blass, Apr. 3, 1955 (div. 1967); children—Andrew H., Jeffrey S.; m. 2d, Barbara Slatko, Feb. 15, 1970. Admitted to Fla. bar, 1951, since practiced in Miami; mem. firm Bittel Langer & Blass, 1965—; lectr., acting dir. Inter-Am. law program U. Miami Sch. Law, 1955-56, adj. prof., 1965—; exchange prof. law U. Havana, Cuba, 1956; also lectr. tax insts.; pres., mng. dir.

Grand Cayman Trust Corp. Ltd. (B.W.I.); dir. several banks. Chmn. programs on doing bus. in Caribbean, Practising Law Inst., 1972—. Mem. The Fla. Bar (chmn. tax sect. com. on fgn. income 1964-68), Am., Inter-Am. (asst. sec. gen. 1956-61), Dade County bar assns., Internat. Fiscal Assn., Am. Fgn. Law Assn. (cht. pres. 1955), Greater Miami Tax Inst. (pres. 1967), Iron Arrow, Zeta Beta Tau (nat. historian, 1959-60), Omicron Delta Kappa, Phi Kappa Phi. Contbr. chpts. to books, articles to profl. jours. Home: 444 Av Rovino Coral Gables FL 33156 Office: 2250 First Federal Bldg Miami FL 33131 also PO Box 1109 Grand Cayman British West Indies

LANGFORD, JOHN SHOLAR, JR., judge; b. Atlanta, July 4, 1931; s. John Sholar and Virginia (Flynt) L.; B.S., Auburn U., 1953; LL.B., Emory U., 1958; m. Margaret Hodgson Ellis, June 9, 1956; children—John Sholar III, Martha Ellen, David Ellis. Law clk. to mem. U.S. Ho. of Reps. from Ga., Washington, 1956; admitted to Ga. bar, 1957; mem. firm Bryan, Carter, Ansley & Smith, Atlanta, 1957-66; judge Civil Ct. Fulton County, Atlanta, 1966-68, Juvenile Ct., 1968-73, Superior Ct., 1973—. Bd. Dirs. Children's Center Met. Atlanta. Served as 1st lt. USAF, 1954-55. Mem. Am., Ga., Atlanta bar assns., Lawyers Club Atlanta, Am. Judicature Soc., Southeastern Conf. Football Ofcls. Assn. Episcopalian (vestryman 1962-68, sr. warden 1968). Club: Touchdown (Atlanta, pres. 1965). Home: 2765 Northside Dr NW Atlanta GA 30305 Office: 801 Fulton County Court House Atlanta GA 30303

LANGLAND, CHARLES ALBERT, systems analyst; b. Manchester, Ia., Mar. 28, 1929; s. Thore and Mary Delight (Robison) L.; B.S. in Math., U. S.D., 1951; m. Betty Lou Good, July 2, 1951; children—Ruth Ann, Marc C., Thomas J. Geophysicist, head geophysics-data processing Gen. Geophys. Co., Rocky Mountain and Gulf Coast area, 1951-63; systems engr. IBM Corp., Houston, 1963-67; co-founder, v.p., dir. Asso. Computer Services, Inc., Houston, 1967-71; sr. profl. systems analyst Exxon U.S.A., 1971—. Recipient award for helping install 1st system 360 in world for IBM Mem. Soc. Exploration Geophysicists, Assn. for Computing Machinery. Mem. Christian Ch. (dir. 1966-68, 70-73, chmn. deacons 1971-72, elder 1972—). Home: 10026 Briar Dr Houston TX 77042 Office: 3616 Richmond Av Houston TX 77027

LANGLAND, OLAF ELMER, dentist, educator; b. Madrid, Ia., May 30, 1925; s. Raymond Fritzoff and Minnie Margaret (Kinsey) L.; D.D.S., U. Ia., 1951, M.S., 1961; m. Carolyn Jean Anderson, Oct. 23, 1955 (div. July 1972); children—Sara, Beth. Practice dentistry, Albert City, Ia., 1951-59; asst. prof. dentistry U. Ia., 1961-64, asso. prof., 1964-69, also head dept. oral diagnosis; prof. dentistry La. State U., New Orleans, 1969—, also head dept. oral diagnosis, 1969—. Vis. dentist Charity Hosp., New Orleans, 1969—; cons. Wilborn Hall Hosp., Lackland AFB, Tex.; dental rotator Ship Hope, Maccio, Brazil, 1973. Served with AUS, 1943-45. Decorated Purple Heart. Fellow Am. Coll. Dentists; mem. Am. Acad. Oral Medicine, Am. Acad. Dental Radiology, Am. Dental Assn., Orgn. Tchrs. Oral Diagnosis, Delta Sigma Delta, Omicron Kappa Upsilon. Methodist. Author: Textbook of Dental Radiology, 1973. Home: 3301 W Esplanade Metairie LA 70002 Office: 1100 Florida Av New Orleans LA 70119

LANGLEY, EARNEST LEE, lawyer; b. Sweetwater, Tex., July 14, 1920; s. Earnest Lee and Willie Eugenia (Pipkin) L.; B.A. with honors, Tex. Tech. U., 1946; J.D. with honors, U. Tex., 1951; m. Helen Richter, Dec. 28, 1941; children—Suzanne (Mrs. Dan G. Wall), Barbara, Camille, Carolyn. Clk., Gulf Oil Corp., 1941-48; admitted to Tex. bar, 1950, practiced in Amarillo, 1951-52, Hereford, 1952—; mem. firms Witherspoon, Aikin, Langley, Woods, Kendrick & Gulley, Hereford; dir. First Nat. Bank, Hereford, Tex., Select Investment Co., Legal Investment Co., First Nat. Co., Legal Bldg. Corp.; city atty., Hereford, 1954—. Bd. dirs. Kings Manor Meth. Home, Inc., Hereford Area Found. Served to capt. AUS, World War II; ETO. Named Citizen of Year, Hereford C. of C., 1969. Fellow Tex. Bar Found.; mem. Am. Judicature Soc., Am. Bar Assn., Order Coif, Alpha Chi, Kappa Kappa Psi, Phi Delta Phi. Methodist. Mason, Lion. Club: Country (Hereford). Editor-in-chief Tex. Law Rev., 1950-51. Home: 502 Star St Hereford TX 79045 Office: Box 1818 Hereford TX 79045

LANGLEY, MAURICE NATHAN, cons. engr.; b. Dorchester, Neb., July 6, 1913; s. Nathan Arthur and Amy Golden (Hansen) L.; B.S., Colo. State U., 1939; postgrad. Dartmouth, 1942; m. Ruby Ellen Frederiksen, June 18, 1939; children—Susan (Mrs. Carl O. Thomas), Gilbert Wayne, Richard Jay. With Soil Conservation Service, U.S. Dept. Agr., 1940-42; with Bur. Reclamation, U.S. Dept. Interior, 1946-73, chief, land div., Yuma, Ariz., 1946-55, chief, operations div., 1956-58, chief, operations br., Washington, 1959-61, asst. chief land use and settlement, 1962-63, chief, div. water and land, 1964-73; mgr. Bookman-Edmonston Engring., Inc., Washington, 1973—. Served to lt. comdr. USNR, 1942-46. Recipient Incentive award, 1947, Outstanding Service award, 1947, Meritorious Service awards, 1956, 69, Distinguished Service award, 1968 (all Dept. Interior). Mem. Internat. Commn. on Irrigation and Drainage (v.p. 1973), Western Soc. Soil Sci. (pres. 1952-53), Am. Soc. Agrl. Engrs., Am. Soc. Agronomy, Am. Soc. Soil Sci. Kiwanian (past pres.). Contbr. articles to profl. jours. Home: 6825 Algonquin Av Bethesda MD 20034 Office: 1000 Vermont Av Washington DC 20005

LANGLYKKE, ASGER FUNDER, assn. exec.; b. Pleasant Prairie, Wis., July 17, 1909; s. Peter Iversen and Anna (Funder) L.; B.S., U. Wis., 1931, M.S., 1934, Ph.D., 1936; Sc.D., Trinity Coll., 1965; m. Margaret Hays Page, Dec. 16, 1939; children—Peter Page, Kristin Margaret, Gerald Page, Cynthia Jane. Research chemist Hiram Walker & Sons, Inc., Peoria, Ill., 1937-40; supt. Butyl Alcohol Plant, Asociacion Azucarera Coop. Lafayette, Arroyo, P.R., 1940-43; sect. head, acting div. head U.S. Dept. Agr., Peoria, Ill., 1943, div. head, 1945-47; chief pilot plants, also chief tech. officer Chem. Warfare Service, 1943-45; successively dir. microbiol. devel., dir. research and devel. labs., v.p. E.R. Squibb & Sons, New Brunswick, N.J., also N.Y.C., 1947-67; exec. dir. Am. Soc. Microbiology, Washington, 1968—. Cons. U.S. Army, 1945-66, Office Defense Research and Engring. Adv. Panel Biol. and Chem. Defense, 1960-63; adj. prof. Rutgers U., 1968—. Recipient Unit award for superior service U.S. Dept. Agr., 1956. Fellow Am. Acad. Microbiology, A.A.A.S., N.Y. Acad. Scis., Am. Inst. Chemists; mem. Am. Soc. Microbiology, Am. Chem. Soc. (div. chmn., councilor 1951-54), Am. Inst. Chem. Engrs., Assn. Research Dirs., Biochem. Soc. London (emeritus), Internat. Union Pure and Applied Chemistry (vice chmn., chmn. 1965-73), Sigma Xi, Tau Beta Pi, Phi Lambda Upsilon, Phi Sigma, Gamma Alpha. Research, publs., patents in field. Home: 6609 Barnaby St Washington DC 20015 Office: 1913 Eye St Washington DC 20006

LANGSTON, JAMES HORACE, educator; b. Garrison, Tex., Oct. 8, 1917; s. James Horace and Jane Ruth (Green) L.; B.A., Stephen F. Austin State U., 1937; M.A., U. N.C., 1939, Ph.D., 1941. Chemist, Columbia Chem. div. Pitts. Plate Glass Co., Barberton, O., 1941-46; asso. prof. textile chemistry Clemson (S.C.) U., 1946-51, prof., 1951-58; prof., head dept. chemistry Samford U., Birmingham, Ala., 1958—. Fulbright lectr. Central Univ. Ecuador, Quito, 1959-60, Nat. Univ. Honduras, Tegucicalpa, 1967-68. Fellow Am. Inst. Chemists; mem. Am. Chem. Soc., Sigma Xi. Club: Birmingham Executive. Contbr. profl. jours. Home: 1008 Vista Circle Birmingham AL 35216

LANHAM, BEN TILLMAN, JR., univ. adminstr.; b. Edgefield, S.C., Apr. 5, 1917; s. Ben Tillman and Mary (Shaw) L.; B.S., Clemson U., 1937; M.S., U. Tenn., 1938; postgrad. Ia. State U., 1938-39; Ph.D., Mich. State U., 1960; m. Bernice Arnold, June 29, 1941; children—Ben Tillman III, Betty Anne. Research asst. U. Tenn., 1937-38, Mich. State U., 1954-55, Ia. State U., 1938-39; asst. prof. Auburn (Ala.) U., 1939-46, asso. prof., 1946-48, prof., 1948-56, prof., head dept. agrl. econs., 1956-64, asso. dir. Agr. Expt. Sta., asst. dean Sch. Agr., 1964-66, v.p. research, 1966-72, v.p. adminstrn., 1972—. Pres. Research Found., chmn. Research Council, chmn. research grant-in-aid com. Auburn U.; chmn. Ala. Water Resources Research Inst. Council; mem. adv. com. Ala. Program Devel. Office. Served from 2d lt. to maj. Inf., AUS, 1942-46. Mem. A.A.A.S., Am. Farm Econ. Assn., Am., So. econ. assns., Am. Marketing Assn., Am. Acad. Polit. and Social Sci., Am. Sociol. Soc., Assn. So. Agrl. Workers, Internat. Conf. Agrl. Economists, Ala. Acad. Sci., Ala. Edn. Assn., Nat. Council U. Research Adminstrs., Council for Research Policy and Adminstrn. Land-Grant Coll. Assn., Sigma Xi, Gamma Alpha Mu, Gamma Sigma Delta, Omicron Delta Epsilon, Phi Delta Kappa, Omicron Delta Kappa. Baptist. Kiwanian. Contbr. articles profl. jours. Home: 536 S Gay St Auburn AL 36830

LANIER, BILL ED, mfg. co. exec.; b. Ada, Okla., Sept. 5, 1937; s. William Franklin and Jewel Ozella (Martin) L.; B.B.A., U. Okla., 1961; m. Janet Gaye McLin, Jan. 30, 1965; children—Jamie Jan, Christin Gaye, Roderick William. Supr. accounting office Southwestern Bell Telephone Co., Topeka, Kan., 1963; financial analyst Continental Pipeline Co., Ponca City, Okla., 1964-67; dir. personnel, plant mgr., mgr. scheduling systems Sequoyah Industries, Oklahoma City, 1967-73, dir. purchasing, 1973—. Bd. dirs. Oklahoma City council Boy Scouts Am., 1969-70. Served with AUS, 1961-63. Mem. Soc. Advancement Mgmt., Davis C. of C. (pres., 1969-70), U.S. Armor Officers Assn. (chmn. 1962-63), Beta Gamma Sigma. Methodist. Elk. Home: 10802 Sunrise Blvd Oklahoma City OK 73120 Office: 4545 N Lincoln Blvd Oklahoma City OK 73105

LANIER, DAVID WILLIAM, lawyer, mayor; b. Newbern, Tenn., Nov. 16, 1934; s. James Parker and Robbye (Sullivan) L.; student Memphis State U., 1952-55; LL.B., U. Tenn., 1958; m. Mary Joan Mills, Dec. 2, 1962; children—Leigh Anne, Robbye Claire. Admitted to Tenn. bar, 1959, since practiced in Dyersburg; mem. firms David W. Lanier 1959—; mayor, Dyersburg, 1966—. Mem. adv. council Peoples Protective Life Ins. Co., Jackson, Tenn., 1965—. Nat. exec. committeeman Parade Am., 1967, Cerebral Palsy Telethon, 1967, 70. Alderman, Dyersburg, 1964-65; Dyer County campaign mgr. Buford Ellington for Gov., 1966; state chmn. Mayor's for Hooker for Gov. com., 1970; v.p. Tenn. Young Democrats, 1962-67, 8th dist. committeeman, 1966-68; chmn. Dyer County Dem. exec. com., 1972—. Served with Air N.G. Col.-Aide de Camp, Gov. Buford Ellington's Staff. Bd. dirs. Vocational Rehab. Tng. Center. Mem. Bar Assn. Tenn., Dyer County Bar Assn. (pres. 1971-72), Tenn. Law Enforcement Officers Assn., Fraternal Order Police, Memphis State U. Alumni Assn. (mem. adv. council 1966-68, nat. dir. 1967-71, mem. legislative relations com. 1967-68), Tenn. Municipal League (dir. 1968-71, pres. 1971-72), Downtown Mchts. Assn. (dir.), Jr. C. of C., C. of C. (dir.), Phi Delta Phi, Kappa Sigma. Mem. Ch. of Christ. Mason (Shriner), Moose, Rotarian. Club: Dyersburg Boosters (dir.). Home: 2117 Starlight Dr Dyersburg TN 38024 Office: First Citizens Nat Bank Bldg Dyersburg TN 38024

LANIER, ERNEST WILSON, physician; b. Elton, La., Oct. 4, 1918; s. Morgan Martin and Lillian (Clements) L.; A.A., Lamar Coll., 1948; M.D., Southwestern Med. Coll., 1953; student U. Tex., 1948-49; m. Maxine Bailey, Nov. 10, 1939; children—Jacquelyn Ruth, Norman Preston, Michael Roland. Tchr. math. Civilian Conservation Corps, 1937-39; shipping, receiving clk. Sears Roebuck & Co., Port Arthur, Tex., 1939; dock man helper terminal dept. Tex. Co., Port Arthur, 1939-43, bulk oil dept., summers 1946-52; intern VA Hosp., Houston, 1953-54; mem. staff St. Mary's Hosp.; mem. staff Park Place Hosp., Port Arthur, v.p. 1970-71, pres. med. staff, 1972-73. Dir. Rainbow Devel. Corp., Port Arthur, 1960—. Dir. Mid-Jefferson County unit Am. Cancer Soc., 1960-61; mem. adv. bd. Jefferson County Chpt. Med. Assts. Assn. Served with USAAF, 1943-46. Fellow Am. Acad. Family Practice, Jefferson County Med. Soc., Am., Tex. med. assns., Am. Heart Assn., C. of C., Nat. Rifle Assn., Phi Beta Pi, Phi Theta Kappa. Democrat. Baptist. Rotarian (past pres.). Clubs: Snorkle Skin Divers (med. examiner 1959—), Sabine Neches Sportsman. Home: 6358 Jefferson St Groves TX 77619 Office: 5700 39th St Groves TX 77619

LANIER, JAMES GIBSON, freight co. exec.; b. Birmingham, Ala., Jan. 7, 1920; s. Russel D'Lyon and Martha Henrietta (Gibson) L.; student Coll. Engring., U. Ala., 1936-40; m. Mildred Jeanett Pipes, Jan. 9, 1943; children—James Gibson Jr., Randolph Houston. Engr., Jones & Donan, Madisonville, Ky., cons. engrs., 1946-48; chief engr. Norton Coal Corp., Nortonville, Ky., 1948-52; with Malone Freight Lines, Inc., Birmingham, 1952—, v.p., 1963-72, exec. v.p., 1972—, dir., 1963—. Served to lt. comdr. USNR, 1940-46. Decorated Silver Star. Mem. Alpha Tau Omega. Clubs: Birmingham Country, Birmingham Sailing, Relay House (Birmingham). Home: 2832 Hastings Rd Mountain Brook AL 35223 Office: 200 S 35th St Birmingham AL 35202

LANIER, JAMES OLANDA, lawyer; b. Newbern, Tenn., Sept. 8, 1931; s. James Parker and Robbye (Sullivan) L.; student U. Tenn., 1949, U. Tenn. Jr. Coll., 1950-51; B.S., Memphis State Coll., 1955, J.D., Memphis State U., 1969; m. Carolyn Holland, June 1, 1950; children—James Elton, Donna Kay, Robbye Ann (dec.), Amy Claire. Indsl. engr. Milan (Tenn.) Arsenal, 1953-54; social worker Dept. Pub. Welfare, Memphis, 1955-57, sr. social worker, appeals examiner, 1957-58; dir. Surplus Commodities, Dyer County, Tenn., 1958; pres., gen. mgr. Main Sporting Goods, Inc., Dyersburg, 1959-62; tech. engr. Milan Ordnance Plant, 1961-63; spl. investigator Tenn. Dept. Pub. Welfare, Nashville, 1963-67; ins. adjuster U.S. Fidelity & Guaranty Co., 1967-69; pvt. practice law, Dyersburg, 1969—; county atty. Dyer County, 1972—. Mem. Tenn. Ho. of Reps., 1959-62, 71-72, chmn. com. on state and local govt.; dir. Dyer County Levee and Drainage Dist. Pres. Dyer County chpt. Muscular Dystrophy Assns. Am., 1958-60. Mem. Jr. C. of C. (past treas.) (hon.) Tenn. Law Enforcement Officers Assn., Am., Dyersburg-Dyer County (sec.-treas.) bar assns., Bar Assn. Tenn., Am., Tenn. trial lawyers assns., Am. Judicature Soc., Dyer County C. of C., Sigma Delta Kappa (pres. 1967-68). Democrat (W. Tenn. pres. Young Democrats of Tenn. 1957-63). Mem. Ch. of Christ. Moose (jr. gov. 1959-60, gov. 1960-62, chmn. com. civic affairs, recipient fellowship degree and gov.'s award of merit 1963). Clubs: Dyersburg Kiwanis, Dyersburg Country. Home: 617 Sunset Blvd Dyersburg TN 38024 Office: Lanier Bldg 208 N Mill St Dyersburg TN 38024

LANIER, THURMAN WAYNE, dentist; b. Batesville, Ark., Sept. 19, 1932; s. Luther Thurman and Ethel (Settle) L.; student Ark. Tech. Coll., 1950-51; B.S., U. Ark., 1958; D.D.S., Washington U., St. Louis, 1962; m. Helen Lorene Barnes, Sept. 4, 1955; children—Lance Littleton, Tara Kaay. Individual practice dentistry. Ft. Smith, Ark., 1962—; cons. dental health, Ft. Smith; mem. staff Sparks Meml. Hosp., Ft. Smith, 1967—. Mem. Ark. Ednl. TV Commn., 1974—. Bd. regents Carnegie City Library, Ft. Smith; trustee Westark Community Coll., 1972—. Served with USN, 1951-54. Mem. Am., Ark. dental assns., Am. Assn. Dental Editors (pres. 1974), Assn. Mil. Surgeons, Ft. Smith C. of C. (dir. 1973—), Am. Soc. Dentistry Children (pres. Ark. unit 1973-74), Xi Psi Phi. Methodist. Mason. Editor Ark. Dental Jour., 1965—. Home: 2920 S 33d St Fort Smith AR 72901 Office: 5422 Euper Lane Ft Smith AR 72901

LANIER, WILLIAM DONALD, engr., municipal ofcl.; b. Albany, Ga., Sept. 25, 1929; s. Jefferson Bradwell and Angeline (Davis) L.; student North Ga. Coll., 1946-48; B.S.C.E., Ga. Inst. Tech., 1951; m. Sylvia Sue Smith, June 15, 1957; children—Lewis Tod, David Charles, Sue Angeline. Chmn. to party chief Marbury Engring. Co., Albany, 1947-51, party chief, 1954-56; project engr. Wright Contracting Co., Columbus, Ga., 1956-57; asst. city engr., dir. pub. works Albany, Ga., 1957—. Served as 2d lt. AUS, 1951-53. Home: 1318 Gail Av Albany GA 31705 Office: 401 11th Av Albany GA 31705

LANSDOWN, ROBERT RAY, museum dir.; b. Bartlesville, Okla., June 28, 1941; s. Robert Lee and Genieve (Holly) L.; B.S. in Zoology, Okla. State U., 1967; m. Cheryl Kay Martin, Sept. 4, 1965; 1 son, Mark Justin. Asst. dir. Woolaroc Mus., Bartlesville, 1967-71, dir., 1971—. Served with AUS, 1961-64; Korea. Home: 105 NW Mulberry Lane Bartlesville OK 74003 Office: Woolaroc Museum Route 3 Bartlesville OK 74003

LANSFORD, DOYLE KEITH, physician; b. Custer City, Okla., Jan. 26, 1931; s. William Harrison and Dorothy Missouri (Baker) L.; B.S., Baylor U., 1951; M.D., Tulane U., 1955; m. Tommie Elizabeth Berry, Feb. 11, 1956; children—James Randal, David Michael, Laura Jean, Elizabeth Ann. Intern, Charity Hosp., New Orleans, 1955-56; practice medicine specializing in family practice, Arlington, Tex., 1959—; mem. staff Arlington Meml. Hosp., Arlington Community Hosp. Served with M.C. USAF, 1956-58. Diplomate Am. Bd. Family Practice. Fellow Am. Acad. Family Practice; mem. A.M.A. Home: 2805 Black Oak Lane Arlington TX 76012 Office: 2306 E Park Row Arlington TX 76010

LANTZ, ALLEN DEAN, elec. engr.; b. Electric Mills, Miss., Dec. 11, 1934; s. Felix Allen and Lena (Wilkins) L.; student Meridian Jr. Coll., 1963-65; B.S., U. Miss., 1968; m. Bobbye Lynn Rasberry, June 3, 1955; children—Allen D. Lantz, Gerald Brian. With Miss. Power Co., Gulfport, 1968—, substation constrn. engr., 1970—. Served with USAF, 1952-66. Mem. I.E.E.E. Mason. Home: 104 St Augustine Dr Long Beach MS 39560 Office: 2992 West Beach St Gulfport MS 39501

LANTZ, JOHN EDWARD, clergyman; b. Edgerton, O., June 7, 1911; s. John M. and Elizabeth (Conrad) L.; A.B., DePauw U., 1934; M.Div., Yale, 1938; M.A., Mich. U., 1942; Litt.D., Evang. Bible Coll. and Sem., 1969; m. Ruth Esther Cox., Aug. 26, 1937; children—Thomas Edward, John Harvey, Alma Esther. Ordained to ministry Meth. Ch., 1939; teaching fellow U. Mich., 1940-42; instr. McCormick Theol. Sem., 1943-45; editorial staff Meth. Ch., 1945-51; pastor Meth. Ch. South Bend, Ind., 1951-55; exec. dir. so. office Nat. Council Chs., Atlanta, 1955-65; vis. instr. Interdenom. Theol. Center, Atlanta, 1959-65, asst. prof. speech and communication, 1965-67, asso. prof. communications and ecumenics, 1967—; lectr. speech Vanderbilt U. Sch. Religion, 1946-50; instr. speech U. Tenn. Extension Div., Nashville, 1948-50; vis. instr. Gammon Theol. Sem., 1957-59; chaplain Ga. Internat. Trade Assn. Mem. Druid Hills Civic Assn. Bd. trustees and visitors DePauw U., 1954-57; trustee Protestant Radio and TV Center, Atlanta, 1955-63; mem. men's com. Japan Internat. Christian U. Mem. Ga. Writers Assn., Dixie Council Authors and Journalists, Nat. Travel Club, Wycliffe Assos., Internat. Platform Assn., UN Assn. U.S.A., Am. Acad. Polit. and Social Sci., Middle East Inst., World Council Christian Edn. (N.Am. regional com. 1960-71, voting del. to gen. assembly, Lima, Peru, 1971), Speech Communications Assn., Atlanta Writer's Club (pres. 1974—). Kiwanian. Author: Speaking in the Church, 1954; Church Councils in the South, 1957; Reading the Bible Aloud, 1959; (with Ruth Cox Lantz) Bible Characters in Action, 1955, Plays for Happier Homes, 1957; also numerous articles in field. Editor: Best Religious Stories, 1948; Stories of Christian Living, 1950; Stories to Grow By, 1953. Home: 1040 Springdale Rd NE Atlanta GA 30306 Office: 671 Beckwith St SW Atlanta GA 30314

LANTZ, ROBERT BRYAN, clergyman; b. Mansfield, O., Jan. 11, 1936; s. William Bryan and Dorothy (Weatherbie) L.; A.B., Wittenberg U., 1958; grad. Hamma Div. Sch., 1961; m. Katherine I. Isenhour, Aug. 10, 1958. Ordained to ministry Luth. Ch., 1961; chaplain Ohio State Tb Hosp., Columbus, 1959, Univ. Hosp., 1960-61, Trinity Luth. Ch., Akron, O., 1961-63, chaplain Med. Coll. Va., 1963-64; dir. chaplain's dept. Balt. City Hosps., 1965-66; chmn. dept. pastoral care U. Tenn. Med. Units, 1967-69; dir. field edn. and pastoral counseling St. Paul's Coll., Washington, 1969-72; dir. Washington Inst. Pastoral Counseling, 1972—; asso. prof. pastoral counselling Memphis Theol. Sem., dir. Inst. Medicine and Religion, Memphis, 1967-69. Chaplain Supr. Council for Clin. Tng., Inc., N.Y.C., Lutheran Council U.S.A., N.Y.C. Fellow Am. Assn. Pastoral Counselors; mem. Assn. for Clin Pastoral Edn., Alpha Tau Omega. Kiwanian. Club: Annapolis Yacht (Md.). Home: 700 Americana Dr Annapolis MD 21403 Office: 3015 4th St NE Washington DC 20017

LANTZ, ROBERT BUTLER, recreation equipment mfg. co. exec.; b. Lincoln, Neb., Nov. 11, 1938; s. Robert Earl and Maxine Louise (Butler) L.; B.S., Ga. Inst. Tech., 1962, M.S. (NASA trainee), 1969; m. Alice Brackett, June 3, 1961; children—Robert Kenneth, William Earl. Materials and process engr. Douglas Aircraft, Santa Monica, Cal., 1962-64; structures engr. Lockheed Aircraft, Marietta, Ga., 1964-68; staff engr. Avco Aerostructures, Nashville, 1969-73; v.p. David L. Federer and Assos., soils and found. engrs., Nashville, 1973; chmn. bd., v.p. Blue Hole Canoe Co., Sunbright, Tenn., 1973—. NASA research asso., 1971. Registered profl. engr., Tenn. Mem. Tenn. Scenic Rivers Assn. (dir., editor newsletter), Am. Soc. Testing and Materials, Sierra Club. Contbr. articles to tech. jours. Home: Route 1 Mill Creek Rd Sunbright TN 37872 Office: Blue Hole Canoe Co Sunbright TN 37872

LANTZ, RUTH COX (MRS. JOHN EDWARD LANTZ), educator; b. Gainesville, Fla., Jan. 11, 1914; d. Harvey Warren and Daisy (Frisbie) Cox; A.B., Emory U., 1934; postgrad. Yale, 1935-36, Pratt Inst., 1936; M.A., U. Mich., 1942; m. John Edward Lantz, Aug. 26, 1937; children—Thomas Edward, John Harvy, Alma Esther. Tchr. Druid Hills Sch., 1934-35; instr. speech Vanderbilt U., 1946-52; speech tchr. St. Mary's Acad., 1952; instr. religious edn. Interdenominational Theol. Center, Atlanta, 1960-69; speaker, dramatic reader various chs., women's groups. Chmn. publicity United Ch. Women of Ga., 1955-56, chmn. individual membership, 1957, chmn. pub. relations, 1961-63, v. pres., 1972—, coordinator regional conf., 1973; dist. camping chmn. Camp Fire Girls, Atlanta council, 1956-58, pres., 1958-60, program chmn., 1961-64, regional exec. com., 1961-72, sec., 1962-66, mem. nat. com. 1966-68; bd. dirs. YWCA, Atlanta, 1963-69, v.p., 1969; Nashville pres. Fellowship of Reconciliation, 1950-51, mem. nat. council, 1950-55; pres. County Sunday Sch. Conv., Monroe, Mich., 1938-39. Mem. women's planning com. Internat. Christian U. Japan. Mem. Am. Assn. U.

Women (chmn. creative writing group Atlanta br. 1969, 74). Clubs: Georgia Writers, Atlanta Writers, Atlanta Artists, Am. Bus. Women's Assn., Wycliffe Assos. Author: (with J. Edward Lantz) Bible Characters in Action, 1955; Plays for Happier Homes, 1957; also numerous poems, articles, plays in field of art and religion. Editor: The Shepherdess, 1950-58. Illustrator: Speaking in the Church, 1954. Home: 1040 Springdale Rd Atlanta GA 30306

LAPIDUS, MORRIS, architect, interior designer; b. Odessa, Russia, Nov. 25, 1902; s. Leon and Eva (Sherman) L.; came to U.S., 1903, naturalized, 1914; B. Architecture, Columbia, 1927; m. Beatrice Perlman, Feb. 22, 1929; children—Richard L., Alan H. With Warren & Wetmore, N.Y.C., 1926-28, Arthur Weiser, N.Y.C., 1928-30; assn. architect Ross-Frankel, Inc. (now Morris Lapidus Assos., N.Y.C., 1930-42, prin., 1942—; pioneered use of modern in mdsg. field; areas of work include hotels, shopping centers, office bldgs., religious instns.; architect-designer Fontainebleau Hotel, 1954, Eden Roc Hotel, 1955, Americana Hotel, 1956 (all Miami Beach, Fla.), Sheraton Motor Inn, N.Y.C., Cadman Plaza, Bklyn., S.W. Urban Redevel., Washington, Americana Hotel, N.Y.C., Cadman Plaza Devel., N.Y.C., Bedford-Stuyvesant Municipal Swimming Pool, N.Y.C., Paradise Island Hotel, Nassau, Mt. Sinai Continuing Care Pavilion; lectr. store hotel design. Mem. Miami Beach Devel. Commn. Named Citizen of Year in Miami Beach, 1961. Mem. A.I.A., Am. Inst. Decorators, Archtl. League, Nat. Inst. Archtl. Edn., Municipal Art Soc., N.Y., Guild for Religious Architecture, Miami/Beach C. of C. Kiwanian, Elk. Author: Architecture—A Profession and A Business. Home: 3 Island Av Miami Beach FL 33139 Office: 641 Lexington New York City NY 10022

LAPO, CECIL ELWYN, musician; b. Flint, Mich., Mar. 12, 1910; s. Clyde E. and Adeline (Draper) L.; student Westminster Choir Coll., Princeton, N.J., 1941; Mus.D., Mt. Union Coll., Alliance, O., 1964; m. Beatrice M. Brodie, Aug. 16, 1931; children—Richard Deane, Carol Anne (Mrs. Roger M. Kunkel). Minister music 1st Presbyn. Ch., Hornell, N.Y., 1934-39, Newtown, Pa., 1939-41, 1st Meth. Ch., Cuyahoga Falls, O., 1941-49, Wichita Falls, Tex., 1949-53, St. Lukes Meth. Ch., Oklahoma City, 1953-61; dir. ministry music United Meth. Ch., Nashville, 1961-70; asso. exec. dir. Choristers Guild, Dallas, 1970-72, exec. dir., 1972—. Bd. dirs. Choristers Guild, Dallas; trustee Westminster Choir Coll. Mem. A.S.C.A.P., Hymn Soc. Am., Woodcarvers Assn. Home: 9805 Audelia Rd Dallas TX 75238 Office: 440 Northlake Center PO Box 38188 Dallas TX 75238

LAPRADE, WILLIAM THOMAS, educator; b. Franklin County, Va., Dec. 27, 1883; s. George Washington and Mary Elizabeth (Muse) L.; A.B., Washington (D.C.) Christian Coll., 1906; Ph.D., Johns Hopkins, 1909; m. Nancy Hamilton Calfee, June 11, 1913; 1 dau., Nancy Elizabeth (Mrs. J.D.T. Hamilton). Prof. history Trinity Coll. (now Duke U.), Durham, N.C., 1909-53, prof. emeritus, 1953—; prof. history U. Ill., summers 1916, 30; lectr. history and politics, tng. sch. for secs., YMCA, held at Blue Ridge, N.C., 1918-19; prof. history U. Pa., summer 1925; prof. history U. Mich., summer 1929. Mem. Am. Hist. Assn., Royal Hist. Soc., Am. Polit. Science Assn., Am. Assn. U. Profs. (mem. exec. com. of council 1934-37; chmn. com. on academic freedom and tenure, 1937-48; pres. 1942-43), N.C. State Lit. and Hist. Assn. (pres. 1937), Phi Beta Kappa. Mem. exec. bd. N.C. Dept. Archives and History, 1944—. Mem. Christian (Disciples) Ch. Author: England and the French Revolution, 1909; British History for American Students, 1926; Public Opinion and Politics in Eighteenth Century England, 1936; also articles in Am. Hist. Rev., English Hist. Rev., Am. Polit. Sci. Rev., and series 18 articles on The Teaching of History and Civics, in N.C. Education, 1921-23. Editor Parliamentary Papers of John Robinson (for Royal Hist. Soc.), 1922. Editor the South Atlantic Quar., 1944—. Home: 1108 Monmouth Av Durham NC 27701

LARABEE, LOTTIE B(ERTHA), coll. cons., lectr.; b. Sprague, Neb.; d. Arthur Henry and Anna (Bartels) Larabee; Mus.B., U. Sch. Music, Lincoln, Neb.; Mus.M., Am. Conservatory Music; M.A., Ph.D., N.Y. U., 1955. Prin. elementary sch., Beatrice, Neb.; music instr. Albion State Normal Sch.; music instr., dir. extension So. State Coll.; music instr., acting head music dept. Lock Haven State Coll.; dir. own sch. Chgo.; research coll. and univ. adminstrn. and coll. cons., 1953-67, 69—; lectr., 1969—; asst. to pres., acad. asst. to pres., prof. higher edn., v.p. acad. affairs Ft. Lauderdale (Fla.) U., 1967-69. Recipient 1st Distinguished Service award Am. Assn. Ind. Coll. and U. Presidents, 1968. Mem. Am. Assn. Higher Edn., Drs. U.S., A.A.A.S., New Eng. Historic Geneal. Soc., Kappa Delta Pi, Sigma Alpha Iota (past nat. editor). Author: Administrators Who Subvert Learning, Their Residence and Education, 1957; A Parent's Guide to Colleges and Universities, 1963. Home: 1201 SE 2d St Fort Lauderdale FL 33301

LARAMORE, DON N., federal judge; b. Hamlet, Ind., Dec. 22, 1906; s. Louis Nelson and Pearl (Stephenson) L.; m. Charlotte M. Schminke, Dec. 29, 1938; 1 dau., Prudence Ann. Admitted to Ind. bar, 1931; judge protempore Starke Circuit Ct. of Ind., 1942-44, judge, 1944-54; judge U.S. Ct. of Claims, Washington, 1954—. Home: 5017 Searsdale Rd Washington DC 20016 Office: US Ct of Claims 717 Madison Pl NW Washington DC 20011

LARDNER, GEORGE EDMUND, JR., newspaper reporter; b. Bklyn., Aug. 10, 1934; s. George Edmund and Rosetta (Russo) L.; A.B. in Journalism summa cum laude, Marquette U., 1956, M.A., 1962; m. Rosemary Schalk, July 6, 1957; children—Helen, Edmund, Richard, Charles, Kristin. Copyboy Milw. Sentinel, 1956-57; reporter Worcester (Mass.) Telegram, 1957-59, Miami (Fla.) Herald, 1959-63; with Washington Post, 1963—, reporter, 1963-64, columnist, originator Potomac Watch column, 1964-66, reporter nat. staff, 1966—. Recipient Byline award Marquette U., 1967. Mem. Am. Newspaper Guild, Congl. Press Gallery, Sigma Delta Chi, Alpha Sigma Nu. Roman Catholic. Contbr. free-lance articles to nat., local mags. Home: 5604 32d St NW Washington DC 20015 Office: Washington Post 1150 15th St NW Washington DC 20015

LAREY, BETHEL BRYAN, U.S. atty.; b. Texarkana, Ark., Nov. 15, 1933; s. Bert Bethel and Mayno (Britt) L.; B.S. in Engring., Henderson State Coll., 1957; J.D., Vanderbilt U., 1959; m. Emma Lee Tomlinson, Aug. 22, 1954; children—Keith, David. Admitted to Ark. bar; law clk. Ark. Supreme Ct., 1959-60; practiced law, 1963-66; commr. of revenue State of Ark., 1967-69; U.S. atty. Western Dist. of Ark., 1969—. Chmn., Ark. Reciprocity Commn., 1967-69; ex officio sec. Ark. Racing Commn., 1967-69. Mem. Ark. Republican Com., 1966-69. Served with USAF, 1960-63. Methodist (ofcl. bd. 1966). Lion (dir. Texarkana 1965-66). Home: 2323 Jefferson St Texarkana AR 75501 Office: Justice Dept 6th and Rogers Sts Fort Smith AR 72901

LARGE, ARTHUR EARL, elec. engr.; b. Alva, Okla., Mar. 12, 1910; s. Alvah Curtis and Nettie Bell (Cofield) L.; student Okla. State U., 1929-31; m. Helen Philena Heath, Sept. 5, 1937; children—Patricia (Mrs. Howard Furlow), Gail (Mrs. Alan Glass), David B. Installer, repairman Southwestern Bell Tel. Co., Ardmore, O., 1937-46, engr., 1946-70; cons. engr., 1970—. Served with AUS, 1940-45, 50-52. Decorated Bronze Star with cluster. Registered profl. engr., Okla. Recipient Meritorious Service medal State of Okla., 1968. Baptist (deacon). Home: 4612 Reeves Dr Oklahoma City OK 73122

LARGE, DEWEY ERNEST, phys. scientist; b. Sevierville, Tenn., May 11, 1922; s. Bernard Marcus and Flora Lee (Atchley) L.; student Berry Coll., 1940-43, Catawba Coll., 1943; B.S., U. Tenn., 1947, M.S., 1952; m. Annie Irene Owens, Apr. 25, 1944; children—Floanna (Mrs. Russell Long), Raynella (Mrs. William Edward Dossett), Marcus Dewey, Robyn Ridgena. Sci. tchr., Knoxville, Tenn., 1946-47; sci. tchr., sch. adminstr., Sevier County Bd. Edn., 1947-54; head spl. services and programs Oak Ridge Inst. Nuclear Studies, 1954-55, curator edn., 1955-56, mgmt. specialist sci. and spl. edn., 1956-57; chemist U.S. AEC, 1957-58, asst. chief engring. and process devel. br., 1958-62, operations analyst, exec. planner, 1962-73, phys. scientist research and tech. support, 1973—. Bd. dirs. So. Appalachian Regional Sci. Fair, 1954-62. Served with USAAF, 1942-45. Decorated Air medal, Purple Heart. Fellow Am. Inst. Chemists, A.A.A.S.; mem. Am. Nuclear Soc., Atomic Indsl. Forum, Am. Chem. Soc., Nat. Sci. Tchrs. Assn., Tex. Acad. Sci., N.Y., Tenn. acads. sci., Phi Delta Kappa, Phi Kappa Phi. Republican. Baptist. Mason. Home: Fox Park Rd Route 17 Knoxville TN 37921 Office: PO Box E US AEC Oak Ridge TN 37830

LARGENT, MAX DALE, ednl. adminstr.; b. Winchester, Va., Feb. 28, 1923; s. Flournoy Leonard and Ethyl Pauline (Riley) L.; student U. Va., 1940-43; D.D.S., Med. Coll. Va., 1950; postgrad., U. Neb., 1950-51; m. Hazel Louise Danner, July 10, 1954; 1 son, Max Dale II. Pvt. practice pedodontics, Charlottesville, Va., 1951-56; faculty Med. Coll. Va., Richmond, 1952-72, prof. pedodontics, 1964-72, chmn. dept., 1969-72; prof. pedodontics Baylor Coll. Dentistry, Dallas, 1972—, asst. dean program devel., 1972—. Served with USNR, 1943-46. Fellow Am. Coll. Dentists; mem. Am., Tex., Va., Dallas, Richmond dental assns., Am., Tex., Va. socs. dentistry for children, Fedn. Dentaire Internationale, Southeastern Soc. Pedodontics, Va. Pedondontic Soc., Am. Assn. Dental Schs., Omicron Kappa Upsilon. Home: 9222 Loma Vista Dr Dallas TX 75231 Office: 800 Hall St Dallas TX 75226

LARGESS, GEORGE JOSEPH, educator; b. Malden, Mass., Oct. 20, 1917; s. James Edmund and Ellen (Hyland) L.; B.S., U.S. Naval Acad., 1939; postgrad. U.S. Naval Postgrad. Sch., 1945; M.S.T., Am. U., 1972; m. Zoe McCombs, Feb. 2, 1942; children—George Joseph, Robert P., Dennis N., Mary Jude, William M. Commd. ensign USN, 1939, advanced through grades to comdr., 1949; comdr. U.S.S. Altair, 1952-53, U.S.S. Keppler, 1957-58; ret., 1961; project engr. Booz-Allen Applied Research, Inc., 1961-68; instr. math. St. Cecilia's Acad., Washington, 1968-69, D.C. pub. schs., 1968, 73—, Bullis sch., Silver Spring, Md., 1969-70, Anne Arundel (Md.) pub. schs., 1970-72. Mem. adv. group on electronic warfare U.S. Dept. Def., 1959-61. Pres., Crestwood Citizens Assn., 1960-61, del. D.C. Fedn., 1961-62; pres. Holy Name Soc., 1962-64, del. Archdiocesan Union, 1961-68; pres. Cath. Youth Orgn., 1958-61; leader Capital council Boy Scouts Am., 1953-56; sec. Archdiocesan Union Holy Name Socs., 1968-71; mem. St. Matthew's Cathedral Council, 1968—, Holy Year com., 1974—; mem. Calvert Sch. bd., 1968-70. Recipient Holy Name Soc. Appreciation award, 1964. Mem. Nat. Council Cath. Men, I.E.E.E., Am. Soc. Naval Engrs., A.A.A.S., Armed Forces Communication-Electronics Assn., Washington Operations Research Council, Internat. Platform Assn., N.E.A., Nat. Council Tchrs. Math., Am. Security Council, Phi Delta Kappa. Club: Serra of Washington (trustee). Home: 1908 Quincy St NW Washington DC 20011 Office: DC Pub Schs 415 12th St NW Washington DC 20004

LARICK, DONALD FRANK, clergyman; b. Los Angeles, July 29, 1932; s. Otto Marvin and Frances Annetta (Burke) L.; B.A., Phillips U., 1959, B.D., 1962; m. Barbara Muriel Buck, Aug. 26, 1955; children—Mark, Karen, Steven. With Lockheed Aircraft, Burbank, Cal., 1951-52; ordained to ministry Christian Ch., 1959; minister First Christian Ch., Medford, Okla., 1959-61; interim minister, Coldwater, Kan., 1962, Lake Jackson, Tex., 1963, Victoria, Tex., 1972; minister First Christian Ch., Bay City, Tex., 1964-72; dir. youth services Youth Services Bur., Bay City, 1971—; minister-at-large Christian Ch. of Tex., 1972—. Active Boy Scouts Am.; v.p. Bay City Elementary P.T.A., 1964-65; mem. County Juvenile Probation Officers, 1967-69. Served with USAF, 1952-56. Mem. Bay City Ministerial Assn. (pres. 1964-66), Tex. Conf. of Chs. (state resource person of ct. vols. 1971—), Tex. Criminal Justice Council (state resource person of ct. vols. 1971—), Blue Key, Pi Kappa Delta. Home: 1707 Pecan St Bay City TX 77414 Office: 3203 Av F Bay City TX 77414

LARIMORE, LEON, clergyman; b. Horse Cave, Ky., July 22, 1911; s. William C. and Myrtie D. (Isenberg) L.; grad. Campbellsville Coll., 1946, D.D., 1962; student Georgetown Coll., 1946; A.B., Western Ky. U., 1949; B.D., So. Bapt. Theol. Sem., 1952; m. Blanche Lile, July 13, 1929; 1 dau., Majorie Bell (Mrs. Levy Ray Broady). Ordained to ministry, Baptist Ch., 1937; pastor Bapt. Chs., Hart, Edmonson, Metcalfe, Green and Monroe Counties, Ky., 1937-57, 3d Av. Bapt. Ch., Louisville, 1957—. Mem. State Mission Bd., 1972—; vice chmn. adminstrv. com. Ky. Bapt. Conv., chmn. assembly and camps, 1972—. Dir. South Central Rural Telephone Coop. Mem. Econ. Security Welfare Commn., 1951-57; chmn. Hart County unit Am. Cancer Soc., 1952-56. Trustee Campbellsville Coll., 1953-70, chmn., 1967-68; trustee Wigginton Bapt. Home for Men; bd. dirs. Bapt. Homes for Elderly. Mem. Liberty Assn. So. Bapts. (moderator 1942-49, 52-57), Ky. Bapt. Conv. (v.p. 1965), Long Run Assn. So. Bapts. (moderator 1971-72; pres. exec. bd. 1971-72). Mason, Rotarian (pres. club 1956). Home: 1041 Eastern Pkwy Louisville KY 40217 Office: 1726 S 3d St Louisville KY 40208

LARKEY, CHARLES SAMUEL, cons. petroleum engr.; b. Hennessey, Okla., Oct. 5, 1891; s. John Ketron and Mary Louise (Nickels) L.; grad. Am. Sch. Law, 1913; grad. Internat. Corrs. Sch., 1915; m. Ruth Marcella Royse, Mar. 8, 1914. Engr., Tulsa County, 1915; admitted to Okla. bar, 1913; with Hughes Engring. Co., Tulsa, 1916-18, Roxana Petroleum Co. (now Shell), Tulsa, 1918-19, Sinclair Cudahy Piple Line Co., Tulsa, 1919; with Sinclair Oil & Gas Co., Tulsa, 1919-56, mgr. econs., 1951-53, mgr. data processing, 1953-56; marketing analyst Douglas Aircraft Co., Tulsa, 1957-58, astrodynamics engr., 1958-59; engring. programmer Earlougher Engring. Co., Tulsa, 1960-62; cons. in petroleum engring. programming, Tulsa, 1960—. Chief systems engr. I-C Computer Corp., Tulsa, 1968-69. Registered profl. engr., Okla. Mem. Okla., Tulsa County bar assns., Okla. (pres. 1943-44), Nat. (dir. 1945-46) socs. profl. engrs., Engrs. Soc. Tulsa. Home and office: 2447 E 6th St Tulsa OK 74104

LARKIN, ROBERT NELSON, heavy truck mfg. co. exec.; b. Buffalo, Dec. 27, 1931; s. James Crate and Florence W. (Daniels) L.; student Hackley Sch., Tarrytown, N.Y., 1949-50; student Williams Coll., 1952; postgrad. U. Wash., 1969; m. Mary Lou Evans, Apr. 25, 1958; children—Robert Nelson, James S., John T., Mary Kathleen. Pres., Constrn. Transport Ltd., Honolulu, 1958-60; gen. mgr. Consol. Freightways, Inc., Honolulu, 1960-63; mng. dir. Peterbilt Australia Pty. Ltd., Sydney, 1963-65; prodn. mgr. Peterbilt Motors Co., Newark, Cal., 1965-71, plant mgr., Nashville, 1971—. Pres. Atherton (Cal.) Little League, 1969-71; active Boy Scouts Am. Bd. dirs. Nashville Boys Club, Middle Tenn. council Boy Scouts Am., Nashville chpt. A.R.C. Mem. Soc. Automotive Engrs., Delta Upsilon. Rotarian. Clubs: Hillwood Country, City (Nashville); Commonwealth (San Francisco); Pacific (Honolulu). Home: 700 Darden Pl Nashville TN 37205 Office: 430 Myatt Dr Madison TN 37115

LARKINS, JOHN DAVIS, JR., judge; b. Morristown, Tenn., June 8, 1909; s. C.H. and Mamie (Dorset) L.; adopted s. John D. and Emma (Cooper) L.; B.A., Wake Forest U., 1929, law student, 1930; LL.D., Belin U., 1957; m. Pauline Murrill, Mar. 15, 1930; children—Emma Sue (Mrs. D.H. Loftin), Polly (Mrs. J.H. Bearden). Admitted to N.C. bar, 1930, gen. practice in Trenton, 1930-61; U.S. dist. judge Eastern Dist. N.C., 1961—. Sec. Larkins Stores, Inc.; dir. Life Ins. Co. N.C. Nat. bd. dirs., vice chmn. Am. Cancer Soc. Del.-at-large Democratic Nat. Conv., 1940, 44, 48, 56, 60; sec. N.C. Dem. Exec. Com., 1952-54, chmn., 1954-58; mem. Dem. Nat. Com., 1958-60; mem. N.C. Senate 7th dist., 1936-44, 48-54, pres. pro tem, 1941-42. Chmn. gov.'s adv. budget commn., 1951-53; gov.'s liaison officer and legislative counsel, 1955. Trustee U. N.C., Bapt. Hosp. Served as pvt. AUS, 1945. Recipient distinguished service award Am. Cancer Soc.; Outstanding Alumni Service award Wake Forest U. Sch. Law, 1968. Mem. Am., N.C. bar assns., N.C. Bar, Inc. Baptist (chmn. bd. deacons 1930-70). Home: Trenton NC 28585 Office: US Post Office and Federal Bldg Trenton NC 28585

LARKS, JACK, engr., educator; b. Chgo., Nov. 16, 1926; s. Israel David and Frieda (Morganstern) L.; student U. Ill., 1947-49; B.S., Mass. Inst. Tech., 1952, M.S., 1953; m. Norma Colwell, Dec. 24, 1957; children—Terri Lynn, Kevin Jon. Research engr. Mass. Inst. Tech., 1953-54; design test engr. Douglas Aircraft, Tulsa, 1955-57, missile operations engr., Cape Canaveral, Fla., 1957-59; facilities engr. Space Tech. Labs., Cape Canaveral, 1959-64; advanced design engr. TRW, Cape Canaveral, 1964-66, dist. rep., Houston, 1966-67, Apollo design engr., 1967-68; marketing rep. Lockheed, Houston, 1968-69, mission planning engr. earth resources, 1969-71; prof. civil tech. U. Houston, 1971—, chmn. dept., 1972—. Cons./instr. NASA/JSC, Houston, 1972-74; mem. Houston adv. bd. AMTRAK, 1973; instr. surveying Mass. Inst. Tech., 1951-52, U. Mass., 1952-53; instr. math. U. Okla., 1955-56, Brevard Engring. Coll., 1964-65, Coll. Mainland, 1968-69. Bd. dirs. United Fund, Brevard, Fla., 1964-66. Served with AUS, 1945-47. Decorated Purple Heart, Belgian Croix deGuerre; recipient Army Res. Components achievement medal. Registered profl. engr., Okla., Fla., Tex. Mem. Research Engrs. Soc. Am., Am. Soc. C.E., Am. Inst. Aeros. and Astronautics, Missiles, Space and Range Pioneers, Mass. Inst. Tech. Assn. South Tex. (pres. 1974-75), Sigma Xi, Phi Delta Kappa (pres. 1974-75). Mason, Kiwanian (pres. 1968-69). Home: 1701 Oleander Dr Dickinson TX 77539 Office: U Houston Coll of Technology Houston TX 77058

LAROCHE, PETER ALFRED, carpet and tile mfg. co. exec.; b. Albany, N.Y., Oct. 30, 1940; s. LeRoy Alfred and Christine (Johnston) L.; B.A., St. Lawrence U., 1962; M.B.A., Syracuse U., 1967; m. Georgia R. Hodge, Mar. 30, 1974. Sales rep. Corning Glass Works (N.Y.), 1965-70; with Sikes Corp., Lakeland, Fla., 1970—, nat. sales mgr. Sikes Carpets div., 1972—. Vice chmn. advt. and publs. com. Tile Council of Am., Princeton, N.J., 1973—; mem. advt. and publicity bd. City of Lakeland, 1973—. Bd. dirs. Lakeland YMCA, 1973—. Served to 1st lt. AUS, 1962-65. Mem. Am. Marketing Assn., Lakeland Jaycees (past pres. 1970), Lakeland C. of C., Sigma Chi. Presbyn. Mason. Home: 2404 New Jersey Rd Lakeland FL 33803 Office: PO Box 447 Lakeland FL 33803

LAROSE, ROBERT LEE, data processing equipment mfg. co. exec.; b. Hudson Falls, N.Y., Jan. 13, 1937; s. Kenneth Lee and Stella (Kokosa) LaR.; student N.Y. State Tchrs. Coll., 1956-58; B.A. in Math. and Physics, Tex. A. and M. U., 1961; D.Computer Sci. (hon.), Marlowe U., 1968; m. Janis Elaine Mahaffey, May 27, 1956; children—Robin Lee, Diana Dawn, Robert Lee Jr. Sr. sales rep. Honeywell EDP Co., Dallas, 1964-67, dist. mgr. information services operations div. Honeywell Corp., Dallas, 1969-71; v.p. marketing Associometrics, Inc., Dallas, 1967-69; mgr. Dallas br. MSI Data Corp., 1971—; chmn. bd. Software Technologies Inc., Dallas. Served with USAF, 1954-58. Mem. Augustan Soc., Conn. Soc. Genealogists. Episcopalian (vestryman). Contbr. to profl. jours. Home: 1206 Northgate Dr Irving TX 75062 Office: 3129 Hwy 67 Suite D Mesquite TX 75149

LARRABEE, CHARLES XAVIER, sci. research exec.; b. Seattle, June 23, 1922; s. Charles Francis and Mary Adele (Brownlie) L.; student Dartmouth, 1940-42; m. Margaret Dwelle, Oct. 8, 1943; children—Giles, Sarah, Meg, Charles, Alexander, Lucy, Jean. Asst. to editor San Francisco Chronicle, 1946-53; adminstrv. asst. to dir. Stanford Research Inst., Menlo Park, Cal., 1953-56; asso. gen. mgr., acting fiction editor Crowell-Collier Pub. Co., N.Y.C., 1956-57; asst. to v.p. United Fruit Co., Boston, 1957-62; mgr. information services Spindletop Research, Lexington, Ky., 1962-64; pub. relations mgr. Research Triangle Inst., Research Triangle Park, N.C., 1964-71, asst. to pres., 1971—. Vice pres. United Fund, 1971. Bd. dirs. Better Bus. Bur. Served with USMCR, 1942-45. Recipient Excellence award Raleigh Pub. Relations Soc., 1968. Mem. Pub. Relations Soc. Am. (pres. N.C. chpt.), Durham C. of C. (task force chmn. 1968-70). Kiwanian. Club: Croasdaile Country (Durham, N.C.). Home: 1114 Woodburn Rd Durham NC 27705 Office: Box 12194 Research Triangle Park NC 27709

LARRICK, ROBERT VERNON, psychiatrist; b. Capon Bridge, W.Va., Feb. 27, 1914; s. James Walter and Myrtle (Powell) L.; A.B., Shepherd Coll., 1941; M.S., W.Va. U., 1943; M.D., Med. Coll. Va., 1946; postgrad. Vanderbilt U., 1953-56; m. Frances Covington; children—Donna, Pamela, Robert Vernon. Sch. tchr., 1934-41; rotating intern Chesapeake and Ohio Hosp., Huntington, W.Va., 1946-48, resident internal medicine, 1947-48; practice of medicine, Winchester, Va., 1950-53; resident psychiatry Vanderbilt U., Nashville, 1953-56; med. dir. Central State Hosp., Nashville, 1959; psychiatrist Hillcrest San., 1958-60; dir. Plateau Mental Health Center, Cookeville, Tenn., 1960-70. Served to maj. AUS, 1948-50. Diplomate Am. Bd. Psychiatry. Mem. Am. Psychiat. Assn., So., Tenn., Middle Tenn., Putnam County med. assns., Phi Chi. Methodist. Home: 855 Loweland Rd Cookeville TN 38501

LARSEN, BRUCE WESTERLY, elec. engr.; b. Everett, Mass., Oct. 25, 1939; s. Nels and Beatrice (Zuercher) L.; B.S., U. Md., 1961; m. Patricia Engstrom, Oct. 5, 1963; children—Sharon Patricia, Wayne Bruce, Sonja Carol. Analog applications engr. Pratt & Whitney Aircraft, West Palm Beach, Fla., 1961-64; recovery engr. manned spacecraft NASA, Houston, 1964-67, unmanned spacecraft project officer Kennedy Spacecenter (Fla.), 1967-70, Skylab expts. mgr. Apollo-Skylab program office, 1970-72; guidance and control systems engr. Unmanned Launch Operations, NASA-Kennedy Space Center, Fla., 1972—. Registered profl. engr., Fla. Mem. Soc. Am. Mil. Engrs., I.E.E.E., Assn. Advanced Med. Instrumentation, U.S. Naval Inst. Methodist. Home: 504 Bianca Ct Altamonte Springs FL 32701 Office: NASA Kennedy Spacecenter FL 32899

LARSEN, GEORGE EDWARD, librarian; b. N.Y.C., Mar. 26, 1912; s. George and Edythe (Keys) L.; A.B., Williams Coll., 1933; diploma Command and Gen. Staff Coll., 1951, Army War Coll., 1957; M.S., Fla. State U., 1968; m. Hope Harrin, Nov. 11, 1949; children—Margo,

Linda, Jeanne, George Edward. Sales mgr. T.M. James & Co., N.Y.C., 1933-43; served from pvt. to col. U.S. Army, 1943-67; faculty Command and Gen. Staff Coll., 1951-54, Army War Coll., 1957-60; ret., 1967; dir. libraries Rollins Coll., Winter Park, Fla., 1968—. Decorated Legion of Merit. Mem. Am., Fla. library assns., Assn. Am. U. Profs., Delta Phi, Beta Phi Mu. Home: 660 Arjay Way Winter Park FL 32789

LARSEN, LAWRENCE EDWIN, neurophysiologist, educator; b. Denver, Apr. 20, 1943; s. John Magnus and Anna (Manning) L.; M.D. magna cum laude, U. Colo., 1968; m. Linda Lee Gorvett, Dec. 28, 1966; children—Adam John, Leanne Gay, Dana Elizabeth. NIH postdoctoral fellow Brain Research Inst., U. Cal. Los Angeles, 1968-70; research physiologist dept. microwave research Walter Reed Army Inst. Research, Washington, 1970-73; asst. prof. physiology Baylor Coll. Medicine, Houston, 1973—. Cons. U.S. Naval Neuropsychiat. Unit, Nat. Inst. Mental Health, Nat. Inst. Child Health and Devel., neurobiology br. NSF. Served to maj. M.C., AUS, 1970-73. Recipient Glaser prize U. Colo. Sch. Medicine, 1968, Lange Med. Publs. award, 1968. Mem. Biometric Soc., Soc. for Neuroscis., Alpha Epsilon Delta, Alpha Omega Alpha. Contbr. articles on neurophysiology to sci. jours. Inventor microwave integrated circuit transducers for brain temperature and EEG measurement. Research in applications of physics and biomath. to physiology of central nervous system. Home: 16463 Parksley Dr Houston TX 77058

LARSH, HOWARD WILLIAM, educator; b. East St. Louis, Ill., May 20, 1914; s. John Edgar and Margaret (Kays) L.; B.A., McKendree Coll., 1936; student mycology Washington U., St. Louis, 1936-37; M.S., U. Ill. at Urbana, 1938, Ph.D., 1941; postgrad. med. mycology Duke, also U. N.C., summer 1946; m. Georgia Lee Thomson, Sept. 4, 1938; 1 son, Jonathan Thomson. Mem. faculty U. Okla., 1941—, prof. med. mycology, 1948—, research prof., 1962—, chmn. dept. botany and microbiology, 1966—; cons. in field, 1950—; asso. dir. labs. Mo. Chest Hosp., 1955; mem. Lunar Quarantine Operations Team; research reviewer immunology and infectious diseases com. VA Hosp., Oklahoma City, 1972. Diplomate Am. Bd. Med. Microbiology. Fellow A.A.A.S., Am. Pub. Health Assn., Okla. Acad. Sci., Am. Acad. Microbiology; mem. Bot. Soc. Am., Soc. Am. Bacteriologists, Am. Soc. Tropical Medicine and Hygiene, Soc. Exptl. Biology and Medicine, Internat. Soc. Human and Animal Mycology, Reticuloendothelial Soc., Med. Mycology Soc. Ams. (pres. 1973-74), Sigma Xi, Phi Sigma, Lambda Tau. Author articles in field. Home: 611 Broad Lane Norman OK 73069

LARSON, BEN JOHN, accountant, state ofcl.; b. Tulsa, July 11, 1927; s. Ben K. and Pearl (Monks) L.; student Ft. Smith Jr. Coll., 1953-54, Tulsa U., 1954-56; m. Evelyna A. A. Liotta, Dec. 15, 1948; children—Ben T., Michael J., Stephen J., Philip A., David P., Marianne. Various civilian, mil. accounting and financial positions, 1946-61; sr. auditor Mercing & Thomas, 1961-66; audit mgr. Nat. Investors Cos., 1966-68; sr. examiner ins. dept. Ark., Little Rock, 1968-71, chief examiner Ark. securities div., 1971-72; sr. ins. examiner Okla. Ins. Dept., Oklahoma City, 1972—. Served with AUS, 1943-46, 47-53. Decorated Bronze Star medal with oak leaf cluster, C.I.B. with star. Croix de Guerre Mem. Am. Inst. C.P.A.'s, Ark. Soc. C.P.A.'s, Accounting Research Assn. Roman Catholic. K.C. Home: 6417 N Nicklas Oklahoma City OK 73132 Office: Will Rogers Memorial Bldg Oklahoma City OK 73105

LARSON, BILL ALLEN, oil field supply co. exec.; b. Bartlesville, Okla., July 14, 1920; s. Albert D. and Blanche (Stover) L.; B.A., Okla. U., 1942, J.D., 1948; m. Laura L. Pratt, Aug. 5, 1950; 1 dau., Kristen K. Admitted to Okla. bar, 1948; practice in Oklahoma City, 1948-51; asst. to v.p. Consol. Gas Utilities Corp., Oklahoma City, 1953-58; v.p., gen. counsel A.D. Larson Supply Co. Oklahoma City, 1958-64, exec. v.p., 1964-68, pres., 1968—, also dir.; pres. Larsco, Inc., 1968—. Mem. boys rehab. com. Okla. County Juvenile Judges. Served to maj. AUS, 1942-46, 51-53; operations officer IX Corps Arty., Korea; lt. col. Judge Advocate, 95th Division (Res.), also hon. marshall. Decorated Air medal with 3 oak leaf clusters; hon. county atty.; hon. justice, practice ct., Okla. U. Coll. Law; hon. mayor Oklahoma City; 95th Div. Outstanding Oklahoman award. Mem. Am., Okla., Oklahoma County bar assns., Am. Petroleum Inst., Res. Officers Assn., Okla. Hist. Soc., Oklahoma City C. of C., Phi Kappa Psi, Phi Alpha Delta. Democrat. Unitarian. Clubs: Petroleum, Oklahoma City Golf and Country (Oklahoma City). Home: 6904 N Grand Blvd Oklahoma City OK 73116

LARSON, JORDAN LOUIS, credit co. exec.; b. Roland, Ia., Jan. 4, 1900; s. Louis and Julia (Johnson) L.; B.A., U. Ia., 1922, M.A., 1931; M.A., Ed.D., Columbia, 1951; m. Mildred Thorson, June 24, 1925; children—Jordan, Jeanne (Mrs. Paul W. Griewe), Marilyn (Mrs. Robert Mau), Leland. Tchr., supt. schs., Littleport, Ia., 1922-24, Garnavillo, Ia., 1924-26, Dunkerton, Ia., 1926-31, Grundy Center, Ia., 1931-36, Ames, Ia. 1936-40, Dubuque, Ia., 1940-46, Mt. Vernon, N.Y., 1946-65; exec. sec. Sch. Facilities Council of Architecture, Edn. and Industry, Prospect Heights, Ill., 1965-70; now pres., chief exec. officer Tower Credit Corp., Tampa, Fla.; vis. prof. Ia. State Coll., summers 1938-40; lectr. N.Y. U., 1947. Chmn. com. on religion and pub. edn. Nat. Council Chs., 1953-61; pres. Asso. Pub. Sch. Systems, 1949-50; mem. U.S. aviation industry adv. panel Air Coordinating Com., 1952-59; v.p. Nat. Aviation Council, 1952-53, pres. 1953-54; adviser to nat. comdr. Civil Air Patrol, 1951-70. Served with U.S. Army, 1918; to lt. col. AUS, 1942-45; ret. col. USAF. Recipient Frank G. Brewer Civil Air Patrol Aerospace award, 1960. Mem. Am. Assn. Sch. Adminstrs. (pres. 1954-55, Distinguished Service award 1973), Ia. Legion Schoolmasters (pres. 1939-40), Ia. Supts. (pres. 1940-41), N.Y. Legion Schoolmasters (pres. 1950-53), European Flying Classroom, Nat. Sch. Facilities Council (pres. 1958-65), Westchester County Chief Sch. Officers (pres. 1957-58), Am. Legion, Alpha Sigma Phi, Phi Delta Kappa. Mason. Club: N.Y. Schoolmasters (pres. 1963), Rotary (pres. 1935-36, 53-54). Contbr. articles to ednl. mags. Home: 5116 San Jose St Tampa FL 33609 Office: 915 Ashley St Suite 306 Tampa FL 33602

LARSON, KERMIT DEAN, educator; b. Algona, Ia., Apr. 7, 1939; s. Loren L. and Hansena Laurena (Andersen) L.; A.A., Fort Dodge Jr. Coll., 1960; B.B.A., U. Ia., 1962, M.B.A., 1963; D.B.A., U. Colo., 1966; m. Nancy Lynne Weber, June 17, 1961; children—Julie Renee, Timothy Dean, Cynthia Lynne. Mem. faculty U. Tex. at Austin, 1966—, prof. accounting, 1971—, chmn. dept., 1971—. Vis. asso. prof. Tulane U., New Orleans, fall 1970-71. Cons. sales tax audit litigation Atty. Gen. Tex., 1973. C.P.A., Tex. Am. Accounting Assn. fellow, 1965-66. Mem. Am. Accounting Assn., Am. Finance Assn., Am. Inst. C.P.A.'s, Am. Inst. Decision Scis., Tex. Soc. C.P.A.'s, Beta Gamma Sigma, Beta Alpha Psi. Baptist. Author: (with C.H. Griffin and T.H. Williams) Advanced Accounting, 1971, Solutions Manual for Advanced Accounting, 1971. Contbr. profl. jours. Home: 5602 Ridge Oak Dr Austin TX 78731 Office: Dept Accounting Univ Texas Austin TX 78712

LARSON, LAWRENCE TILFORD, educator; b. Waukegan, Ill., Dec. 3, 1930; s. Lawrence L. and Margaret (Tilford) L.; B.S. with highest honors, U. Ill., 1957; M.S., U. Wis., 1959, Ph.D., 1962; m. Elizabeth A. Rich, Sept. 7, 1957; children—Jacqueline, Lawrence, Kathleen. Asst. prof. geology U. Tenn., Knoxville, 1961-65, asso. prof., 1965-70, prof., 1970—; partner Applied Exploration Concepts, 1972—. Served with USAF, 1950-54. Wis. Alumni fellow, 1957-59, Union Carbide Ore Co. fellow, 1959-61. Fellow Geol. Soc. Am.; mem. Mineral. Soc. Am., Am. Inst. Mining, Metall. and Petroleum Engrs., Soc. Econ. Geologists, Canadian Inst. Mining and Metallurgy, Internat. Orgn. Genesis Ore Deposits. Home: 5802 Wassman Rd Knoxville TN 37912

LARSON, LEWIS JENNINGS, coll. dean; b. Lincoln, Neb., Sept. 29, 1911; s. Lewis J. and Anna Catherine (Nelson) L.; B.S., Madison Coll., 1938; M.A., George Peabody Coll. for Tchrs., 1947, Ed.S., 1963, Ed.D., 1964; m. Mary Ninaj, Aug. 19, 1934; children—Karl Milan, Elizabeth Ann. Ordained to ministry Seventh-day Adventist Ch., 1956; ednl. and editorial service in India, 1939-61; Ford teaching fellow George Peabody Coll., 1961-62; dean acad. affairs Oakwood Coll., Huntsville, Ala., 1964-69; dean acad. affairs Southwestern Union Coll., Keene, Tex., 1969—, mem. exec. bd., 1969—. Mem. ednl. council Gen. Conf. Seventh-day Adventist Ch., India, Burma, Ceylon and Pakistan, 1945-61, N.Am. Ednl. Adv. Council, 1970—; dep. dir. Ala. Center for Higher Edn., 1968-69. Mem. Am. Sch. Adminstrs., Am. Assn. for Higher Edn., Phi Delta Kappa. Author: Report of First Institute of Scientific Studies-Bombay, 1956; Story Time, vols. I-10, 1952-57. Editor: Selected Messages, 1961; Health and Longevity, 1957. Editor monthly mags. Herald of Health, 1951-59, Our Times, 1958-59. Address: Southwestern Union Coll Keene TX 76059

LARSON, REED EUGENE, assn. exec.; b. nr. Kensington, Kan., Sept. 27, 1922; s. George Christian and Edith Hazel (Whitney) L.; student Kan. Wesleyan U., 1940-41, Ohio State U., 1943-44; B.S. in Elec. Engring., Kan. State U., 1947; m. Majorie Jeanne Hess, Aug. 31, 1947; children—Patricia Kay, Barbara Ann, Marcia Lynn. Design engr. Stein Labs., Atchison, Kan., 1947-48; processing engr. Coleman Co., Wichita, Kan., 1948-54; exec. v.p. Kansans for Right to Work, Wichita, Kan., 1954-58; exec. v.p. Nat. Right to Work Com., Washington, 1959—; exec. v.p. Nat. Right to Work Legal Def. Found., Washington, 1968-73, pres., 1973—. Served with AUS, 1943-46. Recipient Seldon Waldo award U.S. Jr. C. of C., 1956, Silver Anvil award Pub. Relations Soc. Am., 1966. Mem. Am. Soc. Assn. Execs., Farm Bur., Am. Nat. Cattlemen's Assn., C. of C. Methodist. Home: 6149 Beachway Dr Falls Church VA 22041 Office: 1990 M St NW Suite 400 Washington DC 20036

LASALLE, SHELBY PAUL, JR., engring. co. exec.; b. New Orleans, Aug. 11, 1940; s. Shelby Paul and Dolly Rose (Anthony) LaS.; student Delgado Coll., La. State U.; m. Gloria May Lemoine, May 14, 1960; children—Shelby Blair, Jody Gerard, Chad Lee, René Monroe. Sr. engring. insp. Jefferson Parish (La.) Dept. Water, 1959-65; with J.J. Krebs & Sons, Inc., civil engrs. and surveyors, Metairie, La., 1965—, v.p., 1968-73, sr. v.p. engring., 1973—, dir., 1972—; dir. Medmil Meadow, Inc., St. Charles Parish, La. Mem. Jefferson Parish Cultural Attraction Com.; v.p. 3d Dist. Vol. Fire Dept., 1973—. Democratic precinct capt., Jefferson Parish, 1971-72. Mem. Am. Water Works Assn., Am. Pub. Works Assn., La. Engring. Soc., Jefferson Bd. Realtors, La. Realtors Assn., Nat. Assn. Realtors, La. State Firemen's Assn., Vol. Fire Chiefs Assn. La., Am. Motorcycle Assn. Mem. United Ch. of Christ. Club: Jefferson Parish Athletic. Home: 8717 Darby Lane New Orleans LA 70123 Office: 3013 27th St Metairie LA 70002

LASATER, ROBERT EDWARD, structural engr.; b. Erwin, N.C., Feb. 11, 1930; s. Eugene Herndon and Josephine (Stuart) L.; student Campbell Coll., 1948-50; B.C.E., N.C. State U., 1958; m. Julia Elizabeth Henderson, June 17, 1952; children—Elizabeth, Margaret, Helen, Robert Julia. Designer, draftsman Watson Engrs., Greensboro, N.C., 1958, Holloway-Reeves, Raleigh, N.C., 1959-63, M.J. Andrews, Greensboro, 1964-65; cons. structural engr., Raleigh, 1966—. Served with USNR, 1950-54. Registered profl. engr., N.C., Ohio. Mem. Am. Soc. C.E., Nat. Soc. Profl. Engrs., Profl. Engrs. N.C., Constrn. Specification Inst. Democrat. Presbyn. (deacon 1971—). Clubs: North Hills (dir. 1967-69), Optimist (Raleigh); MacGregor Downs Country (Cary, N.C.). Home: 5310 Inglewood Lane Raleigh NC 27609 Office: Hwy 70 West Raleigh NC 17612

LASBURY, LEAH (MRS. CLYDE P. LASBURY), realtor, artist; b. Boca Grand, Fla., Apr. 11, 1915; d. James E. and Nellie (Allen) Bartlett; B.A., Rollins Coll., 1936; B.S., Simmons Coll., 1937; m. Clyde P. Lasbury, Sept. 16, 1939; children—Cherick Pitchford, Dana Lynne, Leah Jean. Exec. trainee G. Fox & Co., Hartford, Conn., 1937-39; real estate broker, Englewood, Fla., 1951—; sec.-treas. Lee Lasbury, Inc., realtors; dir. J. E. Bartlett & Sons, Inc., Englewood; charter mem. adv. bd. Englewood Bank. One-man shows Englewood Bank, 1960, Community Gallery, Venice, Fla., 1960, Corridor Gallery, Asheville, N.C., 1961, Italian Villa, Venice, 1963, Am. Bank, Sarasota, Fla., 1966; exhibited group shows, 1955—, including Nat. Assn. Women Artists, N.Y.C., 1959, N.Y.C. Pen and Brush Club, 1959, Ringling Mus., Sarasota, 1961, South Coast Galleries, Corridor Gallery, 1961, Tampa Fair, 1960-61, Lowe Gallery, Miami, 1963, 68, Fla. Artist Group shows, 1964-74, 1st Rollins Coll. Alumni Show., 1966, 67, 68, New Coll. Artists Group, Sarasota Fla., 1966, numerous others; represented in pvt. collections. Organizer Englewood Teen Club, 1952; pres. P.T.A., Broad Brook, Conn., 1945; mem. Englewood Zoning Commn., 1956-57; mem. adv. bd. Sarasota County Library, 1966—; v.p. Ringling Mus. Mems. Guild, 1960-62; organizer 1st road commn., Englewood, 1956, 1st water commn., 1956; organizer Englewood Library, 1962, bd. dirs., 1962—, pres., 1972-73; mem. Sarasota County Community Goals Council, 1965—; dir. Asolo Theatre Festival Assn., 1963—. Mem. Venice Area Art League (dir.), Englewood Realtors Bd. (organizer, charter pres., dir.), Englewood (past pres.), Sarasota County (publicity com. 1963) chambers commerce, Englewood Women Taxpayers League (organizer, charter pres.), Sarasota Art Assn., Fla. Artist Group Inc. (pres. 1972-74), Internat. Platform Assn., Nat. Assn. Women Artists, D.A.R. (charter Myakka chpt. Venice), Pi Gamma Mu., Phi Mu, Alpha Omega. Republican. Methodist. Clubs: Venice Yacht (charter mem.). Home: 115 Lee Circle Englewood FL 33533 Office: 312 Indiana Av Englewood FL 33533

LASH, ROBERT FREDERICK, physician; b. Danville, Ill., Mar. 3, 1925; s. Fred John and Willa Aileen (Myers) L.; student Wabash Coll., 1942-45; M.D., George Washington U., 1949; m. Katherine Mae Pleune, June 5, 1948; children—Robert Frederick, Kathryn Sue, John Steven. Intern, USPHS Hosp., Staten Island, N.Y., 1949-50; gen. practice medicine, Knoxville, 1952—; med. examiner FAA, 1960—; dir. emergency med. service U. Tenn. Meml. Research Center and Hosp., 1968—, chmn., prof. dept. family practice, 1969—, chief of staff, 1970. Dir. Knoxville Poison Control Center, 1957—; med. dir. Knoxville Methadone and Drug Clinic, 1970; sec., dir. Lost Sea, Inc. Pres., chmn. Physicians Med. Edn. and Research Found.; bd. dirs. Knox County Vol. Rescue Squad. Served with USNR, 1942-45, USPHS, 1949-52. Recipient FAA certificate of commendation, 1965, C.D. Henry award Civil Aviation Med. Assn., 1968; Distinguished Service award U.S. Jr. C. of C., 1968. Diplomate Am. Bd. Family Practice. Fellow Am. Acad. Family Physicians; asso. fellow Aerospace Med. Assn.; mem. A.M.A., Civil Aviation, Pan. Am., So. med. assns., Tenn., Knoxville acads. family practice, Am. Soc. Clin. Hypnosis, A.A.A.S., Flying Physicians Assn., Internat. Soc. Toxinology, Am. Assn. Poison Control Centers, Am. Coll. Emergency Physicians, Am. Acad. Clin. Toxicology, Air Force Assn., Pilots Internat. Assn., Air Traffic Controllers Med. Assn. Club: South Knoxville Optimist (past pres.). Home: 216 Sarvis Dr Knoxville TN 37920 Office: Physicians Office Bldg 1928 Alcoa Hwy Knoxville TN 37920

LASHER, HUMES TRUITT, judge; b. Kittanning, Pa., Oct. 20, 1912; s. John H. and Margaret (Truitt) L.; B.B.A., U. Miami, 1947, LL.B., 1950; m. Evelyn Mae Weitzel, Dec. 21, 1934; children—Humes Truitt, Barry Humes. Admitted to Fla. bar, 1950; practiced in Pitts., 1950-61; partner firm Lasher & Hartwig, Ft. Lauderdale, Fla., 1962-70; judge Ct. of Record, Ft. Lauderdale, 1967—, Circuit Ct., Fla., 1972—. Served with USNR, 1942-47. Mem. Internat. Yachtsmen Assn., Under Seas Edn., Better Yachting Council, Broward Artificial Reef, Phi Kappa Alpha, Delta Theta Phi. Republican. Mason, Elk, Rotarian. Home: 1008 Avocado Isle Fort Lauderdale FL 33315 Office: Broward County Ct House Fort Lauderdale FL 33315

LASLIE, JOHN LEWIS COBBS, banker; b. Montgomery, Ala., May 27, 1917; s. Carney Graham and Isabelle Woodfin (Cobbs) L.; student Phillips Exeter Acad., 1933-35; B.A. magna cum laude, Princeton, 1939; m. Martha Elaine Alexander; 1 dau., Adele Easton. Owner, Cook's Confections, 1950-60; chief adminstrv. officer Continental Barges, Inc., Gentilly Properties, Inc., Financial Securities, Inc., New Orleans, 1957-73; v.p., treas., dir. Delta Capital Corp., 1961-73; pres., chief adminstr. Aladdin Oil Co., Aladdin Prodn. Co., 1963—; pres. First Nat. Bank, Slidell, La., 1967-73; pres. Small Bus. Assistance Corp., Panama City, Fla., 1973—; pres. Panama City Nat. Bank, 1973—; dir. Ceres Devel. Co., So. Cemeteries, Inc., Roane Flying Service, Inc., So. Metal Products, Consmar Corp., Continental Shelf Marine, Panhandle Broadcasting Co. Chmn. adv. council investment div. Small Bus. Adminstrn., Washington. Chmn. St. Tammany Parish Disaster Fund, 1969, St. Tammany Parish United Fund, 1970. Bd. dirs. Family Service Soc., 1950-54, Gaudet Home, 1953-57. Recipient Nat. Venture Capital award, 1966. Mem. Nat. Assn. Small Bus. Investment Cos. Democrat. Episcopalian. Rotarian. Home: 2300 Magnolia Dr Panama City FL 32401 Office: PO Drawer J Panama City Beach FL 32401

LASSETTER, CLARENCE RAY, clergyman; b. Harperville, Miss., May 13, 1926; s. Benjamin Poole and Lola Louise (Lyle) L.; student Miss. Coll., 1944; B.A., also B.S., U. Tex., 1947; B.D., So. Bapt. Theol. Sem., 1950, Th.D., 1954; m. Jean Elizabeth Rasco, Jan. 31, 1951; children—Elizabeth Lee, Leslie Ann, Scott Austin, Steven Lyle. Ordained to ministry Bapt. Ch., 1948; pastor Raymond Ch., Webster, Ky., 1948-51, Glen Allen (Va.) Ch., 1953-55, Ft. Mitchell (Ky.) Ch., 1955-64; exec. sec. No. Ky. Assn. Prot. Chs., Covington, 1964-67; program coordinator Comprehensive Care Center, Covington, 1967-72, clin. specialist, 1972—; lectr. math. and philosophy No. Community Coll. of U. Ky., 1966-70; lectr. philosophy No. Ky. State Coll., 1971—. Pres. No. Ky. Bapt. Pastors Conf., 1960, Ky. Alumni Assn. So. Bapt. Theol. Sem., 1960. Pres. No. Ky. Mental Health Assn., 1961-62; sec., dir. Western Recorder, 1960-66; trustee Greater Cin. Council Alcoholism; dir. No. Ky. Health Council, 1962-67. Served with USNR, 1944-46; chaplain Res. Ky. Col. Mem. Ky. Philos. Soc., No. Ky. Assn. Protestant Chs. (pres. 1960-61), No. Ky. Bapt. Assn. (sec.), Phi Beta Kappa. Democrat. Home: 2003 Pieck Dr Covington KY 41011 Office: 2d and Greenup Sts Covington KY 41011

LASSETTER, JAMES GREEN, realtor; b. Villa Rica, Ga., Sept. 13, 1916; s. John G. W. and Addie (Green) L.; student West Ga. Jr. Coll., 1935-36; B.S., U. Ga., 1940; m. Maggie Samples, Apr. 7, 1939; children—Margaret Anne (Mrs. Charles W. Rushing), Mary Lynn (Mrs. Earl Maxwell), James W. Asst. supr. Farm Security Adminstrn., Carrollton, Ga., 1940; soil conservationist Soil Conservation Service, U.S. Dept. Agr., Marianna, Fla., 1941-43, Chipley, Fla., 1943-52, DeFuniak Springs, Fla., 1952-54; real estate broker James G. Lassetter, DeFuniak Springs, 1954-56, Tallahassee, 1956-58; pres. Tallahassee Realty Co., 1958—; pres. Lassetters of Fla., 1959—. Mem. Tallahassee Bd. Realtors (pres. 1964), Fla. Assn. Realtors (dist. v.p. 1962, 65), Fla. Real Estate Exchangers, Nat., Fla. assns. farm and land brokers, Nat. Inst. Real Estate Brokers, Nat. Assn. Realtors, Phi Kappa Phi. Baptist. Elk. Home: 1101 Kenilworth PO Box 1333 Tallahassee FL 32302 Office: 1215 Thomasville Rd PO Box 1333 Tallahassee FL 32302

LASSETTER, MAGGIE SAMPLES (MRS. JAMES GREEN LASSETTER), realtor; b. Villa Rica, Ga.; d. Moses Monroe and Ethel (Boyd) Samples; student W. Ga. Coll., 1938-39; m. James Green Lassetter, Apr. 7, 1939; children—Margaret Annette (Mrs. Charles W. Rushing), Mary Lynn (Mrs. Earl Maxwell), James William. Pvt. practice real estate broker, DeFuniak Springs, Fla., 1954-55; partner Tallahassee Realty Co., 1958—, v.p., 1963. Mem. Tallahassee Sister City Commn., Popayan, Colombia, Fla. Adult Edn. Adv. Bd. Mem. Nat. Inst. Real Estate Brokers (regional v.p. 1971), Nat. (gov. 1967, nat. dir. 1972—), Fla. (dir. dist. 8, 1972; Fla. pres. women's council 1965, dir. Region 10, 1968, pres. Tallahassee 1971, mem. edn. com.; Woman of Year 1965) assns. realtors, Tallahassee Bd. Realtors (pres. 1970, membership com.; Realtor of Year 1970), Am. Bus. Women's Assn. (Woman of Year 1964, pres. Tallahassee 1966), Capitol (pres. 1968), Dist. II (dir.) bus. and profl. women's clubs, Urban League, Heritage Found. Baptist. Mem. Order Eastern Star. Clubs: Toastmistress, woman's (chmn. Am. homes dept.) (Tallahassee). Home: 1101 Kenilworth Rd Tallahassee FL 32303 Office: 1215 Thomasville Rd PO Box 1333 Tallahassee FL 32302

LASSITER, JAMES WILLIAM, nutritionist, educator; b. Covington, Ga., May 28, 1920; s. Elwood Gray and Georgia Falls (Salter) L.; B.S.A., U. Ga., 1941, M.S.A., 1952; Ph.D., U. Ill., 1955; m. Mary Sue Kitchens, Oct. 5, 1947; children—Mary Lynda (Mrs. Ronnie Monroe Sims), James William. Asst. U. Ill. at Urbana, 1952-54; asst. prof. animal sci. U. Ga., Athens, 1954-61, asso. prof., 1961-70, prof., 1970—. Vis. scholar U. Cambridge, Eng., 1972; cons. Oak Ridge Inst. Nuclear Studies, 1958-63; participant 9th Internat. Congress of Animal Prodn., 1966, 8th Internat. Congress Nutrition, 1966, 1st and 2d Internat. Symposium on Trace Element Metabolism in Animals, 1969, 73. Served to maj., 9th. Cav., USAAF, 1941-46. AEC grantee, 1960, Geigy Corp. grantee, 1970, Gold Kist Inc. grantee, 1972, Ga. Alumni Found. grantee, 1972. Mem. Am. Soc. Animal Sci. (chmn. teaching com. 1972-73, Distinguished Tchr. award 1971), Am. Inst. Nutrition, Am. Dairy Sci. Assn., Nat. (mem. manganese panel nat. research council 1971-73), Ga. acads. sci., Assn. So. Agrl. Workers, Blue Key, Aghon, Sigma Xi (pres. elect 1972-73), Gamma Sigma Delta (Distinguished tchr. award 1969), Phi Kappa Phi, Gamma Sigma Epsilon, Alpha Zeta, Omicron Delta Kappa, Phi Eta Sigma. Methodist. Lion, Toastmaster. Editorial Bd. Am. Jour. Animal Sci., 1972—. Home: 515 Forest Heights Dr Athens GA 30601

LASSITER, WILLIAM EDMUND, physician, educator; b. Wilmington, N.C., July 21, 1927; s. Leroy Irving and Annie Elizabeth (Cummings) L.; A.B. magna cum laude in Physics, Harvard, 1950, M.D. cum laude (Nat. scholar), 1954; m. Diane Irving, June 30, 1956; children—William, Susan, David, John. Intern, resident medicine Mass. Gen. Hosp. and N.C. Meml. Hosp., 1954-57, research fellow, 1957-60; faculty U. N.C. Sch. Medicine, Chapel Hill, 1960—, now prof. medicine; established investigator Am. Heart Assn., 1962-67; vis. investigator Physiol. Inst., Free U., Berlin, 1963-64. Cons. NIH cardiovascular and pulmonary study sect., 1969-73. Served with USNR, 1945-46. John and Mary R. Markle scholar in acad. medicine, 1963-68. Fellow A.C.P.; mem. Am. Soc. Clin. Investigation, Am. Physiol. Soc. (editorial bd.), Phi Beta Kappa, Sigma Xi, Alpha Omega Alpha. Episcopalian. Mem. editorial bd. Jour. Applied Physiology, Am. Jour. Physiology, 1970—, Proc. Soc. Exptl. Biology and Medicine, 1967-73. Contbr. articles profl. jours. Home: 303 Elliott Rd Chapel Hill NC 27514

LASSITER, WRIGHT LOWENSTEIN, coll. adminstr.; b. Vicksburg, Miss., Mar. 21, 1934; s. Wright Lowenstein and Ethel Lee (Franklin) L.; B.S., Alcorn A. and M. U., 1955; certificate in instl. bus. mgmt. Tuckegee Inst., 1956; M.B.A., Ind. U., 1962; postgrad. Auburn U., 1972-74; m. Bessie Loretta Ryan, Oct. 3, 1958; children—Michele Denise, Wright Lowenstein III. Investments accountant Hampton (Va.) Inst., 1956; sr. accountant Tuskegee Inst. (Ala.), 1958-61, dir. aux. enterprises, 1962—, asst. prof. mgmt., 1962—; research asso. Ind. U., Bloomington, 1961-62. Vice pres. Tuskegee Fed. Credit Union, 1971—; cons. Robert R. Moton Devel. Asso., 1973—. Chmn., City of Tuskegee Indsl. Devel. Bd., 1972—; chmn. bd. commrs. Tuskegee Housing Authority, 1965-73; pres. Macon County Heart Fund, 1972—; treas. United Negro Coll. Fund, 1962—; chmn. adv. com. Assn. Ala. Women's Clubs, 1966-73. Served with AUS, 1956-62; now capt. Res. Mem. Nat. Assn. Coll. Aux. Service Officers (charter pres. 1968-70), Council Ednl. Facility Planners, Soc. for Advancement Mgmt., Sigma Pi Phi, Alpha Phi Alpha. Delta Mu Delta, Kappa Delta Pi, Phi Delta Kappa, Alpha Kappa Nu. Mason (Shriner, 33 deg.). Home: 2009 Ethel Dr Tuskegee Institute AL 36088

LASSWELL, SHIRLEY ANN BASSO SLESINGER (MRS. FRED D. LASSWELL JR.), lit. promoting co. exec.; b. Detroit, 1924; d. Michael and Clara (Leasia) Basso; grad. high sch.; m. Stephen Slesinger, Oct. 1949 (dec. 1953); 1 dau., Patricia Ann; m. 2d, Fred D. Lasswell, Jr., June 1964. Appeared with Olsen & Johnson Show, 1941-49; pres. Stephen Slesinger, Inc., N.Y.C., Tampa, Fla., 1953—; pres. Red Ryder Enterprises, Inc., Hawley Publs., Inc., Tele-Comics, Inc.; owner U.S. and Canadian rights Winnie-the-Pooh Mdse., 1929—; owner comic strips Red Ryder, Little Beaver, King of the Royal Mounted, Ozark Ike; asso. Zane Grey, Inc. in motion picture field, promotion sales comic books based on famous Western stories. Mem. Tampa Aux. Power Squadron, Krewe of Venus. Home: 5108 Longfellow Av Tampa FL 33609 Office: 1111 N Westshore Blvd Tampa FL 33607

LASTRA, FRANK TRIBIN, cons. indsl. engr.; b. Tampa, Fla., Sept. 11, 1922; s. Everisto Tribin and Anna Cacciatore (Leto) L.; B.Indsl. Engring., Ga. Sch. Tech., 1948; postgrad. Mass. Inst. Tech., 1941-42; m. Gloria Martin Diaz, Apr. 2, 1950; children—Frank Marcel, Alice Ann. Jr. indsl. engr. Sylvania Elec. Products, Inc., Huntington, W.Va., 1948; mgr. family bus., Tampa, 1948-50; plant estimator Continental Can Co., Tampa, 1950-51, lead indsl. engr., Balt., 1957-58, div. staff indsl. engr., Chgo., 1958-60, Wheeling, W.Va., 1960-61; indsl. engr. ordnance dept. Dept. Army, Conley, Ga., 1951-53, indsl. engring. coordinator, 1953; asst. to pres. Art Furniture Mfg. Co., Macon, Ga., 1953-54; indsl. engr. Kaiser Aluminum Corp., Baton Rouge, 1954-55, supr. procedures and systems, 1955; plant indsl. engr. Crown Cork and Seal Co., Orlando, Fla., 1955-57; indsl. engr. Honeywell Inc., St. Petersburg, Fla., 1961-62, supr. indsl. engring., 1962-67; cons. indsl. engr., Lutz, Fla., 1967—; pres. Apex Bldg. Supplies Co., Inc., Lutz, 1967—. Served with AUS, 1943-46. Registered profl. engr., Fla. Mem. Am. Inst. Indsl. Engrs. (sr., dir. external affairs 1965-66), Nat. Soc. Profl. Engrs., Fla. Engring. Soc. Contbr. articles to profl. jours. Address: 101 Whitaker Rd Lutz FL 33549

LASTRA, JESUS L., dentist; b. La Salud, Havana, Cuba, Jan. 5, 1928 (came to U.S., 1961, naturalized, 1968); s. Patricio and Antonia (Martinez) L.; B.S., Inst. of Havana, 1947; D.D.S., Havana U., 1952; D.M.D., U. Ala., 1966; m. Silvia M. Lopez, Aug. 6, 1950; children—Idalia, Teresa. Practice dentistry, Havana, 1952-61; instr. crown and bridge U. Havana, 1952-59, prof., 1959-61, prof. Summer Sch., 1956; instr., research asso. U. Ala., 1966-68; practice dentistry, Miami, Fla., 1968—. Mem. Am., Mexican, Cuban (past v.p., sec. sci. com.), Havana dental assns., Internat. Assn. for Dental Research, Am. Prosthodontic Soc., Acad. Gen. Dentistry, Latin Am. Dental Study Club (pres. 1973-74), Delta Sigma Delta. Lion (pres. 1972-73). Club: Cuban Sertoma. Contbr. articles to profl. jours. Home: 2100 SW 21st Terrace Miami FL 33145 Office: 2150 SW 21st Av Miami FL 33145

LASWELL, THOMAS CARROLL, JR., realtor; b. Owensboro, Ky., Sept. 27, 1920; s. Thomas Carroll and Lottie (Omer) L.; A.B., Centre Coll. Ky., 1943; m. Martha Hardin Bosley, Sept. 20, 1943; children—Martha Carroll, Janet Bosley. Realtor, real estate appraiser J.R. Laswell & Sons, Owensboro, 1946—, Laswell Ins. Agcy., Owensboro, 1948—; chmn. bd. Citizens Security Life Ins. Co. Instr. real estate courses Brecia Coll., 1969—. Mayor protem, Owensboro, 1954-57. Bd. dirs. Ky. Soc. Crippled Children, Jr. Achievement, Owensboro. Served to lt. (j.g.) USNR, 1943-45; ETO, PTO. Named Realtor of Year Owensboro Bd. Realtors, 1966. Mem. Am. Right of Way Assn., Ky. Assn. Realtors (dir. 1968, pres. 1971), Ky. Assn. Farm Mgrs. and Rural Appraisers, Ownesboro-Daviess County C. of C. (v.p. 1966), Centre Coll. Alumni Assn. (nat. pres. 1969-70). Mem. Christian Ch. (chmn. congregation 1960-61). Rotarian (gov. dist. 371, 1959-60). Clubs: Owensboro (Ky.) Country; Campbell, Investigators. Home: 2110 S Cedar St Owensboro KY 42301 Office: 2309 Frederica St Owensboro KY 42301

LASZLO, JOHN, physician; b. Cologne, Germany, May 28, 1931; s. Daniel and Edith (Vincze) L.; A.B., Columbia, 1951; M.D., Harvard, 1955; m. Nancy Warner, Mar. 19, 1962; children—Rebecca, Jennifer, Daniel Walter. Came to U.S., 1937, naturalized, 1944. Intern, U. Chgo. Med. Center, 1956; sr. asst. surgeon Nat. Cancer Inst., 1957-58; asso. prof. medicine Duke Med. Center, 1960-71, prof., 1971—; chief med. service Durham VA Hosp., 1968-73. Chmn. exptl. therapeutics sect. NIH, 1972-74. Mem. A.C.P., Am. Soc. Hematology, Am. Assn. Cancer Research. Home: Box 266 Route 1 Durham NC 27705 Office: Duke Med Center Durham NC 27710

LATCHAM, FREDERICK CHARLES, JR., publisher; b. Denver, Aug. 17, 1917; s. Frederick Charles and Louise (Newman) L.; B.A., U. Colo., 1942; m. Joyce Elaine Atkins, Oct. 3, 1953; children—Frederick Charles III, George Geoffery. Line forman Colo. Builders Supply Co., Denver, 1942-43; survey party chief Ford, Bacon & Davis, 1947-49; project engr. Brown & Roote, Miss., Ala., Ga. 1949-53; mng. editor Beeville Pub. Co., Inc. (Tex.), 1953-58, pub., 1958—. Bee County drive chmn. United Fund; mem. United Community Services, Corpus Christi, 1971; pres. Bee County Devel. Corp., 1974. Pres. bd. trustees Bee County Coll., 1965-72. Served with AUS, 1943-47. Mem. South Tex. (pres. 1966-67), Tex. (dir. 1965-69) press assns., South Tex. (dir. 1967—), Beeville and Bee County (pres. 1966) chambers commerce, Navy League (Beeville council pres. 1960-61, 71-72), Chi Psi. Methodist. Rotarian (pres. 1959-60). Home: 210 E Hutchinson St Beeville TX 78102 Office: 206 W Corpus Christi St Beeville TX 78102

LATHAM, ALICE FRANCES PATTERSON (MRS. WILLIAM JOSEPH LATHAM), pub. health nurse; b. Macon, Ga., Dec. 18, 1916; d. Frank Waters and Ruby (Dews) Patterson; R.N., Charity Hosp. Sch. Nursing, New Orleans, 1937; student George Peabody Coll. Tchrs., 1938-39; B.S. in Pub. Health Nursing, U. N.C., 1954; M.P.H., Johns Hopkins U., 1966; m. William Joseph Latham, July 21, 1940; children—Jo Alice (Mrs. Samuel Earl Wood), Marynette (Mrs. Myles Shannon Webb), Lauruby Cathleen. Staff pub. health nurse assigned spl. venereal disease study USPHS, Darien Ga., 1939-40; county pub. health nurse Bacon County, Alma, 1940-41; USPHS spl. venereal disease project, Glynn County, Brunswick, 1943-47; county pub. health nurse Glyn County, 1949-51, Ware County, Waycross, 1951-52; pub. health nurse supr. Wayne-Long-Brantley-Liberty Counties, Jesup, 1954-56; dir. pub. health nursing Wayne-Long-Appling Bacon-Pierce Counties, Jesup 1956—, now dist. nursing dir. S.E. health dist., exec. Wayne County and Ware County Home Health Agys. Bd. dirs. Wayne County Mental Health Assn., 1959, 60, 61, Wayne County Tb Assn., 1958-62; a non-alcoholic organizer Jesup group Alcoholics Anonymous, 1962-63; adv. council Ware Meml. Hosp, Sch. Practical Nursing, Waycross, Ga., 1958. Recipient recognition Gen. Service Bd., Alcoholics Anonymous, Inc. Fellow Am. Pub. Health Assn.; mem. Am., 8th Dist. (pres. 1954-58, dir. 1960-62, 1st v.p. 1962), Ga. (exec. bd. 1954-58) nurses assns., Ga. Pub. Health Assn. (chmn. nursing sect. 1956-57). Contbr. to state nursing manuals. Home: 115 Harper St Jesup GA 31545 Office: Southeast Health District Office 1101 Church St Waycross GA 31501

LATHAM, HERALD ROWE, pub. relations co. exec.; b. Durham, N.C., Dec. 13, 1924; s. Romulus Everett and Lucille (Hocutt) L.; student N.C. State Coll., 1945-46, U. N.C., 1946-47, Coll. of William and Mary, 1948-49; m. Emileigh Maxwell, May 26, 1951; children—Lynn and Diann (twins), Herald Jeffrey. Reporter, Norfolk (Va.) Ledger-Dispatch, 1948-51; reporter Charlotte (N.C.) Observer, 1951-52; reporter Norfolk Virginian-Pilot, 1952-54; pub. relations editor Va. State Ports Authority, 1954-55; city editor Kinston (N.C.) Daily Free Press, 1955-60; mng. editor Florence (S.C.) Morning News, 1960-61; copy desk chief Atlanta Jour., 1961-64; asst. mng. editor Indsl. Devel. Mag., Atlanta, 1964-65; pub. relations dir., editor Cin. Mag., Greater Cin. C. of C., 1965-69; pub. relations, v.p., gen. mgr. Harshe-Rotman & Druck, Inc., Memphis office, 1969—; free-lance writer. Sec. Cin. Pub. Observance Assn., 1966-69. Served with USNR, 1942-45; PTO. Mem. Cin. Advertisers Club (v.p., dir.), Memphis Advertisers Club, Pub. Relations Soc. Am. (pres. 1974). Kiwanian. Editor: Memphis Mag., 1970. Home: 5801 Vassar Dr Memphis TN 38138 Office: 100 N Main Bldg Memphis TN 38103

LATHAM, JAMES ARTHUR, oil and coal co. exec.; b. El Dorado, Ark., Feb. 24, 1926; s. Austin Dewitt and Emily (Ross) L.; B.S., U.S. Naval Acad., 1951; B.S., U. Okla., 1955, M.S., 1956; m. Marian Malone, Oct. 25, 1958; children—Laura, Anna, Madeline, James Arthur. Sr. reservoir engr. Ark. Fuel Oil Corp., Shreveport, La., 1956-60; self-employed as petroleum cons., Shreveport, 1960-62; pres., chmn. Latham Oil Co., Inc., 1962-68; pres., dir. Transcontinental Oil Corp., Shreveport, 1968—; chmn., pres. Diamond Coal Co., Inc., Shreveport, 1971—; dir. Tampa Properties, Inc., Pyramid Properties, Inc. Served to lt. USAAF, 1944-45, USAF, 1951-54. Mem. Am. Assn. Petroleum Geologists, Am. Inst. Mining, Metall. and Petroleum Engrs., Am. Petroleum Inst., Am. Mgmt. Assn., U.S., Shreveport chambers commerce, Shreveport Petroleum Club. Methodist (adminstrv. bd. 1966-68, 73—). Clubs: Shreveport, Country, Pierremont Oaks Tennis (Shreveport); Raffles (N.Y.C.). Home: 6936 Gilbert Dr Shreveport LA 71106 Office: 416 Travis St Shreveport LA 71101

LATHAM, JAMES IVAN, elec. engr.; b. Latham, Mo., Dec. 1, 1937; s. James Alexander and Montrie (Elliot) L.; B.S. in Elec. Engring., U. Mo. at Rolla, 1959, M.S. in Physics, 1964, Ph.D. (AEC fellow), 1967; m. Ruby Jane Kusgen, Sept. 1, 1957; children—Paul, Angela, Katrina. Mem. staff Tex. Instruments Co., Dallas, 1967—, now engaged in research and devel. gallium arsenide microwave diodes. Chmn. bd. dirs. Richardson (Tex.) Pub. Library. Curators scholar, 1955-56. Mem. I.E.E.E., Pershing Rifles, Sigma Xi, Tau Beta Pi, Eta Kappa Nu, Blue Key. Mem. Christian Ch. (chmn. elders 1971). Home: 117 N Lois Lane Richardson TX 75080 Office: MS 134 PO Box 6015 Dallas TX 75222

LATHAM, JAMES PARKER, educator; b. Collingdale, Pa., June 2, 1918; s. William Harry and Martha (Curry) L.; B.S., U. Pa., 1949, M.S., 1950; M.A. in Econs., 1951, Ph.D., 1959; m. Eloise McDaniel, Mar. 7, 1945. Lectr. geography and industry Wharton Sch., U. Pa., 1951-59; asst. prof. geography Bowling Green (O.) State U., 1959-61, asso. prof., 1961-64; prof., chmn. dept. geography Fla. Atlantic U., Boca Raton, 1964-70, prof., dir. Remote Sensing Lab., 1970—; prin. investigator Office Naval Research project, 1965—, U.S. Geol. Survey project, 1967—. Mem. com. remote sensing NRC, 1973—. Mem. Bowling Green City Planning Commn., 1963-64, Beach Park Devel. Com., Boca Raton, 1967. Served with USAAF, 1942-46; maj. AUS, Res. Mem. Assn. Am. Geographers, Fla. Soc. Geographers (pres. 1966-67), Am. Geog. Soc., I.E.E.E., Am. Soc. Photogrammetry (pres. Fla. region 1969-70, nat. dir., mem. exec. com. 1971-74), Phi Kappa Phi. Methodist. Kiwanian. Contbr. articles to profl. jours. Home: 830 NE 69th St Boca Raton FL 33432

LATHAM, WILLIAM IGNATIOUS, newspaper editor; b. Washington, May 27, 1911; s. Ola Vincent and Mary Anne (McNamara) L.; B.A. in Journalism, U. S.C., 1932; m. Martha Jane Stark, Apr. 5, 1935; children—Mary Anna (Mrs. Stanley Love), Patricia (Mrs. James Caffey), Nancy Roberts, Peggy Lynn, William Ignatious. Reporter, El Paso (Tex.) and Douglas (Ariz.) newspapers, 1935-41; with El Paso Times, 1941—, city editor, 1942-46, mng. editor, 1946-70, editor, 1970—. Active El Paso Rescue Mission, Family Service El Paso, El Paso Boys Club, S.W. Carnival Assn. Served with AUS, 1942-45. Decorated Bronze Star. Mem. Tex. A.P. Mng. Editors Assn. (past pres.), Am. Soc. Newspaper Editors, Sigma Delta Chi (pres. Rio Bajo chpt.). Baptist. Lion. Club: Press (El Paso). Home: 417 Cincinnati St El Paso TX 79902 Office: 401 Mills St El Paso TX 79999

LATHROP, GEORGE TERRELL, urban planner, educator; b. Asheville, N.C., Aug. 17, 1935; s. Albert Henry and Virginia (Terrell) L.; B.S., N.C. State U., 1957; M. in City Planning, Yale, 1962, certificate Bur. Hwy. Traffic, 1962; postgrad. U. N.C., 1966-69; m. Ann Anthony, Aug. 24, 1957; children—Anthony Terrell, William Park. Urban planner, dir. research Upstate N.Y. Transp. Studies, Albany, 1962-66; lectr. dept. city and regional planning U. N.C., Chapel Hill, 1966-73, dir. met. simulation lab., 1968-73; asso. Kimley-Horn & Assos., Raleigh, N.C., 1973—. Cons. urban and transp. planning agys., 1963—. Served to 1st lt. USAF, 1958-60. Mem. Am. Soc. C.E., Inst. Traffic Engrs., Am. Inst. Planners, Regional Sci. Assn., Tau Beta Pi, Chi Epsilon, Phi Kappa Phi, Sigma Chi. Home: 606 Greenwood Rd Chapel Hill NC 27514

LATHROP, JAY WALLACE, educator; b. Bangor, Me., Sept. 6, 1927; s. Frank H. and Beatrice (Freer) L.; B.S., Mass. Inst. Tech., 1948, M.S., 1949, Ph.D., 1952; m. Marjorie W. Cramton, Sept. 6, 1948; children—Peggy, Vicky, Frank, David. Elec. engr. Nat. Bur. Standards/Harry Diamond Fuze Labs., Washington, 1952-58; mgr. advanced component tech. Tex. Instruments Co., Dallas, 1958-68; prof. elec. engring. Clemson (S.C.) U., 1968—. Cons. Jack Kilby Co., Dallas, 1968-72, Tex. Instruments Co., 1973—. Recipient Meritorious Civilian Service award Dept. Army, 1959. Mem. I.E.E.E. (chmn. acad. affairs parts, hybrid, packaging group), Sigma Xi, Tau Beta Pi, Eta Kappa Nu. Home: 211 Lark Circle Clemson SC 29631

LATIMER, CARLOS GUILLERMO, lawyer; b. Ponce, P.R., Feb. 25, 1926; s. Guillermo A. and Josefina (Lopez de Tord) L.; student U. Va., 1945-47; J.D., U. Miami, 1954; m. Edwina Arsuaga, Nov. 27, 1950; children—Carlos, Karen, Roberto, Ricardo. Admitted to P.R. bar, 1955; law clk. Supreme Ct. P.R., 1955-56; asst. dist. atty. Dept. Justice, San Juan, P.R., 1956-58, asst. solicitor gen., 1959-61; asso., Gutierrez & Ramirez, 1962-63; partner Ramirez, Segal & Latimer, Santurce, P.R., 1963—; asst. sec. U.S.I. P.R., Inc., subsidiary U.S. Industries, 1970—. Mem. adv. com. Gov. P.R. for Judicial Appointments, 1973; mem. adv. com. Gov. P.R. in connection with Natural Resources Commonwealth, 1973. Mem. Am., P.R. bar assns., Phi Alpha Delta. Club: Caparra Country (Guaynabo, P.R.). Home: IA-11 Miramontes Garden Hills Guaynabo PR Office: 208 First Fed Bldg Santurce PR 00909

LATIMER, EDWIN PHINNEY, credit co. exec.; b. Honea Path, S.C., Aug. 20, 1909; s. James Clayton and Corrie V. (Phinney) L.; A.B., The Citadel, 1931; m. Katharine Wharton, Sept. 28, 1934; 1 dau., Kay. Instr., Bailey Mil. Acad., 1931-34; with Comml. Credit Co., Columbia, S.C., 1934-37; with Am. Credit Corp. and predecessor cos., Charlotte, N.C., 1937—, pres., 1947-65, chmn. bd., chief exec. officer, 1965—, dir., 1945—, mem. exec. com., 1965—; dir., mem. exec. com. Wachovia Corp., Winston-Salem, N.C. Mem. adv. bd. Salvation Army, Charlotte; bd. dirs. Mint Mus. Art, N.C. Citizens Assn., Family and Children's Service, Citadel Devel. Found.; vice chmn. Met. Financial Planning Council, Charlotte. Served to maj. AUS, 1941-46. Mem. Charlotte C. of C. (pres. 1969). Methodist. Clubs: Charlotte Country, Charlotte City, Quail Hollow Country (Charlotte). Home: 1927 Cassamia Pl Charlotte NC 28211 Office: PO Box 2665 Charlotte NC 28201

LATIMER, PAUL HENRY, biophysicist; b. New Orleans, Nov. 25, 1925; s. Claiborne Green and Frieda (Hildebrandt) L.; student U. Ky., 1943-44, 46-47; B.S., Northwestern U., 1949; M.S., U. Ill., 1950, Ph.D., 1956; m. Margaret Kinard, Aug. 16, 1952; children—Margaret Gwyn, Marianne Mason, Susan Pauline. Postdoctoral fellow Carnegie Instn., Stanford, Cal., 1956-57; asst. prof. dept. physics, investigator Howard Hughes Med. Inst., Vanderbilt U., Nashville, 1957-62; asso. prof. dept. physics Auburn (Ala.) U., 1962-71, prof., 1971—. Cons. Dept. Justice, 1959; ASEE-NASA fellow Marshall Space Flight Center, Ala., summer 1971. Served with AUS, 1944-46; ETO. Decorated Bronze Star. Mem. Optical Soc. Am., Biophys. Soc., Am. Phys. Soc., Sigma Xi, Kappa Alpha. Presbyn. Kiwanian. Contbr. profl. jours. Home: 530 Forestdale Dr Auburn AL 36830

LATIMER, ROY TRUETT, govt. ofcl.; b. Albany, Tex., Aug. 23, 1928; s. Charles Lee and Zora Neil (Brock) L.; B.A., Hardin-Simmons U., 1951; m. Judith Gail Johnson, Nov. 26, 1955; children—Jeffrey Alan, Laura Gail, Tiffany Claire. Owner, Latimer Ins. Agy., Abilene, Tex., 1952-55; alumni dir. Hardin-Simmons U., Abilene, 1955-62; pub. relations dir. Tex. Real Estate Assn., Austin, 1962-65; exec. dir. Tex. Hist. Commn., Austin, 1965—. Exec. sec. Tex. Antiquities Com., Austin, 1969—; state historic preservation officer for Tex., 1967—. Mem. Ho. of Reps., 1952-62. Mem. bd. devel. Hardin-Simmons U., 1968—. Mem. Hardin-Simmons U. Alumni Assn. (pres. 1967-68). Baptist. Rotarian. Home: 7631 Rockpoint Dr Austin TX 78731 Office: PO Box 12276 Capitol Sta Austin TX 78711

LATIMER, STEVE BENTON, educator; b. Oklahoma City, Nov. 4, 1927; s. Frank Amos and Charlene E. (Smith) L.; B.S., Tuskegee Inst., 1953, M.S., 1955; Ph.D., N.C. State U., 1967; m. Louise Cunningham, May 21, 1952; children—Steve, Ronald Gail. Chmn. dept. chemistry Shaw U., Raleigh, N.C., 1955-62; research asst. N.C. State U., 1962-66; research coordinator, prof. chemistry, dir. arts and scis. Langston (Okla.) U., 1966—. Cons., NIH. Bd. dirs. Langston Devel. Found. Carver Found. fellow, 1953; NSF fellow, 1960-62. Fellow Am. Inst. Chemists, A.A.A.S., Nat. Inst. Sci., Am. Chem. Soc., Okla. Inst. Chemists (sec. 1972), Alpha Phi Alpha, Alpha Phi Omega, Beta Kappa Chi. Mason (Shriner). Contbr. to profl. publs. in field. Home: Box 780 Langston OK 73050

LATTA, HUGH LUSK, designer; b. Corinth, Miss., May 5, 1938; s. Hugh Basil and Ruth (Lusk) L.; B.Design, U. Fla., 1961; M.F.A., Cranbrook Acad. Art, 1963. Instr., Young Peoples Art Center, Cranbrook, Bloomfield Hills, Mich., 1961-62; pres. Design Continuum Inc., Atlanta, 1971—. Asso. prof. Auburn U. Coll. Architecture, 1967—. Mem. Young Men's Round Table, High Mus. Art, Atlanta, 1972—. Named Outstanding Young Man of Atlanta, 1970. Mem. Am. Inst. Designers (nat. gov., chmn. bd. Ga. chpt.), Am. Inst. Interior Designers (nat. edn. chmn. 1971—), Illuminating Engrs. Soc., U. Fla. Alumni Assn., Sigma Chi. Republican. Episcopalian. Contbr. articles to profl. jours. Home: 1857 Walthall Dr NW Atlanta GA 30318 Office: Suite 706 2751 Buford Hwy NE Atlanta GA 30324

LATTA, SARAH FRANCES WHITE (MRS THOMAS H. LATTA), writer; b. Brownwood, Tex., Nov. 8, 1930; d. Todd Rector and Edith (Lloyd) White; B.J., U. Mo., 1951; tchrs. certificate Tex. Woman's U., 1956; librarians certificate Sam Houston State Tchrs. Coll., 1962; M.Ed., Lamar U., 1973; m. Thomas H. Latta, Oct. 2, 1973. Soc. editor Gainesville (Tex.) Daily Register, 1951; tchr. journalism Winters (Tex.) High Sch., 1952, Iraan (Tex.) High Sch., 1953-54, Port Neches (Tex.)-Groves High Sch., 1955-60; librarian Groves (Tex.) Jr. High Sch., 1961-72; free-lance writer 1972—. Mem. Tex. Library Assn., Classroom Tchrs. Assn., Tex. Tchrs. Assn., Alpha Delta Pi, Theta Sigma Phi, Beta Sigma Phi. Democrat. Methodist. Address: Box 146 St Mark's Methodist Ch Parsonage Center TX 75935

LATTIER, JOSEPH MALCOLM, JR., dentist; b. Shreveport, La., Sept. 15, 1938; s. Joseph Malcolm and Ozelle (Hadwin) L.; B.A., La. State U., 1961; D.D.S., Loyola U., New Orleans, 1965; m. Mary Martha Martin, Aug. 15, 1964; 1 son, Joseph Martin. Pvt. practice gen. dentistry, Shreveport, 1967—; vis. staff Confederate Meml. Hosp., Willis-Knighton Hosp. Mem. vis. staff Young Men for Good Govt., 1970. Served to capt. USAF, 1965-67. Mem. Am., La. dental assns., La. 4th Dist. Dental Soc. (sci. program chmn., treas. 1972) Acad. Gen. Dentistry, Am. Soc. Dentistry for Children, Shreveport C. of C., Am. Legion, Blue Key, Delta Sigma Delta, Kappa Sigma. Club: Mid-City Optimist (v.p. 1969). Home: 310 Americana St Shreveport LA 71105 Office: 5803 Youree Dr Shreveport LA 71105

LATTIMER, KENNETH CURTIS, A.R.C. exec.; b. La Porte, Ind., June 6, 1914; s. Chancie Owen and Myrta (Curtis) L.; A.B. maxima cum laude, U. Notre Dame, 1937; student A.R.C. Mgmt. Devel. Sch., Charlottesville, Va., 1956; m. Besse Tyree, Mar. 17, 1945; children—Tyree C., Kenneth D. With Nat. Youth Adminstrn., 1937-41, dir. St. Joseph County, South Bend, Ind., 1937-38, finance supr., Ind., 1941; with Office Emergency Mgmt., 1941-43, asst. regional finance officer, Chgo., 1942-43; with A.R.C., 1943—, dep. dir.

fund raising Southeastern area, 1959-64, fund cons. Southeastern area, 1965-69, dir. office mems. and funds Southeastern area, Atlanta, 1970—. Vice pres. program Blue Ridge Inst. So. Community Service Execs., 1962-62, pres., 1968-69. Recipient Service medal Philippine Nat. Red Cross, 1959. Mem. Nat. Soc. Fund Raisers. Episcopalian. Club: Lake Lanier Sailing (sec. 1969-71, commodore 1972) (Flowery Branch, Ga.). Home: 2114 Fairway Circle NE Atlanta GA 30319 Office: Am Red Cross 1955 Monroe Dr NE Atlanta GA 30324

LAU, LEUNG WANG, nuclear engr.; b. Shekki, Kwongtung, China, Nov. 1, 1936; s. Hin Kwok and Seen Wah (Leung) L.; came U.S., 1957, naturalized, 1971; B.S. in Physics, U. Okla., 1960; M.S. in Physics, U. N.C., 1961; Ph.D., N.C. State U., 1967; m. Florence Fung, Apr. 12, 1963; children—Rita, Serena. Asso. prof. physics U. N.C., Wilmington, 1967-70; nuclear engr. TVA, Knoxville, 1970—. Mem. Am. Nuclear Soc. Author: Elements of Nuclear Reactor Engring. Home: 321 Russfield Dr Concord TN 37720 Office: 303 A-UB Tennessee Valley Authority Knoxville TN 37907

LAU, NORMAN EUGENE, ednl. adminstr.; b. Harvey, Ill., July 8, 1930; s. Lawrence J. and Mary Louise (Parent) L.; B.S., Colo. State U., 1953, M.S., 1955; Ph.D., Rutgers U., 1958; m. Eleanor C. Tardy, June 6, 1970; 1 son, Scott Norman. Entomologist, N.J. Dept. Agr., Trenton, 1958-61; tech. cons. Ratner Pest Control, Atlantic City, 1961-63; product devel. rep. Hooker Chem. Corp., Niagara Falls, N.Y., 1963-65; extension coordinator chems., drugs and pesticides Va. Poly. Inst. and State U., Blacksburg, Va., 1965—. Vice-pres. Niagara County (N.Y.) Mental Health Assn., 1964. Mem. Entomol. Soc. Am., Nat., Va. adult edn. assns., Sigma Xi, Epsilon Sigma Xi. Club: Torch (1st v.p.) (Blacksburg). Home: 17 Laurel Dr Blacksburg VA 24060 Office: Va Poly Inst and State U Blacksburg VA 24061

LAUBSCHER, JAMES ALBERT, chem. co. exec.; b. St. Paul, Nov. 28, 1938; s. Albert Rudolph and Bernice Doris (Schacht) L.; B.S., U. Ariz., 1961, M.S., 1968; m. Geraldine Lee Bird, June 1, 1958; children—Laura Sue, Robert James, Daniel Timothy, Elizabeth Ann. Pilot mill chemist Banner Mining Co., Tucson, Ariz., 1961-64; asst. research engr. Anaconda Co., Tucson, 1964-65; research asso. U. Ariz., Tucson, 1965-69; sr. chemist Carnation Co., Van Nuys, Cal., 1969-71; pres. Woodson-Tenent Labs., Memphis, 1971—. Cons. chemist. Mem. Am. Chem. Soc., Inst. Food Technologists, Assn. Analytical Chemists, Tri-State Oil Mill Supts. Assn., Tenn. Feed Mfrs. Assn., Southeastern Poultry and Egg Assn., Memphis C. of C. Baptist. Republican. Home: 2555 Glenlivet Dr Memphis TN 38138 Office: 345 Adams St Memphis TN 38101

LAUGHEAD, GEORGE JOSEPH, retail trade co. exec.; b. Havertown, Pa., July 8, 1918; s. Horace Goodley and Bella (Young) L.; grad. Taylor Bus. Coll., 1940; m. Margaret Evelyn Ramsdell, July 8, 1942; children—George Ross, James Marshall. Grocery buyer Handy Andy Supermarkets, Inc., San Antonio, 1946-60, asst. to v.p. purchasing, 1960-64, v.p., dir., 1964—; dir. Pan Am. Nat. Bank, 1962—, chmn., 1969—; partner Community Realty Co., 1961—. Alderman, City of Alamo Heights, Tex., 1964—; mayor pro tem City of Alamo Heights, 1965—; Egg Marketing Adv. Bd. of Tex., 1969. Trustee Tex. Presbyn. Found.; bd. dirs. Morningside Manor Nursing Home, vice chmn., 1971—; bd. dirs., vice chmn. Presbyn. Mo-Ranch Assembly, 1969—; mem. exec. bd. Alamo council Boy Scouts Am.; chmn. adv. bd. Salvation Army, 1961—; bd. dirs. Bexar County unit Am. Cancer Soc., 1967—. Served to capt. AUS, 1941-46. Recipient Silver Beaver award Boy Scouts Am., 1971. Mem. Tex. Mchts. Assn. (pres. 1971), S.W. Tex. Frozen Food Assn. (pres. 1960), Tex. Wholesale Grocers Assn. (dir. 1971-72), Navy League U.S. Presbyn. (moderator presbytery 1971, elder 1963—, pres. 1963—, chmn. gen. council 1970-73). Mason, Kiwanian (pres. 1951). Clubs: San Antonio Country, Knife and Fork (dir. 1971—). Home: 336 Tuxedo Av San Antonio TX 78209 Office: PO Box 1161 San Antonio TX 78294

LAUGHLIN, DILLARD CHAPPELL, lawyer; b. N.Y.C., July 6, 1927; s. Samuel Dillard and Sally Julia (Chappell) L.; B.S., U. Va., 1950, LL.B., 1952; m. Jane May Thompson, May 21, 1955; children—Elizabeth Derrick, Dillard Chappell, David Macllwaine, Andrew St. John. Admitted to Va. bar, 1952; practiced in mem. firm Phillips, Kendrick, Gearheart & Aylor, Arlington, Va., 1954—. Served with USCGR, 1945-46, AUS, 1952-54. Decorated Bronze Star medal. Mem. Am., Va. (mem. council 1971—), Arlington County (pres. 1967-68) bar assns. Club: Washington Golf and Country (Arlington). Home: 3715 N Woodrow St Arlington VA 22207 Office: 2009 N 14th St Arlington VA 22201

LAUGHLIN, HAROLD EMERSON, mus. dir.; b. Tulsa, Feb. 11, 1932; s. Walter Emerson and Katherine Barbara (Frnke) L.; B.S., U. Tulsa, 1955; M.A., U. Tex., 1958, Ph.D., 1965; m. Mary Jo Hyatt, Apr. 12, 1952; children—Katherine Jo, Margaret Ellen, Theodore Howard. Asst. prof. biology Southeastern State Coll., Durant, Okla., 1960-65; adminstrv. dir. Heard Natural Sci. Mus. and Wildlife Sanctuary, McKinney, Tex., 1965—. Recipient Elsie M.B. Naumberg award Natural Sci. for Youth Found., 1973. Fellow Tex. Acad. Sci.; mem. Southwestern Assn. Naturalists, Am. Soc. Ichthyologists and Herpetologists. Presbyn. (elder). Home: Route 7 Box 171 McKinney TX 75069 Office: Heard Museum Route 7 Box 171 McKinney TX 75069

LAUGHRIDGE, RICHARD THOMAS, broadcasting exec.; b. Clover, S.C., Oct. 29, 1934; s. Clyde Thomas and Addie Williams (Pursley) L.; B.S., U. S.C., 1957; m. Phyllis Jean Fowke, Jan. 26, 1958; children—Laurie, Richard Thomas, Philip, Stephen. Announcer, WTYC, Rock Hill, S.C., 1952, boom boy, 1953; cameraman WNOK-TV, Columbia, summer, 1954; announcer WKMT, Kingsmountain, N.C., 1954; dir. WNOK-TV, Columbia, 1955-58, prodn. mgr., 1958-59, salesman 1958-59, sales mgr., 1960-69, v.p. sales, 1969—; pres. Swamp Fox Broadcasting Corp., 1967, Seacoast Broadcasting Corp., 1971—. Recipient Printer's Ink Silver Medal award Columbia Advt. Club, 1969. Mem. S.C. Broadcasters Assn. (pres. 1971), Columbia Advt. Club (pres. 1966), Columbia Sales and Marketing Execs. Club, Exec. Assn. Greater Columbia. Rotarian (dir. 1970). Presbyn. (elder 1972). Club: Rockbridge Country. Home: 1482 Florawood Dr Columbia SC 29204 Office: PO Drawer M Columbia SC 29250

LAUNIUS, MELVIN RAY, mfg. co. exec.; b. McLeansboro, Ill., Mar. 4, 1935; s. Jeff H. and Delcie J. (Jenkins) L.; B.A., So. Ill. U., 1956; m. Ardeth Jean Meyer, Mar. 8, 1958; children—Laurie Kay, Melvin Ray, Jeff L., John. Agy. builder All Am. Life and Casualty Co., Greenville, S.C., 1956—; pres. Launius Enterprises Inc.; owner Holiday Apts., Morristown, Tenn., also dental lab., farms in S.C. and Mo. Sec., Ill. Young Democrats, 1954-55. Served to capt. USAF, 1957-67. Named jr. agy. builder of the year All Am. Life & Casualty Co., 1964. Mem. Ch. Jesus Christ of Latter-day Saints (elder 1969—). Mason, Eagle. Home: Route 3 Stevenson Rd Taylors SC 29687 Office: 134 Donaldson Rd Greenville SC 29606

LAURIA, PHILIP CHARLES, city ofcl.; b. Rochester, N.Y., Mar. 6, 1916; s. Stephen and Josephine (Orefice) L.; student U. Md. in Germany, 1958-59, Austin Peay State Coll., 1962-63; m. Mary G. Jackson, June 8, 1943; children—Patricia Ann (Mrs. Martin Eatman), Marilyn J. With U.S. Army, various locations, 1941-64; East Point, Ga., 1967-69; exec. dir. The South Fulton C. of C., East Point, 1969-70; city mgr., City of Riverdale, Ga., 1970—; sec., dir. Sports Mgmt. and Maintenance, Inc., 1973—. Mgmt. cons. assisting small cities. Decorated Commendation medal with 3 oak leaf clusters. Mem. Internat. City Mgmt. Assn., Am. Legion, V.F.W. Lion (pres. 1965-66, zone chmn. 1973-74), Mason (Shriner), Moose. Clubs: Lake Side Country (Atlanta); Fort McPherson Officers. Home: 2459 Ben Hill Rd East Point GA 30344 Office: City Hall Riverdale GA 30274

LAUTENSCHLAGER, EDWARD WALTER, coll. dean; b. Amsterdam, N.Y., Mar. 1, 1927; s. Edward A. and Carolyn (Haas) L.; B.S., Franklin and Marshall Coll., 1950; M.S., U. Va., 1956, Ph.D., 1963; m. Audrey Mae Warner, June 16, 1948; children—Edward Warner, Carolee Anne, Karen Sue, Garrett Brian, Laurence David. Instr. biology U. Va., 1959-63, asst. prof., 1963-65, registrar, 1959-65; dir. data processing U. Va., 1964-65; prof. biology, dean coll., Roanoke Coll., 1965—. Chmn. Salem Redevelopment and Housing Authority. Trustee Marion Coll., Va. Served with USNR, 1944-46, 51-53, comdr. Res. Mem. Va. Assn. Coll. Registrars and Admissions Officers (past pres.), So. Assn. Coll. Registrars and Admissions Officers (past pres.), Am. Soc. Parasitologists, Am. Soc. Tropical Medicine and Hygiene, Salem-Roanoke County C. of C. (past pres.), Sigma Xi, Omicron Delta Kappa, Phi Sigma Kappa. Research in animal parasitology. Home: 530 E Main St Salem VA 24153

LAUTZENHEISER, MARVIN WENDELL, computer systems analysis co. exec.; b. Maximo, O., Feb. 19, 1929; s. Milton Leander and Mary (Keim) L.; B.S. in Math. magna cum laude, Mt. Union Coll., Alliance, O., 1953; m. Jean Bethene Baker, Oct. 26, 1946; children—Constance (Mrs. Paul Dluehosh), Thomas Edward, Jan Stephen. Spl. agt. FBI, Washington and Charlotte, N.C., 1953-59; computer systems analyst Tech. Operations, Inc., Washington, 1959-64; pres., systems analyst Anagram Corp., Springfield, Va., 1964—. Mem. Assn. Computing Machinery, Am. Theatre Organ Soc. (vice chmn. 1970-71). Inventor, designer, builder computer (GENII) to play pipe organ from score, 1972. Home: 7216 Neuman St Springfield VA 22150 Office: 6560 Backlick Rd Springfield VA 22150

LAVENDER, DEWITT EARL, educator; b. nr. Athens, Ga., Nov. 9, 1938; s. DeWitt Edward and Emlyn Alice (Hale) L.; B.S., U. Ga., 1962, M.A., 1963, Ph.D., 1966; m. Karen Ann Wilson, June 15, 1958; children—David Robert, John Edward, Thomas Wilson. Asst. prof. math. Ga. So. Coll., Statesboro, 1966-67, asso. prof., head dept. math., 1967—. Served with AUS, 1956-58. Mem. Am. Math. Soc., Math. Assn. Am., Inst. Math. Statistics, Phi Beta Kappa, Phi Kappa Phi, Pi Mu Epsilon. Methodist (trustee 1972—). Club: Civitan (pres. 1969-70) (Statesboro, Ga.). Home: 310 Wendwood Dr Statesboro GA 30458

LAVENDER, HERBERT JACKSON, elec. engr.; b. Gordon, Ga., Mar. 14, 1916; s. Zollie Cleveland and Emmie Inez (Lyles) L.; B.E.E., Ga. Inst. Tech., 1950; m. Lizzie Lou Hartley, Aug. 2, 1942; 1 dau., Celeste Anne. Design engr. Welker & Assos., Marietta, Ga., 1949-62; facility engr. Lockheed-Ga. Corp., Marietta, 1962-70; jr. asso. Hensley-Schmidt, Inc., Atlanta, 1970—. Registered profl. engr., Ga., Ala. Mem. Ga. Soc. Profl. Engrs. (sec. N.W. Ga. chpt. 1956-58). Home: Route 1 Powder Springs GA 30073 Office: 290 N Interstate Pkwy Atlanta GA 30339

LAVENDER, ROBERT E., justice Okla. Supreme Ct.; b. Muskogee, Okla., July 19, 1926; s. Harold J. and Vergene (Martin) L.; student U. Tulsa, 1946-49, LL.B., 1953; m. Maxine Knight, Dec. 22, 1945; children—Linda, Robert K., Debra, William. Dept. clk. Ct. of Tulsa County, 1946-48, Ct. of Common Pleas, 1949-51; asst. bookkeeper Cain's Coffee Co., 1948-49; claim adjuster Mass. Bond & Ins. Co., Tulsa, 1951-53, U.S. Fidelity & Guarantee, 1953-54; admitted to Okla. bar, 1954; asso. with Joe Francis, Tulsa, 1955-58; practiced in Tulsa, 1958-61; partner firm Bassmann, Gordon, Mayberry & Lavender, Claremore, 1961-65; asst. atty. City of Tulsa, 1954-55; justice Okla. Supreme Ct., 1965—. Served with USNR, 1944-46; PTO. Mem. Am., Okla., Rogers County bar assns., Am. Judicature Soc., Phi Alpha Delta. Republican. Methodist (dir.). Mason, Lion. Home: 2910 Kerry Lane Oklahoma City OK 73120 Office: State Supreme Ct State Capitol Bldg Oklahoma City OK 73120

LAVEY, FREDERICK ADOLPH, lawyer, pub. co. exec.; b. Manchester, Conn., Sept. 15, 1916; s. Frederick Henry and Hilma (Anderson) L.; B.S., Harvard, 1938, postgrad. in bus. adminstrn., 1938-39; postgrad. U. Va. Law Sch. 1940-42, J.D., 1946; m. Evelyn Heatwole, Jan. 16, 1943; 1 son, Frederick Painter. Admitted to Conn. bar, 1946, D.C. bar, 1947; asso. firm Hewes & Awalt, Hartford, Conn., 1946-47, Awalt Clark & Sparks, Washington, 1947-51; with Pub. Utilities Reports, Inc., 1951—, exec. v.p., 1956-61, pres., 1961—, gen. mgr., 1959—, dir., 1968—; exec. sec. Utilities Publ. Com., 1961—; pres. 2d Class Mail Publs., Inc., 1966-70, also dir.; pub. mgmt. com. Am. Bus. Press, Inc., 1965-68, dir., 1968-70. Mem. Postmaster Gen.'s Tech. Adv. Com., 1965-68, 70—; chmn. local troop com. Boy Scouts Am.; pres., chmn. bd. dirs. Shenandoah Retreat Civic Assn., 1958-62, 69-70. Served to lt., USNR, 1942-46. Mem. Am. Bar Assn., Bar Assn. D.C., Raven Soc., Delta Theta Phi. Lutheran. Clubs: Harvard Business School, Harvard, University of Va., Internat., Retreat Golf and Country. Home: 4204 Thornapple St Chevy Chase MD 20015 Office: 1828 L St NW Washington DC 20036

LAVIN, JOHN THOMAS, food co. exec., entertainer; b. Gurdon, Ark., Apr. 5, 1916; s. John T. and Ruby Leah (Black) L.; Mus.B., Ouachita Bapt. U., 1937; Mus.M., So. Coll. Fine Arts, 1952; m. Dorothy M. Carroll, Apr. 28, 1968; 1 dau. by previous marriage, Carolyn (Mrs. Thomas J. Kirk). Instr. music in various pub. schs., colls., 1938-50; mfr.'s rep., entertainer, 1951-53; exec. sec. Natural Food Assos., Atlanta, Tex., 1954—; co-owner Creative Printers, Atlanta, Tex., 1973—. Active as an after dinner entertainer, 1948—. Pres., Tex. Forest Festival, Atlanta, 1969-72; chmn. Centennial Celebration, Atlanta, Tex., 1972. Mason (Shriner, 32 deg.), Lion (pres. 1949-50). Author: A Concept of Laughter, 1961; Laughing All the Way, 1964; Holiday for Fun, 1973. Home: 702 Florence Atlanta TX 75551 Office: Hwy 59 W Atlanta TX 75551

LAW, BRUCE, lawyer, mayor, judge; b. Memphis, Dec. 21, 1925; s. Stanley and Mary (Sheperd) L.; B.S., Memphis State U., 1950, LL.B., 1952; postgrad. U. Tenn., 1952; m. Rebekah Jane Bell, July 1, 1955; 1 dau., Lisa Jane. Admitted to Tenn. bar, 1952; practiced in Memphis, 1952—; city judge, mayor, Germantown, Tenn., 1958—. Instr. U. Memphis, 1961-62. City councilman, Germantown, 1958-60. Served with AUS, 1944-46. Decorated Bronze Star medal, Purple Heart. Mem. Tenn., Memphis, Shelby County bar assns., Delta Theta Phi, Lambda Chi Alpha. Democrat. Methodist. Home: 6922 Great Oakes Rd Germantown TN 38038 Office: Sterick Bldg Memphis TN 38103

LAW, JAMES PIERCE, JR., agrl. scientist; b. Atlanta, Tex., Aug. 4, 1916; s. James Pierce and Eula Elizabeth (Sharrer) L.; B.S., U. Tex., 1939; M.S., So. Methodist U., 1961; Ph.D., Tex. A. & M. U., 1965; m. Miriam Katherine Dacus, Jan. 8, 1941; 1 son, James Fred. Process control chemist Gen. Dynamics Corp., Fort Worth, 1956-61; research asst. and technician Tex. Agrl. Exptl. Sta., College Station, 1961-65; soil scientist Robert S. Kerr Water Research Center, Fed. Water Pollution Control Adminstrn., Ada, Okla., 1965-67, research soil scientist, 1967-72; chief, agrl. wastes sect. U.S. Environmental Protection Agy., Ada, 1973—. Bd. dirs. Ada Fed. Employees Credit Union, 1969—. Served with USAAF, 1944-45. Mem. Am. Soc. Agronomy, Am. Soc. Agrl. Engrs., Soil Sci. Soc. Am., Internat. Soc. Soil Sci., Sigma Xi, Phi Kappa Phi. Contbr. articles to profl. jours. Home: 531 Rebecca Lane Ada OK 74820 Office: Robert S. Kerr Environmental Research Lab PO Box 1198 Ada OK 74820

LAW, JOHN RANDOLPH, orthodontist; b. Morgantown, W.Va., Dec. 16, 1927; s. Harry Randolph and Gail (Davis) L.; A.B., W.Va. U., 1949, M.S. in Zoology, 1951; D.D.S., Georgetown U., 1955; M.S.D. (USPHS, NIH fellow), U. Wash., 1960; m. Margaret T. Hoffman, July 16, 1948; children—John, Carolyn, Christopher, Andrew. Instr. microbiol. technique lab. W.Va. U., 1949-51, instr. ornithology lab. course, 1949-51; asst. curator W.Va. U. Zool. Mus., 1949-51; asso. prof. orthodontics Georgetown U. Sch. Dentistry, 1960-62, asst. clin. prof. orthodontics, 1962-64, guest lectr. dept. anatomy Med. Sch., 1966-68; guest lectr. orthodontics Montgomery Jr. Coll., 1968; asst. prof. orthodontics Howard U. Dental Sch. Grad. Orthodontic Program, 1969; practice orthodontics, Washington, 1962—; partner Drs. Heim & Law, Potomac Real Estate Assos.; cons. Washington Hosp. Center of D.C., Childrens Hosp. Nat. Med. Center. Mem. Alumni Senate, Georgetown U. Served to lt. USN, 1955-58. Mem. D.C. Dental Soc., Middle Atlantic, Balt. Washington socs. orthodontists, Eastern Strang Tweed, Greater Washington (past pres.) orthodontic study clubs, Am. Soc. Dentistry for Children, A.A.A.S., Am. Soc. Preventive Dentistry, Georgetown U. Dental Sch. Alumni Assn., Phi Kappa Psi, Psi Omega. Kiwanian (past pres., dist. lt. gov.). Club: Potomac Swimming and Tennis (Potomac, Md.). Home: 7543 Sebago Rd Bethesda MD 20034 Office: 4633 41st St NW Washington DC 20016

LAW, WILLIAM HOLDEN, JR., city ofcl.; b. Colonie, N.Y., Feb. 23, 1930; s. William H. and Dorothy (Lant) L.; B.A., U. Me., 1953; M.G.A., U. Pa., 1959; m. Shirley F. Findley, Mar. 31, 1972; children—Richard D., William H. III, Robin Elizabeth. City mgr., Guttenberg, Ia., 1959-61; staff asso. J.K. Jacobs & Co., 1961-62; town mgr. Franklin Twp., N.J., 1962-64; bus. adminstr. Town of Irvington (N.J.), 1964-65; city mgr., Pensacola, Fla., 1965-71; staff dir. Fla. Ho. of Reps., Tallahassee, 1971-73; city mgr., Boca Raton, Fla., 1973—; pres. Municipal Cons. Service; trustee Financial Fla. Investors. Bd. dirs. Jr. Achievement; bd. dirs. United Fund, 1966-71, exec. com., 1970-71. Dir. Escambia County Water Devel. Authority, 1969-72; mem. adv. com. to com. rds. and hwys. Legislative Council, 1968-69; mem. space allocation subcom. Fla. Utilities Coordinating Com., 1967-70; mem. resources and adv. com. to com. on transp. Fla. Ho. of Reps, 1969. Served with USNR, 1949-53. Mem. Indsl. Mgmt. Assn., Internat. City Mgmt. Assn., Fla. Mgrs. Assn. (dir.), Fla. League Municipalities, Am. Soc. Pub. Adminstrn., Am. Acad. Polit. Sci. Home: 2975 NE 2d Av Boca Raton FL 33432 Office: City Hall 201 W Palmetto Park Rd Boca Raton FL 33432

LAWHORN, JESS SHERMAN, finance co. exec.; b. Cin., Jan. 20, 1933; s. Jess Sherman and Dorothy E. (Riggs) L.; B.B.A. in Marketing and Econs., U. Miami, 1953; postgrad. Sch. Mortgage Banking Northwestern U., 1960-63, Mich. State U., 1969-70; m. Hilda D. Foxworth, Oct. 12, 1957; 1 son, Jess S. Officer, dir. Shaw Bros. Shipping Co., Miami, Fla., 1964-68, Shaw Marine Co., 1964-68; officer Lon Worth Crow Co., Miami, 1958-64, 69-71; Lon Worth Crow Realty Co., Miami, 1970-71; officer, dir. Southeast Mortgage Co., Miami, 1971—, 75-14 Realty Co., 1971—. Lectr. mortgage banking U. Ga., 1973—, So. Meth. U., 1973—. Chmn. United Fund Div. Served to 1st lt. USAF, 1954-56. Mem. Econ. Soc. South Fla., C. of C., S.A.R., Soc. Real Estate Appraisers (pres. Greater Miami chpt. 1966), Order Founders and Patriots Am., Sigma Alpha Epsilon. Rotarian. Clubs: Riviera Country, University. Home: 500 Perugia Av Coral Gables FL 33146 Office: 75 SE 14th St Miami FL 33131

LAWHUN, D.E. (GENE), civil engr.; b. Holden, W.Va., Nov. 21, 1933; s. Elijah and Fay (Dean) L.; B.Engring.Sci. cum laude, Marshall U., 1960; postgrad. W.Va. U., 1961-62, U. Ill., 1963; m. Peggy Ann Fox, Aug. 11, 1953; children—Debra, Richard Eugene. Civilian with U.S. Army C.E., 1960-70, chief survey reports sect., Huntington, W.Va., 1967-70; alternate army rep. U.S. Water Resources Council, Office Chief Engrs., Dept. Army, Washington, 1971—. Instr. engring. Marshall U., Huntington, part-time 1959-62; v.p. Jones & Lawhun Constrn. Co., Huntington, 1962-66. Sec., Wakefield Chapel Civic Assn., Annandale, W.Va., 1973—. Served with AUS, 1953-56. Registered profl. engr., W.Va. Mem. Am. Soc. C.E. (local sect. student chpt. contact mem. 1969), Nat., Va. socs. profl. engrs., Soc. Am. Mil. Engrs., Engrs. Club Huntington (1st v.p. 1970), Am. Legion. Home: 8114 Briar Creek Dr Annandale VA 22003 Office: 1000 Independence Av Washington DC 20314

LAWLER, EDWARD J., lawyer; b. Chgo., Sept. 15, 1908; s. Edward James and Sarah (Gahan) L.; Ph.B., U. Chgo., 1926-30; LL.B., Harvard, 1933; m. Elizabeth Falls Dunscomb, Dec. 16, 1939. Admitted to Ill. bar, 1933, Tenn. bar, 1941; atty., auditor income tax sect. Office Collector Internal Revenue, Chgo., 1933-34; spl. atty. Bur. Internal Revenue, 1935-36, practicing lawyer, 1937-38, atty. SEC, 1939-40; practiced in Memphis, 1941—. Dir. Mid-South Title Co., Inc., Chickasaw Bldg. Co. Mem. State Dept. Adv. Panel on Internat. Law, 1967—. Served as lt. comdr. USNR, 1942-45. Decorated Bronze Star medal. Fellow Am. Bar Found.; mem. Am., Tenn., Memphis Shelby County bar assns., Phi Beta Kappa. Home: 644 S Belvedere Blvd Memphis TN 38104 Office: 1st Nat Bank Bldg Memphis TN 38103

LAWLER, JAMES JOSEPH, mgmt. cons.; b. Coudersport, Pa., May 31, 1908; s. Martin Joseph and Nellie (Ryan) L.; student St. Bonaventure U., 1927-30, Layfayette U., 1930-31; m. Margaret Mary Heckel. With Sylvania Electric Products, Inc., Emporium, Pa., 1933-62, area safety engr., 1943-52, div. safety engr. radio tube div., 1952-62; loss prevention mgr. Gen. Telephone & Electric Service Corp., N.Y.C., 1962-65; dir. safety City St. Petersburg (Fla.), 1965-72; safety mgmt. cons., St. Petersburg, 1972—. Mem. Boro Authority Sewerage Treatment Program and Sch. Authority for Consol. Sch. Bd., 1959-62; chmn. United Fund, city employees, St. Petersburg, 1966-68; bd. dirs. A.R.C., Tb Chest program, Emporium, Pa., 1950-60. Mem. Soc. Safety Engrs. West Coast Fla., Nat. Safety Council, Compressed Gas Assn., Safety Execs. Met. N.Y.C., Certified Safety Profls., Sigma Chi, Roman Catholic. K.C., Kiwanian. Club: Emporium Country (pres. 1960). Address: 6301 16th St S St Petersburg FL 33705

LAWLER, ROBERT CLAIR, real estate developer; b. Richmond, Ind., May 9, 1902; s. William F. and Mary M. (McManus) L.; student pub. schs.; m. Elizabeth Francis, Apr. 28, 1931; children—Mary Louise, Betty Ann, Nancy C. Owner Lawler's, Inc., Richmond, New Castle and Muncie, Ind.,. 1932-52; real estate developer, builder shopping centers and apts., Clearwater, Fla., 1952—; dir. Pinellas Central Bank & Trust Co., Bank of Indian Rocks (Largo, Fla.); pres. Lawlers, Inc. Elk, Kiwanian. Home and office: 817 Osceola Rd Belleair Clearwater FL 33516

LAWLOR, JAMES JAY, SR., med. instn. adminstr.; b. Washington, Dec. 22, 1928; s. James Joseph and Barbara Lucille (King) L.; A.A., Palm Beach Jr. Coll., 1950; m. Patricia Lindsay Way, Feb. 20, 1966; children—James Jay, James Michael, James Patrick. Analyst Nat. Security Agy., Washington, 1950-51; account exec. Power Advt. Co. West Palm Beach, Fla., 1953-55; agt. Life Ins. Co. of Ga., West Palm Beach, 1956-59; exec. dir. Internat. Eye Found., Washington, 1959—; pres. Spring Valley Opticians, Inc., Washington, 1971—. Bd. dirs. Paul E Casassa Meml. Found. Served as 1st lt. AUS, 1951-53. Mem. Eye Bank Assn. Am. (dir. 1963—, cons. 1961—), Big Brothers Club, Army and Navy Club. Roman Catholic. Lion (dir. 1965—). Clubs: Touchdown, Black Tie, Nat. Capital Sports. Home: 6416 31 Pl NW Washington DC 20015 Office: Sibley Memorial Hospital Washington DC 20016

LAWRENCE, ALEXANDER A., U.S. dist. judge; b. Savannah, Ga., Dec. 28, 1906; s. Alexander A. and Isabel (Paine) L.; A.B. magna cum laude, U. Ga., 1929; pvt. study law; m. Margaret T. Adams, Apr. 18, 1933; 1 son, Alexander A. Admitted to Ga. bar; gen. practice law, Savannah, 1930-68; judge U.S. Dist. Ct. so. dist. Ga., after 1968, now chief judge. Mem. Ga. Bd. Bar Examiners, 1951-58. Mem. Ga. Hist. Commn., 1951-67. Mem. Ga. Bar Assn. (pres. 1949-50), Ga. Hist. Soc. (pres. 1945-50, 66-68), Phi Beta Kappa. Author: James Moore Wayne, Southern Unionist, 1945, 70; Storm Over Savannah, 1951, 69; James Johnston, Georgia's First Printer, 1956; A Present for Mr. Lincoln, 1961; Johnny Leber and the Confederate Major, 1962. Home: 401 E 44th St Savannah GA 31405 Office: PO Box 9029 Wright Sq Post Office Bldg Savannah GA 31402

LAWRENCE, DAVID PAUL, mfg. co. exec.; b. Holdenville, Okla., Feb. 28, 1941; s. Roy Alvin and Eva Marie (Majors) L.; B.S., Abilene Christian Coll., 1962; m. Linda Mayfield, Jan. 29, 1962; children—Linda, Lorri. Cost accountant Flintkote Co., Sweetwater, Tex., 1962-64; financial accountant Milchem. Corp., Houston, 1964-66; auditor Arthur Andersen & Co., C.P.A.'s, Houston, 1967-71; v.p., controller Ruhmann Mfg. Co., Schulenburg, Tex., 1971—. Mem. Capital Area Manpower Planning Council, 1973—. C.P.A., Tex. Mem. Tex. Soc. C.P.A.'s. Rotarian. Home: 903 Texana St Hallettsville TX 77964 Office: 801 N Main St Schulenburg TX 78956

LAWRENCE, DUARD JONES, telephone co. exec.; b. Covington, Ky., July 24, 1923; s. Duard H. and Leona (Jones) L.; student Ohio Mechanics Inst. Applied Sci., 1942; B.S. in Personnel Adminstrn., U. Cin., 1953; grad. Ind. Exec. Program, U. Ind., 1972; m. Loraine Emily Stickling, Apr. 30, 1945; children—Keith C., Denise M., David H. Sales mgr. Cin. & Suburban Bell Telephone Co., 1945-58, marketing sales mgr., 1960-68, gen. labor relations mgr., 1969-73, gen. personnel mgr., 1973—; marketing rep. A.T. & T., N.Y.C., 1958-60. Served with USNR, 1942-46. Mem. Am. Marketing Assn. (mem. bd. control 1960-63), Cin. Exec. Assn. (dir. 1965-68), Campbell County (Ky.) C. of C., Indsl. Relations Research Assn. Republican. Mem. United Ch. of Christ. Home: 33 Riverview St Fort Thomas KY 41075 Office: 225 E 4th St Cincinnati OH 45202

LAWRENCE, FRED PARKER, citriculturist ; b. Lebanon, Tenn., Mar. 13, 1911; s. Euless Smith and Daisy (Parker L.; B.S., U. Fla., 1934, M.A., 1953; m. Ann Kathryn Williams, Dec. 23, 1934; children—Fred Parker II, Stephen Lawson. With Farmers Home Adminstrn., 1933-42, asst. state dir., 1940-42; citriculturist U. Fla., Agrl. Extension Service, U.S. Dept. Agr., Gainesville, 1947—. U.S. Dept. Agr. citrus breeding and variety dir. Whitmore Found., 1958-60. Active Fla. 4-H Found., U. Fla. Senate. Served to comdr. USNR, 1942-46. Recipient Distinguished Service award Fla. Bankers, 1965; Camp McQuarrie Distinguished Service award Fla. Citrus Growers Assn., 1964; Golden Orange award Fla. Citrus Mut., 1973, others. Mem. Am. Soc. Hort. Sci., Soil and Crop Sci. Soc. Am., Tropical Region, Southeastern hort. socs., Fla. State Hort. Soc. (hon. life), Fla. Entomol. Soc., Soil and Crop Soc. Fla., Phi Kappa Phi, Gamma Sigma Delta, Epsilon Sigma Phi. Kiwanian. Club: Gainesville (Fla.) Golf and Country. Contbr. articles to profl. jours. Home: 2805 SW 1st Av Gainesville FL 32601

LAWRENCE, HOMER ALBERT, JR., ednl. adminstr.; b. Texarkana, Tex., June 13, 1930; s. Homer Albert and Earnistene Dawn (Nichols) L.; B.S., East Tex. State U., 1951, M.Ed., 1956; D.Ed., U. Tenn., 1966; postgrad. U. S.C., 1969, U. Ga., 1971; m. Mary Ellen Woodruff, Oct. 6, 1951; children—Marianne, James Albert, Julianna. Instr. engring. U. Tex., Arlington, 1957-60; asst. prof. Memphis State U., 1960-64; research asst. Sch. Planning Lab., U. Tenn., 1964-65; supr. sch. plant div. Tenn. Dept. Edn., Nashville, 1965-67; dir. continuing edn. Jackson (Tenn.) State Community Coll., 1967-70; dir. vocational and adult edn. Jackson City Sch. System, 1970—; ednl. and sch. planning cons. Committeeman West Tenn. area council Boy Scouts Am., 1971. Bd. dirs. YMCA, 1968-70; mem. tech. adv. com. Tenn. Commn. on Aging. Served with Finance Corps, AUS, 1951-53. Named Civitan of Year, 1969. Mem. Adult Edn. Assn. Am., N.E.A., Tenn. Adult Edn. Assn. (pres.), Am. Assn. Sch. Adminstrs., Vocational Indsl. Clubs Am., Am. Indsl. Arts Assn., Acacia, Pi Omega Pi. Methodist. Mason (Shriner). Club: Civitan (v.p., dir.) (Jackson). Author: Standard Repair Manual, 1956; A Study of Tennessee School Property Accounting, 1966; Dynamic Maturity, 1969. Editor: Tenn. Adult Edn. Assn. Newsletter, 1969-71. Home: 1508 N Royal St Jackson TN 38301 Office: 207 Allen St Jackson TN 38301

LAWRENCE, HOWARD S., food packing co. exec.; b. N.Y.C., June 19, 1923; s. Jack and Irene Lillian (Greenman) L.; B.S., N.Y. U., 1946; m. Lila Frances Bilgore, Aug. 26, 1947; children—David Alan, Debra Sue. With David Bilgore & Co., Inc., Clearwater, Fla., 1950—, v.p., 1965—, sec., 1966—. Dir. Northwest Bank of Clearwater. Instr., Dale Carnegie, 1956-58. Pres., Clearwater Festival, 1966-67; mem. adv. bd. Mease Hosp., 1969-70; mem. Sheriffs Adv. Bd., 1971; mem. County Personal Bd., 1969-70; mem. Mchts. Bd., 1971—; pres. Big Bros., 1972-73. Mem. exec. bd. Pinellas County Democratic Com., 1970-73; Dem. state committeeman, 1973—. Bd. dirs. Drug Abuse Hosp., Clearwater. Served with USAF, 1942-45; PTO. Recipient Outstanding Pres. award Sertoma Club, 1958; City of Clearwater medal outstanding community service, 1967. Mem. Fla. Gift Shippers Assn. (dir. Fla. chpt. 1968—, pres. elect 1972-73), Fraternal Order Police (v.p.), Clearwater C. of C. (dir.). Clubs: Sertoma (pres. 1958-59). Jewish religion (pres. temple 1958, bd. dirs. 1959—). Home: 749 Snug Island Clearwater FL 33515 Office: 702 Franklin St Clearwater FL 33517

LAWRENCE, JAMES HAROLD, JR., mech. engr., educator; b. Beatrice, Neb., Feb. 9, 1932; s. James Harold and Doris Edris (Wheeler) L.; B.S. in Mech. Engring., Tex. Tech. U., 1956, M.S. in Mech. Engring., 1960; Ph.D. (Ford Found. fellow), Tex. A. and M. U., 1965; m. Jane Lenore Matthews, Jan. 16, 1955; children—Jenny Ann, Julie Kay. Design engr. Gen. Electric Co., Richland, Wash., 1957; prof. mech. engring. Tex. Tech. U., Lubbock, 1956—. Cons. to various law firms. Mem. Emergency Med. Service Study Group, Lubbock, 1973. Mem. Am. Soc. Engring. Edn. (chmn. ann. conf. 1973), Am. Soc. M.E., Am. Soc. Heating, Refrigerating and Air-Conditioning Engrs., Lubbock C. of C., Pi Tau Sigma, Phi Kappa Phi. Methodist (chmn. bd. trustees 1970—). Home: 6027 Norfolk St Lubbock TX 79413

LAWRENCE, JOHN, corp. exec.; b. Rutland, Vt., Feb. 12, 1911; s. Edwin Winship and Florence (Roby) L.; grad. Phillips Acad., Exeter, N.H., 1928; B.S., Mass. Inst. Tech., 1932; m. Janet Beal, May 28, 1938; children—Carol (Mrs. John Hoffman), Gale, Johanne (Mrs. Ronald La Grange), John Rodney, Ann. Factory mgr. Jones & Lamson Machine Co., 1934-44; gen. factory mgr. SKF Industries, Inc., Phila., 1944-49, tech. v.p. charge mfg., engring. and research, 1950-51; v.p. mfg. Joy Mfg. Co., Pitts., 1951-54, exec. v.p., 1954-55, pres., 1956-57; v.p. Dresser Industries, Inc., Dallas, 1957, exec. v.p., dir., 1957-62, chmn. bd., chmn. exec. com., 1962-70, 72—, pres., 1965-68, 69—; dep. chmn., Class C dir. Fed. Res. Bank Dallas; dir. Keebler Co., Santa Fe Industries, Inc., Western Electric Co., Nat. Life Ins. Co. Vt. Home: 5527 Meaders Lane Dallas TX 75229 Office: Republic Nat Bank Bldg Dallas TX 75221

LAWRENCE, PETER, ballet co. ofcl. Formerly dir. devel. Saratoga Performing Arts Center; exec. dir. Fairfax County Cultural Assn.; adminstr. Garden States Arts Center; gen. mgr. Dick Button's Ice-Travaganza; producer Peter Pan, Let's Make an Opera, Shinbone Alley, Shakespeare's Ages of Man; stage mgr. 6 Broadway shows, 3 U.S.O. shows; stage mgr., producer Ballet Theater, Columbia Artists Mgmt., also other groups; with advt. dept., photographer N.Y. Times, also for subsidiary Wide World Photos; film critic Topeka State Jour.; gen. mgr. Atlanta Ballet, 1972—. Cons., Theater Planning Assos., N.Y.C. Office: 3211 Cains Hill Pl Atlanta GA 30305*

LAWRENCE, RAY VANCE, chemist; b. Ala. July 6, 1910; s. William Monroe and Frances (Ray) L.; B.S., U. Ala., 1931; M.S., U. Tenn., 1933; m. Barbara Frances New, June 22, 1935; children—Robert Craig, Richard Vance. Instr. Marion (Ala.) Mil. Inst., 1932-33; chemist TVA, Muscle Shoals, Ala., 1933-38, Naval Stores Sta., Olustee, Fla., 1938-41, Naval Stores research div., Washington, 1941-43; head rosin research sect., 1950-57, chief Naval Stores Lab., 1958—. Lectr. terpene chemistry U. Fla., 1953, 58. Mem. Am. Chem. Soc. (chmn. Fla. sect. 1965, Fla. award 1970), A.A.A.S., Am. Soc. Testing Materials, T.A.P.P.I. Patentee in field. Home: 621 W De Soto St Lake City FL 32055 Office: Box 1 Olustee FL 32072

LAWRENCE, RICHARD CROMWELL, constrn. co. exec.; b. Hamburg, Germany, Oct. 19, 1933 (parents Am. citizens); s. Newbold Trotter and Evelyn (Cromwell) L.; B.M.E., N.Y. State Maritime Coll., 1955; m. Suzanne Were, Sept. 2, 1955; children—Anne, Richard Cromwell, Elizabeth, Robert, Mark, Denise. Field engr. Sperry Gyroscope Co., 1956-58; dept. head Marine div. Denison Engring. Co., 1958-61; self-employed, St. Thomas, Virgin Islands, 1961-65; with Devcon Internat. Corp., and predecessor, St. Thomas, 1965—, v.p., 1971—; pres. Controlled Concrete Products, 1967—, St. Maarten divs. Bouwbedrijf Boven Winden N.V. Active local Boy Scouts Am. Mem. St. Thomas C. of C. Club: St. Thomas Yacht. Home: 79 Estate Wintberg St Thomas VI 00801 Office: Turpentine Rd PO Box 3368 St Thomas VI 00801

LAWRENCE, TELETE ZORAYDA (MRS. ERNEST LAWRENCE), speech and voice pathologist, educator; b. Worcester, Mass., Aug. 5, 1910; d. James Newton and Cora Valeria (Hester) Lester; A.B. cum laude, U. Cal. at Berkeley, 1932; M.A., Tex. Christian U., 1963; pvt. study voice with Edgar Schofield, N.Y.C., 1936-41, drama with Enrica Clay Dillon, N.Y.C., 1937-40; m. Ernest Lawrence, Oct. 9, 1939; children—James Lester, Valerie Alma. Mem. Am. Lyric Theatre, 1939—; instr. speech Sch. Fine Arts, Tex. Christian U., Ft. Worth, 1959-66, asst. prof., 1966-71, asso. prof., 1971—, univ. speech pathologist specializing in voice disorders Speech and Hearing Clinic, 1959—; individual practice speech and voice therapy, 1960—; cons. voice disorders. Participant, contbr. numerous internat. congresses, 1965—. Bd. dirs. Sunshine Haven, home for retarded children, 1957-59; gen. chmn. Ft. Worth and Tarrant County, Nat. Retarded Children's Week, 1954; mem. family and child welfare div. Community Council of Ft. Worth and Tarrant County, 1955-57; mem. health and hosp. div., 1959-60; mem. women's com. Ft. Worth chpt. Nat. Conf. Christians and Jews, Inc., 1956-59; exec. v.p. Fine Arts Found. Guild of Tex. Christian U., 1955-56, exec. sec., 1956-58, financial sec., 1958-59. Tex. Christian U. faculty research grantee, 1961, on leave to Gt. Britain, Western Europe, Hungary, 1968. Mem. Nat. Council Chs. (bd. dirs. joint com. missionary edn. Pacific Coast area, 1952-55), United Ch. Women of Ft. Worth (chmn. Christian world missions dept. 1955-57, pres., 1957-59), Ft. Worth Area Council Chs. (v.p. 1955-57, exec. com. 1957-59, dir. 1959-60), U. Cal. Alumni Assn., Am., Tex. speech and hearing assns., Ft. Worth Council for Retarded Children, Speech Communication Assn. Am. (sec. speech and hearing disorders interest group 1962, 63), American Dialect Soc., Am. Assn. U. Profs., Internat. Assn. Logopedics and Phoniatrics, Internat. Soc. Phonetic Scis., Tex. Speech Assn., Phi Beta Kappa (pres. chpt. 1973-74), Delta Zeta, Psi Chi, Sigma Alpha Eta. Republican. Mem. Christian Ch. Clubs: Woman's of Fort Worth; Women of Rotary. Author: Handbook for Instructors of Voice and Diction, 1968. Contbr. articles to profl. publs. Home: 3860 South Hills Circle Fort Worth TX 76109

LAWRENCE, WALTER WILLIAM, JR., chem. engr.; b. New Brunswick, N.J., May 8, 1929; s. Walter William and Mildred Irene (Wright) L.; B.S., Rutgers U., 1951; Ph.D., Ia. State U., 1959; m. Hazel Marilyn Hermanson, June 15, 1957; children—Brian, Andrea, Carin. Research chemist Barrett div. Allied Chem. Co., 1951-54; research chemist Ethyl Corp., Baton Rouge, 1959-73, process devel. engr., 1973—. Active Boy Scouts Am. Mem. Am. Chem. Soc. (edn. chmn. Baton Rouge sect. 1971), Wickland Terrace Citizens Assn. (pres. 1962-63), Phi Lambda Upsilon. Republican. Methodist (mem. ofcl. bd. 1969-70). Club: Fairwood Country (Baton Rouge). Home: 12288 Armstrong Dr Baton Rouge LA 70816 Office: PO Box 341 Baton Rouge LA 70821

LAWRENCE, WILLIAM ROBERT, clergyman; b. Gatesville, Tex., Oct. 12, 1906; s. William Henry and Denia (Millsap) L.; student Baylor U., 1932, S.W. Baptist Sem., 1933-35; m. Inez G. Glaze, Aug. 4, 1930; children—William Robert, Jerry Joe, Janice (Mrs. Cyrus Virl Ruth). Ordained to ministry Baptist Ch., 1928; pastor in Lefors, Tex., 1935-41, Dumas, 1942, McLean, 1947, Delhart, Tex., 1947-49, Clarendon, Tex., 1959-73. Head Bible dept. Clarendon Jr. Coll., 1959-73. Mem. exec. bd. Bapt. Gen. Conv. Tex., pres. Dist 10; chmn. Human Devel. Adv. Bd., Clarendon, 1968-73. Trustee Wayland Bapt. Coll., Highland Bapt. Hosp; pres. Panfork Bapt. Encampment, 1963-73. Dep. wing chaplain Tex. Civil Air Patrol; chaplain Fire Dept., Am. Legion, V.F.W. (all Dalhart). Mem. Child Welfare Bd., Juvenile Delinquency Bd., Dalhart. Served as chaplain USAAF, World War 11, also 1952-53, lt. col. Res. Named citizen of year, Dalhart, 1951. Rotarian (pres. Dalhart 1956), Lion (pres. Clarendon 1964.). Office: Box 944 Clarendon TX 97226

LAWS, JAMES TAYLOR, petroleum engr.; b. Kingsville, Tex., Dec. 12, 1926; s. Francis Howison and Lydia Lucinda (Yerick) L.; B.S., Tex. A and I U., 1950; m. Betsy B. Barton, July 12, 1969; children—Linda (Mrs. Glen Arthur Cunha), Shelly Ann. Asst. to measurement engr. Houston Nat. Gas Co., 1950-52; asst. dist. engr. Champlin Petroleum Co., McAllen, Tex., 1952-53, dist. engr., Corpus Christi, 1953-54. asst. div. engr., Enid, Okla., 1954-55, staff engr., Fort Worth, 1955-57, chief engr., 1957-66, dir. engring., 1966-73, v.p. engring., 1973—. Served with USNR, 1944-46. Mem. Am. Petroleum Inst. (exec. com. on drilling and prodn. practice 1969-71), Am. Inst. Mining, Metall. and Petroleum Engrs. (dir. local chpt. 1971-72), Fort Worth Petroleum Engrs. Club, Petroleum Club Fort Worth. Mason. Club: Ridglea Country (Fort Worth). Home: 4321 Winding Way Fort Worth TX 76126 Office: 5301 Camp Bowie Blvd Fort Worth TX 76107

LAWSON, ABRAM VENABLE, univ. adminstr.; b. South Boston, Va., Jan. 9, 1922; s. Abram Venable and Vivien Strudwick (Moseley) L.; B.A., U. Ala., 1946; M.L.S., Emory U., 1950; D.L.S., Columbia, 1969; m. Julia Lee Clark, 1949 (div.); children—Janet Lee, Venable, Mary Vivian. Auditor, Socony-Mobil Oil Co., Denver, 1947-48; teller First Nat. Bank, Altavista, Va., 1948-49; asst. reference dept. Atlanta Pub. Library, 1951, head reference dept., 1954-56, coordinator pub. services, 1956-60; library asst. Harvard Coll. Library, 1951-54; asst. prof. Fla. State U. Library Sch., 1960-65; dir. librarianship Emory U., Atlanta, 1965—. Served with USAAF, 1942-46. Recipient George Virgil Fuller award Columbia, 1964. Mem. A.L.A., Spl. Libraries Assn., Assn. Am. Library Schs., Am. Assn. U. Profs., Am. Soc. for Information Sci. Home: 771 Houston Mill Rd NE Atlanta GA 30329

LAWSON, CHARLES VALENTINE, accountant; b. Pineville, Ky., Feb. 14, 1937; s. Charlie and Elizabeth (Parolari) L.; B.S. in Accounting, Eastern Ky. U., 1960; m. Geraldine Bryant, July 18, 1964; children—Michael, Charlie, Scott. Mgr., Ernst & Ernst, Louisville, 1960-73; controller Alachua Gen. Hosp., Gainsville, Fla., 1973—. Served with inf., AUS, 1954-57. C.P.A., Ky. Mem. Louisville C. of C., Ky. Hosp. Assn., Hosp. Financial Mgmt. Assn. Home: PO Box 927 Williston FL 32696 Office: Alachua General Hospital Gainsville FL 32601

LAWSON, HERBERT RONALD, petroleum co. exec.; b. Beaver, Okla., Apr. 28, 1942; s. Herbert Noble and Gloria Carrolea (Johnson) L.; student U. Okla., 1960-62; m. Della Pearl Judd, June 1, 1965; children—Terri, Denise, Shannon, Lee Ann. With Lawson Title Co., Beaver, 1962-71, v.p. 1971; pres. Ivanhoe Petroleum Co., Beaver, 1972—; v.p. Lobo Exploration Co., Oklahoma City, 1972—. Mem. Beaver Jr. C. of C. (treas. 1968). Democrat. Presbyn. Home: PO Box 130 Beaver OK 73932 Office: 47 W 2nd St Beaver OK 73932

LAWSON, MAURICE ANTOINE, real estate exec.; b. Carbon Hill, Ala., May 20, 1918; s. Ellie Fields and Minnie (Buchanan) L.; student Massey Bus. Coll., 1940; m. Ella Earlene Earnest, Sept. 6, 1941; children—Juanita Maurice (Mrs. Jerry Bruce Case) and Martha Antoinette (Mrs. Larry Hugh Graves) (twins), Thomas Henry. Purchasing agt. McCullough Industries, Birmingham, Ala., 1946-49; prop. Lawson Realty Co., Birmingham, 1950-65; pres. Nat. Mortgage Exchange, Birmingham, 1966—, Commerce Square, Inc., Birmingham, 1967—; real estate broker Johnson-Rase & Hays Co., Birmingham, 1967—, v.p., 1971—. Mem. Birmingham Real Estate Bd., So. Indsl. Devel. Council. Mem. Jefferson County Water Commn., 1971—. Served with USAAF, 1941-45. Baptist. Mason (Shriner). Clubs: The Club, Roebuck Exchange (pres. 1955), Jade Lake (dir. 1969—). Home: 636 Elm St Birmingham AL 35206 Office: 1020 S 22d St Birmingham AL 35205

LAWSON, RALPH IVY, lawyer; b. Grenada, Miss., June 16, 1935; s. Sid Hopkins and Mary Lillie (Ivy) L.; B.A., U. Miss., 1957, LL.B., 1961; m. Patricia Lee Peterson, June 8, 1962; children—Nell Ivy, Rush Denman. Admitted to Miss. bar, 1961, Tenn. bar, 1962; mem. firm Ashley, Ashley & Lawson, Dyersburg, Tenn., 1961—; city judge, Dyersburg, 1963-67. Chmn. Dyer County chpt. A.R.C., 1963-65; fund drive chmn. Reelfoot council Girl Scouts Am., 1973-74. Served to lt. USNR, 1957-59. Mem. Am., Tenn., Miss., Dyer County (pres. 1966-67) bar assns., Tenn. (pres. 1972-73), Am. trial lawyers assns., Phi Alpha Delta, Kappa Alpha. Presbyn. (deacon 1964-73). Moose (gov. 1971-72). Home: 9806 Cooper Dr Dyersburg TN 38024 Office: 322 Church Av Dyersburg TN 38024

LAWSON, WILLIAM E., JR., city ofcl.; b. Newport News, Va., Mar. 19, 1923; s. William E. and Ann (Moore) L.; B.S. in Civil Engring., Va. Mil. Inst.; grad. extension course Technique Municipal Adminstrn; m. Ann Weston, Jan. 24, 1948; children—William E. III, Deborah Ann. City engr., Waynesboro, Va., 1947-48; town mgr., South Boston, Va., 1948-51; city mgr., Buena Vista, Va., 1952-54, Delray Beach, Fla., 1954-60, St. Augustine, Fla., 1960-62; dir. pub. works, Newport News, 1962-65, city mgr., 1965—. Dir. Bank of Hampton Roads, Newport News. Sec., treas. Peninsula Ports Authority. Bd. dirs. Salvation Army. Served with C.I.C., AUS. Home: 51 James Landing Rd Newport News VA 23606 Office: 2400 Washington Av Newport News VA 23607

LAWSON, WILLIAM JENNINGS, data processor; b. Poteet, Tex., Sept. 17, 1927; s. Curty Jennings and Belva Lois (Bramlett) L.; student Tex. A. and I. Coll., Kingsville, 1946-47; m. Mary Lee Selman, Oct. 16, 1948; children—Gail (Mrs. Leslie L. Willoughby), William Jennings, Pamela. Craftsman, Bell Telephone Co., Edinburg, Tex., 1948-52; technician Anchorage Telephone Dept., 1952-56; with Air Force Logistics Command, Kelly AFB, Tex., 1956—, supervisory electronic specialist, 1972—. Served with USNR, 1945-46. Mem. Am. Amateur Inventors Club (founder, dir.). Baptist. Patentee electronic remote control device. Home: 300 Pecan St PO Box 711 Poteet TX 78065 Office: SAAMA/MMPMI Kelly AFB TX 78241

LAWTON, G. CABELL, corp. exec.; b. Richmond, Va., Jan. 4, 1893; s. W. P., Jr. and Sallie Syme (Waddill) L.; ed. high sch.; m. Ruth A. Wells, Oct. 6, 1914; children—G. Cabell, Jr., Floy Leigh, John Courthope. Office mgr. Duplex Envelope Co., 1911-16; treas. Eagle Paper Co., 1916-21, Cushnoc Paper Co., 1917-21, Kennebec Paper Co., 1918-21, Moore and Thompson Paper Co., 1918-21, Hercules Paper Bag Mills, 1919-21, Am. Trust Co., 1928-33; office mgr. Hunton, Williams, Gay Powell & Gibson, 1932-64; pres., dir. Brown Oil Co.; treas., dir. Va.-Ga. Realty Corp., 1935-58; sec., dir. Charles C Haskell and Co., Inc., 1938-58. Clubs: Down Town. Home: 300 W Franklin St Richmond VA 23220 Office: 700 E Main St Richmond VA 23219

LAWTON, MYRTLE HAWKINS (MRS. REED LAWTON), civic worker; b. Phenix City, Ala., Mar. 29, 1908; d. Thomas Jefferson and Carrie (Brown) Hawkins; student pub. schs.; m. A. John Bartram, June 8, 1935 (dec. June 1960); m. 2d, Reed Lawton, Aug. 23, 1966. Office sec. J.D. Thomason Realty Co., Columbus, Ga., 1928; compiler rates for fire ins. Ga. Inspection Rating Bur., 1929-31; sec. Dudley Products Co., 1932, White Realty Co., Phenix City, 1933-35; editorial-clk-typist to dir. instrn. and tng. lit. U.S. Army Inf. Sch., Ft. Benning, Ga., 1942-66. Chmn. Family Services, A.R.C., 1963—; fallout shelter mgr. Civil Def., 1963—. Mem. East Ala. Genealogy Soc. (chmn. publicity com. 1963-65), Assn. U.S. Army, U.D.C. (pres. Phenix City chpt. 1962-66; chmn. Memorian Program and Year Book), Women of Presbyn. Ch. (v.p. 1960-62, sec. 1958-60, treas. 1972—, chmn. spiritual growth 1959, chmn. ch. extension 1962—), Parapsychology Group, Am. Organist Guild. Presbyn. (chmn. music com. 1972—). Home: PO Box 333 1112 28th St Phenix City AL 36867

LAWTON, RICHARD STANLEY, banker; b. Detroit, Aug. 11, 1931; s. Kenneth E. and Gertrude (Van Keulen) L.; B.A. in Bus. Adminstrn., George Washington U., 1956; student Am. Savs. and Loan Inst., 1957., ; m. Dana Marian Hoop, Feb. 18, 1961; 1 dau., Amy. Chief accounting and loan servicing sect. Equitable Life Ins. Co., Washington, 1956-58; asst. treas., mgr. W.W. McCollum, Inc., Arlington, Va., 1958-60; exec. v.p., mgr., dir. Va. Savs. & Loan Assn., Springfield and Fairfax, Va., 1960-64; 1st v.p. Eastern Mortgage Corp., Washington, 1964-65; exec. v.p. Washington-Lee Savs. & Loan Assn., Alexandria, Va., 1965-66, pres., 1966—, also dir.; pres., dir. 1st Financial of Va. Corp., S & L Service Corp. Va.; dir. Data Systems Corp., Home Guaranty Ins. Corp. Served with AUS, 1951-52. Mem. Va. Savs. and Loan League, Kappa Sigma. Club: Washington Golf and Country. Home: 4501 N 35th Rd Arlington VA 22207

LAWTON, THOMAS, art gallery exec.; b. Somerset, Mass., Feb. 5, 1931; student R.I. Sch. Design, 1949-50; B.S. in Design, Durfee Tech. Inst., 1953; postgrad. Chinese Lang. Tng. Center, Stanford U., Taipei, Taiwan, 1963-64; Ph.D. in Fine Arts (Ford Found. fellow, Univ. scholar), Harvard, 1970. Designer, Cheney Bros., Manchester, Conn., 1953-55; asst. prof. Ia. State U., Ames, 1955-57; asso. curator Chinese art Freer Gallery Art, Washington, 1967-70, curator Chinese art, 1970-71, asst. dir., 1971—. Adviser, Nat. Palace Mus., Taiwan, 1965-67; hon. lectr. Chinese art U. Mich.; instr. Chinese art Smithsonian Assos., 1970, George Washington U., 1970-71; lectr. to art museums, clubs, univs. Fulbright fellow, 1963-66; John D. Rockefeller III Fund grantee, 1966-67. Author: (with Li Chu-tsing) The New Chinese Landscape: Six Contemporary Chinese Artists, 1966; (with John A. Pope) The Freer Gallery of Art, Part I, China, 1971, (with Harold P. Stern), Part II, Japan, 1971; Eugene and Agnes E. Meyer Memorial Exhibition, 1971. Translator (from Chinese) Chinese Cultural Art Treasures: National Palace Museum Illustrated Handbook, 1967; A Garland of Chinese Painting, 1967. Contbr. articles to profl. publs. Office: Freer Gallery Art 12th and Jefferson Dr SW Washington DC 20560*

LAWTON, THOMAS OREGON, JR., lawyer; b. Barton, S.C., Nov. 10, 1924; s. Thomas Oregon and Alexania (Easterling) L.; student Wofford Coll., 1941-43; A.B., Duke, 1947, J.D., 1950; m. Bess White Macaulay, July 10, 1952; children—Thomas Oregon, III, Margaret Macaulay, Angus Macaulay. Admitted to S.C. bar, 1950; practiced in Georgetown, 1950-51, Allendale, 1951—; mem. firm McNair and Lawton, 1951-65, Lawton and Myrick, 1965—; city atty., Allendale, 1951—; county atty., Allendale County, S.C., 1951—; county Allendale Recreation Assn., 1958-59, Hampton-Allendale County Community Concert Assn., 1961-65; vice chmn. Allendale County Devel. Bd., 1956-70, chmn., 1970—; vice chmn. Savannah River Basin Devel. Commn., 1966—; chmn. S.C. Tricentennial Commn., 1966-71, Allendale-Hampton Indls. Devel. Commn., 1972—; curator, v.p. S.C. Hist. Soc.; mem. S.C. Dept. Archives and History Commn., 1968—. Chmn., Allendale County Democratic Com., 1968—. Served with AUS, 1943-45. Decorated Bronze Star, Purple Heart. Mem. Am., S.C., Allendale County (pres. 1965-73) bar assns., S.C. City Atty. Assn. (pres. 1967-68), U. S.C. Soc. (dir.), Am. Trial Lawyers Assn., S.C. C. of C. (chmn. tourist and travel council 1960-62), Huguenot Soc. for S.C., Soc. of Cincinnati, Soc. of Columbia, Sons Colonial Wars, Sigma Alpha Epsilon, Phi Delta Phi. Democrat. Episcopalian (sr. warden 1968-70). Clubs: Fairdale Country (past pres.); Plantation (Hilton Head Island); Summit (Columbia). Home: Hampton Grove Allendale SC 29810 Office: Memorial Av Allendale SC 29810

LAY, COY LAFAYETTE, physician, surgeon; b. Carbondale, Ill., Feb. 19, 1923; s. Chester Frederic and Harriet (Lewis) L.; student U. Tex., 1939-42, M.D., 1946; M.S. in Obstetrics and Gynecology, U. Minn., 1952; m. Madeline Randolph, Dec. 19, 1943; children—Lois Gretchen, Coy Lafayette, Joel Randolph, John Chester. Clin. asso. prof. U. Wash. Med. Sch., 1947-49; fellow obstetrics and gynecology Mayo Clinic, Rochester, Minn., 1949-51, gynecol. surgery, 1951-52; partner Watson Clinic, Lakeland, Fla., 1952—; asso. prof. obstetrics and gynecology U. South Fla., Tampa, 1973—; cons. obstetrics and gynecology Polk County Hosp., Bartow, Fla., 1956—; chmn. dept. obstetrics-gynecology Lakeland Gen. Hosp., 1961, chief gynecology, 1967; clin. asso. prof. anatomy Washington U. Sch. Medicine, 1949. Owner citrus groves; pres. Sky View Groves & Ranch, 1967, Ob-Gyn Letters, Inc., 1962-63; pres. Cleveland Heights Properties, Inc.; dir. Fla. Midlands Real Estate Corp. Pres. Polk County unit Am. Cancer Soc., 1961-62. Served as lt. (j.g.), Med. Res., USN, 1943-49. Diplomate Am. Bd. Obstetrics and Gynecology. Fellow A.C.S.; mem. Am., So. (chmn. gynecology sec.), Fla. med. assns., Am. Coll. Obstet. and Gynecol., Fla. Obstetrics and Gynecology Soc., Mayo Clinic Alumni Assn., Am. Fertility Soc. (pres. 1974), So. Gynecol. and Obstet. Soc., South Atlantic Assn. Obstetricians and Gynecologists (exec. bd. 1972-73), Am. Cytology Soc., Chi Phi, Alpha Kappa Kappa, Alpha Epsilon Delta. Rotarian. Editor: Internat. Corr. Soc. Obstetricians and Gynecologists, 1960—. Home: 419 Lake Hollingsworth Dr Lakeland FL 33803 Office: Watson Clinic Lakeland FL 33802

LAY, EMILY M. (MRS. JAMES SELDEN, JR.), psychiat. social worker, educator; b. Shelby, N.C., Feb. 3, 1913; d. Hugh Graham and Margaret (LeGrand) Miller; B.A., Meredith Coll., 1934; M.S.S., Smith Coll. Sch. Social Work, 1936; m. James Selden Lay, Jr., Feb. 27, 1937; children—Carolyn Miller (Mrs. W. J. Dowd), Patricia L. (Mrs. E.C. Dorsey), Emily (Mrs. P.I. O'Connell). Case worker Guilford County Welfare, Greensboro, N.C., 1934-35; psychiat. social worker Children's Meml. Clinic, Richmond, Va., 1936-37, Bklyn. Bur. Charities, 1937-39, Fairfax County Child Guidance Clinic, Falls Church, Va., 1960-64; supr. family counseling Catholic Family and Children's Services of No. Va., 1964-69; asst. prof., dir. admissions Nat. Catholic Sch. Social Service, Catholic U., Washington, 1969-73; mem. faculty program of continuing edn. Smith Coll. Sch. Social Work, 1974. Field instr. Va. Commonwealth U. Sch. Social Work, 1961-68; vol. social worker A.R.C., Arlington, Va., 1942-45. Mem. Juvenile Detention Commn. No. Va., 1961-62; mem. bd. dirs. Fairfax Child Guidance Clinic, Falls Church, 1950-60, sec. 1950-52, v.p. 1952-54, pres., 1954-56; mem. regional bd. Health Welfare Council, 1957-59. Active Camp Fire Girls, 1953-60. pres. Fairfax dist., 1953-54, Potomac area, Washington 1956-57; cons. mental health Potomac area Camp Fire Girls, 1961-67. Mem. Nat. Assn. Social Workers, Acad. Certified Social Workers, Council Social Work Edn., Smith, Meredith (pres. Washington chpt. 1950-54) coll. alumnae. Roman Catholic. Home: 202 Forest Dr Falls Church VA 22046

LAY, JAMES SELDEN, JR., govt. ofcl.; b. Washington, Aug. 24, 1911; s. James Selden and Lillian Lee (Lockhart) L.; B.S., Va. Mil. Inst., 1933; M.B.A., Harvard, 1935; m. Emily Graham Miller, Feb. 27, 1937; children—Carolyn Miller (Mrs. William Joseph Dowd), Patricia Lockhart (Mrs. Edward Carson Dorsey), Emily Graham (Mrs. Paul Ignatius O'Connell). Asst. to gen. sales mgr. Va. Electric & Power Co., Richmond, 1935-37; asst. to v.p. Stone & Webster Service Corp., N.Y. City, 1937-39; sales mgr. Hagerstown (Md.) Gas Co., 1939-41; mgmt. analyst State Dept., Washington, 1945; sec. Nat. Intelligence Authority, 1946, div. chief Central Intelligence Group, 1947, asst. exec. sec. NSC, 1947-50, exec. sec., 1950-61; dep. asst. to dir. Central Intelligence, 1961-64; exec. sec. U.S. Intelligence Bd., 1962-71; cons. Pres.'s Fgn. Intelligence Adv. Bd., 1971—. Mem. Falls Church (Va.) Sch. Bd., 1949-51, 61-64. Served as army officer stationed War Dept., 1941-45, sec., joint intelligence com. Joint Chiefs of Staff, Washington, 1943-45; col. M.I., U.S. Army Res. ret. Decorated Legion of Merit (U.S.); Order Brit. Empire; recipient Career Service award Nat. Civil Service League, 1964, Distinguished Intelligence medal CIA. Roman Catholic. Home: 202 Forest Dr Falls Church VA 22046

LAY, JOE LAFAYETTE, food packing co. exec.; b. Knoxville, Tenn., Jan. 17, 1925; s. Ira Vivian and Ava Edna (Parrott) L.; B.S. in Bus. Adminstrn., U. Tenn., 1948; m. Sarah Randolph Lowry, Oct. 15, 1948; children—Sally, Joe Lafayette, Tillman L. With Lay Packing Co., Knoxville, 1948—, sales mgr., 1958-69, v.p. sales, 1969-70, exec. v.p., 1970—. Bd. dirs. Better Bus. Bur. Served with AUS, 1943-45. Mem. Knoxville C. of C., Knoxville Tourist Bur., Am. Meat Inst., Nat. Ind. Meat Packers Assn., Tenn. Ind. Meat Packers Assn. (dir. 1961—), Sigma Nu, Phi Kappa Phi, Omicron Delta Kappa. Rotarian. Home: 4003 Avon Park Circle Knoxville TN 37918 Office: 400 E Jackson Av Knoxville TN 37915

LAY, LYNDELL EVERETT, mortgage banker; b. Copeland, Ark., Sept. 3, 1933; s. Cecil Melvin and Reta Viola (Patton) L.; student U. Ark., 1951-53; B.B.A., Baylor U., 1957; m. Iona Bernice Casey, Apr. 20, 1954; children—Phillip Lyndell, Mark Melvin, Michelle Rose. Staff accountant John Dornblaser, C.P.A., Little Rock, 1957-60; v.p. Modern Am. Mortgage Corp., Little Rock, 1960-68; chmn. bd., pres. L.E. Lay & Co., Inc., Little Rock, 1968—; dir. First Ark. Bankstock Corp.; guest lectr. Grad. Center, U. Ark. Mem. Little Rock Bd. Realtors. Mem. Nat. Housing Adv. Council, 1973-74. Chmn. bd. Albert Pike Resident Hotel for Elderly; trustee Gulf YMCA Bd. Served with AUS, 1954-56. Mem. Am. Inst. C.P.A.'s, Ark. Soc. C.P.A.'s, Mortgage Bankers Assn. Ark. (pres. 1971), Greater Little Rock Home Builders Assn. (asso.). Baptist. Mason. Office: PO Box 711 Little Rock AR 72203

LAY, THOMAS FOX, lawyer; b. Waller, Tex., July 11, 1928; s. Archie William and Amalia Augusta (Kalbow) L.; B.A., U. Tex., 1949, LL.B., 1950; m. Ruth Jordan Kent, Apr. 24, 1954; children—Alicia Ruth, Margaret Lynette. Admitted to Tex. bar, 1950, practiced in Houston, 1953-54, Pasadena, 1954—; city atty. City of Pasadena, Tex., 1959-63. Dir. Southmore Savs. Assn., HLM Constructors Inc.; pres. T-R Devel. Corp., Pasadena, 1972—. Lectr. real estate law San Jacinto Jr. Coll., 1968-69. Pres. Lewis Elementary P.T.A., 1971-72. Served to 1st lt. AUS, 1950-53. Mem. State Bar Tex., Houston Bar Assn., Am. Judicature Soc., Am. Radio Relay League, Phi Alpha Delta, Theta Xi. Methodist (chmn. bd. 1959-60). Mason (32 deg.), Rotarian (pres. 1969-70). Club: Exchange (pres. 1958-60). Home: 6435 N Haywood St Houston TX 77017 Office: 825 Southmore St Pasadena TX 77502

LAYMAN, BILLY ALLEN, city ofcl.; b. Owensboro, Ky., Aug. 7, 1938; s. Emmett Mitchell and Lillie May (Connor) L.; student pub. schs.; m. Jewell Lou Kelly, Apr. 15, 1960; children—Debra Lynne, Billy Allen, Jeffrey Scott. St. maintenance foreman City Owensboro Dept. Pub. Works, 1961—. Served with USAF, 1956-60. Home: Route 1 Philpot KY 42366 Office: Dept Pub Works City Hall Owensboro KY 42301

LAYMAN, EARL ROBERT, lawyer; b. Knoxville, Tenn., Aug. 5, 1932; s. William Earl and Marie Frances (Little) L.; B.S., U. Tenn., 1955, J.D., 1962; m. Nancy Doris Shaver, Oct. 30, 1953; children—William Douglas, Marilyn Lee, Linda Ann, Sharon Gail. Accountant, East Tenn. Packing Co., Knoxville, 1957-59; admitted to Tenn. bar, 1963; asso. Joyce & Wilson, Oak Ridge, 1962-64, Key, Lee & Layman, Knoxville, 1964—. Part time instr. U. Tenn. Coll. Law, 1966-70. Pres., Knox County Young Republican Club, 1963; mem. Knox County Election Commn., 1967-71; mem. Tenn. Rep. Exec. Com., 1972—. Mem. Knoxville YWCA Adv. Bd., 1966—, chmn., 1972-73. Served as 1st lt. AUS, 1955-57. Mem. Am., Tenn., Knoxville bar assns., Phi Delta Phi. Elk. Club: Sertoma. Home: Route 1 Lakefront Lane Concord TN 37720 Office: 14th Floor Bank of Knoxville Bldg Knoxville TN 37902

LAYMAN, GENE EDWARD, elec. engr.; b. Louisville, Sept. 24, 1938; s. William Edward and Martine Anna (Bittel) L.; B.S. in Elec. Engring., U. Ky., 1965; M.S. in Elec. Engring., Seattle U., 1967; Ph.D., W.Va. U., 1972; m. L. Darlene Jackel, Aug. 8, 1965; children—Dianna Rachelle, Angela Christene. Circuit designer Boeing Co., Seattle, 1965-67; design, research engr. Tex. Instruments, Inc., Dallas, 1967—. U.S. Bur. Mines grantee, 1970-72. Served with USMC, 1955-59. Mem. I.E.E.E., Hon. Order Ky. Cols., Sigma Xi, Eta Kappa Nu, Triangle Frat. Home: 1102 Hillsdale Dr Richardson TX 75080 Office: 13500 N Central Expressway Dallas TX 75231

LAZAR, BENJAMIN EDWARD, engring. educator; b. Vatra Dornei, Romania, Feb. 2, 1930; s. Edward and Victoria (Cassian) L.; C.E., McGill U. (Can.), 1968; M.E., St. George Williams U. (Can.), 1969, D.Engring., 1971; m. Silvia Holtman, July 17, 1954; 1 dau., Victoria. Came to U.S., 1968, naturalized, 1973. Sr. design engr. Found. of Can., 1963-65, Monti Lavoie Nadon, cons. engrs., Montreal, Que., Can., 1965-67, Rust Engring. Co., 1967-68; research asso. Sir George Williams U., Montreal, 1969-71; asst. prof. civil tech. U. Houston, 1971—. Mem. bd. edn. South Tex. Acad., Houston. Pier fellow Nat. Research Council Can., 1969-71. Registered profl. engr., Tex. Mem. Am., Tex. socs. civil engrs., Tex. Soc. Profl. Engrs., Corp. Profl. Engrs., Que. Contbr. articles profl. jours. Home: 5446 Cheena Dr Houston TX 77035

LAZZARI, PIETRO, painter, sculptor; b. Rome, Italy, May 15, 1898; s. Pietro and Maria (Glacomelli) L.; Master Artist, Ornamental Sch. of Rome, 1920; m. Evelyn Cohen, Dec. 1, 1934; 1 dau., Nina. Came to U.S., 1929, naturalized, 1936. Free-lance painter, sculptor; executed murals, fine arts sect. U.S. Treasury Dept., 1936-42; faculty Am. U., Washington, 1943-48; head art dept. Dumbarton Coll., Washington, 1948-50; instr. Corcoran Gallery Sch. Art, Washington, 1966-69; executed sculptured busts of Eleanor Roosevelt, Norman Thomas, Adlai Stevenson, Alexander Kerensky, Pope Paul VI; bronze monuments to Edward Miner Gallaudent, Walter Reuther; exhibited Mus. Modern Art, Whitney Mus. Am. Art, Met. Mus., Acad. Design, Venetian Biennial, Art Inst. Chgo., Musee National d'Art Moderne, Paris, Corcoran Gallery, Pa. Acad. Fine Arts, Parsons Gallery, N.Y.C.; represented permanent collections Am. U., Art Inst. Chgo., Corcoran Gallery, Howard U., Smithsonian Instn., Balt. Mus., Mus. Honolulu, Truman Library, Independence, Mo., San Francisco Mus., Franklin Delano Roosevelt Library, Hyde Park, Whitney Mus., Okla. Art Center, Library of Congress, Nat. Collection Fine Arts, Washington. Fulbright research fellow ancient art media, 1950; recipient prizes Ornamental Sch. Rome, Balt. Mus., Corcoran Gallery, Washington Water Color Soc. Developer of polychrome concrete. Home: 3609 Albemarle St NW Washington DC 20008

LE, NGOC-BOI, elec. engr.; b. Quang Nam, Vietnam, June 15, 1942; s. Dai and The Thi (Nguyen) L.; came to U.S., 1959; B.A., Rockhurst Coll., 1963; B.S., U. Mo., 1967; M.S., U. Tenn., 1973; m. Khanh Lam Pham, Aug. 30, 1969; children—Francoise G.P., Harrison Q.M. Instr., Army Lang. Sch., Monterey, Cal., 1964-66; elec. engr. TVA, Chattanooga, 1967—. Registered profl. engr., Tenn. Mem. I.E.E.E., Alpha Phi Omega. Home: 4201 Forest Plaza Dr Hixson TN 37343 Office: 1023 Chattanooga Bank Bldg TVA Chattanooga TN 37401

LEA, TOM, painter, writer; b. El Paso, Tex., July 11, 1907; s. Tom and Zola (Utt) L.; student Art Inst. Chgo., 1924-26; D.Litt., Baylor U., 1967; L.H.D., So. Methodist U., 1970; m. Sarah Catherine Dighton, July 14, 1938; 1 son, James Dighton. Mural painter, comml. artist, art tchr., Chgo., 1926-33; student in Italy, 1930, N.M., 1933-35; staff Lab. Anthropology, Santa Fe, 1933-35; muralist, easel painter, book illustrator, El Paso, 1936—, writer, 1947—; war corr. Life mag., 1941-46; executed murals pub. bldgs., El Paso, Washington, Dallas, Odessa, Tex., Pleasant Hill, Mo.; easel works represented Dallas Mus. Fine Arts, Life mag. World War II art, collection in Pentagon, also El Paso Mus. Art, pvt. collections. Recipient Distinguished Pub. Service medal for services as war corr. U.S. Navy, 1971. Author and illustrator: Peleliu Landing, 1945; The Brave Bulls, 1949; The Wonderful Country, 1952; The King Ranch, 2 vols., 1957; The Primal Yoke, 1960; The Hands of Cantu, 1964; A Picture Gallery, 1968. Address: 2401 Savannah St El Paso TX 79930

LEA, WALKER ALFRED, JR., physician; b. Port Arthur, Tex., July 31, 1924; s. Walker Alfred and Alice (Townsend) L.; A.A., Lamar Jr. Coll., Beaumont, Tex., 1947; B.S., Baylor U., 1949, M.D., 1954; m. Beverly Barbara Hayes, Dec. 27, 1947; children—Alfred Scott, Walker Alfred III, Jean Kristen. Intern Methodist Hosp., Tex. Med. Center, Houston, 1954-55; resident U. Mich. Hosp., Ann Arbor, 1955-58; clin. instr. U. Mich. Med. Sch., Ann Arbor, 1957-58; chmn. dept. dermatology Scott and White Clinic, Temple, Tex., 1958-69; practice medicine, specializing in dermatology, Waco, Tex., 1970—; mem. staff Hillcrest Hosp., 1970—, Providence Hosp., 1970—; cons. in dermatology G., C & S. F. Ry. Hosp., 1958-69, VA Hosp., Temple, 1962-69, vis. dermatologist Ft. Hood Army Hosp., 1960-69; attending dermatologist Cora Anderson Negro Hosp.; lectr. U. Tex. Postgrad. Sch. Medicine, Temple div., 1960-63, U. Tex. Grad. Sch. Biomed. Scis., Houston, 1964-67. Dir. First Fed. Savs. & Loan Assn., Waco. Trustee Scott and White Meml. Hosp., 1964-69 treas. 1964-67, 69, exec. com., 1964-69, sec., 1968; bd. dirs. Family Counseling Services Waco, Scott and White Employees Credit Union, 1964-66, Waco Symphony Assn., 1973—, Heart O'Tex. council Boy Scouts Am., 1970—; vice chmn exec. Chisholm Trail dist. Boy Scouts Am., 1963-64; bd. dirs. Temple United Fund, 1963, 65, 67-69, v.p., 1968; dir. Bell County Bd. Health, 1967-68, Scott, Sherwood and Brindley Edn. and Research Found.; bd. dirs. Cultural Activities Center, Inc., 1961-67, pres. bd. dirs., 1962-63. Served with AUS, 1943-45; ETO. Recipient Outstanding Citizen award Temple Jr. C. of C., 1963, Taub Internat. award for research in psoriasis, 1959. Diplomate Am. Bd. Dermatology. Fellow Am. Acad. Dermatology, Am. Soc. Geriatrics; mem. A.M.A., Tex. Med. Assn. (pres. 12th dist. soc. 1965), Bell County (pres. 1967), McLennan County med. socs., Soc. Investigative Dermatology, Tex. Dermatol. Assn., N.Y. Acad. Scis., Tex. Hist. Assn., Waco C. of C., Baylor U. Med., U. Mich. alumni assns., Baylor-Waco Found., Baylor U. Ex-Student Assn. (pres. 1972-73), Magna Charta Barons, S.A.R., Sigma Xi, Alpha Omega Alpha, Phi Sigma, Phi Sigma, Phi Theta Kappa, Phi Beta Pi. Presbyn. (chmn. bd. deacons). Mason (32 deg., K.T.), Rotarian (dir. temple 1961-64, 66-67, pres. 1962-63, trustee student scholarship found. 1964-69). Clubs: Bell County Baylor (pres. 1965, past dir.); Rigdwood Country; Hedonia; City (Waco). Contbr. articles to med. jours. Home: 5309 Lake Jackson St Waco TX 76710 Office: 1314 Austin Av Waco TX 76701

LEACH, DAN PAYTON, architect; b. Brooks, Ga., Oct. 30, 1931; s. Dan Payton and Viola (Smith) L.; B.S., Erskine Coll., 1953; B.Arch., Clemson U., 1962; postgrad. U. Tex., 1955-56; m. Mary Ann Kay, Jan. 8, 1951; children—Dan Payton, Donna Victoria. Architect firm James M. Hunt, Elberton, Ga., 1962-65, J. Harold Mack & Asso., Greenville, S.C., 1965—. Mem. Bd. Zoning, Elberton, 1962-65. Served with AUS, 1953-55. Mem. A.I.A. (pub. relations officer S.C. chpt.), Greenville Council Architects (pres.), Nat. Council Archtl. Registration Bd., Constrn. Specification Inst. (pres. chpt.), Nat. Guard Assn. Republican. Baptist. Elk, Lion. Home: Route No 7 Box 247 Grear SC 29651 Office: PO Box 1717 Greenville SC 29602

LEACH, GEORGE WEBSTER, banker; b. Tampa, Fla., Mar. 12, 1942; s. Gilbert de la Matyr and Elizabeth Louise (Webster) L.; B.S. in Bus. Adminstrn., U. Fla., 1964; student Banking Sch. of South, La. State U., 1968-70; m. Karen Marie Keller, Aug. 27, 1963; children—Robin, James, Jane, Anne. Computer operator Atlantic Bank of Tampa, 1964-65, asst. cashier, 1966-67, cashier, 1968-70, v.p., cashier, 1971—. Instr. Am. Inst. Banking, Tampa, 1969—. Mem. Data Processing Mgmt. Assn., Sigma Phi Epsilon (treas. 1959-60). Baptist (deacon 1972—). Kiwanian (treas. 1972-74). Home: 4512 Melrose St Tampa FL 33609 Office: 1506 S Dale Mabry Tampa FL 33609

LEACH, JOSEPH LEE, educator, author; b. Weatherford, Tex., May 2, 1921; s. Austin Felix and Eula Lee (Gose) L.; B.A., So. Methodist U., 1942; Ph.D., Yale, 1948; m. Dorothy Ann Stuart, June 5, 1958; children—Joseph Lee, Jonathan Stuart, Anne Stuart. Prof. English, U. Tex., El Paso, 1947—; prof. U. Ark., Fayetteville, 1957, European div. U. Md., 1957-58. Pres. Festival Theatre, El Paso, 1969, El Paso County Hist. Soc., 1961. Served with inf. AUS, 1946-47. U. Tex. Research grantee, 1969-70. Mem. Modern Lang. Assn. Am., Nat. Council Tchrs. English, Sierra Club (pres. El Paso group 1970-71), Pi Kappa Alpha. Republican. Episcopalian. Club: Yale. Author: The Typical Texan, 1952, Bright Particular Star, 1970. Co-editor: World Literature Written in English, 1969. Contbr. articles on history and English to scholarly publs. Home: 735 DeLeon St El Paso TX 79912

LEACH, LEON AARON, veterinarian; b. Providence, July 29, 1921; s. Hyman and Fannie L.; D.V.M., Middlesex U., 1944; m. Selma Jacobs, Nov. 20, 1947; children—Frederick Ellis, Harvey Irwin, Sharon Fae. Veterinarian Leach Animal Hosp., Portsmouth, Va., 1947-62, Kempsville (Va.) Vet. Clinic, 1962—, Rivershores Vet. Clinic, 1966-72. Pres. Lomar Realty Corp., Bole Realty Corp. Mem. United Fund; counselor Boy Scouts Am. Bd. dirs. Portsmouth Human Soc., 1946-55. Mem. Am. Vet. Med. Assn., Va. Vet. Assn., Tidewater Artificial Breeding Assn., Beta Beta Chi. Mason. Club: Temple Israel Mens (dir. 1965—). Home: 461 Hariton Court Norfolk VA 23505 Office: 5136 Princess Anne Rd Virginia Beach VA 23462

LEACH, MAURICE DERBY, JR., librarian, educator; b. Lexington, Ky., June 23, 1923; s. Maurice Derby and Sallie Eleanor (Woods) L.; A.B., U. Ky., 1945; B.L.S., U. Chgo., 1946; m. Virginia Stuart Baskett, Mar. 16, 1953; 1 dau., Sarah Stuart. Bibliographer, Dept. State, 1947-50; fgn. service officer Dept. State (USIS), vice consul, attache, Cairo and Alexandria, U.A.R., Beirut, Lebanon, 1950-59; chmn. dept. library sci. U. Ky., 1959-66; regional program officer Ford Found., Beirut, 1967-68; librarian, prof. Washington and Lee U., Lexington, Va., 1968—. Library adviser Nat. Library, Egypt, Lebanon and acad. libraries in Middle East. Served with AUS, 1948-49. Mem. English Speaking Union. Episcopalian. Rotarian. Club: Tri-Brook Country (Lexington, Va.). Contbr. articles to profl. jours. Home: 1 Courtland Center Lexington VA 24450

LEACH, PEMBROKE OSCAR, welding engr.; b. Chattanooga, Mar. 19, 1916; s. Lewis Charles and Olga Anna (Czarnowski) L.; student McCallie Sch., 1927-33; B.Chem. Engring., Tulane U., 1937; m. Margaret Alice Divine, Oct. 14, 1950; children—Laura Anna, Lewis Samuel, Margaret Williams. With Tenn. Electric Power Co., summers, 1935-36; chemist, trainee Lookout Oil & Refining Co., Chattanooga, 1937-39; chemist, foreman Chattanooga Glass Co., 1939-40; with Combustion Engring., Inc., 1941—, welding foreman, 1951-54, plant welding engr., 1954—; pres. L.C. Leach & Co., Chattanooga, 1954-56; pres. Reliable Engring., Inc., 1967—. Mem. Tulane U. Alumni Assn. (bd. dirs. 1969-72), Alpha Tau Omega. Episcopalian (lay reader 1960-70). Home: 1002 Ault Dr Chattanooga TN 37404 Office: Combustion Engring Inc 911 W Main St Chattanooga TN 37401 also Reliable Engring Inc 1002 Ault Dr Chattanooga TN 37404

LEACH, THOMAS RICHARD, agrl. engr.; b. Brownwood, Tex., Aug. 26, 1912; s. Grover Cleveland and Della B. (Jones) L.; grad. high sch.; m. Vivian Joyce Knight, Dec. 23, 1942; children—Richard Scott, Shirley (Mrs. Billy Charles Page), Carol (Mrs. John Scott Dismukes). Owner, mgr. Leach Bros. Mfg. Co., Brownwood, Tex., 1936—. Recipient Award of Merit, U-Haul Rental System, 1960. Mem. Brownwood C. of C. Patentee in field. Home: 3512 Austin Av Brownwood TX 76801 Office: 210 N Main Av Brownwood TX 76801

LEACH, WARREN BRUCE, JR., lawyer; b. Houston, July 29, 1926; s. Warren Bruce and Sadie (Warren) L.; LL.B., U. Tex., 1951; m. Mary Wilson, June 20, 1952; children—Betty, Barbara, Warren Bruce III, Brenda. Admitted to Tex. bar, 1951; practiced in Houston, 1953—; asst. county atty. Harris County, 1954-56; atty. Marathon Oil Co., Houston, 1956-67, div. atty., 1967—. Pres., Neighborhood Civic Club, 1958-59; P.T.A., 1960-61. Served with USMCR, 1944-46, 51-53. Mem. Am., Tex., Houston bar assns., Tex. Mfrs. Assn., Tex. Mid-Continent, N.M. oil and gas assns. Methodist. Rotarian (pres. chpt. 1965-66). Home: 810 Flint River St Houston TX 77024 Office: PO Box 3128 Houston TX 77001

LEADERS, WILLIAM MORGAN, chem. engr.; b. Holyoke, Mass., Mar. 18, 1916; s. William Henry and Anna Marie (Fournier) L.; B.S. in Chemistry, Ohio U., 1937; Ph.D., Mass. Inst. Tech., 1940; m. Dorothy Ellen Lint, June 26, 1959; children—William Henry II, Wayne Morgan, Carl Alan. Research chemist Swift & Co., 1941-45; chief chemist Anderson & Clayton Co., 1945-47; research chemist Union Carbide Corp., 1947-50; tech. dir. Mallinckrodt Chem. Works, 1950-59; tech. dir. nuclear fuels Spencer Chem. Co., 1959-62, Kerr-McGee Corp., 1962-71; project mgr. Uranium Recovery Corp., Mulberry, Fla., 1971—. Mem. Phi Beta Kappa, Sigma Xi. Mason. Patentee in field. Home: 4021 Carlisle Rd Lakeland FL 33803 Office: PO Box 765 Mulberry FL 33860

LEAGUE, RICHARD (DOUGLAS), educator; b. Chgo., May 19, 1927; s. Thomas Jefferson III and Gladys Elaine (MacFeely) L.; B.S. in Psychology, Northwestern U., 1951, M.A. in Lang. Pathology, 1952; Ph.D. in Psycholinguistics, U. Fla., 1966, postdoctoral fellow biolinguistics, 1966-68; postdoctoral fellow higher mental processes, U. Minn., 1968; m. Susan Irene Henderson, May 31, 1963; children—Richard Douglas, Thomas Jefferson IV, Charles Morris, Kristin Elizabeth. Manuscript scout Prentice Hall Inc., N.Y.C., 1952-53; indsl. contract specialist Marshall Field & Co., Chgo., 1953-56; lang. master rep. Ellamac Inc., also liaison McGraw-Hill Book Co., 1956-59; v.p., dir. Eloamac Inc., Chgo., 1959-63; mem. faculty U. Fla., Gainesville, 1966-72, asst. prof. Inst. Devel. Human Resources 1968-69; asso. prof. communication Fla. Tech. U., Orlando, 1972—. Chmn. bd. dirs. Tree of Life Press. Served with USNR, 1945-47. Mem. A.A.A.S., Am. Cleft Palate Assn., Am., Southeastern psychol. assns., Assn. Childhood Edn. Internat., Assn. Humanistic Psychology, Biofeedback Research Soc., Fla. Cleft Palate Assn., Psychonomic Soc., So. Soc. Philosophy and Psychology, Am. Speech and Hearing Assn., Southeastern Conf. Linguistics, Am. Optical Soc., Phi Delta Kappa. Author: Assessing Language Skills in Infancy, 1971; Psycholinguistic Matrices, 1973. Mem. editorial bd. Jour. Study Consciousness, 1972. Discoverer sci. prin. of nuclear thought transmission; inventor League projection, mercatorlike math. conception for psycholinguistic mapping of human mind. Home: 88 Tomoka Dr Oviedo FL 32765 Office: Fla Tech Univ Orlando FL 32816

LEAHY, ROBERT JAMES, mgmt. cons.; b. Monroe, Wis., Jan. 28, 1908; s. John H. and Anna (Kundert) L.; B.A., U. Wis., 1932, LL.B., 1935, postgrad., 1937-42, J.D., 1966; m. Neva Jean Gestland, July 1, 1936; children—Robert Gestland, James Wallace, John Lewis. Admitted to Wis. bar, 1935; with legal dept. S.C. Johnson & Son, Inc., Racine, Wis., 1946-52; mgr. tech. service Philip Morris, Inc., Richmond, Va., 1952-56; mng. dir. Philip Morris, Australia, Ltd., Melbourne, 1956-61, also dir.; pres. Benson & Hedges Can., Ltd., Brampton, Ont., 1961-67, vice chmn., 1967-69, cons., 1959—; v.p. Philip Morris Internat., N.Y.C., 1963-69; internat. cons. Robert Leahy & Assos., Richmond, 1969—. Vice pres. parents com. Rollins Coll., 1965-66. Served to lt. comdr. USNR, 1943-46. Mem. Am., Wis. bar assns., Am. Chem. Soc. Clubs: Chemists (N.Y.C.); St. George's Golf and Country (Toronto, Ont.); Victoria, Victoria Golf (Melbourne); Mt. Stephen (Montreal). Home: 208 Berkshire Rd Richmond VA 23221

LEAK, ROBERT E., state ofcl.; b. Charlotte, N.C., Sept. 15, 1934; s. James Pickett and Cornelia (Edwards) L.; B.S., Duke, 1956; M.S., U. Tenn., 1957; m. Martha Councill, Aug. 25, 1956; children—Robert E., James Councill. With Pan Am. Petroleum Co., Lafayette, La., 1957-59, Allied Securities Corp., Raleigh, N.C., 1961-62, Cameron Brown Mortgage Co., Raleigh, also Charlotte, 1962-64; with N.C. Dept. Conservation and Devel., Raleigh, 1959-61, 64—, adminstr. div. commerce and industry, 1964-71, dir. Office Indsl., Tourist and Community Resources, 1971—; mem. N.C. adv. council Small Bus. Adminstrn. Sec.-treas. N.C. Land Use Congress. Bd. dirs. Raleigh YMCA. Episcopalian (pres. men, lay reader). Mem. Am. Indsl. Devel. Council (dir., certified indsl. developer), Nat. Assn. State Devel. Agys. (v.p.), So. Indsl. Devel. Council, N.C. Indsl. Devel. Assn., So. Assn. State Devel. Agys. (pres., mem. indsl. devel. task force Coastal Plains Regional Commn.). Home: 4900 Rampart St Raleigh NC 27609 Office: Administration Bldg Raleigh NC 27611

LEAKE, WOODROW WILSON, govt. ofcl.; b. Rossville, Ga., Dec. 18, 1916; s. James W. and Bertha (Martin) L.; B.S.A., Berry Coll., 1937; postgrad. U. Tenn., 1937, U. Ga., 1938; m. 2d, Lana Mirzayants, Jan. 4, 1957; children—Donald James, Thomas Frank; children of previous marriage—Woodrow Wilson II, Frances Diane. Mgr., owner Leake's Dairy Farm, Chattanooga, 1937-41; supr. FHA, Cartersville, Rossville, Rome, Ga., 1941-47; agr. adviser Army Dept., Chonju, Korea, 1948-49; econ. adviser ECA, Seoul, Korea, 1949-50; agr. adviser, regional dir. ICA, Isfahan, Kerman, Meshed, Iran, 1951-56, chief agr. adviser, Dacca, East Pakistan, 1956-61, chief agrl. adviser, rural devel. officer AID, Blantyre, Nyasaland, 1961-64; chief extension adviser, dep. food and agr. officer AID, Lagos, Nigeria, 1964-66, agrl. specialist instnl. devel. div., Washington, 1966-70, agrl. officer Office North African Affairs, 1970—. Mem. Soc. Internat. Devel. Lion (pres. Dacca 1959-61). Home: 10303 Dickens Av Bethesda MD 20014 Office: AID Dept State Washington DC 20521

LEARD, TERRY SEARS, archtl. engring. and planning firm exec.; b. Hugo, Okla., Sept. 26, 1930; s. Wheeler R. and Katherine (Sears) L.; B.S. in Indsl. Engring., Okla. State U., 1953; m. Marilynn Webb, Aug. 4, 1951; children—Michael Wayne, Vicki Lynn. Sr. staff engr. Southwest Bell Telephone Co., Oklahoma City, 1953-59; project engr. Hudgins, Thompson & Ball, Oklahoma City, 1959-68, v.p., 1969-71, v.p., dir. aviation services div., 1971—; pres., Hudgins, Thompson, Ball Internat., Ltd., Oklahoma City, 1973—, also dir.; dir. Planning Assos., Inc., Project Planners, Inc., Interiors by the Assos., Hudgins, Thompson & Ball & Assos., Inc., Car Rentals, Inc., Profl. Equipment Co., Hudgins, Thompson, Ball Ark., Inc., Mid-Am. Engrs., Inc., Northwest Engrs., Inc. Bd. dirs. Oklahoma City Beautiful, Jr. Achievement Greater Oklahoma City. Served with USAF, 1954-56. Registered profl. engr., Okla. Mem. Cons. Engrs. Council, Nat. Soc. Profl. Engrs., Am. Assn. Airport Execs., Am. Inst. Indsl. Engrs. (dir. 1962-67, Distinguished Service award), Oklahoma City C. of C. (com. chmn. 1970-72). Home: 3117 Briarwood Bethany OK 73008 Office: PO Box 1845 Oklahoma City OK 73101

LEARY, JOSEPH RIVE, JR., osteo. physician; b. Tampa, Fla., July 21, 1908; s. Joseph Robert and Sara (Jones) L.; D.O., Kirksville Coll. Osteopathy, 1930; m. Mary Alice Coppinger, Jan. 1, 1934; children—Alice Patricia Ann (Mrs. C.B. Miller), Joseph Rive III, Elizabeth Roberta (Mrs. William E. Pinder). Technician x-ray dept. Jackson Meml. Hosp., Miami, Fla., 1930-35, Dade County Hosp., Kendell, Fla., 1936-37; x-ray diagnostic practice, Ferguson-McCormick Clinic, Miami, 1937-41; practice medicine, specializing in X-ray diagnosis, Miami, Coral Gables, Fla., 1941—; chief dept. radiology Osteo. Gen. Hosp., North Miami Beach, Fla., 1962—; radiologist N.W. Hosp., Miami; x-ray cons. to gen. practioners. Active Boy Scouts Am., Fla. Civil Def. Mem. Am. Osteo. Assn., Divisional X-ray Soc., Pan-Am. Cancer Cytology Soc., Fla. Soc. Applied Osteopathy, Fla. (1st v.p.) Dade County (hon. life mem., past pres.) osteo.-med. assns., Internat. Platform Assn., Sigma Sigma Phi. Baptist (deacon). Club: Atlas. Home: 2332 SW Fifth St Miami FL 33129 Office: Osteopathic Gen Hosp 1750 NE 167th St North Miami Beach FL 33161

LEAS, A. ROBERT, gas co. exec.; b. Marion, Ind., Mar. 1, 1905; s. Charles Francis and Purlena May (Patterson) L.; ed. pvt. sch.; m. Hazel Louise Miller, Sept. 29, 1929 (dec. Oct. 1964); 1 dau., Hazel Roberta. Pres., Navgas, Inc., Washington, 1960—; pres., dir. Nat. Projects Devel. Corp.; cons. petroleum econs. Mem. Am. Petroleum Inst., Am. Inst. Mining Engrs., Am. Mil. Engrs., Nat. Assn. Corrosion Engrs. Mason (Shriner), Elk. Clubs: Explorers, Kenwood Country. Home: 1711 Massachusetts Av NW Washington DC 20036 Office: 1875 Connecticut Av NW Washington DC 20009

LEASE, FRANCES VICTORIA (MRS. GILLIAN CHARLES LEASE), librarian; b. Lufkin, Tex., Sept. 15, 1918; d. Aurelius Nash and Minnie Emma (Cockroft) Hogue; B.A., Baylor U., 1939; B.S. in L.S., George Peabody Coll. for Tchrs., 1940; m. Gillian Charles Lease, Jan. 23, 1944; children—Agnes (Mrs. Richard Michael Scibelli), Linda (Mrs. Robert Bernard Nelson), Laura. Librarian, Marfa (Tex.) High Sch., 1940-44, Meml. Jr. High Sch., Kingsville, Tex., 1951-53, Premont (Tex.) High Sch., 1955-56, Gillett Jr. High Sch., Kingsville, 1956—. Mem. Tex. (chmn. dist. library sect. 1969-70), Coastal Bend, Am. library assns., Am. Assn. U. Women (v.p. br. 1965-67), Kingsville Bus. and Profl. Women's Club, Delta Kappa Gamma. Baptist. Club: Woman's (Kingsville). Home: 730 Shelton St Kingsville TX 78363 Office: Box 871 Kingsville TX 78363

LEASE, GOLDEN RICHARD, constrn. co. exec.; b. Plainville, Ill., June 10, 1908; s. Henry Woodrow and Lucinda (Cook) L.; student U. Chgo., 1930-33, So. Meth. U., 1957-59; m. Zella Mae Long, Sept. 4, 1926 (dec.); 1 step-son, Bert E. Phillips; children—Marcella June (Mrs. William R. Curry), Richard Wayne. Payroll and cost accountant J.M. Meltezer Co., N.Y.C., 1931-33; asst. shipping clk. Moorman Mfg. Co., Quincy, Ill., 1934-38; asst. to controller Bechtel-McCone-Parsons, Inc., Birmingham, Ala., 1939-45; mgr., officer, dir. Harman Elec. Constrn. Corp., Dallas, 1946—; sec.-treas., dir. Equipment Rental Corp. Div. mgr. Dallas United Fund, 1957-68. Mem. Cost Accountants Assn. Am., Photog. Assn. Am., So. Meth. U. Alumni Assn. Methodist (mem. ofcl. bd.). Home: 4520 Livingston Av Dallas TX 75205 Office: 4311 Belmont St Dallas TX 75204

LEASENDALE, FRANK OTTO, trucking co. exec.; b. Jersey City, May 15, 1921; s. F. Otto and Lydia (Klix) L.; student Clemson Coll., 1942-43; B.Sc., N.Y. U., 1950, M.B.A., 1955; m. Mildred E. Schlenger, June 12, 1949; children—Nancy, Jeffrey. Chief accountant Gen. Aniline & Film Corp., N.Y.C., 1939-64; mgr. corporate accounting Prentice-Hall, Inc., Englewood Cliffs, N.J., 1964-66; treas. Volkswagen North Central Distbr., Inc., Deerfield, Ill., 1966-69; v.p., treas. Burnham Van Services Inc., Columbus, Ga., 1969—. Instr. budgets and forecasting Coll. City N.Y., 1955-57. Served with AUS, 1942-45. Mem. Nat. Assn. Accountants, Assn. U.S. Army, N.Y. U. Alumni Assn., Am. Trucking Assn., Infantry Museum Assn. Presbyn. (elder). Kiwanian. Club: Green Island Country. Home: 5945 Sherborne Dr Columbus GA 31904

LEATHERBURY, JOHN RAYMOND, JR., elec. engr.; b. Balt., June 22, 1942; s. John Raymond and Hester Louise (Hoffecker) L.; B.S. in E.E., U. Tex., 1965; postgrad. Tex. Christian U., 1968. Jr. engr. Phillips Pipe Line Co., Bartlesville, Okla., 1965-66; jr. engr. Tex. Electric Service Co., Fort Worth, 1966-67, asso. elec. engr., 1967—. Mem. scholarship com. David W. Leatherbury Meml. Scholarship, 1968—. Mem. I.E.E.E. Episcopalian. Clubs: Steeplechase, River Crest Country (Fort Worth). Home: 2420 College Av Fort Worth TX 76110 Office: Box 970 Fort Worth TX 76101

LEATHERWOOD, MICHAEL DAVID, basketball coach, educator; b. Century, Fla., Sept. 30, 1947; s. Malcolm David and Jane Carol (Brown) L.; A.A., Pensacola Jr. Coll., 1967; B.S. in Phys. Edn., U. Fla., 1969, M.S. in Phys. Edn., 1970; m. Carolyn De Lucia, July 30, 1973. Grad. asst. U. Fla., varsity basketball, Gainesville, 1969-70; head basketball coach Indian River Jr. Coll., Ft. Pierce, Fla., 1970—. Mem. Am. Assn. U. Profs. Home: 2707 Virginia Av Apt 9 Fort Pierce FL 33450 Office: 3209 Virginia Av Fort Pierce FL 33450

LEAVELL, BYRD STUART, physician, educator; b. Washington, Dec. 29, 1910; s. Byrd and Lucie (Browning) L.; B.S., Va. Mil. Inst., 1931; M.D., U. Va., 1935; m. Nancy Butzner, Oct. 7, 1939; children—Anne (Mrs. Herbert Reynolds), Lucie (Mrs. Scott Vogel), Byrd Stuart Jr. Intern, N.Y. Hosp., N.Y.C., 1935-36, asst. resident, 1936-38; practice medicine, specializing in internal medicine, Charlottesville, Va., 1946—; prof. medicine U. Va. Sch. Medicine, 1954—, chmn. dept. internal medicine, 1966-68, asst. dean Sch. Medicine, 1958-61, head div. hematology, 1945-70. Served to maj. M.C., AUS, 1942-46. Decorated Bronze Star medal. Mem. A.M.A., A.C.P., Internat., Am. socs. hematology, A.A.A.S., So. Soc. Clin. Investigation, Am. Clin. and Climatological Assn., Kappa Alpha, Alpha Omega Alpha, Omicron Delta Kappa. Episcopalian. Clubs: Colonnade (pres. 1960), Farmington Country (Charlottesville). Author: The 8th Evac., 1970; (with O. A. Thorup) Fundamentals of Clinical Hematology, 3d edit., 1971. Home: Box 229 Route 2 Charlottesville VA 22901

LEAVITT, MARY JANICE DEIMEL (MRS. ROBERT WALKER LEAVITT), educator; b. Washington, Aug. 21, 1924; d. Henry L. and Ruth (Grady) Deimel; B.A., Am. U., Washington, 1946; postgrad. U. Md., 1963-65, U. Va., 1965-67, George Washington U., 1966-67; m. Robert Walker Leavitt, Mar. 30, 1945; children—Michael Deimel, Robert Walker, Caroline Ann. Tchr., Rothery Sch., Arlington, Va., 1947; dir. Sunnyside, Children's House, Washington, 1949; asst. dir. Coop. Sch. for Handicapped Children, Arlington, 1962, dir., Arlington, Springfield, Va., 1963-66; tchr. mentally retarded children Fairfax (Va.) County Pub. Schs., 1966-68; asst. dir. Burgundy Farm Country Day Sch., Alexandria, Va., 1968-69; tchr. specific learning problem children Accotink Acad., Springfield, Va., 1970—, now substitute tchr.; also substitute tchr. Children's Achievement Center, McLean, Va. Den mother Nat. Capital Area Cub Scouts, Boy Scouts Am., 1962; troop fund raising chmn. Nat. Capitol council Girl Scouts U.S.A., 1968-69; capt. amblyopia team No. Va. chpt. Delta Gamma Alumnae, 1969, mem. edn. subcom. Va. Comm. Children and Youth, 1973—. Mem. Am. Assn. U. Women (co-chmn. met. area mass media com. 1973-75), Council Exceptional Children, Audubon Naturalist Soc. Central Atlantic States, Delta Gamma (treas. alumnae chpt. 1973-75). Roman Catholic. Club: Arlington Hall Officer's Wives. Home: 4902 Larno Dr Alexandria VA 22301 Office: 8519 Tuttle Rd West Springfield VA 22152

LEBLANC, CLIFFORD HARRIS, machine co. exec.; b. Franklin, La., Nov. 25, 1905; s. Clebert Joseph and Louise (Harris) LeB.; student La. State U., 1925-26, U. Ala., 1926-27; m. Eunice Estella Thompson, Feb. 2, 1930; children—Clifford Harris and George Thompson (twins), Judith Marie. Draftsman, Almo Iron Works, Houston, 1928-32; chief engr. Gulf Coast Machine & Supply Co., Beaumont, Tex., 1933, sec. bd. dirs., 1934-42, v.p., 1943-49, exec. v.p., gen. mgr., 1950-54, pres., gen. mgr., 1955—; chmn. bd. Lemac, Inc., El Campo, Tex.; pres. Gulfco Mfg. Ltd., Edmonton, Alta., Can., Indsl. Lands, Inc., Beaumont; v.p. Tyrrell Hardware Co.; dir. Village State Bank, Beaumont. Gen. campaign chmn. United Appeals Bd. Trustees, 1958, pres., 1959; charter mem. Tex. Big Thicket Com., 1964—; gen. chmn. Beaumont Tb. Christmas Seal Campaign, 1967; mem. Jefferson County Hwy. Com., 1967—; mem. adv. council Small Bus. Adminstrn. of U.S., 1967-68; met. chmn. Golden Triangle Area, Nat. Alliance Businessmen, 1971—. Mayor, Beaumont, 1960-62. Pres., Sabine Dist. Transp. Club, 1942, Young Mens Bus. League, 1947, pres. Key Mens Club, 1949, Camp Fire Girls Assn., 1952; v.p. Port Commn. Jefferson County, 1949-60; bd. dirs. U.S. Selective Service Bd. North Jefferson County, 1946-71, Neches River Festival, Trinity Neches council Boy Scouts Am., 1945-55, Jr. Achievement Golden Triangle, S.E. Tex. Health Found., 1970-72. Recipient Selective Service citation for 20 years continuous service Selective Service Bd. North Jefferson County, 1967, Neches River Festival Ann. Community Progress award, 1966-67, Leadership Progress award Beaumont C. of C., 1966. Mem. Am. Petroleum Inst., Mid-Continent Oil and Gas Assn., Tex. Mfg. Assn. (life), N.A.M., Beaumont (v.p. 1959), East Tex. (dir. 1969), Sabin Neches (council) chambers commerce, Sales and Marketing Execs. Club Beaumont (pres. 1963-64), Southwestern Sales and Marketing Execs. Council (pres. 1966). Episcopalian. Lion. Clubs: Beaumont, Beaumont Country, Business and Professional Mens, Pinewood Country. Home: 1425 Infinity Lane Beaumont TX 77706 Office: PO Box 1914 Beaumont TX 77704

LEBLANC, PAUL EURBY, telephone co. exec.; b. LeRoy, La., Mar. 28, 1925; s. Efis and Lucy (Comeaux) L.; student, Schriener Inst., 1946-47; B.S. in Elec. Engring., U. Tex., 1950; postgrad. U. Kan., 1965, N.Y. U., 1969; m. Billie Ruth Hunt, Sept. 3, 1949; children—Kent, Lisa. With Gen. Telephone Co., 1950—, div. mgr., v.p. staff, v.p. area devel., Tampa, Fla., 1966—. Pres., Tampa World Trade Council, 1973—; chmn. Fla. Coll. Fund drive, 1973; co-ordinator WEDU-TV Auction, Tampa, 1969; chmn. Tampa United Fund drive, 1974, mem. planning com. 1972—, dir., mem. exec. com., 1974—; coordinator Tampa Bay area Internat. Air Service Task Force, 1971—; co-chmn. U. S. Fla. Picasso drive, Tampa; coordinator Boy Scout drive, Tampa, 1973-74; mem. St. Joseph Hosp. Devel. Council, Tampa, Fla., 1969—. Chmn. bd. counselors U. Tampa, Forward Fund drive, 1974—, mem. devel. com. 1972—; trustee MacDonald Tng. Center; bd. dirs. A.R.C. Served with USAAF, 1943-46. Mem. So. Indsl. Devel. Council, Fla. Indsl. Council, Ind. Telephone Pioneer Assn., Com. of 100, Tampa Com. on Fgn. Relations, C. of C. of Ams. (ambassador at large 1971—), U.S. C. of C. (mem. edn. and man power devel. com. 1972—), Greater Tampa C. of C. (energy information council), Phi Theta Kappa. Republican. Roman Catholic. Rotarian (dir. 1967). Clubs: Univ. (Tampa); Palma Ceia Golf and Country, Temple Terrace (Fla.) Golf and Country. Home: 333 Fern Cliff Temple Terrace FL 33617 Office: 610 Morgan St Box 100 Tampa FL 33601

LEBO, DELL, psychologist; b. N.Y.C., Aug. 6, 1922; s. Dell Roy and Marguerite (Bruneel) L.; B.A. cum laude, N.Y. U., 1949; M.A., Fla. State U., 1951, Ph.D., 1956; m. Elaine Pauline Larsen, July 1, 1949; 1 dau., Lea. Asso. prof. Coll. of William and Mary, Richmond, Va., 1955-59; chief psychologist Child Guidance Clinic, Jacksonville, Fla., 1959—; pvt. practice psychol. counseling, Jacksonville, 1959—; sr. psychologist Gender Identity Assn., Jacksonville, 1967—. Community staff mem. Jacksonville Mag., 1972—; lectr. indsl. psychology C. of C., Jacksonville, 1963—. Field rep. Personnel Data Systems, 1967—. Mem. profl. adv. com. Fla. Found. for the Handicapped, Jacksonville, 1972—. Served with USAAF, 1942-45; ETO. Mem. Fla. (historian 1971—), N.E. Fla. (pres. 1962, 66-67) psychol. assns., Arcane Order (founder, preceptor 1950—), C. of C. (com. mem. supervisory tng. program 1969—), Internat. Assn. Torch Clubs (dir. 1970-72). Contbr. numerous articles in field to profl. jours. Home: 5340 Weller Av Jacksonville FL 32211 Office: Child Guidance Clinic 1635 St Paul Av Jacksonville FL 32207

LEBOWITZ, MORTIMER CHARLES, retail co. exec.; b. N.Y.C., Mar. 18, 1912; s. Henry I. and Esther (Roth) L.; A.B., U. Pa., 1932; student N.Y.U. Law Sch., 1933-35; m. Adele Gusack, June 4, 1940; children—John William, Emily (Mrs. Richard Olbrich), Caroline (Mrs. Richard Simon), Petrina (Mrs. Walter Locke). Buyer, The Mart, Paterson, N.J., 1933-35; founder, pres. Morton's, Washington, 1935—. Bd. dirs. Washington Urban League, 1956—, pres., 1960-61; chmn. Washington Commn. Human Resources, 1962-71; chmn. inner city com. Nat. Capital area council Boy Scouts Am., 1967—, mem. Nat. council, 1970—, mem. interim bicentennial com., 1971—. Trustee Va. Coll.; bd. overseers Coll. V.I.; bd. dirs. Center Met. Studies, 1961-71. Recipient Human Relations award Capitol Press Club, 1961; Merit award D.C. C. of C., 1962; Equal Opportunity Day award, 1963, 67; Silver Beaver award Boy Scouts Am., 1968. Mem. D.C. Bd. Trade, D.C. Retail Bur., Am. Jewish Com., Alpha Phi Omega, Tau Epsilon Phi. Mem. B'nai B'rith. Home: 6319 Georgetown Pike McLean VA 22101 Office: 310 6th St S Arlington VA 22202

LEBRON, AMARYLLIS VELILLA (MRS. RAMON CLEMENTE LEBRON), b. San Juan, P.R., July 24, 1937; d. Rafael and Dolores Urrutia (Vega) Velilla; B.B.A., U. P.R., 1958; postgrad. P.R. Inst. Statistics, 1958-65, P.R. Sch. Pub. Health, 1967-69, P.R. Grad. Sch. Pub. Adminstrn., 1971—; m. Ramon Clemente Lebron, Dec. 15, 1962; children—Vanessa, Amaryllis, Ramon Clemente. Statistician II, Bur. Labor Statistics, Dept. Labor, 1958-60, statistician

III, 1960-62; statistician, Caribbean Orgn., 1962-64; statistician IV Office Sci. Research, Dept. Health, 1965-67, statistician V, statistics and econs. studies sect., Planning Research and Evaluation Office, 1967-72; program analyst I, Bur. Budget, Office Gov., San Juan, P.R., 1972-73, program analyst II, 1973—. Pres. pub. relations com. Comprehensive Health Planning Week, 1971; coordinator pharmacy com. State Bd. Health, 1969-71, asst. of exec. dir., 1969-71. Active P.T.A., Al-Anon. Recipient Scholarship, Govt. P.R., 1954. Mem. Am. Statis. Assn. (chpt. sec. P.R. chpt. 1971—), P.R. Statis. Soc. (sec. 1970-71). Home: 1 L-19 Nogal Av Royal Palms Bayamon PR 00619 Office: Bur Budget Office Gov PR Fortaleza St San Juan PR 00904

LECKY, WILLIAM RALSTON III, elec. engr.; b. Richmond, Va., July 8, 1940; s. William Ralston and Allene (Pace) L.; B.S. in Elec. Engring., Va. Poly. Inst., 1963; m. Susan Evans Hearn, June 6, 1964; children—Jennifer Jill, Kathryn Pace, Susan Arrington. Asso. engr., plant engring. Mobile (Ala.) Mill, Internat. Paper Co., 1963-64, project engr., 1966-68, sr. project engr., central design engring., 1968-74, design engr., 1974—. Adviser, Jr. Achievement, 1967-68; active United Fund Canvass, 1971-72; v.p. Mobile Soap Box Derby, Inc., 1972-73. Bd. dirs. Greater Gulf State Fair, Inc., 1972-74, chief engr., mgr. constrn. new fair grounds, 1973. Served to 1st lt. AUS, 1964-66. Registered profl. engr., Ala. Mem. I.E.E.E. (sect. treas. 1971-72, sec. 1972-73, vice chmn. 1973-74), Va. Tech. Alumni Assn., Mobile Jr. C. of C. (sec. 1971-72), Omicron Delta Kappa. Mem. Christian Ch. Home: 5564 William and Mary St Mobile AL 36608 Office: PO Box 2328 Mobile AL 36601

LECLAIR, HUGH GRENVILLE, waste treatment equipment co. exec.; b. Chgo., Nov. 30, 1925; s. Titus George and Alice (Bessee) L.; B.S. in Sci. and Math., U. Mich., 1949, M.S. in Chemistry, 1950; Ph.D. in Chemistry, Harvard, 1954; m. Mary Margaret Dodson, Sept. 1, 1948; children—Kristin Lee, Lewis Titus, Lise Ann, Mary Elizabeth. Teaching fellow U. Mich. at Ann Arbor, 1948-50; research chemist E.I. DuPont de Nemours, Buffalo, 1953-56; v.p. Lewis Dodson Engring. Co., Amarillo, Tex., 1956-66; pres. Triple F. Controls, Inc., Amarillo, 1966—. Mem. Panhandle Regional Planning Commn., Amarillo, 1970—, chmn. environmental com., 1970-74. Bd. dirs. Amarillo Symphony, 1961-62. Served with USNR, 1944-46. Mem. Water Pollution Control Fedn., Am. Water Works Assn., Tex. Water Utilities Assn., Sigma Xi, Phi Beta Kappa, Phi Kappa Phi, Phi Eta Sigma. Episcopalian (mem. vestry bd., del. to diocesan council, sec. diocesan liturgical commn. 1968-74). Club: Amarillo Country. Home: 3206 Hawthorne St Amarillo TX 79109 Office: PO Box 1260 Amarillo TX 79105

LECROY, JAMES ALVIN, communications engr.; b. Maplesville, Ala., Apr. 19, 1936; s. James William and Ethel Inez (Mize) LeC.; B.S. in Elec. Engring., Auburn U., 1958; certificate Bell System regional sch., Clemson U., 1965; postgrad. Samford U., 1971-73; m. Marcia Jann Pitts, Aug. 31, 1958; 1 son, Scott Whitfield. Communications engr. So. Central Bell Telephone Mobile, Ala., 1963-64, Birmingham, Ala., 1964—. Mem. adminstrv. com., pack 26, Birmingham council Cub Scouts Am., 1968-69. Served to 1st lt. Signal Corps, AUS, 1959-62. Named Young Engr. of Year, Nat. Assn. Corrosion Engrs., 1970. Registered profl. engr., Ala. Mem. I.E.E.E., Scabbard and Blade, Theta Chi, Pi Tau Pi Sigma. Baptist (deacon 1966—, Sunday sch. dir. 1966-69, instr. tchr. tng. 1969—). Home: 1408 67th St W Birmingham AL 35228 Office: 600 N 19th St Birmingham AL 35201

LECROY, JAMES FRANKLIN, govt. ofcl.; b. Chattanooga, Mar. 16, 1928; s. John Prior and Ruby Isabella Matilda (Duncan) L.; student George Washington U., 1946-49, 51-52, U. Va., 1962-69, Upper Ia. U., 1973; m. Jackie Blount, Feb. 27, 1955; children—James Lynn, Judy Gail, Jackie Marie, Jenny. Cartographic aid Aero. Chart Bur., USAF, Washington, 1948; phys. scientist aide U.S. Navy, David Taylor Model Basin, Washington, 1948-49, aero. engring. aide, 1950-53; with Metall. Research Lab., Combustion Engring. Co., Chattanooga, 1953-55; project adminstr. fixed wing and convertiplane devel. U.S. Army Chief of Transp., Washington, 1955-56; multiple line ins. agt. State Farm Ins. Co., Alexandria, Va., 1956; devel. engr. Capital Airlines, Washington, 1956-60; aero. engr. United Airlines, Washington, 1960-66; supervisory aerospace engr., asst. project mgr. logistics Naval Air Systems Command Hdqrs., Washington, 1966-69, supervisory aerospace engr., supr. targets, drones, ground electronics and range instrumentation, 1969—. Mem. West Springfield (Va.) Civic Assn., 1965—. Served with USNR, 1949-50. Registered profl. engr., Vt. Recipient Sustained Superior Performance award U.S. Navy, 1973, 74, Award for Invention Disclosure, 1973. Mem. Nat., Va. (dir. Fairfax chpt. 1971-72, membership com. 1973-74) socs. profl. engr., Assn. of Naval Weapon's Scientists and Engrs. (award 1974), Tau Kappa Epsilon, Theta Tau. Methodist (mem. ofcl. bd. 1958—, chmn. builders club 1972-74). Inventor Laser Firing Error Indicator Vector Scoring System. Home: 6406 Charnwood St Springfield VA 22152 Office: Naval Air Systems Command Hdqrs Code Air-41043 Navy Dept Washington DC 20360

LEDBETTER, CHARLES ROLAND, lawyer; b. Ft. Smith, Ark., Mar. 25, 1938; s. John H. and Mary Ethel (Reeves) L.; A.B. in Econs. and Physics, Hendrix Coll., 1960; LL.B., U. Ark., 1963, J.D., 1970; m. Doria Jean Fitzgerald, June 27, 1965; 1 dau., Jennifer Lynn. Admitted to Supreme Ct. Ark. bar, 1963; research asst. U.S. Dist. Judge John Miller, Ft. Smith, 1963-65; sr. partner firm Shaw & Ledbetter, Ft. Smith, 1966—; atty. First Nat. Bank, Ft. Smith, Mansfield Bank, Standard Fed. Savs. and Loan Assn. Mem. Hendrix Coll. Alumni Bd. Govs., 1971—. Bd. dirs. Ft. Smith Art Center. Mem. Am. Bar assn. (chmn. Ark. pub. relations sect. 1969—, chmn. creditors rights sect. 1973-74), Phi Alpha Delta. Methodist. Home: 7800 Dover Circle Fort Smith AR 72901 Office: 212 Mchts Bank Fort Smith AR 72901

LEDBETTER, ROBERT HARBIN, constrn. co. exec.; b. Rome, Ga., Sept. 24, 1935; s. Allison W. and Rosa (Harbin) L.; grad. Darlington Sch., 1953, Culver Mil. Acad., 1954; B.S., Ga. Inst. Tech., 1958; m. Betty D. Wright, Jan. 19, 1963; children—Robert Harbin, Ernest Wright, David Dandridge. Vice pres., dir. Ledbetter Bros., Inc., Rome, 1960-70, pres., dir., 1970—; chmn. Network Bldg. Systems, Inc., Am. Concrete Co.; pres., dir. Sandalwood Corp.; pres. LBI Quarries, Inc.; v.p., dir. Ledbetter Trucks, Inc.; v.p. Lloyds of Rome, Inc.; dir., mem. exec. com. Chesapeake Internat. Corp.; dir. Echota Realty Co., Rome, Shorter Realty Co., Atlanta Hockey, Inc., Ledbetter Indsl. Devel., Coliseum Promotions, Inc. Bd. dirs. Boys Club Rome. Served to lt. (j.g.) USNR, 1958-60. Mem. Nat. Asphalt Pavement Assn., Asso. Gen. Contractors Am., Ala. Rome Builders Assn., Ga. Hwy. Contractors Assn. (dir., mem. exec. com., 1st v.p.), Am. Road Builders Assn. (dir. contractors div.), Ga. Asphalt Pavement Assn. (dir. 1965—, mem. exec. com., past pres.), Carolina Asphalt Pavement Assn. (dir.), Rome C. of C., S.A.R., Sigma Alpha Epsilon. Presbyn. Clubs: Coosa Country (Rome); Commerce (Atlanta). Home: 1121 Kingston Rd Rome GA 30161 Office: 2 W 2d Av Rome GA 30161

LEDFORD, CLAUDE JENNINGS, bank exec.; b. Sevier County, Tenn., Jan. 30, 1925; s. William Floyd and Mae Rachel (Green) L.; B.S., U. Tenn., 1950; grad. Banking Sch. La. State U., 1972; m. Mabel Joseph, Nov. 26, 1953; children—Linda Gay, Joseph Allen. Office mgr. Beneficial Finance Co., Atlanta, 1953-57; v.p., dir. operations Universal Finance Co., Dallas, 1957-66; exec. v.p. Bank of Morristown (Tenn.), 1966—. Dir., sec. Horner Hardware, Inc., 1970—, Woodbendings, Inc., 1973—. Mem. indsl. devel. bd. City of Morristown, Tenn., 1968—, sec. health and ednl. facilities bd., 1970—; mem. indsl. devel. bd. State of Tenn., 1970-74. Bd. dirs. Boys Club, 1970—. Served with AUS, 1943-45. Recipient Silver Star medal. Mem. V.F.W., D.A.V., Morristown C. of C. (dir. 1969-71). Elk, Kiwanian (v.p., treas. 1968-72). Home: 1107 Meadowlark Dr Morristown TN 37814 Office: 1112 W 1st N St Morristown TN 37814

LEDFORD, DEWEY CARL, elec. engr.; b. Cleveland, Tenn., Nov. 8, 1933; s. Canary Bascom and Pauline Anne (Harrison) L.; B.S. in Elec. Engring., U. Tenn., 1960; postgrad. U. Ala., Birmingham, 1969-72; m. Genevieve Fletcher, June 25, 1961; children—Andrew Carl, Darrin Charles, Elizabeth Geneen. Elec. engr. Bowaters Corp., Calhoun, Tenn., 1960-62; elec. engr., project engr., supr. maintenance services Olin Corp., Charleston, Tenn., 1962-68; plant engr. ITT Continental Baking Co., Concord, N.C., 1968-69; elec. engr. Rust Engring. Co., Birmingham, Ala., 1969-72; plant engr. Cutter Labs., Inc., Chattanooga, 1972—. Adviser Jr. Achievement; asst. cubmaster Birmingham area council Boy Scouts Am. Served with USAF, 1952-56. Mem. Am. Inst. Plant Engrs., Tenn. Soc. Profl. Engrs., Cleveland (Tenn.) Creative Arts Guild, Delta Sigma Phi. Home: 3409 Betty Lane Chattanooga TN 37412 Office: 1800 Crutchfield St Chattanooga TN 37406

LEDFORD, JOHN BYRON, clergyman; b. Cadiz, Ky., Jan. 20, 1943; s. James Sidney and Inez Thelma (Cunningham) L.; student Western Ky. U., 1962-65; B.S., Austin Peay State U., 1966; M.Div., Lexington Theol. Sem., 1969; m. Carolyn Cox Ledford, Aug. 6, 1966; children—Jeffrey William, Lisa Deanne. Ordained to ministry Christian Ch., 1969; asso. minister Central Christian Ch., Orlando, Fla., 1969-71; minister Central Christian Ch., Bradenton, Fla., 1971—. Chmn. com. on evangelism and renewal Fla. Christian Chs., mem. regional bd. Chmn. clergy div. United Appeal Orlando, 1971; chmn. religious activities Multiple Sclerosis campaign, Orange County, 1971. Bd. dirs. Manatee County Meals on Wheels. Served as chaplain AUS. Mem. Manatee County Ministerial Assn. (v.p. 1973-74), Ministers Fla. Christian Chs. (pres. 1973-74). Kiwanian. Home: 3804 17th Av W Bradenton FL 33505 Office: 926 15th St W Bradenton FL 33505

LEDFORD, THERON R., pub. relations cons., writer; b. Gainesville, Ga., July 30, 1931; s. Theron Clifton and Nell Rose (Robertson) L.; A.B. magna cum laude, Mercer U., 1954; m. Carol Deane Williams, Dec. 23, 1962; children—Laurie Dianne, Anna Robertson. With pub. relations dept. Ga. Hwy. Dept., Atlanta, 1958-70; free-lance writer, pub. relations cons., Gainesville, 1970—. Served with AUS, 1954-56. Mem. Pub. Relations Soc. Am., Alpha Tau Omega. Baptist (Sunday sch. tchr., dir. intermediate tng. union). Contbr. articles to various publs. Home: 790 Park St Gainesville GA 30501 Office: PO Box 744 Gainesville GA 30501

LEDFORD, WILLIAM LESTER, elec. engr.; b. Cleve., Sept. 12, 1935; s. Canary Bascom and Annie Pauling (Harrison) L.; B.S., U. Tenn., 1959; postgrad. U. Utah, 1961-62; m. Martha Sue Cunningham, Nov. 12, 1960; children—John William, Benjamin James. Elec. engr. trainee TVA, Nashville, 1959-60, Chattanooga, 1962-63, elec. engr., Bowling Green, Ky., 1964-65, Paradise, Ky., 1966-69, Muscle Shoals, Ky., 1970—. Served with Chem. Corps, AUS, 1960-62. Mem. I.E.E.E., Engrs. Assn., Nat. Soc. Profl. Engrs. Baptist (treas. 1962, tchr. 1960-69). Home: 1027 Piedmont St Florence AL 35630

LEDOUX, JACK, author, ret. race track exec.; b. Orlando, Fla., Oct. 4, 1928; s. Leonard K. and Louise (Downs) L.; B.S. in Journalism, U. Fla., 1950; m. Geraldine C. Collins, Sept. 12, 1949; children—Michele, Lance, Stephen, Lola. Sportswriter, columnist Orlando Sentinel-Star, 1948-53; pub. relations dir. Sarasota, Daytona Beach (Fla.) Kennel Clubs, 1953-55; gen. mgr., corp. sec. Sanford-Orlando Kennel Club, 1955-72; gen. mgr., exec. v.p. Black Hills Kennel Club, Rapid City, S.C., 1964-71; ind. editorial columnist, free-lance writer, 1972—. Dir. Combank Casselberry Bank, Tropicana Pools, Inc. Mem. Fla. Golf Assn. (chmn. adv. com. 1964-65, dir., pres.), Am. Greyhound Track Operators Assn. (publ. and supervisory com. Am. Greyhound Racing Ency., pub. 1963; nat. pres.), World Racing Fedn. (chmn.), World Greyhound Racing Fedn. (pres.), Internat. Platform Assn., U. Fla. Alumni Assn. (past pres. Sarasota County chpt.), Sigma Delta Chi, Theta Chi. Democrat. Clubs: University, Country, Touchdown (Orlando); Winter Park (Fla.) Racquet. Home: 877 Brock St Winter Park FL 32789

LEDUC, ALBERT L., educator; b. Vincennes, Ind., June 18, 1911; s. David and Helen (Fish) L.; A.B., Ind. U., 1931, M.A., 1935; Ph.D., U. Wis., 1952; m. Rachel Wineinger, Sept. 1, 1933; children—Albert, Louise (Mrs. Arthur Zierzow), Theodore. Faculty mem. Earlham Coll., 1931-33, Ind. U., 1933-36, Huntingdon Coll., 1936-40, U.S. Mil. Acad., 1942-47; asst. prof. modern langs. Fla. State U., 1947-53, asso. prof., 1953-62; prof. modern langs. Hampden-Sydney (Va.) Coll., 1962-72, prof. emeritus, 1972—. Vis. prof. S.F. Austin State U., summer 1961, Appalachian State U., summers 1965, 68. Served as col. USAAF, World War II. Mem. South Atlantic Modern Lang. Assn. (officer 1948-49, 59-61), Am. Assn. Tchrs. German, Am. Assn. Tchrs. French (state pres. 1950-53, 65-67, 68-70), Am. Assn. U. Profs., Phi Beta Kappa (pres. Alpha Fla. chpt. 1955-56), Pi Delta Phi, Sigma Delta Pi. Methodist. Rotarian (pres. 1967-68). Editor: (with James A. Preu) The Selected Speeches of Robert M. Strozier. Contbr. to French Rev., Am. Travelers Companion, other profl. publs. Home: 2035 Doomar Dr Tallahassee FL 32303

LEDYARD, WALTER WILLIAM, physician; b. Rockford, Ill., Mar. 6, 1915; s. Walter Riley and Vera (Miller) L.; student Rockford Coll., 1935-36; A.B. summa cum laude, U. Ill., 1942, M.D., 1945; m. Margaret Olga McCarthy, June 22, 1943; 1 dau., Shoon. Intern, U.S. Naval Med. Center, Bethesda, Md., 1945-50; resident U. Va. Hosp., Charlottesville, 1950-53; practice medicine, specializing in neurol. surgery, Columbia, S.C., 1953—; chief staff Columbia Hosp.; mem. staff Bapt., Providence hosps., instr. neurol surgery U. Va. Coll. Medicine, 1951-53; cons. VA Hosp., 1954—. Exhibited one man sculpture show Columbia Mus. Art; exhibited in group shows numerous museums and galleries; represented in permanent collections, including S.C. State Art Collection. Pres. bd. trustees Columbia Mus. Art. Served to lt. (j.g.), M.C., USNR, 1945-50. Diplomate Am. Bd. Neurol. Surgery. Mem. A.M.A., S.C., Columbia med. socs., Harvey Cushing Soc., Am. Assn. Neurol. Surgeons, So. Neurosurg. Soc., So. Med. Assn., S.C. Artists Guild (trustee 1965), Phi Beta Kappa, Alpha Chi Sigma. Alpha Kappa Kappa, Phi Lambda Epsilon. Clubs: Torch (pres. 1956), Kosmos (pres. 1969). Editor: Recorder, 1966-67. Home: 3900 McGregor Dr Columbia SC 29206

LEE, AMY FREEMAN (MRS. FREEMAN LEE), artist, educator; b. San Antonio, Oct. 3, 1914; d. Joe and Julie (Freeman) Freeman; grad. St. Mary's Hall, 1931; student U. Tex., 1931-34; student Incarnate Word College, 1934-42, Litt.D., 1965; m. Ernest R. Lee, Oct. 17, 1937 (div. Jan., 1941). Art critic San Antonio Express, 1939-41; staff art critic radio sta. KONO, 1947-51; lectr. art Trinity U., San Antonio, 1954-56, San Antonio Art Inst., 1955-56, Our Lady of Lake Coll., San Antonio, 1969-71; one man shows various Tex. coll., 1969, 70, 71, including Incarnate Word Coll., San Antonio, 1969, U. Tex., 1970, 72, 73; Woman's Forum, Henderson, Tex., 1970; Beaumont (Tex.) Art Museum, 1970, Tex. Tech U. Museum, Lubbock, 1970, Southwestern U., Georgetown, Tex., 1971, L. & L. Gallery, Longview, Tex., Pioneer Meml. Library, Fredericksburg, Tex., 1971, Ojo del Sol Gallery, El Paso, Tex., 1972, Shook-Carrington Gallery, San Antonio, 1972; exhibited numerous group shows including San Antonio Art League, 1969, Nat. Soc. Painters in Casein, N.Y.C., 1969, 71, 72, 73, Water Color Invitational Exhibit Cal. State U. at Chico, 1972, Southwest Watercolor Soc. Regional Exhbn., Dallas, 1969, 72, Silvermine Guild, New Canaan, Conn., 1970, 72, Tex. Fine Arts Assn., 1970, 73, Cal. Nat. Watercolor Soc., 1970, 71, 72, 73, L. & L. Gallery, 1970, Jr. League Ann. Collectors Show, San Antonio, 1970, 6th Miniature Paintings Invitation Exhbn., San Antonio, Tex. Fine Arts Assn. Ann. Travelling Exhbn., 1970, 71, 72, Contemporary Artists Group Ann. Travelling Exhbn., 1970, Contemporary Artists Group Ann. Mems. Exhbn., San Antonio, 1970, Day of Fine Arts Exhbn., Crystal City, Tex., 1970, Virginia Museum Travelling Exhbn., 1971, North Star Mall Gallery, San Antonio, 1971, Western Assn. Art Museums, 1971, San Antonio Artists Assn., 1971, Service League of Port Arthur (Tex.) Exhbn., 1971, Painters and Sculptors Soc. N.J., 1971, Del Mar Coll., 1971, Oklahoma City Art Center, 1971, U. Tex. Art Museum, 1971, San Antonio Art League Gallery, 1971, Pioneer Meml. Library, 1971, Ogunquit (Me.) Art Assn., 1971, Ojo Del Sol Gallery, El Paso, 1972, Contemporary Artists Group Exhbn., 1972, Worcester (Mass.) Mus., 1972, Nash and Jacobs Collection, 1973, Tex. Watercolor Soc., 1973, 2d Biennial 5-State Art Exhbn., Port Arthur, 1973, others; represented in permanent collections Westfall Br. Library, San Antonio, Baylor U. Theater, D.D. Felman Collection, Dallas, Smith Coll. Mus. Fine Arts, Northampton, Mass., Witte Meml. Mus., San Antonio, Ft. Worth Art Center, Norfolk (Va.) Mus. Arts and Scis., U. Tex. Mus. Fine Arts, Beaumont Art Mus., Nathaniel Saltonstall Collection, Boston, Trevira Collection, N.Y.C. Chmn. San Antonio Ad Hoc Humane Com. Chmn. bd. dirs. Incarnate Word Coll.; bd. dirs. Madonna Neighborhood Centers of San Antonio, San Antonio Blind Assn., San Antonio Ballet Co., bd. dirs. Friends of San Antonio Pub. Library, pres., 1969; mem. adv. bd. Coll. Fine Arts, U. Tex., 1957-72; bd. dirs. Pub. Information Corp., Austin, Tex., First Repertory Theater, San Antonio, Cultural Art Assn. San Antonio, Arts Council San Antonio, Cambridge Sch., Weston, Mass.; bd. mgrs. United Colls. San Antonio; mem. consultative bd. Kenwood Community Council, San Antonio; mem. adv. bd. Occupational Edn. and Tech. Dept., Alamo Heights Ind. Sch. Dist. San Antonio. Recipient numerous prizes including 1st prize 18th Ann. Exhbn., Beaumont Art Mus., 1969; Harwood K. Smith award Southwestern Watercolor Soc., Dallas, 1969; Purchase prize 20th Ann. Tex. Watercolor Soc. Exhbn., 1969; Tex. Fine Arts Assn. citation, 1969; Camellia award Joskes of Tex., 1971; Honorable Mention, 5-State Art Exhbn. 1st Biennial, Gates Gallery and Meml. Library, Port Arthur, Tex.; 1st prize Contemporary Artists exhbn., 1973; honored at ann. Woman's Day, Baylor U., Waco, 1967; scholarship given in her name Am. Assn. U. Women, 1973. Mem. San Antonio Art League (pres.), Am. Fedn. Arts, Artists Equity Assn., Nat. Soc. Arts and Letters, Tex. Art Educators, Coll. Art Assn. Am., Poetry Soc. Tex., Am. Soc. Aesthetics, Assn. Internationale des Critiques d'Art (Paris), Tex. Watercolor Soc. (founder, pres., dir.), Nat. Art Edn. Assn., Internat. Soc. for Edn. Through Art, Nat. Soc. Painters Casein, Tex. Council for Wildlife Protection (dir. 1969), Humane Soc. U.S. (dir.). Silvermine Guild Artists, Humane Soc. U.S. (nat. bd. dirs. 1969, bd. dirs. Gulf States region), Laguna Beach Art Assn. (hon.), Philos. Soc. Tex., Am. Civil Liberties Union, Common Cause, Cal. Nat. Watercolor Soc., Laguna Beach Art Assn. (hon.), Barn Gallery Assos., Coll. Art Assn. Am., Contemporary Artists Group, San Antonio Chamber Music Soc., San Antonio Conservation Soc., UN Assn. U.S., Women's Internat. League Peace and Freedom, Am. Assn. U. Profs., Am. Assn. U. Women, Marquis Biog. Library Soc. (adv. mem.), Nat. Assn. R.R. Passengers, Poetry Soc. San Antonio (dir.), Kappa Pi (hon.), Delta Delta Delta, others. Author: Hobby Horses, 1940; A Critic's Notebook, 1943, Remember Pearl Harbor, 1945. Works reproduced in Tex. Quar., 1966, 73, Art & The Creative Teacher, 1971, other mags. Contbr. articles to profl. jours. Address: 127 Canterbury Hill San Antonio TX 78209

LEE, BUDGE VAN, indsl. engr.; b. Checotah, Okla., Nov. 30, 1915; s. Budge Van and Whig (Murray) L.; student Southwestern Coll., 1934-35, Hutchinson Jr. Coll., 1935-36, U. Okla., 1937-38, Tex. Christian U., 1945-62; m. Marguerite Louteen Gower, Aug. 16, 1941; children—Carol (Mrs. Jay Loucks), Linda (Mrs. Sidney Neal Shults). With Gen. Dynamics, Ft. Worth, 1942—, chief procurement planning and control, chief material control, 1960-64, procurement research supr., 1964—. Mem. Ft. Worth City Plan Commn., 1954-55, Ft. Worth City Zoning Commn., 1954-55; team capt. United Fund, 1960-72. Recipient Distinguished Service award City of Ft. Worth, 1955. Mem. Am. Inst. Indsl. Engrs., Soc. Am. Value Engrs., Nat. Mgmt. Assn., Aerospace Industries Assn. (small bus. adv. panel 1966—), Ft. Worth C. of C. (life), Delta Tau Delta. Club: Ridglea Country (Ft. Worth). Home: 3476 Wellington Rd Fort Worth TX 76116 Office: Box 748 Fort Worth TX 76101

LEE, CARROLL DEAN, museum ofcl.; b. Ft. Worth, Apr. 22, 1938; s. Ira D. and Iola Margaret (Magness) L.; B.A., Tex. Christian U., 1961; summer scholar Aspen (Colo.) Sch. Contemporary Art, 1962; M.F.A. (grad. asst.), Tex. Christian U., 1969; m. Tommie Jean North, May 31, 1969; 1 dau., Shelby. Mem. staff Ft. Worth Art Center Mus., 1963—, exhibit designer, 1967-69, asst. to dir., 1969—, mus. coordinator, 1974—; tchr. printmaking, figure drawing and painting mus. sch., 1964-68. Mem. Am. Assn. Museums, Tex. Museums Consortium, Mountain Plains Museums Conf., Tex. Museums Assn. Office: 1309 Montgomery St Fort Worth TX 76107

LEE, CHARLES EDWARD, state ofcl.; b. Asheville, N.C., June 17, 1917; s. Ralph Edwin and Mabel (Robinson) L.; A.B., U. S.C., 1938, A.M., 1939; postgrad. U. Chgo., 1939-41, 46-48; m. Ethel Jane Blizzard, Jan. 20, 1945; children—Christopher Lewes, Janet Castle, Frank Everett Robinson. Editorial asst. Jour. Modern History at U. Chgo., 1939-41; instr. history U. S.C., 1946; asst. prof. history Roosevelt Coll., 1948-50; editor U. S.C. Press, 1952-56, Henry Regnery Co., Chgo., 1956-60; dir. S.C. Dept. Archives and History, Columbia, 1961—. Mem. Nat. Archives Adv. Council, 1968-70, S.C. Parks, Recreation and Tourism Commn., 1967—; v.p. Nat. Conf. State Hist. Preservation Officers, 1969-72, mem. exec. com., 1974—; mem. cons. com. Nat. Survey Historic Sites and Bldgs., Nat. Park Service, 1970—, chmn. S.E. regional adv. com., 1974—; dep. exec. sec. S.C. Revolutionary Bicentennial Commn., 1971—; mem. adv. panel on research and publs. Heritage '76 com. Am. Revolutionary Bicentennial Commn., 1972—; mem. adv. bd. S.C. Heritage Trust, 1974—. Vice pres. Hist. Columbia Found., 1964-70. Served as lt. USNR, 1941-45; PTO. Fellow Soc. Am. Archivists (pres. 1971-72); mem. Am. Assn. State and Local History. Clubs: Columbia Forum (sec. 1966-69, pres. 1974—), Kosmos (pres. 1972-73). Contbr. articles to profl. jours. Home: 1325 Adger Rd Columbia SC 29205 Office: Box 11669 Columbia SC 29211

LEE, CHARLES EDWIN, civil engr.; b. Baton Rouge, Sept 5, 1920; s. Claude Charles and Ida (Furlow) L.; student Miss. State U., 1938-41; student Miss. State Coll. Extension, 1946, C.Z. Jr. Coll., 1946-47, U. Ill. Extension, 1953, Mass. Inst. Tech., 1960; m. Evelyn Bruce, July 6, 1942. Civilian engr. U.S. Army C.E., 1941-70, with spl. engring. div. Panama C.Z., 1946-48, hydraulic design with Detroit Dist., 1948-50, North Central div., Chgo., 1950-55, New Eng. div., Boston, 1955-60, asst. chief hydraulic design Office Chief Engrs., Washington, 1960-70; asso. D & M Research Co., Glen Burnie, Md., 1970—; also farmer, cons. coastal engr. Cons. engr. in pvt. practice, Halbrook, Mass., 1956-60. Mem. Fed. Adv. Com. Water Data, 1967-70; cons. panel wind and seismic design U.S.-Japan Coop. Program Natural Resources, 1968-70; legislative chmn. Floyd County Farm Bur.; mem. resolutions com. Va. Farm Bur., 1973. Mem. planning bd. Town of Halbrook, 1956-60, mem. sch. planning, sch. bldg. coms., 1957-60. Served with USNR, 1942-45. Registered profl. engr., R.I., Mass., Md. Mem. Am. Soc. C.E., Internat. Assn. Hydraulic Research, Coastal Engring. Research Council, Permanent Internat. Assn. Nav. Congresses, Task Com. Small Craft Harbors, Task Com. Groins (chmn.), Washington City Ten Pin Assn. (exec. dir. 1968-70). Research and publs. in field. Address: Ten Pines Farm Rt 1 Box 138 Check VA 24072

LEE, CHARLES HENRY, lawyer, internat. exec.; b. Santiago, Chile, June 28, 1909; s. Charles Henry and Ellen Scott (Wilson) L.; student Columbia, 1927-28; Ph.B. cum laude, Georgetown U., 1931; postgrad. George Washington, Columbia, 1932-33; LL.B., Fordham U., 1937; m. Lulu Vargas-Vila, Aug. 20, 1938; children—Patricia Ellen (Mrs. Lars Schonander), Charles Henry III (dec.), Elisabeth (Mrs. John D. Sevier). Asst. to arbitrator Guatemala-Honduras Boundary Arbitration Tribunal, Washington, 1931-33; admitted to N.Y. bar, 1938, D.C. bar, 1946; practiced in N.Y.C., 1937-41; atty. Coordinator Inter-Am. Affairs, Washington, 1941; atty. Tex. Co., N.Y.C., 1941-46; spl. asst. to asst. sec. state Inter-Am. Affairs Dept. State, Washington, 1946-47; mng. dir. E.R. Squibb & Sons Argentina, Buenos Aires, 1947-49, asst. v.p., asst. to pres., dir. Brazilian subsidiary, 1949-56; mng. dir. internat. practice McKinsey & Co., mgmt. cons., N.Y.C., 1956-58; mng. partner Lee, Altieri, Sisto & Assos., mgmt. cons., Mexico City, 1958-61; partner firm Rado & Lee, N.Y.C., 1958-61; dir. Econ. Mission of U.S. to Chile, Santiago, 1961-64; v.p. gen. mgr. Hooker Mexicana, 1964-73, chmn. bd. dirs., 1972—; partner Sintemex Mgmt. Cons., Mexico City. Mem. Council Fgn. Relations N.Y., 1951—; hon. mem. faculty Catholic U. Chile; chmn. Inter-Am. Council Grad. Sch. Fordham U. With Inter-Am. Def. Bd., Washington, 1942; mil. attache Div. G-2 War Dept., Washington, 1942-43; asst. mil. attache Am. embassy, Argentina, 1943-45. Decorated comdr. Order al Merito (Chile). Mem. Am. C. of C. of Mexico (chmn. bus. adv. council), Mexican-Am. Cultural Inst. (v.p., dir.), Mexican Acad. History and Geography, Am. Mgmt. Assn., Am. Bar Assn. (past sec., chmn. Latin Am. law com.), Assn. Bar City N.Y., Am. Chambers Commerce Latin Am. (v.p.), Pan Am. Soc. U.S. Roman Catholic. Clubs: Military (Santiago); University (Washington); University (N.Y.C.); University, Campestre Churubusco (Mexico City). Internat. relations editor: Handbook of Latin Am. Studies, 1941. Home: Platon 445 Mexico City Mexico Office: Mariano Escobedo 752 Mexico City Mexico

LEE, CLYDE EDWARD, educator, researcher; b. Heathman, Miss., Oct. 2, 1929; s. Gabe Edward and Lela (Ponder) L.; B.S., Miss. State U., 1952, M.S. (Automotive Safety Found. fellow), 1956; Dr. Engring. (Automotive Safety Found. fellow 1957; Am. Bitumals fellow 1959), U. Cal. at Berkeley, 1962; m. Mary Rebecca McGraw, May 20, 1972; children—Mark Stephen, Larry Rheinhardt. Instr. dept. civil engring. Miss. State U., State College, 1955-57; mem. faculty U. Tex. at Austin, 1959—, asso. prof., 1963-68, prof., 1968—, also dir. Center Hwy. Research, 1963—. Mem. Traffic Safety Commn., Austin, 1971—. Served to 1st lt. AUS, 1952-54. Mem. Am. Soc. Civil Engrs., Am. Acad. Transp. (dir. 1967-70), Inst. Traffic Engrs., Hwy. Research Bd., Am. Rd. Builders Assn., Pi Kappa Alpha. Patentee in field. Home: 1703 Cloverleaf Dr Austin TX 78723 Office: 242 ENS Bldg Univ Tex Austin TX 78712

LEE, DANIEL ELMER, govt. ofcl.; b. Mammoth Cave, Ky., Oct. 2, 1927; s. Daniel and Madie Ruth (Zimmerman) L.; student Western Ky. State U., 1948-52; m. Alice Marie Kennedy, Nov. 25, 1948; children—Nancy (Mrs. Keith Mitchell), Linda, Amy, Dana. Park ranger Nat. Park Service, 1952-68; park supt. Custer Battlefield Nat. Monument, Crow Agy., Mont., 1968-70; park supt. Vicksburg (Miss.) Nat. Mil. Park, 1970—. Mem. council A.R.C., Vicksburg, 1973-74. Vice pres. adv. bd. Vicksburg and Warren County Hist. Soc., 1973—. Served with AUS, 1946-48. Mason, Rotarian. Home and office: PO Box 349 Vicksburg MS 39180

LEE, DANIEL WARNELL, retail services co. exec.; b. Alma, Ga., June 23, 1919; s. Daniel Marson and Ida (Hyers) L.; B.S. in Agr., U. Ga., 1941; m. Sallie Elizabeth Davis, Dec. 13, 1942; children—Daniel W., James D., Elizabeth C. Soil scientist U.S. Dept. Agr., Walhalla, S.C., 1941-42; tng. specialist VA, Valdosta, Ga., 1946-50, Swainsboro, Ga., 1952-53; with EBSCO Industries, Inc., Birmingham, Ala., 1953—, v.p., regional mgr., 1958—; sec. treas. Lee Land & Timber Co. Inc. Served to capt. AUS, 1942-46, 50-52; ETO. Decorated Congl. Medal of Honor, Purple Heart. Mem. V.F.W., Congl. Medal of Honor Soc. (v.p. 1973—). Lion. Home: 1123 Melissa Dr San Antonio TX 78213 Office: 8410 Speedway San Antonio TX 78230

LEE, DONALD FRANKLIN, land devel. co. exec.; b. Winchester, Tenn., Jan. 4, 1940; s. Marion Jasper and Minnie Maud (Fuller) L.; B.S. in C.E., U. Tenn., 1961; m. Zonetta Fain, Aug. 21, 1965; children—Mike, Valerie. Pres., Lee Investments, Inc., Atlanta, 1968—. Served to lt. USAF, 1961-65. Registered profl. engr., Tenn., Ga., Fla. Mem. Nat. Soc. Profl. Engrs., Nat. Soc. Homebuilders, Lockridge Forest Civic Assn., Alpha Gamma Rho. Home: 2993 Sumac Dr Doraville GA 30340 Office: 7000 Peachtree Blvd Norcross-Atlanta GA 30071

LEE, FREEMAN GORDON, govt. ofcl.; b. Washington, Dec. 31, 1929; s. Freeman Gaylord and Odessa (Wardlaw) L.; degree U. Md., 1955; high speed aerodynamics degree U. Cal. at Los Angeles, 1957; m. Mildred Marie Potter, July 19, 1952; children—Lucile Jean, Melodie Susan, Celeste Ann, Montgomery Delta. Controls engr. Vanguard project Glenn L. Martin Co., Balt., 1955-56; flight test analysis engr. Lockheed-MSD, Van Nuys, Cal., 1956-57; analysis engr. aero-space systems Marquardt Aircraft Co., Van Nuys, 1957-58; sr. systems analysis engr. Pershing project The Martin Co., Orlando, Fla., 1958-59; tech. staff, asst. to chief engr. aerospace systems Melpar, Inc., Falls Church, Va., 1959-60; sr. physicist ASW research Aerojet-Gen. Corp., Frederick, Md., 1960-61; sr. systems analysis engr. aero-space projects Naval Air Engring. Center, Phila., 1962-64; electronics project engr., tech. expert land combat systems U.S. Army Missile Command, Redstone Arsenal, Ala., 1964-73; gen. engr. Office of Chief of Staff, U.S. Army, 1973—. Committeeman, Explorer Post 280, Boy Scouts Am., Absecond, N.J., 1962-64, roundtable commr. Tennessee Valley council Arrowhead Dist., 1970-73; asst. dist. commr. Nat. Capitol Area Council, 1973—. Served with 88th Blue Devil Div., 1945-49, Italy; with 1092d Combat Engrs., 1951-52, Korea. Recipient Navy commendation for personal contbns. to space effort, 1963; Meritorious award and Medal of Merit, Boy Scouts Am., 1972; Patriotic Civilian Service award Dept. Army, 1971; Humanitarian award Dept. Health, Edn. and Welfare, 1972. Fellow Brit. Interplanetary Soc. (br. chmn. D.C. 1959-61); mem. Am. Rocket Soc. (sect. v.p. 1958), Soc. Am. Mil. Engrs. (nat. award of merit 1966, v.p. 1967-68, 1st dir. 1969-70), Assn. U.S. Army, Am. Astronautical Soc., Am. Legion, Sons Confederate Vets., Order Stars and Bars (vice comdr.-in-chief 1963-64). Conducted controls analysis on all vanguard rockets and post flight analyses of Vikings; designed fuel flow and shock positioning system for BOMARC Missile; system analysis and reentry studies of Pershing Missile; developed airborne radiation analyzer, air def. command and control system, automatic multi-system test equipment for land combat missile systems and support equipment, operational testing of major mil. systems; certified fallout shelter analyst, radiol. officer. Home: 7303 Old Keene Mill Rd Springfield VA 22150 Office: US Army Operational Test and Evaluation Agy Fort Belvoir VA 22060

LEE, GARY EDWIN, lawyer; b. Pampa, Tex., Dec. 15, 1944; s. Walter E. and Nancy (Caudell) L.; B.S., W. Tex. State U., 1967; J.D., U. Houston, 1970; m. Ruth Ocine Chism, Feb. 23, 1962; children—Beverli Jean, Greg Anthony. Admitted to Tex. bar, 1970; mem. firm Funderburk & Funderburk, Houston, 1970-71; partner Lee & Pettitt, Houston, 1971—. Mem. Am., Tex., Houston, Houston Jr. bar assns., U. Houston Coll. Law Alumni Assn. (dir.), Phi Alpha Delta. Home: 9322 Willow Meadow Houston TX 77071 Office: 609 Fannin St Houston TX 77002

LEE, J. D., lawyer; b. Tellico Plains, Tenn., May 3, 1929; student Stetson U.; B.S., East Tenn. State U., 1951; J.D., U. Tenn., 1954. Admitted to Tenn. bar, 1954; mem. firm Lee, McGee, Garrett & Chandler, Knoxville, Tenn.; counsel Lester, Hildebrand, Nolan, Lane, Underhill, Mondelli & Thompson, Nashville; clk., master Chancery Ct., 1954-59. Lectr., Profl. Trial Lawyers Inst., 1969. Sec., Tenn. Conservation Commn., 1963-66. Del., Tenn. Constl. Conv., 1953, Democratic Nat. Conv., 1964. Bd. dirs. South Eastern Trial Lawyers Inst., U. Tenn. Coll. Law, 1965—. Mem. Am., Monroe County (pres. 1965) bar assns., Bar Assn. Tenn., Am. (gov. 1964-66, 68—, vice chmn. tort sect. 1966, 68, chmn. basic trial advocacy com. 1969-70, pres. 1972-73), Tenn. (gov. 1966—) trial lawyers assns., Am. Judicature Soc., Internat. Soc. Barristers, Selden Soc., Phi Delta Phi (province pres. 1957-59). Contbr. articles to legal jours. Office: 205 Clinch Av Knoxville TN 37902 also 200 Sheets Bldg Madisonville TN 37354

LEE, JAMES RODNEY, lawyer; b. Colorado City, Tex., Jan. 28, 1930; s. James Ralph and Mary (Biggerstaff) L.; B.S., Tex. Christian U., 1951; LL.B., Baylor U., 1956; m. Sara Ann Norman, June 9, 1957; children—Rebecca Ann, Ralph Norman, James Curtis. Admitted to Tex. bar, 1956, since practiced in Waco; partner firm Naman, Howell, Smith & Chase; dir. Tex. Nat. Bank of Waco, NCB Co., Waco, Word Music, Inc. Lectr. Baylor U. Law Sch. Pres. U.S.O. council, Waco, 1962-63; pres. Action planning council, Waco, 1969-70; mem. Bd. Adjustment Waco, 1964-68; mem. Heart of Tex. council Boy Scouts Am. Bd. dirs., trustee Greater Waco United Fund. Served to 1st lt. AUS, 1951-54. Mem. Am., Tex., Waco-McLennan County (v.p., dir.), Waco Jr. (past pres.) bar assns., Tex. Bar Found., Waco C. of C., Phi Delta Phi. Democrat. Disciple of Christ. Comments editor Baylor Law Rev., 1955-56. Home: 5307 Chaparral Dr Waco TX 76710 Office: First Nat Bldg Waco TX 76701

LEE, JAMES WIDNER, aero. engr.; b. Birmingham, Ala., Nov. 9, 1935; s. Robert Edward and Pearlie May (Widner) L.; B.S. in Aero. Engring., Auburn U., 1957; m. Ola Ann Sims, Aug. 25, 1956; children—James Edward, David Alan, Gary Richard. Prin. investigator, supr. air augmented propulsion analysis Thiokol Corp., Huntsville, Ala., 1957—. Mem. Joint Army-Navy-NASA-Air Force Working Group on Air Breathing Propulsion, 1968—. Com. chmn. Boy Scouts Am., 1967-71; player agt. Huntsville Internat. Little League Baseball, 1974; chmn. solicitation program Thiokol Democracy in Action, 1970. Registered profl. engr., Ala. Asso. fellow Am. Inst. Aeros. and Astronautics (Martin Schilling award 1960, chmn. Ala. sect. 1971-72, mem. adv. bd. 1972-74); mem. Thiokol Mgmt. Club (pres. 1969), Pi Kappa Alpha. Baptist. Contbr. articles on advanced propulsion tech. to profl. publs. Home: 1004 Appalachee Rd SE Huntsville AL 35801 Office: Thiokol Corp Redstone Arsenal AL 35807

LEE, JOHN HOLMES, constrn. engr.; b. Marion, Ala., Apr. 20, 1919; s. John Holmes and Charlotte (Parks) L.; A.A., Marion Inst., 1939; B.C.E., Ala. Poly. Inst., 1942; m. Sara Frances Yeager, Aug. 10, 1946; children—Eva Frances, John Holmes IV, Sara Louise. Jr. engr. Ky. Dam, 1942-43; elec. engr. Navy Dept., Washington, 1943; constrn. engr. locks and dams U.S. Army C.E., Ala., Ga., 1946-65, asst. resident engr., Millers Ferry Lock and Dam, Camden, Ala., 1965-71; resident engr. Jones Bluff Powerhouse, Selma, Ala., 1972—. Mem. Marion City Bd. Edn. Served with USAAF, 1943-46. Registered profl. engr., Ala. Mem. Chi Epsilon. Baptist (deacon). Home: 503 East St Marion AL 36756 Office: PO Box 222 RFD 3 Selma AL 36201

LEE, JOHN LAWRENCE, ret. army officer, lawyer; b. Albertson, N.C., Aug. 12, 1894; s. Ezekiel and Rosa (Davis) L.; diploma Inf. Sch., Ft. Benning, Ga., 1933, Command and Gen. Staff Sch., Ft. Leavenworth, Kan., 1937; LL.B., Duke, 1949, LL.M., Woodrow Wilson Coll. Law, 1951; m. Mary Harlan, Sept. 17, 1932; 1 dau., Linda Joan (Mrs. James Robert Beacham). Served from pvt. to col. Inf., U.S. Army, 1913-46, ret. phys. disability, 1946; admitted to Ga. bar, 1951, practiced in Atlanta and Dunwoody, Ga.; justice 524th Dist. G.M., DeKalb County, Ga., 1957-65. Mem. Justices and Constables Assn. De Kalb County (pres.), Disabled Officers Assn. (nat. exec. committeeman So. Area 1948-58, 60-68, sr. nat. vice comdr. 1958-60, 68-70), Ga., Gwinnett Circuit bar assns., Ret. Officers Assn., David Crockett and Martha Stroud Lee Desc. Assn. of Old Duplin County (patriarch-pres. 1960—), Sigma Delta Kappa (scholarship award). Mason (50th yr. award). Club: Old War Horse Lawyers (Atlanta). Home: Route 1 Box 445 Westbrook Rd Suwanee GA 30174 Office: Suwanee GA 30174

LEE, LEWIS SWIFT, lawyer; b. Dallas, Nov. 19, 1933; s. Lenoir Valentine and Margaret (Clendon) L.; student Washington and Lee U., 1954-55; A.B., U. of South, 1955; M.A., Emory U., 1956, LL.B., 1960; m. Frances Ann Childress, Mar. 16, 1956; children—Frances Ann, Lewis Swift, George Childress, Lenoir Valentine II. Admitted to Fla. bar, 1960, since practiced in Jacksonville; partner firm Ulmer, Murchison, Ashby and Ball; sec., dir. Can. Dry Bottling Co. of Fla., Inc. Instr. math. Washington and Lee U., 1955; instr. polit. sci. Ga. State Coll., 1955-56; instr. social studies Ga. Inst. Tech., 1956. Pres., Mental Health Clinic Duval County, 1967; pres. Community Planning Council, Jacksonville, 1969-70, dir. Bd. dirs., sec., counselor Childrens Home Soc. Fla., pres. N.E. div., 1972; former trustee Bartram Sch.; trustee Bolles Sch., U. South, Jacksonville Episcopal High Sch. Found., Willing Hands, Inc., Greater Jacksonville Econ. Opportunity, Inc., Jr. Achievement. Served to 1st lt. AUS, 1956-58. Mem. Maritime Law Assn., Am., Fla., Jacksonville bar assns., Phi Beta Kappa, Phi Delta Theta. Republican. Episcopalian. Clubs: Fla. Yacht, Timuquana Country, River, Ponte Vedra. Home: 3733 Ortega Blvd Jacksonville FL 32210 Office: PO Box 479 Fla Nat Bank Bldg Jacksonville FL 32201

LEE, MAJOR CLINTON, elec. engr.; b. Pike County, Miss., Aug. 22, 1942; s. Ellis W. and Liddie Mae (Dallis) L.; B.S. in Elec. Engring., Miss. State U., 1965; M.E.E., U. Va., 1968; m. Kathryn M. Lockard, Feb. 14, 1970. Electronic engr. Langley Research Center, NASA, Hampton, Va., 1965—. Patentee dual resonant cavity absorption cell. Home: 896 Devol Dr Newport News VA 23602 Office: NASA VPO MS159 Langley Research Center Hampton VA 23665

LEE, MARY ANN, journalist; b. Memphis, July 30, 1939; d. Robert Martin and Mattye Veva (Nash) Lee; B.A., Southwestern at Memphis, 1958. Copywriter, John Cleghorn Agy., 1958; continuity dir. WMC-TV, 1959-64; TV columnist Memphis Press-Scimitar, 1964-67, TV-radio editor, 1967—; Memphis corr. Variety, 1968—. Charter mem. Critics Consensus, 1966—. Cons. to Women in Cable Communications Inc. Mem. Am. Newspaper Guild, Women in Communications, Nat. Acad. Rec. Arts and Scis., Memphis Music Inc., Shelby County Democratic Women. Episcopalian. Home: 3771 Waynoka Av Memphis TN 38111 Office: 495 Union Av Memphis TN 38101

LEE, MILTON HORACE, county engr.; b. Carrollton, Ala., May 11, 1919; s. George Lofton and Annie Delma (Carson) L.; B.S. in Mech. Engring., Auburn (Ala.) U., 1951; m. Euna Faye Johnson, June 20, 1944; children—Nelda, Lyndall (Mrs. Leroy Fulton), Milton Horace, Roger. With Allis Chalmers Mfg. Co., Gadsden, Ala., 1951-53, Ala. Hwy. Dept., Tuscaloosa, 1953-54; engr. Pickens County, Ala., 1954—; engring. cons. Served with AUS, 1944-45. Decorated Purple Heart. Registered profl. engr., Ala. Mem. Nat. Assn. County Engrs., Ala. Assn. County Engrs., V.F.W., Am. Legion. Baptist (deacon, past Sunday sch. supt.). Home: Route 1 Carrollton AL 35447 Office: PO Box 367 Carrollton AL 35447

LEE, NEAL EDWARD, civil engr.; b. Corpus Christi, Tex., Aug. 6, 1926; s. John T. and Ethyl (Sears) L.; B.S. in C.E., Tex. A. and M. U., 1950; m. Mona Lasemen, Jan. 17, 1922; children—Gregory D., Tammy T. Timekeeper, P.O.B. Montgomery, Wichita Falls, Tex., 1950-51; layout engr. R.F. Ball, San Antonio, 1951; engr. McKinzie Constrn. Co., San Antonio and Beeville, Tex., 1951-56; engr.-estimator Heldenfels Bros., Corpus Christi, 1956—. Served with AUS, 1944-46. Registered profl. engr. Mem. Tex. Soc. Profl. Engrs. (treas. Nueces chpt. 1968-70), Am. Assn. Cost Engrs. Moose. Club: Aggie (Corpus Christi). Home: 302 Cape Hatteras Corpus Christi TX 78412 Office: PO Box 4957 Corpus Christi TX 78408

LEE, (NELLE) HARPER, author; b. Monroeville, Ala., Apr. 28; d. Amasa Coleman and Frances (Finch) Lee; student Huntingdon Coll., 1944-45, U. Ala., 1945-49. Author: To Kill a Mockingbird, 1960 (Pulitzer prize for fiction 1961). Republican. Methodist. Home: Monroeville AL Office: care Maurice Crain Inc 18 E 41st St New York City NY 10017

LEE, RAYMOND ALTON, bus. machines co. exec.; b. St. Paul, Aug. 29, 1916; s. Phillip E. and Hildur M. (Belisle-Nordstrom) L.; student Lancaster Bus. Coll., 1938, Yale, 1939; grad U. Minn., 1950, Macalester Coll., 1951; m. Katherine R. Ferschweiler, Sept. 18, 1943; 1 son, Christopher Ray. Editor publs. Peavey Co., 1951-53; dir. publs. Agr. Markets Pub. Co., 1953-54; co. editor Dairy Nat. Assn., St. Paul, 1954-55; pub. relations dir. Greater St. Paul Community Chest, 1950; editor, pub. relations mgr. IBM Corp., Austin, Tex., 1956—; tchr. pub. speaking; editor Nat. Assn. Systems; asst. Journalism Inst., Macalester Coll. Chmn. admissions com. Austin United Fund, 1969-70, trustee, 1967—, dir. pub. relations, 1973—; chmn. publicity com. Vol. Bur., 1968-70; coordinator Jr. Achievement, 1969—. Bd. dirs. Am. Cancer Soc., Austin Arts Council; sec. St. Vincent de Paul. Served with USAAF, World War II and Korea. Decorated D.F.C., Air medal with 6 oak leaf clusters, Silver Star, Purple Heart; recipient 4 Art for Industry awards, 1968, 69. Mem. Pub. Relations Soc. Am., St. Theresa-St. Vincent de Paul Soc., Sigma Delta Chi. Clubs: Rochester (Minn.) Country; Great Hills Country, Balcones Country (Austin, Tex.). Contbr. articles profl. jours., gen. mags. Home: 4213 Woodway Dr Austin TX 78731 Office: 1325 F M Rd Austin TX 78759

LEE, ROBERT EDWARD, JR., judge; b. Miley, S.C., May 20, 1922; s. Robert Edward and Edna (Chalker) L.; student U. Fla., 1939-40; LL.D., John B. Stetson U., 1949; m. Shirley Hudson, July 8, 1967; children—Virginia M., Mary Edna. Admitted to Fla. bar, 1949, since practiced in Deland; circuit judge 7th Jud. Ct., 1964—. Mem. Fla. Gov.'s Adv. Commn. to Div. Youth Services, 1965—. Bd. dirs. YMCA, 1966-69. Served with S.C., AUS, 1942-45; PTO. Mem. Am., Fla. bar assns., Am. Judicature Soc., Nat., Fla. assns. juvenile ct. judges, Am. Legion, Phi Alpha Delta. K.C. Club: Deland Toastmasters (pres. 1964-65). Home: 2100 N Thorpe Av Orange City FL 32763 Office: Court House Deland FL 32720

LEE, ROLAND MARION, archtl. and engring. co. exec.; b. Punta Gorda, Fla., Mar. 1, 1923; s. Marion and Elna (Atkinson) L.; B.C.E., U. Fla., 1948; postgrad., Fla. Tech. U., 1971-72; m. Shirley Joyce Harris, Dec. 24, 1944; children—Lucinda (Mrs. Charles Price), Lauren (Mrs. Phillip Thompson), Jonathan. Dist. engr. Ark. La. Gas Co., Shreveport, La., 1948-56; asst. v.p. Hubbard Constrn. Co., Orlando, Fla., 1956-66; v.p. Watson and Co., Orlando, 1966—, also dir. Vice pres. Friends of Univ., Fla. Tech. U., 1972-73. Bd. dirs. Fla. Industries Expn., 1966-71. Served to 1st lt. USAAF, 1942-45; ETO; lt. col. U.S. Army Res. ret. Decorated D.F.C., Air medal with 11 oak leaf clusters, Purple Heart. Registered profl. engr., Fla., La. Mem. Am. Soc. C.E., Fla. Engring. Soc. (pres. 1966-67, Distinguished Service award 1970), Nat. Soc. Profl. Engrs. (dir. 1969-73), Orlando C. of C., Sigma Tau, Phi Kappa Phi, Beta Theta Pi. Republican. Presbyn. (deacon 1957-60, elder 1960—). Kiwanian (dir. 1971-73, sec. 73-74). Clubs: Orlando Country, Orlando University. Office: 2811 E South St Orlando FL 32803

LEE, SAMUEL HUNT, JR., educator; b. Hutchinson, Kan., Sept. 2, 1918; s. Samuel Hunt and Laura Louise (Grant) L.; B.S., U. Tex. at Austin, 1939; Ph.D., Ohio State U., 1944; m. Evalyn Madden, Aug. 25, 1949; children—Gordon Thomas, Gregory Hunt. Chemist Morton Salt Co., Manistee, Mich., Grand Saline, Tex., 1939-40; sr. research chemist Shell Oil Co., Deer Park, Tex., 1944-46; asst. prof. chemistry U. Tex. at Austin, 1946-49; asso. prof. chemistry Okla. A. and M. Coll., Stillwater, 1949-51; chemist U.S. Naval Ordnance Testing Sta., China Lake, Cal., summer 1951; asst. prof. chemistry Tex. Tech. U., Lubbock, 1951-53, asso. prof., 1953-61, prof., 1961—; vis. prof. Birmingham (Ala.)-So. Coll., summer 1961; sr. chemist Amoco Chem. Corp., Brownsville, Tex., summer 1957; instr. NSF Summer Inst., Tex. Tech. U., 1959, Mont. State U., 1963. Cons., instr. U.S. AID Summer Inst. Chemistry, Sardor Patel U., Vallabh Vidyanagar, Gujarat, India, summer 1966; reader, table leader in chemistry Advanced Placement Exams., Coll. Entrance Exam. Bd., Ednl. Testing Service, Princeton, N.J., 1968—. Bd. dirs. Wesley Found. Tex. Tech. U., 1964-70. Fellow Am. Inst. Chemists, A.A.A.S., Tex. Acad. Sci. (vis. scientist 1955-63, chmn. bd. sci. edn.); mem. Am. Chem. Soc. (sec., chmn. South Plains sect. 1970-72), Tex. Interscholastic League (dir. regional sci. contest 1961—), Sigma Xi, Phi Kappa Phi, Tau Beta Pi, Phi Lambda Upsilon, Phi Gamma Delta.

Democrat. Methodist. Club: Lubbock Knife and Fork (dir.). Author: An Approach to Physical Science, 1968. Home: 3303 55th St Lubbock TX 79413

LEE, SHEW KUHN, optometrist; b. Balt., Apr. 24, 1923; s. Mong Har and Gum Tuey (Wong) L.; Dr. Optometry, Ill. Coll. Optometry, 1949; postgrad. Catholic U. Am., 1957, Md. U., 1959; m. Florence Gin Toy, Oct. 29, 1949; children—Wayson Perry, Davin Jeffrey. Pvt. practice optometry, Washington, 1949—. Lectr. D.C. Traffic Safety Sch.; v.p. D.C. Bd. Optometry, 1959-65; mem. D.C. Bd. Examiners in Optometry, 1973—; mem. Eye Bank Council. Bd. dirs. Eye Bank and Research Found., Washington Hosp. Center. Served with AUS, 1942-45. Decorated Purple Heart, Bronze Star medal with oak leaf cluster. Mem. Am. Optometric Assn., Am. Legion (post comdr. D.C. 1960), D.C. Optometric Soc. (sec. 1956-57), Lees Assn. (trustee), Chinese Consol. Benevolent Assn., Beta Sigma Kappa. Lion (charter pres. Chi-Am 1960, zone chmn. 1961, dep. dist. gov. 1963, hon. mem. Capitol Hill). Research, publs. in field. Home: 2939 McKinley St NW Washington DC 20015 Office: 813 7th St NW Washington DC 20001

LEE, WILLIAM IVEY III, oil and gas co. exec.; b. Asheville, N.C., Oct. 8, 1926; s. William I. and Margaret A. (Thrash) L.; student U. Okla., 1946-49; m. Jane Durand, May 28, 1960. Ind. oil producer, 1955-66; pres. Triton Oil & Gas Corp., Dallas, 1966—, chief exec. officer related cos., 1966—, also dir.; dir., chmn. Triton Oil (Australia) Ltd., Triton Oil (Holdings) Australia Ltd., Triton Oil (New Zealand) Ltd., Triton Philippines Oil & Gas Co., Dallas Investments Ltd. (New Zealand); pres., dir. Triton Middle East Oil Co. (Turkey), Antilles Enterprises, Inc., Whalen Corp., Wilco Properties, Inc.; dir. Antilles Enterprises, N.V. Aviation Properties, Inc., Crusader Oil, N.L. (Australia), Inter-Island Devel. Co. (New Zealand), Lubbock Cotton Oil Co., Petroleum Services, Ltd. (New Zealand), Pursuit Oil N.L. (Australia), Sweetwater Cotton Oil Co. Served with USAAF, 1944-45. Clubs: Brook Hollow Golf, Dallas Petroleum, Preston Trail Golf, Dallas (Dallas); N.Y. Athletic (N.Y.C.). Home: 3310 Fairmount St Dallas TX 75201 also 111 E 56th St New York City NY 10022 Office: #One Energy Sq Dallas TX 75206

LEE, WILLIAM JOHN, chem. engr.; b. Lubbock, Tex., Jan. 16, 1936; s. William Preston and Bonnie Lee (Cook) L.; B.Chem.Engring., Ga. Inst. Tech., 1959, M.S. (NSF fellow), 1961, Ph.D., 1963; m. Phyllis Ann Bass, June 10, 1961; children—Anne Preston, Mary Denise. Sr. research specialist Esso Prodn. Research Co., Houston, 1962-68; asso. prof. petroleum engring. Miss. State U., Starkville, 1968-71; div. staff engr. Exxon Co., Houston, 1971—. Registered profl. engr., Miss. Mem. Soc. Petroleum Engrs. of Am. Inst. Mining, Metal. and Petroleum Engrs. (mem. career guidance com. 1971—, chmn. formation evaluation com. 1973; chmn. Gulf Coast sect. student affairs 1972-73, sec. treas. 1973-74). Home: 249 Beauregard St Conroe TX 77301 Office: PO Box 2180 Houston TX 77001

LEE, WILLIAM MUDGE, contracting co. exec., civil-san. engr.; b. Evergreen, Ala., Oct. 17, 1932; s. Alfred Mudge and Gladys Pauline (Dreaden) L.; B.C.E., Auburn U., 1955; m. Carole Anne Bishop, Sept. 28, 1963; children—Chip, Juli-Ann Bishop, Jenifer McLean, Charles Thomas. Pres., Lee, Wainwright and Ham, Inc., civil engring., Dothan, Ala., 1960-65; v.p. Polyengring., Inc., Dothan, 1965-69; pres. Bill Lee Contracting Co., Inc., Dothan, 1969—; v.p. Blankenship and Lee, Inc., Tallahassee, 1973—. Served with U.S. Coast and Geodetic Survey. Mem. Nat. (bd. dirs.), Ala. (pres. 1974—) utility contractors assns. Home: 2911 Briarcliff Rd Dothan AL 36301 Office: PO Box 486 Dothan AL 38301

LEEMAN, HAFFORD RANSOM, savs. and loan exec., educator; b. Morgan County, Ala., Nov. 19, 1907; s. James Ervin and Mary Ella (Ransom) L.; A.B., Athens Coll., 1938; B.S., U. Ala., 1939, M.A., 1942; m. Wilma Sue Sheats, Nov. 1, 1936; 1 dau., Charlotte Dianne (Mrs. John Edwin Knight, Jr.). Tchr., prin. Morgan County Schs., 1925-47, supt., 1947-53; tchr., prin. Decatur (Ala.) City Schs., 1953-56, supt., 1956-69; faculty Florence State Coll. Summer Sch., 1960, 61, 62. Pres. First Fed. Savs. & Loan Assn., 1969—. Mem. bd. control Tchrs. Retirement System Ala., 1965-69; mem. Ala. Savs. and Loan Exec. Com., 1970-73. Mem. So. Assn. Schs. (state secondary com. 1963-69), Ala. Edn. Assn. (chmn. joint com. retirement 1967-69); mem. legislative com.), Ala. Savs. and Loan League (sec. 1973-74), Ala. Savs. Assn. (pub. affairs com. 1972-73). Baptist (Sunday sch. tchr., deacon). Home: 2315 Brookwood Dr SE Decatur AL 35601 Office: First Fed Savs & Loan Assn 255 Grant St SE Decatur AL 35601

LEEPER, JOHN PALMER, museum exec.; b. Denison, Tex., Feb. 4, 1921; s. John Palmer and Maryanne (Platter) L.; B.Journalism, So. Methodist U., 1942; M.A. in Art History, Harvard, 1947; m. Blanche Wheeler Magurn, Sept. 18, 1948; 1 dau., Maryanne M. Keeper W.A. Clark Collection, Corcoran Gallery Art, Washington, 1948, asst. dir. gallery, 1949-50; dir. Pasadena (Cal.) Art Inst., 1950-53; dir. Marion Koogler McNay Art Inst., San Antonio, 1954—. Instr. Dexter Sch., Boston, 1947-48; lectr. Pasadena Sch. Fine Arts, 1952-53, U. So. Cal., Los Angeles, 1952, Trinity U., San Antonio, 1957-59. Pres. San Antonio Little Theatre. Trustee San Antonio Art Inst. Served with USAAF, 1942-45. Mem. Am. Assn. Museums, Assn. Art Mus. Dirs., Tex. Soc. Arts and Letters (hon.). Club: Harvard (San Antonio). Address: 6000 N Braunfels San Antonio TX 78209

LEEPER, ROBERT ROSBOROUGH, editor; b. Hiddenite, N.C., Sept. 8, 1913; s. Donald Harper and Bera (Davis) L.; A.B., U. N.C., 1934; M.A., George Washington U., 1942; Ed.D., Columbia, 1950; m. Sarah Lou Hammond, Dec. 28, 1963. Asso. sec., editor publs. Assn. for Supervision and Curriculum Devel., Washington, 1950—, editor Ednl. Leadership, 1951—. Instr., U. Va., 1956-57, 62-63. Served with AUS, 1943-46. Mem. N.E.A., Assn. for Childhood Edn. Internat., Am. Assn. Sch. Adminstrs., Assn. for Supervision and Curriculum Devel., U.S. Nat. Com. on Early Childhood Edn., John Dewey Soc., Horace Mann League, Ednl. Press Assn. Am., Phi Delta Kappa, Kappa Delta Pi. Methodist. Contbr. articles to profl. jours. Home: 1239 Noyes Dr Silver Spring MD 20910 Office: 1701 K St NW Washington DC 20006

LEER, JAMES MONROE, JR., assn. exec.; b. Millersburg, Ky., May 11, 1921; s. James Monroe and George (McDaniel) L.; B.S., U. Ky., 1946; m. Louise Burris, Dec. 28, 1952; children—Jesse C. Booth II, Molly B., James Monroe III. Cpl., U.S. Army, 1942, advanced through grades to lt. col., 1968; platoon leader 65th div., 1st Cav. Div., 1961-62, chief tactical intelligence div. Intelligence Sch., 1963-64, chief conduct intelligence div. U.S. Army C.Z.; ret., 1968; exec. dir. Nat. Skeet Shooting Assn., San Antonio, 1969—. Decorated Bronze Star, Purple Heart. Mem. Alpha Gamma Rho. Democrat. Methodist. Mason. Home: 5511 Ben Hur St San Antonio TX 78224 Office: Box 28188 San Antonio TX 78228

LEETH, ROY MILTON, JR., elec. engr.; b. Birmingham, Ala., Nov. 13, 1934; s. Roy Milton and Mildred (Hicks) L.; B.S., Auburn U., 1957; m. Carol Wynn Posey, Apr. 6, 1963; children—Scott, Alan, Clark. Elec. engr. Rust Engring. Co., Birmingham, 1957-62, test and devel. engr. Chrysler Corp., Huntsville, Ala., 1962-63, chief elec. engr. Uniroyal, Inc., Opelika, Ala., 1963—. Bd. dirs. Lee County Fair Assn., 1972-73; tech. bd. advisers Opalika State Tech. Sch. Served to lt. AUS, 1958. Registered profl. engr., Ala. Baptist (deacon 1969—). Club: Exchange (pres. 1973-74) (Opelika). Home: 1302 Gwen Hill Dr Opelika AL 36801 Office: Uniroyal Inc PO Box 30 Opelika AL 36801

LEFEBER, EDWARD JAMES, physician; b. Wauwatosa, Wis., June 1, 1911; s. Cornelius George and May (McCord) L.; B.S., U. Wis., 1934, M.D., 1936; m. Ellie Hancock Weisiger, June 4, 1938; children—Edward James, Robert Randolph, John Courtney, Ann Elizabeth, Donald Louis, Nancy Ellen. Intern, resident in medicine Med. Coll. Va. Hosps., Richmond, 1936-40; mem. faculty Med. Br., U. Tex., Galveston, 1940—, clin. asso. prof. medicine, 1951—, dir. Student Health Service, 1943-46; practice medicine, specializing in internal medicine with Internal Medicine Assos., Galveston, 1948—; chief out-patient service Galveston office Houston Regional Office, VA, 1946-48; cons. gastroenterology USPHS Hosp., Galveston, 1952-53; pres. staff St. Mary's Infirmary, Galveston, 1961. Mem. service mil. families com., bd. dirs. Galveston chpt. A.R.C., 1958—; mem. Galveston Civic Orch., 1957-60. Bd. dirs. Moody House, 1964-65, 67-71, med. dir. Diplomate Am. Bd. Internal Medicine. Fellow A.C.P.; mem. Galveston County Med. Soc. (pres. 1954, sec.-treas. 1948-53), A.M.A., Tex., So. med. assns., Am. Soc. Internal Medicine, Am. Soc. Gastro-Intestinal Endoscopy, Tex. Acad. Internal Medicine, Tex. Club Internists, Phi Chi. Episcopalian (vestryman). Mason. Home: 2927 Av P Galveston TX 77550 Office: Sealy Smith Profl Bldg 200 University Blvd Galveston TX 77550

LEFER, ALLAN MARK, research scientist, educator; b. N.Y.C., Feb. 1, 1936; s. Judah and Lillian (Gastwirth) L.; B.A., Adelphi Coll., 1957; M.A., Western Res. U., 1959; Ph.D., U. Ill., 1962; m. Mary Elizabeth Indoe, Aug. 23, 1959; children—Debra Lynn, David Joseph, Barry Lee, Leslie Ann. Instr. physiology Western Res. U. Sch. Medicine, Cleve., 1962-64; asst. prof. U. Va. Sch. Medicine, Charlottesville, 1964-69, asso. prof., 1969-72, prof., 1972—. Vis. prof. Hadassah Med. Sch., Jerusalem, Israel, 1971-72; cons. Nat. Heart and Lung Inst.; lectr. in field. Mem. Am. Physiol. Soc., Am. Soc. Zoologists, Cardiac Muscle Soc., Soc. Exptl. Biology and Medicine, Am. Heart Assn. (basic sci. council; established investigator 1968-73), Israel Physiology and Pharmacology Soc., Internat. Study Group Cardiac Metabolism, Reticuloendothelial Soc., Pancreatic Study Group, Va. Acad. Sci., Council Biology Editors., Am. Profs. Peace in Middle East, Sigma Xi. Editor: Circulatory Stock. Editorial bd. Am. Jour. Physiology. Contbr. articles to profl. jours. Home: 101 Powhatan Circle Charlottesville VA 22901

LEFEVRE, ELBERT WALTER, JR., educator; b. Eden, Tex., July 29, 1932; s. Elbert Walter and Hazie (Davis) LeF.; B.S. in Civil Engring., Tex. A. and M. U., 1957, M.S. in Civil Engring., 1961; Ph.D., Okla. State U., 1966; m. Joyce Ann Terry, Nov. 28, 1957; children—Terry Ann, Charmaine Rene, George Walter, John Philip. Faculty, Tex. A. and M. U., Bryan, 1958, Tex. Technol. Coll., Lubbock, 1959-63, Okla. State U., Stillwater, 1963—; faculty U. Ark., Fayetteville, 1966—, head dept. civil engring., 1971—; head prin. Engring. Services, Inc., Springdale, Ark., 1973—. Served to 1st lt. AUS, 1953-56. Registered profl. engr., Ark., Tex. Mem. Am. Soc. C.E. (pres. Mid-South sect. 1972, mem. hwy. research bd. 1966—), Am. Soc. Engring. Edn., Ark. Soc. Profl. Engrs. (state dir. 1974—), Sigma Xi, Chi Epsilon. Mason, Rotarian (pres. 1973—). Home: 300 Paradise Lane Springdale AR 72764 Office: Dept Civil Engineering University Arkansas Fayetteville AR 72701

LEFILES, ROBERT JULIAN, JR., elec. engr.; b. Valdosta, Ga., Jan. 29, 1938; s. Robert Julian and Clyde Lorena (Senterfit) LeF.; B.S. in Elec. Engring., U. Miami (Fla.), 1962; m. Cynthia Nicholas, May 28, 1970; children—Ann Lynn, Robert Julian, Denise Suzanne. Designer Newport News Shipbuilding & Drydock Co. (Va.), 1962-64; electronics design sr. engr. Fla. Power & Light Co., Miami, 1964—. Owner ranch, Dade County, Fla., 1972—. Registered profl. engr., Fla. Mem. I.E.E.E., Fla. Engring. Soc., Nat. Rifle Assn. Home: 19955 SW 186th St Miami FL 33157 Office: PO Box 3100 Miami FL 33101

LE GARDEUR, GEORGE VERGNES, JR., cons. engr.; b. Shreveport, La., Aug. 4, 1926; s. George Vergnes and Claire (Parkhouse) LeG.; B.S., U. Ala., 1950; postgrad. Tulane U., 1944-45, 58-59; m. Norma Powell, Aug. 24, 1951 (div. Jan. 1970); children—Michael, Susan, Shelley, Deborah; m. 2d, Barbara J. Jett, May 16, 1970. Field constrn. supt. R. P. Farnsworth & Co., Inc., New Orleans, 1950-51; engr. Sverdrup & Parcell, cons. engrs., 1951-53; project engr. H. K. Ferguson & Co., Inc., engrs. and contractors, Cleve., 1953-55; jr. partner, cons. engr. Ewin, Campbell and Gottlieb, cons. engrs., New Orleans, 1955-59; cons. engr. G.V. Le Gardeur, Jr., 1959-66; v.p. H.B. Fowler & Co., Inc., Harvey La., 1966-70, exec. v.p., 1970-72; pres. LeGardeur Internat. Inc., 1972—. Vice pres. Protestant Home for Aged, 1967. Served with AUS, 1943-44. Registered profl. engr. La., Miss., Ala., Tex., Tenn., Ark. Mem. Cons. Engrs. Council La. (sec.-treas. 1962, pres. 1964), Am. Concrete Inst., Prestressed Concrete Inst., Am. Inst. Steel Constrn., Nat. Soc. Profl. Engrs., La. Engring. Soc., Cons. Engrs. Council, Am. Soc. Testing and Materials, Am. Soc. C.E., St. Pat's Engring. Soc., Theta Tau, Mu Epsilon, Beta Theta Pi, Tau Beta Pi, Chi Epsilon, Omicon Delta Kappa. Methodist. Home: 3700 S Pin Oak Dr New Orleans LA 70114

LEGERTON, CLARENCE WILLIAM, JR., physician, educator; b. Charleston, S.C., July 8, 1922; s. Clarence William and Winnie Davis (McMaster) L.; student Davidson Coll., 1939-43; M.D., Med. Coll. S.C., 1946; m. Mitzi Foster Herrin, May 31, 1958; children—Clarence William III, Mary Pringle, Gregg McMaster. Intern University Hosp., Balt., 1946-47, med. resident, 1947-48; instr. medicine Duke U. Sch. Medicine, 1950-53; practice medicine specializing in gastroenterology, Conway, S.C., 1953-56, Charleston, S.C., 1956-66; prof. medicine, dir. div. gastroenterology Med. U. S.C., Charleston, 1966—; dir. Citizens and So. Nat. Bank, Charleston, S.C., chmn. Charleston adv. bd., 1974—. Vice-chmn. Commrs. Pub. Works, Charleston, 1959—; chmn. water supply City of Charleston; pres. Charleston Symphony Orchestra Assn., 1967-68; chmn. bd. dirs. Legerton & Co., Inc. Mem. City Council, Charleston, S.C., 1959—, mayor pro-tem, 1960; pres. Charleston County Democratic Conv., 1960. Trustee Montreat-Anderson Coll., vice-chmn., 1962-74, chmn., 1974—; trustee Queens Coll.; chmn. bd. dirs. Charleston Municipal Auditorium; chmn. adv. bd. Comprehensive Health Planning Council Charleston, Berkeley and Dorchester Counties. Served to capt. AUS, 1948-50. Fellow A.C.P.; mem. S.C. Soc., New Eng. Soc., Alpha Omega Alpha, Sigma Phi Epsilon, Alpha Kappa Kappa. Presbyn. (pres. corp. 1965—). Club: Carolina Yacht (Charleston). Home: 32 Council St Charleston SC 29401 Office: Medical University Hospital Charleston SC 29401

LEGG, WILLIAM BEALE HIBBS, JR., motion picture producer; b. Washington, Sept. 24, 1934; s. William Beale Hibbs and Mary Jane (Nelson) L.; m. Barbara Roemer Blair, Aug. 18, 1956; children—Blair Nelson, Bryce Creighton, Baugham Roemer, Brae Jefferson, Brandt Hibbs. Vice pres. Paragon Prodns., Vienna, Va., 1961-62, pres., owner, 1962—. Served with USAF, 1952-60. Mem. Internat. Quorum, Motion Picture Producers (pres. 1969—), Internat. Film, Tape, Audio-Visual Producers Assn. (dir.), Soc. Motion Picture Technicians and Engrs., Information Film Producers Assn. Recipient several film festival awards. Address: 2363 Hunter Mill Rd Vienna VA 22180

LEGNER, STANLEY GAYLE, physician; b. Paw Paw, Ill., Feb. 28, 1920; s. Ernest and Hazel (Girton) L.; A.B., Drake U., 1943; M.D., St. Louis U., 1947; m. Beulah Clem Grah, Oct. 13, 1946; children—David Michael, Robert Eugene. Intern, St. Mary's Hosp., East St. Louis, Ill., 1947-48; resident Woman's Hosp., Chattanooga, 1948-50; practice medicine specializing in family practice, Perryville, Mo., 1950-68, Rossville, Ga., 1968—; mem. staff Hutcheson Meml. Hosp., Ft. Oglethorpe, Ga. Pres., Perry County Pub. Schs., 1962-67. Served with AUS, 1952-54. Mem. A.M.A., Med. Assn. Ga. Presbyn. (elder 1952—), Elk, Lion. Home: 7816 Stongehenge Dr Chattanooga TN 37421 Office: 214 Andrews St Rossville GA 30741

LEGORRETA, LUIS G., banker; b. Zamora, Mex., Jan. 30, 1898; s. Juan de Dios Legorreta and Guadalupe Garcia de Legorreta; student Instituto Cientifico de Mexico City, 1911; m. Gudalupe Vilchis, Dec. 2, 1926; children—Xavier, Isabel, Ricardo, Fernando. Joined Banco Nacional de Mexico S.A., Mexico City, 1913, mem. fgn. dept., 1916, various depts., 1917-22; sec., 1922-26, v.p., 1926-33, pres., 1934-52, vice-chmn., dir. dels., 1952-58, chmn. bd., dir. dels., 1958-70, hon. chmn., 1970—; dir. Banco de Mexico, Cia Fundidora de Fierro y Acero de Monterrey, Celaneses Mexicana, Fabricas de Papel San Rafael, Industria Electrica de Mexico, and other indsl. and financial cos. Chmn. bd. trustees Fundacion Mier y Pesado, pvt. charity orgn. Clubs: Bankers, University of Mexico, Campestre de la Ciudad de Mexico, Jockey Mexicano, Jr. (Mexico City). Home: Montanas Calizas 490 Mexico City Mexico Office: Isabel Catolica 44 Mexico City Mexico

LEGUM, STANLEY HOWARD, dentist; b. Norfolk, Va., Oct. 19, 1939; s. Albert and Janice (Harris) L.; B.A., U. Va., 1961; D.D.S., Med. Coll. Va., 1965; m. Gayle Sue Jacobson, Aug. 4, 1963; children—Keith Jon, Robin Denise, Paige Allison, Lisa Joy. Individual practice dentistry, Norfolk, Va., 1965-66, Virginia Beach, Va. 1968—. Served to capt. Dental Corps, USAAF, 1966-68. Mem. Am., Va. dental assns., Tidewater, Virginia Beach dental socs., Norfolk Dental Study Club, Virginia Beach Dental Forum, Alpha Omega. Jewish religion (dir. temple 1969—). Home: 533 Gleneagle Dr Virginia Beach VA 23452 Office: 3712 S Plaza Trail Virginia Beach VA 23452

LEHMAN, DAVID JOHN, JR., physician; b. Newark, Oct. 20, 1915; s. David J. and May (Stern) L.; M.D., U. Va., 1939; m. Henrietta Tichenor, Feb. 27, 1943 (div. July 1961); children—Bonnie (Mrs. Bonnie Maierhoffer), David J. III (dec.), Wendi Ann; m. 2d, Mary Ann Pennington, Oct. 19, 1969. Intern, Newark City Hosp., 1939-41; resident medicine Mount Sinai Hosp., N.Y.C., 1946; practice medicine, specializing in internal medicine and cardiology, Newark, 1947-54, Hollywood, Fla., 1954—; sr. attending in medicine Meml. Hosp., Hollywood, Fla., chief medicine, 1963-64, sec., med. staff, 1964; adj. prof. depts. psychology and sociology Fort Lauderdale U., 1971—; founder, mem. EKG panel Meml. Hosp., 1965—; dir. Dangerous Drugs div. Office of Atty. Gen. of Fla., 1968-69; chmn. Broward Country (Fla.) Council on Aging, 1966-67; organized Teenage and Parental Alert, drug edn. program, 1967; founder, pres. Dangerous Substances Guidance Center, Inc., Broward County, 1969-72; The Starting Place Edn. and Guidance Counseling Center, 1969-72; mem. med. adv. staff the Seed, Rehab. Drug Center for Youthful Drug Offenders, Broward County, 1971—. Served with AUS, 1941-46. Recipient Distinguished Service award Kiwanis Club, Fort Lauderdale, Fla., 1967, Meritorious Citizenship award Fla. Assn. Grand Juries, 1969, citizen of the year award Hollywood Elks, 1970. Diplomate Am. Bd. Internal Medicine. Mem. A.C.P., Broward County Med. Assn. (chmn. drug abuse com. 1967—, v.p. 1964), Fla. Med. Assn. (ad hoc drug abuse com. 1970), Hollywood Men's Golf Assn. (pres. 1965), Am. Legion, Fraternal Order of Police. Elk. Home: 3206 Calle Largo Hollywood FL 33021 Office: 2740 Hollywood Blvd Hollywood FL 33020

LEHMAN, GEORGE IRVIN, educator; b. Lancaster, Pa., June 11, 1915; s. George Ernest and Leah Weaver (Martin) L.; B.S., Elizabethtown Coll., 1938; B.D., Eastern Bapt. Sem., 1940; S.T.M. (Jacobus fellow), Hartford Theol. Sem., 1942, postgrad., 1943-45; M.A., N.Y. U., 1960, Ph.D. (Univ. fellow, Dept. Health, Edn. and Welfare fellow), 1964; m. Edith Vander Ploeg, Aug. 22, 1943 (dec. July 1970); children—George, Peter, Timothy, Eunice; m. 2d, Verna M. Yeager, Feb. 24, 1971. Tchr. pub. sch., Lancaster County (Pa.), 1935-37; dir. med. relief Mennonite Central Com., Nazareth, Ethiopia, 1945-47; instr. English, Am. U., Beirut, Lebanon, 1947-50, Anatlia Coll., Salonika, Greece, 1951-52; prof. O.T., Eastern Mennonite Coll., Harrisonburg, Va., 1952—. Pres. adv. bd. Salvation Army, 1973, 74. Mem. editorial com. New International Bible, 1973. Home: 1481 College Av Harrisonburg VA 22801 Office: Eastern Mennonite Seminary Harrisonburg VA 22801

LEHMAN, JAMES LUTHER, univ. exec.; b. Kansas City, Mo., June 24, 1929; s. Luther James and Sherrill L. (Arnold) L.; student Oklahoma City U., 1946-47; B.B.A., U. Tex., Austin, 1955; postgrad. Tex. Christian U., 1960; m. Henrietta Rohrer, June 6, 1954; children—Linda Diane, Jamie Denise, Sheryl Esther. Asst. advt. agt. Gulf, Colo. & Santa Fe Ry., Galveston, Tex., 1954-56; asst. dir. pub. relations Tex. Christian U., Ft. Worth, 1956-67, dir. pub. relations, 1967—. Chmn. service to mil. families com. Tarrant County chpt. A.R.C., 1971—. Served with AUS, 1951-53. Mem. Am. Coll. Pub. Relations Assn. (S.W. dist. dir. 1961-62, nat. trustee 1967-70), Advt. Club Ft. Worth (pres. 1966-67), Religious Pub. Relations Council (pres. Ft. Worth chpt. 1963-64), Pub. Relations Soc. Am., Ft. Worth C. of C. (chmn. pub. relations com. 1967-68), Alpha Phi Omega. Home: 3528 Walton St Fort Worth TX 76133 Office: Box 30776 Tex Christian U Fort Worth TX 76129

LEHMAN, WILLIAM, congressman; b. Selma, Ala., Oct. 5, 1913; s. Maurice M. and Corinne L. (Leva) L.; B.S., U. Ala., 1934; postgrad. Barry Coll., Miami, Fla., Exeter Coll., Oxford U., Harvard, U. Edinburgh; Teaching certificate secondary sch., 1963; m. Joan Feibelman, 1939; children—William, Kathy (Mrs. Donald Weiner), Tom. Owner car sales and finance bus., Miami, 1936-41, 46-56; instr. aircraft mechanics Army cadets J.P. Riddle Co., 1942; transf. to Brazilian Air Force, Sao Paulo, 1943-45; DeSoto-Plymouth dealer, Miami, 1956-59; owner Lehman Pontiac-Buick Dealership, Selma, 1960-66, Lehman Motors, South Miami, 1960—, Lehman Auto Sales, North Miami Beach, Fla., 1962—; Gen. Electric Appliance dealer, Miami, 1963-67; owner William Lehman Buick, North Miami Beach, 1966—; mem. 93d Congress from 13th Dist. Fla. Tchr., Miami Norland Jr. High Sch., 1963-64, Miami Dade Jr. Coll., 1964-66. Mem. Dade County Sch. Bd., Miami, 1966-72, chmn., 1971-72; mem. edn. com. Greater Miami Coalition. Pres., bd. dirs. Muscular Dystrophy Soc.; bd. dirs. Miami Art Center, Am. Jewish Com. Recipient Man of Year award North Miami Beach Jr. C. of C., 1971, Humanitarian of Year award Am. Jewish Congress, 1972. Democrat. Jewish religion (trustee, past sec. temple). Home: 200 NW 143d St North Miami FL 33168 Office: 502 Cannon House Office Bldg Washington DC 20515

LEHMANN, FREDERICK OTTO, JR., accountant; b. Dallas, Apr. 14, 1942; s. Frederick O. and Virginia Jane (Gates) L.; B.S., Austin Coll., 1964. Partner Tom M Hudgins & Co., pub. accountants, Sherman, Tex., 1969—. Instr. Grayson County Jr. Coll., Denison, Tex., 1973. Served with USN, 1966-69. C.P.A., Tex. Mem. Am. Inst.

C.P.A.s, Tex. Soc. C.P.A.s (Grayson county coordinator 1971-73, mem. mgmt. accounting practice com. 1972—), Sherman C. of C. (mem. govtl. affairs com. 1972-73), Sherman Jaycees. Presbyn. Home: 2521 N Travis St Sherman TX 75090 Office: 302 M and P Bldg Sherman TX 75090

LEHNERT, PETER KARL, wholesale co. exec.; b. Rumburku, Czechoslovakia, May 13, 1938 (came to U.S., 1962); s. Franz and Erna (Hentschel) L.; ed. Gymnasium, Cologne, West Germany; m. Heidrun Lingen, May 26, 1969; children—Natasha, Norman. Mgr. br. Pan Am. Trade Devel. Corp., N.Y.C., 1962-65; founder, pres. Lensteel, Inc., Houston, 1966-68, v.p. mcht. and structural steel dept., 1969—. Mem. Tex. Assn. Steel Importers (v.p.). Home: 510 W Forest St Houston TX 77024 Office: 1301 Texas Av Houston TX 77002

LEHRMAN, IRVING, clerbyman; b. Poland, June 15, 1912; s. Abraham and Minnie (Dinowitiz) L.; came to U.S., 1921; B.S., City Coll. N.Y., 1936; Rabbi, M.H.L., Jewish Inst. Rabbis, 1942; D.H.L., Jewish Theol. Sem. Am., 1958, D.D., 1968; m. Bella Goldfarb, 1935; children—David, Rosalind. Rabbi, 1942; rabbi Temple Emanu-El, Miami Beach, Fla., 1943-51, life rabbi, 1951—. Former vis. prof. homiletics Jewish Theol. Sem. Am., mem. rabbinical cabinet and bd. rabbinical visitors; hon. chaplain Jewish War Vets.; pres. Synagogue Council Am., 1971-73, hon. pres., 1973—; pres. South Fla. regional Rabbinical Assembly, 1960-63, hon. pres., 1963—, mem. exec. com., 1950—; v.p. Zionist Orgn. Am., Greater Miami Jewish Fedn.; chmn. dialogue com. Nat. Council Christians and Jews. Active numerous civic orgns.; mem. President's Commn. on Obscenity and Pornography; mem. exec. bd. South Fla. council Boy Scouts Am.; mem. Mayor's Adv. Commn. on Juvenile Delinquency. Bd. dirs. United Fund of Dade County, Citizens Housing Found., Bur. Jewish Edn. Greater Miami; bd. dirs., mem. nat. council United Hebrew Immigrant Aid Service. Mem. Am. Technion Soc. (dir.). Home: 2925 Flamingo Dr Miami Beach FL 33140 Office: 1701 Washington Av Miami Beach FL 33139

LEIDGEN, JAMES ROBERT, armored transport co. exec.; b. Milw., Aug. 11, 1924; s. Charles O. and Marian (Jasperson) L.; student Milw. State Tchrs. Coll., 1942-43; B.S., Marquette U., 1949; m. Virginia Carolyn Coursey, July 13, 1945; children—Linda Eibe (Mrs. Clark C. Eibe), Virginia (Mrs. George E. Duncan), Elizabeth, Patricia. Salesman, Brink's, Inc., Atlanta, 1949-51, J.H. Pence Co., Richmond, Va., 1951-57; sales mgr. Brink's, Inc., Atlanta, 1957-59, marketing v.p., Chgo., 1959-67; pres. Wells Fargo Armored Service Corp., Atlanta, 1967—. Mem. Atlanta Impact Com., 1971—. Served to lt. USNR, 1943-46. Mem. Nat. Armored Car Assn. (pres. 1969-70). Republican. Roman Catholic. Clubs: Cherokee Town and Country, Commodore, Commerce (Atlanta). Home: 8965 River Run Dunwoody GA 30338 Office: PO Box 4313 Atlanta GA 30302

LEIFERMAN, SILVIA WEINER (MRS. IRWIN H. LEIFERMAN), artist, civic worker; b. Chgo.; d. Morris and Annah (Caplan) Weiner; student U. Chgo., 1960-61; m. Irwin H. Leiferman, Apr. 20, 1947. One-woman shows include D'Arcy Galleries, N.Y.C., 1944, Contemporary Gallery, Palm Beach, Fla., 1966, Miami (Fla.) Museum Modern Art, 1966, Schram Galleries, Ft. Lauderdale, Fla., 1966; exhibited group shows include Riccardo Restaurant Gallery, Chgo., 1961-62, Bryn Mawr Country Club, Chgo., 1961-62, Covenant Club Ill., Chgo., 1963, D'Arcy Galleries, 1965, Miami Mus. Modern Art, 1967, Baccardi Gallery, 1967, Hollywood Mus. Art, 1968, Gallery 99, Miami, 1968, Barry Coll. Artist's Equity show, Miami Beach, 1968, Lowe Art Mus., 1968, others; pres. Active Accessories by Silvia, Chgo., 1964—. Organizer women's div. Edgewater Hosp., Chgo., 1954; chairwoman spl. events Greater Chgo. Com. State Israel, founder Ambassador's Ball, 1956; chmn. women's com. Salute to Med. Research City of Hope, 1960; chairwoman Dior-Israel Fashion Preview for State Israel, 1962; founder, chairwoman Presentation Ball State Israel, 1962; mem. Miami Beach Opera Guild Commn. Bd. dirs. Jewish Children's Bur., 1958, Mt. Sinai Hosp., Chgo., 1960, Bradeis U. (life), women's div. Hebrew U., Nathan Goldblatt Soc. Cancer Research, Orgn. Rehab. and Tng. Fox River Sanatorium; co-founder, v.p. bd. dirs. Silvia and Irwin Leiferman Found. Recipient citations for def. bond sales U.S. Govt.; named Woman of Valor (Israel), 1963. Mem. Internat. Platform Assn., Am. Fedn. Arts, Artists Equity Assn., Internat. Council Museums, Nat. Council Jewish Women (dir.), Art Inst. Chgo. (life). Clubs: Standard, Bryn Mawr Country (Chgo.); Westview Country (Miami). Home: Standard Club 320 S Plymouth Ct Chicago IL 60604 also 5255 Collins Av Miami Beach FL 33140

LEIGH, JAMES TILLMAN, antique appraiser and cons.; b. Haines City, Fla., Oct. 21, 1925; s. Samuel Garcia and Ethel (King) L.; student Loyola U., New Orleans, 1946, U. Tampa, 1947-48, U. Pitts. Grad. Sch., 1961, Brookings Inst. Advanced Studies 1962; m. Angela Maria Nistal, May 15, 1948; children—Charles Michael, James Joseph, Phillip Martine, Rita Denise, Ramona Diane. Project mgr. Paul Smith Constrn. Co., Tampa, Fla., 1949-51, v.p., 1963-67, also dir.; v.p. Patrick Gardens, Inc., Patrick AFB, Fla., 1951-54, Nat. Engring. & Devel. Corp., Washington, 1954-57; sr. coordinator Urban Renewal Adminstrn., HHFA, Washington, 1958-60, regional dir., Phila., 1960-63; dir. Am. Nat. Bank, Guaranty Fed. Savs. & Loan, 1963-65; pres., dir. Tampa Plaza, Inc., Heirloom Antiques Ltd., Inc., Waverly Arms, Inc., Tampa; v.p., dir. Golden Eagle Antiques, Inc., Lamplighter, Tampa; Chmn., Mayor's Adv. Com., Tampa, 1963—. Served with F.A., AUS, 1943-46. Decorated Bronze Star. Mem. Nat. Assn. Dealers in Antiques, Antique Appraisal Assn. Am., Suncoast Antique Dealers Assn., El Prado Antique Center, Tampa C. of C., Tau Omega. Kiwanian (pres., dir. Cocoa Beach, Fla.). Author: Management Handbook for Multifamily Rental Projects, 1956. Writer weekly newspaper column on antiques. Home: 4506 San Rafael St Tampa FL 33609 Office: The Leigh Bldg Suite 17 4320 El Prado Blvd Tampa FL 33609 also 3815 Florida Av Tampa FL 33603

LEIGH, THOMAS WATKINS, lawyer; b. Winnsboro, La., Apr. 8, 1903; s. Benjamin Watkins and Olive (Buckingham) L.; LL.B., La. St. U., 1924; m. Louise Grisham, July 7, 1942. Admitted to La. bar, 1924; pvt. practice, 1924-29; mem. firm Theus, Grisham, Davis & Leigh, Monroe, La., 1929—. Dir. 1st Nat. Bank of West Monroe. Mem. Gov.'s Spl. Commn. to Study Needs of Higher Edn. in La., 1954; mem. Gov.'s Spl: Tidelands Adv. Com., 1964-72; mem. exec. com. Pub. Affairs Research Council La., bd. dirs. Council for Better La.; chmn. La. Mineral Bd., 1966-72; del. La. Constl. Conv., 1973. Bd. suprs. La. State U., 1940-60, chmn., 1948-50. Served as lt. comdr. USNR, 1942-45. Mem. Am. (ho. of dels.), La. (pres. 1954-55, gov.) bar assns., Am. Coll. Probate Attys., Am. Coll. Trial Lawyers, Am., La. (council, v.p.) law insts., Order of Coif, Gamma Eta Gamma, Theta Xi. Episcopalian (vestryman). Clubs: Army and Navy (Washington); Boston, Pickwick (New Orleans). Home: 1401 S Grand St Monroe LA 71201 Office: 400 S Grand St Monroe LA 71201

LEIGON, WALTER A., oil co. exec.; b. Morgan, Tex., Nov. 27, 1918; s. Samuel Lindsay and Minnie May (Newton) L.; student, Clifton Jr. Coll., 1939; B.B.A. with honors, U. Tex., 1948; M.B.A. with honors, U. Houston, 1953; m. Lena Mae Windham, Mar. 19, 1943; children—Larry Alan, William Lindsay. With, Humble Oil & Refining Co., 1948—, adminstrv. coordinator, Houston, 1967—. Instr. accounting U. Houston, 1956. Scoutmaster, Cub Scouts Am., Bellaire, Tex., 1956-60; coach Little League Baseball, Bellaire, 1958-60; active United Fund Drs., Houston, 1969—. Served to capt. inf. AUS, 1940-45; ETO. Decorated Bronze Star with cluster, Silver Star. C.P.A., Tex. Mem. Nat. Assn. Accountants, Am. Petroleum Inst., Tex. Soc. C.P.A.'s. Methodist (mem. bd. stewards 1961-64, 67-70). Democrat. Home: 8827 Manhattan St Houston TX 77035 Office: 800 Bell St Houston TX 77001

LEITCH, VINCENT BARRY, educator; b. Hempstead, N.Y., Sept. 18, 1944; s. Eugene Vincent and Lucile (Amplo) L.; student State U. N.Y. Maritime Coll., 1962-64; B.A., Hofstra U., 1966; M.A., Villanova U., 1967; Ph.D., U. Fla., 1972; m. Jill Robin Berman, May 20, 1970; 1 dau., Kristin Meredith. Research asst. Villanova U., 1967; tchr. North Babylon (N.Y.) High Sch., 1968; grad. teaching asst. U. Fla., 1969-72, interim asst. prof., 1972-73; asst. prof. English lit. Mercer U., Macon, Ga., 1973—. Am. Philos. Soc. research grantee, 1974; Mercer U. Research Fund grantee, 1974. Mem. Modern Lang. Assn. Am., South Atlantic Modern Lang. Assn., Renaissance Soc. Am., Southeastern Renaissance Conf., Nat. Council Tchrs. English, Am. Assn. U. Profs. Kiwanian (lt. gov. N.Y. dist. 1963-64). Editor: Marie Magdalens Funeral Teares (Robert Southwell), 1974. Mem. editorial staff Abstracts of English Studies, 1972—. Contbr. articles to mags. Home: 4693 Twin Oaks Dr Macon GA 31204 Office: Mercer U Macon GA 31207

LEITER, BEULAH G. (MRS. ROBERT PAUL LEITER), lawyer; b. Chgo.; d. Jehiel O. and Rose (Rossman) Liebling; J.D., John Marshall U., 1945, LL.M., 1946; spl. student U. Chgo., U. Ga., Emory U.; m. Robert Paul Leiter, May 9, 1936; children—Darryl J., Paula S. Admitted to Ga. bar, 1945, since practiced in Atlanta; mem. firm Leiter & Leiter, 1946—; dep. sheriff, 1958—. Mem. of Iota Tau Tau, 1951—, So. chancellor, 1955-57, internat. supreme chancellor, 1955-59, mem. supreme council, 1955-63, supreme asso. dean, 1959-61, internat. supreme dean, 1961-63. Mem. Nat. Women's Com. Brandeis U., 1961—. Mem. Internat. Fedn. Women Lawyers (legal edn. com. 1958, penal law, outer space law, UN coms. 1959-60), Nat. Assn. Women Lawyers, Am. Judicature Soc., Com. Women in Pub. Service, Ga. Assn. Women Lawyers (past v.p., rec. sec.), Ga. Bar Assn., Fulton County Lawyers Assn. (charter, trustee 1952, rec. sec. 1956—), Nat. Assn. Claimant Attys., Am. Bus. Women's Assn., P.T.A., Internat. Platform Assn., Am. Trial Lawyers Assn., Nat. Geog. Soc., Phi Kappa Delta. Clubs: Equity (publicity com. 1959-60, 63—), Old War Horse Lawyers, Nat. Travel. Home: 1219 Poplar Grove Dr NE Atlanta GA 30306 Office: Equitable Bldg Suite 520 100 Peachtree St NW Atlanta GA 30303

LEITER, GORDON ALBERT, elec. engr.; b. Sedalia, Mo., Feb. 4, 1930; s. Noah Claud and Violet Albertha (Fry) L.; B.S. in Elec. Engring., U. Mo., 1951; m. Ida Marguerite Saville, July 26, 1952; children—Virginia Gayle, Lawrence David, Katherine Sue. With Gen. Electric Co., 1952—, mgr. control design, voltage regulators, Pittsfield, Mass., 1964-66; sr. design engr. load tap changers and controls, Rome, Ga., 1966—; sec.-treas. West Rome Band Buses, Inc., 1973—. Served with AUS, 1953-55. Registered profl. engr., Mo. Mem. I.E.E.E. (chmn. Rome subsect. 1970-71). Methodist. Club: West Rome Chieftains. Home: 9 Wilson Dr Rome GA 30161 Office: Gen Electric Co Redmond Circle Rome GA 30161

LEITNER, PAUL R., lawyer; b. Winnsboro, S.C., Nov. 11, 1928; s. W. Walker and Irene (Lewis) L.; A.B., Duke, 1950; LL.B., McKenzie Coll., 1954; m. Sandra Strickland, Dec. 29, 1972; children by previous marriage—David, Douglas, Gregory, Reid, Cheryl. Admitted to Tenn. bar, 1954; practiced in Chattanooga, 1954; asso. firm Thomas Leitner, Mann, Warner & Owens, and predecessors, 1952-57, partner, 1957—. Treas., dir., Nat. Motor Club of Tenn., Inc., 1956—. Bd. dirs. Family Service Agy., 1957-63; mem. Chattanooga-Hamilton County Community Action Bd.; mem. Juvenile Ct. Commn., Hamilton County, 1955-61, chmn., 1958-59; chmn. Citizens Com. for Better Sch.; mem. Met. Govt. Charter Commn. Bd. dirs. U. Chattanooga Meth. Student Center, Camp Ocoee, YMCA. Served with AUS, 1946-47. Recipient Young Man of Year award, Chattanooga area, 1957. Mem. Jr. C. of C. (pres. 1956-57), Am., Chattanooga, Tenn. bar assns., Am. Judicature Soc., Fedn. Ins. Counsel, Trial Attys. Am., Tenn. Def. Lawyers Assn. (sec.-treas. 1973-74). Methodist (chmn. ofcl. bd., lay leader, dist. bd. lay activities). Home: 1034 Red Robin Lane Chattanooga TN 37421 Office: 330 Pioneer Bldg Chattanooga TN 37402

LEMIEUX, HENRY FISHER, constrn. co. exec.; b. Greenville, Miss., Aug. 20, 1926; s. Frederic Alexander and Elizabeth (Fisher) LeM.; B.E.E., Tulane U., 1946, B.S. in Civil Engring., 1949; m. Marjorie Elizabeth Hunter, May 7, 1954; children—Michelle E., Jolie M., Babette A., Henry Fisher. Engr., field supt. Raymond Internat., Inc., 1949-51, dist. mgr. New Orleans, 1951-57, asst. v.p., New Orleans, N.Y.C., London, Eng., 1957-65, pres., N.Y.C., 1968—, chief exec. officer, 1970—, also dir.; v.p., gen. mgr. Raymond Concrete Pile div., 1965-68, also officer, dir. subsidiary cos.; dir. So. Nat. Bank, Houston. Bd. advisers Tulane Sch. Engring.; adv. com. Coll. Bus. Adminstrn. U. Houston. Served to lt. (j.g.) USNR, 1944-46. Registered profl. engr., N.Y., Fla., La. Mem. Am. Soc. C.E., Am. Soc. Testing Materials, Newcomen Soc. N.Am., Pan Am. Soc. U.S., Engrs. Joint Council, Tau Beta Pi, Sigma Alpha Epsilon. Episcopalian. Clubs: Larchmont (N.Y.) Yacht; Moles, Beavers; American (London); Southern Yacht, Plimsoll (New Orleans); Houston, Ramada, University, River Oaks (Houston); Ocean Reef (Key Largo, Fla.). Home: 19 Courtlandt Pl Houston TX 77006 Office: 2801 S Post Oak Rd Houston TX 77027

LEMING, JOE BILLY, mech. engr.; b. Normandy, Tenn., May 30, 1924; s. Charles Winfred and Pearlean (Troxler) L.; B.S., Vanderbilt U., 1949; m. Lelia Barnes, May 17, 1952; 1 son, Charles William. Field engr. Factory Ins. Assn., Chgo., 1949-63; sr. mech. engr. Tenn. Eastman Co., Kingsport, 1963—. Pres., bd. dirs. Kingsport Safety Council. Served with USNR, 1943-46. Registered profl. engr., Tenn. Mem. Nat. Fire Protection Assn., Soc. Fire Protection Engrs., Am. Soc. Safety Engrs. Elk, Moose, Eagle. Home: 800 Meadow Lane Kingsport TN 37663 Office: Tenn Eastman Co B-18 Kingsport TN 37662

LEMMON, MARK, architect; b. Gainesville, Tex., Nov. 10, 1889; s. William Leonard and Cosette (Lipscomb) L.; B.A., U. Tex., 1912; B.S., Mass. Inst. Tech., 1916; m. Maybelle Reynolds, Nov. 14, 1922; children—Dr. Mark Leonard, George Reynolds. Individual practice architecture, Dallas, 1923—; cons. architect U. of Tex. in Austin and brs. Galveston and Dallas; dir. Nat. City Bank of Dallas. Mem. adv. com. Greater Dallas Planning Council; past mem. council, Highland Park. Served as 1st lt., C.E., U.S. Army, World War I; chmn. contract renegotiations bd. Southwestern div. C.E., AUS, 1943-44. Mem. Newcomen Soc. N.Am.; Tex. Philos. Soc., Dallas Hist. Soc., Am. Legion, Sigma Chi. Presbyn. Clubs: City of Dallas, Dallas Country, Friars. Designs executed include Highland Park Presbyn. Ch., 22-story Corrigan Tower, Perkins Sch. Theology for So. Meth. U., U. Tex. Southwestern Med. Sch., Southland Center (cons.), Sheraton Dallas Hotel (cons.); one of two architects Fed. Courthouse and Office Bldg., Dallas; sole architect St. Luke's Meth. Ch., Houston, also pub. schs., Marshall, Longview, Terrell, Grand Prairie, Port Arthur, Sherman and Dallas, Tex. Home: 3211 Mockingbird Lane Dallas TX 75201 Office: Southland Center Dallas TX 75201

LEMMON, MAYBELLE REYNOLDS (MRS. MARK LEMMON), civic worker; b. Longview, Tex.; d. George Thompson and MayBelle (Bruner) Reynolds; grad. Sullins Coll., 1921; postgrad. U. Tex. at Austin, 1921-22; m. Mark Lemmon, Nov. 14, 1922; children—Mark Leonard, George Reynolds. Exhibited group shows at Dallas Mus. Fine Arts, 1962, 63, 64, Jr. League Art Show, 1963. Mem. bd. Jr. League, Dallas, 1938-43; mem. woman's bd. Dallas Civic Opera, 1960-64; mem. bd. Presbyn. Home and Sch., Itasca, Tex., 1944-52; mem. joint adv. bd. So. Meth. U., 1957-63, YMCA, Dallas, 1940-63; women's com. Met. Opera Co., Dallas, 1962. Mem. First Families Va., Nat. Soc. Colonial Dames Am., Dallas Symphony League, Dallas Art Assn., Kappa Kappa Gamma. Presbyn. (a founder, active Women of Ch.). Clubs: Garden of Am.; Junior League Garden (founder), Dallas Shakespeare (pres. 1963-64), Dallas Garden (bd. mem. 1952-57, v.p. of Founders Garden Club Dallas), Dallas Woman's (pres. 1951-53). Home: 3211 Mockingbird Lane Dallas TX 75205

LEMMONS, STANLEY LEON, civil engr.; b. Rochester, Tex., Aug. 12, 1925; s. Benjamin and Blanche (Ulshen) L.; B.S. in Civil Engring., Tex. Agrl. and Mech. U., 1949; m. Hazel Bernice Pollard, Sept. 3, 1964; children—Robert, Douglas, Samuel, Paul. Liaison engr. J.E. Greiner Co., Balt., 1950-56; office engr. Turnpike Engrs., Inc., Arlington, Tex., 1956-57; pvt. practice engring., 1957-61; with Tex. Water Rights Commn., Austin, 1961—, dir. water rights div., 1965—. Served with USNR, 1943-46. Registered profl. engr., Tex., Ohio. Jewish religion. Home: 2916 Dover Pl Austin TX 78731 Office: PO Box 13207 Capitol Sta Austin TX 78711

LEMON, WILLIAM JACOB, lawyer; b. Covington, Va., Oct. 25, 1932; s. James Gordon and Elizabeth (Wilson) L.; B.A., Washington and Lee U., 1957, LL.B., 1959; m. Barbara Inez Boyle, Aug. 17, 1957; children—Sarah E., William Tucker, Stephen W. Admitted to Va. bar, 1959; asso. Martin, Martin & Hopkins, 1959-61; partner Martin, Hopkins & Lemon, Roanoke, Va., 1961—; pres., dir. Va. Sarshares, Inc.; chmn. bd. Home Savs. & Loan Assn., Inc.; pres., dir. Liberty Nursing Homes, Inc. Served with AUS, 1952-54. Mem. Am., Va., Roanoke bar assns., Kappa Sigma, Phi Alpha Delta. Presbyn. Clubs: Shenandoah, Hunting Hills Country (Roanoke). Home: 160 27th St Roanoke VA 24014 Office: Boxley Bldg Roanoke VA 24011

LEMSER, BERNARD AUGUST, banker; b. St. Joseph, Mo., June 11, 1911; s. August Carl and Edith Marguerite (Dieter) L.; student pub. schs., St. Joseph; m. Mildred Lavon Wadlow, Sept. 18, 1932; children—Lawrence Scott, Daniel Carl. Store mgr. Wohl Shoe Co., St. Louis, 1929-35; mdse. mgr. Sears, Roebuck & Co., Birmingham, Ala., 1935-47; mdse. mgr. Montgomery Ward & Co., 1947-48; gen. mdse. mgr. Aldens, Chgo., 1949-65; v.p. State 1st Nat. Bank, Texarkana, Ark., 1966—; pres. Lake Texarkana Water Supply Corp., Texarkana Manpower & Devel. Corp. Sec.-treas. N.E. Tex. Econ. Devel. Dist.; v.p. Red River Valley Assn. Mem. N.E. Tex. Water Assn., Texarkana C. of C. (past pres., chmn. com. of 15). Lion. Home: 720 W 27th St Texarkana TX 75501 Office: State Line Plaza Texarkana AR 75501

LENCHNER, VICTOR, dentist; b. Bklyn., Feb. 7, 1925; s. Herman and Molly Hildreth (Gerber) L.; D.D.S., N.Y. U., 1948; M.S. in Psychology, U. Miami, 1969; m. Rose Shermer, July 18, 1948; children—Douglas Roy, Julie Claire. Gen. practice dentistry, Bklyn., 1948-50, practice specializing in pedodontics, Miami Beach, Fla., 1953—. Served to capt. Dental Corps, AUS, 1951-53. Recipient Alumni Gold medal N.Y. U., 1948. Diplomate Am. Bd. Pedodontics (examiner 1973). Fellow Am. Coll. Dentists, Am. Acad. Pedodontics, mem. Am. (past pres.), Fla. (past pres.) socs. dentistry for children, Miami Beach Dental Soc. (past pres.), Fla. (past pres.), Southeastern (pres. elect) socs. pedodontists, Psi Chi. Author: What You Should Know About Your Child's Teeth, 1971. Home: 1315 Daytonia Rd Miami Beach FL 33141 Office: 1185 71st St Miami Beach FL 33141

LENNOX, EDWARD NEWMAN, pub. affairs exec.; b. New Orleans, July 27, 1925; s. Joseph Andrew and May Alice (Newman) L.; B.B.A., Tulane U., 1949; m. Joan Marie Landry, Sept. 3, 1949; children—Katherine Sarah, Anne Victoria, Mary Elizabeth, Laura Joan. Marketing service clk. Shell Oil Co., New Orleans, 1949; with W.M. Chambers Truck Line, Inc., 1950-60, exec. v.p., 1953-60; v.p. Radcliff Materials, Inc., New Orleans, 1961-73, So. Industries Corp., New Orleans, 1971—; dir. Mut. Homestead Assn., 1967-73. Mem. La. Bd. Hwys., 1965-67; chmn. New Orleans Aviation Bd., 1960-67; bd. mem. Travelers Aid Soc., 1966-68; pres. Met. New Orleans Safety Council, 1969-70, Bd. Levee Commrs. of Orleans Levee Dist., 1969-72; bd. dirs. Constrn. Industry Legislative Council, 1968—, Miss. Valley Assn., 1969-72; mem. Ala. Gov.'s Adv. Council on Econs., 1971-72, La. Gov.'s Adv. Com. on River Area Transp. and Planning Study, 1971-72; bus. and financial adviser Congregation Sisters of Immaculate Conception, New Orleans, 1964—. Bd. dirs., mem. exec. com. Methodist Hosp.; bd. dirs. New Orleans, Boys' Clubs Greater New Orleans, Inc. Served to capt. AUS, 1943-46. Recipient Industry Service award Asso. Gen. Contractors Am., 1967; New Orleans Jr. C. of C. award, 1960; certificate of merit. City New Orleans, 1964, 67; named hon. citizen, Jacksonville, Fla. Mem. La. Tank Truck Carriers (pres. 1953-54), La. Motor Transport Assn. (pres. 1963-64), Am. (v.p. 1962-63), La. Good Roads Assn. (exec. com. 1972—), Ala. (v.p. 1956-60) trucking assns., So. Concrete Masonry Assn. (pres. 1963-68), Greater New Orleans Ready Mixed Concrete Assn. (pres. 1966-68), Pub. Affairs Research Council La. (area v.p. 1972-73), La. Shell Producers Assn. (pres. 1966-68), C. of C. New Orleans Area (pres. elect 1973, area v.p. external affairs 1969-72), Lakeshore Property Owners Assn., Internat. House, Tulane Alumni Assn. Clubs: Metairie Country, Traffic (New Orleans). Home: 862 Topaz St New Orleans LA 70124 Office: 1010 Common St Suite 1710 New Orleans LA 70112

LENOIR, WILLIAM BENJAMIN, astronaut; b. Miami, Fla., Mar. 14, 1939; s. Samuel S. and Iona (Yann) L.; S.B., Mass. Inst. Tech., 1962, Ph.D., 1965; m. Elizabeth May Frost, July 4, 1964; children—William Benjamin, Samantha Ellen. Elec. engr. Gen. Radio Co., 1964; instr., then asst. prof. elec. engring. Mass. Inst. Tech., 1964—; scientist-astronaut NASA, 1967—; cons. on meteorol. satellites, 1965—. Recipient C.E. Tucker teaching excellence award Mass. Inst. Tech., 1964. Mem. Am. Geophys. Union, A.A.A.S., Am. Astron. Soc., Am. Inst. Physics, Sigma Xi, Eta Kappa Nu, Sigma Alpha Epsilon. Roman Catholic. Research articles on electromagnetic wave propagation, remote sounding planetary atmospheres, meteorol. satellites; investigator sci. satellite experiments, balloon experiments. Address: NASA-MSC 2101 NASA Rd Houston TX 77058

LEON, LEONARD, petroleum co. exec.; b. Chgo., Oct. 13, 1923; s. Harry and Rae (Bolstein) L.; student Tulane U., 1939-41; B.S. in Aero. Engring., Tex. A. and M. U., 1947; student Advanced Mgmt. Program, Harvard, 1972; m. Dora Rose Bernstein, July 31, 1943; children—Barbara (Mrs. Michael Donsky), Roy Nathan, Jack Stephen. Engr. trainee to regional v.p. Halliburton Co., various locations 1948-69, exec. v.p. Halliburton Services div., Duncan, Okla., 1969—; dir. Jet Research Center, Arlington, Tex. Served with USAAF, 1942-45; ETO. Decorated Air medal with 4 oak leaf clusters. Registered profl. engr., Tex., Okla. Mem. Am. Petroleum Inst., Soc. Petroleum Engrs. Elk. Home: 2206 Carolin Dr Duncan OK 73533 Office: 1015 Bois D'Arc Duncan OK 73533

LEONARD, ROBERT BRUCE, physician; b. Cleburne, Tex., July 11, 1910; s. Andy and Mary (Martin) L.; B.S., East Tex. State U., 1947; M.D., Baylor U., 1947; m. Fredleen Power, Feb. 5, 1941; children—Betty Jo (Mrs. G.R. Singleton), Bonnie (Mrs. W.J. Hyson), Robert F., Theodore W. Intern Methodist Hosp., Houston, 1947-48; gen. practice medicine, Houston, 1948-63; staff psychiatrist Terrell (Tex.) State Hosp., 1964—. Tchr. adult bible class First Meth. Ch., Terrell, lesson broadcast over KTER each Sunday, 1968—. Mem. A.M.A., Tex. Med. Assn., Kaufman County Med. Soc., Theta Kappa Psi. Contbr. articles to med. jours. Home: 202 Melody Lane Terrell TX 75160 Office: Terrell State Hosp Terrell TX 75160

LEONARD, STEWART WALLACE, physician; b. Louisville, Nov. 15, 1905; s. William Kirkland and Lena (Stewart) L.; A.B., Harvard, 1927; M.D., U. Louisville, 1931; m. Beatrice Thomasia Goodmonson, Apr. 14, 1944; children—Cathryn Gail, Linda Lee, Deborah Stewart. Jr. rotating intern Louisville Gen. Hosp., 1931-32, sr. intern pathology, 1932-33, internal medicine, 1933-34, surgery, 1934-35, asst. resident pathology, 1935, surgery, 1936-37; gen. practice medicine, Louisville, 1937-42, 46—. Served from capt. to maj. M.C., AUS, 1942-46; PTO. Mem. Am., Ky., So. med. assns., Am. Geriatrics Soc., Jefferson County Med. Soc., Louisville C. of C. (charter), Ky. Hist. Soc. (life), English Speaking Union. Methodist. Clubs: Filson, Eexcutives (Louisville). Home: 1801 Windsor Pl Louisville KY 40204 Office: 1983 Douglas Blvd Louisville KY 40205

LEON-PORTILLA, MIGUEL, author; b. Mexico City, Mexico, Feb. 22, 1926. Dir. Inst. Hist. Research Nat. U. Mexico. Author: Broken Spears: The Aztec Account of the Conquest of Mexico, 1962; Aztec Thought and Culture: A Study of the Ancient Nahuatl Mind, 1963; Pre-Columbian Literatures of Mexico, 1969; Time and Reality in the Thought of the Maya, 1973. Address: care Instituto de Investigaciones Historicas Torre de Humanidades 70 piso Ciudad Universitaria Mexico 20 DF Mexico

LEON-SOTOMAYOR, LUIS ANGEL, physician; b. Ponce, P.R., Aug. 2, 1931; s. Jose Luis Leon-Parra and Olga Sotomayor-Falcon; B.S. cum laude, U. P.R., 1954, Med. Tech. summa cum laude, 1954, M.D. with highest honors, 1958; m. Rosita Fonfria, June 17, 1955; children—Olga Vanessa, Rose Valerie, Louis Angel, Wanda Lisette, Sharon, David. Extern surgery with highest honors Columbia Presbyn. Hosp., N.Y.C., 1957; intern with highest honors Charity Hosp. of La., New Orleans, 1958-59, resident internal medicine Tulane div., 1959-62; fellow in medicine, cardiology Johns Hopkins U., Balt., 1962-63; instr. medicine Tulane U., dir. Alcoholic Research div. Charity Hosp., New Orleans, 1961-62; instr. Med. Coll. Ga., Augusta, 1963-65, U. Tex. Med. Br., Galveston, 1965—; practice medicine, specializing in internal medicine and cardiology, Galveston, 1965—; chmn. dept. medicine Galveston County Hosp., Texas City, 1965-68; mem. staffs John Sealy Hosp., Galveston, St. Mary's Hosp., Galveston, Galveston County Meml. Hosp., Danforth Hosp., Texas City, Clear Lake and Space Center Meml. Hosp., Webster, Tex.; sec. Drs. Clinic, Galveston, 1970—; lectr. in field. Mem. Galveston Bd. Health, 1966-70. Served to capt. M.C., AUS, 1963-65. Recipient grant Tex. Heart Assn., 1969, Bay Area Heart Assn. Diplomate Am. Bd. Internal Medicine, Nat. Bd. Med. Examiners. Fellow A.C.P., Am. Coll. Cardiology, Am. Coll. Angiology, Am. Coll. Chest Physicians, Royal Soc. Medicine (U.K.), Royal Soc. Health; mem. Am. Heart Assn. (council clin. cardiology), Bay Area Heart Assn. (v.p. 1972—), A.M.A., Sigma Xi, Alpha Omega Alpha. Clubs: Galveston Artillery, Galveston Country, Galveston Boat. Author: Myxedema Coma, 1964; Cirrhosis of Liver and Hepatoma, 1966; Epidemic Diencephalomyelytis, 1969. Contbr. articles to profl. jours. Developer cardiac pacemaker catheter with atrial pressure recorder; co-developer heated ultrasound nebulization machine. Home: 4402 Caduceous St Galveston TX 77550 Office: Drs Clinic 1501 Broadway Galveston TX 77550

LEOPOLD, JOSEPH HAROLD, cons. engr.; b. N.Y.C., Dec. 17, 1917; s. Joseph and Mary (Sifter) L.; B.S. in Civil Engring., U. Pa., 1940; postgrad. Columbia Grad. Sch. Bus., 1940-41; m. Johnnie Victoria Correll, June 30, 1956. Student engr. Panama Canal, Balboa, C.Z., 1941-42; draftsman Charles T. Main, Inc., Kingsport, Tenn., 1942-44; engring. designer Kellex Corp., N.Y.C., 1944-46, Chemstrand Corp., N.Y.C., 1946-48; engring. designer Patehen & Zimmerman Engrs., Oak Ridge, 1948-49, dist. mgr., Anniston, Ala., 1951-52, Chattanooga, 1952-54, chief engr., Atlanta, 1954-58; engring. designer Austin Co., Oak Ridge, 1949-51; partner Zimmerman, Evans & Leopold, Atlanta, 1958—. Mem. Nat., Ga. (pres. 1968-69) socs. profl. engrs., Atlanta Exchange Club. Presbyn. Author: The Kingdom of Prosperity, 1964; contbg. editor Ga. Bus. News, 1967—. Home: 1765 Ft Valley Dr SW Atlanta GA 30311 Office: 44 Forsyth St NW Atlanta GA 30303

LEOPOLD, LOUIS, aerospace electronics engr.; b. Boston, Mar. 8, 1918; s. Nathan and Mary (Meyers) L.; B.S., U. Mich., 1941, Ill. Inst. Tech., 1958; postgrad. U. Chgo., 1949-51; m. Wilma Erika Miron, Dec. 27, 1947; children—Robert Louis, Laurence Scott. Electronics devel. engr. Magnecord, Inc., Chgo., 1952-53; sr. electronics project engr., group leader Motorola, Inc., 1953-59; electronics aero. research engr. communications system Project Mercury, NASA, Langley Field, Va., 1950-60, head antennas and microwave systems Project Apollo, Manned Spacecraft Center, Houston, 1961-67; NASA rep. for Project Mercury, McDonnell Aircraft Corp., St. Louis, 1960-61; mgr. NASA office, Apollo High Gain and LEM Steerable High Gain Antennas, Dalmo Victor Co., Belmont, Cal., 1968-69; expt. mgr. NASA Apollo Lunar Orbital Missions, S-band Transponder and Bistatic Radar Expts., 1969—. Cons., A.M.A., Chgo., 1957-59, Motorola, Inc., Thompson Ramo Wooldridge, Inc., 1956-59. Served to capt. USAAF, 1942-46. Recipient NASA Achievement awards, 1963-74. Mem. I.E.E.E. (chmn. aerospace group 1964-65), A.A.A.S., Ill. Acad. Sci., U. Mich. Union, St. Louis Engrs. Club, U. Mich. Alumni Assn. (dir. Houston 1967-68). Home: 7751 El Rancho St Houston TX 77017 Office: NASA Manned Spacecraft Center Houston TX 77058

LERMAN, ALLEN HERBERT, economist; b. N.Y.C., Mar. 21, 1943; s. Louis and Elizabeth (Solomon) L.; A.B., Columbia Coll., 1964; postgrad. (research fellow) The Brookings Instn., 1967-68; M.A., Yale, 1965, M.Philosophy, 1967; m. Barbara Ina Cohen, Aug. 25, 1968. Teaching asso. dept. econs. Yale, 1966-67, asst. instr., 1968-70; cons. to Pres.'s Council Econ. Advisers, 1965-68; cons. in computer systems design, 1970-71; financial economist Office of Tax Analysis, Office of the Sec., U.S. Treasury Dept., Washington, 1971—. NSF fellow, 1964-68. Mem. Am. Econ. Assn. Author: National Income Policy Simulation, 1970. Editor: (with Harold W. Chase) Kennedy and the Press: The News Conferences, 1965. Home: 14905 Waterway Dr Rockville MD 20853 Office: 4051A Main Treasury Bldg US Treasury Dept 15th St and Pennsylvania Av NW Washington DC 20220

LERNER, LOUIS D., accountant; b. Houston, Dec. 15, 1940; s. Hyman A. and Camille Anna (Todaro) L.; B.B.A., U. Tex., 1962; postgrad. U. Houston, 1966; m. Beverly Lewis, Aug. 31, 1961; children—Russell, Jay, Stephanie. Mem. staff Rumsey & Sklar, C.P.A.'s, Houston, 1964-68; partner Rumsey & Lerner, C.P.A.'s, Houston, 1968—. C.P.A., Tex. Mem. Am. Inst. C.P.A.'s, Tex. Soc. C.P.A.'s, Am. Judicature Soc., Beta Alpha Psi. Home: 10015 Briar Dr Houston TX 77042 Office: 3120 Southwest Freeway 414 Houston TX 77006

LERNER, SAMUEL HAROLD, physician; b. N.Y.C., June 6, 1917; s. Isadore and Rebecca (Goldstein) L.; A.B., Columbia, 1939; M.D., U. Cin., 1943; m. Mary Elizabeth Sullivan, Feb. 24, 1943; children—Margaret Judith (Mrs. James Krueger), Jo Ann (Mrs. Jon Steen), Deborah Ellen (Mrs. Jack Sweeney), Robert Tod, Caroline Elizabeth. Intern Cin. Gen. Hosp., 1943-44; sr. clin. instr., Western Res. U., 1957-67, asst. clin. prof., 1967-68; asso. clin. prof. Emory U., 1969—. Served to capt. USMCR, 1943-46. Commonwealth fellow Western Res. U., 1946-47, Rockefeller fellow, 1947-48, Diplomate Am. Bd. Psychiatry. Fellow Am. Psychiat. Assn., Am. Orthopsychiat. Assn.; mem. Am. Psychoanalytic Assn., Center Advanced Psychoanalytic Studies (Princeton), Cleve. Psychoanalytic Soc., Phila. Assn. Psychoanalysis. Contbr. articles to profl. jours. Home: 2117 Bucktrout Pl Atlanta GA 30341 Office: 3400 Peachtree Rd Atlanta GA 30326

LESANSKY, WILLIAM A., statistician, govt. ofcl.; b. N.Y.C., Apr. 22, 1921; s. Harry and Sarah (Dorfman) L.; B.B.A., Coll. City N.Y., 1942; M.A., George Washington U., 1947; m. Filomena Agnelli, May 19, 1966; children—Henry, Lewis, Mendel, David. Statistician, comptroller Dept. Def., Washington, 1942-69; staff statistician Interstate Commerce Commn., Washington, 1969—. Pres. Sleepy Hollow Citizens Assn., 1973—. Bd. dirs. Transp. Research Forum. Mem. Am. Statis. Assn., Am. Soc. Mil. Comptrollers (editor Armed Forces comptroller). Home: 6444 Sleepy Ridge Rd Falls Church VA 22042 Office: 12th and Constitution Av NW Washington DC 20423

LESESNE, EDWARD HUGUENIN, govt. ofcl.; b. Charleston, S.C., Oct. 4, 1920; s. Daniel Somers and Emma Rose (Huguenin) L.; B.S. in Civil Engring., Clemson Coll., 1941; grad. Fed. Exec. Inst., 1972; m. Sarah Frances Brodie, Apr. 12, 1942; children—Edward Huguenin, Sarah M. (Mrs. John M. Craddock), Elizabeth H., Robert H. With TVA, 1941—, asst. dir. water control planning, 1968-74, dir. water control planning, 1974—. Mem. U.S. Nat. Com. of Internat. Hydrological Decade, 1964-70. Served to capt. AUS, 1942-46; maj. Res. ret. Registered profl. engr., N.C. Fellow Am. Soc. C.E.; mem. U.S. Com. on Large Dams Internat. Commn. Large Dams, Internat. Water Resources Assn., Sigma Xi, Tau Beta Pi, Chi Epsilon. Prebyn. (elder). Home: 5817 Marilyn Dr Knoxville TN 37914 Office: Evans Bldg Union Av Knoxville TN 37902

LESHER, ARTHUR CARNEY, JR., judge; b. Ambler, Pa., Mar. 8, 1916; s. Arthur C. and Kathryn Marie (Shannon) L.; student Malvern Prep. Sch., 1934; A.B., U. Ala., 1938; LL.B., St. Mary's U., San Antonio, 1942; m. Marie R. Palmisano, Sept. 2, 1960. Admitted to Tex. bar, 1942, U.S. Supreme Ct. bar, 1946; asso. firm Eskridge, Croce & Chiles, San Antonio, 1942-45; partner firm Blades, Chiles, Moore & Kennerly, Houston, 1945-48, Chiles, Lawler & Lesher, 1948; individual practice, 1948; partner firm Kennerly & Leshner, 1956-62; judge Probate Ct., 1962, Ct. Domestic Relations, Houston, 1963-67, 157th Jud. Dist. Ct., 1967—. Bd. dirs. Homes of St. Mark, Variety Boys Club; trustee St. Mary's U. Sch. Law, San Antonio, 1959-61. Mem. Am. Houston, (dir., 1st v.p.) bar assns., State Bar Tex., Delta Theta Phi. Rotarian. Club: Houson. Home: 10130 Shady River Rd Houston TX 77042 Office: Civil Courts Bldg Houston TX 77002

LESHER, EUGENE ALBERT, household chem. co. exec.; b. Sunman, Ind., Sept. 3, 1914; s. Walter E. and Bertha (Miller) L.; student U. Cin., 1932-34; m. Ella M. Brinegar, May 16, 1936; children—Charles E., Thomas A., Katherine J. Clk., A.S. Boyle Co., Cin., 1930-36, salesman, 1936-40; with Boyle Midway div. Am. Home Products Corp., 1944—, v.p. nat. sales, N.Y.C., 1957-66, v.p. So. region, Atlanta, 1967—. Vice pres. Berkeley Lake Property Owners Assn. Mem. Atlanta Sales and Marketing Execs. (exec. v.p., dir.). Methodist. Clubs: Canadian (N.Y.C.); Cherokee Town and Country (Atlanta). Home: 150 Bayway Circle Berkeley Lake Duluth GA 30136 Office: 4111 Pleasant Dale Rd Atlanta GA 30340

LESKIN, LOUIS WORON, psychiatrist; b. Chernigov, Russia, Mar. 10, 1913; s. Isidore and Clara (Woronov) L.; came to U.S., 1913, naturalized, 1941; B.S., Coll. City N.Y., 1933; M.D., U. Md., 1937; m. Carolyn Hopkins, May 4, 1941; children—Carol Louise (Mrs. Charles Allen), Abigail (Mrs. Stuart W. Royle), Michael C., Jane H., Edyth Eugenia. Intern, Beth David Hosp., N.Y.C., 1937-38; resident VA Hosp., Waco, Tex., 1946-48; practice medicine specializing in psychiatry Murfreesboro, Tenn., 1940-41, Waco, Tex., 1941-42, 46—; camp physician Civilian Conservation Corps, S.C., Ga., 1939-40; staff physician VA Hosps., Augusta, Ga., 1940, Murfreesboro, 1940-41, Waco, 1941-42; staff psychiatrist VA Hosp., Waco, 1946—. Served with AUS, 1942-45; PTO. Recipient 30 Year Service award VA, 1969. Fellow Am. Psychiat. Assn.; mem. A.M.A., Acad. Religion and Mental Health (pres. Waco Tex. br. 1968-69). Res. Officer Assn. Episcopalian. Home: 2706 Glendale St Waco TX 76710 Office: VA Hosp Memorial Dr Waco TX 76703

LESLEY, THEODORE LIVINGSTON, county ofcl.; b. Tampa, Fla.; s. Theodore and Carrie May (Yancey) L.; student U. Tampa, 1932-36; postgrad. U. Aberdeen, 1959. Mgr., Hartsfield Co., Inc., Tampa, 1942-46, Gen. Acceptance Corp., Tampa, 1946-48; estate agt., property mgr., 1948—. Commr. Hillsborough County Hist. Commn. of Records, 1949—, vice chmn., 1955-62, county historian, 1966—; mem. Oaklawn Restoration Com., and asso. mem. Tampa City Park Bd., 1957-58; mem. Fla.'s Gettysburg Battlefield Monument Adv. Com., 1963, Tampa Barrio Latino Commn., 1970—; mem. Fla. Dept. Council Abandoned Mil. Posts, 1973—; museum cons. Arts Council Tampa. Named Knight of Justice, Sovereign Order St. John of Jerusalem, Knight of Malta. Mem. Fla. Hist. Soc. (dir. 1950), Fla. Geneal. Soc. (pres. 1967-68), Territorial Soc. Fla. (pres. 1939), Order Stars and Bars, S.C.V., Soc. of Cincinnati, Braemar Royal Highland Soc. (hon.). Democrat. Episcopalian (past vestryman. jr. warden). Clubs: Sword and Shield, Royal Tennis. Author: The Lesley Family in South Carolina, 1945; The Townsend Memoirs, 1960. Editor: Fla. Geneal. Jour., 1968—. Contbr. numerous hist. and biog. monographs to So. hist. quars. and newspapers. Home: 719 S Delaware Av Tampa FL 33606 Office: County Ct House Tampa FL 33602

LESLIE, HENRY ARTHUR, banker; b. Troy, Ala., Oct. 15, 1921; s. James B. and Alice (Minchener) L.; B.S., U. Ala., 1942, J.D., 1948; J.S.D., Yale, 1959; grad. Sch. Banking, Rutgers U., 1964; m. Anita Doyle, Apr. 5, 1943; children—Anita Lucinda (Mrs. David Miller), Henry Arthur. Admitted to Ala. bar, 1948; asst. prof. bus. law U. Ala., 1948-50, 52-54, prof. law, asst. dean Sch. Law, 1954-59; v.p., trust officer Birmingham Trust Nat. Bank (Ala.), 1959-64; sr. v.p., sr. trust officer Union Bank & Trust Co., Montgomery, Ala., 1964-74, sr. v.p., dir., 1974—. Mem. Ala. State Bd. Bar Examiners. Mem. Water Improvement Commn. of Ala., Ala. Armory Commn. Chmn. bd. dirs. Ala. Bankers Found.; chmn. bd. trustees St. John's Endowment Fund. Served to capt. AUS, 1942-46; now lt. col. Res. Decorated Bronze Star medal. Mem. Fed., Am., Ala. Montgomery bar assns., Am., Ala. (trust div. pres. 1963-65) bankers assns., Farrah Order Jurisprudence (past pres.), Newcomen Soc. N.Am., Delta Sigma Pi, Phi Delta Phi, Omicron Delta Kappa, Pi Kappa Phi. Episcopalian (vestryman). Kiwanian. Club: Montgomery Country. Contbr. articles to profl. jours. Home: 3332 Boxwood Dr Montgomery AL 36111 Office: Union Bank & Trust Co Montgomery AL 36104

LESPIER, WILLIAM, lawyer; b. Ponce, P.R., Dec. 15, 1935; s. Vidal Lespier and Francisca Santiago; B.A. magna cun laude, U. P.R., 1958, LL.B., 1961. Instr. U. P.R., 1957-60; admitted to P.R. bar, 1960; law clk. Supreme Ct. P.R., San Juan, 1960-61; atty. NLRB P.R., 1961-62; partner firm Cohen & Lespier, Hato Rey, P.R., 1965-72; partner firm Lespier & Toro, Hato Rey, 1972—. Instr., Cornell U. P.R. campus, 1972-73; vis. instr. Inter-Am. U. Sch. Banking, 1972-73. Mem. Pub. Personnel Adminstrs. Eastern Regional Ann. Conf., 1971. Mem. Am. Arbitration Assn. (panel arbitrators), Am. Soc. for Personnel Adminstrs. (chpt. award 1972), Hotel and Restaurants Assn. Personnel Mgrs., Colegio de Abogados de P.R., Fed. Bar Assn. Home: RD 3 Buzón 41G Beverly Hills PR 00928 Office: PO Box 1441 Banco Popular Center Bldg Hato Rey PR 00919

LESSENCO, GILBERT BARRY, lawyer; b. Balt., June 19, 1929; s. Jacob David and Sarah (Bank) L.; B.S., Johns Hopkins, 1950; LL.B., Harvard, 1953; m. Elaine Beitler, Sept. 3, 1952; children—Susan Donna, Amy Gail, Robert Howard. Admitted to D.C. bar, 1953; since practiced in Washington; mem. firm Wilner and Bergson, 1953-55; partner Wilner & Scheiner, 1955—. Mem. Democratic Central Com., Montgomery County, Md., 1970—. Bd. dirs. Thanks to Scandinavia, Inc. Found; trustee Meridian House Found. Served to lt. USAF, 1953-55. Mem. D.C. Jr. Bar (mem. exec. council 1962-64, named Outstanding Young Lawyer of Year 1965), Phi Sigma Delta. Home: 7928 Robison Rd Bethesda MD 20034 Office: 2021 L St NW Washington DC 20036

LESSO, WILLIAM GEORGE, educator; b. Cleve., Mar. 23, 1931; s. Andrew Michael and Catherine (Franks) L.; B.S. in Mech. Engring., U. Notre Dame, 1953; M.B.A., Xavier U., 1963; M.S., Case Inst. Tech., 1966, Ph.D., 1967; m. Josephine Marie Parker, Dec. 27, 1952; children—William, David, Mary Ellen, Anne Marie, Julie Jo. Bearing designer Cleve. Graphite Bronze Co., 1953-58; jet engine designer Gen. Electric Co., Evendale, O., 1958-64; asso. prof. U. Tex., Austin, 1967-72, prof. operations research, 1972—, also grad. adviser, 1972—; cons. operations research to pvt., state agys. Served to lt. USAF, 1954-56. Registered profl. engr., Ohio, Tex. Mem. Am. Soc. Engring. Edn., Operations Research Soc. Am., Inst. Mgmt. Scis., Am. Inst. Indsl. Engrs., Sigma Xi. K.C. Author (with R. Harris and M. Maggaro) Computer Models in Operations Research, 1974. Home: 2505 Roxmoor Dr Austin TX 78723

LESTER, BARNETT BENJAMIN, editor, govt. ofcl.; b. Toronto, Ont., Can., Aug. 7, 1912; s. Louis and Lena (Rubenstein) L.; came to U.S., 1917; student Cleveland Coll., Western Res. U., 1933; B.A., Oberlin Coll., 1934; scholarships Oberlin Coll., 1930-34, 1934-35, Nat. Inst. Pub. Affairs, Washington, 1935-36, Syracuse U., Acad. Internat. Law, The Hague, 1936, fellow Fletcher Sch. Law and Diplomacy, 1935-36; student Fgn. Service Inst., Dept. of State, 1952, 56; m. Rita Constance Hatcher, May 31, 1943 (dec. Nov. 1960); m. 2d, Claudette Yvonne Gionet, Apr. 19, 1970. Editorial staff Cleve. Plain Dealer, 1928-30; corr. various newspapers, 1930-38; staff reporter and feature writer Cleve. News, 1931-32; with Cleve. bur. Asso. Press, 1933; feature writer Boston Sunday Post, 1935-38; asso. editor The Writer Mag., 1936-38; mng. editor, later editor Exclusive Features Syndicate, Boston, 1936-38; with U.S. Dept. Justice, 1938-41; assigned to Office of Atty. Gen., Washington, 1938-40, editorial and informational asst., 1940-41, information officer, 1941; with Office of Coordinator of Inter-Am. Affairs, 1941-45, asst. dir. feature div., 1941-45; with U.S. Dept. of State, Washington, as asst. dir. feature div., Interim Internat. Information Service (OIAA), 1945; pub. relations exec. Al Paul Lefton Co., Inc., Phila., 1945-46; information specialist, chief motion picture unit, acting chief audio-visual sect. Office of Health Information, USPHS, Office Surgeon Gen., Washington, 1947-48; information specialist Office Publs. and Reports, FSA, 1948-49; chief editorial and prodn. sect., Nat. Heart Inst., 1949-52; pub. information chief, 1950, information specialist, sci. reports br. NIH, 1949-52; rev. officer Dept. State, 1952-61, supervisory publs. editor, 1961-63; editor-writer, 1963-73, pub. information officer, 1973—, U.S. Fgn. Service Res. officer, 1965—, assigned to policy and pub. information affairs programs, 1962-67, Newsletter and Information officer Office Dir. Gen., 1967—. Career counselor Oberlin Coll., 1940—. Rep. Office Surg. Gen., USPHS, on interdepartmental com. med. tng. aids, 1947-48; invited participant U.S. Commr. Edn. Conf. Audio-Visual Aids to Edn., 1948; mem. information staff Pres.'s Midcentury White House Conf. on Children and Youth, 1950; mem. spl. survey audio-visual teaching and tng. aids Nat. Heart Inst., USPHS and Assn. Am. Med. Colls., 1951. Recipient Meritorious Honor Group award Dept. State, 1967. Hon. mem. Internat. Rho Pi Phi; fellow Am. Geog. Soc.; mem. Oberlin Coll. Alumni Assn., Alumni Assn. Fletcher Sch. Law and Diplomacy, Tufts U. Alumni Assn., Diplomatic and Consular Officers Ret., Am. Polit. Sci. Assn., Am. Fgn. Service Assn., Acad. Polit. Sci., Am. Acad. Polit. and Social Sci., Fed. Editors Assn. Clubs: Oberlin, Nat. Press, Am. Foreign Service, Internat. (Washington). Author: (with others) The Writer's Handbook, 1936. Writer of articles in mags. and profl. jours., radio and motion picture scripts, and biographies. Home: 2507 N Lincoln St Arlington VA 22207 Office: US Dept State Washington DC 20520

LESTER, DARRELL REAKS, constrn. co. exec.; b. Temple, Tex., Mar. 5, 1943; s. Darrell George and Dorothy (Reaks) L.; B.B.A., Tex. Christian U., 1966, M.B.A., 1968; m. Marion Frances Wilkinson, June 26, 1966; children—Darrell Reaks, Jennifer Joy. Programmer, systems analyst, corp. auditor Gen. Dynamics, Ft. Worth, 1966-69; corp. auditor Bonanza Internat. Inc., Dallas, 1969-70; mgmt. cons. Arthur Young & Co., Ft. Worth, 1970-73; sec.-treas., dir. Haws & Garrett Gen. Contractors Inc., Ft. Worth, 1973—. Financial cons. Treas., Miss. Tex. Scholarship Pageant Corp., 1970-72; active fund raising Tex. Christian U., 1966—; budget dir. Colonial Nat. Invitational Golf Tournament, 1973-74. Mem. Am. Inst. C.P.A.'s, Tex. State Soc. C.P.A.'s, Data Processing Mgmt. Assn., Inst. Internal Auditors, Nat. Mgmt. Assn., Tex. Christian U. Lettermans Assn., Phi Kappa Sigma. Home: 5613 Whitman St Fort Worth TX 76133 Office: PO Box 1080 Fort Worth TX 76101

LESTER, EVERARD M., ret. mfg. exec.; b. Norwich, Conn., July 31, 1906; s. Walter Fitch and Rose Eva (Kasche) L.; B.S. in Mech. Engring., Mass. Inst. Tech., 1928, Hayden fellow bus. adminstrn., 1933; m. Helen Louise Jerome, July 19, 1930; children—Jerome Mason, Patricia (Mrs. R.F. Miller). Became asso. with Pratt & Whitney Aircraft, 1929; with Fairchild Engine div. Fairchild Engine and Airplane Corp., 1941-59, asst. gen. mgr., 1950-58, gen. mgr., 1958-59; became dir. mfg. govt. products group Am. Machine & Foundry Co., 1959, asst. group exec. comml. devel., advanced products group, AMF, York, Pa., until 1965; cons., pres. Tri-County Engring. Corp., Harrisburg, Pa., 1965-67; cons. Foster Wheeler Corp., Livingston, N.J., 1966-69, v.p., 1969-71; ret., 1971; past dir. Foster Wheeler John Brown Boilers, Ltd., London. Mem. Inst. Aero. Scis., Quiet Birdmen. Club: Flying Yankee. Contbr. report field. Airplane pilot, Air Corps Advance Tng. Sch., 1929. Address: 190 The Maine First Colony Williamsburg VA 23185

LESTER, HAROLD DEWITT, dentist; b. Parksville, Ky., Aug. 18, 1933; s. Marvin DeWitt and Anna Margaret (May) L.; B.A., U. Louisville, 1956, D.M.D., 1963; certificate in pedodontics Eastman Dental Center, 1965; m. Martha Anne Breland, Dec. 28, 1956; children—Harold DeWitt, Elizabeth Anne. Practice dentistry, specializing in pedodontics, Louisville, 1965—; teaching staff dept. pedodontics U. Louisville Sch. Dentistry, 1971—; mem. active staff Louisville Childrens Hosp.; mem. courtesy staff Kasair Children's Hosp. Served to lt. (j.g.) USNR, 1956-59. Diplomate Am. Bd. Pedodontics. Fellow Am. Acad. Pedodontics; mem. Am., Ky. dental assns., Louisville Dental Soc. (past sec.-treas.), Am. Soc. Dentistry for Children, Ky. Soc. Dentistry for Children (past pres.), Southeastern Soc. Pedodontics, Ky. Med. Assn., Jefferson County Med. Soc., Am. Soc. Pedodontic Diplomates, Psi Omega, Phi Delta. Baptist. Home: 119 Blankenbaker Lane Louisville KY 40207 Office: Semonin Bldg 4812 Hwy 42 Louisville KY 40222

LESTER, HORACE B(AXTER), cons. engr., state legislator; b. Quitman County, Miss., Sept. 5, 1919; s. Simon Edward and Willie (Reid) L.; corr. course in engring.; m. Dora Essie Sanford, May 12, 1942; children—Horace B., Thomas Sanford. With Miss. Hwy. Dept., 1936-40; with U.S., Engrs., 1940-41; with E. I. du Pont de Nemours & Co., 1941-42; engr. City of Jackson, Miss., 1946-47; with EBASCO Services, 1947-49, W. & S. Constrn. Co., 1949-53; cons. engr. as Lester Engrs., Jackson, Miss., 1953—; mem. Miss. Ho. of Reps. Mem. W. Central Miss. Waterway Commn. Served as capt. AUS, 1942-46; col. Res. Mem. Res. Officers Assn. U.S., Am. Soc. C.E., Nat., Miss. socs. profl. engrs., Miss. Water Pollution Control Fedn., Am. Soc. Planning Ofcls., Cons. Engrs. Council U.S., and Miss., Am. Soc. State Legislators, Scabbard and Blade. Rotarian. Home: 1350 Eastover Dr Jackson MS 39211 Office: 555 Yazoo St Jackson MS 39201

LESTER, HUBERT ELISHA, govt. ofcl.; b. Jacksonville, Ala., Jan. 5, 1908; s. Forney Macon and Laura (Dale) L.; student pub. schs.; m. Anne Laurene Harris, Aug., 1929; children—Martha Anne (Mrs. Roy Thomas Ford, Jr.), Cherie (Mrs. Arthur Morris Lockridge), Kirby Lynn (Mrs. William Latham Snowden). Organizer, partner Calhoun Butane & Propane Co., Anniston, Ala., 1947-49; asst. cashier 1st Nat. Bank, Jacksonville, 1930-44; examiner, auditor U.S. Govt. Rent Stblzn. Program, Anniston, 1952, dir. Anniston and Calhoun County, Ala., 1953; partner, v.p., treas. Bethea Furniture Co., Jacksonville, 1954-55; tax assessor Calhoun County, Anniston, 1956—. Dir. Ala. Factoring and Finance Corp. Mayor, Jacksonville, 1941-44; mem. Jacksonville Sch. Bd., 1955-71; mem. Ala. Democratic Exec. Com., 1950-58. Treas., Calhoun County chpt. Nat. Found. for Polio, Birth Defects and Arthritis, 1958—; scholarship adv. com. Anniston Meml. Hosp. Served with USNR, 1944-46. Mem. Tax Assessors and Collectors Assn. Ala. (v.p. 1962-63, pres. 1964-65), chmn. legislative com. 1966—), Internat. Assn. Assessing officers, Anniston, Jacksonville chambers commerce, Am. Legion, V.F.W., 40 and 8, Kiwanian. Home: 401 4th St Jacksonville AL 36265 Office: Calhoun County Ct House Anniston AL 36201

LESTER, JAMES ADAMS, editor, clergyman; b. Edison, Ga., Dec. 18, 1928; s. Paul Edwin and Myrtice (Peters) L.; grad. Norman Jr. Coll., Norman Park, Ga., 1946; B.A., Mercer U., Macon, Ga., 1949; B.D., New Orleans Bapt. Theol. Sem., 1953, Th.M., 1955; children—James Earl, Edwin Oliver. Ordained to ministry Baptist Ch., 1949; tchr. pub. schs., Mitchell County, Ga., 1947, Brooks County, Ga., 1950; dir. News Bur., Mercer U., 1949; mem. staff Times Picayune, New Orleans, 1951-57, copy desk, state news editor, 1955-57; dir. promotion and pub. relations, asso. to exec. sec.-treas. Ga. Bapt. Conv., Atlanta, 1957-68; editor Bapt. and Reflector news jour. Tenn. Bapt. Conv., Brentwood, 1968—; pastor Bapt. Chs., La., Miss., Ga.; pres., owner Lester Enterprises, Inc., Brentwood. Mem. Pub. Relations Soc. Am., So. Bapt. Press Assn., Bapt. Pub. Relations Assn. Author: A History of the Christian Index, 1822-1953, 1955; A History of the Georgia Baptist Convention, 1822-72, 1972. Contbr. articles to profl. jours. Home: Shenandoah Dr Brentwood TN 37027 Office: Tenn Bapt Conv Franklin Rd Brentwood TN 37027 also PO Box 726 Wilson Pike Circle Brentwood TN 37027

LESTER, ROBERT, orthodontist; b. Mt. Vernon, N.Y., Jan. 11, 1932; s. Herman and Eva (Kaplan) L.; A.B., Columbia Coll., 1953; D.D.S., Columbia U., 1957; certificate in orthodontics N.Y. U., 1970; m. Janice Sheila Wechter, June 8, 1957; children—Nina Beth, Jonathan. Gen. practice dentistry, Eastchester and Dobbs Ferry, N.Y., 1959-70, practice limited to orthodontics, Plantation, Fla., 1970—. Chmn., advancement chmn., membership mgmt. chmn. New River Dist. South Fla. council Boy Scouts Am., 1973—. Served with USNR, 1957-59; mem. Res. Mem. Am., Fla., Broward County dental assns., Am. Assn. Orthodontists, Plantation Dental Study Group. Elk. Club: Civitan (treas. 1971-73) (Plantation, Fla.). Home: 1039 E Tropical Way Plantation FL 33314 Office: 7360 Northwest 5th St Plantation FL 33313

LESTER, WILLIAM BERNARD, econ. researcher; b. Havana, Fla., Jan. 9, 1939; s. W.D. and Edith (Blackburn) L.; B.S., U. Fla., 1961, M.S., 1962; Ph.D., Tex. A. and M. U., 1965; m. Elaine Purnell, Mar. 30, 1961; 1 son, Mark. Research asst. Tex. A. and M. U., College Station, 1962-65, agrl. economist, 1965-67; research economist, econ. research dept. Fla. Citrus Commn., U. Fla., Gainesville, 1967-68, econ. research dir., 1969—. Served with AUS, 1956. Mem. Am. Marketing Assn., Am., So. agrl. econs. assns., Blue Key, Alpha Zeta, Gamma Sigma Delta, Phi Kappa Phi. Methodist (mem. adminstrv. bd. 1968-71). Home: 2007 NW 36th Terrace Gainesville FL 32605 Office: Room 1107 McCarty Hall U Fla Gainesville FL 32611

LETERMAN, ELMER GOLDSMITH, ins. cons., author; b. Charlottesville, Va., Jan. 16, 1897; s. Jacob and Bertha (Goldsmith) L.; student pub. schs.; m. Blanche C. Leterman, Dec. 17, 1950. Chmn. bd. Leterman Gortz Stebbins Leterman Gates, N.Y.C., 1948-70; pres. Leterman Gortz Corp., N.Y.C., 1949-70, chmn., 1970-72; ins. cons., Ft. Lauderdale, Fla., 1971—. Named hon. life mayor of Honolulu, 1954. Mem. C. of C. Author: Commissions Don't Fall From Heaven, 1957; Personal Power Through Creative Selling, 1963; Sale Begins When Customer Says No, 1965; How Showmanship Sells, 1965; They Dare to Be Different, 1968; Quotes, 1972. Home: 4280 N Ocean Blvd Fort Lauderdale FL 33308

LETTON, JAMES CAREY, educator; b. Lexington, Ky., June 9, 1933; s. William and Lillie (Lampkins) L.; B.S., Ky. State Coll., 1955; Ph.D., U. Ill., Chgo., 1971; m. Rosaline Stovall, Dec. 14, 1956; children—James A., Alan, Lillian Stacy. Tchr., Bunche High Sch., Glasgow, Ky., 1956-57; chem. foreman, prodn. supt. Julian Labs., Franklin Park, Ill., 1957-64, research chemist Julian Research Inst., 1964-70; prof. chemistry, chmn. dept. Ky. State U., Frankfort, 1970—; instr. Triton Coll., 1969-70. Vice pres. Hearn Elementary Sch. Parent Tchr. Orgn., Frankfort, Ky., 1973—; mem. adv. council Franklin County High Sch., Frankfort, 1973—. Coop. States Research Service grantee, 1972—. Fellow Am. Inst. Chemists; mem. Am. Chem. Soc., Ky. Acad. Sci. (sec. 1974), Omega Psi Phi, Rho Chi. Home: 200 Esperanza Dr Frankfort KY 40601

LETTS, THOMAS CLINTON, ret. educator; b. El Campo, Tex., Mar. 15, 1911; s. Henry Frank and Clara (Spencer) L.; student U. Houston, 1935-36, 47-48; B.S., Sam Houston State U., 1937; M.S., Tex. A. and M. U., 1945, postgrad. 1948-52; m. Margaret Evelyn McDaniel, Oct. 27, 1934; 1 dau., Margaret Sue (Mrs. Rufus Denman Hopper, Jr.). Tchr., prin., supt. pub. schs., Tex., 1929-42; clk. War Dept., 1942; work unit conservationist U.S. Dept. Agr., 1943-46; asso. prof. Sam Houston State U., 1946-58; agriculturist FOA, Tel Aviv, Israel, 1953-54; educationist ICA, Taipei, Taiwan, 1955-57, elementary edn. adviser, Asuncion, Paraguay, 1958-60; tchr. ednl. adviser USOM, Tegucigalpa, Honduras, 1960-62; elementary edn. adviser AID, Recife, Brazil, 1963-65; area devel. officer USOM, Dinh Turong Province, Vietnam, 1965, agrl. edn. officer AID, Saigon, Vietnam, 1966-71. Pres. Asuncion Coop. Commissary, 1959-60. Exec. com. Wharton County Inter-Scholastic League, 1935-37. Mem. Tex. Tchrs. Assn., S.W. Social Sci. Assn., Walker County C. of C. (dir. 1946-49), Kappa Delta Pi. Rotarian. (past pres.). Club: Vocational Agriculture (past pres.). Home: Rt 5 Box 88 Huntsville TX 77340

LE VAN, DANIEL HAYDEN, business exec.; b. Savannah, Ga., Mar. 29, 1924; s. Daniel Hayden and Ruth (Harner) LeV.; grad. Middlesex Sch., 1943; B.A., Harvard, 1950; student Babson Inst., 1950-51. With underwriter's dept. Zurich Ins. Co., N.Y.C., 1951-52; liquified petroleum sales and engring. Gas, Inc., Lowell, Mass., 1952-54; customer relations Lowell Gas Co., 1954-56, in charge LP gas sales and promotion, 1956-58; trustee Colonial Gas Energy System, Boston; dir. Lowell Gas Co., Cape Cod Gas Co., Gas, Inc., Lowell Factors, Mass. Assos., Lowell Appliances, Gas Rentals, Inc., Overseas Properties Ltd., N.Y.C. Served with AUS, 1943-46. Club: Harvard (N.Y.C.). Home: Box 158 DeLeon Springs FL 32028 Office: care Colonial Gas Energy System 50 Congress St Boston MA 02109

LEVELL, JAMES WAYMON, real estate developer; b. Kemp, Tex., Jan. 10, 1940; s. Edward Franklin and Clara Eurilla (Harris) L.; B.B.A., U. Tex., 1963; m. Mary Ann Meland, Nov. 11, 1967; children—Heather Lynn, Holly Ann (dec.). Sr. accountant Haskins & Sells, C.P.A.'s, Dallas, 1963-69; treas., v.p. I.C. Deal Cos., Inc., Dallas, 1969-71; co-owner Pan Western Corp., Dallas, 1972—, also dir. C.P.A., Tex. Mem. Am. Inst. C.P.A.'s, Tex. Soc. C.P.A.'s, Real Estate Financial Execs. Assn. Club: 500 Inc (Dallas). Home: 4417 Echo Glen Dallas TX 75234 Office: 3303 Lee Pkwy Dallas TX 75219

LEVEN, STEPHEN ALOYSIUS, bishop; b. Blackwell, Okla., Apr. 30, 1905; s. Joseph J. and Gertrude (Conrady) L.; student St. Benedict's Coll., Atchison, Kan., St. Mary's Sem., LaPorte, Tex.; student philosophy and theology Cath. U. Louvain (Belgium), 1922-28; Ph.D., Institut Superieur de Philosophie, Louvain, 1938; LL.D. honoris causa, St. Edward's U., Austin, Tex., 1957. Ordained priest Roman Cath. Ch., 1928; consecrated bishop, 1956; asst. pastor St. Joseph's Old Cathedral, Oklahoma City, 1928-32; pastor St. Joseph's Ch., Bristow, Okla., 1932-35; vice rector Am. Coll., Louvain, 1935-38; pastor St. Joseph's Ch., Tonkawa, Okla., 1938-48, St. Francis Xavier Ch., Enid, Okla., 1948-56; aux. bishop of San Antonio, 1956-69; bishop, San Angelo, Tex., 1969—. Home: 223 E Summit St San Antonio TX 78212 Office: 9123 Lorene Lane San Antonio TX 78216

LEVENS, JOHNNY BLACKWELL, JR., physician; b. Gulfport, Miss., Dec. 11, 1932; s. John Blackwell and Blanche (Woodcock) L.; B.S., U. Miss., Oxford, 1954-59, M.D., 1961; m. Gayle Larkin, June 26, 1971; children from previous marriage—Sandra, Tracy, John, Mark, Barbara, Sabrina. Intern, Miss. Bapt. Hosp., Jackson, 1961-62; resident Miss. State Hosp., Whitfield; county health dir. Hancock and Pearl River counties, 1962-63; practice medicine, Bay St. Louis, Miss., 1963—; chief staff Hancock Gen. Hosp., Bay St. Louis, 1963-65, 70—, sec. med. staff, 1963-66, chief internal medicine, 1965—. Pres. Waveland Clinic, Inc., 1971; county health officer cons. Hancock County, 1969-71. Pres. Hancock County chpt. Am. Cancer Soc., 1965-68; pres. Hancock County Heart Assn., 1963-70; chmn. K-O Polio campaign, 1964; pres. Hancock County Port and Harbor Commn. Sustaining mem. Nat. Republican Party; chmn. Hancock County Republican Com., 1968-72. Trustee Hancock Gen. Hosp. Med. Staff Pediatric Fund. Served with Inf. AUS, 1951-54. Fellow Am. Coll. Angiology, Am. Clin. Council Cardiology; mem. A.M.A., So. Med. Assn., New Orleans Grad. Med. Assembly, Coast County Med. Soc., Am., Miss. thoracic socs., Am. Acad. Family Practice, Profl. Practice Assn., Am. Legion, V.F.W. Mason. Home: 118 Whispering Pines Waveland MS 39576 Office: 641 Dunbar Av Bay St Louis MS 39520

LEVERETT, SIDNEY DUNCAN, JR., physiologist; b. Houston, Nov. 27, 1925; s. Sidney Duncan and Evelyn (Bailey) L.; B.S., Tex. A. and M. Coll., 1949; M.S., Ohio State U., 1955, Ph.D., 1960; m. Gladys Musgrove, Sept. 3, 1948; children—Laurie Verne, Thomas DeWitt. Chief acceleration sect. Aerospace Med. Research Lab., Wright-Patterson AFB, O., 1955-58, chief cardiovascular unit Brooks AFB, Tex., 1960-62, chief biodynamics br., 1962—; cons. NASA Manned Space Center; mem. grad. faculty St. Mary's U., Tex. A. and M. Coll., U. Mich., Trinity U. Pres. Shady Oaks Home Owners Assn., 1967. Served to capt. USAF, 1951-72. Recipient Eric Liljencrantz award Aerospace Med. Assn., 1970; award for Scientific Achievement, Air Force Systems Command, 1962; Meritorious Service award USAF, 1972. Fellow Aerospace Med. Assn. (pres. biomed sci. and engring. br. 1973—); mem. A.A.A.S., Sigma Xi. Methodist. Contbr. numerous articles to sci. jours. Contbg. author: Gravitational Stress in Aerospace Medicine, 1961. Home: 103 Encino Blanco San Antonio TX 78216 Office: SAM (VNB) US Air Force Brooks AFB TX 78235

LEVI, G. KENNETH, publisher; b. Berryville, Va., Feb. 22, 1910; s. George H. and Martha Louise (Williams) L.; student Va. Inst. Tech., 1927-30; m. Evelyn Shiles Dean, Sept. 16, 1929; children—Kenneth Dean, Evelyn Page (Mrs. Henry T. Goode Jr.), Wesley Christopher. Engr. Shenandoah Nat. Park, 1930-31; editor The Clarke Courier, Berryville, 1931-52, owner, pub., 1952—; owner, pub. The Blue Ridge Press, Berryville, 1952—, Spur of Va., 1969—; pres. Spur, Inc. Mem. Clarke County Sch. Bd., 1944—; bd. control Dowell J. Howard Vocational Sch., Winchester, Va. Mem. Berryville C. of C. Democrat. Episcopalian. Clubs: Nat. Press, Touchdown (Washington); Millwood Country (Boyce, Va.); Harpers Ferry (W. Va.) Cooking; Hokie; Virginia Tech (Blacksburg, Va.). Address: Berryville VA 22611

LEVIN, ALLEN JAY, judge; b. Bridgeport, Conn., May 27, 1932; s. Simon H. and Adele M. (Rossinoff) L.; B.A., N.Y.U., 1954; J.D., U. Miami, 1957; student Boston U., 1954-55; m. Judith Ann Rubinstein, Aug. 18, 1957; children—Jennifer Suzanne, Miriam Adele, David N., Michael A. Admitted to Fla. bar, 1957, Conn. bar, 1958; practiced in Conn., 1958-60, Port Charlotte, Fla., 1960—; judge Small Claims Ct., Charlotte County, Fla., 1963-72; municipal judge, North Port, Fla., 1972—; atty. bd. commrs. Port Charlotte-Charlotte Harbor Fire Control Dist., 1965—. Instr. Port Charlotte U., 1960-63; legal adviser Port Charlotte Civic Assn., 1960-63, 67—; legal counsel Nat. Police Officers Assn. Am., 1963-67. Bd. dirs. Charlotte County United Way, 1969—, pres., 1973; bd. dirs. Charlotte County Family YMCA, 1971-72. Mem. Am., Charlotte County bar assns., Am. Judicature Soc., Comml. Law League Am., Fla. Bar, Fla. Municipal Judges Assn., Bar and Gavel, Alpha Epsilon Pi, Tau Epsilon Rho. Elk, Kiwanian (2d v.p. Port Charlotte 1968). Jewish religion (v.p. Port Charlotte Jewish Community Group 1965-66, dir. 1961-64, 70—, pres. 1967-69). Home: 834 NE Beacon Dr Port Charlotte FL 33952 Office: 135A S Tamiami Dr NW Port Charlotte FL 33952

LEVIN, DAVID HAROLD, lawyer; b. Pensacola, Fla., Nov. 19, 1928; s. Abe Irvin and Rose (Lefkowitz) L.; A.B., Duke, 1949; J.D., U. Fla., 1952; m. Mona Joyce Lindy, Feb. 16, 1958; 1 dau., Lisa Ann. Admitted to Fla. bar, 1952, since practiced in Pensacola; asst. county solicitor, 1952; asso. Robinson, Roark & Hopkins, 1954-55; partner Levin, Askew, Warfield, Graff & Mabie, 1955—. Pres., dir. Gator Boosters, Inc. Crusade chmn. Pensacola chpt. Am. Cancer Soc., 1964-65, pres., 1966-67; bd. dirs. Pensacola chpt. Am. Heart Assn., 1966-69; chmn. Pensacola United Jewish Appeal, 1967-68; chmn. Fla. Pollution Control Bd., 1971—. Bd. dirs. U. Fla. Found., Inc. Served to capt. USAF, 1952-54. Fellow Fla. Trial Lawyers Assn.; mem. Am., Fla. bar assns., Am. Judicature Soc., Am. Trial Lawyers Assn., Am. Legion, Pensacola U. Fla. Alumni Assn. (pres. 1960), Fla. Council 100. Mason (32 deg., Shriner). Home: 3632 Menendez St Pensacola FL 32503 Office: 9th Floor Seville Tower Pensacola FL 32501

LEVIN, RUBEN, editor; b. Warsaw, Poland, Aug. 2, 1902; s. Benjamin D. and Ida (Gochlik) L.; brought to U.S., 1904, naturalized 1917; B.A., U. Wis., 1930; m. Bertha G. Greenberg, June 7, 1931; children—Hilda (Mrs. Alvin Tanenholtz), David A., Jonathan H. Reporter, copyreader on various dailies, 1924-38; with Labor Newspaper, 1938—, editor, mgr., 1953—. Recipient award for distinguished service to journalism U. Wis., 1965. Mem. Am. Newspaper Guild. Democrat. Jewish religion. Contbr. articles to profl. jours. Home: 2712 Blaine Dr Chevy Chase MD 20015 Office: 400 1st St NW Washington DC 20001

LEVIN, SEYMOUR ARTHUR, nuclear-enriched uranium prodn. co. engr.; b. Newark, Sept. 16, 1922; s. Nathan and Matilda (Horwitz) L.; B.Ch.E., Johns Hopkins U., 1943; postgrad. Columbia, 1945, U. Tenn., 1947-50; m. Patsy Elythe Whitehurst, Mar. 16, 1948; children—Stephen, Natalie, Charles, Margaret. Research asst. SAM Labs. Columbia U., 1943-45; with Nuclear div. Union Carbide Corp., Oak Ridge, 1945—, head long-range planning-prodn. plants, 1968—. Mem. Am. Chem. Soc., A.A.A.S. Expert on isotope separation processes. Contbr. articles to sci., tech. jours. Home: 956 W Outer Dr Oak Ridge TN 37830 Office: PO Box P Oak Ridge TN 37830

LEVIN, SIDNEY HERBERT, broadcasting exec.; b. Balt., May 5, 1935; s. Jack and Ida (Kasoff) L.; B.A., Am. U., 1957; m. Sally Rubin, Feb. 2, 1957; children—Aimee, Ira. Announcer radio sta. WITH-FM, Balt., 1952-53, program dir., 1953-55; sales mgr. WGMS, Washington, 1955-57; asst. mgr. WKAT, Miami, Fla., 1957-62, exec. v.p., gen. mgr., 1962—; founding dir. Third Century Corp. Guest lectr. U. Miami, 1966—. Past pres. Dade County Citizens Safety Council; adviser Dade County Bd. Pub. Instrn. Mem. bd. Tropical council Girl Scouts U.S.A.; bd. dirs. Anti-Defamation League, Greater Miami Progress Found. Mem. Miami Assn. Food Trades (past pres., dir.), Greater Miami Radio Broadcasters Assn. (founder, past pres.), Radio Advt. Bur., Greater Miami C. of C. (pres.), Alpha Epsilon Rho. Jewish religion. Club: Miami Touchdown (past pres.). Home: 21310 NE 24th Ct Miami FL 33160 Office: 1759 Bay Rd Miami Beach FL 33139

LEVIN, WILLIAM COHN, physician, univ. pres.; b. Waco, Tex., Mar. 2, 1917; s. Samuel P. and Jeannette (Cohn) L.; B.A., U. Tex., 1938, M.D., 1941; m. Edna Seinsheimer, June 23, 1941; children—Gerry Lee (Mrs. Eugene Hornstein), Carol Lynn. Intern Michael Reese Hosp., Chgo., 1941-42; resident John Sealy Hosp., Galveston, Tex., 1942-44; mem. staff U. Tex. Med. Br. Hosps., Galveston, 1944—, asso. prof. internal medicine, 1948-65, prof., 1965—, now also Warmoth prof. hematology; pres. U. Tex. at Galveston, 1974—. Dir. hematology research lab., blood bank, clin. study center U. Tex. Med. Br. Cons. Surgeon Gen. U.S. Army, U.S. Air Force; chmn. cancer clin. investigation rev. com. Nat. Cancer Inst. Exec. com., vice chmn. nat. bd. Union Am. Hebrew Congregations. Diplomate Am. Bd. Internal Medicine. Fellow A.C.P., Internat. Soc. Hematology; mem. Phi Beta Kappa, Sigma Xi, Alpha Omega Alpha. Home: 1301 Harbor View Dr Galveston TX 77550 Office: Office Pres U Tex Galveston TX 77550

LEVINE, HAROLD, mfg. co. exec.; b. Newark, Apr. 30, 1931; s. Rubin and Gussie (Lifshitz) L.; B.S., Purdue U., 1954; J.D., George Washington U., 1958; m. Harriet Shapiro, Aug. 17, 1952; children—Linda Ellen, Brenda Sue, Jill Anne, Louise Abby. Admitted to Va. bar, 1958, D.C. bar, 1958, Mass. bar, 1960; marine engr., naval architect Navy Dept., Washington, 1954-55; patent examiner U.S. Patent Office, Washington, 1955-58; with Tex. Instruments Inc., Dallas, 1959—, mgr. corp. patents, 1966—, asst. sec., 1968—, asst. v.p., gen. patent counsel, 1972—. Lectr. Practicing Law Inst. Bd. govs. Pacific Indsl. Property Assn. Mem. Am., Dallas, Fort Worth patent law assns., Assn. Corp. Patent Counsel (sec.-treas. 1971-73), Electronic Industries Assn. (chmn. patents com. 1970-72), Am. Bar Assn. (chmn. com. 407 taxation, patent and trademarks sect. 1971-72), Order of Coif, Alpha Epsilon Pi, Phi Alpha Delta. Kiwanian. Home: 7530 Stonecrest St Dallas TX 75240 Office: 13500 N Central Expressway Dallas TX 75222

LEVINE, JEROME EDWARD, physician; b. Pitts., Mar. 23, 1923; s. Harry Robert and Marian (Finesilver) LeV.; student U. Pitts., 1940-42, 44; M.D., Hahnemann Med. Sch., 1949; postgrad. opthalmology U. Pa., 1951-52; m. Marilyn Toby Hiedovitz, Apr. 14, 1957; children—Loren Robert, Beau Jay, Janice Lyn. Intern St. Francis Hosp., Pitts., 1949-50; resident opthalmologist Jefferson Med. Sch. and Hosp., Phila., 1952-54; opthamologist Leech Farm VA Hosp., 1955-59; chief eye dept. Stanocola Clinic, Baton Rouge, 1959-64; practice medicine specializing in ophthalmology, Baton Rouge, 1964—. Cons. La. State U. Infirmary, Villa Feliciana Geriatric Hosp., Women's Hosp., Dixon Meml. Hosp., Lane Meml. Hosp.; mem. staff Baton Rouge Gen. Hosp., Our Lady of Lake Hosp.; coding cons. div. blind La. State Dept. Pub. Welfare; instr. spl. edn. U. Southeastern La., 1971. Served with M.C., AUS, 1942-44. Fellow Am. Geriatric Soc., Royal Soc. Health; mem. La. Eye, Ear Nose and Throat Soc., New Orleans Acad. Ophthalmology, Inst. Glaucoma Research, A.M.A., So., Internat., Indsl., So. med. assns., La., East Baton Rouge Parish med. socs., Pi Lambda Phi, Phi Delta Epsilon. Home: 5876 Glenwood Dr Baton Rouge LA 70806 Office: 4560 North Blvd Baton Rouge La 70806

LEVINE, LEWIS, structural engr.; b. Glasgow, Scotland, Oct. 30, 1899 (came to U.S. 1905, naturalized 1931); s. Elias and Mary (Rosoffsky) L.; C.E., Bklyn. Poly. Inst., 1936, M.C.E., 1940; m. Pearl Margolett Heirshberg, Feb. 29, 1932. Civil engr., Brazil, W.I., Greece, Turkey, South Burma, 1942-48; fgn. service officer, adviser Ministry of Pub. Works, Greece, 1948-50; structural engr. Tippets, Abbet, McCarthy, Stratton, Greece, 1950-57; chief structural engr. David Volkert & Assos., Washington, 1957—. Served with Royal Brit. Army, 1917-20. Fellow Am. Soc. C.E., Soc. Am. Mil. Engrs. Home: 4221 16th St N W Washington DC 20011 Office: 4701 Sangamore Rd Bethesda MD 20016

LEVINE, RAPHAEL BERG, regional planner; b. Mpls., Dec. 8, 1920; s. Moses N. and Ruth (Berg) L.; B.A., cum laude, U. Minn., 1941, M.A. in Physics, 1950, Ph.D. in Biophysics, 1951; m. Jean Taylor, Apr. 21, 1957; children—Ceila Ruth, Garth Taylor. Research asso. biophysics U. Minn., 1951-54; research asso. neurophysiology U. Ill., 1954-54; asst. prof. psychiatry and research biophysicist Ohio State U., 1957-58; with Lockheed-Ga. Co., Marietta, Ga., 1958-70, mgr. Human Factors Research dept., 1961-63, staff scientist, 1964-70; exec. dir. Met. Atlanta Council Health, 1970-71, also exec. dir. Met. Atlanta Council Health, 1969-70; dir. health and social services planning Atlanta Regional Commn., 1972—. Mem. nat. exec. com., nat. bd. dirs. Planned Parenthood/World Population, 1971-73. Chmn. bd. Ga. Council Voluntary Family Planning, 1972—. Served with USNR, 1944-46. Mem. Biophysical Soc., Human Factors Soc., A.A.A.S., Am. Assn. Comprehensive Heatlh Planning, Am. Assn. Physics Tchrs., Sigma Xi. Author: (with C.N. Wall and F.E. Christensen) Physics Laboratory Manual, 1947, 49, 51, 62, 72. Contbr. articles to profl. jours. Home: 6455 Bridgewood Valley Rd Atlanta GA 30328 Office: 100 Peachtree St Atlanta GA 30303

LEVINE, RICHARD, architect-designer; b. Miami, Fla., June 1, 1933; s. Max and Mae (Mannis) L.; B.Arch., U. Fla., 1953. With Gerber-Paniana, architects, Miami, 1957-65; propr. Richard Levine, architect, Miami, 1965—; partner Bleemer & Levine, interior designs, Miami, 1965—. Chmn. Dade County (Fla.) Library Bd., 1970-71. Served to lt. (j.g.) USNR, 1954-57. Mem. A.I.A., Miami Interior Design Assn., Designers and Decorators Guild. Home: Costa Brava Condominium 11 Island Av Miami Beach FL 33139 Office: 35 NE 39th St Miami FL 33137

LEVINE, ROBERT ERWIN, editor, writer, economist; b. N.Y.C., Sept. 22, 1930; s. Arnold K. and Beatrice (Euer) L.; student Northwestern U., 1948-50; B.S., Wharton Sch., U. Pa., 1952; m. Patience Edge Appel, Feb. 21, 1952; children—Andrew Steven, Gregory Roberts, Elizabeth Rengier, Timothy Edge. Asst. bus. mgr. Billboard Pub. Co., 1954-56; advt. mgr. Rodale Press, Inc., Emmaus, Pa., 1956-59; asst. promotion mgr. House Beautiful mag., 1959-61; copywriter Newsweek mag., 1961-67; market researcher U.S. News and World Report, 1967-68; information and publs. dir. The Urban Land Inst., Washington, 1968-70; asst. editor Bur. Nat. Affairs, Inc., 1971-72; information dir. Opticians Assn. Am., 1972—. Scoutmaster, com. chmn. Washington Irving council Boy Scouts Am., 1956-66; baseball and basketball coach Little League, 1961-66; bd. dirs., officer Battery Park Citizens Recreation Assn., 1967—. Recipient Writer's award Newsweek, 1967; coach award Greenburgh Recreation Commn., 1965. Mem. Soc. Tech. Writers and Pubs., Pub. Relations Soc. Am., Tau Delta Phi. Jewish religion (bd. dir. congregation 1957-58). Clubs: Nat. Press (Washington); Palisades (Potomac, Md.); Battery Park (Bethesda, Md.). Editor: Calvert Party Ency., 1959; Nine Cities-The Anatomy of Downtown Renewal (Leo Adde), 1969. Founding editor Newsweek Communicator, 1961, Land Use Digest, 1968; exec. editor Urban Land, 1968-71; editor RXO Jour. Opticianry, 1972—. Home: 5217 Goddard Rd Bethesda MD 20014 Office: 1250 Connecticut Av NW Washington DC 20036

LEVINE, ROBERT HAROLD, elec. engr.; b. Albany, N.Y., Sept. 11, 1928; s. David Louis and Celia Dorothy (Link) L.; B.S., Purdue U., 1949; postgrad. Rutgers U., 1951-55, Indsl. Coll. Armed Forces, 1969-70; m. Miriam S. Lebedun, June 13, 1954; children—Karen, Amy, Jan. Elec. engr. Underwriters Labs., N.Y.C., 1950; electronic engr. Signal Corps Engring. Labs., Ft. Monmouth, N.J., 1950-60; project leader RCA Systems Lab., N.Y.C., 1960-61; with Def. Communications Agy., Reston, Va., 1961—, asso. engring. dir., 1973—. Served with AUS, 1949-50. Registered profl. engr., N.Y. Mem. I.E.E.E. (sr.), Armed Forces Communications Electronics Assn. Mason; mem. B'nai Brith. Office: 1860 Wiehl Av Reston VA 22090

LEVINE, SAM, concrete mfr.; b. Savannah, Ga., Aug. 13, 1919; s. Jacob Herman and Ida (Hershman) L.; student N.Y.U., 1938-39; m. Marilyn Budovsky Grossman, Dec. 24, 1955; children—Jack Jeffrey, Randie Sue, Michael Edward, Nanci Gale, Robert James, Judith Lynn. Partner, Mursam Block Co., 1946-47, Samson Block Co., 1947—; pres. Samson Concrete Industries, Inc., 1955-68, Samson Block Co., Inc. of Miami, 1957-68; sec., treas. Samson Block Co., Inc. of Homestead, 1957-68; treas., chmn. bd. Builders Finance & Mortgage Co. (name now Samson Realty & Devel. Corp.), 1958—; v.p. Coral Aggregate Corp., 1961-65; pres. Perrine Devel. Co., 1960—. Served as lt. (j.g.) U.S. Maritime Service, 1943-45. Mem. Fla. Home Builders Assn., Engring. Contractors Assn., South Fla. Masonry Assn., C. of C., Zionist Orgn. Am. (pres. Miami Gables dist. 1957-59). Mason (Shriner), Kiwanian; mem. B'nai B'rith. Home: 13575 SW 68th Ct Miami FL 33156 Office: 16300 SW 137th Av Miami FL 33157

LEVINGSTON, ERNEST LEE, engring. co. exec.; b. Pineville, La., Nov. 7, 1921; s. Vernon Lee and Adele (Miller) L.; B.M.E., La. State U., 1960; m. Kathleen Bernice Bordelon, June 23, 1944; children—David Lewis, Jeanne Evelyn (Mrs. James Woltz), James Lee. Gen. foreman T. Miller & Sons, Lake Charles, La., 1939-42; sr. engr., sect. head Cities Service Refining Corp., Lake Charles, La., 1946-57; group leader Bovay Engrs., Baton Rouge, 1957-59; chief engr. Augenstein Constrn. Co., Lake Charles, 1959-60; pres. Levingston Engrs., Inc., Lake Charles, 1961—. Mem. Lake Charles Planning and Zoning Commn., 1965-70; mem. adv. bd. Sowela Tech. Inst., 1969—; mem. Regional Export Expansion Council, 1969-70, chmn. code com. 1966—. Bd. dirs. Lake Charles Meml. Hosp. Served with USNR, 1942-46. Named Jaycee Boss of Year, 1972. Registered profl. engr., La., Tex., Miss., Ark., Tenn., Pa., Md., Del., N.J., D.C. Mem. La. Engring. Soc. (pres. 1967-68, state dir. 1967-68), Lake Charles C. of C. (dir. 1969-73). Baptist (deacon 1955—). Kiwanian. Club: Lake Charles Quarter Horse (pres. 1966—). Home: Levinwood Rd Lake Charles LA Office: PO Box 1865 Lake Charles LA 70601

LEVINSON, DONALD EARL, investment broker; b. Galesburg, Ill., Nov. 19, 1923; s. Erland Leonard and Esther (Clausen) M.; A.A., North Park Coll., 1948; postgrad. Northwestern U., 1948; m. Lorraine Jeanette Rydstedt, July 15, 1947; children—James, John, Lynn. Sales trainee Hornblower & Weeks, Chgo., 1948-49, registered rep., 1949-53; resident mgr. Hornblower & Weeks-Hemphill, Noyes, Rockford, Ill., 1953-69, v.p., regional cons., 1969-72; exec. v.p. Gibbs-Levinson Investments, Inc., Austin, Tex., 1972—; dir. Hook 'n Horn Ltd., Nestor Falls, Ont., Can. Asso. mem. Austin Bd. Realtors, since 1974—. Pres., Friends of North Park Coll., Chgo., 1966-67. Exec. bd. Rockford Coll., 1964-67, counselor, 1958-72. Served with USNR, 1943-46. Mem. Evang. Ch. (chmn. pension fund 1966-67). Rotarian. Club: Mid-Day (pres. Rockford 1965). Home: 4203 Greenridge Pl Austin TX 78759 Office: 900 Forest View Dr Austin TX 78746

LEVINSON, ROBERT PAUL, constrn. co. exec.; b. Buford, Ga., Oct. 7, 1919; s. Joseph and Lena (Harris) L.; student U. Chattanooga, 1937-38, U. Palm Beach, 1955; m. Martha Johnsey, May 8, 1943. Clk., timekeeper Rubin Constrn. Co., Chattanooga, 1938-39, field office mgr., 1939-41, asst. to pres., 1941-45, v.p., gen. mgr., 1946—; dir. Citizens Bank Palm Beach County. Chmn. Palm Beach County Planning, Zoning and Bldg. Commn., 1967-71, Palm Beach County Devel. Bd., 1971—; mem. Palm Beach County Constrn. Industry Licensing Bd. Bd. dirs. Boys Club Am., Goodwill Industries, Palm Beach County Fair Bd., Gulfstream council Boy Scouts Am., Palm Beach Zool. Soc. Recipient Industry Appreciation award State of Fla., 1970. Mem. Fla. Asphalt Contractors Assn. (dir. 1965—, pres. 1967-69), Fla. Rd. Builders, Nat. Asphalt Pavement Assn. Elk, Kiwanian. Home: 34 Country Club Rd West Palm Beach FL 33406 Office: PO Box 15065 West Palm Beach FL 33406

LEVITAS, ELLIOTT HARRIS, lawyer; b. Atlanta, Dec. 26, 1930; s. Louis J. and Ida (Goldstein) L.; A.B., Emory U., 1952, LL.B., 1956; B.A. (Rhodes scholar), Oxford U., 1954, M.A., 1958; postgrad. U. Mich., 1954-55; m. Barbara Hillman, June 8, 1955; children—Karen, Susan, Kevin. Admitted to Ga. bar, 1955; practiced in Atlanta, 1955—; mem. firm Arnall, Golden, Gregory, 1955—; mem. Ga. Ho. of Reps., 1965—, chmn. com. community affairs and planning, chmn. joint house-senate com. on rapid transit overview. Lectr. Emory U., 1959-60, 68-70. Mem. bd. dirs. Atlanta Jewish Community Center, Atlanta Jewish Welfare Fedn. Served to lt. USAF, 1956-58. Mem. Am., Ga., Atlanta bar assns. Democrat. Home: 829 Castle Falls Dr NE Atlanta GA 30329 Office: Fulton Fed Bldg Atlanta GA 30303

LEVITCH, HERMAN HARRY, jeweler; b. Memphis, Dec. 24, 1916; s. Samuel and Lena (Feingold) L.; LL.B. cum laude, So. Law U., 1941; LL.B., Memphis State U., 1967; grad. Gemological Inst. Am., 1965; m. Frances Wagner, May 31, 1936; 1 son, Ronald Wagner. Jeweler, diamond specialist, jewelry designer, Memphis, 1936—. Gen. chmn. United Jewish Appeal Southwest Mo. and No. Ark., 1948-50; del. conf. Am.'s problems, Washington, 1967-69, regional conf. U.S. fgn. policy, Louisville, 1969; mem. Memphis Community Relations Council. Mem. Shelby County exec. bd. Memphis area March of Dimes, 1966—; mem. exec. com. Memphis and Shelby County Music Commn.; mem. adminstrv. com. bd. trustees Leo N. Levi Nat. Arthritic Hosp., Hot Springs Nat. Park, Ark.; mem. exec. bd. B'nai B'rith Home and Hosp. for Aged. Served with USAAF, World War II. Recipient B award Diamonds Internat., 1969. Mem. Memphis area C. of C. (welcoming com. 1965—), Jewelry Industry Council, Retail Jewelers Am., Moose former trustee), Mason (32 deg., Shriner); mem. B'nai B'rith (pres. dist. 7, 1974—, bd. govs. supreme lodge, Vol. of Year 1966-67, del. leadership conf. Israel 1970). Clubs: Petroleum, Summit. Home: 4972 Peg Lane Memphis TN 38117 Office: 147 Union Av Memphis TN 38103

LEVITT, PHILLIP RUSSELL, periodontist; b. Cheyenne, Wyo., July 29, 1926; s. Max P. and Alice (Weinstein) L.; B.A., U. Colo., 1950; postgrad. U. Wyo., 1950-51; D.D.S., Northwestern U., 1954; certificate in Periodontics, U. Ala., 1960; m. Helene Sylvia Rosenthal, Feb. 27, 1955; children—Gail Mandi, Ronald Alan, Jeffrey Miles. Pvt. practice gen. dentistry, Denver, 1955-58, specializing in periodontics, Tuscaloosa, Ala., 1961-63, Birmingham, Ala., 1963—; staff periodontist Ala. State Hosps., 1960-63; clin. instr. dentistry U. Ala., 1966—. Served with AUS, 1944-46. Mem. Am., Ala. dental assns., Birmingham Dist. Dental Soc., Am. Acad. Periodontology, Ala. Soc. Periodontists, Southern Acad. Periodontology, Phi Sigma Delta, Alpha Omega, Zeta Beta Tau. Jewish religion. Mem. B'nai B'rith. Home: 912 Beech Lane Birmingham AL 35213 Office: 1000 S 19th St Birmingham AL 35205

LEVITT, RONALD L., pub. relations cons.; b. Rochester, N.Y., Mar. 23, 1931; s. Maurice and Pearl (Altman) L.; A.B., U. Miami, 1956; m. Geraldine Rita Wortsman, June 20, 1954; children—Lynn Barbara, Howard Jay. Staff corr. UP, 1956-59; news dir., accounts supr. Mandell/Newman, 1959-60; pres. Ronald Levitt Assos. Inc., pub. relations cons., Coral Gables, Fla., 1961—. Lectr. pub. relations colls. throughout U.S.; guest lectr. on pub. relations and politics. Served with USN, 1950-54. Recipient Dept. Def. award, 1953; service awards Pub. Relations Soc. Am., 1966, 67, 68, 69. Mem. Pub. Relations Soc. Am. (pres. Fla. 1966; chmn. Southeastern dist. 1968-70), Internat. Platform Assn., Assn. Indsl. Editors, Am. Assn. Polit. Cons., Fla. Pub. Relations Assn. Clubs: Miami Press, U. Miami Alumni, Palm Bay. Contbr. articles to mags. Home: 7170 SW 119th St Miami FL 33156 Office: 141 Sevilla Av Coral Gables FL 33134

LEVY, JACK BENJAMIN, educator; b. Savannah, Ga., Jan. 17, 1941; s. Hyman Sidney and Minnie (Weitz) L.; A.B., Duke U., 1962; M.S., N.C. State U., 1964, Ph.D., 1967; postdoctoral research Cambridge U. (Eng.), 1967; m. Doris Rose Levy, June 4, 1963; children—Rachel, Matthew Asher. Asst. prof. chemistry U. N.C. at Wilmington, 1968-69, asso. prof., 1969-73, prof., 1973—, dir. Multiple Abilities Program for Gifted Students, 1972-73. Treas. Head Start of New Hanover County, 1972-73. Mem. N.C. Acad. Sci. (chmn. Chemistry sect. 1973—), Am. Chem. Soc., Am. Inst. Chemists, N.Y. Acad. Sci., A.A.A.S., Sigma Xi. Contbr. articles to sci., tech. jours. Home: 1307 Country Club Rd Wilmington NC 28401 Office: Chemistry Dept U NC at Wilmington Wilmington NC 28401

LEVY, JEROME SICKLES, physician; b. Morganfield, Ky., Sept. 27, 1902; s. Phil and Hattie (Sickles) L.; B.S., Washington U., St. Louis, 1923, M.D., 1925; m. Marion Lee, June 15, 1946; children—Carol Lee, Jere-Jane. Intern Jewish Hosp., St. Louis, 1926-27; asst. in surgery Washington U. Sch. Medicine, 1925-26; resident MaPac Hosp., St. Louis, 1927-29; practice medicine, specializing in internal medicine and gastroenterology Little Rock, 1929—; mem. staff St. Vincent Infirmary, U. Ark., Ark. Baptist Med. Center, Mo. Pacific Hosp.; clin. prof. medicine U. Ark. Sch. Medicine, 1945—. Vice pres. S.W. regional bd. Am. Jewish Com. 1960—, also mem. nat. adminstrv. bd.; mem. adminstrv. bd. Leo N. Levi Meml. Hosp., Hot Springs, Ark., 1955—; chmn. Central Ark. Council for Comprehensive Health Planning, 1968-70; adv. bd. Ark. Regional Med. Program. Served with AUS, 1942-46. Diplomate in gastroenterology Am. Bd. Internal Medicine. Fellow A.C.P. (Ark. gov. 1963-71), Am. Coll. Gastroenterology; mem. A.M.A., Pan-Am., Ark. (1st v.p. 1967-68, chmn. com. on medicine and religion 1968-70), So., Pulaski County (pres. 1957) med. assns., Am. Gastroenterol. Assn., Digestive Disease Found. (founding mem.), Zeta Beta Tau. Jewish religion. Mem. B'nai B'rith. Contbr. articles to profl. jours. Home: 3 E Palisades Dr Little Rock AR 72207 Office: 500 S University Av Little Rock AR 72205

LEVY, JOE SIMON, physician; b. Memphis, Jan. 9, 1941; s. Ludwig and Irma (Menkel) L.; B.S. with distinction, Southwestern U. at Memphis, 1963; M.D., U. Tenn., 1966; m. Myrna Jean O'Mell, June 15, 1969; children—Elizabeth Ann, Alan Louis. Intern John Gaston Hosp., Memphis, 1967-68, resident, 1968-69; resident Children's Med. Center, Dallas, 1969-70; practice medicine specializing in pediatrics, Memphis, 1972-73; dir. clin. services Memphis and Shelby County (Tenn.) Health Dept., 1973—; clin. instr. pediatrics U. Tenn. Med. Sch., 1970—, clin. instr. dept. community medicine, 1974—; mem. staff Le Bonheur Children's Hosp., Memphis, Bapt. Meml. Hosp., Memphis, Meth. Hosp., Memphis, St. Joseph Hosp., Memphis. Bd. dirs. West Tenn. Cancer Clinic, Memphis. Fellow Am. Acad. Pediatrics; mem. Tenn. Med. Assn., Tenn. Pub. Health Assn. Jewish religion. Home: 6747 Huntsman Cove Memphis TN 38138 Office: 814 Jefferson Av Memphis TN 38105

LEVY, LARRY, newspaperman; b. Chgo., Nov. 24, 1931; s. Edward Albert and Ruth (Oppenheim) L.; student Colo. Coll., 1950-51; student U. Miami, 1956-57; m. Carole Marie Wolf, Sept. 1, 1962; children—Carrie Ruth, David Jeffrey, Karen Michelle. Reporter, Miami (Fla.) Herald, 1956-57, Southtown Economist, Chgo., 1958-59, Tucson Citizen, 1959, Daily Oklahoman, Oklahoma City, 1959-62, San Bernardino (Cal.) Sun-Telegram, 1962-63; aviation, mil. writer Daily Oklahoman, Oklahoma City, 1963-67, Oklahoma City Times, 1963-67; aviation writer Tulsa Tribune, 1967—; free-lance mag. writer. Past mem. adv. bd. Monte Cassino Sch., Tulsa. Served with USAF, 1951-55. Mem. Aviation Space Writers Assn., Air Force Assn., Sigma Delta Chi, Kappa Alpha Mu. Clubs: Oklahoma City Gridiron, Oklahoma City Press (dir. 1961-66). Home: 7823 S College Pl Tulsa OK 74136 Office: PO Box 1770 Tulsa OK 74102

LEVY, LOUIS, II, cardiologist; b. New Orleans, Nov. 24, 1919; s. Herman and Hannah (Klein) L; B.S., La. State U., 1940, M.D., 1943; m. Dorothy Cobb, Sept. 28, 1945; children—Louis Herman, Larry, Lynda, Leslie, Lizabeth. Intern, resident Charity Hosp., New Orleans, 1943-46, dir. Heart Sta., 1947—; practice medicine specializing in internal medicine, New Orleans, 1946—; mem. staff Touro, Hotel Dieu, Mercy, Flint Goodridge, Charity, St. Charles Gen. hosps.; instr. medicine La. State U., 1946-51, prof., 1961—. Diplomate Am. Bd. Internal Medicine and Cardiology. Fellow A.C.P., Am. Coll. Cardiology, Am. Coll. Chest Physicians; mem. A.M.A., So. Med. Assn., New Orleans Acad. Internal Medicine. Home: 1516 1st St New Orleans LA 70130 Office: 3600 Prytania 81 Schick Ct New Orleans LA 70115

LEVY, S. SANFORD, judge; b. Bastrop, La., Jan. 27, 1902; s. Emile and Melanie (Guggenheim) L.; J.D. cum laude, Loyola U., New Orleans; m. Anna Judge Veters, Feb. 24, 1930 (dec. Mar. 1964); m. 2d, Mary Phene Veters, May 31, 1965. Admitted to La. bar, 1922; exec. v.p., then receiver Ins. Securities Cos.; practiced law, New Orleans, 1933-64; judge First City Ct. New Orleans, 1964-66; judge Civil Dist. Ct., New Orleans, 1966—. Mgr., sec.-treas. Anna Judge Veters Levy Found.; trustee Joseph A. Breaux Scholarship Fund. Home: 832 St Louis St New Orleans LA 70112 Office: 828 St Louis St New Orleans LA 70112

LEWEY, MERLE CREIGHTON, ret. army officer, govt. ofcl.; b. Coffeen, Ill., Apr. 30, 1921; s. Merle Walter and Flos (Roberts) L.; A.B., James Millikin U., 1948, A.M., U. So. Cal., 1959. Announcer radio sta. WSOY, Decatur, Ill., 1941-42; instr. James Millikin U., 1947-48; announcer WCRA, Effington, Ill., 1950-51; commd. 2d lt. U.S. Army, 1942, advanced through grades to lt. col., 1962; chief audio-visual br. Office Chief Information, Dept. Army, Washington, 1964-66; ret., 1966; audio-visual support officer Office Asst. Chief Staff Communications-Electronics, Dept. Army, 1967-72, audio-visual programs officer Office Dep. Chief Staff Personnel, 1972—. Decorated Bronze Star, Legion of Merit. Mem. Soc. Motion Picture and TV Engrs., Acad. TV Arts and Scis., Tau Kappa Epsilon, Alpha Phi Omega, Alpha Epsilon Rho. Home: Cavalier Club 6200 Wilson Blvd Apt 1110 Falls Church VA 22044 Office: Office Dep Chief Staff for Personnel Dept Army Washington DC 20310

LEWINSON, SAM, textile corp. exec.; b. Ashburn, Ga., June 21, 1914; s. Mendel and Annie (Greenberg) L.; B.A., U. Fla., 1935; postgrad. So. Coll. Pharmacy, Atlanta, 1936; m. Alice Lewin, July 3, 1965; children—Nancy Jean, Sally Ann. Mgr. Friendly Dept. Store, Dalton, Ga., 1937-44; partner Blue Ribbon Mills, Dalton, 1944-45; pres. Royal Mills, Inc., Dalton, 1945-67; partner K. & W. Mfg. Co., Dalton, 1960-68; treas. North Ga. Indsl. Devel. Corp., Dalton, 1965-73; Margate Mills, Inc., Dalton, 1968—; sec.-treas. Comml. Mills-Antigua Mills, Inc., Dalton, 1969—; pres. S. & L. Sales Corp., Dalton, 1960—. Mason, Elk. Home: 1410 Belmont Rd Dalton GA 30720 Office: Box 547 Dalton GA 30720

LEWIS, CEYLON SMITH, JR., physician; b. Muskogee, Okla., July 19, 1920; s. Ceylon Smith and Glenn (Ellis) L.; A.B., Washington U., St. Louis, 1942, M.D., 1945; m. Marguerite Dearmont, Dec. 20, 1943; children—Sarah Lee, Ceylon Smith III, Carol D. Intern Salt Lake Gen. Hosp., 1945-46; resident in internal medicine Salt Lake VA Hosp., Salt Lake County Hosp., 1948-51; practice internal medicine and cardiology, Tulsa, 1951—; asst. clin. prof. medicine U. Okla. Sch. Medicine, 1971—; cons. internal medicine USPHS Indian Hosp. Trustee Coll. Ozarks, 1964—; bd. dirs. Am. Heart Assn., 1971—; pres. Med. Mission Fund, 1972. Served to capt. M.C., AUS, 1946-48. Diplomate Am. Bd. Internal Medicine. Fellow A.C.P.; mem. Tulsa County Med. Soc. (pres. 1971), Okla. Soc. Internal Medicine (pres. 1971-72). Presbyn. Contbr. articles to profl. jours. Home: 3747 S Wheeling Tulsa OK 74105 Office: 2021 S Lewis Tulsa OK 74104

LEWIS, CORNELIUS CRAWFORD, educator; b. Appomattox, Va., May 24, 1921; s. Mace R. and Martha Jane (Patterson) L.; B.S., Va. State Coll., 1942; M.S., Mich. State Coll., 1945; Ph.D., U. Mass., 1948; postgrad. (research asso.), Ohio State U., 1961-62, U. Md., 1970-71; m. Martina Hall, Sept. 2, 1949. Prof. chemistry Va. State Coll., Petersburg, 1941-51, chmn. dept. plant sci., 1954-56, head dept., 1956-63, prof. chemistry and soils, 1963—. Soil chemist U.S. Govt., Liberia, 1951-54. Mem. Ettrick (Va.) Improvement Assn. Served with AUS, 1942-43. Research grantee U.S. Dept. Agr., 1964, 66, 72, AEC, 1965. Mem. Am. Soc. Agronomy, A.A.A.S., Am. Chem. Soc., Sigma Xi, Phi Beta Sigma. Baptist (mem. bd.; mem. finance com. 1972-73). Club: Catjemb Investment (Ettrick). Home: 20412 Woodpecker Rd Ettrick VA 23806 Office: Box 43 Va State Coll Petersburg VA 23806

LEWIS, DANIEL CURTIS, JR., paper co. exec.; b. Suffolk, Va., Aug. 26, 1918; s. Daniel Curtis and Frances (Rawls) L.; A.B. cum laude, Washington and Lee U., 1942; M.B.A. with distinction, Harvard, 1948, D.C.S., 1954; m. Elizabeth Shirley Baer, June 5, 1948; children—Lawrence S., Clifford R., Robert D. Jr. staff accountant Lybrand Ross Bros. & Montgomery, Boston, 1948-49; asst. prof. commerce Washington and Lee U., 1949-52; research asso. bus. adminstrn. Harvard Grad. Sch. Bus. Adminstrn., 1952-54; asst. to pres. Lynchburg Foundry Co. (Va.), 1954-56, controller, 1956-60, sec., asst. treas., 1960-63; asst. sec. Woodward Iron Co. Birmingham, Lynchburg, 1961-63; asst. to pres. The Chesapeake Corp. Va., West Point, 1963-66, v.p. adminstrn., 1966—, also dir.; sec. Greenlife Products Co., 1969—, also dir.; pres. Chesapeake Bay Plywood Corp., 1967—, also dir.; dir. York River Oyster Research Corp., Cands Lumber Co. Chmn. West Point Sch. Bd., 1965—; mem. Va. Commn. on Higher Edn., 1964-65, Va. Commn. on State and Local Revenues, Expenditures and Related Matters, 1962-63; chmn. Lynchburg Citizens Sch. Study Commn., 1960-61; treas. Va. Found. for Ind. Colls., 1957-63; mem. Va. State Bd. for Community Colls., 1966—, vice chmn., 1970-71, chmn., 1971—. Pres., bd. dirs. Ednl. Found. for Community Colls. Va., 1968—; mem. West Point Bi-racial Com., 1968—. Bd. dirs. United Fund Lynchburg, 1959-61, v.p., 1960-61; bd. dirs. Lynchburg Guidance Center, 1956-59, pres., 1958-59; bd. dirs. Lynchburg chpt. A.R.C., 1956-59, West Point Improvement Assn., 1964-67; trustee Va. Episcopal Sch., 1960-66, Va. Found. Ind. Colls., 1966-73, Williamsburg Community Hosp., 1967-70; bd. dirs. bus. sch. sponsors Coll. William and Mary. Served with USNR, 1942-46. Mem. Financial Execs. Inst., Newcomen Soc. N.Am., So. Forest Inst. (pres. 1971). Episcopalian (vestryman). Clubs: Harvard of Va., West Point Country (dir.), Downtown, York River Yacht Haven. Home: Tanager Ct West Point VA 23181 Office: The Chesapeake Corp Va West Point VA 23181

LEWIS, DANNY PHEARON, accountant; b. San Diego, Aug. 6, 1942; s. Darrell Preston and Ora (Lee) L.; m. Dorothy Ann Shepherd, Nov. 27, 1968; children—Barbara Ann, Darrell Preston II.

Accountant firm Brown, Graham & Co., Tulia, Tex., 1962-69, partner, 1969-73, mfg. partner, Dimmitt, Tex., 1973—. Mem. City Charter Commn. Tulia, 1972. Exec. bd. dirs. South Plains Council Boy Scouts Am., 1973—. C.P.A., Tex. Mem. Am. Inst. C.P.A.'s, Tex. Soc. C.P.A.'s Kiwanian. Home: 712 Pine St Dimmitt TX 79027 Office: PO Box 895 Dimmitt TX 79027

LEWIS, DAVID WARREN, educator; b. Salem, O., June 16, 1930; s. Fred Summers and Prudence (Foster) L.; B.A., Rice U., 1952, B.S. in Mech. Engring., 1953; Ph.D. (Cabell fellow 1957-58), Northwestern U., 1958; m. Mary Alice Umstott, June 14, 1953; children—Tamara, Rebecca, Amy, Mary. Asst. prof. U.S. Naval Postgrad. Sch., Montery, Cal., 1958-60; staff engr. IBM Corp., Endicott, N.Y., 1960-63; mem. faculty U. Va., Charlottesville, 1963—, prof. mech. and biomed. engring., 1970—. Pres. Ivy Design Engring. And Systems, Inc. (Va.), 1973—; cons. in patent litigation and automotive areas. Registered profl. engr., Va. Mem. Am. Soc. M.E., Am. Soc. Engring. Edn., Am. Thermographic Soc., Sigma Xi. Patentee in field. Home: The Shadows Route 2 Box 198 Charlottesville VA 22901

LEWIS, DOUGLAS, museum curator; b. Centreville, Miss., Apr. 30, 1938; s. Charles Douglas and Beatrice Fenwick (Stewart) L.; diploma cum laude, Lawrenceville Sch., 1956; B.A. in History, Yale, 1959, B.A. in History of Art magna cum laude, 1960, M.A. in History of Art, 1963, Ph.D., 1967; B.A. in Architecture and Fine Arts with 1st class honors (Mellon fellow), Clare Coll. U. Cambridge (Eng.), 1962; m. Carolyn Jo Kolb, June 1, 1969. Asst. instr. Yale, 1962-64; asst. prof., vis. lectr. Bryn Mawr Coll., 1967-68; curator sculpture Nat. Gallery Art, Washington, 1968—; vis. lectr. U. Cal. at Berkeley, 1970, Johns Hopkins, 1973—; co-leader G Folger Renaissance Seminar, Washington, 1972. Bd. dirs. Am. fellowships com. Belgian-Am. Ednl. Found.; trustee John Marshall House, Richmond, Va. Prix de Rome fellow Am. Acad. Rome, 1964-66; Chester Dale fellow Nat. Gallery Art, 1964-65, David E. Finley fellow, 1965-67. Fellow Am. Acad. Rome, Soc. Archtl. Historians, Coll. Art Assn. Am. Clubs: Yale (N.Y.C.); Oxford and Cambridge (London, Eng.); Manuscript Society (New Haven); Falcons (Cambridge); Bucintoro (Venice, Italy). Contbr. articles to profl. jours., also translations from Italian. Home: 319 Constitution Av NE Washington DC 20002 Office: Nat Gallery Art Washington DC 20565

LEWIS, E. CROSBY, lawyer; b. Fairfield County, S.C., Mar. 4, 1934; s. Ernest Vann and Nell (Brooks) L.; student U. S.C., 1952-55, LL.B., 1958; m. Cleo B. Dickerson; children—Lisa LaVelle, Allyson Lee, E. Crosby. Admitted to S.C. bar, 1958, since practiced in Columbia. Dir. Riverland Devel. Corp., First Palmetto State Bank & Trust. Vice chmn. S.C. Bd. Edn., 1965-69. Mem. S.C. Ho. of Reps. from Richland County, 1961-64, chmn. mil., pub. and municipal affairs com.; chmn. S.C. Democratic Party, 1967-69; v.p. Nat. Assn. Dem. State Chmn., 1969—. Bd. visitors The Citadel; bd. dirs. S.C. Med. Coll. Served with AUS. Named Eagle Scout. Mem. Am., S.C., Richland County bar assns., Columbia C. of C. Methodist. Mason (Shriner). Club: Forest Lake. Home: RFD Winnsboro SC 29180 Office: 1717 Gervais St Columbia SC 29201

LEWIS, EARL CALVIN, clergyman; b. St. Joseph, Mo., Dec. 9, 1901; s. General Washington and Letha (Ramey) L.; B.A., Culver-Stockton Coll., 1930; M.Ed., La. State U., 1950; m. Nina Ruby Quidor, July 13, 1950; children—Alice Letha (Mrs. Dorman K. Gunter), Roberta (Mrs. Charles Davis), John Paul. Ordained to ministry Christian Ch., 1932; minister Bucklin (Mo.) Christian Ch., 1937-40, Baton Rouge Christian Ch., 1949-58, West Side Christian Ch., New Orleans, 1958-61, Harahen Christian Ch., New Orleans, 1962-66, Gould (Ark.) Christian Ch., 1966-67, First Christian Ch., North Little Rock, Ark., 1967-69, Carlisle (Ark.) Christian Ch., 1969—. Tchr., Central High Sch., Baton Rouge, 1956-57, Chalmette (La.) High Sch., 1957-66. Pres., Bayou Metro Civic and Recreation Assn., 1969—. Bd. dirs. La. Civic and Moral Found., 1948-58. Served with AUS, 1940-45; ETO. Mason (K.T.); mem. Order Eastern Star. Address: Route 2 Box 299 Jacksonville AR 72076

LEWIS, EDWARD, educator; b. St. Louis, Feb. 10, 1930; s. William and Priscilla (Chambers) L.; B.A., Washington U., St. Louis, 1952, M.A., 1953, Ph.D., 1957; m. Anne Livingston, Oct. 18, 1954; children—William Edward, Patricia Jane, Sophie Eleanor. Asst. prof. U. Kan. at Lawrence, 1953-54; asso. prof. modern langs. U. N.C. at Durham, 1954-60, prof., 1960—, chmn. dept. modern langs., 1962-68. Mem. Modern Lang. Assn., Am. Assn. U. Profs., Phi Beta Kappa, Alpha Tau Omega. Contbr. articles to profl. jours. Home: 7908 Gala Ct Raleigh NC 27609

LEWIS, GEORGE, banker; b. Tallahassee, Fla., Nov. 4, 1913; s. George Edward and Sarah (Davis) L.; B.S., U. Fla., 1935; grad. Grad. Sch. Banking of Rutgers U., 1939; m. Clifton VanBrunt, Sept. 4, 1940; children—George Edward II, William VanBrunt, Clifton Byrd, Benjamin Bridges. With Lewis State Bank, Tallahassee, 1935—, pres., 1955-67, chmn. bd., 1967—, also dir. Chmn. Fla. adv. com. to U.S. Commn. Civil Rights, 1962-64; treas. Fla. Council Human Relations; mem. so. regional council Am. Civil Liberties Union, Center Study of Dem. Instns., Common Cause, Nation Assos., Bus. Execs. Move for New Nat. Priorities, World Assn. World Federalists. Trustee Fla. Bankers Ednl. Found., 1959-65. Recipient Frontiers Human Relations award, 1963. Mem. Fla. Bankers Assn., World Federalists U.S.A., Inst. Am. Democracy, Fellowship of Reconciliation, UN Assn. of U.S., Urban Coalition. Democrat. Episcopalian. Owner Frank Lloyd Wright Fla. House. Home: 3117 Okeeheepkee Rd Tallahassee FL 32303 Office: PO Box 750 Tallahassee FL 32302

LEWIS, GEORGE MCKOY, banker; b. Valley Mills, Tex., Aug. 3, 1902; s. Samuel Knight and Mary Rebecca (Barrett) L.; B.S., Tex. A. and M. U., 1924; M.B.A., Harvard, 1927; postgrad. U. Chgo., 1929-30; m. Mary Gregory Bunting, Feb. 10, 1940. Mem. staff U.S. Dept. Agr., 1924-25; staff Bur. Bus. Research, U. Tex., 1927-29; Inst. Meat Packing fellow U. Chgo., 1929-30; dir. marketing Am. Meat Inst., Chgo., 1939-57, v.p., 1950-63; vice chmn. bd., economist Jefferson State Bank, San Antonio, 1963—. Vice pres. Am. Meat Inst. Found., 1957-63. Mem. Sons Tex. Republic. Mason (Shriner). Clubs: Quadrangle, Union League, University of Chicago, South Shore Country (Chgo.); Argyle (San Antonio). Home: 715 Wiltshire Av San Antonio TX 78209 Office: Jefferson State Bank San Antonio TX 78284

LEWIS, GILBERT LASEINE, drug co. exec.; b. Millen, Ga., Oct. 6, 1923; s. Robert Lee and Fannie (Ethridge) L.; student Ga. So. Coll., 1946-47; B.S. in Pharmacy, U. Ga., 1950; m. Betty Ann Camp, Mar. 4, 1929; children—Michael, Elizabeth. Pharmacist Crystal Pharmacy, Moultrie, Ga., 1950-51, Williford Drug Co., Camilla, Ga., 1951-54; pharmacist Pelham Drug Co. (Ga.), 1954-61, now pres.; owner, pres. Lewis Drug Co., Pelham, 1961—; pres. Meigs Pharmacy (Ga.), 1968—; dir. Farmers Bank Pelham. Mem. Pelham City Adv. Com., 1968—; pres. Pelham Devel. Corp., 1965—; chmn. Pelham Recreation Bd. 1966—. Mem. Sch. Bd., Pelham, 1968—; mem. exec. com. Pelham City Democratic party, 1964—. Bd. dirs. Ravenwood Acad., Meigs, Chickasaw Devel. Corp. Served with USAAF, 1942-46. Mem. Pelham C. of C. (dir.), Ga. Pharm. Assn. Methodist (steward). Rotarian. Home: 3 N Legion Dr Pelham GA 31779 Office: 450 W Railroad St Pelham GA 31779

LEWIS, HENRY HOLMES, city govt. ofcl.; b. Waco, Tex., June 16, 1909; s. William Clarence and Mable (Holmes) L.; grad. high sch.; m. Ruth Johnson, Nov. 23, 1932; children—Lina Ruth (Mrs. Jack Rischer McClintock), William Johnson. Instrument man Tex. Hwy. Dept., 1934-37; chief insp. constrn. Nueces County (Tex.) PWA Project, 1937-40; sr. constrn. insp., civil engr. Bur. Yards and Docks, Navy Dept., 1940-46; street supt. City of Corpus Christi, Tex., 1946—. Recipient Man of Year award Am. Pub. Works Assn., 1970. Presbyn. (deacon 1948, 68, chmn. deacons 1951, elder 1954, 60, 65). Mason. Home: 1334 Tyler St Corpus Christi TX 78415 Office: 2525 Sacky St Corpus Christi TX 78415

LEWIS, HERBERT CLAY, educator; b. Newton, Mass., Aug. 7, 1913; s. Warren Kendall and Rosalind Denny (Kenway) L.; B.A., Bowdoin Coll., 1934; M.S., Mass. Inst. Tech., 1937, postgrad. Center for Advanced Engring. Study, 1971-72; Sc.D., Carnegie Inst. Tech., 1942; spl. student Imperial Coll. Sci. and Tech., 1960-61; m. Isabella Campbell Wilson, Dec. 21, 1949. With Humble Oil and Refining Co., Baytown, Tex., 1937-40; mem. faculty U. Ill., Urbana, 1942-45; research asso. Mass. Inst. Tech., Cambridge, 1945-46; mem. faculty Ga. Inst. Tech., Atlanta, 1946—, prof. chem. engring., 1952—. Vis. prof. Tunghai U., Taichung, Taiwan, 1969. Mem. Am. Chem. Soc., Am. Inst. Chem. Engrs., Am. Soc. Engring. Edn., Zeta Psi, Gamma Alpha. Author: (with W.K. Lewis, A.H. Radasch) Industrial Stoichiometry, 2d edit., 1954. Home: 212 Winnona Dr Decatur GA 30030 Office: Chem Engring Dept Ga Inst Tech Atlanta GA 30332

LEWIS, JACK PEARL, educator; b. Midlothian, Tex., Mar. 13, 1919; s. Pearl Gaunce and Anna Elizabeth (Holland) L.; B.A. summa cum laude, Abilene Christian Coll., 1941; M.A., Sam Houston State Tchrs. Coll., 1944; S.T.B., Harvard Divinity Sch., 1947; Ph.D., Harvard, 1953; Ph.D. (Interfaith fellow 1951-54), Hebrew Union Coll., 1962; m. Lynell Carpenter, Aug. 3, 1943; children—John Robert, Jerry Wayne. Minister, Ch. of Christ, Throckmorton, Tex., 1941-42, Huntsville, Tex., 1942-44, Providence, 1944-51, Garrod St. Ch. of Christ, Covington, Ky., 1951-54, Hwy. 61 South Ch. of Christ, Memphis, 1959-62, Ch. of Christ, Ripley, Tenn., 1962-64, Henning, Tenn., 1964-65; mem. faculty Harding Coll., Memphis, 1954—, prof. Bible, 1957—. Trustee U. Christian Center, Oxford, Miss., 1966—. Recipient Hopkins Share, Harvard Div. Sch., 1947-48; Christian Edn. award 20th Century Christian, 1968. Thayer fellow Am. Schs. Oriental Research, 1967-68. Mem. Nat. Assn. Profs. Hebrew, Soc. Bibl. Lit., Am. Acad. Religion, Evang. Theol. Soc. Author: The Minor Prophets, 1966; The Interpretation of Noah and the Flood in Jewish and Christian Literature, 1968; Historical Backgrounds of Bible History, 1971. Editor: The Last Things, 1972. Mem. editorial bd. Restoration Quar., 1957—, Jour. Hebraic Studies, 1969-70; mem. staff Power for Today, 1960—. Home: 1132 S Perkins Rd Memphis TN 38117

LEWIS, JAMES WOODROW, state supreme ct. justice; b. Darlington County, S.C., Mar. 8, 1912; s. W. J. and Mary Aletha (Bryant) L.; A.B., U. S.C., 1932; m. Alice Lee, Dec. 26, 1936; 1 dau., Barbara (Mrs. Olin D. Haynes). Admitted to S.C. bar 1935; mem. S.C. Hwy. Commn., 1936-40; mem. S.C. Ho. of Reps. from Darlington County, 1935-36, 43-45; judge 4th Jud Circuit S.C., 1945-61; asso. justice Supreme Ct. S.C., 1961—. Address: Darlington SC 29532

LEWIS, JAY FREDERICK, pathologist; b. Albuquerque, Sept. 15, 1931; s. Jay F. and Elizabeth (Holloman) L.; B.S., N.M. State U., 1953; M.D., Vanderbilt U., 1958; m. Joy Smith, July 27, 1957; children—Elizabeth, William, Robert, Barbara. Intern, Vanberbilt Hosp., Nashville, 1958-59; resident St. Thomas Hosp., Nashville, 1963-66; practice medicine specializing in pathology, Wilmington, N.C., 1966-70, Chattanooga, 1970—; mem. staff New Hanover Meml. Hosp., Wilmington, 1967-70; asso. pathologist Baroness Erlanger Hosp., Chattanooga, 1970—. Served to lt. M.C., USNR, 1959-63. Diplomate Am. Bd. Pathology, Am. Bd. Microbiology. Mem. A.C.P., A.M.A., Am. Soc. Clin. Pathologists. Contbr. articles to med. jours. Home: 7465 Preston Circle Chattanooga TN 37421 Office: 261 Wiehl St Chattanooga TN 37403

LEWIS, JESSE CORNELIUS, educator; b. Vaughan, Miss., June 26, 1929; s. Jefferson and Elizabeth (Hollins) L.; B.S., Tougaloo Coll., 1949; M.A., U. Ill., 1959, M.S., 1955; Ph.D., Syracuse U., 1966; m. Emma Goldman, May 5, 1973; 1 dau., Valerie. Instr. math. So. U., Baton Rouge, 1955-57, Prairie View (Tex.) Coll., 1957-58; research asst. computer center Syracuse (N.Y.) U., 1963-66; prof. math. Jackson (Miss.) State Coll., 1966—, dir. computer center, 1966—; sec., dir. State Mut. Savs. & Loan, Jackson, 1969—. Cons., lectr. Am. Math. Assn., 1971—; chmn. faculty senate Jackson State Coll., 1970-73; project dir. NSF Computing Network, 1973—. NSF Sci. Faculty fellow, 1958, 61. Mem. Math. Assn. Am., Assn. Computing Machinery, Am. Math. Soc., Alpha Phi Alpha. Home: 1566 Schoolview Dr Jackson MS 39213

LEWIS, JOHN ALDEN, optometrist; b. Lexington, Ky., Aug. 25, 1946; s. Alden McLean and Mary Frances (Wade) L.; student Morehead State U., 1964-67; B.S. in optometry, U. Houston, 1969, O.D., 1971; m. Mary Rose Abrams, Aug. 4, 1973. Head optometrist Park DuValle Neighborhood Health Center, Louisville, 1971-72; asso. Larry Hoagland, Optometrist, Louisville, 1971-73; asso. Dr. Herma Abel, Optometrist, Lexington, 1973—. Mem. Am. Optometric Found., 1971—. Mem. Louisville (sec., treas. 1972), Blue Grass optometric socs., Am., Ky. optometric assns., Phi Theta Upsilon. Republican. Mem. Christian Ch. Home: Apt 37 260 E Reynolds Rd Lexington KY 40503 Office: 129 E Main St Lexington KY 40507

LEWIS, JOHN MILTON, cable TV co. exec.; b. nr. Slocomb, Ala., Mar. 29, 1931; s. Phil Truman and Vermell Beatrice (Avery) L.; grad. high sch.; m. Mary Lee Robledo, June 9, 1951; children—Janet Lee, Lee Michael. With Gulf Power Co., Panama City, Fla., 1949-56; self employed vehicle service co., Panama City, 1956-58; v.p., dir., Burnup & Sims, Inc., West Palm Beach, Fla., 1958-70; mgr. Cable Antenna TV div. Wometco Enterprises, Inc., Miami, Fla., 1970—; pres. Middlesex Cablevision, East Brunswick, N.J., 1971—; pres. Allstate Cablevision, Plainfield, N.J., 1971—, Plainfield Cablevision, 1971—; v.p. Wometco Communications, Inc., Miami; v.p., dir. LaFourche-Communications, Inc., Thibodaux, La., 1972—, St. Landry Cable TV, Inc., Opelousas, La., 1973—, Ausable Communications, Inc., Plattsburg, N.Y., 1972—. Cons. in field. Democrat. Mason. Home: 8385 SW 143d St Miami FL 33158 Office: 316 N Miami Av Miami FL 33128

LEWIS, JOHN ROBERT, assn. exec.; b. Troy, Ala., Feb. 21, 1940; s. Eddie and Willie Mae Lewis; B.A., Am. Bapt. Theol. Sem., 1961; B.A. in Philosophy, Fisk U., 1967; m. Lillian Miles, Dec. 21, 1968. Chmn., Student Nonviolent Coordinating Con., 1963-66; asso. dir. Field Found., 1966-67; dir. Community Orgn. Project, 1967-70; dir. Voter Edn. Project, Atlanta, 1970—. An organizer Nashville student sit-in movement, 1960; a Freedom Rider, 1961; a leader March on Washington, 1963, March from Selma to Montgomery (Ala.), 1965. Appointee to White House Conf. To Fulfill These Rights, 1966; worker Robert F. Kennedy for Pres. Campaign, 1968. Bd. dirs. So. Christian Leadership Conf., Scholarship Edn. and Def. Fund for Racial Equality; trustee Robert F. Kennedy Meml. Found. Home: 1520 Pinehurst Dr SW Atlanta GA 30311 Office: 52 Fairlie St NW Atlanta GA 30303

LEWIS, JOHN TILLERY, III, ednl. adminstr.; b. Hattiesburg, Miss., Oct. 3, 1930; s. John T. and Jewel (Parkman) L.; B.A., Millsaps Coll., Jackson, Miss., 1953; M.A., U. Miss., 1958, Ph.D., 1963; m. Helen Fay Head, June 10, 1955; children—John Charles, Janis Kay. Clk.-typist USP-FO, Miss., 1948-51; adminstrv. asst. Miss. N.G., 1951-57; asst. to adj. Gen. of Miss., 1957-60; instr. Stephen F. Austin State Coll., Nacogdoches, Tex., 1960-61, asst. prof., 1961-64, head dept. psychology, 1964-67, v.p. acad. affairs, 1967—. Active Boy Scouts Am. Served with AUS, 1961-62. Mem. Am., Southwestern psychol. assns. Kiwanian (pres.). Contbr. articles to profl. jours. Home: 620 Bostwick St Nacogdoches TX 75961

LEWIS, LAWRENCE GLENDON, advt. co. exec.; b. nr. Tuscaloosa, Ala., June 5, 1918; s. Monroe Jordan, Anna (Gardner) L.; student pub. schs.; m. Carrie Mae Hayes, Nov. 7, 1940; children—Robert Jordan, Harriet Anna. Agt., Life & Casualty Ins. Co. Tenn., Nashville, 1939-42, staff mgr. Mobile, 1942-48, tng. supr., 1948, dist. mgr., Jackson, Miss., 1948-56; v.p. Standard Life Ins. Co. of South, Jackson, 1956-65; sales and marketing dir. Mut. Savs. Life Ins. Co., Decatur, Ala., 1965-68; spl. accounts exec., v.p. ins. div. Francis & Lusky Co., Inc., Nashville, 1968—. Served with AUS, 1943-46. Decorated Purple Heart. Past pres. Miss. Assn. Life Underwriters. Baptist. Mason (32 deg., Shriner); mem. Order of Eastern Star (1st worthy patron). Home: 127 Twin Bay Dr Hendersonville TN 37075 Office: 1450 Elm Hill Rd Nashville TN 37210

LEWIS, LEE H(ONLY), constrn. co. exec.; b. Raymond, Wash., Aug. 25, 1917; s. Burt H. and Myrtle B. (Belles) L.; student U. Wash., 1936-40; B.S., Rutgers U., 1947; m. Marcia Eugenia Wagner, Aug. 20, 1960; children—Tricia (Mrs. Norman Hallonquist, Jr.), Laurie (Mrs. Richard Crossman), Barry, Lawrence. Constrn. engr., div. controller Vitro Corp. Am., N.Y.C., 1947-61; v.p. Century Geophysical Corp., Tulsa, 1961-64, now dis.; owner Rochester Photo Supply, Tulsa, 1965-68; v.p., dir. McMichael Concrete Co., Tulsa, 1968—. Served to lt. USNR, 1942-46. C.P.A., Okla. Mem. Am. Inst. C.P.A.'s, Psi Upsilon, Beta Gamma Sigma. Lutheran. Kiwanian. Home: 5301 E 37th St Tulsa OK 74135 Office: McMichael Concrete Co 431 W 23d St Tulsa OK 74107

LEWIS, MARY GENEVIEVE, librarian; b. Vincennes, Ind., Aug. 28, 1911; d. Claudius Ervin and Isa (Hollister) Lewis; B.A., Northwestern U., 1933, M.A., 1935; B.S., Columbia, 1938. Reference asst., reference librarian Oak Park (Ill.) Pub. Library, 1935-37, 38-43, head reference dept., 1938-43, 45-50; instr. English, head dept. Warren Wilson Coll., Swannanoa, N.C., 1950-61; reference librarian Stetson U., DeLand, Fla., 1961-73. Active West Volusia chpt. A.R.C. Served to capt. WAC, 1943-45; ETO. Mem. Am., Fla. library assns. Democrat. Presbyn. Home: 135 W Minnesota Av DeLand FL 32720

LEWIS, OREN RITTER, U.S. judge; b. Seymour, Ind., Oct. 7, 1902; s. John M. and Emma Anna (Crabb) L.; student Hanover (Ind.) Coll., 1920-23; LL.B., Nat. U., 1939; m. Grace Marguerite Wells, Aug. 12, 1925; children—Oren Ritter, Robert Wells. Admitted to Va. bar, 1939; practice in Arlington, 1939-60; U.S. dist. Judge Eastern Dist. Va., 1960—. Mem. Am., Va. Arlington County (pres. 1951) bar assns., Va. State Bar, Phi Delta Theta, Sigma Nu Phi. Kiwanian (lt. gov. 1952). Clubs: Nat. Lawyers, Washington Golf and Country. Home: 3409 N Albemarie St Arlington VA 22207 Office: US Dist Ct Alexandria VA 22314

LEWIS, OREN RITTER, JR., lawyer; b. Washington, Feb. 21, 1929; s. Oren Ritter and Grace Marguerite (Wells) L.; B.A., William and Mary Coll., 1954; LL.B., U. Va., 1957; m. JoAnne Warren, Oct. 5, 1957; children—Oren Ritter III, Jacqueline Claire. Admitted to Va. bar, 1957, since practiced in Arlington; mem. firm Lewis, Wilson, Cowles, Cummings & Lewis, Ltd. (formerly Tolbert, Lewis & FitzGerald, Ltd.), Arlington, 1957—, pres., 1972—, chmn. bd. dirs., 1972—. Dir. First Va. Life Ins. Co., Falls Church, Va. Bd. dirs. Va. Mental Health Found., 1971—, No. Va. Community Coll., Arlington, 1967-71. Served with USAF, 1950-52. Mem. Am., Va., Arlington County (pres. 1972-73), Va. State Bar assns., Conf. Local Bar Presidents (chmn. 1971-72), Conf. La. Bar Assns. (pres. 1972-74), No. Va., Am. Trial lawyers assns. Home: 4525 25th Rd N Arlington VA 22207 Office: 2054 N 14th St Arlington VA 22216

LEWIS, RICHARD HAYES, lawyer, state legislator; b. Hopkinsville, Ky., Dec. 3, 1937; s. Fred T. and Nola (Hayes) L.; B.S., Murray State U., 1960; LL.B., U. Ky., 1965; m. Martha Jane Cunningham, June 24, 1961; children—Laura Elizabeth, Cynthia Jane, Katherine Hayes. Asst. city planner Ky. Dept. Commerce, Owenton, 1963; legal aide Ky. Dept. Labor, Frankfort, 1964; admitted to Ky. bar, 1965; practiced in Benton, 1965—; mem. firm Lovett and Lewis, 1965—. City atty., Benton, 1968-70; exec. dir. Benton Municipal Housing Commn., 1966-68; mem. Ky. Gen. Assembly, 1970—. Trustee, Marshall County Law Library; bd. dirs. Marshall County March of Dimes, Purchase Area Devel. Dist., Purchase Area Crime Council. pres. Epsilon Tau Sigma Chi House Corp., Inc., 1967—. Served to capt. AUS, 1960-62. Named outstanding freshman rep. Ky. Ho. of Reps., 1970; recipient Vet. of Year award D.A.V. Mem. Am., Ky., Marshall County (pres. 1967) bar assns., C. of C. (dir. 1967-69, sec.-treas. 1968-69), Murray State U. Alumni Assn. (dir. 1970-74, v.p. 1974-75), Phi Alpha Delta. Democrat. Baptist. Club: Lions (pres. 1968-69). Home: Merrywood Dr Benton KY 42025 Office: 1114 Main St Benton KY 42025

LEWIS, ROBERT, educator; b. Natchez, Miss., Oct. 11, 1914; s. Robert and Lena (Jones) L.; B.A., Campbell Coll., 1938; B.S., Alcorn Coll., 1952; M.Ed., Ohio State U., 1953; m. Theresa Davis, Nov. 4, 1938; 1 dau., Ra Faye K. Tchr., Winston County (Miss.) pub. schs., 1938-43; Natchez (Miss.) Pub. Sch., 1953-54; supr. Concordia Parish (La.) schs., 1948-51; prin. Brumfield Elementary Sch., Natchez, 1954-61; Anchorage Jr. High Sch., Natchez, 1961-67, Sadie V. Thompson High Sch., Natchez, 1967-70, North-Natchez Adams High Sch., 1970—. Served with USAAF, 1943-46. Mem. N.E.A., Nat. Assn. Secondary Sch. Prins., Nat. Soc. Edn., Miss. Tchrs. Assn., Kappa Alpha Psi. Methodist (trustee). Home: 915 N Union St Natchez MS 39120

LEWIS, ROBERT CLYDE, accountant; b. Marbury, Ala., Oct. 16, 1932; s. Joseph Clanton and Mary (Cook) L.; student Auburn U., 1955-57; B.S., U. Ala., 1958; m. Dorothy J. Goolsby, Nov. 25, 1954; children—Donald E., S. Yvonne, Ronald C., Richard K., Alan G., Deborah J. Accountant, Frank E. Donilon, Jr., C.P.A., Tuscumbia, Ala., 1958-69; partner Donilon & Lewis, C.P.A.'s, Tuscumbia, 1969—. Pres. Howell Graves Sch. P.T.A., 1963-64. Served with USAF, 1951-55. C.P.A., Ala. Mem. Am. Inst. C.P.A.'s, Ala. Soc. C.P.A.'s (mem. council 1970-71). Methodist (chmn. adminstrv. bd. 1973—). Club: Civitan (sec. 1971-72, pres. 1972-73). Home: PO Box 405 Tuscumbia AL 35674 Office: PO Box 405 Tuscumbia AL 35674

LEWIS, STANLEY JOSEPH, record co. exec.; b. Shreveport, La., July 5, 1927; s. Frank L. and Lucille (Scalia) L.; grad. high sch.; m. Pauline Marie Taglivore, July 1, 1947; children—Leonard, Susan Marie. Owner, Stans Record Service, Shreveport, 1948—; pres. Su-Ma Pub. Co., Inc. (BMI), Jewel Record Co., Stan's Record Shop, Stan's Record Service of Fla., Inc., Stan's Record Service of Mo., Inc., Stan's Record Service of Okla., Inc., Stan's Record Service of Tenn., Inc., Shreve Advt. Corp., Lenny Pub. Co., Stan's Record Service of La., Stan's Record Service of Ark., Stan's Record Service of Miss., Stan's Record Service of Tex., Stan's Record Rack Service, Paula Record Co., Ronn Record Co. K.C. Club: Progressive Men's (v.p.). Composer songs. Home: 219 Symphony Lane Shreveport LA 71105 Office: 728 Texas St Shreveport LA 71101

LEWIS, WILLIAM HUBERT, author, govt. ofcl.; b. N.Y.C., June 4, 1928; s. John S. and Lillian (Rome) L.; student U. Ariz., 1947-48; B.A., George Washington U., 1951, M.A., 1953; postgrad. Johns Hopkins, 1953-54; Ph.D., Am. U., 1960; m. Kathleen Moran, Aug. 20, 1949. With dept. African affairs U.S. Dept. State, 1952-65; vis. prof. Middle Eastern and African studies U. Mich., 1965-66; div. dir. U.S. Dept. State, 1966-67; mem. policy planning staff Office Sec. of Def., Washington, 1967-70; dir. planning and analysis staff, bur. polit.-mil. affairs Dept. State, Washington, 1971—; asso. prof. Middle Eastern and African studies Georgetown and Am. Univs., 1960-69. Served as lt. AUS, 1950-52. Fellow African, Middle Eastern studies assns.; mem. Am. Polit. Sci. Assn. Author: New Forces in Africa, 1962; Modern Middle East, 1963; Emerging Africa, 1964; French-speaking Africa, 1966; Islam in Africa, 1969. Contbr. articles profl. jours. Home: 1200 N Nash St Arlington VA 22209 Office: Office Undersec US Dept of State Washington DC 20520

LEWIS, WILLIAM SEXTON, physician; b. Strong, Ark., Mar. 6, 1931; s. William Colvin and Mary Catherine (Hammonds) L.; student La. Poly. Inst., 1949-52; B.S., U. Ark., 1956, M.D., 1956; m. Mary Lynda McCuistion, June 26, 1954; children—John Taylor, Sarah Margaret. Intern, U. Ark. Med. Center, 1956-57, resident, 1957-60; fellow cardiology U. Ark., 1960-61; practice medicine specializing in cardiology, Little Rock, 1961—; co-founder Little Rock Diagnostic Clinic, 1961-72; practice medicine ltd. to cons. cardiology, 1973—; mem. staffs Bapt. Med. Center, Little Rock, St. Vincent's Infirmary, Little Rock, Meml. Hosp., North Little Rock; co-dir., coronary care tng. of nurses Regional Med. Program, 1970—; co-dir. coronary care unit Bapt. Med. Center, Little Rock, 1970—, dir. cardiac lab., 1966—, chief medicine, 1972-73; asso. clin. prof. medicine U. Ark., 1973—; cons. VA Hosp., 1970—; dir. Profl. Underwriters Life Ins. Served with AUS, 1961-62. Mem. Am. (bd. dirs. 1971—, mem. heart Com. So. region 1967-71), Ark. (pres. 1968-71, mem. exec. com. 1970-71) heart assns., Alpha Omega Alpha. Home: 58 River Ridge Rd Little Rock AR 72207 Office: Bapt Med Towers Little Rock AR 72205

LEYDEN, DONALD ELLIOTT, educator; b. Gadsden, Ala., June 26, 1938; s. Elliott Hampton and Vivian Ione (Buckner) L.; B.S., Kent State U., 1960; M.S., Emory U., 1961, Ph.D., 1964; m. Alice Jane Trowbridge, June 10, 1961; children—Mary Dawn, Sean Michael. Research asso. U. N.C., Chapel Hill, 1963-65; asst. prof. U. Ga., Athens, 1965-71, asso. prof. chemistry, 1971—. Recipient several research grants NIH, NSF. Mem. Am. Chem. Soc. Home: 590 Camelot Dr Athens GA 30601

LEYSIEFFER, FREDERICK WALTER, educator; b. Milw., Jan. 30, 1933; s. Walter and Charlotte (Martins) L.; B.A., U. Wis., 1955, M.A., 1956; Ph.D., U. Mich., 1964; m. Annelise Carlsen, Aug. 6, 1964; children—Kirsten, Suzanne. Asst. prof. dept. statistics Fla. State U., Tallahassee, 1964-70, asso. prof., 1970—, also asso. head dept., 1969—; Leverhulme Commonwealth/Am. vis. fellow U. Sheffield (Eng.), 1973-74. Mem. Am. Math. Soc., Math. Assn. Am., Inst. Math. Statistics, A.A.A.S. Home: 3720 Lifford Circle Tallahassee FL 32303 Office: Fla State Univ Tallahassee FL 32306

LHOTKA, JOHN FRANCIS, JR., educator, physician; b. Butte, Mont., May 13, 1921; s. John Francis and Mary (Backowske) L.; B.A., U. Mont., 1942; M.S. in Anatomy, Northwestern U., 1948, M.B., 1949, M.D., 1951, Ph.D., 1953; m. Lois Katherine Clysdale, Sept. 21, 1951. Asst. in anatomy Northwestern U., 1947-50, Stain Commn. fellow summer 1952; asst. prof. anatomy U. Okla. Med. Sch., 1951-55, asso. prof. anatomy, 1955-69, prof. anatomical scis., 1969—. Active in numis. field, especially medieval coinage of Western Europe. Donat Order St. Lazarus Jerusalem. Served to 1st lt. CWS, USAAF, 1942-46; PTO. Recipient 4 Health medals, Medal of Merit, Farran Zerbe award, also initial Newell award Am. Numis. Assn. Fellow Am., Royal, Swiss numis. socs., Asociacion Numismatica Espanola, Am. Geriatric Soc., Internat. Acad. Pathology, Royal Soc. Health; patron Am. Numis. Soc., 1962; mem. Am. Assn. Anatomists, Histochem. Soc., Am. Inst. Biol. Scis., Am. Soc. Zoology, Biol. Stain Commn., Soc. for Exptl. Biology and Medicine, Am. Chem. Soc., Archeol. Inst. Am., East African Wildlife Soc., Nat. Audobon Soc., Wilderness Soc., Nat. Wildlife Fedn., N.Y. Acad. Scis., Co. Mi. Historians, Brit. Museum Soc., Orders and Medals Soc. Am., Midwest Orders and Medals Soc., Am. Soc. Ichthyologists and Herpetologists, Soc. for Promotion of Roman Studies, Sigma Xi, Phi Sigma. Club: Petroleum (Oklahoma City). Author monographs: Introduction to East Roman Coinage, 1957; Medieval Bacteates, 1958; Medieval French Feudal Coinage, 1966; (with P.K. Anderson) Survey of Medieval Iberian Coinages, 1963; also articles. Office: 801 NE 13TH St Oklahoma City OK 73104

LIBERATORE, SALVATORE NICHOLAS, elec. engr.; b. Staten Island, N.Y., Mar. 31, 1923; s. Alexander and Angelina (Laspagnoletta) L.; B.Elec. Engring., Manhattan Coll., 1947; postgrad. Stevens Inst. Tech., 1948; m. Frances Veronica Creedon, May 23, 1953; children—Stephen, James, Thomas, Robert, William, Michael. Elec. engr. Am. & Fgn. Power Co., N.Y.C., 1952-56, Mexico City, Mexico, 1956-60; elec. engr. Export-Import Bank U.S., Washington, 1961-67; electric power engring. specialist Inter-Am. Devel. Bank, Washington, 1968—. Served with USMCR, 1943-46. Registered profl. engr., N.Y., D.C. Mem. I.E.E.E. (sr.). Roman Catholic. Clubs: Eaglehead Golf and Country (Frederick, Md.); Fleetwood Hunt (Caroline County, Va.). Home: 4612 46th St NW Washington DC 20016 Office: 808 17th St NW Washington DC 20577

LIBHART, MYLES LAROY, govt. ofcl.; b. Marietta, Pa., Mar. 8, 1931; s. John Henry and Emily Elizabeth (Jones) L.; student Bklyn. Mus. Art Sch., 1951-53; pvt. instruction, 1954-57. Practicing designer, craftsman Georg Jensen, Inc., N.Y.C., 1959-62; supr. dept. exhbns., publs., and graphics The Bklyn. Mus., 1960-63; instr. enameling Bklyn. Mus. Art Sch., 1961-63; with Indian Arts and Crafts Bd., U.S. Dept. Interior, Washington, 1963—, dir. museums, 1963—. Mem. Am. Assn. of Museums, Am. Crafts Council. Home: 601 19th St NW Washington DC 20006 Office: Room 4004 US Dept of the Interior Washington DC 20240

LICHTENFELD, SEYMOUR L., med., health service exec., mech. engr.; b. Gary, Ind., Jan. 10, 1925; s. Albert I. and Sidell (Korenthal) L.; B.S. in Mech. Engring., Purdue U., 1950; m. Natalie Nora Dunaetz, July 30, 1950; children—Norman, Eileen, Roberta. Chief engr. Midwestco, Chgo., 1952-54; cons. engr., owner Melco Engrs., Chgo., 1954-63; owner, operator Chai Convalescent Home, Miami, Fla., 1963—; pres., 1967—; owner Renn Constrn. Co., Miami, 1966—, owner S.L. Lichtenfeld & Assos. Cons. Engrs., North Miami Beach, 1963—. Pres., Dade County 101 Club, Miami, 1968. Bd. dirs. Health Planning Council, Miami. Served with AUS, 1943-45. Decorated Bronze Star, Purple Heart. Fellow Am. Coll. Nursing Home Adminstrs.; mem. Fla. Nursing Home Assn. (dir.), Am. Arbitration Assn. Mason (Shriner), Elk. Clubs: Dade 100 (Miami); South Florida Purdue (pres. 1970). Address: 19450 NE 21st Ct North Miami Beach FL 33162

LICHTENSTEIN, MURRAY MARC, banker; b. N.Y.C., Apr. 16, 1935; s. Samuel Martin and Laura (Anger) L.; B.B.A., U. Tex. at El Paso, 1966; m. Sharon Lee Heller, Oct. 29, 1959; children—Laura, Diana, Nita, James. Sr. accountant firm Main LaFrentz & Co., El Paso, 1966-68, firm Joshua N. Kahn & Co., El Paso, 1968-69; controller El Paso Nat Bank, 1969—; Controller Trans Tex. Bancorp., Inc., 1974—. Served with AUS, 1958-60. C.P.A., Tex. Mem. Am. Inst. C.P.A.'s, Tex. Soc. C.P.A.'s, El Paso Jr. C. of C. (past dir.), Delta Sigma Pi. Mason (32 deg.). Jewish religion. Club: Sertoma (El Paso). Home: 252 Northwind St El Paso TX 79912 Office: PO Drawer 140 El Paso TX 79980

LIDDELL, FRANK AUSTIN, JR., lawyer; b. Houston, Aug. 25, 1928; s. Frank Austin and Virginia (Roby) L.; B.S., Va. Mil. Inst., 1949; M.A., U. Tex., 1952; LL.B., U. Houston, 1958; m. Lise M. Putnam, Dec. 2, 1961; children—Lise A., Frank A. III, Robert Bruce. Research chemist Monsanto Co., Texas City, Tex., 1952-53; admitted to Tex. bar, 1958; practiced in Houston, 1958—; mem. firm Liddell Sapp, Zivley & Brown, 1964—. Dir. S.W. Chem. & Plastics Co. Served to 1st lt. USAF, 1953-55. Mem. Am., Tex. bar assns., Am. Judicature Soc., Am. Soc. for Oceanography, Am. Chem. Soc., A.A.A.S., Kappa Sigma. Democrat. Methodist. Clubs: Houston, Houston Country. Home: 6050 Crab Orchard St Houston TX 77027 Office: Gulf Bldg Houston TX 77002

LIDDELL, JAMES LARRY, athletic pub. relations exec.; b. Shreveport, La., June 8, 1942; s. William Walker and Vina Belle (Patman) L.; B.A., Delta State Coll., 1964; m. Martha Rae Howell Hinton, May 25, 1973; 1 dau., Stephanie Rae Hinton. Sports information dir. Delta State Coll., Cleveland, Miss., 1960-64; sports editor Clarksdale (Miss.) Press Register, 1964-68; asst. athletic publicity dir. U. Miss., 1968-71; asst. dir. pub. relations New Orleans Saints, 1971-72, dir. pub. relations, 1972—. Served with AUS, 1966. Mem. Nat. Sportscasters and Sportswriters Assn., Miss. Big Eight Conf. Writers Assn., Coll. Sports Information Dirs. Am., Am. Basketball Writers Assn., Coll. Baseball Writers Assn. Am., Profl. Football Writers Assn. Am., Am. Football Writers Assn. Baptist. Lion. Home: 59 40th St Kenner LA 70062

LIDDLE, JOHN ALLEN, banker; b. St. Louis, Nov. 23, 1927; s. Frank M. and Margaret H. (Noble) L.; student U. Tex., 1945-46, Butler U., 1948-49; B.S., Ind. U., 1950; m. Leonardine Smith, July 7, 1951; children—Peggy, John Lee, Suzi, Joan. Accountant Sprole's & Woodard, Fort Worth, 1951-55; with Citizens Nat. Bank, Abilene, Tex., 1955—, sr. v.p., trust officer, 1969—, also dir. Instr. finance and econs. Hardin Simmons U., 1956-58; instr. McMurry Coll., 1970-72. Pres. Abilene Estate Planning Council, 1962. Served with AUS, 1946-48. C.P.A., Tex. Mem. Abilene Soc. C.P.A.'s (pres. 1962). Home: 3126 S Willis St Abilene TX 79605 Office: Box 1251 Abilene TX 79604

LIDE, VINTON DEVANE, lawyer; b. Greenville, S.C., May 4, 1937; s. Theodore Ellis and Elizabeth (DeVane) L.; A.B., Davidson Coll., 1959; J.D., U. Va., 1962; m. Vivian Lucille Feemster, July 1, 1961; children—Jonathan R., Jennifer DeVane. Admitted to S.C. bar, 1962; asso. mem. firm Shamd & Wilmeth, Hartsville, S.C., 1962-63, partner, 1963-64; partner firm Shand & Lide, Hartsville, 1965—. Treas. Farmington Assos., Inc., Hartsville, 1968—; exec. v.p. N.W. Prestwood Inc., Hartsville, 1972—; municipal judge City Hartsville, 1964-69; pub. defender Darlington County, 1969—. Mem. Va., S.C., Am. bar assns., Am. Judicature Soc., Hartsville Jr. C. of C. (past pres.), Hartsville C. of C. (past pres.). Presbyn. (deacon). Home: 113 Loring Dr Hartsville SC 29550 Office: 954 W Carolina Av Hartsville SC 29550

LIEBERMAN, BARNARD LEON, physician; b. Chernigov, Russia, Dec. 13, 1902; s. Israil and Pearl (Jarnofsky) L.; B.S., Wayne State U., 1925, M.B., 1925, M.D., 1926; Sc.D., London Inst. Applied Research, 1973; m. Mary McKinney, Nov. 22, 1944; 1 son, Douglas Lionel. Came to U.S., 1906, naturalized, 1926. Intern Providence Hosp., Detroit, 1925-26; resident Herman Kiefer Receiving Hosp., 1926-28; practice medicine specializing in obstetrics and gynecology, Detroit, 1928-69; attending obstetrician Evang. Deaconess Hosp., Detroit, 1928-43; chief staff North Detroit Gen. Hosp., 1944-65, now mem. staff emeritus. Cons. North Detroit Gen. Hosp., 1965-69; dir. Northwest Realty Co. Bd. trustees North Detroit Gen. Hosp., 1944-65. Recipient Brotherhood Week award Armenian Ch. of North Am., 1962; Religious Leadership award U. Am. Hebrew Congregations, 1969. Mem. A.M.A. (life), Phi Lambda Kappa (v.p. 1939). Jewish religion (pres. Temple Emanu El 1958-60). Mason (Shriner); mem. B'nai B'rith. Address: 668 El Centro Sarasota FL 33577

LIEBERMAN, MELVYN, educator; b. Bklyn., Feb. 4, 1938; B.A. in Zoology, Cornell U., 1959; Ph.D. in Physiology, State U. N.Y. Downstate Med. Center, Bklyn., 1964; married; 2 children. Lectr., lab. instr. dept. biology Queens Coll., City U. N.Y., 1960, 63-64; teaching asst. dept. physiology State U. N.Y. Downstate Med. Center, 1960-64; postdoctoral fellow dept. embryology Carnegie Inst. Washington, Balt., 1964-65, Instituto de Biofisica, Universidade Federal do Rio de Janeiro (Brazil), 1965-67; postdoctoral fellow div. biomed. engring. Duke, 1967, research asso. dept. physiology and pharmacology, 1967-68, asst. prof. Duke Med. Center, 1968-73, asso. prof., 1973—; lectr. U. Miami, 1973, Columbia Coll. Phys. and Surg., 1973; cons. Macy Found., 1970, NIH, 1972, others; participant numerous sci. symposia; established investigator Am. Heart Assn., 1971—. Mem. A.A.A.S., Am. Heart Assn. (basic sci. council 1963), Am. Physiol. Soc., Am. Soc. Cell Biology, Biophys. Soc., Cardiac Muscle Soc., N.C. Heart Assn. (research rev. subcom. 1972-75), Soc. Gen. Physiologists (rep. NRC 1971-74; chmn. session developmental physiology Woods Hole (Mass.) 1970. Editorial cons. Jour. Applied Physiology, Circulation research, Jour. Gen. Physiology, Jour. Molecular Cell Cardiology, Jour. Pharm. Exptl. Therapeutics. Contbr. numerous articles to profl. jours. Home: 1110 Woodburn Rd Durham NC 27705

LIEBLING, HERMAN I., govt. ofcl.; b. Bklyn., Oct. 20, 1916; s. Benjamin and Rose (Levinson) L.; B.A., Bklyn. Coll., 1940; M.A., Am. U., 1945, Ph.D., 1961; m. Mabel B. Rudman, Mar. 6, 1947; children—Lynne Joyce, Lauren Gail. Staff economist Survey of Current Bus., U.S. Dept. Commerce, Washington, 1946-59; dir. econ. studies NSF, Washington, 1959-62; chief bus. economist Dept. of Treasury, Washington, 1962—; asso. prof. U. Md., 1963-73; cons. Ministry of Finance, Govt. of Morocco, 1968. Mem. U.S. delegation to IMF Consultations, 1965-72. Recipient Meritorious Service award for bus. forecasting Dept. Treasury, 1969. Mem. Am. Econ. Assn., Am. Statis. Assn. Author: U.S. Postwar Inflation and the Phillips Curve, 1969. Home: 6317 W Halbert Rd Bethesda MD 20034 Office: Dept of the Treasury Washington DC 20220

LIEBMAN, SEYMOUR BERTRAM, historian, author, ret. lawyer; b. N.Y.C., Mar. 12, 1907; s. Henry and Fannie (Abend) L.; LL.B., St. Lawrence U., 1929; M.A. magna cum laude, U. America, 1963; m. Malvina Weiss, June 25, 1950; 1 son, Charles Seymour. Admitted to N.Y. bar, 1929, Fla. bar, 1950; practice law, N.Y.C., 1929-49, Miami Beach, 1950-60. Tchr., U. America, 1962-66, Fla. Atlantic U., 1968, Miami Dade Jr. Coll., intermittently 1967-71; vis. lectr. at several Am. Univs., also in Eng., Mexico, and Israel; adj. research scholar Inst. Inter-Am. Affairs, U. Miami, 1971—. Mem. nat. exec. com. Am. Profs. Peace in the Middle East, 1970—; mem. bar com. on communist tactics and objectives, 1956-70; mem. Com. on Inter-Am. Affairs, 1966-70; exec. com. Greater Miami Jewish Fedn., 1955-59. Bd. dirs. Miami Beach Taxpayers Assn., v.p., 1955-59. Grantee Meml. Found. for Jewish Culture, 1967, Nat. Found Jewish Culture, 1971, Am. Philos. Soc., 1968, Henry E. Huntington Library, 1966. Mem. Am. Hist. Assn., Haklyut Soc. Eng., Jewish Hist. Soc. Eng., Am. Acad. Polit. and Social Sci., Miami Beach Bar Assn. (dir. 1957-59). Author: Guide to Jewish References in the Mexican Colonial Era, 1964; The Enlightened, 1967; The Jews in New Spain, 1970; The Inquisitors and Jews in the New World, 1974, The Great Auto de Fe of 1649, 1974. Contbr. articles to profl. pubs. Reviewer for Choices, 1969—, Hispanic American Historical Review, 1971, Judaism, 1971, Jewish Social Studies, 1972, Jewish Floridian, 1967. Editor: Report Mid East, 1969—. Address: 8119 SW 82d Pl Miami FL 33143

LIEBMANN, SEYMOUR W., constrn. co. exec.; b. N.Y.C., Nov 1, 1928; s. Isidor W. and Etta (Waltzer) L.; B.S. in Mech. Engring., Clarkson Coll. Tech., 1948; grad. Indsl. Coll. Armed Forces, 1963, Command and Gen. Staff Coll., 1966, Army War Coll., 1971; m. Hinda Adam, Sept. 20, 1959; children—Peter Adam, David W. Area engr. constrn. div. E.I. DuPont de Nemours, & Co., Inc., 1952-54; constrn. planner Lummus Co., 1954-56; prin. mech. engr. Perini Corp., 1956-62; v.p. Boston Based Contractors, 1962-66; v.p. A.R. Abrams, Inc., Atlanta, 1967-74, pres., 1974—, also dir. Mem. U.S.O. Council, Atlanta. Served to 1st lt. C.E., AUS, 1948-52; col. Res. Registered profl. engr., N.Y., Mass., Ga. Mem. Soc. First U.S. Inf., Res. Officers Assn. U.S., Nat., Ga. socs. profl. engrs., Soc. Am. Mil. Engrs., Engrs. Club Boston. Mason (32 deg., Shriner), Elk. Club: Civitan (Atlanta). Author: Military Engineer Field Notes, 1953; Prestressing Miter Gate Diagonals, 1960. Address: 3260 Rilman Dr NW Atlanta GA 30327

LIEPINS, RAIMOND, chemist; b. Plavinas, Latvia, May 19, 1930; s. Otto and Zelma (Murasko) L.; came to U.S., 1949, naturalized, 1956; B.A., So. Ill. U., 1954; M.S., U. Minn., 1956; Ph.D., Kan. State U., 1960; postgrad. U. Akron, 1962-63; m. Norma Leila Zayas, Dec. 26, 1961; children—Elsa Maria, Ilze, Olga Rebecca, Otto Marcelino. Research chemist B.F. Goodrich Co., Brecksville, O., 1960-64; research asso. U. Ariz., Tucson, 1964-66; sr. chemist Research Triangle Inst., Research Triangle Park, N.C., 1966—. Fellow Am. Inst. Chemists; mem. Am. Phys. Soc., N.C. Inst. Chemists (mem. nominations, elections com.), A.A.A.S., Am. Che. Soc., Materials Research Soc., N.Y. Acad. Scis., Phi Lambda Upsilon. Patentee in field. Home: 1714 Wallace St Durham NC 27707 Office: PO Box 12194 Research Triangle Park NC 27709

LIEPMAN, HANS PETER, aerospace engr.; b. Kiel, Germany, Oct. 24, 1913; s. Moritz and Helena (Robert) Liepmann; came to U.S., 1938, naturalized, 1944; Dipl. Ing., Swiss Fed. Inst. Tech., Zurich, 1937; M.S., Harvard, 1939; Ph.D., U. Mich., 1953; m. Nanette Virginia Henry, Feb. 2, 1946; children—Peter Christopher, Robert Henry, Joan, Lise. Instr. aero. engring. U. Cin., 1939-41, asst. prof., 1941-44; sr. aerodynamicist Goodyear Aerospace Co., Akron, 1944-46, chief aerodynamicist, 1946-49; lectr. U. Mich., Ann Arbor, 1949-53, asso. prof. aero. engring., dir. supersonic wind tunnels, 1953-59; sect. head aerophysics TRW Systems Group, Redondo Beach, Cal., 1959-65; asst. dept. mgr. systems devel., 1965-71; pvt. cons. aero engring., edn., tech. translations, Greenbrae, Cal., 1971-73; mem. research staff, sci. and tech. div. Inst. for Def. Analyses, Arlington, Va., 1973—. Coordinator, ground instr. Civilian Pilot Tng. Program, Cin., 1942-44; sci. adviser Karman index project USAF, Europe, 1945. Asso. fellow Am. Inst. Aeros. and Astronautics; mem. Am. Soc. Engring. Edn. Office: 400 Army Navy Dr Arlington VA 22202

LIETZSEY, BARNEY BURR, ednl. adminstr.; b. Newberry, S.C., Aug. 2, 1903; s. Barney Burr and Hanna (Brown) L.; A.B., Newberry Coll., 1925; M.A., U. S.C., 1942; postgrad. Winthrop U., Furman U., Newberry Coll.; m. Marie Sease, June 9, 1926. Prin., Stoney Hill High Sch., Prosperity, S.C., 1925-26, Hartford Elementary Sch., Newberry, S.C., 1926-28; supt. Trenton schs., Edgefield County, 1928-29; supt. schs., Saleme schs., New Zion, S.C., 1929-37; supt. Elim schs., Effingham, S.C., 1937-42; sch. prin. Florence County (S.C.) Dist. No. 1, 1942-46, prin. jr. high sch., 1946-54, asst. supt., 1954-67, including supr. rural schs., 1954-58, supr. high schs., 1958-67, bus. mgr., 1958-67, supr. vocational tng., 1958-67, sup. adult schs., 1958-67; dir. Marion Mullins Vocational Center, Marion, S.C., 1967-73; clk. Marion County Bd. Edn., 1973—. Mem. Florence Bd. Health, 1941-67, chmn. bd., 1951-67; chmn. Marion City Easter Seals, 1971-73, chmn. Marion County, 1937-74. Bd. dirs. Tb. Assn., 1938—, pres., 1961-64; bd. dirs. Cancer Soc. Assn., 1961-67. Recipient honor award Florence County Edn. Assn.; recognition award Florence Sch. Dist. 1 Vocational Tchrs., 1967, named outstanding vocational person, 1972-73; hon. state farmers del. So. States Conf., 1957, 62, 67, 73. Mem. Nat., S.C., Marion County edn. assns., P.T.A. (hon., life); past mem. Nat. S.C. assns. secondary sch. prins., S.C. Adminstrn. Assn., Nat., S.C. adult assns., S.C. Bus. Mgrs. Assn., Nat., S.C. vocational assns. Presbyn. (deacon 1939-52, elder 1952-72). Home: PO Box 695 Marion SC 29571 Office: PO Box 410 Marion SC 29571

LIGHTBOURNE, JAMES HORN, JR., clergyman; b. Dover, Del., Dec. 26, 1921; s. James Horn and Margaret (Benson) L.; B.A., Elon Coll., 1942, D.D., 1951; M.A., Brown U., 1947, B.D., Hartford Theol. Sem., 1950; m. Carolyn Anderson, Aug. 17, 1946; children—James Horn III, Ernest Anderson, Leslie Hope. Ordained to the ministry United Ch. Christ, 1950; pastor United Ch. of Christ, Holland, Va., 1950-57; supt. Southeast Conv. Conglist. Christian Chs., Atlanta, 1957-65; conf. minister So. Conf. United Ch. of Christ, Burlington, N.C., 1966—. Chmn. United Ch. Christ Council Conf. Execs., 1971, mem. exec. com., 1973—; mem. exec. council United Ch. Christ, 1973—, mem. council for Christian social action, 1957-65, stewardship council, 1966-73. Chmn. Alamanace County Human Relations Council, 1970—. Bd. dirs. Elon Coll., Elon Home for Children, United Ch. Retirement Home, Uplands Center, Frandklinton Center. Served with USAAF, 1942-45. Mem. Ga. (pres. 1962-64), N.C. (pres. 1970-72) councils chs. Home: 2903 Amherst Av Burlington NC 27215 Office: PO Box 2410 Burlington NC 27215

LIGHTFOOT, ROBERT HAROLD, SR., banker; b. Brownwood, Tex., Feb. 26, 1942; s. Raymond Harold and Mattie Leona (Serrat) L.; B.B.A., U. Houston, 1968, M.B.A., 1969; m. Betty Joy Atkins, Aug. 24, 1960; children—Robert Harold, Paul Brian. Sr. accountant Peat, Marwick, Mitchell & Co., Houston, 1969-72; v.p., treas. Cullen Savs.

Assn., Houston, 1972—. Served with AUS, 1960-63. C.P.A., Tex. Mem. Am. Inst. C.P.A.'s, Tex., Houston socs. C.P.A.'s, Nat. Soc. Controllers for Financial Instns. Home: 11315 Pompano St Houston TX 77072 Office: 601 Jefferson St Houston TX 77002

LIGHTNER, JAMES RICHMOND, electronics co. exec.; b. Cedar Rapids, Ia., July 20, 1922; s. John W. and Bess (Richmond) L.; B.S. in Mech. Engring., U. Ia., 1944; m. Ida M. Pettigrew, Dec. 22, 1945; 1 dau., Cynthia M. (Mrs. John L. Sullivan). Design engr. Goodyear Tire & Rubber Co., Akron, O., 1944-46, Cherry Burrell Corp., Cedar Rapids, 1946-51, 52-53, Thompson Products Co., Cleve., 1951-52; div. head Collins Radio Co., Cedar Rapids, Dallas, 1953-70; pres., chmn. bd. Electrospace Systems, Inc., Richardson, Tex., 1970—; chmn. bd. Omega-T Systems, Inc., 1971—. City councilman, Parma Heights, O., 1952; pres. Young Republican Club, Linn County, Ia., 1954-56; campaign mgr. William Lynes for Gov. Rep. Primary in State of Ia., 1956. Chmn. adv. com. Bd. Edn., Cedar Rapids, 1956-58. Mem. Armed Forces Communications and Electronics Assn. (dir.), Richardson C. of C. Methodist. Kiwanian, Toastmaster. Club: Brookhaven Country (pres., dir. 1968-71) (Dallas). Home: 1200 Cheyenne Pl Richardson TX 75080 Office: PO Box 1359 Richardson TX 75080

LIGON, KATIE WILLIMAS (MRS. WOODIE C. LIGON), educator; b. Tallassee, Ala.; d. Robert Roland and Katie (Roper) Williams; B.S., Ala. A. and M. Coll., 1947; M.A., N.Y.U., 1953; m. Woodie C. Ligon, July 3, 1937. Tchr. Dallas County Tng. Sch., Selma, Ala., 1931-34, Lane Grammar Sch., Birmingham, Ala., 1935-36, Council Elementary Sch., 1936-52; chmn. guidance, adviser to girls Western High Sch., 1952-64; dean women Ala. A. and M. U., 1964-69, dean students, 1969—, v.p. for student affairs, 1970—. Adv. bd. N. Ala. chpt. Multiple Sclerosis Soc., Harris Home for Children, Madison County Assn. Mental Health. Mem. Nat. Assn. Women Deans and Counselors, Am. Personnel and Guidance Assn., Nat. Assn. Student Personnel Adminstrs., Ala. Tchrs. Assn., Alpha Kappa Delta, Alpha Kappa Alpha (regional pub. relations rep.). Methodist. Home: 56 18th Av S Birmingham AL 35205 Office: Ala A and M Univ PO Box 327 Normal AL 35762

LIGON, ROBERT BROWNING, social worker; b. Mayfield, Ky., Nov. 16, 1912; s. Edward Bolinger and Ethel (Browning) L.; B.S., Washington U., St. Louis, 1934; m. Ruth Green, June 1, 1938; 1 son, Robert Browning. With Radio Sta. WNGO, Mayfield, 1951-57, Ligon Bros. Loose Leaf Floor, Mayfield, 1934-64, Mayfield Coal & Ice Co., 1935-55; social worker Ky. State Welfare Dept., Mayfield, 1968—. Bd. dirs. Mayfield Child Day Care Center, Graves County chpt. A.R.C. Welfare sec. Salvation Army, 1972—. Mem. Am. Pub. Welfare Assn., Ky. Welfare Assn., Travellers Protective Assn. (state pres. 1958-59), Jackson Purchase Hist. Soc. (pres. 1971-72). Methodist (mem. adminstrv. bd. 1936). Woodman of World, Rotarian. Club: Senior Citizens (dir. Mayfield). Home: 603 S 7th St Mayfield KY 42066 Office: 319 S 7th St Mayfield KY 42066

LIGON, RONALD SANDERS, travel agy. exec.; b. Lebanon, Tenn., Jan. 6, 1937; s. H. Raymond and Lucille (Sanders) L.; student Vanderbilt U., 1956-58; m. Mary Francis Schmitt, Aug. 2, 1958; children—Ronald Sanders, John Jefferson, Mathew Courtney. Pres., Union Acceptance Corp., Nashville, 1957-62, Security Realty & Mortgage Corp., Nashville, 1958-62; pres. Christus Gardens, Gatlinburg, Tenn., 1959—; dir. Security Ins. Corp., Nashville, Harpeth Enterprises, Inc., Franklin, Tenn., Handy Hardware Co., Inc., Franklin, Woodlawn Constrn. Corp., Inc., Nashville, Volunteer Realty Corp., Ft. Lauderdale, Fla., Harpeth Nat. Bank, Franklin. Chmn. bd. dirs. Harpeth Acad., Franklin; bd. dirs. Monroe-Harding Children's Home, Nashville, Heritage Found., Tenn. Regional Med. Program. Mem. So. Highland Attractions Assn. (past pres.), Blue Ridge Pkwy. Assn. (past pres.), Discover Am. Travel Orgn. (chmn. U.S. Travel Barometer 1970—), Gatlinburg (past pres.), Williamson County (chmn. heritage com. 1971) chambers commerce, Kappa Sigma. Republican. Presbyn. (deacon). Kiwanian, Elk. Clubs: Carnton (Franklin), Elks, Keeneland, Franklin Men's Breakfast (past pres.), Middle Tenn. Pony (dir. 1971—). Home: Riverside Farm Route 2 Franklin TN 37064 Office: 204 3d Av Box 332 Franklin TN 37064

LIKAN, GUSTAV, artist, educator; b. Yugoslavia, 1912; student Munich (Germany) Art Acad., also in Paris, France, Rome, Italy and Amsterdam, Netherlands. Came to U.S., 1957. One-man shows and group exhbns. in Zagreb and Split, Yugoslavia, also in Paris, Berlin, Germany, Vienna, Austria, other European capitols until 1948; one-man show. Kuenstlerhaus, Salzburg, Austria, 1948; exhibited group shows Galeries Georges Petit, Paris, 1932, Nat. Gallery, Oslo, Norway, 1938, Nat. Gallery, Stockholm, Sweden, 1938, Nat. Gallery, Goeteberg, Denmark, 1938, Nat. Mus., Vienna, Austria, 1941, Narodni Mus., Bratislava, 1942, U. Chgo., 1958, Merrill Chase Galleries, Chgo., 1965, 66; lived in Argentina, 1949-57; commd. by Eva Peron for portraits and murals in schs.; prof., head dept. fine arts Chgo. Acad. Fine Art, 1960-67; instr. Laguna Gloria Mus. Art Sch., Austin, Tex., 1969—. Address: 3203 Shoal Creek Blvd Austin TX 78705

LILIENFIELD, LAWRENCE SPENCER, med. educator; b. Bkyn., May 5, 1927; s. Henry J. and Lee (Markman) L.; B.S., Villanova Coll., 1945; M.D., Georgetown U., 1949, M.S., 1954, Ph.D., 1956; m. Eleanor Marion Russ, Oct. 22, 1950; children—Jan, Adele, Lisa. Intern, Georgetown U. Hosp., Washington, 1949-50, asst. resident internal medicine, 1950, 52-53; instr. dept. medicine Georgetown U. Sch. Medicine, 1955-58, asst. prof., 1958-61, asso. prof. depts. medicine, physiology and biophysics, 1961-64; asst. chief cardiovascular research lab. Georgetown U. Hosp., 1956-63, chmn. dept. physiology and biophysics, 1963—, prof., 1964—; vis. prof. Faculty Medicine, U. Saigon, 1965, Tel Aviv U., 1968. Cons., USPHS, 1964—; mem. NRC-Nat. Acad. Sci., 1965-67. Asso., Com. on Internat. Exchange Persons, 1970—. Served with USNR, 1944-46, with USAF, 1950-52. Fellow A.C.P., A.A.A.S.; mem. A.M.A., Am. Heart Assn., Biophys. Soc., Am. Physiology Soc., Soc. Exptl. Biology and Medicine, Am. Soc. Clin. Investigation, Sigma Xi. Contbr. articles to profl. jours. Home: 6304 Maiden Lane Bethesda MD 20034 Office: 3900 Reservoir Rd NW Washington DC 20007

LILJENQUIST, L(ORENZO) BLAINE, assn. exec.; b. Salt Lake City, Apr. 5, 1912; s. Ezra L. and Mary M. (Wilcox) L.; B.S., U. Ida., 1938; J.D., George Washington U., 1959; m. Sophia Jean Liljenquist, June 1, 1938 (dec. Oct. 1963); children—John Eric, Blaine Lee, David F., Charles Steven, Thomas Richard, Kathryn P., Mark D.; m. 2d, Patricia L. Charters, July 31, 1964. Farmer, agrl. agt. U.S. Dept. Interior, United Pueblos Indian Agy., Albuquerque, 1938-40; agrl. economist Bur, Agrl. Econs., U.S. Dept, Agr., Amarillo, Tex., 1941, with personnel div., 1942-44; Washington rep. Western States Meat Packers Assn., Inc., Washington, 1946-58, v.p., 1958-61, pres., gen. mgr., 1961-70; chmn. Am. Taxpayers and Consumers Assn., Inc., 1970-71; chmn. bd. Com-Trend, Inc. Farmer, rancher, Va., N.Z. Chmn. bd. dirs. Youth Devel. Found., Inc. Served to lt. USNR, 1944-46; PTO. Mem. Nat. Assn. Execs. Club (past pres.), Am., Washington socs. assn. execs., Alpha Zeta. Club: 150. Mem. Ch. of Jesus Christ of Latter-day Saints (bishop 1951—). Home: 1234 Meyer Ct McLean VA 22101

LILLARD, EUGENE PATTERSON, librarian; b. Bowie, Tex., Oct. 6, 1906; s. Orestes Eugene and Julia (Patterson) L.; B.A., Rice U., 1927; M.Ed., So. Meth. U., 1952; M.L.S., Tex. U., 1964. Tchr. Milby High Sch., Houston, 1928-30, Kaufman (Tex.) High Sch., 1930-31, Forney (Tex.) High Sch., 1934-36; mem. faculty Tex. Mil. Coll., Terrell, 1931-34, Edinburg Jr. Coll., 1934-52; prof. Pan Am. Coll., 1952-63; librarian U. Tex. at Austin, 1964-73, cons. humanities research library, 1973—. Served with USAF, 1942-45. Home: 7802 Mullen St Austin TX 78757 Office: Humanities Research Center Library U Tex Austin TX 78712

LILLARD, ROTHWELL JACKSON, lawyer; b. Duet, Va., Sept. 16, 1910; s. James Robert and Sallie Blanche (Finks) L.; B.S., U. Va., 1934, LL.B., 1948; m. Anne P. Eastham, May 5, 1951; children—James Martin, John Eastham. Admitted to Va. bar, 1948, since practiced in Fairfax; mem. firm McCandlish, Lillard & Marsh and predecessors, 1948—; lectr. Sch. Law U. Va., No. Va. Div. Dir. Braddock Land Co., Inc. Trustee, Fairfax Hosp. Assn. Served to lt. comdr. USNR, 1942-46. Fellow Am. Coll. Trial Lawyers; mem. Va. State Bar (council, exec. com.), Raven Soc., Order of Coif. Episcopalian. Clubs: Country of Fairfax; Greene Hills Country. Home: 11109 Pelham Lane Fairfax VA 22030 Office: 4069 Chain Br Rd Fairfax VA 22030

LILLIE, RICHARD RANSOM, city ofcl.; b. Merrill, Wis., Oct. 21, 1930; s. Arthur Ransom and Mildred Rose (Gipple) L.; B.B.A., U. Tex., 1958; M.City Planning, Ga. Inst. Tech., 1964; m. Nelda Stanford, Sept. 1, 1957; children—Elizabeth Suzanne, Julianne Marie. Planner, City of Austin, Tex., 1958-62; with Dept. Housing and Urban Devel. Region III, Atlanta, 1962-63, Harry Adley, planning cons., Atlanta, 1963-64; dir. planning City of Waco, Tex., 1964; asst. dir. planning City of Austin, 1965-70, dir. planning, 1970—. Vis. lectr. community and regional planning U. Tex. at Austin, 1971-73. Served with USN, 1950-54. Recipient Pub. Service award A.I.A., 1973. Home: 4202 Cat Hollow Dr Austin TX 78731 Office: PO Box 1088 Austin TX 78701

LILLIE, WILLIAM HENRY, JR., architect, ret. air force officer; b. Conneaut, O., July 16, 1917; s. William Henry and Kathryn (Green) L.; B.S., Miami U., Oxford, O., 1937-41; m. Janis Crall, July 23, 1942. Commd. 2d lt. U.S. Army Air Force, 1942, advanced through grades to col. U.S. Air Force, 1969; chief architect br. hdqrs., Washington, 1954-58; chief design, Spain, 1958-60; dir. constrn. 3d Air Force, U.K., 1960; chief family housing programs, Washington, 1968-69; base civil engr., Vietnam, 1969-70; chief civil engr. J-4 Office Joint Chiefs Staff, Washington, 1971; ret., 1971; Washington rep. Neuhaus & Taylor, architects, Houston, 1971-72; constrn. monitor Internat. Bank Reconstrn. and Devel., Washington, 1972-73, asst. chief bldg. operations, 1973—. Architect F & Y Bldgs., Columbus, O., 1947-50. Decorated Air medal, Army Commendation medal, Air Force Commendation medal with 2 oak leaf clusters, Bronze Star, Legion Merit; recipient Harvey Hiestand design award Miami U., 1940. Mem. Soc. Mil. Engrs. (pres. chpt. 1969), A.I.A. (corporate), Delta Upsilon. Republican. Conglist. Home: 6717 Bulkley Rd Newington VA 22122 Office: Internat Bank Reconstrn & Devel Washington DC 20433

LILLY, CLYDE ALANSON, JR., utility co. exec.; b. Dallas, Oct. 31, 1919; s. Clyde Alanson and Leila Graumer (Wilson) L.; B.S. in Mech. Engring., Tex. A. and M. U., 1941; m. Dolores Ekren, Dec. 24, 1945; children—Jeffrey A., Gail Elizabeth, Clyde Alanson III. Mgr. generator engring., large steam turbine generator dept. Gen. Electric Co., Schenectady, 1946-62; mgr. marketing Indsl. Equipment div. Baldwin-Lima-Hamilton Corp., Phila., 1962-64; exec. v.p. Gulf Power Co., 1964-65, pres., 1965-69, now dir.; pres. So. Services, Inc., Birmingham, Ala., 1969—, also dir.; v.p. engring. So. Co., Atlanta, 1971—, also dir.; dir. Atomic Indsl. Forum, Inc. Pres. Jr. Achievement of Pensacola (Fla.), 1967; v.p. U. West Fla. Found., 1967. Bd. dirs. United Fund, 1966; mem. exec. bd. Birmingham Area council Boy Scouts Am., 1969-73. Served to capt. AUS, 1941-46. Decorated Bronze Star, Air medal, Purple Heart. Fellow Am. Soc. M.E.; mem. I.E.E.E., Air Force Assn., Newcomen Soc. N.Am., Fla. State C. of C. (dir. 1967). Presbyn. Rotarian. Clubs: Country of Birmingham, Mountain Brook. Home: 3509 S Woodridge Rd Birmingham AL 35223 Office: So Services Inc PO Box 2625 Birmingham AL 35202

LILLY, DENNIS EUGENE, univ. adminstr.; b. Beckley, W.Va., Feb. 20, 1921; s. Ira Bryan and Lessie Ann (Hubbard) L.; student Concord Coll., 1939-40, Bowling Green Bus. U., 1948-49; B.A., Western State U., 1950; Mus.M., W.Va. U., 1952; postgrad. U. Mass., 1962-64, U. Mo., 1966-67; m. Katherine June Donham, Nov. 24, 1952; children—Suzanne (Mrs. Omie James), Marjorie (Mrs. Robert Harvey), David Rene, Michael Eugene, Jason Donham. Asst. engr. Logan Clay Products Co. (O.), 1944; dir. recreation and music Munsey Meml. Meth. Ch., Johnson City, Tenn., 1952-57; asst. dir. Student Union, U. Mass., Amherst, 1957-66, instr. phys. edn., recreation and music 1954-56; dir. student activities Park Coll., Parkville, Mo., 1966-67; dir. religious and fgn. student affairs East Tenn. State U., Johnson City, 1967—. Dir. Recreation and Camping Program, Cecilton, Md., 1950-52; chmn. Concert Assn., 1952; chmn. water safety com. A.R.C., 1952-57; choral and choir dir., 1942-55; scoutmaster, neighborhood commr., leadership tng. chmn. Sequoyah council Boy Scouts Am., 1940—, staff mem. Nat. council, 1973—. Bd. dirs. Girls Club, Amherst, 1963-66. Served with USMC, 1945-46. Mem. Assn. for Coordination U. Religious Affairs (sec.-treas.), Council Student Personnel Assns., Assn. Coll. Unions Internat., Nat. Assn. Student Personnel, Nat. Assn. Fgn. Student Affairs, Phi Delta Kappa. Mason, Kiwanian. Home: 1612 Woodridge Dr Johnson City TN 37601

LILLY, EDWARD GUERRANT, JR., utility exec.; b. Lexington, Ky., Oct. 29, 1925; s. Edward Guerrant and Elisabeth (Frazer) L.; student U. Va., 1944; B.S., Davidson Coll., 1948; M.B.A., U. Pa., 1949; m. Nancy Cobb, Nov. 25, 1961; children—Penelope Read, Edward Guerrant III, Collier Cobb, Steven Clay. With Citizens & So. Nat. Bank Charleston, S.C., 1949-50; with Wachovia Bank & Trust Co., Durham, N.C., 1952-71, sr. v.p., 1960-71; sr. v.p. finance Carolina Power & Light Co., Raleigh, N.C., 1971—, also dir. Wachovia Bank and Trust Co. N.A., Raleigh, Gen. Telephone Co. S.E. Served to ensign USNR, 1944-46, lt. 1950-52. Mem. Durham C. of C. (pres. 1968-69, dir. 1964-69). Home: 612 Scotland St Raleigh NC 27609 Office: PO Box 1551 Raleigh NC 27602

LILLY, JOHN CUNNINGHAM, neurophysiologist, biophysicist; b. St. Paul, Jan. 6, 1915; s. Richard Coyle and Rachel (Cunningham) L.; B.Sc., Cal. Inst. Tech., 1938; student Dartmouth Med. Sch., 1938-40; M.D., U. Pa., 1942; m. Elisabeth Christine Bjerg, June 12, 1959; children—John Cunningham, Charles R., Pamela C., Cynthia R. O. Mem. faculty U. Pa., 1942-56, fellow in biophysics E. R. Johnson Found. of Med. Physics, 1942-46, asso., 1946-49, asst. prof. biophysics, 1949-52, asso. prof. med. physics, 1952-56, asso. prof. exptl. neurology dept. neurology and Grad. Sch. Medicine, 1952-56; chief cortical integration sect. Lab. of Neurophys., Nat. Inst. Mental Health, 1953-58; established Communication Research Inst., St. Thomas, V.I., 1959, Miami, Fla., 1960, chmn. bd. trustees, 1959-60, dir. inst., 1960—; Hixon lectr. Cal. Inst. Tech., 1952; Mayo Found. lectr., 1952; Colloquim lectr. Harvard, 1954; John Kershman Meml. lectr., 1961; lectr. to laity N.Y. Acad. Medicine, 1962; research prof. in medicine U. Miami Med. Sch., 1960; also lectr. numerous univs., learned socs. Condr. research for com. med. research OSRD-USAF, 1942-46 (effective service award 1945); mem. fellowship bd. Nat. Inst. Mental Health, 1954-57; sci. adv. com. for grad. schs. NIH, 1954; bioscis. adv. panel Office Sci. Research, USAF Research and Devel. Command, 1958-61, sci. adv. bd., 1958-63. Recipient John Clark Research prize, 1943. Fellow A.A.A.S., N.Y. Acad. Scis.; mem. Am. Physiol. Soc. (steering com. on neurophysiology 1953-56). Am. Electroencephalographic Soc., I.E.E.E., Biophys. Soc. (charter), Acoustical Soc. Am., Internat. Brain Research Orgn., Aerospace Med. Assn., Washington Acad. Scis., Internat. Fedn. Med. Electronics, Am. Soc. Mammalogists. Assn. Research in Nervous and Mental Diseases, Optical Soc. Am., Soc. Exptl. Biology and Medicine, Sigma Xi, Alpha Mu, Pi Omega. Author: The Mind of the Dolphin, 1961; Man and Dolphin, 1962; Center of the Cyclone, 1971; co-author: The Dolphin in History, 1963. Editor Psychosomatic Medicine, 1957. Contbr. articles to profl. jours. Address: 3670 Hibiscus St Miami FL 33133

LIMBER, D(AVID) NELSON, astronomer, educator; b. Alexandria, Va., May 25, 1928; s. Donald Philips and Phyllis Annette (Dawson) L.; A.B., Ohio State U., 1950, M.Sc., 1950; Ph.D., U. Chgo., 1953; postgrad. (NSF fellow) Princeton, 1956, (Higgins fellow), 1956-57; m. Marian Loretta Ahner, Sept. 20, 1958; children—Ellen, Susan. Asst. prof. U. Rochester (N.Y.), 1957-58; asst. prof. U. Chgo., 1958-62, asso. prof., 1962-68; prof. astronomy U. Va., Charlottesville, 1968—. Served with AUS, 1954-56. Fellow Royal Astron. Soc.; mem. Am. Astron. Soc., A.A.A.S. Contbr. articles to profl. jours. Home: 106 Westminster Rd Charlottesville VA 22901

LIMING, WILLIAM SINGLETON, coll. adminstr.; b. Toms River, N.J., Aug. 23, 1910; s. William Lewis and Esther (Singleton) L.; B.A., Bucknell U., 1933; m. Ruth Elizabeth Rohr, June 26, 1936; children—Ruth Gail (Mrs. David E. Ackroyd), Robert Geoffrey. Editor, Ocean County Sun, Toms River, N.J., 1934-36; editorial staff L.I. Daily Press, Jamaica, N.Y., 1936-42; mgr. sales promotion and publicity Met. Life Ins. Co., N.Y.C., 1945-64; v.p. for devel. Erskine Coll., Due West, S.C., 1964-70, instr. journalism, 1966-70; dir. deferred giving devel. dept. Furman U., Greenville, S.C., 1970—. Trustee Bucknell U., 1964-69. Served to lt. (j.g.) USNR, 1942-45. Recipient Distinguished Service award Bucknell U., 1960. Mem. Am. Coll. Pub. Relations Assn., Am. Assn. Indsl. Editors (pres. 1956-57), Profl. Indsl. Communications Assn. (pres. 1957-59), Bucknell U. Gen. Alumni Assn. (pres. 1962-63), Tau Kappa Epsilon, Pi Delta Epsilon, Sigma Tau Delta. Associate Reform Presbyn. Rotarian. Club: Poinsett (Greenville, S.C.). Home: PO Box 395 Due West SC 29639 Office: Furman U Greenville SC 29613

LIMMER, EZEKIEL, govt. ofcl.; b. Galatz, Roumania, May 1, 1912; s. Morris Solomon and Peppy (Ermowitz) L.; came to U.S., 1920, naturalized, 1926; A.B., Brown U., 1933; M.A., Columbia, 1934; Ph.D., Am. U., 1942; m. Evelyn G. Ifshin, Aug. 10, 1947; children—Beverly (Mrs. Martin Elliot Gordon), Leslie Sue. Transp. economist ICC, Washington, 1935-38, U.S. Dept. Agr., 1938-42, 48-51, 53-56, War Assets Adminstrn., 1946-48, Office of Salary Stablzn., 1951-53, chief domestic cargo rates sect. CAB, 1956—. Lectr. Am. U., 1948-59, Southeastern U., U. Va., U. Md., 1965—. Trustee Washington United Jewish Appeal. Served to capt. AUS, 1942-45. Recipient certificate of hon. award CAB, 1967. Mem. Am. Econ. Assn., Transp. Research Forum, Am. Soc. Traffic and Transp., Phi Beta Kappa. Home: 812 Malcolm Dr Silver Spring MD 20901 Office: 1825 Connecticut Av Washington DC 20428

LIMPUS, LAWRENCE LEROY, elec. engr.; b. Camp Shelby, Miss., July 6, 1945; s. Leroy David and Eileen (Mintyala) L.; B.S. in Elec. Engring., Tex. A. and M. U., 1968; postgrad. S. Tex. Coll. Law, 1970—; m. Patsy Lorraine Longino, June 4, 1966; children—Alicia Lorraine, Christopher Lee. Instrument, elec. maintenance engr. Monsanto Chem. Co., Alvin, Tex., 1968-71, instrument, elec. project engr., 1971—. Registered profl. engr., Tex. Mem. Instrument Soc. Am., Student Bar Assn. S. Tex. Coll. Law, Tex. Soc. Profl. Engrs. (jr. mem.). Home: 1608 Alta Vista Alvin TX 77511 Office: PO Box 711 Alvin TX 77511

LIN, SAN-SU CHEN (MRS. PAUL LIN), educator; b. Hong Kong, China, June 3, 1916; d. L.O. and Nellie (Wong) Chan; B.A., Nat. Peking U., Peiping, China, 1939; M.A., Tchrs. Coll. Columbia, 1950, Ed.D., 1953; m. Paul J.S. Lin, Oct. 8, 1939; children—Betty, Jeannie. Came to U.S., 1949, naturalized, 1966. Instr. English, Provincial Tchrs. Coll., Taipei, Taiwan, China, 1948-49; prof. English, Claflin Coll., Orangeburg, S.C., 1955-64, head English dept., 1957-64; prof. English, So. U., Baton Rouge, La., 1964—, dir. freshman English, 1969—. Cons. U.S. Office Edn. for evaluation project proposals. U.S. Office Edn. research grantee, 1961-64. Mem. Nat. Council Tchrs. English (spl. task force to study English programs for disadvantaged students 1965), Conf. on Coll. Composition and Communication, Commn. on Humanities, Assn. for Supervision and Curriculum Devel. Author: Pattern Practice in the Teaching of Standard English to Students with a Nonstandard Dialect, 1965. Contbr. articles to English Jour., Coll. English, CLA Jour., others. Home: 8107 Branchwood Dr Baton Rouge LA 70811

LIN, YOU-FENG, educator; b. Taiwan, Republic of China, July 31, 1932; s. Hwei-Yen and San (Chen) L.; B.S., Taiwan Normal U., 1957; postgrad. (research fellow) Tulane U., 1959-63; Ph.D. (research fellow 1963-64), U. Fla., 1964; m. Shwu-Yeng Tzeng, July 30, 1960; children—Luke, Halbert, Winston. Research asst. Inst. Math., Academia Sineca, Taipei, Taiwan, 1957-59; instr. Tulane U., New Orleans, 1959-63; mem. faculty U. South Fla., Tampa, 1964—, prof. math., 1969—. Recipient Research award U. So. Fla., 1965, 66. Mem. Am. Math. Soc., Math. Assn. Am. Author: (with Shwu-yeng T. Lin) Set Theory: An Intuitive Approach, 1974. Home: 321 Belle View Av Temple Terrace FL 33617 Office: Dept Math U So Fla Tampa FL 33620

LINAM, RONALD HAMPTON, profl. investor; b. Waco, Tex., Nov. 17, 1935; s. Raymond H. and Evelyn (Brooks) L.; B.B.A., Baylor U., 1958; B.S., So. Meth. U., 1961; m. 2d, Georgia Heath, July 1, 1971; children (by previous marriage)—Daniel Kyle, Michael Ray. Dir. investments Transport Ins. Group, Dallas, 1961-70; cons. portfolio mgr., 1970—; pres. Am. Commonwealth Devel. Corp., dir. Intermed Corp., cons. indsl. engr., 1958—. Trustee Dallas Bapt. Coll. Mem. Am. Inst. Indsl. Engrs., Dallas Assn. Investment Analysts, Financial Analysts Fedn. Am. Home: Linam Ranch Route 1 Box 13A Krum TX 76249 Office: Adolphus Tower Dallas TX 75202

LIND, DON LESLIE, astronaut; b. Midvale, Utah, May 18, 1930; s. Leslie A. and Elizabeth C. (Whitmore) L.; B.S., U. Utah, 1953; Ph.D., U. Cal. at Berkeley, 1964; m. Kathleen Maughan, Apr. 1, 1955; children—Carol, David, Dawna, Douglas, Kimberly, Lisa. Commd. USN, 1954, advanced through grade to comdr., 1969; naval aviator, 1954-57; space physicist devel. plasma expts. Fields and Plasma br. Goddard Space Flight Center, Greenbelt, Md., 1964-66; astronaut NASA Manned Spacecraft Center, Houston, 1966—. Mem. Am. Geophys. Union. Office: Code (CB) NASA Manned Spacecraft Center Houston TX 77058

LINDAHL, ROY LAWRENCE, pedodontist, educator; b. Los Angeles, Aug. 22, 1925; s. Lars and Alice Catherine (Chilstrom) L.; B.S., D.D.S., U. So. Cal., 1950; M.S. (Mott Found. fellow), U. Mich., 1952; m. Gwendolyn Janice Carle, June 18, 1948; children—John Carle, Linda Jean, Lawrence Craige, Carol Ann. Asst. prof. U. N.C. Sch. Dentistry, Chapel Hill, 1952-55, prof., chmn. dept. pedodontics, 1955-69, dir. Office Continuing Edn., Sch. Dentistry, dir. dental demonstration practice Health Services Research Center, 1969—. Vice pres. Delta Dental Plan N.C., Inc.; cons. Womack Army Hosp., Ft. Bragg, N.C. Mem. Chapel Hill Bd. Edn., 1965-71, chmn., 1967-71. Pres. Am. Soc. Dentistry for Children Found. Served with USNR, 1944-46. Recipient citation Boston U. Sch. Grad. Dentistry, 1969; Service to Mankind award Tarheel Sertoma Club, 1965. Fellow Am. Coll. Dentists; mem. Am. Dental Assn., N.C. Dental Soc., Am. Soc. Dentistry for Children (pres.), Am. Acad. Pedodontics (past pres.), Internat. Assn. Dental Research, Am. Pub. Health Assn., Chapel Hill-Carrboro C. of C. (pres. 1967, Distinguished Service award 1964), Blue Key, Psi Omega, Chi Phi, Omicron Kappa Upsilon. Rotarian. Contbr., editor: Dentistry for Children, 1964. Home: 305 Clayton Rd Chapel Hill NC 27514

LINDAUER, MAURICE WILLIAM, educator; b. Millstadt, Ill., Sept. 25, 1924; s. Herbert Johann and Pearl (Maserang) L.; B.A., Washington U., St. Louis, 1949; M.A., Harvard, 1953, M.Ed., 1962; Ph.D., Fla. State U., 1970; m. Janie Ruth Shiver, Feb. 14, 1946; children—Jane (Mrs. Lamar A. Elder, Jr.), Rosemary (Mrs. William M. Brannen), Maurice Jack. Research chemist Mallinckrodt Chem. Works, St. Louis, 1952-55, Allied Chem. & Dye Corp., Hopewell, Va., 1956-57; research engr. Am. Zinc Co., Monsanto, Ill., 1955-56; mem. faculty Valdosta (Ga.) State Coll., 1957—, prof. chemistry, 1971—. Chief radiol. def. Lowndes County Civil Def. Corps, 1962—. Served with USNR, 1943-46. NSF Sci. Faculty fellow, 1964-65; Oak Ridge Asso. Univs. fellow, 1967. Fellow Am. Inst. Chemists; mem. Am. Chem. Soc., Sigma Xi. Contbr. articles to profl. jours. Home: 1401 Miramar St Valdosta GA 31601

LINDEMAN, ROBERT DEAN, educator; b. Fort Dodge, Ia., July 19, 1930; s. Verlus Frank and Dorothy (Cawelti) L.; B.S., N.Y. State Coll. Forestry, 1952; M.D., Upstate Med. Center, State U. N.Y. at Syracuse, 1956; m. Janet Ruth Lyman, Apr. 10, 1954; children—William Douglas, Ann Denise, James Lawrence, Peter Verlus, David Matthew. Intern Blodgett Meml. Hosp., Grand Rapids, Mich., 1956-57; resident Upstate Med. Center, Syracuse, 1957-60; clin. asst. medicine Okla. Med. Center, Oklahoma City, 1960-62; instr. medicine Balt. City Hosp. and Johns Hopkins Coll. Medicine, Balt., 1962-66; mem. faculty Coll. Medicine, U. Okla., 1966—, asso. prof., 1968-71, prof. medicine, physiology, 1971—, also asso. prof. biostatistics, epidemiology Coll. Health, 1966—; chief renal section, asso. chief staff research sectr. VA Hosp., Oklahoma City, 1966—; practice medicine specializing in internal medicine, nephrology, Oklahoma City, 1960-62, 66—, Balt., 1962-66; mem. staff U. Okla. Hosps., Children's Meml. Hosp., Oklahoma City. Mem. nat. med. adv. council Nat. Kidney Found., 1970—; pres. Okla.-South Kan. Kidney Found., 1969-71. Served with USPHS, 1960-66. VA exchange fellow Institut National de la Santé et de la Recherche Medicale (France), 1974; VA grantee, 1967—, NIH grantee, 1967—. Fellow A.C.P.; mem. Central Soc. Clin. Research, So. Soc. Clin. Investigation, Am. Fedn. Clin. Research, Am., Internat. socs. nephrology, Soc. Exptl. Biology and Medicine, A.M.A., Okla. State, Oklahoma County med. socs., Sigma Xi. Asso. editor The Kidney jour. Nat. Kidney Found., 1973—. Contbr. articles to profl. jours. Home: 3621 NW 68th St Oklahoma City OK 73116 Office: 921 NE 13th St Oklahoma City OK 73190

LINDEMANN, ARTHUR WILLIS, aerospace products mfg. co. exec.; b. Enderlin, N.D., Apr. 13, 1924; s. Robert and Alvina (Friedrich) L.; B.S. in Elec. Engring., N.D. State U., 1949; postgrad. Northwestern U., 1950, Bert Rodgers Schs. Real Estate, 1972-73; m. Corrine Mae Erickson, May 15, 1954; children—James, David, Bradley. Devel. and research engr. Honeywell Aero. Products, Mpls., 1951-56; devel. and research engr. Delco div. Gen. Motors Corp., Milw., 1956-61; lead engr. Honeywell Aerospace div., St. Petersburg, Fla., 1961-69, supr. engring. computers guidance systems, 1969—. Asso. mem. realty firm Clearwater/Largo, Largo, Fla., 1973—. Active Indian Guides, Brookfield, Wis., also, Clearwater, 1962-65. Served with USAAF, 1945-46. Mem. I.E.E.E., U.S. Power Squadron, Tau Beta Pi, Kappa Sigma Chi. Club: Western Racquet (Elm Grove, Wis.). Patentee in field. Home: 1520 Keene Rd S Clearwater FL 33516 Office: 13350 Hwy 19 St Petersburg FL 33733

LINDEMANN, LILLIAN CHAMBERS (MRS. BOHN CARL LINDEMANN), physician; b. N.Y.C., Nov. 14, 1922; d. Robert A. and Jean Boalt (Wheeler) Chambers; B.A., Sarah Lawrence Coll., 1944; M.D., Columbia, 1949; m. Bohn Carl Lindemann, Dec. 17, 1948; children—Robert C., A. Louise Laurence, Jean W., Lillian M., Charles S.W. Intern, U. Cal. Hosp., San Francisco, 1949-51; resident Med. Coll. Va., Richmond, 1953-54, 61-64, 64-66; chief maternal and child health Health Dept., City of Richmond, 1955-58; practice medicine, specializing in pediatrics, Richmond, 1958-61, in psychiatry, 1966—; mem. staff Med. Coll. Va., Richmond Meml. Hosp., Grace Hosp.; instr. dept. pediatrics Med. Coll. Va., 1955-59, clin. instr., 1959-60, clin. asso., 1960, instr. dept. psychiatry, 1964-65, asso., 1965-66, asst. clin. prof., 1967—. Diplomate Am. Bd. Pediatrics. Mem. Am. Soc. Adolescent Psychiatry, So. Va. Assn. Adolescent Psychiatry. Club: Deep Run Hunt (Manakin, Va.). Contbr. articles in field to profl. jours. Home: 4708 Cary St Rd Richmond VA 23226 Office: 2223 Monument Av Richmond VA 23220

LINDEMANN, MARCIA ANN RICE (MRS. CHARLES J. LINDEMANN), advt. exec.; b. Huntington, W.Va., Jan. 15, 1931; d. Lloyd Emerson and Beatrice (Odell) Rice; B.A. in English, U. N.C., 1951, M.A. in Comparative Linguistics, 1953; m. Charles J. Lindemann, Feb. 14, 1953; children—Kirstine, Anna Margrethe, Carla. Instr. English, Old Dominion U., 1953-58; copy dir. Atlantic Nat. Adv. Agy., Norfolk, Va., 1961; v.p., co-owner Matthews Advt. Agy. Inc., Norfolk, 1962-71; pres. Hampton Rds. Advt. Inc., 1971—. Mem. bd., dir. pub. relations Tidewater Arts Council, 1961—, founder Norfolk Arts Festival, 1961; mem. Norfolk Commn. Community Programming, 1969—. Mem. Am. Assn. U. Women (dir.), Linguistic Soc. Am., Norfolk C. of C. (dir. women's div. 1967—) Pub. Relations Soc. Am. Home: 5201 Studeley Av Norfolk VA 23508 Office: 610 W 25th St Norfolk VA 23517

LINDENBAUM, SOL, govt. ofcl.; b. Lawrenceville, Ill., June 7, 1915; s. Louis and Hilda (Zelmanovitz) L.; A.B., U. Kan., 1936; LL.B., Harvard, 1939; m. Dorothy Wolk, Sept. 11, 1943; children—Joan Frances (Mrs. Michael M. Stern), David Sage. Admitted to Kan. bar, 1939; practiced in El Dorado, Kan., 1940-42; atty. Dept. Justice, Washington, 1946—, exec. asst. to atty. gen., 1967—. Mem. Adminstrv. Conf. U.S. Served with AUS, 1942-45. Mem. Phi Beta Kappa. Home: 9921 Pinehurst Av Fairfax VA 22030 Office: Dept Justice 10th and Pennsylvania Av Washington DC 20530

LINDENBERG, FREDERICK AUGUST, structural engr.; b. Charleston, S.C., Aug. 9, 1932; s. Maxwell Theodore and Louise (Stender) L.; B.S., Coll. Charleston, 1954; B.S. in Civil Engring., The Citadel, 1959; m. Harriet Diane Payne, Aug. 13, 1963; 1 dau., Andrea Diane. Engr., Am. Bridge div. U.S. Steel Corp., Birmingham, 1959-62, field engr. constrn. dept., 1962-64; design engr. Rust Engring. Co., Birmingham, 1964-69, sr. design engr., 1969—. Served with AUS, 1954-56; Far East. Mem. Am. Soc. C.E. Home: 709 Hoadley Dr Birmingham AL 35213 Office: 1130 S 22d St Birmingham AL 35201

LINDER, ROBERT EUGENE, agrl. agt.; b. Samson, Ala., May 3, 1926; s. Irvin Vuron and Eula Mae (Owens) L.; B.S. in Agr., Auburn U., 1952, M. in Agr., 1967; m. Barbara Ann Northcutt, Dec. 20, 1953; children—Elaine, Annette, Victoria Jean. Pension counsellor Ala. Dept. of Pensions and Security, Geneva, 1954-60; extension farm agt. Coop. Extension Service, Auburn U., Andalusia, 1960—. Treas., Andalusia (Ala.) Civitan Club, 1971-72, v.p., 1972-73. Served with AUS, 1952-53. Clubs: Andalusia Toastmaster (pres. 1971-72, sgt. at arms 1969-70). Home: Route 2 Andalusia AL 36420 Office: PO Box 519 Andalusia AL 36420

LINDHOLM, DALE DAVID, educator, physician; b. Duluth, Minn., Dec. 4, 1931; s. David and Jenny (Lind) L.; B.A., U. Minn., 1953, B.S., 1954, M.D., 1957; m. Dolores Cecil Hennings, June 20, 1953; children—Ronald Dale, Cynthia Sue. Intern St. Luke's Hosp., Duluth, 1957-58; resident USPHS Hosp., Seattle, 1959-62; nephrology fellow U. Wash. Sch. Medicine, Seattle, 1962-64; chief research Seamen's Meml. Research Lab., USPHS Hosp., New Orleans, 1964-66; prof. medicine, head mephrology sect. Sch. Medicine, Tulane U., New Orleans, 1965—; mem. staff Charity Hosp. La., VA Hosp., both New Orleans. Mem. renal planning com. La. Regional Med. Program, 1970—; cons. USPHS, NIH. Mem. med. adv. bd. La. chpt. Nat. Kidney Found., 1968—. Bd. dirs. Trinity Christian Community, New Orleans, 1969—. Served with USPHS, 1958-66. James Wright Hunt scholar, 1953-54; Nat. Heart Inst. fellow U. Wash., Seattle, 1962-64. Mem. Am. Soc. Nephrology, Am., Internat. socs. nephrology, Am. Soc. Artificial Internal Organs, Am. Assn. U. Profs., A.A.A.S., others. Baptist (deacon). Club: Aurora Country (New Orleans). Contbr. profl. jours. Home: 2216 St Nick Dr New Orleans LA 70114 Office: 1430 Tulane Av New Orleans LA 70112

LINDLEY, CLYDE JOE, govt. ofcl.; b. Granite City, Ill., May 7, 1915; s. Clyde Clifford and Lillie Mary (Brady) L.; A.B., U. Mo., 1937; M.A., U. Ia., 1938; postgrad. U. Minn., 1938-41; m. Marie Williams, Dec. 23, 1940; children—Richard Williams, Suzanna (Mrs. Richard D. Summersgill). With VA, Washington, 1946—, asso. dir. planning, dept. medicine and surgery, 1962-66, exec. sec., spl. med. adv. group, 1967-70, exec. sec., mental health and behavioral scis., 1971—; sec.-treas. Am. Bd. Counseling Services, Washington, 1960-63, pres., 1963-66; asso. prof. psychology George Washington U., Washington, 1946-66. Served to maj. AUS, 1941-46. Mem. Am. Psychol. Assn., Am. Personnel and Guidance Assn., Nat. Vocational Guidance Assn. Editor: VA Cooperative Chemotheraphy Studies in Psychiatry, vols. 1-6, 1957-61. Home: 1608 Sanford Rd Silver Spring MD 20902 Office: 810 Vermont Av NW Washington DC 20420

LINDLEY, JAMES ROY, lawyer, city ofcl.; b. Oletha, Tex., Feb. 2, 1931; s. John and Nina Lolene (Archer) L.; B.A., Tex. Technol. U., 1952; J.D., Baylor U., 1962; m. Bernice G. Thibeau, June 30, 1956; children—Cecile Marie, Mary Alexandra. Claim agt. N.Y. Central R.R., Buffalo, 1957-59; admitted to Tex. bar, 1962; mem. firm Splawn & Mayer, Lubbock, Tex., 1962-65, Lindley, Wells & Michalk, Killeen, Tex., 1965—. Mayor City of Killeen, 1970—. Mem. environmental com. Nat. League Cities, 1974. Bd. dirs. Good Will Industries, Inc. Served with USNR, 1952-56. Mem. Am., Bell-Lampasas-Mills Counties bar assns., Am. Judicature Soc., Tex. Trial Lawyers Assn. (dir. 1969), State Bar Tex. K.C. Home: 616 Live Oak Dr Killeen TX 76541 Office: 617 N 8th St Killeen TX 76541

LINDLEY, JOHN ELLIS, physician; b. Macon, Miss., Apr. 23, 1926; s. Ancil Levinson and Brancie Ann (Stuart) L.; student Miss. State U., 1943-44, student U. Miss., 1950; B.S., Harvard, 1952; M.D., Baylor U., 1953; m. Helen Marie Puffenbarger, Aug. 21, 1954; children—Mary Lisa, John Ellis II, Mark Andrew. Intern Jefferson Davis Hosp., Houston, 1952-53, resident, 1953-56; practice medicine specializing in obstetrics, gynecology, Houston, 1956-57; staff obstetrician and gynecologist Jeff Anderson Meml., now chief staff; mem. staff St. Joseph, Riley hosps., Meridian, Miss.; asst. instr. obstetrics, gynecology Baylor U., 1953-57, instr., 1956-57; asst. prof. obstetrics, gynecology U. Miss., 1957-58; pres. Lindley-Jones Clinic Women. Pres. Lindley Enterprises, Inc., Diamond L Beef House, Inc.; owner Lindley Ranch, Lindley's Flowers' & Gift Castle. Mem. exec. staff Gov. of Miss., 1960-72; mayor of Marion, Miss. Bd. dirs. Am. Cancer Soc., Lauderdale County, Miss., 1960-63; pres., bd. dirs. Jefferson Davis Acad. Served with USNR, 1944-46. Diplomate Am. Bd. Obstetrics and Gynecology. Fellow A.C.S., Am. Coll. Obstetrics and Gynecology, Central Assn. Obstetricians and Gynecologists; mem. Miss. Obstet. and Gynecol. Soc. (pres.-elect 1965), Am., Miss., So. med. assns., S.W. Postgrad., East Miss. (pres. 1963), Lauderdale County (pres. 1963) med. socs., Miss. Cattlemen's Assn., Sigma Chi. Democrat. Baptist. Mason (Shriner). Contbr. articles to profl. jours.; inventor of Lindley Newborn Resuscitator. Home: Marion MS 39342 Office: 1410 20th Av Meridian MS 39301

LINDOW, LESTER WILLIAM, telecasters orgn. exec.; b. Milw., Apr. 11, 1913; B.A. in Journalism, U. Wis., 1934; m. Andree de Verdor, Dec. 7, 1946; 1 dau., Suzanne Helene. Asso. editor Advt. Almanac, Hearst Newspapers, N.Y.C., 1934-35; with comml. dept. sta. WCAE, Pitts., 1935-36, nat. sales mgr., 1936-38, comml. mgr., asst. to gen. mgr., 1938-40; sec., gen. mgr. WFBM, Inc., Indpls., 1940-42; gen. mgr. stas. WRNY and WRNY-FM, Rochester, N.Y., 1946-47; sec., gen. mgr. Trebit Corp. operators sta. WFDF, Flint, 1947-60, sec., dir., 1948-60, v.p., 1954-60; sec.-treas. Landsmore Corp., 1952-57, v.p., 1954-57; mem. exec. com. NBC Radio Affiliates, 1955-57, chmn. exec. com., 1956-57; exec. dir. Assn. Maximum Service Telecasters, Inc., 1957—, also dir. asst. sec.-treas.; v.p., dir. Grelin Broadcasting Inc., sta. WWRI, West Warwick, R.I., 1957-69, Radio Buffalo, Inc., sta. WWOL and WWOL-FM, Buffalo, 1959-62. Treas., dir. A.R.C., 1953-56, nat. fund vice chmn. for Mich., 1956-57. Served from 1st lt. to lt. col. AUS, 1942-46; apptd. to Gen. Staff Corps, War Dept., 1946-47; col. Res. ret. Mem. Mich. Assn. Broadcasters, Mich. A.P. Broadcasters' Assn. (dir.), Res. Officers Assn., Nat. Assn. Radio and TV Broadcasters (dir. AM radio com.), Radio Advt. Bur. (Mich. chmn.), A.P. Radio Programming Com. N.Y.C., Assn. Profl. Broadcasting Edn. (dir.), A.P. Radio and TV Assn. (v.p., dir.), TV Allocations Study Orgn. (alternate dir.). Union U. Wis. Alumni Assn., Broadcasters Club of Washington (pres. 1964-65, gov. 1959-61, chmn. bd. 1965-66), Internat. Radio and TV Soc., Radio-TV Pioneers Alpha Chi Rho, Scabbard and Blade, Iron Cross, White Spades, Sigma Delta Chi. Elk, Rotarian (pres.). Clubs: Flint Golf; Radio Executives (N.Y.C.); Nat. Press, Congressional Country, Internat. (Washington). Home: 4000 Massachusetts Av NW Washington DC 20016 Office: 1735 DeSales St NW Washington DC 20036

LINDQUIST, CLARENCE BERNHART, ednl. adminstr.; b. Superior, Wis., Dec. 21, 1913; s. Gust and Hannah (Berentson) L.; B.E., Wis. State U., 1937; M.Philosophy, U. Wis., 1939, Ph.D., 1941; m. Helen Jane Conroy, Dec. 29, 1941; children—Clarence Conroy, Thomas Ward, James Raymond, Robert Michael, Mary Lenore. Instr., U.S. Naval Acad., Annapolis, Md., 1941-42, asst. prof., 1945-46; faculty U. Minn., Duluth, adminstrv. asst. to provost, 1949-51, prof., head math. and engring., 1951-57; program and research adminstr. U.S. Office Edn., Washington, 1957—. Cons. Conf. Bd. Math. Scis. Served to lt. comdr. USNR, 1942-45. Mem. A.A.A.S., N.E.A., Am. Math. Soc., Nat. Council Tchrs. Math., Math. Assn. Am., Res. Officer Assn., Sigma Xi. Lutheran. Author: Mathematics in Colleges and Universities, 1965; Recent Trends in Soviet Scientific and Technical Education, 1964; Soviet Education Programs, 1960; Aspects of Undergraduate Training in the Mathematical Sciences, 1967; NDEA Fellowships for College Teaching, 1971. Home: 6008 Utah Av NW Washington DC 20015 Office: 400 Maryland Av SW Washington DC 20202

LINDSAY, BRYAN EUGENE, educator; b. Bklyn., Sept. 19, 1931; s. Eugene Fenton and Evelyn (Moore) L.; B.A., Troy State Coll., 1956; M.A., George Peabody Coll. Tchrs., 1962, Ph.D., 1966; m. Mary Ray Moore, children—Eric Evan, Christy, Alyson, Tracey, Jason Moore. Choral, stage band dir. Choctawatchee High Sch., Shalimar, Fla., 1956-61; chmn. dept. humanities, dir. music Okaloosa-Walton Jr. Coll., Valparaiso, Fla., 1965-69; chmn. gen. studies humanities program, prof. humanities Eastern Ky. U., Richmond, 1969-72; mem. staff Center Humanities, Converse Coll., Spartanburg, S.C., 1972—. Mem. Specialist workshop for gifted and talented, Gifted Program Devel. Sect., Ill., Dept. Edn., 1970—. Served with USAF, 1951-54. Nat. Def. Edn. Act fellow fine arts and humanities, 1961-64, Inst. fellow in counseling, guidance, 1960; recipient Composer's award A.S.C.A.P., 1963, 65. Mem. A.S.C.A.P., Nat. Acad. Rec. Arts and Scis., Nat. Assn. Jazz Educators (S.E. divisional coordinator 1972—), Nat. Assn. Humanities Edn. nat. dir., nat. membership chmn. 1972—), Am. Film Inst., S.C. Music Educators Assn., Music Educators Nat. Conf., World Poetry Soc. Intercontinental. Author more than 50 published poems; composer more than 50 compositions. Home: 109 Greenbriar Rd Spartanburg SC 29302 Office: Box 381 Converse Coll Spartanburg SC 29301

LINDSAY, CHARLES SIDNEY, architect; b. Tucker, Ga., July 13, 1919; s. Paul Leonard and Gussie (Chewning) L.; B.S., Ga. Inst. Tech., 1942, B.S. in Architecture, 1942; m. Glenna Stubley, Dec. 14, 1946; children—Glenn, Leonard, Carolyn, Richard, Charles. Jr. architect TVA, Knoxville, 1942, 46; partner firm Lindsay & Maples, Inc., Knoxville, 1947—, pres., 1970-74. Dir. Cloverleaf Corp. Adviser Tenn. Arts Commn., 1969-72; mem. Maryville (Tenn.) Bd. of Appeals, 1960-68. Served to capt. USMCR, 1942-46. Decorated Bronze Star. Mem. A.I.A. (pres. East Tenn. chpt. 1963), Tenn. Soc. Architects (pres. 1964). Democrat. Methodist. Club: Green Meadow Country (pres. 1965) (Alcoa, Tenn.). Home: 1318 Young Av Maryville TN 37801 Office: 1301 Hannah St Knoxville TN 37901

LINDSAY, EDWARD WILLIAMS, vacuum system co. exec.; b. Boyce, Va., Aug. 24, 1921; s. Winston Southgate and Marjorie (Harris) L.; student U. Tex., 1939-40; B.S. in Elec. Engring., Ala. Poly. Inst. (now Auburn U.), 1943, postgrad., 1946-47; postgrad. U. Pitts., 1951-52; m. Margaret Ruth Upton, June 24, 1948; children—Edward Williams, Winston, Margaret. Research engr. Westinghouse Electric Corp., Pitts., 1943-50, sr. design engr., 1950-56, sr. engr., 1957-63; chief research, devel. So. States Equipment Corp., Hampton, Ga., 1956; v.p., gen. mgr. Vacu-Maid, Inc., Ponca City, Okla., 1963—. Mem. Penn Hills (Pa.) Com. Republican party, 1958-61. Trustee Lindsay Trust. Named Boss of Year, Ponca City Jr. C. of C., 1973. Registered profl. engr., Pa. Mem. I.E.E.E. (Best Paper award Pitts. chpt. 1956), Built-In Cleaning Systems Inst., Antique Wireless Assn., Antique Radio Club Am., Eta Kappa Nu, Sigma Pi. Kiwanian. Clubs: Cotillion (Wilkinsburg, Pa.), Sylvan Canoe (Verona, Pa.). Home: 21 Hillcrest Rd Ponca City OK 74601 Office: PO Drawer 1708 Ponca City OK 74601

LINDSAY, HAGUE LELAND, JR., educator; b. Fort Worth, Jan. 24, 1929; s. Hague Leland and Rebah (Albright) L.; B.A., Tex. Christian U., 1949; M.A., U. Tex., 1951, Ph.D. (NSF fellow 1957), 1958; m. Elizabeth Anne Maust, Sept. 1, 1956; children—Carol Anne, Robert Landon, Dana Elizabeth, John Leland. Mem. faculty U. Tulsa, 1956—, asso. prof. zoology, 1965—. Fishery biologist Corps Engrs., Tulsa dist., 1961. Chmn. Redbud Valley Project Com., 1973. Served with AUS, 1954-56. NSF grantee, 1958-59, Faculty Research grantee, 1970. Mem. Tulsa C. of C. (mem. com. 1973), Tex. Herpetological So. (sec. 1952), A.A.A.S., Okla. Acad. Sci., Southwestern Assn. Naturalists, Am. Soc. Ichthyologists and Herpetologists, Am. Fisheries Soc., U. Tex. Ex-Students Assn. (pres. Tulsa 1960), Sigma Xi. Democrat. Mem. Ch. of Christ. Home: 8518 E 35th St Tulsa OK 74145

LINDSAY, JOHN CALVIN, concrete products co. exec.; b. Oklahoma City, June 20, 1924; s. Murray Dual and Freda Christine (Nau) L.; student Okla. State U., 1943—; m. Syble Charline Piatt, Mar. 24, 1943; children—Carla (Mrs. Robt. Michael Barber), Calvin Glen, Cindy (Mrs. Griffin West Graham). Draftsman Harter Concrete Products, Inc., 1946-47, chief draftsman, 1947-65, prodn. mgr. 1965-69, div. mgr. 1969—; v.p. Heritage Concrete Products, Inc., Oklahoma City, 1971—. Served with USAAF, 1943-46. Decorated Air medal, D.F.C. Home: 1718 Oxford Way Oklahoma City OK 73120 Office: 1628 W Main Oklahoma City OK 73106

LINDSAY, JOSEPH LLOYD, III, dentist; b. Tulsa, Aug. 25, 1940; s. Joseph Lloyd, Jr. and Gennevive (Hollabaugh) L.; student U. Tenn., 1958-60, 61-64, D.D.S., 1964; student Millsaps Coll., Jackson, Miss., summers 1959-60; m. Sandra Faye Brown, June 12, 1963; children—Jeffery Scott, Christie Delane, Jennifer Lynn, Abby Kathleen. Individual practice dentistry, Slidell, La., 1967—; mem. staff Slidell Meml. Hosp. Adult adviser Com. United for Prevention of Illegal Drugs, 1970—; scoutmaster East Carolina council Boy Scouts Am., 1964-67, cubmaster, 1967-70; Ward 9 mem. St. Tammany Parish Sch. Bd., 1971—. Republican mem. Municipal Exec. Com., 1970-71, now mem. parish Exec. Rep. Com.; campaign mgr. Citizens for Nixon, Slidell, 1968; adult adviser Teenage Republicans, Slidell, 1969—. Served to lt. comdr. Dental Corps, USNR. Recipient Eagle Scout award Boy Scouts Am., 1955, Order of Arrow, 1957, Scouters Leadership and Tng. award, 1966, Green Band award, 1967; named Outstanding Young Man of Year, Jr. C. of C., 1969. Mem. Am., La. dental assns., Acad. Gen. Dentistry, Royal Soc. Health, Sigma Phi Epsilon, Xi Psi Phi. Mem. Christian Ch. (deacon). Kiwanian (Kiwanian of Year 1971), Elk. Club: Slidell Country. Home: 152 Pinewood Dr Slidell LA 70458 Office: 401 Pontchastrain Dr Slidell LA 70458

LINDSEY, D. RUTH, corrective therapist, educator; b. Kingfisher, Okla., Oct. 26, 1926; d. Lewis H. and Kenyon (King) Lindsey; B.S., Okla. State U., 1948; M.S., U. Wis., 1954; P.E.D., Ind. U., 1965. Faculty health phys. edn. and recreation Okla. State U., 1948-50, 56—, Monticello Coll., Godfrey, Ill., 1951-54, DePauw U., 1954-56. Counselor, Camp Waldemar, Hunt, Tex., 1948-56; cons. Payne County Child Welfare Dept. and County Health Dept.; fencing cons. Olympic Devel. Com., 2d Nat. Inst. Girls and Women's Sports, 1965; Okla. liaison Nat. Task Force on Perceptual Motor Devel., 1969-70; dir. Workshop on Phys. Edn. for Mentally Retarded, 1967; mem. Gov.'s Phys. Fitness Council, 1966, 69. Bd. dirs. Payne County Sheltered Workshop. Recipient award Danforth Found., 1944. Mem. Amateur Fencers League Am., Nat. Fencing Coaches Assn. Am., Am.

(nat. membership chmn.), Okla. (past v.p.) assns. health, phys. edn. and recreation, So., Nat. assns. phys. edn. for coll. women, Okla. Bd. Women's Ofcls. (past chmn.), Am. Corrective Therapy Assn. Republican. Baptist. Author: (with Jones, Whitley) Body Mechanics, 1968; (with Corbin, Dowell, others) Concepts in Physical Education, 1970; A Survey and Critical Analysis of Practices Found in Selected Commercial Reducing Salons, 1971. Contbr. articles to profl. jours., mags. Home: 824 Ranch Dr Stillwater OK 74074 Office: Okla State U Stillwater OK 74074

LINDSEY, EDWARD STORMONT, educator, surgeon; b. West Palm Beach, Fla., June 3, 1930; s. Edward Austin and Jane (Stormont) L.; B.S., Tulane U., 1951, M.D., 1958, M.Med.Sci., 1968; m. Margaret Ann Turfitt, Oct. 20, 1953; children—Ann Stormont, Myron Turfitt. Intern Tulane U. Service, Charity Hosp. La., New Orleans, 1958-59, resident, 1959-64, asst. prof. surgery, 1966-69, asso. prof., 1969—; Nat. Heart Inst. fellow U. Edinburgh (Scotland), 1964-65; mem. staff So. Bapt. Hosp., Hotel Dieu Hosp., Touro Infirmary. Cons. several hosps. Served with USNR, 1952-55. Fellow A.C.S.; mem. Am. Assn. Thoracic Surgery, Transplantation Soc., Am. Thoracic Soc., Am. Assn. U. Profs., N.Y. Acad. Scis. Assn. Acad. Surgery, Am. Soc. Artificial Internal Organs, Oscar Creech Surg. Soc. (v.p.), Kappa Sigma. Presbyn. Clubs: Essex, Azalea (New Orleans). Contbr. to profl. jours. Home: 4 Rosa Park New Orleans LA 70115 Office: 1430 Tulane Av New Orleans LA 70112

LINDSEY, H. EDWARD, JR., oil well service co. exec.; b. Atlanta, Dec. 17, 1926; s. Hiram Edward D. and Carolyn (Spraggins) L.; B.S., Ga. Inst. Tech., 1948; m. Vangie Theis, Aug. 14, 1954; children—Kristin, Stephen C. Sales engr. Kobe, Inc., Huntington Park, Cal., 1948-50, Internat. Harvester Co., Chgo., 1950-52; pres., owner MWL Tool & Supply Co., Midland, Tex., 1952—; pres. Diamond Oil Well Drilling Co., Midland, 1961-72, Helco Fishing Tools, Inc., 1969-74, Bond-Coat, Inc., 1969-74. Served with USNR, 1943-46. Mem. Soc. Petroleum Engrs., Aircraft Owners and Pilots Assn., Am. Petroleum Inst. Baptist. Mason (Shriner), Rotarian. Clubs: Midland Petroleum, Midland Country. Home: 1611 Gulf St Midland TX 79701 Office: PO Drawer 631 Midland TX 79701

LINDSEY, JAMES LESLIE, mining engr.; b. Hopkinsville, Ky., May 16, 1910; s. James Leslie and Mamie (Stone) L.; student pub. schs., Hopkinsville; m. Imogene Dunning, Nov. 18, 1934; children—Arkie Hank, James Philip. Mine supt. Nashville & W.Ky. Coal Cos., 1950-57; gen. supt. Chem. Coke Co., Dawson Springs, Ky., 1957-60; supt. Rialto Coal Co., Inc., Madisonville, Ky., 1963-69, receiver, 1970. Mem. Nortonville City Council, 1963-69; mem. Hopkins County Joint Planning Commn., 1967—. Mem. Ky. Mining Inst., Nat., Ky. (past treas.) socs. profl. engrs., Am. Congress on Surveying and Mapping. Mem. Disciples of Christ Ch. Mason (Shriner). Home: Route 1 Nortonville KY 42442

LINDSEY, JAMES LOUIS, civil engr.; b. Statesboro, Ga., Dec. 12, 1922; s. Walter Mason and Birdie Mae (Perkins) L.; B.S., The Citadel, Charleston, S.C., 1949; M.S., Ga. Inst. Tech., 1951; m. Helen Delores Nelson, Apr. 28, 1952; children—James Louis, David J., Mark N., Robert A., Michael P. Engr., W.H. Armstrong, cons. engrs., Atlanta, 1949-56; owner J.L. Lindsey Co. Cons. Engrs., Albany, Ga., 1956-64; pres. Lindsey, Tucker & Ritter, Inc., cons. engrs., Albany, 1964—; partner Dougherty Blueprint Co., Inc., 1957—, Lindsey, Sperry & Lewis, 1963—. Mem. Gov.'s Bd. Engring. Rev., 1961-62, Albany-Dougherty County Planning Commn., 1963-67. Pres., Albany YMCA, 1970-71. Served to capt. USAAF, 1942-46; CBI. Decorated Air medal with oak leaf cluster, D.F.C. Fellow Am. Soc. C.E. (past pres. Albany br.); mem. Nat. Soc. Profl. Engrs., Am. Cons. Engrs. Council. Rotarian (pres. Albany club 1973-74). Club: Flint Skeet and Trap. Important works include Bobs Candy Co., USMC Supply Depot, Albany, Columbus-Muscogee County Courthouse, Columbus, Ga. Home: 1614 Lynwood Lane Albany GA 31707 Office: 423 Pine Av Albany GA 31702

LINDSEY, THOMAS FRANCIS, dentist; b. Frederick, Md., Oct. 6, 1937; s. William Francis and Elizabeth Mae (Cramer) L.; B.A., George Washington U., 1959, M.A., 1964; D.D.S., Georgetown U., 1969; m. Eleanor Jane Hendricks, May 6, 1961; children—Sherrill, Melinda, Von Dubell, Hendricks, Angela. Tchr. pub. schs. Arlington County (Va.), 1959-65; dir. instrn. Reading Dynamics of D.C., Inc., 1965-69; individual practice dentistry, Arlington, Va., 1969—; instr. No. Va. Community Coll. Dental Aux. Continuing Edn. Program, 1970-72; pres. Ernest, Inc., 1969-73. Adv. council for dental programs No. Va. Community Coll., 1973-74; mem. North VA Dental Soc. Speakers Bur., 1970-72. Mem. Am., Va. dental assns., No. Va. Dental Soc., Phi Kappa Delta, Delta Tau Delta. Mem. Ch. of Jesus Christ of Latter-day Saints. Home: 6623 Melrose Dr McLean VA 22101 Office: 5730 Washington Blvd Arlington VA 22205

LINDVEIT, EARL WAYNE, govt. ofcl.; b. Elmont, N.Y., June 6, 1926; s. Alfred and Julie (Jacobsen) L.; A.B., Bethany Coll., 1950; M.A., Am. U., 1954, Ph.D., 1958; m. Sheila Rogers Brown, May 31, 1958; children—Kristin Hill, Eric Brown. Mem. profl. staff U.S. Senate Space Com., Washington, 1959-61; regional mgr. def. systems div. Gen. Motors Corp., Washington, 1961-62; exec. sec. Com. on Sponsored Research, Am. Council on Edn., Washington, 1962-65; sr. scientist Battelle Meml. Inst., Washington, 1965-68; sr. research adminstr. U.S. Dept. Housing and Urban Devel., Washington, 1968—. Cons., Brookings Inst., Inst. for Def. Analyses, Pres.'s Com on Scientists and Engrs. Pres. Westmoreland Citizens Assn., 1970-72; mem. adv. council Aerospace Edn. Found, 1964-66; adv. bd. Washington Colloquium on Sci. and Soc., 1963-66. Served with USAAF, 1944-46. Fellow A.A.A.S.; mem. Acad. Polit. and Social Sci., Am. Polit. Sci. Assn., Am. Soc. for Pub. Adminstrn. Episcopalian. Author: Scientists in Government, 1960. Home: 2 Carvel Circle Washington DC 20016 Office: 451 7th St SW Washington DC 20410

LING, CYRIL CURTIS, ednl. assn. exec., educator; b. Detroit, Jan. 28, 1936; s. Robert Harold and Marie Magdalen (Guilloz) L.; B.S., Wayne State U., 1957, M.B.A. (teaching fellow), 1958; D.Bus. Adminstrn., Ind. U., 1962; m. Beatrice Elaine Panizzoli, Jan. 25, 1957 (div.); children—Robin Kyle, Renee Hollis, Rosyln Elaine. Faculty lectr. mgmt. Ind. U., Bloomington, 1959-60; asst. prof. mgmt. U. Cin., 1960-63, asso. prof., 1963-66; asso. prof. bus. adminstrn. Richmond (Va.) U., 1966-67, also dir. Mgmt. Center; mng. dir. Am. Assembly Collegiate Schs. Bus., 1967-71, exec. v.p., St. Louis, 1971-72, exec. v.p., Washington, 1972—. Cons. in bus. mgmt. to hosps., govt. agys., also tchr. Mem. United Appeal, div. co-chmn., 1964-65; mem. P.T.A., officer, 1969-71. Bd. dirs. Mgmt. Council U.S.; trustee Joint Council on Econ. Edn. Mem. Acad. Mgmt., Beta Gamma Sigma (exec. v.p. 1971—), Psi Chi, Omicron Delta Kappa, Sigma Iota Epsilon, Pi Kappa Alpha. Mason (Shriner). Club: Cosmos. Author: The Management of Personnel Relations: History and Origins, 1965. Editor: Am. Assembly Collegiate Schs. Bus. Bull. Home: 4970 Battery Lane Bethesda MD Office: 1755 Massachusetts Av NW Washington DC 20036

LING, JAMES J., electronics co. exec.; b. Hugo, Okla.; s. Henry William and Mary (Jones) L.; ed. St. John's Coll. Prep. Sch., Shreveport, La. Pres. Ling Electric Co.; pres., chmn. bd., dir. Ling-Temco Electronics, Dallas; chmn. bd., chief exec. officer Ling-Altec Electronics, Dallas, Ling-Temco-Vought, Inc., Dallas; dir. 1st Nat. Bank, Dallas, Dallas Cowboys Football Club. Bd. dirs. Dallas Community Chest, Dallas Symphony Orch., S.W. Center for Advanced Studies; trustee, tech. adv. com. So. Meth. U. Found. for Sci. and Engring.; vice chmn., dir. Dallas Civic Opera Assn.; bd. dirs., mem. chpt. plan com. United Fund Dallas County; dir., mem. council Cotton Bowl Council; trustee St. Mark's Sch. Tex.; mem. adv. council Engring. Found., U. Tex. Served with USNR, World War II; PTO. Mem. Hudson Inst. Home: 10300 Gaywood Rd Dallas TX 75229 Office: PO Box 5003 Dallas TX 75222

LING, JAMES THOMAS, mfg. co. adminstr.; b. Dallas, May 21, 1944; s. James Joseph and Dorothy (Hill) L.; student So. Meth. U., 1962-63, North Tex. State U., 1964, N.Y. Inst. Finance, 1965; m. T. Carole Pavlic, Aug. 15, 1967; 1 son, James Joseph II. Vice pres. Ling & Co., Inc. (name now LCI, Inc.), Dallas, 1964-70, sec., 1966—, also dir.; asst. to chmn., pres. Omega-Alpha, Inc., Dallas, 1971—. Club: Brook Hollow Golf. Office: PO Box 50046 Dallas TX 75250

LING, SUILIN, mgmt. cons.; b. Shanghai, China, Oct. 13, 1930; s. Chunchen and Maisan (Dunn) L.; came to U.S., 1949, naturalized, 1963; B.S., U. Mich., 1952; Ph.D., Columbia, 1961; m. Avril Marjorie Kathleen Button, Apr. 4, 1964; children—Christopher Charles, Charmian Avril. Mech. engr. Ebasco Services, Inc., 1953-54; with research div. Foster Wheeler Corp., 1954-64; mgmt. cons. The Emerson Cons., Inc., 1964-65; sr. economist Communications Satellite Corp., 1965-67; asst. dir. econ. and mgmt. planning Northrop-Page Communications Engrs., Inc., 1967-69, chief economist, 1969-70; dir., chief economist Teleconsult Inc., Washington, 1970—; lectr. econs. Bernard M. Baruch Sch. Bus. and Pub. Adminstrn., City Coll. N.Y. Mem. Am. Mgmt. Assn., Am. Econ. Assn., Am. Soc. M.E., Am. Acad. Polit. and Social Sci. Author: Economies of Scale in the Steam-Electric Power Generating Industry, 1964. Home: 2401 Calvert St NW Washington DC 20008 Office: 2918 M St NW Washington DC 20007

LINGAFELT, CHARLES RICHARD, telephone co. exec.; b. Gretna, Va., Sept. 19, 1934; s. Charles Edwin and Essie Jeanette (Walker) L.; student Danville Tech. Inst., 1954; m. Glenna Tillotson, Aug. 14, 1955; children—Steven, Phillip. With Piedmont Broadcasting Corp., 1953-56, Central Va. Broadcasting Corp., 1956-64; plant supt. Peoples Mut. Telephone Co., Gretna, Va., 1964—. Mem. Gretna Vol. Fire Dept. 1959—, 2d lt., 1965—. Baptist (deacon, supt. Sunday sch.) Home: PO Box 38 Gretna VA 24557 Office: PO Box 367 Gretna VA 24557

LINIADO, RALPH MARTIN, motor transp. co. exec.; b. Sebring, Fla., Sept. 18, 1944; s. Morris and Mildred (Massey) L.; B.S., Commonwealth U., Richmond, Va., 1966; m. Ethel Joy Korn, Oct. 29, 1966; children—Mark Elliot, David Michael. Auditor, Dept. Def., Washington, 1966-68; sr. staff internal auditor Colonial Stores, Inc., Atlanta, 1968-70; sec.-treas., dir. Theatres Service Co., Atlanta, 1970—; sec.-treas., dir. Tri-State Air Cargo Services, Inc., Atlanta, 1973—. Mem. Nat. Assn. Accountants, Am. Trucking Assn. (Nat. Accounting and Finance Council), Data Processing Mgmt. Assn. Home: 2953 Tilton Lane Atlanta GA 30340 Office: 830 Willoughby Way NE Atlanta GA 30301

LINK, ACREE SHREVE, dentist; b. Danville, Va., Mar. 20, 1925; s. Oscar Nathaniel and Lillie May (Shreve) L.; student Va. Poly. Inst., 1946-47; B.S., U. Richmond, 1950; D.D.S., Med. Coll. Va., 1954; m. Barbara DeHardit, Dec. 20, 1952; children—Teresa Joan, Acree Shreve, Michael Joseph. Individual practice dentistry, Newport News, Va., 1954—; mem. staff Riverside Hosp. Bd. dirs. Peninsula United Fund, 1956-59; bd. advs. Mary Immaculate Hosp., 1958-60. Served with AUS, 1943-46. Mem. Am., Va., Peninsula dental assns., Acad. Gen. Dentistry, Omicron Kappa Upsilon, Beta Beta Beta, Phi Kappa Sigma, Psi Omega. Roman Catholic. Club: James River Country. Home: 1201 Mallicotte Lane Newport News VA 23606 Office: 9296 Warwick Blvd Newport News VA 23607

LINK, JOSEPH FRANCIS, dentist; b. Dubuque, Ia., Jan. 9, 1917; s. Nicholas John and Martha (McCullough) L.; student Loras Coll., 1934-35; D.D.S., Coll. Dentistry, State U. Ia., 1939; postgrad. Old Dominion U., 1970-73; m. June Roslyn Murray; 6 children. Individual practice dentistry, Dubuque, 1939-41; commd. lt. (j.g.) U.S. Navy, 1941, advancing through grades to capt., 1955; chief dental service, dental officer U.S.S. Repose, 1947-48; chief dental service Naval Hosp., Camp Lejeune, N.C., 1960-62; chief dental service, cons. instr. dental residency tng. program oral surgery Naval Hosp., Great Lakes, Ill., 1962-67; exec. officer Naval Dental Clinic, Norfolk, Va., from 1967; now instr. dental hygiene old Dominion U., Norfolk; lectr. in field. Diplomate Am. Bd. Oral Surgery (recipient Meritorious Service medal 1971). Fellow Am. Coll. Dentists; mem. Am. Dental Assn., Am. Soc. Oral Surgeons, Am. Dental Soc. Anesthesiology, Inc., Am. Coll. Dentists, Pierre Fauchard Acad., Internat. Assn. Oral Surgeons. K.C. Club: Ryan (pres. 1971—) (Tidewater, Va.). Contbr. articles to profl. jours. Home: 1003 Hanover Av Norfolk VA 23508 Office: Old Dominion U Norfolk VA 23508

LINK, MAE MILLS (MRS. S. GORDDEN LINK), historian; b. Corbin, Ky., May 14, 1915; d. William Speed and Florence (Estes) Mills; B.S., George Peabody Coll. Tchrs., 1936; M.A., Vanderbilt U., 1937; Ph.D., Am. U., 1951; grad. Air War Coll., 1965; m. S. Gordden Link, Jan. 11, 1936. Instr. social sci. Oglethorpe U., 1938-39; instr. English, Drury Coll., 1940-41; asso. dir. edn. Ga. Warm Springs Found., 1941-42; mil. historian Hdqrs. Army Air Forces, 1943-45, Office Mil. History, Dept. Army, 1945-51; spl. asst. to surgeon gen. and sr. med. historian USAF, Washington, 1951-62; cons. documentation and space medicine historian NASA, Washington, 1962-64, coordinator documentation and life scis. historian, 1964-70; research asso. Ohio State U. Found., 1970-72; trustee, dir. history fellows Amos R. Koontz Meml. Found., Riverton, Va., 1972—. Trustee D.C. area Orgn. Advancement Coll. Teaching. Trustee, Univ. Press Fund. Recipient Meritorious Service award USAF, 1955, Outstanding Performance award, 1956, 62; Friday Nighters cup, 1960. Fellow Am. Med. Writers Assn. (dir. Middle Atlantic region); mem. Aerospace Med. Assn. (standing com. sci. communication in bioastronautics and space medicine), Am. Inst. Aeros. and Astronautics (hist. adv. com.), Air Force Hist. Found. (charter), Am. Assn. Med. History, Assn. Mil. Surgeons, Internat. Congress History Medicine, Soc. History Tech., Am. Hist. Assn., Societe International d'Histoire de la Medicine, Am. Assn. U. Women. Republican. Episcopalian. Club: Garden of Va.; Nat. Space. Author: (with others) Medical Support of the Army Air Forces in World War II, 1955; Annual Reports of the U.S. Air Force Medical Service, 1949-62; Space Medicine in Project Mercury, 1965; co-author US/USSR Joint Publ. Foundations of Space Biology and Medicine. Editor: U.S. Air Force Med. Service Digest, 1957-62. Contbr. to Ency. Brit., Collier's Ency., Funk and Wagnall's Standard Reference Ency., New Ency., profl. jours. Home: Dellbrook Riverton VA 22651 Office: Koontz Center Advanced Studies Riverton VA 22651

LINK, S. GORDDEN, educator, author; b. Chgo., Apr. 9, 1907; s. Joseph S. and Florence (Tannenholtz) L.; B.S., N.Y. U., 1929, A.M., 1930; M.Ed., Harvard, 1932; Ph.D., George Peabody Coll. for Tchrs., 1938; postgrad. Yale, 1931, Columbia, 1935, George Washington U., 1956, Washington Sch. of Psychiatry, 1958; m. Dr. Mae Mills, Jan. 11, 1936. Prof. Limestone Coll., 1930-34; vis. prof. Northeastern U., 1932-33; lectr. George Peabody Coll. for Tchrs., 1934-38; asst. pastor McKendree Meth. Ch., Nashville, 1937-38; prof., chaplain Oglethorpe U., 1938-39; vis. prof. St. Lawrence U., 1939-40; dir. tng., personnel Microstat Corp., 1941-42; dir. writing workshop, McCoy Coll., Johns Hopkins, 1947-51; cons. office Chief of Staff, U.S. Army, 1948-49; dir. Washington Counseling Center, 1949-61; chmn. div. humanities Anne Arundel Community Coll., Severna Park, Md., 1962-64, prof. English, poet in residence, 1962-66; dir. liberal arts Southeastern U., Washington, 1966-71; professorial lectr. grad. div. Loyola Coll., Balt., 1962-64. Exec. dir. Orgn. Advancement Coll. Teaching, 1964—; pres. Center for Advanced Studies, Amos R. Koontz Meml. Found., Dellbrook campus, Riverton, Va.; writer in residence Shenandoah Coll. and Conservatory Music, 1971—; dir. Dellbrook-Shenandoah Coll. Writers' Conf., 1969—. Trustee Amos R. Koontz Meml. Found. Chmn. Univ. Press Fund. Served from 2d lt. to lt. col. M.I. AUS, 1942-47; lt. col. Res. ret. Decorated Army Commendation medal with Oak Leaf Cluster, Bronze Star (U.S.), Army-Navy Air Force medal, first class (China), Spl. Breast Order Yun Hui with Rosette, Breast Order Pau Tang with Rosette (China). Fellow Am. Assn. Social Psychiatry (Merrill Moore award 1960); mem. Latin Am. Inst. Washington (past pres.). Poetry Soc. Am. (Lois Ridge award 1948, James Joyce award 1971), Poetry Soc. Va., Baker St. Irregulars, Mil. Order World Wars, Res. Officers Assn. (past v.p. for army, past chaplain D.C. dept.). Republican. Methodist. Author: One Small Unwilling Captain: A Study of the Japanese Mind, 1937; The German Prisoner of War, 1944; The Engineers in the Pacific, 1947; Pocket Guide to Germany, 1951, Three Poems for Now, 1953. Contbr. to poetry anthologies. Home: Dellbrook Riverton VA 22651 Office: Center for Advanced Studies Dellbrook Campus Riverton VA 22651

LINKOVICH, WILLIAM, civil engr.; b. Winsted, Conn., Oct. 7, 1943; s. Michael and Elizabeth Ruth (Houser) L.; student Stetson U., 1962-64; B.S., U. Fla., 1966. Dist. drainage engr. Fla. Dept. Transp., Lake City, 1971—. Registered profl. engr., Fla. Mem. Fla. Engring. Soc., Nat. Soc. Profl. Engrs. Elk. Home: Route 6 Box 629 Lake City FL 32055 Office: PO Box 1089 Lake City FL 32055

LINN, ROBERT JOSEPH, physician; b. Birmingham, July 11, 1926; s. Jesse Edwards and Mary Alif (Mulvehill) L.; student Birmingham So. Coll., 1942-43; B.A., Vanderbilt U., 1946, M.D., 1950; m. Marion Joanne Lovell, Aug. 30, 1949; children—Mary Louise (Mrs. Scott Peyton Fitzhugh), Joseph Lovell, Margaret Ruth, David Robert. Intern Johns Hopkins Hosp., Balt., 1950-51; resident Vanderbilt U., Nashville, 1951-58; practice medicine, specializing in radiology, Nashville, 1958—; partner firm Radiology Consultants Inc., 1972—; radiologist Madison (Tenn.) Hosp., 1962—; mem. staff Parkview Hosp., Westside Hosp., Miller Hosp., all Nashville; clin. instr. radiology Sch. Medicine Vanderbilt U., 1960—. Pres. Radiol. Services Inc., 1972—. Served to lt. USMCR, 1952-54. Diplomate Am. Bd. Radiology. Mem. Am. Coll. Radiology, Tenn., So. med. socs., Tenn., Middle Tenn. radiol. socs., Alpha Omega Alpha, Kappa Alpha. Presbyn. Rotarian. Contbr. articles to profl. jours. Home: 6532 Jocelyn Hollow Rd Nashville TN 37205 Office: 2119 Hayes St Nashville TN 37203

LINNE, AUBREY ARTHUR, prodn. exec.; b. Centralia, Ill., Apr. 19, 1939; s. Aubrey Herman and Mary Lois (Webb) L.; B.S., Tex. Christian U., 1961; m. Peggy Belle Runkle, Jan. 1959; children—Tami Caye, Larry Glen. Profl. football player Balt. Colts, 1961, Toronto (Ont., Can.) Argonauts, 1962, Edmonton (Alta., Can.) Eskimos, 1963; operations research Collins Radio Co., Dallas, 1964-69; owner Creative Bus. Cons., Dallas, 1969-73; bus. systems analyst, prodn. mgr. B.P. Industries, Pubs., Midland, Tex., 1973—; v.p. Creative Mortgage Corp., Dallas; seminar instr. S.B.A.-El Centro Coll., Dallas. Pres., Teen Power, 1971, S.W. Youth Football Conf., 1973; capt. United Fund, 1966-70; mem. Goals for Dallas Com., 1970, YMCA Athletic Com., 1970. Precinct committeeman Democratic Party, 1972—. Mem. Richardson (pres. 1969), Tex. (dir. pub. relations 1971, pres.'s cabinet 1972), Dallas (met. chmn. 1969) jaycees, Jr. Chamber Internat. Senate (sec.-treas. Tex. 1972). Methodist. Club: Optimist. Author: Football Fundamentals Handbook, 1973. Editor: Texas Jaycee mag., 1970. Home: 2405 Seaboard St Midland TX 79701 Office: PO Box 3040 Midland TX 79701

LINNENBERG, CLEM CHARLES, JR., economist; b. Houston, May 20, 1912; s. Clem Charles and Maggie (White) L.; student So. Meth. U., 1930; B.A., M.A., U. Tex., 1933; Ph.D., Yale, 1941; postgrad. Am. U., 1954; m. Marianne Sakmann, Aug. 15, 1942. Economist, Dept. Labor, 1934-35, Social Security Bd., 1936, antitrust div. Dept. Justice, 1938-39, Bur. Budget, 1939-51; program planning officer Office Sec. Commerce, 1951-53; chief econ. analysis sect. Office Internat. Trade, Dept. Commerce, 1953; transp. economist Gen. Services Adminstrn., 1953-54, Dept. Agr., 1954-59; chief div. statistics and studies Office Vocational Rehab., Dept. Health, Edn. and Welfare, 1959-62; economist USPHS, 1962-69; ind. cons. in econs. and statistics, 1969—. Lectr. in transp. Georgetown U., 1956-57. Mem. Am. Pub. Health Assn., Phi Beta Kappa, Pi Sigma Alpha, Sigma Delta Pi. Democrat. Methodist. Author: Twixt Chaos and Conformism, 1950; The Agricultural Exemptions in Interstate Trucking: Mend Them or End Them?, 1960; Economics in Program Planning for Health, 1966; Organizing and Staffing for the Program Planning Function, 1967; other monographs. Home and office: 3812 Benton St NW Washington DC 20007

LINSKIE, GEORGE ANTHONY, constrn. co. exec.; b. Dallas, Nov. 20, 1915; s. John Joseph and Zoda (Dorsa) L.; M.E., Tex. A. and M. U., 1938; m. Helen Dorothy Lee, Apr. 9, 1939. Mech. engr. Rollins & Forrest Cons. Engrs., Dallas, 1939; mech. engr. U.S. Corps Engrs., Denison, Tex., 1940-42, head mech. engring. dept., 1942-45; v.p. Farwell Co., Inc., Dallas, 1946-50; founder, pres. George Linskie Co., Inc., Dallas, 1950—; dir. Grand Ave. Bank and Trust, Dallas, Gibraltar Life Ins. Co. Chmn. budget, finance com. Children's Med. Center, Dallas, 1968-71, 1st v.p., 1968-71, pres., 1971-73; chmn. task force gen. aviation subcom. Dallas Aviation Com., 1968—. Bd. dirs. State Fair Tex. Mem. Am. Soc. Heating, Refrigerating and Air-Conditioning Engrs., Inc (nat. bd. dirs. 1962-64; Nat. Distinguished Pub. Service award 1970), Mech. Contractors Assn. Tex. (pres. Tex. 1958), Dallas A&M Club, Salesmanship Club Dallas, Engrs. Club Dallas (past pres., chmn. bd. 1956-57). Club: Dallas Country. Home: 5346 Edmondson Dallas TX 75209 Office: Linwood Bldg 2608 Inwood Rd Dallas TX 75235

LINTON, CALVIN DARLINGTON, educator, coll. dean; b. Kensington, Md., June 11, 1914; s. Irwin Helfenstein and Helen Pauline (Grier) L.; student Erskine Coll., S.C., 1931-32; A.B., George Washington U., 1935; A.M., Johns Hopkins, 1939, Ph.D., 1940; m. Jeanne Etling LeFevre, Aug. 1, 1951. Lecture reporter, instr. stenotyping Temple Bus. Sch., Washington, 1935-36; instr. English Wheaton (Ill.) Coll. summer 1938, Johns Hopkins, 1939-40; asso. prof., chmn. English dept. Queens Coll., N.C., 1940-41; asst. prof. English, George Washington U., 1945-46, asso. prof., 1946-48, prof. English lit., 1948—, asst. dean Columbian Coll., 1949-56, asso. dean 1956-57, dean, 1957—; lectr. lit. subjects WGMS, Washington,

1953-54, Folger Inst. Renaissance and 18th Century Studies. Cons. various govt. agys. in report writing. Vice chmn. Commn. Instns. Higher Edn., Middle States Assn. Served as lt. (j.g.), Office Sec. of Navy, 1941-43; lt. comdr. Minecraft Tng. Center, Norfolk, Va., 1943-45. Mem. Modern Lang. Assn. (program com.); Coll. English Assn., Modern Humanities Research Assn. (Am. chmn., sec., 1963—), Lit. Soc. Washington (pres. 1973-75), Eastern Assn. Deans (pres. 1965-66), Conf. Christianity and Lit. (pres. 1965-66). Presbyn. Clubs: Tudor and Stuart (Johns Hopkins); Cosmos (pres. 1973) (Washington). Author: Report Construction and Analysis (U.S. Map Service), 1953; How to Write Reports, 1954; Effective Writing, 1958. Contbr. articles to profl. jours. Home: 5216 Farrington Rd Washington DC 20016

LIPCHINSKY, ZELEK LAWRENCE, educator, curator; b. Detroit, June 8, 1938; s. Roy and Evaline (Askowitz) L.; A.A., U. Fla., 1958, B.S., 1960, M.S., 1963; postgrad. Clark U., 1967-68; m. Jacqueline Thomas, June 23, 1969; 1 dau. by previous marriage, Francine Lynn. Map librarian U. Fla., Gainesville, 1960-64; asst. prof., chmn. dept. geology and geography Berea (Ky.) Coll., 1964—; curator Burroughs Geol. Mus., Berea, Ky., 1964—; map librarian Clark U., Worcester, Mass., 1967-68. Mem. Am. Assn. U. Profs., Nat. Assn. Geology Tchrs., Am. Assn. Geographers, Ky. Geologic Soc., Ky. Acad. Scis. Democrat. Jewish religion. Home: 241 S Porter Dr Richmond KY 40475 Office: CPO Box 1105 Berea KY 40403

LIPMAN, IRA ACKERMAN, security service co. exec.; b. Little Rock, Nov. 15, 1940; s. Mark and Belle (Ackerman) L.; grad. Ohio Wesleyan U., 1960; LL.D., John Marshall U., 1970; m. Barbara Ellen Couch, July 5, 1970; children—Gustave K., Joshua S. Salesman and exec. Mark Lipman Service, Inc., Memphis, 1960-63; pres. Guardsmark, Inc., Memphis, 1963—, chief exec. officer, 1966—, also chmn. bd. Mem. Nat. Alliance Businessmen (Metro chmn. Memphis 1970-71), Internat. Assn. Chiefs Police, Am. Soc. Indsl. Security. Republican. Mem. B'nai B'rith. Club: Ridgeway Country (Memphis). Home: 4490 Park Av Memphis TN 38117 Office: 10 E 40th St New York City NY 10016 also 22 S 2d St Memphis TN 38103

LIPMAN, JAMES ALAN, electronics design engr.; b. N.Y.C., June 3, 1946; s. Stanley Arthur and Bernice (Menas) L.; B.E.E., Carnegie Inst. Tech., 1967; M.E.E., Carnegie-Mellon U., 1969. Design engr., semiconductor research and devel. lab. Tex. Instruments Inc., Dallas, 1968—. NSF fellow, 1967-68. Mem. I.E.E.E., Eta Kappa Nu. Home: 14018 Brookgreen Dr Dallas TX 75240 Office: 13500 N Central Expressway Dallas TX 75222

LIPNER, HARRY, educator; b. N.Y.C., Aug. 26, 1922; s. Samuel and Sarah (Linkoff) L.; B.S., L.I. U., 1942; M.S., U. Chgo., 1947; Ph.D., U. Ia., 1952; m. Ethel Lapis, Nov. 11, 1949; children—Laura Jean, Sandra (Mrs. Paul Shang), William Frederick, Michael Allen. Chemist Nat. Oil Products Co., Harrison, N.J., 1942-45; USPHS fellow Nat. Cancer Inst., 1952-54; instr. Chgo. Med. Sch., 1955; asst. prof. endocrinology - reproductive physiology, Fla. State U., Tallahassee, 1955-58, asso. prof., 1958-65, prof., 1965—. USPHS Sr. fellow Harvard Med. Sch., 1969-70. Mem. Soc. for Study Reprodn. (mem. edn. com. 1969-72), A.A.A.S., Am. Physiol. Soc., Endocrine Soc., Am. Soc. Zoologists, Sigma Xi. Author (with E. Frieden, H. Lipner) Biochemical Endocrinology of the Vertebrates. Mem. editorial bd. Endocrinology; rev. editor Biology of Reprodn. Home: 3214 Brookforest Dr Tallahassee FL 32303

LIPSCOMB, ALYS HARRIS, physician; b. Sassafras Ridge, Ky., July 13, 1915; s. Sydney Harris and Myrtle (Pledger) L.; M.S., U. Tenn., 1944, M.D., 1945. Intern, Cleve. Clinic, 1945-46, resident, 1946-48; practice medicine, specializing in internal medicine and nuclear medicine, Memphis, 1951—; instr. physiology U. Tenn. Coll. Medicine, 1942-43, instr. medicine, 1948-50, asst. prof., 1950-59, asso. clin. prof. medicine, 1965—, attending physician Thyroid Clinic, 1949—, asso. clin. prof. medicine, endocrinology, 1965—; cons. nuclear medicine dept. Methodist Hosp., Memphis; mem. staff City of Memphis Hosps., Meth., Baptist Meml., St. Joseph's, VA hosps. (all Memphis). Diplomate Am. Bd. Nuclear Medicine, Am. Bd. Internal Medicine. Fellow A.C.P.; mem. Memphis, Shelby County med. socs., A.M.A., Am. Soc. Internal Medicine, Soc. Nuclear Medicine, Memphis Acad. Internal Medicine (pres. 1966), Tenn. Diabetes Assn., Sigma Xi, Alpha Omega Alpha. Contbr. articles to profl. jours. Home: 35 N Cox Memphis TN 38104 Office: 188 S Bellevue Memphis TN 38104

LIPSCOMB, DAVID MILTON, educator; b. Morrill, Neb., Aug. 4, 1935; s. Roy Milton and Elsie (Schmidt) L.; B.A., U. Redlands, 1957, M.A., 1959; Ph.D., U. Wash., 1966; m. Dixie Lea Johnson, June 28, 1957; children—Scott, Steven, Shari Lea. Asst. prof. West Tex. State Coll., 1960-62; asst. prof. audiology and speech pathology U. Tenn., 1962-64, asso. prof., 1966-73, prof., 1973—; cons. Environmental Protection Agy.; sci. adv. bd. Environmental Def. Fund. Recipient U. Tenn. Alumni Pub. Service award, 1973. Fellow Am. Speech and Hearing Assn.; mem. Acoust. Soc. Am., So. Audiology Soc. (pres.-elect 1973), Am. Speech and Hearing Assn. (mem. legislative council 1972-73). Democrat. Author: Laboratory Techniques in the Study of the Ear, 1974; Noise: The Unwanted Sounds, 1974. Contbr. numerous articles to profl. jours. Home: 4524 Royalview Rd Knoxville TN 37921 Office: U Tenn Knoxville TN 37916

LIPSCOMB, THOMAS ABNER, dentist; b. Mineola, Tex., July 1, 1895; s. Charles Day and Sara Annie (Harris) L.; student North Tex. State U., 1917-18; D.D.S., Baylor U., 1922; m. Bera Oliver Billings, Dec. 2, 1950; 1 son, Thomas Abner. Pharmacist, Dallas, 1918-22; tchr. Baylor Dental Coll., Dallas, 1922-25; dentist, Southwest Med. Clinic, Dallas, 1924-32; individual practice denistry, Dallas, 1932-73. Co-founder Mid-Winter Dental Clinic, Dallas, 1929, mgr., 1938, 39, 40; cons. bd. trustees Baylor Dental Coll., 1949-55. Fellow Am. Coll. Dentistry; mem. Dallas County Dental Soc. (pres., 1942-43; named Dentist of Year 1970-71), Federation Dentaire Internationale, Tex. Dental Soc., Am. Dental Assn., Omicron Kappa Upsilon. Baptist. Mason. Home: 6615 Northport Dr Dallas TX 75230

LIPSEY, JOSEPH, JR., dept. store exec.; b. Selma, Ala., Sept. 12, 1934; s. Joseph and Anna (Bendersky) L.; student U. Colo., 1952; B.A., La. State U., 1955, LL.B., 1957; m. Betty Wellan, June 6, 1960; children—Debora Louise, Joseph III, Elizabeth Ann, Tami Leigh. Admitted to La. bar, 1957, Republic of Korea bar, 1958; practiced in Baton Rouge, 1960-64; mng. dir. Wellan's Dept. Store, Alexandria, La., 1965—; v.p., dir. Steinberg Sporting Center, Baton Rouge, 1967—; partner Gulf Purchasing Co. Lectr. mil. law and cts. martial La. State U., 1961-64; legal cons. U.S. Ambassador to Japan, 1958-59. State chmn. Nat. Library Week, 1967-70; mem. Tulane U. So. Assembly, 1969, Columbia U. Am. Assembly, 1971. Bd. dirs. Alexandria Country Day Sch., Rapides Parish Symphony Orch., Attakapas council Boy Scouts Am., Rapides United Givers Fund, La. State U. Found.; v.p. bd. dirs. Grand Isle Tarpon Rodeo Internat., 1965-73; chmn. COFLEX 1971. Served with USAF, 1957-60. Mem. Baton Rouge Shippers Assn. (pres. 1963), Internat. Bar Assn. Ryukyu Islands, Alexandria-Pineville (pres. 1971), La. (pres. 1974) chambers commerce, La., Parish bar assns., Omicron Delta Kappa, Zeta Beta Tau, Phi Delta Phi. Democrat. Jewish religion. Office: 1200 3d St Alexandria LA 71301

LIPSON, LEONARD BERGER, petroleum co. exec.; b. Chelsea, Mass., Mar. 2, 1922; s. Edward and Sara (Berger) L.; student Colo. Sch. Mines, 1940-41; B.A., U. Tex., 1942, M.A., 1946, Ph.D. in Physics and Math. (teaching fellow), 1953; m. Betty Cecile Hymans, Dec. 9, 1942; children—Lucienne Cecile, Nicole Gay. Sr. research physicist Mobil Oil Co., Dallas, 1948-54; asso. prof. engring. U. Houston, 1954-60; v.p. Mgmt. Decisions Inc., Houston, 1962-64; staff scientist Lockheed Corp., Houston, 1964-65, Atlanta, 1965-69; v.p. staff cons. Guernsey Petroleum Corp., Atlanta, 1969-72, New Orleans, 1972—. Instr., Ga. State U., Atlanta, part-time 1971; spl. lectr. U. New Orleans, 1973—. Mem. Soc. Petroleum Engrs., Am. Inst. Decision Scis., Internat. Assn. Math. Geology, Sigma Xi, Sigma Pi Sigma. Clubs: Petroleum, Plimsoll (New Orleans). Patentee in field. Contbr. articles to profl. jours. Home: 6042 Pontchartrain Blvd New Orleans LA 70124 Office: Oil and Gas Bldg New Orleans LA 70112

LIPTAK, GREGORY JAMES, cable co. exec.; b. Streator, Ill., Jan. 4, 1940; s. Clarence J. Genevieve A. (Comfort) L.; B.S., U. Ill., 1961, M.S., 1964; m. Stephanie Ann Smith, Oct. 29, 1966; children—Christine, Gregory. Newsman sta. WAND-TV, Decatur, Ill., 1965-66; program dir. Cox Cable Communications, Inc., Atlanta, 1966-68; v.p. LVO Cable, Inc., Tulsa, 1968—. Served to 1st lt., Signal Corps, AUS, 1961-63. Mem. Sigma Delta Chi. Roman Catholic. Home: 6762 S 71st St E Av Tulsa OK 74133 Office: PO Box 3423 Tulsa OK 74101

LIPTON, ROBERT ISRAEL, lawyer; b. N.Y.C., Dec. 11, 1920; s. Simon and Sadie (Berger) L.; B.S. in Commerce, U. N.C., 1942, J.D. with honors, 1946; m. Cecille Rosenblum, Sept. 9, 1947; children—Howard Alan, Lawrence Jay, Stuart Samuel. Admitted to N.C. bar, 1946; editor-in-chief N.C. Law Review, U. N.C., 1945-46; vis. prof. law U. N.C., 1959; practicing atty., Durham, N.C., 1946—, mem. firm Bryant, Lipton, Bryant & Battle, P.A., 1955—; dir numerous comml. corps. Pres., N.C. B'nal B'rith Assn., 1960-61; chmn. State N.C. United Jewish Appeal, 1952-54; del. Internat. Econ. Conf., Jerusalem, Israel, 1953. Bd. dirs. Durham United Fund, 1952-54, Silver Leukemia Found., Leo N. Levy Hosp., Duncan-Fletcher Found., Allied Arts, Inc.; vice chmn. B'nai B'rith Found. U.S. Served as pfc., USMC, 1942-43. Mem. Am., N.C., Durham County, Orange County bar assns., Internat. Acad. Law and Sci., Am. Judicature Soc. Beta Gamma Sigma, Order of Coif. Jewish religion (pres. congregation 1962-64). Mem. B'nai B'rith (pres. dist. grand lodge 1964-65, nat. chmn. pres.'s club). Clubs: Nat. Lawyers (Washington); Durham City, Willowhaven Country (Durham); Chapel Hill (N.C.) Country; Le Mirador Country (Lake Geneva, Switzerland). Contbr. articles to law jours. Home: 302 Country Club Dr Durham NC 27705 Office: Wachovia Bank Bldg Durham NC 27701

LISBY, CARROLL EDWARD, editor; B.A., M.A., U. Ala.; m. Mary O'Mary; children—Gregory, Nina, Jeffrey. Editor, Columbus (Ga.) Ledger, Sunday Ledger-Enquirer. Mem. Phi Beta Kappa, Sigma Delta Chi. Home: 2608 Juniper Av Columbus GA 31907 Office: 17 W 12th St Columbus GA 31902

LISELLA, FRANK SCOTT, health adviser; b. Lancaster, Pa., Aug. 11, 1936; s. Frank J. and Bertha (Scott) L.; B.S., Millersville State Coll., 1957; M.P.H., Tulane U., 1961; Ph.D., U. Ia., 1970; m. Beverly Trembath, Dec. 28, 1958. Health adviser Pa. Dept. Health, Harrisburg, Pa., 1957-64; health scientist USPHS, Atlanta, 1964—; adj. instr. DeKalb Community Coll., Clarkston, Ga., 1970—. Recipient certificate appreciation Civil Service Commn., Phila., 1962. Mem. Nat. Environmental Health Assn., Commd. Officers Assn., Am. Pub. Health Assn., Am. Men of Sci., Delta Omega. Contbr. numerous articles to profl. jours. Home: 3042 Hathaway Ct Chamblee GA 30341 Office: 1600 Clifton Rd Alanta GA 30333

LISTON, WILLIAM HARRY, lawyer; b. Natchez, Miss., Mar. 13, 1931; s. William and Hester (Jordan) L.; student Miss. State U., 1950-51, U. Md. Extension (Europe), 1951-52; LL.B., U. Miss., 1958; children—William, III, Lori Layne. Admitted to Miss. bar, 1958; investigator Miss. Dept. Ins., Jackson, 1958; practiced in Winona, Miss., 1958—; former mem. firm Liston & Sumner; mem. firm Liston & Upshaw. Served with USAF, 1951-54. Mem. Am., Miss. State, Montgomery County bar assns., Am. Trial Lawyers Assn., Pi Kappa Alpha, Phi Alpha Delta. Methodist. Home: 810 Michelle Dr Winona MS 38967 Office: 128 N Quitman St Winona MS 38967 also Aven Bldg Greenwood MS 38930

LITHERLAND, JAMES GEORGE, JR., petroleum reservior engr.; b. Shreveport, La., Feb. 19, 1922; s. James George and Madeline Melissa (Worley) L.; B.S., La. State U., 1948; m. Evelyn Dunnam, May 7, 1945; children—James George III, Steven Richard. With Magnolia Petroleum Co., Morgan City, La., Falfurrias, Tex., Midland, Tex., Dallas, 1948-54, petroleum engr., 1948-52, staff engr., 1952-54; with DeGolyer and Mac Naughton, Dallas, 1954—, petroleum engr., 1954-61, v.p., 1961—, treas., 1969—. Precinct chmn. Republican Party, 1956-64, area chmn., 1958-64. Served with USAAF, 1942-46. Mem. Soc. Petroleum Engrs. (dir. 1974—; Engr. of Year award Dallas sect. 1971), Am. Inst. M.E. (chmn. Dallas sect. Soc. Petroleum Engrs. br. 1970), Petroleum Engrs. Club of Dallas (pres. 1967). Clubs: Toastmasters (pres. 1958), Brookhaven Country. Home: 7827 Northaven Rd Dallas TX 75230 Office: One Energy Sq Dallas TX 75206

LITTLE, ALBERT KEIL, ret. lawyer; b. Pitts., May 13, 1885; s. John G. and Sarah (Keil) L.; B.S., Pa. State Coll., 1907; LL.B., U. Pitts., 1910; m. Gladys Ralston, Oct. 17, 1912 (dec. 1927); 1 dau., Sarah (Mrs. A.H. Watson, Jr.); m. 2d, Opal Browder, Dec. 14, 1928; 1 son, William B. Admitted to Pa. bar, 1910; gen. practice law, Pitts., 1910-12; Des Moines, 1913-17; office atty. Hicks Loan & Investment Co., Oklahoma City, 1917-20; gen. counsel Gum Bros. Co., farm and city real estate loans, Oklahoma City, 1920-32; gen. practice law, Oklahoma City, 1932-73; partner firm Little and Hoyt, 1946-72; spl. lectr. bus. adminstrn. U. Okla., 1946-58. Mem. bd. rev. Okla. Employment Security Commn., 1947-53. Mem. Oklahoma City Bd. Realtors, Am., Okla., Oklahoma County bar assns., Oklahoma City Soc. Title Attys., Beta Theta Pi, Phi Kappa Phi. Lutheran. Contbr. articles to legal publs. Home: 1134 NW 37th St Oklahoma City OK 73118

LITTLE, DELMAS CARROLL, instrumentation engr.; b. Bradford, O., Mar. 16, 1907; s. Kenneth and Cora (McCune) L.; B.A., U. Louisville, 1950; m. Gladys Caldwell, Feb. 3, 1955. Chief instrumentation U.S. Army Med. Research Lab., Ft. Knox, Ky., 1945-55; instr. physics U. Louisville, 1953-54; project mgr. Missile Range, N.M., 1955-60; chief instrumentation Army Ballistics Missile Agy., White Sands Missile Range Firing Operations Br., 1960-61; field rep. R & D Directorate, Army Missile Command, Redstone Arsenal, Ala., 1961-63, chief engring. sect. flight operations br., 1963-68. Mem. Instrument Soc. Am. (tech. v.p. 1954, 1st v.p. 1955), Am. Phys. Soc., A.A.A.S., Royal Order of Scotland. Republican. Presbyn. Mason (33 deg.). Home: 4421 Brookhaven Av Louisville KY 40220

LITTLE, JAMES SINGLETON, tax exec.; b. Eatonton, Ga., May 27, 1906; s. William Clarence and Laura (Nance) L.; B.S., Mercer U., 1928; m. Helen Elizabeth Salter, Nov. 18, 1937; children—Helen Elizabeth, James Singleton, David Clarence. Accountant E.F. Taylor, C.P.A., Augusta, Ga., 1928-30; accountant gen. office Texaco, Inc., Houston, 1930-33, traveling auditor, 1933-40; spl. accountant Horton Motor Lines, Inc., Charlotte, N.C., 1940-42; chief accountant So. div. Asso. Transport, Inc., Charlotte, 1942-43; asst. to pres., dir. taxes The Mason Dixon Lines, Inc. affiliated corps., Kingsport, Tenn., 1943—, chmn. trustees Retirement Trusts; dir., sec. The Crown Enterprises, Inc., The Royal Corp. Bd. dirs., sec. The King Found. Mem. Tenn. Soc. C.P.A.'s. Methodist. Home: 1200 Midland Dr Kingsport TN 37664 Office: Hwy 11-W Kingsport TN 37660

LITTLE, JOHN GOODWIN, JR., govt. ofcl.; b. Greenville, Ala., June 10, 1924; s. John Goodwin and Carrie Louise (Hobbs) Little; B.S., U. Ala., 1950; m. Tera Fay Cook, May 2, 1953; children—John Goodwin III, Phyllis Gail. With Little Mfg. Co., Greenville, 1953-54; postmaster City of Greenville, 1954—. Served with AUS, 1943-46, 51-53; now maj. Res. Mem. Nat. Assn. Postmasters U.S.A., Am. Legion, Butler County Hist. Soc. (pres. 1972-73). Baptist. Kiwanian. Home: 108 Brookside Dr Greenville AL 36037 Office: US PO 101 E Commerce St Greenville AL 36037

LITTLE, KENNETH BRUCE, assn. exec.; b. Wasco, Cal., Jan. 2, 1918; s. James and Amy M. (Robertson) L.; A.B., U. Cal. at Los Angeles, 1939, Ph.D., 1951; m. Yvonne Brackbill, July 29, 1959; 1 son, Michael James. Clin. psychologist VA, San Francisco, 1951-52; asst. prof. Stanford, 1952-57; tng. specialist USPHS, 1957-61; prof. psychology, chmn. dept. U. Denver, 1957-69; exec. officer Am. Psychol. Assn., Washington, 1969—, sec. Am. Psychol. Found. Served with USNR, 1941-45. Decorated Bronze Star. Diplomate Am. Bd. Examiners Profl. Psychology. Fellow A.A.A.S., Soc. Personality Assessment (pres. 1969). Office: 1200 17th St NW Washington DC 20036

LITTLE, LAMAR EUGENE, dentist; b. Winnsboro, La., June 22, 1913; s. Eugene Samuel and Carrie Mae (Butler) L.; B.A., La. Coll., 1935; D.D.S., St. Louis U., 1939; postgrad. N.Y. U., 1943-44, U. Miss., 1959; m. Darlyn McCarty, Jan. 22, 1950; children—Stephen Eugene, Charles McHenry, John Thomas. Individual practice dentistry, Winnsboro, La., 1939—. Served to comdr. USNR, 1941-45. Mem. Am., La., Fifth Dist. dental assns. Home: PO Box 509 Crowville Rd Winnsboro LA 71295 Office: 610 Prairie St Winnsboro LA 71295

LITTLE, MARY ALICE ENGLAND (MRS. JOE PERRY LITTLE), librarian; b. Sparta, Tenn., June 22, 1916; d. Dallas Carmichael and Althea (Alcorn) England; B.S., Tenn. Tech. U., 1938; M.A. in English, George Peabody Coll., 1946, M.A. in L.S., 1957; m. Joe Perry Little, Dec. 16, 1938; children—Joe Perry, Mary Elizabeth. Tchr., White County High Sch., Sparta, 1938-39, 44-45, Dover (Tenn.) High Sch., 1940-44, Murfreesboro (Tenn.) Central Sch., 1945-51, Sparta Elementary Sch., 1952-56; regional dir. Caney Fork Regional Library, Sparta, 1957—. Mem. Am. Assn. U. Women (br. pres. 1967-69, topic chmn. Tenn. div. 1973—), N.E.A., Nat. (life), Tenn. (life, state dir. 1959—) congresses parents and tchrs., Gen. Alumni Assn. Tenn. Tech. U. (pres. 1965-67, dir. 1963-68), Pi Gamma Mu, Delta Kappa Gamma (pres. 1968-70). Democrat. Mem. Ch. of Christ. Contbr. articles to profl. jours. Home: Route 4 208 S Spring St Sparta TN 38583 Office: 209 Rhea St Sparta TN 38583

LITTLE, ROBERT WARREN, dentist; b. Blacksburg, S.C., Mar. 19, 1920; s. Adolphus Lamar and Mildred Pratt (Waterson) L.; B.S., La. State U., 1942; D.D.S., U. Tex., 1950; m. Theda Inez Childress, July 11, 1942; children—Robert Warren, Steven Louis, Martha Ann. Individual practice dentistry, Waco, Tex., 1954—. Served with USAAF, 1942-45, with Dental Corps, AUS, 1949-54. Decorated Air medal with two oak leaf clusters. Mem. Acad. Internat. Dentistry, Acad. Gen. Dentistry, Tex. Dental Assn. (mem. ho. of dels. 1969-72), Central Tex. Dist. Dental Soc. (pres. 1962-63), U. Tex. Dental Br. Alumni Assn. (dir. 1968-71), Omicron Kappa Upsilon. Rotarian. Home: 5112 Lake Jackson St Waco TX 76710 Office: 5001 Lakewood Dr Waco TX 76710

LITTLE, THOMAS CHARLES, supt. schs.; b. Moore's Creek, Ky., Jan. 19, 1915; s. Thomas H. and Delila (Dyche) L.; B.A., Eastern Ky. U., 1937; M.A., U. Ky., 1942; Ph.D., George Peabody Coll. Tchrs., 1948; m. Hazel Calico, Oct. 21, 1933. Tchr. Paint Lick Elementary Sch., Garrard County, Ky., 1933-36, Lebanon (Ky.) High Sch., 1937-39; prin. Lebanon Elementary Sch., 1939-40; supt. schs. Columbia, Ky., 1940-44; chmn. edn. div. Ga. So. Coll., Statesboro, 1948-54; asst. supt. bus. affairs Richmond (Va.) Pub. Schs., 1954-69, asso. supt., 1969-72, supt. schs., 1972—. Ednl. cons. various pub. schs. Mem. adv. council Salvation Army Hosp., 1961-72; bd. dirs. Jr. Achievement, Richmond Pub. Library, Central Va. Ednl. TV. Served with USNR, 1944-46. Mem. Am. Assn. Sch. Adminstrs., Va. Edn. Assn., Va. Assn. Sch. Adminstrs., Va. Library Assn., Council Ednl. Facility Planners, Kappa Delta Phi, Phi Delta Kappa. Rotarian (pres. 1966-67). Club: Commonwealth (Richmond). Contbr. articles to profl. jours. Home: 5306 Riverside Dr Richmond VA 23225 Office: Richmond Pub Schs 301 N 9th St Richmond VA 23219

LITTLE, WALDEN PASKEL, ins. co. exec.; b. nr. Groesbeck, Tex., Mar. 14, 1920; s. Wilmer Preston and Georgia (Cates) L.; A.A., Westminister Coll., 1940; m. Billye Jean Bostick, June 9, 1965; children—Gregory, Regina. With Combined Underwriters Life Ins. Co., Tyler, Tex., 1949—, pres., 1956—. City commr. Tyler, 1966—, mayor, 1968—. Bd. dirs. YMCA. Mem. Tyler Sales Execs. Club. Mem. Christian Ch. Mason (Shriner). Home: 3326 Pollard St Tyler TX 75701 Office: 307 N Glenwood St Tyler TX 75701

LITTLE, WILLIAM D., JR., newspaper exec.; b. Ada., Okla., May 22, 1921; s. William Dee and Willie (Faust) L.; grad. McCallie Sch., 1938; A.B., East Central State Coll., Ada, Okla., 1942; m. Mary Louise Osborne, Sept. 13, 1942; children—Helen Jane, Linda Brooks, William D. III. With News Publ. and Printing Co., Ada, 1942—, advt. solicitor, asst. to pub., 1946, v.p., bus. mgr., 1947-66, pres., 1966—; pub. Ada Evening News, 1966—; dir. Home Fed. Savs. & Loan Assn., Ada, Ada Indsl. Devel. Corp., Okla. Gas & Electric Co. Mem. exec. bd. Valley View Hosp., Ada, chmn., 1963—; mem. Okla. Econ. Adv. Council, 1963-66, Gov.'s Capital Expenditures Adv. Council, 1967; pres. E. Central Okla. Bldg. Authority, 1965—; mem. Okla. Health Council, 1968-72; v.p. Okla. Health Scis. Found. Bd. dirs. Scis. and Natural Resources Found. Okla.; trustee Okla. Newspaper Found., E. Central State Coll. Found., Inc.; mem. Okla. Heritage Found. Mem. Am., So. (dir. 1969-72) newspaper pubs. assns., Okla. A.P. Mng. Editors Assn. (pres. 1958), Okla. Press Assn., Ada. (pres. 1954), Okla. (dir. 1971—, v.p.) chambers commerce, East Central Coll. Alumni Assn. (pres. 1949), Newcomen Soc. N.Am. Episcopalian. Home: South-on-Jack Fork PO Box 596 Ada OK 74820 Office: 116 N Broadway Ada OK 74820

LITTLEJOHN, BROADUS RICHARD, supermarket exec.; b. Cedar Springs, S.C., Sept. 24, 1894; s. Wallace W. and Nealie (Willard) L.; student pub. schs., Spartanburg County, S.C.; LL.D. (hon.), Converse Coll., 1966; m. Evelyn Hicks, Oct. 6, 1920; 1 son, Broadus Richard. Formerly with Spartanburg Herald Jour., pres. Community Cash Stores, Spartanburg, S.C., 1921—; dir. First Nat. Bank S.C., Spartan Broadcasting, Liberty Mut. Ins. Co. Mem. Bd. commrs. Cedar Springs Inst. for Deaf and Blind Sch. for S.C.,

1950-70. Councilman, City of Spartanburg. Trustee, vice-chmn. bd. Converse Coll.; trustee Furman U., Spartanburg County Found., Spartanburg Jr. Coll; bd. dirs. Spartanburg County Library. Served with AEF, World War I. Recipient Alernon Sydney Sullivan Medallion Wofford Coll., 1965. Mem. Am. Legion. Baptist (deacon). Kiwanian (Man of Year 1957). Home: 20 Woodburn Rd Spartanburg SC 29301 Office: PO Box 5688 Spartanburg SC 29302

LITTLEJOHN, CAMERON BRUCE, justice S.C. Supreme Ct.; b. Pacolet, S.C., July 22, 1913; s. Cameron and Lady Sara (Warmouth) L.; A.B., Wofford Coll., 1935, LL.D., 1968; LL.B., U.S.C., 1936; m. Inell Smith, Feb. 7, 1942. Mem. S.C. Ho. of Reps., 1937-43, speaker, 47-49; judge 7th Circuit Ct., 1949-67; asso. justice S.C. Supreme Ct., 1967—. Del. Nat. Conf. State Trial Judges, 1964, 65, 66; del. Nat. Appellate Judges Conf., 1967; mem. Spartanburg adv. bd. registrants Selective Service Act, 1960. Sec. Orgn. Young Dem. Clubs S.C., 1935-36, chmn. Spartenburg County, 1936-37. Served to 1st lt. AUS, 1943-46; PTO. Mem. Wofford Coll. Alumni Assn. (dir. 1966—), Am. Legion, Blue Key. Baptist (trustee 1962-67). Home: 450 Connecticut Av Spartanburg SC 29302 Office: Supreme Ct SC PO Box 1924 Spartanburg SC 29301

LITTLEJOHN, JAMES DEWITT, assn. exec.; b. El Paso, Tex., June 21, 1931; s. James Franklin and Mary Kathleen (Badgett) L.; B.A., Tex. Christian U., 1954; m. Sunny Gail Wright, May 25, 1968; 1 son, James Hartwell. Tchr. pub. schs., San Angelo, Odessa, Tex., 1954-60; pres., Marlo Products Co., Odessa, 1960-61; asst. mgr. Greater Florence (S.C.) C. of C., 1961-63; sports editor, bur. chief Florence Morning News, Savannah (Ga.) Morning News, 1963-69; exec. dir. Hilton Head (S.C.) C. of C., 1969—; editor Islander Mag., 1969—; chmn. bd., pres. Sunlit Enterprises Ltd. Mem. Am. C. of C. Assn., S.C. Chamber Execs. Assn., U.S., S.C. State chambers commerce. Rotarian. Clubs: Chatham (Savannah, Ga.); Port Royal Golf, Sea Pines Plantation, Palmetto Dunes Golf and Country (Hilton Head). Home: 7 S Port Royal Dr Hilton Head Island SC 29928 Office: PO Box 5647 Hilton Head Island SC 29928

LITTLEJOHN, TALMADGE DEAN, lawyer; b. Blue Springs, Miss., Oct. 18, 1935; s. Ivy Lee and Annie (Speck) L.; B.A., Miss. Coll., 1957; LL.B., U. Miss., 1960; m. Julia Gray Littlejohn, Sept. 2, 1961; children—Lisa Michele, Christy Madonna. Admitted to Miss. bar., 1960; gen. practice law, New Albany, Miss., 1961—; mem. Miss. Ho. of Reps., 1960-64; mem. senate, 1964-68, dist. atty. 3d Circuit Ct., 1968—. Mem. Miss. Planning Council on Mental Retardation, 1964—; mem. Union County 4-H Adv. Council. Bd. dirs. Regional Rehab. Center, Union County Assn. for Retarded Children. Named outstanding Young Man of Year, New Albany Jr. C. of C., 1963. Mem. Miss., Union County bar assns., Miss. Resource Devel. Com., Miss. Forestry Assn. (dir. 1971), Pi Kappa Delta. Baptist. Club: Civitan (pres. New Albany 1968-69, lt. gov. Miss. dist. 1970-71). Home: 303 Pinecrest Dr New Albany MS 38652 Office: 202 Court Av New Albany MS 38652

LITTLEJOHN, WILLIAM DONALD, physician; b. Oklahoma City, Dec. 30, 1934; s. Arthur Lee and Lucille (Crowe) L.; B.S., Tex. Wesleyan Coll., 1967; M.D., Southwestern Med. Sch., 1967; m. Rosa Louise DuMain, June 13, 1964; children—Linda Joy, Donna Sue, Vicki Lynn, Cynthia Ann. Intern John Peter Smith Hosp., 1967, resident, 1969; practice gen. medicine, Fort Worth, 1969—; mem. staff St. Joseph Hosp., Ft. Worth Children's Hosp., Harris Hosp., All Saints Episcopal Hosp., Ft. Worth; team physician Fort Worth Braves football team, 1970—, Fort Worth Wings hockey team, 1970—. Served with USAF, 1954-61. Mem. A.M.A., Tarrant County Med. Assn., Am. Assn. Gen. Practitioners, Nat. Rifle Assn., Am. Motorcycle Assn., Theta Kappa Psi, Alpha Chi. Home: Rte 1 Box 206 Weatherford TX 76086 Office: 2501 Ridgmar Plaza Fort Worth TX 76116

LITTON, ROBERT BENTON, dentist; b. Shelby, N.C., June 29, 1930; s. Farley Benton and Luta (Smith) L.; student U. N.C., 1948-50; D.D.S., U. Md., 1954; m. Margaret Easom, Aug. 7, 1954; children—Lu, Robert Benton, Margaret S. Oral surgeon intern U. Hosp., Balt., 1954; individual practice dentistry, Shelby, N.C., 1957—; mem. staff Cleve. Meml. Hosp., Shelby. Served with Dental Corps, AUS, 1955-57. Named Shelby's Man of Year, 1960. Mem. 1st Dist. N.C. Dental Soc. (pres. 1970-71), Western N.C. Swim Assn. (pres. 1971-72). Kiwanian (pres. 1961; dir. 1957-62). Club: Bulldog (pres. 1971-72). Home: 1220 Timberland St Shelby NC 28150 Office: 423 W Marion St Shelby NC 28150

LITZENBERGER, SAMUEL CAMERON, govt. ofcl.; b. Calgary, Alta., Can., July 21, 1914; s. Adam and Marie (Gorr) L.; B.Sc. (Union Pacific scholar 1933), Colo. State U., 1937; M.Sc., Mont. State U., 1939; Ph.D., Ia. State U., 1948; m. Hazel Lucille West, May 24, 1941. Came to U.S., 1914, naturalized, 1943. Agronomy research advisor U.S. AID mission Cambodia, Phnom Penh, 1958-63, food and agr. officer, Conakry, Guinea, 1963-66, Tunis, Tunisia, 1966-70; agronomy research specialist Office of Agr. AID, Washington, 1970-72, chief food crops prodn. div., 1972—. Dept. Agr. Research fellow, 1937-39; Quaker Oats Research fellow, 1946-48. Fellow A.A.A.S., Am. Soc. Agronomy; mem. Am. Phytopathology Soc., Am. Forestry Assn. Home: 500 23d St NW Baron 407 Washington DC 20037 Office: Office of Agr Tech Assistance Bur AID Dept State Washington DC 20523

LIU, FRANK CHUNG-WOO, educator; b. Chaohsien, Shantung, China, Apr. 15, 1926; s. Tao-yuan and Yun-ching (Fan) L.; B.S., Nat. Chekian U., 1949; M.S., U. Wash., 1953; Ph.D., U. Tex., 1958; m. Amy Fang-heng Tu, Aug. 7, 1954; children—Tony, Jimmy, Leroy. Came to U.S., naturalized, 1963. Research engr. Boeing Airplane Co., Renton, Wash., 1957-62; mem. sci. staff Marshall Space Flight Center NASA, Huntsville, Ala., 1962-67; asso. prof. U. Ala., Huntsville, 1962-67, prof. engring. mechanics, 1967—. Home: 8906 Valley View Dr Huntsville AL 35802

LIU, FRED WEI-JUI, chemist; b. Canton, China, Jan. 29, 1926; s. Chun Lim and Shou Ying (Chow) L.; came to U.S., 1948, naturalized, 1960; B.S. in Chemistry, St. John's U., Shanghai, China, 1948; M.A. in Chemistry, Temple U., 1950; Ph.D., Lehigh U., 1952; m. Kathleen Elliott, May 12, 1961. Research asso. Lehigh U., Bethlehem, Pa., 1952-53; chief chemist Lester Labs., Atlanta, 1953-64; dir. Continental Cons., Inc., Atlanta, 1964—. Mem. Am. Chem. Soc., Nat. Assn. Corrosion Engrs., Am. Assn. Textile and Colors Chemists, Sigma Xi. Home: 157 Lake Forest Lane Atlanta GA 30342 Office: 792 Windsor St Atlanta GA 30315

LIVELY, GENE, TV news broadcaster; b. Carlsbad, N.M., July 18, 1939; s. Forbis Whitely and Juanita (Bass) L.; student San Antonio Coll., 1958-59; student San Angelo (Tex.) Coll., 1959-61; m. Billie Jean Key, Feb. 18, 1961; children—Robin, Andrea, Kristee. Program dir. radio sta. KWFR San Angelo, 1959-61; anchorman KC TV, San Angelo, 1964-65; anchorman early news KSAT, San Antonio, 1965-68; news dir., anchorman Avco Broadcasting Corp., WOAI-TV, San Antonio, 1968—. Served with AUS, 1962-64. Mem. Radio & TV News Dirs. Assn., Sigma Delta Chi. Home: 335 GoodHue San Antonio TX 78218 Office: 1031 Navarro San Antonio TX 78205

LIVELY, LLOYD LESTER, JR., missile system program mgr.; b. Phila., Sept. 14, 1927; s. Lloyd Lester and Olive (Stoner) L.; B.S., Auburn U., 1949; m. Phyllis Barnes, Sept. 3, 1949; children—Lloyd Lester III, Elizabeth Ann. Quality control engr. Mock, Judson, Voehringer Co., Greensboro, N.C., 1949-51, personnel mgr., 1951-52; supr. dyeing operation Gayley Mills, Marietta, S.C., 1952-53; weapon system engr. U.S. Army Rocket and Guided Missile Agy., Redstone Arsenal, Huntsville, Ala., 1953-57, dep. weapon systems project mgr., 1957-60, dep. chief functional div. indsl. operations, 1960-62, anti-tank, field artillery weapon systems project mgr., 1962-63, nuclear programs mgr., 1963—, high energy laser program mgr., 1967-69, mem. Dept. Army Standardization Task Group, 1955-56, panelist Armed Forces Communication and Electronics Assn. Fellowship Awards Bd., 1965, mem. U.S. Army Missile Comd. Laser Adv. Com., 1967-69; mem. Def. Atomic Support Agy. Dept. Def. Electromagnetic Pulse Test and Evaluation Com., 1968—; mem. U.S. Army Integrated Effects (Nuclear) Com., 1968—; exec. sec. U.S. Army Missile Command Sci. Adv. Group, 1963—. Vice-pres. Rocket City Swimming Assn., 1969. Mem. Nat. Soc. Profl. Engrs., Ala. Acad. Sci., Phi Psi, Sigma Alpha Epsilon. Presbyn. (trustee 1962-64, deacon 1958-62). Lion. Home: 1402 Dale Circle Huntsville AL 35801 Office: US Army Missile Command Attn AMSMI-RR Redstone Arsenal AL 35809

LIVERANCE, SARA VANDIVER (MRS. ROBERT E. LIVERANCE), journalist; b. Anderson, S.C., Feb. 21, 1914; d. Thomas Melvin and Mary M. (Brown) Vandiver; grad. high sch.; m. Robert E. Liverance, Oct. 25, 1944. Writer shopping column, reporter Anderson Independent-Daily Mail, 1933-44; promotion, publicity Radio Sta. WAGA, Atlanta, 1944-45; reporter Kannapolis (N.C.) Independent, 1946; local news editor Radio Sta. WABZ, Albemarle, N.C., 1947-48; local news editor, womens editor Radio Sta. WFGN, Gaffney, S.C., 1948-49; chief Anderson Bur., Greenville (S.C.) News, 1949—. Sec. S.C. Conf. on Status Women, 1956; pres. S.C. Council for Common Good, 1960-62; mem. S.C. Gov.'s Commn. on Status Women, 1965-71, com. chmn., 1965-71; staff mem. Synodical Tng. Sch. Presbyn. Ch., 1965-67, sec. Women of Ch. Piedmont Presbytery, 1966-67; rec. sec. Anderson County Hist. Soc., 1967—, bd. govs., 1966—; mem. S.C. Tri-Centennial Com., 1968-71; sec. Anderson County Arts Council. Trustee State Colls., 1969—, Anderson Heritage, Inc. Recipient Distinguished Service award S.C. Council for Common Good, 1963, Hon. Miss Anderson award Anderson Jr. C. of C., 1967; named Career Woman of Year Anderson Bus. and Profl. Womens Club, 1967. Mem. Anderson Bus. and Profl. Womens Club (past pres., state chmn., conv. del.). Clubs: Altrusa (past pres. Anderson), Anderson County Woman's (pres. 1974). Address: PO Box 479 Anderson SC 29621

LIVINGOOD, MARVIN DUANE, chem. engr.; b. Corning, Kan., Aug. 13, 1918; s. Aldo Morton and Gladys Orda (Peck) L.; B.S., Okla. State U., 1938, M.S., 1940; postgrad. Ill. Inst. Tech., 1940-41; Ph.D., Mich. State U., 1952; spl. courses U. Louisville, 1970; m. Agnes Schasse Dyer II, Apr. 17, 1947; children—Christopher M., Winifred (Mrs. James R. Purcell), Matthew G., Abigail. Chem. engr. Arzone Products Co., Chgo., 1940-41; instr. chem. engring. Mo. Sch. Mines, Rolla, 1941-45; asst. prof. chem. engring. Mich. State U., East Lansing, 1945-49, research asst. prof., engring. experiment sta., 1949-52; research engr. E.I. du Pont de Nemours & Co., Deepwater, N.J., 1952-58, Louisville, 1958—. Cons. agrl./food processing waste recovery and chem. safety. Mem. A.A.A.S., Am. Inst. Chem. Engrs. (mem. nat. com. career guidance, profl. devel. 1965-73), Mensa (proctor 1970-73), Triangle Frat. (hon. life), Alpha Chi Sigma. Patentee in field. Home: 2603 Landor Av Louisville KY 40205 Office: PO Box 1378 Louisville KY 40201

LIVINGOOD, WILLIAM COOK, physician; b. Graysville, Pa., Feb. 3, 1915; s. John Madison and Frances (Cook) L.; B.S., Waynesburg Coll., 1936; M.D., U. Md., 1940; postgrad. U. Pa., 1949-50; m. Lucille Bernadine Donegan, Aug. 21, 1939; children—Frances (Mrs. James J. Castello), William Cook, Carol (Mrs. R. Stinson Swyers), John M., Charles P., Joan L. Intern Mercy Hosp., Balt., 1940-41; commd. lt. jg. U.S. Navy, 1942, advanced through grades to capt., 1955; ret., 1962; chief of otolaryngology service U.S. Naval Hosp., Phila., 1955-62, head Nat. Naval Aural Rehab. Center, 1955-62, naval flight surgeon Marine Air Wings Pacific, World War II, sr. med. officer U.S.S. Wright, 1947-49; otolaryngologist Guthrie Clinic and Robert Packer Hosp., Sayre, Pa., 1962-70; VA Hosp., Fayetteville, N.C., 1970—; clin. asso. prof. surgery Hahnemann Med. Sch., 1956-70; vis. prof. speech pathology and audiology Ithaca Coll., N.Y., 1966-70. Diplomate Am. Bd. Otolaryngology. Fellow A.C.S., Am. Otologicarhinol. and Laryngol. Soc., A.M.A.; mem. Soc. Mil. Otolaryngologists (nat. pres. 1956-57), Am. Council of Otolaryngology. Office: VA Hosp Fayetteville NC 28301

LIVINGSTON, DAVID WARREN, composer; b. Corbin, Ky., Jan. 10, 1925; s. Carl Daniel and Lucy (Darnell) L.; B.S., Western Ky. U., 1951; M.A., U. Ky., 1952; Ph.D., Ohio State U., 1971; m. Joyce E. West, Oct. 5, 1951; children—Pamela, David Timothy. Band dir. Western Ky. U., 1965—; supr. music in Frankfort, Ky., 1953-63. Dir. Civic Symphonette, Frankfort, Ky., 1956-58; dir., arranger Drum and Bugle Corps, 1957-58; tour with band Gemini 15, Europe, 1968. Active Boy Scouts Am. Served with USAAF, 1943-46. Mem. Phi Mu Alpha. Kiwanian. Composer: Theme and Variations, 1952; Adagio for Four Trombones, 1954; How Firm a Foundation, 1956; Saxville, 1962; Prelude and Fugue for Winds, 1963; Pastorale for Winds, 1966. Home: 2325 Bellevue Dr Bowling Green KY 42101

LIVINGSTON, DEAN BENNETTE, newspaper pub., editor; b. North, S.C., Jan. 9, 1933; s. Alex Hamilton and Madge (Rogers) L.; A.B., U.S.C., 1955; m. Grace Dukes, Dec. 22, 1955; children—Donna Grace, Dean. Sports editor Orangeburg (S.C.) Times and Democrat, 1953-55, farm editor, 1955-56, mng. editor, 1959-61, pub., 1961—, editor, 1964—. Served as 1st lt., navagator USAF, 1956-59. Mem. Greater Orangeburg C. of C. (pres. 1967-68), S.C. A.P. Assn. (pres.), S.C. Press Assn. (pres. 1969), Sigma Chi. Mason, Rotarian. Home: 1167 Middleton NE Orangeburg SC 29115 Office: 211 Broughton SE Orangeburg SC 29115

LIVINGSTON, LAWRENCE GORDON, physician; b. Mountain Grive, Mo., Nov. 25, 1905; s. James Harry and Mabel (Beazley) L.; M.D., Washington U. (St. Louis) 1930; m. Gwennie M. Bonham, May 12, 1932 (div. Feb. 1940); adopted children-Janice Mae, Richard Lewis; m. 2d, Alice Jane Pritchett Fletcher, Aug. 19, 1960; children—Phillip Douglas, Harold Arlyn. Intern Okla. State U. Hosp., Oklahoma City, 1930-31, St. Louis Maternity Hosp., 1931-32; practice gen. medicine, surgery, Cordell, Okla., 1933-73; asso. Mesquite (Tex.) Med. and Surg. Clinic, 1973—; mem. staff Cordell Meml. Hosp., also equipment cons.; asso. perceptor Okla. State U. Med. Sch., 1957-58. Dir. Cordell Indsl. Corp., 1960—. Served to lt. col. M.C., AUS, 1940-45; PTO. Mem. A.M.A., Okla. Med. Soc. (councilor 1945-52), Phi Beta Pi, Kappa Sigma. Methodist. Kiwanian. Home: 10615 Seagoville Rd Dallas TX 75217

LIVINGSTON, ORRIN WILLIAM, ret. elec. engr.; b. Roselle Park, N.J., July 11, 1905; s. William Hamilton and Adele (Moller) L.; B.E.E., Rutgers U., 1927; postgrad. Union Coll., 1927-29; m. Teresa Rundle Rankin, July 23, 1932; children—Mary (Mrs. Ralph B. Snyder), William Rankin, David Orrin. Student engr. Gen. Electric Co., Schenectady, 1927-28, devel. engr. research lab., 1928-29, application engr. tube engring. dept., 1930-40, design and devel. engr. control dept., 1940-54, cons. engr. splty. control dept., numerical equipment control dept., 1954-70. Recipient Charles A. Coffin award Gen. Electric Co., 1934; Outstanding Engring. Achievement award Rutgers U., 1973. Fellow I.E.E.E. (mem. nat. com. on electronics 1946-50, mem. com. indsl. control 1946-70, program chmn. conv., Buffalo 1949), Phi Beta Kappa, Tau Beta Pi. Patentee shield grid thyratrons; phase shift circuits; voltage regulators; electric welders; motor controls; automatic machine tool controls, others. Home: PO Box 1092 Waynesboro VA 22980

LIVINGSTONE, DANIEL ARCHIBALD, educator; b. Detroit, Aug. 3, 1927; s. Harrison Lincoln and Elizabeth (Matheson) L.; student McGill U., 1944-45; B.Sc., Dalhousie U., 1948, M.Sc., 1950; Ph.D., Yale, 1953; m. Bertha Griffin Ross, June 21, 1952; children—Laura Ross, Mary Lisa, John Malcolm, Christina Ann, Elizabeth. NRC postdoctoral fellow Cambridge (Eng.) U., 1953-54, NRC postdoctoral fellow, spl. lectr. Dalhousie U., 1954-55; asst. prof. U. Md., 1955-56; mem. faculty Duke, 1956—, prof. zoology, 1967—; limnologist U.S. Geol. Survey, intermittently, 1956—. Guggenheim fellow, 1960-61. Mem. N.S. Inst. Sci., Am. Soc. Icthyologists and Herpetologists, Ecol. Soc. Am., Am. Soc. Limnology and Oceanography, Geochem. Soc., N.C. Acad. Sci., Internat. Assn. Fundamental and Applied Limnology, Canadian Soc. Zoologists, Am., Internat. Quat. assns., Assn. pour L'Etude Taxonomy de la Flore d'Afrique Tropicale, Sigma Xi. Zoology editor Ecol. Monographs, 1961-66. Research, publs. on distbn. freshwater fishes N.S., effects temperature and activity on oxygen consumption salmon embryos, reactions between sedimentary and dissolved phosphorus in lakes, origin and devel. of lakes as ecol. systems, dissolved solids in lake and river water, vegetational changes Pleistocene in Alaska, N.S., E. Africa. Home: 2827 Ridge Rd Durham NC 27706

LIVINGSTONE, RAY(MOND) S., educator; b. Pitts., Feb. 12, 1907; s. Maurice M. and Ella Marie (Villatte) L.; student Case Inst. Tech., 1924-27, Citation, 1953, Dr. Engring., 1954; m. Sylvia Flora, May 5, 1934; children—Raymond S., Barbara Anne (Mrs. Hector Jose Aguirre). With Thompson Products Inc. (Name later changed to TRW Inc.), Cleve., 1929-66, v.p., corp. officer responsible for employee relations, govt. relations, community relations, 1942-66, ret., 1966; vis. prof. Fla. Atlantic U., 1966—, mem. nat. labor-mgmt. manpower policy com., 1966-70; dir. Prodn. Machinery Corp., Mentor, Ohio, 1957—; cons. Harris Intertype Corp., Cleve., 1966-72. Pres. Cleve. Community Chest, 1962-63; pres. Cleve. Welfare Fedn., 1964-65; mem. exec. adv. com. Fla. Atlantic U. Trustee Am. Enterprise Inst., Washington; life trustee Community Chest of Greater Cleve.; life trustee Euclid (Ohio) Glenville Hosp. Recipient Citation for work as Hoover Commn. mem., 1955. Mem. Cleve. Personnel Assn. (pres. 1940-41), Aerospace Industries Assn. (mem. indsl. relations com. 1957-65, nat. chmn. 1962-63), Personnel Round Table. Mason (33 deg., Shriner). Clubs: Economic Round Table, Royal Palm Yacht and Country (Boca Raton, Fla. commodore 1972-73). Home: 282 Fan Palm Rd Boca Raton FL 33432

LJUNGDAHL, LARS GERHARD, educator; b. Stockholm, Sweden, Aug. 5, 1926; s. Karl Axel Gerhard and Ruth Elisabeth (Soderlund) L.; B.S., Stockholm Tech. Inst., 1945; Ph.D., Case Western Res. U., 1964; m. Britt-Marie Swahn, Aug. 28, 1949; children—Ann-Sofie Elisabeth, Lars Per-Olof. Came to U.S., 1958, naturalized, 1969. Research technologist Karolinska Institut, Stockholm, 1943-46; research chemist Stockholm Brewery Co., 1947-58; sr. instr. Case Western Res. U., Cleve., 1964-66, asst. prof., 1967; asst. prof. U. Ga., Athens, 1967-69, asso. prof. biochemistry and microbiology, 1969—. Research grantee NIH, 1968, NSF, 1970. Mem. Am. Soc. Biol. Chemists, Am. Soc. Microbiology, Am. Chem. Soc., A.A.A.S., N.Y. Acad. Sci., Biochem. Soc. (U.K.), Swedish Chem. Soc., Sigma Xi. Contbr. articles in field to profl. jours. Home: 250 Hancock Lane Athens GA 30601

LLANES, CARLOS GILBERTO, physician; b. Havana Cuba, Mar. 31, 1919; s. Carlos G. and Mirtha (Fernandez) L.; B.S. and B.A., Instituto de la Habana, 1938; M.D., Sch. Medicine U. Havana, 1945; m. Martha Maria Borg, Sept. 18, 1948; children—Carlos Gilberto III, Patricia Ann, Mirtha Maria, Diana Lynn. Came to U.S., 1945, naturalized, 1950. Rotating intern St. Joseph's Hosp., Yonkers, N.Y., 1945-46; resident chest diseases Lakeland Chest Diseases Hosp., Blackwood, N.J., 1946-50; resident radiology Roosevelt Hosp., N.Y.C., 1950-53; spl. course radioactive isotopes Oak Ridge Inst. Nuclear Studies, Tenn., 1953; asso. radiologist Doctors' Hosp., Coral Gables, Fla., 1953-55; chief radiologist Murphy Army Hosp., Waltham, Mass., 1955-56; asso. radiologist Gorgas Hosp., Panama Canal Zone, 1956-57; radiologist, chief cobalt div. Mercy Hosp., Miami, Fla., 1957-59; pvt. practice radiology, Coral Gables, 1959-67, Miami, 1964—; dir. dept. radiology Palm Springs Gen. Hosp., Hialeah, Fla., 1965-67; chief dept. radiology Pan Am. Hosp., Miami, also bd. dirs. Served from capt. to maj., AUS, 1955-57. Diplomate Am. Bd. Radiology. Mem. Am., Fla., Dade County med. assns., Radiol. Soc. N.Am., Greater Miami Radiol. Soc., Fla. Radiol. Soc., Am. Coll. Radiology, Heart Assn. Greater Miami. Lutheran (past pres. congregation). Rotarian. Home: 11225 SW 58th Ct Miami FL 33156 Office: 434 SW 12th Av Miami FL 33130

LLEWELLYN, CHARLES ELROY, JR., physician, educator; b. Richmond, Va., Jan. 16, 1922; s. Charles Elroy and Pearl Ann (Shield) L.; B.S., Hampden-Sydney Coll., 1943; M.D., Med. Coll. Va., 1946; M.S. (Psychiat.), U. Colo. Postgrad. Med. Sch., 1953; m. Sara Grace Eldridge, Sept. 25, 1948; children—Charles Elroy III, George Eldridge (dec. July 1970), Richard Shield. Intern, Bellevue, N.Y., 1947-48; resident in psychiatry Colo. Psychopathic Hosp., Denver, 1950-53; asso. in psychiatry, asst. chief adult psychiat. outpatient clinic, dept. psychiatry Duke Med. Center, 1955-56, asst. prof. psychiatry, 1956-63, asso. prof. psychiatry, 1963—, head psychiat. outpatient div., 1956—, dir. student mental health service, 1959-69, dir. Duke study group Inter-Univ. Forum for Educators in Community Psychiatry, 1967-71, dir. Duke Drug Abuse Rehab. Service, 1972—; psychiat. cons., med. services div. Medicaid Program, 1971—; mem. vis. faculty, seminars Lab. Community Psychiatry, Harvard Med. Sch., 1964-67; practice gen. psychiatry, part time 1955—. Sr. psychiat. cons. N.C. Dept. Social Services, 1955—; cons. Family Counseling Service Durham, 1966—, bd. dirs., 1971—; mem. N.C. Mental Health Council, chmn., 1965-69; adv. bd. Durham Drug Rehab. Program, 1973—. Cubmaster, Occoneechee council Boy Scouts Am., 1960-66 (named Cubmaster of Year Shawnee dist. 1962). Served to capt. M.C., AUS, 1953-55. Diplomate Am. Bd. Psychiatry and Neurology. Fellow Am., So. psychiat. assns., Am. Orthopsychiat. Assn., Pan Am. Med. Assn.; mem. A.M.A., Am. Group Psychotherapy Assn., Southeastern Group Psychotherapy Soc. (pres. 1965-66), Am. Acad. Religion and Mental Health, N.C. Neuropsychiat. Assn. (pres. 1971-73), N.C. Group Behavior Soc., N.C., Durham (chmn. med. adv. com. 1957-61) mental health assns. Methodist (pres. Sunday sch. 1957-58; mem. ofcl. bd. 1957-68; chmn. commn. social concerns 1963-68; trustee 1958-59). Office: Duke Univ Medical Center Durham NC 27710 Home: 3550 Hamstead Ct Durham NC 27707

LLEWELLYN, LYNN GRESHAM, psychologist; b. Washington, Aug. 20, 1935; s. Haskell V. and Mae Glenn (Griffin) L.; B.S., Coll. William and Mary, 1957; M.A., George Washington U., 1959; Ph.D., 1969; m. Barbara Ann Best, June 29, 1963. Research asst. Nat. Inst. Mental Health, Bethesda, Md., 1958-59, social sci. analyst, 1959-60; research psychologist, 1964-68; community organizer D.C. Commr.'s Youth Council, 1960-61; research asso. Spl. Operations Research Office, Washington, 1961-62; social psychologist Operations Research Inc., Silver Spring, Md., 1968-71; research psychologist Nat. Bur. Standards, 1971—. Cons. NSF, 1969; vis. prof. U.S. Army War Coll., 1970-71. Trustee Greater Washington Ednl. TV Assn., 1973—. Served to capt. AUS, 1959. Recipient Psi Chi Grad. award George Washington U., 1959. Mem. Am. Psychol. Assn., A.I.A. (cons. mem. regional devel. and natural resources com. 1973—, chmn. endangered species subcom. 1974), Nature Conservancy, Nat. Audubon Soc., Defenders of Wildlife, Friends of Animals, Sigma Xi, Pi Kappa Alpha. Editor: Studies in Environment, 1973. Home: 4209 Aspen Hill Rd Rockville MD 20853 Office: Div 431.00 Bldg 225 Room A122 Nat Bur Standards Washington DC 20234

LLEWELLYN, RAEBURN CARSON, surgeon; b. Corbin, Ky., May 29, 1920; s. Raeburn and Christine (Carson) L.; M.D., U. Va., 1945; m. Carmen Rolon, Sept. 4, 1967. Intern, Touro Infirmary, New Orleans, 1945; resident Ochsner Found. Hosp., New Orleans, 1948-51 practice medicine, specializing in neurosurgery, New Orleans, 1953—; mem. faculty Tulane U. Med. Sch., 1953—, prof., chmn. div. neurosurgery, 1962—. Served with USAF, 1946-48. Diplomate Am. Bd. Neurol. Surgery. Mem. A.M.A., A.C.S., So. Neurosurgery Soc., Acad. Neurol. Surgeons, Assn. Neurol. Surgeons, Orleans Parish Med. Soc., Soc. Neurol. Surgeons, Alpha Omega Alpha. Contbr. articles to med. jours. Home: 32 Versailles Blvd New Orleans LA 70125 Office: Tulane U Sch Medicine 1430 Tulane Av New Orleans LA 70112

LLOYD, BOB MOTLEY, lawyer; b. Teneha, Tex., Mar. 24, 1929; s. Sidney David and Hortense (Motley) L.; B.B.A., So. Meth. U., 1952, LL.B., 1952; m. Joan Kelley, Dec. 7, 1962; children—Donald Baker, Kelley Sidney. Admitted to Tex. bar, 1953, since practiced in Henderson as partner firm Colley & Lloyd. Officer, dir. P.R.F. Co., Delta Container Co., Abel Loan Co., Abel Furnishings Co. Served to 1st lt. USAF, 1953. Mem. Am., Tex. bar assns. Home: 325 McNee St Henderson TX 75652 Office: 125 N Van Buren St Henderson TX 75652

LLOYD, (CHARLES) HAROLD, lawyer; b. Marshall, Tex., May 2, 1936; s. Harvey Thomas and Anna Louise (Fyffe) L.; B.A., North Tex. State U., 1958; J.D., U. Tex., 1961; m. Elizabeth Anne Taylor, June 21, 1958; children—Rebecca Anne, Amanda Catherine, Jennifer Ruth. Admitted to Tex. bar, 1961; asso. McClure and Lucas, Houston, 1961-64; individual practice law, Houston, 1965—. Dir. United Tech. Labs., Inc., Dallas. Mem. Tex. Trial Lawyers Assn. (dir.), Houston Bar Assn. (dir.), Phi Alpha Delta, Pi Kappa Alpha. Mason. Home: 14203 Kellywood Houston TX 77024 Office: Suite #444 Houston 1st Savs Bldg Houston TX 77002

LLOYD, ROBERT AUSTIN, JR., chemist; b. High Point, N.C., May 11, 1940; s. Robert Austin and Nellie Edith (Stone) L.; B.S., High Point Coll., 1962; M.S., Clemson U., 1965, Ph.D., 1968; m. Sara Alyce Ratliff, June 9, 1963; 1 son, Daniel Hamilton. Research chemist R.J. Reynolds Tobacco Co., Winston-Salem, N.C., 1968—. Mem. Am. Chem. Soc., Sigma Xi. Home: 414 Plymouth Av Winston-Salem NC 27104

LLOYD, WILLIAM GILBERT, educator, organic chemist; b. N.Y.C., July 10, 1923; s. John Grainger and Marguerite (Ryalls) L.; A.B. in Chemistry, Kalamazoo Coll., 1947; Sc.M., Brown U., 1950; Ph.D., Mich. State U., 1957; m. Anne M. Henderson, Apr. 6, 1947; children—Susan, David Grainger, Peter Henderson. With Dow Chem. Co., Midland, Mich., 1950-60, research chemist, 1957-60, asso. scientist, 1960-62; sr. process research specialist Lummus Co., Bloomfield, N.J., 1962-67; prof. chemistry Western Ky. U., Bowling Green, 1967—; cons. to univs.; pres., dir. Larox Research Corp., 1972—. Served with AUS, 1942-45. Recipient Distinguished Research award Western Ky. U., 1971. Mem. Am. Chem. Soc., Am. Inst. Chemists, Chem. Soc. (London), Sigma Xi. Unitarian Universalist. Author, patentee in field. Home: 1419 Woodhurst Dr Bowling Green KY 42101

LLOYD, WILLIAM NELSON, lawyer; b. Lewisburg, Tenn., July 24, 1920; s. William Houston and Rhoda (Hastings) L.; student Cumberland U., 1939-40, U. of South, 1941, U. Tenn., 1946; LL.B., Vanderbilt U., 1948, J.D., 1969; m. LaDelle Estes, Sept. 15, 1949; children—William Hastings, Robert Estes. Admitted to Tenn. bar, 1948, since practiced in Lewisburg. Dir. First Nat. Bank of Lewisburg, WSML, Inc. Judge, Ct. of Gen. Sessions, 1950-58; mem. Constl. Conv. Tenn., 1965; del. Democratic Nat. Conv., 1964. Served with USNR, 1942-46. Decorated Silver Star medal, D.F.C. with two oak leaf clusters. Recipient Long Rifle citation Boy Scouts Am., 1960. Mem. Am. Bar Assn., Am., Tenn. (bd. govs.) trial lawyers assns., Am. Judicature Soc., Am. Soc. Law and Sci. Presbyn. (elder). Home: 343 Forrest St Lewisburg TN 37901 Office: 220 W Church St Lewisburg TN 37901

LNENICKA, WILLIAM JOSEPH, educator; b. Hay Springs, Neb., Oct. 16, 1922; s. Joseph William and Lula Mae (Votruba) L.; B.S., U. Neb., 1949; M.S., Kan. State U., 1953; Ph.D. (Sci. Faculty fellow), Ga. Inst. Tech., 1961; m. Georgia Marie Erickson, Dec. 23, 1947; children—Wade, Susan. Mem. faculty U. Neb., 1949-51, Kan. State U., 1952-54, U. Okla., 1954-57, La. State U., 1957-58; mem. faculty Ga. Inst. Tech., 1958—, prof., 1968—. Treas., Vinings Chem. Co., Atlanta, 1964-73; pres. Universal Corporate Services, Inc., Atlanta, 1973—. Registered profl. engr., Ga., Okla., Kan. Mem. Am. Soc. Engring. Edn., Soc. Am. Mil. Engrs. Club: Cochise Riverview (Atlanta). Author: Effective College Teaching, 1970, Programmed Instruction - Statics, 1973. Home: 3235 Laramie Dr NW Atlanta GA 30339

LOCKART, JAMES ELDRIDGE III, accountant; b. Dallas, Apr. 14, 1947; B.B.A., U. Tex., 1969, M.B.A., 1971; m. Katherine Jarmon, May 16, 1970. Accountant, Touche Ross & Co., Austin, Tex., 1970-73, Capital Nat. Bank, Austin, 1973—; dir. High Fidelity, Inc., Austin. Mem. Coll. Bus. Adminstrn. Found. of U. Tex., Austin. Marquis G. Eaton scholar, 1968. Mem. Am. Inst. C.P.A.'s, Tex. Soc. C.P.A.'s. Nat. Assn. Accountants, Heritage Soc. Austin, Laguna Gloria Art Mus., Operation Self-Help, Delta Sigma Pi, Beta Alpha Psi. Home: 4518 Spanish Oak Trail Austin TX 78731 Office: Capital Nat Bank Bldg Austin TX 78701

LOCKE, CLAUDE ELVIN, telephone co. exec.; b. Oxford, Fla., Sept. 11, 1925; s. Coy and Thelma (Perry) L.; grad. high sch.; m. Charleen Clayton, Feb. 27, 1945; 1 dau., Linda. With Fla. Telephone Co., Leesburg, 1946—, v.p. operations, 1969—. Gen. fund dr. chmn. United Appeal, Leesburg, Fla., 1969-70. Served with USNR, 1944-46. Mem. Fla. Telephone Assn. (dir. 1969—, pres. 1970-71), Fla. Waterways Assn., Leesburg, Ocala-Marion County chambers of commerce. Lion (dist. gov. 1964-65), Elk. Club: University (Leesburg). Home: 1540 Normandy Way Leesburg FL 32748 Office: 425 N 3rd St Leesburg FL 32748

LOCKE, HOWARD PALMER, ret. lawyer; b. Charleston, S.C., July 11, 1899; s. Howard Palmer and Annie Hurst (Smith) L.; student Piedmont Coll., Demorest, Ga., 1916-18; B.C.S., Southeastern U., Washington, 1923; J.D., George Washington U., 1927; m. Margaret S. Danhakl, June 17, 1926; children—Henry Preston, John Howard. Admitted to D.C. bar, 1927, N.C. bar, 1927, S.C. bar, 1954; asst. adminstrv. officer Am. Agy. German Claims Commn., 1922-23, atty., adminstrv. officer Mexican Claims Commn., 1924-31; with Dept. Justice, 1931-54, exec. atty. tax div., 1934-54; pvt. practice, Charleston, S.C., 1954-55; clk. Tax Ct. U.S., 1955-66; with law firm Hudson & Creyke, 1967-71; lectr. tax matters U. Ga. Inst. Accountants, La. Poly Inst.; past instr. tax law Nat. U., Washington. Served with AUS, World War I. Mem. Kappa Alpha (past nat. pres.), Delta Theta Phi. Episcopalian. Contbr. articles on taxes to profl. jours. Home: 3901 Connecticut Av NW Washington DC 20008

LOCKE, JOHN FILLMORE, stock market service co. exec.; b. Bklyn., May 10, 1908; s. John Calvin and Adelaide (Fillmore) L.; degrees commerce, chemistry U. Cin., 1936, postgrad. engring.; m. Elsie Jane Nash, Aug. 8, 1942; children—Laura Carolyn, Joy Adelaide, John Noble, Harmon Fillmore. Formerly leader orch., band.; dept. head Avco, Cin., 1942-47; owner, pres. Cyclotron Trading Service, Covington, Ky., 1942—. Lectr. in field; chartist. Mem. child evangelism fellowship YMCA, Cin., 1954-56. Mem. No. Ky. Protestant Assn., Alpha Sigma Phi. Baptist (mem. finance com.). Mason (32 deg.). Author: Cyclotron Stock Market Forecasting, 1946; What is Commodity Trading 1956. Contbr. articles to profl. jours. Home and office: 1081 Montague Rd Park Hills Covington KY 41011

LOCKE, JOHN HOWARD, lawyer; b. Berryville, Va., Sept. 4, 1920; s. James Howard and Mary Elizabeth (Hart) L.; B.S. in Bus. Adminstrn., U. Richmond, 1941; LL.B., U. Va., 1948; m. Frances Rebecca Cook, Feb. 23, 1946; children—Anne Marie (Mrs. John Melton Hudgins), Nancy Lee, Rebecca Howard. Admitted to Va. bar, 1948, U.S. Supreme Ct., 1970; asso. Gentry, Locke, Rakes & Moore, Roanoke, Va., 1948—. Founder, Big Bros. Roanoke, 1958. Served with USNR, 1942-46; PTO. Fellow Internat. Soc. Barristers (pres. 1970), Am. Coll. Trial Lawyers; mem. Internat. Assn. Ins. Counsel, Am. Judicature Soc., Va. State Bar, Am., Va., Roanoke City (pres. 1970-71) bar assns. Clubs: Roanoke Country, Shenandoah (Roanoke). Editor or co-editor various legal jours. Home: 3015 Carolina Av Roanoke VA 24014 Office: Suite 300 Shenandoah Bldg Roanoke VA 24005

LOCKE, WENDELL VERNON, architect; b. Douglas, Kan., Aug. 19, 1924; s. Noel Corbet and Francis (McNutt) L.; student Tex. A. and M. U.; B.A., Okla. State U., 1950, B.Arch., 1953; m. Thyra June Shattuck, Nov. 27, 1947; children—Diane Adele, Jeanne Sharon, Anita Sue, Betty Karen. Draftsman, designer firm Coston, Frankfurt, Short, Oklahoma City, 1953-55; architect firm Caudill, Rowlett, Scott, Oklahoma City, 1955-62; partner, pres. Locke Wright Foster, Inc., Oklahoma City, 1962—. Mem. 1971-72 Sch. of Month jury. Served with AUS to maj., C.E., AUS, World War II, Korea. Recipient several profl. awards, citations. Mem. A.I.A. (mem. nat. com. architecture for edn. 1971-73, vice chmn. 1974), Council Edn. Facility Planners, Sch. Facilities Council, Soc. Coll. and Univ. Planning. Works include Performing Arts Center, Okla. State U., Stillwater, 1970. Home: Route 13 Box 122A Oklahoma City OK 73132 Office: 5700 N Portland St Oklahoma City OK 73112

LOCKE, WILLIAM, physician; b. Morden, Man., Can., Mar. 16, 1916; s. Corbet and Ruby Louise (Brown) L.; M.D., U. Man., 1938; M.S. in Medicine, U. Minn., 1947; m. Katherine Elizabeth Acer, Sept. 29, 1945. Fellow in medicine Mayo Clinic, 1938-40, 46-47; research fellow Harvard, 1948-50; mem. staff Ochsner Clinic, New Orleans, 1950—, now head sect. endocrinology and metabolism; faculty dept. medicine Tulane U., 1951—, clin. prof. medicine, 1969—; sr. active staff Ochsner Found. Hosp., New Orleans, 1955—, pres. staff, 1954-55; sr. vis. physician Charity Hosp., New Orleans. Served to lt. comdr. Royal Canadian Navy, 1940-46. Fellow A.C.P.; mem. Endocrine Soc., Am. Diabetes Assn., Sigma Xi. Club: Roundtable (New Orleans). Editor: (with A.V. Schally) The Hypothalamus and Pituitary in Health and Disease, 1972. Contbr. articles profl. jours. Home: 4815 Dryades St New Orleans LA 70115 Office: 1514 Jefferson Hwy New Orleans LA 70115

LOCKETT, BROOKER THOMAS, ednl. adminstr.; b. Albany, Ga., Aug. 28, 1925; s. Joseph Moselle and Essie Lee (Thomas) L.; B.A., Fisk U., Nashville, 1948; M.A., Atlanta U., 1958; postgrad. Peabody Coll. for Tchrs., Nashville, 1960, Emory U., Atlanta, 1964. Instr. English, Booker T. Washington High Sch., Atlanta, 1948-68; instr., chmn. dept. English, D.M. Therrell High Sch., Atlanta, 1968—; instr. English, W.Ga. Coll., Carrollton, 1972-73. Past exec. sec. Met. Atlanta Assn. for Blind. So. Edn. Found. grantee to Ednl. Adminstrn. Seminar, Peabody Coll. for Tchrs., 1960, Nat. Def. Lang. Inst., Vanderbilt U., 1962, Knoxville (Tenn.) Coll., 1962, Inst. Humanities, Knoxville Coll., 1965. Mem. N.E.A., Nat. Soc. Secondary Edn., Nat. Council Tchrs. English, Ga. Assn. Educators, Atlanta Area English Assn., Nat. Soc. Study Edn., Soc. Negro History and Life, N.A.A.C.P., Alpha Phi Alpha. Episcopalian. Clubs: Fisk University (chmn. constl. com.), Emblem YMCA (Atlanta). Home: 1848 Tiger Flower Dr NW Atlanta GA 30314

LOCKETT, LESLIE STERNE, lawyer; b. Fort Worth, July 14, 1911; s. Joseph Louis and Nellie Lee (Davis) L.; student Washington and Lee U., 1928-29; B.A., U. Tex., 1932, LL.B., 1935; postgrad. U. Wis., 1932, 33; m. Catherine Dinn, July 18, 1966; children—Lee (Mrs. J. Pat Fletcher), Maggie (Mrs. John L. Winters). Admitted to Tex. bar, 1935; practiced in Corpus Christi, Tex., 1935-42, 45—; dir. Citizens State Bank, Corpus Christi, Tex. Served with USNR, 1942-45. Mem. State Bar Tex. (mem. com. on adminstrn. justice 1960-66), Nueces County Bar Assn. (pres. 1958-59). Rotarian. Home: 206 Leming St Corpus Christi TX 78404 Office: Box 2446 Corpus Christi TX 78403

LOCKETT, MARY CLODOVIA, educator; b. Austin, Tex., Jan. 23, 1913; d. Edgar Stevens and Monica Margaret (Mangon) Lockett; B.S. summa cum laude, St. Louis U., 1937, Ph.D., 1952; M.S., DePaul U., 1947. Asst. prof. biology Le Clerc Coll., Belleville, Ill., 1947-49; asso. prof. biology, chmn. dept. Notre Dame Coll., St. Louis, 1950-65; prof. biology, chmn. dept. U. Dallas, Irving, 1965—. Bd. dirs. Am. Cancer Soc., Dallas Human Relations, Dallas Interracial Council. Recipient A.R.C. award, 1964. Piper prof., 1969-70. Mem. A.A.A.S., Am. Inst. Biol. Scis., Soc. Nuclear Medicine. Author: Research Problems in Biology, series 1 and 2, 1971. Contbr. articles to profl. jours. Home: Route 2 Box 4 Irving TX 75062

LOCKROW, ARTHUR LYNN, dir. performing arts; b. Nyskiuna, N.Y., Nov. 21, 1945; s. Arthur Herman and Helen Grace (Thierolf) L.; B.S., East Tenn. State U., 1968; postgrad. U. N.C., Greensboro, 1972-74. Drama tchr. Burke County Pub. Schs., Morgantown, N.C., 1968-69; tchr. jr. high sch., Charlotte, N.C., 1969-72; tech. dir., designer, summers 1968-72; tech. dir. Lost Colony, Manteo, N.C., 1973-74. Mem. Alpha Phi Omega, Alpha Psi Omega. Home and office: PO Box 87 Autumn Forest MHV Brown Summit NC 27241

LOCKWOOD, MRS. CHARLES HOWARD (DOROTHY PYLE LOCKWOOD), newspaper pub.; b. Conway, Ark., Nov. 10; d. Lucas Hilliard and Augusta E. (Manes) Pyle; B.A., Central Coll., 1918; postgrad. piano N.Y.C. Sch. Music, 1919-24; m. James Aloysius McGrath, Oct. 1924 (dec. May 1928); m. 2d, Randall B. Terry, Sept. 17, 1931 (dec. May 1955); 1 son, Randall B. Head piano dept. Ark. State Tchrs. Coll., 1920-24; v.p. Burlington (N.C.) Times News, 1955—, High Point (N.C.) Enterprise, 1955—, The Times, Thomasville, N.C., 1958—. Past bd. dirs. So. Furniture Expn., 1961. Active Heart Assn., United Fund. Bd. dirs. YMCA, Mem. N.C. Soc. Preservation Antiquities, Presbyn. Clubs: Emerywood Country; Blowing Rock (N.C.) Country. Home: 811 Willowbar Terrace High Point NC 27262 also 1015 Riverview Dr Atchison KS 66002 Office: 210 Church Av High Point NC 27261

LODAL, OLAF T., elec. engr.; b. Gordon, Tex., Feb. 9, 1908; s. Martin and Clara (Harward) L.; B.S. in Elec. Engring., Tex. Tech. U., 1932; m. Daisy Warriner, Dec. 14, 1940; children—Jan Martin, Gene Wright. Asst. resident engr., supr. Tex. State Wide Planning Survey, Tex. Hwy. Dept., 1932-39; pres. Lodal & Bain Engrs., Inc., San Antonio 1939—. Mem. exec. bd. Alamo Area council Boy Scouts Am., 1950—. Named San Antonio Engr. of Year, Tex. Soc. Profl. Engrs., 1963. Registered profl. engr., Tex., Okla., N.M., Ariz. Fellow Am. Soc. C.E.; mem. I.E.E.E. (chmn. South Tex. sect. 1946), Nat. (dir. 1967-68), Tex. (pres. 1960) socs. profl. engrs., Tex. Tech. U. Ex-Students Assn. (pres. 1951-52). Presbyn. (clk. of session 1969-70). Lion. Home: 8806 Pineridge Rd San Antonio TX 78217 Office: 8530 Village Dr San Antonio TX 78217

LODGE, WILLIAM DUNKIN, communications equipment mfg. co. exec.; b. Bridgeport, W.Va., July 3, 1927; s. John Dunkin and Mary Tirzah (Hayes) L.; B.S., W.Va. U., 1951; M.B.A., N.Y. U., 1965; m. Pauline Marie Haskins, Aug. 6, 1950; children—David, Linda, Thomas, Daniel. With Western Electric Co. Inc., 1954—, staff mgr., N.Y.C., 1962-68, mgr. So. Tex. area, Houston, 1968—. Served with USNR, 1945-46, AUS, 1951-54. Mem. Am. Mgmt. Assn., I.E.E.E., Sigma Nu. Kiwanian. Home: 311 Yorkchester Houston TX 77024 Office: 601 Lockwood Dr Houston TX 77011

LODOVIC, JOSEPH JAMES, III, securities co. exec.; b. San Antonio, July 17, 1939; s. Joseph James and Jeanne Elizabeth (Spencer) L.; B.B.A., So. Meth. U., 1961; m. Sharon Kay Imes, Apr. 1, 1960; children—Joseph James IV, Whitney Ann. Field rep. Municipal Adv. Council Tex., 1961-63; registered rep., v.p., adv. dir. Russ & Co., Inc., 1963-73; v.p., dir. Russ Securities Corp., San Antonio, 1973—. Mem. bd. Municipal Adv. Council Tex., 1969-71. Mem. San Antonio Municipal Bond Club (pres. 1971-72), Sigma Alpha Epsilon. Methodist (treas. 1971-73). Club: 730 Breakfast (pres. 1972) (San Antonio). Office: 1605 Alamo Nat Bldg San Antonio TX 78205

LOEB, BEN FOHL, JR., lawyer, educator; b. Nashville, May 15, 1932; s. Ben Fohl and Frances (Paysinger) L.; B.A., Vanderbilt U., 1955, J.D., 1960; m. Anne Nelson, Sept. 23, 1961; children—Charles N., William N. Admitted to Tenn. bar, 1960, U.S. Supreme Ct. bar, 1966; asso. firm Crownover, Branstetter & Folk, Nashville, 1960-64; prof. pub. law and govt., asst. dir. U. N.C. Inst. Govt., Chapel Hill, 1964—. Served to 1st lt. AUS, 1955-57. Mem. Am Bar Assn., U. N.C. Faculty Club, Am. Assn. U. Profs., Phi Beta Kappa, Phi Delta Phi, Pi Kappa Alpha (chpt. pres. 1955). Democrat. Baptist. Author: Drivers' License Law, 1965; Regulation of Intoxicating Liquors, 1966; Motor Vehicle Law, 1967; Traffic Law and Highway Safety, 1970. Asso. editor Vanderbilt Law Rev., 1960. Home: 812 Emory Dr Chapel Hill NC 27514

LOEB, WILLIAM SIGFRIED, retail radio store exec.; b. Athens, Ala., June 14, 1925; s. Emil Felix and Addie Louise (Hannah) L.; grad. high sch.; m. Helen Ruth Newsom, Mar. 22, 1944; s. Kenneth N., Beverly (Mrs. Ted L. Bullard), Richard E. Founder, 1946, since pres. Huntsville Radio Service Inc. (Ala.), design, installation and maintenance radio communications and microwave systems; mem. consumer panel parts and service Motorola, Inc. Vice pres. Madison County Govt. Study Commn., 1972-73. Served with USNR, World War II. Mem. I.E.E.E., Nat. Assn. Ind. Bus., Nat. Assn. Bus. and Ednl. Radio, Huntsville Amateur Radio Club (charter, past pres.), Huntsville-Madison C. of C., Am. Radio Relay League (past emergency coordinator). Presbyn. (charter mem. trustees, past deacon). Lion (past pres. Huntsville; past zone chmn.). Contbr. articles to tech. mags. Home: 6619 Chadwell Rd SW Huntsville AL 35802 Office: 2402 Clinton Av W Huntsville AL 35805

LOEBELSON, ROBERT MORRIS, editor, pub.; b. N.Y.C., Feb. 13, 1923; s. Ira and Gertrude (Gordon) L.; student U. Mich., 1943-44; B.A. in Journalism, Ohio State U., 1947; m. Jean Amdur, Jan. 30, 1942; 1 son, Richard Kenneth. Newspaper reporter Ohio State Jour., Cleve. Plain Dealer, Springfield News and Sun, Dayton Herald (all Ohio), 1941-48; editor Tech. Data Digest Mag., Dayton, O., 1948-51; mil. editor Am. Aviation mag., Washington, 1951-56, Space/Aeronautics mag., Washington, 1958-61; mem. pub. relations staff Aerospace Industries Assn., Washington, 1956-58; free-lance writer Washington, 1961-66; editor Vertical World Mag., Washington, 1966-70, pres. Vertical World, Inc., 1968-70; pres. Aerospace Communications, Washington, 1970—; editor Urban Transport News, 1973—; dir. Aerosystems Tech. Corp., Franklin, N.J. Served with M.I. AUS, 1943-46. Recipient 1st prize Trans-World Airlines writing competition, 1958. Mem. Aviation Space Writers Assn. (pres. 1960-61), Nat. Press Club. Home: 10001 Sinnott Dr Bethesda MD 20034 Office: National Press Bldg Washington DC 20004

LOEFFLER, LARRY JAMES, educator; b. Beaver Falls, Pa., May 6, 1932; s. Theodore Paul and Lylian Rosena (Boots) L.; A.B., Princeton, 1954, M.A., 1959, Ph.D., 1961; m. Carol Ann Baker, July 6, 1957; children—Matthew David, Michael Andrew. Organic chemist, USPHS fellow Swiss Fed. Inst. Tech., Zurich, 1961; chemist Merck, Sharp & Dohme Research Labs., West Point, Pa., 1961-69; research asso. in pharmacology NIH, Bethesda, Md., 1969-71; asso. prof. medicinal chemistry U. N.C., Chapel Hill, 1971—. Served with AUS, 1955. Mem. A.A.A.S., Am. Assn. Colls. Pharmacy, Am. Chem. Soc., N.Y. Acad. Scis., Sigma Xi, Phi Beta Kappa. Contbr. articles to sci. lit. Home: 317 Wesley Dr Chapel Hill NC 27514

LOEPPERT, RICHARD HENRY, educator; b. Chgo., Mar. 13, 1914; s. Adam John and Anna (Breslich) L.; B.S., Northwestern U., 1935; Ph.D., U. Minn., 1940; m. Adeline Louise Radtke, Dec. 28, 1940; 1 son, Richard H. Research chemist Richardson Co., Melrose Park, Ill., 1939-40; prof., asst. head dept. chemistry N.C. State U., Raleigh, 1940—. Dir., N.Central N.C. Sci. Fair, 1958, N.C. Sci. Fair, 1960. Mem. Am. Chem. Soc. (chmn. N.C. sect. 1961, sec.-treas. 1957-60), A.A.A.S., N.C. Acad. Sci. (chmn. chemistry sect. 1965-66, vice chmn. 1970-71), Sigma Xi, Phi Beta Kappa, Phi Lambda Upsilon. Home: 1317 Rand Dr Raleigh NC 27608

LOESCH, HAROLD CARL, educator; b. Osage, Tex., Oct. 3, 1926; s. Eldor E. and Martha (Niemeier) L.; student Tarleton State U., 1946-47; B.S., Tex. A. and M. U., 1951, M.S., 1954, Ph.D., 1962; m. Mabel L. Treichler, Oct. 19, 1945; children—Stephen, Gretchen

(Mrs. Dennis Fehler), Jonathon, Frederick. Prin. marine biologist, acting lab. dir. Dept. Conservation, Ala., 1952-57; fisheries officer FAO, Honduras, Guatemala, El Salvador, Ecuador, 1960-68; prof. marine scis. La. State U., Baton Rouge, 1968—. Vis. prof. U. Guayaguil, Ecuador, 1972. Served with USAAF, 1945-46. Research and publs. in field. Home: 1232 Dahlia St Baton Rouge LA 70808

LOEVINGER, LEE, lawyer; b. St. Paul, Apr. 24, 1913; s. Gustavus and Millie (Strouse) L.; B.A. summa cum laude, U. Minn., 1933, J.D., 1936; m. Ruth E. Howe, Mar. 4, 1950; children—Barbara Lee, Eric Howe, Peter Howe. Admitted to Minn. bar, 1936, Mo. bar, 1937, U.S. Supreme Ct. bar, 1941, D.C. bar, 1966; asso. law firm Watson, Ess, Groner, Barnett & Whittaker, Kansas City, Mo., 1936-37; trial atty., regional atty. NLRB, 1937-41; atty. antitrust div. U.S. Dept. Justice, 1941-46, asst. atty. gen. charge antitrust div., 1961-63; partner law firm Larson, Loevinger, Lindquist, Freeman & Fraser, Mpls., 1946-60; asso. justice Minn. Supreme Ct., 1960-61; commr. FCC, 1963-68; partner law firm Hogan & Hartson, Washington, 1968—. Gen. counsel Craig-Hallum, Inc., investment banking, Mpls., 1950-60, v.p., dir., 1968-73; v.p., dir. Craig-Hallum Corp., Mpls., 1968-73; gen. counsel Gen. Securities, Inc., 1951-60; lectr. hosp. and nursing law U. Minn. Med. Sch., 1953-60; vis. prof. jurisprudence, Law Sch., 1961; gen. counsel Minn. Nurses Assn., 1950-60; spl. counsel to subcom. on small bus. U.S. Senate, 1951-52; U.S. del. to com. experts on restrictive bus. practices OECD, 1961-64, vice chmn. com., 1963-64; U.S. del., vice chmn. extraordinary adminstrv. radio conf. Internat. Telecommunications Union, Geneva, 1964, 66; mem. Adminstrv. Conf. U.S., 1972—. Served to lt. comdr. USNR, 1942-45. Recipient Outstanding Achievement award U. Minn. Regents, 1968. Mem. Am. (mem. law and tech. com. 1969—), D.C., Fed., Minn., Hennepin County bar assns., Am. Judicature Soc., A.A.A.S., Broadcast Pioneers, Phi Beta Kappa, Sigma Xi, Phi Delta Gamma, Delta Sigma Rho, Sigma Delta Chi, Tau Kappa Alpha, Alpha Epsilon Rho. Author: The Law of Free Enterprise, 1949; Jurimetrics, 1949; An Introduction to Legal Logic, 1952. Editor, contbr. Basic Data on Atomic Development Problems in Minnesota, 1958; editorial adviser Jurimetrics Jour.; adv. bd. Antitrust Bull., Performing Arts Rev. Contbr. articles to profl. jours. Home: 5669 Bent Branch Rd Washington DC 20016 Office: 815 Connecticut Av Washington DC 20006

LOEWENSTEIN, JOSEPH EDWARD, endocrinologist; b. Crockett, Tex., Nov. 25, 1937; s. Joseph Meyer and Ethel Lois (Fallis) L.; B.A., U. Tex., 1959; M.D., Washington U., 1963; m. Marjorie Marie Thomson, Aug. 16, 1958; children—Sarah Frances, Edward Benjamin. Intern Barnes Hosp., St. Louis, 1963-64, resident internal medicine, 1967-69; research asso. NIH, Bethesda, Md., 1964-66, mem. staff, 1966-67; fellow metabolism Washington U., St. Louis, 1969-70, instr. medicine, 1970; asst. prof. medicine La. State U., Shreveport, 1970-73, asso. prof., 1973—, chief sect. endocrinology, dept. medicine, 1970—. Bd. dirs. Shreveport Civic Opera Assn., 1971—, 2d v.p., 1972-74. Served with USPHS, 1964-67. Diplomate Am. Bd. Internal Medicine with subsplty. in endocrinology. Fellow A.C.P.; mem. Gilbert and Sullivan Soc. Shreveport (dir. 1970—, pres. 1973), Phi Beta Kappa, Alpha Omega Alpha. Home: 616 Linden St Shreveport LA 71104 Office: La State U Med Center Shreveport LA 71130

LOEWENSTEIN, JOSEPH MEYER, physician; b. Houston, May 15, 1910; s. Edward Benjamin and Lena (Kapner) L.; B.A., Rice U., 1931; M.D., U. Tex., 1935; postgrad. N.Y. U., 1954, U. London (Eng.), 1965; m. Ethel Lois Fallis, June 6, 1933; children—Joseph Edward, Robert Fallis. Intern John Sealy Hosp., Galveston, Tex., 1935-36; practice gen. medicine, Lovelady, Tex., 1936-38, Port Arthur, Tex., 1938—; partner Parkside Clinic, Port Arthur, 1938—; chief staff St. Mary's Hosp., Port Arthur, 1953; mem. staff Park Place Hosp., Port Arthur. Pres. Port Arthur Little Theater, 1955-59; med. adviser Draft Bd. No. 75, Jefferson County, Tex., 1967—, Schlesinger Convalescent Home, 1967—. Bd. dirs. Gates Meml. Art Mus., Port Arthur, 1958-59. Mem. A.M.A., Tex. Med. Assn., Am. Assn. Gen. Practitioners, Royal Soc. Medicine (London; affiliate mem.), Phi Beta Kappa, Alpha Omega Alpha. Club: Port Arthur Town. Home: 3045 Eugenia Dr Groves TX 77619 Office: 3048 Procter St Port Arthur TX 77640

LOEWENSTEIN, MORRISON, educator; b. Kearney, Neb., Aug. 21, 1915; s. Daniel J. and Birdie (Leake) L.; B.S., U. Neb., 1938; M.S., Kan. State U., 1940; Ph.D., Ohio State U., 1954; m. Genevieve Kathryn Johnson, Sept. 10, 1939; children—Kentley A., Roger E., Douglas B. Instr. N.M. State U., Las Cruces, 1940-41; grad. asst. U. Neb. at Lincoln, 1946-47; asso. prof. Okla. State U., Stillwater, 1947-55; research dir. Crest Foods Co., Ashton, Ill., 1955-66; prof. dairy sci. U. Ga., Athens, 1966—. Pres. Sutton Crest Proteins, Ltd., Sutton, Que., Can., 1961-65; gen. cons. to dairy industry. Pres., Dist. 275 Sch. Bd., Ashton, 1960-66. Served with AUS, 1941-46; ETO. Decorated Bronze Star medal Mem. Toastmasters Internat. (lt. gov. div. III, 1970), Am. Dairy Sci. Assn., Inst. Food Technologists, Sigma Xi, Gamma Sigma Delta, Alpha Zeta. Presbyn. (elder). Club: Torch International. Contbr. articles to profl. jours. Patentee in field. Home: 173 Beacham Dr Athens GA 30601 Office: Dairy Sci Dept U Ga Athens GA 30602

LOEWER, ERIC GEORGE, JR., accountant; b. Eunice, La., Oct. 23, 1942; s. Eric George and Hattie (Bieber) L.; B.A., U. Southwestern La., 1966; m. Jane Gilchrist, July 17, 1965; children—Laura K., Eric George III. Accountant, Price Waterhouse & Co., Houston, 1966-69; partner Loewer & Zimmerman, Eunice, La., 1969—; dir. Acadiana Bank, Planters Securities Inc., Acadian Bloodstock, Inc.; pres., dir. Reich Enterprises, Inc., Eunice, 1973-74, Streifen, Inc., 1974-75; treas., dir. Hallmad Co., Eunice, 1973-74, Plan Corp., 1973-74, L & L Storage, Inc., Rayne, La., 1966-74, Acadian Acres, 1973-74, Acadiana Bldg. Corp., 1970-74; various farming and ranching activities. Mem. Am. Inst. C.P.A.'s, Soc. La. C.P.A.'s, Tex. Soc. C.P.A.'s, La. Cattlemen's Assn. Baptist. Home: 1401 Betty St Eunice LA 70535 Office: 851 W Park St Eunice LA 70535

LOFROOS, WILLIAM NORMAN, civil engr.; b. Warren, O., June 19, 1931; s. William Eric and Margaret (White) L.; B.E. in Civil Engring., Vanderbilt U., 1954; M.S., U. Fla., 1959; m. Avis Hurst, Aug. 8, 1959; children—Margaret Elizabeth, William Eric. Instr., U. Fla., 1957-59; with Fla. Dept. Transp., Tallahassee, 1959—, now chief bur. planning. Served with USMC, 1954-57, lt. col. Res. Mem. Am. Soc. C.E. (past br. pres.), Fla. Engring. Soc. (past br. pres., past sect. chmn.), Am., Southeastern assns. state hwy. ofcls., Marine Corps Res. Officers Assn. Mason. Home: 1904 Doomar St Tallahassee FL 32303 Office: Fla Dept Transportation Tallahassee FL 32301

LOFTIN, CHARLIE FRANKLIN, JR., petroleum corp. exec.; b. Fort Deposit, Ala., June 2, 1924; s. Charlie Franklin and Lucy (Frazier) L.; B.S. in Mech. Engring., U. Ala., 1949; postgrad. Alexander Hamilton Inst., Inc., 1963; m. Jeanine Cearley, Jan. 17, 1953; children—Lynn, Dean, Vivian. Sales engr. Warren Petroleum Corp., Tulsa, 1950-55, mgr. tech. services, 1959-70, dir. adminstrv. services, 1970—; v.p. Power Motor Fuel Sales, Chgo. and Dallas, 1955-59; Dir. Nat. L.P. Gas Assn., Chgo., 1970-72. Mem. Nat. Def. Exec. Res., Washington, 1973—. Served with USAAF, 1943-45. Decorated Air medal with five clusters. Registered profl. engr., Okla. Mem. Soc. Automotive Engrs., Am. Soc. Testing Materials, Nat. Gas Processors Assn. Patentee in field. Home: 3445 E 75th Pl Tulsa OK 74136 Office: PO Box 1589 Tulsa OK 74102

LOFTON, GENE TRAVIS, curator; b. Healdton, Okla., Mar. 8, 1934; s. J.T. and Era Julia (Cooper) L.; student Okla. A. and M. U., 1952-55, East Central State U., 1953-54; m. Donna Ruth Adair, May 20, 1966; children—Randy Gene, Travis Lynn. Corrision engr. Cities Service Pipe Line, Cushing, Okla., 1955-56; logging engr. Lane Wells Co., Odessa, Tex., 1956-57; spl. test engr. Firestone Tire & Rubber Co., Ft. Stockton, Tex., 1957-61; soil technician State of Okla. Hwy. Dept., Duncan, 1965-69; dir. Tucker Tower Mus., Ardmore, Okla., 1972—. Cons. soil engr., Ada, Okla., 1961-65. Active Boy Scouts Am., 1957-65. Mem. Kappa Kappa Psi. Lutheran. Mason. Home and office: PO Box 1649 Ardmore OK 73401

LOGAN, ALBERT BOYD, lawyer; b. Colorado Springs, Colo., Jan. 27, 1909; s. Glen Hayes and Margaret (McGee) L.; A.B., U. Colo., 1930, J.D., 1932; m. Martha Elizabeth Hutchison, Sept. 28, 1934; children—Marla Lee (Mrs. Al Hollingsworth), Glenda Sue (Mrs. Stephen Harrison). Admitted to Colo. bar, 1932; pvt. practice law, Colorado Springs, 1932-56; with Office Solicitor, U.S. Dept. Interior, Denver, 1956-66; counsel Indian Claims Commn., Washington, 1966-70, Office Gen. Counsel VA, 1970—; lectr. jud. problems. Exec. dir. N.Am. Judges Assn., 1960-67; sec., trustee Jud. Research Found., Washington, 1960-68; cons. Am. Judicature Soc., Nat. Council Alcoholism, U. Colo. Sch. Alcohol Studies, Colo. Commn. Alcoholism, Inst. Law and Psychiatry, Mil.-Jud. Conf. Hwy Safety, Nat. Council Indian Opportunity, Internat. Acad. Metabology. Trustee Harmony Found., Inc. Served with USMCR, 1944-45. Recipient Beyond Call of Duty award Nat. Assn. Municipal Judges, 1961. Mem. Fed., Am., Colo. bar assns., Am. Legion, Am. Judicature Soc., Nat. Inst. Jud. Dynamics (dir.), U.S. Jr. C. of C. (nat. dir.), N.Am. Judges Assn. (hon. life mem., Amicus Curiae award 1964), Phi Alpha Delta, Sigma Delta Chi, Alpha Tau Omega. Clubs: El Paso, Exchange (pres. Colorado Springs); National Lawyers. Author: Struggle For Equal Justice, 1968; Justice in Jeopardy, 1973; With Liberty and Justice for All, 1972. Editor: Municipal Ct. Rev., 1960-67, Municipal Ct. Briefs, 1960-67. Contbr. to legal periodicals. Home: 2727 29th St NW Washington DC 20008 Office: National Institute of Judicial Dynamics 2607 Connecticut Av NW Washington DC 20008

LOGAN, WILLIAM BOYD, coll. pres.; b. Asheville, N.C., June 29, 1910; s. William Erwin and Rose Addie (Deaver) L.; student Mars Hill Coll., 1927-29; B.A., Furman U., 1939; M.S., U. N.C., 1944; Ph.D., Ohio State U., 1952; m. Annie Lou Bell, May 29, 1937; children—Susan Carole, William Boyd. Tchr., Lee H. Edwards High Sch., Asheville, 1936-40, coordinator distributive edn., 1940-44; tchr. Biltmore Coll., Asheville, 1942-44; part-time tchr. Mars Hill Coll., 1944; acting supr. distributive edn. N.C. Dept. Edn., 1944-46; asso. prof. edn. Woman's Coll., U. N.C., 1946-48; successively instr., asst. prof., asso. prof., prof. edn. Ohio State U., 1948-67, dir. distributive edn. mgmt. insts., 1955-67; pres. Webber Coll., Babson Park, Fla., 1967—; vis. prof. summers Colo. A. and M. Coll., 1947, La. State U., 1952, U. N.C., 1955, George Peabody Coll., 1956, U. Mich., 1956, U. Ala., 1957, Ind. U., 1959, Colo. State Coll., 1960, Wayne State U., 1961, U. Wash., 1963, U. Cal. at Berkeley, 1965; edn. cons. Nat. Retail Hardware Assn.; lectr. mgmt. and sales tng. Chmn.; Nat. Tchr. Tng. Conf. Distbn., 1957; instr. first Nat. Adult Distributive Edn. Conf., 1958; mem. vocational edn. survey team Ore. Dept. Edn., 1958; worked with groups fgn. vocational educators, Ohio State U., 1955, 56. Mem. Pres. Kennedy's Panel Cons. Vocational Edn. to Sec. Health, Edn. and Welfare, 1961-62; nat. panel cons. Vocational Edn. Personnel Devel., Dept. Health, Edn. and Welfare, Washington, served on civic coms. Trustee Highlands Sch., Avon Park, Fla. Mem. Am. (chmn. nominating com. 1952, awards com. 1957-60; pres. 1961; editor various publs.), N.C. (sect. v.p. 1943), Ohio (membership sec. 1952-58) vocational assns., N.E.A., Asso. Orgns. for Tchr. Edn. (chmn. 1967), Fla. Assn. Colls. and Univs. (pres. 1974), Lake Wales C. of C. (dir.), Delta Pi Epsilon (nat. historian 1944, nat. v.p. 1946), Phi Delta Kappa, Pi Omega Pi. Mason (32 deg., Shriner). Author: (with Beckley) The Retail Salesperson at Work, 1948; (with Robinson and Blackler) Store Salesmanship, 6th edit., 1966; (with others) Vocational Education in Rural America (yearbook), 1959; (with others) National Business Teachers Association Yearbook, 1947; (with Helen Moon) Facts About Merchandise, 1962, 2d edit., 1967. Co-author: Merchandising Mathematics, 1970; Mathematics in Marketing, 1970. Contbr. articles to profl. jours. Home: Presidents Home Webber Coll Babson Park FL 33827

LOGAN, WILLIAM THOMAS, dentist; b. Dublin, Tex., Dec. 10, 1925; s. James Marvin and Eula (Kiker) L.; B.A., Hardin-Simmons U., 1948; D.D.S., U. Tex., 1952; m. Margaret Elaine Dobbins, May 31, 1947; children—Richard Alan, Diana Lynn. Practice dentistry, Borger, Tex., 1952—. Served with USNR, 1944-46; PTO. Fellow Acad. Gen. Dentistry; mem. Am., Tex. dental assns., Borger (pres. 1959), Panhandle Dist. (pres. 1966-67) dental socs., Am. Acad. Gold Foil Operators, Am. Inst. Oral Biology, Tex. Acad. Gen. Dentistry, Palo Duro (pres. 1960), Clyde Schuyler dental study groups, Tex. Jr. C. of C. (dir. 1954), Psi Omega. Methodist. Mason (Shriner, 32 deg.), Elk, Lion. Clubs: North Plains Knife and Fork (dir. 1962-64). Home: 1400 Bluebonnet Lane Borger TX 79007 Office: 706 S McGee St Borger TX 79007

LOGSDON, GUY WILLIAM, librarian; b. Ada, Okla., May 31, 1934; s. Guy and Mattie Theresa (Marsalas) L.; B.A. in Edn., East Central State Coll., 1957; M.L.S., U. Okla., 1964, postgrad., 1969-70; postgrad. Ind. U., 1968; m. Phyllis Evelyn Landers, Dec. 28, 1953; children—Tamara Lei, Cindy Lou, Susan Elizabeth, Nathalie Marsalas. Photographer Guy Logsdon Studio, Ada, 1954-56; tchr. Norwalk-La Mirada (Cal.) Sch. Dist., 1956-67, Burbank (Okla.) Sch. Dist., 1957-58, Payson (Ariz.) Sch. Dist., 1960-63; salesman Gt. So. Life Ins., Ardmore, Okla., 1958-60; reference librarian Okla. State U., Stillwater, 1964-67; dir. libraries U. Tulsa, 1967—. Mem. Am., Okla., Southwestern library assns., Am., Tex., Cal. folklore socs., Indian Terr. Posse Westerners, Sons of Confederacy, Okla., Western, Rodeo hist. socs., Phi Delta Kappa. Democrat. Methodist. Mason. Editor: Great River and Small (Welborn Hope). Contbr. articles to profl. jours. and encys. Home: 4645 S Columbia St Tulsa OK 74105 Office: U Tulsa 600 S College St Tulsa OK 74104

LOGUE, THOMAS OTTO, JR., hosp. adminstr.; b. Vicksburg, Miss., Oct. 18, 1932; student Vicksburg Sch. Med. Tech., 1951-53; B.S. in Bus. Adminstrn., Withworth Coll., 1971; postgrad. U. Ala., 1971-72; m. Joyce Wilson; children—Tonia, Thomas Edward, Linda. Adminstr., Hancock Gen. Hosp., Bay St. Louis, Miss., 1959-66, Tallahatchie Gen. Hosp., Charleston, Miss., 1966-68, Southwest Miss. Gen. Hosp., McComb, 1968—. Mem. Miss. Manpower Bd., 1970-72; pres. Health Adv. Bd., 1970—; mem. adv. com. Southwest Miss. Jr. Coll., 1970—. Bd. dirs. United Givers Fund. Served to lt. col. AUS, 1966. Named Outstanding Young Man of Yr., Miss. Jr. C. of C., 1961. Fellow Am. Coll. Hosp. Adminstrs. (sec.-treas. 71); mem. Miss. Hosp. Assn. (bd. govs. 1970—), Am. Legion (post comdr. 1970-73), Tallahatchie County C. of C. (pres. 1967-68), Bay St. Louis and Mendenhall Jaycees (pres.). Republican. Rotarian (past pres), Mason. Contbr. articles to profl. jours., mags. Home: 1510 Vermont St McComb MS 39648 Office: PO Box 68 McComb MS 39648

LOH, JOHN KING SING, oil co. adminstr.; b. Shanghai, China, Dec. 24, 1937; s. Finch and Shoutsen (Chao) L.; B.S. in Petroleum Engring., U. Okla., 1960; postgrad. Mo. Sch. Mines, 1960, U. Okla., 1961-63; m. Ingeborg G. Eickert, Feb. 4, 1961; children—Matthew F., Michael E. Came to U.S., 1956, naturalized, 1970. Research group leader Oil Recovery Corp., Norman, Okla., 1962-63; prodn. engr. Mobil Oil Corp., Duncan, Okla., 1964-69, drilling engr., Oklahoma City, 1969, sr. operations engr., Guymon, Okla., 1969-71, asso. operations engr., 1971, asso. prodn. foreman, 1971—. Pvt. cons. in petroleum engring., 1963. Commr. Adobe Walls Council Boy Scouts Am., 1972, scoutmaster, 1973—. Registered profl. engr., Okla. Elk. Home: 6029 Sunset Dr Guymon OK 73942 Office: Box 1227 Guymon OK 73942

LOHNES, GEORGE MANFORD, elec. engr.; b. Dayton, O., Sept. 10, 1908; s. George Conrad and Hagar Shobe (Franz) L.; B.S. in Elec. Engring., George Washington U., 1939; m. Sara Harriet DeWitt, Feb. 8, 1930; children—Sara Ann (Mrs. Donald S. Schneider), Marilyn Louise, George Manfrod Lohnes, Jr. Draftsman-engr. Jansky & Bailey, Washington, 1932-45; partner Lohnes & Culver, cons. engrs., Washington, 1945—. Registered profl. engr., D.C. Mem. I.E.E.E., Am. Radio Relay League, Aircraft Owners and Pilots Assn., Nat. Pilots Assn., Assn. Fed. Communications Cons. Engrs., Theta Tau. Methodist. Mason (Shriner). Club: Nat. Aviation. Home: 5053 Massachusetts Av NW Washington DC 20016 Office: 1156 15th St NW Washington DC 20005

LOHR, DERMOT, physician; b. Lexington, N.C., Sept. 1, 1910; s. Andrew Curtis and Fallie (Curry) L.; B.S., U. N.C., 1932; M.D., Jefferson Med. Coll., Phila., 1934; m. Blanche Grimes, Aug. 18, 1935; children—Loyd D., Jacob A., Sarah Jo. Intern, T.C.I. Hosp., Birmingham, Ala., 1934-35; practice medicine, Lexington, 1937-42, 46-57; health dir. Davidson County Health Dept., Lexington, 1959—. Coroner, Davidson County, 1946-50. Served with USN, 1935-37. USNR, 1942-45. Decorated Purple Heart. Mem. Davidson County Med. Soc. (past pres.). Kiwanian (pres. 1950). Home: 20 Vance Circle Lexington NC 27292 Office: N Main St Lexington NC 27292

LOKEY, CLARENCE WALTERS, clergyman; b. Farmersville, Tex., Aug. 21, 1895; s. Thomas Franklin and Luella (Haskin) L.; A.B., Rice U., 1917; M.S., Tex. A. and M. Coll., 1930; Ph.D., 1947; D.D., Southwestern U., 1947; m. Mary Augustine Kerr, Aug. 31, 1918 (dec. 1962); children—Mary Augustine (Mrs. Warren D. Barton), Althea Anne (Mrs. Arthur B. Kelly), Clarence Walters; m. 2d, Zada Olive Maxwell Hamilton, 1967. Traffic supt. Southwestern Bell Telephone Co., Beaumont, Tex. Dist., 1919, supt. toll traffic. Houston, 1920; ordained to ministry Methodist Ch., 1920; pastor in Beaumont, Tex., 1920-21, Vickery, Tex., 1921-22, Doucette, Tex., 1922-24, Edgewood, Tex., 1925-26, Gilmer, Tex., 1930-32, Nacogdoches, Tex., 1932-38; extension sec. Tex. Conf., Gen. Bd. Missions, M.E. Ch. South, 1926-30; presiding elder Marlin dist. Tex. Conf., 1938-40, dist. supt. Bryan dist., 1940-44; exec. sec. home mission bd. Meth. Ch., N.Y.C., 1944-48, sec. Spanish speaking work Meth. Ch., N.Y.C., Phila., also San Antonio, 1948-66. Mem. com. Spanish-Am. work Nat. Council Chs., 1948-66, Nat., Tex. migrant labor coms., 1950-62, treas. Council on Spanish Am. Work, 1963-66; pres. Interdenominational Council Spanish Am. Work, 1959-61. Served to lt. U.S. Army, 1918-19; AEF in France. Recipient Citation for Distinguished Service, Coll. Bishops, Pastors and Laymen, 1966. Mem. Tex. Acad. Sci., Theta Phi (hon.). Mason, Rotarian. Co-author: Spanish Doorways. Originator, developer Lord's Acre, program of edn. and service for rural and mission chs. and adapted to more gen. application. Home: 7923 Donore Pl San Antonio TX 78229 Office: 535 Bandera Rd San Antonio TX 78228

LOMASNEY, THOMAS LAWRENCE, physician; b. Central Falls, R.I., May 29, 1920; s. Thomas Cornelius and Mary (Parks) L.; A.B., Brown U., 1941; M.D., Boston U., 1944; m. Kate Stewart Rutherford, Dec. 17, 1955; children—Robert Rutherford, William Stewart, Sarah Wright. Intern Mass. Meml. Hosps., Boston, 1944-45; resident Boston City Hosp., 1946, VA Deans' Com. Hosp., Rutland Heights, Mass., 1947-49, Providence, R.I., 1950-52, Dartmouth Med. Group. Hanover, N.H., 1950; practice medicine specializing in thoracic and cardiac surgery, Knoxville, Tenn., 1952—, Middlesboro, Ky., 1952—; attending thoracic surgeon St. Mary's Hosp., Knoxville, 1952—, Ft. Sanders Presbyn. Hosp., Knoxville, 1952—; attending thoracic surgeon U. Tenn. Meml. Research Center and Hosp., Knoxville, 1961—, instr. thoracic surgery, 1961—; cons. thoracic surgeon Meml. Hosp., Middlesboro, 1956—. Served from lt. (j.g.) to lt. M.C., USNR, 1945-46, 53-54. Diplomate Am. Bd. Surgery, Am. Bd. Thoracic Surgery. Mem. A.M.A., Am. Thoracic Soc., So. Thoracic Surg. Assn., Pan Am. Med. Assn. (diplomate mem., sect. on thoracic surgery), Knoxville Surg. Soc., Soc. Thoracic Surgeons. Contbr. articles to med. jours. Home: 6613 Sherwood Dr Knoxville TN 37919 Office: 2209 White Av Knoxville TN 37916

LOMAX, JOHN HARVARD, finance corp. exec.; b. Macon, Ga., Mar. 28, 1924; s. John Howard and Regis (Garrity) L.; B.B.A. cum laude, U. Ga., 1948; postgrad. U. N.C., 1961-62; m. Ann E. Davis, Dec. 30, 1947; children—John H., Jr., Jane Elisabeth. Personnel dir. Schwob Mfg. Co., Columbus, Ga., 1949-51; supr. personnel Burlington Mills, Gastonia, N.C., 1951-55; personnel mgr. Allstate Ins. Co., Charlotte, N.C., 1955-59; with Am. Credit Corp., Charlotte, 1959—, sr. v.p., 1967-73, exec. v.p., 1973—; pres. Home Advt. Agy. subsidiary Am. Credit Corp., 1965—. Founder Great to Be An American program, 1969. Bd. advisers Soc. for Advancement Mgmt., 1973. Served with USAAF, 1942-45. Methodist. Clubs: Carmel County, Athletic (Charlotte, N.C.). Contbr. articles to profl. jours. Home: 5730 Farmbrook Dr Charlotte NC 28201 Office: 201 S Tryon St Charlotte NC 28201

LOMBA-MIRANDA, RAMON ANTONIO, lawyer; b. San Juan, P.R., Oct. 25, 1930; s. Ramon A. and Nuri (Miranda) L.; student, Spring Hill Coll., 1947-49, Cath. U. Am., 1949-52; A.B., U. P.R., 1953; LL.B., U. Miss., 1956; m. Zwlma Sola, Dec. 13, 1958. Admitted to Miss. bar, 1956, P.R. bar, 1957; mem. firm Fiddler, Gonzalez & Rodriguez, San Juan, 1957—. Mem. Phi Alpha Delta, Phi Kappa Theta, Phi Sigma Alpha. Elk, K.C. Club: Nat. Lawyers (Washington). Home: 8 Pedrosa St Villa Caparra Guaynabo PR 00657 Office: GPO Box 3507 San Juan PR 00936

LOMBARDI, LOUIS FELIX, economist; b. Elizabeth, N.J., Aug. 19, 1935; s. Felix Edward and Charlotte Jordan (Morris) L.; B.S. cum laude, Mt. St. Mary's Coll., Emmitsburg, Md., 1958; M.A., Fordham U., 1963; LL.B., LaSalle Extension U., 1970; m. Adrienne Jeanette Wire, Dec. 27, 1958; children—Kathleen Ann, Louis Felix II. Asst. trust officer, estate planning Peoples Trust City Bank, Reading, Pa., 1962-65; financial cons., Reading, Pa., 1965; project adminstr. AMF Corp., York, Pa., 1965-66; prin. economist Va. Water Control Bd., Richmond, 1966—, state coordinator flood ins. and flood plain studies, 1973—. Mem. adj. faculty Va. Commonwealth U., Richmond, 1969-72. Served with AUS, 1958-60. Mem. Am. Econ. Assn., Nat. Economists Club. Author: Regional Analysis and Forecasting for Regional Areas, 1971. Contbr. articles to publs. Home: 9007 Mapleton Rd Richmond VA 23229 Office: 2109 N Hamilton St Richmond VA 23230

LOMBARDI, MAX HABIB, radiation biologist; b. Huanuco, Peru, S. Am., Apr. 25, 1932; s. Maximo David and Maria Eva (Lombardi) L.; B.V.M., U. San Marcos, Lima, Peru, 1958; D.V.M., 1958; M.S., Cornell U., 1961; m. Jeanette Sylvia Dunbar, May 31, 1961; children—Katherine Jeanne, Maria Louisa, David Alexander. Came to U.S., 1963, naturalized, 1970. Instr. exptl. physiology U. San Marcos, Lima, Peru, 1956-59; auxiliar prof. physiology, biochemistry and nutrition, 1960-62, asso. prof. biochemistry, nutrition, radiobiology, 1962-63; scientist Oak Ridge Asso. Univs., 1964-67, sr. scientist, 1967—, coordinator medical radioisotope courses and internat. programs, 1964—. Mem. Am. Vet. Med. Assn., Soc. Nuclear Medicine. Author: (with L. K. Akers) Radioisotopos en Investigacion Basica, 1967, Radiosotopos en Diagnostico Medico, 1967; also numerous articles. Home: Route 17 Guinn Rd Knoxville TN 37921 Office: PO Box 117 Oak Ridge TN 37830

LOMBARDO, THOMAS A., physician; b. Beaumont, Tex., Sept. 10, 1927; s. Anthony and Antionette (Maida) L.; M.D., U. Tex., Dallas, 1951; m. Jean Ming, June 9, 1950; children—Karen, Lauren, Randolph. Fellow U. Ala., Birmingham, 1951-52; intern Peter Bent Brigham Hosp., Boston, 1952-53; resident Barnes Hosp., St. Louis, 1953-54; clin. asso. Nat. Heart Inst., Bethesda, Md., 1954-56; asst. prof. dept. medicine U. Ala., 1956-57; practice medicine, specializing in cardiovascular diseases, Beaumont, Tex., 1957—; dir. cardiovascular labs. St. Elizabeth Hosp., 1962—; cons. cardiologist Orange (Tex.) Meml. Hosp., Tyler County Hosp., Woodville, Tex.; asst. prof. U. Tex., Houston, 1969—. Dir. Beaumont State Bank, First Fed. Savs. & Loan Assn., Beaumont. Served with USPHS, 1954-56. Diplomate in cardiovascular diseases Am. Bd. Internal Medicine. Fellow A.C.P., Am. Coll. Cardiology, Council Clin. Cardiology of Am. Heart Assn.; mem. A.M.A., Am. Fedn. CLin. Research, Alpha Omega Alpha. Club: Beaumont Country. Home: 1875 Thomas Rd Beaumont TX 77706 Office: 3155 Stagg Dr Beaumont TX 77701

LONG, ALFRED B., oil co. exec.; b. Galveston, Tex., Aug. 4, 1909; s. Jessie A. and Ada (Beckwith) L.; student S. Park Jr. Coll., 1928-29, Lamar State Coll. Tech., 1947-56, U. Tex., 1941; m. Sylvia V. Thomas, Oct. 29, 1932; 1 dau., Kathleen Sylvia (Mrs. E.A. Pearson, II). With Sun Oil Co., Beaumont, Tex., 1931—, driller geophys. dept., surveyor engring. dept., engr. operating dept., engr. prodn. lab., 1931-59, regional supr., 1960-69, now ret.; ind. oil cons., Beaumont, Tex., 1969—. Mem. Jefferson County Program Planning Com., 1964. Mem. Soc. Petroleum Engrs., Am. Assn. Petroleum Geologists, I.E.E.E., Houston, Beaumont geol. socs., Gulf Coast Engring. and Sci. Soc. (treas. 1962-65), Am. Petroleum Inst., Soc. Wireless Pioneers, U.S. Power Squadron. Inventor various oil well devices. Home: PO Box 7266 Beaumont TX 77706 Office: PO Box 7266 Beaumont TX 77706

LONG, CHARLES ALLEN, JR., constrn. co. exec.; b. Bessemer, Ala., July 13, 1927; s. Charles Allen and Lois (Mason) L.; B.S., U. Ala., 1950; m. Barbara Ann Porter, June 29, 1948; children—Patricia (Mrs. William S. Staines), William Jacob. Constrn. supt. Long Lewis Hardware Co., Birmingham, 1950—, chmn. bd., 1971—; v.p. Sullivan Long & Hagerty, Birmingham, 1960-71, chmn. bd., 1971—; chmn. bd. Amer-o-Matic Corp., Bessemer, 1973—. Pres. Bessemer Bd. Edn., 1965. Served with USNR, 1945-47. Mem. Kappa Alpha. Ind. Presbyn. (deacon). Mason (Shriner). Clubs: Birmingham Country, The Club. Home: 4144 Sharpsburg Dr Birmingham AL 35213 Office: PO Box 2247 Birmingham AL 35201

LONG, CLARENCE SUMNER, JR., educator; b. Adairsville, Ga., June 5, 1929; s. Clarence Sumner and Catherine (Williamson) L.; B.S. in Geology, Tulane U., 1951; postgrad. Colo. Sch. Mines, 1960-61; Ph.D., U. Colo., 1966; m. Alice Marion Trumbull, Sept. 15, 1956; children—Catherine, Grant, David, Evan. Field, subsurface geologist Gulf Oil Corp., Rocky Mountain region, 1954-57; exploration geologist Pan Am. Petroleum Co., Gulf Coastal region, 1964-66; asst. prof. U. Ga., Athens, 1966-69; asso. prof., head dept. geology West Ga. Coll., Carrollton, 1969-73, prof. geology, chmn. dept., 1973—. Cons. geology Chattahoochee Flint Area Planning and Devel. Commn., 1967-69. Bd. dirs. Wesleyan Found., Carrollton, 1972-73, Carroll Service Council, 1971-73. Served to lt. (j.g.) USNR, 1951-54. Mem. Am. Assn. Petroleum Geologists, Geol. Soc. Am., A.A.A.S., Am. Assn. U. Profs., Ga. Acad. Sci., Ga. Geol. Soc. (pres. 1970-71), Sigma Gamma Epsilon, Kappa Sigma. Methodist (mem. adminstrv. bd. 1972—). Rotarian (dir. 1971-73). Author: Mines and Prospects of the Chattahoochee-Flint Area, Georgia, 1971; (with V.J. Hurst) Geochemical Study of Alluvium in the Chattahoochee-Flint Area, Georgia. Home: 12 Forrest Dr Carrollton GA 30117

LONG, DAVID MARSHALL, concrete products exec., city ofcl.; b. Lexington, Ky., Oct. 23, 1936; s. David Tyler and Edith Thorn (Marshall) L.; B.A., Centre Coll., 1959; m. Claudette Cecile Hulette, Feb. 19, 1972; 1 son, Marshall Tyler. Pres. Long Block & Supply Co., Shelbyville, Ky., 1965—; v.p. Farmers & Traders Bank, Shelbyville, 1972—, 1018 Apts., Inc., Shelbyville, 1970—; sec., treas. C.B.E., Inc., Shelbyville, 1965—. Dir. Citizens Union Bank, Lexington, Farmers & Traders Bank, Shelbyville. Mem. Triple S Planning Comm., Shelby County, Ky., 1972—; Mayor, Shelbyville, Ky., 1973—. Pres. Shelby County Indsl. & Devel. Found., Shelbyville, 1970—. Served to capt. USAF, 1959-66. Recipient Robert M. Kemper award Navy League, 1971; named Outstanding Young Man Jr. C. of C., 1972. Mem. Shelby County C. of C. (pres. 1965), Phi Delta Theta. Presbyn. (elder 1968-73). Democrat. Home: 904 Craig Av Shelbyville KY 40065 Office: PO Box 505 Shelbyville KY 40065

LONG, ERNEST CROFT, med. adminstr.; b. London, Eng., Nov. 5, 1920; s. Ernest Joseph and Annabella (Caw) L.; B.Sc. with honors, U. London, 1949, B.Medicine, 1952, B.Surgery, 1952, Ph.D., 1957; m. Mary Caroline Becker, Feb. 24, 1953; 1 son, Croft Wormald. Came to U.S., 1953, naturalized, 1965. Hanes fellow pediatrics Sch. Medicine, Duke, 1953, asst. prof. dept. physiology, pharmacology, asso. pediatrics, 1956-60, asso. prof., 1960-66, prof. community health scis. Div. Internat. Health, 1966—, also asso. dean, 1967-69, asso. dir., 1969-71; field dir. Div. Internat. Med. Edn., Assn. Am. Med. Colls., Guatemala City, Guatemala, 1971, field rep. div. biomed. scis. Rockefeller Found., 1973—. Vice pres. bd. dirs. Durham Acad. (N.C.). Served with RAF, 1940-45. Fellow Royal Coll. Physicians (Eng.); mem. Royal Coll. Surgeons (Eng.), Am. Physiol. Soc., N.C. Acad. Scis., Med. Library Assn., Am. Assn. History Medicine, A.A.A.S., Assn. Am. Med. Colls., Assn. Computing Machinery, UN Assn. (past pres.), N.Y. Acad. Scis., Am. Pub. Health Assn., Soc. Internat. Devel., Nat. Bd. Med. Examiners (dir.), Royal Soc. Medicine (Eng.), Sigma Xi, Alpha Omega Alpha. Contbr. articles to profl. jours. Home: Box 218 Route 7 Durham NC 27706 Office: Edificio Cruz Azul Sa Avenida Guatemala

LONG, GAIL BAKER, metal mfg. co. exec.; b. Childress, Tex., Nov. 11, 1932; s. Aretas William and Ester (Bussey) L.; B.B.A., Tex. A. and M. U., 1954; M.B.A., Tex. Christian U., 1960; m. Shirley Janice Adams, Aug. 30, 1953; children—Karen J., Catherine F. Accountant Texaco, Inc., Ft. Worth, 1957-58, Dallas, 1958-60; v.p. M.J. Neeley & Co., Inc., Ft. Worth, 1960-69; pres. Mid Tex. Mfg. Co., Ft. Worth, 1969—; chmn. bd. E.L. White & Co., Ft. Worth, 1968—. Instr. corporate finance Tex. Christian U., Ft. Worth, 1962-64. Served to 1st lt. USAF, 1954-57. Mem. Tex. Mfrs. Assn., Am. Ordiance Assn., Greater Richland Jaycees (v.p. 1960-63), Ft. Worth C. of C. (mem. found. com. 1969—). Presbyn. (elder 1966-68). Rotarian. Club: Colonial Country. Home: 2233 Winton Terrace W Fort Worth TX 76109 Office: 993 S Haltom Rd Box 1235 Ft Worth TX 76101

LONG, GEORGE ROBERT, assn. exec.; b. Roachdale, Ind., Feb. 23, 1917; s. George Batman and Stella (Sutherlin) L.; A.B., Wabash Coll., 1939; M.A., Ind. U., 1949; postgrad. U. Va., 1949-53; m. Mary Henley Spencer, Dec. 7, 1968. Instr. govt. Ind. U., Bloomington, 1949-53; research fellow Bur. Pub. Adminstrn., U. Va., Charlottesville, 1949-53; planning adminstr. Henrico County, Richmond, Va., 1953-54; field rep. Va. Div. Planning and Econ. Devel., Abingdon, 1954-57; acting commr. Div. Planning and Econ. Devel., 1957-58; exec. dir. Wilson (N.C.) Indsl. Council, 1958-60; mng. partner Robinson, Long & McDonald, Cons., Charlottesville, 1960-62; field cons. League of Va. Counties, Charlottesville, 1962-64; exec. dir. Va. Assn. Counties, Charlottesville, 1964—. Mem. State Rural Area Devel. Com., 1963, Mental Health Study Commn., 1964-66, Met. Areas Study Commn., 1966-68, Commn. Rights Pub. Employees, 1972-74. Gov.'s Com. on State and Local Cooperation, 1969-74; lectr. on Va. county govt. U. Va., Fed. Exec. Inst., Christopher Newport Coll., George Mason Coll., U. No. Colo. Served with AUS, 1941-45. Mem. Nat. Conf. Execs. State Assns. of Counties (pres. 1969-70), Nat. Assn. Counties (dir. 1969-70), Lambda Chi Alpha. Democrat. Presbyn. (elder). Mason. Home: 2310 Tarleton Dr Charlottesville VA 22901 Office: 402 County Office Bldg Charlottesville VA 22901

LONG, GILLIS WILLIAM, congressman; b. Winnfield, La., May 4, 1923; s. Floyd H. and Birdie (Shumake) L.; B.A., La. State U., 1949, J.D., 1951; m. Mary Catherine Small, June 21, 1947; children—George Harrison, Janis Catherine. Admitted to La. bar, 1951; legal counsel select com. small bus. U.S. Senate, 1951-53; chief legal counsel spl. com. campaign expenditures (elections) U.S. Ho. of Reps., 1952, 56, 58, 60; mem. 88th and 93d Congresses 8th Dist. La.; asst. dir. Office Econ. Opportunity, Exec. Office of Pres., 1964-65. Legislative counsel Spl. Com. Historic Preservation, Spl. Com. Urban Growth Policy. Chmn. La. Support Task Force, pres., 1972; commr. La. Deep Draft Harbor and Terminal Authority, 1973; pres. Lower Mississippi Flood Control Assn., 1973. Assn. counsel adv. com. rules Democratic Nat. Com., 1954-55; del. Dem. Nat. Conv., 1964. Served to capt., inf., AUS, World War II; ETO. Decorated Bronze Star, Purple Heart. Mem. Am., La., Alexandria bar assns., V.F.W., Am. Legion, Omicron Delta Kappa, Delta Kappa Epsilon. Baptist. Lion. Home: 1232 Southampton Dr Alexandria LA 71301 Office: 215 Cannon House Office Bldg Washington DC 20515 also 811 Johnston St Alexandria LA 71301

LONG, HAROLD GLENN, physician; b. Akron, O., July 12, 1933; s. Luke Glenn and Minnie (Caltrider) L.; B.S., North Ga. Coll., 1954; M.D., Med. Coll. Ga., 1958; m. Mary Joel Williams, July 12, 1959; children—Mary Ellyn, Joel Glenn. Intern Athens Gen. Hosp. (Ga.), 1959-60; practice gen. medicine Dahlonega, Ga., 1960—; mem. staff Hall County Hosp., Gainesville, Ga. Active Boy Scouts Am., Ga. Heart Assn. Bd. dirs. Blue Cross and Blue Shield, Columbus, Ga., Named Young Man Year, Dahlonega Jr. C. of C., 1964. Mem. 9th Dist. Med. Soc. Democrat. Methodist. Lion, Elk. Club: Skitts Mountain Golf (Cleveland, Ga.). Home: 2151 Mountain View Dr Dahlonega GA 30533 Office: Memorial Dr Dahlonega GA 30533

LONG, JAMES GRANT, JR., lawyer; b. Greenville, S.C., Mar. 7, 1938; s. James Grant and Beulah (Blythe) L.; A.B., U. S.C., 1960, J.D., 1962; m. Frances Jane Sexton, June 3, 1961; children—James Grant III, William Vincent, Amy Jane. Admitted to S.C. bar, 1962; asso. mem. firm Perrin & Perrin, Spartanburg, S.C., 1963-66; partner firm Ward, Howell, Barnes & Long, Spartanburg, 1966—; dir. Spartanburg County Pub. Defender Corp. Bd. dirs. Spartanburg chpt. Am. Cancer Soc., 1970-72. Mem. Spartanburg County, S.C., Am. bar assns., S.C. State Bar, Spartanburg Young Lawyers Assn. Mason. Club: Country (Spartanburg). Home: 111 Kearse Ct Spartanburg SC 29302 Office: 200 Library St Office Bldg Spartanburg SC 29301

LONG, JAMES VIRDEN, banker; b. Berwyn, Ill.. Nov. 25, 1947; s. Don A. and Reta S. (Staff) L.; B.S. in Accounting, No. Ill. U., 1969; M.Profl. Accounting, U. Tex., 1971. Staff accountant Kerber, Eck & Braeckel, C.P.A.'s, Springfield, Ill., 1967-68; staff accountant Arthur Andersen & Co., C.P.A.'s, Chgo., 1968-69; instr. accounting U. Tex. at Austin, 1969-71; audit sr. Peat Marwick Mitchell & Co., C.P.A.'s, Houston, 1971-73; v.p. Tex. Comml. Bank, Houston, 1973—. Cons. fed. income taxes, 1969—; financial planning and investment adviser to several pvt. businesses, 1970—. Adminstr. C.P.A. exam. Moody Center, Galveston, Tex., 1972—. Recipient Arthur Young & Co. scholarship, 1970. C.P.A., Tex. Mem. Tex. Soc. C.P.A.'s, Am. Inst. C.P.A.'s, Tex. State Bd. Pub. Accountancy, Beta Alpha Psi (pres. 1970—), Sigma Nu (treas. 1965-69). Home: 1855 Fountain View #88 Houston TX 77027 Office: PO Box 2558 Houston TX 77001

LONG, JOSEPH JUDSON, JR., savs. and loan exec.; b. Edenton, N.C., Aug. 16, 1911; s. Joseph Judson and Corinne (Gatling) L.; B.S. in Bus. Adminstrn., N.C. State U., 1935; postgrad. Ind. U., 1958; m. Mildred Woodall, Aug. 17, 1972; 1 son, Joseph Judson III. Pres. Raleigh Savs. & Loan Assn., 1955—; dir. State Bank of Raleigh, Amic Corp., Central Service Corp. Mem. Bd. Adjustment, Raleigh, 1961. Mem. N.C. State U. Edn. Found. Served to col. AUS, 1941-46. Decorated Bronze Star medal; Croix de Guerre (France). Home: 2900 Wycliff Rd Raleigh NC 27607 Office: 219 Fayetteville St Raleigh NC 27601

LONG, LARRY HOWARD, statistician; b. Lockhart, Tex., Oct. 15, 1943; s. G.A. and Olive (DeViney) L.; B.A. with honors, U. Tex., 1966, M.A., 1968, Ph.D., 1969; postgrad. U. Pa., 1969-70. Statistician, U.S. Bur. Census, Washington, 1970—. Mem. Am. Sociol. Assn., Am. Statis. Assn., Population Assn. Am., Internat. Union Sci. Study Population, A.A.A.S. Contbr. profl. jours. Home: 201 I St Washington DC 20024 Office: Population div Bur Census Washington DC 20233

LONG, LESTER CARL, JR., chem. engr.; b. Wheeling, W.Va., May 27, 1938; s. Lester Carl and Mary Jean (Murphy) L.; B.S. in Chem. Engring., W.Va. U., 1960; M.S., U. Ill., 1962, Ph.D., 1965; m. Marie Andree Louise Chatel, Jan. 23, 1965; children—Michelle, Suzanne, Michael, Jennifer. Research engr. E.I. Dupont de Nemours & Co., Richmond, Va., 1968-71, staff engr. film dept., 1971-72, sr. research engr. textile fibers dept., 1972—. Served with USAF, 1965-68. Mem. Am. Chem. Soc. Home: 10120 Epsilon Rd Richmond VA 23235 Office: PO Box 27001 Richmond VA 23261

LONG, OWEN DOUGLAS, cons. civil engr.; b. Kaufman, Tex., Jan. 25, 1932; s. George Boren and Myrl (Nichols) L.; B.S. in Civil Engring., So. Meth. U., 1958; m. Mary Elizabeth McNutt, May 7, 1955; children—Mark Douglas, April Gay. Design engr. Tex. Hwy. Dept., 1958-61; owner Owen D. Long, cons. engr., Hurst, Tex., 1959—; city engr., dir. pub. works, Hurst, 1959-62; constrn. engr. Chaney and James Constrn. Co., Richardson, Tex., 1961-62; sec. D-D Investment Corp., Hurst; dir. Ford Devel. Corp., Hurst, Sixtenn Precinct Inc., Hurst. Pres. Hurst Employees Credit Union, 1965-68. Served with AUS, 1954-56. Registered profl. engr., Tex., Ark. Mem., Nat., Tex. socs. profl. engrs., Am. Soc. C.E., Hurst-Euless-Bedford C. of C. (dir.). Mason, Rotarian (pres. Hurst Mid-City club 1969-70). Home: 1108 Irwin Dr Hurst TX 76053 Office: PO Box 777 1615 Precinct Line Rd Hurst TX 76053

LONG, PAUL JUNIOR, scientist, artist; b. Tellico Plains, Tenn., May 27, 1927; s. Charles Ody and Maggie Lane (Rogers) L.; B.S., Tenn. Tech. U., 1950; M.S., U. Tenn., 1970; m. Willa Mae Williams, Nov. 16, 1952; children—David Paul, Susan Gayle, Gregory Lessel. Asst. to erector Combustion Engring., Newnan, Ga., 1950; foreman radiographic lab. Union Carbide Corp., Oak Ridge, Tenn., 1951-53, supr. spl. pilot plant operations, 1953-55, supr. ultra-sonic and spl. nondestructive testing group, 1955-63, physicist in charge metall. services lab., 1963-69, head engring. test systems dept., 1969—. Exhibited in group shows at Dulin Art Gallery, Knoxville, Tenn. Committeeman, Boy Scouts Am., Oak Ridge, 1969-71; vocational edn. chmn. Jefferson Jr. High Sch. P.T.A., Oak Ridge, 1971-72. Served with USAAF, 1945-46. Registered profl. engr., Tenn. Mem. Soc. Nondestructive Testing (charter mem. Oak Ridge, chpt. dir.), S.A.R. Baptist (deacon). Author: Our Hill Country Heritage, Vol. I, Williams and Related Families, 1970; Our Hill Country Heritage, Vol. II, Longs and Related Families, 1972. Contbr. articles to profl. jours. Home: Route 2 Box 159-A Lenoir City TN 37771 Office: Union Carbide Y 12 Plant Oak Ridge TN 37830

LONG, ROBERT WILLIAM, JR., botanist, educator; b. Ashland, Ky., Nov. 23, 1927; s. Robert William and Naomi I. (Forson) L.; A.B., Ohio Wesleyan U., 1950; A.M., Ind. U., 1952, Ph.D., 1954; m. Gloria A. Overstreet, Aug. 30, 1953; children—Alice, Nancy, Robert William III, Celia. Grad. teaching asst. Ind. U., 1950-53; instr. biology So. Meth. U., 1953-54; asst. prof., asso. prof. botany Ohio Wesleyan U., Delaware, 1954-62; asso. prof., prof. botany, dir. Herbarium, U. South Fla., Tampa, 1962—, chmn. dept. botany and bacteriology, 1966-71. Commr., Commn. on Undergrad. Edn. in Biol. Scis.; cons. Office Biol. Edn. NSF. Bd. dirs. Univ. Chapel Fellowship, Tampa; trustee Fairchild Tropical Garden, Coral Gables, Fla. Recipient Faculty Devel. award U. South Fla., 1968; NSF research grantee, 1957—. Postdoctoral fellow Harvard, 1968. Mem. Bot. Soc. Am. (editor 1970—), Am. Soc. Plant Taxonomists (treas. 1965-70), Fla. Acad. Sci. (sec. 1971—, pres. elect 1973), Internat. Assn. Plant Taxonomy, Sigma Xi, Kappa Sigma. Author: (with Olga Lakela) A Flora of Tropical Florida, 1971; Wild Flowers of Coastal Florida, 1974; Plant Biology, 1975. Contbr. articles to profl. jours. Home: 2802 Samara Dr Tampa FL 33618

LONG, RUSSELL B(ILLIU), U.S. senator; b. Shreveport, La., Nov. 3, 1918; s. Huey Pierce and Rose (McConnell) L.; B.A., La. State U., 1941, LL.B., 1942; m. Carolyn Bason, Dec. 23, 1969; children—(by previous marriage) Katherine (Mrs. Dean Mosely), Pamela Rust (Mrs. Prescott McCardell). Admitted to La. bar, 1942; practiced law, Baton Rouge, 1946-47; exec. counsel to gov. La., May-June, 1948; elected to U.S. Senate from La., for unexpired term ending 1950, reelected 1950—, asst. majority leader, 1965-68, chmn. finance com., alternate chmn. Joint Com. on Internal Revenue, chmn. Mcht. Marine Subcom. of Commerce Com. Del. Democratic nat. conv., 1952. Served to lt. USNR, 1942-45; MTO, NATO. Mem. Am. Legion, Order of Coif, Delta Kappa Epsilon, Pi Delta Phi, Tau Kappa Alpha, Omicron Delta Kappa. Elk, Lion. Home: Baton Rouge LA Office: Senate Office Bldg Washington DC 20510

LONG, SAMUEL SPURGEON, JR., telephone co. exec.; b. Russellville, Ky., Sept. 13, 1917; s. Samuel Spurgeon and Eunice Marie (Brown) L.; B.S., Eastern Ky. U., 1941; postgrad. U. Mich., 1955, Angelo State U., 1969; m. Maxine Alcorn, Aug. 27, 1941; children—Larry, Brenda. With traffic dept. Gen. Telephone Co., Lexington, Ky., 1945-54, operating v.p., 1954-58; marketing dir. Gen. Telephone Co. of S.W., San Angelo, Tex., 1959-72, vendor liaison adminstr., 1972—. Chmn. U.S. Savs. Bond, Tom Green County, San Angelo, 1964. Served to 1st lt. AUS, 1941-44. Mem. Nat. Assn. Suggestors Soc., Nat. Ind. Telephone Pioneers Assn. (dir. 1971-74, regional v.p. 1973-74). Mason (Shriner). Home: 2626 A and M San Angelo TX 76901 Office: Box 1001 San Angelo TX 76901

LONG, STUART MORRISON, editor; b. Portales, N.M., Nov. 15, 1913; s. Jeb Stuart and Elizabeth (Menefee) L.; B.J., U. Tex., 1943; m. Emma Pauline Jackson, July 27, 1936; children—Jeb Jackson, Jefferson Paine. Reporter Austin Am.-Statesman and Internat. News Service, Austin, Tex., 1935-37; pub. Kermit (Tex.) Sun, 1937-40; news editor Austin (Tex.) Statesman, 1940-42; news editor KVET, Austin, 1946-50; editor Long News Service, Austin, Tex., 1946—. Mem. Pres.'s Water Pollution Control Adv. Bd., 1968-71; mem. Tex. Sch. Land Bd., 1970—. Mem. State Democratic Exec. Com., 1948-52. Served with USMCR, 1942-45. Mem. Sigma Delta Chi (chpt. pres. 1967-68, state pres. 1968-70). Mem. Christian Ch. Author: (with Sam Kinch) Allan Shivers: The Pied Piper of Texas Politics, 1973. Home: 1306 Bradwood Rd Austin TX 78722 Office: State Capitol Pressroom Austin TX 78711

LONG, WILLIAM BANKS, JR., lawyer; b. Charlotte, N.C., Dec. 3, 1935; s. William Banks and Elizabeth (Laney) L.; A.B., Davidson Coll., 1958; LL.B., U. S.C., 1962; m. Ann Shields King, July 10, 1965; 1 dau. Anna LeConte. Admitted to S.C. bar, 1962; practiced in Greenville, S.C., 1962—; mem. firms Haynsworth, Perry, Bryant, Marion & Johnstone, to 1970; now firm William B. Long, Atty., Greenville, 1970—; asst. U.S. atty. S.C., Greenville, 1966-69. Chmn. Greenville County March Dimes Campaign, 1968-70, YMCA Campaign, 1970-71; Col. United Fund, 1970. Served to maj. AUS, 1959. Mem. Am., S.C., Greenville County Bar assns., Poinsett Sertoma. Mason (Shriner), Rotarian. Clubs: Cotillion, Metropolitan, Beaux Arts (Greenville). Home: 200 Brookside Way Greenville SC 29605 Office: 1306 E Washington St Greenville SC 29602

LONG, WILLIAM BOWMAN, physician; b. Eddy, Tex., June 19, 1921; s. Roderick John and Ester Margueriete (Bowman) L.; D.D.S., Baylor U., 1945, M.D., 1951; m. Mary Cole Farrow, June 3, 1944; children—William F., Daryl E., Robert J., Linda S. Intern Jefferson Davis Hosp., Houston, 1951-52; practice medicine specializing in family practice, Belton, Tex., 1952-68; mem. staffs Sewell-Long Hosp., Belton, Tex.; physician Mary Hardin Baylor Coll., 1969—; cons. Crestview Manor, 1970—. Trustee, Belton Ind. Sch. Dist., v.p. 1966-72, pres., 1972-74. Served with AUS, 1943-44, USNR, 1945-47. Mem. Am. Acad. Gen. Practice, Am., Tex., Bell County med. assns., Belton C. of C. (pres. 1958, Belton Athletic Assn. (pres. 1955-56). Lion (pres. 1959-60). Home: 415 Downing St Belton TX 76513 Office: 402 N Main St Belton TX 76513

LONG, WILLIAM EVERETT, JR., utility exec.; b. Oklahoma City, Sept. 3, 1919; s. William Everett and Hazel (Stafford) L.; m. Frances Jeanne Baum, Aug. 7, 1942; children—Susan Jeanne, Nancy Lee. Sales rep. Pan. Am. Airways, Houston, 1946-48; with Houston Natural Gas Corp., 1949—, v.p., asst. gen. mgr. distbn. div., 1968-70, v.p., gen. mgr. distbn. div., 1970—. Chmn. Met. div. United Fund, Houston, 1971—. Served with USAAC, 1941-45, USAF, 1951-52. Mem. Am. Soc. Tng. Dirs. (past pres.), Am. Gas Assn. (recipient Indsl.-Comml. Achievement award 1968), So. Gas Assn., Houston C. of C., Phi Kappa Psi. Mem. Disciples of Christ Ch. Mason. Clubs: Houston, Lakeside Country. Home: 5010 Westbriar Lane Houston TX 77027 Office: PO Box 1188 Houston TX 77001

LONGFELLOW, CONRAD DAYTON, steel culvert mfg. co. exec.; b. Siloam Springs, Ark., June 29, 1927; s. Marion Thomas and Evalyn May (Kibbee) L.; B.S., U. Ark., 1952; m. Tommie Cornelia Addington, Feb. 6, 1953; children—Deborah Ann, James Warren. Design engr. Cities Service Co., Shreveport, La., 1952-55; resident constrn. engr. Black & Veatch, Kansas City, Mo., 1955-58; sales engr. Armco Steel Corp., Little Rock, 1958-65; v.p. Caldwell Culvert & Metal Fabricators, Little Rock, also Greenville, Miss., 1965-69; pres. Caldwell Culvert Co., Greenville, 1969—, also dir.; dir. Riverside Land Co. Col., Gov's. Staff, State of Miss., 1972—. Bd. dirs. Greenville Indsl. Found., 1971—, Greenville YMCA, 1973—. Served with USNR, 1945-46. Mem. Nat., Ark. socs. profl. engrs., Nat. Corrugated Steel Pipe Assn. (tech. rev. com. 1973—), U. Ark. Alumni Assn., Greenville C. of C. (v.p. 1970-71, dir. 1970-71). Methodist. Kiwanian. Office: PO Box 4766 Greenville MS 38701

LONGHURST, PHILIP, JR., health adminstr.; b. Idaho Falls, Ida., Sept. 14, 1931; s. Philip Alberto and Anna M. (Bolander) L.; B.A., Ida. State Coll., 1956; postgrad. Stanford, 1967-68; M.S. in Health Adminstrn., U. Colo., 1970; m. Joy E. Pullium, May 15, 1952; children—Suzanne Elizabeth, Philip James. Personnel dir. Ft. Logan Mental Health Center, Denver, 1961-69, asst. to dir., 1969-70; mng. partner Jarett, Rader & Longhurst, Raleigh, N.C., 1970—; pres. Carolina Electrobike Inc., Raleigh, N.C., 1974—. Democratic precinct committeeman, Denver, 1962. Served with AUS, 1951-53. Recipient Forest Found. award Assn. Mental Health Adminstrs., 1970. Fellow Nat. Inst. Pub. Affairs; mem. Am. Coll. Hosp. Adminstrs., Assn. Mental Health Adminstrs., Am. Pub. Health Assn. Home: Route 7 Box 364 Raleigh NC 27609 Office: PO Box 27311 Raleigh NC 27611

LONGLEY, GLENN, JR., educator; b. Del Rio, Tex., June 2, 1942; s. Glenn Lawley and Cleo Mittie (Tipton) L.; student Abilene Christian Coll., 1960-61; B.S. in Biology, Southwest Tex. State U., 1964; M.S., U. Utah, 1966, Ph.D. in Environmental Biology, 1969; m. Frances Van Winkle, Aug. 5, 1961; children—Kimberley Kay, Kelly Frances. Asst. prof. biology Southwest Tex. State U., San Marcos, 1969—. Cons. Southwest Research Found., San Antonio, 1973. Chmn. City of San Marcos Environmental Adv. Com., 1971—; mem. Com. for Master Plan of Devel. San Marcos River, 1971-72. Bd. trustees San Marcos Bicentennial Commn., 1972. NIH grantee U. Utah, 1965-66; Nat. Def. Edn. Act fellow, 1966-69; Univ. Research grantee U. Utah, 1971, 72, 73; Tex. Water Devel. Bd. grantee Southwest Tex. State U., 1972-73. Mem. Am. Fishery Soc. (chpt. sec., treas. 1967-68), Am. Soc. Limnology and Oceanography, A.A.A.S., Water Pollution Control Fedn. (mem. com. 1973-74), Tex. Water Pollution Control Assn., Tex. Acad. Sci., Sigma Xi, Alpha Chi, Phi Sigma. Elk, Lion. Home: Blanco St Route Box 22 A San Marcos TX 78666 Office: Box 46 Southwest Tex State U San Marcos TX 78666

LONGLEY, JAMES WILDON, economist; b. San Saba, Tex., Oct. 29, 1913; s. Leonard and Emily Arementi (Patton) L.; B.A., Tex. Agrl. and Mech. U., 1936, M.S., 1937; M.A., Harvard, 1946, Ph.D., 1947; m. Letitia Jane Robinson, Jan. 19, 1961; 1 son, Roger Wayne. Economist Bur. Labor Statistics, U.S. Dept. Labor, Washington, 1955—. Mem. Econometric Soc., Am. Statis. Assn. Home: 8200 Cedar St Silver Spring MD 20910 Office: Dept Labor 441 G St NW Washington DC 20212

LONGMUIR, IAN STEWART, educator; b. Glasgow, Scotland, Mar. 12, 1922; s. John Bogie and Rita (Stewart) L.; B.A., Cambridge (Eng.) U., 1943, M.A., B.Medicine, B.Surgery, 1948; m. Shirley Anne Wood, Mar. 24, 1949; children—Gavin, Nicola, Diana, Karin. Came to U.S., 1965. Intern St. Bartholomew's Hosp., London, Eng., 1948; research asso. Cambridge U., 1948-51; prin. sci. officer Brit. Ministry of Supply, 1951-54; sr. lectr. in charge biochemistry dept. Inst. Diseases Chest, London, 1954-65; prof. dept. biochemistry N.C. State U., Raleigh, 1965—. Mem. Royal Soc. Medicine, Biochem. Soc., Am. Chem. Soc., Am. Physiol. Soc., A.A.A.S., Undersea Med. Soc. Editor Jour. Polarographic Soc., 1957-62. Contbr. profl. jours. Home: 2408 Tyson St Raleigh NC 27612 Office: 135 Polk Hall NC State U Raleigh NC 27607

LONGNECKER, THOMAS CHRISTOPHER, sci. adminstr.; b. Union City, Ind., Aug. 6, 1913; s. Henry and Bertha (Lacy) L.; B.S. in Agrl. Chemistry, Purdue U., 1935; M.S. in Soil Sci., Rutgers U., 1937, Ph.D., 1941; m. Blanche Blue, Feb. 10, 1940; children—Thomas Christopher, Linda, Charles H., Bradley B. Agronomist N.J. Agrl. Expt. Sta., New Brunswick, 1946-47; soil scientist, asst. dir. Tex. Research Found., Renner, 1947-56; chief soil scientist, dir. High Plains Research Found., Plainview, Tex., 1956—. Mem. Richardson (Tex.) City Council, 1948-56, mayor, 1952-54; pres. Plainview Ind. Sch. Dist. Sch. Bd., 1972—. Served with AUS, 1941-46. Mem. Am. Soc. Agronomy. Elk, Kiwanian. Contbr. articles to profl. jours. Home: 2000 Dallas St Plainview TX 79072 Office: PO Box 1870 Plainview TX 79072

LONGWITH, JEAN MARGUERITE, radio sta. mgr.; b. San Antonio, Mar. 15, 1918; d. Harold Eugene and Anna Frances (Marshall) Longwith; B.A. cum laude, U. Tex., 1937, M.Ed. cum laude, 1945; M.F.A. cum laude (fellow), U. Ia., 1950; Tchr. sr. high sch., San Antonio, 1938-45; dir. Community Players, San Antonio, 1942-46; dir. San Antonio Little Theatre, 1947-49; instr., communications TV Hour, U. Ia., Iowa City, 1949-50; dir. WOC-TV, Davenport, Ia., 1949-51; chmn. drama dept. Jefferson High Sch., San Antonio, 1952-64; gen. mgr. radio sta. KSYM-FM, San Antonio, 1966—; prof. radio, TV, film San Antonio Coll., 1964—. Dir. Summer Dance Festival, San Antonio Recreation Dept., 1952-69; lectr. Our Lady of Lake Coll., San Antonio, 1956-59. Recipient Service citation as entertainment dir. U.S.O., 1945. Mem. Am. Assn. U. Women (v.p., 1964-66), Zeta Phi Eta, Pi Lambda Theta, Phi Theta Kappa. Delta Kappa Gamma (pres. chpt. 1966-68; pres. coordinating council 1968-70). Episcopalian. Club: Zonta. Author: Adaptation of Three Short Stories for Television, 1950; The Community That Cares (play), 1960; Poetry for Interpretation, 1955; Ten Syllabi for Courses in Broadcasting, 1969. Home: 210 Quentin Dr San Antonio TX 78201 Office: 1300 San Pedro Av San Antonio TX 78284

LOONEY, JAMES CULLEN, lawyer; b. Kossuth, Miss., May 8, 1903; s. James Owem and Virginia (Dean) L.; B.A., Vanderbilt U., 1924, LL.B., J.D., 1926; m. Margaret Montgomery, June 15, 1933; children—Margaret L. (Mrs. Robert A. McAllen), D'Ette (Mrs. Clegg Fowlkes), Cullen R. Admitted to Tenn., Tex. bars, 1926; practice in Edinburg, Tex., 1926—; county judge Hidalgo County, Tex., 1941-46. Chmn. bd. First State Bank & Trust Co., Edinburg, Security State Bank, Pharr, Tex.; dir. Dixel Industries, Houston, First Nat. Bank, La Feria, Tex., First Nat. Bank, Mercedes, Tex., Border Bank, Hidalgo, Tex., Valley Transit Co., Harbenito Broadcasting Co. (both Harlingen, Tex.), Edinburg Community Hotel. Mem. Tex. Citrus Commn., 1949-51. Tex. Commn. Higher Edn., 1963-65, Tex. Coordinating Bd. Higher Edn., 1965-68, Tex. Dept. Pub. Safety, 1968; pres. Mental Health and Mental Retardation Bd. Hidalgo County, 1967-70. Chmn. Hildago County Democratic Exec. Com., 1932-40, 54-68. Trustee Looney Found., Edinburg; bd. regents Pan Am. Coll., Edinburg, 1952-58. Mem. Am., Tex., Hidalgo County bar assns., Episcopalian. Kiwanian (pres. Edinburg 1935). Club: McAllen (Tex.) Country. Home: Route 2 211A Edinburg TX 78539 Office: PO Box 237 Edinburg TX 78539

LOONEY, JAMES HOLLAND, clergyman; b. Dallas, May 11, 1944; s. Billy Albert and Helen Dorothy (Holland) L.; B.A., Tex. Christian U., 1967, M.Div., 1970; postgrad., 1970-71; postgrad. New Orleans Baptist Theol. Sem., 1971-72, Inst. for Human Understanding, 1973—; m. Brenda Jo Stone, May 14, 1965; children—James Holland, Brenda Anne, Stephen Brian. Ordained to ministry Christian Ch., 1969; pastor Crestview Christian Ch., Greenville, Tex., 1970-71, Gentilly Christian Ch., New Orleans, 1971—. Dir. Chi Rho Jr. High Camps, La. Assn. Christian Chs., 1972—; mem. religious counsel La. State U., New Orleans, 1971—, finance chmn. of council, 1973. Chmn. interfaith com. United Fund of Greater New Orleans, 1972. Bd. dirs. Parkchester Friendship House, 1971—, Children's Center, Inc., La. Interchurch Conf., 1972—. Mem. Greater New Orleans Fedn. of Chs. (dir. 1971—, v.p. ch. relations div. 1973), Soc. Bibl. Lit., Theta Phi. Home: 6029 Perlita St New Orleans LA 70122 Office: 1551 Mirabeam Av New Orleans LA 70122

LOONEY, JUNE PAIGE MURPHY, coll. dean; b. Ivor, Va., June 9, 1919; d. Henry Patrick and Louisa (Crumpler) Murphy; A.B., Elon Coll., 1942; M.A., E. Carolina U., 1961; postgrad. Atlantic Christian Coll., 1956, N.C. State U., 1959; m. John Joseph Williams Looney, Jr., May 30, 1942 (div. Oct. 1969); children—Carolyn Page, Charlotte Anne. Tchr., Norfolk (Va.) County Schs., 1943-45; guidance counselor Rocky Mount (N.C.) City Schs., 1957-60; dir. guidance services Nash County Schs. Nashville, N.C., 1960-62; dir. guidance services Rocky Mount (N.C.) City Schs., 1962-68; asso. dean students Elon Coll. (N.C.), 1968—. Active Girl Scouts U.S.A.; v.p. Mental Health Assn., 1964-68, chmn. mental illness com., 1963-68; city program chmn. Sub-Deb Bd. Advisors, 1962-64, finance chmn., 1965-67; v.p. Rocky Mount Council Parents and Tchrs., 1952-54, pres., 1954-56; active Rocky Mount Arts Center, 1957-68; mem. N.C. Gov's. Council on Mental Retardation, 1965-69. Mem. N.E.A., Am., N.C. personnel and guidance assns., Assn. for Counselor Edn. and Supervision, Am. Sch. Counselor Assn., Nat. Vocational Guidance Assn., Am., N.C. assns. women deans and counselors, Am. Assn. U. Women, N.C. Edn. Assn., N.C. Council Parents and Tchrs., Delta Kappa Gamma, Pi Gamma Mu. Democrat. Episcopalian. Home: 204 N Holt St Elon College NC 27244 Office: Box 2231 Elon Coll Elon College NC 27244

LOONEY, SEBERT TYLER, safety engr.; b. New Castle, Va., Nov. 6, 1927; s. Roscoe F. and Murphy O. (Looney) L.; m. Christine R. Rose, Nov. 21, 1927; children—Carolyn, Watson, Lynn. With Western Electric, Winston-Salem, N.C., 1950-53, Hake Mfg. Co., Roanoke, Va., 1953-57; prodn. mgr. John Martin & Assos., Balt., 1957-63; indsl. engr. Am. Mut. Ins. Co., Richmond, Va., 1953-71; owner Safety Consultants, Richmond, 1971—. Served with USAAF, 1945-48. Mem. Am. Soc. Safety Engrs. (nat. dir. 1968-69), Va. Safety Assn. Mason. Club: Engineers (Richmond). Home: 10541 Duryea Dr Richmond VA 23235 Office: 7825 Midlothian Turnpike Richmond VA 23235

LOPEZ, ANTHONY, food scientist, educator; b. Quillota, Chile, May 13, 1919; s. Antonio and Flora (Matas) L.; came to U.S., 1952, naturalized, 1956; B.S. in Indsl. Chemistry, Catholic U. of Chile, 1942; Ph.D. in Food Sci. and Tech., U. Mass., 1947; m. Mary Josephine Fellers, Sept. 27, 1947; children—Martita, Anthony, Michael. Chemist S.A. Organa (Drugs), Santiago, Chile, 1942-45; tech. dir. Ipal Foods S.A. Santiago, Chile; asso. prof. food tech. U. Mass., Amherst, 1952-53; asso. prof. food tech. U. Ga., Athens, 1953-54; prof. food sci. and tech. Va. Poly. Inst. and State U., Blacksburg, 1954—. Pres. Progress Apts., Inc., Blacksburg, 1965—. Cons. in food processing. Mem. Inst. Food Technologists (chmn. Carolina-Va. sect. 1969-70, mem. exec. com. 1971-74, nat. councilor 1969-75), Am. Chem. Soc., Packaging Inst. Author: Marine Products and By-Products, 1953; A Complete Course in Canning, 1969. Editor Food Prodn. and Mgmt., 1971—. Contbr. research articles on food tech. to sci. jours. Home: 721 Hutcheson Dr Blacksburg VA 24060

LOPEZ, JOAQUIN, aero. engr.; b. Cienfuegos, Cuba, Feb. 9, 1923 (came to U.S., 1967, naturalized 1972); s. Victorino and Amanda (Garcia) L.; B.S., Tri State Coll. Engring., Angola, Ind., 1946; m. Siria Jimenez, Feb. 14, 1948; children—Joaquin, Oscar, Carlos. Asst. to chief engr. Pub. Works Dept., Cienfuegos Dist., Cuba, 1946-49; pres., owner Tractores Centro S.A., Cienfuegos, 1949-63; supt. machinery Agosa S.A., civil engrs., Santander, Spain, 1965-67; aero. engr. Allstate Diesel Inc., Miami, Fla., 1967-69, Growers Ford Tractor Co., Miami, 1969—. Drafting instr. Miami Sr. High Sch., Adult Edn. Training, 1970—. Mem. Am. Soc. Agrl. Engrs., 1952. Roman Catholic. Tech. translator Internat. div. Allis Chalmers Mfg. Co., 1969—. Home: 9210 S W 57th Terrace Miami FL 33143 Office: 3825 N W 32d Av Miami FL 33142

LOPEZ, RAOUL WELDON, engr., govt. ofcl.; b. Santurce, P.R., Feb. 11, 1943; s. Raoul Pascal and Sarah Louise (Weldon) L.; B.Mech. Engring., Auburn U., 1966; m. Phyllis Jean Winkles, Feb. 1, 1963; children—Felicia Lorraine, Evelyn Paulett. Engr. NASA Marshall Spaceflight Center, Huntsville, Ala., 1967—. Registered profl. engr., Ala. Mem. Sigma Phi Epsilon. Club: Sports Car of America (Huntsville). Home: 3901 Pickett Dr Huntsville AL 35805 Office: NASA - MSFC Structures and Propulsion Lab Thermal Engring Br Huntsville AL 35812

LOPEZ, RUFINO ELIAS, JR., lawyer; b. San Diego, Tex., June 9, 1941; s. Rufino Elias and Elvira (Saenz) L.; B.A., Baylor U., 1962, Sch. Law, 1962-64; m. Rose Mary Moore, Apr. 14, 1963; children—Rufus Lopez III, Raymond, Bettina. Admitted to Tex. bar, 1965, since practiced in Alice; mem. firm Dean, Mullen & Lopez. Pres. Jim Wells County Master Planners Assn., 1973—; commr. dist. Gulf Coast council Boy Scouts Am., 1970—. Mem. Coastal Bend Bar Assn. (v.p.). Lion (v.p.). Home: 1306 Rose Dr Alice TX 78332 Office: 611 E 1st St Alice TX 78332

LOPEZ, SEVERO ALEJANDRO, structural engr.; b. Magangue, Colombia, July 24, 1933; s. Carlos Alberto and Emma Zarela (Alvarez) L.; came to U.S., 1953, naturalized, 1963; A.A., Christian Bros. Coll., 1955; B.S., U. Tenn., 1958; M.S., Memphis State U., 1972; m. Irene Cowan Gamble, May 10, 1958; children—Rebecca, Karla, Teresa, Thomas, Ann, Paula. Designer, Howard, Needles, Tammen & Bergendoff, Kansas City, Mo., 1958-65; project engr. Brown Engring. Co., Huntsville, Ala., 1965-67, Harland Bartholomew & Assos., Memphis, 1967-72; structural engr. Tech. Support Group Internat., Memphis, 1972-73; asso. W.S. Pollard Consultants, Memphis, 1973—. Registered profl. engr., Mo., Ala., Tenn. Mem. Am. Soc. C.E., Nat. Soc. Profl. Engrs., Chi Epsilon, Tau Beta Pi. Roman Catholic. K.C. (3 deg.). Home: 1654 Ivy St Memphis TN 38117 Office: 60 N 3d St Memphis TN 38103

LOPRESTI, BASIL GABRIEL, educator; b. Bklyn., Mar. 6, 1910; s. Philip and Mary Stella (Aidala) LoP.; student civil engring. Rensselaer Poly. Inst., 1929-34; M.A., N.Y. U., 1963; m. Marian Lee Engl, Dec. 22, 1954; children—Maryellen E., Alice E., Philip B., Lisa E. With constrn. co., N.J., N.Y.C., 1934-40; spl. project engr. Sparkman and Stephens, Inc., N.Y.C., 1941-45, 1957-58; self employed cons. engr., land surveyor, N.J., 1946-56; engr. examiner N.Y. Civil Service Dept., Albany, 1959; tchr. math. Midland (N.J.) High Sch., 1960-65, Naples (Fla.) High Sch., 1965-68; prof. engring. and tech. studies Edison Community Coll., Fort Myers, Fla., 1968—; dir., sec. The Shores of Naples, condominium, Naples. Bd. dirs. Gulf Coast council Girl Scouts Am., 1973—. Registered profl. engr. N.J., Fla. Mem. Nat., N.J., Bergen County socs. profl. engrs., Fla. Engring. Soc., Am. Assn. U. Profs., Fla. Assn. Profs. Jr. Colls., Fla. Assn. Community Colls., Sigma Chi. Clubs: Bachelor's, R. Home: 2401 Gulf Shore Blvd N Naples FL 33940 Office: Edison Community Coll College Pkwy Fort Myers FL 33901

LORD, COLUMBUS ELLIS, architect; b. Abbot, Me., Apr. 30, 1897; s. Alvah Brown and Addie Winifred (Colson) L.; student U. Me., 1914-16; B.S. in Arch., Mass. Inst. Tech., 1924; m. Vera Dale Bolan, Feb. 18, 1928; children—Nancy Claire (Mrs. Philip Edwin Graves), Charles Ellis Bolan (dec.). Architect, various firms, Boston, 1924-31; civil engr. City Boston, 1931-34; architect, procurement div. Treasury Dept., Washington, 1934-37; with firm Clarence Wunder, Phila, 1937-38; Quartermaster, U.S. Army, Washington, 1938-41; engr. Corps Engrs. U.S. Army, Washington, 1941-47; chief engr. air facilities Def. Dept., Washington, 1947-67; cons. architect, engr., Arlington, Va., 1967—. Mem. pack council Cub Scouts, Washington, 1953-55; mem. P.T.A., Arlington, Va., 1955-63. Served with Signal Corps, U.S. Army, 1917-19. Registered profl. engr., Va., D.C., Mass., Vt. Registered architect, Va. Mem. A.I.A., Am. Soc. C.E., Nat. Soc. Profl. Engrs., Hwy. Research Bd. of Nat. Acad. Scis., Nat. Aero. Assn., Va. Acad. Sci., Aircraft Owners and Pilots Assn., So. Am. Mil. Engrs. Mason; mem. Order Eastern Star. Clubs: Aero, Mass. Institute Technology (Washington). Home and Office: 2000 N Adams St No 329 Arlington VA 22201

LORD, FONCHEN USHER (MRS. WILLIAM WALCOTT LORD), artist; b. St. Louis; d. Roland Green and Florence (Richardson) Usher; A.B., Harvard, 1933; M.A., Washington U., St. Louis, 1935; m. William Walcott Lord, June 12, 1935; children—Fonya (Mrs. James DeLong), William Pepperell, Carter Usher, Elizabeth Usher. Exhibited invitational one-man shows Stetson U., Deland, Fla., 1969, W.Va. Wesleyan Coll., 1970, Avanti Galleries, N.Y.C., 1970, Miami Mus. Modern Art, 1970, Broward Community Coll., Ft. Lauderdale, 1971, Polk Pub. Mus., 1972, Trendhouse Gallery, 1972, Fla. So. Coll., 1974; exhibited in group shows at Columbia Mus. Art, Columbus Mus. Arts and Crafts, Birmingham Mus. Art, Atlanta High Mus., Norton Gallery, Dulin Gallery Art, Ringling Mus. Art, Butler Inst. Am. Art, Jacksonville Art Mus., many others; represented in permanent collections Miami Mus. Modern Art, W.Va. Wesleyan Coll., Lowe Mus., New Coll., Sarasota, Fla., State of Fla. Pres., Palm Island Corp., Bartow, Fla., 1954-64, Braden River Ranchettes, Bartow, 1964-71; asst. treas. Paris Tanning Co., South Paris, Me., 1944-48. Recipient Merit award Fla. State Fair, 1964; Clearwater Art Seminar award, 1961, 63; 1st prize Sunshine Art Festival, 1962; 1st prize Polk County Ann., 1963, 67, awards, 1965, 66, 70, 73, Chautauqua Nat. award, 1968; awards Festival of States Ann., 1965; Cape Coral Nat. award, 1973. Fellow Royal Soc. Arts (London); mem. Fla. Artists Group, Nat. Assn. Am. Pen Women, Zeta Tau Alpha. Episcopalian. Home: 4305 Oak Glen Rd Lakeland FL 33803

LORD, MARION E. MANNS, educator; b. Ft. Huachuca, Ariz., Dec. 17, 1914; d. George Wiley and Annie (Pellett) Manns; student R.I. State Coll., 1932; B.S., Northwestern U., 1936; postgrad. Breadloaf Coll., summer 1936; M.Ed., Harvard, 1962; M.A., Ph.D. (E. B. Fred fellow), U. Wis., 1968; m. William Shepard Lord, Apr. 29, 1938 (div. May 1965); children—Caroline B. (Mrs. Martin L. Gross), Marion F. (Mrs. Fred W. Steadman), Jane B. (Mrs. Jared Chapin). N.H. State rep. Gen. Ct., Concord, N.H., 1957-62; dean of women, dir. guidance New Eng. Coll., Henniker, N.H., 1962-64; edn. program specialist, asst. to dir. div. coll. support Bur. Higher Edn., Office of Edn., Washington, 1968-71, dir. women's project Nat. Center Ednl. Statistics, 1971—, asst. program mgr. for coop. edn. programs div. coll. support Bur. Higher Edn., 1972—. Vice pres., dir. N.H. Council for Better Schs., 1957-64; county co-chmn. Nat. Found. Infantile Paralysis-March of Dimes, Laconia, N.H., 1958; dir. N.H. Council on World Affairs, 1957-63, Laconia Hosp. Mem. Am. Psychol. Assn., Am. Polit. Sci. Assn., D.C. Sociol. Soc. (treas., mem. com. on status of women), Nat. Council Adminstrv. Women in Edn., Federally Employed Women, Order Women Legislators, N.H. State Soc. in Washington, Am. Personnel and Guidance Assn., Nat. Assn. Women Deans and Counselors, League Women Voters, Am. Assn. U. Women, Bus. and Profl. Womens Club. Republican. Home: 800 4th St SW Washington DC 20024 Office: 400 Maryland Av SW Washington DC 20202

LORENZ, PAUL, architect; b. Joplin, Mo., Jan. 16, 1906; s. Max John and Anna Margaret (Hink) L.; B.S. in Architecture, U. Mich., 1931; m. Mabel Ruth McDuffee, Aug. 19, 1932; children—Marcia (Mrs. John M. Freese), Max Paul, Leni (Mrs. Don Bane). Prin., owner Paul Lorenz, architect, Tulsa, 1937—. Certified Nat. Council Archtl. Registration Bds. Mem. A.I.A. Democrat. Lutheran. Club: Tulsa Country. Home: 4131 S Sandusky St Tulsa OK 74135 Office: Amoco-East Bldg 119 E6 Tulsa OK 74119

LORENZEN, HOWARD OTTO, research lab. adminstr.; b. Atlantic, Ia., June 24, 1912; s. Hans Otto and Eleanor May (Stier) L.; B.S., Ia. State Coll., 1935; postgrad. U. Buffalo, 1936-37, Northwestern U., 1939; m. Etta Mae Owen, May 6, 1936; 1 dau., Susan Ann (Mrs. Claude A. Black, Jr.). Design engr. Colonial Radio Co., Buffalo, 1935-39, Zenith Radio Co., Chgo., 1939-40; electronics design engr. Naval Research Lab., Washington, 1940-48, head countermeasures br., 1948-55, supt. electronic warfare div., 1955-71, supt. space systems div., 1971—. Recipient Meritorious Civilian Service award U.S. Navy, 1946, Distinguished Civilian Service award, 1965. Robert Dexter Conrad award, 1972. Fellow I.E.E.E.; mem. Quarter Century Wireless Assn., Am. Radio Relay League. Home: 3713 Bangor St SE Washington DC 20020 Office: Code 7900 Washington DC 20385

LORENZEN, KENNETH ELBERT, dentist; b. Burlington, Ia., Apr. 16, 1923; s. Harry A. and Lilly (Love) L.; student Tex. Tech. U., 1946-47; D.D.S., Creighton U., 1952; m. Jo Anne Wolaver, Nov. 29, 1944; children—Sandra (Mrs. Richard Barrett), Kenneth R., Malcolm C. Gen. practice dentistry, Arcadia, Neb., 1952-54, Lubbock, Tex., 1954—; occasional clinician. Served with USNR, 1942-46. Mem. Am., Tex., South Plains (past pres.) dental socs., Phi Eta Sigma. Republican. Methodist. Home: 5412 28th St Lubbock TX 79407 Office: 1608 Aven St Lubbock TX 79401

LORENZO, FRANCISCO A., airlines co. exec.; b. N.Y.C., May 19, 1940; s. Olegario and Ana (Mateos) L.; B.A., Columbia, 1961; M.B.A., Harvard, 1963; m. Sharon Neill Murray, Oct. 14, 1972. Financial analyst TWA, 1963-65; mgr. financial analysis Eastern Airlines, 1965-66; founder, chmn. bd. Lorenzo, Carney & Co., financial advisers, New York, 1966—; chmn. bd. Jet Capital Corp., financial advisers, Houston, 1969—; pres. Tex. Internat. Airlines, Inc., Houston, 1972—. Served with AUS, 1963. Home: 10010 Memorial St Houston TX 77024 Office: PO Box 60188 Houston TX 77060

LORIA, FRANK LEO, surgeon; b. Vacherie, La., Jan. 19, 1898; s. Paul and Phyllis (Cipolla) L.; B.S., Tulane U., 1921, M.D., 1923; m. Pauline Ouaglino, Feb. 12, 1924 (dec. Oct. 1966); children—Paul Leonard, Philip Ronald; m. 2d, Octavie Livaudals, July 27, 1968. Gen. surg. practice, 1925—; surg. preceptorships Prof. Rudolph Matas, 1925-27, Prof. Maurice Geipi, 1928-31; asst. in surgery, sch. medicine Tulane U., 1925-27, instr. in surgery, 1927-50, in charge lab. operative surgery, 1932-38, in charge lab. of surg. anatomy, 1938-41, lectr. in anatomy, phys. diagnosis and minor surgery, sch. phys. edn., 1932-52, prof. hygiene Coll. Arts and Scis., 1958-61; chmn. surg. sects. Charity Hosp. La., 1942-44, later sr. vis. surgeon; chmn. surg. sect. Hotel Dieu Hosp., 1956-57, chief of staff, 1959, now sr. attending surgeon; formerly vis. surgeon Sara Mayo, Flint-Goodridge hosps., all New Orleans. Past pres. Virgilian Soc. New Orleans, New Orleans chpt. Dante Allghierl Soc.; past dir. New Orleans chpt. A.R.C., Travelers' Aid Soc., New Orleans Opera House Assn. Served as pvt. U.S. Army, World War I. Decorated silver medal Italian Govt., 1937; named adm. Gt. Navy of State of Neb. Diplomate Am. Bd. Abdominal Surgery. Fellow A.C.S., S.E. Surg. Congress, Am. Soc. Abdominal Surgeons; mem. Am., So. med. assns., La., Orleans Parish med. socs., New Orleans Acad. Sci. (life), Mediaeval Acad. Am., Shakespeare Soc. New Orleans, La. Hist. Soc. (past pres.), Internat. Boswell Inst., Tulane Alumni Assn. (life), Stars and Bars Soc., Alpha Omega Alpha, Alpha Tau Omega. Mason (Shriner). Clubs: Round Table, Metairie Country. Author: Montl's Antonio Scarpa-(a translation), 1957; Historical Aspects of Abdominal Injuries, 1968; also sci. med. and surg. papers. Ex-asso. editor New Orleans Med. and Surg. Jour.; hon. editor LaVoce Coloniale, 1932-40; founder Bull. La. Hist. Soc. Home: 223 Audubon Blvd New Orleans LA 70118 Office: Maison Blanche Bldg 921 Canal St New Orleans LA 70112

LORIA, JOHN CECIL, govt. ofcl.; b. Boston, Jan. 17, 1924; s. Claudio Joaquin and Louise Katherine (Oedell) L.; B.S. in Aero. Engring., Mass. Inst. Tech., 1950, M.S., 1952; m. Maria Adelaida Diez, Apr. 23, 1947; children—Maria (Mrs. Jose Juan Garcia), Teresa, Adele, John, Richard, Elisa, Mark. Project engr. Mass. Inst. Tech., 1950-57; staff engr. Arthur D. Little, Inc., Cambridge, 1957-63; dir. Instnl. Safety and Operating Systems Office, NASA Hdqrs., Washington, 1963—. Served with USAAF, 1942-47. Home: 11042 Ring Rd Reston VA 22090 Office: Code JS NASA Hdqrs Washington DC 20546

LORTON, WILLIAM DAVID, JR., city ofcl.; b. Radford, Va., Feb. 9, 1915; s. William David and Nelia Snow (Howell) L.; student Safety and Security Sch., Anniston, Ala., 1943, Va. Central Police Tng. Sch., 1947; diploma in fingerprinting and photography Chgo. Inst. Applied Sci., 1952; grad. FBI Acad., 1954; m. Pauline Elizabeth Rotenberry, Oct. 7, 1950; 1 dau., Lois (Mrs. Raymond Crockett Horton). With police dept. City of Radford (Va.), 1946-50, police sgt., 1952-57, chief police, 1957—; investigator Hercules Powder Plant, 1950-52. Chmn. Hwy. Safety Com., City Radford, Va., 1969—. Served with AUX. Mil. Police, AUS, 1943-46. Named Boss of Year Jr. C. of C., 1961. Mem. Nat. FBI Acad. Assos. Commonwealth Va. (pres. 1967-68), Va. Assn. Chief Police (mem. exec. com. 1970-71). Mem. Christian Ch. Mason (Shriner), Kiwanian. Home: 611 Calhoun St Radford VA 24141 Office: Radford Police Dept 1st and Wadsworth St Radford VA 24141

LOTHMAN, VICTOR OLIVER, cons. prodn. and inventory control; b. Akron, Aug. 26, 1902; s. Edwin Oliver and Meta Hermina (Fruechtenicht) L.; student Concordia Coll., Fort Wayne, 1917-19; m. Mary Frances Chiles, Sept. 21, 1929; children—Mary Vic (Mrs. Robert Emmet) Mullins, Meta Ann. Accountant, Louisville and Chgo., 1920-35; asst. controller, mdse. controller Butler Bros., wholesalers, Chgo., 1936-49; inventory control mgr. Ford Motor Co., Dearborn, Mich., 1950-67; cons. prodn. and inventory control Vt. Am. Corp., Louisville, 1968—. Cons. WPB, 1942. Ky. col. C.P.A., Ind., Ill., Ky. Mem. Am. Contract Bridge League (life master). Republican. Lutheran. Home: 1048 Cherokee Rd Louisville KY 40204 Office: 100 E Liberty St Louisville KY 40202

LOTT, H.C., JR., indsl. engr.; b. Odell, Tex., Oct. 31, 1931; s. Herman and Elsie (Tomes) L.; B.S. in Civil Engring., Tex. A. and M. U., 1958, M.S. in Civil Engring. (Humble Oil Co. fellow), 1960; m. Jimmie Warren, July 22, 1950; children—Mark, Kris, Kip, Todd, Kimberly. Constrn. engr. E.I. duPont de Nemours & Co., Wilmington, Del., 1960-64; engr., asst. dir. plant engring. and maintenance TWA, Kennedy Space Center, Fla., 1964-71; dir. corporate maintenance So. Industries Corp., Mobile, Ala., 1971-73; mgr. indsl. engring. and maintenance Gen. Portland, Inc., Dallas, 1973—. Speaker on maintenance mgmt. Served with USMCR, 1950-51. Registered profl. engr., Tex., La., Ala. Mem. Nat. Soc. Profl. Engrs., Am. Inst. Plant Engrs. (founder, pres. Mid Gulf Coast chpt. 1972, vice chmn. internat. com. energy conservation), La., Ala., Fla. engring. socs. Home: 1406 Danish Dr Grand Prairie TX 75050 Office: 4400 Republic Nat Tower Dallas TX 75221

LOTT, H(ENRY) ALVIN, constrn. co. exec.; b. Pearl River, La., Sept. 8, 1908; s. John Alexander and Minnie (Till) L.; student Internat. Corr. Schs.; m. Edna Joiner, Feb. 12, 1931; children—Harold Alvin, Edna Inez (Mrs. Harold T. Dokupil). With R.P. Farnsworth Co., New Orleans, 1927-49, supt., 1935-41, gen. supt., 1941-49; v.p. constrn. Farnsworth & Chamber Co., Inc., Houston, 1949-57; organizer H.A. Lott, Inc., Gen. Contractors, Houston, 1957, chmn. bd. Recipient Merit award U.S. Dept. Housing and Urban Devel., 1966. Clubs: Houston, Lakeside Country. Joint contractor of domed stadium, Houston, 1963. Home: 3502 Amherst St Houston TX 77005 Office: 6315 Gulfton Houston TX 77036

LOTT, JAMES ROBERT, educator; b. Houston, Jan. 16, 1924; s. Charles V. and Billie Carmen (Craig) Contella; B.A., U. Tex., 1949, M.A., 1951, Ph.D., 1956; m. Opal Estelle Sowell, July 29, 1942; children—Linda (Mrs. Ray Rogers), Lori Lee, James Robert, John Randall. Lectr. zoology U. Tex. at Austin, 1950-55; microbiologist Breckenridge Hosp., Austin, 1954-55; research scientist Radiobiol. Lab., Balcones Research Inst., Austin, 1955-56; instr. physiology Emory (Ga.) U. Sch. Medicine, 1956-57; faculty North Tex. State U., Denton, 1957—, prof. physiology, 1962—. Mem. research com. Denton County (Tex.) Heart Assn., 1965—. Sr. investigator AEC Contract, 1958-68. Served with USNR, 1942-45. NSF grantee, 1962-63. Mem. Internat. Soc. Biometeorology, Am. Soc. Physiology, Am. Soc. Gen. Physiology, Radiation Research Soc., Tex. Acad. Sci., Sigma Xi. Contbr. articles in field to profl. jours. Research biol. effects electric fields, microwaves and x-irradiation, others. Home: 1907 Locksley Lane Denton TX 76201

LOTT, REUBEN, furniture co., securities, real estate exec.; b. Ararat, Ala., Jan. 8, 1897; s. George Franklin and Carrie (Craft) L.; student North Manchester (Ind.) Coll., 1917-18; m. Blondie Clara Powell, Apr. 20, 1927. Partner, Foster & Lott Retail Furniture Co., Laurel, Miss., 1919; owner, mgr. Lott Furniture Co., Laurel, 1923; pres. Laurel Furniture Co., Inc., 1946—; former pres. Lott Furniture Co. Meridian, Inc. (Miss.), Lott Furniture Co. Brookhaven, Inc. (Miss.), Lott Furniture Co. Jackson, Inc. (Miss.), Lott Furniture Co. Forest, Inc. (Miss.), Lott Furniture Co. McComb, Inc. (Miss.); dir. 1st Nat. Bank, Laurel. Chmn., Laurel Housing Authority; mem. Miss. Econ. Council. Trustee Clarke Coll. Served with U.S. Army, 1919. Mem. Nat., Miss. retail furniture assns., Miss. Mchts. Assn., U.S., Miss., Laurel (past dir.) chambers commerce, Am. Legion. Baptist (deacon). Mason. Home: 1005 15th St Laurel MS 39440 Office: 318-22 Front St Laurel MS 39440

LOTT, TRENT, congressman; b. Grenada, Miss., Oct. 9, 1941; s. Chester P. and Iona (Watson) L.; B.P.A., U. Miss., 1963, J.D., 1967; m. Patricia E. Thompson, Dec. 27, 1964; children—Chester T., Jr., Tyler Elizabeth. Admitted to Miss. bar, 1967; asso. firm Bryan & Gordon, Pascagoula, 1967; adminstrv. asst. to Congressman William M. Colmer, 1968-72; mem. 93d Congress from 5th dist. Miss. Field rep. for U. Miss., 1963-65; acting alumni sec. Ole Miss Alumni Assn., 1966-67. Mem. Am., Jackson County bar assns., Sigma Nu, Phi Alpha Delta. Republican. Baptist. Mason. Office: 1712 Longworth House Office Bldg Washington DC 20515*

LOTT, YANCY DAVIS, railroad exec.; b. Jackson, Miss., Aug. 28, 1906; s. Y. D. and Annette (Heintz) L.; A.B., Spring Hill Coll., 1927; J.D., Georgetown U., 1932; m. Sarah C. Hunter, Nov. 20, 1935; children—Sally, Yancy Davis, Annette, Thomas, Lillis, Catherine. Spl. agt. FBI, 1932-34; admitted to D.C. bar, 1931, Miss. bar, 1934, Ala. bar, 1935; atty. G. M. & N. R.R., 1934-40; gen. atty. G. M. & O. R.R., 1940-50, gen. solicitor, 1950-55, v.p., comptroller, 1956-72; v.p. finance I.C.G. R.R., 1972—; dir. Gulf Transport Co., G. M. & O. Land Co., New Orleans Gt. No. Ry. Co., Mchts. Nat. Bank Mobile. Bd. dirs. Providence Hosp., America's Jr. Miss Pageant. Mem. Spring Hill Coll., Georgetown U. (gov.) alumni assns., Soc. Former Spl. Agts. FBI, Am., Ala., Miss., Mobile bar assns., Assn. Am. R.R.'s (past chmn. accounting div.). Clubs: Touchdown, Internat. Trade, Athelstan, Mobile Country (Mobile); University (Chgo.). Home: 11 E Wimbledon Dr Mobile AL 36608 Office: 104 St Francis St Mobile AL 36602

LOTTERHOS, WILLIAM EAST, physician; b. Crystal Springs, Miss., Nov. 22, 1914; s. Julius L. and Bessie (East) L.; student Millsaps Coll., 1932, Miss. State U., 1934; B.S., U. Miss., 1938; postgrad., 1937-38; M.D., U. Tenn., 1940; m. Elizabeth Teat, Oct. 19, 1943; children—William East, George, Elizabeth, Richard, John Howard. Intern, Miss. Baptist Hosp., Jackson, 1940-41; resident Methodist Hosp., Memphis, Tenn., 1946-47; practice medicine, specializing in family practice Jackson, Miss., 1947—; prof., also chmn. dept. family practice Med. Coll. Ga., Augusta, 1972—; mem. staffs St. Dominic's, Bapt., Doctor's, Hinds Gen., Univ. hosps. (all Jackson). Pres., Jackson Council on Alcoholism, 1959; mem. Nurse's Examining Bd., Miss., 1959-66; mem. Bd. License for Phys. Therapy, 1966-71; mem. Gov.'s Council Comprehensive Health Planning, 1968-72; chmn. Com. Area Wide Health Planning, Gov.'s Com. on Rehab., 1968-72; bd. dirs. Central Miss. Home Health Agy. Served to lt. col. M.C., AUS, 1941-46. Decorated Bronze Star, Purple Heart, Legion of Merit; Italian Mil. Cross of Valor. Diplomate Am. Bd. Family Practice. Fellow Am. Geriatric Soc.; mem. Am. Acad. Gen. Practice (pres. 1970-71, chmn. bd. dirs. 1968-70), Central Med. Soc. (pres. 1958-59), Miss. Med. Assn. (speaker Ho. of Dels. 1968-72), A.M.A., (chmn. sect. gen. practice 1965—, chmn., mem. council sci. assembly 1972-73). Home: 920 Millege Rd Augusta GA 30904 Office: Med Coll Ga Dept Family Practice Augusta Ga 30902

LOTTS, ADOLPHUS LLOYD, metall. engr.; b. Va., June 10, 1934; s. Lloyd Newton and Pinkie Carolyn (Perkins) L.; B.S., Va. Poly. Inst. and State U., 1955, M.S., 1957; m. Grace Frances Howard, Oct. 22, 1954; children—Deborah, Patricia, Michelle, Marcella. Instr. metall. engring. Va. Poly. Inst. and State U., Blacksburg, 1955-57; asso. metallurgist Babcock & Wilcox Co., Lynchburg, Va., 1957-59; metall. engr. Union Carbide Corp., Oak Ridge Nat. Lab., 1959—. Mem. bd. edn., Knox County, Tenn., 1972—; ex-officio mem. Met. Planning Commn., Knoxville, Knox County, Tenn., 1972—. Served with AUS, 1957. Recipient award Sigma Xi, 1957. Mem. Am. Soc. Metals, Am. Nuclear Soc. (mem. exec. com. materials sci. and tech. div. 1972—). Republican. Presbyn. (elder 1964—). Club: Park West Sertoma. Home: 849 Chateaugay Rd Knoxville TN 37919 Office: PO Box X Oak Ridge Nat Lab Oak Ridge TN 37830

LOTZ, MYRON, physician; b. Warren, O., July 10, 1932; s. Michael Theodore and Anastasia (Mundrick) L.; B.S. summa cum laude, Yale, 1954, M.D. cum laude, 1958; Henry fellow, Oxford U., Eng., 1955-56; m. Janice Gay Holler, Feb. 15, 1969; children—Robin Michael, Ariel Lee. Intern, Mass. Gen. Hosp., Boston, 1958-59, resident, 1959-60; research and clin. fellow medicine Harvard Med. Sch. and Mass. Gen. Hosp., 1960-62; resident med. tutor Quincy House, Harvard, 1960-62; clin. asso. Nat. Heart Inst., Bethesda, Md., 1962-65; practice medicine, specializing in internal medicine, Vienna, Va., 1968—; asst. prof. medicine Georgetown U. Sch. Medicine, Washington, 1965—; chief med. officer Georgetown U. Med. Div., D.C. Gen. Hosp., 1965-68; cons. The Med. Letter. Served with USPHS, 1962-65. Diplomate Am. Bd. Internal Medicine. Fellow A.C.P.; mem. Am. Fedn. Clin. Research, Internat., Am. endocrine socs., Phi Beta Kappa, Sigma Xi, Alpha Omega Alpha. Home: 4123 N River St Arlington VA 22302 Office: 301 Maple St W Vienna VA 22180

LOUDEN, LESTER RICHARD, geochemist; b. Monroe, Wash., July 8, 1933; s. Lester A. and Mimi M. (Arnoldt) L.; Ph.D., U. Würzburg, Germany, 1963; m. Edit Margit Toro, Apr. 14, 1963. Came to U.S., 1963, naturalized, 1966. Prof. geology U. Houston, 1963-64; geologist Magcobar, Houston, 1964-65, mgr. x-ray labs., 1965-68, mgr. analytical sect. Dresser Magcobar, 1969-70, tech. adviser research, 1970-72, devel. mgr. Dresser pollution, 1972-73, product mgr. pollution control and equipment, 1973—. Mem. adv. bd. Foundry Research Assn., 1965—. Served with AUS, 1967-68. NASA grantee, 1963-64. Mem. Marine Tech. Soc., Malasian Geol. Soc., German Geol. Soc., Clay Mineral Soc. Club: American Sportsman (Houston). Contbr. articles to tech. lit. Home: 8011 Highmeadow Houston TX 77042 Office: PO Box 6504 Houston TX 77005

LOURIE, ABRAHAM M., retail co. exec.; b. St. George, S.C., July 17, 1926; s. Louis and Ann Gertrude (Friedman) L.; student U. Ga., 1946-47; m. Nancy Jean Elfenbaum, Mar. 7, 1954; children—Allison Beth, Louis Steven, Joan Ellen, Adam Neal. With Lourie's Inc., Columbia, S.C., 1950—, v.p. 1954—. Pres. Loubro Co., Inc., Columbia, S.C., 1959—, Lourie's Dutch Sq., Columbia, 1970, Columbia Jewish Community Center, 1966-67. Team capt. United Fund, 1957-58. Bd. dirs. House of Peace Synagogue, 1957-59, Carolina Assn. Clothiers and Furnishers, 1965-67. Mem. Greater Columbia C. of C. Downtown Bus. Assn. (pres. 1970), Greater Columbia C. of C. (dir. sports com. 1969-70), Phi Epsilon Pi. Mason; mem. B'nai B'rith. Club: Country (Columbia). Home: 6210 Eastshore Rd Columbia SC 29206 Office: 1601 Main St Columbia SC 29201

LOURIE, ISADORE EDWARD, lawyer, state senator; b. St. George, S.C., Aug. 4, 1932; s. Louis and Ann (Friedman) L.; LL.B., U.S.C., 1956; m. Susan Reiner, Nov. 29, 1959; children—Lance, Joel, Neal. Admitted to S.C. bar, 1956, since practiced in Columbia; partner Lourie and Draine, 1966—; mem. S.C. Ho. of Reps., 1965-72, S.C. Senate, 1973—. Dir., First Palmetto State Bank & Trust Co. Pres. S.C. Young Democrats, 1957-58; del. Nat. Dem. Conv., 1972. Pres. Happy Time Center for Mentally Retarded Children. Named Columbia's Young Man of Year, 1960. Mem. Am., S.C., Richland County bar assns., Am. Trial Lawyers Assn., Columbia Jr. C. of C. (past pres.). Jewish religion. Mason; mem. B'nai B'rith. Club: Civitan (Columbia). Home: 6308 West Shore Rd Columbia SC 29206 Office: 1224 Pickens St Columbia SC 29201

LOUSTALOT, ARNAUD JOSEPH, agriculturist; b. New Orleans, July 14, 1913; s. Arnaud J. and Odette F. (Dazette) L.; B.S., La. State U., 1935, M.S., 1936; Ph.D., Cornell U., 1939; m. Mildred D. Franz, Dec. 27, 1937; children—Arnaud J. III, Elaine P., Andre P. Asst. plant physiologist U.S. Pecan Lab., Brownwood, Tex., 1939-43, U.S. Tung Lab., Gainesville, Fla., 1943-45; sr. plant physiologist, asst. dir. Fed. Exptl. Sta., Mayaguez, P.R., 1945-54; prin. plant physiologist U.S. Dept. Agr. Coop. State Research Service, Washington, 1954—. Cons. to AID, Ecuador, 1965, Dahomey, 1966; cons. UN Mission to West Africa, 1970; Nat. Acad. Scis. participant tour to eastern Europe, 1971. Recipient 6 awards Soc. Agrl. Sci., 1946-53. Mem. Am. Soc. Hort. Sci., Am. Soc. Plant Physiologists, Weed Sci. Soc. Am., Sigma Xi, Gamma Sigma Delta. Home: 3165 N 21st St Arlington VA 22201 Office: USDA CSRS Washington DC 20250

LOVAN, CHARLES RONALD, civil engr.; b. Owensboro, Ky., Mar. 1, 1947; s. Alfred Cole and Lena Francis (Best) L.; B.S. in Civil Engring., U. Ky., 1969, M.S. in Civil Engring., 1971. San. engr. Water Pollution Control Commn., Frankfort, Ky., 1971-72; dist. engr. Nat. Clay Pipe Inst., Lexington, Ky., 1972—. Served with AUS, 1970-71. Registered profl. engr., Ky. Mem. Nat. Soc. Profl. Engrs., Am. Soc. C.E., Am. Pub. Works Assn., Water Pollution Control Fedn., Tau Beta Pi, Chi Epsilon. Baptist. Address: 1268 Village Dr Apt 313 Lexington KY 40504

LOVE, JIMMY OSCAR, mech. design engr.; b. Union County, N.C., Oct. 4, 1939; s. Samuel Oscar and Docie Ann (Little) L.; B.S. in Mech. Engring., N.C. State U., 1961; m. Sylvia E. Lisenby, Jan. 20, 1963. Design engr. Roberts Co., Sanford, N.C., 1961-63; textile machinery engring. specialist Monsanto Textiles Co., Pensacola, Fla., 1963—. Served with AUS, 1962. Mem. Am. Soc. M.E. Home: 221 St Barnabas St Pensacola FL 32503 Office: PO Box 12830 Pensacola FL 32575

LOVE, MIRON ANDERSON, dist. judge; b. Houston, Oct. 25, 1920; s. Robert William and Josephine (Moody) L.; student So. Meth. U., 1946-48; LL.B., S. Tex. Law Sch., 1951; m. Marjorie Ruth Skiles, Dec. 21, 1948; children—Mark Lowry, Ross William. Admitted to Tex., bar, 1951; asst. dist. atty., 1952-54; city judge Houston, 1955-58; state dist. judge, Houston, 1958—. Bd. dirs., pres. Tex. Bill of Rights Found., 1960—; bd. dirs. Travelers Aid, March of Dimes. Served to 1st lt. USAAF, 1943-46. Mem. Am. (mem. adv. com. standards for criminal justice 1969—), Tex., Houston bar assns., Internat. Acad. Trial Judges (organizing bd. regents), Delta Theta Phi. Home: 3526 Garrott St Houston TX 77002 Office: Court House 301 San Jacinto St Houston TX 77002

LOVE, RICHARD ARTHUR, aerospace design engr.; b. San Diego, May 8, 1930; s. Arthur and Lora Elizabeth (Dieffenbach) L.; A.A., Boise State Coll., 1951; B.S. in Mech. Engring., U. Washington, Seattle, 1956; m. Mary Verna Eberle, Sept. 20, 1952; children—William Duncan, Robert Douglas. With Boeing Co., Seattle, 1951-63, sr. preliminary design engr., 1961-63; project engr. Brown Engring. Co., Huntsville, Ala., 1963-64; sr. engr. Marshall Space Flight Center, NASA, Huntsville, 1964—. Served with USNR, 1951-53. Teaching fellow U. Washington, 1956-58. Registered profl. engr., Ala. Mem. Marshall Engrs. and Scientists Assn. (v.p. 1970—), Am. Aviation Hist. Soc., Sigma Xi. Home: 2002 Giles Dr Huntsville AL 35811 Office: PD DO SL MSFC Huntsville AL 35812

LOVE, RICHARD HARVEY, lawyer; b. Washington, Aug. 31, 1915; s. Leo Young and Grace Marie (Jett) L.; A.B., U. Md., 1936, LL.B., 1938; m. Betty Zane Schofield, Nov. 14, 1942 (dec. Sept. 1967); children—Richard, Robert, Edward, William, Elizabeth. Admitted to Md., D.C. bars. 1939; legal research asst. to Hon. W. Calvin Chesnut, U.S. dist. judge, Md., 1938-40; pvt. practice law, 1940-41, 46—; counsel Bd. Zoning Appeals, Prince Georges County, Md., 1953-55. Served from pvt. to maj. AUS, 1941-46; ETO; col. Judge Adv. Gen. Corps, Res. Decorated Legion Merit, Am. Def., Am. Service, European, African, Middle East, World War II Victory, Armed Forces Res. medal. Mem. Am., Md. bar assns., Bar Assn. D.C., Judge Advs. Assn. (exec. sec.), Mil. Order Fgn. Wars (vice comdr. gen. Nat. commandery), Assn. U.S. Army, Mil. Law Inst., Phi Kappa Phi, Order of Coif. Republican. Roman Catholic. Club: Army-Navy (Washington). Editor: Judge Adv. Jour. Home: 6905 Carleton Terrace College Park MD 20740 Office: 1010 Vermont Av Washington DC 20005

LOVE, ROBERT MARSHALL, engr.; b. Houston, Jan. 6, 1919; s. Robert Marshall and Sarah Beatrice (Killingsworth) L.; B.S. in Chem. Engring., Rice U., 1941; m. Martha Elizabeth Adams, Nov. 29, 1941; children—Linda (Mrs. John Herff Krueger), Sally. With Exxon Chem. Co., Baytown, Tex., 1941—, engaged in research and devel., 1941-62, lab. dept. head, 1963-70, environmental coordinator, 1970—. Registered profl. engr., Tex. Mem. Am. Inst. Chem. Engrs., Am. Chem. Soc., Water Pollution Control Fedn., Air Pollution Control Assn., Engrs. Council Houston, Houston C. of C. (vice chmn. air conservation com.), Sigma Xi, Tau Beta Pi. Kiwanian (v.p. 1973). Patentee in field petroleum refining. Home: 404 Burnet Baytown TX 77520 Office: PO Box 4004 Baytown TX 77520

LOVE, ROBERT MITCHELL, assn. exec.; b. Chgo., Aug. 7, 1928; s. Quill Horace and Jemma (Mitchell) L.; student Monterey Peninsula Jr. Coll., 1960-61; grad. Inst. for Orgn. Mgmt., U. Houston, 1968, Advanced Mgmt. Studies, Tex. Christian U., 1971; m. Shari Lee Cook, Dec. 12, 1964; children—Mark, Gregory, Wendi. Customer service agt. Am. Airlines, Memphis, 1951-55, customer service mgr., Washington, 1955-59, mgr. mil. traffic office, San Francisco, 1959-63; mgr. customer service and operations Mohawk Airlines, N.Y.C., 1963-65; mgr. conv. and visitors bur. Little Rock C. of C., 1965-67; exec. v.p., also gen. mgr. Jonesboro (Ark.) C. of C., 1967-71; dir. indsl. services Knoxville (Tenn.) C. of C., 1971-72; exec. dir. Melton Hill Regional Indsl. Devel. Assn., 1972-73; exec. v.p. Scott County (Tenn.) Indsl. Devel. Bd., Oneida, 1974—. Served with AUS, USAF, 1946-51. Decorated Bronze Star medal, Purle Heart. Mem. Am. Soc. Assn. Execs., Am., Tenn., Eastern Tenn. indsl. devel. councils. Methodist. Mason. Home: Oneida TN 37841 Office: PO Box 423 Oneida TN 37841

LOVE, ROBERT WORRELL, city ofcl.; b. Madisonville, Tenn., Sept. 5, 1916; s. Robert John and Lillian Dee (Worrell) L.; student Vanderbilt U., 1933-34; B.S., U.S. Mil. Acad., 1938; M.B.A., Harvard, 1948; m. Cornelia Gambill, Sept. 16, 1939; children—Candace (Mrs. E.C. Dimitri), Robert, Wheless, Anne, Jenelle. Commd. 2d lt. U.S., Army, 1938, advanced through grades to col.; div. engr. Mo. River Div., Omaha, 1966-68; ret., 1968; urban renewal project mgr. Nashville Housing Authority, 1968—. Decorated D.S.M., Silver Star, Bronze Star, Legion of Merit (U.S.); Croix de Guerre (France). Fellow Am. Soc. C.E.; mem. Soc. Am. Mil. Engrs., Nat. Assn. Housing, and Redevel. Ofcls., Assn. U.S. Army. Presbyn (elder 1970—). Club: Exchange (Nashville). Home: 4505 Price Circle Rd Nashville TN 37205 Office: 701 S 6th St Nashville TN 37206

LOVE, SAMUEL DAVID, conservation adminstr.; b. Aliceville, Ala., Dec. 4, 1946; s. David Brown and Bessie (Dial) L.; B.A., Miss. State U., 1969. City editor Delta Democrat-Times, Greenville, Miss., 1969-70; So. coordinator Earth Day, 1970; coordinator Environmental Action, Inc., Washington, 1970—; dir. Environmental Coalition N.Am.; adviser Environmental Action Found. Nat. committeeman Young Democrats of Miss., 1969. Mem. Pi Delta Epsilon. Editor: Earth Tool Kit, 1971; Ecotage, 1972. Contbg. editor Mississippi Freelance, 1969. Home: 2200 19th St NW Washington DC 20009 Office: 1346 Connecticut Av Washington DC 20036

LOVE, TERRENCE LESTER, planner, architect, economist; b. Covington, Va., Feb. 6, 1937; s. James Harold and Patsy (King) L.; B.Arch., Va. Poly. Inst., 1961; M.B.A. in Real Estate and Urban Affairs, Ga. State U., 1969, Ph.D. in Land Econs., 1970; m. Valerie Gay LeCraw, Nov. 20, 1965; 1 son, Terrence Lester. Architect Aeck Assos., Inc., Atlanta, 1965-67; urban planner Adley Assos., Inc., Atlanta, 1967-70; asso. prof. Ga. State U., Atlanta, 1970-73; chmn. bd. Land Devel. Analysts, Inc., Atlanta, 1974—; dir. 1st Land Collaborative, Inc. Bd. dirs. Atlanta Arts Festival, 1970—; chmn. Atlanta Inter-Profl. Learning Team, 1970-73. Served with AUS, 1961-62. Mem. A.I.A. (life), Am. Inst. Planners (life mem.; treas. Ga. chpt.), Am. Real Estate and Urban Econ. Assn. (life, editor newsletter), Beta Gamma Sigma, Delta Sigma Pi, Rho Epsilon (nat. treas.). Home: 506 Manor Ridge Dr NW Atlanta GA 30305 Office: Suite 1210 Healey Bldg 57 Forsyth St NW Atlanta GA 30303

LOVELACE, JOHN HENRY, lawyer; b. Waco, Tex., Oct. 26, 1926; s. Carl and Lucile (Hill) L.; B.A., U. Okla., 1948; J.D., U. Tex., 1951; m. Sarah Elizabeth Sadler, Oct. 20, 1951 (dec. May 1973); children—John Henry, Sarah Elizabeth. Admitted to Tex. bar, 1951; with firm Sheehy, Lovelace & Mayfield and predecessors, Waco, 1951—, partner, 1957—. Lectr. Baylor U. Sch. Law, 1965-68. Gen. chmn. Grass Roots Orgn. Waco, 1964; mem. exec. com. Citizens Adv. Com., 1970—. Served with AUS, 1944-46. Fellow Tex. Bar Found.; mem. Assn. Life Ins. Counsel, State Bar Tex., Am. Bar Assn., Kappa Alpha Order (nat. bd. dirs. 1963-69, certificate of honor 1970), Phi Alpha Delta. Home: 3420 Oakridge Lane Waco TX 76708 Office: American-Amicable Bldg Waco TX 76701

LOVELL, JAMES A., astronaut; b. Cleve., Mar. 25, 1928; s. James A. and Blanche Lovell; student U. Wis., 1946-58; B.S., U.S. Naval Acad., 1952; grad. Aviation Safety Sch., U. So. Cal., 1961; hon. D., Ill. Wesleyan U.; D.Sc. (hon.), Rockhurst Coll., 1970; m. Marilyn Gerlach; children—Barbara Lynn, James Arthur, Susan Kay, Jeffrey C. Commd. 2d lt. U.S. Navy, advanced through grades to capt., 1965; test pilot Navy Air Test Center, Patuxent River, Md., 1958-61; then flight instr., safety officer Fighter Squadron 101, Naval Air Sta., Oceana, Va.; astronaut with Manned Spacecraft Center, NASA, 1962—; made 14 day orbital Gemini 7 flight, Dec. 1965, including rendezvous with Gemini 6, Gemini 12 Mission, 1966; command module pilot Apollo VIII, 1968; backup spacecraft comdr. Apollo XI; spacecraft comdr. Apollo XIII, 1970. Spl. cons. President's Council on Phys. Fitness and Sports, 1967—. Recipient Distinguished Service award NASA, 1965, Harmon Internat. Trophy, 1966, 67, Flight Achievement award Am. Astronautical Soc., 1966, 68, DeLaval Medal, 1967, Gold Space Medal, 1967, Gen. Thomas D. White Space trophy USAF, 1968, Robert J. Collier trophy, 1968, Henry G. Bennett Distinguished Service award, 1969, Robert H. Goddard Meml. trophy, 1969, H.H. Arnold trophy, 1969, Golden Plate award Am. Acad. Achievement, 1969, Gold Medal N.Y.C., 1969, Medal for valor City of Houston, 1969, Hubbard Medal Nat. Geographic Soc., 1969, Spl. Trustees award Nat. Acad. TV Arts and Scis., 1969, award Inst. Nav., 1969, Distinguished Alumni Service award U. Wis., 1970, Haley Astronautics award Am. Inst. Aeros. and Astronautics 1970, Presdl. medal for Freedom, 1970, Exceptional Service medal (two) NASA; decorated D.F.C. (two), Distinguished Service medal (Navy). Club: Toastmasters. Address: Manned Spacecraft Center NASA 2101 NASA Rd Houston TX 77058

LOVELL, JAMES GODFREY, JR., banker; b. Birmingham, Ala., Nov. 10, 1939; s. James Godfrey and Annie Lucile (Stone) L.; B.S., Auburn U., 1962; postgrad. Northwestern U., 1965, Am. Inst. Banking, 1963, La. State U. Sch. Banking, 1970-72; m. Sharon Elizabeth Rochambeau, Mar. 17, 1962; children—James Godfrey III, Daniel Guy. With Exchange Security Bank, Birmingham, 1962-66; v.p. corr. banking, marketing Central Bancshares of the South, Birmingham, 1966—. Mem. Pi Kappa Phi, Delta Sigma Pi. Methodist (mem. adminstrv. bd. 1962—, mem. finance com. 1966—). Club: Crestwood Civic (Birmingham). Home: 2305 Ponderosa Circle Vestavia Hills Birmingham AL 35216 Office: Central Bancshares of the South 701 S 20th St Birmingham AL 35233

LOVELL, JOE W., utilities ofcl.; b. Wartrace, Tenn., Oct. 2, 1912; s. Hall and Mattie (Jernigan) L.; student pub. schs., Murfreesboro; m. Flora Mae Qualls, Aug. 4, 1935. House electrician Tenn. Coll., 1926-29; bookkeeper, plumber, steamfitter Standard Plumbing & Heating Co., 1930-32; meter reader, cashier Murfreesboro (Tenn.) Water Dept., 1932-38, supt. Water Dept., 1938-56, Water and Sewer Dept., 1956—. Chmn., Tenn. Water and Wastewater Certification Bd., 1971—, Com. for Tng. Water and Wastewater Plant Operators in Tenn., 1968-72. Bd. dirs. Tenn. Municipal League, 1964-65. Recipient Samuel A. Greeley Service award, 1962; George Warren, Fuller award, 1967. Mem. Am. Water Works Assn. (life mem.; chmn. Ky.-Tenn. sect. 1957-58), Am. Pub. Works Assn. (pres. Tenn. 1964-65), Water Pollution Control Fedn. Presbyn. (elder, treas. 1944-51). Mason. Home: 1115 Houston Dr Murfreesboro TN 37130 Office: PO Box 700 Murfreesboro TN 37130

LOVELL, JOHN, JR., educator; b. Asheville, N.C., July 25, 1907; s. John and Zula (Pope) L.; A.B., Northwestern U., 1926, M.A., 1927; Ph.D., (Rockefeller Found. fellow), U. Cal. at Berkeley, 1938; m. Nancy Merritt, Sept. 6, 1940 (div. Mar. 1951); 1 dau., Taunya Marita; m. 2d, Marian Giles Mouzon, July 31, 1954 (dec. Oct. 13, 1966). Instr. English, W. Va. State Coll., 1927-29; asst. prof. English, Howard U., Washington, 1930-46, asso. prof., 1946-58, prof., 1958—, asso. dean Coll. Liberal Arts, 1964-68, acting head dept. English, 1968-69, chmn. dept., 1972—; vis. prof. in Ia., Cal., Am. Friends Service Com., 1948; vis. prof. U. Pacific, summers 1950, 56; lectr., cons. seminars for exec. devel. U.S. Dept. Agr. Fulbright lectr., Japan, 1960-61. Served to 1st lt. AUS, 1943-46. Mem. Modern Lang. Assn. Am., Am. Lit. Sect., Am. Studies Assn., Am. Soc. for Theatre Research, Am. Ednl. Theatre Assn., Assn. for Asian Studies, Folklore Soc. Greater Washington, Internat. Theatre Inst., ANTA, Authors League Am., Nat. Council Tchrs. English, Washington Urban League, N.A.A.C.P. (sec. 1939-42), Kappa Alpha Psi. Democrat. Author: Digests of Great American Plays, 1961; Black Song: The Forge and the Flame, 1972. Contbr. articles to profl. jours. Research, lectr. native drama and folklore. Home: 201 I St SW Washington DC 20024

LOVING, GEORGE HORACE, architect; b. Abilene, Tex., Aug. 7, 1933; s. Noble Lee and Mary Eleanor (Broyles) L.; B.Arch., U. Okla., 1957; m. Barbara Ann Smith, Oct. 25, 1952; children—Toni Lynn (Mrs. Steve Glenn Arthur), Lori Lee, Sheri Ann. With Tucker & Lindberg, Abilene, 1957, Tittle & Luther, 1958-63, 65; with Tucker & Loving, Kenville, Tex., 1964-65; partner Tittle, Luther, Loving & Lee, Abilene, Tex., 1966-71, Tittle, Luther, Loving, 1971—. Mem. Long Range Planning Com., Abilene, 1967-68; mem. Elec. Bd. Examiners, Abilene, 1967-68; mem. United Fund, 1972—. Bd. dirs. Abilene Fine Arts Mus., 1971—, v.p., 1973—. Served with AUS, 1957-58. Admiral, Okla. Navy. Recipient Archtl. Design awards for Nelson Park Zoo, Recreating and Tng. Bldg. Abilene State Sch., Air Terminal BLdg., Citizens Nat. Bank, all Abilene. Mem. Nat. Council Archtl. Registration Bds. (dir. So. Conf.), A.I.A. (pres., dir. Abilene chpt.), Tex. Soc. Architects (dir., chmn. publs. com.), Tex. Bd. Archtl. Examiners (past chmn.). Clubs: Abilene Country, Abilene Exchange (dir. 1974). Home: 2525 Regent Abilene TX 79605 Office: 340 Beech Abilene TX 79601

LOVING, JOE HILTON, JR., municipal judge; b. Dallas, Dec. 12, 1935; s. Joe Hilton and Lola Julia (Anders) L.; B.A., So. Meth. U., 1958, LL.B., 1960; M.Div., Southwestern Bapt. Theol. Sem., 1973; m. Mary Leone Carpenter, June 8, 1963; children—Donna Michelle, Sheryl Diane, Kimberly Dawn. Admitted to Tex. bar, 1960, practiced in Grand Prairie, 1961; asst. city atty., Dallas, 1961-68; judge municipal ct., Dallas, 1968—. Ordained to ministry Bapt. Ch., 1969. Mem. Tex., Dallas bar assns., Am. Judges Assn., Delta Theta Phi. Home: 10932 Carissa Dallas TX 75218 Office: Police and Courts Bldg Main and Harwood Sts Dallas TX 75201

LOVVORN, MARTIN CRAFT, banker; b. Dallas, Apr. 15, 1928; s. Ben H. and Floyd (Craft) L.; B.B.A., So. Meth. U., 1948; m. Mary Carolyn Goodman, Nov. 18, 1950; children—Janet, Mark, Linda, Laurie. Chmn. bd. Lewisville (Tex.) Nat. Bank, 1963-65, Tex. Nat. Bank, Dallas, 1965—; pres. 1st Nat. Bank, Richardson, Tex., 1964—, Dynamerica Corp., Dallas, Tex., 1969—. Bd. dirs. Bapt. Found. of Tex.; trustee annuity bd. So. Bapt. Conv. Served to lt. (j.g.) USNR, 1951-52. Home: 3820 W Bay Circle Dallas TX 75214 Office: 808 S Central Expressway Richardson TX 75080

LOW, JAMES PATTERSON, orgn. exec.; b. Hartford, Conn., July 25, 1927; s. Marshall and Margaret (Fleming) L.; B.A., U. Md. 1953; M.B.A., Fla. Atlantic U., 1972; m. Patricia Marion Siegman, Nov. 20, 1956; children—Lisa Patricia, Lori Patterson. Mgr., Pulaski County (Va.) Indsl. Devel. Corp. and C. of C., 1953-55; asst. mgr. assn. service dept. C. of C. U.S., Washington, 1956-58, mgr., 1958-66; exec. v.p. Am. Soc. Assn. Execs., 1966—. Instr., Insts. for Ogn. Mgmt., Yale, Mich. State U., Syracuse U., Stanford, 1958—. Mem. Nat. Export Expansion Council. Bd. dirs. Nat. Center for Vol. Action. Served with USMCR, 1945-46; to capt. AUS, 1951-54. Decorated Bronze Star. Mem. Washington Trade Assn. Execs., Am. Soc. Assn. Execs., Nat. Assn. Execs. Club (dir.), Sigma Nu. Clubs: Congressional Country, Metropolitan (Washington). Author: Basic Operating Policies of Trade and Professional Associations, 1960; Association Legislative Handbook, 1962; Association Executive Contracts, 1965. Home: 8463 Brook Rd McLean VA 22101 Office: 1101 16th St NW Washington DC 20036

LOWBEER, LEO, physician; b. Vienna, Austria, May 30, 1901; s. Alfred and Pauline (Sobotka) L.; M.D., U. Vienna, 1927; m. Gertrude Neuhut, Sept. 28, 1940; 1 dau., Carol Ann. Came to U.S., 1938, naturalized, 1944. Intern dept. pathology Vienna Municipal Hosp., 1927-28, rotating intern 1928-29, 1st asst. to Prof. Jakob Erdheim dept. pathology, 1929-32, resident dept. metabolic and nutritional diseases, 1932-33, sr. resident dept. geriatric medicine, 1933-37; pathologist Hillcrest Meml. Hosp., Tulsa, 1939-45; chief pathologist, dir. dept. pathology Hillcrest Med. Center, Tulsa, 1945-67, emeritus, 1967—; chief cons. pathologist Hillcrest Med. Center and Okla. Bd. Medicolegal Investigations, 1967—; cons. pathologist Diagnostic Physicians of Tulsa, 1973—; distinguished lectr. dept. pathology U. Okla. Sch. Medicine, Oklahoma City, 1947—; cons. pathologist FAA; cons. U.S. Dept. Justice; dir. Hillcrest Poison Center, Tulsa, 1961—. Recipient citation for meritorious service North Tulsa Community Service, 1954; certificate appreciation, 1969, Service to Mankind award, 1971 (both Tulsa Sertoma Club). Diplomate Am. Bd. Pathology. Fellow emeritus Am. Assn. Pathologists and Bacteriologists, Coll. Am. Pathologists, Internat. Acad. Pathology; fellow Am. Soc. Clin. Pathologists; mem. Am. (life), So., Okla. med. assns., Tulsa County Med. Soc. (life mem., alternate del., Tulsa Dr. of Yr. award 1973), Am. Acad. Forensic Scis., A.A.A.S. (emeritus), Soc. Exptl. Biology and Medicine, Nat. Assn. Med. Examiners, Am. Assn. Poison Control Centers, Am. Acad. Clin. Toxicology, Okla. Assn. Pathologists (pres. 1950), Tulsa Philharmonic Assn. Democrat. Methodist. Clubs: Tulsa Ski, Concertime, Tulsa Tennis. Contbr. articles to med. jours. Home: 2547 S College St Tulsa OK 74114 Office: Hillcrest Medical Center 1120 S Utica St Tulsa OK 74104

LOWE, DONALD RAY, educator; b. Sacramento, Cal., Sept. 22, 1942; s. Ray Clement and Mary Frances (Thomas) L.; B.S. with honors, Stanford, 1964; Ph.D., U. Ill., 1967; m. Necla Aytug, Sept. 6, 1964; children—Nina, Deniz. Instr. geology U. Ill. at Urbana, 1967-68; postdoctoral research asso. U.S. Geol. Survey, Menlo Park, Cal., 1968-70; prof. geology La. State U., Baton Rouge, 1970—. Mem. Geol. Soc. Am., Soc. Econ. Paleontologists and Mineralogists. Home: 724 Rue Crozat Baton Rouge LA 70810

LOWE, JOHN WILL, mobile home mfg. co. exec.; b. Milltown, Ala., May 23, 1932; s. Marvin Clifford and Bertha L. (Looser) L.; B.S. in Indsl. Engring., Auburn U., 1956; m. June Mary Karnuth, May 9, 1959; children—Stephen, Suzette. Salesman, Armstrong Cork Co., Atlanta, 1956-68; propr. Craftmade Homes, Henderson Tex., 1968-70 (merger with APECO Corp., Evanston, Ill. 1970), pres., gen. mgr., 1970—. Bd. dirs. YMCA. Served to capt. AUS, 1956. Mem. Tex. Mobile Home Assn. (sec. bd. dirs. 1973), Henderson C. of C. (dir.). Republican. Presbyn. (elder, finance chmn.). Lion (dir.). Home: 1100 Slaydon Henderson TX 75652 Office: PO Box 1185 Henderson TX 75652

LOWE, PETER LOFTIS, realtor; b. Pensacola, Fla., July 19, 1938; s. E. Len and Nadis (Loftis) L.; B.S., U. Ala., 1960; m. Elizabeth Jones, Apr. 1, 1961; children—Peter, Carl, Sarah. Exec. v.p. G.W. Jones & Sons, Inc., Huntsville, Ala., 1961—; sec. Jones Valley Devel. Co., 1962—; treas. N. Ala. Mineral Devel. Co., 1967—; partner Jones-Lowe Co., 1970—, Pres. Central City Assn., Huntsville, 1969-71. Served with AUS, 1960. Mem. Am. Inst. Real Estate Appraisers (2d v.p. Ala. 1973), Soc. Real Estate Appraisers, Am. Soc. Farm Mgrs. and Rural Appraisers, Nat. Assn. Real Estate Bds., Ala. Real Estate Assn., Huntsville Bd. Realtors, Phi Gamma Delta. Methodist. Rotarian (pres. Huntsville 1974). Home: 5701 Criner Rd Huntsville AL 35802 Office: 307 Franklin St Huntsville AL 35802

LOWE, MRS. THOMAS JACKSON (ROSE WALKER MAYNE), assn. exec.; b. Athens, Ga.; d. George Stovall and Rosa Montgomery (Walker) Mayne; A.B. in Edn. (U.D.C. scholar), M.S. (U. fellow), U. Ga.; Nat. Soc. Crippled Children and Adults, Inc. and Alpha Chi Omega scholar U. Mich. and Mich. State Normal Coll.; m. Thomas Jackson Lowe; 1 dau., Harriet Rose. Cerebral palsy coordinator S.C. Soc. Crippled Children and Adults, 1949-50, exec. dir., 1951—; adviser, cons. health related tax-supported agys.; vis. lectr. state univs., colls. Sponsored legislation to provide edn. to handicapped children in Ga., S.C. Mem. Gov.'s, Mayor's coms. on handicapped. Named Columbia Career Woman of Year, 1965, S.C. Career Woman of Yr. 1966; recipient State S.C. Rehab. award of yr., 1969. Mem. Internat. Council Exceptional Children (past dist. pres.; former S.C. pres.), Am. Assn. Easter Seal Execs., Nat., S.C. rehab. assns., Daus. Colonial Wars, Colonial Dames 17th Century, Nat. Soc. Magna Charta Dames, S.C. Psychol. Assn., S.C. Acad. Sci., S.C. Conf. Social Work, Jamestowne Soc., Soc. Descs. Knights of Garter, Daus. 1812, Dau. Am. Colonists, D.A.R., U.D.C., Plantagenet Soc., Psi Chi, Xi Phi Xi. Methodist. Home: 4017 MacGregor Dr Columbia SC 29206 Office: 3020 Farrow Rd Columbia SC 29203

LOWE, WILLIAM CLIFFORD, librarian; b. Bklyn., Sept. 18, 1930; s. Clifford Munson and Irene Abby (Reiners) L.; B.A., Colgate U., 1952; M.S., State U. N.Y., 1960; m. Irene Frances Stoll, Dec. 28, 1952; children—James Lawrence, Judith Laura. Physicist, Xerox Corp., Webster, N.Y., 1952-58, sr. tech. librarian, 1958-66; head Tech. Information Center, N.C. State U. at Raleigh, 1966-71, asst. dir. for reference services D.H. Hill Library, 1971—. Mem., chmn. planning bd. Town of Webster, 1961-63; mem. Webster Sch. Dist. Transp. Policy Com., 1963. Served to 2nd lt. USAF, 1952-53. Mem. N.C., Southeastern library assns., Spl. Libraries Assn. (N.Y. chpt. pres. 1961-62, N.C. chpt. pres. 1970-71). Contbr. articles in field to profl. jours. Editor: Rochester Area Union List of Serials, 1966. Home: 4708 Woodridge Dr Raleigh NC 27612 Office: DH Hill Library North Carolina State University PO Box 5007 Raleigh NC 27607

LOWELL, ANTHONY M., statistician; b. Koniuchy, Ukraine, July 22, 1908; s. Anthony and Johanna (Soner) Lotowycz; brought to U.S., 1912, naturalized, 1921; B.S., Alfred U., 1932; postgrad. U. Rochester, 1932-34; M.P.H., Mass. Inst. Tech., 1935, C.P.H., 1935; postgrad. Yale, 1944. Statistician Phila. Health Council, 1937-39; dir. statis. div. N.Y. Tb and Health Assn., N.Y.C., 1939-62; chief statistics and program analysis Tb br. Nat. Center Disease Control, Atlanta, 1962—. Asso. mem. Henry Phipps Inst., Phila., 1937—; cons. in field. Served with AUS, 1943-45. Fellow Am. Pub. Health Assn.; mem. Am. Statis. Assn., Soc. Epidemological Research. Author: Tb in New York City, ann. 1953-62; Advances in Tb Research, 1966; Tuberculosis, 1969. Contbr. to profl. jours. Home: 3645 Peachtree Rd NE Atlanta GA 30319 Office: Center Disease Control Atlanta GA 30333

LOWELL, PHILIP SIVERLY, research co. exec.; b. Manila, Philippines, July 9, 1931; s. Fred R. and Winifred (Smith) L.; B.S. in Chem. Engring., U. Tex., 1954, M.S., 1963, Ph.D., 1966; m. Judith O. Lowell; children—Allison Gardiner, Winifred Piper. With Jefferson Chem. Co., Port Neches, Tex., 1954-55; sr. engr. C.F. Braun & Co., Alhambra, Cal., 1955-60; engr. III, group leader, sect. head Tracor, Inc., Austin, 1960-69; v.p., prin. scientist Radian Corp., Austin, 1969—, also dir. Mem. U.S.-USSR Tech. and Sci. Cooperation Working Group Air Pollution. Registered profl. engr., Tex., Cal. Mem. Am. Inst. Chem. Engring., Air Pollution Control Assn. Home: 6307 Shoal Creek W Austin TX 78731 Office: PO Box 9948 8500 Shoal Creek Blvd Austin TX 78766

LOWENSTEIN, CHARLES DOUGLAS, ednl. services co. exec.; b. Bayonne, N.J., Apr. 22, 1942; s. Irving Eric and Barbara (Goldenberg) L.; B.S. in Commerce and Econs., U. Vt., 1963; m. Leslie Ann Diamond, Sept. 5, 1965; children—Lee Jay, Andrea Michelle, Evan Mitchell and Jaron David (twins). Supt. Lowenstein Metals Inc., Newark, 1964-67; registered prin. Penn Securities Co., East Orange, N.J., 1967-68; asst. dir. Nelson Sch. Securities, Mountainside, N.J., 1968-69; v.p. sales Ga. Internat. Securities Co., Atlanta, 1969-70; pres. Investment Tng. Inst., Inc., Atlanta, 1969—; tng. cons. Wiesenberger Services, Inc., N.Y.C., 1971—. Mem. task force to design new industry tng. standards Nat. Assn. Securities Dealers, 1971; bd. regents Coll. for Financial Planning, Denver, 1972-73. Served with AUS, 1963. Mem. Internat. Assn. Financial Planners (dir. 1973-74), Sales and Marketing Execs. Internat., Jr. C. of C., Nat. R.R. Hist. Soc., Tau Epsilon Phi. Jewish religion. Home: 2974 Cravey Dr Atlanta GA 30345 Office: PO Box 29151 Atlanta GA 30329

LOWENSTEIN, GEORGE WOLFGANG, UN cons.; b. Germany, Apr. 18, 1890; s. Julius Max and Augusta Victoria (Klettschoff) L.; student Royal William Coll., Germany, 1909, Frederik Williams U., Germany, 1919, London (Eng.) Sch. Tropical Hygiene and Medicine, 1939; m. Johanna Sabath, Nov. 27, 1923; children—Peter F. Lansing and Ruth Edith (Mrs. Roger G. Gallagher) (twins). Intern Berlin III U. Clinic, 1919; resident Berlin Charity Hosp., 1920; dir. pub. health Berlin Neubabelsberg, 1920-22; dir. pub. health and welfare, Berlin, Germany, 1923-33; pvt. practice medicine in Berlin, 1933-38, Chgo., 1940-46, Chebeague and Dark Harbor, Me., 1947-58; permanent cons. for Internat. Abolitionists Fedn. at ECOSOC, UN, 1947—; med. cons. German Consulate (Atlanta) for Fla. Social Econs. Research; pres. Aripeka Corp. for Devel., 1958-66; med. cons. Pasco County Civil Def., 1958-66; lectr. Morton Plaut Hosp., Clearwater, also Clearwater campus St. Petersburg Jr. Coll. Vice pres. Allied Art Council West Pasco, 1960-66. Bd. dirs. Aripeka Meml. Library, Rlchey Symphony Assn., West Pasco County Hosp. Assn., 1959-66. Co-founder German Hygiene Mus., Dresden; county chmn. first aid A.R.C., 1958-66, vol. program cons. nat. A.R.C., 1958-66; vol. worker A.R.C., 52 years. Civilian Def., Chebeague and Dark Harbor, Me., 1946-57. Served with German Army, 1914-18. Decorated Cross Merit I Class, Germany, 1965; recipient Commendation awards Pres. U.S., 1945, 70; 50 Year Gold Service Pin, A.M.A. and A.R.C., 1970; Service to Mankind award Sertoma, 1972, others. Fellow Acad. Family Physicians (charter, life mem.), A.A.A.S., Am. Coll. Sport Medicine (emeritus), Am. Pub. Health Assn. (life); mem. A.M.A., Am. Assn. Mil. Surgeons, Steuben Soc. Club: City (Chgo. chmn. hygiene sect. 1946-46). Rotarian, Mason (Shriner, Comdr., 32 deg.). Home: 1007 Woodside Dr Clearwater FL 33516

LOWENTHAL, WERNER, educator; b. Krefeld, Germany, Dec. 20, 1930; s. Kurt and Senta (Seligmann) L.; came to U.S., 1937, naturalized, 1945; B.S. (Borden scholar 1952), Albany Coll. Pharmacy, 1953; M.S., U. Mich., 1955, Ph.D., 1958; m. Jane Sperberg, Dec. 23, 1961; children—John Marc, Julie Dara. Asst., Abbott Labs., North Chicago, Ill., 1958-61; asst. prof. Sch. Pharmacy, Va. Commonwealth U., Richmond, 1961-66, asso. prof., 1966-71, prof., 1971—. Bd. dirs. Beth Sholom Home of Va. Recipient certificate of recognition Va. Edn. Research Assn. Mem. Am. Pharm. Assn., Va. Pharm. Assn., A.A.A.S., Am. Chem. Soc., Nat. Soc. Performance Improvement, Am. Assn. Colls. Pharmacy (chmn. sect. tchrs. pharmacy, 1973-74), Sigma Xi, Rho Pi Phi, Phi Lambda Upsilon. Club: Torch (dir. 1971—) (Richmond). Contbr. to profl. publs. in field. Patentee in field. Home: 2301 Fon-Du-Lac Rd Richmond VA 23229

LOWERY, JAMES HARLTON, city ofcl.; b. Remlig, Tex., July 10, 1923; s. James Frank and Lillian (Mitchell) L.; grad. Port Arthur Bus. Coll., 1944. Clk. Lumus Constrn. Co., N.Y.C., 1944; parts mgr. Hempel Motors Co., Orange, Tex., 1953-54; auditor Tex. Employment Commn., Houston, 1955-56; with City of Port Arthur (Tex.), 1957—, dir. finance, 1964—. Mem. C. of C., Municipal Finance Officers Assn. Baptist (deacon chmn. finance com. 1967—). Home: 2749 31st St Port Arthur TX 77640 Office: 400 4th St Port Arthur TX 77640

LOWERY, LEE LEON, JR., civil engr.; b. Corpus Christi, Tex., Dec. 26, 1938; s. Lee Leon and Blanch (Dietrich) L.; B.S., Tex. A. and M. U., 1960, M.S., 1962, Ph.D., 1966; m. Evelyn Frances Lindsey, Sept. 4, 1960; children—Kelli Lane, Christianne. Asso. research engr. Tex. Transp. Inst., Bryan, 1960—; asso. prof. depts. civil engring., aerospace engring., archtl. engring. Tex. A. and M. U., 1960—; research engr. Albritton Engring. Corp., 1963-66; sr. partner Pile Dynamics, Inc., 1968—; pres. Anderson-Lowery & Assos. Profl. engring. cons. Esso Prodn. Research, Brown & Root, Kaiser Steel Co., Chgo. Bridge & Iron Works. Mem. Am. Soc. C.E., Nat., Tex. socs. profl. engrs., Am. Soc. Engring. Edn., Sigma Xi, Tau Beta Pi, Phi Kappa Phi, Chi Epsilon. Kiwanian. Contbr. articles to profl. jours. Patentee in field. Home: 2404 Wayside St Bryan TX 77801 Office: 4015 Texas Av Bryan TX 77801

LOWERY, RAYMOND, newspaper editor; b. Patterson Springs, N.C., Jan. 13, 1918; s. William and Ida (McBrayer) L.; student Oak Ridge Mil. Inst., 1935-36; A.B., U. N.C., 1936-39; m. Jeanne DeKam, Mar. 13, 1948; children—David, Danny. Mng. editor Los Angeles Comml. News, 1948; telegraph editor Shelby (N.C.) Daily Star, 1948-50; entertainment editor The News and Observer, Raleigh, N.C., 1952-60, Sunday editor, 1960-69, copy editor, feature writer, 1969—. Dir. N.C. State Ballet, Raleigh Concert Music Assn., N.C. Music Assn. Served with USAAF, 1942-46. Home: 4306 Lambeth Dr Raleigh NC 27609 Office: News and Observer 215 McDowell St Raleigh NC 27602

LOWNDES, RICHARD I'ON III, computer service co. exec.; b. Atlanta, June 7, 1936; s. Richard I'On and Elizabeth Hunt (Plumb) L.; B.Aero. Engring., Ga. Inst. Tech., 1958, M.Aero. Engring., 1960; postgrad. (Nat. Def. Edn. Act grantee), Vanderbilt U., 1968-71; m. Laura Gray Parker, Oct. 18, 1958; children—John Parker, Laura Ann. Research and testing engr. ARO, Inc., Arnold Air Force Sta., Tenn., 1960-66; staff engr. TRW Systems, Inc., Houston, 1966-67; chief engr., owner Engring. and Computer Services, Estill Springs, Tenn., 1970—. Mem. faculty Ga. Inst. Tech., 1958-60, U. Tenn., 1969-71; cons. Investigative Design Assos., Estill Springs, 1973. Chmn., Franklin County Regional Planning Commn., 1971-73. Mem. Nat., Tenn. socs. profl. engrs., Franklin County C. of C. (dir. 1970-73), Sigma Xi, Phi Sigma Kappa. Episcopalian (layreader). Lion. Home: Route 1 Estill Springs TN 37330 Office: Box 186 Estill Springs TN 37330

LOWREY, AMOS CLARK, JR., city ofcl.; b. Little Rock, July 12, 1916; s. Amos Clark and Nettie May (Dean) L.; student U. Md., European extension, Frankfurt, German, 1952-53; corr. Internat. Accountants Soc., 1963; m. Hazel Marie Sweat, Sept. 4, 1938; 1 dau., Sandra Gail (Mrs. Julian Reed Hodges, Jr.). Bookkeeper, Eli Witt Cigar Co., Tampa, Fla., 1937-42; mem. internat. dept. Marine Bank & Trust Co., Tampa, 1963-66; finance dir. City of Pinellas Park (Fla.), 1966-69, City of Clearwater (Fla.), 1969—. Served to maj. USAF, 1942-63. Decorated Air medal with 5 oak leaf clusters (U.S.); Croix de Guerre avec palme (France). Mem. Municipal Finance Officers Assn., Municipal Treasurers Assn., Ret. Officers Assn., Nat. Assn. Uniformed Services. Club: Officers (MacDill AFB, Fla.). Home: 4415 Vasconia St Tampa FL 33609 Office: PO Box 4748 Clearwater FL 33515

LOWREY, CHARLES BOYCE, educator; b. New Orleans, Mar. 15, 1941; s. Horace Rutherford and Delma Ree (Chambers) L.; B.S. cum laude, Centernay Coll., 1963; Ph.D., U. Houston, 1968; m. Nita Jean Madden, June 23, 1961; children—Charles Boyce II, Barry Morris, Paul Scott, Peyton Dale. Asst. prof. chemistry Centenary Coll., Shreveport, La., 1966-73, registrar coll., 1972-73, asso. prof., registrar, 1973—, also cons. to pres. for long-range planning. Cons., Gould Battery, Inc., Shreveport, 1968—. Mem. Am. Chem. Soc. (pres. N.W.La. sect.), Chem. Soc. London, Kappa Sigma (faculty adviser). Home: 9396 Garfield Shreveport LA 71108

LOWREY, RUSSELL HARMON, dentist; b. Montgomery, Ala., Mar. 21, 1942; s. Allen Benjamin and Lillian Anna (Russell) L.; student Huntingdon Coll., 1959-61; B.S., U. Ala. at Tuscaloosa, 1963, D.M.D. cum laude, 1967, certificate orthodontics, 1971; m. Sheryl Delane McCain, May 25, 1968. Practice orthodontics, Huntsville, Ala., 1971—. Served to capt. USAF, 1967-69. Mem. Am., Ala. dental assns., Am. Assn. Orthodontists, Ala., So. socs. orthodontists, Royal Soc. Health, Psi Omega, Lambda Chi Alpha. Baptist Home: 1901 Crapemyrtle Green Huntsville AL 35803 Office: 2319 Whitesburg Dr Huntsville AL 35801

LOWREY, THOMAS JEFFERSON, physician; b. Slick, Okla., July 4, 1927; s. Estel Jack and Bertha Vineta (Conner) L.; student Okla. U., 1944-45, Northeastern State Coll. (Okla.), 1945-46; B.S., So. Methodist U., 1950; M.D., U. Tex., 1954. Intern Univ. Hosps., Oklahoma City, 1954-55, resident, 1955-56; resident internal medicine VA Hosp., Oklahoma City, 1956-57; practice gen. medicine, Yukon, Okla., 1957—; mem. staff Parkview Hosp., El Reno, Okla., chief staff, 1966-68, Deaconess, Baptist hosps., both Oklahoma City. Served with AUS, 1946-48. Diplomate Am. Bd. Family Practice. Fellow Am. Acad. Family Practice; mem. A.M.A., Am. Acad. Family Practice, Okla., Canadian County med. assns., Alumni Assn. U. Tex. Med. Br., Alpha Omega Alpha, Theta Kappa Psi. Lion. Mem. Christian Ch. (elder). Home: 716 Kingston Dr Yukon OK 73099 Office: 331 Main St Yukon OK 73099

LOWRIMORE, GENE RAY, data processor; b. nr. Tabor City, N.C., Feb. 10, 1937; s. Asbound Lundy and Geneva Zena (Ray) L.; B.S. in Applied Math., N.C. State U., 1959; M.S. in Statistics, Va. Poly. Inst. and State U., 1968, Ph.D., 1972; m. Julia Marie Norman, Aug. 31, 1958; children—Gene Ray, Kerry Dean, Jill Alison, Amy Beth. Statistician, Hercules, Inc., Radford, Va., 1960-62, area supr., 1962-69; chief data processing sect. Human Studies Lab., U.S. Environmental Protection Agy., Research Triangle Park, N.C., 1969—. Sec., bd. dirs., vice chmn. Raleigh Wesley Found. Mem. Am. Statis. Assn., Inst. Math. Statistics, Pi Mu Epsilon, Phi Kappa Phi. Democrat. Methodist. Home: 1007 Indian Trail Raleigh NC 27609 Office: NERC Bldg Research Triangle Park NC 27711

LOWRY, IVAN, chem. engr.; b. Prentiss, Miss., Jan. 14, 1937; s. Ivan and Annabelle (Wallace) L.; B.S. in Chem. Engring., Miss. State U., 1959; M.S., La. State U., 1966; m. Helen E. Armstrong, Oct. 15, 1961; children—Elizabeth, Michael. Process devel. engr. DuPont Co., Chattanooga, 1966-69; plant engr. GAF Corp., Chattanooga, 1969-73, High Point Chem. Corp. (N.C.), 1973—. Air Force Res. adviser to Civil Air Patrol, High Point, 1973—. Served to maj. USAF, 1959-64. Registered profl. engr., Tenn., N.C. Mem. Am. Inst. Chem. Engrs., Phi Lambda Upsilon. Club: Exchange (High Point). Home: 215 Cloverbrook Dr Jamestown NC 27282 Office: Box 608 High Point NC 27261

LOWRY, KERMIT, JR., surgeon; b. Kinston, N.C., May 30, 1935; s. Kermit and Pattye Moye (Richardson) L.; B.A., U. Va., 1955; M.D., Emory U., 1959; m. Sarah Eleanor Hardy, Dec. 30, 1961; children—Sarah Lynn, Kermit II, Pattye Tera. Intern, Grady Meml. Hosp., Atlanta, 1959-60; surg. resident Emory U. Hosps., Atlanta, 1960-64; mem. staff Bristol (Tenn.) Meml. Hosp., 1966—, chief of surg. sect., 1968, dir. Tumor Clinic, 1969-70. Bd. dirs. Salvation Army, United Fund, Bristol Cancer Assn. Served to maj. M.C., AUS, 1964-66. Diplomate Am. Bd. Surgery. Fellow A.C.S., Am. Coll. Angiology, Southeastern Surg. Congress; mem. J.C. Thoroughman Surg. Soc., Central Assn. Dentists and Physicians, Southeastern Med.-Dental Assn. (dir.). Home: 133 Fairfield Dr Bristol TN 37620 Office: 2D Doctors Bldg Bristol TN 37620

LOWRY, LEO ELMO, petroleum exec.; b. Utopia, Kan., Dec. 4, 1916; s. Nim Roderick and Marticia (Veach) L.; B.A., Okla. A. and M. Coll., 1937; m. Elizabeth Watson, Sept. 5, 1940; children—Richard Clark, John Christopher, Janet Kaye. With Creole Petroleum Corp., Caracas, Venezuela, 1937-71, exec. v.p., 1961-64, pres., 1964-71; pres. Esso Inter-Am., Inc., Coral Gables, Fla., 1971—. Office: 396 Alhambra Circle Coral Gables FL 33134

LOWRY, ROY FRANK, supt. county schs.; b. Pasqualank, N.C., Dec. 21, 1907; s. William and Daisy E. (White) L.; A.B., U. N.C., 1930, M.A. in Sch. Adminstrn., 1936; m. Mary Katherine Goodson, 1932; children—Katherine (Mrs. D.R. Donovan), Roy Frank. Tchr., coach Union Grove High Sch., Iredell County (N.C.), 1930-31, prin., 1931-33; prin. Cameron High Sch., Moore County (N.C.), 1933-42, Thomasville (N.C.) High Sch., 1942-44, Wakelon High Sch., Zebolon, N.C., 1944-47; supt. Washington (N.C.) County Schs., 1947-61, Northampton (N.C.) County Schs., Jackson, 1961—. Past pres. Albemarle Sch. Masters Club, Wake County Sch. Masters Club. Mem. N.C. Assn. Educators (past pres. Moore and Wake counties; past pres. supts. N.E. dist.; past chmn. N.C. elementary edn. com.). Rotarian, Lion. Home: Box 503 Jackson NC 27845 Office: Box 158 Jackson NC 27845

LOWRY, WALLACE DEAN, educator; b. Medford, Ore., Oct. 5, 1917; s. Bert Bebe and Neva May (Britten) L.; B.S. with honors, Ore. State U., 1939, M.S., 1940; m. Marian Dorothea Wyckoff, Nov. 20, 1942; 1 son, Robert Edward. Geologist, Ore. Dept. Geology and Mineral Industries, Portland, 1942-47, Texaco, Taft, Cal., 1947-49; prof. structural geology Va. Poly. Inst. and State U. Dept. Geol. Scis., Blacksburg, 1949—. Fellow Geol. Soc. Am. (v.p. S.E. sect. 1962-63); mem. Am. Assn. Petroleum Geologists (acad. adv. com. 1970—), Va. Acad. Sci., Sigma Xi. Editor: Tectonics of the Southern Appalachians, 1964, Guidebook to Appalachian Tectonics and Sulfide Mineralization of Southwestern Virginia, 1971, Guidebook to Contrast in Style of Deformation of the Southern and Central Appalachians of Virginia, 1971. Home: 607 Rose Av Blacksburg VA 24060

LOWRY, WALLACE EDWIN, coll. adminstr.; b. Holliday, Tex., Sept. 3, 1903; s. Jasper A. and Flora A. (Blakemore) L.; B.A. in Math. and Spanish, Southwestern U., 1923, B.S. in Chemistry and Physics, 1928; M.A. in Adminstrn. and English, U. Tex., 1935, D. Ed., 1951; m. Julia M. Wallace, June 4, 1932; children—Wallace Edwin, Burt Lewis. Prin., Huntsville (Tex.) High Sch., 1929-35; supt. schs., Orange, Tex., 1936-39; dir. pub. services Sam Houston State Coll., 1940-42, dean of college, 1951-65, v.p. acad. affairs, 1965—; asst. commr. edn., State of Tex., 1945-50. Mem. com. armed forces edn. Dept. Def., 1949-52; mem. nat. commn. for vocational edn. U.S. Dept. Health, Edn. and Welfare, 1969—. Bd. visitors U.S. Marine Corps Inst., 1959-62. Served to maj. USAAF, World War II. Decorated Bronze Star; recipient Silver Beaver award. Mem. Scabbard and Blade, Order of the Arrow, Pi Kappa Alpha (nat. pres. 1968—), Phi Delta Kappa, Kappa Kappa Psi, Alpha Kappa Delta, Alpha Phi Omega. Methodist. Rotarian. Author: Evaluative Study of Veterans Education Contiguous to Texas, 1947. Editor: Texas State Plan for Vocational Education, 1947; Bull. of So. Conf. Tchr. Edn., 1961-66. Home: 2020 Av O Huntsville TX 77340

LOWTHER, JAMES DAVID, mech. engr., educator; b. Jackson, Miss., June 22, 1939; s. James Thomas and Alma Iona (Robertson) L.; B.S., Miss. State U., 1961, M.S. (NSF fellow), 1962; Ph.D. (NASA trainee), U. Tex., 1968; m. Dorothy Gayle Griffin, May 31, 1961; children—Linda Carol, Lisa Karen, Laura Marie. Engr. Exxon Corp., Baton Rouge, 1962-63; asst. prof. mech. engring. La. Tech. U., Ruston, 1963-68, asso. prof., 1968-73, prof., 1973—. Engring. cons. Exxon Corp. NSF Research grantee, 1970-71. Recipient Ralph R. Teetor Ednl. award Soc. Automotive Engrs., 1969. Registered profl. engr., La. Mem. Am. Soc. M.E., La. Engring. Soc., Instrument Soc. Am., Am. Soc. for Engring. Edn., Sigma Xi (treas. 1970-71, sec. 1972-73, pres. 1974-75), Phi Kappa Phi (pres. 1973-74), Pi Tau Sigma, Tau Beta Pi. Democrat. Baptist (deacon 1972—, ch. clk. 1969-73). Lion. Home: 2105 Greenbriar Dr Ruston LA 71270

LOYD, LOYE CARROLL, glass co. exec.; b. Yantis, Tex., May 19, 1926; s. Edward M. and Ava (Gilbreath) L.; student So. Meth. U., 1949-50; m. Barbara Ray, Feb. 16, 1952; children—Stanley Alan, Terry Ray. Mgr., Mid-West Glass Co., Midland, Tex., 1955-62; owner Glasco Glass Co., Midland, 1962—; pres. Temple Glass & Mirror Co., Inc. (Tex.), 1969—, Bell Glass & Mirror Co., Killeen, Tex., 1970—, El Paso Glass & Mirror Co., Inc. (Tex.), 1970—; sec.-treas. Barber Glass & Mirror Co., Inc., Big Spring, Tex., 1968—; dir. Tex. Glass Distbrs., Inc., Ft. Worth, Odessa Glass & Mirror Co., Inc. (Tex.), El Paso Glass & Mirror Co., Inc., Eastex Glass Co. Inc., Nacogdoches, Tex., Gateway Glass Co. Inc., Laredo, Tex.; mem. adv. panel Dodge div. McGraw-Hill. Served with USNR, 1943-46. Mem. Assembly of God Ch. Rotarian (sec. 1965-66). Home: 2503 Dartmouth St Midland TX 79701 Office: 24 Industrial Loop Midland TX 79701

LOZZIO, BISMARCK BERTO, med. researcher, hematologist; b. Patagones, Buenos Aires, Argentina, Jan. 27, 1931; s. Bartolo and Haydee Angela (Piucill) L.; B.S., Bernardino Rivadavia Coll., Buenos Aires, 1949; Physician, U. Buenos Aires, 1955, M.D., 1957; m. Carmen Irene Bertucci, Mar. 10, 1955; 1 dau., Graciela Irene. Came to U.S., 1965, naturalized, 1971. Asso. gastroenterologist, instr. internal medicine Tornu Hosp., U. Buenos Aires, 1955-58; asso. hematologist NIH, Buenos Aires, 1958-65; research asso. U. Tenn. Meml. Research Center, Knoxville, 1965-67, asst. prof. research, 1968-71, asso. prof., 1971—. Lectr., U. Tenn. dept. microbiology, 1971—; cons. Oak Ridge Asso. Univs. Served with Argentine Marine Corps, 1952-53. Nat. Council for Sci. and Tech. Research fellow, 1958-60; U. Tenn. grantee, 1964-65, 66-70, NSF grantee, 1966, Am. Heart Assn. grantee, 1966, NIH grantee, 1966—, Am. Cancer Soc. grantee, 1969—, Nat. Found. Neuromuscular Disease grantee, 1969. Mem. Reticuloendothelial Soc., Internat. Soc. Hematology, Am. Soc. Hematology, Am. Soc. Lab. Animal Sci., A.A.A.S., Soc. Exptl. Biology and Medicine, Am. Fedn. Clin. Research, Internat. Soc. Exptl. Hematology, N.Y. Acad. Scis., Am. Assn. for Cancer Research, Southeastern Cancer Research Assn., Asociacion Medica Argentina, Sociedad Argentina de Biologia, Sociedad Argentina de Immunologia, Sociedad Argentina de Investigación Clinica, Sociedad Argentina de Hematologia y Hemoterapia, Sigma Xi. Home: 9709 Tunbridge Lane Concord TN 37922 Office: U Tenn Meml Research Center 1924 Alcoa Hwy Knoxville TN 37920

LU, JIMMY KIEN-TEH, physician; b. Shanghai, China, May 26, 1937; s. Yun Chun and Shu Yun (Peh) Lu (came to U.S. 1958, naturalized 1970); student Centenary Coll. La., 1959-61, East Tex. Baptist Coll., 1958-59; M.D., Tulane U., 1965; m. Sandra Lee Anderson, Sept. 17, 1966; children—Monica, Jimmy K., Jason, Stephanie Intern Methodist Gen. Hosp., Dallas, 1965-66, resident surgery, 1966-67; practice gen. medicine, Dallas, 1967—; mem. staff Meth. Hosp. Mem. A.M.A., Tex., Dallas County med. soc. Home: 1116 Kensington St Dallas TX 75208 Office: 214 Westcliff Profl Bldg Hampton Rd at Ledbetter St Dallas TX 75224

LUBBE, CATHERINE CASE (MRS. JOHN A. LUBBE), author; b. Villa Park Ill., Sept. 24, 1898; d. John Joseph and Frances A. (Darmstadt) Case; student No. Ill. State Normal Coll., 1917; grad. Columbia Conservatory, 1923; L.H.D., l'Universitie Libre (Asie), 1970; m. John Andrew Lubbe, 1929; children—John Andrew, Kaye Don. Tchr. pub., pvt. schs., Ill., 1916-25; author poems pub. in numerous mags., newspapers, anthologies, including Poets Am., Book of Year, Poetry Soc. Tex., Child Welfare, Dallas Morning News, Colo. Springs Gazette and Telegraph, Kaleidograph, Elmhurst Press, South and West, Encore, Hawk & Whippoorwill Recalled, others; dramatic reader poetry on various radio, television programs, 1922-57. Active A.R.C. Recipient World Fair Gold Medal Poetry Day award, 1940; Nyogen Senzaki Meml. Haiku award, 1966; UN day Leadership award (P.I.), 1967; gold medal award United Poets Laureate Internat., 1968 Leadership in Poetry award Internat. Acad. Leadership, Philippines, 1970. Mem. Poetry Soc. Tex. (hon. life mem., corr. sec. 1952-56, dir. 1957—, librarian, poetry critic, mem. poetry day com. editorial com.; Old South award 1971, Edsel Ford Meml. award 1971), Nat. Fedn. State Poetry Socs. Inc. (2d v.p. 1972-73, 1st v.p. 1973—, awards chmn. 1972—), La. Poetry Soc., St. Edward's Altar Soc., Eugene Field Soc. (hon.), United Poets Laureate Internat. Roman Catholic. Clubs: Lakewood Garden, Competriots. Home: 419 Clermont Av Dallas TX 75223

LUBESKI, DAVID THOMAS, sports dir.; b. St. Louis, Aug. 24, 1946; s. Thomas Reed and Lorayne (Hanna) L.; student South Tex. Jr. Coll., 1964-65; m. Judy Ann Lawler, Dec. 28, 1968; 1 dau., Maureen Elizabeth. With radio sta. KTRH, Houston, 1969—, sports announcer, 1970-71, sports dir., 1971—. Served with M.C., AUS, 1967-69. Home: 12410 Bexley Dr Houston TX 77072 Office: 510 Lovett Blvd Houston TX 77006

LUBIN, SAMUEL, govt. ofcl.; b. Washington, Sept. 16, 1914; s. Israel H. and Annie (Cohen) L.; B.S., Wilson Tchrs. Coll., 1936; M.S.W., Nat. Cath. Sch. Social Work, 1947; m. Frances C. Reichman, Nov. 5, 1945; children—Michael Evan, Amy Ilene. Dir. UNRRA operations, U.S. Zone Germany, 1945-47; adminstr. Jewish Social Service Agys., 1949-63; regional dir. Am. Jewish Com., 1956-58; regional dir. Council Jewish Fedns. for S.E. States, 1958-63; manpower adminstrn. rep., regional youth and program cons. S.E. region U.S. Dept. Labor, Atlanta, 1963—. Served with AUS, 1942-45. Mem. Acad. Certified Social Workers. Home: 1602 Adelia Pl NE Atlanta GA 30329 Office: 1371 Peachtree St NE Atlanta GA 30306

LUBKE, GEORGE WILLIAM, JR., mortgage banker; b. Yonkers, N.Y., Dec. 10, 1919; s. George William and Valeska (Kostka) L.; student N.Y.U., Columbia, N.Y. Tech. Inst., Newark U., 1938-42, Stetson U., 1946-47, Northwestern U., 1953-56; LL.D., Fla. Research Inst., 1970; m. Alice Myra Painter, Jan. 26, 1944; children—Robin Alice, George William III. Salesman, Mut. Benefit Life Ins. Co., Daytona Beach, Fla., 1946-49; founder George W. Lubke, Inc., Daytona Beach, 1949, pres., 1949—. Chmn., Tax Study Com., Volusia County, 1954; commr. on aging, State of Fla., 1962-67, chmn. exec. com., 1963-68. Vice pres. Young Democratic Clubs Fla., 1953-55. Chmn. bd. Daytona Beach Housing Authority, 1958-69. Served with N.Y. State N.G., 1941-42; with AUS, 1942-46. Named Man of Year, Daytona Beach Jr. C. of C., 1949. Mem. Am., Fla. mortgage bankers assns., Nat. Housing Conf. (dir.), Nat. Housing Research Council (dir.), Nat., Fla. (past pres.) assns. housing and redevel. ofcls., D.A.V. (past treas. Fla.). Home: 311 Shady Pl Daytona Beach FL 32014 Office: PO Box 5726 Daytona Beach FL 32020

LUCAS, ALFRED SPEAR, JR., banker; b. Birmingham, Ala., Jan. 10, 1921; s. A. S. and Angela (McCaffrey) L.; student St. Bernard Jr. Coll., Cullman, Ala., 1938-40; B.S., Auburn U., 1942; m. Winifred Strohmeyer, Oct. 22, 1949; children—Thomas William, Alfred John, Mary Angela, Winifred Loretta, Michael Joseph, William Patrick, Cecelia Anne. With Birmingham Trust Nat. Bank, 1942—, v.p. in charge nat. accounts, 1957-67, v.p. bus. devel., 1967—. Mem. Downtown Improvement Assn.; chmn. comml. div. United Appeal, 1969; adv. bd. mem. Jefferson County Community Chest; 1968—; nat. trustee Leukemia Soc., Am. Inc., 1968—, pres. Ala. chpt. Bd. dirs. Vol. Bur., Girls' Club, Nat. Conf. Christians and Jews; pres. bd. Catholic Charities Found. Ala. Served with AUS, 1942-46. Bestowed Knight of St. Gregory by Pope Pius XII, 1961. Life mem. Birmingham Area C. of C.; mem. Bank Marketing Assn. (past nat. membership chmn., past dir.), Pub. Relations Assn. Ala., Ala. Bankers Assn. (chmn. pub. relations com., 1965-66), So. Indsl. Council, Asso. Industries Ala., Sales and Marketing Execs. Club Birmingham, Delta Sigma Pi. Roman Catholic (past pres. Diocesan Holy Name Union). Kiwanian. Home: 106 Azalea Rd Birmingham AL 35213 Office: 112 N 20th St Birmingham AL 35202

LUCAS, AUBREY KEITH, coll. pres.; b. State Line, Miss., July 12, 1934; s. Keith Caldwell and Audelle Margaret (Robertson) L.; B.S., U. So. Miss., 1955, M.A., 1956; Ph.D., Fla. State U., 1966; m. Ella Frances Ginn, Dec. 19, 1955; children—Margaret Frances, Keith Godbold (dec.), Martha Carol, Alan Douglas, Mark Christopher. Asst. dir. reading clinic U. So. Miss., 1955-56, dir. admissions, 1957-61, registrar, 1963-69, dean Grad. Sch., 1970-71; pres. Delta State Coll., Cleveland, Miss., 1971—; instr. Hinds Jr. Coll., Raymond, Miss., 1956-57. Pres. Gulf South Athletic Conf. Bd. dirs. Cross-Tie Arts Council, United Givers Fund, Delta area council Boy Scouts Am. Mem. Am. Assn. Higher Edn., Newcomen Soc. N.Am., P.T.A., Cleveland C. of C. (dir.), Miss. Forestry Assn., Omicron Delta Kappa, Phi Kappa Phi, Pi Gamma Mu, Pi Tau Chi, Kappa Delta Pi, Phi Delta Kappa, Kappa Pi, Sigma Phi Epsilon. Rotarian. Clubs: Red Red Rose, Delta Revelers, Metropolitan Dinner Greater Delta Area. Author: The Mississippi Legislature and Mississippi Public Higher Education, 1890-1960; contbg. author: A History of Mississippi, 1973. Home: Box 1952 Delta State Coll Cleveland MS 28732

LUCAS, EARL STANCIL, mayor; b. Mound Bayou, Miss., Jan. 1, 1938; s. William Hymon and Lillie Bell (Rushing) L; B.S., Dillard U., 1957; postgrad. Depauw U., 1963, Beloit (Wis.) U., 1964; m. Marilee Lewis, Sept. 13, 1959; children—Eric, Vicki, Carla, Tina, Mark. Dir. pub. edn., Mound Bayou, 1965—, dir. adult edn., 1965—; mayor, Mound Bayou, 1969—. Bd. dirs. Mound Bayou Devel. Corp., Delta Found., Fund for Edn. and Community Devel., Am. Civil Liberties Union; bd. dirs., steering com. Nat. Council Chs.; chmn. bd. Delta Ministry. Elk. Home: PO Box 476 Mound Bayou MS 38762 Office: Drawer H Mound Bayou MS 38762

LUCAS, GEORGE BLANCHARD, educator; b. Philipsburg, Pa., Mar. 8, 1915; s. Reuben and Rebie (Jodon) L.; B.Sc., Pa. State U., 1940; M.Sc., La. State U., 1942, Ph.D., 1946; m. Jennie Elizabeth Boyd, Dec. 27, 1940 (dec. Nov. 1950); children—Irvin, Glenn, Guy; m. 2d, Vernelle Violet Vaughan, July 16, 1955; children—Candace, George Blanchard, stepchildren—Woodson, Lee. Asst. prof. plant pathology N.C. State U. at Raleigh, 1946-55, asso. prof., 1955-63, prof., 1963—. Served with USNR, 1942-46. Mem. Am. Phytopath. Soc., Phi Beta Kappa, Sigma Xi. Author: Diseases of Tobacco, 1958, 3d edit., 1974. Home: 3040 Churchill Rd Raleigh NC 27607

LUCAS, GEORGE JOSEPH, physician; b. Bridgeport, Conn., Oct. 25, 1929; s. George Michael and Louise (Dziack) L.; B.S., Georgetown U., 1951, M.D., 1955; m. Margaret E. Droyd, June 25,

1955; children—George M., Rosemary A., Brian J. Intern, D.C. Gen. Hosp., Washington, 1955-56; resident Mt. Alto VA Hosp., Washington, 1956-57, U. Wis., Madison, 1959-61; asst. chief neurology D.C. Gen. Hosp., Washington, 1964-65; practice medicine, specializing in neurology, Washington, 1964-69; chief neurol. service VA Hosp., Little Rock, 1969—; mem. staff St. Elizabeth Hosp.; clin. asst. prof. neurology Georgetown U., 1966-69; asst. prof. neurology and psychiatry U. Ark. Med. Center, 1969—. Chmn., Potomac Valley chpt. Myas Thenia Gravis Found., Washington, 1968-69. Served with USAF, 1957-64. Diplomate Am. Bd. Neurology and Psychiatry. Fellow A.C.P., Am. Acad. Neurology; mem. A.M.A., Am. Psychiat. Assn., Pulaski County, Med. Soc., Ark. State Med. Soc., A.A.A.S., Am. EEG Soc. (asso.). Home: 5320 Edgewood Rd Little Rock AR 72207 Office: 300 E Roosevelt Rd Little Rock AR 72206

LUCAS, J. LYNN, lawyer; b. Luray, Va., Dec. 27, 1898; s. Edwin L. and Minnie C. (Strickler) L.; A.B., Roanoke Coll., 1925; grad. law U. Va., 1928; m. Vivian D. Shenk, July 21, 1931. Admitted to Va. bar, 1928, since practiced in Luray. Past chmn. Democratic Com. of Page County, Va. Mem. Am., Va. (v.p. 1937, mem. council 1972—), Page County (pres. 1957-60), Luray bar assns., Columbia Hist. Soc., S.A.R. (past pres. Shenandoah Valley chpt.), Internat. Assn. Ins. Counsel, Va. Trial Lawyers Assn., Am. Judicature Soc., Sigma Chi, Phi Alpha Delta. Lutheran. Mason (Scottish Rite, York Rite, Shriner), Lion (past pres. Luray). Died Apr. 29, 1974. Home: 165 S Court St Luray VA 22835

LUCAS, JAMES ARTHUR, JR., lumber co. exec.; b. Grand Prairie, Tex., July 5, 1917; s. James Arthur and Mattie Lou (Eden) L.; B.S., Tex. Tech U., 1947; m. Prudence Howard, Mar. 10, 1945; children—Nancy, Prudence. Engr., Lone Star Gas Co., Fort Worth, 1947-52; with Hurst Lumber Co., (Tex.) 1952—, pres., 1968—; dir. First Nat. Bank of Hurst. Tchr. math. Tex. Christian U., Fort Worth, 1959-60. Mem. Met. Regional Hwy. Com., Fort Worth Region, 1966—. Served to maj. AUS, 1944-47. Mem. Euless C. of C. (pres. 1960-61). Lion (pres. 1959-60). Home: 1213 Greenbriar Lane Arlington TX 67013 Office: 104 E Hurst Blvd Hurst TX 76053

LUCAS, ROSEMARY DEAN, broadcasting exec.; b. Los Angeles; d. Roy and Juarita (Damer) Dean; grad. Ind. U., 1953; m. children—Kim, Jim. Hostess, producer Mid-Day, also weather girl WAPI-TV, Birmingham, Ala., 1962—. Mem. Birmingham Press Club. Office: WAPI-TV Box 1310 Birmingham AL 35201

LUCAS, WILLIAM RAY, govt. ofcl.; b. Newbern, Tenn., Mar. 1, 1922; s. William S. and Dona (Ray) L.; B.S., Memphis State U., 1943; M.S., Vanderbilt U., 1950, Ph.D., 1952; m. Polly Jean Torti, Sept. 11, 1948; children—Donna Jeanne, William Ray, Michael Lee. Chemist, materials engr. Redstone Arsenal, U.S. Army, Huntsville, Ala., 1952-55, chief engring. materials br. Army Ballistic Missile Agy., 1955-60; with Marshall Space Flight Center, NASA, Huntsville, 1960—, dep. dir., 1971-74, dir., 1974—. Trustee, Mobile (Ala.) Coll., 1971—. Served with USNR, 1943-46. Recipient medal exceptional sci. achievement NASA, 1964, Exceptional Service medal, 1969, Distinguished Service medal, 1972; Herman Oberth award Am. Inst. Aeros. and Astronautics, 1965. Fellow Am. Soc. for Metals, Am. Astronautical Soc., Am. Inst. Aeros. and Astronautics (asso.); mem. Am. Chem. Soc., Sigma Xi. Contbr. articles in field to profl. jours. Patentee in field. Home: 6805 Criner St Huntsville AL 35802 Office: Marshall Space Flight Center AL 35812

LUCKAM, THOMAS GRANT, dentist; b. Newport News, Va., Jan. 7, 1935; s. Grant Hiram and Mary (Thompson) L.; student Randolph Macon Coll., 1953-56; B.S., D.D.S., Med. Coll. Va., 1960; m. Elizabeth Madison Hargrave, Sept. 12, 1959; children—Thomas G., Mary Elizabeth, Sarah Madison. Pvt. practice dentistry, Gloucester Point, Va., 1962—; asso. State Health Dept., 1969—. Den leader Boy Scouts Am., Gloucester Point, 1971—. Served as lt. comdr. USNR. Mem. Am., Va. dental assns., Peninsula Dental Soc., Acad. Gen. Dentistry, Am. Analgesia Soc., C. of C., Omicron Delta Kappa. Episcopalian. Lion. Clubs: York River Yacht (commodore 1968-69) (Gloucester Point); Ware River Yacht (dir. 1971—) (Gloucester, Va.). Address: Box 112 Gloucester Point VA 23062

LUCKETT, PAUL HERBERT, III, fiber and textile co. exec.; b. El Paso, Tex., Feb. 6, 1935; s. Paul Herbert and Maxine Revelle (Mooney) L.; B.S. in Chem. Engring., Mass. Inst. Tech., 1956; grad. Advanced Mgmt. Tng. Program, U. Tex., 1970; m. Caroline Curtis Foisie, Oct. 6, 1956; children—Elizabeth Winkler, Christopher Lloyd. Process engr. El Paso Products Co., Odessa, Tex., 1956-59, sales rep., 1960-65, marketing exec., 1966-69, asst. v.p., 1969-70; exec. v.p. operations Beaunit Corp., 1970-72, exec. v.p., gen. mgr. Fibers div., Research Triangle Park, N.C., 1972-73, exec. v.p., gen. mgr. Textiles div., 1973—. Bd. dirs. Odessa-Midland Symphony Assn., 1967-70, Odessa Jazz Assn., 1966-70. Served with AUS, 1957. Mem. Man-Made Fiber Assn., Am. Textile Mfrs. Inst., Tau Beta Pi, Delta Kappa Epsilon. Republican. Episcopalian. Home: 821 Faulkner Pl Raleigh NC 27609 Office: PO Box 12234 Research Triangle Park NC 27709

LUCKEY, CARL FREEMAN, physician; b. Jackson, Tenn., July 16, 1914; s. David William and Mabel Dent (Freeman) L.; B.A., Union U., 1936; M.D., Vanderbilt U., 1941; m. Althea Ann Colvin, Dec. 31, 1938; children—Carl Freeman, George DeLansone. Intern, John Gaston Hosp., Memphis, 1941-42; resident Vanderbilt U. and VA Hosp., Nashville, 1947-50; practice medicine, Franklin, Tenn., 1945-47, Florence, Ala., 1950—; mem. staffs Coffee and Colonial Manor hosps., Florence. Bd. dirs. Colonial Manor Hosp., Florence, 1970—. Served to maj. M.C., AUS, 1941-45. Fellow A.C.P.; mem. A.M.A., Ala., So. med. assns., Sigma Xi, Phi Beta Pi, Alpha Tau Omega. Episcopalian. Club: Turtle Point Yacht and Country. Home: 2101 Arlington Blvd Florence AL 35630 Office: 211 Cloyd Blvd PO Box 2309 Florence AL 35630

LUCKEY, GEORGE PAUL, ret. bus. exec.; b. Ontario, Cal., Apr. 4, 1891; s. George W. A. and Bertha (Musson) L.; A.B., U. Neb., 1910, M.A., 1912, D.Engring. (hon.), 1952; postgrad. U. Goettingen, Germany, 1912-14; m. Olive Lehmer, July 12, 1922; children—George William, Helen L. Staff, Mt. Wilson Solar Obs., Pasadena, Cal., 1915; Charles E. Brush fellow Nela Research Lab., Cleve., 1916; physicist Westinghouse Research Lab., East Pittsburgh, Pa., 1917-19-20; physicist, instrument and equipment sect. McCook Field, Dayton, O., 1920-26, asst. chief equipment sect., 1926-27; with Hamilton Watch Co., Lancaster, Pa., 1927-54, head tachometer div., 1927-30, dir. research, asst. gen. supt., 1930-33, factory mgr., 1933-40, v.p. charge mfg., 1940-52, pres., chmn. bd., 1952-54, dir., 1947-54, ret., 1954; dir. Nuclear Research Chems., Orlando, Fla., 1960-67. Mem. adv. bd. Phila. Ordnance Dist., 1950-54. Served with AC, U.S. Army, 1918. Recipient certificate of Appreciation, Joint Chiefs of Staff, 1951. Mem. A.A.A.S., Am. Ordnance Assn., Horological Inst. Am. (hon.), Am. Phys. Soc., Winter Park C. of C., Sigma Xi. Clubs: Orlando Country; University (Winter Park, Fla.). Patentee in field. Home: 461 Virginia Dr Winter Park FL 32789

LUCKFIELD, CHARLES FERDINAND, cons. engr.; b. Rawlins, Wyo., June 7, 1903; s. William Richard and June R. (Wells) L.; B.S. in Civil Engring., U. Mo., 1927; postgrad. Ia. State U., 1927; m. Gertrude A. Ward, Sept. 7, 1929 (dec. Feb. 1966); children—Charlene (Mrs. Ted L. Ernst), Linda (Mrs. L.L. Beaver). Adminstrv. asst. Standard Oil Co. Ind., Tulsa, until 1966; cons. engr. pipeline design, Tulsa, 1966—. Mem. Kappa Sigma, Theta Tau, Theta Nu Epsilon. Elk, Mason. Clubs: Harvard, Southwood (Tulsa). Home and office: 1703 S Jamestown Tulsa OK 74112

LUCKIE, CHARLES ADAMS, circuit judge; b. Montgomery, Ala., Nov. 27, 1906; s. Arche Carter and Orlene (Goodwyn) L.; LL.B., Stetson U., 1931; m. Suzanne Knox, Nov. 27, 1963. Admitted to Fla. bar, 1931; practiced law, Jacksonville, Fla., 1931-50; partner Rogers, Towers & Bailey, 1931-50; mem. Fla. Ho. of Reps., 1941, 47, 49; circuit judge, Jacksonville, 1950—. Served to col. AUS, 1941-46. Decorated Legion of Merit, Bronze Star, Army Commendation medal. Mem. Fla. Bar, Jacksonville Bar Assn. Democrat. Presbyn. (elder). Home: Ortega Blvd Apts Jacksonville FL 32210 Office: County Courthouse Jacksonville FL 32202

LUDDEN, FOREST EDWIN, state ofcl.; b. Lewiston, Me., July 10, 1932; s. William Robinson and Dorothy (Barry) L.; B.S., So. Ill. U., 1959, M.S., 1960; M.P.H., U. Mich., 1962; Ed. D., U. Ala., 1970; m. Theresa Marie Shotts, Nov. 27, 1954; children—Sandra Ann, William Roger, James Alan. Dir. Bur. Primary Prevention, Ala. Dept. Pub. Health, Montgomery, 1962-69, dir. div. narcotics and dangerous drugs, 1969—; asst. to state health officer, 1968-72, dir. Spl. Services Adminstrn., 1972—. Treas., Montgomery Council Indsl. Editors, 1965—; field supr. Nat. Health Council, 1959; pres. Jackson County (Ill.) Health Council, 1960. Served with USNR, 1951-55. Fellow Soc. Pub. Health Educators; mem. Am., Ala. pub. health assns., N.E.A., Ala. Heart Assn., Phi Delta Kappa. Lion. Club: Bonnie Crest Country. Home: 1012 High Point Rd Montgomery AL 36109 Office: State Office Bldg Montgomery AL 36104

LUDDEN, JOHN FRANKLIN, economist, govt. ofcl.; b. Michigan City, Ind., May 6, 1930; s. Charles Franklin and Marie Bernadette (Kelley) L.; B.S., U. Wis., 1952, M.S., 1955; postgrad. U. Mich., 1955-58; m. Edna Adriana Abadie-Abarca, Dec. 13, 1964; children—Charles Robert, Anne Marie, John Michael, James Edward. Storekeeper, U.S. Army Corps Engrs., 1947-48; wage and hour investigator U.S. Dept Labor, Washington, 1960, mgmt. intern, 1960-61, economist, tng. instr., 1961-63, labor economist, 1963; industry economist Internal Revenue Service, Treasury Dept., Washington, 1963—. Served with AUS, 1952-54. Recipient Spl. Service award Treasury Dept., 1967, 69. Mem. Am. Econ. Assn. Home: 8503 Fairburn Dr Springfield VA 22152 Office: Audit Div US Internal Revenue Service Washington DC 20224

LUDLUM, BOBBY RAY, electronic engr.; b. Whiteville, N.C., Mar. 9, 1942; s. John Lency and Ora Blanch (Reeves) L.; B.S. in Elec. Engring. with honors, N.C. State U., 1964; m. Sharlet Joy Young, July 26, 1969; 1 dau., Holly Denise. Electronic engr. Naval Coastal Systems Lab., Panama City, Fla., 1964—. Recipient Sustained Superior Performance award Navy Dept., 1966, Outstanding Performance award 1973. Mem. I.E.E.E., Aircraft Owners and Pilots Assn., Exptl. Aircraft Assn., Mooney Assn. Am., Eta Kappa Nu. Baptist (deacon, Sunday sch. tchr.). Patentee in field. Research and devel. high resolution sonar systems and mine counter measures systems. Home: 1101 W 22d St Panama City FL 32401 Office: Code 721 NCSL Panama City FL 32401

LUDWIG, JOHN TRUMAN, elec.-mech. engr.; b. Portland, Ore., Aug. 11, 1926; s. Clarence Columbus and Virginia Myrtle (Copenhaver); B.E.E., U. Minn., 1948, M.S., 1952, Ph.D., 1954; m. Harriet Laura Mullan Johnson, Feb. 23, 1961 (div. 1969); children—James R. Johnson, Eric W., Mark E., Karl M., Barbara A. Elec. engr., Minn. Mining Mfg., St. Paul, 1951; sr. research scientist Honeywell Corp., Mpls., 1954-59; prin. engring. scientist Electronic Communications, Inc., St. Petersburg, Fla., 1960-62; sect. mgr. ITT Research Inst., Chgo., 1962-63; engr. Argonne Nat. Lab. U. Chgo., 1963-66; pvt. profl. practice, Clearwater, Fla., 1966-71; engr. Fla. Div. Health, Jacksonville, 1971—. Extension instr. U. Fla. at St. Petersburg, 1960-62. Mem. Wilderness Soc., 1964-68, Am. Civil Liberties Union, 1960—, Ams. for Democratic Action, 1964-66, Upper Pinellas Council Human Relations, 1968-71, LaGrange (Ill.) Interracial Fellowship, 1962-66, N.A.A.C.P., 1964-69; mem. commn. for social responsibility Chgo. Area Council Liberal Chs., 1964-65, fair housing com. Hinsdale Area Human Relations Council, 1964-66; active Boy Scouts, 1938—; mem. steering com. Harbor Opportunities Promotion Efforts, Safety Harbor (Fla.), 1966-70, v.p., 1967—. Precinct chmn. Democratic party, Hinsdale, Ill., 1965-66, Clearwater, Fla., 1969-71. Bd. dirs. Adult Mental Health Clinic, Pinellas County, 1967-70, Carver Nursery Assn. Dunedin (Fla.), 1967-68, Head Start Pinellas County, 1968. Served with USNR, 1944-46. Research fellow U. Minn., 1949-50, 51-54. Mem. A.A.A.S., Am. Phys. Soc., Am. Vacuum Soc., I.E.E.E. (sr.), Am. Inst. E.E. (sect. exec. com. 1958-59), I.R.E. (sect. exec. com. 1961-62), Nat., Minn. (dir. 1958-60), Ill. socs. profl. engrs., Fla. Engring. Soc. (chpt. sec.-treas. 1961-62), Assn. Advancement Med. Instrumentation, Am. Soc. Hosp. Engrs. Home: PO Box 238 Jacksonville FL 32201 Office: PO Box 210 Jacksonville FL 32201

LUDWIG, WILLIAM MICHAEL, physician; b. N.Y.C., July 6, 1937; s. Saul and Blanche (Ober) L.; B.A., U. Pa., 1957; M.D., N.Y.U., 1961; m. Carolee Ann Frum, June 20, 1964; children—Adam Nathan, Alexandra. Intern, U. Pitts., 1961-62, resident medicine, 1964-66; NIH postdoctoral fellow in gastroenterology, 1967; practice medicine, Miami Beach, Fla., 1968—; clin. instr. medicine U. Miami. Served with USPHS, 1962-64. Fellow A.C.P.; mem. Phi Beta Kappa. Home: 7441 Wayne Av Miami Beach FL 33141 Office: 1680 Meridian Av Miami Beach FL 33139

LUEBKE, EMMETH AUGUST, physicist; b. Manitowoc, Wis., Aug. 1, 1915; s. Herman W. and Hedwig (Lippert) L.; B.A., Ripon Coll., 1936; Ph.D., U. Ill., 1941; m. Nora V. Weyer, Sept. 4, 1938; children—Dennis Otto, Dorothy (Mrs. Joseph Trusz). Group leader radiation lab. Mass. Inst. Tech., Cambridge, 1941-45; research asso. Gen. Electric Co., Schenectady, 1945-50, mgr. reactor evaluation Knolls Atomic Power Lab., Schenectady, 1950-55, physicist, 1955-63; physicist TEMPO, Santa Barbara, Cal., 1963-72; adminstrv. law judge presiding as tech. mem., atomic safety and licensing bd. AEC, Washington, 1972—. Mem. joint liquid metals com. U.S. Navy/AEC, 1950-55. Fellow Am. Phys. Soc.; mem. Am. Nuclear Soc. Research with microwave radar components, design and evaluation of reactor power plants, submarine propulsion, nuclear weapons effects. Home: 5500 Friendship Blvd Chevy Chase MD 20015 Office: AEC Washington DC 20545

LUECKE, FRANK MARTIN GEORGE, JR., journalist; b. Mountain Grove, Mo., July 17, 1931; s. Frank Martin George and Mabel Clare (Bedingfield) L.; B.J., U. Mo., 1953; m. Janet Emma Wright, Oct. 29, 1953; children—Leslie Ruth, Martin Wright. News editor, adman Purcell (Okla.) Register, 1955-56; pub. Grand Prairie (Tex.) Banner, 1956-57; owner, editor, pub. Cameron (Tex.) Herald, 1957—. Pres., Cameron Pub. Library Bd.,1966-67. Bd. dirs. Central Tex. Symphony Assn., 1965-67, pres., 1968-69; bd. dirs. Cultural Activities Center, Temple, Tex., Cameron Indsl. Found., St. Edward Hosp. Devel. Fund. Served to 1st lt. AUS, 1953-55. Recipient 1st prize editorials Okla. Press Assn., 1955, hon. mention editorials, 1956; Golden Pen award 1970; Golden Dozen editorialist award Internat. Conf. Weekly Newspaper Editors, 1970. Mem. Cameron C. of C. (dir. bd.), Cameron Jr. C. of C. (dir. 1958-59), Nat. Newspaper Assn. (com. chmn. 1969-72), Tex. Press Assn. (prizes 1958, 62, dir. 1964-65, 72-73, sec., treas. 1968-69, co-chmn. legislative com.), Dallas Press Club. Rotarian (pres. 1966-67). Club: Cameron Country. Contbr. articles to mags. Home: 806 E 7th St Cameron TX 76520 Office: 108 E 1st St Cameron TX 76520

LUECKE, GERALD, elec. engr.; b. Will County, Ill., Apr. 10, 1925; s. Edwin Henry and Alma (Westenfeldt) L.; B.A. (Westinghouse fellow), U. Ia., 1950; M.S., Northwestern U., 1951; m. E. Mary Ashton, June 16, 1956; children—Gerald, Douglas, Stephen, Margaret Mary. Asst., Computer Center, Northwestern Technol. Inst., 1950-51; electronic engr. Victor Adding Machine Co., Chgo., 1951-56; applications engr. Tex. Instruments, Inc., Dallas, 1957-59, design engring. mgr., 1959-65, engring. mgr., 1965-71, mgr. advanced tech., 1971—. Troop com. chmn. Circle Ten council Boy Scouts Am., 1970-72; pres. Rockwall High Sch. Band Booster Club, 1973-74. Served with USNR, 1943-46. Mem. I.E.E.E., Sigma Xi, Tau Beta Pi, Eta Kappa Nu. Lutheran (past pres.). Author: (with J.P. Mize and W.N. Carr) Semiconductor Memory Design and Applications, 1973. Patentee in field. Home: 1415 Alamo Rd Rockwall TX 75087 Office: Box 5012 MS 16 Dallas TX 75222

LUEDECKE, WILLIAM HENRY, engring. co. exec.; b. Pittsburg, Tex., Apr. 5, 1918; s. Henry Herman and Lula May (Abernathy) L.; B.S., U. Tex., 1940; m. Mary Anne Copeland, June 3, 1939; children—William Henry III, John Copeland. Mech. engr. Columbian Gasoline Corp., Monroe, La., 1940-41; supr. ship bldg., mech. entr. USN, Orange, Tex., 1941-42; gen. supr. factory mgrs. N. Am. Aviation Co., Dallas, 1942-44; air conditoning engr. Westinghouse Elec. Corp., Dallas, 1944-46; mech. engr., charge Chrysler Airtemp. div. Chrysler Corp., Los Angeles, 1946-50; owner Luedecke Engring. Co., Austin, Tex., 1950—, also Luedecke Investment Co.; dir. City Nat. Bank, Austin, Mut. Savs. Instn., Austin, 1st Tex. Financial Corp., Dallas. Bd. Dirs. Travis County Heart Fund. Austin YMCA. Named Man of Yr., Tex. Barbed Wire Collectors Assn. Registered profl. engr., Tex. Mem. Am. Soc. Heating, Refrigerating, Air Conditioning Engrs. (dir., pres. Austin chpt.), Tex., Nat. socs. profl. engrs., C. of C., Econ. Devel. Council, Better Bus. Bur., Nat. Fedn. Ind. Bus. (nat. adv. council). Methodist. Rotarian. Club: Westwood Country (treas., dir.). Home: 3403 Foothills Pkwy Austin TX 78731 Office: 1007 W 34th St Austin TX 78705

LUESSENHOP, ALFRED JOHN, educator; b. Chgo., Feb. 6, 1926; s. Alfred Lewis and Gertrude (Meuller) L.; B.S., Yale, 1949; M.D., Harvard, 1952; m. Elizabeth Connell, June 15, 1952; children—Cynthia, Constance, Alfred John, Charles. Intern, U. Chgo. Clinics, 1952-53; resident neurosurgery Mass. Gen. Hosp., Boston, 1953-59; vis. scientist Nat. Inst. Neurol. Diseases and Stroke, Bethesda, Md., 1960; faculty neurosurgery Georgetown U. Med. Sch., Washington, 1960—, asso. prof., 1968-73, prof., 1973—. Served with AUS, 1943-46. Mem. Am. Assn. Neurol. Surgeons, Congress Neurosurgery, Soc. Neurol. Surgeons. Author: Pathogenesis and Treatment of Cerebrovascular Disease, 1961; Progress in Neurological Surgery, 1969; Cisternography and Hydrocelphalus, 1972. Contbr. articles to profl. publs. Home: 1021 Basil Rd McLean VA 22101 Office: Georgetown U Hosp 3800 Reservoir Rd Washington DC 20007

LUGINBYHL, THOMAS TERENCE, govt. ofcl.; b. Stinnett, Tex., Feb. 20, 1923; s. Oliver Wesley and Cleo Zell (Ingram) L.; B.A., William Jewell Coll., 1946; M.B.A., U. Chgo., 1963; M.S., George Washington U., 1966; postgrad. Air War Coll., 1965-66; m. Frankie Anne White, Nov. 21, 1945; children—Cynthia Anne, Terri Lynn, Alan Kurt, Karen Sue. Aviation cadet USAF, 1943, advanced through grades to lt. col., 1970; chief engring. and testing electronics countermeasures research USAF, 1954-58, chief phys. scis. missile guidance and trajectory calculation, 1958-62; chief scis. and resources div. def. intelligence Dept. Def., 1963-65; dep. dir. sci. and tech. information USAF, 1967-69, dir. sci. and tech. information, 1969-70; chief tech. information Nat. Inst. Occupational Safety and Health, Dept. Health, Edn. and Welfare, Rockville, Md., 1970—. Guest lectr. USAF Inst. Tech., 1966-70; mem. mgmt. panel Com. Sci. and Tech. Information, Office Pres. Sci. Adviser, Exec. Office Pres., 1967-70; chmn. Internat. Conf. on Tech. Information, Geneva, 1973. Decorated Air medal with five cluster, Air Force Commendation medal. Mem. Am. Soc. Information Scis., Am. Indsl. Hygienists Assn., Am. Conf. Govt. Indsl. Hygienists, Sigma Pi Sigma. Methodist (mem. adminstrv. bd. 1972-74). Mason. Editor Occupational Safety and Health Thesaurus, 1973. Asso. editor Toxic Substances List, 1972, 73, 74. Home: 8425 Porter Lane Alexandria VA 22308 Office: 5600 Fishers Lane Rockville MD 20852

LUH, JIANG, educator; b. Haining, Chekiang, China, June 24, 1932; s. Hseih Tang and Hsin Su (Wu) L.; B.S., Taiwan Normal U., 1956; M.S., U. Neb., 1959; Ph.D., U. Mich., 1963; m. Tsu-yunn Ma, July 25, 1956; children—Albert, Ellice, Michael. Came to U.S., 1957, naturalized, 1972. Asso. prof. Ind. State U., Terre Haute, 1963-66; asso. prof. Wright State U., Dayton, O., 1966-68; prof. math. N.C. State U., Raleigh, 1968—. Reviewer, Math. Revs., 1968—. Mem. Am. Math. Soc., Math. Assn. Am. Contbr. to profl. publs. in field. Home: 5613 Deblyn Av Raleigh NC 27612

LUHRS, CARO ELISE, physician; b. Dover, N.J., Jan. 21, 1935; d. Albert Weigand and Ethel Adelaide (Voss) L.; A.B., Swarthmore Coll., 1956; M.D., Harvard, 1960. Intern U. N.C., Chapel Hill, 1960-61, resident, 1961-62; fellow hematology Georgetown U. Med. Sch., Washington, 1962-64, instr. medicine, 1964-67, dir. hematology labs. and blood bank, 1966-68, asst. prof. medicine, 1967—; med. adviser Sec. Agr., Washington, 1968-73; health and mgmt. cons., 1973—. Dir. Pillsbury Co. Bd. dirs. U. S. Dept. Agr. Grad. Sch., 1971—. Recipient Superior Service award U.S. Dept. Agr., 1971. Diplomate Am. Bd. Internal Medicine. Fellow Royal Soc. Health, A.C.P., Royal Soc. Medicine; mem. Am. Soc. Hematology, Internat. Soc. Hematology, A.M.A., Am. Med. Women's Assn., D.C. Med. Soc., Internat. Assn. Agrl. Medicine. Club: Zonta. Home: 2939 Van Ness St NW Washington DC 20008

LUIGS, CHARLES RUSSELL, mfg. exec.; b. Evansville, Ind., Apr. 4, 1933; s. Charles Anthony and Agnes (Russell) L.; student St. Edwards U., 1951-52; B.S., U. Tex., 1957; m. Mary M. McClaine, Sept. 7, 1957; children—Charles Edwin, James Russell, Carol Lynn, Susan Nadine, Michael Allan. Vice pres. sales U.S. Industries De Venezuela, Anaco, Venezuela, 1958-63; v.p. engring. petroleum equipment div. U.S. Industries, Inc., Longview, Tex., 1963-66, v.p. marketing petroleum-chem. equipment group, Houston, 1966-67, v.p. corporate devel. So. U.S.A. group, Dallas, 1967-68, chmn. furnishings group, Dallas, 1968-69, exec. chmn. Northeast group, v.p. parent co., 1969-70, exec. group chmn. So. U.S.A. group, 1970-73, exec. v.p., dir. corp., 1971—, exec. v.p. bldg. and furnishings, 1973—; dir. Delwood Furniture Co., Inc., 1972—. Mem. Nat. Soc. Profl. Engrs., Am. Inst. Mining Metall. and Petroleum Engrs. Home: 4475 Royal Lane Dallas TX 75229 Office: Expressway Tower Dallas TX 75206

LUKE, JAMES LINDSAY, physician; b. Cleve., Aug. 29, 1932; s. James Lindsay and Parthenia (Burke) L.; student Yale, 1950-52; B.S., cum laude, Columbia, 1956; M.D., Case Western Res. U., 1960; m. Marcia Gene Alley, Oct. 5, 1957; children—Lindsay Jean, Sarah Chisolm, Alexandra Blair. Intern, Yale Med. Center, New Haven, 1960-61; resident, then chief resident in pathology Univ. Hosps. of Cleve., 1961-63; staff researcher Lab. Exptl. Pathology, Nat. Inst. Arthritis and Metabolic Diseases, NIH, Bethesda, Md., 1963-65; asso. med. examiner Office Chief Med. Examiner, N.Y.C., 1965-67; state med. examiner, Okla., Oklahoma City, 1967-71; chief med. examiner, D.C., 1971—; prof. forensic pathology U. Okla. Med. Center, 1967-71; prof. pathology George Washington U., 1971—, Georgetown U., 1971—, Howard U., 1971—. Served with USPHS, 1963-65. Recipient Distinguished Faculty award U. Okla. Med. Center, 1969. Fellow Am. Acad. Forensic Scis. (pres. 1966); mem. Am. Assn. Pathologists and Bacteriologists, Nat. Assn. Med. Examiners (exec. com. 1970—). Contbr. articles to profl. jours. Home: 5240 Loughboro Rd NW Washington DC 20016 Office: 1901 E St SE Washington DC 20003

LUKHARD, WILLIAM LEE, govt. ofcl.; b. Richmond, Va., June 14, 1927; s. Horace Clinton and Florence (Shuler) L.; B.S., U. Richmond, 1949, M.Commerce, 1966; m. Mary Louise Ragland, Apr. 2, 1955; children—Ralph, Lee, Beth, Bobby. Ins. examiner, underwriter Am. Casualty Co., Richmond, 1949-51; sec., treas. The Corley Co., Richmond, 1951-57; with State Dept. of Welfare and Instns., Richmond, 1957—, dir. welfare and instns., 1972—. Lectr. finance and mgmt. U. Richmond, 1967-73. Served with USNR, 1945-46. Mem. Am. Pub. Welfare Finance Officers Assn., Sigma Phi Epsilon, Tau Alpha. Methodist (mem. adminstrv. bd. 1963-72). Home: 5 Dogwood Dr Manakin-Sabot VA 23103 Office: 429 S Belvidere Richmond VA 23220

LUMB, ROBERT MONTY, dentist; b. Vancouver, B.C., Can., July 9, 1928; s. Robert John and Anna Margaret (Burgess) L.; student Staunton Mil. Acad., 1947, U. Houston, 1954-56, Emory U. Sch. Dentistry, 1956-60; m. Shirlee Anne Young, Sept. 12, 1958; children—Julie Anne, Linda Lee, Robert Scott. Individual practice dentistry, Miami, Fla., 1960-65, Homestead, Fla., 1965—. Mem. staff Dade County Research Clinic, Miami, 1961-63. Served with AUS, 1951-53. Mem. Am. Dental Assn., Fla., East Coast, South Dade dental socs., C. of C. (essay chmn. 1966-67). Baptist. Mason (Shriner). Clubs: Civitan (dir. 1969) Toastmaster (Homestead). Home: 28550 SW 172d Av Homestead FL 33030 Office: 1555 N Krome Av Homestead FL 33030

LUMLEY, JOHN MORRIS, educator; b. Vineland, N.J., Feb. 10, 1906; s. John and Flossie (Zaner) L.; B.A., Muhlenberg Coll., 1928; M.Ed., Pa. State U., 1945; D.Ed., Waynesburg Coll., 1955; m. Kathryn Wentzel; 1 son, Joe Ernie. Tchr.-prin. Eagles Mere (Pa.) Sch., 1928-30; prin. Dushore (Pa.) High Sch., 1930-32; supervising prin. Dushore Borough schs., 1932-38; supt. schs., Sullivan County, Pa., 1938-52; dep. supt. pub. instrn. Pa., 1952-55; supt. city schs., Wilkes Barre, Pa., 1955-57; exec. asst., dir. div. fed. relations N.E.A., Washington, 1957-67, asst. exec. sec. for legislation and fed. relations, 1967-71, also mem. nat. legislative commn., now nat. legislative cons., lectr., 1971—. Pres. Pa. Edn. Assn., 1951. Chmn. Sullivan County Tb Soc., 1940-51, Sullivan County Tb and Heart Assn., 1950-51, Sullivan County council Boy Scouts Am., 1950. Trustee Mansfield (Pa.) Tchrs. Coll.; bd. dirs. Multiple Sclerosis Soc. Washington, 1949-53. Recipient Alumni Achievement award Muhlenberg Coll., 1955. Mem. N.E.A., Am. Assn. Sch. Adminstrs., Phi Delta Kappa. Lutheran. Mason. Home: 3100 Wisconsin Av NW Washington DC 20016 Office: 1201 16th St NW Washington DC 20036

LUMPKIN, ALVA M., lawyer; b. Columbia, S.C., Nov. 25, 1921; A.B., U. S.C., 1943, LL.B., 1947. Admitted to S.C. bar, 1947; since practiced in Columbia; mem. firm Lumpkin and Lafaye; spl. atty. S.C. Legislative Research Council, 1950-51; spl. asst. U.S. atty., trial atty. OPS, 1951-52. Vice chancellor Episcopal Diocese of Upper S.C., 1956-65. Fellow Am. Coll. Probate Counsel; mem. Am., S.C. bar assns., Am. Counsel Assn., Am. Law Inst., Am. Judicature Soc., Assn. Bar City N.Y. Office: 507 Barringer Bldg Columbia SC 29201*

LUMPKIN, ROBERT PIERCE, banker; b. Culpeper, Va., Mar. 16, 1913; s. Robert Pierce and Inez (King) L.; B.A., U. Richmond, 1948; A.M., Harvard, 1950, Ph.D., 1955; m. Katherine Willis Green, Apr. 4, 1947; children—Margaret (Mrs. Robert S. Forrester), Robert Pierce III, Willis Green, Richard King. Economist Fed. Res. Bank, Richmond, Va., 1952-60; prof., chmn. econs. dept. Va. Commonwealth U., 1961-68; cons. economist Bank Va., Richmond, 1960-68, sr. v.p., treas., 1968—; dir. Bank Va. Properties, Inc., Bank Va. Internat., BVA Credit Corp. Mem. Gov. Va. Commn. Port Unification, 1969, Gov. Va. Commn. Port Financing, 1971; dir. Richmond Better Bus. Bur. Served with AUS, 1942-46. Mem. Am., So. econ. assns., Am. Finance Assn., Financial Mgmt. Assn., Phi Beta Kappa. Presbyn. Rotarian. Club: Harvard of Va. Author: Readings on Money, 1956; (with Harold Leith) Economics, USA, 1968. Home: 8414 Yolanda Rd Richmond VA 23229 Office: 7 N 8th St Richmond VA 23260

LUMSDEN, (MARY) ISABEL, educator; b. Nacoochee, Ga., May 6, 1915; d. Walter B. and Minnie (Turk) Lumsden; student Piedmont Coll., 1932-35; B.S., U. Ga., 1936, M.S. in Edn., 1941, postgrad., 1961-64, Duke, 1938. With Habersham County Schs., Clarkesville, Ga., 1958-69, curriculum dir. schs., 1958-69; asso. prof. edn. North Ga. Coll., Dahlonega, 1969-72; part-time tchr. U. Ga., 1972—; cons., 1972—. Mem. Habersham County Bus. and Profl. Women's Club (charter, pres. 1968-69), Nat., Ga. edn. assns., Delta Kappa Gamma, Kappa Delta Pi. Presbyn. (elder 1971—). Home: Sautee GA 30571

LUNARDINI, ROBERT CHRISTOPHER, cons. engr.; b. Holyoke, Mass., Feb. 18, 1933; s. Virgil Joseph and Christine (Cavanaugh) L.; B.S. in Civil Engring., Mich. Tech. U., 1954; M.S., U. Mich., 1957; m. Susan Haywood, Nov. 22, 1968; children—Karen Ann, Robert C., Victoria, William, Maria, Kathleen, Thomas, Michael, John. Field engr. Testing Service Corp., Villa Park, Ill., 1957-59; chief planning engr. Michael Baker, Jr., Inc., Jackson, Miss., 1959-64; owner, pres. So. Cons., Inc., Jackson, 1964—; sec.-treas. C4V Corp., Jackson; dir. Lime Research, Inc., Jackson. Served with C.E., AUS, 1954-56. Mem. Nat., Miss. socs. profl. engrs., Am. Water Works Assn., Fed. Water Pollution Control Assn., Am. Inst. Planners, Soc. Am. Mil. Engrs., Delta Sigma Phi. K.C. Home: 3747 Crane Blvd Jackson MS 39216 Office: 114 Office Plaza Jackson MS 39206

LUNDBLADE, HOBERT PHILIP, dentist; b. Sandstone, Minn., Oct. 12, 1929; s. Joseph M. and Hilda C. (Nordgren) L.; B.S., U. Minn., 1952, D.D.S., 1954, M.S. in Dentistry, 1955; m. Evelyn Eleanore Parvey, Sept. 12, 1953; children—Deborah Diane, Gregory Scott. Practice dentistry, St. Paul, 1954-55; teaching asst., clin. instr. U. Minn., Mpls., 1954-55; practice endodontics, San Antonio, 1958—; instr. dental assisting San Antonio Coll., 1961-68. Sec., dir. Beverage Consultants Am., Inc. Alderman, mayor City of Castle Hills, Tex. Served to capt. Dental Corps, AUS, 1955-58. Fellow Internat., Am. colls. dentists; mem. Am., Tex. dental assns., San Antonio Dist. Dental Soc. (bd. dirs. 1967—, pres.), Am. Assn. Endodontists, U.S. Power Squadron, Omicron Kappa Upsilon, Psi Omega. Research with isotopes on root canal sealers. Home: 503 Squires Row San Antonio TX 78213 Office: 1019 Shook Av San Antonio TX 78212

LUNDE, DAVID ARLAND, coll. adminstr.; b. Pittsfield, Mass., Oct. 12, 1938; s. Harold Theodore and Bernice (Bradway) L.; student Ill. Inst. Tech., 1956-57; B.Arch., U. Pa., 1961; m. Carol Lee Buckley, Dec. 22, 1962; 1 dau., Laura Lee. Apprentice, Aeck Assos., Atlanta, 1964-67, architect, 1967-68; campus architect U. Ga., Athens, 1968—. Served with USN, 1961-64. Mem. A.I.A., Soc. Coll. and Univ. Planners, Delta Tau Delta. Presbyn. (deacon, supt. Sunday sch.). Toastmaster (pres.). Archtl. works include Walton House, Northrope House, both 1969, Jefferson (Ga.) City Hall, 1972, Lunde House, 1972, N.E. Ga. APDC Office Bldg., 1973. Home: 245 Bishop Dr Athens GA 30601 Office: New Coll Bldg U Ga Athens GA 30602

LUNDIEN, JERRY RAY, elec. engr.; b. Humboldt, Ia., Jan. 20, 1938; s. Raymond Andew and Lois Maxine (Early) L.; B.S. in E.E., Ia. State U., 1960; M.S. in E.E., U. Kan., 1967; m. Sheryl Ruth Severson, Aug. 23, 1959; children—David Andrew, Matthew Carl. Elec. engr. Ia.-Ill. Gas & Electric Co., Davenport, 1960-61; research elec. engr. U.S. Army Engrs. Waterways Expt. Sta., Vicksburg, Miss., 1963—. Served with AUS, 1961-63. Recipient Fellowship award Army Advanced Study Program for Engrs. and Scientists, 1966; Spl. Service award, 1972, Sustained Superior Performance award, 1972, Dir.'s Research and Engring. Achievement award, 1973 (all U.S. Army Engrs. Waterways Expt. Sta.). Registered profl. engr., Miss. Mem. I.E.E.E., Engrs. Club Vicksburg, Ia. State U. Alumni Assn., Mensa. Democrat. Lutheran. Elk. Home: 117 Signal Hill Dr Vicksburg MS 39180 Office: PO Box 631 Vicksburg MS 39180

LUNDQUIST, GEORGE HOWARD, apparel mfg. co. exec.; b. Willmar, Minn., Apr. 21, 1939; s. Warren Sanford and Margaret (Barnett) L.; E.E., U. Minn., 1960, B.A., 1965; postgrad. U. Dallas, 1968—; m. Alija Metra, Jan. 21, 1960; children—Eric George, Dana Jon. Lineman, Northwest Bell Telephone Co., St. Cloud, Minn., 1957-58; draftsman IBM Corp., Rochester, Minn., 1960-62; electro mechanical designer Tachtronic Inst., Inc., St. Paul, 1962; electrical design engr. Continental Machines, Inc., Savage, Minn., 1963-64; area mgr. Tex. Instruments, Inc., Dallas, 1965-68; plant mgr. Greenville Pant Mfg. Co. (Tex.), 1968-71; v.p., gen. mgr. Edinburg Mfg. Co. (Tex.), mfr. Haggar slacks, 1971—. Active Boy Scouts Am. Recipient citation Gov. Tex., 1973; name Jaycee of Year Greenville Jr. C. of C., 1971. Mem. Am. Personnel and Guidance Assn., Greenville Jr. C. of C. (1st v.p. 1970-71), C. of C. (dir. 1970-71), Rodeo Assn. (pres. 1970-71), Phi Kappa Theta (pres. adv. bd. 1972—). Home: 1205 S Canna St Pharr TX 78577 Office: 1407 E Freddy Gonzalez Dr Edinburg TX 78539

LUNDQUIST, MERTON LAVERNE, JR., radio and television broadcasting exec.; b. Duluth, Minn., July 17, 1940; s. Merton LaVerne and Arda Christine (Thompsen) L.; B.A., Tex. Luth. Coll., 1962; postgrad. Luth. Sch. Theology, 1962-63, U. Tex., 1964; m. Kathy Lynn Vernon, Mar. 10, 1972. Sports dir. KTBC-TV, Austin, Tex., 1964-66; newscaster WOAI-TV, San Antonio, 1966-67; sports dir. WFAA-TV, Dallas, 1967—; color announcer Dallas Cowboy Radio Network, 1968-71, play-by-play announcer, 1972—. Instr. speech dept. Tex. Luth. Coll., 1964-65. Served with USAF, 1965. Recipient award U.P.I., 1972, Best TV Sportcast award Dallas Press Club, 1972. Lutheran. Home: 3904 Deepwood Colleyville TX 75230 Office: Communications Center Dallas TX 75202

LUNDY, CLARENCE HAROLD, architect; b. Rhone, Tex., Dec. 22, 1932; s. Jesse Lee and Pearl Lena (Mooney) L.; B.Arch., Tex. A. and M. U., 1961; m. Marcia Sue Banks, Aug. 2, 1959 (div. Dec. 1963); 1 dau., Lisa Gail. Prin., C.H. Lundy, architect, Dallas, 1965-72; architect, pres. IBS Architects, Dallas, 1972—, also dir.; sec., treas., dir. Internat. Bldg. Systems, 1972—; mgr. IBS Devel., Dallas, 1973—. Served with USMCR, 1953-56; Korea. Mem. A.I.A. (student archtl. award 1961), Nat. Council Archtl. Registration Bds., Phi Kappa Phi, Tau Beta Pi. Kiwanian (dir. 1971—, pres. 1972-73, named Kiwanian of Year 1969-70). Principal works: Chapel Mausoleum, Decatur, Ill., 1968, Garden Mausoleum, Sunset Burial Park, 1970, St. Louis Married Med. Student Housing, 1973, Presbyn. Hosp. Dallas, 1973, Pleasant Grove Med. Center, Dallas, 1973. Home: 4405 Hyer St Dallas TX 75205 Office: 3000 Diamond Park Suite 900 Dallas TX 75247

LUNGER, HAROLD LEHMAN, educator; b. Williamsport, Pa., Nov. 5, 1910; s. George Lee and Mabel Clara (Griggs) L.; B.A., Hiram Coll., 1932; M.A., Oberlin Grad. Sch. Theology, 1936; B.D., Yale, 1938; Ph.D., Yale, 1949; m. Alberta Mae Huff, July 17, 1933; children—Norman Lee, Constance Grace (Mrs. Constance Grace Couts). Ordained to ministry Christian Ch., 1931; minister Wooster Av. Ch. of Christ, Akron, O., 1931-36, Union Congregational Ch., West Haven, Conn., 1936-39, Austin Blvd. Christian Ch., Oak Park, Ill., 1939-50, First Christian Ch., Tucson, 1950-56; faculty Brite Div. Sch., Tex. Christian U., Ft. Worth, 1956—, prof. Christian ethics, 1956—, acting dean Brite Div. Sch., 1973-74. Bd. dirs. Internat. Conv. of Christian Chs., 1949-52. Am. Assn. Theol. Schs. fellow, 1965-66. Mem. Am. Acad. Religion, Am. Assn. U. Profs., Am. Soc. Christian Ethics (dir. 1963-67), Am. Soc. Ch. History. Author: Political Ethics of Alexander Campbell, 1954; Pocket Full of Seeds, 1954; Finding Holy Ground, 1957; Bible and Our Social Responsibility, 1958; Being Christian in Our Times, 1963; Citizen Under God, 1973; Editor: Foundations of Ecumenical Social Thought (J.H. Oldham), 1966. Home: Glen Rose Star Route Box 52 Granbury TX 76048 Office: Brite Divinity School Texas Christian University Fort Worth TX 76129

LUNGER, IRVIN EUGENE, univ. pres., clergyman; b. Williamsport, Pa., June 28, 1912; s. George Lee and Mabel Clara (Griggs) L.; A.B. magna cum laude, Bethany Coll., 1934; B.D., U. Chgo., 1935, A.M., 1936, Ph.D., 1938; student U. Munich, Germany, 1936-37; Litt.D., Bethany Coll., 1959, Eastern Ky. U., 1974; L.H.D., U. Ala., 1965; m. Eleanor Jeanne Zink, Feb. 10, 1939 (dec. Aug. 1955); children—Susan Ann (Mrs. Lee C. Brown) (dec.), Kathryn Elizabeth (Mrs. Bob Willis); m. 2d, Kay Walsh Ritchey, June 19, 1957; foster son, Owsley Ritchey. Ordained to ministry Disciples of Christ Ch., 1932; minister Christian Ch., Morristown, O., 1930-34, University Ch. Disciples of Christ, Chgo., 1939-55; prof. religion, dean Morrison Chapel, Transylvania U., Lexington, Ky., 1955-56, acad. dean, 1956-57, pres., 1958—. Dir. United Fund, 1959-65, pres. bd. dirs., 1962-64; pres. dirs. Bd. Higher Edn., Disciples of Christ, 1963-64; pres. bd. dirs. Henry Clay Found., Lexington, 1968—; chmn. exec. com. Ky. Ind. Coll. Found., 1967-68; Ky. chmn. Rhodes Scholarship Selection Com., 1960-67; mem. Ky. Gov.'s Commn. Higher Edn., 1964-69; mem. Lexington-Fayette Found., 1960—; chmn. bd. dirs. Living Arts and Sci. Center, Inc., 1968-69; bd. dirs. Ednl. Adv. and Reference Corp., N.Y.C., 1965-70; chmn. bd. dirs. Lexington Pub. Library, 1966-70; bd. dirs. Fund Advancement of Edn. and Research of U. Ky. Med. Center. Named Ky. col., 1959. Mem. Council Ind. Ky. Colls. and Univs. (pres. 1966, 68), Civil War Roundtable, Conf. Ch.-Related Colls. of South (pres. 1970), Omicron Delta Kappa, Tau Kappa Alpha, Beta Theta Pi. Democrat. Kiwanian. Clubs: Informal, Lafayette (Lexington); Spindletop, Idle Hour Country, Filson. Contbr.: Faith of the Free, 1940. Home: 469 N Broadway Lexington KY 40508

LUNNON, BETTY SHEEHAN (MRS. JAMES LUNNON), librarian; b. Montgomery, Ala., May 29, 1908; d. Merrill Ashurst and Martha (Guice) Sheehan; student U. Ala., 1928, 30, 32-34; A.B., George Washington U., 1938; M.A., Appalachian State Tchrs. Coll., 1959; m. David White, Nov. 27, 1927 (div. 1936); m. 2d, James Lunnon, May 13, 1939 (dec. Nov. 1954); 1 dau., Penelope Anne (Mrs. Darrell F. Fleeger). Tchr., librarian Hayneville (Ala.) Pub. Sch., 1927-29, Seale (Ala.) Pub. Sch., 1929-31, Dadeville (Ala.) Pub. Sch., 1931-32; case worker Ala. Dept. Pub. Welfare, Fed. Emergency Relief Adminstrn., 1933-35; statis. cataloger U.S. Govt., 1937-38; librarian Miami Edison Sr. High Sch., 1938-42, Fairlawn Elementary Sch., 1952-54; supr. Dade County Sch. Libraries, Miami, 1954-68; supr. libraries Dept. Edn., Pago Pago, American Samoa, 1968—; asst. prof. U. Miami, summer 1960, evening sch., 1961, 63-66; prof. summer workshop Drexel Inst., 1965; library com. cons. Field Enterprises Ednl. Corp. Gray Lady, A.R.C., 1949-52; dir. Fla. Hearing and Speech Center, 1962-63. Mem. Am. Assn. U. Women (br. v.p. 1950-51), D.A.R., Nat., Fla. edn. assns., Am. (nat. chmn. sch. library suprs. 1966-67), Fla. (pres. 1961-62) library assns., Dade County Sch. Library Assn. (pres. 1953), Am. (dir. southeastern states 1962-64, chmn. suprs. sect. 1966-67, dir. 1962-64), Fla. (pres. 1956) assns. sch. librarians, Kappa Delta Pi, Delta Kappa Gamma. Club: Quota (lt. gov. 27th dist.). Author: Jacarezinho Vadico, 1946; Two Shoes, 1951. Contbr. articles profl. jours. Home: 1002 Granada Blvd Coral Gables FL 33134

LUNSFORD, CARL DALTON, research co. exec.; b. Richmond, Va., Feb. 11, 1927; s. Edward Burpee and Mable (Harris) L.; student Coll. William and Mary, 1944-45; B.S. in Chemistry, U. Richmond, 1949, M.S., 1950; Ph.D. (E.I. duPont fellow), U. Va., 1953; m. Audrey Ann Strong, Jan. 11, 1947; children—Bonnie (Mrs. G. Russel Moyar), Debra (Mrs. Rogers S. Webb), Jan Dalton. Research chemist A.H. Robins Co., Inc., Richmond, Va., 1953-57, asso. dir. chem. research, 1957-59, dir., 1959-62, dir. labs. and chem. research, 1962-64, dir. research, 1964—, asst. v.p., Richmond, Va., 1966-73, v.p., 1973—. Instr. chemistry U. Va., 1952. Served with AUS, 1945-46. Mem. A.A.A.S., Am. Inst. Chemists, Am. Chem. Soc., Va. Acad. Sci. (chmn. chemistry sect. 1965-66), Sigma Xi, Sigma Pi Sigma, Gamma Sigma Epsilon, Phi Beta Kappa. Contbr. articles to profl. publs. Patents in field. Home: 8209 Diane Lane Richmond VA 23227 Office: 1211 Sherwood Av Richmond VA 23220

LUPINE, ELMER ALAN ROY, civil engr.; b. Pasadena, Cal, Nov. 19, 1908; s. Joseph Edward and Philipa Anne (Caracaus) L.; B.S., U. Ala., 1931; C.E., Roosevelt Grad. Coll., Chgo., 1944; postgrad. Columbia U., 1936-38; m. Mary Mac Smith, Aug. 2, 1955. Civil engr. Ala. State Hwy Dept., Tuscaloosa, 1931-32, Carl B. Call, Architect, N.Y.C., 1933-34, Office of the Borough Engr., N.Y.C., 1934-39, mem. staff of Dept. Engr., San Juan, P.R., 1939-40; civil engr. design div. Dept. of Navy, Atlantic Div. Naval Facilities Engring. Command, 1940-60, fecilities mgmt., 1961-69, facilities planning, 1969—. Registered profl. engr., Va. Fellow Am. Soc. C.E. (mem. various coms.). Club: Norfolk Boat. Home: 212 86th St Virginia Beach VA 23451 Office: Atlantic Division Naval Facilities Engineering Command Norfolk VA 23511

LUPO, ROBERT MAXCY, JR., indsl. engr.; b. Hendersonville, N.C., Nov. 17, 1928; s. Robert Maxcy and Dessie (Dixon) L.; B. Indsl. Engring., Ga. Inst. Tech., 1949; m. Carolyn Simpson, Sept. 5, 1954 (div. May 1969); children—Douglas Robert, Carol Lynne; m. 2d, Gretchen Minnich, Jan. 30, 1970; step-children—John L. Kaufmann, Paul M. Kaufmann, Elizabeth K. Kaufmann. Engr., So. Bell Tel. & Tel. Co., Augusta, Ga., 1949-63; tech. study mgmt. advanced engring. and planning br. NASA, Kennedy Space Center, Fla., 1963—. Served with USNR, 1952-54. Mem. Ga., Ala., Fla., S.C. socs. profl. engrs., Am. Inst. Indsl. Engrs., Air Force Communication Electronics Assn., Sigma Chi. Republican. Methodist. Club: Cape Kennedy Ga. Tech. Home: PO Box 731 Titusville FL 32780 Office: Kennedy Space Center FL 32899

LUSK, CLU FLU, physician; b. Eros, La., June 26, 1921; s. Frank E. and Helen (Remington) L.; B.S., La. Tech. U., 1942; M.D., Tulane U., 1950; m. Betty Morse, Jan. 1, 1944 (div. June 1945); 1 son, Frederick; m. 2d, Shirley C. Dieterich, June 17, 1950; children—Alan, Jane, John, Claire. Intern Shreveport (La.) Confederate Memorial Hosp., 1950-51, resident H.P. Long Hosp., Pineville, La., 1951-52; practice medicine, specializing in family practice, Weimar, Tex., 1952-53, Gainesville, Tex., 1953—; chief staff Gainesville Mem. Hosp., also bd. dirs. Served with USCGR, 1942-45; ETO, PTO. Diplomate Am. Bd. Family Practice. Mem. Kappa Sigma, Phi Chi, Omicron Delta Kappa, Alpha Omega Alpha. Home: Woodbine Rd Gainesville TX 76240 Office: 314 N Grand St Gainesville TX 76240

LUSS, DAN, chem. engr., educator; b. Tel Aviv, Israel, May 5, 1938; s. Manfred and Gertrude (Weinstein) L.; B.S., Technion Inst. Tech., Haifa, Israel, 1960, M.Sc., 1963; Ph.D., U. Minn., 1966; m. Amalia Rubin, Sept. 4, 1966; children—Michal, Noya. Came to U.S., 1963, naturalized, 1973. Asst. prof. chem. engring. U. Minn., Mpls., 1966-67; asst. prof. chem. engring. U. Houston, 1967-69, asso. prof., 1969-72, prof., 1972—. Cons. to several chem. cos. Registered profl. engr., Tex. Mem. Am. Inst. Chem. Engrs. (Allan P. Colburn award 1973, mem. editorial bd. jour.), Am. Chem. Soc. (Honor Scroll award of indsl. engring. chemistry div. 1961). Home: 5467 Imogene St Houston TX 77035

LUSSKY, WARREN ALFRED, librarian; b. Chgo., Apr. 16, 1919; s. Arthur W. and Alma (Proegler) L.; B.A., U. Colo., 1946; M.A., U. Denver, 1948; student U. Ill., 1941-42;; m. Mildred Joann Island, June 12, 1948. Asst. librarian Pacific Luth. Coll., Parkland Wash., 1948-49; librarian Hopkins Transp. Library, Stanford, 1950, Rocky Mountain Coll., Billings, Mont., 1950-55; head librarian Neb. Wesleyan U., Lincoln, 1955-56; dir. library, asso. prof. Tex. Luth. Coll., Sequin, 1956—. Mem. accrediting team Tex. Edn. Agy., U. Corpus Christi, Tex., 1961. Mem. Am., Tex. (dist. vice chmn. 1965, chmn. 1966), Pacific N.W. (personnel adminstrn. com. 1951-53), S.W. library assns. Prin. contbr. to design new Tex. Luth. Coll. Library; research and publs. on design and functions coll. library bldgs. Home: 357 Irvington Dr San Antonio TX 78209 Office: Texas Luth College Library Seguin TX 78155

LUSZKI, MARGARET BARRON (MRS. WALTER A. LUSZKI), psychologist; b. Washington, Mar. 24, 1907; d. Charles Henry and Helena (Johnson) Butler; A.B., U. Mich., 1928; M.A., U. Md., 1930; postgrad. Cath. U. Am. Sch. Social Work, 1939-40, Wash. Sch. Psychiatry, 1945-47, Mass. Inst. Tech., 1947-48; Ph.D., U. Mich., 1951; m. Walter A. Luszki, Mar. 15, 1950. Employee counselor Social Security Bd. and FSA, 1939-43; chief employee relations sec. U.S. Dept. Health, Edn. and Welfare, 1943-50; lectr. U.S. Dept. Agr. Grad. Sch., 1945-47; lectr. Am. U., 1951; project coordinator work confs. in Mental Health Research, Nat. Tng. Labs., 1951-57; cons. in student personal adjustment Paine Coll., Augusta, Ga., 1957-58; psychologist VA Hosp., Augusta, 1958-59; psychol. cons. Crippled Children's div. Ga. Dept. Health, 1958-59; study dir. Research Center for Group Dynamics, Inst. for Social Research, U. Mich., 1960-61; clin. psychologist and vocational counselor VA Hosp., Ann Arbor, Mich., 1961-66; research asso. Center for Research on Utilization of Sci. Knowledge, Inst. for Social Research, U. Mich., 1961-66; clin.

psychologist VA Hosp., Charleston, S.C., 1966-72 clin. asso. in psychiatry (psychology) dept. psychiatry S.C. Med. U., 1968—; cons. psychologist, 1962—. Fellow Am. Psychol. Assn., Soc. for Psychol. Study Social Issues, Am. Sociol. Assn.; mem. Nat. Rehab. Assn. Unitarian. Author: Interdisciplinary Team Research: Methods and Problems, 1958; (with Fox and Schmuck) Diagnosing Classroom Learning Environments, 1966. Contbr. articles to profl. jours. Home: Box 361 Folly Beach SC 29439 Office: 165 Maple St Charleston SC 29403

LUTHER, EDWARD TURNER, geologist, state ofcl.; b. Nashville, Feb. 11, 1928; s. Eligah Turner and Margaret Matilda (McCall) L.; B.A., Vanderbilt U., 1950, M.S., 1951; m. Patricia Ann Worthy, Sept. 17, 1955; children—Margaret Kennedy, Daniel Edward. Geologist Tenn. Div. Geology, State Geol. Survey, Nashville, 1951-54, sr. geologist, 1954-57, prin. geologist, 1958-61, asst. state geologist, 1961-66, chief geologist research and areal geology, 1966—; fuels engr. TVA, Chattanooga, 1957. Cons. on coal geology; instr. geology U. Tenn., Nashville, 1955-57. Served with USN, 1946-48. Fellow Geol. Soc. Am. (chmn. coal geology div. 1970-71, sec. 1973—); mem. Am. Inst. Profl. Geologists, Tenn. Acad. Sci. (chmn. geology sect. 1959-60). Methodist. Contbr. articles and maps on geology to sci. publs. Home: 838 Summerly Dr Nashville TN 37209 Office: G 5 State Office Bldg Nashville TN 37219

LUTHER, HOMER LEE, JR., trust co. exec.; b. Houston, Apr. 4, 1939; s. Homer Lee and Rose (White) L.; B.B.A., U. Tex., 1961, M.B.A., 1962; M.B.A., Harvard, 1964; m. Helen Patterson Dayvault, Dec. 22, 1961; children—Homer Lee III, Michael Casey, Alan Dayvault. Trainee, Haskins & Sells, Houston, Boston, 1962, 63; asso. Dean Witter & Co., Los Angeles, 1964-66; v.p., dir. Fayez Sarofim & Co., Houston, 1966-69; a founder, chmn., dir. Eagle Mgmt. and Trust Co., Houston, 1969—. Dir., CML Group, Inc., Boston. Advance rep. White House serving Pres. Nixon, 1972—. Trustee, Chinquapin Sch.; bd. dirs. S.W. YMCA. Mem. Jr. C. of C., Houston Soc. Financial Analysts, U. Tex. Alumni (life), Harvard Sch. Alumni Assn., Sigma Alpha Epsilon. Republican. Presbyn. (ruling elder, past deacon). Mason. Clubs: Ramada, Houston Country (Houston); Harvard (Boston). Home: 3661 Wickersham Houston TX 77027 Office: 1206 River Oaks Bank Tower Houston TX 77019

LUTHER, MONROE MARTIN, trust co. exec.; b. Houston, June 8, 1940; s. Homer Lee and Rose (White) L.; B.B.A., U. Tex., 1962; M.B.A., Harvard, 1964; m. Toy Kay Crocker, Feb. 3, 1962; children—Stephanie Kay, Marie Lanae, Monroe Martin. With Manned Spacecraft Center, NASA, Houston, 1963; accountant Touche, Ross & Co., C.P.A.'s, Houston, 1964-66; v.p., dir. Fayez Sarofim & Co., Houston, 1966-69; pres., dir. Eagle Mgmt. & Trust Co., Houston, 1969—. Bd. dirs. Alley Theatre, Florence Crittiton; trustee South Tex. Coll. Law. Mem. Beta Alpha Psi, Sigma Alpha Epsilon. Presbyn. (deacon). Home: 607 Shartle Circle Houston TX 77024 Office: 1206 River Oaks Bank Bldg Houston TX 77019

LUTHER, WILLIAM BROWNING, lawyer; b. Independence, Va., July 23, 1932; s. Eugene Littleton and Pauline (Browning) L.; B.S., U. Tenn., 1954, LL.B., 1959, S.J.D., 1959; m. Shirley Jean Sauls, Feb. 5, 1960; children—Susanna, Diana, Bill. Admitted to Tenn. bar, 1960, since practiced in Chattanooga; mem. firm Cunningham, Crutchfield & Luther, 1960-70, Luther, Anderson & Ruth, 1970—; judge City Ct., East Ridge, Tenn., 1960—; corporate sec. East Ridge City Bank, 19—. Served with USNR, 1950-54. Mem. Am., Tenn. bar assns., Chattanooga C. of C. (co-chmn. legislative coms. consolidation of schs. 1970), Phi Alpha Delta. Lutheran. Club: Rivermont Golf and Country (Chattanooga). Home: 4012 Patton Edwards Dr East Ridge TN 37412 Office: 8th Floor Blue Cross Bldg Chattanooga TN 37402

LUTIN, PHILIP ALBERT, cons. environmental engr.; b. Nashville, Aug. 21, 1941; s. Joseph Judah and Ethel (Wolfe) L.; B.Engring., Vanderbilt U., 1964, M.S., 1966; m. Linda Himes, Sept. 15, 1965; children—Joseph Benjamin, Susan Elizabeth. Instr. san. engring. Tenn. Tech. U., Cookeville, 1965-66; hydrologist, project leader U.S. Geol. Survey, Tampa, Fla., 1966-67; staff research engr. U. Mass., Amherst, 1967-69; head environmental engring. div. Hensley-Schmidt, Inc., cons. engrs., Chattanooga, 1969—. Pres. Coop. Pre-sch., Chattanooga. Undergrad. ind. research fellow NSF 1963; grad. research fellow Fed. Water Quality Adminstrn., 1965. Registered profl. engr., Tenn., Fla., N.C. Mem. Am. Soc. C.E., Nat. Soc. Profl. Engrs., Water Pollution Control Fedn., Sigma Xi. Contbr. profl. papers. Home: 1905 Bella Vista Dr Chattanooga TN 37421 Office: 1212 America Nat Bank Bldg Chattanooga TN 37402

LUTON, FRANK HARPER, psychiatrist; b. Decaturville, Tenn., Oct. 18, 1898; s. William Oliver and Corilla (Harper) L.; M.D., Vanderbilt U., 1927; m. Milbrey Young, June 8, 1927; children—Deborah (Mrs. Thomas Randolph Cate), Melissa (Mrs. William H. Bradford). Intern, Phipps Psychiat. Clinic, Johns Hopkins Hosp., Balt., 1927, resident, 1929-31; clin. clk. Queen's Sq. Hosp., London, 1931, Judge Baker Found., Boston, 1932, Boston City Hosp., 1933; practice psychiatry, Nashville, 1931—; cons. VA Hosp., Thayer, State Hosp., Nashville, 1947-60, clin. dir., 1960-69; vis. psychiatrist Mental Health Clinic Vanderbilt U. Hosp., Nashville, 1947-60; commr. Tenn. Dept. Mental Health, Nashville, 1969-71, dir. tng. and research, 1971—; Instr. psychiatry Johns Hopkins, 1930-31; asst. prof. Vanderbilt U., 1931-37, asso. prof., 1937-42; prof. psychiatry, 1942-64, prof. emeritus, 1964—. Mem. A.M.A. So. Med. Assn., Am. Assn. Mental Deficiency, Am. Psychiat. Assn., Am. Coll. Psychiatrists, Assn. for Research Nervous and Mental Disorders, Nat. Assn. Mental Health. Home: 5401 Stanford Dr Nashville TN 37215 Office: Central State Psychiatric Hospital 1501 Murfreesboro Rd Nashville TN 37217

LUTON, NORMAN SMITH, surgeon; b. Dover, Tenn., Jan. 21, 1916; s. James Wesley and Mable Willie (Smith) L.; B.S., Western Ky. U., 1939; M.D., Ark. Med. Sch., 1944; m. Kate Durham, Apr. 29, 1944; children—Norman Smith, Patricia (Mrs. Thomas L. Murphy). Intern, City Hosp., Columbus, Ga., 1943-44; resident U.S. Army Hosps., 1944-46; practice medicine, specializing in surgery, Phenix City, Ala., 1946—; mem. staff Cobb Meml. Hosp. Bd. dirs. Cobb Meml. Hosp. Served to capt. AUS, 1944-46. Mem. A.M.A., Russell County Med. Assn., Ala. Med. Soc., Am. Legion, Phenix City C. of C., Theta Kappa Psi. Methodist. Club: Tenn. Walking Horse Association (Lewisburg, Tenn.). Home: 3009 Summerville Rd Phenix City AL 36867 Office: 1400 Broad St Phenix City AL 36867

LUTS, HEINO ALFRED, educator; b. Torva, Estonia, Dec. 18, 1919; s. Hermann and Liisa (Kirbus) L.; came to U.S., 1945, naturalized, 1954; B.A., Upsala Coll., 1952; M.S., U. Miss., 1958, Ph.D., 1967; m. Marie Rogers, Dec. 19, 1954; children—Heino, Mary, Ellen, Liisa, Kai. Research chemist Ciba Pharms., Summit, N.J., 1956-57; project leader Horizon, Inc., Cleve., 1958-60; pres. Structure-Activity Research, Inc., Oxford, Miss., 1960-67; prof. chemistry Eastern Ky. U., Richmond, 1967—. Founder, Esto Assos., Oxford, Miss., 1954, SAR, Inc., Oxford, 1960. Pres. Estonian Student Assn., 1952. Recipient Lunsford award Mallinckrodt Corp., 1957. NSF fellow, 1958; Am. Pharm. Assn. fellow, 1957-58; Am. Lutheran Ch. fellow, 1952—; Fulbright-Hays grantee, Finland, 1974-75. Mem. Am. Chem. Soc., Am. Pharm. Assn., Fed. Internationale Pharmacetique, Sigma Xi. Lion. Research, publs. in field. Home: 213 Eastway Dr Richmond KY 40475

LUTTRELL, LESTER LEE, dentist; b. Columbus, Ga., June 22, 1933; s. Lester Lee and Alice Eloile (Brinson) L.; B.S., North Ga. Coll., 1954; D.D.S., Emory U., 1958, certificate in orthodontics, 1966; m. Jo Beth Rice, July 11, 1959; children—Dena Jan, David Reed, Linda Dayle. Intern Brooke Gen. Hosp., San Antonio, 1958-59, rotating intern, 1964-66; practice dentistry, specializing in orthodontics, Griffin, Ga., 1966—; mem. staff, chief dental service Griffin Spalding County Hosp. Bd. dirs. Am. Cancer Soc. Served to maj. Dental Corps, AUS, 1958-64. Mem. Ga. Soc. Orthodontists, So. Soc. Orthodontists, Am. Assn. Orthodontists, Am. Dental Assn., Ga. Conservancy, Orthodontic Edn. and Research Found., Am. Soc. Preventive Dentistry, Profl. Practice Assn., Nature Conservancy, Wilderness Soc., Smithsonian Assos., Environmental Def. Fund, SANE, Consumers Union, Am. Civil Liberties Union, Center for Study Dem. Instns., Am. Humanist Assn., Common Cause, Nat. Trust for Historic Preservation, Soc. Archtl. History, Griffin Spalding County Hist. Soc., Forum for Contemporary History, Griffin Spalding County Art Assn., C. of C., Griffin Touchdown Club, Internat. Platform Assn., Delta Sigma Delta. Baptist. Clubs: Exchange (pres. 1971-72) (Griffin, Ga.); Sierra. Home: 1005 Springer Dr Griffin GA 30227 Office: 218 Addevale St Griffin GA 30223

LUTZ, CHARLES EDMUND, broadcasting exec.; b. Groveport, O., Jan. 11, 1928; s. Clarence Milton and Agnes M. (Ellinger) L.; E.E., Franklin U., Columbus, O., 1951; m. Helen Rosetta Howard, Aug. 13, 1950; children—Kurt, Mark, Eric, Kara. Engr. Avco Broadcasting Co., Columbus, 1950-67, producer, facilities supr., 1967-69, prodn. mgr., San Antonio, 1969—. Sec., dir. Ohio Archery Assn., 1950-60; parliamentarian, pres., dir. U.S. Archery Assn., 1960-70; mgr., coach local Little League, 1960—. Served with USN, 1946-47. Editorial bd. Archery mag., 1968-72. Office: PO Box 2641 San Antonio TX 78299

LUTZ, KEITH WILLIAM, state ofcl.; b. Shannon, Ill., Feb. 22, 1922; s. Otis and Ada Marie (Boyd) L.; B.S., U. Okla., 1948; grad. Central Flight Instr. Sch.; m. Suzannelle Hall, June 10, 1952; 1 son, Kenneth W. Formerly flight instr., faculty pilot U. Okla., corporate pilot, pilot Air Transport Command United Airlines; dir. Okla. Aeros. Commn., 1963—. Vice chmn. Gov.'s Aerospace Edn. Com. Served with USAF. Recipient Certificate of Merit Aviation Distbrs. and Mfrs. Assn., 1971. Mem. Am. Assn. Airport Execs., Aircraft Owners and Pilots Assn., Nat. Pilots Assn., Nat. Assn. State Aviation Ofcls., Quiet Birdmen, Phi Delta Theta. Club: Air and Indsl. Kiwanis Oklahoma City (pres.). Home: 6809 Ann Arbor Terrace Oklahoma City OK 73132 Office: 424 United Founders Tower Oklahoma City OK 73112

LUTZ, PAUL EUGENE, educator; b. Hickory, N.C., June 25, 1934; s. Cy Emmet and Ruth May (Karriker) L.; A.B., Lenoir Rhyne Coll., 1956; M.S., U. Miami, 1958; Ph.D., U. N.C., 1962; m. Alice Elaine Patterson, June 8, 1957; 1 dau., Carol Susan. Instr., U. N.C., Greensboro, 1961-62, asst. prof., 1962-66, asso. prof., 1966-70, prof. biology, 1970—. Mem. Guilford County Adv. Bd. Environmental Quality, 1972—; mem. environmental com. Piedmont Triad Council Govts., 1970—. Trustee, Lenoir Rhyne Coll.; mem. bd. social ministry Lutheran Ch. Am. NSF grantee, alumni teaching excellence award U. N.C. at Greensboro, 1966, outstanding educator award U. N.C. at Greensboro, 1968, distinguished service citation Lenoir Rhyne Coll., 1971. Mem. Ecological Soc. Am., Am. Soc. Zoologists, A.A.A.S., Am. Inst. Biol. Scis., Sigma Xi. Author: (with H. Paul Santmire) Ecological Renewal, 1972. Home: 4001 Cascade Dr Greensboro NC 27410

LUTZ, RAYMOND PRICE, educator; b. Oak Park, Ill., Feb. 27, 1935; s. Raymond Price and Sibyl Elizabeth (Haralson) L.; B.S. in Mech. Engring., U. N.M., 1958, M.B.A., 1962; Ph.D., Ia. State U., 1964; m. Nancy Marie Cole, Aug. 22, 1958. With Sandia Corp., Albuquerque, summers 1958-63; instr. mech. engring. U. N.M., 1958-62; asst. to asso. prof. indsl. engring. N.M. State U., 1964-68; prof., head indsl. engring. U. Okla., 1968-73; prof., head, mgmt. and adminstrv. scis. U. Tex. at Dallas, 1973—. Dir., OMEC, Norman, Okla.; cons. Bell Telephone Labs., Tex. Instruments, Kennecott Corp., City of Dallas, Oklahoma City, U.S. Army, USAF, U.S. Dept. Transp., Los Angeles and Seattle pub. schs. Registered profl. engr., N.M., Okla. Fellow A.A.A.S.; mem. Am. Soc. Engring. Edn. (Eugene L. Grant award 1972, chmn. engring. economy div.), Am. Inst. Indsl. Engrs. (dir. engring. economy div., systems engring. group, Operations Research Soc. Am., Inst. Mgmt. Sci. Editor, asso. editor for manuscripts Engring. Economist, 1971—. Home: 10275 Hollow Way Dallas TX 75229

LUTZ, THERESA PENCE (MRS. C. RALPH LUTZ), ednl. adminstr.; b. nr. Greensboro, N.C.; d. Claude S. Stroud and Lelia (Powell) Pence; B.A., Mary Washington Coll., 1947; M.Ed., U.Va., 1956, postgrad., 1956-57; postgrad. George Washington U., summer 1961, 61-62, Am. U., 1963, Coll. William and Mary, 1964-71; m. C. Ralph Lutz, May 30, 1931; children—Patricia (Mrs. Edward L. Plummer, Jr.), Philip (dec.). Tchr., New Market (Va.) Elementary Sch., 1944-46, New Market High Sch., 1946-47, Wilson Meml. High Sch., Fishesville, Va., 1947-57; tchr., counselor Mt. Vernon High Sch., Alexandria, Va., 1957-58; dir. guidance Lee High Sch., Springfield, Va., 1958-67; counselor, instr. grad. edn. No. Va. Center, U. Va., also instr., counselor West Springfield High Sch. Trustee, Marion Coll. Mem. N.E.A. (life), Va. (chmn. tchr. and profl. standards com. 1966—), Fairfax edn. assns., Am., Va., No. Va. personnel and guidance Assns., Nat. Vocational Guidance Assn., Va., Guidance Assn., Delta Kappa Gamma (chpt. pres. 1972-74). Lutheran (counselor Luther League 1961-63). Author: (with Lillian W. Eisenberg) Central Evangelical Lutheran Church and Christ Evangelical Lutheran Church, 1953. Home: 5803 Accomac St Springfield VA 22150 Office: 6100 Rolling Rd Springfield VA 22152

LUXENBERG, MALCOLM NEUWAHL, ophthalmologist; b. Philipsburg, Pa., July 29, 1935; s. Maurice and Henrietta (Neuwahl) L.; student Tulane U., 1953-56; M.D., U. Miami, Fl., 1960; m. Sandra Diane Rosen, June 16, 1957; children—Steven Neuwahl, Cathy Ann. Intern, Cin. Gen. Hosp., 1960-61; resident neurology U. Vt. Affiliated Hosps., Burlington, 1961-63; resident ophthalmology Bascom Palmer Eye Inst., U. Miami-Jackson Meml. Hosp., Miami, Fla., 1963-66; practice medicine, specializing in ophthalmology, West Palm Beach, Fla., 1970-72; asst. prof. ophthalmology U. Ia. Coll. Medicine, Iowa City, 1968-70; chief ophthalmology service VA Hosp., Iowa City, 1968-70; prof., chmn. dept. ophtholomology Med. Coll. Ga., Augusta, 1972—. Sr. surgeon USPHS, 1966-68. Diplomate Am. Bd. Ophthalmology. Mem. A.M.A., Am. Acad. Ophthalmology and Otolaryngology, Assn. for Research in Vision and Ophthalmology. Home: 512 Scotts Way Augusta GA 30904 Office: Dept Ophthalmology Med Coll Georgia Augusta GA 30902

LYBRAND, RAYMOND DONOVAN, bank exec.; b. Columbia, S.C., Sept. 9, 1922; s. Fritz Otis and Elizabeth A. (Murphy) L.; student U. S.C., 1947-48, Am. Inst. Banking, 1954-64, Carolinas Sch. Banking U. N.C., 1962-65; m. Doris Louise Eastman, June 2, 1945; children—Ted D., Donna Dee. With Citizens and So. Nat. Bank, Columbia, 1941-51; store auditor Edens Food Stores, Columbia, 1951-52; teller First Nat. Bank S.C., Spartansburg, 1952-53, head teller, 1953-55, asst. cashier, 1955-61, cashier operations, 1961-66; with First State Nat. Bank, Jackson, S.C., 1966—, v.p., cashier in charge operations, 1966—. Served with USNR, 1942-45, 50-51; Korea. Mem. Bank Adminstrn. Inst. (dir. 1957-58). Methodist (chmn. finance commn., 1959-62, bd. trustees, 1963-65, vice chmn. bd., 1964-65, financial sec., 1967-69). Clubs: Silverton Agricultural (Jackson); Civitan (pres. 1961-62, dir., 1957-63, lt. gov., 1964) (Union, S.C.). Home: Lions Club Rd Jackson SC 29831 Office: First State Nat Bank PO Box 128 Jackson SC 29831

LYDA, HAP, educator; b. Nampa, Ida., Dec. 25, 1932; s. Thomas Shelton and Martha (Grueneich) L.; B.Th., N.W. Christian Coll., 1954; M.Div., Tex. Christian U., 1957; M.A. (fellow 1967-71), Vanderbilt U., 1971, Ph.D., 1972; m. Julia Anne Whiteman, June 23, 1960; children—Marc Grayson, Jay Shelton, Lance Emerson. Ordained to ministry Christian Ch., 1954; pastor Crestview Christian Ch., Greenville, Tex., 1956-58; asso. pastor First Christian Ch., Corpus Christi, Tex., 1958-61; pastor Northside Christian Ch., St. Louis, 1961-67; chaplain VA Hosp., Nashville, 1967-71; prof. philosophy and religion Tarrant County Jr. Coll., Ft. Worth, 1971—. Founding partner Criminal Justice Press, Ft. Worth, 1973—. Mem. Am. Assn. U. Profs., Am. Soc. Ch. History, Tex. Jr. Coll. Tchrs. Assn., Am. Acad. Religion, Cambell Inst. Club: Century (Fort Worth). Co-editor: Jour. of Expression, 1973—. Office: Tarrant County Jr Coll South Campus Fort Worth TX 76119

LYERLY, PAUL JUNIOR, ednl. adminstr.; b. Granite Quarry, N.C., Feb. 24, 1918; s. Paul Jacob and Leona Sarah (McCombs) L.; B.S., N.C. State U., 1938; M.S., Ia. State U., 1940, Ph.D., 1942; m. Mary Lucille Ludwig, June 20, 1942; children—Bonnie (Mrs. Ron Fowler), Vickie Ann (Mrs. Richard Valera). Asst. corn investigation Ia. State U., Ames, 1938-41; agronomist Expt. Sta., Tex. A. and M. U., 1942-45, cotton breeder, 1945-47, supt. expt. sta., 1947-59, research coordinator trans Pecos Area, 1959-72, resident dir. research center, El Paso, 1973—. Mem. Am. Soc. Agronomy, Weed Soc. Am., Am. Soc. Plant Physiology, Am. Phytopathol. Soc., Am. Genetic Soc., Sigma Xi, Alpha Zeta, Gamma Sigma Delta, Phi Kappa Phi. Lion (pres. 1947). Methodist (chmn. bd. 1949). Address: 10601 North Loop Rd El Paso TX 79927

LYLES, WILLIAM GORDON, architect; b. Whitmire, S.C., Oct. 23, 1913; s. John Thomas and Maggie (Livingston) L.; B.Arch., Clemson Coll., 1934; m. Louise Stork, Jan. 15, 1937; children—William Gordon, Robert Thomas. Apprentice several archtl. offices, 1934-38; architect Stork and Lyles, Columbia, S.C., 1938-41, 45-47; pres., chmn. bd. Lyles, Bissett, Carlisle & Wolff, Columbia, 1947—; chmn. bd. Asso. Investments, Inc., 1952—; dir. Bankers Trust, Columbia, Bank Commerce, Prosperity, S.C. and Chapin, S.C. Chmn. Columbia and Richland Country's Indsl. Devel. Commn., 1958-61; co-chmn. Columbia Community Relations Council, 1963-70, chmn., 1970—; co-chmn. ad hoc com. on design and constrn. evaluation study for Gen. Services Adminstrn., Washington, 1963-64, mem. pub. adv. panel on archtl. services, 1965-67; mem. Gov.'s Adv. Com., 1964-70; mem. Mayor's Adv. Coms., 1958-70; mem. Richland County Historic Commn., 1962—; mem. S.C. Devel. Bd., 1973—. Mem. adv. bd. Commn. on Higher Edn., 1965-68; trustee United Community Services, 1968—; co-chmn. Columbia Guidance Center, 1965-70. Served to col. C.E. AUS, 1941-45. Decorated Legion of Merit; recipient 27 awards and citations for excellence in design. Fellow Nat. Am. Inst. Architects (mem. govt. affairs com. 1964-70, chmn. 1970; mem. interprofl. com. architects and engrs. concerning fed. procurement A-E services 1966—, vice chmn. 1969—; chmn. interregional com. on fees and practices 1970—; mem. Columbia Council Architects 1956—); mem. S.C. chpt. A.I.A. (chmn. com. to publish regulations and booklets governing practice architecture S.C. 1952, 61, 69-70), Columbia C. of C. (dir. 1958-62, 70—), U.S. C. of C. (constrn. and civic devel. com. 1961-63), Newcomen Soc. N.Am. Lutheran (mem. ch. council 1954-57, 60-64, 66-70; chmn. pastor's selection com. 1963). Clubs: Cosmos (Washington); City (Raleigh); Forest Lake Country; Spring Valley Country; Palmetto (Columbia). Archtl. works include Langley Bath Clearwater Sch.; Russell House U. S.C., also Undergrad. Library; Elmwood Cemetery Meml. Tower; libraries at S.C. State Coll. and Wofford Coll.; Orangeburg-Calhoun TEC, U. S.C. Coliseum, U. S.C. Humanities Center, numerous others. Home: 5625 Lakeshore Dr Columbia SC 29206 Office: 1301 Gervais St Columbia SC 29202

LYMAN, JOHN, oceanographer, educator; b. Berkeley, Cal., Oct. 28, 1915; s. Theodore Benedict and Rowena (Wilson) L.; B.S., U. Cal. at Berkeley, 1936; M.S., U. Cal. at Los Angeles, 1951, Ph.D., 1957; m. Mitchell Forrest, May 4, 1946; children—John F., Richard D. Chemist Union Oil Co., Oleum, Cal., 1937; research asst. Scripps Instn. Oceanography, La Jolla, Cal., 1937-41; oceanographer U.S. Navy Hydrographic Office, Washington, 1946-59; program dir. for oceanography NSF, Washington, 1959-64; oceanographic coordinator Bur. Comml. Fisheries, Washington, 1964-66; program dir. chem. oceanography Office Naval Research, Washington, 1966-68; prof. oceanography U. N.C., Chapel Hill, 1968-73. Mem. Atomic Safety and Licensing Bd. panel, AEC., 1972—. Served to lt. (j.g.) USNR, 1941-45. Fellow Am. Geophys. Union; mem. Soc. Nautical Research, Nautical Research Guild, N.Am. Vexillogical Assn., Am. Names Soc. Home: 404 Clayton Rd Chapel Hill NC 27514

LYNCH, ALMA MARTHA HIRSCH (MRS. WILLIAM WRIGHT LYNCH), civic worker; b. Wheeling, W.Va.; d. Conrad and Alma (Hanszen) Hirsch; B.A., U. Tex.; grad. Sullins Coll.; m. William Wright Lynch, Oct. 18, 1930; children—William Wright, Harry Hanszen. Dir., Ins. Bldg. Corp. Chmn. exec. com. Dallas Council World Affairs, 1963-66, chmn. West Dallas Scholarship Com., 1962-66; dir. Soc. Animal Protection, 1964-66, W. Dallas Community Centers, 1962-66; mem. exec. com. Dean's Club So. Meth. U., 1964-66; trustee Lynch Found., Ednl. Opportunities, Dallas; mem.-at-large, mem. steering com. Nat. Com. Children and Youth, 1966-73; chmn. women's bd. Dallas Civic Opera, 1967-68; mem. bd. devel. Bishop Coll. Bd. dirs. Tex. Women's Council Dallas County, 1967-71, North Tex. Arthritis Found.; Dallas Theater Center, Dallas Symphony Orch., Dallas Civic Ballet, Dallas County Heritage Soc., Douglas MacArthur Acad. Freedom, Brownwood, Tex.; adv. bd. Crystal Charity Ball. Recipient Honor award Nat. Jewish Hosp., 1963, Zonta Service award, 1967. Mem. Chi Omega, Sigma Alpha Iota. Episcopalian. Clubs: Brook Hollow Golf, Dallas Woman's. Office: 1710 Jackson St Dallas TX 75201

LYNCH, BROTHER DANIEL MATTHEW, educator; b. Detroit, June 28, 1921; s. Daniel Matthew and Claire Marie (Langlois) L.; A.B., U. Detroit, 1943; M.S., Mich. State U., 1948; Ph.D., Wash. State U., 1952. Joined Brothers Holy Cross, 1952; from instr. to asso. prof. biology St. Edward's U., Austin, Tex., 1954-64, prof., 1965—, premed. adviser, 1959-73. Served with USAAF, 1945-46. Fellow Tex. Acad. Sci.; mem. Bot. Soc. Am., Ecol. Soc. Am., A.A.A.S., Farmhouse, Sigma Xi. K.C. Contbr. articles to sci. lit. Home and office: 3001 S Congress Austin TX 78704

LYNCH, HOWARD WAYNE, banker; b. Hamilton, Tex., Mar. 2, 1902; s. William Warner and Martha Isabella (Miller) L.; B.A., Centre Coll., Danville, Ky., 1925; M.A., U. Ky., 1933; m. Dolly Gretna Hanna, Nov. 2, 1925; children—William Hanna, Howard Wayne, Dan Winsett. Prin., tchr., coach Franklin (Ky.) High Sch., 1925-30;

tchr., asst. football coach Amarillo (Tex.) High Sch., 1930-37, head football coach 1937-50, asst. prin., 1950-58; prin. Tascosa High Sch., Amarillo, 1958-67; asst. v.p. Tascoasa Nat. Bank, Amarillo, 1967-68, v.p., 1968—. Mem. Panhandle Sports Hall of Fame, 1964. Mem. Tex. High Sch. Coaches Assn. (Hall of Honor, 1963), Tex. Tchrs. Assn., N.E.A., Tex. Assn. Secondary Sch. Prins., Nat. Assn. Secondary Sch. Prins., Phi Kappa Tau, Omicron Delta Kappa, Phi Delta Kappa. Methodist. Rotarian. Home: 1000 Western St Amarillo TX 79106 Office: 3601 W 15th St Amarillo TX 79106

LYNCH, JOSEPH P., newspaper advt. exec.; b. Grand Rapids, Mich., May 27, 1919; s. Joseph Patrick and Ellen Joan (Lynch) L.; ed. Northwestern U., Harvard Grad. Sch. Bus.; m. Patsy Elizabeth Ashbolt, Apr. 29, 1944; children—Joseph P. III, Michael L., David, Pamela E., Anthony J. Mdse. mgr. asst. to advt. mgr., promotion mgr. Grand Rapids Press, 1946-54; promotion mgr. Washington Post, 1954-61, classified advt. mgr., 1961-67, advt. mgr., 1967-69, v.p. advt., 1969—. Mem. plans bd. Bur. Advt.; dir. Advt. Council. Active Boy Scouts Am. Bd. dirs. Cath. Youth Orgn., Met. Boys Club. Served to 1st lt. AUS, 1941-45. Mem. Internat. Newspaper Promotion Assn. (past pres.), Assn. Newspaper Classified Advt. Mgrs. (past v.p.), Internat. Newspaper Advt. Execs. (dir.). Clubs: University (Washington); Burning Tree; Talbot Country. Home: 5215 Portsmouth Washington DC 20016 also New Scotland Farm Trappe MD Office: 1515 L St Washington DC 20005

LYNCH, KENNETH CLYDE, physician; b. New Tazewell, Tenn., Oct. 13, 1926; s. Brownlow M. and Pearl (Sowder) L.; student Lincoln Meml. U., 1946-47; M.D., U. Tenn., 1961; m. Bobbie Lee Ryder, Sept. 24, 1948; children—Elizabeth Jean, Donald Wayne. Intern, Holston Valley Community Hosp., Kingsport, Tenn., 1961-62, co-dir. diabetic clinic, 1962—, dir. med. staff out-patient clinic, chmn. dept. gen. practice, mem. med. staff exec. com., 1967—, pres. med. staff, 1971; operator Blomingdale Med. Clinic, Kingsport, 1962—. Bd. dirs. Indian Path Hosp., 1973—. Served with AUS, World War II. Fellow Royal Soc. Health; mem. Am., Tenn. med. assns., Sullivan-Johnson County Med. Soc. (pres. 1972), Am. Acad. Gen. Practice, Am. Diabetic Assn. Republican. Kiwanian. Home: 1417 Linville St Kingsport TN 37664 Office: 2901 Bloomingdale Pike Kingsport TN 37660

LYNCH, MINNIE-LOU CHITTICK (MRS. WELDON JEROME LYNCH), lectr., civic leader, library cons.; b. Cutler, Inc., Feb. 28, 1916; d. Loren Maconn and Mae (Callane) Chittick; student Maryville Coll., 1934-36; m. Weldon Jerome Lynch, Mar. 24, 1940; children—Jenny Callane (Mrs. Robert L. Royer), Bridget Dorn (Mrs. Matt V. Hargrove IV). Book reviewer for audiences, 1938—; Book Theater presentations, 1950—; lectr., Can., U.S. Organizer, Allen Parish (La.) Com. Library Devel., 1950, chmn., 1950-57; pres. Allen Parish Library Bd. Control, 1957-65, v.p., 1968—; mem. com. library standards State Dept. Edn., 1965-67; chmn. La. Library Devel. Com., 1964-68, mem. library survey sub-com., 1967-69; cons. Coastal Bend Planning Commn., Corpus Christi, Tex., 1969; cons. inservice tng. La. Central Dist. Libraries, 1968-69; coordinator spl. programs La. State Library, 1968-70; dir. S.W. Libraries Motivation Study Project, 1971-72; chmn. com. to advise Students to Dallas project, 1970-72; mem. exec. com. La. Adv. Council on Libraries, 1971—; dir. La. Gov.'s Conf. on Libraries, 1973; mem. U.S. com. for Am. Library in Paris, 1970—; lectr. Cath. U., Washington, 1973. Adv. bd. Bank of S.W. La., 1973—. Recipient citation La. Soil and Water Conservation Commn., 1971-72. Mem. A.L.A. (Trustee citation 1964, adv. com. to pub. relations office 1964-68, membership com. exec. bd. 1966-68, network legislative cons. 1973—), La. Council Performing Arts, Am. Library Trustee Assn. (nat. pres. 1961-63), Southwestern, La. (Modisette award 1963, sect. chmn. 1960) library assns., Nat. Book Com. (nat. bd.), Internat. Platform Assn., Psi Iota Xi, Pi Kappa Delta. Methodist (ofcl. bd.). Clubs: Matinee Music, Oakdale Garden (organizer). Author monograph: Guidelines for Holding a Governor's Conference on Libraries, 1963, rev., 1968; contbg. author: The Library Trustee, 1968, Ency. Library and Info. Sci., 1974. Home: 404 E 6th Av Oakdale LA 71463

LYNCH, ROBERT RAMSAY, JR., newspaper editor; b. Mansfield, O., Jan. 30, 1935; s. Robert R. and Muriel (Parker) L.; B.S. in Journalism, U. Fla., 1956; m. Joan Halberstadt, Dec. 26, 1957; 1 dau., Donna. Sports writer Fort Lauderdale (Fla.) News, 1958-62, sports editor, 1962-64, news and feature editor U. Fla., 1964-65, dir. information services, 1965-73; mng. editor So. Beacon, Statesboro, Ga., 1973—. Fla. advt. rep. Golf World Mag., 1961-64. Served with AUS, 1956-58. Recipient Pompano Beach Jr. C. of C. award 1962. Mem. Am. Coll. Pub. Relations Assn. (trustee 1971-73, sec. 1971-73, dist. dir. 1970-71), Fla. Pub. Relations Assn. (v.p. 1969-71, chpt. pres. 1969), U. Fla. Alumni Assn. (pres. Alachua County 1968, dist. v.p. 1970-72), Delta Chi, Sigma Delta Chi. Home: 205 Pitt-Moore Rd Statesboro GA 30458 Office: 14 S Main St Statesboro GA 30458

LYNCH, WILLIAM CHARLES, theater chain exec.; b. Halifax County, Va., Aug. 5, 1922; s. John Henry and Annie Lee (Gilliland) L.; m. Beulah Boyd, Nov. 17, 1945; children—Larry Allen, Libby Carol (Mrs. Ray K. Heskett). With Martinsville Theater Mgmt. Corp. (Va.), 1947—, gen. mgr., 1961-73, v.p., gen. mgr., 1973—. Bd. dirs. NATO of Va., 1963—. Served with AUS, 1942-45. Mem. United Comml. Travelers, Travelers Protective Assn., Am. Legion. Presbyn. Elk, K.P. Home: 1204 Spruce St Martinsville VA 24112 Office: 215 E Church St Martinsville VA 24112

LYND, JAMES PAUL, social worker; b. Ironton, O., Jan. 16, 1928; s. Ben H. and Frances (Schmitt) L.; student Rio Grande Coll., 1948-49, Cedarville Coll., 1949-51, Miami U. (Ohio), 1952; B.I.S., U. Mid-Fla., 1971, M.S., 1973; m. Ann Wilkes, June 1, 1973. Supr., Cal. Youth Authority, Norwalk, 1954-55; field counselor Ohio Juvenile Placement Bur., Dayton, 1955-59; supt. Butler County Juvenile Center, Hamilton, O., 1959-63, Orange County Juvenile-Parental Homes, Orlando, Fla., 1963—. Bd. dirs. Edgewood Boys Ranch, Gil-Lyn Guest Home, Drug Abuse Treatment Center. Served with USNR, 1945-46. Mem. Fla. (chpt. pres. 1965-66), Nat. councils on crime and delinquency, Nat. Juvenile Detention Assn. (sec.-treas. 1971-72), D.A.V. Lutheran. Mason (32 deg., Shriner). Club: Sertoma (dir. 1966-68). Address: 1540 George Av Orlando FL 32806

LYNE, JAMES ANTHONY, JR., civil engr.; b. Nashville, Dec. 29, 1928; s. James Anthony and Anne Briggs (Evans) L.; grad. Mercersburg Acad., 1947; student (Ky. Regional scholar) Mass. Inst. Tech., 1947-49; B.S. in Civil Engring. (Ky. Assn. Ins. Agts. scholar), U. Ky., 1952; m. Mary Rae Tucker, Oct. 27, 1950; 1 son, James Evans. Draftsman, Howard K. Bell, Lexington, Ky., 1949-52; v.p., dir. in charge civil engring. projects Howard, Nielsen, Lyne, Thomas, Aldred, Henry & O'Brien, Inc., engrs., architects, Nashville, 1952-73; v.p., sec., dir. Morton-Lyne & Assos., Inc., Nashville, 1973—; dir. Hoblyn Corp., Nashville. Chmn., Franklin Rd. Area fund drive Boy Scouts Am., 1968-73. Mem. Nat. Soc. Profl. Engrs., Nashville Engrs. Assn., Water Pollution Control Fedn., Am. Water Works Assn., Phi Kappa Sigma, Tau Beta Pi. Democrat. Methodist (adminstrv. bd. 1974—). Club: Wildwood Swim and Tennis (Nashville, vice chmn. bd.). Home: 730 Elysian Fields Rd Nashville TN 37204 Office: 217 24th Av N Nashville TN 37203

LYNE, JAMES COLEMAN, lawyer; b. Logan County, Ky., Aug. 7, 1908; s. Coleman Sandford III and Myrtle (Thomerson) L.; A.A., Bethel Coll., 1928; J.D., U. Ky., 1932; m. Lucy L. Linton, Nov. 10, 1936; children—June Carolyne, James Coleman; m. 2d, Lucille Nunn Forcum, June 16, 1961. Admitted to Ky. bar, 1933, since practiced in Russellville; mem. firm Felts & Lyne, 1935-37; atty. City of Russellville, 1943-48, Logan County, Russellville, 1948-57; atty. 7th jud. dist. Commonwealth of Ky., Russellville, 1962—; pres., dir. 1st Fed. Savs. & Loan Assn., Russellville, 1934—. Trustee Logan-Todd Bookmobile Commn.; chmn. bd. trustees Logan County Hosp. Mem. Am., Ky., Logan County bar assns., Tenn. Valley Golf Assn. (pres. 1959, 65, 73), Phi Alpha Delta, Sigma Alpha Epsilon, Phi Mu Alpha. Democrat. Baptist. Kiwanian (pres Russellville 1963). Home: Daleview Circle Cloverland Russellville KY 42276 Office: First Federal Bldg Russellville KY 42276

LYNHAM, JOHN MARMADUKE, lawyer, banker; b. Washington, Feb. 19, 1908; s. Edgar Hardwicke and Mera Elsie (Marmaduke) L.; B.S. in Govt., Am. U., 1935; J.D., George Washington U., 1931, LL.M., 1932; m. Adele Randolph Pugh, May 22, 1947; children—Adele Cameron (Mrs. Robert B. Shanks), John Marmaduke, Mary Hardwicke, Gale Randolph. Admitted to D.C. bar, 1931; Md. bar, 1953; mem. firm of Drury, Lynham & Powell (formerly Minor, Gatley & Drury), Washington, 1930-69; v.p., trust officer Nat. Savs. & Trust Co., Washington 1969—. Bd. mgrs. Chevy Chase Village, 1963-73, vice chmn., 1969-73. Trustee Nat. U., 1947-54; trustee Landon Sch., 1966—, chmn. bd., 1967—; dir. Gunston Hall Sch., 1941-46; sponsor Ophthalmic Research Found., 1973—; trustee Nat. Ballet Soc., 1969-72. Served from lt. (j.g.) to comdr., USNR, 1941-45. Fellow Am. Bar Found.; mem. Am., D.C., Md. bar assns., Bar Assn. D.C., Am. Judicature Soc., Inst. Jud. Adminstrn., Lawyers Club, The Barristers (pres. 1960). Clubs: Chevy Chase (gov. 1949-55, 59-65, pres. 1954-55); Metropolitan (gov. 1968-73, pres. 1972-73), Nat. Lawyers (Washington). Author: The Chevy Chase Club—A History, 1958. Home: 14 Oxford St Chevy Chase Village MD 20015 Office: 719 15th St NW Washington DC 20005

LYNN, JAMES HERMAN, museum curator; b. Gastonia, N.C., May 2, 1938; s. Samuel Alexander and Lola Naomi (Robinson) L.; A.B., Pfeiffer Coll., 1960; m. Shirley Anne Dellinger, June 19, 1959; children—James Ross, Andrea Elizabeth. Tchr. Gastonia City Schs., 1960-67; curator planetarium, curator minerals Schiele Museum Natural History and Planetarium, Gastonia, 1967—. Democrat. Methodist. Home: 1422 Cambrdge St Gastonia NC 28052 Office: PO Box 953 Gastonia NC 28052

LYNN, JAMES THOMAS, retailer; b. Fordyce, Ark., Nov. 3, 1928; s. James Nathawial and Birthal Mae (Johnson) L.; student Ouachita Bapt. Coll., 1946-47, Kan. State U., 1950-51; m. Lois Marie Kennedy, Oct. 17, 1953; 1 son, James T. With West & Co. of La. Inc., 1953—, mgr., 1958-60, buyer, 1960-63, discount store mgr., 1963-66, v.p., mdse. mgr., 1966-72, v.p., dir. operations, Minden, La., 1972—. Served with inf. AUS, 1950-53; Korea. Mem. Delta Sigma. Baptist. Lion. Clubs: Pines Hills Country, Minden Tennis (Minden); Shreveport, Metropolitan Dinner (Shreveport). Home: 1406 E Todd Minden LA 71055 Office: PO Drawer G Minden LA 71055

LYNN, JAMES THOMAS, govt. ofcl.; b. Cleve., Feb. 27, 1927; s. Fredrick Robert and Dorothea Estelle (Petersen) L.; A.B. summa cum laude, Western Res. U., 1948; LL.B. magna cum laude, Harvard, 1951; m. Joan Miller, June 5, 1954; children—Marjorie, Peter, Sarah. Admitted to bar; partner firm Jones, Day, Cockley & Reavis, Cleve., 1951-69; gen. counsel Dept. Commerce, Washington, 1969-71, undersec., 1971-73; sec. housing and urban devel., Washington, 1973—. Hon. mem. Nat. council Boy Scouts Am. Bd. govs. A.R.C. Served with USNR, 1945-46. Mem. Am., Fed., Ohio, Cleve. bar assns., Council Fgn. Relations. Republican. Episcopalian. Home: 6736 Newbold Dr Bethesda MD 20034 Office: Dept Housing and Urban Devel Washington DC 20410

LYNN, MELVYN STUART, mathematician; b. London, Eng., July 7, 1937; s. Richard and Julie (Shavick) L.; B.A., Oxford U., 1958, M.A., 1964; M.A., U. Cal. at Los Angeles. 1960. Ph.D., 1962; m. Barbara Berkson, Aug. 26, 1960; children—Monica Georgette, Anthea Suzanne, Matthew David. Open exhibitioner Merton Coll., Eng., 1955-58; research asst. numerical analysis research, U. Cal. at Los Angeles, 1959-62; research fellow Nat. Phys. Lab., Teddington, Eng., 1962-63, sr. sci. officer, 1963-64; staff mem. IBM, Los Angeles Sci. Center, 1964-65, mgr. math. dept. Houston Sci. Center, 1965-66, mgr. research dept., 1966-67, mgr. center, 1967-71; prof. math. scis., dir. Inst. for Computer Services and Applications, Rice U., Houston, 1971—. Mem. Assn. for Computing Machinery (editor in chief Communications of the ACM 1968-73, chmn. editorial com. 1971-73), Soc. Indsl. and Applied Math., Am. Fedn. Info. Processing Socs. (chmn. publs. com. 1973—). Editorial bd. Acta Informatica, 1973—. Contbr. articles to profl. jours. Home: 931 Magdalene St Houston TX 77024 Office: Rice Univ Houston TX 77001

LYNN, PHILLIP WAYNE, utility exec.; b. Woodbury, Tenn., Sept. 23, 1942; s. Luther Britton and R.A. (Burks) L.; student Middle Tenn. State U., 1960-62; B.S. in Civil Engring., U. Tenn., 1966, M.S., 1967; m. Mary Evelyn Harris, Nov. 4, 1967; 1 son, Britton Earle. Research asst. U. Tenn. Water Resources Research Center, Knoxville, 1966-67; engr. Shell Oil Co., Norco, La., 1967-70; chief engr. Frank Foster and Assos., Inc., Kenner, La., 1970-72; dir. waste water control system City of Knoxville, 1972—. Chmn., Knoxville Tech. Soc. Environmental Resources Subcom. for Water, 1973—, Pub. Tech. Inc. Water/Wastewater mgmt. user requirements com. Registered profl. engr. Mem. Am. Soc. C.E., Water Pollution Control Fedn., Nat. Soc. Profl. Engrs., La. Engring. Soc., Ky.-Tenn. Operators Assn., Chi Epsilon. Mem. Ch. of Christ. Republican. Home: 5404 Shenandoah Dr Knoxville TN 37919 Office: Box 33 2015 Neyland Dr Knoxville TN 37901

LYNN, ROBERT DEWESE, headmaster; b. Brighton, Tenn., Oct. 20, 1913; s. Lucius Ross and Edith Lenora (DeWese) L.; A.B., Presbyn. Coll., 1934; M.S. in Social Work, Coll. William and Mary, 1935; M.A., Memphis State U., 1961, Ed.D., 1968; m. Evelyn McDowell, June 28, 1941; children—Sara Frances, Robert DeWese, Elizabeth Jane. Athletic dir. Dublin (Ga.) High Sch., 1935-36; engaged in business, Clinton, S.C., 1937-38; asst. to pres. Thornwell Orphanage, Clinton, 1938-40; auto salesman, Laurens, S.C., 1941-43; instr. econs. Presbyn. Coll., Clinton, S.C., 1943-45; field sec. Pi Kappa Alpha frat., Atlanta, 1945-46, exec. sec., Memphis, 1946-59; headmaster The Hutchison Sch., Memphis, 1959—. Adminstr. Nat. chpt. House Loan Fund; exec. v.p. Pi Kappa Alpha Meml. Found., 1948-59, chmn. scholarship com., 1960—. Mem. Coll. Frat. Secs. Assn. (pres.), Coll. Frat. Editors Assn. (pres.), Memphis Assn. Ind. Schs. (pres.), Nat. Assn. Prins. Schs. for Girls, Nat. Interfrat. Conf. (exec. com. 1962—, pres. 1970—), So. (exec. com. 1963—, pres. 1965-66), Mid-South (pres. 1969-70, exec. com. 1965—) assns. ind. schs., Am. Assn. Sch. Adminstrs., Newcomen Soc. N.Am., English Speaking Union, Blue Key. Presbyn. (elder; lectr. Men's Bible Class). Clubs: University, Executive. Editor Shield and Diamond mag., 1949—. Home: 1738 Ridgeway Rd Memphis TN 38138 Office: 1740 Ridgeway Rd Memphis TN 38138

LYNN, ROSS MCCAIN, headmaster; b. Jacksonville, Fla., Apr. 1, 1911; s. Lucius Ross and Edith (DeWese) L.; A.B., Presbyn. Coll., 1931, LL.D., 1952; M.A., U. N.C., 1948; m. Halcyon Roach, July 20, 1960; stepsons—Richard Charlton Moore, Jr., Thurston Roach Moore. Tchr., coach Dublin (Ga.) High Sch., 1931-32; tchr., coach Darlington Sch., Rome, Ga., 1932-41, tchr., dean, 1946-51; headmaster Presbyn. Day Sch., Memphis, 1951-55, Memphis U. Sch., 1955—. Trustee William R. Moore Sch.; bd. dirs. Ednl. Records Bur.; sec. bd. Memphis U. Sch. Served from 2d lt. to lt. col. USAAF, 1942-46. Decorated Bronze Star. Mem. Memphis, So., Mid-South assns. ind. schs., Tenn. Edn. Assn., N.E.A., Nat. Assn. Secondary Sch. Prins., Nat. Assn. Ind. Schs. (dir.), Country Day Sch. Headmasters Assn., Mil. Order World Wars, Am. Legion, Blue Key, Pi Kappa Alpha. Presbyn. (elder). Clubs: University, Memphis Country (Memphis). Home: 1288 Ridgeway Rd Memphis TN 38138 Office: 6191 Park Rd Memphis TN 38138

LYNN, SHERWOOD CHANG, physician; b. Anju, Korea, Oct. 4, 1904 (came to U.S. 1921, naturalized 1954); s. Dong Shang and En Sang (Park) C.; B.A., U. Dubuque (Ia.), 1930; M.D., Emory U., 1935; m. Martha Owen Hood, Aug. 25, 1931 (dec. Aug. 1970); children—Jennie (Mrs. John Watts Jamison), Mary (Mrs. Laurence George Jenewein), Sherwood Chang, Leigh (Mrs. Jimmie Edward McClendon). Intern Quincy (Mass.) City Hosp., 1936; resident Norfolk County Hosp., South Braintree, Mass., practice medicine, specializing in family practice, Savannah, Ga., 1939-55, Houston, 1957—. Hon. pres. Korean-Am. Friendship Assn. Houston, 1961-70, pres., 1970—; chmn. bd. Korea-Am. Edn. Found., Houston; pres. Korean Sunday Sch., South Main Baptist Ch., Houston, 1969—; hon. pres. officers Korea Community Ch., Houston, 1973—; bd. dirs. Korea Tex. Trade Promotion Council, 1973—. Mem. A.M.A., Tex. Med. Assn. Presbyn. Mem. Slavonic Benevolent Order State Tex. (supreme lodge). Home: 4502 University Oaks Blvd Houston TX 77004 Office: 1520 Capitol Av Houston TX 77002

LYNN, WILLIAM SANFORD, JR., physician, educator; b. Clarendon, Va., June 14, 1922; s. William Sanford and Lois (Law) L.; M.D., Columbia, 1946; m. Mary E. Gilbert, Nov. 29, 1947; children—David, Peter, Melanie, Leslie. Intern Duke, 1948, resident, 1949-52, mem. faculty, 1952—, prof. medicine and biochemistry, 1965—. Served with AUS, 1942-46. Markle scholar, 1955-60. Democrat. Baptist. Contbr. articles to sci. lit. Home: Route 1 Hillsborough NC 27278

LYNN, WOODROW LAWRENCE, design engr.; b. Tampa, Fla., Mar. 7, 1914; s. Swettzy Eugene and Ethel Jane (McCain) L.; B.S. in Civil Engring., U. Fla., 1935; m. Ina Margaret Robinson, Apr. 19, 1941; children—Marsha Anne, Lawrence W. Jr. engr. U.S. Navy, Pensacola, Fla., 1935-37, Am. Bridge Co., Ambridge, Pa., 1937-38, Fla. State Bridge Dept., Tallahassee, 1938-39; with U.S. Navy, Pensacola, 1946—, head, engring. dept., 1947—. Vice chmn. Pensacola chpt. A.R.C., 1965—; chmn. City Planning Bd., 1967-73; mem. adv. com. Engring. Coll., U. Fla., 1960—. Served to lt. col. AUS, 1941-46; col. Res. ret. Decorated Legion of Merit, Bronze Star medal; recipient Distinguished Service award Nat. Health Agys., 1970. Mem. Nat. Soc. Profl. Engrs., Fla. Engring. Soc. (pres. chpt., state bd. dirs.), Res. Officers Soc. (pres. chpt.), Phi Delta Theta. Home: 604 W Blount St Pensacola FL 32501 Office: Navy Pub Works Center Pensacola FL 32508

LYNSKEY, WILLIAM WALLACE, corp. exec.; b. Huntsville, Ala., Jan. 20, 1927; s. Randall William and Katherine (Drake) L.; student U. Chattanooga, 1946-47, Ga. Inst. Tech., 1948-49; m. Ruby Thompson, Mar. 14, 1956; children—Mark Edward, William David, Theresa Anne, Christopher Paul, Timothy Joseph. Teller, The Hamilton Nat. Bank, Chattanooga, 1950; salesman Vance Iron & Steel Co., 1951; purchasing agt. Chattanooga Boiler & Tank Co., 1952-67; pres. Threadco, Inc., 1962—, Tenn. Machine Works, 1967—. Served with USNR, 1945-46. Mem. Nat. Rifle Assn., Pi Kappa Alpha. Roman Catholic. Clubs: Chattanooga Yacht, Loret Yacht (dir.) (Chattanooga). Home: 6400 Bayshore Dr Harrison TN 37341 Office: Latta St PO Box 8035 Chattanooga TN 37411

LYON, HENRY LOUIS, JR., clergyman; b. Tuscaloosa, Ala., Aug. 1, 1907; s. Henry L. and Dorothy (Lucius) L.; A.B., Samford U., 1930, D.D. (hon.), 1948; Th.M., So. Bapt. Theol. Sem., 1932; LL.D., U. Ala., 1964; m. Louise Jackson, Dec. 23, 1929; 1 son, Henry Louis III. Ordained to ministry Bapt. Ch., 1929; pastor Powderly Bapt. Ch., Birmingham, Ala., 1932-38, 66th St. Bapt. Ch., Birmingham, 1938-43; pres. Highland Av. Bapt. Ch., Montgomery, Ala., 1946-73, pastor emeritus, 1973—; chaplain Jackson Meml. Hosp., Montgomery, 1974—. Pres., Ala. Bapt. Conv., 1955-56; mem. home bd. missions So. Bapt. Conv., 1950-56, mem. relief and annuity bd., 1963-69. Mem. Ala. Textbook Com., 1966-71. Bd. dirs. Montgomery Bapt. Hosp. Served to capt. USAAF, 1943-46. Recipient Cross of Mil. Service U.D.C., 1959. Mem. S.C.V., S.A.R., Kappa Phi Kappa. Mason (32 deg., K.T., Shriner). Club: Exchange (pres. 1954). Home: 2606 Oxford Dr Montgomery AL 36111 Office: 1931 Highland Av Montgomery AL 36111

LYON, JAMES FRANK, JR., bottling co. exec.; b. Little Rock, May 13, 1941; s. James Frank and Marion Rose (Bradley) L.; student Davidson Coll., 1959-61; B.A., U. Ark., 1963; M.B.A., Harvard, 1967. With Frank Lyon Co., Little Rock, 1967-69; chmn. bd., chief exec. officer Coca-Cola Bottling Co. Ark., Little Rock, 1969—. Dir. Frank Lyon Co., Twin City Bank, Interstate Hwy. Sign Co., Datamatics Services, Inc., Twin City Agy.; pres. Lyon Realty Co., Little Rock, 1968—. Exec. bd. Quapaw council Boy Scouts Am., 1968—, treas., 1970-71; bd. dirs. Goodwill Industries Ark., 1969—, 1st v.p., 1972-73, pres., 1974—; mem. adv. council Opportunities Industrialization Center, 1970—; trustee Hendrix Coll., Conway, Ark., 1970—, mem. finance com., 1970—; bd. dirs. Presbyn. Family and Child Service Agy., 1970—, Epilespy Found., 1972—, Ark. Red Cross, 1972—. Served with AUS, 1963-65. Decorated Army Commendation medal. Mem. C. of C., Young Presidents' Orgn., Ark. Soft Drink Assn. 1970—), Blue Key, Scabbard and Blade, Beta Gamma Sigma, Sigma Alpha Epsilon, Alpha Kappa Psi. Home: 5608 Hawthorne St Little Rock AR 72207 Office: 6901 Murray St Little Rock AR 72203

LYON, JOHN BLAKESLEE, JR., educator; b. Auburn, N.Y., Mar. 17, 1925; s. John Blakeslee and Margaretta Olive (Owen) L.; A.B., Hamilton Coll., 1950; M.Sc., Brown U., 1952, Ph.D., 1954; m. Elizabeth Anne Mack, June 12, 1948; children—Paul Douglas, Deborah Elizabeth. Life Ins. Med. Research fellow biochemistry Emory U., Atlanta, 1954-56, mem. faculty, 1956—, prof. biochemistry, 1970—. Served with USNR, 1943-46. Recipient Lederle Med. Faculty award, 1956-59, Career Devel. award NIH, 1959-69. Mem. Am. Assn. Biol. Chemists, A.A.A.S., Sigma Xi. Home: 8 Leeward Lane Flowery Branch GA 30542

LYON, THAYER CLAUDE, JR., dentist, army officer; b. Cairnbrook, Pa., Mar. 10, 1931; s. Thayer Claude and Ethel (Kennedy) L.; B.S., Bucknell U., 1952; D.D.S., U. Pitts., 1958; M.S., Georgetown U., 1967; m. Norma Ruth Morrison, June 14, 1958; children—Margaret Thayer, Holly Elizabeth. Research chem. technician Neville Chem. Co., Pitts., 1952-54; commd. 2d lt. U.S. Army, 1957, advanced through grades to lt. col., 1968; chief dept.

microbiology U.S. Army Inst. Dental Research, Walter Reed Army Med. Center, Washington, 1967—; cons. microbiology First U.S. Army, 1968—. Mem. Am. Dental Assn., Internat. Assn. Dental Research, Am. Soc. Microbiologists, N.Y. Acad. Sci., A.A.A.S., Delta Upsilon, Delta Sigma Delta, Phi Sigma. Home: 101 Bluff Terrace Silver Spring MD 20902 Office: US Army Inst of Dental Research Walter Reed Army Med Center Washington DC 20012

LYONS, DENNIS GERALD, lawyer; b. Passaic, N.J., Nov. 20, 1931; s. Denis A.G. and Agnes C. (Dyt) L.; A.B., Holy Cross Coll., 1952; J.D., Harvard, 1955; children—Andrew, Sarah, Tessa. Admitted to D.C. bar, 1955, N.Y. bar, 1956, U.S. Supreme Ct., 1960; law clk. to justice U.S. Supreme Ct., Washington, 1958-60; asso. Arnold & Porter, Washington, 1960-62, partner, 1963—. Vice pres., gen. counsel, dir. Gulf Life Holding Co., Jacksonville, Fla., 1968—; asst. sec. Braniff Airways, Dallas, 1966—; trustee Gulf Mortgage and Realty Investments, Boston. Served with USAF, 1955-58. Mem. Am. Law Inst., Am. Bar Assn. Pres., Harvard Law Rev., 1954-55. Home: 700 New Hampshire Av NW Washington DC 20037 Office: 1229 19th St NW Washington DC 20036

LYONS, PHILLIP MITCHELL, ins. exec., real estate broker; b. Gueydan, La., Nov. 22, 1941; s. Joseph Bosman and Elder (Richard) L.; student McNeese State Coll., 1959-62, Alvin Jr. Coll., 1964; m. Wynona Faye Meyers, Apr. 28, 1962; children—Phillip M., Wilton J. Adminstrv. trainee Am. Nat. Ins. Co., Galveston, Tex., 1965, asst. mgr., acting mgr. policy issue dept., 1966-67, mgr., 1967—, systems analyst, 1971-72, div. mgr., policyholders service div., 1972—; partner Lyons Real Estate, Sulphur, La., 1966—. Solicitor, United Fund, 1966-69. Mem. Jr. C. of C. (dir. 1972, state dir. 1972—, Sparkplug of Year 1972-73, Roadrunner of Year 1972-73). Elk. Club: Neuman. Home: 1602 Bayou Shore Galveston TX 77550 also 1012 S Stanford St Sulphur LA 70663 Office: 1 Moody Plaza Galveston TX 77550 also 1339 Cypress St Sulphur LA 70663

LYONS, THOMAS WILLIAM, clergyman; b. Washington, Sept. 26, 1923; s. Thomas William and Nora (Bagley) L.; student St. Charles Coll., 1937-43; A.B., St. Mary's Sem., Balt., 1945, S.T.B., 1946, postgrad. 1946-48. Ordained priest Roman Catholic Ch., 1948; served at St. John the Evangelist Ch., Silver Spring, Md., 1948-49, St. Matthew's Cathedral, Washington, 1949-53; dir. Mackin High Sch., Washington, 1953-57; asst. dir. edn. archdiocese Washington, 1954-64, dir., 1964-73, sec. for Christian edn., 1972—; pastor St. Francis de Sales Ch., Washington, 1963-66, St. Thomas Apostle Ch., Washington, 1966—. Chmn. Archdiocesan Commn. on Sacred Music, 1966-71. Mem. Nat. Cath. Ednl. Assn. (v.p. 1965-69), Assn. Cath. Sch. Supts. (chmn. 1968-70). Home: 2665 Woodley Rd NW Washington DC Office: 1200 17th St NW Washington 20036

LYSTAD, MARY HANEMANN (MRS. ROBERT LYSTAD), sociologist; b. New Orleans, Apr. 11, 1928; d. James and Mary (Douglass) Hanemann; A.B. cum laude, Newcomb Coll., 1949; M.A., Columbia, 1951; Ph.D., Tulane U., 1955; m. Robert Lystad, June 20, 1953; children—Lisa Douglass, Anne Hanemann, Mary Lunde, Robert Douglass, James Hanemann. Postdoctoral fellow social psychology S.E. La. Hosp., Mandeville, 1955-57; field research social psychology, Ghana, 1957-58, South Africa and Swaziland, 1968; chief sociologist Collaborative Child Devel. Project, Charity Hosp. La., New Orleans, 1958-61; cons. spl. operations research office Am. U., Washington, 1962; feature writer African div. Voice Am., Washington, 1964-73; program analyst Nat. Inst. Mental Health, Washington, 1968-72; spl. asst. to dir. div. spl. mental health programs Nat. Inst. Mental Health, 1973—. Cons. on youth Nat. Goals Research Staff, White House, Washington, 1969-70. Fellow Am. Sociol. Soc. Author: Millicent the Monster, 1968; Social Aspects of Alienation, 1969; Jennifer Takes Over P.S. 94, 1972; James the Jaguar, 1972; As They See It: Changing Values of College Youth, 1972; That New Boy, 1973; Halloween Parade, 1973; Violence at Home, 1974; A Child's World As Seen in His Stories and Drawings, 1974. Home: 4900 Scarsdale Rd Washington DC 20016 Office: 5600 Fishers Lane Rockville MD 20852

LYSTAD, ROBERT ARTHUR, educator; b. Milw., Aug. 10, 1920; s. Arthur Frederick and Lulu (Lunde) L.; B.A., U. Wis., 1941; B.D., Drew Theol. Sem., 1944; Ph.D., Northwestern U., 1951; m. Mary Agnes Hanemann, June 21, 1953; children—Lise Douglass, Anne Hanemann, Mary Lunde, Robert Douglass, James Hanemann. Ordained to ministry Meth. Ch., 1945; minister Meth. Chs., Columbus, O., 1944-47, also Millersport, O.; prof. anthropology Tulane U., New Orleans, 1951-61; prof. African studies, Sch. Advanced Internat. Studies, Johns Hopkins, Washington, 1961—. Author: The Ashanti: A Proud People, 1958; The African World: A Survey of Social Research, 1965. Home: 4900 Scarsdale Rd Washington DC 20016 Office: 1740 Massachusetts Av NW Washington DC 20036

LYTLE, ROY COBB, lawyer; b. Pitts., Oct. 18, 1902; s. Louis Edward and Emma Elizabeth (Cobb) L.; A.B., Cornell U., 1924; J.D., Harvard, 1927; m. Virginia Baugh, Oct. 12, 1927; children—Camilla (Mrs. Alex P. Aven), Margaret (Mrs. John A. Griner III); m. 2d, Joanne Harper, May 16, 1966. Admitted to Okla. bar, 1927, since practiced in Oklahoma City; mem. firm Lytle, Soule & Emery, 1927—; counsel Better Bus. Bur., 1930—; prof. emeritus Okla. U. Sch. Medicine. Chmn. bd. Va. Blue Ridge Ry., Lynchburg; dir. Swanson's Tire Co., Governair Corp. Past pres. Greater Oklahoma City United Appeal; mem. adv. com. St. Anthony Hosp. Mem. A.M.A. (affiliate), Okla. Med. Hall of Fame, Okla. Bar Assn., Am. Law Inst., Am. Judicature Soc., Phi Beta Kappa, Phi Kappa Phi, Alpha Tau Omega. Republican. Episcopalian. Mason (32 degree). Clubs: Oklahoma City Country, Beacon. Home: 6806 NW Grand Blvd Oklahoma City OK 73116 Office: 2210 First Nat Center Oklahoma City OK 73102

LYTTON, JACK LESTER, educator; b. Los Angeles, Aug. 4, 1933; s. Lester Charles and Charlotte (Starbuck) L.; B.S. in Mech. Engring. with honors, U. Cal. at Berkeley, 1956, M.S. in Engring. Sci., 1957; Ph.D. in Materials Sci., Stanford, 1962; m. Ruth Lovena Hutchinson, June 18, 1954; children—Lisa, Russell, Gary, Michael. Research scientist Lockheed Missiles & Space Co., Palo Alto, Cal., 1960-65; asso. prof. dept. metall. engring. Va. Poly. Ins. and State U., Blacksburg, 1965-71, prof., chmn. dept., 1971—. Served with USAF, 1957-59. Decorated Air Force Commendation medal. Mem. Am. Soc. Metals, Am. Inst. Mining, Metall. and Petroleum Engrs., Sigma Xi, Sigma Gamma Epsilon, Alpha Sigma Mu. Contbr. profl. jours. Home: 602 Forest Hill Dr Blacksburg VA 24060

MAAS, ROY WALTER, engring. co. exec.; b. Utica, Mich., Nov. 12, 1931; s. Walter C. and Eleanor (Pruehs) M.; B.C.E., Valparaiso U., 1955; M.S., U. Louisville, 1973; m. Barbara Jean Strombeck, June 4, 1955; children—David, Caron, Roger. Field engr. J. S. Watkins Cons. Engrs., Valparaiso, Ind., 1955-56, design engr., Lansing, Mich., 1958, Charleston, W.Va., 1958-62, Ind. Dept. Hwys., Indpls., 1962-63; v.p. Watkins & Assos. Inc., Cons. Engrs., Louisville, 1963—, dir., 1968—. Served to lt. USNR, 1956-57. Registered profl. engr., Ill., Ind., Ky., W.Va., Va. Mem. Am. Soc. C.E.'s, Nat. Soc. Profl. Engrs., Am. Road Bldrs. Assn., Cons. Engrs. Council Ky. (treas. 1973-74), Am. R.R. Engrs. Assn., Am. Water Works Assn., Ky., Louisville chambers commerce. Lutheran (pres. ch. council 1970-71). Home: 9813 Longwood Circle Anchorage KY 40223 Office: 834 E Broadway Louisville KY 40204

MABRY, ARMON ERCELL, architect; b. Roanoke, Va., Dec. 19, 1899; s. James David and Ida Lee (Brown) M.; B.S. in C.E., U. Wis., 1923; Ecole Nationale Superieure des Beaux Arts de Paris, 1926-31; Diplome De Paris, 1931; m. Wally Bergliot Fredriksen, June 18, 1927; 1 dau., Mary Jacqueline; m. 2d, Irene Hester Majors, Feb. 16, 1948. Draftsman, Holabird & Root, Chgo., 1924-25; pvt. practice architecture, Houston, 1931—. Asst. prof. archtl. engring. U. Fla., Gainesville, 1948-49; vis. prof. U. Tex., Austin, 1950-52. Served with USNR, 1918-19. Recipient Am. Field fellowship, 1930. Mem. Sigma Phi. Works include Austin Co., Freeport, Tex., 1941-43, Loomis Co., Nederland, Tex., 1943-45. Address: 5058 Navarro Lane Apt C Houston TX 77027

MABRY, CHARLES EDWARD, JR., agr. exec.; b. Talala, Okla., June 4, 1920; s. Charles Edward and Janie Ann (Strange) M.; B.S. in Agr., Okla. State U., 1941, M.S., 1946; m. Doris Lorene Meggs, Aug. 8, 1942; children—Merle Charlene (Mrs. John Neumeier), Charles E., John W. Supr. vets. agrl. tng. Stillwater (Okla.) High Sch., 1946-47; asst. dir. in charge U. Ark. Livestock and Forestry Expt. Sta., Batesville, 1947—. Owner, operator Mabry Farm, 1950—, Rogers Co., 1950—. Vice chmn. No. Ark. Conf. Bd. Edn., 1970-71, mem., 1965—. Bd. dirs. Independence County Fair, 1948—. Served to capt. AUS, 1941-45; ETO. Decorated Bronze Star. Recipient Service award U. Ark., 1967; Diamond Clover award 4-H, 1970. Mem. Ark. Hampshire Swine Breeders Assn. (pres. 1968-73; a founder 1954), Batesville Livestock Marketing Assn. (organizer 1957, pres. 1957-60). Methodist (lay leader 1970-72, lay del. 1972-73). Kiwanian (chmn. com. 1947-62). Inventor portable hay conveyor, cattle gate. Address: Route 4 Box 166 Batesville AR 72501

MABRY, NELLOISE JOHNSON, educator; b. Valdosta, Ga., Sept. 8, 1921; d. Hansford Duncan and Maudelle (Williams) Johnson; student Bethel Woman's Coll., 1938-39, Wesleyan Conservatory, 1941; A.B., Mercer U., 1943, M.Ed., 1949; m. William Herbert Mabry, Mar. 5, 1942 (div. Nov. 1947); 1 son, William Herbert. Tchr., Cynthia H. Weir Elementary Sch., Macon, Ga., 1950—. Mem. Nat., Ga., Bibb edn. assns., Ga. Assn. for Childhood Edn. (pres. 1964-66), Delta Kappa Gamma (chpt. scrapbook chmn. 1966-68), Am. Assn. U. Women, Alpha Delta Pi, Alpha Psi Omega. Democrat. Baptist. Home: 1575 Adams St Macon GA 31204

MACALUSO, CHARLES ANTHONY, environmental products co. exec.; b. Paterson, N.J., Sept. 1, 1928; s. Vincent J. and Virginia (Pasqualletti) M.; M.E., Stevens Inst. Tech., 1950, M.S., 1958; m. Arlene DeYoung, Jan. 26, 1952; children—Steven C., Nancy L., Marc D. Chief engr. Worthington Corp., capital goods machinery products, Harrison, N.J., 1950-63; mgr. advanced product planning, Buffalo, N.Y., 1963-68; v.p. corporate devel. Ecological Sci. Corp., environmental products and services, Miami, Fla., 1969—; pres., chief exec. officer Dyna Technology, Inc., 1972—; dir. Adache Assos., Inc., Cleve., Dyna Tech., Inc., Sioux City, Ia. Dir., sec. Episcopal Charities of Western N.Y., 1966-68. Served with Ordnance Corps, AUS, 1951-53. Registered profl. engr., N.J., Fla. Mem. Am. Soc. M.E. (bd. chmn. Turbomachinery Inst. 1970—), Tau Beta Pi. Episcopalian (lay reader 1960-68). Patentee in field. Home: 7450 N W 7th Court Plantation FL 33317 Office: 20215 NW 2d Av Miami FL 33169

MACARTHUR, ALLEN GRANT, banker; b. Detroit, Aug. 2, 1939; s. Alexander Grant and Corrinne Ann (Mellon) MacA.; student Provincial Inst. Mining, 1955-57; A.A., St. Petersburg Jr. Coll., 1962; B.S. in Bus. Adminstrn., Fla. State U., 1965; m. Mary Paula Karlavage, Nov. 29, 1969; children—Allen Joseph, Ann Marie, John Allen. Nat. bank examiner Tallahassee, Fla., 1965-68; exec. v.p. Southeast Nat. Bank, Dunedin, Fla., 1968, pres., 1968—; dir. Plasti-Craft Corp., Dunedin, Fla. Bd. dirs. Anclote Psychiat. Centre, Tarpon Springs, Fla. Mem. Dunedin C. of C. (dir. 1971—), Delta Sigma Pi. Presbyn. Home: 2307 Jones Ct Dunedin FL 33528 Office: 2494 Bayshore Blvd Dunedin FL 33528

MACARTHUR, DIANA TAYLOR, public affairs cons.; b. Santa Fe, July 7, 1933; d. Antonio J. and Elizabeth (Steele) Taylor; B.A., Vassar Coll., 1955; student U. Geneva, 1953-54; children by previous marriage—Elizabeth Tschursin, Alexander Tschursin; m. 2d, Donald Malcolm MacArthur, Mar. 31, 1962. Cons. economist Checchi & Co., Washington, 1957-61; v.p., dir. Washington office Thomas J. Deegan Co., 1961-62; dep. chief West Africa, Peace Corps, 1963, regional program officer North Africa, Near East, South Asia, 1964, dir. div. pvt. and internat. orgns., 1965-66; coordinator Nat. Youth Conf. on Natural Beauty and Conservation, 1966-68; self-employed cons. pub. affairs to corps., assns., Washington, 1968—. Mem. citizens adv. bd. Pres.'s Council on Youth Opportunity, 1968-69. Bd. dirs. Washington area Council Alcohol and Drug Abuse, 1973—, chmn., 1974—; trustee Menninger Found., 1972—. Mem. Phi Beta Kappa. Home: 5313 Albemarle St NW Washington DC 20016

MACARTHUR, DONALD MALCOLM, corp. exec.; b. Detroit, Jan. 7, 1931; s. Donald J. and Margaret (MacAuley) MacA.; B.Sc. with honors, St. Andrews (Scotland) U., 1954; Ph.D., Edinburgh (Scotland) U., 1957; m. Diana Taylor, Mar. 31, 1962; children—Elizabeth, Alexander. Mem. faculty U. Conn., 1957-58; mgr. research center Malpar Inc., subsidiary Westinghouse Air Brake Co., 1958-66; dep. dir. research and tech. Office Sec. Def., 1966-70; pres. Enviro Control, Inc., Washington, 1970—; dir. Module Systems and Devel., Inc., Diversition, Inc., Enviro Control, Inc.; cons. water pollution Dept. Interior, Dept. Def. Fellow Am. Inst. Chemists; mem. Am. Chem. Soc., A.A.A.S., Am. Water Works Assn., N.Y. Acad. Scis. Contbr. articles to tech. jours. Home: 5313 Albemarle St Washington DC 20016 Office: 960 Thompson Av Rockville MD 20852

MACAULAY, ANGUS HAMILTON, lawyer; b. Spartanburg, S.C., Apr. 1, 1928; s. Angus H. and Margaret (White) M.; A.B., The Citadel, 1950; LL.B., Yale, 1955; m. Amanda C. Tevepaugh, May 12, 1962; children—Angus H., Alexander M., Katherine. Admitted to S.C. bar, 1955, Va. bar, 1956, since practiced in Richmond, Va.; mem. firm Mays, Valentine, Davenport & Moore, 1961—. Dir. Colonial Life & Accident Ins. Co., Columbia, S.C. Mem. Richmond Air Pollution Control Bd., 1965—; pres. Richmond Community Action Program, 1969-70. Mem. Richmond 3d Dist. and State Central Democratic Coms. Trustee Richmond Forward, 1965-70; bd. dirs. United Givers Fund, 1969-72, Maymont Found. (v.p. 1973—). Served with AUS, 1946-47, to 1st lt., 1951-53. Mem. Am. (exec. council jr. bar conf. 1960-62), Va. (chmn. young lawyers sect. 1959-60, chmn. joint com. pub. information 1966-68), Richmond bar assns. Presbyn. Kiwanian. Club: Downtown (Richmond). Home: 502 Henri Rd Richmond VA 23226 Office: Ross Bldg Richmond VA 23219

MACBRIDE, DEXTER DUPONT, assn. exec.; b. Elizabeth, N.J., Aug. 18, 1917; s. Charles Munnerlyn and Flora T. (Jerome) MacB.; student William & Mary Coll., 1936-37; LL.B., Cumberland U., 1938; J.D., Samford U., 1970; m. Grace Anderson, Dec. 23, 1963; 1 son, Charles Dexter. Admitted to Va. bar, 1939; practiced in Norfolk, 1939-41; sr. right of way agt. City of Los Angeles, 1946-47; supervising right of way agt. State of Cal., Sacramento, 1948-63, asst. chief right of way agt., 1963-70; exec. v.p. Am. Soc. Appraisers, Washington, 1970—. Dir. Nat. Valutape Program ASA. Mem. Am. Right of Way Assn. (nat. sec.; exec. com., sr. mem.), Am. Arbitration Assn. (nat. panel arbitrators), Audubon Soc., Am. Soc. Assn. Execs., Am. Soc. Appraisers. Author: Power and Process. Editor: Valuation Quar.; The Bibliography of Appraisal Literature, 1974. Home: 11457 Washington Plaza W Reston VA 22070 Office: Dulles Internat Airport PO Box 17265 Washington DC 20041

MACCONNELL, JOHN GRIFFITH, chemist; b. Chgo., Oct. 14, 1942; s. Norman Darrell and Daisy (Whitehead) MacC.; B.S., U. Ill., 1964; M.S., U. Mich., 1968, Ph.D., 1969. Chemist, Staley's, Inc., Decatur, Ill., 1963, Velsicol Chem. Co., Chgo., 1964-65; teaching fellow dept. chemistry U. Mich., 1965-67; research asso. Coll. Forestry, Syracuse, N.Y., 1970-72; research asso., dept. entomology U. Ga., Athens, 1969-70, 72-73; asst. prof. chemistry Dalton (Ga.) Jr. Coll., 1973-74; research asso. depts. chemistry and psychiatry Emory U., Atlanta, 1974—. Recipient honored student award Am. Oil Chemists' Soc., 1968. Mem. Internat. Soc. Toxicology, A.A.A.S., Am. Chem. Soc., Chem. Soc. (London), Common Cause, Consumers Union, Council for a Livable World. Home: 986 Greenwood Av NE Atlanta GA 30309

MACDONALD, CLAUDE RUSSELL, clergyman; b. Paw Paw, W.Va., May 31, 1913; s. George Cleveland and Nannie Pearl (Alderton) MacD.; B.A., Transylvania Coll., 1947; B.D., Lexington Theol. Sem., 1950; m. Thelma Virginia Reckley, May 18, 1941; children—John R., Nancy Ann (Mrs. Bobby C. Long). Tax accountant Kelly-Springfield Tire Co., Cumberland, Md., 1934-44; ordained to ministry Christian Ch., 1947; pastor in Petersburg, Ky., 1944-49, Pfraftown, N.C., 1950-56, Strasburg, Va., 1956-62, Erlanger, Ky., 1962-65, Williamston, N.C., 1965—. Del., World Student Christian Fedn., Netherlands, 1948; past mem. bd. Christian Ch. in N.C.; chmn. Citizens Adv. Com. Williamston, 1970-71. Trustee Atlantic Christian Coll., Wilson, N.C. Named Rural Minister of Yr. in N.C., Prog. Farmer mag. and Candler Sch. Theology, 1955. Mem. N.C. Christian Ministers Assn. (pres. 1955, 66). Home: 105 E Liberty St Williamston NC 27892 Office: First Christian Ch Williamston NC 27982

MACDONALD, L(ELAND) LLOYD, lawyer; b. Marfa, Tex., July 19, 1931; s. John E. and Myrtle (Barnett) MacD.; B.B.A., Baylor U., 1952, LL.B., 1957; m. Juanice Koen, Nov. 22, 1958; children—David Allen, Kathryn Ann. Tchr. pub. sch., San Antonio, 1954-55; admitted to Tex. bar, 1957; title analyst Shell Oil Co., Midland, Tex., 1957-60; practiced law, Midland, 1960—; mem. firm L.L. MacDonald, 1960-64, Kerr, Fitz-Gerald & Kerr, 1964-74, Turpin, Smith, Dyer, Harmon & Dawson, 1973—. Mem. youth council YMCA, 1963-64; chmn. adv. bd. Salvation Army, 1969-72; bd. dirs. United Fund, 1973—. Served to 1st lt. 1952-54. Mem. Midland County Bar Assn. (v.p. 1964), State Bar Tex., Baylor Law Alumni Assn. (dir. 1967-69). Baptist. Mason, Rotarian. Home: 1515 Community Lane Midland TX 79701 Office: First Nat Bank Bldg Midland TX 79701

MACDONALD, RODERICK, JR., ophthalmologist, educator; b. Charleston, S.C., Oct. 16, 1926; s. Roderick and Ada Jean (Cunningham) M.; B.S. in Chemistry and Biology, Davidson Coll., 1947; M.D., Med. Coll. S.C., 1950; postgrad. basic sci. course in ophthalmology Tulane U. Postgrad. Sch. Medicine, 1950-52; m. Helen Rosemary Codington, Dec. 22, 1951; children—Roderick III, Anne C., Alexandra C., Elizabeth G., Margaret C. Rotating intern Balt. City Hosps., 1950-51; resident in ophthalmology New Orleans Eye, Ear, Nose and Throat Hosp., 1952-53, 55-56; asst. in ophthalmology Tulane U. Sch. Medicine, New Orleans, 1952-53, 55-56, instr., 1956-57; asst. prof. ophthalmology U. Louisville Sch. Medicine, 1957-61, asso. prof., 1961-65, prof., 1965-73, exec. dir. sect. ophthalmology, 1957-65, chmn. dept., 1965-73, asso. in pharmacology, 1969-73, asso. dean for clin. affairs, 1969-70, vice dean Sch. Medicine, 1970-72; prof. ophthalmology, chmn. dept. Med. Coll. Va., Richmond, 1973—; chief ophthalmology Med. Coll. Va. Hosps., 1973—, McGuire VA Hosp., Richmond, 1974—; active staff Richmond Eye Hosp.; med. dir. Ky. Lion's Eye Found. Eye Bank, Louisville, 1958-73. Cons. in ophthalmology Ky. Dept. Health, 1960-67, Leroy Stevens Sch. for Handicapped Children, Louisville, 1960-73; mem. Gov.'s Commn. for Ky. Blind Sch., 1961; mem. vision research tng. com. NIH, 1968-72. Bd. dirs. Ky. Soc. for Prevention Blindness, Old Dominion Eye Bank and Research, Richmond; chmn. bd. trustees Clin. Services Assn. U. Louisville. Served as 1st lt. M.C., AUS, 1953-55. Diplomate Am. Bd. Ophthalmology (asso. examiner 1968-70). Mem. A.C.S., A.M.A. (program com. sect. ophthalmology 1972), Ky. Med. Assn., Jefferson County Med. Soc., Am. Acad. Ophthalmology and Otolaryngology, A.A.A.S., Assn. for Research in Ophthalmology, Am. Ophthal. Soc., Contact Lens Assn. Ophthalmologists (dir.), Internat. Assn. Secs. Ophthalmology and Otolaryngol. Socs., Pan Am. Assn. Ophthalmology, Midwestern, So. ophthalmic pathology socs., Richmond Acad. Medicine, Louisville, New Orleans acads. ophthalmology, Richmond Eye, Ear, Nose and Throat Soc., Ophthalmic Microbiology and Immunology Group, Royal Soc. Health, Med. Soc. Va., Va. Ophthal. and Otolaryn. Soc., Louisville Eye and Ear Soc. (pres. 1962-63), Ky. Eye, Ear, Nose and Throat Soc., Medico-Chirurg. Soc., Innominate Soc. for Study Med. History, St. Andrews Soc. of Williamsburg, S.A.R., Medieval Acad. Am., Sigma Xi, Alpha Kappa Kappa, Beta Theta Pi. Presbyn. (elder). Contbr. articles to med. jours. Home: 8 Berkshire Dr Richmond VA 23229 Office: Box 262 MCV Station Richmond VA 23298

MACDONALD, THOMAS COOK, JR., lawyer; b. Atlanta, Oct. 11, 1929; s. Thomas Cook and Mary (Morgan) MacD.; B.S., U. Fla., 1951, LL.B., 1953; m. Gay Anne Everiss, June 30, 1956; children—Margaret Anne, Thomas William. Admitted to Fla. bar, 1953; practiced in Tampa, 1953—; mem. firm Shackleford, Farrior, Stallings & Evans, 1953—. Legislative counsel Gov. of Fla., 1963. Mem. Fla. Student Scholarship and Loan Commn., 1963-67, Hillsborough County Pub. Edn. Study Commn., 1965. Bd. dirs. Univ. Community Hosp. Served to 1st lt. Judge Adv. Gen. Corp., USAF, 1953-55. Mem. Am. Law Inst., Am. Bar Assn. (com. on ethics and profl. responsibility 1972—), Fla. Bar (mem. com. on profl. ethics 1964-72, chmn. 1966-70, bd. govs. 1970-74), Fla. W. Coast Sports Assn. (sec. 1965—), Gasparilla Krewe, U. Fla. Alumni Assn. (pres. 1973), Phi Kappa Phi, Phi Delta Phi, Fla. Blue Key, Kappa Alpha. Episcopalian. Home: 1904 Holly Lane Tampa FL 33609 Office: PO Box 3324 Tampa FL 33601

MACDONALD, WARREN HARDING, govt. ofcl.; b. Prince William County, Va., Mar. 31, 1921; s. George H. and Esther (Stiles) MacD.; student George Washington U., 1939-41, postgrad. 1970-71; B.S. in Social Sci. with distinction, Am. U., 1955, postgrad. 1955-56; m. Martina H. Connors, Jan. 10, 1944. Accredited rep. Vet.'s Claims and Appeals, Am. Legion, Washington, 1945-51, supr. appeals sect. Nat. Rehab. div., 1951-55, research analyst, 1955-59, dep. dir. Nat. Rehab. Com., 1959-61, dir. research and fgn. relations, 1961-69; spl. asst. to adminstr. vets. VA, 1969—. Served with USAAF, 1943-45. Decorated Air medal. Mem. Am. Legion. Republican. Author numerous research reports for Am. Legion. Home: 4619 Edgefield Rd Bethesda MD 20014 Office: 810 Vermont Av NW Washington DC 20240

MACDORMAN, LITTLETON CORBIN, transp. and mgmt. cons.; b. Chgo., Dec. 1, 1930; s. George Edwin and Hilda Villars (Corbin) MacD.; B.S. in Civil Engring., U. Md., 1952; M.Civil Engring., Cath. U. Am., 1967; m. Dorothy Janice Fisher, Feb. 17, 1956; children—John, James, Susan. With Whitman, Requardt & Assos., cons. engrs., Balt., 1953-58, Buchard-Horn, cons. engrs., York, Pa., 1958-63; hwy. research engr. D.C. Govt., 1963-66; prin. project engr. Traffic Research Corp., Washington, 1966; transp. and mgmt. cons. Peat, Marwick, Mitchell & Co., Washington, 1967—, prin. firm, 1968—. Served with USAF, 1952-53. Registered profl. engr., Ariz., D.C., Fla., Ga., Md., N.C., N.Y., Pa., Tenn., Va., W.Va. Mem. Am. Soc. C.E., Nat. Soc. Profl. Engrs., Inst. Traffic Engrs., Hwy. Research Bd., Am. Soc. Planning Ofcls. Contbr. to profl. jours. Home: 4808 N 29th St Arlington VA 22207 Office: 1025 Connecticut Av NW Washington DC 20036

MACDOUGALL, ROBERT DOUGLAS, geologist; b. McVille, N.D., Jan. 2, 1922; s. Rollo Dixon and Nettie Corinne (Syvertson) MacD.; student N.D. State Sch. Sci., 1939-41, U. N.D., 1946-47; B.A., U. Mont., 1949; M.S., U. Minn., 1952; m. Ingrid Margarete Heemann, Sept. 30, 1961; children—Jerome W., James F. Surface geologist Arabian Am. Oil Co., Saudi Arabia, 1952-56, subsurface geologist, 1956-59; cons. geologist, N.D. and Mont., 1959-62; geologist U.S. Geol. Survey, Washington, 1962-70, Metairie, La., 1970—. Served with USNR, 1941-45. Fellow Royal Geog. Soc.; mem. Am. Assn. Petroleum Geologists, New Orleans Geol. Soc. Home: 646 Oak St Mandeville LA 70448 Office: US Geol Survey Gulf of Mexico Area 3301 N Causeway Blvd PO Box 7944 Metairie LA 70011

MACEK, HELEN DOROTHY, banker; b. Damon, Tex., July 28, 1931; d. Otto and Ella (Lacina) Macek; student Southwestern Bus. U., 1948, U. Houston, 1950, 63, 64, 65, Am. Inst. Banking, 1964, 67, 68, 69. With Alltex Mortgage Co., Inc., Houston, 1949-63, asst. sec., 1959-63; with Med. Center Bank, Houston, 1963—, asst. cashier, 1963-73, asst. v.p., 1973—. Mem. Nat. Assn. Bank Women, Slavonic Benevolent Order State of Tex., Phi Eta. Presbyn. Home: 2004 Southgate Blvd Houston TX 77025 Office: 6900 Fannin St Houston TX 77025

MACFARLAND, ALFRED T., govt. ofcl., lawyer; b.Lebanon, Tenn., Apr. 23, 1917; B.A., U. Ala., 1940; J.D., Cumberland U., 1941. Admitted to Tenn. bar, 1942, U.S. Ct. Customs and Patent Appeals bar, 1948, U.S. Dist. Ct. bar, 1948, U.S. Tax Ct. bar, 1948, U.S. Ct. Appeals bar, 1949, U.S. Supreme Ct. bar, 1950, U.S. Ct. Mil. Appeals bar, 1953. Prof. law, Cumberland U., 1947-48; gen. counsel, R.R. and Pub. Utilities Commn., 1951-55; vice chmn. Interstate Commerce Commn., 1972—. Mem. Tenn. Ho. of Reps., 1945-47, Tenn. Senate, 1951-53; commnr. Revenue Dept. Tenn., 1959-61. Mem. Am., Tenn., Lebanon bar assns.; Barristers Club, Blue Key. Office: Interstate Commerce Commn Room 5211 12th and Constitution Av NW Washington DC 20423

MACFARLANE, IAN, mgmt. cons.; b. Chgo., Sept. 6, 1931; s. William and Helen Burns (Smith) MacF.; A.B., Princeton, 1953; M.B.A., Stanford, 1958; m. Dorothy Lee Carl, June 30, 1956; children—Jennifer Jeanne, Meredith Anne, Catherine Ella, David Bruce. Engaged in chem. sales and marketing Dow Chem. Co., Indpls., 1958-64; indsl. products mgr. Armour Agrl. Chem. Co., Atlanta, 1965-67; mng. prin. Fry Cons., Inc., Atlanta, 1967-72; pres. MacFarlane and Co., Inc., Avondale Estates, Ga., 1972—. Speaker before profl. groups; distinguished vis. lectr. marketing U. Ga. Sch. Bus., 1973—. Mem. Ga. Indsl. Devel. Council, 1970—; vice chmn. bus. unit United Way Greater Atlanta, 1971—. Served with USNR, 1953-56. Mem. Chem. Marketing Research Assn., Am. Marketing Assn. (past pres. Atlanta chpt.), Newcomen Soc., Princeton Club Ga. (schs. com. chmn.). Republican. Methodist (Sunday Sch. gen. supt., adult supt.). Club: Burns (pres.) (Atlanta). Home: 3 Berkeley Rd Avondale Estates GA 30002 Office: PO Box 657 Avondale Estates GA 30002

MACFARLANE, JOHN SYDNEY, electronics engr.; b. Shreveport, La., Jan. 27, 1923; s. John Wycliffe and Evelyn Frances (Wright) MacF.; student La. Poly. Coll., 1942; m. Sammie Joyce Hendley, Sept. 17, 1955; children—Farlane John, Bruce Duncan. With Booth Furniture Co., Shreveport, 1940-42; aircraft radio technician Barksdale AFB, La., 1944-45; traffic controller technician So. Signals Co., Shreveport, 1945-46; radio technician Electric Supply Co., Shreveport, 1946-49; service rep. Pitney-Bowes Mailing Machines, Shreveport, 1949-52; static test supr. Universal Match Corp., Karnack, Tex., 1952-54; TV technician Westinghouse Electric Co., Shreveport, 1954-56; constrn. supr., telecontrol Tex. Eastern Transmission, Shreveport, 1956-62; electronic technician Southwestern Electric Power Co., Shreveport, 1962-63; sr. technician Pennzoil Research Lab., Shreveport, 1963—. Cons. TV interference Shreveport Jour. Action Line. Vol. tchr. radio classes, 1965-67; theory instr. emergency communications A.R.C., 1964-66; emergency communications work Naval Res., 1968—; chmn. TV Interference Com., Shreveport-Bossier City, 1966—; counselor Boy Scouts Am., 1968—. Vol. worker Rep. polit. campaigns, 1964, 66-72. Served with Signal Corps, USAAF, 1942-44. Recipient pub. service award Amateur Radio Relay League, 1964, 65. Mem. I.E.E.E., Am. Chem. Soc., Amateur Radio Relay League (emergency coordinator 1961-64), Am. Legion. Democrat. Presbyn. (deacon 1956—). Elk. Clubs: Caravan Radio (pres. 1965-67). Inventor electronic traffic controller, 1946. Home: 175 Richard St Shreveport LA 71105 Office: 8015 St Vincent St Shreveport LA 71106

MACGREGOR, ALICIA AMORY DUPONT (MRS. GEORGE PURNELL MACGREGOR), bus. exec.; b. Wilmington, Del., Aug. 1, 1903; d. Alfred Irenee and Alicia (Bradford) duPont; pvt. edn.; m. Harold Sanford Glendening, June 27, 1922 (div.); 1 son, Alan Sanford; m. 2d, Frank Leslie Fraser, Oct. 11, 1947 (dec. 1962); m. 3d, George Purnell MacGregor, Mar. 29, 1965. Pres., Fla. Paper Converters, 1962-68; dir. Am. Nat. Bank, 1962-69. Pres. women's aux. St. Anthony Hosp., 1954-55; founder Queen of Hearts Ball, fund-raising event for Sun Coast Heart Assn., 1959. Recipient certificates of appreciation Am. Heart Assn., 1956, 57, 63, Silver medal, 1958, 59, Gold medal, 1960, 61; citation Nat. Assn. for Mental Health, 1962. Home: 700 Beach Dr NE St Petersburg FL 33701

MACGREGOR, GEORGE LESCHER, utilites exec.; b. Little Rock, Oct. 29, 1901; s. Arthur William and Irene (Lescher) MacG.; B.S., U. Tex., 1923; LL.D., Southwestern U.; m. Jean Edge, Dec. 7, 1929; children—Gregor Carmichael, George Lescher. Joined Dallas Power & Light Co., 1929, mgr., pres., 1940-53, chmn. bd., 1944-53, dir. until 1968; v.p., dir. Tex. Utilities Co., Dallas, 1945-53, pres., 1953-57, chmn. bd., 1967-72; chmn. Tech. Services, Inc., until 1967. Bd. dirs. State Fair Tex.; pres., trustee Southwestern Med. Found.; trustee, past pres. Tex. Research Found.; bd. dirs., chmn. Hobilitzele Found., Childrens Med. Center; past pres. Community Chest, Citizens Council. Recipient Distinguished Engring. Grad. award U. Tex., Dallas County Hosp. award, 1969. Registered profl. engr. Mem. Edison Electric Inst. (past dir.), Philos. Soc. Tex., Tex. State, Dallas hist. socs., Sons Republic Tex., Electric Club, Phi Gamma Delta, Episcopalian, Mason. Kiwanian. Clubs: Dallas Country, Brook Hollow Golf, The Dallas, City (Dallas); Recess (N.Y.C.). Home: 6322 Westchester Dr Dallas TX 75205 Office: 1506 Commerce St Dallas TX 75201

MACHEN, BILLY RAY, coll. adminstr.; b. Magnolia, Ark., July 2, 1933; s. Ray Lewis and Lessie May (Looney) M.; student So. State Coll., 1951-53; B.S., La. Tech. U., 1955; m. Dorothy Ann Hamilton, Apr. 7, 1955; children—Steven Ray, Billy Randall. Plant engr. So. Bell Telephone Co., Shreveport, La., 1955-56; elec. engr. Cal. Co., New Orleans, 1956-58; dist. engr. La. Power & Light Co., West Monroe, 1958-63; asst. to pres. So. State Coll., Magnolia, Ark., 1963—. Pres. Eastside Elementary P.T.A., Magnolia, 1965; sec., treas. Magnolia (Ark.) City Council of P.T.A.'s, 1966-67, pres. 1967-68; chmn. Magnolia (Ark.) Sewer Commn., 1969—. Alderman, City of Magnolia, Ark., 1965-66. Registered profl. engr., Ark., La. Mem. Nat. Soc. Profl. Engrs., Am. Soc. Heating, Refrigeration and Air Conditioning Engrs., Assn. Phys. Plant Adminstrs. Mason. Home: Box 1384 Magnolia AR 71753

MACIEL-AGUILAR, SERGIO ROMAN, educator, physician; b. Guadalajara, Mex., Oct. 18, 1933; s. Ramon Maciel-Marin and Maria Aguilar de Maciel; M.D., U. Guadalajara, 1957; m. Virginia Medina-Elizondo, Nov. 6, 1965; children—Cecilia, Sergio, Virginia. Resident in anesthesiology Sud-Pacifico Hosp., Guadalajara, Mex., 1958-59, State U. Ia. Hosps., Iowa City, 1961-63; intern Good Samaritan Hosp., Phoenix, 1959-60; asst. prof. anesthesiology Escuela de Medicine, U. Guadalajara, 1966—. Mem. Am. Soc. Anesthesiologists (affiliate), Associacion de Anestesiologos de Jalisco Soc. (sec. 1958-59, pres. 1973—), Football Club Asociacion Civil. Home: 2702 Bogota Frac Providencia Guadalajara Jal Mexico Office: U Guadalajara Guadalajara Mexico

MACINTYRE, A(LFONSO) EVERETTE, lawyer; b. nr. Burlington, N.C., Feb. 3, 1901; s. William Seymour and Ella Mary (Clark) MacI.; A.B., U. N.C., 1926; LL.B., George Washington U., 1929; m. Reita Jane Lyons, Aug. 20, 1930; 1 son, Miles Everette. Admitted to N.C. bar, 1929, Va. bar, 1938, D.C. bar, 1930, U.S. Supreme Ct., 1933; practiced in Washington, 1929—; mem. legal staff FTC, Washington 1930-55, chief antimonopoly trial staff, 1945-50, asst. dir. antimonopoly bur., 1950-55, chief div. investigation and litigation, 1950-54, adviser on antimonopoly, 1954-55, commr. FTC, 1961-73; mem. firm McKean, Whitehead & Wilson, Washington; staff dir., gen. counsel select com. on small bus. U.S. Ho. Reps., Washington, 1955-57, gen. counsel, 1957-61. Mem. Am., Fed. bar assns., Am. Acad. Polit. and Social Scis., Acad. Polit. Sci. (life), Nat. Lawyers Club. Home: 1564 Colonial Terrace Arlington VA 22209 Office: 888 17th St NW Washington DC 20006

MACIVER, PEGGE FARMER (MRS. DONALD GORDON MACIVER), monodramatist, educator; b. Colon, C.Z.; d. Alfred Gibson and Minnie (Cuckler) Farmer; B.A., Ohio U., 1935; B.L.L., Cin. Conservatory Music, 1938; M.A., George Washington U., 1964; m. Donald Gordon MacIver, June 7, 1957; 1 stepson, Neil. Monodramatist, lectr., writer touring U.S., Can. writing, performing own plays for one woman theatre presentations, 1938-59; speech therapist D.C. Pub. Schs., 1959-67, tchr. in-service tng. programs, program coordinator Ednl. Resources Center, 1967-70, asst. dir. Developmental Center for Spl. Edn., 1970-72, supervising dir. Div. Spl. Edn., 1972—; tchr. in-service tng. programs D.C. Tchrs. Coll. TV moderator, panelist Its Your World and World Headliner programs; mem. speakers burs., Dayton (O.) Council World Affairs, League Women Voters, 1950-57. Mem. Nat. League Am. Pen Women, Am., D.C. speech and hearing assns., N.E.A., D.C. Edn. Assn., Internat. Platform Assn., Phi Beta Kappa, Pi Beta Phi, Alpha Delta Kappa, Delta Kappa Gamma. Contbr. articles to profl. publs. Home: 8500 New Hampshire Av Silver Spring MD 20903 Office: DC Pub Schs Washington DC 20007

MACK, THEODORE, lawyer; b. Fort Worth, Tex., Mar. 5, 1936; s. Henry and Norma (Harris) M.; A.B. cum laude, Harvard, 1958, J.D., 1961; m. Ellen Feinknopf, June 19, 1960; children—Katherine Norma, Elizabeth Ellen, Alexandra. Admitted to Tex. bar, 1961, U.S. Supreme Ct. bar, 1971; asso. firm Mack & Mack, Fort Worth, 1961-62, partner, 1963-70; partner Wynn, Irby, Brown, McConnico & Mack, 1970—. Dir. So. Plow Co., Dallas, 1966—, v.p., 1968—. Bd. dirs. Jewish Fedn. Fort Worth, 1965-72, sec., 1967-68, 3d v.p., 1968-69; bd. dirs. Suicide Prevention of Tarrant County, Tex., 1963-64, Tarrant County Sr. Citizens Center, Inc., 1969—; trustee several pvt. trusts. Mem. Am., Fort Worth Tarrant County bar assns., State Bar Tex. (chmn. dist. grievance com. 1973), Harvard Alumni Assn., Harvard Law Sch. Assn., Harvard Law Sch. Assn. Tex. (dir. 1970-73, treas. 1973-74). Democrat. Jewish religion (dir. congregation 1964-73, sec. 1968-69, 72-73). Editor: Bar News of Fort Worth Tarrant County Bar Assn., 1963-64. Home: 2817 Harlanwood St Fort Worth TX 76109 Office: Schick Bldg Fort Worth TX 76102

MACK, WILBUR OLLIO, educator; b. Seward, Okla., Aug. 11, 1919; s. Colister L. and Addie Lee (Lowe) M.; B.S., Langston (Okla.) U., 1947; M.S., Okla. State U., 1954; m. Julia Mae Hobbs, May 19, 1945 (dec. Mar. 6, 1968); children—Ronald Wilbur, Waymond Ollio, Larry Wayne, Wilma Denise; m. 2d, Martha Margaret Mayo, Aug. 11, 1970. Tchr., Prairie View (Tex.) Coll., 1953-57, So. U., Baton Rouge, 1957-62; asst. prof. engring. Fla. A. and M. U., Tallahassee, 1962—. Served as 1st lt., AUS, 1941-45. Registered profl. engr., Tex., La. Mem. Am. Soc. Agrl. Engrs., Nat. Safety Council, Kappa Alpha Psi. Democrat. Baptist. Mason (32 deg.). Home: 710 Stafford St Tallahassee FL 32304

MACKAY, JAMES LESTER, psychologist; b. St. Louis, Sept. 23, 1891; s. James T. and Clara L. (Messmer) MacK.; B.S., U. Mo., 1920, M.A., 1924; Ph.D., N.Y. U., 1944; student U. Tex., summer 1956, Mills Coll., summer 1946; m. Mabel G. Crouch, Jan. 28, 1920; children—William Robert, Edward James. Sch. adminstrn., Philippine Islands, 1914-16; prin. Elias Michael sch. for Crippled Children, St. Louis, 1925-30, Carondelet Sch., 1930-37; Exptl. edn., St. Louis, 1920-46; chief VA Guidance Center, U. Ariz. at Tucson, 1946-48; dir. guidance South San Antonio (Tex.) Schs., 1949-59; practice of psychology, San Antonio, 1948—. Pres., Mental Health Assn. Bexar County, 1959; del. White House Conf. on Aging, 1971; chmn. San Antonio Inst. on Lifetime Learning; chmn. adv. bd. Alama area Adminstrn. on Aging. Served with inf. 1918. Mem. Acad. Religion and Mental Health, World Fedn. Mental Health, Am. Personnel & Guidance Assn., Nat. Vocation Guidance Assn., Am. Psychology Assn., Nat. Soc. Study Edn., Phi Delta Kappa. Episcopalian. Home: 3737 Fredericksburg Rd San Antonio TX 78201

MACKECHNIE, HORACE KNIGHT, elec. engr.; b. Somerville, Mass., Jan. 26, 1909; s. Arthur North and Marion Ardelle (Knight) MacK.; B.S., Mass. Inst. Tech., 1933; postgrad., Harvard, 1943, N.Y. U., 1942; m. Prudence Smith, Oct. 10, 1931; children—Margaret (Mrs. Richard Skillman), Joan North. Research asso. Harvard Radio Research Lab., 1942-46; lab. chief Air Materiel Command, Cambridge (Mass.) Field Sta., 1946-47, sr. engr. Mass. Inst. Tech., 1947; cons., mgr. various indsl. electronics cos., 1947-58; project mgr. Sylvania Elec. Products, Inc., Buffalo, N.Y., 1958-62; design rev. mgr. RCA, Camden, N.J., 1962-64; program mgr. Product Engring. Services Office, Dept. Def., Alexandria, Va., 1964—. Mem. Town Meeting, Lexington, Mass., 1956-57. Served with AUS Res., 1933-40. Registered profl. engr., Mass., Ohio. Mem. I.E.E.E. (sr.), Nat. Soc. Profl. Engrs., Soc. Am. Valve Engrs., Mason. Club: Mass. Institute of Technology (Washington). Patentee elec. blanket control, high current switch. Home: 8315 Bound Brook Lane Alexandria VA 22309 Office: Product Engring Services Office Dept Def Alexandria VA 22314

MACKEL, DONALD CHARLES, microbiologist; b. Madison, S.D., Nov. 29, 1927; s. Sylvester Charles and Elsie May (Zink) M.; B.S., U. Fla., 1950, M.S., 1951; M.P.H., Tulane U., 1965; m. Rose Rita Donahue, Sept. 11, 1952; children—James Charles, Anne Marie, Joan Marie. Microbiologist, Fla. Bd. Health, Jacksonville, 1950-51; chief bacteriologist Armed Forces Epidemiological Bd., Korea, 1951-52; commd. officer USPHS, 1952; chief microbiologist enteric investigations USPHS, Phoenix, also Atlanta, 1952-65, chief Hosp. Infections Labs., Atlanta 1966—, dep. chief Epidemiology Labs., 1973—. Cons. to state and local health depts.; tchr. hosp. personnel, 1965—. Treas., Civic Assn., 1971-72. Mem. Am. Soc. Microbiology, Sci. Research Soc. Am., Royal Soc. Health. Author: Manual Enteric Disease Studies, 1964. Contbr. articles to sci. publs. Home: 1742 Timothy Dr Atlanta GA 30329 Office: 1600 Clifton Rd NE Atlanta GA 30333

MACKENTHUN, KENNETH MARSH, aquatic biologist, govt. ofcl.; b. Bushong, Kan., May 15, 1919; s. William Henry and Cora (Marsh) M.; B.A., Coll. of Emporia, 1941; M.A., U. Ill., 1946; m. Dorothy I. Gebhardt, Feb. 28, 1942; 1 son, Kenneth M. Aquatic biologist Wis. Com. on Water Pollution, Madison, 1946-62, chief Aquatic Nuisance Control, 1949-62; chief biology and chem. sect. Environmental Protection Agy., Washington, 1962-69, dir. div. tech. support, 1969-72, dir. tech. support staff, 1972—. Served with AUS, 1942-45. Recipient Superior Performance award U.S. Dept. Interior, 1970. Mem. Midwest Benthological Soc. (pres. 1958), Fed. Water Quality Assn. (pres. 1973). Author: Water Pollution Control, Sewage Treatment, Water Treatment, 1963; Limnological Aspects of Recreational Lakes, 1964; Nitrogen and Phosphorus in Water, 1965; Biological Field Investigative Data for Water Pollution Surveys, 1966; Biology of Water Pollution, 1967; The Practice of Water Pollution Biology, 1969; Toward a Cleaner Aquatic Environment, 1973; also articles. Home: 2000 S Eads St Arlington VA 22202 Office: Environmental Protection Agency Washington DC 20460

MACKENZIE, JAMES DONALD, clergyman; b. Detroit, Nov. 17, 1924; s. James and Ida (Conklin) M.; student Moody Bible Inst., 1946-49, Union Theol. Sem., 1952; m. Elsie Joan Kerr, May 7, 1960; children—Janet Eileen, Kayly Kathleen, Christy Carol, Kenneth Kerr. Ordained to ministry Presbyn. Ch., 1953; pastor Calvary Ch., Swan Quarter, N.C., 1952-60, Kirkwood Ch., Kannapolis, N.C., 1960-64, Barbecue and Olivia Ch., Olivia, N.C., 1964-71, Elise Ch., Robbins, N.C., 1971—. Founder, Conf. on Celtic Studies, Campbell Coll., Buies Creek, N.C., 1972—; councillor Conf. on Scottish Studies (Can.), 1968—. Served with AUS, 1943-45; ETO. Decorated Purple Heart. Mem. N.C. Presbyn. Hist. Soc. (pres. 1972—, Author's award 1970), Harnett Hist. Soc. (pres. 1968-71, Distinguished Service award 1970), Irish Uilleann Pipers Osc., Gaelic Soc. of Inverness. Author: Colorful Heritage, 1970. Contbr. articles in field to profl. jours. Home: PO Box 867 Robbins NC 27325

MACKENZIE, ROLAND REDUS, realtor; b. Washington, Mar. 13, 1907; s. Albert Redus and Mary J. (Hummer) MacK.; grad. Brown U., 1929; m. Louise Parker Fownes, May 11, 1940; children—Clark Fownes, Margot Fownes. Rep. U.S. Walker Cup Golf Team, 1926, 28-30; with Dupont Laundry, Washington, 1930-32; golf profl. Colorado Springs Country Club (Colo.), Congl. Country Club, Washington, 1933-37; pres., dir. Shamrock Properties, Inc., Balt., 1938—, pres. Shamrock Realty Co., Greentree Realty Co., Towson, Md.; pres., dir. S.E. Airmotive, Charlotte, N.C., 1958—. Pres., dir. Big Pebble Assn., Pinehurst, N.C. Presbyn. Club: Foxfire Golf and Country (chmn. bd.) (Pinehurst, N.C.); Gulf Stream Golf (Del Ray Beach); Elkridge-Greenspring (Balt.). Home: McCaskill Rd Pinehurst NC 28374 also Shamrock Farm Cockeysville MD Office: MacKenzie Bldg Southern Pines NC 28387

MACKEY, BENJAMIN FRANK, judge; b. Atlanta, Dec. 1, 1904; s. James M. and Dora (Gaddy) M.; student pub. schs., Little Rock, Ark.; m. Maxie Walker, Feb. 12, 1928; children—Mary Frances (Mrs. Robert E. Phillips), B. Frank, Maxilee (Mrs. John J. Williams). Policeman, Little Rock, Ark., 1937-58; agt. 1st Pyramid Life Ins. Co., Little Rock, Ark., 1958-62; sheriff Pulaski County, Little Rock, Ark., 1963-68, county judge 1969—. Mem. Little Rock Sch. Bd., 1959-62. Mem. central bd., YMCA, 1963-65; mem. chmn. bd. Pulaski County March of Dimes, 1969—. Mem. Ark. Sheriffs Assn. (pres. 1968), Ark. Law Enforcement Assn. (1st v.p. 1962-69), Nat. Sheriffs Assn. (dir. 1967-68). Methodist. Mason (33 deg.). Home: 819 McAdoo Little Rock AR 77205 Office: Pulaski County Courthouse Little Rock AR 72204

MACKEY, LYLA THRASHER (MRS. ALEXANDER B. MACKEY), ret. librarian; b. Highway, Ky.; d. John D. and Myrtie (Smith) Thrasher; A.B., Central State Coll., Edmond, Okla., 1934; M.A., George Peabody Coll., 1937, B.S. in L.S., 1943; m. Alexander B. Mackey, Feb. 15, 1935. Tchr. pub. schs., Clinton County, Ky., 1929-32; asso. prof. Trevecca Coll., Nashville, 1935-43, librarian, 1944-72, spl. counselor young women, 1950-64. Mem. N.E.A., Am. (Tenn. recruitment network), Southeastern, Tenn., Nashville library assns., Am. Assn. U. Women, Ladies' Hermitage Assn. Mem. Ch. of Nazarene. Home: 700 Harding Pl Nashville TN 37211

MACKEY, M(AURICE) CECIL, JR., univ. pres.; b. Montgomery, Ala., Jan. 23, 1929; s. M. Cecil and Annie Laurie (Kimrey) M.; B.A., U. Ala., 1949, M.A., 1953, LL.B., 1958; Ph.D., U. Ill., 1955; postgrad. Harvard, 1958-59; m. Clare Siewert, Aug. 29, 1953; children—Carol, John, Ann. Asst. prof. econs. U. Ill., 1955-56; asso. prof. econs. USAF Acad., 1956-57; admitted to Ala. bar, 1958; asst. prof. law U. Ala., 1959-62; with FAA, 1963-65, U.S. Dept. Commerce, 1965-67; asst. sec. U.S. Dept. Transp., 1967-69; exec. v.p., prof. law Fla. State U., Tallahassee, 1969-71; pres. U. South Fla., Tampa, 1971—. Asst. counsel sub-com. on antitrust and monopoly U.S. Senate, 1958-62. Recipient Arthur S. Flemming award Washington Jaycees, 1967. Mem. Artus, Chi Alpha Phi. Home: 10410 Butia Pl Tampa FL 33618

MACKEY, OSCAR POWELL, III, state ofcl.; b. Memphis, Aug. 13, 1938; s. Oscar P. and Lucy C. (Wallace) M.; B.B.A., U. Miss., 1960, LL.B., 1963, J.D., 1968. Admitted to Miss. bar, 1963; practiced in Coffeeville, 1963-65, Water Valley, 1965-70; mem. firm Oscar P. Mackey III, 1965-70; asst. atty. gen. State Miss., 1970—. Mem. Miss. Ho. of Reps., 1967-70. Mem. Am., Yalobusha County bar assns., Miss. State Bar, Order of DeMolay, Water Valley Jr. C. of C. (pres. 1965), Delta Kappa Epsilon, Alpha Phi Omega. Presbyn. Home: 5155 Wayneland Dr Apt B-8 Jackson MS 39211 Office: State Office Bldg Room 1007 Jackson MS 39205

MACKEY, PAUL RETTIG, ednl. adminstr.; b. Galion, O., Apr. 22, 1912; s. Charles Alvan and Minnie (Rettig) M.; B.A., Emory and Henry Coll., 1935; M.A., Ohio State U., 1940; postgrad. George Washington U., 1950-51; m. Kathryn Campbell Scott, Oct. 26, 1935. Coach, tchr., Johnson City, Tenn., 1935-36, Norton, Va., 1936-39,

Galion, O., 1940-41, Bristol, Tenn., 1941-43; tchr.-coach, Alexandria, Va., 1943-48, tchr. guidance, 1948-56, asst. supt. constrn.-planning, 1956-69; dir. bldgs. and constrn. Loudoun County Schs., Leesburg, Va., 1969—. Mason, Lion, Kiwanian. Home: Rural Route 1 Box 1R Purcellville VA 22132 Office: 30 W North St Leesburg VA 22075

MACKEY, WILLIAM STURGES, JR., med. co. exec.; b. St. Louis, May 27, 1921; s. William S. and Dorothy Frances (Allison) M.; B.A., Rice U., 1943; M.B.A., U. Tex., 1950; m. Margaret Wescot Powell, Dec. 10, 1943; children—Dorothy (Mrs. Thomas Robben), John, James. Asso. prof. accounting Rice U., Houston, 1946-62; partner Simons & Mackey, Houston, 1946-62; v.p., treas. Mandrel Industries, Houston, 1962-66; v.p. finance Tex. Internat. Airlines, Houston, 1966-69; chmn., pres. Medenco, Inc., Houston, 1969—. Served to 1st lt. USAAF, 1946. C.P.A., Tex. Mem. Am. Inst. C.P.A.'s, Tex. Soc. C.P.A.'s, Beta Gamma Sigma. Clubs: Lakeside Country, University, Plaza. Episcopalian. Home: 11335 Holidan St Houston TX 77024 Office: 5 Greenway Plaza E Houston TX 77046

MACKHARDT, LUCILLE ALMA HILL, real estate broker; b. Marion, La., May 7; d. Robert Lee and Cornelia Ann (Haile) Hill; student pub. schs.; grad. bus. coll., 1940; m. Fred R. Mackhardt, July 19, 1937 (dec.). Real estate broker Lucille Mackhardt, realtor, Dallas, 1953—, Richardson, Tex., 1965—. Vice pres. City Council of Women, Hot Springs, Ark., 1946-47; mgr. Community Chest, A.R.C. drives, Hot Springs, Ark., 1945-46; with War Price Adminstrn. Bd., Garland County, Ark., 1945-46; sec. Ark. State Symphony, 1946-47. Mem. Bus. and Profl. Womens Club (ways and means chmn., personal service chmn.), Nat., Tex., Dallas real estate bds., Nat. Inst. Real Estate Brokers Farms Brokers and Traders Club, Dallas Council on World Affairs Womens Group (sec. 1954-55), Women's Council Realtors, Ladies Elks Aux., Phi Sigma Alpha (corr. sec. Delta Eta chpt. 1968-69, extension chmn. 1970-71, v.p. 1972—). Home: 4719 Cole Av PO Box 8291 Dallas TX 75205 Office: 8700 Chancellor St Dallas TX 75247

MACKIN, JOHN GILMAN, JR., constrn. co. exec.; b. Ada, Okla., July 17, 1930; s. John Gilman and Dorothy Doris (Hatchett) M.; B.S. in Civil Engring., Tex. A. and M. U., 1955; m. Mary Louise Bunch, May 29, 1949; children—Jana (Mrs. Gary Cathy), Ina Carol, Renata Diane, John Gilman. Offshore constrn. engr. Cal. Co., 1955-56; project engr. Brown & Root, Inc., Houston, 1957-61, mgr. marine industries group, 1962-67; v.p. Divcon, Inc., also pres. Descon Engrs., Houston, 1968; v.p., gen. mgr. Fluor Ocean Services, Inc., Houston, 1969-70, exec. v.p., 1970-73; pres. J.G. Mackin & Assos. Tech. and Mgmt. Services, 1973—. Vice pres. Maplewood North-South Community Improvement Assn., 1962-66, pres., 1966, dir., 1962-65. County and Tex. del. Democratic Conv., 1958, 59, 68. Served with AUS, 1950-51. Registered profl. engr., Tex., La. Mem. Am. Soc. C.E., Am. Soc. Oceanography-Marine Tech. Soc., Houston C. of C. (mem. sci. com. 1967—), Nat. Oceanography Assn. (dir. 1970—). Patentee offshore structural system for offshore regions with ice flow, guidance structure for deepwater pipeline constrn. Home: 13138 Trail Hollow Houston TX 77024 Office: 2050 North Loop West Suite 228 Houston TX 77018

MACKLIN, ANDERSON DELANO, educator; b. Luther, Okla., Jan. 17, 1933; s. Herman Randolph and Alice (Anderson) M.; B.S., Lincoln U., 1954; M.A., U. Mo., 1956; Ed.D., Pa. State U., 1969; m. Georgia Gaye Day, Dec. 4, 1971; children—Anderson Delano, Cheryl, Rahn, Armand. Teaching asst. Pa. State U., 1967-68; asst. instr. art Lincoln U., Jefferson City, Mo., 1954-58; instr. art Wiley Coll., Marshall, Tex., 1958-60; prof. art Va. State Coll., Petersburg, 1962—, chmn. dept. fine arts, 1969—; artist-in-residence Richmond (Va.) Pub. Schs., 1971-72. Recipient So. Fellowships Found. award, 1967-68, Asian Studies fellowship, 1969-70. Mem. Va. Art Edn. Assn. (v.p. 1973-74), Kappa Alpha Psi. Baptist (v.p. Men's fellowship 1973-74). Home: 11200 Rosewood Lane Petersburg VA 23803

MACLEAN, HECTOR, banker, lawyer; b. Balt., Sept. 15, 1920; s. Angus W. and Margaret (French) McL.; B.S., Davidson Coll., 1941; LL. B., U. N.C., 1948; m. Lyl Francis Warwick, Dec. 18, 1944; 1 dau., Lyl Billings. Admitted to N.C. bar, 1948; pvt. practice, 1948—; pres. So. Nat. Bank of Lumberton, 1955—, So. Nat. Bank of N.C.; director, pres. Lumberton Implement Co., Va. and Carolina So. R.R.; dir. Kay & Co. Mem. N.C. Senate. Mayor of Lumberton 1949-53. Dir. N.C. Tb Assn., Med. Found. of N.C.; trustee St. Andrews Presbyn. Coll. Served from lt. to capt., AUS, 1942-46. Decorated Bronze Star medal. Mem. Robeson County Hist. Soc. (pres. 1955), C. of C., Am., N.C. bar assns., Omicron Delta Kappa, Phi Delta Phi. Home: 2101 Elm St Lumberton NC 28358 Office: 550 N Chestnut St Lumberton NC 28358

MACLEAN, PAUL D(ONALD), neurophysiologist; b. Phelps, N.Y., May 1, 1913; B.A., Yale, 1935, M.D., 1940; postgrad. U. Edinburgh, 1935-36; m. 1942; five children. Intern Johns Hopkins Hosp., 1940-41; asst. resident medicine New Haven Hosp., 1941-42; research asst., pathologist Yale Med. Sch., 1942; clin. instr. medicine Washington Med. Sch., 1946-47; resident fellow psychiatry USPHS, Harvard Med. Sch., also Mass. Gen. Hosp., 1947-49; asst. prof. physiology, Yale Med. Sch., 1949-51, asst. prof. psychiatry, 1951-53, asso. prof. psychiatry, physiology and neurology, 1953-56, asso. prof. physiology, 1956-57; chief Limbic Integration and Behavior Sect., NIH 1957-71, chief Lab. Brain Evolution and Behavior, 1971—. Dir., Electroencephalographic Lab., New Haven Hosp., 1951-52; attending physician Grace-New Haven Hosp., 1953-56. Trustee Prof. Percival Bailey Ednl. Project. Served to maj., M.C., AUS, 1942-46. Recipient Distinguished Res. award Assn. Research Nervous and Mental Disease, 1964, Thomas William Salmon Lectureship award N.Y. Acad. Medicine, 1966, Salmon Medal for Distinguished Service to Psychiatry, Superior Service award DHEW, 1967, Clarence M. Hincks Meml. Lectureship Ont. Mental Health Found., 1969, Spl. award Am. Psychopathological Assn., 1971, G. Burroughs Mider award NIH, 1972, Karl Spencer Lashley award Am. Philos. Soc., 1972; NSF sr. resident fellow, Switzerland, 1956-57. Mem. Electroencephalogical Soc., Soc. Neuroscience, Pavlovian Soc. N.Am., Cajal Club, Internat. Soc. Psychoneuroendocrinology, Assn. Hist. Med., Am. Neurol. Assn. Physiol. Soc. Office: Lab of Brain Evolution and Behavior Nat Inst Mental Health Bethesda MD 20014

MACLEAY, DONALD, lawyer; b. Tacoma, Dec. 27, 1908; s. Lachian and Mabel (Nye) M.; student Hill Mil. Acad., Portland, Ore., 1922-24, Phillips Acad., Andover, Mass., 1924-25; LL.B., U. Colo., 1931; m. Elizabeth Hall Fesser, Jan. 27, 1934; children—Donald, Linda (Mrs. J. L. Dewell), Murdo Lachlan. Admitted to Colo., Ill., D.C. bars, 1931-33; com. prevention and punishment of crime Chgo. Assn. Commerce, 1931-32; gen. practice law, 1933—; now mem. firm Macleay, Lynch, Berhard & Gregg. Served to lt. USNR, 1943-45. Mem. Am., Maritime Administrv. bar assns., Bar Assn. D.C., Am. Judicature Soc., Assn. Interstate Commerce Practitioners Maritime Law Assn. U.S., Phi Delta Phi, Chi Psi. Episcopalian. Clubs: University, Propeller (Washington); Belle Haven Country (Alexandria, Va.); Pickwick, Internat. House (New Orleans); Jefferson Island, Nat. Lawyers (Washington). Home: 1800 Edgehill Dr Belle Haven Alexandria VA 22307 Office: 1625 K St Washington DC 20006

MACMILLAN, CHARLES JAMES BARR, educator; b. Auburn, N.Y., Apr. 30, 1935; s. John Walker and Margaret Ethel (Barr) M.; B.A., Cornell U., 1957, Ph.D., 1965; M.A., Colgate U., 1960; m. Joan Tyler Reinberg, June 15, 1958; children—Ann Tyler, Tyler Lash. Acting asst. prof. U. Cal. at Los Angeles, 1962-64; asst. prof., asso. prof., dir. Gen. Edn. Program for Tchrs., Temple U., 1964-70; asso. prof., head dept. foundational studies in edn. Fla. State U., Tallahassee, 1970—. Mem. Philosophy Edn. Soc. (mem. exec. com.), Seal and Serpent Soc., Sherwoods of Cornell, Phi Kappa Phi, Phi Delta Kappa. Bd. editors Studies in Philosophy and Education, 1970. Editor: (with B. Paul Komisar) Psychological Concepts in Education, 1966; (with Thomas W. Nelson) Concepts of Teaching, 1968. Home: 2316 Armistead Rd Tallahassee FL 32303

MACMILLAN, ROBERT RANKIN, lawyer; b. Johnson City, Tenn., June 13, 1923; s. Jason L. and Nelle Theresa (Rankin) MacM.; B.A., U. N.C., 1947; M.A., U. Ala., 1949; LL.B., U. Va., 1951; m. Katherine James Olinger, Oct. 4, 1952; children—R. Rankin, David H., Martha T., John M. Admitted to Va. bar, 1951; asso. Breeden & Hoffman, Norfolk, 1951-53; partner Breeden, Howard & MacMillan, 1953—. Chmn., Norfolk Redevel. and Housing Authority, 1969—; pres. Norfolk YMCA. Trustee Union Theol. Sem., Richmond, Va. Served to lt. (j.g.) USNR, 1943-46. Decorated Bronze Star medal with oak leaf cluster. Rockefeller Found. fellow So. Regional Tng. Program in Pub. Adminstrn., 1948-50. Presbyn. (elder, gen. exec. bd.). Clubs: Virginia, Norfolk Yacht and Country, Harbor, Virginia (Norfolk). Home: 1953 Twin Cove Rd Virginia Beach VA 23454 Office: Va Nat Bank Bldg Norfolk VA 23510

MACNABB, ALEXANDER STUART, govt. ofcl.; b. Bay Shore, L.I., N.Y., Aug. 24, 1929; s. Francis Patrick Glennon and Helen Theresa (Monahan) MacN.; A.B., Colgate U., 1956; J.D., Washington and Lee U., 1959; postgrad. N.Y. U. Law Sch., 1960-61; m. Kathleen Marie Noonan, June 29, 1963; children—Helen Marie, Margaret Ann, Mary Alice, Ian Christopher, Joshua Finlay. Pres., Alexander MacNabb Assos., Advt., Bay Shore, 1960-67; pres. Town Almanac Pub. Co., Bay Shore, 1960-67; mem. Pres.'s Com. on Manpower, U.S. Office Econ. Opportunity, 1966-67, spl. asst. to dir. Community Action Program, 1967-69; Office Econ. Opportunity rep. to presidentially established Nat. Program for Vol. Action, Washington, 1969-70; dir. Office Operating Services, U.S. Dept. Interior, Bur. Indian Affairs, Washington, 1970-72, dir. Office Engring., 1972-73; dir. Office Indian and Territorial Devel. U.S. Dept. Interior, 1973-74; dep. dir. office of fed. contract compliance Employment Standards Adminstrn., Dept. of Labor, 1974—; v.p. Newmark, Posner & Mitchell, N.Y.C., 1961; dir. Munston Electronic Mfg. Corp., Islip, N.Y., 1962. Chmn., Boy Scouts Am. fund drive, L.I., 1960, Arlington, Va., 1968-69, mem. exec. bd. Nat. Capital Area Council; asso. adviser Explorer Post, Arlington, commr. Boy Scout Roundtable, Arlington, mem. Scout World Jamboree Com. 1971, mem.-at-large nat. council; chmn. Girl Scouts U.S.A. fund drive, 1968; chmn. Washington and Lee Law Sch. fund drive, 1967-69. Bd. dirs. Nat. Capital Area Big Bros. Served with USNR, 1952-54. Mem. Am. Polit. Sci. Assn., Am. Sociol. Assn., Am. Acad. Polit. and Social Scis., Nat. Congress Am. Indians (Micmac Tribe), Am. Indian Movement, Nat. Indian Youth Council, Canoe Cruisers Assn., Blue Ridge Voyaguers, Nat. Speleological Soc., Am. Motorcycle Assn. (competitor), New Eng. Trail Riders, Phi Alpha Delta, Pi Sigma Alpha. Roman Catholic. Clubs: Potomac Speleological (Arlington); Potomac Appalachian Trail (Washington). Home: 129 N Oakland St Arlington VA 22203 Office: Office Fed Contract Compliance Employment Standards Adminstrn US Dept Labor Washington DC 20210

MACNAMARA, THOMAS EDWARD, physician, educator; b. Airdrie, Scotland, May 23, 1929; s. Edward Francis and Bridget Monica (Fawcett) M.; Paisley Tech. Coll., Glasgow (Scotland) U., 1947, M.B., Ch.B., 1952; postgrad. Mass. Gen. Hosp., 1956-57; m. Julia B. Caulfield, Sept. 22, 1956; children—Edward, Brian, Mary, Bridget, Anne. Came to U.S., 1956, naturalized, 1962. Intern Victoria Infirmary, Glasgow, 1953, Leith Hosp., Edinburgh, Scotland, 1954, Bellsdyke Hosp., Laybert, Scotland, 1954; resident St. Martin's Hosp., Bath, Eng., 1954, Birmingham Accident Hosp. (Eng.), 1955; practice medicine, specializing in anesthesia, Washington, 1957-59, 62—, Boston, 1960-62; instr. anesthesia Georgetown U., 1957-60; asst. anesthesia Mass. Gen. Hosp., Harvard Med. Sch., Boston, 1960-62; mem. faculty Georgetown U. Med. Center, Washington, 1962—, prof. anesthesiology, 1962—, chmn. dept. anesthesia, 1962—; cons. VA Hosp., Washington, D.C. Gen. Hosp., Nat. Naval Med. Center, Bethesda, Md., Charles Town Gen. Hosp., Ransom, W.Va. Dir. Georgetown U. Fed. Credit Union, 1972—; med. senator faculty senate Georgetown U., 1967—, v.p., 1967-70, pres., 1973—. Diplomate Am. Bd. Anesthesiology. Fellow Am. Coll. Anesthesiologists (asso. examiner 1966—); mem. Brit., Mass., D.C. med. socs., Am. Soc. Anesthesiology, Am. Coll. Sports Medicine, Royal Soc. Medicine, Assn. Am. Med. Colls., Soc. Acad. Anesthesia Chairmen, Soc. for Obstetrics Anesthesiology and Perinatology, D.C. Soc. Anesthesiology (pres. 1966-67), Am. Assn. U. Profs. Editor: Surgical Digest, 1966—. Home: 2736 N Nelson St Arlington VA 22207 Office: Dept Anesthesia Georgetown U Hosp 3800 Reservoir RD NW Washington DC 20007

MACNAUGHTON, WILLIAM ALEXANDER, lawyer; b. Winchester, Ky., Jan. 18, 1922; s. Archibald John and Anne (Epperson) MacN.; B.B.A., U. Tex., 1943, LL.B., 1948; m. Anne Cherlene O'Hair, Aug. 23, 1943; children—Anne Lynn, Virginia Sue, William Alexander, James Robert, Charles Thomas. Admitted to Tex. bar, 1948; since practiced in Houston, 1948—; mem. firms MacNaughton & Levevidge, 1948-50, Townes & Townes, 1950-54; pvt. practice law, 1958-66; gen. atty. Ginther, Warren & Ginther, 1955-58; city judge Bellaire, Tex., 1951-56; partner MacNaughton, Brady & Marlatt, Houston, 1966-68, MacNaughton & McWhorter, 1968-72; pres., So. Cross Inc., 1967—, MacNaughton Lands, Inc., 1973—; gen. partner MacNaughton & Assos., Ltd., 1963—, Loop 610 West, Ltd., 1972—; sr. resident Portuer, Nelson, Harding, Morchetti, Leonard & Tate, 1974—. Mem. Houston Bar Assn. (v.p. 1958). Home: 2148 Inwood St Houston TX 77019 Office: Suite 330 1100 Wilson Bldg Houston TX 77002

MACNEES, VALERIE CATHERINE KOOPS (MRS. JAMES BARRY MACNEES), journalist; b. LaCrosse, Wis., Sept. 11, 1912; d. Edward Charles and Minnie (Morley) Koops; B.A., Wis. State U., 1933; postgrad. U. Wis., 1936-37; m. James Barry MacNees, June 5, 1940; children—Valerie Ann (Mrs. Robert Van Meter), James Michael. Tchr. pub. schs., Wis., 1933-40; clk. U.S. Census Bur., Washington, 1940-42; classification clk. WPB, Washington, 1942-43; editor Fgn. Broadcast Intelligence, Washington, 1944-45; mem. editorial staff N.C.W.C. News Service, Washington, 1946-51; womens editor Catholic Standard, Washington, 1951-63, feature editor, 1963—. Weekly columnist Prince Georges Post, Hyattsville, Md., 1969—. Author: Catholic Churches in Montgomery County, 1966. Home: 2007 Brighton Rd Washington DC 20018 Office: 1711 N St Washington DC 20006

MAC NERNEY, JOHN SHERIDAN, educator; b. N.Y.C., Jan. 10, 1923; s. John Sheridan and Lillian (Egelhofer) MacN.; student Trinity Coll., 1939-41; B.A. with highest honors, U. Tex., 1948, Ph.D., 1951; m. Kathleen Mary O'Connor, Dec. 8, 1945. Vibration analyst, United Aircraft Corp., E. Hartford, Conn., 1941-43; instr. pure math. U. Tex. 1948-51; instr. math. Northwestern U., 1951-52; asst. prof. math., U. N.C., 1952-56, asso. prof. 1956-62, prof., 1962-67; prof. math. U. Houston, 1967—. Served as cpl. USAAF, 1943-46. Mem. A.A.A.S., Am. Math. Soc., Elisha Mitchell Sci. Soc., Math. Assn. Am., N.C. Acad. Sci., Circolo Matematico di Palermo, Phi Beta Kappa, Sigma Xi (pres. N.C. chpt. 1966-67). Home: 2016 Main St Houston TX 77002

MACON, SETH CRAVEN, ins. co. exec.; b. Climax, N.C., Mar. 22, 1919; s. Oren T. and Kate (Craven) M.; A.B., Guilford Coll., 1940; grad. Am. Coll. Life Underwriters, 1949; attended So. Meth. U. Inst. Ins. Marketing, 1947, U. N.C. Exec. Program, 1958; m. Hazel Lee Monsees, June 27, 1942; children—Carol Susan, Randall Seth. With Jefferson Standard Life Ins. Co., 1940—, supt. agys., 1946, sales dir., Greensboro, N.C., 1956-58, asst. agy. mgr., 1958-62, 2d v.p., asso. agy. mgr., 1962-64, v.p., asso. agy. mgr., 1964-67, v.p., agy. mgr., 1967-70, sr. v.p. agy., 1970—, also dir. Trustee Guilford Coll. Served with USA-AF, 1942-46. Baptist (deacon, mem. finance com.). Clubs: Greensboro Rotary, Starmount Forest Country, Piedmont Sales Execs. Home: 3803 Madison Av Greensboro NC 27403 Office: P O Box 21008 Greensboro NC 27420

MACPHERSON, JANET TAYLOR WOLFENDEN (MRS. HERBERT GRENFELL MACPHERSON), civic worker; b. Phila.; d. Edward Musker and Annette (Robertson) Wolfenden; B.S., M.A., U. Pa.; m. Herbert Grenfell MacPherson, June 5, 1937; children—Janet Lynne, Robert Duncan. Pres., Franklin Sch. P.T.A., Lakewood, O., 1954-56; chpt. dir. Am. Assn. U. Women, Oak Ridge, 1957-59; pres. League Women Voters, Oak Ridge, 1961-63, Tenn., 1967-69; pres. Oak Ridge Civic Music Assn. Women Guild, 1963-64; pres. Friends Oak Ridge Pub. Library, 1966-67; mem. Nat. Com. for Support Pub. Schs., 1967-70; mem. Comm. 100 Found. for Better Govt. for Tenn., 1968-70, Oak Ridge Charter Commn., 1972-74; mem. salary structure study com. Bd. Edn. Oak Ridge, 1969-71; bd. dirs. Awareness House of Oak Ridge, Inc., 1970-73; mem. Tenn. com. for 1970 White House Conf. on Children and Youth, 1969-70; mem. state planning com. Air Quality Project for Tenn., 1970-71. Editor: This Is Oak Ridge, Tenn., 1961. Home: 102 Orchard Circle Oak Ridge TN 37830

MACRAE, BRUCE FARQUHAR, retail food exec.; b. Detroit, Nov. 28, 1923; s. Keith William and Geraldine (Starr) M.; student Wayne U., 1942-43; B.S., U. Md., 1951; m. Laura Belle Wyatt, Sept. 6, 1952; 1 son, Stuart Wyatt. Asst. chief tariff compilations Am. Trucking Assn., Washington, 1951-53; asst. terminal mgr. Davidson Transfer and Storage, Washington, 1953-55; traffic analyst Ryder Truck Lines, Jacksonville, Fla., 1955-57; inco alloy salesmgr. J.M. Tull Metal and Supply Co., Jacksonville, 1957-60; traffic and distbn. mgr. Food Fair Stores, Inc., Jacksonville, 1960—. Instr. transp. Fla. Jr. Coll., Jacksonville, 1968—; lectr. transp. U. North Fla., Jacksonville, 1972—. Served with USNR, 1943-46. Recipient Transp. Man of Yr. award Traffic Club, Jacksonville, 1972. Mem. Traffic Clubs Internat., Traffic Club Jacksonville, Navy League U.S., Nat. Rifle Assn. (life), Nat. Def. Transp. Assn. (1st v.p. 1970-72), Delta Nu Alpha (nat. regional v.p. 1964-66), Sigma Pi, Delta Sigma Pi. Club: University (Jacksonville). Home: 6896 Howalt Dr Jacksonville FL 32211 Office: PO Box 2605 Jacksonville FL 32203

MACRAE, CECIL DUNCAN, economist; b. St. Louis, Apr. 14, 1940; s. Cecil Duncan and Winifred Henry (Carroll) MacR.; A.B., Harvard, 1962; Ph.D. (Univ. Research scholar), Cambridge U., 1965; m. Elizabeth Studley Chase, May 24, 1969. Tutor Christ's Coll., Cambridge U., Eng., 1965; asst. prof. econs. Mass. Inst. Tech., Cambridge, Mass., 1965-69; Research economist Urban Inst., Washington, 1969-70, sr. research, economist, 1971—, project mgr., 1972—. Vis. lectr. econs. Tech. U. Berlin, 1967; cons. U.S. Dept. Labor, 1968-69. Mem. Am. Econ. Assn., Am. Polit. Sci. Assn., Am. Sociol. Assn., Am. Statis. Assn., Econometric Soc., Inst. Mgmt. Sci., Soc. Govt. Economists. Author: (with other) The Unemployment-Inflation Dilemma, 1971. Contbr. articles to profl. jours. Home: 314 N St SW Washington DC 20024 Office: 2100 M St Washington DC 20037

MACY, ARTHUR WARREN, lawyer; b. Phila., July 1, 1919; s. Arthur Warren and Marietta (Nyland) M.; student U. Colo., 1939-41, 45-48; J.D., La. State U., 1952; m. Frances Walts, Sept. 7, 1948 (div. 1973); children—Patricia Ann, Susan Lyn, Mary Jane, Barbara Warren. Research asst. history dept. U. Colo., 1947-48; tchr. San Carlos (Ariz.) Apache Reservations, 1948-49; research asst. legal biography La. State U., 1949-50; admitted to La. bar, 1952; practiced in Hammond, La., 1952—; mem. firm Reid & Reid, 1952-54, Reid & Macy, 1955-68, Macy, Kemp and Newton, 1969-71, Macy & Kemp, 1971—; law clk. 1st Circuit Ct. of Appeal, State of La., 1962—. Served with USNR, 1941-45. Mem. Am., La., 21st Jud. Dist. La. (pres. 1965-67), bar assns., Order of Coif, Phi Kappa Phi, Phi Delta Phi, Pi Gamma Mu, Phi Kappa Psi. Democrat. Episcopalian. Mason (K.T.), Rotarian, Lion, Kiwanian. Asso. editor: La. Law Rev., 1951-52. Home: Route 4 Box 171M Hammond LA 70401 Office: 220 W Thomas St Hammond LA 70401

MACY, JOSEPH, educator; b. Bklyn., Mar. 29, 1927; s. John and Anna Maria (Maurer) M.; A.A., Palm Beach Jr. Coll., 1962; B.A., Fla. Atlantic U., 1966, M.Ed., 1967; postgrad. FBI Nat. Acad., 1961; m. Shirley Walden, Oct. 15, 1949; children—Michael Joseph, John Francis, Kathryn Ann, Ralph William. With Palm Beach Police Dept., 1950-51; patrolman to asst. chief West Palm Beach Police Dept., 1951-68; prof. law enforcement Palm Beach (Fla.) Jr. Coll., adj. prof. law enforcement Fla. Atlantic U., 1969—. Founder traffic violators sch. Palm Beach County, 1968. Mem. adv. com. State Dept. Edn. on Higher Edn. for Police Officers, 1966—; mem. Gov.'s Police Standards Council, 1967—; police tng. coordinator Palm Beach County, 1973—. Bd. dirs. Palm Beach County Mental Health Assn., 1963—, Comprehensive Community Mental Health Center, 1966—, Gulfstream council Boy Scouts Am., 1951—. Served with USNR, 1944-48. Recipient J. Edgar Hoover medal for excellence, 1961. Mem. Fla. Peace Officers Assn., Am. Assn. Jr. Colls., Internat. Assn. Chiefs of Police, Palm Beach County Police and Firemans Guild, Phi Theta Kappa. Democrat. Roman Catholic. K.C. Home: 224 Belmonte Rd West Palm Beach FL 33405 Office: 4200 S Congress Av Lakeworth FL 33460

MADAMBA, JORGE JUDY, dentist; b. Central Tinunga Isabelia, Negros Occidental, P.I., Jan. 26, 1936 (parent Am. citizen); s. Jorge Arzaga and Iva (Harrison) M.; B.S., Okla. State U., 1960; D.D.S., U. Mo., 1967; m. Drucilla Pemberton, Oct. 25, 1969; children—Ryan Koby, Karla Marie. Instr., U. Mo. Dental Sch., Kansas City, 1967; pvt. practice dentistry, Tulsa, 1967—. Mem. Dental Health Edn. Com., Tulsa, 1971—, Vocational Edn. Com., Tulsa, 1971—, adv. com. Tulsa Pub. Health Dept., 1971—. Mem. Am. Dental Assn., Okla., Tulsa County dental socs., Am. Soc. Preventive Dentistry, Acad. Gen. Dentistry, Am. Soc. Clin. Hypnosis (sec.-treas. Okla. chpt.), Endodontics Study Club (pres. 1970), Central Okla. Soc. Clin. Hypnosis (sec.-treas. 1973), Okla. State U. Alumni Assn. (chpt. pres. 1972), Sigma Chi. Kiwanian. Home: 2931 E 77th St Tulsa OK 74136 Office: 2865 E Skelly Dr Tulsa OK 74135

MADDEN, EDWARD BINGHAM, cons.; b. Newton, Miss., Dec. 11, 1912; s. Oscar Edwards and Carrie Lee (Bingham) M.; student La. Coll., 1929-30; B.S., Ga. Sch. Tech., 1934; postgrad., State U. Ia., 1941, U. Ark., 1952, 59, 60; m. Margaret Hughes Witherspoon, May 7, 1937; children—Margaret Donna (Mrs. Gerald Zolton Jacobi), Edward Bingham. Engring. aide to jr. engr. TVA, Murphy, N.C., 1934-39; with U.S. Army C.E., Little Rock, Ark., 1939-60, Dallas, 1960-71, chief sect. hydraulic design, 1967-71; pvt. cons. on hydraulic, river engring. and sediment transport studies in the U.S. and Argentina, 1971—. Recipient Superior Performance award U.S. Army C.E., 1960. Registered profl. engr., Ark., Tex. Mem. Internat. Assn. for Hydraulic Research, U.S. Com. on Large Dams, Nat. Soc. Profl. Engrs., Permanent Internat. Assn. Nav. Congresses, Am. Soc. C.E., Soc. Am. Mil. Engrs., Tau Beta Pi. Presbyn. Home: 10109 McCree Rd Dallas TX 75238

MADDEN, MARTHA ANN, coll. dean; b. Shreveport, La., Apr. 5, 1937; d. James H. and Velma (Fletcher) Madden; B.S., So. Methodist U., 1959; M.A., 1963. Tchr. math. Dallas Ind. Sch. Dist., 1959-62; guidance counselor Thomas Rusk Jr. High Sch., Dallas, 1962-65; dir. Florence Moore Hall, dean student staff Stanford, 1965-67; dean of women N.E. La. U., Monroe, 1967—. Dean students World Campus Afloat, spring 1970; N.E. La. U. adviser, mem. exec. bd. World Campus Afloat Assn., 1971—, mem. exec. council 1971-73, asst. counselor, summer 1972. Hon. mem. adv. bd. vol. workers VA Hosp., Palo Alto, Cal., 1967; mem. San Francisco Symphony Found., 1965-67; rep. Monroe Panhellenic Council, 1969—. Bd. dirs. Methodist Wesley Found., N.E. La. U., bd. govs. Ouachita Parish chpt. A.R.C., 1971. Mem. La. Tchrs. Assn., La. Assn. Deans of Women (v.p. 1969), Am., La. personnel and guidance assns., Nat. Assn. Women Deans and Counselors (La. membership chmn.), La. Vocational Guidance Assn. (membership chmn. 1972), So. Coll. Personnel Guidance Assn., Nat. Vocational Guidance Assn., Am. Assn. U. Women, Internat. Platform Assn., Zeta Tau Alpha, Alpha Lambda Delta, Pi Lambda Theta. Clubs: Altrusa; Toastmistress. Home: 1604 Shannon St Monroe LA 71201

MADDEN, ROBERT BOWMAN, airline co. exec.; b. Sharon, Pa., Aug. 28, 1912; s. Edward Aloysius and Nannie Aletta (Bowman) M.; B.S., U.S. Naval Acad., 1933; M.S., Mass. Inst. Tech., 1938; postgrad. Harvard, 1947; m. Mary Norman Hopkins, June 18, 1935; children—Nancy Helen (Mrs. Linwood Banks Simmons), Robert Hopkins. Commd. ensign USN, 1933, advanced through grades to capt., 1953; adminstrv. asst. to chief Bur. Ships, 1953-54; head marine engring. dept. U.S. Naval Acad., 1954-57; dir. ship design Bur. Ships, 1957-59; comdr. Charleston Naval Shipyard, 1959-60; v.p. engring. Am. Pres. Lines, San Francisco, 1961-63; mgr. marine engring. Pan Am. World Airways, Inc., Patrick AFB, Kennedy Space Center, Fla., 1963-65, mgr. facilities engring., 1964-70; project mgr. engring. support services project NASA, 1970—. Mem. bd. control U.S. Naval Inst., 1954-59. Registered profl. engr., D.C. Mem. Am. Soc. Naval Engrs. (asst. sec.-treas. 1950-59), Soc. Naval Architects and Marine Engrs., Soc. Am. Mil. Engrs. (pres. Canaveral post 1971-72), Sigma Xi. Republican. Methodist. Asst. editor Jour Am. Soc. Naval Engrs., 1950-59. Home: 102 W Bay Dr Cocoa Beach FL 32931 Office: Pan Am World Airways Inc Kennedy Space Center FL 32899

MADDEN, TOM J., clergyman; b. Enid, Okla., Apr. 14, 1919; s. Thomas J. and Ama (Sigmon) M.; A.B., Okla. Bapt. U., 1943; postgrad. Baylor U., 1943-44; Th.M., Southwestern Bapt. Theol. Sem., 1948; m. Edna Earle Parker, June 27, 1946; children—Thomas J. III, Jane Elizabeth. Ordained to ministry Bapt. Ch., 1941; prof. Bible, Arlington State U., Tex., 1947-48; pastor Calvary Bapt. Ch., Mexia, Tex., 1948-51, Greenbrier (Tenn.) Bapt. Ch., 1951-54, 1st Bapt. Ch., Tullahoma, Tenn., 1954—. Pres., Tenn. Bapt. Conv., 1968—, Tenn. Bapt. Found., 1963—, Tullahoma Ministerial Alliance, 1957-58; exec. com. So. Baptist Conv., 1966—. Trustee Bapt. Hosp., Nashville. Rotarian. Home: 124 Oak Park Tullahoma TN 37388 Office: Grundy at Washington Tullahoma TN 37388

MADDOX, DAN WAITE, credit corp. exec.; b. Easonville, Ala., June 9, 1909; s. William Notley and Minnie (Waite) M.; student Ga. Sch. Tech., 1925-29; m. Margaret Huffman, June 21, 1969; children—Judith E. (Mrs. Frank Isbel Nebhut), Ellen King (Mrs. Norman Christianson), James Notley. With Universal C.I.T. Corp., N.Y.C., 1930-41; founder, chief exec. officer Assos. Capital Corp., Nashville, Tenn., 1943—; dir. Assos. Corp. North Am., South Bend, Ind., mem. exec. com., 1964—; dir. Capital Life Ins. Co., Denver, Colo., Shoney's Big Boy Enterprises, Nashville, Commerce Union Bank, Nashville, Assos. First Capital Corp., N.Y.; chmn. bd. Cumberland Life Ins. Co., Nashville. Mem. Economic Devel. Com., State of Tenn., 1971—, Tenn. Agrl. and Indsl. Commn., 1972—. Trustee, African Wildlife Leadership Found., Washington; trustee Childrens Museum, Nashville, v.p., 1971—; trustee Maddox Found. Recipient Weatherby award Shikar Safari Internat., 1967. Mem. East African Profl. Hunters Assn. Clubs: Mill Reef (Antigua, West Indies); Explorers (N.Y.C.). Home: 1228 Chickering Rd Nashville TN 37215 Office: 1 Park Plaza Nashville TN 37203

MADDOX, EUGENE PERRY, JR., dairy co. exec.; b. Appalachia, Va., Sept. 29, 1944; s. Eugene Perry and Flora Margaret (Asbury) M.; B.S., E. Tenn. State U., Johnson City, 1966, M.B.A., 1968; m. Linda R. Lowe, Apr. 21, 1966; 1 dau., Karen. With dairy div. Pet Inc., Johnson City, 1967—, financial systems mgr., 1971-73, adminstrv. asst. to pres., 1973—. Lutheran (mem. council, chmn. finance com. 1970-72). Home: 2704 Oak Cliff Ct Johnson City TN 37601 Office: PO Box 0-CRS Johnson City TN 37601

MADDOX, JERALD CURTIS, curator; b. Decatur, Ind., June 9, 1933; s. William Vance and Martha Geraldine (Moser) M.; student Ball State Tchrs. Coll., 1951-52; A.B., Ind. U., 1955, M.A., 1960; postgrad. Harvard, 1960-61; m. Janet Frerichs, Jan. 24, 1959; children—David Curtis, Andrew Frerichs. Instr. art history N.Y. State U. Coll. at New Paltz, 1962-63; asst. to dir. U. Neb. Art Galleries, Lincoln, 1963-66; head curatorial sect., curator photography, prints and photographs div. Library of Congress, Washington, 1966—. Served with AUS, 1955-58. Mem. Coll. Art Assn. Am., Am. Assn. Museums, Soc. for Photog. Edn. (dir. 1968-73, treas. 1968-73), Phi Beta Kappa. Home: 4514 Highland Av Bethesda MD 20014 Office: Library of Congress 10 1st St SE Washington DC 20540

MADDOX, LESTER GARFIELD, lt. gov. Ga.; b. Atlanta, Sept. 30, 1915; ed. Atlanta pub. schs.; student accounting and engring.; m. Virginia Cox; children—Linda (Mrs. Don Densmore), Lester Garfield, Virginia Louise, Larry. Formerly supr. Atlanta indsl. plant; entered retail bus. and opened Pickrick Restaurant; formerly engaged in real estate sales, devel., grocery field; established Pickrick Furniture; later gov. of Ga., now lt. gov. Mem. U.S., Ga. chambers commerce, Atlanta Better Bus. Bur., Nat. Retail Furniture Assn., Travelers Protective Assn., Ga. Sheriffs Assn. (hon.), Peace Officers Assn. Ga. (hon.), Justices of Peace and Constables Assn. Ga. (hon.), Westgate Mchts. Assn. (pres.). Baptist. Mason (Shriner). Moose; mem. Jr. Order United Am. Mechanics. Club: Buckhead Fifty. Address: Office of Lt Gov Atlanta GA 30334

MADDOX, MILTON T., architect; b. Benbrook, Tex., July 14, 1924; s. Alexander Calvin and Nettie Frances (Page) M.; student U. Tex., 1944-45; m. Geneva Estell Denton, Sept. 5, 1942; 1 son, Michael Louis. Draftsman, 1945-52; prodn. co-ordinator Preston M. Geren Architects, Fort Worth, 1953-66; prodn. and field mgr. Olin Boese & Assos. Architects, Fort Worth, 1966-70; pvt. practice, Fort Worth, 1971-72; prodn. and field mgr. Growald Schutts Architects, Ft. Worth, 1972—. Served with USAAF, 1945. Mem. A.I.A. Lion (treas. Southside Ft. Worth 1971-72, sec. 1972-73, program chmn. 1973-74). Patentee ice heading machine. Home: 829 Edna Dr Everman TX 76140 Office: Fort Worth National Bank Bldg Fort Worth TX 76102

MADDOX, THOMAS EMMETT, agrl. engr.; b. Dalton, Ga., Dec. 3, 1938; s. Gordon Issac and Miriam (Smith) M.; B.S., U. Ga., 1961; M.S., U. Tenn., 1965; m. Betty Ann McChesney, Sept. 5, 1965; children—Amy Miriam, James Daniel. Grad. research asst. U. Tenn., 1964-65; residential sales engr. Ga. Power Co., Cornelia, 1966-67; agrl. engr. TVA, Nashville, 1968—. Served with AUS, 1962-63. Registered profl. engr., Tenn. Mem. Am. Soc. Agrl. Engrs. (v.p. Tenn. sect.). Baptist (deacon). Mem. Gideons, Lion. Club: Toastmasters (pres. Nashville 1970). Home: 3408 Oak Cliff Dr Nashville TN 37214

MADER, HELOISE CROWNOVER, educator; b. Winchester, Tenn., Feb. 7, 1914; d. Arthur and Emma (Sims) Crownover; student Ward Belmont Coll., 1934; B.S., George Peabody Coll., 1937, M.A., 1949; postgrad. Oxford U., 1955, U. Tenn., 1959, 67, Middle Tenn. State U., 1962, 63, 71, Abilene Christian Coll., 1964, Samford U., 1966, Tenn. State U., 1973-74; m. Perry Wesley Mader, Oct. 23, 1939 (div. July 1943); children—Heloise Crownover, Arthur Crownover. Tchr., John Early Sch., Nashville, 1949-59; tchr. Berry Sch., Nashville, 1959—, now prin. Fulbright exchange tchr. St. Paul's Ch. of Eng. Sch., Bolton, Eng., 1954-55. Pres. Murphy Sch. P.T.A., Nashville, 1948-49. Vice pres. Democratic Women's Club of Davidson County, 1969, mem. bd., 1970; mem. Dems. for Gore, 1971. Freedoms Found. at Valley Forge grantee, 1966; Mem. N.E.A. (life), Tenn. (chmn. upper elementary sect. 1964-65, 66-67), Middle Tenn. (sec.-treas. upper elementary sect. 1962-63), Met. Nashville (v.p. upper elementary assn. 1958-59, mem. profl. cooperation council 1968-72, honor award 1969, 71, negotiation council 1968-76) edn. assns., Nat. Aerospace Edn. Assn., Civil Air Patrol, Am. Assn. U. Women (v.p. 1958-59, pres. 1974—, Tenn. legislative chmn. 1971-72), Am. Legion Aux. (post pres. 1953), Internat. Platform Assn., English-Speaking Union, Tenn. Hist. Soc., Tenn. Bot. Gardens and Fine Arts Soc., Tenn. Fedn. Dem. Women. Episcopalian. Club: Query (Nashville). Home: 912 Tower Pl Nashville TN 37204 Office: 2200 Winford Av Nashville TN 37211

MADIGAN, JOHN ALPHONSUS, JR., lawyer; b. Monesson, Pa., Apr. 15, 1919; s. John Alphonsus and Edna L. (Scales) M.; B.S., U. Miami, 1940; J.D., George Washington U., 1948; postgrad. U. Fla., 1940-42; m. Mary Louise Green, Sept. 29, 1946; children—John Raymond, Terrell Courtney. Mem. staff U.S. War Dept., Washington, 1942-43, 46-48, U.S. Dept. Air Force, 1948-50; admitted to Fla. bar, 1948, D.C. Bar, 1948; practiced in Tallahassee, 1950—; asst. atty. gen., Fla., 1950-53; mem. firm Madigan, Parker, Gatlin, Truett & Swedmark and predecessor firms, Tallahassee, 1958—, sr. partner, 1970—; pres. Seminole Ventures, Inc., Tallahassee, 1970—; dir. Univ. Bus. Asso., Univ. Comml. Asso., Tallahassee; chmn. Tallahassee Bd. Fla. Fed. Savs. & Loan Assn.; chmn. Parkway Nat. Bank, Tallahassee. Pres. United Fund, Tallahassee, 1965. Vice pres. Tallahassee C. of C.; chmn. bd. trustees Tallahassee Community Coll. Served to comdr. USNR, 1943-46. Mem. Fla., Tallahassee bar assns., 2d Jud. Bar Assn. (pres. 1964), Phi Delta Phi, Pi Kappa Alpha. Clubs: Capital City Country (pres. 1970), Killearn Golf and Country, Tiger Bay (Tallahassee). Home: 1410 Alban Av Tallahassee FL 32301 Office: PO Box 669 Tallahassee FL 32302

MADIGAN, ROBERT JOSEPH, lawyer; b. Washington, Feb. 28, 1938; s. Joseph F. and Nettie (Merando) M.; B.S., George Washington U., 1960, J.D., 1963; m. Claudia C. Cooper, Dec. 22, 1962; children—Mark, Christopher, Jennifer. Admitted to Va. bar, 1964, D.C. bar, 1965; atty. Fed. Housing Adminstrn., Washington, 1966-67; mem. firm Batrus, Foldenauer, Madigan & Scott, Inc., Bailey's Cross Roads, Va., 1968—. Dir. Hunter Constrn. Co. Commr. in chancery Fairfax County Circuit Ct., 1970—. Served to capt. USMCR, 1962-66. Mem. Prince William County, Fairfax County, D.C. bar assns., Sigma Alpha Epsilon, Delta Theta Phi. Home: 1905 Westfield St Alexandria VA 22308 Office: 5205 Leesburg Pike Suite 206 Bailey's Crossroads VA 22041

MAECHLING, CHARLES, JR., lawyer, educator; b. N.Y.C., Apr. 18, 1920; Charles and Eugenie (Hirschborg) M.; B.A., Yale, 1941; LL.B., U. Va., 1949; m. Janet Leighton, Sept. 2, 1944; children—Philip Leighton and Eugenie Elisabeth. Admitted to N.Y. bar, 1949, D.C. bar, 1957; asso. Sullivan & Cromwell, N.Y.C., 1949-51; atty. Office Sec. Air Force, 1951-52; mgr. govt. relations dept., counsel Electronics Industries Assn., Washington, 1953-56; partner firm Shaw, Pittman, Potts & Maechling, 1956-61; dir. for internal def. Dept. State, Washington, 1961-63; spl. asst. to undersec. for polit. affairs, 1963-65, spl. asst. to ambassador-at-large, 1965-66; dep. gen. counsel NSF, 1966-71, spl. asst. to dir., 1972-74; prof. law U. Va., Charlottesville, 1974—. Legal adviser internat. matters Nat. Acad. Scis., 1972; gen. counsel Fairways Corp., 1959-61. Served to lt. comdr. USNR, 1941-46; mem. secretariat Joint Chiefs Staff, 1943-44, del. to Cairo Conf., 1943. Recipient Ross Essay award Am. Bar Assn., 1969. Editor-in-chief Va. Law Rev., 1948-49. Contbr. articles to profl. jours. Home: 627 Park St Charlottesville VA 22901

MAEHL, WILLIAM HENRY, JR., educator; b. Chicago Heights, Ill., June 13, 1930; s. William Henry and Marvel Lillian (Carlson) M.; B.A., U. Minn., 1950, M.A., 1951; postgrad. (Fulbright fellow), King's Coll., U. Durham (Eng.), 1955-56; Ph.D., U. Chgo., 1957; m. Audrey Mae Ellsworth, Aug. 25, 1962; 1 dau., Christine Amanda. Asst. prof. Montclair (N.J. State Coll., 1957-58; asst. prof. Washington Coll., Chestertown, Md., 1958-59; asst. prof. U. Okla., Norman, 1959-64, asso. prof., 1964-70, prof. English history, 1970—; vis. prof. U. Neb., summer, 1965. Served with AUS, 1953-55. Leverhulme Research fellow, 1961-62; grantee Am. Philos. Soc., 1961-62, 67-68, 71. Fellow Royal Hist. Soc.; mem. Am. Hist. Assn., Conf. on Brit. Studies, Soc. for Study Labour History, Southwestern Social Sci. Assn., Econ. History Soc., Am. Assn. U. Profs. Author: The Reform Bill of 1832, 1967; also articles. Home: 2601 Meadowbrook Dr Norman OK 73069 Office: Room 406 455 W Lindsey St Norman OK 73069

MAGARIAN, ROBERT ARMEN, educator; b. East St. Louis, Ill., July 27, 1930; s. Leon and Pauline (Struel) M.; student Washington U., St. Louis, 1951-52; A.B., U. Miss., 1956, B.S. in Pharmacy with honors, 1960, Ph.D. (Am. Found. Pharm. Edn. fellow), 1966; m. Charmaine V. Kugler, June 24, 1950; children—Paula, Cindy, Leslie, Robert D. NIH postdoctoral fellow U. Kan. Coll. Pharmacy, 1966-67; asst. prof. St. Louis Coll. Pharmacy, 1967-70; asso. prof. Coll. Pharmacy, U. Okla., Norman, 1970—. Served with AUS, 1952-54; Korea. Mead Johnson research grantee, 1968-69, NSF grantee, 1969-70. Mem. Am. Chem. Soc., Chem. Soc. (London, Eng.), Acad. Pharm. Scis., Am. Pharm. Assn., Smithsonian Instn. (nat. mem.), Sigma Xi, Phi Kappa Phi, Rho Chi, Kappa Psi. Home: 311 N Mercedes Dr Norman OK 73069

MAGEE, DENNIS ELTON, physician; b. Picayune, Miss., Aug. 18, 1931; s. Cooper Ray and Wilder (Patten) E.; B.S., U. So. Miss., 1955; M.D., U. Miss., 1958; m. Jamis Calhoun, July 4, 1952; children—Don, Mary Kathryn, Denise. Intern, Miss. Bapt. Hosp., Jackson, 1958-59; gen. practice medicine, Pearl, Miss., 1960-61, Picayune, Miss., 1962—; mem. staff Crosby Meml. Hosp., chief staff, 1962-63. County health officer Miss. Bd. Health, Picayune, 1960-62. Mem. Pearl River County Med. Soc., Miss. Med. Assn., A.M.A. Club: Civitan International (past pres.). Home: 529 River Rd Picayune MS 39466 Office: 220 E Canal St Picayune MS 39466

MAGEE, JOHN MELVIN, clergyman; b. Mize, Miss., Sept. 24, 1915; s. John Grenaid and Emma Catherine (Carr) M.; B.A., Maryville Coll., 1941; B.D., Columbia Theol. Sem., 1944, postgrad., 1948-50, M.Div., 1971; m. Margaret Christine Sisk, May 20, 1943; children—Connie Louise, Mary Rebecca, Nancy Christine. Ordained to ministry Presbyn. Ch., 1944; pastor, Nettleton, Saltillo, Plantersville, Tupelo, Bucy Garden chs. (all Miss.), 1944-48, Decatur, Ga., 1948-51, Union City, Tenn., 1951-55, Norris Memphis Ch., Memphis, 1955-62; asst. minister Covenant Ch., Memphis, 1962; pastor 1st Presbyn. Ch., Hammond, La., 1962-65, Concord (Tenn.) Presbyn. Ch., 1965-69; stated supply Chota Presbyn. Ch., Concord, 1965-69; pastor 1st Presbyn. Ch., Union City, Tenn., 1969—. Past moderator Memphis Presbytery, Knoxville Presbytery; chmn. com. evangelism, mem. interch. relations com. Synod Tenn.; chmn. interch. relations com. Memphis Presbytery; chmn. com. TV, radio and vis. synod of Appalachia; chmn. wom's. work Presby. of Knoxville; mem. com. on Christianity and health New Orleans Presbytery. Chmn. advancement com. Chickasaw council S.W. Dist., Boy Scouts Am. Served with USMC, 1933-37; lt. col., dep. wing chaplain Tenn. Wing, Civil Air Patrol, 1969, wing chaplain, 1971—. Mem. Memphis, Union City (past pres.), Tangepahoa Parish (v.p.), Obion County (treas. 1970) ministerial assns., Knoxville Presbyn. Ministers Assn. (sec.-treas. 1967). Mason (K.T., illustrious grand chaplain) Kiwanian. Home: 609 E Main St PO Box 898 Union City TN 38261

MAGEE, NELSON MOORE, constrn. exec.; b. nr. Wakefield, Va., Oct. 10, 1930; s. E. Daniel and Elva (Laine) M.; B.S., Va. Poly. Inst., 1952; m. Edna Yolanda Perez, Jan. 30, 1953; children—Gregory Nelson, Shane Bradford, Karen Yolanda. Partner, Magee & Son, Gen. Contractors, Wakefield, 1954-55; estimator, engr. Reid & Hope Constrn. Co., Suffolk, Va., 1955-57; field estimator E.I. DuPont de Nemours & Co., Inc., Waynesboro, Va. and Old Hickory, Tenn., 1957-58; estimator, engr. Harbert Constrn. Corp., Birmingham, Ala., 1958-60; v.p., gen. mgr. Constructors of Fla., Inc., Orlando, 1960-62; v.p., chief engr., dir. Ledbetter-Johnson Co. and Ledbetter Bros., Inc., Rome, Ga., 1962—; exec. v.p. LBI Quarries, Inc.; dir. Network Bldg. Systems Inc.; adv. dir. Zenith Devel. Co. Cubmaster, Boy Scouts Am., 1962-68; chmn. Berry Acad. Parents Orgn.; bd. mgmt. YMCA. Served to 1st lt. AUS, 1952-54. Mem. Asso. Gen. Contractors, Nat. Asphalt Paving Assn., Am. Rd. Builders, Nat. Soc. Profl. Engrs., Am. Legion. Kiwanian. Home: 341 Mt Alto Rd Rome GA 30161 Office: 2 W 2d Av Rome GA 30161

MAGEE, WILLIAM ALBIN, ins. co. exec.; b. Lexington, Va., Nov. 18, 1925; s. Joseph Gardner and Maggie Boude (Humphries) M.; B.S. in Commerce, Washington and Lee U., 1947; m. Virginia Gill Watson, Sept. 25, 1954; children—Annette, Mary Sue. With Shenandoah Life Ins. Co., Roanoke, Va., 1947—, 2d v.p. securities, 1970-72, v.p. investments, 1972—. Bd. dirs. Better Bus. Bur., Roanoke, Blue Cross S.W. Va. Served with USNR, 1944-46. Fellow Life Mgmt. Inst.; mem. Richmond Soc. Financial Analysts, Bond Club Va. Methodist (chmn. edn. commn. 1966-68, adult coordinator 1969-70, lay leader 1971-72, chmn. council on ministries 1973). Kiwanian (chmn. various coms. 1966—). Club: Hunting Hills Country. Home: 2374 Howard Rd Roanoke VA 24015 Office: 2301 Brambleton Av Roanoke VA 24015 also PO Box 2421 Roanoke VA 24010

MAGER, GERALD, judge; b. Bklyn., June 1, 1934; s. Morris David and Adele (Lapter) M.; B.A., U. Miami, 1956, J.D., 1959; postgrad. George Washington U., 1959; m. Naomi Himmelstein, Aug. 24, 1956; children—Mark Adam, Scott Alan, Russ Evan, Seth Lee. Admitted to Fla. bar, 1959; asst. atty. gen. State of Fla., Tallahassee, 1959-67, gen. counsel to gov., 1967-70; judge 4th Dist. Ct. Appeals Fla., West Palm Beach, 1970—. Chmn. Inter-agy. Com. on Mental Retardation Planning, 1964-66; mem. Adv. Council on Mental Retardation, 1965-66, chmn., 1966-67; mem. Fla. Oil Compact Com., 1967-70, Fla. Law Enforcement Planning Council, 1968-70, Fla. Jud. Council, 1970—. Recipient Outstanding Legislative Service award Fla. Psychology Assn., 1961; spl. recognition for legislative service Fla. Jud. Council, 1963; State Govtl. Affairs award Fla. Jaycees, 1965; certificate of appreciation Radio Free Europe, 1963-66; named Jaycee of Month, Tallahassee Jaycees, 1965. Mem. Am. (appellate judges sect.), Broward County, Palm Beach County, Orange County, Brevard County bar assns., Fla. Bar (com. on jud. selection, tenure and compensation), Am. Judicature Soc., Fla. Govt. Bar, Tau Delta Phi (founder), Tau Epsilon Rho, Omicron Delta Kappa (hon.). Jewish religion. Kiwanian, Elk, Woodmen of World, Toastmaster. Home: 3105 Palm Aire Dr Pompano Beach FL 33060 Office: 1525 Palm Beach Lakes Blvd West Palm Beach FL 33402

MAGGARD, JAMES ELMER, engr.; b. Cumberland, Ky., Dec. 25, 1933; s. James Elmer and Hazel (White) M.; B.C.E., U. Ky., 1956, student, 1951-56; student U. Cin., 1962-64; m. Lois Ann Grove, Aug. 19, 1961; children—James Joseph, Kimberly Monette. Constrn. engr. Balt. & Ohio R.R. Co., Cin., 1959-62; design engr. Larson, McKinney & Miller, Cin., 1962-64; engr. Watkins & Assos., Cons. Engrs., Lexington, Ky., 1964-72, v.p., dir. 1972—. Served to capt. USAF, 1956-59. Registered land surveyor, Ky. Asso. mem. Am. Inst. Planners; mem. Nat., Ky. socs. profl. engrs., Cons. Engrs. Council, Am. Legion, Ky. C. of C. Home: 673 Bayswater Way Lexington KY 40503 Office: 446 E High St Lexington KY 40508

MAGILL, HENRY FRASER, army officer; b. Badin, N.C., May 3, 1928; s. Ora Basel and Sally (Jenkins) M.; B.S. in Engring., Clemson A. and M. Coll., 1951; M.S. in Engring., U. Ala., 1960; advanced arty. officer course, 1952, electronic fire control, 1955, guided missile course, 1957, advanced ordnance officer course, 1961; student Army Command and Gen. Staff Coll., Army War Coll.; m. Janice Francis Kirby, June 27, 1964; 1 dau. Engr., Owens-Corning Fiberglas Corp., N.Y.C., 1952; commd. maj. AUS, 1963, advanced through grades to col.; arty. officer, Korea, 1953, comdr. officer ordnance co., 1954; aide-de-camp Maj. Gen. J.B. Medaris, Army Ballistic Missile Agy. and mil. asst. to Dr. Wernher von Braun, 1956-58; chief plans br. Antimissile and Space Def. Projects. Office, Redstone Arsenal, Ala., 1960-62; project officer Atomic Task Force High Altitude Atomic Tests, Down Range Antimissile Measurement Program, Atlantic Missile Range, 1963; project officer phys. scis. div. Army Research Office, Arlington, Va., 1963-67; battalion comdr. 3d Armored div., Germany, 1968; ordnance officer U.S. Forces, Berlin, Germany, 1969; office sec. def. advanced research projects agy., Vietnam, 1970-72; dir. Kwajalein Missile Range, Marshall Islands Trust Ty. Pacific Islands, 1972; chief requirements div. Safeguard System Command, 1973-74; project mgr. All Weather Short Range Air Def. System, Redstone Arsenal, 1974—. Mem. Community Concert Series, Huntsville, Ala., 1956. Mem. Am. Inst. Indsl. Engrs., Soc. Profl. Engrs., Am. Inst. Aeros. and Astronautics, Am. Ordnance Assn. Methodist. Club:

Army-Navy Country. Contbr. articles to profl. jours. Home: 7744 Mallard Rd Huntsville AL 35802 Office: Hq US Army Missile Command Redstone Arsenal AL 35807

MAGILL, RICHARD VINCENT, JR., ins. co. exec.; b. Greenville, S.C., Mar. 13, 1941; s. Richard Vincent and Kathryn Audrey (McKnight) M.; B.S., Clemson U., 1962; postgrad. Mich. State U., 1962-63; M.S., Fla. State U., 1968; m. Frances Carolyn Burgess, Mar. 8, 1969; 1 son, Richard Travis. Guide, U.S. Capitol Guide Force, 1963; circulation asst. Greenville County (S.C.) Library, 1966-69, head of spl. collections, 1969-71, head gen. reference, 1971-72; with Keys Printing Co., 1972-74; sales rep. Liberty Life Ins. Co., Greenville, 1974—. Served with AUS, 1963-65. Mem. Christian Ch. (bd. deacons 1970—). Home: 107 Burgess Av Greenville SC 29609 Office: 101 Camperdown Way Greenville SC 29602

MAGILL, VERNON ROY, mech. engr.; b. McCook, Neb., June 18, 1933; s. Van H. and Leila (Hoffman) M.; B.S. in Mech. Engring., U. Neb., 1956; M.S. in Indsl. Engring., U. Okla., 1965; m. Connie Jean Lindly, Aug. 15, 1954; children—Michael A., Scott L., Lee A. Jr. engr. Boeing Co., Wichita, Kan., 1956; asso. engr. Chance Vought Aircraft Co., Dallas, 1958-60; project engr. USAF, Tinker AFB, Okla., 1960-66, sr. engr., 1966-70, supr. prodn. mgmt., 1970—. Served to 1st lt. C.E., AUS, 1956-58. Registered profl. engr., Okla. Mem. Tinker Mgmt. Club, Sigma Xi, Delta Sigma Phi. Episcopalian. Author: Simplified Method for Preliminary Design of Thermal Anti-Icing Systems, 1960; Emergency Escape From High Performance Aircraft, 1965; Awakening of Middle Management to Value Engineering, 1967. Home: 7308 NW 19th St Bethany OK 73008 Office: OCAMA Tinker Air Force Base OK 73145

MAGINNISS, HOWARD PICHON, JR., aircraft co. exec.; b. Phila., Feb. 25, 1912; s. Howard Pichon and Mary Leona (Meyers) M.; student U. Kan., 1931-32; m. Muriel A. Starbecker, Feb. 1, 1964; children—Vicki Mae, Lee Kirk. Reporter, editor Tulsa Tribune, 1933-42; plant pub. relations mgr. Douglas Aircraft Co., Tulsa, 1942-46, pub. relations exec., Tulsa, also Santa Monica, Cal., 1951-60; Washington mgr. for pub. relations Douglas Aircraft, also McDonnell Douglas Corp., 1960—; dir. advt. and pub. relations Nat. Bank of Tulsa, 1946-51. Mem. Pub. Relations Soc. Am., Aero Club of Washington, Nat. Aviation Club, Nat. Space Club. Clubs: Nat. Press, Washington Golf and Country; Chesapeake Country (Lusby, Md.). Home: 3987 N River St Arlington VA 22207 Office: 1150 17th St NW Washington DC 20036

MAGLIO, M. MARTIN, chem. co. exec.; b. Bklyn., July 1, 1914; s. Charles and Phyllis (Aquino) M.; B.S., Manhattan Coll., 1937; M.S., Cath. U. Am., 1939; m. Alma Regina Roberts, Apr. 7, 1945; children—Janet Ellen (Mrs. John Madison Harris), Martin Brian. Research and development chemist Am. Cyanamid Co., Bound Brook, N.J., 1939-41; asst. prof. chemistry St. John's U., Bklyn., 1941-44; head Jersey City Labs. Advance Solvents Chems., Jersey City, 1944-47; research dir. Vestal Labs., St. Louis, 1947-53; pres. MCS Co., Riviera Beach, Fla., 1953—, Tropical Rentals, Inc., Riviera Beach, 1955—; exec. v.p. PCI Industries, Inc., Riviera Beach, 1972—; dir. First Marine Bank & Trust Co., Riviera Beach. Bd. dirs. A.R.C., Palm Beach County, Fla., 1965—. Mem. Am. Chem. Soc. (sect. alternate councilor 1944-45), Southeastern Terazzo Assn., Alpha Chi Sigma, Epsilon Sigma Pi. Club: PGA Golf (Palm Beach Gardens, Fla.). Contbr. articles to tech. publs. Home: 392 Golfview Rd Townhouse C North Palm Beach FL 33408 Office: 925 W 17th St Riviera Beach FL 33404

MAGNANT, KENNETH KARL, mech. engr.; b. Rhinelander, Wis., Aug. 2, 1937; s. Earl Hamilton and Elsie (Segerlund) M.; B.M.E., U. Fla., 1960; student U. Ala., 1968-71; m. Catherine Anne Slater, Dec. 22, 1962; children—Lance Kenneth, Mark Raymond. Mech. engr. Brookley AFB, Mobile, Ala., 1960; mech. engr., aerospace technologist NASA, Huntsville, Ala., 1961-64; mech. engr. U.S. Army Missile Command, Redstone Arsenal, Ala., 1964—; partner L & M Cons., Huntsville, 1967—. Registered profl. engr., Ala. Patentee air bourne missile launcher. Home: 3616 Crestmore Av Huntsville AL 35805 Office: US Army Missile Comd Redstone Arsenal AL 35809

MAGNES, WILLIAM DAVID, advt. agy. exec.; b. N.Y.C., May 22, 1916; s. Isaac David and Stella (Haberman) M.; student Yale, 1934-36, Columbia, 1936-38; m. Mary Rutherford Bull, Oct. 17, 1946. With Gussow, Kahn & Co., N.Y.C., 1946-48, Doherty, Clifford & Shenfield, N.Y.C., 1948-50; pub. relations dir. Columbia Artists Mgmt., N.Y.C., 1952-56; creative dir. Larrabee Assos., Washington, 1956-60; creative dir., exec. v.p. Robert Gamble, Jr., Inc., Washington, 1960-65; pres. William Magnes Advt., Inc., Washington, 1965—. Instr. advt. copy Am. U., Washington, 1959-60; pub. relations cons. to various orgns. Pres. Georgetown Workshop Theatre, Inc., 3020 Tilden St N.W., Inc. Served to capt. AUS, 1942-46, 50-52. Mem. Met. Washington Bd. of Trade, Am. Advt. Fedn., English-Speaking Union. Author short stories, novelettes. Home: 3020 Tilden St NW Washington DC 20008 Office: 1775 K St NW Washington DC 20006

MAGOFFIN, JAMES EDWARD, chem. co. exec.; b. Buffalo, Dec. 31, 1910; s. James A. and May Belle (Miller) M.; B.Chemistry, Cornell U., 1932, Ph.D., 1936; m. Dorothy Elizabeth Seay, Sept. 9, 1937; 1 dau., Elizabeth S. (Mrs. D. Bruce Shine). Asso. prof. indsl. chemistry U. N.C. at Chapel Hill, 1936-40; dir. research Thompson & Co., Oakmont, Pa., 1940-41; with Tenn. Eastman Co., Kingsport, 1941-53; with Eastman Chem. Products, Inc., Kingsport, 1953—, pres., 1973—. Mem. Am. Chem. Soc., Am. Inst. Chem. Engrs., Sigma Xi, Tau Beta Pi, Phi Kappa Phi. Episcopalian. Mason. Clubs: Ridgefields Country (Kingsport); The Chemists' (N.Y.C.). Home: 1433 Linville St Kingsport TN 37664 Office: Eastman Chem Products Inc PO Box 431 Kingsport TN 37662

MAGUIRE, CARY MCILWAINE, oil co. exec.; b. Ardmore, Pa., May 30, 1928; s. John Russell and Luna Neal (Ambler) M.; B.S., U. Pa., 1950; m. Ann Thompson, Feb. 27, 1960; children—Cary McIlwaine, Melinda Ambler, Ann Blaine. Mgr. Russell Maguire Oil Operations, Wichita Falls, also Dallas, Tex., 1955-67; chmn. bd., pres. Maguire Oil Co., Dallas, 1968—; pres. Camm Realty Co., St. Louis, 1967-71, Columbia Producing Co., N.Y.C., 1967-70; v.p. Alco Controls, St. Louis, 1956-69, Weber Dental Mfg. Co., Canton, O., 1956-69; dir. Components Corp. Am., Mt. Carmel, Ill. Mem. Nat. Rep. Finance Com., 1971—; chmn. Dallas County Rep. Finance Com., 1969-70. Mem. Nat. Petroleum Council, Ind. Petroleum Producers Assn. Am. (dir. 1956—, mem. gas com. 1970—), Tex. Ind. Producers and Royalty Owners Assn. (v.p. 1969-71), Dallas Wildcat Assn. (mem. exec. com. 1969-71). Clubs: Brook Hollow Golf, Dallas Petroleum, Idlewild, Terpsichorean (Dallas). Home: 5146 Kelsey St Dallas TX 75229 Office: 4200 First Nat Bank Bldg Dallas TX 75283

MAGUIRE, JACK RUSSELL, univ. ofcl.; b. Denison, Tex., Apr. 10, 1920; s. Jeff Edward and Elizabeth (Russell) M.; student N. Tex. State Coll., 1940-41; B. Journalism, U. Tex. at Austin, 1944; m. Patsy Jean Horton, Aug. 11, 1946; children—Jack Russell, Kevin Maguire. Reporter AP, Austin, 1943-44; pub. relations rep. M.-K.-T. R.R., St. Louis, 1945-50, T.P. & P. Ry., Dallas, 1950-51; dir. pub. relations Tex. Ins. Adv. Assn., Austin, 1950-56; exec. dir. U. Tex. Ex-Students' Assn., 1956—; pvt. practice as pub. relations cons., Austin, 1950—. Dir. Univ. State Bank, Austin; trustee Ednl. Projects for Edn., Inc., Washington. Mem. Am. Ry. Mag. Editors Assn., Pub. Relations Soc. Am., Am. Alumni Council (dir.), Am. Soc. Assn. Execs., Sigma Delta Chi. Presbyn. Clubs: Rotary, Westwood Country, Headliner. Author: Talk of Texas, 1973. Editor: A President's Country. Columnist: Talk of Texas. Contbr. articles profl. jours. Home: 1306 Belmont Pkwy Austin TX 78703 Office: Box 7278 Univ Station Austin TX 78712

MAGUIRE, JOHN NORRIS, computer software co. exec.; b. Brockton, Mass., May 4, 1930; s. John Norris and Helenor Mary (Hurley) M.; B.S. in Elec. Engring. summa cum laude, U. R.I., 1958; S.M. in Indsl. Mgmt., Mass. Inst. Tech., 1960; m. Ann Louise Connolly, June 6, 1956; children—Norrie, Alicia, Marty, Michael. Design engr., supr. Raytheon Corp., Waltham, Mass., 1956-59; computer system designer Lockheed Missiles & Space Co., Sunnyvale, Cal., 1960-66; sr. v.p., dir. tech. operations Consol. Analysis Center, Inc., Washington, 1966-72; pres. Software AG of N.Am., Inc., Reston, Va., 1972—. Served with USN, 1951-55. Mem. Assn. Computing Machinery (chmn. ann. tech. symposium DC chpt. 19—), Inst. Mgmt. Scis. (chmn. San Francisco chpt. 1965). Club: Mass. Inst. Tech. (pres. 1972-73, bd. dirs. 1973) (Washington). Home: 12124 Basset Lane Reston VA 22091 Office: 11800 Sunset Valley Dr Reston VA 22091

MAGUIRE, PAT HORTON (MRS. JACK RUSSELL MAGUIRE), editor; b. Houston, Apr. 23, 1926; d. Pat Arthur and Hilda (West) Horton; B.A., U. Tex., 1946; m. Jack Russell Maguire, Aug. 11, 1946; children—Jack, Kevin. Free lance writer, researcher St. Louis, Dallas, Austin, 1946-56; dir. pub. relations Austin Presbyn. Theol. Sem., 1956-61; acting mng. editor U. Tex. Alumni Mag., ALCALDE, 1961, mng. editor, 1961—, dir. alumni publs., 1964—; dir. communications Ex-Students' Assn. U. Tex., 1971—. Mem. Internat. Assn. Bus. Communicators, Women in Communications (regional v.p.), Alpha Phi. Clubs: Westwood Country, The Headliners (Austin). Home: 1306 Belmont Pkwy Austin TX 78703 Office: 2110 San Jacinto St Austin TX 78712

MAHAFFEY, WILLIAM EDGAR, elec. engr.; b. Anniston, Ala., Dec. 16, 1944; s. William Morris and Ada Lucille (Clark) M.; B.E.E., Auburn (Ala.) U., 1968, M.S. in Elec. Engring., 1972; m. Peggy Jo Wade, Aug. 10, 1968. With Ala. Power Co., Anniston, 1968-70, 72-74, Birmingham, 1974—, sr. engr., 1972—; grad. teaching asst. Auburn U., 1970-71. Registered profl. engr., Ala. Mem. Ala. Power Co. Nat. Mgmt. Assn. (treas. Eastern div. 1972-73), Eta Kappa Nu. Baptist. Home: 813 19th Av NW Birmingham AL 35215 Office: 600 N 18th St Birmingham AL 35203

MAHAN, OSCAR LELAND, lawyer; b. Chatham, Va., Mar. 26, 1939; s. John Ray and Virginia Atwood (Blair) M.; B.S., Va. Poly. Inst., 1961; postgrad. Wake Forest Law Sch., 1961-62; LL.D., U. Richmond, 1964; m. Cecelia Ann Stiff, July 18, 1964; children—Eric Leland, Stanley Patrick, Karen Cecelia. Admitted to Va. bar, 1964; partner firm Hall, Monahan, Engle, Mahan & Mitchell, Leesburg, 1967—, Winchester, 1967—. Chmn. Loudoun County Campaign for Atty. Gen. Andrew Miller, State Va., 1969-73. Served to capt. USAF, 1964-67. Decorated Air Force Commendation medal. Mem. Am., Va. bar assns., Va. State Bar., Va. Trial Lawyers Assn. (dir. 1970—), Am. Legion (post comdr. 1973—), Loudoun C. of C. Presbyn. (chmn. bd. deacons 1969-72, trustee 1972—). Kiwanian (pres. 1971-72). Home: 11 White Pl Leesburg VA 22075 Office: 3 E Market St Leesburg VA 22075

MAHAN, STANLEY MICHAEL, JR., dentist; b. Montevallo, Ala., June 29, 1934; s. Stanley Michael and Mary Ethyl (Wood) M.; B.S., Auburn U., 1956; M.A., Ala. Coll., 1961; D.M.D., U. Ala., 1966; m. Linda Chambers, Sept. 1, 1962; children—Susan Margaret, Stann Melinda. With H.H. Tchakarian & Sons, organ builders, part-time, 1952-56; dir. faculty-student services Ala. Coll., 1957-61; sales rep. Upjohn Drug Co., 1961-62; bass player Birmingham Symphony Orch., 1965-66; practice dentistry, Montevallo, 1966—; mem. faculty U. Ala. Sch. Dentistry, 1966-69. Chmn. Montevallo Community Chest, 1970. Dep. sheriff Shelby County, Ala., 1961-72; sec.-treas. Montevallo Fire Dept., 1958-61, asst. chief, 1970-71, chief, 1971—; Shelby County finance chmn. Albert P. Brewer campaign for gov., 1970. Bd. dirs. Musemont Fine Arts Camp, Birmingham Area council Boy Scouts Am. Recipient Vulcan award Boy Scouts Am., 1970. Mem. Ala. Fire Chiefs Assn., Montevallo C. of C., Ala. Conservancy, North-South Skirmish Assn., Phi Mu Alpha, Beta Beta Beta, Delta Sigma Delta (dep. 1966-72), Delta Tau Delta. Democrat. Methodist (mem. adminstrv. bd.). Mason, Lion (1st v.p. Montevallo 1961), Rotarian (dirs. Montevallo 1968, 71). Home: Montebrier Brierfield AL 35035 Office: 266 Salem Rd Montevallo AL 35115

MAHANEY, R. DAN, govt. ofcl.; b. Dubois, Pa., Dec. 23, 1918; s. Daniel Thomas and Nora (Hepburn) M.; m. Lois C. Campbell, June 28, 1952; children—Michael, Patricia. Chief operations and safety CAA, Washington Nat. Airport, 1945-57; chief operations and safety FAA, Bur. Nat. Capital Airports, Washington, 1957-65, mgr. Dulles Internat. Airport, 1965-72, mgr. Nat. Capital Airports, 1972—. Served with USAAF, 1940-45. Mem. Am. Soc. Safety Engrs., Am. Assn. Airport Execs., Nat. Aviation Club, Washington Aero. Club. Home: 3466 Roberts Lane Arlington VA 22207 Office: Hangar 9 Washington Nat Airport Washington DC 20001

MAHER, ALVIN MICHAEL, research co. exec.; b. Houston, Aug. 9, 1929; s. Alvin Michael and Lucille Germaine (Guillaume) M.; B.S., Tulane, 1957; postgrad. U. Md., 1957, George Washington U., 1958; m. Renate Erika Betterman; children—Christopher, Katherine, Robert, Wayne, Debra, Karina. Supr. applied reliability engring. Melpar, Inc., Arlington, Va., 1957-60; dir. quality assurance div. Keltec Industries, Inc., Alexandria, Va., 1960-64; pres. Gen. Environments Corp., Springfield, Va., 1972—; pres., dir. M-S Marine Corp., Annapolis, Md., 1970—; tech. expert on shock and vibration U.S. Internat. Electrotech. Commn., 1967-73; dir. constrn. Injun II Earth Satellite, 1961. Served with USAF, 1951-55. Mem. Am. Council Ind. Labs., Am. Ordnance Assn., Inst. Environmental Scis. (sr. pres. 1966-67, nat. bd. dirs. 1967-68), Soc. Automotive Engrs., Am. Soc. Testing and Materials, Pi Kappa Alpha. Patentee in field. Home: 8301 Weller Av McLean VA 22101 Office: 6840 Industrial Rd Springfield VA 22151

MAHLMAN, HARVEY ARTHUR, utility co. exec.; b. LaCrosse, Wis., Aug. 8, 1923; s. Arthur Alvin and Marie (Putzier) M.; B.S. in Chemistry, U. Minn., 1946, B.B.A., 1949; Ph.D., U. Tenn., 1956; m. Nancy Taylor, June 30, 1945; children—Janice Lee (Mrs. James Moore), John Arthur. Lab. asst. Gen. Electric Co., Schenectady, 1949-52; sr. research staff Oak Ridge Nat. Lab., 1952-73; power resource specialist Fla. Power & Light Co., Miami, Fla., 1973—. Active Little League Baseball, Knoxville, Tenn., 1965—. Served with C.E., AUS, 1943-46. NIH fellow, 1963-64. Mem. Am. Chem. Soc., Tenn. Acad. Sci., Sigma Xi. Mason. Contbr. articles on radiation chemistry to sci. jours. Patentee in waste water treatment. Home: 7006 Downing Dr Knoxville TN 37919 Office: PO Box 3100 Florida Power and Light Co Miami FL 33101

MAHLMANN, JOHN JAMES, assn. exec.; b. Washington, Jan. 21, 1942; s. Charles Victor and Mary Elizabeth (Deye) M.; B.F.A., Boston U., 1962, M.F.A., 1963; postgrad. U. Notre Dame, 1962; Ed.D., Pa. State U., 1970; m. Ning Ning Chang, Feb. 5, 1972; 1 son, Justin Geeng Ming. Grad. asst. Boston U., 1962-63, instr., supr. student tchrs., 1964-66; grad. asst., research asst. Pa. State U., University Park, 1963-64, instr., 1966-67; asst. prof. Tex. Tech. Coll., Lubbock, 1967-69; dir. publs., asst. exec. sec. Nat. Art Edn. Assn., Washington, 1969-71, exec. sec., 1971—, editor Art Edn. Jour., 1970—, Art Tchr. Mag., 1971—; exhibited in one-man shows at Botolph Gallery, Boston, 1965, also Salem (Mass.) State Coll., Loft Gallery, San Antonio, Harvard; exhibited group shows Boston U., Cushing Gallery, Dallas, Lubbock Art Assn.; represented in permanent collections at S.W. Tex. State Coll., San Marcos, Salem State Coll., Pa. State U., others. Mem. N.E.A., Nat. Art Edn. Asn., Am. Soc. Assn. Execs., Washington Soc. Assn. Execs. Contbr. articles in field to profl. jours. Home: 11702 Indian Ridge Rd Reston VA 22070 Office: 1201 16th St NW Washington DC 20036

MAHON, GEORGE HERMAN, congressman; b. Mahon, La., Sept. 22, 1900; s. John Kirkpatrick and Lola Willis (Brown) M.; A.B., Simmons U., 1924; LL.B., U. Tex., 1925; postgrad. U. Minn., summer 1925; LL.D. (hon.), Waynesburg Coll., 1951, Wayland Coll., 1960, Tex. Technol. Coll., 1962, Hardin Simmons U., 1964, Pepperdine Coll., 1965; m. Helen Stevenson, Dec. 21, 1923; 1 dau., Daphne. Began practice at Colorado City, Tex., 1925; elected county atty. Mitchell County, Tex., 1926; apptd. dist. atty. 32d Jud. Dist. Tex., 1927, elected without opposition, 1928, 30, 32; mem. 74th to 93d Congresses, 19th Tex. Dist., chmn. house appropriations com., 1964—, chmn. house subcom. def. appropriations, 1949-52, 55—, author ann. def. appropriation bills, chmn. joint senate-house com. on reduction of fed. expenditures. Recipient Distinguished Pub. Service award Am. Legion, 1973. Democrat. Methodist. Mason (33 deg.). Home: Lubbock TX 79408 Office: House Office Bldg Washington DC 20515

MAHONEY, VERNON LLOYD MIKE, city planner, cons.; b. Asheville, N.C., Feb. 14, 1925; s. Vernon Litsinger and Esther (Newberg) M.; student U. Ariz., 1942-43; B.S., U. N.M., 1945; postgrad. U. Tex., 1947, U. Okla., 1949, 50-51; children—Lloyd S., Molly F., D. Kirkman, Ellen N. Instr. civil engring. U. Ariz., 1947-48; planning asst. Tucson-Pima County, Ariz., 1948; asst. planning dir., 1951-53; asst. planning engr. City of El Paso, Tex., 1948-50; research asst. U. Okla., 1950-51; planning dir. Austin, Tex., 1953-58, City and County of Yuma, Ariz., 1958-62; asst. planning dir., City of Phoenix, 1962-64; planning dir. Ft. Worth, 1964-69; pres. Mike Mahoney & Assos., Inc., urban planning cons., Ft. Worth, 1969—; lectr. urban studies Tex. Christian U., 1965-70, real estate, regional plng. So. Meth. U., 1970—. Pres., Austin Council Chs., 1958, Yuma council Camp Fire Girls, 1961, chmn. long range planning com. Maricopa council, 1963, mem. bd. Tarrant County council, 1965, pres., 1966, 67. Bd. dirs. Ft. Worth-Tarrant County Community Council, 1968-70, Fort Worth Chamber Devel. Corp., 1968-70. Served with USNR, 1943-46. Mem. Am. Inst. Planners, Am. Soc. C.E., Am. Soc. Planning Ofcls., Phi Delta Kappa, Theta Chi. Office: 3221 Cockrell Av Fort Worth TX 76109

MAHONY, BERNARD JOSEPH, petroleum engr.; b. Chgo., June 29, 1927; s. Myles Aloysius and Anne Frances (Gaughan) M.; B.S. in Petroleum Engring., N.M. Sch. Mines, 1952; m. Vonna Belle Hendren, Dec. 16, 1950; children—Bernard, Colleen, Kevin. Field petroleum engr. Texaco, Inc., Panwell, Tex., 1952-59; petroleum engr. Creole Petroleum Co., Venezuela, S.Am., 1954-58; prin. B.J. Mahony cons. petroleum engr., Chanute, Kan., 1958-65; drilling engr. Drilling Well Control Inc., Midland, Tex., 1965-69; drilling specialist Sinclair Oil Co., Midland, 1969—; div. mgr. Inexco Oil Co., Midland, 1970-73. Cons. deep drilling, Falcon Engring. Co. Served with USNR, 1945-46. Registered profl. engr., Kan. Mem. Am. Assn. Profl. Engrs., Am. Inst. Mining Engrs., Soc. Petroleum Engrs. Contbr. articles on engring. to tech. mags. Home: 3529 Imperial St Midland TX 79701 Office: 2002 W Wall St Midland TX 79701

MAI, LUDWIG HUBERT, educator; b. Mannheim, Germany, Mar. 27, 1898; s. Hubert C. and Anna Maria (Specht) M.; Diploma, U. Manneheim, 1920; Diploma Com. Ed, Goethe U., 1921, Dr. Rer. Pol., 1924; came to U.S., 1950; m. Ilse Behrend, Feb. 12, 1927; children—Veronica (Mrs. J.R. Reynolds), Klaus L., Ursula (Mrs. Gordon White). Instr. Fressl Coll., Augsburg, Germany, 1922; mgr. DEFAG, Shanghai, China, 1923-45; lectr. Tientsin (China) Coll., 1945-49; prof. econs. St. Mary's U., San Antonio, 1950—, dean grad. sch., 1959-68, Univ. prof., 1968—, dir. Inst. Internat. and Pub. Affairs, 1968—; cons. Southwest Research Inst., San Antonio, 1956-66. Mem. Am. Econ. Assn., Assn. for Social Econs. (v.p. 1970), Royal Econ. Soc., S.W. Social Sci. Assn., Tex. Internat. Trade Assn. (dir. edn. 1955-60), Assn. Evolutionary Econs., Omicron Delta Epsilon, Pi Gamma Mu. Author: Approach to Economics, 1966; On the Formation of Political Economy, 1969. Home: 343 Shadwell Dr San Antonio TX 78228

MAIKEN, PETER TRUEBLOOD, editor; b. Washington Island, Wis., Sept. 9, 1934; s. John Andrew and Grace (Trueblood) M.; B.A. in History, Beloit Coll., 1955; M.A. in History, Northwestern U., 1966; m. Gail Bradley, Dec. 19, 1959; children—Eric Bradley, Terrence Trueblood, Steven Chancellor. Reporter, Freeport (Ill.) Jour.-Standard, 1961; staff writer Rockford (Ill.) Register-Republic, 1962; asst. editor Chgo. Tribune Mag., 1963-68, mng. editor, 1969-70; editor Washington mag. of The Sunday Star, 1970—. Served to lt. USNR, 1956-60. Mem. Sigma Alpha Epsilon. Presbyn. Home: 2290 Dunster Lane Rockville MD 20854 Office: 225 Virginia Av SE Washington DC 20003

MAILEN, JAMES CLIFFORD, chem. engr., b. Colorado Springs., Colo., Aug. 19, 1937; s. Clifford Philman and Ruth Lorine (Richeson) M.; B.S. in Chem. Engring., Kan. State U., 1959; Ph.D. (NSF fellow, Univ. fellow), U. Fla., 1964; m. Ima Jean Hester, June 8, 1963; children—Kim Hamilton Bolick, John Edward. Devel. engr. Oak Ridge Nat. Lab., 1963-71, coordinator engring. fast analyzer, 1971-73, coordinator chem. devel. fuel reprocessing, 1973—. Mem. A.A.A.S., Am. Chem. Soc., Am. Inst. Chem. Engrs., Phi Kappa Phi. Contbr. tech. articles on chem. engring. to profl. jours. Patentee in field. Home: 134 Cumberland View Dr Oak Ridge TN 37830 Office: PO Box Oak Ridge TN 37830

MAILEN, TYSON HARVEY, oil co. exec.; b. Cottonwood Falls, Kan., Jan. 26, 1911; s. Francis Charles and Jennie Bird (Harvey) M.; B.A., Kan. U., 1939; M.S., Okla. State U., 1941; m. Caroline Watson, Nov. 15, 1963; children—Tarry Watson, Tyson Harvey. Research fellow Okla. State U., 1939-41; with Phillips Petroleum Co., Bartlesville, Okla., 1941—, mgr. agrl. chems. Analyst Marketing Research Chem. Dept., 1963—. Asst. commr. Cherokee Area council Boy Scouts Am., 1954-57. Served to 1st lt., AUS, 1941-45. Mem. Entomological Soc. Am., Sons of God Evangelistic Assn. (dir. 1971—), Sigma Phi Epsilon. Presbyn. (ruling elder). Mason (32 deg., Shriner), K.T., Elk. Club: Frank Phillips Mens. Patentee in field. Home: 101 N Seneca St Bartlesville OK 74003 Office: 16 C 1 Phillips Bldg Bartlesville OK 74004

MAILMAN, DAVID SHERWIN, educator; b. Chgo., June 29, 1938; s. Louis Leo and Harriette (Churnkoff) M.; B.S. in Physiology, U. Chgo., 1958; Ph.D. (fellow), U. Ill. Med. Sch., 1964; postgrad. (postdoctoral fellow), U. Md. Med. Sch., 1963-64; m. Mary Louise Malakoff, Sept. 19, 1960; children—Daniel Stephen, Douglas Raymond, Dennis Michael, Duane Edward. Asst. prof. biology dept. U. Houston, 1964-70, asso. prof., 1970—. Adj. asso. prof. physiology U. Tex., Houston, 1973. Active Boy Scouts Am. NSF grantee, 1966-68, Gulf Oil Co. grantee, 1971, Office Naval Research grantee, 1968-73. Mem. Am. Soc. Zoology, Soc. Exptl. Biol. Medicine, A.A.A.S., Sigma Xi, Phi Sigma Delta. Research in mechanisms of salt and water transport, regulation of body water and cardiovascular system. Home: 4414 Roseneath St Houston TX 77021 Office: Biology Dept Univ Houston TX 77004

MAINS, THOMAS PHILLIP, JR., lawyer; b. Denver, Sept. 17, 1934; s. Thomas Phillip and Louise (Rankin) M.; student, Williams Coll., 1952-54; U. Colo., 1954-59; LL.B. magna cum laude, Am. U., 1963; m. Diana Elizabeth Dabbelt, Jan. 31, 1959; children—Jon F., Thomas Phillip III, Courtney M. Admitted to Va. bar, 1963; asso. T. Brooke Howard, Alexandria, Va., 1963-65; partner Howard, Morris, Hancock, Mains & Howard, Alexandria, 1965-68; pvt. practice, Alexandria, Va., 1968—. Cons. to various med., para-med. and medico-legal groups, 1968—. Mem. Assn. Trial Lawyers, Va., No. Va. trial lawyers, Delta Kappa Epsilon, Phi Rho Sigma, Sigma Delta Phi. Presbyn. Home: 4790 Old Dominion Dr Arlington VA 22207 Office: 421 King St Alexandria VA 22314

MAJOR, ALEXANDER DAVID, physician; b. Madison, Wis., Nov. 18, 1916; s. David Maggard and Leta Elliot (Allen) M.; A.S., U. Tex. at Arlington, 1935; M.D., Baylor U., 1939; m. Mabel Kathryn Chandler, Dec. 9, 1941; children—Kay (Mrs. Tom Telle), Carol (Mrs. Tom Grow), Mike, Chan, Sandy, Brent, Kris. Intern City County Hosp., Ft. Worth, 1939-40; resident, 1940-43; practice medicine, specializing in surgery, Nocona, Tex., 1946—; mem. staff Major Clinic Hosp., Bowie Meml. Hosp.; med. dir. Consol. Aircraft Co., Fort Worth, 1943-44; owner, dir. Major Clinic Hosp., 1946-71. Pres., Nocona Sch. Bd., 1949-60. Served to lt. col. M.C., AUS, 1943-46; PTO. Recipient Man of Year award from Nocona C. of C., 1950. Decorated Bronze Star medal. Diplomate Am. Bd. Family Practice. Mem. Tri-County Med. Soc. (past pres.), Tex. Med. Assn., A.M.A., Am. Acad. Family Practice. Home: Route 3 Nocona TX 76255 Office: Box 239 Nocona TX 76255

MAJOR, JAMES BROOKS, clergyman; b. Hopkinsville, Ky., Sept. 1, 1928; s. Robert Howard and Harriett (Steger) M.; M.A., Austin Peay State U., 1953; M.Div., Vanderbilt U., 1957, Ph.D., 1966; m. Martha Stuart Hutchison, Sept. 19, 1948; 1 son, Robert Boyd. Ordained to ministry Christian Ch., 1953; minister, Liberty, Elkton, Millbrooke Ch., Hopkinsville, 1948—. Coordinator acad. affairs U. Ky., Hopkinsville Community Coll., 1967—. Chmn. bd. Eagle U. Consortium, Ft. Campbell, Ky., 1972—, Hopkinsville Pub. Library, 1970—. Recipient Great Tchr. award U. Ky. Alumni Assn., 1968. Mem. Phi Kappa Tau. Democrat. Club: Athenaeum (Hopkinsville). Home: 303 Deepwood Hopkinsville KY 42240 Office: North Dr Hopkinsville KY 42240

MAJOR, LAWRENCE ELLIOTT, lawyer; b. Cannonsburg, Pa., Apr. 12, 1942; s. David and Tillie (Finkel) M.; student Washington and Jefferson Coll., 1960-62; B.A., Ohio No. U., 1965, J.D., 1968; m. Linda Ruth Brett, Dec. 26, 1964; children—Dania, David. Admitted to Ohio bar, 1968, Fla. bar, 1972; with office gen. counsel U.S. Dept. Agr., 1968; trial atty. Navarre, Rizor & DaPore, Lima, O., 1968-72, Wolfson & Diamond, Miami Beach, Fla., 1972—. Cons. Tradeway of Kokomo, Inc. (Ind.). Mem. Am. Trial Lawyers Assn., Am., Fla., Ohio, Allen County bar assns., Ohio Acad. Trial Lawyers, Am. Judicature Soc., Phi Alpha Delta, Alpha Epsilon Pi. Home: 6757 SW 40th St Fort Lauderdale FL 33314 Office: 407 Lincoln Rd Miami Beach FL 33139

MAKANSI, MUNZER, chem. co. exec.; b. Aleppo, Syria, Dec. 23, 1923; s. Ismail and Amina (Khudari) M.; B.Sc. with honors, Fouad-I U., Cairo, Egypt, 1943; M.A., Columbia, 1950, M.S., 1951, D. Engring. Sci., 1957; m. Nellie M. Kotsakis, Jan. 2, 1951; children—Delal, Antar, Jason, Tarek. Tchr. Alma-Amoun High Sch., Aleppo, 1947-49; with Dupont Co., 1954—, Wilmington, Del., 1954-66, supr. research and devel., Chattanooga, 1966—. Mem. Sigma Xi, Phi Lambda Upsilon. Author: Periodic Classification of Chemical Elements, 1949. Patentee in field. Home: 106 Stratford Rd Signal Mountain TN 37377 Office: Chattanooga Nylon Plant Access Rd Chattanooga TN 37343

MAKOVER, SYLVAN AARON, clothing co. exec.; b. Baltimore, Jan. 28, 1914; s. Thomas and Mollie Eva (Land) M.; LL.B., Atlanta Law Sch., 1933; m. Frances Katz, Sept. 26, 1940; children—Marilyn (Mrs. Mitchell Shapiro), Bette (Mrs. Bernard Bell). With Shirley of Atlanta, Inc., mfr. ladies and childrens sportswear, Atlanta, Ga., 1928—, pres., 1964—. Vice pres. Jewish Nat. Fund of Atlanta, 1970—. Vice pres., bd. dirs. Atlanta Jewish Community Center; bd. dirs. Jewish Home of Atlanta; bd. overseers Jewish Theol. Sem., 1972—. Recipient Louis Marshall Meml. medal, 1972. Mem. Jewish religion (pres. congregation 1968-69, bd. dirs. 1958—). Mem. B'nai B'rith. Clubs: Standard, Progressive. Home: 3020 Nancy Creek Rd NW Atlanta GA 30327 Office: 4200 Shirley Dr SW Atlanta GA 30336

MALACARA, RAYMUNDO AMPUDIA, editor; b. Mexico City, Mexico, Nov. 24, 1946; s. Raymundo Ampudia and Aurora Malacara (de Ampudia) Del Valle; ed. bus. adminstrn. Instituto Tecnologica de estudios Superiores de Monterrey, 1965-69; m. Elsie C. de Ampudia, Jan. 26, 1973. Adminstrn. mgr. Hoy S.A., Mexico City, 1967-69, dir. gen., 1972—; gen. mgr. editorial Caballero S.A., Mexico City, 1969-72; dir. gen. Condominios Conar, Mexico City. Clubs: Mexico Athletic, Club de Golf (Mexico, D.F.). Home: 358 Augusto Rodin Mexico DF 19 Mexico Office: 9 Amores Mexico DF 12 Mexico

MALCOM, JOHN PAUL, lumber co. exec.; b. Okolona, Ark., Dec. 3, 1918; s. John Franklin and Nellie C. (Hare) M.; grad. high sch.; m. Frances Jane Hardin, June 9, 1945; children—Mary Karol (Mrs. Edwin Dale), Paula Jane (Mrs. John L. Griffin). With Gurdon (Ark.) Lumber Co., 1939—, sales mgr., 1958—. Mem. Gurdon City Council, 1962-66; mem. Gurdon Sch. Bd., 1964—. Served with USAAF, 1942-45. Baptist. Mason, Rotarian. Club: Hoo Hoo Lumbermens. Home: 903 E Main St Gurdon AR 71743 Office: Gurdon Lumber Co Hwy 67 Gurdon AR 71743

MALETTE, WILLIAM GRAHAM, educator; b. Springfield, Mo., Mar. 27, 1922; s. Harry Lomison and Olive (Graham) M.; student Drury Coll., 1940-42, Fresno State Coll., 1947-49; M.D., Washington U. (St. Louis), 1953; m. Darleen Roberta Sullenger, May 25, 1943; children—Diane (Mrs. John Henry), William Graham II. Intern Letterman Army Hosp., San Francisco, 1953-54; resident Denver VA Hosp., 1954-58; commd. U.S. A.F., 1953, advanced through grades to maj., 1953; chief exptl. surgery dept. Sch. Aviation Medicine, Brooks AFB, Tex., 1958-61, chief unit 2, Gen. Surg. Service, Wilford Hall USAF Hosp., Lackland AFB, Tex., 1961-63; ret. 1963, asso. prof. dept. surgery Med. Center, U. Ky. at Lexington, 1963-71, prof., 1971-73, also asso. dean VA affairs, 1971-73; prof. surgery, chmn. emergency med. dept. U. Fla., Jacksonville, 1973—; chief surg. service VA Hosp., Lexington, 1963-71, chief staff, 1971-73; mem. staff University Hosp., Jacksonville. Cons. Nat. Inst. Mental Health, and others. Served with USAAF, 1942-46. Diplomate Am. Bd. Surgery, Am. Bd. Thoracic Surgery. Fellow A.C.S., Am. Coll. Cardiology, Am. Coll. Chest Physicians; mem. Soc. Thoracic Surgery, A.M.A., Aerospace Med. Assn., So. med. assn., Central Surg. Soc., So. Thoracic Surg. Assn., Pan-Pacific Surg. Assn., Am. Soc. Artificial Internal Organs, Internat. Cardiovascular Soc., Am. Assn. Thoracic Surgery, Assn. Advancement Med. Instrumentation (pres.), Sports Car Club Am. Mason. Contbr. profl. jours. Home: 4965 Long Bow Rd Jacksonville FL 32210 Office: 655 8th St W Jacksonville FL 32203

MALIK, ANAND KUMAR, educator; b. Main Channu, India, Apr. 10, 1924; came to U.S., 1954; s. Arjan Das and Kartar (Kaur) M.; F.Sc., Panjab U., India, 1942, B.A., 1944, M.A., 1946; P.G.C.E., U. London (Eng.), 1952, D.Ed., 1954; Ed.D., Columbia, 1955; m. Vik Chandler, Sept. 20, 1958; children—Arun Kumar, Ashwin Kumar, Avinash Chankumar. 1954. Lectr. Govt. Coll., Rohtak, India, 1949-52; vis. prof. edn. U. Ida., 1957-60; head div. Asiatic studies U. Bahia, Salvador, Brazil, 1960-63; head Sch. Edn. of Panjab U., 1963-64; asst. prof. U. Sask. (Can.), 1964-67; prof. philosophy of edn. U. Tenn., 1967—; cons. Sch. Planning Lab., Knoxville, Tenn., 1960, Fla. Sch. Desegregation Center, Coral Gables, 1971. Mem. Brit. Mus. Soc. Recipient research award Can. Council Humanities and Social Scis., 1965-67, postgrad. research award U. Tenn., 1970; named Top Tchr. of Year U. Tenn., 1971, lectr. of year Phi Kappa Phi, 1972. Fellow Philosophy of Edn. Soc.; mem. Delta Tau Kappa, Phi Delta Kappa. Author: From the Five Continents, 1956; Current Themes in Philosophy of Education, 1967; Social Foundations of Canadian Education, 1969; Comparative Theories of Knowledge, 1971. Editor of Internat. Edn. Home: 7709 Sussex Circle Knoxville TN 37919

MALIK, DHARAM DEV, educator; b. Bhainsval, India, June 20, 1931; s. Chet Ram and Amar Kaur M.; B.V.Sc., Coll. Vet. Medicine, Hissar, India, 1956; M.S., Tex. A. & M. U., 1962, Ph.D., 1964; m. Bimla Devi, Apr. 24, 1951; children—Kapil, Rishi, Came to U.S., 1967. Instr. Coll. Vet. Medicine, Hissar, India, 1956-60; research asso., then asst. Tex. A. & M. U., College Station, 1960-64; asso. prof. Punjab Agrl. U., Hissar, 1964-67; mem. faculty Jarvis Christian Coll., Hawkins, Tex., 1967—, prof. biology, 1969—, head dept., 1967—. Veterinarian Punjab State, India, 1956-60. Research grantee, 1965-67; Teaching fellow, 1968-69. Mem. Poultry Sci. Assn. Natural History Assn., Sigma Xi. Contbr. articles to profl. jours. Home: PO Box 463 Hawkins TX 75765

MALKANI, MOHAN JETHMAL, educator; b. Hyderabad, Pakistan, Sept. 17, 1933; s. Jethmal Hukmatrai and Gobindi Jethmal (Chablani) M.; M.S., U. Baroda, India, 1955; M.S. in Elec. Engring., Miss. State U., 1964; m. Duru Vaswani, Dec. 31, 1967; children—Sunil, Tony. Came to U.S., 1960. Mem. faculty Tenn. State U., Nashville, 1967—, prof. elec. engring., 1967—, head elec. engring. dept., 1967—; vis. scientist Mass. Inst. Tech. Lincoln Lab., summers 1970-73. Cons. Arnold Engring. Research Center, Tullahoma, Tenn., 1973. NSF Summer fellow Utah State U., 1964, Rennselaer Poly. Inst., 1967. Mem. I.E.E.E., Am. Soc. Engring. Edn. Home: 246 White Bridge Rd Nashville TN 37209 Office: 3500 Centennial Blvd Nashville TN 37203

MALKEMUS, JOHN DAVID, chem. co. exec.; b. Louisville, Sept. 6, 1913; s. David S. and Catherine (Carr) M.; B.S., DePaul U., Chgo., 1934, M.S., 1936; Ph.D., Northwestern U., 1939, postgrad., 1939-40; m. Deidre DeVries, June 11, 1939; children—Deirdre (Mrs. Gary Norton), David W., Douglas S., Dean, Diana. Chemist, Colgate-Palmolive-Peet Co., Jersey City, 1940-46; dir. products application div. Jefferson Chem. Co., Austin, Tex., 1946-59; asst. gen. mgr., tech. dir. specialty chems. div. Reichhold Chems., Inc., Austin, 1959—. Mem. Am. Chem. Soc., Soc. Plastics Engrs. Contbr. articles profl. jours. Patentee in field. Home: 4603 Crestway Dr Austin TX 78731 Office: PO Box 9405 Austin TX 78766

MALL, MYRON MERRIELL, banker; b. St. Louis, Dec. 5, 1940; s. Martin A. and Lorraine H.E. (Flamm) M.; B.A. in Bus. Adminstrn., Parsons Coll., 1964; m. Barbara Louise Heinz, Aug. 24, 1963; children—Elizabeth Gould, Frederick Andrew. Portfolio mgr. St. Louis Union Trust Co., 1964-67; v.p. Nat. Bank of Commerce, Memphis, 1967—; dir. Delightful Living, Inc., Memphis, 1970—. Bd. dirs. Educare Child Care Centers, Inc., Memphis, 1969—. Mem. St. Louis Soc. Financial Analysts, Ark. Soc. Financial Mgrs., Brooks Art League, Les Amis du Vin. Club: Memphis Petroleum. Home: 235 Kimbrough St Memphis TN 38104 Office: One Commerce Square Memphis TN 38150

MALLALIEU, FRANK ARTHUR, architect; b. Springfield, Mass., Apr. 14, 1937; s. Herbert and Charlotte Alden (Howe) M.; B.S. (Edward W. Edwards scholar) in Arch., U. Cin., 1963; postgrad. George Washington U., 1964-66; m. Judith Ann Conover, June 15, 1963; children—Todd Stephen, Lori Elizabeth. Asst. sect. chief Office Constrn. and Preliminary Planning Service, VA, Washington, 1963-69; sr. asso. William Phillips Brown & Assos., Alexandria, Va., 1969-71; project mgr. Enviro-Med, Ind. med., ednl. facility planners, LaJolla, Cal., Washington, 1971-72; project coordinator Office of Operating Programs Gen. Services Adminstrn., Washington, 1972—. Archtl., constrn. mgmt. cons. Gerald A. Schwab, Alexandria, Va. Mem. Arlington (Va.) Community Action Com., 1966—, Civic Assn. Hollin Hills (Va.), 1967—. Served with USNR, 1954-62. Recipient 3d award Illuminating Engring. Soc., 1961; named Outstanding Young Architect in Washington D.C. area D.C. Council Engring. and Archtl. Socs. and Washington Acad. Scis., 1966. Mem. A.I.A., Acacia, Delta Phi Delta. Club: Hollin Meadows Swim and Tennis (bd. dirs.) (Alexandria). Prin. archtl. works include Gar-Field Sr. High Sch., Prince William County, Va., 1970; Stafford Sr. High Sch., Stafford County, Va., 1971. Home: 2115 Mason Hill Dr Alexandria VA 22306 Office: 19th and F Sts NW Washington DC 20405

MALLAN, JOHN POWERS, polit. scientist; b. Cambridge, Mass., Dec. 20, 1922; s. Thomas Francis and Anna (Powers) M.; B.S., U. N.H., 1942; M.A., U. Chgo., 1948; Ph.D., Harvard, 1964; m. Lucy Margaret Bunzl, Aug. 7, 1965; 1 son, Thomas Walter; stepchildren—Elizabeth Augustine, Margaret Augustine. Instr., Boston U., 1948-50; asst. prof. Simmons Coll., 1950-51; teaching fellow Harvard, 1952-55; instr., asst. prof. Smith Coll., 1955-57, 60-65; dir. Mass. Audit of State Needs, 1957-60; trustee Mass. Bd. Community Colls., 1960-65; mem. sr. staff Am. Assn. Jr. Colls., 1965-68, 69-73; dir. govtl. relations Am. Assn. State Colls. and Univs., 1973—; mem. sr. research staff Urban Inst., Washington, 1968-69. Mem. Northampton (Mass.) Sch. Com., 1962-63; sec. Mass. Higher Ednl. Facilities Commn., 1964-65. Served with AUS, 1944-46. Mem. Am. Polit. Sci. Assn. Home: 3235 38th St NW Washington DC 20016 Office: 1 Dupont Circle NW Washington DC 20036

MALLE, ALBERT LEON, educator; b. Pittsburg, Kan., Sept. 30, 1914; s. Albert Edward and Maude Florence (Guthrie) M.; D.V.M., Kan. State U., 1939; m. Thela Fern Chesnut, June 28, 1936; children—Diane Lee (Mrs. Martin Jon Beeman), Kathy Jo (Mrs. Thomas John Dearinger). Pvt. practice vet. medicine, Pierson, Ia., 1939-51; mem. faculty Okla. State U., Stillwater, 1951—, prof. pathology, 1968—, dir. extension Coll. Vet. Medicine, 1968—. City councilman, Pierson, Ia., 1940-47; mayor, Pierson, 1949-51. Mem. Am., Okla. vet. med. assns., Am. Assn. Avian Pathologists, Phi Zeta. Methodist. Mason. Home: 1819 W 5th St Stillwater OK 74074 Office: Okla State U Coll Vet Medicine Stillwater OK 74074

MALLEN, SAUL TWOM, textile mfg. exec.; b. Boston, Dec. 18, 1914; s. Joseph and Ida (Seltzer) M.; LL.B., Northeastern U., 1937, J.D., 1972; m. Muriel S. Goldberg, June 10, 1939; children—Ted A., Steven L. (dec.), Peter J. Admitted to Mass. bar, 1938; with Sport-Wear Hosiery Mills, Inc. (co. name changed to Sport Wear Mills, Inc., 1968), Phila., 1938—, exec. mgr., Etowah, Tenn., exec. v.p., sec. treas., dir., chmn. 1942—; officer, chmn. bd. dirs. Windsor Hosiery Mills, Inc., Etowah; co-founder, exec. v.p., treas., chmn., Internat. Yarn Corp., San Juan, P.R., 1963, Cleveland, Tenn., 1967—; co-founder, dir., chmn. Knitco, Inc., N.Y.C., 1966-69, Amtex, Inc., Cleveland, Tenn., 1972—. Pioneer drive to establish first blood bank in McMinn County, Tenn.; mem. Jewish Community Center; active Ochs Meml. Temple, Chattanooga, 1941—, dir. 1965-67; patron Bright Sch., Chattanooga, 1946—; charter mem., dir. Cleveland Regional Speech and Hearing Center (Tenn.), 1971—. Bd. dirs., McCallie Sch., 1953-61, patron, 1953—. Mem. Nat. Assn. Am. Hosiery Mfrs., Am. Sci. Yarn Mfrs. Mason (32 deg., Shriner), Elk; mem. B'nai B'rith. Club: Valleybrook Golf and Country. Home: 3408 Harcourt Dr Chattanooga TN 37411 Office: Amtex Inc 240 1st St SW Cleveland TN 37311

MALLERY, WILLIAM HENRY, III, city ofcl.; b. McComb, Miss., Dec. 15, 1935; s. William Henry and Tot (McManus) M.; B.Pub. Adminstrn., U. Miss., 1958; postgrad. So. Meth. U.; m. Cecil Nolan, July 12, 1958; children—David, Mark, Kathy, William Henry 1V, John Paul, Beth. Asst. to city mgr., Farmers Branch, Tex., 1958-59; mgr. C. of C., Farmers Branch, 1959; self-employed as pub. relations counsellor, Pub. Relations Council, 1960; dir. pub. relations, asst. sales mgr. Magnolia Mobile Homes Sales Corp., 1961; purchasing agt., Vicksburg, Miss., 1962; program officer Program of Advances for Pub. Works Planning, U.S. Dept. Housing and Urban Devel., 1963-66; city mgr., Punta Gorda, Fla., Belle Glade, Fla., 1966—. Chmn. PBJC Glades area steering com., 1972—. Mem. Internat., Fla., Palm Beach County (past pres.) city mgrs. assns. Unitarian. Home: 930 NW 4th St Belle Glade FL 33430 Office: 33 W Av A Belle Glade FL 33430

MALLIN, JAY, journalist; b. N.Y.C., Dec. 10, 1927; s. Albert Milton and Cecilia (Jaffe) M.; A.B., Fla. So. Coll., 1949; m. Caroll Sue Driftmeyer, Jan. 31, 1959; children—Jay, Linda Anne. News editor Havana (Cuba) Herald, 1951-53; stringer corr. Time and Life, 1956—; columnist Copley News Service, 1972—. Research scientist Center for Advanced Internat. Studies, Miami, 1967-69; cons. various corps., 1970—. Author: Fortress Cuba, 1965; Caribbean Crisis, 1965; Terror in Viet Nam, 1966; Guevara on Revolution, 1969; Strategy for Conquest, 1970; Terror and Urban Guerrillas, 1972. Contbr. gen., acad., mil. jours. Home: 406 Savona Av Coral Gables FL 33146

MALLING, HEINRICH VALDEMAR, geneticist; b. Copenhagen, Denmark, Apr. 21, 1931; s. Henry Valdmar and Jenny Theodora (Jensen) M.; came to U.S., 1963, naturalized, 1969; B.S. in Chemistry and Physics, U. Copenhagen, 1951, M.S., 1953, Ph.D. in Biochem. Genetics, 1957; m. Martha Hale Shackford, July 18, 1969; children—Tove, Soren, Jakob, Richard, Kevin, Mikael, Kirsten. Research staff mem. Leo Pharm. Factory, Copenhagen, 1957-61; asso. prof. biochem. genetics U. Copenhagen, 1961-63; sr. scientist biology div. Oak Ridge Nat. Lab., 1963-72; sect. head Nat. Inst. Environmental Health Scis. Research Triangle Park, N.C., 1972—. Dir. Environmental Mutagen Information center, Oak Ridge, 1968-72; adj. prof. N.C. State U., Raleigh, 1972—. Mem. Senator's Com. on Mercury, 1972—. Predoctoral fellow Danish Research Found, 1953-57, postdoctoral fellow, 1958-61. Mem. N.Y. Acad. Sci., Genetic Soc. Am., Environmental Mutagen Soc. (council mem. 1968—), Indian Guides (nation chief 1971-72). Editorial Bd. Environmental Health Perspective, since 1972—. Discovered mutagenic activity of immulogical process. Home: 4208 Galax Dr Raleigh NC 27609 Office: PO Box 12233 Research Triangel Park NC 27709

MALLON, ARTHUR HENRY, civil engr.; b. Worcester, Mass., Apr. 27, 1912; s. Arthur Peter and Flora (Madden) Malboeuf; B.S. in Civil Engring., Worcester Poly. Inst., 1940; M.S., Northeastern U., 1959; m. Helen Karpawich, Nov. 23, 1940; children—Robert, Nancy (Mrs. William J. Hetzel), Maureen (Mrs. Lawrence T. Lawler), James, Pamela, Kathy. Staff engr., indsl. polution control div., research and devel. Environmental Protection Agy., Washington, 1970—. Adj. prof. Washington Tech. Inst., 1969—. Registered profl. engr., Mo., Mass. Mem. Am. Soc. C.E., Nat. Soc. Profl. Engrs., Am. Wildlife Soc., Am. Concrete Inst., Water Pollution Control Fedn., Am. Soc. Engring. Edn. Home: 3034 Battersea Lane Alexandria VA 23309 Office: EPA Washington DC 20460

MALLON, LAWRENCE MICHAEL, accountant; b. St. Joseph, Mo., May 2, 1941; s. Charles Leo and Lillian Elizabeth (Ryan) M.; B.B.A., McMurry Coll., 1964; m. Kathleen Louise King, Dec. 21, 1963; children—Melissa Louise, Laura Kay. Staff accountant Weaver & Tidwell, C.P.A.'s, Fort Worth, Tex., 1964-70; comptroller Alamo Mfg. Co., 1970; partner Wilson & Mallon, C.P.A.'s, Fort Worth and Breckenridge, Tex., 1971—. Dir. Pembleton Co., Inc., Hootie's Pucker Bag Co. (both Breckenridge). Named Jaycee of Month, Breckenridge Jr. C. of C., 1972. Mem. Am. Inst. C.P.A.'s, Tex. Soc. C.P.A.'s, Breckenridge Jr. C. of C. (v.p. 1971-72, pres. 1973-74), Breckenridge C. of C., Am. Legion. Republican. Mem. Christian Ch. (sec. bd. deacons 1972—). Elk, Lion (treas. 1972—). Home: 307 W 3d St Breckenridge TX 76024 Office: 117 S Breckenridge St Breckenridge TX 76024

MALLORY, JAMES GUY, JR., dentist; b. Cairo, Ill., Jan. 8, 1914; s. James Guy and Birdie Elizabeth (Clutts) M.; student Tulane U., 1932-33, St. Louis U., 1933-34; D.D.S., Loyola South U., 1939; m. Grace Lenore Chapman, Sept. 7, 1940; children—Nancy (Mrs. John Christian Archer), Jamie (Mrs. Watson Van Benthuysen), Janet, Susan. Pvt. practice dentistry, New Orleans, 1939—; mem. staff Mercy Hosp. Active Young Men's Bus. Club. Served with Dental Corps, USNR, 1941-46. Fellow Internat. Coll. Dentistry; mem. Am., La., New Orleans dental assns., Mil. Order World Wars, Psi Omega, Phi Kappa Sigma. Democrat. Baptist. Mason. Home: 8001 Sycamore St New Orleans LA 70118 Office: Maison Blanche Bldg New Orleans LA 70112

MALLOY, BERNARD MATHIS, psychiatrist; b. Chgo., Sept. 2, 1928; s. John Cyril and Jennie (Mathis) M.; A.B., Lambuth Coll., 1950; M.D., Vanderbilt U., 1954; m. Dorothy Davis, July 1, 1958; children—John Davis, Bernard Mathis Jr., Elizabeth Grace. Intern Vanderbilt Hosp., Nashville, 1954-55, resident 1955-56; resident Payne Whitney Clinic, N.Y.C., 1956-58, Nat. Hosp. Neurol. Diseases, London, 1958; practice psychiatry, Washington, 1959—; mem. staff Sibley Memp. Hosp., Washington; asst. clin. prof. Georgetown U., Washington, 1961—; chief psychiat. staff CIA, Washington, 1958. Served with AUS, 1946-48. Diplomate Am. Bd. Psychiatry. Mem. D.C. Med. Soc. A.M.A., Washington, So., Am. Psychiat. assns., Balt.-D.C. Psychoanalytic Inst., Am. Psychoanalytic Assn., Acad.

Religion and Mental Health, Sons Am. Revolution. Office: 2520 L St NW Washington DC 20037

MALMI, A. CARL, govt. ofcl.; b. Duluth, Minn., Oct. 20, 1917; s. Andrew and Mary (Ojaniemi) M.; student Duluth Bus. U., 1936; B.C.S., Columbus U., 1949, M.F.A., 1950; m. Bobbie Grace Simmons, Oct. 18, 1942; children—Carol L., Robert A. File clk. Social Security Agy., Balt., 1941; payroll clk. State Dept., Washington, 1941-46, group supr., 1946-47, orgn. and methods examiner 1947-51; area budget officer USIA, Nr. East, South Asia, Africa, 1951-56, 60-62; adminstrv. officer Voice of Am., 1962-65; exec. officer, 1965—; budget planning and procedures officer, Washington, 1956-58; budget and finance Officer Am. Nat. Exhbn. in Moscow, Dept. of Commerce, 1958-59, adminstrv. officer in Washington, U.S. Sci. Exhibit, Century 21 Exposition, 1959-60. Pres. Fernwood Citizens Assn., 1961-62. Served with AUS, 1942-45, ETO. Democrat. Methodist. Home: 9705 Holmhurst Rd Bethesda MD 20034 Office: 1776 Pennsylvania Av Washington DC 20006*

MALOAN, WALTER THOMAS, banker; b. Harlingen, Tex., June 26, 1933; s. Walter Gleason and Ruth (Wright) M.; student Tex. U., 1950-53; B.B.A., So. Meth. U., 1959, M.B.A., 1964; m. Suzanne Stanford, Sept. 30, 1960; children—Michael Thomas, Kathryn. Accountant Boyd Young Gano & Stallings, C.P.A.'s, Dallas, 1959-61; asst. cashier Republic Nat. Bank, Dallas, 1961-66; v.p. Hibernia Nat. Bank, New Orleans, 1966-71; sr. v.p. Union Nat. Bank, Little Rock, 1971—. Instr., U. Ark., Little Rock; tchr., various grad. schs. banking, 1969—. Mem. met. com. New Orleans 1969-71; asst. treas. Greater New Orleans Fedn. Chs., 1969-71; treas. New Orleans Housing Devel. Corp., 1970-71. Served with USAF, 1954-57. C.P.A., Tex., La., Ark. Mem. Tex., La., Ark. socs. C.P.A.'s, Robert Morris Assos. (chpt. pres. 1973-74), Am. Bankers Assn. (mem. exec. com. comml. lending div. 1971-74), Am. Inst. Banking, New Orleans, Little Rock chambers commerce, Beta Alpha Psi. Clubs: Pleasant Valley Country (Little Rock), Little Rock. Contbr. articles to accounting jours. Office: PO Box 1541 Little Rock AR 72203

MALOF, JOSEPH FETLER, educator; b. Riga, Latvia, May 26, 1934; s. Basil Fetler and Barbara (Kovalevsky) M.; came to U.S., 1939, naturalized, 1947; B.A., Kenyon Coll., 1956; M.A., U. Cal. at Los Angeles, 1957, Ph.D., 1962; m. Delores Ann Kildare, Dec. 21, 1957; children—Andrew, Jessica, Peter. Asst. in English, U. Cal. at Los Angeles, 1959-61; instr. U. Tex. at Austin, 1961-65, asst. prof. English, 1965-68, asso. prof., 1968-73, prof., 1973—. Recipient E. Harris Harbison prize for outstanding teaching Danforth Found., 1970. Kenyon Prize scholar, 1952-56; Nat. Woodrow Wilson fellow 1956-57. Mem. Modern Lang. Assn. Author: A Manual of English Meters, 1970. Home: Box 8617 Austin TX 78712

MALONE, CHARLES RANDALL, ecologist; b. Sweetwater, Tex., May 9, 1938; s. Raymond Cortez and Laura Emilia (Neie) M.; B.S., Tex. Tech. U., 1963, M.S. (NIH fellow), 1965; Ph.D. (NSF fellow 1966-68), Rutgers U., 1968; m. Laura Kay Gray, July 18, 1964; children—Susan Lynn. Ecologist, AEC postdoctoral fellow, Oak Ridge Nat. Lab., 1968-70, sr. ecologist, environmental sci. div., 1973; prin. staff officer, environmental studies bd. Nat. Acad. Scis., Washington, 1970-73, 73—. Served with USMCR, 1957-60. Mem. Ecol. Soc. Am. (program chmn. 1971-74), Am. Inst. Biol. Scis., A.A.A.S., Brit. Ecol. Soc., Water Pollution Control Fedn., Am. Chem. Soc. Contbr. profl. to jours. Home: 5621 N 9th Rd Arlington VA 22205 Office: Environmental Studies Bd Nat Acad Scis 2101 Constitution Av Washington DC 20418

MALONE, JAMES LEONARD, elec. contractor; b. McDavid, Fla., Nov. 6, 1918; s. Mannie A. and Seola (Roach) M.; student Coyne Elec. Sch., 1939; Asso. Elec. Engring., Bliss Elec. Sch., 1947; m. Kathryn Brock, June 15, 1940; children—Gloria (Mrs. J.D. McNeil), Carolyn (Mrs. Hubert Williams), Faye (Mrs. Larry E. Carlton), Richard Glenn. Electrician, White Elec. Constrn. Co., Columbus, Ga., 1942-46, mgr. motor repair and sales, 1946-50; founder Ga. Elec. Co., Albany, 1950, pres., gen. mgr., 1950-69; founder J.L. Malone and Assos., Inc., Albany, 1969, pres., mgr., 1969—. Sec., S.W. Ga. Constrn. Tng. Council, Inc., Albany, 1973-74; mem. City Albany Elec. Examining Bd., 1964—, pres., 1972-73. Served with AUS, 1944-46. Mem. I.E.E.E., Nat. Elec. Contractors Assn., Ga. Soc. Profl. Engrs. Baptist. Home: 1724 Pineknoll Lane Albany GA 31707 Office: PO Box 3367 Albany GA 31706

MALONE, MICHAEL JOSEPH, neurologist, educator; b. Portland, Me., Apr. 28, 1930; s. Patrick Joseph and Margaret Marie (Ridge) M.; A.B. cum laude, Boston Coll., 1951; M.D., U. Georgetown, 1956; m. Dorothy Helen Corcoran, July 4, 1957; 1 son, Michael Patrick. Intern, Detroit Receiving Hosp., 1956-57; resident in neurology Boston VA and Boston U., 1960-63; fellow neurochemistry Harvard Med. Sch., Cambridge, Mass., 1963-65, asso. neurology, 1965-67, lectr., 1969-70; asst. biochemist McLean div. Mass. Gen. Hosp., Boston, 1965-69; asst. prof. neurology and biochemistry Boston U. Sch. Medicine, 1967-70; prof. neurology and child devel. George Washington U. Sch. Medicine, 1970—; chmn. dept. neurology Children's Hosp., Washington, 1970—. Cons. Dept. Army, Dept. Navy, NIH, U.S. Army Hosp. Walter Reed, U.S. Naval Hosp., Bethesda, Md., Clin. Center NIH; clin. investigator VA, Boston, 1965-68. Served with AUS, 1957-60. Recipient Career Devel. award NIH, 1969-70, NIH Research grantee, 1967-70. Mem. A.A.A.S., N.Y. Acad. Sci., A.M.A., Am. Acad. Neurology, Am. Soc. Neurochemistry, Internat. Soc. Neurochemistry, Mass., D.C. med. socs. Contbr. articles on neurology to med. jours. Home: 4614 N 33d St Arlington VA 22207 Office: 2125 13th St NW Washington DC 20009

MALONE, WAYNE WEAR, banker; b. Russellville, Ala., Apr. 8, 1943; s. Hayes Wear and Dorothy Allen (Whitlock) M.; student U. Ala., 1960-65; m. Pamela Antoinette Smith, Mar. 29, 1970; 1 son, Jeffrey Wayne. Nat. bank examiner U.S. Treasury Dept., 1966-70; pres. First Nat. Bank, Russellville, Ala., 1971—. Mem. C. of C. Club: Civitan. Home: PO Box 666 Russellville AL 35653 Office: PO Box 850 Russellville AL 35653

MALONE, WILLIAM WARREN, JR., lawyer; b. Athens, Ala., Feb. 12, 1916; s. William Warren and Daisy (Warren) M.; student Birmingham-So. Coll., 1933-34; A.B., U. Ala., 1937, LL.B., 1939; m. Mitzi Browning Chambers, Nov. 18, 1946; children—Miriam Lane, William Warren III, Patrick B. Admitted to Ala. bar, 1939; since practiced in Athens. Dir. East Lauderdale Banking Co. Mem. Ala. Legislature, 1950-53. Past pres. N.Ala. Tb. Assn., Athens Jr. C. of C. Presdl. elector Ala., 1960. Served with USAAF, 1942-45. Mem. Am., Ala., Athens (past pres.) bar assns., Am. Legion (past post comdr.). Home: 400 S Beaty St Athens AL 35611 Office: PO Box 711 Athens AL 35611

MALONEY, CHARLES G., bishop; b. Sept. 9, 1912. Ordained priest Roman Cath. Ch., 1937; titular bishop of Capsa and aux. to archbishop of Louisville, 1954—. Address: 212 E College St Louisville KY 40203

MALONEY, CLEMENT GARLAND, corp. and govt. cons.; b. Hot Springs, Ark., July 4, 1917; s. James C. and Dorothy (Clement) M.; student Northwestern U., 1937-40; 1 son, Thomas C. Vice pres. Kollsman Instrument Corp., N.Y.C., 1961-64; cons. to sec. def., Washington, 1964-66; internat. marketing cons. Philco Corp. div. Ford Motor Co., 1966-67; cons. internat. sales and export financing Office Sec. Def., 1967-69; spl. asst. to the pres. Control Data Corp., 1969—. Served as col. USAAF, World War II; now col. USAF Res. Recipient Exceptional Civilian award U.S. Air Force. Mem. Nat. Security Indsl. Assn., Air Force Assn. U.S. Mil. Order of Carabao, Am. Ordnance Assn., Am. Mgmt. Assn. Clubs: Fort Myers Officers; Bolling AFB Officers; Nat. Aviation, Army Navy (Washington). Home: Crystal Plaza Apt 405 S 2111 Jefferson Davis Hwy Arlington VA 22202

MALONEY, FRANK CAMPBELL III, lawyer; b. Richmond, Va., Apr. 27, 1931; s. Frank Campbell, Jr. and Iola Virginia (Johnson) M.; A.B., Yale, 1953; J.D., U. Va., 1956; m. Ellen Mayo Smith, Dec. 14, 1957 (dec. Mar. 1967); children—Frank Campbell IV, Tucker Mayo, John Waller; m. 2d, Virginia Pegram Baskerville, Aug. 2, 1968; 1 dau., Virginia Pegram. Admitted to Va. bar, 1956, since practiced in Richmond; partner firm Maloney & Yeatts, 1971—; lectr. U. Richmond Law Sch., 1972-73. Mem. Am., Va., Richmond (exec. com. 1971-74) bar assns., Va. State Bar, Assn. Trial Lawyers Am., Va. Trial Lawyers Assn., Va. Tennis Assn. (pres. 1965), Richmond Tennis Patrons Assn. (pres. 1964), Delta Theta Phi. Clubs: Yale of Va. (pres. 1964); Country of Va., Bull and Bear (Richmond). Contbr. legal jours. Home: 8 Oak Lane Richmond VA 23226 Office: 326 Ross Bldg Richmond VA 23219

MALONEY, MICHAEL OTTO, architect; b. Grandfield, Okla., Aug. 25, 1936; s. William Oscar and Theodora Barbara (Mundkowski) M.; B.Arch., U. Okla., 1960. With James Marshall, architect, Lawton, Okla., 1961-62; asso., project architect Pardue, Read and Dice, architects and engrs., Wichita Falls, Tex., 1962-69; pvt. practice as Michael O. Maloney, architect, Wichita Falls, 1970—. Mem. Wichita Falls Land Use Adv. Bd., Flood Plain Adv. Bd. Bd. dirs. Wichita Falls Symphony, Wichita Falls Civic Ballet Theatre, McCutchen Day Nursery, Backdoor Civic Playhouse, Wichita Falls Museum and Art Center. Rotary fellow, New Zealand, 1969. Mem. Tex. Soc. Architects. Roman Cath. (past pres. N. Tex. deanery). Prin. works include Waverly, 1971, Orchid br. Wichita Falls First Savs. and Loan Assn., 1973; project architect Notre Dame High Sch., Wichita Falls, 1966. Address: 1803 Midwestern Pky Wichita Falls TX 76302

MALOOF, LOUIS NASSIR, architect; b. Copperhill, Tenn., Feb. 27, 1935; s. Nassir Ackle and Adline (Ferris) M.; B.S., Ga. Inst. Tech., 1957, B.Arch., 1962; m. Sue Ann Thomason, June 7, 1958; children—Noel, Gabriel. With Heery & Heery, Inc., Atlanta, 1960—, exec. v.p., 1967—. Served to lt. (j.g.) USNR, 1957-59. Mem. A.I.A., Pi Kappa Alpha. Roman Catholic. Kiwanian. Home: Route 3 Buford GA 30518 Office: 880 W Peachtree St Atlanta GA 30309

MALOOLY, DONALD ALBERT, physician; b. El Paso, Tex., May 9, 1930; s. Elias A. and Mamie (Coury) M.; student Rice U., 1947-49; B.A., Tex. Western Coll., 1950; M.D., U. So. Cal., 1954; m. Mary Hill, July 9, 1955; children—Donald Ellis, Mary Elizabeth, Mark Hill. Intern, William Beaumont Army Hosp., Ft. Bliss, Tex., 1954-55; resident Scott and White Clinic, Temple, Tex., 1957-59, Long Beach (Cal.) VA Hosp., 1959-60; fellow Mayo Clinic, Rochester, Minn., 1960-61; practice medicine, specializing in cardiology, El Paso, 1962—; mem. staff Providence Meml., St. Joseph's, Sun Towers hosps., Hotel Dieu. Served to capt. M.C., AUS, 1954-57. Diplomate Am. Bd. Internal Medicine, also cardiovascular bd. Fellow Am. Coll. Chest Physicians, Am. Coll. Cardiology, Royal Soc. Promotion Health; mem. A.M.A., Am. Heart Assn. (fellow council on clin. cardiology, mem. council high blood pressure research, arteriosclosis, basic sci.), Tex. Acad. Internal Medicine, Tex. Med. Assn., Alpha Omega Alpha, Phi Rho Sigma, Phi Kappa Phi, Tau Kappa Epsilon. Episcopalian. Contbr. articles to profl. jours. Home: 6249 Westwind Dr El Paso TX 79912 Office: 1100 N Stanton St El Paso TX 79902

MALOY, THEODORE HASKELL, pub. relations exec.; b. nr. Delhi, Okla., Aug. 26, 1907; s. Pumphrey Angelo and Nettie Josephine (McGowen) M.; A.B., U. Okla., 1929; m. Dorothy Inez Fluck, June 2, 1929 (dec. Oct. 1971); 1 dau., Amy Lynn (Mrs. Richard R. Lindsly). Editor Elk City (Okla.) Daily News, 1929-32; staff corr., bur. mgr., S.W. div. news editor UP, 1932-44; br. mgr. Braun & Co., Dallas, 1944-57; Dallas region pub. relations mgr. Safeway Stores, 1957-62; sr. partner VanCronkhite & Maloy, Inc., Dallas, 1962—; v.p. Suburban Newspapers, Inc., Ft. Worth. Named one of five Friends of Tex. Press award, Tex. Press Assn., 1956. Mem. Pub. Relations Soc. Am., Sigma Delta Chi. Ind. Democrat. Presbyn. Clubs: Dallas Press, Dallas Rotary. Home: 3710 Granada St Dallas TX 75205 Office: 506 Stemmons Tower N2710 Stemmons Freeway Dallas TX 75207

MALZAHN, RAY ANDREW, ednl. adminstr.; b. Ft. Madison, Ia., July 8, 1929; s. Arnold Frederick and Inez Zoe (Russel) M.; B.A., Gustavus Adolphus Coll., 1951; M.S., U. N.D., 1953; Ph.D., U. Md., 1962; m. Elizabeth Mae Barrett, Aug. 23, 1953; children—Karen Louise, Janet Elizabeth. Research asso. U. Ariz., Tucson, 1961-63; asst. prof. chemistry West Tex. State U., Canyon, 1963-65, asso. prof., 1965-67, prof., 1967-71, also dean coll. arts and scis., v.p. acad. affairs, 1971—. Served with AUS, 1954-56. Mem. Am. Chem. Soc., Tex. Assn. Coll. Tchrs., Sigma Xi. Rotarian. Home: 1700 Hillcrest Dr Canyon TX 79015

MAMALAKIS, MARIE J., educator, news corr.; b. Shreveport, La., Sept. 15, 1913; d. John and Demetria (Passadakis) Mamalakis; A.B., Southwestern La. Inst., 1933; B.S. in L.S., La. State U., 1940; postgrad. U. Chgo., 1948. Tchr. St. Landry Parish Schs., 1934-40; librarian and tchr. St. Landry Parish Opelousas High Sch., 1938-41; circulation librarian U. Southwestern La., Lafayette, 1941-65, dir. publs., prof. 1965—; mng. editor Lafayette Progress, 1951-54, editor, 1954-62. Free-lance feature story writer local papers. Field work disaster relief A.R.C., 1940. Mayor's rep. Community Action Council, 1973—. Mem. Nat. Fedn. Press Women, A.L.A., La. Library Assn., La. Tchrs. Assn., La. Press Women's Assn. (treas. 1957-58), Pi Gamma Mu, Beta Phi Mu, Phi Kappa Phi, Sigma Sigma Sigma, Phi Alpha Theta, Omicron Delta Epsilon. Mem. Order Eastern Star. Contbr. articles to profl. jours. Home: 1018 Auburn Av Lafayette LA 70501

MAN, EUGENE HERBERT, univ. adminstr.; b. Scranton, Pa., Dec. 14, 1923; s. E. Lester and Celia (Cohen) M.; A.B., Oberlin Coll., 1948; Ph.D. (Office Naval Research fellow, E.I. duPont fellow), Duke, 1952; m. Gladys Greenberg, Mar. 7, 1945; children—Elizabeth Sue (Mrs. Carl B. Eichenberger), Barbara Ruth, Linda Jeanne, Bruce Jonathan. Research chemist E.I. duPont de Nemours & Co., Inc., Wilmington, Del., 1952-60, supr. tech. sect., Chattanooga, 1960-61, sr. supr., 1961-62; coordinator research U. Miami, Coral Gables, Fla., 1962-66, dean research coordination, 1966—. Vis. investigator Scripps Instn. Oceanography, 1971-72. Bd. dirs. Health Planning Council, Dade County, Fla., 1970-71; mem. Mental Health Consortium, Dade County, pres., 1970-71; dir., chmn. Gulf Univs. Research Consortium, 1969-71; trustee, v.p. Community Mental Health Services, Dade County, 1968-72; trustee United Fund Dade County, 1967-69; council mem. Oak Ridge (Tenn.) Asso. Univs., 1973—. Served to 1st lt. AUS, 1943-46. Recipient Harry N. Holmes award in chemistry, Oberlin Coll., 1948. Fellow Am. Inst. Chemists; mem. Am. Chem. Soc., A.A.A.S., Nat. Council Univ. Research Adminstrs. (exec. com. 1967-72), Sigma Xi, Phi Beta Kappa, Phi Lambda Upsilon. Contbr. articles profl. jours. Patentee in field. Home: PO Box 248542 U Miami Coral Gables FL 33124 Office: Ferre Bldg U Miami Coral Gables FL 33124

MANCEAUX, WILSON JOHN, physician; b. Kaplan, La., Jan. 6, 1935; s. Elias and Nessie (Hebert) M.; B.S., Southwestern U., 1956; M.D., La. State U., 1960; m. Priscilla Pate, Oct. 11, 1969; children—Wilson John, Derrell, Michael, Cheryl. Intern, Confed. Meml. Hosp., Shreveport, La., 1960-61; pvt. practice medicine, Kaplan, La., 1964—; mem. staff Abram Kaplan Meml. Hosp. Served with AUS, 1962-64. Lion (pres. 1967-68). Home: Route 2 Box 396-H Kaplan LA 70548 Office: 801 N Cushing St Kaplan LA 70548

MANCHESTER, MONTE JAMES, radio broadcaster; b. Clarendon, Tex., Jan. 13, 1945; s. Monte Franklin and Mildred Elizabeth (Love) M.; grad. high sch.; m. Kay White, June 21, 1962; children—Lisa, Scott, Tony; m. 2d, Mary Lou Howard, July 27, 1973. Announcer, KBIB, Monette, Ark., 1964; with KTLO, Mountain Home, Ark., 1965—, Announcer, sales mgr., 1970—. Mem. Mountain Home City Council, 1970-72. Named Outstanding Drive chmn. March of Dimes, 1971. Mem. Ark. (v.p. 1970), Mountain Home (pres. 1969) jr. chambers commerce. Home: Route 4 Mountain Home AR 72653 Office: Box C Mountain Home AR 72653

MANDELL, GERALD LEE, educator; b. N.Y.C., Aug. 20, 1936; s. Herman H. and Sylvia L. (Keller) M.; B.A., Cornell U., Ithaca, N.Y., 1958, M.D., 1962; m. Judith H. Rensin, Dec. 20, 1960; children—James, Pamela, Scott. Instr. Cornell U. Med. Coll., N.Y.C., 1968-69; asst. prof. medicine U. Va., Charlottesville, 1969—, asso. prof. internal medicine, 1972—, head div. infectious diseases, 1969—. Served with Indian Health Service, USPHS, 1963-65. Recipient Research Career Devel. award NIH. Mem. So. Soc. Clin. Investigation, Infectious Disease Soc. Am., Soc. for Exptl. Biology and Medicine, Am. Soc. Immunologists, Phi Beta Kappa, Alpha Omega Alpha. Contbr. articles to profl. jours. Home: 106 Powhatan Circle Charlottesville VA 22901 Office: Box 251 Univ Va Sch Medicine Charlottesville VA 22901

MANGE, EDWARD CARL, corp. exec.; b. N.Y.C., Jan. 12, 1941; s. Ralph A. and Edith (Gogel) M.; student Del Mar Coll., 1958-59, Tex. A. and M. Coll., 1959-60; m. Heleen Simon, Nov. 9, 1962; children—Jody Lynn, Andrew Martin. Pres., gen. mgr. Metals Inc. div. Western Metal Co., 1961-71, Metals Inc., Metals Inc. Overseas Export Corp., 1971—. Mem. acquisition com. United Fund Corpus Christi. Bd. dirs. Jewish Community Council Corpus Christi. Mem. Nat. Assn. Secondary Material Industries. Jewish religion (tchr. temple Sunday sch.). Mem. B'nai B'rith (treas.). Patentee wire stripper. Home: 338 Palmetto St Corpus Christi TX 78412 Office: 3000 Agnes St Corpus Christi TX 78403

MANGER, MARTIN CLARENCE, educator; b. Bethlehem, Pa., Sept. 20, 1937; s. Martin Fredrick and Hazel (Tiel) M.; B.S., Muhlenberg Coll., 1959; M.S., St. Lawrence U., 1961; M.S., Rutgers U., 1964; Ph.D., U. Sheffield (Eng.), 1968; m. Elizabeth Clara Zulalian, July 13, 1963. Research fellow Rutgers U., New Brunswick, N.J., 1961-64; research chemist E.R. Squibb & Sons, New Brunswick, 1964-65; asso. prof. dept. chemistry Ala. A. and M. U., Normal, 1968-72, prof., 1972—. NASA grantee, 1972—. Fellow Am. Inst. Chemists; mem. Am. Chem. Soc. (chmn.), N.Y. Acad. Socs., Ala. Acad. Sci., Am. Assn. U. Profs., Sigma Xi, Gamma Sigma Epsilon. Club: Huntsville Kennel (Ala.). Home: 11005 Donneita Dr Huntsville AL 35810 Office: PO Box 134 Normal AL 35762

MANGRUM, FRANKLIN MAYER, educator; b. Mayfield, Ky., June 1, 1925; s. Louis Varon and Harriet Elizabeth (Mayer) M.; A.B., Washington U., St. Louis, 1949; Ph.D., U. Chgo., 1957; m. Jessie Graves, Aug. 25, 1945. Tchr. philosophy, chmn. humanities div. Shimer Coll., Mt. Carroll, Ill., 1956-59; mem. faculty Morehead (Ky.) State U., 1959—, prof. philosophy, 1962—, head dept., 1966—. Tchr. Rockford (Ill.) Coll., summers, 1958, 59. Faculty mem. bd. regents Morehead State U., 1968-71. Served with AUS, 1944-46. Decorated Bronze Star Medal. Recipient Distinguished Faculty award Morehead State U. Alumni Assn., 1969. Mem. Ky. Philos. Assn. (pres. 1966-67), Am. Philos. Assn., Metaphysical Soc. Am., N.E.A., Ky. Edn. Assn., Ky. Col., Blue Key, Delta Tau Delta. Baptist. Home: 416 Allen Av Morehead KY 40351

MANGU, JOHN, JR., truck lines co. exec.; b. Akron, O., Nov. 4, 1925; s. John and Elizabeth (Stoica) M.; B.C.E., U. Akron, 1950; m. Donna Jean Smith, Sept. 24, 1951; children—Pamela Beth, Jean Marie, Linda Ann. Field engr. Clemmer Constrn. Co., Akron, 1950-55, MileHi Constrn. Co., Akron, 1955-56; dir. properties Roadway Express, Inc., Akron, 1956-69; dir. properties and real estate Ryder Truck Lines Inc., Jacksonville, Fla., 1970-73, v.p., 1973—; chmn. bd. Terminal Properties Exchange. Served with AUS, 1944-46. Registered profl. engr., 28 states; registered land surveyor La., Ky., S.C. Fellow Am. Soc. C.E., Nat. Soc. Profl. Engrs. Home: 3857 Musket Trail Jacksonville FL 32211 Office: PO Box 2408 2050 Kings Rd Jacksonville FL 32211

MANGUM, GRADY GARDNER, realtor; b. nr. Magee, Miss., Sept. 26, 1906; s. Cooper Haywood and Letha (Gardner) M.; student U. Miss., 1927-31, Tulane U., 1942; m. Hilda Hughey, July 6, 1935; children—Charles Grady, David Haywood. With U.S. Civil Service Commn., 1934-65, engr. rep. Fed. Land Bank, New Orleans, 1934-37, New Orleans Port of Embarkation, 1942-45, C.E. 8th Service Command, Dallas, 1945-46, USAF Tng. Command, Randolph AFB, Tex., 1946-65, ret. as engr., dep. dir. base facilities 1965; pvt. practice as real estate broker and cons., San Antonio, 1966—. Recipient Outstanding Service award USAF, 1965. Mem. I.E.E.E. Mason (Shriner). Home: 4531 Waikiki Dr San Antonio TX 78218

MANGUM, NEIL CLAYTON, historian; b. Farmville, Va., Oct. 12, 1948; s. Ralph Decator and Nellie Clay (Hardy) M.; A.A. (scholar), Richard Bland Coll., 1970; B.S., Va. State Coll., 1972. Historian Petersburg (Va.) Nat. Battlefield, 1971—, librarian, 1971—, museum curator, 1971—. Mem. Civil War Roundtable, Sons Confederate Vets. Home: Box 549 Petersburg VA 23803 Office: Box 549 Petersburg VA 23803

MANGUM, OLLIE MACK, electric utility exec.; b. Magee, Miss., Sept. 8, 1913; s. Lee E. and Frances (Stroud) M.; Elec. Engr., Internat. Corr. Schs., 1957; m. Johnora Keith, Apr. 11, 1942; 1 dau., Frances Grace (Mrs. Larry F. Turner). Supervising engr. Bowman & Bowman, cons. engrs., Greenwood, Miss., 1937-54; chief engr. Twin County Electric Power Co., Hillandale, Miss., 1954-60; asst. gen. mgr. Natchez Trace Electric Power Co., Houston, Miss., 1960-68, gen. mgr., 1968—. Served with USNR, 1942-45. Registered profl. engr., Miss., Tenn. Mem. Nat., Miss. socs. profl. engrs., Electric Power Assn. Miss. (sec., dir.), TVP Power Assn. (dir.), N. Miss. Indsl. Devel. Assn., (dir., past pres.), N. Miss. Pub. Power Assn. (dir., past pres.), V.F.W., Am. Legion. Mason, Lion. Address: 108 Carol Dr Houston MS 38851

MANLEY, LILLIAN CARDWELL (MRS. RICHARD SHANNON MANLEY), educator; b. Birmingham, Ala., Oct. 22, 1932; d. William Whitt and Grace (Cameron) M.; B.S., U. Ala., 1953, M.S., 1958, Ph.D., 1961; m. Richard Shannon Manley, Aug. 23, 1953; children—Richard Shannon, Alyce Hughes. Research asst. So. Research Inst., 1953-54; teaching fellow U. Ala., 1957-58; instr. Demopolis (Ala.) High Sch., 1958-59; asso. prof. biology Livingston U., 1959-63; chmn. div. sci., prof. biology Judson Coll., 1963-70; exec. dir. Ala. Consortium for Devel. of Higher Edn., 1970—; lectr. vis. scientists program, 1966-68. Sec. Ala. Spl. Edn. Study Commn., 1968-69; vice chmn. Ala. Commn. on Higher Edn., 1970-72; mem. Gov.'s Commn. on Status Women, 1962-66. Trustee, Troy State U., 1968-70. Named Distinguished Young Woman, Demopolis Jayceettes, 1968. Mem. Am. Assn. U. Women (pres. Ala. div. 1964-66, mem. Internat. fellowships awards com. 1962-68, ednl. found. devel. com. 1968—), Ala. Acad. Scis. (counselor West Ala. region 1964-70, com. on pub. relations 1966-68, v.p. 1968-69, mem. exec. com. 1966-70), U. Ala. Nat. Alumni Assn. (v.p., chmn. women's div. 1970-71; Distinguished alumna 1971), Assn. Southeastern Biologists, A.A.A.S., Mortar Bd., Phi Beta Kappa, Sigma Xi, Alpha Epsilon Delta, Alpha Lambda Delta, Alpha Chi Omega, Lambda Tau (charter; adviser Sigma chpt.). Club: Women of Demopolis Country. Methodist (mem. adminstrv. bd.). Home: Country Club Dr PO Box 338 Demopolis AL 36732 Office: 305 N Main St Demopolis AL 36732

MANLEY, RICHARD SHANNON, lawyer, state legislator; b. Birmingham, Ala., June 23, 1932; s. Richard Sabine and Alice (Hughes) M.; B.S., U. Ala., 1953, LL.B., 1958; m. Lillian Grace Cardwell, Aug. 23, 1953; children—Richard Shannon, Alyce Hughes. Admitted to Ala. bar, 1958, U.S. Dist. Ct. So. Dist. Ala., U.S. 5th Circuit Ct. of Appeals, U.S. Supreme Ct., U.S. Ct. Mil. Appeals; practiced in Demopolis, 1958—; mem. Ala. Ho. of Reps., 1967—. Dir. New Southland Nat. Ins. Co.; v.p. Demopolis Cable TV Co., Inc. Pres. Bd. Edn., Demopolis, 1969-70, Demopolis Jr. C. of C., 1961-62; v.p. Ala. Jr. C. of C., 1960-61; dir. U.S. Jr. C. of C., 1962-63. Bd. dirs. Marengo County Hist. Soc., Marengo County Mental Health Assn.; bd. advisers Ala. Hist. Commn., Gen. Holland M. Smith Meml. Served with USMCR, 1953-56. Mem. Am., Ala. (mem. bd. of bar commrs. 1972—), 17th Judicial Circuit (past pres.) bar assns., Am. Trial Lawyers Assn., Comml. Law League Am., Am. Judicature Soc., Demopolis C. of C. (dir., past pres.), Marine Corps Res. Officers Assn., U. Ala. Nat. Alumni Assn. (v.p. 1967-68), Farrah Law Soc., Phi Delta Phi, Delta Chi. Methodist (trustee). Rotarian. Clubs: Demopolis Country (past pres., dir.), Demopolis Athletic, U. Ala. Alumni (pres. Marengo County 1965-66); Indian Hills Country (Tuscaloosa, Ala.); The Club (Birmingham, Ala.). Home: 1501 Country Club Dr SW Demopolis AL 36732 Office: 105 S Walnut Av Demopolis AL 36732

MANLEY, WILLIAM TANNER, govt. ofcl.; b. nr. Owingsville, Ky., Aug. 18, 1929; s. Nathan and Flora (Whaley) M.; B.S., U. Ky., 1951, M.S., 1955; Ph.D., U. Fla., 1958; m. Vertna Jane Alexander, Oct. 29, 1951; 1 son, William Conway. Asst. prof. U. Fla., 1958-63, asso. prof., 1963-65; economist U.S. Dept. Agr., Gainesville, Fla., 1960-65, dep. dir., marketing econs. div., Washington, 1966-68, dir., 1968-73, dir. nat. econ. analysis div., 1973—. Served to 1st lt. USAF, 1951-53. Recipient Certificates of Merit, U.S. Dept. Agr., 1963, 69. Mem. Am. Agrl. Econs. Assn., Gamma Sigma Delta, Omicron Delta Epsilon. Home: 6928 Girard St McLean VA 22101 Office: 14th and Independence Sts Washington DC 20205

MANN, CHARLES SCOTT, dentist; b. Lufkin, Tex., Apr. 17, 1926; s. David L. and Blanche Catherine (Scott) M.; student Stephen F. Austin U., 1942-44; D.D.S., U. Tex., 1947; postgrad. U. Tenn., 1959, U. Ala., 1959; m. Leah Catherine Mann, Sept. 1949; children—Charles Scott, Barbara Kay. Individual practice dentistry, Lufkin, Tex., Amarillo, Houston, now Austin, Tex.; dentist Gary Job Corps, San Marcos, Tex. Served to lt. col. Dental Corps, AUS, World War II, Korea; lt. col. Res., comdr. 425th Med. Detachment, Ft. Sam Houston, Tex. Mem. Royal Soc. Health, Army Dental Surgeon. Mem. Am., Tex. dental assns., Austin Dental Soc., Assn. Mil. Surgeons, Res. Officers Assn., Xi Psi Phi. Methodist. Kiwanian. Home: 4204 North Hills Dr PO Box 9709 Austin TX 78766 Office: 103 W 5th St Austin TX 78701

MANN, DAVID PERRY, JR., furniture co. exec.; b. Woodville, Tex., Apr. 18, 1927; s. David Perry and Hattie Lucille (Barclay) M.; student U. Tex., 1945; B.B.S., So. Meth. U., 1952; m. Alpha Jane Bazzoon, July 25, 1964; 1 son, Lee Perry. Owner, Mann Furniture Co., also Direct Furniture Co., Woodville, Tex., 1964—; v.p., dir. Citizens State Bank, Woodville. Served with USNR, 1945-47. Mem. Retail Furniture Assn. Tex. (dir.), Kappa Sigma. Methodist. Kiwanian. Home: PO Box 626 Woodville TX 75979 Office: 206 W Bluff St Woodville TX 75979

MANN, EDWARD CULLEE, physician, educator; b. Laredo, Tex., Nov. 21, 1923; s. George Cullee and Olivette (Landrum) M.; B.S., Tulane U., 1946, M.D., 1950; m. Sandra Gail Whatley, Dec. 28, 1970. Intern Walter Reed Gen. Hosp., Bethesda, Md., 1950-51; resident psychiatry Johns Hopkins Hosp., 1951-54; resident obstetrics and gynecology Cornell U. Hosp., 1954-58; instr. psychiatry Johns Hopkins Med. Sch., 1953-54; psychiatrist, attending obstetrician and gynecologist N.Y. Lying-In Hosp., 1959-67; pvt. practice, N.Y.C., 1958-67; faculty Cornell U. Med. Sch., 1957-67, asso. prof. clin. obstetrics N.Y. Lying-In Hosp., 1962-67; asso. prof. obstetrics and gynecology La. State U. Sch. Medicine, Baton Rouge, 1967—. Served to capt. USAAF, 1942-46. Decorated D.F.C., Air medal with clusters, Purple Heart; recipient Sidney K. Simon award Tulane U., 1950, Found. prize Am. Assn. Obstetricians and Gynecologists, 1958, bronze medal Am. Roentgen Ray Soc., 1959, Cum Laude award Radiol. Soc. N.Am., 1959. Diplomate Am. Bd. Obstetricians and Gynecologists. Fellow Am. Coll. Obstetricians and Gynecologists; mem. Am. Psychiat. Assn. Contbg. author: Comprehensive Textbook of Psychiatry, 1973. Home: 9895 Florida Blvd Baton Rouge LA 70815

MANN, EDWARD NEWTON, JR., savs. and loan co. exec.; b. Carrboro, N.C., Feb. 12, 1932; s. Edward Newton and Bessie (Bock) M.; B.S. in Bus. Adminstrn., U. N.C., 1955; m. Evelyn Jean Stanford, Feb. 25, 1956; children—Jennifer Willcox, Edward Newton III, Charles Stanford. Partner Mann Constrn. Co., Chapel Hill, N.C., 1960-64; treas. Orange Savs. & Loan Assn., Chapel Hill, 1964—, also dir. Chmn. Chapel Hill Recreation Commn., 1962-66, Orange County Recreation Com., 1973—; commr. Chapel Hill Pub. Housing Authority, 1968-70, Chapel Hill Draft Bd., SSS, 1971—. Served with AUS, 1955-57. Mem. Am. Savs. and Loan Inst. (N.C. dir.), Chapel Hill Jr. C. of C. (past pres.). Club: Chapel Hill Tennis. Home: Route 1 Box 126 Chapel Hill NC 27514 Office: 101 E Rosemary St Chapel Hill NC 27514

MANN, FRANK EUGENE, lawyer, city ofcl.; b. Mart, Tex., Jan. 15, 1909; s. Cary and Pearl (Alden) M.; m. Janice Jones, Aug. 28, 1948;children—Frank Eugene, Donna (Mrs. Addison Thornhill), Sharon (Mrs. Neal Kinholt), Patricia (Mrs. Joseph W. Warfield). Admitted to Tex. bar, 1932, since practiced in Houston; fire commr., dir. fire def. Houston and Harris County, 1939-42; mem. Houston City Council, 1959—. Mem. Tex. Ho. of Reps., 1937-38, 57-58. Served from pvt. to capt. AUS, 1942-45. Mem. Tex., Harris County, Houston bar assns., Am. Legion, V.F.W., Sons of Herman, Harris County Mounted Sheriff's Posse (life mem., past pres.). Eagle (past pres.), Nat. Rifle Assn. (life), Bayou Rifles. Lion. Home: 5430 W 43d St Houston TX 77018 Office: Chronicle Bldg Houston TX 77002

MANN, GEORGE JOSEPH, univ. ofcl.; b. Vienna, Austria, Jan. 29, 1938; s. Lazar and Helene (Schwartz) M.; came to U.S., 1940, naturalized, 1946; B.Arch., Columbia, 1961, M.S., 1962; m. Amy Elisabeth Waldman, June 20, 1965; children—Daniel Jonathan, Deborah Karen. With I.M. Pei & Assos., N.Y.C., 1961; asst. prof. Kan. State U., Manhattan, 1963-64; with Isadore & Zachary Rosenfield, Architects, N.Y.C., 1964-65, Skidmore Owings & Merrill, N.Y.C., 1965-66; dir. health facilities research Tex. A. and M. U., College Station, 1966—. Pres., Resource Planning & Devel., Bryan, Tex., 1971—. Mem. A.I.A. pres. Brazos chpt. 1971, mem. nat., Tex. coms. on architecture for health, Tau Sigma Delta. Author numerous publs. on architecture, environmental design, resource planning. Home: 201 Redbud St Bryan TX 77801 Office: Texas A and M U Sch Architecture College Station TX 77843

MANN, GEORGE PATRICK, elec. engr.; b. Baytown, Tex., Nov. 5, 1934; s. Carl Ronald and Agnes Patricia (Bracken) M.; B.S. in Elec. Engring., U. Tex., 1956, M.S., 1957; m. Nancy Ann Shoup, Aug. 31, 1957; children—Michael Patrick, Ronald Joseph, Brian David. Distbn. engr. Roy Krezdorn, Cons. Engrs., Austin, Tex., 1959-62; distbn. engr., later chief engr. N.M. Electric Service Co., Hobbs, 1962-66; part-owner Baytown Engring. Co., 1966-72; mgr. elec. engring. dept. Caudill Rowlett Scott, architects and engrs., Houston, 1972—. Chmn. E. Harris Dist. council Boy Scouts Am., 1971-72. Registered profl. engr., Tex., La. Mem. I.E.E.E., Nat., Tex. (pres. Baytown chpt. 1971-72) socs. profl. engrs., Illuminating Engring. Soc. Elk. Home: 1403 Idaho St Baytown TX 77520 Office: PO Box 22427 Houston TX 77027

MANN, JACK MATTHEWSON, bottling co. exec.; b. Marshall, Tex., Apr. 14, 1932; s. Jack Slater and Mary (Matthewson) M.; student N.M. Mil. Inst., 1952; B.B.A., U. Tex., 1954; M.B.A., Harvard, 1960; m. True Sandlin, Sept. 4, 1954; children—Jack, Robert, Daniel, Nathaniel. Asst. sales mgr. MadeRite Co. (Dr. Pepper Bottling Co.), Marshall, 1957-58, gen. mgr., Longview, Tex., 1961—, pres., 1972—; chem. coordinator Humble Oil and Refining Co., Baytown, Tex., 1960-61. Credit analyst Republic Nat. Bank, Dallas, summer 1959; dir. Met. Savs. and Loan Assn., Longview. Pres., Trinity Episcopal Day Sch., Longivew, 1967-70; mem. exec. bd. Episcopal Diocese Tex., 1974—. Mem. exec. com. 2d Senatorial Dist. Tex., Republican party, 1963-66. Served to 1st lt., AUS, 1954-56. Mem. Longview C. of C. (dir. 1965-68), Tex. Soft Drink Assn. (pres. 1972). Episcopalian (past sr. warden). Mason, Rotarian (past dir.). Home: 1203 Montclair Longview TX 75601 Office: Box 3283 Longview TX 75601

MANN, JAMES ROBERT, congressman; b. Greenville, S.C., Apr. 27, 1920; s. Alfred Cleo and Nina (Griffin) M.; B.A., The Citadel, 1941; LL.B. magna cum laude, U. S.C., 1947; m. Virginia Thomason Brunson, Jan. 15, 1945; children—James Robert, David Brunson, William Walker, Virginia Brunson. Admitted to S.C. bar, 1947; practice in Greenville, 1947-69; partner firm Mann, Foster & Richardson, 1969-73; del. S.C. Ho. of Reps. from Greenville County, 1949-52; solicitor 13th Jud. Circuit, 1953-63; mem. 91st thru 93d Congresses from 4th Dist. S.C. Dir. Palmetto State Life Ins. Co. Sec., Greenville County Planning Commn., 1963-67; chmn. Greenville County Heart Assn., 1952; mem. bd. devel. New Orleans Bapt. Theol. Sem. Bd. dirs. Family Service Agy., 1952; trustee Greenville Hosp. System, 1965-68; bd. visitors Presbyn. Coll. Served to lt. col. AUS, 1941-46. Mem. Am., S.C., Greenville County bar assns., Am. Judicature Soc., Greater Greenville C. of C. (pres. 1965), V.F.W. (dep. comdr. 1951-52), Am. Legion, Phi Beta Kappa, Omicron Delta Kappa. Democrat. Baptist. Mason (Shriner), Kiwanian, Elk; mem. Woodmen of the World. Home: 118 W Mountain View Av Greenville SC 29609 Office: Longworth House Office Bldg Washington DC 20515

MANN, JANEAN LEE, adminstrv. asst.; b. Riverdale, Md., Sept. 14, 1943; d. Francis Lee and Jean (Hughes) Mann; B.A. in Journalism, U. S.C., 1966. With Americana Corp., 1962-63; staff writer Birmingham (Ala.) Post-Herald, 1966-69; press sec. U.S. Rep. John H. Buchanan, Jr. (Republican-Ala.), 1969-71, exec. asst., 1971-73, adminstrv. asst., 1973—. Recipient pub. service award U.S. Treasury Dept.; newswriting award A.P. Mem. House Republican Communications Assn. Theta Sigma Phi. Republican. Club: Greater Birmingham. Home: 608 6th St NE Washington DC 20002 Office: Longworth House Office Bldg Washington DC 20515

MANN, ROBERT TRASK, appellate judge; b. Tarpon Springs, Florida, June 5, 1924; s. William Edgar and Eunice (Trask) M.; B.S., in Bus. Adminstrn., U. Fla., 1946, LL.B., 1951; M.A. in Govt., George Washington U., 1948; LL.M., Harvard, 1953; LL.M., Yale, 1968; m. Elizabeth Brown, Dec. 27, 1947; children—Robert Trask, Margaret Elizabeth. Instr. bus. organization and control U. Md., 1947-48; admitted to Fla. bar, 1951, Mass. bar, 1952; asst. prof. law Northeastern U., 1951-53; practice law, Tampa, Fla., 1953-68; mem. firms Graham & Mann, 1956-58, Whitaker, Mann & Stagg, 1959-63; Campbell, Mann & Hampton, 1964-66; now judge Dist. Ct. of Appeal, Lakeland, Fla. Mem. Fla. Ho. of Reps., 1956-68. Served with AUS, 1943-45. Named Young Man of Year, Tampa, Jr. C. of C., 1958; recipient outstanding rep. award, St. Petersburg Times, 1967. Mem. Am. Law Inst. Methodist (mem. gen. conf., 1960, 64, 68, 72, World Council 1965, Southeastern jurisdictional council 1960-68). Home: Lake Weeks SeFrier FL 33584 Office: District Court Appeal Lakeland FL 33802

MANNHEIMER, WALTER HERBERT, physician; b. Mainz, Germany, June 24, 1911; s. Eugene and Hedwig (Weiss) M.; B.S., U. Freiburg, 1931, M.D., U. Basel, 1934; m. Ilse Holz, Jan. 20, 1937; children—Irene (Mrs. Gabriel Mirkin), Hedy (Mrs. Richard B. Dunn). Came to U.S., 1936, naturalized, 1942. Intern, Wichita Gen. Hosp., Wichita Falls, 1936-37; resident Charity Hosp., New Orleans, La., 1949-50; practice medicine, specializing in anesthesiology, Seguin, Tex., 1937-49; chief anesthesia sect. VA Hosp., Houston, 1955—; asso. prof. anesthesia Baylor Coll. Medicine, 1955—. Served with M.C., AUS, 1944-46. Author: Histopathologic Effects of Local Anesthetic Drugs, 1961. Contbr. articles to profl. pubs. Home: 5114 Jackwood St Houston TX 77035 Office: VA Hospital Houston TX 77031

MANNING, ALLEN BRYANT, physician; b. Mills County, Tex., Nov. 21, 1936; s. Marvin H. and Artiste Cozette (Bryant) M.; student McMurry Coll., 1955-57, Hardin-Simmons U., 1956-58, Abilene Christian Coll., 1958; M.D., U. Tex., Galveston, 1962; m. Vivian Gay Holmes, Aug. 23, 1958; children—Debra Gay, Jeffrey Holmes. Rotating intern John Peter Smith Hosp., Ft. Worth, 1962-63, resident, 1963-64, vice chmn. dept. gen. practice, 1970—; gen. practice medicine, Arlington, Tex., 1964—; pres. med. staff Arlington Community Hosp., 1969-70; sec. med. staff Arlington Meml. Hosp., 1972-73; aviation med. examiner FAA, 1966—. Bd. dirs. Arlington Boys Club, 1967-70. Recipient NSF research grant U. Tex. Med. Br., 1959-61, Mead Johnson award gen. practice residency, 1963-64, Physicians Recognition award A.M.A., 1969; NSF fellow, 1969-71. Diplomate Am. Bd. Family Practice. Mem. A.M.A., Tex. Med. Assn., Tarrant County Med. Soc., Am., Tex., Tarrant County acads. gen. practice, Am. Assn. Physicians and Surgeons, Am. Coll. Emergency Physicians, N.Central Tex. Council Med. Staffs Pvt. Hosps., Phi Chi, Mu Delta. Home: 1008 Live Oak Lane Arlington TX 76013 Office: 1300 S Fielder Rd Arlington TX 76013

MANNING, ALMA SQUIRES (MRS. T. WESLEY MANNING), nursing adminstr.; b. New Middleton, Tenn., Sept. 9, 1912; d. James T. and Florence (Hays) Squires; diploma St. Thomas Sch. Nursing, Nashville, 1941; certificate Middle Tenn. Tchrs. Coll., Murfreesboro, 1931; B.S. in Nursing Edn., Cath. U. Am. 1955; m. T. Wesley Manning, Aug. 26, 1947. Substitute tchr. Smith County Schs., Carthage, Tenn., 1931-38; instr. nursing St. Thomas Sch. Nursing, Nashville, 1941-44, St. Mary's Sch. Nursing, Knoxville, Tenn., 1944-48; dir. nursing Nashville Met. Gen. Hosp., 1948—. Mem. bd. examiners Tenn. Com. on Nursing Edn. and Nursing Practice, 1945-50; mem. Tenn. Bd. Nursing, 1952-54; Named one of 5 outstanding execs. of year Davidson County, Bus. and Profl. Women's Club, 1963. Methodist. Club: Zonta (charter). Home: 2514 Joya Dr Nashville TN 37214 Office: Nashville Met Gen Hosp Nashville TN 37210

MANNING, ARTHUR BREWSTER, newspaper editor; b. Atlanta, Mar. 31, 1913; s. James Arthur and Rose (Word) M.; m. Mildred J. Dalton, July 11, 1945; children—March Word, James Brewster, William Dalton. Editorial positions Atlanta Constn., 1932-55; press-radio dir. Ga. War Finance Com., 1944-46; copy chief Robert Scott Advt. Agy., Atlanta, 1943-50; with Jacksonville (Fla.) Times-Union, 1955—, mng. editor, 1959—. Mem. Alpha Kappa Psi. Rotarian. Club: University. Home: 414 Oglethorpe Rd Jacksonville FL 32216 Office: PO Box 1949 Jacksonville FL 32201

MANNING, BILLY RANDOLPH, ednl. adminstr.; b. Roanoke, Va., Apr. 27, 1934; s. Daris William and Irma (Hundley) M.; B.S., Va. Poly. Inst., 1955; m. Shirley Ann Scott, Sept. 10, 1955; 1 son, Michael Scott. Designer Newport News (Va.) Shipbldg. and Dry Dock Co., 1957-61; structural engr., Fort Lee, Va., 1961-63, Office Civil Def., Olney, Md., 1963-65; civil engr. C.E. U.S. Army, Olney, 1965-68; dir. profl. adv. center Auburn U., Birmingham, 1968—. Mem. Birmingham Area Manpower Planning Council, 1972—. Served to lt. AUS, 1955-57. Registered Profl. Engr., Ala., W.Va., Ga. Mem. Profl. Soc. Nuclear Def., Nat. Soc. Profl. Engrs. (course dir., instr. 1969—), Ala., Ga. civil def. assns. Lutheran (deacon 1972-73). Clubs: Shades Valley Optimist, Green Valley Country. Home: 1616 Colesbury Circle Birmingham AL 35226 Office: Vulcan Life Bldg Birmingham AL 35209

MANNING, DOUGLAS HERMIT, leather co. exec.; b. nr. Yoakum, Tex., June 13, 1912; s. Martin Hermit and Janie Amanda (Ridgway) M.; grad. high sch.; m. Mary Edna Manning, Apr. 18, 1936; children—Norman Leland, Ronald Bryan, Gordon Lester, Melva Don (Mrs. Donald Ray Brown). With Tex Tan Western Leather Co., Yoakum, Tex., 1932-70, v.p. charge sales, 1945-70, dir., 1955-70; v.p. Tandy Corp., Ft. Worth, 1970—. Clubs: Lakeside Country (Yoakum); Shady Oaks Country, Petroleum (Ft. Worth). Home: 2921 Overton Park E Fort Worth TX 76109 Office: 2727 W 7th St Fort Worth TX 76107

MANNING, FRANK WILLIAM, electronic engr.; b. Chariton, Ia., July 26, 1917; s. Frank Eli and Margaret (Fowler) M.; B.E. in Elec. Engring., Ia. State Coll., 1938; m. Margaret Elizabeth Rollins, Mar. 2, 1946; children—Margaret Elaine, William Frank, Susan Amy, Jane Elizabeth. With Central States Power & Light Corp., West Union, Ia., 1938-41; engr. Interstate Power Co., Dubuque, 1941; mem. aircraft radio lab. staff U.S. War Dept., Dayton, O., 1942-47; with Oak Ridge Nat. Lab., 1947—, supervising engr. electronics sect., 1949—. Engring. cons. Democritus Nuclear Center, Greece, 1963-64; v.p. Hilltop Corp., Norris, Tenn., 1960—. Commr., Norris Water Commn., 1952-54; mem. Norris Municipal Pub. Works Com., 1954-66, chmn. 1956-65. Councilman, City of Norris, 1969-70, vice mayor, 1971-74. Mem. Anderson County Republican Exec. Com., 1960-72. Registered profl. engr., Ohio, Tenn. Mem. I.E.E.E., A.A.A.S., Am. Nat. Standards Inst., Am. Nuclear Soc. Rep. Episcopalian (warden ch. 1959-64, 65-66). Mason. Patentee in field. Home: 32 Deer Ridge Rd Norris TN 37828 Office: PO Box X Oak Ridge TN 37830

MANNING, GLENN FRANKLIN, lawyer; b. Huntsville, Ala., July 10, 1922; s. Frank C. and Lucile (Davis) M.; student Auburn U., 1940-41; student U. Ala., 1941-43, LL.B., 1948; student Georgetown U., 1943-44; LL.M., George Washington U., 1949; m. Mary Elizabeth Kirkpatrick, Oct. 16, 1954; children—Frank R., Mary K., Alice E., Sam D. Admitted to Ala. bar, 1948; atty. FTC, 1948-49; practice law, Huntsville, Ala., 1949-50, 58-74; state dist. atty. 23d Jud. Circuit of Ala., 1951-58; partner firm Watts, Salmon, Roberts, Manning & Noouin. Instr. polit. sci. U. Ala., 1952-55. Mem. Madison County (Ala.) Democratic Exec. Com., 1958-64, Madison County Republican Exec. Com., 1965-70; del. Ala. Rep. Conv., 1968, 70; mem. Ala. State Rep. Com., 1969-70. Bd. dirs. U. Ala. Law Sch. Found. Mem. Am., Ala. (bd. commnrs.), Huntsville-Madison County (pres. 1969-70) bar assns., Farrah Order Jurisprudence, Ala. Trial Lawyers Assn., Am. Trial Lawyers Assn. Episcopalian. Home: 2603 Ridgeview Circle SE Huntsville AL 35803 Office: Terry-Hutchens Bldg Huntsville AL 35804

MANNING, JAMES HOWARD, electronic design engr.; b. Raymondville, Tex., Apr. 8, 1946; s. William Maurice and Astrid Marie (Sundling) M.; student Tex. Luth. Coll., 1964-65; B.S. in Elec. Engring., Tex. Arts and Industries U., 1969; m. Dorothy Louise Jones, Aug. 7, 1971. Elec. inspection engr. Transcontinental Gas Pipeline Co., Houston, 1968; electronic design engr. Tex. Instruments, Dallas, 1969—, tchr. tng. classes on metastable helium magnetometer, 1972—. Republican. Baptist. Home: 1902 Mission Dr Garland TX 75042 Office: 13500 N Central Dallas TX 75222

MANNING, JOHN W., educator, physiologist; b. New Orleans, Nov. 14, 1930; s. John W. and Dorothy (Baylor) M.; B.S. in Physiology, Loyola U. of South, New Orleans, 1951; M.S., Tulane U., 1955; Ph.D., Loyola U., Chgo., 1958; m. Cynthia Satterlee, Jan. 9, 1954; children—Kathleen, Michael, Donald, Edward, Cheryl Ann, Robert. Research asso. physiology Tulane U., 1952-54, research asso. ophthalmology, 1955-56; USPHS postdoctoral fellow pharmacology Emory U., also instr., 1960-61, advanced research fellow physiology Am. Heart Assn., 1961-63, mem. faculty, 1964—, prof. physiology, 1970—, dir. grad. studies physiology, 1969—; vis. scientist pharmacology Karolinska Inst., Stockholm, Sweden, 1964-66, Schinshu U. Med. Sch., Matasumoto, Japan, 1972—. Mem. A.A.A.S., Am. Physiol. Soc., Am. Assn. Anatomists. Soc. Neurosci., Sigma Xi. Contbr. articles to med. jours. Editorial bd. Cardiology, 1970. Home: 1406 Council Bluff Dr Atlanta GA 30306

MANNING, MELVIN RAY, lawyer; b. Smithfield, N.C., Nov. 20, 1937; s. Ray Eugene and Emily (Edwards) M.; J.D., U. Richmond, 1964; m. Judith Guy Morris, Oct. 25, 1958; 1 son, Ray Bradford. Admitted to Va. bar, 1964; mem. firm McCaul, Grigsby & Pearsall,

Richmond, Va., 1964—. Instr. Law Sch., U. Richmond, 1965-66; dir. Import Autohaus, Bon Air Realty Co., Berckman Corp.; counsel Va. Senate Commerce and Labor Com., 1968-72. Mem. bd. St. Michael's Episcopal Sch., Richmond, 1969-72, chmn. bd., 1971-72; dir. U. Richmond Law Sch. Alumni Assn., 1966-69. Recipient Charles T. Norman medal in law, U. Richmond, 1964. Mem. Am., Va. (chmn. bar news media relations 1972—), Richmond, Chesterfield bar assns., McNeill Law Soc., Omicron Delta Kappa, Delta Theta Phi. Democrat. Episcopalian. Clubs: Commonwealth, Stonehenge Golf and Country, Bull and Bear (Richmond). Editor: U. Richmond Law Rev., 1963-64. Home: 1522 N Bon View Dr Bon Air VA 23235 Office: 1005 United Virginia Bank Bldg 9th and Main Sts Richmond VA 23219

MANNING, ROBERT LISBON, TV cinematographer; b. Nashville, May 18, 1933; s. Robert Lisbon and Katherine (Kallock) M.; student Vanderbilt U., 1952-54. With WSM-TV, Nashville, 1950-54, 56—, news cinematographer, reporter, 1956-60, chief cinematographer, 1960—. Bd. dirs. Cath. Communication Commn. Tenn. Served with Signal Corps, AUS, 1954-56. Mem. Radio-TV News Dirs. Assn., Nat. Press Photographers Assn., Soc. Motion Picture and TV Engrs., Mid-Tenn. News Photographers Assn., Sigma Delta Chi (chpt. dir.). Roman Catholic. Home: 6668 S Upton Ct Nashville TN 37209 Office: 5700 Knob Rd PO Box 100 Nashville TN 37202

MANNING, WALTER SCOTT, educator; b. nr. Yoakum, Tex.; B.B.A., Tex. Coll. Arts and Industries, 1932; M.B.A., U. Tex., 1940; m. Eleanor Mary Jones, Aug. 27, 1937; children—Sharon Frances, Walter Scott, Robert Kenneth. Asst. to bus. mgr. Tex. Coll. Arts and Industries, Kingsville, 1932; tchr., Sinton (Tex.) High Sch., 1933-37, Robstown (Tex.) High Sch., 1937-41; prof. Tex. A. and M. Coll., College Station, 1941—. Cons. C.P.A. Mem. athletic council Tex. A & M U. C.P.A., Tex. Mem. Am. Assn. U. Profs., Am. Accounting Assn., Am. Inst. C.P.A.'s Tex. Soc. C.P.A.'s, College Station C. of C. (past pres.), Tex. Assn. U. Instrs. in Accounting (pres. 1963-64), Knights York Cross of Honor, Alpha Chi. Democrat. Presbyn. (elder). Mason (32 deg., Shriner, K.T.), Kiwanian. Home: 405 Walton Dr E College Station TX 77840

MANNONI, RAYMOND, univ. adminstr.; b. Pittsburg, Kan., July 11, 1921; s. Espartero U. and Mary Katherine (Scalet) M.; B.S., Kan. State U., 1944; M.Ed., U. Mich., 1946; postgrad. Northwestern U., 1947-48; D.Mus. Edn., Chgo. Mus. Coll., 1956; m. Karen Whittet, June 2, 1956; 1 dau., Barbara Gwen. Dir. bands U. Tulsa, 1946-48; 1st hornist Tulsa Symphony Orch., 1946-48; dir. bands, instr. music Kan. State Tchrs. Coll., Emporia, 1949-50; prof. music, dean Sch. Fine Arts, U. So. Miss., Hattiesburg, 1960—. Cons. music edn. dept. Lyon & Healy, Chgo., 1949-50; mem. LeBlanc Music Educators Nat. Adv. Bd., 1958-68. Served with USN, World War II. Recipient Alumni Certificate of award U. So. Miss., 1954-55, Award of Merit, Nat. Fedn. Music Clubs, 1962. Mem. Music Educators Nat. Conf. (life), Phi Kappa Phi, Phi Delta Kappa, Kappa Kappa Psi, Alpha Psi Omega, Phi Mu Alpha Sinfonia, Phi Kappa Lambda. Mason (Shriner), Elk. Club: Exchange (Hattiesburg). Co-author: Music Theory for Beginners, 1956. Home: 45 Fairlake Dr Country Club Estates Hattiesburg MS 39401

MANOR, HAROLD CARL, coll. pres.; b. Ft. Wayne, Ind., Sept. 20, 1913; s. Carl E. and Mabel (Timmis) M.; B. Music Edn., Ind. U., 1936, M.A., 1938, Ed.D., 1947; postgrad. U. Fla., 1954-56; D. Humane Letters, Fla. Atlantic U., 1972; m. Dorothy Beatrice McCormick, June 6, 1937; 1 dau., Marcia Lee. Supr. music, Rockville, Ind., 1936-38, Winchester, Ind., 1938-44; instr., critic Ind. U., 1944-47; chmn. fine arts dept. Ark. State Coll., 1947-53; instr. St. Petersburg Jr. Coll., 1953-55, dean evening div., 1955-57; asst. pres. Palm Beach Jr. Coll., Lake Worth, Fla., 1957-58, pres., 1958—. Mem. Assn. for Higher Edn. Am., So. Assn. Colls. and Schs. (v.p. 1944; mem. commn. on colls.), Phi Delta Kappa, Phi Mu Alpha. Presbyn. Mason, Rotarian. Home: 3570 S Ocean Blvd Palm Beach FL 33480 Office: 4200 Congress Av Lake Worth FL 33460

MANRIQUE, JOSÉ ANGEL, educator; b. León, Guanajuato, Mexico, Jan. 22, 1942; s. José Andel and Concepción (Váladez) M.; B.S. in Mech. Engring., Tecnológico de Monterrey (Mexico), 1965; Ph.D., U. Wis., 1969. Asso. prof. thermal engring. Tecnológico de Moterrey, 1969-73, prof., 1973—. Cons., Desarrollo Industrial Mexicano, S.A. de C.V., 1969—. Recipient Premio al Saber, Mención Honorífica, Tecnológico de Monterrey, 1965. Mem. Soc. Automotive Engrs. (Ralph R. Teetor award, 1972, Distinguished Service award, 1973), Am. Soc. Engring. Edn., Am. Inst. Chem. Engrs., Am. Soc. M.E., Sigma Xi. Author textbook on Thermodynamics, 1973, also articles. Home: Mazatlán 4224 Col Valle de las Brisas Monterrey NL México Office: ITESM Dept Thermal Engring Monterrey NL México

MANSBACH, HARRY HIRSCH, lawyer; b. Norfolk, Va., Sept. 10, 1911; s. Charles Milton and Regina (Rosenbaum) M.; grad. Philips Acad., 1927; A.B., Yale, 1931; LL.B. magna cum laude, Harvard, 1934; m. Marie Altschul, Apr. 16, 1935; children—Charles Milton II, Benjamin Thomas, Sally Jean (Mrs. Stephen A. Herman). Admitted to Va. bar, 1934; practiced in Norfolk, 1934-42; mgr. The Hub, Mansbach Bros., Inc., 1945-50, pres., 1950-66; mem. firm Kaufman, Oberndorfer & Spainhour, Norfolk, 1967—; dir. Va. Nat. Bank, Ocean Electric Corp., Investment Funds, Inc. Pres. Health, Welfare and Recreation Planning Council, 1959-61; chmn. Norfolk Area Med. Center Authority, 1970—, commr., 1966—. Bd. dirs., mem. exec. com. United Communities Fund; bd. dirs. Tidewater Regional Health Planning Council, DePaul Hosp., Norfolk Symphony Assn. Served with USNR, 1942-45; PTO. Mem. Am., Va bar assns., Nat. Conf. Christians and Jews, Norfolk C. of C. (pres. 1962), Norfolk Retail Mchts. Assn. (pres. 1965-66), Phi Beta Kappa. Club: Harbor (Norfolk). Home: 7429 Shirland Av Norfolk VA 23505 Office: 2030 Virginia Nat Bank Bldg Norfolk VA 23510

MANSBERGER, ARLIE ROLAND, surgeon; b. Turtle Creek, Pa., Oct. 22, 1922; s. Arlie R. and Mayne M. (Smith) M.; A.B., Western Md. Coll., 1944; M.D., U. Md., 1947; m. Anna Ellen Piel, July 27, 1946; children—Ellen Lynn, John Arlie, Leigh Ann. Intern U. Md. Hosp., Balt., 1947-49, research fellow, 1949-50, resident in surgery, 1950-54, instr., 1956-59, asst. prof., 1959-61, asso. prof., 1961-69, prof. surgery, 1969-73, head div. gen. surgery, 1971-73, dir. clin. research shock-trauma unit, 1962-66, adviser, 1966-72; prof., chmn. dept. Surgery Med. Coll. Ga., 1973—; practice medicine specializing in surgery; cons. Montebello St. Hosp., Balt., 1957-73, chief cons. VA Hosp., Augusta, Ga., Ft. Gordon Army Hosp., 1973—. Alumni rep. Western Md. Coll., 1968-71, life-time trustee, 1968—. Served with AUS, 1943-46, to capt. M.C., 1954-56; col., comdg. officer 136th Evacuation Hosp. Md. Army Nat. Guard. Recipient Golden Apple award SAMA, 1968, 72; Man of Yr. award Student Council U. Md., 1970, 72. Diplomate Am. Bd. Surgery. Fellow A.C.S. (cons. shock-trauma unit 1957—); mem. Soc. Univ. Surgeons, So. Surg. Assn., Am. Assn. Surgery of Trauma, Southeastern Surg. Conf. (forum com. 1967—), Soc. for Surgery of Alimentary Tract, Soc. Consultants to Armed Forces, Am. Surg. Assn., Alpha Omega Alpha. Republican. Contbr. articles on ammonia metabolism, metabolic changes in shock, water and electrolyte shifts in disease to profl. jours. Editor: Am. Surgeon, 1973—. Chmn. editorial bd. Bull. U. Md. Sch. Medicine, 1971-73. Home: 3128 Walton Way Augusta GA 30904 Office: Eugene Talmadge Meml Hosp Atlanta GA 30902

MANSCHOT, WILLIAM GEORGE, JR., TV exec.; b. Milw.; s. William George and Gertrude (Gordon) M.; student Northwestern U., 1946-47; m. Beverly Hubinger, May 31, 1947; children—Jill Ann (Mrs. Robert W. Lewis), William George III. Designer, Port Players, Oconomowoc, Wis., 1947; scenic artist Midwest Scenic Studio, Milw., 1947-48; designer sta. WTMJ-TV, Milw., 1948-50; artist Wilding Pictures, Chgo., 1950; dir. photography Apollo Pictures, Ltd., Milw., 1951; prodn. mgr. WBAY-TV, Green Bay, Wis., 1951-54; with WTTW, Chgo., 1955-67, program mgr., 1966-67; dir. programming WYES-TV, New Orleans, 1967-69; pres. Gateway Prodns., Inc., New Orleans, 1970—; dir. nat. advt. sales Mecca mag., New Orleans; corr. UPI TV News; cons. Am. Personnel and Guidance Assn. Asst. prof. Northwestern U.-NBC TV Inst., Chgo., 1958; profl. faculty Loyola U. Communications Inst., 1969. Bd. dirs. Internat. Jazz Festival, Inc., New Orleans Community Relations Council. Recipient award for best TV series on alcoholism U.S. Com. on Alcoholism, 1966; award for best TV series on mental health Ill. Dept. Mental Health, 1966. Mem. Nat. Assn. Ednl. Broadcasters, Am. Film Inst., Information Film Producers Am. Club: New Orleans Press. Exec. producer nat. TV series including: Three Faces of Cuba, 1964, Fine Arts Quartet Plays Beethoven, 1960, Alcoholics Are People, 1966, The New Biology, 1962. Home: 8312 Pritchard Pl New Orleans LA 70118 Office: 860 St Charles Av New Orleans LA 70130

MANSFIELD, JIM HOLLAND, mgmt. cons.; b. Bandera, Tex., Oct. 8, 1936; s. James Roy and Beverly Jenny (Boles) M.; B.S. in Indsl. Engring., Okla. State U., 1959; postgrad. So. Ill. U., 1959-60; m. Sue Jane Kallenberger, Aug. 25, 1956; children—Sherry Lynn, Melanie Sue. Sr. mgmt. cons. Lifson, Wilson, Ferguson & Winick, Dallas, 1961-68; dir. operations Internat. Optical Co., Dallas, 1968-69; v.p. mfg. Home Metal Products Co., Plano, Tex., 1969-72; v.p., gen. mgr. Internat. Optical, Dallas, 1972-73; mgmt. cons., 1973—. Cons. county hosps. Bd. dirs. Collin County United Fund, 1971-72. Registered profl. engr., Tex. Mem. Am. Inst. Indsl. Engrs. (sr. mem.), Sigma Phi Epsilon (treas. 1954). Republican. Methodist. Home: 7039 Town Bluff Dallas TX 75240 Office: 4230 LBJ Freeway Dallas TX 75240

MANSKE, WALLIS HENRY, lawyer; b. Oldenburg, Tex., Jan. 30, 1922; s. Herbert G. and Eleanora (Ahlhorn) M.; student Tex. Luth. Coll., 1940-42; LL.B., U. Louisville, 1949; m. Ethel Mae Price, May 19, 1946; 1 dau., Patricia Ann. Admitted to Ky. bar, 1950; practiced in Louisville, 1950—. Served with USAAF, 1942-45. Decorated Bronze Star medal. Mem. Am., Ky., Louisville bar assns., World Peace Through Law, Nat., Ky. assns. trial attys., Ky. Hist. Soc. Mason. Home: 3318 Autumn Way Louisville KY 40218 Office: Marion E Taylor Bldg Louisville KY 40202

MANUCCIA, HERBERT, cons. engr., educator; b. N.Y.C., Sept. 15, 1905; s. Louis and Constance (Speciale) M.; City Coll. N.Y., Cooper Union, George Washington U.; m. Marie Serena, Jan. 27, 1928; 1 son, Herbert Louis. With Herbert Manuccia, P.E. and Assos., cons. engrs., Washington; prof., staff asso. prof. Sch. Engring. and Architecture Cath. U. Am. Prin. works include design multi story bldgs., subways, Ind. Subway System, N.Y.C.; bridges, ships, Maritime Commn.; stress analysis N.Y. World's Fair; mil. structures, including Pentagon Bldg., Arlington, Va.; engr. cons. foreign mil. installations; overseas engring. cons. mil. installations. Vice chmn. Alexandria City Bd. Zoning Appeals. Past rep. D.C. council Archtl. and Engring. Socs., former officer and past chmn. various coms. in these socs. Former chmn. No. Va. com. Boy Scouts Am. Registered profl. engr., Va., D.C., Md., N.C. Certified by Nat. Council State Bds. Engring. Exams. Recipient Outstanding Engr. award D.C. Soc. Profl. Engrs., 1955, Va. Soc. Profl. Engrs., 57. Mem. Am. Assn. U. Profs., Am. Soc. Engring. Edn., A.A.A.S., Soc. Am. Mil. Engrs., Municipal Engrs. Soc. City N.Y., Nat. (past nat. dir.; past nat. sec. cons. engineers, nat. gov.), Va. (past dir.), No. Va. (past pres.), D.C. (past pres., now state chmn.) socs. profl. engrs., Holy Name Soc. Roman Catholic. Home: 716 Pryor St Alexandria VA 22304 Office: Shirlington Trust Bldg 2740 S Randolph St Arlington VA 22206

MANUEL, JOHN WILLIAM III, city mgr.; b. Front Royal, Va., Apr. 13, 1947; s. John William, Jr., and Bernice Vera (Boyce) M.; A.A., Brevard Community Coll., 1970; B.A., Fla. Technol. U., 1972; m. Vonya LaRene Ferrell, May 26, 1973. Asst. city mgr., Largo, Fla., 1972-73, acting city mgr., 1973; city mgr., Palm Springs, Fla., 1973—. Served with Airborne Div., AUS, 1966-69. Decorated Purple Heart, Combat Infantryman's badge. Mem. Internat. City Mgmt. Assn., Fla. City and County Mgrs. Assn. Rotarian. Home: 300 Vienna Dr Palm Springs FL 33460 Office: 225 1st Av SW Largo FL 33540

MANUEL, MAURICE, JR., dentist; b. Mamou, La., Dec. 24, 1930; s. Maurice and Armida (Young) M.; B.S., U. Southwestern La., 1951; postgrad. U. Ill., summers 1951, 52; D.D.S., Loyola U., 1955; m. Lois Lorene Henderson, Aug. 23, 1955; children—Maurice III, Charles Cary. Instr. crown and bridge dentistry Loyola U. Sch. Dentistry, New Orleans, 1955; practice dentistry, Lafayette, La., 1959—. Served to maj. Dental Corps, USAF, 1955-59. Mem. Am., La., Lafayette dental assns. Roman Catholic. K.C. Rotarian (pres. 1969). Home: 1003 Greenbriar Rd Lafayette LA 70501 Office: Bldg E 1144 Collidge St Lafayette LA 70501

MANUEL, SADAY J., city ofcl.; b. Basile, La., Mar. 28, 1922; s. Valentin and Valentine M.; student Jefferson Davis Vocational-Tech. Sch., 1951-52; m. Ellen Ardoin, Nov. 26, 1946; children—Brenda Joy, Sidney Joel, James Steven. Owner store, Jennings, La., 1939-52, G. B. Zigler Shipyard, Jennings, 1952-56; city clk. City of Jennings, sec.-treas. Jennings Vol. Fire Dept., 1956—; asst. fire chief. Mem. Democratic Exec. Com., 1957—. Served with AUS, 1942-45. Mem. Am. Legion, V.F.W. Roman Catholic. K.C., Lion. Home: 523 W Division St Jennings LA 70546 Office: City Hall Jennings LA 70546

MANYAN, DAVID RICHARD, research scientist; b. Providence, Nov. 9, 1936; s. George and Gladys (Nalbandian) M.; A.B., Bowdoin Coll., 1958; postgrad. U. Vt., 1958-59; M.S., U. R.I., 1965, Ph.D., 1967; m. Janet Ruth Conlon, Oct. 9, 1965; children—Aram David, Jessica Conlon. Asst. chemist Tex. Instruments, Inc., Attleboro, Mass., 1959-60; NIH postdoctoral fellow U. Miami (Fla.) Med. Sch., 1967-69, sr. fellow hematology, 1969-71, instr. medicine, 1971-72; dir. heart attack and stroke prevention program Am. Heart Assn., Miami, 1972-73; vis. investigator Howard Hughes Med. Inst., Miami, 1973—. Served with USNR, 1958. Research grantee NIH, 1967-69, Am. Cancer Soc., 1971. Mem. A.A.A.S., Am. Chem. Soc., Biochem. Soc. (Eng.), Fedn. European Biochem. Socs., Am. Inst. Chemists, Am. Fedn. Clin. Research, N.Y. Acad. Scis., Sigma Xi, Phi Kappa Phi. Home: 2200 N Greenway Dr Coral Gables FL 33134 Office: PO Box 605 Biscayne Annex Miami FL 33152

MANZO, JOSEPH PAUL, cons. engr.; b. Providence, Aug. 17, 1936; s. Constanzo and Gelsomina (Ruggieri) M.; B.S., N.Y. U., 1958; M.S., U. R.I., 1959. Cons. engr., Providence, 1959-62; instr. N.C. State U., 1962-66; cons. in mfg., bus., constrn., finance, Washington, 1966-71; founder, pres. Engring. Arts, Inc., Alexandria, Va., 1971—. Mem. President's Com. on Employment of Handicapped, 1970—. Registered profl. engr., Fla., Va., D.C. Mem. Nat. Soc. Profl. Engrs., Am. Soc. M.E. Roman Catholic. Home: PO Box 407 Alexandria VA 22313

MAPLES, JOHN, JR., banker; b. Omaha, Ga., Dec. 21, 1913; s. John and Mary (Portis) M.; student Auburn U., 1932-35, Rutgers U., 1945-47; m. Susie Hayes, Apr. 24, 1937; 1 dau., Mary Sue (Mrs. J. Donald Thornburgh). Sr. v.p. Birmingham Trust Nat. Bank (Ala.), 1935-64; exec. v.p., dir. Union Bank & Trust Co., Montgomery, Ala., 1964—; dir. Fed. Reserve Bank, Birmingham. Treas., Ala. Heart Assn., 1958-65, chmn. bd., 1966—; Ala. treas. Radio Free Europe, 1964-68, state chmn., 1968; mem. budget com. Am. Heart Assn., 1967-68; bd. dirs. United Appeal, Montgomery, Downtown Unlimited, Montgomery Baptist Hosp. Mem. Theta Chi. Baptist. Club: Montgomery Country, Kiwanis (bd. dirs.). Home: 3107 Pinehurst Dr Montgomery AL 36111 Office: 60 Commerce St Montgomery AL 36103

MAPLES, JOHN CLIFTON, civil engr.; b. Cromwell, Ky., Oct. 18, 1921; s. Orson C. and Pearl (Renfrow) M.; B.S. in Civil Engring., U. Ala., 1951; postgrad. Okla. State U., 1969—; m. Florence Utley, Apr. 6, 1946; children—Stephen J., Patricia. Civil engr. design TVA, Knoxville, 1951-53, constrn. engr. Johnsonville Steam Plant, 1956-58; constrn. engr. U.S. C.E., Wilmington Dist., N.C., 1953-56, constrn. engr., designer, Tulsa Dist., 1958-60, project engr. Keystone Dam, Tulsa Dist., 1960-62, constrn. mgmt. engr., Tulsa Dist., 1962-66, resident engr. Ark. Navigation Project, Locks Dam 18, Tulsa Dist., 1966-71, chief navigation br., Tulsa dist., 1971—. Cubmaster, Boy Scouts Am., 1955-56, scoutmaster, 1959-61, explorer leader, 1961-62. Served with AUS, 1942-45; ETO. Registered profl. engr., Okla. Mem. Am. Soc. C.E., Chi Epsilon. Baptist (supt. Sunday Sch. 1967—). Home: 14660 E 11th Pl Tulsa OK 74108 Office: Box 61 Tulsa OK 74108

MAPP, FREDERICK EVERETT, educator, biologist; b. Atlanta, Oct. 12, 1910; s. Thaddeus Henry and Willie Anne (Johnson) M.; B.S., Morehouse Coll., Atlanta, 1932; M.S., Atlanta U., 1934; M.A., Harvard, 1942; Ph.D., U. Chgo., 1950; m. Betty Lewis, Mar. 31, 1963; children—William M. Boyd II, Robert A. Boyd. Tchr., Washington High Sch., Atlanta, 1933-40; mem. faculty Knoxville (Tenn.) Coll., 1944-46, Roosevelt U., Chgo., 1948-50, Tenn. State U., Nashville, 1951-52; mem. faculty Morehouse Coll., 1952—, prof. developmental biology, 1952—; tchr. NSF, Dillard U., summer 1958. Past chmn. Southeastern Assn. Advisers for Health Professions. Mem. adv. bd. Atlanta Zoo, Ga. Zool. Soc.; bd. dirs. Atlanta Humane Soc., Soc. Prevention Cruelty to Animals. Mem. A.A.A.S., Am. Zool. Soc., N.Y. Acad. Sci., Am. Microscopic Soc., Am. Inst. Biol. Scis., Southeastern Electron Microscopy Soc., Phi Beta Kappa, Sigma Xi. Home: 703 Waterford Rd NW Atlanta GA 30318

MAPP, LOUIS EDGAR, concrete pipe co. exec.; b. Hattiesburg, Miss., June 30, 1937; s. William Claud and Mary Elizabeth (Faulkner) M.; student U. Miss., 1955-56, U. So. Miss., 1957-58, La. State U., 1958-59; m. Melinda McWilliams, Aug. 18, 1959; children—Louis E., Claude M., Leslie Lynn. With Faulkner Concrete Pipe Co., Hattiesburg, Miss., 1958—; v.p., 1960-72, pres., 1972—, also dir., v.p., dir. Carter Bldg., Inc.; dir. First Miss. Nat. Bank. Chmn. Forrest County Savs. Bond Drive, 1970. Bd. dirs. Forrest County Indsl. Bd., Pine Burr Area council Boy Scouts Am., Southeastern Miss. Air Ambulance Dist., Hattiesburg Boys Brotherhood, Hattiesburg YMCA, Sch. Engring. U. Miss., U. So. Miss. Found.; trustee Forrest Gen. Hosp. Served with AUS, 1957. Mem. Am. Concrete Pipe Assn. (region bd. dirs. 1969—), Young Pres.'s Orgn., Hattiesburg C. of C. (pres. 1971, bd. dirs. 1969—). Presbyn. (deacon 1970—). Kiwanian (bd. dirs. 1970—), Elk. Club: Hattiesburg Country (pres. 1971—, bd. dirs. 1969—). Office: Drawer F Hattiesburg MS 39401

MARBURY, RITCHEY MCGUIRE, III, civil engr.; b. Albany, Ga., May 18, 1938; s. Ritchey McGuire and Kathryn (Van Houten) M.; B.C.E., Ga. Inst. Tech., 1960, M.C.P., 1966; m. Fonda Gayle Starnes, June 16, 1962; children—Mary Kathryn, Ritchey McGuire IV. Planning intern Wichita-Sedgwick County Met. Planning Dept., 1961; partner Marbury Engring. Co., Albany, 1965—; pres. Marbury, Ritter, Scott; Turner, Inc., cons. engrs. Instr. algebra Albany Area Tech. and Vocational Sch., 1966. Served with C.E., AUS, 1963-65. Mem. Am. Soc. C.E. (pres.), Ga. Soc. Registered Profl. Land Surveyors (sec.-treas., dir.), Surveying and Mapping Soc. Ga. (v.p.), Cons. Engrs. Councils Ga., U.S., Am. Congress Surveying and Mapping, Phi Gamma Delta, Phi Kappa Phi. Mem. Ch. of Jesus Christ of Latter-day Saints (pres. br.). Rotarian. Home: 1824 Green Valley Lane Albany GA 31705 Office: 2330 Whispering Pines Rd Albany GA 31705

MARBURY, WILLIAM ARDIS, JR., banker, ins. exec.; b. Ruston, La., July 22, 1917; s. William Ardis and Leola R. (Ridgdill) M.; B.A., La. Poly. Inst. 1936; m. Virginia Lomax, Sept. 5, 1943; children—Rebekah, Caroline. Organized William A. Marbury & Co., Ruston, 1944; pres. Am. Home Plan Corp., Marbury Investment Corp., Bankers Life of La., Marbury Bldg. Corp., So. States Gen. Agy.; pres., dir. Homer Nat. Bank (La.), Ruston State Bank & Trust Co. (La.); dir. La. Bank & Trust Co., Shreveport. Chmn. Am. Cancer Soc. Pres. (first) Greater Tech Club, Inc.; bd. dirs. Lincoln Gen. Hosp., Ruston; mem. Alumni bd. La. Poly. Inst.; former mem. Lincoln Parish Sch. Bd. Mem. Young Pres.' Orgn., Homer (dir., exec. com.), Ruston (past pres., dir.) chambers commerce, Beta Gamma Sigma, Kappa Sigma. Episcopalian. Home: N Trenton St Ruston LA 71270 Office: 605 N Vienna St Ruston LA 71270

MARBUT, SYRIAN ERASMUS, lawyer; b. Verona, Mo., Apr. 30, 1907; s. John Franklin and Viola Ann (Walker) M.; B.A., U. Okla., 1930, LL.B., 1932; m. Elizabeth Caroline Gardner, Apr. 1, 1933. Admitted to Okla. bar, 1931, Tex. bar, 1932; asso. C.C. Triplett, Lubbock, 1932-35, pvt. practice, 1935-40; partner Anderson & Marbut, 1940-42; county atty., Lubbock County, 1942-46; asst. city atty., Lubbock, Tex., 1946-49; mem. firm Crenshaw, Marbut & Charness, 1950-52; pvt. practice, Lubbock, 1952—. Mem. Tex., Lubbock County bar assns., Sigma Mu Sigma, Phi Alpha Delta. Democrat. Episcopalian (vestryman 1944-47). Mason (32 deg., Shriner, K.T.), K.P. Club: Optimist (pres. 1941-42). Home: 1922 24th St Lubbock TX 79411 Office: Myrick Bldg Lubbock TX 79401

MARCHANT, TRELAWNEY ESTON, lawyer; b. Columbia, S.C., Dec. 9, 1921; s. Trelawney Eston and Lila (Cave) M.; B.S., U. S.C., 1942, LL.B., 1947; m. Caroline Melton Bristow, Nov. 10, 1951; children—Trelawney Eston III, Walter Bristow, Caroline Melton, Nancy Lila. Admitted to S.C. bar, 1947; practiced in Columbia, 1948—; mem. firm Marchant, Bristow & Bates, 1952—; judge Municipal Ct., Columbia, 1956-61. Dir., 1st Palmetto Bank & Trust Co. Chmn., Richland County chpt. Nat. Found., 1954-55. Chmn., Richland County Democratic Party, 1963-68. bd. dirs., v.p. U. S.C. Ednl. Found.; trustee U. S.C., 1965-70, chmn. bd. trustees, 1970—. Served to capt. USMCR, 1942-46, now brig. gen. S.C. Nat. Guard. Mem. Am., S.C., Richland County (pres. 1970-71) bar assns., Am. Judicature Soc., Acad. Polit. Sci., U. S.C. Alumni Assn. (past pres.), Am. Legion, Mil. Order of World Wars (past pres.), Omicron Delta Kappa, Sigma Nu. Episcopalian. Kiwanian (dir.). Clubs: Forest Lake Country; Cotillion, Columbia Ball, Torch. Home: 5046 Courtney Rd Columbia SC 29201 Office: 830 Laurel St Columbia SC 20201

MARCHBANKS, JERRY LEE, bus. exec.; b. San Antonio, Oct. 26, 1935; s. James Lee and Neva R. (Dixon) M.; B.S., Tex. A. and M. U., 1959; M.B.A., St. Marys U., 1965; m. Janice E. Lancaster, Sept. 2, 1961; children—Deborah Lynne, Michael Lee, Stephen Lance. Chief indsl. engr. Kelly AFB, Tex., San Antonio, 1960-64; mgr. Ernst & Ernst, San Antonio, 1964-68; v.p., dir. Computer & Bus. Mgmt., Inc., San Antonio, 1968-70; v.p., dir. CBM Edn. Centers, San Antonio and Baton Rouge, 1968—; chmn. Marchbanks & Parker, San Antonio, 1973—; mem. faculty Grad. Sch. Bus. St. Mary's U., San Antonio. Served with USAF, 1959-60. Mem. Am. Inst. Indsl. Engrs. (chpt. pres. 1964-65), Tex. Soc. Profl. Engrs., Data Processing Mgmt. Assn. Contbr. articles to profl. jours. Home: 129 Meadowbrook Dr San Antonio TX 78232 Office: 4438 Centerview San Antonio TX 78228

MARCHFIELD, RUDOLPH L., author; b. Chgo., May 29, 1907; s. Ignatius and Sali (Fleischer) M.; grad. pub. high sch.; m. Gloria Adams, June 22, 1937 (div. Feb. 1941) remarried, Oct. 27, 1963. Author, mfr., poet, musician, lyricist, free-lance reporter. Mem. A.S.C.A.P., Voltaire Soc. (pres.). Patentee kitchen and recreational products field. Recordings include Who Am I to Say, Line of Life, Your Bright Red Lips, If I Could Have You Back Again, Sinner and Saint, and others. Home: Route 4 PO Box 1837 Azalea St Basswood Okeechobee FL 33472

MARCOM, ORVAL WELDON, coll. adminstr.; b. Royse City, Tex., Jan. 2, 1908; s. George Ralph and Hattie (Jones) M.; student So. Meth. U., 1926-27; B.A., Tex. Tech. U., 1936, M.A., 1949, Ed.D., 1961; m. Laura Lucille Latimer, Mar. 15, 1929; children—Patsy (Mrs. William B. Methvin), George W., Marilyn (Mrs. Robert F. Wham). Tchr., prin. pub. schs., Tex., 1928-47; supt. schs., Levelland, Tex., 1947-61; academic dean San Jacinto Coll., Pasadena, Tex., 1961-67, academic v.p., 1967—. Mem. Tex. State Tchrs. Assn. (dist. past pres.), C. of C., Phi Delta Kappa. Mason, Rotarian. Home: 2611 Shenandoah St Pasadena TX 77502

MARCOTT, PAUL, pub. relations exec.; b. Buffalo, Mar. 8, 1915; s. Samuel C. and Elsa (Newman) M.; student U. Buffalo, 1933; m. Lorena M. Smith, Aug. 30, 1941. Indsl. editor Am. Optical Co., 1946-47; prodn. mgr., account exec. Warman & Co., 1947-48; copy chief Lansheft, Inc., 1947-48; indsl. editor Western Electric Co., 1948-50 (all Buffalo), asst. dir. pub. relations Bell Helicopter Co., Buffalo, 1950-56, advt. mgr., Fort Worth, 1956—. Vice pres. bd. Community Hosp. Planning Bd., 1965-67. Served with USAAF, 1942-46. Mem. Am. Helicopter Soc., Am. Marketing Assn., Assn. U.S. Army, Dallas Ad League, Ft. Worth Ad Club, Hurst-Euless C. of C. (pres. 1967, dir. 1965-67), Sigma Delta Chi (past dir.). Republican. Mason (Shriner). Patentee in field. Home: 4625 Mackey Dr Fort Worth TX 76118 Office: PO Box 482 Fort Worth TX 76101

MARCUS, IRWIN M., psychoanalyst, educator; b. Chgo., Mar. 18, 1919; s. Max U. and Belle (Rothbaum) M.; B.S., U. Ill., 1939, M.D., 1943; postgrad. Columbia, 1946-49; m. Dorothy Mann, June 29, 1948; children—Randall, Sherry, Melinda. Asso. psychoanalyst dept. psychiatry Columbia, 1949-51; asso. prof. Tulane U., 1951-56, also adj. prof. sch. Social Work and Tchr. Edn. Center; clin. prof. La. State U. Med. Center, New Orleans, 1956—; pres. New Orleans Psychoanalytic Inst., 1967-71, now dir. Child Psychoanalysis Div.; chmn. dept. psychiatry Touro Hosp., 1972-74; Charity Hosp. sr. vis. physician Children's Bur., Dept. Pub. Welfare, Orleans, Jefferson and St. Bernard parishes. Served to capt. AUS, World War II. Diplomate Am. Bd. Psychiatry and Neurology. Fellow Bd. Profl. Standards, Am. Psychoanalytic Assn., Am. Group Psychotherapy Assn. (past dir.), Am. Coll. Psychoanalysts, Am. Orthopsychiat. Assn., Am. Psychiat. Assn., Am. Acad. Child Psychiatry (chmn. program com. 1971-73); mem. Internat. Assn. Child Psychiatry, Assn. Child Psychoanalysis (councillor), Sigma Xi. Author: Costume Play Therapy, 1966; Learning Problems, 1967. Co-editor: Family Book Child Care, 1957, Masturbation: From Infancy to Senescence, 1974. Editor Currents in Psychoanalysis, 1972. Contbr. articles to profl. jours. Home: 4231 Vendome Pl New Orleans LA 70125 Office: 3619 Prytania St New Orleans LA 70115

MARCUS, MARIE SARTALAMACHIA, educator; b. New Orleans; d. John and Theresa (Ranatza) Sartalamachia; B.A., Tulane U., 1955, M.A., 1959; Ed.D., George Peabody Coll., 1964; m. William M. Marcus, Aug. 9, 1941 (div. Nov. 1952); 1 son, John William. Tchr. elementary schs., New Orleans, 1953-62; instr. George Peabody Coll. for Tchrs., Nashville, 1963-64; asst. prof. La. State U., New Orleans, 1964-66, asso. prof., 1966-70, prof., 1970—, dir. Lang. Arts Center, 1966—. Lang. arts cons. St. Bernard, Lafayette, Washington parishes schs. Mem. Internat. Reading Assn. (state chmn. 1966-72), Nat. Council Tchrs. English, Assn. Supervision and Curriculum Improvement. Author: A Handbook for Individualizing Reading Instruction, 1974. Mem. editorial bd. Reading Improvement; mem. adv. bd. Elementary English. Contbr. arteiles on lang. arts and reading to profl. jours. Home: 821 Angela Av Arabi LA 70032 Office: Lakefront New Orleans LA 70122

MARCUS, ROBERT BROWN, educator; b. Phila., Dec. 1, 1918; s. Henry Fisher and Mary Emma (Brown) M.; B.S., West Chester State Coll., 1940; M.A., U. Fla., Gainesville, 1953, Ed.D., 1956; m. Catherine Lucille Davis, Feb. 28, 1942; children—Robert B. Marcus, Pamela Jane. Chemistry and physics tchr. high sch., Elizabeth City, N.C., 1941-42; head sci. dept. The Pennington Sch., (N.J.), 1946-51; instr. phys. scis. and geography U. Fla., Gainesville, 1954-57, asst. prof., 1957-65, asso. prof., 1965-68, prof., 1968—, asst. dir. counseling University Coll., 1965—. Served to capt. AUS, 1942-46; now Col. res. Mem. Fla. Soc. Geographers (pres. 1971-72), Assn. Am. Geographers, Nat. Council Geog. Edn., Phi Delta Kappa, Kappa Delta Pi. Author: A Geography of Florida, 1964. Home: 4821 NW 20th Place Gainesville FL 32601

MARCUS, STANLEY RAYMOND, govt. research dir.; b. Providence, Feb. 29, 1916; s. Lyon A. and Mabel (Phillips) M.; B.S., U. R.I., 1938; M.S. in Engring. Adminstrn., George Washington U., 1958; postgrad. Mass. Inst. Tech., Pa. State U.; m. Beatrice Perry, Sept. 26, 1942; 1 son, Malcolm Jeffrey. Mech. engr. U.S. Naval Torpedo Sta., Newport, R.I., 1940-45; asst. chief engr. div. war research Columbia U., Newport, 1945-56; ind. practice, Providence, 1946-51; project engr. Bur. Ordnance, Washington, 1951-56, coordinator underwater Office Naval Research, 1956-59, coordinator anti-submarine warfare weapons Dep. Chief Naval Operations, 1959-60, asst. tech. dir. systems planning, 1960-63, dir. research div. Bur. Naval Weapons, Washington, 1963-66, exec. dir., chief scientist research and tech. directorate Naval Ordnance Systems Command, Washington, 1966—. Recipient Distinguished Civilian Service award U.S. Navy, 1973. Registered profl. engr., R.I. Mem. Acoustical Soc. Am., Am. Inst. Physics, Operations Research Soc. Am., Wash. Operations Research Council, Nat. Soc. Profl. Engrs., A.A.A.S., Am. Soc. of Cybernetics, Am. Ordnance Assn., Philos. Soc. Washington, Alpha Epsilon Pi. Mem. editorial bd. Navy Tech. Forum. Home: 2111 Jeff Davis Hwy Arlington VA 22202 Office: Naval Ordnance Systems Command Dept Navy Washington DC 20360

MARDAN, OMAR, newspaperman; b. Richmond, Va., June 21, 1924; s. Omar and Willoughby (Hull) M.; B.A., U. Richmond, 1945; m. Jacqueline Mae Lewis, 1969. With Richmond Times-Dispatch, 1945—, news editor, 1960-69, asst. mng. editor, 1969—. Mem. Sigma Phi Epsilon, Omicron Delta Kappa, Sigma Delta Chi (chpt. pres. 1965). Clubs: Willow Oaks Country. Home: 607 W 25th St Richmond VA 23225 Office: 333 E Grace St Richmond VA 23219

MARDER, ESTELLE ROTHENBERG, mus. ofcl.; b. Bklyn.; d. Max and Ida (Milman) Rothenberg; student Alpha Bus. Sch., State U. N.Y., 1926-28; m. David Marder, July 3, 1932 (dec. Sept. 1965); 1 dau., Rita Muriel (Mrs. Alan Barton). Med. sec. Dr. Herman Besser, N.Y.C., 1928-29; exec. sec., advt. mgr. Thrift Service and Thrista Holding Co., Bklyn., 1929-33; exec. sec. Winsoney Furnishers, Inc., N.Y.C., 1933-34; exec. sec., curator edn., Asheville (N.C.) Art Mus., 1966—. N.C. rep. Nat. Zionist Emergency Council, 1942-48; chmn. Citizens Food Conservation Com., 1947-48. Mem. Nat. Council Jewish Women (v.p. 1948-49), Hadassah (pres. Asheville chpt. 1942-45), Sigma Beta Sigma. Jewish religion (pres. temple sisterhood 1946-48). Home: 16 Maplewood Rd Asheville NC 28804 Office: Civic Center Haywood St Asheville NC 28801

MARIE, SISTER JOAN, coll. pres.; b. Nebraska City, Neb., July 25, 1913; d. John G. and Mary (Tongish) Lechner; A.B., Loras Coll., Dubuque, Ia., 1950; Ph.D., St. Louis U., 1960. Joined Soc. of Ursulines, 1934; instr. English, Latin and commerce St. Joseph's High Sch., Owensboro, Ky., 1936-48, St. Catherine's High Sch., New Haven, 1948-50; instr. English, Latin and bus., also prin. St. Francis' High Sch., Loretta, 1950-53; instr. English and bus., also treas. Brescia Coll., Owensboro, 1953-56, pres., 1960—. Recipient merit award St. Louis U. Alumni, 1968; Citizen of Yr. award, 1969; Liberty Bell award Daviess County Bar Assn., 1969, Woman of Achievement of the Yr. award Bus. and Profl. Women, 1973. Address: Brescia Coll Owensboro KY 42301

MARINACCIO, ANTHONY, educator; b. Bridgeport, Conn., Aug. 26, 1912; s. Paul and Louisa (DeLibero) M.; B.E., Conn. State Coll., 1937; M.A., Ohio State U., 1939; Ph.D., Yale, 1949; LL.D., Parsons Coll., 1961; m. Elsie Kleps, Sept. 5, 1936 (dec. Sept. 1964); children—Warren, Karen (Mrs. John Beacon), Dianna (Mrs. Joseph Carlisi), Nancy (Mrs. David Wilber), Linda, Lee; m. 2d, M. Maxine Reynolds, Oct. 15, 1965. Tchr. Jr. High Sch., Hartford, Conn., 1935-41; elementary sch. prin., 1941-46; prof. edn., prin. campus sch. Tchrs. Coll., State U. N.Y. at Oswego, 1946-49; asst. supt. charge instrn. and supervision pub. schs., Peoria, Ill., 1949-53; supt. schs., Mexico, Mo., 1953-55, Kankakee, Ill., 1955-59, Davenport, Ia., 1959-64; dean Parsons Coll., 1964-65; pres. The Hiram Scott Coll., Scottsbluff, Neb., 1964-69; prof. grad. edn. George Washington U., Washington, 1969—; professorial lectr. edn. George Washington U., summers, 1952-69; prof. edn. Bradley U., part time, 1949-53, supervision of instrn. research extension courses, 1956-58; vis. prof. secondary edn. Ohio State U., summers, 1953-54. Speaker various civic and ednl. groups. Active various local civic, religious and ednl. groups; organized South End Council, Hartford, Conn., 1944-46, Peoria Citizens' Council for Pub. Schs., 1951-52, in service tchr. edn. program, Peoria, 1949-53; pres. Kankakee Community Chest (Ill.), 1957-58. Mem. Davenport (Ia.) Planning Commn., 1960-63. Bd. dirs. Peoria Council Boy Scouts Am., 1951-53, A.R.C., Peoria, 1951-53; trustee Hiram Scott Coll., 1964-69. Mem. Sheldon Forum, Phi Delta Kappa, Epsilon Pi Tau, Phi Sigma Phi, Psi Phi. Mason (Shriner). Author: Exploring the Graphic Arts, 1959; Human Relations: The New Dimension in American Education, 1974. Contbr. articles to profl. pubs. Home: 13919 Turnmore Rd Silver Spring MD 20906 Office: The George Washington University Washington DC 20006

MARINER, HOBART GRAHAM, oil pipeline co. exec.; b. Fredonia, Kan., Nov. 9, 1914; s. Ralph Edwin and Geneva Frank (Beeson) M.; B.S., Kan. State U., 1937; m. Janice Taylor, Jan. 16, 1965; 1 dau. by previous marriage, Wendy (Mrs. Paul Garn Whitby). Jr. engr. Phillips Petroleum Co., Kansas City, Kan., 1937-38, Okla. Pipeline Co., Tulsa, 1938-40; with Amoco Pipeline Co., 1940—, div. mgr., Ft. Worth, 1966—. Served to lt. C.E., USNR, 1942-46. Registered profl. engr., Okla., Mo. Mem. Nat. Soc. Profl. Engrs., Am. Petroleum Inst., Okla. Soc. Profl. Engrs. Republican. Mason (Shriner). Clubs: Ridglea Country, Petroleum (Ft. Worth). Home: 3816 Trails Edge Fort Worth TX 76109 Office: 2300 Continental Nat Bank Bldg Fort Worth TX 76102

MARINO, SALVADOR ANTHONY, elec. engr.; b. Birmingham, Ala., Dec. 28, 1927; s. Joseph Salvador and Mary (Raia) M.; student Birmingham So. Coll., 1946-48; B.E.E., Auburn U., 1951; m. Josephine Musso, Sept. 17, 1951; children—Joseph, Anthony, Salvador. Design engr. Ala. Power Co., Birmingham, Ala., 1951-55, system planning engr., 1955-65, sr. system planning engr., 1965-72, asst. mgr. system planning, 1972—. Active Boy Scouts Am., 1961-70; pres. St. Joseph Sch. P.T.A., 1960-61. Served with USNR, 1945-46. Registered profl. engr., Ala. Mem. I.E.E.E., Tau Beta Pi, Eta Kappa Nu, Phi Kappa Phi. Roman Catholic (pres. St. Joseph Holy Name Soc., 1960-61, chmn. finance com. 1969-70, pres. Parish council 1970—). Home: 1437 27th St Birmingham AL 35218 Office: 600 N 18th St Birmingham AL 35291

MARISCAL, RICHARD NORTH, marine biologist, educator; b. Los Angeles, Oct. 4, 1935; s. Joseph Francis and Janet (Whittemore) M.; B.A., Stanford, 1957, M.A., 1961; Ph.D., U. Cal. at Berkeley, 1966. Lectr. in zoology U. Cal., Berkeley, 1966; vis. instr., researcher Hawaii Inst. Marine Biology, 1967; asst. prof. biol. sci. Fla. State U., Tallahassee, 1968-71, asso. prof., 1972—; vis. asst. prof., U. Cal., Santa Barbara, 1968; vis. asst. prof. Marine Sci. Center, Ore. State U., Corvallis, 1969; vis. asst. prof., Friday Harbor Labs., U. Wash., Seattle, 1970; vis. asst. prof. Bodega Marine Lab., U. Cal., Berkeley, 1971, vis. asso. prof., 1972. Bd. dirs. Fla. Trail Assn.; trustee Fla. Defenders Environment. Served to lt. USNR, 1957-59, NIH postdoctoral fellow, 1967-68; NSF research grantee, 1973. Mem. A.A.A.S., Am. Soc. Zoologists, Am. Inst. Biol. Scis., Ecol. Soc. Am., Animal Behavior Soc., Cal., N.Y., Fla. acads. scis., Assn. for Tropical Biology, Western Soc. Naturalists, Assn. Southeastern Biologists, Am. Soc. Ichthyologists and Herpetologists, Wilderness Soc., Nat. Audubon Soc., East African Wildlife Soc., Wildlife Fedn., Sierra Club, Stanford Alumni, Phi Sigma Kappa. Contbr. articles on marine biology to sci. publs. Editor: Experimental Marine Biology, 1974. Home: Route 3 Box 574 Tallahassee FL 32303

MARK, JEROME ALBERT, govt. ofcl.; b. Pitts., Apr. 16, 1924; s. Jacob and Ida (Albert) M.; B.S. in Mgmt. Engring. (Buhl Found. scholar 1941-42, Carnegie scholar 1941-43), Carnegie Inst. Tech., 1948; M.A. in Econs., U. Chgo., 1957; m. Frances Munz, Apr. 12, 1951; 1 dau., Karen. With Bur. Labor Statistics, Labor Dept., Washington, 1951—, dep. asst. commr., 1962-66, asst. commr. productivity, tech., 1966—. Served with C.E., AUS, 1943-46. Recipient distinguished service award Dept. Labor, 1965, eminent achievement award Commr. Labor Statistics, 1973. Fellow Am. Statis. Assn.; mem. Am. Econ. Assn. Indsl. Relations Research Assn. Home: 11207 Lombardy Rd Silver Spring MD 20901 Office: Bur Labor Statistics Washington DC 20212

MARK, SIDNEY CARL, broadcasting exec.; b. N.Y., Feb. 27, 1914; s. Henry and Sarah (Berkowitz) M.; B.A., Coll. City N.Y., 1934; m. Patricia Greenfield, Jan. 18, 1946; children—Priscilla, Jonathan Greenfield, Mary Alice, Sarah Edna, Henry Greenfield. Announcer, producer radio sta. WHN, N.Y., 1935; spl. events prodn. mgr., radio sta. WHK-WCLE, Cleve., 1937-43; radio-TV dir. Al Paul Lefton Co., 1943-48; pres., gen. mgr., radio sta. WTTM, Trenton, N.J., 1948-53; pres. Swern & Co. (Lit Brothers), Trenton, 1954-62; chmn., pres. Mark/way, Inc. (radio sta. KAKC AM-FM, Tulsa, WAKC, Bloomington-Normal, Ill., KFUN AM-FM, Las Vegas, N.M.); dir. Bankers Bond & Mortgage Co. Am. Instr. radio-TV announcing and prodn. Western Res. U., Cleve., also Coll. City N.Y., 1937-53. Chmn. Trenton Planning Bd., 1955-59; v.p. Trenton Philharmonic Soc., 1953-63; v.p. Del. Valley United Fund, 1954-56; bd. dirs. Greater Phila.-S. Jersey Council, 1949-53; trustee Greater Trenton Council, 1956-62; bd. dirs. Tulsa chpt. A.R.C., Tulsa Recreation Center for Physically Ltd.; bd. dirs., v.p. Tulsa Civic Ballet; v.p. Jr. Achievement of Tulsa, Inc.; pres. Concertime, Inc. of Tulsa; bd. dirs. Tulsa Philharmonic Soc., Inc.; chmn. Tulsa Met. YMCA; finance chmn. Boy Scouts; treas. adv. council Salvation Army, Tulsa; trustee Fenster Gallery of Judaica; mem. Jewish Community Council, Tulsa. Pres. N.J. Broadcasters Assn., 1951-52. Mem. Mensa (chmn. Tulsa). Clubs: Petroleum, Tulsa Tennis. Home: 6766 S Columbia Av Tulsa OK 74136 Office: KAKC Bldg 51st and S Peoria Box 970 Tulsa OK 74101

MARKEN, DONALD GLENN, metal products co. exec.; b. Topeka, Kan., Dec. 10, 1937; s. Ronald Glenn and Lillie Ruth (Fox) M.; Indsl. Engr., Washburn U., 1962; postgrad. Arlington U., 1966-67, So. Methodist U., 1970—; m. Patricia L. Whiteside, Aug. 27, 1957; children—Mike G., Dan G., David G., Doug G. Mfg. mgr. Triple S. Dynamics, Dallas, 1965-68; v.p. Reddy Metal Products Co., Dallas, 1969-70; pres. D'Mark Assn., Garland, Tex., 1970—; v.p. mfg. Mesco Metal Bldg. Corp., Grapevine, Tex., 1970—; trustee Tex. Bank, Dallas. Cons. indsl. mgmt. and sales; guest lectr. Purdue U., So. Meth. U., Long Beach (Cal.) State U., Spring Garden (Pa.) Coll., Mesa Jr. Coll., Grand Junction, Colo.; mem. faculty Metal Fabricating Inst., Rockford, Ill. Bd. dirs. New World Homeowners Assn., Garland, Tex., 1969-71. Mem. Cleve. Engring. Soc. K.C. Home: 1121 Mill River Dr Garland TX 75049 Office: PO Box Drawer G Grapevine TX 76051

MARKER, HOWARD WILLIAM, physician; b. Dallas, Nov. 16, 1932; s. Al B. and Menah (Rubinsky) M.; A.A., Tyler Jr. Coll., 1951; B.A., U. Tex., 1953, M.D., 1958; m. Fay Bussel, Aug. 16, 1956; children—Michael Barry, Jeffrey Harold, Edward Andrew, Cynthia Elaine. Intern, Memphis (Tenn.) Hosps., 1958-59, resident in internal medicine, 1961-65; pvt. practice specializing in internal medicine, Memphis, 1966—; mem. staff Bapt. Meml., St. Joseph, Meth., William Bowld hosps.; clin. asst. prof. internal medicine U. Tenn. Med. Units, Memphis, 1966—; physician in chief B'nai B'rith Home and Hosp., Memphis, 1967—. Chmn. med. and sci. com. West Tenn. chpt. Arthritis Found., 1969—. Served with USAF, 1959-61. NIH fellow, 1963-65. Diplomate Am. Bd. Internal Medicine. Fellow Am. Coll. Physicians, Am. Geriatric Soc.; mem. A.M.A., Tenn. Med. Soc., Am. Rheumatology Assn. Mem. B'nai B'rith (v.p. 1970—, treas. 1970-71). Home: 90 Grovedale St Memphis TN 38117 Office: 210 Jackson St Memphis TN 38105

MARKERT, WILLIAM NORMAN, fabricated metal products mfg. co. exec.; b. Louisville, May 14, 1923; s. William Reese and Anna (Gruner) M.; B.M.E., U. Ky., 1949; m. Marie LaVerne Bauer, June 27, 1949; children—Janice Kaye, Suzanne Marie. Design engr. Schmutz Mfg. Co., Louisville, 1949-52; sr. engr. Tube Turns div. Chemetron, Louisville, 1952-66; chief mgr. engring. Grinnell Corp., Princeton, Ky., 1966—. Chmn. bd. dirs. Caldwell County Airport, 1971—. Served with AUS, 1943-46. Registered Profl. Engr., Ky. Mem. Soc. Mech. Engrs., Order Ky. Cols. Home: 33 Dogwood Lane Princeton KY 42445 Office: ITT Grinnell Corp Welding Products Div PO Box 647 Princeton KY 42445

MARKEY, GENE, author; b. Jackson, Mich., Dec. 11, 1895; s. Eugene Lawrence and Alice (White) M.; B.S., Dartmouth, 1918; student Art Inst. Chgo., 1919-20; L.H.D., Rollins Coll., 1957; m. Joan Bennett, 1932 (div. 1937); 1 dau., Melinda; m. 2d, Hedy Lamarr, 1939 (div. 1940); m. 3d, Myrna Loy (div. 1950); m. 4th, Lucille Parker Wright, 1952. Served as 1st lt., 19th Inf., AUS, 1917-19; with USNR 1930-55; on active duty, 1941-46; promoted comdr., 1945; ret. rear adm., 1955. Spl. asst. Sec. of Navy, 1944, 1946. Decorated Legion of Merit, Bronze Star Medal, Navy Commendation Medal; star of solidarity (Italy); Legion of Honor (France). Mem. Delta Kappa Epsilon. Roman Catholic. Clubs: Buck's, White's (London); Jockey, Knickerbocker, Brook (N.Y.C.); Travellers (Paris, France). Author: Literary Lights, 1923; Men About Town, 1924; (with Charles Collins) The Dark Island, 1928; The Pumpkin Coach, 1928; Stepping High, 1929; The Road to Rouen, 1930; His Majesty's Pyjamas, 1934; The Great Companions, 1949; Kingdom of the Spur, 1953; Kentucky Pride, 1956; That Far Paradise, 1960; Women, Women, Everywhere, 1964; (plays) Right You Are, 1925; (with Samuel Hoffenstein) The Eskimo, 1926. Contbr. short stories to mags. Home: Calumet Farm Lexington KY 40501

MARKEY, LUCILLE PARKER, thoroughbred horse breeder and owner; b. Maysville, Ky., Dec. 14, 1896; d. John W. and Sarah B. (Owens) Parker; ed. Weston Sch.; m. Warren Wright, Mar. 26, 1919 (dec. Dec. 1950); 1 son, Warren; m. 2d, Gene Markey, Sept. 27, 1952. Owner, propr. Calumet Farm, breeding establishment and racing stable, Lexington, Ky., 1950—; 8 winners Ky. Derby. Address: Calumet Farm PO Box 1810 Lexington KY 40501

MARKHAM, ANNIE CATHERINE PARRISH (MRS. OSCAR C. MARKHAM), librarian; b. McNeill, Miss., Sept. 23, 1905; d. Robert Alexander and Daisy (Terry) Parrish; B.A., Belhaven Coll., 1925; M.A., Tulane U., 1928; postgrad. Peabody Coll., 1939, U. London, 1942; Ed.M. (Sch. Edn. scholar), Harvard, 1944; postgrad. U. Edinburgh, 1962, Hellenic Inst., Athens, Greece, 1966; m. Oscar C. Markham, Feb. 15, 1957. Tchr., Arlington (Ky.) High Sch., 1925-28; faculty Bethel Woman's Coll., Hopkinsville, 1929-42, 46-55, dean faculty, 1946-47; faculty various schs., colls., 1942-45, 55-58; exchange tchr. Avery Hill Coll., Eltham, Eng., 1953-54; faculty Murray (Ky.) State U., 1958-68, asso. prof. English, 1967-68; librarian Mid-Continent Baptist Bible Coll., Mayfield, Ky., 1968—. Del. Baptist World Alliance, Tokyo, Japan, 1970. Active Am. Cancer Soc. drives, Mayfield, 1962-67. Mem. Nat. Council Tchrs. English, Christian Librarians' Fellowship, Am. Theol. Library Assn. Am. Assn. U. Women (historian 1965-68), Chi Delta Phi, (nat. sec. 1941-42, 67-70). Baptist (pres. Woman's Missionary Union 1966-67, ch. librarian 1961—). Home: 101 Wilson Av Mayfield KY 42066 Office: 15th and Dunbar Sts Mayfield KY 42066

MARKHAM, JOHN STEWART, hosp. adminstr.; b. Richmond, Va., May 4, 1933; s. Curtis Owen and Lucy Mildred (Hall) M.; student U. Va., 1952-53; B.S., U. Richmond, 1958; M.H.A., Med. Coll. Va., 1967.; m. Betty Ann Johns, Feb. 13, 1954; children—Mary Lucy, Catherine Ann, Ernest Owen. Pub. accountant, Va., 1958-65; asst. adminstr. Meml. Mission Hosp., Asheville, N.C., 1967-68; adminstr. Culpeper (Va.) Meml. Hosp., 1968-72, Nat. Orthopaedic and Rehab. Hosp., Arlington, Va., 1972-73; asst. prof. Dept. Health Care Adminstrn. MCV Div. Va. Commonwealth U., Richmond, 1973—. Lectr.; prof. in residence Lynchburg (Va.) Tng. Sch. and Hosp., spring 1972. Mem. com. on income Va. White House Conf. on Aging, 1971. Bd. dirs. Culpeper chpt. Va. Heart Assn., Am. Cancer Soc. Served with AUS, 1953-55. C.P.A., Va. Fellow Va. Soc. C.P.A.'s; mem. Am., Va. (dir.) hosp. assns., Am. Coll. Hosp. Adminstrs. Author: Cost Accounting in Health Care Management, 1971. Home: 8117 Lethbridge Rd Richmond VA 23235 Office: PO Box 264 MCV Sta Richmond VA 23298

MARKHAM, MEELER, religious assn. exec.; b. Fort Worth, Mar. 8, 1914; s. Henry Nathan and Mattie Viola Jane (Sanders) M.; student Howard Payne Coll., 1934-35, U. Tex., 1936, Tex. Christian U., 1943, Southwestern Bapt. Theol. Sem., 1943-45, summer 1947; m. Myrtie Lesselle Manlove, June 18, 1937; 1 son, Edwin Meeler. With Soil Conservation Service, U.S. Dept. Agr., Kenedy, Tex., 1937-40; insp. Q.M.C., 1941, chief insp., 1942-43; ordained to ministry Bapt. Ch.; asst. pastor, choir dir. First Bapt. Ch., Beeville, Tex., 1945; pastor First Bapt. Ch., Carrizo Springs, 1945-51; pastor First Bapt. Ch., Mercedes, 1951-55; supt. missions Lower Rio Grande Bapt. Assn., Tex., 1955-60; missions sec. Kan. Conv. So. Bapts., Wichita, 1960-65; sec. Mission Property Services, Home Mission Bd., So. Bapt. Conv., Atlanta, 1966-70, dir. associational pubs., 1971—. Trustee Valley Bapt. Acad., Harlingen, Tex., 1953—, sec., 1954—; bd. dirs. Alto Frio Bapt. Encampment, Tex., 1953-57, pres., 1954-57. Mem. Winter Garden Bapt. Assn. (moderator 1947-48), Bapt. Gen. Conv. Tex. (exec. bd. 1950-51), So. Tex. Pastor's Conf. (pres. 1960). Mason, Rotarian (pres.). Author: This Confident Faith, 1968; contbg. author: Every Day: Five Minutes with God, 1969. Contbr. articles, writer column profl. pubs. Home: 678 E Paces Ferry Rd NE Atlanta GA 30305 Office: 1350 Spring St NW Atlanta GA 30309

MARKLE, DONALD M., judge; b. Palestine, Tex., July 9, 1911; s. Frank Barrows and Carrie (McDonald) M.; A.B., LL.B., U. Tex., 1937. Admitted to Tex. bar, 1937; formerly asso. with Wayman & Kleinecke; mem. firm McDonald & Markle, 1946-50; judge Tenth Dist. Ct., Tex., 1950—. Mem. Ho. of Reps., Tex., 1941-48. Mem. Beta Theta Pi. Episcopalian. Home: 2903 Dominique Dr Galveston TX 77550 Office: County Courthouse Galveston TX 77550

MARKLEY, SALLIE ANN PRICE (MRS. HOWARD WESLEY MARKLEY), educator; b. Magazine, Ark., Dec. 26, 1903; d. William Henry and Willie Ann (Cobb) Price; student Ark. Poly. Coll., summers 1930-38, Neb. State Tchrs. Coll., 1941-42; B.S., Ark. State Tchrs. Coll., 1946, M.S., 1957; postgrad. U. Ark., 1954; m. Howard Wesley Markley, Nov. 23, 1940; 1 stepson, J. Howard; 1 dau., Laura Ann. Tchr. pub. schs., Logan County, Ark., 1923-28, Paris, Ark., 1929-41; supr. English dept., tchr. Booneville (Ark.) Jr. and Sr. High Schs., 1946—; librarian Booneville High Sch., 1951-53. Vol. worker Child Devel. Center, Bonneville; vol. adminstrv. asst. adult basic edn. Ark. Dept. Edn., 1973—. 1st v.p. local P.T.A., 1946-50; mem. Ark. Library Bd., 1964—. Trustee Logan County Library, 1950—, Ark. River Valley Regional Library, 1959—. Mem. N.E.A., Ark. Edn. Assn., Nat., Ark. councils tchrs. English, A.L.A., Ark., N.W. Regional library assns., Rotary Anns (pres. 1968). Methodist (adminstrv. bd, past Sunday sch. tchr., pres. Wesleyan Service Guild 1970). Home: 214 W 4th St Bonneville AR 72927

MARKMAN, SHERMAN, jewelry mfg. co. exec.; b. Denver, Aug. 21, 1920; s. Abe and Julia (Rosen) M.; student So. Methodist U., 1962-64; m. Sande Kartus, July 24, 1942; children—Stephen Michael, Joan Susan, Lori Ann. Vice pres. Lester's, Inc., Oklahoma City, 1940-59; exec. v.p. Besco Enterprises, 1960-61; sr. v.p. Zale Corp., Dallas, 1962-69; pres. Designcraft Jewel Industries, N.Y.C., 1969—, chief exec. officer, 1969—. Mem. Dallas Council World Affairs, 1962—. Served with USMCR, 1942-45; PTO. Mem. Jewelry Mfrs. Assn. N.Y., Nat. Assn. Christians and Jews. Clubs: Press, Columbian, City (Dallas). Home: 7207 Joyce Way Dallas TX 75225 Office: 380 2d Av New York City NY 10010

MARKS, DOROTHY LOUISE AMES (MRS. LEONARD H. MARKS), journalist; b. Washington, Sept. 18, 1919; d. Frank Diman and Mary (Gannett) Ames; A.B., George Washington U., 1940; postgrad. U. N.C., 1941; m. Leonard H. Marks, June 3, 1948; children—Stephen Ames, Robert Evan. Asst. dir. pub. information FCC, Washington, 1941-45; Washington corr. Variety, San Diego Jour., Sioux Falls (S.D.) Argus Leader, 1945-50; contbg. editor Democratic Nat. Com., Washington, 1952-60; corr. N.Am. Newspaper Alliance and Women's News Service, Washington, 1969—. Mem. exec. com. Fgn. Student Service Council, 1968-69. Pres., Woman's Nat. Democratic Club, 1965-67. Bd. governance George Washington U., 1970-71. Clubs: Washington Press, Am. Newspaper Women's (v.p.), 1925 F St. Home: 2833 McGill Terrace NW Washington DC 20008

MARKS, EDWARD ARCHIBALD, JR., lawyer; b. Newark, June 25, 1909; s. Edward A. and Mary C. (Blodgett) M.; B.S., U. Va., 1931, LL.B., 1933; m. Irene Dwight Patterson, June 21, 1932; children—Irene (Mrs. Rowland Anthony Rupp, Jr.), Edward Archibald III. Admitted to Va. bar, 1932; practiced in Richmond, 1933—; mem. firms King & Marks, 1936-42, Sands, Marks & Sands, 1945-61, Sands, Anderson, Marks & Clarke, 1961—; commr. in chancery Chancery Ct. of Richmond, Circuit Ct. of Henrico County, Va. Dir. Hankins & Johann, Inc., Central Va. Shippers Assn., J.M. Fry Co., Inc., Nat. Cab Co., Inc. (all Richmond), Hoofprint Hill Stables, Inc., Goochland, Va. Bd. dirs. Richmond Natural History Soc. Recipient Order of Merit, Boy Scouts Am., 1946. Fellow Am. Coll. Trial Lawyers; mem. Va. State Bar, Am., Richmond City bar assns., Internat. Assn. Ins. Counsel, Def. Research Inst., U.S. Power Squadron, Va. Soc. Ornithology, Nat. Trust for Historic Preservation, Wilderness Soc., Order of Coif, Nat. Wildlife Fedn., Nat. Audubon Soc., Phi Beta Kappa, Phi Alpha Delta. Episcopalian (trustee). Home: 7200 W Franklin St Richmond VA 23226 Office: Fidelity Bankers Life Bldg 9th and Main Sts Richmond VA 23219

MARKS, HENRY MORTIMER, JR., ret. surg. supply co. exec., farmer; b. Augusta, Ga., May 18, 1900; s. Henry Mortimer and Jane Oliver (Henry) M.; grad. Richmond Acad., 1918; student Eastman Bus. Coll., 1919-21; m. Virginia Clark, June 16, 1937; children—Henry Mortimer, John Mulford, Charles Rainsford. Clk., Marks Drug Co., Augusta, Ga., 1919-22, pres., 1923-31; pres. Marks & Marks Wholesale Drug Co., Augusta, 1931-36; pres. Marks Surg. Supplies, Augusta, 1936-68, chmn. bd., 1968-70; owner, mgr. cattle and grain farm Burke County, Ga., 1968—; dir. Owens, Minor & Bodeker, Inc., Richmond, Va., Surg. Leasing Corp., Augusta. Presbyn. (elder). Kiwanian. Club: Augusta Country, Pinnacle. Home: 3122 Walton Way Augusta GA 30904 Office: 1815 15th St Augusta GA 30901

MARKS, HENRY SEYMOUR, historian, educator; b. Greensboro, N.C., May 26, 1933; B.B.A. in Mgmt. U. Miami (Fla.), 1955, M.A. in History (Food Fair Found. fellow), 1956; postgrad. U. Ala. 1960-61, 62-64; m. Marsha Kass. Faculty, U. Miami (Fla.), 1955-56, Jacksonville (Ala.) State Coll., 1958-60, U. Ala., 1960-61, Florence (Ala.) State Coll. 1961-62, U. Ala., Huntsville, 1964-68, Ala. A. & M. Coll. 1968-69. Lectr. ednl. subjects; judge social sci. fairs, Ala. Pres. so. region Popular Culture Assn., also mem. nat. adv. council. Mem. Am., Ala. So., Fla. hist. assns., Orgn. Am. Historians, Huntsville Hist. Soc., Rotary Internat., Hist. Assn. S. Fla., Hakluyt Soc., Am. Soc. Pub. Adminstrn., Phi Alpha Theta, Phi Delta Kappa. Jewish religion (pres. temple). Author: The Failure of the United States to Maintain the Independence of Korea and the Effect of the Failure upon Americans in Korea. Contbr. book reviews and abstracts to Huntsville (Ala.) Times and numerous publs. in field. Address: 102 Clinton Av W Huntsville AL 35801

MARKS, HERBERT EDWARD, lawyer; b. Dayton, O., Nov. 3, 1935; s. I.M. and Sarah (Schiff) M.; A.B., U. Mich., 1957; LL.B., Yale, 1960; postgrad. George Washington U., 1966-69; m. Marcia Frager, June 5, 1966; children—Jennifer Lynn, Susan Elizabeth. Admitted to Ohio bar, 1960, D.C. bar, 1964; law clk. to chief judge U.S. Ct. Claims, Washington, 1964-65; practiced in Washington, 1965—; partner firm Wilkinson, Cragun & Barker, 1969—. Lectr. bus. law Am. U. Extension, 1962-63. Asso. gen. counsel Presdl. Inaugural Com., 1969, 73. Sec., gen. counsel Am. Historic and Cultural Soc., Inc. Served to capt. USAF, 1961-64. Mem. Bar Assn. D.C., Am., Fed. bar assns., Fed. Communications Bar Assn., Phi Beta Kappa, Pi Sigma Alpha. Republican. Jewish religion. Clubs: Lawyers, Army and Navy. Home: 5317 Cardinal Ct Spring Hill Bethesda MD 20016 Office: 1735 New York Av NW Washington DC 20006

MARKS, JAMES JOHN, restaurateur, developer; b. Chgo., Aug. 23, 1911; s. Nicholas John and Stella (Gourety) M.; B.S., U. Mich., 1936; m. Christine Constance Tampary, Nov. 11, 1939; children—Lianna Sandra, James John. Forestry technician U.S. Forestry Service, Ava, Mo., 1934; forest supr. Mich. Conservation Dept., Lansing, 1934-35; cons. forester, Ann Arbor, Mich., 1936-37; owner Martine's Restaurant, Pensacola, Fla., 1942—, Martine's Ice Cream Co., Pensacola, 1942—; pres. Esquire House, Inc., Warrington, Fla., 1934—, Martine's Corp., Pensacola, 1947—, Marwood Motors, Inc., Pensacola, 1955—, Ky. Fried Chicken, Biloxi and Gulfport, Miss., 1964—, Martines Ky. Fried Chicken Corp., 1964—, New Orleans, 1967—, Col. Sander's Ky. Fried Chicken Corp., Martine's KFC Corp.; sec.-treas. Circle Sanitation, Pensacola, 1959—. Mem. adv. bd. Fla. Hotel and Restaurant Commn., 1961-62; mem. bd. Fla. Hospitality Edn. Program, 1962-63; chmn., pres. Fla. Tourism Council, 1962-63; mem. Fla. Council of 100, 1963—, mem. exec. com. Served to comdr. USNR, 1937-45. Mem. Am. Restaurants Hall of Fame, 1961. Mem. Nat., Fla. (pres. 1961-62) restaurant assns., Sales Execs. Club. Mem. Hellenic Orthodox Ch. Rotarian (past local pres.). Clubs: Toastmasters; Mobile Country, Pensacola Country. Home: 4002 Marlane Dr Pensacola FL 32506 Office: 4101 Mobile Hwy Pensacola FL 32506

MARKS, LEONARD HAROLD, lawyer; b. Pitts., Mar. 5, 1916; s. Samuel and Ida (Lewine) M.; B.A., U. Pitts., 1935, LL.B., 1938, L.D., 1965; m. Dorothy Ames, June 3, 1948; children—Stephen Ames, Robert Evan. Admitted to Pa. bar, 1938, D.C. bar, 1946; asst. prof. law U. Pitts. Law Sch., 1938-42; prof. law Nat. U., 1943-55; asst. to gen. counsel FCC, 1942-46; partner firm Cohn & Marks, Washington, 1946-65; 69—; head USIA, 1965-68; dir. Communications Satellite Corp., 1963-65. Dept. State lectr. adminstrv. and constl. law, India, 1958, Pakistan, Afghanistan, Iran, Turkey, 1961; Am. del. Internat. Broadcasting Conf., Mexico City, 1948, N.Am. Regional Broadcasting Conf., Montreal, 1949; mem. U.S. delegation Internat. Telecommunications Conf., Geneva, Switzerland, 1959, 63, Summit conf., Honolulu and Manila, 1966, Latin Am. Presidents Conf., Punta del Este, Uruguay, 1967; chmn. U.S. delegation, ambassador, chmn. Internat. Conf. on Communication Satellites, Washington, 1969; pres. Internat. Rescue Com., 1974; chmn. U.S. Adv. Commn. Internat. Ednl. and Cultural Affairs, 1974. Mem. Am. (mem. ho. of dels. 1962-64), Fed. Communications (pres. 1959-60), Allegheny County, Inter-Am., Internat. bar assns., Bar Assn. D.C., Order of Coif, Phi Beta Kappa, Omicron Delta Kappa, Sigma Delta Chi. Clubs: Cosmos, Metropolitan, Federal City, Internat., Broadcasters (pres. 1957-59) (Washington). Home: 2833 McGill Terrace NW Washington DC 20008 Office: 1920 L St NW Washington DC 20547

MARKS, MEYER BENJAMIN, pediatric allergist; b. Chgo., Feb. 16, 1907; s. Simon and Rose (Block) M.; B.S., U. Ill., 1929, M.D., 1933, M.S., 1934; m. Golda A. Nathan, Sept. 27, 1932; children—Linda, Stephen. Intern Cook County Hosp., 1934-35, resident, 1935-36; practice medicine specializing in pediatrics, 1937-57; cons. pediatric allergist Mt. Sinai Hosp., Miami Beach; dir. pediatric allergy clinic Jackson Meml. Hosp.; pediatric allergy and gen. allergy, 1957—; chief med. officer Asthmatic Children's Found. Residential Treatment Center, North Miami Beach; clin. prof. pediatrics U. Miami Sch. Medicine. Hon. pres. med. div., Southeastern div. Am. Friends Hebrew U. Pres. Asso. Convalescent Homes and Hosp. for Asthmatic Children, 1971. Diplomate in pediatric allergy Am. Bd. Pediatrics, Am. Bd. Allergy and Immunology. Fellow Am. Acad. Pediatrics, Am. Coll. Allergists, Am. Acad. Allergy; mem. A.M.A., Fla., Dade County med. assns., Fla., Miami (pres. 1954-55) pediatric socs., Fla. Allergy Soc. (pres. 1970), Sigma Xi. Jewish religion. Contbr. articles to med. books and jours. Home: 105 E San Marino Dr Miami Beach FL 33139 Office: 333 Arthur Godfrey Rd Miami Beach FL 33140

MARKS, MORTON, JR., interior designers co. exec.; b. Richmond, Va., July 31, 1926; s. Morton and Hannah (Dombrower) M.; student N.C. State U., 1943-44, Va. Poly. Inst., 1944, Biarritz-Am. U., France, 1945; B.A., U. Richmond, 1949; m. Helen Lucille Wallerstein, June 30, 1949; children—Linda H., Robert M., Kathryn A., Morton Marks III. Asst. dir. pub. relations Am. Fidelity and Casualty Co., and affiliate Markel Service, Inc., Richmond, Va., 1948-51; exec. v.p.-treas. Morton Marks & Sons, Inc., contract furnishings and interior designers, 1951—. Pres. Kanawha Recreation Assn., 1971—, Tuckahoe Elementary P.T.A., 1964, Harry F. Byrd Middle Sch. P.T.A., 1971. Bd. dirs. Credit Bur. of Richmond, Inc., Rainbow Found. Served with AUS, 1944-46. Decorated, D.S.M., Bronze Star medal, Purple Heart, Cross of Mil. Service; recipient Key Man award Richmond Jr. C. of C., 1956. Mem. Am. Inst. Interior Designers, Inst. Bus. Designers (internat. v.p. 1973—), Retail Mchts. Assn. Greater Richmond (vice chmn. 1972—), Va. Retail Mchts. Assn. (treas. 1973—), Va. Mus. Fine Arts, Va. Congress of Parents and Tchrs. (hon. life mem.), Rainbow Div. Vets. (nat. exec. com. 1952-53), Omicron Delta Kappa, Pi Delta Epsilon. Mem. Jewish religion. (bd. mgrs. temple 1965-69). Mason. Clubs: Bull and Bear, Kanawha, Richmond First. Contbr. articles to profl. pubs. Home: 411 Westham Pkwy Richmond VA 23229 Office: Main at 13th St Richmond VA 23211

MARKS, PAUL H., lawyer; b. Key West, Fla., Feb. 8, 1908; s. Herman and Pauline (Rosenthal) M.; J.D., U. Fla., 1930; m. Martha Gilchrist Frame, 1949; children—Patricia, Paul, Stephen. Admitted to Fla. bar, 1930, since practiced law in Miami; counsel to M.A. Smith, state bank liquidator, 1933-38, HOLC, Miami, 1934-36; gen. counsel Overseas Bridge Commn., 1937-39; counsel Gulf Life Ins. Co., 1934—; chmn. bd. Flagler Fed. Savs. & Loan Assn., Miami. Pres. Miami Downtown Bus. Council, 1959-62; dir. Crime Commn.; chmn. Orange Bowl Stadium Com., 1961—. Served to lt. comdr. USNR 1942-45. Recipient City of Miami Outstanding Citizen award, 1964; citations from City of Miami, Orange Bowl Com., USN, Pi Lambda Phi, U. Fla. Alumni, State of Fla., Miami-Dade C. of C., Fla. Savs. and Loan League. Charter mem. Orange Bowl Com. and Adv. Council. Mem. Fla. Savs. and Loan League (pres. 1964-65), Dade County Bar Assn. (past dir.), U. Fla. Alumni (past pres. Miami), Fla. Blue Key, Miami-Dade C. of C. (past dir., mem. adv. council). Home: 6464 Caballero Blvd Coral Gables FL 33146 Office: 101 NE 1st Av Miami FL 33132

MARKS, WILLIAM BURNELL, ednl. adminstr.; b. Warsaw, Va., Apr. 4, 1903; s. Henry Thomas and Elizabeth (France) M.; A.B., Coll. William and Mary, 1925; Ed.M., Duke U., 1932; M.A., U. Mich., 1936; postgrad. Ohio State U., 1947, U. Tenn., 1948, U. Wis., 1950, George Washington U., 1955, U. Md., 1957; m. Fanny Elizabeth Young, Dec. 26, 1928; children—William Burnell, Kenneth Livingston. Asst. prin. Herndon High Sch., Fairfax, Va., 1925-26; tchr.-coach Washington-Lee High Sch., Arlington, Va., 1926-28; prin. Fincastle (Va.) High Sch., 1928-30; vice-prin., coach Sandy Spring High Sch., Montgomery County, Md., 1930-34; counselor Bethesda-Chevy Chase (Md.) Sr. High Sch., 1934-35; prin. Takoma Park Jr. High Sch., Silver Spring, Md., 1935-46; supr. Montgomery County (Md.) Schs., 1946-52; counselor Montgomery Blair Sr. High Sch., Silver Spring, 1952-61; prin. Lively (Va.) pub. schs., 1961-72. Bd. govs. Fed. Schoolmen, Washington; patron Found. for Econ. Edn. Asso. Smithsonian Instn. Washington. Mem. Lancaster, Va. edn. assns., Va. PTA, Phi Beta Kappa, Kappa Phi Kappa, Phi Delta Kappa. Methodist (chmn. pastor parish relations com. 1965—). Mason (32 deg., Shriner), Lion. Mem. Order Eastern Star. Club: Ruritan (past dist. gov. 1967-68, dist. dir. 1969-72). Home: Rt 2 Box 280 Lancaster VA 22503 Office: PO Box 17 Lively VA 22507

MARKWELL, DICK R(OBERT), educator; b. Muskogee, Okla., Feb. 20, 1925; s. Alex J. and May (Albright) M.; B.S., Wichita State U., 1948, M.S., 1950; Ph.D., U. Wis., 1956; m. Virginia Ann Gass, Aug. 28, 1949; children—Steven R., Scot L., Eric R., Cheryl F. Commd. 2d lt. U.S. Army, 1951, ret. lt. col., 1967, with Office Chief Research and Devel.; asso. prof. chemistry San Antonio Coll., 1967—. Served with USMCR, 1942-45. Mem. Am. Chem. Soc., Sigma Xi. Home: 1406 Haskin Dr San Antonio TX 78209

MARLATT, ABBY LINDSEY, food scientist, educator; b. Manhattan, Kan., Dec. 5, 1916; d. Frederick Albert and Annie Elsie (Lindsey) Marlatt; B.S. in Home Econs., Kan. State U., 1938; certificate in Hosp. Dietetics, U. Cal. at Berkeley, 1940, Ph.D. in Animal Nutrition, 1947. Asso. prof. foods and nutrition Kan. State U., Manhattan, 1945-52, prof., 1952-56; dir. Sch. Home Econs. U. Ky., Lexington, 1956-63, prof., 1963-68, prof. nutrition and food sci., 1968—. Vis. prof. Beirut (Lebanon) Coll. for Women, 1953-54; vis. research prof. Ky. State Coll., Frankfort, 1968-71. Chmn. Lexington Youth Devel. Center, 1973; bd. dirs. Emerson Center, 1972—. Mem. bd. Community Action Lexington Fayette County, 1967-71, sec. 1970-71; mem. bd. Micro-City Govt., 1972—. Fellow A.A.A.S.; mem. Am. Dietetic Assn., Am. Home Econs. Assn. Soc. for Nutrition Edn., Am. Sch. Health Assn., Ky. Nutrition Council, Am. Assn. U. Profs., Am. Assn. U. Women, Nat. Council Christians and Jews (mem. Lexington chpt.), Am. Civil Liberties Union, Sigma Xi, Phi Kappa Phi, Omicron Nu, Phi Upsilon Omicron, Iota Sigma Pi. Unitarian-Universalist (Ohio Valley council pres. 1972—). Contbr. articles on research in nutrition to profl. jours. Home: 256 Tahoma Rd Lexington KY 40503

MARLIN, CLIFTON BOYD, educator; b. Dorsey, Miss., Oct. 24, 1920; s. Gordon and Minnie (Farris) M.; B.S., Miss. State U., 1943; M.F., Duke, 1949; m. Dorothy Ree Moore, Mar. 20, 1945; 1 son, Roger B. With Forestry Dept., Miss. State U., 1949-50; with Miss. Forestry Commn., Jackson, 1951-61, dir. forest mgmt., 1953-56, state forester, 1956-61; asst. prof. La. State U., Baton Rouge, 1961-72, asso. prof., 1973—. Mem. exec. com. Smokey Bear program Nat. Coop. Forest Fire Prevention, 1957-60; chmn. So. Group State Foresters, 1960. Served from cpl. to capt. AUS, World War II; ETO. Decorated Purple Heart. Mem. La., Miss. (past dir.) forestry assns., Am. Assn. U. Profs., Soc. Am. Foresters, Scabbard and Blade, Sigma Xi, Gamma Sigma Delta, Sigma Pi, Beta Beta Beta, Alpha Zeta. Baptist. Contbr. articles to profl. jours. Home: 5822 Clematis Dr Baton Rouge LA 70808

MARLIN, ERVIN R., assn. ofcl.; b. 1909; ed. Trinity Coll., Dublin. Personnel officer Farm Credit Adminstrn., Washington, 1935-36, Social Security Bd., 1936-39; asst. dir. personnel FSA, 1939-42; spl. asst. to U.S. ministr., Dublin, to U.S. ambassador, London, 1942-44; adminstrv. analyst Bur. Budget, Washington, 1944-45; external relations officer, dir. Tech. Assistance Bur., Internat. Civil Aviation Orgn., Montreal, 1945-62; sr. dir. UN High Commr. for Refugees, Geneva, Switzerland, 1962-65; dir. Office Internat. Orgn. Recruitment, Dept. State, Washington, 1965-71; dir. internat. relations Am. Assn. Retired Persons, Washington, 1971; gen. sec. Internat. Fedn. on Ageing, Washington, 1973—. Office: 1909 K St NW Washington DC 20006

MARLOW, H(OBSON) MCKINLEY, lawyer; b. Cookeville, Tenn., Sept. 20, 1931; s. H.M. and Birtha (Bryant) M.; B.S., Tenn. Tech. U., 1954; J.D., Vanderbilt U., 1957; m. Dorothy Fay Teal, June 18, 1960; children—Darryl McKinley, Stephen Teal, Eric Martin. Admitted to Tenn. bar, 1957; gen. practice, Nashville, 1957—; pres. Motivation Mgmt. Inc., Image Pub. Co., Ashwood Music Co.; treas. Music Industries Corp. Mem. Am. (copyright com.), Nashville bar assns., Am. Trial Lawyers Assn., Bar Assn. Tenn. Mason (Shriner). Author: ABC's of Copyright Law for Songwriters, 1960. Home: Lynn Dr Nashville TN 37211 Office: Parkway Towers Nashville TN 37219

MARLOW, W(ILLIAM) H(ENRY), mathematician, educator; b. Waterloo, Ia., Nov. 26, 1924; s. Clifford William and Ella Louise (Murphy) M.; B.S., St. Ambrose Coll., Davenport, Ia., 1947; M.S., U. Ia., 1948, Ph.D., 1951; m. Delphine Elizabeth Meisch, Aug. 9, 1948; children—William J., David T., Michael L., Mary D., Anne T. Research asso. logistics research project George Washington U., 1951-56, prin. investigator, 1956-69, dir. Inst. for Mgmt. Sci. and Engring., 1969—, prof. applied sci., 1969-71, prof., chmn. operations research, 1971—. Asso. research mathematician U. Cal. at Los Angeles, 1954-55. Served to lt. (j.g.) USNR, 1943-46. Mem. Math. Soc., Math. Assn., Navy Inst., Washington Operations Research Council, Operations Research Soc. Am., Inst. Mgmt. Scis., Soc. for Indsl. and Applied Math., Am. Soc. for Engring. Edn., Sigma Xi. Asso. editor Navy Research Logistics Quart., 1956—. Home: 4038 27th Rd N Arlington VA 22207 Office: George Washington U Washington DC 20006

MARLOWE, EDGAR EARL, JR., physician; b. Shelby, N.C., Apr. 3, 1937; s. Edgar Earl and Alliwee (McDaniel) M.; student Appalachian Coll., 1955-56, Wake Forest Coll., 1956-57, N.C. State U., 1957-59; M.D., U. Tenn., 1962; m. Donne Ruth Broadwell, July 6, 1965; children—John Cohron, Caroline Wade. Intern, Roanoke (Va.) Meml. Hosp., 1962-63; gen. practice medicine, Gastonia, N.C.; mem. staff Garrison Gen. Hosp.; sec. med. services Gastonia Meml. Hosp., 1967-68. Mem. chorus com. Charlotte Opera Chorus, 1968-72, chmn., 1970-71. Served with USNR, 1963-65. Mem. Am., N.C., Gastonia med. assns., Delta Sigma Phi. Episcopalian. Club: Cowens Ford Country. Home: 1030 S Belvedere Gastonia NC 28052 Office: 213 1/2 W Main St Gastonia NC 28052

MARLOWE, JAMES MILTON, physician; b. Jacksonville, Fla., Aug. 15, 1930; s. Thomas Lee and Ola (Cannte) M.; B.S., Fla. So. Coll., 1955; M.D., U. Miami, 1959; m. Selma Paterson, Nov. 1, 1952;

children—Robert Charles, Ronald Jack, Richard James, Russell George. Intern, U.S. Naval Hosp., Portsmouth, Va., 1959-60; pvt. practice medicine, specializing in family practice, New Port Richey, Fla., 1963—; sr. mem. Richey Med. Center, New Port Richey, 1970-73; chief staff West Pasco Hosp., New Port Richey, 1968-69; sec., treas. New Port Richey Community Hosp., 1970-72, dir. edn., 1970-72; v.p., dir. Richey Manor, Inc., 1964-74; mem. staffs Tarpon Springs (Fla.) Gen. Hosp., Morton Plant Hosp., Clearwater, Fla. Instr. sex edn. and drug edn. Pasco County Sch. System, 1968-74; team physician dept. athletics Gulf High Sch., New Port Richey, Fla., 1963-72. Mem. exec. bd. Pinellas Area council Boy Scouts Am., 1968-73, council rep. to Nat. and Regional councils, scoutmaster, 1964-72. Mem. pres.'s council Fla. So. Coll., Lakeland, 1969-74. Served with USNR, 1950-53, 1959-63. Diplomate Am. Bd. Family Practice. Mem. Pasco-Hernandos-Citrus County Med. Soc. (pres. 1972), Fla. Med. Assn., A.M.A., Am. Acad. Family Physicians, Am. Diabetes Assn. Democrat. Methodist (trustee 1968-71, del. ann. conf. 1963-71). Home: 917 River Rd N New Port Richey FL 33552 Office: PO Box 1058 New Port Richey FL 33552

MARMET, ROBERT ARTHUR, lawyer; b. Omaha, Jan. 25, 1925; s. Robert and Helen (Anderson) M.; student Oberlin Coll., 1942-43; B.S., U.S. Naval Acad., 1946; LL.B., Georgetown U., 1951, LL.M., 1954; m. Barbara Jean Driscoll, June 21, 1947; children—Lynne, Robert G., Richard A., Roger D. Commd. ensign USN, 1946, advanced through grades to lt., 1952; radar officer, U.S.S. Portsmouth, 6th Fleet, 1946-47; communications officers, trial counsel Naval Base Kenitra, Morocco, 1951-53; naval aide to vice dir. Nat. Security Agy., Washington, 1953-55; ret., 1955; admitted to D.C. bar, 1951; practiced in Washington, 1955—; mem. firm Marmet & Schneider, 1961-70, Marmet & Webster, 1970-73, Marmet Profl. Corp., 1973—. Mem. exec. com. Boys Club, Washington, 1962-65. Bd. dirs. YMCA Day Camp, 1964-65. Mem. Fed. Communications Bar Assn. (treas. 1964-65, exec. com. 1965), Am. Judicature Soc., Washington Assembly, Georgetown U. Alumni Assn. (v.p. 1965-66), Delta Theta Phi. Presbyn. Home: 5120 Cammack Dr Washington DC 20016 Office: 1822 Jefferson Pl Washington DC 20036

MARMION, CHARLES GRESHAM, bishop; b. Houston, Aug. 19, 1905; s. Charles Gresham and Katherine Angie (Rankin) M.; B.B.A., U. Tex., 1930; B.D., P.E. Theol. Sem. in Va., 1933, D.D. (hon.), 1954; D.D. (hon.), U. of South, Sewanee, Tenn., 1954; m. Doris Anita Dissen, July 1, 1937; children—Beverley Anne, Sara Katherine, Dana Elizabeth. Bank clk., Houston, 1921-26; rector Christ Episcopal Ch., Eagle Lake, also St. John's Ch., Columbus, Tex., 1933-37; asst. rector St. Alban's Ch., Washington, 1937-40; rector St. George's Ch., Port Arthur, Tex., 1940-45, Ch. of Incarnation, Dallas, 1945-54; bishop Diocese of Ky., P.E. Ch., 1954-74, bishop emeritus, 1974—; pres. Province of Sewanee, Episcopal Ch., 1969-71. Mem. nat. council P.E. Ch., 1948-54, dep. to gen. conv., 1943, 52. Chmn. Port Arthur chpt. A.R.C., 1942-45. Trustee U. of South, 1954—, Ch. Home and Infirmary, Louisville, 1954—. Mem. Beta Alpha Psi, Theta Xi. Mason, Rotarian. Mem. Legion of Honor, Order of DeMolay. Club: Pendennis (Louisville). Home: 147 W Wind Rd Louisville KY 40207 Office: 421 S 2d St Louisville KY 40202

MARMION, WILLIAM HENRY, bishop; b. Houston, Oct. 8, 1907; s. Charles Gresham and Katherine (Rankin) M.; A.B., Rice Inst., 1929; B.D., Va. Theol. Sem., 1932, D.D. 1954; m. Mabel Dougherty Nall, Dec. 28, 1935; children—William Henry, Roger Mills Nall. Ordained deacon Episcopal Ch., 1932, priest, 1933; priest in charge St. James, Taylor, Tex., and Grace Ch., Georgetown, 1932-35; asso. rector St. Mark's Ch., San Antonio, 1935-38; rector St. Mary's-on-Highland, Birmingham, Ala., 1938-50; St. Andrew's Ch., Wilmington, Del., 1950-54; consecrated bishop Episcopal Diocese of Southwestern Va., Roanoke, 1954—. Former dir. diocesan camps for young people in Tex. and Ala., headed diocesan youth work several years; dep. to Gen. Conv. Episcopal Ch., 1943, 46, alternate dep., 1949, 52; del. to Provincial Synod; mem. exec. council Episcopal Ch., 1963—. Chmn. Ala. Com. on Interracial Cooperation, 4 yrs. Trustee Va. Theol. Sem. Rotarian. Home: 2730 Avenham Av SW Roanoke VA 24014 Office: 1000 1st St SW Roanoke VA 24016

MARNEY, SAMUEL ROWE, JR., physician; b. Bristol, Va., Feb. 15, 1934; s. Samuel Rowe and Frances (Moorman) M.; B.A., U. Va., 1955, M.D., 1960; m. Elizabeth Ann Bingham, Oct. 1, 1966; children—Samuel Rowe III, Annis Morison. Intern Vanderbilt Hosp., Nashville, Tenn., 1960-61, resident, 1961-62, 64-66; resident Nashville VA Hosp., 1966-67; research fellow hematology Radcliffe Infirmary, Oxford (Eng.) U., 1967-68; practice medicine, specializing in infectious disease and allergy, Nashville, 1969—; mem. staff Vanderbilt U. Hosp., Nashville; asst. prof. medicine, chief allergy clinic Vanderbilt U., 1970—. Infectious disease trainee Vanderbilt, Nashville VA hosps., 1968-71; clin. investigator VA, 1971-74; guest investigator Scripps Clinic and Research Found., 1973-74. Served with USAF, 1962-64. Diplomate Am. Bd. Internal Medicine. Mem. Am. Fedn. Clin. Research, Raven Soc., Phi Beta Kappa, Omega Delta Kappa. Contbr. to profl. jours. Home: 4340 Sneed Rd Nashville TN 37215 Office: Vanderbilt Hosp Nashville TN 37232

MARQUEZ-DIAZ, NESTOR, educator, lawyer; b. Caquas, P.R., Mar. 7, 1936; s. Mario and Angela (Diaz) M.-D.; B.S., U. P.R., 1955; M.A., Ind. U., 1956; Ph.D., U. Madrid, 1958; LL.B., Tulane U., 1961; 1 son, Nestor II. Admitted to La. bar, 1961; economist P.R. Treasury Dept., 1954-55; economist P.R. Econ. Devel. Adminstrn., 1956-59; lectr. Loyola U., New Orleans, 1959-61, co-dir. Inter-Am. Labor Mgmt. Center, 1961; partner firm Pilie, Nelson & Limes, New Orleans, 1961-62; prof. bus. adminstrn. Nicholls State Coll., Thibodaux, 1961-70; prof. bus. adminstrn. Tex. A & I U., Laredo, 1970-74; dir. Office Econ. Research for Continental and Overseas Operations Econ. Devel. Adminstrn. P.R., 1974—; pvt. practice law, New Orleans, 1962—; sr. partner Marquez-Diaz & Parker, 1967-70; legal and econ. cons.; asst. atty. gen. State of La. Vice pres. Inter-Am. Pub. Corp., New Orleans, 1961-62, Interam. Shipbldg. Corp., La. Rose, La., 1961-63; sec.-treas. All-state Marine & Investment Services, Inc., New Orleans; pres. Marquez-Diaz & Parker Arms Co. Lectr. L. P.R., 1958; tech. adviser to rector U. of Central Am., Managua, Nicaragua, 1961—; indsl. promotion and econ. devel. cons. AID, San Jose, Costa Rica, 1963; econs. cons., New Orleans, 1961—. Spl. agt. La. State Police; dep. sheriff Lafourche Parish; dep. policy insp., Nuevo Laredo, Mexico. Pres. New Orleans West Civic Assn. Vice pres. Spanish Am. Union of La., 1963. Chmn. Seven Eighty Niners Dem. Orgn., 1963; pres. Citizens for Democratic Action. Bd. dirs. U. Coahuila, Torreon, Mexico. Recipient Juarez award Govt. of Mex.; Order of Quetzal medal Govt. of Guatemala. Mem. Am., La., Inter-Am. bar assns., Am. Econ. Assn., Nat. Planning Assn., Acad. Polit. Sci., Phi Alpha Delta, Phi Delta Gamma. Roman Catholic. Clubs: Pass Christian Yacht; International House, New Orleans Press, Import-Export, Young Mens Business; Bayou Country. Author: An Analysis of the Banking System of Costa Rica, 1962; The Furniture Industry of Puerto Rico; Notes and Comments on the Ministry of Industry of Costa Rica; Foreign Capital and Its Role in Economic Development; LAFTA Aims and Achievements, 1973. Home: 2311 Victoria Villa Angela Apts Laredo TX 78040 Office: 1290 Av of the Americas New York City NY 10019

MARRIOTT, ALICE SHEETS (MRS. JOHN WILLARD MARRIOTT), restaurant chain exec., Rep. nat. committeewoman; b. Salt Lake City, Oct. 19, 1907; d. Edwin Spencer and Alice (Taylor) Sheets; A.B., U. Utah, 1927; m. John Willard Marriott, June 9, 1927; children—John Willard, Richard Edwin. Partner Hot Shoppes, Inc. (name changed to Marriott Corp. 1967), Restaurant chain, Washington, 1927—; v.p., dir., 1929—. Mem. Republican Nat. Com., 1959—, vice chmn., 1965—; mem. Rep. Coordinating Com., 1965-69; exec. com. D.C. Rep. Com.; treas. Rep. Nat. Conv., 1964, 68, 72; vice chmn. inaugural com., 1969, hon. vice chmn., 1973; chmn. distinguished ladies reception for the inaugural, 1969. Mem. Nat. Adv. Commn. Children and Youth; chmn. Pres.'s Adv. Com. on Arts of John F. Kennedy Center for Performing Arts, 1970—, trustee, 1972—. Bd. dirs. Washington Ballet Guild, Goodwill Guild, Washington Home Rule Com., Arthritis and Rheumatism Found. of Met. Washington. Mem. League Republican Women D.C. (v.p. 1957-61), Nat. Symphony Orch. Assn., Am. Newspaper Womens Club, Chi Omega, Phi Kappa Phi. Mem. Ch. of Jesus Christ of Latter-day Saints. Clubs: Capitol Speakers (membership chmn.), Washington, Capitol Hill, Women's Nat. Republican, F Street, Welcome to Washington Internat. (treas.). Home: 4500 Garfield St Washington DC 20007 Office: 5161 River Rd Washington DC 20016

MARRIOTT, JOHN WILLARD, restaurant and motel exec.; b. Marriott, Utah, Sept. 17, 1900; s. Hyrum Willard and Ellen (Morris) M.; grad. Weber Coll., Ogden, Utah, 1922; A.B., U. Utah, 1926; LL.D. (hon.), Brigham Young U., 1958; m. Alice Sheets, June 9, 1927; children—John Willard, Richard Edwin. Franchise holder A. & W. Root Beer Co., Washington, 1926-28; pres. Marriott Corp. (formerly Hot Shoppes, Inc.), 1928-64, now chmn., dir.; dir. Am. Motors Corp., Detroit, Riggs Nat. Bank, Chesapeak & Potomac Telephone Co. Mem. commrs. adv. planning bd. Fed. City Council. Bd. govs. United Service Orgns. Recipient Hall of Fame award Am. Restaurant Mag., 1954; Achievement award Advt. Club, 1957; award Am. Marketing Assn., 1959; U. Utah, 1959; Chain Store Age award, 1961; Businessman of Yr. award Religious Heritage Am., 1971; Capt. of Achievement award Am. Acad. Achievement, 1971. Mem. N.A.M. (dir.), Com. for Econ. Devel. (trustee), Washington Bd. Trade (dir.), Nat. (pres. 1948), Washington (pres. 1939, 43) restaurant assns. Mem. Ch. of Jesus Christ of Latter-Day Saints (pres. Washington stake 1948-57). Clubs: Burning Tree (Bethesda, Md.); Indian Creek Country (Miami Beach, Fla.); Bald Peak Colony (Melvin Village, N.H.); Columbia Country (Chevy Chase, Md.); Paradise Valley Country (Ariz); Washington Admirals, Capitol Hill (Washington). Home: 4500 Garfield St NW Washington DC 20007 Office: care of Marriott Corp 5161 River Rd Bethesda MD

MARRIOTT, J(OHN) WILLARD, JR., restaurant-hotel chain, cruise ship exec.; b. Washington, Mar. 25, 1932; s. John Willard and Alice (Sheets) M.; B.S. in Banking and Finance, U. Utah, 1954; m. Donna Garff, June 29, 1955; children—Deborah, Stephen Garff, John Willard III, David Sheets. Pres. Marriott Motor Hotels, 1957-65; v.p. Hot Shoppes Inc., 1959-64, exec. v.p., 1964; pres. Marriott-Hot Shoppes, Inc. (now Marriott Corp.), 1964-72, chief exec. officer, 1972—, also dir.; dir. Southeast Banking Corp. Bd. dirs. Met. Washington Bd. Trade, Downtown Progress, Washington, Washington Nat. Symphony; apptd. by Pres. Nixon to Adv. Council for Minority Enterprise; mem. Pres.'s Nat. Tourism Resources Rev. Commn. Bd. govs. St. Alban's Sch., Washington. Served to lt. USNR, 1954-56. Mem. Fla. Council 100, Am. Hotel and Motel Assn., Nat. Alliance Businessmen (bus. adv. bd.), Am. Mgmt. Assn. (dir.), Sigma Chi. Clubs: Burning Tree, Columbia Country (Bethesda, Md.). Home: 5214 Parkway Dr Chevy Chase MD 20015 Office: 5161 River Rd Washington DC 20016

MARS, DORSIE LEE, radio and TV announcer, wholesale trade co. exec.; b. El Dorado, Ark., May 30, 1927; s. Dorsie Benjamin and Lula Elizabeth (Burney) M.; student E. Tex. State Tchrs. Coll., 1950-51; m. Patsy Ruth Alexander, Mar. 11, 1949; children—Dorsie Lynn, Tommy Lee, Darrell Ray, Charles Edwin. Announcer KIMP Radio, Mount Pleasant, Tex., 1951-54, KNOE Radio, Monroe, La., 1954-55, KTBS Radio and TV, Shreveport, La., 1955-71; pres. Sportsman's Services, Inc., Shreveport, 1971—; announcer numerous radio, TV commls. First v.p. Northwood High Sch. P.T.A., Shreveport, 1969-70; pres. North Highlands Sch. Athletic Council, Shreveport, 1965-66. Bd. Dirs. Caddo Wildlife Fedn. Served with USNR, 1944-48, 50-51. Home: 5960 North Market St Shreveport LA 71107 Office: 3306 Youree Dr Shreveport LA 71105

MARSDEN, ELIZABETH HARLOW, educator; b. Nashville, Mar. 17, 1923; d. Frank Ernest and Harriet Ellsworth (Rees) Harlow; Mus.B., U. Miami, 1944; M.A., Columbia, 1945; m. Edward Derwood Marsden, Dec. 23, 1946 (div. Jan. 1971); children—Elizabeth Rhys, Margaret Lee, Catherine Harlow, Harriet Ann. Tchr., Southeastern La. Coll., 1945-47; asst. prof. music U. Miami, 1947-52; supr. music Penn Hills Sch., Pitts., 1954-59; tchr. piano, voice, Pitts., 1959-61; judge Music Educators Nat. Conf., Miami, 1953, Tampa, Fla., 1953; tchr. Dade County (Fla.) Schs., 1964, Brevard County (Fla.) Schs., 1966-72; minister of music Coral Way Presbyn. Ch., Miami, 1964-66, First Presbyn. Ch., Titusville, 1966-72; music cons. Marietta (Ga.) City Schs., 1972—. Lectr. U. South Fla., 1967-72, Rollins Coll., 1971, U. Ga., 1972—. Mem. Am. Assn. U. Profs., Am. Assn. U. Women, Am. Guild Organists, Music Educators Nat. Conf., N.E.A., Classroom Tchrs. Assn., Fla. Elementary Tchrs. Assn., Brevard Edn. Assn., Ga. Music Educators Assn., Ga. Assn. Curriculum and Instrnl. Suprs., Brevard Music Edn. Assn. (v.p.), Delta Kappa Gamma, Chi Omega, Sigma Alpha Iota. Presbyn. (v.p. women's guild). Clubs: College, Tuesday Music, Mt. Lebanon Women's (Pitts.); Coral Gables Garden, Flamingo Dinner. Home: Box 584 Marietta GA 30060 Office: 145 Dodd St Box 6066 Marietta GA 30060

MARSH, ELEANOR MILLER HACK (MRS. GARNETT S. MARSH), former social worker; b. Indpls., Mar. 23, 1913; d. Oren Stephen and Elizabeth (Miller) Hack; B.S., Butler U., 1934, M.S. in Edn., 1939; M.A. in Social Service, Ind. U., 1947; m. Garnett S. Marsh, Feb. 27, 1972. Elementary sch. tchr., Boggstown, Ind., 1935-39; probation officer Marion County Juvenile Ct., 1939-40, div. spl. services, 1940-42; case worker Children's Bur., Indpls., 1943; supr. med. care and eye treatment pub. assistance div. Ind. Dept. Pub. Welfare, 1944-52; dir. admissions and asst. to med. dir. Ind. U. Med. Center, Indpls., 1953-66; supr. field service sect., div. pub. assistance Ind. Dept. Pub. Welfare, 1966-72. Pres. Ind. Conf. Social Work, 1955, dir., 1952-55, 57-63; chmn. Com. Registration Social Workers, 1950-53; program chmn. Am. Pub. Welfare Assn. Central Regional Conf., 1973. Sec. Women's Aux. YMCA, Henderson County. Mem. Am. Pub. Welfare Assn. (Ind. membership chmn. 1952-55), Indpls. Social Workers Club (pres. 1951-53, chmn. legislative com., 1953-55, James L. Fieser award for distinguished service 1968), Kappa Alpha Theta, Phi Kappa Phi, Kappa Delta Pi. Presbyn. Editor: Health and Welfare Legislative Information Service, 1949-52. Address: 924 N Main St Henderson KY 42420

MARSH, HOMER ELLSWORTH, assn. exec.; b. Plymouth, Ind., Apr. 19, 1912; s. Marion Oscar and Pearl Ione (Ritter) M.; B.S., Ind. U., 1935, postgrad., 1935-36; m. Hazel Gladys Monce, May 24, 1941. Instr. sch. bus. adminstrn. Ind. U., 1935-36; dir. research and statistics Unemployment Compensation div. State of Ind., 1936-44; cons. bur. labor statistics U.S. Dept. Labor, 1942-44; dir. research Nat. Tax Equality Assn., Chgo., 1944-48, 49-62, exec. sec., 1962-70, cons., 1970—; dir. research Nat. Asso. Businessmen, Inc., Washington, 1948. Mem. Govtl. Research Assn., Nat. Tax Assn., Internat. Fiscal Assn., Am. Acad. Polit. and Social Sci., Beta Gamma Sigma. Author: Bibliography of Public Employment Offices (with Thomas W. Rogers), 1935; Solvency of Ind. Unemployment Compensation Fund, 1943; Cooperative Expansion in the Petroleum Industry, 1944; Super-Cooperatives in the Field Purchasing, 1944; Tax Free Manufacturing Cooperative Corporations, 1945; Subsidized Cooperatives in the Marketing Field, 1945; Cooperative Competition in New England, 1946; The Facts in the Matter, 1947; The Other Tax Exempts, 1947; Tax Escaping Cooperatives Engaged in Grocery Distribution, 1949. Contbr. to trade publs. Home: PO Box 485 Plymouth IN 46563 Office: 1000 Connecticut Av Washington DC 20036

MARSH, WARREN ELDON, banker; b. DuBois, Neb., Mar. 9, 1925; s. Daniel Booker and Katherine Molly (Hartman) M.; ed. USN spl. courses, Southwestern Grad. Sch. Banking; m. Alpha Mae Holt, Jan. 28, 1956; children—Stephanie Yvonne, Ronald Eugene, Angelia Dean. Sr. v.p. 1st Pasadena State Bank (Tex.), 1945—. Served with USNR, 1943-45. Mem. Am. Inst. Banking, Pasadena C. of C. Mem. Reorganized Ch. Jesus Christ of Latter-day Saints. Mason, Elk. Club: Pasadena Optimist (past pres.). Home: 1804 Glencrest St Pasadena TX 77502 Office: 1001 Southmore St Pasadena TX 77502

MARSH, WINSTON WILLIAM, assn. exec.; b. Dayton, Aug. 11, 1909; s. William Raymond and Audrey (Elleman) M.; A.B., Wittenberg U., 1931; M.B.A., George Washington U., 1955; LL.D., Findlay Coll., 1963; m. J. Eleanor Baumgartner, Sept. 24, 1931; children—Winston W., Julia (Mrs. Gundersdorff). Pres. Marsh Gen. Tire Service, Dayton, 1938-41; partner Marsh Schneider Tire Co., Hamilton, O., 1941-49; exec. v.p. Nat. Tire Dealers and Retreaders Assn., Washington, 1949—. Served to lt. (s.g.) USNR, 1944-45; PTO. Mem. Am. Marketing Assn. (past pres.), Am. Soc. Assn. Execs. (pres.), Am. Mgmt. Assn., Res. Officers Assn. (past pres.), Navy League, Psi Chi, Lambda Chi Alpha. Mason (Shriner), Elk, Rotarian (mem. internat. fellowship commn.). Clubs: University (Washington); West River Yacht (Mayo, Md.). Author: Sales Reporting, 1956. Contbr. profl. jours. Home: 2637 Colston Dr Chevy Chase MD 20015 Office: 1343 L St NW Washington DC 20005

MARSH, WOODROW LEE, JR., supt. schs.; b. Pinson, Ala., July 5, 1924; s. Woodrow Lee and Pearl (Loggins) M.; B.A., Miss. Coll., 1947; M.A., U. Miss., 1949, Ed.D., 1968; postgrad. Nat. Acad. Sch. Adminstrs., 1969, Tchrs. Coll. Columbia U., 1971; m. Adelia Bell Rogers, Apr. 29, 1944; children—Carol (Mrs. Charles Felix Humphrey), James Rogers, Barbara Elaine. Tchr., coach Canton (Miss.) High Sch., 1947-49; prin. Yazoo City High Sch., 1949-53, Greenwood High Sch., 1953-57; asst. supt. Greenwood pub. schs., 1957-61; supt. schs., Moss Point, 1961-66; dir. consultative services for schs. U. Miss., 1966-67; supt. schs. Bolivar Sch. Dist. IV, Cleveland, Miss., 1967—. Vis. prof. Miss. State U., summer 1958, Delta State Coll., summer 1968, 70. Mem. Legislative Recess Ednl. Study Com., chmn. Policies and Procs. Com. 1970—. Served with AUS, 1943-46. Decorated Bronze Star medal. Mem. Am. (bicentennial commn. 1971—), Miss. assns. sch. adminstrs., Nat., Miss., Bolivar County edn. assns., Miss. Assn. Sch. Supts. (pres. 1965-66), Miss. High Sch. Activities Assn. (state councilman 1969—), Cleveland C. of C. (bd. dirs. 1967—), Bolivar County Farm Bur. Mason, Rotarian (pres. 1964-65). Home: 512 Hillcrest Circle Cleveland MS 38732 Office: 305 Merritt Dr Cleveland MS 38732

MARSHALL, C(HARLES) HERBERT, physician; b. Washington, June 26, 1898; s. Charles H. and Pauline L. (Jennings) M.; Sc.B., Howard U., 1921, M.D., 1924; m. Esther Ophelia Tibbs, July 21, 1939; 1 son, Charles Herbert 3d. Intern Freedman's Hosp., Washington, 1924-25; pvt. practice medicine, Washington, 1925—; asst. instr. dept. medicine Howard U., Washington, 1928-32. Mem. Jr. Police and Citizens' Corps; mem. exec. bd. Nat. Capital area Boy Scouts Am.; mem. bd. Whipper Maternity Home; vice chmn. Commr.'s Youth Council, D.C., Citizens Joint Com. on Nat. Rep. D.C.; mem. Mayors Com. for Employment of Handicapped. Bd. dirs. Citizens Assn. of Georgetown, Citizens' Crime Commn. Met. Washington, So. Conf. Ednl. Fund, Met. Police Boys Club. Served with SATC, 1918. Recipient SSS Medal. Mem. Rock Creek Citizens Assn. (pres. 1935—), D.C. Fedn. Civic Assns. (pres. 1952-54), Nat. Med. Assn. (chmn. bd. trustees 1944-47, pres. 1949-50), N.A.A.C.P. (D.C. pres. 1941-43). Baptist. Club: Pigskin (v.p.).Home: 2710 P St NW Washington DC 20007

MARSHALL, DONALD IRVING, chem. engr.; b. Houston, Jan. 22, 1924; s. Elmer Daniel and Grace (Crossman) M.; B.S., Sam Houston State Coll., 1944; M.A., U. Tex., 1946, Ph.D., 1948; m. Elaine Ann Kautz, 1948; children—Eric Donald, Scott Alan, Todd Alden; m. 2d, Mary Penton, Feb. 24, 1973. Devel. asso. plastics div. Union Carbide Corp., Bound Brook, N.J., 1948-58; mem. research staff, research leader Engring. Research Center Western Electric Co., Princeton, N.J., 1958-71, sr. staff devel. engr., Atlanta, 1971—. Com. chmn. George Washington council Boy Scouts Am., 1961. Trustee, treas. Plastics Inst. Am., 1967-72. Recipient Annual Tech. Writing award Western Electric Co., 1966. Mem. Soc. Plastics Engrs., Am. Chem. Soc., Soc. Rheology, Sigma Xi. Editor: (Imrich Klein) Computer Programs for Plastics Engineers, 1968. Editorial adv. bd. Polymer Engring. and Sci., 1967—. Home: 275 Mark Trail Norcross GA 30071 Office: 2000 NE Expressway Norcross GA 30071

MARSHALL, JAMES STANLEY, univ. pres.; b. Cheswick, Pa., Jan. 27, 1923; s. Walter and Mildred (Crawford) M.; student Pa. State Tchrs. Coll. at Slippery Rock, 1940-43, U. Chgo., 1943-44; B.S., Pa. State Tchrs. Coll., Slippery Rock, 1947; M.S., Syracuse U., 1950, Ph.D., 1956; m. Ruth Cratty, June 10, 1944 (div. Apr. 1966); children—David Stanley, Sue Ellen, John Dodds; m. 2d, Shirley Slade, Sept. 10, 1966; children—Kimberly, James Andrew. Tchr. sci. Mynderse Acad., Seneca Falls, N.Y., 1947-52; asst. prof. sci. State U. N.Y. Coll. Edn. at Cortland, 1953-55, asso. prof., 1956, prof., 1957-58; instr. Syracuse U., 1955-56; prof. sci. edn., head dept. Fla. State U., Tallahassee, 1958, asso. dean Sch. Edn., 1965-67, dean Coll. Edn., 1967-69, acting pres., 1969, pres., 1969—; cons. Turkish Ministry Edn.; dir. Turkish Nat. Sci. High Sch. Project, 1963-67; ednl. cons. state, local sch. dists. Vice pres., bd. dirs. So. Scholarship and Research Found.; bd. dirs. Southeastern Ednl. Corp. Fellow A.A.A.S. (mem. commn. sci. edn. 1962-67); mem. Am. Inst. Physics, Nat., Fla. sci. tchrs. assn., N.E.A., Fla. Edn. Assn., Am. Assn. Physics Tchrs., Nat. Assn. Research Sci. Teaching, Fla. Acad. Scis., Sigma Xi, Phi Delta Kappa. Contbg. author: Curriculum Planning for the Gifted, 1960; New Curricula, 1963. Editor: Jour. Research in Sci. Teaching, 1963-67, Co-author: Current Trends in Science Education. Contbr. articles to sci., ednl. jours. Home: 1030 W Tennessee St Tallahassee FL 32304

MARSHALL, JEROME BENJAMIN, JR., dentist; b. Wilkes-Barre, Pa., Sept. 27, 1929; s. Jerome Benjamin and Anna Montford (Stoneham) M.; student Wyo. Sem., 1943-47; B.A., Princeton U., 1951; D.D.S., U. Pa., 1955, postgrad. 1965-66; m. Nancy Elisabeth Brader, Dec. 27, 1955; children—Elisabeth

Stoneham, Jerome Benjamin III, Sarah Atherton. Chief oral surgery Wilkes-Barre (Pa.) Gen. Hosp., 1959-61; commd. 2d lt. Dental Corps, USAF, 1961, advanced through grades to lt. col., 1970, resigned, 1970; pvt. practice dentistry specializing in oral surgery, Alexandria, Va., 1970-72, ret.; owner The Drawknife specializing in restoration 18th century furniture, 1972—; instr. in oral surgery U. Pa. Sch. Dentistry, 1957-58, Med. Sch., 1966-67; dir. The Shonk Land Co. Chmn. The Alexandria Lyceum Restoration Campaign, 1971, Alexandria Candlelight Historic House Tour, 1974; chmn. Greater Washington Area 125th anniversary dr. Wyo. Sem., 1971. Bd. dirs. The Hist. Alexandria Found. Mem. Am., Alexandria dental assns., Va., Alexandria (dir.) dental socs., Delta Sigma Delta, Omicron Kappa Upsilon. Episcopalian. Mason. Clubs: Belle Haven Country (Alexandria, Va.); Irem Temple Country (Dallas, Pa.); Westmoreland (Wilkes-Barre, Pa.). Home: 213 Prince St Alexandria VA 22314

MARSHALL, JOHN DAVID, librarian; b. McKenzie, Tenn., Sept. 7, 1928; s. Maxwell Cole and Emma (Walpole) M.; B.A. summa cum laude, Bethel Coll., McKenzie, Tenn., 1950; M.A., Fla. State U., 1951, postgrad., 1951-52. Grad. asst. Office of Dean of Sch. of Library Sci., Fla. State U., 1951-52; reference librarian Clemson (S.C.) U. Library, 1952-55; head reference dept. Auburn (Ala.) U. Library, 1955-57; head acquisitions div. U. Ga. Library, Athens, 1957-67; univ. librarian Middle Tenn. State U., Murfreesboro, 1967—. Cons. Library Sci. Inst., Tenn. Tech. U., 1971-72. Mem. Am., Southeastern (chmn. coll. and univ. section, 1972-74), Tenn. (chmn. intellectual freedom com. 1969-70) library assns., Am. Library History Round Table (sec. 1969-72), Assn. Coll. and Research Libraries (pub. com. 1957-62), Tenn. Edn. Assn., Phi Kappa Phi, Beta Phi Mu. Author: Books in Your Life, 1959; A Fable of Tomorrow's Library, 1965; Louis Shores: A Bibliography, 1964. Editor: Of, By, and For Librarians, 1960, 2d series, 1974; An American Library History Reader, 1961; In Pursuit of Library History, 1962; Mark Hopkins' Log and Other Essays of Louis Shores, 1965; Approaches to Library History, 1966; Library in the University, 1967; (with Louis Shores and Wayne Shirley) Books, Libraries, Librarians, 1955. Book rev. editor Jour. of Library History, 1966—; gen. editor Shoe String Press contbrns. to Library Literature series, 1963—; contbg. editor So. Observer, 1953-66. Editorial bd. Alabama Librarian, 1956-57. Book reviewer Library Jour., 1953-64. Home: 802 E Main St Apt 34 Murfreesboro TN 37130

MARSHALL, LAWRENCE MARCELLUS, JR., computer software engr.; b. Pine Bluff, Ark., Mar. 23, 1944; s. Lawrence Marcellus and Mary (Williams) M.; B.S. in Elec. Engring., Rensselaer Polytech. U., 1968; m. Patricia C. Hogue, May 5, 1973; 1 son, Paul L. Navigation systems engr. Control Data Corp., Bethesda, Md., 1967-70; asso. engr. applied physics lab. Johns Hopkins, Silver Springs, Md., 1970—. Mem. I.E.E.E., Zeta Beta Tau. Democrat. Assisted in devel. C-LAD, low cost navigation assist device. Home: 4915 12th St NE Washington DC 20017

MARSHALL, MARA BLUMBERG (MRS. SYLVAN MITCHELL MARSHALL), artist; b. Nice, France, July 21, 1926 (parents Am. citizens); d. Joseph and Leah (Kristeller) Blumberg; grad. Scudder-Culver Jr. Coll., 1945, N.Y. Sch. Interior Decoration, 1946; Student Art Students' League, N.Y.C., 1945-46; m. Sylvan Mitchell Marshall, Feb. 11, 1951; children—Douglas Wayne, Bradley Ross. One-man show First Fed. Gallery, Chgo., 1971, Nat. League Pen Women, Washington, 1972; exhibited group shows Cosmos Club, Washington, Am. Art League Exhibit, Washington, Exhibit for Kennedy Center for Performing Arts, Washington, Julius Garfinckel & Co., Am. Art League Gallery, Washington, Washington Gallery Art, Nat. League Am. Pen Women, 1970, 72, Pres. Park Exhibit, Washington; represented in permanent collections. Mem. bd. Salvation Army Aux., 1954-56; mem. Pan Am. Liaison Com. of Women's Orgns., 1954—; mem. White House Spanish-Portuguese Study Group, 1953—, mem. bd., corr. sec., 1956-57. Mem. Nat. League Am. Pen Women (Ann. award Biennial Contest in Art, D.C. br. 1967, 69, Ann. award, 1st prize oils nat. biennial contest 1969, exec. bd. D.C. br. 1968-70, corr. sec., 1968-70, pres. D.C. br. 1970-72, 1st prize accryllics 1971), Artists Equity Assn. Am. Art League. Club: International. Home: 2929 Ellicott St NW Washington DC 20008

MARSHALL, MELVIN D., author; b. San Antonio, Oct. 8, 1911; s. Carl S. and Della (Duncan) M.; grad. high sch.; m. Aldine Thompson, May 17, 1937. Newspaper, radio writing, 1928-35, broadcast mgmt., 1936-45; owner, pub. Pittsburg (Cal.) News weekly, editor, pub. Pittsburg Daily News, 1945-49; owner, gen. mgr. KECC, Pittsburg Broadcasting Co., 1949-57; owner, pres. KENL, Humboldt Broadcasters, Inc., Arcata, Cal., 1957-63, KPLY, Del Norte Broadcasting Co., Inc., Crescent City, Cal., 1958-62; free lance writer books, articles in Am., fgn. mags., photographer, Phillips, Tex., 1964—, recent books include Valley of Death, Trail of Vengeance, 1966; Guns on the Pedernales, 1967; The Delectable Egg, 1968; Riders of Tierra Roja, Longhorns North, 1969; Buffalo!, McQuade, Long Rider, Drift Fence, Cooking Over Coals, Fish Cookery, 1971; Hell Canyon, Steelhead, Two Funerals for Tombstone, Family Cookout Cookbook, Family Chicken and Fowl Cookbook, Family One-Pot Cookbook, 1973. Mem. Western Writers Am. Republican. Rotarian. Address: 330 1st St Phillips TX 79071

MARSHALL, RICHARD TREEGER, lawyer; b. N.Y.C., May 17, 1925; s. Edward and Sydney (Treeger) M.; student Queens Coll., 1942-43; B.S., Cornell U., 1948; LL.B., Yale, 1951; m. Dorothy M. Goodman, June 4, 1950; children—Abigail Ruth, D. Brooks. Admitted to Tex. bar, 1952, since practiced in El Paso; asso. firm Fryer and Milstead, 1951-52; sr. partner Marshall and Wendorf, 1959-61. Instr. Am. govt. U. Tex., El Paso, 1961-62; lectr. legal seminars. Chmn. El Paso Vols. for Stevenson, 1956; co-chmn. Tex. Citizens for Kennedy, 1960. Mem. Yale Alumni Bd., 1959-60. Served with Signal Corps, AUS, 1943-45; ETO. Fellow Am. Acad. Matrimonial Lawyers; mem. Am. Trial Lawyers Assn. (nat. sec. 1969-70), Tex. Civil Liberties Union (sr. legal counsel 1968-73), El Paso Trial Lawyers Assn. (pres. 1965-66), Am. Arbitration Assn. (panelist 1966—). Author numerous articles in field. Editor: El Paso Trial Lawyers Quar., 1973—. Home: 309 Rainbow Circle El Paso TX 79912 Office: 4141 Pinnacle-Executive Center El Paso TX 79902

MARSHALL, SYLVAN MITCHELL, lawyer, TV producer; b. N.Y.C., May 14, 1917; s. Louis H. and Kitty Markowitz; B.A., Coll. City N.Y., 1938; LL.B., Harvard, 1941; m. Mara Byron, Feb. 11, 1951; children—Douglas Wayne, Bradley Ross. Admitted to N.Y. bar, 1946, Washington bar, 1953; mem. firm Garey & Garey, N.Y.C., 1946-51; spl. asst. to chief counsel OPS, Washington, 1951-53; partner Granik & Marshall, Washington, 1953-58; asst. producer Youth Wants To Know and Am. Forum, NBC-TV and radio, 1953-58; spl. dep. atty. gen., N.Y., 1946-50; pvt. practice Washington, 1958—; sr. partner law firm Marshall & Soll, Washington; partner Soll, Connelly & Marshall, N.Y.C.; Washington counsel Community Fed. Savs. & Loan Assn., St. Louis, First Fed. Savs. & Loan Assn., Chgo., First Fed. Savs. & Loan of Miami, First Fed. Savs. & Loan Assn., Jacksonville, Fla., Standard Fed. Savs. & Loan Assn., Cin., First Fed. Savs. & Loan Assn. of Wis., Milw., Sooner Fed. Savs. & Loan Assn., Tulsa, Am. Bancshares, Inc., Fla., Diamond & Precious Stone Bourse, Idar-Oberstein, West Germany. Hon. dep. police commr. N.Y.C., 1950-53; hon. consul Finland. Served from 2d lt. to lt. col., AUS, 1941-46. Decorated knight comdr. Order of the Falcon (Iceland); Knight comdr. Order of Vasco Nunez de Balboa (Republic of Panama); comdr. Order of Lion (Finland); Order of Taj (Iran); Order of So. Cross (Brazil); Order of Ruben Dario (Nicaragua). Mem. Acad. Television Arts and Scis. Clubs: International, Cosmos (Washington). Home: 2929 Ellicott St NW Washington DC 20008 Office: 1825 K St NW Washington DC 20006 also 230 Park Av New York City NY 10017

MARSHALL, THURGOOD, asso. justice U.S. Supreme Ct.; b. Balt., July 2, 1908; s. William & Norma A. (Williams) M.; A.B., Lincoln U., 1930, LL.D., 1947; LL.B., Howard U., 1933, LL.D., 1954; LL.D., Va. State Coll., 1948, Morgan State Coll., 1952, Grinnell Coll., 1954, Syracuse U., 1956, N.Y. Sch. Social Research, 1956, U. Liberia, 1960, Brandeis U., 1960, U. Mass., 1962, Jewish Theol. Sem., 1962, Wayne U., 1963, Princeton U., 1963, U. Mich., 1964; m. Vivian Burey, Sept. 4, 1929 (dec. Feb. 1955); m. 2d, Cecilia A. Suyat, Dec. 17, 1955; children—Thurgood, John. Admitted to Md. bar 1933, individual practice, Balt., 1933-37; asst. spl. counsel N.A.A.C.P., 1936-38, spl. counsel, 1938-50, dir., counsel legal def. and ednl. fund, 1940-61; U.S. circuit judge for 2d jud. circuit, 1961-65; solicitor gen. of U.S., Dept. Justice, Washington, 1965-67; asso. justice Supreme Ct. U.S., Washington, 1967—. Civil rights cases argued include: Tex. Primary Case, 1944; Restrictive Covenant Cases, 1948; U. Tex. and Okla. Cases, 1950; sch. segregation cases, 1952-53; visited Japan and Korea to make investigation of ct. martial cases involving Negro soldiers, 1951. Mem. N.Y. State Commn. World's Fair. Cons. Constl. Conf. on Kenya, London, 1960; rep. White House Conf. Youth and Children. Bd. dirs. John F. Kennedy Meml. Library; mem. coll. electors Hall of Fame N.Y. U. Recipient Spingarn medal, 1946; Living History award Research Inst. Mem. Am., Nat. bar assns., Assn. Bar City N.Y., N.Y. County Lawyers Assn., Alpha Phi Alpha. Episcopalian. Mason (33 deg.). Home: 6233 Lakeview Dr Falls Church VA 22041 Office: Supreme Court US Washington DC 20543

MARSHALL, VIRGIL HARRISON, dentist; b. Newport News, Va., May 7, 1922; s. Albert Holman and Vera Adel (Hall) M.; student Va. Poly. Inst., 1942-43, 45-46; D.D.S., Med. Coll. Va., 1950; m. Evelyn Ruth Gardner, June 16, 1947; children—Virgil Harrison, Marilyn Gardner, David Randolph. Intern in oral surgery Med. Coll. Va. Hosp., 1950-51; practice of gen. dentistry, Charlottesville, Va., 1951—; pres. Beaver Dam Land Corp., Charlottesville, 1964, V.H.M. Corp., 1962; v.p. M & O Corp. 1967; dir. Farmington, Inc., 1971—; Va. Nat. Bank, Farmington Property Owners, Inc. Bd. dirs. United Givers Fund, 1961-66, vice chmn. campaign, 1965, chmn. campaign, 1966. Served to 1st lt., USAAF, 1943-45. Fellow Va. Dental Assn.; mem. Am. Dental Assn. (mem. at large exec. council 1968-70), Va. Artificial Kidney Assn. (pres. 1967—), Atwood Wash Soc., Omicron Kappa Upsilon, Psi Omega. Episcopalian (vestryman 1968-71). Mason (Shriner), Rotarian. Contbr. to ency. Home: 3 Oak Circle Farmington Charlottesville VA 22901 Office: 306 E Jefferson Charlottesville VA 22901

MARSHALL, WALLACE, physician, surgeon; b. Appleton, Wis., July 19, 1904; s. Victor F. and Fanny (Levy) M.; B.A., U. Wis., 1930; B.M., Northwestern U., 1932, M.D., 1933; m. Louise Marjorie Clayton, Aug. 14, 1953; 1 dau., Victoria Louise. Intern, Wesley Hosp., Wichita, Kan., 1932, Los Angeles County Gen. Hosp., 1932-33; pvt. practice medicine, Two Rivers, Wis., 1949-59, Watertown, Wis., 1959-61, Florala, Ala., 1961-62, Heflin, Ala., 1962, Anniston, Ala.; instr. physiol. chemistry, medicine U. Ala., 1936-37; asso. prof. physiol. chemistry Spring Hill Coll., 1947; lectr. sci. research St. Norbert Coll., 1953; fellow psychiatry La. State U.-Charity Hosp. of La., New Orleans, 1966-67; med. cons. to pharm. firms; prof. psychology Auburn U., Montgomery, 1971—; staff psychiatrist Bapt. Hosp., Montgomery, Jackson Hosp., Montgomery. Recipient certificate of award Med. Econs., 1967. Fellow A.A.A.S., Am. Med. Writers Assn. (life), Miss. Valley Med. Soc. (life dir., Wis. v.p. 1959-61), Royal Soc. Health, Acad. Psychosomatic Medicine; mem. Indian Assn. Dermatologists and Venereologists (life), Nat. Writers Club, A.M.A., Am. Fedn. Clin. Research, Wis., (sec., program chmn. 5th councillor dist., 1956-57), Montgomery County med. socs., Med. Assn. State Ala., So. Med. Assn., Am. Acad. Gen. Practice (past chpt. pres.). Mason (32 deg., Shriner). Author: Noise of Great Waters (1st prize Am. Physicians Literary Guild), 1947; Essentials of Medical Research, 1953; numerous med., surg. articles. Asso. editor: Med. Times, 1943-63; cons. editor gen. practice of Med. Digest, 1957—; abstract editor Psychol. Reviews, 1938-40; book review editor Mississippi Valley Med. Jour., Clin. Medicine, 1959-61; hon. cons. editor Med. Digest, Bombay, India, 1960—. Discovered and produced microcirculatory constrictor from crude liver, Kutapressin, 1950; co-discoverer Marshall-White syndrome, 1965; originator theory of psychoimmunology. Address: 2326 Winchester Rd Montgomery AL 36111

MARSHALL, WILLIAM JAMES ALOYSIUS, ednl. adminstr.; b. Boston, Sept. 19, 1941; s. John Gerald and Florence Blanche (Zaporowicz) M.; B.S., Stonehill Coll., 1964; M.Ed., Gallaudet Coll., 1965; Ed.D., (U.S. Office Edn. fellow), U. Ill., 1970; m. Mardi Lee Meyers, Sept. 5, 1966; children—Jennifer Allison, Geoffrey Alexander, Stephanie Ann, Anastasia. Research asst. prof. U. Ill. at Urbana, 1970; asst. prof. U. Wash., Seattle, 1970-72; dir. research Project Life/N.E.A., Washington, 1972; liaison officer Nat. Center on Ednl. Media and Materials for the Handicapped/Model Secondary Sch. for the Deaf, Gallaudet Coll., Washington, 1972—, cons. advanced edn. program, 1964-65. Cons., Project Life, 1972—, Ohio State Dept. Edn., Bur. Edn. to Handicapped, U.S. Office Edn., 1957-70. Recipient Daniel T. Cloud award for acad. excellence Gallaudet Coll., 1965. Mem. Nat. Assn. of Deaf, Am. Ednl. Research Orgn., Council of Exceptional Children, Conv. Am. Instrs. of Deaf, Assn. for Ednl. Communications and Tech., Phi Delta Kappa. Author: Analysis of Written Language Production of Deaf Children, 1970; Behavioral Objectives in the Classroom, 1971; Research Field Manual, 1972. Home: 114 E Columbia St Falls Church VA 22046 Office: Model Secondary Sch for Deaf Gallaudet Coll Washington DC 20002 also Model Secondary Sch for Deaf 220 W 12th Av Ohio State Univ Columbus OH 43210

MARSHALL, WILLIAM LEITCH, chemist; b. Columbia, S.C., Dec. 3, 1925; s. William Leitch and Georgia (Kittrell) M.; B.S., Clemson U., 1945; Ph.D., Ohio State U., 1949; m. Joanne Fox, Apr. 16, 1949; children—Nancy Diane, William Fox. Teaching asst. Clemson U., 1944-45, Ohio State U., 1945-46; Naval research fellow Ohio State U., 1947-49; mem. sr. research staff Oak Ridge Nat. Lab., 1949—, research group leader, 1957—. Guggenheim fellow van der Waals Lab., U. Amsterdam, 1956-57. Mem. Am. Chem. Soc. (nat. council 1968—, chmn. nat. subcom. on high sch. chem. edn. 1970—), A.A.A.S., Geochem. Soc., Sci. Research Soc. Am., Sigma Xi, Phi Kappa Phi. Contbr. articles to profl. jours. Patentee in field. Home: 101 Oak Lane Oak Ridge TN 37830 Office: Chemistry Div Oak Ridge Nat Lab Oak Ridge TN 37830

MARSHBURN, JOSEPH HANCOCK, educator; b. Josselyn, Ga., Jan. 11, 1890; s. M. Thomas and Alice Verina (Hendricks) M.; A.B., U. Ga., 1911, A.M., 1912; A.M., Harvard, 1919; Yale fellowship, 1923; Ph.D., Cornell, 1927; m. Mary Amoss, Jan. 17, 1919; 1 son, Joseph Hancock. Instr. English, U. Ga., 1912-14; head dept. English, Ga. Mil. Coll., 1914-16, v.p., 1916-17, pres., 1917-20; prof. English, U. Okla., 1920—, ret. chmn. dept. Reader, Folger Shakespeare Library, 1936, Brit. Mus., 1948-49; David Ross Boyd prof. English lit., 1949. Mem. Royal Soc. Lit., Modern Lang. Assn., Am. Assn. U. Profs., Sigma Chi, Phi Beta Kappa. Democrat. Episcopalian. Mason (K.T., Shriner), Lion. Author: Murder and Witchcraft in England, 1550-1640, 1972; (with Alan Velie) Blood and Knavery, 1973. Home: 652 Reed Av Norman OK 73069

MARSTON, JOHN PARK, journalist, assn. adminstr.; b. Montgomery, W.Va., Sept. 21, 1939; s. John Edward and Mary Park (Nease) M.; B.S. in Journalism W. Va. U., 1962; postgrad. in Journalism, U. N.C., 1964-66; m. Shelby Purser, Sept. 11, 1966; children—John Purser, Margaret Ann. News reporter Daily Mail, Charleston, W. Va., 1962-64; asst. dir. News Bur., U. N.C. at Greensboro, 1966-67; dir. communications N.C. Bd. Sci. and Tech., Raleigh, 1967-68; asst. dir. N.C. Hosp. Assn., Raleigh, 1968—. Served with USAF, 1962. Mem. Raleigh Pub. Relations Soc. (dir. 1971—, first prize for profl. excellence 1970), Raleigh Jaycees (com. chmn. of year 1973), Sigma Delta Chi. Home: 1000 Wofford Lane Raleigh NC 27609 Office: PO Box 10937 Raleigh NC 27605

MARTENS, WILLIAM STEPHEN, chemist; b. Pitts., June 14, 1935; s. James Hart Curry and Vivian (Stone) M.; B.S. (Henry Rutgers scholar), Rutgers U., 1956, Ph.D. (AEC research fellow), 1960; m. Mary Adams Anderson, May 13, 1973. Sr. research chemist Internat. Minerals & Chem. Corp., Mulberry, Fla., 1960-62; scientist Allied Chem. Corp., Hopewell, Va., 1962-69; cons. Va. State Health Dept., Richmond, 1969-70; research chemist U.S. Naval Weapons Lab., Dahlgren, Va., 1970—. Mem. Am. Chem. Soc., Sigma Xi, Phi Lambda Upsilon. Clubs: U.S. Power Squadron, Richmond Ski. Home: PO Box 697 Dahlgren VA 22448 Office: US Naval Weapons Lab Dahlgren VA 22448

MARTENSON, HERBERT ERIC, state ofcl.; b. Bklyn., Aug. 25, 1925; s. Anton and Thyra (Eklund) A.; B.S. in Indsl. Engring., Lehigh U., 1951; m. Elizabeth Zini, Mar. 9, 1967; children—Michael, Keith. Dir. data processing Greyhound Corp., Chgo., 1965-67, Signode Corp., Chgo., 1967-68; dir. data processing So. Airway, Atlanta, 1970-71; prin. Tech. Resources, Inc., Atlanta, 1971-72; chief data processing S.C. Dept. Social Services, Columbia, 1973—. Served with USNR, 1943-46. Mem. Assn., Computing Machinery. Kiwanian. Home: 558 Westover Rd Woodland Hills Columbia SC 29210 Office: Box 1520 Columbia SC 29202

MARTH-SNADER, ELLA CAROLYN MARTH, educator; b. Alton, Ill.; d. Louis George and Elizabeth (Krauskopf) Marth; A.B., Harris Tchrs. Coll., 1930; M.S., St. Louis U., 1935, Ph.D., 1944; m. Daniel W. Snader, July 28, 1956 (div. Aug. 1972). Tchr. pub. schs., St. Louis, 1930-44; asst. prof. math. Harris Tchrs. Coll., 1945-47, dean of women, asso. prof., 1947-52; prof., chmn. div. math. and bus. edn. D.C. Tchrs. Coll., 1952-56, prof., 1960—; asso. prof. div. math. Chgo. Tchrs. Coll., 1956-59; specialist elementary math. U.S. Office of Edn., Washington, 1959. Cons. elementary math. Mem. St. Louis Assn. for Human Relations, 1950. Mem. Am. Math. Soc., Nat. Council Tchrs. Math., Central Assn. Sci. and Math. Tchrs. (dir. 1949, 51-53), Am. Math. Assn., Internat. Platform Assn., Sigma Xi, Pi Mu Epsilon, Delta Kappa Gamma. Unitarian. Contbr. articles to profl. jours. Home: 3701 Connecticut Av NW Washington DC 20008 Office: 1100 Harvard St NW Washington DC 20009

MARTIN, ALBERT ERSKINE, JR., fiber producer exec.; b. Rome, Ga., Jan. 22, 1919; s. Albert Erskine and Pauline (Taylor) M.; B.S., Tulane U., 1945, M.S., 1946; postgrad. Brown U., 1947-50; m. Rosemay Yvonne Carrere, Aug. 22, 1958; 1 son, Albert Erskine III. Sr. physicist U.S. Dept. Agr., So. Regional Research Lab., New Orleans, 1950-57; head textile physics sect. textile research and devel. Courtauld, Inc., Mobile, Ala., 1957-62; mgr. tech. services Firestone Synthetic Fibers Co., Hopewell, Va., 1962—, now mgr. applications research. Spl. lectr. physics Spring Hill Coll., Mobile, 1957-59; instr. physics Tulane U., 1945-47, 52-57, Brown U., 1947-50; mem. research adv. council Auburn U. Textile Sch., 1959-61. Committeeman, merit badge counsellor Boy Scouts Am., Richmond, Va., 1962—. Pres. bd. dirs. Old Dominion chpt. Nat. Cystic Fibrosis Research Found. Mem. Fiber Soc., Am. Soc. for Testing Materials, Am. Assn. Textile Technologists, Am. Radio Relay League. Patentee in field. Home: 4221 Stratford Rd Richmond VA 23225 Office: PO Box 450 Hopewell VA 23860

MARTIN, ALLEN JACKSON, JR., hosp. adminstr.; b. Ruffin, N.C., Sept. 12, 1931; s. Allen Jackson and Pearl (Kennedy) M.; A.B., Elon Coll., 1958; m. Mary Anne Ward, June 18, 1954; children—Allen Jackson, Jeffrey Ward, Mary Celeste. Asst. adminstr. Meml. Hosp., Danville, Va., 1959; adminstr. Washington County Hosp., Plymouth, N.C., 1959-66, Lower Florence County Hosp., Lake City, S.C., 1966-69; cons. for planning Edgefield (S.C.) County Hosp., 1969-71, adminstr., 1971-73; adminstr. Davie County Hosp., Mocksville, N.C., 1973—. Bd. dirs. Albemarle Area Devel. Corp., 1964-66. Mem. N.C. (dist. pres. 1965-66), S.C. hosp. assns., Plymouth and Washington County C. of C. (pres. 1965). Presbyn. (deacon, elder, lay minister). Rotarian. Home: 718 Magnolia Av Mocksville NC 27028 Office: Davie County Hosp PO Box 908 Mocksville NC 27028

MARTIN, BENJAMIN FRANKLIN III, pathologist; b. Memphis, Mar. 25, 1938; s. Benjamin Franklin and Margaret Eugenia (Rather) M.; B.A., U. Miss., 1960, M.D., 1966; m. Linda Lee Morgan, May 30, 1971; 1 son, Benjamin Franklin. Intern Methodist Hosp., Memphis, 1966-67, resident, 1967-70; practice medicine, specializing in pathology, Columbus, Miss., 1970—; cons. pathologist Columbus Hosp., Ivy Hosp., West Point, Miss., Noxubee Hosp., Macon, Miss., Webster Gen. Hosp., Eupora, Miss., Oktibbeha Hosp., Starkville, Miss.; dir. Columbus Pathology Labs., Columbus, 1970—, labs. Lowndes Gen. Hosp., Columbus, 1970—. Diplomate Am. Bd. Pathology. Fellow Coll. Am. Pathologists, Am. Soc. Clin. Pathologists; mem. Am., So., Miss. med. assns., Miss. Soc. Pathologists. Rotarian. Home: Route 6 Box 193 Columbus MS 39701 Office: 425 Hospital Dr Columbus MS 39701

MARTIN, BENNY WORTH, dentist; b. High Point, N.C., May 9, 1931; s. Jesse Worth and Murphy Irene (Joyce) M.; B.S., High Point Coll., 1954; D.D.S., U. N.C., 1958; M.S.D., U. Minn., 1964; m. Shirley Goodale Purinton, July 25, 1959; children—Jesse Worth, George Kinner, Dennis Vernon, Gordon Hunter, Amy Purinton. Clin. Instr. Sch. Dentistry, U. N.C. Dept. Oral Surgery, 1958-59, cons., part time instr., 1970—; intern oral surgery Mayo Clinic, Rochester, Minn., 1961-62, resident oral surgery, 1962-64; practice dentistry specializing in oral surgery, Raleigh, N.C., 1954—. Oral surgery cons. N.C. Dept. Correction, Raleigh, 1964—, Wayne County Meml., Johnston County Meml., Wilson Meml. hosps.; mem. staff Wake County Meml. Hosp., Rex Hosp., Raleigh. Chmn. dental div. N.C. Cancer Soc., 1967, 68; mem. exec. com., bds. dirs. N.C. div. Am. Cancer Soc., 1967, 68. Served to capt. Dental Corp, USAF, 1959-61. Diplomate Am. Bd. Oral Surgery. Mem. Am., N.C. dental assns., Am., N.C. socs. oral surgeons, Am., N.C. socs. dental anesthesia, Sigma Phi Epsilon, Psi Omega. Methodist. Home: 5424 Thayer Dr Raleigh NC 27609 Office: Building E Glenwood Professional Village Raleigh NC 27608

MARTIN, BROOKS, architect; b. Colorado, Tex., Sept. 23, 1913; s. A.D. and Ury (Brooks) M.; B.Arch., Tex. A. and M. Coll., 1940; B.Arch., Harvard, 1952, M.Arch., 1953; m. Orabel Foster, May 16, 1941. Pvt. practice, Bryan, Tex., 1948-51, San Antonio, 1959—, Mexico, 1962—; asst. architect Tex. A. and M. Coll. system, 1945-48; cons. architect Fehr & Granger, Austin, Tex., 1950; designer-architect Carl Kock, Boston, 1952; asso. architect Hugh Stubbins, Jr., Boston, 1952-54; architect Samuel Glaser Assos., Boston, 1955; sr. research architect Southwest Research Inst., San Antonio, 1956-58; vis. critic design Harvard, 1953, Boston Archtl. Center, 1955; group exhbn. San Antonio Press Club, 1962; prin. works include St. Mary's U. Law Sch., 1959, Cambridge Oval Apts., Alamo Heights, 1959, Canyon Creek Country Club, 1959, St. Cecelia's, also St. Margaret Mary parish schs. and rectory, 1959, McDavitt Lester Ins. Bldg., 1958, residences for John Fonveilles, 1959, Elbert DeCourseys, 1959, W. S. Lights, 1960, Navarro Houses restoration, 1962-64, Aransas Pass subdiv., 1962, Cambridge Oval Duplex, 1964, McCullough Med. Center, 1962, Dougherty Tea House, also Dougherty Office Bldg., 1964, town houses Cambridge Oval, 1964, Chandler Bldg. remodeling, 1964; resident architect W.S. Light Devel. Co., 1959—; archtl. adviser, pres. Jackson Todd Memorial Found. Cancer Research; interior design project Dempsey-Tegler, 1960, N. Star Mall and McCrelless Shopping Center, 1960; coordinating architect St. Mary's U., 1964; resident architect Fomento Economico Monterrey, S.A., Mexico, 1959; prin. works in Mexico City include Cine Tacubaya, 1963, apt. house project, 1963. Recipient Guptill certificate Tex. A. and M. Coll., 1941; winner U.S. Plywood Co. regional competition, 1940, Fenestra Co. regional competition, 1940. Sec. Savannah Corp., San Antonio, Argyle Investment Co., San Antonio. Bd. dirs. Jackson Todd Cancer Research Found., 1960—, La Prensa, 1959-61. Served with AUS, World War II. Decorated Purple Heart. Fellow A.I.A. (2d prize nat. journalism award 1959), mem. Tex. Soc. Architects (award merit 1963), San Antonio Conservation Soc. (hon.), San Antonio C. of C. (chmn. projects com.), Alpha Rho Chi (medal 1952). Democrat. Episcopalian. Kiwanian. Home: 122 Downing Dr San Antonio TX 78209 Office: L-28 Cypress Tower San Antonio TX 78212 also Hamburgo Mexico City 6 Mexico

MARTIN, CHARLES ALVIN, JR., frozen food industry exec.; b. Nashville, Sept. 5, 1923; s. Charles Alvin and Maude (Cameron) M.; grad. pub. schs.; m. Mary Virginia Tate, Oct. 22, 1946; children—Charles Douglas, Harriett Julia (Mrs. James P. Bennett), Deborah Tate. Vice pres., gen. mgr. Polar Refrigerated Services, Inc., Nashville, 1946-66, asst. to pres., 1966-72, pres., 1972—, also dir.; v.p. Frozen Foods Inc., Nashville, 1952-57; pres. Frozen Food Distbrs., Inc., St. Petersburg, Fla., 1959-69; v.p. Winter Garden Freezer Co., Inc., Bells, Tenn., 1969-71; gen. mgr., dir. Agrl. Services Assn., Bells., 1971—; comml. warehouse service officer Dept. Def., Chgo., 1950-51. Served with 1st Inf. Div., AUS, 1942-46. Decorated with two Bronze Star medals. Mem. Nat. Assn. Refrigerated Warehouses (mem. exec. com. 1960-63), Am., So. (dir. 1959-62) frozen food assns., Am. Mgmt. Assn., Nat. Council Phys. Distbn. Mgmt. Club: Exchange (Nashville). Home: 5821 Beauregard Dr Nashville TN 37215 Office: Polar Refrigerated Services Inc PO Box 1174 Nashville TN 37202

MARTIN, CHARLES EDWARD, educator; b. Mantee, Miss., Sept. 3, 1930; s. James Aaron and Armenda (Vaughn) M.; B.A., Miss. Coll., 1951; M.A., Tulane U., 1958, Ph.D., 1965; m. Anne Armstrong, Aug. 7, 1953; children—Carol Anne, James Charles, Ellen Elaine. Asst. prof., asso. prof., prof. Spanish, Miss. Coll., Clinton, 1957—, head dept. fgn. langs., 1966—, v.p. for acad. affairs, 1969—. Danforth asso. Served with AUS, 1951-54. Mem. Am. Assn. Honors Councils, Am. Assn. Tchrs. Spanish and Portuguese, Am. Council Tchrs. Fgn. Langs., South Central, Miss. (v.p.) modern lang. assns., Am. Assn. U. Profs. (past chpt. pres., sec. state conf.), Omicron Delta Kappa, Phi Sigma Iota, Phi Delta Kappa. Baptist (deacon). Home: 107 Billy Byrd Dr Clinton MS 39056

MARTIN, CHARLES THOMAS, elec. engr.; b. Charleston, S.C., July 25, 1942; s. Calvin Sanford and Faye Elizabeth (Jameson) M.; B.S. in Elec. Engring., Clemson U., 1965; m. Linda Lee Shell, Dec. 18, 1971. With Newport News Shipbldg. & Dry Dock Co. (Va.), 1965—, mgr. power sect., 1972-73, mgr. power and lighting sect. for surface ships, 1973—. Registered profl. engr., Va. Mem. I.E.E.E., Va. Soc. Profl. Engrs. Home: 29 Richland Dr Newport News VA 23602 Office: 4101 Washington Av Newport News VA 23607

MARTIN, MRS. CHESTER E., club woman; b. College Park, Ga., June 29, 1902; d. James Franklin and Etta (Doyal) Lambert; student U. Ga., 1919, Draughon's Bus. Coll., 1920; m. Chester Earle Martin, Nov. 4, 1922; 1 dau., Elsie Lambert (Mrs. John Wen Lundeen Jr.). Hon. consul for Guatemala to Atlanta, 1955-65. Pres., Hapeville Woman's Club, 1926, woman's council First Christian Ch., Atlanta, 1927, United Ch. Women Atlanta 1950-51, United Ch. Women Ga., 1952-53, Ga. Fedn. Women's Clubs, 1952-54, life dir.; southeastern council Gen. Fedn. Women's Clubs, 1954-56, gardens chmn., 1954-58, chmn. dept. fine arts, 1960-62, treas., 1964-66, pres. Past State Presidents Club, 1962-64; chmn. UN Day Observance, Atlanta, 1951, mem. bd. Atlanta UN, 1967—; bd. mem. Atlanta Goodwill Industries, 1948-58, Atlanta Girls' Club, 1955-57, United Ch. Women Atlanta, 1946-70; pres. Atlanta Music Club guild, 1972—; bd. mem. Atlanta Council Girl Scouts, 1948-57, mem. Juliett Low Regional Commn., 1954-66; mem. adv. bd. Fulton County Juvenile Ct., 1954-65; pres. bd. dirs. Savannah St. Mission Inc., 1958-65, finance chmn., 1965—; pres. Ga. Roadside Council, 1966—; pres. Peachtree unit Parliamentary Law, 1969-71; parliamentarian women's com. Atlanta Symphony Guild, 1966-68; chmn. Japanese Internat. Christian U. Ga. Recipient Woman of Year in Civic Service award, Atlanta, 1950, master certificate for flower show judging Nat. Council State Garden Clubs, 1961, Commendation for Conservation award Pres. Nixon, 1971. Life mem. Disciples of Christ Hist. Soc., Garden Club of Ga. Mem. Christian Ch. (pres. Altar guild). Club: Pan American (pres. Atlanta 1960-62). Author: Reverend James Franklin Lambert, 1965. Home: 300 Blackland Rd NW Atlanta GA 30342

MARTIN, CORA ARLETA, equal opportunity specialist; b. Dean, Tenn., Sept. 30, 1923; d. Thomas Crawford and Florice (Gardner) Martin; certificate Bowling Green Bus. U., 1943. Clk. typist War Dept., Tullahoma, Tenn., 1943-46; payroll clk. VA and U.S. Dept. Agr., Atlanta, 1946-51; personnel rep. U.S. Army Corps of Engrs., Tullahoma, Tenn., 1951-60; placement and employee mgmt. relations specialist Army Rocket and Guided Missile Agy. and U.S. Army Missile Support Agy., 1960-69; personnel staffing specialist, equal opportunity specialist and fed. women's program coordinator U.S. Army Missile Command, 1969—. Chmn. Bedford County Heart Unit, 1964-67, vice chmn., 1967—. Mem. Internat. Personnel Mgmt. Adminstrn., Shelbyville Bus. and Profl. Women's Club, Tenn. Fedn. Bus. and Profl. Women's Clubs, Inc. (pres. 1963, parliamentarian 1965-66, 71-72), Bedford County African Violet Soc., Federally Employed Women (chpt. pres. 1971-72). Home: 502 Riverview Dr Shelbyville TN 37160 Office: Equal Opportunity Office Redstone Arsenal AL 35809

MARTIN, DAVID BOUCHER, city ofcl.; b. New Orleans, Nov. 7, 1925; s. Edmund Butts and Dora Odile (Musson) M.; B.Engring., Tulane U., 1947; certificate hwy. traffic, Yale, 1949. Asst. traffic engr. City of New Orleans, 1947-52; traffic engr. City of Savannah, also Chatham County, Ga., 1953-54; traffic engr. Palmer & Baker Engrs., Inc., Mobile, Ala., 1954-72; city traffic engr., Jackson, Miss., 1972—. Served with USNR, 1945-46; PTO. Registered profl. engr., La., Ala., Miss. Fellow Inst. Traffic Engrs.; mem. Nat. Soc. Profl. Engrs., Beta Theta Pi. Roman Catholic. Home: 1620 Brecon Dr Jackson MS 39211 Office: PO Box 17 Jackson MS 39205

MARTIN, DEAN FREDERICK, educator; b. Woodburn, Ia., Apr. 6, 1933; s. Herman A. and Frances (Rausis) M.; B.A., Grinnell Coll., 1955; Ph.D., Pa. State U., 1958; m. Barbara Bursa, Dec. 22, 1956; children—Diane, Bruce, John, Paul, Brian, Eric. Research fellow chemistry Pa. State U., 1955-58; NSF fellow Univ. Coll., London, Eng., 1958-59; instr. inorganic chemistry U. Ill. at Urbana, 1959-61, asst. prof., 1961-64; asso. prof. chemistry U. South Fla., Tampa, 1964-69, prof., 1969—; cons. in field. U. Ill. Research Bd. grantee, 1960, USPHS grantee, 1961-66, 69—, U.S. Dept. Interior grantee, 1966-68, Fla. Bd. Conservation grantee, 1968-69, S.W. Water Mgmt. Dist. grantee, 1969-70, Fla. Dept. Natural Resources grantee, 1972—, Mote Marine Lab. grantee, 1972—, Proctor & Gamble Co. grantee, 1972—. Mem. Am. Chem. Soc., The Chem. Soc. (London), N.Y. Acad. Sci., Am. Soc. Limnology and Oceanography, A.A.A.S., Phi Beta Kappa, Sigma Xi, Alpha Chi Sigma. Roman Catholic. Author: (with Barbara B. Martin) Coordination Compounds, 1964; (with Theodore Moeller) Laboratory Chemistry, 1964; Marine Chemistry, 1968, 70, 72. Editor (with G.M. Padilla) Marine Pharmacognosy, 1973. Contbr. articles to profl. jours. Home: 3402 Valencia Rd Tampa FL 33618

MARTIN, DONALD THOMAS, ry. exec.; b. Richmond, Va., Dec. 6, 1913; s. Clarence Vincent and Pearl (Thirston) M.; B.S. in Bus. Adminstrn., Va. Poly. Inst., 1934; m. Louise Whitehurst, June 12, 1937; children—Donald Thomas, Robert Eugene, Charles David. Terminal mgr., Brooks Transp. Co., Washington, 1935-41; mgr. Ft. Terminal VA, Richmond, Va., 1946-48; gen. mgr. Cabell Eanes Advt. Agy., Richmond, 1947, v.p., 1954-56; pvt. practice pub. relations cons., Richmond, 1955-58; dir. pub. relations, advt., A.C.L. R.R., Jacksonville, Fla., 1958-60, asst. v.p., 1961-67; asst. v.p. pub. relations and advt. Seaboard Coast Line R.R. Co., Jacksonville, 1967-73; v.p. pub. relations and advt. Seaboard Coastline Industries, Inc., 1973—; dir. Fla. Pub. Co. Jacksonville, Southeast First Bank of Jacksonville. Active various community drives; past pres. Duval county unit Am. Cancer Soc.; mem. univ. council Jacksonville U. Bd. dirs. Children's Home Soc., North Fla. council Boy Scouts Am., United Community Services, U.S.O., St. John's Country Day Sch.; chmn. bd. trustees Fla. Jr. Coll. at Jacksonville. Served to lt. col. AUS, 1941-46. Mem. Assn. Am. R.R.'s, R.R. Pub. Relations Assn., Fla., Ga. pub. relations assns., Pub. Relations Soc. Am., Assn. R.R. Advt. Mgrs., Nat. Alliance Businessmen (met. chmn.). Roman Catholic. Rotarian. Club: Timuquana Country. Home: 4620 Avon Lane Jacksonville FL 32210 Office: 500 Water St Jacksonville FL 32202

MARTIN, DWIGHT WESLEY, co. exec.; b. Kalamazoo, June 16, 1910; s. Arba and Virgie (Frantz) M.; A.B., Ohio Wesleyan U., 1931; LL.B., U. Cin., 1934; m. Jeannette B. Nichols, Sept. 7, 1936; children—Sally N., Jeannette F., Dwight Wesley (dec.). Admitted to Ohio bar, 1934; with trust dept. Central Trust Co., Cin., 1934-35; asso. Dinsmore, Shohl, Sawyer & Dinsmore, 1935-45, partner, 1945-46; v.p. Crosley Broadcasting Corp., 1946-52; v.p., dir. Gen. Teleradio, Inc. 1952-55, RKO Teleradio, 1955-56; exec. v.p. Lion Television Corp., 1956-59; chmn. bd. Modern Broadcasting Co. of Baton Rouge, Inc., 1956-64; exec. v.p., treas., dir. Royal St. Corp., 1962—; chmn. bd., dir. Royal St. Investment Corp., New Orleans, Interchange Realty Co., Inc., 1963—; dir. Mission Hills Ranch, Inc., Royal St. Devel. Co., Inc., Broadcast Music, Inc., Elec. Industries, Inc., The Urban Corp., Greater Park City Co., DASA Corp. Bd. dirs. Met. Crime Commn. Served as lt. comdr. USNR, 1943-45. Mem. Nat. Assn. Broadcasters (dir. 1958-62), Order of Coif, Phi Beta Kappa, Omicron Delta Kappa. Home: 415 Park Rd Metairie LA 70005 Office: 521 Royal St New Orleans LA 70130

MARTIN, EDMUND CLYDE, state ofcl.; b. Gainesville, Ga., Mar. 8, 1923; s. Webster W. and Winnie (Wood) M.; B.S., U. Ga., 1943, M. Edn., 1951, Ed.D., 1964; m. Leila Carolyn Langford, July 28, 1946; children—Barbara Joan (Mrs. Loren H. Hill), Edmund Clyde. Tchr., Hall County Bd. Edn., Gainesville, Ga., 1946-49; prin., Maysville High Sch., 1949-51, Ila High Sch., 1951-54, Hart County High Sch., Hartwell, 1954-59, Cartersville High Sch., 1959-61; supt. schs., Cartersville City Schs., 1961-65; exec. dir. Ga. Ednl. Improvement Council, Atlanta, 1965—. Mem. Ga. Edn. Coordinating Com., 1966—, Lunch Room Council, 1969—, Ga. Regional Med. Program Regional Adv. Group, 1970—, Treas. Health Careers Council, Inc., 1968-70. Bd. dirs. Ga. State League for Nursing, 1969—. Served with AUS, 1943-46. Mem. N.E.A., Ga. Assn. Educators, Am. Assn. Sch. Adminstrs., Phi Delta Kappa, Kappa Delta Pi. Democrat. Baptist (ordained deacon, chmn. bd. deacons, 1950-60, supt. Sunday sch. 1963-64, Bapt. tng. union dir. 1964-65). Author: College Enrollment of Georgia's 1968 High School Graduates, 1969; Directory of Educational Opportunities in Georgia, 1972-73. Home: 2289 Shasta Way NE Atlanta GA 30345 Office: 7 Hunter St Bldg Atlanta GA 30334

MARTIN, EDWARD, physician; b. Atlanta, Nov. 24, 1910; s. John and Rosemarie (Claxton) M.; B.S., Cornell U., 1931; M.D., Chgo. Med. Sch., 1933; m. Alice Cartwright, Sept. 25, 1935; children—Edward, Benjamin, Hamilton, Intern Presbyn.-St. Lukes Hosp., Chgo., 1933-34, resident, 1934-35; pvt. practice medicine, Decatur, Ga., 1935—. Cons. Decatur Bd. Pub. Health, 1956—. Served as capt. M.C., AUS, 1944-46. Diplomate Am. Bd. Family Practice. Fellow A.C.P.; mem. Ga., Decatur med. socs., A.M.A., Sigma Chi, Alpha Omega Alpha. Address: 3978 Phylis Pl Decatur GA 30032

MARTIN, EDWARD CURTIS, JR., educator; b. Albany, Ga., Aug. 21, 1928; s. Edward Curtis and Mildred Lee (Tyler) M.; B.F.A., U. Ga., 1950, M. Landscape Architecture, 1969; m. Roberta Inman Parker, Mar. 18, 1967; children—Edward Curtis III, Andrew Parker. Landscape architect, Norman C. Butts, Landscape contractor, Atlanta, 1950, M. Thomas Brooks, landscape architect, Birmingham, Ala., 1950-56; univ. landscape architect Miss. State U., Mississippi State, 1956-70, prof. landscape architecture, 1970—. Instr. Nat. Landscape Design Study Courses Nat. Council State Garden Clubs, Inc., 1960—. Mem. Miss. State Bd. Landscape Architects for Profl. Registration, 1973—. Mem. Starkville (Miss.) Park and Recreation Bd., 1973—. Recipient Silver Seal award Nat. Council State Garden Clubs, 1969. Mem. Am. Soc. Landscape Architects (chmn. chpt. edn. com. 1960-61), Garden Clubs Miss. (dir. 1958—), Am. Hort. Soc., Miss. Design Collaborative, Blue Key, Alpha Tau Omega. Presbyn. Rotarian (dir. 1961). Home: 104 Edgewood Dr Starkville MS 39759 Office: PO Drawer MQ Mississippi State MS 39762

MARTIN, FRANCIS LINTON, lawyer; b. Chattanooga, Jan. 6, 1891; s. Francis and Lydia (Linton) M.; Ph.B., Yale, 1912; LL.B., Columbia, 1915; m. Emily T. Kelley, Aug. 17, 1933; 1 dau., Caroline T. (Mrs. Erwin Brady Bartusch). Admitted to Tenn. bar, 1916, since practiced Chattanooga; mem. firm Miller, Martin, Hitching, Tipton, Lenihan & Waterhouse, 1923—. Served as 1st lt., 17th F.A., 2d Div., U.S. Army, 1917-19; AEF in France. Decorated Silver Star (U.S.); Fourragere of Croix de Guerre (France). Mem. Am. Bar Assn., Assn. Life Ins. Counsel. Clubs: Mountain City, Chattanooga Half Century. Home: 1914 Poplar Av Memphis TN 38104 Office: Volunteer Bldg Chattanooga TN 37402

MARTIN, GEORGE DAN, lawyer, state sen.; b. Jackson, Miss., Nov. 29, 1936; s. George Drew and Maggie Lee (O'Quinn) M.; student Ind. U., 1955-56; LL.B., Jackson Sch. Law, 1961; m. Marianna McLain, Dec. 27, 1959; children—Dana Virginia, Garron Patrick. With First Nat. Bank, Jackson, Miss., 1958-59, U.S. P.O., Jackson, 1959-60; admitted to Miss. bar, 1961; practiced in Brandon, 1961—; mem. firm Martin & Martin, 1966—. Partner Farm Bur. Ins. Cos., Rankin County, 1960-67; mem. Miss. Senate, 1968—. Vice chmn. Miss. Central Data Processing Authority, 1970-71; mem. Miss. Soverignty Commn., 1972—. Mem. State Democratic Exec. Com., 1972—. Served with USAF, 1955-58. Recipient Distinguished Service award Brandon Jaycees, 1962. Mem. Am., Miss., Rankin County bar assns., Miss. Jr. C. of C. (state pres. 1966-67), Rankin County C. of C., Sigma Delta Kappa. Baptist (chmn. bd. deacons 1969-70). Home: Bentonwood Dr Brandon MS 39042 Office: Box 9 Corner Hwy 18 and 80 Brandon MS 39042

MARTIN, GEORGE WILLIAM, research scientist; b. Youngstown, O., Apr. 10, 1936; s. George Wendell and Mary Francis (Donald) M.; B.S., Mich. State U., 1959; postgrad. U. Mich. (fellow), 1960, U. Va. (fellow), 1965-70, U. Del., 1967. Research scientist Ingersoll-Rand, Paint Post, N.Y., 1960-62, NASA, Wallops Island, Va., 1962-63, 64—, Am. Electric Power, 1963-64; cons. GWM Works, Wallops Island, 1967—, also dir. Mem. I.E.E.E. (exec. officer eastern shore sect. 1973—). Home: H-20 Wallops Island VA 23337 Office: NASA Wallops Island VA 23337

MARTIN, GLENN CARSON, JR., mfg. co. exec.; b. San Antonio, Dec. 7, 1922; s. Glenn Carson and Sarah Rubye (Robinson) M.; grad. high sch.; m. Mildred Marie Beck, June 20, 1946; children—Glenn Carson III, Becky Ann, Kathleen Marie. With Tex. Scenic Co., Inc., San Antonio, 1946—, pres., 1954. Cons. planning, design of tech. requirements for auditoriums, theatres, civic centers, various sch. systems and archtl. firms in U.S. Mem. Alamo Area council Boy Scouts Am., 1938-68; active San Antonio Archdioce Cath. Com. on Scouting, 1962— (award 1963); fire chief Castle Hills (Tex.) Vol. Fire Dept., 1959-61. Mem. Castle Hills City Council, 1961-69. Served with USAAF, 1941-46. Recipient Distinguished Community Service award City of Castle Hills, 1969. Mem. San Antonio Mfrs. Assn., Tex. Sch. Bus. Ofcls. Assn., USAF Assn., Illuminating Engring. Soc., Soc. Am. Mil. Engrs., Soc. Motion Picture and TV Engrs., Constrn. Specifications Inst., San Antonio C. of C. (chmn. red carpet com. 1967-69, awards 1968, 69). Republican. Rotarian. K.C. Contbr. articles to profl. jours. Home: 118 Herweck Dr Castle Hills San Antonio TX 78213

MARTIN, JAMES GLASGOW, JR., govt. ofcl.; b. Hendersonville, Tenn., May 8, 1918; s. James Glasgow and Edith (Coolidge) M.; student Falls Bus. Coll., Nashville, 1937-38, Internat. Accounting Soc., Chgo., 1949-52; m. Marjorie Collins, Nov. 9, 1942; children—James Glasgow III, John S. Formerly with Gen. Shoe Corp., Gallatin, Tenn.; revenue officer Internal Revenue Service, Chattanooga, 1945-51, div. chief spl. tax fraud squad, Nashville, 1951-52, acting chief Delinquent Accounts and Returns br., Nashville, 1952-54, chief, 1954-59, chief collection div., 1959-62, asst. to dist. dir., 1962-63, asst. dist. dir., Jackson, Miss., 1963-64, dist. dir., 1964-71, asst. regional commr. accounts, collection and taxpayer service, southeast region, Atlanta, 1971—. Chmn. finance and fund raising com. Hiawatha dist. Boy Scouts Am., 1967-68, mem. Andrew Jackson council, 1966-68; chmn. Combined Fed. Campaign, Fed. agys., 1969. Pres. bd. dirs. Interagy. Bd. U.S. Civil Service Com. for Miss.; trustee United Givers Fund. Served to capt. AUS, 1941-45. Decorated Bronze Star medal with bronze oak leaf cluster, Purple Heart, Silver Star; recipient Superior and Outstanding Performance awards Internal Revenue Service. Mem. Jackson Fed. Execs. Assn. (pres.). Presbyn. Kiwanian (pres. 1969). Club: Colonial Country (Jackson). Home: 119 Fairways Dr Hendersonville TN 37075 Office: Federal Office Bldg Peachtree Baker St Atlanta GA 30301

MARTIN, JOHN BEISEL, JR., dentist; b. Freeland, Pa., Oct. 25, 1927; s. John Beisel and L. (Virgil) M.; student Va. Poly. Inst., 1945-46, Ursinus Coll., 1947-49; D.D.S. U. Pa., 1953; m. Sandra Arline Anderson, Dec. 26, 1965. Instr., U. Pa., 1953-55; dentist Saucer Dental Clinic, Phila., 1953-55, Boston-Miami (Fla.) Clinic, 1955—; pvt. practice dentistry, Phila., 1953-55, Coconut Grove, Fla., 1955—. Minister of dissent Soverign Nation of New Atlantis, apptd. by Pres. Leicester Hemingway, 1965—. Bd. dirs. Charity Dental Clinic, Coconut Grove Cares, 1970—; supt. Dade County Youth Fair, 1970—; pres. Miami Indoor Aircraft Assn., 1964—; asso. Salvation Army Charity Clinic, 1964—, Smithsonian Instn., 1968—. Served with AUS, 1945-47. Mem. Psi Omega. Republican. Mem. Christian Ch. Club: Miami Sports Car (pres. 1958-60). Editor Pa. Dental Jour., 1951-53. Address: 3227 Darwin St Coconut Grove FL 33133

MARTIN, JOHN THOMAS, govt. ofcl.; b. N.Y.C., Apr. 29, 1920; s. John Thomas and Bertha (Howard) M.; A.B., Howard U., 1940; student Sch. Law, 1940-41; student U. Wis. Sch. Jour., 1962; m. Hestlene Lee Brooks, June 15, 1941; children—Joan (Mrs. John T. Teaiwa), John Thomas III (dec.), Alan, Theresa, Charles. Commd. 2d lt., U.S. Army, 1941, advanced through grades to col., 1966-68, exec. to counsellor Office Sec. Defense, Washington, 1952-53, 1956-62, 1965-66; ret., 1968; dir. Selective Service, Washington, 1966—. Dir. Met. Capital Corp., Tyroc Constrn. Co. Mem. Capital Health and Welfare Council, 1969; dir. Capitol USO, 1967-70; dir. Nat. Capitol Area council Boy Scouts Am., 1968-69. Decorated Bronze Star medal with one oak leaf cluster. Mem. Am. Soc. Pub. Adminstrs., Retired Officers Assn., Kappa Alpha Psi. Republican. Baptist. Home: 5026 10th St NE Washington DC 20017 Office: 441 G St NW Washington DC 20001

MARTIN, OKIE RAYMOND, architect; b. Memphis, Jan. 13, 1924; s. Okie Raymond and Willie Martha (Peterson) M.; student Southwestern Coll., 1946, Tulane U., 1950; M.S. in Architecture, Va. Poly. Inst., 1953; m. Hazel Mae Brown, Jan. 29, 1949; children—Vann Raymond, Catherine Lynne, Dorothy Leigh. Owner, Raymond Martin. Architect, Memphis, 1955-57; partner Martin & Adams, Architects, Memphis, 1957-61; pres., treas. Martin & Adams Architects, Inc., Memphis, 1961-62; pres., treas. Raymond Martin & Assos. Architects, Inc., Memphis, 1962-73; pres., treas. Martin/Barnett/Assos., Memphis, 1973—. Vice pres. Century Bldg. Corp., 1962—. Gen. chmn. Shelby and Crittenden counties Muscular Dystrophy Assn. Am., 1963, pres. Mid-South chpt., 1970-72, nat. v.p., 1970-72; col., aide de camp on staff Gov. Winfield Dunn, 1971—; chmn. Joint Fire Study Code com. State Tenn., 1971-73, v.p. Bldg. & Fire Code Tenn. Appeals Bd., 1973—. Served to 1st lt. AUS, 1942-46, 50-52. Mem. A.I.A. (Silver medal award 1952, chpt. pres. 1962), Guild for Religious Architecture Tenn. Soc. Architects (pres. 1973, dir.), Memphis C. of C., Tau Sigma Delta, Sigma Nu. Baptist (chmn. deacons 1971-73). Clubs: Executives; Park Woodland Civic (past pres.). Important works include Century Bldg., Memphis, 1959, First Assembly of God Ch., Memphis, 1962, Liberty Nat. Bank-Suburban Bldg., Louisville, 1962, Memphis State U. Sch. Edn. and Campus Sch., 1963, Univ. Center, 1967, Wooddale High Sch., Memphis, 1967,

Activities Bldg. for Walnut St. Bapt. Ch., Louisville, 1970, Memphis State U. Engring Sci. Bldg., 1970, Engring. Tech. Bldg., 1971, Law Sch. addition, 1974. Home: 180 S Goodlett St Memphis TN 38117 Office: 3294 Poplar Av Memphis TN 38111

MARTIN, PATRICK GLENN, fire chief; b. Childress, Tex., Apr. 3, 1930; s. John Middleton and Ila May (Waller) M.; grad. high sch.; m. Jacqueline Pearl Hargett, Nov. 29, 1969; children—Patrick Glenn, Jr., Alana, Barbara, Brenda, Cheri. Fireman, Arlington, Tex., 1952-56, Capt., 1956-58, tng. officer, 1958-62, asst. chief, 1962-65, fire chief, 1965—. Asst. field supr. fire fighting course Tex. A. and M. U., 1970-71. Mem. adv. com. fire protection Tarrant County Jr. Coll., 1968-71. Served with AUS, 1947-50; Korea. Recipient Civil Def. Award Merit Ft. Worth, Tarrant County Civil Def. Office, 1957. Mem. N. Tex. Firemans Assn. (pres. 1970-72), Tex. Fire Chiefs, Southwestern Fire Chiefs, Internat. Fire Chiefs. Baptist. Home: 2611 Monterrey St Arlington TX 76015 Office: 403 W Main St Arlington TX 76010

MARTIN, RACHEL SANGSTER, librarian; b. Mt. Olive, N.C., Aug. 18, 1918; d. Leon Forrest and Bertha (Reaves) Martin; B.A., Brenau Coll., 1939; B.S. in L.S., U. N.C., 1949; M.A., State U. Ia., 1955. Tchr. pub. schs., N.C., 1939-49; asst. reference librarian Auburn (Ala.) U., 1949-51; librarian Mary Baldwin Coll., Staunton, Va., 1951-56; head humanities div. library Fla. State U., Tallahassee, 1956-57; reference and serials librarian Furman U., Greenville, S.C., 1957-66, asso. librarian, 1966—. Mem. Am. (reference and subscription books rev. Com. 1968—, Southeastern (chmn. nominating com. reference services div. 1960, vice chmn., chmn. reference services div. 1964-66), S.C. (sec. 1959, chmn. membership com. 1960-61) library assns., Am. Assn. U. Profs. (pres. Furman U. chpt. 1962-63), Delta Kappa Gamma, Beta Phi Mu, Zeta Tau Alpha. Baptist. Club: Altrusa (rec. sec. Greenville, 1959-61, archivist 1961-63, pres. 1966-68, parliamentarian 1970-71). Compiler index to articles Furman Studies 1959. Home: 220 Covington Rd Greenville SC 29609 Office: Furman U Library Greenville SC 29613

MARTIN, RICHARD BLAZO, chemist; b. Winchendon, Mass., July 1, 1917; s. William Butler and Elizabeth (Ela) M.; A.B., Clark U., 1939, M.A., 1940, Ph.D., 1949; m. Dorothy Mae Holway, Sept. 20, 1941; children—Lawrence Sanborn, Richard Holway, Janet Lois, Jean Leslie. Instr. chemistry Clark U., Worcester, Mass., 1946-49, asst. prof., 1949-53; chemist research br., research and devel. div. AEC, Oak Ridge operations, 1953-56, chief research br., 1956-59, dep. dir. research and devel. div., 1959-66, dep. dir. lab. and univ. dir., 1966-72, asst. br. chief waste mgmt. br., research and tech. support div., 1972-73, phys. scientist classification and tech. support br., research and tech. support div., 1973—. Pack com. chmn. Great Smoky Mountain Council Boy Scouts Am., 1964; pres. Cedar Hill P.T.A., 1962. Served to lt. comdr. USNR, 1941-46; capt. Res. ret. Mem. Am. Chem. Soc. (treas. Central Mass. sect. 1952-53), Res. Officers Assn. (pres. chpt. 1971-72), Am. Nuclear Soc., Sigma Xi, Lambda Chi Alpha. Republican. Clubs: Nat Campers and Hikers Association (pres. 1966-67) (Oak Ridge); Smoky Mountain Coachmen (v.p. 1972-74) (Knoxville). Home: 117 Meadow Rd Oak Ridge TN 37830 Office: PO Box E Oak Ridge TN 37830

MARTIN, SHEDRICK MICHAEL, JR., city ofcl.; b. Savannah, Ga., Jan. 5, 1927; s. Shedrick Michael and Hattie Mae (Mew) Martin; B.S., Savannah State Coll., 1951; grad. FBI Nat. Acad., 1970; m. Laura Bernice Randolph, Jan. 11, 1956; children—Beverly Anne (Mrs. Felipe Alou), Brenda Annette. Clk., U.S. P.O., Atlanta, 1951-52; tchr., Chatham County, Ga., 1952-57; detective Savannah (Ga.) Police Dept., 1957-70; personnel asst. City of Savannah, 1971-72, adminstr. Dept. Pub. Services, 1972—. Served with AUS, 1945-46. Mem. Am. Pub. Works Assn., N.A.A.C.P., Fraternal Order of Police, Holy Name Soc. Roman Catholic. Club: Wolves (Savannah). Home: 17 E Stillwood Circle Savannah GA 31406 Office: PO Box 1027 Savannah GA 31402

MARTIN, THOMAS FLOYD, clergyman; b. Tullahoma, Tenn., Aug. 9, 1942; s. Homer Lee and Carrie Mae (Mangrum) M.; B.A., Vanderbilt U., 1964; M.Divinity, Lexington Theol. Sem., 1968; m. Suzanne DeMoss, June 19, 1965; 1 son, Terry Lee. Ordained to ministry Christian Ch., 1968; minister 1st Ch., Pikeville, Ky., 1968-69, 1st Ch., Dawson Springs, Ky., 1969-72, Shelbyville, Tenn., 1972—. Pres., Dist. 14, Christian Ch. in Ky., 1971-72. Chmn., Dawson Springs Community Center Bd., 1971-72; mem. Mayor's Citizens Adv. Com., Shelbyville, 1973—. Mem. Common Cause, Disciples Peace Fellowship, various ministerial assns. Democrat. Rotarian (pres. 1971-72). Home: PO Box 631 Shelbyville TN 37160 Office: 309 Madison St Shelbyville TN 37160

MARTIN, VERNON NORTHFLEET, educator; b. Benham, Ky., Mar. 25, 1930; s. Oscar F. and Nancy Ellen (Burkhart) M.; B.A., U. Ky., 1955, M.A., 1958, Ph.D., 1968; m. Jessie Mae Worley, Oct. 15, 1950; children—Rebecca, Mark, John. Head polit. sci. dept. Cumberland Coll., Williamsburg, Ky., 1956-63; head. govt. dept. Western Ky. U., Bowling Green, 1963-73, asst. dean Coll. Bus. and Pub. Affairs, 1973—. Served with USNR, 1948-49, 52-53. Home: 2031 Honeysuckle St Bowling Green KY 42101

MARTIN, WADE OMER, JR., state ofcl.; b. Arnaudville, La., Apr. 18, 1911; s. Wade O. and Alice (Mills) M.; B.A., Southwestern La. Inst., 1932, LL.B., La. State U., 1935; m. Juliette Bonnette, Oct. 25, 1938; children—Merle Mary, Marcelle, Wade O., III, David, Wallace, Gregory. Admitted to La. bar, 1935; asst. atty. gen., Baton Rouge, 1935-40; practice of law, Baton Rouge, 1940-44; sec. of state of La., 1944—. Mem. Am., La., East Baton Rouge Parish bar assns., Nat. Assn. Secs. of State (past. pres.; exec. com.), Nat. Assn. Ins. Commrs. (past pres.), Gamma Eta Gamma, Kappa Sigma. K.C. Home: 210 LSU Av Baton Rouge LA 70808 Office: State Capitol Baton Rouge LA 70804

MARTIN, WESTON JOSEPH, educator; b. Church Point, La., Jan. 15, 1917; s. Camile Joseph and Ada Marie (Daigle) M.; B.S., Southwestern La. U., 1937; M.S., La. State U., 1939; Ph.D., U. Minn., 1942; m. Aimie Norma Miller, Feb. 9, 1948; children—Jeanne Weslyn, Wayne Mark, Carol Ann, Grace Ellen, Blair James. Asso. pathologist U.S. Dept. Agr., Mexico and Central Am., 1942-47; asso. pathologist La. Agrl. Exptl. Station, 1947-54; prof. plant pathology La. State U., Baton Rouge, 1954—. Fellow A.A.A.S.; mem. Am. Phytopathol. Soc. (div. pres. 1960, councilor 1961-62), Helminthological Soc. Washington, La. Acad. Sci., Sigma Xi, Gamma Sigma Delta. Contbr. to profl. publs. in field. Home: 1944 Richland Av Baton Rouge LA 70808

MARTIN, WILLIAM ARNOLD, machinery co. exec.; b. Many, La., Nov. 26, 1932; s. James Thomas and Ida Elizabeth (Cobb) M.; student Centenary Coll., 1952-54; B.B.A., Baylor U., 1961; m. Alice Hargis, June 3, 1951; children—Karl David, Kevin Dean. Sr. office clk. Caterpillar Tractor Co., Shreveport, La., 1950-55; with Darr Equipment Co., 1955—, v.p., Dallas, 1969—. Chmn. adv. dirs. Am. Bank & Trust, Irving, Tex., 1973-74. Pres. Traffic Safety Commn., Irving, 1973—; pres. Greater Carpenter Freeway Improvement Assn., Irving, 1966—; mem. adv. council Ind. Sch. Dist. Technical-Vocational Edn., Irving, 1973-74. Mem. Dallas County Democratic Exec. Com., 1970-74; Dem. precinct chmn., 1970-74. Recipient Boss of Year award Irving Jr. C. of C., 1974. Mem. Dallas Data Processing Mgmt. Assn., Sales and Marketing Execs. Internat., Irving C. of C. (div. V pres. 1970-74). Baptist (deacon 1951-74). Kiwanian (dir. 1970-72, 74—). Home: 424 E Northgate Dr Irving TX 75062 Office: PO Box 20737 Dallas TX 75220

MARTIN, WILLIAM ARTHUR, JR., librarian; b. Burlingame, Kan., May 11, 1922; s. William Arthur and Edna LaVerne (Harris) M.; A.B., Coll. Emporia, 1949; M.L.S., Kan. State Tchrs. Coll., 1953; divorced; children—William Arthur III, Margaret Angela. Stacks supr., undergrad. librarian U. Kan., 1953-58; head circulation dept., dir. reader services U. Mo., 1958-68; dir. library Okla. Coll. Liberal Arts, Chickasha, 1968—. Mem. adv. bd. Okla. Title III; mem. Okla. Gov.'s Conf. on Libraries; cons., creative writing program Am. Assn. U. Women. Served with AUS, 1942-45. Mem. Am., Okla. (pres. coll. div. 1972-73), Southwestern (v.p. coll. div. 1973-74), Mo. (pres. 1967-68) library assns., Okla. Edn. Assn. (chpt. pres. 1971-72), N.E.A., Grady County, Okla. hist. socs., D.A.V. Episcopalian (vestry). Lion (Sight Conservation award, dir.). Contbr. to profl. jours. Home: 504 S 6th St Chickasha OK 73018

MARTIN, WILLIAM HAYWOOD III, life scientist; b. Bath Springs, Tenn., Nov. 29, 1938; s. William Haywood and Mary (Isbell) M.; B.S., Tenn. Technol. U., 1960; M.S., U. Tenn., 1966, Ph.D., 1971; m. Sybil Ann Hendrix, Aug. 29, 1965; children—Thomas McMillan, Marianne Hendrix. Asso. prof. dept. gen. studies Eastern Ky. Univ., Richmond, 1969—. Dir. Ky. Jr. Acad. Sci. Eastern Ky. Univ. grantee, 1971-73. Mem. Tenn., Ky. acads. sci., A.A.A.S., Assn. Southeastern Biologists, Ecol. Soc. Am., Sigma Xi. Independent. Methodist. Mason (Shriner). Home: 403 Springfield St Richmond KY 40475 Office: Dept Gen Studies Eastern Ky Univ Richmond KY 40475

MARTIN, ZENON AGUSTIN, constrn. co. exec.; b. Havana, Cuba, Apr. 12, 1921; s. Agustin P. and Matilde S. (Jimenez) M.; B.A., Havana U., 1944, M.A., 1946, C.E., 1948; m. Olga Freyre, Feb. 26, 1951; 1 son, Zenon B. Architect, Obras Publicas de Cuba, 1946-48; pres. Zenon Martin & Asso., architect, Havana, 1948-60; insp. Reed, Basorsa & Menendez, San Juan, P.R., 1961-63; with Diaz & Asso., Ponce, P.R., 1964—, v.p., 1974—; pres. T.D. City Constrn. Corp., Ponce, 1968—. Mem. Am. Soc. for Testing and Materials, Am. Concrete Inst., Exile Architects Assn. Roman Catholic. Club: Ponce (P.R.) Yacht and Fishing. Home: Americas Bldg Ponce City Apt #706 Ponce PR 00731 Office: TD Construction Corp PO Box 230 Ponce PR 00731

MARTINEZ, ANITA (MRS. ALFRED MARTINEZ), city ofcl.; b. Dallas, Dec. 8, 1925; d. Joe Franco and Anita Trevinio (Mongaras) Nanes; student Dallas Coll. So. Meth. U., 1945; m. Alfred Martinez, Jan. 27, 1946; children—Alfred Joseph, Steve Dan, Patricia Ann, Rene Orlando. Mem. Dallas City Council, 1969—. Mem. Dallas Community Action Head Start Program, 1969—; fund solicitor West Dallas Youth Center, 1965—; mem. criminal justice com. N. Tex. Central Council Govts.; mem. text book adv. com. Dallas Ind. Sch. Dist.; mem. designs of city com. Goals for Dallas; active fund raising Children's Med. Center; founder Mexican-Am. Block Partnership Program; mem. gen. council Dallas Young Adult Inst.; mem. Jesuit Parents Club, Children's Sch. Safety Com.; active Mobility Adjustment Retrained Workers, So. Meth. U.; initiated Weekly Council Report column in El Sol newspaper. Bd. dirs. Met. YWCA, Nat. Center for Vol. Action. Recipient Worthy Woman award Citizens Nat. Bank, 1968; named One of Ten Outstanding Women News Shapers, Dallas Times Herald, 1968, 69, 70. Mem. ladies aux. Dallas Restaurant Assn. (promoter Tasting Bee for charity), Women's Council Dallas County, St. Monica Spanish Lit. Guild, Tex. Municipal League. Home: 3866 Beutel Ct Dallas TX 75229 Office: City Hall Dallas TX 75201

MARTINEZ, AUGUSTO JULIO, physician; b. Camagüey, Cuba, Apr. 12, 1930; s. Augusto M. and Aurora (Avila) M.; B.Sc., Inst. Camagüey, 1950; M.D., U. Havana (Cuba), 1959; postgrad. Case Western Res. U., 1967-69; m. Josephine Bridget O'Donnell, Oct. 16, 1968; children—Killeen Josephine, Bridget Elizabeth, Mary Ondina. Came to U.S., 1962, naturalized, 1968. Intern Univ. Hosps., Havana, 1960-61; resident St. Alexis Hosp., Cleve., 1962-64; resident, fellow in pathology U. Tenn., Memphis, 1964-66, asso. prof., 1971-72; practice medicine, specializing in neuropathology, Richmond, 1969-71, Memphis, 1971-72; asst. prof. neuropathology Med. Coll. Va., Richmond, 1969-71, asso. prof., 1972—. USPHS spl. fellow, 1967-69. Diplomate Am. Bd. Pathology. Fellow Am. Acad. Neurology; mem. Am. Coll. Pathologists, Am. Soc. Clin. Pathologists, Am. Assn. Neuropathologists, So. Med. Assn., A.M.A. Contbr. to profl. jours. Home: 8041 Ammonett St Richmond VA 23235 Office: 1100 Marshall St Richmond VA 23298

MARTINEZ, LUIS APONTE, archbishop, univ. chancellor; b. Lajas, P.R., Aug. 4, 1922; s. Santiago E. Aponte and Rosa (Martinez) M.; student San Idlefonso Sem., San Juan, P.R., 1944, St. John's Sem., Boston, 1950; LL.D. (hon.), Fordham U., 1965. Ordained priest Roman Catholic Ch., 1950; asst. pastor in Patillas, P.R., 1950-51; pastor in Maricao, P.R., 1951-53, Santa Isabel, P.R., 1953-55, Aibonito, P.R., 1957-60; sec. to bishop of Ponce, P.R., 1955-57; aux. bishop of Ponce, 1960-63, bishop, 1963-64; archbishop of San Juan, 1964-73; created cardinal, 1973; chancellor Cath. U. P.R. at Ponce, 1964—. Served as chaplain P.R. N.G., 1957-60. Lion. Address: 50 Cristo St Box 1967 San Juan PR 00903

MARTINEZ, OLIMPIO R(AMON), constrn. mgmt. cons.; b. Santurce, P.R., July 26, 1926; s. Oscar O. and Soledad (Munoz) M.; B.S. in Civil Engring., Va. Poly. Inst., 1946; m. Isabel Llado, Dec. 18, 1948; children—Amalia I., Elisa S., Lucia M. Jr. structural engr. P.R. Water Resources Authority, San Juan, 1946-47, asst. structural engr., 1947-48, asst. constrn. engr., 1948-59, structural design engr., 1952-54; constrn. engr. Oscar Martinez, Inc., San Juan, 1950-51; structural design engr. Robert L. Brown & Assos. Co., Roanoke, Va., 1951-52; asst. project engr. Raymond Internat., Inc., San Juan, 1954-56, project engr., 1956-58, asst. dist. mgr., 1958-63; project mgr. Frederick Snare Corp., San Juan, 1963-64, Interstate Gen. Contractors, Inc., San Juan, 1964-66, Glenwal Constrn. Corp., San Juan, 1966-67; prin. partner Martinez & Torres Constrn. Mgmt. Cons., Santurce, P.R., 1967—. Mem. P.R. Inst. Architects, Engrs. and Surveyors, Am. Soc. C.E., Soc. Am. Mil. Engrs., Nat., Va. socs. profl. engrs., Constrn. Specification Inst. Home: 9-B 4 St Parkside Guaynabo PR 00920 Office: El Monte Mall Hato Rey PR 00918

MARTINEZ, ROBERT, assn. exec.; b. Tampa, Fla., Dec. 25, 1934; s. Serafin M. and Ida (Carreno) M.; B.S., U. Tampa, 1957; M.A., U. Ill., 1964; m. Mary Jane Marino, Dec. 19, 1954; children—Sharon Marie, Robert Alan. Tchr. social studies Hillsborough County (Fla.) Bd. Pub. Instrn., Tampa, 1957-62, 63-66, dept. head, 1957-62; exec. dir. Hillsborough Classroom Tchrs. Assn. Inc., Tampa, 1966—; sec.-treas. CTA River Apts., Inc. Instr. econs. U. Tampa, summer 1965; mgmt. cons. labor and indsl. relations, 1964-67. Sec., Hillsborough Polit. Action Com. for Edn., 1966—; lobbyist for edn. Fla., 1967—. Mem. Model Cities Adv. Com. on Edn. Mgmt. trustee Employee Welfare Trust Fund, Tampa, 1965—; v.p. West Tampa Little League, 1973. Mem. N.E.A. (task force commn. on urban edn. 1968), Fla. Edn. Assn., Hillsborough Classroom Tchrs. Assn., U. Ill., U. Tampa alumni assns., Urban Com. Exec. Secs., Greater Tampa C. of C., Fla. Council on Urban Edn. Assns. (sec.-treas.). Democrat. Clubs: Tampa Bay Boulevard School Dad's, Suncoast Illini (pres.). Contbr. articles to publs. Home: 4647 San Jose St Tampa FL 33609 Office: 4505 N Rome Av Tampa FL 33603

MARTINEZ-LOPEZ, JORGE IGNACIO, physician; b. Santruce, P.R., Oct. 5, 1926; s. Jorge and Dolores (Lopez) Martinez; student U. P.R., 1943-44; M.D., La. State U., 1950; m. Mona Hagan, June 12, 1950; children—Jorge Alan, Anthony James, Ricardo, Matthew Joseph. Intern Arecibo (P.R.) Dist. Hosp., 1950-51; practice gen. medicine, Elizabeth, La., 1953-54; resident Charity Hosp., New Orleans, 1954-57; cardiovascular trainee Med. Center, La. State U., New Orleans, 1957-59, mem. faculty, 1957—, asso. prof. medicine, 1963-70, prof., 1970—; practice medicine, specializing in cardiology, New Orleans, 1957—; mem. staff Charity Hosp., Hotel Dieu, Delgado Rehab. Center (all New Orleans). Pres. Club de P.R., New Orleans, 1972-73; mem. council Boy Scouts Am. Served with M.C., AUS, 1951-53; Germany. Diplomate Am. Bd. Internal Medicine. Fellow Am. Coll. Cardiology, Am. Coll Chest Physicians, A.C.P., Am. Heart Assn. Council Clin. Cardiology; mem. La. Heart Assn. (pres. elect), New Orleans Acad. Internal Medicine (pres. 1970), La., Orleans Parish med. socs., Res. Officers Assn., Southeastern Clin. Club (pres 1972-73), Alpha Omega Alpha. Contbr. to profl. jours. Home: 3712 James Dr Metairie LA 70003 Office: 1542 Tulane Av New Orleans LA 70112

MARTINEZ-MALDONADO, MANUEL, physician; b. Yauco, P.R., Aug. 25, 1937; s. Manuel and Josefa M. (Maldonado) Martinez Crespo. B.S., U. P.R., 1957; M.D. (Nat. Found. fellow), Temple U., 1961; m. Nivia Elean Rivera, Dec. 13, 1959; children—Manuel, David, Ricardo, Pablo. Intern, St. Charles Hosp., Toledo, 1961-62; resident San Juan VA Hosp., also U. P.R. Hosp., 1962-65; fellow nephrology U. Tex., Southwestern Med. Sch., 1965-67; med. dir. dialysis unit Parkland Hosp., 1967-68; chief nephrology sect. Houston VA Hosp., 1968-73; faculty medicine Baylor Coll. Medicine, Houston, 1968-73, prof., 1973, asso. dir. nephrology sect., 1968-73; practice medicine specializing in nephrology, Houston, 1968-73, San Juan, 1973—; asso. chief staff San Juan (P.R.) VA Hosp., 1973—. Pres.-elect Inst. Hispanic Culture Houston, 1972-73; v.p. Bio-Med. Applications Houston, 1972-73. Lederle Internat. fellow, 1967. Fellow A.C.P.; mem. Am. Soc. Clin. Investigation, Am. Fedn. Clin. Research, Central Soc. Clin. Research, So. Soc. Clin. Investigation, Alpha Omega Alpha. Democrat. Roman Catholic. Home: 7 Petunia St Santa Maria Rio Piedras PR 00927 Office: PO Box 4867 San Juan PR 00936

MARTINSONS, HERMANIS, architect; b. Riga, Latvia, Mar. 22, 1919; s. John and Klara (Veveris) M.; student U. Riga, 1940-44; Certified Engr., Sch. Principles Architecture, Tech. U. Hanover, Germany, 1949; m. Mirdza Zandmanis, Apr. 5, 1952; 1 dau., Clara Ann. Came to U.S., 1951, naturalized, 1958. Pvt. archtl. practice, Hanover, Germany, 1949-50; architect E.A. Fretz, architects. Dallas, 1951-55; pvt. archtl. practice, Dallas, 1955—. Mem. A.I.A. (asso.), Tex. Soc. Architects (asso.), Dallas C. of C., Latvian Student Assn. (chmn. 1947-48). Lutheran (v.p. brotherhood 1959-62, deacon, councilman). Home: 5507 Winston Ct Dallas TX 75220 Office: 4515 Prentice St Dallas TX 75206

MARTONE, PETER WAYNE, lawyer; b. Norfolk, Va., May 2, 1941; s. Alexander L. and Filomena Virginia (Console) M.; A.B., Duke U., 1964; LL.B., Washington and Lee U., 1967; m. Nancy Charlton Sugg, Aug. 13, 1966; children—Susan Kelly, Peter Wayne. Admitted to Va. bar, 1967, since practiced in Norfolk; partner Canoles, Mastracco, Martone, Barr & Russell, 1969—; dir. corps. Lectr. estate planning Va. Bankers Assn., 1971. Campaign treas. incumbent Va. State Legislature, 1973. Mem. Va., Norfolk-Portsmouth bar assns., Va. State Bar, Phi Beta Kappa, Omicron Delta Kappa, Order of Coif. Roman Catholic. Clubs: Norfolk Yacht and Country; Cedar Point (Nansemond, Va.); Harbor (Norfolk). Editor in chief Washington and Lee Law Rev., 1966-67. Contbr. to profl. publs. Home: 1509 Runnymede Rd Norfolk VA 23508 Office: 1620 Virginia Nat Bank Bldg Norfolk VA 23510

MARTZ, GLENN EVERETT, journalist, author, lectr.; b. Livonia, Mo., Sept. 1, 1900; s. Seth Thomas and Lydia Dea (Speak) M.; student Kirksville (Mo.) State Tchrs. Coll., 1924, No. State Tchrs. Coll., S.D., 1926-27; m. Beverly Margaret Smith, June 4, 1936 (dec.); children—Dale Ellsworth, Glenn Eldon, Sally Ann (Mrs. Edward Southgate), Mary Lou (Mrs. Malcolm Minor); m. 2d, Annie Louise Monan, June 2, 1972. Editor Am.-News, Aberdeen, S.D., 1930-36, A.P., Bismarck, N.D., 1945-46, U.P.I., Washington, 1947-53; asso. editor Banner, Nashville, 1965-69; staff writer Look Mag., Des Moines, 1940; pub. Washington News Beat, 1954-63; editorial writer Pensacola (Fla.) New-Jour. Field mgr. Office Def. Transp., Minn., N.D., 1943-45; dir. pub. relations Marine Resources div. Ala. Dept. Conservation, 1971-74. Republican. Roman Catholic. Home: 534 Jackson St Summerdale AL 36580

MARUYAMA, KOSHI, pathologist, virologist, educator; b. Sapporo, Hokkaido, Japan, Feb. 19, 1932; s. Kotaro and Eiko (Nakamura) M.; M.D., Hokkaido U., 1957, D.Med. Sc., 1962; m. Rumy Misawa, May 6, 1961; children—Nariyuki, Narihiro, Yumie. Came to U.S., 1967. Intern Sapporo (Japan) Municipal Gen. Hosp., 1957-58; resident Hokkaido U. Sch. Medicine, Sapporo, 1958-62; asso. mem. staff dept. medicine Sapporo (Japan) Municipal Gen. Hosp., 1961-62; mem. staff Nat. Inst. for Leprosy Research, Tokyo, Japan, 1963-65; mem. staff Nat. Cancer Center, Tokyo, 1965-67; asst. prof. virology U. Tex. M.D. Anderson Hosp. and Tumor Inst., Houston, 1967—; asso. faculty mem. U. Tex. Grad. Sch. Biomed. Scis., Houston, 1968—. Fellow N.Y. Acad. Scis., Japanese Pathological Soc.; mem. Japanese Cancer Assn., Japanese Leprosy Assn., Japanese Soc. Reticuloendothelial System, Japanese Soc. Electron Microscopy, A.A.A.S., Am. Assn. Cancer Research, Am. Assn. Pathologists and Bacteriologists, Leukemia Soc. Am. (scholar 1968-73), Electron Microscopy, Soc. Am., Internat. Assn. for Comparative Research on Leukemia and Related Diseases, Am. Soc. Microbiology, Soc. Exptl. Biol. Medicine. Contbr. numerous articles on pathology and virology to med. and sci. jours. Home: 7923 Pella Dr Houston TX 77036 Office: 6723 Bertner St Houston TX 77025

MARVEL, MASON EDWIN, univ. adminstr.; b. Brewton, Ala., Dec. 11, 1921; s. Mason Edward and Augusta Teresa (Ellis) M.; B.S., U. Mass., 1950; M.S., Va. Poly. Inst., 1952; Ph.D., W.Va. U., 1970; m. Audrey Louise Jones, Sept. 21, 1945; children—Daniel, Priscilla, Margaret. Asst. in horticulture W.Va. U., 1951-56; tech. salesman Cal. Chem. Co., 1956-57; prof. extension U. Fla., Gainesville, 1957-70, chief party, team Vietnam, 1970-72, asst. dir. tech. assistance internat. programs, 1972—. Cons. United Fruit Corp., 1967-70, U.S. AID, 1969-70, Hanover Brands, 1973—, also to firms in Latin Am., Caribbean and S.E. Asia, 1966—. Instl. rep. N. Fla. Boy Scouts Am., 1960-66; mem. local com. Farmers Home Adminstrn., 1973—. Served to 1st lt. USAAF, 1942-45; PTO. Recipient Outstanding Service award Nat. Jr. Vegetable Growers Assn., 1963, First Class Merit award Govt. Vietnam, 1972. Mem. Am. Soc. Hort. Scis., Fla. State Hort. Soc. (v.p. 1964), Gamma Sigma Delta, Epsilon Sigma Phi.

Republican. Methodist (trustee, chmn. bd. 1960-68). Home: 2030 NW 71st St Gainesville FL 32605

MARVIN, DANIEL EZRA JR., ednl. adminstr.; b. East Stroudsburg, Pa., Apr. 25, 1938; s. Daniel Ezra and Hazel Elizabeth (Meitzler) M.; student Susquehanna U., 1956-58; B.S. in Edn., East Stroudsburg State Coll., 1960; M.S. in Zoology, Ohio U., 1962; Ph.D. in Physiology, Va. Poly. Inst., 1967; m. Maxine James, June 15, 1958; children—Bryan, Laurie, Amy. Grad. asst. Ohio U., Athens, 1960-61, instr. biology, 1961-62; asst. prof. biology Radford Coll., Va., 1962-66, prof., 1966-67, dean div. natural scis., 1967-68, v.p. acad. affairs, 1968-70, acting pres. 1970; asso. dir. State Council Higher Edn. for Va., Richmond, 1970-72, dir., 1972—. Pres. Appalachia Ednl. Lab.; mem. Gov's. Manpower Planning Council; mem. Va. Drug Abuse Control Council. Mich. State U. grantee, 1965, NSF grantee, 1966-67, Theodore Roosevelt Research Found., 1964, Ford Found. Program, U. Cal. at Berkeley, 1970. Mem. Sigma Xi., Phi Kappa Phi, Chi Beta Phi. Contbr. articles to profl. jours. Home: 916 Elaine Av Richmond VA 23235 Office: 911 E Broad St Richmond VA 23219

MARVIN, JOHN GEORGE, clergyman, ch. orgn. exec.; b. Summit, N.J., May 8, 1912; s. George and Caroline (Whitman) M.; B.S., Davidson Coll., 1933; Th.B., Princeton, 1936; D.D., Coll. Emporia, 1964; LL.D., Tarkio Coll., 1964; m. Elizabeth Anne Wheater, June 30, 1944; children—Caroline Wheater (Dorney), Elizabeth Anne, Martha Jane, Frances Alice. Ordained to ministry Presbyn. Ch., 1936; pastor, Windsor, N.Y., 1936-37, Montrose, Pa., 1937-44, Lewistown, Pa., 1944-52, Denton, Tex., 1952-61; presbytery exec. Greater Kansas City, Mo., 1961-65; pastor 1st Presbyn. Ch., Bartlesville, Okla., 1965-69; sr. minister Chevy Chase Presbyn. Ch., Washington, 1969—. Mem. exec. com. Pa. Council Chs., 1949-52, Tex. Council Chs., 1953-61; mem. exec. com., long range chmn. Greater Kansas City Council Chs., 1962-65; chmn. campus Christian Life Tex. Synod, 1958-61; chmn. nat. mission Pa. Synod, 1949-52; sec. nomination com. Gen. Assembly U.P. Ch., 1955-58, chmn. com. on baptized children, 1969-70, mem. com. of nine on synod boundaries, 1970-72; bd. dirs. Midwest Christian Counseling Center, 1963-69, Presbyn. Homes of Okla., Inc., 1966-69; mem. jud. commn. Synod of Okla.-Ark., 1966-69; mem. strategy com. Bd. Nat. Missions, 1968-70. Bd. dirs., mem. exec. and acad. coms. Tarkio Coll., 1961-67; bd. dirs. Westminster Found., Pa. State U., 1945-52, N. Tex. State U., 1952-61; chmn. constnl. procedures Washington City Presbytery, 1969-72; bd. visitors Warren Wilson Coll. Mem. Beta Theta Pi. Republican. Rotarian. Contbr. articles to religious publs. Home: 11912 Gregerscroft Rd Potomac MD 20854 Office: One Chevy Chase Circle Washington DC 20015

MARVIN, MURRAY JOSEPH, life ins. co. exec.; b. Green County, O., June 15, 1913; s. Murray Joseph and Iona (Gee) M.; B.S., W.Va. State Coll., 1936; M.B.A., U. Chgo., 1960; m. Delores Kathleen Jackson, Dec. 31, 1946. Partner with wife Marvin & Marvin, pub. relations and advt. agy., Chgo., 1947-52; exec. dir. Nat. Ins. Assn., Chgo., 1950-61; dir. planning N.C. Mut. Life Ins. Co., Durham, 1961-71, v.p. planning and communication, 1971—; instr. Grad. Sch. Bus. N.C. Central U., Durham, part time, 1962-66. Mem. 3 man cons. team reviewing activities local anti-poverty agy. Operation Breakthrough, 1965-66; mem. Pres. Nixon's Urban Renewal Task Force, 1969; mem. budget com. United Fund, 1966-71, v.p., 1973. Bd. dirs. Children's Mus. Served with USNR, 1944-46. Recipient Crosthwait award Chgo. Ins. Assn., 1961, 40th Anniversary award Nat. Ins. Assn., 1961. Mem. Am. Mgmt. Assn., Am. Ins Mgmt., Pub. Relations Soc. Am., Life Advertisers Assn., Kappa Alpha Psi. Republican. Episcopalian. Rotarian. Home: 909 Dupree St Durham NC 27701 Office: Mutual Plaza Durham NC 27701

MARX, DONALD HENRY, plant pathologist; b. Ocean Falls, B.C., Can., Oct. 3, 1936; s. Edmund N. and Frances (Gorski) M.; B.S., U. Ga., 1962, M.S., 1963; Ph.D., N.C. State U., 1966; m. Selina Van Giesen, Dec. 21, 1957; children—Selina, Teresa, Beth, Donald, Frank. Plant pathologist, project leader U.S. Dept. Agr. Forest Service, S.E., Athens, Ga., 1963—. Mem. grad. faculty U. Fla., 1973—, N.C. State U., 1973, Pa. State U., 1972, U. Ga., 1967—. Served with USMC, 1953-57. Recipient Superior Service award U.S. Dept. Agr., 1970, Regional awards in forestry and agr. Sears Roebuck, Forest Disease Workshop, 1970. Mem. Am. Phytopath. Soc. (com. chmn. 1971—), Phytophthora Work Group (co-chmn. 1970—), Internat. Union Forest Research Orgn., Sigma Xi. Club: Bass Anglers Sportsman Soc. (Montgomery, Ala.). Home: 465 Camelot Dr Athens GA 30601 Office: Carlton St Athens GA 30602

MARX, JAMES HENRY, govt. ofcl.; b. Green Bay, Wis., Sept. 29, 1925; s. Henry and Alvina (Mueller) M.; student Newberry Coll., 1943-45; B.S., Duke U., 1946; M.B.A., Harvard, 1958; m. Eddie Beatrice Owen, Feb. 9, 1952; children—Marilyn, Owen, James Jr., Barbara. Commd. ensign USN, 1946, advanced through grades to comdr., 1963; chief emergency supply operations, Def. Supply Agy.; pres., chmn. Navy Fed. Credit Union, 1961-63; pres. United Nat. Bank, Washington, 1963-67; treas. Overseas Service Corp., Washington, 1967-68; sr. v.p., treas. Young World Corp., Washington, 1968-70; financial cons., Washington, 1970-71; dir. capital devel. U.S. Dept. Commerce, Washington, 1971—; dir. Wellmar, Inc., Antaya Bros. Inc., Techmod Corp. Lectr. U. Va., Charlottesville, 1961-64, George Washington U., Washington, 1961-64, Howard U., Washington, 1963-68. Active Boy Scouts Am., 1962-72; mem. curriculum com. Alexandria (Va.) Sch. System, 1973-74; pres. Alexandria P.T.A. Council, 1971—. Dir. D.C. chpt. Am. Cancer Soc., Piccard Found., Lucerne, Switzerland. Decorated Legion Merit. Mem. Bus. Profl. Assn. N.E., Washington Soc. Investment Analysis, Financial Fedn., D.C. C. of C. (dir.). Home: 4709 Surry Pl Alexandria VA 22304 Office: Dept Commerce Washington DC 20230

MASCIOCCHI, PIUS JAMES, bldg., constrn. exec.; b. Dudley, Pa., Nov. 25, 1913; s. Joseph and Paulina (Mosca) M.; B.S. in C.E., Drexel U., 1937. With E.I. duPont de Nemours & Co., Wilmington, Del., 1936—, cost contract supr. engring. dept., Wilmington, 1941-47, project closing supr., 1947-51, engring. office supt. Savannah River Plant, AEC, Augusta, Ga., 1951—. Chmn. United Fund, 1968. Fellow Am. Soc. C.E. (mem. local qualifications com. 1954—, br. pres. 1954, state dir. 1957, 69); mem. S.C. Soc. Engrs. (dir. 1966). Roman Catholic (pres. Holy Name Soc. 1960). K.C. (4 deg.). Home: 2426 Kings Way Augusta GA 30904 Office: E I DuPont de Nemours & Co PO Box 117 Augusta GA 30903

MASDEN, HOWARD SEEFELD, social work exec.; b. Milw., Feb. 15, 1909; s. Charles Pitman and Louise (Seefeld) M.; student Lawrence Coll., 1929-30; B.A., U. Ia., 1953; M.S. in Social Work, U. Tex., 1955; children—(by previous marriage) Sally Louise (Mrs. Horace Houston), Nancy Lee (Mrs. J.O. Duncan, Jr.); m. 2d, Annie Laurie Davis, Dec. 22, 1950. With Tex. Dept. Pub. Welfare, 1950-63, asst. dir. child welfare, 1958-63; dir. child care, edn. and tng. Tex. Youth Council, Austin, 1964-72, dir. ednl. program adminstrn., 1972—. Active United Fund, 1958; Sponsor S.W. Tex. Ednl. TV Council, 1969. Bd. dirs. Tex. Social Welfare Assn., 1960-64, treas., 1963-64. Recipient Gov.'s citation for service to mentally retarded, 1966. Mem. Nat. Assn. Social Workers, Acad. Certified Social Workers, Nat. Assn. Tng. Schs. and Juvenile Agys., A.A.A.S., Phi Alpha Delta. Methodist. Home: 2005 Mimosa Dr Austin TX 78745 Office: 201 E 14th St Austin TX 78701

MASELLA, ROGER PAUL, prosthodontist; b. N.Y.C., Sept. 21, 1941; s. Aristide Bartholomew and Ruth Theresa (Garfinkel) M.; B.S., Coll. City N.Y., 1962; D.D.S., N.Y. U. Sch. Dentistry, 1966; M.Sci. in Dentistry, Mayo Grad. Sch. Medicine U. Minn., 1972; m. Marie Marthe Helene Therrien, June 4, 1966; children—Brigitte Tina, Erik Roger. Intern U.S. Naval Hosp., Camp Pendleton, Cal., 1966-67; resident in prosthodontics Mayo Clinic, Rochester, 1969-72; practice dentistry specializing in maxillofacial prosthodontics, Biloxi, Miss., 1972—; mem. staff Coastal Med. Center. Served with Dental Corps, USN, 1966-69. Recipient Dr. Samuel Hess Meml. award N.Y. Sch. Dentistry, 1966. Mem. Am. Dental Assn., Omicron Kappa Upsilon. Home: 3409 Nottingham Rd Ocean Springs MS 39564 Office: PO Box 4080 Biloxi MS 39531

MASHBURN, MARIAN GRIFFIN, realtor, civic worker; b. Tallapoosa, Ga., June 13, 1919; d. Charter W. and Emma (MacDonald) Griffin; U. Ala., 1942; m. John Blaine Mashburn, Oct. 24, 1942; 1 dau., Marsha Anita. Sales rep. W.C. and A.N. Miller Devel. Co., Washington, 1955-60; asso. realtor Belle Harris Realtor, Jacksonville, Fla., 1961-64, Stockton, Whatley, Davin & Co., 1964-69; realtor, 1970—. Publicity dir. Girl Scouts Am. Wilmington, N.C., 1953; bus. mgr. Jr. League Children's Theatre, Wilmington, 1954; docent Smithsonian Inst. Washington, 1955; mem. advt. staff Antique Show, Washington, 1959; mem. Jr. League Am., 1949. Recipient White House Youth Conf. award, 1959. Mem. Jacksonville Bd. Realtors. Home: 4613 Waverly Lane Jacksonville FL 32210 Office: 2000 Corporate Sq Blvd Jacksonville FL 32216

MASHMAN, JOSEPH, aircraft co. exec.; b. Chgo., Apr. 17, 1916; s. Samuel and Rebecca (Lechman) M.; student Armour Inst. Tech., 1933-37; postgrad. U. Buffalo, 1943-45; m. Barbara Bridges, Apr. 3, 1965; children (by previous marriage)—Joanne Susan, Barbara Jean (Mrs. Merrick H. Reese), Steve Edgar, Sally Elizabeth (Mrs. Richard Feffer). Sr. exptl. test pilot Bell Aircraft Corp., Niagara Falls, N.Y., 1943-45; chief exptl. test pilot Bell Helicopter Corp., Niagara Falls, 1945-51, dir. market devel., Fort Worth, 1951-60, asst. v.p. marketing projects, 1960-68, v.p. spl. projects, 1968—. Rep. U.S. Vertical Lift Industry on FAA Com., 1958-63; cons. on helicopters to White House, Washington, 1964-69; mem. research engring. adv. com. Nat. Security Indsl. Assn., 1970—. Decorated Gold Medal Award for Valor (Peru); Presidential Cavaliere dell'Ordinae (Italy); recipient Golden Plate award Am. Acad. Achievement, 1965. Fellow Am. Helicopter Soc. (hon.), Australian Helicopter Soc. (hon.), Helicopter Soc. India (hon.), Am. Inst. Aeronautics and Astronautics (asso.), Royal Aero. Soc. Great Britain (asso.); mem. Am. Helicopter Soc. (pres. 1970-71, chmn. bd. 1971-72), Am. Acad. Achievement (bd. govs. 1965—), Assn. U.S. Army, Army Aviation Assn. Am., Quiet Birdmen, Internat. Order Characters, Soc. Exptl. Test Pilots, Helicopter Assn. Am., Twirly Birds Soc. (founding mem.). Home: 3310 Fairmount St Dallas TX 75201 Office: PO Box 482 Fort Worth TX 76101

MASIKO, PETER, JR., coll. pres.; b. Vera Cruz, Pa., Mar. 18, 1914; s. Peter, Sr., and Sophia (Baker) M.; B.A. with highest honors, Lehigh U., 1936; M.A. (fellow), U. Ill., 1937, Ph.D., 1939; m. Anne E. Fetterolf, July 9, 1932; children—Elaine Irene (Mrs. James Salapatas), Peter, III. Instr. U. Ill., 1936-39; with Wright Jr. Coll., Chgo., 1939-56, successively instr., chmn. social sci. dept., asst. dean, became dean, 1950; exec. dean Chgo. City Jr. Coll., 1956-62; pres. Miami-Dade Community Coll., Miami, Fla., 1962—; economist Bd. Investigation and Research, Washington, summer 1942. Mem. U.S. Dept. Def. adv. com. on edn. in armed forces; mem. edn. commn. Dade County Community Relation Bd. Mem. exec. bd. S. Fla. council Boy Scouts Am.; bd. dirs. Dade County Med. Research and Health Services Found., United Fund, S. Fla. Comprehensive Health Planning Council; mem. Dade County Oceanographic Sci. Park Adv. Com. Mem. steering com. mental health tng. and research So. Regional Edn. Bd. Mem. Am. Econ. Asso., Am. Assn. Sch. Adminstrs. (mem. com. on founds.), Am. Assn. Community and Jr. Colls. (chmn. bd., mem. jr.-sr. coll. com., mem. constl. revision com.; dir., mem. adv. com. new instrs.), N.E.A., N. Central Assn. (commr. commn. on colls., univs. 1956-60), Am. Council on Edn. (dir., sec., mem. commn. on fed. relations), Fla. Community Coll. Pres.'s Council, Greater Miami C. of C., Phi Beta Kappa, Phi Kappa Phi. Lutheran. Kiwanian. Author: Introduction to Social Sci. (with Atteberry, Auble and Hunt), rev. edit., 1951. Home: 10270 SW 102d Terrace Miami FL 33156 Office: 11011 SW 104th St Miami FL 33156

MASINTER, RALPH, lawyer; b. Marietta, O.; s. Elias Michael and Rachel Leah (Shereshefsky) M.; LL.B., Washington and Lee U., 1926; LL.M., N.Y. U., 1929; m. Miriam Beilin, Apr. 16, 1939 (dec. Sept. 1970); 1 dau., Enid Renee. Admitted to W.Va. bar, 1927, N.Y. bar, 1933, Va. bar, 1956; gen. practice Roanoke, Va., 1956—; spl. asst. to atty. gen. N.Y., 1933, Va., 1956-64; fed. adminstrv. judge N.Y., Pa., N.J., Del., Md., D.C., 1943-44; asso. editor Am. Trial Lawyers Jour., 1962—. Lectr. advanced legal tng. Past pres. Midway Jewish Community Center, Forest Hills, N.Y. Past mem. Democratic County Com., N.Y. County; past pres. Mid-Manhatton Dem. Club; past mem. speakers bur. Dem. Nat. Com.; alt. del. Dem. Nat. Conv., 1960; mem. exec. cof. Dem. City Com. Bd. dirs. Va. Assn. for Mental Health. Mem. Va., Roanoke, N.Y. State bar assns., Va. trial lawyers assns., Va. State Bar, Am. Judicature Soc., Comml. Law League Am., Ground Hog Club Am. (v.p. Roanoke), Jewish Nat. Council, C. of C., Delta Sigma Rho, Phi Epsilon Pi. Jewish religion (past chmn. bd. synagogue; past pres. Men's Club). Mason (32 deg., Shriner); mem. B'nai B'rith (past v.p., exec. mem. Tristate Anti-Defamation League). Contbr. articles to profl. jours. Home: 1867 Blenheim Rd SW Roanoke VA 24015 Office: State and City Bldg Roanoke VA 24011

MASON, ALVIN HUGHLETT, cons. scientist and engr.; b. Harborton, Va., Feb. 3, 1905; s. Alvin T. and Elizabeth (Hughlett) M.; B.S. with honor in Civil Engring., U. S.C., 1929; M.S., U. Pa., 1931, Ph.D., 1953; m. Mary R. Crow, Sept. 3, 1937. Physicist Nat. Bur. Standards, Washington, 1937-39; stress analyst, torsional vibration analyst U.S. Navy and U.S. Maritime Commn., 1939-48; physicist Office of Chief of Staff, U.S. Army, 1953-63. Registered profl. engr., Washington. Fellow A.A.A.S.; mem. Am. Geophys. Union, Va. Acad. Sci., Philos. Soc. Washington, Washington Soc. Engrs. Democrat. Methodist. Author: The Journal of Charles Mason and Jeremiah Dixon, 1969; History of Steam Navigation to the Eastern Shore of Virginia, 1973. Contbr. articles to profl. jours. Home: 2407 N Kenmore St Arlington VA 22207

MASON, CHARLES NATHAN, ret. govt. ofcl.; b. Billings, Mont., Mar. 9, 1909; s. Joseph E. and Anna E. (Ganser) M.; B.A., Mont. State U., 1930, M.A., 1934; postgrad. U. Wis. Extension, 1940, advanced mgmt. program Harvard, 1959; m. Mabel Rebecca Smith, Dec. 24, 1929; children—Charles Nathan, Gary F., Kent W., Mark S. Laborer, Gt. Western Sugar Co., Billings, 1924-25; bookkeeper Midland Nat. Bank, Billings, 1926; clk. to asst. registrar Mont. State U., Missoula, 1927-35, instr., 1934-35; various adminstrv. positions U.S. Dept. Agr., Missoula, Milw., Indpls., 1935-42, chief div. accounting Office Budget and Finance, Dept. Agr., Washington, 1942-46; budget officer CCC, Washington, 1946-50; systems accountant Gen. Accounting Office, Washington, 1951-52; budget officer CIA, Washington, 1952-62, asst. dir. finance, 1962-69; ret. Instr. Dept. Agr. Grad. Sch., 1943-55, 65-69; professorial lectr. accounting George Washington U., 1953, 54. Pres. Chevy Chase Citizens Assn., 1970-72. Recipient CIA Merit medal, 1959. Mem. Am. Accounting Assn., Fed. Govt. Accountants Assn., Nature Conservancy (treas. 1960-69, bd. 1969-70), Wilderness Soc., Am. Ornithologists Union, Wilson Ornithol. Soc., Wis. Soc. for Ornithology, Nat. Audubon Soc., Audubon Soc. of Central Atlantic States (treas. 1961-63), Fed. Union, Md. Ornithol. Soc. (v.p. Montgomery County 1964-67), Alpha Kappa Psi (silver service award, 1951; dist. dir. 1957-68). Episcopalian. Home: 6432 31st St NW Washington DC 20015

MASON, CLINTON KENNETH, investment co. exec.; b. Boston, May 22, 1931; s. Clinton Kenneth and Irene Mary (Perham) M.; A.B., Dartmouth, 1953; M.B.A., N.Y. U., 1957; m. Elaine Durham, Aug. 3, 1962;children—Lauren Irene, Clinton Kenneth III, Scott Thomas. Buyer, Western Electric Corp., 1953-60; account exec. F.I. Du Pont, Oklahoma City, 1960-68; v.p. Parker Bishop & Welsh, Oklahoma City, 1969-70; v.p. instl. sales Parker Welsh & Hadden, 1970-71; officer Lenz-Newton, Oklahoma City, 1971—; v.p., sec., treas., dir. Gamma Financial Assn., Oklahoma City. Officer, United Fund, Oklahoma City, 1967-68. Bd. dirs. Oklahoma City Jr. Symphony, 1967-68. Mem. Opera Guild, Oklahoma City C. of C. Republican. Methodist. Clubs: Sportsmans, Dartmouth (Oklahoma City). Financial columnist Pulse mag., 1971—. Home: 3828 N W 69th Terrace Oklahoma City OK 73116 Office: Suite 822 Fidelity Plaza Oklahoma City OK 73102

MASON, DONALD GREY, banker; b. Ferrum, Va., Oct. 11, 1927; s. Able Grey and Roxie (Buckner) M.; B.S., Coll. William and Mary, 1957; m. Mary Clay Nichols, Dec. 23, 1956; children—Donald Grey, Nancy Elizabeth, Ellen Kay. Asst. v.p. Va. Nat. Bank, Norfolk, 1957-69; v.p. First Va. Bankshares, Springfield, 1969—. Served with AUS, 1950-52. Home: 3825 King Arthur Rd Annandale VA 22003 Office: 6400 Arlington Blvd Falls Church VA 22042

MASON, FRANKLIN GASQUE, dentist; b. Mullins, S.C., Nov. 20, 1924; s. Edison I. and Mary (Gasque) M.; B.S., Clemson U., 1949; D.D.S., Emory U., 1953; m. Lucy Farrow Reames, June 18, 1947; children—Mary Lydia, Lucy Anne, Deborah Lynn, Francis Elizabeth. Practice dentistry, Mullins, S.C., 1953—. Adv. com. Florence Darlington Tech. Sch., 1969—; vis. lectr. Sch. Dental Medicine, Med. U. S.C., 1970—. Pres., Mullins United Fund, 1965; chmn. Mullins Recreation Bd., 1960-61. Trustee Baptist Coll. at Charleston (S.C.); v.p. S.C. Eye Bank. Served with C.E., AUS, 1943-46. Named Mullins Young Man of Year, 1959. Mem. Am., S.C. (pres. 1965) dental assns., Pee Dee Dental Soc. (pres. 1959), S.C. Soc. Dentistry for Children, S.C. Lions Sight Conservation Assn. (v.p. 1970). Baptist (deacon, chmn., supt. Sunday sch. 1960-64, mem. bldg. com. 1960-70, chmn. finance com. 1969-70). Lion (dist. gov. 1967-68). Club: Pinewood Country. Home: S Main St Mullins SC 29574 Office: 160 E Wine St Mullins SC 29574

MASON, GILBERT RUTLEDGE, physician; b. Jackson, Miss., Oct 7, 1928; s. Willie Atwood and Adlean (Jackson) M.; B.S., Tenn. State U., 1949; M.D., Howard U., 1954; m. Natalie Lorraine Hamlar, July 29, 1950; 1 son, Gilbert Rutledge. Intern Homer G. Phillips Hosp., St. Louis, 1954-55; gen. practice medicine, Biloxi, Miss., 1955—. Med. dir. Harrison County Head Start, 1969—; mem. tissue and drug coms. Howard Meml. Hosp., Biloxi, 1967—, chief family practice sect., 1971—. Vice chmn. bd. Greater Gulf Coast Land Devel. Corp., 1970—; dir. Miss. Indsl. Spl. Services, Inc. Pres. N.A.A.C.P., Biloxi, 1960—; chmn. USO, 1959-60, 70—; chmn. Community Action Program, 1966-69; mem. City Planning Commn., 1969—; mem. state adv. com. U.S. Civil Rights Comm., 1965—; mem. Gov.'s Emergency Council, 1969-71; vice chmn. state adv. com. to Cabinet Com. on Pub. Edn., 1970—; mem. state adv. com. Div. Comprehensive Health Planning, 1969—; vice chmn. Harrison County Regional Econ. Commn., 1973—; scoutmaster Boy Scouts Am., 1959-72; pres. Biloxi Civil League, 1960-69. Mem. Harrison County Democratic Exec. Com., 1968-72. Recipient Silver Beaver award Boy Scouts Am., 1963; Outstanding Alumnus citation Semi-centennial Celebration Tenn. State U., 1962; named Citizen of Year, 1959, 64; Outstanding Citizen, 1970. Fellow N.Y. Research Found. Diplomate Am. Bd. Family Practice. Fellow Am. Acad. Family Physicians; mem. A.M.A., Nat. Med. Assn., Alpha Phi Alpha. Baptist. Elk, Mason (32 deg.). Home: 119 Alicia Dr Biloxi MS 39531 Office: 433 E Division St Biloxi MS 39530

MASON, GORDON LEE, ophthalmologist; b. Portsmouth, Va., Jan. 25, 1931; s. Lee Arnold and Hazel Marie (Simpson) M.; B.S., Coll. of William and Mary, 1952; M.D., Med. Coll. Va., 1957; M.S., U. Mich., 1961; m. Betty Joyce Nuckols, May 4, 1958; 1 dau., Linda Marie. Intern Norfolk (Va.) Gen. Hosp., 1957-58; resident U. Mich., Ann Arbor, 1958-61; practice medicine, specializing in ophthalmology, Johnson City, Tenn., 1961—; partner Johnson City Eye Hosp., 1961—. Diplomate Am. Bd. Ophthalmology. Fellow Am. Acad. Ophthalmology and Otolaryngology; mem. Phi Beta Kappa, Omicron Delta Kappa, Alpha Omega Alpha, Sigma Zeta. Kiwanian. Home: 1606 Hickory Court Johnson City TN 37601 Office: 207 E Watauga Av Johnson City TN 37601

MASON, JAMES MIDDLETON, investment co. exec.; b. Augusta, Ga., Mar. 19, 1908; s. James Middleton and Daisy Claire (Bacon) M.; student Augusta Coll., 1926; m. Emma Louise Lester, Sept. 29, 1934; 1 son, Benjamin Lester. With Johnson, Lane, Space, Smith & Co., Augusta, 1933—, salesman, 1944-61, v.p., 1961—, also dir. Asso. mem. N.Y. Stock Exchange. Served with AUS, 1943-44. Charter mem. Augusta Assembly. Episcopalian. Elk. Clubs: Augusta Country, Pinnacle. Home: 1211 Milledge Rd Augusta GA 30904 Office: 721 Broad St Augusta GA 30904

MASON, JOSEPH BARRY, educator; b. Memphis, Mar. 24, 1941; s. Rufus Crawford and Joyce (Fontenot) M.; B.S. in Bus. Adminstrn., La. Poly. U., 1963; M.A. in Marketing, U. Ala., 1964, Ph.D. in Bus. Adminstrn. (Loveman's scholar 1964-65), 1967; m. Linda Sue Fairchild, Dec. 20, 1961; children—Michael Barry, Michele Rene. Mem. faculty dept. marketing, urban studies U. Ala., University, 1967—, asso. prof., 1969-71, prof., 1971—, also dir. research, spl. program Grad. Sch. Bus., 1971—; research asso. Ala. Hwy. Research Project, 1964-67, project dir., co-principal researcher, 1967-72. Partner Market Research Asso., Tuscaloosa, 1970—; mem. hwy. research bd. Nat. Acad. Scis., since 1967—. Mem. community adv. com. Family Services Task Force, Tuscaloosa (Ala.) Community Council, 1972. Mem. Assn. Consumer Research, Am. Marketing Assn., Am., So. marketing assns., Ala. Acad. Sci., Regional Sci. Assn., Delta Sigma Pi, Beta Gamma Sigma. Home: 4921 10th Ct E Tuscaloosa AL Office: PO Box 2312 University AL 35486

MASON, (MARY) THOMASINE GRAYSON (MRS. E. FLEMING MASON), lawyer, state ofcl.; b. Summerton, S.C., Nov. 7, 1918; d. James Fulton and Anne (Gentry) Grayson; A.B., U. S.C. 1938, LL.B., 1942; m. Edgar Fleming Mason, June 30, 1939. Recruiter, personnel worker U.S. Civil Service Commn., Ga., also S.C., World War II; admitted to S.C. bar, 1941, since practiced in Manning; asso. Grayson-Elliott, Inc., 1952-63, sec. bd. dirs., 1947—;

trial atty. civil div. U.S. Dept. Justice, Washington, 1968-72; adminstrv. law judge Bur. Hearings and Appeals, Social Security Adminstrn., Dept. Health, Edn. and Welfare, 1972—. Dist. vice chmn. A.R.C., 1955-56; chmn. TB seals dr., 1965-67. Del. nat. conv., Democratic party, 1960; mem. S.C. Senate, 1966-68. Bd. dirs. Palmetto Girls State; trustee Clarendon Meml. Hosp. Mem. Clarendon County Farm Bur., Clarendon County C. of C. D.A.R., Am. Legion Aux. (v.p. S.C. dept.), Am., S.C. (v.p. 3d jud. circuit 1965-67) bar assns., Am. Trial Lawyers Assn., Am. Bar Assn., Alpha Delta Pi. Clubs: Booster; Garden (Summerton); Business and Professional Women's, Executive (Sumter, S.C.). Home: Apt 106 Chateau de Ville Apts 3600 Chateau Dr Columbia SC 29204 also Summerton SC Office: 221 Middleburg Plaza Columbia SC 29204

MASON, RICHARD ALLEN, banker; b. Little Rock, July 15, 1934; s. Thomas Allen and Pauline (Thompson) M.; B.S. in Commerce, Tex. Christian U., 1957; m. Janford Smith, Aug. 30, 1956; children—Tracy, Leslie, Hilary. With data processing div. IBM, 1958-66; with Ft. Worth Nat. Bank, 1966—, sr. v.p. gen. banking div., 1969—. Mem. faculty Tex. Christian U., 1968—, bd. dirs. Ft. Worth C. of C. Devel. Corp., 1969-71. Chmn. bus. div. United Fund Campaign Cabinet, 1968; group dir. Tex. Christian U. Research Found., 1969-70. Served to 1st lt., Transp. Corps, AUS, 1956. Mem. Am. Bankers Assn., Bank Pub. Relations and Marketing Assn., Sales and Marketing Execs., Tex. Christian U. Alumni Assn. (dir. 1969-72, pres. elect), Tex. Christian U. M.J. Neeley Sch. Bus. Alumni Assn. (pres. 1969-70), Kappa Sigma. Republican. Baptist. Home: 2309 Medford Ct E Fort Worth TX 76109 Office: PO Box 2050 Fort Worth TX 76101

MASON, ROBERT, editor; b. Charlotte, N.C., Sept. 1, 1912; s. Walter L. and Irene (Peterson) M.; A.B., U. N.C., 1933; m. Frances Fulton, Feb. 11, 1939; 1 dau., Frances Fulton II (now Mrs. Robert Baldwin, Jr.). City editor Sanford (N.C.) Herald, 1933-35, editor, 1952-57; reporter Raleigh (N.C.) News & Observer, 1935-37; city editor Durham (N.C.) Herald, 1937-41; Sunday editor Norfolk (Va.) Virginian-Pilot, 1941-43, 46-52, asso. editor, 1957-59, mng. editor, 1959-62, editor, 1962—. Chmn. Norfolk Civil War Centennial Commn.; mem. Pres.'s Nat. Citizens Com. for Community Relations. Trustee, Chrysler Mus., Norfolk. Served to lt. USNR, 1943-46. Mem. Am. Soc. Newspaper Editors, N.C. Hist. Soc., N.C. Editorial Writers Conf. (chmn. 1955-56), Va. Press Assn., Norfolk Assembly, Navy League, Newcomen Soc., Alpha Tau Omega. Democrat. Episcopalian. Clubs: Princess Anne Country, Harbor, Virginia; Federal City, Nat. Press (Washington). Home: 1412 Trouville Av Norfolk VA 23505 Office: 150 W Brambleton Av Norfolk VA 23510

MASON, ROBERT EDWARD, banker; b. Madison, Ga., Apr. 27, 1938; s. Charles Levingston and Sarah Ernestine (Ponder) M.; B.S., Ga. Inst. Tech., 1960; postgrad. indsl. mgmt. Grad. Sch. of Banking of South, 1970-73; m. Carole Brannon, Aug. 5, 1967; children—George Ross, Robert Brannon. Gen. mgr. Mason Gin & Fertilizer Co., Madison, 1963-67; v.p. First Nat. Bank of Gainesville (Ga.), 1967—; incorporator, dir. Bank of Banks County, Homer, Ga. Bd. dirs. Hall County unit Am. Cancer Soc., 1971; bd. dirs. Gainesville Civic Theater, 1967-70, treas., 1969-70; bd. dirs. Gainesville Hall County Community Chest. Served to lt. (j.g.) Supply Corps, USNR, 1961-63. Mem. Robert Morris Assos., Ga. Inst. Tech. Alumni Assn. (pres. Gainesville area 1973-74), Fellowship Christian Athletes (chpt. trustee), C. of C. (dir.). Baptist (deacon 1973—). Kiwanian (pres. 1971-72). Club: Chattahoochee Country. Home: 158 Piedmont Av Gainesville GA 30501 Office: PO Drawer 937 Gainesville GA 30501

MASON, ROBERT ELIJAH, II, profl. engr.; b. Charlotte, N.C., Apr. 24, 1906; s. Edwin Lowell and Mamie (Badgett) M.; B.S., U. N.C., 1930; m. Sallie Wilfong Schenck, June 13, 1931; children—Robert Elijah, Lucinda Lewis. Engr. air conditioning dept. Gen. Electric Co., N.Y.C., Atlanta, 1931-39; owner Robert E. Mason & Co., Charlotte, N.C., 1940—; pres., treas. Robert E. Mason & Assos., Inc., Charlotte, 1955—. Mem. Profl. Engring. Soc. N.C., Am. Soc. Heating, Refrigerating and Air Conditioning Engrs., Instrument Soc. Am. Episcopalian (sr. warden). Clubs: Charlotte City, Charlotte Country. Died Apr. 10, 1968. Home: 3811 Bonwood Dr Charlotte NC 28211

MASON, WALTER LAWRENCE, surgeon; b. Memphis, Jan. 15, 1933; s. Lawrence and Donie Lynne (McCallum) M.; student Washington U., 1951-52, Memphis State U., 1952-54; M.D., U. Tenn., 1957; m. Nancy Elizabeth Moran, Mar. 21, 1968; 1 son, Andrew. Intern Roanoke (Va.) Meml. Hosp., 1957-58; resident UA Teaching Group Hosp., 1962-66; practice medicine, specializing in surgery, Memphis, 1966-69, Greeneville, Tenn., 1969—; mem. staffs Laughlin Meml. Hosp., Takoma Hosp., Greeneville Hosp. Diplomate Am. Bd. Surgery. Mem. A.C.S., Southeastern Surg. Congress. Home: 105 Fairway Lane Greeneville TN 37743 Office: 6 Spencer Square Greeneville TN 37743

MASQUELETTE, PHILIP ABBOTT, lawyer; b. Port Arthur, Tex., Jan. 16, 1926; s. Philip Reddington and Nelia Elizabeth (Wilkins) M.; student Tex. A. and M. Coll., 1942-43, Harvard Bus. Sch., 1944-45; B.B.A., Tulane U., 1945; M.B.A., U. Tex., 1947; LL.B., U. Houston, 1952; postgrad. Southwestern Grad. Sch. Banking, So. Meth. U., 1960; m. Elizabeth Daggett Simmons, Mar. 17, 1948; children—Laura (Mrs. Robert Selig), Philip E., Pamela A., David S. Admitted to Tex. bar, 1952; accountant Masquelette Bruhl & Co. accountants, Houston, 1947-53; asso. firm Butler, Binion, Rice & Cook attys., Houston, 1953-57; v.p., dir. Bank Tex., Houston, 1957-61, sr. v.p., 1961-62; pres., dir. Perpetual Corp., Houston, 1962-65; individual practice law, Houston, 1965-71; partner Masquelette, Bailey, Donisi & Haynes, Houston, 1971-72, Dillingham, Schleider & Masquelette, 1973—. Trustee Episcopal Ch. Pension Fund, N.Y.C., 1967, S. Tex. Law Found., Houston, 1964. Served with USNR, 1943-46. C.P.A., Tex. Mem. Am., Houston bar assns., State Bar Tex., Am. Coll. Probate Counsel, Am. Inst. C.P.A.'s, Tex. Soc. C.P.A.'s, Sigma Alpha Epsilon, Beta Gamma Sigma, Beta Alpha Psi, Phi Delta Phi. Republican. Episcopalian. Home: 6239 Lynbrook Dr Houston TX 77027 Office: 802 Capital National Bank Bldg Houston TX 77002

MASSEL, GARY ALAN, govt. ofcl.; b. Trenton, N.J., May 5, 1939; s. Oliver and Rose (Litt) M.; B.S. in Physics, N.C. State U., 1961, Ph.D. (Ford Found. fellow, AEC fellow), 1967; m. Janet Lynn Markley, Dec. 27, 1959; children—Kathryn Leigh, Suzanne Jane. Aerospace engr. NASA, Hampton, Va., 1965-67; sr. staff mem. Inst. for Def. Analysis, Arlington, Va., 1967-70; operations research analyst Office Asst. Sec. Def., Washington, 1970-71, dir. land force program, 1971-72; dir. naval force programs Office Asst. Sec. Def. for Systems Analysis, 1972-73; asso. adminstr. Social Rehab. Service U.S. Dept. Health, Edn. and Welfare, Washington, 1973—. Mem. Operations Research Soc., Am. Soc. Pub. Adminstrn., Phi Kappa Phi, Sigma Pi Sigma, Pi Mu Epsilon, Tau Beta Pi. Home: 8020 Birnam Wood Dr McLean VA 22101 Office: 330 C St Washington DC 20201

MASSELL, SAM, realtor; b. Atlanta, Aug. 26, 1927; s. Sam and Florence (Rubin) M.; student Emory U., 1944-45, U. Ga., 1947-48; LL.B., Atlanta Law Sch., 1949; B.C.S., Ga. State U., 1951, postgrad. certificate in selling, 1952, postgrad. diploma in real estate, 1953; m. Doris M. Middlebrooks, Oct. 25, 1952; children—Cynthia Diane, Steven Alan, Melanie Denise. Chief publs. Nat. Assn. Women's and Children's Apparel Salesmen, Inc., 1949-51; with Allan-Grayson Realty Co., 1951-69, v.p., 1955-69; v.p. Mallin Developers, Inc., 1956-65; vice mayor, pres. Atlanta Bd. Alderman, 1962-69; mayor City of Atlanta, 1970-74; pres. Allan-Grayson Devel. Assos., 1974—. Instr. in real estate Smith-Hughes Atlanta Vocational Sch., 1956. Councilman, City of Mountain Park (Ga.), 1950-52; sec., Atlanta City Exec. Com., 1953-61. Served with USAAF, 1946-47. Mem. U.S. Conf. Mayors (dir. 1971-74), Nat. League Cities (pres. 1972, chmn. adv. council 1973), Inter-Am. Municipal Orgn. (v.p. 1972). Democrat. Jewish religion. Clubs: Standard, Commerce. Home: 2750 Wyngate NW Atlanta GA 30305 Office: 400 Colony Square Tower 1201 Peachtree St NE Atlanta GA 30361

MASSENGALE, R. GLENN, clergyman, educator; b. Stewart, Ala., June 4, 1915; s. Warren Grover and Mattie (Spencer) M.; A.B., Birmingham-So. Coll., 1935; B.D., Yale, 1939, Ph.D., 1950; m. Lessie Elizabeth Clements, Aug. 16, 1938; 1 dau., Ellona Lois. Jr. sec. YMCA, Ansonia, Conn., 1936-39; dir. religious and social life Emory U., Atlanta, 1939-41; dir. Wesley Found., Yale, 1941-43; ordained to ministry Methodist Ch., 1941; pastor Meth. Ch., Decatur, Miss., 1943; chaplain U. S.C., Columbia, 1946-49; prof. religious edn. Scarritt Coll., Nashville, 1949-51; prof. religion and philosophy, dean of men Huntingdon Coll., Montgomery, Ala., 1951-57, prof. religion and philosophy, dir. library, 1957—. Served as chaplain USNR, 1944-46; comdr. USNR. Mem. A.L.A., Am. Acad. Religion, Soc. Bibl. Lit., Sigma Alpha Epsilon, Omicron Delta Kappa. Rotarian. Contbr. to ch. publs. Home: 1346 Wedgewood Dr Montgomery AL 36111

MASSENGILL, MYERS NEWTON, lawyer; b. Bristol, Va., July 12, 1941; s. Raymond McClellan and Mary Louise (Myers) M.; B.A., E. Tenn. State U., 1963; J.D., U. Tenn., 1964; m. Janet Chase Tallman, June 11, 1967; 1 son, Myers Newton II. Admitted to Tenn. bar, 1965, since practiced in Bristol; mem. firm Caldwell, Johnson, Winston, Haynes, Grayson & Massengill, Bristol, 1965—, partner, 1973—; asst. city atty. Bristol, 1965—; asst. dist. atty. gen. 26th Jud. Circuit Tenn., 1971-72. Mem. adv. bd. Va. Highlands Community Coll., Abingdon, Va., 1970-71; chmn. adv. bd. Salvation Army, Bristol, 1973—; bd. dirs. Bristol Regional Speech and Hearing Center, Inc., 1969-73, chmn. 1971-72. Served with USAF, 1965. Mem. Bristol, Sullivan County, Tenn. bar assns., Tenn. Protective Assn., Am. Legion, Bristol Jr. C. of C. (internat. v.p. 1971), Tenn. Jr. C. of C., Phi Alpha Delta, Phi Sigma Kappa. Democrat. Methodist. Elk. Club: Bristol Country. Home: 507 Brookwood Dr Bristol TN 37620 Office: PO Box 745 Bristol TN 37620

MASSENGILL, RAYMOND MCCELLAN, JR., educator, researcher; b. Bristol, Va., Dec. 8, 1937; s. Raymond McCellan and Mary Louise (Myers) M.; B.S., U. Tenn., 1959, M.S., 1959; Ed.D., U. Va., 1968; m. Harriet Hargreave, Dec. 20, 1958; children—Kimberely, Deborah, Raymond McCellan III, Andrew. Dir. med. speech pathology Duke U. Med. Center, Durham, N.C., 1964—, asso. prof. dept. surgery, 1971—, chmn. campus Christian Life com., 1970—. Dept. Health, Edn. and Welfare trainee, 1963; Nat. Elks Found. scholar, 1963, Vocational Rehab. Assn. scholar, 1963, research grantee Nat. Insts., 1966. Fellow Am. Speech and Hearing Assn.; mem. Am. Cleft Palate Assn., So. Speech Communication Assn. (chmn. speech pathology sect. 1971). Author: Hypernasality: Considerations in Causes and Treatment Procedures, 1971. Contbr. articles to sci. publs. Editorial cons. Am. Jour. Speech and Hearing Disorders, 1971—. Home: 2734 Spencer St Durham NC 27775

MASSEY, CECIL EARL, city mgr.; b. Stamford, Tex., Sept. 16, 1921; s. Hugh Thomas and Ella May (Grisby) M.; student Washington and Lee U., 1945; B.B.A., Baylor U., 1949, M.A. 1950; postgrad. West Tex. State Coll., 1951; m. Mary Ann Burton, Dec. 30, 1949; children—Cleve, Neal, Mark, Linda. Mgr., Canyon (Tex.) C. of C., 1950-51, Deaf Smith County C. of C., Hereford, Tex., 1951-53; mgr. City of Hereford (Tex.), 1953-56, City of Haltom City (Tex.), 1956-57, City of Weatherford (Tex.), 1957-62, City of Weslaco (Tex.), 1962—. Active Boy Scouts Am.; bd. commrs. Waco Methodist Children's Home; past pres. Hereford Lions Club: past zone chmn., Lions Internat., dist. gov., 1960-61, now internat. counselor, pres. gov.'s council Tex. Lions Clubs, 1960-61, past officer Canyon and Haltom City Lions Clubs. Served with AUS, 1942-45. Named Man of Year, Weslaco, 1967. Rockefeller Found. Fellow, N.Y.C., Nat. Theatre Conf. fellow, N.Y.C. Mem. Baylor Ex-Lettermen's Assn. (chmn. bd. dirs. 1953-57), State Hwy. 60 Assn. (sec. 1952), Internat., Tex. city mgrs. assns., S.W. Conf. Football Ofcls. Methodist (mem. ofcl. bd., asso. dist. lay leader). Mason. Home: 904 Border Weslaco TX 78596 Office: City Hall Bldg Weslaco TX 78596

MASSEY, DONALD WAYNE, microfilm cons.; b. Durham, N.C., Mar. 7, 1938; s. Gordon Davis and Lucille Alma (Gregory) M.; student U. Hawaii, 1959, U. Ky., 1965; m. Violet Sue McIlvain, Nov. 2, 1958; children—Kimberly Shan, Leon Dale, Donn Krichele. Head microfilm sect. Ky. Hist. Soc., Frankfort, 1961; dir. microfilm center U. Ky., Lexington, 1962-67; dir. photographic services and graphics U. Va., Charlottesville, 1967-73; owner Micrographics II, 1973—. Instr., U. Va. Sch. Continuing Edn., 1971-72; cons. Microform Systems and Copying Centers. Owner, Massland Farm, Shadwell, Va. Served with USMCR, 1957-60. Recipient Key award Workshop V, for handicapped, Charlottesville, Va., pres. bd., 1972-73. Mem. Am., Va. library assns., Soc. Reprodn. Engrs., Nat. (library relations com. 1973—), Va. (Pioneer award 1973, pres. 1971, v.p. 1973-74, program chmn. ann. conf. 1974), Ky. (Outstanding award 1967, pres. 1964-67) microfilm assns. Mem. Christian Ch. (elder, chmn. bd.). Contbg. editor Va. Librarian, 1970-71, Micro-News Va. Microfilm Assn., 1970-71. Contbr. articles to profl. publs. Address: Route 7 Box 258G Charlottesville VA 22903

MASSEY, EDWIN DWIGHT, hosp. adminstr.; b. Leslie, Ark., Feb. 11, 1926; s. Daniel B. and Louisa Belle (Stephenson) M.; student McNeese State Coll., 1968, La. State U., 1969-70, U. Ala., 1970-71; m. Bonnie Lucile Williams, Aug. 7, 1946; children—Linda (Mrs. William Riley Milner II), Larry D., Paul D., Michael Edwin. Computer, Petty Geophys. Engring. Co., San Antonio, 1947-53; party chief Liberty Exploration Co., Houston, 1953-59; bus. mgr. Beauregard Meml. Bapt. Hosp., DeRidder, La., 1959-60, adminstr., 1960—. Named col. Staff La. Gov., 1969—. Mem. Am. Acad. Med. Adminstrs., La. Hosp. Assn., La. Nursing Home Assn., DeRidder C. of C. Baptist. Kiwanian. Club: DeRidder Duck. Home: 105 Henderson St DeRidder LA 70634 Office: 502 S Pine St DeRidder LA 70634

MASSEY, JACK TAYLOR, life ins. co. exec.; b. Frederick, Okla., May 7, 1927; s. James A. and Viola (Taylor) M.; B.B.A., U. Okla., 1951, LL.B., 1957; m. Sue Neal, Nov. 10, 1951; children—Sarena L., Cynthia S., J. Taylor, Neal E. Admitted to Okla. bar, 1957; agt. Mass. Mut. Life Ins. Co., Oklahoma City, 1951-62; self employed ind. ins. agt., ins. cons., Oklahoma City, 1962-64; with United Founders Life Ins. Co., Oklahoma City, 1964—, exec. v.p. 1966—, also dir., mem. exec. com.; dir. United Founders Life Ins. Co. of Ill., Chgo., Reis Corp., Oklahoma City, United Founders Life Ins. Co. of Tex., Dallas, Am. Capital Corp., Am. Computer Service Corp., EPIC Corp., Investors Equity Corp. Served with USNR, 1945-46. C.L.U. Mem. Am. Soc. C.L.U.'S, Okla.-Oklahoma County Bar Assn., Lawyers Tax Group, Beta Theta Pi, Phi Alpha Delta. Methodist (adminstrv. bd.). Lion. Club: Quail Creek Golf and Country, Beacon, Oklahoma City Boat. Home: 2308 NW 58th St Oklahoma City OK 73112 Office: 5900 Mosteller Dr Oklahoma City OK 73112

MASSEY, LUTHER M., dentist; b. Wakefield, N.C., July 4, 1895; s. Daniel D. and Eldora Frances (Hood) M.; student Wake Forest Coll., 1913-16; D.D.S., Med. Coll. Va., 1918; grad. implant dentistry Inst. Grad. Dentists, N.Y.C., 1969; m. Vivian Dawson, June 24, 1927; 1 dau., Carolyn Vivian. Practicing dentist, Zebulon, N.C., 1919—; farmer; dir. N.C. Farm Bur. Service Co.; mem. exec. com., dir. N.C. Farm Bur. Mut. Ins. Co. Mem. N.C. Bd. Edn., 1939-44; chmn. Wake County Bd. Elections, 1939-41. Chmn. bd. trustees Meredith Coll., 1952-68, trustee, 1968—; bd. dirs. Wake County Opportunities, Inc., State N.C. Tchrs. and State Employees Retirement System; trustee agrl. found. State Coll., N.C., chmn. research fund; trustee dental found. U.N.C. Served with Dental Co. No. I, World War I; 1st lt. Dental Res., until 1936. Mem. Am., 4th Dist. (pres.) dental assns., D.C. Dental Soc., N.C. (pres. local county unit, dir.), Four County (past pres.) heart assns., Internat. Soc. Implant Dentistry, N.C. Farm Bur. Fedn. (exec. com.), Am. Legion. Baptist (chmn. finance com.). Mason (32 deg.), Rotarian (pres.). Club: Carolina Country. Home: Zebulon NC 27597

MASSEY, MARION LAWRENCE, lawyer; b. Fort Worth, May 17, 1932; s. Marion Lawrence and Willie (Neely) M.; B.S., N.Tex. State U., 1954; J.D., So. Methodist U., 1957; m. Margaret Ann Parker, Dec. 27, 1955; children—Kyle Massey, Kevin, Kay. Admitted to Tex. bar, 1957, since practiced in Fort Worth; mem. firms Spurlock, Schattman & Jacobs, 1959-63, Crumley & Hooper, 1963-64, King & Massey, 1964—. Judge City North Richland Hills, Tex., 1960-65, atty., 1966-69; mayor, North Richland Hills, 1970-74. Served with USMCR, 1957-59. Mem. Am., Tex., Fort Worth-Tarrant County bar assns., Am., Tex. trial lawyers assns. Home: 4916 Weyland St Hurst TX 76053 Office: 2701 Airport Freeway Fort Worth TX 76111

MASSEY, ROBERT LEE, dentist; b. Detroit, Tex., Dec. 24, 1902; s. Robert Price and Frances Elizabeth (Coleman) M.; D.D.S., Baylor U., 1927; m. Agnes High, Apr. 19, 1930; children—Roberta (Mrs. Jack B. Ramsey), Elizabeth (Mrs. Mac Kehoe), Carole (Mrs. E.E. Dean). Gen. practice dentistry, Tulia, Tex., 1928—. Recipient Order Good Fellow, 1955. Mem. Am. (life), Tex. (life) dental assns., Panhandle Dental Soc., Xi Psi Phi. Baptist. Home: 507 N Donley St Tulia TX 79088 Office: First Nat Bank Bldg Tulia TX 79088

MASSEY, THOMAS CADE, lawyer, state legislator; b. San Angelo, Tex., Mar. 5, 1931; s. Guilford M.C. and Villa (Ault) M.; student San Angelo Coll., 1949-50, Tex. A. and M. U., 1954-55; B.A. in Govt., U. Tex., 1959, J.D., 1960; m. Mary Anna Byrom, Dec. 22, 1957; children—Julie, Alyson, Byrom Cade, Will Truitt. Admitted to Tex. bar, 1960; city atty. City of Graham, 1960-63; master in chancery Rio Grande Water Rights Suit, McAllen, Tex., 1963-64; practice in San Angelo, 1964—; mem. firm Logan, Lear, Massey and Gossett, 1964—. Mem. Tex. Ho. of Reps., 1972—. Co-founder Char-Swiss Breeders Assn., exec., 1970—; mem. San Angelo Com. on Status of Women, 1970-72, state legacy com. Am. Cancer Soc., 1965-67. Chmn. Tom Green County Dem. Com., 1970-71. Bd. dirs. West Tex. Therapy Center. Served with AUS, 1951-53. Rotarian (pres. 1965). Methodist (chmn. bd. trustees 1971—). Home: 1909 Douglas Dr San Angelo TX 76901 Office: PO Box 1663 San Angelo TX 76901

MASSEY, WILLIAM WALTER, JR., automobile agy. exec.; b. Lawrenceburg, Tenn., Sept. 21, 1928; s. William Walter and Bess Ann (Brian) M.; B.B.A., U. Miami, 1949; B.F.A., U. Fla., 1969; m. Virginia Claire Smith, Aug. 16, 1952; children—William Walter III, Laura Ann, Lynn Smith, Lisa Claire. Vice pres. Massey Motors, Inc., Jacksonville, Fla., 1950—, Atlantic Discount Co., Inc., Jacksonville, 1954-64; pres. Owners Surety Corp., Jacksonville, 1959—, Gen. Services Corp., Jacksonville, 1960-69, Fla. Properties, Inc., Jacksonville, 1961-66; pres. Owners Guaranty Life Ins. Co., Phoenix, 1960-64, Securities Guaranty Life Ins. Co., Phoenix, 1961-64; pres. Chi-Cha, Inc., Jacksonville, 1965-70; v.p., dir. Massey Dodge, Inc., Jacksonville, Regency Dodge, Inc., Jacksonville, Westside Dodge, Inc., Jacksonville, Massey-Mixon Chrysler-Plymouth, Inc., Jacksonville, Biscayne Dodge, Inc., North Miami Beach, Massey-Andrews, Inc., Clearwater, Brooks-Massey, Inc., Tampa, Univ. Dodge, Inc., Tampa, Massey Motors, Inc., Daytona Beach, Massey-Yardley, Inc., Ft. Lauderdale; owner Univ. Sq. Properties; dir. Southside Atlantic Bank, Jacksonville. Exhibited group shows N.Y. Internat. Art Show, 1970; Ball State U., Muncie, Ind., 1972; Artists/U.S.A., 1974. Vice pres. bd. dirs. Southside Country Day Sch., 1963-68. Served to 1st lt. USAF, 1950-52. Mem. Conn. Acad. Fine Arts, Sigma Chi. Methodist. Clubs: River, Deerwood (Jacksonville). Home: 7080 San Fernando Pl Jacksonville FL 32217 Office: 2434 Atlantic Blvd Jacksonville FL 32207

MASSIE, IRA EVAN, educator; b. Lexington, Ky., Nov. 13, 1919; s. William Goebel and Bess Mae (Parker) M.; B.S., U. Ky., 1951, M.S., 1958; m. Clarice Virginia Claiborne, Nov. 9, 1952; children—Ira Evan II, Kevin Claiborne, Diane Mae. Asst. mgr. Ky. Seed Improvement Assn., Lexington, 1950-51; asst. county agt. U. Ky., Maysville, 1952; mem. faculty U. Ky., Lexington, 1952—, agronomist, tobacco specialist, 1953—. Cons., Philip Morris, Inc., 1969-71, Proctor and Gamble Co., 1966-73, Chicopee Mill, Inc., N.Y.C., 1972; adviser tobacco com. Ky. Farm Bur.; mem. Burley Farmers Adv. Council. Served with USMC, 1940-47. Decorated D.F.C. with oak leaf cluster, Air medal with several oak leaf clusters. Recipient grant Philip Morris, Inc., N.Y.C., 1971, certificate of service Ky. Dept. Agr., 1963, meritorious service award Epsilon Sigma Phi. Mem. Am. Soc. Agronomy. Democrat. Baptist (mem. ch. nominating com. 1971—, chmn. 1972). Mason. Author: Plantbed Management, 1966; Tobacco Production, 1968; Harvesting and Curing Burley Tobacco, 1968; Marketing Burley Tobacco, 1969. Tobacco editor Ky. Farmer mag., 1952—, Rural Kentuckian mag., 1971—. Home: 544 Claymont Dr Lexington KY 40503

MASSIEU, GUILLERMO HELGUERA, research exec.; b. San Luis Potosi, Mexico, Oct. 7, 1920; s. Wilfrido Massieu and Maria Helguera Ceballos; B.Sc., Nat. Sch. Biol. Scis., Nat. Poly. Inst. Mexico, 1945, Sc.D., 1963; m. Yolanda M. Trigo, Aug. 11, 1951; children—Yolanda M., Lourdes M. Mem. research staff Nat. Inst. Nutrition Mexico, 1945-55; prof. Inst. Biology, Nat. U. Mexico, 1956-64; dir. gen. Nat. Poly. Inst. Mexico, 1965-70; prof. biochemistry, dir. Center Research and Advanced Studies, Nat. Poly. Inst., 1971—; cons. Nat. Council Sci. and Tech., Mexico, 1971—. Rep. Mexico to exec. com. Interam. Council Sci., Edn. and Culture, Orgn. Am. States, 1969—. Decorated comdr. Order Merit (Italy); comdr. Order Roi Leopold (Belgium); comdr. Order Gt. Cross (West Germany); officer Palmes Academiques (France); recipient Gold medal French Soc. Encourgement Sci. Research and Innovation, 1973. Brit. Council scholar, 1954-55. Mem. Nat. Acad. Medicine Mexico, Acad. Sci. Research Mexico, Mexican Chem. Soc., Mexican Soc. Biochemistry, Internat. Soc. Neurochemistry, Am. Soc. Neurochemistry. Contbr. articles on nutrition, neurochemistry, sci. policy to profl. jours. Home: 20 Ret P de la Llave 18 Mexico DF Z-22 Mexico Office: Apdo Postal 14-740 Mexico DF Z-14 Mexico

MASSMAN, RICHARD ALLAN, lawyer; b. Beaumont, Tex., Aug. 19, 1943; s. Irwin and Sylvia (Schmidt) M.; B.S. cum laude, U. Pa., 1965; J.D. cum laude, Harvard, 1968; m. Barbara Elaine Kessler, July 7, 1968; 1 son, Jason. Admitted to Tex. bar, 1968; asso. firm Coke & Coke, Dallas, 1968-70; asso., partner Hewett, Johnson, Swanson & Barbee, 1970—. Lectr. Law Sch., So. Methodist U., 1973. Mem. Am., Dallas bar assns., State Bar Tex. Club: Dallas. Home: 4950 Mill Run Dallas TX 75234 Office: 211 N Ervay Bldg Dallas TX 75201

MAST, STEWART DALE, airport exec.; b. Kalamazoo, Mich., May 10, 1924; s. Virgil S. and Sarah L. (Rippey) M.; student U. Mich., 1942, Argubright Coll. Bus. Adminstrn., 1946, Spartan Sch. Aeros., 1947; m. Mary F. Smith, Aug. 1, 1945; children—Peter S., Frances A. Mgr. city airport, Battle Creek, Mich., 1948-60; airport dir., County of Milw., 1960-66; mgr. airports Hillsborough County Aviation Authority, Tampa, Fla., 1966—. Mem. bd. review Milw. council Boy Scouts Am., 1964-65. Served to 2d lt. USAAF, 1943-45. Mem. Am. Assn. Airport Execs. (dir. 1965-67, 74—). Mason. Home: 5114 Homer Av Tampa FL 33609 Office: PO Box 22287 Tampa FL 33622

MASTEN, JOHN TALBOT, educator; b. Newark, Mar. 13, 1914; s. Glenn Arnold and Janet (Turner) M.; student Springfield (Ill.) Jr. Coll., 1932-34; B.S., U. Ill., 1936, M.S., 1937; Ph.D., U. N.C., 1942; m. Elizabeth Ida Bluemke, Aug. 17, 1938; children—Patricia Sue (Mrs. Charles Judd Barnes), John Talbot. Regional price economist Bur. Labor Statistics, Chgo., 1945-47; chmn. dept. econs. Kalamazoo Coll., 1947-48; asso. prof. U. Ky., Lexington, 1948-57, prof. econs., 1957-67, dir. grad. studies in econs., 1963-66, chmn. dept., 1964-66; Ga. Bankers Assn. prof. banking U. Ga., Athens, 1967—. Cons. Ky. Bankers Assn., 1964—; ednl. dir. Ga. Banking Sch., Athens, 1968—; faculty Banking Sch. of South, Baton Rouge, 1964-69. Mem. Fayette County Recreation Bd., Lexington, 1957-62. Mem. Am., So. econ. assns., Am. Finance Assn., Beta Gamma Sigma. Author: (with W. Warren Haynes) Programmed Text in Money and Banking, 1969. Contbr. articles to profl. jours. Home: 130 Devereux Dr Athens GA 30601

MASTEN, MICHAEL KEITH, research engr.; b. Gainesville, Tex., Nov. 11, 1939; s. Raleigh Lee and Dollye (McFarlin) M.; B.E.E., U. Tex., 1963, M.E.E., 1965, Ph.D., 1968; m. Roma Yvonne Mayo, June 6, 1964; 1 dau., Rhonda Michelle. Mem. tech. staff Tex. Instruments, Dallas, 1968—, project mgr. pattern recognition study, 1970-73, lead engr. Stblzn. Tech. Center Equipment Research and Devel. Lab., 1973—. Part-time instr. U. Tex., 1963-67; instr. computer programming I.E.E.E., 1972. Ford Found. fellow, 1964-67. Mem. I.E.E.E., Tau Beta Pi, Eta Kappa Nu. Club: Toastmasters Internat. (v.p. Richardson Noon chpt. 1971, pres. 1972, area ednl. gov. 1973). Patentee pattern recognition area. Office: 13500 N Central Av Dallas TX 75222

MASTERS, GEORGE R., utility co. exec.; b. Pickens, S.C., Dec. 2, 1924; s. George Dewey and Ina (Cannon) M.; B.S., Ind. Inst. Tech., 1948; m. Dorothy Alice Sorrells, June 26, 1949; children—Ronald, Karen, David. With Duke Power Co., Charlotte, N.C., 1949—, mgr. system communications, 1972—. Served with USNR, 1943-45. Registered profl. engr., N.C. Mem. I.E.E.E. (sr.). Home: Route 1 Box 373 Denver NC 28037 Office: 422 S Church St Charlotte NC 28242

MASTERS, ROBERT WAYNE, elec. products co. exec.; b. Ft. Wayne, Ind., May 25, 1914; s. Thomas Osgood and Elsie Mabel (Masten) M.; B.S. in Elec. Engring., U. Ala., 1938; M.S. in Communications, Ohio State U., 1941; Ph.D. in Elec. Engring., U. Pa., 1957; m. Audrey June Holstein, Oct. 11, 1941; 1 son, Robert Wayne. Adv. devel. engr. RCA, Camden, N.J., 1941-49; research asso., asst. prof. circuit theory antennas Ohio State U., Columbus, 1949-58; research supr. Boeing Airplane Co., Seattle, 1958-60; mgr. antenna dept. Melpar, Inc., Falls Church, Va., 1960-64; cons. fellow engr. Westinghouse Corp., Leesburg, Va., 1965-68; v.p., sec. Antenna Research Assos., Inc., Beltsville, Md., 1968—, also dir. Chief elec. cons., mem. primary com. Empire State TV Tower, 1949-52; cons. at large TV transmitting systems and antennas, 1964-65. Registered profl. engr., Ohio. Fellow I.E.E.E.; mem. Sigma Xi, Tau Beta Pi, Eta Kappa Nu, Delta Chi. Presbyn. Mason (Shriner). Inventor TV transmitting antennas. Home: 6423 Walters Woods Dr Falls Church VA 22044 Office: 11317 Frederick Av Beltsville MD 20705

MASTRAN, DAVID VINCENT, systems analyst; b. El Paso, Tex., Dec. 14, 1942; s. Joseph Lee and Mary (Black) M.; B.S., U.S. Mil. Acad., 1965; M.S., Stanford, 1966; Sc.D., George Washington U., 1973; m. Shelley Ellen Smith, June 12, 1965; children—David Bruce, Susannah Mary. Commd. 2d lt. U.S. Air Force, 1965, advanced through grades to capt. 1971; reliability analyst Directorate of Spl. Weapons, San Antonio, 1966-67; operations research analyst Hdqrs. 7th Air Force Operations Analysis Office, Tan Son Nhut Air Base, Viet Nam, 1967-68, Hdqrs. Air Force Operations Analysis Office, Washington, 1968-71; ret., 1972; operations research analyst Office Asst. Sec. Def. (Systems Analysis), 1972-73; dir. research Dept. Health, Edn. and Welfare, 1973—. Decorated Bronze Star, Air Force Commendation medal. Mem. Operations Research Soc. Am., Washington Operations Research Council, Inst. Mgmt. Sci. (treas., newsletter editor D.C. chpt.), West Point Alumni Assn., Sigma Xi. Home: 933 Mackall Av McLean VA 22101 Office: Immediate Office Adminstr Social and Rehab Service Dept Health Edn and Welfare Washington DC 22010

MASTRO, NICK, state ofcl.; b. Jacksonville, Fla., Jan. 9, 1924; s. L.K. and Mary (Gionis) Mastrogianakis; B.C.E., U. Fla., 1946; M.P.H. in Engring., U. Mich., 1952; m. Eva Yeatropoulos, Oct. 4, 1953; children—Mary Christine, Elain Sophia. Jr. engr. Smith & Gillespie, cons. engrs., Jacksonville, 1946-47; with Fla. Bd. Health, Jacksonville, 1947—, regional san. engr., 1949-67, dir. div. indsl. waste, 1967-68, asst. chief bur. san. engring., 1968—. Dir. Div. Health Employees Credit Union. Mem. Gov.'s Environmental Coordinating Council. Registered profl. engr., Fla. Fellow Water Pollution Control Fedn.; mem. Fla. Pub. Health Assn., Nat. Soc. Profl. Engrs., Air Pollution Control Assn., Fla. Water Pollution Control Operators Assn., Fla. Engring. Soc., Sigma Tau, Sigma Phi Epsilon. Mem. Greek Orthodox Ch. (trustee, v.p.). Clubs: University Park Country, University Park Civic (dir. 1965-68) (Jacksonville). Home: 5413 Coppedge Av Jacksonville FL 32211 Office: Fla Div Health 1217 Pearl St Jacksonville FL 32201

MATEKER, EMIL JOSEPH, JR., geophysicist; b. St. Louis, Apr. 25, 1931; s. Emil J. and Lillian A. (Broz) M.; B.S., St. Louis U., 1956, M.S., 1959, Ph.D., 1964; m. Lolita A. Winter, Nov. 25, 1954; children—Mark Steven, Anne Marie, John David. Geophysicist, Stanolind Oil & Gas Co., Midland, Tex., 1956, Standard Oil Co. of Cal., Salt Lake City, 1957, 58-60; instr. geophysics St. Louis U., 1960-63; asst. prof. geophysics Washington U., St. Louis, 1963-66, asso. prof., 1966-69; mgr. geophys. research Western Geophys. Co., Houston, 1969-70, v.p. research and devel., 1970—. Cons. U.S. Army C.E., St. Louis Met. Sewer Dist., Fred Weber Constrn. Co., Traylor Bros. Constrn. Co., Pan Am. Petroleum Co., others. Served to 2d lt., inf. AUS, 1952-54. Mem. Soc. Exploration Geophysicists, Seismol. Soc. Am., Am. Geophys. Union, European Assn. Exploration Geophysicists, A.A.A.S., Sigma Xi. Author: A Treatise on Modern Exploration Seismology, 1965, also others. Asst. editor Geophysics, 1968-69. Home: 419 Hickory Post Houston TX 77024 Office: PO Box 2469 Houston TX 77001

MATHENY, CHARLES WOODBURN, JR., engr., city ofcl.; b. Sarasota, Fla., Aug. 7, 1914; s. Charles Woodburn and Virginia (Yates) M.; B.S. in Civil Engring., U. Fla., 1936; grad. Army Command and Gen. Staff Coll., 1944; m. Jeanne Felkel, July 12, 1942; children—Virginia Ann, Nancy Carolina, Charles Woodburn III. Civil engr. Fla. East Coast Ry., 1939-41; commd. 2d lt. U.S. Army Res., 1936, 1st lt. U.S. Army, 1941, advanced through grades to col., 1955; gen. staff Dept. Army, 1948-51; arty. bn. comdr., Germany, 1945-46; aviation officer 25th Inf. Div., Korea, 1952; dep. comdt., dir. combat devel. Army Aviation Sch., 1954; dep. dir., research dir., dept. tactics Arty. Sch., 1955-57; aviation officer 7th U.S. Army, 1957-58; Munich sub area comdr. So. Area Command, Europe, 1959, dep. chief staff for information, 1960; Mich. sector comdr. VI Army Corps, 1961-62; ret., 1962; asst. supt. Dept. Pub. Works and Engring., City of Tampa (Fla.), 1963—. Active Boy Scouts Am., various community and ch. activities. Decorated Bronze Star with oak leaf cluster, Air Medal with three oak leaf clusters. Registered profl. engr., Ga. Mem. Assn. U.S. Army, Army Aviation Assn., Am. Helicopter Soc., S.A.R., Alpha Tau Omega. Episcopalian. Initiator tactical use of helicopters in Army, 1949. Home: 4802 Beachway Dr Tampa FL 33609 Office: 404 Jackson St Tampa FL 33602

MATHENY, TOM HARRELL, lawyer; b. Houston; s. Whitman and Lorene (Harrell) M.; B.A., Southeastern La. U., 1954; J.D., Tulane U., 1957. Admitted to La. bar, 1957; partner firm Pittman & Matheny, Hammond, La., 1957—; trust counsel 1st Guaranty Bank, Hammond; v.p. Edwards & Assos., So. Brick Supply, Inc. Faculty, Southeastern La. U., 5 years, Holy Cross Coll., New Orleans, 3 years; lectr. Union Theol. Sem., Law Sci. Acad.; mem. com. on conciliation and mediation of disputes World Peace through Law Center. Chmn. advancement com. Boy Scouts Am., Hammond, 1960-64, mem. dist. council, 1957-66, mem. exec. bd. Istrouma council, 1966—, adv. com. to dist. area council; pres. Tangipahoa Parish Mental Health Assn.; sec. Chep Morrison Scholarship Found.; mem. men's com. Japan Internat. Christian U. Found.; chmn. speakers com., mem. com. on community action and crime prevention La. Commn. on Law Enforcement and Adminstrn. Criminal Justice. Bd. dirs. La. Moral and Civic Found., Tangipahoa Parish A.R.C., 1957-67, Hammond United Givers Fund, 1957-68, La. Council Chs., Southeastern Devel. Found., La. Mental Health Assn., Wesley Found., La. State U., 1965-68, 70—; sec. Chep Morrison Scholarship Found.; trustee Centenary Coll., 1964-70; hon. trustee John F. Kennedy Coll. Recipient Man of Year award, Hammond, 1961, 64, also La. Jr. C. of C., 1964. Fellow Harry S. Truman Library Inst. (hon.); mem. Am. (La. com. on probate and trust), La. (past gen. chmn. com. on legal aid), 21st Jud. Dist. (past sec.-treas., v.p. 1967-68, 71—) bar assns., Comml. Law League Am. (past mem. com. on ethics), La. Alumni Council (past pres.), Acad. Religion and Mental Health, La. Assn. Claimant Compensation Attys., Southeastern La. U. (dir., pres. 1961-62, dir. spl. fund 1959-62, past dir. Tangipahoa chpt.), Tulane Sch. Law alumni assns., Am. Trial Lawyers Assn., Am. Judicature Soc., Law-Sci. Inst., World Peace Through Law Acad., Acad. Polit. Sci., Am. Acad. Polit. and Social Sci., Internat. Acad. Law and Sci., Common Cause, Internat. Platform Assn., UN Assn., La. Hist. Assn., Friends of Cabildo, Gideons Internat., Nat. Assn. Conf. Lay Leaders (pres.), Assn. Conf. Lay Leaders South Central Jurisdiction (pres.), Hammond Assn. Commerce (dir. 1960-65), Phi Delta Phi, Phi Alpha Delta. Democrat. Methodist (steward, adminstrv. bd., dist. lay leader 1960-64, past co-chmn. conf. bd. lay activities, lay minister, lay leader La. area conf., numerous other ch. activities). Mason, DeMolay (Legion of Honor), Kiwanian (v.p., dir.). Home: Pleasant Ridge Hammond LA 70401 Office: Guaranty Bank Bldg Hammond LA 70401

MATHEWS, JAMES KENNETH, bishop; b. Breezewood, Pa., Feb. 10, 1913; s. James Davenport and Laura Mae (Wilson) M.; A.B., Lincoln Meml. U., 1934, D.D. (hon.), 1954; S.T.B., N.Y. Theol. Sem., 1937; grad. student Boston U. Sch. Theology, 1937-38; spl. student Cambridge (Eng.) U., 1955; Ph.D., Columbia, 1957; D.D., Wesleyan U., 1965, Colby Coll., 1971; L.H.D., Lycoming Coll., 1966, Ohio Wesleyan U., 1969, Norwich U., 1970; m. Eunice Jones, June 1, 1940; children—Anne (Mrs. Robert W. O'Connor), Janice (Mrs. William R. Stromsem), James Stanley. Ordained to ministry Methodist Ch., 1938; missionary to India, 1938-42; asso. sec. div. world missions Meth. Bd. Missions, 1946-52, asso. gen. sec., 1952-60; bishop United Meth. Ch., resident in Boston Area, 1960-72, Washington area, 1972—. Mem. United Meth. Bd. Global Ministries; chmn. United Meth. Div. Ecumenical and Interreligious Concerns; mem. exec. com. and governing bd. Nat. Council Chs.; chmn. Meth. Corp.; mem. central com. World Council Chs.; exec. com. World Conf. Religion for Peace; chmn. United Christian Ashrams. Trustee, Boston U., Am. U., Western Md. Coll., Wesley Coll., Sibley Meml. Hosp., Asbury Meth. Home, Morgan Christian Center United Meth. Home, Providence, Claflin Coll., Nur Manzil Psychiat. Center, Lucknow, India; chmn. trustees Santiago (Chile) Coll.; bd. govs., mem. exec. com. Wesley Theol. Sem.; bd. dirs. North Conway (N.H.) Inst., Friends of WCC Inc., Wesley Found., U. Del. Served to maj. AUS, 1942-46. Author: South of the Himalayas, 1955; To the End of the Earth, 1959; Eternal Values in a World of Change, 1960; A Church Truly Catholic, 1969; (with Eunice J. Mathews) Selections from E. Stanley Jones, 1972. Contbr. articles to jours., mags. Home: 4120 48th St NW Washington DC 20016 Office: 100 Maryland Av NE Washington DC 20002

MATHEWS, THOMAS RICHARD, assn. exec.; b. Salt Lake City, Aug. 1, 1921; s. Wesley Chase and Edith Blanche (Alm) M.; B.A., U. Utah, 1942; m. Bonnie Johnson, Dec. 27, 1942; children—Thomas Richard, Colin Dee, Anne. Sunday editor Salt Lake City Tribune, 1946-51; reporter San Francisco Chronicle, 1951-60; dir. information Peace Corps, Washington, 1961-62; dep. asst. sec. for congl. relations U.S. Dept. State, Washington, 1963-64, also White House cons., 1963; dir. pub. relations Lincoln Center for Performing Arts, N.Y.C., 1965-68; v.p. communications Urban Coalition, Washington, 1969; v.p. Common Cause, Washington, 1970—. Washington press sec. Robert Kennedy for Pres. campaign, 1968. Served as 1st lt. 10th Mountain Div., AUS, 1943-45. Decorated Air medal with 4 oak leaf clusters. Recipient Christopher award for outstanding journalism, 1960. Democrat. Clubs: Brooklyn Heights Casino (Bklyn.), St. Albans Tennis (Washington). Home: 2311 Connecticut Av NW Washington DC 20008 Office: Common Cause 2030 M St NW Washington DC 20036

MATHEY, F(ABYAN) COURTENAY, newspaper exec.; b. N.Y.C., July 14, 1932; s. C. Fabyan and Edith (Barber) M.; student Princeton, 1950-53; B.S., U. Ark., 1957, M.B.A., 1960; m. Emily Gail O'Rear, July 12, 1958; children—Fabyan Courtenay II, C. Robinson. Cons., Peat, Marwick, Mitchell & Co., Dallas, 1960-64; accountant E.L. Gaunt & Co., Little Rock, 1964-65; partner Rothwell & Mathey, C.P.A.'s, Dallas, 1965-69, Travis, Ramsey & Mathey, C.P.A.'s, Dallas, 1969-70; controller Dallas Times Herald, 1970—; treas., dir. Systems Devel., Inc. Pres., George B. Dealey Elementary Sch. Dad's Club, 1969-70; asst. scoutmaster Boy Scouts Am., 1973—. Served with AUS, 1953-55. C.P.A., Tex., Ark. Mem. Am. Inst. C.P.A.'s, Tex. Soc. C.P.A.'s. Clubs: Princeton (v.p.), Exchange of North Park (past pres.) (Dallas). Home: 6429 Orchid Lane Dallas TX 75230 Office: Herald Sq Dallas TX 75202

MATHIS, DAWSON M., congressman; b. Nashville, Ga., Nov. 30, 1940; s. Marvin W. and Nell Dawson (Abel) M.; student South Ga. Coll., 1958-60; m. Patricia Ann Connell, July 26, 1959; children—Anthony Dawson, Craig Steven, Jason Everett, Russell Dean. News dir. sta. WALB-TV, Albany, Ga., 1964-70; mem. 92d-93d congresses from 2d Dist. Ga., mem. House Com. Agr. Active Chehaw Boy Scouts Am., 1967-70. Mem. Ga. Assn. Newscasters, Fraternal Order Police. Elk, Toastmaster. Home: 1203 Forestwood Dr McLean VA 22101 also 1124 Stuart Av Albany GA 31701 Office: Cannon House Office Bldg Washington DC 20515

MATHIS, EVAN THOMAS, JR., mining co. exec.; b. Americus, Ga., Dec. 23, 1925; s. Evan Thomas and Lois (McMath) M.; student Ga. Southwestern Jr. Coll., 1942-43; B.S., U.S. Naval Acad., 1946; m. Nell McGehee, June 24, 1950; children—Lane, Nell, Carol. Commd. ensign U.S. Navy, 1946, advanced through gardes to lt., 1950; shipboard officer in U.S.S. Stormes, 1946-48, U.S.S. Patrol Craft Escort 903, 1948; naval aviator, Atlantic and Caribbean, 1948-54; with Marble Products Co., Atlanta, 1954—, sales mgr., 1954-58, treas., 1958-59, v.p., 1959-62, dir., 1959—, pres., 1962—; exec. v.p., dir. Fla. Terrazzo Supplies, Inc., Miami, Fla., 1960-65, pres., 1965—; exec. v.p., dir. Bilbrough Marble Co., Austin, Tex., 1964—; treas. Imperial Chems., Inc., West Palm Beach, 1960-65, pres., 1965—; co-owner Peachtree Park Office Bldg., Atlanta, 1963—; v.p., dir. Citizens Bank of Americus; adv. dir. Citizens & So. Nat. Bank, Atlanta; dir. Conseehee Carpets, Inc., Ellijay, Ga.; partner MSM Farms, Whitestone, Ga. Mem. Atlanta Freight Bur. (dir.), Young Pres.'s Orgn. Methodist (steward). Kiwanian. Clubs: Capital City, Gyro, Piedmont Driving. Home: 547 Spring Valley Rd NW Atlanta GA 30318 Office: 67 Peachtree Park Dr Atlanta GA 30309

MATHIS, ROBIN HOOD, broadcasting exec.; b. Houlka, Miss., Nov. 29, 1929; s. Henry Lacy and Annie Nina (Cole) M.; B.S. in Agronomy, Miss. State U., 1952; postgrad. Elkins Radio Sch., 1958; m. Shirley Lorraine Carroll, June 29, 1958; children—Melanie Carol, Leslie, Sharon. Announcer WHOS, Decatur, Ala., 1955; partner, mgr. WCPC-AM/FM, Houston, Miss., 1955-67, pres., gen. mgr., 1967—; partner WSJC-AM-FM, Magee, Miss., 1957—, WXTN, Lexington, Miss., 1958—, WDXE-AM/FM Lawrenceburg, Tenn., 1974—, WTPR-AM/FM, Paris, Tenn., 1974—, WSAO, Senatobia, Miss. Bd. dirs. Chickasaw Devel. Found.; trustee radio and TV commn. So. Bapt. Conv., 1973—. Served from 2d lt. to 1st lt., USAF, 1952-54. Recipient Silver Beaver award Boy Scouts Am. Mem. U.P.I., Nat. Assn. Broadcasters, Daytimers (nat. dir.), Miss. (state dir.) broadcasters assns. Miss. Econ. Council (dir. 1967-69), U.S. Jr., Miss. Jr. (pres. 1962-63) chambers commerce. Baptist. Club: Exchange (pres. Houston 1967-68). Home: Route 2 Box 29 Houston MS 38851 Office: PO Box 569 Houston MS 38851

MATLOCK, KENNETH JEROME, bldg. materials co. exec.; b. Oak Park, Ill., May 30, 1928; s. Harvey and Lillian (Sivertsen) Samuelson; student James Millikin U., 1946-48; B.S. in Accountancy, U. Ill., 1950; postgrad. Northwestern U. Inst. Mgmt., summer 1963; m. Dorothy Belowski, Nov. 3, 1956; children—Geoffrey, Barbara, Gail, Paul. Sr. audit mgr. Price Waterhouse & Co., Chgo., 1950-64; with Celotex Corp., Chgo., 1964-65, v.p. financial operations, Tampa, Fla., 1965-70; asst. to v.p. Jim Walter Corp., Tampa, 1966-70, controller, 1970—, v.p., 1972—; v.p. Jim Walter Research Corp., St. Petersburg, Fla., 1967—; controller, dir. Walter Land Co., Tampa, 1970—. Adviser, Jr. Achievement, Chgo., 1958-60; active Heart Fund, United Fund, Chgo., 1956-58. Served with USNR, 1945-46. C.P.A., Ill., Fla. Mem. Am. Inst. C.P.A.s, Ill., Fla. socs. C.P.A.s, Financial Execs. Inst. Home: 1401 87th Av N St Petersburg FL 33702 Office: 1500 N Dale Mabry Hwy Tampa FL 33607

MATLOCK, ROBERT JOE, dentist; b. Dumas, Ark., July 20, 1940; s. Robert Gray and Josephine (Edington) M.; B.A., U. Ark., 1962; D.D.S., U. Tenn., 1965; m. Darlene Burnett, July 19, 1969; 1 dau., Jennifer Gray. Dentist, Wayne County Health Dept., Greenville, Mo., 1965; individual practice dentistry, Rogers, Ark., 1969—; mem. staff Rogers Meml. Hosp. Served to maj. Dental Corps, AUS, 1965-69. Mem. Am., Ark., Northwest Ark. dental assns., Ozark Dental Study Club, Am. Soc. Dentistry for Children, Rogers C. of C., Delta Sigma Delta. Methodist. Elk (exalted ruler), Kiwanian (dir.). Home: 904 S 14th Pl Rogers AR 72756 Office: 1107 W Elm St Rogers AR 72756

MATOUSEK, ELIZABETH GRAW (MRS. O. RALPH MATOUSEK), lawyer; b. Homestead, Fla., Nov. 9, 1925; d. G. LaMonte and Lillian I. (Mills) Graw; student Stetson U., 1943-45; B.S., Northwestern U., 1947; J.D., U. Miami, 1968; m. O. Ralph Matousek, Dec. 28, 1946; children—Robert, Charles, Martha Lynne. Catalog copywriter Sears, Roebuck & Co., Chgo., 1947-50; admitted to Fla. bar, 1968; since practiced in Homestead. Pres. Avocado Elementary P.T.A., 1964; sec. Homestead Pioneer Mus., 1972-73. Mem. Dade County Commn. Status Women, 1973—. Mem. Fla. Assn. Women Lawyers, Fla. Bar, Homestead Bar Assn. (pres. 1972-73), C. of C. (pres. 1972-73, dir. 1972-75). Delta Delta Delta. Presbyn. (pres. women of the ch. 1951-52). Elk Women. Clubs: Woman's (pres. 1953-54), Soroptomist (pres. 1972-73) (Homestead). Home: 4 NW 22d St Homestead FL 33030 Office: 234 N Krome Av Homestead FL 33030

MATOUSEK, O(TTO) RALPH, lawyer; b. Chgo., May 29, 1923; s. Otto J. and Helen (Filip) M.; B.A., Stetson U., 1944; postgrad. Harvard, 1944-45; J.D., Northwestern U., 1949; m. Lillian Elizabeth Graw, Dec. 28, 1946; children—Robert, Charles, Martha Lynne. Admitted to Ill. bar, 1949, Fla. bar, 1949, U.S. Supreme Ct. bar, 1961; practiced in Chgo., 1949, Homestead, Fla., 1949—; spl. asst. atty. gen., Homestead, 1952-64; city atty., Homestead, 1953-61; dir., gen. counsel First Nat. Bank, Fla. Title Co.; pres., chmn. Homestead Radio Sta. WIII; founding dir. Fla. Title Co., Miami, First Nat. Bank of Princeton-Naranja. Served to lt. comdr. USNR, 1943-46. Named Boss of Yr., Homestead Secs. Assn., 1959. Mem. Fla. Bar, Am., Ill., Homestead (pres. 1968-70) bar assns., Am. Legion, V.F.W., Sigma Nu, Delta Theta Phi, Phi Alpha Theta, Pi Gamma Mu. Democrat. Presbyn. Elk (exalted ruler 1953, state v.p. 1958, dist. dep. 1959), Rotarian (pres. 1963), Moose (gov. Homestead 1971, dist. pres. 1972-73). Home: 4 NW 22d St Homestead FL 33030 Office: 234 N Krome Av Homestead FL 33030

MATSON, JESSIE BALDWIN, ret. govt. ofcl.; b. Omaha, July 18, 1904; d. William Arthur and Elizabeth M. (Bratt) Baldwin; student Grinnell Coll., 1922-25; A.B., U. Neb., 1926; postgrad. U. Utah, 1945-47; children—John Hanthorn (dec.), Joanne Sandra. Writer Omaha Daily Jour. Stockman, 1926-30; syndicate writer Corn Belt Farm Dailies, 1930-34; state dir. women's div. Ia. Emergency Relief Adminstrn., 1934-35; Ia. dir. women's and profl. projects WPA, 1935-40; with Archives Security, Air Force, 1942; faculty mem. U. Utah, 1945-46; tchr. Guam, Marianas Islands, 1946-47; coordinator women's activities St. Paul Civil Def., 1950-70; now ret.; tchr. So. Cross Sch., Miami, Fla., 1971-72; substitute tchr. Charlotte County Schs., Lee County Schs. Former comdr. Ramsey County Cancer Soc.; founder St. Paul Council Human Relations, 1948; former chmn. Nat. Thanksgiving Day Assn.; past v.p. pub. affairs Soroptimist Fedn.

Ams.; life mem. past pres. St. Paul Club. State chmn. Luther W. Youngdahl campaign for gov., 1949-50. Recipient certificate of merit Gov. of Minn., 1961, 70, numerous awards on retirement. Mem. V.F.W. Aux., Am. Legion Aux., Bus. and Profl. Womens Clubs, Nat. Assn. Ret. Govt. Profl. Employees (asst. editor News), Inter-Club Council (founder 1944, pres. 1948-49, bd. mem.), League Women Voters, P.E.O., Theta Sigma Phi, Alpha Phi, Gamma Alpha Chi. Christian Scientist. Clubs: University, Toastmistress (founder 1st St. Paul and Peace River clubs). Home: 234 SE Beeney Rd Port Charlotte FL 33950

MATSON, MORRIS CHARLES, city ofcl.; b. Smackover, Ark., Sept. 24, 1928; s. George Loval and Della Banks (Cox) M.; M.B.A., Tex. Christian U., 1968; A.B., Bethany Nazarene Coll., 1951; m. Kathryn Chisholm, Dec. 17, 1948; children—Dana Kay, Paula. Budget dir., chief accountant, mgr. systems planning Western Co., Fort Worth, 1956-66; cons., mgr. Peat, Marwick, Mitchell, Dallas, 1966, 69-71; pres. AID Computing, Inc., 1967; v.p. marketing Computer Statistics, Inc., 1968; asst. city mgr., dir. finance City of Fort Worth, 1971—. Adj. asst. prof. Tex. Christian U., 1963—; faculty mem. continuing edn. program Nat. Assn. Accountants, 1966—; cons. City of New Orleans, Tex. Dept. Pub. Welfare. Loaned exec., mem. budget com. United Fund, Fort Worth, 1967-72; trustee, mem. exec. com. United Way of Tarrant County, 1973; treas., mem. exec. com. Casa Manana Musicals, Inc., 1971-73. Served to capt. USAF, 1951-56. Recipient Outstanding Alumnus award Bethany Nazarene Coll., 1962, 71, Outstanding Performance award Tex. Mid-Continent Oil and Assn., 1966. Mem. Nat. Assn. Accountants (mem. nat. com. edn. 1973-74), Am. Soc. Pub. Adminstrn., Municipal Finance Officers Assn., Assn. Systems Mgmt., Data Processing Mgmt. Assn., Beta Gamma Sigma. Ch. Rotarian. Contbr. to profl. publs. in field. Home: 5616 Woodway Dr Fort Worth TX 76133 Office: City Hall Fort Worth TX 76102

MATTESON, LEWIS WHITFORD, JR., data processing co. exec.; b. Houston, Nov. 24, 1924; s. Lewis Whitford and Lillian (Hall) M.; B.S. in Elec. Engring., Rice U., 1949; m. Betty Irene Dykes, Dec. 16, 1954; children—Sherry, Whit, Debbie, Ricky. Partner, Matteson S.W. Co., Houston, 1950-62, v.p., 1962-67; chmn. bd., 1967-71; owner, chmn. bd., pres. Matteson Transformers Inc., Houston, 1957-70; owner, mgr. Matteson Devel. Co., Houston, 1970—; v.p., sec., treas., dir. Plaza Lincoln-Mercury, Inc., Houston, 1971—; chmn. bd., pres. Matteson's Motorcycles, Inc., Kerrville, Tex., 1973—. Served with Signal Corps, AUS, 1943-46. Mem. I.E.E.E., Phi Theta Kappa. Episcopalian. Club: Racquet (Houston). Home: 211 Paul Revere Dr Houston TX 77024 also Casa del Rio Hunt TX 78024 Office: 9426 Old Katy Rd Houston TX 77055

MATTHEIS, FLOYD ELLIOTT, educator, ednl. adminstr.; b. Ellendale, N.D., Dec. 21, 1931; s. John and Katherine (Ammon) M.; B.S. in Edn., U. N.D., 1952; M.Ed., U. N.C., 1959, Ed.D., 1962; m. Clarice Pauline Skeie, Aug. 21, 1955; children—David, John, Mary, Joseph, Jane. Tchr. sci. and math. Granite Falls (Minn.) High Sch., 1954-58; asst. prof. sci. East Carolina U., Greenville, N.C., 1960-63, asso. prof., 1963-66, prof., 1966—. Cons. on Sci. Curriculum Improvement Study program. Served with AUS, 1952-54. Mem. Nat. Sci. Tchrs. Assn., Assn. Edn. Tchrs. Sci., Nat. Assn. Research in Sci. Teaching, N.E.A., N.C. Assn. Educators, Phi Delta Kappa. Lutheran (mem. exec. bd. 1967-73). Home: 1402 Evergreen Dr Greenville NC 27834 Office: Sci Edn Dept East Carolina Univ Greenville NC 27834

MATTHEWS, CARL LEWIS, supt. schs.; b. Smiths Grove, Ky., Mar. 17, 1924; s. Jerman Walter and Lula D. (Rountree) M.; A.B., Westery Ky. State U., 1951, M.A., 1954; m. Dorothy Coop, Sept. 9, 1950; children—Monie, Sheila, David, Mark. Social studies tchr., Hopkinsville, Ky., 1951-52, Park City, 1952-54; asst. prin. high sch., Hilliard, Fla., 1954-56, Munfordville, Ky., 1956-60; supt. schs., West Point, Ky., 1960—. Active Boy Scouts Am., Girl Scouts Am., local Heart Fund. Chmn. Recreation Commn., West Point, 1961-72; chmn. Zoning Appeals Bd., West Point, 1969-72. Served with USAAF, 1942-46. Mem. Nat., Ky. edn. assns., Am., Ky. assns. sch. adminstrs., Internat. Platform Soc., Ky. Hist. Assn. Republican. Mem. Ch. of Christ. Home: 1502 Geoghegan St West Point KY 40177 Office: PO Box 367 West Point KY 40177

MATTHEWS, CHARLES SEDWICK, petroluem co. exec.; b. Houston, Mar. 27, 1920; s. Charles James and Zadoc (Sedwick) M.; B.S. in Chem. Engring., Rice U., 1941, M.S., 1943, Ph.D., 1944; m. Miriam Ormerod, June 2, 1945; children—Joan, Wendy. With Shell Devel. Co., San Francisco, 1944-48, Houston, 1948-65, N.Y.C., 1965-67, dir. research, Houston, 1967-72, mgr. engring., 1972—. Mem. Shell Found., 1967—, engring. adv. council Rice U., Houston, 1971—; chmn. Tex. Engrs. for Conservation, 1973—. Registered profl. engr., Tex. Mem. Soc. Petroleum Engrs. (distinguished lectr.), Am. Petroleum Inst. Clubs: Houston, Meyerland (Houston). Author: (with D.G. Russell) Pressure Buildup and Flow Tests in Wells, 1967. Patentee in field. Contbr. profl. jours. Home: 5307 S Braeswood Blvd Houston TX 77035 Office: PO Box 2463 Houston TX 77001

MATTHEWS, DORIS BOOZER (MRS. CHARLES L. MATTHEWS), educator; b. Lexington, S.C., Aug. 18, 1932; d. Otto Raymond and Ruth (Sox) Boozer; B.S., Newberry Coll., 1952; M.Ed., U.S.C., 1955, 6-Yr. Certificate, 1971, Ph.D., 1972; m. Charles L. Matthews, Aug. 20, 1952; children—Shirley Ruth, Carles Ray, Sylvia Ann. Tchr., Brennen Sch., Columbia, S.C., 1952-64; supr. counseling S.C. State Employment Service, Columbia, 1964-66; counseling supr. and basic edn. specialist S.C. Com. for Tech. Edn., Columbia, 1966-68; instr. elementary edn. U. S.C., Columbia, 1968-72; asst. prof. S.C. State Coll., Orangeburg, 1972—. Chmn. Columbians Youth Com., 1968-72, chmn. Cayce Neighborhood Center, 1967-70. Mem. Nat., S.C. edn. assns., Nat., S.C. assns. supervision and curriculum devel., Audio-Tutorial Congress, Employment Counselors Assn., Am. Vocational Guidance Assn., Am., S.C. personnel and guidance assns., S.C. Dept. Audio-Visual Instrn., Am. Vocational Assn., Am. Assn. U. Profs., S.C. State Employees Assn., Internat. Platform Assn. Lutheran. Clubs: Cayce Womens (pres. 1965-67), Fashion Rose Garden (pres. 1962-64). Home: 101 Deliesseline Rd Cayce SC 29033 Office: SC State Coll Orangeburg SC 29115

MATTHEWS, JAMES HARVEY, physician; b. Liberty, Mo., June 11, 1916; s. Ollie G. and Antoinette Thompson (Craig) M.; B.S., Okla. Baptist U., 1937; M.D., Vanderbilt U., 1941; m. Doris Marie Parish, June 11, 1939; children—Annette (Mrs. Ray M. Woodlief), Rebecca (Mrs. Michael H. Barnes), Jeanne (Mrs. Ward B. Masden, Jr.). Physician VA Hosps., Asheville, N.C. and Nashville, 1946-60; chief, pulmonary disease research, VA Central Office, Washington, 1960-68, asst. dir. research service, 1968-72; clinician Va. Tb Control Bur., 1972—. Served with M.C., AUS, 1942-46. Fellow A.C.P., Am. Coll. Chest Physicians; mem. Am. Thoracic Soc., Alpha Omega Alpha. Editor: Transactions, VA Armed Forces Pulmonary Disease Conferences, 1960-68. Home: 3030 Stratford Rd Richmond VA 23225 Office: 109 Governor Rd Richmond VA 23219

MATTHEWS, JAY ARLON, JR., publisher, editor; b. St. Louis, Apr. 13, 1918; s. Jay Arlon and Mary (Long) M.; student San Jose State Coll., 1939-41, U. Tex., 1946-47; m. May Clark McLemore, Jan. 16, 1944; children—Jay Arlon III, Emily Cochrane, Sally McLemore. Asst. dir. personnel Adj. Gen.'s Dept. Tex., 1947-53, dept. adj., 1957-65, mil. support plans officer, 1965-69, chief emergency operations, 1965-71; pub. Presidial Press, Mil. History Press. Past dir. Civil Def., Austin; mem. adv. bd. Confed. Research Center, Hill Jr. Coll. Served with AGC, Tex. N.G., 1946—, brig. gen. ret., 1973. Mem. Austin (state v.p. 1951-52) U.S. (chmn. nat. security com. 1952-53) jr. chambers commerce, Tex. Safety Assn. (dir. traffic safety), N.G. Assn. U.S. (chmn. publicity 81st Gen. Conf.), Instituto Internationale de Historia Militar (hon. life), Co. Mil. Historians, Assn. U.S. Army. Episcopalian. Club: Exchange. Editor: Mil. History of Tex. and S.W. Quar. Home: 1807 Stamford Lane Austin TX 78703 Office: 6529 South Interregional US 35 Austin TX 78744 and PO Box 5248 Austin TX 78703

MATTHEWS, JOHN LOCKETT, accountant; b. Dallas, Mar. 15, 1911; s. Roy Mancil and Katherine (Tate) M.; LL.B., Dixie U., 1932, LL.D., 1942, J.D., 1966; m. Mary Cathryn Fullerton, Sept. 30, 1939; children—John Frederick, Margaret Anne, Roy Richard. Admitted to Ark. bar, 1932; practice law, Little Rock, 1932-35; practice income tax law, accountant, 1938-51; asst. mgr. lab. furniture mfg. co., 1951-53; gen. mgr., sec.-treas. Taylor Mfg. Co. (Tex.), 1953-73, also dir.; now pub. accountant. Pres. E. Williamson County Cancer Soc., 1966, TB Assn., 1965-66. Served to 1st lt., U.S. Army, 1935-38. Licensed pub. accountant. Mem. Ark. Bar Assn., A.I.M. (fellow pres.'s council 1969-70), Nat., Tex. socs. pub. accountants. Mason (Shriner, 32 deg.). Home: 1720 Kimbro St Taylor TX 76574 Office: 1007 N Main St Taylor TX 76574

MATTHEWS, MARTIN, accountant, educator; b. nr. Timmonsville, S.C., June 30, 1915; s. Martin L. and Elizabeth (Sansbury) M.; B.S., U. S.C., 1938, M.Accountancy, 1971; grad. LaSalle Extension U., 1944. Accountant, U.S. Govt., 1938-39, Standard Oil Co. of N.J., 1939-42; pub. accountant, 1946-54; gen. practice C.P.A., 1954-60; partner Matthews & Yates, C.P.A.'s, Columbia, S.C., 1960-64, owner, mgr., 1964-72, partner, 1972—; asso. prof. accounting S.C. State Coll., 1967—. Sec., Columbia Covenant Council of Lutheran Chs., Mo. Synod. Served with AUS, 1942-46. Mem. S.C. Assn. C.P.A.'s, Am. Inst. C.P.A.'s, Nat. Assn. Accountants, Am. Assn. Univ. Profs., S.C. Assn. Accounting Instrs. (sec.-treas.), S.C. C. of C. Lutheran (past pres.). Mason, Elk. Clubs: Optimist (past dist. lt. gov., S.C. dist. gov. 1970-71), Columbia Breakfast Optimist (past pres.). Home: 2931 Forest Dr Columbia SC 29204 Office: 2230 Devine St Columbia SC 29205

MATTHEWS, RITA SUE, assn. exec.; b. Durant, Okla., Dec. 18, 1925; d. Edward Sam and Lois (Sharpless) Matthews; A.A., No. Okla. Jr. Coll., 1946; B.A. in Journalism, U. Okla., 1949. News editor Sentinel (Okla.) Leader, 1949-50, Tonkawa (Okla.) News, 1950-51; women's editor radio sta. KWHW, Altus, Okla., 1951-54; health information sec. Tulsa County Pub. Health and Heart Assn., 1954-56; field rep. Okla. Heart Assn., 1956-64, exec. dir., 1965—. Mem. Gov.'s Com. on Rehab., 1966-67, Gov's Council on Regional Med. Program, 1966-73; mem. nat. com. on rehab. Am. Heart Assn., 1968-70. Bd. dirs. Oklahoma City Vis. Nurse Assn., 1973—. Mem. Okla. Pub. Health Assn. (v.p. 1969-70), Okla. Health and Welfare Assn., Okla. Assn. Voluntary Health Agys. (pres. 1970-72), Theta Sigma Phi. Republican. Presbyn. Home: 1845 Westminster Pl Oklahoma City OK 73120 Office: 800 NE 15th St Oklahoma City OK 73104

MATTHEWS, THOMAS A., lawyer; b. Chgo., Aug. 3, 1901; s. Thomas Henry and Lorena (Stewart) M.; A.B., Northwestern U., 1922, J.D., 1925; m. Elsie S. Spears, June 27, 1925; children—Thomas Alexander, Byron Stewart. Admitted to Ill. bar, 1925; practiced in Chgo., 1926-71; specialist on municipal law; editor Edward Thompson Law Pub. Co.; counsel for Ill. Municipal League, 1927-65. Presbyn. Author complete code of ordnances for about 150 cities and villages in Ill. Author: Municipal Ordinances, 4 vols.; pamphlets: Handbook for Municipal Officials; How To Levy Taxes; Municipal Licensing Powers; Forms for Special Assessment Proceedings. Contbr. to Ill. Municipal Rev. Editor: Current Municipal Problems Mag. Home and Office: 926 Sandstone Dr Bartlesville OK 74003

MATTHEWS, THOMAS LEROY, JR., aluminum co. exec.; b. Phila., Nov. 5, 1918; s. Thomas LeRoy and Elsie (Von Zingraf) M.; B.A., U. Va., 1941, M.A., 1950; mgmt. certificate U. Richmond, 1954; B.S. (hon.), Ga. Inst. Tech., 1958; m. Nellie Louise Early, June 7, 1941; 1 dau., Carol Loraine. Research asso. Dept. Air Force, 1948-50; head psychology VA Center Va., Charlottesville, 1948-50; with Reynolds Metals Co., 1950—, personnel mgr., mgr. personnel research, Richmond, Va., 1957-61, div. personnel mgr. cable and can divs., 1961-67, dir. manpower planning and devel., 1967-74, gen. dir. personnel services, 1974—. Mem. adj. faculty Va. Commonwealth U.; mem. vis. faculty U.S. Army Logistics Mgmt. Center; vis. lectr. U. Va., U. Minn. Served to capt. AUS, 1942-46. Mem. Am., Southeastern psychol. assns., Am. Mgmt. Assn., Va. Acad. Sci., A.A.A.S., Am. Soc. Personnel Adminstrn., Sigma Xi, Sigma Nu, Theta Kappa Psi. Contbr. articles to profl. jours. Home: Beechwood Box 216 Route 1 Doswell VA 23047 Office: 6601 W Broad St Richmond VA 23218

MATTHEWS, WILLIAM BUSH, lawyer; b. Memphis, Feb. 12, 1931; s. Joseph Warren and Jewel (Bush) M.; B.A., U. Tenn., 1952; LL.B., Vanderbilt U., 1956; m. Florence Carroll, Jan. 22, 1955; children—William Bush, Maurine Carroll, Warren Carroll. Admitted to Ala. bar, 1956; practice law, Ozarks, Ala., 1956—; asst. dist. atty. Dale County, 1959—. Dir. Bank of Ozark. Mem. Ala. Bar Commn., 1966—. Chmn., Dale County March of Dimes, 1957-58, Dale County Red Cross, 1959-60. Served with AUS, 1953-55. Mem. Delta Sigma Phi, Phi Delta Phi. Rotarian (pres. 1966-67); Ozark Quarterback. Methodist. Home: Squirrel Dr Ozark AL 36360 Office: PO Box 1145 Ozark AL 36360

MATTHEWS, 'WILLIAM HENRY III, geologist, educator; b. Henryetta, Okla., Mar. 1, 1919; s. William Henry and Douglass (Fain) M.; B.A., Tex. Christian U., 1946, M.A., 1948; m. Jennie Anzalone, Sept. 7, 1942; children—William Henry, James Douglas. Asst. prof. geology Tex. Christian U., 1948-52; subsurface geologist Texaco, Inc., Midland, Tex., 1952-55; prof. geology Lamar U., Beaumont, Tex., 1955—. Research scientist Tex. Bur. Econ. Geology, Austin, summers 1962-70; dir. edn. Am. Geol. Inst., Washington, 1972-73; chief sci. adviser Ency. Brit. Films. Served with USNR, 1942-45. Fellow Geol. Soc. Am., Tex. Acad. Sci., mem. Nat. Assn. Geology Tchrs. (pres. 1969-70, Neil Miner award 1965), Nat. Sci. Tchrs. Assn., Paleontol. Soc., Geosci. Information Soc., Sigma Xi, Phi Kappa Phi. Author: Fossils, 1962; Wonders of Dinosaur World, 1963; Geology Made Simple, 1967; Story of the Earth, 1968; Wonders of Fossils, 1968; Guide to the National Parks, 1968; Story of Volcanoes and Earthquakes, 1969; Science Probes the Earth, 1969; Invitation to Geology, 1971; Soils, 1971; Earth's Crust, 1971; Introducing the Earth, 1972. Home: 5795 Sul Ross Beaumont TX 77706 Off'ce: Box 10031 Lamar Univ Beaumont TX 77710

MATTHEWS, WILLIAM MCGILL V, dept. store exec.; b. Gastonia, N.C., July 17, 1940; s. Henry Belk and Evelyn (McArver) M.; B.S., Presbyn. Coll., 1962; m. Frances Augusta Flournoy, Sept. 10, 1966; children—William McGill, Evelyn Flourncy, Carson Henry Belk. With Belk Matthews Co., dept. stores, Macon, Ga., 1964—, sec.-treas., 1966—, v.p., 1972—, also dir.; v.p., sec.-treas., dir. stores in Warner Robins, Milledgeville, Dublin, Cordele and Vidalia, Ga.; dir. First Nat. Bank & Trust Co., Macon. Chmn., Macon Downtown Council, 1971. Served with AUS, 1962-64. Mem. Macon C. of C. (dir. 1972—), Presbyn. Coll. Nat. Alumni Assn. (pres. 1974), Kappa Alpha. Presbyn. (deacon 1971—, trustee day sch.). Rotarian. Club: Idle Hour Country (Macon). Home: 3185 Vista Circle Macon GA 31204 Office: 464 3d St Macon GA 31202

MATTINGLY, JAMES WILLIAM, JR., apparel mfg. co. exec.; b. Lexington, Ky., Nov. 9, 1920; s. James William and Geneva (White) M.; A.B., U. Ky., 1949; m. Kitty Richardson, Oct. 6, 1950; children—John Basil, Laura Lee, Todd Davenport. With Cowden Mfg. Co., Lexington, Ky., 1951—, salesman, 1954-61, account exec., 1961-67, v.p. merchandising, 1968—, also dir. Served with USMCR, 1942-45. Episcopalian (vestryman). Clubs: Lafayette, Lexington Country, Lansdowne (Lexington). Home: Route 5 Evans Mill Rd Lexington KY 40507 Office: 300 New Circle Rd NW PO Box 2500 Lexington KY 40501

MATTINGLY, THOMAS K., astronaut; b. Chgo., Mar. 17, 1936; s. Thomas K. Mattingly; B. Aero. Engring., Auburn U., 1958. Commd. officer U.S. Navy, 1958, now lt.; astronaut NASA Manned Spacecraft Center, Houston; pilot command module Apollo XVI, 1972. Address: NASA Manned Spacecraft Center Houston TX 77001*

MATTISON, CHARLES RAY, city ofcl.; b. Belton, S.C., July 13, 1929; s. Clyde Calhoun and Carrie Lucinda (Fant) M.; grad. Cecil's Inst. Accountancy, Greenville, S.C., 1949; m. Betty Lucille Vaughn, Aug. 20, 1954; 1 dau., Connie Faye. Shipping clk. Textron, Inc., Belton, 1949-51; city clk., treas. Town of Belton, 1951-52; teller, internal control accountant S.C. Nat. Bank, Belton, 1952-57; mgr. Greer & Campbell Ins. Agy., Belton, 1957-59; accountant J. Marion Campbell & Co., Anderson, S.C., 1960-61; city clk., treas. City of Belton, 1962—. Sec., Belton Jr. C. of C., 1956-57, treas., 1957-58. Recipient Outstanding Civic Leaders of Am. award, 1967. Mem. Internat. Inst. Municipal Clks., Anderson County Municipal Assn. (asst. sec., treas.). Baptist. Home: 437 Forest Lane Belton SC 29627 Office: PO Box 520 201 O'Neal St Belton SC 29627

MATTOX, HOYT TOBIAS, pub. relations dir.; b. Los Angeles, July 11, 1938; s. Harry Emmitt and Cloie Phyrne (Stich) M.; B.A. in Journalism, Tex. A. and M. U., 1959; m. Rachel Anne Zimmerman, July 15, 1967; 1 dau., Anne Meredith. Pub. relations with Foley's, Houston, 1962-68, Sakowitz, Houston, 1968-70; exec. dir. Houston Area Forum, 1970-71; adminstrv. mgr. Houston Symphony, 1971-72; pub. relations dir. Houston Symphony Soc., 1973-74; mgr. pub. relations Prudential Ins. Co., 1974—. Mem. adv. bd. Miller Theatre; mem. Country Playhouse, Theatre Suburbia. Served with USAF, 1959-62, capt. Res. Mem. Pub. Relations Soc. Am., Tex. Soc. Fundraisers, Houston C. of C. (cultural affairs and civic affairs coms.). Republican. Presbyn. Home: 12619 Trail Hollow Houston TX 77024 Office: PO Box 2075 Houston TX 77001

MATTOX, JOSEPH HERBERT, JR., univ. pub. relations exec.; b. Chillicothe, O., Sept. 5, 1914; s. Joseph Herbert and Mary Olive (Blaney) M.; student La. State U., 1934-37, 49-51; m. Mary Bertha Willis, Dec. 20, 1940; 1 dau., Ilse. Writer, editor Baton Rouge State-Times and Morning Adv., 1936-37; pub. relations counsel La. Welfare Dept., also La. Hosp. Bd., 1937-40; editor Monroe (La.) Morning World, 1940-41, Memphis Comml. Appeal, 1941-42; dir. pub. relations La. State U. System, Baton Rouge, 1948-72, coordinator information services, communications counsel, 1972—. Pub. relations cons. Chillicothe Sesquicentennial Commn., 1946-47. Served from pvt. to lt. col., inf. AUS, 1942-46; ETO. Decorated Bronze Star. Mem. Am. Coll. Pub. Relations Assn. (dist. pres. 1952), Pub. Relations Soc. Am. (pres. Baton Rouge chpt. 1961-63). Democrat. Episcopalian. Author: The Future of Educational Public Relations, 1951. Editor: Welfare, 1937-40. Contbr. articles profl. jours. Home: 2425 June St Baton Rouge LA 70808 Office: Louisiana State University, Baton Rouge LA 70803

MATUSZKO, ANTHONY JOSEPH, chemist; b. Hadley, Mass., Jan. 31, 1926; s. Joseph Anthony and Kathryn (Narog) M.; B.A., Amherst Coll., 1946; M.S., U. Mass., 1951; Ph.D., McGill U., 1953; m. Anita Carolyn Colley, Oct. 26, 1966; children—Martha, Mary, Stephen, Richard. Mem. faculty Lafayette Coll., Easton, Pa., 1952-58, asso. prof., 1956-58; asso. head chemistry div., head fundamental process div., head polymer div. Naval Ordnance Sta., Indian Head, Md., 1958-62; program mgr. chemistry Air Force Office Sci. Research, Arlington, Va., 1962—. Pres., Forest Hts. Elementary Sch. P.T.A., 1966-67. Served with AUS, 1946-48. Recipient superior performance award USAF, 1966. Fellow A.A.A.S., Am. Inst. Chemists; mem. Am. Chem. Soc., Am. Ordnance Assn. Clubs: Cosmos, Torch. Contbr. articles to profl. publs. Patentee in field. Home: 4210 Elizabeth Lane Annandale VA 22003 Office: 1400 Wilson Blvd Arlington VA 22209

MAUDERLI, WALTER, educator; b. Aarau, Switzerland, Mar. 8, 1924; s. Jakob and Bertha (Hofer) M.; M.S. in Physics, Fed. Inst. Tech., Zurich, Switzerland, 1949, D.Sc., 1956; m. Lottie Leuw, Apr. 15, 1950; children—Claudine, Patricia, Priska, Pamela, Walter. Came to U.S., 1956, naturalized, 1962. Research asst. isotope, betatron labs. U. Zurich, 1950-56; asst. prof. isotope lab. U. Ark., Little Rock, 1956-60, also radiation safety officer Med. Center, 1956-60, asst. prof. math., physics, 1958-60; asso. prof. dept. radiology U. Fla., Gainesville, 1960-64, prof., 1965—. Served to 1st lt. Swiss Army, 1944-56. Mem. Am. Assn. Physicists in Medicine, Soc. Nuclear Medicine, Societe Helvetique des Naturelles, Soc. Fed. Inst. Tech., Swiss. Soc. Physics, A.M.A., Air Force Assn., Sigma Xi. Home: PO Box 13916 Gainesville FL 32604

MAUNDER, ADDISON BRUCE, agrl. products co. exec.; b. Holdrege, Neb., May 13, 1934; s. Addison Haynes and Marie (Luebs) M.; B.Sc. with high distinction, U. Neb., 1956; M.Sc., Purdue U., 1958, Ph.D., 1960; m. Marvel Lee Garrison, June 10, 1957; 1 dau., Lynda. Plant breeder Dekalb Ag Research Inc., Lubbock, Tex., 1960-61, dir. sorghum research, 1961—. Named Master, U. Neb., 1973. Mem. Am. Soc. Agronomy (founding pres. Tex. chpt. 1971), Council Agrl. Sci. and Tech., Tex. Technol. Univ. Agronomy Club (hon.), Sigma Xi, Farmhouse fraternity. Contbr. to profl. jours. Developed 51 comml. sorghum hybrids. Home: 4511 9th St Lubbock TX 79416 Office: Route 2 Lubbock TX 29415

MAURICE, ROBERT WELDON, architect, landscape architect; b. Houston, July 7, 1925; s. Charles Ernest and Minnie (Butler) M.; B.A., Rice U., 1946, B.S. in Architecture, 1946, M.A., (Mary Alice Elliott fellow), 1947; m. Beverly Taylor, Dec. 23, 1952; (div. Mar. 1970); children—Dianne Michelle, Robert W. II. Pvt. practice architecture, planning cons., 1948-61; partner firm Robert W. Maurice - Richard S. Wilkins & Assos., Houston, 1961—. Lectr., Sch. Architecture, U. Houston, 1956. Founder Zool. Soc. Houston, 1966; treas. Arts Council Houston, 1956-57. Bd. dirs. Music Guild, Houston. Decorated Compagnia dell'Arte dei Brentatori Soci d'Onore (Italy); recipient numerous awards Tex. Soc. Architects, A.I.A., others. Mem. A.I.A., Tex. Soc. Architects, Houston C. of C. Rotarian. Author: The Juveniles of Harris County. Contbr. articles to zool. jours. Home: 4040

San Felipe Rd #27B Houston TX 77027 Office: 3222 Mercer St Houston TX 77027

MAUZY, OSCAR HOLCOMBE, state senator; b. Houston, Nov. 9, 1926; s. Harry Lincoln and Mildred (Kincaid) M.; B.B.A., U. Tex., 1950, LL.B., 1952; m. Aglaia Dixie, Dec. 22, 1957; children—Catherine Anne, Charles Fred, James Stephen. Admitted to Tex. bar, 1951; partner firm Mullinax, Wells, Mauzy & Baab, Inc., Dallas, 1952—. State senator 23d Dist., 1967—; pres. pro tempore 63d Legislature, 1973—; acting gov. Tex., 1973—. Mem. nat. com. for Tex., Young Democrats, 1954-56; precinct chmn. Dem. party, Dallas, 1962-66; vice-chmn. Dem. Exec. Com. Dallas County, 1964-66. Served with USNR, 1944-46; PTO. Mem. Am., Dallas bar assns., State Bar Tex., Am. Trial Lawyers Assn., Am. Bd. Trial Advocates, V.F.W., Delta Theta Phi. Kiwanian. Home: 1338 Acapulco Dr Dallas TX 75232 Office: 8204 Elmbrook Dr Suite 200 Dallas TX 75247

MAVRIS, NICHOLAS BENNIE, pipe line co. exec.; b. Oklahoma City, Nov. 23, 1923; s. George and Ada Virginia (Diles) M.; B.S. in Mech. Engring., Okla. State U., 1948, M.S., 1949; m. Elizabeth Ann Shaver, July 3, 1943; children—Virginia Ann (Mrs. Earl Eugene Humes), George Samuel, Kathryn Ann, Nicola Ann. Instr., Okla. State U., 1948-49; engr. Interstate Oil Pipeline Co., 1949-51; asst. regional mgr. Rocky Mountain region Continental Oil Co., 1963-67, mgr. transp., 1967-68; with Continental Pipe Line Co., 1951-63, 68—, pres., chief exec. officer, Ponca City, Okla., 1969—, also dir.; dir., pres. Yellowstone Pipe Line Co., 1969—, Cherokee Pipe Line Co., Glacier Pipe Line Co., 1969—; dir. Butte Pipe Line Co., Platte Pipe Line Co., West Shore Pipe Line Co., Explorer Pipeline Co., Seadock, Inc. Served with AUS, 1943-46. Mem. Rocky Mountain Oil and Gas Assn. (dir.), Am. Petroleum Inst. (div. transp. central com. 1968—), Assn. Oil Pipe Lines. Club: Sugar Creek Country. Home: 802 Longview Dr Sugarland TX 77478 Office: PO Box 2197 Houston TX 77001

MAX, PETER, economist; b. Utica, N.Y., Mar. 19, 1933; s. Theodore Louis and Marian (Smith) M.; B.A., Williams Coll., 1955; postgrad. Cornell U., 1955-59; m. Susanne Widtman, Aug. 10, 1953;children—Eric, Gregg, Peter. With Cornell U., 1955-59, Carnegie Inst. Tech., 1959-60; sr. cons. Boni Watkins Jason & Co., N.Y., 1960-61, Nat. Econ. Research Assos., N.Y.C., 1961-63; chief bus. econs. Battelle Meml. Inst., Columbus, O., 1963-65; sr. cons. NERA, Inc., Washington, 1965-69; v.p. Nat. Econ. Research Assos., 1970—. Mem. Am. Econ. Assn., Am. Statis. Assn., Nat. Assn. Bus. Econ., Phi Beta Kappa, Phi Gamma Delta, Phi Kappa Phi. Clubs: International, Williams (Washington); Nat. Economists (pres. 1970, chmn. bd. govs. 1971, gov. 1972—). Address: 1211 Connecticut Av NW Washington DC 20036

MAXEY, JACK U., YMCA exec.; b. Oilton, Okla., Aug. 23, 1925; s. Jack and Ann (Miller) M.; student Salt City Bus. Coll., 1946-48, Hutchinson (Kan.) Jr. Coll., 1948-49, Bethany Coll., Lindsborg, Kan., 1949-51, George Williams Coll., Chgo., 1951-52; m. Melba Aleen Sims, Aug. 19, 1944; children—Ronald, Rommie Lee, Lynda, Danny, Randy. Phys. dir. YMCA, Chgo., 1951-53; phys. dir., program dir. YMCA, Streator, Ill., 1953-56; men's phys. dir. YMCA, Topeka, 1956-60; exec. dir. YMCA, Perryton, Tex., 1960-63, Greenville, Tex., 1963-69, Enid, Okla., 1969—. Served with A.C., USNR, 1942-46. Recipient Distinguished Service awards Perryton Lions Club, 1962, Perryton YMCA, 1960, Greenville YMCA, 1969. Mem. Assn. of Dirs., Sigma Delta Alpha. Methodist. Rotarian. Home: 119 S Watson St Enid OK 73701 Office: 415 W Cherokee St Enid OK 73701

MAXSON, ALBERT LEROY, airline exec.; b. Erie, Pa., Dec. 27, 1935; s. Walter LeRoy and Emily (Sabol) M.; B.S. in Bus. Adminstrn., Pa. State U., 1957; M.B.A., Ga. State U.; m. Linda Kay Kiger, Apr. 18, 1964; children—Barbara, Janet, Patricia. With Price Waterhouse & Co., Pitts., 1957-66; v.p. finance, treas. So. Airways, Inc., Atlanta, 1966—. C.P.A., W.Va., Penn. Home: 2663 Canna Ridge Circle NE Atlanta GA 30345 Office: Atlanta Airport Atlanta GA 30320

MAXWELL, CHESTER ARTHUR, radio exec.; b. San Antonio, Mar. 29, 1930; s. Chester A. and Clara A. (Olle) M.; student Trinity U., San Antonio, 1948-51; m. Carolyn King, Aug. 7, 1969; children by previous marriage—Sheryl Ann, Karen Kay (Mrs. Charles Cervantes). With advt. dept. Joskes of Tex., dept. store, San Antonio, 1952-56; account exec., sales mgr. KBAT radio, 1956-63; account ext. KILT radio, Houston, 1964-68; asst. gen. mgr. KBOX/KTLC radio, Dallas, 1969-71, v.p., gen. mgr., 1972—. Instr. summer student clinic Tex. Assn. Broadcasters, Howard Payne U., Abilene, Tex., 1962. Pres., Greater Dallas chpt. Muscular Dystrophy Assn., 1972-73. Trustee Dallas Multiple Sclerosis Soc. Served with USMC, 1946-48. Mem. Dallas Advt. League, Assn. Broadcast Execs. Tex. (sec. 1971, pres. 1974), Marketing and Communications Execs. Am. Club: Los Colinas Country (Dallas). Home: 9304 Raeford Dr Dallas TX 75231 Office: 9900 McCree Rd Dallas TX 75238

MAXWELL, GEORGE ENGLE, cons. engr.; b. Ft. Worth, Dec. 23, 1924; s. Roscoe Conklin and Stella Lillian (Shaw) M.; B.S. in Archtl. Engring., U. Tex., 1953, M.A., 1955; m. Yvonne Hensley, Dec. 23, 1947 (div. July 1969); children—Georgia, Scott, Kent. With bridge div. Tex. Hwy. Dept., Austin, 1952-54; with design and constrn. div. Tex. Bd. Control, Austin, 1954-63; architect, engr. Lumbermen's Investment Corp., Austin, 1963-67; individual practice archtl. engring., Austin, 1967—. Served to 2d lt. USAAF, 1943-47. Mem. Am. Soc. Heating, Refrigeration and Air Conditioning Engrs., Tex. Soc. Profl. Engrs., Am. Soc. C.E., Nat. Fire Protection Assn., Chi Epsilon. Club: Headliners (Austin). Home: 8220 Research Blvd Austin TX 78758 Office: 1201 W 24th St Austin TX 78705

MAXWELL, GROVER CLEVELAND, ret. retail exec.; b. Resaca, N.C., Nov. 6, 1887; s. Gilbert Motier and Mary Jeannette (Grady) M.; student pub. schs.; m. Corrie Ann Meares, Sept. 22, 1926; children—Grover Cleveland, George Motier, William Thomas. Former pres. Maxwell Bros., Inc., Augusta, Ga., ret., 1968; chmn. bd. emeritus Ga. R.R. Bank & Trust Co. Bd. visitors Presbyn. Coll.; chmn. Augusta Coll. Found. Served with Q.M.C., 1918. Mem. Augusta C. of C., Augusta Retail Assn., Ga. Bankers Assn. Mason. Clubs: Augusta Country, Augusta National, Pinnacle; Highland Country (N.C.); La Coquille (Palm Beach, Fla.). Author: Maxwell Brothers Furniture Business, 1968. Home: 2353 McDowell St Augusta GA 30904 Office: Ga R R Bank Bldg Augusta GA 30902

MAXWELL, HENRY FAVILLE, educator, clergyman; b. Esidumbini, Natal, South Africa, Mar. 18, 1908; s. Charles Henry and Katherine L. (Sullivan) M.; B.A., Carleton Coll., 1929; B.D., M.Div., Chgo. Theol. Sem., U. Chgo., 1932; M.F.C. in Theology, Mansfield Coll., Oxford, Eng., 1934; B.Litt., St. Catherine's Coll., Oxford, 1935, Oxford U., 1935; m. Mary Elizabeth Ketron, Sept. 30, 1934; 1 son, Henry Ketron. Ordained to ministry United Ch. of Christ, 1934; pastor 1st Congl. Ch., Ashland, Wis., 1934-37, Ladysmith, Wis., 1937-40, Flossmoor (Ill.) Community, Ch., 1940-44; commd. lt. (j.g.) U.S. Navy, 1944, advanced through grades to lt. comdr., 1954; staff chaplain Philippine Sea Frontier, 1945-46, 1st Marine Div., Tientsin, China, 1946-47, in U.S.S. Lake Champlain, 1957-59, U.S.S. F.D. Roosevelt, 1953-54; ret., 1965; asso. prof. sociology Limestone Coll., Gaffney, S.C., 1965-70; prof. sociology Dakota Wesleyan U., Mitchell, S.D., 1970-71; prof. ethics, dir. pastoral services Med. Univ. of S.C., Charleston, 1971—. Chaplain to students, interim prof. sociology, econs. Northland Coll., Ashland, Wis., 1934-47. Mem. Ill. Conf. United Ch. of Christ, Oxford Soc., Corinthian Lit. Soc. Kiwanian. Home: 1412 Burning Tree Rd Charleston SC 29412

MAXWELL, JUNIUS, sales exec.; b. Kinston, N.C., Oct. 15, 1931; s. Ernest Roscoe and Glenn (Sutton) M.; student U. N.C., 1949-50; B.S., N.C. State U., 1953, M.A., 1960; m. Virginia Clark Ihrie, June 22, 1957; children—Glenn Elizabeth, Junius Kenneth, William Ernest, Virginia Lynne. Farmer, Pink Hill, N.C., 1956-64; tech. rep. Daly-Herring Co., Kinston, 1964-65, mgr. animal health dept., 1965—. Served with AUS, 1954-56. Club: Methodist Men's (v.p. Pink Hill). Home: 201 Kinston Blvd PO Box 87 Pink Hill NC 28572 Office: PO Box 127 Teachey NC 28464

MAXWELL, OLEN DALE, psychiatrist; b. Tulsa, Oct. 3, 1939; s. Arlie Warren and Edna Pearl (Dees) M.; B.A., Tulsa U., 1962; M.D., Vanderbilt U., 1966; m. Sherry Caumissar, Apr. 2, 1971; 1 dau., Kelly Rebecca. Intern, U. Ky. Med. Center, 1966-67; resident psychiatry Vanderbilt U. Hosp., 1967-70; instr. dept. psychiatry Vanderbilt U., 1970-71; dir. student health psychiatry Okla. State U., Stillwater, 1971—; psychiat. cons. Payne County Guidance Center, 1971—, Osage County Guidance Center, 1972-73, Psychol. Guidance Center, Okla. State U., 1972—; mem. active staff Ponca City (Okla.) Hosp., 1971—, Stillwater Municipal Hosp., 1973—; guest lectr. Okla. State Guidance Center Assn., 1972. Bd. dirs. Sooner unit Am. Contract Bridge League. Diplomate Nat. Bd. Med. Examiners. Mem. A.M.A. (Physicians Recognition award 1970-72), Okla., Kay-Nobel Counties med. assns. Home: 6622 Coventry St Stillwater OK 74074 Office: 2324 W 7th Pl Stillwater OK 74074

MAXWELL, WILLIAM JAMES, dentist; b. Florence, S.C., Feb. 27, 1935; s. William James and Hannah (Harrell) M.; B.S., The Citadel, 1957; D.D.S., Med. Coll. Va., 1961; m. Mary Nell Wilson, Dec. 27, 1957; 1 son, William James, Jr. Dir. dental assisting program Florence-Darlington Tech. Edn. Center, 1967-69; pvt. practice gen. dentistry, Florence, 1963—. Bd. dirs. Am. Cancer Soc., 1969; mem. Pee Dee Comprehensive Health Planning Council, 1968—. Served to capt., Dental Corps, AUS, 1961-63. Mem. Am., S.C. dental assns., Pee Dee Dental Soc. (pres. 1969—), Pee Dee Dental Study Club (sec. 1968—), Psi Omega. Baptist. Kiwanian (dir. 1966-69). Home: 1019 Park Av Florence SC 29501 Office: 614 W Palmetto St Florence SC 29501

MAY, ALAN MUTNICK, restaurant chain exec.; b. N.Y.C., Apr. 23, 1935; s. Jack and Madeline (Mutnick) M.; S.B., Mass. Inst. Tech., 1957; M.B.A., N.Y. U., 1959; m. Marcia Wolfson, June 6, 1963; 1 dau., Alexandra Nicole. Asst. treas. Bankers Trust Co., N.Y.C., 1957-60, asst. v.p., 1960-65; v.p. finance Elcor Chem. Corp., Midland, Tex., 1965-69; exec. v.p., dir. Steak and Ale Restaurants of Am., Inc., Dallas, 1970—. Mem. Financial Execs. Inst. Home: 3601 Turtle Creek Blvd Dallas TX 75219 Office: 12890 Hillcrest St Dallas TX 75220

MAY, ALETHA BARRETT (MRS. DONALD W. MAY), advt. exec.; b. Trenton, Tex., July 11, 1911; d. James Absalom and Lois (Adams) Barrett; student Tex. Women's U., 1928-29; B.S., E. Tex. State Coll., 1940; m. Donald Wright May, Sept. 3, 1944; 1 dau., Janis Susan. Tchr. pub. schs., Tex., 1930-31; county home demonstration agt. Brooks County, Tex., 1941-44; editor, staff home economist Producer-Consumer, Amarillo, Tex., 1944-48; v.p. Don May Advt., Inc., Dallas 1958—. Home: 6149 Brandels Lane Dallas TX 75214 Office: PO Box 9736 Lakewood Station Dallas TX 75214

MAY, CLIFFORD HORTON, engring. co. exec.; b. Nokesville, Va., Feb. 29, 1924; s. Grover Thomas and Amelia (Horton) M.; B.S. in Mech. Engring., U. Md., 1950; m. Lucile Garnett Hinshaw, Jan. 31, 1948; children—Penelope (Mrs. James Thayer), Carolyn (Mrs. Lee Parrish, Jr.), Clifford Horton. Design engr. Westinghouse Corp., 1952-54; sr. project engr. U.S. Govt., Ft. Belvoir, Va., 1954-57; dir. research Bowser, Inc., 1957-65; chief engr. indsl. div. Fram Corp., Tulsa, 1965-68; founder, pres., chmn. bd. Banner Engring. Corp., Sapulpa, Okla., 1968—. Served with AUS, 1942-45; ETO; served to lt. USAF, 1951-52. Decorated Purple Heart. Registered profl. engr., Okla. Mem. Soc. Automotive Engrs., Am. Soc. Lubricating Engrs. Methodist (trustee). Patentee in field. Home: 702 S Muskogee St Sapulpa OK 74066 Office: 120 S Water St Sapulpa OK 74066

MAY, DONALD WRIGHT, advt. agy. exec.; b. Leonard, Tex., June 18, 1911; s. Robert C. and Mary Agnes (Wright) M.; m. Aletha Barrett, Sept. 3, 1944; children—Janis Susan, Robert Arthur. Editor, Memphis Democrat, Bay City Tribune, 1933-38; asso. prof. journalism Tex. A. and M. Coll., 1938-43; became dir. pub. relations and edn. Consumers Coops. Asso., 1943; dir. sales Farmers Coop. Exchange, Raleigh, N.C., 1952-54; asso. McCarty Co., advt. counselors, Dallas, 1954-58; pres. Don May Advt., Inc., Dallas, 1958—. Mem. Am. Assn. U. Profs., Tex., Panhandle press assns. A.I.M. (pres.'s council). Republican. Home: 6149 Brandeis Lane Dallas TX 75214 Office: PO Box 9736 Lakewood Sta Dallas TX 75214

MAY, FRANCIS BARNS, educator; b. Cascilla, Miss., Dec. 24, 1915; s. James Marshall and Hallye (Rice) M.; B.B.A. with highest honors, U. Tex., 1941, M.B.A., 1943, Ph.D., 1957; m. Janice Evelyn Christensen, June 9, 1956. Instr. bus. statistics U. Tex., Austin, 1941-43, asst. prof., 1947-58, asso. prof., 1958-61, prof. 1961—, chmn. dept. gen. bus., 1964-68, research scientist Bur. Bus. Research, 1954-57, statistician, 1958-64, cons. statistician, 1964—. Vis. prof. statistics U. Minn., Mpls., 1960; dir. San Antonio br. Dallas Fed. Res. Bank, 1966-71, chmn. bd., 1968, 70. Served from pvt. to capt., USAAF, 1943-46. Mem. Am. Statis. Assn. (council, pres. Austin chpt. 1964-66), Southwestern Social Sci. Assn. (chmn. bus. research sect. 1956-57, editor 1958, pres. 1968-69), Econometric Soc., Operation Research Soc., Inst. Mgmt. Scis., Phi Kappa Phi, Phi Eta Sigma, Beta Gamma Sigma, Sigma Iota Epsilon, Beta Alpha Psi. Club: Social Science (pres. Austin 1965-66). Author: Introduction to Games of Strategy, 1970. Asso. editor Tex. Bus. Rev., 1963-64. Contbr. numerous articles to profl. jours. Home: 6504 Auburnhill Austin TX 78723

MAY, HOWARD M., accountant; b. Ashland, Ky., June 18, 1917; s. Ruben N. and Dora Belle (Mutters) M.; grad. high sch.; m. Hilda Cooper, Nov. 2, 1946; 1 dau., Rhondda Lee. Clk. Laynes Pharmacy, Ashland, Ky., 1936-38; jr. accountant Estil W. Smith, C.P.A., 1939-41, 45-49; self-employed as C.P.A., Ashland, Ky., 1950—. Mem. Ashland (Ky.) Bd. Edn., 1965-72, pres., 1968-69. Served with AUS, 1941-45. C.P.A., Ky., W.Va. Mem. Am. Inst. C.P.A.'s, Ky., W.Va. socs. C.P.A.'s. Baptist (chmn. trustees 1968—). Kiwanian. Home: 2116 Mantz St Ashland KY 41101 Office: 2741 Winchester St Ashland KY 41101

MAY, JOHN LAWRENCE, bishop; b. Evanston, Ill., Mar. 31, 1922; s. Peter Michael and Catherine (Allare) M.; M.A., St. Mary of Lake Sem., Mundelein, Ill., 1945, S.T.L., 1947. Ordained priest Roman Catholic Ch., 1947; asst. pastor St. Gregory Ch., Chgo., 1947-56; chaplain Mercy Hosp., Chgo., 1956-59; v.p., gen. sec. Catholic Ch. Extension Soc. U.S., 1959-67, pres., 1967—; tchr. St. Gregory High Sch., Chgo., 1949-56, Loyola U., Chgo., 1948-49; lectr. Cana Conf. Chgo., 1949-65; defender of bond, met. tribunal Archdiocese of Chgo., 1949-58, prosynodal judge, 1958-69; aux. bishop of Chgo., 1967-69; bishop Diocese of Mobile (Ala.), 1969—. Office: Office of Bishop Diocese of Mobile Mobile AL 33601

MAY, WINSTON CHARLES, optometrist; b. Cin., Apr. 16, 1943; s. E. Winston and Ann Burnett (Cummings) M.; student Defiance (O.) Coll., 1961-64; B.S., M.Optometry, Ind., U., 1967; m. Helen Neumann, Sept. 3, 1966. Pvt. practice optometry, Manassas, Va., 1967—. Diplomate Nat. Bd. Examiners in Optometry. Fellow Am. Acad. Optometry; mem. Am., Va. optometric assns., No.Va. Optometric Soc. (pres. 1973). Home: 8313 Irongate Way Manassas VA 22110 Office: 8721 Digges Rd Manassas VA 22110

MAYBORN, FRANK WILLIS, newspaper editor and publisher; b. Akron, O., Dec. 7, 1903; s. Ward C. and Nellie C. (Welton) M.; B.A., U. Colo., 1927. With Dallas News, 1926, N. Tex. Traction Co., Ft. Worth, 1927-29; bus. mgr. Temple (Tex.) Telegram, 1929-45, editor, pres., pub., 1945—; founder, pres., 1936-70, operator radio sta. KTEM, Temple; founder, pres., 1953—, operator KCEN-TV, Temple; owner Sherman (Tex.) Democrat, 1945—; pres., part owner, operator Killeen (Tex.) Herald, 1952—, Taylor (Tex.) Press, 1959—; founder, operator radio sta. WMAK, Nashville, 1947-54; pres., dir. Bell Pub. Co., Temple, 1945—, Bell Broadcasting Co., Temple, 1936-70, Sherman Democrat Co., 1945—, Killeen (Tex.) Herald Pub. Co., 1952—, Taylor (Tex.) Pub. Co., 1959—, Channel 6, Inc., 1962—, County Developers, Inc., 1967—, FWM Properties, 1965—, Community Enterprises, Inc., 1959—; dir. 1st Nat. Bank, Temple. Mem. Tex. Democratic Com., 1948. Dir. Temple Indsl. Found., 1956, 59-61, 64-66, 68-70, pres., 1963; mem. Tex. Hist. Found., 1967-68, Tex. Hist. Survey Com., 1966-69; mem. adv. council U. Tex. Journalism Found., 1964-66, Tex. A. and M. U. Dept. Journalism, 1958-59; mem. adv. and devel. bds. Tex. Indsl. Commn., 1958-64; mem. Ft. Hood Civilian Adv. Com., 1963—, Baylor U. Broadcast Council, 1964-65; mem. adv. bd. Scott and White Hosp. Found., Temple; bd. dirs. Temple Boys Choir, 1969, Waco Symphony Assn., 1968-69, Frank W. Mayborn Found., 1964—; trustee Peabody Coll., 1970—, Central Tex. Med. Found., 1970—; chmn. bd. trustees Kinsolving Youth Center, 1971—. Served from pvt. to maj., AUS, 1942-45; ETO. Decorated Bronze Star Medal; recipient Outstanding Citizens award, Temple, 1948, Tex. award for outstanding service V.F.W., 1955, award for contbn. to soil and water conservation Soil Conservation Service, 1959; Citizenship award Jr. C. of C., 1951, Man of Year award, 1971, 4-H award for outstanding service to 4-H Clubs, 1971. Mem. Am. Soc. Newspaper Editors (past dir.), Tex. Daily Press League (dir. Tex. Sunday comic sect.), Temple C. of C. (dir., past pres.), Retail Mchts. Assn. Temple, Tex. Daily Newspaper Assn. (past pres.; award 1946), Am. (fed. laws com.), So. (pres. 1962, chmn. bd. 1963) newspaper pubs. assns., Tex. Council Higher Edn., Assn. U.S. Army (life, mem. mil. affairs com., certificate of achievement 1969), Broadcast Pioneers, Phi Kappa Psi, Sigma Delta Chi. Presbyn. (elder). Mason, Rotarian (hon.). Clubs: Nat. Press (Washington); Advertising (past pres.) (Ft. Worth); Dallas Athletic, Lancers (Dallas); Headliners (Austin); Temple Country. Office: 17 S 3d St Temple TX 76501

MAYBURY, PAUL CALVIN, educator; b. Rio Grande, N.J., July 20, 1924; s. Byron Harris and Mildred Abigail (Bower) M.; B.S., Eastern Nazarene Coll., 1947; Ph.D., Johns Hopkins, 1952; m. Rebecca Lillian Palmer, July 27, 1949; children—Paul Calvin, James Palmer, Anne Elizabeth, Lynn Marie, Susan Gail. Chemist, Applied Physics Lab., Silver Spring, Md., 1951-52; research asso. Johns Hopkins, Balt., 1952-54; faculty Eastern Nazarene Coll., Quincy, Mass., 1954-61; faculty U. South Fla., Tampa, 1961—, prof., chmn. dept. chemistry, 1963—. Sci. ednl. cons. AID, U. Gorakpur, India, 1966; vis. prof. Tufts U., Medford, Mass., 1967; vis. scholar U. Cal. at Los Angeles, 1973; cons. Am. Chem. Soc., 1973-76. Served with AUS, 1944-46. Fellow Am. Inst. Chemists; mem. Sigma Xi, Am. Chem. Soc., A.A.A.S. Home: 10607 Carrollbrook Lane Tampa FL 33618

MAYER, GLENN WALDO, data processor; b. Chgo., May 27, 1923; s. Waldo Edgar and Mae Martha (Schaer) M.; B.A., U. N.M., 1948; M.B.A., Air Force Inst. Tech., 1959; M.S. in Adminstrn., George Washington U., 1973; m. Patricia Thomasa Belt, June 3, 1947; children—Barbara Ann (Mrs. Joseph A. Fiorillo, Jr.), Robert Glenn, John Thomas Belt. Comml. rep. Mountain States Tel. & Tel. Co., 1947-51; commd. 2d lt. USAF, 1944, advanced through grades to lt. col., 1966; supply mgmt. officer, Albuquerque, 1951-53; wing supply staff officer Manston RAF Sta., Eng., 1953-56; inspector gen. Shelby (O.) Air Force Depot, 1956-58; supply staff officer USAF, London, Eng., 1959-61, Ramstein, Germany, 1961-63; systems planning officer Def. Atomic Support Agy., Albuquerque, 1963-66; logistics planning officer USAF, Washington, 1966-70; ret., 1970; computer systems specialist U.S. Postal Service, Washington, 1970-72, program mgr. computer systems adminstrn., 1973—. Pres. Am. Schs. P.T.A., Eastcote, Eng., 1960-61; committeeman Kit Carson council Boy Scouts Am., 1963-66. Decorated Meritorious Service medal, Air medal, Joint Services Commendation medal, Air Force Commendation medal with oak leaf cluster. Mem. Fed. Govt. Accountants Assn., Soc. Logistics Engrs., N.M. State Soc., Kappa Alpha. Methodist. Home: 4312 Southwood Dr Alexandria VA 22309 Office: 475 L'Efant Plaza W Washington DC 20260

MAYER, JOHN PROSPER, govt. ofcl.; b. Binghamton, N.Y., May 10, 1922; s. Prosper Aloysius and Grace (Sheehan) M.; B.S. in Aero. Engring., U. Mich., 1944; m. Geraldine Couch, July 30, 1949; children—Dale John, Cynthia Lynn, Gwenn Ellen. Mem. staff NASA, 1944—, asst. chief flight operations div., 1961-63, chief mission planning and analysis div., Johnson Space Center, Houston, 1963-74, asst. dir. datasystems and analysis directorate, 1974—. Recipient superior achievement award Johnson Space Center, 1966, Exceptional Service medal NASA, 1968, 69, Distinguished Alumni award U. Mich., 1970, Thurlow award Inst. Nav., 1971. Asso. fellow Am. Inst. Aeros. and Astronautics (mechanics and control flight award 1969). Home: 1018 Willowvale St Seabrook TX 77586 Office: LB Johnson Space Center Houston TX 77058

MAYER, PAUL GUSTAV WILHELM, educator; b. Frankfurt, Germany, Nov. 3, 1923; s. Fritz and Alice Lucie (Walldin) M.; student Staedtische Berufsschule, Frankfurt-Main, Germany, 1938-41; B.S. in C.E., U. Cin., 1953; M.S., Cornell U., 1955, Ph.D., 1957; m. Virginia Wagner, July 2, 1955; children—Frederick, Marianne, Laura, Donald. Came to U.S., 1947, naturalized, 1952. Apprentice, journeyman Heinrich Thielemann, Frankfurt, 1938-45; technischer asst. Deutsche Bundesbahn, Frankfurt-Main, 1945-47; engring. aid. City Cin., 1950-52; research asst. U. Cin., 1953; research asst. Sch. Civil Engring., Cornell U., 1953-54, hydraulic engr., 1954-55, instr., 1955-57, asst. prof., 1957-59; designer, cons. Wallace Steel & Supply Co., Ithaca, N.Y., 1955-57; hydraulic engr. U.S. Geol. Survey, research sect., Atlanta, 1959-67; asst. prof. civil engring. Sch. Civil Engring. Ga. Inst. Tech., Atlanta, 1959-66, prof. civil engring., 1966—. Cons. Ga. Power Co., Atlanta, 1963—; vis. prof. U. Wales, Swansea, 1964-65; cons., Allied-Gulf Nuclear Services, Barnwell, S.C., 1970—. Recipient Alfred M. Cohen award U. Cin., 1952; Dean Pershing Trophy, Ga. Inst. Tech., 1963, Faculty award Ga. Inst. Tech., 1968, Distinguished Service award Anak, 1970, Outstanding Faculty award Ga. Inst. Tech., 1973. Registered profl. engr., Ga.

Mem. Am. Soc. C.E., Am. Soc. Engring. Edn. (chmn. applied hydraulics com. 1967), Internat. Assn. Hydraulic Research, Am. Geophys. Union, Nat. Soc. Profl. Engrs., N.Y. Acad. Scis., Sigma Xi, Phi Kappa Phi, Omicron Delta Kappa, Tau Beta Pi, Chi Epsilon, Sigma Sigma. Contbr. articles to profl. jours. Home: 1126 Lullwater Rd NE Atlanta GA 30307

MAYES, RICHARD LEON, candy co. exec.; b. Earlsboro, Okla., Oct. 29, 1928; s. Sterling L. and Alberta Beatrice (Follmar) M.; B.B.A., U. Okla., 1952; postgrad. N.Y.U., 1958-59, Central State U., 1971-72; m. Jo Ann McKibben, July 14, 1951; children—Cynthia Ann, Deborah Sue, Beverly Gayle, Julie Kay. Asst. mgr. Oklahoma City Safety Council, 1952-55; with pub. relations dept. Assn. Casualty and Surety Cos., 1955-57; account supr. Batten, Barton, Durstine & Osborn, N.Y.C., 1957-62, account group supr., Boston, 1962-64; v.p. sales and marketing, dir. Bunte Candies Inc., Oklahoma City, 1964—; partner Sheridan Assos. Instr. Oklahoma City U., 1954, mem. tennis adv. com., 1970—. Served with AUS, 1946-48. Mem. Oklahoma City All Sports Assn. (dir.). Unitarian. Club: Quail Creek Golf and Country. Home: 2713 NW 59th St Oklahoma City OK 73112 Office: 129 E California St Oklahoma City OK 73104

MAYES, SAMUEL HUBERT, JR., lawyer; b. Little Rock, Sept. 6, 1931; s. S. Hubert and Charlotte (McIntosh) M.; J.D., U. Ark., 1954; m. L. Susan Harrell, Dec. 30, 1971; children by previous marriage—Jean, Charlotte, Melissa. Admitted to Ark. bar, 1954; atty. Ark. Revenue Dept., 1954; dep. pros. atty. 6th Jud. Dist., Little Rock, 1957-58; spl. asst. atty. gen. State of Ark., 1963; partner firm Fulk, Lovett & Mayes, Little Rock, 1960—. Asst. sec. Ark. Senate, 1953. Served with USAF, 1955-57. Mem. Delta Theta Phi, Omicron Delta Kappa, Sigma Chi. Democrat. Methodist. Home: 2021 Beechwood St Little Rock AR 72207 Office: 807 W 3d St Little Rock AR 72201

MAYES, WENDELL WISE, JR., radio exec.; b. San Antonio, Tex., Mar. 2, 1924; s. Wendell Wise and Dorothy Lydia (Evans) M.; student Schreiner Inst., 1941-42, U. Tex. at Austin, 1942, Daniel Baker Coll., 1946; B.S., Tex. Tech. Coll., 1949; m. Mary Jane King, May 11, 1946; children—Cathey (Mrs. Joe Rollins), Sarah (Mrs. Bill Yost), Wendell Wise III. Program dir., sta. mgr. KBWD, Brownwood, Tex., 1949-57; mgr. KCRS, Midland, Tex., 1957-63, pres., 1965—; pres. KNOW, Austin, 1970—, KVIC, Victoria, 1970—; chmn. bd. Cablevision Constrn. Corp., Houston; dir. Western United Life Ins. Co., Midland. Vice pres. Am. Diabetes Assn.; pres. Tex. Broadcast Edn. Found., 1973—. Served with USNR, 1943-46. Mem. Tex. Assn. Broadcasters (pres. 1964), Nat. Assn. Broadcasters (dir. 1969-72), Broadcast Edn. Assn. (dir. 1973—). Episcopalian (clk. of vestry 1968). Home: 4014 Sierra St Austin TX 78731 Office: Box 2197 Austin TX 78767

MAYLE, FRANCIS CARL, JR., physician; b. Newark, June 5, 1928; s. Francis C. and Pauline (Finkbeiner) M.; B.S., Georgetown U., 1949, M.D., 1953, M.S. in Neurophysiology, 1959; m. Barbara Mollach, May 30, 1953; children—Marjorie, Francis Carl III, Katherine, Paul. Intern U.S. Naval Hosp., St. Albans, N.Y., 1953-54; resident Georgetown U. Hosp., Washington, 1956-59, Mt. Alto VA Hosp., Washington, 1956-59, D.C. Gen. Hosp., 1957; practice medicine specializing in neurology, Bethesda, Md., Washington, 1959—; mem. staffs Providence, Georgetown U. Children's, Sibley hosps., Washington Hosp. Center (all Washington), Suburban Hosp., Bethesda; Holy Cross Hosp., Silver Spring, Md.; asst. clin. prof. neurology Georgetown U. Sch. Medicine, 1959—. Chmn. regional adv. com. Met. Washington Regional Med. Programs, 1969-73; chmn. bd. Md. Med. Polit. Action Com. Served with USNR, 1953-56. Diplomate Am. Bd. Neurology. Fellow A.C.P., Am. Geriatric Soc.; mem. A.M.A., Am. Epilepsy Assn., So. Med. Assn., Montgomery County (v.p. 1972-73, pres. elect 1974—), D.C. med. socs., St. Luke's Soc., Georgetown Clin. Soc., Washington Med. and Surg. Soc., Am. Acad. Neurology (press and pub. relations chmn. 1969-73), Council Med. Chirurgical Faculty Md., Georgetown U. Alumni Assn. (senate). K.C. Home: 4903 Scarsdale Rd Washington DC 20016 Office: 8218 Wisconsin Av Bethesda MD 20014

MAYNARD, JOHN GARY, JR., dentist; b. Bennettsville, S.C., Apr. 14, 1936; s. John Gary and Grace Evelyn (Lee) M.; A.B. in Econs., Davidson Coll., 1958; D.D.S., Med. Coll. Va., 1958-62; certificate of periodontics U. Ky., 1967; m. Sara Jean Mason, Aug. 2, 1958; children—Sara Grason, Catherine Mason, John Gary, Walter Mason. Intern, Walter Reed Hosp., 1962-63; practice periodontics, Richmond, Va., 1967—; part-time faculty dept. periodontics U. Ky., 1966-67, U. Pa., 1969-70; asso. clin. prof. periodontics Med. Coll. Va., Richmond, 1970—. Served to capt. Dental Corps, AUS, 1962-65. Decorated Army Commendation medal. Mem. Am., Va. dental assns., Richmond Dental Soc. (treas. 1971-73), Am., Va. (organizer, pres. 1968-70) socs. periodontists, Am. Acad. Periodontology (chmn. membership com., student loan fund com.), So. Acad. Periodontology (mem. membership com. 1969-71, exec. council 1972—). Presbyn. (deacon, elder). Rotarian. Club: Westwood Racquet (Richmond). Home: 29 Twin Lake Lane Richmond VA 23229 Office: 4909 Grove Av Richmond VA 23226

MAYNARD, W. NEIL, banker; b. Winthrop, Ark., Jan. 22, 1942; s. J. D. and Eurby (Abney) M.; B.S., U. Ark., 1963; postgrad. Ark. Law Sch., 1963-65, La. State U. Sch. Banking, 1968-70; m. Marianne Crank, June 15, 1963; children—Eric Neil, Jason Hunter. Trainee, Worthen Bank & Trust Co., Little Rock, 1963-66; asst. cashier First Nat. Bank, Stuttgart, Ark., 1967, cashier, 1968, exec. v.p., 1969, pres., 1970—, also dir. Pres., Stuttgart Indsl. Devel. Corp., 1970; chmn. Boy Scout Fund drive, 1969, Ark. County chpt. Crippled Childrens Assn., 1969-71. Bd. dirs. Grand Prairie Home Builders Assn. Named Outstanding Young Man, 1971. Mem. Am. Inst. Bankers (chmn. Grand Prairie), Life Underwriters Assn., Ark. Bankers Assn. (vice chmn.), Ark. Polled Hereford Assn., Stuttgart C. of C. (pres.), Acacia. Lion. Home: 2110 Strait Pl Stuttgart AR 72160 Office: PO Drawer 908 Stuttgart AR 72160

MAYNE, ALVIN, mgmt. and econ. cons. co. exec.; b. Chgo., May 14, 1914; s. Oscar A. and Sahra (Greenberg) M.; B.A., U. Chgo., 1936; M.B.A., U. Chgo., 1940; m. Jeannette Ladin, June 20, 1937; 1 dau., Evelyn. With NRA, Washington, 1934-36; adviser to Q.M. Gen., 1942-45; economist Moody's Investor Service, 1945-48; faculty Wharton Sch., U. Pa., Phila., 1948-51, 53-54; dep. asst. adminstr. Nat. Prodn. Authority, Washington, 1951-53; adviser Exec. Office of Pres., Washington, 1953-54; econ. adviser Govt. P.R., 1954-61; adviser U.S. coordinator Alliance for Progress, 1962-64; pres. Clapp & Mayne, Inc. of P.R., Santurce, 1965—. Mem. Soc. Internat. Devel. (chpt. pres. 1970—), Am. Econ. Assn., Econometric Soc., Am. Statis. Assn., Sigma Xi. Contbr. articles to various publs. Home: 61 Kings Ct San Juan PR 00911 Office: 1606 Ponce de Leon Av Santurce PR 00909

MAYO, EDWARD BURNETT, mus. ofcl.; b. Houston, July 13, 1918; s. Henry M. and Mary (Sweeney) M.; B.S. in Architecture, Rice U., 1942. Architect firm Thompson McCleary, Houston, 1943-51; draftsman M.D. Anderson Hosp. and Tumor Inst., Houston, 1954-57; sales Coblar Book Stores, Houston, 1956-60, Handmakers Splty. Shop, Houston, 1955-59; mus. registrar Mus. Fine Arts, Houston, 1961—. Served with USAAF, 1942-45. Roman Catholic. Home: 1511 California St Houston TX 77006 Office: 1001 Bissonnet St PO Box 6826 Houston TX 77005

MAYO, WALLACE C., dentist; b. Century, Fla., Feb. 10, 1914; s. James Lawrence and Lula Mae (Tompkins) M.; student U. Fla., 1932-33; D.D.S., Emory U., 1937; m. Jean Kingsbery, Jan. 11, 1941; children—Donna Jean, Susan, Clair, Howard. Intern Ft. Oglethorpe, Ga., 1938; pvt. practice dentistry, Pensacola, Fla., 1939-41, specializing in periodontics, 1945—. Chmn. adv. council Emory U. Sch. Dentistry; mem. adv. com. U. Fla. Sch. Dentistry, Pensacola Jr. Coll. Sch. Dental Hygiene; mem. dental adv. com. Dept. Def. Served with Dental Corps, AUS, 1941-45; ETO; NATOUSA. Fellow Internat. Coll. Dentists, Am. Coll. Dentists; mem. Fla. Soc. Peridontology, Am. Dental Assn. (ho. of dels.), Fla. (past pres., chmn. council on dental edn.), N.W. Fla. Dist. (past pres.), Pensacola (past pres.) dental socs., Am., So. (past pres.) acads. peridontology, Acad. Internat. Dentistry, Fedn. Dentaire Internationale, Res. Officers Assn. (past pres. Fla. dist.), Pensacola C. of C., USCG Aux. (insp. examiner). Baptist. Clubs: Exchange (past pres.), Yacht, Scenic Hills Country. Home: 2920 E Blackshear St Pensacola FL 32503 Office: 901 N 12th Av Pensacola FL 32501

MAYORAL-BIGAS, JORGE WALTER, physician; b. Adjuntas, P.R., Sept. 5, 1927; s. Angel Maria and Felicia (Bigas) Mayoral; B.S. magna cum laude, U. P.R., 1947; M.D., Boston U., 1951; m. Nilda Maldonado, June 16, 1962; children—Georyanna, Jorge Walter, Michael, Nilmarie. Intern, resident internal medicine San Juan City Hosp., 1951-53; resident internal medicine San Juan VA Hosp., 1953-54; resident gastroenterology Kennedy VA Hosp., Memphis, 1956-58; practice medicine, specializing in gastroenterology, Ponce, P.R., 1958—; head dept. medicine Damas Hosp., Ponce. Served with USAF, 1954-56. Mem. A.C.P., P.R. Med. Assn., P.R. Soc. Gastroenterology. Author: Dubib-Johnson Disease, 1967. Home: Santa Maria A-51 Ponce PR 00731 Office: 33 Concordia Ponce PR 00731

MAYS, AVERY, constrn. co. exec.; b. Morgan County, Ala., Mar. 11, 1911; s. Walter Ernest and Millie Ann (Blankenship) M.; ed. pub. schs., Tex.; m. Eva Blanche Ponder, Mar. 27, 1932; children—Evelyn Joyce (Mrs. Tom C. McClellan), Gerald Avery. Retail lumberman, 1929-42; residential builder and land developer, 1943-55; gen. contractor, 1955—; treas., dir. Red Bird Indsl. Devel., Inc., Dallas, 1963—; dir. Lone Star Gas Co., Great Am. Res. Ins. Co., Oak Cliff Bank and Trust Co., State Fair of Texas. Mem. Dallas Ind. Sch. Dist., 1947-53; chmn. Dallas County A.R.C., 1965-66; pres. Greater Dallas Planning Council, 1966-67; bd. dirs. Dallas Citizens Council, pres., 1968; pres. Dallas United Fund; bd. dirs. Dallas County Boys Home; past pres. bd. Meth. Hosp., Dallas. Recipient Constrn. Industry Brotherhood citation Nat. Conf. Christians and Jews, 1962; named Oak Cliff Man of Year, 1962. Mem. Dallas Home Builders Assn. (pres. 1949; Hugh Prather Distinguished Service trophy 1960), Nat. Assn. Home Builders (dir. 1949-52), Dallas C. of C. (pres. 1961-62), Dallas Real Estate Bd. (Easterwood trophy 1960), Asso. Gen. Contractors (pres. Dallas 1967). Mason (32 deg., Shriner), Kiwanian (past pres. Oak Cliff). Home: 950 Kessler Pkwy Dallas TX 75208 Office: 625 Frito Lay Bldg PO Box 35612 Dallas TX 75235

MAYS, MAX CARROLL, dentist; b. Beaumont, Tex., Dec. 2, 1935; s. Ed Kellie and Edith Joan (Miller) M.; B.S., So. Methodist U., 1958; D.D.S., U. Tex., 1963; m. Laura Lee Alvis, June 4, 1960; children—Roy Kellie, Matthew Carroll, Amanda. Gen. practice dentistry, Silsbee, Tex., 1965-67, Lake Jackson, Tex., 1967—. Mem. City Charter Rev. Commn., 1971. Served to lt. Dental Corps, USNR, 1963-65. Mem. Am., Tex. dental assns., 9th Dist. Dental Soc., Brazoria County Dental Study Club (pres.), Brazosport C. of C., Alpha Tau Omega, Xi Psi Phi, Omicron Kappa Upsilon. Republican. Methodist. Kiwanian. Home: 316 Forest Dr Lake Jackson TX 77566 Office: 82 Flag Lake Rd Lake Jackson TX 77566

MAYS, RICHARD DUDLEY, judge; b. Dallas, Dec. 28, 1939; s. Carl Cecil and Bonnie Jean (Troutt) M.; B.B.A., U. Tex., 1963, LL.B., 1965; m. Patricia Ridgway, Dec. 23, 1960; children—Allison Lynn, Erik Reagan. Admitted to Tex. bar, 1965; partner firm Mays & Mays, Dallas, 1965-67; asst. dist. atty. Dallas County, Dallas, 1967-74; judge 204th Dist. Ct., 1974—. Precinct chmn. Dallas Democratic Com., 1966-68. Served with USCGR, 1959-60. Mem. Am., Dallas, Dallas Jr. bar assns., State Bar Tex., Delta Tau Delta. Club: Dallas Athletic. Home: 3804 Villanova St Dallas TX 75225 Office: Dallas County Courthouse Dallas TX 75202

MAYS, WILLIAM V., hosp. assn. exec.; b. Fordyce, Ark., Dec. 1, 1922; B.B.S., U. Ark., 1954; M.H.A., Northwestern U., 1956. Adminstrv. resident Parkland Hosp., Dallas, 1956-57; asso. adminstr. Methodist Hosp., Dallas, 1957-68; exec. dir. Dallas Hosp. Council, 1968—. Mem. health panel Community Council Greater Dallas; ex-officio mem. Dallas Health Planning Council; mem. regional health rev. Council Govts., 1969—, regional health planning council, 1970—; mem. adv. bd. Vis. Nurses Assn., Dallas. Fellow Am. Coll. Hosp. Adminstrs.; mem. Blackland Area Hosp. Council (chmn. 1961), Tex. Hosp. Assn. (chmn. council adminstrv. practice 1961-63). Rotarian, Toastmaster. Office: 2608 Inwood Rd #230 Dallas TX 75235

MAZO, EARL, writer; b. Warsaw, Poland, July 7, 1919; s. Samuel George and Sonia (Portugal) M.; grad. Clemson Coll., 1940; m. Rita Vane, 1941; children—Judith Frances, Mark Elliot. Staff Charleston (S.C.) News and Courier, also Greenville News, 1939-41; editor, editorial page Camden (N.J.) Courier Post, 1945-50; staff N.Y. Herald Tribune, 1950-64, nat. polit. corr.; with N.Y. Times, N.Y.C., 1964-65, Reader's Digest, 1965—; polit. commentator WTOP-TV, CBS, Washington, 1969—. Sr. fellow Woodrow Wilson Internat. Inst. for Scholars, Smithsonian Instn., 1972. Served to lt. AUS, World War II; combat corr. European Star and Stripes. Decorated Air medals, Bronze Star medal, Presidential citations. Mem. Acad. Polit. Sci., Sigma Delta Chi. Clubs: Overseas Press (N.Y.C.); Nat. Press (Washington). Author: Richard Nixon, A Political and Personal Portrait, 1959; The Great Debates, 1961; The Mindreaders, 1964; Nixon, 1968; The History of Exim, A Bureaucracy That Improves With Age, 1973. Home: 5915 Nebraska Av NW Washington DC 20015

MAZUR, EDWARD THOMAS, JR., mfg. co. exec.; b. Newark, Apr. 4, 1930; s. Edward Thomas and Mary Estelle (Kozakewicz) M.; B.S., U.S. Mcht. Marine Acad., 1952; m. Lillian Trusivick, July 2, 1955; children—Lisa, Christopher, Suzanne, Nancy. Marine engr., Texas Co., N.Y.C., 1952-54; with Worthington Corp., Harrison, N.J., 1956-69, dist. engr., 1959-67, regional engr., 1967-69; service mgr. Am. Air Filter, Louisville, 1969-72, Schilling Trane, Indpls., 1972—. Mgr., coach girls softball team YMCA, 1966-67; mem. P.T.A., 1960—. Served with USNR, 1954-56. Registered profl. engr., Kan. Mem. Nat. Soc. Profl. Engrs., Nat. Mgmt. Assn. Toastmaster. Home: 7511 Lanfair Dr Louisville KY 40222

MAZURSKY, MORRIS DAVID, lawyer; b. Columbia, S.C., June 10, 1923; s. Abraham Isaac and Mary (Blatt) M.; B.A., U. S.C., 1943, LL.B., 1945; m. Marcia Jane Weisbond, Oct. 28, 1951; children—Don, Leigh, Jon. Admitted to S.C. bar, 1945; asso. mem. firm Lee & Moise, Sumter, S.C., 1945-52; pvt. practice, 1952-71; partner firm Mazursky & Evans, Sumter, 1971—. Chmn. Commrs. Gen. Election, Sumter, 1953-59; mem. Sumter City Council, 1958, mayor, 1965, mayor pro tempore, 1960—. Trustee Toumey Hosp. Mem. Sumter, Am., S.C. bar assns., Sumter Jr. C. of C. (past pres.). Mason, Elk, Optimist. Home: 222 Mason Croft Dr Sumter SC 29510 Office: 19 N Harvin St Sumter SC 29150

MAZYCK, HAROLD EUGENE, JR., educator, ednl. adminstr.; b. Charleston, S.C., July 7, 1922; s. Harold E. and Esther B. (Spencer) M.; B.S., S.C. State A. and M. Coll., 1944; M.A., N.Y. U., 1948; Ph.D., U. N.C., 1971; m. Aurelia A. Chaney, Sept. 3, 1959; children—Carla, Harold. Asst. dean of men, counselor Clark Coll., Atlanta, 1948-52; asst. prof. guidance Prairie View (Tex.) A. and M. Coll., 1952-59; coordinator student activities Hampton (Va.) Inst., 1959-60; asst. prof. guidance N.C. Agr. and Tech. State U., Greensboro, 1960-69, prof. child devel., counselor edn., 1971-72, chmn. home econs. dept., 1972—. Mem. Interagy. Com. on Child Devel., 1971—; treas. N.C. Assn. for Children Under Six. Bd. dirs. Family Life Council, Greater Greensboro, N.C. Served with U.S. Army, 1944-46. Ford Found. grantee, 1969-71. Mem. Am. Assn. U. Profs., Assn. Home Econs. Adminstrs., Am., N.C. home econs. assns., Am.; N.C. personnel and guidance assns., So. Assn. Children Under Six, Soc. Research Child Devel., Alpha Phi Alpha. Home: 2007 Chelsea Lane Greensboro NC 27406 Office: N Dudley St Greensboro NC 27411

MAZZOLI, ROMANO LOUIS, congressman, lawyer; b. Louisville, Nov. 2, 1932; B.S. in Bus. Adminstrn. magna cum laude, U. Notre Dame, 1954; J.D. with honors, U. Louisville, 1960; m. Helen Dillon, Aug. 1, 1959; children—Michael, Andrea. Admitted to Ky. bar, 1960; with law dept. L.&N. R.R., Louisville, 1960-62; mem. firm Goldberg & Lloyd, Louisville, 1962-69; individual practice law, Louisville, 1969-71; mem. 92d to 93d congresses from 3d Ky. Dist., mem. Com. on Labor, 1970-72, Edn. and Labor Com., 1973—, Com. on D.C., 1973—. Lectr. bus. law Bellarmine Coll., Louisville, 1963-67. Mem. Ky. Senate, 1967-70; alternate del. Democratic Nat. Conv., 1968; co-chmn. Louisville and Jefferson County Dem. Campaign Com., 1969; mem. commn. on del. selection Dem. Nat. Com. Named Outstanding Freshman Senator, 1968, Best Senator from a Pub. Standpoint, 1970 (both Capitol Press Club). Mem. Am., Ky. State, Louisville bar assns., Louisville C. of C., Notre Dame Club of Ky. (past pres.). Home: 939 Ardmore Dr Louisville KY 40217 Office: House Office Bldg Washington DC 20515

MCADAMS, HERBERT HALL, banker; b. Jonesboro, Ark., June 6, 1915; s. H.H. and Stella (Patrick) McA.; B.S., Northwestern U., 1937; postgrad. Harvard, 1937-38, Loyola U., Chgo., 1938-39; LL.B., U. Ark., 1940; m. Sheila Wallace, Nov. 27, 1970; children by previous marriage—Judith (Mrs. Walter A. DeRoeck), Sandra (Mrs. Robert C. Connor), Hall, Penny (Mrs. Timothy Hodges). Admitted to Ark. bar, 1940, since practiced in Jonesboro; pres., chmn. bd. Citizens Bank, Jonesboro, chmn. Home Fed. Savs. & Loan Assn.; dir. Ark. La. Gas Co., 1964-72; chmn. bd., chief exec. officer Union Nat. Bank, Little Rock, 1970—. Dir. Fed. Res. Bank, Little Rock br., 1974—. Chmn. Ark. Indsl. Devel. Commn., 1965—, chmn., 1967-72; chmn. Metrocentre Improvement Dist.; gen. chmn. capital funds dr. Heifer Project Internat. Bd. dirs. Ark. Children's Hosp., Little Rock, Fifty for the Future; trustee John Brown U., Siloam Springs, Ark.; chmn. bd. Ark. chpt. Nat. Council Christians and Jews. Served with USNR, World War II. Recipient Top Mgmt. award Sales and Marketing Execs. Club, 1972. Mem. Am., Ark. bar assns., Am., Ark. bankers assns., Little Rock C. of C. (dir.), Little Rock Unltd. Progress (dir.). Baptist. Clubs: Little Rock Country, Little Rock, Pleasant Valley Country, Capital, Racquet (Little Rock); Summit, Tennessee (Memphis). Home: 47 Edgehill Rd Little Rock AR Office: Citizens Bank Bldg Jonesboro AR 72401 also #1 Union Plaza Little Rock AR 72201

MCADAMS, JOHN M., internat. ofcl.; b. Vega Baja, P.R., July 15, 1916; s. Walter Q. and Barbara (Martinez) McA.; A.B., U. P.R., 1937; A.M., Fordham U., 1938, Ph.D., 1952; grad. Inf. Sch., Ft. Benning, Ga., Command and Gen. Staff Coll., Ft. Leavenworth, Kan.; m. Elizabeth L. Simmons, Apr. 14, 1948; children—Elizabeth B., John M., Walter L., Mary E., Michael P. Instr., U. P.R., 1939-42; acting mil. attache Am. embassy, Paraguay, 1942-44; instr., editor Command and Gen. Staff Coll., Ft. Leavenworth, 1945-47; chief tech. information office Dept. Army, Pentagon, 1947-49; dir. publs. office, gen. secretariat OAS, Washington, 1949—. Lectr. personnel mgmt. for execs. Army Tng. Center, Washington, 1962—, Washington Internat. Center, 1966—. Pres., Bethesda (Md.) Fire Bd., 1967—. Served from lt. to maj. AUS, 1940-49. Decorated Orden Nacional del Merito (Paraguay). Mem. Am. Polit. Sci. Assn. Roman Catholic. K.C. Home: 5606 Forest Pl Bethesda MD 20014 Office: 19th and Constitution Av NW Washington DC 20006

MCADAMS, KELLY ROY, educator; b. Huntsville, Tex., Feb. 28, 1929; s. Kelly Edgar and Ina (Ogletree) McA.; B.Arch., U. Tex. at Austin, 1951, M.Arch., 1970; m. Nancy Carolyn Reeves, Aug. 12, 1950; 1 dau., Diana Claire. Asso. architect firm R. Gommel Roessner, Austin, 1954-60; prin. firm K.R. McAdams, Austin, 1960-62; instr. dept. architecture U. Tex., Austin, 1960-71, asst. prof., 1971—. Dir. Western Digital Systems, Inc., Austin. Bd. dirs. Austin Symphony Soc., 1966-69, McAdams Found. Mem. A.I.A., Tex. Soc. Architects, Constrn. Specification Inst., Assn. Computing Machinery, Nat. Guard Assn. Tex. (dir. 1968-71). Asso. editor: Military History of Texas and the Southwest, 1961. Home: 2607 Great Oaks Pkwy Austin TX 78756 Office: PO Box 7907 Austin TX 78712

MCALISTER, DURWOOD, newspaper editor; b. Bolivar, Tenn., June 16, 1927; s. Turner D. and Mary (Brown) McA.; B.A., Howard Coll., 1949; m. Dorris Fay Curenton, June 15, 1950; children—David Bruce, Jane Kimberly, Donald Kent. Reporter, Birmingham (Ala.) Age-Herald, 1948-50; reporter, news editor Anniston (Ala.) Star, 1950-54; with Atlanta Jour., 1954—, news editor, 1957-63, asst. mng. editor, 1967-68, mng. editor, 1968—; Sunday editor Atlanta Jour.-Constn., 1963-67. Served with USNR, 1945-46. Mem. A.P. Mng. Editors Assn. (nat. dir.), Sigma Delta Chi. Home: 2491 Glenrock Dr Decatur GA 30032 Office: PO Box 4689 Atlanta GA 30302

MCALLISTER, HORACE ALEXANDER, JR., city mgr.; b. Waynesville, N.C., Apr. 4, 1921; s. Horace Alexander and Anne Ruby (Alexander) McA.; B.S., C.E., Carnegie Inst. Tech., 1950; postgrad. Columbia, 1950-51, Manhattan Coll., 1961; m. Rachel Eleanor Nelms, July 18, 1942; 1 dau., Katherine Helen. Cons. engr. bridges and soil mechanics, N.Y.C., 1950-58; town engr., Oyster Bay Twp., L.I., N.Y., 1959-63; pub. works dir., Scotia, N.Y., 1964-66; city adminstr., Meadville, Pa., 1966-67; dir. pub. works, Morganton, N.C., 1967-69; city mgr., Newton, N.C., 1969—. Served with USNR, 1944-46. Fellow Am. Soc. C.E., Internat. City Mgmt. Assn. Presbyn. (elder). Lion. Home: 113 W 7th St Newton NC 28658 Office: City Hall Newton NC 28658

MCALLISTER, RAYMOND FRANCIS, educator; b. Ithaca, N.Y., June 26, 1923; s. Raymond Francis and Jessie Idell (Pinder) McA.; B.S. cum laude, Cornell U., 1950; M.S., U. Ill., 1951; postgrad. U. Cal. Scripps Inst. Oceanography, 1951-54; Ph.D., Tex. A. and M. Coll., 1958; m. Joan Margaret Simonson, Sept. 1, 1951; children—Keith, Karen, Kevin. Researcher, Columbia Geophys. Field Sta., Bermuda,

1958-63; marine technologist N.Am. Aviation, Miami, Fla., 1963-65; prof. ocean engring. Fla. Atlantic U., Boca Raton, 1965—; owner McAllister Marine Consultants, Pompano Beach, 1965—; dir. C&J Assos., Pompano Beach, Explorations, Inc., Mpls. Bd. dirs. Santa Maria Found., Sea Camp Assn. Served with AUS, 1943-45. Mem. Marine Tech. Soc., World Dredging Assn., Fla. Shore and Beach Preservation Assn., Sigma Xi, Alpha Zeta, Sigma Gamma Epsilon, Phi Kappa Phi. Co-editor: Handbook of Ocean and Underwater Engineering, 1969. Home: 987 SW 13th Pl Boca Raton FL 33432

MCALLISTER, ROY L., chem. co. exec.; b. Dundee, Fla., Apr. 23, 1928; s. John William and Hattie (Pate) McA.; A.B., U. Ala., 1954; m. Zedell Ward, Jan. 24, 1948; children—William, Richard, James, Donald. Mgr. WJRD radio, Tuscaloosa, Ala., 1952-57; editor Monsanto, Decatur, Ala., 1957-61, community relations and govt. affairs rep., 1961—. Publicity dir. Morgan County chpt. United Way, 1973—. Served with USAAF, 1946-48. Mem. pub. relations socs. Am., Ala. (Distinguished Service award 1969), Decatur C. of C. (dir., pres. 1974). Baptist (deacon). Lion. Home: 2204 12th St SE Decatur AL 35601 Office: Monsanto Courtland Hwy Decatur AL 35601

MCALLISTER, RUSSELL GREENWAY, JR., physician; b. Richmond Va., Nov. 23, 1941; s. Russell Greenway and Kathryn (Young) McA.; B.S., Hampden-Sydney Coll., 1963; postgrad. St. Thomas Hosp.-Med. Sch., London, Eng., 1966; M.D., Med. Coll. Va., 1967; m. Ann Elizabeth Parks, Nov. 9, 1968. Intern Vanderbilt Hosp., Nashville, Tenn., 1967-68, resident, 1968-69, clin. pharmacology, cardiology fellow, 1969-72; practice medicine, specializing in cardiology, Lexington, Ky., 1972—; mem. staff U. Ky. Hosp., Good Samaritan Hosp., Lexington VA Hosp., (all Lexington); asst. prof. medicine U. Ky., Lexington, 1972—. Vice chmn. Va. Fedn. Young Republicans, 1962-63. Diplomate Nat. Bd. Med. Examiners, Am. Bd. Internal Medicine. Mem. A.C.P., Am. Fedn. Clin. Research, Am. Heart Assn. Presbyn. Contbr. to profl. jours. Home: 322 S Turner St Midway KY 40347 Office: Univ Ky Med Center Lexington KY 40506

MCALLISTER, WALTER WILLIAMS, savs. and loan exec.; b. San Antonio, Mar. 26, 1889; s. Frank Williams and Lena (Stumberg) McA.; E.E., U. Tex., 1910; m. Lenora Alexander, Mar. 26, 1913 (dec. May 1969); children—Elizabeth (Mrs. O. J. Solcher, Jr.), Walter Williams, Gerald N. Chmn. bd. San Antonio Savs. Assn., 1921—, South States Oil Co., San Antonio, 1961—; dir. Mortgage Guaranty Ins. Corp., Milw.; mayor City of San Antonio, 1961-71. Chmn., Fed. Home Loan Bank Bd., Washington, 1953-56. Pres. Tex. Municipal League, 1965; mem. San Antonio River Beautification Commn., 1933, Tex. Finance Commn., 1952-53; hon. co-chmn. Hemis Fair; commr. Urban Renewal Agy. Bd. dirs. Research and Planning Council, Ednl. TV, Channel 9, Austin; chmn. bd. dirs. Witte Mus., 1952-53; trustee Internat. Union Bldg. Socs. and Savs. and Loan Assn.; pres. bd. trustees San Antonio Union Jr. Coll., 1945-60. Recipient Golden Deeds award San Antonio Exchange Club, 1956; Outstanding Citizen award San Antonio Council of Presidents, 1964. Mem. U.S. (mem. legislative com., past pres.), Southwestern (past pres.), Tex. (past pres.) savs. and loan leagues, San Antonio C. of C. (past pres.). Mason (33 deg., Shriner), Kiwanian (past pres. San Antonio). Clubs: Argyle; San Antonio Country. Home: 103 Bushnell Pl San Antonio TX 78212 Office: PO Box 1810 San Antonio TX 78296

MCALPINE, ROBERT GOODING, forestry program adminstr.; b. Union, S.C., Nov. 30, 1921; s. Laurens Elliot and Joe Cummings (Ketchin) M.; B.S. in Math., U. S.C., 1943; M.F., U. Ga., 1957; m. Ellen Lorena Cate, Apr. 23, 1946; children—Mary Ellen (Mrs. Richard Gates Elm), Robert Gooding, Martha Cate. Researcher, U.S. Forest Service, Athens, Ga., 1957-72, research adminstr. Triangle Park, N.C., 1972—. Instr. dendrology U. Ga., Athens, 1970. Served with USNR, 1943-46. Mem. Forest Farmers Assn., Ga. Acad. Scis., Soc. Am. Foresters, Forest Products Research Soc., Sigma Xi, Phi Kappa Phi, Xi Sigma Pi. Contbr. articles to profl. jours. Home: 4712 Metcalf Dr Raleigh NC 27612 Office: Forestry Science Lab Research Triangle Park NC 27709

MCANDREWS, HARRY, geologist, govt. ofcl.; b. Brownsville, Pa., Oct. 5, 1926; s. Harry G. and Nellie Viola (Snyder) McA.; B.S., W.Va. U., 1955, M.S., 1956; m. Lucille Marie Haregsin, Nov. 23, 1950; children—Ellen M., H. Scott, Susan D. Geologist, U.S. Geol. Survey, Casper, Wyo., 1956-64, dist. geologist, Salt Lake City, 1964-67, dist. geologist, Casper, 1967-68, regional geologist, Washington, 1968-71, staff geologist, Washington, 1971-73, area geologist, Metairie, La., 1973-74, area oil and gas supr. resource evaluation and analysis, Metairie, 1974—. Served with USAAF, 1945-46. Mem. Am. Assn. Petroleum Geologists, Geol. Soc. Am., Am. Inst. Profl. Geologists. Home: 118 Wilow Dr Covington LA 70433 Office: PO Box 7944 Metairie LA 70011

MCARTHUR, LAURIN CURRIE, JR., supt. schs.; b. Bennettsville, S.C., May 5, 1918; s. Laurin Currie and Nova Belle (Drake) McA.; A.B., U. S.C., 1939, A.M., 1942; Ed.D., Columbia, 1950; m. Anne Chisolm Barron, June 18, 1949; children—Laurin, John, Sara. Tchr. Darlington (S.C.) City Schs., 1939-42, prin., 1946-49; mem. staff Inst. Field Studies Columbia, 1949-50; asst. supt. elementary edn. Orangeburg (S.C.) City Schs., 1950-53; supt. Beaufort (S.C.) Schs., 1953-59; supt. Sumter (S.C.) City Schs., 1959—; cons., lectr. in field. Pres. S.C. Com. Progress, 1973; vice-chmn. S.C. Com. Econ. Edn. Bd. dirs. Lab. for Higher Edn. U.S. Served with USNR, 1942-46; PTO. Decorated Bronze Star with combat V. Mem. S.C. Com. Tchr. Certification (chmn. 1967-68), Sumter C. of C. (dir. 1972-73), S.C. Assn. Sch. Adminstrn., S.C. Adult Edn. Assn., N.E.A., S.C. Edn. Assn., Nat. Assn. Secondary Sch. Prins., Am. Ednl. Research Assn., U. S.C. Alumni Assn., Kappa Delta Pi, Phi Delta Kappa, Kappa Sigma. Author: Selective Teacher Recruitment, 1950—; Seeking Better Ways to Serve, 1972. Home: 311 Haynsworth St Sumter SC 29150 Office: Drawer 1180 Sumter SC 29150

MCASHAN, S.M., JR., business exec., 1904; A.B., Princeton, 1927; m. Chmn. bd., chief exec. officer, chmn. exec. com. Anderson, Clayton & Co., 1966—; dir. Houston & Shell Oil Co. Address: Tennessee Bldg Houston TX 77002*

MCATEE, ROBERT LINDLOFF, accountant; b. San Antonio, Jan. 18, 1946; s. Robert Harrison and Lila Ruth (Lindloff) McA.; B.S. magna cum laude, Trinity U., 1968. Owner Robert McAtee, C.P.A., San Antonio, 1968—. Cons. bus. and real estate mgmt., 1968—; mem. faculty Trinity U., part time, 1970—, San Antonio Coll., 1971-73. Patron, Witte Mus., San Antonio, 1971-73. C.P.A., Tex. Mem. Nat. Assn. Accountants (employment dir., 1971—), Jr. C. of C., Packard Internat. Motor Car Club (v.p., 1972-73, sec.-treas. 1973—), Tex. Soc. C.P.A.'s, Am. Inst. C.P.A.'s, Trinity Alumni Assn. Kaiser-Frazer Owners Club. Optimist. Home: 11103 West Av San Antonio TX 78213 Office: 6836 San Pedro Pedro St 210 San Antonio TX 78216

MCAULEY, JAMES ARTHUR, petroleum co. exec.; b. Pampa, Tex., Aug. 18, 1930; s. James Arthur and Lillie (Robertson) McA.; B.S. in Petroleum Engring., Tex. Technol. U., 1953; m. Joanne Elaine Guest, Sept. 1, 1952; 1 son, James Kelly. Engr., Sun Oil Co., 1953-56, Nortex Oil & Gas Corp., 1956-60, Ryan Consol. Petroleum Corp., 1958-60 (all Dallas); partner, petroleum engr. Gandy-McAuley, Dallas, 1960-68; pres. Oilfield Prodn. Services, Inc., 1964-71, also dir., v.p. parent co.; pres. Halliburton Resource Mgmt., Inc., Dallas, 1971—. Served with AUS, 1953-55. Mem. Am. Inst. Mining and Metall. Engrs., Ind. Petroleum Assn. Am., Soc. Petroleum Engrs., Am. Petroleum Inst., Tex. Mid-Continent Oil and Gas Assn., Tex. Tech. Ex-Students Assn. (pres. 1960). Clubs: Red Raider (pres., dir. Dallas 1969-70), Dallas Athletic. Contbr. articles to profl. jours. Home: 11524 E Ricks Circle Dallas TX 75230 Office: 211 N Ervay Bldg Dallas TX 75201

MCAVOY, BLANCHE, educator; b. Mitchell, Ind., Sept. 11, 1885; d. George and Mary (McIntire) McAvoy; B.A., U. Cin., 1909; M.A., Ohio State U., 1912; postgrad. Columbia, 1916; Ph.D., U. Chgo., 1930. Tchr., Kennedy Heights (O.) Pub. Sch., 1909-11; teaching fellow Ohio State U., 1911-14; tchr. Watterman (Ill.) Hall, 1914-15, Mt. Healthy (O.) High Sch., 1915-18, Wyoming (O.) High Sch., 1918-21; asst. prof. Ball Tchrs. Coll., 1921-25; substitute tchr. Western Coll. for Women, 1925; instr. Ill. State Normal U., 1926-31, asst. prof., 1931-45, asso. prof., 1945-51, prof., 1951-54, prof. emeritus, 1954—. Fellow A.A.A.S.; mem. Am. Bot. Soc., Ecol. Soc. Am., Acad. Sci. Ind. and Ill., Sigma Xi, Sigma Delta Epsilon, Gamma Theta Upsilon (nat. sec.-treas.). Author: Biology A Study Guide, 1939. Home: 3701 N Cincinnati Av Tulsa OK 74106

MCBAY, ARTHUR JOHN, educator; b. Medford, Mass., Jan. 6, 1919; s. Arthur and Virginia (Davito) McB.; B.S., Mass. Coll. Pharmacy, 1940, M.S., 1942; Ph.D., Purdue U., 1948; m. Avis L. Botsford, Aug. 24, 1946; children—John, Robert. prof. chemistry Mass. Coll. Pharmacy, Boston, 1953-55; supr. labs. Mass. Dept. Pub. Safety, Boston, 1955-69; asst. in legal medicine Harvard Med. Sch., 1953-69; prof. dept. pathology, prof. Sch. Pharmacy U. N.C., 1973—; chief toxicologist Office of Chief Med. Examiner for N.C., Chapel Hill, 1969—. Served to capt. USAAF, 1943-45. Mem. Am. Acad. Forensic Sci. (chmn. toxicology sect. 1966-68), Am. Pharm. Assn. (sec.-treas. sci. sect. 1954-57), Sigma Xi, Rho Chi, Phi Lambda Upsilon. Contbr. numerous articles to sci. jours. Home: 102 Kings Mountain Ct Chapel Hill NC 27514 Office: PO Box 2488 Chapel Hill NC 27514

MCBEE, J.D., dentist; b. Brady, Tex., July 26, 1932; s. Gussie Daymon and Julia M. (Carlson) McB.; student N. Tex. State Coll., 1949-52, 55-56; D.D.S., U. Tex., 1960; m. Ruth Junell Carlson, Jan. 26, 1952; children—Kay Lynn, Gregory Scott. Practice dentistry, Smithville, Tex., 1960—. Dental cons. Smithville Ind. Sch. Dist.; dir. Smithville Light and Water Dept. Alderman, Smithville, 1963-73. Chmn., Bastrop County Community Action, 1966-67. Served with inf. AUS, 1952-54. Mem. Am., Tex., Austin Dist. dental assns., C. of C. (dir. 1963-64). Baptist (deacon). Lion (pres. 1962-63). Home: 801 Whitehead St Smithville TX 78957 Office: 601 E 9th St Smithville TX 78957

MCBRIDE, JAMES ALBERTUS, II, architect; b. Marion, Tex., Oct. 24, 1934; s. James Albertus and Laura (Kainer) M.; B.Arch., U. Tex., 1958; m. Marjorie Harkrider, July 13, 1956; children—Laura Lynn, Susan Marie, Charlotte Ann; m. 2d, Charlotte Hardin, Dec. 21, 1971. Project mgr. McBride Agys., Houston, 1961-65; prin. James A. McBride II, Architect, Aspen, Colo., 1965-67, Houston, 1971—; architect Williams & Tazwell, Norfolk, Va., 1967-69; design and project mgr. Mills Petticord & Mills, Washington, 1969; archt. cons. Guatemala, 1969-71. Principal works include apt. projects Aspen and Houston, ski lodges, Aspen, Norfolk Yacht and Country Club, Norfolk Cultural and Convention Center, Norfolk. Mem. A.I.A., Tex. Soc. Architects, Alpha Rho Chi, Tau Sigma Delta, Sphinx, Houston C. of C., Delta Tau Delta. Exhibited collections Mayan Rubbings Houston Pub. Library, Wilson Meml. Mus., Beaumont, Tex., Laguna Gloria Mus., Austin, Tex., Alexandria, La., Lubbock, Tex.; two selected for permanent exhibit Mus. Fine Arts, Houston. Home: 4744 Cashel Forest St Houston TX 77069 Office: 1102 Leeland St Houston TX 77002

MCBRIDE, JAMES CLIFTON, edn. cons.; b. Houston, Aug. 12, 1932; s. William Bryan and Mary Elizabeth (Guimont) McB.; A.A., U. Houston, 1952, B.S., 1953, M.Ed., 1958, Ed.D., 1965; postgrad. North Tex. State U., 1965; m. Grace Marian Reed, June 20, 1952 (div.); children—John, Michael, Margory, Callie, Mary; m. 2d, Barbara Betterton DeVillier, Mar. 16, 1974. Comdt. R.O.T.C., tchr. Bellaire (Tex.) High Sch., 1956-64; lectr. U.S. history U. Houston, 1960-61; chmn. history dept., tchr. U.S. and modern history Kinkaid Sch., Houston, 1964-65; prin. Lincoln High Sch., LaMarque, Tex., 1965-66; exec. dir. Region IX Edn. Service Center, Wichita Falls, Tex., 1966-69; cons. instructional systems Aboussie Electronic Systems, Inc., Dallas, 1969-71; owner, cons. McBride & Asso. Edn. Cons., Wichita Falls and Atlanta, 1971—. Pres. Mainland Council for Retarded Children, Texas City, 1966. City councilman City of Bellaire (Tex.), 1960-62, 64-65; mem. Tex. State Republican. Platform Com., 1962. Bd. mgrs. S.W. YMCA, Houston, 1960-64; bd. dirs. Individual Devel. Center, Wichita Falls, 1968-69, Wichita County Cancer Soc., 1969. Served with AUS, 1953-56; lt. col. Res. Mem. Am. Arbitration Assn. (mem. panel of arbitrators 1972—), Council Edn. Facilities Planners, Tex. Assn. Sch. Adminstrs. (life), Phi Kappa Phi, Kappa Delta Pi, Phi Delta Kappa. Episcopalian. Mason (K.T.). Contbr. articles to profl. jours. Home: 3200 Peckham St Wichita Falls TX 76308 Office: Suite 254 Dover Sq 120 Copeland Rd NE Atlanta GA 30342

MCBRYDE, MYRON HOMER, banker; b. Sanford, N.C., July 27, 1923; s. Forrest Glenn and Anne (Stone) McB.; B.A., Rollins Coll., 1950; J.D., U. Miss., 1964; m. Ann Elizabeth Garner, Aug. 4, 1950; children—Bruce Garner, Lory Joan. Spl. agt. FBI, 1951-61; admitted to Miss. bar, 1964, U.S. Supreme Ct. bar, 1968; atty., Columbus, Miss., 1964-67; dir. N.C. Bur. Investigation, 1967-69; dir. security Wachovia Bank & Trust Co., Winston-Salem, N.C., 1969—. Faculty criminology Miss. State Coll. for Women, 1964. Bd. dirs. Youth Service Bur., Winston-Salem. Served with AUS, 1943-46. Mem. Am. Bar Assn., Bank Adminstrn. Inst. (chmn. security commn. 1970—, dir. 1970—), N.C. Bankers Assn. (chmn. protective com. 1970—), Kappa Alpha, Phi Alpha Delta. Rotarian. Home: 4007 Beaver Brook Rd Clemmons NC 27012 Office: Box 3099 Winston Salem NC 27102

MCCABE, DESOTO BEN, JR., civil engr.; b. Kansas City, Mo., Nov. 15, 1919; s. DeSoto Ben and Nedetta (McPherson) McC.; B.C.E. cum laude U. Mo., 1943; m. Katheryn Elizabeth Welch, Sept. 9, 1939; children—Edward Glen, Kathleen (Mrs. Alan Ray Lamarche)), Colleen. Engr.-in-charge Fed. Pub. Housing Authority, Sioux City, Ia., 1946; city mgr. Clarinda, Ia., 1947-49, Park Ridge, Ill., 1950-52; chief engr. McCabe Assos., Engrs., Chgo., 1953-65; project mgr. World Bank Water and Sewer Project, East Pakistan, 1966-68; chief san. engr. Barnhouse-McCabe Engrs., Columbus, O., 1969-70; chief san. engr. Rader & Assos., Miami, Fla., 1970-71; chief engr. McCabe Assos. Ltd., Miami, 1971—. Served with USNR; P.T.O. Registered profl. engr., Fla., W.Va., Tenn., Ky., Mo., Ill., Ga., Ariz., Ind., Ia., Ohio. Mem. Inst. Engrs. of Pakistan, Am. Soc. C.E., Am. Water Works Assn., Am. Pub. Works Assn., Am. Water Resources Assn., Water Pollution Control Fedn., Am. Soc. Pub. Adminstrn., Am. Soc. Planning Ofcls., Internat. City Mgrs. Assn. Home and office: 521 San Servando Coral Gables FL 33143

MCCABE, GERARD BENEDICT, univ. library adminstr.; b. N.Y.C., Jan. 22, 1930; s. Patrick Joseph and Margaret Irene (McDonald) McC.; B.A. in English, Manhattan Coll., 1952; A.M. in L.S., U. Mich., 1954; M.A. in English, Mich. State U., 1959; m. Jacquelyn L. Maloney, Aug. 3, 1963; children—Theresa Marie, Rebecca Mary. Library service scholar U. Mich., 1952-53, library service fellow, 1953-54; asst. acquisitions dept. U. Neb. Library, Lincoln, 1954-56; chief bibliog. acquisitions dept. Mich. State U. Library, East Lansing, 1956-58, librarian Inst. for Community Devel. and Service, Mich. State U., 1958-59; acquisitions librarian U. S. Fla., Tampa, 1959-66, asst. dir. planning and devel., 1967-70; asso. dir. U. Ark. Library, Fayetteville, 1966-67; dir. univ. libraries Va. Commonwealth U., Richmond, 1970—. Mem. A.L.A., Va., Southeastern library assns., Bibliog. Soc. Am. Home: 1519 Village Grove Rd Richmond VA 23233 Office: 901 Park Av Richmond VA 23284

MCCAFFERTY, ROBERT MICHAEL, civil engr., govt. ofcl.; b. Lee's Summit, Mo., Nov. 28, 1940; s. Hugh Efton and Mary Elizabeth (Alley) McC.; B.S., (research fellow), U. Mo. at Columbia, 1962, M.S., 1963; Ph.D. (NSF fellow), U. Colo., 1972; m. Kerrelyn Lee Starr, June 3, 1962; children—Michael Shane, David Ryan. Structural engr. Bur. Reclamation Dept. Interior, Denver, 1963-72; civil engr., advanced systems div. Fed. R.R. Adminstrn., Washington, 1972—. Mem. Am. Soc. C.E., Am. Concrete Inst. Home: 5007 Gadsen Dr Fairfax VA 22030 Office: 2100 2d St SW Washington DC 20590

MCCAFFREY, JOSEPH FRANCIS, broadcasting co. journalist; b. Poughkeepsie, N.Y., May 9, 1920; s. Philip Francis and Kathryn (Shally) McC.; student State U. N.Y., 1939; m. Mildred M. Barrington, Oct. 27, 1945; children—Sally Ann (Mrs. Dennis Shumaker), Michael. With Poughkeepsie (N.Y.) Courier, 1939-41; corr. CBS, Washington, 1944-48, MBS, Washington, 1948-54; chief corr., commentator Evening Star Broadcasting Co., Washington, 1954—. Chmn. standing com. Congl. Radio-TV Galleries, 1956, 71. Chmn. No. Va. Easter Seal drive, 1964; chmn. No. Va. Christmas Seal Dr., 1970. Served to 1st lt. AUS, 1941-44. Recipient Ted Yates award Washington Acad. Tv Arts and Scis., 1971, Emmys, 1960, 61, 64, 68. Mem. Radio Tv. Correspondents Assn. (pres. 1955-56, 70-71). A.F.T.R.A. (local v.p. 1957-58). Author: Election Guide, 1954. Home: 1309 Sunnyside Lane McLean VA 22101 Office: 4461 Connecticut Av Washington DC 20008

MCCAIN, DAVID L., state justice; b. Sebastian, Fla., July 23, 1931; LL.B., U. Fla., 1955; m. Helen Champion; 8 children. Admitted to Fla. bar, Fed. bar; asso. firm Thad H. Carlton, Ft. Pierce, Fla.; with firm Carlton & McCain, Carlton, McCain, Brennan & McAliley, to 1967; judge Fourth Dist. Ct. Appeal, 1967-70; justice Fla. Supreme Ct., Tallahassee, 1970—. Co-dir. United Fund Dr., St. Lucie County, Fla. Served to capt. USAF, 1955-57. Mem. Fla. Acad. Trial Lawyers, Am. Trial Lawyers Assn., Nat. Assn. Municipal Law Officers, Jaycees (dir.; Good Govt. award), Am. Legion. Moose. Home: 2317 Killarney Way Tallahassee FL Office: Supreme Ct Bldg Tallahassee FL 33504

MCCAIN, MAURICE EDWARD, uniform co. exec.; b. Denver, Feb. 14, 1909; s. Thomas C. and Fannie (Burke) McC.; grad. high sch.; m. Florence Inez Snowden, Dec. 27, 1927. With McCain Tailoring Co., 1927-34; mgr. uniform dept. Yielding Bros., 1934-39; with McCain Uniform Co., Inc., Birmingham, Ala., 1939—, pres., 1954—; v.p., dir. Decatur Transit Truck Lines (Ala.), 1954-61; chmn. bd. dirs. Banner Uniform Co., Inc., Atlanta, 1962—; v.p., dir. Burke Uniform Co., Houston, 1967—. Served with USAAF, 1943-45. Mem. Nat. Assn. Uniform Mfrs. (dir.), Birmingham C. of C., Birmingham Traffic and Transp. Club, Birmingham Motor Truck Club, Aero Club. Baptist. Mason (Shriner). Clubs: Civitan, City Salesmen's (pres. 1967-68), Birmingham Area, Vestavia Country, The Club, Downtown. Home: 3756 Locksley Dr Birmingham AL 35223 Office: 2208 3d Av N Birmingham AL 35203

MCCAIN, VIRGIL BOWDEN, JR., coll. pres.; b. Oneonta, Ala., Mar. 9, 1910; s. Virgil Bowden and Jessie (Roberts) McC.; B.A., Birmingham-So. Coll., 1932; exchange fellow Lycee David, Angers, France, 1932-33; M.A., U. Ala., 1934; postgrad. (Austin grad. fellow) Harvard, 1934-35, Auburn U., 1970; L.H.D., Athens (Ala.) Coll., 1957; LL.D., Jacksonville U., 1973; m. Martha Elizabeth Freeman, May 28, 1938; children—Virgil Bowden III, Robert Freeman. Tchr., asst. coach Corinth (Miss.) High Sch., 1935-38; techr. Lanier (Ala.) High Sch., 1938-40; prin. Pine Level Sch., also Pike Rd. High Schs., Montgomery County, Ala., 1940-42; supt., bus. mgr. Methodist Childrens Home, Selma, Ala., 1942-48; dean men, head edn. dept., dir. pub. relations Huntingdon Coll., Montgomery, Ala., 1948-54; pres., bus. mgr. Snead Coll., Boaz, Ala., 1954-59; pres. Athens Coll., 1959-65, Pershing Coll., Beatrice, Neb., 1965-67, Snead State Jr. Coll., Boaz, 1967—. Pres. So. Methodist Childrens Home Workers, 1944, Ala. Conf. Child Caring Instns. and Agys., 1945; mem. conf. bd. lay activities Meth. Ch., 1954-66, commn. promotion and cultivation, 1960-64; del. Gen. Conf. Meth. Ch., 1960, 64. Chmn. bd. dirs. Emanual Brown Tng. Sch., Minter, Ala., 1952-65. Recipient Man of Year award Boaz Civitan Club, 1958, Athens Civitan Club, 1960; Eyes Upon You award Ala. Optometric Assn., 1959. Mem. Ala. Edn. Assn. (pres. div. higher edn. 1953-59), Am. Coll. Pub. Relations Assn. (nat. dir. 1957-59, pres. Southeastern dist. 1953), Assn. Am. Colls., Ala. Assn. Ind. Colls. (pres. 1963-66), Omicron Delta Kappa, Kappa Phi Kappa. Club: Civitan. Home: 308 Mann Av Boaz AL 35957

MCCAIN, WILLIAM DAVID, univ. pres.; b. Bellefontaine, Miss., Mar. 29, 1907; s. Samuel Woodward and Sarah Alda (Shaw) McC.; B.S., Delta State Coll., Cleveland, Miss., 1930; A.M., U. Miss., 1931; Ph.D., Duke U., 1935; Litt.D., Miss. Coll., 1967; m. Minnie Leicester Lenz, Oct. 3, 1931; children—William David, John Woodward (dec.), Patricia. Teaching fellow history U. Miss., 1930-31; head math. dept. East Central Jr. Coll., Decatur, Miss., 1931-32; head social sci. dept. Copiah-Lincoln Jr. Coll., Wesson, Miss., 1932-33; fellow history Duke U., 1933-35; historian Morristown (N.J.) Nat. Hist. Park, 1935; asst. archivist Nat. Archives, Washington, 1935-37; acting asso. prof. history U. Miss., summers 1942, 46, 47; lectr. history Millsaps Coll., 1941-42, 46-48; historian Miss. dept. V.F.W., 1946—; historian dept. Miss., Am. Legion, 1946-55; dir., sec. bd. trustees Miss. Dept. of Archives and History, 1938-55; pres. U. So. Miss., Hattiesburg, 1955—. Chmn. Miss. Library Commn., 1941-43, Miss. Hist. Commn., 1948-55; mem. Miss. Geol. Commn., 1938-55. Served as 1st lt. A.A.A., Coast Arty., AUS, 1943-45, 51-53; maj. gen. Res. Mem. Soc. Am. Archivists (founding, council 1939-44, pres. 1951-53), Miss. Hist. Soc., Miss. Library Assn. (pres. 1941-44), Miss. N.G. Assn., Alpha Tau Omega. Baptist. Author: The United States and the Republic of Panama, 1937; The Story of Jackson: A History of the Capitol of Mississippi, 1821-1951, 1953. Editor: Jour. Miss. History, 1939-56. Contbr. to jours. and newspapers. Address: Southern Sta Box 1 Hattiesburg MS 39401

MCCALEB, JOHN HENRY, real estate broker; b. Saline County, Ark., Feb. 17, 1934; s. William Harvey and Laura Mildred (McCright) McC.; B.S., U. Ark., 1956; m. Annette Woodard Watts, Oct. 23, 1962; children—Jonathan J., Suzanna E., Sarah L. Engr. U.S. Army C.E., Little Rock, 1958-65; owner John H. McCaleb Constrn. Inc., Little Rock, 1965—. Dir. Quadrangle Enterprises, Inc., Little Rock, 1971-74, Minerva Enterprises, Inc., Little Rock, 1971-74.

Committeeman Republican party Pulaski County, 1969-71. Served with USNR, 1956-58. Registered profl. engr., Ark. Mem. Am. Soc. M.E., Home Builders Assn. of Greater Little Rock. Home: 4600 Annette Lane Little Rock AR 72206 Office: 4600 Annette Lane Little Rock AR 72206

MCCALEB, STANLEY BERT, clay mineralogist; b. Santa Barbara, Cal., Oct. 29, 1919; s. Herbert Stanley and Louise Marie (Grande) McC.; B.S., U. Cal. at Berkeley, 1942; M.S., Cornell U., 1948, Ph.D., 1950; m. Regina B. Berta, Sept. 12, 1947; chidlren—Bruce R., Robert Stanley, Pamela Louise. Asst. prof. soil sci. N.C. State Coll., Raleigh, 1950-52, asso. prof., 1952-56; sr. soil correlator, soil conservation service U.S. Dept. Agr., Berkeley, 1956-58; sr. research geologist Sun Oil Co., Richardson, Tex., 1958-69, supr. chem. engring., specialist x-ray mineralogy and environmental conservation, 1969—. Mem. Richardson Ind. Sch. Dist. Trustees, 1964-72, pres., 1969-72; 3d congl. dist. mem. Tex. Bd. Edn., 1972—. Served to 1st lt. AUS, 1942-46. Mem. Soil Sci. Soc. Am., Am. Soc. Agronomy, Clay Minerals Soc., Internat. Soil Sci. Soc., Nat. Sch. Bd. Assn., Nat. Assn. States Bds. Edn., Tex. Commn. on Sch. Accreditation, Sigma Xi, Phi Kappa Phi, Sigma Gamma Epsilon, Alpha Zeta. Republican. Contbr. to profl. publs. Patentee in drilling tech., x-ray automation. Home: 200 W Shore Dr Richardson TX 75080 Office: 503 N Central Expressway Richardson TX 75080

MCCALL, BENNY GORDON, physician; b. Maryville, Tenn., Dec. 29, 1933; s. Benjamin Harrison and Isa (Porter) McC.; M.D., U. Tenn., 1963; m. Judy Ann Mills, Apr. 25, 1965; children—Kimberly Ann, Christy Lynn, Sherri Leigh. Intern, Univ. Hosp., Knoxville, Tenn., 1963-64, resident, 1964-67; pvt. practice medicine, specializing in internal medicine, Maryville, 1967—; mem. staff Blount Meml. Hosp., Maryville. Served with AUS, 1955-57. Mem. A.M.A., Tenn. Med. Assn., Blount County Med. Soc., Knoxville Soc. Internal Medicine. Baptist. Home: 403 Sherwood Dr Maryville TN 37801 Office: Chilhowee Med Park Maryville TN 37801

MCCALL, CHARLIE CAMPBELL, lawyer; b. Causeyville, Miss., Mar. 23, 1895; s. Charles Edward and Mary Rebecca (Collins) McC.; ed. bus. coll., prep. sch., Starkes (Ala.), Edgar's (Ala.), Denna's (N.Y.) and Ga. Mil. Acad.; LL.B., Georgetown U., 1921, LL.M., 1922, M.P.L., 1922; LL.M., Nat. U., 1922, M.P.L. 1922, S.J.D., 1936; LL.M. in Dp., Am. U., 1923; student U. Ala., 1915, 17; grad. Sch. Mil. Govt. U.S. Army, Charlottesville, Va., 1944, AAF Sch. Applied Tactics, (Orlando, Fla.), Sch. Applied Personnel Mgmt., 1945; m. Nellie Curtis Cave, Apr. 16, 1924; 1 dau. (by previous marriage), Dorothy. Admitted to bar D.C., 1920, Ala. 1920, U.S. Supreme Ct., 1926, Va., 1957, also U.S. Ct. Claims, Tax Ct., FCC, ICC, Treasury Dept.; pvt. sec. to Congressman John McDuffie of Ala., 1919-20; capt. judge adv. Judge Adv. Gen.'s Dept. Washington, 1921-23; examiner pub. accounts, Ala., 1924-27; atty. gen. of Ala., 1927-31; spl. asst. atty. gen. of Ala., 1931-32; counsel RFC, Washington, 1932-33; chief counsel pub. bodies sect. legal div. Fed. Emergency Adminstrn. Pub. Works, 1933-34, chief legal adviser N.Y. State office, 1934-35; counsel PWA, 1935-38, asst. gen. counsel, 1938-39, acting gen. counsel, 1939-40, gen. counsel, 1940-42; acting gen. counsel P.R. Reconstrn. Adminstrn., San Juan, 1937; spl. asso. gen. counsel Fed. Works Agy., 1941-42, asst. gen. counsel, 1945-48; practiced in Birmingham, Ala., 1948-49; chief financing atty. div. law Slum Clearance Staff, HHFA, Washington, 1949-58, spl. counsel, office gen. counsel, 1954-57, spl. asst. to gen. counsel, 1957-58; pvt. law practice, 1958—. Served as 1st lt., cav., U.S. Army, 1917-19, capt. 1920-24, capt. to maj. cav., U.S.R. and Ala. N.G., 1925-34; maj. to lt. col., AC, U.S. Army, 1942-45; lt. col. USAF Res. (ret.). Fellow Internat. Biog. Assn.; mem. Am., Va., Fed., Birmingham bar assns., Bar Assn. D.C., Nat. Assn. Attys. Gen. (pres. 1929), Mil. Order World Wars, Nat. Antivivisection Soc., Animal Protective Assn., Sigma Nu Phi, Chi Psi Omega. Mason (32 deg., Shriner). Home: 8525 Crestview Dr Fairfax VA 22030

MCCALL, DANIEL THOMPSON, JR., justice Supreme Ct. Ala.; b. Butler, Ala., Mar. 12, 1909; s. Daniel Thompson and Caroline (Bush) McC.; B.A., U. Ala., 1931, LL.B., 1933; m. Mary Edna Montgomery, Apr. 3, 1937; children—Mary Winston (Mrs. Rogers Neilson Laseter), Daniel Thompson III, Nancy (Mrs. John Worrell Poynor). Admitted to Ala. bar, 1933; practiced in Mobile, 1933-60; partner firm Johnston, McCall & Johnston, 1943-60; circuit judge 13th Circuit, 1960-69; asso. justice Ala. Supreme Ct., Montgomery, 1969—. Mem. Mobile County Bd. Sch. Commrs. 1950-56, 58-60. Trustee U. Ala., nat. alumni pres., 1963. Served to lt. USNR, World War II. Mem. Am., Ala., Mobile County (past pres.) bar assns., Jr. Bar Assn. Ala. (past pres.), Am. Judicature Soc., Nat. Conf. State Trial Judges, Ala. Assn. Circuit Judges, Inst. Jud. Adminstrn., Ala. Law Inst., Am. Trial Lawyers Assn., Farrah Law Soc., Ala. Hist. Soc., Wildlife and Conservation Assn., Navy League U.S., Am. Legion, 40 and 8, S.A.R., Sons of Confederacy, Sigma Nu, Phi Delta Phi, Omicron Delta Kappa. Democrat. Episcopalian. Clubs: Bienville, Indian Hills Country, Athelstan, Hickory Hill Hunting. Home: 118 Ryan Av Mobile AL 36607 Office: PO Box 218 Montgomery AL 36101

MCCALL, DAVID BENJAMIN, JR., banker, ins. co. exec.; b. Farmersville, Tex., Mar. 31, 1924; s. David Benjamin and Lela (Kemp) McC.; B.A., La. Tech., 1944; M.Ed., So. Meth. U., 1949; m. Nellie V. Hutchins, May 28, 1945; children—David B., James Brian. Prin. Plano Elementary Sch., Plano, Tex., 1946-55; prin. David McCall Ins. Agy., Plano, 1955—; pres. Plano Savs. & Loan Assn., 1963—; exec. dir. First Nat. Bank of Plano, 1967—. Pres. Plano Centennial, Inc., 1973. Mayor City of Plano, 1956-60; dir. North Tex. Municipal Water Dist., Wylie, 1973—. Bd. dirs. Institutional Devel. Baylor U., Waco, Tex., 1971—. Served to lt. USMCR, 1942-45. Mem. Plano C. of C. (pres. 1955, Man of Year award 1958). Mason, Rotarian (pres. 1955). Baptist (deacon 1956—). Home: 1704 N Place Plano TX 75074 Office: PO Box :5 Plano TX 75074

MCCALL, HAZEL BRADFIELD (MRS. JOHN DEAN MCCALL), club woman; b. Fiskville, Tex.; d. Thomas Bascom and Martha (Colvin) Bradfield; grad. Kenilworth Hall, Austin, Tex.; student U. Tex.; m. John Dean McCall, June 21, 1933; children—Paul Bradfield Horton, Mary Helen Horton (Mrs. Frederic H. Brownell), John Dean, Thomas Screven. Pres. Dallas Lawyers Wives' Club, 1952-53, Dallas Soc. Meml. Assn., 1956-57; dir. Women's Council Dallas County, 1959—; mem. scholarship com., 1963-64, 72; dir. Dallas Fedn. Women's Club Girl's Found., Inc., 1962—; bd. mem. women's bd. Dallas Civic Opera, Dallas Civic Ballet, Friday Forum. Pres. Dem. Women Dallas County, 1949-50. Mem. D.A.R., U.D.C., Dallas Fedn. Women's Clubs, Dallas Women's Symphony League, Dallas Pan Am. Round Table Number 1, Shakespeare Followers (pres. 1963-64). Clubs: Dallas Woman's (auditor 1972-73), Marianne Scruggs Garden, Dallas Country. Home: 3628 Beverly Dr Dallas TX 75205

MCCALL, LEMUEL ALLSOBROOK, museum trustee; b. Florence, S.C., June 29, 1913; s. Lemuel Allsobrook and Irene (French) McC.; B.A., Presbyn. Coll. (Clinton, S.C.), 1935; m. Carolyn Elizabeth Heriot, Apr. 22, 1949; children—Ann Richards (Mrs. E.D. Crenshaw II), Elizabeth Allsobrook, Susan Heriot. Asst. state dir. Nat. Youth Adminstr., S.C., 1935-37; pres. Fairfield Dairy, Florence, S.C., 1937-45; owner Fairfield Farms, Florence, 1938-71; pres. Darlington Motor Co., (S.C.), 1946-53; lay Hi-Y dir. Florence (S.C.) YMCA, 1940-70; trustee Florence (S.C.) Museum, 1954—. Pres. Florence County Farm Bur., 1960; mem. S.C. State Mental Health Bd., 1967; mem. Florence County Mental Health Bd., 1964-70. Served with AUS, 1936-37. Accredited flower judge. Mem. Florence Garden Council (pres. 1970-71), S.C. Huguenot Soc., S.C. Hist. Soc., Florence Choral Soc., Florence County Hist. Soc., Pi Kappa Alpha. Democrat. Club: Country of S.C. Home: Cashua Ferry Rd Route 8 Florence SC 29501 also (summer) Litchfield Beach SC Office: Cashua Ferry Rd Route 8 Florence SC 29501

MCCALLIAN, RICHARD JONES, engring. cons.; b. Dayton, O., Jan. 5, 1913; s. Edwin Lewis and Mary (Marsh) M.; B.S., Tri-State Coll., 1934; postgrad. U. Ga., 1963-65; m. Louise Garnett, Aug. 4, 1969. Metallurgist, U.S. Steel Corp., Gary, Ind., 1936-44; engring. cons., Phila., 1945-48; dist. sales mgr. Stulz-Sickles Co., Elizabeth, N.J., 1949-62; indsl. devel. cons., Port Richey, Fla., 1963—; pres., Florestate Park, Inc., Oceanographic Minerals, Inc., Port Richey, 1967—; dir. Chasco Fiesta, Inc., Port Richey. Bd. dirs. Boy Scouts Am., Port Richey. Mem. Fla. Travel Council, Fla. Indsl. Devel. Council, Am. Marketing Assn., Fla. C. of C. Methodist (certified lay speaker 1967—, asso. dist. lay leader 1968—). Author: Potential Economic Benefits of Cross Florida Barge Canal, 1965. Patentee in field. Home: 30 Gulf Breeze N Port Richey FL 33568 Office: 19 N Main St Port Richey FL 33568

MCCAMMON, CURTIS PAUL, physician; b. Knoxville, Tenn., Nov. 6, 1922; s. William Howard and Trula (Reynolds) McC.; B.A., U. Tenn., 1946; M.D., Temple U. (Phila.), 1949; M.P.H., Harvard, 1958; m. Doris Marie Meggs, May 22, 1954; children—NanMarie, Stanley Paul, Janet Lee, Daniel Kevin. Intern Brooke Gen. Hosp., San Antonio, 1949-50; asst. health officer Bur. Health, Knoxville, 1950-52; practice medicine specializing in gen. practice, Wartburg, Tenn., 1954-57; dir. indsl. hygiene Tenn. Dept. Pub. Health, Nashville, 1957-68; med. dir. U. Tenn. Med. Research Center and Hosp., Knoxville, 1968—, also clin. prof. Med. Sch., Memphis, 1958-67; clin. prof. Vanderbilt U., Nashville, 1960-66; mem. staff U. Tenn. Med. Research Center. Mem. Am. Pub. Health Assn., Indsl. Med. Assn., A.M.A., Tenn. Med. Assn. Methodist. Mason (32 deg.). Club: Holston Hills Country (Knoxville). Home: 320 Essex Dr Concord TN 37720 Office: 1924 Alcoa Hwy Knoxville TN 37920

MCCAMPBELL, BRUCE RANKIN, surgeon; b. Knoxville, Tenn., Jan. 15, 1916; s. Bruce Philip and Mary Isabel (Rankin) McC.; student Maryville Coll., 1933-35; B.A., U. Tenn., 1937; M.D., 1941; m. Erma Faye Williams, Mar. 16, 1941; children—Mary (Mrs. John M. Bell), Patricia (Mrs. David C. Thompson), Bruce, Janet, Rebecca, Rachael. Intern, U.S. Naval Hosp., San Diego, 1941-42; commd. lt. (j.g.) M.C., USN, 1941, advanced through grades to comdr., 1945; chief surgery U.S. Naval Hosp., Beaufort, N.C., 1948-49, asst. chief surgery, Oakland, Cal., 1950-51; chief surgery U.S.S. Consolation, 1951-52, U.S. Naval Hosp., St. Albans, N.Y., 1952-53; pvt. practice medicine specializing in surgery, Knoxville, 1953—; now chief surgery St. Mary's Meml. Hosp., Knoxville; mem. staff E.T. Baptist Hosp., U. Tenn. Meml. Research Center and Hosp., Ft. Sanders Presbyn. Hosp. (all Knoxville). Bd. dirs. Shannondale Health Care Center. Diplomate Am. Bd. Surgery. Fellow A.C.S.; mem. Knoxville Acad. Medicine, Knoxville Surg. Soc. Presbyn. (elder). Home: Route 23 Knoxville TN 37920 Office: 1831 W Clinch Av Knoxville TN 37916

MCCAMY, ROBERT JULIAN, textile co. exec.; b. Lindale, Ga., July 18, 1911; s. Robert and Bernice (Herring) McC.; grad. Darlington Sch., 1928; B.S. in Textile Engring., Ga. Inst. Tech., 1932; m. Charlotte Powers, June 5, 1936; children—Robert J., Donald Howard, Mary Deane, Charles Powers. Trainee, Pepperell Mfg. Co., Lindale, Ga., 1932-37, 38-39, supt. dyeing, 1939-42, asst. plant supt., 1942-47, plant supt., 1947-55, asst. mgr., 1955-61, v.p., 1961-65, v.p. West Point-Pepperell, Inc., 1965—; tech. sales So. Dyestuff Corp., Charlotte, N.C., 1938-39. Pres., TB Assn., Rome, Ga., 1963—. Trustee Darlington Sch.; bd. dirs. Textile Edn. Found. Mem. C. of C. (dir. 1960), Phi Psi, Tau Beta Pi, Pi Kappa Phi. Methodist (trustee). Mason. Club: Riverside Country. Home: 209 Hamilton Dr West Point GA 31833 Office: West Point-Pepperell Inc West Point GA 31833

MCCANDLESS, BRUCE II, astronaut; b. Boston, June 8, 1937; s. Bruce and Sue (Bradley) McC.; B.S., U.S. Naval Acad., 1958; M.S. in Elec. Engring., Stanford, 1965; m. Alfreda Bernice Doyle, Aug. 6, 1960; children—Bruce III, Tracy. Commd. ensign U.S. Navy, 1958, advanced through grades to comdr., 1972; naval aviator, 1960, with Fighter Squadron 102, 1960-64; astronaut Manned Spacecraft Center, Houston, 1966—. Mem. I.E.E.E., U.S. Naval Inst., Nat. Geog. Soc. Episcopalian. Home: 314 Whitecap Dr Seabrook TX 77586 Office: Code CB NASA Johnson Space Center Houston TX 77058

MCCANDLESS, CHARLES EMERY, educator; b. Dallas, July 26, 1931; s. Dewey Taylor and Clara (Askins) McC.; B.S., Tex. A. and M. U., 1956, M.Ed., 1958; Ed.D., North Tex. State U., 1966; m. Joyce Elaine Thompson, Apr. 8, 1951; children—Cathy, Sharon, Debra. Head coach Silsbee (Tex.) Jr. High Sch., 1956-58; counselor Silsbee High Sch., 1958-60; part-time instr. health, phys. edn., recreation North Tex. U., Denton, 1960-61; asst. prof. health and phys. edn., intramural athletics dir. Tex. A. and M. U., College Station, 1963-66, chmn. freshman courses dept. edn. and psychology, 1964-66, dir. adj., chmn. counselor edn., 1966-67, asso. prof. edn. and psychology, 1967—, asso. dean liberal arts, 1966-74, coordinator univ. self study, 1971-73, dir. acad. planning and services, 1974—. Pres., College Station Recreation Council, 1968-73, College Station United Chest, 1973-74; pres. adv. bd. Central Brazos Valley Mental Health Center. Served with USAF, 1951-53. Recipient Student-Faculty Relations award Coll. Liberal Arts, 1969. Mem. College Station Progress Assn. (dir. 1969-71), Am. Personnel and Guidance Assn., Am. Coll. Personnel Assn., Assn. Counselor Edn. and Supervision, Tex. Personnel and Guidance Assn., Tex. Psychol. Assn. Assoc. dir. several profl. jours. Home: 212 Redmond Dr College Station TX 77840

MCCANLESS, GEORGE FOLSOM, ret. justice Supreme Ct. Tenn.; b. Morristown, Tenn., June 8, 1904; s. Michael C. and Nannie Louise (Folsom) McC.; A.B., Vanderbilt U., 1926, LL.B., 1928; m. Sarah Gaut Hardcastle, Apr. 9, 1929; children—Sarah, George Folsom. Admitted to Tenn. bar., 1928, practiced in Morristown, 1928-37, 46-54; chancellor 13th Chancery Div. Tenn., 1937-38, commr. finance and taxation Tenn., 1939-46; atty. gen. Tenn., 1954-69; justice Supreme Ct. Tenn., Nashville, 1969-74. Mem. Tenn. Hist. Commn., 1961—. Mem. Tenn. Hist. Soc. (pres. 1959-61), Phi Kappa Sigma, Phi Delta Phi. Presbyn. Home: 700 Crescent Rd Nashville TN 37205

MCCANN, KELLY FRANKLIN, battery mfg. co. exec.; b. Oklahoma City, Apr. 3, 1928; s. Ralph Williamson and Thelma Jane (Franklin) McC.; B.B.A., Baylor U., 1949; m. Ethel Hurr, Dec. 23, 1949; children—Kelly Franklin, James Ralph, William Lee. Reporter, Dun & Bradstreet, Inc., 1949-50; with Continental Battery Mfg. Corp., 1950—, pres., 1960—, also dir.; dir. Tex. Nat. Bank, Dynamerica Corp. (all Dallas). Bd. mgmt. Town North YMCA, Dallas, 1967—. Mem. Ind. Battery Mfrs. Am. (past trustee). Baptist (deacon). Rotarian. Club: Preston Trail Golf (dir. Dallas). Home: 6805 Midcrest Dr Dallas TX 75240 Office: 4919 Woodall St Dallas TX 75247

MCCANN, RALPH WILLIAMSON, battery mfg. co. exec.; b. Jacksonville, Fla. Mar. 28, 1897; s. William A. and Joanna (Williamson) McC.; student comml. law U. Tex. Extension, 1922-23; m. Thelma J. Franklin, Nov. 29, 1922; children—Joanna (Mrs. John G. Heard), Kelly F., Ralph Williamson. Comml. reporter R.G. Dun & Co., Jacksonville, Fla., Denver, 1916-19; salesman, dist. and zone mgr. Firestone Tire & Rubber Co., Akron, O., 1920-42; co-founder Continental Battery Mfg. Co., Dallas, 1932—, pres., 1950—; chmn. bd. Continental Battery Co., 1959—, McCann-Continental Bldg. Co., Dallas, 1963—. Mem. Dallas Council Social Agys., 1946-48; adv. council Dallas Community Chest Trust Fund. Mem. Dallas Sch. Dist. Bd., 1950-52. Founder Thelma J. McCann 4-year scholarship Baylor U., 1962. Recipient certificate of distinguished service Dallas Sch. Bd., 1952. Mem. Am. Assn. Battery Mfrs., Dallas C. of C. Baptist (deacon). Clubs: Rotary, Dallas Athletic, Dallas Salesmanship (past v.p., camp bd. chmn.), Glen Lakes Country (past pres.). Donor (with wife) dept. of electrocardiology and electroencephalography to Baylor U. Med. Center, 1967, also Presbyn. Hosp. Devel. Fund, Dallas Bapt. Coll. Home: 7501 Rambler Rd Dallas TX 75231 Office: 4919 Woodall St Dallas TX 75247

MCCANN, RALPH WILLIAMSON, JR., battery co. exec.; b. Dallas, Aug. 1, 1932; s. Ralph Williamson and Thelma Jane (Franklin) McC.; B.B.A., Baylor U., 1954; m. Bobbie Louise Barclay, May 22, 1954; children—Ralph Williamson III, Charles B. Credit reporter Dun & Bradstreet, Inc., Houston, 1954-55; marketing mgr. Continental Battery Co., Dallas, 1957—. Pres., Northwood P.T.A., 1969-70; commr. Little League, 1971. Served to capt. USAF, 1955-57. Baptist. Club: Canyon Creek Country (Richardson, Tex.). Home: 2500 Cedar Elm Lane Plano TX 75074 Office: 4919 Woodall St Dallas TX 75247

MCCANTS, DONALD GLENN, computer mgr.; b. Charleston, S.C., Dec. 20, 1931; s. Rudolph Chesleigh and Lillian Gertrude (Hare) McC.; B.S. in Elec. Engring., Va. Poly. Inst., 1958; M.B.A., Lynchburg Coll., 1973; m. Jacqueline Anne Matthews, Dec. 31, 1957; children—Glenna, Donald Glenn, Matthew. Account rep., IBM Corp., Lynchburg, Va., 1958-66; gen. mgr. Ednl. Computer Center, Lynchburg, 1966—; also dir. Asst. prof. Lynchburg Coll., 1968—. Served with USAF, 1951-54. Mem. Assn. Computing Machinery, Nat. Assn. Accountants, Data Processing Mgmt. Assn., Eta Kappa Nu, Omicron Delta Kappa, Tau Beta Pi. Editor, pub. Synergism newsletter, 1971—. Home: 2408 Indian Hill Rd Lynchburg VA 24503 Office: 1201 Kemper St Lynchburg VA 24505

MCCARLEY, CAROLYN JOSEPHINE SPENCE (MRS. CLINT WELDON MCCARLEY), shoe store exec.; b. Emporium, Pa., Oct. 16, 1919; d. Charles Burnell and Marguerite (Schoenbohm) Spence; student West Tex. State U., 1938-40; B.A., Tex. Arts and Industries U., 1942; postgrad. U. Guadalajara, 1944; m. Clint Weldon McCarley, June 8, 1945; children—Clint Weldon, Philip Allen, Charles Aubra, Kelvyn Joe. Tchr., Kingsville, Tex., 1942-43, Falfurrias, Tex., 1943-44, Gregory, Tex., 1944-45, Clarkwood, Tex., 1948-49, Harlingen, Tex., 1952-53; co-owner Carolyn's Shoe Store, Harlingen, 1954—. Vice pres. Stephen F. Austin Sch. P.T.A., Harlingen, 1964-65; sec. St. Paul's Luth Sch. P.T.A., 1966-68; chmn. Project Goodwill, 1966-68. Recipient citation State Fine Arts Commn., 1966-67. Mem. South Tex. Dist. (pub. affairs dept. chmn. 1968-70, pres. 1970-72, sec. scholarship fund com. 1973-74, chmn., internat. hostess 1972-74), Rio Grande Valley (conv. coordinator 1969-71, hospitality chmn. 1971—) fedns. women's clubs. Presbyn. (chmn. Christian edn. com., regional chmn. Women of Ch. 1973-75). Clubs: Zonta (pres. 1968-70, service chmn. 1971-72), Afflatus (sec. 1969-70, pres. 1970-72), City Federation Past Presidents (sec. 1969) (all Harlingen). Home: 102 Wildwood St Harlingen TX 78550 Office: 705 Coronado Village Harlingen TX 78550

MCCARROLL, EARL LUCAS, banker; b. Holly Springs, Miss., May 2, 1915; s. John Ramsay and Marie (McKie) McC.; extension student Northwestern U.; certificate Am. Inst. Banking, 1941; grad. Rutgers U. Grad. Sch. Banking, 1949; m. Helen Shannon, Oct. 15, 1938; children—Earl Lucas, Eileen (Mrs. James J. McDonald), Michael Shannon. With Union Planters Nat. Bank, Memphis, 1933-52, asst. vice pres. charge comml. loans, 1950-52; with First Nat. Bank, Little Rock, 1952-59, exec. v.p., 1955-58, pres., 1958-59; exec. v.p. Union Nat. Bank, Little Rock, 1959-63, pres., 1963-68, also dir. mem. exec. com., chief exec. office; 1967-68; pres. Farmers Bank & Trust Co., Blytheville, Ark., 1968—. Treas. Little Rock Sch. Dist., 1956-64; former sec. bd. trustees Little Rock U., 1963—; pres. Blytheville United Fund; dist. chmn. U.S. Savs. Bond Program. Mem. Am., Ark., (exec. council) bankers assns., Am. Inst. Banking (pres.), Memphis (1946-48), Little Rock C. of C. (pres. 1961), Blytheville Unltd. Episcopalian (past vestryman, chmn. finance com.). Rotarian. Club: Blytheville Country (pres.). Home: 710 N 16th St Blytheville AR 72315 Office: PO Box 688 Blytheville AR 72315

MCCARTER, GRADY SYLVESTER III, clergyman; b. Shreveport, La., Mar. 5, 1945; s. Grady Sylvester and Virginia Ann (Wolfe) McC.; B.A., Tex. Christian U., 1967; M.Div. (Bernice Hanson scholar), Brite Div. Sch., 1971; postgrad. La. State U. Law Sch., 1971; m. Judith Frances Keator, Sept. 2, 1967; children—Nancy Ann, David Ross. Ordained to ministry Christian Ch., 1971; minister First Christian Ch., Crockett, Tex., 1967-71, First Christian Ch., Levelland, Tex., 1972—. Bd. dirs. Hockley County Community Action Agy., 1973—, Hockley County Youth Center, 1973—, Brite Div. Sch. Found., 1973—. Mem. Hi Plains Assn. Christian Chs. (dir. 1973—), Phi Delta Theta. Editor Perspective, lit. jour., 1966-67. Home: 407 Poplar St Levelland TX 79336 Office: 311 Club View Levelland TX 79336

MCCARTER, JAMES THOMAS, engring. co. exec.; b. Greenville, S.C., Sept. 24, 1932; s. Thomas Avery and Emily (Street) McC.; B.M.E., Clemson U., 1954; m. Patricia Marie Hood, Feb. 14, 1959; children—Steven Thomas, Bruce Hood, David Christopher. Engr., Western Electric Co., Burlington, N.C., 1954-55, J.E. Sirrine Co., Engrs., Greenville, 1957-58; resident engr. U.S. Army, Charlotte, N.C., 1958-59; project engr. Davis Mech. Contractors, Greenville, 1959-64; v.p. Piedmont Engrs., Architects and Planners, Greenville, 1964-73, exec. v.p., 1973—, also dir. Served to 1st lt. AUS, 1955-57. Registered profl. engr., S.C., N.C., Ga., Ala., Tenn., N.J., Me. Mem. Am. Soc. M.E. (vice-chmn. 1962-63, chmn. 1963-64), Am. Soc. Heating, Refrigeration and Air Conditioning Engrs. (chpt. treas. 1964-65, 2d v.p. 1965-66, 1st v.p. 1966-67, pres. 1967-68), Nat. Soc. Profl. Engrs. (chpt. pres. 1968-69), Phi Kappa Phi, Tau Beta Pi. Baptist (deacon 1965—). Patentee in field. Home: 228 McSwain Dr Greenville SC 29607 Office: PO Box 1717 Greenville SC 29602

MCCARTHA, WALTER HAYNE, civil engr.; b. Batesburg, S.C., May 13, 1908; s. Walter Jacob and Henryetta (Towill) McC.; B.S. in Civil Engring., The Citadel, 1930, C.E., 1936; postgrad. in econs. George Washington U., 1930-31, in architecture, 34-35; postgrad. U. Mo. at Rolla, 1963, 64, 68, Civil Service Commn., 1966, USPHS, 1969, U. Md., 1962; m. Virginia Jean Ritchhart, June 3, 1957. Valuation engr. aide ICC Washington, 1930-31; archtl. engr. Pub. Bldgs. Service, Washington, 1931-40; engr., chief materials engring. group, 1950-57; chief specifications engr. for constrn. VA, Richmond,

Va., 1946-49; archtl. gen. engr. charge specification standards for constrn. Directorate of Civil Engring., Hdqrs. U.S. Air Force, Washington, 1957—. Dir. Joint Bd. on Sci. Edn., Washington, 1955-64, 72—, chmn., 1958-59; mem. tri-service com. for constrn. research Nat. Bur. Standards, 1971—, chmn., 1973-74. Served to col. USAAF, 1940-46. Recipient Civil Engring. Meritorious Achievement award Dept. Air Force, 1962. Registered profl. engr., D.C. Mem. Nat., D.C. (pres. 1954-55, dir. 1963-66) socs. profl. engrs., Soc. Am. Mil. Engrs., Washington Soc. Engrs. (dir. 1969-70, 74—, 1st v.p. 1972, pres. 1973), D.C. Council Engring. and Archtl. Socs. (chmn. 1956-57), Am. Soc. Testing and Materials. Baptist. Mason (32 deg. Shriner). Clubs: Chantilly Nat. Golf and Country (Centerville, Va.). Contbr. constrn. chpts. to Air Force Manuals, 1960, 61, 64-74). Home: 3804 14th St N Arlington VA 22201 Office: Engring Div Directorate of Civil Engring Hdqrs US Air Force Bolling AFB Washington DC 20332

MCCARTHY, THOMAS JAMES, JR., lawyer, real estate exec.; b. Pulaski, Va., Nov. 24, 1943; s. Thomas James and M. Jane (Osborne) McC.; grad. The Episcopal High Sch., Alexandria, Va., 1963; B.A. in Econs., Washington and Lee U., 1967; J.D., U. Va., 1970. Admitted to Va. bar, 1970, since practiced in Pulaski; asso. firm Gilmer, Sadler, Ingram, Sutherland & Hutton, 1970—; pres. Pulaski Bus. Plaza, Inc., 1969—; pres. Turnpike Enterprises, Inc., Pulaski, 1970—; dir. Count Pulaski Realty. Mem. Pulaski County Democratic Com., 1971—. Served with AUS, 1970; capt. Res. Mem. Pulaski County C. of C. (dir. 1971—), Va., Pulaski County (sec.-treas. 1973-74) bar assns., Sigma Chi. Episcopalian. Elk. Home: 612 Cardinal Dr Pulaski VA 24301 Office: Midtown Professional Bldg 65 E Main St Pulaski VA 24301

MCCARTNEY, RICHARD THOMAS, pub. relations co. exec.; b. Ozark, Ark., Aug. 18, 1927; s. Herbert Earl and Carrie (Adcock) McC.; B.A., John Brown U., 1947, L.H.D., 1967; B.D., Southwestern Theol. Sem., 1956, M.Div., 1973; postgrad. Baylor U., 1967-68; m. Barbara Anne Treadwell, Oct. 1, 1947; children—Judith Anne, Mary Kathleen, Michael David. Mem. staff radio and TV stas., 1947-57; dir. pub. relations Baptist Gen. Conv. of Okla., Oklahoma City, 1957-62, Bapt. Gen. Conv. of Tex., Dallas, 1962-68; exec. v.p. Arthur Davenport Assos., Inc., Oklahoma City, 1968-69, pres., 1969—. Mem. fund campaign team Okla. Bapt. U., 1969-70; mem. pub. relations com. United Appeal, 1970-72. Recipient Distinguished Service in Religious Journalism award Lambda Lambda Lambda, 1959. Mem. Pub. Relations Soc. Am. (accredited pres. Oklahoma City chpt., 1969—, chmn. S.W. dist. 1971, vice chmn. honors and awards com. 1972; chmn.'s citation 1971, nat. dir. 1973—), John Brown U. Alumni Assn. (nat. pres., 1967-69, Oklahoma City C. of C. (pub. relations div. 1973). Democrat. Lion. Home: 7328 Hammond Circle Oklahoma City OK 73132 Office: Arthur Davenport Assos Inc 13 NW 41st St Oklahoma City OK 73118

MCCARTY, CHARLES CLYDE, statistician; b. Little Rock, Apr. 2, 1943; s. James L. and Dora Louise (Morton) McC.; B.S., U. Ark. at Little Rock, 1965; postgrad. St. Marys U., 1967-71, Tex. A. and M. U., 1968; m. Carol L. Coots, Jan. 6, 1967; 1 dau., Jenny L. Statis. cons., USAF Sch. Aerospace Medicine, Brooks AFB, Tex., 1966-70; research dir. Crime Commn. Ark., Little Rock, 1970-73; mgr. statistics Ark. Criminal Justice Information Center, Little Rock, 1973—. Served with USMCR, 1960. Mem. Am. Statis. Assn., Nat. Assn. Criminal Justice Statistics Dirs. Exec. bd. Project Search, 1970-74. Home: 2720 N Pierce St Little Rock AR 72207 Office: Box 7445 Little Rock AR 72207

MCCAUL, THOMAS VADEN, JR., lawyer, securities co. exec.; b. Clemson, S.C., Dec. 30, 1911; s. Thomas Vaden and Waldine Byrd (Scearce) McC.; LL.B., U. Fla., 1935; m. Sammy Anne Wills, Apr. 26, 1957. Admitted to Fla. bar, 1935; practiced in Miami, Fla., 1936-54; mem. firm Bouvier, Helliwell & McCaul, Miami, Fla., 1948-50; spl. asst. to atty. gen. of Fla., Tallahassee, 1941-43; prin. Wall St. Corp. Am., Inc. security dealers, Miami, 1963-73, v.p., treas., 1965-73, also dir.; v.p. Fremont & Co., Miami Shores, Fla., 1973—. Mem. Nat. Assn. Security Dealers. Pi Kappa Alpha. Democrat. Home: 530 N E 133rd St North Miami FL 33161 Office: 9301 NE 6th Av Miami Shores FL 33138

MCCAULEY, HAROLD HOMER, mech. engr.; b. Stockton, Kan., Aug. 26, 1923; s. Homer Wilson and Hilda (Moore) McC.; B.S., Kan. State U., 1949; m. Patricia June Canfield, July 22, 1951; children—Carol Linn, Barbara Jean, Avis Dee, Allan Wade. Civilian engr. U.S. Army Corps Engrs., Kansas City Dist., 1949-54; elec.-mech. engr. Servis, Van Dorn & Hazard, cons. engr., Topeka, 1954-59; supr. engr. Corps Engrs., ICBM Launcher Sites, 1959-63; mech. engr. Office Chief of Engrs., Washington, 1963-70, supervisory engr., 1970—. Mem. Am. Nat. Standards Inst. B31.4 sect. com.; adviser Jr. Engr. Tech. Soc. local high sch., 1965-69. Treas., P.T.A., 1965-66, 68-71, pres. Woodlawn Citizens Assn., 1971. Served with USNR, 1945-46. Recipient letters of commendation, certificates of achievement Dept. Army, 1962, 64. Mem. Nat. Soc. Profl. Engrs., Sigma Tau, Pi Tau Sigma. Presbyn. Home: 5017 Rosemont Av Alexandria VA 22309 Office: Forrestal Bldg Washington DC 20314

MCCAULEY, LOYD CECIL, dentist; b. Canton, Tex., Sept. 2, 1913; s. Sidney James and Florence Eva (Prater) McC.; student N. Tex. State Tchrs. Coll., 1930-32; D.D.S., Baylor U., 1936; m. Claudia Alethe Moore, Aug. 30, 1934; children—Phillip Ray, Ronald Cecil, Danny Paul. Pvt. practice dentistry, Alba, Tex., 1938-42, Mt. Pleasant, Tex., 1942—; courtesy staff Titus County Meml. Hosp., Mt. Pleasant. Pres., Mt. Pleasant Ind. Sch. Bd., 1952-56. Fellow Royal Soc. Health; mem. Am. Dental Assn., Tex., First Dist. (pres. 1954) dental socs., Pierre Fauchard Acad., Order of Goodfellow. Mem. Ch. of Christ. Home: 303 Chester St Mount Pleasant TX 75455 Office: PO Box 508 Mount Pleasant TX 75455

MCCLAIN, DAVID H., lawyer, state senator; b. Macon, Ga., June 4, 1933; s. Joseph A. Jr. and Laura (Burkett) McC.; B.A., Duke, 1957; M.A. (Scottish Rite fellow 1958), George Washington U., 1961; LL.B., Stetson Coll. Law, 1961; m. Leslie McNevin, Dec. 20, 1968; 1 dau., Linda N. (Mrs. Wheeler). Partner, MacFarlane, Ferguson, Allison & Kelly, Tampa, Fla., 1961-73; individual practice, Tampa, 1973—; legislative liason Fla. Gov.'s office, 1967; mem. Fla. Senate, 1970—. Mem., Fla. Law Revision Council, 1970-72. Vice chmn. Bd. Pub. Relations and Conf. Facilities, Tampa, 1969-70. Served with AUS. Recipient Outstanding Leadership and Service award Bd. Pub. Relations and Conv. Facilities, 1970; Green Cross award Greater Tampa Safety Council, 1972, numerous others. Mem. Fla. (constrn. com. 1970, 72), Am., Tampa, Hillsborough County (chmn. unauthorized practice of law com. 1969) bar assns., Tampa Jr. C. of C. (Good Govt. award 1971), Beta Theta Pi, Delta Theta Phi. Mason (Shriner). Clubs: Interbay Sertoma (sec. 1970-71), Highlights. Home: 4611 Fig St Tampa FL 33609 Office: PO Box 1253 310 N Jefferson St Tampa FL 33602

MCCLAIN, WILLIAM FRANCIS, mfg. co. owner; b. Atlanta, June 14, 1922; s. Clarence Oliver and Ottie Loraine (Davis) McC.; B.S. in Mech. Engring., Clemson U., 1949; m. Mary Edity Stone, Feb. 8, 1946; children—Frances (Mrs. Charles M. Wallace), Randolph Stone. Chief project engr. Studebaker-Packard Corp., Detroit, 1953-56; mgr. engine overhaul Curtiss-Wright Corp., Utica, Mich., 1956-60; owner, pres. McClain Internat., Inc., College Park, Ga., 1962—; also dir.; pres., owner, dir. Tecni Flame Coatings, Inc., College Park, 1970—; partner various real estate ventures. Bd. dirs. Arlington Schs., Inc., Atlanta. Served with USAF, 1941-46, 51-53. Decorated D.F.C., Air medal with oak leaf cluster, Purple Heart. Mem. Am. Soc. M.E., South Fulton County C. of C. (dir. 1972, pres. 1974—). Elk. Clubs: Lakeside Country (dir.), Commerce (Atlanta). Home: 3470 Somerset St Atlanta GA 30331 Office: 4785 Roosevelt Hwy College Park GA 30349

MCCLANAHAN, JOHN HOWARD, city utility exec.; b. Hartselle, Ala., Sept. 22, 1921; s. William Alexander and Trannie (Cooper) McC.; B.E.E., Auburn U., 1943; m. Mary Evelyn Irons, Aug. 3, 1947; children—William Alexander, Timmons Smith. Coop. student electricity dept. City of Florence, Ala., 1939-43, distbn. engr., 1946-64, mgr., 1964—; cons. elec. engr., 1954-68. Chmn., Cerebral Palsy Telethon, 1966-67. Bd. dirs. YMCA, N.W. Ala. Cerebral Palsy Assn. Served to capt. C.E., AUS, 1943-46. Mem. No. Ala. Indsl. Devel. Assn. (v.p. 1972-73), Florence C. of C. (v.p. 1972-73), Eta Kappa Nu. Democrat. Mem. Disciples of Christ (chmn. bd. 1966, trustee 1970—, elder, 1959—, supt. Sunday sch., 1958-65). Clubs: Florence Civitan (sec. 1949-62, pres. 1963, lt. gov. Ala. dist. 1964), Quad-Cities Quarterback (capt. 1966), Quad-Cities Auburn (pres. 1961). Home: 318 Deer Point Lane Florence AL 35630 Office: 110 W College St Florence AL 35630

MCCLANAHAN, LARRY DUNCAN, civil engr.; b. Franklin, Ky., July 30, 1938; s. Ernest William and Anne Isabelle (Henderson) McC.; B.S. in Civil Engring., Tenn. Poly Inst., 1965; M.S. in Civil Engring., Tenn. Tech. U., 1974; m. Betty Jane Marquess, Mar. 16, 1963; children—Michael Curtis, Marta Suzette, Meredith Angela. Engr., Texaco, New Orleans, 1965; sr. civil engr. Tenn. Aeros. Commn., Nashville, 1965-67; sr. engr. airports Eastern Airlines, Miami, 1967; airport planning engr. FAA, Memphis, 1967-68; sr. staff mem. R. Dixon Speas Assos., Atlanta, 1968-70; pvt. practice, Cookeville, Tenn., 1970-71; asso. Wilbur Smith & Assos., Columbia, S.C., 1971; v.p. Aviation Systems, Inc., Nashville, 1971-73; pres. Enviroplan, Inc. cons. engrs., Hendersonville, Tenn., 1973—. Instr. civil engring. Tenn. Tech. U., Cookeville, part time 1970-74. Chmn. bd. commrs. Hendersonville Mcpl. Airport Authority, 1973—. Served with USAF, 1956-59. Recipient Sustained Superior Performance award FAA, 1968, Pres.'s award R. Dixon Speas Assos., 1969. Registered profl. engr., Tenn., Ala., S.C., Ky., N.C., Ga. Mem. Am. Soc. C.E. (chmn. nat. landing area facilities com. 1970-72), Tenn., Nat. socs. profl. engrs. Mason, Elk. Home: 124 Country Club Dr Hendersonville TN 37075 Office: 699 W Main St Hendersonville TN 37075

MCCLARRIN, WILLIAM OTTO, govt. ofcl.; b. Atlanta, Ga., Apr. 11, 1918; s. Mozell and Geneva (Radden) McC.; B.A., Howard U., 1949; postgrad. Am. U., evenings 1949-55, New Sch. Social Studies, N.Y.C., 1953, U. Notre Dame, 1969; m. Frances Justine Morsell, Feb. 14, 1942; children—Vaughn Otto, Lynn Frances. Reporter, artist Afro-Am., newspaper, Balt., 1936-40, copy editor, artist, 1940-41; publicity agt. Howard U., Washington, 1941-43, dir. pub. relations, 1947-56, 69-70; sr. artist, designer OPA, 1943; editor Newspic mag., Birmingham, Ala., N.Y.C., asst. editor Consumers Union Pubs., N.Y.C., 1946-47; pub. affairs officer USIA, Indonesia, 1956-58; chief information office, illustrator U.S. Commn. on Civil Rights, 1958-62; pvt. practice pub. relations, U.S., Africa, 1962-66; dir. community relations community action program U.S. Office Econ. Opportunity, Washington, 1966-69, dir. spl. communications programs Office Pub. Affairs, 1970-72, dir. editorial div., 1972-74; coordinator agy.-wide recruitment Health Service Adminstrn. Dept. Health, Edn. and Welfare, 1974—. Pub. relations cons. various businesses, profl. orgns. Pub. relations com. Washington chpt. A.R.C., 1965—; chmn. pub. relations com. Health and Welfare Council Nat. Capital area, 1967-69, UN Assn., Washington, 1971—; mem. citizens adv. com. Washington Zoning Commn., 1966—. Served with USAAF, 1943-45. Lucy E. Moten Travel fellow Howard U., 1941. Mem. Nat., Capital (Ann. awards 1948, 50, Newsman trophy 1960) press clubs, Pub. Relations Soc. Am., Coll. Pub. Relations Assn., Am. Alumni Council (Merit award 1949, 52), Advt. Club Met. Washington, Omega Psi Phi. Episcopalian. Clubs: Gourmets, Consorts (Washington). Editor: Oracle mag., 1970—. Home: 1712 Allison St NW Washington DC 20011 Office: 5600 Fishers Lane Rockville MD 20852

MCCLARY, GEORGE OSCAR, ednl. psychologist; b. Rapidan, Va., June 27, 1923; s. Haywood Oscar and Jane Irene (Hopkins) McC.; B.A., U. Richmond, 1949; M.S., Pa. State U., 1954; Ph.D. in Psychology, George Washington U., 1969. Office mgr., personnel supr., shipwright dept. Newport News Shipbldg. & Dry Dock Co. (Va.), 1940-44; publs. analyst VA, Richmond, Va., summer 1946; case record asst. Va. Dept. Corrections, 1947-48; psychiat. aide Western State Hosp., Staunton, Va., summer 1949; counselor Norfolk (Va.) Consultation Service, Va. Bd. Edn., 1949-52; dir. student workshop John Marshall High Sch., Richmond, summers 1957-58; instr. Richmond Profl. Inst., Coll. William and Mary, 1957-59; instr. U. Va. Extension Div., 1959; psychometrist, sch. psychologist, dir. guidance and psychol. services, supr. guidance services Richmond Pub. Schs., 1952-66, dir. pupil personnel services, 1966—. Instr., George Washington U., 1961, U. Va., 1962, 64, 68, 70, U. Richmond, 1966, 71, 72, William and Mary Coll. Extension, 1963; mem. Govs. Com. on Employment of Physically Handicapped, 1961-62; edn. com. Richmond Mental Health Assn., 1961-64, 65-67, bd. dirs., 1967-71; bd. dirs. Meml. Guidance Clinic, Richmond, 1966-69; bd. dirs. Va. Council on Social Welfare 1968-71, mem. exec. com., 1969-71; bd. dirs., 1968-71; bd. dirs. Va. Inst. Pastoral Care, 1970—; mem. Richmond Youth Com., 1963-67; mem. Mental Health Execs. Roundtable, Richmond Area Community Council, 1964-67; bd. dirs. Speech Center, Med. Coll. Va., 1956-60, Big Sister Assn. Richmond, 1956-60, Shakespeare Players, Inc., 1963-65. Served with AUS, 1944-46. Diplomate in sch. psychology Am. Bd. Profl. Psychology. Mem. Am. (exec. council 1963-66), Va. (pres. elect 1960-61, pres. 1961-62), Richmond (treas. 1955-56, v.p. 1958-60, pres. 1960-61) personnel and guidance assns., Am. Sch. Counselor Assn. (pres. elect 1963-64, pres. 1964-65, gov. 1960-66), Nat. Vocational Guidance Assn., Assn. for Measurement and Evaluation in Guidance, N.E.A., Assn. for Counselor Edn. and Supervision, Am., Va., Richmond psychol. assns., Nat. Assn. Pupil Personnel Adminstrs. (editor news bull. 1969, 70, pres. 1972—). Presbyn. Club: Va. Boat. Author: Interpreting Guidance Programs to Pupils, 1968. Home: 213 N Plum St Richmond VA 23220

MCCLEARY, EDGAR THOMAS, ednl. adminstr.; b. Ordway, Colo., Sept. 22, 1925; s. Ernest Otis and Edna Frances (Woodard) McC.; B.A., Yale, 1946. With Asheville (N.C.) Sch., 1946-60, asso. dir. admissions and studies, 1951-60; headmaster Berkeley Preparatory Sch., Tampa, Fla., 1960—. Treas. Fla. Council Ind. Sch. Recipient George Washington Honor medal Freedoms Found., 1970, 71. Mem. Nat. Assn. Biology Tchrs., Republican. Episcopalian. Clubs: Palma Celia Golf and Country, Bay Area Yale (Tampa); Yale (N.Y.C.); University. Home: 4 Sandpiper Rd Tampa FL 33609 Office: 102 Biscayne Tampa FL 33606

MCCLEARY, WILLIAM ERNEST, librarian, educator; b. Alexandria, La., May 29, 1927; s. Ernest Earl and Laura (Hearte) McC.; B.A., Centenary Coll. La., 1948; M.A. in Journalism, La. State U., 1950, M.S. in L.S., 1958; Certificate Advanced Studies in Librarianship U. Ill., 1971. Tchr., Caddo Parish Sch. Bd., Shreveport, La., 1950-58; catalog, acquisitions librarian Shreve Meml. Library, 1958-60; librarian Union Producing Co., 1961-67; reference librarian La. State U., Shreveport, 1967-72, documents librarian, 1972—, instr., Baton Rouge, summer 1972. Served with USMCR, 1945-46, 50-51. Recipient scholarship City of Oslo, Norway, 1953, assistantship La. State U., 1957-58, U. Ill., summer 1970, grantee La. State U., summer 1971. Mem. Am. Assn. U. Profs., Spl. Libraries Assn., Am., Southwestern, La. (treas. 1964-65; chmn. subject specialist sect. 1971-72; chmn. intellectual freedom com. 1972-73; La. Lit. award com. 1973-74) library assns., Common Cause, Am. Civil Liberties Union. Democrat. Episcopalian. Club: Caddo Bossier Library (pres. 1964-65, 70-71) (Shreveport). Bull. editor La. Library Assn., 1965-66, La. chpt. Spl. Libraries Assn., 1965-66, 68, 72-73. Home: 6147 Creswell Rd Shreveport LA 71106 Office: 8515 Youree Dr Shreveport LA 71105

MCCLELLAN, JOHN LITTLE, U.S. senator; b. Sheridan, Ark., Feb. 25, 1896; s. Isaac Scott and Belle (Suddleth) McC.; ed. pub. schs.; m. Eula Hicks, Nov. 2, 1913 (dec.); children—Max Eldon, Doris; m. 2d, Lucille Smith, Nov. 8, 1922 (dec.); children—John L., James, Mary Alice; m. 3d, Norma Myers Cheatham, Nov. 10, 1937. Admitted to Ark. bar, 1913, and began practice at Sheridan; pros. atty. 7th Jud. Dist. of Ark. 2 terms, 1927-30; mem. 74th and 75th Congresses from 6th Ark. Dist.; U.S. senator from Ark., 1942—. Served at 1st lt., A.S.S.C., World War I. Recipient Distinguished Pub. Service award, Nat. Tax Found., 1957; George Washington award, Am. Good Govt. Soc., 1959; Hatton W. Sumners award, S.W. Legal Found., 1959. Democrat. Baptist. Home: Little Rock AR Office: Dirksen Office Bldg Washington DC 20510 also Union Life Bldg 212 Center Little Rock AR 72201 also Federal Office Bldg 700 W Capitol Little Rock AR 72201

MCCLELLAND, GEORGE JOSEPH, clergyman; b. Wilmington, N.C., Aug. 10, 1937; s. Charles William and Shirley Lee (Eichorn) McC.; B.A., Atlantic Christian Coll., 1961; M.Div. (grantee) Lexington Theol. Sem., 1969; m. Golda Sue Page, June 2, 1962; children—Carlton Lee, Sara Elizabeth. Ordained to ministry Christian Ch., 1964; minister, Springfield, Ill., 1966-68, La Grange, N.C., 1969-70; social worker O'Berry Center, Goldsboro, N.C., 1970-71, chaplain, 1971—; minister First Christian Ch., Mt. Olive, N.C., 1972—. Bd. govs. Jacksonville (Ill.) Meml. Hosp., 1964-66. Mem. Wayne County, Mt. Olive ministerial assns., N.C. Employees Assn., N.C. Chaplains Assn., Sigma Phi Epsilon. Mem. Woodsmen of World. Home: 107 Perry Dr Goldsboro NC 27530 Office: O'Berry Center Goldsboro NC 27530

MCCLELLAND, ROBERT NELSON, educator; b. Gilmer, Tex., Nov. 20, 1929; s. Robert Hilton and Verna (Nelson) McC.; B.A., U. Tex., 1952, M.D., 1954; m. Connie Logan, May 5, 1958; children—Robert Christopher, Alison, Julie. Intern, U. Kan. Med. Center, Kansas City, 1954-55; resident Parkland Meml. Hosp., Dallas, 1957-62; instr. gen. surgery U. Tex. Southwestern Med. Sch. at Dallas, 1962-63, asst. prof., 1963-67, asso. prof., 1967-71, prof., 1971—; mem. staff Parkland, Presbyn., VA hosps., all Dallas; cons. Baylor, St. Paul, Methodist hosps., Dallas, John Peter Smith Hosp., Ft. Worth, Tex., 4th Army, Ft. Hood, Tex. Served to capt. USAF, 1955-57. Mem. Dallas County Med. Soc., Tex., Am. med. assns., Western Surg. Assn., Soc. for Surgery Alimentary Tract (mem. membership com. 1972-73), Am. Gastroenterol. Assn., A.C.S., Tex., Southwestern surg. socs., Phi Beta Kappa, Alpha Omega Alpha, Theta Kappa Psi. Editor: Audio-Jour. Review-Gen. Surgery, 1971—. Contbr. numerous articles, chpts. to surg. med. texts. Home: 3601 Potomac St Dallas TX 75205 Office: 5323 Harry Hines Blvd Dallas TX 75235

MCCLELLAND, WILLIAM AGNEW, psychologist; b. N.Y.C., Nov. 8, 1918; s. William Cecil and Charlotte (Brooks) McC.; A.B., Brown U., 1941; M.A., U. Minn., 1946, Ph.D., 1948; m. Dorothy Ann Nelson, Sept. 16, 1942; children—Katherine E., Richard B. Instr., dept. psychology U. Minn., Mpls., 1946-48; asst. prof., dept. psychology Brown U., Providence, 1948-51; research psychologist U.S. Air Force, 1951-55; dir. research, dept. dir., asso. dir. Human Resources Research Office, George Washington U., Washington, 1955-69, profl. lectr. dept. psychology, 1966—; exec. v.p. Human Resources Research Orgn., Alexandria, Va., 1969—. Served from pvt. to capt. USAAF, 1942-46. Fellow Am. Psycholol. Assn., A.A.A.S.; mem. Am. Edn. Research Assn., Psychonomic Soc., D.C. Psychol. Assn. Home: 7813 Accotink Pl Alexandria VA 22308 Office: 300 N Washington St Alexandria VA 22314

MCCLENDON, CARLEE THOMAS, ednl. TV network ofcl.; b. Edgefield, S.C., Aug. 15, 1940; s. Ralph Thomas and Sadie (Jackson) M.; B.A. in Journalism, U. S.C., 1965; m. Juliet McCreary Refo, June 10, 1967; 1 dau., Julie R. Tchr. history Langley-Bath-Clearwater High Sch., Aiken County, S.C., 1965-66; asst. historic resources coordinator S.C. Dept. Archives and History, 1966-67; mng. editor Edgefield Adv., 1967-68; coordinator local events S.C. Tricentennial Commn., Columbia, 1968-71; edn. editor SC ETV Network, Columbia, 1971—. Organizer historic homes tours, 1966-71; restoration cons. Edgefield's Magnolia Dale, 1965-68; founder Pottersville Mus., 1970. Mem. Edgefield Jr. C. of C., Am. Assn. State and Local History (merit award for Edgefield County Hist. Soc. 1967, state membership chmn. 1969), Nat. Trust Historic Preservation, S.C., Edgefield (v.p. 1960—) hist. socs., Nat. Assn. Ednl. Broadcasters, S.C. Press Assn., Assn. Ednl. Communications Tech. (publs. chmn. S.C. 1974), South Caroliniana Soc., Sigma Delta Chi, Sigma Phi Epsilon. Methodist (Sunday Sch. tchr.). Author: 1790 and 1800 Federal Census Records of Edgefield District, 1960; Edgefield Marriage Records, 1970. Cons. editor Teacher's Guide and Adminstrator's Guide for Ednl. TV series Your Future is Now, 1974. Home: 138 Wembley St Columbia SC 29209 Office: Drawer L 2712 Millwood Av Columbia SC 29250

MCCLENDON, JAMES LOWELL, dentist; b. Houston, Jan. 29, 1927; s. Ezra James and Bessie Edith (Day) McC.; student Tex. A. and M. U., 1943-44; B.A., U. Tex., 1950, D.D.S., 1954; m. Anne Cecelia Glavin, Apr. 24, 1957; children—Theresa Ann, James Lowell. Fellow in oral surgery Mayo Clinic, 1954-57; pvt. practice oral surgery, Houston, 1954—; clin. asso. clin. prof. dept. pathology U. Tex. Dental Br., Houston, 1957—. Cons. oral pathology M. D. Anderson Hosp. and Tumor Inst., Houston, 1964-72; chief oral surgery Meml. Baptist Hosp. Systems, 1967-72. Bd. dirs. Harris County and Tex. chpts. Am. Cancer Soc. Served with USNR, 1945-48. Recipient Bronze Exhibit award Am. Acad. Dermatology. Diplomate Am. Bd. Oral Surgery. Fellow Internat. Assn. Oral Surgeons; mem. Am. Soc. Oral Surgeons, Am. Dental Assn., U. Tex. Dental Br. Alumni Assn. (trustee 1959-62), Omicron Kappa Upsilon. Republican. Roman Catholic. Optimist (pres. Houston 1960). Contbr. articles to profl. jours. Home: 11835 Stuckey Lane Houston TX 77024 Office: 1118 Meml Profl Bldg 1019 Lamar St Houston TX 77002

MCCLENDON, JOAN PARSONS (MRS. CLAUDE M. MCCLENDON), banker; b. Boston, Apr. 21, 1925; d. Jack and Victoria Muriel (Adams) Parsons; student Long Beach Jr. Coll., 1942-43, Los Angeles City Coll., 1944; grad. U. Miss. Sch. Banking, 1973-74; m. Claude M. McClendon, Nov. 17, 1945; 1 dau., Joan

Diane (Mrs. Glenn Wayne Kuykendall). Teller, bookkeeper S.W. Miss. Bank (formerly Magnolia Bank), Magnolia Miss., 1953-59, asst. cashier, 1960—, asst. to pres., 1974—, also exec. sec. Pres., Pike County chpt. Am. Cancer Soc., 1971-72. Del. Democratic State Conv., 1968—; sec. Pike County Dem. Exec. Com., 1966—. Mem. Nat. Assn. Bank Women (state chmn. 1971-72), Banking Adminstrn. Inst. (dir. S.W. Miss. chpt. 1972—), Am. Inst. Banking (study group chmn.), Miss. Bankers Assn. (v.p. banking edn. com.), Magnolia Area C. of C. (sec., dir.). Episcopalian. Home: Route 4 Magnolia MS 39652 Office: PO Box 109 Magnolia MS 39652

MCCLENDON, RUPERT, record co. exec.; b. Roanoke, Ala., Mar. 27, 1907; s. John Allen and Mary (Pruett) McC.; student pub. schs.; m. Adelle Bassett, Mar. 6, 1927; 1 son, Ernest Calvin. Owner, Trepur Record Co., 1952—; part-owner McClendon Enterprises, 1959—. Mem. Am. Fedn. Musicians, Life Underwriters, Country Music Assn. Presbyn. Mason. Composer songs: Plant Some Flowers By My Grave, 1938; Honky Tonk Swing, 1938; The Moon Won't Tell, 1955; others. Home: Route 3 LaGrange GA 30240

MCCLINTOCK, SIMMS, polit. scientist, educator; b. Lake Village, Ark., July 10, 1927; s. William Richey and Lilly (Simms) McC.; B.A., Hendrix Coll., 1951; M.A., Columbia, 1953. Coordinator social studies Crossett (Ark.) High Sch., 1953-65; asso. prof. history and polit. sci. State Coll. Ark., Conway, 1966—. Faculty adviser State Coll. Ark. Young Democrats, 1966—. Faulkner County Hist. Soc. Sec., bd. dirs. Carmichael Found. Served with USNR, 1945-48, 51-52. Recipient Distinguished award Ark. Jr. C. of C., 1962; named Ark. Tchr. of Year, U.S. Office Edn. and Look Mag., 1963. John Hay fellow Columbia, 1965-66. Mem. Classroom Tchrs. Ark. (pres.), N.E.A., Ark. Edn. Assn., Faulkner County Hist. Soc. (pres.), Phi Delta Kappa. Episcopalian. Author: Guide To Teaching Citizenship, 1961; Guide To Teaching Economics, 1965. Home: 120 Baridon St Conway AR 72032

MCCLUNEY, JOE ALFRED, assn. exec.; b. Oxford, Ala., Sept. 9, 1924; s. Olin A. and Myrtle (Hartline) McC.; B.S. in Gen. Bus., U. Ala., 1949; postgrad. U. N.C., 1956-62, Mich. State U., 1963-65; m. Margaret Elizabeth Locke, May 13, 1949; children—Sandra Etoile, Margaret Judson, Joe A. Mgr. Geneva (Ala.) C. of C., 1956-58, Ozark (Ala.) C. of C., 1958-59, Atmore (Ala.) C. of C., 1959-63, mgr., exec. v.p. Jasper (Ala.) area C. of C., 1963—. Chmn. Geneva County (Ala.) March of Dimes, 1957; adviser Jr. Achievement, Opelika, Ala., 1954; active United Fund. Bd. dirs. Community Service Council; treas. Birmingham Regional Planning Commn. Served with AUS, 1944-46; ETO. Mem. Am., So., Ala. (pres. 1963-64, sec.-treas. 1964—) chamber commerce execs. assns. Methodist (mem. bd., past treas.). Rotarian (treas. Atmore, Ala. 1962). Home: 816 8th Av Jasper AL 35501 Office: Chamber Bldg PO Box 972 Jasper AL 35501

MCCLUNG, CLOYD HARRELL, librarian; b. Waco, Tex., Sept. 11, 1916; s. Sampson Reece and Ethel (Reding) McC.; B.A., Baylor U., 1938; M.R.E., Southwestern Theol. Sem., 1941; M.A. in L.S., Fla. State U., 1953; m. Doris Wilson, July 3, 1943; 1 son, Reece Alfred. Ednl. dir. Calvary Bapt. Ch., Fort Worth, 1940-42, Allapattah Bapt. Ch., Miami, 1945-48, 1st Bapt. Ch., Fort Pierce, Fla., 1948-49, Panama City, Fla., 1949-54; Tidwell Bible librarian Baylor U., Waco, 1954-64; head librarian Polk Jr. Coll., Winter Haven, Fla. 1964-68, Eckerd Coll., St. Petersburg, 1968—. Reference librarian, U.S.A. World Fair, summer 1965. Served with USAAF, 1941-46. Mem. Am., Tex., Southwestern, Southeastern Fla. library assns. Baptist. Home: 2667 Granada Circle St Petersburg FL 33712

MCCLUNG, DORIS LOUISE (MRS. CLOYD HARRELL MCCLUNG), librarian; b. Laurel, Miss., Feb. 5, 1920; d. Oscar Alfred and Nona Alma (Wilder) Wilson; B.A., Miss. Woman's Coll., 1940, B.S., 1940; M.R.E., Southwestern Bapt. Theol. Sem., 1942; M.L.S. (fellow 1966), La. State U., 1972; m. Cloyd Harrell McClung, July 3, 1943; 1 son, Reece Alfred. Sec. to dean and acting registrar Miss. Woman's Coll., 1938-40; sec., editorial asst. Bapt. Sunday Sch. Bd., Nashville, 1942-44; ednl. sec. First Bapt. Ch., Grand Prairie, Tex., 1944, Panama City, Fla., 1949-51, Allapattah Bapt. Ch., Miami, Fla., 1946-48; credit interviewer Burdine's, Miami, 1944-46; owner, mgr. The Book Mark, Waco, Tex., 1955-62; media specialist Lena Vista Elementary Sch., Auburndale, Fla., 1964—. Mem. A.L.A., Fla., Polk County assns. sch. librarians, United Teaching Profession, Orchid Soc., Am. Assn. U. Women, Alpha Psi Omega. Republican. Baptist. Home: 2667 Granada Circle E St Petersburg FL 33712 Office: 208 S Berkley Rd Auburndale FL 33823

MCCLUNG, JAMES COWAN, newspaper pub.; b. Kerens, Tex., May 17, 1912; s. Luther Thurman and Carrie J. (Miller) M.; grad. high sch.; m. Evelyn Louise Terry, Nov. 19, 1936; children—James Cowan, Katrina Sue (Mrs. James Thomas Williams). With Dallas Dispatch, 1930-37; with Dallas Times Herald, 1937—, prodn. mgr., 1956-73, v.p., 1973—. Mem. Am., So. newspaper pub. assn., Tex. Daily Newspaper Assn. Mason (32 deg., Jester, Shriner). Home: 4128 Drowsy Lane Dallas TX 75233 Office: 1101 Pacific Av Dallas TX 75202

MCCLUNG, JERRY CLARK, banker; b. Homer, La., June 28, 1933; s. Joe Brooks and Thelma Lois (Wyatt) McC.; pre-standard and standard degrees Am. Inst. Banking, 1963, 69; student La. State U. Banking Sch. of South, 1967-69, Grad. Sch. Consumer Banking, U. Va., 1970-72; m. Lacey Edgerton, Apr. 20, 1968; children—Margaret Alayne, Debra Diane, Jerry Clark, Chadwick Edgerton, Rowdy Wyatt. With Rapides Bank and Trust Co., Alexandria, La., 1957—, asst. cashier, 1964-69, asst. v.p., 1969-70, v.p., 1970—, head installment loan dept., 1973—. Notary, La., 1961—. Adviser Jr. Achievement, 1963-65; treas. Rugg Elementary Sch. P.T.A., 1966-67. Served with AUS, 1955-57. Mem. Am. Inst. Banking (pres. Central La. chpt. 1964-65), Alexandria-Pineville C. of C., Am. Legion. Democrat. Baptist. Rotarian (sec.-treas., dir. 1971—). Home: 5603 Skylark Alexandria LA 71301 Office: PO Box 31 Alexandria LA 71301

MCCLUNG, NORVEL MALCOLM, educator; b. McClungs, W.Va., June 9, 1916; s. Virgil Edward and Mary (Anderson) McC.; A.B., Glenville State Coll., 1936; M.S., U. Mich., 1940, Ph.D., 1948; m. Delia Rainey, Aug. 31, 1945 (div. Sept. 1966); children—Charles E., Margaret L., Ralph A., Susan E.; m. 2d, Hermine Friedson, Oct. 16, 1966. Tchr. Webster Springs (W.Va.) High Sch., 1936-41; asst. prof. biology U. Kan., Lawrence, 1948-57; asso. prof. U. Ga., Athens, 1957-66; prof. U.S. Fla., Tampa, 1966—. Vis. prof. Kyoto (Japan) U., 1962-63; cons. Fla. Dept. Health, 1968, Ocean Products, Plant City, Fla., 1968-69. Served to capt. USNR, 1941-46. Decorated Purple Heart. La. State U. tropical medicine fellow, 1960; Fulbright Research award, Japan, 1961-62; recipient grants U. Kan. Found., 1950-53, NIH, 1954-57, Massengill Corp., 1956-58, NSF, 1960-61, 50-65, travel award Sigma Xi, 1961, Am. Soc. Microbiology, 1963. Mem. Southeastern Electron Microscopy Soc. (chmn. 1970-72), A.A.A.S., Am. Assn. U. Profs., Am. Inst. Biol. Scis., Am. Soc. Microbiology, Bacteriol. Soc. Japan, Bot. Soc. Am., Internat. Soc. Human and Animal Mycoses, Kan. Acad. Scis., Med. Mycology Soc. Am. (charter), Mycol. Soc. Am., Soc. Gen. Microbiology (Brit.), Am. Acad. Microbiology, Sigma Xi, Phi Kappa Phi, Phi Sigma. Author: (with A.J. Mix) Mycology for Students of Bacteriology and Medicine, 1955; (with R.G. Eagon and W.J. Payne) A Laboratory Manual for Intruductory Bacteriology, 1960. Contbr. to profl. jours. Home: 2701 Varsity Pl Tampa FL 33612

MCCLUNG, RALPH CLAY, dentist; b. Collinsville, Ala., Apr. 21, 1907; s. James Newton and Virginia Ida (Jones) McC.; student Auburn U., 1925-26, Birmingham So. Coll., summer 1926; D.D.S. cum laude, Emory U., 1930; m. Olive Ann Greagan, Aug. 8, 1950; 1 son, Ralph Clay. Practice dentistry, Birmingham, Ala., 1930—. Pres. Bachelors Cotillion, 1933; king Christmas Carnival, 1940, Linly Heflin Festival, 1933. Served to capt. Dental Corps, AUS, 1943-44; ETO. Fellow Acad. Internat. Dentistry, Am. Dental Assn., Internat. Coll. Dentists (pres. 1972-73), Pierre Fauchard Acad.; mem. Acad. Anesthesiology, Am. (life), Ala. (life) dental assns., Birmingham Dist., Chgo. dental socs., Am. Acad. Restorative Dentistry (pres. 1958-59), Am. Assn. Dental insultants (pres. 1971-73), Psi Omega, Omicron Kappa Upsilon. Methodist. Rotarian. Clubs: Birmingham Country, Birmingham Aero (pres. 1943); Ace Flying (pres. 1942); The Club; Hole-in-one; Quarterback (hon., charter). Home: Overhill Rd Birmingham AL 35223 Office: Profl Arts Bldg Birmingham AL 35205

MCCLURE, HARLAN EWART, architect, coll. dean; b. Delaware, O., Oct. 19, 1916; s. Alexander Ewart and Mary Jeanette (Huffman) McC.; A.B., B.Arch., George Washington U., 1937; Archtl. Diploma, Royal Swedish Acad., 1938; M.Arch., Mass. Inst. Tech., 1941; m. Virginia Withers Varney, Mar. 13, 1942 (dec. Nov. 1973); children—Christopher Ewart, Wesley Alexander, Barbara Beth. Asst. prof. U. Minn., 1946-47, asso. prof. architecture, 1947-51, prof., 1952-55; prof., head archtl. faculty Clemson (S.C.) U., 1955-58, prof., dean Sch. Architecture, 1958-69, prof., dean Coll. Architecture, 1969—. Town planner; pvt. practice architecture; cons. architect, designer Clemson Engring. Center, Clemson U. Master Plan; vis. prof. A.A. Sch. Architecture, London. Pres. S.C. Bd. Archtl. Examiners, 1959—; sec. Nat. Archtl. Accrediting Bd., 1965-69, pres., 1969-70; mem. S.C. Fine Arts Commn., S.C. Tricentennial Commn; sec.-treas. Clemson Archtl. Found., 1945—; adviser to mayors of Greenville and Charleston. Bd. dirs. Nat. Council Arts in Edn., 1960—; mem. Interprofl. Task Force on Environmental Design; mem. design adv. panel Gen. Service Adminstrn., 1969—; design and planning cons. Redevel. Commn. City Charlotte, 1966—. Served ensign to lt. comdr. USNR, 1941-45. Fulbright sr. fellow, U. K., 1952-53. Fellow A.I.A. (dir. Mpls. 1948-50, sec. 1950-51, mem. task force on social responsibilities 1969-70, mem. commn. on edn); mem. Am. Assn. U. Profs., Assn. Coll. Schs. Architecture (chmn. publ., editor vol. 11-2, nat. pres. 1959-61), Minaret Soc., Plumb Bob, Scarab, Tau Sigma Delta (nat. grand chpt. master 1970—), Phi Kappa Phi, Alpha Rho Chi. Episcopalian. Clubs: University, Campus, Gown-In-Town (Mpls.); Archtl. Assn. (London, Eng.). Author: Study of an Evolving Architectural Design, 1946; Beginning Architectural Design, 1948; Guide to Architecture of the Twin Cities, 1955. Co-author: South Carolina Architecture, 1670-1970. Editor: Architecture South Carolina, 1960-62. Contbr. articles to profl. publs. Home: Boxwood House E Queen St Pendleton SC 29670 Office: Clemson U Clemson SC 29631

MCCOACH, BLAKE ALEXANDER, JR., newspaper editor; b. Middletown, N.Y., Oct. 17, 1920; s. Blake A. and Kathleen A. (Cute) McC.; student pub. schs.; m. Dorothy M. Marshall, May 16, 1943; children—Gary Alexander Alan Jeffrey. News, announcer Sta. WENY, Elmira, N.Y., 1945-46, WSLB, Ogdensburg, N.Y., 1946-47, WENT, Gloversville, N.Y., 1947-50, WABY, Albany, N.Y., 1950-57; columnist Hearst Times Union, Albany, 1955-57; pub. Dade County Times Union, Miami, Fla., 1960-64; became v.p., editor Hialeah (Fla.) Miami Springs Jour., 1965; pres., pub.-editor Greater Miami Jour., 1965—. Pub. relations Democratic Registration drive State of Fla., 1964. Served with USAAF, 1940-45. Mem. Broadcast Music. Methodist. Lyricist for songs, including Take Care of My Heart, Save the Last Waltz for Me, Lawrence Welk Polka, Forever and Ever and Ever, others. Home: 10271 SW 49th St Miami FL 33165 Office: 45 E 9th Ct Hialeah FL 33010

MCCOLLOCH, LAWRENCE EDGAR, athletic adminstr.; b. Burlington, Ia., Aug. 20, 1920; s. Clarence Henry and Bertha Mable (Dietsch) McC.; B.S., Tex. Technol. U., 1943, M.Ed., 1948; postgrad. Ariz. U., 1968, 70; m. Jean Marie Hyde, Feb. 16, 1952. Tchr., coach Memphis (Tex.) High Sch., 1946-49, Big Spring (Tex.) High Sch., 1949-52; athletic dir., coach Odessa (Tex.) Coll., 1952—. Bd. dirs. Wrangler Club Scholarship Fund. Served with USAAF, 1943-46. Mem. Nat. Coaching Assn., Nat. Assn. Coll. Dirs. Athletics, Nat. Assn. Watch and Clock Collectors, West Tex. Gem and Mineral Soc. (pres. 1970-71), Tex. Archeol. Soc., Order of Arrow. Baptist. Mason. Home: 1615 E Everglade St Odessa TX 79762

MCCOLLOM, KENNETH ALLEN, elec. engr., educator; ednl. adminstr.; b. Sentinel, Okla., June 17, 1922; s. Walter William and Irene Pearl (Allen) McC.; B.S., Okla. State U., 1948; M.S. (Westinghouse fellow), in Elec. Engring., U. Ill., 1949; Ph.D., Ia. State U., 1964; m. Helen Katherine Tompkins, Jan. 4, 1944; children—Alan Tompkins, Neal Norman. Research engr. Phillips Petroleum Co., Bartlesville, Okla., 1949-51, 54-57, Idaho Falls, 1951-54, chief atomic energy div. Phillips Petroleum Co., 1957-60, br. mgr., 1960-62; asso. prof. elec. engring. Okla. State U., Stillwater, 1964-68, prof., 1968—, also asso. dean Coll. Engring., 1973—. Cons. to AEC. Asst. condr. Idaho Falls Civic Symphony, 1957-60; mem. Atomic Safety and Licensing Bd. panel., 1972—. Bd. dirs. Will Rogers council Boy Scouts Am.; bd. dirs. Stillwater United Fund Campaign, chmn., 1969-72. Served with Signal Corps, AUS, 1942-46. Registered profl. engr., Okla. Mem. Am. Soc. Engring. Edn. (Chester F. Carlson award 1973), I.E.E.E., Am. Nuclear Soc., Nat. Soc. Profl. Engrs., Okla. Soc. Prfl. Engrs. (dir. 1972—). Methodist (chmn. edn. commn. 1970-72, dir. 1966—). Lion. Patentee in electronic instrumentation. Home: 1107 W Knapp St Stillwater OK 74074

MCCOLLUM, PAUL ALLEN, educator; b. Helena, Okla., Oct. 19, 1919; s. Alva Allen and Etta Viola (Christen) McC.; B.S., Okla. State U., 1947, M.S., 1953; m. Lona Mae Wiggins, Apr. 17, 1940; children—Phillip Allen, Linda (Mrs. Ronald A. Marten), Betty (Mrs. Jimmie Shields). Dir. radio instrn. No. Okla. Jr. Coll., Tonkawa, 1941-42; mem. faculty Okla. State U., Stillwater, 1942—, prof. elec. engring., 1954—, research engr. guided missile instrumentation, 1947-48, supr. Air Force Electronics Sch., 1951, research engr. radar confusion, 1953-54, project dir. unconventional power sources, 1954-57, dir. engring. computing lab., 1962—. Chief engr. radio sta. KSPI, Stillwater, 1946-60; cons. in field, 1949—. Computer grantee NSF, 1962, 64. Registered profl. engr., Okla. Mem. Nat., Okla. socs. profl. engrs., I.E.E.E., Eta Kappa Nu, Sigma Tau. Mem. Ch. of Christ (deacon 1966—). Author: Laplace Transform Tables and Theorems, 1965. Home: 2203 Arrowhead Dr Stillwater OK 74074

MCCOMBS, HAROLD KELLY, JR., former govt. ofcl.; b. Pitts., Dec. 30, 1950; s. Harold Kelly and Florence Amy (Davis) McC.; student U. Mich., 1968-69; B.J. in Radio-TV News, B.A. in Econs. (both with honors), U. Tex., 1972; postgrad. George Washington U., 1972—. Reporter, prodn. asst. stas. KUT-FM and KLRN-TV, Austin, Tex., 1969-70; disc jockey, sta. KMFA-FM, Austin, 1970-71, 71-72; regional news editor, Voice of Am., USIA, Washington, 1971, 72, 73—, regional news editor, 1971, 72, fgn. policy program officer Information Center Service, Washington, 1973; law clk. Marmet Profl. Corp., 1973—. Mem. Sigma Delta Chi. Home: 211 Walnut Way Euless TX 76039 Office: 1822 Jefferson Pl NW Washington DC 20036

MCCONNELL, BEN HARRISON, physician; b. Kansas City, Mo., Mar. 14, 1918; s. Ben H. and Lucile A. (Huckin) McC.; B.S., U. Okla., 1939; A.B., U. Denver, 1947; M.D., Georgetown U., 1950; m. Drucilla Baca, June 12, 1950; children—Lila T., Irma G., Alice I., Ben Harrison III. Intern, Gorgas Gen. Hosp., Balboa, C.Z., 1950-51; dir. Hudson Stuck Meml. Hosp., Ft. Yukon, Alaska, 1951-53; med. officer D.C., Washington, 1953-56; practice medicine, specializing in diagnosis, Lakeland, Fla., 1956—. Mem. Assn. Internat. Med. Study (sec. 1966—). Home: 901 S Jefferson St Lakeland FL 33801 Office: 1040 E McDonald St Lakeland FL 33801

MCCONNELL, ELLIOTT BONNELL, JR., petroleum co. exec.; b. Elizabeth, N.J., June 2, 1928; s. Elliott Bonnell and Mildred Alice (Snibbe) McC.; A.B., Duke, 1951; M.S., Pa. State U., 1953; grad. Advanced Mgmt. Program, Harvard, 1973; m. Sara K. Gerber, Aug. 16, 1952; children—Marilyn B., James D. Explorationist, Mobil Oil Corp., Midland, Tex., 1953-64, exploration supr., Calgary, Alta., Can., 1964-69, exploration mgr., Casper, Wyo., 1967-69, corporate planner, N.Y.C., 1969-70; planning mgr. Gen. Crude Oil Co., Houston, 1970-71, v.p., 1971—. Mem. Am. Assn. Petroleum Geologists, Soc. Exploration Geophysicists, Wyo. Geol. Assn., Alta. Soc. Petroleum Geologists, Am. Petroleum Inst., Ind. Petroleum Assn. Am. Clubs: Houston, Lakeside Country. Home: 13315 Perthshire St Houston TX 77024 Office: PO Box 2252 Houston TX 77001

MCCONNELL, RICHARD LEON, chemist; b. Gate City, Va., Mar. 23, 1926; s. Robert F. and Janie (Broadwater) McC.; student Carson Newman Coll., 1944-45; U. Ill., 1945-46; B.S., U. Ky., 1948; M.S., U. Va., 1950, Ph.D., 1952; m. Carolyn C. McMeekin, July 17, 1948; children—Richard Leon, Ann Craig, Elizabeth Lee. With Tenn. Eastman Co., Kingsport, Tenn., 1951—, sr. research chemist, 1957-70, research asso., 1970—. Served with USNR, 1944-46. Mem. Am. Chem. Soc., Sigma Xi, Alpha Chi Sigma. Presbyn. Contbr. to profl. jours. Patentee chemicals. Home: 421 Manderley Rd Kingsport TN 37660 Office: Tenn Eastman Co Kingsport TN 37662

MCCONNELL, RONALD CLEO, dentist; b. Stafford, Kan., Apr. 29, 1937; s. Cleo Carl and Jenny Lois (Wagner) McC.; Asso. Sci., Arlington State Jr. Coll., 1957; student Tex. Christian U., 1957-58; B.S., Tex. Wesleyan Coll., 1959; D.D.S., Baylor U., 1963, M.S.D., 1965; m. Patricia Anne Schmid, July 2, 1960; children—Ronald Todd, Patrick Sean. Resident in pedodontics Children's Med. Center, Dallas, 1963-65; practice dentistry for children, Richardson, Tex., 1965—. Asso. prof. pedodontics Baylor U. Coll. Dentistry, 1965-70. Active YMCA. Bd. dirs. Richardson Pub. Library, 1967-69. Diplomate Am. Bd. Pedodontics. Mem. Internat. Assn. Orthodontics, Am. Soc. Preventive Dentistry, Am., Tex., Dallas County (dir. 1972—, dir. continuing edn. programs 1970-71) dental assns., Am. (certificate of merit 1963), Tex. (pres. 1970-71) socs. dentistry for children, Southwestern Soc. Dental Analgesia (pres. 1970-71), Southwestern Soc. Pedodontists, Greater Dallas (pres. 1968-69), Richardson (pres. 1970-71) dental study research groups, Baylor U. Grad. Pedodontic Alumni Assn. (pres. 1967-68), Delta Sigma Delta (dep. supreme grand master Baylor chpt. 1963—). Rotarian. Club: Toastmasters (Richardson); Royal Oaks Country, Lancers (Dallas). Home: 1222 Mohawk Trail Richardson TX 75080 Office: 400 S Cottonwood TX 75080

MCCORD, GUYTE PIERCE, JR., judge; b. Tallahassee, Sept. 23, 1914; s. Guyte Pierce and Jean (Patterson) McC.; student Davidson Coll., 1933-34; B.A., J.D., U. Fla., 1940; m. Laura Elizabeth Mack, Dec. 16, 1939; children—Florence Elizabeth, Guyte Pierce III, Edward LeRoy. Admitted to Fla. bar, 1940; practiced in Tallahassee, 1940-60; dep. commr. Fla. Insl. Commn., 1946-47, pros. atty. Leon County, 1947-48, asst. gen. counsel Fla. Pub. Service Commn., 1949-60; judge 2d Jud. Circuit Fla., Tallahassee, 1960-74, Ct. Appeal 1st Dist. Fla., 1974—. Pres. Murat House Assn., Inc., 1967-69; bd. dirs. Fla. Heritage Found., 1969-70, mem. exec. com., 1965-69. Served to comdr. USNR, 1942-46, 52-53. Mem. Res. Officers Assn. (v.p. Tallahassee 1961-64), Tallahassee C. of C., Am. Legion, Fla. Conf. Circuit Judges (sec.-treas. 1970, chmn. 1972), Phi Delta Phi, Sigma Alpha Epsilon. Presbyn. (elder 1960—). Kiwanian (dir. 1958-59). Home: 502 S Ride St Tallahassee FL 32303 Office: PO Box 1028 Tallahassee FL 32302

MCCORD, MOLLIE ROYALL, lawyer, clubwoman; b. Atlanta; d. Claude Manley and Mollie (McCormick) McCord; B.A., Southwestern at Memphis; LL.B., Memphis State U., 1954. Owner, mgr. Meter Splty. Co., Memphis, 1941—; admitted to Tenn. bar, 1954; priorities and indsl. analyst WPB, Civilian Prodn. Adminstrn., Memphis, 1942-47; dir. Memphis Legal Aid Office, 1954-55; practiced in Memphis, 1954—. Pres. Memphis Art League, 1958-59, 63-64, Josephine Circle, 1954-55, Memphis Panhellenic Assn., 1946-47, Mid-Day Study Club, 1956-57, Women's Inter-Club Golf Assn., 1970; mem. Royal Club of Cotton Carnival, Soc. Preservation Tenn. Antiquities, Memphis Symphony League, In His Name II Circle, King's Daus. Mem. Tenn., Memphis, Shelby County bar assns., Brooks Art Gallery League, Delta Delta Delta (pres. local alumnae 1940-41, woman of year 1954), Phi Delta Delta. Presbyn. Clubs: Review (pres. 1967-69), Memphis Country (chmn. orgn. women golfers 1967); Chickasaw Garden; Women's Interclub Golf Assn. (pres. 1971). Home: Country Club Apts 3170 Southern Av Memphis TN 38111

MCCORD, ROBERT SANFORD, editor; b. Camden, Ark., Apr. 4, 1929; s. Mose Sanford and Myrtle (Hutchinson) McC.; B.J., U. Ark., 1951; M.S. in Journalism, Columbia, 1954; m. Muriel Helene Stuck, Dec. 16, 1951; children—Kim Sanford, Jeffrey Sanford, Stacey Elise. Reporter, Sunday mag. editor Ark. Democrat, Little Rock, 1954-57, asso. editor, 1968-74, exec. editor, 1974—; editor, pub. North Little Rock (Ark.) Times, 1957-68; dir. First Nat. Bank of Little Rock. Trustee Little Rock U., 1965-70. Served with AUS, 1951-53. Mem. Ark. Press Assn. (treas. 1963—), Am. Soc. Newspaper Editors, Fgn. Policy Assn., North Little Rock C. of C., Blue Key, Kappa Sigma, Sigma Delta Chi (regional dir. 1968-72, nat. treas. 1972-73, sec. 1973-74). Methodist. Rotarian. Home: 2039 Topf Rd North Little Rock AR 72116 Office: 5th and Scott Sts Little Rock AR 72203

MCCORKLE, CHARLES HOWARD, supt. schs.; b. Elizabethton, Tenn., Apr. 8, 1909; s. Arthur Emmert and Bessie D. (Williams) McC.; B.S., Milligan Coll., 1931, LL.D. (hon.), 1972; postgrad. E. Tenn. State U., 1932, State U. Ia., 1952, George Peabody Coll., 1938; M.A., Vanderbilt U., 1936; m. Elizabeth L. Connell, June 9, 1936; children—Nancy Williams (Mrs. Olan W. Hay), Elizabeth Louise (Mrs. Michael Ludwig). Elementary tchr. Johnson City (Tenn.) Pub. Schs., 1932-34, elementary prin., 1934-36, asst. prin. jr. high, 1936-41, prin. jr. high, 1941-42, prin. sr. high, 1942-52, supr., 1952-56, supt., 1956—. Mem. exec. com. Assn. Drug Edn., 1969-70; mem. Gov's. Com. for Mentally Retarded, 1967-70. Bd. dirs. Johnson City United Fund, 1950-60; trustee, mem. exec. com. Milligan Coll. Mem. N.E.A. (life), City Supts. Assn. (pres. 1960-62), Tenn. (pres. 1953), E. Tenn. (pres. 1964-65) edn. assns., Tenn. Secondary Sch. Athletic Assn.

(legislative council 1958-64), Tenn. Supts. Study Council (chmn. curriculum com. 1963-70), Am., Tenn. (pres. 1964) assns. sch. adminstrs., Kappa Sigma. Mem. Christian Ch. (Bible Sch. supt. 1944-50). Kiwanian. Home: 427 Highland Av Johnson City TN 37601 Office: S Roan St Johnson City TN 37601

MCCORMACK, AUSTIN FRANCIS, JR., pollution control co. exec.; b. Bklyn., Feb. 9, 1924; s. Austin Francis and Irene (Halligan) McC.; M.E., Stevens Inst., 1945; m. June Doyle, June 25, 1949; children—Austin III, William, Kathryn, Daniel, Thomas, Ann. Dist. engr. Permutit Co., Rochester, N.Y., 1946-49, dist. engr., Dallas, 1961-63; chief engr. Comml. Chem Products, Midland Park, N.J., 1959-61; formed McCormack Equipment Co., Dallas, 1963; pres. McCormack Corp., Dallas, 1967—; chmn. bd., dir. Automation Equipment & Controls Co. Inc., Dallas, 1968—. Neighborhood commr. Boy Scouts Am., 1961-67; co-chmn. Jesuit Sustentation Fund, 1968, 69, 71; chmn. bd. advisers Jesuit Coll. Prep., 1973; pres. Bishop Lynch Athletic Assn., 1970. Served as ensign USNR, 1945-46. Registered profl. engr., Tex., Okla. Mem. Am. Water Works Assn., Water Pollution Control, Fedn., Tex. Soc. Profl. Engrs., Dallas C. of C. (water pollution com. 1969). Roman Catholic. Club: Dallas Athletic. Patentee in field. Home: 9424 Sherwood Glen Dallas TX 75228 Office: 3505 Turtle Creek Blvd Dallas TX 75219

MCCORMACK, CAROL HARTFORD, financial exec.; b. Redfield, S.D., Jan. 15, 1920; s. Elliott Hartford and Inger Dorthea (Stapp) McC.; B.S., Drake U., 1953; postgrad. La. State U. Sch. Banking, 1957; m. Virginia Dare Rothgeb, June 12, 1946; 1 dau., Patricia Ann. Dist. mgr. Universal C.I.T. Credit Corp., Des Moines, 1946-50; v.p., controller La. Nat. Bank, Baton Rouge, 1953-56; cons. mgr. Ernst & Ernst, St. Louis, 1956-59; exec. v.p., dir. Am. Nat. Bank, Portsmouth, Va., 1959-60; treas. Merc. Mortgage Co., St. Louis, 1960-62; sr. industry analyst IBM, N.Y.C., 1962-67; financial v.p. Waddell & Reed, Inc., Kansas City, Mo., 1967-68; self-employed as financial cons., Kansas City, Mo., 1968-69, Houston, 1969—; founder, owner, operator C.H. McCormack & Assos., Inc., Houston, 1971—. Cons. various banks and domestic corps. Bd. dirs., trustee Low Heywood Sch., Stamford, Conn. Served to capt. AUS, World War II; PTO. Decorated Bronze Star with oak leaf cluster. Clubs: Stamford (Conn.) Yacht, Brookridge Country (Overland Park, Kan.). Author: Bank Investment Portfolio, 1964; Bond Trade Analysis Program, 1964; Optimum Bond Bidding Program, 1966; Accounting for Debt Securities, 1972; Managing and Trading Debt Securities, 1972. Inventor portfolio control system, inter-portfolio trade locater. Home: 811 Patchester Dr Houston TX 77024

MCCORMICK, EDWARD MACK, govt. ofcl.; b. Neck City, Mo., June 7, 1920; s. Edward Franklin and Ida (McKay) McC.; B.S., Kan. State Coll. at Pittsburg, 1941, M.S., 1947; Ph.D., Am. U., 1970; m. Cleta Gail Steward, Nov. 7, 1943; children—Susan, Patti. Tech. editor Nat. Radio Inst., Washington, 1946-49; electronic engr. Goodyear Aircraft Corp., Akron, O., 1949-51; with U.S. Naval Ordnance Lab., Corona, Cal., 1951-59, head data assessment div., 1955-59; asso. program dir. NSF, Washington, 1959-64, head data processing center 1964-68; with Office Information Systems, Dept. Agr., Washington, 1968—. Lectr. U. Cal. at Los Angeles, 1955-59; profl. lectr. Am. U., 1960—. Served with USAAF, 1943-46. Mem. Assn. for Computing Machinery. Democrat. Mem. Disciples of Christ Ch. Author: Digital Computer Primer, 1959. Contbr. chpt. to book, articles to profl. jours. Home: 8720 Ewing Dr Bethesda MD 20034 Office: Office Information Systems Dept Agr Washington DC 20250

MCCORMICK, HERMAN MONTGOMERY, JR., city ofcl.; b. Abingdon, Va., Nov. 10, 1928; s. Herman Montgomery and Flossie Lee (Ball) McC.; student pub. schs.; m. Dora Mae Lawson, May 31, 1947; children—Patricia (Mrs. James Dove), Linda (Mrs. Ronnie South), Donna, Mark, John. Employed with Town of Abingdon, 1947—, supt. pub. works, 1958—; mem. Abingdon Fire Dept., 1951—, chief, 1964—. Capt. Washington County Life Saving Crew, 1961-64. Baptist. Moose. Home: 486 Oak Hill Abingdon VA 24210 Office: 160 A St Abingdon VA 24210

MCCORMICK, JAMES EDWARD, geologist; b. Providence, Nov. 5, 1927; s. James Edward and Edna Josephine (Smith) McC.; A.B. in Geology, Boston U., 1953; m. Catherine Sullivan, Aug. 31, 1952; children—Daniel, Catherine, Bernard, Michael, Eileen, Robert. Exploration geologist Sun Oil Co., Lafayette, La., 1953-61, Beaumont, Tex., 1961-63; div. offshore geologist, Beaumont, 1963-70, regional geologist, Dallas, 1970-71, exploration programs mgr., Dallas. 1972—. Served with USAAF, 1945-48. Mem. Marine Tech. Soc., Am. Assn. Petroleum Geologists, Nat. Acad. Sci. Club: Dallas Athletic. Home: 9436 Angleridge St Dallas TX 75238 Office: 12850 Hillcrest Rd Dallas TX 75230

MCCORMICK, JOHN HOYLE, lawyer; b. Pensacola, Fla., July 30, 1933; s. Clyde H. and Orrie B. (Frink) McC.; B.S., U. Fla., 1955; J.D., Stetson U., 1958. Admitted to Fla. bar, 1958, U.S. Supreme Ct. bar, 1964; practice law, White Springs, Fla., 1958-60, Jasper, Fla., 1960—; mayor White Springs, 1959-60; county judge Hamilton County, Fla., 1960-72; atty. Hamilton County Bank, Jasper, 1966—, v.p., 1968—; also dir.; dir. First Fed. Savs. & Loan Assn., Live Oak, Fla.; local counsel So. Ry. System, 1967—; atty. Hamilton County Devel. Authority, 1966—; approved loan closing atty. First Fed. Savs. & Loan Assn., Live Oak, Fed. Land Bank of Columbia, S.C., VA, Farmers Home Adminstrn., John Hancock Mut. Life Ins. Co.; approved atty. Lawyers Title Ins. Corp., Richmond, Va., Lawyers' Title Guaranty Fund, Orlando, Fla., Title & Trust Co. Fla., Jacksonville, Peninsular Title Ins. Co., Jacksonville. Mem. Hamilton County C. of C. (pres. 1961), Am. Bar Assn., Fla. Bar, Am. Arbitration Assn., Phi Delta Phi. Methodist. Kiwanian, Mason. Club: Suwanee River Valley Country (dir. Jasper). Address: PO Drawer O Jasper FL 32052

MCCORMICK, MICHAEL PATRICK, physicist, govt. ofcl.; b. Canonsburg, Pa., Nov. 23, 1940; s. Arthur John and Mary Ann (Nestor) McC.; B.A., Washington and Jefferson Coll., 1962; M.A., Coll. William and Mary, 1964, Ph.D., 1967; m. Judy Kay Moyer, June 30, 1962; children—Lynn Ann, Michael Patrick. Research physicist Nat. Bur. Mines, Pitts., 1962; physicist, head photoelectronic instrumentation sect. NASA, Hampton, Va., 1967—. Served to capt., Ordnance Corps, AUS, 1968-70. Mem. Optical Soc. Am., Am. Meteorol. Soc. (mem. com. on Laser atmospheric sensing 1973—), Nat. Wrestling Ofcls. Assn. (sec.-treas. 1973—), Va. Wrestling Coaches and Ofcls. Assn., Phi Kappa Psi. Contbr. articles on laser radar and atmospheric measurements of pollution. Home: 1 NEFF Hampton VA 23669 Office: Langley Research Center MS 475 Hampton VA 23665

MCCORMICK, RONALD ROBERT, psychologist; b. Chgo., June 19, 1929; s. Robert D. and Gladys (Swain) McC.; B.S., Northwestern U. 1951, M.A., 1952; postgrad. North Tex. State U., 1959-62; m. Shirlee B. Boggs, Sept. 5, 1952 (div. 1964); children—Brian, Kelly, Melinda; m. 2d, Barbara Anderson, Aug. 30, 1968; children—Daniel, Mark. Psychologist, Dallas County Juvenile Ct., Dallas, 1957-61; sr. human factors psychologist System Devel. Corp., Paramus N.J., 1961-62; lead human factors psychologist Ling-Temco-Vought Corp., Dallas, 1962-66; engr.-scientist Tracor., Inc., Austin, Tex., 1966-67; vocational rehab. psychologist Fla. Dept. Edn., Ft. Lauderdale, 1967; research asso. and asst. dir. testing and evaluation Fla. Atlantic U., Boca Raton, 1967—; cons. Western Union Computer Utilities Corp., Ft. Lauderdale, 1968—; pres., founder Internat. Data Interchange, Inc., Boca Raton, Fla., 1969—, Trademark Design Products, Inc., Boca Raton, 1970—. Personnel cons. Broward County Mfrs. Assn., Ft. Lauderdale, 1967-69. Served to capt. USAF, 1952-57. Mem. Am. Psychol. Assn., Am. Ednl. Research Assn., Phi Delta Kappa. Co-author: Broward County Computer-Assisted Wage and Salary Survey; author, Mastery-Commitment Education; The McCormick Job Performance Measurement Rate-S-Scales; Journal Oriented Educational Update Program. Home: 97 NW 12th Av Boca Raton FL 33432 Office: Testing and Evaluation Center Fla Atlantic U Boca Raton FL 33432

MCCORMICK, SANFORD ELLIOTT, petroleum co. exec.; b. N.Y.C., July 18, 1931; s. Robert Elliott and Helen (Roberts) McC.; B.A., Yale, 1953; Certificat d'Etudes Politique, L'Ecole des Politique, Paris, France, 1955; m. Inez Balene Cross, Dec. 31, 1956; children—Peter, Carolyn. Landman, Zapata Petroleum, Midland, Tex., 1956-58; with Tex. Crude Oil Midland, 1958-59; landman Chambers & Kennedy, Midland, 1959-64; ind. oil operator, Houston, 1964-69; chmn., pres. McCormick Oil and Gas Corp., Houston, 1969—. Bd. dirs. Cardio Pulmonary Inst., Houston, Houston Ballet, Robert Joffrey Ballet, N.Y.; trustee Mus. Fine Arts, Houston. Served with USAF, 1954-56. Mem. Houston Petroleum Club. Clubs: Country, University (Houston); Racquet and Tennis (N.Y.C.); Maidstone (East Hampton, N.Y.). Home: 275 Pine Hollow Lane Houston TX 77027 Office: 1204 Tenneco Bldg Houston TX 77002

MCCORMICK, WILLIE MAE WARD (MRS. WALTER WITTEN MCCORMICK), city ofcl., ret. tech. specialist; b. Centerville, Tex. Oct. 17, 1908; d. William Sylvester and Lucy (Marshall) Ward; B.A., Mary Hardin Baylor Coll., 1929; M.A., Hardin Simmons U., 1931; postgrad. So. Methodist U., Tex. Woman's U.; m. Walter Witten McCormick, May 29, 1929; 1 dau., Elizabeth Ward (Mrs. Billy Joe Wilcox). Tchr. chemistry and algebra Big Spring (Tex.) High Sch., 1941-44, 45-48; weather observer for Dept. Commerce, Big Spring, 1943-44; analytical chemist Dow Chem. Co., Freeport, 1944-45; calculator Chance Vought (now Ling-Temco-Vought), Dallas, 1951-55, structural engr., 1955-63, sci. programmer, 1963-67, tech. specialist, 1967-69; sr. program analyst Univ. Computing Co., Arlington, Tex., 1970-73. Mem. Euless (Tex.) City Council, 1973—. Mem. A.A.A.S., Assn. Computing Machinery, Math. Assn. Am., Fedn. Am. Scientists, Am. Assn. U. Women (treas.), Am. Soc. Information Sci., Trainmen's Aux. (pres. 1940-41, Internat. Platform Assn., League Women Voters (publicity chmn.). Democrat. Baptist (supt. adult dept. Sunday sch.). Mem. Order Eastern Star (past worthy matron). Home: Route 1 Box 66 Euless TX 76039 Office: Computer Technology Arlington TX 76010

MCCOTTER, BURNEY RICHARD, life ins. co. exec.; b. Grantsboro, N.C., Feb. 9, 1920; s. John Lawrence and Flora (Tingle) M.; A.B., Atlantic Christian Coll., 1941; grad. exec. program U. N.C., 1965; m. Margaret R. Palmer, June 21, 1946; children—Richard, Karen. Tchr. high sch., N.C., 1941-42; agt. Jefferson Standard Life Ins. Co., 1946-47, 48-50; gen. agt. Franklin Life Ins. Co., 1947-48; mgr. Occidental Life Ins. Co., N.C., 1950-52, agy. asst., Raleigh, 1952-55, agy. sec., 1955-60, asst. v.p., 1960-64, v.p., 1964, v.p., sec., 1964-66, v.p. operations, 1966-70, sr. v.p., 1970—; pres. Mgmt. Services Corp., Wade Properties Inc., Piedmont Proprietary, Ltd. Trustee Occidental Charitable Found. Served to 1st lt. USAAF, 1942-46. Decorated Air medal with two oak leaf clusters. C.L.U. Mem. Am. Soc. Chartered Life Underwriters (chpt. pres. 1961), Atlantic Christian Coll. Alumni Assn. (past pres.). Democrat. Presbyn. (deacon 1960-64, elder 1969-73). Kiwanian. Club: Carolina Country. Home: 332 Buncombe St Raleigh NC 27609 Office: 1001 Wade Av Raleigh NC 27605

MCCOTTER, MARGARET ROSEMOND PALMER (MRS. BURNEY RICHARD MCCOTTER), librarian; b. Thomasville, N.C., Nov. 7, 1921; d. Jacob Alexander and Etna (Little) Palmer; A.B., Catawba Coll., 1942; B.S., U. N.C., 1944; m. Burney Richard McCotter, June 21, 1946; children—Richard Palmer, Karen Ellen. Librarian So. Pines (N.C.) Sch. System, 1944-47; post librarian Fort Story (Va.), 1950-51; librarian LeRoy Martin Jr. High Sch., Raleigh, N.C., 1959-62, 65—; library cons. N.C. Dept. Pub. Instrn., Raleigh, 1963-65. Mem. N.E.A., United Daus. Confederacy, N.C. Library Assn., N.C. Assn. Educators, N.C. Soc. for Preservation of Antiquities, Beta Phi Mu, Sigma Pi Alpha, Delta Kappa Gamma. Democrat. Presbyn. Club: Carolina Country (Raleigh). Author: (with others) AV Cataloging and Processing Simplified, 1971. Editor: Reference Materials for School Libraries, 1965. Home: 332 Buncombe St Raleigh NC 27609 Office: 1701 Ridge Rd Raleigh NC 27607

MCCOUN, FRED CORBETT, clergyman; b. Campton, Ky., Nov. 9, 1931; s. Glenn Rynolds and Grace Dorcas (Coldiron) McC.; student U. Ky., 1949-51; A.B., Transylvania Coll., 1954; B.D., Lexington Theol. Sem., 1958; m. Margaret Jane Giltner, June 24, 1956; children—Beth, Amy, Laura. Ordained to ministry Christian Ch., 1958; minister Mt. Carmel Christian Ch., Bourban County, Ky., 1954-56, Floyd's Knobs (Ind.) Christian Ch., 1956; sr. minister Southport Christian Ch., Indpls., 1958-65, Gordon St. Christian Ch., Kinston, N.C., 1965-67, First Christian Ch., Tyler, Tex., 1967—. Pres. Perry Twp. Ministerial Assn., 1958-59, Indpls. Ministerial Assn., 1961-62, Ind. Christian Ministers Assn., 1963-64, Christian Ch. Union of Greater Indpls., 1964-65, Tyler Ministerial Alliance, 1971, Northeast Area of Christian Chs. (dist. 14, 16), 1971-73; mem. Gen. Bd. Christian Ch., 1973—. Bd. dirs. East Texas Urban Housing Found. Corp. (chmn. 1969—). Recipient Distinguished Service award Indpls. Jaycees, 1962. Mason, Rotarian. Home: 803 Watkins Tyler TX 75701 Office: 4202 S Broadway Tyler TX 75701

MCCOURT, JAMES WILLIAM, JR., dentist; b. Hartford, Conn., Oct. 1, 1940; s. James William and Katheryn (Kane) McC.; B.S., St. Mary's Coll. of Cal., 1962; D.M.D., Pitts. U., 1966; certificate in pediatric dentistry Harvard, 1971; m. Martha Krepp, June 11, 1966; children—David James, Kelly Lynn. Resident, Children's Hosp., Boston, 1969-71; practice dentistry, specializing in pediatric dentistry, Charleston, S.C., 1971—. Asst. prof. dept. pediatric dentistry Dental Coll., Med. U. S.C., Charleston, 1971-72. Served with USAF, 1966-69. Mem. Am. Dental Assn., Internat. Assn. Orthodontics, Am. Soc. Dentistry for Children. Kiwanian. Home: 835 Mikell Dr Charleston SC 29412 Office: 80 Barre St Charleston SC 29401

MCCOWN, JAMES KIMBOL, dentist; b. Philadelphia, Miss., Sept. 14, 1915; s. James Monroe and Lou Ada (Green) McC.; student Miss. State U., 1935-37, U. Miss., 1937-38; D.D.S., Loyola U. of South, New Orleans, 1943; m. Mary Victoria Lee, Sept. 8, 1940 (dec. Jan. 1972); m. Mabel Page Yarber, Feb. 24, 1973. Practice dentistry, Amory, Miss., 1946—; pres. Glendale, Inc., Amory, 1970—; owner Glendale Shopping Center, Amory, 1970—. Served with Dental Corps, AUS, 1943-46. Mem. Am. Dental Assn., Miss., Northeast Miss. dental socs. Democrat. Baptist. Home: 808 Town and Country Lane Amory MS 38821 Office: 107 N 3d St Amory MS 38821

MCCOWN, THEODORE VEDELL, JR., govt. ofcl.; b. Johnson City, Tenn., Jan. 14, 1932; s. Theodore Vedell and Sarah (Brown) McC.; B.S., E. Tenn. State U., 1953; m. Jane Rector McCown, Jan. 6, 1955; 1 dau., Sarah Jane. Office mgr. Gen. Shale Products Corp., Kingsport, Tenn., 1956-62; adminstrv. asst. to city mgr. City of Kingsport, 1962-69, dir. personnel and pub. relations, 1969—, asst. city mgr., 1972—. Chmn. comml. div. United Fund Campaign, 1970, gen. chmn., 1971. Chmn. bd. Appalachian Preaching Mission, 1967, area chmn., 1968—; bd. dirs., area chmn., publicity dir. Nat. Found.-March of Dimes; bd. dirs. A.R.C., Community Aid Agy., Community Chest of Kingsport. Served with AUS, 1954-56. Mem. United Comml. Travelers, Alpha Phi Omega. Presbyn. (deacon, elder). Moose Club: Sertoma (pres. 1963, chmn. bd. 1964). Home: 3833 Telstar Dr Kingsport TN 37664 Office: 225 W Center St Kingsport TN 37660

MCCOY, FRANCIS TYRONE, educator; b. N.Y.C., Oct. 15, 1922; s. Francis Thomas and Gladys (Parker) McC.; B.A. Fla U., 1944, M.A., 1947, J.D., 1955; postgrad. (fellow) Yale Law Sch., 1963-64. Admitted to Fla. bar 1955; vice consul U.S. Frgn. Service, 1947-52; asst. law librarian U. Fla., Gainesville 1955-56, law librarian, 1956-62, asst. prof. law, 1956-65, asso. prof., 1965-70, prof., 1970—. Served to 2d lt. AUS, 1943-45; lt. col. Res. Mem. Fla. Bar, Phi Beta Kappa, Kappa Alpha. Episcopalian. Home: 28 NW 36th St Gainesville FL 32601

MCCOY, GENE GUY, advt. exec; b. Oskaloosa, Ia., May 11, 1926; s. Guy Gene and Edith (Seaman) McC.; B.B.A., U. Wis., 1951; M.A. in Marketing, State U. Ia., 1952; m. Idella Maria Brown, Aug. 8, 1947; children—Gene Guy III, Vicki V., Randi R., S. Sherman. Advt. mgr. W.M. McAllister Co., Sycamore, Ill., 1952-53; account exec. Gerald T. LeFever & Assos., Little Rock, 1953-55, partner, 1956-57; pres. Ad Craft of Ark., Inc., Little Rock, 1958—. Asst. prof., chmn. dept. advt. U. Ark. at Little Rock. Mem. Ark. Atty. Gen.'s Study Com. for Consumer Protection Legislation; state vice chmn. Ark. Better Bus. Bur., 1973; cons. Model Cities Program. Served with AUS, 1944-47. Recipient Advt. Educator of Year award G.D. Crain Found., 1972. Named Ark. Traveler, 1969. Mem. Am. Advt. Fedn. (dir. 10th dist. 1958—, gov. 10th dist. 1969-70, nat. dir. 1969-70, lt. gov. 1968-69, Advt. Educator of Year 1972, Silver Medal award 1966), Pub. Relations Soc. Am. (sec. Ark. chpt. 1972-73), Little Rock Advt. Club (pres. 1958-60), A.I.M. (pres. council), Am. Marketing Assn., Alpha Delta Sigma (nat. v.p. 1971-72), Alpha Kappa Psi, Sigma Alpha Epsilon. Author publs. in field. Home: 12000 Rivercrest Dr Little Rock AR 72207 Office: 3d and Cross St Little Rock AR 72203

MCCOY, IDELLA MARIA THERESA BROWN (MRS. GENE GUY MCCOY), bus. exec.; b. Woodriver, Ill., July 21, 1928; d. Mayo Clinton and Loretta (Weisaupt) Brown; student Shurtleff Coll., Ill., 1946-48; m. Gene Guy McCoy, Aug. 8, 1948; children—Gene Guy III, Vicki V., Randall R., S. Sherman. Prodn. mgr. Ad Craft of Ark., Inc., Little Rock, 1958, sec.-treas., 1958-65, exec. v.p., 1965—. Residential chmn. United Fund Pulaski County, 1962-63, pub. relations, 1969. Mem. Am. Advt. Fedn. (dir. S.W. dist.), Little Rock Advt. Club (pres. 1970-71), Gamma Alpha Chi (Spl. Service award 1969). Home: 12000 Rivercrest Dr Little Rock AR 72207 Office: 1122 W 3d St Little Rock AR 72201

MCCOY, JOSEPH HENRY, JR., dentist; b. Norfolk, Va., Feb. 15, 1933; s. Joseph Henry and Frances Louise (Rogers) McC.; A.A., Coll. William and Mary, 1953; B.S., Med. Coll. Va., 1956, D.D.S., 1957; m. Shirley Mae Perry, Mar. 31, 1956; children—Yvonne Vicki, Sheryl Anne; m. 2d, Diana Lee Freeman, July 26, 1973; stepchildren—Kevin Keith, Kimberly Kay, Joy Marie. Pvt. practice dentistry, Virginia Beach, Va., 1959—. Pres., Haven Heights Civic League, 1965-68. Mem. Virginia Beach City Council, 1974—. Bd. visitors Old Dominion U., 1968—; bd. dirs., chmn. Tidewater Community Coll. Served to capt. Dental Corps, USAF, 1957-59. Mem. Virginia Beach (pres. 1970), Tidewater (exec. committeeman 1970—, rec. sec. 1973-74) dental socs. Mason (Shriner), Lion (pres. 1972). Home: 5167 Fallsmead Downs Virginia Beach VA 23462 Office: 4920 Virginia Beach Blvd Virginia Beach VA 23462

MCCOY, WILLIAM HENRY, III, coll. pres.; b. Jacksonville, Fla., Feb. 8, 1928; s. William Henry and Thelma (Windham) McC.; B.A. in History, U. Fla., 1949, M.Ed. in Adminstrn., 1966, Specialist's Certificate in Adminstrn., 1967, Ed.D. in Coll. Adminstrn., 1968; m. Diane Christine Grieco, June 9, 1962. Tchr. Fla. pub. schs. Dade County, 1955-56, Duval County, 1957-61; dir. news bur. Jacksonville U., 1961-62, dir. placement, 1962-64, registrar, 1964-66; spl. asst. to pres., asst. prof. edn. U. Fla., Gainesville, 1968-69; pres. Lord Fairfax Community Coll., Middletown, Va., 1969—. Pres. St. Thomas Chapel Trust, Middletown, 1971—; pres. Shenandoah Area council Boy Scouts Am. Bd. dirs. Nat. Trust for Hist. Preservation, Winchester Apple Blossom Festival. Served with AUS, 1950-53; Far East. Mem. So. Coll. Placement Assn., Phi Delta Kappa, Phi Kappa Phi, Phi Delta Theta, Blue Key. Rotarian. Home: Route 2 Box 172B Berryville VA 22611 Office: PO Drawer E Middletown VA 22645

MCCRACKEN, BOBBIE ADKINS (MRS. WILLIAM O. MCCRACKEN), civic worker; b. Clarksville, Ark., May 15, 1920; d. Robert E. and Elzada (Storm) Adkins; student Coll. Ozarks, 1937-41, Am. Conservatory of Music, Chgo., 1944, U. Ark., 1943; postgrad. U. Ark., 1969-70; m. William O. McCracken, Apr. 13, 1945; 1 dau., Kay Lynn. Clk., Ark. State Selective Service System, 1941-46; sec., clk. FBI, 1940; tchr. Little Rock Pub. Sch. System, 1953-54. Pres., Little Rock Dist. Ark. Fedn. Women's Clubs, 1966—, state bd. dirs.; pres. Meml. chpt. U.D.C., 1966—, Ark. Pioneers Pulaski County Assn., 1967—; mem. President's Com. on Safety, 1959-62, Gov.'s Commn. on Status of Women; v.p. Sears Civic Center; chmn. Gov.'s Commn. Ark. Childrens Hosp.; bd. mem. Ark. Safety Commn.; mem. Gov.'s Consumer Affairs Commn., State Econs. Commn.; adv. bd. Ark. Nurses Assn., 1972—; mem. housing subcom. women and men in Services Dept. Def., 1973—. Mem. Ark. Women in Pub. Affairs (pres. 1970—), Greater Little Rock Fedn. Women's Clubs (past pres.), Nat. Jr. Fedn. Music Clubs (past pres.). Clubs: Women's City (pres. 1968-70, 1st pres. 1969-70, dir. 1972—, editor directory 1972), Women's (organizer) (Little Rock). Home: 90 Indian Trail Little Rock AR 72207

MCCRACKEN, FRANKLIN ALLEN, banker; b. Covington, Ky., Sept. 6, 1901; s. Clarence C. and Lucy (Swindler) McC.; grad. high sch.; m. Margaret Teegarden, Aug. 30, 1930; children—Joyce (Mrs. Robert B. Patrick), Ruth Ann (Mrs. Gilbert D. Cheatham). With Fifth Third Bank, Cin., 1920-29; chmn. bd., trust officer Newport (Ky.) Nat. Bank, 1929—. Mem. No. Ky. C. of C. Mason, Optimist. Club: Highland Country (Ft. Thomas, Ky). Home: 234 S Fort Thomas Av Fort Thomas KY 41075 Office: PO Box 190 Newport KY 41072

MCCRACKEN, JARRELL FRANKLIN, pub. co. exec.; b. Wartburg, Tenn., Nov. 18, 1927; s. Leonard Oren and Hazel (Rowe) McC.; B.A., Baylor U., 1950, M.A., 1953; LL.D. (hon.), John Brown U., 1969; m. Judith Murray, Aug. 21, 1953; children—Lisa, Timothy. Founder, pres. Word Inc., Waco, Tex., 1951—; dir. Nat. City Bank, Waco, Eaton Internat., Phoenix. Vice pres. Youth for Christ Internat.; chmn. civic affairs Waco Advancement Com.; pres. Waco Symphony Assn., 1969; pres. Baylor Stadium Com. Bd. dirs. San Marcos Acad.,

Dag Hammarskjold Coll. Named one of Five Outstanding Young Texans, 1961. Mem. Waco C. of C. (chmn. cultural affairs com. 1971), Record Industry Assn. Am. (pres. 1970-71). Baptist. Home: 4820 Hillcrest St Waco TX 76708 Office: 4800 W Waco Dr Waco TX 76710

MCCRACKEN, JOSEPH GLENN, supt. schs.; b. Fairview, N.C., Oct. 21, 1913; s. Cicero McAfee and Laura Helen (Clayton) McC.; A.B., Wake Forest U., 1938; M.A., U. N.C., 1942; LL.D., Limestone Coll., 1957; m. Katherine Frenger Mason, Dec. 16, 1939; children—Katherine Mason, Jo Ann. Tchr. high sch., Greensboro, N.C., 1938-40; dean of boys Needham Broughton High Sch., Raleigh, 1940-41; prin. Elizabeth City High Sch., 1941-44, supt., Elizabeth City pub. schs., 1944-49; dir. div. ins. N.C. State Bd. Edn., 1949-50; supt. schs., Spartanburg, S.C., 1950—. Edn. cons. sch. dist. reorgn. finance, architecture.; commr. Edn. Commn. of States, Compact for Edn., 1966-68. Mem. Spartanburg Planning Commn., 1965-69. Bd. dirs., mem. planning bd. Spartanburg YMCA; council assos. Wofford Coll.; bd. dirs. S.C. Blue Cross-Blue Shield. Recipient outstanding service certificate Am. Econ. Found., 1962, citizen's distinguished service award Wofford Coll., 1968, outstanding service award Spartanburg Civitan Club 1969. Mem. S.C. Edn. Assn. (pres. 1967-68), S.C. (pres. 1944-45), Am. (bd. dirs. nat. acad. sch. execs. 1968—) assns. sch. adminstrs., Appalachian Regional Ednl. Adv. Com., S.C. Congress Parents and Tchrs., Wake Forest U. Alumni Assn. (pres. 1961-62; spl. merit award 1961-62). Methodist. Rotarian (pres. 1957-58). Author: (with Am. Assn. Sch. Adminstrs. Commn.) State Associatons of School Administrators, 1968. Contbr. articles to profl. pubs. Home: 144 Shoreham Rd Spartanburg SC 29302 Office: Spartanburg City Schools PO Box 970 Spartanburg SC 29301

MCCRACKEN, JOSEPH HILL, III, lawyer; b. Dallas, June 12, 1927; s. Joseph Hill and Mary Frances (Hall) McC.; B.S., Okla. A. and M. Coll., 1950; LL.B., So. Methodist U., 1956. Admitted to Tex. bar, 1956; asso. firm Carrington, Gowan, Johnson, Bromberg & Leeds, Dallas, 1956-58; partner firm Hughes, Donosky, McCracken & Hunt, Dallas, 1958-63, McCulloch, Ray, Trotti & Hemphill, Dallas, 1963-66; practiced in Dallas, 1966—. Mem. com. edn. Southwestern Law Jour., So. Meth. U., 1955-56, now cons, Mem. S.A.R., Sons Republic of Tex., Tex. Bar, Dallas Bar Assn. (sec-treas., dir. 1958), Nat. (dir. 1965-69), Tex. (hon. life dir.) skeet shooting assns. Huguenot Soc., Am. Soc. Arms Collectors, Barristers, Sigma Alpha Epsilon, Delta Theta Phi. Methodist. Clubs: Dallas Gun (dir. 1963—), Terpsichorean, Idlewild. Contbg. biog. author Tex. State Hist. Assns.'s. Handbook of Texas-Supplement, 1969. Home: 3028 Potomac Dallas TX 75205 Office: 211 North Ervay Bldg Dallas TX 75201

MCCRACKIN, EARL WINDELL, lawyer; b. Conway, S.C., June 17, 1929; s. John Mayo and Donnie Bell (Small) McC.; A.B., Wofford Coll., 1951; LL.B., U. S.C., 1955; m. Johann Temple Mishoe, Nov. 28, 1957; children—Sidney M., Mary Ann, James F. Admitted to S.C. bar, 1955; atty. U.S. Justice Dept., Washington, 1955-56; law clk. to U.S. Dist. Judge, Charleston, 1956-57; mem. firm Urner, Farlow & McCrackin, 1957-59; pvt. practice, 1959—. Mem. S.C. Ho. of Reps., 1960-64. Served with USMCR, 1946-48, AUS, 1951-52. Decorated Combat Infantryman's bdge. Mem. Greater Myrtle Beach C. of C. (dir. 1972-73), Am. Legion, Am., S.C. (exec. com. 1967-70) Horry County (pres. 1969-72) bar assns., Am. Judicature Soc., Phi Delta Phi, Blue Key, Wig and Robe, Delta Sigma Phi, Pi Gamma Mu. Mason. Presbyn. (elder). Home: Star Route 2 Myrtle Beach SC 29577 Office: 1002 N King's Hwy PO Box 1182 Myrtle Beach SC 29577

MCCRARY, DENNIE LOCKHART, real estate devel. co. exec.; b. Macon, Ga., Mar. 7, 1938; s. Dennie Lockhart and Mary Marguerite (Barksdale) McC.; B.S., U.S. Naval Acad., 1960; M.B.A., Harvard, 1966; m. Frances Roberta Parker, June 24, 1961; children—Jennifer Lane, Thomas Parker, Catherine Barksdale. Asst. to pres. Sea Pines Co. real estate devel., resort operations, Hilton Head Island, S.C., 1966-68, v.p. finance, 1968-70, v.p. finance, gen. mgr., 1970-71, exec. v.p., 1971-72; pres. Hilton Head Beach Properties, 1972—; dir. Sea Pines Co., First Carolina Bank, Beaufort, S.C. Chmn. bd. trustees Sea Pines Acad. Served to 1st lt. USAF, 1960-64. Decorated Air Force Commendation Medal. Mem. Hilton Head C. of C. (pres.). Presbyn. (deacon). Rotarian, Toastmaster. Home: 8 Surf Scoter Rd Hilton Head Island SC 29928 Office: Hilton Head Beach Properties PO Box 5685 Hilton Head Island SC 29928

MCCRARY, GEORGE AUTREY, physician; b. Nashville, Ark., Aug. 31, 1939; s. Matthew Marcellus and Addie Mae (Young) McC; student U. Ark., 1957-60, M.D., 1964; m. Mary Ann Frizzell, Aug. 25, 1961; children—George Autrey, Jr., Mary Lynn. Intern, Bapt. Med. Center, Little Rock, 1964-65; physician Johnson Durham Clinic, Jacksonville, Ark., 1967-71, Durham-McCrary, P.A., Jacksonville, 1971—; mem. staffs Rebsamen Meml. Hosp., Jacksonville, Ark. Mem. Ark. Merit System Council, 1969-71. Served with USNR, 1965-67. Mem. Jacksonville C. of C. (dir. 1968-72) Ark., Pulaski County med. socs., A.M.A. Baptist (trustee). Home: 1 Red Fox Lane Jacksonville AR 70276 Office: 2 Crestview Plaza Jacksonville AR 70276

MCCRAY, ARTHUR WHITE, educator; b. Rouseville, Pa., Feb. 10, 1913; s. William Arthur and Hilma Amelia (Nelson) McC.; B.S., Pa. State U., 1940, M.S., 1942; Ph.D., Okla. State U., 1968; m. Mary Estella Watson, Nov. 20, 1946; children—John Arthur, Katherine Mary (Mrs. Leon Samuel Hatcher), David William. Instr. petroleum engring. Pa. State U., 1940-42; engr. Atlantic-Richfield Co., Dallas, 1946-50; prof. petroleum engring. U. Okla., Norman, 1950—. Served to lt. USNR, 1943-46. Registered profl. engr., Okla. Mem. Nat., Okla. socs. profl. engrs., Soc. Petroleum Engrs. of Am. Inst. Mining, Metall. and Petroleum Engrs., Am. Soc. Engring. Edn., Delta Tau Delta, Pi Epsilon Tau. Democrat. Methodist. Author: (with Frank W. Cole) Oil Well Drilling Technology, 1959. Home: 1110 Grover Lane Norman OK 73069 Office: 865 Asp Av Norman OK 73069

MCCREARY, JOSEPH ROBERT, city ofcl.; b. Tarpon Springs, Fla., Aug. 5, 1915; s. Harry and Pearle Davona (Swartsel) McC.; student St. Petersburg Jr. Coll., 1932-33; B.S. in Civil Engring., Auburn U., 1938; m. Clara Winifrede Sawyer, Sept. 3, 1939; children—Joseph Robert, Martha Sawyer (Mrs. David Robert Baldry). Mgr. So. Coast Fisheries West Palm Beach, Fla., 1938-42; supr. shipbuilding USN, Jacksonville, Fla., 1942-47; city mgr. Tarpon Springs, 1947-52, 61—; chief engr. Tampa Marine Co., 1952-60. Bd. dirs. Tarpon Springs Hosp. Found. Mem. Lambda Chi Alpha (treas. v.p. 1935-37). Elk, Mason, Lion, Rotarian. Club: Tarpon Springs Yacht (commodore 1950). Home: 15 Central Court Tarpon Springs FL Office: City Hall Pinelles Av Tarpon Springs FL 33589

MCCREARY, JOSEPH SAMUEL, JR., dentist; b. Buffalo, Tex., Jan. 7, 1934; s. Joseph Samuel and Edna Emma (Jones) McC.; B.S., Baylor U., 1954, D.D.S., 1958; m. Linda Frances Severin, June 21, 1958; children—Melissa Lynn, Joseph Samuel III, Jon Patrick and Christina (twins). Pvt. practice dentistry, Fort Worth, 1960—. Dental dir. Head Start, 1969. Served to capt. Dental Corps, AUS, 1958-60. Mem. Nat. Fedn. Ind. Bus., Am. Soc. Dentistry for Children, Am. (alternate del. 1973-74), Tex. (del. 1968-69, 71-72, 74-75) dental assns., Fort Worth Dist. Dental Soc. (v.p. 1971-72, pres. 1974-75), Fort Worth C. of C., Psi Omega. Methodist (bd. mem. 1956—). Kiwanian. Home: 3932 Thistle Lane Fort Worth TX 76109 Office: 6013 Wedgwood Dr Fort Worth TX 76109

MCCRIGHT, WILLIAM ROBERT, TV broadcasting co. producer; b. Tulsa, Mar. 26, 1948; s. William Francis and Margaret Belle (Roberts) McC.; B.F.A., U. Okla., 1972. Founder, dir., producer Tulsa Children's Theatre, 1967-73; contract player Universal City (Cal.) Studios, 1968-69; producer, dir. Tulsa Cable TV, 1973—. Cons. theatre equipment and design., 1967—. Prin. W.R. McCright tchr. dramatic arts, Tulsa, 1967-73. Bd. dirs. Arts and Humanities Council of Tulsa, 1967-73. Served with U.S. Army, 1969-70. Recipient World Premiere Talent Search award NBC, 1968. Mem. Am., Children's theatre assns., Screen Actors Guild, Assn. Internat. du Theatre pour les enfants and la Jeunnesse, Zeta Phi Eta. Author: (play) Little Witch's Christmas, 1967. Home: 4442 S Harvard Tulsa OK 74135 Office: 6650 E 44th St Tulsa OK 74145

MCCRORY, ELLANN, radiologist; b. Butler Springs, Ala., Mar. 22, 1936; d. William Bryant and Eva Estelle (Stabler) McCrory; B.S., U. Ala., 1956; M.D., Med. Coll. Ala., 1960. Rotating intern Univ. Hosp., Birmingham, Ala., 1960-61; resident Bapt. Meml. Hosp., Memphis, 1961-64; instr. radiology U. Fla., 1964-65; practice medicine specializing in radiology, Andalusia, Ala., 1964-66, Langdale, Ala., 1966—; speaker. Recipient Bausch and Lomb sci. award, 1953. Mem. Am. Coll. Radiology, Radiol. Soc. N.A., A.M.A., Am. Med. Women's Assn., So. Radiol. Assn., Med. Assn. Ala., Chambers County (pres. 1970) med. socs., So. Med. Assn., Ala. Radiol. Soc., Valley C. of C., Phi Beta Kappa, Alpha Lambda Delta. Methodist. Home: PO Box 425 Lanett AL 36863 Office: Lanier Hospital Langdale AL 36864

MCCRORY, HARVEY FRED, veterinarian, state ofcl.; b. Kosciosko, Miss., Oct. 6, 1921; s. Harvey Lee and Hettie (Adams) McC.; B.S. in Animal Husbandry, Miss. State U., 1942; postgrad., 1967-68; D.V.M., Tex. A and M U., 1949; m. Nadine Elizabeth Weaver, May 20, 1944; children—Sharon Lee, Kathy Ann, Virginia Ruth, John Charles. Mem. dept. vet. sci. Miss. State U., State College, 1949-71, prof., acting head dept., 1966-69; dir. Vet. Diagnostic Lab., state veterinarian Miss. Bd. Animal Health, Jackson, 1971—. Vice chmn. Internat. Anaplasmosis Workers Conf., Guatemala, 1967. Bd. dirs., pres. Felix Long Meml. Hosp., Starkville, Miss., 1960-71. Served with A.C., AUS, 1943-45. Named Miss. Veterinarian of Year, 1971. Mem. Am. (alt. del. 1972—), N.E. Miss. (sec. 1960), Miss. (exec. sec. 1961) vet. medicine assns., So. Animal Health Assn. (pres. 1974), Am. Legion, Oktibbeha County C. of C. (1st v.p. 1969-70, pres. 1970-71), Acacia. Mason (Shriner), Rotarian (past pres. Starkville). Club: Pearl (sec.). Home: 17 Cedar Cove Brandon MS 39042 Office: Veterinary Diagnostic Lab PO Box 4356 Jackson MS 39216

MCCRORY, MARTHA, educator; b. Quincy, Ill.; d. Joseph W. and Florence (Bastert) McCrory; student Northwestern U., 1937-38; B.M., U. Mich., 1941; M.M., Eastman Sch. Music, 1944, also artists diploma; postgrad. U. London, summer 1955, Berkshire Music Center, 1941, Music Acad. of West, 1952. Cellist, All Am. Youth Orch., 1940, U. Mich. Little Symphony, 1940, Rochester Philharmonic, 1942-46; asst. prof. music Drake U., 1946-47, Trinity U., San Antonio, 1947-52; asst. prin. cello San Antonio Symphony, 1947-53, Chattanooga Symphony, 1955-62, mgr., 1958-62; asst. prof. music U. of South, Sewanee, Tenn., 1962-69, asso. prof., 1969—; dir. Sewanee Summer Music Center, 1963—; cellist Chattanooga, Nashville, Knoxville symphonies, Cumberland Trio, 1967—. Mem. adv. panel Tenn. Arts Commn. Mem. Nat. Sch. Orch. Assn. (chpt. chmn, chpt. pres.), Tenn. Fedn. Music Clubs (dir.), Tenn. String Tchrs. Assn. (pres.), Pi Beta Phi, Sigma Alpha Iota, Pi Kappa Lambda. Republican. Conglist. Home: Sewanee TN 37375 Office: U of the South Sewanee TN 37375

MCCULLOUGH, EUGENE FREDERICK, lawyer; b. Hagerman, N.M., Nov. 7, 1909; s. James Isaac and Blanche (Wagoner) McC.; B.A., Sul Ross State Coll., 1930; M.A., U. N.C., 1933; postgrad. U. Colo., 1935; m. Margaret Walker Bell, Aug. 6, 1932; children—Graham Eugene, James Albright. Admitted to Tex. bar, 1943; prin., athletic coach Seagraves (Tex.) High Sch., 1933-34, Aztec (N.M.) High Sch., 1934-35; supt. schs., Seagraves, 1936-44; practice law, Harlingen, Tex., 1944—; sr. mem. firm McCullough, Murray & McCullough, Harlingen, 1965—. Mayor City Harlingen, Tex., 1950-52; candidate U.S. Congress, Tex. 15th Congl. Dist., 1964; chmn. Cameron County Child Welfare Bd., 1960-67; mem. Tex. State Democratic Exec. Com., 1962-66. Mem. Am., Tex., Cameron County (pres. 1959-60) bar assns. Presbyn. (elder 1944-71). Rotarian (dist. gov. Internat. Dist. 593, 1971-72). Home: 309 Arroyo Dr Harlingen TX 78550 Office: 320 E Van Buren St Harlingen TX 78550

MCCULLOUGH, GRAHAM EUGENE, lawyer; b. Clovis, N.M., Dec. 6, 1935; s. Eugene F. and Margaret (Bell) McC.; B.A., U. Tex., 1957, LL.B., 1958; postgrad. (Rotary Found. fellow), U. Sydney (Australia), 1959; m. Anne Klein, Aug 6, 1960; children—Gretchen, Margaret, Arthur Eugene. Admitted to Tex. bar, 1960, since practiced in Harlingen; mem. firm McCullough, Murray and McCullough, 1965—. Chmn. bd. dirs. Rio Grande Title Co., 1973—. Instr. Southmost Coll., Brownsville, Tex., 1961. Mem. Cameron County Bar Assn. (pres. elect 1974-75). Rotarian (pres. 1973-74). Clubs: Harlingen Tennis Assn., Harlingen Country. Home: 917 East Taylor St Harlingen TX 78550 Office: 320 E Van Buren St Harlingen TX 78550

MCCUNE, WILLIAM STANLEY, surgeon; b. Petoskey, Mich., June 4, 1909; s. William George and Helen (Allen) McC.; B.A. summa cum laude, Swarthmore Coll., 1931; M.D. cum laude, Harvard, 1935; m. Doris Douglas, July 8, 1936; children—Carol, Cynthia (Mrs. Philip Allen III), Barbara, Mary. Intern, Mass. Gen. Hosp., 1935-37; resident Peter Bent Brigham Hosp., Boston, 1937-39; house physician Boston Lying-in Hospital, 1939-40; practice medicine specializing in surgery, Mich., 1940-43, Washington, 1946—; research grantee for vascular surgery, 1954-58, pancreatic x-ray visualization, 1960-64, NIH research on duo-denoscopy pancreatic surgery, 1965-68; clin. prof. surgery George Washington U. Sch. Medicine, 1958—; cons. in surgery Walter Reed Hosp. NIH VA Hosp., D.C. Mem. adv. bd. Care-Medico, 1964—; bd. dirs. Medico, Bloedorn Found., Washington. Served to maj., M.C., AUS, 1943-46. Fellow Am. (v.p. 1963), So. (v.p. 1971) surg. assns., Royal Soc. Medicine; mem. Soc. Surg. Alimentary Tract (founder), Med. Soc. D.C. (pres. 1968, chmn. exec. bd. 1972), A.C.S. (chmn. state adv. com, 1969), Southeastern Surg. Congress (v.p. 1973), Internat. Soc. Surgery, Orgn. State Med. Soc. Presidents (steering com. 1967-68), A.M.A., Soc. Alumni and Friends of Care/Medico (pres. 1966-67), N.Y. Acad. Sci., Washington Acad. Surgery, (pres. 1972-73), Phi Beta Kappa, Alpha Omega Alpha. Episcopalian (sr. warden 1968-73). Author: (with B. Blades) Nash's Surg. Physiology, 1953; Cancer of Digestive Tract, 1968. Contbr. articles to profl. jours. Home: 2510 Virginia Av NW Washington DC 20037 Office: 2520 L St NW Washington DC 20037

MCCUTCHEN, JOSEPH KELLY, JR., carpet co. exec.; b. Chattanooga, Nov. 14, 1939; s. Joseph Kelly and Christine Mercier (Bandy) McC.; grad. McCallie Sch., 1958; B.S., Ga. Inst. Tech., 1962; m. Elizabeth Mills McDonald, Dec. 19, 1964; children—Joseph Kelly III, Elizabeth Shannon. Asst. to pres. J & C Carpet Co., Inc., Ellijay, Ga., 1962-64, nat. sales mgr., 1964-69; pres., dir. Universal Carpets, Inc., Ellijay, 1969—; dir. 1st State Bank Gilmer County. Served with AUS, 1963-69. Mem. Carpet and Rug Inst., Young Pres.'s Orgn., Sigma Alpha Epsilon. Republican. Methodist (adminstrv. bd.). Lion. Clubs: Cotillion, Quarterback, Piedmont Driving. Home: Blue Ridge Rd Ellijay GA 30540 Office: Indsl Blvd Ellijay GA 30540

MCCUTCHEN, SAMUEL PROCTOR, govt. ofcl.; b. Corinth, Miss., May 2, 1928; s. Samuel Proctor and Lineta (Price) McC.; B.E.E., Vanderbilt U., 1950; LL.B., LaSalle Extension U., 1966; m. Mary Carmella Pugliese Gleason, May 6, 1972; children—Kathleen, Kyle, Proctor, Winfield, Timothy. Product engr. magnetic head design Brush Electronics, Inc., Cleve., 1953-55; project engr. infrared system Aerojet-Gen. Corp., Azusa, Cal., 1955-58; group supr. Polaris system design Lockheed Missiles & Space Div., Sunnyvale, Cal., 1958-59; supr. countermeasures studies Sylvania, Inc., Mountain View, Cal., 1959-60; tech. staff classified studies Inst. for Def. Analysis, Arlington, Va., 1960-63; engring. mgr. air def. systems Philco-Ford, Inc., Bluebell, Pa., 1963; sr. staff engr. command-control systems Burroughs Corp., Paoli, Pa., also Colorado Springs, Colo., 1963-66; sr. staff mem. ASW System Studies, TRW Systems, Washington, 1966-69; chief, systems engring. and computation support office U.S. Army Mobility Equipment Research and Devel. Center, Ft. Belvoir, Va., 1969—. Founder, pres. local civic assn., 1967-68; scoutmaster, troop com. chmn. Nat. Capital Area council Boy Scouts Am., 1971—. Served to lt. (j.g.) USN, 1950-53. Mem. Tau Beta Pi. Patentee in field. Home: 6022 Florence Lane Alexandria VA 22310 Office: USAMERDC Fort Belvoir VA 22060

MCCUTCHEN, THOMAS ENGLISH, lawyer; b. Bishopville, S.C., June 20, 1919; s. Thomas English and Cornelia (Lavender) McC.; A.B., U. S.C., 1940, LL.B., 1946; m. Jane Perry, Sept. 25, 1943; children—Thomas English III, Jane Perry, Grace Perry. Admitted to S.C. bar, 1941, since practiced in Columbia. Chmn. bd. dirs. Perry-Mann Elec. Co., Columbia, 1960—. Pres. S.C. Mental Health Assn., 1961-62. Served to maj. USAAF, 1941-45. Fellow Am. Coll. Trial Lawyers; mem. Richland County Bar Assn. (pres. 1969-70), Columbia Jr. C. of C. (pres. 1951-52). Rotarian (pres. Columbia 1968-69). Home: 6 Heathwood Circle Columbia SC 29205 Office: 1414 Lady St Columbia SC 29201

MCCUTCHEON, CHESTER MYERS, investment co. exec.; b. Monroeville, Pa., Oct. 30, 1907; s. William Erwin and Margaret Kelso (Myers) McC.; student Westinghouse Tech. Night Sch., East Pittsburgh, Pa., 1926-30, La Salle Extension U., 1933-35, Am. Savs. and Loan Inst., Atlanta, 1947-54; m. Hellen Sophia Clawson, Nov. 3, 1944; children—Ronald R., Brian L., Brenda (Mrs. Ernest Mosley), Lynn Ellis, Bruce A., Curtis W. Cost accountant Westinghouse Electric & Mfg. Co., Pitts., 1926-33; tax collector No. Huntingdon Twp., Westmoreland County, Pa., 1934-40; examiner Fed. Home Loan Bank Bd., Washington, 1941-47; comptroller Fulton Fed. Savs. & Loan Assn., Atlanta, 1947-73; tech. adviser Bolivian Savs. & Loan Industry; v.p. Fulton Investment Co., 1958-60, pres., 1960-65; dir. Southeastern Capital Co.; pres. Cherokee Enterprises, Tuxedo, Inc. Chmn. Cobb County Republican Exec. Com., Marietta, Ga., 1964-66; co-chmn. finance com. Callaway for Gov. Campaign, 1966. Mem. thesis rev. bd. Grad. Sch. Savs. and Loan, Ind. U., 1960—. Mem. Nat. Soc. Controllers and Financial Officers (past pres.). Presbyn. (deacon). Contbr. articles to profl. jours. Home: 96 Whitlock Av Marietta GA 30060 Office: Fulton Fed Bldg 11 Pryor St NE Atlanta GA 30303

MCCUTCHEON, ERNEST PARRISH, physician; b. Durham, N.C., May, 7, 1933; s. Ernest Parrish and Mary Hazel (Pleasants) McC.; B.S., Davidson Coll., 1955; M.D., Duke, 1959; m. Susan Angel Strader, Aug. 4, 1956; children—Mary Elizabeth, Ernest Parrish, James Sydnor. Intern, resident internal medicine and cardiovascular physiology, Atlanta, Durham, Seattle, 1959-61, 63-66; asst. prof. U. Ky., 1966-71, asso. prof., 1971—, chmn. Biomedical Engring. Council, 1972-73; vis. asso. prof. Stanford Med. Center, 1973—. Nat. Acad. Scis.-NRC research asso. NASA-Ames Research Center, 1973—. Served as capt. M.C., USAF, 1961-63. NIH Sr. Research fellow, 1963-66. Mem. I.E.E.E., A.A.A.S., Am., Ky. heart assns., Biomedical Engring. Soc., N.Y. Acad. Scis., Instrument Soc. Am., Sigma Xi, Kappa Alpha. Democrat. Presbyn. Editor: Chronically Implanted Cardiovascular Instrumentation, 1973. Office: Wenner-Gren Research Lab U Ky Lexington KY 40506

MCCUTCHEON, NANCY SUSAN, educator; b. Columbia, S.C., July 10, 1937; d. Samuel Durant and Nancy (Milford) McCutcheon; B.A., U. S.C., 1957, M.Ed., 1966, Ph.D., 1969; diploma, tchrs. certificate in piano Sherwood Music Sch., Chgo., 1959. Tchr., Belvedere Elementary Sch., Columbia, 1957-65; grad. teaching asst. Sch. Edn., U. S.C., Columbia, 1965-68, instr., 1968-70, asst. prof., 1970—. Pvt. piano tchr., 1955—; cons. substitute teaching program Williamsburg County, S.C., 1969-70; coordinator Career Opportunities Program, Williamsburg County, 1970-73, dir., 1973—. Mem. N.E.A., S.C. Edn. Assn., S.C. Assn. Student Teaching, Assn. Supervision and Curriculum Devel., Soc. Research Child Devel., Am. Ednl. Research Assn., Columbia Music Tchrs. Assn. (sec. 1964-66), So. Assn. Schs. and Colls. (vis. com.) Nat. Assn. Edn. Young Children, S.C. Fedn. Music Clubs (adjudicator piano festivals 1960—), Nat. Council Tchrs. English, Nat. Soc. Study Edn., So. Assn. Children Under Six, Phi Beta Kappa (sec.-treas. Alpha of S.C. chpt. 1970—), Kappa Delta Epsilon, Alpha Delta Kappa, Delta Kappa Gamma, Beta Sigma Phi (chpt. pres. 1961-62), Baptist. Club: Sherwood Music School Seminar (pres. 1967, 68). Contbr. to profl. publs. Home: 2911 Devine St Columbia SC 29205

MCDANIEL, BOYD JACK, city ofcl.; b. Abilene, Tex., Aug. 18, 1924; s. Boyd Joseph and Myrtle (Snodgrass) McD.; B.S., Agrl. and Mech. Coll. Tex., 1948; m. Elizabeth Ann Talbott, June 4, 1947; children—Boyd John, Bonnie Beth. Resident engr. Freese & Nichols, cons. engrs., Beaumont, San Angelo, Tex., 1948-52; constrn. engr. Boyd J. McDaniel Co., Abilene, Tex., 1953-62; dir. pub. works City of Abilene, 1962-66, City of Corpus Christi, Tex., 1966-72; dir. solid waste mgmt. City of Houston, 1972—. Served to 1st lt. C.E., AUS, 1943-46, 52-53. Registered profl. engr., Tex. Mem. Nat., Tex. socs. profl. engrs., Am. Pub. Works Assn. (pres. Tex. chpt. 1966, chmn. ho. of dels. 1974), Presbyn. (deacon 1956-57, elder 1958-66). Home: 9827 Vogue Lane Houston TX 77055 Office: City Hall Annex Houston TX 77001

MCDANIEL, CLAUDETTE BLACK (MRS. SYLVESTER W. MCDANIEL), broadcasting exec.; b. Richmond, Va., Dec. 12, 1939; d. Lawrence Nicklos and Leolia C. (Cheatham) Black; B.A., Va. Union U., 1964; postgrad. Va. Commonwealth U., 1965—; m. Sylvester W. McDaniel, Mar. 21, 1969; 1 dau., Claudine Renee. With radio sta. WANT, Richmond, 1950-68; pub. service dir. radio sta. WENZ, Richmond, 1968—, Spl. activities supr. Dept. Occupational Therapy, Health Sci. Center, Med. Coll. Va., 1970—; publicity chmn. Nat. Council of Coll. Women. Recipient Music Scholarship, Va. State Coll., 1957. Mem. Va. Recreational and Parks Soc., Nat. Recreational Soc., Alpha Phi Zeta chpt. Zeta Phi Beta. Home: 105 E 15th St Richmond VA 23224 Office: 111 N 4th St Richmond VA 23219

MCDANIEL, ESTES CRUDEN, farmer, state legislator; b. Pontotoc, Miss., June 28, 1909; s. Thomas L. and Janie (Inzer) McD.; B.S., U. Okla., 1931; M.A., George Peabody Coll., 1941; m. Grace B. Gary, June 30, 1951. Supt. schs., Trinity, Ala., 1932-42; supervising high sch. prin. Morgan County (Ala). Bd. Edn., 1942-52; farmer nr. Greenwood Miss., 1952—; mem. Miss. Ho. of Reps. from 15th Dist., 1964—. Bd. dirs. Lower Yazoo River Basin Dist., Cottonlandia Ednl. and Recreational Corp. Mem. Nat. Soc. State Legislators (charter mem., del. nat. conv. 1966, 68-70, charter pres. Miss. chpt. 1968-69, nat. gov. 1969-72), Farm Bur., Am. Miss. Angus assns., Rivers and Harbors Assn., Am. Soybean Assn., Miss. Forestry Assn., Miss. Cattlemen's Assn., Greenwood C. of C., S.A.R., Kappa Phi Kappa. Democrat. Presbyn. Mason (32 deg. Shriner), Elk, Lion, Odd Fellow, Woodman of World; mem. Order Eastern Star. Home: 301 E Claiborne St Greenwood MS 38930

MCDANIEL, FELIX CARSON, food service co. exec.; b. Lake Lure, N.C., Sept. 2, 1939; s. Donald Gordon and Jessie C. (Flynn) McD.; asso. Lees McRae Jr. Coll., 1957-59; B.S. in Bus. Adminstrn., Berea Coll., 1961; M.B.A., Ind. U., 1962; m. Janice Mayhall, Aug. 26, 1961; children—Stanley, Brian. Staff accountant, Arthur Young & Co., C.P.A.'s, 1963-65; controller Pepsi-Cola Bottling Co., Inc., Springfield, O., 1965-68; treas. All Am. Beverages, Winston-Salem, N.C., 1968-73; with Shoney's Big Boy Enterprises, Inc., Nashville, 1973—. Mem. Springfield Golf Commn., 1969—. C.P.A., N.C., Ohio. Mem. Am. Inst. C.P.A.'s, Beta Gamma Sigma, Beta Alpha Psi. Lion (pres. 1970—). Home: Route 2 High Lea Rd Brentwood TN 37027 Office: 1727 Elm Hill Pike Nashville TN 37122

MCDANIEL, HERMAN, ednl. adminstr.; b. Chattanooga, Apr. 17, 1938; s. Wiley Samuel and Amy Jane (Long) McD.; grad. high sch., 1955. Mem. staff Fgn. Service Inst., U.S. Dept. of State, Washington, 1962-64; instr. Computer Tng. br. U.S. Bur. of Census, Washington, 1964-67; with Automatic Data Processing Mgmt. Tng. Center, U.S. Civil Service Commn., Washington, 1968—, asso. dir., 1968—. Lectr. univs. and profl. groups, U.S. and abroad; cons. to numerous bus. firms. Served with AUS, 1959-62. Author: An Introduction to Decision Logic Tables, 1968; Applications of Decision Tables, 1970; Decision Table Software, 1970. Home: 1625 25th St SE Washington DC 20020 Office: The ADP Management Training Center US Civil Service Commission 1900 E St NW Washington DC 20415

MCDANIEL, THOMAS ZERE, gas co. engr.; b. St. Petersburg, Fla., July 27, 1925; s. Robert H. and Susie J. (Lovelace) McD.; B.S., Auburn U., 1950; postgrad. Rice U., 1963, U. Houston, 1960-64; m. Olga M. Caceres, Sept. 5, 1970; 1 dau., Dorothy B. Designer chs., homes, pub. bldgs., salesman Phillips Bros., Inc., Roanoke, Ala., 1950-54; jr. engr. Transcontinental Gas Compressor Sta., Roanoke, 1954-55; constrn. engr. Transco Gas Corp., Linden, N.J., 1955, div. pipeline engr., Baton Rouge, 1956-57, acting dist. pipeline supt., Laurel, Miss., 1958-59, engr. meter sta. design, Houston, 1959-62, sr. engr. in charge Tex., La., Ga. Pa., N.J., N.Y. stas., 1963—. Mem. instructional staff W.Va. U., 1962-71, U. Okla., 1966-68, U. Houston, 1968. Served with inf., AUS, World War II; ETO. Decorated Bronze Star medal, French and Belgian Fourragere. Mem. Instrument Soc. Am. (past edn. dir.), Nat. Gas Measurement Assn., Nat. Soc. Profl. Engrs., Engrs. Council Houston (past councilor), Am. Soc. M.E., U.S. Jr. C. of C. (past v.p. and acting pres.), V.F.W., Dramatic Order Knights of Khorassan. Mason, K.P., Rotarian. Contbr. articles to profl. jours. Home: 2119 DeMilo St Houston TX 77018 Office: PO Box 1396 Transco Gas Corp Houston TX 77001

MCDANIEL, WILLIAM ROBERT, tool co. exec.; b. Fayetteville, Ark., June 26, 1924; s. Aubrey and Minnie (Scott) McD.; B.S. in Mining Engring., Va. Poly. Inst., 1950; m. Janice Ruth Heineman, Nov. 7, 1959; children—Jeffrey, Mike. Pres., Prodn. Equipment Co., Milw., 1961-66; v.p. sales Mehl Machinery Co., Houston, 1966-69; pres. Tool Technologist Corp., Houston, 1968—. Served with AUS, World War II. Club: Houston Racquet. Home: 109 Sage Rd Houston TX 77027 Office: 400 Bringhurst St Houston TX 77020

MCDAVID, FREDERICK RHODES, cons. mech. engr.; b. Sanford, N.C., Dec. 26, 1924; s. James Philip and Nora (Foy) McD.; B. Mech. Engring., N.C. State U., 1948; postgrad. Carnegie Inst. Tech., 1949; m. Janet Frances Smiley, Jan. 19, 1950; children—Frederick R., Philip A., Susan K., Nora J., Robert J. Process engr. U.S. Steel Corp., Pitts., 1947-49; design engr. Walter Hook & Assos., Charlotte, N.C. 1950-51, H.K. Ferguson Co., Cleve., 1951-53; partner McDavid Co., Washington, 1954—. Cons. engr. master plan Haile Selassie I Univ., Ethiopia. Chmn., Fairfax County (Va.) Bd. Plumbing Examiners and Appeals, 1968—. Organizer, troop com. chmn. Nat. Capitol Area council Boy Scouts Am. Served with AUS, 1944-46. Registered profl. engr., D.C., Va., Md., Pa., Ohio, Fla., Conn., N.Y., Ga., Tex., N.J., Minn. Mem. Am. Soc. M.E., Cons. Engrs. Council, Am. Legion. Republican. Methodist (dir. 1960-61). Elk. Home: 9321 Convento Terrace Fairfax VA 22030 Office: 2430 Pennsylvania Av Washington DC 20037

MCDAVID, JOEL DUNCAN, clergyman; b. Georgetown, Ala., June 10, 1916; s. Harry and Ola Elizabeth (McCaskill) McD.; B.A., Millsaps Coll., 1941; B.D., Emory U., 1944; D.D., Birmingham So. Coll., 1959, Fla. So. U., 1973, Bethune-Cookman Coll., 1973; m. Milah Dodd Gibson, Aug. 29, 1942; children—Ben A., Joel G., Karen Anne. Ordained to ministry Meth. Ch., 1944; pastor Grand Bay, Ala., 1944-46, Toulminville, Ala., 1946-50, Auburn, Ala., 1950-58, First Meth. Ch., Montgomery, Ala., 1958-66, Dauphin Way Ch., Mobile, Ala., 1966-72; bishop United Meth. Ch., 1972—; faculty Auburn U., 1950-58. Mem. Ala. State Ethics Commn., 1966-67, Bi-racial Com. Montgomery, 1964-66, Mobile, 1970-72; v.p. United Meth. Southeastern Jurisdictional Council, 1968-72. Trustee Fla. So. Coll. Named Man of Year, Montgomery, 1965. Mason, Kiwanian. Author: Waiting, 1969. Home: 127 Lake Hollingsworth Dr Lakeland FL 33801 Office: 968 Callahan Ct Lakeland FL 33801

MCDEVITT, ELLEN, physician; b. Shubuta, Miss., Sept. 3, 1907; d. James Andrew and Alma (McManus) McDevitt; A.B., Miss. State Coll., 1930; M.D., U. Utah, 1949. Chief technician vascular clinic N.Y. Post Grad. Hosp., 1934-46; intern Meadowbrook Hosp., Hempstead, N.Y., 1949-50; asst. resident Hackensack (N.J.) Hosp., 1950-51, Bellevue Hosp., N.Y.C., 1953-54; research asso. medicine N.Y. Hosp.-Cornell U. Med. Coll., 1951-52; provisional asst. physician out patient dept. N.Y. Hosp., 1951-52; mem. staff, chief 2d med. div. vascular clinic Bellevue Hosp.; instr. medicine Cornell U., 1954-56, asst. prof., 1957-63, asso. prof., 1963-72; asso. attending N.Y. Hosp., dir. vascular sect., 1968-72, courtesy staff, 1972—; cons. staff Watkins Meml. Hosp., Quitman, Miss. Fellow Am. Soc. Geratics; mem. A.M.A., Am. (fellow council on circulation, fellow council on stroke), N.Y., Miss. heart assns., Miss. Med. Assn., East Miss. Med. Soc., Altrusa Internat., Sigma Xi. Contbr. articles to profl. jours. Home: 1520 Olive St Gulfport MS 39501

MCDILL, EDWIN BRANDAO, librarian; b. New Orleans, June 11, 1936; s. James Delph and Esther Mary (Brandao) McD.; B.S., Spring Hill Coll., 1958; M.S., La. State U., 1960; m. Lucinda Lanning, July 12, 1963; 1 dau., Lucinda Amy. Librarian, Cranwell Sch., Lenox, Mass., 1960-62; reference librarian Holy Cross Coll., Worcester, Mass., 1962-64; reference asst. Greensboro (N.C.) Pub. Library, 1964-67; asst. librarian Guilford Tech. Inst., Jamestown, N.C., 1967—. Active Buten Mus. Wedgwood, Merion, Pa., Dyson Perrins Mus., Worcester, Eng., Friends Salisbury (Eng.) Cathedral. Mem. Am. Vocational Assn., Southeastern, N.C. library assns., Guilford Library Club, Greensboro Preservation Soc., Wedgwood Soc. London. Contbr. articles to mags. Home: 1705 Efland Dr Greensboro NC 27408 Office: Box 309 Jamestown NC 27282

MCDONALD, ALVIS EDWARD, mathematician; b. Clarksville, Tex., June 12, 1935; s. Cecil Edward and Edith Mae (Roberts) McD.; B.S. in Math. (Inst. Alumni Fund scholar), N.M. Inst. Mining and Tech., 1959, B.S. in Petroleum Engring. (Socony Mobil scholar), 1960; M.A., Wash. State U., 1962; Ph.D. (Mobil Oil fellow), U. Tex., 1970; m. JoAnn Rotunno, June 4, 1960; children—James Patrick, Belinda Kathleen, Maureen Elizabeth. Tchr. math, physics Socorro (N.M.) High Sch., 1960; research technologist Mobil Research & Devel., Dallas, 1963-65, sr. research mathematician, 1968-73, research asso., 1973—. Precinct chmn. Republican party, 1969-70. Ford Found. scholar, 1954-55. Mem. Soc. Petroleum Engrs., Soc. Computer Simulation. Republican. Roman Catholic. Home: 1805 Egyptian Dr Dallas TX 75232 Office: PO Box 900 Field Research Lab Dallas TX 75221

MCDONALD, CHARLES DONALD, JR., physician; b. Athens, Ga., July 23, 1937; s. Charles Donald and Kathleen Lou (Henderson) McD.; B.S. in Biology magna cum laude, N.Ga. Coll., 1959; M.D., Med. Coll. Ga., 1963; m. Janet Cleo Whitfield, July 23, 1960; children—Charles Donald III, Timothy Whitfield, David Patrick. Intern, USPHS Hosp., Balt., 1963-64; resident USPHS Hosp., New Orleans, 1964-66, dep. chief medicine, also chief cardiology, 1968-70; fellow in cardiology Tulane Med. Sch., New Orleans, 1966-68, instr. in medicine, 1966-70; practice medicine specializing in cardiology, Chattanooga, 1970—; clin. instr. internal medicine and cardiology Erlanger Hosp., Chattanooga, 1970—; mem. staffs Meml., Hutchinson Meml., Diagnostic hosps. (all Chattanooga), Tri-County Hosp., Ft. Oglethorpe, Ga. Trustee Christian Counseling Service, Chattanooga. Served with USPHS, 1963-70. Decorated Commendation medal. Diplomate Am. Bd. Internal Medicine, Am. Bd. Cardiovascular Disease. Fellow Am. Coll. Cardiology, A.C.P.; mem. Am. Heart Assn. (fellow council clin. cardiology), Alpha Omega Alpha. Presbyn. (deacon). Contbr. articles on cardiovascular disease to med. jours. Home: 1116 Cumberland Rd Elder Mountain TN 37409 Office: 2410 McCallie Av Chattanooga TN 37404

MCDONALD, CLARENCE JACKSON, mfg. co. exec., lawyer; b. Junction, Tex., Dec. 12, 1926; s. Clarence Grenville and Minnie Ila (Dunning) McD.; B.S., Trinity U., San Antonio, 1950; J.D., So. Meth. U., 1966; m. Barbara June Kennon, Apr. 9, 1950; children—Zane Jay, Laurie Jill. Electronics engr. San Antonio Air Material Command, 1950-54; chief engr. Mathes Co., Marble Falls, Tex., 1955-62; exec. v.p. Folsom Co., Dallas, 1962-66; admitted to Tex. bar, 1966; since practiced in Dallas; pres., co-founder Electric Products Mfg. Corp., Mesquite, Tex., 1968—. Served with USNR, 1942-44; PTO. Mem. I.E.E.E. Mason, Kiwanian. Methodist. Home: 2523 Greenport Dr Dallas TX 75228 Office: 800 E Kearney St Mesquite TX 75149

MCDONALD, CLIFFORD WILLIAM, clergyman; b. Chgo., June 7, 1931; s. Clifford William and Irene May (Krampe) McD.; student U. Ill., 1950-51, Chgo. Tchrs. Coll., summer 1956; A.B., Anderson Coll. and Theol. Sem., 1959; postgrad. Emory U., 1961; m. Ruth A. Lee, Aug. 2, 1952; children—David L., Connie L., Judith A. With C.W. McDonald & Son, accountants, Blue Island, Ill., 1954-56; ordained to ministry Ch. of God, 1960; pastor Bay Shore Chapel Ch. of God, Clearwater, Fla., 1959-62, Community Ch. of God, Melbourne, 1962-67, First Ch. of God, Bradenton, 1967—. Mem. exec. com., historian Gen. Assembly of Ch. of God in Fla., 1971-72, chmn. bd. Christian edn., chmn. state program com., 1968-69. Chapalin C.A.P. Brevard County and Sarasota County, 1970-71, Manatee County Cancer Assn., 1973; pres. Manatee High Sch. P.T.A., 1973—. Bd. dirs. Manatee Safety Council, 1973—. Served with AUS, 1952-54. Mem. Fla. Ministerial Assn. Ch. of God (sec.-treas. 1960-63), Manatee County Ministerial Assn. (pres. 1972-73). Kiwanian (chmn. citizenship com. 1974—). Home: 5411 14th Av Dr W Bradenton FL 33505 Office: 2520 43d St W Bradenton FL 33505

MCDONALD, EDGAR HASKELL, state ofcl.; b. Cloud Chief, Okla., Sept. 18, 1907; s. James Edgar and Corda McDonald; B.S., Southwestern State Coll. Weatherford, Okla., 1933; M.A., Western State Coll., Gunnison, Colo., 1939; m. Kathryn O'Hara Waggoner, May 13, 1944; children—Stephen, Deborah. Tchr., adminstr. pub. schs., Carter, Walters, Vimson, Verden, Gracemont, Noble (all Okla.); dep. and asst. supt. edn. State of Okla., Oklahoma City. Served with AUS. Mem. Okla. Assn. Sch. Adminstrs., N.E.A. Mason (32 deg.), Lion. Home: 4508 NW 32d St Oklahoma City OK 73122 Office: Room 328 State Capitol Bldg Oklahoma City OK 73105

MCDONALD, ERWIN LAWRENCE, clergyman, editor; b. London, Ark., Oct. 31, 1907; s. Frank Floyd and Rebecca Geneva (Powell) McD.; grad. Ark. Poly. Coll., 1932; A.B., Ouachita Coll., 1943; B.D., So. Baptist Theol. Sem., 1947; Litt. D., Georgetown Coll., 1958; m. Mary Elsie Price, Mar. 1, 1930; children—Avis Jeannine (Mrs. Sam H. Jones, Jr.), Judy Carole (Mrs. J. W. Lucas). Press corr., Russellville, Ark., 1932-37; city editor Daily Courier-Democrat, 1937-41; ordained to ministry Baptist Ch., 1938; editor So. Standard, Arkadelphia, Ark., 1941-43; instr. Ouachita Coll., 1943-44, pastor Washington (Ark.) Bapt. Ch., 1942-44, Sligo Ch.Pendleton, Ky., 1944-47; dir. pub. relations So. Bapt. Theol. Sem., 1944-51, editor The Tie, 1947-51; dir. pub. relations Furman U. and editor Furman U. Mag., 1951-54; exec. sec. edn. Gen. Assn. Bapts. in Ky., 1954-57; editor Ark. Bapt., Little Rock, 1957-72; religion editor Ark. Democrat, Little Rock, 1972—. Chmn., Ark. Literacy Com., 1965; mem. Ark. adv. com. U.S. Commn. on Civil Rights. Dir. Christian Civic Found. Ark., Inc.; bd. dirs. Asso. Ch. Press, 1969-72; asso. dir. Scotland Bapt. Evangelistic Crusade, 1961. Recipient Distinguished Alumnus award Ouachita Coll., 1960, Distinguished Bapt. Minister award So. Bapt. Coll., 1963; hon. Ky. col., 1963; named Alumnus of Yr., So. Bapt. Theol. Sem., 1972. Mem. C. of C., So. Bapt. Press Assn. (pres. 1965), Greater Little Rock Ministerial Assn. (pres. 1965), Inst. Fundamental Communication (rec, sec. 1965). Democrat. Rotarian. Author: The Church Using the Newspaper, 1961; 75 Stories & Illustrations from Everyday Life, 1964; (with Ralph Creger) A Look Down the Lonesome Road, 1964; Across the Editors Desk, 1966; Stories for Speakers and Writers, 1970. Editor: The Church Proclaiming and Witnessing, 1966. Home and Office: 1419 Garland Av North Little Rock AR 72116

MCDONALD, FRANK GOODALL, appellate judge; b. Meridian, Tex., Apr. 9, 1916; s. John Francis and Helen Leonese (Tomlinson) McD.; student Hillsboro Coll., 1933-34; B.A., Baylor U., 1936; LL.B., U. Tex., 1938; m. Artie Louise Vanderford, Dec. 22, 1948; 1 dau., Luann Leonese. Admitted to Tex. bar, 1938; practiced in Hillsboro, 1938-40; judge 66th Jud. Dist. Tex., Hillsboro, 1947-52; chief justice Ct. Civil Appeals, Waco, 1953—. Served from pvt. to col., AUS, 1940-46. Mem. Am., Waco bar assns., State Bar Tex., Am. Legion, V.F.W., Delta Theta Phi. Democrat. Episcopalian. Mason (K.T., Shriner), K.P., Odd Fellow, Lion. Home: 2407 Starr St Waco TX 76710 Office: Courthouse Waco TX 76701

MCDONALD, HENRY BURNSIDE, constrn. co. exec.; b. Yatesville, Ga., June 15, 1912; s. John Braxton and Henrietta May (Burnside) McD.; student U. Ga., 1929-32; m. Margaret Lee Wade, Sept. 12, 1943; children—Betty Ann (Mrs. M. John Thomas), Henry Burnside, James Malcolm. Jr. engr. U.S. Dept. Agr., 1932-35; party chief surveys W.S. Lee Engring. Co., 1935-37; design engr. J.E. Greiner Co., 1937-40; gen. supt. Blythe Bros., 1940-42, 51-53; asst. mgr. Koppers Co., 1946-50; v.p. Wright Contracting Co., Columbus, Ga., 1954—, also dir.; v.p., dir. Concrete Pavers, Inc.; pres., dir. Wright C.Am. Gov., Md. Safety Council, 1961-64. Served to lt. comdr. USNR, 1942-46. Registered profl. engr., Md. Mem. Am. Soc. M.E., Am. Soc. C.E., Am. Soc. Hwy. Engrs., Nat. Asphalt Paving Assn. (dir.), Am. Rd. Builders Assn. (nat. safety com.), Ga. Asphalt Assn. (dir., exec. com.), Moles. Rotarian. Home: 15 Greensland Vista Standing Boy Rd Columbus GA 31904 Office: Box 1580 506 Coolidge Av Columbus GA 31902

MCDONALD, JACK WILLIAM, govt. ofcl.; b. San Francisco, May 26, 1918; s. Jack Shire and Pine Lorraine (Hawkes) McD.; grad. high sch.; m. Phyllis Irene Bowen, Feb. 10, 1950; children—Jack Robert, William Forrest. Enlisted U.S. Army, 1937, advanced through grades to lt. col., 1954, ret., 1959; with Dept. Def., Washington, 1959-62; with Def. Communications Agy., Washington, 1962—, dep. chief plans div. Plans and Programs Directorate, 1970—. Mem. Assn. U.S. Army, Armed Forces Communications Electronics Assn., I.E.E.E., Ind. Telephone Pioneers Assn. Club: internat. Town and Country (Fairfax, Va.). Home: 1100 N Powhatan St Arlington VA 22205 Office: Code 410 Defense Communications Agency Washington DC 20305

MCDONALD, JAMES CLIFTON, educator; b. Oklahoma City, Apr. 2, 1930; s. James C. and Dorothy E. (Cox) McD.; A.B., Washington U., St. Louis, 1952; M.A., U. Mo., 1957, Ph.D., 1960; m. Caroline Jane Rush, Aug. 29, 1954; children—Ben, David, Kathryn. Asst. prof. biology Wake Forest U., Winston-Salem, N.C., 1960-65, asso. prof., 1965—, chmn. biology dept., 1971—. Served with AUS, 1952-54. Mem. A.A.A.S., N.C. Acad. Sci., Assn. Southeastern Biologists (sec. 1973-76), Mycol. Soc. Am., Am. Inst. Biol. Scis., Sigma Xi. Home: Box 416 Route 1 King NC 27021

MCDONALD, LAURIER BERNARD, lawyer; b. Memphis, Oct. 3, 1931; s. Laurier Bernard and Mary Eva (Covington) McD.; B.A. in History, Tex. Arts and Industry U., 1957; J.D., U. Tex., 1961; m. Juanita Littleton, June 11, 1960; children—James, Rebecca, John, Susan. Admitted to Tex. bar, 1961; spl. agt. FBI, Quantico, Va., 1961, Tampa, Fla., 1961-62, Washington, 1962-63, San Juan, P.R., 1963-65, N.Y.C., 1965-66; partner firm Pena, McDonald, Gutierrez & Prestia, Edinburg, Tex., 1966—. U.S. commr. So. Dist. Tex., Edinburg, 1966-71; adj. prof. drug abuse and organized crime Pan Am. U., Edinburg, 1972. Chmn. Hidalgo County Hist. Commn., 1966-73. Turstee Haggar Student Fund, Edinburg. Served with USMCR, 1951-53. Mem. Assn. Immigration and Nationality Lawyers (gov.), Edinburg C. of C. (pres. 1973), Alpha Chi, Phi Alpha Theta. Roman Catholic. Club: Rotary of Edinburg. Home: 1027 S 12th St Edinburg TX 78539 Office: PO Drawer 54 Edinburg TX 78539

MCDONALD, LAWRENCE LOWN, petroleum co. exec.; b. Omaha, Jan. 17, 1913; s. Paul Tamble and Kittie Belle (Lown) McD.; B.S. in Mech. Engring., Purdue U., 1934; grad. exec. devel. program, Cornell U., 1956; m. Mary Alice Montgomery, July 3, 1935. Various positions, including mgr. operations Pure Oil Co., Palatine, Ill., 1935-65; v.p. prodn. Champlin Petroleum Co., Ft. Worth, 1965—. Served to maj. AUS, 1942-46; ETO. Decorated Bronze Star. Registered profl. engr., Tex. Mem. Am. Petroleum Inst. (mem. gen. com., exec. com. drilling and prodn. practices; certificate of appreciation 1968, citation for service 1964), Soc. Petroleum Engrs., Tex. Midcontinental Oil and Gas Assn., Ind. Petroleum Assn., W. Central Tex. Oil and Gas Assn. Clubs: Fort Worth Boat, Petroleum (dir.), Shady Oaks Country (Ft. Worth). Home: Rural Route 9 Box 187 Fort Worth TX 76179 Office: Box 9365 Fort Worth TX 76107

MCDONALD, OLIN KENNETH, sch. adminstr.; b. Marshville, N.C., Apr. 7, 1919; s. John Norman and Ruth (Dees) McD.; A.B., U. S.C., 1941, M.Ed., 1949; m, Ann McCutchen, July 12, 1942; children—John Michael, Robert Norman. Tchr. pub. sch., Camden, S.C., 1947-55; prin. Willow Dr. Elementary Sch., Sumter, S.C., 1955-60, McLaurin Jr. High Sch., Sumter, 1960-69; coordinator instructional media Dist. 17, 1969—. Instr. extension div. U. S.C., 1949—. Mem. bd. advisers Am. Security Council, 1972—. Bd. dirs. Art Mus. Served to capt. USAAF, 1941-47; lt. col. Res. Decorated Air medal with three oak leaf clusters, D.F.C, with oak leaf cluster. Mem. Nat. Assn. Secondary Prins., S.C. Edn. Assn., S.C. Assn. Elementary Tchrs. (dir. 1971-73), Am. Legion, Blue Key, Pi Kappa Phi. Democrat. Presbyn. (supt. sr. dept. 1964-65). Elk (youth com.). Home: 120 Willow Dr Sumter SC 29150

MCDONALD, OWEN PETER, govt. ofcl.; b. Yankton, S.D., June 5, 1916; s. Peter Joseph and Beatrice (Cogan) McD.; teaching certificate Black Hills Tchrs. Coll., 1936; B.A., Neb. State Coll., 1939; M.A., Am. U., 1954; m. Elinor Dawn Johnson, Sept. 24, 1942; children—Kathleen Ann, John Owen, Lawrence Edward. Tchr., adminstr. Shannon County Pub. Schs., Denby, S,D., 1939-41; personnel classification analyst WPB, 1941-42; mem, planning staff, asst. adminstr, for constrn., supply and real estate VA, Washington, 1946-48; analyst mgmt. div. Hdqrs. USAF, Washington, 1948-51, chief systems and procedures br. mgmt. div., 1951-55; specialist for analysis and rev. properties and installations Office Asst. Sec. Def., Washington, 1955, staff asst., 1955-56, chief mgmt. div., 1957-58, realty officer Dept. Def., 1958-65, chief mgmt. and reporting div. contract support services directorate, 1965-70, contract specialist, 1970—; spl. asst. to adminstr. Gen. Services Adminstrn., Washington, 1956. Served from 2d lt. to capt., AUS, 1942-46; CBI; col. USAF Res, Decorated Bronze Star medal, Air Force Commendation medal. Mem. Am. Polit. Sci. Assn. Roman Catholic. K.C. Home: 9000 Linton Lane Stratford on the Potomac Alexandria VA 22308 Office: Pentagon Washington DC 20330

MCDONALD, ROBERTSON, advt. agy. pres.; b. Nashville, May 12, 1927; s. Hunter and Clara Hendon (Gilliland) McD.; student U. of South, 1946-48; m. Patricia Herbert Potter, Jan. 22, 1954; children—William D., Edward P., Robertson, Donald. Account exec. Ruthrauff & Ryan Advt., Chgo., 1948-51; account exec., mgr. br. Griswold Eshleman Advt., Nashville, 1951-53; pres. McDonald & Assos., Nashville, 1953—. High commr., Clan Donald, U.S.A., 1970—. Trustee, Isle of Skye, Scotland; pres. bd. govs. Sewanee Acad., 1973—. Mem. Nashville Advt. Fedn. Clubs: Harbor Island Yacht (commodore 1971-72), Bellemeade Country, Cumberland, Nashville City. Patentee non-breakable thermometer. Home: 4905 Franklin Rd Nashville TN 37220 Office: 1220 McGavock St Nashville TN 37203

MCDONALD, WILLIAM CHARLES, educator; b. Chgo., Feb. 14, 1933; s. Justin Joseph and Avis Margaret (Pillsbury) McD.; B.S., U. Okla., 1955; Ph.D., U. Tex., 1959; m. Matilda Jane Metz, Oct. 19,

1957; children—Kathryn, Judith, Susan, Laura. Research asso. Children's Hosp., Buffalo, 1959-60; asst. prof. Wash. State U., Pullman, 1962-65; asso. prof. biology Tulane U., New Orleans, 1965-72, prof. 1972-73; prof., chmn. dept. biology U. Tex., Arlington, 1973—. Served to 1st. lt. Chem. Corps, AUS, 1960-62. NSF grantee, 1963-67. Fellow Am. Acad. for Microbiology; mem. Am. Soc. Microbiology (sec. treas. south central br. 1969-71, v.p. 1971-73), A.A.A.S., Sigma Xi. Home: 1708 Tennyson St Arlington TX 76013

MCDONALD, WILLIAM HENRY, JR., broadcasting co. exec.; b. Corpus Christi, Tex., Jan. 26, 1944; s. William Henry and Ruth Cock (Sturdivant) M.; student Del Mar Jr. Coll., 1962-63; journalism scholar Pan Am. Coll., Edinburg, 1964; m. Dorothy Joann Ewing, Feb. 1, 1964; children—Darin, Jeff, Dianna. News editor Radio Stas. KTSA and KONO, San Antonio, Tex., 1964-65; news dir. KEYS Radio, Corpus Christi, 1966-70; news dir. KIII-TV, Corpus Christi, 1970—. Gen. chmn. Leadership Corpus Christi, 1974—. Mem. U.P.I. Broadcasters Assn. Tex. (pres. 1970, 73). Mem. Christian Ch. Club: Corpus Christi Press (pres. 1971). Home: 215 Blanco Portland TX 78437 Office: 4645 Ocean Dr Corpus Christi TX 78412

MCDONALD, WILLIAM LINDSEY, govt. ofcl.; b. Florence, Ala., June 7, 1927; s. William Ervin and Pauline McRann (Lindsey) McD.; B.S., Florence State U., 1952; m. Dorothy Evelyn Carter, Nov. 3, 1945; children—Nancy Carter (Mrs. Marvin McDaniel Buttram), Suzannah Lee. Cost engr. TVA, Muscle Shoals, Ala., 1953-64, editor, reports writer, 1964-67, planner and supr. scheduling and records, nat. fertilizer devel. center, 1967—. Adviser Ala. Hist. Commn., 1968—; mem. Am. Bicentennial Com. of Florence, 1973-74; mem. com. on restoration of historic Wesleyan hall Florence State U., 1973—; chmn. city hist. bd., head city museums City of Florence (Ala.), 1968—. Served with AUS, 1945-47, 51-53; now lt. col. Res. Mem. Tenn. Valley Hist. Soc. (pres. 1963), N. Ala. Hist. Assn. (pres. 1969-72), S.R., Sons of Confederacy. Methodist (ordained to ministry 1949). Bd. editors Historic Muscle Shoals, 1962. Contbr. articles to various publs. Home: 2207 Berry Av Florence AL 35630 Office: Tennessee Valley Authority Muscle Shoals AL 35660

MCDONOUGH, THOMAS JOSEPH, bishop; b. Phila., Dec. 5, 1911; s. Michael Francis and Margaret Mary (Nolnan) McD.; A.B., St. Charles Sem., Phila., 1935; J.C.D., Catholic U. Am., 1941. Ordained priest Roman Cath. Ch. in Cathedral of Phila, May 26, 1938; asst. pastor, Cathedral and St. Charles parish, Phila., 1938-40; vice-chancellor, chancellor, vicar gen. officialis, diocese of St. Augustine, Fla., 1941-48; pastor of Cathedral, St. Augustine, 1943-45; apptd. domestic prelate, 1945; consecrated bishop, St. Augustine, 1947; bishop of St. Augustine, 1947-57; aux. bishop of Savannah, Ga., 1957-60, archbishop, 1960-67; archbishop of Louisville, 1967—. Author: Apostolic Administrators, 1941. Home: 40 Cathedral Place Louisville KY 40203 Office: 212 E College St Louisville KY 40203

MCDOWELL, ALFRED NORMAN, petroleum exporation co. exec.; b. Tulsa, Feb. 15, 1915; s. George Madison and Bettie (Joplin) McD.; B.S., Colo. Sch. Mines, 1940; M.S., Tex. A. & M. U., 1951; m. Esta Lee Hazlewood, May 9, 1962; children—Linda Nuttall, Mary Lee (Mrs. Roland Bandy), Jean, James. Geophysicist, Creole Petroleum Co., Caracas, Venezuela, 1940-48; asso. prof., geol. research asso. Tex. A. & M. U., 1948-51; geologist Tex. Gulf Sulphur Co., Houston, 1951-55; geologist, mgr. Tenneco Oil Co., Houston, 1955—. Trustee Wilchester Assn. Served with USNR, 1942-46. Mem. Am. Assn. Petroleum Geologists, Soc. Exploration Geophysicists, Houston Geol. Soc., Tau Beta Pi. Presbyn. (deacon 1965). Kiwanian. Clubs: Lakeside Country (Houston); Lakeway Yacht (Austin, Tex.). Home: 355 Cinnamon Oak Houston TX 77024 Office: Tenneco Oil Co PO Box 2511 Houston TX 77001

MCDOWELL, JOHN HOLMWOOD, security analyst; b. Buffalo, Feb. 6, 1932; s. William Harold and Marion (Holmwood) M.; B.A., Hiram Coll., 1953; postgrad. U. Buffalo, 1958-60, U. Richmond, 1965-67; m. Stasia T. Mayfield, Nov. 11, 1967. Registered rep. Doolittle & Co., Buffalo, 1958-63; security analyst United Va. Bank, Richmond, 1963-68; dir. regional research Abbott, Proctor & Paine, Richmond, 1968-71; sr. securtiy analyst Wheat, First Securities, Richmond, 1971—. Served with AUS, 1953-55. Mem. N.Y., Richmond socs. financial analysts, Home Furnishings Splinter Group. Presbyn. (deacon 1967—). Club: Bull and Bear. Contbr. articles on home furnishings to mags. Home: 602 Baldwin Rd Richmond VA 23229 Office: 801 E Main St Richmond VA 23219

MCDOWELL, JOHN WILLIS, educator; b. Honolulu, Dec. 12, 1921; s. James Rhea and Sarah Elizabeth (Willis) McD.; student Loyola U., Chgo., 1939-43; B.S., Colo. State U., 1947, M.S., 1948; postgrad. Okla. State U., 1948-49; M.P.H., U. N.C., 1950; Ph.D., Okla. State U., 1953; m. Hazel Gilchrist, Aug. 6, 1950; children—Jean Carol, Kenneth Edward. Parasitologist, Mut. Security Agy., USPHS, Cambodia, Laos and Vietnam, 1951-53, chief malaria control ICA, Iran, 1954-56, chief malariologist, Philippines, 1956-60, regional malaria adviser Western Pacific region, 1960-61, asst. chief Vector Control Tng. sect. Center for Disease Control USPHS, 1961-64; chief of evaluation Aedes Aegypte Eradication Project, Center for Disease Control, 1964-66, asst. chief of evaluation Malaria Eradication Project, 1966-69; asso. prof. biology Berry Coll., Mt. Berry, Ga., 1969-72, prof. biology, 1972—. Cons., WHO, 1964, AID, 1964-69. Served with AUS, 1943-46. Mem. Ga. Acad. Sci., Nat. Environmental Health Assn., Commd. Officers Assn. USPHS. Contbr. articles profl. jours. Home: 5 Beaver Run Rome GA 30161 Office: Dept Biology Berry Coll Mount Berry GA 30149

MCDOWELL, WILETT EDWIN, pulpwood co. exec; b. Damascus, Ga., Dec. 9, 1914; s. Edd C. and Nancy Lou (Wiley) McD.; student pub. schs; m. Pearl Willis, Jan. 18, 1941; children—Ladon, Dolores Ann, Janis Regina. Farmer, Damascus, 1937—; owner McDowell's Garage & Service Sta., Damascus, 1951—; partner Harper Lumber Co., Blakely, Ga., 1954-73; dealer Gt. No. Paper Co., Cedar Springs, Ga., 1963—; pres., owner W.E. McDowell Pulpwood Co., Inc., Damascus, 1967—. Mem. Early County Bd. Edn., 1966—. Mem. Cattlemens Assn., Early County Farm Bur. Baptist. Mason (Shriner). Home: Route 1 Box 163 Damascus GA 21741 Office: Route 1 Damascus GA 31741

MCDOWELL, WILLIAM LEWIS, JR., archivist; b. Chester, S.C., Sept. 3, 1926; s. William Lewis and Carrie Jane (White) McD.; B.S., Clemson Coll., 1949; M.A. (R. Means Davis fellow), U. S.C., 1953; m. Martha Isabel Rowell, Sept. 10, 1956; children—Martha Ellen, William Lewis III. Archivist, Hist. Commn. S.C. and S.C. Archives Dept., Columbia, 1953-60; asst. dir. S.C. Archives Dept., Columbia, 1961-68; dep. dir. S.C. Dept. Archives and History, Columbia, 1968—. Served with USNR, 1945-46. Recipient award of merit Am. Assn. State and Local History, 1971. Fellow Soc. Am. Archivists; mem. Am. Records Mgmt. Assn., S.C. Soc., S.C. Hist. Assn., S.C. Hist. Soc., Nat. Microfilm Assn. Methodist. Editor: Journal of Commissioners of Indian Trade, 1710-18, 1955; Documents Relating to Indian Affairs, 1750-1754, 1958; Documents Relating to Indian Affairs, 1754-65, 1970. Home: 3304 Oakdale Rd West Columbia SC 29169 Office: 1430 Senate St Columbia SC 29201

MCDOWELL, WILLIAM RALSTON, lawyer; b. Shreveport, La., Jan. 18, 1917; s. Milas R. and Mollie (Ayres) McD.; B.B.A., U. Tex., 1940, LL.B., 1940; m. Fern Bronstad, Sept. 15, 1939; children—Rebecca Gail (Mrs. W. Lionel Carver), Mollye Aleda (Mrs. F. Folson Bell) (dec.). Admitted to Tex. bar, 1940; spl. agt. FBI, Washington, 1940-41; adminstrv. asst to dir., 1941-45; asso. law firm McBride & Johnson, Dallas, 1945-47; asst. dist. atty. Dallas County, 1947-48; atty. gen. atty. T. & P. Ry., Dallas, 1948-58. v.p., gen. counsel, 1959—; gen. counsel So. Lines, M.P. R.R., Dallas, 1962—; dir. Abilene & So. Ry., Gt. S.W. R.R., Mchts. Cold Storage, Tex-N.M. Ry. Co., Tex. Pacific R.R. Co. Mem. Fed., Am., Dallas, Inter-Am. bar assns. State Bar Tex. Am. Judicature Soc., ICC Practioners, Soc. Former Agts. FBI. Lutheran. Home: 5353 Edmondson St Dallas TX 75209 Office: Fidelity Union Tower Dallas TX 75201

MCELHANEY, JOHN HESS, lawyer; b. Milw., Apr. 16, 1934; s. Lewis Keck and Sara (Hess) McE.; B.B.A., So. Methodist U., 1956, J.D., 1958; m. Jacquelyn Masur, Aug. 4, 1962; children—Scott, Vicky. Admitted to Tex. bar, 1958; asso. law firm Woodgate, Richards & McElhaney, Dallas, 1958-62; partner firm Turner, Rodgers, Sailers, Jordan & Calloway, Dallas, 1962—; lectr. law So. Meth. U. Sch. Law, 1967—. Mem. Tex. State (chmn. com. on substantive law changes and advancements 1969-70), Am. (regional chmn. com. on automobile reparations, 1973—, mem. com. on achievement justice through adversary system 1971-72), Am. Bd. Trial Advocates, So. Meth. U. Law Alumni Assn. (dir. 1970-73, pres. 1972-73). Presbyn. Mason. Clubs: Town and Gown, Calyx, So. Meth. U. Mustang (dir. 1969-71). Contbr. articles to legal jours. Home: 7138 Lakehurst St Dallas TX 75230 Office: 2400 Republic Nat Bank Bldg Dallas TX 75201

MCELHINNEY, JOHN, physicist; b. Phila., Mar. 25, 1921; s. Joseph and Mary (Kearney) McE.; B.S., Ursinus Coll., 1942; M.S., U. Ill., 1943, Ph.D., 1947; m. Geraldine E. Walters, Dec. 28, 1942; children—Ruth Elaine, Barbara Jill (Mrs. Chester Garner). Spl. research asso. U. Ill., Urbana, 1947-48; research asso. Los Alamos (N.M.) Sci. Lab., 1948-49; supervisory scientist Nat. Bur. Standards, Washington, 1949-55; br. head Naval Research Lab., Washington, 1955-66, supt. nuclear scis. div., 1966—. Recipient Superior Accomplishment award Nat. Bur. Standards, 1954; Presdl. citation Naval Research Lab., 1964. Fellow Am. Phys. Soc., Wash. Acad. Scis.; mem. Am. Nuclear Soc., I.E.E.E., A.A.A.S., Philos. Soc. Wash., Research Soc. Am. Home: 11601 Stephen Rd Silver Spring MD 20904 Office: Naval Research Lab Washington DC 20375

MCELRATH, ROBERT LEE, supt. schs.; b. Candler, N.C., July 4, 1928; s. Alonzo and Nova (Peebles) McE.; student Mars Hill Jr. Coll., 1945-49; A.B., Baldwin-Wallace Coll., 1951; M.P.H., U. N.C., 1957; Ed.D., U. Tenn., 1968; m. Betty A. Duck, Dec. 24, 1948; children—Richard S., Robin L. Tchr., Buncome County Schs., Asheville, N.C., 1951-56, prin. elementary sch., 1958-59, prin. sr. high sch., 1956-66; asso. dir. sch. planning lab. U. Tenn., 1966-68; supt. schs., Greeneville, Tenn., 1968—. Vis. lectr. U. Tenn., summers 1969-70, Tusculum Coll., 1969—; sch. plant cons. Bd. dirs. Greeneville YMCA. Served with AUS, 1946-48. Mem. Am. Assn. Sch. Adminstrs., N.E.A., Council Ednl. Facility Planners. Lion. Home: 208 Sasong Lane Greeneville TN 37743 Office: PO Box 30 Greeneville TN 37743

MCELREATH, JESSE DALE, assn. exec.; b. Big Spring, Tex., Nov. 7, 1938; s. Jesse James and Myrtle Estelle (Lancaster) McE.; A.A., Howard County Jr. Coll., 1959; B.A., Tex. Tech. U., 1961, postgrad., 1961-62; postgrad. U. Tenn., Nashville, 1964-74; m. Frances Darlene Williams, Aug. 15, 1959; children—Dana Danise, Marcus Dale. Asst. to dir. branded sales Cosden Petroleum Corp., Big Spring, 1962-63, Am. Petrofina, Inc., Dallas, 1963-64; sr. research analyst Bapt. Sunday Sch. Bd., Nashville, 1964-68, Broadman Press marketing planning coordinator 1968—. Asst. to prof. marketing Tex. Tech. U., 1961-62. Mem. Am. Marketing Assn. (pres. Lubbock chpt. 1962). So. Baptist (minister music, deacon). Home: Route 7 Foxwood Lane Franklin TN 37064 Office: 127 9th Av N Nashville TN 37203

MCELROY, B. THOMAS, lawyer; b. Dallas, Nov. 22, 1922; s. Howard D. and Ruby (Dyess) McE.; grad. Phillips Acad., 1940; B.A., Yale U., 1945; LL.B., U. Tex., 1949; m. Linda Lee Harris, July 11, 1959; children—Elizabeth Lynn, B. Thomas, Leslie Jane, Andrew Harris. Admitted to Tex. bar, 1949; legislative asst. to U.S. Congressman Lloyd Bentsen, 1949-50; asst. atty. gen. of Tex. to Price Daniel, 1950-51; asso. law firm Estes & Cantwell, Dallas, 1952-54; asso. firm Turner, White, Atwood, Meer & Francis, Dallas, 1955-56, partner, 1957-62; partner firm White, McElroy, White & Sides, Dallas, 1963—; mem. grievance com. 5th Dist. State Bar of Tex., 1967-69. Candidate for Republican nomination for Gov. of Tex., 1972; active participant in fund drives for Community Chest, United Fund, St. Michael's Episcopal Ch., St. Paul Hosp., Cotton Bowl Council, Park Cities Y.M.C.A. Sec., bd. dirs. Dallas Summer Musicals, Inc. Served with USNR, World War II. Research fellow Southwestern Legal Found., 1970-73. Mem. Dallas Bar Assn. (dir. 1965-68, chmn. bar candidates 1962, finance 1966), Internat. Assn. Ins. Counsel, Beta Theta Phi, Skull & Bones. Clubs: Dallas Country, Garden of the Gods (Colorado Springs, Colo.). Home: 4428 Lorraine St Dallas TX 75201 Office: 2505 Republic Bank Tower Dallas TX 75201

MCELROY, EDGAR HOOD, JR., mfg. co. exec.; b. Waxahachie, Tex., June 20, 1921; s. Edgar Hood and Myrle (Anderson) McE.; B.S in Mech. Engring., Tex. Tech. U., 1947; m. Dorothy Clift, Apr. 25, 1948; children—Edgar Hood III, Oliver C. Power engr. Tex. Power & Light Co., Dallas, 1947-55; dir. area devel., 1955-57; v.p., gen. mgr. Tex. div. Capitol Products Corp., Sherman, Tex., 1957-63; dir. indsl. div. Hardwicke-Etter Co., Sherman, 1963-64; pres. Medco, Inc., Sherman, 1961—, Day Mfg. Co., Sherman, 1964—, Bodie Corp., Sherman, 1964—, DMC Bus. Forms, Inc. Sherman, 1968—; mgr.-partner Grayco Investments, Sherman, 1969—; dir. Grayson County State Bank, Sherman, Recovery Co., Sherman. Served with USNR, 1945-47. Decorated Air medal. Registered profl. engr., Tex. Mem. Sherman C. of C. (past pres.), Tex. Mfrs. Assn. (past v.p., dir.), Nat. Paperboard Box Assn., Tex. Soc. Profl. Engrs. Rotarian. Home: 610 N McKown St Sherman TX 75090 Office: Box 907 Sherman TX 75090

MCELROY, WILLIAM TYNDELL, JR., educator; b. Shreveport, La., Sept. 29, 1924; s. William Tyndell and Effie Lavonia (Shaw) McE.; B.S., La. State U., 1949; M.S., U. Minn., 1954; Ph.D. (honors fellow 1954-55), Stanford, 1956. Asst. prof. physiology S.D. State Coll., Brookings, 1956-59, Hahnemann Med. Coll., Phila., 1959-67; asso. prof. La. State U. Med. Center, Shreveport, 1967-70, prof. physiology, 1970—, asso. dean, 1970—. Mem. research awards com. La. Heart Assn., 1972—. Served with M.C., USNR, 1943-46. Am. Physiol. Soc. fellow, 1957, 58. Mem. Am. Physiol. Soc., A.M.A., Assn. Am. Med. Colls., Kappa Alpha. Research in cardiovascular allergic shock. Home: 4727 Richmond St Shreveport LA 71106 Office: 510 E Stoner St Shreveport LA 71101

MCELVEEN, THOMAS M(ELVIN), ins. adjuster, appraiser, marine surveyor; b. Florence, S.C., July 6, 1902; s. Joseph McSwain and Frances (Hicks) McE.; grad. Spartan Acad., 1921; B.S., Furman U., 1925; m. Alice Senn, June 20, 1929 (dec.); children—Thomas Melvin, William Lawrence, Allice Palmer. Gen. adjuster Travelers Ins. Co. of Hartford, Conn., Charlotte, N.C., 1926-36, Glens Falls Ins. Group, Columbia, S.C., 1934-39; organized Thomas M. McElveen Co., Miami, Fla., 1939, pres., 1939—; pres. Thomas M. McElveen Bolivia, S.A., Thomas M. McElveen Internat. Corp., Miami, Fla. Mem. Fla. Assn. Ind. Ins. Adjusters, (past pres.), S. Fla., S.C. claims men assns., Internat. Chartered Inst. Loss Adjusters (founder, pres. 3 terms), Nat. Assn. Ind. Ins. Adjusters, C. of C., Hon. Order Ky. Cols. Baptist. Mason (Shriner). Contbr. articles trade mags. Home: 5867 SW 49th St Miami FL 33155 Office: 121 SW 8th St Miami FL 33130

MCENNIS, LEONARD J., JR., govt. ofcl.; b. Houston, Oct. 10, 1912; s. Leonard J. and Marie Ida (Whips) McE.; B.J., U. Mo., 1934; m. Bernice A. Thoma, June 21, 1941; children—Michael J., Mary Beth, Thomas C. Reporter The Herald-Post, Louisville, 1934-35; publicist, writer, editor Nat. Safety Council, Chgo., 1935-40; dir. publs. The Traffic Inst., Northwestern U., Evanston, Ill., 1940-59; dir. pub. relations Ins. Inst. for Hwy. Safety, Washington, 1959-69, asst. v.p. communications, 1969-70; dep. dir. information FTC, Washington, 1970—. Served with USNR, 1942-46. Mem. Pub. Relations Soc. Am. Home: 6517 Wilmett Rd Bethesda MD 20034 Office: Fed Trade Commn Washington DC 20580

MCEVER, VIRGLE WASHINGTON, JR., physician; b. Moultrie, Ga., May 11, 1925; s. Virgle Washington and Mary Elizabeth (Johnson) McE.; B.S cum laude, North Ga. Coll., 1948; M.S., U. Ala., 1949; M.D., Med. Coll. Ga., 1953; m. Amelia Elizabeth Calabrese, Aug. 20, 1945; children—Michael Paul, Joseph Anthony, Virgle Washington, III. Intern Brooke Army Med. Center, 1953-54; resident surgery St. Joseph's Infirmary, 1959-63; pres., chmn. bd. Warner Robins (Ga.) Clinic, Inc., 1960—, med. dir., 1954-65; pres., chmn. bd. Doctors Clinic Profl. Assn., Warner Robins, 1966—; pvt. practice medicine specializing in surgery, Warner Robins, Ga., 1963—; chief surgery Houston County Hosp., Warner Robins, 1964—; dir. med. services Pabst Brewing Co. (Ga.), 1970—; mem. staffs Houston County, Ga. Peachbelt, Hallmark hosps. Dir., mem. exec. com. Citizens & So. Bank, Warner Robins, 1966—; dir. Burke Corp., Warner Robins, 1967—. Mem. Houston County Bd. Health, Perry, Ga., 1957-59, 68—; mem. Warner Robins City Council, 1957-59; Houston County Commr., 1973—; mem. Robins AFB Community Council, 1958-59; pres. Warner Robins Library Bd., 1965-71. Mem. Houston County Republican Com., 1964—, del. Rep. Nat. Conv., 1972. Served with AUS, 1943-46, 53-54; PTO. Fellow A.C.S., Southeastern Surg. Congress, Pan-Pacific Surg. Assn.; mem. Peach Belt Med. Soc. (pres. 1970-71), Med. Assn. Ga. (del. 1966—), A.M.A., So. Med. Assn., Phi Chi. Episcopalian (sr. warden 1956-58, 1970—, del. Diocesan Council 1964-70, mem. exec. bd. Diocese Ga. 1968). Mason (32 deg., Shriner), Elk. Clubs: Lake Country (Houston); Optimist (distinguished pres. 1956-57, chmn. bd. 1958) (Warner Robins). Home: 108 Tanglewood Dr Warner Robins GA 31093 Office: 212 Hospital Dr Warner Robins GA 31093

MCEWIN, JOHN BEN, mech. engr.; b. Paris, Tex., Feb. 22, 1914; s. Fernie Fae and Cora (Weikel) McE.; B.S., Tex. Technol. Coll., 1942 Test engr. Gen. Electric Co., Schenectady, 1942-43; mech. engr. Humble Oil & Refining Co., Baytown, Tex., 1943-46; field engr. Peerless Pump Div., Oklahoma City, 1946-51; project engr. Sandia Corp., Albuquerque, 1951-55; mech., elec. engr. U.S. Army C.E., Perrin AFB, Tex., 1956-57, USAF, 1957-64, Goodfellow AFB, Tex., 1964—. Cons. engr., 1963—. Mem. Nat., Tex. socs. profl. engrs., Nat. Rifle Assn. Methodist. Club: San Angelo Gun (treas. 1966). Home: 3354 Cumberland Dr San Angelo TX 76901 Office: Goodfellow AFB San Angelo TX 76901

MCFADDEN, HENRY BERNARD, JR., tool mfg. co. exec.; b. Covington, Va., Mar. 17, 1935; s. Henry Bernard and Blanche Marie (Wells) McF.; B.S., Va. Poly. Inst., 1962; m. Josephine Ann Metts, Apr. 17, 1970; 1 son, Robert E. Machinist, Gen. Electric Co., Salem, Va., 1956-57; tool and die designer Poly-Scientific Corp., Blacksburg, 1957-60; tool engring. supt. Inland Motors, Radford, 1960-64; cons. engr. McFadden Engring. Co., Radford, 1964-65; pres. McFadden Tool & Engring. Corp., Roanoke, 1965—; dir. Masterbar Electronics, Inc., Roanoke. Chmn. Roanoke Valley Machine Trades Council, 1967—. Served with USNR, 1952-56. Mem. Am. Soc. Metals, Am. Soc. Tool and Mfg. Engrs. (state chmn. 1967-68), Am. Ordinance Assn., Soc. Mfg. Engrs. (state chmn. 1971-72), Fluid Power Soc., Air Force Assn. Moose, Elk. Inventor computerized bartending machine, 1968. Home: 2401 Mt Vernon Rd Roanoke VA 24015 Office: 3316 Aerial Way Roanoke VA 24015

MCFADDEN, JAMES DOUGLAS, govt. ofcl.; b. Winchester, Va., Feb. 19, 1934; s. Samuel Donald and Ruth Henrietta (Douglas) McF.; B.S., Va. Poly. Inst., 1960; Ph.D., U. Wis., 1965; m. Sharon Mary Joan Maloney, Aug. 26, 1956; children—Kerry Anne, James Douglas, Sheila Mary, Brian Landis. Research meteorologist Environmental Sci. Services Adminstrn., Silver Spring, Md. and Miami, 1965-68; research meteorologist, coordinator sci. programs, Nat. Oceanic and Atmospheric Adminstrn., Miami, 1968-71, chief data mgmt. br., research meteorologist, 1971-73, dir. research flight facility, 1973—. Served as lt., arty. AUS, 1956-58. Fellow Am. Geog. Soc.; mem. Am. Meteorol. Soc., Am. Geophys. Union, Miami Meteorol. Soc. (v.p. 1969-70), Sigma Xi, Sigma Gamma Epsilon. Roman Catholic. Research with application of airborne infra-red sensing techniques to oceanographic studies and studies of effects of hurricanes on thermal structure of surface layers of ocean. Home: 4423 Toledo St Coral Gables FL 33146 Office: Nat Oceanic and Atmospheric Adminstrn Research Flight Facility Box 480 197 IAB Miami FL 33148

MCFALL, ROBERT WILLIAM, clin. psychologist; b. Endicott, N.Y., Mar. 9, 1938; s. Robert S. and Ruth (Sutton) McF.; B.S., U. Ky., 1961, M.A., 1963, Ed.D., 1965; m. Gene Ann Carter, Aug. 12, 1967. Research, teaching asst. U. Ky., 1961-65; dir. psychology Frankfort (Ky.) State Hosp., 1965-67; asst. dir. diagnosis and evaluation service Dept. Mental Health, Frankfort, 1967-68; clin. research psychologist Nat. Inst. Mental Health Clin. Research Center, Lexington, Ky., 1968-71, chief male treatment service, 1971-74; chief male treatment Fed. Treatment Facility, Justice Dept., Lexington, 1974—. Vis. prof. U. Ky., 1968-70; cons. Ky. Dept. Mental Health, 1968—. Mem. Am., Ky. psychol. assns., Am., Ky. speech and hearing assns., A.A.A.S., Central Ky. Mental Health Assn. Home: 3045 Montavesta Rd Lexington KY 40502 Office: Leestown Pike Lexington KY 40507

MCFARLAN, EDWARD, JR., geologist; b. Bklyn., Mar. 25, 1921; s. Edward and Marjorie (Walker) McF.; B.A. in Geology, Williams Coll., 1943; M.A. in Petroleum Geology, U. Tex., 1948; m. Bettie Simonton, Oct. 8, 1949; children—Kathleen Simonton, Edward III. Geol. exploration Humble Oil & Refining Co., 1949, div. stratigraphic supr., New Orleans, 1960-64, area geologist, New Orleans, 1964-66, div. stratigrapher supr., Corpus Christi, Tex., 1966-67; geol. research Esso Prodn. Research Co., 1949-60, mgr. stratigraphic geology div., Houston, 1967-73; exploration adviser hdqrs. Exxon Corp. U.S.A., Houston, 1973—. Served to lt. (j.g.) USNR, 1943-46. Mem. Soc. Econ. Paleontologists and Mineralogists (program chmn. 1964), Am. Assn. Petroleum Geologists (chmn. subcom. research activities 1968—; Best Paper of Yr. award 1952). Presbyn. (adult Sunday sch. supt., deacon, elder). Clubs: Lake Vista (New Orleans); Houston Yacht; Corpus Christi Yacht. Author: Geologic Framework of the

Modern Mississippi Delta, 1954. Home: 10631 Gawain St Houston TX 77024 Office: PO Box 2180 Room 3977 Houston TX 77001

MCFARLAND, CHARLES KEITH, historian, educator; b. Frostburg, Md., May 12, 1934; s. Charles Marshall and Maria Blanche (Fike) McF.; B.A., Bridgewater Coll., 1960; M.A., U. Ariz., 1962, Ph.D., 1965; m. Linda Gayle Miller, May 30, 1970; 1 dau., Melissa Gayle. Asst. prof. U.S. history U. Southwestern La., Lafayette, 1965-66; asso. prof. Tex. Christian U., Ft. Worth, 1966-71; prof. history Ark. State U., State University, 1971—. Served with USNR, 1954-56. Mem. Am. Hist. Assn., Orgn. of Am. Historians, Am. Assn. Sch. Adminstrs. Elk. Author: Roosevelt, Lewis and the New Deal, 1970; Intellectual History: The Modern American Tradition, 1972. Contbr. articles on Am. history to profl. publs. Home: 2017 Indian Trails Jonesboro AR 72401 Office: Arkansas State University State University AR 72467

MCFARLAND, H(AROLD) RICHARD, food co. exec.; b. Hoopeston, Ill., Aug. 19, 1930; s. Arthur Bryan and Jennie (Wilkey) McF.; B.S. in Agr., U. Ill., 1952; m. Sarah Forney, Dec. 30, 1967. Mgr. purchasing Campbell Soup Co., Camden, N.J., 1957-67; dir. procurement Keebler Co., Elmhurst, Ill., 1967-69; v.p. purchasing and distbn. Ky. Fried Chicken Corp., Louisville, 1969—; dir. Fountain Trust Co., Covington Service Corp. (Ind.), Spring Valley Foods, Inc., Empire, Ala. Served to 1st lt. USAF, 1952-54. Decorated Korea Sygman Rhee unit citation, UN medal. Recipient Ky. Fried Chicken Pres.'s award, 1970. Mem. Ky., Louisville chambers commerce, Ky. Restaurant Assn. (dir.), Nat. Broiler Council (dir. 1972—), Am. Mgmt. Assn., Am. Shorthorn Cattle Assn., World Poultry Congress (chmn. process fund), Delta Upsilon. Presbyn. Club: Wildwood Country. Home: 4110 Lime Kiln Lane Louisville KY 40222 Office: 1441 Gardiner Lane Louisville KY 40213

MCFARLAND, M. ROBERT, lawyer; b. Oskaloosa, Ia., June 12, 1941; s. Millard Robert and Mildred Fern (VanBibber) McF.; B.B.A., U. Tex. at Arlington, 1963; J.D., So. Meth. U., 1966; m. Helen Jane Highfill, Aug. 10, 1963; children—Theresa Jane, Sandra Diane, Millard Robert. Admitted to Tex. bar, 1966; spl. agt. FBI, Washington, New Orleans and Atlanta, 1966-69; security adminstrv. specialist LTV, Inc., Dallas, 1969; partner Cribbs, McFarland & Holman, Arlington, Tex., 1969—. Bus. chmn. Dallas County United Fund, 1965; mem. adv. bd. Arlington Tarrant County YWCA, 1971-72; pres., 1972, Young Men of Arlington; chmn. profl. sect. Tarrant County United Fund for Arlington, 1971; group leader Tarrant County Cancer Crusade, 1972. Bd. dirs. Arlington Boys Club, 1971—, Young Men of Arlington, 1970—; trustee Arlington Boys Club Endowment Fund, 1973—. Mem. State Bar Tex., Am., Arlington (pres. 1973), Fort Worth-Tarrant County bar assns., Phi Delta Phi. Roman Catholic. Home: 1205 Canterbury Ct Arlington TX 76013 Office: PO Box 668 Arlington TX 76010

MCFARLAND, PAUL HEDRICH, JR., oral surgeon, educator, ret. army officer; b. Hagerstown, Md., Dec. 11, 1925; s. Paul Hedrich and Beulah Lee (McDonald) McF.; B.A., Gettysburg Coll., 1948; D.D.S., U. Md., 1952; B.S. in Dentistry, Baylor U., 1960, M.S. in Dentistry, 1962; m. Mabel Louise Gardner, Aug. 24, 1951; children—Stephen Scott (dec.), Richard Paul, Pamela Lee. Served with AUS, 1944-46; commd. 1st lt., Dental Corps, U.S. Army, 1952, advanced through grades to col., 1971; chief oral surgery Murphy Army Hosp., Waltham, Mass., 1954-55, 130th Sta. Hosp., Heidelberg, Germany, 1956; oral surgeon, Ft. Sam Houston, Tex., 1957-59; resident in oral surgery Brooke Gen. Hosp., Ft. Sam Houston, 1960-62; chief dental service, also chief oral surgery 121st Evacuation Hosp., Ascom, Korea, 1962-63, asst. chief oral surgery Ireland Army Hosp., Ft. Knox, Ky., 1963-65; chief oral surgery, 1965-68, chief hosp. dental service, 1966-68; chief dept. dentistry and oral surgery service 97th Gen. Hosp., also cons. oral surgery Frankfurt (Germany) Med. Service Area, 1968-71; asst. chief profl. br. Office of Asst. Surgeon Gen. for Dental Services, Dept. of Army, Washington, 1971-72, chief profl. br., 1972-73; ret., 1973; prof. surgery U. Tex. Dental Br., Houston, 1973—. Instr. oral surgery U. Md. Sch. Dentistry, 1952-54; faculty ann. post-grad. course oral surgery Walter Reed Gen. Hosp., Washington, 1967-68, 72, Letterman Gen. Hosp., San Francisco, 1968, 72; cons. oral surgery 8th U.S. Army, also Surgeon Gen. Republic of Korea Army, 1962-63, 1st U.S. Army, 1968; chmn. program com. U.S. Army Europe Ann. Dental Tng. Conf., Garmisch, Germany, 1969, gen. chmn., 1970. Pres. bd. govs. Officers' Open Mess, 121st Evacuation Hosp., Korea, 1962-63, 97th Gen. Hosp., Frankfurt, 1969-70. Decorated Legion of Merit, Army Commendation medal with oak leaf cluster. Diplomate Am. Bd. Oral Surgery (adv. com. 1967-68, 74). Fellow Am. Coll. Dentists, Internat. Assn. Oral Surgeons; mem. Am., Brit. socs. oral surgeons, Am., Korean (hon.) dental assns., Assn. Mil. Surgeons, Assn. U.S. Army. Methodist (mem. ofcl. ch. bd. 1960-62, chmn. commn. on edn. 1961-62). Contbr. articles to dental jours., chpts. to Current Therapy in Dentistry. Lectr. profl. meetings, hosps., seminars. Home: 3610 La Costa Dr Quail Valley Missouri City TX 77459 Office: Dept Surgery U Tex Dental Branch PO Box 20068 Houston TX 77025

MCFARLIN, RICHARD FRANCIS, chem. co. exec.; b. Oklahoma City, Oct. 29, 1929; s. Loy Lester and Julia Mae (Collins) McF.; B.S., Va. Mil. Inst., 1951; M.S., Purdue U., 1953, Ph.D. (Purdue Research Found. fellow), 1956; certificate Grad. Sch. Bus. Adminstrn., Columbia, 1968; m. Clare Jane Burroughs, Apr. 4, 1953; children—Robin Sue, Richard Prescott, Rebecca Lynn, Rogert Whitsitt. Research chemist Monsanto Chem. Co., St. Louis, 1956-61; mgr. inorganic research Internat. Minerals & Chems., Mulberry, Fla., 1961-62; tech. dir. Armour Agrl. Chem. Co., Atlanta, 1962-65, v.p., 1965-68; v.p. USS Agri-Chemicals div. U.S. Steel, Atlanta, 1968—. Recipient Bausch & Lombe Sci. award, 1951, M.M. Cohn scholarship award, 1951, L.D. Wall award, 1952, Gaston DuBois Research award, 1959. Mem. Va. Mil. Inst. Alumni Assn. (pres. 1968), Am. Chem. Soc., A.A.A.S., Sigma Xi, Phi Lambda Upsilon. Republican. Presbyn. Patentee in field. Home: 455 Forestdale Dr NE Atlanta GA 30342 Office: 30 Pryor St SW Atlanta GA 30301

MCFEE, ARTHUR STORER, physician; b. Portland, Me., May 1, 1932; s. Arthur Stewart and Helen Knight (Dresser) McF.; B.A. cum laude, Harvard, 1953, M.D., 1957; M.S., U. Minn., 1966, Ph.D., 1967; m. Iris Goeschel, May 13, 1967. Intern U. Minn. Hosp., 1957-58, resident in surgery, 1958-65; asst. prof. surgery U. Tex. Med. Sch., San Antonio, 1967-70; asso. prof., 1970-74, prof., 1974—; co-dir. surg. intensive care unit Bexar County Hosp., San Antonio, 1968—. Served with USNR, 1965-67. Diplomate Am. Bd. Surgery. Fellow A.C.S.; mem. Am. Assn. History Medicine, Assn. Acad. Surgery, A.C.S., A.M.A., Tex. Med. Assn., Bexar County Med. Soc., San Antonio Surg. Soc., Soc. Surgery Alimentary Tract, So. Med. Assn., N.Y. Acad. Scis., Royal Soc.-Medicine, Allen O. Whipple Soc. Contbr. to profl. jours. Home: 131 Brittany Dr San Antonio TX 78212 Office: 7703 Floyd Curl Dr San Antonio TX 78212

MCGALLIARD, HARRY WOODROW, state ofcl.; b. Connelly Springs, N.C., July 19, 1911; s. William Theodore and Agnes (Presson) McG.; A.B., U. N.C., 1929, J.D., 1935; postgrad. Harvard, 1929-30; m. Ac Ruble, Apr. 17, 1937; 1 dau., Ac Ann (Mrs. W. D. Brunson, Jr.). Admitted to N.C. bar, 1935; asst. dir. N.C. Inst. Govt., 1935-40; mem. N.C. atty. genls. staff, Raleigh, 1940-51, asst. N.C. atty. gen., 1951-63, dep. atty. gen., 1963-70, chief dep. atty. gen., 1970—. Commr. on uniform state laws, 1946-55; mem. N.C. jud. council, 1959-61, 62-66. Served with AUS, 1943-46. Home: 408 Glascock St Raleigh NC 27604 Office: N C Atty Gen Office Raleigh NC 27602

MCGARITY, THOMAS WAYNE, mfg. co. exec.; b. Como, Tex., Aug. 21, 1936; s. Thomas Edgar and Crystal Lee (Jones) McG.; Asso. in Sci., Arlington State Coll., 1957; B.B.A., So. Meth. U., 1959, M.B.A., 1968; m. Patricia Ann Whitis, Oct. 3, 1953; children—Mollie, Sara, Patrick, Ginger, Timmy. Mem. staff Dranquet, Foote & Co., C.P.A.'s, Dallas, 1959-60; accounting supr. Oilwell div. U.S. Steel, Inc., Dallas, 1960-65; with Luminator div. Gulton Industries, Inc., Plano, Tex., 1965—, v.p. finance, 1971—. Tax cons., 1960—. C.P.A., Tex. Mem. Tex. Soc. C.P.A.'s, Am. Inst. C.P.A.'s. Presbyn (active youth work). Home: 501 S Greenville Av Allen TX 75002 Office: Box 278 Plano TX 75074

MCGAVOCK, POLLY P(OLITT), realtor; b. Walton, Ky., Feb. 7, 1904; d. Flor S. and Shirlie (Tucker) Politt; student Marshall Coll., 1921-22; A.B., Randolph-Macon Women's Coll., 1925; m. John Fulton McGavock, June 9, 1925 (div.); 1 dau., Shirley (Mrs. Richard Estabrook McConnell), Asso. H. T. Van Nostrand & Co., 1948; realtor, 1948—. Mem. exec, bd, Charlottesville A.R.C., 1943-46, rotating mem. bd,, 1948—; pres. Charlottesville and Albemarle Child Welfare Assn., 1944-46; co-chmn. Community Chest Campaign, 1955; bd. dirs. Charlottesville div. Am. Cancer Soc., 1956-57. Head A.R.C. Motor Corp, World War II. Asso. U. Va. Library. Mem. Nat. Assn. Real Estate Appraisers, C. of C., Charlottesville and Albermarle Real Estate Bd. (pres. 1954), Nat., Va. (regional v.p. 1961, bd. dirs. 1965) real estate assn., Va. Assn. Realtors (legislative com. 1972, Most Ethical Realtor award 1973), Internat. Real Estate Fedn., Nat. Inst. Real Estate Brokers (state membership chmn. 1962), Nat. Inst. Farm and Land Brokers, Nat. Assn. Real Estate Bds. (women's council), Internat. Platform Assn., Kappa Delta. Episcopalian. Clubs: Farmington Hunt, Farmington Country (Charlottesville); Greencroft. Home: 314 Kent Rd Charlottesville VA 22903 Office: 1 Boar's Head Lane Charlottesville VA 22901

MCGAW, JESSIE BREWER, author, educator; b. Clarksville, Tenn., Oct. 17, 1913; d. Lewis Vernon and Birdie (Basford) Brewer; A.B., Duke, 1935; M.A., Peabody Coll., 1940; postgrad. Columbia, 1948-50; student (Fulbright scholar) Am. Acad. Rome, 1959; m. Howard Franklin McGaw, Dec. 28, 1939 (div. 1958); children—Miriam Katherine, Vernon Howard; m. 2d, Harold L. Geis, Aug. 1964 (div. Mar. 1972). Tchr. Latin, Ward Belmont Sch., Nashville, 1938-40; tchr. Lausanne Sch., Memphis, 1940-42; tchr. English and Latin, U. Houston, 1952—. Bd. dirs. YWCA, 1957-59, Day Care Assn., 1956-61, Houston Civic Music Assn., 1958-60, Houston Council Human Relations. Recipient Cokesburg Juvenile award; Theta Sigma Phi lit. award; research grant, 1964; Delta Kappa Theta study grantee, 1972. Mem. Tex. Folklore Soc., South Central Modern Lang. Assn., Houston Council. Tchrs. Fgn. Lang. (treas.), League Women Voters, Am. Assn. U. Women, Tex. Inst. Letters, U. Houston Women's Assn. (pres. 1967-68), Kappa Kappa Gamma. Democrat. Methodist. Club: University Houston Woman's (pres. 1954-55). Author: How Medicine Man Cured Paleface Woman, 1956; Painted Pony Runs Away, 1958; Little Elk Hunts Buffalo, 1961; History of Houston YWCA; translator Heptaplus. Home: 2405 Dickey Pl Houston TX 77019

MCGAW, ROBERT ARMISTEAD, ednl. adminstr.; b. Nashville, Mar. 25, 1914; s. Samuel Marshall and Bonnie Louise (Howard) McG.; student Vanderbilt U., 1931-32; m. Elizabeth Early, May 25, 1937; 1 son, John Early. Sports writer Nashville Banner, 1932-36; editor Meth. Pub. House, Nashville, 1936-40, advt. mgr., 1940-43, dir. personnel and pub. relations, 1946-48; asst. to chancellor Vanderbilt U., Nashville, 1948-51, alumni sec., 1951-56, dir. information and publs., 1956-64, sec. of univ., 1964—. Mem. Tenn. Hist. Commn., 1953—, chmn., 1969—; mem. Met. Nashville Hist. Commn., 1967—. Trustee Children's Museum of Nashville, 1972—. Served with USMCR, 1943-46. Mem. Nat. Trust for Historic Preservation (mem. adv. bd. 1972—), Tenn. Hist. Soc. (pres. 1969-71). Methodist. Author: A Brief History of Vanderbilt University, 1973. Home: 3803 Brighton Rd Nashville TN 37205 Office: Vanderbilt U Nashville TN 37240

MCGEE, BOBBYE REX, lawyer; b. West Point, Tenn., Dec. 1, 1926; s. James Leonard and Edna Ona (Moore) McG.; LL.B., U. Tenn., 1950; m. Edith Rhea Lundy, May 25, 1949; children—Bobby Ray, Vickie Lynn. Admitted to Tenn. bar, 1950; mem. firm Duncan, Duncan and McGee, Knoxville, Tenn., 1950-58; asst. atty. gen., Knoxville, 1956-58; mem. firm Clement and McGee, Knoxville, 1958-62, Lee, McGee and Garrett, Knoxville, 1962-67, Lee, McGee, Garrett and Chandler, Knoxville, 1967—. Bd. dirs. Vol. Rescue Squad, also legal adviser, 1971—. Served with USNR, 1944-46. Mem. Am., Tenn. trial lawyers assns., Knoxville Bar Assn., Tenn. Assn. of Criminal Def. Lawyers (dir. 1973—). Elk. Home: 7920 Stratton Dr Knoxville TN Office: 205 Clinch Av Knoxville TN 37902

MCGEE, NEALE STRATTON, banker; b. Oklahoma City, Nov. 18, 1924; s. Leonard Kyle and Thelma (Selcer) McG.; student U. Colo., 1943; B.S. magna cum laude, Oklahoma City U., 1948, J.D., 1954; grad. Stonier Grad. Sch. Banking Rutgers, 1968; m. Ruth Rauch, June 22, 1946; children—Melanie Alison, Patrick Neale, Valerie Ann. Sales mgr. Gen. Motors Acceptance Corp., Oklahoma City, also Amarillo, N.Y.C., Denver, 1948-59; area mgr. Ford Motor Credit Co., Dallas and Detroit, 1960-64; asst. v.p. Bank Commonwealth, Detroit, 1965-67; v.p. Republic Nat. Bank Dallas, 1967-72, v.p. and rep.-Mexico; pres. Greenville Av. State Bank, Dallas, 1972—; dir. Greenville Av. State Bank. Am. Transfer & Storage Co., Dallas Clearing House. Served to lt. comdr. USNR, 1943-46. Mem. Sales and Marketing Internat., Robert Morris Assos., Am. Inst. Banking, Naval Res. Assn., Navy League, Naval Order U.S. Club: Dallas Athletic and Country. Presbyn. Republican. Clubs: University (Mexico City); Dallas Athletic, Dallas Athletic Country. Home: 9775 Wisterwood St Dallas TX 75238 Office: 1827 Greenville Av Dallas TX 75206

MCGEE, RONALD ALEXANDER, educator; b. Marydell, Miss., Nov. 30, 1910; s. James LeRoy and Edith Matilda (Shields) McG.; B.A., Miss. Coll., 1937; M.A., U. Miss., 1948; postgrad. U. Tex., 1952, Kan. State Coll., 1960, U. Okla., 1961, U. Kan., 1962; m. Isabel Black, Dec. 23, 1939; children—James LeRoy II, Carolyn Isabel (Mrs. Michael Kittredge), Edith Catholine (Mrs. Stuart Tribble), Marjorie Catherine. Prin., tchr. County Line Sch., Union, Miss., 1937-39; tchr. Houston (Miss.) High Sch., 1940-41; instr. electronics Air Forces Tech. Sch., Scott Field, Ill., 1942-47; tchr. Kosciusko (Miss.) High Sch., 1947-48; asst. prof. Physics U. Miss., Oxford, 1948-53; asst. prof. physics So. State Coll., Magnolia, Ark., 1953—, head dept., 1953-70. Mem. Miss. Ho. of Reps., 1940-44. Mem. Columbia dist. com. Boy Scouts Am., 1953—; founder, dir. S.W. Ark. Regional Sci. Fair, 1955—. Mem. Am. Phys. Soc., Am. Inst. Physics, Ark. Acad. Sci., N.E.A., Alpha Epsilon Delta, Sigma Pi Sigma. Republican. Baptist. Home: 1236 S State Coll Magnolia AR 71753

MCGEE, TOM G., supt. schs.; b. Bison, Okla., May 23, 1904; s. Jess and Mary Chesley (Van Dusen) McG.; B.S., Phillips U., 1952, M.E., 1953; m. Margaret Irene Burns, Aug. 13, 1944 (div. July 1952). Tchr., 1927-46; supt. schs. Kingfisher County, Okla., 1946—; local corr. newspapers, 1932—. Mem. Okla. Edn. Assn. (co-chmn. area planning bd.), Okla. County Supts. Assn., Okla. County Officers Assn. Author. An Incident on the Chisholm Trail, 1938; Tom's Rules of English Grammar, 1969. Author, dir.: Pat Hennessey Massacre Pageant, 1939; Who Killed Pat Hennessey, 1941; Auntie's Money, 1940; Buddy the Boomer, 1939; The Ruby Knot, 1942; Pat Hennessey Story, 1956; Songs Turkey Creek, 1957; Half Past Noon, 1957; Trails Past Oklahoma, 1958; Their Children's Hour of Verse, 1958; The Revised Pat Hennessey Massacre, 1963. Home: 302 S Main St Hennessey OK 73742 Office: Court House Kingfisher OK 73750

MCGEHEE, BENJAMIN HARRIS, wholesale trade co. exec.; b. Wilmington, Va., July 7, 1918; s. Thomas Harris and Kate (Winston) McG.; B.B.A., U. Richmond, 1941; m. Sarah Glen Callan, July 7, 1951; children—Susan (Mrs. Donald A. Tucker). Reporter, salesman Dun & Bradstreet, Richmond, Va., 1942-48; gen. credit mgr. Stephen Putnam Shoe Co., Richmond, 1948-49, treas., 1949-50; credit mgr. Noland Co., Newport News, Va., 1950-59, asst. treas., 1958-59, treas., 1959—, v.p. finance, 1964—, also dir.; v.p. finance, treas., dir. Noland Credit Co.; dir. United Virginia Bank, Citizens & Marine Bank, Virginia Indsl. Devel. Corp. Mem. Financial Execs. Inst. Clubs: Peninsula Kiwanis, James River Country, Williamsburg Country. Home: 403 Woodroof Rd Newport News VA 23606 Office: 2700 Warwick Blvd Newport News VA 23607

MCGEHEE, REGINALD BEN, food broker; b. Summit, Miss., Oct. 4, 1911; s. Louis Hooker and Stella (Scott) McG.; student Southwest Jr. Coll., Summit, 1930-32; m. Rebecca Felder, Oct. 18, 1933; children—Reginald Ben, Millie. Soda mgr. Liggett Drug Co., Washington, 1934-40; salesman Rumford Chem. Corp. (R.I.), 1940-50; mgr. R. B. McGehee Co., food brokers, Jackson, Miss., 1950-54; sec.-treas., partner McGehee Brokerage Co., Inc., Jackson, 1954—, now pres. Mem. Jackson Food Brokers Assn. (sec.-treas. 1957, pres. 1958), Grocers-Mfrs. Assn. Jackson. Democrat. Baptist. Clubs: Shady Oaks Country, Central Miss. Traffic, Liveoaks Golf. Home: 5358 S Venetian Way Jackson MS 39211 Office: 126 Ricks St Jackson MS 39211

MCGETTRICK, WILLIAM JOSEPH JOHN, cons. engr.; b. Whitesboro, N.Y., Nov. 2, 1921; s. William J. and Florence (Avery) McG.; B.S., Fordham U., 1942; postgrad. Stevens Inst., 1948, Tri-State Coll., 1953; m. Ruth Margaret Sheppard, Oct. 17, 1945; children—Judith Ann (Mrs. William Leon Barfield), Craig William. Engr., scientist Norden Bombsight Co., Elmira, N.Y., 1945-48; project engr. Bendix Aviation Co., Teterboro, N.J., 1948-53; pres. Pomac Industries, Alfred, N.Y., 1953-55; program mgr., research staff Link Aviation Co., Binghamton, N.Y., 1955-60; chief scientist Carib-Orient Cons., Largo, Fla., 1960-66; pres. Sci. Pollution Control Co., Orlando, Fla., 1966-72; cons. engr. Am. Cons. Assn., Chgo., 1972—. Partner Craig's Scuba Shop, Burlington, N.C., 1966—. Mem. exec. com. Cherokee council Boy Scouts Am., 1966-70; capt. expansion drive Morton F. Plant Hosp., Clearwater, Fla., 1964-65. Served to lt. comdr. USNR 1941-45. Mem. Marine Tech. Soc., Internat. Oceanographic Found. Kiwanian, Rotarian, Lion. Home: 72 Nancy Lee Av Orlando FL 32807 Office: Am Cons Assn 5680 N Elston Av Chicago IL 60646

MCGILL, JOHN CHARLES, physician; b. Clover, SC., Aug. 3, 1922; s. Waldo Knox and Elsie (Sullivan) McG.; B.A., Erskine Coll., 1943; M.D., Vanderbilt U., 1946; m. Mabel Lindsay Hamilton, Oct. 6, 1950; children—Frances, Meredith, John, Elizabeth, Hamilton. Intern, Med. Coll. Va., Richmond, 1946-47, Charlotte (N.C.) Meml. Hosp., 1949-50; practice medicine specializing in family practice, Williamston, S.C., 1950-51, Kings Mountain, N.C., 1951—; mem. staff Kings Mountain, Gaston Meml. hosps. Pres., Kings Mountain Savs. & Loan Assn., 1971—. Served with AUS, 1947-49. Mem. A.M.A., So. Med. Assn., N.C. Med. Soc., Am. Bd. Family Practice (charter). Presbyn. (elder). Rotarian. Home: 703 Hillside St Kings Mountain NC 28086 Office: 103 Watterson St Kings Mountain NC 28086

MCGIMSEY, CHARLES ROBERT, III, educator; b. Dallas, June 18, 1925; s. Charles Robert, Jr. and Ellen (Parks) McG.; student Vanderbilt U., 1942-43, U. of South, 1943-44; B.A. in Anthropology, U. N.M., 1949; M.A. (teaching fellow), Harvard, 1954, Ph.D. in Anthropology, 1958; m. Mary Elizabeth Conger, Dec. 20, 1949; children—Charles Robert, Brian Keith, Mark Douglass. Instr., U. Ark. at Fayetteville, 1957, asst. prof., 1958-62, asso. prof., 1962-67, prof. anthropology, 1967—, chmn. dept., 1969-72, asst. curator U. Ark. Mus., 1957-59, dir., 1959—. Dir. Ark. Archeol. Survey, 1967—; chmn. Ark. Mus. Study Commn., 1967-71; mem. Ark. rev. com. Ark. Historic Preservation Program, 1969—; collaborator Nat. Park Service, 1972-74, adviser, 1974—. Served to lt. (j.g.) USNR, 1943-47. Fellow Am. Anthrop. Assn.; mem. Am. Assn. Museums, Ark. Archeol. Soc. (editor 1960—), Soc. Am. Archeology (exec. com. 1971—, pres. 1974—), Southeastern Museums Conf. (council 1962-71, editor 1964-71). Author: (with G.R. Willey) Monagrillo Culture of Panama, 1954; Mariana Mesa, 1958; Indians of Arkansas, 1969; Public Archeology, 1972. Research in archeology, N.M., 1948-51, Panama, 1952, 55-56, 61-62, Ark., 1957—. Home: 435 Hawthorn St Fayetteville AR 72701

MCGINNES, FRANKLIN PIERCE, seafood co. exec., automobile dealer; b. Mollusk, Va., Feb. 22, 1927; s. Thomas Dix and Aileen (Poole) McG.; B.S., U. Va., 1947; postgrad. Gen. Motor Inst., Flint, Mich., 1948; m. Nancy Madison Crawford Hubbard, Aug. 14, 1965; 1 stepdau., Anne C. Hubbard. Gen. mgr. T.D. McGinnes, Inc., Kilmarnock, Va., 1948-64, pres., 1964—; pres. Va. Seafoods, Inc., Irvington, 1964—; pres. MCCO Enterprises, Inc., Kilmarnock, Va. Pet Foods, Inc., Irvington; pres. Kilmarnock Motor Sales, Inc. Served with USNR, 1944-46, 52-53. Mem. No. Neck Automobile Dealers Assn. (past pres.), Va. Canners Assn. (past pres.), Shellfish Inst. N.Am. (past pres.), Mid-Atlantic Food Processors Assn. (past pres.). Rotarian. Home: Bell Tower Irvington VA 22480 Office: Irvington VA 22480

MCGINNIS, HERMAN GARRARD, constrn. co. exec.; b. Cedartown, Ga., Mar. 16, 1924; s. John Henry and Rosie (Miller) McG.; student U. Ga., 1946-48; m. Virginia Lee Brannon, Aug. 25, 1946; children—Kathy, Herman G., Mary Ann. With Ledbetter Bros., Inc., Rome, Ga., 1942—, sec.-treas., 1960—. Served with AUS, 1943-45. Baptist. Home: 304 Lavendar Dr Rome GA 30161 Office: 2 W 2d Av Rome GA 30161

MCGINTY, JOHN MILTON, architect; b. Houston, Apr. 24, 1935; s. Milton Bowles and Ruth Louise (Dreaper) McG.; B.S., Rice U., 1957; M.F.A., Princeton, 1961; m. Juanita Jones, May 4, 1957; children—Christopher Harold, Jacqueline Ruth. With Barnes, Landes & Goodman, architects, Austin, Tex., 1957-58, Ingram & Harris, architects, Beaumont, Tex., 1958-59, McGinty Partnership, architects, Houston, 1961—. Instr. archtl. design U. Houston, 1965-67; White House fellow, asst. to sec. interior, 1967-68; vis. prof. Rice U. Sch. Architecture, 1969-70. Mem. A.I.A. (mem. U.S. delegation to USSR 1972, pres. Houston chpt. 1973, nat. v.p. 1973-74). Home: 5403 John Dreaper Dr Houston TX 77027 Office: 3501 W Alabama St Houston TX 77027

MCGLAMERY, GERALD GARRIS, pollution control engr.; b. North Wilkesboro, N.C., Aug. 31, 1937; s. George Allen and Ruby W. (Landreth) McG.; B.S. in Chem. Engring., Auburn U., 1959; m. Barbara Ann Coggins, Nov. 26, 1960; children—Gerald Garris, George Lee. Tech. service engr. Olin Corp., Brevard, N.C., 1959-62; process design engr. Monsanto Co., Decatur, Ala., 1962-65, sr. planning engr., 1965-67; chem. engr. TVA, Muscle Shoals, Ala., 1967-70, supr. conceptual designs, 1970-73, asst. dir. stack gas emission study staff, 1973—. Lectr. on polution control U. Ala., 1972, Florence (Ala.) State U., 1971. Head adviser Jr. Achievement, Florence, 1971—; baseball coach Underwood Dixie Youth League, Florence, 1971—; active Boy Scouts Am. Registered profl. engr., Ala. Mem. Am. Inst. Chem. Engrs., Tau Beta Pi, Phi Lambda Upsilon. Presbyn. Clubs: Quad-Cities, Auburn Alumni (Florence). Home: 214 Robin Hood Dr Florence AL 35630 Office: TVA Nat Fertilizer Devel Center Bldg Muscle Shoals AL 35660

MCGLAMERY, WILLIAM MARSHALL, mfg. co. exec.; b. Toms Creek, Va., Mar. 18, 1913; s. Lee Roy and Della (Autry) McG.; student Emory and Henry Coll., 1933; m. Mary Cornelia Holt, Nov. 23, 1939. Asst. chief accountant Pocahontas Fuel Co. (Va.), 1946-57; office mfg. Coppinger Machinery Service, Inc., Bluefield, Va., 1957-66, sec., dir., 1966—. Mem. Bluefield Town Council, 1960-66; mayor of Bluefield, 1966-68. Served with finance dept. AUS, 1943-45. Methodist (chmn. ofcl. bd. 1957-58, ch. treas. 1959-67). Mason, Kiwanian (pres. Bluefield 1958). Clubs: Metropolitan Dinner, University, Fincastle Country (Bluefield). Home: Route 3 Box 254 Bluefield VA 24605 Office: Coppinger Machinery Service Inc US 52 N Bluefield VA 24701

MCGLAMRY, MAX REGINALD, lawyer; b. Wilcox County, Ga., Sept. 12, 1928; s. Edgar Lee and Allie Bea (Faircloth) McG.; B.S., Auburn U., 1948; J.D. cum laude, Mercer U., 1952; m. Jean Louise Hilyer, Dec. 28, 1950; children—Sharon Kay, Michael Lee. Admitted to Ga. bar, 1953; individual law, practice law, Columbus, Ga., 1954-64; partner Swift, Pease, Davidson & Chapman, Attys., 1964-70, Swift, Page & Chapman, 1971-73, Page, Scranton, Harris, McGlamry & Chapman, 1973—. Exec. com. Muscogee County Democratic party, 1956-60. Served with USNR, 1948-49. Fellow Am. Coll. Probate Counsel; mem. Am., Ga. bar assns., State Bar Ga., Am. Judicature Soc., Blue Key, Phi Kappa Phi, Phi Alpha Delta, Alpha Epsilon Delta, Pi Kappa Alpha. Democrat Baptist. Clubs: Columbus Lawyers (pres. 1964), Lions (pres. 1967), Green Island Hills Country. Home: 2937 Lynda Lane Columbus GA 31906 Office: 1043 3d Av Columbus GA 31902

MCGLOHON, LOONIS, broadcasting co. exec.; b. Ayden, N.C., Sept. 29, 1921; s. Max Cromwell and Bertha (Andrews) McG.; B.S., East Carolina U., 1942; m. Nan Lovelace, June 19, 1943; children—Reeves, Fan, Laurie. With Jefferson Pilot Broadcasting Co., Charlotte, N.C., 1949—, music dir., 1954—, dir. community relations, 1972—; freelance producer, 1950—; composer numerous compositions and works, including many recorded jazz and popular pieces; various commns. for religious works; film scores; new mus. version of Land of Oz, 1970-73; syndicated TV feature mus. scores, including Come Blow Your Horn, 1966, others; score for symphonic drama The Hornets Nest, 1965; guest performer N.C. Symphony. Organizer N.C. agy. Big Bros. Am., 1972, v.p., 1972-73; producer, chmn. March of Dimes Telerama, 1972. Bd. dirs. Cultural Arts Com. of Charlotte. Served with USAAF, 1942-45. Mem. A.S.C.A.P., Broadcast Music Inc., Pub. Relations Soc. Am. Club: Charlotte Athletic. Home: 222 Wonderwood Dr Charlotte NC 28211 Office: 1 Julian Price Pl Charlotte NC 28208

MCGOWAN, E(DGAR) L(EON), state ofcl., lawyer; b. Conway, S.C., June 1, 1920; s. Edgar L. and Francis (Mishoe) McG.; student U. Ala., 1938-41; B.S., U. S.C., 1947, M.S., 1950, LL.B., 1957; m. Mildred Parris, Apr. 3, 1941; 1 son, E. Linden. Instr. U. S.C., 1947-50, asst. prof., 1950-57, asso. prof., 1957-71; practice accounting Columbia, S.C., 1947-57; pvt. practice law, 1957—, v.p., dir. Investment Life & Trust Co., Mullins, S.C.; commr. labor State of S.C., 1971—. Sec.-treas. S.C. Democratic party; sec. Richland County Dem. party. Mem. Am. Accountants Assn., Am., S.C., Richland County bar assns. Methodist. Mason (Shriner), Lion. Club: Palmetto. Home: 5067 Hillside Rd Columbia SC 29201 Office: 3600 Forest Dr Columbia SC 29211

MCGOWAN, SANDY LEE (MRS. JAMES ROBERT MCFARLAND), horse trailer mfg. co. exec.; b. Cleve., Sept. 12, 1947; d. Albert Edward and Clara Arlene (Wright) Jenkins; B.B.A., Tex. Tech U., 1969; m. James Robert McFarland, Dec. 31, 1973. Accountant North Central Tex. Council Govts., Arlington, 1969-70, Constrn. Analysts, Inc., Ft. Worth, 1970-71; with Miley Trailer Co., Ft. Worth, 1971—, sec.-treas., 1972—; sec.-treas. McVean Steel Co. subsidiary Miley Trailer Co., Ft. Worth, 1972—, Rite Weld Supply Co. div., Ft. Worth, 1972—. C.P.A., Tex. Mem. Nat. Assn. Accountants, Beta Alpha Psi. Home: 7440 Vanessa Dr Fort Worth TX 76112 Office: 2501 Decatur Av Fort Worth TX 76106

MCGRAIL, THOMAS HUGH, lawyer; b. Albany, N.Y., Sept. 6, 1920; s. Thomas H. and Katherine (Fischer) McG.; A.B., Harvard, 1947, LL.B., 1950; m. Ruth Ann Hutton, June 15, 1957; children—Mary Ann, Katherine, Margaretha, Elizabeth. Admitted to D.C. bar, 1956; trial atty. U.S. Dept. Justice, 1951-55; mem. com. counsel, judiciary com. U.S. Ho. of Reps., 1955-56; asst. U.S. atty., Washington, 1956-59; individual law practice, 1959-61; partner Thompson, McGrail & O'Donnell, Washington, 1962—. Served to capt., inf. AUS, 1941-46. Home: 9730 Schreiner Lane Great Falls VA 22066 Office: Union Trust Bldg Washington DC 20005

MCGRAIN, PRESTON, geologist; b. Corydon, Ind., Dec. 10, 1917; s. Albert M. and Eva (Shuck) McG.; student Antioch Coll., 1935-39; A.B., Ind. U., 1940, M.A., 1942, postgrad., 1946-47; m. Magdalene Schlotthauer, Feb. 16, 1959. Field asst., geologist Ind. Geol. Survey, Bloomington, summers 1940, 46, 47; geologist Ind. Flood Control and Water Resources Commn., Indpls., 1947-50; asst. state geologist Ky. Geol. Survey, U. Ky., Lexington, 1950—. Teaching asst. dept. geology Ind. U., Bloomington, 1940-42. Co-chmn. steering com. Forum on Geology of Indsl. Minerals, 1972-73. Served to capt. C.E., AUS, 1942-46. Fellow Geol. Soc. Am., Ind. Acad. Sci.; mem. Am. Assn. Petroleum Geologists, Geol. Soc. Ky. (pres. 1955-56), Am. Inst. Mining, Metall. and Petroleum Engrs. Christian Scientist. Contbr. articles to profl. jours. Home: 1221 Providence Rd Lexington KY 40502 Office: Ky Geol Survey U Ky Lexington KY 40506

MCGRATH, HAROLD MORRIS, educator; b. Cortez, Colo., June 1, 1916; s. Michael A. and Bernice (Holt) McG.; B.A., No. Colo. U., 1956, M.A., 1957, Ed.D., 1964; m. Mildred M. Taylor, Mar. 26, 1950; children—Patricia Ann., Michael Arthur. Prin., Kuner Sch. Dist., Kersey, Colo., 1951; with Ideal Grocery Inc., Greeley, Colo., 1952-56; salesman Miller Supermarkets, Greeley, 1956-58; faculty E. Carolina U., Greenville, 1957—, prof. bus. edn., 1964—. Served with USCGR, 1942-45. Mem. N.E.A., N.C. Edn. Assn., Greeley Numis. Soc. (pres. 1948-51), Pi Omega Pi (hon.), Phi Delta Kappa, Delta Pi Epsilon, Beta Gamma Sigma. Moose. Club: Civitan. Home: 103 Deerwood Dr Greenville NC 27834

MCGRATH, JAMES RUSSELL, physicist; b. Chgo., Dec. 2, 1932; s. James Gerard and Irene Veronica (Grogan) McG.; B.Aero. Engring., Cath. U. Am., 1957, M.S. in Physics, 1965, Ph.D., 1971; A.B. in Physics, George Washington U., 1963; m. Anne Marie Finnegan, Aug. 29, 1959; children—Eileen, James, Michael, Kathleen. Aero. research engr., bur. aeros. U.S. Dept. Navy, Washington, 1957-61, staff physicist underwater acoustics research, naval research lab., Washington, 1962—. Served with USNR, 1952-53; maj. USMCR, 1972—. Mem. Acoustical Soc. Am., Brit. Acoustical Soc., Inst. Physics, Engring. and Sci. Assn. Ireland, Washington Acad. Sci., Sigma Pi Sigma. Home: 5900 Madawaska Rd Washington DC 20016 Office: Code 8168 US Naval Research Laboratory Washington DC 20375

MCGRATH, KYRAN MURRAY, assn. exec., lawyer; b. Chgo., Aug. 24, 1934; s. George E. and Annabelle (Colten) G.; B.S. cum laude Georgetown U., 1956, LL.B., 1959; m. Rosemary McVeigh, June 16, 1956; children—Kyran Murray, Jr., Eileen, Thomas, Roseann. Admitted to D.C. bar, 1959; gen. practice, Washington, 1959-61; legislative counsel Senator Paul H. Douglas, Washington, 1961-65; chief Ill. Dept. Bus. and Econ. Devel., Washington, 1965-67; spl. asst. to chmn. Nat. Adv. Commn. on Civil Disorders, Washington, 1967-68; dir. Am. Assn. Museums, Washington, 1968—. Lectr., cons. U.S. Dept. Labor, 1967; mem. U.S. nat. commn. to UNESCO, 1970—, chmn. cultural com. Pres., P.T.A., Washington, 1967. Roman Catholic. Club: Happy Hour Investment (pres. 1965-67) (Washington). Office: Am Assn Museums 2233 Wisconsin Av NW Washington DC 20007

MCGRATH, ROGER GREGORY, III, oil co. exec.; b. Greenwood, Miss., Feb. 19, 1930; s. Roger Gregory and Xavier (Brickell) McG.; student St. Bernard Coll., 1947-48, Miss. State U., 1948-49; m. Barbara Peaster, July 14, 1956; children—John Gregory, Barbara Lynn. With Southland Oil Co., Yazoo City, Miss., 1949—, v.p., 1965-72, v.p., dir., 1972—. Chmn., Yazoo County United Givers Fund, 1966. Served with AUS, 1951-52. Mem. Am. (bd. dirs.). Miss. (bd. dirs., pres. 1972) trucking assns., Yazoo County C. of C. (pres. 1969). Club: Yazoo Country (pres. 1969). Home: 2254 Wildwood Terrace Yazoo City MS 39194 Office: 112 E Broadway St Yazoo City MS 39194

MCGRAW, JACK ELMER, ednl. fund exec.; b. Barwick, Ga., July 8, 1928; s. Henry Harris and Carrie (Vanlandingham) McG.; B.S., Fla. State U., 1950; m. Lynnette Emily Forrester, June 26, 1949; children—Jacquelyn Carol, Russell Howard, Lynnette Elise. Asst. mgr. bookstore Fla. State U., Tallahassee, 1950-52; administrv. asst. Fla. State U. Alumni Assn., 1952-54, asst. exec. sec., 1957-60; dir. pub. relations Valdosta (Ga.) State Coll., 1954-57; asst. sec. Pickett & Hatcher Ednl. Fund, Inc., Columbus, Ga., 1960-63, sec., 1963—. Bd. dirs. Goodwill Industries; sec. Columbus chpt. A.R.C., 1972-73. Served with AUS, 1946-47. Mem. Ga. Assn. student Financial Aid Adminstrs. (v.p. 1968-70). Baptist (chmn. bd. deacons). Kiwanian (pres. 1969. dist. lt. gov. 1969-70, dist. sec.-treas. 1973-74). Home: 2646 Edgewood Rd Columbus GA 31906 Office: 1800 Buena Vista Rd Columbus GA 31902

MCGREEVY, MARTIN KENNETH, ins. co. exec.; b. Central Falls, R.I., Jan. 17, 1931; s. John Martin and Elizabeth Mary (Coderre) McG.; A.B., Providence Coll., 1952; M.A., Boston U., 1953; m. Amy Whitfield Jones, Feb. 19, 1955; children—Brian Kenneth, Marion Elizabeth. Tchr. pub. schs., Pawtucket, R.I., 1953; ins. agt. various cos., Atlanta, 1956-60; br. sales mgr. Am. Mut. Fire Ins. Co., 1960-63, multi peril underwriting mgr., Charleston, S.C., 1963-66, underwriting mgr., 1966-67, v.p. underwriting, 1967-73, sr. v.p., 1973—; v.p. underwriting Carolina Am. Life Ins. Co., 1969—. Active United Fund, Citadel Enll. Found. Served to 1st. lt. AUS, 1953-55. Mem. Soc. C.P.C.U.'s (chpt. pres. 1970-72, regional adv. bd. 1971-72, nat. research activities com. 1973—), S.C. Windstorm and Hail Underwriting Assn. (chmn. bd. dirs. 1971—), Ga. Property Ins. Facility (vice chmn. 1973—, dir.), Ga. Automobile Ins. Plan (dir.), S.C. Hist. Soc., Carolina Art Assn., Charleston Symphony Assn., Phi Alpha Theta. Episcopalian (sr. warden 1969-71, 73, conv. del. 1970). Rotarian (chmn. internat. youth projects com. 1971-72). Club: Charleston Country. Home: 221 Shady Lane Charleston SC 29407 Office: 100 Broad St PO Box 838 Charleston SC 29402

MCGREGOR, WILLIAM HENRY DAVIS, coll. dean; b. Florence, S.C., Mar. 25, 1927; s. Garland and Mary (Davis) McG.; B.S., Clemson Coll., 1951; B.S.F., U. Mich., 1953, M.F., 1953; Ph.D., Duke U., 1958; m. Mary Monica Jackson, Dec 27, 1950; children—William Henry Davis, Mary Monica. Research forester U.S. Forest Service, Lake City, Fla., 1953-57, plant physiologist, 1957-60; research asst. Duke U., 1955-57; asso. prof. dept. forestry Clemson U., 1960-69, prof., 1969—, dean Coll. Forest and Recreation Resources, 1970—. Mem. Clemson City Planning Commn., 1969-70. Served with USNR, 1945-46. Registered Forester, S.C. Mem. Soc. Am. Foresters (chmn. S.C. subsect. 1973), Am. Soc. Plant Physiologists, Am. Forestry Assn., Nat. Parks and Conservation Assn., Sigma Xi, Xi Sigma Pi, Phi Kappa Phi, Phi Eta Sigma (faculty adviser 1964-70). Presbyn. (elder 1967—). Club: Forum. Contbr. articles to forestry jours. Home: 210 Thomas St Clemson SC 29631

MCGRUDER, CHARLES E., physician; b. Wedgeworth, Ala., July 25, 1925; s. Alphonso and Dora (Coleman) McG.; student Ala. A. & M. Coll., 1942-43, Xavier U., 1946-48; M.D., Meharry Med. Coll., 1952; m. Curlie Haslip, June 16, 1952; children—Charles E., Jeffery W. Intern, Maumee Valley Hosp., Toledo, 1952-53, resident, 1953-56; practice medicine, specializing in obstetrics and gynecology, Nashville, Tenn., 1956—; faculty Meharry Med. Coll., 1956—, asso. prof. obstetrics and gynecology, 1968—; staff Hubbard Hosp., Vanderbilt Hosp., Nashville Gen. Hosp., Riverside Hosp. (all Nashville). Asst. troup scoutmaster Middle Tenn. council Boy Scouts Am., 1962-72, scoutmaster, 1973—. Served with USAAF, 1943-46. Recipient Nat. Med. Fellowships grant, 1963. Fellow Am. Coll. Obstetricians and Gynecologists, Phi Beta Sigma. Home: 908 32d Av N Nashville TN 37209 Office: 1104 C 14th Av N Nashville TN 37208

MCGUFFEY, CARROLL WADE, educator; b. nr. Nora, Ky., May 8, 1922; s. Logan Herschel and Kate Ida (Wade) McG.; B.S., Eastern Ky. State U., 1948; M.A., George Peabody Coll. for Tchrs., 1949; D.Ed., Fla. State U., 1957; m. Dorothy Jane Landers, Sept. 2, 1950; children—Carroll Wade, Janie Sue, Linda Lou, Patrick William, Donald Eugene. Math. tchr. Fitzgerald (Ga.) High Sch., 1949-50; survey cons. Ga. Dept. Edn., 1950-51, coordinator field studies, 1952-53, supr. sch. plant services, 1953-54, chief Office Sch. Plant Service, 1956-58; grad. research asst. Fla. State U., 1954-55; sch. plant adminstr. Fla. State Dept. Edn., 1958-60, asst. dir. sch. plant adminstrn., 1960-64; exec. dir. Asso. Cons. Edn., Inc., Tallahassee, 1964-68; prof. edn., dir. ednl. planning and devel. studies U. Ga., Athens, 1968—. Vis. prof. Fla. State U., 1962-68; pres. Ednl. Cons., Inc., Athens, Ga., 1969—; pres. Interstate Sch. Bldg. Service, 1962; adviser Fla. Sch. Plant Mgmt. Assn., 1960-64. Served to capt. AUS, 1942-46, 51-52. Recipient citation Exec. Office Pres. U.S., 1964; certificate of Merit, Fla. Civil Def. Council, 1964. Mem. Council Ednl. Facility Planners Internat. (Distinguished Service award 1971, pres. 1972-73), Am. Assn. Sch. Adminstrs., Assn. U. Profs., Assn. Sch. Bus. Ofcls., Southeastern Council Ednl. Facility Planners (chmn. 1970-71), Phi Delta Kappa. Contbr. articles to profl. jours. Home: Route 1 Deerfield Rd Bogart GA 30622 Office: Coll Edn U Ga Athens GA 30601

MCGUIRE, DONALD CHARLES, govt. ofcl.; b. Clearwater, Kan., Sept. 29, 1915; s. Joseph Tillman and Ruth Anna (Moon) McG.; B.A., U. Wash., Seattle, 1946; Ph.D., U. Cal. at Davis, 1950; m. June Vivian Leet, June 20, 1942; children—Donald Marshall, Kathleen (Mrs. Howard B. Warren), Douglas Joseph, Patrick Arthur. Prof. humanities U. Hawaii, Honolulu, 1957-61, chmn. dept. tropical crop sci., 1961-62; with NSF, Washington, 1962—, sci. edn. adminstr., 1966-73, program mgr. exptl. programs group, 1973—. Mem. environmental scis. adv. com. Washington Tech. Inst., 1973—. Precinct committeeman, chmn. Democratic party, Honolulu, 1952-58. Served to lt. F.A., AUS, 1939-45. Decorated Silver Star. Recipient research grants Hawaiian Acad. Sci., U. Hawaii, 1958-62. Fellow A.A.A.S.; mem. Hawaii Acad. Sci. (chmn. sch. sci. edn. com., 1959-61), Am. Inst. Biol. Scis., Am. Ednl. Research Assn., No. Va. Probability Soc., Assn. Ednl. Tchrs. in Sci. Club: Potomac Appalachian Trail (Washington). Contbr. to profl. jours. Home: 4206 N 35th St Arlington VA 22207 Office: NSF Washington DC 20550

MCGUIRE, FRANK JOSEPH, basketball coach; b. N.Y.C., Nov. 8, 1916; s. Robert J. and Anne (Lynch) McG.; B.S., St. John's U., 1936; M.S. in Phys. Ed., N.Y. U., 1949; L.H.D., Belmont Abbey Coll., 1961; m. Patricia Johnson, Apr. 14, 1941; children—Patricia Jeanne (Mrs. Stephen F. Johnson), Carol Anne, Frank Joseph. Asst. football coach, baseball coach St. Xavier High Sch., N.Y.C., 1937-47; basketball coach, baseball coach St, John's U., N.Y,C,, 1947-52; head basketball coach U, N.C., Chapel Hill, 1952-61, Phila. Warriors, Nat. Basketball Assn., 1961-62; head basketball coach, asso. athletic dir. U. S.C., 1964—. Lectr. basketball various clinics. Pres. N.C. Cerebral Palsy Found., 1958-59; chmn. N.C. Heart Fund Campaign, 1959-60; state dir. S.C. Multiple Slerosis Drive, 1965. Bd. dirs. Nat. Cerebral Palsy Found.; adv. bd. Fellowship of Christian Athletes. Served to lt. USNR, 1942-46. Named U.S. Basketball Coach of Yr., Met. N.Y.C. Writers, 1952, U.P.I., A.P., U.S. Basketball Coaches Assn., 1957. Roman Catholic. Author: Offensive Basketball, 1958; Defensive Basketball, 1959. Home: 268 Sandhurst Rd Columbia SC 29210

MCGUIRE, HUBERT EVERETT, elec. equipment co. exec.; b. Littlefield, Tex., Dec. 6, 1927; s. Albert Roger and Maude (Hutton) McG.; B.S. in Elec. Engring., Tex. Technol. U., 1952; m. Marilyn Swanson, Sept. 27, 1948; children—Thomas Michael, Diana (Mrs. Michael T. Wright). Project engr. Melpar, Inc., Fairfax, Va., 1953-58; engring. mgr. Martin Marietta Corp., Orlando, Fla., 1958-66, NASA programs mgr., 1966-67; v.p. Airtronics Internat. Corp., Fort Lauderdale, Fla., 1966; v.p. Ground/data Corp., Fort Lauderdale, 1967-71, pres., 1971—, also dir.; pres., dir. McGuire Devel. Corp., 1973—; dir. John McGuire Builders, Inc., Fort Lauderdale. Scoutmaster Cub Scouts Am., Fairfax, Va., 1958. Served with USNR, 1946-48. A.I.M. Patentee in field. Home: 5780 SW 4 Ct Plantation FL 33314 Office: 4014 NE 5 Terr Fort Lauderdale FL 33308

MCGUIRK, TERRENCE, TV sta. exec.; b. Bklyn., Apr. 2, 1925; s. William and Loretta (Lanigan) McG.; student Cornell U., 1942—; B.A., Fordham U., 1950; m. Gloria Geoghan, June 17, 1950; children—Terry, Sara (Mrs. Steven Duncan), Susan, Elizabeth, Melissa, Bryan, Michelle. With CBS TV Network, N.Y.C., 1950-61, asst. sales service mgr., 1952-53, sales mgr. extended market planning, 1953-54; With WAGA-TV, Atlanta, 1961-67, 69—, nat. sales mgr., 1964-67, sta. mgr., 1969—; eastern sales mgr. Storer TV Sales, N.Y.C., 1967-69. Sec. Ga. chpt. Leukemia Soc. Am., 1969—; mem. adv. bd. Salvation Army, Atlanta, 1970—. Bd. dirs. Vol. Action Atlanta. Served with AUS, 1943-46. Mem. Atlanta Broadcasting Execs. Club (past pres.). Roman Catholic (lector). Clubs: Cherokee Town and Country (Atlanta); Babylon Yacht (N.Y.). Home: 4390 Sentinel View NW Atlanta GA 30327 Office: PO Box 4207 Atlanta GA 30302

MCGURN, BARRETT, govt. ofcl.; b. N.Y.C., Aug. 6, 1914; s. William Barrett and Alice (Schneider) McG. ; A.B., Fordham U., 1935, Litt.D., 1958; m. Mary Elizabeth Johnson, May 30, 1942 (dec. Feb. 1960); children—William Barrett III, Elizabeth (Mrs. John J. Hehn), Andrew; m. 2d, Janice Ann McLaughlin, June 19, 1962; children—Summers, Martin Barrett, Mark Barrett. With N.Y. Herald Tribune, 1935-66, reporting staff, N.Y.C., 1936-41, 62-66, asst. corr., Rome, 1939, bur. chief Rome 1946-52, 55-62, bur. chief, Paris, 1952-55, acting chief bur., Moscow, 1958, assignments in Morocco, Algeria, Tunisia, Hungary (1956 revolution), Egypt, Greece, Yugoslavia, Poland, Austria, Switzerland, French Equatorial Africa; press attache Am. embassy, Rome, 1966-68; dep. dir. U.S. Govt. Press Center, Vietnam, 1968, dir., 1968-69; counselor for press affairs U.S. embassy, Vietnam, 1968-69; dep. spokesman Dept. of State, press liaison between White House, Dept. of Def., Dept. of State, 1969-72; information dir. U.S. Supreme Ct., 1972—. Mem. State Dept. Com. to Determine Policy on Computerization of Files of Pub. Policy Statements, 1970; mem. interagy. task force to rescue Americans in danger in Amman, Jordan, 1970; mem. White House Com. for Drug Control Information, 1971-72. Mem. Am. embassy com. to select Italian fellowship winners for study in U.S., 1950-52. Trustee Corrs. Fund, 1965-68, trustee Overseas Press Club Found.; adv. council, Fordham U.; journalism adv. council Iona Coll. Served to sgt. AUS, 1943-45; corr. Yank, covered assignments Peliliu Invasion in Marianas, Solomon Islands, New Hebrides, New Zealand and Hawaiian Islands. Decorated Purple Heart, Italian Order of Merit; recipient Polk award for outstanding fgn. reporting L.I. U., 1955; named best press corr. abroad Overseas Press Club, 1957; recipient Christopher award for one of ten most inspiring books of yr., 1960; named man of yr., Cath. Inst. Press, 1962; Fordham U. Alumnus of Yr. in communications, 1963; co-winner ann. Golden Typewriter award N.Y. Newspaper Reporters Assn., 1965, outstanding pub. service award N.Y. chpt. Sigma Delta Chi, 1965; Page One award, 1966; Silurians award, 1966; award N.Y. Newspaper Reporters' Assn. 1966, Meritorious Honor award State Dept., 1972, numerous others. Mem. Fgn. Press Assn. Italy (pres. 1961-62), SHAPE Corrs. Assn. (treas. Paris 1955). Roman Catholic. Clubs: Overseas Press (pres. 1963-65, life gov.) (N.Y.C.); Kenwood (Washington); The Anglo-American Press (Paris); Cercle Sportif (Saigon); Circolo del Ministero degli Affari Esteri (Rome). Author: Decade in Europe, 1959; A Reporter Looks at the Vatican, 1962; A Reporter Looks at American Catholicism, 1967. Contbg. author: The Best from Yank, 1945; Yank, The GI Story of the War, 1946; Highlights from Yank, 1948; Combat, 1950; Overseas Press Club Cook Book, 1962; I Can Tell it Now, 1964; How I Got that Story, 1967; Heroes for Our Times, 1968; also numerous mags. Author initial study N.Y., Herald Tribune series, New York City in Crisis. Early life papers on deposit in U.S. journalism collection Wis. State Hist. Soc. Home: 5229 Duvall Dr Westmoreland Hills Washington DC 20016 Office: Supreme Ct US 1st St NE Washington DC 20543

MCGURN, JOHN MARTIN, utilities exec.; b. El Paso, Tex., Oct. 25, 1913; s. Martin James and Margaret (McGovern) McG.; student St. Edward's U., Austin, Tex. 1930-32; B.S., N.M. State U., 1934; m. Catherine Pinner, Nov. 12, 1946; children—John Martin, Katrina C., Arthur S., Teresa C., Christopher P., Monica N. With El Paso Electric Co., 1934-41; with Vepco Co., Richmond, Va., 1941—, v.p., 1963-66, sr. v.p., 1966-67, pres., chief exec. officer, dir., 1967-70, vice chmn. bd., 1970-71, chmn. bd., chief exec. officer, 1971—; dir. Bank of Va.-Central, Bank of Va. Co., Robertshaw Controls Co. Chmn. Va. Gov.'s Adv. Bd. on Indsl. Devel. Mem. Va., Greater Richmond (v.p.) chambers commerce, So. Electric Exchange (pres.), N.A.M. Pub. Utilities Assn. Virginias (mem. exec. com.), Edison Electric Inst. (mem. adv. com.), Electric Power Research Inst. Roman Catholic. Kiwanian. Home: 4100 W Franklin St Richmond VA 23221 Office: PO Box 26666 Richmond VA 23261

MCHARD, JAMES DALE, govt. ofcl.; b. Blackwell, Okla., Oct. 28, 1933; s. William Carl and Ruby (Thomas) McH.; B.S., Okla. State U., 1956; M.P.H., U. Mich., 1962; m. Mary Janett Bush, Aug. 20, 1961; children—Dale, Janet Marie. Jr. engr. Alcoa, Point Comfort, Tex., 1956-58; asst. engr. Okla. State Dept. Health, Oklahoma City, 1958-61, engr., 1962-69, dir., div. occupational and radiol. health, 1969—. Served with AUS, 1957. Registered profl. engr., Okla. Mem. Am. Air Pollution Control Assn., Am. Pub. Health Assn., Conf. on Radiol. Health, Am. Conf. Govtl. Indsl. Hygienists, Acad. Environmental Health Scientists. Republican. Methodist. Home: 812 NW 42 St Oklahoma City OK 73118 Office: NE 10th and Stonewall St Oklahoma City OK 73105

MCHENRY, RICHARD JOSEPH, pub. relations counselor, publisher; b. Parkersburg, W.Va., June 15, 1934; s. Edward E. and Ethel (Wood) McH.; student Ohio State U., 1952-54; B.A., Marshall U., 1958; m. Eleanor B. McRae, Feb. 19, 1961; children—Richard J., Karen M. Reporter, Orlando (Fla.) Sentinel-Star, 1959-65; pub. relations dir. Botts Advt. Inc., Orlando, 1965-66; pres. Dick McHenry Pub. Relations, Orlando, 1966—, also McHenry Pub. Co., Inc.; pub. Fla. Industries Guide, 1971—, Fla. Golf Guide, 1972—, Fla. Football Annual, 1973—. Television producer WFTV Apt. Guide, Orlando, 1969. Bd. dirs. Miss Fla. Pageant. Served with USNR, 1954-56. Mem. Fla. Pub. Relations Assn. (chpt. pres. 1969-70), Pub. Relations Soc. Am., Sigma Alpha Epsilon. Presbyn. Rotarian. Home: 910 S Osceola Av Orlando FL 32806 Office: 20 W Lucerne Circle Orlando FL 32801

MCHENRY, SILAS LEE, govt. ofcl., educator, agrl. specialist; b. Spokane, Wash., Aug. 30, 1918; s. Silas Laura and Marian C. (Rodibaugh) McH.; B.S., U. Del., 1939, M.S., 1958; Ed.D., Pa. State U., 1960; m. Myrtle Alice Tull, Feb. 20, 1943; children—Silas Lee, Linda Jane. Tchr. vocational agr. Greenwood High Sch., Del., 1939-40; tng. officer U.S. VA, Newark, 1946-47; agrl. agt. Rutgers U., Bridgeton, N.J., 1947-49; extension poultry specialist U. Del., Newark, 1949-51, 53-58; state specialist in poultry sci. U. Hawaii, Honolulu, 1959-64, asso. prof., 1959-62, grad. faculty, 1962-63, prof., 1963-64, chmn. poultry sci. dept., supr. research, teaching, extension, 1963-64; pub. information specialist div. industry advice, bur. edn. and vol. compliance FDA, U.S. Dept. Health, Edn. and Welfare, Washington, 1964-65, industry information officer div. industry edn., program leader chem. contamination, 1966-68, bur. vol. compliance div. industry services, 1968-70, industry relations br. bur. vet. medicine, 1970—. Chmn. food task group Hawaiian Civil Def., 1962-63; participant numerous seminars and workshops U.S., 1966-68; presented results of nation-wide survey extension teaching methods at World's Poultry Congress, Sydney, Australia, 1962. Scoutmaster Boy Scouts Am. Served to lt. comdr. USNR, 1940-45, 51-53. Mem. Am. Assn. U. Profs., Am. Assn. Agrl. Coll. Editors, World's Poultry Sci Assn., Res. Officers U.S., S.A.R., Am. Legion, V.F.W., Fed. Editors Assn., Gamma Sigma Delta. Contbr. numerous articles in field to profl jours. Home: PO Box 9811 Chevy Chase MD 20015 Office: US Food and Drug Adminstrn Washington DC 20204

MCHENRY, WILLIAM PAUL, petroleum refining co. exec.; b. Conway, Ark., June 23, 1913; s. Martin Josiah and Beulah (Denison) McH.; A.B., Hendrix Coll., 1933; student U. Tex., 1934; m. Odell Lawson, Dec. 25, 1937; children—Margaret (Mrs. Jerry D. Collar), Linda (Mrs. Karl Otto). With Macmillan Ring Free Oil Co. Inc., El Dorado, Ark., 1934—, div. mgr., 1960, v.p., 1961—, also dir. Mem. El Dorado C. of C. (pres. 1968). Methodist. Club: El Dorado Country. Home: PO Box 103 Norphlet AR 71759 Office: PO Box 1623 El Dorado AR 71730

MCILVAIN, ERNEST HADLEY, JR., govt. ofcl.; b. Prescott, Ariz., Oct. 29, 1918; s. Ernest Hadley and Ellen (Throne) McI.; B.S., Colo. State U., 1940; M.S., Utah State U., 1948; m. Mary Jane Covey, Mar. 1, 1941; children—Ruth Ann, Michael J. Range ecologist Agrl. Research Service, U.S. Dept. Agr., Woodward, Okla., 1940-54, research agronomist, supt., 1954—. Research cons. Rockefeller Found., 1958—. Scoutmaster Boy Scouts Am., Woodward, 1946-50, 65—. Served with AUS, 1942-46. Decorated Bronze Star medal. Mem. Am. Soc. Range Mgmt., Woodward C. of C. Mem. Christian Ch. Address: So Great Plains Field Sta Woodward OK 73801

MCILVAIN, JESS HALL, architect; b. Denton, Tex., Mar. 29, 1933; s. Charles Lee and Edith (Hall) McI.; B.Arch., Tex. Tech. U., 1959; m. Joni Wimberley, Aug. 23, 1959; children—James Sean, Sheila Maria. Designer Nesmith & Lane, Architects, El Paso, Tex., 1959, Garland & Hilles, Architects, El Paso, Tex., 1960-63; designer, project mgr. William Metcalf Architect, Washington, 1963, Cooper & Auerbach, Architects, Washington, 1963-65, Bucher-Meyers Architects, Washington, 1966-67, project mgr. Weihe, Black, Kerr, Architects, Washington, 1967-68, designer Callmer & Milstead, Architects, Washington, 1968. Archtl. dir. Tile Council of Am., Inc. 1969. Treas., Woodacres Citizen's Assn. Mem. Tex. Tech. U. Century Club. Bd. dirs. Conduit Rd. Fire Bd., 1972—. Served with AUS, 1953-55. Recipient Horizon Homes Regional award for residential design, 1962. Mem. A.I.A. (chpt. exec. bd. 1968, chmn. house com. 1969), Constrn. Specifications Inst. (D.C. Met. chpt. award for excellent service 1973, program chmn. 1972-74, 3d v.p. 1974—), Tex. Tech. U. Alumni Assn. (pres. Washington chpt. 1971-72), Sigma Chi. Clubs: Kenwood (Bethesda, Md.); Loughborough Lions. Author publs. on ceramic tile. Address: 6012 Woodacres Dr Washington DC 20016

MCINNIS, JOHN ROBERT, physician, surgeon; b. Moore County, N.C., July 15, 1908; s. James Dalton and Florence Elizabeth (Blue) McI.; student Davidson Coll., 1927-29, U. Okla., 1931; A.B., U. N.C., 1933; M.D., U. Tenn., 1956; m. Esther Alice Hurley, Dec. 26, 1941; children—John Robert, Charles Hurly, Marilyn Esther, Nancy Catherine. Vice pres., mgr. Caroline Handerchief Co., Inc., West End, N.C., 1935-42; accountant, office mgr. Sandhill Furniture Corp., 1947-51; intern. surgery resident Mercy Hosp., Oklahoma City, 1956-58; pvt. practice medicine and surgery, 1956—; mem. staffs Mercy, Bapt. Meml., Doctors Gen. South Community hosps. (all Oklahoma City). Chmn. sch. bd. West End (N.C.) Pub. Schs., 1959-61. Served from pvt. to capt. AUS, 1942-47; col. M.C. Res. ret. Mem. A.M.A., Am. Acad. Family Practice, Okla., Oklahoma County med. socs., Oklahoma City Clin. Soc., Ret. Officers Assn., Capitol Hill, Oklahoma City chambers commerce. Presbyn. (elder, trustee). Mason (32 deg., Shriner); mem. Order Eastern Star (past patron). Club: Hillcrest Golf and Country (Oklahoma City). Home: 7008 S Country Club Dr Oklahoma City OK 73159 Office: 4515 S Pennsylvania St Oklahoma City OK 73119

MCINTOSH, EDWARD DALTON, lawyer; b. Marlin, Tex., Dec. 19, 1932; s. Ed and Audie (Allen) McI.; B.B.A., U. Tex., 1956, LL.B., 1960. Admitted to Tex. bar, 1960; asst. county atty. Wichita County, Tex., 1960-61; asso. Banner & McIntosh and predecessor firm, Wichita Falls, Tex., 1962-65, partner, 1965—. Served with AUS, 1956-57. Mem. Wichita County Bar Assn. (pres. 1972-73), Delta Theta Phi, Sigma Nu. Home: 2020 Santa Fe St Wichita Falls TX Office: 1200 Hamilton Bldg Wichita Falls TX 76301

MCINTOSH, NEVA TRICE (MRS. OTHO R. MCINTOSH), dept. store exec.; b. Louisville, Miss., Nov. 9, 1921; d. John Milton and Viola (Futrell) Trice; grad. high sch.; m. Otho R. McIntosh, Sept. 28, 1940; 1 dau., Mattie (Mrs. Reynolds R. Smith, Jr.). Cosmetic buyer L. Hammel Dept. Stores, Inc., Mobile, Ala., 1953-62, accessory and cosmetic buyer, 1968-73, area mgr. cosmetics and fashion accessories, 1973—; sales rep. Helena Rubinstein Cosmetics, 1962-68. Baptist. Club: Marvella Garden (Chickasaw, Ala.). Home: 262 5th Av Chickasaw AL 36611 Office: 3300 Bel Air Mall Mobile AL 36623

MCINTOSH, ROY THOMAS, mech. engr.; b. St. Joseph, Mo., Aug. 28, 1910; s. Paul Augustus and Amanda Mae Rose (Sowards) McI.; student N.M. Sch. Mines, 1949-50; A.S., Oscar Rose Jr. Coll., 1972; m. Billie Jo Berlin, Sept. 4, 1953; 1 dau., Julie Margo. Electrician, machinist Smith Brothers Mfg. Co., St. Joseph, 1931-40; journeyman mechanic Consol. Aircraft Co., San Diego, Cal, 1940-42; supervisory inspector, instr. tech. writer N.Am. Aviation, Inglewood, Cal., 1942-44; dept. head (hydraulics) Escola Tecnica de Aviacao, Brazil, 1944-48; with Boeing Co., various locations, 1950-66, Cape Kennedy, Fla., 1966-67, Everett, Wash., 1968-70; flightline mechanic Lockheed-Cal. Co., Palmdale, 1971—. Recipient Appreciation certificate USAF, 1963, Achievement award Lockheed, 1972. Registered profl. engr., Okla. Mem. Soc. Tech. Writers and Editors (banquet chmn. 1964), Am. Soc. M.E., Am. Inst. Aeros. and Astronautics, Am. Soc. Tech. Edn., Nat., Okla. socs. profl. engrs. Mason (Shriner). Home: 9813 Chesterton Pl Oklahoma City OK 73120

MCINTYRE, BRUCE MARTIN, oil co. exec.; b. Denver, Aug. 1, 1927; s. Paul Joseph and Alice Herschel (Martin) M.; A.B., Harvard, 1950, M.B.A., 1952; m. Mary Ellen Neale, Nov. 20, 1954; children—Betsy, John. Dist. landman Sinclair Oil & Gas Co., Denver, 1952-63; mgr. oil and gas investments, chmn. investment com. Jenney Oil Co., Chestnut Hill, Mass., 1963-69; v.p. finance C. & K. Petroleum Inc., Houston, 1969—. Gen. partner Pegasus Fund Ltd., Houston, 1971—. Served with USNR, 1945-46. Mem. Boston Soc. Security Analysts, Financial Execs. Inst. Episcopalian. Clubs: Country Brookline, Mass., Harvard of N.Y., Denver, Mile High of Denver. Home: 6154 San Felipe Rd Houston TX 77027 Office: 608 First City National Bank Bldg Houston TX 77002

MCINTYRE, MARY SHELLEY, musician; b. Good Pine, La.; d. Archibald Ormsby and May (Rawlings) McIntyre; student Ward-Belmont Jr. Coll., 1 year, New Orleans Conservatory; 1 year; grad., also postgrad. Juilliard Inst. Mus. Art, N.Y.C.; student Columbia, 1 summer, pupil Vlado Kolitsch, N.Y.C. Solo violinist concert ensemble The Homestead, Hot Springs, Va., 8 years; solo violinist concert ensemble Lauderdale Beach Hotel, Ft. Lauderdale, Fla., 5 winters; solo violinist concert ensemble Grindstone Inn, Winter Harbor, Me., 3 summers; violinist Houston Symphony, 1943—; violist Brevard (N.C.) Festival 2 seasons. Mem. Am. Fedn. Musicans. Presbyn. Home: 2724 Nottingham Rd Houston TX 77005 Office: Houston Symphony Soc Jesse H Jones Hall for Performing Arts 615 Louisiana St Houston TX 77001

MCINTYRE, ROBERT ALLEN, JR., biologist, educator; b. Lumberton, N.C., Feb. 25, 1926; s. Robert Allen and Margaret (Pope) M.; B.S., Wake Forest U., 1946; M.A., U. N.C., 1948. Asst. prof. biology Coker Coll., Hartsville, S.C., 1948-51; asso. prof. biology Presbyn. Coll., Clinton, S.C., 1955-62, Campbell Coll., Buies Creek, N.C., 1962—. NSF grantee, 1960, 69. Mem. Am. Assn. U. Profs., Sigma Xi. Baptist (deacon). Home: PO Box 201 Buies Creek NC 27506

MCINTYRE, STANLEY DONALD, govt. ofcl.; b. Evanston, Ill., Feb. 4, 1938; s. Donald Sharvy and Daisy Katherine (Barrett) McI.; B.S. in Mech. Engring., U. Ill., 1961; m. Joan Carol Daugherty, Aug. 24, 1957; children—Michael Stanley, David John, Sharon Lynne. Asso. research engr. Boeing Co., Seattle, 1961-62, Huntsville, Ala., 1962-65; sr. engr. Brown Engring. Co., Huntsville, 1965-66; subsystem mgr. Marshall Space Flight Center, NASA, Huntsville, 1966—. Team coach Little League, 1972; team mgr. Babe Ruth League, 1973. Registered profl. engr., Ala. Democrat. Methodist. Clubs: Northern Ala. Amateur Retriever (pres. 1965-69), Rocket City Radio Controllers. Home: 10001 Hickory Hill Lane SE Huntsville AL 35803 Office: NASA Marshall Space Flight Center Huntsville AL 35803

MCIVER, RICHARD DONALD, organic geochemist, oceanographer; b. South Haven, Mich., Dec. 1, 1929; s. William Kenneth and Irene (Cooper) McI.; A.B., John Brown U., 1951; Ph.D., Ohio State U., 1954; m. Virginia Elaine Schmidt, Sept. 7, 1951; children—Richard William, David Walter, Cheryl Elaine. Research chemist Carter Oil Co., Tulsa, 1956-58; sr. research chemist Jersey Prodn. Research Co., Tulsa, 1958-64, sect. head, 1964; sect. supr. Esso Prodn. Research Co., Houston, 1965-67, sr. research asso. 1970—. Planning specialist Humble Oil & Refining Co., Houston, 1968-69. Served with AUS, 1954-56. Mem. Am. Chem. Soc., Geochem. Soc. (chmn. organic geochemistry div. 1972), Am. Assn. Petroleum Geologists (asso. editor Bull. 1969—). Contbr. articles to sci., tech. jours. Home: 6203 Rutherslenn St Houston TX 77035 Office: PO Box 2189 Houston TX 77001

MCKAMIE, EDGAR MORAN, electric supply co. exec.; b. Moody, Tex., June 14, 1925; s. William Henry and Nancy Ida (Permenter) McK; grad. high sch.; m. Lura Fay Snowden, May 20, 1949; children—William Michael, David Edgar. Trainee Celanese Corp., Kingsville, Tex., 1947; salesman Corpus Christi (Tex.) Hardware, 1948-50; with Dealers Elec. Supply Co., Waco, Tex., 1950—, sales mgr., 1955-58, store mgr., 1958-61, v.p. sales and purchasing, 1961—; partner Eimak Industries, Waco, 1971—. Active United Fund drive, 1959-70; cubmaster Boy Scouts Am., 1959, scoutmaster, 1966-68, explorer adviser, 1968-73, dist. commr., 1961-64, 1968-71, council explorer chmn., 1970-71, council commr., 1972-73; v.p. Waco Teenage Baseball, 1969-71; pres. Dist. 15 Christian Mens Fellowship, 1963-65; pres. Northwestern Little League, 1965; pres. elect Christian Mens Fellowship Tex., 1972-73, pres., 1973-74. Del., Democratic County Conv., 1956, 58. Bd. dirs. Lake Air Little League. Served with U.S. Mcht. Marine, 1943-46. Recipient Silver Beaver award Boy Scouts Am., 1966. Mem. Christian Ch. (chmn. bd. 1961-62, 1968, 70, 73, 74, mem. state bd. 1972-74). Club: Woodland West Country (Waco). Home: 5409 Edinburgh St Waco TX 76710 Office: 1808 Washington St Waco TX 76703

MCKAY, CHARLES FLINT, bus. cons.; b. St. Johnsbury, Vt., Nov. 18, 1930; s. Littleton Kirk and Mabel (Flint) McK.; B.B.A., U. Miami, 1954; m. Margaret Eileen Mund, June 14, 1956; children—Lisa Charlene, Sharon Lee. U.S. fgn. service officer Am. embassy, Quito, Ecuador, 1956-57, Am. consulate, Puerto la Cruz, Venezuela, 1957-59, Am. embassy, Uruguay, 1959-62; pres. chmn. bd. North & Latin Am. Devel. Corp., 1962—; pres., founder Charles McKay & Assos., Inc., Miami, Fla., 1964—. Mem. exec. res. U.S. Dept Commerce, 1967; mem. Regional Export Expansion Council, del. to nat. council conf., Washington, 1970, vice chmn. S. Fla. council, 1971, 72. Founding mem., bd. dirs. Nat. Fedn. Export Mgmt. Cos., 1972—, Internat. Center, Inc., 1972—, bd. dirs. Bd. Internat. Trade, 1969—. Served to 1st lt. AUS, 1955-56. Mem. Dominican-Am. C. of C. (pres.) Fla. Colombia Alliance, Miami-Dade County C. of C. (bd. dirs.), C. of C. of Ams. (dir. 1970, 71, chmn. world trade com. 1972), Center for Advanced Internat. Studies (mem. council), Fla. World Trade Assn. (founder, pres. 1968—). Rotarian. Contbg. author: Guidelines to Operating in Latin America, 1970. Author: A Profile of International Business in Dade County, Florida, 1972; Caribbean Yachting Facilities, 1972; Exporter Profiles, 1973; Florida's World Trade Companies, 1974. Home: 7550 SW 141 St Miami FL 33158 Office: 299 Alhambra Circle Coral Gables FL 33134

MCKAY, CONNALLY, judge; b. Eddy, Tex., Sept. 22, 1914; s. Daniel Sparks and Lila (Connally) McK.; LL.B., Baylor U., 1937; m. Glee McCrary, Mar. 26, 1938; children—Diane (Mrs. Thomas W. Gilliam), Elaine (Mrs. Walker Harman), Robert Connally. Admitted to Tex. bar, 1937; county atty., Wood County, Tex., 1941-43, 46; dist. atty. Smith, Wood & Upshur Counties, Tex., 1946-49; referee in bankruptcy, 1949-52; dist. judge 114th Jud. Dist., Tyler, Tex., 1953-69; asso. justice Ct. of Civil Appeals, 12th Supreme Jud. Dist. of Tex., Tyler, 1969—; dir. Citizens First Nat. Bank of Tyler, E. Tex. Savs. & Loan Assn. Mem. Tex. Jud. Qualifications Commn. of Tex., 1965-69. Pres., East Tex. Fair Assn., 1960, Tyler Indsl. Found., 1966-67, East Tex. Hosp. Found. 1970—, Tex. Rose Festival Assn., 1974; mem. devel. council Baylor U., 1971—; mem. Human Welfare commn. Baptist Gen. Conv. of Tex., 1971—. Bd. dirs. Bapt. Found. Tex.; trustee Baylor Coll. Dentistry. Served to lt. USNR, 1943-46. Recipient T.B. Butler award as outstanding citizen, T.B. Butler Pub. Co., 1965. Mem. Tyler C. of C. (pres. 1965-66), Baylor U. Ex-Students' Assn. (pres. 1963), State Bar Tex. Baptist (chmn. bd. deacons 1959-60). Mason (Shriner). Home: 3110 Belmead St Tyler TX 75701 Office: 306 County Courthouse Tyler TX 75701

MCKAY, DOUTHITT ELIZABETH MELUGIN (MRS. JAMES MARVIN MCKAY), ret. librarian; b. Bonham, Tex., Jan. 3, 1904; d. William Stephen and Etta Elizabeth (Ballew) Melugin; student U. Tex., 1924-27; B.A., Our Lady of the Lake, 1961, provisional library certificate, 1964; m. James Marvin McKay, Nov. 15, 1930; (dec. Apr. 1955). Sec. to civilian supt., Randolph AFB, 1943-47; with Tex. Pub. Schs., 1925-73; tchr. San Antonio Ind. Sch. Dist., 1968-73; genealogy record searcher. Mem. N.E.A., Tex. State Tchrs. Assn., D.A.R., Tenn., Decatur geneal. socs. Democrat. Baptist. Mem. Order Eastern Star. Home: 618 Rayburn Dr San Antonio TX 78221

MCKAY, EGBERT ROBINSON, police chief; b. Mecklenburg County, nr. Charlotte, N.C., Nov. 3, 1911; s. Elmer Ranson and Mary Arlena (Benfield) McK.; student Mecklenburg County Police Tng. Sch., 1946-47, 67-68; m. Edith Isenhour, Dec. 17, 1935; 1 son, James Carroll (dec.). Mgr. Vicks Lunch, Concord, N.C., 1931-36; agt. Pilot Life Ins. Co., Concord, 1936-41; Weave room Cannon Mills, Concord, 1942; with Concord (N.C.) Police Dept., 1943—, police chief, 1969—. Served with USNR, 1943-45. Mem. Piedmont Law Enforcement Acad. (dir. 1966—), N.C. Law Enforcement Officers Assn. (dir. 1969—), N.C. Police Execs. Assn., Internat. Assn. Chiefs Police, Inc. Lutheran (stewardship chmn. 1970-71, mem. council, congl. v.p.). Lion, Mason. Home: 629 Propston St NW Concord NC 28025 Office: 8 Barbrick Av SW Concord NC 28025

MCKAY, GORDON BUSH, educator; b. Bangor, Me., Apr. 4, 1919; s. Hugh Gordon and Elizabeth (Jellison) McK.; B.S., U. Me., 1941; M.S., Columbia, 1946, Ph.D., 1951; m. Florence Morrissette, Dec. 25, 1941 (dec. 1964); children—Carol Ann, Sally Lou (Mrs. Curtis Hedman), Candie Jane (Mrs. Charles Lamb), Ruth Lynn (Mrs. Michael Channell), Donald Douglas, Ginger Sue; m. 2d, Roberta Smith Hopper, Aug. 31, 1966. Engr., Wright Aero. Corp., Wood-Ridge, N.J., 1941-48; asso. prof. mech. engring. Columbia, 1948-59; prof., head mech. engring. U. Wichita (Kan.), 1959-64; prof. U. Ala., University, 1964—. Cons., Curtis Wright Corp., N.Y., 1948-59, Bergen Research Engring. Corp., N.J., 1950-62, Kennecott Copper Corp., N.Y., 1953-55, Boeing Airplane Co., Wichita, 1960-61, Beach Aircraft Corp., Wichita, 1962-64, Hayes Internat. Corp., Birmingham, Ala., 1965-70, Que. Metal Poweders Ltd. (Can.), Sorel, 1967-71, Remtech Corp., Birmingham, 1970-73. Registered profl. engr., N.Y. Mem. Am. Soc. M.E., Am. Helicopter Soc., Nat. Soc. Profl. Engrs., Am. Inst. Aeros. and Astronautics, N.Y. Acad. Scis., Am. Soc. U. Profs., Sigma Xi, Tau Beta Pi, Sigma Nu. Episcopalian. Kiwanian. Home: 2728 Claymont Circle Tuscaloosa AL 35401 Office: Dept Mechanical Engineering Univ Alabama University AL 35486

MCKAY, GRIFFITH HEAD, cons. engr.; b. Jackson, Miss., Oct. 20, 1907; s. John Peyton and Alice Rose (Strait) McK.; B.S. in Civil Engring., Miss. State U., 1930, Jr. engr. Ark.-La. Gas Co., Shreveport, La., 1930-32, natural gas engr., 1932-42; cons. engr. WPB, Washington, 1942-43; asst. to v.p. Tenn. Gas Transmission Co., Houston, 1943-45, mgr. sales, 1945-47, v.p., 1947-48; v.p., dir. East Tenn. Natural Gas Co., Chattanooga, 1948-49; cons. engr., mgmt., gas, fuels, real estate leasing, rentals, financing, Houston, 1959—. Tchr. gas engring. Centenary Coll., 1939-41. Registered profl. engr., Tex. Mem. Nat., Tex. socs. profl. engrs., Houston Engring. and Sci. Soc, Democrat. Club: Houston. Contbr. articles to trade mags. Designer (with R.M. Hutchins) Slide Rule-High Gas Transmission. Home: 1220 Southmore St Houston TX 77004 Office: 1215 Oakdale St Houston TX 77004

MCKAY, JAMES ALVIN, JR., judge; b. San Antonio, Nov. 22, 1917; s. James Alvin and Margaret (Basala) McK.; LL.B., U. Tex. 1941; m. Ida Lucille Camiade, Dec. 4, 1941; children—Michael, Madelyn, Patrick, Dennis, Marie. Admitted to Tex. bar, 1943, practiced in San Antonio, 1946-62; judge 150th Dist. Ct., Bexar County (Tex.), San Antonio, 1963—. Participant nat. conf. Justice for the Child, U. Chgo., 1961, Nat. Inst. for Juvenile Ct. Judges, U. Okla., 1963, Nat. Inst. Juvenile Ct. Judges, U. Minn., 1966. Mem. Tex. Ho. of Reps., 1959-60. Pres., Community Welfare Council San Antonio, 1955-56; chmn. San Antonio Planning and Zoning Commn., 1957-58; chmn. Bexar County Juvenile Bd., 1963-69. Recipient citation for outstanding service Pres.'s Com. on Nat. Employ the Physically Handicapped Week, 1951. Served from pvt. to capt. AUS, 1942-46; PTO; lt. col. Res. (ret.). Recipient Papal award Pro Ecclesia et Pontifice, 1973. Mem. San Antonio Bar Assn. (pres. 1955), State Bar Tex., Harp and Shamrock Soc. Tex., Am. Legion (comdr. 20th Dist. 1952-54, judge adv. Tex. 1948-49), Cath. Lawyers Guild, Roman Catholic (past legislation chmn. Archdiocesan Council Cath. Men.). Home: 807 Patricia Dr San Antonio TX 78216 Office: Bexar County Courthouse San Antonio TX 78204

MCKAY, JOHN JUDSON, JR., lawyer; b. Anderson, S.C., Aug. 13, 1939; s. John Judson and Polly (Plowden) McK.; A.B., U. S.C., 1960, J.D. cum laude, 1966; m. Jill Hall Ryon, June 3, 1961; children—Julia Plowden, Katherine Henry, William Ryon, Elizabeth Hall. Admitted to S.C. bar, 1966; atty. Haynsworth, Perry, Bryant, Marion &

Johnstone, Greenville, 1966-70; partner Rainey, Fant & McKay, Greenville, 1970—. Served to lt. (j.g.) USNR, 1961-63; lt. comdr. Res., 1973. Mem. Am., S.C. (sec. young lawyers 1969, pres. 1971, mem. exec. com. 1972), Greenville County bar assns., S.C. Def. Lawyers Assn., Blue Key, Phi Delta Phi, Chi Psi. Episcopalian. Clubs: Poinsett, Greenville Country, Western Carolina Sailing. Editor-in-chief S.C. Law Rev., 1965-66. Home: 188 Chapman Rd Greenville SC 29605 Office: 118 Broadus Av Greenville SC 29601

MCKAY, LAWRENCE BRIAN, sales promotion co. exec.; b. Bronx, N.Y., Feb. 19, 1924; s. William Leo and Lillian (Treacey) McK.; student U. Cal. at Los Angeles, 1947-49; B.B.A., N.Y. U., 1943; m. Lola Merle Reagan, Mar. 10, 1948. Partner, dir. marketing Marketing Innovations Co., Arlington, Va., Washington, 1967—; dir. several cos. Mem. Arlington Ridge Civic Assn., 1973—; co-founder South Arlington Coalition, 1973. Served with 11th AAF, World War II; PTO. Mem. Am. Marketing Assn., Am. Inventors Assn. Methodist (mem. adminstrv. bd.). Patentee robbery prevention device. Home and office: 1400 S Joyce St Arlington VA 22202

MCKAY, SAMUEL LEROY, clergyman; b. nr. Charlotte, N.C., Oct. 15, 1913; s. Elmer Ranson and Arlena (Benfield) McK.; A.B. cum laude, Erskine Coll., 1937; B.D. cum laude, Erskine Theol. Sem., 1939; postgrad. U. Ga., 1941-42, Union Theol. Sem., 1957; m. Martha Elizabeth Caldwell, Apr. 29, 1939; children—Samuel LeRoy, Mary Louise, William Ranson. Ordained to ministry of Presbyn. Ch., 1940; pastor Prosperity Asso. Ref. Ch., Fayetteville, Tenn., 1942-46, Bethel Asso. Ref. Ch., Oak Hill, Ala., 1946-50, 1st Asso. Ref. Ch., Salisbury, N.C., 1950-53, 1st Ch. U.S., Dallas, N.C., 1953-60, First Ch., Kernersville, N.C., 1960-66, Cooleemee (N.C.) Presbyn. Ch., 1966-69, Broadway-Salem Presbyn. Ch., Broadway, N.C., 1969—. Stated clk. Gen. Synod Asso. Ref. Presbyn. Ch., 1950-53; commr. Gen. Assembly Presbyn. Ch. U.S., 1960, 69; permanent clk. Winston-Salem Presbytery, 1961-69, chmn. leadership edn. com., 1962-66, chmn. Christian edn. com., 1967-68; supr. chaplaincy program Davie County Hosp., 1968-69. Pres. Dallas P.T.A., 1955-56. Bd. mgrs. Kernersville YMCA, 1962-66, chmn. membership com., 1963, treas., 1964, pres., 1965-66; bd. dirs. Winston-Salem-Forsyth County YMCA, 1965-66. Mem. Kernersville Area Ministers Assn. (pres. 1963-64), N.C. Poetry Soc. (dir. 1971—, chmn. poetry contests 1970-72, pres. 1972-74), Clan MacKay Soc. N.Am. (pres. 1971—). Lion. Contbr. articles and sermons to periodicals and publs. Home: PO Box 268 Broadway NC 27505 Office: Broadway Presbyn Ch Main at Mcleod Broadway NC 27505

MCKEE, ARTHUR, JR., treasure hunter, museum ofcl.; b. Bridgeton, N.J., Nov. 2, 1910; s. Arthur and Mabel A. (Chain) McK.; grad. Bridgeton High Sch., 1931; m. Janet Gay Bodden; children—Wayne Norris (dec.), Patricia D., Richard A., Arthur III, Terry (dec.), Karen T., Kevin D. Recreational dir., Bridgeton, 1935-36; city recreation dir., Homestead, Fla., 1940-50; deep sea Diver USN pipe line, Fla., 1941-43; organized McKee's Museum Sunken Treasure, Inc., Homestead, 1949; founder, operator McKee's Treasure Mus., Treasure Harbor, Plantation Key, Fla., 1950—; founder, operator divers' tng. sch. underwater archaeology, Treasure Harbor, 1960—; condr. 32 expdns., Bahamas, Fla. Keys, Caribbean, including McKee-Smithsonian Instn. expdn. to recover treasure from Spanish ship wrecked 1733; evacuated Sunken City Port Royal with Link expdn., Kingston Harbor; guest appearances numerous TV shows, Of Land and Seas, To Tell the Truth, Danger is My Business, Mike Douglas Show, others, Named Mr. Treasure Hunter Am. Treasure Trove Club, N.Y.C., 1966, Pioneer in Underwater Archaeology in Western Hemisphere Nat. Geog. Soc., 1973-74. Mem. Islamorada (pres. 1967-68), Upper Keys Fla. (dir. 1973-74) chambers commerce. Elk. Clubs: Ocho Rios Reef (Jamaica); Caribbean Yacht (Grand Cayman). Patentee underwater motion picture camera, underwater metal detector, system excavating wreck site, others. Recoveries include gold, silver, doubloons, Spanish Coins and artifacts. Home: Treasure Harbor Plantation Key FL 33070

MCKEE, LARRY ABRAHAM, civil engr., engring. co. exec.; b. Folsom, La., Sept. 3, 1932; s. Jules B. and Carrie Roberta (Wilkins) McK.; B.S. in Civil Engring., La. State U., 1958; m. Betty Jo Thaxton, July 23, 1960; children—Karen Tracey, Michael Kevin. Pres., Profl. Engring. Cons. Corp., Baton Rouge, 1969—, S.E. Aerial Mappers, Inc., Baton Rouge, 1973—. Democratic exec. committeeman East Baton Rouge Parish, 1970—. Served with AUS, 1953-55. Registered profl. engr., La., Tex., Miss., Ala., Mo. Mem. Am. Soc. C.E. (v.p. Baton Rouge chpt. 1973—), La. Engr. Soc. (legislative chmn. 1972-73). Methodist (trustee). Home: 1045 Verdun Dr Baton Rouge LA 70810 Office: PO Box 64785 3340 Convention St Baton Rouge LA 70806

MCKEE, MELVIN JAY, editor; b. Webb City, Mo., June 22, 1934; s. Daniel H. and LaVeta (Cook) McK.; B.A. cum laude, Tenn. Temple Coll., 1958; M.A., U. Ga., 1959; postgrad. (fellow) Emory U., 1962-64, Ga. State U., 1969. Founder, editor DeKalb Lit. Arts Jour., Clarkston, Ga., 1966—; founder, editor, publisher This Issue, The Magazine of the New Creative, Atlanta, 1971—. Mem. faculty Young Harris Coll., 1959-61, U. Tenn., 1961, West Ga. Coll., 1961-62, DeKalb Coll., 1964—. Served with Air Force USNR, 1952-54. Named Ga. Young Writer of Year So. Festival, U. Ga., 1959. Mem. South Atlantic Modern Lang. Assn., Modern Lang. Assn., Nat. Council Tchrs. English, Internat. Composers Guild, Poetry Soc. Am. Home: 110 E Maple St Decatur GA 30030 Office: 555 Indian Creek Rd Clarkston GA 30021

MCKEE, REUEL STEWART, JR., hwy. constrn. co. exec.; b. Phila., Feb. 13, 1932; s. Reuel Stewart and Elizabeth Ann (Cochran) McK.; B.S. in Civil Engring., Drexel Inst. Tech., 1958; m. Joan E. Jurgensen, June 8, 1957; children—Heather, Matthew, Piper. Vice pres. John R. Jurgensen Co., contractors, Cin., 1958-66; gen. supt. Gallaqter Asphalt Corp., Chgo., 1966-68; owner, v.p. McGouney and McKee, Inc., Portsmouth, O., 1968-72; v.p. Dickerson, Inc. Monroe, N.C., 1972—. Served with AUS, 1953-55. Mem. Am. Soc. C.E. Presbyn. Mason. Home: Route 9 Box 36A Rolling Hills Dr Monroe NC 28110 Office: Box 400 Monroe NC 28110

MCKEE, WILLIAM E., educator; b. Apr. 15, 1924; s. Elmer W. McK.; B.M., Syracuse; M.M., Eastman Sch. Music; Ph.D., N. Tex. State U.; m. Margaret Ruby; children—George, Jonathan, Timothy, Robin. Faculty, U. Tulsa, 1950—, presently prof. music. Mem. Am. Musicological Assn., Phi Mu Alpha, Lambda Chi Alpha. Composer: Introduction and Dance. Contbr. articles to profl. journals. Office: Sch Music U Tulsa 600 College Av S Tulsa OK 74104*

MCKELLAR, DOUGLAS HOWARD, railroad exec.; b. Louisville, June 17, 1917; s. Robert Lide and Mattie-Sevier (Bonnie) McK.; grad. Hotchkiss Sch., 1935; B.S., Yale, 1939; m. Jessie Barker, May 4, 1943; 1 son, Douglas Howard. Salesman, Campbell Soup Co., Camden, N.J., 1939-41, Ky. Color & Chem. Co., Louisville, 1945-51; with sales, marketing dept. Reynolds Metals Co., Louisville, 1951-58; pres. Louisville Flying Service, Inc., 1958—; v.p. freight traffic L. & N. R.R. Co., Louisville, 1961—. Served to lt. col. USAAF, 1941-45; ETO. Decorated D.F.C., Air medal with four clusters. Home: 160 Westwind Rd Louisville KY 40207 Office: 908 W Broadway Louisville KY 40201

MCKELPIN, JOSEPH PRYCE, coll. dean; b. Highlandale, Miss., May 6, 1914; s. Kirby and Lula (Smith) McK.; B.A., So. U., 1943; M.S., U. Wis., 1948, Ph.D., 1952; m. Peggy Ann Jones, Oct. 24, 1972; children by previous marriage—Joseph Pryce, Emmett Osceola. Tchr. Richard Sch., New Orleans, 1938-52; faculty So. U., Baton Rouge, 1952-62; prof. edn., dir. of ednl. research N.C. Central U., Durham, 1962-67; dir. research and evaluation Edn. Improvement Program, So. Assn. Colls. and Schs., Atlanta, 1967-73; acad. dean Morris Brown Coll., Atlanta, 1973—. Mem. Durham (N.C.) Council on Human Relations, 1964-67, treas. 1966-67. Served to 2d lt. AUS, 1943-46. Mem. Nat. Soc. for Study Edn., Nat. Council on Measurement in Edn., Am. Ednl. Research Assn., Am. Assn. U. Profs., Phi Delta Kappa, Kappa Delta Pi, Kappa Phi Kappa, Omega Psi Phi. Home: 794 Casplan St SW Atlanta GA 30310 Office: Morris Brown College 643 Hunter St Atlanta GA 30314

MCKENNA, THOMAS ADAM, JR., analytical chemist; b. Natchez, Miss., Mar. 14, 1922; s. Thomas Adam and Blanche (Korndorffer) McK.; student Copiah-Lincoln Jr. Coll., 1938-39; B.S. in Chemistry, La, State U., 1944; student U. Miss., 1955, Podbielniak Inst., 1956; m. Peggy Marie McCrosky, June 2, 1949; children—Mary Lucille, Thomas Adam III, Michael Gerard, Patrick Joseph. With Motor Fuels Lab., Dept. Revenue, State La.; with Firestone Tire & Rubber Co., Orange, Tex., 1944—, successively shift control chemist, spl. problems chemist, spl. problems chemist, lab., mgr. and chief chemist, 1956—; owner, dir. work Marian Labs., Lake Charles, La., 1955—, Lectr. Lamar Coll. Tech., 1963. Mem. dist. advancement com. Boy Scouts Am.; pres. St. Mary's Home and Sch. Assn., 1963-64; active Community Concert Assn. Fellow Am. Inst. Chemists; mem. Gulf Coast Spectroscopic Group (chmn.), Am. Soc. Quality Control (area dir. S. Tex. sect. 1959—; chmn. membership com. Sabine subsect.; sr. mem.), Am. Chem. Soc. (chmn. S.W. La. 1954—; sec. Tex.-La.-Gulf sect. 1961-62), Am. Soc. Testing Materials (com. chmn.), A.A.A.S., C. of C., Alpha Tau Omega. K.C. Editor: The Newletter, 1949-54. Author numerous articles in profl. jours.; also papers. Home: 2001 W Rio Grande Pl Orange TX 77631 Office: PO Box 1269 Orange TX 77631

MCKENNA, WILLIAM FRANCIS, lawyer; b. Meriden, Conn., May 14, 1910; s. Frank Joseph and Alice (Downes) McK.; Ph.B., Yale, 1930, J.D., 1932; m. Catherine Agnes Donahue, June 25, 1935; children—William Francis (dec. 1966), Daniel Joseph. Admitted to Conn, bar, 1932; with Buckley, Creedon & Danaher, Hartford, 1932-35; counsel, acting chief pub. loans sect. legal div. RFC, Washington, 1935-42; counsel Def. Supplies Corp., 1942; chief airports br. War Assets Adminstrn., 1945-47; counsel com. banking and currency U.S. Senate, 1947-57, U.S. Joint Com. Def. Prodn., 1950-51; administrv. asst. U.S. Senator William Benton, 1950; asso. Ford Motor Co., Washington Office, 1957-58; house counsel Nat. Assn. Mut. Savs. Banks, N.Y.C., 1958-59; dir-counsel Washington office Nat. Assn. Mut. Savs. Banks, Washington, 1959-63; gen. counsel, v.p. Nat. Savs. and Loan League, Washington, 1963—, sec., 1973—; sec. Nat. League Internat., Inc., 1974—. Comdg. officer USNR Law Co. 5-11, Washington, 1956-57, 64-65. Pres. Conn. Democrats D.C., 1939-40. Served from lt. (j.g.) to lt., USNR, 1943-45, capt. USNR ret. Mem. Am. Inter-Am., Fed., Md., D.C. bar assns., Bar Assn. D.C., Yale Law Sch. Assn., U.S. Senate Assn. Adminstrv. Assts. and Secs., Assn. Former Senate Aides, Assn. Bar City N.Y., Nat. Lawyers Club, Lambda Alpha. Roman Catholic (lector, servor). Clubs: Yale, University, Exchequer (past chancellor) (Washington); Yale (N.Y.C.); Men's (Silver Spring, Md.). Editor in chief Nat. League Mgrs. Manual; writer Nat. League legal bulls; lectr. savs. and loan topics. Home: 8004 Park Crest Dr Silver Spring MD 20910 Office: 1200 17th St NW Washington DC 20036

MCKENNEY, THOMAS WILLIAM, biologist; b. Livermore, Me., Dec. 2, 1928; s. Hartson William and Jeanette Isabelle (MacCarlie) McK.; B.Sc., Tufts U., 1951; M.Sc., U. Miami (Fla.), 1958, Ph.D., 1965; m. Mary Elizabeth Marmion, June 4, 1960. Research asst. Rosensteil Sch. Marine and Atmosphere Sci., U. Miami, Fla., 1955-58, research instr., 1958-63; asst. prof. biology Meml. U. Nfld., St. John's, Can., 1964-67; fishery biologist Nat. Marine Fisheries Service, Brunswick, Ga., 1967-69, Beaufont, N.C., 1969-70, Miami, Fla., 1970—. Served with USN, 1951-54. Mem. Am. Soc. Ichthyologists and Herpetologists, A.A.A.S., Am. Soc. Zoologists, Can. Soc. Zoology, Marine Biol. Assn. U.K. Office: 75 Virginia Beach Dr Miami FL 33149

MCKENZIE, BENJAMIN FRANKLIN, JR., gas engr.; b. Nowata, Okla., June 6, 1921; s. Benjamin Franklin and Lucille (Powell) McK.; B.S.M.E., U. Mo., 1950; m. Shirley Rose Day, Sept. 13, 1969; children—Mark Allen, Scott Wayne. Welding instr. Mo. Sch. Mines & Metallurgy, 1947-50, maintenance welder, 1950; layout welder Apex Machine & Mfg. Co., Tulsa, Okla., 1950-51; asst. to chief engr. Manning, Maxwell & Moore, Inc., Tulsa, 1951-54; office engr. Gaso Pump & Burner Mfg. Co., Tulsa, 1954-61; project engr. T.D. Williamson, Inc., Tulsa, 1961-62, quality control engr., 1962, staff asst. to gen. mgr., 1962-63, mgr. materials dept., 1963-69; dist. engr. So. Union Gas Co., Austin, Tex., 1969—. Registered Profl. Engr., Okla. Mem. Nat. Assn. Corrosion Engrs., Engrs. Soc. Tulsa (dir. 1969-70, pres. 1968-69). Club: Thunderbird Toastmasters Club of Tulsa (pres. 1964-65). Home: 11309 Indianhead Dr Austin TX 78753

MCKENZIE, MILTON DEAN, oil producer; b. Chanute, Kan., Apr. 10, 1937; s. Frank Lloyd and Maxine Mae (Hunt) McK.; B.S., U. Tulsa, 1960; J.D., U. Denver, 1965; m. Areta Marceline Bartlett, June 10, 1961; children—Bart Bryan, Bret Alan. Area supt. Layton Oil Co., Tulsa, 1960-61; area sales mgr. Byron-Jackson, Denver, 1962-68; pres. Viking Petroleum, Inc., crude oil producer, Tulsa, 1968—; dir. Mohawk Rock & Sand Co., Inc. B & B Trading Co., Tiger Trucks, Inc., Protective Coating & Sand Blasting Co. Mem. Okla. Energy Adv. Council, 1973-74. Mem. Okla., Colo. bar assns., Tulsa C. of C., Am. Petroleum Inst. (chpt. chmn. 1973), Okla. Ind. Petroleum Assn., Order St. Ives, Pi Epsilon Tau. Elk. Clubs: Cedar Ridge Country, Summit (Tulsa). Home: 3420 E 61st Pl Tulsa OK 74105 Office: 2005 E Skelly Dr Tulsa OK 74105

MCKENZIE, SAM PHILLIPS, superior court judge; b. Blytheville, Ark., Oct. 30, 1920; s. William Morrell and Rose Elizabeth (Phillips) McK.; J.D. with 1st honors, U. Ga., 1944; m. Margaret Mundy, Nov. 20, 1948; children—Sam Phillips, Judith Ann, Michael Morrell, Margaret Mundy. Admitted to Ga. bar, 1944; mem. firm Carter, Carter & McKenzie, Atlanta, 1944-49, McKenzie, Kaler & Shulman, Atlanta, 1949-56; individual practice in Atlanta, 1956-62; judge Superior Ct., Atlanta Jud. Circuit, 1962—. Lectr., Atlanta Law Sch., 1944-64; faculty Nat. Coll. State Trial Judges, U. Nev., Reno, 1966-68, 72, bd, dirs., 1970-73. Pres., Atlanta Tb Assn., 1956-58, bd. dirs., 1963-64; pres. Cath. Social Services, 1956-59; Ga. mem. Council for Christian Unity, 1963; pres. bd. dirs. Holy Family Hosp. 1962-64. Named Atlanta Young Man of Year, Jr. C. of C., 1948. Mem. Am. (mem. adv. coms. on judges function, pre-trial intervention, standards for juvenile justice), Ga., Atlanta bar assns., Nat. Conf. State Trial Judges (exec. com.; chmn. 1971-72), Am. Law Inst., Inst. Jud. Adminstrn. (com. on standards criminal justice), Phi Delta Theta (internat. pres. 1962-64). Clubs: Atlanta Lawyers; Cherokee Town and Country; Atlanta Athletic. Co-author: State Trial Judge's Book, 2d edit., 1969. Home: 3370 E Wood Valley Rd NW Atlanta GA 30327 Office: Fulton County Court House Atlanta GA 30303

MCKIE, EDWARD F., JR., lawyer; b. Albany, N.Y., Oct. 29, 1924; B.E.E., Rensselaer Poly. Inst., 1948; LL.B., Georgetown U., 1952. Admitted to D.C. bar, 1952; now with Schuyler, Birch, Swindler, McKie & Beckett, Washington. Adj. prof. Georgetown Law Sch., 1963-67; chmn. Nat. Counsel Patent Law Assns., 1969-70; sr. adviser U.S. Del. Diplomatic Conf., on Patent Cooperation Treaty, 1970. Mem. Bar Assn. D.C., Am. Bar Assn. (chmn. sect. patent, trademark, copyright law, 1967-68), Am. Patent Law Assn. (1st v.p. 1973-74), Phi Delta Phi. Asso. Editor: Georgetown Law Jour., 1951-52. Office: Schuyler Birch Swindler McKie & Beckett 1000 Connecticut Av Washington DC 20036*

MCKIM, CHARLOTTE B., civic worker; b. Bklyn., Apr. 20, 1899; d. David Peyton and Maude (Logan) Bevans; student Art Student's League, 1920-23, Harvard, summer 1934; m. William Lee McKim, Oct. 15, 1924. Sec. Soc. Four Arts, 1951-56, dir,, 1951—. Mem. Norton Gallery Art, Mus. Modern Art N.Y.C., English-Speaking Union Palm Beach. Compiler: The Salles Letters 1825-50, 1957. Address: 322 Eden Rd Palm Beach FL 33480

MC KIM, WILLIAM LEE, civic worker; b. Cooperstown, N.Y., Oct. 19, 1894; s. William J. A. and Maud Stewart (Lee) McK,; grad Hill Sch., Pottstown, Pa., 1913; B.A., Yale, 1918; m. Charlotte Frances Bevans, Oct. 15, 1924. Salesman, Blair & Co., Inc., stocks and bonds, 1919-29; art collecting and assembling art exhbns. in Palm Beach, 1939-54. Dir. Soc. Four Arts, Palm Beach, 1941—, v.p., 1952-73. Served cpl. to sgt. 1st class, CWS, AEF, 1917-19. Mem. Palm Beach Civic Assn., English-Speaking Union (dir.), Soc, Colonial Wars. Episcopalian. Clubs: Knickerbocker (N.Y.C.); Baltusrol Golf (Springfield, N.J.); The Beach, Everglades (Palm Beach, Fla.). Address: 322 Eden Rd Palm Beach FL 33480

MCKINNEY, JAMES DAVID, chemist; b. Gainesville, Ga., Dec. 28, 1941; s. William Boyd and Dorothy Mae (Ferguson) McK.; B.S., U. Ga., 1963, Ph.D. (NIH scholar), 1968; m. Peggy Jean Jones, June 6, 1970; children—Alan, Joseph. Pub. health scientist, pesticide toxicology lab. FDA, Atlanta, 1967-69; research scientist, chief organic chem. biomechanisms unit, environmental biology and chemistry br. Nat. Inst. Environmental Health Scis., Research Triangle Park, N.C., 1969—. Served with USPHS, 1967-69. Mem. Am. Chem. Soc., Ga. Acad. Scis. Contbr. articles to profl. jours. Home: 7025 Robbie Dr Raleigh NC 27607 Office: Environmental Biology and Chemistry Branch PO Box 12233 Research Triangle Park NC 27709

MCKINNEY, JOHN ROBERT, hosp. exec.; b. Chattanooga, Dec. 2, 1928; s. Charles Dana and Kathryn (Simmons) McK.; B.S., U. Chattanooga, 1950; postgrad. U. Va., 1955-56; M.H.A., Med. Coll. Va., 1959; m. Marion Teresa Coan, Aug. 29, 1959; children—John Robert, Susan K., Maureen S., Collin C., Catherine C. Asst. dir. U. Va. Hosp., Charlottesville, 1959-60, Hosp. Council Nat. Capital Area, Washington, 1960-62; exec. dir. Health Facilities Planning Council for Met. Washington, 1962-72; pres. Inst. for Health Care Research, Washington, 1972-73; adminstr. Nat. Orthopaedic and Rehab. Hosp., Arlington, Va., 1973—. Clin. asst. prof. dept. community medicine Georgetown U. Sch. Medicine, 1969-72; guest lectr. Med. Coll. Va. Sch. Hosp. Adminstrn., 1965—. Pres. citizens adv. bd. Arlington County (Va.) Mental Health Clinic, 1966-69. Served to lt. USNR, 1951-55. Fellow Am. Coll. Hosp. Adminstrs. mem. Am. Assn. Hosp. Planning. Home: 1214 N Columbus St Arlington VA 22205 Office: 2455 Army-Navy Dr Arlington VA 22206

MCKINNEY, THOMAS ANDREW, lawyer; b. Greenville, S.C., July 16, 1940; s. Raymond Andrew and Ruby (Moss) McK.; student Furman U., 1958-60; Southeast Mo. State Coll., 1961; B.A., U. S.C., 1962, J.D., 1965; m. Nancy Camille Hopkins, Aug. 26, 1961; children—Brent Andrew, Mark William. Admitted to S.C. bar, 1965; asso. law firm Ridley, Simrill & McKinney, Rock Hill, S.C., 1965—, partner, 1967—. Dir. Murdock Sign Co. Inc., River Pines Inc.; cons. Carowinds, Inc. Gen. counsel S.C. Republican Party, 1970—; mem. Rock Hill Mayor's Community Council, 1968—. Bd. dirs. Rock Hill chpt. A.R.C., Rock Hill YMCA; bd. dirs. Rock Hill Come See Me, chmn., 1971; bd. dirs. Speech and Hearing Center, chmn., 1972. Mem. York County (pres. 1972), Am. bar assns., Am., S.C. trial lawyers assns., S.C. Def. Lawyers Assn., Phi Delta Phi, Sigma Chi. Republican. Baptist. Clubs: Elks, Sertoma. Home: 2080 Hayes St Rock Hill SC 29730 Office: 310 E Black St Rock Hill SC 29730

MCKINNEY, WILTON JOHNSON, textile exec.; b. Greer, S.C., Apr. 14, 1921; s. Boyd Brown and Alice (Johnson) McK.; B.S. in Accounting, U. S.C., 1947. Accountant, S.D. Leidesdorf & Co., C.P.A.'s, 1947-50, Ely & Walker Mills, 1950-55; with Burlington Industries, Inc., 1955—, controller Burlington Cotton Co., Greenville, S.C., 1968-73; treas. Horizon Apts. Ltd., 1973—. Varsity tennis coach Greenville (S.C.) Sr. High Sch., 1948-73. Treas., Greenville Fine Arts Festival; 1966-73; chmn. Selective Service Bd., Greenville, 1963—. Bd. dirs. YMCA, 1974—. Served to lt. USNR, 1943-46. Mem. Adminstrv. Mgmt. Soc., So. Lawn Tennis Assn. (v.p. 1963-65), S.C. Tennis Assn. (pres. 1963, sec.-treas. 1964—), Sigma Alpha Epsilon, Omicron Delta Kappa. Presbyn. (deacon). Rotarian (sec. 1964-68). Club: Greenville Country (hon.). Home: 238 Byrd Blvd Greenville SC 29605 Office: PO Box 3846 Greenville SC 29608

MCKINNIS, GEORGE EDEN, JR., lawyer, business exec.; b. Shawnee, Okla., July 23, 1901; s. George E. and Mary (Dickson) McK.; student Okla. Bapt. U., 1919-22; A.B., U. Wis., 1923; LL.B., Harvard, 1927; m. Marion Harris, June 7, 1935; children—George Courtney, Sarah Ann. Admitted to Okla. bar, 1928, since practiced in Shawnee; v.p. Shawnee Realty & Investment Co., 1935—; v.p. First Fed. Savs. & Loan Assn., 1947-57, pres., 1957-72, chmn. bd., gen. counsel, 1972—. Atty., Shawnee Bd. Edn., 1954-62; hearing officer SSS, Dept. Justice, 1946-50. Chmn. adv. bd. Salvation Army, 1965; mem. adv. com. 4th Army, 1948-54; vice chmn. Okla. Election Bd., 1950-54; pres. Shawnee Community Concert Assn., 1946-50; dir. Shawnee YMCA, 1948-60; mem. Greater Seminole Area council Camp Fire Girls, 1950-54; mem. Shawnee Bicentennial Commn., 1973—. Mem. Shawnee Bd. City Commrs., 1946-50, mayor, 1946-48; mem. Shawnee Planning Commn., 1972—. Trustee Okla. Bapt. U., 1949-52, Shawnee Indsl. Found., 1970-73. Served as lt. comdr. USNR, 1941-45; PTO. Mem. U.S. (com. on Fed. Home Loan Bank system 1969-70), Okla. (v.p. 1964-66, pres. 1967-68) savs. and loan leagues, S.W. Savs. and Loan Conf. (dir. 1964-68), Am., Okla. (ho. dels.), Pottawatomie County (pres. 1962) bar assns., Shawnee C. of C. (dir. 1970—), Am. Legion, V.F.W., Delta Upsilon, Phi Delta Phi, Pi Kappa Delta, Theta Alpha Phi. Presbyn. (trustee, former elder). Mason (K.T.), Elk (exalted ruler Shawnee 1962), Lion (pres. Shawnee 1938, dist. gov. 1950). Club: Knife and Fork (pres. 1949-50). Home: 1506 N Union St Shawnee OK 74801 Office: 330 N Broadway Shawnee OK 74801

MCKINNON, MORRIS HARVEY, ednl. adminstr.; b. ElDorado, Ark., Mar. 17, 1933; s. Harvey Gratis and Lettie Grace (Lewis) McK.; B.S., So. State Coll., 1957; M.Ed., U. Ark., 1961; m. Mary Ledbetter, Sept. 2, 1955; children—Kathy, Rhonda, Randall, Steve. Coach, Mt.

Holly Sch. Dist. 10, (Ark.), 1957-60, supt. schs., 1960—. Served with AUS, 1953-55. Mem. Am. Edn. Assn., Am. Assn. Sch. Adminstrs., South Ark. Schoolmasters Assn., Nat., Ark. edn. assn., Ark. Adminstrs. Assn., Union County Tchrs. Assn. (pres.). Mason. Home: PO Box 68 Mount Holly AR 71758 Office: PO Box 68 Mount Holly AR 71758

MCKISSACK, WILLIAM DEBERRY, architect; b. Nashville, Aug. 29, 1925; s. Moses Andrew and Miranda (Winter) McKissack; B. Arch., Howard U., 1951; m. Leatrice Harriett Buchanan, Oct. 31, 1949; children—Andrea (Mrs. Charles L. Franklin II), Cheryl Joan, Deryl Kaye. With, McKissack & McKissack, Architects & Engrs., Inc., Nashville, 1951—, pres., 1968—, chmn. bd. dir., 1968—. Instr., guest lectr. Tenn. State U., Nashville, 1959-61; pres., chmn. bd. dir. Coll. Hill Realty Co., Nashville, 1968. Served with USNR, 1943-46. Mem. Nat. Council of Registration Bds., A.I.A., Nat. Tech. Assn., Frontiers of Am., Sigma Pi Phi, Omega Si Phi. Home: 3610 Batavia St Nashville TN 37209 Office: Morris Memorial Bldg Nashville TN 37201

MCKITTRICK, JAMES LIVINGSTON, mfg. exec.; b. Saluda, S.C., Mar. 6, 1914; s. James R. and Carrie (Parks) M.; B.A., Furman U., 1933; postgrad. Benjamin Franklin U., 1939-40 ; m. Nancy Katherine Buntin, June 9, 1956; 1 dau., Nancy Rebecca. Tchr. schs. and colls., until 1947; mgr. C.E. Luttrell & Co., Greenville, S.C., 1947-52; sec. Franklin Nat. Life Ins. Co., 1953-57; gen. mgr. Acme Cloth Reel Co., 1958—. Served with USAAF, 1942-43. Democrat. Baptist. Lion. Home: 401 Garrison Rd Simpsonville SC 29681 Office: 214 W McBee Av Greenville SC 29601

MCKNIGHT, COLBERT AUGUSTUS, newspaper editor; b. Shelby, N.C., Aug. 19, 1916; s. John Samuel and Norva (Proctor) McK.; B.S., Davidson Coll., 1938; LL.D., Colby Coll.; m. Margaret Belle Henderson, Mar. 29, 1941 (div. 1968); children—John Peter, Margaret C., David P.; m. 2d, Gail Oliver Ehle, Oct. 30, 1968; 1 dau., Colby Augusta. Reporter Charlotte News, 1939-42, news editor, 1944-48, mng. editor, 1948-49, editor, 1949-54; editor San Juan (P.R.) World Jour., also Asso. Press war corr., 1942-44; exec. dir. So. Edn. Reporting Service, 1954-55; editor Charlotte (N.C.) Observer, 1955—; v.p., dir. Knight Pub. Co., 1956—. Pres. N.C. Fund, 1963-65; chmn. bd. So. Edn. Reporting Service, 1963-65; trustee Charlotte Coll., 1960-65; bd. dirs. Found. of U. N.C. at Charlotte, 1974—. Mem. Am. Soc. Newspaper Editors (dir. 1965-73, pres. 1971-72), Nat., N.C. confs. editorial writers, N.C. Press Assn. (dir. 1973—). Presbyn. Home: 1627 Beverly Dr Charlotte NC 28207 Office: 600 S Tryon St Charlotte NC 28202

MCLAFFERTY, CHARLES LOWRY, mfg. co. exec.; b. Evanston, Ill., Apr. 11, 1927; s. Joel Edward and Margaret (Keifer) McL.; B.Sc., U. Neb., 1949; B.S., Bowling Green Bus. U., 1950; M.B.A., Northwestern U., 1952; m. Dee Hartmann; children—Ardith Ann, Karen Dee, Charles Lowry Jr., Kevin Paul. EDP systems analyst Genesco, Inc., Nashville, 1954-59; controller Martin Stove & Range Co., Florence, Ala., 1959-60; dir. finance Alamet div. Universal Oil Products Co., Selma, Ala., 1961-70; pres. So. Shelter, Inc., Selma, 1970-71; controller Southbridge Plastics div. W.R. Grace & Co., 1971-72; controller Utica Tool Co. Inc., Orangeburg, S.C., 1972—; dir. Dalco, Inc. Instr. U. Tenn., Nashville, 1959-61. Mem. Gov.'s Com. to Save USS Alabama, 1962-63, treas., commr. USS Ala. Battleship Commn., 1963—; zone chmn. major gifts Lurleen Wallace Cancer Hosp. Fund, 1969; sec. Dallas County Pvt. Sch. Found., Selma, 1968-70. Del. Ala. Republican Conv., 1962. Chmn. bd. trustees John T. Morgan Acad., Selma, 1965-67. Served with USNR, 1944-46. Mem. Financial Execs. Inst., Nat. Assn. Accountants, Nat. Assn. Homebuilders (nat. dir. 1970-71), Asso. Industries Ala., Mil. Order Loyal Legion (nat. commandery-in-chief), Beta Alpha Psi, Sigma Chi. Kiwanian, Toastmaster. Club: Orangeburg Country. Office: Cameron Rd Orangeburg SC 29115

MCLAIN, EUGENE MILTON, lawyer, state senator; b. Cragford, Ala., Feb. 14, 1931; s. Eugene Milton and Louise (Leftwich) McL.; B.S., Auburn U., 1953; postgrad. Cambridge (Eng.) U., 1953-54; LL.B., U. Ala., 1959; m. Geraldine Phillips, Aug. 23, 1953; children—David Scott, Caroline. Admitted to Ala. bar, 1959, practiced in Huntsville; former partner firm Bell, Richardson, Cleary, McLain & Tucker; mem. Ala. Ho. of Reps., 1966-70; mem. Ala. Senate, 1970—. Served with USAF, 1954-56. Recipient George Washington Honor medal, 1955; named One of Four Outstanding Young Men of Ala., 1960, Huntsville's Young Man of Year, 1961. Mem. Ala. Bar Assn. (past pres. young lawyers sect.). Democrat. Baptist. Rotarian, Elk, Mason (Shriner). Home: 4101 Piedmont Dr SE Huntsville AL 35802 Office: PO Box 2209 Huntsville AL 35801

MCLAIN, JACK, aerospace co. exec.; b. Jackson, Miss., Nov. 18, 1923; s. Cas Vincent and Tura (Miley) McL.; student Belhaven Coll., 1946, U. Ga., 1946-47; B.S., Millsaps Coll., 1949; M.S. (fellow), U. Miss., 1951; postgrad. Birmingham So. Coll., 1952; m. Hazel Irene Garrett, June 4, 1950; children—Ellen Denise, Sharon Grace. Asso. physicist U. Miss., Oxford, 1950, Philco Corp., Phila., 1951, So. Research Inst., Birmingham, 1952-54; with LTV Aerospace Corp., Dallas, also Hampton, Va., 1954—, div. mgr., Hampton, 1961—. Served with AC, USMCR, 1942-46. Decorated Air medal. Mem. Am. Inst. Aeros. and Astronautics, I.E.E.E., Am. Def. Preparedness Assn. (life), Nat. Contract Mgmt. Assn., Air Force Assn., Peninsula C. of C., Theta Nu Sigma, Omicron Delta Kappa. Baptist. Kiwanian (pres. 1973). Club: Williamsburg Country (York County, Va.). Home: 706 Antrim Dr Newport News VA 23601 Office: 3221 N Armistead Av Hampton VA 23666

MCLAIN, LEE ROY, drilling co. exec.; b. Normangee, Tex., Mar. 29, 1927; s. Etcil and Evie Irene (Hamilton) McL.; B.B.A., U. Houston, 1949; m. Ima Jean Mathis, June 4, 1949; 1 dau., Cindy. Exec. v.p. Butler Drilling Co., Houston, 1964—, aslo dir.; dir. Prodn. Maintenance Co., Tex. Gulf Coast Leasing, Inc. Bd. dirs. Com. Sound Am. Edn., pres. council Houston Bapt. Coll. Served with C.E., AUS, 1945-47; ETO. Mem. Internat. Assn. Drilling Contractors (dir.). Baptist (deacon 1954-72). Clubs: University, Racquet (Houston). Office: PO Box 14291 7440 Cullen Blvd Houston TX 77021

MCLANE, H. ARTHUR, lawyer; b. Valdosta, Ga., Apr. 2, 1939; s. Carson H. and Philena (Tyson) McL.; B.A., Emory U., 1961; J.D., U. Ga., 1963; m. Jane Campbell Bennet, June 17, 1961; children—Mary Campbell, Paul Corbett. Admitted to Ga. bar, 1963; practiced in Valdosta, Ga., 1963—; county atty. Lowndes County (Ga.), 1965-73; atty. Echols County Bd. Edn., 1966—; judge State Ct., 1974—. Adv. bd. Valdosta Area Vocational Tech. Sch., 1967—. Bd. dirs. Valdosta Boys Club, 1966—, pres., 1971-72; bd. dirs. Valdosta Entertainment Assn., 1968-71. Named Outstanding Young Man, 1972. Mem. State Bar Ga., Valdosta Bar Assn. (pres. 1974), Am. Judicature Soc., Sigma Alpha Epsilon, Phi Delta Phi, Phi Kappa Phi. Methodist. Elk, Rotarian (dir. 1973). Club: Valdosta Country (dir., pres. 1971). Office: 504 N Patterson St Valdosta GA 31601

MCLARRY, LACY, concertmaster; b. Tex.; student of violin with Philip Williams, Dallas; grad. So. Meth. U., also Master's degree. Currently concertmaster Okla. City Symphony Orch.; prof. violin U. Okla.; former concertmaster N.H. Music Festival Orch.; mem. string quartet Western Arts Summer Music Festival, Laramie, Wyo.; violin tchr. Kan. State Tchrs. Coll., Emporia. Served with USN. Office: Oklahoma City Symphony Orch Civic Center Music Hall Oklahoma City OK 73102*

MCLARTY, CLEYLON LEE, educator; b. Oxford, Miss., Apr. 10, 1923; s. Walter Eugene and Ada (Livingston) McL.; B.Mus., U. Miss., 1951, M.Ed., 1958, Ed.D., 1963; m. Mildred Hale, Feb. 26, 1948; children—Michael, Patricia, Dianne, Phillip. Tchr., counselor pub. schs., Miss., 1949-59; grad. asst. U. Miss., Oxford, 1959-60; asst. to dean of students, dir. devel. U. Ga., Athens, 1960-61; instr. Miss. State U., Starksville, summer 1962, U. Miss., summer 1964; asso. prof. Delta State Coll., Cleveland, Miss., 1962-66; prof. edn., coordinator rehab. counseling program Ark. State U., Jonesboro, 1966—. Mem. Am. Ednl. Research Assn., N.E.A., Am. Personnel and Guidance Assn., Assn. for Counselor Edn. and Supervision, Assn. for Measurement and Evaluation in Guidance, Nat. Rehab. Assn., Mid-South Ednl. Research Assn. (dir.), Ark. Personnel and Guidance Assn., Ark. Sch. Counselors Assn., Assn. for Higher Edn., Phi Delta Kappa, Kappa Delta Pi. Home: Hasbrook Rd Jonesboro AR 72401 Office: Box 898 Ark State U State University AR 72467

MCLAUGHLIN, CHARLES BORROMEO, clergyman; b. N.Y.C., Sept. 26, 1913; ed. St. Joseph Sem., St. John Sem. Ordained priest, Roman Catholic Ch., 1941; titular bishop Risinium and aux. of Raleigh (N.C.), 1964; bishop St. Petersburg, Fla., 1968—. Address: 4960 Bogie Av N St Petersburg FL 33710*

MCLAUGHLIN, DAVID, protozoologist, educator; b. Sumter, S.C., Nov. 1, 1934; s. Arthur S. and Iris (Ladson) McL.; B.S., Clark Coll., Atlanta, 1956; M.S., Howard U., 1962, Ph.D., 1965; m. Pauletta Fellows, Sept. 7, 1963. Research asst., USPHS grantee Howard U., Washington, 1957-62, teaching and research supr. NSF Summer Research Participant for High Sch. Tchrs., 1957-58, NSF Summer Research Participant for High Sch. Students, 1958-64, research asso., USPHS grantee, 1962-65, supr. summer undergrad. research participation, 1965-66, prof. zoology, coordinator Ind. Research Lab., 1965—. Postdoctoral studies Bio-Space Tech. Tng. Program NASA Wallops Sta., 1965, Gemini Summary Conf. NASA Manned Space Craft Center, Houston; participant 3d Internat. Congress on Protozoology, Leningrad, USSR, 1969. Mem. Soc. Protozoologists, Am. Inst. Biol. Sci., A.A.A.S., Am. Micros. Soc., Am. Soc. Zoologists, N.A.A.C.P., Sigma Xi, Beta Kappa, Omega Psi Phi. Baptist. Contbr. articles to profl. jours. Home: 907 Cox Av Hyattsville MD 20783 Office: 415 College St NW Washington DC 20001

MCLAUGHLIN, DONALD JOSEPH, electronics engr.; b. Sioux Falls, S.D., Feb. 17, 1915; s. Lysle Wayne and Ida Luella (Opperud) McL.; B.S., Ia. State Coll., 1940; postgrad. Ohio State U., 1966; m. Clara Lebsack, Apr. 26, 1942; 1 son, Dennis Eugene. Regional service supr., field engr. Montgomery Ward & Co., Chgo., 1940-42; with Naval Research Lab., Washington, 1942—, head applied physics br., 1969-71, head optical engring. br., 1972—. Vice pres., dir. Radio Control Corp., Denver, 1960-62. Pres. Summit Park (D.C.) Citizens Assn., 1955-57. Registered profl. engr., D.C. Recipient Incentive award Naval Research Lab., 1955. Sr. mem. I.E.E.E. (chmn. aerospace electronics systems group Washington chpt. 1967-68), Sigma Xi. Republican. Methodist (chmn. adminstrv. bd. 1964—). Mason (32 deg.). Home: 3730 Camden St SE Washington DC 20020 Office: Code 6560 Naval Research Lab Washington DC 20375

MCLAUGHLIN, EDWARD, educator; b. Ballymena, Ireland, Oct. 16, 1928; s. Patrick Joseph and Helena Mary (Leonard) McL.; B.Sc., Queen's U., Belfast, 1953, M.Sc., 1954; Ph.D., Imperial Coll. U. London, 1956, diploma, 1957; m. Annie Kathleen Friel, Apr. 3, 1956; children—Fiona, Declan, Don, Bronagh. Came to U.S. 1970. Mem. faculty Imperial Coll. U. London, 1956-70, sr. lectr. chem. engring., 1962-66, reader, 1966-70; asst. to dir. Salter's Inst., London, 1960-70; prof. La. State U., Baton Rouge, 1970—. NSF sr. fgn. scientist, 1967-68. Mem. Am. Inst. Chem. Engrs., Faraday Soc., Am. Chem. Soc., Sigma Xi. Roman Catholic. Contbr. articles to profl. jours. Home: 358 Dunstan Circle Baton Rouge LA 70815 Office: Dept Chemical Engring La State Univ Baton Rouge LA 70803

MCLAUGHLIN, (EDWARD) BRUCE, lawyer; b. Omaha, Apr. 2, 1921; s. Charles F. and Margaret (Bruce) McL.; student Mercersburg Acad., 1935-38; B.S., Georgetown U., 1943; postgrad. George Washington U., 1950-51; J.D., U. Miami, 1953. Announcer Sta. KTSM, El Paso, Tex., 1943-44; news editor KFRE, Fresno, Cal., 1944; with McKesson-Robbins, San Francisco, 1945-46; radio prodn. Sta. KOSA, Odessa Tex., 1947-49, Sta. KPHO, Phoenix, 1949; TV prodn. Sta. WITV, Miami-Ft. Lauderdale, Fla., 1953-55; admitted to Fla. bar, 1955, since practiced in Miami. Served with Signal Corps, AUS, World War II. Mem. Fla. Bar, Am., Dade County bar assns., Lawyers Club Dade County (dir. 1969-70), Screen Actors Guild (pres. Fla. br. 1965-69, mem. Fla. council 1962—, mem. nat. bd. dirs. 1968—), Am. Legion, Gamma Eta Gamma. Democrat. Roman Catholic. Clubs: Coral Gables (Fla.) Country; Jockey (Miami, Fla.); University (Washington). Home: 45 Antilla Av Coral Gables FL 33134 Office: Ainsley Bldg Miami FL 33132

MCLAUGHLIN, JAMES OSCAR, JR., finance co. exec.; b. Atlanta, Aug. 4, 1924; s. James O. and Myrtle Lee (Humphries) McL.; B.A., U. Ga.; grad. Sch. Exec. Devel., U. Ga., 1964; grad. Grad. Sch. Savs. and Loan, Ind. U., 1971; m. Ethyl Velma Pierce, Mar. 2, 1947; children—Vicki Lee, Tracie Elizabeth. Treas. Campbell Coal Co., Atlanta, 1947-57; with Atlanta Fed. Savs. and Loan Assn., 1957—, asst. v.p., 1962-66, v.p. service div., 1966-73, v.p. operations, 1973—. Instr. Am. Savs. and Loan Inst., Atlanta, 1964—. Vol. worker various charitable orgns. Served with USAF, 1943. Mem. Am. Savs. and Loan Institute (pres. 1969). Optimist (sec.-treas. chpt.). Home: 3543 Summitridge Dr Doraville GA 30040 Office: 20 Marietta St NW Atlanta GA 30303

MCLAUGHLIN, MAX VICTOR, physician; b. Blue Springs, Ala., Nov. 4, 1928; s. James Daniel and Dovie Alma (Whigham) McL.; B.S., U. Ala., 1952; M.D., Med. Coll. Ala., 1956; m. Sally Girard Schofield, Dec. 23, 1954 (dec. July 1968); 1 son, Max Victor. Intern Mobile (Ala.) Gen. Hosp., 1956-57, resident, 1957-58; practice gen. medicine, Mobile, 1958—. Mem. Ala. Bd. Corrections, 1963—, chmn., 1972—. Bd. dirs. Doctors Hosp., Mobile. Served with AUS, 1946-48. Mem. Med. Assn. State of Ala., Med. Assn. Mobile County, Am. Acad. Family Practice, Phi Gamma Delta, Phi Beta Pi, Omicron Delta Kappa. Episcopalian. Mason, Kiwanian (charter mem. West Mobile). Home: 13 N Springbank Rd Mobile AL 36608 Office: 2218 Fulbrook Center Mobile AL 36605

MCLAUGHLIN, SHIRLEY BURDEN (MRS. LOGAN HAROLD MCLAUGHLIN), librarian; b. Knoxville, Tenn., May 11, 1943; d. Jess W. and Alva Leona (Patterson) Burden; B.S., Western Carolina U., 1965; M.L.S., Appalachian State U., 1969; m. Logan Harold McLaughlin, Sept. 21, 1963. Head librarian Mt. Holly (N.C.) High Sch., 1965-66, West Henderson High Sch., Hendersonville, N.C., 1966-68, Asheville Buncombe Tech. Inst., Asheville, N.C., 1969—. Mem. Am., Southeastern, N.C. library assns. Home: Route 8 Box 41 Hendersonville NC 28739 Office: 340 Victoria Rd Asheville NC 28801

MCLEAN, AUGUSTUS ALEXANDER, JR., physician; b. Lenoir, N.C., Feb. 2, 1920; s. Augustus Alexander and Hallie (Hall) McL.; B.S., Davidson Coll., 1942; M.D., Med. Coll. Va., 1945; m. Margaret Stephenson, Sept. 30, 1944; children—Margaret (Mrs. James Womble), Patricia, Augustus Alexander III, Gay, Benjamin. Intern, U. Va. Hosps., 1945-46; practice family medicine, Lenoir, 1948-50, Murfreesboro, N.C., 1950—; mem. staff Roanoke Chowan Hosp., Ahoskie, N.C. Farmer, Murfreesboro. Mem. Tri County Airport Authority. Bd. dirs. Pine Forest Rest Home. Served to capt. AUS, 1946-48. Mem. Am., So., N.C. (del. 1961-62), Seaboard (v.p. 1970-71, pres. 1973-74) med. assns., Hertford County (pres. 1956-58), 1st Dist. (sec.-treas. 1955-56) med. socs., Murfreesboro Hist. Assn., Murfreesboro C. of C. Rotarian (pres. 1969-70). Home: 615 Woodridge Dr Murfreesboro NC 27855 Office: 200 S Wynn St Murfreesboro NC 27855

MCLEAN, JAMES MARION, clergyman; b. Lebanon, Ind., May 8, 1944; s. William Stegal and Fern Bernice (Hodson) McL.; Asso. in Sci., Purdue U., 1964; A.B., Lynchburg (Va.) Coll., 1966; M.Div., Lexington (Ky.) Theol. Sem., 1970; m. Patrae Ellen Filson, July 24, 1970. Ordained to ministry Christian Ch., 1970; asst. pastor Chauncy, O., 1966-68, Margarita, C.Z., 1968-69, Falmouth (Ky.) Christian Ch., 1970—; pastor Am. Bible Soc., 1969-70; family and personal counselor, 1970—. Chmn. Regional Devel. Disabled Task Force, 1973—; mem. cabinet on youth work Christian Ch. in Ky., 1971—; mem. Pendleton County Drug Abuse Com., 1971—. Bd. dirs. No. Ky. Health and Social Planning Council, Pendleton County Assn. Mentally Retarded. Beargrass Christian Ch. scholar, 1968-70. Home: 311 Maple St Falmouth KY 41040 Office: 303 W Shelby St Falmouth KY 41040

MCLEAN, LEON MOORE, supt. schs.; b. Rowland, N.C., Dec. 15, 1928; s. Arless Lester and Maggie Mae (McRimmon) McL.; B.S., Appalachian State U., 1949; M.Ed., U. N.C., 1957, advanced supt. certificate, 1967; m. Janie Rae Britt, June 22, 1951; children—Steven, Donna. Tchr., coach Massey Hill Sch., Fayetteville, N.C., 1949-52, Littlefield Sch., Lumberton, N.C., 1955-57; prin. Garland (N.C.) Sch., 1957-63; supt. sch. system, Fairmont, N.C., 1963—. Chmn. Robeson County March of Dimes Campaign, 1963. Served with AUS, 1952-55. Mem. N.C. Edn. Assn. (pres. supt.'s div. Southeastern N.C. dist. 1966). Rotarian. Home: 701 Gertrude St Fairmont NC 28340 Office: 106 Trinity St Fairmont NC 28340

MCLEAN, WILLIAM YOUMANS, architect; b. Vidalia, Ga., Aug. 9, 1927; s. John Archibald and Alma (Tod) McL.; student U.S. Naval Acad., 1945-47; B.S., Ga. Inst. Tech., 1947, B.Arch., 1950; m. Larue Jane Wells, June 9, 1951; children—William Youmans, Jonathan Wells, Amanda Jane. Archtl. draftsman, designer Wm. J.J. Chase & Assos., Atlanta, 1951-52, 55-58; architect Harvey & Elliott, Rome, Ga., 1959-60, M.G. Turner, Rome, 1960-61; partner Turner & McLean, Architects, Rome, 1961-62; asso. Hugh Gaston Assos., Albany, Ga., 1962-63; owner William Y. McLean, Architect, Albany, 1963-67, Tifton Ga., 1967—. City commr., vice mayor Tifton, 1972. Served as lt. (j.g.) USNR 1952-55. Mem. A.I.A. (organizer, 1st pres. S.W. Ga. chpt. 1965-66, dir. Ga. council, 1966-67, dir. s. Atlantic regional council 1966). Democrat. Episcopalian (mem. diocesan council 1971-72). Elk, Rotarian. Home: 202 W 26th St Tifton GA 31794 Office: 215 N Central Av Tifton GA 31794

MCLELLAN, JOHN S., lawyer; b. Kingsport, Tenn., Nov. 19, 1921; grad. U. Ky. Admitted to Tenn. bar, 1944, U.S. Appeals Ct. bar, 6th Circuit, 1955, 7th Circuit, 1956, 1st, 5th Circuits, 1957, 4th Circuit, 1967; practice law, Kingsport, Tenn. Chmn., TVA bd. commrs. for Fed. Ct., Eastern Dist. Tenn., 1968—. Mem. Kingsport (pres. 1973), Tenn. (del. 6th Circuit Judicial Conf. 1969-70, chmn. labor law sect. 1970), Am. (chmn. com. on devel. law of union adminstrn. and procedure) bar assns., Am. Judicature Soc., Am., Tenn. trial lawyers assns. Author: Trends in Labor Relations Law, 1961. Office: 421 E Market St Kingsport TN 37660

MCLEMORE, ANDREW JACKSON, III, librarian; b. Memphis, Feb. 6, 1932; s. Andrew Jackson and Willia (Rogers) McL.; A.B., Morehouse Coll., 1954; M.S. in Library Sci., Atlanta U., 1960; grad. Ga. So. Coll., 1970; m. Willie George Scott, July 30, 1964; children—Mignon, Andrew, Victor. Asst. librarian Atlanta U., 1958-62; librarian Miles Coll., Birmingham, Ala., 1962-66, Savannah (Ga.) State Coll., 1966—. Served with AUS, 1955-57. Recipient fellowship Nat. Urban League, 1969. Mem. Am., Ga., Southeastern library assns., Alpha Phi Alpha. Mason. Editor faculty research bull. Savannah State Coll., 1966—. Home: 1412 Stillwood Dr Savannah GA 31406 Office: PO Box 20394 Savannah State Coll Savannah GA 31404

MCLEMORE, BOBBIE FRANK, plant physiologist; b. Jasper, Tex., May 22, 1932; s. Ivy Augustus and Kate Elizabeth (Sims) McL.; B.S. (Julia-Ball Lee fellow), Tex. A. and M. U., 1953; postgrad. Mich. State U., 1955-56; M.F., La. State U., 1957, Ph.D., 1967; postgrad. U. Md., 1961-62; m. Bobbiline Marshall, Aug. 27, 1950; children—Kent Robert, Brenda Lynn. Research technician Tex. Agrl. Expt. Sta., Beaumont, 1955; forester Internat. Paper Co., Jasper, 1956; research forester So. Forest Expt. Sta., Pineville, La., 1957—. Outdoor chmn. Attakapas council Boy Scouts Am., 1968—, chmn. troop com., 1969-70; chmn. Sch. Parents Club, 1963-64, 69-70. Served as 1st lt. AUS, 1953-55; lt. col. Res. Named One of Top 3 Fed. Employees in Central La., 1964. Mem. Soc. Am. Foresters, Scandinavian Soc. Plant Physiology, La. Forestry Assn., Sigma Xi, Phi Eta Sigma, Xi Sigma Pi. Baptist. Contbr. articles to profl. jours. Home: 1750 Georgia Dr Pineville LA 71360 Office: 2500 Shreveport Hwy Pineville LA 71360

MCLEMORE, ETHEL WARD, research geophysicist, mathematician; b. Sylvarena, Miss., Jan. 22, 1908; d. William Robert and Frances Virginia (Douglas) Ward; B.A., Miss. Woman's Coll., 1928; M.A., U. N.C., 1929; postgrad. U. Chgo., 1931, Colo. Sch. Mines, 1941-42, So. Meth. U., 1962-64; m. Robert Henry McLemore, June 30, 1935; 1 dau., Mary Frances. Head math. dept. Miss. Jr. Coll., 1929-30; instr. chemistry, math. Miss. State Coll. for Women, 1930-32; research mathematician Humble Oil & Refining Co., Houston, 1933-36; ind. geophys. research, Tex. and Colo., 1936-42, Ft. Worth, 1946—; geophysicist United Geophys. Co., Pasadena, Cal., 1942-46; tchr. chemistry, physics Hockaday Sch., Dallas, 1958-59, tchr. math., 1959-60, tchr. chemistry, 1968-69; tchr. chemistry Ursuline Acad., Dallas, 1964-67. Mem. Am. Math. Soc., Math. Assn. Am., Am. Geophys. Union, Seismol. Soc. Am., Soc. Exploration Geophysicists, A.A.A.S., Soc. Indsl. and Applied Math., Tex. Acad. Sci., Sigma Xi. Contbr. articles to profl. jours. Home: 11625 Wander Lane Dallas TX 75230

MCLEMORE, RICHARD AUBREY, author; b. Perry County, Miss., June 6, 1903; s. Hezekiah and Tabitha (Small) McL.; A.B., Miss. Coll., 1923, Litt.D., 1969; A.M., George Peabody Coll., 1926; Ph.D., Vanderbilt U., 1933 (fellow in history, 1930-33); m. Nannie Pitts, 1927; 1 son, Harry Kimbrell. Supt. village schs., Miss., 1923-26; instr. history, and dean, Jones County Jr. Coll., 1926-30, 33-34; prof. history and dean Judson Coll., 1934-38; prof. Miss. So. Coll., 1938-57, dean, 1945-54, 55-57, acting pres., 1955; pres. Miss. Coll., Clinton, 1957-68; dir. Miss. Dept. Archives and History, 1969-73. Mem. Am., So., Miss., So. Bapt. hist. assns. Baptist (deacon). Mason (33 deg.,

Shriner), Lion (past dist. gov., state historian, internat. counselor). Author: The Natchez County, 1936; Franco-American Diplomatic Relations, 1816-1836, 1940; Mississippi Through 4 Centuries (with wife), 1945, rev., 1949, 60, Outline of Mississippi History, 1941, rev., 1944, 46, 51, 59, 69; (with Blough and Switzer) Fundamentals of Citizenship, 1950, rev., 1957; Our Nation's Story (with Everett Auguspurger), 1954, rev., 1962; (with Boyd C. Shafer and Everett Augspurger) A United States History for High Schools, 1966, rev., 1969, 1865 to the Present: A United States History for High Schools, 1966; A History of Mississippi Baptists, 1970. Contbr. to encys., hist. jours. Hist. editor Official Map of Mississippi, 1953; editor in chief Jour. Miss. History, 1969-73; editor A History of Mississippi, 2 vols., 1973. Home: 224 Kitchings Dr Clinton MS 39056

MCLEMORE, MRS. RICHARD AUBREY, educator, author; b. Harvest, Ala., Sept. 21, 1900; d. James Ervin and Lola (Sanderson) Pitts; A.B., Athens Coll., 1921; M.A., George Peabody Coll. Tchrs., 1927; postgrad. Vanderbilt U., 1930-31; m. Richard Aubrey McLemore, June 2, 1927; 1 son, Harry Kimbrell. Instr. history Northport (Ala.) High Sch., 1921-22, Escambia County High Sch., 1922-24, Monrovia High Sch., 1924-25; head dept. history McComb (Miss.) High Sch., 1925-27; prof. history Jones County Jr. Coll., 1927-30, 33-34; instr. history Perry County High Sch., Ala., 1936-37. Mem. Miss. Hist. Soc., Am. Assn. U. Women (Miss. div. pres. 1950-52), Miss. Geneol. Soc. Democrat. Baptist. Author: (with Richard Aubrey McLemore) Outline of Mississippi History, 1941; Mississippi Through Four Centuries, 1944; the Mississippi Story, 1959, rev. 1969; also articles in field. Address: 224 Kitchings Dr Clinton MS 39056

MCLENDON, BILLYE BURRELL, psychologist; b. Copperas Cove, Tex.; d. Norwood W. and Lena Mae (McGonagill) McLendon; A.A. with 1st Honors, Temple Jr. Coll., 1948; B.A. magna cum laude, U. Tex., 1950, M.A., 1956, Ph.D., 1965. Secretarial positions, 1946-50, 52; classroom tchr. Ind. Sch. Dist., Port Arthur, Austin, Tex., 1950-54; research and teaching asst. dept. psychology U. Tex., 1955-56, asst. psychologist, intern Testing and Counseling Center, 1957-59, teaching asst., lectr. dept. ednl. psychology, 1959-61; psychologist Austin Community Guidance Center, 1956-57; sch. psychologist St. Andrews Episcopal Sch., 1958; clin. psychologist Child Psychiatry Center, Milw. Children's Hosp., also instr. psychology depts. psychiatry and pediatrics Marquette U. Sch. Medicine, Milw., 1964-67; practice counseling and clin. psychology, 1965—; elementary multi-school counselor and psychologist San Antonio Ind. Sch. Dist., 1969-70; psychologist Harlandale Ind. Sch. Dist., 1970-71, Lebe Hoch Learning and Treatment Center, Fredericksburg, Tex., 1972-73. Delta Delta Delta scholar U. Tex., 1949. Mem. Am., Southwestern, Tex. psychol. assns., UN Assn., Nat. Council on Family Relations, Internat. Platform Assn., Am. Mus. Natural History, Nat. Wildlife Fedn., Phi Beta Kappa, Pi Lambda Theta, Psy Chi. Democrat. Methodist. Contbr. articles to profl. jours. Research on origins of the person, creativeness, student-centered teaching, psychotherapy, community mental health. Home: 1205 S 27th St Temple TX 76501

MCLENDON, R.D., coll. pres.; b. Quitman, Miss., May 23, 1905; s. Rosier Alexander and Mary Ann (McLemore) McL.; B.S., Miss. So. Coll., 1929; M.S., U. Tex., 1938; m. Corinne Hipps, May 1, 1938. Prin. Leaksville (Miss.) High Sch., 1929-31, Waynesboro High Sch., 1931-33, Madison-Ridgeland High Sch., 1933-35; supt. Lumberton (Miss.) High Sch., 1935-40, Woodville High Sch., 1940-42; pres. Pearl River Jr. Coll., Poplarville, Miss., 1942-53, N.W. Miss. Jr. Coll., Senatobia, 1953—. Named col. gov.'s staff. Mem. Instns. Higher Learning Miss. (trustee), Miss. Jr. Coll. Assn. (pres. 1947-49), Miss. Assn. Colls. (pres. 1953-54), Mason, Rotarian. Address: Senatobia MS 38668

MCLENDON, ROBERT BURNS, lawyer; b. Frankston, Tex., Apr. 19, 1937; s. Robert Blakely and Mary (Moss) McL.; B.A., Baylor U., 1959, J.D., 1961; m. Margery Hamilton, Feb. 16, 1963; children—Blake, Steven. Admitted to Tex. bar, 1961; spl. agt. FBI, Justice Dept., various locations, 1961-66; atty. Gen. Telephone and Electronics, Tampa, Fla., 1966-67; partner firm Fisher, Roch, McLendon & Gallagher, Houston, 1967—. Pres. Tex. Gulf Coast chpt. Leukemia Soc. Am., 1973. Mem. Am., Fla. bar assns., State Bar Tex. (mem. grievance com.), Am., Tex., Houston trial lawyers assns. Home: 10626 Del Monte Dr Houston TX 77042 Office: 723 Main St Houston TX 77002

MCLEOD, JOHN PURL UTTLEY, physician; b . Fayetteville, N.C., Nov. 5, 1911; s. James Luther Torquil and Geneva Gertrude (Allran) McL.; premed. student So. Missionary Coll.; M.D., Loma Linda U., 1939; m. Wilma Georgia Dickerson, July 30, 1935; children—Geneva Irene (Mrs. Donald Ellis Blood), John Purl Uttley, Wayne Torquil. Intern, Glendale (Cal.) Sanitarium and Hosp., 1938, Highsmith Hosp., Fayetteville, N.C., 1938-39; practice family medicine, Marshville, N.C., 1939—; dir. McLeod Clinic, 1941-45; pres. Bio-Factor Labs., Marshville, 1956—; pres. McLeod Airport, Wingate, N.C., 1948-62; acting dir. Anson County Health Dept., 1968—; coronor Union County, N.C., 1957-58; med. examiner, 1958-60; justice of peace, 1967-69. Comdr., capt. Civil Air Patrol, 1945-48; active A.R.C. Diplomate Nat. Bd. Med. Examiners. Fellow Am. Assn. Family Practice; mem. A.M.A., So. Med. Assn. (life), N.C., Union County (past pres.) med. socs., N.Y. Acad. Scis., N.C. Art Soc. (life). Lion (charter mem. Marshville, treas. 1963—). Contbr. articles to med. jours., newspapers, mags. Author: Ish and Isha, 1967. Home: 301 White St Marshville NC 28103 Office: 103 S Elm St Marshville NC 28103

MCMAHON, CHARLES ALEXANDER, TV sta. exec.; b. Knoxville, Tenn., Mar. 22, 1912; s. Charles Perry and Parley (Lett) McM.; student U. Tenn., 1929-30, Carnegie Inst. Tech., 1930-31; m. Evelyn Eve Jones, Oct. 10, 1936; 1 son, Charles Alexander III. Dir. programming, reporter, dir., actor WNOX radio, Knoxville, 1946-62; anchorman, editor-producer WATE-TV, Knoxville, 1962-68; anchorman, dir. pub. affairs, moderator-producer WXEX-TV, Richmond, Va., 1968—. Bd. dirs. Carousel Theatre, U. Tenn., Knoxville, 1956-60. Served with USNR, 1944-45; ETO. Methodist (chmn. bd. stewards). Mason (Shriner, K.T.). Home: Apt H 6231 Sloan Ct Richmond VA 23234 Office: 623 E Main St Richmond VA 23219

MCMAHON, JOHN MARTIN, physician; b. Buffalo, Dec. 24, 1915; s. Charles A. and Mary (Fox) McM.; B.S., Georgetown U., 1936, M.D., 1940; M.S. in Medicine, U. Minn., 1950; m. Virginia Mary Tracy, Mar. 21, 1942; children—John Martin, Edward, Barbara, Robert, Bruce, Tommy. Intern, Georgetown U. Hosp., Washington, 1940-41; practice medicine specializing in internal medicine, Bessemer, Ala.; asso. Browne-McHardy Clinic, New Orleans, 1950-52; partner Bessemer Clinic, 1952—; prof. clin. medicine U. Ala., 1952—, dir. Arthritis Clinic Med. Center; attending cons. VA Hosp., Birmingham; chief of medicine Bapt. Med. Center-Princeton, Birmingham; mem. staff Carraway Med. Center. Served to capt. AUS, World War II; PTO. Recipient Benemerenti award Pope Paul VI, 1968. Diplomate Am. Bd. Internal Medicine. Fellow A.C.P., Am. Coll. Gastroenterology (past pres.). Contbr. articles to profl. jours. Home: 106 Waverly Circle Bessemer AL 35020 Office: 800 Clinic Lane Bessemer AL 35020

MCMAHON, RHETT RUSSELL, rental property co. exec.; b. Baton Rouge, La., Nov. 16, 1916; s. Rhett Gustav and Pearl F. (Fridge) McM.; student La. State U., 1934-35; B.S., Tulane U., 1939; m. Yvonne Marie Barbe, May 29, 1941; children—Rhett, Claudia Barbe, Diane Marie. Owner, mgr. rental properties, Baton Rouge, 1946—; dir. Baton Rouge Water Works Co. Served as sgt. M.C., AUS, 1941-45; ETO. Mem. Baton Rouge C. of C., Kappa Sigma. Kiwanian (pres. 1952). Club: Baton Rouge Country. Address: 1645 Perkins Rd Baton Rouge LA 70808

MCMAHON, RICHARD WARREN, motel corp. exec.; b. Memphis, Aug. 12, 1939; s. Warren Greenway and Ometra (Simpson) McM.; B.S., Memphis State U., 1962; m. Linda Bentley, Apr. 10, 1974; 1 dau. by previous marriage, Valerie Jones. With Holiday Inns, Inc., Memphis, 1962—, dir. sales for operations, 1963-66, dir. nat. sales, 1966-69, dir. marketing western region, 1969-70, dir. sales and promotion, inns and restaurants, 1970-73, div. asst. v.p. market devel., 1973—. Recipient Distinguished Sales award Memphis Sales Execs. Assn., 1968; named Salesman of Year, Holiday Inns, Inc., 1968. Mem. Hotel Sales Mgmt. Assn. Internat. (dir. 1971—), Discover Am. Travel Orgn., Am. Marketing Assn., Memphis Sales and Marketing Execs. Club, Mid-South Football Ofcls. Assn., Touchdown Club Memphis, Pi Sigma Epsilon, Psi Chi, Omicron Delta Kappa, Chi Beta Phi, Sigma Alpha Epsilon. Home: 3924 Springfield Dr Memphis TN 38128 Office: 3796 Lamar Av Memphis TN 38118

MCMAKIN, WILLIAM ISAAC, JR., wholesale trade exec.; b. LaGrange, Ky., June 7, 1912; s. William Isaac and Elizabeth (Emerson) McM.; student Eastern U., 1931, U. Ky., 1932, Transylvania U., 1932-33; m. Kathryn Hardin, Oct. 17, 1940; children—William Isaac III, Ronald Albert. Salesman, Belknap, Inc., No. Ky., 1936-62, buyer wholesale hardware, 1962-72, v.p., 1972—, also dir.; dir. Bank of Oldham County, LaGrange, Ky. Mem. Christian Ch. (chmn. bd. 1969-70). Mason (32 deg. Shriner, dist. dep. grand master 1956), Rotarian. Home: Route 1 Box 55 LaGrange KY 40031 Office: 111 E Main St Louisville KY 40202

MCMANUS, SAMUEL PLYLER, chemist, educator; b. Edgemoor, S.C., Oct. 29, 1938; s. Henry Plyler and Louise (Sanders) McM.; B.S. in Chemistry, The Citadel, 1960; M.S., Clemson U., 1962, Ph.D. in Chemistry, 1964; m. Nancy Fincher, Mar. 26, 1959; children—Samuel Plyler, Robert Adair. Research chemist Du Pont, Phila., 1964; asst. prof. chemistry U. Ala. at Huntsville, 1966-68, asso. prof., 1968-73, prof., 1973—, also chmn. dept. chemistry, 1970-72. Cons. to govt. and indsl. firms. Committeeman Tenn. Valley council Boy Scouts Am., 1973—; radio com. chmn. U.S. Power Squadrons, 1973—. Served to capt., AUS, 1964-66. Petroleum Research Fund grantee, 1968—. Named Outstanding educator U. Ala. at Huntsville, 1971. Alumni Fellow Clemson U., 1961. Mem. Am. Chem. Soc. (chmn. north Ala. sect. 1969), Ala. Acad. Sci. (v.p. 1973-74), A.A. A. S., Sigma Xi. Clubs: Lake Guntersville Yacht, U. Ala. Huntsville (pres. 1970-71). Editor: Organic Reactive Intermediates. Contbr. articles on chemistry to sci. jours. Home: 2513 Norman Terrace Huntsville AL 35810 Office: Dept of Chemistry Univ of Alabama Huntsville 35807

MCMASTER, CLIFFORD FRANKLIN, lawyer; b. Kansas City, Mo., Aug. 8, 1935; s. Clifford Montgomery and Esther (Osborn) McM.; B.M.E., U. Tex., 1958, LL.B., 1961; m. Margie Ann Vaden, Aug. 19, 1961. Admitted to Tex. bar, 1961, since practiced in Ft. Worth. Mem. State Bar of Tex., Am. Bar Assn., Ft. Worth-Tarrant County Jr. Bar, Nat. Rifle Assn. Methodist. Mason. Home: 5652 Wedgmont Circle Fort Worth TX 76133 Office: 206 Ft Worth Club Bldg Ft Worth TX 76102

MCMASTER, JOHN GREGG, lawyer; b. Florence, S.C., Mar. 16, 1914; B.S., U. S.C., 1936, LL.B., 1938. Admitted to S.C. bar, 1938; since practiced in Columbia; mem. firm Tompkins, McMaster and Thomas. Code commr. State of S.C., 1953-54; vice chmn. S.C. Aeros. Commn., 1952-56, chmn., 1956-67; exec. dir. Assn. S.C. Life Ins. Cos., 1956—. Mem. ho. reps. S.C. Gen. Assembly, 1945-48. Fellow Am. Coll. Trial Lawyers; mem. Am., S.C., Richland County (dir. 1941, sec. 1945) bar assns., Nat. Assn. R.R. Trial Counsel, S.C. Def. Attys. Assn., Omicron Delta Kappa. Office: Security Fed Bldg Columbia SC 29201*

MCMILLAN, ANN ALTA, psychologist; b. Tallahassee, May 16, 1936; d. Robert Alton and Margaret (Smith) McMillan; B.A., Blue Mountain Coll., 1958; M.Ed., U. Miss., 1966, Ed.D., 1967; m. J.R. Null, June 26, 1958 (div. Mar. 1960); children—Robert Alton, David Bruce. Dir. guidance Keystone High Sch., Keystone Heights, Fla., 1963-65; instr. counselor U. Miss. Counseling Center, Oxford, 1965-67; dir. student personnel services Blue Mountain Coll., Miss., 1967-68; sch. psychologist Orange County (Fla.) Sch. System, 1968-69; clin. psychologist Guidance Center, Inc., Daytona Beach, Fla., 1969—. Cons. psychol. services. Mem. Volusia County Mental Health Assn., Am., Fla. personnel and guidance assns., Nat., Fla. assns. women deans and counselors, Nat. Assn. Sch. Psychologists, Kappa Delta Pi. Home: 1109 Richardson Rd Tallahassee FL 32301 Office: 1220 Willis Av Daytona Beach FL 32014

MCMILLAN, CAMPBELL WHITE, educator, physician; b. Soochow, China, Jan. 10, 1927 (parents Am. citizens); s. Henry Hudson and Leila (Memory) McM.; B.S. summa cum laude, Wake Forest U., 1948; M.D., Bowman Gray Sch. Medicine, 1952; m. Florence Jean MacKenzie, June 11, 1955; children—Ian J., Sally H., Donna J., Andrew D., Bridget W., Wendy M. Intern Harvard Med. Service Boston City Hosp., 1952-53; pediatric resident Children's Hosp. Med. Center, Boston, 1953-55; pediatric registrar St. Mary's Hosp. Med. Sch., London, Eng., 1955-56; asst. in medicine Nemazee Hosp., Shiraz, Iran, 1956-58; research fellow Harvard Med. Sch., Boston, 1958-61; practice medicine, specializing in pediatrics, Laurinburg, N.C., 1961-63; asst. prof. pediatrics, U. N.C., Chapel Hill, 1963-68, asso. prof., 1968-72, prof., 1972—. Served with Hosp. Corps, USNR, 1944-46. Recipient Lederle Med. Faculty award Lederle Labs. div. Am. Cyanamid Co., 1964, Distinguished Alumnus award Bowman Gray Sch. Medicine, 1972, Professor award U. N.C. Sch. Medicine, 1967, 70. Diplomate Am. Bd. Pediatrics. Mem. A.M.A., Soc. for Pediatric Research, Am. Pediatric Soc., Am. Acad. Pediatrics, Phi Beta Kappa, Sigma Xi, Omicron Delta Kappa, Alpha Omega Alpha, Sigma Phi Epsilon, Phi Rho Sigma. Democrat. Episcopalian. Rotarian. Contbr. to profl. publs. Home: 408 Ridgecrest Dr Chapel Hill NC 27514 Office: Dept Pediatrics NC Meml Hosp Chapel Hill NC 27514

MCMILLAN, ED LEIGH II, timber co. exec.; b. Brewton, Ala., July 8, 1940; s. Thomas Edward and Elvire Minge (Cochrane) McC.; B.S. in Forest Mgmt., N.C. State Coll., 1962; B.S. in Finance, U. Ala., 1964; m. Mary Anne Self, June 22, 1958; children—Ed Leigh III, Daniel Webster. With woodlands div. T.R. Miller Mill Co., Inc., Brewton, Ala., 1964—, v.p., 1968—; forester D.W. McMillan Trust, Brewton, 1964—; sec., dir.-treas. Neal Land & Timber Co., Blounts Town, Fla., 1969—. Vice pres. Gulf Coast council Boy Scouts Am., 1970-73. Chmn. Young Republican Com., Escambia County, Ala., 1970-72. Named An Outstanding Young Man in Am., Ala. Jaycees, 1968. Mem. Kappa Alpha, Delta Sigma Pi. Home: 805 Evergreen St Brewton AL 36426 Office: T R Miller Mill Co Inc Deer St Brewton AL 36426

MCMILLAN, HUGH DIX, JR., mfrs. rep.; b. Shreveport, La., Sept. 15, 1925; s. Hugh Dix and Edna (Self) McM.; B.S., Tex. A. and M. Coll., 1947; m. Dorothy Jean Sawyer, May 10, 1952; children—Hugh Dix III, Janet Lynn. Design engr. Coastal Equipment Co., Houston, 1947-48; design and sales engr. D & S Sales, Inc., 1948-49; sales engr, J.R. Dowdell & Co., 1949-55; pres. McMillan Equipment Co., 1955—. Dir. F.E. Giesecke Meml. Fund Austin, Tex. Served with AC, AUS, 1944-45. Mem. Am. Soc. Heating, Refrigerating and Air Conditioning Engrs. (past pres. Houston chpt., nat. dir., regional chmn. Houston Engring. and Sci. Soc., Nat., Tex. socs. profl. engrs. Baptist. Mason (Shriner). Club: Pine Forest Country. Home: 13302 Apple Tree Houston TX 77024 Office: 1336 W Clay Houston TX 77019

MCMILLAN, JAMES BRYAN, judge; b. Goldsboro, N.C., Dec. 19, 1916; s. Robert Hunter and Louise (Outlaw) McM.; grad. Presbyn. Jr. Coll., 1934; A.B., U. N.C., 1937; LL.B., Harvard, 1940; m. Margaret Blair Miles, Feb. 27, 1944; children—James Bryan, Marjorie Miles. Admitted to N.C. bar, 1941; mem. staff N.C. atty.-gen., 1940-42; partner Helms, Mulliss, McMillan & Johnston, Charlotte, 1946-68; U.S. dist. judge Western Dist. N.C., 1968—; judge pro tem Charlotte City Ct., 1947-51. Mem. N.C. Cts. Commn., 1963-71. Pres. Travelers Aid Soc., 1957-59; bd. visitors Davidson Coll. Served from apprentice seaman to lt. (s.g.), USNR, 1942-46; ETO. Fellow Internat. Acad. Trial Lawyers; mem. Am., 26th Dist. (pres. 1957-58), N.C. (pres. 1960-61) bar assns., United World Federalists, Newcomen Soc., St. Andrews Coll. Alumni Assn. (pres. 1965-66), Omicron Delta Kappa. Democrat. Presbyn. Clubs: Charlotte City, Charlotte Country. Home: 1930 Mecklenburg Av Charlotte NC 28205 Office: US Dist Ct Charlotte NC 28201

MCMILLAN, JOHN ALEXANDER, III, holding co. exec.; b. Charlotte, N.C., May 9, 1932; s. John Alexander and Mildred Elizabeth (Shepherd) McM.; A.B. in History, U. N.C., 1954; M.B.A., U. Va., 1958; m. Caroline Hill Houston, Nov. 21, 1959; children—Elizabeth Houston, John Alexander IV. Vice pres. Carolina Paper Bd. Corp., Charlotte, 1958-60; v.p. John C. Shepherd Lumber Corp., Charlotte, 1960-63; v.p. R.S. Dickson & Co., Charlotte, 1963-68; v.p., treas. Ruddick Corp., Charlotte, 1968—; dir. Am. & Efird Mills, Charlie's Girls, Inc., Harris-Teeter Supermarkets, Jordan Bus. Forms, Inc., Asso. Auto Parts, Inc., Lowndes Hill Realty Co., Knapdale Properties, Ltd. Mem. child and family care com. social planning council United Community Services. Mem. Mecklenburg County Bd. Commrs., 1972-74, Mecklenburg County Social Services Bd., 1974—. Served with AUS, 1954-56. Mem. Sigma Alpha Epsilon. Republican. Presbyn. (deacon 1965—, treas. 1971, elder 1972—). Mem. Order of Gimghoul. Clubs: Charlotte Country, Charlotte City. Home: 754 Museum Dr Charlotte NC 28207 Office: First Union Jefferson Tower Charlotte NC 28282

MCMILLAN, JOHN LANNEQU, former congressman; b. Mullins, S.C.; s. M. L. and Mary Alice (Keith) McM.; ed. Mullins High Sch., U. S.C., U. N.C.; m. Margaret English, Oct. 31, 1936; 1 son, John L. Mem. 76th-93d Congresses, 6th S.C. Dist., chmn. D.C. com., vice chmn. agr. com. Mem. Am. Legion. Democrat. Baptist. Mason, Elk. Home: Florence SC 29501

MCMILLEN, LARRY BYRON, prosthodontist; b. Defiance, O., Apr. 18, 1942; s. Nelson Guy and Beulah Martha (Belden) McM.; D.D.S., Ohio State U., 1966, M.S., 1970; m. JoEllen Vinsel, June 14, 1964; children—Jeffrey Daron, Jason Derek. Instr. Ohio State U. Coll. Dentistry, Columbus, 1969-70; pvt. practice prosthodontics, Metairie, La., 1970—. Asst. prof. Sch. Dentistry, La. State U., New Orleans, 1970—; vis. staff Charity Hosp., New Orleans; cons. staff Ochsner Found. Hosp., 1973; adivser Kenner (La.) Hosp. Bd., 1973. Served with AUS, 1966-68. Mem. Ohio State U. Alumni Assn. (pres. 1971-73), Aircraft Owners and Pilots Assn., Psi Omega. Kiwanian. Club: Chateau Estates Golf and Country. Home: 35 Antiqua Dr Kenner LA 70062 Office: 4300 Houma Blvd Metairie LA 70002

MCMILLON, REGNAL LUTHER, ins. co. exec., pub. speaker; b. Guion, Tex., Apr. 23, 1921; s. James Luther and Tennessee Jones (Haynie) McM.; student Tarleton State Coll., 1938; m. Elsie Eugenia Roberts, Dec. 14, 1941; children—Toni Karen, Steven Grant. Internat. speaker for convs., clubs, other orgns.; with Bus. Men's Assurance Co., Abilene, Tex., 1946-71, dist. mgr., 1956-60, br. mgr., Abilene, Tex., 1961-71; gen. agt. Washington Nat. Ins. Co., Lubbock, Tex., 1971—. Dir. Nat. Gen. Agts. and Mgrs. Conf.; trustee Life Underwriters Tng. Council U.S., pres., 1965-66. Served with USAAF, 1942-46. Named Ins. Field Man of Yr. in Life Ins. in U.S., 1962; Internat. Health Ins. Man of Yr., 1965; recipient Harold R. Gordon Meml. award Internat. Assn. Health Underwriters, 1965, Distinguished Service award Vocational Agr. Tchrs. Tex., 1965; John Newton Russell award, 1967. Mem. Nat. (pres, 1961-62), Tex. (pres. 1956-57) assns. life underwriters, Tex. Assn. Health Underwriters (pres. 1954-55), Author numerous articles on selling, human relations. Home: 3508 37th St Lubbock TX 79413 Office: 2321 50th St Lubbock TX 79412

MCMORDIE, WARREN C., JR., chem. products co. exec.; b. Austin, Tex., May 14, 1929; s. Warren C. and Mamie Ailene (Jones) McM.; B.A., Tex. Christian U., 1950, M.A., 1960; Ph.D., U. Tex., 1963; m. Betty Ann Armstrong, June 24, 1952; children—Robert Bruce, William Douglas, Mary Ann, Warren Claud. Jr. chemist Gen. Dymanics, Ft. Wroth, 1951-53, chemist, 1953-56, sr. chemist, 1956-58, asst. supr., 1958-61; research chemist DuPont Co., Deepwater, N.J., 1963-67; lab. mgr. Oil Base, Inc., Houston, 1967-72, dir. research and devel., 1972—. Mem. Am. Chem. Soc., Am. Petroleum Inst. Chem. Soc. (London), Soc. Petroleum Engrs., Am. Inst. Mining Engrs., Sigma Xi. Presbyn. Patentee in field. Home: 220 Caruthers St Houston TX 77024 Office: P O Box 22753 Houston TX 77027

MCMORRIES, BILLY RAY, civil engr.; b. Anson, Tex., Jan. 9, 1927; s. James Oscar and Nellie (Marbut) McM.; B.S. in Civil Engring., U. Okla., 1949, M.C.E., 1950; LL.B., Am. Sch. Law, 1951; m. Billie Jean Blanton, Aug. 27, 1949; children—Kim, Stephani, Marcia. Office engr. Hasie & Green Engrs., Lubbock, Tex., 1950-52; civil engr. McMorries & Assos., Amarillo, Tex., 1952—. Vice-chmn. CL & I Trust, Amarillo, 1967—. Served with AUS, 1944-46. Registered profl. engr., Tex., Okla., N.M. Mem. Am. Soc. C.E., Nat., Tex. (sec. Panhandle chpt. 1954—) socs. profl. engrs. Home: 2907 Harmony St Amarillo TX 79106 Office: 6300 Canyon Dr Amarillo TX 79109

MCMURRAY, JAMES EDWIN, hotel exec.; b. Hubbard, O., Dec. 7, 1931; s. Homer Dewey and Edith (Mason) McM.; student Youngstown Coll., 1956-58; m. Ellen Wagner, Feb. 10, 1952; 1 dau., Bess Marla. Owner, mgr. Lakeside Lodge, Geneva-on-the-Lake, O., 1956-62; v.p., gen. mgr., dir. Wedgewood South Corp., Hilton Inns of N.C., Winston-Salem, 1959-72; gen. mgr. Winston-Salem Hyatt House, 1973—; treas., dir. Wedgewood Enterprises, Inc. Served with AUS, 1952-54. Mem. N.C. (pres. elect), Winston-Salem (past pres.)

innkeepers assns., N.C. Travel Council, Am. Hotel and Motel Assn., Winston-Salem C. of C. (dir.). Home: Route 2 Clinedale Rd Pfafftown NC 27040 Office: 300 W 5th St Winston-Salem NC 27102

MCMURTRY, EDWARD HOYSE, architect; b. Silverton, Tex., July 11, 1912; s. Edward Dawson and Ollie Mae (Smithee) McM.; B.A. in Arch., Tex Tech U., 1937; m. Esther Lloyd Jones, Sept. 4, 1938; children—Kathryn (Mrs. Warren E. Hunt), Allan Edward, Steven Lloyd. Draftsman, Robert E. Merrell, architect, Clovis, N.M., 1938-41, Wyatt C. Hendrick, Houston, 1941-42, Atcheson & Atkinson, architects, Lubbock, Tex., 1946-51; chief draftsman O.R. Walker, Lubbock, 1951-53; partner McMurtry & Craig, architects and engrs., Lubbock, 1953—. Vice pres. Friends of Tex. Libraries, 1969-71, pres., 1971-73. Trustee W. Tex. Mus. Assn., Lubbock; bd. dirs. Lubbock Boys Club. Served with USAAF, 1944-46. Mem. A.I.A. (pres. Lubbock chpt. 1966), Tex. Soc. Architects, Tau Beta Pi. Democrat. Baptist. Lion (dist. gov. 1972-73). Prin. works: Tulia (Tex.). High Sch., 1956; Evans Jr. High Sch., Lubbock, 1958, Tex Tech U. Mus., Lubbock, 1968, Dormitory Bldgs., 1957-63; George and Helen Mahon Library, Lubbock, 1973; various chs. Home: 3813 27th St Lubbock TX 79410 Office: 3014 50th St Lubbock TX 79413

MCNAB, M(AHON) TERRY, lawyer, corp. exec.; b. Tampa, Fla., Feb. 1, 1927; s. Robert Calvin and Hazel (Kirkconnel) McN.; B.S. in Bus. Adminstrn., U. Fla., 1950; J.D., Stetson U., 1958; m. Marjorie Katherine Huddleston, Apr. 6, 1963. Staff accountant Ernst & Ernst, C.P.A.'s, Tampa, 1950-53; instr. accounting U. Fla., Gainesville, 1953-55; admitted to Fla. bar, 1958; partner firm Mabry, Reaves, Carlton, Fields & Ward, Tampa, 1958-62; practice in Tampa, 1962-66; v.p., gen. counsel, dir. Kenflo Corp., Tampa, 1966-71; exec. v.p., founder EDCO, Inc., Tampa, 1971—. Lectr. law Stetson U., 1958. Served to lt. (j.g.), USNR, 1945-46. C.P.A., Fla. Mem. Am., Fla., Tampa, Hillsborough County bar assns., Am., Fla. insts. certified pub. accountants, Aircraft Owners and Pilots Assn., Tampa C. of C., Phi Delta Phi, Alpha Kappa Psi, Phi Delta Theta. Episcopalian (instr. Sunday Sch. 1964-65, bd. ushers 1965—). Clubs: Merrymakers (pres. Tampa 1958); Tampa Yacht and Country; Ye Mystic Krew of Gasparilla. Home: 3109 Watrous Av Tampa FL 33606 Office: 512 Florida Av Tampa FL 33602

MCNABB, ROBERT EUGENE, state ofcl.; b. Newport, Tenn., June 20, 1932; s. Hugh F. and Lena Mae (Kennedy) McN.; B.A., Carson-Newman Coll., 1955; M.S. in Social Work, U. Tenn., 1960; m. Mary Hu Medlin, Oct. 8 1955; 1 dau., Lora Annette. Staff social worker Central State Psychiat. Hosp., Nashville, 1960-62, VA Hosp., Murfreesboro, Tenn., 1962-64; chief psychiat. social worker Clover Bottom Hosp. and Sch., Nashville, 1964-66; dir. psychiat. social work Tenn. Dept. Mental Health, Nashville, 1966—. Mem. Nat. Assn. Social Workers, Acad. Certified Social Workers, Am. Pub. Health Assn., Conf. Social Workers in State and Territorial Mental Health Programs (chmn.), Tenn. Conf. Social Welfare, Am. Assn. on Mental Deficiency. Baptist. Mason. Home: 2709 Western Hills Dr Nashville TN 37214 Office: Cordell Hall Bldg Nashville TN 37219

MCNAIR, GROVER CLEVELAND, JR., constrn. co exec.; b. Winston-Salem, N.C., May 17, 1924; s. Grover Cleveland and Renna (Klinetob) McN.; student Mass. Inst. Tech., 1943-44; B.S. in Archtl. Engring., N.C. State U., 1949; m. Jane Marilyn Casstevens, Dec. 8, 1951; children—Grover Cleveland III, Julia Owen, Mary Lyn. Pres., McNair Constrn. Co., Inc., Winston-Salem, 1954—. Pres., Casstevens Hosp. Corp., 1964—; founder Med. Park Hosp., 1969— (both Winston-Salem). Served with AUS, World War II, ETO. Decorated Combat Inf. Badge. Mem. Nat. Assn. Home Builders (nat, dir.), Fedn. Am. Hosps. (dir.), Sigma Phi Epsilon, Mu Beta Psi. Democrat. Presbyn. (deacon). Kiwanian. Club: Old Town (Winston-Salem). Home: 130 Pine Valley Rd Winston-Salem NC 27104 Office: 747 Summit St Winston-Salem NC 27102

MCNAIR, LARRY DELANO, profl. engr.; b. Macon, Ga., June 21, 1934; s. William Oscar and Annie (Buchannan) McN.; B.Ch.E., Ga. Inst. Tech., 1956; student Okla. A. and M. U., 1956, U. Chattanooga, 1959; m. Mary Lee Padgett, Aug. 3, 1953; children—Jennifer Scott, Mary Shannan, Jeffery Webb, Andrew Buchannan. Process engr. Continental Oil Co., Ponca City, Okla., 1956-57; design engr. Combustion Engring. Inc., Chattanooga, Tenn., 1957-61, research engr., Windsor, Conn., 1961-65; sr. engr. So. Services Inc., Birmingham, Ala., 1965—. Mem. Midwest Benthol. Soc., Nat. Soc. Profl. Engrs., Am. Inst. Chem. Engrs., Am. Chem. Soc., A.A.A.S., Air Pollution Control Assn., Nat. Fire Protection Assn., So. Services Leadership Assn. (v.p. 1971). Patentee furnace explosion prevention systems. Home: 804 Vestavia Lake Dr Birmingham AL 35216 Office: PO Box 2625 Birmingham AL 35202

MCNAIRY, SIDNEY ARCHIE, JR., educator; b. Memphis, Oct. 16, 1937; s. Sidney Archie and Mary Lee (Hayslette) McN.; B.S., LeMoyne Coll., 1959; M.S., Purdue U., 1965; m. Bobbie Lee Nelson, June 2, 1965; children—Alicia Yvette, Sidney III. Mem. faculty So. U., Baton Rouge, 1965—, dir. health research center, 1971—, dir. biomed. support program, 1972—, prof. chemistry, 1968—. Mem. Scotlandville Area Adv. Com., 1969—, Park Vista Improvement Assn., 1968—. U.S. Dept. Agr. Research grantee, 1972-75. Mem. A.A.A.S., Am. Chem. Soc., Alpha Phi Alpha, Beta Kappa Chi, Alpha Chi Sigma. Home: 10571 Birchwood Dr Baton Rouge LA 70807 Office: PO Box 9921 Southern Univ Baton Rouge LA 70813

MCNAMARA, DOLORES MABEL LACOUME (MRS. ROBERT J. MCNAMARA), editor; b. Galveston, Tex., Apr. 26, 1913; d. James G. and Lucille (Rizzo) LaCoume; student pub. and parochial schs.; m. Robert J. McNamara, Apr. 27, 1938; 1 dau., Linda Ann (Mrs. Joseph Paul Polivka, Jr.). With Tex. Prudential Ins. Co., Galveston, Tex., 1930-32; clk.-typist Am. Nat. Ins. Co., Galveston, 1932-39, asst. supr., 1940-44; asso. editor Star Bull., Galveston, 1946—. Club: Altrusa (corr. sec. 1966-67) (Galveston, Tex.). Home: 2714 John Dr LaMarque TX 77568 Office: One Moody Plaza Galveston TX 77551

MCNAMARA, EDWARD PAUL, ceramic tile mfg. co. exec.; b. Troy, N.Y., Sept. 27, 1911; s. John Vincent and Josephine (McChristian) McN.; student Rensselaer Poly. Inst., 1930-32; B.S., Alfred U., 1935; M.S., Pa. State U., 1937, postgrad., 1937-41; postgrad. U. Cin., 1954; m. Alma May Falle, Apr. 18, 1933; children—Imelda (Mrs. John H. Way), Edward Paul. Research asst. Pa. State U., 1935-36, supr. ceramics extension, 1936-42; head dept. ceramics Rutgers U., 1942-45; pres., gen. mgr. Pfaltzgraff Pottery Co., York, Pa., 1945-46; dir. ceramics Shenango China Co., New Castle, Pa., 1946-53; v.p. Cambridge Tile Mfg. Co., Cin., 1953-69; pres., chief exec. officer Monarch Tile Mfg. Inc., San Angelo, Tex., 1969—. Trustee Alfred U. Fellow Am. Ceramic Soc.; mem. Ceramic Tile Mfrs. U.S. (v.p. 1972—, treas. 1972—), Tile Council Am. (dir. 1972), Nat. Inst. Ceramic Engrs. (pres. 1972-73), Am. Soc. for Testing and Materials, Sigma Xi, Phi Lambda Upsilon. Republican. Presbyn. Clubs: Keramos, San Angelo Country. Author: Ceramics, 3 vols., 1937-40. Contbr. numerous articles to tech. jours. Home: 2644 W Twohig St San Angelo TX 76901 Office: Box 2041 San Angelo TX 76901

MCNAMARA, NEDRA, univ. exec.; b. New Castle, Pa., Mar. 4, 1914; d. John Fleming and Ann (Hartland) McNamara; student U. Miami, Coral Gables, Fla., 1931-34; A.B., Fla. State U., 1935. Reporter, Miami (Fla.) Herald, 1932-35; tchr. English, head journalism dept. Coral Gables High Sch., 1935-42; exec. asst. Pleasantville Constrn. Co., Nassau, B.W.I., 1942-44; adminstrv. asst. Office Personnel Narratives, USAF Intelligence, Orlando, Fla., N.Y.C., 1944-45; exec. asst., editor house organ First Nat. Bank Miami, 1945-49; staff writer U. Miami Pub. Information Office, 1949—, news editor, 1951, asst. dir., 1958-62, acting dir., 1962-64, dir. pub. information, 1964-66, dir. news bur., 1966—; asst. to editor U. Miami Press, 1949-57; free-lance contbr. Rendezvous, 1940-41. Mem. Am. Coll. Pub. Relations Assn., Alpha Epsilon Rho, Women in Communications (v.p. Greater Miami 1959-60), Mortar Board, Kappa Alpha Theta. Office: U Miami Coral Gables FL 33124

MCNEELY, ROBERT LEWIS, educator; b. Morganton, N.C., June 5, 1938; s. Ralph Ballew and Lillie (Oxford) McN.; B.S., Duke U., 1960; student Cal. Inst. Tech., 1960-62; Ph.D., U. N.C., 1969. Peace Corps vol. Government Coll., Ibadan, Nigeria, 1962-65; asso. prof. chemistry U. Tenn., Chattanooga, 1969—; chem. and environmental cons. Mem. Hamilton County Democratic Party Task Force on Crime, 1972—. Trustee Ipetu-Ijesha Hosp., Nigeria. Mem. Am. Assn. U. Profs., Am. Chem. Soc. (chmn. com. on profl. relations 1973), A.A.A.S., Chattanooga C. of C. (mem. task force on water pollution 1971—), Phi Beta Kappa, Sigma Xi. Methodist (chmn. commn. on social concerns 1973—). Home: Yacht Relevance Gold Point Marina Gann Rd Hixson TN 37343 Office: Chemistry Dept U Tenn Chattanooga TN 37401

MCNEIL, ALLIE SPENCER, warehousing exec.; b. Wilkes County, N.C., Apr. 20, 1933; s. Wiley Estel and Golda (Hurt) McNeil; grad. high sch.; m. Dollie Parsons, July 25, 1953; 1 dau., Nancy Gail. Funeral dir. Reins Sturdivant Funeral Home, North Wilkesboro, N.C., 1951-53; with D.D. Jones Transfer & Warehouse Co., Inc., Chesapeake, Va., 1955—, v.p., 1966—, also dir. Served with AUS, 1953-55. Mem. Tidewater Motor Carriers Traffic Assn. (pres. 1973—), Norfolk Portsmouth Traffic Club (dir. 1971, 72, 2d v.p., 1974—), Hampton Rds. Maritime Assn. (inland transp., hazardous cargo coms. 1972—). Baptist (treas. 1961-69, trustee). Clubs: Cavalier Yacht and Country (Virginia Beach, Va.); Propeller U.S.; Harbor, Port Norfolk, Virginian. (Norfolk, Va.). Home: 6419 Bridle Way Norfolk VA 23518 Office: 630 22 St Chesapeake VA 23324

MCNEIL, MARSHALL, newspaper corr.; b. San Antonio, Mar. 29, 1904; s. Clarence W. and P. Jane (Taylor) McN.; ed. pub. schs.; m. Blanche Venable, May 2, 1925 (dec. Feb. 1962); 1 son, Neil Venable; m. 2d, Jennie June Langer, Sept. 11, 1963. Newspaperman, San Antonio and Beaumont, Tex., to 1926, later Pensacola and Jacksonville, Fla.; city editor Houston Press, 1926-29; mng. editor Jacksonville Jour., 1929-30; corr., mng. editor Scripps-Howard Newspaper Alliance, Washington, 1930-34, corr., 1937—; editor Knoxville (Tenn.) News-Sentinel, 1934-37. Episcopalian. Club: Gridiron (pres. 1954). Home: 2845 29th Pl NW Washington DC 20008

MCNEIL, NORMAN LAIRD, univ. pres.; b. San Antonio, Oct. 3, 1915; s. Bert and Annie (Fite) McN.; B.A., U. Tex., 1937, M.A., 1944, Ph.D., 1956; m. Kathleen Howard, Feb. 7, 1941; children—Laird Howard, John Robert. Instr. English, U. Tex., 1954-56; prof. English, Tex. A. and I. U., Kingsville, 1956-65; pres. Sul Ross State U., Alpine, Tex., 1965—; field collector folk materials Library of Congress, 1940-41; Am. specialist lectr. Dept. of State, 1962. Served with USAAF, 1943-44. Recipient E.D. Farmer Internat. fellowship award for collection folklore in Mexico, U. Tex., 1941. Mem. Tex. Folklore Soc. (pres. 1946-49). Episcopalian. Spl. research British folk ballad in Am., folk ballad in Mexico. Home: President's Home Sul Ross State U Alpine TX 79830

MCNEIL, WALTER HARVE, sales rep.; b. Harlan, Ky., Apr. 21, 1920; s. John Charles and Marie E. (McBrayer) McN.; student Pikeville Coll., 1956-59; grad. Squadron Officer Sch., 1955, Air Command and Staff Coll., 1960; m. Nellie Dean, June 1, 1946; children—Kay Francis (Mrs. Barry Runyon), Paula Jean (Mrs. Freddy Branham). With Sycamore Coal Corp., Patterson, Va., 1937-42; enlisted pvt. USAAF, 1942, commd. 2d lt. U.S. Army, 1943, advanced through grades to capt., 1946; staff communication officer Hdqrs. ETO; trans. to USAF Res., 1946, advanced through grades to lt. col., 1967, ret., 1970; liaison officer Air Force Acad. coordinator W.Va., Ky., So. Ohio, 1961-70; with Foster Thornburg Hardware Corp., Huntington, W.Va., 1946-61; sales rep. Banks-Miller Supply Co., 1961—. Named Outstanding Liaison Officer Coordinator in South, USAF Acad., 1965. Charter mem. Armed Forces Communications and Electronics Assn.; mem. Air Force Assn., U.S. Capitol Hist. Soc., USAF Hist. Found. (life), Met. Opera Guild, Res. Officers Assn. Democrat. Baptist (deacon). Mason. Club: Army and Navy (Charleston, W.Va.). Home: 508 5th St Pikeville KY 41501 Office: PO Box 2097 Pikeville KY 41501

MCNEILL, RICHARD REID, soft drink co. exec.; b. Phila., Nov. 23, 1940; s. Alfred Mason and Elizabeth A. (McCaughan) McN.; B.S., U. Ariz., 1963; M.B.A., U. Pa., 1967; postgrad. Ga. State U., 1970; m. Nancy Philips McDonald, Aug. 23, 1963; children—Andy, David, Melissa. With Coca-Cola Co., Atlanta, 1967—, area market planner, 1970-71, mgr. sales analysis and market planning, 1971-72, nat. account exec., 1972—. Group chmn. Atlanta United Way, 1973; active local YMCA, Indian Guides. Served to 1st lt. AUS, 1964-66. Decorated Army Commendation medal. Mem. Am. Marketing Assn., Wharton Sch. Alumni Club. Episcopalian. Office: PO Drawer 1734 Atlanta GA 30301

MCNELIS, THOMAS ANTHONY, JR., editor; b. Kingston, N.Y., Feb. 8, 1929; s. Thomas Anthony and Marjorie (O'Reilly) McN.; B.S., Fordham U., 1952; M.S., Columbia, 1953; m. Victoria Zakseski, Aug. 22, 1953; children—Marilyn Judith, Robert Thomas, James William. Sports writer Binghamton (N.Y.) Press, 1953-54, Evening Sun, Balt., 1954-55; communications and pub. relations specialist Bayonne (N.J.) Refinery, Standard Oil Co. (N.J.), 1955-59, Bayway Refinery, Linden, N.J., 1959-61; editor Exxon Extra service sta. pub. Exxon Co., U.S.A., Houston, 1961—. Pres., Green Brook Twp. Republican Club, 1959-60. Chmn., Green Brook Recreation Com., 1960-61; dist. dir. Bronco div. Boys Baseball, 1968-72. Served with AUS, 1946. Mem. Spring Br. Meml. Sports Assn. Roman Catholic. Kiwanian, Lion. Home: 12803 Traviata St Houston TX 77024 Office: PO Box 2180 Houston TX 77001

MCNICHOLS, GERALD ROBERT, govt. ofcl.; b. Cleve., Nov. 21, 1943; s. Charles Wellington and June Beatrice (Kalal) McN.; B.S. cum laude, Case Inst. Tech., 1965; M.S., U. Pa., 1966; postgrad. George Washington U., 1967—; m. Paula Kay Austin, Dec. 26, 1964; children—Gerald Robert, Katherine Lynn, Melissa Sue. Computer cons., Cleve., 1963-65; mgmt. research analyst Wharton Sch., Phila., 1965-66; cons. Corning Glass Works Co. (N.Y.), 1965-67; operations research analyst Hdqrs. Air Force, Washington, 1967-70; dir. strategic aircraft, office dep. asst. sec. def. Def. Dept., Washington, 1970-72, dir. cost research office sec. def., 1972—. Professorial lectr. Am. U., Washington, 1967—; lectr. engring. George Washinton U., Washington, 1969-72. Served to capt. USAF, 1967-70. Mem. Washington Operations Research Council (sec. 1973-74), Inst. Mgmt. Scis. (sec. 1973-74), Operations Research Soc. Am., Assn. Pub. Program Analysis, Mil. Operation Research Soc., Phi Beta Kappa. Presbyn. (elder). Author: (with Ignizio Gupta) Operations Research in Decision-Making, 1973. Editor Cost-Effectiveness Newsletter, 1972—; referee Operation Research, 1968-72. Mgmt. Sci., 1969-71. Home: 8101 Rondelay Lane Fairfax Station VA 22039 Office: Office Sec Defense (ODDPA & E) Washington DC 20301

MCNIEL, GEORGE WILLIAM, state ofcl.; b. San Marcos, Tex., Feb. 21, 1931; s. William and Lora Mae (Riley) McN.; B.B.A., Baylor U., 1952; student S.W. Tex. State U., 1948-50; m. Barbara Jo Metz, June 12, 1953; children—Mark William, Earl Wayne, Glen Daniel. Staff auditor Arthur Andersen & Co., Houston, 1955-56; staff auditor firm Mulholland & Conklin, Austin, Tex., 1956-57; treas. Rich Plan of Austin Inc., 1957-60; partner firm Mulholland, McWhirter & McNiel, Austin, 1960-62; staff auditor Tex. Auditor's Dept., 1962-64, supervising asst., 1964-66, 1st asst., 1966-68, state auditor, 1968—. Served to 1st lt. USAF, 1952-54. Mem. Beta Alpha Psi, Delta Sigma Pi. Baptist (deacon, chmn. bd.). Home: 6507 NE Dr Austin TX 78723 Office: 319 Sam Houston State Office Bldg Austin TX 78711

MCNIEL, NORBERT ARTHUR, educator; b. Moody, Tex., Dec. 22, 1914; s. Arthur A. and Gertrude (Burt) McN.; B.S., Tex. A. and M. Coll., 1935, M.Ed., 1952, Ph.D., 1955; m. Jane Edith Richter, Aug. 13, 1939; children—Rebecca (Mrs. Joe W. Lindley), Ruth (Mrs. Charles W. Garner, Jr.), Fred Larkin. Tchr. high sch., Alvin, Tex., 1935-41; supr. McLennan County Vocational Sch., Waco, Tex., 1946-51; adviser fgn. programs Tex. A. and M. Coll. System, Pakistan, 1955-56; mem. faculty Tex. A. and M. U., 1957—, prof. genetics, 1972—. Del. Tex. Republican Conv., 1968, 70, 72; precinct chmn., 1968—. Served to lt. col. AUS, 1941-46. Decorated Bronze Star; recipient Distinguished Faculty award Assn. Former Students Tex. A. and M. U., 1964. Mem. Am. Genetic Assn., Am. Legion (post comdr. 1946-50). Mem. Ch. of Christ. Kiwanian. Home: 100 Dexter St College Station TX 77840

MCNITT, HAROLD AUSTIN, internat. economist; b. Dec. 6, 1924; s. Harold Anson and Margaret (Austin) McN.; student Western Res. U., 1945; A.B., U. Mich., 1949, M.A., 1953, Ph.D., 1956; postgrad. (Fulbright fellow) U. Copenhagen, 1954-55, (SSRC fellow) U. Uppsala, Sweden, 1957-58; m. Roberta Frank, June 8, 1946. Instr. philosophy U. Mich., 1955-56, Western Res. U., 1956-57, Johns Hopkins, 1958-59; European area specialist Dept. of Commerce, Washington, 1961—; trade devel. officer U.S. Trade Mission to Sweden, 1963, dir., 1972. Served to 2d lt. USAAF, 1943-45. Mem. A.A.A.S., Am. Econ. Assn., Am. Assn. U. Profs., Am. Philos. Assn., Am. Fgn. Service Assn., Phi Beta Kappa, Phi Kappa Phi. Club: Washington Philosophy. Contbr. articles to profl. jours. Home: 4918 Belt Rd NW Washington DC 20016 Office: US Dept Commerce Washington DC 20230

MCNIVEN, JAMES ANGUS, pollution co. exec.; b. New Orleans, Nov. 15, 1917; s. John Alexander and Ella Linton (Mahaffy) McN.; B.Engring., Tulane U., 1939; postgrad. electronics engring., N.Y. U., 1944. Elec. engr. La. Power & Light Co., New Orleans, 1939-42; Link Radio Co., N.Y.C., 1943-45; with USCG, N.Y.C., 1949-62, chief, mech. and elec. sect. 1949-62; application engr. McGraw Edison Co., New Orleans, 1962-70; with La. Air Pollution Controls, New Orleans, 1971—, project mgr., 1971—. Served to 2d lt. Signal Corps, AUS, 1942-43. Mem. I.E.E.E., Phi Kappa Sigma. Home: 224 E Livingston Place Metairie LA 70005 Office: 1150 Camp St New Orleans LA 70005

MCNIVEN, MALCOLM ALBERT, soft drink co. exec.; b. Oceanside, N.Y., Dec. 8, 1929; s. William and Hazel (Summers) McN.; B.A., Denison U., 1951; M.S. Ohio U., 1952; Ph.D., Pa. State U., 1955; m. Elaine Vellacott, June 12, 1954; children—Geoffrey David, Susan Leslie, Jane Elizabeth. Asst. prof. U. Md., College Park, 1956-57; supr. indsl. testing Pa. State U., University Park, 1957-59; research psychologist advt. research sect. E.I. du Pont de Nemours, Wilmington, Del., 1957-59, sect. mgr., 1959-67; mgr. marketing research dept. The Coca Cola Co., Atlanta, 1967-71, v.p., 1968—, v.p. marketing services Coca-Cola U.S.A., 1971-72, v.p., dir. planning, 1972—. Vis. prof. U. Pa., Phila., 1966-67, Ga. Inst. Tech., Atlanta, 1969—. Trustee Denison U. Fellow Am. Psychol. Assn.; mem. Inst. Mgmt. Sci., Nat. Indsl. Conf. Bd. (mem. council on marketing research 1967—), Audit Bur. Circulations (dir.), Lambda Chi Alpha. Editor: How Much to Spend for Advertising, 1969—. Home: 810 Edgewater Trail NW Atlanta GA 30328 Office: 310 North Av NW Atlanta GA 30313

MCNULTY, JOSEPH PETER, dist. ct. appeals judge; b. N.Y.C., May 11, 1925; s. Peter J. and Charlotte (Morton) McN.; student Slippery Rock State Tchrs. Coll., 1943-44, St. Petersburg Jr. Coll., 1947-48, St. John's U., 1948-50; LL.B., Stetson U., 1952; m. Norma Virginia McInerney, Feb. 3, 1962; children—Maura Rose, Joseph Peter, Stephen Edward, Colleen Marie. Admitted to Fla. bar, 1952; practice law St. Petersburg, 1952-57; atty. Pinellas County Legislative Delegation, 1955; asst. U.S. atty., So. Dist. Fla., 1955-56; judge Civil and Criminal Ct., Pinellas County, 1957-62; circuit judge, Clearwater, Fla., 1963-68; judge Dist. Ct. Appeals, 1968—. Served to lt. USAAF, 1943-45. Mem. Pi Kappa Alpha, Phi Alpha Delta. K.C., Eagle, Moose, Elk. Club: West Side Exhange (St. Petersburg). Home: 2001 16th Av SW Largo FL 33540 Office: District Court of Appeals Lakeland FL 32202

MCNULTY, MATTHEW FRANCIS, JR., educator, health sci.-service adminstr.; b. Elizabeth, N.J., Nov. 26, 1914; s. Matthew Francis and A. Helen (Dwyer) McN.; B.S., St. Peters Coll., 1938; law student Rutgers U., 1939-41; M. Hosp. Adminstrn., Northwestern U., 1949; M.P.H., U. N.C., 1952; Sc.D., U. Ala., 1969; m. Mary Nell Johnson, May 4, 1946; children—Matthew Francis III, Mary Lauren. Contract writer, mgmt. trainee actuarial div. Prudential Life Ins. Co. of Am., N.J., 1938-41; dir. med. adminstrn. VA, 1946-54; adminstr. U. Ala. Hosp., Birmingham, 1954-63; gen. dir. U. Ala. Hosps. and Clins., 1963-66; prof. hosp. adminstrn. U. Ala. Grad. Sch., 1954-69, vis. prof., 1969—, dir. grad. program hosp. adminstrn., 1964-66, prof. epidemiology and preventive medicine U. Ala. Sch. Medicine, Birmingham, 1964-69, vis. prof., 1969—, dean Sch. Health Services Adminstrn. 1966-68; dir. Council Teaching Hosps., 1966-69; prof. community medicine and internat. health Georgetown U., Washington, 1969—, v.p. for med. center affairs, 1969-72, exec. v.p. med. center affairs, 1972—; chmn. bd. dirs. Univ. Affiliated Health Plan, Inc., 1974—; chmn. bd. trustees Georgetown U. Community Health Plan, Inc., 1972—, W.K. Kellogg Found. Vis. prof. Central U. Venezuela, 1967; hosp. cons., 1953—; preceptor hosp. adminstrn. George Washington U., U. Ia., U. Minn. Mem. nat. adv. com. health research projects Ga. Inst. Tech., 1959-65; nat. adv. com. health research projects U. Pitts., 1956-60; adv. com. W.K. Kellogg Found., 1960-65; vis. cons., lectr. Ministry of Health and Social Welfare, Venezuela, 1967-69. Bd. dirs. Blue Cross-Blue Shield of Ala., 1960-61, 65-68, Greater Birmingham United Appeal, 1960-66; trustee Jefferson County Tb Sanatorium, 1958-64; mem. Health Services Research Study Section, NIH, 1963-67; cons. com. on profl. nurse traineeships USPHS, 1959, 63; mem. White House Conf. on Health, 1965, White

House Conf. on Medicare Implementation, 1966, Sec. Labor Conf. on Health Manpower, 1966, Nat. Conf. on Group Practice, 1967, Nat. Conf. on Costs of Health Care Facilities, 1967, mem. health services devel. grants study sect. NIH, 1971—. Trustee Group Hospitalization, Inc., Washington, 1973—; bd. dirs., mem. exec. com. Nat. League Nursing. Served from pvt. to lt. col. USAAF, 1941-46. Recipient Northwestern U. Alumni Assn. Distinguished award, 1973. Fellow Am. Pub. Health Assn., Am. Coll. Hosp. Adminstrs. (bd. regents and council of regents 1961-67); mem. Am., Ala. (past pres.) hosp. assns., Nat. (bd. dirs. 1971—), Ala. (past dir.) leagues for nursing, Internat. Hosp. Fedn., Jefferson County Vis. Nursing Assn. (past pres.), Ala. Pub. Health Assn. (past chmn. med. care sect.), Southeastern Hosp. Conf. (past dir.), Birmingham Hosp. Council (past pres.), Assn. Univ. Programs in Hosp. Adminstrn., Greater Birmingham Area C. of C., Soc. Advancement Mgmt., Am. Assn. Med. Colls. (chmn. teaching hosp. council 1964-65), Royal Soc. Health, Orgn. Univ. Health Center Adminstrs., A.A.A.S., Santa Gertrudis Breeders Internat. Author articles in field. Clubs: University (Ala.); Cosmos, City Tavern, Nat. Press (Washington); Bethesda (Md.) Country. Home: 10000 Carter Rd Bethesda MD 20034 Office: 3800 Reservoir Rd NW Washington DC 20007

MCNUTT, BILLY JOE, cosmetic mfg. exec.; b. Paris, Tenn., May 29, 1930; s. Thomas L. and Lena (Barton) McN.; student Murray State U., 1948-50; B.S., U. Tenn., 1953, postgrad., 1960, 63, 66; m. Mary Ann Coursey, June 15, 1952; children—Debra Ann, Randall Joe. Pharmacist, Hamlet Drug Co., Paris, 1954-57; chemist Golden Peacock, Inc., Paris, 1957-60, chief chemist, 1960-62, tech. dir., 1962-66, v.p. tech. div., 1966; v.p. tech. div. Mitchum Co., Paris, 1966-72; v.p. tech. operations Etesal Mfg. Corp., Paris, 1972-73. Mem. Toilet Goods Assn., Tenn., 8th Dist. (pres. 1961) pharm. assns., Soc. Cosmetic Chemists, Kappa Psi (treas. 1951), Rho Chi. Baptist. Mason, Lion (past pres.), Elk. Club: Paris Country. Home: Anderson Dr Route 2 Paris TN 38242

MCNUTT, CHESTER RAYMOND, govt. ofcl.; b. Kingsville, O., Nov. 29, 1912; s. Amos Lindsay and Fannie Eliza (McGoun) McN.; B.S. in Edn., Miami U., Oxford, O., 1934; A.M., U. Mich., 1939; Ed.D., Case-Western Res. U., 1952; m. Beth Critchfield, Feb. 8, 1942; 1 son, Michael Chester. Tchr. pub. schs., Marion and Cin., O., 1934-42; instr., then asst. prof. edn. Case-Western Res. U., 1946-53; ednl. adviser Provost Marshal Gen.'s Sch., Augusta, Ga., 1953-55; ednl. adviser Internal Revenue Service, Washington, 1955-57, mgmt. tng. specialist, 1957-64, fgn. tax assistance tng. officer, 1964—. Lectr. extension edn. courses U. Ga., 1955, George Washington U., 1958-61; vis. asso. prof. pub. adminstrn. U. So. Cal., 1962; edn. adviser Treasury Law Enforcement Sch., 1962-63. Mem. Leadership tng. commn. Mt. Vernon Baptist Assn., 1970-73; leader on Christian leadership Bapt. state summer confs. Bd. dirs. Cedarville Coll., 1952-53; charter mem. bd. dirs. Luther Rice Coll., chmn., 1966-69. Served to capt. F.A., AUS, 1942-46; ETO. Decorated Bronze Star medal. Mem. N.E.A., Nat. Soc. Study Edn. Contbr. articles to ch. publs. Home: 1600 Ridge Rd Woodbridge VA 22191 Office: 1111 Constitution Av NW Washington DC 20224

MCPHEETERS, HAROLD LAWRENCE, physician; b. N.Y.C., Mar. 10, 1923; s. Harry Halstead and Ethel (Brush) McP.; A.B., Lafayette Coll., 1945; M.D., U. Louisville, 1948; m. Phyllis Merrill, Dec. 24, 1951; children—David, Doris, Thomas, Amy. Intern, City Hosp., Springfield, O., 1948-49; resident U. Louisville (Ky.) Hosp., 1949-52; asst. psychiatrist Ellis Hosp., Schenectady, N.Y., 1954-55; asst. commr. Ky. Dept. Mental Health, Louisville, 1955-57, commr., 1957-64; dep. commr. N.Y. Dept. Mental Hygiene, Albany, 1964-65; dir. mental health So. Regional Edn. Bd., Atlanta, 1965—; instr. Albany Med. Coll., 1954-55; asst. prof. psychiatry U. Louisville, 1955-64; clin. asso. prof. psychiatry Emory U., 1970—. Bd. dirs. Louisville Child Guidance Clinic, 1957-64, Atlanta Area Community Council, 1970-73, Inst. for Social Research, 1974—. Served with AUS, 1943-46; served to lt. M.C., USNR, 1952-54. Mem. Am., Ky. (pres. 1960), Ga. psychiat. assns., A.M.A., Am. Pub. Health Assn. Contbr. articles in field to profl. jours. Home: 435 Forest Valley Rd NE Atlanta GA 30342 Office: 130 6th St NW Atlanta GA 30313

MCPHERON, ALAN BEAUMONT, judge; b. McAlester, Okla,, July 6, 1914; s. Robert Lee and Jeannette (Kridler) McP.; LL.B., U. Okla., 1937; m. Mary Jane Bass, Apr. 8, 1938; 1 dau., Jill. Admitted to Okla. bar, 1937; practice law, Durant, 1946-65, dist. judge 1965—; asst. county atty., 1939-43; judge 19th Jud. Dist. Okla. Chmn. War Vets. Commn. of Okla., 1949-51; chmn. Bd. Review, Okla. Employment Security Commn., 1951-59. Served with U.S. Army, 1943-46. Recipient Bronze Star, Croix de Guerre. Home: 2010 W Liveoak Durant OK 74701 Office: Bryan County Court House Durant OK 74701

MCPHERSON, DAVID LEE, banker; b. Wellston, Okla., Nov. 11, 1942; s. D. D. and J. D. (Holt) McP.; student Okla. State U., 1960, U. Tulsa, 1961-62; grad. Okla. Sch. Banking, 1968; m. Sandra Lynn Dollins, Sept. 22, 1963; children—Cynthia Kay, Paul Gavin, Ryan Gregor. Salesman, Petty's Shoes and Trippett's Shoes, 1961-62; teller Security Nat. Bank, Sapulpa, Okla., 1962-64, asst. cashier, 1964-67; cashier 1st Nat. Bank, Edmond, Okla., 1967-73, v.p., 1972-73; exec. v.p. Exchange Nat. Bank, Del City, Okla., 1973-74, pres., 1974—. Treas., Edmond, 1973—. Bd. dirs., state dir., treas., 1st v.p., pres. Sapulpa Jr. C. of C., 1962-67; treas., bd. dirs. Sapulpa Campfire Girls Assn., 1965-67. Mem. Bank Adminstrn. Inst., Okla. Bankers Assn., Edmond (v.p., treas., dir. 1967—), Edmond Jr. (pres., dir. 1967—) chambers commerce. Republican. Home: 4801 Woodview Dr Del City OK 73115 Office: 1221 S Sunnylane Del City OK 73115

MCQUADE, WILLIAM MICHAEL, editor; b. Ann Arbor, Mich., Nov. 11, 1943; s. Thaddeus B. and Clarissa (Palmer) McQ.; B.Sc., Ohio State U., 1965; J.D., Nat. Law Center George Washington U., 1972; m. Jane Ellen Wales, Sept. 12, 1964; 1 son, Thadd Michael. Naturalist Ohio Dept. Natural Resources, 1964; foreman R.B. Stout Landscaping Inc., Bath, O., 1969; staff asst. Whiteman Digest Internat. Law, Office Legal Adviser, U.S. Dept. State, 1970-71, atty.-adviser, 1973—; adminstrv. editor Jour. Internat. Law and Econs., George Washington U. Nat. Law Center, Washington, 1970-71, editor in chief, 1971-72. Served to capt. AUS, 1966-69. Home: 3619 S 7th St Arlington VA 22204 Office: State Dept Washington DC 20520

MCQUAID, WILLIAM RAVENEL, JR., sales engr.; b. Jacksonville, Fla., July 23, 1924; s. William Ravenel and Henrietta (Murray) McQ.; grad. Hill Sch., 1942; M.E., Stevens Inst. Tech., 1948; m. Elizabeth Ann Tiffany, June 12, 1948; children—William Ravenel III, Elizabeth Lorimier, Douglas Murray. Jr. engr. Am. Locomotive Co., Schenectady, 1948-50; sales rep., also dist. sales mgr. Alco Products, Inc. (formerly Am. Locomotive Co), Chgo., 1950-60; owner Transdustrial Sales Co., Jacksonville, 1960—. Chmn. marine events com. Jacksonville Sesquicentennial Commn., 1971-72. Trustee, past pres. bd. St. Johns Country Day Sch. Served to ensign USNR, 1944-46; PTO. Mem. So. and Southwestern Ry. Club, Fla. Sailing Assn., Delta Tau Delta. Republican. Presbyn. Rotarian (dir. Jacksonville 1973—). Club: Fla. Yacht (past commodore). Home: 3547 Richmond St Jacksonville FL 32205 Office: 1419 Seaboard Coast Line Bldg Jacksonville FL 32202

MCQUAY, GEORGE WASHINGTON, tech. mgmt. services co. exec.; b. Charleston, S.C., May 24, 1927; s. George Washington and Lorena Geneve (Bennett) McQ.; B.S., Loyola Coll., Balt., 1953; m. Bettie Mae Martin, Aug. 16, 1947; children—Michael, Mark. Finance supr. Joseph E. Seagrams & Sons, Balt., 1953-58; controller Air Mod div. Cook Elec., Balt., 1958-62, Pic N Pay Shoes, Inc., Charlotte, N.C., 1962; dir. finance and adminstrn. Am. Brewery, Inc., Balt., 1962, asst. sec., 1962-63; asst. sec., v.p. adminstrn. Lear Siegler, Inc., Oklahoma City, 1963—. Coach, Little League Baseball, 1966-71. Served with AUS, 1945-47; ETO. Mem. Nat. Accounting Assn., Responsible Businessmen for Better Govt., C. of C. K.C. Home: 8404 Surrey Pl Oklahoma City OK 73120 Office: 4001 Lincoln Blvd Oklahoma City OK 73105

MCQUEEN, DORIS JANICE, sch. exec.; b. Marshall, Tex., May 27, 1930; d. Alvy Lee and Cora (Jones) McQueen; student Kilgore Coll., 1954-55. Sec., Office of Supt. Schs., Longview (Tex.) Ind. Sch. Dist., 1948-55, financial sec. Sch. Bd., 1955-58, dir. bus. services, 1958—. Dir. East Tex. Tchrs. Credit Union, 1953—. Mem. Am. Bus. Women's Assn., Am., Tex. assns. sch. bus. ofcls., Tex. Tchrs. Assn., N.E.A. Presbyn. Home: 2600 Dogwood Lane Longview TX 75601 Office: 515 N Court St Longview TX 75601

MCQUEEN, JAMES LEE, microbiologist, veterinarian; b. Jefferson City, Mo., Dec. 28, 1932; s. Malloy James and Frances (Johnson) McQ.; B.S., U. Mo., 1957, D.V.M., 1957; M.P.H., U. Mich., 1961, D.P.H., 1964; m. Shirley Ann Perry, Aug. 30, 1958; children—Shawna Maureen, Cristin Eileen, Peri Lyn. Practice vet. medicine, Little Rock, 1957; commd. capt. USPHS, 1957, with Center for Disease Control, Atlanta, 1957-73, NASA Johnson Space Center, Houston, 1967—. Adj. asso. prof. environmental health Sch. Pub. Health, U. Tex., Houston, 1972—. Mem. A.A.A.S., Am. Pub. Health Assn., Am. Soc. Microbiology, Aerospace Med. Assn., Sci. Research Soc. Am., Alpha Zeta. Contbr. articles to profl. jours. Home: 406 Cedar Lane Seabrook TX 77586 Office: Johnson Space Center Code DD52 Houston TX 77058

MCRAE, VINCENT VERNON, govt. ofcl.; b. Columbia, S.C., Sept. 2, 1918; s. Thomas Tyson and Clireta (Avery) McR.; student U. Chgo., 1944-45; B.S., Miner Tchrs. Coll., 1940; M.S., Cath. U., 1944, Ph.D. in Math., 1955; m. Mae Agnes Smith, June 27, 1941; children—Vincent Vernon, Ronald G.S. Tchr., D.C. Pub. Schs., 1940-42; operations analyst Operations Research Office, Johns Hopkins, Balt., 1952-61; chief strategic div. Operations Research Office, chief air def. div. chmn. armour group and stratspiel group, 1952-61; chief strategic div. Research Analysis Corp., McLean, Va., 1962-64; cons. Office Spl. Asst. to Pres. for Sci. and Tech., Washington, 1962-64; tech. asst. Office Sci. and Tech., The White House, Washington, 1964-73; adviser for systems requirements Fed. Systems div. IBM Corp., 1973—. Cons., Nat. Security Council, State Dept., Def. Dept. Mem. staff Gathier Commn., 1956, Coolidge Arms Control Com., 1958; mem. U.S. delegation Conf. on Surprise Attack, Geneva, Switzerland, 1957. Sec., Brookland Civic Assn., Washington. Served to 2d lt. U.S. 1944-47. Fellow A.A.A.S.; mem. Am. Math. Soc., Operations Research Soc., N.E.A., N.A.A.C.P., D.C. Fedn. Civic Assn., Sigma Xi, Rho Delta Rho. Home: 1501 Emerson St NW Washington DC 20011 Office: 10215 Linwood Rd Bethesda MD 20034

MCRAE, WILLIAM HOLLAND, lawyer; b. Dallas, June 1, 1937; s. Colin E. and Virginia Saffel (Holland) McR.; B.A. magna cum laude, So. Meth. U., 1959, J.D. cum laude, 1962; m. Lucy Ashcroft Carothers, Nov. 19, 1966; children—Holland Carothers, Ashley Ashcroft. Admitted to Tex. bar, 1962; asso. firm Coon, Dedman, May & Hoffman, Dallas, 1962-64, Strasburger, Price, Kelton, Miller & Martin, Dallas, 1964-66; asso. firm Stroud & Smith, Dallas, 1966-69, partner, 1969—. Mem. Am., Tex., Dallas bar assns., Barristers, Order Woolsack, Phi Beta Kappa, Phi Delta Theta. Republican. Conglist. Clubs: Toastmasters (pres. 1970), North Dallas Racquet, Terpsichorean, Calyx, City. Home: 4565 Belclaire Av Dallas TX 75205 Office: 1407 Main St Dallas TX 75202

MCREE, JOE RICHARD, ret. purchasing agt.; b. Soddy, Tenn., Mar. 21, 1911; s. Frederick Emmett and Winifred (Thomas) McR.; student U. Chattanooga, 1947-49; B.S., U. Tenn., 1950; m. Onah Leneve Wilcox, Dec. 12, 1963; 1 dau., Renee Elisabeth (Mrs. David Rhodes Hunter). Engr., Tenn. Hwy. Dept., Chattanooga, 1928-40, 45-50; purchasing agt. TVA, Chattanooga, 1951-72. Served to lt. col. AUS, 1940-45. Registered engr., Tenn. Mem. Internat. Platform Assn., Am. Mus. Natural History, Ret. Officers Assn., Phi Eta Sigma, Sigma Pi Sigma. Home: 19 Caddy Rd Rotonda West FL 33947

MCREYNOLDS, EDWARD WAYNE, educator; b. Bristol, Va., Dec. 6, 1944; s. Hobart Evans and Lena (Brewer) McR.; B.S., U. Tenn., 1965, M.D., 1968; m. Sherry Sue Clark, June 15, 1968; children—Holly Lynn, Wendy Anne. Intern City Memphis Hosps., 1969-70; resident, 1970-71, Daland fellow Am. Philos. Soc., 1972; instr. dept. pediatrics, Med. Sch., U. Tenn., Memphis, 1973—; practice medicine, specializing in pediatrics, Memphis, 1972—; mem. staff Tobey Children's Hosp. (dir. pediatric intensive care unit 1973—), LeBonheur Children's Hosp. Recipient Pediatrics award U. Tenn., 1968, Physicians Recognition award Am. Med. Assn., 1972. Diplomate Am. Bd. Pediatrics. Mem. Phi Eta Sigma, Sigma Phi Epsilon. Lutheran (mem. council). Club: Stokley Athletic Center. Home: 3249 Ridgecrest St Memphis TN 38127 Office: 860 Madison St Memphis TN 38103

MCSPADDEN, CLEM ROGERS, congressman; b. Bushyhead, Okla., Nov. 9, 1925; s. Herbert T. and Madalyn (Pope) McS.; student U. Redlands, Cal., 1944-46, Arlington (Tex.) State Coll., 1946-47, U. Tex., 1947-48; B.S., Okla. A. and M. U., Stillwater, 1948; m. Donna Marie Casity, Feb. 11, 1962; 1 son, Barton Casity. Dir. First Nat. Bank, Claremore, 1964—; v.p., dir. Cattlemens Ins. & Investment Co., Oklahoma City, 1962—; owner, operator cattle ranch, Chelsea, Okla., 1950—; mem. 93d Congress from 2d dist. Okla. Pres. Rodeo Cowboys Assn., 1970-71; gen. mgr. Nat. Finals Rodeo, Oklahoma City, 1967-73. Mem. Okla. Senate, 1954-72, pres., 1966-70, appropriations chmn., 1972. Served with USNR. Recipient Man of Yr. award Claremore C. of C., 1972. Mem. Am. Legion, V.F.W., Sigma Alpha Epsilon. Democrat. Methodist. Lion, Kiwanian. Home: Route 1 Chelsea OK 74016 Office: 1233 Longworth House Office Bldg Washington DC 20515

MCSTAY, JOHN DEWITT, found. exec.; b. Vernon, Tex., Oct. 26, 1942; s. John DeWitt and Mary Belle (Sams) McS.; B.B.A., U. Tex., 1965, M.B.A., 1966; m. Mary Ellen Shields, Jan. 23, 1965; children—Dee Ellen, Judge Michael. Trust investment officer portfolio mgr., analyst Republic Nat. Bank, Dallas, 1966-69; analyst, v.p., Underwood Neuhaus & Co., Dallas, 1969-74; dir. research and equity investments U. Tex. Endowment Fund, Austin, 1974—. Active Greater Dallas Planning Council, Dallas Forum, Jr. Achievement. Mem. Dallas Assn. Investment Analysts (v.p. 1972—, dir. 1972—), Financial Analyst Fedn. (edn. com.), Kappa Alpha. Presbyn. Home: 1616 Gaston St Austin TX 78703 Office: 210 W 6th St Austin TX 78712

MCSWEEN, DONALD MURDOCH, recreation co. exec.; b. Newport, Tenn., May 18, 1915; s. William Daniel and Rowena (Jones) McS.; ed. U. Tenn., 1933-37, Cumberland U., 1939-40; m. Louise Valentine, Aug. 20, 1938. Admitted to Tenn. bar, 1942; practiced in Newport, 1945-62, Nashville, 1959-62; atty. City of Newport, 1946-49; v.p. Diversified Mgmt. Corp. (now Downtowner Corp), Memphis, 1959; pres. Diversified Securities Corp., Memphis, 1959-61, With TVA, VA, War Manpower Commn., 1940-45; Tenn. commr. of employment security, 1953-59; Tenn. commr. of conservation, 1963-67; S.C. dir. state parks and recreation, 1967-71; pres. Travel Retreats Internat., also Holiday Camps Am., Inc., Alcoa, Tenn., 1971—. Served with Signal Corps, AUS, World War II. Named Outstanding Young Man Yr., Tenn. Jr. C. of C., 1947. Mem. Am., Cocke County bar assns., Bar Assn. Tenn., S.E. State Park Dirs. Assn. (pres. 1968-69), Nat. Conf. State Parks (chmn. legislative com. 1968—, bd. dirs. 1969—), Am. Legion (Tenn. comdr. 1947-48), also numerous employment security, conservation, recreation and travel orgns. Presbyn. Mason (32 deg., K.T., Shriner), Elk, Kiwanian. Home: Old Glory Rd Smoky View Estates Rt 2 Maryville TN 37801 Office: 243 Calderwood St Alcoa TN 37701

MCWANE, KENNETH GOODWIN, hwy. engr.; b. Lynchburg, Va., Oct. 29, 1900; s. Charles William and Cora Lee (Wilkinson) McW.; student U. Va., 1919-21; m. Ruth Leon Henson, Oct. 30, 1926; 1 dau., Ruth (Mrs. Robert Lee Mason). Successively instrumentman, resident engr., dist. engr., state traffic and planning engr. Va. Dept. Hwys., 1921-52; engr. traffic and operations Hwy. Research Bd., Nat. Acad. Scis. NRC, Washington, 1952-64. Registered profl. engr., Va. Fellow Am. Soc. C.E., Inst. Traffic Engrs. (mem. tech. council 1960-64); mem. Va. Assn. Traffic Engrs. Thomas Jefferson Soc. Alumni Assn. U. Va. Democrat. Methodist (past mem. adminstrv. bd.). Elk. Home: 4011 Morrison Dr Lynchburg VA 24503

MCWHIRTER, WELDON HAYS, SR., bank exec.; b. Gainesville, Tex., Oct. 30, 1931; s. Sidney Hays and Olive Roberta (Ballard) McW.; B.S., So. State Coll., 1953; m. Billie Jean Boyd, May 7, 1953; children—Weldon Hays, Pamela Jean. Asst. cashier First Nat. Bank Magnolia, Ark., 1955-62; v.p. First Nat. Bank Warren, Ark., 1962-68, pres., 1968-69; pres., dir. Met. Nat. Bank, Little Rock, 1969—. Mem. Bd. Edn., Warren, 1967-69. Served with AUS, 1953-55. Mem. Warren C. of C. (pres. 1967). Lion (treas. 1964—, v.p. 1965-66, dir. 1966-69). Home: 8621 Oman Rd Little Rock AR 72209 Office: 5601 S University St Little Rock AR 72209

MCWHORTER, JOHN ALEXANDER, JR., lawyer; b. Greensboro, Ga., July 19, 1925; s. John Alexander and Annie (Sanders) McW.; A.B., Washington and Lee U., 1947, LL.B., 1950; LL.M., George Washington U., 1956. Admitted to Va. bar, 1950, D.C. bar, 1955; atty. Office Chief Engrs., Dept. Army, Washington, 1950-55; practiced in Washington, 1955—; mem. firm King & King, 1955—. Mem. Fed., Am. (chmn. pub. contracts sect. 1972—), D.C., Va. bar assns., Phi Delta Phi, Phi Kappa Sigma. Club: Nat. Lawyers. Home: 2301 E St NW Washington DC 20037 Office: 1320 19th St NW Washington DC 20036

MCWHORTER, THOMAS OSBORNE, lawyer; b. Lawrenceburg, Ky., Sept. 27, 1920; s. Thomas Afton and Helen (Ripy) McW.; student U. Houston, 1936-37; B.S., U.S. Naval Acad., 1941; J.D., U. Tex., 1955; m. Louise Duvall Day, Sept. 2, 1953 (div. Mar. 1969); children—John Charles, Anne Stuart, Thomas Duvall, James Barry; m. 2d, Ina Claire Killgore, June 1, 1973. Commd. ensign USN, 1941, advanced through grades to comdr.; served in U.S.S. Sterett, 1941-43, U.S.S. Black, 1943-44, U.S.S. Sherburne, 1944-46; staff Transport Div. 21, 1946-47, staff comdr. in chief, Atlantic, 1947-49; staff comdt. 1st. Naval Dist., 1949-50; served in U.S.S. Kimberly, 1950-52; staff Fleet Tng. Center, Norfolk, Va., 1953; resigned commn., 1953; admitted to Tex. bar, 1955; practiced in Houston, 1955-59, 65—, Midland, Tex., 1959-65; mem. firm Smith & Lehmann, Houston, 1955-59, Perkins, Bezoni, Kirwan & McWhorter, Midland, 1959-62, MacNaughton & McWhorter, Houston, 1965-73; individual practice, 1973—. Mem. Am., Houston bar assns., Tex. State Bar, S.A.R. (founder, pres. Permian chpt. 1961, chmn. Americanism com. Tex. soc. 1964-66, v.p. 1973-74, pres. Houston chpt. 1967), Phi Alpha Delta. Republican. Presbyn. Author: Res Publica, 1966. Home: 11 315 Coloma Lane Houston TX 77024 Office: 2000 W Loop South Houston TX 77027

MCWHORTER, WILLIAM HORACE, ednl. adminstr.; b. Montgomery, Ala., Jan. 9, 1928; s. Abbott Milton and Leona Estelle (White) McW.; B.S., Jacksonville State U., 1949; M.A., George Peabody Coll. for Tchrs., 1956; Ed.D., U. Ala., 1969; m. Kathleen Story, Jan. 31, 1954; children—William Timothy, Lillian, Suzanne. Tchr., coach high sch., Oxford, Ala., 1949-51; instr. Jacksonville State U., 1952-53; tchr., coach high sch., Blue Springs, Ala., 1951-52, Wildwood, Fla., 1956-57; prin. high sch., White Springs, Fla., 1957-59; dir. Colegio Internat., Valencia, Venezuela, 1959-66; dean Faulkner State Jr. Coll., 1966-68; pres. Lurleen B. Wallace State Jr. Coll., Andalusia, Ala., 1969—. Cons. research and higher edn. State of Ala., 1968—. Served with AUS, 1953-55. Mem. Am. Assn. Sch. Adminstrs., Andalusa C. of C. (dir.), Phi Delta Kappa, Kappa Delta Pi, Beta Beta Beta. Methodist (adminstrv. bd. 1969—). Rotarian. Home: 1409 Sunset Dr Andalusia AL 36420 Office: PO Drawer 1418 Andalusia AL 36420

MCWILLIAMS, JETTIE MANNING CRISP (MRS. WILEY E. MCWILLIAMS, JR.), educator; b. nr. Mt. Creek, Ala., May 5, 1928; A.B., Berea Coll., 1958; postgrad. Bluffton Coll., 1957, Ohio State U., 1964; M.A. (Haggin fellow), U. Ky., 1963, Ed.D., 1966; m. Robert Alton Crisp, Jr., May 5, 1949 (dec. Mar. 1961); children—Jane Rae, Victoria Anne, Kathryn Dianne, Yvonne Nell; m. 2d, Wiley E. McWilliams, Jr., June 4, 1967 (dec. Apr. 1972). Pub. high sch. English tchr., Wheelwright, Ky., 1950-52, Pandora, O., 1959-61; guidance counselor Bryan St. Jr. High Sch., Lexington, Ky., 1963-64; instr. U. Ky., Lexington, 1965-66; asst. prof. ednl. psychology and guidance, then asso. prof. Tenn. Tech. U., Cookeville, 1966—. Cons. ednl. systems and Project Upper Cumberland, Cookeville, 1967—. Leader, Girl Scouts U.S.A., Beaverdam, O. 1959-61; sec. Cookeville P.T.A., 1966-67, 2d v.p., 1967-68. Bd. dirs. Tenn. Vocational Tng. Center, Cookeville, 1967-74, Wesley Found., Tenn. Tech., 1972—. Recipient Outstanding Alumnus award Bluffton Coll., 1971. Mem. Am. Assn. U. Women, Am. Personnel and Guidance Assn., Nat. Vocational Guidance Assn., Am. Coll. Personnel Assn., Am. Assn. U. Profs. (v.p. Tenn. Tech. U. chpt. 1973-74, pres. 1974—), Cumberland Personnel and Guidance Assn. (pres. 1974—), Tenn. Assn. Counselor Educators and Suprs., Nat. Tenn. edn. assns., Internat. Platform Assn., Kappa Delta Pi, Beta Sigma Phi. Contbr. articles to profl. jours. Home: 1131 Flatt Circle Cookeville TN 38501

MCWILLIAMS, ROBERT WHEALTON, life ins. co. exec.; b. Portsmouth, N.C., July 8, 1910; s. Charles S. and Annie T. (Toler) McW.; student U. N.C., 1930-31, Eastman Coll., 1932-33; m. Dorothy J. Osborne, May 20, 1950; children—Robert Wheelton, Ann Cullen. With Life Ins. Co. Va., Portsmouth, 1933—, successively agt., staff mgr., Portsmouth, mgr. Staunton, Lynchburg, Newport News, Norfolk and Portsmouth, divisional supr., asst. v.p., 1946-50, 2d v.p., 1955-56, now dist. mgr. Past dir. Lynchburg Staunton, Norfolk Life Underwriters. Pres., Norfolk Found., Inc.; trustee Va. Bapt. Homes.

Mem. Peninsular Assn. Life Underwriters (past pres.), Portsmouth Assn. Life Underwriters (pres., dir.). Baptist. Mason (Shriner). Clubs: Cosmopolitan (past pres.), Norfolk (Va.) Yacht and Country; Virginia; Cedar Point Country (Crittenden, Va.). Home: 1215 S Fairwater Dr Norfolk VA 23508 Office: 808 Loudoun Av Portsmouth VA 23707

MEACHAM, ELLIS KIRBY, judge; b. Chattanooga, Sept. 5, 1913; s. Cowan White Kirby and Jean (Ellis) M.; A.B., U. Chattanooga, 1935; LL.B., Vanderbilt U., 1937, J.D., 1969; m. Jean Bevan Austin, Feb. 12, 1940; children—G.B. Kirby, Jere Ellis. Admitted to Tenn. bar, 1937; gen. practice civil law, Chattanooga, 1937-72; atty. City of Chattanooga, 1948-72; judge Chattanooga Municipal Ct., 1972—. Served as comdr. USNR, 1941-45. Recipient award for fiction Friends of Am. Writers, 1969. Mem. Am., Tenn., Chattanooga bar assns., Authors Guild, Authors League Am. Episcopalian. Club: Fairyland (Lookout Mountain, Tenn.). Author: The East Indiaman, 1968; On the Company's Service, 1971. Home: 414 S Crest Rd Chattanooga TN 37404 Office: 1000 Lindsay St Chattanooga TN 37402

MEAD, DAYTON RICHARD, mortgage banker; b. Rockford, Ill., Sept. 17, 1899; s. Durand Raymond and Jeanette (Wisegarver) M.; B.A., U. Wis., 1922; m. Catharine Chadbourn, June 7, 1924; 1 son, Dayton Richard. Chmn. D.R. Mead & Co., Miami, Fla., 1973—; adv. bd. dirs. First Nat. Bank, Miami; dir. Consol. Papers, Inc., Wisconsin Rapids, Wis., First Nat. Bank & Trust Co., Eustis, Fla., Bank of Mont Dora, Fla. Trustee James Deering Hosp. Trust, Miami. Served with inf. U.S. Army, 1918. Conglist. Home: 2755 N Bay Rd Miami Beach FL 33140 Office: 1900 Biscayne Blvd Miami FL 33132

MEAD, ROBERT EVERETT, oil co. exec.; b. Cleburne, Tex., Nov. 30, 1920; s. Everett K. and Ruth (Ransone) M.; A.B. cum laude, Princeton, 1942; m. Mary McLain, Jan. 25, 1962 (div. Sept. 1973); children—Robert E. II, Susan (Mrs. Loftus Jestin), Peyton P. Geologist, Geochem. Surveys, Tex., Okla., Ill., 1946-51; founder, pres. Macdonald Oil Corp., Dallas, Okla., Midland, Tex., 1955—. Chief exec. officer Hart Furniture Co., Dallas, 1965—. Mem. Dallas Citizens Council, 1969—; v.p. Dallas County Mental Health Assn., 1971—. Trustee St. Mark's Sch. Tex. Served from pvt. to capt., C.E., USAAF, 1942. Mem. Ind. Petroleum Assn. Am. (pres. 1968), Tex. Mid-Continent Oil and Gas Assn. (past v.p.), West Central Tex. Oil and Gas Assn. (dir.). Home: 8626 Douglas Dallas TX 75225 Office: 4805 Republic Nat Bank Tower Dallas TX 75201

MEADE, EDWARD GRANT, educator; b. Phila., Apr. 6, 1914; s. Edward and Elizabeth (Grant) M.; A.B., Dartmouth, 1935; M.A., U. Wis., 1936; M.A.L.D., Fletcher Sch. Law and Diplomacy, 1938; Ph.D., U. Pa., 1948; postgrad. Harvard, 1945, Air War Coll., 1960-61; m. Courtenay Frances Etheridge, Oct. 21, 1949; children—Elise Stokes, Courtenay Etheridge, Sydney Ingram, Elizabeth Grant, Celestia Loyall. Chmn. polit. sci. dept. Haverford Coll., 1946-48; U.S. cultural attache, Bangkok, Thailand, 1955-56, U.S. pub. affairs attache, Thailand, 1956-60, Lagos, Nigeria, 1961-64; coordinator book program USIA, Europe, Africa, Washington, 1964-65; prof., chmn. polit. sci. dept. Old Dominion U., Norfolk, Va., 1965—. Spl. prof. polit. sci. faculty Chulalongkorn U., Bangkok, Thailand, 1956-60. Dir. pub. relations Norfolk (Va.) A.R.C., 1954-55; vice chmn. Fulbright Found., Thailand, 1955-60; bd. dirs. John E. Peurifoy Found., Bangkok, 1956-60, Social Sci. Assn. Thailand, 1957-60, Norfolk Forum, 1969-72. Served with USNR, 1941-46, 48-55. Fletcher fellow, 1936-38. Mem. Am. Hist. Assn., Am. Acad. Polit. and Social Sci., Am. Polit. Sci. Assn., Am. Soc. Internat. Law, Am. Soc. Pub. Adminstrn., Am. Assn. U. Profs., Am. Fgn. Service Assn., Cum Laude Soc., Mil. Order Fgn. Wars, Pa. Soc., S.R., Pub. Relations Soc. Am., Delta Kappa Epsilon. Clubs: Norfolk Yacht and Country; Merion Cricket (Haverford, Pa.). Author: American Military Government in Korea, 1951. Contbr. articles to profl. jours. Home: 1000 Cambridge Crescent Norfolk VA 23508

MEADE, EVERARD WILSON, ednl. adminstr.; b. Pohick, Va., Jan. 2, 1914; s. Emmett Augustus and Katie Elizabeth (Wilson) M.; B.A., U. Va., 1935; m. Virginia Valentine Walker, Mar. 28, 1935; 1 dau., Elizabeth Valentine (Mrs. John Winship Howard). Asst. to pres. Am. Tobacco Co., 1945-48; v.p. Young & Rubicam, Inc., 1948-53, Ogilvy Benson & Mather, Inc., 1955-57; spl. asst. to dean U. Va. Grad. Sch. Bus. Adminstrn., Charlottesville, 1956—. Served with USNR, 1942-45; PTO. Mem. Kappa Alpha. Episcopalian. Clubs: Farmington Country, Farmington Hunt (Charlottesville). Author: The Golden Geese, 1968. Contbr. articles to profl. jours. Home: 1 Blue Ridge Lane Farmington Charlottesville VA 22901

MEADE, GEORGE PETERKIN, ret. sugar refiner; b. Cumberland, Md., Dec. 26, 1883; s. Philip Nelson and Sarah (Rannells) M.; B.S., N.Y.U., 1905, Chem.E., 1921, D.Eng. (hon.), 1955; student U. Mich., 1914; D.Sc., La. State U., 1954, Tulane U., 1970; m. Eleanore Felicia Hussey, Aug. 7, 1912 (dec.). Asst. chemist Nat. Sugar Refinery, Yonkers, N.Y., summers 1901-05, full time, 1905-07; asst. chemist Fajardo (P.R.) Sugar Co., 1908; chemist and asst. supt. Colonial Sugars Co., Gramercy, La., 1909-13; supt. and mgr. Cuban Sugar Refining Co., Cardenas, also dir. Central Control Lab. Cuban-Am. Sugar Co., 1913-23; gen. supt. Colonial Sugars Co., 1923-28, mgr., 1928-56, dir., 1950-59. Mem. sugar com. 8th Internat. Congress Applied Chemistry, N.Y., 1912; chmn. U.S. Nat. Com. on Sugar Analysis, 1953-60; del. Internat. Commn. Uniform Methods of Sugar Analysis, London, 1936, Brussels, 1949, Paris, 1954, v.p. Internat. Commn., 1954-62, hon. v.p. Internat. Commn., Hamburg, 1962, chmn. U.S. Nat. Commn., Washington, 1958. Mem. tech. adv. com. Sugar Research Found.; trustee Pub. Affairs Research Council La.; mem. Bur. Govtl. Research, New Orleans. Pres. St. James Parish (county) Sch. Bd., 1932-56. Recipient Dyer award Sugar Man of Yr., 1961; award Sugar Industry Technologists, 1963. Fellow A.A.A.S., Am. Inst. Chemists, Herpetologists League, N.Y. Acad. Scis.; mem. Am. Chem. Soc. (named man of year carbohydrate div. 1953), La. Engring. Soc., Am. Inst. Chem. Engrs., Internat. Soc. Sugar Cane Technologists (hon.), Am. Soc. Icthyologists and Herpetologists tv.p.), N.Y. Zool. Soc., S.C.V., Phi Beta Kappa, Tau Beta Pi, Alpha Chi Sigma. Democrat. Episcopalian. Clubs: Chemists (N.Y.C.); Round Table, Louisiana, (New Orleans). Pres. Bone Char Research Project, Inc. 1948-49. Author: Cane Sugar Handbook 9th edit., 1963; Athletic Records: The Whys and Wherefores, 1966. Contbr. tech. articles to Indsl. and Engring. Chemistry, Internat. Sugar Jour., Sports Illustrated, Sci. Monthly, Ency. Brit., etc.; also articles on Habits of La. Harmless Snakes; Asso. editor Sugar Jour. (New Orleans), monthly column, The Proof Stick. Home: Pontchartrain Hotel New Orleans LA 70140

MEADOR, BRUCE BARNES, newspaper exec.; b. Haskell, Tex., Aug. 27, 1910; s. Clay Bruce and Sarah (Alsbrook) M.; B.S., McMurry Coll., 1932; m. Margaret Henson, Jan. 28, 1932; 1 dau., Margie Ann (Mrs. Robert E. Shackelford). C.P.A., Abilene, Tex.; dir., chmn. exec. com., sec. Harte Hanks Newspapers, Inc., San Antonio; dir. Times Pub. Co., Wichita Falls, Tex. Trustee Bernard Hanks Estate, Abilene, Eva May Hanks Estate, Abilene. Mem. Am. Inst. C.P.A.'s, Tex. Soc. C.P.A.'s. Democrat. Methodist. Home: 2703 Marlborough St San Antonio TX 78230 Office: PO Box 269 San Antonio TX 78291

MEADOR, CHARLES EDWIN, accountant; b. Kissimmee, Fla., Nov. 22, 1940; s. Charles Finney and Myrtle Lilly (Thompson) M.; B.A. (scholar), Rice U., 1963; postgrad. So. Methodist U., 1966-67; m. Mary Carole Pistole, June 2, 1963; children—Kyle Randall, Bret Alexander, Brook Temple. Accountant, Arthur Andersen & Co., Dallas, 1967—. Com. chmn., local P.T.A., 1972-74; vice-chmn. accountant com. ann. fund drive Rice U., 1972-73. Bd. dirs. Houston Lighthouse for Blind. Served to lt. (j.g.) USN, 1963-67. C.P.A., Tex. Mem. Am. Inst. C.P.A.'s, Tex. Soc. C.P.A.'s, Financial Mgmt. Assn. Clubs: Houston; Dallas Athletic. Home: 11237 Ferndale Rd Dallas TX 75238 Office: 2100 One Main Pl Dallas TX 75250

MEADOR, CLIFTON KIRKPATRICK, physician, educator; b. Selma, Ala., Sept. 7, 1931; s. Daniel John and Mabel (Kirkpatrick) M.; B.A., (Walter O. Parmer scholar), Vanderbilt U., 1952, M.D., 1955; m. Helen Allen, June 17, 1955; children—Clifton Kirkpatrick, Aubrey Allen, Ann Graham, Elizabeth Garrett. Intern, Presbyn. Hosp., N.Y.C., 1955-56, asst. resident medicine, 1956-57; asst. resident medicine Vanderbilt U. Hosp., 1959-60; fellow endocrinology Vanderbilt U., 1960-61, instr. dept. medicine Sch. Medicine, 1960-61; practice medicine, specializing in endocrinology, Selma, 1961-62, pvt. practice; asst. prof. medicine Sch. Medicine, U. Ala., 1962-64, asso. prof., 1964-66, prof., 1966—; asst. chief-of-staff U. Ala. Hosp., 1966-68; dean Sch. Medicine, U. Ala., 1968-73; prof. medicine Sch. Medicine, Vanderbilt U., Nashville, 1973—; chief medicine St. Thomas Hosp., Nashville, 1973—. Served as capt., M.C., AUS, 1957-59. Recipient Founders medal for scholastic honors Vanderbilt Sch. Medicine, 1955. John and Mary R. Markle scholar, 1963. Fellow A.C.P.; mem. Am. Diabetes Assn., Am. Fedn. for Clin. Research, Endocrine Soc., N.Y. Acad. Sci., Phi Beta Kappa, Sigma Xi, Alpha Omega Alpha. Mem. editorial bd. So. Med. Jour., 1969—. Contbr. articles profl. jours. Home: 222 Robin Hill Rd Nashville TN 37205

MEADOW, CHARLES TROUB, computer scientist; b. Paterson, N.J., Dec. 16, 1929; s. Abraham and Florence (Troub) M.; B.A., U. Rochester, 1951; M.S., Rutgers U., 1954; m. Mary Louise Shinskey, June 24, 1972; children—Debra Lynne, Sandra Lee, Alison Maria. Mathematician USN Dept., Washington, 1954-55; asst. mathematician RAND Corp., Lexington, Mass., 1955-56; unit mgr., cons. analyst Gen. Electric Co., Phoenix, also Washington, 1957-60; sr. systems analyst IBM Corp., Washington, 1960-68; chief, systems devel. div. Nat. Bur. Standards, Washington, 1968-71; asst. dir. div. mgmt. information and telecommunications U.S. AEC, Washington, 1971—. Pres. Washington Communications Inc., Washington, 1972—. Served with USMCR, 1951-53. Mem. Assn. for Computing Machinery, Am. Soc. Information Sci. (chmn. spl. interest group on tech., information and soc. 1971-73), A.A.A.S. Author: The Analysis of Information Systems, 1967, 2d edit., 1973; Man-Machine Communication, 1970; The Story of Computers, 1970. Co-editor: Interactive Bibliographic Systems, 1973. Home: 3300 McKinley St NW Washington DC 20015 Office: Ca 434 US AEC Washington DC 20545

MEADOWS, CLAUDE RILEY, JR., savs. and loan exec.; b. Jacksonville, Tex., May 29, 1917; s. Claude Riley and Eugenia (Gladney) M.; A.A., Jacksonville Coll., 1937; m. Frances Elizabeth Aber, Apr. 5, 1940; children—Michael Lynn, Patrick Jerome, Deborah (Mrs. Larry Joe Jackson). Sec., Jacksonville Bldg. & Loan Assn., 1938-47; owner Meadows Ins. Agy., Kilgore, Tex., 1947-59; exec. v.p. First Savs. & Loan Assn., Burkburnett, Tex., 1959-62; pres. Briercroft Savs. & Loan Assn., Lubbock, Tex., 1962—; pres., dir. Potomac Corp., Trust Co. of Am., Lubbock. Bd. dirs. Lubbock Meal on Wheels; bd. dirs., asst. adminstr. West Tex. Home Health Agy.; trustee Jacksonville Coll., Missionary Bapt. Found. Served with USNR, 1943-45. Baptist (trustee, deacon). Mason (32 deg.), Lion. Home: 1913 54th St Lubbock TX 79412 Office: 5002 Av Q Lubbock TX 79412

MEADOWS, DANIEL THOMAS, dentist; b. Salem, Ala., June 5, 1917; s. Daniel Porter and Gemmie Bruce (Browning) M.; B.S., Auburn U., 1939; D.M.D., U. Ala., 1953; m. Agatha Joan Fischer, Mar. 31, 1944; children—Gemma (Mrs. Thomas W. Stanford, Jr.), Daniel Thomas. Pvt. practice dentistry, Birmingham, Ala., 1953; resident in prosthodontics U. Ala., 1955-57; staff dentist Birmingham VA Hosp., 1954-55, 57-62, chief dental service, 1962-68, 69—. Prof. clin. dentistry U. Ala., Birmingham, 1968—. Served to col. Dental Corps, AUS, 1942-46, 68-69. Decorated Army Commendation medal with oak leaf cluster. Fellow Am. Coll. Dentists; mem. Am. Prosthodontic Soc., Am., Ala. dental assns., Am. Legion, Southeastern Acad. Prosthodontics, Birmingham Dist. Dental Soc. (exec. council 1968-72), Phi Kappa Phi, Gamma Sigma Delta, Kappa Delta Pi, Xi Psi Phi. Editor: Ala. Farmer, 1939. Home: 4309 Corinth Dr Birmingham AL 35213 Office: 700 S 19th St Birmingham AL 35233

MEADOWS, JACK EDWARD, lumber and mfg. co. exec.; b. Tulsa, Sept. 2, 1919; s. Noel Etter and Nellie (Connolly) M.; B.S. in Chem. Engring., U. Tex., 1941; grad. Advanced Mgmt. Program Harvard, 1960; m. Jane Worthington Duls, Mar. 10, 1944; children—Jack E., William Noel. Asst. to supt. power and recovery Crossett (Ark.) Paper Mills, 1945-49, asst. to mgr., 1949-52, asst. prodn. mgr., 1952-56, asst. mgr., 1956-62; asst. mgr. Georgia-Pacific Corp., 1962-63, mgr., Toledo operations, 1964, mgr. paper operations, Crossett, 1964-68, v.p., gen. mgr. Crossett div., 1968-72, sr. v.p., gen. mgr., 1972—; dir. First Nat. Bank Crossett. Pres. So. Forest Inst., 1973. Mem. Ark. State Bd. Edn., 1969—; chmn. Ark. Careers, 1972; vice-chmn. Crossett Health Center, 1973—. Served with USNR, 1941-45. Recipient C.E. Palmer award distinguished service to Ark., 1953. Mem. Ark. C. of C. (pres. 1973), Pi Kappa Alpha. Methodist. Home: 1004 Walnut St Crossett AR 71635 Office: PO Box 520 Crossett AR 71635

MEADOWS, LARRY GROVES, golf course ofcl.; b. Winchester, Ky., Apr. 17, 1942; s. Roscoe T. and Nellie (Kennon) M.; grad. high sch.; m. Viola Faye Bentley, May 29, 1965; children—Shawna Demarron Leif, Cody Flint. Carpenter, Meadows Constrn. Co., Clay City, Ky., 1961-72; golf pro, gen. mgr. Meadows Golf Course, Clay City, 1972—. Mem. Red River Hist. Soc. (dir. 1967-74), Jr. C. of C. Lion. Author: Abner Shelter, 1969. Home: Main St Clay City KY 40312 Office: PO Box 246 Clay City KY 43012

MEADS, MANSON, ednl. adminstr.; b. Oakland, Cal., Mar. 25, 1918; s. Albert Manson and Romilda (Paroni) M.; A.B., U. Cal. at Berkeley, 1939; M.D., Temple U., 1943; D.Sc., Temple U., 1956; m. Helen Wheeler Belding, May 26, 1945; 1 dau., Elizabeth Manson. Intern medicine U. Cal. Hosp., San Francisco, 1943; resident medicine Permanente Found. Hosp., Oakland, Cal., 1943-44; research fellow medicine Thorndike Meml. Lab., Harvard Med. Sch., 1944-46, resident medicine, 1945-46, Ernst fellow bacteriology, 1946-47; instr. medicine The Bowman Gry Sch. Medicine, Winston-Salem, N.C., 1947-50, asst. prof. medicine, 1951-57, asso. prof. preventive medicine, chmn. dept. preventive medicine, 1951-55, prof., chmn. dept. preventive medicine, 1955-57, asso. dean, 1955-58, prof. medicine, 1957—, acad. dean, 1958-59, exec. dean, 1959-63, dean, 1963-67, v.p. med. affairs, dean medicine, 1967-71, v.p. med. affairs, 1971—; sr. surgeon, visiting prof. medicine, adv. med. edn. USPHS, Thailand, 1953-55. Bd. dirs. Joint conf. com. med. care State N.C., 1968—; bd. dirs. Piedmont Triad Regional Comprehensive Health Planning Council, 1970—, mem. com. finance and legislation, 1972—; mem. review com. teaching facilities Bur. Health manpower, 1967-70; cons. Facilities Survey of Health Professions Schs., 1971—. Bd. dirs. United Health Found., 1962-65, mem. exec. com., 1963-65. Recipient Markle Found. scholarship, 1948-53. Diplomate Am. Bd. Internal Medicine. Mem. A.C.P., Am. Soc. Clin. Investigation, A.M.A., Assn. Am. Med. Colls., Assn. Academic Health Centers, Med. Soc. N.C., Forsyth County Med. Soc., Alpha Omega Alpha, Sigma Xi, Winston Salem C. of C. (bd. dirs. 1967-70, 73—). Rotarian. Contbr. to profl. publs. in field. Home: 1855 Meadowbrook Dr Winston-Salem NC 27104 Office: The Bowman Gray Sch Medicine Winston-Salem NC 27103

MEAGHER, CHARLES FRANKLIN, engring. co. exec.; b. Sayreton, Ala., Nov. 29, 1925; s. Arch Webster and Winnie Davis (Layne) M.; B.S. in Mech. Engring., St. Mary's (Cal.) Coll., 1946; postgrad. U. Tenn., 1950, U. Chgo., 1957; m. Francis June Coffman, Dec. 19, 1946 (div. Mar. 1964); children—Vicki Jo, Chareece Lee, David Jonathan; m. 2d, June Elizabeth Jones, Sept. 26, 1964; children—Beth Carol, Nancy Jean, Ellen Lee. Supervising trainee Combustion Engring. Co., Chattanooga, 1950-53; gen. foreman Atlas Powder Co., Tyner, Tenn., 1953-55, engr. in charge layaway, 1955-57; gen. foreman Cramet Titamium Facility, Chattanooga, 1957-58; chief engring. services NASA, Huntsville, Ala., 1960-66; owner, cons. engr. Jonathan Engring. Service, Prospect, Tenn., 1966—. Mil. service, 1944-46. Registered profl. engr., Tenn. Mem. Am. Soc. M.E., Am. Rocket Soc., Nat. Soc. Profl. Engrs. Methodist (steward 1953-66, Sunday sch. supt. 1963-65). Mason. Author: Layaway Manual for Decontaminating TNT Plants, 1955; How to Recover Airplanes, 1958. Address: Box 124 Prospect TN 38477

MEAKIN, JOHN LEONARD, lighting products distbr.; b. Washington, Dec. 8, 1918; s. Frances Hardie and Marguerite (DeSale) M.; B.A., U. Md., 1941; m. Betty R. Korbel, Sept. 18, 1941; 1 son, John William. Commd. 2d lt. U.S. Army, 1941, advanced through grades to maj., 1956; assigned to Hdqrs. U.S. European Command, Heidelberg, Germany, 1950-53, Office Dep. Chief Staff Logistics, Dept. Army, 1954-56; resigned, 1956; commd. col. Res., 1967; exec. v.p. Mason Mortgage & Investment Corp., Washington, 1955-61; gen. mgr. Reed A. Thursby & Co., St. Petersburg, Fla., 1961; owner, pres. Howlen Assos., Inc., St. Petersburg, 1961-63; v.p. Hardee's Food Systems, Inc., Rocky Mount, N.C., 1963-68, Unico Corp., Virginia Beach, Va., 1968-70; owner Eterna S of Tidewater, Norfolk, Va., 1970—. Mem. Am. Drive-In Operators' Assn. (pres. 1970), Aircraft Owners and Pilots Assn., Eastern Carolina Airmen's Assn. Republican. Presbyn. Home: 504 Sandy Valley Ct Virginia Beach VA 23452 Office: 4991 Cleveland St Virginia Beach VA 23462

MEALING, ISABEL THORPE, social worker; b. Townsend, Ga., Oct. 4, 1907; d. Elisha McDonald and Maude (Davis) Thorpe; student Ga. State Tchrs. Coll., 1924-26; A.B., Randolph-Macon Woman's Coll., 1928; M.S.W., Tulane U., 1943; postgrad. U. Va., 1929; m. John Pace Mealing, Jr., Aug. 15, 1929 (div. Dec. 1939); children—Elisha Thorpe, Margaret Mae (Mrs. Wayne Frederick Orlowski). Visitor Fulton County Dept. Pub. Welfare, Atlanta, 1937-38; dir. McIntosh County Dept. Pub. Welfare, Darien, Ga., 1938-40; child welfare cons. State of Ga., Atlanta, 1941-44; social worker A.R.C., Lawson Gen. Hosp., Atlanta, 1944-45; asst. field dir. Lawson Gen. Hosp., and Station Hosp., Ft. Benning, Ga., 1945-46; chief social work service VA Regional Office, Ft. Jackson, S.C., 1947-48; pub. welfare officer Dept. Army, Japan, 1949-51; sr. social worker Valley Forge Army Hosp., 1951; chief social work service VA Hosp., Richmond, Va., 1951-52, VA Center, Wadsworth, Kan., 1952-68, Dublin, Ga., 1968—. Mem. Social Planning Council, Leavenworth, Kan., 1952-68, v.p., 1955-56, 67-68, pres., 1956-57; bd. dirs. A.R.C., Leavenworth, Kan., 1960-68; bd. govs. United Fund, Leavenworth, 1967-68; bd. dirs. YWCA, Leavenworth, 1962-68, pres., 1964-65; chmn. welfare com. Mayor's Adv. Com., Leavenworth, 1968; mem. organizational bd. Leavenworth Community Action Program, 1966; adviser Explorer Scouts Am., 1972; bd. dirs. Dublin Mental Health Assn., v.p., 1972-73, pres., 1973—. Mem. Nat. Assn. Social Workers (exec. bd. Mo.-Kan. chpt. 1954-56, pres. central Ga. chpt. 1970-71, del. to assembly 1971), Am. Assn. Med. Social Workers (pres. Mo.-Kan. chpt. 1954-55), Nat., Internat., Ga. (nominating com. 1945) confs. on social welfare, Daus. Am. Colonists, Colonial Dames, Community Resource Forum (pres. 1971-73), Pilot Club Dublin (charter). Address: VA Center Dublin GA 31021

MEANEY, DANIEL D., civil engr.; b. Corpus Christi, Tex., Nov. 7, 1924; s. William Patrick and Mary Ann (Dunn) M.; B.S. in Civil Engring., U. Notre Dame, 1947; postgrad. Mexico City Coll., U. Ams., 1947; m. Margaret Ann Clarkson, July 2, 1949; children—Patrick, Bernadette, Catherine, Mary M. Civil engr., rancher, real estate broker. Vatican observer World Methodist Council, London, Eng., 1966; mem. Vatican-Meth. Unity Conversations, 1966-68; dir. ecumenism Roman Catholic Diocese, Corpus Christi, 1966-72, chmn. adminstrv. bd., 1972—; mem. state bd. Tex. Conf. Chs., 1966-72. Bd. mgrs. Nueces County Hosp. Dist., Meml. Hosp., Corpus Christi, Vatican Secretariat for Christian Unity, 1966-68; nat. trustee Nat. Conf. Christians and Jews, 1970—. Served with USNR, 1942-46. Mem. Am. Soc. C.E., Tex. Soc. Profl. Engrs., Nat. Council Cath. Men (nat. sec. 1962-66), Serra Club (pres., dist. gov.). Democrat. K.C. Home: 1201 Lantana St Corpus Christi TX 78407 Office: PO Box 4322 Corpus Christi TX 78408

MEANS, WILLIAM WALTER, judge; b. Sand Springs, Okla., Mar. 29, 1933; s. Paul Willard and Marie (Conkey) M.; student U. Okla., 1951-53, 55-57; J.D., U. Tulsa, 1961; m. Mary Ellen Faulkner, Aug. 6, 1960; children—Karl W., Karen A. Admitted to Okla. bar, 1961; practice law, Tulsa, 1961-62; asst. dist. atty., Tulsa, 1962-66; chief civil asst. dist. atty., Tulsa, 1966-67; judge Ct. Common Pleas, Tulsa, 1967-68; asso. judge, 14th dist., Tulsa, 1969-71, dist. judge, 1971—. Served with AUS, 1953-55. Mem. Am., Okla., Tulsa County bar assns., Jud. Conf. Okla. (pres. 1973). Presbyn. Kiwanian. Home: 5519 S Marion St Tulsa OK 74135 Office: Tulsa County Court House Tulsa OK 74103

MEANY, GEORGE, labor ofcl.; b. N.Y.C., Aug. 16, 1894; s. Michael Joseph and Anne (Cullen) M.; ed. pub. and high sch., N.Y.C.; recipient of numerous honorary degrees; m. Eugenia A. McMahon, Nov. 26, 1919; children—Regina Clare (Mrs. Robert C. Mayer), Eileen (Mrs. Ernest S. Lee), Genevieve (Mrs. John S. Lutz). Began career as apprentice plumber, 1910, journeyman plumber, 1915; business rep. Plumbers Local Union No. 463, N.Y.C., 1922-34; pres. N.Y. State Fedn. of Labor, 1934-39; sec.-treas. AFL, 1940-52, pres. from 1952; pres. new combined orgn. AFL-CIO, 1955—. Mem. Nat. War Labor Bd., 1942—. Del. 12th, 14th Gen. Assembly UN. Democrat. Catholic. Home: 8819 Burdette Rd Bethesda MD 20034 Office: AFL-CIO Washington DC 20006

MEARES, ROMULUS LINNEY, JR., lawyer; b. Knoxville, Tenn., Apr. 15, 1941; s. Romulus Linney and Lucile Elizabeth (Goyne) M.; student U.S. Naval Acad., 1959-61; J.D., U. Tenn., 1964; m. Susan Katherine Harry, June 9, 1963; children—Jennifer Katherine, Judith Price, Romulus Linney. Admitted to Tenn. bar, 1964; practice in Maryville, 1964—. Mem. Am. (com. environmental law), Tenn., Blount County (pres. 1973) bar assns., Am. Judicature Soc., Tenn.

Def. Lawyers Assn., Phi Delta Phi. Office: PO Box 407 111 E Broadway Maryville TN 37801

MEARS, ALLEN LAVERN, JR., county agt.; b. Haynesville, La., Dec. 18, 1925; s. Allen Lavern and Icy (Martin) M.; B.S., La. State U., 1951, M.S., 1962; postgrad. U. Ark., 1955; m. Joyce Cockrell, June 24, 1951; children—James, John. Asst. county agt. Webster Parish, Minden, La., 1951-53, county agt., area livestock agt., 1967—; asst. county agt. Beauregard Parish, De Ridder, La., 1953-66; asso. county agt. Caddo Parish, Shreveport, La., 1966-67. Served with AUS, 1945-46; PTO. Mem. Farm Bur. (dir.), Cattlemens Assn. (dir.), Hog Marketing Assn. (dir.), Cattle and Pasture Demonstration (dir.), Feed and Pig Assn. (dir.), County Agt. Assn., Hon. Coop. Extension Orgn., V.F.W., Am. Legion. Mason. Club: Civitan (Minden). Home: 910 Nella St Minden LA 71055 Office: Box 836 Minden LA 71055

MEDFORD, FRANK ELDRIDGE, physician; b. Asheville, N.C., July 18, 1935; s. Clarence Columbus and Madell Elizabeth (Hardin) M.; B.S., Wake Forest Coll., 1957; M.D., Bowman Gray Sch. Medicine, 1961; m. Eva Sharon Phillips, Oct. 27, 1962; 1 dau. Cheryl Dawn. Intern, Charleston (W.Va.) Meml. Hosp., 1961-62, resident, 1962-65; fellow W. Va. U. Hosp., Morgantown, 1964-65; med. dir. Tech. Center, Union Carbide Corp., South Charleston, W. Va., 1965-68; practice medicine, specializing in internal medicine, Newport News, Va., 1968-74, Brevard, N.C., 1974—; mem. staff Transylvania County Hosp., Brevard. mem. staff Riverside Hosp., Newport News. Diplomate Am. Bd. Internal Medicine, Nat. Bd. Med. Examiners. Mem. Newport News Med. Soc. Home: Route 4 Millbrook Estates Brevard NC 28712 Office: Gallemore Rd Brevard NC 28712

MEDLEN, AMMON BROWN, educator; b. Lockhart, Tex., Sept. 12, 1908; s. Robert Milton and Caledonia Frances (Brown) M.; B.A., Baylor U., 1930, M.A., 1932; Ph.D., Tex. A. and M. U., 1952; m. Sue Myrtle Williams, June 6, 1936; children—Robert Byron, Suzanne Isabelle. Instr., Baylor U., 1932-34; tchr. prin. pub. schs., Tex., 1935-40; asst. prof. Ouachita Coll., 1940-43; instr. U. Houston, 1946; instr. dir. Tex. A. and M. Coll., 1946-41; asst. prof., 1951-54, asso. prof., 1954-65; prof., head biology dept. Tarleton State Coll., Stephenville, Tex., 1965—. Served with USNR, 1942-45. Fellow Tex. Acad. Scis.; mem. A.A.A.S., Am. Assn. U. Profs., N.Y. Acad. Scis., Am. Soc. Zoologists, Sigma Xi, Beta Beta Beta. Lion (pres. 1955-56, dep. dist. gov. 1956-57). Home: 881 Rome Av Stephenville TX 76401

MEDLER, ROWLAND, ednl. broadcasting exec.; b. St. Louis, Oct. 1, 1917; s. Ira B. and Mary Lethia (Nichols) M.; student U. East Tenn., 1957-58, U. Fla., 1961-62; m. Elaine Starr, June 20, 1948; children—Janice (Mrs. Michael Heidingsfield), Marilee, Jennifer Sue. With Callaway Mills, textiles, Manchester, Ga., 1935-39; with Sta. WJHL, Johnson City, Tenn., 1939-58; engr. WVFT TV, U. Fla., Gainesville, 1958—. Instr. electronics Steed Coll., Johnson City, 1956-58. Served with AUS, 1951-54; PTO. Mem. I.E.E.E., Soc. Broadcast Engrs. (charter, sr.), Am. Radio Relay League. Methodist. Clubs: Amateur Radio, Quarter Century Wireless (Gainesville). Home: 1041 NE 20th Av Gainesville FL 32601 Office: 234 Stadium Bldg Gainesville FL 32601

MEDLEY, PAUL, JR., librarian; b. San Angelo, Tex., Mar. 9, 1936; s. Paul and Lucille (Cauble) M.; B.A., So. Meth. U., 1958; M.S. in L.S., U. Tex., 1969, postgrad. Law Sch., 1961-62; m. Margaret Sue Robbins, Sept. 30, 1960; children—Mark, Marshall, Meredith. With Vari-Typer Corp., Austin, Tex., 1962-64; library asst. U. Tex. Library, Austin, 1964-66; pub. services librarian Abilene (Tex.) Pub. Library, 1966-67; dir. Waco-McLennan County Library, Waco, Tex., 1967—. Team capt. local United Fund. Pres., dir. W. Tex. Library Film Circuit. Mem. Am., Tex., Southwestern, Waco (pres.) library assns. Rotarian. Home: 1717 Mountainview Dr Waco TX 76710 Office: 1717 Austin Av Waco TX 76701

MEDLOCK, JULIUS LESTER, poet, educator; b. Mexia, Tex., Nov. 7, 1894; s. Oscar and Biddie Ophelia (Sloan) M.; life certificate, E. Central State Coll., Ada, Okla., 1921-23; B.S., Okla. State U., 1925; Ed.M., U. Okla., 1937; m. Alma Wendt, June 2, 1926 (dec. Nov. 1966). Tchr. high schs., Okla., Center, 1921-22, El Reno, 1923-24, McAlester, 1925-27, Pauls Valley, 1927-38, Poteau, 1938-41; instr. Okla. Indsl. Coll. Diversified Occupations, Weatherford, 1941, Elmore City High Sch., 1946-50; now engaged in ranching. Served from pvt. to pfc., U.S. Army, 1917-18. Fellow Internat. Inst. Arts and Letters (life); mem. Am. Poets Fellowships Soc., Okla. Writers Assn. (merit award 1963), Poetry Soc. Okla. (pres. 1958-60), Avalon World Arts Acad., Okla. Hist. Soc., Alumni Assn. U. Okla., Kappa Delta Pi, Phi Delta Kappa. Presbyn. (past chmn. com. pensions Washita Valley Presbytery). Mason, Rotarian. Author: Stray Hearts, 1956; Threads of Flame, 1960; When Swallows Fly Home, 1962; Fragments of Forever, 1964; Trumpets in Eden, 1966; Pearls and Tears, 1967; Tryst With the Stars, 1972; Winds in the Willows, 1974. Contbr. articles to mags. Address: Route 1 Box 227 Pauls Valley OK 73075

MEECE, O'LEARY MELROSE, supt. schs.; b. nr. Somerset, Ky., Mar. 20, 1911; s. George Linville and Eva E. (Silvers) M.; A.B., Western Ky. U., 1938; M.A., U. Ky., 1948; m. Marjorie Elaine Sears, June 23, 1942; 1 dau., Anne Louise (Mrs. Charles Bennett Farris). Elementary tchr. Pulaski County Schs., 1933-35; elementary prin. Somerset (Ky.) Pub. Schs., 1936-39; secondary tchr. Somerset High Sch., 1939-42, 47-50; dir. instrn. Somerset Pub. Schs., 1950-54, supr., 1954—. Bd. mgrs. Ky. P.T.A.; adv. bd. Somerset Community Coll.; adv. com. Ky. Ednl. TV. Served with USAAF, 1942-47. Decorated Bronze Star medal with 2 oak leaf clusters. Mem. Ky. (dir.), Middle Cumberland Dist. (sec.) edn. assns., Am. Legion, Phi Delta Kappa. Methodist (trustee). Rotarian. Contbr. articles profl. jours. Home: 306 College St Somerset KY 42501 Office: Somerset Schs College St Somerset KY 42501

MEEKER, CHARLES RUTHERFORD, JR., mgmt. cons.; b. Parkersburg, W.Va., Apr. 30, 1913; s. Charles R. and Estella (Tate) M.; student So. Meth. U., 1932-36; m. Doris Alton Shaw, Feb. 4, 1939; 1 son, Charles Rutherford III. With Interstate Theaters, 1936-44, successively publicity dir. Palace and Majestic Theatres, Dallas, mgr. State Theater, Amarillo, asst. city mgr. Dallas theaters; mng. dir. State Fair Musicals, Dallas, 1944-59, v.p., 1951-59; gen. mgr. Cary Schneider Investment Corp., 1961-62; cons. to pres. Gt. S.W. Corp. and Six Flags over Tex., 1961-68; pres. Miss Teenage Am., Inc., producer Miss Teenage Am. Pageant, 1962—; gen. partner Charles R. Meeker, Jr. & Assos., 1968—; cons., chmn. bd. Cedar Point, Inc., Sandusky, O., 1968—; cons., pres. Dr. Pepper Co., Dallas; cons. 1st Fed. Savs. & Loan Assn., Dallas. Mem. Christian Ch. Clubs: Salesmanship, Dallas Country, Conferie Des Chevaliers Du Tastevin, Cipango, Les Amis d'Escoffier. Author articles in field. Home: Park Towers 3310 Fairmount Dallas TX 75201 Office: 1165 Empire Central Place Dallas TX 75247

MEEKS, JAMES ROGER, savs. and loan exec.; b. Scottsville, Ky., Feb. 13, 1938; s. Roger A. and Billie L. (Dale) M.; student (Ogden scholar) Western Ky. U., 1960-64; m. Emma J. Walker, July 13, 1960; children—Jennifer, Stephanie, Jim. Asst. v.p. First Fed. Savs., Bowling Green, Ky., 1962-69, v.p., 1969-71; exec. v.p., dir. Hopkinsville Fed. Savs. and Loan Assn. (Ky.), 1971—; pres., dir. Sports Systems, Inc., Hopkinsville, 1972—. Lectr. money and credit Western Ky. U., 1969-71. Pres., Jr. Achievement, 1972-73; co-chmn. Salvation Army, 1972; co-chmn. Hobson House Nat. Restoration Project, 1971—. Served with USAF, 1956-57. Recipient awards Salvation Army, 1972, Hobson House, 1971, Distributive Edn. Found., 1970. Mem. U.S. Savs. and Loan League, Hopkinsville Jr. C. of C. (dir. 1967). Episcopalian (dir. 1971). Kiwanian (dir. 1973). Home: 116 Remington Rd Hopkinsville KY 42240 Office: Hopkinsville Fed Savings and Loan Assn 7th and Main Sts Hopkinsville KY 42240

MEGGINSON, ROBERT MITFORD, mortgage banker; b. Jackson, Miss., Aug. 2, 1932; s. Oscar Gray and Gladys (Lindsey) M.; student Millsaps Coll., 1965-66; B.S., Miss. State U., 1958; grad. Northwestern U. Mortgage Banking Sch., 1965-67; m. Joanne Jenkins, Jan. 8, 1953; 1 dau., Laurie Anne. Mem. acctg. dept. First Nat. Bank, Jackson, Miss., 1951-53; bookkeeper Ross & Hurst, C.P.A.'s, Jackson, Miss., 1958-59; mem. loan servicing, processing and acctg. dept. Reid-McGee & Co., Jackson, Miss., 1959-61; v.p. loan origination Wortman & Mann, Inc., Jackson, Miss., 1961-69; exec. v.p. Milton & Megginson Mortgage Co., Inc., Jackson, Miss., 1969—; pres. Milton, Megginson & Spencer, Inc., Jackson, Miss., 1970—; treas., dir. First Am. Savs. & Loan Assn., Clinton, Miss., 1972—. Mem. adv. bd. dirs., bd. dirs. Youth for Christ, Jackson, Miss. Served with AUS, 1953-55. Licensed Real Estate Broker, Miss. Mem. Soc. Real Estate Appraisers (chpt. v.p. 1968-69), Jackson Bd. Realtors, Nat. Assn. Real Estate Bds., Miss. Assn. Realtor Bds. Inc., Mortgage Bankers Assn. of Miss., Nat., Miss. assns. home bldrs., Jackson C. of C. (past pres.; recipient Spark Plug award, Speak Up award, Spoke award). Baptist. Club: Jackson Civitan. Home: 17 Rob Lane Jackson MS 39212 Office: 1456 Ellis Av Jackson MS 39204

MEHALLIS, GEORGE, educator; b. Wheeling, W.Va., Feb. 14, 1923; s. Gus and Eva (Bizakis) M.; B.S., Ohio State U., 1945, M.A., 1948, Ph.D., 1963; m. Ruth Jane Gaddy, Apr. 23, 1957; children—Constance West, George. Tchr., Ashtabula (O.) Harbor High Sch., 1945-48, Miami Beach (Fla.) Sr. High Sch., 1948-50; asst. prof. indsl. edn. U. Miami, 1950-56, asso. prof., 1956-60, chmn. dept. indsl. edn., 1961-64; instr. Ohio State U., 1960-61; dir. tech.-vocational studies Miami (Fla.)-Dade Jr. Coll., 1964—; Ed.D. cluster coordinator Nova Coll., 1972—. Mem. Fla. State Supts. Adv. Council Indsl. Arts, 1963-68; cons. Am. Assn. Jr. Colls.; mem. com. occupational edn. instns. So. Assn. Colls. and Schs.; mem. editorial adv. bd. Prakken Pubs., 1970-73; cons. Gen. Learning Corp., 1968-70; evaluator N. Central Assn. Colls. and Schs. Chmn., Occupational Program Coordinating Council Dade County, 1971. Served with USNR, 1942-44. Mem. Am. (pres. 1971-72), Fla. tech. edn. assns., Am., Fla. vocational assns., Am. Indsl. Arts Assn., Nat. Aerospace Edn. Council, Greater Miami Aviation Assn., Am. Soc. for Tng. and Devel., Phi Delta Kappa, Kappa Delta Pi, Epsilon Pi Tau. Contbr. articles to profl. jours. Home: 614 Aledo Av Coral Gables FL 33134 Office: 11380 NW 27th Av Miami FL 33167

MEI, HARRY THOMAS, educator, mech. engr.; b. Chekiang, China, Mar. 15, 1928; s. Tson-Yeh and Mary (Tsia) M.; came to U.S., 1954, naturalized, 1968; B.S., Nat. Taiwan U., 1953; M.S., U. Tex. at Austin, 1956, Ph.D., 1960; m. Betty Yuen, Dec. 15, 1962; children—Christine, Michael. Mech. designer Devenco Inc., N.Y.C., 1956-57; research engr. U. Tex. at Austin, 1957-60; mem. faculty Lamar U., Beaumont, Tex., 1960—, prof. mech. engring., 1966—; cons. in field. Registered profl. engr., Tex., La. Mem. Am. Soc. M.E., Am. Soc. Engring. Edn., Am. Soc. Heating, Refrigerating and Aircconditioning Engrs., Sigma Xi, Tau Beta Pi, Pi Tau Sigma. Author: Fortran IV for Engineers and Scientists, 1969. Home: 1955 Carson Dr Beaumont TX 77706

MEIER, WILLIAM LUDWIG, JR., dentist; b. Teague, Tex., Apr. 12, 1924; s. William Ludwig and Irene Emma (Senter) M.; student Tex. Tech. U., 1941-43, 46-47; D.D.S., Northwestern U., 1951; meteorology certificate Cal. Inst. Tech., 1944; m. Juanita Champion, Oct. 18, 1952; children—Clark, Carolyn. Pvt. practice dentistry, Austin, Tex., 1951—. Mem. adv. bd. Central Tex. Dist. Campus Crusade for Christ, 1965—, chmn., 1970. Served with USAAF, 1943-46. Mem. Austin Dist. Dental Soc. (pres. 1967-68). Kiwanian. Home: 405 Almarion St Austin TX 78746 Office: 7030 Village Center Dr Austin TX 78731

MEINKE, ROY WALTER, elec. engr.; b. Cleve., Aug. 7, 1929; s. George F. and Marie (Reyer) M.; B.S., Miami U., Oxford, O., 1952; postgrad. Ohio State U., 1952-53, 67-68. Asst. instr. dept. math. Ohio State U., Columbus, 1953; tchr. high sch., Edgerton, O., 1953-54, Kingman, Ariz., 1954-56; aerodynamics engr. N. Am. Aviation, Los Angeles, 1956-57; instr. physics dept. Central State Coll., Edmond, Okla., 1957-58; elec. engr. engr. Boeing Co., Seattle, Wash., 1958-62, Huntsville, Ala., 1962—. Co-pilot Mercy Flight Systems, 1973-74. Recipient Apollo Achievement award NASA, 1970. Mem. I.E.E.E., Am. Inst. Aeronautics and Astronautics, Nat. Soc. Profl. Engrs. Mem. United Ch. of Christ (dir. S.E. conf. 1969-73). Home: Mountain View Ct Route 4 Madison AL 35758 Office: PO Box 1470 Huntsville AL 35807

MEIROWSKY, ARNOLD MAX, neurol. surgeon; b. Cologne, Germany, Apr. 7, 1910; s. Emil and Clara (Wedel) M.; M.D., U. Cologne, 1937. Intern in surgery Martin Luther Hosp., Berlin, Germany, 1935-36; rotating intern St. Francis Hosp., Santa Barbara Cal., 1938-39; asst. resident, then resident neurol. surgery Albany (N.Y.) Hosp., Albany Med. Coll. of Union U., 1939-42; fellow neurol. surgery Barnes Hosp., also St. Louis Children's Hosp. and Washington U. Sch. Medicine, St. Louis, 1940; chief sect. neurol. surgery, dir. surg. research VA Med. Teaching Group, Kennedy Hosp., Memphis, 1946-50; research fellow neurosurgery U. Cin. Coll. Medicine, 1952-53; pvt. practice specializing in neurol. surgery, Nashville, 1953—; mem. attending staff Vanderbilt U., St. Thomas, Park View, Nashville Gen. hosps.; cons. staff Nashville Meml., Mid State Bapt., Williamson County hosps.; asst. prof. clin. neurol. surgery Vanderbilt U. Sch. Medicine, 1954—, neurol. surgery cons. U.S. Army, 1955—; vis. prof. Nat. Naval Med. Center, Bethesda, Md., 1967, 68. Served to lt. col. M.C., AUS, 1942-46, 50-52. Decorated Legion of Merit with oak leaf cluster; Chungmu Distinguished Mil. Service cross with gold star (Korea); recipient Outstanding Civilian Service medal U.S. Army, 1973. Diplomate Am. Bd. Neurol. Surgery. Mem. So. (pres. 1971-72, gov. 1970—), Tenn. neurosurg. socs., Am., Tenn., Middle Tenn. (pres. 1965-66, sec. 1961-64, gov. 1961-71) med. assns., Am. Assn. Neurol. Surgeons, Assn. Mil. Surgeons, Nashville Acad. Medicine, Nat. Rehab. Assn., Nashville Surg. Soc., Soc. Med. Cons. to Armed Forces. Editor, co-author: Neurological Surgery of Trauma, 1965. Contbr. to med. jours. Home: Etzelhof Old Hillsboro Rd Franklin TN 37064 Office: 401 Medical Arts Bldg 1211 21st Av S Nashville TN 37212

MEISTER, JOHN DAVID, diversified mfg. co. exec.; b. Miami, Fla., Apr. 16, 1939; s. Clarence Raymond and Rose E. (Dasch) M.; B.S. in Elec. Engring., U. N.M., 1962; m. Martha Elizabeth Terwilliger, June 30, 1962; children—John David, James Christopher. Exploration geophysicist Humble Oil Co., Houston, 1962; mgr. systems engring. TRW, Inc., San Bernardino, Cal., 1965-68; research and devel. program mgr. Tracor, Inc., Austin, Tex., 1968—. Active U. Tex. Internat. Student Host Family Program, 1969—; adult vol. Capitol Area council Boy Scouts Am., 1972—. Served to 1st lt. USAF, 1962-65. Mem. I.E.E.E., Kappa Alpha. Republican. Presbyn. (deacon 1971-73). Research, publs. in systems engring. field. Home: 6815 Willamette Austin TX 78723 Office: 6500 Tracor Lane Austin TX 78721

MELENDEZ, EFRAIN SANTIAGO, clergyman, business exec.; b. Comerio, P.R., Feb. 17, 1930; s. Jose Antonio and Justina (Melendez) Santiago; student Defenders Theol. Sem., 1957-61, Psychol. Inst. P.R., 1967-69; m. Gwendolyn Page, July 18, 1953; children—Jeffery Lee, Brian Mallory, Lorinda Sue, Merikay. Ordained to ministry Methodist Ch., 1961; pastor Wesleyan Meth. Ch. of P.R., 1957-64; pres. Weleyan Conf. P.R., 1962-64; pres. Safway Sales Co., Rio Piedras, P.R., 1959-63; v.p. Halco Sales Co., Rio Piedras, 1960-68, 73—; pres. Andamios, Inc., 1965-68, 73—; sec. Social Services of P.R., Santurce, 1969-72. Coordinator, dir. Billy Graham Evangelistic Assn. in Latin Am., 1964-68. Mem. adv. com. Columbia U.; mem. Samaritan Found.; mem. exec. bd. council Boy Scouts Am. Vice pres., mem. presdl. bd. Progressive Party of P.R., 1967—. Served with USNR, 1953-57. Recipient various honors. Mem. Nat. Council Family Relations, Nat. Rehab. Assn., Am. Pub. Welfare Assn., Nat. Council Illegitimacy, Acad. Polit. Scis., Am. Legion, Internat. Platform Assn., Logia Soberana de P.R., P.R. League against Cancer. Internat. Platform Assn. Home: Calle Tulipan 178 Urb San Francisco Rio Piedras PR 00927 Office: Box B Carolina PR 00630

MELICH, EDWARD IDEL, physician; b. N.Y.C., May 17, 1906; s. Morris and Esther (Schwartz) M.; student Columbia, 1926-27; A.B., George Washington U., 1929, M.D., 1932; m. Virginia Miller Param, Oct. 23, 1971; children by previous marriage—Henry A., Arthur E., Karen Marie (Mrs. Marvin Solomon). Intern, Jersey City Med. Center, 1932-34; physician VA, 1936-68, chief sect. gastroenterology VA Center, Bay Pines, Fla., 1946-48; pvt. practice medicine, St. Petersburg, Fla., 1969—; mem. staff Palms Pasadena, St. Petersburg Gen. hosps. Served to capt. M.C., AUS, 1942-46. Fellow A.C.P., Am. Coll. Gastroenterology (past gov. Fla., past chmn. bd. govs., past v.p.); mem. Am. Heart Assn. Contbr. articles to profl. jours. Home: Box 6755 St Petersburg FL 33756 Office: 1609 Pasadena Av S St Petersburg FL 33707

MELLADO, RAMON, govt. ofcl.; m. Rosario G. Mellado; children—Elena, Ramon, Ricardo, Manuel. Pub. sch. adminstr., 1931-41; under-sec. edn., Govt. of P.R., 1941-43; prof., dir. dept. pedagogy Coll. Edn., U. P.R., 1943-48, dean of adminstrn., 1948-56, prof. grad. sch. edn., 1957-68; sec. edn. Commonwealth of P.R., 1968-72; mem. P.R. Senate, 1972—. Mem. Constl. Covn., Commonwealth of P.R., 1952. Mem. Am. Acad. Social and Polit. Sci., P.R. Tchrs. Assn. Author: Designing a Science Curriculum, 1941; Culture and Education in Puerto Rico, 1948; Puerto Rico y Occidente, 1963. Home: Centrum Plaza Condominium Hato Rey PR 00919 Office: Capital Bldg San Juan PR 00901

MELLICHAMP, NELL VAUGHAN, music educator; b. Blythewood, S.C., June 15, 1890; d. Saint Lo H. and Amelia (MacMillian) Mellichamp; studied with Paul de Launey of Paris Conservatoire, also Philipps Standish Gilman, George Sumner Kittredge; summer student Juilliard Sch. Music, Columbia. Dir. music Heathwood Hall, Episcopal Sch., 1950—, Mellichamp Music Studio, Columbia, S.C., 1918—. Faculty Nat. Guild Piano Tchrs., Sherwood Music Sch., Chgo. Active vol. USO, Travelers Aid. Mem. Soc. Prevention Cruelty Animals, Am. Guild Organists, Am. Coll. Musicians, Hugenot Soc. N.C., S.C. Poetry Soc., Colonial Dames Am., S.C. Fedn. Humane Socs. (bd. dirs.). Club: Altrusa. Author: How to Begin (tchrs. manual); also several study books. Composer: Hymn Melodies for Children to Play; Children's Pieces; Record books. Contbr. poems American Anthology. Home: 726 Queen St Columbia SC 29205 Studio: 3504 Main St Columbia SC 29203

MELLO, JAMES FRANCIS, mus. exec.; b. Providence, Aug. 24, 1936; s. Frank Anthony and Elena Marguerite (Primiano) M.; A.B., Brown U., 1958; M.Sc., Yale, 1960, Ph.D., 1962; m. Sally Ann Cameron, Aug. 24, 1957; children—Jeanne, Frank, Craig, Roger. Paleontologist, U.S. Geol. Survey, Washington, 1967-70; spl. asst. to dir. Automatic Data Processing Nat. Mus. Natural History, 1970-73, asst. dir., 1973—. Mem. Fairfax City (Va.) Planning Commn., 1972—. Mem. A.A.A.S., Paleontol. Soc. Home: 10700 Orchard St Fairfax VA 22030 Office: Room 421 Nat Mus Natural History Washington DC 20560

MELLON, PAUL, art gallery exec.; b. Pitts., June 11, 1907; s. Andrew W. and Nora (McMullen) M.; A.B., Yale, 1929, L.H.D., 1967; A.B., Cambridge (Eng.) U., 1931, M.A., 1938; Litt.D. (hon.), Oxford U., 1961; LL.D., Carnegie Inst. Tech., 1967; m. Mary Conover, Feb. 2, 1935 (dec. Oct. 1946); children—Catherine Conover (Mrs. Catherine Warner) Timothy; m. 2d, Rachel Lambert Lloyd, May 1, 1948. Dir. Mellon Nat. Bank & Trust Co., Pitts. Pres., trustee Nat. Gallery Art, Washington; trustee Va. Mus. Fine Arts, Richmond, A.W. Mellon Ednl. and Charitable Trust, Pitts.; trustee Andrew W. Mellon Found., N.Y. Asso. fellow Berkeley Coll., Yale; hon. fellow Clare Coll., Cambridge, Eng., St. Joh. 's Coll., Annapolis; Benjamin Franklin fellow Royal Soc. Arts, London, 1969. Served from pvt. to 1st lt. Cav., AUS, 1941-43, 1st lt. to maj. overseas service with OSS, 1943-45. Recipient Yale medal award, 1953; Horace Marden Albright Scenic Preservation medal, 1957; award for distinguished service to arts Nat. Inst. Arts and Letters, 1962; Benjamin Franklin medal Royal Soc. Arts, London, 1965; Skowhegan Gertrude Vanderbilt Whitney award, 1972. Mem. Scroll and Key Soc., Am. Philos. Soc.; hon. mem. English Jockey Club, London. Clubs: Metropolitan (Washington); Racquet and Tennis, Grolier, Links, Knickerbocker, Jockey, Nat. Steeplechase and Hunt Assn. (N.Y.C.). Office: 1729 H St NW Washington DC 20006

MELLOWN, WILLIAM EWING, JR., state ofcl.; b. York, Ala., Jan. 17, 1931; s. William Ewing and Mildred (Harris) M.; B.S., Livingston State Coll., 1952; M.A., U. Ala., 1953; postgrad. Columbia, 1956, Syracuse U., 1964; m. Jeanette Steedley, Aug. 31, 1952; 1 son, William Ewing III. Grad. asst. dept. history U. Ala., 1953-54; tchr. Bibb County Bd. Edn., Centerville, Ala., 1954-55; tchr., asst. prin. Alexandria (Ala.) Sch., 1955-57; prin. Saks High Sch., Anniston, Ala., 1957-64; asst. ednl. TV coordinator State Dept. Edn., Montgomery, Ala., 1964-67; asst. coordinator Title I, Elementary and Secondary Edn. Act, 1965-67, coordinator, 1967-71, coordinator Title III, 1965-71, Title V, 1967-71, Title VII and VIII, fed. projects coordinator, 1971—. Bd. dirs. Prattville (Ala.) YMCA. Mem. Ala. Edn. Assn., Am. Assn. Sch. Adminstrn., N.E.A., Phi Delta Kappa. Kappa Phi Kappa. Club: Civitan (sec.-treas. 1963-64). Home: 116 Heritage Hills Dr Prattville AL 36067 Office: State Office Bldg Montgomery AL 36104

MELNICK, JOHN LATANE, lawyer, state legislator; b. Alexandria, Va., Apr. 19, 1935; s. Norbert and Myrtle Gray (Waring) M.; student Roanoke Coll., 1953-55; B.S. in Commerce, U. Va., 1958, J.D., 1961; m. Marjory Mary Helter, Apr. 28, 1962; children—John Latane, Paul Helter, Marjory Kathleen. Admitted to Va. bar, 1961, since practiced in Arlington; asso. firm Kinney, Whitaker, Smith and Barham, 1961-64; asst. commonwealth atty., 1962-63; mem. firm Ball, McCarthy, Ball and Melnick, 1964-67, Berryman, Melnick and

Sanders, 1970—; mem. Va. Ho. of Dels., 1971—. Dir. United Savs. and Loan Assn., Arlington Yellow Cab Co., Transp., Inc., Arlington. Dem. committeeman, Arlington, 1964-68; pres. Arlington Young Dems., 1965-66. Bd. dirs. Arlington YMCA, Boy Scouts Am., 1964-67. Recipient Humane Socs. of Va. award, 1973. Mem. Am., Va., Arlington (pres. 1969-70) bar assns., Am. Judicature Soc. Methodist (dir. 1964—, trustee 1972—). Kiwanian (dir. 1965—), Mason. Home: 4710 N Dittmar Rd Arlington VA 22207 Office: 2400 Wilson Blvd Arlington VA 22201

MELSA, JAMES LOUIS, educator; b. Omaha, July 6, 1938; s. Louis Fred and Ann (Pelnar) M.; B.S., Ia. State U., 1960; M.S., U. Ariz., 1962, Ph.D., 1965; m. Katherine Rose Smith, June 25, 1960; children—Susan, Elisabeth, Peter, Jon, Jennifer. Mem. tech. staff RCA, Vail, Ariz., 1960-61; asst. prof. elec. engring. U. Ariz., 1965-67; prof. elec. engring. So. Methodist U., 1967—. Mem. I.E.E.E., Am. Soc. Elec. Engrs., Sigma Xi, Eta Kappa Nu. Author: State Functions and Linear Control Systems, 1967; Linear Control Systems, 1969; Estimation Theory, 1971; Computer Programs for Computational Assistance in the Study of Linear Control Theory, 1971; System Identification, 1972; Introduction to Probability and Stochastic Processes, 1973. Contbr. numerous articles to tech. jours. Home: 9751 Larchcrest Dallas TX 75238

MELTON, CARLTON EARL, JR., physiologist; b. Allen, Tex., June 1, 1924; s. Carlton Earl and Sallie (Cate) M.; B.S., N.Tex. State Coll., 1948; M.S., U. Ill., 1950, Ph.D., 1953; m. Frances Joanne Jones, Nov. 9, 1957; children—Edith Cate, Carlton Eric, Matthew Edward. Research asst. biology N.Tex. State Coll., Denton, 1947-48; research asst. elec. engring. U. Ill., Urbana, 1949-51, teaching asst. physiology, 1951-53; instr. physiology Western Res. U., Cleve., 1953-55; asst. prof. U. Tex., Southwestern Med. Sch., Dallas, 1955-61; chief electrophysiology research Civil Aeromed. Inst., Oklahoma City, 1961—. Research prof. physiology Okla. U. Med. Center, 1961—; adjunct prof. zoology Okla. U., 1973—. Served with USNR, 1943-47. Mem. Am. Physiol. Soc., Am. Assn. Anatomists, Aerospace Med. Assn., Order Quiet Birdmen. Contbr. to profl. publs. in field. Home: 2710 Walnut Rd Norman OK 73069 Office: PO Box 25082 Oklahoma City OK 73125

MELTON, CHANCELLOR GARLAND, optometrist; b. Yellville, Ark., Apr. 28, 1899; s. William Thomas and Mary Elizabeth (Sims) M.; O.D., No. Ill. Coll. Optometry, 1923; m. Josephine McGill, Dec. 31, 1924; children—Garland, Betty Jo (Mrs. James H. Bennett). Practice optometry, Fayetteville, Ark., 1923-73. Organizer, sr. v.p., mem. bd. Investors Preferred Life Ins. Co., Little Rock, 1959-73. Mem. Ark. Bd. Optometric Examiners, 1937-68, pres. bd., 1940-50. Mem. Washington County Bd. Health, 1928-45, Fayetteville City Hosp., 1928-40, Washington County A.R.C., 1928-45, Fayetteville Boys Club, 1941-48, U.S.O., 1942-45, Ark. Savs. Bond, 1941—; organizer Washington County Crippled Children, 1933, 1933-54, pres., mem. bd., 1933-54; mem. bd., 1st v.p. Fayetteville Community Chest, 1933-34; Washington County War Bond chmn., 1941-48. Mem. central com. Washington County Democrats, 1937-40. Trustee So. Coll. Optometry, 1962-70, chmn. bd., 1964-70; mem. Fayette Sch. Bd., 1935-54, Huntsville Vocational, 1940-55. Named Ark. Optometrist of Year, 1971; Optometrist of Yr., So. Council Optometry, 1971; hon. crew mem. U.S.S. John F. Kennedy, 1970. Fellow Am. Acad. Optometry, Am. Research Council Optometry; mem. Am. (mem. council edn. 1946-62, mem. legal-legislative com. 1934-60), Ark. (pres. 1935-36) optometric assns., Grad. Clinic Found., Am. Optometric Found. (mem. original bd. 1952-54), Fayetteville C. of C., Beta Sigma Kappa. Methodist (bd. stewards 1924-73, chmn. 1933-40, chmn. bd. edn. 1946-48, dist. lay leader 1929-32, conf. rep. 1933-40). Lion (pres. 1930-31, dep. dist. gov. 1930-31, hon. life mem.), Mason (Shriner). Died Nov. 30, 1973. Home: 418 Ila St Fayetteville AR 72701

MELTON, CHANCELLOR GARLAND, optometrist; b. Fayetteville, Ark., May 22, 1920; s. Josephine (McGill) M.; student U. Ark., 1947-48; B.S., Pacific U., 1951, Dr. Optometry, 1952, M.S., 1957; m. Beverly Joan Brooks Melton, Jan. 22, 1956; children—Marsha Jan, Melissa Jeanne. Individual practice optometry, Fayetteville, Ark., 1957—; pres. Metrocenter Devel. Corp., Fayetteville, 1973-74. Mem. bd. adjustment City of Fayetteville, 1965, mem. bd. dirs., 1966-70, mayor, 1968-70, mem. indsl. park commn., 1970-74, chmn. parking authority, 1973-74; chmn. N.W. Ark. Regional Planning Commn., 1966-74. Bd. dirs. Fayetteville Boys Club, 1959-65, pres., 1964. Served with USNR, 1952-56; now capt. Res. Recipient State Lions Sight award, 1958, gold medallion Boys Club Am., 1964; Distinguished Service award Fayetteville Jaycees, 1965. Mem. Am. (mem. nominating com. 1966), Ark. (pres. 1966) optometric assns., So. Council Optometry (trustee 1966-67), Am. Optometric Found., Leonardo da Vinci Contact Lens Inst., Fayetteville C. of C. (dir. 1973-74). Democrat. Methodist. Mason (32 deg.), Lion. Home: 927 Applebury Dr Fayetteville AR 72701 Office: 230 N Block St Fayetteville AR 72701

MELTON, FREEMAN H., JR., supt. schs.; b. Wellington, Tex., Jan. 15, 1926; s. Freeman H. and Sudie (Stephens) M.; B.S., West Tex. State Coll., 1950, M.S., 1952; m. Rosemary Phillips, Aug. 14, 1949; children—Stephen Earl, Julie Carol, Margaret Joyce, Paul Freeman. Coach, tchr. pub. schs., Earth, Tex., 1950-51, McLean, Tex., 1951-52; sch. prin., McLean, 1952-54, supt. schs., 1954-60; supt. schs., Panhandle, Tex., 1960—. Mem. Panhandle Bd. City Devel.; chmn. A.R.C., Panhandle. Served with USNR, 1944-46. Recipient service citation A.R.C., 1958. Mem. N.E.A., Am., Tex. assns. sch. adminstrs., Tex. Tchrs. Assn. Mason. Lion. Home: 1406 Maple St Panhandle TX 79068 Office: Box 68 Panhandle TX 79068

MELTON, HOWELL WEBSTER, circuit ct. judge; b. Atlanta, Dec. 15, 1923; s. Holmes and Alma (Combee) M.; LL.B., U. Fla., 1948; m. Margaret Catherine Wolfe, Mar. 4, 1950; children—Howell Webster, Carol Anne. Admitted to Fla. bar, 1948, since practiced in St. Augustine; with firm Upchurch, Melton & Upchurch, 1948-61; circuit ct. judge 7th Jud. Circuit of Fla., 1961—. Mem., past sec. St. Johns County Blood Bank; mem. St. Johns County Welfare Fedn.; Trustee Flagler Coll., St. Augustine. Served with AUS, 1943-46. Recipient Distinguished Service award Fla. Jaycees, 1953. Mem. Am., St. Johns County bar assns., Fla. Bar (past chmn. council of bar presidents), Am. Judicature Soc., U. Fla. Alumni Assn., Phi Delta Theta, Phi Delta Phi. Methodist (past chmn. ofcl. bd.). Mason. Club: Ponce de Leon Country (St. Augustine). Home: 41 Carrera St St Augustine FL 32084 Office: County Courthouse St Augustine FL 32084

MELTON, OLIVER QUIMBY, JR., newspaper editor, state rep.; b. Americus, Ga., Feb. 12, 1922; s. Oliver Quimby and Mary (Davenport) M.; A.B. in Journalism, U. Ga., 1942; LL.D., John Marshall Law Sch., Atlanta, 1956; LL.B., LaSalle Extension U., 1958, Woodrow Wilson Coll. Law, 1961; m. May Wingfield, June 30, 1943; children—Oliver Quimby III, Mary W., Laura, Leila. Editor, mng. editor Griffin Daily News, 1945-72, editor, pub., 1973—; mem. Ga. Ho. of Reps., 1959-72; admitted to Ga. bar, 1961. Mem. bd. regents Univ. System Ga., 1955-60. Served as lt., cav., AUS, World War II. Decorated Purple Heart; recipient George Washington honor medals for editorials (two), Freedoms Found., 1951, 55; citations for editorials on religious understanding Nat. Conf. Christians and Jews, 1947, 48; citation for work with handicapped people Nat. Am. Legion, 1949; H.H. Dean trophy for best editorial in daily Ga. newspaper Ga. Press Assn., 1952; Salvation Army War Cry awards, 1945, 46; citation for fire prevention campaign Nat. Bd. Fire Underwriters, 1947; named Ga. Citizen of Yr., 1955; Most Fearless Editorial award Ga. Press Assn., 1955, 60. Mem. Ga. Press Assn. (bd. mgrs. 1952-56, pres. 1955-56), 4th Dist. Press Assn. (pres. 1953), Kappa Alpha. Methodist (steward). Mason, Elk. Clubs: Commerce, Griffin Country, Deer Trail Golf. Author: History of Griffin, 1959. Home: RFD Route 2 Box 176 Griffin GA 30223 Office: Griffin Daily News Griffin GA 30223

MELTON, ROSSER B., educator; b. Appleby, Tex., Nov. 21, 1910; s. William B and Rosa Belle (Blacksher) M.; B.S., Stephen F. Austin State U., 1934; M.A., U. Tex., 1937, Ph.D., 1940; m. Frances Elizabeth Couch, Dec. 21, 1938; children—Rosser B., Lynn Ayres, William C. Prof. sociology Sam Houston State U., 1940-45; asso. prof. econs. U. Ark., 1945-47; prof. econs. North Tex. State U., 1947—. Mem. Am., S.W. econ. assns., S.W. Social Sci. Assn., A.A.A.S., Assn. Evolutionary Econs., Alpha Chi, Alpha Kappa Delta, Pi Gamma Mu. Contbr. articles to profl. jours. Home: 1605 Kendolph St Denton TX 76201

MELTZER, MILTON, physician, psychoanalyst; b. Rochester, N.Y., May 11, 1923; s. Louis and Clara (Ratner) M.; B.A. cum laude, Ohio State U., 1943, M.D., 1946; grad. Washington Psychoanalytic Inst., 1960; m. Sallie Rabinoff, Mar. 23, 1946; children—Gail Miriam, Steven Marc. Intern, St. Elizabeth's Hosp., Washington, 1946-47, resident psychiatry, 1947-50; chief med. officer Alcatraz Fed. Penitentiary, 1951-52; gen. practice psychoanalysis and psychiatry Washington, 1952—; psychiatric cons. D.C. Dept. Vocational Rehab., 1953-73; tng. and supervising analyst Washington Psychoanalytic Inst., 1965—; clin. prof. psychiatry and behavioral scis. George Washington U. Sch. Medicine and Health Scis., 1973—. Served with USPHS, 1951-53. Fellow Am. Psychiat. Assn., A.A.A.S.; mem. Am. Psychoanalytic Assn. (mem. exec. council 1967-73), Washington Psychiatric Soc. (pres. 1967-68), Phi Beta Kappa, Alpha Omega Alpha. Address: 2934 Fessenden St NW Washington DC 20008

MELTZER, MORTON FRANKLIN, aircraft co. exec.; b. New Bedford, Mass., Apr. 15, 1930; s. Eli Newton and Bessie Estelle (Mackler) M.; B.S. in Journalism summa cum laude, Boston U., 1957; M.B.A., Rollins Coll., 1964. Mgr. tech. information center Martin Marietta Corp., Orlando, Fla., 1959—. Prof. bus communication Crummer Sch. Finance and Bus. Adminstrn., Rollins Coll., 1968—; mgmt. cons. bus. communication to govt. and industry; lectr. Served with AUS, 1953-55. Recipient George Washington Honor medal Freedoms Found., 1954. Mem. Internat. Soc. Gen. Semantics, Internat. Communication Assn., Am. Bus. Communication Assn., Am. Soc. Information Sci., Spl. Libraries Assn., A.L.A., Internat. Platform Assn. Author: The Information Center: Management's Hidden Asset, 1967; The Information Imperative, 1971. Home: 2722 Paseo St Orlando FL 32805 Office: PO Box 5837 Orlando FL 32805

MELVIN, ERNEST EUGENE, educator; b. Monmouth, Ill., May 15, 1923; s. Glenn Ivan and Susan Maurine (Perrine) M.; B.S., Western Ill. U., 1947; M.A., Syracuse U., 1949; Ph.D., Northwestern U., 1952; m. Carolyn Mae Hameister, Sept. 19, 1952; 1 dau., Carol Lynn. Geographer, Office of Engr. for Far Eastern Command, Tokyo, Japan, 1952-54; economist Kincaid & Assos., Chgo., 1954-56; planning asst. Evanston (Ill.) Planning Dept., 1956-57; city planner Chgo. Dept. City Planning, 1957-61; prof., dir. Inst. Community and Area Devel., U. Ga., Athens, 1961—; sec.-treas. Ga. Planning Assos., 1973—. Vice chmn. Athens Model City Policy Bd., 1972-73. Served with USNR, 1943-46. Recipient fellowship Office Naval Research, 1951-52. Mem. Am. Inst. Planners, Assn. Am. Geographers, Community Devel. Soc., A.A.A.S., Sigma Xi. Methodist. Mason (Shriner, 32 deg.). Home: 355 Ashton Dr Athens GA 30601

MELVIN, WILLIAM THOMAS, seed oil processing co. exec.; b. Durham, N.C., Nov. 7, 1910; s. Joshua Love and Sarah (Conoley) M.; grad. pub. schs.; m. Mary Baker Jenkins, Nov. 20, 1937; children—Samuel Jenkins, Sarah Anne (Mrs. Ronald Clingman Green). Bookkeeper, Planters Nat. Bank & Trust Co., Rocky Mount, N.C., 1928-30; with Planters Cotton Oil & Fertilizer (now Planters Industries Inc.), 1930-68, bookkeeper, 1930-35, mgr. cotton gins, 1935-41, mgr. oil mill dept., 1941-50, v.p., 1950-68; gen. mgr., v.p., dir. Planters Oil Mill Inc., Rocky Mount, 1968—. Mem. Nat. Soybean Processors Assn. (dir.), Nat. Cottonseed Products Assn. (pres. 1963-64), Southeastern Cottonseed Crushers Assn. (dir.), Nat. Cotton Council (dir.), Cotton Council Internat. (dir.). Episcopalian. Clubs: Elks, Rotary, Benvenue Country (pres. 1957). Home: 1625 Pinecrest Rd Rocky Mount NC 27801 Office: 1004 Cokey Rd Rocky Mount NC 27801

MENAKER, EDWARD GOWARD, elec. engr.; b. Newark, Apr. 10, 1919; s. George and Sara (Goward) M.; A.B., Columbia Coll., 1938; M.A., Columbia, 1939; postgrad. Union Coll., Schenectady, 1947-49; m. Elizabeth Dresbold, Sept. 6, 1941; children—Richard Glen, Lawrence James. Tchr. Altaraz Sch., Monterey, Mass., 1940-41; with Gen. Electric Co., Schenectady, N.Y. and Waynesboro, Va., 1946—, product reliability and service analyst numerical equipment control dept., 1968—; mgr. value control Compagnie Bull-Gen. Electric, computer, Paris, France, 1967. Pres. Waynesboro Council P.T.A.'s, 1957-58; leader, scouter Boy Scouts Am., 1948—; fencing instr., ofcl. Blue Ridge Fencing Club, 1961—, Amateur Fencers League Am., 1961—. Chmn. Waynesboro and 15th Legislative Dist. Democratic Com., 1968-72; del. Dem. Nat. Conv., Chgo., 1968; mem., chmn. Waynesboro Recreation Commn., 1972—. Trustee, chmn. bldg. com. Waynesboro Pub. Library, 1965-67; bd. dirs. Stonewall Jackson Area council Boy Scouts Am., 1961—. Served to maj. USAAF, 1942-46. Decorated Bronze Star medal; recipient Silver Beaver award Boy Scouts Am., 1967. Registered profl. engr., N.Y. Mem. I.E.E.E., Va. Soc. Profl. Engrs., Columbia Alumni Assn., 14th Air Force Assn., Va. Council Human Relations. Club: Waynesboro (Va.) Country. Home: 1824 Westminster Rd Waynesboro VA 22980 Office: General Electric Co Waynesboro VA 22980

MENDELL, DAVID, psychiatrist; b. N.Y.C., May 10, 1909; s. Morris H. and Sarah (Kahn) M.; B.S., Coll. City N.Y., 1929; M.D., U. Vienna, 1934; m. Miriam Wydra, June 27, 1944; children—Jeffrey V., Mark Judson. Intern, Bellevue Hosp., N.Y.C., 1934-35, St. Joseph Infirmary, Houston, 1935-36; pvt. practice medicine, Houston, 1937-42; resident fellow psychiatry Langley Porter Clinic, San Francisco, 1946-47, asst. chief child psychiatry dept., 1947-48; practice medicine, specializing in psychoanalysis, San Francisco, 1948-50, specializing in psychiatry, psychoanalytic group and family, Houston, 1950—; candidate, clin. asso. San Francisco Inst. Psychoanalysis, 1946-50; instr. psychiatry U. Cal. Med. Sch., San Francisco, 1947-48; clin. asso. prof. psychiatry U. Tex. Grad. Sch. Bio-Med. Sci., 1953—, Baylor Coll. Medicine, 1959—; clin. prof. psychiatry U. Tex. Sch. Med. Houston, 1972—; cons., dir. group therapy program Baylor Coll. Medicine, 1963-70; cons. staff VA Mental Hygiene Clinic, San Francisco, 1948-50; cons. USAF Hosp., San Antonio. Served from capt. to lt. col. USAAF, 1942-46. Diplomate Am. Bd. Psychiatry and Neurology. Fellow Am. Group Psychotherapy Assn., Am. Psychiat. Assn.; mem. Am. Acad. Psychotherapists (pres. 1967-68), Group for Advancement Psychiatry (com. on family 1956—, chmn. com. on family 1971-72), Internat. Group Therapy Assn. (dir. 1973—), UN Assn. of U.S.A. (mem. chpt. adv. com.). Contbr. articles to profl. jours. Home: 3611 N Braeswood Blvd Houston TX 77025 Office: Medical Towers Houston TX 77025

MENDELL, HENRY ELIAS, physician; b. Key West, Fla., Feb. 27, 1925; s. Julius and Clara (Rothman) M.; M.D., U. Tex., 1947; m. Muriel Friedman, Dec. 6, 1958; children—Jeffrey Neal, Robin Sheryl. Rotating intern St. Louis City Hosp., 1947-48; intern in medicine Barnes Hosp., St. Louis, 1948-49; resident in internal medicine Baylor U. Affiliated Programs, Houston, 1949-51; practice medicine, specializing in internal medicine, Houston, 1954—; asso. internist M. D. Anderson Hosp. and Tumor Inst., Houston, 1954—; mem. staff Ben Taub, Hermann, Meth., Meml., St. Luke's, St. Joseph, Bellaire Gen. hosps., Houston; clin. asso. prof. internal medicine Baylor Coll. Medicine, Houston, 1964—. Served to capt. M.C., USAF, 1951-53. Diplomate Am. Bd. Internal Medicine. Mem. A.M.A., A.C.P., Tex. Acad. Internal Medicine, Houston Soc. Internal Medicine, Alpha Omega Alpha. Republican. Jewish religion. Home: 5735 Ariel St Houston TX 77035 Office: 5401 Dashwood St Suite 2C Bellaire TX 77401

MENDELSSOHN, RUDOLPH CHRISTIAN, govt. ofcl.; b. N.Y.C., Nov. 20, 1914; s. Erich Micheal and Barbara Josephine (Willike) M.; A.B., U. Chgo., 1938, postgrad., 1939; postgrad. George Washington U., 1946; m. Ruth Lorell Royce, June 25, 1950; children—Lorell, Barbara. With bur. labor statistics U.S. Dept. Labor, Washington, 1940—, asst. commr., 1968—. Served with AUS, 1942-46. Mem. Assn. Computing Machinery, Am. Statis. Assn. Unitarian. Contbr. to profl. publs. in field. Home: 4106 Elizabeth Lane Fairfax VA 22030 Office: 441 G St NW Washington DC 20212

MENDENHALL, JOHN RYAN, accountant; b. Des Moines, Jan. 17, 1928; s. Merritt Blake and Elizabeth (Ryan) M.; B.Sc., U. Notre Dame, 1950; LL.B., Harvard, 1953; m. Joan Lois Schaefer, June 20, 1953; children—Thomas, James, Jane, Julie, Robert. With tax dept. Arthur Andersen & Co., C.P.A., Cleve., 1953-66, partner, 1963—, dir. taxes, Chgo., 1966—. Served with AUS, 1946-47, C.P.A., Ohio, Mich., Ia., Ill. N.C. Mem. Ohio Soc. C.P.A.'s, Am. Inst. C.P.A.'s, Roman Catholic. Clubs: University, Harvard (N.Y.C.); Internat. (Washington). Contbr. articles to tech. tax jours. Office: 1666 K St NW Washington DC 20006

MENDENHALL, LESLIE WARD, JR., wholesale co. exec.; b. Fort Worth, Sept. 20, 1920; s. Leslie Ward and Viola (Herring) M.; student Tex. Christian U., 1938-41, 45-48; m. June Helen McCord, May 5, 1942; children—Leslie Ward III, June Anne, Melinda Kaye (Mrs. Bill E. Blair). Accountant, Patterson, Leatherwood & Miller, Fort Worth, 1945-47; accountant, office mgr. J.P. Bowlin Co., Fort Worth, 1947-48; head accounts payable dept., accounting dept., mgr. budget control Montgomery Ward, Fort Worth, 1948-51; accountant, Fort Worth, 1951-59; sec.-treas., controller, dir. Nationwide Advt. Specialty Co. and related cos., Arlington, Tex., 1959—; dir. Arlington Fraternal Builders, Inc.; sec.-treas., dir. Newbern Corp., 1959—, SRI Publ. Co., 1968—, Texad Specialty Co., 1964—, NACO Advt. Specialty Co., 1973—, Nat. Calendar & Advt. Co., 1972—(all Arlington), Heritage Mfg. Corp., Fort Worth, 1959—. C.P.A., Tex. Episcopalian. Elk, Rotarian. Home: 1510 W Lavender Lane Arlington TX 76013 Office: 2025 S Cooper St Arlington TX 76010

MENDENHALL, WILLIAM, III, educator; b. Williamsport, Pa., Apr. 20, 1925; s. William and Helen (Hempfield) M.; B.S. in Engring., Bucknell U., 1946, M.S. in Math., 1950; Ph.D. in Statistics, N.C. State U., 1957; m. Joan S. Fleming, June 19, 1949; children—William M., Charles M. Research asso. N.C. State U. and London (Eng.) Sch. Econs., 1957-58; asst. prof. N.C. State U., 1958-59; asso. prof. Bucknell U., 1959-63; prof. statistics, chmn. dept. U. Fla., 1963—. Served with USNR, 1943-46, 50-52. Mem. Royal Statis. Soc., Am. Statis. Assn., Inst. Math. Statistics. Author: Introduction to Linear Models and The Design and Analysis of Experiments, 1968; (with R.I. Ott and R.L. Scheaffer) Elementary Survey Sampling, 1971; Introduction to Probability and Statistics, 3d edit., 1971; (with J. Reinmuth) Statistics for Business and Management, 1971; (with R. L. Ott) Understanding Statistics, 1972, 2d edit., 1974; (with M. Ramey) Statistics for Psychology, 1973; (with R. L. Scheaffer) Mathematical Statistics with Applications, 1973; (with R.L. Ott and R. Larson) Statistics: A Tool for The Social Sciences, 1974. Home: 2021 NW 23d Terrace Gainesville FL 32601

MENDEZ, ALFRED F., clergyman; b. Chgo., June 3, 1907; ed. U. Notre Dame, Holy Cross Coll. Ordained priest Roman Catholic Ch., 1935; 1st bishop of Arecibo (P.R.), 1960—. Address: Box 606 Arecibo PR 00613*

MENDEZ, FELIX GILBERTO, pub. relations exec.; b. Lares, P.R., July 31, 1932; s. Edelmiro Mendez and Inocencia Soto M.; B.S., U. P.R., 1954; postgrad. Am. U., Cornell U., Lares Sch. Commerce; m. Antonia Gonzalez, Dec. 21, 1953; children—Felix Antonio, Mercedes, Rosa, Francisco, Marife. Med. rep. Endo Pharm. Co., 1956-59, Armour Pharm. Co., 1959-61; supr. Smith, Miller & Patch, 1961-62; pub. relations dir. Interstate Gen. Contractor, 1962-63; mgr. govt. relations, asst. dir. pub. relations, I.T.T., 1963-69; dir. Econ. Devel. Adminstrn. P.R. Office Information and Pub. Relations 1969-70; pub. relations counsellor Coop. Devel. Adminstrn. and Govt. Housing Bank, 1970—; v.p. Admakers, also pres., owner San Juan Pub. Relations, Inc. (P.R.), 1971—. Cons. Served as 2d lt. AUS, 1954-56. Mem. Pub. Relations Soc. P.R. (past pres.), InterAm. Pub. Relations Soc. (dir.), Pub. Relations Soc. Am., Casino de P.R., San Juan Pub. Relations (pres.), P.R. C. of C., Alpha Beta Chi (nat. past pres.). Roman Catholic. K.C., Lion (sec.). Home: C-29 Rufino Rodriguez Villa Clementina Guaynabo PR 00657 Office: 1106 FD Roosevelt Av Puerto Nuevo San Juan PR 00907 also GPO Box 2114 San Juan PR 00936

MENENDEZ-MONROIG, JOSE M., state senator; b. San Juan, P.R., June 22, 1917; s. Albert Seaman Menendez and Agustina Monroig; B.A., U. P.R., 1939, LL.B., 1941; m. Lyda M. Cortada, Aug. 3, 1946; children—Jose Antonio, Michele Marie. Admitted to P.R. bar, 1941; asso. atty. Pub. Service Commn., 1946; adjudicator VA, 1947. Mem. P.R. Senate, 1969—; sec. gen. New Progressive party. Mem. Am. Bar Assn., Colegio de Abogados de P.R. Roman Catholic. Home: 54 Krug St Santurce PR 00911 Office: PO Box 3183 San Juan PR 00904

MENGER, GARNET CARPENTER, accountant; b. Corpus Christi, Tex., Apr. 8, 1921; s. Garnet and Lottie (Schoenbohm) M.; student Del Mar Coll., 1939; B.S., Tex. A. & M. U., 1944; m. Faith Lowell Anderson, May 15, 1943; children—Garnet, Tarana Belle. Office clk. C.P.A. firm Collier, Johnson & Woods, Corpus Christi, Tex., 1947-58, C.P.A., 1958-63, partner, 1963—. Bd. dirs. YMCA. Served to lt. AUS, 1943-46. Decorated Bronze Star. C.P.A., Tex. Mem. C.P.A.'s (sec. Corpus Christi chpt. 1969), Am. Inst. C.P.A.'s, Am. Legion. Presbyn. Clubs: Eagles, Revelaires (pres. 1973—), Carousel. Home: 3312 Santa Fe Corpus Christi TX 78411 Office: 618 Guaranty Nat Tower Corpus Christi TX 78401

MENIUS, ESPIE FLYNN, JR., elec. engr.; b. New Bern, N.C., Mar. 5, 1923; s. Espie Flynn and Sudie Grey (Lyerly) M.; B.E.E., N.C. State U., 1947; M.B.A. U. S.C., 1973; adopted children—James Benfield, Ruben Hughes. With Carolina Power & Light Co., 1947-63, asst. to dist. mgr., Raleigh, Henderson, N.C., Sumter, S.C., 1947-50, elec. engr., Asheville, Southern Pines, Dunn, N.C., 1950-52, dist. engr. Hartsville, S.C., 1952-63; sr. elec. engr. Sonoco Products Co., Hartsville, 1963—. Instr. Florence-Darlington Tech. Ednl. Center. Mem. Hartsville Vol. Fire Dept., 1958—; Eagle Scout, Boy Scouts Am., 1938, scout troop leader New Bern, N.C., 1940-41, Raleigh, N.C., 1941-47, Henderson, N.C., 1948-49, Asheville, N.C., 1950, Southern Pines, N.C., 1951-52, Sumter, S.C., 1949-50, Hartsville, S.C., 1952-64. Served with AUS, 1943-46. Recipient Silver Beaver award Boy Scouts Am., 1959; named Hartsville's Citizen Yr., Rotary, 1960. Registered profl. engr., N.C., S.C., Tenn., Ga. Mem. I.E.E.E., A.A.A.S., Nat. Assn. Engrs., Knight of St. Patrick, Scabbard and Blade, Eta Kappa Nu, Pine Burr, Phi Eta Sigma, Theta Tau, Beta Gamma Sigma. Presbyn. (elder, tchr. men's Bible class). Club: Civitan (past dir.). Author articles in field. Home: 423 Richardson Circle W Hartsville SC 29550 Office: Sonoco Products Co N 2d St Hartsville SC 29550

MENN, HUBERT L., JR., state ofcl.; b. Yorktown, Tex., Mar. 1, 1921; s. Hubert L. and Martha (Poch) M.; student Tex. Lutheran Coll., 1938-40; B.B.A., U. Tex., 1942, M.B.A., 1943, Ph.D., 1957; m. Marciel Elizabeth Mueller, Mar. 31, 1946; children—Maricel (Mrs. Donald Maschmeyer), Mark. Auditor, Price Waterhouse & Co., Houston, 1946-48; asst. prof. accounting U. Tex., Austin, 1948-51; budget officer Tex. Dept. Mental Health, Austin, 1951-55, fiscal officer 1956-59, chief budget and finance, 1960—; dir. Augsburg Publishing House, Mpls. Bd. dirs. Lutheran Social Service Tex. Served with AUS, 1943-46. Mem. Tex. Lutheran Coll. Ex-Students Assn. (pres. 1952-53), Am. Lutheran Ch. Men (dist. pres. 1961-62, nat. sec. 1963-69), Am. Inst. C.P.A.'s, Assn. Mental Health Adminstrs., Tex. Soc. C.P.A.'s. Author: Cost Accounting and Budgeting for State Mental Hospitals 1957; Accounting Procedures Manual, 1958. Home: 4501 Erin Lane Austin TX 78756 Office: PO Box 12268 Capital Station Austin TX 78711

MENSCHER, BARNET GARY, steel co. exec.; b. Laurelton, N.Y., Sept. 5, 1940; s. Samuel and Louise (Zaimont) M.; student Centenary Coll., 1958-59; B.B.A., U. Tex., 1963; m. Diane Elaine Gachman, June 12, 1966; children—Melissa Denise, Corey Lane. Vice pres. marketing Ella Gant Mfg., Shreveport, La., 1964-66; warehouse mgr., dir. material control Gachman Steel Co., Fort Worth, 1966-68, gen. mgr., Houston, 1968-70, v.p., sales mgr. Gulf Coast, 1971—. Investment cons. D & L Enterprises, 1966—. Mem. solicitation com. United Fund, 1969-73; mem. Nat. Alliance of Businessmen Jobs Program, 1969—. Served with AUS, 1963-65. Mem. Assn. Steel Distbrs., Tex. Assn. Steel Importers, Purchasing Agts. Assn. Houston, Credit Assn. Houston, Am. Mgmt. Assn., Phi Sigma Delta, Alpha Phi Omega. Democrat. Jewish religion. Home: 314 Tealwood Dr Houston TX 77024 Office: PO Box 40448 Houston TX 77040

MENZEL, ROBERT WINSTON, educator; b. James City County, Va., Jan. 29, 1920; s. George Ernest and Susie Francis (Gary) M.; B.S., Coll. William and Mary, 1940, M.A., 1943; postgrad. U. Va., 1945-46; Ph.D., Tex. A. and M. U., 1954; m. Margaret Young, Apr. 9, 1949; children—Robert Winston, Gary, Mary Linda. Research asst. Va. Fisheries Lab., Yorktown, 1940-42, asst. biologist, 1942-46; oyster biologist Tex. A. and M. Research Found., Houma, La., and College Sta., Tex., 1947-51; asst. prof. marine biology Fla. State U., Tallahassee, 1954-58, asso. prof., 1958-70, prof., 1970—. Vis. prof. marine biology Tex. A. and M. U., 1972-73. Cons. Lamont Dougherty Geol. Lab., U.S. Nat. Marine Fisheries Service, and to industry; judge Fla. State Sci. Fair. Mem. bd. rev. and cons. oceanography Boy Scouts Am., 1966-70. Recipient saltwater conservation award Fla. Wildlife Fedn., 1964. Fellow Tex. Acad. Scis.; mem. A.A.A.S., Am. Fisheries Soc., Am. Soc. Ichthyology and Herpetology, Am. Soc. Limnology and Oceanography, Am. Soc. Zoologists, Assn. Southeastern Biologists, Fla. Acad. Scis., Gulf and Caribbean Fisheries Inst., Nat. Shellfisheries Assn. (pres. 1971-73), World Mariculture Soc., Sigma Xi, Phi Sigma. Contbr. to profl. publs. in field. Home: 1605 Kolapakin St Tallahassee FL 32301

MENZEL, RONALD GEORGE, soil scientist; b. Independence, Ia., Jan. 23, 1924; s. Raymond Gerald and Bonnie (Dillard) M.; B.S., Ia. State U., 1947; Ph.D., U. Wis., 1950; m. Elsie Gray Burke, Feb. 23, 1952; children—Martha Jean, Robert Gray. Soil scientist U.S. Dept. Agr., Beltsville, Md., 1950-69, lab. dir. Water Quality Mgmt. Lab., Durant, Okla., 1969—. Fellow Am. Soc. Agronomy; mem. Am. Chem. Soc., A.A.A.S. Kiwanian. Research on behavior of radioactive fission products in soils and uptake by plants. Home: 1216 Alma St Durant OK 74701 Office: Rt 2 Box 322A Durant OK 74701

MERCER, GERALD DEAN, chemist; b. Bushnell, Neb., Apr. 9, 1926; s. Harry Virgil and Ardath Marie (Brestel) M.; B.Sc., U. Neb., 1952, M.Sc., 1955, Ph.D., 1956; m. Elfriede Anna Spitzenberger, Mar. 13, 1948; children—Herald Dean, Kim Ione. Research chemist Dow Chem. Co., Midland, Mich., 1956-69; research chemist Buckman Labs, Inc., Memphis, Tenn., 1969—. Served with AUS, 1944-48. Decorated Bronze Star medal. Standard Oil Co. fellow, 1954, NIH fellow, 1955. Mem. Am. Chem. Soc. Home: 3216 Ancroft Cove Memphis TN 38128 Office: 1256 N McLean St Memphis TN 38108

MERCER, JOHN YAGER, banker; b. Leitchfield, Ky., Jan. 9, 1922; s. James Jones and Emma Mae (Yager) M.; A.B., Centre Coll., Danville, Ky., 1943; M.A., Western Ky. U., 1949; postgrad., Sch. Banking of South, La. State U., 1967; m. Juanita Church, Dec. 22, 1946; children—Michael Evans, Sarah Bishop, Marjorie Mae. Tchr., Butler High Sch., Princeton, Ky., 1946-48; prin. Bartow (Fla.) Jr. High Sch., 1949-51, Bartow Elementary Sch., 1951-58; supervising prin. Ft. Meade (Fla.) Sch. Area, 1958-62; loan officer 1st State Bank, Ft. Meade, 1962-63; pres., dir. U.S. Bank of Seminole, Sanford, Fla., 1964—. Pres., Polk County Edn. Assn., 1957-59; chmn. Sanford Airport Authority, 1973—. Bd. dirs. United Fund Seminole County. Served with AUS, 1943-46. Decorated Air medal, Combat Inf. badge; named Hon. State Farmer Future Farmers Am., 1960. Gen. Elec. Sci. fellow Case Inst. Tech., 1947. Mem. Sanford C. of C. (pres. 1971, dir. 1970-73), Sanford Plaza Mchts. Assn. (sec.-treas.), Sigma Alpha Epsilon. Democrat. Baptist. Rotarian (pres. 1974—). Clubs: Seminole High School Booster (pres. 1971), Mayfair Country. Home: 201 W 19th St Sanford FL 32771 Office: 3000 Orlando Dr Sanford FL 32771

MERCER, RONALD EUGENE, assn. exec.; b. Ipava, Ill., June 17, 1938; s. Clifford Irwin and Ila (Onion) M.; student Humboldt Inst., 1956-57, U. Colo., 1966-68, U. Okla., 1967-69, Tex. Christian U., 1969-71, 73; m. Janet Sue Adcock, Jan. 27, 1957; children—Ronald Eugene, Pamela Sue. Rate clk. Central Transfer Co., Peoria, Ill., 1957-58; freight bill auditor, Burlington Truck Lines, Inc., Galesburg, Ill., 1958-62, asst. traffic mgr., 1962-63, asst. traffic mgr. marketing, 1963-65; chief exec. C. of C., Sidney, Neb., 1965-67, Scottsbluff, Neb., 1967-68, Helena, Ark., 1969-72; Big Spring, Tex., 1972—; dir. econ. devel., Salina, Kan., 1968-69. Exec. dir. Nat. River Acad. U.S.A., Helena, Ark., 1970—. Asst. scoutmaster Ark. Area council Boy Scouts Am., 1969-72; Scoutmaster Buffalo Trail Area council, 1972—; mgr. Little League Baseball, Sidney, Scottsbluff, 1965-68; chmn. Ark. Task Force for Continuing Edn., Inst. for Orgn. Mgmt., Tex. Christian U., 1972—; pres. Moss P.T.A., 1973-74; mem. Tex. Indsl. Devel. Council, Tex. Tourist Council. Bd. dirs. Big Spring United Fund. Mem. Am., So. indsl. devel. councils, Am. C. of C. Execs., So. Assn. C. of C. Execs., Tex. C. of C. Mgrs., C. of C. Execs. of West Tex. (dir.), Permian Basin C. of C. Mgrs. (pres. 1974). Home: 1718 Yale Big Spring TX 79720 Office: 215 E 3d Big Spring TX 79720

MERCER, THEODORE CHELTON, coll. pres.; b. Spring City, Tenn., Sept. 3, 1920; s. Robert and Minerva Jane (Lewis) M.; A.B., Bob Jones U., 1943, M.A., 1944; postgrad. U. Chgo., 1946; Litt. D., Houghton Coll., 1952; m. Ora Alice Moore, Aug. 24, 1944; children—Theodore Chelton, John Moore, David Mark. Licensed to preach Meth. Ch., 1938; ordained to ministry Bapt. Ch., 1942; mem. faculty in English, Bob Jones U., 1943-53, dean men, 1944-47, registrar, 1947-53, asst. to pres., 1949-53; dir. publicity, also asst. in devel. Muskingum Coll., 1953-56; mem. Dayton Indsl. Devel. Bd., 1972-74; pres. Bryan Coll., Dayton, Tenn., 1956—. Local historian Rhea County; mem. Council Advancement Small Colls.; bd. dirs. Tenn. div. Am. Cancer Soc., 1962-68, Appalachian Regional Arthritis Center Found., 1974—; chmn. county United Fund, 1968—. Mem. Am. Assn. Higher Edn., Am. Coll. Pub. Relations Assn., Newcomen Soc. N. Am., Tenn. Hist. Soc. Dayton C. of C. (dir. 1971—), Rhea County Hist. Soc. (founding pres. 1972—). Rotarian (pres. 1972-73). Home: Bryan Coll Dayton TN 37321

MERCER, WILLIAM AUSTIN, JR., pub. relations, mgmt. cons.; b. Metter, Ga., Feb. 10, 1927; s. William Austin and Seola Louise (Miller) M.; B.S. in Journalism, N.Y. U., 1955, postgrad., 1955-56; m. Elizabeth Jane Eggleston, July 3, 1954. Pres., Mercermedia, Inc., Washington, publisher Black Viewpoint Newsletter and operator Minority Exec. Matchmakers, Inc., 1972—; pres. Newark Cable TV, Inc., 1970-72; dir. Broad Nat. Bank, Newark; founder-dir. Medic Enterprises, Inc., 1968-72, chmn. bd., 1970-72. Vice chmn. pub. relations United Way of Met. Washington, 1973. Communications coordinator Kenneth A. Gibson Mayoral campaigns, 1966, 70. Mem. exec. com. Council Social Agys. of Essex and West Hudson counties, N.J., 1968-69; mem. adv. com. Charles Engelbard Found., 1967-71; mem. Nat. YMCA's Assn. Press, 1963-73. Served with AUS, 1950-52; ETO. Recipient numerous community service, Man of Year and civic citations and awards. Mem. Pub. Relations Soc. Am., Capital Press Club. Mason. Clubs: Newark, Frontiers International, Newark Downtown. Author: The Labor Management Manpower Training Project, 1966. Home: 1436 Hemlock St NW Washington DC 20012 Office: 1832 Jefferson Pl NW Washington DC 20036

MERCHANT, DONALD JOSEPH, scientist; b. Biltmore, N.C., Sept. 7, 1921; s. Oscar Lowell and Bess (Clark) M.; A.B., Berea Coll., 1942; M.S., U. Mich., 1947, Ph.D., 1950; m. Marian Adelaide Yeager, May 31, 1943; children—Nancy Adele, Barry Scott, Karen Ruth. Instr. bacteriology U. Mich., 1948-51, asst. prof., 1951-58, asso. prof. microbiology, 1958-64, prof., 1964-69; dir. W. Alton Jones Cell Sci. Center, Lake Placid, N.Y., 1969-72; prof. microbiology U. Vt., 1969-72; prof., chmn. dept. microbiology and cell biology Eastern Va. Med. Sch., Norfolk, 1973—. Cons. research lab. U.S. VA Hosp., Ann Arbor, Mich., 1954-62, process devel. div. U.S. Army Biol. Labs., Ft. Detrick, Md., 1966-68; mem. sci. adv. bd. Found. for Research on Nervous System, Boston, 1965-69, Masonic Med. Research Lab., Utica, N.Y., 1971—; mem. adv. com. to animal cell culture collection Am. Type Culture Collection, 1966-70; mem. prostatic cancer task force NCI, 1972—. Bd. dirs. N.Y. State div. Am. Cancer Soc., 1972. Mem. Portage Trails council Chippewa dist. Boy Scouts Am., 1965-67; mem. pub. health sect. Detroit Office Civil Def., 1958-62. Bd. dirs. Northeastern N.Y. Ednl. TV. Served with AUS, 1944-46. Mem. Tissue Culture Assn. (pres. 1964-68), Am. Soc. Microbiology (mem. council 1968), A.A.A.S., Soc. for Exptl. Biology and Medicine, Am., Internat. socs. cell biology, N.Y. Acad. Sci., Sigma Xi, Phi Kappa Phi. Author: (with R.H. Kahn, W.H. Murphy) Handbook of Cell and Organ Culture, 1960, 2d edit., 1964. Home: 2433 Spindrift Rd Virginia Beach VA 23451 Office: Eastern Va Med Sch 358 Mowbray Arch Norfolk VA 23507

MERCHANT, WALTER MAYFIELD, orgn. exec.; b. Haskell, Tex., Feb. 1, 1927; s. Walter Herbert and Gladys Adelia (Mayfield) M.; student Southwestern U., 1944-45, 46-47; B.A., U. Tex., 1949; m. Charles Rhea Blocker, Nov. 26, 1947; 1 dau., Donna Rhea. Incorporator, sec. Am. Coll. Musicians, Austin, Tex., 1947-51; salesman Western Auto Co., Austin, 1951-54; owner Self-Merchant's Service Stas., Austin, 1954-59; owner-operator Self-Merchant's Student House for U. Tex. Boys, 1959-62; sales Prudential Life Ins. Co., Austin, 1961-64; editor, v.p. pub. relations, chmn. account schedule Am. Coll. Musicians, 1962—; incorporator Coll. Aid Agy., Austin, sec.-treas., 1969—, editor Piano Guild Notes, 1964—. Served with USNR, 1944-45. Named to Hall of Fame, Am. Coll. Musicians, 1969. Mem. Tex. Ex's, Kappa Alpha. Methodist (treas, 1950-54, mem. bd. 1950—, pres. Sunday sch. class 1969—). Home: 5801 Marilyn Dr Austin TX 78731 Office: 808 Rio Grande St Austin TX 78767

MERCIECA, CHARLES, educator; b. Malta, Feb. 3, 1933; s. Carmel and Julia (Brincat) M.; came to U.S., 1961, naturalized, 1971; A.B. in English, Loyola Coll., Malta, 1955; A.B. in Philosophy, Istituto Filosofico, Milan, Italy, 1958; M.S. in Sch. Adminstrn., Kan. State U., 1964; B.S. in Social Work, St. Louis U., 1965; Ph.D. in Social Founds., U. Kan., 1966; D.D., U. Remo (Nigeria), 1973; m. Sherry Jean Watson, May 28, 1970; 1 dau., Juliette Ruth. Instr. elementary teaching Loyola Coll., Malta, 1951-55; instr., supr. St. Aloysius' Coll., Malta, 1958-61; tchr. St. Marys (Kan.) Pub. High Sch., 1962-64; asso. prof. Chgo. State U., 1966; asso. prof. Cal. State U., Fresno, 1967; prof. edn. Ala. A. and M. U., Huntsville, 1967—, dir. Center for Intercultural Studies, 1971—. Named African Chief of Idarne, Nigeria, 1973. Fellow Philosophy Edn. Soc.; mem. Internat. Edn. Assn. (pres. Ala. 1970-73), Soc. Profs. Edn., Am. Assn. U. Profs., Internat. Council Edn. for Tchrs., Comparative and Internat. Edn. Soc., Internat. Assn. Educators for World Peace (founder 1969), Delta Tau Kappa (U.S. chancellor 1968—). Contbr. articles to profl. jours. Home: 3713 Fox Trail Circle NW Huntsville AL 35810

MEREDITH, OWEN NICHOLS, pub. relations ofcl.; b. Etowah, Tenn., Mar. 27, 1924; s. Owen Habner and Ora (Nichols) M.; B.A., U. Va., 1946; postgrad. Fla. State U., 1949, U. Mo., 1950, Alliance Francaise (Paris), 1951; M.A., Syracuse U., 1952; Editor, Circuit Rider, sub-features editor Together mag. Meth. Pub. House, Nashville, Chgo., 1953-57; pub. information dir. Nasvhile-Davidson County chpt. A.R.C., 1957-70; dir. Tenn. State Mus., Nashville, 1970-72; owner, mgr. Gazetteer Typesetters, Nashville, 1973-74; pub. info. dir. Nashville-Davidson County chpt. A.R.C., 1974—. Sec., Tenn. Exec. Residence Preservation Found. Mem. Inter-Mus. Council of Nashville and Davidson County (pres. 1970-72), Tenn. Assn. Museums (arrangements chmn. 1971 state conv.), Confederate Meml. Lit. Soc. (Tenn. regent 1972—). Address 413 Chesterfield Av Nashville TN 37212

MEREDITH, WENDELL CLARK, lawyer; b. Alcoa, Tenn., Mar. 26, 1942; s. George Clifton and Helen Mae (Moody) M.; student U. Tenn., 1960-63; A.B., Emory U., 1966, J.D., 1966; m. Rosalyn Bible, Apr. 18, 1964; children—George Mark, Joan Elizabeth. Admitted to Tenn. bar, 1967; mem. Joyce, Andersen, Wood & Meredith and predecessor firm, Oak Ridge 1967—, partner, 1970—. Mem. Oak Ridge Charter Commn., 1972—. Named outstanding young man of year Oak Ridge C. of C., 1972. Mem. Tenn., Ga., Anderson County (pres. 1970) bar assns. Elk. Club: Oak Ridge Country. Home: 106 Normandy Rd Oak Ridge TN 37830 Office: Town Hall Oak Ridge TN 37830

MERGELER, HANS DANIEL, computer-graphics co. exec.; b. Dortmund, Germany, Aug. 14, 1932; s. Hans and Gertrud (Kreutzer) M.; came to U.S., 1956, naturalized, 1964; B.A., U. Wuerzburg, (Germany), 1952; postgrad. U. Wis., 1953, U. Adelaide (South Australia), 1955, So. Methodist U., 1973; m. Ingrid R. Misterek, Aug. 14, 1955; children—Sylvia, Robert. Typographer, Milw. Jour., 1956-62; owner Hanin Photographer, Dallas, 1962-67; v.p., gen. mgr. Computer Composition, 1967-70; v.p. Cybergraphics, Inc., Dallas, 1972—. Asst. scoutleader Circle Ten council Boy Scouts Am., 1968-73. Contbr. to profl. publs. in field. Home: 8421 Hunnicut St Dallas TX 75228 Office: 3727 Dilido 106 Dallas TX 75228

MERIDA, FREDERICK AUSTIN, art dealer; b. Indpls., Mar. 10, 1936; s. Arthur and Lelia Mae (Bristol) M.; student Kansas City Art Inst., 1954-57, New Sch. Social Scis., 1957-59, (Max Beckmann fellow) Bklyn. Mus. Sch., 1957-59; m. Margaret Louise Braden, June 11, 1962; 1 son, Frederick James Craven. Asst. dir. Ky. Guild Artists and Craftsman Train, Berea, 1963; dir. Corner Gallery, Anchorage, Ky., 1964-65, Merida Gallery, Louisville, 1965-69, Frame House Gallery, Inc., Louisville, 1969—. Lectr., U. Louisville, 1969. Served with AUS, 1959-61. Fulbright fellow, 1959. Editor, pub. Art Gallery Guide Louisville, 1968-69. Home: 1278 Bassett Av Louisville KY 40204 Office: Frame House Gallery 110 E Market St Louisville KY 40202

MERIN, SIDNEY JULIUS, psychologist; b. Altoona, Pa., Jan. 22, 1927; s. Morris and Lillian (Foreman) M.; B.S., Pa. State U., 1950, Ph.D., 1956, M.A., Temple U., 1952; m. Arlene R. Merrow, Dec. 31, 1945; children—Cheryl Ann, Debra Kay, Michele Lee, Jeffrey Michael. Psychol. asst. Psychol. Clinic, Temple U., 1950-51; psychol. intern Elgin (Ill.) State Hosp., 1952; psychologist Child Guidance Clinic St. Petersburg, Fla., 1953-54; psychol. asst., asst. supr. Psychol. Clinic, Pa. State U., 1954-55; clin. psychologist Child Guidance Clinic, St. Petersburg, 1955-56; staff psychologist Byron Harless & Assos., Tampa, Fla., 1956-60; sr. psychologist Samuel G. Hibbs, M.D. & Assos., Tampa, 1960-64; pvt. practice as clin. psychologist, Tampa, 1964—. Cons. to Clearwater Adult Mental Health Clinic, 1961—, Reading Edn. and Devel. Clinic, 1962—, dir. Ednl. Services Clinic; faculty U. South Fla., 1962—; dir. psychology, pres. Clin. Center for Reading and Learning, Inc. Mem. profl. services com. Community Resources Council; co-chmn. Mayor's Com. to Investigate Civil Service Practices, 1969. Bd. dirs. Hillsborough County Assn. Mental Health, Inter Profl. Family Council. Served with AUS, 1945-46; ETO. Diplomate Am. Bd. Examiners Profl. Psychology. Mem. Am., Fla. (pres. 1970-71, chmn. standards and ethics com.), Tampa Bay (pres. 1957, chmn. standards and ethics com.) psychol. assns., Council on Exceptional Children, Council on Family Relations, Hillsborough County Soc. Clin. Psychologists, Internat. Acad. Law and Sci., Fla. Bd. Examiners Psychology, Sigma Alpha Eta, Phi Delta Kappa. Contbr. articles to profl. jours. Research in psychol. factors in identical twins, wives of men on hazardous duty, psychol. and psychiat. influence in ct. decisions regarding child custody. Home: 4509 San Rafael St Tampa FL 33609 Office: 41 Davis Blvd Tampa FL 33606

MERIWETHER, CHARLES MINOR, drug co. exec.; b. Memphis, Feb. 15, 1911; s. Charles Minor and Leslie Allen (Stevens) M.; student U. Tenn., 1932; LL.B., Cumberland U., 1933; J.D., Samford U., 1969; m. Beverly Alston, June 7, 1939; children—Leslie Ann (Mrs. Albert M. Shuler, Jr.), Beverly (Mrs. Frank Lockridge, Jr.), Charles Minor. Engaged in ins. law and ins. mgmt., Memphis, 1933-42, in retail and wholesale drug bus., Birmingham, Ala., 1944-58; dir. finance, Ala., 1958-61; bd. dirs. Export-Import Bank Washington, 1961-65; v.p. Dewberry Drug Co., Inc., Birmingham, Ala., 1965—. Pres. Ala. Ednl. Authority, 1958-61, Ala. Hwy. Authority, 1958-61; chmn. investment com. Tchr. Retirement Fund and Employees Retirement Fund, Ala., 1958-61; dir. Ala. Adjustment Bd., 1958-61. Chmn. dirs. Ala. chpt. Nat. Multiple Sclerosis Soc., 1958-59. Served with U.S. Mcht. Marine, 1942-43. Mem. Birmingham City Salesmen's Club, Phi Gamma Delta. Methodist. Odd Fellow. Clubs: Nat. Press (Washington); Birmingham Downtown, Birmingham Relay House. Home: 4331 Little River Rd Birmingham AL 35213 Office: City Fed Bldg Birmingham AL 35203

MERIWETHER, RICHARD EARL, hosp. adminstr.; b. Clarksville, Tenn., July 31, 1920; s. William Douglas and Doris (Crosman) M.; B.S., Austin Peay State U., 1943; M.S., Northwestern U., 1959; m. Pauline Keller, Jan. 30, 1949; children—William Walton, Margaret Ann, John Barker. Farmer, nr. Guthrie, Ky., 1946-50; buyer Covington Grain Co., Guthrie, 1950-52; office mgr. Tenn. Roofing Co., Clarksville, 1952-55; asst. adminstr. Western State Hosp., Hopkinsville, Ky., 1955-57, adminstr., 1957-62; dir. hosp. adminstrn. Ky. Dept. Mental Health, Louisville, 1962-65; adminstr. Muhlenberg Community Hosp., Greenville, Ky., 1965-70, Bowling Green (Ky.)-Warren County Hosp., 1971—. Mem. adv. council Ohio Valley Regional Med. Program, 1966-73; dir. Western Ky. Hosp. Services, Inc., 1968-70; mem. bd. Blue Cross Hosp. Plan, 1968-69. Mem. adv. bd. Freed-Hardeman Coll., Henderson, Tenn., 1961-68; bd. dirs. Mid-Western Mental Health Mental Retardation, Madisonville, Ky., 1965-69, vice chmn., 1968. Served with USAF, 1943-46. Recipient William A. Wycoff Meml. award Twin Lakes dist. Ky. Hosp. Assn., 1967. Mem. Greenville C. of C. (sec., treas. 1968-70, pres. 1967-68), S.A.R. (chpt. pres. 1969), Am. Coll. Hosp. Adminstrs., Nat. Assn. Hosp. Purchasing Agts. (regional v.p. 1961), Ky. Hosp. Assn. (trustee 1966-68, pres. 1968-69), Nat. League Nursing, Ky. League Nursing (mem. bd. 1962). Kiwanian (pres. 1969). Contbr. articles to profl. jours. Home: 1412 Scottsville Rd Bowling Green KY 42101 Office: PO Box 56 Bowling Green KY 42101

MERLO, THOMAS JOHN, public accountant; b. Scranton, Pa., Dec. 3, 1930; s. Vito and Mildred (Gatto) M.; student U. Scranton, 1953-54; B.B.A., U. Miami, 1957; m. Ann Piccioni, May 18, 1957; children—Robin, Thomas, Kim Marie, William, Lisa. Utilities cons. Morgan, Altemus & Barrs, Miami, Fla., 1963-66; dir. fiscal affairs Jackson Meml. Hosp., Miami, 1966-68; dir. internal auditing Dade County, Miami, Fla., 1968-71; sr. partner Thomas J. Merlo, C.P.A., Miami, 1971—; utilities cons.; dir. Nat. Properties, Inc., Miami, Biscayne Bank. Chmn. Dade County Employees United Fund Campaign, 1968-69; bd dir. Dade County United Fund, 1969—. Served with USN, 1949-52. Mem. Am. Inst. C.P.A.'s, Fla. Inst. C.P.A.'s, Internal Auditors Assn. Fla., Nat. Assn. Accountants, Unico Southwest (pres. 1971). Clubs: Serra (treas.), Southwest Lions (treas. 1962). Home: 2010 Alhambra Circle Coral Gables FL 33134 Office: 2138 Biscayne Blvd Miami FL 33137

MEROS, GEORGE NICHOLAS, lawyer; b. Abbeville, S.C., Mar. 21, 1923; s. Nicholas G. and Pearl (Peterson) M.; B.S., U. Fla., 1950, LL.B., 1953; m. Anne Shropshire, Nov. 30, 1946; children—Peter, Dede, George Nicholas, John. Admitted to Fla. bar, 1953, since practiced in St. Petersburg; mem. firm Meros, Wells, Edman, Meros & Rouse and predecessor firms, 1956—; pres. Jebb, Inc., St. Petersburg; lectr. Stetson Law Sch.; dep. commr. Fla. Indsl. Commn., 1953-58. Bd. dirs. Mound Park Hosp. Served with AUS, 1941-45. Mem. Am., Fla. bar assns., Com. of 100, Alpha Tau Omega, Phi Delta Phi. Clubs: Lakewood Country, St. Petersburg Yacht. Kiwanian. Contbr. articles to profl. jours. Home: 4627 Sunrise Dr S St Petersburg FL 33705 Office: 432 7th St S St Petersburg FL 33701

MERRELL, CURTIS HARLAN, supt. schs.; b. Crawfordsville, Ark., Feb. 18, 1935; s. William and Golda (Barks) M.; B.A., Ouachita Baptist U., 1957; M.S., La. State U., 1960; Ed.D., U. Ark., 1969; m. Virginia Ramona Moody, Aug. 28, 1954; children—Scott Carleton, Stephen Craig, Drew Christopher. Grad. teaching asst. La. State U., 1959-60; coach, athletic dir., asst. prin., math. tchr. Central High Sch., Helena-West Helena, Ark., 1960-67; head resident Pomfret Hall, U. Ark., 1967-69; dir. S.E. Ark. Ednl. Service Center, Monticello, 1969-71; supt. schs., Monticello, 1971—. Chmn. Phillips County Assn. Crippled Children; pres. Drew County Mental Retardation Council, 1972-73. Served with AUS, 1957-59. Named Outstanding Young Educator, Helena-W. Helena, 1966. Mem. Nat., Ark. (chmn. legislative com. dept. classroom tchrs. 1962-64) edn. assns., Am., Ark. assns. sch. adminstrs., Ark., S.E. Ark. sch. study councils, S.E. Ark. Schoolmasters, Drew County C. of C., Phi Delta Kappa. Baptist. Club: Monticello Country. Home: 211 McKnight Dr Monticello AR 71655 Office: 136 W College St Monticello AR 71655

MERRICK, EUNICE PEACOCK (MRS. GEORGE E. MERRICK), civic worker; b. Coconut Grove, Fla.; d. Alfred and Lillian (Frow) Peacock; student pvt. and pub. schs.; m. George Edgar Merrick, Feb. 5, 1916. Treas. George E. Merrick, Inc., real estate, 1934-42, pres., 1942-45. Active in establishing Dade County Schs., Coral Gables, 1922-25. Recipient Book of Golden Deeds, Exchange Club Coral Gables, 1957. Mem. Hist. Soc. So. Fla., Fla. Hist. Soc., Nat. League Am. Pen Women (patroness), Sigma Alpha Iota (patroness). Christian Scientist. Clubs: Coral Gables Woman's (charter mem., dir.), Coral Gables Garden (past pres.). George E. Merrick, the original owner, founder Coral Gables, Fla. Home: 1015 Coral Way Coral Gables FL 33134

MERRILL, MARY ANN, biologist, author; b. Toledo, Dec. 10, 1930; d. George L. and Dorothy (Borton) Merrill; B.A., U. Ariz., 1953; M.A., U. Miami (Fla.), 1957; grad. De Vry Tech. Inst., 1966, Locksmithing Inst., 1969. Operator marine biol. and fresh water labs., Ray, Ind. and Coral Gables, Fla., 1953; tchr. Shenendoah Jr. High Sch., Miami, 1958-59, Exmoor Sch., Miami, 1959-60; exhibited in group shows at Lowe Art Gallery, Miami, 1955—. Fellow Internat. Oceanographic Found. (life); mem. Audubon Soc., D.A.R., Toledo Art Mus., Lowe Art Gallery, Film Soc., Am. Radio Relay League, Delta Delta Delta. Methodist. Author: Angels & Corners, 1958; Hermit, 1965; Chaborus, 1965; Shadows, 1969; Synathidae, Vols. I, II, III, 1968-70; Melon Patch, 1969; Survey, 1969; New Mama for Christmas, 1969; Diary of a Lady Spy, 1970; Toledo to Miami by Train, 1970; Richard Basehart, Vols. I-IV, 1970. Home: 1210 S Alhambra Circle Coral Gables FL 33146 Office: 372 Spitzer Bldg Toledo OH 43604

MERRILL, PATRICIA KOKEN (MRS. JACK H. MERRILL), civic worker; b. Toronto, Ont., Can., Jan. 12, 1926; d. Frank W. and Violet (Vernon) Koken; B.J., Ohio State U., 1948; m. Jack Hilton Merrill, Aug. 7, 1948; children—Jeffrey Leeson, Lisa Marie. Adviser, Kappa Delta, 1948-59, province pres., 1960-63, nat. press dir., 1963-65, nat. v.p., 1965-67, nat. pres., 1967-71, mem. evaluation com., 1972-73, membership chmn. Cleve. chpt. 1962-63, v.p., 1963-64, pres., 1964-65; den mother Cub Scouts Am., 1961-63, area adviser to den mothers, 1962-63; sec. Ohio State U. Alumnae Assn., Toledo, 1958; room mother Avon (O.) Elementary Sch., 1960-61, Crestwood Elementary Sch., Richmond, 1970; room mother Rocky River (O.) Elementary Sch., 1963-64, chmn. ways and means, 1965-66; del. Va. Congress Parents and Tchrs. Conv., 1971; 3d alternate area adviser, for 35 colls., N.C., Va., W. Va., chmn. quota-limitation com. Nat. Panhellenic Conf., 1971—. Del., Chesterfield County Republican Conv., 1971, 72, 73, Va. Rep. Conv. 1971, 72; canvass chmn. Crestwood Precinct Rep. Com., 1971, 72; precinct chmn. Crestwood Rep. party; mem. Chesterfield County Rep. Com., 1971-74. Conglist (asst. dir. Bible sch. 1957-58, sec. Couple's Club 1958—). Home: 1620 Creekside Rd Richmond VA 23235

MERRILL, WARNER JAY, JR., govt. ofcl.; b. Springfield, Ill., Jan. 27, 1923; s. Warner Jay and Ida Virginia (Millard) M.; B.A., U. Del., 1947; Ph.D., Ohio State U., 1956; m. Colleen Bryan, Dec. 23, 1945; children—David B., Marsha J. Staff statistician Am. Power Jet Co., Ridgefield, N.J., 1951-53; asso. mathematician IBM, Endicott, N.Y., 1953-56; statistician Gen. Electric Co., Schenectady, 1956-61; prof. mgmt. Rensselaer Poly. Inst., Troy, 1961-64; mgmt. scientist Dunlap & Assos., Darien, Conn., 1964-65; mem. tech. staff Hughes Aircraft Co., Washington, 1965-66; sr. asso. Planning Research Corp., 1966-68; operations research analyst Nat. Inst. Law Enforcement and Criminal Justice, Law Enforcement Assistance Adminstrn., 1968—. Lectr. George Washington U., 1968-70; adj. prof. Am. U., 1969-72. Mem. law enforcement adv. group Nat. Commn. on Productivity, 1973. Served with AUS, 1943-46. Mem. Am. Statis. Assn., Inst. Mgmt. Scis., Sigma Xi, Kappa Alpha. Contbr. to profl. publs. in field. Home: 9904 Inglemere Dr Bethesda MD 20034 Office: Dept Justice LEAA Washington DC 20530

MERRIMAN, JERRY JOHNSON, religious ofcl.; b. Lufkin, Tex., Jan. 10, 1939; s. Gratton Johnson and Audrey Faye (Beasley) M.; B.S., (Baseball scholar), Miss. State U., 1961; M.R.E., Southwestern Bapt. Theol. Sem., 1963; postgrad. Southwestern Bapt. Sem., 1965, European Bapt. Sem., 1967; m. Rhonda Jean Cox, June 27, 1970; 1 son, John David. Religious youth counselor Christian Life Crusade, 1963-69; dir. Bapt. Student Union, Miss. State U., Mississippi State, 1969—. Soloist for religious, sch., civic groups, 1963—. Counselor, tribal dir. Camp Rockmont for Boys, Black Mountain, N.C., summers 1961, 66. Mem. Miss. State Alumni Assn. Baptist (deacon 1971—, mem. long range planning com., bldg. com.). Club: M (Miss. State). Author: (with Chester E. Swor) The Teenage Slant, 1963, Youth at Bat, 1968, To Enrich Each Day, 1969. Home: PO Box 4035 Mississippi State MS 39762

MERRITT, HARRY WARNER, JR., chem. engr.; b. Houston, Aug. 25, 1934; s. Harry Warner and Marian Elizabeth (Farrenkopf) M.; B.S., Yale, 1956, U. Tex., 1961; M.S. in Chem. Engring., U. Minn., 1963; Ph.D., U. Okla., 1966. With E.I. du Pont de Nemours and Co. Inc., 1956-71, research engr., Wilmington, Del., 1966-71; sr. research engr. Houston Research, Inc., 1971-73; sr. devel. engr. Ciba-Geigy Corp., Mobile, Ala., 1973—. Instr. math. Houston Community Coll., 1972—. Registered profl. engr., Tex. Mem. Am. Inst. Chem. Engrs., Sigma Xi, Tau Beta Pi, Phi Lambda Upsilon. Home: 1811 Sunset Blvd Houston TX 77005 Office: Ciba-Geigy Corp McIntosh AL 36553

MERRITT, LUCIAN GERALD, instrument mfg. dir.; b. Waco, Tex., Aug. 8, 1936; s. Lucian Henry and Hester Novel (Perdue) M.; B.B.A., Baylor U., 1958, M.S., 1960; postgrad. St. Mary's U., 1960-62; m. Tommie Pierce, Dec. 22, 1956; 1 dau., Lezli Diane. Mgr. div. purchasing, space and information systems div. N.Am. Aviation, Inc., Downey, Cal., 1962-67; dir. material services Tracor, Inc., Austin, Tex., 1967-71, dir. mfg. operations, 1971—; dir. Merritt, Inc. Past pres. Austin Gideon Camp; past bd. dirs. Campus Crusade for Christ. Served from 2d lt. to 1st lt. USAF, 1959-62; capt. Res. Mem. Am. Mgmt. Assn., Nat. Purchasing Mgmt. Assn., Gideons, Order of Artus, Alpha Chi. Mason. Home: 100 Wallis St Austin TX 78746 Office: 6500 Tracor Lane Austin TX 78721

MERRITT, MARION WILLIAM, retail store exec.; b. Belton, S.C., Apr. 20, 1921; s. Marion Shafter and Nell Blyth (Williamson) M.; B.S., The Citadel, 1943; m. Inez Hill Bussey, Dec. 4, 1943; children—Marion William, Kathy (Mrs. Harry Stinson), Inez. With Winn-Dixie Stores, Inc., Greenville, S.C., 1946-55, Jacksonville, Fla., 1955-58, Louisville, 1958-63, div. mgr., v.p., Atlanta, 1969—. Served with AUS, 1942-45. Decorated Bronze Star medal. Home: 3825 Dumbarton Rd NW Atlanta GA 30327 Office: 5400 Fulton Indsl Blvd Atlanta GA 30336

MERRITT, PAUL BURWELL, ins. exec.; b. Chincoteague, Va., Dec. 23, 1924; s. Leslie Uphsur and Aletia (Tarr) M.; student LaSalle U., 1949-53; m. Helen Mae Potts, June 3, 1943; 1 son, Gregory Paul. Comptroller, Naval Air Sta., Fed. Civil Service, 1947-59; owner Paul B. Merritt Co., Chincoteague, 1959—; pres. Pony Penninl Enterprises, Inc., 1962—, also dir.; pres. Misty Meadows Devel., 1970—. Vice-mayor Chincoteague, 1952-54, mem. Accomack County Bd. Suprs., 1963—. Served with USNR, 1943-45; PTO. Mem. V.F.W. (comdr. 1949-52), Chincoteague C. of C. (exec. sec. 1953-57, 63-68). Democrat. Baptist (Sunday sch. supt. 1957-71). Mason, Kiwanian. Home: 111 Maddox Blvd Chincoteague VA 23336 Office: 201 Maddox Blvd Chincoteague VA 23336

MERRY, FRANCES ROBINSON (MRS. ERNEST BRISCOE MERRY, JR.), civic worker; b. Jacksonville, Fla., May 15, 1914; d. Philip Frank and Lorene (Youngblood) Robinson; student Ward-Belmont Sch., Nashville, 1930-32, Mary Baldwin Coll., 1932-33; m. Ernest Briscoe Merry, Jr., Nov. 1, 1933; children—Frances Robinson (Mrs. George Bryan Simkins), Ernest Briscoe III, Philip Robinson, Anne Somers. Bd. dirs. Girl Scouts U.S.A., Augusta, Ga. area, 1938-40; bd. dirs. Jr. League, 1936-41, 50-53; pres. Episcopal Day Sch. Assn., 1951-52; with Gray Ladies A.R.C., 1942-44; bd. dirs. Augusta Assembly, 1955-56; chmn. meml. petit point furnishing St. Paul's Episcopal Ch., 1957-66, dir. Jr. Dau. King, 1954-55, pres. Women's Aux., 1943-44. pres. Augusta Symphony Orch. Guild, 1961-64; bd. dirs. Augusta Symphony and Historic Augusta, Inc.; trustee Augusta Prep. Sch., 1961-71. Clubs: Augusta Country; Town and Country Garden (pres. 1951-52, 66-67). Pinnacle. Home: 16 Indian Cove Rd Augusta GA 30904

MERSCH, EDWARD BERNARD, surgeon; b. Covington, Ky., Nov. 20, 1908; s. Bernard H. and Mary C. (Kruetzman) M.; B.S., Xavier U., 1931; M.B., U. Cin., 1935, M.D., 1936; m. Margaret W. Rettig, Sept. 11, 1940; 1 dau., Mary Margaret. Surg. resident Louisville Gen. Hosp., 1936-39; asst. surg. clinician Cin. Gen. Hosp., 1940-53; practice medicine specializing in surgery, Covington, 1953—; mem. surg. staff St. Elizabeth Hosp., 1940—, Booth Meml. Hosp., 1940—, St. Luke's Hosp., Ft. Thomas, Ky., 1954—. Fellow A.C.S.; mem. A.M.A., Ky. Med. Assn. (pres. 1957-58), Southeastern Surg. Congress, Cin. Surg. Soc. Lion (past pres. Covington). Club: Art (Cin.). Home: 3261 Turkeyfoot Rd S Fort Mitchell KY 41017 Office: 722 Scott St Covington KY 41011

MERSKY, ROY MARTIN, lawyer, educator; s.; Irving and Rose (Mendelson) M.; B.S., U. Wis., 1948, J.D., 1952; M.A. in L.S., 1953; m. Deena Hersh, Feb. 3, 1951; children—Alisa Judith, Deborah Ann, Ruth Elizabeth. Admitted Wis. bar, 1952, Tex. bar, 1970; practiced law, Wis., 1952-54; municipal reference librarian, Milw., 1953-54; asst. librarian Yale, 1954-59; dir. Washington State Law Library, 1959-63; exec. sec. Washington Jud. Council, 1959-63; commr. Wash. Supreme Ct. Reports, 1959-63; prof. law, law librarian U. Colo., 1963-65, U. Tex. 1965—; acting dir. Jewish Nat. and U. Library, Hebrew U., Jerusalem, 1972-73. Bd. dirs. Tex. bd. Am. Civil Liberties Union. Served with AUS, 1944-46. Decorated Bronze Star Medal. Mem. Am., Wis. bar assns., Tex. Library Assn., State Bar Tex., Am. Assn. Law Schs., Am. Assn. Law Libraries, Am. Judicature Soc., Am. Soc. Legal History, A.L.A., Spl. Libraries Assn., N.A.A.C.P., Am. Assn. U. Profs., Tex. Assn. Coll. Tchrs. Jewish religion. Author: Louis Dembitz Brandeis, 1856-1941; A Bibliography, 1958; Water Law Bibliography 1947-65; Sources Book on U.S. Water and Irrigation Studies, 1966; Law Books for Non-Law Libraries and Laymen, A Bibliography, 1966; Index to Periodical Articles Related to Law, 1970; (with others) Fundamentals of Legal Research. Editor publs. in field. Contbr. articles legal jours. Book review editor Law Library Jour., 1965-72, Criminal Law Bull., 1972—; asso. editor Bankers Law Jour., Real Estate Law Jour., Securities Regulation Law Jour. Cons. various law libraries. Home: 1419 Gaston Av Austin TX 78703

MERTINS, CHRISTIAN CARL, JR., banker; b. Pensacola, Fla., July 10, 1926; s. Christian Carl and Helen (Bond) M.; B.S., U. Fla., 1950; m. Dorothy Gertrude Nobles, Jan. 4, 1952; children—Clifton Karl, Laura Marie, David Laurence. Mgmt. trainee Newport Industries, Inc., Pensacola, 1950-51; v.p., cashier First Bank & Trust Co., Pensacola, 1953—, also dir.; pres. Barnett Bank Pensacola, 1953—. Dir. Fla. Sch. of Banking. Pres. Jr. Achievement of Pensacola. Bd. dirs. Children's Home Soc. W. Fla., Children's Home Soc. of Fla., Pensacola Port Authority; bd. dirs. Children's Home Soc. West Fla., pres., 1973-74. Served with AUS, 1944-46, 51-53. Mem. Assn. for Bank Audit, Control and Operations, Unit Bankers W. Fla., Pensacola C. of C. (pres. 1973), Scabbard and Blade, Pi Kappa Alpha. Clubs: Exchange, Pensacola Country. Home: 777 Tanglewood Dr Pensacola FL 32503 Office: 100 W Garden St Pensacola FL 32502

MESH, HOWARD ALAN, accountant; b. Chgo., Oct. 3, 1933; s. William B. and Rose (Kanter) M.; B.B.A., U. Miami, 1955; m. Sandra Ann Rosen, June 26, 1955; children—Ronna Fern, Scott Everett. Sr. accountant Pentland, Purvis, Keller & Co., 1955-60; pvt. practice accounting, 1960-61; partner H.N. Miller & Co., 1961-63, Miller, Beer & Co., 1963-68; mgr. Peat, Marwick, Mitchell & Co., Miami, Fla., 1969-70; sr. partner Mesh, Dick & Baum, 1970—. Mem. leaders div. United Jewish Appeal, 1966—. Bd. dirs. United Fund of Dade County; bd. dirs., treas. V.I.P. Sch., Inc. Served with AUS, 1956-58. Mem. Am., Fla. (chmn. com. on mgmt. services 1967-68, chpt. v.p.) insts. C.P.A.'s, Accounting Soc. U. Miami (founder, charter pres.). Jewish religion (dir., youth commr. congregation). Club: Optimist of Southwest Miami (charter, pres. 1961-62). Home: 12240 SW 89th Av Miami FL 33156 Office: 8740 N Kendall Dr Miami FL 33156

MESSENGER, STEVE, accountant; b. Friona, Tex., Sept. 24, 1923; s. George C. and Ruth (Kirk) M.; B.B.A., West Tex. State U., 1953; m. Narcia Evelyn Finney, July 18, 1954; children—Michael Brent, Jay Corwin, Troy Wayne. Self-employed accountant, Friona, 1953-66; sr. partner firm Steve Messenger & Co., Hereford, also Friona, 1966-70; partner Kernaghan, Harvey & Co., Dallas, also Friona, Hereford, Amarillo, 1970-72; with Harvey, Messenger & Co., 1973—. Gen. chmn. United Fund, 1966, city chmn., 1967—; mem. Amarillo Area Estate Planning Council, 1966—, treas., 1974—. Bd. dirs. Greater S.W. Music Festival, 1973—; mem. council Tex. Panhandle Library System, 1973—. Recipient Golden Rule award United Fund. C.P.A., Tex. Mem. Am. Inst. C.P.A.'s, Tex. (state dir. Panhandle chpt. 1971-72), Amarillo socs. C.P.A.'s, Accounting Research Soc., Tex. Tech. Tax Inst. (v.p. 1969), Friona (dir., sec. 1960-61, v.p. 1961-62, 68-69, pres. 1969-70), West Tex. (mem. legislative, ednl. coms. 1970—) chambers commerce, Tex. Cattle Feeders Assn. Baptist. Mason, Lion (pres. 1969, Hi-Plains Eye Bank dir. 1965-70). Home: 6203 Jameson St Amarillo TX 79106 Office: Am Nat Bank Amarillo TX 79101

MESSER, H(ARRY) DONALD, mgmt. and tech. cons. co. exec.; b. N.Y.C., Apr. 19, 1931; s. Harry Andrew and Sue (Metzger) M.; B.S., N.Y. U., 1952; M.S., Cornell U., 1955; Dr. Engring., Johns Hopkins, 1963; m. Jeanine Louise Aline Sizorn, Mar. 28, 1956; children—Michael Alan, Philip Daniel. Physicist, Hughes Aircraft Co., Los Angeles, 1954-55; sr. engr. Martin Co., Balt., 1957-61; mgr. systems engring. Fairchild-Hiller Corp., Hagerstown, Md., 1961-63; prin. scientist Booz Allen Applied Research, Inc., 1963-64, research dir., 1964-66, v.p., 1966-67; v.p. Booz Allen and Hamilton, Inc., Washington, 1967-70; v.p. Orkand Corp., Silver Spring, Md., 1970-71; pres. Messer Assos., Inc., Silver Spring, 1971—. Served with AUS, 1955-57. Mem. Operations Research Soc. Am., Inst. Mgmt. Cons. (founding), A.A.A.S. Club: University (Washington). Home: 6425 31st Pl NW Washington DC 20015 Office: 8555 16th St Silver Spring MD 20910

MESSERSMITH, LLOYD LOWELL, ret. educator; b. Francisco, Ind., Jan. 29, 1905; s. Martin Lewis and Amelia (Rogers) M.; B.A., DePauw U., 1928; M.A., Columbia, 1932; Ed.D., Ind. U., 1942; m. Fae Elizabeth Houston, Aug. 22, 1929; children—Martha Ann (Mrs. Lindsay B. Smith), Betty Jean (Mrs. James Cole), Alice Kay (Mrs. James Collins). Tchr. pub. schs., Francisco, Ind., 1922-24, Shortridge High Sch., Indpls., 1928-30; instr. history, basketball coach DePauw U., Greencastle, Ind., 1930-45; prof. phys. edn. So. Meth. U., Dallas, 1945-70. Mem. evaluation team Nat. Council Accreditation Tchr. Edn., 1965-66, Tex. Edn. Agy., 1966-67. Chmn. group work div. Council Social Agys. Dallas, 1949-50; mem. phys. edn. com. S.W. area YMCA, 1950-68; mem. adv. com. Dallas Mus. Health and Sci., 1960-68. Bd. dirs. YMCA, Dallas, 1946-56. Recipient Honor awards Ind. Assn. Health, Phys. Edn. and Recreation, 1950, So. dist., 1956, Tex. Assn. Health, Phys. Edn. and Recreation, 1956, A.A.H.P.E.R., 1961. Fellow A.A.H.P.E.R. (v.p. phys. edn. div. 1962-63, chmn. recognition awards com. 1967-69, dist. pres. 1959-61), Am. Coll. Sports Medicine, Am. Pub. Health Assn., Am. Sch. Health Assn.; mem. Ind. (pres. 1936-37), Tex. (pres. 1955-56) assns. health, phys. edn., recreation, Am. Acad. Phys. Edn., Am. Assn. U. Profs., Lambda Chi. Methodist. Author: (with others) Physical Education Handbook, 1954, 6th rev. edit., 1974. Mem. editorial com. Tex. Assn. Health, Phys. Edn., Recreation Jour., 1968-71. Contbr. articles to profl. jours. Home: 3513 Purdue St Dallas TX 75225

MESSMER, H(ERMAN) PAUL, govt. ofcl.; b. Columbus, O., Aug. 7, 1913; s. Herman L. and Doris (Fishinger) M.; B.A., B.S. in Edn., Ohio State U., 1937; m. Clara Kathryn Stuckey, May 14, 1936; children—Barbara Kay (Mrs. John L. Stevens), Lawrence P. Tchr., Fairfield Twp Schs., Huron County, O., 1937-42, supt., 1942-46; supr. counseling and services to handicapped Ohio Employment Service, Columbus, 1946-50, chief counseling, 1950-61, chief community projects Manpower Devel. and Tng., 1961-64; employment adviser, liaison officer President's Com. on Employment Handicapped, Washington, 1964-68, dep. asst. exec. sec., 1968-70, asst. exec. sec., 1970-73, dir. state relations, 1974—. Exec. dir. Ohio Worker Tng. Com., 1961-64; exec. sec. Ohio Gov.'s Com. Employment Handicapped, 1954-63. Mem. Nat. Rehab. Assn. (charter treas. Ohio; pres. job placement div. 1970; mem. bd. 1970-72), Internat. Assn. Personnel in Employment Security (past pres. Ohio), Nat. Vocational Guidance Assn., Am. Personnel and Guidance Assn., Internat. Platform Assn. Home: 6006 16th St N Arlington VA 22205 Office: President's Com on Employment of Handicapped Washington DC 20210

MESTER, JORGE, condr.; b. Mexico City, Mexico, 1935; came to U.S., 1945; studied with Jean Morel, Leonard Bernstein, Albert Wolff. Condr. concerts Mozart Festival, Lincoln Center, N.Y.C., summers 1966, 67; condr. Nat. Symphony, Mexico City, 1966, Boston Symphony, 1967, Pitts. Symphony, 1968; prin. condr. Aspen (Colo.) Music Festival, 1969, now music dir.; guest condr. Boston, New Orleans, Indpls. orchs., Japan Philharmonic, Trieste Philharmonic, Los Angeles Philharmonic; now condr., music dir. Louisville Philharmonic Soc. Home: 3200 Tucker Station Rd Louisville KY 40299 Office: 321 W Broadway Louisville KY 40202

METCALFE, ALBERT GALLATIN, JR., petroleum co. exec.; b. Greenville, Miss., Dec. 29, 1927; s. Albert Gallatin and Ruth (Reynolds) M.; B.S., Tex. A. and M. U., 1950; m. Catherine Lehnen, Apr. 7, 1951; children—Gail, Albert Gallatin III, Elizabeth. With Tidewater Oil Co., Kilgore, Tex., 1952-53, Conroe, Tex., 1954-57, Victoria, Tex., 1957-61; mgr. James G. Brown & Asso., Corpus Christi, Tex., 1961-63; with Tamarack Petroleum Co., Inc., Midland, Tex., 1963—, v.p. prodn., 1966—. Served to 1st lt. AUS, 1950-52. Registered profl. engr., Tex. Clubs: Midland Petroleum, Midland Country. Home: 1603 Gulf St Midland TX 79701 Office: 910 Bldg of the Southwest Midland TX 79701

METCALFE, JOSEPH DAVIS, constrn. co. exec.; b. Pearsall, Tex., Sept. 29, 1916; s. Joseph Davis and Mary (Hudson) M.; B.S., Tex. A. and M. U., 1937; m. Antoinette Barnwell Mazyck, Aug. 11, 1939; children—Joseph Davis, Marilyn (Mrs. Douglas L. Inhofe), John Barnwell. Engr. Ark. Natural Gas Corp., 1937-41, Bucyru-Erie Co., 1946-48; v.p. Tecon Corp., 1948-55; with Standard Industries, Inc., Tulsa, 1955—, pres., dir., 1967—; pres., dir. J.D. Metcalfe, Inc., Tulsa, 1962—. Served to lt. col. C.E., AUS, 1941-46; ETO. Decorated Bronze Star. Registered profl. engr., Okla., Tex. Mem. Assn. Gen. Contractors (br. v.p. 1967), Nat. Crushed Stone Assn. (v.p. S.W. region 1972—), Okla. Asphalt Pavement Assn. (dir. 1972—, chmn. 1974); Tulsa Indsl. Execs. Council (chmn. 1973—), Nat. Soc. Profl. Engrs. Episcopalian (vestryman 1963-66). Home: 2128 E 31st Pl Tulsa OK 74105 Office: Box 15670 Tulsa OK 74115

METHVIN, EUGENE HILBURN, editor; b. Vienna, Ga., Sept. 19, 1934; s. Claude McKee, Jr., and Madge (Hilburn) M.; B.A. cum laude, U. Ga., 1955; postgrad. Youngstown U., Am. U., George Washington U.; m. Barbara Lester, Sept. 2, 1958; children—Helen Lester, Claudia Hilburn. Reporter, Washington Daily News, 1958-60; staff writer Washington bur. Reader's Digest, 1960-64, asso. editor, 1965-71, sr. editor, 1972—. Occasional lectr. Internat. Police Acad., Fgn. Service Inst. Served with USAF, 1955-58. Mem. Phi Beta Kappa, Soc. Profl. Journalists (pres. Washington chpt. 1966-67, nat. bd. dirs. 1967-69; award for pub. service mag. journalism 1965), Sigma Nu, Phi Kappa Phi, Blue Key. Baptist. Author: The Riot Makers, 1970; The Rise of Radicalism, 1973. Home: 8111 Old Georgetown Pike McLean VA 22101 Office: 1730 Rhode Island Av NW Washington DC 20036

METHVIN, MYRON ALBERT, lawyer; b. Drew, Miss., Feb. 1, 1934; s. Martin Luther and Flora Alcie (McCain) M.; B.A., U. Miss., 1960, LL.B., 1961; diploma Def. Lang. Inst., 1963; postgrad. N.Y. U., 1964-67, Bernard M. Baruch Sch. Bus., 1966-67; 1 son, Marc Andrew. Spl. agt. FBI, 1961-66; tax specialist Alexander Grant & Co., C.P.A.'s,

Dallas, 1967-68; chief gen. accounting Army and Air Force Exchange Service, Vietnam, 1969-70; admitted to Tex. bar, 1971; mem. firm Blanchette, Shelton & James, Dallas, 1970-73; gen. counsel Coley Properties, Houston, 1973—. Served with AUS, 1954-56. Mem. Miss., Tex., Dallas bar assns., Ex-FBI Agts. Assn. Author: Love and Other Fables in the Disconnectivist Form, 1973. Home: 3333 Cummins St Houston TX 77027 Office: 3333 W Alabamo St Houston TX 77006

METKO, GERALD EARL, bus. adminstr.; b. Evanston, Ill., Oct. 23, 1930; s. John Arthur and Blanche (Heinz) M.; student Lake Forest Coll., 1948-50; B.S., No. Ill. U., 1957; postgrad. Stetson U., 1957-58; m. Ann Sumer, June 14, 1952; children—LorAnn, Scott. Asst. pub. relations mgr. Allstate Ins. Co., St. Petersburg, Fla., 1959-64; exec. dir. St. Petersburg Housing Authority, 1964-68; mgr. bus.-govt. relations and community devel. St. Petersburg Area C. of C., 1969—; devel. dir. All Childrens Hosp., 1969-71; v.p. First St. Petersburg Service Corp., 1971—. Mem. Mayor's Adv. Com. for Elimination of Slums and Blight, 1966-69; moderator, participant Gov.'s Conf. on Cities, Tallahassee, Fla., 1968; mem. Mayor's Com. for Relocation of Displaced Persons, 1966-69; mem. St. Petersburg Ann. Christmas Parade Com., 1967-68; chmn. St. Petersburg Motorcade Com. honoring President Kennedy, 1963; mem. Mayor's Green Spot Com., 1968-69; mem. Mayor's Goals Com. leading to All Am. City Award, 1973; mem. Community Alliance. Vice pres. Vis. Nurses Assn.; dir. CACEP, Presbyn. Social Ministries, Villa Maria Housing, Inc., Project Find. Neighborly Center; commr. St. Petersburg Housing Authority. Served with USNR, 1950-54. Recipient Outstanding Service award City of St. Petersburg, 1969, 71, Key to City St. Petersburg, 1968, 71. Mem. Fla. Assn. Housing and Redevel. Ofcls. (past pres.). Club: St. Petersburg Exchange (past pres.). Home: 5120 Huntington Circle NE St Petersburg FL 33703 Office: First Federal Savings & Loan Bldg 4th and Central Av St Petersburg FL 33701

METTS, DANIEL LAMAR, JR., librarian; b. Pulaski, Tenn., June 9, 1925; s. Daniel Lamar and Ruth MacMurray (Feagin) M.; A.B., Emory U., 1947, M.A., 1948, M.L.S., 1950; m. Evelyn Bates, Aug. 26, 1949; children—Martha, Catherine, Marguerite. Asst. in acquisitions Fla. State U., Tallahassee, 1950-53, head serial acquisitions, 1954-56; asst. head acquisitions Library U. Minn., St. Paul, 1956-63; librarian Mercer U., Macon, Ga., 1963—. Served with USNR, 1943-46. Mem. Southeastern, Ga. library assns., Am. Soc. Information Sci. Alpha Tau Omega. Home: 3020 Clairmont Av Macon GA 31204 Office: Stetson Memorial Library Mercer U Macon GA 31207

METZ, LEON CLAIRE, archivist, author; b. Parkersburg, W.Va., Nov. 6, 1930; s. Leon and Velma Mae (Balderson) M.; student U. Tex., 1949-69; children—Velma Marlene, Leon Samuel, Matthew Claire; m. 2d, Cheryl Lynn Schilling, June 12, 1970; 1 son, James David. Patrolman, El Paso Police Dept., 1953; deliveryman Prices Milk Co., El Paso, 1953; operator Standard Oil Co. Tex., El Paso, 1953-67; univ. archivist U. Tex., El Paso, 1967—. Cons., Suncountry Mag., El Paso, 1973—. Pres., Tex. Consortium for Microfilming Mexican Archives, 1970-74; pres. El Paso County Hist. Soc., 1971-72, El Paso Council Arts and Humanities, 1973—; mem. exec. bd. El Paso Zool. Soc., 1973-74, Soc. S.W. Archivists, 1972; treas. Mayor's Heritage Found., El Paso, 1974—; active United Fund, El Paso, 1970-73; v.p. Dowell P.T.A., El Paso, 1973. Served with USAF, 1948-52. Recipient El Paso C. of C. award, 1973. Mem. Western Writers Am., Nat. Soc. Arts and Letters, Soc. Am. Archivists, Border Regional Library Assn. Club: Westerners Corral (El Paso). Author: John Selman: Texas Gunfighter (Tex. Writers Roundup prize 1966), 1966; Dallas Stoudenmire: El Paso Marshal, 1969, Pat Garrett: The Story of A Western Lawman, 1974, also articles revs. Home: 5235 Rushing Dr El Paso TX 79924

METZGER, SIDNEY, elec. engr.; b. N.Y.C., Feb. 1, 1917; s. Julius and Molly (Gottesman) M.; B.S. in Elec. Engring., N.Y. U., 1937; M.E.E., Poly. Inst. Bklyn., 1950; m. Miriam M. Lipstein, Dec. 3, 1944; children—David, Sally (Mrs. Zachary D. Fasman), Philip. Mgr. radio relay br. Signal Corps Labs., Ft. Monmouth, N.J., 1939-45; div. head radio relay div. ITT Labs., Nutley, N.J., 1945-54; mgr. communications engring., astroelec. div. RCA, Princeton, N.J., 1954-63; asst. v.p., chief scientist Communications Satellite Corp., Washington, 1963—. Mem. joint tech. adv. council I.E.E.E.-Electronics Industries Assn., com. telecommunications Nat. Acad. Engrs. Fellow I.E.E.E.; asso. fellow Am. Inst. Aeros. and Astronautics, Sigma Xi, Tau Beta Pi. Home: 9505 Barroll Lane Kensington MD 20795 Office: 950 L'Enfant Plaza Washington DC 20024

METZGER, SIDNEY M., bishop; b. Fredericksburg, Tex., July 11, 1902; s. Francis and Ida (Dietz) M.; student St. Mary's Sch., Fredericksburg, 1910-15, St. John's Sem., San Antonio, 1915-22; Th.D., North Am. Coll., Rome, Italy, 1925; Dr. Canon Law, Pontifical Inst. of Canon and Civil Law, Rome, 1928; LL.D., St. Edwards U., 1940. Ordained priest St. John Lateran Basilica, Rome, 1926; prof. St. John's Sem., San Antonio, 1928-33, rector, 1933-40; regent St. Mary's U. Law Sch., San Antonio, 1935-40; consecrated aux. bishop of Santa Fe (titular bishop of Birta), 1940; installed as coadjutor of El Paso, with the right of succession, 1942; succeeded to the See of El Paso, 1942; asst. to Papal Throne, 1965. Decorated Knight Comdr. Equestrian Order of Holy Sepulchre of Jerusalem; Grand Cross of King Alfonso X, The Wise (Spain). Doctor Mundunae Sapientiae of Boswell Soc., 1963; recipient St. Joseph the Worker award Tex. AFL-CIO; John Casey Labor Man of Year award Cath. Labor Inst.; award Amalgamated Clothing Workers Am., 1973. Address: 1012 N Mesa Av El Paso TX 79902

MEWHORTER, WILLIAM JOSEPH, banker; b. Mpls., May 17, 1925; s. William Henry and Cathryn Mary (Dwyer) M.; B.B.A., Tex. Coll. Mines, 1948; m. Anne Beys, Feb. 17, 1950; children—William Paul, Anne Lynn. Asst. v.p. State Nat. Bank, El Paso, 1948-62; v.p. First Nat. Bank, Roswell, N.M., 1963-66, First Nat. Bank, Midland, Tex., 1966-72; pres., dir. Western State Bank, Midland, 1972—. Served with USNR, 1942-45. Democrat. Roman Catholic. Home: 1700 Culver Dr Midland TX 79701 Office: 1030 Andrews Hwy Midland TX 79701

MEYER, ALBERTA LOUISE, ednl. assn. adminstr.; b. St. Louis, Mar. 4, 1913; d. Otto H. and Alvina (Schnellbacher) M.; A.B., Harris Tchrs. Coll., 1933; M.A., Columbia, 1943. Tchr. St. Louis Elementary Schs., 1936-48, 49-50; Assn. for Childhood Edn. Internat. fellow, 1948-49; audio-visual cons. St. Louis Pub. Schs., 1950-59; exec. sec. Assn. for Childhood Edn. Internat., Washington, 1959—, vice-chmn. Women's Joint Congl. Com., 1960-61, chmn., 1961-62; sec. U.S. Nat. Com. on Early Childhood Edn., 1960-71; mem. exec. com. Council of Nat. Orgns. for Children and Youth, 1960-72, chmn., 1968-70; mem. nat. adv. com. on Exchange of Teachers U.S. Office of Edn., 1959—; mem. tech. asst. com. White House Conf. on Children, 1970; chmn. planning com. Nat. Com. on Children and Youth for Citizen's Conf. on Priorities and Action for Children and Youth, 1971. Mem. Assn. for Childhood Edn. Internat., Adminstrv. Women in Edn., Am. Speech and Hearing Assn. (mem. nat. adv. council on prevention of speech and language handicaps 1971-72), Nat. Audubon Soc., Kappa Delta Pi, Delta Kappa Gamma, Sigma Sigma Sigma. Home: 3201 Wisconsin Av NW Washington DC 20016 Office: 3615 Wisconsin Av NW Washington DC 20016

MEYER, ALPHONSE HERMAN, JR., surgeon, educator; b. Memphis, Feb. 3, 1919; s. Alphonse Herman and Eulalie (Ashner) M.; student U. Va., 1936-38; S.B., Harvard, 1940, M.D., 1943; m. Janis Floe Hays, Aug. 13, 1949; children—James Hays McIntosh (stepson), Gregory Allison, Andrew Hays. Intern Barnes Hosp., St. Louis, 1944; asst. resident surgery Barnes Hosp., 1946-48, Albany Hosp., 1948-49; asst. in surgery Washington U. Med. Sch., 1946-48, Albany Med. Coll., 1948-49; chief resident surgery Queens Gen. Hosp., 1949-51; mem. faculty U. Tenn. Sch. Medicine, Memphis, 1951—, asst. clin. prof. surgery, 1962—; practice medicine specializing in surgery, Memphis, 1951—; mem. staffs Bapt. Meml., Meth., St. Joseph, LeBonheur Children's, City of Memphis hosps. (all Memphis). Served with M.C., USNR, 1944-46. Diplomate Am. Bd. Surgery, Am. Bd. Abdominal Surgery. Mem. A.C.S., Southeastern Surg. Congress, Am. Soc. Abdominal Surgeons, Am. Coll. Gastroenterology. Contbr. articles to profl. jours. Home: 79 W Galloway Dr Memphis TN 38111 Office: 20 S Dudley St Memphis TN 38103

MEYER, ALVIN FELIX, JR., govt. ofcl.; b. Shreveport, La., Sept. 3, 1920; s. Alvin Felix and Bertha (Weil) M.; B.S., Va. Mil. Inst., 1941; postgrad. George Washington U., 1962; m. Vivian Burford, June 13, 1942; children—Alvin Felix III, Carolyn Burford (Mrs. Ronald Rhode). Commd. 2d lt. USAAF, 1941, advanced through grades to col., 1960; chief biomed. sci. corps, 1965-69, chmn. Dept. Def. Environmental Pollution Control Com., 1965-69; spl. asst., legislative affairs Consumer Protection and Environmental Health Service, U.S. Dept. Health, Edn. and Welfare, Washington, 1969-70; dep. asst. adminstr. for noise abatement and control U.S. Environmental Protection Agy., Washington, 1970—. Chmn. bd. Abe Meyer Corp., Shreveport, 1969—. Fellow Am. Soc. C.E., Am. Pub. Health Assn., Aerospace Med. Assn. (asso.); mem. Nat. Soc. Profl. Engrs. Contbr. articles to profl. jours. Home: 1600 Longfellow St McLean VA 22101 Office: Environmental Protection Agency Washington DC 20460

MEYER, ANDRE BERNARD, air force officer; b. Chgo., May 21, 1938; s. Max Bernard and Josephine Virginia (Daley) M.; B.S. in Elec. Engring., Christian Bros. Coll., Memphis, 1964; postgrad. in Indsl. Engring., U. N.D., 1966-67; grad. Air Command and Staff Coll., 1973; postgrad. Indsl. Coll. Armed Forces, 1973—; m. Marie Carroll Strong, Apr. 27, 1963; children—Andrea Bridget, Adrienne Bernadette, Annette Beverly. Mem. Cath. Fgn. Mission Soc. Am., 1957-61; commd. 2d lt. USAF, 1965, advanced through grades to 1st lt., 1967, capt., 1968; mem. missile combat crew, 1965-69, comdr. crew, 1967-69; tng. mgr. Airborne Electronics Div., Hdqrs. Air Tng. Command, 1969-71; single service tng. mgr. World Wide Mil. Command and Control System, 1971-73; alt. rep. Def. Satellite Communications System Personnel and Tng. Panel, 1969-73; lead engr. Kelly AFB, Tex., 1973—. Instr. Confrat. Christian Doctrine, State Dist., 1971-72. Judge, Sci. Fair, Minot, N.D., 1966; asst. scoutmaster troop Boy Scouts Am., Minot 1966-67, com. chmn., 1967-69; mem. Children Have a Potential, 1969—, pres., 1969-71, mem. council, 1969-71; mem. Live Oak Vol. Fire Dept., 1970—, pres., 1970-73, tng. chief, 1973-74, asst. chief, 1974—; mem. Bexar County Fire Fighters Assn., 1970—; mem. St. Monica's Sch. Bd., 1971—, v.p., 1971-72, pres., 1972-73, treas., 1973—; 1st first aid A.R.C., 1974—. Nominee for Presdl. citation as Outstanding Mil. Mgr. Year, 1974; recipient Certificate of Appreciation, Live Oak Vol. Fire Dept., 1973. Mem. I.E.E.E., U.S.A.F. Officers Club. Roman Catholic (pres. parish council 1971-72). K.C. Home: 566 Shin Oak Dr San Antonio TX 78233 Office: SAALC MMEEE Kelly AFB TX 78241

MEYER, CHARLES EDWARD, constrn. co. exec.; b. New Orleans, Aug. 20, 1938; s. Elbert J. and Ruth (Thomas) M.; B.S. in Mech. Engring., Tulane U., 1960; M.B.A., Loyola U., 1965; m. Myrna Knight, Dec. 29, 1956; children—Richard Charles, Randall James, Ronald Scott. Engr., U.S. Gypsum Co., 1960-62; sr. tool engr. Boeing Co., 1962-65; sec., treas. Hamilton, Meyer & Assos., Inc., Metairie, La., 1964—; pres. La. Housing & Urban Devel. Corp., Metairie, La., 1967—, La. Housing & Urban Devel. Constrn. Co., Metairie, 1968—. Registered profl. engr., La. Mem. Am. Soc. M.E., La. Engring. Soc., Am. Pilots Assn. Home: 6 Shady Oak Lane New Orleans LA 70123 Office: PO Box 763 Metairie LA 70004

MEYER, FLOYD RAYMOND, librarian; b. Oak Park, Ill., Dec. 4, 1915; s. Roman N. and Cecil (Ayers) M.; B.Sc. in Edn., U. Neb., 1938, Ed.D., 1957; M.A. in L.S., U. Denver, 1949; m. Marjorie Marie Carie, June 7, 1938; children—Philip R., Karen M. (Mrs. Danny Eugene Myers). Tchr., prin. jr. high sch. Howells (Neb.) Pub. Schs., 1938-40, Cedar Bluffs (Neb.) High Sch., 1940-41, Stratton (Neb.) High Sch., 1946-47; librarian North Platte (Neb.) Pub. Schs., 1947-48; asst. edn. librarian, instr. dept. secondary edn. U. Neb., 1948-50, asst. librarian social studies div., instr. secondary edn., 1950-53, asst. librarian tech. services div., asst. prof. secondary edn., 1953-56, librarian U. High Sch., asst. prof. secondary edn. in charge library edn., 1956-57; dir. East St. Louis Residence Center Library, So. Ill. U., 1957-58; dir., prof., chmn. dept. library sci. Kan. State Coll., Pittsburg, 1958-66; library dir. Stephen F. Austin State U., Nacogdoches, Tex., 1966-71, documents librarian, 1971-72, serials recs. librarian, 1972—. Chmn. Resident Center Libraries, East St. Louis, Ill., 1957-58. Served from 1st lt. to lt. col. AUS, 1941-46. Mem. Am. Legion. Democrat. Roman Catholic. Club: Piney Woods Country (Nacogdoches). Author: Nebraska School Library Handbook, 1952; Look to Your Library, 1953, rev., 1956. Home: 4104 Forest Lane Nacogdoches TX 75961

MEYER, GARY GORDON, banker; b. Pulaski, Tenn., Oct. 22, 1941; s. Clarence Leslie and Margret Kathleen (Gordon) M.; B.S., U. Tenn., 1963; M.B.A. (Bus. Found. fellow), U. N.C., 1969; m. Angela A. Upchurch, July 11, 1964. Market analyst Commerce Union Bank, Nashville, 1969, adminstrv. officer, marketing coordinator, 1970, asst. v.p., mgr. marketing dept., 1971-73, v.p., sec., treas., Chattanooga, 1973—. Instr. marketing U. Tenn., Nashville, 1970-72. Served to lt. comdr. USNR. Mem. Am. Marketing Assn., Bank Marketing Assn., Beta Gamma Sigma, Omicron Delta Kappa, Phi Kappa Phi. Home: 200 Windmere Chattanooga TN 37411 Office: 401 Chestnut Chattanooga TN 37402

MEYER, GEORGE GOTTHOLD, physician; b. Frankfurt, Germany, Nov. 13, 1931; s. Hans and Hilda (Lesser) M.; came to U.S., 1941, naturalized, 1946; B.A., Johns Hopkins, 1951; M.D., U. Chgo., 1955; m. Paula Saslaw, June 17, 1953; children—Bruce Alan, Brian Lee, Barry Dale. Intern USPHS Hosp., S.I., N.Y., 1955-56; resident psychiatry U. Chgo. Hosps. and Clinics, 1958-60, chief resident, 1960-61, chief psychiat. inpatient service, 1966-69; mem. faculty U. Chgo. Med. Sch., 1961-69, asso. prof. psychiatry, 1968-69; asso. prof. psychiatry U. Tex. Med. Sch., San Antonio, 1969-71; prof. psychiatry U. Tex. Health Sci. Center, San Antonio, 1971—; dir. N.W. San Antonio Mental Health Center, 1969-74; mem. exec. bd. Crisis Center, San Antonio, 1971—; cons. VA Hosp., Kerrville, Tex., Kerrville State Hosp., San Antonio State Hosp., Santa Rosa Med. Center; cons. in field, 1961—. Mem. med. adv. bd. for driver licensing Tex. Dept. Health, 1973—. Mem. bd. Econ. Devel. Corp., Mexican-Am. Unity Council, San Antonio, 1971—. Bd. dirs. Jewish Social Service Fedn., San Antonio. Served with USPHS, 1955-58. Nat. Inst. Mental Health career tchr. grantee, 1961-63; vis. lectr. psychiatry U. Edinburgh (Scotland) Med. Sch., 1966; recipient OKIE award by gov. Okla., 1969. Diplomate Am. Bd. Psychiatry and Neurology. Fellow Am. Psychiat. Assn., Am. Orthopsychiat. Assn.; mem. Am., Tex., Bexar County med. assns., Tex., Bexar County, World psychiat. assns., Am. Group Psychotherapy Assn., San Antonio Group Process and Group Psychotherapy Soc., Am. Assn. Med. Colls., Am. Coll. Psychiatrists, Sigma Xi, Alpha Omega Alpha, Phi Lambda Upsilon. Contbr. numerous articles to med. jours. Home: 2907 Marlborough Dr San Antonio TX 78230

MEYER, GERALD, hydrologist, govt. ofcl.; b. Newport News, Va., Dec. 31, 1922; s. Louis and Sophie (Superior) M.; B.S., U. N.C., 1948; m. Libby Alterman, Aug. 31, 1947; children—Helen (Mrs. Sam Brand), Peggy. Lab. instr. U. N.C., Chapel Hill, 1947-48; field asst. Va. Geol. Survey, Charlottesville, 1948; with U.S. Geol. Survey, Balt., also Morgantown, W.Va., 1948-64, asst. chief, ground water br., Washington, 1964-72, chief, ground water br., 1973—. Served with USAF, 1943-46. Fellow Geol. Soc. Am. (chmn. hydrogeology div. 1973-74); mem. Am. Geophys. Union, Am. Water Resources Assn., Am. Water Works Assn., Am. Water Well Assn., Sigma Xi. Contbr. articles to sci. jours. Home: 8224 Stonewall Dr Vienna VA 22180 Office: U S Geol Survey Nat Center Reston VA 22092

MEYER, HENRY ALBERT, state ofcl.; b. St. Louis, June 15, 1904; s. Albert George and Mary Gertrude (Bruns) M.; B.S., U. Ill., 1930, M.E., 1938; Ed.M., U. Fla., 1963, Ed.S., 1964, Ed.D., 1966; m. Elizabeth M. Shea, Oct. 2, 1931. Commd. ensign USCG, 1930, advanced through grades to capt., 1952; with USCG Dist. 3, 1955-57, Dist. 5, 1957-61; ret., 1961; dir. evening program Edson Jr. Coll., 1966-68; dir. operations research Vocational Rehab., Fla. Dept. Health and Rehab. Services, Tallahassee, 1968—. Mem. Am. Assn. Sch. Adminstrs., Assn. for Supervision and Curriculum Devel., Ret. Officers Assn., Fla. Vocational Assn., Nat., Fla. rehab. assns., Am. Legion, U. Ill. Alumni Assn., Phi Delta Kappa, Kappa Delta Pi, Alpha Kappa Delta. Home: 420 E Park Av Tallahassee FL 32301 Office: 1309 Winewood Blvd Tallahassee FL 32304

MEYER, JOHANNES HORST, physicist; b. Berlin, Germany, Mar. 1, 1926; s. Kurt Heinrich and Gertrude (Hellwig) M.; B.Sc., U. Geneva (Switzerland), 1949; Ph.D., U. Zurich, 1953; m. Ruth Mary Hunter, Mar. 28, 1953; children—Richard, Christopher. Came to U.S., 1957. Nuffield fellow Oxford U., 1953-57; lectr. Harvard U., 1957-59, asst. prof., 1959-60, asso. prof., 1960-64; prof. physics Duke, 1964—; vis. prof. Technische Hochschule, Munich, Germany, fall 1965; cons. NSF. Served with Swiss Army, 1946-56. Alfred P. Sloan fellow, 1960-64; vis. fellow Japanese Soc. Promotion of Sci., 1971. Fellow Am. Phys. Soc. Contbr. numerous articles on low temperature physics to sci. jours. Home: 2716 Montgomery St Durham NC 27705 Office: Dept Physics Duke U Durham NC 27706

MEYER, JOHN VINCENT, elec. products mfg. co. exec.; b. St. Louis, Sept. 25, 1938; s. Vincent and Jimmie Ckarice (Weitinger) M.; B.S. in Bus., U. Kan., 1960. Trust adminstr. Republic Nat. Bank, Dallas, 1960-65; pres. Edge-Rite Corp., Brownwood, Tex., 1965—. Pres. Brown County United Fund, 1973; chmn. J. Clements Work Center for Mentally Retarded, Brownwood, 1972—. Clubs: Willow Bend Polo and Hunt (Dallas); North Dallas Racquet. Office: Box 1448 Brownwood TX 76801

MEYER, JOHN WILLIAM, drainage and flood control engr.; b. Bismarck, Mo., Sept. 20, 1898; s. George Frederick and Wilhelmina Rosine (Godau) M.; student engring. Internat. Corr. Schs., 1918-20; m. Hazel Fleeman Killian, June 1, 1960; children by previous marriage—Annetta, Severin Poirot. With U.S. Geol. Survey, Wis., 1915-17; resident engr. Drainage Dist. 17, Mississippi County (Ark.), 1918-28, chief engr., 1928-42, cons. engr., 1961—; chief engr. Lee Wilson & Co., Wilson, Ark., 1942-51; cons. engr., Blytheville, Ark., 1951—. Chmn. Blytheville San. Sewer Commn., 1971—; exec. sec. Blytheville Planning Commn., 1958-67. Chmn. Mississippi County March of Dimes, 1943. Alderman, City of Blytheville, 1963-66. Served with U.S. Army, 1918. Recipient plaque appreciation Nat. Assn. Real Estate Bds., 1955. Registered profl. engr., Ark. Life mem. Am. Soc. C.E.; mem. Nat. Soc. Profl. Engrs. Club: Blytheville Country (dir. 1966-68). Home: 1800 Country Club Rd Blytheville AR 72315 Office: PO Box 446 Blytheville AR 72315

MEYER, JOSEPH WILLIAM, airline exec.; b. St. Louis, Aug. 24, 1908; s. Fred L. and Elizabeth (Bastian) M.; grad. high. sch.; m. Lorraine Buchmann, Oct. 15, 1936; children—Jerry, Robert, John. Bookkeeper, Smith, Moore & Co., St. Louis, 1927-31, R. E. Funsten Co., St. Louis, 1931-36; with Delta Air Lines, St. Louis, Memphis, Atlanta, 1936—, asst. v.p. customer relations, 1967—. Episcopalian. Home: 3132 Argonne Dr NW Atlanta GA 30305 Office: Atlanta Airport Atlanta GA 30320

MEYER, JULIEN H(ERMAN), surgeon, obstetrician, gynecologist; b. Enfield, N.C., May 7, 1914; s. Joseph and Hennye (Lehman); B.S., U. N.C., 1935; M.D., Med. Coll. Va., 1937; m. Dorothy Rose Kahn, July 14, 1940; children—Julien Herman, Carol Joan. Intern. Greater Balt. Med. Center, 1937-38; resident in obstetrics and gynecology St. Joseph's Hosp., Balt., 1938-40; postgrad, course gynecol. pathology Johns Hopkins Hosp., 1940; practice obstetrics and gynecology, Roanoke, Va., 1940—; attending obstetrician, gynecologist Roanoke Meml. Hosps., 1940—, chief obstetrics and gynecology, 1961-62; cons. gynecology VA Hosp., 1946—; staff Community Hosp. of Roanoke Valley. Fellow A.C.S., Am. Coll. Obstetricians and Gynecologists; mem. A.M.A., Med. Soc. Va., Va. Obstet. and Gynecol. Soc., Roanoke Acad. Medicine, So. Med. Assn., Roanoke Valley Assn. Obstetricians and Gynecologists (pres. 1965-66). Home: 4925 Crossbow Circle SW Roanoke VA 24014 Office: Med Center Bldg 127 McClanahan St SW Roanoke VA 24014

MEYER, KENNETH LEON, JR., banker; b. Woodward, Okla., Feb. 22, 1926; s. Kenneth Leon and Coralie Florence (Fisher) M.; J.D., U. Okla., 1950; m. Elaine Kathleen Nesbitt, Aug. 6, 1950; children—Kenneth Leon III, Michael M., Kathleen, Suzanne. Admitted to Okla. bar, 1950; practice in Checotah, Okla., 1952; with 1st Nat. Bank & Trust Co., Muskogee, Okla., 1952—, v.p., trust officer, 1958-73, exec. v.p., 1973—, also dir.; dir. Three Rivers Nat. Bank, Muskogee, Three Rivers Finance Co., First of Muskogee Corp. Mem. faculty So. Meth. U., Dallas, 1962-67, Okla. State U., Stillwater, 1965-73, Southwest Grad. Sch. Banking. Served with USNR, 1943-51. Mem. Am., Fed., Okla. (asso. examiner bd. bar examiners 1965-67), Musogee County (pres. 1972-73) bar assns., Okla. Bankers Assn. (pres. trust div. 1957), Okla. Soc. Financial Analysts, Phi Delta Phi. Democrat. Methodist. Mason, Rotarian (pres. 1969). Home: 1500 W Okmulgee St Muskogee OK 74401 Office: PO Box 68 Muskogee OK 74401

MEYER, LAWRENCE JOSEPH, lawyer; b. Chgo., July 7, 1927; s. Joseph Benjamin and Sarah (Peilet) M.; student Roosevelt Coll., Chgo., 1948-50; LL.B., U. Miami, 1954; m. Roslyn Simon, Mar. 28, 1953; children—Sandra Leigh, Janice Beth, Pamela Sue. Admitted to Fla. bar, 1955; individual practice law, Hollywood, Fla., 1955—; small claims judge Broward County, 1963-73. Past chmn. T-Y Park Bd. Broward County. Served with USNR, 1945-48. Mem. Broward mem. exec. com.), South Broward (past dir.) bar assns. Mason (Shriner).

Home: 5000 McKinley St Hollywood FL 33021 Office: 2435 Hollywood Blvd Hollywood FL 33020

MEYER, LEO FRANCIS, tobacco research co. exec.; b. Pitts., July 19, 1929; s. Jacob John and Teresa Bernardine (Bayer) M.; B.S., Duquesne U., 1956; postgrad. Carnegie Inst. Tech. Evening Sch., 1956-60; M.S., U. Richmond, 1966; m. Jean Lorraine Enard, Jan. 28, 1954; children—Leo R., Beth A., Susan J., Maria C. Research chemist Gulf Research and Devel. Co., Harmarville, Pa., 1956-61; asso. chemist Philip Morris Research Center, Richmond, Va., 1961-63, research chemist, 1963-69, mgr., 1969—. Served with USMCR, 1950-52. Mem. Am. Chem. Soc. Roman Catholic (tchr. sch. religion 1969-72). K.C. (4 deg., state program dir. 1970-71). Patentee in field. Home: 8526 Hanford Dr Richmond VA 23229 Office: Philip Morris Research Center PO Box 26583 Richmond VA 23261

MEYER, PHILIP EDWARD, journalist; b. Deshler, Neb., Oct. 27, 1930; s. Elmer Edward and Hilda (Morrison) M.; B.S., Kan. State U., 1952; M.A., U. N.C., 1963; postgrad. Harvard, 1966-67; m. Mary Sue Quail, Aug. 5, 1956; children—Caroline, Katherine, Melissa, Sarah. Asst. state editor Topeka (Kan.) Daily Capital, 1954-56; grad. asst., part-time instr. U. N.C., 1956-58; reporter Miami (Fla.) Herald, 1958-62; Washington corr. Knight Newspapers, 1962-69, 70—; project dir. Russell Sage Found., 1969-70; dir. Negro attitude surveys, Detroit, Miami, 1967-68. Served with USNR, 1952-54. Recipient Pub. Affairs Reporting award Am. Polit. Sci. Assn., 1960; Distinguished Service award Sigma Delta Chi, 1974; Nieman fellow, 1967. Mem. Am. Polit. Sci. Assn. Episcopalian. Club: Harvard (N.Y.C.). Author: Precision Journalism, 1973. Contbr. articles on social scis. to profl. jours. Home: 11650 Mediterranean Ct Reston VA 22090 Office: Nat Press Bldg Washington DC 20004

MEYER, RAYMOND WAYNE, ins. co. exec.; b. Victoria, Tex., Oct. 31, 1941; s. Raymond Frank and Leona (Holy) M.; A.A., Victoria Coll., 1961; B.B.A., Tex. A. and I. U., 1963; m. Rosalee Frances Hauboldt, May 31, 1963; children—Ronald Wayne, Rachelle Anne. Staff accountant Ernst & Ernst, C.P.A.'s, San Antonio, 1963-64; sr. accountant Peat, Marwick, Mitchell & Co., San Antonio, 1964-69, audit supr., Austin, Tex., 1969-71; dir. internal auditing United Services Automobile Assn., San Antonio, 1971—. Mem. Inst. Internal Auditors (chpt. pres. 1973-74), Am. Inst. C.P.A.'s, Tex. Soc. C.P.A.'s (mem. industry com. 1972-74), Nat. Assn. Accountants, Am. Accounting Assn., San Antonio C. of C. (mem. finance com. 1973-74), Alpha Chi. Club: Serra (treas. 1970-71, 73-74). Home: 5919 Forest Cove San Antonio TX 78240 Office: USAA Bldg San Antonio TX 78288

MEYER, VAUGHAN BENJAMIN, lumber co. exec.; b. Eagle Pass, Tex., Dec. 13, 1920; s. Otto C. and Genevieve C. (Vaughan) M.; B.S., Rice U., 1941; postgrad. Cal. Inst. Tech., 1941-42; m. Courtenay Langdon Lyon, May 25, 1946 (div. Feb. 1969); children—Catherine (Mrs. Richard Abbott Lange), Beverly; m. 2d, Alice Gerturdis King Klebrg, Dec. 23, 1972. Exec. v.p. Alamo Lumber Co., San Antonio, 1948-61; pres. Eagle Lumber Co., San Antonio, 1956—, Eagle Lumber Co. of Tex., 1961—; dir. George C. Vaughan & Sons, San Antonio, Lumbermen's Underwriters, Austin, Tex. Councilman, mayor pro tempore City of Terrell Hills, 1965-68. Trustee S.W. Found. for Research and Edn., Vaughan Found., Raymond Dickson Found., St. Marys Hall. Served to lt. comdr. USNR, 1942-46. Mem. S.A.R., Soc. Colonial Wars, Tex. Cavaliers, Sigma Xi. Episcopalian. Clubs: Argyle, San Antonio Country, Pilon. Home: 3714 Mary Mont San Antonio TX 78217 Office: PO Box 6985 San Antonio TX 78209

MEYER, WILLIAM AUGUST PETER, oil co. exec.; b. Rheydt, Germany, June 20, 1923; s. Ernst and Eva (Peltzer) M.; brought to U.S., 1924, naturalized, 1929; student U. Conn., 1941-43; B.Engring. with honors, Yale, 1944, M.Engring., 1947, Dr.Engr., 1959; m. Gladys Shirley Bach, Dec. 21, 1946; children—Wendelyn (Mrs. Robert F. Thill), Sally (Mrs. Donald B. Grimm). Engr., Standard Oil Co. (Ind.), Whiting, Ind., 1947-50; asst. instr. Yale, 1950-51; engr. Gulf Research and Devel. Co., Harmarville, Pa., 1953-56, group leader, 1956-61, supr. automotive research sect. 1961-68, supr. research and devel. section, 1968-69, sr. scientist, project mgr., 1969-70; dir. tech. services Gulf Oil Co.-U.S., Houston, 1970-73, mgr. lube oils marketing, 1973—. Served to lt. USNR, 1943-46, 51-53. Mem. Soc. Automotive Engrs. (chmn. fuels and lubricants activity 1971), Am. Petroleum Inst., Nat. Petroleum Refiners Assn., Ind. Oil Compounders Assn., Nat. Lubricating Grease Inst., Sigma Xi, Tau Beta Pi. Contbr. to profl. publs. in field. Home: 815 Glenchester St Houston TX 77024 Office: Gulf Oil Co-US PO Box 1519 Houston TX 77001

MEYERCORD, EDWARD BERNARD, door mfg. co. exec.; b. Chgo., June 21, 1912; s. George Rudolph and Agnes (Adams) M.; B.L.S., Northwestern U., 1934; m. Carol Duffield, Nov. 13, 1937; children—Edward Bernard, Jr., Susan (Mrs. Patrick J. Rice), Francis D., Pamela Ann (Mrs. Michael P. Mitchell). Unit mgr. Comml. Credit Co., Chgo., 1935-37; sec. Meyercord Compound Lumber Co., Mobile, Ala., 1937-40, pres., 1940-49; owner Meyercord Sales Co., Mobile, 1949—; pres., treas. Meyercord Door Corp., Mobile, 1957—. Bd. dirs., v.p. Mobile Symphony, 1957-67; bd. dirs. Providence Hosp., Mobile, 1959—, chmn., 1968-69. Club: Country (pres. 1946-47) (Mobile). Home: 8 Springbank St S Mobile AL 36608 Office: Box 7187 Mobile AL 36607

MEYERHOFF, JOHN WESLEY ELWOOD, educator; b. Rochester, N.Y., June 21, 1943; s. Elwood George and Margaret Isabelle (Childs) M.; B.A., Colgate U., 1964; M.S., Old Dominion U., 1973; m. Tempie Lou Williford, Oct. 8, 1966; children—Kristen Lee, Kimberly Rae. Athletic dir., basketball coach, tchr. Chesapeake (Va.) Coll., 1970-73; basketball coach, tennis coach, tchr. Brevard (N.C.) Coll., 1973—. Mem. basketball com. NJCAA Region X, 1972-73. Served with USNR, 1965-70; now lt. comdr. Res. Mem. Fellowship of Christian Athletes (dir. 1970-73, v.p. 1972-73), NJCAA Coaches Assn., Nat. Assn. Basketball Coaches. Great Bridge Jr. C. of C., Phi Kappa Tau. Club: Chesapeake College Athletic Boosters (dir. 1971-73). Address: Brevard Coll Brevard NC 28712

MEYERS, GRANT ULYSSES, foundry co. exec.; b. Moline, Ill., May 1, 1913; s. George C. and Lillian (Rommel) M.; B.S.C., Northwestern U., 1933; M.B.A., U. Chgo., 1955; m. Doris M. Fraser, Jan. 23, 1953; children—Stuart, Joan, Glen, Eric, Marcia. Mgr. accounting dept. Wis. Steel Works div. Internat. Harvester Co., Chgo., 1933-55; v.p., comptroller Radiant Mfg. Corp., Morton Grove, 1955-59; sec.-treas. Security-Columbian Banknote Co., N.Y.C., 1959-60, financial v.p., sec., 1960-65; owner, chmn., pres., chief exec. officer Oil City Iron Works, Inc., Corsicana, Tex., 1965—. Mem. Financial Execs. Inst., Nat. Assn. Accountants (internat. pres. 1969-70), Acacia, Beta Gamma Sigma, Beta Alpha Psi. Mason. Clubs: Metropolitan (N.Y.C.); Cipango, Lancers (Dallas); Corsicana Country; Chicago Yacht; Canyon Creek Country (Richardson, Tex.). Home: 2514 Big Horn Lane PO Box 725 Richardson TX 75080 Office: PO Drawer 1560 Corsicana TX 75110

MEYERS, TEDSON J., lawyer; b. Bayonne, N.J., May 6, 1928; A.B., N.Y. U., 1949, M.A., 1950; J.D., Harvard, 1953. Admitted to D.C. bar, 1953, N.Y. State bar, 1957; since practiced in Washington; govt. regulation counsel ABC, 1958-61; adminstrn. asst. to chmn. FCC, 1961-62; spl. asst. to dir. Peace Corps, 1963-68. Mem. D.C. City Council, 1972—; mem. White House Task Force on Ednl. TV Overseas, 1966-68; pub. mem. Criminal Justice Coordinating Bd., D.C., 1970—. Mem. Bar Assn. D.C. (mem. adminstrv. law sect.), Am., FCC bar assns. Home: 1828 Wyoming Av NW Washington DC 20009 Office: 1200 18th St NW Washington DC 20036

MEYERS, TIMOTHY CERVERA, JR., orthodontist; b. Austin, Tex., Feb. 13, 1938; s. Timothy Cervera and Mildred Inez (Stone) M.; A.B., Lincoln U., 1959; M.S., Worcester Poly. Inst., 1961; D.D.S., Howard U., 1966, certificate in orthodontics, 1970; m. Carolyn Tonsler Winstead, Dec. 28, 1968; children—Timothy Cervera III and Leslie Carroll (twins), Lisa Ann-Marie. Research chemist Pennsalt Chem. Corp., Chestnut Hill, Pa., 1961-62; pvt. practice in orthodontics, Atlanta, 1970—. Orthodontist Atlanta Southside Comprehensive Health Center, 1971—; clin. instr. orthodontics Emory U., Atlanta, 1972—. Vol. clinician Ben Massell Dental Clinic, Atlanta, 1970-73. Served with USAF, 1966-68. Mem. Am., Ga. dental assns., Am. Assn. Orthodontists, So., Ga. socs. orthodontists, Ga., N. Ga., No. Dist. dental socs., Alpha Phi Alpha, Omicron Kappa Upsilon, Chi Delta Mu. Club: Falcons (Atlanta). Home: 2764 Landrum Dr SW Atlanta GA 30311 Office: Suite 408 75 Piedmont Av NE Atlanta GA 30303

MEYERS, WILTON ANDREW, chem. co. exec.; b. Sulphur, La., Sept. 19, 1943; s. Wilton John and Sarah Leona (Olsen) M.; B.S., La. State U., 1966, M.B.A., 1968; m. Janet Sue Pack, Jan. 24, 1967; children—Michael Scott, Debra Louise. Financial analyst City Nat. Bank, Baton Rouge, 1967-68, Continental Oil Co., Houston, 1968-70; sr. auditor Tex. Instruments Dallas, 1969-70; asst. controller Occidental Chem. Co., Houston, 1970—. Oil and gas developer, realtor. Auditor United Fund, 1970-71. C.P.A., Tex. Mem. Am. Inst. C.P.A.'s, Tex. Soc. C.P.A.'s, Am. Mgmt. Assn., Upsilon Pi Tau. Home: 5728 W Airport St Houston TX 77035 Office: PO Box 35571 Houston TX 77035

MEYERSON, MELVIN RAYMOND, govt. ofcl.; b. Portsmouth, Va., Oct. 27, 1921; s. Louis and Rose (Weprin) M.; B.S., Va. Poly. Inst., 1942; M.S., U. Md., 1953, Ph.D., 1962; m. Eva Dominitz, June 11, 1944; children—Mark Daniel, Andrew Philip. Research metallurgist, project leader Nat. Bur. Standards, Washington, 1946-69, chief, engring. metallurgy sect., 1965-69, asst. chief, metallurgy div., 1968-69, chief, product evaluation tech. div., 1969—. Profl. lectr. George Washington U., 1957-58; lectr. U. Md., 1962-66; dir. engring. dept. U.S. Army Reserve Sch., Washington, 1951-65. Conferee 2d World Metall. Congress, 1957. Served with AUS, 1942-46. Recipient Silver medal U.S. Dept. Commerce, Washington chpt. Am. Soc. Fellow Washington Acad. Scis.; mem. Am. Soc. for Testing and Materials (Dudley medal), Am. Soc. for Metals (Burgess Meml. award Washington chpt.), Soc. Standards Engrs., Alpha Sigma Mu. Contbr. numerous articles to sci. jours. Home: 611 Goldsborough Dr Rockville MD 20850 Office: Nat Bur Standards A349 Polymer Bldg Washington DC 20234

MIA, ABDUL JABBAR, educator; b. Dacca, Bangladesh, Feb. 1, 1929; s. Kader Baksh and Nasimun (Chaudhury) M.; B.S., Dacca U., 1950, M.S., 1952; postgrad. La. State U., 1956; Ph.D., N.C. State U., 1959; m. Virginia S. Novais, Oct. 24, 1970. Came to U.S., 1956. Botanist, Jute Research Inst., Dacca, Bangladesh, 1959-61; U.S. exchange prof. Bishop Coll., Dallas, 1961-63, prof. biology, 1971—; NRC Can. fellow Carleton U., Ottawa, 1964-66; research scientist Canadian Dept. Fisheries and Forestry, Ottawa, Ont., 1966-70. Mem. adv. council Profl. Inst. Pub. Service of Can., 1968-69; mem. exec. com. Munshigunj Cultural Assn., Dacca, Bangladesh, 1960-61. Mem. Canadian Soc. Cell Biologists (founding mem.), Bot. Soc. Am., Tex. Acad. Sci., Tex. Soc. Electron Microscopy, Internat. Bot. Congress, Internat. Assn. Wood Anatomists, English Speaking Union Am. Contbr. to profl. publs. Home: 6122 Woodcrest Lane Dallas TX 75214 Office: Dept Life Scis Bishop Coll Dallas TX 75241

MICHA, DAVID ALLAN, physicist, educator; b. V. Mercedes (San Luis), Argentina, Sept. 12, 1939; s. Simon David and Catherine (Cohen) M.; Licenciate in Physics, U. Cuyo, Bariloche, Argentina, 1962; Filosofie Licenciat, U. Uppsala, Sweden, 1965, Filosofie Dr., 1966, Docent, 1968; m. Anna Margaretha Samuelsson, Aug. 29, 1966; children—Michael Fredrik, Anna Katherine. Came to U.S., 1966, naturalized, 1974. Research asso. U. Wis., 1966-67; asst. research physicist U. Cal. at La Jolla, 1967-69, vis. prof., 1973; asso. prof. chemistry and physics U. Fla., Gainesville, 1969-74, prof., 1974—. vis. prof. Harvard, 1972; vis. Lamberg prof. U. Gothenburg, Sweden, 1970. Petroleum Research Fund grantee, 1969-72, NSF grantee, 1970—; Alfred P. Sloan Found. fellow, 1971-73. Mem. Am. Phys. Soc., Am. Chem. Soc., Sigma Xi. Asst. editor: Internat. Jour. Quantum Chemistry, 1971-73. Contbr. articles to profl. jours. Office: Quantum Theory Project Williamson Hall U Fla Gainesville FL 32601

MICHAEL, FRANZ HENRY, educator; b. Freiburg, Germany, Mar. 10, 1907; s. Wolfgang and Elizabeth (Wehrenpfennig) M.; Referendar, U. Freiburg, 1931; J.D., U. Berlin, 1933; m. Dolores M. Tewell, Dec. 30, 1966; children—Peter Michael, Ingred Vera (Mrs. John Osterhaug). Came to U.S., 1939, naturalized, 1944. Mem. German Diplomatic Service, 1933; prof. Nat. Chekiang U., Hangchow, China, 1934-38; research asso., Charles Lathrope fellow Walter Hines Page Sch., Johns Hopkins, 1939-42; prof. Chinese History and Govt. U. Wash., 1942-64, acting chmn. Far Eastern dept., 1942-47, asst. dir. Far Eastern and Russian Inst., 1947-62, chmn. Modern Chinese History project, 1947-64; dir. Inst. for Sino-Soviet Studies George Washington U., 1969-72, prof. Internat. Affairs and Far Eastern History, 1964—; cons. U.S. State Dept. and Dept. Def. Recipient Republic of China Order of the Brilliant Star First Class. Rockefeller Found. grantee, Ford Found. grantee, Japan Found. grantee. Author: The Origin of Manchu Rule in China, 1942; The Far East in the Modern World, 1956-73; The Taiping Rebellion, 3 vols., 1964-70. Contbr. numerous articles to learned jours., chpts. in books. Home: 121 Princess St Alexandria VA 22314 Office: Inst for Sino-Soviet Studies George Washington U Washington DC 20006

MICHAEL, JAMES HARRY, JR., lawyer, state senator; b. Charlottesville, Va., Oct. 17, 1918; s. James Harry and Reuben (Shelton) M.; B.S., U. Va., 1940, LL.B., 1942; m. Barbara E. Puryear, Dec. 18, 1946; children—Jarrett, Victoria. Admitted to Va. bar, 1942; since practiced in Charlottesville; mem. firm Michael and Musselman, 1946-54, J.H. Michael, Jr., 1954-59, Michael and Dent, 1959-72, Michael, Dent & Brooks Ltd., 1972—; asso. judge Juvenile and Domestic Relations Ct., Charlottesville, 1954-68; mem. Va. Senate, 1968—. Exec. dir. Inst. Pub. Affairs, U. Va., 1952; mem. governing bd. Council State Govts., mem. exec. com. So. conf.; vice chmn. So. Legislative Conf., 1973—. Mem. Charlottesville Sch. Bd., 1951-62; bd. govs. St. Anne's Sch. Bd., 1954—; sec. Charlottesville Com. Fgn. Relations, 1950—. Served with USNR, 1942-46, comdr. Res. ret. Wilton Park fellow Wilton Park Conf., Sussex, Eng., 1971. Mem. Am., Va. State (v.p. 1957-58), Charlottesville-Albemarle (pres. 1966) bar assns., C. of C., Am. Judicature Soc., Nat. Consumer Finance Assn., 4th Jud. Conf., Va., Am. trial lawyers assns., Raven Soc., Sigma Nu Phi, Omicron Delta Kappa. Episcopalian (vestryman). Elks. Clubs: Downtown (Richmond, Va.); Farmington Country (Charlottesville); Redland. Home: 900 Rugby Rd Charlottesville VA 22903 Office: 414 Park St Charlottesville VA 22901

MICHAEL, WILLIAM HERBERT, JR., physicist; b. Richmond, Va., Dec. 10, 1926; s. William Herbert and Alice (Anderson) M.; B.S., Princeton, 1948; M.S., U. Va., 1950; M.A. in Physics, William and Mary Coll., 1962; Ph.D., Princeton, 1967; m. Marjorie May Boswick, June 28, 1952; children—Alice Caroline, Cynthia Boswick. With NASA, Langley Research Center, Hampton, Va., 1948—, head lunar and planetary scis. br., 1969-71, chief environmental and space scis. div., 1971—; also leader Viking radio sci. team for Mars Missions, 1975. Served with USNR, 1944-46. Recipient Spl. Service award for Exceptional Service NASA, 1967, Spl. Achievement award, 1969. Fellow Am. Inst. Aeros. and Astronautics (asso.); mem. Am. Geophys. Union, Internat. Astron. Union (mem. commn. on the moon, 1969—). Contbr. articles to profl. jours. Home: 29 Haughton Lane Newport News VA 23606 Office: M/S 401 NASA Langley Research Center Hampton VA 23665

MICHAELIAN, CHARLES THOMAS, accountant; b. Jersey City, Nov. 23, 1927; s. Karekin P. and Katharine (Sprauer) M.; student Drexel Inst. Tech., 1945-46; B.B.A. cum laude, Pace Coll., 1952; m. Joan Morledge, July 20, 1957; children—Thomas J., Richard C., Paul K., Margaret J. Sr. staff accountant Arthur Andersen & Co., N.Y.C., 1952-56; asst. controller Am. Export Lines, Inc., N.Y.C., 1956-62; controller Adam Young, Inc., N.Y.C., 1962-63; divisional accountant C.F. Braun & Co., Murray Hill, N.J., 1964-65; mgr. financial analysis Newport News (Va.) Shipbldg. & Dry Dock Co., 1966—. Instr. Sch. World Trade, N.Y.C., 1960-62. Treas., Hidenwood Presbyn. Kindergarten Bd., Newport News, 1966-69, Richard T. Yates P.T.A., Newport News, 1969-70. Served with ordnance dept. AUS, 1946-49. C.P.A., N.Y. Mem. Am. Inst. C.P.A.'s. Republican. Presbyn. (elder). Kiwanian. Home: 97 Stonewall Pl Newport News VA 23606 Office: 4101 Washington Av Newport News VA 23607

MICHAELIS, FRED JACOB, JR., ins. and finance exec.; b. New Orleans, Nov. 15, 1919; s. Fred Jacob and Louise (Beck) M.; student pub. schs.; m. Ruth Louise Holls, Oct. 14, 1946; 1 son, Jonathan Frederick. Clk., Marshall J. Smith & Co. Ltd., New Orleans, 1937-39; spl. agt. Gottschalk Gen. Ags., New Orleans, 1939-40, Fire Assn. Phila., La. and Miss., 1945-50, R. Kirk Moyer Agy., Shreveport, La., 1950-54; ins. agt. Love Ins. Agy., Shreveport, 1954-57, Allied Services, Shreveport, 1957—; exec. asst. to dir. La., Office of Emergency Planning, 1965-67; econ. planner Coordinating and Devel. Council N.W. La., 1968—, exec. dir., 1968—. Mem. Shreveport Regional Am. Revolution Bicentennial Celebration Commn.; pres. Muscular Dystrophy Assn., Shreveport, 1960-64. Served to capt. AUS, 1940-45. Decorated Purple Heart with oak leaf cluster. Mem. Nat. Assn. Ins. Agts., Home Builders Assn. Shreveport. Democrat. Lutheran. Clubs: Kiwanis (pres. 1962), Shreveport Progressive Mens (pres. 1964-65), Riverside Swimming (pres. 1967-68). Home: 216 E Southfield Blvd Shreveport LA 71105 Office: 2942 Youree Dr Shreveport LA 71104

MICHAELS, ROBERT PHILLIP, JR., tobacco co. exec.; b. nr. Morrisville, N.C., Jan. 11, 1917; s. Robert Phillip and Caroline (Searcy) M.; student U. N.C., Chapel Hill, 1935-37; m. Margaret Brown Martin, Apr. 27, 1946; children—Robert Phillip III, Margaret Martin, Gail Brown, Richard Gregory. Vice-pres., dir. Venable Tobacco Co., Inc., Durham, N.C., 1949-54; v.p. gen. sales A.C. Monk & Co., Inc., leaf tobacco, Farmville, 1954—. Mem. Pitt County (N.C.) Devel. Commn., 1962—. Mem. Bethel Twp. (N.C.) Sch. Bd., 1962—. Served with USAAF, 1941-45. Decorated 3 Air Medals, D.F.C. Methodist (ofcl. bd. 1960-64). Home: PO Box 396 Bethel NC 27812 Office: A C Monk & Co Farmville NC 27828

MICHAELSON, LOUIS HENRY, ind. oil operator; b. Wichita, Kan., Feb. 22, 1919; s. I.T. and Regula (Schenebricker) M.; B.S., Wichita State U., 1941; m. Ruth Foster White, Mar. 30, 1946; children—Eric Lance, Kristin Rae. With Gulf Oil Corp., Wichita, 1936-42; exptl. geologist Skelly Oil Co., Midland, Tex., 1946-48; div. geologist Tex. Gulf Producing Co., 1948-65; v.p. Green & Michaelson Producing Co., Midland, 1965-74, Texam Oil Corp., 1965-67, Michaelson Producing Co., Midland, 1974—. Vice pres. Permian Basin council Girl Scouts U.S.A., 1969. Served with USAAF, 1942-45. Recipient Silver Beaver award Boy Scouts Am., 1969. Mem. Am. Assn. Petroleum Geologists, Geol. Soc. Am., W. Tex. Geol. Soc., Soc. Econ. Paleontologists and Mineralogists. Presbyn. (deacon 1959-62, 65-67, treas. 1961-62, 67). Home: 2008 Douglas St Midland TX 79701 Office: Midland Savs Bldg Midland TX 79701

MICHALOWICZ, JOSEPH CASIMIR, educator; b. Washington, Mar. 4, 1916; s. Roch and Pelagia (Sniegoski) M.; B. Elec. Engring., Cath. U., 1940, M. Elec. Engring., 1951; m. Louise M. Anselmo, Oct. 5, 1940; children—Joseph V., John A., Jean (Mrs. Jay Gerdes), Joan L., James A. Engr. Rural Electrification Adminstrn., Washington, 1940-42; mem. faculty dept. elec. engring. Cath. U. Am., Washington, 1942—, asso. prof., 1951—, chmn. dept., 1952-69, asst. dean Sch. Engring. and Architecture, 1969-70, dean admissions and financial aid, registrar, 1973—. Cons., NSF, Capitol Radio Engring. Inst., Internat. Brotherhood Elec. Workers. Served with USNR, 1944-46. Recipient numerous awards and grants for research in field elec. engring. Fellow I.E.E.E.; mem. Am. Soc. Engring. Edn. (sect. chmn. 1954-55), Sigma Xi, Tau Beta Pi. Contbr. articles to profl. publs. in field. Patentee in field. Home: 7409 Wyndale Rd Chevy Chase MD 20015 Office: Admissions and Records Cath U Washington DC 20017

MICHALOWICZ, JOSEPH VICTOR, mathematician; b. Washington, Oct. 23, 1941; s. Joseph Casimir and Louise Mary (Anselmo) M.; B.A. summa cum laude, Cath. U., 1963, Ph.D. (Nat. Def. Edn. Act fellow), 1967; postgrad. (NSF fellow) Bowdoin Coll., 1965, 69; m. Karen Dee Shuman, June 8, 1963; children—Joleen Marie, Michael J. Mathematician, Research Analysis Corp., McLean, Va., 1966-67; asst. prof. math. Cath. U., Washington, 1967-73; mathematician Harry Diamond Lab. U.S. Army, Washington, 1970—. Treas., Glen Forest Civic Assn., Falls Church, Va., 1973. Bd. dirs. No. Va. Boys Club, Fairfax County, 1972. Mem. Am. Math. Soc., Math. Assn. Am., Phi Beta Kappa, Sigma Xi, Delta Epsilon Sigma. Roman Catholic. Club: Senators (Washington). Home: 5855 Glen Forest Dr Falls Church VA 22041 Office: Harry Diamond Lab Washington DC 20438

MICHALSKI, EDWARD MATTHEW, engring. sales corp. exec.; b. Orange, N.J., Sept. 29, 1926; s. Matthew Joseph and Katherine (Zachariziewicz) M.; B.S., U.S. Mcht. Marine Acad., 1947; postgrad. Hays Sch. Combustion, 1953; m. Carol Swafford, Nov. 9, 1949. Third engr. Mcht. Marines, 1948; service engr. Combustion Engring., Inc., N.Y.C., 1949-54, burner engr. engring dept., 1954-55, supr. Fuels Equipment Engring. div., 1955-58, mgr., 1958-62; pres., owner Matthew Engring. Co., Chattanooga, 1962-64; v.p., treas. P-V-F Suppliers, Inc., 1964-65; pres., chmn. bd. dirs. Mike Michalski & Co., Chattanooga, 1965—. Served with USNR, 1945-46. Registered profl. engr., Tenn. Mem. Nat. Tenn. socs. profl. engrs., Chattanooga Engrs. Club, Am. Soc. M.E., Instrument Soc. Am., Am. Inst. Plant Engrs. Methodist. Clubs: Chattanooga Golf and Country, Rivermont Golf and Country. Patentee in field. Home: 1234 Dallas Rd Chattanooga TN 37405 Office: 1203 Hixson Pike Chattanooga TN 37405

MICHEL, BURLYN EVERETT, educator; b. Ladoga, Ind., Mar. 7, 1923; s. Roy Wesley and Ella (Scharer) M.; student Purdue U., 1941-43, S.D. State Coll., 1943-44; B.S., U. Chgo., 1948, Ph.D., 1950; m. Florence Mary Schalkle, May 29, 1946; children—Linda Jean, Douglas Roy, Donald Henry. Asst. prof. botany State U. Ia., Iowa City, 1951-58; asso. prof. U. Ga., Athens, 1958-64, prof., 1964—. Cons. plant physiologist U.S. Dept. Agr., 1959-61. Scoutmaster Northeast Ga. council Boy Scouts Am., 1965—. Served with AUS, 1943-46. NSF grantee, 1959, 62, 64, 66, 70, Interior Dept. grantee, 1973-74. Mem. Am. Soc. Plant Physiologists (exec. com., 1970-72), Bot. Soc. Am., Assn. S.E. Biologists, Ga. Acad. Sci., Sigma Xi. Methodist. Contbr. articles to profl. jours. Home: 344 Beechwood Dr Athens GA 30601 Office: Dept Botany U GA Athens GA 30602

MICHEL, HARDING BOEHME OWRE (MRS. JOHN F. MICHEL), educator; b. Louisville, Aug. 17, 1924; d. Henry Oscar and Mary Cornell (Inman) Boehme; B.S., Duke, 1946; Ph.D., U. Mich., 1957; m. Oscar T. Owre, Aug. 4, 1948 (div. Dec. 1967); 1 dau., Caroline Harding; m. 2d, John F. Michel, Nov. 24, 1970. Mem. faculty U. Miami (Fla.), 1952—, asso. prof. Rosenstiel Sch. Marine and Atmospheric Sci., 1967-70, prof., 1970—. Teaching fellow U. Mich., 1950-52; research grantee NSF, NIH, Office Naval Research. Mem. Marine Biol. Assn. U.K., Soc. Systematic Zoology, Phi Beta Kappa, Sigma Xi. Club: Key Biscayne Yacht. Author: Copepods of the Florida Current, 1967; (with F.M. Bayer) The Free-Living Lower Invertebrates, 1968. Home: 5000 Hammock Lake Dr Miami FL 33156 Office: Rosenstiel Sch Marine and Atmospheric Science 10 Rickenbacker Causeway Miami FL 33149

MICHEL, MARSHALL LOUIS, JR., physician; b. Biloxi, Miss., July 11, 1913; s. Marshall Louis and Mary Louise (Meant) M.; M.D., Tulane Coll., 1937; m. Nancy Shaw, Apr. 16, 1941; children—Marshall Louis III, Helen (Mrs. W.J. Smith), Mary Louise. Intern, Touro Infirmary, New Orleans 1937-38, resident, 1938-40; practice medicine specializing in gen. surgery, New Orleans, 1941—; chief surgery Touro Infirmary, 1963-66, sr. surgeon, 1966-73; vis. surgeon Charity Hosp.; cons. Crippled Children's Hosp.; prof. surgery Tulane U., 1971—. Chmn. bd. Oscar Lee Putnam Cultural Found. Mem. Tulane Med. Alumni Assn., Sociedad Columbia de Pediatrica and Puericultura (hon.), Alpha Epsilon Delta, Alpha Omega Alpha. Clubs: Boston; Stratford (New Orleans). Contbr. to profl. publs. in field. Home: 208 Brockenbrough Court Metairie LA 70105 Office: Tulane Sch Medicine Dept Surgery 1430 Tulane Av New Orleans LA 70112

MICHELIS, ADOLPH NEWTON, dredging co. ofcl.; b. Port Clinton, O., July 2, 1937; s. Adolph and Elizabeth (Newton) M.; student Armstrong Jr. Coll., 1955-56; A.S., So. Tech. Inst., 1959; m. Sara Glenda Bevill, Apr. 5, 1958; children—Lisa Lynn, Pamela Ann. Civil technician Ga. Hwy. Dept., Moultrie, 1959-60; asst. engr. Savannah & Atlanta Ry. Co., 1960-63, So. Ry. Co., Atlanta, 1963-64; v.p. dredging Parkhill-Goodloe Co., Inc., Jacksonville, Fla., 1964—. Served with USMC, 1955-56. Mem. World Dredging Assn. Clubs: Jacksonville Propeller. Home: 7646 Holiday Rd S Jacksonville FL 32216 Office: PO Box 8707 Jacksonville FL 32211

MICHELL, GENE SAUL, psychologist; b. Astoria, N.Y., Jan. 15, 1928; s. Gino and Marie (Bartolomel) M.; B.A., N.Y. U., 1949, Ph.D., 1966; M.A., Fordham U., 1952; m. Evelyn Chatterton, Nov. 1, 1958; children—Jacquelyn, Robert. Research psychologist Met. Life Ins. Co., N.Y.C., 1953-59, Naval Tng. Device Center, Orlando, Fla., 1959—. Served to lt. AUS, 1951-53. Mem. Am. Psychol. Assn., A.A.A.S., Human Factors Soc. Research in field. Home: 703 Albertson Pl Orlando FL 32806 Office: Naval Tng Device Center Orlando FL 32813

MICHELS, KENNETH M., univ. adminstr.; b. Chgo., Sept. 17, 1922; A.B., Emory U., 1949, M.A., 1950; Ph.D., U. Wis., 1953; m. Esther Eloise Baker, Feb. 1, 1946; children—Kenneth M., Jeanne Ann. Asst. prof. Purdue U., 1953-56, asso. prof., 1956-60, prof., 1960-64, coordinator off-campus grad. programs, 1960-62, asst. dean univ. extension adminstrn., 1962-64; prof. psychology, chmn. dept. Fla. Atlantic U., Boca Raton, 1964-67, dean Coll. Social Sci., 1967-68, dean Coll. Sci., 1968-71, v.p. acad. affairs, 1971—; research scientist summer faculty program Mil. Operations Research div. Lockheed Aircraft Corp., Marietta, Ga., 1957; summer vis. investigator Roscoe B. Jackson Meml. Labs., 1962; vis. prof. U. Cal. at Berkeley, summer 1964. Cons., Courtney and Co., Phila., 1957-58, Aircraft Armaments, Inc., Cockeysville, Md., 1956-60, VA, 1959-64, System Scis. Affiliates, Columbus, O., 1960—, Columbus div. North Am. Aviation, 1962-63, behavioral scis. tng. com. Nat. Inst. Gen. Med. Scis., 1964-68, Northrop Corp., 1966-69, USPHS, 1967-69. Served with USAAF, 1941-45; now lt. col. Res. Mem. Psychonomic Soc., A.A.A.S., Phi Beta Kappa, Sigma Xi, Phi Kappa Phi, Blue Key. Contbr. articles to profl. jours. Office: Florida Atlantic Univ Boca Raton FL 33432

MICHELSON, AARON IVAN, librarian; b. Cleve., Oct. 3, 1927; s. William and Florence Beatrice (Slesnick) M.; B.S., Case-Western Res. U., 1949, M.S. in L.S., 1950; postgrad. U. Chgo., 1956-59; m. Fairlie A. Brown, Aug. 27, 1955; children—Katherine, Mary, Susanna, Sarah. Reference asst. Detroit Pub. Library, 1950-51; librarian, instr. library sci. N.D. State Coll., 1954-56; reference asst. U. Chgo. Library, 1956-59; dir. Okla. Library-Community Project, 1959-60; asst. prof., asso. prof. U. Okla. Sch. Library Sci., 1960-65; directing editor, head librarian Scott, Foresman & Co., ednl. pubs., Glenview, Ill., 1965-66; library dir. U. South Ala., Mobile, 1966—. Mem. Library Services and Constrn. Act Adv. Com. Ala., 1971. Served with AUS, 1951-54. Mem. A.L.A., Ala. (chmn. coll., univ. and spl. libraries div.), Southeastern library assns., Adult Edn. Assn. U.S., Editor: Oklahoma Library-Community Project Newsletter, 1959-60. Contbr. articles profl. jours. Home: 1107 Fribourg St Mobile AL 36608 Office: Library U South Ala Mobile AL 36688

MICHELSON, EDWARD J., newspaper corr.; b. Northampton, Mass., Apr. 3, 1915; s. Isadore Henry and Fannie (Avrich) M.; B.A., Williams Coll., 1937; m. Dorothea Adair Pohlman, Feb. 3, 1938; children—Kathleen (Mrs. Frederick D. Meloan), Paul, Emily (Mrs. Thomas D. Crews). Reporter St. Louis Post-Dispatch, 1937-38; writer pub. relations div. Westinghouse Electric Co., 1939-40; day editor, internat. shortwave news div. CBS, 1941-44; spl. asst. Office Sec. War, 1946; mem. hist. sect. strategic services unit War Dept., 1946; asso. Robert S. Allen, syndicated columnist, 1946-50; Washington corr. N. Am. Newspaper Alliance, also New Eng. dailies, 1946—; Washington editor Forbes mag., 1956-63, Printer's Ink mag., 1958-63; mag. editor Ocean Sci. News, 1968-69; Washington editor Sci. and Tech. mag., 1969—. Exec., Enterprises Publs. Research dir. pub. works subcom. on water Resources U.S. Ho. of Reps., 1951. Served with OSS, AUS, 1944-46. Mem. Aviation/Space Writers Assn., White House Corrs. Assn., Washington Soc. Investment Analysts, Gargoyle Soc. Clubs: Williams (N.Y.C.); Nat. Press (Washington). Contbr. to gen. financial and spl. bus. periodicals. Editor: Our American Government (Wright Patman) 1948. Home: 2153 Florida Av NW Washington DC 20008 Office: Nat Press Bldg Washington DC 20004

MICHELSON, RONALD KEITH, oral surgeon; b. San Francisco, July 10, 1936; s. Charles Dean and Mary (Bettencourt) M.; student Coll. San Mateo, 1954-56, Georgetown U. Coll. Arts and Scis., 1959-61; D.D.S., Georgetown U., 1965; m. Susan Valarie Michelson; 1 son, David Keith. Intern oral surgery Norfolk (Va.) Gen. Hosp., 1965-66; individual practice dentistry, Virginia Beach, Va., 1967-71; 2d year resident oral surgery Jackson Meml. Hosp., U. Miami, 1971-72, chief resident, 1972-73; oral and maxillofacial surgeon, Virginia Beach, 1973—. Served with AUS, 1956-59. Mem. Tidewater, Va., Am. dental assns., Virginia Beach Dental Soc., Am. Rose Soc., Norfolk Bot. Garden Soc., Mass. Hort. Soc., Delta Sigma Delta. Episcopalian. Contbr. articles to profl. jours. Home: 3050 Comte Ct Virginia Beach VA 23456 Office: 794 Independence Blvd Virginia Beach VA 23455

MICHENER, JOHN WILLIAM, fiberglass co. exec.; b. Wilkinsburg, Pa., May 14, 1924; s. William Henry and Edna (Cornell) M.; B.S., Carnegie Inst. Tech., 1946, M.S., 1953, Ph.D., 1953; m. Ruth Lois Kistler, Dec. 27, 1953; children—William K., Sue Ann. Physicist, Owens-Corning Fiberglas Corp. Research Center, Newark, O., 1950-58, mgr. materials research, 1959; mgr. physics and electronics dept. Deering Milliken Research Corp., Spartanburg, S.C., 1959—, research and teaching asst. Office Naval Research and Manhattan projects Carnegie Inst. Tech., 1942-50. Chmn. elect Greater Spartanburg Environmental Council, 1973; dir. Glendale Acad., 1971-72. Fellow A.A.A.S.; mem. Am. Phys. Soc., S.C. Acad. Sci. (pres. 1971), S.C. Jr. Acad. Sci., Sigma Xi, Tau Beta Pi, Phi Kappa Phi. Home: Route 1 Moore SC 29369 Office: Box 1927 Spartanburg SC 29301

MICHERO, WILLIAM HENDERSON, retail trade exec.; b. Ft. Worth, June 19, 1925; s. William Alvin and Lela Belle (Henderson) M.; B.S., Tex. Christian U., 1948; m. Nan Elaine Henderson, July 9, 1948; children—Jane Elaine (Mrs. Stephen A. Christie), William Sherman, Thomas Edward. With Tandy Corp., 1948—, warehouse mgr., Ft. Worth, 1949-50, credit mgr., 1950-52, div. gen. mgr., Hoboken, N.J., 1952-55, asst. to pres., Boston and N.Y.C., 1958-60, sec., Ft. Worth, 1960-71, v.p., sec., 1971—. Sec. Tandy Found.; trustee Tex. Christian U., Ft. Worth Museum Sci. and Industry. Served with USNR, 1943-46. Named Valuable Alumnus Tex. Christian U., 1969. Mem. Am. Soc. Corporate Secs., Newcomen Soc. N.Am. Clubs: Fort Worth, Fort Worth Boat; Colonial Country. Home: 1300 Mistletoe Dr Fort Worth TX 76110 Office: 2727 W 7th St Fort Worth TX 76107

MICHIE, LUCILE EASTHAM (MRS. J. TEVIS MICHIE), psychologist; b. Charlottesville, Va., Jan. 22, 1907; d. Rosser J. and Helen H. (George) Eastham; student Coll. William and Mary, 1924-26; B.S. in Edn., U. Va., 1929, M.Edn., 1960, advanced grad. student, 1963-72; m. J. Tevis Michie, Aug. 6, 1929; children—Robert Kinloch, Martha Tevis. Tchr. pub. schs. Wakefield, Va., 1929-30, Clark Sch., Charlottesville, 1931-39; sec.-treas., dir. Helen G. Eastham Shop, Inc., 1931-50; tchr. Lane High Sch., Charlottesville, 1931-45, counselor, 1957-60, counselor-psychometrist, 1960-63; sch. psychologist Charlottesville Pub. Schs., 1963-72; cons. Children and Youth Center, Pediatric Dept., U. Va. Hosp., 1972—; sch. psychologist Fluvanna County (Va.) Pub. Schs.; supr. sch. psychology practicum students, 1968-72. Cons. Nat. Guidance Inst., U. Va., Charlottesville, 1960-61; treas. Country Day Sch., 1948-54; v.p. Va. Assn. Mental Health Parliamentarian. Pres. bd. dirs. Children's Service Center, Charlottesville, 1954-56, bd. dirs., 1954-57; bd. dirs. Charlottesville, Albemarle County community chests. Recipient service award Charlottesville Mental Health Assn., 1959. Mem. Nat., Va., Charlottesville (past pres., dir., parliamentarian) edn. assns., Nat. Vocational Guidance Assn., Va., Piedmont (past pres.), Am. personnel and guidance assns., U. Va. Edn. Alumni Assn., Am. Assn. U. Women, League Women Voters, Bus. and Profl. Women's Club (pres. Charlottesville 1939-41, pres., dir. Va. Fedn. 1944-46; dir. nat. fedn.), Charlottesville Mcht. Assn. (treas. 1946-49), Alumni Assn. Coll. William and Mary, U. Va. Alumni Assn. (life mem.), Am. (asso.), Va. psychol. assns., Va. Assn. Sch. Psychologists (mem. profl. affairs com. 1970-72), Nat. Assn. Sch. Psychologists, Delta Kappa Gamma, Kappa Delta Pi (life mem., chpt. treas. 1959-69, service award 1969). Republican. Episcopalian. Club: Colony (Richmond, Va.). Author articles on mental health and handling children's problems. Home: PO Box 3445 Charlottesville VA 22903

MICHOT, LOUIS J., state ofcl.; b. Lafayette Parish, La., Nov. 5, 1922; s. Louis J. and Mary Adele (Doumas) M.; ed. U. Southwestern La., Lafayette; m. Patricia Smith, Sept. 7, 1945; children—Anne Michot Keating, Rick, Tommy, Timmy, Bobby, Mike, Yvonne, David. Formerly dir. franchise sales Burger Chef Systems, La., Miss.; exec. v.p., gen. mgr. Greater Lafayette C. of C.; asst. to v.p. fed. affairs Air Transport Assn. Am., Washington; mem. La. State Bd. Edn., 1968-72, supt. edn., 1972—. Mem. La. Ho. of Reps., 1960-64; candidate Gov. La., 1964. Trustee Pub. Affairs Research Council. Served with USMC, World War II. Mem. Council Devel. French in La. K.C., Kiwanian (gov. La., Miss., West Tenn. dist.). Home: PO Box 52169 Lafayette LA 70501 Office: PO Box 44064 Baton Rouge LA 44064

MICKAL, ABE, physician; b. Talia, Lebanon, June 15, 1913; s. Kalil and Hadda (Abihidar) M.; brought to U.S., 1920, naturalized, 1920; B.S., La. State U., 1936, M.D., 1940; m. Lois Mildred Barnes, May 23, 1942; children—Annette (Mrs. Coleman Alder), Marie (Mrs. Alfred Abaunza), Joanne (Mrs. Henry Kinney), Schaffer L. Intern, Touro Infirmary, New Orleans, 1940-41; resident Charity Hosp., New Orleans, 1946-49; practice medicine, specializing in obstetrics and gynecology, New Orleans, 1949-59; instr. anatomy and pathology La. State U. Sch. Medicine, 1945-46, clin. instr. obstetrics and gynecology, 1949-53, clin. asst. prof., 1953-57, clin. asso. prof., 1957-59, prof., head obstetrics and gynecology, 1959—, obstetrician and gynecologist in chief La. State Unit, 1959—; sr. vis. surgeon Charity Hosp.; mem. staff So. Bapt. Hosp.; cons. VA Hosp., New Orleans. Served to maj. USAAF, World War II. Diplomate Am. Bd. Obstetrics and Gynecology. Fellow Am. Coll. Surgeons; mem. New Orleans Obstetrics and Gynecology Soc. (pres. 1957-58), Central Assn. Obstetrics and Gynecology, Soc. Gynecol. Oncologists, Assn. Profs. of Obstetrics and Gynecology, Am. Coll. Obstetrics and Gynecology, A.M.A., Am. Assn. Obstetricians and Gynecologists, La. State, Orleans Parish med. socs. Contbr. numerous articles to med. jours. Home: 40 Nassau Dr Metairie LA 70005 Office: 1542 Tulane Av New Orleans LA 70112

MICKENS, RONALD ELBERT, educator; b. Petersburg, Va., Feb. 7, 1943; s. Joseph and Daisy (Brown) M.; B.A., Fisk U., 1964; Ph.D., Vanderbilt U., 1968; postgrad. Mass. Inst. Tech., 1970. Research asso. Mass. Inst. Tech., Cambridge, 1968-70; asso. prof. high nuclear physics Fisk U., Nashville, 1970—. Vis. prof. Stanford Linear Accelerator Center, summers 1971, 72; cons. AEC. Woodrow Wilson fellow, 1964-65, Danforth Found. fellowship 1965-68, NSF fellowship, 1968-70, NSF grantee, 1971-73. Mem. Am. Phys. Soc. (mem. com. minorities 1972—), A.A.A.S., Am. Assn. Physics Tchrs., Phi Beta Kappa, Sigma Xi, Beta Kappa Chi, Alpha Phi Alpha. Contbr. to profl. publs. in field. Home: 1809 Morena St Nashville TN 37203 Office: Box 15 Physics Dept Fisk Univ Nashville TN 37203

MICKISH, VIRGINIA LEE JOHNSON (MRS. VERLE LEON MICKISH), educator; b. Torrington, Wyo., Mar. 26, 1935; d. Francis Morris and Della Mae (Wright) Johnson; student Colo. State Coll., 1953-55; B.S. with spl. honors, U. Colo., 1963, M.A., 1967; m. Verle Leon Mickish, May 29, 1955; 1 dau., Valerie Lynn. Elementary tchr. Columbine Sch., Boulder Valley Sch. Dist., 1963-66; research asst. U. Colo., 1967, sect. leader reading conf., summers 1969, 70; reading cons. Boulder Valley Sch. Dist., 1967-71; reading specialist DeKalb County (Ga.) Schs., 1971-72, gen. supr., 1972—. Instr., DeKalb Coll., 1972. Active Girls Scouts U.S.A. Colo. Tchrs. scholar, 1967; Fellowship grantee U. Colo., 1967-68. Mem. Boulder Valley Kindergarten Tchrs. (chmn. 1964-65), Assn. Childhood Edn. Internat. (local corr. sec. 1965-67, state research chmn. 1968, U. Colo. student br. adviser 1969), Internat. Reading Assn. (state council 1969, local pres. 1969-70), Alpha Delta Kappa (v.p. 1970-71, pres. elect 1974-75, parliamentation 1972-73), Kappa Delta Pi. Mem. United Ch. Home: 3537 Sandy Woods Lane Stone Mountain GA 30083

MICKLE, JAMES BURKET, educator; b. Lincoln, Neb., May 19, 1927; s. Robin Stewart and Bessie Ora (Burket) M.; B.Sc., U. Neb., 1949, M.S., 1950; Ph.D., Mich. State U., 1953; postgrad. U. Cal. at Davis, 1961; m. Lois Ann Thorfinnson, Dec. 18, 1949; children—Mary Ann, David Robin, Laura Elizabeth. Asst. prof. animal sci. Okla. State U., Stillwater, 1953-57, asso. prof., 1957-62, prof., 1962—, mgr. foods research lab., 1953—. Cons. to several Okla. food companies. Chmn. aquatic com. Okla. Amateur Athletic Union, 1973. Served with USNR, 1945-46. Mem. Okla. Dairy Tech. Soc. (pres. 1973), Am. Dairy Sci. Assn. (active various coms., student award 1963), Stillwater C. of C. (chmn. cheese festival com. 1953-72), Farmhouse, Sigma Xi (pres. 1965), Alpha Zeta, Gamma Sigma Delta. Lion. Club: Toastmasters (pres. 1959). Contbr. articles to profl. publs. Home: 620 Ranch Dr Stillwater OK 74074

MICKUM, GEORGE BRENT, III, lawyer; b. Washington, Jan. 13, 1928; s. George Brent and Anna (Love) M.; B.S. cum laude, Georgetown U., 1949, LL.B., 1952; m. Lora Ann Mattare, June 27, 1953; children—George Brent, Luke Anthony, Ann Elizabeth, Paul Christopher, Joseph Benedict, Mark Andrew. Admitted to D.C. bar, 1952; clk. Charles Fahy, U.S. Ct. of Appeals, D.C. Circuit, Washington, 1952-53; clk. Stanley F. Reed, Supreme Ct. of U.S., Washington, 1953-54; practiced in Washington, 1954—; mem. firm Steptoe & Johnson. Served with AUS, 1945-47. Mem. Delta Theta Phi, Pi Gamma Mu. Democrat. Roman Catholic. Home: 44 Grafton St Chevy Chase MD 20015 Office: 1250 Connecticut Av NW Washington DC 20036

MIDDENDORF, WILLIAM HENRY, educator; b. Cin., Mar. 23, 1921; s. William J. and Mary J. (Frommeyer) M.; B. Elec. Engring., U. Va., 1946; M.S., U. Cin., 1948; Ph.D., Ohio State U., 1960; m. Evelyn B. Taylor, Nov. 20, 1946; children—Judy (Mrs. Michael L. Marlowe), Mark E., Jeffrey W., Craig A., Susan A. Mem. faculty U. Cin., 1948—, prof. elec. engring., 1960—; with Wadsworth Elec. Mfg. Co., Covington, Ky., 1966—, dir. engring. and research, 1966—. Dir. research Cin. Devel. and Mfg., Inc., 1960-66. Pres., Diocese of Covington Bd. Edn., 1972-73. Trustee, St. Elizabeth Hosp., Covington, 1967—. Served with USNR, 1943-46. NSF fellow, 1958-59. Fellow I.E.E.E.; mem. Am. Soc. Elec. Engrs. Author: Electric Circuit Analysis, 1956; Introductory Network Analysis, 1966; Engineering Design, 1969. Contbr. to profl. publs. in field. Patentee in field. Home: 1941 Provincial St Fort Mitchell KY 41011 Office: Loc 30 Univ Cin Cincinnati OH 45221

MIDDLEBROOK, GEORGE BRUCE, textile, fiber co. exec.; b. Milbank, S.D., Apr. 8, 1913; s. Bruce Smeed and Auretta Hoyt (Agnew) M.; B. Chem. Engring., U. Minn., 1939, M.S., 1941; m. Ione Lageson, Oct. 16, 1941; children—J. Michael, Stephen, Mark. Chemist, Allied Chem. Corp., Buffalo, 1941-55, supr. engring. research, 1955-58, mgr. application research, 1958-62, mgr. chem. research, 1962-63, mgr. process devel., 1963-67, dir. adminstrn., 1967-70, group mgr. operations services, 1970—. Mem. Sigma Xi, Delta Kappa Epsilon. Club: Richmond (Va.) Engineers (pres. 1971-72). Home: 4724 Stornoway Dr Richmond VA 23234 Office: Allied Chem Corp PO Box 31 Petersburg VA 23803

MIDDLETON, DOUGLAS FRANK, petroleum engr.; b. Sedalia, Mo., July 24, 1928; s. Douglas Miles and Florence Elizabeth (Youse) M.; B.S. in Mining Engring., U. Mo., 1950; m. Grace Alice Brigham, Oct. 20, 1956; children—Jane, Grace. Reservoir engr. Texaco Co., 1959; reservoir and prodn. engr. Aramco Co., 1959-63; engring. cons., 1964-65; dist. reservoir engr. Mobil Oil Co., Venezuela, 1965-67; sr. reservoir engr. Coastal States Gas Producing Co., Houston, 1967—. Mem. sch. bd. Escuela Araco, Venezuela, 1965-66. Served with AUS, 1950-52. Registered profl. engr., Tex., Okla., La. Mem. Soc. Petroleum Engrs., Colegio Ingenieros de Venezuela. Methodist. Mason. Home: 4434 Twinkle Ct Houston TX 77072 Office: 5 Gateway Plaza E Houston TX 77046

MIDDLETON, ELWYN LINTON, lawyer; b. Pomona, Fla., Oct. 16, 1914; s. William Spencer and Lizzie A. (Williams) M.; LL.B., Stetson U., 1939; m. Annie L. Fielding, Dec. 7, 1942; children—Elwyn Linton, Mary Ann, John David, Phillip Fielding. Admitted to Fla. bar, 1939, since practiced in Palm Beach; asso. E. Harris Drew, 1939-42; mem. firm Burns, Middleton, Farrell & Faust (formerly Burns, Middleton, Rogers & Farrell), 1946—; town atty., Palm Beach, 1953—. Dir. Bank of Palm Beach & Trust Co., Palm Beach. Trustee Fla. Presbyn. Coll. Served from ensign to lt. USNR, 1942-46. Mem. Am., Palm Beach County (pres. 1951) bar assns., Fla. Bar (gov. 1954-56), Phi Alpha Delta. Democrat. Presbyn. Home: 242 Dunbar Rd Palm Beach FL 33480 Office: 205 Worth Av Palm Beach FL 33480

MIDDLETON, JOHN ALBERT, coll. pres.; b. Foreston, S.C., Jan. 2, 1914; s. Brewington and Lula (Hayes) M.; A.B., Allen U., 1939, LL.D., 1966; B.D., Howard U., 1942; Th.M., Iliff Sch. Theology, 1956; LL.D., Payne Coll., 1966, Bethune-Cookman Coll., 1967, Payne Theol. Sem-Wilberforce U., 1970; m. Merlissie Tyson, Dec. 24, 1943; children—Ann Fay (Mrs. Ronald Reed), Johnsy Althea, Phillip Brewington. Ordained minister A.M.E. Ch., 1938; pastor churches in Va. and Md., 1942-47; prof. Morris Brown Coll. and Turner Theol. Sem., Atlanta, 1947-56; pastor Allen Temple A.M.E. Ch., Atlanta, 1956-65; pres. Morris Brown Coll., Atlanta, 1965-73. Campaign dir. United Negro Coll. Fund; mem. Ga. Council on Human Relation. Mem. Atlanta Bd. Edn., 1969—. Bd. dirs. Interdenominational Theol. Center, Atlanta, Carrie Steel Pitts Home, Atlanta, Atlanta U. Center Corp., Atlanta council Boy Scouts Am. Mem. Frontiers Internat., Sigma Phi Pi, Alpha Phi. Home: 601 University Pl NW Atlanta GA 30314

MIDDLETON, NORWOOD CRONK, newspaper editor; b. Sumter, S.C., May 26, 1918; s. Walter P. and Mattie (Cronk) M.; A.B., Roanoke Coll., 1939; m. Lucille Hood, June 28, 1941; children—Kenneth Norwood, David Lynn. Reporter Roanoke (Va.) World-News, 1940-46; mng. editor Pulaski (Va.) Southwest Times, 1946-49; with Roanoke (Va.) Times, 1949—, successively swing deskman, city editor, news editor, 1949-57, mng. editor, 1957—. Mem. exec. bd. Blue Ridge council Boy Scouts Am., pres. 1966-67. Moderator Montgomery Presbytery, Presbyn. Ch. U.S., 1967. Served from pvt. to capt. USAAF, 1942-45. Mem. Salem C. of C. (past dir.), Va. Press Assn. (pres. 1966-67). Presbyn. (elder). Kiwanian. Home: 1149 Forest Lawn Dr Salem VA 24153 Office: 201 Campbell Av SW Roanoke VA 24010

MIDGETT, ELWIN WILBURN, educator; b. Watertown, Tenn., Dec. 31, 1911; s. Edell Wilburn and Martha (Ellis) M.; B.S., Tenn. Tech. U., 1934; M.A., U. Ky., 1938; m. Margaret Nell Grandstaff, Oct. 28, 1933; children—Don Carter, Dan Earl. Tchr., Lebanon (Tenn.) High Sch., 1934-36, Castle Heights Mil. Acad., Lebanon, 1936-38; mem. faculty Middle Tenn. State U. at Murfreesboro, 1939—, now prof. bus. Proprietor, Home Bakery, Murfreesboro, 1950-54; cons. accounting, 1970—. Served to lt. (j.g.) USNR, 1944-45. Danforth Found. asso., 1953—. Mem. Middle Tenn. Edn. Assn. (pres. 1940), Administrv. Mgmt. Soc., Tenn. Edn. Assn., Nat. Bus. Edn. Assn., Alpha Kappa Psi, Pi Omega Pi. Methodist. Mason, Lion. Author: An Accounting Primer, 1968; Corkus (Punt, Pass, Pitch, Putt) Subtitled, 1970. Home: 510 Woodmore Dr Murfreesboro TN 37130 Office: Dept Bus Edn Middle Tenn State Univ Murfreesboro TN 37130

MIDGETT, LORIMER WILLARD, banker; b. Mann's Harbor, N.C., Feb. 9, 1911; s. Ellis Bradford and Matilda (Tillett) M.; A.B., U. N.C., 1932; m. Margaret White, June 3, 1933. Tchr., Elizabeth City, N.C., 1937-54; owner ins. agy., Elizabeth City, 1937-54; pres. Peoples Bank & Trust Co., Elizabeth City, 1954—, also dir. Mem. N.C. Ho. Reps., 1943, N.C. Senate, 1947. Bd. dirs. Elizabeth City State U. Served to lt. comdr. USNR, World War II. Mem. U.S. C. of C. (dir. 1952-54). Kiwanian (lt. gov. 1941), Elk. Address: E Main St Elizabeth City NC 27909

MIDLEN, JOHN HOLBROOK, lawyer; b. Phila., June 2, 1910; s. Edward B. and Lilian (Lewis) M.; B.S. in Econs., U. Pa., 1931; J.D., Georgetown U., 1938, LL.M., 1954; m. Gertrude H. Robertson, Oct. 12, 1940; children—John H., Margaret R. (Mrs. Manda). Admitted tp D.C. bar, 1935; gen. counsel Delta Sigma Phi, 1940-47, 51-53; practice law in Washington, 1945—; sr. partner Midlen & Reddy, 1968—. Mem. FCC Nat. Industry Adv. Com., 1960-68, FCC Industry Adv. Group U.S.-Mexico Standard Broadcast Agreement Negotiations, 1966-70; communications counsel Nat. Religious Broadcasters, 1968—. Pres., Spring Valley-Wesley Heights Citizens Assn., Washington, 1959-60. Served to lt. col. AUS, 1941-45. Decorated Army Commendation ribbon with oak leaf cluster. Mem. Fed. Communications Bar Assn. (sec., treas., exec. com.), Am. Bar Assn., Bar Assn. D.C. Presbyn. (elder). Home: 4800 Tilden St NW Washington DC 20016 Office: 1990 M St NW Washington DC 20036

MIER, MARIANO JOSÉ, banker; b. Ponce, P.R., Apr. 19, 1941; s. Mariano L. and Gladys (Tous) M.; B.B.A. magna cum laude, U. P.R., 1962; postgrad. N.Y. U. Sch. Bus., 1963-64; grad. Inst. of Investment Banking, U. Pa. Wharton Sch. Finance and Commerce, 1969; m. Ana C. Romeu, June 1, 1963; children—Nicole Marie, Mariano Andrew, Carlos José. With Hilton Hotels Corp., N.Y.C., 1963-64; asst. credit mgr., financial analyst Talcott Interam. Corp., San Juan, P.R., 1964-65; v.p., investment officer Banco Popular de P.R., San Juan, 1965—. Tchr. investment and securities U. P.R., Rio Piedras, 1968-71; tchr. bank investment Am. Inst. Banking, 1973-74. Mem. Nu Sigma Beta. Clubs: Bankers, Caparra (San Juan). Home: Calle Jardin AA-2 Garden Hills Guaynabo PR 00619 Office: GPO Box 2708 San Juan PR 00936

MIERS, MILEY L., II, dentist; b. Montgomery, Ala., Feb. 6, 1927; s. Miley L. and Luna (Browder) M.; A.B., Washington U., St. Louis, 1953, D.D.S., 1953; m. Patricia Malloy, Sept. 5, 1959; children—Melanie Anne, Michael Lawrence, Michelle Lynn, Miley L. III. Practice gen. dentistry, St. Louis, 1953-54, Tallahassee, 1954—; mem. dental staff Tallahassee Meml. Hosp., 1954—; asst. sec. Fla. Bd. Dental Examiners, 1963-67. Pres., Boys Club Leon County, 1969—; head dental div. Leon County United Fund, 1958-61. Mem. Fla. Ho. of Reps., 1966—. Founder, pres. Fla. Reading Research Found., 1973. Bd. dirs. Tallahassee YMCA. Served with USNR, 1944-46. Recipient George Washington Gold medal award Freedoms Found. at Valley Forge, 1968; voted one of most outstanding mems. Fla. Legislature, 1969, 70. Fellow Am., Internat. coll. dentists; mem. Leon County (pres. 1958-59), N.W. Dist. (pres. 1962-63) dental socs., Am. (mem. Fla. delegation 1964-67), Fla. dental assns., Am., Fla. acads. gen. dentistry, Fla. Acad. Dental Practice Adminstrn., Fla. Prosthodontic Soc., North Fla. Dental Research Com. (pres. 1965), Am. Acad. Dental Practice Adminstrn., Am. Equilibration Soc., Am. Soc. Oral Physiology and Occlusion, Pierre Fauchard Acad., Fedn. Dentaire Internationale, Southeastern Acad. Prosthodontics, Am. Prosthonodontic Soc., Tallahassee C. of C. Episcopalian (mem. ofcl. bd.). Mason (32 deg., Shriner), Toastmaster (dir., past pres. Tallahassee), Rotarian (dir. Tallahassee). Clubs: Seminole Booster, Tip-Off (Fla. State U.); Century (Washington U. Dental Sch.). Home: Moccasin Gap FL 32303 Office: 1213 Miccosukee Rd Tallahassee FL 32303

MIGAKI, GEORGE, scientist; b. Troy, Mont., Apr. 26, 1925; s. Kinhichi and Hisano (Omato) M.; student Gonzaga U., 1946-48; B.S., Wash. State U., 1952, D.V.M., 1952; m. Riyoko Hayashi, June 7, 1952; children—Barbara, Karen. Practice vet. medicine, Missoula, Mont., 1952-53, Bremerton, Wash., 1953-54; vet. meat insp. U.S. Dept. Agr., Portland, Ore., 1954-57, vet. pathologist, Beltsville, Md., 1957-68; chief comparative pathology br. Armed Forces Inst. Pathology, Washington, 1968—. Chmn. tennis clinic Clifton Park Citizens Assn., Silver Spring, Md., 1969—; chmn. ofcls. com. Silver Spring YMCA Swim Team Parents Assn., 1971—. Served with AUS, 1945-46. Recipient Outstanding Performance award U.S. Dept. Agr., 1962, certificate of merit, 1965. Mem. Am. Coll. Vet. Pathologists (com. on exams. 1970-73), Am., D.C. (v.p. 1967, pres. 1969, sec.-treas. 1971—) vet. med. assns., Internat. Acad. Pathology, Internat. Assn. Aquatic Animal Medicine, Wildlife Disease Assn., Am. Assn. Avian Pathologists, Wash. State U. Alumni Assn. (community co-ordinator Silver Spring 1970—). Author: (with P.J. Brandly and K.E. Taylor) Meat Hygiene, 1966. Contbg. author: Swine Diseases, 1970. Co-editor: Handbook: Animal Models of Human Disease, 1972. Editor Comparative Pathology Bull. Contbr. numerous articles to sci. pubs. Home: 9200 Daleview Ct Silver Spring MD 20901 Office: Armed Forces Inst Pathology Washington DC 20306

MIGDOL, MARVIN JACOB, pub. relations and personnel exec.; b. Rochester, N.Y., Jan. 11, 1937; s. Frank and Dorothy (Krieger) M.; B.A., U. Buffalo, 1959; postgrad. U. Miami, 1959-60; M.S., Boston U., 1961; m. Sharon Grace Miron, 1970. Sec. for communications Rensselaer Poly. Inst., Troy, N.Y., 1963-64; pub. relations cons., pres. Migdol Assos., New Orleans, Buffalo, 1964-68; pres. Snelling & Snelling, Dallas, 1968—, Internat. Distbrs., Inc., 1974—. Lectr. inst. Boston U., 1960-61, Pa. State U., 1961-63, State U. N.Y., 1966-68. Active Jewish Welfare Fedn. Bd. dirs. Acad. Hosp. Pub. Relations, Inst. Information and Communication in Israel. Mem. Am. Assn. Indsl. Editors, Am. Coll. Pub. Relations Assn., U. Buffalo Alumni Assn. (pres. 1964-65), N.W. Pa. Internat. Council Indsl. Editors, Pub. Relations Assn. Western N.Y., Alpha Epsilon Pi (regional gov. 1966-67). Author: Public Relations Handbook, 1962; Comics as a Public Relations Tool in Communications, 1970. Contbr. numerous articles to profl. jours. Home: 7853 La Casa Dr Dallas TX 75240 Office: Noel Page Bldg Dallas TX 75206

MIGHELL, RICHARD HENRY, elec. engr.; b. Aurora, Ill., Mar. 18, 1907; s. Ray and Ouida Lillian (Henry) M.; B.S., U. Denver, 1929; m. Ruth Aline Simon, June 12, 1930; children—Kenneth, Donald, Robert. Meter and instrument design engr. Gen. Electric Co., Lynn, Mass., 1935, salesman, Schenectady, 1935-38, meter and instrument specialist, Dallas, 1938-43, meter and instrument transformer sales engr., 1943-71. Instr. electric meter schs. Tex. A. and M. U., 1938-71, U. Ark., 1938-71. Capt. United Fund, Dallas, 1966. Mem. Dallas Electric Club. Methodist (mem. ofcl. bd. 1971-73). Club: Brookhaven Country (Dallas). Home: 6705 Golf Dr Dallas TX 75205

MIGLIORE, PHILIP JOSEPH, physician; b. Pitts., Dec. 18, 1931; s. Salvatore and Clara (Pergola) M.; B.S., U. Pitts., 1954, M.D., 1956; m. Ann Nixon, July 20, 1957; children—Philip Victor, Cynthia Ann, Todd Nixon. Intern West Pa. Hosp., Pitts., 1956-57, resident, 1959-60; resident U. Pitts. Presbyn. Hosp., 1960-61; fellow M.D. Anderson Hosp., 1961-64; practice medicine specializing in pathology, Houston, 1964—; asst. pathologist Meth. Hosp., 1969—; asst. prof. pathology Baylor Coll. Medicine, 1969—; asst. pathologist, asst. prof. pathology M.D. Anderson Hosp. and Tumor Inst., 1964-69. Served to capt. USAF, 1957-59. Diplomate Am. Bd. Pathology. Mem. A.M.A., A.A.A.S., Am. Soc. Clin. Pathologists, N.Y. Acad. Scis., Phi Beta Kappa, Alpha Omega Alpha. Presbyn. (elder). Contbr. articles to med. jours. Home: 3602 Grennoch St Houston TX 77025 Office: Meth Hosp Houston TX 77025

MIHALCZO, JOHN THOMAS, nuclear engr.; b. Yonkers, N.Y., May 30, 1931; s. John and Mary (Ferguson) M.; B.A., N.Y. U., 1953, M.S., 1956; Ph.D., U. Tenn., 1970; m. Arlene Marie Howard, May 30, 1952; children—John, Jo Ann, Robert, David, Paul. Physicist, Curtiss Wright Corp., Woodridge and Clifton, N.J., and Quehanna, Pa., 1953-58; physicist Oak Ridge Nat. Lab., 1958-68, mem. research staff, 1973—, mem. research staff Y-12 Plant, 1968-73. Ford Found. prof. nuclear engring. U. Tenn., Knoxville, 1971—. Mem. Am. Nuclear Soc. Roman Catholic. K.C. Contbr. articles to profl. jours. Home: 114 Lehigh Lane Oak Ridge TN 37830

MIHALYKA, EUGENE ERNST, surgeon, bus. exec.; b. Richmond, Va., Nov. 21, 1917; s. Daniel A. and Elizabeth R. (Kristopher) M.; A.B., Johns Hopkins, 1940; M.D., Med. Coll. Va., 1950; m. Jean Beaumont Merritt, Mar. 25, 1942; children—George Kristopher, Jane Beaumont. Intern, Sewickley Valley Gen. Hosp., Pitts., 1950-51; resident Crile VA, Western Res. U. hosps., Cleve., 1953-57; practice medicine specializing in surgery, Cleve., 1953-71; head and neck surgeon, sr. clin. instr. Case Western Res. U. Sch. Medicine, 1953-71, now sr. vis. lectr.; mem. active staff dept. surgery U. Hosps.; asso. staff head and neck surgery Fairview Gen. Hosp., Cleve., 1971—; dir. med. edn. and med. affairs Edward McCready Meml. Hosp., Crisfield, Md., 1972—, also mem. active surg. staff; cons. med. programs State Md. Chmn. bd. Chesapeake Systems Corp., 1964—, Tru-Har Products Inc., Lakewood, O.; dir. Pandor Coal Corp. Physician, Met. Opera Assn. Northeastern Ohio, 1960—; chmn. bd. SSS local bd., 1971—. Fellow Internat. Oceanographic Found. Served to maj. USAAF, 1941-46. Research grantee for head and neck cancer work, 1960. Mem. A.M.A., Ohio, Va., Md. med. socs., Cleve. Acad. Medicine, Johns Hopkins Surg. Assn., Ohio Surg. Soc., Am. Mgmt. Assn., Save the Chesapeake Bay Found., Gt. Lakes Found. Presidents Club. Contbr. articles to profl. jours. Home: Cherry-Core Cheriton VA 23316 Office: Cheriton VA 23316

MIKI, ROBERT T., govt. ofcl.; b. Honolulu, Sept. 21, 1930; s. Thomas L. and Alice (Terada) M.; B.B.A., U. Hawaii, 1952; M.A., U. Ill., 1954; Ph.D., U. Minn., 1957. Instr. econs. U. Minn., 1955-57; prof. Williams Coll., 1957-63; with U.S. Dept. Commerce, Washington, 1963—, research, 1963-65; spl. asst. to dep. asst. sec. econ. devel., 1965-66; dep. dir. Office Econ. Research, 1966-67, sr. economist Office Asst. Sec. Commerce for Econ. Affairs, 1967—; prof. grad. dept. econs. Georgetown U.; cons. in field. Mem. Am. Econ. Assn., Econometric Soc., So. Regional Sci. Assn. (pres. 1971-72), Omicron Delta Gamma. Contbr. articles in field to profl. jours. Editor, Rev. Regional Studies. Home: 4701 Willard Av Chevy Chase MD 20015 Office: Office Asst Sec Econ Affairs US Dept Commerce Washington DC 20230

MIKITEN, TERRY MICHAEL, educator; b. N.Y.C., June 1, 1937; s. Walter Donald and Vera (Rouba) M.; B.A., N.Y. U., 1960; Ph.D., Albert Einstein Coll. Medicine, 1967; m. Jacqueline Tannert, Apr. 30, 1960; children—Shawn, Brian, Erick. Research asso. Schering Pharm. Corp., Bloomfield, N.J., 1960-61; NIH fellow, dept. physiology Columbia Coll. Phys. & Surg., N.Y.C., 1967-69; asst. prof. dept. physiology U. Tex. Health Sci. Center, San Antonio, 1969—. Cons. S.W. Research Inst., 1973; lectr. Nat. Acupuncture Research Soc., 1973; South Tex. chmn. Osteogenesis Imperfecta Found., 1972. Recipient Outstanding Tchr. award U. Tex. Med. Sch. at San Antonio, 1971, USPHS research grantee, 1969—. Mem. A.A.A.S., Soc. Neurosci., N.Y. Acad. Sci. Office: U Tex Health Sci Center San Antonio TX 78284

MIKKELSON, DEAN HAROLD, geol. engr.; b. Devils Lake, N.D., July 25, 1922; s. John Harold and Theodora (Eklund) M.; student N.D. State Coll., 1940-42, U.S. Naval Acad., 1942-45; B.S., U. N.D., 1956; m. Delphene Doss, May 30, 1946; 1 dau., Lynn Dee (Mrs. Kirk Laughbaum). Second officer U.S. Lines, Quaker Lines-States Lines, S.S. Co., 1945-48; partner Mikkelson's, J.I. Case farm machinery, Devils Lake, N.D., 1948-52; oil and gas lease broker, N.D., 1952-54; geologist Sohio Petroleum Co., Oklahoma City, 1956-58; geol. engr. Brazilian Govt., 1958-60; pvt. practice as geol. engr., Oklahoma City, 1960—. Republican candidate for Okla. Legislature, 1958; del. numerous state and county convs., N.D., Okla. Served with USNR, 1942-45, U.S. Maritime Service, 1945-48. Mem. Oklahoma City Geol. Soc. Mason. Contbr. to profl. publs. Home: 4725 NW 59th Terrace Oklahoma City OK 73122 Office: Leininger Bldg 3545 NW 58th St Oklahoma City OK 73112

MIKULECKY, DONALD CASIMIR, educator; b. Chgo., Mar. 23, 1936; s. Elmer Frank and Valerie (Urbick) M.; B.S., Ill. Inst. Tech., 1957; Ph.D., U. Chgo., 1963; m. Tamera Francom Strunk, Apr. 1, 1973; children (from a previous marriage)—Joel David, Elizabeth Ann. Fellow, polymer dept. Weizmann Inst., Rehovoth, Israel, 1963-65; asst. prof. biophysics State U. N.Y. at Buffalo, 1965-68; vis. scholar math., physics Philander Smith Coll., Little Rock, 1958-69; vis. lectr. biophysics Harvard Med. Sch., Boston, 1969-71; asso. prof., div. dir. biophysics Meharry Med. Coll., Nashville, 1971-73; asso. prof. physiology Med. Coll. Va., Richmond, 1973—. Rep., Scientists and Engrs. for Social and Polit. Action, 1971-73; vis. lectr. 1st Winter Sch. on Biophysics of Membrane Transport, Sklavska, Poreba, Poland, 1974. Served to lt. USMCR, 1957-60. NSF fellow, 1960-61, USPHS fellow, 1961-63, 1963-65. Mem. Biophys. Soc. (chmn. biology of survival com. 1973—, edn. com. 1974—), Am. Chem. Soc., Am. Assn. U. Profs. Contbr. articles to profl. publs. Home: 9303 Redborne Rd Richmond VA 23235

MILAM, JOHN THOMAS, physician; s.; Benjamin Burl and Bessie Mable (Crites) M.; B.S., W.Va. U., 1936; postgrad. W.Va. U., 1938-39; grad. Command and Gen. Staff Sch., 1943; M.D., Tulane U. Sch. Medicine, 1946-50; m. Helen Carolyn Graham, May 27, 1946; children—John Benjamin, James Thomas, Lynn Elise. Sci. tchr. Sissonville (W.Va.) High Sch., 1936-37, Charleston (W.Va.) High Sch., 1938-39; intern Charity Hosp., New Orleans, 1950-51; practice gen. medicine, Cleveland, Miss., 1951—. Pres., Russel Bldgs. Corp., Cleveland, 1964—; sec. Cleveland Clinic Bldg. Corp., 1966—; pres. Holiday Enterprises, 1973—; v.p. Arcade Shoes, Inc., Cleveland; dir. Exec. Services, Jackson, Miss. Chief of staff East Bolivar County Hosp., Cleveland, 1962, 65. Served from 2d lt. to maj. AUS, 1940-46. Mem. A.M.A., Am. Acad. Gen. Practice, Miss. State Med. Assn., Delta Med. Soc. Methodist. (steward 1968—), Rotarian. Home: 1108 Farmer St Cleveland MS 38732 Office: Cleveland Clinic Hwy 8 E Cleveland MS 38732

MILANA, FREDERICK IGNATIUS, physician; b. Bklyn., Sept. 16, 1907; s. Pasquale and Anna (Russo) M.; Ph.G., Bklyn. Coll. Pharmacy, 1928; M.D., N.Y. Med. Coll., 1934; m. Theresa Gretchen Noerr, Nov. 13, 1929; 1 dau., Eileen Patricia (Mrs. Harvey Miller). Intern Flower Hosp., N.Y.C., 1934-35; practice medicine, Bklyn., 1935-70; mem. courtesy staff Methodist Hosp., Samaritan Hosp., Bklyn. Cons. blood irradiation therapy for treatment viral diseases. Mem. N.Y. Cardiological Soc. Home: 1200 SW 12th St Fort Lauderdale FL 33315 Office: 368 5th St Brooklyn NY 11215

MILBRODT, PAUL EUGENE, electronic engr.; b. Wilson, Ark., Mar. 21, 1923; s. Paul and Ola (Sanders) M.; student Ark. State Coll., 1946-49; B.S. in Elec. Engring., U. Ark., 1951; M.S., George Washington U., 1969; m. Edna Louise Lindenberg, Aug. 3, 1951; 1 dau., Cathy Louise. Electronic engr. Nat. Union, 1951-54, Melpar Inc., 1954-57; prin. electronic engr. Budd Co., 1963-65; sr. electronic engr. Control Sci. Corp., 1965-67; engring. mgr. Airtronics, Inc., Chantilly, Va., 1968—. Digital cons., Va., 1967-69. Served with USAAF, 1941-45. Registered profl. engr. Home: 12001 Central Dr Fairfax VA 22030 Office: 3001 Centerville Rd Chantilly VA 22021 also Box 17186 Dulles Airport Washington DC 20041

MILES, ALGENE STEVENS, JR., banker; b. Louisville, Nov. 30, 1929; s. Algene Stevens and Edna May (Rietze) M.; B.A., Washington and Lee U., 1951; grad. Grad. Sch. Banking Rutgers-State U., 1964; m. Ann Berry Houston, Nov. 6, 1954; children—Frank, Elizabeth. Trainee First Nat. Bank Louisville, 1954-59, asst. cashier, 1959-61, asst. v.p., 1961-64, v.p., 1964-68, sr. v.p., 1968-70, exec. v.p., 1970-72, pres., 1972—, also dir.; dir. Louisville Title Ins. Co. Campaign dir. Planned Parenthood dr., 1968, Easter Seal dr., 1969; active Explorer div. Boy Scouts Am. Bd. dirs. United Way, 1970, treas., 1970; bd. dirs. Salvation Army Boys Club; bd. dirs. St. Joseph's Infirmary, 1968-70, vice chmn., 1970; bd. dirs. Louisville Central Area, Ky. Historic Homes Found.; Bd. overseers U. Louisville. Served to 2d lt. AUS, 1951-53. Mem. English-Speaking Union (dir.). Episcopalian (vestryman). Clubs: Louisville Country (dir. 1969-71); Pendennis (Louisville). Home: 613 Club Lane Louisville KY 40207 Office: PO Box 1019 101 S 5th St Louisville KY 40201

MILES, CATHERINE E. (MRS. JAMES R. MILES), educator; b. Reform, Ala.; d. Leven Handy and Mary (Sibley) Ellis; B.S., U. Ala., 1949, M.S., 1950, Ph.D., 1953; J.D., Emory U., 1963; m. James R. Miles, Mar. 1952; children—Jeannette (Mrs. B. L. Smith), Maxine (Mrs. J.A. Bayly). Indsl. accountant Batson-Cook Co., West Point, Ga., 1937-42; prof., chmn. dept. Ga. State U. at Atlanta, 1952—. Named Atlanta's Woman of Yr. in Edn., 1967. Mem. Nat. Assn. Accountants, Ga. Soc. C.P.A.'s, Am. Accounting Assn. (sec.-treas. 1969-71), Am. Soc. Women Accountants, State Bar Ga., Am., Atlanta bar assns., Beta Gamma Sigma, Beta Alpha Psi. Author: (with Joe Lane) Business and Personnel Taxes, 1967, rev. edit., 1974. Office: Ga State U Dept Accounting 33 Gilmer St Atlanta GA 30303

MILES, FERDINAND WASHINGTON, nuclear engr.; b. Murfreesboro, Tenn., Feb. 3, 1921; s. Harry Hicks and Annie Luby (Hays) M.; B.S., U. Tenn., 1943, M.S., 1956; postgrad. Oak Ridge Sch. Reactor Tech., 1958-60, Ohio State U., 1949; m. June Elizabeth Cline, June 25, 1948; children—Junene (Mrs. Edward Anderson McCrary), William Harry. With Tenn. Copper Co., Copperhill, 1943-48, Battelle Meml. Inst., Columbus, O., 1948-52; nuclear researcher Oak Ridge Nat. Lab., 1952-70; nuclear fuel processor Gen. Electric Co., Morris, Ill., 1970-71; nuclear engr. TVA, Knoxville, 1971—. Mem. Am. Inst. Chem. Engrs., Profl. Engr. Tenn., TVA Engrs. Assn., Kappa Alpha, Tau Beta Pi, Phi Kappa Phi. Mem. Ch. of Christ. Contbr. to profl. publs. in field. Home: 8212 Corteland Dr Knoxville TN 37919 Office: TVA Room 304 Union Bldg Annex Knoxville TN 37902

MILES, FRANKLIN, city engr.; b. Jacksonville, Fla., July 7, 1924; s. Patrick Hines and Harriet Helena (Seewing) M.; student U. Fla., 1942-43, U. N.C., 1944-45; m. Margie Cater Keen, Mar. 3, 1945; children—Jennifer (Mrs. Edward Allen Cain), Cecelia (Mrs. William Glosson), Franklin, William Patrick, Margaret Ann, Debra Jane, Myra Louise. With Fla. Hwy. Dept., 1946-50; constrn. engr. B.B. McCormick & Sons, Jacksonville Beach, Fla., 1950-51; engring. designer Smith & Gillespie Engrs., Jacksonville, 1953-60; city engr., dir. pub. works City of Waycross, Ga., 1960—. Instr. night sch. Waycross Ware Tech. Sch., cons. engr. and land surveyor, 1965—. Bd. dirs. Waycross chpt. A.R.C., 1960—, chmn. bd., 1968—. Served with USMCR, 1943-46, 51-53. Registered profl. engr., Fla., Ga. Mem. Ga. Soc. Profl. Engrs. Mason, Lion. Club: Engineering Professions (Jacksonville, Fla.). Home: 611 N Nicholls St Waycross GA 31501 Office: City Hall Waycross GA 31501

MILES, GEORGE BENJAMIN, educator; b. Erin, Tenn., May 14, 1926; s. George Gideon and Neva Alice (Tarwater) M.; B.S., U. Tenn. at Knoxville, 1950, Ph.D., 1958; postdoctoral U. Cal. at Berkeley, 1967-68; m. Ida Forbes Robertson, June 3, 1956; 1 dau., Margaret Ann. Chemist, Naval Ordinance Lab., Corona, Cal., 1953-54; research chemist E.I. duPont, Kinston, N.C., 1958-61; mem. faculty Appalachian State U. at Boone, N.C., 1961—, prof. chemistry, 1969—, chmn. dept., 1968—. Served with USN, 1944-46, 51-53. NSF faculty fellow, 1967-68. Mem. Am. Chem. Soc., Am. Assn. U. Profs., Sigma Xi, Phi Kappa Phi. Home: Route 5 Box 14 Boone NC 28607

MILES, HENRY HARCOURT WATERS, physician; b. Burnside, La., Sept. 18, 1915; s. William Porcher and Harriette (Waters) M.; B.S., Tulane U., 1936, M.D., 1939; m. Margaret Bemis Hart, Nov. 29, 1939; children—Sarah Beirne, Robert Hart. Intern, Touro Infirmary, New Orleans, 1939-40, Johns Hopkins Hosp., 1940-41; resident Med. Coll. Va., 1941-42, Mass. Gen. Hosp., 1946-52, Boston Psychoanalytic Inst., 1947-52; individual practice psychiatry and psychoanalysis, New Orleans, 1952—; tng. and supervising analyst New Orleans Psychoanalytic Inst., 1957—; prof. psychiatry Tulane U., 1966—. Mem. La. Hosp. Planning Adv. Council, 1964—, med. adv. bd. Dept. Pub. Welfare, 1966—. Served with M.C. AUS, 1942-46. Fellow Am. Psychiat. Assn.; mem. A.M.A., Am., Internat. psychoanalytic assns., A.A.A.S., Am. Psychosomatic Soc., Alpha Omega Alpha. Author: (with S. Cobb and H. Shands) Case Histories in Psychosomatic Medicine, 1952. Contbr. articles to profl. jours. Home: 1446 Arabella St New Orleans LA 70115 Office: 1430 Tulane Av New Orleans LA 70112

MILES, HUGH SMITH, JR., educator; b. Newsoms, Va., Mar. 11, 1916; s. Hugh Smith and Pearl (Murrell) M.; B.S., Va. Poly. Inst., 1938, M.S., 1947; m. Mary Helen Jeffries, June 14, 1941; children—Hugh Smith III, John Jeffries, William Murrell. Mem. sales staff Internat. Harvester Co., Richmond, Va., 1939; asst. engr. Lummis & Co., Suffolk, Va., 1940; with Va. Poly. Inst. & State U., 1946—, asst. prof., 1946-50, asso. prof., 1950-56, prof. mech. engrs., 1956—, dir. mech. engring. lab., 1947-64, asst. dept. head mech. engring. dept., 1970—. Served to lt. col. AUS, 1941-46. Mem. Va. Poly. Inst. German Club, Omicron Delta Kappa, Tau Beta Pi, Pi Tau Sigma. Episcopalian (sr. warden 1962-65). Home: 506 Skyview Blacksburg VA 24060 Office: Randolph Hall Va Poly Inst Blacksburg VA 24061

MILES, JAMES WILLIAM, analytical chemist; b. Henderson, Ky., Sept. 19, 1918; s. James William and Isabel Teresa (Scherer) M.; B.S. in Chemistry, Western Ky. U., 1940; M.S. in Chemistry, U. Ill., 1947, Ph.D. in Analytical Chemistry, 1953; m. Evalyn Hall Willey, Sept. 8, 1951; 1 dau., JoAnn. Instr. chemistry Louisville Coll. Pharmacy, 1941-42; from asst. prof. to prof. pharm. chemistry, head dept. U. Ky., 1947-58; with USPHS, 1958—, chief chemistry sect., tech. devel. labs., Savannah, Ga., 1963-73, research chemist, tropical disease program Center Disease Control, Atlanta, 1973—. Mem. expert adv. bd. insecticides WHO, 1971—. Served to capt. AUS, 1942-46. Mem. Am. Chem. Soc., Research Soc. Am., Sigma Xi, Phi Lambda Upsilon. Contbr. articles to profl. jours. Home: 915 Starlight Dr NE Atlanta GA 30342 Office: Center Disease Control Tropical Disease Program VBC 1600 Clifton RD NE Atlanta GA 30333

MILES, JOHN BENJAMIN, lawyer; b. Greensboro, N.C., Oct. 19, 1930; s. John Richard and Lois (Wilson) M.; A.B., Guilford Coll., 1952; LL.B., Wake Forest Coll., 1955; m. Daphne Adele Rees, June 25, 1960; children—Lois Rose, John Benjamin, Jr. Admitted to N.C. bar, 1958, practiced in Greensboro, 1958-61, 68—; judge Municipal-County Ct., Greensboro, 1961-68. Bd. dirs. Greensboro Oratorio Soc. Served with CIC, AUS, 1955-58. Mem. N.C., Greensboro bar assns., Wake Forest U. Lawyers Alumni Assn. (exec. com. 1968-70), Phi Delta Phi. Presbyn. (elder). Home: McLeansville NC 27301 Office: Southeastern Bldg Greensboro NC 27401

MILES, LOVICK PIERCE, JR., lawyer; b. Fort Smith, Ark., Nov. 8, 1909; s. Lovick Pierce and Kate Thompson (Crawford) M.; B.A., Yale, 1932, LL.B., 1935; m. Mary Virginia Capell, June 19, 1941; 1 dau., Mary Capell. Admitted to Tenn. bar, 1935, since practiced in Memphis; mem. firm Miles and Miles, 1935—. Mem. Memphis, Shelby, Tenn., Am. bar assns., Delta Kappa Epsilon, Phi Delta Phi. Episcopalian. Club: Memphis Country. Home: 2941 Robin Rd Memphis TN 38111 Office: Sterick Bldg 1031 Memphis TN 38103

MILES, MELVIN HENRY, educator; b. St. George, Utah, Jan. 18, 1937; s. Maurice Jarvis and Mary Hanna (Lyon) M.; B.A., Brigham Young U., 1962; Ph.D., U. Utah, 1966; m. Viola Joyce Cook, July 21, 1962; children—David Lyon, Jolene Carol. Research chemist Naval Weapons Center, Corona, Cal., 1967-69; mem. faculty Middle Tenn. State U., Murfreesboro, 1969—, asso. prof. chemistry, 1972—. Vis. prof. Naval Weapons Center, China Lake, Cal., summers 1971-73. NATO research fellow, 1965-66. Mem. Am. Inst. Chemists, Electrochem. Soc., Sigma Xi. Mem. Ch. Jesus Christ of Latter-day Saints. Patentee in field. Contbr. to profl. publs. in field. Home: 614 Woodhill Dr Murfreesboro TN 37130

MILES, MIKE EDWARD, realtor; b. Austin, Tex., June 8, 1946; s. Burton Edward and Margaret (Jackson) M.; B.S., Washington and Lee U. (Leadership scholar), 1968; M.B.A., Stanford, 1971; m. Elston Downs, June 28, 1968; children—Wendy Jackson, Alexandra Catherine. Operations research analyst Ames Research Lab., NASA, San Francisco, 1970-71; mem. staff Peat Marwick Mitchell & Co., C.P.A.'s, Dallas, 1971-72; sec., financial v.p. Alpert Corp., Dallas, 1972—. Financial cons. Developers Services Inc. Capt. Dallas Cancer Crusade, 1972. Served with AUS, 1969. C.P.A., Tex. Mem. Am. Inst. C.P.A.'s, Tex. Soc. C.P.A.'s, Kappa Sigma, Beta Gamma Sigma. Home: 7766 Goforth Circle Dallas TX 75238 Office: 2766 One Main Pl Dallas TX 75275

MILES, OSCAR LANDON III, constrn. co. exec.; b. Monroe, La., Apr. 5, 1920; s. Oscar Landon and Gladys (Skinner) M.; B.S., La. Tech. U., 1940; m. Virginia Anita Vaughan, Dec. 9, 1944; children—Margaret Ann (Mrs. Oscar P. Barnes), Michael Landon. Mgr. payrolls U.S. Contrn. Q.M., Alexandria, La., 1940; chief project accountant Ford, Bacon & Davis, Monroe, La., 1941-61, mgr. sealants dept., 1962-67, v.p. bus. devel., 1968—; sec.-treas., dir. Sealants Internat., Inc., West Chester, Pa., 1965—; dir. F.B. & D., Engenharia E Construcoes Ltda., Sao Paulo, Brazil. Exec. adviser Jr. Achievement, Monroe, 1970-71; pres. Little League Baseball, Joliet, Ill., 1960. Served with USNR, 1942-46; lt. comdr. Res. (ret.). Mem. T.A.P.P.I., Nat. Assn. Accountants, Am. Gas Assn., La. Engring. Soc., Alpha Phi Omega. Episcopalian. Mason (32 deg., Shriner, K.T.). Clubs: New York Athletic (N.Y.C.); Lotus (pres. 1969-70), Bayou De Siard Country (Monroe). Home: 1305 Glenmar St Monroe LA 71201 Office: 3901 Jackson St Monroe LA 71201

MILES, RAYMOND CARL, mgmt. cons.; b. Indpls., May 6, 1920; s. Samuel Raymond and Marie Henrietta (Ginkel) M.; B.S. in Elec. Engring., Purdue U., 1942; M.S., Pa. State U., 1951; m. Genevieve B. Licato, Dec. 3, 1944; children—Stephen Raymond (dec.), Jeanne-Marie, Roy Christopher (dec.), Michele Gae. Engr., Internat. Tel. & Tel. Co., Newark, 1942-47; chief engr. HRB-Singer Co., State College, Pa., 1947-50; sci. research and devel. engring. supr. Cutler-Hammer, Inc., Deer Park, N.Y., 1950-59, chief engr., 1959-61, div. dir., 1961-65, v.p. AIL div., 1965-69; mgmt. cons., Northport, N.Y., 1969-71, Ft. Lauderdale, Fla., 1971—. Mem. I.E.E.E. (sr.), Made in Europe (world trade orgn.), Theta Chi. Contbr. articles to profl. jours. Patentee electronic devices, machine tool controls. Home: 2643 SW 30th Terrace Fort Lauderdale FL 33312 Office: 305 S Andrews Av Fort Lauderdale FL 33301

MILES, ROBERT IRVING, dentist; b. Glenside, Pa., Aug. 2, 1917; s. William Schooley and Jennie Mae (Keller) M.; student Duke, 1935-36; D.D.S., Med. Coll. Va., 1940; m. Katherine Elizabeth Scherer, Nov. 29, 1941; children—Robert Irving, Elizabeth Scherer, Margaret Carolyn, William Scherer. Pvt. practice dentistry, Richmond 1940-41, 1945—. Tchr. dept. operative dentistry Med. Coll. Va., Richmond, 1940-59. Served to capt. 9th Inf. Div., AUS, 1941-45. Decorated Bronze Star. Mem. Richmond Dental Soc., Va., Am. dental assns., Va. Assn. Professions, McKee Study Club, Delta Sigma Delta, Omicron Kappa Upsilon. Lutheran. Home: 2215 Wedgewood Av Richmond VA 23228 Office: 3604 Monument Av Richmond VA 23230

MILES, RUSS (HAYWARD ALLEN HALL), actor; b. Marion, N.C., Mar. 31, 1944; s. Horace James and Ruby (Owens) Hall; grad. Carolina Sch. Broadcasting, 1964; A.A., King's Coll., 1966; m. Judy Gwin, Dec. 15, 1968; children—Lisa, Russ and Keith (twins). Announcer WGTL, Kannapolis, N.C., 1963-65; announcer WYCL, York, S.C., 1965-66; announcer, music dir. WIST, Charlotte, N.C., 1966-67; announcer, program dir. WQIK, Jacksonville, Fla., 1967-69, 1971-73; announcer, prodn. dir. WVOJ, Jacksonville, 1969-71; pres. Fla. Broadcasters Coll. Inc., 1969-71; active Jax Little Theatre, Jacksonville, Fla., 1967—; now stage and film actor. Nominated for Best Actor, 1972; named Outstanding Personality Sterling Mags., MacFadden-Bartell Publs. Democrat. Baptist. Home: 3333 Kegler Dr Jacksonville FL 32216 Office: 5590 Rio Grande Jacksonville FL 32205

MILES, STANLEY JOE, petroleum co. exec.; b. Levita, Tex., Mar. 14, 1946; s. William Stanley and Floy (Webb) M.; B.B.A., Baylor U., 1968; m. Jo Freeman, June 4, 1966 (div. Mar. 1971); 1 son, Michael Joe. Sr. accountant Price Waterhouse & Co., Houston, 1968-73; financial v.p. Tex. Internat. Petroleum Corp., Shreveport, La., 1973—. C.P.A., Tex. Mem. Am. Inst. C.P.A.'s, Tex. Soc. C.P.A.'s, Houston Soc. C.P.A.'s. Home: 2010 W Algonquin St Shreveport LA 71107 Office: 2625 Line Av Shreveport LA 71104

MILES, THOMAS PEYTON, lawyer, judge; b. Appling County, Ga., Dec. 20, 1921; s. Thomas Peyton and Elizabeth (Faulkner) M.; LL.B., Mercer U., 1950, A.B., 1951; m. Mary Jacqueline Fennell, Sept. 2, 1944; children—Mary Cathy, Constance Ann, Elizabeth Paulette, Thomas Peyton Miles III. Admitted to Ga. bar, 1950; practice law, Baxley, 1950—; solicitor State Ct. of Appling, 1955-58, judge, 1959—; judge Juvenile Ct., Appling County, 1963—. Dir. Appling Devel. Corp. Mayor, Surrency, Ga., 1953-60. Served with USAAF, 1940-45. Decorated Air Medal with 10 oak leaf clusters, Purple Heart. Mem. Am., Ga., Brunswick (pres. 1963-64) bar assns., V.F.W., Am. Legion, Delta Theta Phi. Mason, Moose, Elk, Kiwanian (past pres. Baxley, past lt. gov. 4th div.). Home: PO Box 412 Baxley GA 31513 Office: PO Box 412 Baxley GA 31513

MILES, WAYNE ROBERT, govt. ofcl.; b. Torrance, Cal., Sept. 27, 1930; s. James Henry Orem and Ila Margaret (Jones) M.; B.S. in Civil Engring., U. Miss., 1953; m. Rosemary Cain, Jan. 10, 1953; children—Kristyne, Robyne. With TVA, Knoxville, Tenn., 1953-55, Hall & Norwood, engrs. and architects, Greenville, Miss., 1955-57, Sverdrup & Parcel, St. Louis, 1957-64, Allem & Hoshall, Memphis, 1964-70; asst. chief airports dist. office FAA, Miami, Fla., 1970—. Home: 15925 SW 83d Ct Miami FL 33157 Office: Internat Airport Miami FL 33159

MILEWICH, LEON, educator; b. Buenos Aires, Argentina, Mar. 26, 1927; s. Abraham and Szosza (Zilberdick) M.; B.S., U. Buenos Aires, 1956, M.S., 1958, D.Sc., 1959; m. Renate Nothman, Nov. 29, 1959; children—Susana Ruth, Daniel Abram, David Reuben. Came to U.S., 1961, naturalized, 1964. Postdoctoral fellow, U. Md. Sch. Pharmacy, 1961-64, Johns Hopkins Sch. Medicine, Balt., 1964-66, instr. obstetrics and gynecology, 1966-67; scientist S.W. Found. for Research and Edn., San Antonio, 1967-72; asst. prof. obstetrics and gynecology U. Tex. Southwestern Med. Sch., Dallas, 1972—. Adj. asst. prof. biochemistry U. Tex. Med. Sch. at San Antonio, 1971-72. Served with Argentine Army, 1950-51. Mem. Sociedad Quimica Argentina, Am. Chem. Soc., A.A.A.S., Am. Soc. Pharmacognosy, Chem. Soc. (London), N.Y. Acad. Scis., Am. Inst. Chemists, Sigma Xi, Rho Chi. Jewish religion (pres. congregation, 1971-72). Mem. B'nai B'rith. Contbr. articles to profl. jours. Home: 6331 Prestoncrest St Dallas TX 75230 Office: 5323 Harry Hines St Dallas TX 75235

MILEY, WILLIAM GETTIS, civil engr.; b. Plant City, Fla., Dec. 29, 1933; s. William Manual and Connie Viola (Collins) M.; B.C.E., U. Fla., 1957; m. Joan Beverly Chambers, Nov. 3, 1958; children—Katherine Elizabeth, Barbara Leah, Noel Alan. Mass properties engr., Martin Marietta Corp., Orlando, Fla., 1957-69; civil engr. Fla. State Engrs., Inc., Ocala, Fla., 1969—. Mem. Fla. Engring. Soc. (sr.), Am. Soc. C.E. Home: 716 NE 41st Av Ocala FL 32670 Office: PO Box 1171 Ocala FL 32670

MILFORD, DALE, congressman; b. Bug Tussle, Tex., Feb. 18, 1926; s. Homer Dale and Mary Gladys (Mann) M.; student Baylor U., 1953-57; m. Mary Michaelle Shattuck, June 24, 1967; children—Stephen Craig, Shari. Aircraft communicator CAA, 1942-44; served from pvt. to capt., inf., Signal Corps, AUS, 1944-53; meteorologist, TV weathercaster, 1953-56; meteorologist, aviation fixed-base operator, 1956-58; cons. aviation and meteorology, Dallas, 1958-72; mem. 93d Congress from 24th dist. Tex., 1972—. Mem. aviation adv. com. Dallas Ind. Sch. System, 1970-72. Bd. dirs. Dallas County Dept. Pub. Welfare. Mem. Am. Meteorol. Soc., Quiet Birdmen, Confederate Air Flying Mus. Home: 211 W Main St Grand Prairie TX 75050 Office: 427 Cannon House Office Bldg Washington DC 20515

MILFORD, GEORGE NOEL, JR., chemist; b. Victoria, P.E.I., Can., May 4, 1924; s. Geoge Noel and Anna Beatrice (MacLeod) M.; B.Sc., Mt. Allison U., 1944; M.Sc., Dalhousie U., 1948; Ph.D., McGill U., 1953; m. Margaret Florence Murray, Sept. 25, 1948; children—Murray A., John M., Alan M. Came to U.S., 1953, naturalized, 1965. Chemist. Dominion Steel & Coal, Sydney, N.S., Can., 1948-50; chemist, DuPont, Waynesboro, Va., 1953-61, sr. research chemist textile fibers, 1961—. Mem. Am. Chem. Soc., Sigma Xi. Lion. Patentee in field. Home: 1208 Shamrock Lane Waynesboro VA 22980 Office: Dept Textile Fibers DuPont Co Waynesboro VA 22980

MILFORD, MURRAY HUDSON, educator; b. Honey Grove, Tex., Sept. 29, 1934; s. Murray Lane and Vivian Ione (Hudson) M.; B.S., Tex. A. and M. U., 1955, M.S., 1959; Ph.D., U. Wis., 1962; m. Marsha Ann Rasmussen, July 21, 1961; children—Rebecca Ione, Murray Daniel. Research asso. Cornell U., Ithaca, N.Y., 1962-63; asst. prof., dept. agronomy, 1963-68, asso. prof., 1968; asso. prof., dept. soil and crop scis., Tex. A. and M. U., College Station, 1968-74, prof., 1974—. Served to 1st lt. AUS, 1955-57. Recipient prof. of merit award Agrl. Student Council of Tex. A. and M. U., 1969-70, faculty distinguished achievement award, 1971-72. Mem. Am. Soc. Agronomy, Soil Sci. Soc. Am., Clay Minerals Soc., Soil Conservation Soc. Am., Sigma Xi, Alpha Zeta, Phi Kappa Phi, Gamma Sigma Delta. Democrat. Presbyn. (ruling elder 1964—). Author: Introduction to Soils and Soil Science, 1970. Home: 3606 Tanglewood Dr Bryan TX 77801 Office: Dept Soil and Crop Sciences Tex A and M Univ College Station TX 77843

MILHAM, ROBERT CARR, chemist; b. Grand Haven, Mich., June 20, 1922; s. Clinton Pomeroy and Eleanor (Carr) M.; B.Sc., Alma Coll., 1943; student U. Wyo., 1943-44; Ph.D., U. Wis., 1952; m. Elizabeth Reynolds Deloach, Apr. 7, 1956. Chemist environmental effect div. Savannah River Lab. DuPont, Aiken, S.C., 1952—. Served with AUS, 1943-46. Mem. Am. Chem. Soc., Am. Nuclear Soc., Health Physics Soc. Home: 1474 Lyon Av Aiken SC 29801

MILHOUSE, PAUL WILLIAM, bishop; b. St. Francisville, Ill., Aug. 31, 1910; s. Willis Cleveland and Carrie (Pence) M.; A.B., Ind. Central Coll., 1932; D.D., 1950; B.D., Am. Theol. Sem., 1937, Th.D., 1946; L.H.D., Westmar Coll., 1965; S.T.D., Oklahoma City U., 1969; D.D., So. Meth. U., 1969; m. Mary Frances Noblitt, June 29, 1932; children—Mary (Mrs. R.L. Hauswald), Pauline (Mrs. Arthur Vermillion), Paul David. Ordained to ministry Methodist Ch., 1931; pastor, Birds, Ill., 1928-29, Mt. Vernon, Ill., 1932, Elliott, Ill., 1932-37, Olney, Ill., 1937-41, Decatur, Ill., 1941-51; asso. editor Telescope-Messenger, Harrisburg, Pa., 1951-59; exec. sec. Gen. Council of Adminstrn., Dayton, O., 1959-60; bishop, Kansas City, 1960-68, Oklahoma City, 1968—. Pres., Decatur (Ill.) Council of Chs., 1945-49, Bd. of Arbitration, Decatur, 1946, Bd. of Evangelism, Dayton, 1960-68. Trustee So. Meth. U., Oklahoma City U., United Sem., Meth. Home, Boys Ranch. Mem. Epsilon Sigma Alpha. Author: Enlisting and Developing Church Leaders, 1946; Come Unto Me, 1946; Doorways to Spiritual Living, 1950; Except the Lord Build the House, 1949; Christian Worship in Symbol and Ritual, 1953; Lift Up Your Eyes, 1955; Laymen in the Church, 1957; At Life's Crossroads, 1959; Philip William Otterbein, Pioneer Preacher to German Speaking Americans, 1968. Editor Facing Frontiers, 1960. Contbr. articles to profl. jours. Home: 2213 NW 56th Terrace Oklahoma City OK 73112 Office: 606 Gravens Bldg Oklahoma City OK 73102

MILICI, ROBERT CALVIN, geologist; b. New Haven, Aug. 8, 1931; s. Pompeo Scipio and Margaret Theresa (Koren) M.; A.B., Cornell, 1954; M.S., U. Tenn., 1955, Ph.D., 1960; m. Patricia Ann Hankley, Aug. 9, 1958; children—Pamela Anne, Robert Craig. Instr. geology U. Tenn. at Knoxville, 1955-58; geologist Div. Geology, Tenn. Dept. Conservation, 1958-62, 63—, Va. Div. Mineral Resources, Charlottesville, 1962-63. Fellow Geologic Soc. Am.; mem. Tenn. Acad. Sci. (chmn. geology-geography sect. 1967), A.A.A.S., Am. Assn. Petroleum Geologists, Soc. Econ. Paleontologists and Mineralogists, Carolina, Ga. geologic socs. Contbr. articles to profl. jours. Home: 8101 Normandy Dr Knoxville TN 37919 Office: 4711 Old Kingston St Knoxville TN 37919

MILITELLO, SAM, civil engr.; b. Tampa, Fla., Sept. 24, 1937; s. Angelo and Lily (Giglio) M.; student U. Tampa, 1956-58; B.C.E., U. Fla., 1961; m. Anne C. Butler, Aug. 12, 1972. Asst. design engr. J.E. Greiner Co., Tampa, 1961-64, design engr., 1964-66, project engr., 1966—, asso., 1971. Registered profl. engr., Fla., Ga. Mem. Am. Soc. C.E. (Fla. 1st v.p. 1973-74), Fla. Engring. Soc. (chpt. v.p. 1973-74). Roman Catholic. Club: Sertoma. Home: 2906 Tampa Bay Blvd Tampa FL 33607 Office: 5601 Mariner Dr Tampa FL 33622

MILLARD, JAMES ABIA, JR., clergyman, ch. ofcl.; b. Bristol, Tenn., Apr. 8, 1912; s. James Abia and Elsie Minor (McCutchan) M.; B.A., Hampden-Sydney Coll., 1932; B.D., Union Theol. Sem. in Va., 1935, Th.M., 1936, Th.D., 1942; D.D., Ark. Coll., 1951; m. Sunshine Hooper, June 12, 1937; children—Eleanor Hooper (Mrs. Steuart E. Vest), Pamela Anne, Lora O'Cain. Ordained to ministry Presbyn. Ch., 1936; pastorates in Va., La., Ark., 1935-52; prof. ch. polity and adminstrn. Presbyn. Theol. Sem., Austin, Tex., 1952-55, homiletics, 1956-59; clk., treas. Presbyn. Ch. U.S., Atlanta, 1959-73. Home: 455 Boone Lane Fairhope AL 36532

MILLARD, TIMOTHY ERNEST, lawyer; b. Ada. Okla., May 3, 1945; s. Ernest Mills Spear and Dorothea (Lewis) M.; B.B.A., So. Meth. U., 1967, J.D., 1969; m. Jill Annette Eaton, May 21, 1966; children—Stephanie Kyle, Jennifer Leigh. Admitted to Tex. bar, 1969; pvt. practice, Dallas, 1969-73; asso. mem. firm Locke, Purnell, Boren, Laney & Neely, Dallas, 1973—. Legal counsel, mem. exec. com. Minority Bus. Advisors, 1969—; cons. Dallas Alliance for Minority Enterprise, 1969—, Venture Advisors, 1969—; legal counsel, mem. exec. com. Native Am. League, 1972—. Mem. Dallas, Am. bar assns., State Bar Tex., Dallas Forum, Phi Alpha Delta, Kappa Sigma. Home: 7508 Wellcrest St Dallas TX 75230 Office: 3600 Republic National Bank Tower Dallas TX 75201

MILLARD, WALTER JOHN, JR., architect; b. Shreveport, La., Sept. 6, 1927; s. Walter John and Beulah Bell (Long) M.; B.A. cum laude, Southwestern Coll., Memphis, 1949; B.Arch., U. Pa., 1953; postgrad. Ecole des Beaux Arts, Fontainebleau, France, 1953; m. Blanche Kaiser, June 6, 1959; 1 dau., Blanche Boysen. Draftsman, A.L. Aydelotte & Assos., Memphis, 1953-54; asso. mem. firm Walk C. Jones, Jr., Memphis, 1954-61; prin. John Millad, Jr., Memphis, 1962—. Chmn. div. Shelby United Neighbors Campaign, 1968-71; guarantor Met. Opera and Memphis Opera Theatre, 1971, 72, 73; patron Brooks Art Gallery, Art Today, 1970-73; mem. Pres.'s Council Southwestern Coll. at Memphis, 1971-73. Bd. dirs. Memphis Orchestral Soc., 1973-74. Mem. A.I.A. (sec. 1960, del. 1960-61), U. Pa. Alumni (v.p. 1968-70), Sigma Alpha Epsilon, Omicron Delta Kappa. Presbyn. (deacon). Club: University. Work published in House Beautiful, 1968, 69; architect Bach-A-Nal House, Memphis Orchestral Soc., 1972. Home: 5675 Glade View Dr Memphis TN 38117 Office: 4646 Poplar Av Suite 208 Memphis TN 38117

MILLEDGE, SARAH FRANKLIN (MRS. STANLEY MILLEDGE), civic worker; b. Melrose, Mass., July 8, 1906; d. Albert Barnes and Edith (Bradbury) Franklin; B.A., Wellesley Coll., 1927; m. Stanley Milledge, Sept. 1, 1928 (dec. Oct. 1965); children—Allan Francis, Sarah Woodman (Mrs. Harold S. Nelson), Eleanor Franklin (Mrs. Barry Decker). Dir. women's community affairs WCKT-TV, Miami, Fla., 1962—, also dir. community service; dir. Sunbeam TV Corp. Pres. Miami Shores P.T.A., 1938-39; pres. Girl Scouts U.S.A., Dade County, 1948-50, chmn. region 6, 1952-56, nat. dir., 1952—, chmn. nat. nominating com., 1963-66, mem. nat. exec. com., 1958, council pres., 1961-62; pres. Children's Service Bur., 1950-52, Vis. Nurse Assn., 1952-54; chmn. Dade County recreation div. Welfare Planning Council, 1949-51, chmn. health div., 1956-60; mem. Children's Com., 1951-56; sec. Community Chest, 1953-55; v.p. Council Community Relations, 1954-56, Civil Liberties Assn., 1954-57; sec. Protestant Service Bur., 1955-56 (all Dade County); v.p. James E. Scott Community Assn., 1957-70; mem. state bd. Fla. Council Human Relations, 1958-62; sec. Fla. Co-operating Council Children and Youth; chmn. Fla. Com. for Children and Youth, 1968; bd. St. Petersburg Community Welfare Council, 1958-62; sec. South Pinellas Mental Health chpt., 1959-62; bd. dirs. Girl Scouts Tropical Fla., Dade County Welfare Planning Council, Vis. Nurse Assn., Miami Travellers Aid, United Cerebral Palsy Assn., United Ch. Women Greater Miami; chmn. Miami Wellesley Club Fund; trustee Everglades Sch. Girls, Miami, Fla., 1955-60; bd. dirs. Miami YWCA, pres., 1968-72; sec. Womens Com. of 100, Miami; chmn. Miami Council for Continuing Edn. of Women, 1971-72. Recipient Fla. regional award Nat. Conf. Christians and Jews, 1957; named Woman of Achievement, Dist. 12 Fla. Bus and Profl. Women, 1967. Mem. Am. Assn. U. Women. (chpt. bd. 1958—, local chpt. treas. 1959-62, vice chmn. Miami 1971—), Am. Women in Radio and TV (v.p. chpt.), UN Assn. (pres. chpt. 1972—), Soc. Mayflower Descs., Theta Sigma Phi. Conglist. Clubs: Miami Wellesley (pres. 1947-49). Home: 1600 Bayshore Dr Miami FL 33133 Office: Station WCKT Miami FL 33138

MILLER, AGNES CHAMBLESS (MRS. FRED MAHER MILLER), univ. dean; b. Ruston, La., Apr. 8, 1918; d. Marion Christopher and Rhoda (Liner) Chambless; B.S., La. Tech. U., 1938; M.S., La. State U., 1944; Ph.D., Fla. State U., 1964; m. William L. Cofer, Aug. 17, 1949 (div. 1959); children—Rhenda Scott, Claire Frances; m. 2d, Fred Maher Miller, Aug. 7, 1965. Tchr. high sch., Belcher, La., 1938-40; asst. dining hall dir. La. State U., 1941; food service dir. Standard (Oil) Restaurant Co., Baton Rouge; tchr. high sch., Start and Rayville, La., 1942-44; supr. nutrition and lunchroom edn. A.E. Phillips Tchr. Tng. Sch., La. Tech. U., Ruston, 1944-46, instr. food and nutrition, 1946-49, prof. home econs., 1955-59, 61-62, 64—, dean Coll. Home Econs., 1970—; parish sch. lunch supr. Natchitoches, La., 1949-50, Lake Charles, La., 1954-55. Mem. Am., La. home econs. assns., Nat., Gulf Coast sect. assns. inst. food technologists, Am. Dietetic Assn., La. Tchrs. Assn. (chpt. v.p.

1967-68), Coll. and U. Tchrs. Food and Nutrition (sect. pres. 1968-69), Soc. Nutrition Edn., Am. Assn. Adminstrs. Home Econs., La. Acad. Sci., La. Coll. Conf. (sec. home econs. sec. 1971-72). Alpha Tau Delta, Phi Kappa Phi, Delta Zeta. Baptist. Home: 503 S Sparta Ruston LA 71270

MILLER, ALBERT HENDERSON, cons. engr.; b. Newport, Ark., Nov. 30, 1932; s. Albert Jackson and Dovie (Murphy) M.; student Ark. State Tchrs. Coll., 1950-51; B.S. in Agrl. Engring., U. Ark., 1955; M.S. in Agrl. Engring., U. Mo., 1957; m. Lynette Alexander, Dec. 31, 1957; children—Alison Lyn, Albert Alexander. Sales engr. Delta Irrigation Co., Memphis, 1955; grad. asst. U. Mo., 1955-57; field engr. Short & Brownlee Constrn. Co., Inc., Newport, Ark. and Kansas City, Mo., 1957-59; br. mgr. Brownlee & Rogers, Inc., El Dorado, Ark., 1960; v.p. H.D. Kantor & Son, Inc., Clarksdale, Miss., 1961; pres. Miller Engring. Co., Inc., Clarksdale, 1961-63, Miller-Newell Engrs., Ltd., Newport, Ark., 1963—; owner A.H. Miller Farms, Newport, 1973—; sec.-treas. Miller-Newell Abstract Co., Inc., Newport, 1967—; partner Village Realty & Devel. Co., Newport. Registered profl. engr., Ark., Miss., Mo., Ala. Mem. Am. Soc. Agrl. Engrs. (chmn. Ark. chpt. 1971), Nat. Soc. Profl. Engrs., Newport Area C. of C. (pres. 1971), Phi Delta Theta (chpt. pres. 1954, pres. alumni club 1967), Gamma Sigma Delta, Kappa Kappa Psi, Gamma Alpha (chpt. pres. 1957). Episcopalian. Rotarian (dir. 1964-68, pres. 1973). Home: 1001 Walnut St Newport AR 72112 Office: 308 Walnut St Newport AR 72112

MILLER, ALFORD DONALD, city ofcl.; b. Shamokin, Pa., Sept. 14, 1928; s. Alford Franklin and Edna (Arbogast) M.; student Charlotte Fire Coll., 1958-61, U. N.C., 1969, 71; m. Amanda Damaris Francis, Jan. 15, 1949; children—Nancy Damaris, Karen Diane. Armature winder Electro Motive div. Gen. Motors Corp., Halethorpe, Md., 1948-51; control tower operator Piedmont Airlines, Winston-Salem, N.C., 1955-64; vol. fire chief Pilot Fire Dept., Thomasville, N.C., 1956-64; fire chief Tarboro, N.C., 1964-67; civilian fire chief Pacific Architects and Engrs., Los Angeles, Vietnam, 1967-69; fire chief Shelby, N.C., 1969—; fire rescue instr. N.C. Field Service. Dir. Davidson County Little League Football, 1962-64; chmn. Edgecombe County March of Dimes, 1966. Served with USAF, 1951-55. Mem. N.C. Firemens Assn., N.C. Fire Chief's Assn. (v.p. 1966-67), Nat. Fire Prevention Assn., Am. Legion. Baptist (deacon). Home: 305 S Poston St Shelby NC 28150 Office: 16 Graham St Shelby NC 28150

MILLER, ANN B. (MRS. EDWARD W. YANDRE), lawyer; b. Chattanooga, Dec. 22, 1897; d. Jeremiah T. and Rachel E. (Callahan) Miller; student Tampa U., Wash. Coll. Law, Am. Inst. Banking, 1938-48; m. Richard D. Morales, June 29, 1921 (dec. 1931); m. 2d, Edward W. Yandre, Mar. 4, 1954 (dec. Sept. 1967). Admitted to Fla. bar, 1946; asso. with husband in gen. practice law, Tampa, Fla., 1921-31; asso. firm Lewis H. Hill, Jr. & Robert D. Hill, attys., Tampa, 1931-37; legal sec., office mgr. trust dept. Exchange Nat. Bank Tampa, 1938-48; pvt. practice law, Tampa, 1948—, Orlando, Fla., 1954-70. Mem. Am., Fla., Tampa, Hillsborough and Orange Counties bar assns., Estate Planning Council Tampa (v.p., past sec., treas.), Central Fla. Estate Planning Council, Nat. (past state dir.; S.E. regional dir.), Fla. (past sec., past dir., past pres.), assns. women lawyers, Am. Inst. Banking (pres. Tampa chpt. 1946—), U.S. Council Bus. and Financial Cons. (asso. counsel), Phi Alpha Delta. Presbyn. Clubs: Tampa Yacht and Country; Orlando (Fla.) Country. Address: 2426 Sunset Dr Tampa FL 33609

MILLER, BANNER ISOM, meteorologist; b. Lansing, N.C., Aug. 20, 1917; s. Isom S. and Maude (Davis) M.; B.S., Appalachian State Tchrs. Coll., 1938; M.S., N.Y. U., 1947; Ph.D., U. Chgo., 1963; m. Sue Rice, July 17, 1948. Observer and forecaster U.S. Weather Bur., Charlotte, N.C., 1939-40, Atlanta, 1940-42, Washington, 1942, Brady, Tex., 1942-43, Elizabeth City, N.C., 1943-45, Balt., 1945-46, N.Y.C., 1946-48, San Juan, P.R., 1948-52, San Antonio, 1952-51; research meteorologist Nat. Hurricane Center and Nat. Hurricane Research Lab., Coral Gables, Fla., 1956-71, chief research and devel. Nat. Hurricane Center, 1971—. Recipient Silver Medal award Dept. Commerce, 1968, Distinguished Alumnus award Appalachian State Tchrs. Coll., 1971. Mem. A.A.A.S., Am. Meteorol. Soc., Meteorol. Soc. Japan, Sigma Xi. Author: (with Gordon E. Dunn) Atlantic Hurricanes, 1960. Home: 991 Apache St Miami Springs FL 33166 Office: National Hurricane Center PO Box 8286 Coral Gables FL 33124

MILLER, BARBARA ANN KAUFMAN (MRS. HAROLD I. MILLER), lyric soprano; b. Morgantown, W.Va., Aug. 2, 1932; d. Nathan and Ethel (Ritchin) Kaufman; student U. Mich., 1950-51, Pa. State U., 1951-53; A.B., U. Pitts. 1955; m. Harold I. Miller, Feb. 10, 1963; 1 son, Bruce. Lyric soprano appearing with popular mus. shows, including Call Me Madam, 1953, Blossom Time, 1953, Gentlemen Prefer Blondes, 1953, The Mikado, 1953, Louisiana Purchase, 1953, Naughty Marietta, 1953, Three Wishes for Jamie, 1953, Music In The Air, 1953, Lady In The Dark, 1953, The Great Waltz, 1953. Performer for community and charity orgns., Altonna, Pa., 1954—, Danville, Ky., 1963—. Mem. Council Jewish Women (gen. chmn. spl. projects Lexington 1963—), Sisterhood Adath Israel Temple, Lexington, Ky., Ohio Valley Fedn. Temple Sisterhoods (mem. bd. 1968—, program chmn.), Little Garden Club of Danville, Am. Assn. U. Women, Women Guild Lexington Philharmonic, Sigma Delta Tau, Hadassah (bd. mem. 1963-64). Home: 470 Boone Trail Danville KY 40422

MILLER, CARL EDWARD, retail trade co. exec.; b. Adeline, Ky., Dec. 17, 1915; s. Julius Frederick and Arvilla (Taylor) M.; grad. pub. high sch., 1933; m. Marjorie Lillian Ross, June 30, 1937; children—Gaynelle, Carl Edward. Traffic mgr. Ashland Oil Refining Co., Ashland, Ky., 1941-44; v.p. Vogel-Birch Distributing Co., Ashland, 1944-49, also appliance sales mgr.; pres., mgr. Better Home Appliance O., Inc., Ashland, 1949—. Mem. Ind. Sch. Bd., 1970-72. Bd. dirs. Ashland YMCA, 1970—, Salvation Army, 1970—. Named Ky. Small Businessman of Year Small Bus. Adminstrn., 1973. Mem. Ashland Area (pres. 1972-73), Ashland Jr. (pres. 1945-46) chambers commerce. Republican. Methodist (trustee 1968—). Mason, Elk. Club: Bellefonte Country. Home: 119 Country Club Dr Ashland KY 41101 Office: 2260 Winchester Av Ashland KY 41101

MILLER, CARTER FAKES, JR., pathologist; b. Asheville, N.C., July 10, 1934; s. Carter Fakes and Martha (Franks) M.; B.S., U. Tenn., 1955, M.D., 1958; m. Margaret Sue Moffett, Apr. 13, 1960; children—Randall Carter, Craig Spencer, Kyle Howard, Michelle Moffett. Intern, U. Tenn. Hosp., Knoxville, 1959; resident surgery VA Hosp., Memphis, 1962-64, resident pathology, 1964-67; asst. chief lab. VA Hosp., Atlanta, 1968-69; practice medicine, specializing in pathology Ft. Sanders Presbyn. Hosp., Knoxville, 1969—; chief lab. East Tenn. Children's Hosp., 1969—. Asst. prof. Emory U. Sch. Medicine. 1968-69. Bd. dirs. East Tenn. Heart Assn., 1973; alumni mem. publications bd. U. Tenn., 1972-73. Served as capt. USAF, 1960-62. Diplomate Am. Bd. Pathology. Mem. Am. Cancer Soc., Am. Med. Tennis Assn., Knoxville Acad. Medicine, Am. (Physicians Recognition award 1969), Tenn. med. assns., Et Soc. Pathologists, Am. Soc. Clin. Pathologists, Alpha Kappa Kappa. Clubs: Century, Knoxville Racquet (dir.), Park West Sertoma. Contbr. to profl. publs. in field. Home: 8717 Farmington Dr Knoxville TN 37919 Office: 1901 W Clinch St Knoxville TN 37916

MILLER, CHARLES F., oil co. exec.; b. Lake Charles, La., June 12, 1918; s. Edgar and Ruth (Williams) M.; B.S. in Petroleum Engring., Tex. A. and M. Coll., 1940; m. Marijo Brigham, May 22, 1948; children—Charles B., Lucy Lee, Mary E. Petroleum engr. Gulf Oil Co., Fannett, Tex., 1940-41, from petroleum engr. to dist. engr., Tex., So. La., Houston, 1947-53; with Kerr-McGee Corp., Oklahoma City, 1953—, gen. supt., gen. mgr. prodn., 1953-60, mgr. fgn. drilling and prodn., 1961, gen. mgr. fgn. and domestic prodn., oil and gas operations, 1968—, v.p. Oil and Gas div., v.p. oil and gas operations, 1973— v.p. Kerr-McGee Pipeline Corp., White Shoal Pipeline Corp., Triangle Refineries, Inc. Served to maj. AUS, 1941-46; CBI. Mem. Am. Inst. Mining Engrs., Am. Petroleum Inst., Mid-Continent Oil and Gas Assn. Episcopalian. Home: 6317 Paschall Ct Oklahoma City OK 73132 Office: Kerr-McGee Corp McGee Tower Oklahoma City OK 73102

MILLER, CHARLES VALENTINE, physician; b. Omaha, Apr. 23, 1915; s. Lloyd Herman and Jennette L. (Wiegand) M.; B.S., U. Wyo., 1938; M.D., U. Rochester, 1942; m. Ann Clark, Apr. 28, 1945; 1 son, John Allyn. Intern U. Neb. Hosp., 1942-43, fellow U. Rochester Sch. Medicine, 1946-48; resident and instr. U. Tenn. Coll. Medicine, 1948-51; fellow hematology Pratt Diagnostic Clinic, Boston, 1958-59; practice medicine, Chattanooga, 1954-58, Ft. Worth, 1959-61; dir. labs., hematologist Mary Washington Hosp., Fredericksburg, Va., 1961—. Bd. dirs. Fredericksburg chpt. A.R.C., Fredericksburg bd. Am. Cancer Soc.; med. bd. Va. chpt. Leukemia Soc. Am. Served from 1st lt. to maj., AUS, 1943-46; as maj. USAF, 1951-53; ETO. Diplomate Nat. Bd. Med. Examiners, Am. Bd. Pathology. Fellow Am. Soc. Clin. Pathologists, Internat. Soc. Hematology, Assn. Clin. Scientists, Soc. Nuclear Medicine; mem. A.M.A., Va. Med. Assn., Sigma Chi, Gamma Sigma Epsilon. Presbyn. Kiwanian. Research in field. Home: 1109 Westwood Dr Fredericksburg VA 22401 Office: Med Arts Bldg Fredericksburg VA 22401

MILLER, CLARENCE WILLIAM, hosp. adminstr.; b. Erwin, Tenn., July 5, 1918; s. Hyder Robert and Cecil (Miller) M.; student U.S. Naval Sch. Hosp. Adminstrn., 1952, Mercer U., 1955-56; m. Sharlene Ruth Hansen, May 3, 1969; 1 son Wayne Preston. Commd. officer, USN, 1937; served with Hosp. Corps; ret., 1957; asst. adminstr. Lake Wales (Fla.) Hosp., 1957-59, adminstr., 1959—. Elk. Club: Lake Wales Country. Home: 1104 Circle Dr Lake Wales FL 33853 Office: 410 11th St Lake Wales FL 33853

MILLER, CONRAD HENRY, educator; b. Lowell, W.Va., July 28, 1926; s. Richard Watson and Margaret Eleanor (Holmes) M.; B.S., Va. Tech. Inst., 1954, M.S., 1955; Ph.D., Mich. State U., 1957; m. Sarah Lee Meadows, July 28, 1947; children—Susan Ellen, Samuel Albert. Grad. asst. Va. Tech. Inst., 1954-55; grad. asst., then asst. prof. botany and plant pathology Mich. State U., 1955-57; mem. faculty N.C. State U., Raleigh, 1957—, prof. horticulture, 1969—. Pres. Wake County chpt. Muscular Dystrophy Assn., 1968—, Health Affairs Round Table, 1972-73; chmn. adv. bd. Wake Information Center, 1973-74; v.p. West Raleigh Civic Assn., 1973. Precinct chmn. Wake County Democratic party, 1973-74. Served with AUS, 1944-46. Mem. Am. Soc. Hort. Sci. (chmn. vegetable crops sect. 1973-74). Contbr. articles to profl. jours. Home: 4406 Driftwood Dr Raleigh NC 27606

MILLER, DAVID EDMOND, physician; b. Biscoe, N.C., June 6, 1930; s. James Herbert and Elsie Dale (McGlaughon) M.; A.B., Duke, 1952, M.D., 1956; m. Marjorie Willard Penton, June 4, 1960; children—Marjorie Dale, David Edmond. Intern, Duke Med. Center, Durham, N.C., 1956-57, resident in internal medicine, 1957-58, 59, 60, research fellow cardiovascular disease, 1958-59, 61, asso. internal medicine and cardiology, 1963—; practice medicine, specializing in internal medicine and cardiology, Durham, 1964—; attending physician internal medicine div. cardiology Watts Hosp., Durham, 1964—, also chmn. med. staff patient care com. Served to lt. comdr., USNR, 1961-63. Diplomate Am. Bd. Internal Medicine. Fellow A.C.P., Am. Coll. Cardiology; mem. Am., So. med. assns., Am. Heart Assn. (fellow council clin. cardiology 1963—), N.C., Durham-Orange County med. socs., Am., N.C. socs. internal medicine, Am. Fedn. Clin. Research. Methodist (mem. chancel choir, adminstrv. bd.; pres. men's group; chmn. pastor-parish relations com.; lay del. N.C. ann. conf.). Contbr. articles profl. jours. Home: 1544 Hermitage Ct Durham NC 27707 Office: 1200 Broad St Durham NC 27705

MILLER, DONALD LANE, pub. relations co. exec.; b. Pitts., May 14, 1918; s. Donald Edwin and Arvilla (Lane) M.; A.B., Kenyon Coll., 1940; Russian interpreter certificate U. Colo., 1946; postgrad. U. Pitts., 1947-48; m. Norma Reno, Feb. 2, 1951. Reporter, Pitts. Sun-Telegraph, 1940-42, Washington Post, 1946; pub. relations Westinghouse Electric Corp., Pitts., 1947-51; reporter Billboard and Tide, 1953; pub. relations dir. Nat. Agrl. Chem. Assn., Washington, 1954-58; sec. Donald Larch & Co., Washington, 1958-61; pres. Asso. Pub. Relations Counselors, Washington, 1961—. Exec. dir. All Am. Conf., Washington, 1962—. Editor, GOP Nationalities News, Rep. Nat. Com., 1960; pub. relations nationalities div. Rep. Nat. Com., 1964; coordinator life underwriters sect. Citizens for Nixon-Agnew, 1968. Served from ensign to lt. USNR, 1942-46; from lt. to lt. comdr. 1951-53. Mem. S.A.R., Am. Legion, V.F.W., Amvets, Phi Beta Kappa, Delta Tau Delta. Clubs: National Press, Capital Hill (Washington). Author: Strategy for Conquest, 1966. Contbg. editor Washington New Approach, 1971—. Home: 309 Green St Alexandria VA 22314 Office: 1028 Connecticut Av NW Washington DC 20036

MILLER, DOYLE ELMO, steel co. exec.; b. Klondike, Tex., Oct. 14, 1913; s. Claude Lawrence and Vivian Adell (Moore) M.; B.S., Tex. A. and M. U., 1938; m. Mary Pauline Daniel, June 21, 1935. Design engr., Fort Worth Structural Steel Co., 1939-41, chief engr., 1941-48; chief engr. Gen. Steel Co., Fort Worth, 1948-64, v.p., 1964—; also dir. Mem. Fort Worth Tech. Club (pres. 1946). Home: 2721 Harlan Wood Dr Fort Worth TX 76109 Office: 3001 W Pafford St Fort Worth TX 76109

MILLER, EARL LEWIS, adhesive co. exec.; b. Etowah, Tenn., Mar. 4, 1921; s. Enoch Earl and Lockey (Derrick) M.; grad. high sch.; m. Mildred Toomey, June 2, 1940; children—Gary Earl, Timothy Lewis. Brakeman L & N R.R., 1938-47; salesman H.B. Fuller Co., Atlanta, 1947-51, Empire Labs., Atlanta, 1951-52, Polymer So., Springdale, Conn., 1952-61, Holt Mfg., Birmingham, Ala., 1961-62; with Big Bear Adhesive & Chem. Co., Inc., Etowah, 1962—, pres. train plant personnel, 1968—. Camping chmn. Unaka dist. Boy Scouts Am., 1968-69, scoutmaster, 1969-70, recipient Order of Arrow; pres. P.T.A., Etowah, 1952. Baptist (tchr., Sunday sch. dir. 1973-74). Mason (32 deg., Shriner). Club: Senators (Knoxville, Tenn.). Home: 306 Louisiana St Etowah TN 37331 Office: Hwy 30 W Etowah TN 37331

MILLER, EARL WILLIAM, JR., elec. engr.; b. Mpls., Feb. 1, 1922; s. Earl William and Cecile Alvira (Perkins) M.; student U. Cin., 1943-44; student elec. engring. U. Minn., 1947, 48; m. Goldie Louise Felty, May 2, 1961; children—Ruth Carolyn Suzan Kay. Design engr. supervisory control and telemetering equipment Control Corp., Mnpls., 1945-55; sr. communications engr. Tampa Electric Co. (Fla.), 1955—. Mem. adv. com. electronics Hillsborough Community Coll., 1970—; mem. Hillsborough County Civil Def. Communications Unit, 1965—. Trustee Amateur Radio Club Sta., Hillsborough High Sch., Tampa. 1968—. Served with AUS, 1942-45. Decorated Purple Heart, Bronze Star medal. Registered profl. engr., Fla. Mem. I.E.E.E. (chmn. Fla. West Coast sect. 1969-70), Nat. Soc. Profl. Engrs. Club: Tampa Torch. Home: 943 Cimmeron Dr Tampa FL 33603 Office: PO Box 111 Tampa FL 33601

MILLER, EDMOND TROWBRIDGE, educator; b. Pitts., Dec. 9, 1933; s. George Ellsworth and Billie (Watson) M.; B.C.E., Ga. Inst. Tech., 1955, M.S.C.E., 1957; C.E., Mass. Inst. Tech., 1963; Ph.D., Tex. A. & M. U., 1967; m. Nancy Lee Cooper, July 21, 1956; children—Carol Anne, Nancy Ruth, Laura Elizabeth. Found. engr. Law Engring. Testing Co., Atlanta, 1956-57, found. engr., br. mgr., Tampa, Fla., 1957-61; asst. prof. civil engring. U. Ala., 1963-64; instr. civil engring. Tex. A. & M. U., 1965-67; asso. prof. civil engring. U. Ala., 1967-71, prof., 1971—, acting head dept., 1973; pvt. practice cons. traffic engring. and computer sci. Mem. Tuscaloosa Urbanized Area Transp. Study Tech. Coordinating Com., 1967—. Served with AUS, 1967. Automotive Safety Found. fellowship, 1964-65. Mem. Am. Soc. Civil Engrs., Hwy. Research Bd., Nat. Soc. Profl. Engrs., Ala. Soc. Profl. Engrs., Inst. Traffic Engrs., Assn. Computing Machinery, Phi Kappa Phi, Chi Epsilon, Scabbard and Blade, Phi Gamma Delta. Mem. Ch. Christ Scientist. Home: 78 Woodland Hills Tuscaloosa AL 35401 Office: PO Box AC University AL 35486

MILLER, EDWARD TITUS, geophysicist; b. Englewood, N.J., Apr. 15, 1927; s. Haydock Harvey and Elizabeth May (Titus) M.; B.S., Mass. Inst. Tech., 1949; M.A., Columbia, 1952, Ph.D., 1955; m. Lois Martin Vaetsch, Sept. 30, 1950; children—Katharine E., Emily V., Brian H. Research asso. Lamont Geol. Obs., Columbia U., N.Y.C., 1949-56; sr. research geophysicist Humble Oil & Refining Co., Houston, 1956-65; dir. data processing and research Alpine Geophys. Assos., Norwood, N.J., 1965-68; exploration geophysicist Exxon Co., Houston, 1968—. Mem. Soc. Exploration Geophysicists, Am. Geophys. Union, Acoustical Soc. Am., Seismol. Soc. Am., European Assn. Exploration Geophysicists, I.E.E.E., A.A.A.S., Sigma Xi. Republican. Home: 4674 Merwin St Houston TX 77027 Office: PO Box 2180 Houston TX 77001

MILLER, ERNEST BARGER, III, investment counselor; b. Tyler, Tex., May 15, 1938; s. Ernest Barger Jr. and Dorothy (Bryan) M.; B.S., Stanford U., 1960; M.B.A., Northwestern U., 1962; m. Dale Porter, June 25, 1966; children—Ernest Barger IV, Margaret Dale. Engr., analyst Humble Oil Co., Baton Rouge, La., 1962-66; staff economist, Houston, Tex., 1966-68; portfolio mgr., security analyst Funds, Inc., 1968-69; portfolio mgr., security analyst, v.p., dir. Investment Advisors, Inc., 1969—; dir. Finomic Research Assos., Finomic Investment Fund, Inc. Recipient fellowship Northwestern U., 1962. Mem. Am. Chem. Soc., Am. Inst. Chem. Engrs., Financial Analysts Fedn., Houston Soc. Security Analysts, Baton Rouge Jr. C. of C. (bd. dirs. 1963-65, v.p., 1964-65), Stanford Houston Alumni Assn. (bd. dirs., pres. 1966), Kappa Sigma. Clubs: Charnwood Civic Club, Inc. (pres. 1973-74) (Houston); River Oaks Country (Houston). Home: 7513 Middlewood St Houston TX 77042 Office: 600 Jefferson St Houston TX 77002

MILLER, FLOYD FREEMAN, physician; b. Skiatook, Okla., Mar. 15, 1930; s. Floyd Edwin and Elsie Hazel (Rader) M.; B.S., U. Okla., 1953; M.D., 1956; m. Mary Adeline Fowler, Aug. 16, 1953; children—Michael Floyd, Steven Fowler. Intern, Univ. Hosp., Ann Arbor, Mich., 1956-57, resident internal medicine, 1957-60, allergy fellow, 1960-61; practice medicine specializing in allergy, Tulsa, 1963—; mem. staff St. John's, St. Francis hosps., Tulsa. Instr. U. Mich. Sch. Medicine, 1960-61. Bd. visitors U. Okla. Sch. Medicine, Oklahoma City, 1970-72. Served with USAF, 1961-63. Fellow A.C.P., Am. Acad. Allergy, Am. Coll. Allergy; mem. Tulsa County Med. Soc. (pres. 1973), Tulsa Internists Soc. (pres., 1971), Tulsa C. of C., Okla. Soc. Internal Medicine (sec.-treas. 1970-72), Am. Thoracic Soc., Phi Beta Kappa, Phi Eta Sigma, Alpha Omega Alpha. Club: Southern Hills Country, Philcrest Hills Tennis. Home: 3736 E 43d Pl Tulsa OK 74135 Office: 3233 E 31st St Tulsa OK 74105

MILLER, FORRESTT ALLEN, coll. dean; b. Pinetop, Ariz., July 15, 1931; s. Joseph L. and Allyne Elizabeth (Kendrick) M.; B.A., Chico State Coll., 1956; M.A., U. Cal. at Berkeley, 1959, Ph.D., 1962; m. Suzanne Joy Schneebeli, June 25, 1955; children—Bradford Edwin, Kristina Suzanne. Instr. history U. Mass. at Amherst, 1961-62; mem. faculty Vanderbilt U., Nashville, 1962—, prof., 1971—, asso. dean Coll. Arts and Scis., 1971—. Cons. Random House, 1962-63, Dept. Health, Edn. and Welfare, 1970-71. Rapporteur Nashville Com. Fgn. Relations, 1967—. Served with USAF, 1950-55. Mem. So. Conf. Slavic Studies (pres., 1970, exec. com., 1967-70), Am. Hist. Assn., Am. Assn. Advancement Slavic Studies, Am. Acad. Social and Polit. Sci. Author: Dmitrii Miliutin and the Reform Era in Russia, 1968. Home: 6813 Cloudland Dr Nashville TN 37205

MILLER, FREDERICK WARREN, chem. co. exec.; b. Pitts., Nov. 19, 1935; s. Warren Jennings and Grace Elizabeth (Sawhill) M.; B.S. in Chem. Engring. (H.H. Geist scholar, Pa. Senatorial scholar), Pa. State U., 1957; Ph.D. (fellow), Rice U., 1965; m. Ann Louise Sutton, Jan. 30, 1960; children—Karinne Adele, David Sutton, Diane Elizabeth. With E.I. du Pont de Nemours & Co., Inc., 1957—, research supr., Old Hickory, Tenn., 1970—; pres., co-owner Wine Celler, Inc., Hendersonville, Tenn., 1973—. Com. chmn. Brandywine Hundred Republican Orgn., 1967; mem. exec. com. Sumner County (Tenn.) Rep. Exec. Com., 1969—; regional dir. Henderson Rep. Party, 1970—; vice chmn. Tenn. 4th Congl. Dist., 1972—; mem. Capitol Club Tenn., 1973—. Mem. Am. Inst. Chem. Engrs., Hendersonville C. of C. Clubs: Toastmasters (pres. Wilmington, Del. 1967, Distinguished Achievement award 1967); Hendersonville Seroma (sec. 1970-71). Author, patentee in field. Home: 103 Hillcrest Dr Hendersonville TN 37075 Office: Research and Devel Lab Du Pont Co Old Hickory TN 37138

MILLER, GENE EDWARD, newspaper reporter; b. Evansville, Ind., Sept. 16, 1928; s. Paul E. and Irene (Hudson) M.; A.B. in Journalism, Ind. U., 1950; Nieman fellow, Harvard, 1967-68; m. Electra Sonia Yphantis, Apr. 13, 1952; children—Janet Irene, Theresa Jean, Thomas Raphael, Roberta Lynn. Reporter, Jour.-Gazette, Ft. Wayne, Ind., 1950-51, Washington bur. Wall St. Jour., 1953-54, Richmond (Va.) News Leader, 1954-57, Miami (Fla.) Herald, 1957—. Served with AUS, 1951-53. Recipient Headliner award, 1966, 69, Heywood Broun award, 1966, Pulitzer prize, 1967. Author: 83 Hours till Dawn. Investigative reporting led to freedom and exoneration of two persons wrongly convicted of murder in separate cases. Home: 8831 SW 20th St Miami FL 33165 Office: 1 Herald Plaza Miami FL 33101

MILLER, GEORGE A., TV exec., state senator; b. Montrose, Colo., Apr. 3, 1927; s. George A. and Verdie (Sallee) M.; student East East State Coll., 1946-48, Okla. State U., 1948-50; m. Mary E. Cox, June 11, 1948; children—George E., John D., Robert W., Mary Ann. Chief engr. KADA Broadcasting, Inc., Ada, Okla., 1950-60; news dir. Eastern Okla. Television, Inc., Ada, 1955—; mem. Okla. State Senate, 1964—, chmn. senate com. edn., 1968-72, com. on higher edn., 1972—. Okla. commr. Edn. Commn. of the States. Served with

USNR, 1945-46. Mem. Nazarene Ch. Optimist. Home: 1021 E 6th St Ada OK 74820 Office: 1600 Arlington St Ada OK 74820

MILLER, GEORGE CARPENTER, banker; b. Columbus, O., July 16, 1918; s. Orlando Carpenter and Susan (Siebert) M.; B.Sc. in Bus. Adminstrn., Ohio State U., 1940; m. Mary M. Kritser, Nov. 4, 1947; children—Shelby, Jack, Martha. With Armstrong Cork Co., 1941-51; with Time Motor Freight Co., Lubbock, Tex., 1953-60, dir. sales and traffic, 1955-60; with Citizens Nat. Bank, Lubbock, 1963—, sr. v.p., trust officer, 1965—, dir., 1966—. Chmn., Lubbock Symphony, 1960, Lubbock Tb Assn., 1958, Lubbock Urban Renewal Commn., 1969, Citizens Traffic Commn., 1968. Trustee Methodist Hosp., Lubbock, chmn., 1970-71. Served to maj. USAAF, 1942-46. Decorated Bronze Star medal (U.S.); Croix de Guerre (France). Mem. Phi Gamma Delta. Episcopalian. Home: 3213 43d St Lubbock TX 79413 Office: Box 841 Lubbock TX 79408

MILLER, GEORGE EDWARD, judge; b. Akron, O., Aug. 23, 1920; s. George Dewey and Etta May (Hagerman) M.; B.S., U. Houston, 1949, J.D., 1951; m. Edith M. Booker, Apr. 4, 1944; children—Jackie (Mrs. Dale Davenport), Pamela (Mrs. Steve Sziy). Admitted to Tex. bar, 1951; practiced in Houston, 1951-54; asst. dist. atty. Harris County, Houston, 1954-58; partner firm Tynes, Turk & Miller, Houston, 1958-61; judge County Criminal Ct. at Law 1, Harris County, 1961-67, 113th civil dist. ct., 1967—. Served to 1st lt. USAAF, 1942-46; ETO. Recipient St. John Garwood award U. Houston Law Sch., 1949, Mem. State Bar Tex., Houston, Am. bar assns. Democrat. Methodist. Mason (Shriner). Home: 4948 Post Oak Timber Lane Houston TX 77027 Office: Civil Courts Bldg Houston TX 77002

MILLER, GEORGE HAROLD, supt. schs.; b. Beteravia, Cal., Feb. 23, 1917; s. James Allen and Effie (Shell) M.; B.S., East Tenn. State U., 1940; M.A., Appalachian State U., 1951; m. Elizabeth Alberta Helton, Oct. 12, 1940; children—Gwen, Penny. Tchr. Gastonia (N.C.) city schs., 1940-42, 1947-48, elementary prin., 1948-61, asst. supt., 1961-68; asst. supt. Gastonia county schs., 1968—. Served to lt. (j.g.) USNR, 1943-46; PTO. Mem. N.C. Edn. Assn., Am. Assn. Sch. Adminstrs., N.E.A., Assn. Childhood Edn. (state pres. 1969—), Phi Delta Kappa. Methodist. Club: Civitan (sec. 1964-66) (Gastonia). Home: 806 St Michaels Lane Gastonia NC 28052 Office: Gastonia County Schs Gastonia NC 28052

MILLER, GILES EDWIN, lawyer; b. Dallas, Aug. 2, 1920; s. Clarence R. and Esther (Connell) M.; A.A., Terrill Jr. Coll., 1940; B.A., So. Meth. U., 1941; m. Betty Jane Stewart, Oct. 25, 1941 (div.); children—Giles Edwin, Stewart Ransom, Donovan Connell; m. 2d, Narene McGough, Dec. 13, 1960; children—Sonya, Scott Leonard, Jonathan Edwards Bryan. Admitted to Tex. bar, 1944; exec. v.p. Conro Mfg. Co. and Miller Bros. Fabrics, 1945-50; pres. Tex. Textile Mills, 1950-55; pres. Miller Cotton and Investment, 1955-58; pub., editor Park Cities News, 1958-62; chmn. bd. Legal Security Life Ins., Co., Dallas, 1959-65; pres., treas. Radio KPCN, Inc., Dallas, 1962-68, Radio KBUY, Inc., Amarillo, 1960-66; now engaged in writing and research; civil asst. dist. atty. Chmn. bd. Goins Found. Mem. Am., Dallas bar assns., State Bar Tex., Soc. Advancement Mgmt., Dallas Mgmt. Assn., Terrill EX-students Assn. (pres. 1974—), Navy League. Club: Rock Creek (mem. bd.). Home: 3312 Dartmouth St Highland Park TX 75205 Office: Records Bldg Dallas TX 75202

MILLER, GLENN CURREY, ins. co. exec.; b. Chattanooga, Oct. 13, 1946; s. Willard and Fonza (Swafford) M.; student U. Tenn., 1964-66. With Vol. State Life Ins. Co., Chattanooga, 1967—, advt. asst., 1967-68, mgr. advt. and promotion, 1968-70, dir. advt. and promotion, 1970—. Mem. pub. relations com. United Fund, 1969-70; spl. gifts com. Am. Cancer Soc., 1971; actor Chattanooga Little Theatre, 1967—. Mem. campaign staff U.S. Sen. Albert Gore, 1970. Mem. Chattanooga Advt. Fedn. (pres. 1972-73), Chattanooga Assn. Bus. Communicators (pres. 1969-70), Life Advertisers Assn., Greater Chattanooga C. of C. (jr. adventure adviser, mem. pub. relations com. 1973-74). Democrat. Episcopalian. Home: 3314 Pinewood Terrace Chattanooga TN 37411 Office: PO Box 1369 Chattanooga TN 37411

MILLER, GORDON SMITH, ednl. adminstr.; b. Parkin, Ark., Aug. 23, 1917; s. Maurice Leroy and Jessie Dyle (Smith) M.; B.A., Southeastern La. U., 1940; M.A., La. State U., 1947; m. Margaret Frances Seale, Nov. 16, 1940; 1 dau., Margaret (Mrs. Thomas McCarty). Head sci. dept. high sch., Bogalusa, La., 1940-47, adminstr., 1942-47; asso. prof. chemistry Southeastern La. U., 1947-51; asso. prof. chemistry Mercer U., Macon, Ga., 1951-52; prof. phys. sci. Tift Coll., Forsyth, 1952—, dept. head, 1952-57, dean, 1960-73, asst. to pres., 1971—. Mem. Am. Chem. Soc. Democrat. Baptist. Kiwanian (dist. sec.-treas. 1949). Home: 460 Sunset Circle Forsyth GA 31029

MILLER, HARVEY ALFRED, educator; b. Sturgis, Mich., Oct. 19, 1928; s. Harry Clifton and Carmen (Sager) M.; B.S., U. Mich., 1950; M.S., U. Hawaii, 1952; Ph.D., Stanford U., 1957; m. Marjorie Rosemary Bunge, Sept. 12, 1952; children—Valerie Yvonne, Harry Alfred. Instr. in botany U. Mass., 1955-56; instr. botany Miami U., 1956-57, asst. prof., 1957-61, asso. prof., curator herbarium, 1961-67; prof., chmn. program in biology Wash. State U., 1967-69; vis. prof. botany U. Ill., 1969-70; prof., chmn. dept. biol. scis. Fla. Tech. U., 1970—; v.p. Marine Research Assos. Ltd., Nassau, 1962-65; botanist U. Mich. Expdn. to Aleutian Islands, 1949-50; prin. investigator Systematic and Phytogeol. Studies Bryophytes of Pacific Islands NSF, 1959; prin. investigator Miami U. Expdn. to Micronesia, 1960; dir. NSF-Miami U. Expdn. to Micronesia and Philippines, 1965; vis. prof. U. Guam, 1965; cons. tropical botany. Recipient Acacia Order of Pythagoras; Acacia Nat. award of Merit; Guggenheim fellow, 1958. Mem. Pacific Sci. Assn. (mem. scientific com. 1965—), Assn. for Tropical Biology, Am. Soc. Limnologists and Oceanographers, Am. Inst. Biol. Scis., A.A.A.S., Am. Bryol. Soc. (v.p. 1962-63, pres. 1964-65), British Bryol. Soc., Botan. Soc. Am., Botan. Soc. Japan, Internat. Assn. Plant Taxonomists, Mich. Acad. Sci. Arts and Letters, Hawaiian Acad. Sci., Am. Soc. Plant Taxonomists, Fla. Acad. Sci., Nordic Bryol. Soc., Acacia. Club: Explorers Club of N.Y. Editor: Florida Scientist, 1973—. Contbr. numerous articles to sci. jours. Home: 2300 Cady Way Winter Park FL 32789 Office: Florida Technol U Orlando FL 32816

MILLER, HENRY BATES, chem. co. exec.; b. Muldrow, Okla., June 5, 1910; s. Ernest Ary and Leila Adine (Bates) M.; student Middle Tenn. State U., 1939-42; certificate in electronics and chem. engring. Vanderbilt U., 1945; m. Bessie Pearl Oliver, Aug. 13, 1938; children—Oliver Bates, Frances C. (Mrs. Ralph Bartholomew), Ernest A., Anne J. (Mrs. David Robinson), Rebecca L. (Mrs. Russel Prince). Devel. chemist Genesco, Nashville, 1941—; with Life & Casualty Ins. Co., 1943-45; Genesco, 1941—; owner H.B. Miller Electronic Organ Service, Nashville, 1950—. Mem. Tenn. N.G., 1933-41. Recipient Silver Star, Gen. award Genesco, 1965. Mem. Am. Guild Organists, Am. Assn. Textile Chemists and Colorists, Nat. Investigations Com. on Aerial Phenomena. Kiwanian. Home: 550 Croley Dr Nashville TN 37209 Office: 6100 Centennial St Nashville TN 37209

MILLER, HERBERT LYNN, coll. adminstr.; b. Newark, Oct. 7, 1923; s. Herbert Arthur and Harriette Dorothy (Niebuhr) M.; B.S., Ga. Inst. Tech., 1948, M.S., 1955; postgrad. (fellow) U. Fla., 1959-60; m. Barbara Joyce McKerrow, Sept. 16, 1956; 1 son, Michael Andrew. Financial analyst Citizens and So. Nat. Bank, Atlanta, 1948-54; instr. corp. finance Ga. Inst. Tech., Atlanta, 1956-62; mem. faculty, Central Fla. Community Coll., Ocala, 1962—, dir. div. bus. and social scis., 1968—, dir. instnl. self study, 1972-74. Dir. Marion County Tchrs. Credit Union, 1964—, sec., 1967—. Served with AUS, 1943-46. Mem. Ocala-Marion County C. of C. (chmn. pub. affairs com., 1964-65), Am., So. econs. assns. Democrat. Episcopalian. Rotarian. Contbr. book reviews to Choice mag. Home: 1119 NE 16th Av Ocala FL 32670 Office: PO Box 1388 Ocala FL 32670

MILLER, ISRAEL BERNARD, scrap metal co. exec.; b. Huntsville, Ala., June 11, 1926; s. Louis and Elsie (Ratner) M.; B.S. in Indsl. Mgmt., Ga. Inst. Tech., 1948; m. Dolores Evelyn Katz, Feb. 6, 1947; children—Joy (Mrs. Kenneth Jay Greenberg), Solomon Ira, Sara Gayle. Partner, L. Miller & Son, Inc., Huntsville, 1948-58, treas., mgr., 1958-66, pres., 1966—; bus mgr. Technique, Ga. Inst. Tech., 1947. Mem. Huntsville United Jewish Appeal Com., 1948-59, Huntsville United Jewish Fund, 1959—. Nat. Joint Distbn. Com., 1964—. Bd. dirs. region Anti-Defamation League, B'nai B'rith, 1967—. Served with USNR, 1944-46. Mem. Indsl. Mgmt. Soc., Inst. Scrap Iron and Steel, Am. Welding Soc., Nat. Welding Supply Assn., Alpha Epsilon Pi, Pi Delta Epsilon. Jewish religion (past pres. and trustee temple). Mason (Shriner); mem. B'nai B'rith (pres. 1956, 67). Rotarian. Home: 1101 Fraser Av SE Huntsville AL 35801 Office: PO Box 1207 Huntsville AL 35807

MILLER, JACK EVERETT, lawyer; b. Monroe, La., Dec. 10, 1921; s. Herman M. and Syble (Harrison) M.; student Ga. Tech., 1942-43; grad. Gilbert Johnson Law Sch., 1948; m. Vivian Geraldine Bagby, May 13, 1945 (div.); children—Jack E., John A.; m. 2d, Kathryn Woodard Garriss, Dec. 23, 1970. Admitted to Ga. bar, 1948; formerly mem. firm Duffy, Miller, Duffy; now individual practice, Savannah. Served with USAAF, 1943-45, with USAF, 1951-53, lt. col. Res. Judge Adv. Gen. Dept. Mem. Am. Trial Lawyers Assn., Am., Ga., Savannah bar assns., Am. Legion. Elk. Club: American Business (chpt. pres. 1959, dist. gov. 1964-65). Home: 2 Stillwood Ct S Savannah GA 31406 Office: 122 E Oglethorpe Av Savannah GA 31401

MILLER, JAMES BRYAN, lawyer; b. Roanoke, Va., Aug. 12, 1932; s. Bryan Marcellius and Lillian Rucker (Dent) M.; B.A., U. Va., 1954; LL.B., Am. U., 1960; postgrad. Georgetown U. Law Sch., 1960-61; m. Anne Moore Hutton, Dec. 12, 1963; children—Kathryn Maureen, Leigh Anne. Admitted to Va. bar, 1961, D.C. bar, 1961, U.S. Supreme Ct. bar, 1968; individual practice law, Arlington, Va., 1961-62; partner Johnson, Miller & Zabriskie, Arlington, 1963-67; individual practice Arlington, 1967-72; partner Miller, Miller & Patterson, Arlington, 1973—. Instr. No. Va. Police Acad., Fairfax, 1969—. Coach, Little League Baseball, 1965-68. Served with AUS, 1954-56. Mem. Am. Judicature Soc., C. of C., Am. Arbitration Assn. (arbitrator), Am., Va. trial lawyers assns., Am., Va., D.C., Arlington bar assns. Clubs: Washington Golf and Country; Racquet (Miami Beach, Fla.). Optimist. Home: 4608 N 26th St Arlington VA 22207 Office: 2701 N Pershing Dr Arlington VA 22201

MILLER, JAMES ICEM, JR., tobacco co. exec.; b. Henderson, N.C., Feb. 18, 1908; s. James I. and Mary Lucile (Davis) M.; student Fishburne Mil. Acad., 1925-26, U. N.C., 1926-28; m. Betsy Jane Lamm, Feb. 20, 1932; children—Betsy Jane (Mrs. Walter W. Blake), Mary Lucile (Mrs. William L. Montague). Vice-pres. James I. Miller Tobacco Co., Springfield, Ky., 1950-61; pres., partner Springfield Redrying Co., 1961—; partner So. Tobacco Storage Co., Wilson, N.C., 1966—; pres., mgr. Miller Storages, Inc., Springfield, Ky., 1971—; pres., mgr. Springfield Tobacco & Storage Co., 1948—; partner Fla. Groves, Leesburg, 1943—. Mayor, City of Springfield, 1948-64. Served with AUS, 1945. Mem. Phi Gamma Delta. Home: 419 N Walnut St Springfield KY 40069 Office: 100 Lebanon Hill Springfield KY 40069

MILLER, JAMES MAXWELL, educator; b. Kosciusko, Miss., Sept. 20, 1937; s. James Hoyt and Nora Gladys (Cagle) M.; A.B., Millsaps Coll., 1959; Ph.D., Emory U., 1964; m. Alice Julene King, Aug. 11, 1962; children—David Weldon, Charles Dushan. Mem. faculty Birmingham-So. Coll., Birmingham, Ala., 1964-67; mem. faculty Emory U., Atlanta, 1967—, prof. Hebrew history and archaeology, 1967—. Participant several archaeol. excavations in Israel and Jordan; Ann. prof. Albright Inst. Archaeol. Research, Jerusalem, 1974-75. Mem. Soc. Bibl. Lit. (pres. Southeastern sect. 1970). Contbr. articles to profl. jours. Home: 1927 N Akin Dr NE Atlanta GA 30345

MILLER, JAMES QUINTER, physician; b. Lakewood, O., July 6, 1926; s. J. Quinter and Mae (Hooker) M.; B.A., Haverford Coll., 1949; M.D., Columbia, 1953; m. Alice-Marie March, July 29, 1951; children—Judy, Nancy, Susan, Janice. Intern, then resident internal medicine Mary Imogene Basset Hosp., Cooperstown, N.Y., 1953-57; resident medicine and neurology U. Va. Hosp., Charlottesville, 1957-60; teaching fellow Harvard Med. Sch., 1960-62; mem. faculty U. Va. Med. Sch., Charlottesville, 1962—, prof. neurology, 1973—, asst. dean, 1965-70. Served to capt. USAF, 1953-55. Fellow Am. Acad. Neurology; mem. Am. Epilepsy Soc. Presbyn. (elder). Home: 2505 Hillwood Pl Charlottesville VA 22901

MILLER, JAMES ROBERT, life ins. exec.; b. Live Oak, Fla., Feb. 10, 1903; s. Marion Paschal and Hattie (Williams) M.; student pub. schs.; m. Laurel Armstrong, May 5, 1930; children—James Robert, Martha June, Donald Kay. Agt., Met. Life Ins. Co., Jacksonville, Fla., 1933-37, asst. mgr., Macon, Ga., 1937-45; free-lance salesman chems., 1945-46, 47-49; partner Modern Heating Co., Macon, 1946-47; gen. agt. Guarantee Mut. Life Ins. Co., Omaha, 1949-55; organizer chmn. Cherokee Nat. Life Ins. Co.; organizer, pres. CNL Financial Corp. Mem. Macon Assn. Life Underwriters (past pres.), Macon Gen. Agts and Mgrs. Assn. (past pres.), U.S., Ga., Macon chambers commerce. Baptist (deacon). Mason (Shriner), Kiwanian. Home: 2959 Crestline Dr Macon GA 31204 Office: 1122 Gray Hwy Macon GA 31201

MILLER, JARVIS ERNEST, research adminstr.; b. Orange Grove, Tex., May 30, 1929; s. Richard C. and Ethel (DuBose) M.; B.S., Tex. A. and M.U., 1950; M.S., Purdue U., 1951, Ph.D., 1954; m. Alma Howell, June 20, 1952; children—Susan, Kathleen, Margaret, Carolyn. Asst. prof., asso. prof. agrl. econs. Tex. A. and M. U., College Station, 1955-61; chief of AID party Santo Domingo, Dom. Rep., 1965-67, asst. dir. Agr. Expt. Sta., 1967-71, asso. dir., 1971-72, dir., 1972—; agr. economist, acting rural devel. officer AID, Buenos Aires, Argentina, 1961-65. Served to lt. USAF, 1953-54. Mem. A.A.A.S., Am. Acad. Arts and Scis., Am. Agr. Econs. Assn., Internat. Assn. Agrl. Economists. Home: 3502 Stillmeadow Dr Bryan TX 77801 Office: Tex Agrl Expt Sta College Station TX 77843

MILLER, JOHN DAVID, agronomist; b. Todd, N.C., Aug. 9, 1923; s. Reuben Patterson and Chessie (Graham) M.; B.S., N.C. State U., 1948, M.S., 1950; Ph.D., U. Minn., 1953; m. Frances McCollum, June 9, 1946; children—John David, Glenn, Mary. Research fellow U. Minn., 1953; asst. prof. Kan. State Coll., 1953-57; research agronomist Agrl. Research Service USDA, Blacksburg, Va., 1957—, research leader, 1972—. Dist. commr. Boy Scouts Am., 1971-73. Served with AUS, 1943-46. Decorated Bronze Star medal. Mem. Am. Soc. Agronomy, Phi Kappa Phi, Sigma Xi. Toastmaster, Lion. Home: 806 Draper Rd Blacksburg VA 24020 Office: Agrl Research Service USDA 337 Smyth Bldg Blacksburg VA 24021

MILLER, JOHN EDWARD, ednl. adminstr.; b. McKeesport, Pa., Dec. 9, 1921; s. Thomas and Millie (Price) M.; B.S. in Math., Randolph Macon Coll., 1948; M.A., in Physics, U. Va., 1950, Ph.D., 1952; m. Virginia Lee Bazile, Feb. 25, 1943 (dec. Mar. 1972); 1 dau., Renee (Mrs. Stuart Holmes). Prof. physics Clemson U., 1952-62, 63-66; v.p. academic affairs Fla. Inst. Tech., Melbourne, 1966—. Trustee Caanan (N.H.) Coll. Served with AUS, 1943-47. Mem. V.F.W., Phi Beta Kappa. Contbr. articles on physics to sci. publs. Home: 801 Atlantic St Melbourne Beach FL 32951

MILLER, JOHN MELVILLE III, medical educator; b. Cordova, Ala., Dec. 3, 1931; s. John Melville and Minnie (Holloway) M.; A.B., Vanderbilt U., 1952; M.D., Med. Coll. Ala., 1956; m. Sheila Moffatt, July 11, 1959; children—John, Amanda. Rotating intern Bklyn. Hosp., 1957; resident phys. medicine and rehab. Presbyn. Hosp., N.Y.C., 1966; asst. prof. rehab. medicine Columbia Coll. Phys. and Surg., 1968-70; asst. attending physician Presbyn. Hosp., 1967; cons. physician Englewood Hosp., Englewood, N.J., 1966-70, acting chief dept. phys. medicine and rehab., 1968-70; prof., chmn. dept. rehab. medicine U. Ala. Med. Sch., Birmingham, 1970—; dir. Spain Rehab. Center, 1971—; project dir. Rehab. Research and Tng. Center, also Spinal Cord Injury Center, 1971—. Served with USAF, 1957-59. Named Birmingham Area Physician of Yr., 1973. Mem. Royal Soc. Health, Am. Spinal Injury Assn., Am. Congress Rehab. Medicine, Am. Acad. Phys. Medicine and Rehab., Internat. Med. Soc. Paraplegia, Ala. Acad. Neurology and Psychiatry, A.M.A., Nat. Rehab. Assn., Com. Employment Handicapped. Home: 3908 Old Leeds Rd Birmingham AL 35213

MILLER, JOHN RICHARD JOSEPH, textile products co. exec.; b. Hickory, N.C., Nov. 16, 1933; s. Henry Grady and Anna Barbara (Haase) M.; B.S., N.C. State Coll., 1956; m. Exia Lorraine Boliek, May 20, 1961; 1 dau., Regena Lorraine. Supt. processing, mng. dir. Hickory Dyeing & Winding Co., Hickory, N.C., 1958-59, v.p. charge prodn., 1959—, also dir. Served to 1st lt. AUS, 1956-58. Mem. Hickory Jr. C. of C. (sec. 1963), Tau Kappa Epsilon. Lutheran (tchr. Sunday sch. 1964-71). Designer, supr. constrn. complete plant expansion facility doubling work area and new office location, 1966-67. Home: Route 10 Box 701 Hickory NC 28601 Office: PO Box 1975 Hickroy NC 28601

MILLER, JOHN ULMAN, clergyman; b. N.Y.C., Dec. 9, 1914; s. Clarence John and Edythe Gladys (Shaffer) M.; B.A. cum laude, Taylor U., 1937; M.A., Butler U., 1942; D.D., Geneva Theol. Coll., 1968; m. Marcella E. Hubner, June 12, 1937; children—John U., Mark C., Mary Kay (Mrs. Charles Bolin), Gretchen (Mrs. Ernest Micka). Ordained to ministry Bapt. Ch., 1937; pastor 1st Bapt. Ch., Bluffton, Ind., 1946-49, Boston, 1949-56, Tabernacle Ch., Utica, N.Y., 1956-63, United Ch. of Christ, Hagerstown, Ind., 1963-66, St. John's Evang. Ch., Louisville, 1967—. Participant, Churchmen Weigh News, WNAC, Boston, 1953-56; Meml. Chapel preacher, instr. religion N.Y. State Masonic Home, Utica, 1957-62; broadcast weekly services WKBV, Richmond, Ind., 1965-66; preacher Fellowship Chapel WHAS, Louisville, 1967—; maintains 24 hour Dial-A-Prayer, Louisville, 1968—. Chmn. campaigns Crippled Children, Tb, U.S.O., 1946-49. Served to capt. USAAF, 1942-45; PTO. Named Community Leader Am., News Pub. Co., 1969; Ky. col. Mem. Ind.-Ky. Conf. United Ch. of Christ, Bach Soc. Louisville. Home: 3404 Kirby Lane Louisville KY 40299 Office: 637 E Market St Louisville KY 40202

MILLER, JOSEPH LEWIS, JR., govt. ofcl.; b. Boothbay Harbor, Me., Aug. 21, 1913; s. Joseph Lewis and Addie T. (Perkins) M.; B.S., U. N.H., 1936; student Am. U., 1954-55, Advanced Mgmt. Program, Harvard, 1961; m. Alice Ruth Boyer, June 17, 1939; 1 son, Donald Earl. Exec. trainee Jordan Marsh Co., Boston, 1936-37; food broker J. R. Poole Co., 1937-40; commd. ensign, USN, 1940, advanced through grades to comdr., 1954; invasion Casablanca, 1942, Philippines. 1944; attached cruiser 3d Fleet invasion and surrender Japan. 1944-45; served in Pacific, 1951; exec. officer Large Supply Depot, 1948-51; capt. res.; chief VA br. Bur. of Budget, Washington, 1954-56; dir. mgmt. engring, office FCDA, Battle Creek, Mich., 1956-58; spl. asst. to asst. dir. resources and prodn. OCDM, Washington, 1958-61; asst. chief resources moblzn. br. Office Emergency Planning, Exec. Office of Pres., Washington, 1961-63, officer-in-charge Ghana-Sierra Leone Desk, AID, Dept. State, Washington, 1963-64, asst. dir. mgmt. support Bur. Africa, 1964-67, dir. Office Adminstrv. Services, 1967—. Vice pres. Barcroft Terrace Citizens Assn.; active Boy Scouts Am., Little League Baseball. Recipient Am. Legion Citizenship award, Bklyn., 1928; Eagle Palm, Boy Scouts Am., 1929. Mem. Am. Fgn. Service Assn., Res. Officers Assn. (pres. Battle Creek, Mich.), Am. Soc. Pub. Adminstrn., Potomac River Power Squadron, Harvard U. Alumni Assn., Harvard Advanced Mgmt. Assn., Ret. Officers Assn., Alpha Tau Omega. Clubs: Harvard (Boston and Washington); New Hampshire University Alumni (Washington); Rotary; Annapolis (Md.) Country. Home: 140 E Lake Dr Annapolis MD 21403 Office: US Dept State (AID) Washington DC 20520

MILLER, JOSEPH SIDNEY, wire co. exec.; b. Vancouver, B.C., Can., June 30, 1921; s. Sidney Wilfred and Phyllis Elizabeth (Laidlaw) M.; B.A.Sc. in Mech. Engring., U. B.C., Vancouver, Can., 1950; m. Dorothy Masters Hebb, June 17, 1942; children—Malcolm, Carlyle, Marion, Andrew, Ian. Mgr., Johnson Wire Products, Montreal, Que., Can., 1950-56; gen. mgr. West Coast Wire Works, Vancouver, 1957-58; pres., dir. Atlanta Wire Works, Jonesboro, Ga., 1959—; Johnson Foils, Inc., Springfield, Mass., 1970—, Drytex, Inc., Jonesboro. Served with RCAF, 1942. Mem. Clayton County C. of C. (v.p. 1968-70). Clubs: Capital City, Cherokee Town and Country (Atlanta). Home: 2888 Habersham Rd Atlanta GA 30305 Office: 1117 Battle Creek Rd Jonesboro GA 30236 Mailing Address 1117 Battle Creek Rd Jonesboro GA 30236

MILLER, KENNETH EUGENE, diversified co. exec.; b. Black Fork, O., Apr. 20, 1924; s. James Henry and Nora Estelle (Queen) M.; B.S., Am. Inst. Tech., 1950; m. Gretchen Elizabeth Everhart, May 14, 1948; children—James Henry, Robert Leslie, Richard Everhart, Amelia Jo, Kenneth Alan. With Lear Siegler, Inc., Oklahoma City, 1953—, pres., gen. mgr. 1966—; dir. Tech. Devel. Co., Saigon, Vietnam, 1971—, chmn. bd., 1973—. Served with Signal Corps, AUS, 1943-46. Mem. Oklahoma City C. of C. Republican. Methodist. Club: Keyman (Oklahoma City). Home: 4932 NW 30th Pl Oklahoma City OK 73122 Office: 4001 Lincoln Blvd Oklahoma City OK 73105

MILLER, KENNETH FREDERICK, civil engr.; b. Rochester, N.Y., Aug. 5, 1928; s. Herman Roman and Mary Catherine (Kassman) M.; student Syracuse U., 1949-50; B.S. in Civil Engring., Tri-State Coll., 1954; m. Ruth Lorraine Taylor, Nov. 25, 1955; children—Laura Lee, Kenneth Frederick, Mary Katherine. Sr. draftsman, N.Y. State Dept. Pub. Works, Rochester, 1954-55; paving engr. C.E., Homestead, Fla., 1955-56; designer Radar & Assos., Miami, 1956-58; boundary surveyor Gen. Devel. Corp., Miami, 1958-62, dir. design engring., 1963—, also, Vero Beach, Fla.; office engr. John F. Michell & Assos., Miami, 1962-63; dir. Instr. Miami Dade Community Coll., Miami, 1973-74. Served with AUS, 1946-49, with USAF, 1950-51. Registered profl. engr., Fla. Mem. Fla. Soc. Profl. Land-surveyors, Civil Engring. Program Applications Group Fla. Engring. Soc., Am. Congress Surveying and Mapping. Home: 1836 71st Av Vero Beach FL 32960 Office: Gen Devel Engring Co 2095 SW US #1 Vero Beach FL 32960

MILLER, KENNETH RAY, educator; b. San Antonio, Tex., June 11, 1944; s. Edward and Meta (Blank) M.; B.B.A. with honors, U. Tex., 1967, M.P.A., 1969; m. D'Angelon Koranek, Sept. 2, 1967; 1 son, Kenneth Jason. Accountant, Peat, Marwick, Mitchell & Co., C.P.A.'s; San Antonio, Tex., 1967-70; mem. faculty San Antonio Coll., 1970—, asst. prof., 1973—; pvt. practice as C.P.A., 1970—. Recipient fellowship Humble Oil Co. Mem. Am. Inst. C.P.A.'s, Tex. Soc. C.P.A.'s, Tex. Jr. Coll. Tchrs. Assn., Beta Alpha Psi, San Antonio Jr. C. of C. Home: 201 Harrison Av San Antonio TX 78209 Office: 203 Harrison Av San Antonio TX 78209

MILLER, KENT D., educator, physician; b. Detroit, May 9, 1925; s. Don S. and Alice D. (Dalzell) M.; A.B., Oberlin Coll., 1949; M.S., Wayne State U., 1951, Ph.D., 1954; M.D., Albany Med. Coll., 1962; m. Joanne G. Tucker, July 8, 1950; children—Geoffrey, Joelle, Julie. Research scientist N.Y. State Dept. Health, 1954-58, sr. research scientist, 1958-62, asst. dir., 1962-68; prof. medicine and microbiology U. Miami (Fla.) Med. Sch., 1968—. Cons. to industry, 1970—. Mem. adv. com. plasma protein research A.R.C., 1968-73, bd. dirs. Dade County chpt., 1973—; mem. com. plasma and plasma substitutes NRC, 1965-68. Served with AUS, 1943-46. Decorated Bronze Star with oak leaf cluster. Brown-Hazen study grantee, 1958-62. Mem. Am. Soc. Biol. Chemists, Am. Soc. Hematology, Soc. Exptl. Biology and Medicine, Am. Chem. Soc., Sigma Xi. Home: 7380 SW 123d Terrace Miami FL 33156

MILLER, LEE STEPHEN, research co. pres.; b. Jacksonville, Fla., June 5, 1930; s. Oscar Lee and Elsie Beecher (Simpson) M.; B.S., Ind. Inst. Tech., 1952; Ph.D., Clemson U., 1967; m. Diana B. Sheppard, Aug. 5, 1950; children—Stephen, Jeanette. Scientist TRW Corp., Cocoa Beach, Fla., 1961-64; sr. scientist Research Triangle Inc., Raleigh, N.C., 1967-72; pres. Applied Sci. Assos., Inc., Raleigh, 1972—. Cons., Def. Dept., Washington, 1972—; prin. investigator Skylab program NASA, 1972—. Mem. I.E.E.E., A.A.A.S. Designer antennas used in 1st global space telemetry network, 1957. Home: 615 E Chatham St Apex NC 27502 Office: Box 949 Apex NC 27502

MILLER, LESLIE, contractor; b. Hamilton, Tex., Apr. 18, 1901; s. McDonough and Willie Caroline (Mueller) M.; student Tex. Christian U., 1936; m. Oma Lee Isham, Nov. 10, 1922; 1 dau., June (Mrs. Miller McClung). Pres. Leslie Miller Contractors Co., Ft. Worth, 1941-50; pres. Leslie Miller, Inc., Ft. Worth, 1950—. Recipient U.S. Army Commendation awards C.E., 1960, Dept. Def., 1960. Mem. Ft. Worth Assn. Mech. Contractors (chmn. labor-mgmt. com. 1955-60). Methodist. Mason (Shriner). Clubs: Shady Oaks Country, Colonial Country, Century II. Home: 2000 Indian Creek Dr Fort Worth TX 76107 also McDonough Farm Hamilton TX Office: PO Box 8158 Fort Worth TX 76112

MILLER, LUTHER TABOR, JR., bldg., constrn. co. exec.; b. Ft. Worth, Nov. 13, 1914; s. Luther Tabor and Hulda Estelle (Franklin) M.; B.S., (scholar), Tex. Christian U., 1935, M.A., 1937; m. Grace Nichols, Apr. 2, 1941; children—Cliff, Steve, Janis Ann. C.P.A., Fort Worth, 1939; faculty, acting dir. Tex. Christian U. Sch. Bus., 1939-40; partner Patterson, Leatherwood, Miller, Talkington & Ward, Ft. Worth, 1943-47; sec., treas., v.p., controller, dir. McVean & Barlow, Inc., Odessa, Tex., 1952-73, owner, pres., 1973—. Prof., McMurrey Coll., 1948; cons. Casualty Ins., 1960-70. Bd. dirs. Indsl. Found., Odessa, 1960-70, pres., 1968-69. C.P.A., Tex. Recipient Spl. award Odessa C. of C., 1957, Mem. C. of C. (chmn. com. 1960-65), Tex. Soc. C.P.A.'s, Am. Inst. C.P.A.'s, Am. Assn. Ins. Mgrs., Tex. Mfg. Assn. (past ofcl.), Am. Mgmt. Assn. Club: Optimist (Fort Worth). Home: 3103 Eastover Dr Odessa TX 79760 Office: Box 4517 Odessa TX 79760

MILLER, MALCOLM DRENNAN, lawyer; b. Waverly, Ill., May 26, 1909; s. Malcolm Foote and Ethel May (Pease) M.; B.A., Grinnell Coll., 1931; postgrad. U. Ill. Coll. Law, 1932-34; LL.B., Georgetown U., 1935; m. Martha Ann Riggs, Aug. 26, 1937; children—William (dec.), Malcolm, Margaret (Mrs. Philip Filiatrault), Winifred (Mrs. Robert Payne). Admitted to D.C. bar, 1935, Va. bar, 1945; atty. ICC, 1936-43; atty., chief counsel, common carrier sect. OPA, 1943-46; practice administrv. law, Washington, 1946-56; trial atty. P.O. Dept., Washington, 1947-50; atty., asst. gen. counsel Gen. Services Adminstrn., Washington, 1956-61, asst. commr., Transp. and Communications Service, 1961-62, dep. commr., 1962-66, dep. gen. counsel, 1966-67, mem. bd. contract appeals, 1967-69. Lectr., Am. U., Washington, 1947-58. Mem. Arlington (Va.) Citizens Com. for Sch. Improvement, 1946-52; chmn. Arlington Com. of 100, 1969-70. Recipient Star Cup award Arlington County Civic Fedn., 1950; Meritorious Service award Gen. Services Adminstrn., 1962. Mem. Fed. Bar Assn., Va. State Bar. Club: National Lawyers (Washington). Home: 1701 N Huntington St Arlington VA 22205

MILLER, MARY FRANCES (MRS. SHANNON O. MILLER), office mgr.; b. Richards, Tex., June 11, 1919; d. Albert Nolan and Lynn (Wood) Cecil; high sch. grad.; m. Shannon, O. Miller, Jr., Apr. 7, 1944 (dec. 1960); children—Shannon O. III, Martha. Office mgr. Navarra Motors, Key West, Fla., 1945-49. Peebles Motor Co., South Norfolk, Va., 1949-52, Can. Dry Bottling Co., New London, Conn., 1952-55, Crippo Motor Co., 1955-57, Snelling Motor Co., Houston, 1957-60, Pores, Inc., Ft. Pierce, Fla., 1960-68, also sec.; past office mgr. Taylor Buick Corp., Ft. Pierce; sec.-treas. Dave Snelling Lincoln, Mercury, Inc., Houston, from 1968, now office mgr. Leo Jarnagin Pontiac Center, Houston. Presbyn. Home: 1370 Country Pl Houston TX 77024 Office: Leo Jarnagin Pontiac Center Co 2600 Travis St Houston TX 77006

MILLER, MARY RUTH, educator; b. Bartow, Fla., Dec. 22, 1926; d. Willie Boyd and Ruth (Anderson) Miller; A.B. in Edn., Fla. State U., 1948; M.A., George Peabody Coll., 1951; Ph.D., Duke, 1966; postgrad. Columbia, summer 1953, U. So. Cal., summer 1954, Shakespeare Inst., Stratford-on-Avon, Eng., summer 1955, U. Edinburgh (Scotland), summer 1969. Tchr. elementary sch., Palatka, Fla., 1948-49; tchr. high schs., Bell, Fla., 1949-50, Brandon, Fla., 1950-51, Webster, Fla., 1951-53; tchr. English, dir. pub. relations Reinhardt Coll., 1953-59; asst. prof. English, Fla. So. Coll., 1962-67; prof. English and chmn. dept. Tenn. Wesleyan Coll., Athens, 1967—. Recipient Lewis State Tchr.'s Scholarship, Fla. State U., 1945-48; Danforth Tchrs. Summer Scholarship, U. So. Cal., 1954; Cokesbury award in Coll. Teaching, Duke U., 59-60, 61-62, grad. research assistantship, 1960-61. Mem. South Atlantic Modern Lang. Assn., Coll. English Assn., Modern Lang. Assn., S.E. Renaissance Conf., Tenn. Coll. English Assn. Democrat. Methodist. Home: 422 Gettys Lane Athens TN 37303

MILLER, MAURICE LEON, architect, real estate broker; b. Great Bend, Kan., Sept. 19, 1933; s. Maurice A. and Elsie V. (Spring) M.; B.S., U. Kan., 1960; grad. Tex. Realtors Inst., 1970; m. Fannie Lou Garrison, Feb. 17, 1962; children—Douglas Kyle, Marilyn Kay, Bryan Arthur. Draftsman Thomas, Jameson and Merrill, architects and engrs., Dallas, 1960-61; constrn. supr. Harwood K. Smith & Partners, architects, Dallas, 1961-67; prin. M.L. Miller, architect, Dallas, 1967—; real estate broker Bob Hamilton Realtors, Dallas, 1968—. Served with AUS, 1953-55. Mem. A.I.A., Tex. Soc. Architects, Oak Cliff, Dallas chambers commerce, Dallas Bd. Realtors, Am. Legion. Methodist. Lion (dir. 1973—). Home: 3408 Wentwood St Dallas TX 75225 Office: 2855 Irving Blvd Dallas TX 75207

MILLER, MEREDITH, chemist; b. Murfreesboro, Tenn., Jan. 2, 1922; s. Robert Cleveland and Mary Elizabeth (Smith) M.; B.A., Vanderbilt U., 1943, M.S., 1944; Ph.D., U. Wis., 1950; m. Theresa Alice Stockett, Aug. 31, 1946; children—David A., Beverly A., James M. Prof. Middle Tenn. State U., Murfreesboro, 1946-47; instr., research fellow U. Wis.-Madison, 1948-50; research chemist, staff scientist E.I. Du Pont de Nemours & Co., Buffalo and Richmond, Va., 1950-63; prin. chemist, program mgr. Thiokol Chem. Corp., Huntsville, Ala., 1963—. Vice pres. Symphony Orch. Assos., Huntsville, 1973; active local Boy Scouts Am., Little League, YMCA. Bd. dirs. Presbyn. Apts. for Elderly, 1970—. Served to lt. (j.g.) USNR, 1944-46. Presbyn. (deacon 1965, 68, elder 1969—). Kiwanian (v.p. Huntsville 1973—). Home: 5718 Criner Rd SE Huntsville AL 35802 Office: Huntsville Div Thiokol Chem Corp Huntsville AL 35807

MILLER, META HELENA, educator; b. Balt., Jan. 29, 1897; d. Charles A. A. J. and Mary (Bonnet) Miller; A.B., Goucher Coll., 1917; M.A., Johns Hopkins, 1919, Ph.D., 1922; postgrad. Columbia, Sorbonne; certificat d'etudes pratiques de prononciation Institut de Phonetique, 1931. Instr. French, Wells Coll., 1919-21; with U. N.C., Greensboro, 1922—, successively asst. prof. Romance langs., asso. prof., 1927-37, prof., 1937-66, prof. emeritus, 1966—, acting head dept., 1953-56, head dept., 1956-62. Active Am. aid to France, 1940-45. Mem. Modern Lang. Assn., South Atlantic Modern Lang. Assn., Am. Assn. Tchrs. French, Am. Assn. Tchrs. Spanish, N.C. Edn. Assn., Am. Archaeol. Soc., World Federalists, Alliance Francaise, Luth. Acad. Scholarship, P.E.O., Kappa Kappa Gamma, Alpha Delta Pi, Tau Psi Omega. Democrat. Lutheran. Club: Johns Hopkins. Author: Chateaubriand and English Literature, 1925; (with Chinard, Gilbert, others) Les Natchez, 1932; (with Hooke, Malcolm) French Review Grammar, 1945. Home: 1908 Walker Av Greensboro NC 27403

MILLER, MIKE MYRON, TV news reporter; b. Tulsa, Oct. 9, 1937; s. Lew and Pauline (Erwood) M.; B.A. in Speech, Tulsa U., 1960; m. Mary Elizabeth Jasper, Sept. 3, 1961; children—Gregory, Lorayne. Cameraman, KTUL-TV, Tulsa, 1957-59, news reporter, 1970-73; disc jockey, newsman KTUL radio, 1959-64; TV reporter KVOO TV, Tulsa, 1964-66; congl. corr. WTTG TV Washington, 1969-70; TV reporter WFAA-TV, Dallas, 1973—. Club: Press. Office: WFAA-TV News Communications Center Dallas TX 75202

MILLER, MILLAGE CLINTON, III, educator; b. Enid, Okla., Aug. 28, 1932; s. Millage Clinton and Beatrice Elizabeth (Geis) M.; B.S., U. Okla., 1954, M.A., 1960, Ph.D., 1961; m. H. Kathryn Hamit, Dec. 18, 1965. Asst. prof., dept. preventive medicine and publ. health U. Okla. Med. Sch., 1962-66, asso. prof. preventive medicine and pub. health, 1966-67; asso. prof., div. biostatistics Sch. Medicine, Tulane U., New Orleans, 1967-69; prof., chmn. dept. biometry Med. U. S.C., Charleston, 1969—. Cons. VA Hosp., S.C. Regional Med. Program, State Okla., Okla. Pub. Welfare Commn., S.C. Expanded Nutrition Edn. Program. Bd. dirs., v.p., treas. Med. U. S.C. Credit Union, 1971. Recipient fellowship NIH, 1961-62. Mem. Biometric Soc., Am. Statistical Assn., Inst. Math. Statistics, Assn. Computing Machinery, A.A.A.S., Am. Pub. Health Assn., Soc. Computer Medicine, Soc. Wang Applications and Programming, Nat. Center Health Services Research and Devel., Sigma Xi, Phi Beta Pi, Phi Sigma. Contbr. to profl. publs. in field. Home: 667 Coinbow St Mount Pleasant SC 29464 Office: 80 Barre St Charleston SC 29401

MILLER, MINOS D., JR., judge; b. Jennings, La., Sept. 9, 1920; s. Minos D. and Ruth (Ingram) M.; B.S., La. State U., 1947, J.D., 1947; m. Ruth Means Loyd, Dec. 22, 1942; children—Bonner, Minos D. III, J. Valcour. Admitted to La. bar, 1947; mem. firm Adams & Miller, 1947-53; dist. judge 31st Jud. Dist. Ct. La., 1953-69; judge Ct. Appeal 3d circuit, 1969—; spl. assignment judge La. Supreme Ct., 1958, La. Appeals, 1961-62. Active Boy Scouts; chmn. Jefferson Davis Parish Planning Bd., 1963. Vice-pres. Am. Legion Hosp., Jennings. Served to lt. (sr. grade) USNR, 1941-46. Decorated Purple Heart. Mem. Am., La., S.W. La., Jefferson Davis Parish bar assns., La. Dist. Judges Assn. (past pres.), Am. Judicature Soc., V.F.W., Am. Legion, Lambda Chi Alpha, Phi Eta Sigma, Omicron Delta Kappa, Phi Delta Phi. Democrat. Methodist. Home: PO Box 1309 Jennings LA 70546

MILLER, MONTE MACK, banker; b. Winchester, Va., June 12, 1933; s. George Franklin and Reatha (Hubbard) M.; B.A. in Biology, U. Va., 1956, M.B.A., 1963; m. Carolyn Winn Miller, Sept. 12, 1961; children—Virginia Corydon, Elizabeth Carter, Meredith Winn. Asst. to headmaster Christ church (Va.) Sch., 1958-60; staff Virginian-Post, Norfolk, Va., 1960-61; joined Nat. Bank Commerce of Norfolk, 1962, staff methods and systems div., 1962, (merger Va. Nat. Bank 1963) staff marketing div., 1963-64, nat. accounts div., 1964, asst. cashier, 1964, asst. v.p., 1966-67, v.p. loans, 1967-69, v.p. charge card, 1969-72, sr. v.p. real estate finance dept., 1972—. Chmn. Azalea Festival, Norfolk, 1970, Norfolk Community Concerts, 1968—. Commr. Model Cities Commn., Norfolk, 1969—; mem. adv. com. Norfolk City Council, 1969—. Bd. dirs. Ghent Neighborhood League, Va. Student Aid Found., Friends of Juvnile Ct., Tidewater Health Found., Longwood Coll. Mem. U. Va. Alumni Assn., Norfolk, Va. chambers commerce Tidewater Horse and Pony Assn., Kappa Alpha. Episcopalian (vestryman). Clubs: Norfolk Yacht and Country, Princess Ann Country, Harbor (Norfolk). Home: 535 Fairfax Av Norfolk VA 23507 Office: 1 Commercial Place Norfolk VA 23510

MILLER, NATHAN, govt. ofcl., author; b. Balt., May 26, 1927; s. David and Jennie (Miller) M.; B.A., U. Md., 1950, M.A., 1951; m. Jeanette Martick, Feb. 22, 1963. With Balt. Sun., 1954-69, corr. Rio de Janeiro, 1962-66, Washington Bur., 1966-69; asso. editor Editorial Research Reports, Washington, 1970-71, Kiplinger Washington Letters, 1971; profl. staff mem. U.S. Senate com. on appropriations, 1971—. Served with USNR, 1945-46. Recipient award for pub. service reporting Am. Polit. Sci. Assn., 1961. Mem. White House, State Dept. corrs. assns. Club: Overseas Press (N.Y.C.). Author: Sea of Glory, 1974; contbr. to Inside the System, 1970. Home: 4916 Western Av Chevy Chase MD 20016 Office: New Senate Office Bldg Washington DC 20006

MILLER, NATHAN ANDERSON, educator; b. Dandridge, Tenn., May 24, 1914; s. Thomas Norman and Leutitia (Davis) M.; A.B. magna cum laude, Carson-Newman Coll., 1936; M.S., U. Tenn., 1944; m. Alfreda Rowena Reed, July 5, 1949; children—Gwenna, Thomas. Tchr. grammar sch., Jefferson City, Tenn., 1936-38, prin. high sch., 1943-44; tchr. O'Keefe High Sch., Atlanta, 1938-43; dir. tchr. internes Carson-Newman Coll., 1944; dean Little River Sch., Miami, Fla., 1945-55; dean of boys Madison Jr. High Sch., 1955-56; cons. Reader's Digest, Pleasantville, N.Y., 1956-58; tchr. North Miami (Fla.) High Sch., 1958-65; asst. prin. North Dade High Sch., 1965-67, Miami Springs (Fla.) Jr. High Sch., 1967—; owner, dir. Camp Sky-Top, Rosman, N.C., 1950—; cons. Ednl. Testing Service, Princeton, N.J., 1955—; chmn. interviewing com. for Exchange Tchrs., U.S. Office Edn., 1952—. Chmn., Jefferson County A.R.C. Fund, 1943-44; v.p. Little River Youth Center Found.; bd. dirs. Fla. Youth Found. Mem. Nat. Council Tchrs. English (dir., chmn. audio visual aids com. 1942-50, co-editor Speak-Look-Listen 1943), Dade County Classroom Tchrs. Assn. (hon. life; pres. 1948-49), Nat. Soc. for Study Communication (charter mem.), Jefferson County Bapt. Assn. (Sunday sch. supt.), Phi Kappa Phi, Phi Delta Kappa. Rotarian. Editor: Atlanta Teacher, 1941-43; co-founder, editor: Dade County, Fla. Teacher, 1946-48; editorial collaborator Reading Skill Builders, 1957-58. Home: 570 Hunting Lodge Dr Miami Springs FL 33166 Office: 150 Royal Poinciana Blvd Miami Springs FL 33166

MILLER, NORMAN, lawyer; b. Boston, Dec. 6, 1925; s. Harry and Ethel (Feldman) M.; student Northeastern U., 1942-44, U. Glasgow (Scotland), 1945-46, Boston Coll., 1946-47; LL.B., U. Miami, 1952; m. Constance Hope, Nov. 23, 1952; children—Clifford Michael, Debra Caryl, Edward Harris; m. 2d, Patricia Ann Miller; 1 son, Jason William. Admitted to Fla. bar, 1952; asst. to the city atty., Miami, Fla., 1951-52; practice law, Miami, 1952—; judge Town of Medley, 1960-65. Served as cpl. AUS, 1944-46, ETO. Decorated Bronze Star medal. Mem. Nat. Assn. Claimants Compensation Attys. (state v.p. 1959-60, asso. editor bar jour.; past pres. South Fla.), Fed. (Fla. rep. 1956—), Am., Fla., Dade County bar assns., U. Miami Law Alumni Assn., Fla. Municipal Judges Assn. (pres. 1964-65), Acad. Fla. Trial Lawyers, Am. Arbitration Assn., Am. Trial Lawyers Assn. (safety liaison officer), D.A.V., Jewish War Vets. (local comdr.). Mason (32 deg.). Home: 422 Bargello Coral Gables FL 33146 Office: 299 Alhambra Circle Coral Gables FL 33134

MILLER, NORMAN BRUCE, TV exec.; b. Toronto, Ont., Can., Aug. 9, 1933; s. Norman M. and Elizabeth (Valenti) M.; grad. N.Y. Sch. Radio, TV Technique, 1955; m. Mary Jane Grow, July 27, 1952; children—Teri, Bruce, Laura, Jennifer, Scott, Peter. News dir. sta. WTVR-TV, AM-FM, Richmond, Va., 1957-70; news, pub. affairs dir. WCVE-TV, Richmond, 1970—. Bd. dirs. Richmond Area Safety Council, Glen Allen Youth Assn. Recipient citizen honor award Richmond Police Dept., 1968; George Washington Honor medal Freedom Found., 1970-73; also several awards journalism. Mem. Richmond Met. News Assn. (founder), Va. Press Photographers Assn. (past pres.), Radio TV News Dirs. Assn. Home: Route 5 Box 252 Glen Allen VA 23060 Office: 23 Sesame St Box 23 Bon Air Br Richmond VA 23235

MILLER, PAUL EDWARD, city ofcl.; b. El Campo, Tex., Nov. 10, 1932; s. Edward Frank and Lydia Barbara (Venglar) M.; student pub. schs.; m. Patricia Mozisek, Oct. 18, 1955; children—Paula, Suzanne, Chris, Nancy, Brenda, Randall, Phylis, Phillip. Dir. health and sanitation City of El Campo, 1956-63; sanitation supt. City of Mesquite (Tex.), 1969—. Served with USNR, 1951-55. Mem. Nat., Tex. environmental health assns., Nat., Tex. pub. works assns. Roman Catholic. Home: 2705 Mark Dr Mesquite TX 75149 Office: 711 N Galloway Mesquite TX 75149

MILLER, PAUL JACKSON, JR., lawyer; b. nr. Phenix City, Ala., Mar. 2, 1924; s. Paul J. and Maori (Jackson) M.; student Auburn U., 1946-47; J.D., U. Ala., 1951; m. Agnes Frances Zagar, Apr. 21, 1946; children—Paul, Scott, Leigh, Claire, Dawn, Gwen. Admitted to Ala. bar, 1951; spl. agt. FBI, 1951-54; practice law, Phenix City, Ala., 1954—; judge Russell County Ct., 1956-59. Chmn., Ala. Milk Control Bd., 1959-62; active Springer Theatre. Served with USMCR, 1942-46. Decorated D.F.C., Air medal with 3 gold stars. Mem. Phenix City Jr. C. of C. Mem. Am., Ala. bar assns., Am. Trial Lawyers. Roman Catholic. Home: 1306 32d St Phenix City AL 36867 Office: Phenix Girard Bank Phenix City AL 36867

MILLER, PHILIP HERBERT, lawyer; b. Toms River, N.J., Apr. 16, 1941; s. Herbert Frederick and Pauline Minerva (Shirey) M.; B.S., Hampden-Sydney Coll., 1963; J.D., Washington and Lee U., 1969; m. Carolyn Ann Buscemi, Aug. 17, 1963; children—Paul Herbert, Christine Elliott, Lisa Ann. Admitted to Va. bar, 1966; asso. Joseph Snyth, Arlington, Va., 1966-67; partner Bumgardner, Bumgardner & Miller, Staunton, Va., 1967—. Atty., Augusta County Bd. Suprs., 1972—. Bus. chmn., Heart Fund, 1970. Bd. dirs. Am. Cancer Assn., Staunton-East Augusta, 1969—. Mem. Am., Va., Staunton-Waynesboro bar assns., Jr. C. of C. (regional chmn., 1972). Presbyn. (deacon). Club: Westside Swim (pres. 1971). Home: 240 Wayt St Staunton VA 24401 Office: PO Box 235 Staunton VA 24401

MILLER, RALPH ALEXANDER, aviation co. exec.; b. Washington, May 28, 1935; s. Ralph G. and Marie Therese (Von Degenfeld) M.; B.A., U. Va., 1957; m. Katharin S. Lloyd-Rees, Dec. 16, 1961; children—Ralph George, Mary Lloyd, Robert Alexander, Anthony Otto. Pres., Ram Aviation, Newport News, Va., 1963-69, chmn. bd., 1969-70, pres., 1971—; vice-chmn., dir. First City Bank Newport News. Served to lt. USNR, 1957-62. Mem. Va. Aviation Trades Assn. (pres. 1968-69), Internat. Order Characters. Episcopalian. Rotarian. Club: Metropolitan (Washington). Home: 1042 Algonguin Rd Norfolk VA 23505 Office: Patrick Henry Airport Newport News VA 23602

MILLER, RICHARD MARTIN, civil engr.; b. Allentown, Pa., Aug. 30, 1934; s. Martin Henry and Dorothy Laura (Sell) M.; C.E., Lehigh U., 1960; m. Lois Elaine Bauman, Jan. 25, 1958; children—Susan Ann, Michael. Designer, Bartholomew, Moyer & Horlacher, Allentown, 1958-62; chief structural engr. Fogarasi & Moyer, Allentown, 1962-66; v.p. Gee & Jensen cons. engrs., West Palm Beach, Fla., 1966—. Served with USAF, 1952-56. Registered profl. engr., Fla., Pa., Ga., Ala., S.C., Ill. Mem. Fla. Engring. Soc. (v.p., 1974, pres. elect), Nat. Soc. Profl. Engrs., Am. Soc. C.E. (pres., 1971), Am. Concrete Inst., Prestressed Concrete Inst., Am. Inst. Steel Constrn., Portland Cement Assn., Am. Soc. Testing and Materials. Methodist. Club Sertoma (pres. 1973). Home: 9722 Heather Circle Palm Beach Gardens FL 33403 Office: 2019 Okeechobee Blvd West Palm Beach FL 33401

MILLER, ROBERT JAMES II, coll. dean; b. Dunn, N.C., Jan. 14, 1933; s. Robert James and Edith Irene (Crockett) M.; B.S., N.C. State U. at Raleigh, 1956; M.F., Yale, 1962, M.S., 1965, Ph.D., 1967; m. Rebecca Louise Ballantine, Nov. 28, 1959; children—Patricia A., Susan B., Nancy C. Pub. relations forester W.Va. Pulp & Paper Co., Manteo, N.C., 1956-59; chief forester Tilghman Lumber Co., Sellers, S.C., 1959-61; asst. research and introduction Yale, 1961-65; mem. faculty Radford (Va.) Coll., 1965—, prof. biology, 1965-72, dean, 1968-70, v.p., 1971-72; dean St. Mary's Coll., Raleigh, 1972—. Mem. Radford Forestry Commn., 1971-72. Mem. Ecol. Soc. Am., Am. Soc. Plant Physiologists, Smithsonian Assos., Sigma Xi, Phi Kappa Phi, Xi Sigma Pi. Episcopalian. Mason (Shriner, 32 deg.). Home: 7805 Blackwing Ct Raleigh NC 27609

MILLER, ROBERT TREADWELL, physician; b. N.Y.C., Mar. 8, 1920; s. Edward Grover and Hattie (Robson) M.; B.S., Tufts U., 1942, M.D., 1945; m. Mary Catharine Bolster, Nov. 3, 1945; children—Marjorie Bolster, Christopher Robson. Intern Nat. Naval Med. Center, Bethesda, Md., 1945-46; resident Boston City Hosp., 1948, D.C. Gen. Hosp., Washington, 1948-50; med. dir., also bd. dirs. Orange Grove Center, 1958—, United Cerebral Palsy Child Devel. Center, 1960—, Team Evaluation Center, 1962—; med. adv. staff United Cerebral Palsy Tenn., Siskin Found., 1958—. Bd. dirs. Tenn. Camp for Diabetic Children. Served to lt. (j.g.), M.C., USNR, 1945-47, to lt., 1953-54. Recipient citation, 1954. Diplomate Am. Bd. Pediatrics, Nat. Bd. Med. Examiners. Fellow Am. Acad. Pediatrics, Am. Acad. Cerebral Palsy; mem. Tenn. Pediatric Soc., A.M.A. Tenn., County med. socs. Home: 4100 Tacoma Av Chattanooga TN 37405

MILLER, ROBERT VICTOR, biologist, govt. ofcl.; b. Batavia, N.Y., Apr. 30, 1936; s. James Joseph and Josephine (Brunovsky) M.; B.S., Cornell U., 1958, Ph.D., 1964; M.S., U. Ark., 1961; m. Mildred Rose Canne, June 8, 1956; children—Stephen, Cheryl, Eric, Elizabeth. Research asst. prof. fishery biology U. Md., Solomons, 1963-65; zoologist (fishes) Nat. Marine Fisheries Service, Miami, Fla., 1965-71, staff asst. Washington, 1971—. Active Boy Scouts Am. Mem. Am. Soc. Ichthyologists and Herpetologists, Soc. Systematic Zoology, Am. Soc. Zoologists, Gulf and Caribbean Fisheries Inst., Am. Inst. Fishery Research Biologists, Sigma Xi. Contbr. articles to sci. publs. Home: 11202 Hunting Horn Lane Reston VA 22091 Office: National Marine Fisheries Service Washington DC 20235

MILLER, ROBERTA LEMONS, librarian; b. Penrod, Ky., Oct. 8, 1941; d. James William and Ina (Dickinson) L.; B.S., Murray State U., 1962; M.S. (King grantee 1962), George Peabody Coll., 1963; m. Charles D. Miller, Apr. 20, 1968. Catalog librarian Vanderbilt U. Med. Library, Nashville, 1963-66; reference librarian U. Ky. Med. Library, Lexington, 1966-67; automation librarian U. Va. Med. Library, Charlottesville, 1967-68; chief tech. processing Henrico County Pub. Library, Richmond, Va., 1968-71, dir., 1971—. Instr. library sci. Va. Commonwealth U., Richmond, 1971. Recipient K. T. Distbr. Scholarship award, 1959. Mem. Am., Southeastern, Va. library assns., Potomac Tech. Processing Librarians (chmn. 1970-72). Club: Soroptimist. Home: 103 Chickahominy Bluffs Rd Richmond VA 23227 Office: PO Box 27032 Richmond VA 23273

MILLER, TELLY HUGH, educator; b. Henderson, Tex., June 18, 1939; s. George and Vernon (Jones) M.; B.A., Wiley Coll., 1962; B.D., Interdenominational Theol. Center, 1965; postgrad. Roosevelt U., summer 1969; m. Glory Deen Bennett, Jan. 3, 1963; 1 dau., Alanna Camille. Ordained to ministry Baptist Ch., 1965; pastor St. Paul Bapt. Ch., St. Albans, W.Va., 1965-68; coll. pastor, instr. Wiley Coll., Marshall, Tex., 1968—. Religious counselor Baptists, W.Va. State Coll. Inst., 1967. Chmn. membership dr. N.A.A.C.P., 1967, mem. exec. com. Kanawha County chpt., 1967; vice moderator Mt. Olivet Assn. W.Va., 1966-67; chmn. Christmas Baskets for Needy, St. Albans, 1967—. Bd. dirs. YMCA, St. Albans, 1966-67. Mem. Am. Assn. U. Profs., Alpha Phi Alpha. Mason. Home: 2700 University Av Marshall TX 75670

MILLER, THOMAS LLOYD, galvanizing co. exec.; b. Wilmington, Del., June 30, 1915; s. Thomas W. and Katharine Marie (Tallman) M.; grad. Choate Sch., 1933; B.S., U.S. Naval Acad., 1937; m. Madeleine Bridgeford Russel, Oct. 7, 1939; children—Russel T., Lloyd, Lindsay (Mrs. E. Garrett Colson), Bruce W. Commd. ensign USN, 1937, advanced through grades to comdr., 1947; with submarine forces Atlantic and Pacific, 1940-47; ret., 1947; pres. Miller Ford Co., Inc., Stonington, Conn., 1950-62; pvt. investor, 1962-70; v.p., sec. U.S. Mfg. & Galvanizing Corp., Miami, 1970—. Founder, pres. Pine Point Sch., Stonington, Conn., 1948-52. Justice of the Peace, Stonington, Conn., 1950-63. Trustee Marine Hist. Assn., Mystic Seaport, Conn., 1948—. Mem. Am. Legion, V.F.W., U.S. Naval Acad. Alumni Assn. (trustee 1950-52). Clubs: New York Yacht; Storm Trysail (Larchmont, N.Y.); Ocean Reef (Key Largo, Fla.); Palm Bay, Bath, Biscayne Bay Yacht, Coral Reef Yacht (Miami). Home: 3570 Matheson Av Coconut Grove FL 33133 Office: US Manufacturing & Galvanizing 7320 NW 43d St Miami FL 33166

MILLER, THOMAS WAINWRIGHT, JR., county ofcl.; b. Clearwater, Fla., Nov. 28, 1927; s. Thomas Wainwright and Grace Ellen (Gilbert) M.; B.C.E., Ga. Inst. Tech., 1952; m. Mavis Stinson, Dec. 25, 1952; 1 son, Thomas Wainwright III. With Fla. State Bd. Health, 1952-56; dir. Lee County Mosquito Control Dist., Ft. Myers, Fla., 1956—. Chmn. govt., edn. United Fund, 1970. Served with AUS, 1946-47. Registered profl. engr., Fla., La., Mass. Mem. Fla. Anti-Mosquito Assn. (pres. 1962), Am. (bd. dirs. 1963-72; policy council 1964-72, chmn. 1970; rec. sec. 1965-72), Cal., Tex., La., Va., N.J., Utah, Ill., Ohio, Northeastern, Northwestern mosquito control assns., Am., Fla. pub. health assns., Fla. Engring. Soc. (pres. Calusa chpt. 1967; chmn. engrs. in govt. 1968; v.p. 1969), Nat. Soc. Profl. Engrs. (del. engrs. in govt. 1969), Am. Soc. C.E., Fla. Entomol. Soc., Entomol. Soc. Am., Hyacinth Control Soc. (pres. 1961, sec. 1973—, editor jour. 1965), Weed Sci. Soc. Am., S.W. Fla. Conservation Clearinghouse (sec. 1966—), Ft. Myers-Lee County C. of C. Baptist. Mason, Rotarian. Club: Fort Myers Rod and Gun (pres. 1969). Home: 1314 Florida Av Fort Myers FL 33901 Office: Lee County Mosquito Control Dist PO Box 2237 Fort Myers FL 33902

MILLER, TOM POLK, architect; b. Houston, Nov. 17, 1914; s. Enoch Lester and Willie Elvie (Chumley) M.; B.A., Rice U., 1936, B.S. in Arch., 1937; m. Isabel Mount, Aug. 10, 1947; children—Crispin Mount, Abigail Mount. Architect, Salisbury & McHale, Houston, 1937-38, H.B. Tucker, Nacogdoches, Tex., 1938, Nunn & McGinty, Houston, 1939-40, Robert & Co., Corpus Christi, Tex., 1940-41, Kemper Nomland, Los Angeles, 1946-48, DeWitt & Swank, Dallas, 1952-54; pvt. practice architecture, Denton, Tex., 1954—. Mem. Denton Municipal Research League, 1958-61, com. chmn., 1959. Mem. Denton County Democratic Exec. Com., 1962-68. Mem. A.I.A. (chmn. historic preservation com. Dallas chpt. 1965, mem. Tex. historic preservation com. 1965-68), Fellowship of Reconciliation, War Resisters League, Nat. Trust for Hist. Preservation, North Tex. Assn. Unitarian Universalist Socs. (pres. 1968-69), Denton Community Chorus, Denton Forum, Anthropology Club Dallas. Unitarian Universalist (pres. Denton fellowship 1962-63). Mem. editorial bd. The Voice, 1970-73. Home and office: 711 W Sycamore St Denton TX 76201

MILLER, WESLEY, lawyer; b. Jay, Okla., Mar. 28, 1918; s. William W. and Leah (Boyd) M.; B.A., Northeastern State Coll., 1939; postgrad. U. Okla. Sch. Law, 1939-41; m. Louise Heflebower, Mar. 30, 1963; children—Teresa Lynn, Mark Wesley. Admitted to Okla. bar, 1945; practice law, Tahlequah, Okla., 1945—. Referee, Nat. Mediation Bd., Kansas City, Mo., 1961, Honolulu, 1961, Mpls., 1965, Nat. R.R. Adjustment Bd., Chgo., 1962-71. Pres., Okla. League Young Democrats, 1949-50. Served to capt. AUS, 1941. Recipient 20 Year Selective Service medal, 1969. Mem. Okla. (mem. ho. of dels. 1967—), Cherokee County (pres. 1952-55) bar assns., Tahlequah C. of C., Am. Legion, V.F.W., Phi Beta Epsilon, Phi Delta Phi. Democrat. Methodist. Kiwanian (pres. 1955). Home: 100 Bluff Av Tahlequah OK 74464 Office: 214 S Muskogee St Tahlequah OK 74464

MILLER, WILLIAM ANDREW, JR., judge; b. West Newton, Pa., June 21, 1904; s. William Abraham and Maggie May (Knopp) M.; LL.B., South Tex. Sch. Law, 1936; m. Ruby Allen Miller, June 6, 1932; children—Daryl Marie, William Stephen. Admitted to Tex. bar, 1936; judge, Harris County, Tex., 1954—. Mem. Tex. Ho. Reps., 1946-54. Mem. Houston Democratic Exec. Com., 1940-42. Mem. bd. regents South Tex. Coll., 1953—. Served from 2d lt. to capt., AUS, 1942-46, Res. ret. Mem. Houston Fat Stock Show, Am. Legion, Tex. Christian Endeavor Union (trustee), Delta Theta Phi. Mem. Christian Ch. (licensed minister). Mason (K.T., Shriner), Eagle. Clubs: Houston Yacht, Ellington Air Force Base Officers Farm and Ranch. Home: 6504 Auden St Houston TX 77005 Office: County Civil Ct at Law Civil Sts Bldg Houston TX 77002

MILLER, WILLIAM BARRETT, elec. engr.; b. Galveston, Tex., Nov. 22, 1926; s. William Herman and Margaret (Steinbach) M.; B.S., Tex. A. and M. U., 1948; postgrad. U. Houston, 1949, So. Meth. U., 1951-52, Tex. U., 1957, 62; m. Bernice A. Smith, June 25, 1949; children—William Barrett, Margaret Ann. Asst. rate engr. Houston Light & Power Co., 1948-50; electronic design engr. Convair, Ft. Worth, 1950-52; project engr. Bovay Engrs., Houston, 1953-62; individual practice elec. engr., 1962-63; elec. engr. H. Wayne Holland, 1963; project elec. engr. CRS Design, Houston, 1963-64; sr. elec. design engr. Tellepsen Petro Chem. Constructors, Houston, 1964-70; owner Universal Energy Systems, 1970—, M C Ever Engring., 1970-71, Miller Engring., 1970—, Miller Enterprises, 1970—; elec. engr. B & R, Inc., 1971-73. Sec. cub scouts Sam Houston Area council Boy Scouts Am., 1961; bus. mgr. sr. div. Little League, 1964. Bd. dirs. Ross Sterling Athletic Dad's Club. Mem. Nat., Tex. socs. profl. engrs., Am. Inst. Elec. Engrs. (past sec.), I.E.E.E., A.A.A.S., Instrument Soc. Am., Inst. Radio Engrs., Tex. Talkers Toastmasters Internat., Internat. Platform Soc., Holy Name Soc. Clubs: St. Philip Neri Men's; Crestmont Park Civic. Home: 5503 Grace Point Lane Houston TX 77048 Office: 1775 Saint James Place Houston TX 77048

MILLER, WILLIAM BOYNTON, JR., physicist, educator; b. Atlanta, Aug. 7, 1923; s. William Boynton and Christine (Stone) M.; B.S. in Elec. Engring., Emory U., 1947; m. Ethel Mae Adams, June 30, 1948; children—Barbara Lynn, William Boynton. Research asso. dept. surgery Emory U., Atlanta, 1947-52, instr., dir. clin. radioisotope lab., 1952-56, instr. radiology, 1957-59, asso. radiology, 1959-63, asst. prof. radiology, 1963-68, asso. prof., 1968—, asst. dir. div. allied health professions Med. Sch., 1973—. Mem. I.E.E.E., N.Y. Acad. Sci., Ga. Acad. Sci., Sigma Xi. Research in devel. of radiation detection instruments and study of radiation exposure pertaining to x-ray procedures. Home: 956 Mt Vernon Rd NE Atlanta GA 30328

MILLER, WILLIAM ERNEST, fed. judge; b. Johnson City, Tenn., Feb. 3, 1908; s. Samuel Ernest and Grace (Barlow) M.; A.B., U. Tenn., 1930, J.D. (hon.), 1968; LL.B., Yale, 1933; m. Carolyn Gies, Dec. 1, 1934; 1 dau., Susan Barlow (Mrs. Charles E. Wright, Jr.). Admitted to Tenn. bar, 1933; mem. firm Cox, Epps, Miller & Weller, Johnson City, 1933-55; chancellor First Chancery Div. Tenn., 1939; U.S. dist. judge Middle Dist. Tenn., 1955-70; judge U.S. Ct. Appeals, 6th Circuit, 1970—; lectr. Vanderbilt Law Sch. Chmn. Washington County chpt. A.R.C., 1938-40; chmn. Tenn. Rhodes Scholarship Com.; mem. Tenn. Adv. Council, Higher Edn. Act, 1965. Presdl. elector, 1940; mem. Constl. Conv. Tenn., 1953. Mem. athletic bd., trustee U. Tenn. Served as maj. USAAF, World War II. Recipient award of merit U. Tenn. Law Sch., 1966. Mem. Internat. Platform Assn., Tenn. Hist. Soc., Am., Fed. (hon.), Tenn., Va. (hon.), Nashville bar assns., Am. Judicature Soc., Am. Counsel Assn., Am. Law Inst., Order of Coif, Am. Legion, Phi Beta Kappa, Phi Alpha Delta, Sigma Alpha Epsilon. Republican. Methodist. Rotarian. Clubs: Johnson City Country, Hurstleigh (Johnson City, Tenn.); Cumberland, Belle Meads Country, Round Table (Nashville); Nat. Lawyers (Washington); University (Cin.). Contbr. to law revs. Home: 228 Vaughans Gap Rd Nashville TN 37205 Office: US Courthouse Nashville TN 37203

MILLER, WILLIAM FRANKLIN, physician; b. Stone Creek, O., Jan. 16, 1920; s. Karl R. and Helen A. (Miller) M.; B.A., Wittenberg U., 1942; M.D., Case-Western Res. U., 1945; m. Laura Barker, Nov. 22, 1942 (dec. Mar. 1957); children—Laura Leslie, Karla Jon, William Christopher, Lisa Diane; m. 2d, Jean Stevens, Jan. 12, 1958; 1 dau., Katy Cork. Intern City Hosp., Cleve., 1945-46; resident VA Hosp., Dayton, O., 1946-48; resident VA Hosp., Dallas, 1948-50, fellow, 1950-51; mem. faculty Southwestern Med. Sch., U. Tex., Dallas, 1951—, asso. prof. medicine, 1957-67, prof., 1967—; dir. pulmonary sect. Cardiopulmonary Inst., Methodist Hosp., Dallas, 1967—; mem. staff cons. staff Presbyn., St. Paul, Baylor, VA Hosps. (all Dallas); cons., NIH, med. dir. respiratory therapy tng. program El Centro Coll., Dallas, 1967-69. Chmn. bd. med. advisers Am. Assn. Inhalation Therapy, 1966-68. Served to maj. M.C., AUS, 1946-48. Diplomate Am. Bd. Internal Medicine. Fellow Am. Coll. Chest Physicians (gov. Tex.; chmn. respiratory therapy com.; recipient best movie award 1967), A.C.P.; mem. Am. Fedn. Clin. Research, So., Central socs. clin. research, A.A.A.S., Tex., Am. thoracic socs., Am. Heart Assn., A.M.A., Assn. Schs. Allied Health Professions, Assn. for Advancement Med. Instrumentation, Pan. Am. Med. Assn., Am. Med. Writers Assn., Sigma Xi. Med. editor Respiratory Care jour. Am. Assn. Respiratory Therapy, 1966-72. Home: 1473 Bar Harbor St Dallas TX 75237 Office: PO Box 5999 Dallas TX 75222

MILLER, WILLIAM WADD, III, educator; b. Starkville, Miss., Oct. 4, 1932; s. William Wadd and Nettie M. (Sanders) M.; B.S., Miss. State U., 1954, M.S., 1957; Ph.D., Auburn U., 1962; m. Jane Pierce, July 21, 1957; children—William Wadd IV, Eva Montgomery. Asso. prof. biology Samford U., Birmingham, Ala., 1962-67; asso. prof. biology N.E. La. U., Monroe, 1967-73, prof., 1973—. Served with inf., AUS, 1954-56. NSF grantee, 1969. Mem. A.A.A.S., La. Acad. Scis., Am. Inst. Biol. Scis., Am. Soc. Reproductive Physiology. Club: Clearwater Bass. Home: 43 Jana St Monroe LA 71201 Office: Dept Biology Northeast La Univ Monroe LA 71201

MILLIGAN, RAY KEITH, computer co. exec.; b. Carmi, Ill., Oct. 17, 1934; s. Ray and Margaret Ethel (Barbre) M.; B.A. in Econs., Fla. State U., 1957; postgrad. in finance Wayne State U., 1958-59, Chrysler Inst. Engring., 1958-59; m. Dian Helene Hoskins, May 24, 1956; children—Miachel Keith, Dian Kimberly, Sean Hoskins, Wade Ferrell, Melissa Davis. Systems analyst Chrysler Corp., 1957-59; asst. to pres. Soroban Engring., Melbourne, Fla., Soroban Engring. Co., 1959-61; nat. sales mgr. electronics research and devel. Geo Space Corp., Melbourne, 1962-65; dir. systems div. D. Brown Assos., Melbourne, 1965-67; mgr. computer tech. Quantum Sci. Corp., N.Y.C., 1967-68; pres., chmn. bd. founder, mfr. computer systems HETRA Computer & Communications Industries, Inc., Melbourne, 1968—. Mem. Brevard County Overall Econ. Devel. Program Com., 1970—. Mem. Melbourne C. of C., Soc. for Information Display, Am. Ordnance Orgn., Phi Delta Theta. Episcopalian. Contbr. articles to tech. jours. Home: 915 S Riverside Dr Indialantic FL 32901 Office: 1151 S Eddie Allen Rd Melbourne FL 32901

MILLINGTON, CLAYTON BLAKE, ednl. adminstr.; b. Elk City, Okla., Dec. 4, 1927; s. Chester B. and Fay (Abernathy) M.; B.S., Okla. State U., 1951, M.S., 1956; Ph.D., Mich. State U., 1964; m. Patsy Darlene Unterkircher, June 28, 1951; children—Philip Allen, Eric Lee. Tchr. high sch., Claremore, Okla., 1953-54; instr. Okla. State U., 1954-56, 56-57, Mich. State U., 1957-60; asst. prof. Okla. State U., Stillwater, 1960-61, asso. prof., 1964-69, prof., 1969—, exec. dir. Okla. Council on Econ. Edn., 1960—, dir. Bus. Extension Service, 1961—, dir. Center for Econ. Edn., 1967—; exec. sec. Okla. Dept. Edn. Curriculum Com. on Econ., 1964—; asso. program dir. NSF, Washington, 1971-72. Chmn. Nat. Council Econ. Edn. Dirs., 1971-72. Mem. Nat. Steering Com. for Econ. Edn. Curriculum; chmn. United Fund, 1965, 1st v.p. 1966, pres. 1967; chmn. Stillwater Sales Tax Dr., 1964. Served to 1st lt. with USAF, 1951-53, lt. col. Res. Mem. Nat. Bus. Edn. Assn., Nat. Council for Social Studies, Okla. Assn. Soc. Execs., Nat. Council for Small Bus. Mgmt. Devel. (v.p. 1965, mem. adv. bd. 1966-71), Delta Pi Epsilon (chpt. pres. 1957, 61), Phi Delta Kappa. Methodist. Contbr. articles in field to profl. jours. Home: 1111 S Kings Hwy Stillwater OK 74074

MILLOWAY, JOHN EUGENE, real estate appraiser and cons., shopping center developer; b. High Point, N.C., May 11, 1931; s. John E. and Eugenia (Bennett) M.; B.B.A., U. Miami, Coral Gables, Fla., 1954. Asso., W. L. Harris, real estate appraiser and cons., Miami, Fla., 1951-56; mem. firm Milloway & Coulter, appraisers, consultants, 1956-62; practice as real estate appraiser and cons., 1963—, shopping center developer, 1971—. Alternate del. Nat. Democratic Conv., 1956. Served as 1st lt. USAF Res., 1954-60. Mem. Am. Inst. Real Estate Appraisers, Am. Soc. Appraisers, Soc. Real Estate Appraisers, Am. Right-of-Way Assn., Pi Kappa Alpha. Presbyn. Clubs: Palm Bay, Jockey, University (Miami); LaGorce Country (Miami Beach, Fla.). Home: 1086 NE 91st St Miami FL 33138 Office: Greater Miami Fed Bldg Miami FL 33131

MILLS, ALFRED PRESTON, educator; b. Fallon, Nev., Jan. 8, 1922; s. Percy Edward and Ruth (Candee) M.; B.S. in Chemistry, U. Nev., 1943; Ph.D., Tulane U., 1949; m. Josephine Elizabeth Sullivan, Aug. 6, 1946; children—James Everett, Nancy Louise. Instr. chemistry U. Miami, 1949-51, asst. prof., 1951-56, asso. prof., 1956—, acting asst. dean Grad. Sch., 1964-65, adj. asst. dean for curricula Grad. Sch., 1973—, chmn. div. natural sci. and math., 1960-61, dir. Radioisotopes Lab., 1954-62, pres. U. Miami Credit Union, 1965-68; S.E. regional dir. U. Profs. for Acad. Order, 1971-72. Dir. South Fla. Regional Sci. Fair, 1954-58; mem. sci. edn. panel NSF. Bd. dirs. Fla. Found. Future Scientists, 1960-63; dir. Fla. State Sci. Talent Search, 1967. Served to lt. comdr. USNR, 1943-46, 52-53, now capt. Res.; comdg. officer Naval Res. Officers Sch., 1965-68; South Fla. coordinator Naval Acad. Information Program, 1970—. Mem. Am. Chem. Soc. (nat. council 1956-58, 61-70, 72—, chmn. personnel com., chmn. South Fla. subsect., chmn. phys. chemistry exams. com. 1963—, chmn. Fla. sect. 1971), Am. Phys. Soc., A.A.A.S., Fla. Acad. Sci. (pres. 1962), U.S., Fla. (pres. 1964-65, jr. ranking chmn. 1967, jr. tournament chmn. 1968—) lawn tennis assns., Naval Res. Assn. (chpt. pres. 1966-67), Res. Officers' Assn. (chpt. pres. 1959-60), Am. Assn. U. Profs., Sigma Xi (pres. U. Miami chpt. 1973-74), Phi Kappa Phi (pres. U. Miami chpt. 1965-66). Club: Royal Palm Tennis (pres. 1968; sec. 1971, 72). Author: Laboratory Manual in Physical Chemistry, 1953. Abstractor Chem. Abstracts, 1933—. Editor Fla. Acad. Scis. Newsletter; Fla. regional editor Tennis, USA. Home: 7540 SW 28th St Miami FL 33155 Office: Dept Chemistry U Miami Coral Gables FL 33124

MILLS, CHARLES WINFRED, elec. engr.; b. Newport, Tenn., Aug. 10, 1923; s. William Mitchel and Nora Mae (Holt) M.; B.S., Tri State Coll., Angola, Ind., 1948; m. Elizabeth Parker, Jan. 31, 1945; children—Connie (Mrs. Larry Tew), Larry Mitchel, Samuel Parker, Wendy Elizabeth. Engr., Jefferson Standard Broadcasting Co. WBTV, Charlotte, N.C., 1948-59; project engr. Cryovac div. W.R. Grace & Co., Duncan, S.C., 1959-66; pres., gen. mgr. Control Systems, Inc., Greenville, S.C., 1967—. Served with USAAF, 1942-45. Mem. I.E.E.E., Instrument Soc. Am. Club: Sertoma Sunrisers. Patentee electronic devices. Home: 300 Rockmont Rd Greenville SC 29607 Office: Box 315 Greenville SC 29602

MILLS, DALE JOHNSON, business exec.; b. Landis, N.C., Dec. 20, 1932; s. Andrew Johnson and Mary Elizabeth (Upright) M.; B.S. in C.E., N.C. State U., 1956; m. Joyce Messer, Nov. 11, 1966; children—Dale Johnson, Joyce. City engr., Albemarle, N.C., 1956-58; dir. pub. works Gastonia, N.C., 1955-66; instr. U. Nev., Reno, 1966-67; dir. pub. works Independence, Mo., 1967-68; dir. pub. works Council Bluffs, Ia., 1968-70; city mgr., Haines City, Fla., 1970-74; project mgr. Sverdrup & Parcel & Assos., Inc., Gainesville, Fla., 1974—. Registered profl. engr., N.C., Mo., Ia., Fla. Mem. Am. Soc. C.E., Nat. Soc. Profl. Engrs., Am. Pub. Works Assn., Internat. City Mgrs. Assn. Address: 3924 NW 37th Pl Gainesville FL 32607

MILLS, DONALD ALEXANDER BARNES, environmental engr.; b. Atlanta, May 1, 1937; s. Donald and Elizabeth Barnes (King) M.; B.S. in Civil Engring., U. Ala., 1959; M.S. in Engring., U. Fla., 1960; m. Jane Chapman Clark, Dec. 22, 1959; children—Elizabeth, Jane, Eve. Project engr. Hercules Powder Co., Wilmington, Del., 1960-63; partner Donald Mills, cons. engrs., Selma, Ala., 1963—. Pres. Dallas County Historic Preservation Soc., 1973. Bd. dirs. Sturdivant Mus. Assn., 1972-75, Selma Community Concert Assn., 1973—. Registered profl. engr., Ala., Miss., La., Tex. Mem. Am. Soc. C.E., Am. Waterworks Assn., Cons. Engrs. Council, Water Pollution Control Fedn., Phi Delta Theta (dir. 1959—), Chi Epsilon. Episcopalian (vestry 1972-75). Home: 1106 Keithway Dr Selma AL 36701 Office: PO Box 534 Selma AL 36701

MILLS, EARL WAYNE, publisher; b. Valliant, Okla., July 18, 1912; s. James Walter and Annie Newman (Ward) M.; grad. high sch.; m. Ethel Alma Mason, Sept. 9, 1933; 1 son, Larry Earl. Printer, Valliant (Okla.) Tribune, 1928, pub., 1932-39; printer McCurtain Democrat, Idabel, Okla., 1928-32; pub. Boswell (Okla.) News, 1939-63; pub. Broken Bow (Okla.) News, 1964—; dir. First Nat. Bank, Broken Bow. Treas. Sch. Dist. 1, Boswell, 1940-56; jury commr., Choctaw County, Okla., 1949; sec. Choctaw County Election Bd., 1953-61; chmn. McCurtain County Election Bd., 1967—. Democrat. Methodist. Mason, Lion. Home: 304 S Wallace St Broken Bow OK 74728 Office: 108 Broadway Broken Bow OK 74728

MILLS, GEORGE THOMAS, physician; b. Memphis, Sept. 25, 1920; s. Charles Gilbert and Ina Ruby (Davis) M.; M.D., Loma Linda U., 1949; m. Fay Adele Vaughan, Sept. 10, 1946; children—George Thomas, Joan Marie, Robert Charles, Carolyn Elizabeth. Intern Nashville Gen. Hosp., 1948-49; practice medicine with Dr. B.E. McLarty, Memphis, 1949—, Mills, McLarty and McLarty, 1973—; mem. staff Meth. Hosp., Le Bonheur, Children's, St. Joseph, John Gaston hosps. Bd. dirs. Highland Acad., Portland, Tenn., 1967-72, Madison (Tenn.) Acad., 1967-72. Served with USNR, 1955-57. Fellow Am. Assn. Abdominal Surgeons. Seventh Day Adventist (elder). Home: 1600 Peabody Av Memphis TN 38104 Office: 220 S Claybrook St Memphis TN 38104

MILLS, GORDON CANDEE, educator; b. Fallon, Nev., Feb. 13, 1924; s. Percy Edward and Ruth (Candee) M.; B.S., U. Nev., 1946; M.S., U. Mich., 1948, Ph.D., 1951; m. Mary Jane Medlin, June 13, 1947; children—David Gordon, John Steven, Melinda Jane. Research asso. U. Tenn. Med. Sch., 1950-55; asst. prof. div. biochemistry U. Tex. Med. br., Galveston, Tex., 1955-61, asso. prof., 1961-67, prof., 1967—. Coach YMCA-sponsored Youth Sports Activities, 1965-73.

NIH, USPHS Research grantee, 1956-70. Mem. Am. Soc. Biol. Chemists, Am. Chem. Soc., Am. Assn. U. Profs., Galveston Research Club, Phi Kappa Phi, Sigma Xi (pres. Galveston chpt. 1972-73). Presbyn. (elder 1964-73). Contbr. numerous articles to sci. jours. Home: 118 Barracuda St Galveston TX 77550 Office: Biochemistry Div U Tex Med Br Galveston TX 77550

MILLS, JIM TOM, garment mfg. co. exec.; b. San Angelo, Tex., July 24, 1939; s. William Thomas and Irene (Parker) M.; B.S., Tex. A. and M. U., 1961. With Haggar Slacks, Corsicana, Tex., 1964-71, mgr., 1966-71; owner McAllen Contract Sewing Co., McAllen, Tex. 1971—. Served with AUS, 1962-64. Baptist. Mason. Home and office: PO Box 5007 Station 2 McAllen TX 78501

MILLS, JOHN NORMAN, educator; b. Neenah, Wis., Sept. 29, 1932; s. Norman John and Ruth Marion (Anderson) M.; B.A. in Chemistry, Wis. State Coll., Oshkosh, 1954; M.S. in Biochemistry, Okla. State U., 1956; Ph.D., U. Okla., 1965; m. Glenda Gaye Miller, Nov. 28, 1958; children—Nancy, Robert, Scott, Eric. Sr. investigator Okla. Med. Research Found., 1965-66; mem. faculty Okla. Bapt. U., Shawnee, 1958—, prof. chemistry, 1971—. Active local Boy Scouts Am. Served with USAF, 1958. Predoctoral fellow Okla. Med. Research Found., 1962-65; NIH research grantee proteolytic enzymes, 1967-73. Mem. Am. Chem. Soc. (treas. Okla. sect. 1966-71), Sigma Xi, Phi Sigma, Phi Lambda Upsilon. Democrat. Baptist (deacon). Elk. Home: 2714 Frank Buck Dr Shawnee OK 74801

MILLS, JOHN PARDON, JR., state ofcl.; b. Binghamton, N.Y., Jan. 29, 1911; s. John Pardon and Maude (Brooker) M.; B.S. in Civil Engring., Va. Poly. Inst., 1936; m. Lena Reaves, Apr. 15, 1938; children—Gerald, Dennett. With Va. Dept. Hwys., Richmond, 1936—, asst. traffic and planning engr., 1950-52, state traffic and planning engr., 1952-71, state traffic and safety engr., 1971—; mem. No. Va. Transp. Commn., 1965—, Va. Hwy. Research Bd., 1952—. Registered profl. engr., Va. Mem. Inst. Traffic Engrs. Home: 7614 N Pinehill Dr Richmond VA 23228 Office: 1221 E Broad St Richmond VA 23219

MILLS, ROBERT LEE, coll pres.; b. Erlanger, Ky., Nov. 13, 1916; s. John Clifford and Dixie Lee (Morris) M.; A.B. in Math. and Physics, U. Ky., 1938, M.A. in Ednl. Adminstrn., 1941, Ed.D., 1951; m. Mildred Sizer, June 24, 1942; children—Robert Lee, Dixie Louise, Barbara Jean. Tchr., Covington (Ky.) Pub. Schs., 1938-41; head hydraulics br. Air Force Tech. Sch., Lincoln, Neb., 1942-44; mem. supervisory staff electromagnetic plant, Oak Ridge, 1944-48; research asst. U. Ky., 1948-51, dean admissions, registrar, 1954-57; dir. research, head bur. adminstrn. and finance Ky. Dept. Edn., 1951-54; chmn. dept. ednl. adminstrn. U. Tex., 1957-59; pres. Georgetown (Ky.) Coll., 1959—. Exec. sec. Ky. Adv. Commn. Ednl. Policy 1952-54; v.p. Ky. Assn. Colls. and Secondary Schs., 1962-63, mem. exec. com., 1959-64, pres., 1963-64; chmn. exec. com. Ky. Ind. Coll. Found.; mem. Ky. Commn. on Higher Edn., 1967—; mem. Ky. Govt. Council, 1968—; adviser Tex. Assn. Sch. Bds., 1957-59; cons. Pres. Com. White House Conf. Edn., 1955; mem. Ky. Devel. Council, 1961—. Mem. Nat., Ky. edn. assns., Newcomen Soc., So. Assn. Baptist Colls. (pres. 1965-66), Baptist World Alliance (chmn. mens dept. 1965-70), Kappa Delta Pi, Phi Delta Kappa, Phi Kappa Tau. Democrat. Baptist. Kiwanian. Contbr. articles to profl. jours. Home: 444 E Main St Georgetown KY 40324

MILLS, VERENT JOHN, charitable orgn. exec.; b. Birmingham, Eng., May 12, 1913; s. John William and Ruth (Timms) M.; grad. Western Bible Coll., Winnipeg, Man., Can., 1938; Ph.D., Ewha U., Korea, 1971; m. Alma Eunice Kenney, Apr. 2, 1932; children—Ruth (Mrs. Gale Erickson), Muriel (Mrs. Donald Strum), Beverley (Mrs. Donald MacLeod). Came to U.S., 1949, naturalized, 1956. Ordained to ministry Baptist Ch., 1937; with Missions in China, 1931-40, Am. Adv. Com. in China, 1940-47; overseas dir. Christian Children's Fund, Richmond, Va., 1947-70, exec. dir., 1970—. Mem. Welfare Adv. Com. to Hong Kong Govt.; bd. examiners for Hong Kong Govt. Recipient citations Govts. of China and Japan, 1947-54; decorated Order of Cultural Merit Nat. Award, Order of Camelia (Korea). Republican. Rotarian. Club: Downtown. Home: 507 Ridge Top Rd Richmond VA 23229 Office: 203 E Cary St Richmond VA 23219

MILLS, WILBUR DAIGH, congressman; b. Kensett, Ark., May 24, 1909; s. Ardra Pickens and Abbie Lois (Daigh) M.; student Hendrix Coll., 1926-30, Harvard Law Sch., 1930-33; m. Clarine Billingsley, May 27, 1934; children—Martha Sue, Rebecca Ann. Admitted to Ark. bar, 1933, began practice in Searcy; county and probate judge, White County, Ark., 1934-38; cashier Bank of Kensett, 1934-35; mem. 76th-93d Congresses from 2d Ark. dist.; chmn. House Ways and Means Com. Democrat. Methodist. Mason (33 deg.). Home: Kensett AR 72082 Office: House Office Bldg Washington DC 20515 also Searcy AR 72143 also Little Rock AR 72203

MILLS, WILLIAM ANDREW, accountant; b. nr. Sandersville, Ga., Apr. 7, 1910; s. Oscar L. and Willie Mae (Griffin) M.; B.S. in Commerce, U. Ga., 1934; m. Ruth H. Waters, Aug. 31, 1940. Staff accountant M.H. Barnes & Co., C.P.A.'s, Savannah, Ga., 1934-43; partner Barnes, Askew, Mills & Co., C.P.A.'s, Savannah, 1947-61, Haskins & Sells, pub. accountants, Savannah, 1961—. Served to capt. AUS, 1943-46, C.P.A., Ga., La., N.C. Mem. Am. Inst. C.P.A.'s, Ga. Soc. C.P.A.'s, Beta Gamma Sigma, Phi Kappa Phi, Beta Alpha Psi. Kiwanian. Home: 802 E 41st St Savannah GA 31402 Office: 1st Fed Bldg Savannah GA 31402

MILLS, WILLIAM HAROLD, gen. contractor; b. Birmingham, Ala., Feb. 19, 1911; s. Charles W. and Mary (Parker) M.; student Woodberry Forest Sch. (Va.), 1928-29, U. Fla., 1929-30; B.S. in Civil Engring., Mass. Inst. Tech., 1934; m. Helen D. Cooper, Nov. 16, 1963; children—William Harold, Susan Ann, Caroline Bridget, Mary Danforth. Partner Clarson & Mills, St. Petersburg, Fla., 1935-46; pres., chief exec. officer Mills & Jones Constrn. Co., 1946—; dir. St. Louis Nat. Baseball Club, Inc., Gen. Telephone Co. Fla., Fla. Fed. Savs. and Loan Assn., Founders Life Assurance Co. Mem. vis. com. dept. civil engring. Mass. Inst. Tech.; trustee Museum Fine Arts, St. Petersburg. Mem. Fla. Council 100, St. Petersburg Com. 100, Newcomen Soc., Tampa Horse Show Assn., Greater St. Petersburg C. of C. (past pres.), Suncoasters, Delta Tau Delta. Episcopalian. Clubs: St. Petersburg Yacht, Dragon, Lakewood Country; Jockey (Miami, Fla.); Pasadena Country. Home: 901 40th Av N St Petersburg FL 33703 Office: PO Box 1257 St Petersburg FL 33731

MILLS, WILLIAM HAROLD, JR., bldg. exec.; b. St. Petersburg, Fla., July 24, 1939; s. William Harold and Caroline (Bonfoey) M.; B.C.E., U. Fla., 1961; m. Sylvia Carol Ludwig, Mar. 2, 1962; children—William Harold III, Robert Michael, Leslie Anne. Vice pres. bus. devel. Mills & Jones Constrn. Co., St. Petersburg, 1964-68; v.p. Wellington Corp., Atlanta, 1968-71; v.p. Mills & Jones Constrn. Co., 1971—. Pres. Pinellas Marine Inst. Chmn. blue ribbon zoning com., City St. Petersburg, 1965-68; mem. Tampa Bay Aviation Adv. Com., 1967-68. Bd. dirs. United Fund, Pinellas County, 1966-68. Served to lt. (j.g.) USPHS, 1962-64. Mem. St. Petersburg C. of C., Am. Soc. C.E., Nat. Soc. Profl. Engrs., Am. Mgmt. Assn., Am. Inst. Contractors, Mensa, Sigma Alpha Epsilon. Democrat. Episcopalian. Clubs: St. Petersburg Yacht, Dragon (St. Petersburg); Jockey (Miami, Fla.). Home: 220 Maron St NE St Petersburg FL 33704 Office: 400 23d St S PO Box 1257 St Petersburg FL 33731

MILLS, WILLIAM RAYMOND, JR., physicist; b. Dallas, Feb. 14, 1930; s. William Raymond and Edna Catherine (Rankin) M.; B.A., Rice U., 1951; Ph.D. (Rockefeller scholar), Cal. Inst. Tech., 1955; m. Betty Bellows, Sept. 13, 1952; children—Alison, Amy, Alan. Research asst. Knolls Atomic Power Lab., Schenectady, N.Y., 1955-56; research asso. Mobil Research & Devel. Corp., Dallas, 1956—. Adj. prof. physics So. Meth. U., Dallas, 1969—. Mem. Am. Phys. Soc., Am. Nuclear Soc. Contbr. to profl. jours. Patentee in field. Home: 3914 Picturline Circle Dallas TX 75233 Office: PO Box 900 Mobil Research and Development Corp Dallas TX 75221

MILLWEE, ROBERT MILES, JR., investment banker; b. Oil City, La., May 3, 1924; s. Robert Miles and Ada Belle (Jackson) M.; student U. Ark., 1941-48; B.S., U. Houston, 1949; m. Patricia Jeanne Hale, Mar. 18, 1949; children—Jan, Nancy, Miles, Patrick, Charles. Mgr. engring. Browne & Root, Houston, 1953-67; exec. dir. Ark. Indsl. Devel. Commn., Little Rock, 1967-69; tech. dir. Stephens, Inc., Little Rock, 1969—; v.p., dir. DLM, Inc., Oklahoma City, Midwest Castings Corp., Little Rock. Registered profl. engr., Ark., La., Tex. Served to 1st lt. USAAF, 1942-45. Decorated Air medal with 4 clusters. Mem. Nat., Ark. socs. profl. engrs. Home: 504 McAdoo St Little Rock AR 72205 Office: 114 E Capitol St Little Rock AR 72201

MILNE, DOUGLAS BISSET, food co. exec.; b. The Dalles, Ore., July 9, 1915; s. John J. and Mary (Thompson) M.; B.S., U. Ore., 1938, B.B.A., 1938; m. Betty Lucille Fagerland, Oct. 4, 1941; children—Douglas John, Mary Susan, Jack Fagerland. Salesman, Closset & Devers Coffee Co., Portland, Ore., 1938-42; owner, pres. Doug Milne Co., Inc., Jacksonville, Fla., 1946—; dir. Five Points Guaranty Bank, Jacksonville. Chmn. bd. dirs. YMCA, Jacksonville Univ. Athletic Assn. Served with inf., AUS, 1942-46. Mem. Phi Delta Theta. Elk, Rotarian. Home: 3632 Pine St Jacksonville FL 32205 Office: 1357 W Beaver St Jacksonville FL 32209

MILNER, CHARLES FREMONT, univ. adminstr.; b. Leesburg, O., Aug. 18, 1909; s. Fremont Beverly and Ella Margaret (Walker) M.; student Earlham Coll., 1926-27; B.A., Guilford Coll., 1933; M.A., U. N.C., 1941; m. Eloyse Sargent Postlethwaite, Aug. 21, 1936 (dec. Apr. 1958); children—Charles Fremont, Beverly, Clyde A. II; m. 2d, Evelyn Ogburn Petway Mowery, June 12, 1959. Tchr. sci., coach Sedgegarden High Sch., 1933-36, Central Jr. High Sch., Greensboro, N.C., 1936-37; head bur. visual instrn. U. N.C., Chapel Hill, 1937-42, asso. dir. extension div., 1945-56, acting dir., 1956-59, dir., 1959—. Vis. instr. visual edn. Clemson Coll., summer 1939; cons. audiovisual program U.S. War Dept., Japan, 1948; vis. prof. U. Teheran; U.S. Dept. of State cons. to Ministry of Edn., Iran, 1952-53. Sec. adv. conf. com. off-campus services N.C. Bd. Higher Edn., 1960-61; mem. Chapel Hill Sch. Bd., 1955-61; chmn. adv. com. N.C. Recreation Commn., 1957-63; mem. adminstrv. bd. Inst. Outdoor Drama, 1964—, chmn. 1974—. Served with USNR, 1942-45, comdr. Res. Mem. Nat. Univ. Extension Assn. (pres. 1966-67), Guilford Coll. Alumni Assn. (v.p. 1961). Democrat. Mem. Soc. of Friends. Kiwanian (pres. Chapel Hill 1949). Home: 8 Woodhaven Rd Chapel Hill NC 27514

MILONE, CHARLES LOUIS, educator, dentist; b. Olney, Ill., Jan. 19, 1920; s. Ray and Nellie (Streich) M.; student Eastern Ill. U., 1938-40; B.S., U. Ill., 1948; D.D.S., Northwestern U., 1951; M.P.H., U. N.C., 1968; m. Barbara Elinor Namias, Dec. 24, 1968; 1 son, John E. Practice dentistry, Effingham, Ill., 1952-61, West Palm Beach, Fla., 1962-67; dental dir. Hill Health Center, New Haven, 1968-72; asst. prof. Sch. Dentistry, U. N.C., Chapel Hill, 1972—. Lectr. pub. health Med. Sch., Yale, 1968-72; dental dir. Orange Chatham Comprehensive Health Services, Inc. Served to capt. USMCR, 1942-47. Decorated D.F.C. with star, Air medal with star. Mem. Am. Dental Assn., Am. Acad. Dental Practice Adminstrn. Unitarian. Elk. Home: Cedar St Chapel Hill NC 27514

MILWIT, SANFORD CHARLES, orgn. exec.; b. Vancouver, Wash., Dec. 1, 1939; s. Herbert H. and Ida (Nusbaum) M.; B.S., U. Md., 1963; postgrad. George Washington U., 1968, Washington U., 1972, Ind. U., 1974; m. Ada Josephine Gritz, Aug. 11, 1963; children—Daniel, Kyle. Spl. asst. S.M., Vinocour, pub. relations cons., Washington, 1962-63; advt. mgr., asst. to pub. relations dir. Am. Automobile Assn., Washington, 1963-65; dir. pub. relations D.C. div. Am. Cancer Soc., 1965-69, dir. pub. relations and pub. edn., 1969-73, dep. exec. v.p., 1973—. Pub. relations chmn. Nat. Diabetic Detection Week Met. D.C. Area, 1964. Mem. Georgetown Village Civic Assn., 1965-67; vol. bowling instr. U. Md. Named Best Athlete of Year, Alpha Epsilon Pi, 1961-62; recipient award of merit Am. Diabetes Assn., 1965; Distinguished Service citation Nat. Assn. and Council Bus. Schs., 1966. Mem. Pub. Relations Soc. Am., D.C. Pub. Health Assn. (chmn. pub. relations 1974), Advt. Club Met. Washington, Sigma Delta Chi, Tau Mu Epsilon, Alpha Epsilon Pi. Prepared spl. project for Am. Cancer Soc. Home: 1909 Snowdrop Lane Silver Spring MD 20906 Office: 1825 Connecticut Av NW Washington DC 20009

MIMS, LAMBERT CARTER, city ofcl.; b. Uriah, Ala., Apr. 20, 1930; s. Jeff and Carrie (Lambert) M.; grad. high sch.; m. Reecie Philips, Aug. 17, 1946; children—Dale, Danny. Engaged in retail and wholesale food bus., 1949-65; owner, Mims Brokerage Co., Mobile, Ala., 1958-70; pub. works commr., City Mobile, 1965-68, 69—. Mayor, City Mobile, 1968-69, 72—. Chmn. Sts. and Hwys. Com., Ala. League Municipalities, 1966-68, now chmn. Human Resources Com.; mem. Human Resources Com. Nat. League Cities. Trustee Judson Coll., Marion, Ala. Named Mobile's Most Outstanding Young Man, 1965. Mem. Ala. Pub. Works Assn. (pres. 1969-70, 72—). Baptist (deacon; chmn. bd. 1950-65; 1st v.p. Ala. Bapt. State Conv. 1969-70, 70-71; mem. Mobile Camp Gideons, pres. 1962-65; mem. christian businessmen's com. internat. 1965-70; bd. dirs. Mobile rescue mission). Kiwanian. Author: For Christ and Country, 1969. Address: PO Box 1827 Mobile AL 36601

MIMS, NANCY CROCKETT (MRS. MATTHEW HANSFORD MIMS), editor, librarian; b. Stony Point, Tenn., Nov. 6, 1909; d. Stuart Raper and Marie Langley (Ramsey) Crockett; A.B., Agnes Scott Coll., 1931; postgrad. Grensboro Coll. for Women, 1932; m. Charles R. McCarty, Dec. 27, 1933 (dec. Mar. 1936); m. 2d, Matthew Hansford Mims, Feb. 21, 1940; children—Julian Landrum III, Matthew Hansford, Marie Crockett. Tchr. English dept. Waynesville (N.C.) High Sch., 1931-33, Wilkes County (Ga.) pub. schs., 1935-37, Edgefield High Sch., 1937-39, Franklin (N.C.) High Sch., 1939-40; editor Edgefield Advertiser, county weekly, 1942-45, Johnston Herald, 1942-45, Palmetto White Ribbon, W.C.T.U. publ., 1945—; corr., feature writer Augusta (Ga.) Chronicle, Augusta Herald, 1949—, Columbia (S.C.) Record, 1949-59; head librarian Edgefield County Aiken-Barnwell-Edgefield Regional Library, 1958—. Dir. Civic League Courtesy Center, 1967—. S.C. exec. dir. Nat. Library Week, 1967; Edgefield County chmn. Tricentenary. Chmn. bd. trustees D.A. Tompkins Meml. library, 1943—; Edgefield County chmn. White House Conf. on Children and Youth, 1960. Vice chmn. County Democratic Conv., 1956. Recipient spl. grant Porter Fleming Found., 1964, Community Leader of Am. award, 1968. Mem. Edgefield County Hist. Soc. (sec. 1960—), S.C. Library Assn. (sec. pub. library sect. 1960-61), Caroliniana Soc., Clan Campbell Am., D.A.R. (chpt. regent 1964-66), Daus. Colonial Wars, Daus. Am. Colonists, Nat. Soc. So. Dames Am., U. Archives Inst. Contbr. to Chronicle Sunday Mag., 1953-55. Home: 610 Buncombe St Edgefield SC 29824

MIMS, THOMAS JEROME, ins. co. exec.; b. Sumter, S.C., Dec. 12, 1899; s. Lazarus and Sarah Rebecca (White) M.; A.B., Furman U., 1921; m. Valma Gillespie, Dec. 14, 1926; children—Thomas Jerome, George Franklin. Apprentice, Rec. & Statis. Corp. of N.Y., Detroit, 1921, N.Y.C., 1921-22, asst. mgr., Phila., 1922-25, mgr., Indpls., 1925-27, Boston, 1927-29; salesman Burroughs Adding Machine Co., Detroit, Boston, 1929-31; ins. spl. agt. State N.J., Morley Gen. Agy., Camden, N.J., 1931-32; mgr. William R. Timmons Agy., Greenville, S.C., 1933—; v.p., sec., dir. Canal Ins. Co., Greenville, 1942-48, pres., treas., dir., 1948—; dir., pres. Canal Indemnity Co.; v.p. Century-Lincoln Mercury, Inc. Gov. Internat. Ins. Seminar. Bus. mgr. Greenville Little Theater, 1951-53, 64-66, council, 1951—, v.p., 1956-57, pres., 1957-58, 72—; pres. Rotary Charities, Inc., 1964-65; mem. adv. bd. S.C. Safety Council, 1969-70, pres., 1970—. Bd. dirs. United Fund Greenville, 1970-74; vice-chmn. Found. Modern Liquor Regulations and Control; adv. council Furman U. Named Boss of Yr., Greenville Jr. C. of C., 1964, Greenville Assn. Ins. Women, 1966. Mem. Nat., S.C., Greenville (past pres.) assns. ins. agts., S.C. Motor Transp. Assn. (chmn. ins. com. 1951-63), S.C., U.S. (membership com. 1961-62, 64-68, ins. co. 1959-61, 63-65, dir. 1973-74), Greenville (chmn. community relations com. 1964-68, dir. 1969-72) chambers commerce, Am. Mgmt. Assn., A.I.M. (fellow pres.'s council), Truck and Heavy Equipment Claims Council (charter mem., chmn. membership com.), Assn. S.C. Property and Casualty Ins. Cos. (pres. 1962-63, mem. exec. com. 1963-68), Internat. Platform Assn., Presidents Assn., Am. Acad. Polit. and Social Sci. Baptist (mem. finance com.) Elk, Rotarian (dir. Greenville 1957-58, pres. 1963-64, v.p. 1964-65). Clubs: Touchdown (charter mem.; pres. 1963-64), Greenville City (pres. 1965, dir. 1964, chmn. bd. dirs., 1966-67), Poinsett, Forum (Greenville): Palmetto (Columbia, S.C.). Home: Knollwood Dr Route 6 Greenville SC 29602 Office: 417 E North St Greenville SC 29602

MIMS, WILLIAM HENRY, mech. engr.; b. Beatrice, Ala., May 6, 1909; s. Henry Bart and Clara (Boroughs) M.; B.S. in Elec. Engring., Auburn (Ala.) U., 1932; m. Nelle Martin, Nov. 15, 1927; children—William Edwin, Nancy Elizabeth (Mrs. Billy Greene Walls). Draftsman, Ga. R.R., Augusta, 1942-43, N.C. & St.L. R.R., Nashville, 1943-44; shop engr. Central of Ga. Ry., Macon, 1944-46, asst. mech. engr., Savannah, 1946-48, asst. gen. foreman Savannah Shops, 1948-49, elec. engr., Savannah, 1949-55, supt. motive power and equipment, Savannah, 1955-64; supt. maintenance and operations, dept. bldgs. and grounds Auburn U., 1964—. Chmn. Zoning Bd. of Appeal, Auburn, 1968—. Registered profl. engr., Ala., Ga. Mem. Nat. Soc. Profl. Engrs., Am. Soc. M.E., Ry. Air Conditioning Club (pres. 1953), So. and Southwestern Ry. Club (pres. 1959). Methodist (chmn. bd. trustees). Home: 418 Sehoy Circle Auburn AL 36830 Office: Dept Bldgs and Grounds Auburn U Auburn AL 36830

MIN, HONG SHIK, educator; b. Seoul, Korea, July 18, 1932; s. Young Wook and Soon (Heung) M.; B.A., W.Va. U., 1957, M.S., 1958; Ph.D., U. Ga., 1963; m. Nungsun Choi, Dec. 21, 1964; children—Christopher, Eunice, Janice. Asst. prof. Ga. Inst. Tech., 1963-66, asso. prof., 1967-72; prof. zoology, head dept. Clemson U., 1972—; cons. Nicholson-Brown, Inc. NIH grantee, NASA grantee, Research Corp. grantee. Mem. A.A.A.S., Am. Inst. Biol. Sci., Am. Soc. Cell Biologists, Am. Soc. Zoologists, Assn. Southeastern Biologists, Sigma Xi, Phi Sigma. Contbr. research articles to sci. jours. Home: 115 Knight Circle Clemson SC 29631 Office: Dept Zoology Clemson U Clemson SC 29631

MINCH, VIRGIL ADELBERT, civil and san. engr.; b. Cleve., Dec. 24, 1923; s. Henry Joseph and Mary (Terlaak) M.; B.S., N.D. State U., 1946; S.M. in San. Engring., Mass. Inst. Tech., 1948; m. Elma Queen, Jan. 6, 1947; children—David, Philip. Research asso. Mass. Inst. Tech., 1948-49; sr. asst. san. engr. USPHS, Cin., 1949-53; staff engr. Mead Corp., Chillicothe, O., 1953-55, group leader, 1956-59, mgr. pollution control activities, 1960-65, asso. dir. tech. services, 1966-68, coordinator environmental resources, 1969—; v.p., dir. Asso. Water and Air Resources Engrs., Nashville, 1973—; project mgr. Stanley Cons., Muscatine, Ia. Recipient Indsl. liaison service award Ohio River Valley Water Sanitation Commn., 1959. Mem. Scioto Conservancy dist. (v.p., dir. 1959—), Am. Meteorol. Soc., Am. Water Works Assn., Air Pollution Control Assn., T.A.P.P.I., Ga. Pulp and Paper Assn. (sec. 1955-65), Nat. Council Air and Stream Improvement (chmn. S. Central region 1963—), Nat. Rivers and Harbors Congress (chmn. S.E. Ohio sect. 1968—), Sigma Xi, Tau Beta Pi, Sigma Phi Delta. Contbr. articles profl. jours. Patentee plastic film trickling filter. Office: Main St Union Mills NC 28167

MINDLIN, ALBERT, govt. ofcl.; b. Chgo., Dec. 7, 1917; s. Albert and Lena (Bronstein) M.; B.A., U. Cal. at Los Angeles, 1940; M.A., U. Cal. at Berkeley, 1949; m. Dorothea Friedlander, Feb. 21, 1946; children—Marcel, Melanie. Math. statistician Census Bur., Washington, 1949-53; tech. asst. to chief statistics br. Bur. Old Age and Survivors Ins., Washington, 1953-59; chief statistician Govt. D.C., Washington, 1959—. Instr. dept. statistics U. Balt., 1953-59. Fellow Am. Statis. Assn. (chmn. com. small area statistics); mem. Washington Statis. Soc. (pres. 1968), Urban and Regional Information Systems Assn., Am. Soc. Pub. Adminstrn., Nat. Assn. Housing and Redevel. Ofcls. Contbr. to profl. jours. Home: 6408 Bannockburn Dr Bethesda MD 20034 Office: Rm 117 District Bldg Washington DC 20004

MINER, MARYALICE FAIRBANK (MRS. JOHN H. K. MINER), civic leader; b. Ft. Sam Houston, Tex., Apr. 30, 1925; d. Leigh Cole and May (Romig) Fairbank; student Washington Conservatory Music, 1941-42; A.A., Endicott Jr. Coll., 1945; m. John Hanson Kennard Miner, June 5, 1946; children—David Christopher, Steven Kennard, John Hanson Fairbank, Merileigh Fairbank. Vol. coach swimming Pascagoula (Miss.) Recreation Dept., 1955-65; co-founder Aquatic Club of Jackson County, Pascagoula, 1965, sec., 1965—; leader sr. scouts Girl Scouts U.S.A., 1953-56; den mother Cub Scouts Am., 1956-60; mem. Pasagoula Civic Guild, 1953—, v.p., 1966-67; dir. PasPoint Little Theatre, 1955—, sec., 1964-67, dir., drama coach jr. players, 1960-71; dir. aquatics, St. Andrews-on-Gulf, Ocean Springs, Miss., 1969-71; ofcl. hostess for Pascagoula, Mardi Gras, 1970; founder, pres. Marmin Enterprises, 1972. Recipient Keys to City, Baton Rouge, 1964, New Orleans, 1964; commendatory resolution Pascagoula City Council, 1968. Mem. Am., Nat. Inter-scholastic swimming coaches assns., Internat. Platform Assn., Amateur Athletic Union (chmn. So. women's swimming com. 1964-69, sr. swimming com. 1973—). Author: Dolly the Dolphin's Do's and Don't's for Swimming. Home: 103 St Andrews Dr St Andrews-on-the-Gulf Ocean Springs MS 39564 Office: 1810 Government St Ocean Springs MS 39564

MINGE, JERRY LEE, lawyer; b. Rome, Ga., Sept. 23, 1934; s. Willie Lee and Mary (Moore) M.; B.B.A., U. Ga., 1959, LL.B., 1959; m. Carol Bland, Mar. 27, 1958; children—Mary Angela, Jennifer Bland, Anne Marquerite. Admitted to Ga. bar, 1958; partner Scoggin & Minge, Attys., Rome, 1959-63, Hamilton, Anderson & Minge, Attys., Rome, 1963—; judge City Ct. of Floyd County, Ga., 1967-69. Mem. Ga. Ho. of Reps., 1965-67. Mem. Am., Ga., Rome (pres.) bar assns., Jr. C. of C. (past pres.), Phi Delta Phi, Sigma Nu. Baptist. Mason, Elk. Clubs: Coosa Country, Nine O'Clock Cotillion, Exchange. Home: 10 Saddle Mountain Rd Rome GA 30161 Office: PO Box 746 237 N 5th Av Rome GA 30161

MINGER, JOHN WILSON, realtor; b. Caryville, Fla., May 4, 1918; s. John William and Esther Anna Lee (Dixon) M.; student Tulane U., 1947; m. Aloma Faye Early, Nov. 26, 1946; children—John Wilson, Linda (Mrs. Linda Minger Norris). Co-owner, mgr. Minger Bros. restaurant, Niceville, Fla., 1937-42, Valparaiso Drug Mart (Fla.), 1946-62; pres., owner M & K Drugs, Niceville, 1962-66; owner, mgr. Wilson Minger Agy., real estate, 1963—; pres. 1st Fed. Savs. & Loan Assn., 1971, now dir.; sec., dir. Edgewater Village Corp. subdivision developer, Valparaiso, 1965—; pres. P.S.C. Inc., ins. premium finance co., Ft. Walton Beach, 1961—, Casual Finance Co., Inc., Ft. Walton Beach, Minger Constrn. Co., Inc., Valparaiso. Pres., Niceville High Sch. Athletic Club, 1965-66. Chmn. Democratic party Okaloosa County, 1966-72; mem. Fla. Dem. Com., 1966-72; mem. Nat. Electoral Coll. Dem. party, 1968; alt. del. Dem. Nat. Conv., 1968. Bd. dirs. YMCA Okaloosa County, TB and Health Assn., Playground Humane Soc.; W. Fla. Heart Assn., trustee Okaloosa County Pub. Schs., Okaloosa Walton Jr. Coll. Served with AUS, 1942-45. Mem. Ft. Walton Beach Bd. Realtors, Nat., Fla. real estate bd. assns. Presbyn. Mason (Shriner). Clubs: Krewe of Bowlegs (Ft. Walton Beach); Los Caballeros Español (Crestview). Home: 257 E Ferndell St Valparaiso FL 32580 Office: 203 John C Sims Pky Niceville FL 32578

MINGES, COYTE ROSCOE, dentist; b. Catawba, N.C., Nov. 5, 1912; s. Franklin Alexandria and Mittie Naome (Setzer) M.; student U. N.C., 1930-32; D.D.S., Med. Coll. Va., 1936; m. Jean Lewis, Feb. 5, 1952; children—Clyde, Franklin, Laura. Gen. practice dentistry, Rocky Mount, N.C., 1936—. Dir. First Union Bank, Rocky Mount. Mem. Nash County (N.C.) Bd. Health, 1959—. Served with AUS, 1942-47. Fellow Am. Coll. Dentists; mem. Am., N.C. dental assns., Am. Legion (past post comdr., dist. comdr.), N.C. Res. Officers Assn. (past pres.), Delta Sigma Delta. Democrat. Lutheran. Mason, Elk. Clubs: Civitan (past pres.), Benvenue County (both Rocky Mount). Home: 3305 Hawthorne Rd Rocky Mount NC 27801 Office: PO Box 192 Rocky Mount NC 27801

MINGIONE, ANN DISSINGER (MRS. DONALD LEO MINGIONE), clin. psychologist; b. Berwyn, Ill., Mar. 6, 1936; d. Clarence and Geneva (Hutton) Dissinger; B.A., DePauw U., 1958; M.A., U. N.C., 1961, Ph.D., 1961; m. Donald Lee Mingione, Jan. 16, 1964; 1 son, Daniel Jeffrey. Intern clin. psychology Inst. Living, Hartford, Conn., 1961-62; asst. prof. U. Hartford, 1962; clin. psychologist Guidance Clinic, Portsmouth, Va., 1962-64; practice clin. psychology, Portsmouth, 1964—. Cons. psychologist U.S. Naval Hosp., Portsmouth, 1964-66, Community Psychiat. Clinic, 1964-66. Saint Mary's Infant Home, Norfolk, 1968—, Catholic Family and Children's Service, Norfolk, Child and Family Service Agy., Portsmouth, 1969—. Bd. dirs. Kirk-Cone Rehab. Center, Chesapeake, Va. 1965-67. Served as lt. MSC USNR, 1963-65. Mem. Va., Am. psychol. assns., Soc. for Psychol. Study of Social Issues, Portsmouth Service League, Alpha Phi. Home: 2840 Meadow Wood Dr W Chesapeake VA 23321 Office: The Pass House Crawford at London Sts Portsmouth VA 23704

MINGIONE, DONALD LEO, physician; b. Paterson, N.J., Aug. 10, 1933; s. John R. and Mary (Brown) M.; M.D., Creighton U., 1957; m. Dorothy Ann Dissinger, Jan. 16, 1964; children—Daniel Jeffery, Margaret Mary. Intern, also resident in medicine Med. Centre, Jersey City, N.J., 1957-59; fellow in psychiatry Inst. of Living, Hartford, Con., 1959-62; staff mem. Maryview Hosp., Portsmouth, pres. gen. med. staff, 1970; Portsmouth (Va.) Gen. Hosp., Norfolk (Va.) Gen., Louise Obici, Suffolk, Va., 1963—; gen. practice psychiatry, Portsmouth, Va., 1964—; clin. asst. psychiatry N.J. Coll. Medicine, 1958-59; asst. prof. U. Hartford, 1960-62; cons. Child and Family Service, Catholic Charities; cons. psychiatry USPHS Hosp., Norfolk, Va.; mem. faculty Eastern Va. Med. Sch., Norfolk; cons. child psychiatry St. Mary's Infant Hosp., Norfolk; cons. U.S. Naval Hosp., Portsmouth. Adv. bd. Chrysler Museum, Norfolk. Served as lt. comdr. USNR, 1962-64. Mem. Portsmouth Acad. Medicine, Am. Acad. Adolescent Psychiatry, Neuropsychiat. Soc. Va., Am. Psychiat. Assn., Phi Rho Sigma. Elk, Kiwanian. Home: 2840 W Meadowwood Dr Chesapeake VA 23321 Office: The Pass House Crawford at London Sts Portsmouth VA 23704

MINHAS, KAREEM BUX, med. educator; b. Nairobi, Kenya, Oct. 24, 1918; s. Allah Bux and Igbal (Begum) M.; student U. London, 1934, Met. Coll. St. Albans, England, 1937-70; asso. Inst. Bankers London, 1940; B.Medicine, B.Surgery, King Edward Med. Coll., Lahore, Pakistan, 1946; M.D., U. Punjab, Lahore, 1952; m. Marie Partin, Oct. 26, 1969. Came to U.S., 1953, naturalized, 1963. House physician, fellow Mayo Hosp., Lahore, 1946-52; student Hammersmith Hosp. and Inst. Cardiology, London, 1953, Mass. Gen. Hosp., Boston, 1953-54; chief resident physician Faulkner Hosp., Boston, 1954-55, House of Good Samaritan, Children's Hosp., Boston, 1955-56, Cook County Hosp., Chgo., 1956-58, Presbyn. St. Luke's Hosp., Chgo., 1958-59; teaching fellow, Harvard Med. Sch., 1955-56; mem. faculty U. Ill., 1957-63; faculty U. Louisville Sch. Medicine, 1963—, prof. pediatric cardiology, 1970—; dir. cardiology Norton Children's Hosp., 1964—, cardiac care program Commn. for Handicapped Children, 1964—, WHAS Crusade Heart Lab., 1964—, Kay. Children's Heart Clinics, 1964—; cardiologist Louisville Meml. Hosp., 1971—; cons. cardiologist Kosair Crippled Children Hosp., Louisville, 1970—. Named Ky. col. Fulbright scholar, 1953-54. Fellow Am. Coll. Cardiology; mem. Am. Acad. Pediatrics, Am. Assn. U. Profs., A.M.A., Ky. Med. Assn., Jefferson County Med. Soc., Am., Chgo., Louisville and Jefferson County heart assns., Louisville Pediatric Soc. Clubs: Jefferson (Louisville); Doe Valley Country (Brandenburg, Ky.). Contbr. profl. jours. Home: 4120 Elmwood Av Louisville KY 40207 Office: 200 E Chestnut St Louisville KY 40202

MINK, JOHN ROBERT, educator; b. Peru, Ill., Sept. 8, 1927; s. Monte Franklin and Marcella (White) M.; B.A., Ind. U., 1951, D.D.S. with honors, 1956, M.S. in Pedodontics, 1961; m. Barbara Joanne Merrell, June 21, 1952; children—Sarah, Teresa, Kathleen, Mary, James, Elizabeth. Instr. Ind. U., Indpls., 1957-60, asst. prof., 1960-62; dir. dental Clinic Handicapped Children, James Whitcomb Riley Hosp. for Children, Indpls., 1957-62; mem. faculty U. Ky., Lexington, 1962—, prof. pedodontics, 1966—. Cons. pedodontics USPHS, 1969-72, U.S. Army Ft. Knox, 1969—, Am. Dental Assn., 1972—. Pres. Vols. Bur. Lexington, Ky., 1972-73. Served with AUS, 1946-47. Diplomate Am. Bd. Pedodontics. Fellow Am. Acad. Pedodontics, Internat. Coll. Dentists; mem. Am. Soc. Dentistry for Children (bd. dirs. 1969-72), Ky. Soc. Dentistry for Children (pres. 1967—), Am. Assn. Dental Schs., Internat. Assn. Dental Research, Delta Upsilon. Office: Coll Dentistry U Ky Lexington KY 40506 Home: Rural Route 2 Parkers Mill Rd Lexington KY 40504

MINNICK, ROBERT WOOD, JR., banker; b. Plainfield, N.J., July 12, 1938; s. Robert Wood and Nedra (Alexander) M.; B.S., Fla. State U., 1965; m. Mary Alice Leonard, Dec. 29, 1964; children—Mary Louise, John Alexander. With Pan Am. Bank Miami (Fla.), 1966-71, asst. v.p., 1968-71, v.p., 1971; v.p., cashier Citizens Nat. Bank Orlando (Fla.), 1971—. Instr. Am. Inst. Banking, Miami, 1971. Served with USN, 1955-59. Mem. Nat. Assn. Accountants, Am. Inst. Banking, Orlando C. of C. Republican. Christian Scientist. Club: Rio Pinar Country (Orlando). Home: 5128 Dorian Av Orlando FL 32809 Office: 250 N Orange Av Orlando FL 32802

MINNICK, WILLIAM DAVID, metal co. exec.; b. Boston, Pa., Oct. 30, 1924; s. Harry Atwater and Sarah Jane (Carnahan) M.; B.S., So. Meth. U., 1950; m. N. Jeanne Cole, Aug. 5, 1945; children—Susan Lynn (Mrs. Michael Downie), Barbara Jean. With A.O. Smith Corp., various locations, 1952-73, sales mgr., Milw., 1962-68, dir. marketing Houston, 1968-73; mgr. sales line pipe Armco Steel Corp., Houston, 1973—. Served with AUS, 1943-46. Decorated Combat Infantryman Badge. Clubs: Houston Petroleum, Lakeside Country. Home: 2209 Fulham Ct Houston TX 77042 Office: 1455 W Loop S Houston TX 77027

MINOR, WILLIAM HAROLD, machinery co. exec.; b. Roanoke, Mo., Jan. 19, 1928; s. Julius Harold and Sarah Virginia (Markland) M.; student Central Mo. State Coll., 1945, Brown U., 1945-46; B.S., U. Mo., 1950; m. Joan Garner, Feb. 3, 1950; children—Sandra Lynn, William Markland. Cons., Pate Engring. Co., Tulsa, 1950-56, Sverdrup & Parcel Engring. Co., St. Louis, 1956-58; engr. contracting Standard Industries, Tulsa, 1958-63; engr. Portland Cement Assn., Tulsa, 1963-68; v.p. sales CMI Corp., Oklahoma City, 1968—. Served with USNR, 1945-46. Registered profl. engr., Okla. Mem. Nat., Okla. socs. profl. engrs., Am. Mil. Engrs., Chi Epsilon. Home: 5900 Tiffany Circle Oklahoma City OK 73132 Office: Box 1985 Oklahoma City OK 73101

MINOR, WILLIAM RICHARD, securities broker; b. Keokuk, Ia., Mar. 2, 1942; s. William Frederick and Edna Mitchell (Holsteen) M.; B.B.A., U. Miami, 1964; m. Patricia Anne Brown, Jan. 12, 1966 (div. Apr. 1971); children—William Richard, Stacey Michelle. Actuarial cons. Wyatt Co., actuaries, Dallas, 1963-66; account exec. Merrill Lynch, Pierce, Fenner & Smith, Miami, Fla., 1966-69; resident mgr., v.p. Walston & Co., Inc., Clearwater, Fla., 1969-71; resident mgr. Shearson, Hammill & Co., Dunedin, Fla., 1971—. Cons. corporate finance, trusts, estate planning. Mem. Am. Mgmt. Assn., C. of C. Greater Clearwater, Downtown Clearwater Assn., U. Miami Alumni Assn., Omicron Delta Kappa, Sigma Phi Epsilon, Alpha Kappa Psi. Republican. Methodist. Clubs: St. Petersburg Stock and Bond, Commerce (St. Petersburg, Fla.). Home: 409 Lotus Path Clearwater FL 33516 Office: 748 Broadway Dunedin FL 33528

MINSHEW, ROBERT WILSON, lawyer; b. Sherman, Tex., June 25, 1938; s. Charles Beach and Eloise Winston (Tyler) M.; B.A., Austin Coll., 1960; LL.B., So. Meth. U., 1963; m. Ruth Ann Altman, July 13, 1963; children—Marshall Altman, Monica Ann. Admitted to Tex. bar, 1963, since practiced in Sherman; mem. firm Kennedy & Minshew, 1970—. Instr. comml. law Am. Inst. Banking, 1967-68. County campaign chmn. Nixon Reelection Com., 1972; mem. Sherman Planning and Zoning Commn., 1973—. Bd. dirs. Grayson County Easter Seal Soc. for Crippled Children and Adults, pres., 1972—; adv. bd. Salvation Army, chmn., 1972—; adv. bd. Texoma Valley council Boy Scouts Am. Served as capt. USMCR, 1964-67. Mem. State Bar Tex., Grayson County Bar Assn. (v.p. 1971—), Phi Alpha Delta. Clubs: Lions (dir. Sherman 1970-72), 300 (pres. 1972) (Sherman). Contbr. articles to law jours. Home: 1506 Ridgeway Dr Sherman TX 75090 Office: Professional Bldg 320 N Travis St Sherman TX 75090

MINTER, JAMES CARL, banker; b. Thomasville, Ga., Sept. 10, 1906; s. John Arthur and Sarah (Tomilnson) M.; grad. high sch.; m. Miriam G. Garrison, Aug. 6, 1941; children—Sarah M., Timmerman Carl, John Gorham. With Bank of Thomasville, 1926-32; pres., 1955—. Dir. S.W. Ga. Planning Commn., 1964-68, Ga. Municipal Assn., 1965-68; chmn. Grady County Hosp. Authority, 1953-63, Mayor pro-tem City of Cairo, 1958-68. Trustee Ga. Bapt. Children's Home, 1958-62; Norman Coll., 1968, Cairo High Sch., 1953—; bd. dirs. Grady County Recreation Commn., 1968—. Recipient U.S. Treasury award, 1941-45. Mem. C. of C. (pres. 1955). Democrat. Baptist (deacon). Kiwanian (pres. 1942), Elk, Mason. Club: Country (Cairo). Home: 540 S Broad St Cairo GA 31728 Office: PO Box 28 Cairo GA 31728

MINTER, RICHARD C., mcht., lawyer; b. Monticello, Ga., Apr. 28, 1922; s. Chester Lane and Bessie (Hardin) M.; LL.B., Mercer U., 1950; m. Elizabeth K. Thompson, Oct. 27, 1963; children—Wanda Faye Thompson (Mrs. Hamilton), Jay Wall Thompson. Admitted to Ga. bar, 1950, practiced law, Eastman, 1951; v.p. Stuckey's Inc., Eastman, 1951-57; sec., treas., dir. Pecan Shoppe of Dinwiddie, Fredericksburg, Va., 1957—. Served with USNR, 1942-46. Mem. Am., Ga. bar assns., Phi Alpha Delta, Kappa Sigma. Methodist. Lion, Mason (32 deg., Shriner). Home: PO Box 387 Eastman GA 31023

MINTER, VANCE CECIL, concrete co. exec.; b. Fort Worth, Tex., Nov. 11, 1935; s. Arlie Cecil and Victoria (Dieb) M.; B.S. in Econs. and Bus., U. Tex., 1957. Account exec. firm Goodbody & Co., Fort Worth, 1963-65; with Prater Concrete Co., Fort Worth, 1965-66; pres. Express Concrete Co., Fort Worth, 1966—, also dir.; dir. Continental Security Life Ins. Co., Fort Worth; pres., dir. Rios Sand & Gravel Co., Fort Worth, 1968—. Bd. dirs. Am. Cancer Soc., Fort Worth. Served to lt. AUS, 1957-59. Mem. Kappa Sigma. Mason. Clubs: Colonial Country (pres. 1974), Century II (Fort Worth). Home: 3416 Winifred Dr Fort Worth TX 76133 Office: PO Box 16340 Fort Worth TX 76133

MINTON, LEE ROY, ophthalmologist; b. Baxter, Tenn., Aug. 15, 1929; s. Zealous and Edith Marie (White) M.; B.S., Tenn. Tech. U., 1951; M.D., U. Tenn. Med. Sch., 1958; postgrad. Inst. Neurology, London, Eng., 1964. Intern Cottage Hosp., Santa Barbara, Cal., 1959; resident in ophthalmology Vanderbilt U. Sch. Medicine, 1961-64; practice ophthalmology, Nashville, 1964—. Cons. Vets. Hosp., Nashville, 1964-73; asst. clin. prof. ophthalmology Vanderbilt U. Med. Sch., Nashville, 1967—. Mem. Exec. Council Middle Tenn., Boy Scouts Am., 1973. Served to capt. Signal Corps, AUS, 1952-54. Diplomate Am. Acad. Ophthalmology and Otolaryngology. Fellow A.C.S., Nashville Acad. Ophthalmology and Otolaryngology (pres. 1971), Nashville (pres. 1968), Tenn. (pres. 1969) lawn tennis assns. Home: 7 Peach Blossom Square Nashville TN 37205 Office: 121 21st Av N Nashville TN 37203

MINTZ, A. AARON, physician; b. Houston, July 29, 1922; s. Morris and Rebecca (Mintz) M.; B.A., Rice U., 1943; M.D., U. Tex., 1948; m. Helen Frances Brenner, June 22, 1947; children—Steven, Richard, Beverly. Intern U. Ia. Hosp., 1948-49; resident VA Hosp., Houston, 1949-50, Baylor Affiliated Hosps., Houston, 1950-52; pvt. practice medicine, specializing in pediatrics, Houston, 1952—; asso. prof. pediatrics Baylor Coll. Medicine, 1952—; dep. chief pediatrics Harris County Hosp. Dist., Houston, 1960—; mem. staff Tex. Children's Hosp., Hermann, Ben Taub Gen., Jefferson Davis, Methodist, St. Joseph's, Meml. hosps. Pres. South Tex. Hebrew Acad., Houston, 1971-72; pres. United Orthodox Synagogues Houston, 1969-71. Bd. dirs. Jewish Community Council, Houston, Jewish Home for Aged. Served to capt. AUS, 1952-53. Grantee, Lakeside Labs., 1960-61, E.R. Squibb & Sons, 1961, 1971-72, Plough, Inc., 1961, Johnson & Johnson, 1971, Eaton Labs., 1963, Hoffman-LaRoche, 1963-64, 1965, Ayerst Labs., 1967, 1967-68, Eli Lilly Labs., 1969-70, Wyeth Labs., 1970-72. Diplomate Am. Bd. Pediatrics. Mem. Harris County Med. Soc., Soc. Adolescent Medicine, Ambulatory Pediatric Soc., Houston Pediatric Soc., So. Soc. Pediatric Research, Am. Acad. Pediatrics, Alpha Omega Alpha. Jewish religion. Contbr. numerous articles to sci., med. jours. Home: 3605 S Braeswood Houston TX 77025 Office: Baylor Coll Medicine Houston TX 77025

MINTZ, DONALD DEAN, mortgage banker; b. Houston, May 3, 1937; s. Sam and Eula Lea (Reynolds) M.; B.S. in Econs., U. Houston, 1962; m. Loretta Gowen, Dec. 5, 1959; children—David, Donna Lee. Engaged in elec. constrn. industry, 1962-69; v.p. Center Savs. Assn., Houston, 1971—, mgr. mortgage loan center, 1972—. Active local Little League, Youth Football. Mem. Soc. Real Estate Appraisers (asso.), Greater Houston Home Builders Assn. Club: Houston Power Squadron. Home: 11014 Sage Berry St Houston TX 77034 Office: 1200 Milam St Houston TX 77002

MINTZ, MORTON ABNER, newspaper reporter; b. Ann Arbor, Mich., Jan. 26, 1922; s. William and Sarah (Solomon) M.; A.B. in Econs., U. Mich., 1943; m. Anita Inez Franz, Aug. 30, 1946; children—Margaret Ruth, Elizabeth Diane, Roberta Joan, Daniel Robert. Reporter, St. Louis Star-Times, 1946-50; reporter, asst. city editor St. Louis Globe-Democrat, 1951-58; reporter Washington Post, 1958—. Recipient Heywood Broun, Raymond Clapper, George Polk Meml. awards for journalism, 1962. Author: The Therapeutic Nightmare, 1965; By Prescription Only, 1967; (with Jerry S. Cohen) America, Inc., 1971. Home: 3022 Macomb St NW Washington DC 20008 Office: 1150 15th St NW Washington DC 20005

MINTZER, JULIUS, social orgn. adminstr.; b. Bklyn., Aug. 3, 1913; B.S. in Edn., N.Y. U., 1934, M.A. in Sociology, 1935; M.S. in Social Work, Columbia, 1941; m. Rhoda Dorothy Glick, July 20, 1942; children—Susam Louise (Mrs. Fred Davidow), Amy Helene (Mrs. Joel Abramovitz), Kenneth Louis. Social worker Westchester County, N.Y., 1935-39; field dir. Am. Service Inst., Pitts., 1941; asst. dir. Jewish Community Council, Dayton, O., 1945-49; asst. dir. Jewish Fedn., Cin., 1949-53; dir. Richmond (Va.) Jewish Community Council, 1953—. Served with AUS, 1942-46. Named Man of the Month Am. Jewish Times Outlook mag., 1961. Mem. B'nai B'rith. Home: 4507 Park Av Richmond VA 23221 Office: 5403 Monument Av Richmond VA 23226

MINYARD, JAMES PATRICK, JR., chemist, educator; b. Greenwood, Miss., May 11, 1929; s. James Patrick and Mary Lou (Duke) M.; B.S. in Chemistry, Miss. State U., 1951, Ph.D. (Gen. Edn. Bd. scholar), 1967; postgrad. Cal. Inst. Tech., 1951-52; m. Mary Louise Whitesell, Aug. 11, 1956; children—Mary Susan, Thomas James, Barbara Lynn, Carol Ann, William Patrick. Field engr. Minyard Well Co., Belzoni, Miss., 1954-58; asst. chemist Mississippi State (Miss.) Chem. Lab., 1958-59, chemist, 1959-64, state chemist, 1967—; research chemist Boll Weevil Research Lab., Agrl. Research Service, Dept. Agr., 1964-67. Faculty Miss. State U., 1961—, prof. chemistry, 1967—. Served with AUS, 1952-54. Mem. Am. Chem. Soc., A.A.A.S., Miss. Acad. Scis., Newcomen Soc. Am., Am. Oil Chemists Soc., Assn. Ofcl. Analytical Chemists, Assn. Am. Feed Control Ofcls., Am. Assn. Fertilizer Control Ofcls., Assn. Am. Pesticide Control Ofcls., Assn. Food and Drug Ofcls., Sigma Xi. Democrat. Methodist. Contbr. to profl. jours. Home: Box 2198 Mississippi State MS 39762 Office: Mississippi State Chem Lab Box CR Mississippi State MS 39762

MIREE, BENJAMIN KYSER, engring. co exec.; b. Jackson, Miss., Jan. 25, 1944; s. Royal Richardson and Sarah Belle (Kyser) M.; B.S. in Civil Engring., U. Ala., 1966. Design engr. Rust Engring. Co., Birmingham, Ala., 1966-68, field engr. Brice Bldg. Co., 1969-71, project mgr. MacClary Contracting Co., 1971-72, pres. Miree Constrn. Co., 1973—, chmn. bd. dirs., 1973—. Sec. Custom Packaging Co., Inc. Birmingham, also dir., owner Crow's Next Apts., Birmingham. Registered profl. engr. ALA. Home: 3057 Sterling Rd Birmingham AL 35213 Office: 2621 Arlington Av Birmingham AL 35205

MIRES, A(LBERT) HAROLD, accounting firm exec.; b. Kaplan, La., Jan. 15, 1928; s. Ivy and Rose (Bourque) M.; student U. Southwestern La., 1948-50; m. Rosie Mae Pellesier, Nov. 26, 1953. Accountant, office mgr. Vinton Co-Op Drier, Inc. (La.) 1950-57; pvt. practice accounting, Sulphur, La., 1957—; sr. partner Mires & Broussard, C.P.A.'s, Sulphur, 1967—. Lectr. McNeese State Coll., Lake Charles, La., 1967; mem. S.W. La. Estate Planning Council. Exec. bd. Calcasieu area council, Boy Scouts Am., 1969—, dist. chmn., 1972-73. Served with USNR, 1946-48. C.P.A., La. Mem. Am. Inst. C.P.A.'s. La. Soc. C.P.A.'s, West Calcasieu Assn. Commerce (dir.). Rotarian (pres.). Office: 1633 Arizona St PO Draw W Sulphur LA 70663

MIRUSKI, MICHAEL, elec. products mfg. co. exec.; b. Auburn, N.Y., Dec. 5, 1932; s. Michael and Sadie (Zalopany) M.; B.C.E., Cornell U., 1955; M.B.A., Oklahoma City U., 1968; m. Elizabeth Ann Lowman, Oct. 29, 1955; 1 dau., Michele Ann. Constrn. engr. E.I. duPont de Nemours & Co., Topeka, Kan., also Parlin, N.J., Wilmington, Del., 1957-60; facilities engr. Gen. Electric Co., Syracuse, N.Y., Oklahoma City, 1960-66, supr., Oklahoma City, 1966-70; mgr. Honeywell, Inc., Oklahoma City, 1970—. Instr. indsl. mgmt., marketing M.B.A. program Oklahoma City U., 1968-70. Served from 2d lt. to 1st lt. C.E., AUS, 1955-57. Recipient Grad. Faculty award Oklahoma City U. Sch. Bus., 1968. Mem. Am. Inst. Plant Engrs., Nat. Fire Protection Assn. Home: 6440 N Sterling Dr Oklahoma City OK 73132 Office: 4000 NW 39th St Oklahoma City OK 73112

MISHELEVICH, DAVID JACOB, computer center exec., physician; b. Pitts., Jan., 1942; s. Benjamin and Sarah (Bachrach) M.; B.S., U. Pitts., 1962; M.D. (Henry Strong Denison scholar), Johns Hopkins, 1966, Ph.D. in Biomed. Engring., 1970; m. Elaine Carol Grumer, Aug. 18, 1963. Post-sophomore research fellow Johns Hopkins Sch. Medicine, 1964-65, NIH spl. fellow in biomed. engring. and medicine, 1969-71; intern Balt. City Hosps., 1966-67; sr. asst. surgeon USPHS, 1967-68, surgeon, 1968-69; staff asso. NIH, Bethesda, Md., 1967-69; v.p. Nat. Ednl. Cons., Inc., Balt., 1970-71, chief computing and profl. records div., 1970-72, exec. v.p., 1971-72, dir. Med. Computing Resources Center, U. Tex. Health Sci. Center at Dallas, 1972—, asst. prof. med. computer sci., 1972-74, asso. prof., 1974—, chmn. dept., 1973—, also asst. prof. internal medicine, 1972—. Mem. A.A.A.S., Am. Physiol. Soc., Am. Soc. Information Sci., Assn. for Computing Machinery, I.E.E.E., Phi Beta Kappa, Omicron Delta Kappa. Democrat. Jewish religion. Contbr. articles, abstracts to profl. jours. Home: 12866 Noel Rd Dallas TX 75230 Office: Med Computing Resources Center Univ Tex Health Sci Center 5323 Harry Hines Blvd Dallas TX 75235

MISKIMEN, CARMEN MILAGROS RIVERA-BATLLE DE, educator; b. Mayaguez, P.R., Mar. 15, 1933; d. Benigno and Maria Anna (Batlle-Morella) Rivera-Cintron; B.S., U. P.R., 1953; Ph.D., U. Wis., 1962; m. George William Miskimen, Apr. 19, 1963; children—Kathryn Ann, Teresa Marie, Elizabeth Joan, Carmen Mildred. Tchr. sci. P.R. Dept. Edn., Mayaguez, 1953-55; plant pathologist Crops Research Div., U.S. Dept. Agr., Mayaguez, 1962-63; asst. prof. U. P.R., Mayaguez, 1963-67, asso. prof., 1967-73, prof. biology, coordinator med. tech. program, 1973—. Mem. Central Com. New Progressive Party, P.R., 1968—, sec., 1968-72. Mem. Am. Phytopathol. Soc., Sigma Xi, Gamma Sigma Delta, Beta Beta Beta. Mem. Anglican Ch. Clubs: Boqueron Yacht, Deportivo de Oeste, Casino de Mayaguez. Home: Box 1420 Km 40 Miradero Rd Villa Sonsire Mayaguez PR 00708

MISKIMEN, GEORGE WILLIAM, educator; b. Appleton, Wis., May 21, 1930; s. George Oscar and Gladys Matilda (Burns) M.; B.S., Ohio U., 1953, M.S., 1955; Ph.D., U. Fla. at Gainesville, 1966; m. Carmen Milagros Rivera-Batlle, Apr. 19, 1963; children—Kathryn Ann, Teresa Marie, Elizabeth Joan, Carmen Mildred. Entomologist V.I. Agrl. Program U.S. Dept. Agr., St. Croix, 1958-61; research entomologist, investigations leader entomology research div. U.S. Dept. Agr. Mayaguez, P.R., 1962-66; dir., prof. biology Entomol. Pioneering Research Lab. U. P.R. at Mayaguez, 1966—. Served with AUS, 1947-51. U. Fla. Academic fellow; Hatch Scientific grantee, NSF grantee. Mem. Entomol. Soc. Am., Internat. Orgn. Biol. Control, Soc. Systematic Zoology, Internat. Soc. Sugarcane Technologists, Coleopterist's Soc., Assn. Tropical Biology, Soc. Study Coleoptera, U.S. Coast Guard Aux. (Flotilla comdr. 1968—, div. tng. officer 1970), Sigma Xi, Gamma Sigma Delta, Delta Upsilon (sec. 1954, pledge pres. 1953). Episcopalian. Mason, Rotarian. Clubs: Boqueron Yacht (Boqueron, P.R.); Deportivo del Oeste (Mayaguez, P.R.); Casino de Mayaguez (P.R.). Contbr. articles to scientific jours. Home: Box 1420 Km 4 O Miradero Rd Villa Sonsire Mayaguez PR 00708 Office: Entomol Pioneering Research Lab University PR at Mayaguez Mayaguez PR 00708

MISKOVSKY, GEORGE, lawyer, ex-state senator; b. Oklahoma City, Feb. 13, 1910; s. Frank and Mary (Bourek) M.; LL.B., U. Okla., 1936; m. Nelly Oleta Donahue, Dec. 30, 1932; children—George, Gary, Grover, Gail Marie. Admitted to Okla. bar, 1936, since practiced in Oklahoma City; sr. mem., head firm Miskovsky, Sullivan, Embry & Miskovsky, Oklahoma City; pub. defender Oklahoma City, 1936; county atty. Oklahoma County, 1943-44; mem. Okla. Ho. of Reps., 1939-42; mem. Okla. Senate, 1950-60. Sec. Economy Square, Inc. and Penn 74 Inc. Shopping Centers. Mem. Am., Okla., Oklahoma County bar assns., Am. Judicature Soc., C. of C., Am., Okla. trial lawyers assns., U. Okla. Law Assn., Order of Coif, Pi Kappa Alpha, Phi Alpha Delta. Democrat. Episcopalian. Mason (Shriner). Clubs: Lions, Oklahoma City Golf and Country, Oklahoma City Press. Sooner Dinner. Home: 1511 Drury Lane Oklahoma City OK 73116 Office: Hightower Bldg Oklahoma City OK 73102

MITCHAM, DONALD, physicist; b. Hazlehurst, Miss., Nov. 15, 1921; s. Eddie Carroll and Ethel (Crisco) M.; B.S., Tulane U., 1948. Physicist, So. Regional Research Center, U.S. Dept. Agr., New Orleans, 1948—. Served to lt. USNR, 1942-46. Mem. Am. Oil Chem. Soc., Am. Crystallographic Assn., Soc. Applied Spectroscopy. Contbr. articles to profl. jours. Home: 3326 Marigny St New Orleans LA 70122 Office: PO Box 19687 New Orleans LA 70179

MITCHELHILL, JAMES MOFFAT, indsl. adminstr., b. St. Joseph, Mo., Aug. 11, 1912; s. William and Jeannette (Ambrose) M.; B.S., Northwestern U., 1934, C.E., 1935; m. Maurine Hutchason, Jan. 9, 1937 (div. 1962); children—Janis Maurine (Mrs. Ross W. Johnson), Jeri Ann (Mrs. Charles T. Riney). Engring. dept. C., M., St. P. & P.R.R. Co., Chgo. and Miles City, Mont., 1935-45; asst. mgr. Ponce & Guayama R.R. Co., Aguirre, P.R., 1945-51, v.p., gen. mgr., 1969-70; mgr. Central Cortada, Santa Isabel, P.R., 1951-54; r.r. supt. Braden Copper Co., Rancagua, Chile, 1954-63; staff engr. Coverdale & Colpitts, N.Y.C., 1963-64; asst. to exec. v.p. Central Aguirre Sugar Co., 1964-67; v.p., gen. mgr. Coddea, Inc., Dominican Republic, 1967-68; asst. to gen. mgr. Land Adminstrn. of P.R., La Nueva Central Aguirre, 1970-71, for Centrals Aguirre Lafayette and Mercedita, 1971-72; asst. to gen. mgr. Corporacion Azucarera de P.R., 1973—. Registered profl. engr., Mont., licensed civil engr., P.R. Fellow Am. Soc. C.E., Am. Geog. Soc. N.Y.; mem. Am. Ry. Engring. Assn., Colegio de Ingenieros Arquitectos Y Agrimensores de P.R., Asociacion de Technicos Azucareros de P.R. Sigma Xi, Tau Beta Pi. Home: PO Box 137 Aguirre PR 00608 Office: Central Aguirre Aguirre PR 00608

MITCHELL, ALFRED TAYLOR, univ. adminstr.; b. Rockford, Ia., Mar. 10, 1912; s. Theron Harmon and Bessie (Hanchett) M.; student Ia. State U., 1929-30; B.A., U. Ia., 1946; m. Hazel Margaret Ashley, July 7, 1942; children—Peter Ashley, John Harmon. Mng. editor Student Publs. Inc., Iowa City, Ia., 1931-33; sports and news dir. Mason City (Ia.) Globe-Gazette, KGLO Radio, 1933-40; asst. dir. news service Ia. State U., 1940-42; news editor Iowa City (Ia.) Press-Citizen, 1946-52; sr. tech. writer, publs. mgr. Collins Radio Co., Cedar Rapids, Ia., 1952-57, Dallas, Tex., 1957-62; devel., univ. relations dir. U. Tex. at Dallas, 1962—. Served with USNR, 1942-62. Mem. Am. Coll. Pub. Relations Assn., Retired Officers Assn., Ia. State U., U. Ia. Alumni assns., Press Club of Dallas, Pi Kappa Alpha, Scabbard and Blade. Methodist. Mason. Kiwanian (dist. editor, pub. relations chmn. Tex.-Okla. dist. 1971-72, pub. relations com., counselor Eastern U.S., Eastern Can., Caribbean area 1972-73). Author numerous tech. handbooks for Collins Radio; editor Ki-Notes, 1971-72; editor Advance U. Tex. at Dallas, 1964—. Home: 628 Sherwood Dr Richardson TX 75080 Office: U Tex at Dallas Box 30365 Dallas TX 75230

MITCHELL, DOLPHUS BURL, optometrist; b. Birmingham, Ala., Sept. 9, 1922; s. Allen T. and Gertrude (Robinson) M.; student Alcorn A. and M. Coll., 1941-43, Monroe Coll. Optometry, 1946; Dr. Optometry, No. Ill. Coll. Optometry, 1949; LL.D., Union Bapt. Sem., 1952; m. Rebecca Woodfin, Mar. 16, 1960; children—Dawn Bonita, Dolphus Burl II (dec.), Donald Brian, Dora Bertine. Individual practice optometry, Birmingham, Ala., 1949—, asso. prof. optometry U. Ala., part-time 1970-71. Vol. staff mem. U. Ala. Child Devel. and Learning Disabilities Center, 1969-71. Commr. Boy Scouts Am., Birmingham, 1951-53; v.p. North Smith Civic League, 1971-72. Served with AUS, 1943-46. Recipient Service Award Booker T. Washington Bus. Coll., 1971. Fellow Royal Soc. Health; mem. Ala. Optometric Assn., Nat. Assn. Retarded Children, Am. Pub. Health Assn., Nat. Assn. Children with Learning Disabilities, Am. Acad. Polit. and Social Scis., Internat. Platform Assn., N.A.A.C.P., Fraternal Order Police (asso. mem.). Baptist (deacon). Mason (32 deg., Shriner). Home: 2130 Leola Circle Birmingham AL 35207 Office: 507 17th St N Birmingham AL 35203

MITCHELL, EARL DOUGLASS, JR., educator; b. New Orleans, May 16, 1938; s. Earl Douglass and Mary (Duncan) M.; B.S., Xavier U. of La., 1960; M.S., Mich. State U., 1963, Ph.D., 1966; m. Bernice Elva Compton, Oct. 31, 1959; children—Karen Yvette, Earl Douglass III, Michael Troy. Research asso. Mich. State U., 1966-67; research asso. Okla. State U., 1967-69, asst. prof. biochemistry, 1969-72, asso. prof., 1972—. Mem. Okla. Black Polit. Caucus; pres. Payne County N.A.A.C.P., 1969—; chmn. Stillwater chpt. Okla. Am. Civil Liberties Union, 1970-71, vice-chmn. Am. Civil Liberties Union of Okla., 1972—. Chmn. bd. dirs. Stillwater Neighborhood Nursery. Mem. Danforth Assos., Am. Chem. Soc., Am. Soc. Biol. Chemistry, A.A.A.S., Am. Soc. Plant Physiology, Sigma Xi. Home: 3 Summit Circle Stillwater OK 74074 Office: Dept Biochemistry Okla State U Stillwater OK 74074

MITCHELL, EARL NELSON, educator; b. Centerville, Ia., Aug. 30, 1926; s. Earl Nelson and Nina (Swank) M.; B.A., State U. Ia., 1949, M.S., 1951; Ph.D., U. Minn., 1955; m. Marlys Marie Panning, July 23, 1955. Research scientist Remington-Rand Univac, St. Paul, 1955-58; prof. physics U. N.D. at Grand Forks, 1958-62; prof. physics, asst. chmn. dept. U. N.C. at Chapel Hill, 1962—. Served with USNR, 1945-46. Mem. Am. Phys. Soc., Am. Assn. Physics Tchrs., Phi Beta Kappa, Sigma Xi. Home: 220 Glenhill Lane Chapel Hill NC 27514

MITCHELL, EDGAR DEAN, astronaut; b. Hereford, Tex., Sept. 17, 1930; s. Joseph T. and Ollidean (Arnold) M.; B.S. in Indsl. Mgmt., Carnegie Inst. Tech., 1952; B.S. in Aero. Engring., U.S. Naval Postgrad. Sch., 1961; Sc.D. in Aeros. and Astronautics, Mass. Inst. Tech., 1964; Sc.D., N.M. State U., 1971; D.Eng., Carnegie Mellon U., 1971; m. Louise Elizabeth Randall, Dec. 21, 1951 (div. Jan. 1972); children—Karlyn Louise, Elizabeth Randall. Joined U.S. Navy, 1952, commd. ensign, 1953, advanced through grades to capt., 1966; naval aviator, 1954, with patrol squadron 29, Okinawa, 1955, pilot heavy attack squadron 2, U.S.S. Bon Homme Richard also U.S.S. Ticonderoga, 1957-58, research project pilot air devel. squadron 5, 1958-59, chief project mgmt. div. Navy Field Office Manned Orbiting Lab., Los Angeles, 1964-65, assigned to Aerospace Research Pilot Sch., Edwards AFB, Cal., 1965-66; astronaut Manned Spacecraft Center, Houston, 1966—, prime crew Apollo XIV Lunar Exploration, 1970. Explorer scout leader West Newton (Mass.) council Boy Scouts Am., 1962-63. Decorated D.A.R. Naval Aviator award, Presdl. Medal Freedom, D.S.M. NASA, D.S.M. USN. Mem. Parapsychol. Assn., Soc. Exptl. Test Pilots, Am. Inst. Aeros. and Astronautics, Sigma Xi, Kappa Sigma. Mailing Address: Manned Space Center Houston TX 77058

MITCHELL, GEORGE ERNEST, JR., nutritionist, educator; b. Duoro, N.M., June 7, 1930; s. George Ernest and Alma Thyrza (Hatley) M.; B.S., U. Mo., 1951, M.S., 1954; Ph.D., U. Ill., 1956; m. Billie Carolyn McMahan, Mar. 14, 1952; children—Leslie Dianne, Karen Leigh, Cynthia Faye. Asst. prof. U. Ill., 1956-60; asso. prof. U. Ky., Lexington, 1960-67, prof., 1967—, also coordinator animal nutrition. Partner, Mitchell Livestock Farms, Green Forest, Ark. Served to capt. USAF, 1951-53. Recipient Sang award for contbns. to grad. edn., 1966, Ky. Research Found. Research award, 1969, Thomas Poe Cooper Agrl. Research award, 1969. Sr. Fulbright Research scholar to New Zealand, 1973—. Mem. Am. Soc. Animal Sci. (sec. So. sect. 1969-70, v.p. 1970-71, pres. 1971-72), Am. Dairy Sci. Assn., Am. Inst. Nutrition, A.A.A.S. (life), Sigma Xi, Gamma Sigma Delta, Phi Eta Sigma, Omicron Delta Kappa, Alpha Zeta. Methodist. Contbr. articles to profl. jours. Home: 690 Hill'n'Dale Lexington KY 40503

MITCHELL, GEORGE WILLIAM, IV, chem. co. exec.; b. High Point, N.C., Oct. 22, 1928; s. George William, III, and Frances Minerva (Jones) M.; B.S., Duke; m. Billie Richard, Apr. 16, 1948; children—William Richard, Millicent Ann. Pres., treas. Caro Chem. Corp., Charlotte, N.C., 1966-72; chmn. bd. Chemicaland Corp., Caro Chem. So. Corp., and United Filler & Chem. Co., all Calhoun, Ga., 1970—, Cloray N.J. Corp., Newark, 1971—; dir. Randolph Mills, Inc.; conducted research for USN. Served with AUS. Mem. High Point (pres. 1955—), Duke (treas. 1953) alumni assns. Republican. Mem. Soc. of Friends. Club: Charlotte Athletic. Home: 2600 Roswell Av Charlotte NC 28209 Office: 80 Lister Av Newark NJ 07105

MITCHELL, GERA ALONZA, fire chief; b. Opelika, Ala., Oct. 13, 1915; s. William Osborn and Sallie Lou (Wright) M.; student pub. schs., Opelika; m. Golden Garrett, June 11, 1936; children—William Ellis, Earl Franklin. With City of Opelika Fire Dept., 1928-42, fire chief, 1947—, fire chief Army Depot, Anniston, Ala., 1942-45; Mem. Internat. Assn. Fire Chiefs (treas., dir.). Presbyn. Office: PO Box 629 Opelika AL 36801

MITCHELL, JACK HARRIS, JR., educator, research scientist; b. Auburn, Ala., Sept. 15, 1911; s. Jack Harris and Ethel (Blasingame) M.; B.S., Clemson U., 1933; postgrad. Columbia, 1936-37; Ph.D. in Biochemistry, Purdue, 1941; m. Annie Lee Knox, Oct. 7, 1944; children—Jack H., Scott K., Lee W., Miriam U. Research chemist Am. Meat Inst., Chgo., 1941-42; head biochem. sect. So. Research Inst., Birmingham, Ala., 1947-50; asst. chief stability div. Q.M. Food & Container Inst., Chgo., 1950-55, chief chem. and microbiology div., 1955-57; head food tech. and human nutrition dept. Clemson U., 1957-64, prof. food sci. and biochemistry, 1964—. Served to capt. AUS, 1942-46. Mem. Inst. Food Technologists (chmn. Dixie sect. 1972-73), A.A.A.S., Am. Inst. Chemists (pres. S.C. Inst. 1974—), Assos. U.S. Army Natick (Mass.) Labs. (bd. dirs. 1964-67), Sigma Xi, Gamma Sigma Delta. Methodist. Contbr. articles to profl. publs. Patentee in field. Home: 101 Bradley St Clemson SC 29631

MITCHELL, JOHN MURRAY, JR., climatologist; b. N.Y.C., Sept. 17, 1928; s. John Murray and Lanier Walcott (Comly) M.; S.B., Mass. Inst. Tech., 1951, S.M., 1952; Ph.D., Pa. State U., 1960; grad. Nat. War Coll., 1971; m. Pollyanne Bryant, May 5, 1956; children—John Murray III, Brian Harrison, Katherine Comly, Anne Stuart. Resident observer Blue Hill Meteorol. Obs., Harvard, Milton, Mass., 1946-52; research meteorologist U.S. Weather Bur., Washington, 1955-65; project scientist for climatic change Nat. Oceanic and Atmospheric Adminstrn., Silver Spring, Md., 1965—. Vis. lectr., prof. U. Cal. at Berkeley, 1965, U. Wash., 1969, U. Del. Summer Inst. Climatology, 1970, 71, Woods Hole (Mass.) Oceanographic Instn., 1963-64. Mem. Air Pollution Control Bd. Fairfax County, Va., 1971—. Served with USAF, 1952-55. Recipient Silver medal Commerce Dept., 1969, Gold medal, 1973. Fellow Am. Meteorol. Soc.; mem. Am. Geophys. Union, A.A.A.S., Arctic Inst., Internat. Glaciol. Soc., Royal Meteorol. Soc., U.S. Assn. Quaternary Research, Sigma Xi, Delta Psi. Republican. Episcopalian. Clubs: Cosmos (Washington); Wianno (Osterville, Mass.). Editor, Meteorol. Monographs, 1965—; editorial bd. Am. Geophys. Union Geophys. Monographs, 1970—, Jour. Quaternary Research, 1970—. Contbr. articles to profl. jours. Home: 1106 Dogwood Dr McLean VA 22101 Office: Nat Oceanic and Atmospheric Administration Gramax Bldg Silver Spring MD 20910

MITCHELL, JOHN PATRICK, dentist; b. Butte, Mont., Sept. 8, 1904; s. Frank Joseph and Mary Margaret (McVeigh) M.; student Carroll Coll., 1923-25; D.D.S., Craighton U., 1929; postgrad. Baylor U., 1965-66, Creighton U., 1971, Northwestern U. Individual practice dentistry, Dallas, 1929—. Clinic research tchr., cons. numerous dental meetings. Mem. Am., Tex. (recipient Order of Good Fellow), Mont., Chgo., Dallas County dental assns., Omnicron Kappa Upsilon. K.C. Club: Mustang (So. Meth. U.). Patentee magnetic repelling teeth. Research in vertical-horizontal denture magnetic occlusal balance and retention of artificial teeth. Home and office: 3301 Greenville St Dallas TX 75206

MITCHELL, JOSEPH BRADY, mil. historian, author; b. Ft. Leavenworth, Kan., Sept. 25, 1915; s. William A. and Margery (Brady) M.; B.S., U.S. Mil. Acad., 1937; m. Vivienne French Brown, Aug. 20, 1938; children—Sherwood N., J. Bradford. Mem. operations div. War Dept. Gen. Staff, 1945-49; chief historian Am. Battle Monuments Commn., 1950-61, hist. cons., 1969—; curator Ft. Ward Mus., Alexandria, Va., 1964—. Trustee Nat. Temple Hill Assn. Served from 2d lt. to lt. col., 5th inf. div., AUS, 1937-45; ETO. Decorated Bronze Star medal. Recipient Am. Revolutionary Round Table prize for best book in field, 1962. Mem. Soc. of Cin., Civil War Round Table Alexandria and D.C. Episcopalian. Author: Decisive Battles of the Civil War, 1955; Decisive Battles of the American Revolution, 1962; Twenty Decisive Battles of the World, 1964; Discipline and Bayonets, 1967; The Badge of Gallantry, 1968; Military Leaders in the Civil War, 1972. Contbr. articles to encys. and mags. Home: 606 Beverly Dr Alexandria VA 22305 Office: 4301 W Braddock Rd Alexandria VA 22304

MITCHELL, JOSEPH MCDOWELL, city ofcl.; b. Chevy Chase, Md., Mar. 25, 1922; s. Rossel and Alyne (McDowell) M.; B.S., U. Md., 1956; student Am. U., 1956-57; student U. So. Cal., 1957-58; m. Dorothy Louise Hayes, Nov. 3, 1940; children—Joseph Bronson, Elizabeth Anne. Adminstrv. staff War Prodn. Bd., Washington, 1941-44; adminstrv. officer, intelligence aide Nat. Bur. Standards Nat. Security Agy., Washington, 1946-51; comptroller, adminstrv. officer Dept. Army, Kaiserslautern, Germany, 1953-57; twp. mgr. Marple Twp., Pa., 1958-60; city mgr., Newburgh, N.Y., 1960-63; borough mgr. Hollidaysburg, Pa., 1965-71; city mgr. Lake Alfred, Fla., 1971—. Served with USAAF, 1944-46, AUS, 1951-53. Mem. Internat. City Mgmt. Assn., Fla. City and County Mgmt. Assn., Am. Soc. Pub. Adminstrn., Ridge League of Municipalities (v.p. 1973). Mason. Contbr. articles to mags., jours. Home: 105 S Ilakee Av Lake Alfred FL 33850 Office: 120 E Pomelo St Lake Alfred FL 33850

MITCHELL, JOSEPHINE GRAY (MRS. T. A. MITCHELL), musician, past owner lumber bus.; b. Bonham, Tex.; d. Moses Vashti and Bertie (Hoy) Gray; B.S., Tex. Women's U., 1926, M.A., 1971; m. T.A. Mitchell, Mar. 21, 1929 (dec. 1964); children—Richard Gray, Thomas Albert. Pianist profl. concerts, Tex., Okla., Colo., 1927—; tchr. music Port Arthur (Tex.) High Sch., 1928-29; formerly owner, operator T. A. Mitchell Lumber Co., Ft. Worth. Condr. Statewide Tex. Composers Contests, 1952-72; judge piano auditions Nat. Piano Guild, 1964-72; Music of Tex. Composers lecture recitals. Bd. dirs. Ft. Worth Civic Music, Tex. Girls Choir, Ft. Worth Youth Symphony. Recipient citation Nat. Fedn. Music Clubs, 1962, 68, Nat. Fedn. Musicians, 1966, 69; named 1st lady of music Ft. Worth, 1966, Tex. State citation composers, 1956, 71. Mem. Fort Worth League Composers (founder, chmn. 1958-68, pres.), Nat. Fedn. Music Clubs (nat. citation; asst. nat. folk music archivist 1963-66, archivist, chmn. folk music research S. Central region 1966-68, nat. chmn. folk music 1970-74), Tex. Fedn. Music Clubs (pres. 4th dist. 1964-66), Tex. Composers Guild (state chmn. 1952-58, 62-72), Tex. Women's U. Alumnae Assn. (past pres.), Ft. Worth Ballet Assn., Symphony League, Opera Guild, Sigma Alpha Iota (pres. 1961-62; recognition award), Lady Lions. Episcopalian. Clubs: Fort Worth Women's (chmn. Joint Twilight Musicales 1970-72), Fort Worth Piano Forum, E. Clyde Whitlock Music, Euterpean Music (pres. 1952-54). Author: Texas Composers and Their Works, 1950-70. Compiler: (with others) Texas Composers Catalogue of Works, 1964, 68, 2d edit., 1974. Editor: Tex. Composers Guild Handbook, 1955. Home: 5120 Malinda Lane S Fort Worth TX 76112

MITCHELL, KENNETH LAMAR, cotton buyer; b. Fort Payne, Ala., Nov. 6, 1949; s. Wyatt Barrett and Jessie Faye (Lacy) M.; grad. Murdock Internat. Cotton Sch., Memphis, 1971. Cotton buyer Mitchell-Huntley Cotton Co., Huntsville, Ala., 1971—, also pilot and dir. Mem. Aircraft Owners and Pilots Assn. Republican. Baptist. Mason (Shriner). Home: Route 2 Box 254 Fort Payne AL 35967 Office: 801 Oster Dr Huntsville AL 35801

MITCHELL, LAWRENCE DU-WAYNE, physician; b. Henderson, Ky., Feb. 23, 1925; s. Edward Preston and Martha Alma (Martin) M.; B.B.A., Sam Houston U., 1948; B.A., U. Tex., 1952; M.D., Baylor U., 1956; M.A., Sam Houston U., 1966; m. Ethel Clark, July 3, 1964; children—Michael Warren, Melissa Ann. Intern Midstate Baptist Hosp., Nashville, 1957; practice of gen. medicine, San Jacinto County, Tex., 1957-65, Grimes County, 1965—; med. staff Tex. Dept. Corrections, Huntsville, 1967—; mem. staffs Grimes Meml. Hosp., Navesota, Tex., Huntsville Meml. Hosp., Tex. Served with USNR, 1943-46. Decorated with Bronze Star medal. Mem. Am., Tex. med. assns., Tri-Med. Soc., Royal Soc. Health, The Smithsonian Assos., Tex. Farm Bur., Lambda Alpha Epsilon, Phi Chi. Mason. Home: Route 2 Box 250 Huntsville TX 77340 Office: Navasota Hwy Box 1056 Anderson TX 77340

MITCHELL, MARTHA JOY, librarian; b. Rome, Ga., Mar. 29, 1925; d. John T. and Edith (Terrell) Mitchell; B.A., Tenn. Temple Coll., 1954; B.A., George Peabody Coll. for Tchrs., 1958, M.A. in Library Sci., 1960. Head librarian Tenn. Temple Coll., Chattanooga, 1954-57, 60-64; librarian Dalewood Jr. High Sch., Chattanooga, 1964-66; head librarian Franklin High Sch., Nashville, 1966—. Named Ky. Col. Mem. N.E.A., Tenn. Edn. Assn., Tenn., Am. library assns., Women's Nat. Book Assn. (pres. 1971-73). Home: 2406 Blair Blvd Nashville TN 37212 Office: Franklin High Sch Franklin TN 37064

MITCHELL, MEMORY F. (MRS. T.W. MITCHELL), editor; b. Raleigh, N.C., Jan. 21, 1924; d. James S. and Foy (Johnson) Farmer; A.B., Meredith Coll., 1944; postgrad. Cornell U. Law Sch., 1944-45; J.D., U. N.C., 1946, A.M., 1949; m. B. W. Blackwelder, July 14, 1955 (div. Feb. 1960); m. 2d, Thornton W. Mitchell, Sept. 7, 1963; children—James Thornton and David Wingate (twins). Tchr., Meredith Coll., 1949-50; adminstrv. asst. N.C. Bd. Pub. Welfare, 1950-54; judge Cabarrus County (N.C.) Domestic Relations Ct., 1954-55; supr. N.C. div. Archives and History, 1956-61, chief hist. publs., 1961—, editor N.C. Hist. Rev., 1962—. Trustee Olivia Raney Library, 1961-69. Named Woman of Yr., Raleigh, 1961. Mem. N.C. Bar, Orgn. Am. Historians, Hist. Soc. N.C., So., Wake County hist. socs., Am. Assn. U. Women (pres. Raleigh 1961-63), N.C. Lit. and Hist. Assn. Democrat. Baptist. Author: Legal Aspects of Conscription and Exemption in North Carolina, 1861-1865, 1965. Editor: Messages, Addresses and Public Papers of Terry Sanford, Governor of North Carolina, 1961-65, 1966; Messages, Addresses and Public Papers of Daniel Killian Moore, Governor of North Carolina, 1965-69, 1971. Chmn. editorial bd. American Archivist, 1972—. Contbr. articles to various publs. Home: 2431 Medway Dr Raleigh NC 27608 Office: 109 E Jones St Raleigh NC 27611

MITCHELL, R(ICHARD) GLEN(WOOD), urban designer; b. Oxford, Miss., Oct. 3, 1940; s. Jefferson George and Mary Taylor (Jones) M.; B.S., La. State U., 1966; m. Margaret Gaynell Montagnino, Sept. 1, 1962; children—Glenna, Melissa. Planner, landscape architect Ewald Assos., land planners and landscape architects, Memphis, 1966-67; project planner Ellers & Reaves, Inc., engrs. and planners, Memphis, 1967-68; project planner Reynolds, Smith & Hills, Architects-Engrs.-Planners, Inc., Jacksonville, Fla., 1968-70, head dept. urban and devel. design, 1970-73, asso. v.p.

planning, dir. design, 1973—. Land planning instr. landscape design Nat. Council State Garden Clubs, 1973. Served with USNR, 1962-63. Recipient award of excellence in land planning for maj. center Fla. chpt. Am. Soc. Landscape Architects, 1969, merit award in community planning for maj. center, nat. soc., 1970, award of excellence for Crystal lake, Fla. chpt., 1973. Mem. Am. Soc. Landscape Architects (asso.), Am. Inst. Planners, Delta Sigma Phi. Home: 5830 Michigan Av Jacksonville FL 32211 Office: 4019 Boulevard Center Dr Jacksonville FL 32207

MITCHELL, RICHARD SCOTT, educator; b. Longmont, Colo., Jan. 28, 1929; s. Clarence Floyd and Margaret May (Hartman) M.; student Scottsbluff Jr. Coll., 1946-47, U. Neb., 1947-48; B.S., U. Mich., 1950, M.S., 1951, Ph.D., 1956. Mem. faculty U. Va., Charlottesville, 1953—, acting chmn. dept. geology, 1964-69, prof. environmental scis., 1969—. Sesquicentennial asso. U. Ill., 1973. Fellow Geol. Soc. Am., Mineral. Soc. Am.; mem. Am. Cyrstallographic Assn., Geochemical Soc., A.A.A.S., Clay Minerals Soc., Mineral. Assn. Canada, Sigma Xi, Sigma Gamma Epsilon. Contbr. articles to profl. jours. Home: 1500 Grady Av #8 Charlottesville VA 22903 Office: Lewis Brooks Museum Univ Virginia Charlottesville VA 22903

MITCHELL, ROBERT HARTWELL, physician; b. Plainview, Tex., Dec. 6, 1911; s. Robert Hartwell and Eudora (Alexander) M.; M.D., U. Tex., 1935; m. Vernon Richardson Mitchell, June 1, 1935; children—Martha Elizabeth, Leah Jane. Intern, U. Ia. hosps., 1935-36; individual practice, Fort Worth, 1946-55, Plainview Tex., 1955—; dir. diagnostic div. Terrell's Labs., Fort Worth, 1946-55, chmn. dept. medicine John Peter Smith Hosp., All Saints Hosp., Cook Meml. Hosp. Center for Children, 1946-55; med. dir. Fort Worth Heart Assn. and Heart Lab., 1953-55; chmn. dept. medicine, dir. coronary unit, chief of medicine Central Plains Gen. Hosp., Plainview, 1955—; clin. prof. medicine Tex. Tech. U. Med. Sch., 1973—. Fort Worth Lab. for Surg. Research, Southwestern Med. Sch., 1953-55. Served from 1st lt. to col. M.C., AUS, 1941-46. Diplomate Am. Bd. Internal Medicine. Fellow A.C.P., Am. Coll. Cardiology; mem. Am. Heart Assn. (fellow council clin. cardiology; dir., mem. exec. com., central com., past v.p.), Tex. Heart Assn. (dir. and mem. exec. com. 1961—, pres. 1964), A.M.A., Tex. Med. Assn., Tex. Rheumatism Assn. (past pres. and dir.), Tex. Acad. Internal Med. (pres. 1960), Inter-Am. Congress Cardiology (dir. 1968-72). Episcopalian. Clubs: Fort Worth, Ridglea Country (Ft. Worth); Plainview (Tex.) Country; Lancers (Dallas); 40 Acres (Austin). Contbr. articles to med. jours. Office: Skaggs Bldg Plainview TX 79072

MITCHELL, ROY DEVOY, mgmt. engr., govt. ofcl.; b. Hot Springs, Ark., Sept. 11, 1922; s. Watson W. and Marie (Stewart) M.; B.S., Okla. State U., 1948, M.S., 1950; B.Indsl. Mgmt., Auburn U., 1960; m. Jane Caroline Gibson, Feb. 14, 1958; children—Michael, Marilyn, Martha, Stewart, Nancy. Instr., Odessa (Tex.) Coll., 1953-56; prof. engring. graphics Auburn (Ala.) U., 1956-63; field engr. HHFA, Community Facilities Adminstrn., Atlanta, Jackson, Miss., 1963-71; area engr. Met. Devel. Office, Dept. Housing and Urban Devel., 1971-72, chief architecture and engring., 1972—. Cons., Army Balistic Missile Agy., Huntsville, Ala., 1957-58, Auburn Research Found., NASA, 1963; mem. state tech. action panel Coop. Area Manpower Planning System. Mem. Central Miss. Fed. Personnel Adv. Council. Served USNR, 1943-46. Commended by Sec. of Dept. Housing and Urban Devel., Outstanding Achievement award Dept. Housing and Urban Devel. Registered profl. engr., Ala., Miss. Mem. Nat. Soc. Profl. Engrs., Am. Soc. for Engring. Edn., Miss. Soc. Profl. Engrs., Nat. Assn. Govt. Engrs. (charter mem.), Jackson Fed. Execs. Assn., Central Miss. Safety Council, Am. Water Works Assn., Iota Lambda Sigma. Methodist (trustee, mem. bd. 1959-60). Home: 324 Valley Vista Dr Jackson MS 39211 Office: Dept Housing and Urban Development 300 Woodrow Wilson W Jackson MS 39213

MITCHELL, ROY SHAW, lawyer; b. Sherwood, N.Y., Jan. 16, 1934; s. Malcolm Douglas and Ruth (Holland) M.; B.S. in Indsl., Labor Relations, Cornell U., 1957; J.D. with honors, George Washington U., 1959; m. Nancy Elizabeth Bishop, Aug. 27, 1955; children—Mark, Jeffrey, Jennifer. Admitted to Va. bar, 1967, Ohio bar, 1960, D.C. bar, 1959, U.S. Ct. Mil. Appeals, 1959, U.S. Circuit Ct., 1959, U.S. Supreme Ct., 1965; atty. firm Squire, Sanders & Dempsey, Cleve., 1960-61; partner firm Hudson & Creyke, Washington, 1961-67; founding partner firm Lewis, Mitchell & Moore, Vienna, Va., and Washington, 1967—. Dir. several corps., including McLean Bus. & Profl. Assos., McLean, Va. Mem. Safety Com. No. Va. Builders Assn., 1973—, Dranesville Dist. Council, 1973—, Pine Hill Citizens Assn., 1973—. Mem. Dranesville Dist. Democratic Com., 1973—. Fairfax County Dem. Com., 1973—. Mem. Am. (chmn. current fed. procurement com.), Fed., D.C., Va. bar assns., Am. Arbitration Assn. (mem. nat. panel arbitrators), Nat. Contract Mgmt. Assn. Presbyn. (ruling elder). Contbr. profl. jours. Home: 1014 Shipman Lane McLean VA 22101 Office: 8224 Old Courthouse Rd Vienna VA 22180

MITCHELL, WALTER M., county ofcl., textile industry exec.; b. Cordele, Ga., Aug. 22, 1901; s. James Northern and Rosalie Wade (Marshall) M.; A.B., Ga. Mil. Coll., 1919; B.S., Ga. Inst. Tech., 1923; m. Ethel Niall, Oct. 16, 1926; children—Walter M., William N., Wade T. Dir., v.p., Draper Corp., Atlanta; dir., chmn. Pan Am. Investment Co., Fed. Res. Bank of Atlanta; dir. Alpha Mut. Fund, Alpha Investors Fund, Am. Resorts, Inc. Rich's Inc., Bank of Ga. Commr. roads and revenue Fulton County (Ga.), now chmn. commrs. Trustee, pres. Ga. Tech. Found; trustee Atlanta Childs Home, Lewis H. Beck-Ga. Tech. Scolarship Fund; chmn. Ga. Conservancy. Mem. Am. Cotton Mfrs. Assn., Cotton Mfrs. Assn. Ga., Phi Delta Theta. Rotarian (past pres.). Clubs: Capital City, Piedmont Driving, North Fulton Dads' (past pres.), Peachtree Racket (Atlanta); Piedmont (Spartanburg, S.C.). Home: 45 Montclair Dr NE Atlanta GA 30309

MITCHELL, WILLIAM ALEXANDER, govt. ofcl.; b. Clemson, S.C., May 29, 1917; s. Jack Harris and Ethel (Blasingame) M.; B.S., Clemson U., 1938; M.A., U. N.C., 1939; fellow Duke, 1939-41; M.A., Princeton, 1942, Ph.D., 1948; m. Helen Warner Dart, June 5, 1950. Instr., Princeton U., 1941-42, 46-47; asst. prof. U. Va., 1947-49; asso. prof. U. Mass., 1949-52; mem. staff CIA, Washington, 1952-63; mem. staff Office Mgmt. and Budget, Exec. Office of Pres., Washington, 1963—. Served from 2d lt. to maj. AUS, 1942-46. Home: 6202 Winston Dr Bethesda MD 20034 Office: Exec Office Bldg Washington DC 20503

MITCHINER, J(OSEPH) ELTON, lawyer; b. Smithfield, N.C., Apr. 29, 1919; s. Edwin Joseph and Lola (Talton) M.; A.B., Wake Forest Coll., 1940; postgrad. U. N.C. Law Sch., 1940-42; m. Gretchen Parrish, July 18, 1942; children—Carol Leigh, Judy, Joe. Admitted to N.C. bar, 1943, Fla. bar, 1956; asst. clk. Superior Ct. Johnston County (N.C.), 1943-44; pvt. law practice, specializing in taxation and estates, Smithfield, 1944-54; spl. trial atty. regional counsel Internal Revenue Service, 1954-56; pvt. practice law, specializing in taxation, estates, corporate law, Raleigh, N.C., Ft. Lauderdale, Fla., 1956—; dir., gen. counsel Cook & Pruitt Masonry Contractors, Inc., Miami, Fla., MA-Leek Woodcrafts, Inc. and affiliates, Wingate, N.C., Charles McArthur Dairies and affiliated corps., Okeechobee, Fla. Republican. Baptist. Mason (Shriner). Home: 1200 Kimberley Dr Raleigh NC 27609 Office: Branch Bank and Trust Bldg Raleigh NC 27601 also Bayview Bldg Ft Lauderdale FL 33304

MITLIN, NORMAN, educator, entomologist; b. Bklyn., Feb. 13, 1918; s. Joseph and Fannie Rachel (Goldfein) M.; B.S., N.Y. U., 1945; postgrad. U. Md., 1957-60; m. Luceille Liston, Mar. 14, 1942; 1 son, Laurance R. Research entomologist, U.S. Dept. Agr., State Coll., 1949—; asso. prof. entomology, Miss. State U., State College, 1969—. Trustee Starkville Pub. Library, chmn. bd., 1968—. Served with USAAF, 1942-43. Mem. A.A.A.S., Entomological Soc. Am., Am. Chem. Soc., Miss. Acad. Scis., Miss. Entomological Assn., Miss. Library Assn. (chmn. trustees section 1970-71). Home: 513 Poplar Rd Starkville MS 39759 Office: Box 5367 State College MS 39762

MITTENDORF, THEODOR HENRY, paper mfg. cons.; b. Clay Center, Kan., Jan. 14, 1895; s. Theodor Henry and Antonie (Carls) M.; B.S., Okla. State U., 1917; m. Dorothy E. Solger, May 18, 1919; 1 dau., Laone M. (Mrs. D. R. Hoerl) Lectr. extension div. Okla. State U., 1917; lectr., free-lance writer, 1919-20; dept. supt. Armour & Co., Chgo., 1920-22; sec., dir. sales and advt. Mid-States Gummed Paper Co., Chgo., 1922-38; v.p. charge sales Indsl. Tng. Inst., 1938-39, v.p., gen. mgr. Gummed Products Co., Troy, O., 1940-48; v.p. charge sales Hudson Pulp and Paper Corp., N.Y.C., 1948-56, exec. v.p., 1956-58, cons., 1958—; dir. 5 East 71st St. Corp. Bd. dirs. Muscular Dystrophy Assn. Served from 2d lt. F.A. to 1st lt. AS, U.S. Army, World War I, AEF. Named to Okla. State U. Alumni Hall of Fame, 1961. Mem. Kraft Paper Assn. (dir., mem. exec. com. 1951-58), Gummed Industries Assn. (pres. 1955-56). Paper Bag Inst. (pres. 1955-56). Paper Club N.Y., Am. Legion, Symposiarchs, Kappa Sigma, Alpha Zeta, Pi Kappa Delta. Republican. Methodist. Mason; mem. Order Eastern Star. Clubs: Mt. Dora (Fla.) Golf, Mt. Dora Yacht; Ponte Vedra (Fla.); African Safari of Fla. Home: PO Box 1138 Mount Dora FL 32757 Office: 477 Madison Av New York City NY 10022

MITTENTHAL, FREEMAN LEE, lawyer; b. Dallas, Dec. 29, 1917; s. Albert Harry and Rae (Goldstein) M.; student U. Tex., 1934-36; LL.B., So. Methodist. U., 1940; m. Evelyn Naomi Gates, May 3, 1947; children—Richard Charles, Brian Lee. Admitted to Tex. bar, 1940, U.S. Supreme Ct., U.S. Ct. Mil. Appeals, 1954; pvt. practice law, Dallas, Tex., 1940-42; enforcement atty. Office of Price Adminstrn., Dallas, 1946-47; lawyer U.S. VA, Dallas, 1947-49; pvt. practice law, Dallas, 1949—. Mem. Young Democrats State Exec. Com., 1940; mem. Tex. Economy Commn., 1950. Served to maj. USAAF, 1942-46. Mem. Dallas Bar Assn. (mem. publs. com. 1965—), State Bar of Tex., Am., Fed. bar assns. Mason (32 deg.). Clubs: Dallas Athletic, Metropolitan, Elks. Home: 820 Overglen Dr Dallas TX 75218 Office: 1403 Dallas Fed Savs Bldg Dallas TX 75201

MITTON, JOHN HERBERT, civil engr.; b. Washington, July 28, 1911; s. Philip Francis and Mary Lillian (Gibbons) M.; B.S. cum laude, U. Md., 1931, C.E., 1935; LL.B., Catholic U. Am., 1934; m. Josephine Elizabeth Locraft, Nov. 24, 1938; children—John Herbert, Josephine M. (Mrs. Thaddeus E. Kowynia), Joanne E., Jeanne B. (Mrs. John Van der Vossen), Judith E. (Mrs. John Martucci). Traffic engr. D.C. Govt., 1931-69, asst. dir. Dept. Vehicles and Traffic, 1953-59, chief traffic planning and design Dept. Hwys. and Traffic, 1959-69; cons. traffic engr., Washington, 1969—. Lectr., Cath. U.Am., 1961-70; admitted to D.C. bar, 1934; U.S. Ct. Appeals for D.C., U.S. Supreme Ct.; expert witness before Fed. and State Cts., ICC, Pub. Service Commns., County Councils. Mem. Nat. Com. on Uniform Traffic Laws and Ordinances, Hwy. Research Bd.; tech. cons. to Pres.'s Com. for Traffic Safety, 1955-58; mem. St. Vincent de Paul Soc., 1951—, past pres. St. Martins Conf.; mem. Presdl. Inaugural Coms., 1949, 53, 57, 61, 65. Recipient award of merit D.C. Govt., 1969. Mem. Washington Soc. Engrs. (past pres.), Inst. Traffic Engrs. (trustee Pension Plan, past sect. pres., com. chmn.), Road Gang and Lamplighters, Tau Beta Pi, Phi Kappa Phi. Club: Cosmos (Washington). Contbr. articles to profl. jours. Address: 1736 Holly St NW Washington DC 20012

MITZ, M. A., chemist, govt. ofcl.; b. Milw., May 24, 1921; s. Joe and Sara (Kochman) M.; B.S. in Chemistry, U. Wis., 1940, M.S., 1945; Ph.D. (Ciba fellow), U. Pitts., 1949; m. Virginia Irene Rattin, Apr. 12, 1946; children—Owen David, Andrew Rattin, Jonathan, Daniel. Research chemist Ciba Pharm. Co., Summit, N.J., 1945-46; group leader research div. Armour & Co., Chgo., 1949-59; dir. Melpar, Inc., Falls Church, Va., 1959-67; chief advance sci. planning planetary programs NASA, Washington, 1967—. Cons. NSF, 1972—, Nat. Artificial Heart Program, NIH, 1967-73. Mem. Am. Soc. Biol. Chemists, Am. Chem. Soc., Inst. for Study of Origin of Life, A.A.A.S., Sigma Xi, Phi Lambda Upsilon. Contbr. research articles on organic chemistry, biochemistry to sci. jours. Patentee in field. Home: 5522 Uppingham St Chevy Chase MD 20015 Office: NASA Code SL 400 Maryland Av SW Washington DC 20546

MIXON, ALVIN, farmer, mcht., cattleman; b. Georgiana, Ala., Dec. 19, 1908; s. Samuel Henderson and Lela (Cook) M.; grad. Massey Bus. Sch., Birmingham, Ala., 1930; m. Frances Brassell, May 15, 1936; 1 son, Alvin. Salesman, interior decorator Morgan Bros. Dept. Stores, Birmingham, Georgiana and Evergreen, Ala., 1930; founder, owner S. H. Mixon's Store, Gin & Milling Co., Georgiana, Alvin Mixon Merc., Harper Merc. Co., Belleville; cattleman, Georgiana, 1952—. Organizer So. Pine Electric Co-op, Brewton, Ala., 1938; pres. So. Electric Co-op, Brewton, 1957—; dir. Ala. Electric Power Generation Plants and High Voltage Transmission Lines, Andalusia. Mem. Ala. Energy Adv. Council. Asso. dir. SSS, Conecuh County, 1938-42; organizer Conecuh County United Fund. Organizer Conecuh County Hosp., 1954, bd. dirs., 1954—. Mem. Ala. Forest Products Assn., Am., Ala. Angus assns., Ala., Conecuh County cattlemens assns., Conecuh County Hist. Soc., Conecuh Farm Bur. (dir.), Georgiana, Evergreen chambers commerce, Internat. Platform Assn., Woodmen of World. Methodist (steward, layman). Mason (Shriner), Rotarian, Kiwanian. Club: Quarterback (Georgiana). Address: Route 1 Georgiana AL 36033

MIXSON, THOMAS GOODWIN, banker; b. Levy County, Fla., Oct. 12, 1893; s. Archibald James and Mattie Ella (Mims) M.; grad. Draughon's Bus. Coll., Atlanta, 1910; m. Alma Claire Odell, Aug. 27, 1917; 1 son, James G. With Roess Lumber Co., Ocala, Fla., 1910-12; bookkeeper Ocala Nat. Bank, 1912-15; cashier Greek Am. Bank of Tarpon Springs, Fla., 1915-18; with Exchange Nat. Bank, Tampa, Fla., 1918-45, successively clk., asst. cashier, cashier, v.p., 1940-45, dir., 1935-45; pres., dir. The First Nat. Bank, St. Petersburg, Fla., 1945-56; pres., The Sun Bank and Trust Co. of St. Petersburg, 1959-71, dir., 1959—, chmn. bd., 1971—; chmn. bd., dir., The Sun Coast Bank, 1970—, pres., 1970-73. Chmn. com. Tampa Taxpayers Assn., 1944-45; campaign chmn. Tampa chpt. A.R.C., 1945—. Mem. St. Petersburg (com. of 100), Tampa (pres. 1943-44) chambers commerce. Baptist. (deacon 1962—). Clubs: St. Petersburg Yacht, Lakewood Country (St. Petersburg); Commerce; Tower of Tampa. Home: 501 Bayview Dr NE St Petersburg FL 33704 Office: 301 4th St N St Petersburg FL 33701 also PO Box 13504 St Petersburg FL 33733

MIYAGAWA, ICHIRO, physicist, educator; b. Hiratsuka, Japan, Mar. 5, 1922; s. Shigejiro and Tsuma (Itoh) M.; B.S., Nagoya U., 1945; D.Sc., U. Tokyo (Japan), 1954, postgrad., 1954-56; postgrad. Duke, 1956-59; m. Mitsuko Yamada, Feb. 10, 1950; children—Shigeru, Haruyo, Mari. Came to U.S., 1962. Asst. prof. chem. physics U. Tokyo, 1959-62; vis. asst. prof. Duke, 1963-65; asst. prof. U. Ala., University, 1965-66, asso. prof., 1966-70, prof. physics, 1971—. Cons. to Redstone Arsenal, 1966-72. Chmn. Southeastern Magnetic Resonance conf., 1973. USPHS grantee, 1967. Fellow Am. Phys. Soc.; mem. A.A.A.S., Sigma Xi. Contbr. articles on magnetic resonance to sci. jours. Home: 4905 10th Court E Tuscaloosa AL 35401 Office: Box 1921 University AL 35486

MIZE, GILBERT, supt. schs.; b. Viola, Ark., Nov. 6, 1908; s. William Aaron and Sarah Elizabeth (Johns) M.; B.A., Sul Ross State U., 1932; M.A., Tex. Tech. U., 1939; m. Dannie Brown Stark, May 30, 1936; children—Dennie Jean (Mrs. A. L. Schnell, Jr.), Sara Elizabeth (Mrs. Charles Lovett), Gilbertine. High sch. tchr., athletic coach, Dunn, Tex., 1932-35; high sch. prin., coach, Fluvanna, Tex., 1935-42; jr. high sch. prin., Perryton, Tex., 1942-48, supt. schs., 1948—. Pres. United Fund, 1970. Bd. dirs. YMCA. Served with AUS, 1944-46. Mem. C. of C. (dir. 1967-69). Methodist (chmn. bd. 1964-66). Home: 1705 Drake St Perryton TX 79070 Office: 821 SW 17th St Perryton TX 79070

MIZE, JIMMY ROY, retail exec.; b. Tuscumbia, Ala., Jan. 23, 1937; s. Roy Curtis and Mildred (Davis) M.; student David Lipscomb Coll., 1954-56; B.S., Florence State Coll., 1958; M.S. (research fellow), Auburn U., 1963; m. Ophelia Ann Shook, Aug. 22, 1958; children—Michelle, Matthew, Mark. Tchr., minister Mars Hill Bible Sch., Florence, Ala., 1958-60; audit mgr. Arthur Andersen & Co., Houston, 1963-69; financial v.p. Southwest Growth Mgmt. Co., Houston, 1969-71; stockholder, financial exec. Houston Tube Products, Inc., 1971—, also 3 Honda dealerships. Officer, dir. various corps., Houston, 1969—. Instr. Auburn (Ala.) U., 1962-63. C.P.A., Tex. Mem. Am. Inst. C.P.A.'s, Tex. Soc. C.P.A.'s, Am. Accounting Assn., Phi Kappa Phi. Mem. Ch. of Christ. Home: 930 Circle Bend Missouri City TX 77459 Office: 4822 Ramus St Houston TX 77018

MIZELL, WILMER DAVID, congressman; b. Vinegar Bend, Ala., Aug. 13, 1930; s. Walter David and Addie (Turner) M.; grad. Leaksville (Miss.) High Sch.; m. Nancy Ruth McAlpine, Nov. 16, 1952; children—Wilmer David, James Daniel. Major league baseball pitcher with St. Louis Cardinal orgn., Pitts. Pirates and N.Y. Mets; engaged in sales and pub. relations Winston-Salem Pepsi-Cola Bottling Co. (N.C.); chmn. Davidson County (N.C.) Commnrs.; mem. 91st-93d Congresses, 5th Dist. N.C. Commr. Little League Baseball. Mem. N.C. Republican Exec. Com., Forsyth County Young Reps.; chmn. N.C. Fedn. Teen-age Reps., Nat. Fedn. Teen-age Reps. Served with AUS, 1953-55. Named Distinguished Citizen George Washington U., 1969, Christian Athlete of Year, So. Bapt. Sports Assn., 1951. Mem. U.S. Army Athletic Assn. (hon.), Am. Legion (nat. distinguished guests com.), U.S. Naval Acad. Athletic Assn. (hon.). Home: RDF 5 Winston-Salem NC 27101 Office: 429 Cannon House Office Bldg Washington DC 20515

MMAHAT, JOHN ANTHONY, lawyer; b. New Orleans, Sept. 5, 1931; s. Joseph and Mary (Bertucci) M.; B.A., Tulane U., 1956, J.D., 1958; m. Arlene Cecile Montgomery, Aug. 12, 1967; children—Arlene Cecile, Amy Montgomery, John Anthony. Admitted to La. bar, 1958, since practiced in Metairie; sr. partner Mmahat, Gagliano, Duffy & Giordano, 1958—. Chmn. bd. Medallion Realty, Inc., 33 Flavors of South, Inc.; pres. Gulf Fed. Savs. & Loan Assn., Exec. House Bldg., Inc. Vice chmn. New Orleans Aviation Bd., 1964—; mem. Gov.'s Task Force Com. to Draft Goals for La., 1969. Mem. La. Democratic Central Com., 1960-64; judge ad hoc First Parish Ct., Jefferson Parish, 1965. Bd. dirs. Muscular Dystrophy Assn. Am.; mem. men's adv. com. League Women Voters. Served with USAF, 1951-53. Recipient Glendy Burke medal for oratory Tulane U., 1956; Distinguished Service award as outstanding young man of Greater New Orleans Jr. C. of C., 1965. Mem. Am., La. bar assns., La. Landmarks Soc., Friends of Cabildo, Delgado Art Mus., Metairie Bus. Assn. K.C. Club: New Orleans Athletic. Home: 1239 First St New Orleans LA 70130 Office: 5416 Veterans Meml Blvd Metairie LA 70003

MOBERLY, LUKE EARL, film producer; b. Richmond, Ky., Nov. 1, 1925; s. Harland and Pearlene (Baker) M.; student, U. Cin., 1947-48, U. Miami, 1949-50; m. Mondalee Neihoff, June 5, 1948; children—Paula (Mrs. Dave Salzlien), Pam (Mrs. Kenny Kencheloe), Rick, Penny, Laurie, Belinda. Pres. Luke Moberly Prodns., Inc., Ft. Lauderdale, Fla., 1964—; Clay Teeter, 1974; writer, editor producer, dir. Little Laura and Big John, 1970, Clay Teeter, 1973, The Sweet Talker, 1974; designer film studios, TV studio. Served with USMCR, 1944-47. Home: 4800 SW 54th Terrace Fort Lauderdale FL 33314 Office: 4810 SW 54th Terrace Fort Lauderdale FL 33314

MOBLEY, CARROLL WADE, supt. schs.; b. Williamston, N.C., Jan. 1, 1927; s. William Leonard and Fonnie (Harrison) M.; B.A., Atlantic Christian Coll., 1950; M.Ed., U. N.C., 1954, advanced adminstrn. certificate, 1964; m. Jean Ewing Bellingrath, Mar. 12, 1949; children—Larry Wade, Julia Elizabeth. Athletic dir., coach, Bolivia (N.C.) High Sch., 1950-52; prin. Long Creek Grady Sch., Rocky Point, N.C., 1953-54; prin. Red Springs (N.C.) Schs., 1954-59; prin. Aberdeen Dist. Schs. (N.C.), 1959-63; supt. Montgomery County (N.C.) schs., 1963-71, Rowan County (N.C.) schs., 1971—. Served as sgt. AUS, 1945-46; ETO. Mem. Nat., N.C. (exec. com., past pres. div. prins.) edn. assns., Nat. Assn. Secondary Sch. Prins. Democrat. Presbyn. (elder). Mason, Lion, Rotarian. Address: 227 Camelot Dr Salisbury NC 28144

MOBLEY, ELGIE RONALD, JR., banker; b. Red Rock, Tex., July 8, 1930; s. Elgie R. and Mary (Wright) M.; B.B.A., U. Tex., 1951; m. Billie Marie Conrad, Nov. 23, 1950; children—Elgie Ronald, Melanie Marie, Kevin Reid, Darren Fendall. Asst. cashier Jefferson State Bank, San Antonio, 1952; asst. examiner Tex. State Banking Dept., Austin, 1952-54; office mgr. South Tex. White Truck Service, Corpus Christi, 1954-56; with Victoria Bank & Trust Co. (Tex.), 1956—, v.p., cashier, 1969-72, sr. v.p., cashier, 1972—. Bd. dirs. Tex. Gulf Coast chpt. The Arthritis Found., Houston. Lutheran. Home: 404 Cannon Rd Victoria TX 77901 Office: PO Box 1698 Victoria TX 77901

MOBLEY, FREEMAN FRANCIS, banker; b. New Haven, Ill., Aug. 9, 1901; s. Solan Henry and Clara (Henson) M.; student pub. schs. Mo. and Ark.; m. Wilma C. Moseley, May 21, 1923; 1 son, Freeman Keith. Owner, operator F.F. Mobley Lumber Mill, Williford, Redfield and Batesville, Ark., 1923-45; co-owner, mgr. F.F. Mobley & Son Lumber Mfg. Co., Batesville, Ark., 1945-60; dr. v.p., dir. 1st Nat. Bank, Batesville, Ark., 1944—. Pres., dir. Bank Evening Shade (Ark.), 1964—, Evening Shade Devel. Corp., 1964—. Chmn. financial drive and exec. dir. White River Med. Center, 1969—. Chmn. Batesville Sewer Commn., 1957-71. Bd. dirs. Alcoholic Anonymous, 1968—; exec. bd. Quapaw Area council Boy Scouts Am., 1967—, 1st Ark. Devel. Finance Corp., Little Rock, 1959. Mem. C. of C. (past dir.). Presbyn. Mason (32 deg., past master). Clubs: Batesville Country; Capital (Little Rock). Home: PO Box 112 Batesville AR 72501 Office: 250 S Broad St Batesville AR 72501

MOBLEY, JOHN HOMER, II, lawyer; b. Shreveport, La., Apr. 28, 1930; s. John H. and Beulah (Wilson) M.; A.B., U. Ga., 1951, J.D., 1953; m. Sue Lawton, Aug. 9, 1958; children—John Lawton, Anne Davant. Admitted to Ga. bar, 1952; practiced in Atlanta, 1955; mem. firm Kelley & Mobley, 1956-63, Gambrell & Mobley, 1963—. Served as 1st lt. Judge Adv. Gen. Corps, USAF, 1953-55. Mem. Am., Atlanta bar assns., State Bar Ga., Am. Judicature Soc., Phi Delta Phi, Kappa Alpha Order. Episcopalian. Clubs: Lawyers, Atlanta Athletic, Piedmont Driving, Atlanta Country, Commerce. Home: 4348 Sentinel Post Rd NW Atlanta GA 30327 Office: 1st Nat Bank Bldg Atlanta GA 30303

MOBLEY, JOSEPH CLINTON, obstetrician and gynecologist; b. Memphis, Apr. 22, 1911; s. John Clinton and Julia Catherine (Foppiano) M.; B.S., Southwestern at Memphis, 1932; M.D., U. Tenn., 1935; m. Thirza Lurline Smith, June 12, 1936; children—Thirza L. (Mrs. Theodor B. Sloan), Martha A. (Mrs. Ronald S. Baumann), Mary J. (Mrs. Anthony Viscovich). Intern Memphis Gen. Hosp., 1935-37; preceptorship John Gorton Hosp., 1937-42; pvt. practice obstetrics and gynecology, Memphis, 1937—; mem. staff Meth., St. Joseph, Baptist Meml., City of Memphis hosps., asst. prof. U. Tenn. Med. Sch. 1970—. Served to lt. comdr. M.C., USNR, World War II. Diplomate Am. Bd. Obstetrics and Gynecology. Fellow A.C.S., Am. Coll. Obstetricians and Gynecologists. Mason (33 deg.; past grand master grand lodge Tenn.). Home: 2240 N Parkway Memphis TN 38112 Office: 1196 Peabody Av Memphis TN 38104

MOCHRIE, RICHARD DOUGLAS, educator; b. Lowell, Mass., Feb. 17, 1928; s. William Blair and Helen (Stephens) M.; B.S., U. Conn., 1950, M.S., 1953; Ph.D., N.C. State U., 1958; m. Helene Mary Buchanan, Aug. 19, 1950; children—Barbara Jean, Steven Howard, Lois Ann. Research technician U. Conn., 1950-53; grad. asst. N.C. State U., 1953-54, instr., 1954-58, asst. prof., 1958-61, asso. prof., 1961-72, prof. lactational physiology and nutrition, 1972—. Precinct committeeman, County conv. del. Cary and Wake County Democratic Party, 1972—. Bd. dirs. Raleigh YMCA. Served with AUS, 1946-47. Mem. Nat. Mastitis Council (dir. 1973—), Am. Dairy Sci. Assn., Internat. State Milk Shippers, Sigma Chi, Pi Alpha Sigma, Sigma Xi. Democrat. Presbyn. (deacon 1959-61). Clubs: Cary Exchange (pres. 1963-64), Dairy Shrine. Author: Lactation Laboratory Outline, 1971. Contbr. numerous articles to sci. jours.; contbr. Ruminant Nutrition and Metabolism to Ency. Biochemistry, 1967. Home: 505 S Dixon Av Cary NC 27511 Office: NC State U Raleigh NC 27607

MOCK, PRESLEY JOE, physician; b. Hillsboro, Tex., May 17, 1910; s. Presley Miller and Ina May (Coleman) M.; A.A., Hillsboro Jr. Coll., 1928; B.A., U. Tex., 1931, M.D., 1935; m. Hazel Estell Barger, June 20, 1937; children—Presley Joe, Sue Gale (Mrs. Wesley Wayne Kooken). Rotating intern Jefferson Davis Hosp., Houston, 1935-37; gen. practice medicine and surgery, LaPorte, Tex., 1937—; mem. staffs Pasadena-Bayshore, Southmore hosps., Pasadena, Tex., Baptist Meml. Hosp., Houston. Dir. Medico Investment, Ltd., Pasadena, Medico Investment Co., Inc., Pasadena. Trustee LaPorte Ind. Sch. Dist., 1953-57. Bd. dirs. Pasadena Civic Music Assn. Recipient Meritorious medal N.G., 1947. Fellow Am. Acad. Family Physicians; mem. A.M.A., Tex Med. Assn., Harris County Med. Soc., Houston Acad. Medicine, Harris County, Tex. acads. family physicians, LaPorte Bayshore C. of C. (dir. 1945-64, v.p. 1956). Mason (32 deg., Shriner), Rotarian (pres. 1942-43). Home: 410 S 1st St LaPorte TX 77571 Office: 815 S Broadway La Porte TX 77571

MODENBACH, DONALD JOSEPH, banker; b. New Orleans, Oct. 17, 1931; s. Joseph Carl and Yvonne (Decker) M.; B.S., La. State U., 1958, postgrad., 1958-60; grad. Northwestern U. Sch. Banking and Mktg., 1970; m. Peggy Ann Graefenstein, Apr. 25, 1953; children—Donald Joseph, Leslea Ann, John Carl, Lee Robert. Account analyst Esso Standard Oil Co., Baton Rouge, La., 1958-60; mgmt. analyst Smith Kline & French Labs., Phila., 1960-62; planning adminstr., asst. to v.p. Celanese Fibers Co., Charlotte, N.C., also N.Y.C., 1962-65; mgr. adminstrv. services Arthur Andersen & Co., Atlanta, 1965-67; v.p. N.C. Nat. Bank, Charlotte, N.C., 1967—. Football coach Clairmont-Atlanta and Park Sharon-Charlotte, 1965-70, baseball coach, 1962-73. Served with USN, 1951-54. Club: Charlotte Athletic. Home: 3332 Cotillion Av Charlotte NC 28210 Office: Box 120 Charlotte NC 28201

MODISETTE, JERRY LEE, educator; b. Minden, La., July 28, 1934; s. Purnell James and Velma (Baker) M.; B.S., La. Inst. Tech., 1956; M.S., Va. Poly. Inst., 1960; Ph.D., Rice U., 1967; m. Anne Mary Damerel, June 20, 1959; 1 son, Jason Perry. Aerospace engr. Langley Research Center NASA, 1956-61, chief Space Physics div. Manned Spacecraft Center, 1962-64; prof. physics, dir. research, asso. dean Coll. Sci. and Health Professions Houston Baptist Coll., 1969—; pres. Kemah Marina, Inc.; cons. energy conversion; pollution control; drilling tech. Recipient NASA Apollo Achievement award, 1969. Asso. fellow Am. Inst. Aeros. and Astronautics; mem. Am. Geophys. Union, A.A.A.S., Am. Assn. Physics Teachers, Am. Astron. Soc. Baptist. Contbr. numerous articles to sci. jours. Patents in field pending. Home: 18323 Hereford Lane Nassau Bay TX 77058 Office: 7502 Fondren Rd Houston TX 77036

MODRALL, AUGUSTUS WILLIAM, JR., architect; b. Dallas, Dec. 24, 1930; s. Augustus William and Corinne (Sowell) M.; B.Arch., U. Tex., 1953; m. Janis Marie Dechman, Dec. 4, 1954; children—Gayle Lynn, Gretchen Ellen. Draftsman, architect, Golemon & Rolfe, Houston, 1953-59; architect Cowell & Neuhaus, Houston, 1959-63; with Koetter, Tharp & Cowell, Houston, 1964—, architect, 1964-65, asso. partner, 1965-70, v.p., 1970-72, sr. v.p., 1972—. Mem. A.I.A. (sec. Houston), Tex. Soc. Architects. Presbyn. (elder, deacon). Home: 6126 Reamer St Houston TX 77036 Office: 1535 W Loop South Houston TX 77027

MOE, JOHN LOCKWOOD, electronics engr.; b. Flushing, N.Y., Feb. 29, 1928; s. Franklin Lockwood and Helen Langdon (Bates) M.; B.Indsl. Elec. Engring., Pratt Inst., 1948; m. Julia Dabelstein, Oct. 26, 1953. Mgr. Midwestern div. Filtron Co., Inc., Dayton, O., 1953-63; engring. supr. Gen. Dynamics, Ft. Worth, 1963—. Served with AUS, 1951-53. Recipient certificate of appreciation Soc. Automotive Engrs., 1973. Mem. Soc. Automotive Engrs. (nat. vice chmn. electromagnetic compatibility com. 1965—), S.A.R. Mason (Shriner), Elk. Home: PO Box 12494 Fort Worth TX 76116 Office: Gen Dynamics PO Box 748 Fort Worth TX 76101

MOEHLMAN, WILLIAM FREDERICK, metals co. exec.; b. Madison, Wis., Aug. 7, 1897; s. William Frederick and Dorothea (Niederer) M.; B.S., U. Wis., 1922; m. Constance Kennedy, Sept. 3, 1969. Dist. engr. Armco Drainage & Metal Products, Middletown, O., 1927-30, municipal and airport engr., 1930-33; sales mgr. Tenn. Metal Culvert Co., Nashville, 1934-45, v.p., mgr., dir., 1945-62, chmn., sec., 1962—; dir. Home Fed. Savs. & Loan Assn., Knoxville, Tenn., 1950—; chmn., sec. Knox Concrete Products Inc., Knoxville, 1962—, Southeastern Inc., Knoxville, 1962—. Served with AUS, 1918-19. Mem. Gt. Smoky Mountain Conservation Assn. (pres.), Nat. Soc. Profl. Engrs., Am. Soc. C.E., Knoxville C. of C. (pres. 1947-50), Am. Heart Assn. (dir. 1959-62), Tau Beta Pi. Mason. Home: Route 5 Sevierville TN 37862 Office: Box 1030 Knoxville TN 37901

MOELTER, GREGORY MARTIN, mfg. co. exec.; b. Dover, N.J., Aug. 14, 1919; s. George Bernard and Edna (Schlig) M.; B.S. cum laude, Newark Coll. Engring., 1941; M.S., N.Y. U., 1944; m. Aneta L. Feuerbach, June 20, 1942; children—Christopher Forbes, Jacqueline (Mrs. Otto Brown). Chemist, Barrett Chem. Co., Phila., 1940; with Celanese Corp., Summit, N.J., 1941-63, research engr., 1941-59, sect. head, 1959-63; tech. mgr. Celanese Fibers Co., Charlotte, N.C., 1963-72, tech. adminstr., 1972—. Treas., Mint Museum Drama Guild, 1972-73. Mem. Am. Chem. Soc., Am. Inst. Chem. Engrs., Am. Soc. Engring. Edn. (sect. chmn. 1971), Tau Beta Pi, Alpha Sigma Phi. Presbyn. Patentee in synthetic fibers and plastics. Home: 3637 Henshaw Rd Charlotte NC 28209 Office: Box 1414 Charlotte NC 28209

MOFFAT, DAVID CARL, retail sewing center exec.; b. Chatham, Ont., Can., June 1, 1943; s. Carl Emerson and Velma (Armentrout) M.; A.B., So. Methodist U., 1964, B.B.A., 1965; M.A., Northwestern U., 1969. Vice-pres. Carl's Sewing Center, Inc., Dallas, 1964—; dir. forensics Sunset High Sch., Dallas, 1966-69; dir. drama Richmond (Cal.) High Sch., 1970-71; asst. prof. speech and drama Sauk Valley Coll., Dixon, Ill., 1971-72; prodn. mgr. Orpheum Theater, San Francisco, 1972-73; numerous roles in plays, motion pictures, commercials; founding mem. Dallas Repertory Theatre. Mem. Actors Equity Assn., Screen Actors Guild, Am. Fedn. Radio & TV Artists, Speech Communication Assn., Am. Theatre Assn., Nat. Thespians, Am. Forensic Assn., Nat. Forensic League, Delta Sigma Phi, Blue Key, Delta Psi Omega.

MOFFITT, FRANKLYN MONROE, oil co. exec.; b. Lynbrook, N.Y., Aug. 24, 1914; s. John J. and Olive (Brower) M.; B.A., Duke, 1938; m. Nancy Webb, Apr. 21, 1937; children—Earle W., F. Brower. With Ashland Oil, Inc. (Ky.), 1940—, chemist, terminal mgr., Coraopolis, Pa., salesman, div. mgr., Pitts., sr. salesman, mgr. light oil sales, mgr. nat. account sales, 1940-57, v.p., 1957—; pres. Ashland Ltd., Bermuda, 1973—, Ashland Oil Shipping Co., 1973—, Bluegrass Ins. Co., 1973—, Bluegrass Internat. Ins. Co., 1973—. Bd. dirs. Ry. Progress Inst., Adhesive and Sealant Council, Am. Coke and Coal Chems. Inst. Served as lt. USNR, 1943-45. Mem. Nat. Petroleum Refiners Assn. (chmn. petrochem. div.), Q.M.'s Assn. U.S., Engrs. Soc. Western Pa., Ry. Club Pitts., Am. Petroleum Inst., Ky., Huntington chambers commerce, Newcomen Soc., Sigma Phi Epsilon. Episcopalian. Clubs: Dunes Beach and Golf (Myrtle Beach, S.C.); Bellefonte Country (Ashland). Home: Spithead Harbour Rd Warwick 7-26 Bermuda Office: Ashland Ltd Washington Mall Hamilton 5-31 Bermuda

MOFFITT, ROY BRATTON, lawyer, engr.; b. Greensboro, N.C., Sept. 11, 1927; s. Royall Brower and Janet (Bratton) M.; B. Geol. Engring., N.C. State U., 1952, profl. degree in Ceramic Engring., 1957, B.S. in Chem. Engring., 1961; J.D., George Washington U., 1966; m. Hilda Marie Geide, July 8, 1967. With coal mine works U.S. Steel Co., Fairfield, Ala., 1952-54; instr. engring. N.C. State U., Raleigh, 1955-57, asst. prof. research, 1957-63; with Office Legislative Planning, U.S. Dept. Commerce, Patent Office, Washington, 1963-68; coordinator patent activities Superior Continental Corp., 1968-69, patent counsel, 1969-73, sec., legal counsel, 1973—. Admitted to D.C. bar, 1967, N.C. bar, 1968; engring cons., 1957-63. Republican precinct capt., Birmingham, Ala., 1952. Served with USMC, 1946-47. Mem. Profl. Engrs. N.C., D.C., N.C., Catawoa bar assns. Kiwanian. Contbr. articles to profl. jours. Patentee in field. Home: Box 675 Route 10 Hickory NC 28601 Office: Superior Continental Corp PO Box 489 Hickory NC 28601

MOFIELD, WILLIAM RAY, coll. adminstr.; b. Hardin, Ky., July 3, 1921; s. Kelzie E. and Zela (Irvan) M.; A.B., Murray State Coll., 1943; M.A., Columbia, 1958; Ph.D., So. Ill. U., 1964; LL.D., Ida. Christian Coll., 1962; m. Janie Belle Bloomingburg, July 24, 1953; 1 dau., Ruth Ann. Tchr., Vienna (Ill.) High Sch., 1944-45; with WPAD-AM-FM, Paducah, Ky., 1945-59, mgr., 1959; mgr. WCBL-AM-FM, Benton, 1959; dir. acad. affairs radio-tv dept. So. Ill. U., 1959-64; exec. pres. Murray (Ky.) State U., 1964-68, chmn. dept. communications, 1968—. Stringer, CBS News, 1945-64; sportscaster Ashland Oil Network, 1946-59; radio-tv mgmt. cons., 1945—; alternate mem. Ky. Commn. Higher Edn., 1965—. Bd. dirs. to Assn., Paducah, Ky., 1956-59; commr. Boy Scouts Am., 1965, 66—, bd. dirs., 1965—; bd. dirs. Benton (Ky.) Hosp., Ky. State Penitentiary, Eddyville. Served with USNR, 1942-43. Recipient Duke of Paducah Civic award Mayor Paducah, 1956; named Ky. Col. CBS Found. News fellow, 1958. Mem. Nat. Assn. Broadcasters, Am. Soc. Disk Jockey Newscasters, Sportscasters, Ky. Broadcasters Assn., Ky. Edn. Assn., Alpha Phi Omega, Alpha Phi Gamma, Sigma Delta Chi, Tau Kappa Alpha, Sigma Beta Gamma. Democrat. Mem. Ch. of Christ. Rotarian. Home: RFD 1 Hardin KY 42048 Office: Murray State U Murray KY 42071

MOHLHENRICH, JOHN SIDNEY, govt. ofcl.; b. Balt., Oct. 12, 1931; s. Eugene and Marjorie (Moss) M.; A.A., Towson State Coll., 1950; B.S., U. N.M., 1957, M.S., 1959; postgrad. George Washington U., 1966-67; m. Sherry Livermore, Nov. 24, 1955; children—David John, Eugenia, Mark Moss. With Nat. Park Service, U.S. Dept. Interior, 1959—, chief naturalist Lassen Volcanic Nat. Park, Mineral, Cal., 1968-72, chief park interpreter Natchez Trace Pkwy., Tulepo, Miss., 1972—. Exec. sec. Loomis Mus. Assn., Lassen Volcanic Nat. Park, Mineral, 1968-72; scoutmaster Boy Scouts Am., Mineral, 1967-68. Served with USAF, 1940-54. Mem. Assn. Interpretive Naturalists, Phi Sigma. Club: Toastmasters (Hungry Horse, Mont.). Home: Rural Route 1 NT-34 Tupelo MS 38801 Office: Rural Route 1 NT-143 Tupelo MS 38801

MOHR, JULIAN BOEHM, chem. mfg. co. exec.; b. Atlanta, Apr. 29, 1930; s. Samuel and Marian (Boehm) M.; B.A., Washington and Lee U., 1952; m. Teena Stern, June 24, 1956 (div. Aug. 1970); children—Julie Lin, Greg Eugene; m. 2d, Sandra Simmons, Jan. 31, 1973; children—Leslie, Julian. With Momar, Inc., Atlanta, 1952—, treas., 1956—, pres., 1965—; v.p. Momar (Can.) Ltd., Toronto, 1961—, treas. Momar Export, Inc., Atlanta, 1960, pres. 1965—; v.p. J. & B. Enterprises, real estate devel. and apt. mgmt. co.; dir. Cansa div. Momar South Africa, Capetown, Monar Indsl. Services Ltd., Manchester, Eng., Monar (London) Ltd., Monar div. Caral, Paris, France. Pres. exec. bd. Atlanta Civic Ballet, Inc., 1964-69. Jewish religion (trustee temple Sinai 1968-73). Mem. B'nai B'rith. Clubs: Civitan of Atlanta, Toastmasters (pres. 1959). Home: Box 20224 Station N Atlanta GA 30325 Office: 1830 Ellsworth Industrial Dr NW Atlanta GA 30318

MOISE, FRANCIS DAVIS, brokerage co. exec.; b. Sumter, S.C., Dec. 31, 1935; s. Francis Marion and Ella Pauline (Blanding) M.; B.S., U. S.C., 1958; postgrad. Wharton Inst. Finance, 1972-74; m. Helen Frances Fisher, June 30, 1960; children—Helen Penina, Francis Davis. Registered rep. Bache & Co., Inc., Charlotte, N.C., 1959-70, resident mgr., Fort Worth, 1970—. Solicitor United Fund, 1968-72; sect. chmn. United Way, 1973. Bd. dirs. Boystown, Charlotte, 1968—, founder, 1968. Mem. Leadership Ft. Worth, 1972. Served with inf. AUS, 1958. Mem. Nat. Assn. Securities Dealers, Sigma Nu. Presbyn. (deacon 1970—). Clubs; Petroleum Ft. Worth, Charlotte Athletic. Home: 3804 Branch Rd Fort Worth TX 76109 Office: 810 Commerce Bldg Fort Worth TX 76102

MOLAISON, HENRI JEAN, profl. engr.; b. Opelousas, La., Dec. 12, 1911; s. John and Marie (Godefroy) M.; B.E. in Chem. Engring., Tulane U., 1932, postgrad., 1938, 43-44. In charge routine lab. Jefferson Lake Sulphur Co., Lake Peigneur, La., 1932-36; with asphalt lab. Shell Oil Co., Inc., Norco, La., 1937-39; sales and office work Indsl. Chem. & Processing Co., New Orleans, 1939-40; asst. engring. aide U.S. Engrs., War Dept., New Orleans, 1940; chem. engr. with U.S. So. Regional Lab., U.S. Dept. Agr., New Orleans, 1940-57; design engr. in charge elec. dept. Joseph E. Leininger & Assos., New Orleans, 1957-64; design engr. J. Ray McDermott & Co., Inc., New Orleans, 1964—. Instr. elec. engring. lab., Tulane U., part time 1943-46. Registered profl. engr., La., Tex. Mem. Am. Inst. Chem. Engrs. (N.O. sect. chmn. 1953), Am. Soc. M.E., Nat. Soc. Profl. Engrs., L'Athénée Louisianais, Geneal. Research Soc. New Orleans, La. Geneal. and Research Soc., Société Généalogique Canadienne-Francaise, Société Historique Acadienne, Holy Name Soc., West Baton Rouge Hist. Soc., Greater New Orleans Round Dance Teachers Council (pres. 1965, 73), K.C. Clubs: Swiss-American Society, Swing 'N Turn Square Dance (pres. 1952, 69), Dance-A-Round (instr.) (New Orleans). Home: 5531 Marshal Foch St New Orleans LA 70124 Office: 1010 Common St New Orleans LA 70112

MOLANDER, WILLIAM AUSTIN, electronic co. exec.; b. Boston, Mar. 23, 1926; s. William A. and Ellen (Baron) M.; B.S. in Elec. Engring., Tufts U., 1951; M.Elec. Engring., Stevens Inst. Tech., 1956; postgrad. Poly. Inst. Bklyn., 1951-54; m. Sally Ann Stone, Aug. 2, 1969; children—(from previous marriage) William A., Darlene. Engr., Curtiss-Wright Corp., Caldwell, N.J., 1951-54; mgr. computer br. Kearfott div. Gen. Precision, Inc., Clifton, N.J., 1954-62; dir. communication engring. Honeywell, Inc., Tampa, Fla., 1962-67; chmn. bd., pres. Fla. Communications & Electronics, Inc., Clearwater, 1967—. Registered profl. engr., Fla., N.J. Mem. Armed Forces Communications and Electronics Assn., Tau Beta Pi. Patentee hydraulic valve. Home: 1458 S Jefferson Av Clearwater FL 33516 Office: 3120 44th Av N St Petersburg FL 33714

MOLHOLM, ALICE BURNS (MRS. HANS BARSO MOLHOLM), social worker; b. Glasgow, Scotland, Aug. 21, 1911; d. John Thomas and Alice Gallagher (Corcoran) Burns; came to U.S., 1924, naturalized, 1943; B.S., St. Xavier's Coll., 1932; M.A. (Univ. scholar) Loyola U. Sch. Social Work, 1935; m. Hans Barso Molholm, Feb. 6, 1949 (dec. June 1971); stepchildren—John T. Thomas B. With Cook County Bur. Pub. Welfare, 1933-35; supr. field work, instr. advanced casework Loyola U. Sch. Social work, Chgo., 1935-42; dist. supr. home service dept. Chgo. chpt. A.R.C., 1942-44; dir. intramural service Chgo. State Hosp. for Mentally Ill, 1944-45; exec. dir. Forest Park Children's Center, St. Louis, 1945-47; asst. chief social service Inst. Juvenile Research Chgo., 1947-49; with East St. Louis Child Guidance Clinic, 1949; asso. prof. social work Washington U., St. Louis, 1950-54; ednl. dir. Columbus (O.) State Hosp. for Mentally Ill, 1954-57; dir. social services dept. Mental Health Inst., Independence, Ia., 1958; asst. dir. social service dept. U. Ark. Med. Center, Little Rock, 1957-65, 66-67, mem. child protection com., asso. prof. social work, 1966-67; asso. prof. social work U. Ark. Grad. Sch. Social Work, 1970—; dir. casework services Ark. State Hosp., Little Rock, 1967-72, dir. social service dept., 1973—. Cons. social work to various pub. pvt. instns., agys. Fellow Am. Orthopsychiat. Assn.; mem. Acad. Certified Social Workers, Nat. Assn. Social Workers, Ark. Conf. Social Welfare, Council Social Work Edn. Home: 7318 Ouachita Dr Little Rock AR 72205 Office: 4313 W Markham St Little Rock AR 72201

MOLINARY, SAMUEL VICTOR, educator; b. Dante, Va., Jan. 15, 1939; s. Francis Dominick and Pauline Elizabeth (Starnes) M.; B.A., U. Va., 1961; Ph.D. (A. D. Williams fellow 1964-68), Med. Coll. Va., 1968; m. Elizabeth Walker Burruss, July 5, 1959; children—Elizabeth Suzanne, Mary Helen, John Laneve. Research instr. U. Tenn. at Memphis, 1968-69, asst. prof., chief biochemistry Child Devel. Center, 1969-72, asso. prof., chief dept. biochemistry, 1972—. Cons. State Tenn. Dept. Pub. Health, 1972—. Mem. Community Band, Memphis, 1973—. Pres. med. units Faculty Club, Memphis, 1973-75. Mem. Am. Assn. Clin. Chemists, N.Y. Acad. Sci., Am. Soc. Microbiology, Soc. Neurosi., A.A.A.S., Sigma Xi, Kappa Psi, Sigma Phi Epsilon. Home: 2517 Monette Av Memphis TN 38127 Office: 711 Jefferson Av Memphis TN 38105

MOLL, ROBERT HARRY, educator; b. Lackawanna, N.Y., July 17, 1927; s. Harry John and Pearl Katherine (Bixler) M.; B.S., Cornell U., 1951; M.S., U. Ida., 1953; Ph.D., N.C. State U., 1957; m. Alice Irene MacMillan, June 17, 1950; children—John, Gregory, Glenn, Sandra. Mem. faculty N.C. State U., Raleigh, 1957—, asst. prof., 1957-62, asso. prof., 1962-65, prof. genetics, 1965—. Served with AUS, 1945-47. Mem. Am. Soc. Agronomy, Am. Soc. Naturalists, Am. Soc. Genetics, Sigma Xi, Gamma Sigma Delta, Phi Kappa Phi. Home: 5908 Woodcrest Dr Raleigh NC 27603

MOLL, WILHELM, librarian; b. Vienna, Austria, June 2, 1920 (came to U.S., 1939, naturalized, 1945); s. Leopold and Marie (Schlesinger) M.; B.A., Denison U., 1943; J.D., U. Chgo., 1945; M.S. in Library Sci., Catholic U. Am., 1956; m. Margot Weith, Dec. 14, 1951; 1 son, Kenneth Carl. Polit. analyst War Dept., Frankfurt, Germany, 1945-49, fgn. affairs specialist, Bonn, Germany, 1949-51; research asso. war documentation project Columbia U., N.Y.C., 1951-55; asst. documents librarian Ind. U., Bloomington, 1956-60; asst. med. librarian Med. Center, U. Ky., Lexington, 1960-62; dir. med. library U. Va., Charlottesville, 1962—, asso. prof., 1962-70, prof., 1971—. Mem. Phi Beta Kappa. Contbr. articles on med. history and med. library sci. to profl. jours. Home: 2217 Greenbrier Dr Charlottesville VA 22901

MOLLER, PALMI, educator; b. Sandar-Krok, Iceland, Nov. 4, 1922; s. Johann Georg and Thorbjorg (Palmadottiv) M.; D.M.D., Tufts U., 1948; M.S., U. Ala., 1962; Dr. Odontics, U. Iceland, 1971; m. Malfridur Oskarsdottir, June 12, 1945; children—Palmi, Oskar, Johann. Came to U.S., 1958. Gen. practice dentistry, Iceland, 1948-58; instr. U. Ala., Birmingham, 1958-60, asst. prof., 1960-63, asso. prof., 1963-70, prof. dentistry, 1970—, clin. investigator Inst. Dental Research, 1968—. Mem. Icelandic Dental Assn., Internat. Assn. Dental Research, Sigma Xi, Omicron Kappa Upsilon, Delta Sigma Delta. Home: 1548 Panorama St Birmingham AL 35216

MOLONEY, JOHN FREDERICK, trade assn. exec.; b. Huntington, N.Y., Feb. 28, 1909; s. John And Catherine Genevieve (Mackesy) M.; B.A., Columbia, 1931, M.A. in Econs., 1935; m. Margaret Carlene Treadaway, July 30, 1938; children—Richard, Robert, Walter. Statistician Inst. Am. Fats & Oils, Washington, 1936; economist Nat. Assn. Margarine Mfrs., Columbus, O., 1936; economist Nat. Cottonseed Products Assn., Memphis, 1936-55, sec., treas., 1955—. Mem. Memphis Soc. Assn. Execs. (pres. 1959-60), Am. Soc. Assn. Execs. (mem. com. 1957-58), The Egyptians (pres. 1966-67), Phi Kappa Sigma. Contbr. articles to profl. jours. Home: 2538 N Edwin Circle Memphis TN 38104 Office: PO Box 12023 Memphis TN 38104

MOLONY, MICHAEL JANSSENS, JR., lawyer; b. New Orleans, Sept. 2, 1922; s. Michael Janssens and Marie (Perret) M.; J.D., Tulane U., 1950; m. Jane Leslie Waguespack, Oct. 21, 1951; children—Jane Leslie, Michael Janssens III, Megan, Kevin, Sara, Brian, Ian, Duncan. Admitted to La. bar, 1950; partner Molony & Baldwin, attys., 1950; asso. partner Jones, Flanders, Waechter & Walker, 1951-56; partner Jones, Walker, Waechter, Poitevent, Carrere & Denegre, New Orleans, 1956—; instr., lectr. Med. Sch. and Univ. Coll., Tulane U., 1953-59. Asst. sec.-treas. La. Law Inst., 1958-70. Mem. Eisenhower Legal Com., 1952; chmn. Gov.'s Task Force on Space Industry, 1971-72; chmn. Gov.'s Adv. Com. River Area Transp. and Planning Com., 1971-73; mem. Gov.'s Task Force on Natural Gas Requirements, 1971-72; mem. Mayor's Adv. Com. on City Charter; mem. goals found. council, ex-officio mem. goals found. Met. New Orleans Goals Program, 1969-72; vice chmn. ad hoc planning com. Goals for Met. New Orleans, 1969-72; vice chmn. Port of New Orleans Operation La. Impact Com., 1969-70; mem. Met. Area Com., New Orleans, 1970-73. Trustee, Pub. Affairs Research Council La., 1970-73; mem. corporate bd. Boys Clubs Greater New Orleans, 1969-71; bd. dirs., exec. com. New Orleans Tourist and Conv. Com., 1973, chmn. family attraction com. 1973), Served from aviation cadet to staff sgt., AUS, USAAF, 1942-46, PTO. Mem. Am. (mem. anti-trust law com. 1968, mgmt. co-chmn. com. devel. law union adminstrn. and procedures 1969, mem. com. equal employment opportunity practice and procedure labor relations law sect.), La. (sec.-treas. 1957-59, gov. 1957-60, editor 1957-59), New Orleans (dir. legal aid bur. 1954, chmn. com. legislature 1968, vice chmn. standing com. pub. relations 1970-71), Fed. bar assns., Am. Judicature Soc., Internat. House, So. Inst. Mgmt. (a founder), U.S. (labor relations com. 1965, urban and regional affairs com. 1970-72, blue-ribbon com. lawyers for labor law reform), La. (dir. 1963-66), New Orleans Area (chmn. employer-employee relations council 1962-63, dir. 1963, v.p. bus. climate div. 1966-69), v.p. met. devel. and urban affairs 1969, pres.-elect 1970, pres. 1971, exec. com. bd. dirs. 1972, dir. 1973) chambers commerce, Sigma Chi (pres. New Orleans alumni 1956). Roman Catholic. Clubs: Pickwick, Southern Yacht, Serra, Plimsoll, Bienville (New Orleans). Home: 3039 Hudson Pl New Orleans LA 70114 Office: 225 Baronne St New Orleans LA 70112

MONAGHAN, BERNARD ANDREW, business exec.; b. Birmingham, Ala., Jan. 28, 1916; s. Bernard Andrew and Mary Frances (Jackson) M.; B.A., Birmingham-So. Coll., 1934, L.H.D., 1967; LL.B., Harvard, 1937; B.A. (Rhodes scholar), Oxford U., 1939; m. Margaret Miles Rushton, Jan. 29, 1941; 1 dau., Margaret. Admitted to Ala. bar, 1937, U.S. Supreme Ct. bar, 1944; practiced in Birmingham until 1958; mem. firm White, Bradley, Arant, All and Rose, 1939-48, partner, 1948-58; with Vulcan Materials Co., Birmingham, 1958—, pres., chief exec. officer, 1959—, also dir., chmn. exec. com.; dir., mem. exec. com. Protective Life Ins. Co., Birmingham, 1950—. Beatrice Foods Co., Chgo., South Central Bell Telephone Co., Birmingham; dir. Birmingham Trust Nat. Bank. Bd. dirs. Internat. Exec. Service Corps N.Y.C., Baptist Hosp. Found., Birmingham Urban League, Nat. Conf. Christians and Jews; bd. advisers St. Bernard Coll.; bd. govs. Indian Springs Sch.; trustee Birmingham-So. Coll., Ireland Found., Rushton Lectures, So. Research Inst. Served to capt. USMCR, 1942-45; counselor for Dept. Army, 1952-53. Decorated Purple Heart, Bronze Star; recipient Exceptional Civilian Service medal War Dept., 1953. Mem. Newcomen Soc., Relay House, Ala. C. of C. (dir.), Phi Beta Kappa, Alpha Tau Omega. Clubs: Chicago; University (N.Y.C.). Duquesne, Downtown, Mountain Brook. Home: 14 Beechwood Rd Birmingham AL 35213 Office: PO Box 7497 Birmingham AL 35223

MONAGHAN, PATRICK HENRY, chemist; b. Memphis, July 25, 1922; s. Matthew Laurence and Blanche Frances (Wolf) M.; B.S. in Chem. Engring., La. Poly. Inst., 1943; M.S., La. State U., 1949, Ph.D., 1950; m. Martha Jane Key, Dec. 27, 1943; children—Patricia (Mrs. Vigen Ohanian), Michael Henry. Field engr. Sperry Gyroscope Co., New Orleans, 1946-47; instr. chemistry La. State U., Baton Rouge, 1949-50; research engr. prodn. research div. Humble Oil & Refining Co., Houston, 1950-65; research asso. Esso Prodn. Research Co., Houston, 1965-73, research adviser, 1973—. Served with USMC Reserves, 1943-46. Registered profl. engr., Tex. Mem. Am. Chem. Soc., Soc. Econ. Paleontologists and Mineralogists, Soc. Petroleum Engrs. Home: 13627 Queensbury St Houston TX 77024 Office: Box 2189 Houston TX 77001

MONAHAN, THOMAS VINCENT, lawyer; b. Washington, Apr. 22, 1924; s. Vincent Thomas and Isabel Ann (Garges) M.; student Princeton, 1941-43; B.S., U.S. Mil. Acad., 1947; LL.B., U. Va., 1951; m. Eleanor Hotchkiss Pendleton, June 12, 1951; children—Clare Pendleton, Eleanor Page, Thomas V., Paul Edward, William Gibson. Admitted to Va. bar, 1950, practiced in Winchester and Leesburg, 1954—; partner Hall, Monahan, Engle, Mahon and Mitchell, 1964—. Instr. U. Va. Law Sch., Charlottesville, 1956-58. Served to capt. USAAF, World War II. Fellow Am. Coll. Trial Lawyers; mem. Va. Bar Assn. (pres. elect 1973—), Va. Trial Lawyers Assn. (pres. 1969-70). Home: 457 Merrimans Lane Winchester VA 22601 Office: 9 E Boscowen St Winchester VA 22601 also 3 E Market St Leesburg VA 22075

MONBERG, LAWRENCE, architect; b. Copenhagen, Denmark, June 5, 1900; s. Lauritz C. and Anna (Thelsen) M.; student Armour Inst. Tech., 1917-19; m. Evelyn Schold, June 21, 1937; children—Lawrence John, Bror Carl, Sven Helge. Came to U.S., 1909, naturalized (Act by Congress), 1909. Asso. Lawrence G. Hallberg, architects, 1921-33; own practice, 1934—; pres. Bay Islands Investments, Ltd., Nassau; designer Edgewater Hotel, Madison, Wis., Kungsholm Restaurant, Chgo., U. Wis. Extension Center, Kenosha, Carthage Coll. Sci. Library and Adminstrn. Bldg., Kenosha, West Lakes Housing Devel., The Bridge Hotel and Sheraton Motor Inn, Boca Raton, Fla., and others. Served in U.S. Navy, 1917. Mem. A.I.A., Am. Legion, Navy League. Lutheran. Mason (32 deg.). Clubs: Maple Bluff Country (Madison); Ill. Athletic (Chgo.). Home: 301 Spanish Trail SE Boca Raton FL 33432

MONCRIEF, EVERETTE WHITFIELD, JR., dentist; b. Montgomery, Ala., Nov. 8, 1930; s. Everette Whitfield and Ruth (Mathews) M.; student Emory U., 1948-50, Huntingdon Coll., 1950-51; D.M.D., U. Ala., 1955; M.P.H., U. N.C., 1968; m. Jane McFaden, July 18, 1953; children—Bonnie, Randall. Dental surgeon USAF, Alexandria, La., 1955-57; pvt. practice gen. dentistry, Montgomery, 1957-66; dental cons. Ala. State Health Dept., Montgomery, 1968—; dental dir. Ala. Medicaid Program, 1973—. Served with USAF, 1955-57. Recipient USPHS grant, 1967. Mem. Am. Dental Assn., Am. Assn. Pub. Health Dentists, Am., Ala. pub. health assns., Phi Delta Theta, Psi Omega. Home: 2420 Belcher Dr Montgomery AL 36111 Office: State Office Bldg Montgomery AL 36104

MONCRIEF, JOHN ARTHUR, physician; b. Manila, P.I., July 22, 1924; s. William Henry and Ulah (Ensley) M.; student The Citadel, 1942-43; Cornell U., 1943-44; M.D., Emory U., 1948; m. Constance Jane Knudsen, June 17, 1949; children—John A., Christian Lee, Constance Helen. Commd. 1st lt. U.S. Army, 1948, advanced through grades to col., 1968; intern Brooke Gen. Hosp., Ft. Sam Houston, Tex., 1948-49; resident gen. surgery Barnes Hosp., St. Louis, 1949-50, 51-54; chief gen. surgery 8054th Evacuation Hosp. and 10th Sta. Hosp., Korea, 1950-51, chief gen. surgery U.S. Army Hosp., Ft. Sill, Okla., 1954-55, chief clin. div. U.S. Army Surg. Research Unit, Ft. Sam Houston, 1955-57, chief surg. research br. U.S. Army Med. Research and Devel. Command, 1960-61, comdr., dir. Surg. Research Unit, 1961-68; ret., 1968; pvt. practice medicine, specializing in surgery, Charleston, S.C., 1968—; prof. surgery Med. U. S.C., 1968—; cons. research, surgery VA Hosp., Charleston, 1970—; instr. surgery Emory U. Med. Sch., 1957-60, mem. attending staff Emory U. Hosp., 1957-60; mem. attending staff Grady Meml., Henrietta Egleston Children's, Piedmont hosps., 1957-60; clin. prof. surgery U. Tex. Med. Sch., 1966-68; mem. study sect. on surgery NIH, 1960-68; clin. asso. prof. surgery U. Tex. Med. br., Galveston, 1962-68; vis. prof. surgery Marquette, Wis., Louisville, Syracuse, Rochester, Vt., Okla., Albany, Tex., N.C., S.D., Cin., Ala., Va., Minn., Stanford, Cal., Colo., Kan., Md., Johns Hopkins, Neb., Miami med. schs. Mem. Am. Assn. Surgery of Trauma (councilor at large 1965-66, pres. 1973-74), A.C.S. (mem. trauma com.), Am. Fedn. Clin. Research, Am. Surg. Assn., A.M.A., Assn. Mil. Surgeons, Moyer Surg. Soc., N.Y. Acad. Scis., San Antonio Surg. Soc., Soc. U. Surgeons, Western Surg. Assn., Halsted Soc., Charleston County Med. Soc., Soc. Med. Consultants to Armed Forces, Nat. Acad. Scis., So. Surg. Assn., Am. Burn Assn. (pres. 1970-71). Contbr. numerous articles to med. jours. Home: 715 Knotty Pine Rd Charleston SC 29412 Office: 80 Barre St Charleston SC 29401

MONETTI CALANCHE, JOSE, utility equipment co. exec.; b. Puebla, Mexico, Jan. 4, 1940; s. Jose Monetti A. and Carolina Calanche de Monetti; student Technol. Inst. Chihuahua, 1956-59; E.E., Nat. Poly. Inst. Mexico 1965; m. Maria Del Carmen Castellanos Limon, Oct. 9, 1965; children—Gabriela, Jose. Constrn. engr. Mex. transmission line project Indsl. Electrica Mexicana, S.A., Mexico City, 1964, chief asst. Mexico transmission lines, 1964-66; operations chief Fed. Commn. Electricity, Mexico Nat. Utility, Mexico City, 1966-68; gen. mgr. Preformados de Mexico, S.A. de C.V., Mexico City, 1969—. Mem. Internat. des Grandes Reseaux Electriques, Am. Mgmt. Assn., I.E.E.E. Home: 902-1 Cuzco Mexico 14 DF Mexico Office: Poniente 140 No 526 Col Industrial Vallejo Mexico 14 DF Mexico

MONEY, HENRY THOMAS, clergyman; b. Louisville, Apr. 13, 1933; s. Milton Thomas and Ethel Mae (Heft) M.; A.B., Translyvania U., 1955; M.Div., Lexington Theol. Sem., 1958; M.A., East Carolina U., 1962; m. Suzanne Lewis Silverman, June 15, 1957; children—Terri Lynn, Henry Thomas. Ordained to ministry Disciples of Christ Ch., 1958; minister, Greenville, N.C., 1958-64, Peachtree Christian Ch., Atlanta, 1965—. Vice pres. Christian Council Met. Atlanta, 1971-73. Trustee Christian Coll. Ga., Athens. Mem. Phi Delta Theta. Rotarian (dir. Atlanta). Home: 3991 Whittington Dr NE Atlanta GA 30342 Office: 1580 Peachtree St NW Atlanta GA 30305

MONEY, JOHN MARSHALL, constrn. co. exec.; b. Carrollton, Miss., June 20, 1900; s. John Clark and Annie Laura (Marshall) M.; student Massey Bus. Coll., 1916-17, U. Va., 1918-21; m. Lorraine Lloyd, June 26, 1923; 1 dau., Betty Anne (Mrs. Robert Frances Arenz). With Hardaway Contracting Co., Columbus, Ga., 1921—, engr., 1921-25, supt., 1925-37, v.p., 1937-42, v.p. and gen. mgr., 1942-52, pres. 1952-69, chmn. bd., 1969—; chmn. bd. Internat. Incinerators, Inc., Atlanta; Cone Bros. Contracting Co., Tampa, Fla.; mem. adv. bd. First Nat. Bank. Served with AUS, 1918; Mem. Am. Soc. Civil Engrs. Meth. Clubs: Columbus Country, Atlanta Commerce. Home: 2222 Wildwood Av Columbus GA 31906 Office: 300 Eleventh St Columbus GA 31902

MONEY, LLOYD JEAN, govt. ofcl.; b. Lawton, Okla., Sept. 14, 1920; s. Royce Jennings and Mary Oma (Godwin) M.; B.S., Rice U., 1942; M.S. in E.E., Purdue U., 1950, Ph.D., 1952; m. Ruth Rowntree, May 3, 1944; children—Jeffrey Stewart, Meredith Anne, Jeannette (Mrs. Eric Langdon). Instr. elec. engring. Tulane U., New Orleans, 1945-46, Rice U., Houston, 1946-48. With Hughes Aircraft Co., Culver City, Cal., 1952-68, mgr. European operations, aero. systems div., Paris, 1962-64, asso. mgr. advanced projects and mgr. advanced strike systems div., Culver City, 1964-68; staff mgr. advanced programs TRW Systems Group, Redondo Beach, Cal., 1968-71; asst. dir. systems devel., office systems engring. U.S. Dept. Transp., Washington, 1971—, also acting dir. office univ. research Office of Sec. Transp. Served to lt. comdr. USNR, 1943-45. Mem. I.E.E.E., N.Y. Acad. Scis., Sigma Xi, Tau Beta Pi. Patentee radar antenna. Contbr. profl. jours. Home: 367 O St SW Washington DC 20024 Office: 400 7th St SW Washington DC 20590

MONEY, ROY WILSON, physician; b. Winchester, Tenn., Apr. 9, 1913; s. William Reuben and Ollie (West) M.; B.S., Tenn. Technol. U., 1936; student U. Tenn. Sch. Pharmacy, 1938-39, Memphis State U., 1939-40; M.D., U. Tenn., 1944; m. Ferrell Elizabeth Tisdale, Dec. 19, 1943; children—Roy Wilson, James, David. Intern, Nashville Gen. Hosp., 1944; pvt. practice medicine, Lumberton, Miss., 1947-48, Pulaski, Tenn., 1948-60; mem. staff Giles County Hosp., Pulaski, 1948-60; plant physician Ford Motor Co. Glass Plant, Nashville, 1960—. Served with AUS, 1945-47. Fellow Indsl. Med. Assn.; mem. Nashville Acad. Medicine, Tenn. Med. Assn., A.M.A., Nashville C. of C., Nashville Mental Health Assn. (mem. exec. com. 1973—). Methodist (mem. ofcl. bd. 1972—). Mason. Home: 700 Brownlee Dr Nashville TN 37205 Office: Ford Motor Co Centennial Blvd Nashville TN 37209

MONGER, JAMES ARNOLD, instrumentation engr.; b. Lenoir City, Tenn., Sept. 14, 1924; s. George Elmer and Zona Edna (Denney) M.; student Ga. Inst. Tech., 1946, U. Tenn., 1946-47, Internat. Corr. Schs., 1957-58; diploma engring. sci. U. Tenn., 1964; m. Dorothy Sue Conner, Apr. 18, 1959; 1 son, James Michael. With RCA, Indpls., 1947-52; owner Radio and TV shop, Chattanooga, 1952-54; with Union Carbide Corp., Oak Ridge, 1954-56, Cramet, Inc., Chattanooga, 1956-58; test methods engr. Sperry Farragut Co., Bristol, Tenn., 1958-61; instrument supt., design engr. Am. Saint Gobain Co., Kingsport, Tenn., 1961-66; project engr., missile system div. Raytheon Co., Bristol, 1966—; tchr. courses instrumentation and automation. Served with AUS, 1943-45. Registered profl. engr., Tenn. Sr. mem. Instrument Soc. Am.; mem. Am. Radio Relay League. Republican. Baptist (Sunday sch. and tng. union tchr.). Mason. Designer spl. automatic machine tools. Home: Route 4 Box 30 Bluff City TN 37618 Office: Raytheon Co Bristol TN 37620

MONGET, HENRY SCHORTEN, dentist; b. Baton Rouge, May 1, 1899; s. Joseph William and Annie Elizabeth (Schorten) M.; D.D.S., Tulane U., 1925; m. Emma Jean Monget, Feb. 12, 1924; 1 dau., Jean (Mrs. A.M. Beveridge). Practice dentistry, specializing in anesthesia, Baton Rouge, 1935—. Mem. Nat., La., East Baton Rouge Parish dental socs., Internat. Assn. Anesthesiologists, Sigma Nu. Elk. Address: 1541 Ingleside Dr Baton Rouge LA 70808

MONGLE, BRUCE WILLIAM, physician; b. Holston, Va., Mar. 13, 1905; s. Samuel Anderson and Carrie (Huff) M.; A.B., Emory and Henry Coll., 1929; M.D., Med. Coll. Va., 1933; m. Mary Pauline Glenn, Dec. 25, 1934, (dec. Apr. 1956); children—Samuel Anderson, Mary Bruce (Mrs. David Carr). Intern, Carroway Meth. Hosp., Birmingham, 1933, resident, 1937; pvt. practice medicine, specializing in surgery, Bristol, Tenn., 1937—; mem. surg. staff Bristol Meml. Hosp., 1937—. Mgr. Mongle Angus Cattle Farm, Blountville, Tenn., Mongle Springs Angus Cattle Farm, Abingdon, Va. Reserve dep. sheriff Sullivan County, Tenn., 1973. Served to capt. AUS, 1941. Mem. Am. Coll. Surgeons, Internat. Coll. Surgeons, Am. Soc. Abdominal Surgeons, Am. Bd. Abdominal Surgeons, A.M.A., Va., Tenn. State, Sullivan County med. socs. Clubs: Rotary, Elks. Home: Route 2 Blountville TN 37617 Office: Doctors Bldg Bristol Meml Hosp Bristol TN 37620

MONK, BILLIE W. CARTER (MRS. SAMUEL E. MONK), collection agy. owner; b. nr. Milan, Ga., Oct. 20, 1916; d. William Daniel and Emma M. (Alligood) Carter; student pub. schs.; m. Samuel E. Monk, Aug. 29, 1954. With Jeffersonville (Ga.) New Era, 1935-36; foreman U.S. Naval Ordnance, Macon, Ga., 1941-45; owner, operator coffee shop, 1946-49; co-owner Collection Service & Med. Credits, Savannah, Ga., 1949—; dir. Southeastern Adjustments, Charlotte, So. Credit Counselors, Atlanta. Bd. dirs. Drs. and Mchts. Bur., Mobile, Ala. Consumer Credit Counseling Service, 1966-67. Fellow Certified Am. Collectors Assn., mem. Oglethorpe Bus. and Profl. Club (treas.), Am. Collectors Assn. (nat. dir. 1961-64, nat. v.p. 1962-64, regional v.p. 1964-66), Asso. Credit Bur. Ga. (pres. 1965-66), Tri-State Collectors Assn. (pres. 1955-56, dir.), Retail Credit Men's Assn., Savannah Area C. of C. (chmn. women's div. 1964-65). Methodist. Club: Zonta (pres. 1963-64). Home: 4637 Oakview Dr Savannah GA 31402 Office: 1601 Abercorn St Savannah GA 31402

MONK, CARL DOUGLAS, educator; b. Hurdles Mill, N.C., July 28, 1933; s. Andrew Jackson and Ruth Elizabeth (Phelps) M.; A.B., Duke, 1955, Ph.D., 1959; m. Laura Lynn Swader, Dec. 21, 1957; children—Michael Lawrence, Jonathan Drew. Asst. prof. botany U. Fla. at Gainesville, 1959-64; mem. faculty U. Ga. at Athens, 1964—, asso. prof., 1967-71, prof., 1971—. NSF, 1959-64, 68-70, AEC, 1971-73. Fellow A.A.A.S.; mem. Ecol. Soc. Am. (program chmn. 1966-69), Brit. Ecol. Soc., Zocl. Soc. Am., Bot. Soc. Am., Soc. Naturalists, Am. Assn. Biol. Scientists, Assn. Southeastern Biologists, Torrey Bot. Club. Asso. editor Am. Midland Naturalists, 1971—. Contbr. articles to profl. jours. Home: Route 3 Box 230-1 Athens GA 30601 Office: Dept Botany Univ Georgia Athens GA 30602

MONK, GEORGE EDWARD, lawyer; b. Washington, July 18, 1907; s. John Edward and Anna (Tripp) M.; A.B., George Washington U., 1928, LL.B., 1930, LL.M., 1934; m. Mary Clark deLashmutt, Apr. 16, 1937; children—George Edward, Paul deLashmutt, David Hinton. Admitted to D.C. bar, 1930, Md. bar, 1939; practiced in Washington, 1930—; partner firm Hogan & Hartson, 1949—. Lectr. law George Washington U., Washington, 1947-67; dir. Woodward & Lothrop; gen. counsel D.C. Bankers Assn. 1967—. Served from capt. to lt. col., AUS, 1941-45; ETO. Mem. Am. Bar Assn., Bar Assn. D.C. (pres. 1969-70), Am. Soc. Internat. Law, Order of Coif. Delta Theta Phi. Lutheran. Rotarian. Clubs: Barristers, Nat. Lawyers, University, Columbia Country, Metropolitan (Washington). Home: 4020 Franklin St Kensington MD 20795 Office: Hogan & Hartson 815 Connecticut Av Washington DC 20006

MONK, JAMES FLOYD, banker; b. Moultrie, Ga., July 29, 1914; s. John Franklin and Rachel Matilda (Clark) M.; grad. high sch.; m. Mildred Harris, Jan. 15, 1942; children—Jamie Nell, Lynn Alison. Clerk, Friedlander's Dept. Store, Moultrie, Ga., 1932-33; sec. to prin. Moultrie High Sch., 1933-34; sec. to supt. Moultrie Pub. Schs., 1934-36; with Moultrie Banking Co., 1936-37; with Fla. Nat. Bank & Trust Co., Miami, 1937—, v.p., 1967—. Served with C.E., AUS, 1944-46. Mem. Hist. Assn. So. Fla. (treas. 1961-65), Fla. Anthrop. Soc. (pres. 1967), Fla. Hist. Soc., Soc. History of Discoveries, Nat. Hist. Soc., Nat. Aubudon Soc., Nat. Geog. Soc. Democrat. Presbyn. Home: 1960 S W 61st Court Miami FL 33155 Office: 169 E Flagler St Miami FL 33131

MONROE, DORIS DRIGGERS, editor, author; b. Mt. Pleasant, Tex., July 11, 1916; d. Samuel Wyatt and Leola (Harris) Driggers; student Mary-Hardin Baylor Coll., 1934-35, William Jewell Coll., 1935-37, Southwestern Bapt. Theol. Sem., 1937-38, So. Bapt. Theol. Sem., 1938-39, 44-45, George Peabody Coll., 1947-50; m. Edwin Ulys Monroe, Aug. 6, 1937; children—Leola Fran (Mrs. Dudley B. Burton), Billie Barbara (Mrs. William F. Hardy, Jr.). Music dir., pastor's asst. Bethany Bapt. Ch., Kansas City, Mo., 1945-47; asso. editor Story Hour Leader, Bapt. Sunday Sch. Bd., Nashville, 1947-50, editor Primary Leader, Every Day with Primaries, 1950-68, cons. Work with Exceptional Persons, 1968—. Mem. Sunday sch. bd. So. Bapt. Conv. Mem. Nat. Assn. for Retarded Children, Am. Camping Assn., Am. Pen Women, Beta Lit. Soc. Author: When Marcia Goes to Church, 1966; The Come-and-Go Village, 1967; A Church Ministry to Retarded Persons, 1971. Co-author: The Primary Leadership Manual, 1957; co-author, co-editor Adventures in Christian Living and Learning, Exploring Life Curriculum Series, 1968-72. Home: 2308 Donna Hill Ct Nashville TN 37214 Office: 127 9th Av N Nashville TN 37203

MONROE, DOUGLAS DURRELL, JR., banker; b. Norfolk, Va., Aug. 18, 1933; s. Douglas Durrell and Margaret (Norvell) M.; grad. The Lawrenceville Sch., 1951; B.S., Washington & Lee U., 1955; M.S., Purdue U., 1960; student Stonier Grad. Sch. Banking Rutgers U., 1969; m. Katherine Willis, Sept. 3, 1954; children—Douglas, Margaret, Katherine, Wende, Mark. Asso. prof. Purdue U., 1957-59; with Wachovia Bank & Trust Co., Winston-Salem, N.C., 1960-64, asst. v.p., 1963-64; with Chesapeake Nat. Bank, Kilmarnock, Va., 1965—, exec. v.p., chief exec. officer, 1965-67, pres., 1967-71, vice-chmn., chief exec. officer, 1971—, dir., 1965—; dir. Fed. Res. Bank Richmond, 1969-71; mem. adv. council Sm. Bus. Assn., 1972—. Trustee Chesapeake Acad.; trustee St. Margaret's Sch. Served to lt. USNR, 1955-59. Mem. Kilmarnock C. of C. (dir. 1967). Presbyn. (deacon 1968-70, elder 1971-73). Clubs: Lancaster Lions, Bull & Bear (Richmond, Va.); Chesapeake, Rapp River Yacht (Irvington, Va.); Indian Creek Yacht & Country (Kilmarnock, Va.). Home: PO Box 182 Irvington VA 22480 Office: Box 638 Kilmarnock VA 22482

MONROE, THOMAS CONNELIUS, JR., obstetrician and gynecologist; b. Glenmora, La., Nov. 17, 1925; s. Thomas Connelius and Mary Cooper (Smith) M.; student Tex. A. and M. Coll., 1945-46, La. Coll., 1946-48; M.D., La. State U., 1952; m. Helen Lois Martin, Dec. 24, 1946; children—Thomas Connelius III, Fay Martin. Intern, Mid-State Bapt. Hosp., Nashville, 1952-53, resident, 1955-57; gen. practice medicine, South Pittsburg, Tenn., 1953-55; chief resident Nashville Gen. Hosp., 1957-58; practice medicine, specializing in obstetrics and gynecology, Chattanooga, 1958—; mem. staff Baroness Erlanger Hosp. Vice pres. Tenn. div. Am. Cancer Soc., 1967, pres. Hamilton unit, 1968-69, pres. elect Tenn. div., 1970. Bd. dirs. East Ridge Community Hosp. Served with USAAF, 1942-45. Decorated Air medal with 9 oak leaf clusters. Diplomate Am. Bd. Obstetrics and Gynecology. Fellow Am. Coll. Obstetrics and Gynecologists; mem. Am., Tenn. med. assns. Home: 124 Hilldale St Chattanooga TN 37411 Office: 404 Franklin Bldg Chattanooga TN 37411

MONSON, WARREN GLENN, agronomist, govt. ofcl.; b. Clay Center, Neb., Dec. 24, 1926; s. Elmer Ralph and Gladys Marie (Johnson) M.; B.S., U. Neb., 1951, M.S., 1955, Ph.D., 1958; m. Charlene Anne Campbell, Oct. 4, 1958; children—Christie, Cynthia.

Asst. in agronomy U. Neb., Lincoln, 1955-58; research agronomist U.S. Dept. Agr., Ithaca, N.Y., 1958-66, Tifton, Ga., 1966—. Served with AUS, 1951-53. Mem. Am. Soc. Agronomy, Crop Sci. Soc. Am., Am. Soc. Plant Physiology, Am. Forage and Grassland Council, Assn. So. Agrl. Scientists, Sigma Xi, Gamma Sigma Delta, Alpha Zeta, Alpha Gamma Rho. Republican. Methodist. Elk. Contbr. articles on agronomy to sci. publs. Home: 1411 N College Av Tifton GA 31794 Office: Coastal Plain Experiment Station Tifton GA 31794

MONSOUR, ANDREW R., dept. store exec.; b. Treveskyn, Pa., Aug. 28, 1915; s. Abe and Anise (Bitar) M.; student Duffs City Coll., 1932; m. Alyce Gayle Monsour, Apr. 6, 1940; children—Geoffrey, Andrea, Kriste, Trey. Dept. mgr. Wohl Shoe Co., Toledo, 1940, Cin., 1941, Wheeling, W.Va., 1946, Galveston, Tex., 1947; leased shoe dept. Eiband's Dept. Store, Galveston, 1949-64, owner store, 1964—, now pres., gen. mgr.; owner Monsour Shoes; pres. Geoffrey Shoes, Inc. Chmn. retail div. United Fund, 1969-70, mem. exec. bd., 1970—; vice chmn. Beach Park Bd., 1963-71. Bd. dirs. Family Service Bur.; mem. adv. bd. Goodwill Industries, Salvation Army. Served to capt. AUS, 1941-46; ETO, PTO. Recipient Distinguished Service award Jr. C. of C., 1966; named Most Outstanding Citizen, 1966. Mem. Tex. Retail Fedn. (dir.), Galveston C. of C. (past pres., dir.), Galveston County Council C. of C. (past pres.), Am. Legion, Galveston County Research Council (dir.), So. Fedn. Syrian-Lebanese Am. Clubs (vice chmn. bd. dirs.). Episcopalian (vestryman). Rotarian (pres.). Club: Galveston Country. Home: 62 Colony Park Circle Galveston TX 77550 Office: Central Plaza St Galveston TX 77550

MONSOUR, VICTOR, educator; b. Shreveport, La., Aug. 28, 1922; s. Willie Mike and Mary (Hajj) M.; B.S., La. State U., 1948, M.S., 1950; Ph.D., U. Tex. at Austin, 1954; m. Billie Rae Weeks, Dec. 16, 1950; children—Victor, Vicki Melisa. Bacteriologist Shreveport (La.) Charity Hosp., 1950-51; head microbiology dept. Confederate Meml. Med. Center, Shreveport, La., 1954-57; asst. dir. Bur. Labs. div. Health of Mo., Jefferson City, 1957-59; prof., chmn. dept. microbiology McNeese State U., 1959—; cons. microbiology. Served with USN, 1943-46. AEC grantee, 1951-53; Office Naval Research grantee, 1963-64. Mem. Am. Soc. for Microbiology, Am. Chem. Soc. (dir. 1963-64, chmn. Southwest La. sect. 1964-65), Am. Pub. Health Assn., Nat. Environmental Health Assn. (dir. La. sect. 1973-76), Sigma Xi. Home: 206 McVay St Lake Charles LA 70601

MONTAG, MILLER, accountant; b. Henderson, Tex., Nov. 18, 1919; s. Victor Hugo and Mildred Ardella (Kinnebrew) M.; student Kilgore Jr. Coll., 1937-39; B.B.A., U. Tex., 1941; m. Marjorie L. Stille, May 4, 1946; children—Mark, Jeffrey, Bruce. Staff accountant Leon O. Lewis, accountant, San Antonio, 1946-54; partner Lewis and Montag, accountants, San Antonio, 1954-70; partner Haskins and Sells, accountants, San Antonio, 1970—; dir. Tex. Wis. Oil Co., San Antonio. Vice chmn. United Fund Allocation Com., 1972—. Mem. Bexar County Retirement Bd., 1960-68. Bd. dirs. San Antonio Estate Planners Council, treas., 1959—. Served with USAAF, 1941-45; PTO. Decorated Bronze Star. C.P.A., Tex., N.M., La., Okla., N.C. Mem. Tex. Soc. C.P.A.'s. (pres. 1970-71, trustee ednl. found. 1969-70), San Antonio Council Presidents, Am. Inst. C.P.A.s. (mem. council 1969-71, 72—), Am. Accounting Assn. Kiwanian (pres. 1971-72). Clubs: Oak Hills Country, St. Anthony, San Antonio. Home: 2706 Marlborough St San Antonio TX 78230 Office: 337 Travis Park West San Antonio TX 78205

MONTAGUE, BERT LARRY, wholesale co. exec.; b. Sumter, S.C., Sept. 30, 1943; s. Larry Dupree and Virginia (Thorne) M.; student U. S.C., 1961-65; m. Linda Edens, Jan. 30, 1965; 1 dau., Nancy Lynn. Prodn. planning B.L. Montague Co. Inc., Sumter, 1961-62, accountant, 1962-64, indsl. supply salesman, 1964-67, br. mgr., 1967-70, dir. towmotor div., 1970-71, pres. mill supply-towmotor div., 1971—. Mem. Com. of 100. Mem. Am. Inst. Plant Engrs. (pres. Palmetto chpt. 1970-71), Sertoma Internat. (Centurion award 1973, dist., state sec. treas. 1973—), Columbia C. of C., So. Indsl. Distbrs. Assn., S.C. Buyers and Suppliers Assn. (sec. treas. 1970—), Pi Kappa Phi. Home: 1004 Quail Run Apt Columbia SC 29206 Office: 1230 Bluff Rd Columbia SC 29202

MONTAGUE, DAVID NICHOLLS, lawyer, mayor; b. N.Y.C., Aug. 23, 1936; s. Edgar Sclater and Suzanne (Garrett) M.; B.A., U. Va., 1958, LL.B., 1961; m. Carolyn Stewart Day, June 21, 1958; children—Suzanne Stewart, David Nicholls. Admitted to Va. bar, 1961; mem. firm Montague, Cumming & Watkins, Hampton, Va., 1962-67, Montague & Montague, Hampton, 1967—; mayor, Hampton, 1971—. Mem. Va. Council Higher Edn., 1970-72. First vice chmn. Republican Party of Va., 1968-72; chmn. Rep. Party of Hampton, 1968-70; mem. Hampton City Council, 1971. Served to 1st lt. AUS. 1958-62. Mem. U.S. Conf. Mayors (resolutions com. 1973—), Hampton Retail Mchts. Assn. (pres. 1970). Episcopalian (mem. vestry 1965-72). Home: 29 Hampton Rds Av Hampton VA 23361 Office: 3 E Queen St Hampton VA 23369

MONTAGUE, ROBERT LATANE, III, lawyer; b. Washington, Sept. 18, 1935; s. Robert Latane and Frances Breckinridge (Wilson) M.; B.A., U. Va., 1956, LL.B., 1961; m. Prudence Mason Darnell, June 20, 1964; children—Anne Steele Mason, Robert Latane IV. Asst. atty. gen. State Ky., Frankfort, 1961-64; asso. law with Howard W. Smith, Alexandria, Va., 1964-66; asso. firm Lambert, Broun & Furlow, Washington, 1965-69; asso. John Howard Joynt, Alexandria, 1970—. Pres. Historic Alexandria Found., 1968-70, exec. sec., 1971—; chmn. Alexandria Environmental Policy Commn., 1970—; chmn. Nat. Capital Area chpt. Nat. Found., 1972—; pres. No. Va. Conservation Council, 1973—. Democratic nominee Alexandria city council, 1973. Trustee Assn. Preservation Va. Antiquities, Richmond. Served to comdr. USNR. Mem. Am., Va., Ky., D.C. bar assns., Am. Judicature Soc., Soc. Cin. Clubs: Army and Navy Town; Antique Automobile Am. Contbr. articles to legal jours. Home: 207 Prince St Alexandria VA 22314 Office: 1007 King St Alexandria VA 22314

MONTALVO, ROBERTO SANTIAGO, disc jockey; b. Mayaguez, P.R., July 29, 1947; s. Ramon Santiago and Felicita Montalvo (Rodriguez) Santiago; Dpto. Bellas Artes, Colegio Agricultura y Artes Mecanicas, 1967; m. Mirna Pagan Pagan, June 26, 1966; children—Jeffrey Roberto, Sharon Myrna. Disc Jockey WBMJ, San Juan, P.R., 1973—. Active vol. Campaign Against Drugs, 1971; Selective Service, 1972; Campaign Against Cancer, 1973. Home: DK 3 Lago Cidra Catano PR 00636 Office: WBMJ Penthouse One Hotel Borinquen San Juan PR 00936

MONTAMAT, RONALD HERBERT, chem. engr.; b. Houston, Apr. 23, 1935; s. Gus Herbert and Hazel (Torrence) M.; B.Ch.E., Rice U., 1956; B.Ch.E., Tex. U., 1958; m. Gerry Lynn Barber, Apr. 19, 1958; children—Stephen Craig, Michael Edward, Matthew August. Chem. engr. Celanese Corp., Houston, 1957, Chemstrand Corp., Pensacola, Fla., 1958-62; sr. engr. Monsanto Co., Pensacola, Fla., 1962-67; tech. supr. Amoco Chemicals Corp., Texas City, Tex., 1967—. Instr. data processing Pensacola Jr. Coll., 1966; instr. data processing Coll. of Mainland, 1968, adv. com. data processing, 1973. Mem. orgn. and extension com. Gulf Coast council Boy Scouts Am., 1965; conf. rep. League City Little League Football, 1971; dir. Dickinson Little League Baseball, 1972. Served with AUS, 1959. Mem. Am. Inst. Chem. Engrs., Instrument Soc. Am., Indsl. Mgmt. Assn. Rebublican. Episcopalian. Clubs: Pensacola Sailing Assn. (pres. 1965), Pines. Home: 404 Old Bayou Dr Dickinson TX 77539 Office: 2800 FM 519 East Texas City TX 77590

MONTEITH, LARRY KING, educator; b. Bryson City, N.C., Aug. 17, 1933; s. Noah Earl and Essie Ruth (King) M.; B.S., N.C. State U., 1960; M.S., Duke, 1962, Ph.D., 1965; m. Nancy Carol Alexander, Apr. 19, 1952; children—Carol, Larry, Steve. Systems engr. Bell Telephone Labs., Burlington, N.C., 1960-62; research engr., sr. scientist, group leader Research Triangle Inst., Research Triangle Park, N.C., 1962-68; prof., head dept. elec. engring. N.C. State U. at Raleigh, 1968—. Counselor, Youth Assn., Durham, N.C., 1964-68. Served with USNR, 1952-56. RCA grantee, 1959, Sr. award engring. N.C. State U., 1960. Mem. I.E.E.E., Am. Soc. Engring. Edn. Contbr. articles to profl. jours. Home: 5000 Larchmont Dr Raleigh NC 27612

MONTES, LEOPOLDO FELICIANO, physician, educator; b. Buenos Aires, Argentina, Nov. 22, 1929; s. Leopoldo A. and Celia (Gaztambide) M.; M.D., U. Buenos Aires, 1954; M.S., U. Mich., 1959; m. Maria Mercedes Pfeiffer, Nov. 25, 1961; children—Carolina, Mercedes, Ana, Leopoldo, Teresa, William. Came to U.S., 1955. Intern, City of Buenos Aires Hosps., 1954-55; resident dermatology Pa. Hosp., Phila., 1955-56; resident U. Mich. Med. Center, Ann Arbor, 1956-58, instr. dermatology, 1958-60; practice medicine, specializing in dermatology, Buenos Aires, 1960-63, Houston, 1963-66, Birmingham, Ala., 1966—; asst. prof. dermatology Baylor U. Coll. Medicine, 1963-66; asso. prof. dermatology U. Ala. Med. Center and Med. Coll. Ala., Birmingham, 1966-69, prof. dermatology, 1969—, asso. prof. microbiology, 1968—. Recipient Research Career Devel. award USPHS, 1965-70. Fellow Am. Acad. Dermatology; mem. A.M.A., Am. Soc. Microbiology, Soc. Investigative Dermatology, Histochem Soc., Am. Soc. Cell Biology, A.A.A.S., Am. Fedn. Clin. Research, Am. Acad. Microbiology, Electron Microscopy Soc. Am., Internat. Soc. Tropical Dermatology (asst. sec. gen. 1969—), Am. Dermatol. Assn., Am. Acad. Microbiology, Sigma Xi. Editor: Jour. Cutaneous Pathology, 1973—. Home: 4319 Kennesaw Dr Birmingham AL 35213 Office: 1919 7th Av S Birmingham AL 35233

MONTGOMERY, ALEX BROOKS, govt. ofcl.; b. Hopkinsville, Ky., Sept. 25, 1926; s. William Bruce and Catherine (Markham) M.; A.B., U. Mo., 1954, A.M., 1956; m. Placida Mary Brazinski, Aug. 26, 1951; children—Alex Brooks, Lisa Catherine, Robert Clay. Fishery biologist Ga. Game and Fish Commn., Tifton, 1956-58; dir. aquatic devel. Chem. Insecticide Co., Metuchen, N.J., 1958-60; with U.S. Bur. Sport Fish and Wildlife Service, 1960—, asst. regional supr. fed. aid, Atlanta, 1960-63, asst. regional supr. fishery services, Atlanta, 1963-68, regional supr., 1968—. Served with AUS, 1950-52. Mem. Am. Fisheries Soc. (pres. So. div. 1965-66). Home: 2845 Redding Rd NE Atlanta GA 30319 Office: 17 Executive Park Dr Atlanta GA 30329

MONTGOMERY, GILLESPIE V., legislator; b. Meridian, Miss.; s. Gillespie M. and Emily (Jones) M.; B.S., Miss. State U. Mem. Miss. Senate, 1956-66; mem. 90th-93d congresses, 3d Dist. Miss.; v.p. Greater Miss. Life Ins. Co. Mem. Miss. Agrl. and Indsl. Bd., 1957-60; pres. Miss. N.G. Assn., 1959; pres. Miss. Heart Assn., 1967-68. Served with AUS, World War II, Korean War. Decorated Bronze Star medal, Combat Inf. Badge; recipient Miss. Magnolia award, 1966; certificate of merit for saving a life A.R.C., 1947. Mem. V.F.W., Am. Legion, 40 and 8, Miss. Farm Bur., Congl. Prayer Breakfast Group (pres. 1970), Miss. State U. Alumni Assn. (past pres.), Kappa Alpha. Episcopalian. Mason (Shriner), Moose. Home: PO Box 1009 Meridian MS 39301 also 2000 S Eads St Arlington VA 22202 Office: 208 Cannon House Office Bldg Washington DC 20515

MONTGOMERY, JOHN DENNY, lawyer; b. Hobart, Okla., June 27, 1928; s. Robert Place and Theitis (Curreathers) M.; B.A., U. Okla., 1950, LL.B., 1955; m. Martha Carolyn Flow, June 9, 1950; children—John Denny, Mary Ann. Admitted to Okla. bar, 1955; since practiced in Hobart, Okla.; mem. firm Montgomery & Montgomery, 1955—. Pres., United Fund, Hobart, 1959; chmn. Kiowa County chpt. A.R.C., 1967—; sec. Hobart Planning Commn., 1964-65. Dir. S.W. Okla. Devel. Council, 1964, Hobart Industries, Inc., 1965; trustee Kiowa County Indsl. Trust, 1970-74. Served from ensign to lt. (j.g.) USNR, 1950-53; capt. Res. Mem. Am., Okla., Kiowa County (pres. 1960) bar assns., S.W. Okla. Bar Inst. (v.p. 1965), S.W. Okla. Legal Inst. (pres. 1966-67), Okla. Bar. Found. (trustee), C. of C. (pres. 1962, 73), Kappa Alpha, Phi Alpha Delta. Republican. Presbyn. (elder). Rotarian (pres. 1958-59). Clubs: Hobart Country (pres. 1959), Quarterback (sec. 1965). Home: 107 E Dogwood St Hobart OK 73651 Office: Montgomery Bldg 325 S Main St Hobart OK 73651

MONTGOMERY, LUCIUS KENNEDY, JR., engring. co. exec.; b. Columbia, S.C., Sept. 27, 1938; s. Lucius Kennedy and Mattie Pauline (Shaw) M.; B.S. in Applied Math., Clemson U., 1961; M.S. in Math. (Hughes Aircraft Co. fellow), U. So. Cal., 1963, Ph.D. in Elec. Engring., 1967; m. Muriel Catherine Zaal, July 15, 1962; children—Erik Gordon, Lori Ann, Patricia Lyn. Mem. tech. staff Hughes Aircraft Co., Fullerton, Cal., 1961-63; mgr., performance analysis and simulation br. Teledyne Brown Engring., Huntsville, Ala., 1969—. Cons. Research Inst., U. Ala., Huntsville, 1971-72. Served to capt., AUS, 1967-69. Mem. I.E.E.E., Sigma Xi, Phi Kappa Phi, Sigma Pi Sigma, Eta Kappa Nu. Home: 313 Spring Valley Ct Huntsville AL 35802 Office: 300 Sparkman Dr Huntsville AL 35807

MONTGOMERY, PAUL VAUGHAN, cons. actuary; b. Ft. Worth, Oct. 10, 1886; s. John Thirison and Sallie (Vaughan) M.; B.A., U. Tex., 1907; m. Mabel Chilton, Apr. 8, 1914 (dec. Aug. 19, 1971); children—Mary Vaughan (Mrs. Richard G. Fuller), Jean (Mrs. C.Z. Stevens III). Actuarial clk. Ft. Worth Life Ins. Co., 1907-09, v.p., actuary, 1914-23; actuarial clk., asst. actuary Southwestern Life Ins. Co., Dallas, 1909-14, v.p., actuary Southland Life Ins. Co., Dallas, 1923-49; cons. actuary, Dallas. 1949—. Dep. commr. Ins. div. Bur. War Risk Ins., Washington, 1918. Mem. town council, Highland Park, Tex., 1928-34, mayor, 1930-34. Fellow Conf. Actuaries Pub. Practice, Soc. Actuaries; mem. Acad. Actuaries, Kappa Sigma. Democrat. Episcopalian. Mason (32 deg.), Rotarian. Clubs: City, Dallas Country. Home: 4242 Lomo Alto Dr Dallas TX 75219 Office: Adolphus Tower Dallas TX 75202

MONTGOMERY, PHILIP O'BRYAN, physician; b. Dallas, Aug. 16, 1921; s. Philip O'Bryan and Frances Rebecca (Hench) M.; B.S., So. Meth. U., 1942; M.D., Columbia, 1945; m. Ruth Ann Rogers, June 20, 1953; children—Philip O'Bryan III, Carter Rogers, Will Stuart, Harold Hench. Intern Mary Imogene Bassett Hosp., Cooperstown, N.Y., 1945-46; mem. faculty Southwestern Med. Sch., Dallas, 1952—, asso. dean, 1968-70, prof. pathology, 1961—; sr. staff mem. pathology dept. Parkland Meml. Hosp.; cons. pathologist Lisbon VA Hosp., St. Paul's Hosp., Dallas. Spl. asst. to chancellor U. Tex. system, 1971—; med. adviser to bd. dirs. Damon Runyon-Walter Winchell Meml. Fund for Cancer Research, 1973—. Trustee St. Mark's Sch. Tex., Dallas, 1959—. Served to capt., M.C., AUS, 1946-49. Recipient Career Devel. award NIH, 1962-68, Silver Snoop award profl. excellence from astronauts, 1970. Mem. Biol. Humanics Found. Eagle. Clubs: Petroleum, Northwood Country. Asso. editor Cancer Research, 1970-73. Editorial bd. Space Life Scis., 1967—. Contbr. articles to profl. jours. Home: 6343 Kalani Pl Dallas TX 75240 Office: Dept Pathology Med Coll Univ Tex Southwestern Med Sch Dallas TX 75235

MONTGOMERY, ROBERT MUNGER, real estate broker; b. Birmingham, Ala., June 17, 1916; s. Alexander Cochran and Ruby (Munger) M.; A.B., Birmingham-So. Coll., 1936; postgrad. U. Va., 1937; J.D., U. Ala., 1939; m. Betty Mary Reeves, Oct. 31, 1941; children—Mary (Mrs. Phillip O. Hurst), Virginia (Mrs. John P. Martin), Marlin Elizabeth, Robert Munger. With FBI, 1941-45; pres. Montgomery Real Estate & Ins. Co., Birmingham, 1945—, Munger Realty Co., Montcreek Land Co., Center Ct. Apts., Inc., Signal Land & Investment Co., Englewood Land Co., Manhattan Land Co. Vice pres. Birmingham Boys Club, 1973—. Chmn., Jefferson County Bd. Zoning Adjustment, 1970—. Bd. dirs. Carraway Med. Center. Mem. Nat., Ala., Birmingham assns. realtors, Ala. (dir. 1945-46), Birmingham (pres. 1956) bds. realtors, Birmingham C. of C. (dir. 1965-66), Sigma Alpha Epsilon. Episcopalian (sr. warden 1974). Clubs: Birmingham Country, The Club, Downtown (dir. 1958-62, treas. 1963—) (Birmingham, Ala.). Kiwanian (pres. 1960). Home: 2728 Woodridge Rd Mountain Brook AL 35243 Office: 528 N 20th St Birmingham AL 35201

MONTGOMERY, ROYCE LEE, educator; b. Hartsville, Tenn., Nov. 8, 1933; s. Erby Lee and Jimmie (Belcher) M.; A.B., U. Va., 1955; M.S., W.Va. U., 1960, Ph.D., 1963; m. Jane Hansford, Oct. 3, 1966; children—Royce Todd, Scott Hansford. Asso. prof. anatomy W.Va. U., 1964-65; with U. N.C., 1965—. Served to lt. AUS, 1955-57. Home; 11 Shadylawn Ct Chapel Hill NC 27514 Office: Dept Anatomy U NC Chapel Hill NC 27514

MONTGOMERY, WILDER PERCIVAL, physician; b. Washington, Aug. 10, 1910; s. Wilder Percival and Ethel Mineola (Pearson) M.; A.B., Dartmouth, 1931; M.D., U. Chgo., 1935; postgrad. U. Pa., 1936; m. Doris Mae Auter, July 4, 1942; children—Stephen Wilder, Gordon James. Intern Youngstown Hosp. Assn., resident Henry Phipps Inst. U. Pa.; practice medicine specializing in internal medicine, Washington, 1936—; mem. staff Freedmen's Hosp., Washington, Washington Hosp. Center, Rogers Meml. Hosp., Washington; asst. surgeon res. USPHS, 1946-41; attending physician Washington Chest Clinics, 1936-58; asst. clin. prof. medicine Med. Coll. Howard U., Washington, 1949-73. Mem. Washington Bd. Police and Fire Surgeons, 1961-69; cons. appeals council Social Security Adminstrn., 1968— . Past bd. dirs. Washington Tb Assn., Diplomate Am. Bd. Internal Medicine. Fellow A.C.P.; mem. D.C. Med. Soc., Medico-Chirurgical Soc., D.C., D.C., Am. thoracic socs., D.C. Heart Assn., Phi Beta Kappa, Alpha Omega Alpha. Home: 1728 Shepherd St NW Washington DC 20011 Office: 2570 Sherman Av NW Washington DC 20001

MONTGOMERY, ZENO HART, accountant; b. Kingstree, S.C., June 1, 1935; s. Samuel John and Meta (Bookhardt) M.; B.S., U. S.C., 1957; m. Helen Runita Milling, Apr. 5, 1958; children—Michael Hart, Pamela Elizabeth. Sr. accountant McKnight, Frampton & McKnight, C.P.A.'s, 1957-63; comptroller So. Plastics Co., 1963-65; partner Kight, Beale & Montgomery, C.P.A.'s, Columbia, S.C., 1965-70, Finch, Kight & Jackson, C.P.A.'s, 1970-71; pvt. practice Z.H. Montgomery, C.P.A., 1972-73; partner Montgomery, Wallace & Co., C.P.A.'s, 1973—. C.P.A., S.C. Mem. Am. Inst. C.P.A.'s, S.C. Assn. C.P.A.'s (chpt. pres. 1969-71). Presbyn. (ruling elder 1972—, trustee 1968—, ch. extension com. 1972—). Clubs: Richland Sertoma (treas. 1973—), Congaree Toastmasters (pres. 1965). Home: 158 Dorset Dr Columbia SC 29210 Office: 1916 Assembly St Columbia SC 29201

MONTIEGEL, BARTLIN, civil engr.; b. Wheeling, W.Va., Feb. 12, 1924; s. Bartlin and Ethel Charlotte (Schnell) M.; student Columbia, 1942-45; B.Sc., Brown U., 1946; m. Margaret H. Cupp, Feb. 10, 1949; children—Susan, Bartlin, Kevin. Power engr., mgr. Am. Electric Power Co., W.Va. and Ohio, 1949-68; desalting water and power engr., mgr. V.I. Water and Power Authority, St. Thomas, 1968—. Served with USNR, 1945; PTO. Registered profl. engr., Ohio, W.Va., V.I. Mason (32 deg.), Moose, Lion, Rotarian. Address: PO Box 1492 St Thomas VI 00801

MONTIN, JOHN ERNEST, refrigerating appliances co. exec.; b. Alexandria, Va., Aug. 3, 1918; s. Alfred Constance and Mary Marie (Ceppi) M.; B.S., Okla. A. and M. Coll., 1947; m. Lillian Stout, June 23, 1945; children—John, Jean, Robert, With Frigidaire Sales Corp., Oklahoma City, 1948-49; v.p. W.A. Landers Co., Oklahoma City; v.p. Mid Continent Constructors. Scoutmaster, Boy Scouts Am., 1956-62. Served with AUS, 1941-45; PTO. Decorated Legion of Merit. Registered profl engr., Okla. Mem. Am. Soc. Heating, Refrigerating and Air Conditioning Engrs., Nat. Soc. Profl. Engrs., C. of C., Okla. State U. Alumni Assn. Methodist (trustee). Mason (Shriner, Jester), Kiwanian. Club: Oklahoma City Golf and Country. Home: 1400 Canterbury Pl Oklahoma City OK 73116 Office: 100 NE 25th St Oklahoma City OK 73105

MOODY, ADRIAN BRADLEY, assn. exec.; b. Munfordville, Ky., Apr. 28, 1935; s. Allen Hunter and Ethel (Sturgil) M.; B.S., Ky. Wesleyan Coll., 1957; postgrad. Springfield Coll., 1963; m. Frances Dillehay, June 1, 1957; children—Deborah, David, Stephanie. With YMCA, 1956—, asso. gen. sec., Augusta, Ga., 1959-64, gen. sec., Moultrie, Ga., 1964-69, exec. dir., Bristol, Tenn., 1969—. Exec. dir. United Funds of Colquitt County (Ga.), 1964-66; chmn. Greater Bristol Area Preaching Mission, 1972-73. Bd. dirs. Tenn. Partner to Americas. Recipient Outstanding Citizen's award for pub. service Pilot Club, Moultrie, Ga., 1968. Mem. Am. Camping Assn., Nat. Assn. Profl. Dirs., Tenn. Assn. Profl. Dirs. Baptist (deacon). Rotarian (pres. Bristol 1973-74), Elk (mem. com. selection youth leadership awards 1964—). Club: Industrial Management. Home: 205 Earlway Rd Bristol TN 37620 Office: 400 Edgemont Av Bristol TN 37620

MOODY, JAMES SHELTON, circuit judge; b. Plant City, Fla., Dec. 29, 1914; s. Thomas Edwin and Anna (Herron) M.; student Washington and Lee U., 1932-33; B.S. in Bus. Adminstrn. with honors, LL.B. with honors U. Fla., 1939; m. Irma Cone, Nov. 29, 1939; children—Carole Ann, James Shelton, William C. Admitted to Fla. bar, 1939; practice law Plant City, 1939-57; mem. Fla. Ho. of Reps., 1948-57; asst. atty. Hillsboro County, Fla., 1941-57; circuit judge, Tampa, Fla., 1957—, presiding judge 13th Jud. Circuit, 1963-65. Dir. 1st Fed. Savs. & Loan Assn., Plant City, Hillsboro Bank Plant City. Bd. dirs. East Hillsborough County Fair; chmn. Circuit Judges Conf. Fla., 1968-70; vice chmn. Jud. Qualifications Commn. State Fla. Served with CIC, AUS, USAAF, 1943-46; ETO. Named Most Valuable Legislator, Allen Morris Poll, Most Valuable mem. of legislature St. Petersburg Times Poll, 1957. Mem. Am. (dir.), Tampa bar assns., Fla. Bar, Am. Legion, Pi Kappa Alpha, Phi Kappa Phi, Phi Delta Phi. Democrat. Presbyn. (elder). Elk. Club: Plant City Golf and Country (dir.). Home: 803 N Collins St Plant City FL 33566 Office: Ct House Tampa FL 33602

MOODY, MAX DALE, microbiologist; b. Onaga, Kan., Sept. 29, 1924; s. Harry F. and Cora (Deveny) M.; A.B., U. Kan., 1948, M.A., 1949, Ph.D., 1955; m. Mildred B. Brooks, Apr. 30, 1950; children—Steven, Janet, Marcia. Commd. in USPHS, 1954, advanced through grades to scientist dir., 1971; chief streptococcus unit Center for Disease Control, Atlanta, 1966-70, chief reagents evaluation unit, 1970-71; ret., 1971; tech. dir. reagents div Burroughs Wellcome Co., Research Triangle Park, N.C., 1971—. Served with USNR, 1943-46. Co-recipient Kimble Methodology Research award, 1967. Mem. expert com. bacterial disease WHO, 1966—. Diplomate Am. Bd. Med. Microbiology. Fellow Am. Acad. Med. Microbiology (sec. internat. subcom. streptococci and pneumococci 1960—). Home: 115 Dunedin Ct Cary NC 27511 Office: 3030 Cornwallis Rd Research Triangle Park NC 27709

MOODY, WILLIS ELVIS, JR., educator; b. Raleigh, N.C., Mar. 30, 1924; s. Willis Elvis and Inez Marie (McDade) M.; B.S. in Ceramic Engring., N.C. State U. at Raleigh, 1948, M.S., 1949, Ph.D., 1956; postgrad. in nuclear metallurgy Ia. State U., 1957; m. Mary Susan McAfee, Mar. 22, 1947 (div. June 1967); children—Susan E., Michael T., Peggy A., Willis Elvis III, William S. Ceramic engr. Spark Plug div. Electric Auto Lite Co., Fostoria, O., 1949-50; ceramic engr. Lab. Equipment Corp., St. Joseph, Mich., 1950-51; instr. ceramic engring. and metallurgy N.C. State U. at Raleigh, 1951-56; faculty Ga. Inst. Tech., Atlanta, 1956—, prof. ceramic engring., 1960—. Research participant Oak Ridge Nat. Lab., summers 1954, 55; cons. to clay and ceramic industries, 1951—. Served with AAC, 1943-46; ETO. Decorated Air medal with two oak leaf clusters. Registered profl. engr., Ga. Fellow Orton Ceramics Found., mem. Am. Ceramic Soc. (trustee 1965-68, dir. Southeastern sect. 1962), Ceramic Ednl. Council (pres. 1963), Am. Soc. Engring. Edn. (chmn. materials div. 1971), Am. Phys. Soc., A.A.A.S., Assn. for Applied Solar Energy, Nat. Inst. Ceramic Engrs., Clay Minerals Soc. (councillor 1969-71), Keramos, Sigma Xi, Sigma Pi Sigma, Tau Beta Pi. Contbr. articles to tech. jours. Patentee in field. Home: 1101 Collier Rd Atlanta GA 30318 Office: School of Ceramic Engineering Georgia Institute of Technology Atlanta Ga 30332

MOOK, CONRAD PAYNE, meteorologist, ret. govt. ofcl.; b. Titusville, Pa., May 2, 1914; s. Raymond L. and Ella (Payne) M.; A.B., Coll. of Wooster, 1939; M.S., N.Y. U., 1943; m. Barbara Heer Held, Sept. 6, 1941; children—Patricia Ann (Mrs. Thomas J. Harris), Mary Ann (Mrs. William Douglas Barnum). Instr., N.Y. U., 1941-43; meteorologist U.S. Weather Bur., Washington, 1943-57; geophysicist Harry Diamond Labs., Washington, 1957-61; hurricane forecaster U.S. Weather Bur., Washington, 1961-62; program mgr., space vehicle thermal control and vacuum tech. NASA Hdqrs., Washington, 1962-70; ret. Mem. Am. Meteorol. Soc., Am. Geophys. Union, Am. Inst. Aeros. and Astronautics. Home: 5222 26th Rd N Arlington VA 22207

MOON, JOHN HENRY, banker; b. Van Buren, Ark., Aug. 19, 1937; s. B.R. and Alma (Witte) M.; A.A., Delmar Coll., Corpus Christi, 1956; B.B.A., Tex. A. and I. Coll., 1958; m. Agnes Rose Dickens, Aug. 16, 1958; children—John Henry, Randall Allen. Sr. accountant Tex. Eastern Transp. Co. and subsidiaries, 1958-63; exec. v.p., dir. Houston Research Inst., 1963-68; sr. v.p., asst. to chmn. bd., dir. Main Bank, 1968; vice chmn. bd., dir. N.E. Bank, 1969; chief exec. officer, chmn. bd., dir. Pasadena (Tex.) Nat. Bank, 1970—; dir. Rosenberg Bank & Trust Co., San Jacinto Ins. Co., Houston. Bd. dirs. Pasadena Heart Assn., Salvation Army, Tex. Assn. for Prevention Blindness. Named Outstanding Young Man of Year, Pasadena Jr. C. of C., 1973, Outstanding Young Man of Am., 1973. Mem. Pasadena C. of C. (dir.), Am. Inst. C.P.A.'s, Tex. Soc. C.P.A.'s, Tex. Bankers Assn. Rotarian. Home: 3901 Peru Circle Pasadena TX 77504 Office: PO Box 992 Pasadena TX 77501

MOON, JOSEPH BENJAMIN, physician; b. Chattanooga, Nov. 10, 1936; s. Joseph Worley and Charlotte (Fry) M.; B.S., Lincoln Meml. U., 1957; M.D., U. Tenn., 1961; m. Julia Ann Elkins, June 21, 1958; children—Alexandria Stephanie, Cynthia Lea. Intern U. Tenn. Hosp., Knoxville, 1961-62, resident, 1964-66; pvt. practice family medicine, Knoxville, 1966—; mem. staff Ft. Sanders, U. Tenn., East Tenn. Children's hosps. (all Knoxville); instr. family practice U. Tenn. Hosp. at Knoxville, 1966—. Bd. mgrs. Westside YMCA, 1968—. Served to capt. USAF, 1962-64. Recipient Mead Johnston Family Practice award, 1966. Mem. Knox County, Tenn. med. assns., A.M.A., Knox County Family Practice, Tenn., Am. acads. family practice, Phi Rho Sigma. Presbyn. (deacon). Home: 4802 Tomache Dr Knoxville TN 37919 Office: 6209 Kingston Pike Knoxville TN 37919

MOON, JOSEPH KAY, physician; b. Chariton, Ia., July 28, 1934; s. Harold Leslie and Margaret Jane (James) M.; student Simpson Coll., 1952-53, U. Ia., 1953-55, U. Houston, 1957-58; B.S., Drake U., 1959, postgrad., 1959-63; M.D., U. Tex. at Galveston, 1967; m. Marybeth Blasdel, Apr. 2, 1958; children—Shari Kathleen, Tari Ann, Jodi Kay, Jacki Jo (dec.), Joseph K. Tchr. sci. and math. Irving (Tex.) Ind. Sch. Dist., 1959-60, Galveston (Tex.) Ind. Sch. Dist., 1961-63; intern Meml. Baptist Hosp., Houston, 1967-68; practice medicine specializing in gen. practice and surgery, Tomball, Tex., 1968-70, Houston, 1970—; mem. staff Meml. Baptist, Parkway, N.W. Med. Center hosps.; chief staff Pinewood Meml. Hosp., Houston, 1970-71; health officer, Tomball, Tex., 1968—. Organizer, dir. Montgomery County Nat. Bank, Spring, Tex. Mem. Tex. Polit. Action Com., 1967—. Am. Polit. Action Com., 1967—. Served with M.C., AUS, 1955-57. Mem. Am. Profl. Practice Assn., A.M.A., Tex. Med. Assn., Harris County Med. Soc., Am. Assn. Family Practice, Assn. Am. Physicians and Surgeons, Lambda Chi Alpha, Theta Kappa Psi. Methodist. Mason. Home: 711 Barbara St Tomball TX 77375 Office: Northwest Medical Center 710 FM-1960W at 803 Judiwood Houston TX 77090

MOON, RALPH MARKS, JR., physicist; b. Bombay, India, Oct. 11, 1929; s. Ralph Marks and Lorene Eleanor (Jeffery) M.; B.A., U. Kan., 1950, M.A., 1952; Ph.D., Mass. Inst. Tech., 1963; m. Barbara Katherine Longfellow, Dec. 27, 1950; children—Katherine B., Laura J., Mary Ann, David L. Physicist, U.S. Naval Ordnance Test Sta., China Lake, Cal., 1952-54; physicist Lincoln Lab., Lexington, Mass., 1958-63, Oak Ridge Nat. Lab., 1963—. Pres., Friends of Oak Ridge Pub. Library, 1972-73; v.p. Friends of Responsible Edn., 1970-72. Served to lt. (j.g.) USNR, 1954-59. Fellow Am. Phys. Soc.; mem. Phi Beta Kappa, Sigma Xi, Beta Theta Pi. Unitarian. Home: 865 W Outer Dr Oak Ridge TN 37830 Office: Solid State Div Oak Ridge Nat Lab Oak Ridge TN 37830

MOON, WILLIAM HAROLD, educator; b. Columbus, Ga., Oct. 4, 1931; s. John L. and Elizabeth (Lavender) M.; B.S., Auburn U., 1956; Ph.D., Fla. State U., 1962; m. Kay Thiel, Sept. 14, 1957; children—Alison, Brian Harold. Clin. psychology intern U. Tenn. Med. Sch. Memphis, 1961-62; clin. psychologist Lee County Mental Health Center, Opelika, Ala., 1962-64; mem. faculty Auburn (Ala.) U., 1964-71, asso. prof. psychology, 1967-71; prof., chmn. dept. psychology Augusta (Ga.) Coll., 1972-73, asso. acad. dean, dir. grad. studies, 1973—. Cons. psychologist E. Ala. Comprehensive Mental Health Center, Opelika, 1964-71, Ala. VA Hosp., Tuskegee, 1965-69, Augusta, 1972—. Mem. Ala. Bd. Examiners Psychology, 1968-71, vice chmn., 1969-71. Pres., Auburn Bi-racial Self Study Group, 1965, Augusta-Richmond County Council Alcohol and Drug Abuse, 1973-74. Served with AUS, 1952-54. Mem. Am., Southeastern, Ga., Ala. (editor newsletter 1964-67, sec.-treas. 1967-69, pres. 1970-71) psychol. assns., Am. Assn. U. Profs. (chpt. pres. 1968-69), Gerontological Soc., Phi Kappa Phi, Psi Chi. Home: 3058 Westwood Ct Augusta GA 30904

MOONEY, JOSEPH FRANCIS, JR., flood control engr.; b. Boston, Feb. 6, 1929; s. Joseph Franics and Margaret Gertrude (Clements) M.; student Memphis State Coll., 1950-51; B.S., Miss. State U., 1954; m. Bobbie Katheryn Spencer, May 23, 1948; children—Marilyn Lee, Joseph Spencer. Asst. engr. St. Francis Levee Bd., West Memphis, Ark., 1954-63; chief engr. Yazoo-Miss. Delta Levee Bd., Clarksdale, Miss., 1964—. Mem. Sunflower River Devel. Commn., 1970—, Gov.'s Com. on Long Range Water Planning, 1969; dist. dir. Delta Area council Boy Scouts Am., 1970, 71. Served with USNR, 1946-48, with USAF, 1951-52. Registered profl. engr., Ark., Miss. Mem. Miss. Engring. Soc. (chpt. pres. 1970), Lower Mississippi Valley Flood Control Assn. (chmn. engring. com. 1974), Water Resources Congress (chmn. flood control and flood plain mgmt. 1974). Baptist. Rotarian. Home: 506 Catalpa St Clarksdale MS 38614 Office: PO Box 610 Clarksdale MS 38614

MOONEY, PRENTISS, govt. ofcl.; b. McLoud, Okla., July 18, 1905; s. Jesse and Ella (Ridley) M.; student Okla. Bapt. U., 1923-25, U. Okla., 1925-28; m. Betty J. Robinson, Feb. 25, 1944; children—Gretchen F., Prentiss R. Newspaper reporter, editor, radio broadcaster, St. Joseph, Mo., 1936-42; dir. Mo. Div. Resources and Devel., Jefferson City, 1946-56; dir. Ohio Div. Econ. Devel. and Publicity, Columbus, 1956-59; dir. pub. relations Am. Motor Hotel Assn., Kansas City, Mo., 1959-63, exec. v.p., 1963-65; indsl. devel. specialist U.S. Bur. Indian Affairs, Washington, 1966-69, chief div. indsl. and tourism devel., 1969—. Recipient Young Man of Yr. award St. Joseph Jr. C. of C., 1941. Mem. Nat. Assn. Travel Orgns. (pres. 1955), Soc. Am. Travel Writers, Am. Indsl. Devel. Council, Discover Am. Travel Orgn. (dir.), Outdoor Writers Am., Sigma Chi. Presbyn. Mason, Lion. Clubs: Nat. Aviation (Washington); International Town and Country (Fairfax, Va.). Home: 3627 1st Rd S Arlington VA 22204 Office: US Bur Indian Affairs 1951 Constitution Av NW Washington DC 20242

MOOR, RALPH CARL, state ofcl.; b. Waycross, Ga., Dec. 18, 1912; s. Arthur Fisk and Eva (Frey) M.; B.S., Ga. State U., 1937; M.S.A., George Washington U., 1947; m. Ruth Sanders, July 10, 1937 (div. Oct. 1957); children—Ralph Carl, Larry Sanders; m. 2d, Nadine Penney, June 11, 1965. Dean, prof. econs. S.Ga. Coll., Douglas, 1948-51; educationist U.S. Office Edn., 1951-52; dep. dir. State Merit System Personnel Adminstrn., Atlanta, 1953-73, merit system dir., 1973—. Trustee, sec. Christian Ch. Counseling, Inc., Atlanta, 1968—; trustee Ga. State U. Found., 1969—. Served from 2d lt. to col. AUS; brig. gen. N.G. ret. Mem. Ga. State U. Alumni Assn. (dir. 1969—), Internat. Personnel Mgmt. Assn. (sec.-treas. So. region 1969-70, 2d vice chmn. 1970-71, 1st vice chmn. 1971-72, chmn. 1972-73). Home: 3649 Peachtree Rd NE Atlanta GA 30319 Office: 244 Washington St SW Atlanta GA 30334

MOORE, ALEXANDER BISHOP, educator; b. Knoxville, Tenn., Jan. 31, 1935; s. Thomas Heyward and Nancy Ethel (Bishop) M.; B.S. in Civil Engring., U. Tenn., 1961, M.S. in Engring., 1966; m. Carole June Quillen, June 9, 1965; children—Thomas, Stephen, Cynthia, Douglas; stepchildren—Shawn Fisher, Kelly Fisher. Research instr. Tenn. Hwy. Research Program, U. Tenn., Knoxville, 1961-67, asst. prof., also asst. dir. hwy. research program, 1967-70, acting dir. hwy. research program, also asst. prof. dept. civil engring. U. Tenn., 1970-71, asso. prof. civil engring., 1971—. Cons. to lawyers, ins. cos. and bus. firms in skid resistance and accident reconstrn.; also expert court witness; mem. Hwy. Research Bd. com. on surface properties and vehicle interaction Nat. Acad. Sci., 1963—. Served as communications specialist AUS, 1955-57. Mem. Am. Soc. Testing and Materials (mem. coms. on road and paving materials and skid resistance, chmn. subcom. standard surfaces 1966-70), Am. Soc. C.E., Sigma Xi, Phi Kappa Phi, Tau Beta Pi, Chi Epsilon. Contbr. articles on hwy. materials and pavement performance to tech. jours. Home: 9325 Carlton Circle Concord TN 37720 Office: Berry Hall University of Tennessee Knoxville TN 37916

MOORE, ALFRED, lawyer, banker; b. Hattiesburg, Miss., May 28, 1912; s. Henderson Alfred and Lucy (Currie) M.; student U. So. Miss., 1931-32; B.A., U. Miss., 1934, LL.B., 1936; m. Mary Cleo Barnes, June 16, 1946; children—Betty Barnes, Henderson Alfred III, Lucy Currie. Admitted to Miss. bar, 1936; since practiced in Hattiesburg; pros. atty. Hattiesburg, 1938-41, 47-49; judge Hattiesburg, 1941-42, city atty., 1949-53; mem. firm Moore, Jones & Moore, 1961—; exec. v.p., dir. First Fed. Savs. & Loan Assn., Hattiesburg, 1961-70, pres., 1970—; dir. Fed. Home Loan Bank of Little Rock. Mem. Gov.'s staff, 1964, 72; adv. com. personnel Miss. Employment Security Commn., 1962—. Bd. dirs. U. So. Miss. Found.; past pres. Miss. Savs. & Loan League; past trustee S. Miss. Presbytery. Served to lt. USNR, 1942-46. Mem. Am., South Central bar assns., Miss. State Bar (past pres.), Miss. Bar Found., Miss. Folklore Soc., Miss. Econ. Council, Hattiesburg Civic Assn. (past pres.), C. of C. (past pres.), Alumni Assn. U. So. Miss., Alumni Assn. U. Miss., Newcomen Soc., Soc. War of 1812, Phi Alpha Delta, Pi Kappa Alpha. Presbyn. (elder). Elk. Club: Hattiesburg Country. Home: 2312 Carriage Rd Hattiesburg MS 39401 Office: 130 W Front St Hattiesburg MS 39401

MOORE, ALVIN EDWARD, patent lawyer; b. Auburn, La., Sept. 3, 1904; s. William Absalom and Mahala (Scoggins) M.; student U.S. Naval Acad., 1921-24, George Washington U. Law Sch., 1925, John Marshall Law Sch., Atlanta, 1945; B.S. in History, Am. U., 1949, M.A. in History, 1958; postgrad. U. Fla., 1955-56, La. State U., 1958-61, Tulane U., 1961-62; m. Laura Belle Van Zandt, May 26, 1925. Seaman, U.S. Shipping Bd., 1924; nautical scientist U.S. Hydrographic Office, 1924; patrol insp. U.S. Border Patrol, 1926-27, immigration insp. U.S. Immigration Service, 1927-28; Am. vice consul, Guaymas, Mex., 1928-29; examiner U.S. Patent Office, 1924-25, 30-42, 45-49, 56-58; intelligence officer CIA, 1949-50, 53-56; admitted to Ga. bar, 1945, U.S. Ct. Customs and Patent Appeals bar, 1947; patent atty. Army Ordnance Missile Command, 1958-60; practice as patent atty., Waveland, Miss., 1960—. Co-founder Friends U.S. of Latin Am., 1950. Served with USN, 1921-24; from lt. to lt. comdr. USNR, 1942-46, comdr., 1950-53. Mem. Fed. Bar Assn., U.S. Naval Acad. Alumni Assn., Ret. Officers Assn. Club: Nat. Travel. Author: The World Republic, 1942; History of Hardy County, 1963. Contbr. articles, short stories, poems to various mags. Patentee in various fields. Address: 916 Beach Blvd Waveland MS 39576

MOORE, BERNICE MILBURN (MRS. HARRY E. MOORE), mental health cons., author; b. San Antonio, June 17, 1904; d. Ted Hatton and Carrie (Coley) Milburn; B.J., U. Tex., 1924, M.A., 1932; Ph.D., U. N.C., 1937; m. Harry Estil Moore, Nov. 27, 1924 (dec. July 1966). Reporter, Austin Am. and Statesman, 1924-26; dir. Child Welfare Survey Tex., Tex. Relief Commn., 1933-34; asst., Inst. Research Social Sci., U. N.C., 1934-37; asst. dir. Austin Regional Office, Profl. Projects, Work Projects Adminstrn. Tex., 1938-41; cons., Hogg Found. Mental Hygiene (name now Hogg Found. Mental Health), U. Tex., 1941-55, asst. to pres. community programs, 1955-72, exec. asso., 1972—, asso. dir. philanthropy in S.W., 1964-71; cons. home and family edn., counseling Tex. Edn. Agy., 1941-64, state adv. com. innovation and assessment edn., 1968—; cons. inter-disciplinary program Nat. Inst. Child Health and Human Devel., NIH, 1963-67. Task force on youth Joint Commn. Mental Health of Children; coordinator Tex. Coop. Youth Study; dir. seminars for chaplains in counseling human factors USAF, sponsored by Hogg Found. Mental Health, 1956-66; spl. cons. research utilization br. Nat. Inst. Mental Health, 1963-64; adv. bd. children Children's Bur., U.S. Office Health, Edn., and Welfare, 1963-66, ad hoc com. for youth services, 1968-69. Chmn. adv. com. on med. and dental edn., coordinating bd. Tex. Coll. and U. System, 1973—. Recipient Nat. Headliner award Theta Sigma Phi, 1956; Spl. Service award Tex. Soc. Mental Health, also Ft. Worth-Tarrant County Soc. Mental Health; spl. merit award Am. Vocational Assn., 1963; Bernice Milburn Moore Scholarship established U. Tex. at Austin, 1970. Fellow Am. Sociol. Assn., Am. Assn. Marriage and Family Counselors (hon.); mem. Nat. Assn. Mental Health, Am. Home Econs. Assn., Southwestern Social Sci. Assn., Tex. Assn. Mental Health, Tex. Council Mental Health (past pres.), Tex. Council Mental Health Research, Future Homemakers Am. (nat. hon. mem.), Alpha Kappa Delta, Theta Sigma Phi, Delta Kappa Gamma, Phi Upsilon Omicron. Democrat. Mem. Disciples of Christ Ch. Author: (with Harry Estill Moore) Through Your Own Front Door, 1945; (with Dorothy M. Leahy) You and Your Family, 1948, rev. 1954; (with Robert L. Sutherland) Family, Community and Mental Health, 1950: Juvenile Delinquency, Research, Theory, Comment, 1959; (with W. H. Holtzman) Tomorrow's Parents, 1965; (with Robert L. Sutherland) Our Youngest Children, 1971; pamphlets and study guides on mental health and the family. Contbr. to edn. yearbooks. profl. jours. Home: 1215 W 22 1/2 St Austin TX 78705 Office: Hogg Found Mental Health Will C Hogg Bldg U Tex Austin TX 78712

MOORE, BESSIE B., educator, civic leader; B.A., State Coll. Ark.; M.A., U. Conn.; LL.D., U. Ark., 1958. Organizer county library, Pine Bluff, Ark., 1926; now dir. econ. and environmental edn. Ark. Dept. Edn.; exec. dir. State Council Econ. Edn. Dir. 1st Nat. Bank, Little Rock. Mem. adv. com. library services act U.S. Commr. Edn., 1954-59; mem. Ark. Library Commn., 1941—, chmn., 1949—; mem. U.S. com. Am. Library in Paris, 1970-72; mem. Nat. Library Adv. Commn., 1967-70; vice chmn. Nat. Commn. on Libraries and Information Services, 1970—; mem. Nat. Book Com.; mem. Gov.'s Adv. Com. on Status of Women, 1968-70, Gov.'s Adv. Com. on Aging, 1968—; mem. adv. com. women in services Dept. Def. Mem. Ark. Democratic Com., 1932-36; del. Dem. Nat. Conv., 1936. Mem. Ark. Congress Parents and Tchrs. (life), A.L.A. (chmn. jury citation trustees 1969-70, chmn. trustees state libraries 1970), Am. Library Trustees Assn. (pres. 1958-60), Am. Assn. U. Women, Delta Kappa Gamma. Office: Ark Dept Edn Little Rock AR 72201

MOORE, CARL LEE, physician; b. Dayton, Ky., Dec. 16, 1935; s. Louis Edward and Marie Anna (Knapp) M.; B.A., Hanover Coll., 1958; M.D., U. Cin., 1962; m. Mureen Foster, July 25, 1959; children—Judith Marie, Scot Edward, Steven Wayne. Intern, Mound Park Hosp., St. Petersburg, Fla., 1962-63, resident, 1963-64; practice medicine, St. Petersburg, 1964—. Chmn., Suncoast Tarpon Roundup, 1968-72. Mem. A.M.A., Fla., Pinellas County med. socs., Am., Fla. (pres. 1974) diabetes assns. Mason. Home: 7127 2nd Av S Saint Petersburg FL 33707 Office: 1609 Pasadena Av S Saint Petersburg FL 33707

MOORE, CHARLES GRAY, accountant; b. Franklin, Ky., July 7, 1916; s. Charles Thomas and Stella (Gray) M.; B.S., U. Ky., 1939; m. June Brown, June 21, 1953; children—Marcia Brown, Alan Gray. Auditor Dept. Revenue, Commonwealth of Ky., Frankfort, 1939-41; mem. exec. tng. program Sears, Roebuck & Co., Louisville and Chgo., 1946-48; auditor, mgr., partner Albert B. Maloney & Co., 1948-56; mgr. Ernst & Ernst, Murfreesboro, Tenn., 1956-63, Nashville, 1963-73; sec.-treas. 3d Nat. Corp., 1973—. Tchr. accounting Middle Tenn. State U., Murfreesboro, 1955. Treas. Murfreesboro Community Chest, 1955, Hillsboro High Men's Club, 1972-73. Bd. dirs. Goodwill Industries Nashville, 1968-69, treas., 1969, pres. elect, 1972, chmn. bd., 1973—. Served to lt. col. USAAF, 1941-46. C.P.A., Tenn. Mem. McMinnville Jr. C. of C. (sec. 1951), Nashville C. of C., Nat. Assn. Accountants (dir. Nashville chpt. 1969), Tenn. Soc. C.P.A.'s (chpt. treas. 1954-55, state treas. 1969-71, state council mem. 1972-74), Am. Accounting Assn., Nat. Soc. Accountants for Co-ops., U. Ky. Alumni Assn., Hon. Order Ky. Cols., Am. Inst. C.P.A.'s, Beta Gamma Sigma. Presbyn. (elder 1968-69). Rotarian (sec. Murfreesboro 1960-62; sec. Donelson club 1968-69, pres. 1970-71). Clubs: McMinnville Exchange (sec. 1953-54); Murfreesboro Stone River Country (sec. 1960-62, dir. 1960-62); Frankfort Wisemen's; Richland Country, Nashville City (Nashville); Stewart Air Force Base Officers (Smyrna, Tenn.). Home: 1605 Tynewood Dr Nashville TN 37215 Office: 3d Nat Bank Bldg Nashville TN 37244

MOORE, DANA CLIFTON, JR., lawyer; b. Shaw, Miss., Aug. 4, 1931; s. Dana Clifton and Malvina Yerger (Walker) M.; LL.B., U. Miss., 1957; m. Julia Gibert, Apr. 19, 1958; 1 dau., Julia Kilby. Admitted to Miss. bar, 1957, since practiced in Cleveland; mem. firm Cox & Moore, 1957—; mem. Miss. Ho. of Reps., 1964-71. Bolivar County youth counsellor, 1964—; chmn. Bolivar County Voters League, 1965-67; pres. Boliver County Cancer Soc., 1961-68. Past dir. Delta area council Boy Scouts Am.; pres. Episcopal Laymen Miss., 1972—; lay del. gen. conv. P.E. Ch., Louisville, 1973. Past dir. Miss. div. Am. Cancer Soc., bd. dirs. Cleveland Recreation Assn.; past dir. Bolivar County Conservation League. Mem. Am., Miss. Bolivar County (pres. 1969-70) bar assns., C. of C. (v.p. 1965, dir. 1962—), Phi Delta Theta, Phi Alpha Delta. Episcopalian (past sr. warden). Democrat. Rotarian (past dir., pres. 1968-69, treas.). Home: 208 S Leflore St Cleveland MS 38732 Office: 116 S Court St Cleveland MS 38732

MOORE, DARROW HAYWOOD, realtor; b. Wyatt, La., Aug. 31, 1907; s. Joshua Louis and Rose Demeris (Pierce) M.; B.S., La. State U., 1933; m. Ellen Bryan, Jan. 27, 1944; children—L'Mell (Mrs. Kimbal Robert Smith III), Ellen Victoria (Mrs. Gary Spurlock). Tchr., coach Doyline (La.) High Sch., 1933-34; investigation La. State Dept. Revenue, 1934-44; salesman Franklin Life Ins. Co., 1944-53; owner Haywood Moore, Realtor, Baton Rouge, 1952—; asst. register La. State Land Office, 1972—. Served with AUS, 1943-44. Mem. Nat. Assn. Real Estate Bds., Baton Rouge Bd. Realtors (pres. 1970). Methodist (bd. Stewards). Mason (Shriner), Lion (pres. 1957). Club: Sherwood Forest Country, Bocage Racquet, Camelot (Baton Rouge). Home: 2222 Government St Baton Rouge LA 70806 Office: 2202 Government St Baton Rouge LA 70806

MOORE, DAVE, assn. exec.; b. Pine Bluff, Ark., Jan. 28, 1920; s. William O. and Mary Lou (Wylie) M.; B.J., U. Mo., 1942; postgrad. Washington and Lee U., U. So. Cal., Northwestern U.; m. Martha Owen, Apr. 30, 1943; children—Marnee (Mrs. Pat Loftin), Becky, Davy, Mike. Asst. indsl. mgr. Little Rock C. of C., 1945-46; mgr. C. of C., Fordyce, Ark., 1946-47, Weslaco, Tex., 1947-49, Laredo, Tex., 1950-53, Borger, Tex., 1953-63; gen. mgr. Baytown (Tex.) C. of C., 1963—. Sec. adv. bd. Sterling Municipal Library, 1965-66, pres., 1966—. Served to capt. USAAF, 1942-45. Mem. Tex. C. of C. Mgrs. Assn. (past dir., past editor News), Sigma Alpha Epsilon. Methodist (lay speaker Tex. Conf.). Office: 2 W Texas Av Baytown TX 77520

MOORE, DAVID CLINTON, judge; b. Gladewater, Tex., June 7, 1922; s. Clinton Harvey and Alma (Wood) M.; B.S., North Tex. U., 1942; J.D., U. Tex., 1948; m. Billie Louise Newton, Oct. 12, 1942; children—David, James, Lynda. Admitted to Tex. bar, 1948. Fed. bar, 1950; asst. dist. atty. Gregg County, Longview, Tex., 1949-51, dist. atty., 1952-55; judge 124th Jud. Dist. Longview, 1955—. Dir. First State Bank, Gladewater, Gladwater Fed. Savs. & Loan. Active Boy Scouts Am., 1950—. Served as sgt. USAAF, 1942-46. Mem. Am., Tex. bar assns. Mason (32 deg.), Lion. Home: 308 E Commerce St Gladewater TX 75647 Office: Court House Longview TX 75601

MOORE, DON, JR., lawyer, county judge; b. Chattanooga, Nov. 27, 1928; s. Don M. and Frances (Wolfe) M.; student U. Chattanooga, 1948-49; J.D., U. Tenn., 1952; m. Sarah Mosley; children—Lisa Michele, Deidre Le Ayne. Admitted to Tenn. bar, 1953, Ga. bar, 1959; partner Crutchfield, Moore & Jenkins, attys. Partner Moore & Moore, contractors, 1966—; dir., gen. counsel Wright Systems Internat. Corp. Mem. Tenn. Ho. of Reps., 1956-58, 64-66, Tenn. Senate, 1966-68; chmn. fiscal rev. com. Tenn. Gen. Assembly, 1967-69; county judge, 1974—. Served as staff sgt. U.S. Army Res., 1950-51. Named Legislative Conservationist of Yr., 1968. Mem. Am., Chattanooga bar assns., Am. Legion, Bar Assn. Tenn., Tenn. Trial Lawyers Assn. Democrat. Methodist. Mason (Shriner), Elk. Clubs: Chattanooga Flyers, Moccasin Flying, Brainerd Saddle. Home: 1802 Skyline Dr Chattanooga TN 37421 Office: 509 Cherry St Chattanooga TN 37402

MOORE, EDWARD TOWSON, mfg. co. exec.; b. Wytheville, Va., Feb. 26, 1937; s. Robert Brent and Jane Courtney (Oewel) M.; B.S., Va. Poly. Inst., 1958; Ph.D., Duke, 1963; m. Linda Ernette Lunsford, June 27, 1965; children—Alan Towson, Jennifer Lynn. Pres., Wilmore Electronics Co., Inc., Durham, N.C., 1963—. Bd. dirs. Goodwill Industries Research Triangle Area, Inc., 1967-73. Served to 1st lt. AUS, 1958-59. Mem. I.E.E.E. Kiwanian. Registered profl. engr., N.C., Va. Patentee in electronic circuits. Contbr. profl. jours. Home: 5030 Green Oak Dr Durham NC 27705 Office: PO Box 2973 Durham NC 27705

MOORE, ELLEN BRYAN, state ofcl., bus. exec.; b. Baton Rouge, Apr. 13, 1912; d. Alex Dunn and Louise (Rhodes) Bryan; B.A., La. State U., 1933, M.A., 1950; grad. student Tulane U., 1935; m. Darrow Haywood Moore, Jan. 27, 1944; children—Margaret L'Mell, Ellen Victoria. Tchr. pub. schs., Baton Rouge, 1933-40; builder, personal property mgmt., 1935—; register state lands State of La., 1952—. Vice chmn. La. Office Bldg. Corp. Mem. State Recreation and Park Commn., 1952; bd. dirs. Nat. Park Conf., 1953-60, 69-72; mem. State Park and Recreation Com., 1960—; chmn. La. Gov.'s Commn. Status of Women; rep. Bur. Outdoor Recreation Council; gov.'s rep. Pub. Land Law Commn.; state rep. Nat. Civilian Def. Women's Adv. Council, Washington, 1955. Area rep., bd. dirs. United Democrats La.; bd. dirs. Operation Crossroad (So. div.) Nat. Democratic Com. 1956. Bd. dirs. United Givers Fund, La. Hist. Assn., Capitol Region Planning Commn.; zone chmn. March of Dimes, 1957; mem. budget com. Community Services Council; pres. East Baton Rouge Lioness orgn., 1950-51; bd. dirs. Girl Scouts U.S.A., 1954-55, Camp Fire Girls, 1957. Served to capt. AUS, 1941-45. Hon. mem. Pelican Girls State. Mem. Nat. Assn. Real Estate Bds. (publicity dir. women's council), Am. Legion (del. nat. conv. 1953-54), Nat., La. edn. assns., Am. Assn. U. Women, Amvets, Am. Right of Way Assn., Nat. Conf. State Parks (membership chmn.), La. Council Music and Performing Arts (sec.), Bus. and Profl. Womens Club, Delta Zeta, Phi Lambda Phi, Psi Chi, Alpha Delta Kappa. Clubs: Pilot (pres. Baton Rouge 1940-41). Home: 2222 Government St Baton Rouge LA 70806 Office: State Land and Natural Resources Bldg Baton Rouge LA 70804

MOORE, ERIC BAYLES, sch. headmaster; b. Mt. Vernon, N.Y., Jan. 1, 1935; s. Oscar Fitzland and Mary Adair (Childress) M.; grad. St. Mark's Sch., 1952; A.B., Yale, 1956; M.A. in Teaching (Ford Found. fellow), Harvard, 1964; M.S., Ind. U., 1968; m. Margaret Elizabeth Hunter, Nov. 13, 1957; children—Rebekah, Ruth Anne, Sarah. Researcher dept. biochemistry Dartmouth Med. Sch., 1959-63; tchr. sci. Hanover (N.H.) High Sch., 1964-66; chmn. sci. dept. Shipley Sch., Bryn Mawr, Pa., 1966-71; headmaster St. Luke's Sch., New Canaan, Conn., 1971-74; headmaster Charlotte (N.C.) Latin Sch., 1974—. Tenor soloist Phila. Mendelssohn Club, 1966-68, Haverford-Bryn Mawr Chorus, 1968, Phila. Chorale, 1970. Trustee New Canaan Nature Center. Served with AUS, 1957-59. Mem. Nat. Assn. Ind. Schs., New Eng. Assn. Chemistry Tchrs., Am. Chem. Soc. Contbr. articles to profl. jours. Home: 3165 Pendleton Av Charlotte NC 28210

MOORE, ERMAN MALCOLM, marketing exec.; b. Jasper, N.Y., Jan. 20, 1924; s. Leo K. and Inez (Schoonover) M.; B.S., Cornell U., 1952, M.S., 1956; m. Eleanor J. Gordon, Apr. 26, 1944; 1 son, Sheldon E. Marketing specialist Cornell U., Ithaca, N.Y., 1952-56; gen. mgr. Eastern Market Research Service, Ithaca, 1956-65; sr. market research analyst Pet Inc., St. Louis, 1965-66, group research mgr., 1966-69, marketing research mgr., 1969; dir. marketing research Swift Grocery Products Co., Chgo., 1969-72; pres. Creative Marketing Group Inc., 1972—. Served with AUS, 1944-46. Home: 5230 Ariel St Houston TX 77035 Office: 3336 Richmond Av Houston TX 77006

MOORE, FRANK HUGH, JR., dentist; b. Corpus Christi, Tex., June 10, 1940; s. Frank Hugh and Betty (Hedrick) M.; student U. Notre Dame, 1958-60; B.A., Tex. Christian U., 1963; postgrad. U. Tex., 1963-64; M.A., Southwestern Med. Sch. of U. Tex., 1966; D.D.S., Baylor U., 1969; m. Judy Ann Richter, Sept. 20, 1963; children—Frank Hugh III, Trevor Scott, Angie Catherine. Vice pres. Moores, Inc. and Moore's Saxet Center, Corpus Christi, 1965—; individual practice dentistry, Garland, Tex., 1971—. Served with USNR, 1969-71. Recipient Bernard Gottlieb Meml. award in oral pathology, 1969. Mem. Omicron Kappa Upsilon, Psi Omega, Sigma Chi. Republican. Roman Catholic. Home: 9824 Robin Hill Lane Dallas TX 75238 Office: 500 Eastgate Garland TX 75040

MOORE, GEORGE CARROLL, motel exec.; b. Van Buren, Ark., July 23, 1937; s. Nelson C. and Blanche (Hood) M.; student Ft. Smith Jr. Coll., 1959-61; m. Nola Diane Cress, June 14, 1963; children—Melinda Renee, George Kevin, Geoffrey Grant, Cindy Michelle. Desk clk. Holiday Inn, Ft. Smith, Ark., 1959, mgr., 1962-65; mgr. Holiday Inn, Colorado Springs, Colo., 1966-67; gen. mgr. Holiday Inn, Oklahoma City, 1967—. Adviser State Dept. Vocational and Tech. Edn., 1971; chmn. adv. bd. Hotel and Restaurant Sch., Okla. State U. Extension, 1971-72. Vice chmn. Oklahoma City Conv. and Tourism Commn., 1973—; treas. Meridian Improvement Assn. Served with USAF, 1955-59. Mem. Oklahoma City Hotel and Motel Assn. (pres.), Okla. Lodging Assn. (dir.), Career Devel. Inst. (pres.). Kiwanian (sec. 1974). Address: 801 S Meridian St Oklahoma City OK 73108

MOORE, GLENN EDWARD, chemist; b. Petersburg, Va., Jan. 23, 1930; s. George E. and Nell (Dance) M.; B.S., U. Richmond, 1961; m. Eloise Vick, Feb. 9, 1951 (dec. 1969); children—Glenn E., Thomas H., Cara E., m. 2d, Dorothy F. French, July 25, 1970; 1 stepdau., Pamela J. French. Chemist, Dan River Mills, Danville, Va., 1961-65; dir. survey div. Bur. Survey and Field Studies, Va. Water Control Bd., Richmond, 1965—. Active Boy Scouts Am. Served with USMCR, 1950-51. Mem. Am. Assn. Textile Chemists and Colorists, Water Pollution Control Fedn., Am. Chem. Soc., Va. Water Pollution Control Assn., Am. Legion. Mem. Christian Ch. Home: 302 Winston Av Colonial Heights VA 23334 Office: 2111 Hamilton Av Richmond VA 23230

MOORE, GLOVER, educator; b. Birmingham, Ala., Sept. 22, 1911; s. Glover and Maud (Mims) M.; B.A., Birmingham-So. Coll., 1932; M.A., Vanderbilt U., 1933, Ph.D., 1936. Teaching fellow Vanderbilt U., 1935-36; instr. history Miss. State U., 1936-38, asst. prof., 1938-46, asso. prof., 1946-53, prof., 1953—. Pres. Miss. Hist. Soc., 1970-71. Served with Adj. Gen.'s Dept., AUS, 1942-46. Mem. Am., So. hist. assns., Orgn. Am. Historians. Episcopalian. Author: The Missouri Controversy, 1819-1821, 1953; William Jemison Mims, Soldier and Squire, 1966. Home: 404 Myrtle St Starkville MS 39759 Office: Box 5326 Mississippi State MS 39762

MOORE, GORDON SIDNEY, accountant; b. Midlothian, Tex., Sept. 11, 1922; s. James Hayden and Eleanor (Rouse) M.; B.A., E.Tex. U., 1941; M.S., Tex. A. and M. U., 1943; m. Dorothy Geraldine Evans, Feb. 11, 1943; children—Robert E., Paul L. Instr., Tex. A. and M. U., 1942-43; revenue agt., regional analyst Internal Revenue Service, Dallas, 1946-55; partner Arthur Young & Co., Houston, 1955—. Served with AUS, 1943-46. Mem. Am. Inst. C.P.A.'s, Tex. Soc. C.P.A.'s, Houston Chpt. C.P.A.'s, Houston Bus. and Estate Planning Council. Clubs: Sugar Creek Country, Petroleum (Houston). Home: 3006 Bucknell Ct Sugarland TX 77478 Office: 4800 One Shell Plaza Houston TX 77002

MOORE, HARVEY DANIEL II, clergyman; b. Aurora, Ill., Oct. 29, 1942; s. Harvey Daniel and Ruth Mae (Chase) M.; B.A., Chapman Coll., 1964; B.D., Tex. Christian U., 1967, M.Th., 1967, D. Ministries, 1972; certificate alcoholism counseling Western N.M. U., 1965; children—Daniel Richard, David Irl. Ordained to ministry Christian Ch., 1967; pastor First Christian Ch., Rockwall, Tex., 1965-67, Westridge Christian Ch., Roswell, N.M., 1967-69, First Christian Ch., Wylie, Tex., 1969-74, First Christian Ch., Mineral Wells, Tex., 1974—. Prof. O.T., Eastern N.M. U., Roswell, 1968-69; tchr. Bibl. history Wylie (Tex.) High Sch., 1972-73. Mem. state bd. Christian Chs. N.M., 1967-69; pres. Bd. Hosp. Chaplains, Roswell, 1967-69. Pres. Citizens for Decent Lit., Roswell, 1968-69; counselor Suicide Prevention, Roswell, 1967-68; pres. Wylie Pub. Library Bd., 1972-74. Pres. bd. dirs. New Am. Coffee House, drug rehab., Roswell, 1968-69. Mem. Wylie Ministerial Assn. (pres. 1969-72), Adelphos, Alpha Phi Omega. Mason (32 deg.). Author: Christian Churches of New Mexico, 1966; Little Threads and Other Children's Sermons, 1974. Home: 316 NW 10th St Mineral Wells TX 76067 Office: 302 NW 6th St Mineral Wells TX 76067

MOORE, JAMES ALFRED, lawyer; b. Madisonville, Ky., Oct. 20, 1915; s. Virgil Y. and Ina (Price) M.; A.B., U. Ky., 1936; LL.B., Harvard, 1939; m. Dorothy Marie Kelly, Sept. 27, 1941 (div. Oct. 1968); children—Marjorie Y., James Kelly, Kathleen; m. 2d, Lucile Carpenter, June 29, 1970. Admitted to Pa. bar, 1940; with Pepper, Hamilton & Sonertz, Phila., 1939-72, partner, 1951-72; partner firm Martin, Moore, Thaler & Whifield, Washington, 1972—; pres. Camelback Ski Corp., 1962—, Eagle Land Co., 1967—, Kappa Lannock Ski Corp., 1972; dir. Selby, Bettersby & Co., Phila. Iron Works Co., Ski Roundtop, Inc. Bd. dirs. Phila. Soc. for Crippled Children and Adults. Served from ensign to lt. comdr. USNR, 1942-45. Mem. Am. Bar Assn., Am. Law Inst. Clubs: Marion Cricket (Hayerford, Pa.); Columbia Country (Chevy Chase, Md.). Home: PO Box 1241 Front Royal VA 22630 Office: 1701 Pennsylvania Av NW Washington DC 20006

MOORE, JAMES FRANCIS, educator, accountant; b. Paducah, Ky., July 16, 1925; s. Robert Allen and Robbie (Tatom) M.; M.B.A., Tulane U., 1948; B.S., Bowling Green Coll. Commerce, 1947; m. Sara Ann Swords, June 14, 1957; 1 son, John Craig. Reporter Park City Daily News, Bowling Green, Ky., 1942-45; instr. U. Fla., 1948-53, asst. prof. accounting, 1953-65; pvt. practice as pub. accountant, Gainesville, 1953—; partner Moore, Cobb & Co., C.P.A.'s. Mem. Fla. Bd. Accountancy, 1967-71, chmn., 1968-71. Mem. Fla. Legislature SCOPE Com., 1967-71; Fla. pres. Nat. Muscular Dystrophy Research Found., Inc., 1954-60. Mem. Am., Fla. insts. C.P.A.'s, Nat. Assn. State Bds. Accountancy, U.S. Jr. C. of C. (Gainesville treas. 1958, bd. dirs. 1958; Jaybird editor 1959), Beta Alpha Psi, Alpha Kappa Psi. Republican. Baptist. Contbr. articles to profl. jours. Editor: Fla. C.P.A. Jour., 1960-65. Home: 1418 NW 17th St Gainesville FL 32601

MOORE, JAMES LEWIS, newspaper pub.; b. Greenwood, S.C., Feb. 16, 1908; s. James Walker and Minnie (Thompson) M.; student Brevard Coll., 1934-35, U. Mo., 1935; m. Betty Propst, Sept. 7, 1929 (dec. May 1963); m. 2d, Eloise Tucker Carriker, May 13, 1965. Pub. The Toweler, Kannapolis, N.C., 1927, The China Grove (N.C.) Press, 1930; pres., treas. Kannapolis Pub. Co., now chmn. bd.; pub. gen. mgr. The Daily Independent, Kannapolis. Trustee Independent Student Aid Assn. Mem. Kannapolis C. of C. Methodist. Author: Cabarrus Re-Born. Home: 205 East E St Kannapolis NC 28081 Office: 119-125 N Main St Kannapolis NC 28081

MOORE, JAMES NORMAN, educator; b. Vilonia, Ark., June 10, 1931; s. James Lee and Mittie Elizabeth (Terrell) M.; student Ark. Poly. Coll., 1949-51; B.S., U. Ark., 1956, M.S., 1957; Ph.D., Rutgers U., 1961; m. Janita Faye Fitzgerald, Mar. 1, 1953; children—Pamela Moore, David Moore. Research asso. Rutgers U., New Brunswick, N.J., 1957-61; research horticulturist agr. research sta. U.S. Dept. Agr., Beltsville, Md., 1961-64; mem. faculty U. Ark., Fayetteville, 1964—, asso. prof. horticulture, 1964-69, prof., 1969—. Served with USAF, 1951-53. Mem. Am. Soc. Hort. Sci. (Woodbury award 1958, Gourley award 1963, Ware award 1972), Am. Genetic Assn., Am. Pomological Soc., Sigma Xi, Gamma Sigma Delta. Contbr. articles to profl. jours. Developer 2 blueberry varieties and 1 strawberry variety. Home: 1552 Stephens St Fayetteville AR 72701 Office: Dept Horticulture Univ Ark Fayetteville AR 72701

MOORE, JAMES RUSSELL, lawyer; b. Seven Mile Ford, Va., Feb. 23, 1918; s. George C. and Nita (Rector) M.; student Berea Coll., 1935-37; B.S., U. Va., 1939, LL.B., 1942; m. Lorraine Ratliff, June 28, 1973; children—Anita (Mrs. Martin Thiel), Joseph W. Admitted to Va. bar, 1942; partner firm Florance, Forance & Moore, Richmond, Va., 1950-53; chief asst. U.S. atty. Eastern Dist. Va., 1953-56; partner firm Moore & Browning, Abingdon, Va., 1972—. Mem. Va. Ho. of Dels., 1964-66; chmn. Richmond Republican Com., 1948-52; chmn. 9th Dist. Va. Rep. Com., 1960-62; mem. Va. Rep. Central Com., 1969-72; del. Rep. Nat. Conv., 1952, alternate-at-large, 1968. Mem. Am., Va. bar assns., Am. Judicature Soc., Assn. Trial Lawyers Am., Va. Trial Lawyers Assn. (v.p. 1971-73), Washington County Bar Assn. (v.p. 1973). Clubs: Kiwanis, Elks, Moose. Home: 161 E Main St Abingdon VA 24210 Office: 212 E Main St Abingdon VA 24210

MOORE, JAMES WALLACE, educator; b. Birmingham, Ala., Feb. 19, 1923; s. Felix Tyre and Mary (Ingraham) M.; student Berea Coll., 1941-42; B.A., Tenn. Poly. Inst., 1951; M.S., U. Ky., 1952; Ph.D., Purdue U., 1962; m. Doris Jean Livingston, Sept. 3, 1948; children—Karen Sue, Joyce Ann, James Wallace II. Project engr. Carbide and Carbon Chem. Co., South Charleston, W. Va., 1952-55; sr. project engr. Allison div. Gen. Motors Corp., Indpls., 1955-57; research asst. Purdue U., West Lafayette, Ind., 1958-62; sr. research engr. Jet Propulsion Lab., Cal. Inst. Tech., summers 1960-61; asso. prof. U. Va., Charlottesville, 1962-67, prof., 1967—, mem. univ. senate, 1967-71, U. Va. Sesquicentennial fellow, Barcelona, Spain, 1971-72. Co-chmn. Automatic Control Group, 1967—; cons. automatic controls U.S. Army; cons. automobile accident and failure analysis, various legal and ins. firms.; program chmn. Joint Automatic Control Conf., 1965. Pres., Woodbrook P.T.A., 1966. Mem. Albemarle County Republican Com., 1966-71. Served with AUS, 1943, 45-46; USAF, 1944. Mem. Am. Soc. M.E. (chmn. exec. com. automatic control div. 1971, paper rev. chmn. automatic control div. 1965-67, mem. exec. com. automatic control div. 1967-72, chmn. honors com. 1973-74), Am. Automatic Control Council (dir. 1972—), Sigma Xi, Pi Tau Sigma, Tau Beta Pi. Baptist (deacon 1969-72). Contbr. articles to profl. jours. Patentee automotive safety screen, jet engine variable nozzle; research in reading machine for the blind, learning control and patterns. Home: 3409 Indian Spring Rd Charlottesville VA 22901

MOORE, JAMES YOUNG, mcht.; b. Florence, Ala., Jan. 24, 1913; s. Charles Wallace and Ada Jane (Young) M.; student U. Tenn., N.Y. U.; m. Elizabeth Lumpkin, Jan. 8, 1938; children—James Young, Mary Jane (Mrs. Timothy J. Cambias), Elizabeth Diane (Mrs. James D. Cone), Susan Wallace, Molly Ann. Mfg. rep. Schloss Bros., Balt., 1936-39; organizer, chmn. bd. Jim Moore Co., Lawrenceburg, Tenn., 1939—; organizer Quality Cleaners, 1940—; owner Double M Ranch, 1972—; organizer Lawrence County Bank, Lawrenceburg. Rep. exec. seminar men's wear store mgmt. N.Y. U., 1967. Past Internat. dir. Boy Scouts Am.; past dir. Am. Cancer Soc.; exec. com. Citizens for Ct. Modernization; sponsor Citizens for Decent Lit., Help Hospitalized Vets.; nat. adv. bd. Am. Security Council; hon. citizen Boys Town. Presdl. elector at large for Tenn., 1936; nat. committeeman Young Republican Fedn., 1938-48; del. Rep. Nat. Conv., 1940; sustaining mem. Republican Nat. Com. Mem. Menninger Found. Mem. C. of C. (past nat. counselor, past dir.), Internat. Platform Assn., Farm Bur., Men's Wear Retailers Am., Tenn. Conf. to Improve Adminstrn. Justice, Delta Tau Delta (life). Republican. Mem. Ch. of Christ. Club: Wally Byam Caravan. Home: 5 Locust St Hwy 43 Lawrenceburg TN 38464 Office: 39 NW Public Square Lawrenceburg TN 38464

MOORE, JENNY MCKEAN, author; b. Boston, Mar. 12, 1923; d. Q.A. Shaw and Margaret (Sargent) McKean; B.A., Barnard Coll.; m. Nov. 26, 1944; children—Honor, Paul, Adelia, Rosemary, George, Marian, Daniel, Susanna, Patience. Author: The People On Second St., 1968. Address: 3319 Newark St NW Washington DC 20008

MOORE, JOHN EDWARD, educator; b. Kirkersville, O., Mar. 7, 1935; s. John Harris and Lucinda Pearl (Palmer) M.; B.S., Ohio State U., 1957, M.S., 1958, Ph.D., 1961; m. Geraldine Rittenhouse, June 9, 1957; 1 dau., Tracie Ann. Mem. faculty U. Fla. at Gainesville, 1961—, asso. prof. animal sci., 1966-73, prof., 1973—. Recipient Gamma Sigma Delta Jr. Faculty award, 1972; Ralston Purina Research fellow, 1957. Mem. Am. Soc. Animal Sci., Am. Dairy Sci. Assn., Am. Forage and Grassland Council (dir. 1971-73), Sigma Xi, Gamma Sigma Delta. Contbr. articles to profl. jours. Home: Route 3 Box 191 K Gainesville FL 32601

MOORE, JOHN FRANKLIN, JR., radio producer; b. Dyersburg, Tenn., Nov. 24, 1942; s. John Franklin and Mary Sue (Moody) M.; B.E.E., Ga. Inst. Tech., 1964, grad. student indsl. mgmt., 1969-70; m. Nancy Moore Crissman, Dec. 19, 1970; stepchildren—David, Jennifer, Laura, Drew. Announcer radio sta. WDSG, Dyersburg, 1958-59; announcer, chief engr. radio sta. WTRO, Dyersburg, 1959-62; announcer, engr. radio sta. WLAY, Muscle Shoals, Ala., 1962-64; air personality, coordinator FM radio sta. WSB, Atlanta, 1964—, producer, 1973—. Mem. Tau Beta Pi, Eta Kappa Nu. Home: 1970 Fisher Trail Atlanta GA 30345 Office: 1601 W Peachtree St NE Atlanta GA 30309

MOORE, JOHN HENRY, newspaper exec.; b. N.C., June 7, 1916; s. Odus Lee and Sue (Parker) M.; student Presbyn. Jr. Coll., 1934-35; student Wake Forest U., 1935-37; m. Carolyn Scudder Lindsay, June 1, 1946; children—Susan Lindsay (Mrs. Charles Wentz, Jr.), Karen Elizabeth, Carolyn Anne. With Laurinburg (N.C.) Exchange newspaper, 1937—, mgr. advt., 1937-41, mgr. bus., 1946-66, editor, pres., 1966—. Pres., chmn. campaign Scotland County United Fund, Laurinburg, 1965, 66. Chmn. Zoning Commn., Laurinburg, 1950-63. Bd. dirs. Scotland Meml. Hosp. Served to lt. (j.g.) USNR, 1944-45. Mem. N.C. Press Assn. (past officer), Laurinburg C. of C. (v.p. 1965). Baptist (bd. deacons). Lion (pres. Laurinburg 1965). Home: McLaurin Acres Laurinburg NC 28352 Office: The Laurinburg Exchange 214-18 Cronly St Laurinburg NC 28352

MOORE, JOHN PAUL, lawyer, state senator; b. Louisville, Miss., Aug. 4, 1930; s. Clinton and Birdie (Clay) M.; student Miss. State U., 1954-55; B.B.A., U. Miss., 1957, LL.B., 1959, J.D., 1969; m. Evelyn Jackson, Jan. 31, 1957; children—Teresa Ann, John Stuart, Bruce Alan, Ronald Scott. Admitted to Miss. bar, 1959; practiced in Columbus, Miss. 1959-60; pvt. practice Starkville, 1960—; mem. Miss. Senate, 1968—. Lectr. Miss. State U., 1960-68; dir. Golden Triangle Savs. and Loan Assn., Starkville, Starkville Steaks, Inc. (Miss.). Served to sgt. USAF, 1950-54. Mem. Comml. Law League Am., Phi Alpha Delta. Club: Rotary Internat. Home: 205 Woodlawn St Starkville MS 39759 Office: 207 1/2 E Main St Starkville MS 39759

MOORE, JOHN ROBERT, cons. civil engr.; b. Kewanee, Ill., July 25, 1924; s. John Elmer and Alice (Twing) M.; B.S. with high honors in Civil Engring., U. Ill., 1948; m. Juanita Donnewald, Nov. 23, 1950; children—Kim, Robin, Gary, Lisa, Chris, Kamlin, Alison. With B.P. Thacker & Co., Waukegan, Ill., 1948-49; asst. supr. hwys. Clinton County (Ill.), 1949-50; with James G. Cooney & Assos., Carlyle, Ill., 1950-56; with Harland Bartholomew & Assos., Honolulu, 1956-57, Memphis, 1957—, asso. partner, 1958-66, partner, 1966—; chief exec. officer, dir. Harland Bartholomew & Assos. Internat., Inc. 1966—. Mem. Nat. Def. Exec. Res., U.S. Dept. Transp. Adv. com. civil engring. curriculum U. Ill., 1968—. Served as lt. A.C., AUS, 1943-45. Fellow Am. Soc. C.E.; mem. Am. Water Works Assn., Nat. Soc. Profl. Engrs., Cons. Engrs. Council, Am. Ry. Engring. Assn., Hwy. Research Bd., Water Pollution Control Fedn., Am. Inst. Cons. Engrs., Chi Epsilon. Methodist. Rotarian. Home: 5401 Collingwood Cove Memphis TN 38117 Office: 188 Jefferson Av Memphis TN 38103

MOORE, JOHN STERLING, JR., clergyman; b. Memphis, Aug. 25, 1918; s. John Sterling and Lorena (Bounds) M.; student Auburn U., 1936-37; A.B., Samford U., 1940; Th.M., So. Baptist Theol. Sem., 1944; m. Martha Louise Paulette, July 6, 1944; children—Sterling Hale, John Marshall, Carolyn Paulette. Ordained to ministry Bapt. Ch., 1942; pastor in Pamplin, Va., 1944-48, Amherst, Va., 1949-57, Manly Meml. Bapt. Ch., Lexington, Va., 1957—. Mem. hist. commn. So. Bapt. Conv., 1968—, vice chmn., 1973-74; mem. sesquicentennial com. Bapt. Gen. Assn. Va., 1972-73; pres. Va. Bapt. Pastor's Conf., 1963. Chmn. Lexington Mayor's Com. Race Relations, 1962-65. Bd. dirs. Rockbridge Mental Health Assn., 1962-72; bd. dirs. Rockbridge Mental Health Clinic, 1967—, treas., 1971—; bd. dirs. Stonewall

Jackson Hosp., Lexington, 1967-71, pres., 1969-70. Mem. Soc. Bib. Lit., Va. (exec. com. 1964—), So. (dir. 1972—) Bapt. hist. socs. Mason. Co-author: Meaningful Moments in Virginia Baptist Life, 1972. Contbr. articles to profl. jours. Editor: Va. Bapt. Register, 1972—; Va. editor Ency. So. Bapts., vol. 3, 1971. Home: 463 2444 30 Sellers Av Lexington VA 24450 Office: 463 4181 Main at Preston Sts Lexington VA 24450

MOORE, JOHN TRAVERS, poet, author; b. Wellston, O., Aug. 24, 1908; s. Thomas Emmet and Mary (Tripp) M.; LL.B., U. Dayton, 1933; m. Margaret Rumberger, June 16, 1928. Admitted to Ohio bar, 1933; gen. practice, Dayton, 1933-38; editor several youth and juvenile publns., 1938-42; mng. editor Plane Facts, Army Air Force publ., 1943-45. Author: (with wife Margaret Moore) Sing-Along, Sary, 1951; The Three Tripps, 1959; The Little Band and the Inaugural Parade, 1969; Certainly Carrie, Cut the Cake, Poems A to Z, 1971; Pepito's Speech at the United Nations, 1971; author: Poems, 1955; (poetry) God's Wonderful World, 1964; The Story of Silent Night, 1965; (poetry) When You Walk Out in Spring, 1965, Cinnamon Seed, 1967, Town and Countryside Poems, 1968, There's Motion Everywhere, 1970; Poems: On Writing Poetry, 1971; (poetry) We Are Like Wine, 1972, Around The Corner From Our House, 1972, All Along The Way, 1973; also contbr. to numerous periodicals and anthologies.

MOORE, JOSEPH HENRY, historian; b. Fayetteville, Ga., Oct. 25, 1943; s. James Marion and Josephen Waldrop (Hightower) M.; student Emory U., 1961-62, Phoenix Coll., 1962-63, U. Ga., 1963-65, Armstrong Coll., 1973—. Exec. dir. Hist. Jonesboro, Inc. (Ga.), 1970-72, historian, 1970—, also dir. Lectr., Clayton Jr. Coll., Morrow, Ga., 1971-72; historian Ships of Sea Mus., Savannah, 1973—. Served with USAF, 1966-70. Mem. S.A.R., Sons Confederate Vets., Order Stars and Bars, Victorian Soc. Savannah, Telfair Acad. Arts and Scis., Ga. Writers Assn., Savannah Hist. Research Assn., English Speaking Union, Ga., Fayette County hist. socs., Assn. for Preservation Va. Antiquities. Home: 222 E Jones St Savannah GA 31401

MOORE, JOSEPH HERBERT, univ. adminstr.; b. Spartanburg, S.C., May 13, 1922; s. Henry Stoney and Eulalia (Lewis) M.; B.C.E. (Clark Williams scholar 1939-43), The Citadel, 1943; M.S., Pa. State U., 1949; Ph.D., Purdue U., 1961; m. Mary Julia Kelley, May 29, 1943; children—Mary Janis, Lynda Jean. Asst. prof. The Citadel, 1946-50; asst. prof. Pa. State U., 1950-55; project bridge engr. Joseph K. Knoerle & Assos., Chgo., 1955-56; asso. prof. Pa. State U., 1956-62; prof., head dept. civil engring. Clemson U., 1962-67; head div. engring. and tech. Pa. State U., 1967-72; dir. div. engring. tech. Va. Poly. Inst. & State U., 1972—; cons. Hwy. Research Bd. on Continuously Reinforced Concrete Pavements. Served to lt. AUS, 1943-46. Standard Oil Found. fellow, 1959-60; NSF Sci.-Faculty fellow, 1960-61. Registered profl. engr., Pa., S.C., Va. Fellow Am. Soc. C.E.; mem. Nat. Soc. Profl. Engrs., Am. Concrete Inst., Am. Soc. Engring. Edn., Sigma Xi, Phi Kappa Phi, Chi Epsilon, Citadel Honor Soc. Contbr. articles to tech. jours. Home: 506 Forest Hill Dr Blacksburg VA 24060 Office: Va Poly Inst and State U Blacksburg VA 24061

MOORE, KENNETH BURT, lumberman; b. Red Oak, Tex., May 12, 1913; s. Alvah and Beulah (Russell) M.; student Trinity U., 1930-32, 35, night classes 4C Coll., Waco, Tex., 1938, So. Meth. U., 1943; m. Ruth Wilcher, Mar. 26, 1937; children—Kenneth B. II, William James. Tchr. pub. schs., 1935-37; tchr., prin. William Cameron & Co., Inc., Waco, Tex., 1937-48; part owner, pres. Simms-Moore Lumber Co., Carrollton, Tex., 1948—; pres. Redwood Lumber Co., Dallas; v.p. Wheat Lumber Co., Dallas, Builders Supply Co., Grand Prairie, Tex.; owner Simms-Moore Lumber, Dallas; part owner, v.p. Redwoods, Inc., Waco, Tex.; v.p. Hill Country Lumber, Kerrville, Blanco Lumber, Tex.; dir. Carrollton State Bank (Tex.). Mem. Lumbermans Assn. Tex. Mem. Christian Ch. Clubs: Dallas Athletic, Brookhaven Country, Royal Oaks Country (Dallas). Home: 5838 Belt Line Dallas TX 75240

MOORE, LARRY S., lawyer; b. Thomaston, Ala., Oct. 12, 1913; s. Samuel P. and Addie (Barkley) M.; LL.B., Wake Forest Coll., 1938; m. Dorothy Wallace, Sept. 9, 1939; children—Dorothy Barkley (Mrs. Numa Lee Absher, Jr.), Larry Wallace, Patricia Foster. Admitted to N.C. bar, 1940; since practiced in North Wilkesboro; claims mgr. Hartford Accident & Indemnity Co., Greensboro, N.C., 1941-45. Chmn., Wilkes County Bd. Elections, 1958-62. Mem. N.C. (dist. councilor 1965-68), 23d Jud. Dist. (pres. 1962) bar assns. Democrat. Baptist. Elk, Kiwanian. Office: Moore & Rousseau Bldg 311 9th St North Wilkesboro NC 28659

MOORE, LEE FULTON, architect; b. Lexington, Ky., Mar. 23, 1924; s. John V. and Albertine (Lee) M.; B.C.E., U. Ky., 1948; B.Arch., U. Tex., 1951; m. Marjorie Johnson, Dec. 28, 1950; 1 dau., Leanne. Partner archtl. firm Moore, Stansbury & Vaught, Architects, Port Arthur, Tex., 1957—. Bd. dirs. Lower Neches Valley Authority; bd. dirs. Pleasure Island Commn. City of Port Arthur. Served with USAAF, 1942-46. Mem. Port Arthur C. of C. (pres. 1970), Tex. Soc. Architects (pres. 1964), A.I.A. Mem. Ch. of Christ. Kiwanian (pres. 1962). Home: 8601 Willow Bend Ct Port Arthur TX 77640 Office: 3100 25th St Port Arthur TX 77640

MOORE, LEE PERMENTER, agr. co. exec. mayor; b. Palmetto, Fla., Dec. 8, 1923; s. James Harrison and Lois (Permenter) M.; student U. Fla., 1946-48; m. Ann Leffler Wiggins, Sept. 7, 1946; children—Kathleen Lois (Mrs. Larry Lovell), Analee, Thomas Wiggins, Carolyn, Jere Elizabeth. Account exec. Goodbody & Co., Orlando, Fla., 1956-57; resident mgr. A.M. Kidder & Co., Winter Park, Fla., 1957-61, So. regional mgr., 1961-63; regional mgr. Reynold & Co., Winter Park, 1963-65; exec. v.p., gen. mgr. Chase & Co., Sanford, Fla., 1965—; mayor, Sanford, 1969—. Dir. Fla. State Bank, Sanford. Chmn. United Fund Seminole County, 1965, v.p., 1971; chmn. Seminole County Port Authority, 1968-69. Served to capt. AUS, 1942-46. Mem. Winter Park C. of C. (pres. 1961-62). Episcopalian. Mason, Rotarian. Home: 2456 Mellonville Av Sanford FL 32771 Office: PO Box 1697 Sanford FL 32771

MOORE, LESTER REYNOLDS, petroleum co. exec.; b. Newark, Feb. 24, 1910; s. Lester Reynolds and Emma (Neis) M.; student N.Y. U., 1930-34; grad. exec. session Columbia Grad. Sch. Bus. Adminstrn., 1955; m. Margaret Ramsay Dunlop, Sept. 11, 1936; children—Margaret Ramsey (Mrs. Clyde W. Henry, Jr.), Nancy Reynolds (Mrs. Eppa C. Pace III), Barbara Anderson, Susan Kirk. Asst. treas. Standard Oil of N.J., 1927-44; treas. Esso Standard Oil Co. of N.J., N.Y.C., 1944-49, now treas. Exxon Co. U.S.A., Houston; treas., dir. HSL Corp., Phila.; treas. Exxon Shipping Co., Houston, 1973—, DC HSL Corp., Phila., 1970—; dir. Pacific HSL Corp., Phila., HTS Devel. Corp., Houston, Friendship Devel. Co., Houston, HSL D-C Co., Phila., Petroleum Casualty Co., Houston. Chmn. bd. trustees Exxon USA Found.; trustee, past pres. Hedgecroft Hosp. Mem. Am. Petroleum Inst., Financial Execs. Inst., Am. Mgmt. Assn., Better Bus. Bur. Met. Houston (dir., exec. com. 1968; 1st v.p. 1970). Home: 5905 Green Tree Rd Houston TX 77027 Office: Exxon Co U SA 800 Bell Av Box 2180 Houston TX 77002

MOORE, LOUIS M., lawyer; b. Fajardo, P.R., Mar. 28, 1921; B.A., Marietta Coll., 1946; LL.B., Baylor U., 1951, J.D., 1969; m. Carolann Pinson; children—Robert L., John C., James P. Admitted to Tex. bar, 1951; practiced in Big Lake, 1951-54; mem. firm Patterson, McDaniel, Moore & Browder, Houston, 1954-69, Moore, Morris & Payne, Houston, 1969—. Active Boy Scouts Am., 1954—, YMCA, 1964-69. Legal adviser Planned Parenthood, Houston, 1970-72, bd. dirs., 1970-72; govt. coordinator Houston Assn. for Children with Learning Disabilities, 1969-73, bd. dirs., 1970-73; govt. coordinator Greater Houston chpt. Nat. Soc. Autistic Children, 1969-73; mem. Houston Council Human Relations, 1969—. Served with USNR, 1942-46. Mem. Am., Tex., Houston bar assns., Am., Tex., Houston (sec. 1970-71) trial lawyers assns. Presbyn. (deacon 1970—). Mason. Home: 6714 Redding St Houston TX 77035 Office: 400 Houston Bar Center Bldg 723 Main St Houston TX 77002

MOORE, LUTHER WILLIAM, lawyer, accountant; b. Minden, La., Nov. 20, 1930; s. Luther Carter and Ida (Wallace) M.; B.S. cum laude, La. Poly. Inst., 1952; J.D., La. State U., 1957; m. Claire Drake, June 28, 1958; children—William Drake, Cynthia Claire. Admitted to La. bar, 1957; practice pub. accounting and law, Minden, 1957—; asst. prof. accounting and law La. Poly. Inst. Sec.-treas. Webbo, Inc.; dir. Peoples Bank & Trust Co. Chmn., Minden Municipal Fire and Police Civil Service Bd., 1965-67, Minden Heart Fund, 1966; pres., sec.-treas. La. Tech. Alumni Found.; pres. Minden Indsl. Devel. Corp. Served with AUS, 1953-55. Mem. Am. Inst. C.P.A.'s, La. Soc. C.P.A.'s, La., Webster Parish (sec.-treas.) bar assns., Tax Inst. Ark.-La.-Tex., Am. Legion (trustee post comdr.), Minden C. of C. (dir.), La. Tech. Alumni Assn. (exec. com.), Lambda Chi Alpha, Omicron Delta Kappa, Beta Gamma Sigma, Phi Kappa Phi. Methodist. Lion. Home: 1301 Drake Dr Minden LA 71055 Office: PO Box 896 Minden LA 71055

MOORE, MARGARET RUMBERGER (MRS. JOHN TRAVERS MOORE), librarian, author: b. DuBois, Pa.; d. George F. and Mary E. (Means) Rumberger; B.S. in L.S., Syracuse U., 1926; m. John Travers Moore, June 16, 1928. Children's librarian Dayton (O.) Pub. Library, 1926-41; freelance writer, 1942—; asst. library dir., asst. prof. Xavier U., Cin., 1947-68, cons., 1968-71; author: They Saw Him Fly, 1966; Pretty Kitty, 1966; Guess What I Am, 1974; (with John Travers Moore); Sing Along Sary, 1951; Little Saints, 1953; Big Saints, 1954; The Three Tripps, 1959; On Cherry Tree Hill, 1960; The Little Band and the Inaugural Parade, 1968; Certainly, Carrie, Cut the Cake, 1971; Pepito's Speech at the United Nations, 1971. Mem. Pi Lambda Sigma, Zeta Tau Alpha. Contbr. articles, fiction to profl. jours., children's mags.

MOORE, MARION EDWARD, educator; b. Boise City, Okla., May 22, 1934; s. Floyd Ollie and Bobbie Edith (Bivens) M.; B.S., W.Tex. State U., 1957; M.S., Tex. Tech. U., 1960; Ph.D., U. N.M., 1968; m. Cleta Joy Sappenfield, Jan. 24, 1953; 1 dau., Leslie Ann. Instr., W.Tex. State U., Canyon, 1958-61; instr. U. N.M., 1961-66; asst. prof. U. Tex., Arlington, 1966-70, asso. prof. math., 1970—. Dir. State Com. on History Math. Served with U.S. Army, 1953-55. Mem. Am. Math. Soc., Math. Assn. Am. Contbr. articles to profl. jours. Home: 3207 Canongate Dr Arlington TX 76015

MOORE, MCKENZIE PARKER, JR., pathologist; b. Sumter, S.C., Nov. 7, 1919; s. McKenzie Parker and Elizabeth Brearley (Dargan) M.; B.S., Coll. Charleston, 1941; M.D., Med. Coll. S.C., 1944; m. Amy Ashborn Lofton, Nov. 6, 1948; children—McKenzie Parker, III, Marion Lofton, Dargan Lucas. Intern St. Louis City Hosp., 1944-45; resident in pathology Med. Coll. S.C., Charleston, 1947-50, instr., 1950-55, asst. prof., 1955-62, asso. prof., 1962-67; asso. pathologist Charlotte (N.C.) Meml. Hosp., 1967—. Served with M.C., AUS, 1945-47. Home: 2831 Wickersham Rd Charlotte NC 28211 Office: PO Box 2554 Charlotte NC 28201

MOORE, MICHAEL MUSE, city ofcl.; b. Houston, July 28, 1942; s. William Samuel and Elizabeth Louise (Brown) M.; B.B.A., Tex. Tech. U., 1965; m. Linda Louise Cathcart, Jan. 29, 1966; children—Meredith Louise, Michelle Linn. Field sales rep. Cameron Iron Works, Houston, 1965-68, customer service mgr., 1968-70, asst. mgr. marketing services, 1970-71, coordinator corporate planning, 1971-73; mgr., chief exec. rev. and comment dynamic policy planning Office of mayor City of Houston, 1973—. Vice chmn. Houston/Harris County United Fund, 1971, 72, co-chmn., 1969. Bd. dirs. Houston Livestock Show and Rodeo Assn., 1971-72; trustee Americana Center, 1971-73, pres., 1971-72; trustee Musuem Med. Sci., Houston, 1973—; trustee Jaycee Urban Devel. Found., 1972—; adv. bd. Explorers, Boy Scouts Am., 1972-73. Named Most Outstanding Local Pres. in Tex., U.S. Jaycees, 1972. Mem. Am. Marketing Assn. (dir. 1972, 73), Am. Soc. Metals, Houston C. of C. (dir. 1971-72), U.S. (v.p. 1973-74), Tex. (state metro chmn. 1972-73), Houston (pres. 1971-72, life mem.), Internat. (senator 1973—; life mem.) jaycees, Soc. for Advancement of Mgmt. (charter mem. Tex. Tech U. chpt.), Kappa Alpha Order Alumni Assn. (treas. 1970). Episcopalian. Home: 12126 Rip Van Winkle St Houston TX 77024 Office: City Hall Houston TX 77002

MOORE, MILTON BRITTAIN, JR., physician; b. Jacksonville, Fla., Sept. 2, 1930; s. Milton Brittain and Octavia (McNair) M.; student S. Ga. Coll., 1948-50; A.B., Emory U., 1951, M.D., 1956; m. Ann Martin, Aug. 9, 1953; children—Mary Martin, Laura Brittain. Intern, Atlanta VA Hosp., 1956-57; dir. venereal disease control Louisville-Jefferson County, Ky., 1957-59; resident dermatology Baylor U., Houston, 1959-62; dir. Veneral Disease Research Lab. Communicable Disease Center USPHS, 1962-64; pvt. practice medicine specializing in dermatology Watson Clinic, Lakeland, Fla., 1964—; mem. staff Lakeland Gen. Hosp. Cons. Center for Disease Control USPHS, 1964—. Pres., Am. Cancer Soc., Polk County, 1968-69. Served to sr. surgeon USPHS, 1957-64. Mem. A.M.A., Fla. Med. Assn., Am. Acad. Dermatology, Fla. Soc. Dermatology, Am. Venereal Disease Assn. (sec.-treas. 1967-70), S.E. Allergy Assn., Phi Chi, Sigma Alpha Epsilon, Alpha Omega Alpha. Contbr. articles to profl. jours. Home: 2327 Hawthorne Trail Lakeland FL 33803 Office: 1600 Lakeland Hills Blvd Lakeland FL 33802

MOORE, NOLAN AUBREY, JR., banker; b. Wichita Falls, Tex., June 9, 1917; s. Nolan Aubrey and Fan (Wiley) M.; B.B.A., U. Tex., 1938; m. Frances Morgan, Oct. 26, 1940; children—Nolan Aubrey III, Danny Morgan, Thomas Wiley, Nancy Ann. With City Nat. Bank, Wichita Falls, 1940—, loan officer, 1971—, sr. v.p., 71—. Pres. United Fund Wichita Falls, 1967. Bd. dirs. A.R.C., 1969-71. Mem. Am. Inst. Banking (nat. v.p. 1963-64; nat. pres. 1964-65), C. of C. (dir. 1965-68). Lion (past pres.). Named Outstanding Alumni Midwestern U., 1967. Home: 1401 Tilden St Wichita Falls TX 76309 Office: City Nat Bank 8th and Scott St Wichita Falls TX 76307

MOORE, PAUL MEADOWS, lawyer; b. French Camp, Miss., June 24, 1914; s. Arthur Monroe and Nancy E. (Meadows) M.; LL.B., U. Miss., 1938; m. Mary Nell Sheffield, July 26, 1941; children—Nancy Elizabeth, Mary Sue, Barbara Kay, Paul M., Patricia Lynn, Jerry. Admitted to Miss. bar, 1938; practiced in Calhoun City, Miss., 1938—. Vice pres., atty., dir. Bank of Miss., Tupelo, 1958—; dir. 1st Fed. Savs. & Loan Assn., Grenada, Miss. Mem., past pres. bd. trustees Calhoun City Sch. Dist., 1950-58; mem., past pres. Pushmataha council Boy Scouts Am., 1948-68. Served with USAAF, 1942. Mem. Am., Miss., Calhoun County bar assns., Phi Alpha Delta. Democrat. Presbyn. Rotarian (past pres.). Home: 311 N Main St Calhoun City MS 38916 Office: NW Corner Pub Sq Calhoun City MS 38916

MOORE, RAYBURN SABATZKY, educator; b. Helena, Ark., May 20, 1920; s. Max Sabatzky and Sammie Lou (Rayburn) M.; A.B., Vanderbilt U., 1942, M.A., 1947; Ph.D., Duke, 1956; m. Margaret Elizabeth Bear, Aug. 30, 1947; children—Margaret Elizabeth, Robert Rayburn. Vice pres. Interstate Grocer Co., Helena, 1947-50; research asst. Duke, 1952, grad. asst., 1952-54; asst. prof. English Hendrix Coll., Conway, Ark., 1954-55, asso. prof., 1955-58, prof., 1958-59; asso. prof. English U. Ga., Athens, 1959-65, prof., 1965—, dir. grad. studies in English, 1964-69. Vis. scholar Duke, 1958, 64. Mem. troop com. Boy Scouts Am., Athens, 1973—. Served to capt. AUS, 1942-46. Mem. Soc. for Study So. Lit. (mem. exec. com. 1968, 74—), Modern Lang. Assn. Am. (exec. com., Gen. Topics VI 1972—), South Atlantic Grad. English Coop. Group (exec. com. 1969—, chmn., 1972—), Sigma Chi. Presbyn. (deacon, elder 1962—). Author: Constance Fenimore Woolson, 1963; For the Major and Selected Short Stories of Constance Fenimore Woolson, 1967; Paul Hamilton Hayne, 1972. Contbr. articles to profl. jours. Home: 106 St James Dr Athens GA 30601

MOORE, RAYMOND TILLETT, dentist; b. Mt. Holly, N.C., Nov. 23, 1920; s. Burmah Dixon and Marigold (Gallup) M.; B.S., Wake Forest Coll., 1941; D.D.S., Med. Coll. Va., 1946; m. Betty Palmer, Nov. 27, 1943; children—Mary Ellen (Mrs. Cyril Alfred Wright III), Betty Ann (Mrs. C. Eldridge Lee). Practice dentistry, Greenville, N.C., 1946-48, Mt. Holly, N.C., 1948-71; practice exodontia and denture prosthesis, Charlotte, N.C., 1971—. Councilman, City of Mt. Holly, 1961-65, mayor, 1969-71. Served to lt. USNR, 1944-46, 51-53. Mem. Am. Dental Assn., N.C., N.C. Second Dist. dental socs., Am. Legion, Delta Sigma Delta. Democrat. Episcopalian. Mason (Shriner), Rotarian (past pres.). Home: 145 Oakland St Mount Holly NC 28120 Office: 921 Elizabeth Av Charlotte NC 28204

MOORE, REID FRANCIS, JR., lawyer; b. Chattanooga, Sept. 27, 1934; s. Reid Francis and Corinne (Milton) M.; B.A., Yale, 1956; LL.B., U. Va., 1959; m. Janice Griffin, July 20, 1963; children—Allyson, Ramsey, Carter, Hiram. Admitted to Fla. bar, 1959; practiced in Palm Beach, 1959—; mayor, West Palm Beach, 1967-68. Commr., West Palm Beach, 1965-69. Recipient Distinguished Service award West Palm Beach Jr. C. of C., 1965, Good Govt. award, 1967. Mem. Am., Palm Beach County (chmn. TV program 1972-73) bar assns., Fla. Bar, C. of C. (dir.), West Palm Beach Jr. C. of C. (pres. 1963-64), Phi Alpha Delta. Episcopalian. Republican. Mason (Shriner). Home: 343 Seabreeze Av Palm Beach FL 33480 Office: Worth Av Nat Bank Bldg Palm Beach FL 33480

MOORE, RICHARD BRENNAN, lawyer; b. Aberdeen, S.D., June 19, 1934; s. Ivan Richard and Honnora (Brennan) M.; B.A. cum laude, Vanderbilt U., 1956; LL.B., Tex. U., 1960; m. Patricia Louise Burns, Dec. 22, 1961; children—Richard Brennan, Jettie McMillan, Edward Ayshford. Admitted to Tex. bar, 1960; asso. mem. firm Gresham, Davis, Gregory, Worthy & Moore (and predecessor firm), San Antonio, 1960-67, partner, 1967—; municipal judge City Terrell Hills, Tex., 1971—. Pres., Children Service Bur., 1969-71, YMCA, San Antonio, 1974. Bd. dirs. United Way, 1972-73, Bexar County Child Welfare Unit, 1972-73. Mem. Am., Tex. (cochmn. 1974 conv.), San Antonio bar assns. Episcopalian. Clubs: Blue Wing Hunting and Fishing (dir.), Conopus (sec.), San Antonio German, Order Alamo, San Antonio Country. Home: 403 Terrell Rd San Antonio TX 78209 Office: 1800 Frost Bank Tower San Antonio TX 78205

MOORE, RICHARD DANA, biologist, educator; b. Battle Creek, Mich., Feb. 11, 1926; s. Jay Scott and Mae V. (Prine) M.; B.S., Olivet Coll., 1948; M.S., Mich. State U., 1952, Ph.D., 1956. Grad. asst. biology Olivet (Mich.) Coll., 1948-49; grad. asst. anatomy Mich. State U., East Lansing, 1951-55; asst. prof. biology Hardin Simmons Coll., Abilene, Tex., 1955-66; asso. prof. Albright Coll., Reading, Pa., 1966-67; prof. biology McMurry Coll., Abilene, 1967—. Fellow Tex. Acad. Sci.; mem. Sigma Xi. Club: Am. Contract Bridge. Home: 1717 N 6th St Abilene TX 79603 Office: Biology Dept McMurry College Abilene TX 79605

MOORE, RICHARD V., coll. pres.; b. Quincy, Fla., Nov. 20, 1906; B.E., Knoxville Coll., 1932, LL.D., 1950; M.Ed., Atlanta U., 1944; postgrad. N.Y.U.; LL.D., Syracuse U., 1948; m. Beauford J. Jones, 1934; 9 children. Tchr. social studies Pinellas High Sch., Clearwater, Fla., 1932-34; prin. Union Acad., Tarpon Springs, Fla., 1934-37, Rosenwald High Sch., Panama City, Fla., 1937-44, Washington High Sch., Pensacola, Fla., 1944-46; supr. Negro secondary schs., Tallahassee, 1946-47; pres. Bethune-Cookman Coll., Daytona Beach, Fla., 1947—. Mem. Fla. Citizen's Com. Edn.; sec. Fla. Ind. Colls. and Univs. Mem. Halifax commn. Halifax Med. Center; mem. Civic League Daytona Beach. Recipient medallion and citation for 25 yrs. service Bethune-Cookman Coll.; certificate for meritorious services Daytona Beach Planning Bd.; many other awards. Mem. N.E.A. (life), N.A.A.C.P. (life), Council Negro Coll. Presidents (Fla. scholarship com.), Alpha Phi Alpha, Sigma Pi Phi Boule. Mason (Shriner), Rotarian, Elk (Lovejoy award 1972), K.P. Address: Bethune-Cookman Coll Daytona Beach FL 32015

MOORE, RICHARD WAYNE, educator; b. Lamar, Mo., Aug. 15, 1926; s. Ralph Waldo and Mary Jane (Arner) M.; D.V.M. (Borden fellow 1954), Tex. A. and M. U., 1955, M.S., 1956; postgrad. U. Tex. at Galveston, 1960; m. Betty Jo Leath, Dec. 12, 1948; children—Robert Wallace, Nancy Elizabeth, Randle Winfield. Research veterinarian DeKalb Agr. Assn., Sycamore, Ill., 1956-58; mem. faculty Tex. A. and M. U., College Station, 1958—, asso. prof. vet. microbiology, 1960-67, prof., 1967—. Leader, 4H, 1968—. Served with USAF, 1945-47. Recipient Faculty Achievement award in research, 1970. Fellow Am. Coll. Vet. Microbiologists; mem. Am., Tex. vet. medicine assns., Am. Soc. Microbiologists, N.Y. Acad. Sci., C. of C., U.S. Animal Health Asn., Sigma Xi, Phi Kappa Phi, Phi Eta Sigma, Phi Zeta. Elk. Contbr. articles to profl. jours. Home: Box 3568 Bryan TX 77801 Office: Dept Veternary Microbiology Texas A and M Univ College Station TX 77843

MOORE, ROBERT ARNOLD, JR., agriculturist; b. Fayette, Ala., Sept. 4, 1936; s. Robert Arnold and Gertrude (Hocutt) M.; B.S., Auburn U., 1957, M.Agr., 1963; m. Sarah Elene Matthews, Sept. 4, 1960; children—Roger Alan, Cynthia Renee. With cotton classing div., agr. marketing service U.S. Dept. Agr., Atlanta, 1957-58; asst. supt. Upper Coastal Plain Substation Auburn U., Winfield, Ala., 1959-69, supt., 1969—. Mem. Winfield Ambulance and Rescue Squad, 1973—. FFA State Star farmer, 1954, Am. Farmer degree, 1956. Mem. Ala., Am., Fayette County (sec.-treas. 1969) cattlemens assns., Gideons, Alpha Beta Alpha. Methodist. Kiwanian (pres. 1969). Home: PO Box 706 Winfield AL 35594 Office: Upper Coastal Plain Agriculture Substation Auburn Univ Winfield AL 35594

MOORE, ROBERT EDWARD, research co. exec.; b. Winsted, Conn., July 29, 1923; s. Alfred Edward and Elizabeth (Clark) M.; B.S. in Mech. Engring., U. Wis., 1948; m. Georgiana Muriel Moore, Dec. 22, 1946; children—Kathleen Mary, Brian Robert, John Craig. Chief insp. Rockwell-Standard Corp., Newark, O., 1948-51; sec.-treas. A.E. Moore Co., Oshkosh, Wis., 1951-53; v.p. John I. Thompson & Co., Washington, 1953-65; pres. Potomac Research, Inc., McLean, Va., 1965—. Served with AUS, 1943-46. Registered profl. engr., D.C. Mem. Am. Soc. M.E. Republican. Episcopalian. Home: 3610 Bent Branch Ct Falls Church VA 22041 Office: Westgate Research Park McLean VA 22101

MOORE, ROY SANDERS, optometrist; b. Waco, Tex., July 24, 1925; s. Roy Sanders and Ruth (Holden) M.; student La. Poly. Inst., 1943-44, Baylor U., 1946-47; D.Optometry, So. Coll. Optometry, 1949; m. Grace Szekely, Mar. 7, 1959; children—Diane, William, Andrew, Paul. Optometrist, Tex. Optical, Beaumont, 1951-65; pvt. practice optometry, Harlingen, Tex., 1965—. Served with USNR, 1943-46. Mem. Optometric Progress Fund, Tex. Assn. Optometrists, Harlingen C. of C., Harlingen Credit Bur. Home: 1016 Ebony St Harlingen TX 78550 Office: 105 E Jackson Harlingen Tx 78550

MOORE, SAMUEL JAMES TILDEN, JR., lawyer; b. Deltaville, Va., Apr. 26, 1913; s. Samuel J.T. and Nettie (Powell) M.; A.B., Washington and Lee U., 1935; student U. Richmond Law Sch., 1936-39; m. Mary Frances Edmunds, Apr. 13, 1963; 1 son, Samuel J.T. III. Claim supr. Liberty Mut. Ins. Co., Boston, 1940-50, div. v.p., 1950-51; admitted to Va. bar, 1950; partner Sands, Marks & Sands, Richmond, Va., 1951-61, Shewmake & Gary, Richmond, 1960-70, Moore & Pollard, 1970—. Instr. history Va. Commonwealth U., 1963-70. Mem. St. Peter's Ch. Restoration Assn., New Kent, Va., 1955, v.p., 1960—; mem. adv. bd. Salvation Army, Richmond, 1958—. Pres., Young Democratic Club, 1956-57. Mem. Am., Va., Richmond bar assns., Am. Judicature Soc., Internat. Assn. Ins. Counsel, Assn. Ins. Attys., Def. Research Inst. (v.p.), Va. Trial Lawyers Assn., Sons Confederate Vets. (Va. commdr. 1957-63), Richmond Civil War Roundtable (pres. 1956), Va. Hist. Soc., Va. Mus. Fine Arts, English Speaking Union, U.S. Naval Inst., Navy League, Am. Legion, Chesapeake Bay Yacht Racing Assn., Internat. Platform Assn., N.Am. Yacht Racing Union, U.S. Internat. Sailing Assn., Sigma Delta Chi, Sigma Alpha Epsilon. Episcopalian. Clubs: Fishing Bay Yacht (Deltaville, Va.); Capes Beach and Cabana (Virginia Beach, Va.); Virginia Boat, Bull and Bear, (Richmond). Author: The Jefferson Hotel-A Southern Landmark, 1940. Home: 2216 Park Av Richmond VA 23220 Office: 1001 E Main St Richmond VA 23219

MOORE, SHELLEY WENDELL, mfg. co. exec.; b. Paducah, Tex., Apr. 3, 1931; s. Shelley B. and Gladys D. (Biddy) M.; B.A., Weatherford Coll., 1949; B.A., Tex. Christian U., 1955; m. Lola D. Briden, Feb. 3, 1951. With La Gorse Oil Co., Fort Worth, 1955-57; with Spencer Constrn. Co., Fort Worth, 1957-69; with Woldert Enterprises, Tyler, Tex. 1969—, gen. mgr. automotive mfg. plant, 1974—. Served with USAF, 1950-54. Decorated Air medal. Mem. Tex. Safety Assn., Soc. Mfg. Engrs. Home: 408 Rockwood Lane Longview TX 75601 Office: PO Box 4050 Tyler TX 75701

MOORE, THOMAS JUSTIN, JR., utility co. exec.; b. Richmond, Va., Apr. 15, 1925; s. Thomas Justin and Carrie (Willingham) M.; A.B., Princeton, 1947; LL.B., U. Va., 1950; m. Mary Elizabeth Pearson, Oct. 22, 1954; children—Mary Elizabeth, Thomas Justin III. Admitted to Va. bar, 1949; asso. firm Hunton, Williams, Gay & Gibson, Richmond, 1950-54, mem. firm., 1955-67; asso. gen. counsel Va. Electric and Power Co., Richmond, 1958-67, sr. v.p., 1967-69, exec. v.p., 1969-70, pres., 1970—, also dir.; dir. Central Nat. Bank of Richmond, Philip Morris, Inc., Richmond Corp. Bd. govs. Richmond United Givers Fund, 1962; mem. met. bd. Richmond YMCA; trustee, chmn. bd. Va. Found. for Ind. Colls.; Colonial Williamsburg (Va.) Found., U. Richmond, Richmond Meml. Hosp. Served to lt. (j.g.) USNR, 1943-46; PTO. Mem. Am. (mem. council pub. utility law sect. 1968—), Fed., Va. (chmn. exec. com. 1967), Richmond (pres. 1966) bar assns., Bar Assn. City N.Y., Phi Alpha Delta. Episcopalian. Clubs: Princeton, Knickerbocker (N.Y.C.); Metropolitan (Washington); Country of Va., Commonwealth, Downtown (Richmond). Home: 700 E Franklin St Richmond VA 23219 Office: 9 Maxwell Rd Richmond VA 23226

MOORE, THORNTON BIDGOOD, govt. ofcl.; b. Mobile, Ala., Feb. 15, 1909; s. John Payne and Lucille (Bidgood) M.; B.S. in Bus. Adminstrn., U. Ala., 1930; m. Elizabeth Charlton, Apr. 8, 1966; 1 son (by previous marriage), Thornton Bidgood. Asst. dir. marketing research Appliance div. Westinghouse Electric Corp., Mansfield, O., 1930-36, 37-42; asst. dir. marketing Hearst Mags., N.Y.C., 1936-37; statistician consumer durable goods div. WPB, U.S. Navy, War Assets Adminstrn., U.S. Govt., 1942-48; with Dept. Commerce, 1948—, dep. dir. consumer durable goods div., 1953-57, asst. dir. Office Indsl. Moblzn., 1958-64, dir. gen. indsl. equipment and components div., 1965-68, dir. consumer products div., 1968-72, asst. dir. Office Bus. Assistance, 1973—. Exec. com. Greater Washington Tennis Assn., 1954-62, pres., 1956-59; exec. com. Middle Atlantic Lawn Tennis Assn., 1958-60; bd. dirs. Washington Area Tennis Patrons Found. Served as lt. USN, 1944-46. Recipient Meritorius Service award U.S. Dept. Commerce, 1959. Unitarian. Clubs: University, (Washington); Edgemoor (pres. 1955-57, bd. govs. 1951-57) (Bethesda, Md.). Home: 5508 Cornish Rd Bethesda MD 20014 Office: Main Commerce Bldg 14th and Constitution Av NW Washington DC 20230

MOORE, TOM WHITE, JR., lawyer; b. Nevada City, Cal., July 19, 1943; s. Tom White and Jeanice (Byrne) M.; B.S., U. Tenn., 1967; J.D., Samford U., 1970; m. Linda Blankinship, Aug. 20, 1967; children—Tom White III, Heather Lucille. Admitted to Tenn. bar., 1970; asso. firm Moore, Henry, Henry, Lewis & Cain, Pulaski, Tenn., 1970-71, partner, Columbia, Tenn., 1971—. Treas. Young Democrats of Maury County, 1972-73. Mem. Am., Tenn. bar assns., Assn. Trial Lawyers of Am., Tenn. Trial Lawyers Assn. (bd. govs. 1973—), Columbia Jaycees (dir. 1973—). Home: 1506 Jewell Dr Columbia TN 38401 Office: South Garden St Columbia TN 38401

MOORE, VERNON LEWIS, cons. engr.; b. Erlanger, Ky., Aug. 5, 1925; s. Charles Milton and Bessie L. (Wade) M.; B.S. in Civil Engring., U. Ky., 1950; m. Mary Ellen Massey, Sept. 10, 1955; children—Anne, Mary Clare, Patrick, Murray, Rita, Thomas, Daniel, Adele. Engr., McDowell Co., Cleve., 1950-54, Cleve. Electric Illuminating Co., 1954-55; v.p. Turnbull, Inc., Dallas, 1955-64; pres. Moore Engrs., Inc., Dallas, 1964—; v.p. cement div. Centex Corp., Dallas, 1971—; v.p., dir. Delta Mining Corp., Mill Creek, Okla., 1967—. Fellow Am. Soc. C.E.; mem. Tau Beta Pi. Home: 4311 Northview Lane Dallas TX 75229 Office: 2614 Freewood Dr Dallas TX 75220

MOORE, WALTER GUY, educator; b. Detroit, June 21, 1913; s. Guy Walton and Elizabeth Lillie (Blondin) M.; B.A., Wayne State U., 1934; M.A., U. Minn., 1938, Ph.D., 1940; m. Elizabeth Geneva Parsons, Sept. 19, 1939; children—Judith (Mrs. Robert Caswell), David, Joel, Elizabeth (Mrs. Sidney Valadie), Eleanor (Mrs. Harold Wright), Virginia. Instr. Wayne State U., Detroit, 1934-35; mem. faculty Loyola U., New Orleans, 1940—, instr., 1940-41, asst. prof., 1941-46, asso. prof., 1946-51, prof. biology, 1951—. Bd. dirs. Loyola U., 1972—. Research grantee Carnegie Found., 1946-52; NSF grantee, 1955-68. Fellow A.A.A.S.; mem. Am. Inst. Biol. Sci., Ecol. Soc. Am., Am. Soc. Limnology and Oceanography, Southwestern Assn. Naturalists (sec. 1967-73; pres. 1974—). Contbr. articles to profl. jours. Home: 5231 S Derbigny St New Orleans LA 70125

MOORE, WALTER VOGLER, JR., lawyer; b. Richmond, Va., July 20, 1928; s. Walter Vogler and Josephine (Peacock) M.; grad. Woodberry Forest Sch. (Va.), 1947; student Hampden Sydney Coll., 1948-50; J.D., U. Richmond, 1954; m. Elizabeth Gilmer Evans, Aug. 28, 1954; children—Mary Easley, Walter W. II, Francis Hudson II. Admitted to Va. bar, 1954; since practiced in Orange; partner firm Somerville Moore & Joyner, 1956—. Pres., sec., treas., dir. Orange Youth Improvement Assn; campaign chmn. March of Dimes; pres. March of Dimes County Found.; mem. Orange County Indsl. Devel. Corp. Mem. Va. State Bar, Va., Am. bar assns., Orange County C. of C. Presbyn. (past deacon, elder). Home: 135 Landon Lane Orange VA 22960 Office: Va Nat Bank Bldg Orange VA 22960

MOORE, WEST TABB, physician; b. Richmond, Va., July 5, 1933; s. Roderick Dunn and Virginia Underwood (Tabb) M.; B.A., U. Va., 1955; M.D., Johns Hopkins, 1959; m. Rosaline Lovett Nowland, Jan. 13, 1961; children—Jonathan Tabb, Ann Lovett. Intern Johns Hopkins, Balt., 1959-60, resident, 1960-61, 63-64; fellow endocrinology Mass. Gen. Hosp., Boston, 1961-63; practice medicine specializing in endocrinology, Washington, 1964—; mem. staff Washington Hosp. Center. Clin. instr. George Washington U. Hosp., Washington, 1964-70, asst. clin. prof., 1970-73; asst. clin. prof. medicine Georgetown U. Hosp., 1973—; dir. endocrine clinic Columbia Hosp. for Women, 1966—. Trustee Johns Hopkins U., Balt., 1970—. Diplomate Am. Bd. Internal Medicine. Fellow A.C.P.; mem. Am. Clin. and Climatol. Assn. Clubs: University, Chevy Chase. Home: 5188 Palisades Lane NW Washington DC 20016 Office: 2001 Eye St NW Washington DC 20006

MOORE, WILLIAM LEE, physician; b. Somerset, Pa., Jan. 12, 1935; s. John Brown and Rebecca (Kaufman) M.; A.B., Washington & Jefferson Coll., 1956; M.D., Hahnemann Med. Coll., 1960; m. Isabel Carmen Fernandez, Sept. 18, 1966; children—Heidi Anne, William Lee II. Intern Bayfront Med. Center, 1961-62; practice as family physician, Saint Petersburg, Fla., 1965—; chief of infection com. Palms of Pasadena Hosp., 1966—; chief of gen. practice Saint Petersburg Gen. Hosp., 1969—, exec. com., 1969—. Mem. Pinellas County Com. of 100. Served to lt. USNR, 1962-64. Mem. A.M.A., St. Petersburg C. of C., Phi Kappa Sigma Phi Chi. Republican. Episcopalian. Mason (Shriner), Rotarian. Clubs: Bath, Yacht (Saint Petersburg, Fla.). Home: 7211 4th Av S St Petersburg FL 33707 Office: 6707 1st Av S St Petersburg FL 33707

MOORE, WILLIAM MICHAEL, civil engr.; b. Houston, July 31, 1934; s. A.B. and Mildred (Ankle) M.; B.S., Tex. A. and M. U., 1956, M.E., 1958, Ph.D,, 1965; m. Randa Kunzman, Sept. 3, 1955; children—Gina Berniece, Michael Joseph, Lisa Anne, Randa Elizabeth, Patrick Alastair, Laura Jean, Alexander Ribiere. Grad. asst. Tex. A. and M. U., 1956-57, instr., 1957-61; asst. city engr. College Station, Tex., 1956-62; asst. research engr. Tex. Transp. Inst., 1962-67, asso. research engr., 1967—; pres. Martin Trucker Corp., College Station, 1968—; pvt. practice engring. cons., College Station, 1961—. Served from 2d lt. to 1st lt., C.E., U.S. Army Res., 1956-64. Automotive Safety Found. fellow, 1961-62. Registered profl. engr., Tex. Mem. Sigma Xi; Phi Eta Sigma, Tau Beta Pi. Republican. Roman Catholic. Author research papers in pavement design and soil mechanics. Research in field. Home: 125 Lee St College Station TX 77840 Office: Pavement Design Dept Texas Transportation Institute Texas A and M Univ College Station TX 77843

MOORE, WILLIAM MOULTRIE, JR., bishop; b. Mt. Pleasant, S.C., June 11, 1916; s. William Moultrie and Jennie Verdier (Edmondston) M.; B.A., Coll. Charleston (S.C.), 1937; S.T.B., Gen. Theol. Sem., N.Y.C., 1941, S.T.D., 1957; D.D. U. of South, 1967; m. Florence Muirhead Porcher, 1941; children—Jennie, Caroline, Anne. Ordained priest Episcopal Ch., 1941; minister-in-charge St. Alban's Ch., Kingstree, S.C., St. Stephen's (S.C.) Ch., St. Luke's Ch., Andrews, S.C., Mission Ch., Rhems, S.C., 1940-42; rector Ch. of Epiphany, Leaksville, N.C., St. Thomas Epis. Ch., Reidsville, N.C., 1942-44, St. Luke's Ch., Salisbury, N.C., 1944-52, St. Martin's Ch., Charlotte, N.C., 1952-67; suffragan bishop Diocese of N.C., 1967—. Exam. chaplain Diocese of N.C., 1948-59, 65-67, mem. standing com., 1962, 63, 65-67, pres. 1966, mem. exec. council, 1948-51, 54-61. Bd. mgrs. Thompson Orphanage, 1954-64; bd. dirs. Penick Home for the Ageing, 1960-67; trustee Gen. Theol. Sem., 1960-67, U. of South, 1967—, St. Augustine's Coll., 1968—; pres. bd. dirs. Kanuga, 1973—. Address: Box 17025 Raleigh NC 27609

MOORE, WILLIAM T(AYLOR), journalist; b. Rossville, Ill., Jan. 3, 1901; s. William Taylor and Jennie (Meridith) M.; student U. Chgo., 1924-28; m. Eloise Tasher, June 1, 1929. Feature writer Chgo. Herald and Examiner, 1924-36; mem. editorial staff Chgo. Tribune, 1936-66, mem. Washington bur., 1942-56, corr. Chgo. Tribune Press Service, Moscow, 1956-57, congl. corr., 1957-66; writer Ft. Lauderdale (Fla.) News, 1966-69; lectr. on Russia. Mem Phi Gamma Delta. Republican. Presbyn. Clubs: Cliff Dwellers (Chgo); University, Nat. Press, Arts (past pres.), City Tavern Assn. (Washington). Home: 145 Ocean Av Palm Beach Shores Singer Island FL 33404

MOORE, WOODVALL RAY, librarian; b. Flatwoods, Ky., May 19, 1942; s. Clyde Raymond and Erma (Gallion) M.; student U. Ky., 1960-62, Ashland Oil fellow, 1966-67; A.A., So. Bible Coll., 1964, B.S., 1965; M.S.L.S., U. Ky., 1972; m. Sarah Ellen Markham, Dec. 14, 1963; 1 dau., Tamra Sheri. Head librarian So. Bible Coll., Houston, 1968—, asso. prof. Christian edn. dept., 1968-70; ordained to ministry Pentecostal Ch. of God of Am., 1969. Precinct chmn. Republican Party, 1969-70, 72—. Mem. A.L.A., Tex. Library Assn., Christian Librarians Fellowship, S.W. Basketball Ofcls. Assn., So. Bible Coll. Alumni Assn. (pres. Houston chpt. 1973—). Address: 10950 Beaumont Hwy Houston TX 77028

MOORES, RUSSELL RAY, physician, educator; b. St. Louis, Feb. 25, 1935; s. Floyd Russell and Dorothy Inis (Campbell) M.; B.S., Ark. State U., 1955; B.S., M.D., U. Ark., 1958; m. Helen Dorothy Byrnes, Aug. 3, 1957; children—Russell Ray, Darryl, Cheryl, Sean, Christian, Duane, Doreen. Intern, Strong Meml. Hosp., 1958-59, resident, 1959-60; resident Barnes Hosp., St. Louis, 1960-61; hematology fellow NIH, 1961-63; practice medicine, specializing in internal medicine, Augusta, Ga., 1965—; asst. prof. medicine Med. Coll. Ga., 1965-67, asso. prof., 1967-71, prof. humanities and medicine, 1971—, asso. dean for curriculum, 1972-74, asso. dean for spl. programs, 1974—. Served to lt. comdr. USN, 1963-65. Diplomate Am. Bd. Internal Medicine. Mem. Am. Fedn. for Clin. Research, Am. Assn. for Cancer Edn., Am., Internat. socs. hematology, Am. Soc. for Psychical Research. Home: 2204 Kings Way Augusta GA 30904 Office: Med Coll Ga Augusta GA 30902

MOORHEAD, WILLIAM DAVID, mech. engr.; b. Lynchburg, Tenn., 1908; s. David F. Robertson and Sallie (Ashby) M.; student Ga. Sch. Tech., 1926-29, Vanderbilt U., 1941; m. Virginia Wood, Jan. 3, 1938; 1 son, William David III. Project engr. Manhattan Project, Tenn. Eastman Corp., Oak Ridge, 1944-46; div. engr. Kellex Corp., N.Y., 1948; pres. Atlas Engring. Co., Oak Ridge, 1951-53; chief of design Olin-Matheson Co., Balt., 1953-55; project engr. Arthur G. McKee Co., Cleve., 1955-58; supt. engring. Pan Am. World Airways, Patrick AFB, Fla., 1958-66; prin. engr. Bendix Corp., Kennedy Space Center, Fla., 1966—. Mem. Melbourne (Fla.) Planning and Zoning Bd., 1965—, chmn., 1971-72. Named Engr. of Year, Bendix, 1968; recipient commendation for work on Manhattan Project, Sec. War, 1946. Mem. Nat. Assn. Corrosion Engrs. Mason. Home: 2420 S Scenic Dr Melbourne FL 32901 Office: Kennedy Space Center FL 32899

MOORMAN, GEORGE ROBERTSON, lawyer; b. Ft. Worth, Nov. 17, 1919; s. Richard Harry and Della Gray (Clark) M.; B.S.C., So. Meth. U., 1939, J.D., 1941; m. Billie Scoggin, Nov. 17, 1946; children—Richard Hal IV, Robert Lawson. Admitted to Tex. bar, 1941; spl. agt. FBI, Washington, 1942; with U.S. VA, Lubbock and Waco, Tex., 1946-55; mem. firm Biggers Baker & Lloyd, 1941, Moorman & Tate, 1955—. Dir. Citizens State Bank, Somerville, Tex., South Central Savs. Assn., Breham, Tex. Served with USNR, 1942-45. Mem. Am., Tex., Washington County bar assns., C.of C. (pres. 1961), Naval Res. Assn. (v.p. 1954-55), Res. Officers Assn. (pres. Tex. dept. 1953-54). Home: Navasota Hwy Brenham TX 77833 Office: PO Box 497 212A E Main St Brenham TX 77833

MOOSE, PHILIP ANTHONY, artist; b. Newton, N.C., Jan. 16, 1921; s. James Samuel and Sallie Emma (Anthony) M.; student N.A.D., 1940-42, Columbia, 1946-47, Taxco Sch. Art, Mexico, 1951, Acad. Fine Arts, Munich, Germany, 1953-54. Asso. prof. fine arts Davidson (N.C.) Coll., 1951-53, Queens Coll., Charlotte, N.C., 1956-57; exhibited in one-man shows at Mint Mus., Charlotte, Corcoran Mus., Washington; exhibited in group shows at Met. Mus., Gallery Contemporary Art, Salem, N.C.; represented in permanent collections at Norfolk (Va.) Mus., N.C. State Mus., High Mus., Atlanta, Mint Mus. Served with USAAF, 1942-45. Recipient Pulitzer art award, 1948, Tiffany award, 1949. Fulbright grantee 1953, Fulbright award, 1963. Illustrator: History of Catawba County, 1953; Exploring the Mountains of N.C., 1972. Address: Blowing Rock NC 28605

MOQUIN, JOSEPH CHARLES, aerospace co. exec.; b. Middleboro, Mass., July 7, 1924; s. Joseph Alfred and Sarah (Bump) M.; student Miss. State Coll., 1943-44; B.S., Washington U., 1949; postgrad., 1949-51; m. Margaret Jane Claiborne, Jan. 9, 1948; children—Michael James, Stephen Charles, Claiborne Lee, Margaret Mary, Sarah Jo, William Alfred, Paul Benedict, Thomas Joseph Ousley. Indsl. engr. Beltex Corp., St. Louis, United Wood Heel Co., 1949-50, Rice-Stix Co., 1950-52; program dir. ordnance mgmt. engr. tng. program Rock Island (Ill.) Arsenal, 1952-56; chief mgmt. services Army Ballistic Missile Agy., Redstone Arsenal, Ala., 1956-58; chief mgmt. engring. Army Ordnance Missile Command, 1958-59; exec. v.p. Brown Engring. Co., Inc., Huntsville, Ala., 1959-66, pres., 1966—; dir. 1st Nat. Bank. Bd. dirs. United Givers Fund, Huntsville and Madison County, Ala., 1962-70, pres., 1964—; bd. dirs. Madison County Council Community Orgns., 1959-65, Huntsville Indsl. Expansion Com., 1965-70; mem. local govt. study commn., 1971—; exec. bd. Huntsville Boys Club, Inc., 1956—, Tenn. Valley council Boy Scouts Am., 1970-72. Served to 1st lt. C.E., AUS, 1943-46. Mem. Ala. Soc. Profl. Engrs., Am. Inst. Indsl. Engrs., Assn. U.S. Army, Am. Ordnance Assn., Am. Inst. Aeros. and Astronautics (chmn. Ala. sect. 1965-66), C. of C. (dir. 1964-68), Sigma Nu. Kiwanian (pres.). Home: 1904 Chippendale Dr Huntsville AL 35801 Office: Research Park Huntsville AL 35807

MORACK, JOHN F., coll. adminstr.; b. New Brighton, Pa., Sept. 1, 1931; s. Eugene James and Mary (Bosco) M.; Asso. Engring., Cleve. Inst. Engring., 1957; B.S. in Bus. Adminstrn., Geneva Coll., Beaver Falls, Pa., 1959; M.A. in Edn., Duquesne U., 1964; Ph.D., U. Pitts., 1970; m. Rose Marie Signore, May 7, 1955; children—Kathleen Ann, Daniel Eugene. Asst. to supt. for bus. Hopewell-Independence-Racoon Joint Schs., Aliquippa, Pa., 1958-66; dean financial affairs Community Coll. of Beaver County, Freedom, Pa., 1966-68; asst. to supt. for bus. North Hills Sch. Dist., Pitts., 1968-70; v.p. bus. affairs Broward Community Coll., Ft. Lauderdale, 1970—. Sec. study com. on sch. bus. Tri State Area Sch. Study Council, 1966-68; mem. com. for revision fed. handbook 2 Pa. Dept. Edn., 1969. Ednl. div. chmn. Lower Beaver County United Fund, 1965-67, bd. dirs. Central Beaver County, 1968; bd. dirs. Aliquippa Exchange Club, 1963. Treas. Hopewell Twp. Sch. Bd., 1959-66, Hopewell-Independence-Racoon Joint Sch. Bd., 1959-66. Served with USAF, 1949-52. Mem. Assn. Sch. Bus. Ofcls. of U.S. and Can. (mem. nat. nominating com. 1969), Pa. Assn. Sch. Bus. Ofcls. (pres. 1969-70), Western Pa. Assn. Sch. Bus. Ofcls. (co-founder program chmn. 1966-67), Pa. Sch. Bds. Assn. (adminstrs. adv. com. 1969-70), Am. Assn. Sch. Adminstrs. Home: 7201 NW 5th St Plantation FL 33317 Office: Broward Community Coll 225 E Las Olas Blvd Fort Lauderdale FL 33301

MORA-FARIA, LUIS ENRIQUE, educator, cons.; b. Santurce, P.R., Oct. 10, 1937; s. Felipe N. Mora and Dolores L. Faria; B.S., Rensselaer Poly. Inst., 1959, Ph.D., 1964; M.S., Tex. A. and M. U., 1961; m. Belkis Antongiorgi, Mar. 18, 1960; children—Luis Mora-Antongiorgi, David Mora-Antongiorgi, Belkis Mora-Antongiorgi. Instr., U. P.R., 1959, asst. prof., 1964-67, asso. prof. civil engring., 1967—; lectr. Inter Am. U., 1962; pvt. practice cons. engr., 1964—. Pres. housing com. Popular Democratic Party, 1972. Served with P.R. N.G., 1953-57. Ford Found. grantee 1962. Mem. Am. Soc. C.E., Am. Soc. Engring. Edn., Am. Concrete Inst., Am. Assn. U. Profs., Sigma Xi. Chi Epsilon, Phi Eta Mu, Phi Iota Alpha. Rotarian. Home: 7 Santiago St San German PR 00753 Office: Civil Engring Dept U P R Mayaguez PR 00708 also Cond Las Nereidas 3A Mayaguez PR 00708

MORALES, CECILIO JOSE, banker; b. Buenos Aires, Argentina, Mar. 18, 1921 (came to U.S., 1952); s. Luis C. and Jacinta (Magliano) M.; student U. Buenos Aires, 1936-43; m. Ann M. Kiesewetter, Dec. 11, 1971; children—Cecilio Jose, Maria Helena, Christian Francis. Dir. pub. health statistics, Argentina, 1945-52; econ. counsellor Argentine Delegation to UN, N.Y.C., 1952-57; dir. econ. and social affairs OAS, Washington, 1959-61; tech. mgr. Inter. Am. Devel. Bank, Washington, 1962—. Mem. Am. Econ. Assn., Inst. Mgmt. Scis. Home: 5622 Massachusetts Av Washington DC 20016 Office: 808 17th St Washington DC 20577

MORALES, MANUEL, JR., advt. agy. exec.; b. San Juan, P.R., May 23, 1945; s. Manuel and Miriam (Lopez) Morales-Davila; B.B.A., Pace U., 1968; M.B.A., N.Y. U., 1969; m. Ligia Lema, July 21, 1967; children—Manuel Antonio, Luis Manuel. Account exec. West Indies Advt. Co., San Juan, 1969-71; spl. asst. to adminstr. Econ. Devel. Adminstrn., Commonwealth of P.R., 1971-72; v.p. West Indies Advt. Co., Inc., San Juan, 1972—. Advt. cons. United Fund P.R., 1973, bd. dirs., 1974—; adj. instr. econs. and statistics InterAm. U., 1970-71. Mem. P.R. and The Sea - A Program for Marine Affairs, Report to Gov., 1972. Mem. Advt. Agy. Assn. P.R. (sec.-treas. 1973-74), C. of C. P.R. (chmn. internat. relations com. 1970). Lion (v.p. 1973-74). Club: Overseas Press (San Juan). Contbr. articles to various publs. Office: Box 1443 San Juan PR 00903

MORALES-SANCHEZ, JULIO, lawyer, govt. ofcl.; b. Caguas, P.R., Oct. 11, 1940; s. Julio and Gladys (Sanchez-Diaz) Morales-Ortiz;

B.A., U. P.R., 1962, LL.B., 1965; m. Ilia Miranda-Cassanova, Dec. 16, 1967; children—Gladymar Morales-Miranda, Julio Enrique Morales-Miranda. Admitted to P.R. bar, 1965; asst. atty. gen. for legislation Commonwealth of P.R., San Juan, 1965-66, chief legal counsel Communications Authority, 1966-69, spl. aide, atty. gen., 1969-70; asst. U.S. atty. Dist. of P.R., U.S. Dept. Justice, San Juan, 1970, U.S. atty., 1970—. Prof. comml. English, U. P.R., 1965-67. Recipient medal for excellence and leadership Nat. Exchange Club, 1962. Home: 206 Hija del Caribe Hato Rey PR 00918 Office: PO Box 3391 San Juan PR 00904

MORAN, ANN ELIZABETH, librarian; b. Franklin, Tenn.; d. James Walker and Emma Mai (Fly) Moran; B.S., Middle Tenn. State U., 1940; B.S. in L.S., George Peabody Coll. for Tchrs., 1943, M.A., 1953. Librarian various schs., Tenn., 1943-61; tchr. Franklin City Schs., 1961-65; tchr., librarian Williamson County (Tenn.) Schs., Franklin, 1940-43, library supr., 1965—, Chmn. fund drive Heart Assn., Franklin, 1969, chmn. bus., 1970, co-chmn. rural fund dr., 1972; vice-chmn. Williamson County Heart Council, 1974-75. Mem. Nat. Tenn., Middle Tenn. edn. assns., Am., Tenn. library assns., Bus. and Profl. Women's Club (sec. 1969-70), Women's Nat. Book Assn. (sec. 1971-73), Delta Kappa Gamma (treas. 1972-74). Home: Route 3 Franklin TN 37064 Office: Columbia Av Franklin TN 37064

MORAN, NEIL CLYMER, med. scientist, educator; b. Phoenix, Oct. 12, 1924; s. Francis Joseph and Ethel (Clymer) M.; student Long Beach City Coll., 1942-43, La. State U., 1943-44, U. Mo., 1944, Creighton U., 1945-46, U. Kan., 1946; A.B., Stanford, 1949, M.D., 1950; m. Charlotte Jean Davidson, June 19, 1948; children—Michael Neil, Margaret Lois, James Duncan. Intern, Stanford U. Hosps., Cal., 1949-50; Irving fellow in physiology, 1950-51; asso. prof. pharmacology Emory U., 1956-62, prof., chmn. dept. pharmacology, 1962—; vis. scientist Karolinska Institutet, Stockholm, Sweden, 1960-61. Mem. Am. Civil Liberties Union of Ga., Ga. Heart Assn. Served with AUS, 1943-46; served with USPHS, 1951-56. Mem. Am. Soc. Pharmacology and Exptl. Therapeutics, A.A.A.S., Am. Assn. U. Profs., Am. Heart Assn., Sigma Xi, Alpha Omega Alpha. Contbr. numerous articles in field to profl. jours. Editor, Jour. of Pharmacology and Exptl. Therapeutics, 1961-65; asso. editor Pharm. Reviews, 1966-69; mem. editorial bd. Circulation Research, 1968-72. Home: 1802 E Clifton Rd NE Atlanta GA 30307 Office: Dept Pharmacology Emory U Atlanta GA 30322

MORAN, THOMAS FRANCIS, educator; b. Manchester, N.H., Dec. 11, 1936; s. Francis Leo and Mamie Marie (Morin) M.; B.A., St. Anselm's Coll., 1958; Ph.D., Notre Dame U., 1962; m. Joan Elinor Belliveau, June 25, 1960; children—Dorothy, Michael, Linda, Mary. Postdoctoral fellow Brookhaven Nat. Lab., U.S. AEC, Upton, N.Y., 1962-64, asso. scientist, 1964-66; asst. prof. Ga. Inst. Tech., Atlanta, 1966-68, asso. prof., 1968-72, prof. chemistry, 1972—. Recipient Ferst Research award Ferst Found., Atlanta, 1970. Mem. Am. Phys. Soc., Am. Chem. Soc., A.A.A.S., Ga. Acad. Sci., Sigma Xi. Contbr. articles to profl. jours. Home: 2324 Annapolis Ct NE Atlanta GA 30345 Office: Sch Chemistry Ga Inst Tech Atlanta GA 30332

MORAN, THOMAS JAMES, pathologist; b. Rennerdale, Pa., Oct. 14, 1912; s. Charles Anthony and Agnes Mildred (McCaffery) M.; B.S., U. Pitts., 1936, M.D., 1936; m. Katherine Barbara Fetterman, Feb. 27, 1941; children—Barbara (Mrs. Lloyd Kreuzer), Margaret (Mrs. Daniel Morrow), Thomas J., Sara E. Intern Mercy Hosp., Pitts., 1936-37; resident Pitts. City Hosp., 1937-41; dir. labs. Presbyn-Univ. Hosp., Pitts., 1954-62; chief pathology Meml. Hosp., Danville, Va., 1962—; prof. pathology U. Pitts. Sch. Medicine, 1950-62; prof. biology Averett Coll., Danville, 1971—. Vice chmn. Stratford Coll., Danville, 1973—, chmn. exec. com., 1973—. Served to lt. comdr. USNR, 1942-46. Mem. Am. Assn. Pathologists and Bacteriologists, Am. Soc. Exptl. Pathology, Coll. Am. Pathologists, Am., Pa. (pres. 1956) socs. clin. pathologists, Path. Soc. Gt. Brit. and Ireland, Va. Soc. Pathology (pres. 1972). Club: Golf (Danville). Contbr. articles to profl. jours. Home: Creekside Danville VA 24541 Office: The Meml Hosp Danville VA 24541

MORAN, THOMAS MAURICE, oil co. exec.; b. Boston, Sept. 21, 1923; s. Luke and Julia (Spillaine) M.; B.S., Boston Coll., 1948; M.B.A., U. Mich., 1951; m. Louise Stepat, Sept. 13, 1958 (div. Mar. 1973); children—Dona Marie, Thomas Maurice, Robert M., John M. Tech. rep. Shell Chem. Corp., N.Y.C., 1951-55; chem. rep. Eastern States Petroleum & Chem. Corp., 1955-58; dist. mgr. Signal Oil & Gas Co., Houston, 1958-60, asst. mgr. chem. sales, 1961-63, domestic sales mgr. petrochems. dept., 1963-66, gen. mgr. petrochems. dept., 1966-71; v.p. petrochem. sales Charter Internat. Oil Co., Houston, 1971—; pres., dir. Charter Export Co., 1971—; v.p. Ind. Petrochem. Corp., 1967-72, pres., 1972—. Served to lt. (j.g.) USNR, 1943-46. Mem. Nat. Petroleum Refiners Assn. (chmn. petrochems. com. 1970-72, dir.), Nat. Paint, Varnish and Lacquer Assn. Republican. Roman Catholic. Clubs: Champions Golf (Houston); Houston. Home: 14517 Misty Meadow Houston TX 77024 Office: 8938 Manchester St Houston TX 77012

MORE, PHILIP JEROME, mfg. co. exec.; b. Chgo., Dec. 11, 1911; s. Louis Eli and Anna Leah (Kahn) M.; B.S., Heidelberg (Germany) U., 1933; postgrad. Ill. Inst. Tech., 1936; LL.D., Roosevelt U., 1967; m. Sylvia Sally Bernstein, Oct. 16, 1937; children—Andrea (Mrs. Bernard Williams), Michael E., William M. Owner, pres. Feris Flying Service, Chgo., 1936-38; metallurgist Standard Dental Labs., Chgo., 1938-39; project design engr. Birtman Electric Co., Chgo., 1939-41; sr. design engr. Hotpoint div. Gen. Electric Co., Cicero, Ill., 1950-68; dir. purchasing Modern Maid, McGraw Edison, Chattanooga, 1968—. Cons. primitive monies, museums and univs.; sponsor numismatic studies Roosevelt U., Chgo., 1966-67. Presdl. appointee Assay Commn., 1965. Chmn. Engrs. for Senator Brock, 1970—, Engrs. for Senator Baker, 1972—. Served to comdr. USNR, 1950-58. Decorated Navy Cross. Recipient Gen. Electric citation for cost saving, 1966. Mem. Gas Appliance Engring. Soc. (pres. 1970-71). Clubs: North Shore Coin (founder, pres. 1950-58; Chgo.); Chgo. Coin (pres. 1964-65); Central States Numismatic Society (pres. 1965-66). Author: The Lure of Primitive Money, 1960; Odd and Curious Monies of The World, 1963. Contbr. articles on monies and engring. design to profl. jours. Patentee in field. Home: 404 Tunnell Blvd #H9 Chattanooga TN 37411 Office: PO Box 1111 Chattanooga TN 37401

MOREHEAD, DAVID WASHINGTON, govt. ofcl.; b. Greensboro, N.C., Sept. 9, 1918; s. Wheeler Sylvester and Elizabeth Marian (Johnson) M.; B.S. in Sociology, A. and T. State U., 1948-53; m. Ophelia Cole, Dec. 18, 1942; children—David, Jerome, Marion (Mrs. Oscar Jeter), Faye (Mrs. George Nock). With Hayes-Taylor YMCA, Greensboro, 1942-71, exec. dir., 1944-71; relocation specialist U.S. Dept. Housing and Urban Devel., Greensboro, 1972—. Chmn. Greensboro (N.C.) Pub. Utilities Bd., 1965-69; mem. adv. bd. Am. Savs. & Loan Assn., 1968—. Chmn. adv. bd. Manpower Devel. Tng. Act, 1972—. Trustee A. & T. State U., 1965—, L. Richardson Hosp., 1969-73; bd. dirs. Greensboro Coliseum, 1968—; bd. dirs. Nat. Conf. Christians and Jews, 1965—, chmn., 1971—. Recipient Nat. Greene award Greensboro C. of C., 1969; Man of Year award Sigma Frat., 1970. Mem. Phi Beta Sigma. Methodist (mem. adminstrn. bd. 1971—). Mason (Shriner). Club: Greensboro Emcees. Home: 625 S Florida St Greensboro NC 27406 Office: 2309 W Cone Blvd Greensboro NC 27408

MORELAND, THOMAS DOUGLAS, civil engr.; b. Chatsworth, Ga., July 12, 1933; s. J.L. and Georgia Evelyn (Terry) M.; student North Ga. Coll., 1950-52; B.S., Ga. Inst. Tech., 1955, M.S. (Automotive Safety Found. grant), 1962; m. Evelyn Jesse Kilgore, Dec. 26, 1954; children—Stephen T., Vickie E., Melissa L., Jennifer H. With Ga. Dept. Transp., and predecessor agy., 1957—, state hwy. materials engr., to 1973, state hwy. engr., 1973—. Served to lt. C.E., AUS, 1955-57. Mem. Am. Assn. State Hwy. and Transp. Ofcls. (chmn. subcom. on materials), Ga. Hwy. Dept. Engrs. Assn. Baptist. Home: 1831 Hebron Hills Dr Tucker GA 30084 Office: Number 2 Capitol Square Atlanta GA 30034

MORELOCK, JAMES CRUTCHFIELD, mathematician; b. Martin, Tenn., Feb. 7, 1920; s. Joseph Fletcher and Lura Martha (Crutchfield) M.; student Bethel Coll., McKenzie, Tenn., 1937-39; B.S., Memphis State Coll., 1941; M.A., U. Mo., 1948; Ph.D. (fellow), U. Fla., 1952; m. Eugenia Scott Browne, Apr. 29, 1945; children—Elinor (Mrs. William Lester Smith), Constance Evelyn, Diana Louise. Instr. astronomy and math. U. Fla., Gainesville, 1949-52; asst. prof. math. Auburn (Ala.) U., 1952-56; head math. dept. King Coll., Bristol, Tenn., 1956-60; mathematician U.S. Naval Computation Lab., Dahlgren, Va., 1960-61; mem. staff Computation Center Gen. Electric, Huntsville, Ala., 1961-63; mathematician computation lab. Marshall Space Flight Center, Huntsville, Ala., 1963—. Instl. rep. to Boy Scouts, Civitan Club, Auburn, Ala., 1952-56; v.p. Huntsville Concert Band, 1963—. Served with USAAF, 1941-45; PTO. Manning scholar, 1940-41; recipient U.S. Treasury award, 1968, NASA 10 yr. Achievement award, 1969, NASA Apollo Achievement award, 1969. Mem. Am. Math. Soc., Math. Assn. Am., Assn. Computing Machinery, Bristol Astronomy Soc. (pres. 1956-60). Methodist. Club: Pistol. Home: 2917 Garth Rd SE Huntsville AL 35801 Office: Marshall Space Flight Center S&E COMP-T Huntsville AL 35812

MORELOCK, JONATHAN EDWARD, III, research co. exec.; b. Opelika, Ala., June 20, 1939; s. Jonathan Edward and Edna C. (Gass) M.; B.S., Auburn U., 1961; postgrad. Nashville Law Sch., 1962-63; m. Janet Landers, Dec. 17, 1960. Legal rep. Liberty Mut. Ins. Co., Nashville, 1962-65; contract adminstr. Boeing Co., Huntsville, Ala., 1965-66; contract adminstr. Wyle Labs., Huntsville, 1966-69, adminstrv. mgr., 1969—. Lectr., Calhoun Jr. Coll., 1971; adviser minority businesses. Head div. United Givers Fund, 1970-73; permanent Madison County chmn. U.S. Savs. Bond Program, chmn. Madison County payroll savs., 1968-71; mem. Huntsville Madison County Youth Leadership Program, 1969—, Huntsville Indsl. Expansion Com. Served with USAF, 1961-62. Recipient Merit citation Outstanding Service to Madison County, 1968-72; Patriotic Service award Treas. Dept., 1969-71. Mem. Auburn Alumni Assn., Huntsville Madison County C. of C., Madison Jr. C. of C., Nat. Contract Mgmt. Assn. (sec. 1971), Omicron Delta Kappa, Lambda Chi Alpha, Alpha Phi Omega. Elk. Clubs: Huntsville Quarterback, Huntsville Country (pres. 1973, dir. 1970-73), Valley Hills Country, Ala. Internat. Country, Madison County Auburn (pres. 1972—). Home: 1400 Toney Dr SE Huntsville AL 35802 Office: 7800 Governors Dr W Huntsville AL 35807

MORENO, LEOPOLD SEGISMUNDO, physician; b. Corrientes, Argentina, Feb. 6, 1927; s. Leopoldo Sixto and Espectacion Blasia (Saling) M.; B.S., Colegio Nacional Gen. San Martin, 1944; M.D., Buenos Aires Med. Sch., 1951; m. Susan Elizabeth Kinne, May 27, 1972; chilren—Karen, L. Bryan, Mark. Came to U.S., 1952, naturalized, 1957. Practicante Adscripto, Hosp. Alvarez, Buenos Aires, 1950-51; practicante Hosp. Espanol, Buenos Aires, 1950-52; resident tng. Tampa (Fla.) Municipal Hosp., 1952, St. Marys Hosp., Troy, N.Y., 1953, Suffolk Sanatorium, L.I., N.Y., 1954, Jackson Park Hosp., Chgo., 1955, Lincoln (Ill.) State Sch., 1956; practice medicine, specializing in family practice, Norfolk, Va., 1957—; mem. staff, asst. dir. dept. family practice DePaul Hosp.; mem. staff Med. Center Hosp. Diplomate Am. Bd. Family Practice, Pan Am. Med. Assn. Charter fellow Am. Acad. Family Practice; mem. A.M.A., Am. Thoracic Soc., Va., Norfolk County med. socs., Tidewater Acad. Family Practice (corr. sec. 1970-71) Am. Geriatric Soc., Va. Tb. Assn. Home: 441 Harriton Ct Norfolk VA 23505 Office: 7927 Old Ocean View Rd Norfolk VA 23518

MORET, ANDRES MANUEL, physician; b. Arroyo, Puerto Rico, Apr. 23, 1935; s. Andres Antonio and Gervasia (Velazquez) M.; student Universidad de Puerto Rico, 1952-54, Marquette U., 1954-56; Licenciado in medicine and surgery, Universidad de Barcelona, 1964; m. Amalia Perez, Jan. 5, 1961. Rotating intern, Teacher's Hosp., Hato Rey, Puerto Rico, 1964-65; physician for San Juan City Hosp. and San Juan Municipal Govt., 1965-67; house physician San Jorge Hosp., Santurce, Puerto Rico, physician for Hilton Internat. Hotels of Puerto Rico, med. examiner John Hancock Life Ins. Corp., Equitable Life Ins. Corp., Great Commonwealth Life Ins. Corp., Ga. Life Ins. Corp., New England Life Ins. Corp. Served to maj. M.C., Puerto Rico Nat. Guard. Fellow Royal Soc. Health, Puerto Rico Med. Assn., Assn. of Military Surgeons of the U.S.A., Nat. Guard Assn. U.S.A. Democrat. Roman Catholic. Home: 256 Rosario St Santurce PR 00912 Office: San Jorge St Santurce Puerto Rico 00912

MORETTA, ERNEST, JR., city ofcl.; b. Memphis, Jan. 6, 1937; s. Ernest and Theresa (Faccaro) M.; B.S., Christian Bros. Coll., 1958; m. Patricia Ann Danovi, Aug. 4, 1958; children—John, Gina, Anthony. With Pub. Works Div., City of Memphis, 1955—, adminstrv. asst., 1972-74, adminstrv. mgr. div. pub. works, 1974—. Instr. Center for Tng. and Career Devel., U. Tenn., Knoxville, 1973—. Chmn. pub. works div. Shelby United Neighbors, 1970—; mem. City of Memphis Pension Bd., 1971—. Mem. Am. Pub. Works Assn. Home: 3797 Ladue St Memphis TN 38127 Office: 125 N Main St Room 602 Memphis TN 38103

MORETZ, WILLIAM HENRY, surgeon, educator; b. Hickory, N.C., Oct. 23, 1914; s. Joseph A. and Elizabeth (Leonard) M.; B.S., Lenoir Rhyne Coll., 1935, D.Sc. (hon.), 1960; postgrad. Med. Sch. U. N.C., 1935-37; M.D., Harvard, 1939; m. Laura Thelma Schlums, Dec. 5, 1947; children—William Henry, John D., Robert L., Richard E., Elizabeth L., David L. Intern, also asst. resident surgery, resident surgery Strong Meml. Hosp., Rochester, N.Y., 1939-43; instr. surgery U. Rochester Sch. Medicine, 1944-47; asst. prof. surgery U. Utah Coll. Medicine, 1947-49, asso. prof., 1949-55; prof. surgery, chmn. dept. Med. Coll. Ga., Augusta, 1955-72, pres. coll., 1972—. Cons. surgery VA Hosp., Augusta, U.S. Army Hosp., Augusta, Ga. Served from lt. to capt. M.C., AUS, 1944-47. Fellow A.C.S.; mem. Soc. U. Surgeons, Western, Am., So. surg. assns., Soc. Surgery Alimentary Tract, A.M.A., Richmond County Med. Soc., Ga. Surg. Soc., Internat. Soc. Surgery, Internat. Cardiovascular Soc. Contbr. articles to surg. lit. Home: 2345 McDowell St Augusta GA 30904

MOREY, PHILIP STOCKTON, JR., educator; b. Houston, July 11, 1937; s. Philip Stockton and Helen Holmes (Wolcott) M.; B.A. with honors, U. Tex., 1959, M.A., 1961, Ph.D., 1967; m. Jeri Lynn Snyder, Sept. 5, 1964; 1 son, William Philip. Asst. prof. math. U. Neb., Omaha, 1967-68; asso. prof. math. Tex. A & I U., Kingsville, 1968—. Vice pres. Kingsville Amateur Radio Club, 1973—. Mem. Am. Math. Soc., Math. Assn. Am., Tensor Soc., Sigma Pi Sigma, Phi Kappa Phi. Home: 1514 Lackey Av Kingsville TX 78363

MORGAN, ALBERT RICHARD, JR., industrial exec.; b. Oakland, Cal., Feb. 1, 1922; s. Albert Richard and Genevieve Henrietta (Overman) M.; B.S. in Chemistry, U. Cal. at Berkeley, 1943, postgrad., 1947-48; m. Alice Marie Hill, Jan. 5, 1944; children—Richard John, Jacqueline Diane. Dir. research FMC Corp., Princeton, N.J., 1948-68; v.p. Panacon Corp., Cin., 1968-72; asst. to pres. Jim Walter Corp., Tampa, Fla., 1972-73; v.p. Ecological Scis. Corp., Tulsa, 1973—. Served to capt., Ordnance Corps, AUS, 1943-46. Mem. Am. Inst. Chem. Engrs., Am. Inst. Chemists, Am. Chem. Soc. Chemists Club. Club: Nassau (Princeton). Patentee in field. Home: 145 Center Plaza Tulsa OK 74119 Office: 424 N Boulder Tulsa OK 74101

MORGAN, ALBERT RUFUS, JR., elec. co. exec.; b. Rutherfordton, N.C., Sept. 22, 1916; s. Albert Rufus and Madeline Mahala (Prentiss) M.; B.A., U. S.C., 1937; B.S. in Civil Engring., Ga. Inst. Tech., 1940; m. Irene Elizabeth Mitchell, June 11, 1949; children—Albert Rufus III, Anna Chipman. Prin. naval architect Charleston (S.C.) Navy Yard, 1940-43; engr. Commonwealth and So. Corp., N.Y., 1946-49; depreciation engr. So. Services, Inc., Birmingham, Ala., 1949-63, asst. to tax adviser, 1963-65, asst. mgr. tax dept., Atlanta, 1965-71, mgr. depreciation accounting services 1971—. Treas., Christian Council of Met. Atlanta, 1968. Served to staff sgt. AUS, 1943-46; CBI. Recipient First prize student chapters S.E. Conf. Am. Soc. C.E., 1940; san. engr. summer fellowship W. K. Kellogg Found., 1940; Naval Architect Certificate, The Citadel, 1941. Mem. The Edison Electric Inst. (mem. depreciation accounting com., chmn. 1966-67), Isaak Walton League (sec.-treas., dir. Greater Atlanta chpt.), Sigma Alpha Epsilon, Delta Phi Alpha, Omicron Delta Kappa. Home: 6558 Roswell Rd NW Atlanta GA 30328 Office: 64 Perimeter Center E P O Box 720071 Atlanta GA 30346

MORGAN, ANTONIA BELL (MRS. WILLIAM J. MORGAN), psychologist; b. London, Eng., Oct. 5, 1914; d. James Young and Jean (Macnair) Bell; B.A., U. Oxford, 1936, M.A., 1945; tchrs. diploma U. London, 1938; m. William James Morgan, Nov. 2, 1944; children—William James, Jean Elizabeth, Robert Macnair. Came to U.S., 1946, naturalized, 1948. Chmn. dept. classical studies St. Albans Sch., Hertfordshire, Eng., 1938-41; Walter Hines Page scholar, lectr. English-Speaking Union, 1941-42; lectr. Brit. Ministry of Information, 1942-43, asst. prin., India Office, 1943-45; sec. Aptitude Assos., 1946-49, asso. dir. 1949—; cons. ch. schs. Diocese Va.; lectr. mental health topics to civic groups, schs. Vice pres. No. Va. Mental Health Assn., 1959-61. Licensed clin. psychologist, Va. Mem. A.A.A.S., Am. Personnel and Guidance Assn. Episcopalian. Author psychol. and projective tests, articles on edn. of gifted children. Home and office: 2816 Gallows Rd Vienna VA 22180

MORGAN, ARTHUR C., sculptor, sch. dir.; b. Ascension Parish, La., Aug. 3, 1904; s. H. Arthur and Cora (Carmene) M.; ed. pub. and pvt. schs.; pvt. study with Gutzon Borglum, 1920-21; student Beaux Arts Inst. Design, N.Y., 1921-23; m. Gladys Butler, Mar. 2, 1929; children—Diana, Cynthia (dec.). Sculptor, N.Y.C., 1923, New Orleans, 1924-26; dir. Centenary Coll., Shreveport, 1928-33; founder Southwestern Inst. Arts, dir., 1934—. Works include: heroic figure chief Justice Edward Douglas White, in U.S. Capitol; Morehead Meml., E. L. Kurth Meml. Hosp., Lufkin; E. K. Long momument, Winnfield, La.; basreliefs and monolith Civic Theater, Shreveport, Paul Gersler Meml., Berwick, monumental, archtl. garden and portrait sculpture; bust Judge Robert B. Butler, Ct. House, Houma, La. Henry Miller Shreve monument, Shreveport, La.; busts Paul M. Brown, Dr. George S. Sexton, Dr. John B. Entrikin, Centenary Coll.; marble bust Dr. James M. Owens, stone carving St. Mark's Episcopal Ch.; heroic stone carving Ch. Holy Rosary, Shreveport; Van Cliburn medallion; Henry Schuyler Thibodaux bust, Municipal Auditorium, Thibodaux; represented many pvt. collections. Mem. Nat. Arts Club, (N.Y.C.). Episcopalian. Rotarian. Writer, lectr. in field. Home: 657 Jordan St Shreveport LA 71101 Office: Southwestern Inst of Arts Shreveport LA 71101

MORGAN, CHARLES, JR., lawyer, assn. adminstr.; b. Cin., Mar. 11, 1930; s. Charles and Ethel (Mitchell) M.; B.S., U. Ala., 1953, J.D., 1955; m. Camille Walpole, Sept. 5, 1953; 1 son, Charles III. Admitted to Ala. bar, 1955, D.C. bar, 1972; practiced in Birmingham, Ala., 1955-63; asst. gen. counsel Am. Assn. U. Profs., 1963-64; spl. counsel N.A.A.C.P. Legal Def. and Ednl. Fund, 1963-64; dir. So. regional office Am. Civil Liberties Union, 1964-72, dir. nat. office, Washington, 1972—. Instr. Am. econ. History U. Ala., 1954-55. Nat. committeeman Ala. Young Democrats, 1951-55; nat. committeeman Nat. Democratic Party of Ala., 1968-69; chmn. Kennedy-Johnson speakers campaign, 1960. Pres., Jefferson County Heart Found., 1963; bd. dirs. Ala. Assn. for Mental Health, 1958-63. Named Man of Yr., Utility Club N.Y., 1964; hon. fellow U. Pa. Sch. Law, 1964. Mem. Phi Alpha Delta, Delta Tau Delta (pres. chpt. 1951-52, v.p. So. region 1962-63). Author: A Time To Speak, 1964. Contbr. anthologies; writer for periodicals. Home: 604 Independence Av SE Washington DC 20003 Office: 410 1st St SE Washington DC 20003

MORGAN, CHARLES DAVID, mech. engr.; b. Spring Valley, N.Y., Nov. 7, 1934; s. Charles Elias and Florence Verlene (Smith) M.; M.E., Stevens Inst. Tech., 1956; M.S., Rensselaer Poly. Inst., 1960; Ph.D., Lehigh U., 1965; m. Carolyn Ann Seeback, Dec. 29, 1956; children—Charles David, Gary Allen, John Louis, Andrew Merrill. Engr., Combustion Engring., Windsor, Conn., 1956-60; instr. mech. engring. Bethlehem Pa., Lehigh U., 1960-64; prin. engr. Babcock & Wilcox, Lynchburg, Va., 1964-67, unit mgr., 1967—. Lectr. U. Va. extension at Lynchburg, part time, 1965—. Bd. dirs. Community Concert Series, 1973. Recipient Alumni Service award Stevens Inst. Tech., 1971. Mem. A.A.A.S., Am. Soc. M.E., Delta Tau Delta. Club: Boonsboro Country. Contbr. articles to profl. jours. Home: 1444 Northwood Circle Lynchburg VA 24503 Office: Box 1260 Lynchburg VA 24501

MORGAN, CLYDE NATHANIEL, physician; b. nr. Belton, Tex., Nov. 2, 1923; s. Xenophen William and Rhoda Ella (Deck) M.; B.S., Abilene Christian Coll., 1948; M.D., U. Tex., 1953; m. Birdie Joyce Palmer, Mar. 3, 1951; children—Clyde Nathaniel, Reinette, Nancy. Intern, Robert B. Green Meml. Hosp., San Antonio, 1953-54; resident Cook County Hosp., Chgo., 1967-68; practice gen. medicine, 1954-66, practice speciailizing in dermatology, Abilene, Tex., 1968—; asso. prof. biology Abilene Christian Coll., 1954-56; instr. Hendrick Meml. Hosp. Sch. Nursing, 1954-59. Chmn. Taylor County Republican Party, 1965-70; del. Rep. Nat. Conv., 1968. Served to 1st lt. USAAF, 1943-45; ETO. Recipient Med. Econs. award, 1963, Physicians Recognition award A.M.A., 1969. Mem. Tex. Dermatologic Soc., Ibero Latin Am. Coll. Dermatology, A.M.A., Tex., So. med. assns., Taylor-Jones County Med. Soc., Am., Tex. assns. gen. practice, Aircraft Owners and Pilot Assn., Abilene C. of C. Kiwanian. Author: (with others) The Forbidden Apple, 1965. Home: 1718 Cedarcrest St Abilene TX 79601 Office: 1166 Merchant St Abilene TX 79603

MORGAN, DAVID L., transp. co. exec.; b. High Point, N.C., May 24, 1935; s. David Early and Polly Anne (Whitley) M.; student Wake Forest Coll., 1962-63, U. N.C., 1966-68; m. Betty Jo Robinson, June 16, 1960; children—Michael David, Deborah JoAnn, Nancy Elizabeth, Joel Wesley. Sec.-treas. Buck Young Oil Co., Inc., Lexington, N.C., 1960-69, Maybelle Transport Co., 1969—; also dir. Bd. dirs. Buck Young Found. Served with USNR, 1956-60. Mem. Jr. C. of C. (Outstanding Mem. 1964), Indsl. Mgmt. Club (v.p. 1968). Mason. Club: Sertoma. Home: 504 Queens Rd Lexington NC 27292 Office: 1820 S Main St Lexington NC 27292

MORGAN, DONALD CLINTON, hosp. adminstr.; b. Salisbury, N.C., Aug. 14, 1927; s. Walter C. and Neta (Cranford) M.; A.B., Catawba Coll., 1950; certificate Charlotte Meml. Hosp. Sch. Adminstrn., 1954; m. Peggy Jean Wolfe, Oct. 14, 1951; children—Brad, Andrew, Jeffery. Asst. adminstr. Good Samaritan Hosp., Charlotte, N.C., 1951-52; asst. adminstr. Anderson Meml. Hosp., 1954-58; adminstr. C. J. Harris Community Hosp., Sylva, N.C., 1958—. Mem. regional adv. com. N.C. Med. Program. Served with AUS, World War II. Named Citizen of Year, Jackson County C. of C., 1970. Mem. Am. Coll. Hosp. Adminstrs., Am., N.C. (dir.) hosp. assns. Presbyn. Rotarian. Home: Route 1 Box 97 Sylva NC 28779 Office: 59 Hospital Rd Sylva NC 28779

MORGAN, EDWARD P., writer, broadcaster; b. Walla Walla, Wash., June 23, 1910; s. Arthur H. and Pansy Eledice (Paddock) M.; B.A. cum laude, Whitman Coll., 1932, L.H.D., 1957; grad. student U. Wash., 1932-33; m. Jane Stolle, Dec. 31, 1937 (div. 1945); 1 dau., Linda; m. 2d, Katharine Burden Sohier, July 18, 1960. Reporter Seattle Star, 1932-34; corr. U.P.I., 1934-43, Chgo. Daily News Fgn. Service, 1943-46; corr., asso. editor Collier's Weekly, 1946-48; free lance writer Europe, 1948-50; corr. CBS, 1951-54, dir. news for radio and TV, 1954; news commentator ABC, Wash., 1955-67, 69—; newspaper columnist for Newsday Syndicate, 1966—; sr. corr. Pub. Broadcast Lab., 1967-69. Recipient Peabody award for radio news, 1956; Sidney Hillman Found. award for radio news analysis, 1959; Alfred I. du Pont award best broadcast commentary, 1960; George Polk Meml. award for outstanding radio reporting, 1965; Overseas Press Club citation, 1966; Capital Press Club Journalism Excellence award, 1966. Bd. overseers Whitman Coll.; trustee Howard U. Mem. Overseas Writers, Radio and TV Corrs. Assn. Wash. (pres.), Assn. Radio News Analysts, Am. Civil Liberties Union, Phi Beta Kappa, Sigma Delta Chi, Beta Theta Pi. Clubs: Federal City, Nat. Press (Washington); Century (N.Y.C.). Co-author: Candidates, 1960; The Press in Washington, 1966. Editor: This I Believe, vol. 1, 1952, contbg. author, vol. 2, 1954; Clearing the Air, 1963. Office: 1124 Connecticut Av NW Washington DC 20036

MORGAN, EDWIN BUFORD, hosp. adminstr.; b. Marlow, Okla., Dec. 11, 1918; s. William Pruitt and Sarah Elizabeth (Nevins) M.; student Ark. Tech. Coll., 1938-39, U. Okla., 1940; m. Mary Merle Arline, Sept. 30, 1944; children—Edwin Buford, Dennis Wayne, William Randolph. Asst. adminstr. Angus Hosp., Lawton, Okla., 1945-49; mgr. Double-Cola Bottling Co., Ardmore, Okla., 1949-51; adminstr. Lawton Clinic, 1951-66, John Buist Chester Hosp., also Chester Clinics, Dallas, 1966—; pres. Dallas Credit Consultants, Inc. Vice pres. Dallas Hosp. Council, 1971; pres., 1972; dir. Regional Health Planning Council of N. Central Tex. Council Govts., exec. com., 1973. Mem. Dallas Fire Council, Dallas Health Planning Council. Served with USCG, 1941-44. Recipient Silver Beaver award Boy Scouts Am. Fellow Am. Acad. Med. Adminstrs.; mem. Tex. Hosp. Assn. (chmn. Blacklands div. 1971), Okla. Anthropol. Soc. (pres. S.W. chpt. 1961, 65-66), Southwestern Okla. Hist. Soc. (sec.-treas. 1963-66). Author: Wichita Mountains, Ancient Oasis of the Prairie, 1973. Home: 1540 Driftwood Dr Dallas TX 75224 Office: 3330 S Lancaster St Dallas TX 75216

MORGAN, GARY L., pub. relations and assn. exec.; b. Nashville, Oct. 16, 1935; s. Alec L. and Alva Jane (Kington) M.; B.A., Vanderbilt U., 1959; m. Christine Binkley, July 7, 1953; 1 son, Gary L. With WSM Radio-TV, 1953-58; writer, producer, dir. KGGM-TV, 1959-60; writer, dir. and producer for TV, 1953—; founder Digne Enterprises, Nashville, 1960, Nashville Insta-Print, Inc., 1965; sec. Coronada Stone Co., Inc., 1970—, also dir.; exec. dir. Home Builders Assn. of Tenn., 1968—; chmn. bd. dirs. Image Devel. Assos., 1966—; pres. Association Services, 1970—. Served with AUS, 1958-60. Mem. Pub. Relations Soc. Am., Nat. Assn. of Home Builders (v.p. exec. officers council, 1971), Tenn. Soc. Assn. Execs. (v.p. 1972, pres. 1973). Club: Orange Motor (dir. 1973—). Home: Rt 2 River Oaks Brentwood TN 37027 Office: Capitol Hill Bldg Nashville TN 37219

MORGAN, GEORGE EMIR, dentist; b. Waynesville, Mo., Jan. 28, 1895; s. John Bunyan and Ida Belle (Rollins) M.; student Southwest State Coll., 1911-13; D.D.S., Washington U., 1916; m. Lee Mary Burchard, Apr. 28, 1919; children—Dorothy Lee (Mrs. Claude S. Hayes), George Emir. Practice of pedodontics, Milw., 1918-60; prof. pedodontics Marquette U., 1929-49; hon. mem. med. staff Boca Raton Community Hosp., 1967—. Trustee, Boca Raton Community Hosp., 1967—, treas. exec. com., 1968—. Mem. Am. Dental Assn. (trustee 1935-41), Wis. State Dental Soc. (pres. 1935), Milw. County Dental Soc. (pres. 1926), Fla. Soc. of Dentistry for Children (hon.), Sturdy Oaks Bowling Club for Retired Men (founder 1963), Retired Physicians and Dentists Club (co-founder 1966), Delta Sigma Delta. Methodist (trustee 1970—). Mason. Club: Deerfield Country (Deerfield Beach, Fla.). Address: 632 SW 4th St Boca Raton FL 33432

MORGAN, GEORGE ROBERT, petroleum corp. exec.; b. Baton Rouge, Oct. 30, 1897; s. Thomas O. and Mattie H. (Joor) M.; student La. State U., 1920-21; m. Nell M. Boddeker, Aug. 5, 1925. Stenographer traffic dept. Gulf Coast Lines, 1916-17; chief clk. land dept. Sinclair Oil & Gas Co., 1918-19; clk.-stenographer Am. Petroleum Co., Tex., 1921-22, asst. sec., 1922—, dir., 1940—; asst. treas. Am. Republics Corp., 1932-51, chief communications div., 1951-56, ret., 1956. Democrat. Methodist. Home: RFD 4 Box 432 Baton Rouge LA 70805

MORGAN, HARCOURT ALEXANDER, JR., physician; b. Knoxville, Tenn., Aug. 20, 1909; s. Harcourt Alexander and Sara Elizabeth (Fay) M.; B.A., U. Tenn., 1931, M.D., 1933; M.P.H., Johns Hopkins U., 1941; m. Sarah Lanier Stone, Aug. 9, 1934; children—Harcourt Alexander, III, Sarah Lanier (Mrs. Phillip Howard Davis), Lucy Fay (Mrs. James Connelly Hinds). Intern Memphis Gen. Hosp., 1933-35; resident U.S. Marine Hosp., Balt., 1936-37, Detroit, 1937; gen. practice medicine, Sparta, Tenn., 1937-39; pub. health physician Tenn. Dept. Pub. Health, 1939—; mem. staff Parkview Hosp., Dyersburg; health officer Dyersburg County. Dir. Bank Belfast, Tenn., Middle Tenn. Heart Assn., Nashville, 1970—; med. adviser Selective Service, Lewisburg, Tenn., 1948—; dir. Marshall County Farm Bur., Lewisburg, 1955—. Served to 1st lt. AUS, 1935-36; served with USPHS, 1936-37. Diplomate Am. Bd. Preventive Medicine. Fellow Am. Pub. Health Assn.; mem. Am. Assn. Pub. Health Physicians (charter), Northwest Tenn. Med. Assembly, Tenn. Med. Assn., A.M.A., Delta Omega. Methodist (mem. ofcl. bd. 1948-72). Elk, Lion (pres. 1956-57). Home: 1525 White Dr Lewisburg TN 37091 Office: 1629 Woodlawn St Dyersburg TN 38024

MORGAN, HERMAN WILTON, educator; b. Brooksville, Fla., Apr. 13, 1925; s. Soloman Arleigh and Alice (Lee) M.; B.S., Fla. So. Coll., 1949; M.S., Fla. State U., 1958; m. Florence Harrison, Sept. 7, 1949 (dec. 1964); children—Laura Ann, Herman Wilton; m. 2d, Willette Phillips, Feb. 27, 1965. Linotype operator Dade City (Fla.) Banner, 1949-52; asso. editor Zephyrhills (Fla.) News, 1952-54; printing instr. Brewster Vocational Sch., Tampa, Fla., 1954-62; evening trade extension coordinator Evening Vocational Sch., Tampa, 1962-63; prin. Adult Tech. Sch., Tampa, 1963—. Pres., Printing Industry Tampa, 1960-62; bd. dirs. Printing Industries Fla., 1960-62. Served with USNR, 1943-46. Mem. Fla. Vocational Assn. (v.p. 1961-63, 73—, sec.-treas. 1963-66, 68-71, pres. 1967), Indsl. Edn. Assn. Fla. (pres. 1961-62, 73-75), Am. Vocational Assn., Am. Assn. Sch. Adminstrs., Theta Chi, Phi Delta Kappa, Iota Lambda Sigma. Democrat. Methodist. Home: 410 Island Rd Temple Terrace FL 33617 Office: 105 W Ross Av Tampa FL 33602

MORGAN, HORACE C., JR., veterinarian, educator; b. Piedmont, Ala., July 3, 1928; s. Horace C. and Clancey Eleanor (Moore) M.; D.V.M., Auburn U., 1955, M.S., 1958; m. Dorothy May Thomas, Sept. 2, 1956; children—Diane, Laura. Practiced vet. medicine, Murfreesboro, Tenn., 1959-60; asso. prof. pathology U. Ga., Athens, 1960-70; asst. dean Auburn (Ala.) U., 1970—. Cons. WHO, 1972. Mem. Jury Commn. Clarke Co., Athens, 1970. Served with USAF, 1946-49. Named Ga. Veterinarian of Year, Ga. Vet. Med. Assn., 1970. Mem. Am. Vet. Med. Assn., Am. Soc. Vet. Clin. Pathologists (pres. 1967-68), Am. Animal Hosp. Assn., Alpha Psi (pres. nat. council 1970-72), Phi Zeta, Alpha Psi. Rotarian. Home: Box 1907 Auburn AL 30608 Office: School of Veterinary Medicine Auburn University Auburn AL 30630

MORGAN, HUGH JACKSON, JR., natural gas exec.; b. Nashville, Aug. 10, 1928; s. Hugh Jackson and Robert Ray (Porter) M.; grad. Episcopal High Sch., Alexandria, Va., 1946; A.B., Princeton, 1950; LL.B., Vanderbilt U., 1956; m. Ann Moulton Ward, Aug. 28, 1954; children—Ann, Grace, Caroline, Hugh Jackson III. Admitted to Tenn. bar, 1956; practiced in Chattanooga, 1956-60; with So. Natural Gas Co., Birmingham, Ala., 1960—, asst. gen. counsel, asst. sec., 1965-66, gen. atty., asst. sec., 1966-70, asst. v.p., gen. atty., asst. sec., 1970-71, v.p. pipeline affairs, 1971-73, v.p. pipeline affairs, v.p. So. Natural Resources, Inc., 1973—; dir. S.Ga. Natural Gas Co., Thomasville; dir. Sea Robin Pipeline Co., Houston. Trustee Brooke Hill Sch., Children's Hosp., Birmingham. Served from ensign to lt. (j.g.) USNR, 1950-53. Recipient Bennett Douglas Bell Meml. award Vanderbilt Law Sch., 1956. Mem. Am., Tenn. bar assns., Am., So. gas assns., Ind. Natural Gas Assn. Am., Order of Coif. Episcopalian. Clubs: Mountain Brook, Downtown, Relay House (Birmingham); Boston (New Orleans); Army-Navy (Washington); University Cottage (Princeton); Linville (N.C.) Golf. Home: 3121 Brookwood Rd Mountain Brook AL 35223 Office: First Nat-So Natural Bldg PO Box 2563 Birmingham AL 35202

MORGAN, JACK COCHRAN, lawyer; b. Sweetwater, Tex., Mar. 17, 1928; s. John Franklin and Tommie Lee (Cochran) M.; B.A., Tex. U., 1948, LL.B., 1950; m. Millicent Edmunds, Jan. 24, 1953; children—Millicent, Jack C. Admitted to Tex. bar, 1950, practiced in Kaufman, 1950—; asst. count atty., Kaufman, 1951; mem. firm Morgan and Shumpert. Dir. Farmers & Merchants Nat. Bank, Kaufman. Dem. county chmn., 1965; mem. Tex. legislature, 1955. Mem. State Bar Grievance Com. Chmn. Bd. Regents Tyler State Coll., 1970—; trustee Tyler State Coll. Found., 1970—. Served to capt. USAF, 1951-60. Mem. Kaufman County, (past pres.), Tri-County bar assns., Sigma Chi. Mason, Rotarian. Home: 1506 S Houston St Kaufman TX 75142 Office: 201 W Mulberry St Kaufman TX 75142

MORGAN, JAMES BAKER, lawyer; b. Fort Worth, Tex., Dec. 14, 1940; s. James N. and Ruth Alice (Baker) M.; B.B.A., Baylor U., 1963, J.D., 1964; m. Sherry Diane Rawls, Dec. 28, 1962; children—James Michael, Marshall Wayne. Admitted to Tex. bar, 1964; asst. city atty. Fort Worth, 1964; atty., Office Chief Counsel, IRS, Washington, 1965-66, Jacksonville, Fla., 1966-69; partner Handy & Morgan, Inc., Hurst, Tex., 1969—; dir. 1st Nat. Bank, Hurst, Forest Hill State Bank (Tex.). Mem. adv. council Tarrant County Hosp. Dist., 1973—. Mem. Sch. Bd. Hurst Euless Bedord Ind. Sch. Dist., 1971—. Bd. mgrs. YMCA, 1971—. Mem. Am., Tex., N.E. Tarrant County bar assns., Phi Delta Phi. Rotarian (pres. 1973-74). Club: Woodhaven Country (Fort Worth). Baptist. Home: 428 Billy Creek Circle Hurst TX 76053 Office: 440-A W Pipeline Rd Hurst TX 76053

MORGAN, JAMES HARRIS, lawyer; b. Greenville, Tex., Sept. 17, 1926; s. James Benton and Almarine (Harris) M.; B.A., U. Tex., 1947, LL.B., 1950; m. Barbara Ellen Knox, Apr. 5, 1952; children—Marshall Benton, Florence Lynn, James Brian. Admitted to Tex. bar, 1950, since practiced in Greenville; partner Morgan, Smith & Crough, 1969—. Dir. Citizens Nat. Bank of Greenville. Lectr. in profl. legal econs., univs. and bar assns., 1966—. Bd. dirs. Greenville Entertainment Series, pres., 1951—. Served with AUS, 1945-46. Fellow Tex. Bar Found.; mem. State Bar Tex. (chmn. profl. efficiency and econs. research com. 1966—; recipient Award of Merit 1965, 66, Pres.'s award 1967), N.Tex. (pres. 1961-62, dean skills course for young lawyers 1969—), Hunt County (pres. 1960-61) bar assns., Phi Beta Kappa. Democrat. Presbyn. (elder 1957—). Editor; (with others) American Bar Handbook, 1973, The Efficient Practice of Law, 1966. Home: 7 Oak Village Rd Greenville TX 75401 Office: 2610 S Stonewall St Greenville TX 75401

MORGAN, JOE LEE, librarian; b. nr. Marshall, N.C., May 14, 1931; s. Frank Woodard and Effie Mae (McDaris) M.; A.B. in History and Polit. Sci., Berea Coll., 1954; postgrad. No. Ill. U., 1955, U. Hawaii, 1956, U. Colo., 1957, 58, U. N.C., 1957-58, Asian Affairs Inst., Duke, summer 1959, East Tenn. State U., summers 1960-63, 68-69, 71-72; diploma hotel-motel tng. LaSalle Extension U. Farmer, Marshall, 1945-71; tchr. pub. schs., Mendota, Ill, 1954-55, Charlotte, N.C., 1957-59; tchr.-librarian Madison County (N.C.) Schs., 1959-65; tchr. history Capt. Riverside Mil. Acad., Gainesville, Ga., 1967-69; librarian Vardell Hall Girls' Prep. Sch., Red Springs, N.C., 1969-72; mgr. Cavalier Motel, Asheville, N.C., 1972—. Regional rep. N.C. Sch. Performing Arts; mem. library council, chmn. adult lit. program French Broad Bapt. Assn., 1964-66, clk., 1965-69, contbr. minutes, 1965-69; Sunday Sch. sec., tchr., supt., librarian Peek's Chapel Bapt. Ch., Marshall, 1946-65; mem. Arts and Humanities Commn., Council So. Mountains, 1966-69, edn. commn., 1970-73; mem. Citizens Com. for Free Cuba; bd. policy of Liberty Lobby; mem. Am. Friends Vietnam, Inc.; mem. Civic Arts Council, Inc. Asheville, N.C., 1964-67; active A.R.C. Broadcasting bd. sponsors Radio Free Asia. Precinct chmn., mem. Mecklenburg County Republican Exec. Com., 1958-59; temporary chmn. White County (Ga.) Rep. Conv., 1966; 1st vice chmn. White County Rep. party 1966-67; del. Ga. congl. and state convs., 1966, N.C., 1958, 62, 64, 70, 71, 73; mem. United Reps. Am.; chmn. Robeson County Young Reps., 1970-71; chmn. community services com. N.C. Fedn. Young Reps., 1971, also mem. exec. bd.; del. Young Reps. Fedn. nat. conv., Phoenix, 1971; chmn. Madison County Rep. Com., 1971-73; mem. 11th Dist. N.C. Rep. exec. com., 1971-73; mem. exec. com. N.C. Rep. Com., 1971-73; mem., sec. Madison County Bd. Elections, 1974—. Served with AUS, 1955-57. Recipient certificate appreciation N.C. Rep. party, founding supporter's certificate Radio Free Asia; named Young Am. Day radio sta. WWNC, Asheville, N.C. Mem. N.E.A. (del. assembly), N.C. Edn. Assn., N.C. Librarians Assn., Korean Cultural and Freedom Found., Young Ams. for Freedom, N.C. Literary and Hist. Assn., RCA Victor Soc. Great Music (founding mem.), N.C. Farm Bur., Nat. Congress Parents and Tchrs., Western N.C. (chmn. awards com. 1973-74), Roanoke Island (chmn. Madison County 1971-72) hist. assns., Madison County Classroom Tchrs. Assn. (sec.-treas. 1959-63), N.C. Soc. Preservation Antiquities, U.N. Assn. U.S., Ashville (N.C.) Community Concerts Assn., Am.'s Future, Inc., Internat. Platform Assn. Author: A Librarian's Handbook, 1964; Reflection on the Scopes Evolution Trial, 1965; North Carolina and The Admission of Kansas, 1966. Contbr. to profl. publs. Home: East Fort Route 2 Marshall NC 28753

MORGAN, JOHN EMILE, banker; b. Bay St. Louis, Miss., Aug. 15, 1910; s. Thomas Frank and Carmen Eunice (Hutton) M.; student Loyola at New Orleans, 1936-38; m. Rosalie Roddy, Nov. 1, 1942; Clk., Hibernia Nat. Bank, New Orleans, 1925-38; examiner Fed. Deposit Ins. Corp., Atlanta, 1938-41; with 1st Nat. Bank Commerce, 1947—, trust officer, 1948—, v.p., 1970—. Served to maj., Air Corps, AUS, 1941-46. Clubs: Bienville, Lamplighter, Iris (New Orleans). Home: 300 Jefferson Av Metairie LA 70005 Office: PO Box 60279 New Orleans LA 70160

MORGAN, JOHN KNIGHTON, city ofcl.; b. Dallas, Oct. 28, 1913; s. Boniar Stewart and Clara Louise (Reynolds) M.; student San Antonio Jr. Coll., 1932; m. Josephine Alice Winslow, Dec. 25, 1935; children—John Knighton, Dale S. Asst. mgr. Dickason Goodman Co., Pawhuska, Okla., 1935-40; mgr. Peoples Furniture Co., Odessa, Tex., 1940-42; foreman Continental Motors, Inc., Garland, 1942-45; mgr. Murphy Automotive, Inc., 1945-48; v.p., gen. mgr. Rudy-Patrick Seed Co., 1948-61; city sec., City of Graham, Tex., 1961—. Mem. Internat. Inst. Municipal Clerks, Municipal Finance Officers Assn., Internat. Assn. Assessing Officers (sec. Red River chpt. 1962—), C. of C. Episcopalian (vestryman, treas.). Mason (32 deg., Shriner), Lion (sec. 1962-63). Home: 1411 Scenic Dr Graham TX 76046 Office: City Hall Graham TX 76046

MORGAN, MARIE GRIFFIN (MRS. LOY WESTON MORGAN), club woman, civic worker, editor-pub.; b. Hickox, Ga., Dec. 1, 1914; d. Raiford Avant and Carrie (Higginbotham) Griffin; certificate Abraham Baldwin Agrl. Coll., 1937; B.S. in Home Econs., U. Ga., 1939; postgrad. U. Kan., 1948; m. Loy Weston Morgan, Aug. 29, 1944; children—Raiford Gordon, Linda Marilyn Thursby, Patricia Marie. Tchr. home econs. Lockhart (S.C.) High Sch., 1939-40; asst. home mgmt. supr. FSA, U.S. Dept. Agr., Quitman, Ga., 1940, home supr. Farmers Home Administrn., Donalsonville, Ga., 1940-44, acting farm supr., 1944-46, home supr., Olathe, Kan., 1946; sec., receptionist U.S. Bur. Entomology and Plant Quarantine, Tifton, Ga., 1948-51; tchr. Omega (Ga.) High Sch., 1955-56; reporter for radio, news editor The News Examiner, Tifton, 1960-61; asst. women's news reporter Radio and News Examiner, Tifton, 1962-65; women's news reporter radio sta. WWGS and News Examiner, 1965-69; photographer Live Wire Press Assn.; owner, operator Red Oak Springs Farm; agt. Am. Nat. Ins. Co., 1971-73; editor-pub. News-Examiner, Tifton, 1973—. Mem. resource instrs. com. Tifton Jr. High Sch. Retarded Children's Class; v.p. Hillcrest Neighborhood Garden Club, Tifton, 1949-50, pres., 1951-52, social chmn., 1962-63, civil def. chmn., 1963-64, devotional chmn., 1970-71, publicity chmn., 1971-72; Tift County (Ga.) sec. Am. Legion Aux., 1955-57, 2d v.p., 1957-58, 1st v.p., 1958-59, pres., 1959-61, 70-71, chmn. numerous coms., 1955—, unit 2d v.p., 1968-70, chmn. rehab. com., 1969-70, mem. unit fair com., 1962—, membership chmn. 1968-70, 2d. dist. historian, 1960-61, dist. chmn. nat. security com., 1962-63, dist. 1st v.p., 1963-64, dist. pres. 1965-66, Ga. chmn. community service com., 1961-62, mem. dept. radio-TV com., 1962-64, 2d dist. pres., 1964-65, chmn. dept. child welfare, 1965-66, dist. sec. and jr. activities chmn., 1968-69, communications chmn., 1969-70, chaplain, publicity, radio-TV, rehab. chmn., pres. unit 21, 1965-66, Dept. Ga. civil def. chmn., 1967-68, rehab. com. and field service vol. dir., 1968-69, communications chmn., 1969-70, dept. legislative chmn., 1970-71, dept. jr. activities chmn., 1971-72, chmn. dept. emergency fund 1972-73, dept. communications chmn. 1973-74; sec. Annie Belle Clark P.T.A., Tifton, 1958-60, hospitality chmn., 1960-62; membership chmn. Tifton Jr. High Sch. P.T.A., 1961-62; chmn. bldg. and grounds com., 1962-64, publicity chmn., sec. Tift County High Sch. P.T.A., 1967-68; neighborhood cookie chmn. Girl Scouts; den mother Cub Scouts, Tifton 1957-60, mem. leadership tng. com., 1960-62; key woman Ga. Civil Def.; pres. Tift County Civil Def. Women's Activities Council, 1961-63; coordinator women's activities Civil Def., 1963-64, 67—, radiol. monitor, instr., 1964; charter mem. Scout Mothers Aux., Tifton, 1960-61, pres., 1962-64; councilor Bapt. Girls Aux. Jrs., Tifton, 1961-62, adviser, 1962-63; fund chmn. A.R.C., 1962, chpt. publicity chmn., 1962—; publicity chmn. Blood Bank Program, Tifton, 1961-62, adult leader 4-H Club, 1961-62; publicity chmn, VA Vol. Services Subcom., Thomasville, Ga.; chmn. courtesy and civil def. coms. Hillcrest Neighborhood Garden Club, 1961-62; mem. Tifton Music Assn., 1961-62; mem. com. of Tift County Gifted Children, 1968-70; mem. Ga. Youth and Children's Com.; chmn. 2d dist. Child Welfare Com.; chmn. Dept. Ga. Civil Def.; sec.-treas. Tift County Community Council, 1971—. Recipient longevity service awards Thomasville (Ga.) VA Domiciliary, Dublin VA Center; Baldwin Alumni Homemaker of Yr. award, 1963, Community Leader of Am. award, 1969. Mem. Confederate Hist. Soc. Eng., Book Browsers Club Am., Colonial Dames 17th Century (chpt. directory chmn., chmn. hist. restoration and marking sites com. chpt. 3d v.p., treas. state soc.), U.D.C. (chpt. pres. 1969-74; organizer, sr. chmn., adviser Children of Confederacy chpt. 1964, 2d v.p. chpt. 1966—, program chmn.; chmn. Ga. div. Jefferson Davis Meml. Park com., Ga. chaplain, dist. dir.), Internat. Platform Assn., D.A.R. (chmn. mag. com., vice regent 1966-68, sch. good citizen chmn. 1968-70, registrar 1968-74), Bus. and Profl. Womens Clubs (pres. 1970-71, Woman of Year 1972), Tift County Band Parents Assn. (sec., publicity chmn. 1969-70), Am. Forestry Assn., Tifton Art Assn. (publicity com.), Ga. Retarded Children's Assn., U. Kan., U. Ga., Abraham Baldwin Agrl. Coll. alumni socs. Baptist (asso. missionary So. Bapt. Radio and TV Commn.). Clubs: Twentieth Century Woman's (edn. chmn. 1970-72, librarian); Friends of the Library. Home: Route 3 607 Davis Rd Tifton GA 31794 Office: PO Box 1189 Tifton GA 31794

MORGAN, OMAR JOHN, physician; b. Muskogee, Okla., June 19, 1933; s. Charles Grandison and Nannie Ruth (Freese) M.; student Okla. State U., 1951-52, Northeastern State Coll., 1952-54, 56-58; M.D., Okla. U., 1962. Intern, Wesley Hosp., Oklahoma City, 1962-63; gen. practice medicine, Tahlequah, Okla., 1963—; sch. physician Northeastern State Coll., 1968—; mem. staff Tahlequah (Okla.) City Hosp. Mem. bd. electors Okla. Athletic Hall of Fame, Served with USAF, 1954-56. Mem. A.M.A., Okla. Med. Assn., Am. Assn. Gen. Practice, Am. Coll. Sports Medicine, Cookson Hills Med. Soc. (pres., del. state conv.), Tahlequah C. of C., Okla. U. Sch. Medicine Alumni Assn., Kappa Sigma, Rho Theta Sigma, Phi Sigma Epsilon, Phi Lambda Chi. Republican. Episcopalian. Club: Muskogee Country. Address: 220 N Muskogee Av Tahlequah OK 74464

MORGAN, OSCAR PAUL, mfg. co. exec.; b. Haynesville, La., Nov. 9, 1929; s. Oscar Paul and Amelia (Stephens) M.; B.A. in Petroleum Engring., La. Tech. U., 1954; m. Mary Jane Turnley, June 6, 1953; children—Paula Katherine, Margaret Stacy, Dorothy Lisa. Field engr., then dist. equipment engr. Mobil Oil Corp., Brownfield, Tex., 1954-57; with C-E Natco. div. Combustion Engring. Inc., 1957—, asst. to v.p. mfg., 1966-67, mgr. mfg., Tulsa, 1967—; extension instr. Sch. Prodn. Tech., U. Tex., 1959-72. Mem. indsl. tech. adv. com. Tulsa Jr. Coll.; bd. dirs. Tulsa Area Mfrs. Club. Served with USMCR, 1950-52. Registered profl. engr., La., Okla. Mem. Am. Inst. Mining Engrs., Am. Welding Soc. Republican. Presbyn. (elder, trustee, adult tchr.). Home: 7611 E 55th St Tulsa OK 74145 Office: PO Box 1710 Tulsa OK 74101

MORGAN, PAUL NOLAN, microbiologist; b. Konawa, Okla., Jan. 15, 1927; s. John S. and Elizabeth (Gist) M.; student E. Central State Coll., Ada, Okla., 1946-48, U. Ark., 1948-49; B.S. in Med. Tech., U. Ark. Med. Center, 1952, M.S., 1956; Ph.D., U. Okla. Med. Center, 1963; m. Bobby Kay Bingham, Nov. 27, 1952; children—Jay W., Kay E., Paul K. Research technician in microbiology U. Ark. Med. Center, Little Rock, 1952-54, instr., 1956-59, asst. prof. microbiology, 1963-69, asso. prof., 1969—; microbiologist VA Hosp., Little Rock, 1963—. Served with USNR, 1945-46; PTO. Contbr. articles on virology to sci. jours. Home: 2208 N Garfield St Little Rock AR 72207 Office: Veterans Administration Hospital 300 E Roosevelt Rd Little Rock AR 72206

MORGAN, ROBERT LEWIS, research physicist; b. Fayetteville, Tenn., Jan. 6, 1932; s. Joseph and Clara (Looney) M.; B.S. in Physics, U. Tex., 1953; postgrad. Tex. Christian U., 1958; M.S. in Physics, U. Ala., 1971; m. Beverly Lou Hammersley, Sept. 20, 1957; children—Janet Claire, Robert David. Physicist, U.S. Naval Ordnance Test Sta., China Lake, Cal, 1953-56, Convair, Ft. Worth, 1956-60, Chrysler Corp., Huntsville, Ala., 1960-62; research physicist U.S. Army Missile Command, Redstone Arsenal, Ala., 1962—; dir. Norman & Assos., Inc., Huntsville. Bd. dirs., trustee Huntsville Scottish Rite Temple Corp. Mem. Am. Phys. Soc., Am. Inst. Physics. Presbyn. (elder 1967). Mason. Contbr. articles to profl. jours. Inventor nonlinear optimal control system for small missles, automatically controlled T.O.F. mass spectrometer. Home: 2209 N Rose Dr Huntsville AL 35805 Office: AMSMIRRX Bldg 7770 Redstone Arsenal AL 35809

MORGAN, RUFUS SAMUEL, physician; b. Chattanooga, Mar. 15, 1920; s. Edward Oliver and Anna Lee (Wall) M.; student U. Chatanooga, 1945-48; M.D., U. Tenn., 1950; m. Elizabeth Ann Boyette, Dec. 22, 1948; children—Julia Ann (Mrs. John L. Wilhoit III), Constance Lee. Intern, Baroness Erlanger Hosp., Chattanooga, 1951-52; mem. staff Pikeville (Tenn.) Clinic Profl. Corp., 1952—; mem. staff Rhea County Gen. Hosp., Dayton, Tenn., Cumberland County Hosp., Crossville, Tenn. Mayor of Pikeville, 1960-61. Served with USAAF, 1942-45. Home: PO Box 156 Pikeville TN 37367 Office: Pikeville Clinic Main St Pikeville TN 37367

MORGAN, SAMUEL CLARENCE, dentist, army officer; b. Erwin, Tenn., Sept. 30, 1927; s. Clarence Decatur and Bessie Lou (Woods) M.; D.D.S., U. Tenn., 1952; B.A., E. Tenn. State U., 1964; M. Pub. Health, U. Cal. at Berkeley, 1964; m. Arete Joyce DuVall, Jan. 27, 1951; children—Richard Scott, Melissa Kay. Mem. faculty U. Tenn. Coll. Dentistry, Memphis, 1952-55; pvt. practice dentistry, Knoxville and Memphis, 1955-57; commd. capt. U.S. Army, 1957, advanced through grades to col., 1971; dep. comdr. Dental Co., U.S. Army, Med. Dept. Activity, Ft. Knox, Ky., 1971—; cons. preventive dentistry Brooke Army Med. Center, San Antonio, Tex., 1967-68; cons. to Med. Command U.S. Army Europe, 1968-71. Served with USNR, 1945-46. Fellow Am. Coll. Dentists; mem. Am. Dental Assn., Am. Pub. Health Assn., Am. Assn. Pub. Health Dentists. Home: 1119 Chaffee Av Fort Knox KY 40121 Office: Dental Company US Army MEDDAC Fort Knox KY 40121

MORGAN, SARA RUTH, educator; b. Andrews, N.C., May 11, 1915; d. Garland Temple and Willabelle (Sandlin) Posey; B.S., Asheville Coll., 1942; M.S., U. Tenn., 1944; postgrad. Women's Coll., U. N.C., 1945, Case Inst. Tech., 1956; J.D., Samford U., 1969; m. Frank McConaughy Morgan, Apr. 6, 1946; 1 son, George William. Asst. cashier Citizens Bank & Trust Co., Murphy, N.C., 1935-41; tchr. Chapel Hill (N.C.) High School, 1942-43; teaching fellow U. Tenn., 1943-44; instr. Ala. Coll., Montevallo, 1944-45, asst. prof., 1948-54, asso. prof., 1954-71, prof. U. Montevallo, 1971—; coordinator distributive edn. Asheville (N.C.) City Schs., 1945-46; admitted to Ala. bar, 1969. Program specialist distbn. and marketing U.S. Office Edn., Washington, summer 1966. Recipient certificate merit Ala. Fedn. Women's club. Mem. Am. Assn. U. Women, United Bus. Edn. Assn., Southeastern Bus. Writers Assn., Am., Shelby County bar assns., Ala. Bar, D.A.R., Sigma Alpha Sigma, Pi Omega Pi, Phi Delta Delta. Democrat. Contbr. articles to profl. jours. Home: 346 Moody St N Montevallo AL 35115

MORGAN, SHELDON LEGRANDE, banker; b. Thomasville, Ala., Oct. 9, 1929; s. Stevy Moore and Floy (Brasell) M.; student U. Ala., 1952-53; B.S., Auburn U., 1955, M.Ed., 1956; postgrad. Tulane U., U. Ga., U.N.C., U. Okla., 1958—; m. Joyce Hardwick Morgan, Jan. 31, 1957; children—Ann, Jane, Jack, Steven LeGrande. Adminstrv. trainee Ala. Docks Dept., Mobile, 1957, asst. dir. pub. relations, 1957-60; world trade mgr. Mobile Area C. of C., 1960-63, mgr. indsl. devel., 1963-72; v.p., mgr. indsl. devel. Merchants Nat. Bank Mobile Hon. consul of Nicaragua. Pres., Mobile Azalea Trail and Festival, 1961; sec. Sr. Citizens Services Ala.; chmn. Ala. Indsl. Devel. Conf. Adv. bd. Providence Hosp. Sch. Nursing; bd. dirs. Am. Jr. Miss Pageant, 1961, Mobile County Tb and Health Assn., 1960-63. Served with USAF, 1948-52. Mem. C. of C., Am., So. (dir.) indsl. devel. councils, Indsl. Developers Assn. Ala. (pres.), Phi Delta Kappa. Baptist. Kiwanian. Clubs: International Trade; Dauphin Island Country. Home: 4 Graf Ct Mobile AL 36606 Office: 408 Merchants Nat Bank Bldg Mobile AL 36601

MORGAN, THOMAS EUGENE, educator; b. Guthrie, Ky., Sept. 10, 1929; s. Eugene and Virginia (Lannom) M.; B.S., Austin Peay State U., 1951; M.S., U. Tenn., 1954, Ed.D., 1968; m. Marylou Johnson, July 15, 1954; children—Mary, Thomas Eugene, Patrick. Engr. Lou & Nash Railroad, Louisville, 1954-57; part time instr. in engring. graphics U. Louisville, 1956-57; instr. gen. engring. U. Ky., 1957-60, asst. prof. civil engring., 1960-66; research asso. U. Tenn., 1966-68; asso. prof. edn. and dir. ednl. planning services, Auburn (Ala.) U., 1968—; cons. in ednl. planning. Scoutmaster Boy Scouts of Am., 1963—. Mem. Council of Ednl. Facilities Planners, Internat. Soc. Ednl. Planners, Southeast Council of Ednl. Facilities Planners (bd. govs. 1970—, sec. treas. 1970-72, chmn. 1972-74), Iota Lambda Sigma, Phi Delta Kappa. Mem. Disciples of Christ (deacon 1959-72, elder 1973—). Mason. Home: 913 Terrace Auburn AL 36830

MORGAN, WILLIAM JAMES, psychologist; b. Rochester, N.Y., Apr. 30, 1910; A.B., U. Rochester, 1933; Ph.D., Yale, 1937; m. Antonia Mary Farquharson Bell, Nov. 2, 1944; children—William James, Jean Elizabeth, Robert Macnair. Chief clinician Vineland (N.J.) Tng. Sch., 1936-38; psychologist Bd. Edn., Rochester, N.Y., 1939-41; dir. Psychol. Test Bur., Rochester, 1941-42; dep. chief tng., chief psychol. assessment CIA, 1947-52; mem. Psychol. Strategy Bd., White House, 1952-53; pres. Aptitude Assos., Merrifield, Va., 1953—; mem. Army Research Com.; cons. Dept. Justice, Dept. Def., other agys. Mem. Va. Bd. Certification Clin. Psychologists. Served from pvt. to maj. AUS, 1942-47; OSS, ETO. Diplomate in clin. psychology Am. Bd. Examiners Profl. Psychology. Mem. Va. Psychol. Assn. (pres. 1957-58), Sigma Xi. Author: Spies and Saboteurs (Gollancs-London), 1955; The O.S.S. and I, 1957; numerous articles and tests. Home: 2816 Gallows Rd Vienna VA 22180

MORIN, LEO GREGORY, biochemist; b. Berlin, N.H., May 9, 1941; s. Cleophas Louis and Annette (LaFrance) M.; B.S., Spring Hill Coll., 1965; Ph.D., Boston Coll., 1968; m. Beverly J. Ragona, Sept. 2, 1968; children—Gregory T., Stephanie N. Asst. prof. chemistry Rollins Coll., Winter Park, Fla., 1968-70; sr. research biochemist Sunland Hosp., Orlando, Fla., 1970-71; v.p. research Kiess Instruments, Inc. Miami, Fla., 1971-73; asst. prof. pathology Emory U. Sch. Medicine, Atlanta, 1973—. NASA fellow, 1965-68, NSF fellow, 1968. Mem. Am. Assn. Clin. Chemists, Am. Chem. Soc., A.A.A.S., Sigma Xi. Contbr. profl. jours. Office: Lab Service VA Hospital 1670 Clairmont Rd Decatur GA 30033

MORIN, ORAM JOSEPH, mech. engr.; b. Bristol, Conn., Oct. 31, 1939; s. Oram Joseph and Rose (Salafia) M.; B.S., U. Conn., 1961; postgrad. U. Bridgeport, 1962-65; m. Paula Christene Ploski, July 25, 1959; children—Randal, Andrea, Kristen. Jr. engr., Conn. Light & Power Co., Norwalk, 1961-64; engr., Rayex Corp., Plainville, 1964-65; project engr. marine desalination design AMF/CUNO, Meriden, Conn., 1965-66; supr. mech. engr. Westinghouse, Orange, Cal., 1966-68; v.p., prin. engr. DSS Engrs., Inc., Fort Lauderdale, Fla., 1968—; also dir. Registered profl. engr., Fla., Conn., Pa. Mem. Am. Soc. Mech. Engrs., Nat. Soc. Profl. Engrs., Fla. Engring. Soc., Nat. Water Supply Improvement Assn., Nat. Assn. Corrosion Engrs. Democrat. Roman Catholic. K.C. Home: 9161 NW 24th Ct Sunrise FL 33313 Office: 2701 E Sunrise Blvd Fort Lauderdale FL 33304

MORIN, RICHARD DUDLEY, educator; b. Quincy, Ill., Oct. 5, 1918; s. George Leslie and Mabel Boyd (Reed) Morin; B.S., U. Mich., 1940, M.S., 1942, Ph.D., 1943; m. Margaret Emogene Broughton, July 28, 1967; children—Lynn, Scott, Jay, Kim. Research chemist Battelle Meml. Inst., Columbus, O., 1943-52, asst. div. chief, 1952-61, research asso., 1961-62; asso. prof. medicinal chemistry, dept. psychiatry U. Ala. Med. Sch., Birmingham, 1963-70, prof., 1970—. Mem. Am. Chem. Soc. (chmn. Columbus sect. 1959), A.A.A.S., Sigma Xi, Phi Lambda Upsilon, Phi Kappa Phi. Contbr. articles to profl. jours. Home: 2020 Montreat Pkwy Birmingham AL 35216 Office: 1919 7th Av S Birmingham AL 35233

MORITZ, WALLACE ALBERT, realtor; b. Milw., Apr. 21, 1913; s. Leopold and Theresa (Bauer) M.; student Marquette U., 1931; m. Ruth Kalle, Jan. 2, 1945; children—Judith (Mrs. Donald Phillips), Diana (Mrs. Dan R. Hill), Arthur Lee. Founder Wallace Labs. Inc., San Angelo, Tex., 1940, now pres.; pres. W. Tex. Bus. Music Co., San Angelo, 1953; owner Wallace A. Moritz and Assos., San Angelo, 1960—. Chmn. Nat. Wool Pageant, 1958-59; pres. Crippled Children's Center, San Angelo, 1958, United Fund, San Angelo, 1963, Lighthouse, San Angelo, 1965. Named San Angelo Citizen of Year, 1958. Mem. Nat. (dir.), Tex. (dir. 1969, 1st v.p. 1972) assns. realtors, San Angelo Bd. Realtors (pres. 1967). Presbyn. Mason, Kiwanian. Home: 166 Moritz Circle San Angelo TX 76901 Office: 1900 Sherwood Way San Angelo TX 76901

MORKOVSKY, JOHN L(OUIS), clergyman; b. Moulton, Tex., Aug. 16, 1909; s. Alois J(oseph) and Marie (Raska) M.; grad. St. John's Sem., San Antonio, 1930; student N. Am. Coll., Rome, Italy, 1930-36; S.T.D., Pontifical Gregorian U., 1936; A.M., Cath. U. Am. 1943; LL.D., St. Edward's U., 1958. Ordained priest Roman Cath. Ch. in Rome, 1933; asst. pastor St. Michael's, Weimar, Tex., 1936-39, St. Ann's, San Antonio, 1940; prof. canon law St. John's Sem., San Antonio, 1940-41; archdiocesan supt. of schs., 1941-56; pastor St. Leo's Parish, San Antonio, 1945-54, St. Mary Magdalen Parish, 1954-56; titular bishop of Hieron and aux. bishop of Amarillo, 1956-58, vicar gen., chancellor Amarillo, Diocese, 1956-58, bishop, Amarillo, 1958-63; coadjutor bishop, apostolic adminstr., Galveston-Houston, 1963—. Apptd. Papal Chamberlain with title of Very Reverend Monsignor, 1944, Domestic Prelate with title Right Rev. Monsignor, 1954. Judge, Archiocesan Tribunal, 1946-56; mem. Archdiocesan Bd. Consultors, 1947-56; pres. Tex. Conf. Chs., 1970-72. K.C. (4 deg.). Address: Catholic Chancery 1700 San Jacinto St Houston TX 77002

MORLAND, ALVIN WESLEY, assn. exec.; b. Birmingham, Ala., July 29, 1914; s. Howard Canon and Ethel May (Cowan) M.; B.S., Auburn U., 1937; postgrad. Acad. Orgn. Mgmt., U. Notre Dame, 1972; m. Gretchen Bickelhaupt, Feb. 15, 1947; children—Douglas Verne, Timothy Easton. With U.S. Steel Corp., Birmingham, 1937-41, 46-47; adminstrv. asst. U.S. Congressman L.C. Battle, 1947-49; city mgr. Mountain Brook, Ala., 1949-51; mgr. trade devel. Birmingham C. of C., 1951-53; mgr. Dothan (Ala.) C. of C., 1953-55, Ft. Pierce (Fla.) C. of C., 1955-62; exec. v.p. Pompano Beach (Fla.) C. of C., 1963—. Served with AUS, 1941-46. Decorated Purple Heart, Bronze Star. Mem. Am. C. of C. Execs., So. Assn. C. of C. Execs. (dir. 1971-72), Am., Ala. (dir. 1954), Fla. (pres. 1964-65) chambers commerce execs., Sigma Alpha Epsilon, Omicron Delta Kappa (pres. Auburn U. chpt. 1936-37). Republican. Rotarian (dir. Pompano Beach club 1967, officer, dir. 1969-71). Home: 2326 N E 29th St Lighthouse Point FL 33064 Office: Chamber of Commerce 2200 E Atlantic Blvd Pompano Beach FL 33062

MORLAND, RICHARD BOYD, educator; b. Huntsville, Ala., June 27, 1919; s. Howard Canon and Ethel May (Cowan) M.; A.B., Birmingham-So. Coll., 1940; M.Ed., Springfield Coll., 1947; Ph.D. (So. Fellowships Fund fellow 1957-58), N.Y. U. 1958; m. Jessie May Parrish, Mar. 17, 1949; 1 dau., Laura. Phys. dir. YMCA, Frankfort, Ky., 1940-41; dir. athletics, Fla. So. Coll., 1947-50; lect. in edn., N.Y. U., 1950-51; chmn. dept. phy. edn., Stetson U., Deland, Fla., 1952-60, asso. prof., 1958-63, prof., 1963—, chmn. grad. council, 1962-69, chmn. dept. edn., 1969—. Served to lt., USNR, 1941-45. Mem. Am. Assn. Higher Edn., Philosophy of Edn. Soc. (pres. region 1963-64), Am. Ednl. Research Assn., Am. Edn. Studies Assn., Omicron Delta Kappa, Phi Alpha Theta, Kappa Delta Pi, Kappa Alpha. Methodist. Contbr. articles to profl. jours. Home: 524 N McDonald St DeLand FL 32720

MORLEY, RICHARD E., coll. pres.; b. Nixon, Tex., May 30, 1915; s. Lester H. and D. Lee (Wingfield) M.; B.S., Trinity U., 1954, M.Ed., 1955; Ed.D., U. Houston, 1957; postgrad. U. Tex., Tex. A. and M. U., Fla. State U.; m. Ellenor Rooks, Aug. 13, 1943; 1 dau., Donna Ruth. Prodn. and pub. numerous Tex. weekly and daily newspapers including Nixon News, Gonzales Daily Inquirer, San Antonio Express-News, 1933-49; counselor, tchr. pub. schs., Houston, San Antonio, 1949-57; dean Pensacola (Fla.) Jr. Coll., 1957-60; pres. Gulf Coast Community Coll., Panama City, Fla., 1960—. Cons. psychol. services and mgmt. devel., 1950—; lectr. to clubs, chambers commerces, industry; auctioneer. Chmn. United Fund Drive. Served with USCGR, 1942-45. Named Outstanding Indsl. Tchr., State of Tex. Mem. Am. Council Higher Edn., Nat., Fla. auctioneer assns., Panama City C. of C., So. Assn. Colls. and Schs. (past sec. commn. on colls. and univs., trustee), Internat. Platform Assn., Kappa Delta Pi, Iota Lambda Sigma, Phi Delta Kappa. Baptist (lay speaker). Rotarian (past pres. Panama City). Author: Can You Ask the Intelligent Question?, 1967. Contbr. numerous articles to mags. and newspapers. Home: PO Box 13327 Mexico Beach Sta Panama City FL 32401

MORLEY, STANLEY MALCOLM, lawyer; b. Cheyenne, Wyo., Jan. 9, 1912; s. William and Marion (Stirrit) M.; student Georgetown U., 1930-32; LL.B., Cath. U. Am., 1937, B.C.S., 1940; m. Irene Helen Lipscomb, Jan. 18, 1935; children—Mary Jane (Mrs. Steven Joseph Conway), Betsy Anne (Mrs. John Gerard Swanhaus). Admitted to D.C. bar, 1937, U.S. Supreme Ct. bar, 1945; mem. firm Shannon & Morley, Washington, 1945—. Dir. Ala.-Tenn. Natural Gas Co. Mem. Nat. Lawyers Club, Fed. Power (pres.), Am. bar assns., Bar Assn. D.C. Club: Congressional Country. Home: 6405 Garnett Dr Chevy Chase MD 20015 Office: 1700 K St NW Washington DC 20006

MORONEY, JAMES MCQUEEN, JR., pub. and broadcasting exec.; b. Dallas, July 10, 1921; s. James McQueen and Maidie (Dealey) M.; B.B.A., U. Tex. at Austin, 1943; m. Helen Claire Wilhoit, Mar. 2, 1954; children—Mary Molly, James McQueen III, Melinda Ann, Michael Wilhoit. Reporter, Dallas Morning News, 1946; with radio and TV depts. sta. WFAA, 1948-49; treas. A.H. Belo Corp., Dallas, 1955-60, v.p., treas., 1960-70, exec. v.p., 1970—. Bd. dirs. Catholic Family and Childrens Services, Cistercian Prep. Sch., Community Council Greater Dallas, Cotton Bowl Council, Dallas Area Respiratory Health Assn., Dallas Council on World Affairs, Dallas Summer Musicals, State Fair of Tex., YMCA Met. Dallas. Served to lt. (j.g.) USNR, 1943-46. Mem. Sigma Alpha Epsilon. Roman Catholic. Clubs: Salesmanship, Serra, Dallas Country, Brook Hollow Colf, Preston Trail Golf, Petroleum, Terps and Idlewild. Home: 4425 Bordeaux St Dallas TX 75205 Office: Dallas Morning News Communications Center Dallas TX 75222

MORPHOS, DIANE BELOGIANIS (MRS. PANOS PAUL MORPHOS), civic worker; b. Chgo., d. Demetrios and Alice (Rousseas) Belogianis; B.S., U. Chgo., 1937, M.A., 1938; m. Panos Paul Morphos, Dec. 11, 1948; children—Evangeline, Paul. Mem. faculty U. Chgo. Orthogenic Sch., 1938-45, U. Chgo. Remedial Reading Clinics, 1945-48; vis. lectr. Tulane U., 1947. Bd. dirs. S.E. La. council Girl Scouts U.S., New Orleans, 1959-65, v.p., 1965-68, pres., 1968—; mem. bd. Am. Assn. U. Women, New Orleans, 1969, v.p., 1970—; chmn. legislative com., bd. Reading is Fun program, New Orleans. Mem. Athenee Louisianais, France-Amerique, Maison Hospitaliere, League Women Voters. Mem. Greek Orthodox Ch. Clubs: Greek Women's University (Chgo.); Tulane University Women's (New Orleans, La.). Home: 1404 Audubon St New Orleans LA 70118

MORR, ALEXANDER, theater exec.; b. Cleve.; ed. Western Res. U., Free U Berlin. Stage mgr., dir. Cleve. Playhouse, 1958-61; pub. relations Hanna Theater, Cleve., 1961-62; gen. mgr. Mineola (N.Y.) Playhouse, 1962-64, Colonial and Wilbur theaters, Boston, 1964-72; gen. mgr. theater complex John F. Kennedy Center for Performing Arts, Washington, 1972—. Office: John F Kennedy Center for Performing Arts Washington DC 20566

MORRILL, JOHN BARSTOW, educator; b. Chgo., Nov. 20, 1929; s. John Barstow and Doris Martha (Tirrell) M.; A.B., Grinnell Coll., 1951; M.S., Ia. State Coll., 1953; Ph.D., Fla. State U., 1958; m. Ann Stillman, Mar. 21, 1953; children—Sandra Ann, Martha Elizabeth. Asst. prof. biology Wesleyan U., Middletown, Conn., 1958-66; asso. prof. Coll. William and Mary, Williamsburg, Va., 1966-68; prof. Div. Natural Scis., New Coll., Sarasota, Fla., 1968—. Environmental cons. Siesta Devel., 1969-73, Curtiss-Wright Co., 1970-72, Portofino, 1970 vis. prof. embryology U. Ore. at Charleston, 1967, U. Wash. at Friday Harbor, 1970, U. N.H. at Durham, 1971. Mem. Marine Biol. Lab., Am. Zoologists, Internat. Soc. Embryology, Soc. Devel. Biology. Contbr. articles to profl. jours. Home: 2641 49th St Sarasota FL 33581 Office: Div Natural Scis New College Sarasota FL 33578

MORRIS, ALLEN COVINGTON, state ofcl., columnist, photographic archivist; b. Chgo., Dec. 3, 1909; s. Gustave Allen and Anna (Hunter) M.; student pub. schs.; m. Dorothy Elizabeth Hedley, Nov. 1, 1932 (dec.); children—Martha (Mrs. Kermit Bernard Marsh), David Allen; m. 2d, Joan Lee Perry, Dec. 28, 1966. Photographer, writer Miami (Fla.) News, 1925-33; corr. A.P., Miami, 1933-37; writer Miami (Fla.) Herald, 1937-43; free-lance polit. columnist, Tallahassee, 1943—; photographic archivist Fla. State U., 1951—. Vice-chmn. Fla. Advt. Commn., 1949; mem., sec. Jud. Council Fla., 1953-63; mem. Fla. Library Bd., 1963—; cons. procedure Fla. Ho. of Reps., Tallahassee, 1947—, clk., 1966—. Served to lt. (j.g.) USCGR, 1943-45. Mem. Spl. Libraries Assn., Legislative Corrs. Assn. (pres. 1947-49). Author: The Florida Handbook, 1947, rev. biennially; Florida Facts and Figures, 1954; Florida Business Handbook, 1956; Florida Business Year Book, 1961; Our Florida Government, 1961; Florida Industrial Case Book, 1963; Florida Place Names, 1974. Co-author: How To Win in Politics, 1948; Legal Background to the Government of Florida, 1961; Your Florida Government, 1965; Florida Business Profiles, 1965; The Speaker's Manual, 1965; Florida Under Five Flags, 1967; Florida Place Names, 1974. Home: 2015 E Randolph Circle Tallahassee FL 32303 Office: The Capitol Bldg Tallahassee FL 32304

MORRIS, BARTON WISTAR, JR., publisher; b. Roanoke, Va., Oct. 10, 1922; s. Barton Wistar and Mary Wilkinson (Buckner) M.; A.B., Washington and Lee U., 1943; m. Margaret Jarrett, May 7, 1949; children—Anna J., Barton Wistar III. Reporter Roanoke World-News, also legislative corr., 1945-50; asst. to gen. mgr. Times-World Corp., Roanoke, 1950-52, corporate sec., promotion mgr., 1952-55, exec., editor, v.p., 1960-73; pub. Roanoke Times and World-News, 1973—; dir. Peoples Fed. Savs. & Loan Assn. Chmn. Roanoke Community Fund, 1954. Trustee Va. Western Community Coll., 1969-72. Served with USAAF, 1943-45. So. Nieman Assn. fellow, 1957. Mem. Am., So. newspaper pubs. assns., Am. Soc. Newspaper Editors, Roanoke Washington and Lee Alumni Assn. (chmn. 1952), Sigma Delta Chi. Presbyn. Clubs: Shenandoah; Roanoke Country. Home: 2644 Robin Hood Rd Roanoke VA 24014 Office: 201-209 W Campbell Av Roanoke VA 24010

MORRIS, BENJAMIN HUME, lawyer; b. Louisville, Sept. 25, 1917; s. Ben F. and Mary B. (Hume) M.; J.D., U. Louisville 1941; m. Lacy Hibbs Abell, July 7, 1942; (div. 1968); children—Ben Hume, Lacy Wayne; m. 2d, Mary Fowler Gatlin, Nov. 9, 1968. Admitted to Ky. bar, 1940; mem. firm Doolan, Helm, Stites & Wood, Louisville, 1941-50; atty. Brown-Forman Distillers Corp., Louisville, 1950-55, resident counsel, 1955-59, resident counsel and asst. sec., 1959-64, v.p., mem. exec. com., 1964—, gen. counsel, 1974—; pres., dir. Canadian Mist Distillers, Ltd., 1971—; dir. Licensed Beverage Industries, Inc., 1966-73, vice chmn. bd., 1968-73. Chmn. adv. com. Jefferson County Social Service, 1961-64, mem., 1964-68. Bd. dirs. Distilled Spirits Inst., 1966-73, chmn. exec. com., 1969-70, chmn. bd., 1971-72; bd. dirs. Assn. Canadian Distillers, 1971—; chmn. bd., pres. Distilled Spirits Council U.S., 1973—; bd. dirs. Better Bus. Bur., Louisville, 1969-72, sec., trustee W.L. Lyons Brown Found. Served from aviation cadet to capt., pilot AC, AUS, 1941-45; ETO; col. USAF Res. ret. Decorated Air medal (Army) with oak leaf cluster. Mem. Ky. C. of C. (dir. 1969-72), Soc. Colonial Wars (registrar 1969—), Ky. Distillers Assn. (dir. 1966—, pres. 1969, chmn. 1970), Am., Ky. State, Louisville bar assns., Am. Judicature Soc., Ky. Hist. Soc., Louisville Health and Welfare Council, S.A.R. (pres. Thruston chpt. 1965-66), Kappa Alpha, Omicron Delta Kappa. Presbyn. (elder). Clubs: Filson, Louisville Boat, Midland Trail Golf. Home: 2005 High Ridge Rd Louisville KY 40207 Office: 850 Dixie Hwy Louisville KY 40210

MORRIS, CARLOSS, title guaranty co. exec.; b. Houston, June 7, 1915; s. W.C. and Willie (Stewart) M.; B.A. with distinction, Rice Inst., 1936; J.D. with highest honors, U. Tex., 1939; m. Doris Poole, Dec. 2, 1939; children—Marietta (Mrs. Morgan Maxfield), William Carloss, Malcolm Stewart, Melinda Louise (Mrs. Glen Ginter). Admitted to Tex. bar, 1938; with Stewart Title Guaranty Co., Houston, 1939—, pres., 1951—, also dir.; sr. partner firm Morris, Termini Harris and McCanne, Houston. Pres. Star of Hope Mission, 1951—, Tex. Safety Assn., 1950-51. Bd. dirs. Goodwill Industries; bd. dirs., mem. exec. com. Billy Graham Evangelistic Assn.; trustee Baylor U., 1952-72, Oldham Little Church Found., B.M. Woltman Found., Baylor Coll. Medicine. Fellow State Bar Tex. Found., Am. Bar Assn.; mem. Tex. Bar. Baptist (deacon 1950). Clubs: Downtown Kiwanis (atty. 1945—), River Oaks Country, Sugar Creek Country, University. Home: 3996 Inverness Lane Houston TX 77019 Office: 2200 W Loop S Houston TX 77027

MORRIS, CHARLES ROBERT, educator; b. Houston, Nov. 21, 1924; s. Earl Luckett and Hazel (Hemphill) M.; student Southwestern U., Georgetown, Tex., 1942-44, 46; Columbia, 1944; D.D.S., U. Tex., 1950, postgrad. certificate oral surgery field, 1960; m. Evelyn Barbee Williams, Sept. 13, 1947; children—Charles Robert, Jane (Mrs. Lonnie E. Longmire), Margaret Ann (Mrs. Ronald Huff), Claire Christine, Amy Frances, Earl Leslie. Commd. 2d lt. U.S. Air Force, 1950, advanced through grades to col., 1968; chief oral surgery Air Force Hosp., Wiesbaden, Germany, 1962-66; chief outpatient surgery Willford Hall Air Force Hosp., Lackland AFB, Tex., 1966-67, chief inpatient oral surgery, 1967-68; chief div. dentistry br. dental scis. div. Sch. Aerospace Medicine, Brooks AFB, Tex., 1968-71, dep. chief dental scis. div., 1969-71; ret., 1971; mem. faculty Dental Sch., U. Tex. at Houston, 1966-69, at San Antonio, 1968—, clin. prof. dept. diagnosis and radiology, 1970-71, prof., chmn. dept., 1971—. Cons. various depts. U.S. Air Force, 1960—. Active Boy Scouts Am., 1959—; pres. N.D. chpt. P.T.A., 1961-62, hon. life mem., 1962—. Decorated Legion of Merit; recipient certificate of achievement Surgeon Gen. Air Force, 1970. Diplomate Am. Bd. Oral Surgery. Fellow Internat. Assn. Oral Surgeons, Am. Coll. Dentists; mem. Am. Soc. Oral Surgeons, Tex., Am. dental assns., Internat. Assn. Dental Research, Western Germany Armed Forces, San Antonio Dist. dental socs., Am. Assn. Dental Schs., Kappa Sigma, Psi Omega, Omicron Kappa Upsilon. Baptist (deacon). Contbr. articles to profl. jours. Home: 3119 War Arrow Dr San Antonio TX 78238 Office: 7703 Floyd Curl Dr San Antonio TX 78284

MORRIS, CLETUS EUGENE, chemist, govt. ofcl.; b. nr. Rienzi, Miss., Jan. 30, 1935; s. Van Buren and Jessie Ray (Green) M.; A.S., Northeast Miss. Jr. Coll., 1952-54; B.S., Auburn U., 1959, Ph.D. (NSF fellow, Nat. Def. Grad. fellow), 1966; m. Nancy Carole Mitchell, June 5, 1962; 1 son, Kendall Eugene. Research chemist So. Regional Research Center U.S. Dept. Agr., New Orleans, 1965—. Served with AUS, 1954-57. Mem. Am. Chem. Soc., Am. Assn. Textile Chemists and Colorists, Sci. Research Soc. Am., Phi Lambda Upsilon. Home: 3816 Metairie Ct Metairie LA 70002 Office: PO Box 19687 New Orleans LA 70179

MORRIS, CLIFTON HOWINGTON, JR., boat co. exec.; b. Ft. Worth, July 26, 1935; s. Clifton Howington and Lois (Woods) M.; B.B.A., U. Tex., 1958; m. Andrea Ruhl. With McCammon, Morris, Pickens & Mayhew, C.P.A.'s, Ft. Worth, 1958-61, Arthur Young & Co., C.P.A.'s, 1961-66; with Service Corp. Internat., Houston, 1966-71, financial v.p., 1970-71, also dir.; chmn. bd. C.H.M. Inc., C.B. Delhomme Parts Co. Inc., Houston. Mem. Am. Inst. C.P.A.'s. Episcopalian. Home: 5616 Winsome Houston TX 77027 Office: PO Box 1312 Houston TX 77001

MORRIS, DAVID HARGETT, broadcasting exec.; b. Paris, Tex., Mar. 28, 1920; s. Eugene F. and Elizabeth F. (Hargett) M.; student U. Tex.; m. June Morris, Oct. 23, 1942; children—David Hargett II, Elizabeth Anne. Page Tex. Senate, Austin, 1930-31; with advt. staff Am. Statesman newspaper, 1936-41; with radio sta. K-NUZ, 1948—, now pres.; pres. stas. KQUE, KAY-C, KAY-D, also Musi-King Background Music System. Vice pres. Houston Livestock Show; past pres. Houston Conv. council. Bd. dirs. Boy's Harbor, Inc.; mem. communications bd. U. Tex. Served with USAF. Decorated D.F.C., 5 Air medals. Mem. Tex. Assn. Broadcasters, Assn. Met. Stas., Tex. Hereford Certified Bull Test Assn., Houston Hereford Club. Home: 11706 Monica Lane Houston TX 77024 Office: PO Box 188 Houston TX 77001

MORRIS, DONAL FRANKLIN, chem. engr.; b. Bixby, Okla., June 8, 1932; s. Troy Franklin and Mary Belle (Mulkey) M.; A.S., Connors State U., 1952; B.S. in Chem. Engring., Okla. State U., 1955; m. Delores Joan Marshall, July 31, 1953; children—Randall, Karen, Ron. Process engr. Phillips Petroleum, Borger, Tex., 1955-58; process engr. Dresser Engring. Co., Tulsa, 1958-68, chief process and project engr., 1968—. Registered profl. engr., Okla. Mem. Nat., Okla. socs. profl. engrs., Am. Inst. Chem. Engrs., Engrs. Club Tulsa. Home: 4730 S Irvington Pl Tulsa OK 74135 Office: PO Box 2968 Tulsa OK 74101

MORRIS, EARLE ELIAS, JR., banker, lt. gov. S.C.; b. Greenville, S.C., July 14, 1928; s. Earle Elias and Bernice (Carey) M.; B.S., Clemson Coll., 1949; m. Carol Telford Morris; children—Lynda Lewis, Carey M., Elizabeth, Earle E. III. Owner, operator Morris & Co., Inc., wholesale grocers, Pickens, S.C., 1949-56; v.p., dir. Pickens Bank, 1956—, Bankers Trust S.C., 1968—; pres. Gen. Ins. Agy.; sec. Carolina Investors, Inc.; partner Morris Realty Co., Pickens; dir. Brunswick Worsted Mills. Mem. S.C. Ho. of Reps., 1950-54, S.C. Senate, 1954-70; lt. gov. S.C., 1970—. S.C. rep. So. Regional Council Mental Health. Mem. Crippled Children's Soc. S.C.; mem. S.C. Gov.'s Adv. Group Mental Health Planning; mem. Nat. Adv. Mental Health Council; mem. S.C. Interagy. Council Mental Retardation. Del. S.C. Democratic Conv., 1950, 52, 54, 56, 58, 60, 62, 64, 66, 68, 70, nat. conv., 1952, 56, 68; state chmn. S.C. Dem. Party. Mem. Jr. C. of C., S.C. Vocational Rehab. Assn. (v.p.), S.A.R., Blue Key, Phi Kappa Phi. Presbyn. Mason (32 deg., Shriner), Elk, Moose, Lion. Home: 407 Hampton Av Pickens SC 29671 Office: Bankers Trust Main St Pickens SC 29671

MORRIS, EUGENE TAYLOR, city ofcl.; b. Albemarle, N.C., Dec. 23, 1919; s. Joe and Bessie Mae (Blaylock) M.; student Inst. Govt., U. N.C., 1953-55; m. Mary Hazel Underwood, Jan. 5, 1943; children—Barbara (Mrs. Edward Perrell), Kay (Mrs. Johnny Billings), Eugene Taylor. Vets. service officer Davidson County, N.C., 1951-53; mgr., 1953-60; city mgr., City of Lexington, N.C., 1960—. Chmn., Davidson County Bd. Elections, 1965-66; chmn. March of Dimes, 1954. Bd. dirs., YMCA. Served with AUS, 1940-46; lt. col. Res. Decorated Bronze Star medals (2); recipient Outstanding Public Service award Kiwanis Internat., 1968. Mem. Piedmont Electric Cities Assn. (treas. 1968-70), V.F.W. (comdr. 1951-52), Am. Legion (comdr. 1954-55). Kiwanian, Moose (gov. 1953), Mason (32 deg., Shriner). Home: 207 Woodhaven Dr Lexington NC 27292 Office: PO Box 649 Lexington NC 27292

MORRIS, FRED JOHN, research co. exec.; b. Chgo., Dec. 6, 1919; s. Harry and Lillium (Richardson) M.; B.S., Tex. A. and I., 1942; M.A., U. Tex. at Austin, 1944, Ph.D., 1951; m. Vera Walsh, Sept. 5, 1942; children—Nansi, Gary Kim. Instr. physics U. Tex. at Austin, 1946-51; pres., dir. research Electro-Mechanics Co., Austin, 1951—. Sci. adviser Joint Chiefs Staff, Washington, 1959; cons. Colgate U., 1951, research and engring. program Def. Dept., 1962. Served to lt. (j.g.) USNR, 1944-46. Mem. Am. Phys. Soc., Soc. Am. Mil. Engrs., Am. Geophys. Union, A.A.A.S., I.E.E.E., Optical Soc. Tex., Soc. Exploration Geophysicists, Sigma Xi, Sigma Pi Sigma, Rotarian. Contbr. articles to profl. jours. Patentee magnetic field measurement instruments. Home: Route 7 Box 718E Austin TX 78703 Office: PO Box 1546 Austin TX 78767

MORRIS, JACK AUSTIN, JR., art dir.; b. Macon, Ga., Sept. 29, 1939; s. Jack Austin and Mattie Wise (Elliott) M.; A.B. in Fine Arts, U.S.C., 1962; certificate arts adminstrn., Harvard, 1970; m. Mary Sylvia Emanuel, Mar. 31, 1961; children—Dana Lynn, Jack Austin III. Trainee Columbia (S.C.) Museum Art, 1962-63, lectr., 1963-64, asst. to dir., 1964-65; dir. Greenville County (S.C.) Museum Art, 1965—; founder, pres. Concept II, Inc., Greenville, S.C., 1969—; instr. art. Richland Art Sch., Columbia, 1962-65; lectr. Museum Sch. Art, Greenville, 1965—; juror art exhbns. S.C. chmn. Liberty Life scholastic art award, 1967—; chmn. Star Student Program Congl. Dist., 1969. Chmn., S.C. Arts Commn. Bd. dirs. Greenville Symphony, Greenville Civic Choral. Named Young Man of Yr., Greenville, 1973. Mem. S.E. Museums Conf., Am. Assn. Museums, S.C. Craftsman's Council (mem. exec. bd. 1965—), Guild of S.C. Artists (pres. 1968), S.C. Fedn. Museums (founder 1970, pres. 1973). Rotarian. Author: Contemporary Artists of South Carolina, 1970; William M. Halsey: Retrospective, 1972. Home: 22 Selwyn Dr Greenville SC 29607 Office: 420 College St Greenville SC 29601

MORRIS, JAMES KENNETH, psychologist, clergyman; b. Bessemer, Ala., Jan. 26, 1896; s. Charles Ellis and Rosa (Allenton) M.; B.A., U. Ala., 1917; postgrad. Columbia, 1923; M.Div., Episcopal Theol. Sem., 1925, D.D., 1965; postgrad. Japanese Lang. Sch., Tokyo, 1925-28; M.A., U. S.C., 1957; L.H.D., St. Augustine Coll., 1964; D.Hum., Voorhees Coll., 1972; m. Esther Jones, Sept. 9, 1925; children—Elizabeth (Mrs. J.F. Feltus), James Kenneth, John Robert. Partner, Morris-Howard Lumber Co., Camden, Ala., 1920-22; ordained to ministry Episcopal Ch., 1925; missionary, Kyoto, Japan, 1925-40; rector St. Johns Episcopal Ch., Columbia, S.C., 1941-43, 45-60; psychologist, marriage and family counselor, lectr., Columbia, 1960—. Mem. Council of Advice, trustee Missionary Dist. of Kyoto; pres. Central Japan Missionary Assn., mem. Kagawa Fellowship; sec. Fellowship of Christian Missionaries in Japan, 1925-40; mem. Diocesan Exec. Council; chmn. Dept. Christian Social Relations, Com. on State of Ch., Com. on Ch. Architecture, Com. on Constn. and Canons; dean Central Convocation; dep. Provincial Synod; del. Gen. Conv., 1945-60, N. Am. Conf. on Ch. and Family, 1961, 66. Chmn. merit system council S.C. Bd. Health, 1970—; hon. mem. S.C. Planned Parenthood; adviser Parents without Partners; past chmn. Meml. Youth Center. Trustee Voorhees Coll., Denmark, S.C., 1951—, chmn. bd., 1961-71; trustee Episcopal Ch. Home for Children, Heathwood Hall Sch., Episcopal Ch. Found. Diocese Upper S.C. Served to 1st lt. U.S. Army, World War I; to lt. col. AUS, World War II. Decorated Army Commendation medal with pendant. Diplomate Am. Assn. Pastoral Counselors. Fellow Am. Assn. Marriage and Family Counselors; mem. Assn. for Clin. Pastoral Edn., Am., S.C. psychol. assns., Nat. Council on Family Relations, Phi Beta Kappa, Phi Gamma Delta. Mason, Rotarian. Author: Noda, A Story of Redemption, 1938; Premarital Counseling-A Manual for Ministers, 1960; My Strength and My Shield, 1963; Marriage Counseling-A Manual for Ministers, 1965; The Windows of St. John's, 1971. Contbr. articles profl. jours. Home: 2433 Monroe St Columbia SC 29205 Office: 1316 Main St Columbia SC 29201

MORRIS, JAMES RUSSELL, assn. economist; b. Lakeland, Fla., Nov. 27, 1922; s. Scott and Blanche Gladys (Dicus) M.; A.A., U. Fla., 1943; B.A., Oberlin Coll., 1945; M.B.A., U. Chgo., 1947, Ph.D., 1957; m. Grace Fanes, June 1946. Cons. economist, Chgo., 1953-57, Winter Haven, Fla., 1958-59, Gainesville, Fla., 1959-60; sr. economist Am. Enterprise Inst. for Pub. Policy Research, Washington, 1960-61; cons. economist, Alexandria, Va., 1961-65; sr. asso. C. of C. U.S., 1965—; staff economist Task Force on Econ. Growth and Opportunity, Washington, 1965-70. Instr. U. Ill., Chgo., 1946-57; lectr. U. Chgo., winter 1950; asst. prof. U. Ark., Fayetteville, Ark., 1957-58. Mem. Am. Econ. Assn., A.A.A.S., Am. Acad. Polit. and Social Sci., Phi Eta Sigma, Beta Gamma Sigma. Episcopalian. Author: Employment Opportunities in Later Years, 1960; (with T. Johnson, J. Butts) Renewing America's Cities, 1962; also reports, booklets. Co-editor: Decisions for the Seventies, 1971. Contbr. to econ. jours. Home: 7600 Range Rd Alexandria VA 22306 Office: 1615 H St NW Washington DC 20006

MORRIS, JOSEPH WILSON, lawyer; b. Rice County, Kan., Apr. 28, 1922; s. J. Bertrand and Hazel Mary (Sluder) M.; B.A., Washburn U., 1943, LL.B., 1947; LL.M., U. Mich., 1948, S.J.D., 1955; m. Deane Conklin, Nov. 6, 1948; children—Jeffrey David, Marilyn, Cynthia. Admitted to Kan. bar, 1947, Okla. bar, 1949; staff atty. Shell Oil Co., Tulsa, and N.Y.C., 1948-60; asso. gen. counsel Amerada Petroleum Corp., Tulsa, 1960-67, gen. counsel, 1967-69, gen. counsel Amerada div. Amerada Hess Corp., 1969-71, v.p., asso. gen. counsel Amerada Hess Corp., 1971-72; adj. prof. law Coll. Law U. Tulsa, 1950-72, dean, 1972-74; U.S. dist. judge Eastern Dist. Okla., 1974—. Mem. Okla. State Regents for Higher Edn., 1969-72. Served to lt. (j.g.) USNR, 1944-46. Mem. Am. (council, natural resources law sect. 1970-73), Okla., Tulsa County (pres. 1971) bar assns., Phi Delta Theta, Delta Theta Phi. Republican. Episcopalian. Mason (32 deg. Shriner), Royal Order of Jesters. Contbr. articles in field to profl. jours. Home: 3617 Club Estates Dr Muskogee OK 74401 Office: PO Box 828 Muskogee OK 74401

MORRIS, KENNETH WAYNE, dentist; b. Lynchburg, Va., Mar. 12, 1939; s. Ulysses Bernice and Louise Elvira (Adams) M.; B.A., U. Va., 1961; D.D.S., Med. Coll. of Va., 1965; m. Judy Faye Atkins, May 31, 1964; children—Jeffrey Wayne, Kenneth Christian. Gen. practice dentistry South Hill, Va., 1967—; mem. staff Community Meml. Hosp., South Hill, 1967—. Served to lt., USNR, 1965-67. Mem. Gideons Internat. (pres. S.Central camp 1969-72, meml. bible sec.), Am., Va. dental assns., Southside Dental Soc., Alumni Assn. Med. Coll. Va., Alumni Assn. U. Va., South Hill C. of C. (dir. 1971—). Baptist (deacon, tchr. Sunday sch.). Clubs: Woodfield, Tanglewood Shores Golf and Country. Home: 509 Raleigh Av South Hill VA 23970 Office: 604 N Thomas St South Hill VA 23970

MORRIS, LEO, bio-statistician; b. Boston, Apr. 22, 1935; s. Philip and Esther (Butler) M.; B.S., U. Fla., 1959; M.P.H., U. Mich., 1963, doctoral student, 1970-72; m. Jane Simbulan, May 26, 1962; children—Kimberly, Lorinda, Eliana. With Center Disease Control, Atlanta, 1959—, statistician, epidemiology program, 1959-65, smallpox program, 1966-70, family planning evaluation br., 1970—; adviser ministry Health, Brazil, 1967-70. Served with USCGR, 1954-56. Recipient Incentive award Center Disease Control, 1960, Superior Performance award, 1970. Mem. Am. Statis. Assn., Am. Pub. Health Assn., Population Assn. Am. Contbr. profl. jours. Home: 3232 Leslie Lane NE Atlanta GA 30345 Office: Center Disease Control Atlanta GA 30333

MORRIS, MANFORD DONALD, educator; b. Kamiah, Ida., Apr. 18, 1926; s. James Nathaniel and Ella Katherine (Pfannebecker) M.; student San Mateo Jr. Coll., 1945-47; B.S., U. San Francisco, 1949, M.S. in Chemistry, 1951; Ph.D. in Biochemistry, U. Cal. at Berkeley, 1958; m. Betty Mae Zelezny, Aug. 5, 1951; children—Cheryl Ann, Mary Katherine, James William. Mem. faculty U. Ark. Med. Center, Little Rock, 1961—, prof. pediatrics, biochemistry, 1972—, project dir. Grad. Sch. in Interdisciplinary Toxicology, 1973—. Chmn. edn. com. Ark. Heart Assn., Little Rock, 1972-73. Served with USNR, 1944. Mem. So. Pediatric Soc., Am. Inst. Nutrition, Soc. Exptl. Medicine and Biology, Am. Heart Assn. Home: 9721 Treasure Hills Road Little Rock AR 72205 Office: U Ark Med Center 4301 W Markham St Little Rock AR 72201

MORRIS, MARTIN EUGENE, judge; b. Anderson, Ind., Mar. 26, 1929; s. James Minton and Inez (Clark) M.; B.A., U. South, 1949; LL.B., Wash. Coll. Law, 1959; m. Gwendolyn Strangways-Jones, Jan. 17, 1951; children—Carol Anne, Diane Lucile. Pub. relations asst. N.E.A., 1955-57; asst. to dir. pub. relations Am. Trucking Assns., 1956-59; admitted to Va. bar, 1959; atty. McLean, Va., 1959-67; judge Fairfax County Gen. Dist. Ct., 1967—. Sec., dir. Vega Precision Labs., Vienna, Va., 1964-70. Served with AUS, 1951-53. Episcopalian (vestryman 1966-68). Home: 9117 Falls Run Rd McLean VA 22101

MORRIS, OLIN FRANKLIN, broadcasting exec.; b. Inman, S.C., Nov. 23, 1935; s. Richard Marion and Bonnie (Miller) M.; student Maryville Coll., 1955; student U. Tenn., 1958-60, 1963; m. Jo Anne Benedict, Sept. 5, 1953; children—Lindle Richard, Stacy Anne. Staff announcer, newsman WATE Radio and TV, Knoxville, Tenn., 1958-60; program prodn. mgr. WPTA TV and WPTH FM Radio, Ft. Wayne, Ind., 1960-62; mem. exec. staff South Central Broadcasting Corp., Evansville, Ind., 1962-63; sales mgmt. trainee Armour Grocery Products Co., Memphis, 1963-64; v.p., dir. pub. affairs WREC-TV, Memphis 1964—. Chmn. TV Prodn. and Distbn. of Shelby United Neighbors, 1967-73; chmn. pub. relations com. Memphis Heart Assn., 1969-72; radio and TV chmn. Tenn. Heart Assn., 1972-73; mem. radio and TV com. Am. Heart Assn., 1972-73; mem. exec. com. Shrine Circuses, 1969-73; vice chmn. Thomas B. Davis Y.M.C.A., Memphis, 1966-67; Scout Show chmn. Chickasaw council Boy Scouts Am., 1972. Mem. exec. bd. Muscular Dystrophy Assn. Memphis; nat. v.p. Muscular Dystrophy Assn.; bd. dirs. Mid-South Fair Inc.; trustee Memphis Ecumenical Children's Assn.; bd. dirs. Project Memphis. Served with AUS, 1956-58. Recipient Kiwanis Club Layman of the Yr. award, 1970; Whitehaven Jaycees Distinguished Service award, 1970. Presbyn. (deacon 1969-71, chmn. bd. deacons 1971, elder 1973—, chmn. worship com. 1972-73). Mason (32 deg., Shriner, dir. pub. relations Al Chymia Shrine Temple 1968-73), Rotarian. Writer, exec. producer You In a Patrol Car, documentary nominated for Freedom's Found. award, 1969. Home: 3285 McCorkle St Memphis TN 38116 Office: Hotel Southern Peabody Memphis TN 38103

MORRIS, OWEN GLENN, govt. ofcl.; b. Shawnee, Okla., Feb. 3, 1927; s. Vestus and Myrtle (Lindsey) M.; B.S. in Mech. Engring., U. Okla., 1947, M. Aero. Engring., 1948; postgrad. U. Va., 1952-53, Va. Poly. Inst., 1955-56, Coll. William and Mary, 1957-58; m. Clifton Moree Glover, Aug. 4, 1948; children—Deborah Moree, Janine Inez. With NASA, Houston, 1948—, aero. research scientist, 1948-61, mgr. mission engring. Apollo, 1961-64, mgr. reliability and quality assurance Apollo, 1964-66, chief project engr. Lunar Module, 1966-69, mgr. Lunar Module, 1969-72, mgr. Apollo Spacecraft Program, 1972-73, dep. mgr. Space Shuttle Orbiter, 1973—. Engring. cons. in mech. engring. and aerodynamics, 1966-68. Mem. Tex. Water Control Improvement Dist. Bd., 1969—. Served with USNR, 1943-46. Recipient U.S. Medal of Freedom, NASA, 1972, Distinguished Service medal, 1973, Exceptional Service medal, 1969. Fellow Am. Inst. Aeros. and Astronautics (asso.); mem. Am. Aviation Hist. Soc., Am. Soaring Soc., Acad. Model Aeros., Tau Beta Pi, Tau Omega. Presbyn. (elder 1964—). Rotarian, Elk. Home: 130 Driftwood Dr Seabrook TX 77586 Office: Manned Spacecraft Center NASA Houston TX 77058

MORRIS, PHILIP BROWDER, lawyer; b. Richmond, Va., Sept. 2, 1935; s. James Watson, Jr. and Anne Florence (Browder) M.; B.S. in Bus. Adminstrn., U. Richmond, 1958, LL.B., 1960; m. Jeanne Elizabeth Black, Aug. 4, 1956; children—Lori Page, Susan Barrs, David Philip Browder. Admitted to Va. bar, 1960, practice in Richmond, 1961; partner firm Browder, Russell, Little & Morris, 1964—; mem. Va. Gen. Assembly from Richmond, 1972—; instr. bus. law U. Richmond, 1963-64. Pres. Richmond Jr. Bar Assn., 1969-70. Bd. dirs. Richmond Cerebral Palsy Center. Served to 1st lt. AUS, 1960-61. Mem. Am., Va., Richmond (exec. com. 1969-70) bar assns. Episcopalian. Clubs: Westwood Racquet (past pres.), Downtown (Richmond). Home: 8 Iris Lane Richmond VA 23226 Office: 1510 Ross Bldg 801 E Main St Richmond VA 23219

MORRIS, ROBERT CALDER, entomologist; b. Wellsville, O., May 28, 1912; s. William Llewellyn and Annie Bell (Davidson) M.; B.S., Coll. Forestry State U. N.Y., 1948; M.S., U. Fla., 1968; m. Ora Bee Stuckey, Apr. 4, 1943; children—Brian Deric, Ian David, Adrian Craig. Entomologist U.S. Agr. Dept., 1948-53, Gulfport, Miss., 1951, Panama Canal Zone, 1951-53; with U.S. Forestry Ser., Gulfport and Stoneville, Miss., 1953—, supervisory research entomologist, Stoneville, 1968-71, project leader so. hardwood and insect disease research, 1971—. Leader Delta area concil Boy Scouts Am., 1970, 4-H, Leland, Miss., 1965; mem. Leland (Miss.) Beautification Com., 1962—. Served with AUS, 1940-45. Decorated Combat Infantryman Badge. Recipient Best Insect Forestry Publ. award So. Forest Insect Work Conf., 1967. Mem. Entomol. Soc. Am., Internat. Soc. Tropical Foresters, Internat. Poplar Commn. (chmn. insect com.), Miss. Archeol. Assn. (pres. 1966-67), Poplar Council Am. (sec.-treas., 1970—), Sigma Xi. Home: 205 Lakeview Dr Leland MS 38756 Office: Southern Hardwoods Lab Stoneville MS 38776

MORRIS, ROBERT NELSON, banker; b. Glasgow, Ky., Sept. 5, 1926; s. Ralph P. and Myrtle (Gillock) M.; B.S., U. Ky., 1952, postgrad., 1953; m. Mary Elizabeth Galloway, June 3, 1953; children—Robert Michael, Marcus Allen, Timothy Ray. Tchr. Park City (Ky.) High Sch.; with Conservation Service. U.S. Dept. Agr., Lexington, Ky., 1953; asst. county agt. Fla. Agrl. Extension Service, Tampa, 1953-54; v.p. First Nat. Bank, Tampa, 1954-67; adminstr. Fla. Soil and Water Conservation Bd., 1967—; dir., v.p. M. & M Supply Co. of Fla., Inc., 1961—; v.p. Exchange Nat. Bank of Tampa. Supr. Hillsboro Soil Conservation Dist., 1956-67; sec., dir. Hillsboro County Farm Bur., 1961-67. Mem. Fla. Assn. Soil Conservation Suprs. (pres. 1962-64), Hillsboro Cattlemens Assn. (dir. 1956-67). Home: 5622 Oakland Dr Tampa FL 33617 Office: PO Box 1809 Tampa FL 33601

MORRIS, ROBERT WESLEY, hosp. adminstr.; b. Pasadena, Cal., July 21, 1924; s. John W. and Esther (Brown) M.; B.A., LaSierra Coll., 1948; M.S., Northwestern U., 1961; m. Caroline M. Gibson, Mar. 9, 1948; children—James Olin, Esther Lynn, Constance Estelle, Cynthia Faye, Deborah Ann. Adminstrv. asst. Chgo. Wesley Meml. Hosp., 1957-59; adminstr. Madison (Tenn.) Hosp., 1960—. Treas., Edn. and Research Found., 1969—; v.p. Mid-Cumberland Health Planning

Council, 1969-71; mem. Gov.'s Emergency Med. Services Council, 1972—. Trustee, So. Missionary Coll., Madison Acad., Takoma Hosp., Riverside Hosp., Fla. Hosp. Corp.; bd. dirs. So. Adventist Health and Hosp. System. Served with AUS, 1946-47. Mem. Middle Tenn. Hosp. Council (pres. 1964-65), Tenn. Hosp. Assn. (trustee 1969-74, pres. 1971-72), Am. Hosp. Assn., 7th Day Adventist Hosp. Assn. (pres. 1970-71), Am. Protestant Hosp. Assn. (ho. of dels.), Am. Coll. Hosp. Adminstrs., C. of C. (pres. 1965). Rotarian (past pres.). Home: 225 Peeler Trail Madison TN 37115 Office: Madison Hosp Madison TN 37115

MORRIS, SAMUEL BARRY, supt. schs.; b. Horry, S.C., June 22, 1920; s. Samuel C. and Hattie Lee (Haynes) M.; diploma Ferrum Jr. Coll., 1941; A.B., Duke, 1943; M.A., U. N.C., 1950; postgrad. Fla. State U., 1959-61; m. Elizabeth M. Mullinix, June 24, 1949; children—John B., Robert H., David W., Lee Ann. Tchr. pub. schs., High Point, N.C., 1943-45, Honolulu, 1945-46; tchr. Armed Forces Inst., 1951-58; dir. audio visual edn. Durham County (N.C.) Schs., 1949-51, Asheville (N.C.) City Schs., 1951-58, Fla. Dept. Edn., 1958-62; asst. supt. Fairfax (Va.) County Schs., 1962-70, area supt., 1970—; faculty Appalachian State U., Boone, N.C., 1959, Fla. State U., 1960, U. Va. Sch. Gen. Studies, 1963—. Pres. Nat. Council Chief State Audio Visual Officers, 1961; investigator States Audio Visual Edn. Survey, 1962-63; mem. media specialists panel of advisers U.S. Office Edn., 1968-72. Bd. mgrs. Fla. Congress P.T.A., 1961. Mem. Am. Assn. Sch. Adminstrs., Assn. for Edn. Communications and Tech., N.E.A. (life mem., adviser Ednl. Policies Commn. 1960-66, chmn. legislative commn. dept. audio visual instrn. 1962-65), N.C. Audio Visual Assn. (past pres., chmn. bd. dirs.), Assn. Sch. Bus. Ofcls., Va., Fairfax edn. assns., Nat. Acad. Sch. Execs. (dir. 1970-72), Phi Delta Kappa. Home: 7408 Bull Run Dr Centreville VA 22020 Office: 730 Marshall Rd Vienna VA 22180

MORRIS, SETH IRWIN, architect; b. Madisonville, Tex., Sept. 1, 1914; s. Seth Irwin and Carrie (Holleman) M.; B.A., Rice Inst., 1935; m. Suzanne Kibler, Dec. 29, 1945; children—Mark Peter, Maria, David Kibler, Laura Houston, John Hampson. Practice architecture, Houston, 1935—; partner Wilson, Morris, Crain & Anderson, 1954-72, S.I. Morris Assos., 1972—. prin. works include U.S. Post Office, Houston, 1968, World Trade Center, Houston, 1960. Western Nat. Bank, 1964, Southwestern Bell Telephone Co. Area Hdqrs., 1966, Harris County Domed Stadium, 1965, Houston Lighting & Power Co., 1967, Bd. dirs. Houston Museum Fine Arts, 1960-68, pres., 1967-68. Served to comdr. USNR, 1942-46. Decorated Legion of Merit; Order Cloud and Banner (China); recipient honor awards Tex. Soc. Architects; 5 Nat. awards, 16 awards Houston chpt. A.I.A. 2 awards. Fellow A.I.A. (pres. Houston 1961); mem. Tex. Soc. Architects, Houston C. of C. (dir. 1964-75), Presbyn. (elder). Home: 2 Waverly Pl Houston TX 77005 Office: 3465 W Alabama St Houston TX 77027

MORRIS, STEWART, lawyer, title co. exec.; b. Houston, Oct. 28, 1919; s. William Carloss and Willie (Stewart) M.; B.A., U. Tex., 1943; L.L.B., So. Meth. U., 1943; m. Joella Mitchell, July 17, 1943; children—Carlotta, Stewart, Caralisa. With Stewart Title Co., Houston, 1935—, pres., 1950— admitted to Tex. bar, 1943, since practiced in Houston; partner, Morris, Termini, Harris & McCanne, 1946—; dir. Nassau Bay Nat. Bank, First Nat. Bank of Stafford, Houston Bank & Trust Co., Stewart Title Guaranty Co., Stewart Title Co., Stewart Trust Co., Admiral Investment Co., Inc.; chmn. bd. Stewart Info Services. Co-founder, past chmn. bd. trustees Houston Bapt. Coll.; chmn. bd. trustees Space Center Meml. Hosp. Found.; trustee Star of Hope Mission; adv. bd. Nat. Trust for Historic Preservation; trustee Oldham Little Ch. Found. Served to lt. (j.g.), USNR, 1943-46; PTO. Fellow Tex. Bar Found.; mem. State Bar Tex., Delta Theta Phi, Alpha Tau Omega. Clubs: River Oaks Country, Sugar Creek Country. Home: 5 E Rivercrest Dr Houston TX 77042 Office: 1302 Rusk Av Houston TX 77002

MORRIS, WILLIAM COKE, editor; b. Columbia, S.C., Feb. 21, 1922; s. Robert F. and Frances G. (Green) M.; A.B., Emory U., 1948; m. Mary Walker Leatherwood, Oct. 11, 1949; children—Mary C., William B., Susan F. Publicity dir. Wofford Coll., Spartanburg, S.C., 1949-51; staff writer Greenville (S.C.) Piedmont, 1951-63, city editor, 1963-65, mng. editor, 1965—. Mem. bd. Greenville High Sch. P.T.A., 1966—; treas. Greenville County Mental Health Assn., 1962. Treas. Greenville Republican Com., 1963-64; mem. Greenville County Republican Exec. Com., 1956-65; del. S.C. Rep. convs., 1960, 62, 64, 66. Trustee, Greenville Rescue Mission, S.C. Methodist Center, Columbia, 1957-64; chmn. adv. bd. S.C. Methodist Adv., 1960-65. Served with AUS, 1942-46; ETO. Recipient awards for writing S.C. Press Assn., 1955, 56, 57, 58, 68. Mem. Alston Wilkes Soc. (dir. Greenville County chpt. (1968—, state dir.), Greenville Jr. C. of C., Sigma Delta Chi. Methodist (ofcl. bd.). Author series on survey of S.C. prison camps which resulted in law requiring state inspection all prisons, jails, 1967. Home: 132 Fernwood Lane Greenville SC 29607 Office: News-Piedmont Co PO Box 1688 Greenville SC 29602

MORRISON, EDWARD WALTER, JR., milling co. exec.; b. Wichita, Kan., Feb. 22, 1921; s. Edward Walter and Myrtle (Lane) M.; B.S., N.Tex. State U., Denton, 1939; postgrad. Kan. State U., 1939-42; m. Virginia Ann Boydston, Aug. 21, 1965; 1 son, Edward Walter III. Pres. Morrison Milling Co., Denton, 1942—. Past pres., dir. Self Rising Flour and Corn Meal Program. Served with AUS, 1944-45. Mem. Millers Nat. Fedn. (dir.), Am. Corn Millers Fedn. (dir.), Denton C. of C. (past dir.), Alpha Mu. Mem. Christian Ch. (elder, trustee). Rotarian. Club: Denton Country (dir., pres. 1973). Home: 414 Mimosa St Denton TX 76201 Office: 319 E Prairie St PO Box 719 Denton TX 76201

MORRISON, ESTON ODELL, educator; b. Sabinal, Tex., Sept. 18, 1932; s. Eston William and Maxine (Whitlock) M.; B.S., Tex. A. and I. U., 1957; M.S., Tex. A. and M. U., 1960, Ph.D., 1963; m. Alice Faye Hunt, Feb. 14, 1958; children—Geoffrey Thomas, Gregory Neil, Gary Wade. Instr. biology Tex. A. and I. U., 1960-61; asst. prof. biology Lamar U., 1963-66; prof. biol. sci. Tarleton State U., 1966—. Cubmaster, Stephenville, Tex., 1968-70. Served with USN, 1951-55. Fed. Inst. grantee, 1965; NSF grantee, 1966, 67. Mem. Tex. Acad. Sci., Helminthol. Soc. Washington, Nat., Tex. field archery assns., Am. Soc. Parasitologists, Sigma Xi, Beta Beta Beta. Optimist. Editor: Lonestar Bow Hunter. Contbr. articles to sci. jours. Home: 1895 N McCart St Stephenville TX 76401 Office: Tarleton Sta 219 Stephenville TX 76402

MORRISON, FRED GILBERT, JR., lawyer; b. Memphis, 1939; s. Fred Gilbert and Ethel V. (Hazelwood) M.; B.A., High Point Coll.; LL.B. cum laude, Wake Forest U., 1963; m. Detra Carter, July 20, 1961. Admitted to N.C. bar, 1963; asso. E.W. Hooper, Atty., Thomasville, N.C., 1963-65; solicitor Thomasville Recorder's Ct., 1965-69; legal counsel to Gov. N.C., Raleigh, 1969—. Mem. Gov.'s Study Commn. on Automobile Liability Ins. and Rates, 1969-71. Recipient Distinguished Service award Thomasville Jr. C. of C., 1966, 67; named Tar Heel of Week, Raleigh News and Observer, 1971. Mem. Am., N.C., Thomasville, Davidson County, Wake County bar assns., Am. Judicature Soc., Nat. Legal Aid and Defender Assn., N.C. Jr. (pres.), Thomasville Jr. chambers commerce. Methodist (trustee). Home: 900 Indian Trail Raleigh NC 27602 Office: Box 1305 Raleigh NC 27602

MORRISON, HARRY, lawyer, state ofcl.; b. Crawfordville, Fla., Sept. 21, 1917; s. Angus and Marie (Walker) M.; grad. high sch.; pvt. study law; m. Estelle Mills, Apr. 23, 1953; children—James D., Harry, Angus II. Admitted to Fla. bar, 1940; spl. agt. FBI, 1940-47; gen. practice Tallahassee, 1947-72; first asst. state atty. 2d Jud. Circuit Fla., 1949-72, state atty., 1973—. Dir. Alligator Point Water Resources Dist. Mem. Am., Tallahassee (past pres.) bar assns., Fla. Bar (grievance com. mem. 2d circuit, 1957-67), Soc. Former Spl. Agts. FBI. Democrat. Baptist. Mason (Shriner), Elk. Clubs: Capital City Contry. Home: 2011 E Randolph Circle Tallahassee FL 32303 Office: Leon County Courthouse Tallahassee FL 32301

MORRISON, HUGH MARTIN, health services co. auditor; b. Rockport, Tex., Dec. 2, 1946; s. Hugh Lacey and Dorothy (Rhodes) M.; B.B.A. cum laudg, Tex. A. and I. U., 1969; m. Sara Green White, June 19, 1971. Staff accountant Peat, Marwick, Mitchell & Co., Dallas, 1969-70, sr. and supervising accountant, El Paso, 1970-72; auditor Tex. Instruments, Inc., Dallas, 1972-73; auditor Medenco, Inc., Houston, 1973—. C.P.A., Tex. Mem. Am. Inst. C.P.A.'s, Tex. A. and I. U. Alumni Assn., Delta Sigma Pi. Presbyn. Home: 10010 Memorial Dr 114 Houston TX 77024 Office: 5 Greenway Plaza E Suite 1600 Houston TX 77046

MORRISON, JOHN COULTER, physician; b. Mayfield, Ky., Sept. 11, 1943; s. John William and Dorothy Joyce (Curlin) M.; B.S., Memphis State U., 1965; M.C., U. Tenn., 1969; m. Rita Lucille Dickey, Mar. 4, 1967; children—Paul Alan, John Coulter III, Lisa Hollidae. Intern City Memphis Hosps., 1968-69, resident obstetrics and gynecology, 1969-72; instr. obstetrics and gynecology U. Tenn. at Memphis, 1971-72, asst. prof., 1972—. Pres., Physicians' Placement, Inc., 1970; v.p. Bluff City Testing, Inc., 1971. Diplomate Am. Bd. Obstetrics and Gynecology. Mem. A.C.S., Am. Coll. Obstetrics and Gynecology, Am. Fertility Soc., Am. Chem. Soc., Am. Cancer Research, A.M.A., Tenn., Shelby County med. assns., A Soc. Obstetricians, Anesthesiologists and Pediatricians, So. Med. Assn., Sigma Xi. Contbr. profl. jours. Home: 421 Vescovo Dr Memphis TN 38117 Office: Dept Obstetrics and Gynecology Univ Tenn Memphis TN 38103

MORRISON, JOHN ELLIOTT, aerospace co. exec.; b. Greely, Colo., Jan. 20, 1927; s. Robert Carnine and Lenore Belle (Hiatt) M.; B.S. in Mech. Engring., U. Ariz., 1952; m. Imogene Mayben Woodward, Mar. 20, 1948; 1 son, Robert Michael. Asso. engr. Seattle City Light, 1952-57; with Boeing Co., various locations, 1957—, constrn. and activation mgr. Apollo program, NASA Miss. Test Facility, Bay St. Louis, 1962-68, sky lab mgr., mgr. launch facilities, Kennedy Space Center, Cocoa Beach, Fla., 1968—. Pres., chmn. bd. Brevard Electronics, Inc., Merritt Island, Fla., 1972—. Served with USNR, 1944-46: PTO, ETO. Registered profl. engr., Fla., Wash. Mem. Fla. Electronic Service Assn., Am. Soc. Ichthyologists and Herpetologists, Herpetologists League, C. of C. Home: 235 E Via Havarre Merritt Island FL 32952 Office: Boeing Co Cocoa Beach FL 32931

MORRISON, LONNY DEE, lawyer; b. Victoria, Tex., May 17, 1942; s. Max K. and Amy Louise (Draper) M.; B.A., Washburn U., 1964; M.B.A., Okla. State U., 1965; J.D., U. Tex., 1968; m. Janet J. Harvey, July 1, 1962; children—Sara Jane, Amy Elizabeth. Admitted to Tex. bar, 1968; practiced in Wichita Falls, 1968—; asso. firm Eggers, Sherrill and Pace, 1968-71, mem. firm Sherrill, Pace and Rogers, 1971—. Partner Buffalo Creek Ranch, Wichita County, Tex., 1972—. Chmn. attys. div. United Fund, 1971. Alderman, City of Wichita Falls, 1973—. Bd. dirs. March of Dimes, 1972—. Mem. State Bar Tex., Am. Bar Assn., State Jr. Bar Tex. (dir. 1968-73). Home: 2404 Speedway Wichita Falls TX 76308 Office: 1100 Hamilton Bldg Wichita Falls TX 76301

MORRISON, LUCILE YOUNG (MRS. MERLE JOHN MORRISON), educator; b. Beallsville, O.; d. Howard O. and Margaret (McVay) Young; B.S., Bliss Coll., 1929; M.E., Wayne State U., 1958; Edn. Specialist, Wayne State U., 1964; student Oberlin Conservatory Music, 1923-24; m. Merle John Morrison, May 26, 1934; 1 son, Roger Kent. Tchr. pub. high schs., Ohio, 1929-35; asst. prof. P.T. Wayne State U., Detroit, 1952-56; cons. tng. pub. relations and communications Nat. Bank Detroit, 1952-55; guidance counselor Berkley (Mich.) High Sch., 1956-62, asst. prin., instrn. and guidance, 1962-70. Mem. Assn. Coll. Admissions Counselors, Am. Personnel and Guidance Assn., Mich., Nat. assns. secondary sch. prins., Mich. Edn. Assn., Sigma Tau Delta, Alpha Delta Kappa. Clubs: Detroit Yacht; Venice (Fla.) Yacht. Contbr. articles in field to profl. jours. Home: 1150 Tarpon Center Dr Venice FL 33595 also 1014 Lake Rd Marblehead OH 43440

MORRISON, MAMON L., pianist; b. Coffeyville, Kan., Jan. 8, 1933; s. Hilliard and Galatha (Morrison) M.; Mus.B. Edn., B.Mus., U. Colo., 1957; M.A., Western Res. U., 1958. Faculty, Cleve. Mus. Settlement, 1957-59; asst. prof., chmn. piano Fla. A. and M. U., Tallahassee, 1959-60; asso. prof., chmn. piano Va. State Coll., Petersburg, 1961—; also mem. faculty dept. music Va. Commonwealth U., Richmond. Concert tour of Europe, 1967, 69; soloist Colo. Summer Symphony, 1957, Rochester Symphony, 1963, Va. Symphony, 1965. Served with AUS, 1953-55. Mem. Am. Assn. U. Profs., Phi Mu Alpha. Home: 20908 3d Av Ettrick VA 23803 Office: Va State Coll Petersburg VA 23803

MORRISON, RICHARD SCRUGGS, JR., physician; b. Nashville, Feb. 8, 1916; s. Richard Scruggs and Mary Anderson (Yancey) M.; student Vanderbilt U., 1933-34; B.A., U. Tenn., 1953, M.D., 1956; m. Elizabeth Ann Crew, Oct. 1, 1942; children—Richard Scruggs, Marion, Thomas, Elizabeth (Mrs. Larry Tipton), Patricia, Robert; m. 2d, Betty Lou Hughes, Dec. 15, 1972. Intern Roanoke (Va.) Meml. Hosp., 1956, 1956-57; practice medicine specializing in family practice, Johnson City, Tenn., 1957—; mem. staff Meml. Hosp., Johnson City. Served to lt. col. Med. Service Corps., AUS, 1940-46. Decorated Bronze Star. Home: 905 Forest Av Johnson City TN 37601 Office: 701 B S Roan St Johnson City TN 37601

MORRISON, WALTON S., lawyer; b. Big Spring, Tex., June 16, 1907; s. M. H. and Ethel (Jackson) M.; student Texas A. and M. Coll., 1926-28; J.D., Texas U., 1932; m. Mary Bell, Dec. 19, 1932. Admitted to Tex. bar, 1932: asso. Morrison & Morrison, Big Spring, 1932-37; county atty. Howard County, Tex., 1937-39; county judge Howard County, 1941-42; pvt. practice, 1946-47; county judge Howard, 1947-48; partner Morrison & Morrison, 1949-53; pvt. practice, 1953—; city atty. Big Spring, 1949-58. Served with USAF, 1942-46. Mem. Am., state, local assns. Rotarian. Home: 1501 11th Pl Big Spring TX 79720 Office: 113 E 2d St Big Spring TX 79720

MORRISS, LELA MAE PATTERSON (MRS. JAMES HENRY MORRISS), educator; b. Palo Pinto, Tex., Apr. 9, 1923; d. George Leroy and Henry (Davis) Patterson; student North Tex. State U., 1940-41; B.S. in Edn., U. Houston, 1957; M.Ed., McNeese State U., 1966, Counselor Certificate, 1971; m. James Henry Morriss, Aug. 23, 1941; children—Betty (Mrs. Carl Amos), Nancy (Mrs. Fred Wallace). Tchr. pub. elementary sch., Pearland, Tex., 1952-56, Houston, 1956-61, Lake Charles, La., 1961—. Cooperating tchr. McNee State U., 1965-71. Recipient Key to City, Monroe, La., 1971. Mem. La. (state pres. assn. classroom tchrs. sect. 1971), Calcasieu (past v.p.) tchrs. assns. Assn. Classrooms Tchrs. (state pres. 1971), Assn. Childhood Edn., N.E.A., Alpha Delta Kappa, Omicron. Home: Box 5717 Drew Sta Lake Charles LA 70601 Office: 3618 Ernest St Lake Charles LA 70601

MORRISSETTE, MAURICE CORLETTE, educator; b. Clyde, Kan., Aug. 27, 1921; s. Archil Francis and Anna Marie (LeCuyer) M.; B.S. with honors, Kan. State U., 1954, D.V.M. with honors, 1954; M.S., Okla. State U., 1956, Ph.D., 1964; m. Stella Marie Meyer, May 5, 1945; children—Raymond F., Donald J., Stephen M. Asst. prof. vet. medicine Okla. State U., 1954-57, asso. prof., 1959-64, prof., 1964-69; asst. prof. physiology and pharmacology Kan. State U., 1957-59; mem. faculty La. State U., Baton Rouge, 1969—, prof., head dept. vet. physiology and pharmacology and toxicology Sch. Vet. Medicine, 1969—. Served with USCG, 1942-45. NIH grantee, 1964-69. Mem. Soc. Study Fertility, Soc. Study Reprodn., Am. Soc. Vet. Physiology and Pharmacology (pres. 1971-72), World Assn. Vet. Physiologists, Pharmacologists and Biochemists, Conf. Research Workers in Animal Diseases, Animal Disease Research Workers in So. States, Sigma Xi, Phi Kappa Phi, Alpha Zeta, Gamma Sigma Delta. Contbr. articles to profl. jours. Home: 8956 Tallyho Av Baton Rouge LA 70806

MORRISSEY, ROBERT WILLIAM, air force pathologist; b. Ottumwa, Ia., June 4, 1914; s. John Joseph and Lila (Fulton) M.; B.S., St. Ambrose Coll., 1936; M.S., U. Ia., 1939; M.D., Albany Med. Coll., 1948; m. Florence Loretta Vorwick, June 9, 1945; children—Susan, Nancy (Mrs. Donald Levings), Janet, Robert William, Patricia, Alice Margaret. Intern Ia. Luth. Hosp., Des Moines, 1948-49; commd. 1st lt. USAF, 1948, advanced through grades to col., 1973; resident Walter Reed Army Hosp., Washington, 1952-56; chmn. dept. pathology USAF Hosp., Lackland AFB, Tex., 1965-69, AR dep. dir. Armed Forces Inst. Pathology, Washington, 1969-71, dir., 1971-73; asso. pathologist St. Anthony's Hosp., Louisville, 1973—. Clin. asso. prof. pathology Georgetown U. Sch. Medicine and Dentistry, Washington, 1970-73; sr. cons. to surg. gen. USAF, Washington, 1972-73. Decorated Legion Merit with oak leaf cluster. Diplomate Am. Bd. Pathology. Fellow Coll. Am. Pathologists, Am. Soc. Clin. Pathologists; mem. A.M.A., Air Force Assn., Aerospace Med. Assn., Internat. Acad. Pathology, Assn. Mil. Surgeons, Acad. Medicine Washington. Contbr. articles to profl. jours. Home: 6504 Gunpowder Lane Prospect KY 40059 Office: 1313 St Anthony Pl Louisville KY 40204

MORROW, GENEVIEVE BOWMAN, author; b. Hillsboro, Tex.; d. Oliver Green and Juli (Johnson) Bowman; student Randolph Macon Womans Coll., 1912-13; Litt.B., Howard Payne U., 1953; m. Wright Morrow, Apr. 27, 1916; children—Genevieve Morrow (Mrs. Hans Bohlmann), Nancy Morrow Fagg. A founder Houston Symphony Soc., Orch., bd. dirs., 1935-52; charter mem. Music Guild; mem. Grey Ladies, Ellington AFB, Houston, 1942-46, Vets. Hosp., Houston, 1947-49; vol. Jefferson Davis Charity Hosp., 1950-51; past pres. dir. Girl Town, Whiteface, Tex. Recipient citation of honor Randolph Macon Women's Coll., 1967; Genevieve Morrow Chapel Trinity Epis. Ch. dedicated in her honor, 1972. Mem. Alpha Omicron Pi. Democrat. Episcopalian. Clubs: Houston, Houston Country, Warwick, (Houston). Author: Colored Stories, 1951; Decisions, 1960; Our Patsy, 1969. Home: 3028 S MacGregor Way Houston TX 77021

MORROW, GLENN DAVIS, govt. ofcl.; b. Madisonville, Ky., Mar. 4, 1911; s. Charly and Willie (Hughes) M.; A.B., Murray State Coll., 1933; M.A., George Peabody Coll., 1940; postgrad. U. Ky., 1941-43, U. Chgo., 1966-67; m. Mary B. Folwell, Nov., 1935; 1 son, Dan F. Research asst. Bur. Bus. Research, U. Ky., Lexington, 1941-44, prof. Coll. Commerce, 1945-49; mem. Am. Finance Mission to Iran, Tehran, 1944-45; tax specialist U.S. Army Occupation Japan, Tokyo, 1949-51; spl. asst. to commr. Ky. Dept. Revenue, Frankfort, 1951-52, exec. asst. to commr. Dept. Finance, 1952-54; research asso. Commn. Intergovtl. Relations, Washington, 1954-55; cons. govt. survey and reorgn. commn. Republic Philippines, Manila, 1955-56; tax adminstrn. adviser ICA Mission to Korea, Seoul, 1957; social sci. analyst, finance studies Social Security Adminstrn., Washington, 1958-63; financial economist Office Econ. Adviser, Small Bus. Adminstrn., Washington, 1963-67, supervising economist Office Planning, Research and Analysis, 1967—. Cons. to mayor Louisville, 1953, Legislative Reference Service, Library Congress, Washington, 1954, Com. Econ. Devel., Washington, 1958. Recipient certificate Appreciation, Govt. Survey and Reorgn. Commn. Philippines, 1956. Mem. Beta Gamma Sigma. Club: University of Kentucky Research (Lexington). Contbr. articles to financial jours. Home: 4848 Chevy Chase Dr Chevy Chase MD 20015 Office: 1441 L St NW Washington DC 20416

MORROW, JACOB ISAAC, petroleum co. exec.; b. Quitman, Tex., June 3, 1936; s. Kenneth A. and Alma Irene (Folmer) M.; B.B.A., U. Tex., 1962; m. Sandra Neil Stewart, Mar. 14, 1959; children—Julie Elizabeth, Jennifer Lee. With Atlantic Refining Co., 1962-65, Samedan Oil Corp., 1965-68; with A.J. Wessely Co., Dallas, 1968-71, v.p. Wessely Energy Corp., Dallas, 1971—. Chmn. Landmen's Inst., Southwestern Legal Found., 1971—. Pres. Forest Meadows Community Assn., 1973-74. Served with USNR, 1954-56. Mem. Am., Dallas (v.p. 1973-74) assns. petroleum landmen. Home: 9336 Loma Vista St Dallas TX 75231 Office: 2001 Bryan Tower Dallas TX 75201

MORROW, ROBERT PROSSER, JR., physician; b. Faunsdale, Ala., Jan. 11, 1916; s. Robert Prosser and Mary (McConnell) M.; B.S., Davidson Coll., 1936; M.D., Tulane U., 1940; M.S. in Urology, U. Minn., 1951; m. Lelia Henry Terry, Apr. 5, 1941; children—Lelia Terry, Robert Prosser III. Intern, Touro Infirmary, New Orleans, 1940-41, resident in urology, 1941-42, sr. and chief urology service, 1962—; fellow in urology Mayo Found., Rochester, Minn., 1948-51; practice medicine specializing in urology, New Orleans, 1951—; asst. prof. urology La. State U., New Orleans, 1946-58, asso. prof., 1961-68, prof., 1968—; asso. prof. urology Tulane U., New Orleans, 1958-61; vis. surgeon So. Bapt., Sara Mayo, Flint-Goodridge hosps.; sr. surgeon Charity Hosp; cons. in urology La. Cripple Children's Service, USPHS Hosp. Served to capt. M.C., AUS, 1941-46. Diplomate Am. Bd. Urology. Mem. Am. (Southeastern sect. exec. com., La. rep. 1964-67, chmn. sci. awards com. 1966-67, chmn. advancement sci. com. 1966-68, sec. 1967—, pres. 1971-72), La. urol. assns., A.C.S., Urologist Corr. Club, Pan-Am. (diplomate in urology), Orleans Parish med. socs., So. Med. Assn., New Orleans Grad. Med. Assembly, Am. Med. Soc. Vienna, Royal Soc. Health, Sigma Xi, Kappa Delta Phi, Omicron Delta Kappa, Nu Sigma Nu, Kappa Sigma. Presbyn. (elder). Contbr. articles to med. jours. Home: 1536 Webster St New Orleans LA 70118 Office: Med Arts Bldg 3439 Prytania St New Orleans LA 70115

MORROW, WILLIAM SLATER, printing co. exec.; b. Marshall, Tex., Nov. 16, 1913; s. Spurgeon P. and Ottomease (Brown) M.; grad. high sch.; m. Willie V. Layton, July 1, 1967; 1 son, James M. With Wade H. Taylor Printing Co., Ft. Worth, 1930-35, Dudley Hodgkins Printing Co., Ft. Worth, 1935-44; chmn. bd. Thomason & Morrow Co., Inc., Ft. Worth, 1944—. Mason (32 deg.). Home: Rural Route 4 Granbury TX 76048 Office: 2924 Bledsoe Box 9043 Fort Worth TX 76107

MORSE, BURT JULES, mathematician, govt. ofcl.; b. N.Y.C., June 17, 1926; s. Alexander and Frieda (Langman) M.; B.S., Coll. City N.Y., 1949; A.M., Columbia, 1952; Ph.D., N.Y. U., 1963. Mathematician, Vitro Corp. Am., West Orange, N.J., 1952-54, IBM, N.Y.C., 1954-59; asst. prof. math. U. N.M., Albuquerque, 1963-66; research mathematician Nat. Oceanic and Atmospheric Adminstrn., Washington, 1966—. Served with USNR, 1944-46. Mem. Am. Math. Soc., Soc. for Indsl. Applied Math. Contbr. articles on wave propagation and numerical analysis to sci. jours. Home: 6621 Wakefield Dr No 910 Alexandria VA 22307 Office: NOAA NESS CPDB DAPAD FOB4 S117 Suitland MD 20233

MORSE, F. D., JR., dentist; b. Glen Lyn, Va., Apr. 5, 1928; s. Frank D. and Ida Estell (Davis) M.; B.S., Concord Coll., 1951; D.D.S., Med. Coll. Va., 1955; m. Patsy Lee Apple, Feb. 4, 1967; 1 son, Fortis Davis. Free lance photographer, 1950-56; practice dentistry, Pearisburg, Va., 1958—; mem. staff Giles Hosp., Pearisburg, 1958—. Served from asst. dental surgeon to sr. asst. dental surgeon USPHS, 1955-57; assigned to USCG, 1957-58. Mem. Am., S.W. Va. dental assns., Assn. Mil. Surgeons, A.A.A.S., Nat. Assn. Advancement Sci., Fedn. Dentaire Internat., Internat. Platform Assn., W.Va. Collegiate Acad. Sci., Beta Phi. Kiwanian. Home: Bicuspid Acres Pearisburg VA 24134 Office: Giles Profl Bldg Pearisburg VA 24134

MORSE, FREDERICK TRACY, educator, engr.; b. Unadilla, N.Y., Sept. 11, 1902; s. Ralph and Estella (Rifenbark) M.; E.E., M.E., U. Va., 1924; m. Mary Genevieve Forbes, Jan. 1, 1926; 1 son, Robert Frederick. Practiced engring., Boston, 1924-26; asst. prof. mech. engring. La. Poly. Inst., 1926-33; asst. prof. U. Va., Charlottesville, 1933-43, asso. prof., 1943-46, prof. mech. engring., 1946-72, dir. spl. on-campus aviation tng. for mil. services, 1941-44, chmn. dept. mech. engring., 1957-63. Cons. mech. engr., 1938—. Registered profl. engr., Va. Mem. Am. Soc. Engring. Edn., Am. Soc. M.E. (nat. medalist for contbns. to permanent lit. engring. 1963), Nat. (dir., com. chmn.), Va. (past pres.) socs. profl. engrs., Raven Soc., Sigma Xi, Tau Beta Pi, Theta Tau. Author: Power Plant Engineering and Design, 1932, rev. edits., 1942-53; Elements of Applied Energy, 1947; (with J. P. Raney) Computation and Instrumentation, 1962; Introduction to Engineering, 1965; Professional and Business Environment for Engineers, 1966. Engring. editor, contbr. to Van Nostrand's Sci. Ency., 1928, rev. 1947. Home: Box 6127 Charlottesville VA 22906

MORSE, GENEVIEVE FORBES (MRS. FREDERICK TRACY MORSE), club woman; b. New Rochelle, N.Y., June 8, 1905; d. James and Mabel (Sabin) Forbes; B.A., La. Poly. Inst., 1932; m. Frederick Tracy Morse, Jan. 1, 1926; 1 son, Robert Frederick. Pres., U. Va. Hosp. Circle, 1947-49, bd. dirs., 1945-66; Va. corr. sec. D.A.R., 1953-56, editor Va. News Bull., 1953-59, vice regent, 1956-59, regent, 1959-62, v.p. gen. from Va., 1962-64, curator gen. nat. soc., 1965-68, adviser D.A.R. Museum, 1968—, state chmn. Va. Room, in Washington, 1968-71, mem. com., 1971—, nat. chmn. resolutions com., 1971—; Va. rec. sec. Daus. Colonial Wars, 1953-56, chaplain, 1959-62, pres., 1956-59; nat. chmn. nat. def. com., 1959-62, nat. pres., 1962-65, nat. chmn. historic research and preservation com., 1968-71, chmn. by laws com., 1971—. Mem. Colonial Daus. 17th Century, Order of Crown Am., Daus. Am. Colonists, Daus. Barons Runnemede, Order Descs. Colonial Clergy, Hereditary Order Descs. Colonial Govs. (registrar gen. 1961-67, gov. gen. 1967-70), Soc. Descs. of William I, the Conqueror, Albemarle Hist. Soc., Nat. Soc. Am. Royal Descent, Nat. Trust Hist. Preservation, Ky. Hist. Soc., Sigma Tau Delta, Kappa Delta (nat. council 1953-67, nat. editor The Angelos 1953-59, pres. Alpha South province 1950-54, nat. pres. 1959-67, nat. historiographer 1967-73, nat. dir. archives 1973—). Episcopalian. Editor: Monticello Cook Book, 3d edit., 1950. Author: Through the Years, and Other Poems, 1945; A History of Kappa Delta Sorority, 1897-1972, 2 vols. 1973. Contbr. poetry to various anthologies. Home: Retreat Albemarle County Charlottesville VA 22903 Office: 3426 University Station Charlottesville VA 22903

MORSE, WILLIAM EUGENE, lawyer; b. Newton, Miss., Dec. 1, 1893; s. Joshuah Marion and Annie (McDonald) M.; B.S., Millsaps Coll., 1913; LL.B., U. Miss., 1915; postgrad. Columbia, 1916; m. Annie Wilkinson, Apr. 12, 1917; children—Ruth (Mrs. C.B. Yarborough), William Eugene II, Dan W., Ann S. (Mrs. George F. Woodliff). Admitted to Miss. bar, 1917; pvt. practice law, Jackson, Miss., 1917—, now mem. Morse & Morse; city pros. atty. Jackson, 1926-28, city atty. 1928-54; former spl. judge circuit and chancery ct. Mem. Miss Oil & Gas Bd., 1956-60; pres. Jackson YMCA, 1932-33. Trustee Miss. Dept. Archives and History. Mem. Am. (ho. of dels. 1940-44), Miss. (pres. 1940-41), Hinds County bar assns., Am. Judicature Soc., Am. Law Inst., Jackson C. of C., Kappa Sigma, Sigma Epsilon. Democrat. Episcopalian. Mason (Shriner), Lion. Club: Scribes. Author: Revised City Ordinances of City of Jackson 1929, 38; Form Book, 1940; Form Book, 1950; Supplement to Form Book, 1965; Divorce and Separation in Mississippi, 1957; Wills, Probate of Estates, 1967; The Fight of Jefferson Davis to Recover His Home "Brierfield"; Treatise on Edward Mayes, 1941. Home: 782 Belhaven St Jackson MS 39202

MORTADA, MOHAMED, petroleum corp. exec.; b. Alexandria, Egypt, Mar. 14, 1925; s. Ahmad Fouad and Eniat (Koraim) M.; B.S. with honors in Chem. Engring., U. Cairo, 1946; M.S. in Petroleum Engring., U. Cal. at Berkeley, 1949, Ph.D., 1951; m. Donna Evelyn Davis, Oct. 10, 1958. Came to U.S., 1947, naturalized, 1961. Sr. research engr. Mobil Oil, Dallas, 1954-59; chief reservoir engr. Mobil Internat., N.Y.C., 1960-62, sr. operations research asso., 1962-64; advisor Ministry Oil and Finance, Kuwait, 1964-69; pres. Mortada Internat., Dallas, 1969—. Prof. math. Tex. Christian U., 1959-60. Recipient Alfred Noble prize, 1956; Rossiter W. Raymond award Am. Inst. M.E., 1957; named Distinguished lectr. Soc. Petroleum Engrs., 1971-72. Registered profl. engr., Tex. Mem. Research Soc. Am., Am. Inst. Mech. Engrs. Home: 4820 Millcreek St Dallas TX 75234 Office: 7616 LBJ Freeway Dallas TX 75240

MORTON, ANSELM HERBERT, JR., sales exec.; b. Cullman, Ala., June 17, 1910; s. Anselm Herbert and Florence (Felter) M.; B.S., Ala. Poly. Inst., 1945; m. Clara Crenshaw, June 6, 1935; children—Geralyn Crenshaw (Mrs. John G. Austin, Jr.), Anselm Herbert III; m. 2d, Magdalene Eck, Aug. 3, 1949; children—Elizabeth Ellen (Mrs. Robert Brasington III), John Eugene. San. engr. Ala. Health Dept., Montgomery, 1934-36; civil engr. ARMCO Steel Co., Atlanta, 1936-41; commd. 2d lt., USAF (Res.), 1934, advanced through grades to lt. col., 1945; ret., 1962; pres. Morton Sales Co., 1946-65; owner Herbert Morton, Sales Engr., Montgomery, 1965—. Dir. Montgomery Choral Soc., 1962-67; mem. Arts Council Montgomery, Montgomery County Bd. Revenue, 1964-68. Vice chmn. Montgomery County Rep. Party, 1961-64, now sec. Registered profl. engr., Ala. Mem. Montgomery Bldg. Material Dealers Assn. (past pres.), Soc. Am. Mil. Engrs., Nat., Ala. socs. profl. engrs., Res. Officers Assn. Episcopalian. Lion (past pres.). Clubs: Auburn, Woodley Country (Montgomery). Home: 1605 E Fairview Av Montgomery AL 36106

MORTON, CHARLES BRINKLEY, clergyman, former state rep. and state senator; b. Meridian, Miss., Jan. 6, 1926; s. Albert Cole and Jean (Brinkley) M.; J.D. with distinction, U. Miss., 1949; M.Div. optime merens, U. South, 1959; m. Virginia Roseborough, Aug. 26, 1948; children—Charles Brinkley, Mary Virginia. Admitted to Miss. bar, 1949, also Tenn. bar; practiced in Senatobia, Miss., 1949-56; mem. firm Thomas & Morton, 1952-56; ordained to ministry P.E. Ch. as deacon and priest, 1949; priest-in-charge Ch. of Incarnation, West Point, Miss., 1959-62; rector Grace-St. Luke's Ch., Memphis 1962—. Mem. Miss. Commn. Interstate Cooperation, 1952-56, Miss. State Hist. Commn., 1952-56, Miss. State Sovereignty Commn., 1955-56. Chmn. N. Miss. Polio Fund, 1954. Mem. Miss. House of Reps., 1948-52, Miss. Senate, 1952-56. Served with AUS, World War II, Korea; now col., chaplain Res. Decorated Silver Star, Bronze Star medal with cluster, Purple Heart, Combat Inf. Badge; recipient Freedoms Found. Honor medal, 1967, 68, 72. Mem. Miss. State Bar (complaint commr. 1953), Internat. Soc. Bibl. Lit. and Exegesis, Mil. Order World Wars. Am. Legion (past post comdr.), Phi Delta Phi, Tau Kappa Alpha, Omicron Delta Kappa, Phi Delta Theta. Democrat. Rotarian. Contbr. articles law and hist. jours. Home: 500 S Belvedere Blvd Memphis TN 38104 Office: 1720 Peabody Av Memphis TN 38104

MORTON, H. LEE, physician; b. El Paso, Tex., Dec. 26, 1928; s. Coye Lynn and Alta Mae (Perkins) M.; B.A., U. Tex. at El Paso, 1951; M.D., U. Tex. at Galveston, 1956; m. Dawn Allison Peacock, July 29, 1968; 1 son, Michael Cody. Extern Marine Hosp., Galveston, 1953-56; intern El Paso Gen. Hosp., 1956-57; gen. practice medicine, Anthony, Tex., 1957—; cons. Latuna Fed. Correctional Inst., 1957—. Tex. local health officer, Anthony, 1958-71; maker jewelry and stringed musical instruments; gemologist, owner Anthony Jewelers Co.; sports physician Gadsden, Anthony high schs. Mem. Assn. Am. Physicians and Surgeons, Tex. Numismatic Assn., Phi Chi. Club: El Paso International Coin (dir.). Home: PO Box 6 Anthony TX 88021 Office: 108 E Washington St Anthony TX 88021

MORTON, HERBERT CHARLES, govt. ofcl.; b. Mpls., July 19, 1921; B.A., U. Minn., 1942, M.A., 1950, Ph.D., 1964; m. Doris B. Liebenberg, Apr. 25, 1946; children—Janet, Martha. Information specialist War Assets Adminstrn., Mpls., 1946-47; staff writer, telegraph news editor St. Paul Pioneer Press and Dispatch, 1947-53; asst. prof. Amos Tuck Sch., Dartmouth, 1953-56; dir. publs. Brookings Instn., Washington, 1956-68; dir. publs. Bur. Labor Statistics, U.S. Dept. Labor, Washington, 1968-71, asso. commr. Bur. Labor Statistics, 1971—. Cons. Ford Found., 1964-65; vis. lectr. Amos Tuck Sch., 1966; professorial lectr. Am. U., Washington, 1970. Served with AUS, 1942-46. Mem. Am. Econ. Assn., Sigma Delta Chi. Author: Public Contracts and Private Wages, 1965; (with M.A. Robinson) An Introduction to Economic Reasoning, rev. edit., 1967. Editor: Brookings Papers on Public Policy, 1965; (with Eli Goldston) The American Business Corporation, 1972. Home: 7304 Nevis Rd Bethesda MD 20034 Office: 441 G St Washington DC 20212

MORTON, JAMES HARRY, tax and bus. cons.; b. Charlotte, N.C., Feb. 18, 1939; s. John Harry and Mary Elizabeth (Stikeleather) M.; grad. Am. Inst. Banking, 1964; m. Yvonne Marie Haigler, Nov. 14, 1958; children—Tina Marie, Tressa Yvonne. Staff accountant N.C. Nat. Bank, Charlotte, 1955-65; pub. accountant Conrad, Hoey, East & Co., Charlotte, 1965-69; controller, sec.-treas. Aabco Industries, Inc., Gaffney, S.C., 1969-71, pres. AABS/Nat. Tax Service Gaffney, 1971—, Gaffney Distbg. Co., Inc., 1971-73, Morris Constrn. & Devel. Corp., Gaffney. Nat. v.p. pub. relations Distributive Edn. Clubs Am., 1955-57, pres. N.C. State, 1955-57, pres. N.C. Western Region, 1955-57. Chmn. bd. dirs. Gaffney Day Sch., 1972-73. Mem. Nat. Assn. Accountants. Methodist (mem. adminstrv. bd., finance com.). Club: Cherokee Sertoma (dir.). (Gaffney). Home: 123 Greenbriar Dr Gaffney SC 29340 Office: PO Box 1116 Grant Plaza Gaffney SC 29340

MORTON, RICHARD ALBERT DUNLAP, JR., physician; b. El Paso, Tex., Sept. 6, 1932; s. Richard Albert Dunlap and Julianne (More) M.; student Tex. Western Coll., 1950-53, U. Colo., 1952; M.D., Tulane U., 1957; postgrad. N.Y. U., 1959-61; m. Margaret A. Brown, Dec. 27, 1954; children—Priscilla, Richard Albert Dunlap III, Margaret and Maria (twins), Arthur and Andrew (twins). Intern, St. Vincent's Hosp., N.Y.C., 1957-58; resident otolaryngology Bellevue Hosp., N.Y.C., 1958-61; instr. otolaryngology N.Y. U. Coll. Medicine and U. Hosp., 1959-61; chief Eye, Ear, Nose and Throat Clinic, USAF Hosp., Maxwell Afb. Montgomery, Ala., 1961-63; cons. dept. hearing and speech N.M. State U., Las Cruces; cons. otolaryngology So. Pacific R.R., T. & P. R.R., Santa Fe R.R., Wm. Beaumont Army Hosp., 1963—; mem. active staff Providence Meml. Hosp., Hotel Dieu Hosp.; courtesy staff Southwestern Gen. Hosp., Sun Towers Hosp. Cons. ear, nose and throat USAF, Southeastern U.S., 1961-63, Holloman Air Force Base; chief, ear, nose and throat service Providence Meml. Hosp., 1964-65, Hotel Dieu Hosp., 1965-66, 69-70. Mem. Boy Scout Council, El Paso. Bd. trustees Pan Am. Tumor Inst.; chmn. alumni fund for excellence U. Tex. at El Paso, 1970; trustee El Paso Ind. Sch. Dist. Served to capt. USAF, 1961-63. Diplomate Am. Bd. Otolaryngology. Fellow Am. Acad. Ophthalmology and Otolaryngology; mem. Am., Tex., El Paso County med. assns., Tex. Otolaryn. Assn. (trustee 1966-68), A.C.S., Am. Cancer Soc. (chmn.), Phi Chi, Sigma Alpha Epsilon. Home: 5520 Westside Dr El Paso TX 79932 Office: 1501 Arizona El Paso TX 79902

MORTON, ROGERS CLARK BALLARD, sec. of interior; b. Louisville, Sept. 19, 1914; s. David C. and Mary (Ballard) M.; A.B., Yale, 1937; m. Anne Jones, May 27, 1939; children—David C., Anne McCance. Vice pres. Ballard & Ballard, flour miller and food mfr., Louisville, 1946-47, pres., 1947-51 (co. merged with Pillsbury Co., 1951), v.p. Pillsbury, 1951-53, dir., 1953-71; mem. 88th to 91st Congresses, 1st dist. Md., 1963-71; sec. interior, 1971—. Bd. govs., bd. visitors Washington Coll., Chestertown, Md. Chmn. Republican nat. com., 1969-71. Served as capt. F.A., AUS, 1941-45. Mem. Soc. Cin., Md. Agrl. Soc. Talbot County (trustee). Clubs: Minneapolis (Mpls.); Chesapeake Bay Yacht (Easton). Home: RD 1 Easton MD 21606 Office: Dept Interior Washington DC 20240

MORTON, RONALD GREY, pub. health officer; b. Lilesville, N.C., Feb. 9, 1938; s. Eugene Lynn and Anna Mozella (Harrington) M.; A.A., Campbell Jr. Coll., 1958; B.F.A., Va. Commonwealth U., 1968; m. Suzanne Prince, Sept. 8, 1973. Asst. tech. dir. theatre div. Va. Mus. Fine Arts, Richmond, 1959-61; immunization programs cons.-regional Va. Health Dept., 1968-70; health information officer Norfolk Family Planning Project, 1971—. Mem. Norfolk Tidewater Assembly for Family Life Edn.; mem. adv. com. WHRO-TV Jr. High Mental Health Series. Served with C.E., U.S. Army, 1962-64. Named Outstanding Theatre Technologist, Va. Commonwealth U., 1968. Mem. Am., Va. (chmn. health edn. sect.) pub. health assns., Nat. Assn. Human Services Pub. Information Officers. Baptist. Home: 489 Southside Rd Virginia Beach VA 23451 Office: 1015 E Princess Anne Rd Norfolk VA 23504

MORTON, TOMMIE WINSTON, airline co. exec.; b. Scranton, Tex., Feb. 15, 1921; s. William Bascom and Leona (Barker) M.; student Weatherford Coll., 1938-39; B.A., Emory and Henry Coll., 1944; postgrad. Bus. Sch. Harvard, 1944-45; m. Betty Jo Kirby, June 20, 1945; children—James Winston, David Kirby, Gerald William. With R.L. Wilmoth pub. accounting, Winston-Salem, N.C., 1946-48; with Piedmont Aviation, Inc., Winston-Salem, 1948—, sec., 1966—, sr. v.p., 1972—; also dir. Served to lt. USNR, 1941-46. Mem. Newcomen Soc., Airline Finance and Accounting Conf., C. of C. Home: 1729 Brookwood Dr Winston-Salem NC 27106 Office: PO Box 2720 Winston-Salem NC 27102

MORVANT, HENRY FERDINAND, elec. engr.; b. Crowley, La., Nov. 3, 1925; s. Henry F. and Madeline (Jeanis) M.; B.S., U. Southwestern La., 1951; m. Connie Stewart, June 20, 1959; children—Michael, Michelle. Electronic engr. Michoud plant Chrysler Corp., New Orleans, 1951-52; elec. engr. Kaiser Aluminum & Chem. Corp., Chalmette, 1952—, sr. engr., power dept., 1955—. Served with USNR, 1944-46. Mem. I.E.E.E. (asso.). Home: 76 Carolyn Ct Arabi LA 70032 Office: PO Box 1600 Chalmette LA 70043

MOSBY, JOHN SINGLETON, judge; b. Holly Springs, Miss., Aug. 4, 1903; s. Edward Littleberry and Alta Dandridge (Shackleford) M.; student Ark. Law Sch., 1925; m. Catherine Corinne Mellard, Apr. 8, 1938; 1 son, John Singleton. Admitted to Ark. bar, 1925, U.S. Supreme Ct. bar, 1936; city atty., Lepanto, 1925-63; Caraway, 1949-59, Tyronza, 1950-63; judge 2d jud. dist. Ark., 1963. Mayor, Lepanto, Ark., 1927-30; mem. Ark. Ho. of Reps., 1943-44; mem. senate, 31st Dist., 1945-49; bd. pub. utilities, Lepanto, 1961-65; commr., exec. sec. Lepanto Park Commn., 1953-65. Chmn. County Welfare Bd., 1943-49; dir. Ark. Assn. for Crippled, 1957—; founder Lepanto Student Aid, Inc., 1956; chmn. City Planning Commn., 1960-64; sec. Lepanto Indsl. Devel. Corp., 1956—. Pres., Ark. Young Democrats Club, 1942-50. Named Lepanto Man of Year, 1964. Mem. Lepanto C. of C. (pres. 1959-62), Am., Ark., N.E. Ark. (pres. 1955-56), Poinsett County (pres. 1942-54) bar assns., S.A.R. (Ark. pres. 1972, chpt. pres. 1970—, nat. v.p. 1973—), Sons Confederacy. Methodist. Mason (K.T., Shriner). Clubs: Rivermont, Memphis Yacht, Summit (Memphis); Lions (pres. 1932-34), Rotary (pres. 1962-63). Home: 400 Berney St Lepanto AR 72354 Office: 111 Berney St Lepanto AR 72354

MOSCA, LOUIS, fire chief; b. Lake Charles, La., Aug. 21, 1925; s. Bernardo and Lucia (Saltaformaggi) M.; grad. high sch.; m. Mary Irona Fruge, Oct. 18, 1947; children—Paula Jane (Mrs. Kelley Vigo), Vincent Lee, Emelie E. With Fire Dept., Lake Charles, 1955—, driver, 1957-67, capt., 1967-68, chief, 1968—. Served with USAAF, 1943-46; PTO. Mem. S.W. La. Mut. Aid Soc. (past pres.), Internat. Fire Chiefs Assn., La. Arson and Fire Prevention Assn., La. Fire Chiefs Assn. (pres.), La. Firemens Assn. Home: 3434 Kingham Rd Lake Charles LA 70601 Office: PO Box 1703 Lake Charles LA 70601

MOSELEY, CARL MORRIS, JR., architect; b. Bessemer, Ala., Dec. 23, 1917; s. Carl Morris and Anneola (Bingham) M.; B.S. in Aero. Engring., U. Ala., 1941; B.Arch., Ga. Inst. Tech., 1948; m. Mary Florentine Schuyler, Aug. 1, 1940. With Glenn L. Martin Co., Balt., 1940-41, Bush-Brown, Gailey, Heffernan, Architects, Atlanta, 1947-48, Don. B. Schuyler, Architect, Tuscaloosa, Ala., 1948-49; pvt. practice architecture, Tuscaloosa, 1950—. Served to maj. C.E., AUS, 1941-45. Decorated Bronze Star. Mem. A.I.A., Phi Kappa Phi, Tau Beta Pi, Chi Epsilon. Mason (Shriner), Rotarian. Clubs: Tuscaloosa Country; Millwood (Sawyerville, Ala.). Prin. works include banks, schs. Home: 23 Beech Hills Rd Tuscaloosa AL 35401 Office: 1438 22d Av Tuscaloosa AL 35401

MOSELEY, HARRISON MILLER, educator; b. Dundee, Tex., Dec. 14, 1921; s. John Harrison and Mildred Lucille (Miller) M.; B.A., Tex. Christian U., 1943; Ph.D. (AEC fellow 1948), U. N.C., 1950; m. Doreen Dene Johnson Bussey, Jan. 28, 1967; children—Denise (Mrs. Michael Burgess), Karen, Cheryl. Mem. faculty Tex. Christian U., Ft. Worth, 1950—, prof. physics, 1956—. Served with USNR, 1944-45. Mem. Tex. Acad. Sci. (v.p. 1954), Am. Phys. Soc., Am. Assn. Physics Tchrs., A.A.A.S. Episcopalian. Mason, Elk. Home: 6016 Wrigley Way Fort Worth TX 76133 Office: Physics Dept Tex Christian U Fort Worth TX 76129

MOSELEY, MARY LYDA, dept. store exec.; b. Picayune, Miss., July 20, 1922; d. George Harry and Maye (Williams) Mitchell; grad. pub. high sch.; m. William L. Moseley, Jan. 26, 1939 (dec. Nov. 13, 1968); children—Mary (Mrs. Billy W. Miller), Linda (Mrs. Travis R. Simmons). Owner, prin. M L M Co., Picayune, 1965—, Lane's Dept. Store, Picayune, 1949—; founder, owner radio sta. WRJW, Picayune, 1948-51, Picayune Transp. Co., 1950-54, Picayune Air Service, 1963-66, Pine Hill Apts., Carriere, Miss., 1965—. Mem. Nat. Assn. Theatre Owners. Baptist. Home: 420 Elmwood St Picayune MS 39466 Office: PO Box 370 Picayune MS 39466

MOSELEY, SHERRARD THOMAS, graphic arts co. exec.; b. Roanoke, Va., May 16, 1921; s. Sherrard Alston and Marie Frances (Carr) M.; B.S. in Elec. Engring., Va. Poly. Inst., 1942; M.E.E., Syracuse U., 1952; m. Jean Dreher Willis, Apr. 27, 1941; 1 dau., Judith (Mrs. Philip Edward Tomes). Engr. Gen. Electric Co., Syracuse, N.Y., 1946-48; instr. research asso. Syracuse U., 1948-53; engr. Signal Corps, U.S. Army, Hawaii, 1954-57; asso. prof., chmn. dept. elec. engring. U. S.C. at Columbia, 1957-61; prof. Va. Poly. Inst., Blacksburg, 1961-62; pres. Wytheville (Va.) Community Coll., 1962-67; research asso. Fla. Dept. Edn., Tallahassee, 1967-68; sales mgr. Caldwell-Sites Co., Roanoke, Val., 1968—. Served to capt. AUS, 1942-46: PTO. Kellogg fellow, Fla. State U., 1967. Registered profl. engr., S.C. Mem. I.E.E.E. (sr.), Am. Soc. Profl. Engrs., Adminstrv. Mgmt. Soc., Sigma Xi, Eta Kappa Nu, Sigma Pi Sigma. Club: Roanoke Country. Home: 2310 Stanley Av Roanoke VA 24014 Office: 105 S Jefferson St Roanoke VA 24010

MOSELEY, WILLIAM WARD, architect; b. Lawrenceville, Va., Mar. 26, 1930; s. William Stuart and Anne Gray (Duke) M.; B.S., Va. Poly. Inst., 1952, postgrad., 1952; m. Jewel Mason Moncure, Aug. 22, 1959; children—William Ward, Robert Moncure. Project mgr. Merrill C. Lee, Richmond, Va., 1955-59; project mgr. Marcellus Wright & Son, Richmond, 1959-65; partner Marcellus Wright & Partners, 1965-70; prin. William Ward Moseley, architect-planner, Richmond, 1970-72; pres. Moseley-Hening Asso., Inc., Richmond, 1972—; faculty interior design dept. Va. Commonwealth U., 1970-71. Pres. Highland Hills Community Corp., Bon Air, Va., 1964-65. Served with USAF, 1952-54. Recipient Design award of merit for Richmond Residence, 1966. Mem. A.I.A., Am. Soc. Planning Ofcls., Constrn. Specifications Inst., Va. Citizens Planning Assn., Va. Assn. Professions, Va. Poly. Inst. Alumni Assn., Pi Delta Epsilon, Omicron Delta Kappa. Methodist. Rotarian. Club: Salisbury Country (Midlothian, Va.). Contbr. articles profl. jours. Home: 8410 Halidan

Dr Bon Air VA 23235 Office: 2922 Hathaway Rd Richmond VA 23225

MOSER, CARL GILMORE, JR., elec. engr.; b. Yanceyville, N.C., June 25, 1920; s. Carl Gilmore and Eliza McNeil (Turner) M.; student Radford State Tchrs. Coll., 1943, Richmond Profl. Inst., 1958, Va. Poly. Inst., 1960, Ia. State U., 1963; m. Ann Geraldine Eggleston, Oct. 31, 1939; children—Carl Gilmore III, Patricia Ann (Mrs. Andrew Carter Wickham). With Outlet Shoe Store, Winston-Salem, N.C., 1937, Producers Warehouse, also Stephenson's Drug Store, Danville, Va., 1937-38, Bassett Furniture Co., also Bassett Theater, Bassett, Va., 1939-41; with Chesapeake & Potomac Telephone Co., 1941-66, 68—, engr., Richmond, Va., 1952-66, 68—; engring. con. Def. Communications Agy., S.E. Asia, 1966-68; engr. Western Electric Co., S.E. Asia, 1966-68. Sec. Hanover County Assn. Vol. Fire Depts., 1964—; pres. Ashland Vol. Fire Dept., 1965-66, 70-72. Bd. dir. YMCA Camp Weyanoke Branch, Richmond, Va., 1954-63. Served with USMCR, 1943-46. Mem. I.E.E.E., Armed Forces Communications and Electronics Assn., S.R., Nat. Rifle Assn., Telephone Pioneers, Va. Firemans Assn. Presbyn. (deacon 1954-60, elder 1961—). Lion (pres. 1958-59), Mason (Shriner). Club: Central Va. Engineers (Richmond) (pres. 1964-65). Home: 303 Duncan St Ashland VA 23005 Office: 703 E Grace St Richmond VA 23219

MOSER, CHARLES EDWARD, elec. engr.; b. Shidler, Okla., Feb. 22, 1923; s. Frank James and Margaret May (Christy) M.; B.S. in Arts and Scis., Okla. State U., 1949, B.S. in Elec. Engring., 1949; postgrad. Ohio State U., 1951-52, Trinity U., 1953-54; M.S., So. Meth. U., 1958; m. Dolores Bernice Myers, Dec. 17, 1948; children—Charlene Denise, Susan Kay, Janice Louise, Anita Jean. Engr., Wright Patterson AFB, O., 1949-51; asst. group engr. Beech Aircraft Corp., Wichita, Kan., 1953; research engr. S.W. Research Inst., San Antonio, 1953-54; asst. project engr. Gen. Dynamics Corp., Ft. Worth, 1954—. Served with AUS, 1943-45; served to 1st lt. USAF, 1951-53. Registered profl. engr., Kan. Mem. Scabbard and Blade, Sigma Tau, Eta Kappa Nu. Home: 7113 Willis Av Fort Worth TX 76116 Office: PO Box 748 Fort Worth TX 76101

MOSER, PAUL HOMER, geologist; b. Burity, Brazil, July 23, 1931 (parents Am. citizens); s. Homer Oliver and Edith (Lahr) M.; B.A., Berea Coll., 1954; M.S., U. Ky., 1961; m. I. Delphine Cody, June 7, 1954; 1 son, Cody. Cons. geologist, co-owner Carser Consultants, Lexington, Ky., 1956-60; engring. geologist Stokley & Assos., Lexington, 1959-66; petroleum geologist Texaco Inc., Midland, Tex., 1966-68; environmental geologist Geol. Survey Ala., University, 1968—. Served with C.E., AUS, 1954-56. Registered profl. engr., Ala., Ky. Mem. Ky., Ala. socs. profl. engrs., Am. Inst. Profl. Geologists, Geol. Soc. Am., Ala. Geol. Soc., Sigma Gamma Epsilon. Presbyn. (elder). Home: 10-T Northwood Lake Northport AL 35476 Office: Geological Survey Ala PO Box O University AL 35486

MOSHMAN, JACK, mgmt. cons.; b. Richmond Hill, N.Y., Aug. 12, 1924; s. Morris and Sadye (Posner) M.; B.A., N.Y.U., 1946; M.A., Columbia, 1947; Ph.D., U. Tenn., 1953; m. Annette Gordon, Aug. 10, 1947; children—Gordon, Marc, Esther, Ira. Sr. statistician Oak Ridge Nat. Lab., 1948-54; mem. tech. staff Bell Telephone Labs., Murray Hill, N.J., 1954-57; v.p. C-E-I-R, Inc., Washington, 1957-66; mng. dir. EBS Mgmt. Cons., Washington, 1966-68; sr. v.p. Leasco Systems & Research Corp., Bethesda, Md., 1968-70; pres. Moshman Assos., Inc., Washington, 1970—; adj. prof. Eagleton Inst. Politics, Rutgers U., 1971-73; professorial lectr. George Washington U., 1955-59; instr. Queens Coll., 1946-47, U. Tenn., 1947-53. Mem. adv. com. on statis. policy Office Mgmt. and Budget, 1973—; mem. Com. to Evaluate Nat. Center for Health Statistics. Served with AUS, 1943-46. Fellow Am. Statis. Assn.; mem. Assn. for Computing Machinery, Inst. Math. Statistics, Operations Research Soc. Am., Inst. Mgmt. Sci., Soc. Advancement Mgmt., Biometric Soc. Home: 7008 Carmichael Av Bethesda MD 20034 Office: 6400 Goldsboro Rd Washington DC 20034

MOSKO, SIGMUND WEINER, elec. engr.; b. Phila., June 9, 1936; s. Maurice and Ida (Weiner) M.; B.S. in Elec. Engring., Drexel U., 1958; postgrad. U. Tenn., 1958-60; m. Brenda Charlotte Krauss, Aug. 25, 1963; children—Joel Mark, Tammy Dee, Beth Anne. Elec. engr. Oak Ridge Nat. Lab., 1958—. Mem. exec. com. Democratic party, Anderson County, Tenn., 1969-70. Mem. I.E.E.E. (sr.), Tau Epsilon Phi. Jewish religion (dir. congregation 1968-70, v.p. 1973). Mem. B'nai B'rith. Contbr. articles to tech. lit. Home: 104 Windgate Rd Oak Ridge TN 37830 Office: Box X Oak Ridge TN 37830

MOSKOVITES, JAMES, clergyman; b. Peabody, Mass., Dec. 19, 1945; s. John and Helen (Dallas) M.; B.A., Hellenic Coll., 1967; B.D., Holy Cross Sch. Theology, 1970, M.Div., 1973; m. Diana Niki Lalooses, June 29, 1969; 1 dau., Helen. Youth dir. Annunciation Greek Orthodox Cathedral, Boston, 1969; lay asst. St. Nicholas, Lexington, Mass., 1970; ordained as priest Greek Orthodox Ch., 1970; priest St. George Greek Orthodox Ch., Oklahoma City, 1970—. Chaplain, Greek Orthodox VA Hosp., Oklahoma City, 1970—; civilian aux. chaplain Ft. Sill, Lawton, Okla., 1970—; dir. Diocesan Youth Commn., 1971—; cons. Agy. for Christian Coop. Ministry, 1971—. Mem. Okla. Conf. Chs. (1st presider faith and dialogue group 1971-72), Greek Orthodox Clergyman's Assn., Am. Mgmt. Assn., Okla. Episcopalian Clericus (hon.), Alumni Assn. Holy Cross. Contbr. articles, book revs. to mags. Home: 1102 NW 8th Oklahoma City OK 73106 Office: 1102 NW 8th Oklahoma City OK 73106

MOSLEY, ELLIS GREENLEE, educator; b. Mayflower, Ark., Jan. 30, 1901; s. Wiley Thornton and Maude (Greenlee) M.; A.B. magna cum laude, Hendrix Coll., 1923; B.D., Austin Theol. Sem., 1926; M.A., U. Tex., 1949; D.D., Ark. Coll., 1956; m. Mary Elizabeth Newton, May 19, 1926; children—James, Edward. Ordained to ministry Presbyn. Ch., 1926; minister, Hamilton, Tex., 1926-29, Clifton, 1929-30; asso. Wiley Mosley Bus. Interests, Faulkner County, Ark., 1931-46; tchr. Mayflower (Ark.) High Sch., 1946-48; faculty Ark. Coll., Batesville, 1948—, asso. prof. religion and social studies, 1953-73, prof. emeritus, 1973—, acting pres., summer 1952. Minister part time supply chs. E. Ark. Presbytery, 1948-67; commr. Gen. Assembly Presbyn. Ch. U.S., 1956; chaplain Ark. S.A.R., 1955-57. Recorder, Mayflower, 1940-47; mem. Ark. Gov.'s Citizen's Adv. Com., 1967—. Recipient Citizenship award Batesville Civitan Club, 1973. Mem. Am. Acad. Polit. and Social Sci., Am. Acad. Religion, Am., Ark. hist. assns., Southwestern Sociology Assn., Ark. Acad. Sci., Independence County Hist. Soc. (pres. 1964-65). Democrat. Mason (Shriner). Home: 1950 Maple St Batesville AR 72501

MOSLEY, MARY MAC, librarian; b. Rome, Ga., Nov. 11, 1926; d. William McKinley and Mary Eunice (Caldwell) Howell; student Ga. Coll., 1943-45; B.S., Auburn U., 1947; M.L.S., Emory U., 1968; m. Samuel Adolphus Mosley, June 12, 1946 (div. Jan. 1964); children—Samuel Adolphus, Pamela Ann, James Irwin. Tchr. sci. pub. schs., Rome, Ga., 1964-66; extension librarian, 1966-67; head librarian Shorter Coll., 1968—, asst. prof. library sci., 1968—. Instr. swimming A.R.C., Decatur, Ala., 1956-60; chmn. Floyd County (Ga.) March of Dimes, 1966. Mem. Am., Ga., Southeastern, Coosa Valley library assns., Nat., Ga. edn. assns., Am. Assn. U. Women (pres. chpt. 1973-75). Home: Lyons Bridge Rd Cave Spring GA 30124 Office: Box 346 Shorter College Rome GA 30161

MOSS, ALFRED JEFFERSON, JR., research scientist; b. Little Rock, Nov. 22, 1940; s. Alfred Jefferson and Carolyn (Dobson) M.; B.S., Little Rock U., 1962; M.S. (NIH fellow), U. Ark., 1965, Ph.D., 1970; m. Susan Ellen Wood, Dec. 28, 1965; children—Susan Elizabeth. Research chemist Dow Chem. Co., Freeport, Tex., 1965-68; research chemist Little Rock VA Hosp., 1970—; scientist U. Ark. Med. Center, Little Rock, 1970—. Asst. prof. div. nuclear medicine and radiation biology, also dept. physiology and biophysics U. Ark., Little Rock, 1970—. Nat. Cancer Inst. grantee, 1972—. Mem. Biophys. Soc., Radiation Research Soc., Sigma Xi. Contbr. articles to profl. jours. Home: 1309 Pine Valley Rd Little Rock AR 72207

MOSS, BRIAN HART, youth orgn. exec.; b. Salt Lake City, July 15, 1944; s. Frank E. and Phyllis (Hart) M.; B.A. in Econs. and Spanish, U. Utah, 1970; m. Carol Brennan, June 3, 1972. Exec. dir. Allied Youth, Arlington, Va., 1971—. Mem. Phi Kappa Alpha. Mem. Ch. of Jesus Christ of Latter-day Saints (dir. athletics Washington area). Home: 6015 Goldsboro Rd Bethesda MD 20034 Office: 1901 Fort Myer Dr Arlington VA 22209

MOSS, CHARLES BASIL, physician; b. Medicine Park, Okla., Sept. 13, 1925; s. Robert Frank and Lovie Vitula (Williamson) M.; B.S., Southwestern La. U., 1947; M.D., U. Okla., 1949; m. Pauline Joyce Montgomery, June 15, 1947; children—Paulette Cecilia, Leslie Charlene, Anita Louellen. Intern St. Joseph's Hosp., Fort Worth, 1949-50; gen. practice medicine, Lubbock, 1952—; mem. staff West Texas, Methodist hosps. Med. dir., disaster program A.R.C., 1970. Mem. City-County Child Welfare Bd., 1953-56. Del., Tex. Republican Convention, 1966, precinct chmn., fund raiser, 1966-67. Bd. dirs. W. Tex. Hosp. and Med. Arts Clinic, Lubbock, 1952—, Drug Crisis Center, 1970-72, Parkdale Sick Children's Clinic, 1960-72, Wesley Found., 1969, chmn., 1970—. Served with USNR, 1943-45, 50-52. Mem. Acad. Gen. Practice (pres. 1956), Sons of Republic of Tex. (pres. 1971). Club: Lubbock Riders. Methodist. Med. dir., panelist, prodn. 4 shows TV, 1968, panelist drug abuse, 1969, 71; lectr. sex edn., 1955—. Home: 5508 Av T Lubbock TX 79412 Office: 1318 Broadway St Lubbock TX 79401

MOSS, CLAUDE WAYNE, microbiologist; b. nr. Winston-Salem, N.C., Mar. 20, 1935; s. Walter Jefferson and Sadie Emily (Aldridge) M.; B.S., N.C. State U., 1957, M.S. (Nat. Def. Edn. fellow 1960-63), 1962, Ph.D., 1965; m. Helen Marian, Jan. 4, 1958; children—Sherrie, Barry, Gary, Susan. Microbiologist N.C. Dept. Agr., Raleigh, 1958-60; research asso. N.C. State U., Raleigh, 1960-65; research microbiologist Center for Disease Control, Atlanta, 1965—. Bd. dirs. Internat. Purificiation System, Inc., Atlanta, 1971-73. Served with AUS, 1958-59. USPHS research grantee, 1965. Mem. Phi Kappa Phi, Sigma Xi. Baptist (deacon 1970-72). Home: 5160 Antelope Lane Stone Mountain GA 30083 Office: 1600 Clifton Rd Atlanta GA 30333

MOSS, DONOVAN DEAN, educator; b. Bunker Hill, Ind., Feb. 28, 1926; s. William L. and Laura (Shively) M.; B.S., Auburn U., 1949, M.S., 1950; Ph.D., U. Ga., 1960; m. Carolyn Eleanor Lamb, Apr. 9, 1948; children—Jerry L., Deborah Carrol. Fisheries biologist Ala. Conservation Dept., Montgomery, 1951-57, asst. chief fisheries, 1957-58; research asst. U. Ga., Athens, 1958-60; fisheries adviser U. Ky. at Bogor, Indonesia, 1961-65; asso. prof. biology Tenn. Tech. U., Cookeville, 1965-67; prof. fisheries, asst. dir. Internat. Center for Aquaculture, Auburn (Ala.) U., 1967—. Cons. fisheries, AID, World Bank, various univs. Served with USAAF, 1944-46. Mem. Am. Soc. Limnology and Oceanography, Am. Fisheries Soc., A.A.A.S., World Mariculture Soc., Sigma Xi (sec.-treas. 1973—), Mason. Home: 2623 Orchard Circle Auburn AL 36830

MOSS, GEORGE JOSEPH, JR., elec. engr.; b. Washington, Mar. 24, 1938; s. George Joseph and Joyce Elizabeth (Warren) M.; B.S., Mass. Inst. Tech., 1959; M.S., U. Md., 1964; m. Mary Elizabeth Lawrence, May 4, 1963; children—Mary Monica, William Joseph. Elec./electronic engr. U.S. Naval Ordnance Lab., White Oak, Md., 1959-66; electronic engr. U.S. Naval Oceanographic Office, Washington, 1966-73, head research and devel. br., 1973—. Registered profl. engr., Md. Mem. I.E.E.E., Nat. Soc. Profl. Engrs., Marine Tech. Soc. Republican. Roman Catholic. Contbr. articles to profl. jours. Patentee in field. Home: 5701 Harwick Rd Bethesda MD 20016 Office: Code 6222 US Naval Oceanographic Office Washington DC 20373

MOSS, HENRY PARKS, JR., city ofcl.; b. Gainesville, Ga., May 9, 1939; s. Henry Parks and Sarah Elizabeth (Eberhardt) M.; B.B.A., U. Ga., 1964; m. Ann Margaret DeWitt, Aug. 19, 1960; children—Henry Parks III, Elizabeth Ann, Mary Margaret. Asst. city engr., Brunswick, Ga., 1959-62, asst. city mgr., 1964-65; comptroller Durham (N.C.) Redevel. Commn., 1965-66, dep. dir., 1966-68, exec. dir., 1968-72; city mgr., Beaufort, S.C., 1972—. Dir. Sea Horizons Corp., Beaufort. Bd. dirs. Beaufort United Way, Beaufort Salvation Army. Mem. Internat. City Mgrs. Assn., Nat. Assn. Housing and Redevel. Ofcls., Navy League, Pi Kappa Alph. Clubs: Beaufort Sertoma, Beaufort Rotary (pres. 1973—). Home: 107 Fort Marion Rd Beaufort SC 29902 Office: Office of the City Manager Beaufort SC 29902

MOSS, HOWARD, elec. co. exec.; b. N.Y.C., June 14, 1921; s. Harry and Rose (Reisel) M.; B.S., City U. N.Y., 1941; M.S. in Elec. Engring., Rutgers U., 1953; m. Bernice Catherine Blutter, May 2, 1955; children—Terri Ellen, Robin Jo. Chief, solid state devices br. Evans Signal Lab., Belmar, N.J., 1942-56; v.p. semicondr. group Tex. Instruments, Inc., Dallas, 1956—. Pres., chmn. bd. Semicondr. Equipment and Materials Inst., Inc., Mountain View, Cal., 1970—. Mem. adv. coms. to Dept. Commerce, 1973—. Served with AUS, World War II. Mem. I.E.E.E. (sr.). Home: 5919 Williamstown Rd Dallas TX 75230 Office: 13500 N Central Expressway Dallas TX 75230

MOSS, JAMES MERCER, physician; b. Bradley, Ga., Dec. 15, 1917; s. Fred August and Rosa (Mercer) M.; M.D., U. Va., 1941; m. Rachel Scott Bybee, Sept. 6, 1941; children—James Marion, Fred Aubrey (dec.), William Wallace, Robert Edward. Intern U. Va. Hosp., 1941-42, resident medicine, 1947-49; fellow, instr. endocrinology Duke U., 1946-47; pvt. practice internal medicine, Alexandria, Va., 1949—; instr. clin. medicine Georgetown U., 1949-51, clin. asst. prof. medicine, 1952-56, clin. asso. prof., 1956-62, clin. prof., 1962—; dir. diabetic clinic Georgetown U. Hosp., 1949—, D.C. Gen. Hosp., 1950-55; active staff Circle Terrace Hosp., pres., 1965-68. Dir. City Bank & Trust, 1963-71, Circle Terrace, Inc., 1965— (all Alexandria, Va.). Treas. No. Va. Med. Com. Good Govt., 1960, 62. Chmn. Va.-Med. Polit. Action Com., 1966-67; chmn. Va. Physicians for Reelection of the President, 1972; mem. Alexandria Republican Com., 1972—. Served from lt. to maj., M.C., AUS, 1942-46. Recipient awards for sci. exhibits. Fellow A.C.P., Am. Coll. Cardiology; mem. Am. (pharm. com.), Va. (pres. 1962-63) socs. internal medicine, Am. Heart Assn., Am., Va. (pres. 1971-72) diabetes assns., Endocrine Soc., So. Med. Assn., Med. Soc. Va. (pres. 1970-71), A.M.A. (mem. council sci. assembly 1971—), Diabetes Assn. D.C. (pres. 1956-57), Med. Council Washington Met. Area (pres. 1958-59), Heart Assn. No. Va. (pres. 1964-65), Am. Podiatry Assn. (hon.), Am. Med. Writers Assn., Alexandria Med. Soc. (pres. 1958-59), Med. Alumni Assn. U.Va. (pres. 1965-66), Phi Chi, Alpha Omega Alpha. Editorial bd. Va. Med. Monthly, 1961-70. Editorial cons. Am. Acad. Family Practice, 1969—, Author: Fundamentals of Diabetic Management. Contbr. articles to profl. jours. Home: 319 Mansion Dr Alexandria VA 22302 Office: 1707 Osage St Alexandria VA 22302

MOSS, JAMES THOMAS, devel. co. exec.; b. Youngsville, N.C., July 3, 1927; s. William Thomas and Lula (Wade) M.; B.S., N.C. State U., 1947, M.S., 1949; m. Margaret McLeod Bunn, Dec. 18, 1948; children—James Thomas, William Howard, David Bunn. Co-owner Mosswood Farms, Youngsville, 1949—; v.p. 1st Union Nat. Bank, Raleigh, N.C., 1968—, Pres. N.C. Found. Seed Producers, 1968, Mem. N.C. Banking Commn., 1966—. Pres. N.C. Soil and Water Conservation Dist., 1966, Youngsville Devel. Corp., 1967—. Mem. Sigma Xi, Alpha Zeta, Alpha Gamma Rho, Phi Kappa Phi. Mason, Lion. Home: PO Box 268 Youngsville NC 27596 Office: 1st Union Nat Bank Raleigh NC 27602

MOSS, JOE ALBAUGH, oil co. exec.; b. Waco, Tex., July 26, 1925; s. Robert Edwin and Winnie (Hughes) M.; B.B.A., U. Tex., 1948, LL.B., 1950; m. Anna Lee Reese, May 30, 1947; 1 son, Joe David. Admitted to Tex. bar, 1950; practiced in Austin, 1950; atty. Tex. Bd. Hosps. and Spl. Schs., Abilene, 1952; sec., asst. gen. counsel Cosden Petroleum Corp., 1953-63; v.p., sec., chief counsel Cosden Oil & Chem. Co., Big Spring, Tex., 1963—; chief counsel Am. Petrofina, Inc., 1971—; dir., v.p., chief counsel Am. Petrofina Co. Tex., 1971—; dir., v.p., sec. Trust Pipe Line Co., 1956—; v.p., sec. River Pipeline Co., 1958—; dir., sec. Spencer & Co., 1959-64; sec. Cosden Pipe Line Co., 1961—; v.p., dir. Amdel, Inc., 1973—, Amdel Pipeline Inc., 1973—, Petro Gas Corp., 1973—. Vice chmn. Lone Star dist. Boy Scouts Am., 1961-68; pres., trustee Big Spring Ind. Sch. Dist., 1961-71; trustee Permian Basin Petroleum Mus. Bd. dirs. W. Tex. Boys Ranch, Cosden Credit Union. Served with USNR, 1942-46, 50-52. Mem. Am., Tex., Howard County (past pres.) bar assns., Am. Petroleum Inst., Tex. Research League, Navy League U.S. Presbyn. (elder). Mason. Club: Big Spring Hunting and Fishing (trustee). Home: 5230 Royal Crest Dr Dallas TX 75229 Office: Fina Plaza Dallas TX 75221

MOSS, JOSEPH RODNEY, chief justice S.C. Supreme Ct.; b. York, S.C., July 15, 1903; s. James L. Sr. and Janie E. (Ford) M.; student Erskine Coll., 1920-23, LL.D., 1963; A.B., U. S.C., 1924, M.A., LL.B., 1927; LL.D., 1966, J.D., 1970; m. Rosa Dill, June 11, 1931 (dec. Dec. 1966). Admitted to S.C. bar, 1927; mem. firm Hart & Moss, York, 1927-48; judge 6th Circuit Ct. of S.C., 1948-56; asso. justice S.C. Supreme Ct., 1956-66, chief justice, 1966—. Mem. York County Democratic Exec. Com., 1933-48; mem. S.C. Senate, 1944-48. Presbyn. (elder). Home: PO Box 259 York SC 29754

MOSS, MILTON, economist; b. N.Y.C., Feb. 3, 1915; s. Edward and Fannie (Ostrow) M.; B.S., Coll. City N.Y., 1935; M.S., Columbia, 1937, Ph.D. (Fed. Res. Bd. fellow), 1962; m. Tatyana Jasny, May 31, 1941; children—Lynda Marie, Philip Ira. Instr. sociology U. Conn., 1939; economist Bd. Govs. Fed. Res. System, Washington, 1941-42, 46-62; asst. dir. econ. accounts Office Statis. Policy, Bur. Budget and Office Mgmt. and Budget, Washington, 1962-72; sr. adviser econ. research Nat. Planning Assn., Washington, 1972—. Sr. research con. Inst. Social Research U. Mich., Ann Arbor, 1973—; sr. research asso. Nat. Bur. Econ. Research, N.Y.C., 1972—; professorial lectr. statistics Am. U., Washington, 1958-64. Fed. Exec. fellow, Brookings Instn., Washington, 1967-68. Mem. expert group on system of demographic and social statistics UN, 1972-73; mem. exec. com. Conf. on Research in Income and Wealth, Nat. Bur. Econ. Research, 1965-67. Mem. Am. Statis. Assn. (dir. 1970-72), A.A.A.S., Internat. Assn. Research in Income and Wealth. Club: Cosmos (Washington). Home: 8504 Whittier Blvd Bethesda MD 20034 Office: National Planning Assn 1666 Connecticut Av NW Washington DC 20009

MOSS, RACHEL SCOTT BYBEE (MRS. JAMES MERCER MOSS), civic worker; b. Charlottesville, Va., Feb. 2, 1920; d. Aubrey Walker and Wirtie (Williams) Bybee; R.N., U. Va. 1941; m. James Mercer Moss, Sept. 6, 1941; children—James Marion, Fred Aubrey (dec.), William Wallace, Robert Edward. Head nurse on medicine U. Va. Hosp., 1941-42. Dir. Security Savs. and Loan Assn., Alexandria. Mem. ladies bd. Georgetown U. Hosp., 1954—, Heart Assn. No. Va., 1963—; treas. Alexandria Crew Booster's Club, 1965-67; sec. Va. Med. Polit. Action Com., 1967-68; pres. Mansion Drive Club, 1968-69; chmn. Alexandria Tiny Tots Concert, 1965; mem. nurses com. on continuing edn. Va. Heart Assn., 1969—; mem. ARCS Found., Inc., 1969—; mem. Va. Med. Polit. Action Com. Mem. Alexandria (Va.) Democratic com., 1954-55; mem. Finance Com. to Re-elect Pres. Nixon, 1972. Mem. Woman's Aux. Med. Soc. Va. (pres. 1963-64, dir. 1964-67, finance chmn. 1972-73), Am. Med. Edn. Found., Woman's Aux. So. Med. Assn. (v.p. 1965-66), Woman's Aux. A.M.A. (del. from Va. 1954-64), Woman's Aux. Alexandria Med. Soc. (pres. 1961-62), Alumni Assn. U. Va. Hosp. Sch. Nursing. Presbyn. Clubs: Mansion Drive Garden, Beverly Hills Women's (pres. 1973-74). Home: 319 Mansion Dr Alexandria VA 22302

MOSS, ROBERT SHERIFFS, lawyer; b. Milw., July 15, 1908; s. Roy M. and Cornelia M. (Sheriffs) M.; B.S., Northwestern U., 1929; J.D., U. Wis., 1932; LL.M., Georgetown U., 1964; m. Bernice M. Pfeifer, Aug. 24, 1946; children—Marilyn, Karen. Admitted to Wis. bar, 1932, D.C. bar, 1947; pvt. practice Milw., 1932-43, Washington, 1947—; counsel materials div. Office Gen. Counsel, Navy Dept., 1946-47; with Elmore, Moss & Moore, Washington, 1948-50; partner firm Hart, Moss & Tavenner, 1962-70; pvt. practice, 1970—; gen. counsel Graphic Arts Assn. Wis., 1936-43; lectr. Columbus U., 1950-54, Cath. U., 1945-55, Tax Practice Inst., 1955-58. Sec. Mayor's Adv. Council, Milw., 1936-37; pres. Milw. YMCA Toastmasters Club, YMCA Speakers' Bur. Mem. Am. (chmn. regional program com. 1965-67, chmn. pub. contracts com. 1953-55; mem. council, sect. pub. contract law 1968-71, sec. 1971-72), Wis., Fed. (mem. nat. council 1968-69, 71-72) bar assns., Bar Assn. D.C. (chmn. taxation com. 1954-55, mem. council adminstrv. law sect. 1972—), Wranglers, Scribes, Phi Delta Phi. Clubs: University, Army and Navy, National Lawyers. Author: Cases and Materials on The Law of Government Contracts; Flaherty's District of Columbia Practice; articles on law. Home: 8521 Doter Dr Waynewood Alexandria VA 22308 Office: 1819 H St NW Washington DC 20006

MOSS, THERON CHARLES, textile mfg. co. exec.; b. Cleve., Apr. 6, 1940; s. Theron Victor and Anna Marie (Prevost) M.; B.A., Grinnell Coll., 1962; m. Anne Louise Primo, July 10, 1965; children—Susan Janet, Jennifer Anne. With SECO Industries div. South Eastern Cordage Co., Cleveland, Tenn., 1963—, gen. mgr., 1963—, sec.-treas., 1965—. Served with USCGR, 1962-70. Mem. Cleveland Jaycees (pres. 1973-74), Cleveland Asso. Industries, Coast Guard Aux., Cleveland Personnel Club. Episcopalian. Elk. Club: Cleveland Country. Home: 1205 Greenridge Dr Cleveland TN 37311 Office: PO Box 234 Cleveland TN 37311

MOSS, WILLIAM MONROE, food co. exec.; b. Biloxi, Miss., Dec. 1, 1918; s. Joseph Alayosis and Zellamae (Martin) M.; student St. Stanislaus Coll., 1931-35; m. Betty Ann Keister, Sept. 15, 1942;

children—Pamela Ann, David Martin. Clk. Strauss-Stallings Jewelry Co., Jackson, Miss., 1940-43; salesman Eutectic Welding Co., Jackson, 1945-47; dist. mgr. Gen. Food Corp., Kansas City, Mo., 1947-65; pres. Russell-Moss & Assos., Inc., Dallas, Tex., 1965—. Served with USMCR, 1943-45. Lutheran. Home: 10238 Woodford St Dallas TX 75229 Office: 2714 Bomar St Dallas TX 75235

MOSS, WILLIAM WALTER, constrn. co. exec.; b. Birmingham, Ala., Sept. 7, 1935; s. John Parker and Mariellen (Nottingham) M.; B.S., U. Ala., 1959; m. Marie Francis Sain, June 9, 1956; children—John W., Thomas S., Allison Marie. With Moss-Thornton Co., Inc., Leeds, Ala., 1951—, engr., 1961—, v.p., 1963-73, pres., 1973—. Chmn. bd. dirs. Ala. Sheriffs Boy's and Girl's Ranch, 1973. Served to 1st lt. C.E., AUS, 1959-61. Mem. Asso. Gen. Contractors Am. (pres. Ala. 1968), Am. Soc. C.E., Am. Soc. Mil. Engrs., Chi Epsilon. Clubs: Birmingham Ski, Birmingham Aero, Birmingham Hanger QB's. Mason (Shriner, Jester). Office: 1710 Spruiell St NE Leeds AL 35094

MOSSMAN, REUEL WALLACE, geophys. services co. exec.; b. Fresno, Cal., Aug. 18, 1914; s. Niles Roy and Lois (Coffey) M.; A.B., Columbia, 1935, M.A., 1939; m. Elizabeth Hosmer, Sept. 1, 1940. County supr. Okla. State Geol. Survey, Norman, 1935-36; computer Geophys. Research Corp., Tulsa, 1936-37; with Seismograph Service Corp., Tulsa, 1939—, asst. v.p., 1952—. Mem. Soc. Exploration Geophysicists, Am. Assn. Petroleum Geologists, European Assn. Exploration Geophysicists, Am. Geophys. Union. Club: Tulsa Downtown Sertoma (pres. 1971-72). Home: 5860 S Joplin St Tulsa OK 74135 Office: PO Box 1590 Tulsa OK 74102

MOSTELLER, BETTE VAUGHAN, librarian; b. Amelia County, Va., Feb. 1, 1937; d. Lawson Paul and Rosa Vaughan (Mottley) Mosteller; B.A., Longwood Coll., 1958; M.A. in L.S. (Va. State Library fellow), George Peabody Coll., 1959; now postgrad. Coll. William and Mary. Cataloger, Va. State Library, Richmond, 1959-62; readers adviser Richmond Pub. Library, summer 1962; head librarian Christopher Newport Coll., Newport News, Va., 1962—. Library adv. com. State Council Higher Edn., 1971—; mem. Eastern Va. Hist. Orgn. for the Bi-Centennial Celebration, 1970—. Mem. Va. (exec. asst. nat. library week com. 1969-71), Southeastern library assns., Jr. League Hampton Roads. Home: 163 Yeardley Dr Newport News VA 23601 Office: PO Box 6070 Newport News VA 23606

MOSTILER, THOMAS WAYNE, dentist; b. Forest City, N.C., Feb. 27, 1941; s. Joe Thomas and Katherine (Page) M.; B.S., Wofford Coll., 1963; D.D.S., Med. Coll. Va., 1966; m. Barbara Ann Copenhaver, Oct. 20, 1961; children—Teresa Lynn, Thomas Wayne, Ann Catherine. Resident oral surgery Med. Coll. Va. Hosp., Richmond, 1966-69, chief resident oral surgery, 1969; chief dental service, chmn. dept. oral surgery U.S. Naval Hosp., Lemoore, Cal., 1969-71; pvt. practice oral surgery, Norfolk, Va., 1971—. Dir. dept. dentistry DePaul Hosp. Recipient A.D. Williams Scholarship award Med. Coll. Va., 1964-65, Psi Omega award, 1966. Diplomate Am. Bd. Oral Surgery. Mem. Atwood Wash Oral Surgery Soc., Am., Va. socs. oral surgeons, Am., Va. Tidewater dental assns., Psi Omega, Kappa Sigma, Sigma Zeta, Omicron Kappa Upsilon, Alpha Sigma Chi. Lion. Home: 224 Upperville Rd Virginia Beach VA 23462 Office: DePaul Med Bldg Norfolk VA 23505

MOTARD, RODOLPHE LEO, chem. engr., educator; b. Ottawa, Ont., Can., May. 26, 1925; s. Leo Rodolphe and Flora Mathilda (Lowden) M.; B.Sc. in Chem. Engring., Queen's U., Kingston, Ont., 1947; M.S. in Chem. Engring., Carnegie Mellon U., 1948, D.Sc. in Chem. Engring., 1952; m. Coreen Gertrude Hunt, Sept. 6, 1947; children—Mark, Paul, John, Louise. Came to U.S., 1947, naturalized, 1961. Research engr. Shell Oil Co., Deer Park, Tex., 1951-57; asso. prof. chem. engring. U. Houston, 1957-68, prof., 1968—. Chmn. Bd. Edn. Diocese of Galveston-Houston, 1970-71. Bd. dirs. Houston Council on Human Relations, chmn. edn. com., 1963-67. Registered profl. engr., Tex. Mem. I.E.E.E., Am. Inst. Chem. Engrs., Assn. Computing Machinery, Soc. for Computer Simulation, A.A.A.S., Sigma Xi. Roman Catholic. Home: 4375 Harvest Lane Houston TX 77004

MOTES, JESSE HOGAN, III, missiles mfg. co. exec.; b. Long Beach, Cal., July 11, 1936; s. Jesse Hogan, Jr., and Elizabeth (Lewis) M.; B.S. in Elec. Engring., Princeton, 1958; m. Margaret Peckham, June 19, 1958; children—Kathleen, Sharon, Robert. Reliability engr. IBM, Owego, N.Y., 1958-62, product assurance mgr., Huntsville, Ala., 1962-72, operations exec. mgr., 1972-74, engring. exec. mgr., 1974—. Bd. dirs. Huntsville Art League and Mus. Assn. Served with USNR, 1959. Recipient Outstanding Contbn. award for devel. Saturn hardware IBM, 1966, NASA award for support to Apollo 16, 1972. Mem. I.E.E.E., Internat. Soc. Hybrid Microelectronics, Sigma Xi. Club: Rocket City Aquatic (Huntsville). Home: 205 Winthrop Dr Huntsville AL 35801 Office: 150 Sparkman Dr Huntsville AL 35805

MOTHERSHED, GEORGE LLOYD, lawyer, oil co. exec.; b. Phoenix, June 12, 1943; s. Caldwell C. and Elizabeth Louise (Jagow) M.; B.S. in Econs. History, No. Ariz. U., 1965; J.D., U. Okla., 1968; m. Carrilee Abernathy, Apr. 11, 1963; children—Robert Stuart, Kelsey Ann. Vice pres. Post Oak Oil Co., Oklahoma City, 1966-72, pres., 1972—, also dir.; admitted to Okla. bar, 1968, since practiced in Oklahoma City; of counsel Howell & Smith, Attys., Oklahoma City, 1968—; asst. sec. Big Chief Drilling Co., 1969-71; sec. Chiefs Corp. of Okla., Inc., 1971-72; sec., treas. Shaft Drillers, Inc., 1971-73 (all Oklahoma City); dir. Southwestern Bank & Trust Co., Oklahoma City, Big Chief Internat. Corp., Chieftain Petroleum, Inc. Oklahoma City. Bd. dirs. region 9 exploring com. Boy Scouts Am., chmn. exploring Last Frontier council, 1971-73, mem. nat. exploring com., 1971—, mem.-at-large Nat. council. Mem. Am. Petroleum Inst., Okla. Ind. Petroleum Assn., Ind. Petroleum Assn. Am., Am., Okla., Oklahoma County bar assns., N.A.M., Oklahoma City Zool. Soc., S.W. Legal Found., Okla. Heritage Assn. U.S. C. of C., Am. Assn. Petroleum Landmen, Phi Alpha Delta, Delta Sigma Phi. Presbyn. (deacon). Rotarian. Clubs: Economics, Petroleum. Home: PO Box 116 Oklahoma City OK 73111 Office: 2900 Liberty Tower 100 N Broadway Oklahoma City OK 73102

MOTT, CHARLES DAVIS, civil engr.; b. Phila., Aug. 30, 1914; s. Charles Hilliard and Emma (Davis) M.; B.S. in Civil Engring., U. Pa., 1936; M. Engring. Adminstrn., George Washington U., 1967; m. Ellen Mary Hooge, July 15, 1938; children—Ellen H., Charles H., Joseph W.H. With Cruse Kemper Co., Ambler, Pa., 1936-37, Central Aircraft Mfg. Co., 1941-45; commd. ensign USN, 1937, advanced through grades to capt., 1959; dir. missile, ammunition, astronautics prodn. Navy Dept., Washington, 1960-63; ret., 1963; system engr. Analytic Services, Inc., Falls Church, Va., 1963—. Decorated Purple Heart, Navy Commendation medal, Cloud and Banner (China). Mem. Am. Inst. Aeros. and Astronautics, Am. Def. Preparedness Assn., Am. Ordnance Assn., Armed Forces Communication Electronics Assn., Mil. Operations Research Soc., Naval Inst., Smithsonian Assos., Flying Tiger Assn., U.S. Chess Fedn. Home: 2522 Rocky Branch Rd Vienna VA 22180 Office: 5613 Leesburg Pike Falls Church VA 22041

MOTT, DOROTHY HALE WILLIAMS (MRS. GEORGE FOX MOTT), editor; b. Mpls., Oct. 3, 1910; d. Edward Hale and Margaret (Ladd) Williams; student Ginling Coll., Nanking, China, 1932-33; A.B., U. Minn., 1937; postgrad. Columbia, 1941; m. George Fox Mott, Feb. 12, 1944; children—David Edward Way, Jonathan Loren Gould. Librarian, tchr. social studies Marine Corps Children's Sch., Quantico, Va., 1941-43; adminstrv. asst. Mott of Washington & Assos., 1950-53, tech. writer, research asst., 1953-64, supervising editor, 1964—. First v.p. Friends of D.C. Youth Orch., 1964-70; treas. Chevy Chase Community Council, 1965—; mem. bd. Children's Theatre Washington, 1966-72; bd. dirs. Noyes Sch. Rhythm Found.; dancer, tchr. Noyes Summer Sch., Portland, Conn., 1970—. Home: 3745 Kanawha St NW Washington DC 20015 Office: Dupont Circle Bldg Washington DC 20036

MOTT, GEORGE FOX, mgmt. cons.; b. Riverside, Cal., June 4, 1907; s. George Fox and Alice (Way) M.; A.B., Stanford, 1929, A.M., 1931; Ph.D., U. Minn., 1938; grad. Army Mgmt. Sch., 1959; m. Dorothy Hale Williams, Feb. 12, 1944; children—David Edward Way, Jonathan Loren Gould. Dean Jr. Coll., San Diego, Chgo., 1929-35; asst. to pres. Hancher Orgn., 1935-36; instr. U. Minn., 1936-38; dean N.M. A. & M. Coll., 1938-39; cons., asst. dir. Kansas City Sch. Survey, 1939: cons. Mayors Survey Coms., St. Louis, Houston, 1939-40; chief cons. analyst, adv. council War Assets Adminstrn., 1946-48; mng. partner, sr. cons. Mott of Washington & Assos., 1948—; chmn. Mott Research Group, 1952—; adj. prof. journalism and pub. relations Am. U. Founding dir. Am.-Korean Found.; internat. dir., also chmn. Greater Washington Council; united bd. Christian Higher Edn. in Asia. Commd. Arty., U.S. Army Res., 1928; served as col. AUS, 1940-46, with Insp. Gen.'s Office, 1941-44, insp. gen. combat units S.W. Pacific, 1944-45, Am. Forces-in-Korea, 1945-46, U.S. Army Res., 1946-63, detailed SSS, 1960-63. Decorated Bronze Star medal with cluster, Commendation medal, Distinguished Service citation (Korea), 1962. Mem. A.I.M. (pres.'s council), Am. Acad. Polit. Social Sci., Am. Polit. Sci. Assn., Nat. Def. Transp. Assn., Res. Officers Assn. (past pres. dept. Md., also dept. D.C.; nat. councilman D.C., past nat. councilman dept. Va., past chmn. nat. army affairs, nat. resolutions, nat. budget, nat. rules and finance coms.; nat. minuteman), Am. Rifle Assn., Mil. Order World Wars (editor hist. record, past chpt. comdr.), Mil. Order Fgn. Wars, Am. Legion (past dept. comdr.), Am. Symphony Orch. League, Phi Delta Kappa. Elk. Club: Army and Navy. Author: San Diego Politically Speaking, 1932; History of Middle Ages, 1933, rev. 1958; Survey of Journalism, 1937; New Survey of Journalism, 1950, rev. 1959; Survey of U.S. Ports, 1951; Miami's Marine Destiny, 1955. Editor: Transportation Renaissance, 1963; editor, sr. author Transportation Century, 1967; editor, contbr. Urban Change and the Planning Syndrome, 1973. Home: 3745 Kanawha St NW Washington DC 20015 Office: Dupont Circle Bldg Washington DC 20036

MOTT, HAROLD, educator; b. Harris, N.C., June 16, 1928; s. Volna Logan and Lela Jane (Jackson) M.; B.E.E., N.C. State U., 1951, M.S., 1953, Ph.D., 1960; m. Elizabeth Irene Hunter, May 23, 1959; 1 son, John. Engr., radio sta. WORD, Spartanburg, S.C., summers 1950-51; engr. Wright Machinery Co., Durham, N.C., 1953-54; instr. N.C. State U., Raleigh, 1954-60; engr. Oak Ridge Nat. Lab., summers 1960-61; engr. Bell Telephone Labs., Winston-Salem, N.C., summer 1956; engr. Boeing Co., Seattle, summer 1962; asso. prof. elec. engring. U. Ala., Tuscaloosa, 1960-64, prof., 1964—. Dir. research in antennas NASA. Served with USNR, 1946-47. Registered profl. engr., Ala. Mem. I.E.E.E., Am. Soc. Engring. Edn. (research award Southeastern sect. 1972). Contbr. articles to profl. jours. Home: 248 Woodland Hills Tuscaloosa AL 35401 Office: Box 6169 University AL 35486

MOTT, HUGH B., county ofcl.; b. Nashville, Aug. 14, 1920; grad. Marion Mil. Inst.; m. Mildred Latimer; 3 daus. Entered N.G., 1942, advanced through grades to maj. gen., 1968; comdr. 30th Armored Div., 1968—; adj. gen. State of Tenn., 1968-71; chief staff for pub. safety Met. Nashville-Davidson County (Tenn.), 1971-72, chief policy, 1972—. Chmn. Wautauga Dist., Middle Tenn. council Boy Scouts Am. Mem. Am. Legion, 40 and 8. Mem. Christian Ch. Address: 110 Public Sq Nashville TN 37201

MOTT, LEO JOHN, computer co. exec.; b. Wilkes Barre, Pa., Aug. 24, 1930; s. Leo Joseph and Martha Jane (Dravage) M.; B.S., Kent State U., 1955; postgrad. Washington U., 1962-63; m. Constance Alter, Sept. 6, 1952; children—Devin, Robert, Julie. Sales rep. Addressograph-Multigraph Corp., Cleve., 1955-60; dist. mgr. Gen. Electric Co., St. Louis, 1960-63, Memphis, 1963-65, Dallas, 1965-68; pres. Univ. Computing Co., Dallas, 1968-72; pres. Computer Utility Network Am., Dallas, 1972—, also dir. Served with USAF, 1951-54. Mem. North Dallas C. of C., Phi Delta Theta. Presbyn. Home: 7023 Briar Cove Dallas TX 75240 Office: 7540 Fwy Dallas TX 75240

MOTT, MARVIN LEE, assn. exec.; b. Galveston, Tex., Dec. 28, 1937; s. Louis Arthur and Susie Ellen (Kahla) M.; B.S., Tex. Wesleyan Coll., 1960; postgrad. So. Meth. U., 1960-61; m. Juanita Margaret Smith, June 18, 1960; children—Rhonda Renee, Michael Stephen. Ordained to ministry Methodist Ch., 1961; pastor Meier Settlement Meth. Ch., Riesel, Tex., 1957-59; asso. pastor Grand Prairie (Tex.) 1st Meth. Ch., 1959-62; program dir. Irving (Tex.) YMCA, 1962-65, exec. dir., 1968—; exec. dir. Garland (Tex.) YMCA, 1965-68; area dir. Dallas YMCA, 1972—, supr. YMCA's, Denton, Grand Prairie, Irving. Named Man of Year, Jr. C. of C., 1972. Mem. Assn. Profl. Dirs. YMCA, Symphony Assn. Rotarian. Home: 3905 Boise Ct Irving TX 75062 Office: 2200 W Irving Blvd Irving TX 75061

MOTTOLA, ALEXANDER CARL, chem. engr.; b. Frankfort, N.Y., Aug. 2, 1922; s. Ralph and Theresa (Dunadee) M.; B.A. in Chemistry, Syracuse U., 1950; B.S. in Chem. Engring., U. N.M., 1952; m. Mary Laura Mazzacua, Apr. 9, 1950; 1 dau., Alexis Corrine. Chem. engr. Nav. Ordnance Test Sta., China Lake, Cal., 1952-54; chief process sect. Picatinny Arsenal, Dover, N.J., 1954-58; mem. staff chem. engring. div. U. Cal., Los Alamos, also Livermore, Cal., 1958-63; research chem. engr. U.S. Dept. Agr., Albany, Cal. also Athens, Ga., 1963—. Served with S.C., AUS, 1943-45; ETO. Decorated 2 Bronze Star medals; recipient Superior Service award U.S. Dept. Agr., 1972. Mem. Am. Chem. Soc., Cal. Soc. Profl. Engrs., Sigma Tau. Contbr. profl. jours. Home: 125 Homestead Dr Athens GA 30601 Office: Richard Russell Research Lab College Station Rd Athens GA 30601

MOULTON, FRANK RAY, JR., petroleum co. exec.; b. Winthrop, Mass., June 17, 1924; s. Frank Ray and Mildred Pauline (Hendrickson) M.; student Northeastern U., 1942-43, Tufts Coll., 1943-44; B.S., Brown U., 1946; Geophys. Engr., Colo. Sch. Mines, 1951; m. Louise Pearl Kiser, May 10, 1952; children—Catherine Eugenie, Thaddeus Ray. Trainee, Superior Oil Co., Bakersfield, Cal., 1951, geophysicist, Andrews, Tex., 1952; geophysicist Carter Oil Co., Colo., Mont., 1952, Internat. Petroleum Co., Colombia, 1952-56; staff seismologist Petroleo Brasileiro (PETROBRAS) S.A., Rio de Janeiro, Brazil, 1956-60; staff asst. to mine mgr. Newgulf, Texasgulf, Inc., 1961, sr. geophysicist, Houston, 1962-67, regional mgr. exploration, 1967-69, asst. gen. mgr. exploration, 1969-70, gen. mgr., 1970, v.p., 1971—, also officer various subsidiaries. Served to lt. (j.g.) USNR, 1943-48. Mem. Am. Assn. Petroleum Geologists, Geol. Soc. Am., Soc. Exploration Geophysicists, Sigma Nu, Tau Beta Pi. Conglist. Clubs: Petroleum (Houston); East India and Sports (London, Eng.). Home: 6315 Glenhill St Spring TX 77373 Office: 811 Rusk Av Houston TX 77002

MOULTRIE, H. CARL, judge; b. Charleston, S.C., Apr. 3, 1915; s. William Edward and Annie Elizabeth (Boree) M.; B.A., Lincoln U., 1936; M.A., N.Y. U., 1952; J.D., Georgetown Law Center, 1956; Certificate Jud. Coll., U. Neb., 1973; m. Sara-Ellyn Avant, Dec. 24, 1941; 1 son, H. Carl, II. Admitted to D.C. bar, 1957; columnist Wilmington (N.C.) Jour., 1938-43; exec. dir. Wilmington Boys' Club, 1938-40; probation officer, New Hanover County, N.C., 1940-41; mgr. Hillcrest Housing Project, Wilmington, 1941-49; nat. exec. sec. Omega Psi Phi Frat., Washington, 1949-72; judge Superior Ct. D.C., Washington, 1972—. Vice chmn. Washington Urban Coalition, 1969-72; mem. Hackers' Appeal & Rev. Bd., Washington, 1963—; mem. Criminal Law and Procedure Policy Bd., 1965-69; mem. Mayor's Econ. Devel. Com., Washington, 1970-73; chmn. nominating com. Health and Welfare Council, 1971-73; chmn. D.C. Commn. Human Rights, Washington, 1971-72; v.p. Bur. Rehab. Bd., Washington, 1972. Bd. dirs. Neighborhood Legal Services Project, Washington, 1968-71, Nannie Burroughs Sch. for Girls, Washington, 1969—, D.C. Lung Assn., 1969-73, Commn. Acad. Facilities, Washington, 1968—. Recipient Silver Keystone award Boys' Club Am., 1949; Anacostia Bus. and Profl. Assn. award, 1971; Service award Conf. Christians And Jews, 1972; Community Service award Health and Welfare Council, 1973. Mem. D.C. Bar Assn. (bd. dirs. 1969-70, mem. com. 1966-67), N.A.A.C.P. (dist. pres. 1964-69). Mason (Shriner), Rotarian. Home: 3915 17th St NE Washington DC 20018 Office: 613 G St NW Washington DC 20001

MOULTRIE, ROY DEAN, judge; b. Hamilton, Ga., Apr. 2, 1932; s. Alvah C. and Osie (Richardson) M.; terminal certificate West Ga. Coll., 1950; J.D., Mercer U., 1953; m. Ann Williams, Feb. 1, 1959; children—Charles Dean, Elizabeth Ann. Admitted to Ga. bar, 1953; county atty. Harris County, Ga., 1958-62; owner Roy D. Moultrie Ins. Agy., 1958-73; judge Ct. Ordinary, Harris County, Ga., 1957—; pres. Southern, Inc.; pres. Harris County Realty, Inc.; dir. Farmers & Mchts. Bank, Pine Mountain, Ga. Treas. Chattahoochee Devel. and Planning Commn., 1965-67; atty. Harris County Bd. Edn., 1973—. Bd. dirs. Ga. YMCA, 1960-64, Pine Mountain Soil and Water Dist.; exec. bd. Chattahoochee council Boy Scouts Am. Mem. Am., Ga., Chattahoochee Circuit (pres. 1960-61) bar assns. Baptist (deacon). Mason (32 deg.), Lion (dep. dist. gov. 1962-63; devel. and retention chmn. dist. 18E 1963-64). Address: Courthouse Hamilton GA 31811

MOUNT, CHARLES LE MEAR, JR., physician; b. Holdenville, Okla., June 19, 1912; s. Charles Le Mear and Lela Evelyn (Roseboom) M.; B.S., U. Okla., 1935; M.D., Johns Hopkins, 1940; m. Susan Mae Berry, Jan. 13, 1968; children—Charles Le Mear III (dec.), Susan, Peter. House staff Johns Hopkins Sch. Medicine, 1940-43; asst. resident medicine Vanderbilt U. Hosp., 1944; resident medicine Johns Hopkins Hosp., 1945; chief of medicine and cardiology Winter Gen. Hosp., Topeka, 1946-50; pvt. practice medicine, specializing in internal medicine, Okla., 1951-54; indsl. cardiologist E.I. duPont de Nemours & Co., Charleston, W. Va., 1954-56; chief of geriatrics Central State Griffin Meml. Hosp., Norman, Okla., 1959—; instr. medicine Johns Hopkins Sch. Medicine; lectr. Kellogg Center Continuing Edn. U. Okla.; lectr. psychosomatic medicine and heart disease Winter Gen. Hosp., Menninger Psychiat. Inst.; lectr. geriatrics Okla. Dept. Mental Health; chief med. dir. Central Okla. Vets. Center; med. cons. State Nursing Home Assn.; cons. Southwestern Okla. Soil Conservation Commn. Served as maj. AUS, 1956-58. Mem. U. Okla. Alumni Assn., Balt., Johns Hopkins med. and surg. socs., Okla. Johns Hopkins Alumni Assn., Royal Soc. Health (London, Eng.), Am. Gerontol. Soc., Am. Psychiat. Assn. (hon.), Okla. Arts and Scis. Found., Phi Beta Kappa, Sigma Zi, Sigma Alpha Epsilon, Nu Sigma Nu. Methodist. Home: 2610 Cypress St Norman OK 73069 Office: Box 151 Norman OK 73069

MOUNT, GARY ARTHUR, entomologist; b. Bristow, Okla., Oct. 8, 1936; s. Stanley Arthur and Cylania Paralee (Borthick) M.; B.S., Okla. State U., 1958, M.S., 1960, Ph.D., 1963; m. Edna Lavelle Gottschall, May 30, 1963; children—Jason Arthur, Brian Welton; m. 2d, Sirkka Marketta Makela, June 15, 1973. Research entomologist Insects Affecting Man Lab., U.S. Dept. Agr., Gainesville, Fla., 1963—. Contbr. articles to various publs. Home: 4911 NW 40th Terrace Gainesville FL 32601 Office: PO Box 14565 Gainesville FL 32604

MOUNTAIN, CLIFTON FLETCHER, physician; b. Toledo, Apr. 15, 1924; s. Ira Fletcher and Mary (Stone) M.; A.B., Harvard, 1947, postgrad., 1946-47; M.D., Boston U., 1954; postgrad. U. Chgo., 1954-59; m. Marilyn Isabelle Tapper, Feb. 28, 1945; children—Karen Lockerby, Clifton Fletcher, Jeffrey Richardson. Dir. dept. statis. research Boston U., 1947-50; cons. research analyst Dept. Pub. Health, Commonwealth of Mass., 1951-53; intern U. Chgo. Clinics, 1954, resident, 1955-58, instr. surgery, 1958-59; practice medicine, specializing in thoracic surgery, Houston, 1959—; mem. staff M.D. Anderson Hosp. and Tumor Research Inst.; asst. prof. thoracic surgery U. Tex., 1960-63, chmn. program in biomath. and computer sci., 1962-64, asso. prof. surgery, 1963—; Mike Hogg vis. lectr. in S. Am., 1967; mem. sci. mission on cancer USSR, 1974. Mem. com. health, research and edn. facilities Community Council, Houston, 1964—; cons. Am. Joint Com. for Cancer Staging and End Result Reporting, 1966—; mem. NIH Working Party on Lung Cancer, 1971—, chmn. com. surgery, 1971—, mem. plans and scope com. cancer therapy Nat. Cancer Inst., 1972—, chmn. steering com., 1973—. Chmn. profl. adv. com. Harris County Mental Health Assn.; bd. dirs. Harris County chpt. Am. Cancer Soc. Served to lt. (j.g.) USNR, 1942-46. Diplomate Am. Bd. Surgery. Fellow Am. Coll. Chest Physicians (chmn. com. cancer 1967—), Inst. Environmental Scis., N.Y. Acad. Sci., A.C.S.; mem. A.A.A.S., Am. Assn. Cancer Research, Am., So. med. assns., Am. Thoracic Soc., Soc. Thoracic Surgeons, Soc. Biomed. Computing, Biomed. Information Processing Orgn., Am. Fedn. Clin. Research, Assn. Computing Machinery, Am. Radium Soc., Pan-Am. Med. Assn., Am. Congress Rehab. Medicine, Houston Surg. Soc., Southwest Cancer Chemotherapy Study Group, James Ewing Soc., Sigma Xi. Editor: The New Physician, 1955-59. Editorial bd. Yearbook of Cancer, 1960—. Contbr. articles to profl. jours. Home: 1612 South Blvd Houston TX 77006 Office: 6723 Bertner Av Houston TX 77025

MOUSER, EDWARD MILNER, lawyer; b. Columbia, La., May 28, 1933; s. Vinson M. and Helen (Holmes) M.; B.A., La. State U., 1958, LL.B., 1959, J.D., 1968; m. Erma Del Jones, Aug. 24, 1958; children—Christopher Michael, Patrick Daniel. Admitted to La. bar, 1959; practiced in Oakdale, 1959-63, Kinder, 1963-69; mem. firm Mouser & Mouser, 1959-63; dist. judge 33d Jud. Dist., Allen Parish (La.), 1969—. Served with USMCR, 1954-56. Methodist. Rotarian. Address: PO Drawer AB Kinder LA 70648

MOUSHEGIAN, GEORGE, neurophysiologist; b. Detroit, Jan. 19, 1923; s. Zakar Ardash and Nazig Satennig (Kougasian) M.; B.S., Wayne State U., 1947, M.A., 1951; Ph.D., U. Tex., 1957; m. Lillian Lorraine Whitfield, Aug. 16, 1952; children—Susan Elizabeth, Van. Chief sensory psychology Walter Reed Med. Center, Washington, 1962; sr. research fellow Lab. Sensory Communication, Syracuse U., Syracuse, N.Y., 1964-68; prof. psychology Syracuse (N.Y.) U.,

1964-68; dir. research Callier Hearing & Speech Center, Dallas, 1968—; prof. physiology Southwestern Med. Sch., Dallas, 1969—. Served with AUS, 1943-46. Fellow Acoustical Soc. Am.; mem. Am. Physiol. Soc., Am. Psychol. Assn., Soc. Neurosci.; A.A.A.S., Am. Assn. U. Profs., Sigma Xi. Contbr. articles to various publs. Home: 4507 Mill Run Rd Dallas TX 75234 Office: 1966 Inwood Rd Dallas TX 75235

MOUTON, GROVER ERNEST, III, architect, artist; b. Lafayette, La., Nov. 18, 1946; s. Grover Ernest, Jr. and Elaine Elizabeth Mouton; student U. Southwestern La., 1966-67, Skowhegan (Me.) Sch. Painting, 1969, Archtl. Assos. London (Eng.), 1970; B.Arch., Tulane U., 1971; fellow Am. Acad. Rome (Italy), 1971—. Exhibited one-man shows, New Orleans, 1968, Circle Gallery, New Orleans, 1970; exhibited in group shows U. Southwestern La., Lafayette, 1967, Dublin Nat. Print and Drawing Competition, Dublin Gallery of Art, Knoxville, Tenn., 1970. Recipient Prix de Rome, 1971. Mem. A.I.A., Kappa Sigma. Roman Catholic. Ind. research, design non-gravitational environment. Home: 140 Oakview Blvd Lafayette LA 70501 Office: Am Acad in Rome Via Angelo Masina 5 00153 Rome Italy

MOWERY, CALVIN L., elec. engr.; b. Fort Smith, Ark., Feb. 14, 1912; s. Calvin L. and Agnes (Combs) M.; B.S. in E.E., U. Ark., 1933; m. Lois M. Tongier, Mar. 30, 1935; 1 dau., Mary Louise (Mrs. Kermit Tanzey). With Nat. Refining Co., Coffeyville, Kan., 1933-44; with Coop. Refinery Assn., Coffeyville, 1944-50, chief engr., 1948-50; with Phillips Petroleum Co., Bartlesville, Okla., 1950—, project adminstr., cons., 1960-72, safety dir., 1972—. Registered profl. engr., Okla. Mem. Tau Beta Pi, Lambda Chi Alpha. Methodist. Mason, Elk, Lion (past dist. officer). Home: 3608 Woodland Rd Bartlesville OK 74004 Office: 14 Phillips Bldg Bartlesville OK 74004

MOWERY, WILLIAM EDWARD, dentist; b. Cairo, Ill., Apr. 20, 1919; s. Hugh Lloyd and Adah Belle (Little) M.; student U. Louisville, 1937-40, D.M.D., 1943; postgrad. U. Mich., Ohio State U., U. Pa., Georgetown U.; m. Nancy Wilds Baskett, June 21, 1942; children—Marilyn Elizabeth (Mrs. David W. Bryant), James Taylor, Lois Evelyn. Pvt. practice dentistry, Richmond, Ky., 1946-47; staff dentist VA, Louisville, 1947-50; VA guest worker, dental research labs. Nat. Bur. Standards, Washington, 1950-52; chief Central Dental Lab., VA Regional Office, Louisville, 1952-56, VA West Side Hosp., Chgo., 1956-63; asst. chief dental service VA Center, Dayton, O., 1963-71; chief Central Dental Lab., VA Hosp., Washington, 1971-72; asst. chief dental service VA Hosp., Louisville, 1972—. Mem. faculty U. Louisville Sch. Dentistry, 1953-56, 72—, Loyola U., Chgo., 1956-63, Ohio State U., Columbus, 1964-71. Served with USNR, 1943-46; capt. res. (ret.). Diplomate Am. Bd. Prosthodontics; Fellow Am. Coll. Prosthodontists; mem. Louisville, Ky., Am. dental assns., Am. Prosthodontic Soc. Baptist (deacon). Contbr. articles to profl. jours. Home: 2250 Wynnewood Circle Louisville KY 40222

MOYANT, GEORGE CARL, educator; b. Bklyn., May 30, 1928; s. John B. and Mary (Van Remoortere) M.; B.S. in Elec. Engring. magna cum laude, Lehigh U., 1951; postgrad. Syracuse U., 1951-53; m. Olivera Sajkovic, June 9, 1960. Project mgr. Rome Air Research Center (N.Y.), 1951-56; cons. engr. Kirk Engring., Phila., 1957, Lehigh Engring., Newark, also Ardé Engring., Paramus, N.J., 1958-66; hospitalization with polio, 1967-68; founder, pres., instr. constrn. theory Allstate Constrn. Coll., Inc., Hollywood, Fla., 1968—. Served to 1st lt. USAF, 1951-53. Registered profl. engr., N.J., Fla. Home and office: 7170 Lee St Hollywood FL 33024

MOYER, PAUL KENNETH, ins. co. exec.; b. Hamburg, Pa., May 29, 1936; s. Paul Frederick and Verna (Miller) M.; B.B.A., Tex. Luth. Coll., 1962; postgrad. U. Houston, 1966; M.B.A., So. Meth. U., 1971; m. Betty Louise Scheffer, Aug. 25, 1962; children—Mark Kevin, Kayla Marie. Auditor Ernst & Ernst, C.P.A.'s, Houston, 1962-65; asst. to asst. treas. Gulf & Western Industries, Inc., N.Y.C., 1965-68, asst. treas., 1968-69; v.p., controller UCC Financial Corp., Dallas, 1969-73; v.p. investment services Gulf Ins. Co., Dallas, 1973—. Mem. devel. bd. Tex. Luth. Coll., 1972—. Served with USAF, 1954-58. C.P.A., Tex. Mem. Am. Inst. C.P.A.'s, Nat. Assn. Accountants, Tex. Soc. C.P.A.'s. Lutheran. Home: 12515 Ruthdale Dr Dallas TX 75234 Office: PO Box 1771 Dallas TX 75221

MOYER, ROBERT EARL, broker; b. Frankfort, Ind., Mar. 18, 1916; s. Samuel Earl and Ruby Inis (Maish) M.; student Purdue U., 1933, U. Ill., 1937; m. Mary Stuckey, Sept. 3, 1939; children—James R., Suzanne (Mrs. Joseph F. Keeslar), Marilyn. Chief engr. Moore Enameling & Mfg. Co., West Lafayette, O., 1942-45; with Tappan Co., Mansfield, O., 1945-69, v.p., gen. mgr. Murray (Ky.) div., to 1969; ret., 1969-72; broker I.M. Simon & Co., Murray, 1972—. Cons. Internat. Exec. Service Corps, Teheran, Iran, 1971; mem. adv. com. industry and tech. Murray State U., 1967-69. Chmn. A.R.C., Murray, 1970-73. Chmn. Murray Planning Commn., 1970-73; vice chmn. Murray Human Rights Commn., 1967-73. Named Man of Year Murray C. of C., 1969. Mem. C. of C. (pres. 1968-69, 72-73. Methodist. Mason, Rotarian (past pres.). Home: 1231 Dogwood St Murray KY 42071 Office: Box 87 Murray KY 42071

MOYERS, RALPH WATSON, accountant; b. Houston, Apr. 5, 1937; s. Cecil Henry and Julia Inez (Hargrove) M.; B.B.A., Lamar U., 1962; m. Gracie Jane Johnson, Mar. 26, 1959; children—Melissa Kaye, Jeffrey Watson. With Price Waterhouse & Co., Houston, 1962—, mgr. auditing, 1969—; dir. S.W. Electronics, Inc., Houston. Co-chmn. United Fund, 1972; adviser Jr. Achievement, 1966-67. C.P.A., Tex. Mem. Am. Inst. C.P.A.'s, Tex. Soc. C.P.A.'s, Contemporary Arts Assn., Kappa Alpha. Home: 11210 Valley Stream Rd Houston TX 77043 Office: 1200 Milam St Houston TX 77002

MOYLAN, THOMAS PATRICK, JR., stock broker; b. Hartford, Conn., Oct. 2, 1936; s. Thomas Patrick and Katherine (Hickey) M.; B.S., U.S. Naval Acad., 1960; postgrad. Boston U., 1960-63; m. Joan E. Murphy, July 17, 1965; children—Elizabeth, Meridith, Thomas IV, Meghan. With Barrows & Wallace, Real Estate, West Hartford, Conn., 1963-64; account exec. Merrill, Lynch, Pierce, Fenner & Smith, Inc., N.Y.C., 1964-68, sales mgr., 1968-73, resident mgr., Huntsville, Ala., 1973—. Mem. bd. speakers New York Stock Exchange. Mem. Mayor's Com. on Transp., 1971-72. Bd. advisers Ala. A. and M. Coll. Served with USMCR, 1953-58. Mem. Huntsville C. of C. (pub. relations com.). Rotarian. Clubs: New York Athletic; Valley Hills Country (Huntsville). Home: 4026 Lucerne Dr SE Huntsville AL 35802 Office: 2100 Franklin St SE Huntsville AL 35801

MOZINGO, JAMES DELBERT, ednl. adminstr.; b. Toxey, Ala., Mar. 9, 1935; s. Lewis Weslen and Maggie (Burnham) M.; student Whitworth Coll., 1960-61; B.S., Livingston State Coll., 1967, M.Ed., 1969; m. Gracie Evelyn Hendrix, June 28, 1953; children—James Carlos, Dwight Delbert, Gerald Frank. Store operator, Butler, Ala. also Forest, Miss., 1953-60; bus. mgr. Whitworth Coll., 1960-61; minister Methodist Protestant Ch., Toxey, Ala., 1953-72, pres. Gen. Conf. Bd. Missions, 1965-67, treas. Miss. Conf., 1971-72; tchr. English, speech So. Choctaw High Sch., Silas, Ala., 1967-69; prin. Gilbertown (Ala.) Jr. High Sch., 1969—. Adviser Gilbertown council Boy Scouts Am., 1969-72. Mem. Choctaw County (pres. 1968-69), Am. (del. 1969) edn. assns., Pi Tau Chi, Alpha Rho Tau. Author: Storm and Sunshine, 1972. Home: Drawer C Gilbertown AL 36908 Office: Drawer C Gilbertown AL 36908

MUDD, ALVIN CARL, aircraft co. exec; b. Alvin, Tex., Dec. 23, 1943; s. Alvin and Joyce Josephine (Cooksey) M.; B.B.A., St. Edward's U., 1965; m. Betty Marie Olsovsky, Jan. 30, 1965; children—Jason Todd, Leslie Leigh. Sr. accountant Price Waterhouse & Co., Houston, 1965-71; controller Mitsubishi Aircraft Internat., Inc., San Angelo, Tex., 1971—. C.P.A., Tex. Mem. Am. Inst. C.P.A.'s, Tex. State Soc. C.P.A.'s (Houston, San Angelo chpts.). Home: 2910 Briargrove Lane San Angelo TX 76901 Office: PO Box 3848 San Angelo TX 76901

MUDD, SISTER HILDA, librarian; b. New Haven, Ky.; d. Edward D. and Estelle (Howard) Mudd; A.B., St. Mary of the Woods, Ind., 1938; B.S. in L.S., Catholic U. Am., 1953; M.A., Creighton U., 1972. Tchr., librarian St. Charles High Sch., Lebanon, Ky., 1938-45; librarian Brescia Coll., Owensboro, Ky., 1949—. Mem. Am., Cath. Ky. library assns. Address: Brescia Coll 120 W 7th St Owensboro KY 42301

MUDD, JOHN PHILIP, lawyer, real estate exec.; b. Washington, Aug. 22, 1932; s. T. Paul and Frances M. (Finotti) M.; B.S., Georgetown U., 1954, J.D., 1956; m. Barbara E. Sweeney, Aug. 10, 1957; children—Laura, Ellen, Philip, Clare, David. Admitted to Fla. bar, 1964, Md. bar, 1956, Washington bar, 1963, Cal. bar, 1973; practice law, Upper Marlboro, Md., 1956-66; chief corporate counsel Deltona Corp., Miami, Fla., 1966-68, chief corp. counsel, sec., 1968-72, v.p., 1972-73; sec. Nat. Community Builders, San Diego, 1972-73; gen. counsel Continental Advisers, Continental Mortgage Investors, Coral Gables, Fla., 1973—; dir. 1st Bank Deltona. Sec., Marco Island Devel. Corp., Miami, 1968-72. Mem. internat. land devel. adv. com. N.Y. State, 1971—. Mem. Fla., Am., Dade County bar assns., State Bar Cal. Republican. Roman Catholic. Home: 1211 Hardee Rd Coral Gables FL 33146 Office: 5915 Ponce de Leon Blvd Coral Gables FL 33146

MUDIE, JOHN HOWARD, banker; b. Hackensack, N.J., July 13, 1927; s. John A. and Rose C. (Schwager) M.; A.B., Dartmouth, 1949; M.B.A., U. Pa., 1951; Ph.D., U. Tex., 1960. Asst. prof. Tex. A. and M. Coll., College Station, 1954-55; with Govt. Devel. Bank for P.R., San Juan, 1956—, v.p., 1967—; prof. econs. and bus. adminstrn. Inter-Am. U. P.R., Hato Rey, 1968—, chmn. dept., 1968-70. Served with AUS, 1946-47. Mem. Am. Econ. Assn., Soc. for Internat. Devel. Home: 83 Cervantes St Santurce PR 00907 Office: GPO Box 4748 San Juan PR 00905

MUEHLENBECK, THOMAS HOWARD, city ofcl.; b. Saginaw, Mich., June 6, 1941; s. Howard Paul and Evelyn (Cummings) M.; B.S., Lamar U., 1964; M.P.A., U. Kan., 1966; m. Myrtle Evelyn Brown, July 13, 1963; children—Brian Allan, Brenda Kay. Asst. city mgr. City of Parsons, Kan., 1966-67; city mgr. City of Atchison, Kan., 1967-69; city mgr. City College Park, Ga., 1969—. Mem. Municipal Finance Officers Assn., Internat. City Mgmt. Assn. Rotarian. Home: 1714 Suzanne Way College Park GA 30337 Office: City Hall College Park GA 30337

MUELLER, ALFRED JEROME, physician, county ofcl.; b. Worcester, Mass., Sept. 15, 1928; s. Alfred Don and Marie (Struve) M.; B.S., U. Tenn., 1950, M.D., 1952; m. Margaret Jo Coleman, Feb. 1, 1953; children—Daniel Jerome, Margaret Ann, William Don, Charles Gregory, Molly Marie. Intern, John Gaston Hosp., Memphis, 1952-53; resident obstetrics, gynecology Vanderbilt U. Hosp., Nashville, 1955-57, U. Ark. Med. Center, Little Rock, 1957-58; practice medicine, specializing in obstetrics and gynecology, Lexington, Ky., 1958-59; dir. Jackson-Madison County Health Dept., Jackson, Tenn., 1959—; Madison County health officer, 1960—; asst. Div. Preventive Medicine, U. Tenn., 1962—. Cons. preventive medicine and pub. health Jackson-Madison County Gen. Hosp., 1964—, mem. med. staff exec. com., 1970—; surgeon Cocks-Danuiels Post, V.F.W., 1962-70; mem. C. of C. Task Force for Health Services, 1973—. Dir. V.F.W. Recreation Center, 1963-73. Bd. dirs. Jackson YMCA, 1967-70, Goals for Jackson, 1970—. Served from 1st lt. to capt. M.C., USAF, 1952-55. Mem. Am., Tenn. (chmn. maternal-child health com. 1963, 64, 66; chmn. health officers' sect. 1967-68, pres. 1971-72) pub. health assns., Tenn. Med. Assn., Consol. Med. Assembly W. Tenn., Am. Assn. Pub. Health Physicians, Am. Legion, Alpha Epsilon Delta, Pi Kappa Alpha, Phi Chi, Alpha Omega Alpha. Presbyn. Rotarian. Home: 137 Shadowlawn Dr Jackson TN 38301 Office: 745 W Forest St Jackson TN 38301

MUELLER, JOHN A., JR., ins. co. exec.; b. Cin., June 28, 1940; s. John A. and Marjorie R. (Dhonau) M.; B.B.A., U. Cin., 1962; m. Eileen A. Gavin, Mar. 2, 1962 (div. Aug. 1967); 1 son, John A. III. Intern to sr. supervising auditor Arthur Young & Co., Cin., 1959-64; accountant Atico Financial Corp., Miami, Fla., 1964-65, asst. treas., 1965-67, v.p., controller, 1967-71; v.p., treas. Am. Title Ins. Co., Miami, 1971—. Mem. Am. Land Title Assn. (standing accounting com.). Office: 150 SE 3d Av Miami FL 33131

MUELLER, MARK CHRISTOPHER, lawyer, accountant; b. Dallas, June 19, 1945; s. Herman August and Hazel Deane (Hatzenbuehler) M.; B.A. in Econs., So. Meth. U., 1967, M.B.A. in Accounting, 1969, J.D., 1971. Admitted to Tex. bar, 1971, since practiced in Dallas; accountant A.E. Krutilek, Dallas, 1968-71, Arthur Young & Co., Dallas, 1967-68; asso. L. Vance Stanton, Dallas, 1971-72. Instr. legal writing and research So. Meth. U., 1970-71. C.P.A., Tex. Mem. Am., Tex. bar assns., Tex. Soc. C.P.A.s, Order of Coif, Beta Alpha Psi, Phi Delta Phi, Sigma Chi. Mason (32 deg., Shriner). Club: Nat. Rifle Assn. Home: 7023 Wild Grove Dallas TX 75214 Office: 400 Adolphus Tower TX 75202

MUELLER, ROBERT ARTHUR, pharmacologist, educator; b. Fondulac, Wis., July 24, 1938; s. Gustave Gotlieb and Edith Hulda (Schoenberg) M.; B.S., U. Wis., 1960, M.S. in Pharmacology, 1963; M.D., U. Minn., 1965, Ph.D. in Pharmacology, 1966; m. Marian Schiller, June 22, 1962; children—Kraig, Gustave, Kurt. Intern U. Minn. Hosps., 1966-67; resident Northwestern U. Med. Center, 1969-70; asso. prof. pharmacology and anesthesiology U. N.C., Chapel Hill, 1970-73, dir. anesthesiology research, 1973—. Guest prof. U. Basel (Switzerland), 1973-74. Served with USPHS, 1967-69. Phar. Mfrs. Found. Faculty Devel. award in clin. pharmacology U. N.C. Mem. Am. Soc. Pharmacology and Exptl. Therapeutics, Sigma Xi, Phi Beta Kappa. Home: 712 Kenmore Rd Chapel Hill NC 27514

MUELLER, ROBERT LOUIS, physician; b. Granite City, Ill., Sept. 2, 1929; s. Louis Jacob and Mildred (Fegley) M.; A.B. magna cum laude, Carthage Coll., 1951; M.D., U. Ill., 1955; m. Dorothy Jane Grant, Apr. 28, 1956; children—Deborah Jean, Mary Jane, Allan Louis, Catherine Grant. Intern Ill. Central Hosp., Chgo., 1955-56; resident obstetrics and gynecology U. Tenn. and City of Memphis Hosps., 1957-60; practice medicine, specializing in obstetrics and gynecology, Morristown, Tenn., 1964—; mem. staff Morristown Hamblen Hosp., chief staff, 1969-70, 73—. Served to maj. AUS, 1956-64. Diplomate Am. Bd. Obstetrics and Gynecology. Fellow Am. Coll. Obstetrics and Gynecology; mem. A.M.A., Tenn., So. med. assns., Hamblen County Med. Soc. (pres. 1974). Lutheran. Home: 1420 Doyal Dr Morristown TN 37814 Office: 705 McFarland St Morristown TN 37814

MUES, FLAVIO JORGE, elec. engr.; b. Mexico City, Mexico, Aug. 26, 1930; s. Eric and Marta (Becker) M.; M.S., Nat. U. Mexico 1963; student Grad. Sch., U. Ibero Americana, 1971-73; m. Teresa Zepeda, Jan. 5, 1966; 1 dau., Astrid. Project engr. Continental Engring. N.V., Amsterdam, Holland, 1965, Ingenieria Continental S.A., Mexico City, 1966-67; project mgr. Condumex S.A., wire and cable mfrs., Mexico City, 1968-73; project mgr. Ludwig Saenger Cons., Mexico City, 1974—; Tchr. systems Grad. Sch., U. Ibero Americana, 1973-74. Mem. I.E.E.E., Nat. Geog. Soc., Roda Automobile Club. Club: Cuicacalli (Satellite City). Contbr. articles to profl. jours. Home: 791 Cali Av Mexico City DF 14 Mexico Office: 165 Hamburgo St Mexico City DF 6 Mexico

MUIJE, CORNELIUS SCHULF, tobacco co. exec.; b. Salt Lake City, July 18, 1925; s. Cornelis and Elisabeth (Schuif) M.; B.S. in Mech. Engring., U. Utah, 1956, postgrad., 1956-57; advanced mgmt. program Harvard Bus. Sch., 1971; m. Lilian Siebert, Oct. 22, 1946; 1 dau., Susan A. Supr. operations research, advt. dept. Procter & Gamble, Cin., 1957-64; dir. marketing research Brown & Williamson Tobacco Corp., Louisville, 1964—. Mem. Cin. World Front TV Com., 1961-64. Served with CIC, AUS, 1946-53. Mem. Am., Cin. (pres., 1962-64) philatelic socs., Nat. Indsl. Conf. Bd., Council Marketing Research Dirs., Am. Civil Liberties Union. Home: 4700 Trowbridge Terrace Louisville KY 40207 Office: 1600 W Hill St Louisville KY 40201

MUIR, HELEN, author; b. Yonkers, N.Y., Feb. 9, 1911; d. Emmet A. and Helen T. (Flaherty) Lennehan; student Yonkers pub. schools; m. William Whalley Muir, Jan. 23, 1936; children—Mary (Mrs. Frederick W. Burrell), William Torbert. With Yonkers Herald Statesman, 1929-30, 31-33, N.Y. Eve. Post, 1930-31, N.Y. Eve. Jour., 1933-34, Carl Byoir & Assos., 1934-35; syndicated columnist Universal Service, 1935-38, Miami Daily News, 1935-39; broadcaster stas. WIOD, WQAM, 1935, 42; columnist Miami Herald, 1941-42; woman's editor Miami Daily News, 1943-44; free lance mag. writer, Sat. Eve. Post, This Week, Nations Bus., Woman's Day, 1944—; children's book editor Miami Herald, 1949-56; drama critic Miami News, 1960-65. Trustee Coconut Grove Library Assn., Friends U. Miami Library, Met. Dade County Library Bd. Recipient award Delta Kappa Gamma, 1960; Trustees and Friends award Fla. Library Assn., 1973. Mem. Women in Communications (Community Headline award 1973). Club: Fla. Women's Press (award 1963). Author: Miami, U.S.A., 1954. Home: 3855 Stewart Av Miami FL 33133

MUIR, J. LAWRENCE, geologist; b. Enid, Okla., Apr. 4, 1903; s. Alexander and Lillie (Vaught) M.; B.S., U. Okla., 1930, M.S., 1933; m. Hazel Munhall, Apr. 22, 1930; children—Vivian (Mrs. Leo C. Varian), Robert L., Carolyn (Mrs. Charles R. Gasaway), Gordon K. Geologist, Gulf Refining Co., Shreveport, La., 1930; geologist, then dist. geologist Amerada Petroleum Corp., 1933-48; chief geologist Champlin Refining Co., Enid, Okla., 1948-51, v.p. exploration and devel., 1951-54; cons. geologist, Enid, 1954-62; petroleum geologist SEC, Washington, 1962-68, chief petroleum geologist, chief sect. oil and gas, 1968-72, chief Office Oil and Gas, 1972—. Vis. asso. prof. petroleum geology U. Okla., 1955-56. Pres., U. Okla. Dad's Assn., 1957-58. Mem. Am. Assn. Petroleum Geologists, Am. Inst. Mining and Metall. Engrs., Geol. Soc. Am., Soc. Exploration Geophysicists, Soc. Econ. Paleontologists and Mineralogists, Phi Beta Kappa, Sigma Xi, Sigma Gamma Epsilon. Methodist. Home: 533 W Great Falls St Falls Church VA 22046 Office: Securities and Exchange Commn 500 N Capitol St Washington DC 20549

MUIR, JOHN ANDERSON, metal fabricating co. exec.; b. Springfield, Ill., Jan 24, 1926; s. John Anderson and Irene (Davis) M.; B.S., U. Ill., 1953; m. Sue Crawford, Aug. 1, 1945; children—Sherryl S. (Mrs. Morrow), Marcia S. Tool and die maker Sangamo Electric Co., Springfield, 1946-50, sales engr., 1953-55, plant mech. engr., Pickens, S.C., 1956-59, asst. plant mgr., 1959-62, plant mgr., 1962-64; pres. Metal Fabricators, Inc., Greenville, S.C., 1964—, also dir.; v.p. Gantt Mfg. Corp., Greenville, 1967—, also dir.; pres. Gantt Bldg., Inc., Greenville, 1967, now dir., v.p.; v.p. Golden Tye Corp., Pickens, 1967—, also dir.; sec., treas. Pickens R.R. Co., 1968—, also dir.; dir. Thermal Engring. Corp., Columbia, S.C. Chmn., Oconee County Republicans for Strom Thurmond, 1968. Served with USMCR, 1942-46. Methodist. Mason (Shriner). Clubs: Poinsett, Green Valley Country. Home: 129 Chisolm Trail Greenville SC 29607 Office: PO Box 1946 Greenville SC 29602

MUIRHEAD, JEAN DENMAN, lawyer; b. nr. Charleston, Miss., May 12, 1929; d. Joe M. and Eva (Bufkin) Denman; student Delta State Coll., 1945-47; LL.B., Jackson Sch. Law, 1967; children—Mike, Scott, Melissa. Legal sec. Office Atty. Gen., State of Miss., Jackson, 1947-50; legal sec. firm Overstreet, Kuykendall, Perry & Phillips, Jackson, 1962-64, Satterfield, Shell, Williams & Buford, Jackson, 1967; admitted to Miss. bar, 1967; pvt. practice in Jackson, Miss., 1967—; mem. Miss. Senate, 1968-72. First v.p. Hinds County Kidney Found.; mem. 1970 Assay Commn.; mem. Law Enforcement Assistance Regional Council No. 3. Bd. dirs. Hinds County Mental Health Assn. Mem. Am., Miss., Hinds County bar assns., Nat. Assn. Women Lawyers, Nat. Orgn. Women (state legislative coordinator), Jackson Bus. and Profl. Womens Club (Woman of Achievement 1970). Home: 4035 Redwing Av Jackson MS 39216 Office: Suite 203 Highland Village Jackson MS 39211

MULDOON, PATRICK JOHN, orgn. adminstr.; b. Niagara Falls, N.Y., Oct. 15, 1937; s. Thomas William and Audrey Owen (Hardy) M.; B.S., Mich. State U., 1960; M.S., U. Ida., 1966; Ph.D., Purdue U., 1969; m. Patricia Elaine Turner, Aug. 4, 1962; children—Shaena, Patrick, Meghan, Bronwyn, Sean. Prodn. supr. Internat. Dairy Supply Co., San Francisco, 1960-64; research asst. U. Ida., Moscow, 1964-66, Purdue U., Lafayette, Ind., 1966-69; mem. faculty Va. Poly. Inst. and State U., Blacksburg, 1969-73; exec. dir. New River Community Action, Inc., Christiansburg, Va., 1973—. Pres. Va. Poly. Inst. and State U. Fed. Credit Union, 1973-74; cons. food and dairy industry, 1969-73. Vice pres. Giles County Republican Club, 1973. Pres. Holy Family Ch. Council, 1972—. Grantee Va. Agr. Found., 1971-72. Mem. Pearisburg Jr. C. of C. (treas. 1971-73), Inst. Food Technologists (mem. com. 1970—), Internat. Assn. Milk, Food and Environmental Sanitarians, Am. Chem. Soc., Am. Dairy Sci. Assn., Va. Dairy Shrine, Phi Tau Sigma. Home: Route 1 Box 79 Pembroke VA 24136 Office: PO Box 332 Christiansburg VA 24073

MULHALL, LAWRENCE JOSEPH, wholesale co. exec.; b. Louisville, May 27, 1908; s. Joseph Horace and Elizabeth (Shea) M.; student U. Ky., 1927, U. Louisville, 1928, 29; m. Louise Gillespie, Sept. 13, 1936; 1 dau., Elizabeth Mulhall. Pres., dir. McWhorter Weaver & Co., Nashville, 1946—; pres., dir. Grayson Corp., 1958—. Chmn., Nashville Mayor's adv. com. Housing and Urban Devel., 1968-69; pres. Nashville Symphony Assn., 1969; chmn. adv. bd. St. Thomas Hosp., Nashville, 1970-72. Served with USNR, 1942-45; ETO, MTO, PTO. Mem. Nashville Sales Exec. Counsel (pres. 1948), Nashville C. of C. (pres. 1957). Kiwanian (pres. 1947). Club: Belle Meade Country, Cumberland, Amateur Chefs Soc. (Nashville).

Home: 1616 Chickering Rd Nashville TN 37215 Office: 1101 Menzler Rd Nashville TN 37210

MULHOLLAND, ROBERT JOSEPH, JR., educator; b. St. Louis, Jan. 18, 1940; s. Robert Joseph and Margaret Agnes (Lallinger) M.; B.S., Washington U., St. Louis, 1961, M.S., 1964, D.Sc., 1968; postgrad. (NSF fellow) U. Cal. at Los Angeles, 1968-69; m. Simone Denise Adams, Apr. 15, 1972. Engr., Westinghouse Electric Corp., Balt., 1961-62; teaching asst. Washington U., St. Louis, 1962-64, 66-68, instr., 1964-66, asst. prof., 1969-72; asso. prof. engring. Okla. State U., Stillwater, 1972—. Cons., U.S. Army C.E., TRW Environmental Services. Mem. I.E.E.E., A.A.A.S., Am. Math. Soc., Sigma Xi, Eta Kappa Nu. Contbr. articles to profl. jours. Home: 1126 N Lincoln St Stillwater OK 74074

MULLEN, ANDREW JUDSON, physician; b. Selma, Ala., June 23, 1922; s. Andrew J. and Helen (Johnson) M.; A.B., Vanderbilt U., 1948; M.D., Jefferson Med. Coll., 1952; children—J. Thomas, Debbie, Gail, Andrea, Shawn, Connie, Beth. Intern, U.S. Marine Hosp., Galveston, Tex., 1952-53; resident Tex. Med. Center, Houston, 1954-57; chief neurology and psychiatry service VA Hosp., Jackson, Miss., 1957; dir. Mobile (Ala.) Mental Health Center, 1957-58; practice medicine, specializing in psychiatry and neurology, Shreveport, La., 1958—; chief female service Confederate Meml. Med. Center, 1959-63, bd. dirs., chmn. pub. relations com., 1964; med. dir. Shreveport Child Guidance Center, 1961—; mem. med. adv. bd. Extendicare Corp.; cons. psychiatry and neurology Barksdale AFB, Methodist Children's Home, VA Hosp.; chief staff Brentwood Neuro-Psychiatric Hosp., Shreveport, 1970—; asso. clin. prof. psychiatry La. State U. Sch. Medicine, 1961—. Dep. coroner, cons., Caddo Parish, La., 1964; chmn. mental health com. Community Council, 1964—. Served with RCAF, 1941-42, AUS, 1942-45. Decorated Purple Heart with oak leaf cluster, Bronze Star. Diplomate Am. Bd. Psychiatry and Neurology (asst. examiner). Fellow Am., So. psychiat. assns.; mem. A.M.A., So. Med. Assn., Shreveport Med. Soc. (dir. 1971-72), Flying Physicians Assn., Alpha Tau Omega, Nu Sigma Nu. Episcopalian. Home: 333 Berkshire Pl Shreveport LA 71101 Office: 902 Olive St Shreveport LA 71104

MULLEN, JOHN O'KEEFE, religious goods supplier; b. New Haven, Mar. 13, 1919; s. Arthur Daniel and Katherine Leola (O'Keefe) M.; grad. Phillips Andover Acad., 1936; B.Engring., Yale, 1940, M.E., 1948; m. Ann McNally, Apr. 14, 1956; children—Mark, Christopher, John O'Keefe, Kate, Desmond. Engr., Fed. Shipbldg. & Dry Dock Co., 1940-41; asso. prof. naval architecture U. Tampa, 1941-42; cons. engr. Westcott & Mapes, New Haven, 1946-51; research and devel. engr. Am. Paper Goods Co., Kensington, Conn., 1953-55; gen. mgr. research and devel. Continental Can Co., 1955-56; owner Mullen Religious Supplies, Tampa, Fla., 1956—. Active Tampa Bay Art Center, Tampa Symphony; mem. devel. council St. Joseph's Hosp., Tampa. Served as comdr. USNR, World War II. Mem. Mil. Order World Wars. K.C. Clubs: Bay Area Yale (dir.), Tampa Yacht and Country, Tampa Torch. Devel. 1st plastic lined paper cup, 1954. Home: 901 S Delaware St Tampa FL 33606 Office: 1812 JF Kennedy Blvd Tampa FL 33606

MULLENS, RICHARD ARNOLD, lawyer; b. Cheyenne, Wyo., Apr. 15, 1918; s. Arnold R. and Ada (Brook) M.; B.A., U. Wyo., 1940, LL.B., 1942; m. Barbara Nelson, Apr. 5, 1942; children—Sherry, Joan, Elizabeth. Admitted to Wyo. bar, 1942, D.C. bar, 1954; atty. Internal Revenue Service, 1946-50, legal adv. staff Treasury Dept., 1953-54; asso. firm Hogan & Hartson, Washington, 1954-60; partner firm Silverstein & Mullens, Washington, 1960—. Trustee Nat. Cathedral Sch. for Girls, Washington. Served with AUS, 1942-46, 50-52. Mem. Am. Bar Assn. (com. adminstrv. practice, sect. on taxation 1954—), Wyo. State Bar, Bar Assn. D.C. Episcopalian. Asso. editor Tax Exec. mag., 1963-71. Home: 4030 51st St NW Washington DC 20016 Office: 1776 K St NW Washington DC 20006

MULLER, BERT, assn. exec.; b. Jersey City, Dec. 6, 1926; s. Albert and Sally (O'Gorman) M.; student U. Fla., 1960; m. Rita Jean Sebacher, Feb. 23, 1957; children—Leslie Jean, David Thomas, Christine Louise, Michele Lynn, Albert John. Pres., Muller Ins., Inc., St. Petersburg, Fla., 1952-63; exec. dir Pinellas Assn. for Retarded Children, Pinellas Park, Fla., 1963—, also mental retardation planning coordinator for Pinellas County; dir. Peter Pan Sch. for Retarded Children. Mem. Day Care Adv. Com., Fla. Dept. Pub. Welfare, 1965—; mem. Gov's Conf. of Dirs., Tallahassee, 1964-65, Gov.'s Adv. Council Mental Retardation, 1967—, Gov.'s Hire Handicapped Com. Served with USNR, 1944-46. Recipient Service to Mankind award Seratoma, 1973. Mem. Am. Assn. Mental Deficiency, Council Exceptional Children, Nat. Assn. for Pvt. Residential Facilities for Mentally Retarded, Fla. Assn. Retarded Children. Rotarian, Optimist. Contbr. articles to profl. jours. Author Fla. PKU legislation. Home: 7148 9th St S St Petersburg FL 33705 Office: 3100 75th St N St Petersburg FL 33710

MULLER, CHARLES JULIUS, architect; b. Commerce, Tex., Feb. 24, 1918; s. Charles Julius and Nora Bradley (Cockerham) M.; B.S., East Tex. State U., 1938; B.Arch., Mass. Inst. Tech., 1941; postgrad. U. Tex., 1939; M.Ed., East Tex. State U., 1962; m. Linda Moody, May 18, 1943; children—Charles Julius, Jamie (Mrs. H. Jack Lassiter). Gen. mgr. Muller Ice Co., Commerce, Tex., 1945-58; pvt. practice architecture, 1946—; dir. First Nat. Bank. Chmn., Commerce Bd. Adjustment, 1967—, Housing Authority of Commerce, 1949—. Served to maj. AUS, 1941-45. Mem. A.I.A., Tex. Soc. Architects. C. of C. (pres. 1951), E. Tex. State U. Alumni Assn. (bd. dirs. 1970—), Phi Delta Kappa. Episcopalian. Lion (pres. 1951). Home: 2505 Washington St Commerce TX 71428 Office: 2507 Washington St Commerce TX 75428

MULLER, MERVIN EDGAR, data processor; b. Hollywood, Cal., June 1, 1928; s. Emmanuel and Bertha (Zimmerman) M.; A.B. in Math., U. Cal. at Los Angeles, 1949, M.A., 1951, Ph.D., 1954; m. Barbara Jane McAdam, July 13, 1963; children—Jeffrey McAdam, Steven McAdam, Todd McAdam. Instr. math. Cornell U., 1954-56; research asso. statis. techniques research group, math. dept. Princeton, also cons. IBM Corp., 1956-59; successively sr. corp. statistician, control planning asso., dept. dir. IBM Corp., 1959-62; sr. research scientist depts. statistics and elec. engring. Princeton, 1968-69; prof. computer scis. and statistics, dir. computing center U. Wis.-Madison, 1964-70, spl. asst. to chancellor for long-range planning, 1970; dir. computing activities dept. World Bank, Washington, 1971—. Chmn. adv. com. computing Princeton, 1973—; mem. adv. com. computing to gov. Wis., 1967-68; adv. panel computing Dept. Transp., 1967-70; spl. cons. Ford Found., 1964-71. Thesis fellow Nat. Bur. Standards, 1952; NSF grantee, 1968, Office Naval Research grantee, 1950. Mem. Am. Fedn. Information Processing Socs. (dir. 1971—), Am. Statis. Assn., Inst. Math. Statistics, Assn. Computing Machinery (chmn. spl. interest group univ. computing centers), Royal Statis. Soc., Am. Math. Assn., Math. Soc. Am., A.A.A.S. Contbr. books, author revs., articles, reports. Home: 5303 Mohican Rd Washington DC 20016 Office: 1818 H St NW Washington DC 20433

MULLER, NORMA MARIE ESTES (MRS. RICHARD LOUIS MULLER), social worker; b. Stuttgart, Ark., Aug. 29, 1939; d. Lloyd Tabor Estes and Beryl (Wiest) Estes Becker; student U. Colo., 1957; B.S., State Coll. Ark., 1961; M.S.W., U. Md., 1965; m. Richard Louis Muller, Aug. 7, 1960; 1 son, Richard Louis. With Balt. City Dept. Social Services, 1961-70, social worker III, Western dist., 1969-70; case work supr. Harford County Dept. Social Services, Bel Air, Md., 1970-71; clin. social worker Guidance Clinic Fla. Keys, Key West, after 1972—; now practice social work, counseling. Active Muscular Dystrophy Assn. fund drives. Mem. Acad. Certified Social Workers, Nat. Assn. Social Workers, Am. Pub. Welfare Assn., Md. Conf. Social Welfare, Alpha Sigma Alpha. Methodist (chmn. commn. Christian social concerns 1968-71, mem. adminstrv. bd. 1968-71, mem. council ministries 1969-70). Clubs: Key West Officers' Wives, Carriage Hills Golf and Country. Home: 5576 Charbar Dr Pensacola FL 32506

MULLER, RICHARD LOUIS, govt. ofcl.; b. Chgo., Jan. 26, 1935; s. Ludwig Oboe and Lilyan (Gershan) M.; student U. Ark., 1958-59; B.S. (Gilman fellow), State Coll. Ark., 1961; M.Ed., Johns Hopkins, 1965; postgrad. George Peabody Coll. Tchrs., 1965; D.Sc., London Insts., 1973; m. Norma Marie Estes, Aug. 7, 1960; 1 son, Richard Louis. Tchr. sci. Gwynn Falls Jr. High Sch., Balt., 1961-62, Balt. City Coll., 1962-65, No. High Sch., Balt., 1965-66; edn. specialist U.S. Army Ordnance Center and Sch., Aberdeen, Md., 1966-71; ednl. adviser Dept. Navy Fleet Sonar Sch. Key West, Fla., 1971-73; edn. specialist Chief Naval Edn. and Tng., Pensacola, Fla., 1973—; Mem. WEBB radio panel show Educators Look at, Balt., 1963. Mem. Edgewood Meadows (Md.) Civic Assn., 1966-71, Key Haven (Fla.) Civic Assn., 1973; Harford County (Md.) Sch. Bd. Nominating Caucus, 1968-70. Served with USN, 1953-58. NSF fellow, 1965. Recipient Chem. Rubber Co. Physics Achievement award, 1960-61, U.S. Jr. C. of C. Distinguished Service award, 1968; named Edgewood (Md.) Jaycee of Year, 1968-69, Young Man Md., 1968. Mem. Nat. Sci. Tchrs. Assn. (life), Am. Assn. Sch. Adminstrs., Am. Ednl. Research Assn., Assn. Supervision and Curriculum Devel., Alpha Chi, Phi Delta Kappa (life). Methodist (asst. ch. sch. supt.). Kiwanian; mem. Arturus. Author research pamphlets. Contbr. articles to profl. jours. Home: 5576 Charbar Dr Pensacola FL 32506 Office: Chief Naval Edn and Tng Naval Air Sta Pensacola FL 32508

MULLER, ROBERT ALBERT, educator; b. Passaic, N.J., Dec. 5, 1928; s. Albert Rudolph and Anna Helen (Jurgens) M.; B.A., Rutgers U., 1958; M.A., Syracuse U., 1959, Ph.D., 1962; m. Jeanne Valerie Underhill, Apr. 15, 1950; children—Lisa Ann, John Henry. Forest Climatologist U.S. Forest Service, Berkeley, Cal., 1962-64; asso. prof. Rutgers U., New Brunswick, N.J., 1964-69; prof. geography La. State U., Baton Rouge, 1969—. Lectr. U. Cal. at Berkeley, 1963-64, U. Del., Newark, summers 1970-73. Served with AUS, 1951-53. Mem. Assn. Am. Geographers, Am. Meteorol. Soc., Am. Geog. Soc., Am. Geophys. Union, Sigma Xi, Phi Beta Kappa. Contbr. profl. jours. Home: 865 Seyburn Ct Baton Rouge LA 70808

MULLIKIN, HARWOOD FRANKLIN, educator; b. Balt., June 27, 1908; s. Harwood F. and Ethel (Griffith) M.; B.S., Johns Hopkins, 1930; M.S., Yale, 1931, M.E., 1932, Ph.D., 1934; m. Angela Giardina; children—Patricia, Christine. Mech. engr. Gen. Electric Co., Schenectady, 1934-35; analytical engr. Babcock & Wilcox, N.Y.C., 1935-44; mech. engr. Ebasco Services, N.Y.C., 1944-47; prof. Mont. State U., Bozeman, 1947-66; prof. mech. engring. Herff Coll. Engring., Memphis State U., 1966—. Mem. Am. Soc. M.E., Am. Soc. Engring. Edn. Research in thermodynamics, heat transfer, space tech., civil def. Home: 371 N Highland St Memphis TN 38122

MULLIN, RALPH FILLMORE, assn. exec.; b. Topeka, Mar. 5, 1932; s. Ralph Waldo and Effie J. (Banghart) M.; B.A., Washburn U., 1954; m. Doris K. Reid, Dec. 26, 1954; children—Janet Kay, Judith Ann. Mgr. Wellington (Kan.) C. of C., 1958-60, Leavenworth (Kan.) C. of C., 1960-63; dist. mgr. U.S. C. of C., Sioux Falls, S.D., also Syracuse, N.Y., 1963-68; exec. v.p. Pinellas Suncoast C. of C., St. Petersburg, Fla., 1968—. Republican congl. campaign organizer, 1964, 66. Served to 1st lt. USAF, 1954-57. Named Boss of Year, Secretarial Assn., 1972. Mem. Fla. C. of C. Execs. (pres. 1974), Kappa Sigma. Episcopalian (vestryman, supt. ch. sch.). Home: 7973 10th Av S St Petersburg FL 33707 Office: PO Box 1371 St Petersburg FL 33731

MULLINAX, OTTO B., lawyer; b. Clearwater, Tex., June 28, 1912; s. Clayton Napoleon and Essie Ruth (Shelby) M.; B.A., U. Tex., 1937; LL.B., 1937; m. Ernestine Maxey, July 20, 1941; 1 son, Michael Lewis. Admitted to Tex. bar, 1937; with firm Mandell & Combs, Houston, 1938-40; sr. partner firm Mullinax, Wells, Morris and Mauzy, Dallas, 1947-71; pres. Mullinax, Wells, Mauzy & Baab Inc., Dallas, 1971-72. Dir. Capital Eye Co., 1970-72; trustee KERA-Channel 13, Dallas, 1973—. Pres. Dallas UN Assn., 1971-72. Bd. dirs. Americans for Dem. Action, 1952-71. Served to maj. AUS, 1941-46. Fellow Am. Law-Sci. Acad.; mem. Internat. Acad. Law and Sci., Dallas Trial Lawyers Assn. (pres. 1956), Tex. Trial Lawyers Assn. (dir.). Asso. editor N.A.C.C.A. Law Jour., 1952-65. Home: 11806 Cheswick St Dallas TX 75218 Office: 8204 Elmbrook Dr Dallas TX 75247

MULLINEAUX, RICHARD DENSION, oil co. exec.; b. Portland, Ore., Feb. 23, 1923; s. Lester Ray and Mary Lorene (Drew) M.; B.S., U. Wash., 1948; Ph.D., U. Wis., 1951; m. Karen Andersen, Sept. 14, 1947; children—Karl R., Marie F. Chemist, Shell Devel. Co., Emeryville, Cal., 1951-60, research supr., 1960-63, dir. gen. sci., 1968-69; with Shell Oil Co., various locations, 1963-68, 69—, asst. mgr., mfg. tech., N.Y.C., 1966-67, gen. mgr. research and devel. marketing, transp. and supplies, mfg., Houston, 1969—. Mem. Am. Chem. Soc., Catalysis Soc., Am. Soc. Advanced Sci., Sigma Xi, Phi Beta Kappa, Phi Lambda Upsilon. Patentee in field. Home: 2 Hunters Branch Houston TX 77024 Office: PO Box 2463 Houston TX 77001

MULLINS, DAVID WILEY, univ. pres.; b. Ash Flat, Ark., Aug. 11, 1906; s. Roscoe C. and Emma Matilda (Roberts) M.; B.A. cum laude, U. Ark., 1931; M.A., U. Colo., 1934; Ed.D., Columbia, 1941; LL.D., Hendrix Coll., Conway, Ark., 1965; m. Eula Elizabeth Harrell, Aug. 9, 1935; children—Carolyn Jeanne, David Wiley, Gary Eugene. Tchr. high sch. Williford (Ark.) Consol Schs., 1931-32, supt., 1932-35; supt. schs., Lepanto, Ark., 1935-41; asso. prof. Sch. Adminstrn. Ala. Poly. Inst., 1941-43, research prof. edn., 1946-47, acting dir. div. instrn., 1947-49, exec. v.p., 1949-60; pres. U. Ark., Fayetteville, 1960—. Mem. council on grad. edn. in agrl. scis. So. Regional Edn. Bd., mem., 1960—, mem. exec. com., 1966, vice chmn., 1969—; mem. Ala. Study Com., 1957-59; mem. fed. relations commn. Am. Council on Edn., 1970—, bd. dirs., 1971—; mem. So. regional panel for selection White House Fellows; adv. com. Inst. Internat. Edn.; mem. Higher Edn. Adv. Com. on Wages and Prices, 1971—; mem. adv. panel R.O.T.C. Bd. dirs. Grad. Research Center S.W.; trustee Ark. Coll., 1970—. Served as lt. USNR, 1943-46. Named Ark. Man of Yr., Ark. Democrat newspaper, Little Rock, 1969. Mem. So. Assn. Land Grant Colls. and State Univs. (pres. 1962-63), Ark. Edn. Assn., Nat. Planning Assn. (nat. planning council), Internat. Assn. U. Presidents, N.E.A., Am. Assn. Sch. Adminstrs., Ark. C. of C. (dir. 1960-63), Nat. Assn. State Univ. and Land-Grant Colls. (exec. com. 1969—, com. on fed. legislation 1970—, pres. 1971-72, chmn. exec. com. 1973—), So. Univ. Conf. (pres. 1968), Atlantic Council, Ala. Edn. Assn. (pres. 1955-56), Phi Beta Kappa, Phi Kappa Phi, Phi Delta Kappa, Omicron Delta Kappa, Phi Eta Sigma, Kappa Delta Pi, Pi Mu Epsilon, Phi Alpha Theta, Alpha Kappa Psi. Democrat. Rotarian (dist. gov. 1950-51). Contbr. articles to profl. publs. Home: 2781 Elizabeth Fayetteville AR 72701

MULLINS, JOHN WILLIAM, supt. schs.; b. Newport, Ark., Jan 17, 1921; s. John William and Trula Elnora (Mayfield) M.; student Ouachita U., 1940, N.E. Okla. State U., 1941; B.S., Ark. State U., 1949; M.A., Peabody Coll., 1953; advanced Adminstrs. certificate, U. Tenn., 1965; m. Mary Jane Foster, June 22, 1946; 1 dau., Patti Jo. Athletic dir. Illmo (Mo.) High Sch., 1949-50; coach, instr. history Corning (Ark.) High Sch., 1950-53; supt. Pucico (Mo.) Pub. Schs., 1953-55; supt. Portageville (Mo.) Sch. Dist., 1955-60; supt. Hayti (Mo.) Sch. Dist., 1960-62; supt. Newport (Ark.) Sch. Dist., 1962—. Pres. City Beautiful Com., Newport, 1968. Served with USAAF, 1942-45; ETO. Decorated Air medal, Purple Heart. Mem. Am. Assn. Sch. Adminstrs., Ark. Sch. Adminstrs. Assn. (pres.), Ark. (dir.), Newport (pres.) edn. assns., Area Methodist Men (pres.), Region 3AA Athletic Assn. (pres.), Dist. XII Activities Assn. (pres.), Phi Delta Kappa. Mason, Rotarian. Home: 4 Sue Circle Newport AR 72112 Office: Remmel Park Newport AR 72112

MULLINS, LESLIE MORRIS, lawyer; b. Coeburn, Va., Apr. 19, 1917; s. George Milburn and Willie (Boyd) M.; A.B., Emory and Henry Coll., 1940; J.D., U. Va., 1942; m. Dorothy Ann McGlothlin, June 24, 1943; children—Leslie Wayne, Michael Morris, Elizabeth Ann. Admitted to Va. bar, 1942; practiced in Norton, 1946—; mem. firm Mullins, Winston & Roberson, and predecessors, 1946—. Chmn. Eastern Wise County chpt. A.R.C., 1947-53; chmn. adv. bd. Clinch Valley Coll. of U. Va.; bd. visitors Emory and Henry Coll. Served with USNR, 1942-46. Fellow Am. Coll. Trial Lawyers; mem. Am., Va. State bar assns., Am. R.R. Trial Lawyers Assn., Norton C. of C. (pres. 1949). Democrat. Methodist. Mason, Kiwanian. Club: Lonesome Pine Country. Home: 315 Henry St Norton VA 24273 Office: Law Bldg 7th St Norton VA 24273

MULLINS, LESLIE P., city ofcl.; b. Webbville, Ky., Aug. 10, 1909; s. Fleming Lewis and Sara Jane (Pennington) M.; student Ky. Christian Coll., 1932, Law Sch., U. Balt., 1934-35, W.Va. State Police Recruit Sch., 1938; m. Judy Elizabeth Clay, July 9, 1946; children—Jane (Mrs. Robert Stephen O'Rear). With Island Creek Coal Co., Holden, W.Va., 1929-38; with W.Va. State Police, 1938-60; chief of police, Ocoee, Fla., 1960-61, Lake City, Fla., 1961—. Mem. Fla. Gov.'s Council Criminal Justice. Bd. dirs. Goodwill Industries. Region 11, North Fla. council Boy Scouts Am., 1964-72, Keep Fla. Beautiful. Served with USNR, 1943-46; PTO. Mem. Internat. Chiefs of Police Assn., Fla. Police Chiefs Assn. (pres. 1971-72), Fla. Peace Officers Assn., W.Va. State Police Retired Members Assn., Columbia County Law Enforcement Assn., Am. Legion, Fraternal Order Police, V.F.W. Mason (32 deg., Shriner), Lion; mem. Order of DeMolay (hon.). Home: 1611 S Division St Lake City FL 32055 Office: 150 N Alachua St Lake City FL 32055

MULLINS, LYNN DALTON, research physicist; b. Dallas, Feb. 18, 1923; s. William Henry and Dora (Taylor) M.; B.S., Tex. A. & M. U., 1948, M.S., 1950; m. Jimmie Beatrice O'Harro, Apr. 17, 1944; children—James William, Janet Lynn, Haskell Paul. With Mobil Oil Co., Dallas, 1950—, supr. reservoir mechanics tech. service, 1953-60, research asso., 1961—. Served with USAAF, World War II. Decorated Air medal, D.F.C. Develped world-largest passive analog computer; developed two-phase flow algorithum; developed dynamid sand detector to detect solids in flow stream. Patentee electronic instrumentation. Home: 206 Roaring Springs DeSoto TX 75115 Office: 3600 Duncanville Rd Dallas TX 75221

MULLINS, NEAL, broadcasting exec.; b. Lubbock, Tex., Jan. 28, 1946; s. Emmett Neal and Bonnie Elizabeth (Davis) M.; ed. pub. schs.; m. Edwina Boone, Dec. 21, 1972; children—Jeannia, Rene. With radio stas. KLLL, Lubbock, 1963-66, KCKN, Kansas City, Mo., 1966-69; with radio sta. WINN, Louisville, 1969—, program dir., 1972—. Home: 2833 Bexley Ct Louisville KY 40206 Office: WINN 3d and Broadway Louisville KY 40202

MULLINS, ROLAND THOMAS, educator; b. Gainesville, Ark., May 20, 1932; s. Ray Marshall and Mae Vella (McDaniel) M.; B.S., Ark. State Coll., 1956; M.B.A., U. Ark., 1957, Ph.D., 1960; m. Billie Ann Laffoon, Aug. 18, 1954; children—Joel Wayne, Gary Alan. Economist TVA, Chattanooga, 1959; chmn. dept. econs., finance Memphis State U., 1960-65; chmn. dept. gen. bus., econs. Ark. State U. at State University, 1965-69, prof. econs., finance, 1969—. Tchr., cons. bus. and banking groups. Served to sgt., USMCR, 1951-52. Decorated Purple Heart, Bronze Star. Gen. Electric Corp. fellow U. Chgo., 1967. Mem. Am., So., Ozark (pres. 1965) econ. assns., Ark. Coll. Tchrs. of Econs. and Bus. (pres. 1967), Alpha Kappa Psi, Phi Gamma Mu. Lion. Home: 1000 Sylvan Hill Dr Jonesboro AR 72401

MULLINS, WILLIAM BROWNING, finance co. exec.; b. Cin., Aug. 15, 1943; s. LeCompt Browning and Mary Louise (Clark) M.; student Internat. Data Processing Inst., 1963, Internat. Accountants Soc., 1966; m. Linda Sue Duchemin, Aug. 3, 1963; children—Michelle Lynn, Monica Lee. Computer operator Cin. and Suburban Bell Telephone Co., 1961-63; supr. data processing Robert Becht Co., Cin., 1963-64; dir. data processing Ky. Finance Co., Inc., Lexington, 1964—. Tchr. future data processors, Fayette County (Ky.) pub. high schs., 1966-69. Active youth work in field of baseball. Mem. Data Processing Mgmt. Assn., Univac Users Assn. Republican. Mem. Ch. Christ. Home: 609 Rogers Rd Lexington KY 40505 Office: 200 E Main St Lexington KY 40507

MUMFORD, LAWRENCE QUINCY, librarian; b. Ayden N.C., Dec. 11, 1903; s. Jacob Edward and Emma Luvenia (Stocks) M.; A.B. magna cum laude, Duke, 1925, A.M., 1928, Litt.D. (hon.), 1957; M.L.S., Columbia, 1929; Litt.D. (hon.), Bethany Coll., 1954, Rutgers U., 1956, Belmont Abbey Coll., 1963; LL.D. (hon.), Union Coll., 1955, Bucknell U., 1956, U. Notre Dame, 1964, U. Pitts., 1964, U. Mich., 1970; L.H.D. (hon.), Kings Coll., 1970; m. Permelia Catharine Stevens, Oct. 4, 1930 (dec. Apr. 1961); 1 dau., Kathryn; m. 2d, Betsy Perrin Fox, Nov. 28, 1969. Mem. staff Duke Library, 1922-28; acting chief reference and circulation, 1928; student asst. Columbia U. Library, 1928-29; staff N.Y. Pub. Library, 1929-45, gen. asst. charge dir.'s office, 1932-35, exec. asst., chief preparation div., 1936-43, exec. asst., coordinator gen. services divs., 1943-45; asst. dir. Cleve. Pub. Library, 1945-50, dir., 1950-54; dir. processing dept. Library of Congress, Washington, 1940-41, librarian, 1954—. Chmn. Fed. Library Com.; bd. advisers Dumbarton Oaks Research Library and Collection; mem. sponsors com. Papers of Woodrow Wilson; mem. Pres.'s Com. on Libraries, 1966-68; mem. Carolina Charter Corp.; mem. adv. commn. for publ. Papers of George Washington; chmn. ex officio Permanent Com. for Oliver Wendell Holmes Devise; mem., sec. ex officio Library of Congress Trust Fund Bd.; mem. ex officio adv. bd. Nat. Park Service's Historic Am. Bldgs. Survey; mem. ex officio Nat. Commn. Libraries and Information Sci.; mem. Lincoln Sesquicentennial Commn., 1958-60, Sci. Information Council, Fed. Council on Arts and Humanities, Nat. Hist. Publs. Commn.; mem. nat. adv. com. Am. Antiquarian Soc.; mem. U.S. com. for Am. Library Paris; corr. mem. internat. adv. com. on bibliography UNESCO.

Mem. adv. bd. Cafritz Found.; bd. regents Nat. Library Medicine; trustee John F. Kennedy Center for Performing Arts, Woodrow Wilson Internat. Center for Scholars; hon. fellow Harry S. Truman Library Inst. for Nat. and Internat. Affairs. Benjamin Franklin fellow Royal Soc. for Encouragement of Arts, Manufactures and Commerce (London). Mem. U.S. Nat. Book Com., Brit. Mus. Soc., Mass. Hist. Soc. (corr.), U.S. Capitol Hist. Soc. (hon. trustee), A.L.A. (pres. 1954-55), Ohio Library Assn. (pres. 1947-48), Manuscript Soc. (pres. 1968-70), D.C. Library Assn., Phi Beta Kappa, Omicron Delta Kappa, Beta Phi Mu. Club: Cosmos (Washington). Home: 3721 49th St NW Washington DC 20016 Office: Library of Congress Washington DC 20540

MUMFORD, LEE WARREN, banker; b. Harriman, Tenn., Jan. 18, 1941; s. John Phillip and Jane Eleanor (Becker) M.; student U. Va., 1964-66; B.S., Frederick Coll., 1964; m. Carol Mancuso, Aug. 28, 1965; children—Keith Warren, Christopher Lee. With Bank Ashland (Ky.), 1966-73, v.p., 1971-73; v.p. So. Bankshares Inc., Richmond, Va., 1973—. Mem. Ky. Citizens Commn. on Consumer Protection, 1970-71. Bd. dirs. Ashland (Ky.) Community Concert Assn., 1967. Served with USAF, 1960-61. Mem. Small Bus. Adminstrn. (regional adviser 1971—), Am. Inst. Banking (dir. Tri-State chpt. 1968-69), Ashland Jr. C. of C. (dir. 1967). Episcopalian (treas. 1971—). Home: 2110 Leavey Lane Midlothian VA 23113 Office: 2d and Grace Sts Richmond VA 23223

MUMMA, ALBERT GIRARD, JR., architect; b. Long Beach, Cal., July 2, 1928; s. Albert Girard and Carmen (Braley) M.; B. Architecture, U.Va., 1951; Medal, A.I.A., 1951; m.; children—Eugenia Suzanne, Albert Girard III, Peter Brenaman. Designer, McLeod, & Ferrara, Architects, Washington, 1951-56; asso. Deigert & Yerkes, Architects, 1956-62; prin. Mumma & Assos., Washington, 1962—. Served with USMCR, 1945-47. Recipient Design award Washington Bd. or Trade, 1964. Mem. A.I.A. Presbyn. Prin. archtl. works include; Nat. Arboretum Headquarters Bldg., 1961, Finnmark Square, Silver Spring, Md., 1964, Post Office and Fed. Bldg., Elkins, W.Va., 1971, Dept. Commerce Trade Fairs, Spain, Finland, Japan, El Salvador, USSR, 1963-72, Fallswood housing project, Falls Church, Va., 1972, Bristow Village townhouses, Annandale, Va., 1972-73, pvt. residences, Subdivision and Townhouse projects, Washington, Md., Va., Penn., 1962-71. Address: 1071 Wisconsin Av NW Washington DC 20007

MUMPHREY, ANTHONY, coll. dean; b. St. Rose, La., Oct. 9, 1921; s. Joseph and Lena (Yenni) M.; B.S., La. State U., 1943, M.S., 1949, Ph.D., 1956; m. Amelie Marie Robert, Apr. 26, 1948; children—Linda Marie, Peggy Jane, Joseph Scott, Robbie Ann, Ray Anthony, Terri Geralyn, Michael Louis, Robert Neil. Tchr. vocational agr., 1945-56; prin. Dutchtown (La.) High Sch., 1956-63; prof. La. State U., Baton Rouge, 1963-65; dean La. State U. at Eunice 1965—. World War II. Recipient hon. state farmer degree, 1965. Mem. Am., La. vocational assns., La. Tchrs. Assn., Nat. Vocational Agr. Tchrs. Assn., La. Agr. Tchrs. Assn., Future Farmers Am., Phi Eta Sigma, Alpha Tau Alpha, Alpha Zeta, Phi Kappa Phi, Kappa Phi Kappa. Rotarian, Lion. Co-author: Essential Aspects of Career Planning and Development. Home: Route 2 Box 73-B Eunice LA 70535

MUNCIE, DOUGLAS JENNINGS, physician; b. Bklyn., Oct. 8, 1916; s. Curtis Hamilton and Louise (Jennings) M.; student U. N.C., 1937-38; D.O., Kirksville Coll. Osteopathy and Surgery, 1942; M.D., Kansas City U., 1944; m. JoAnn Tenney, Dec. 22, 1966; children (by previous marriage)—Curtis Hamilton II, Douglas Newson. Intern, Orange Meml. Hosp., Orlando, Fla., 1944; practice medicine, specializing in deafness, Miami, Fla., 1946—; founder Muncie Inst. for Hearing, Miami, 1946. Served with AUS, 1945. Recipient Optimist Club award, Lakeland, Fla., 1958. Mem. Am. Acad. Osteo. Surgeons, Am. Acad. Medicine and Surgery, Dade County Osteo. Med. Soc., Am., Dade County osteo. assns. Research and publs. on treatment of deafness. Home and office: 150 NE 96th St Miami Shores FL 33138 Office: 1940 E Charleston St Las Vegas NV 89104

MUNDEN, KENNETH WHITE, archivist, editor; b. Elizabeth City, N.C., Feb. 16, 1912; s. Joshua Warren and Elizabeth Jane (White) M.; student Duke, 1929-31; A.B., Geoege Washington U., 1943; m. Lia Ghezzi, Aug. 24, 1946; children—Robin Ghezzi, Gordon Ghezzi. Statistician, War Dept., 1934-39; archivist Nat. Archives, 1939-43, 58-68; archivist Dept. Army, 1948-50, 52-57; archivist Fed. Civil Def. Adminstrn., 1958; editor Am. Film Inst., 1968-72; archival cons. Dept. Army, 1972—; historian Office Econ. Opportunity, 1972-73. Lectr. archival methodology Temple U., Am. U., 1951-68. Served with AUS, 1942-48, 51-52; lt. col. Res. ret. Recipient Waldo G. Leland prize Soc. Am. Archivists, 1963, Meritorious Achievement award Gen. Services Adminstrn., 1963; Meritorious Service award Civil War Centennial Commn., 1966; decorated Bronze Star. Mem. Internat. Council Archives, Soc. Am. Archivists, Am. Hist. Assn., Theater Library Assn., Am. Assn. State and Local History, Soc. Cinema Studies. Author: Combined British-American Records of Mediterranean Theater of Operations in World War II, 1948; Preservation of Records Essential to Continuity of State and Local Government, 1958; (with H.P. Beers) Guide to Federal Archives Relating to the Civil War, 1967. Editor: Archives & The Public Interest: Selected Essays by Ernst Posner, 1967; The American Film Institute Catalog of Motion Pictures Produced in the United States: Feature Films 1921-30, 1971. Editor, The American Archivist, 1960-68. Home: 2673 N Upshur St Arlington VA 22207

MUNDT, PHILIP AMOS, geologist, petroleum refining co. exec.; b. Sioux Falls, S.D., Oct. 2, 1927; s. John Carl and Marie Dorothy (Jacobsen) M.; B.S. in Geol. Engring., S.D. Sch. Mines, 1951; M.A. in Geology, Washington U., 1953; Ph.D. in Geology (Standard Oil Cal. fellow), Stanford, 1955; m. Lorraine Jean Blom, Dec. 12, 1951; children—Alan, Larry, Sheryl. Geologist Mobil Oil Co., Billings, Mont., 1954-58, subsurface supr., Ankara, Turkey, 1958-63, staff geologist, N.Y.C., 1963-65, exploration supr., Tripoli, Libya, 1965-67, geol. supr., Los Angeles, 1967-69, mgr. geol. and geochem. research, Dallas, 1972—; exploration mgr. U.S. Natural Resources, Inc., Menlo Park, Cal., 1969-72. Served with AUS, 1946-48. Mem. Am. Assn. Petroleum Geologists (sec. Eastern sect. 1964-65, v.p. 1965), Wyo. Geol. Assn., Dallas Geol. Soc., Independent Petroleum Assn. Am., Sigma Xi, Sigma Tau. Republican. Presbyn. Club: Woodland Hills. Home: 1221 Rock Springs Rd Duncanville TX 75116 Office: PO Box 900 Dallas TX 75221

MUNDY, ROY LEE, educator, pharmacologist; b. Charlottesville, Va., Mar. 4, 1922; s. Johnny Lee and Mary Beulah (Gilbert) M.; B.S., Howard Coll., Birmingham, Ala., 1949; M.S., U. Ala., 1950; Ph.D., U. Va., 1957; m. Maudine Taylor, Nov. 14, 1942; children—Phillip R., Mitchell L., Julia L. Joined U.S. Army, 1940, commd. 2d lt., 1942, advanced through grades to lt. col., 1960; chief pharmacology dept. Walter Reed Army Inst. Research, 1953-66, adviser to dir. on toxicology, 1955-66; ret., 1966; prof. pharmacology U. Ala. Schs. Medicine and Dentistry, 1966—. Liason mem. toxicology study sect. NIH, 1961-66. Pres. band aux. Hewett High Sch., Trussville, Ala., 1969-72. Mem. Am. Soc. Pharmacology and Exptl. Therapeutics, Soc. Exptl. Biology and Medicine, Soc. Toxicology, Radiation Research Soc., Sigma Xi. Contbr. to profl. publs. Office: Dept Pharmacology Univ Ala Medical Center Birmingham AL 35233

MUNIER, RONALD ALAN, mfg. co. exec.; b. St. Louis, Nov. 4, 1933; s. Joseph Charles and Margaret Flora (Wilde) M.; B.S., U. Miami, 1959; M.Mech. Engring., Stevens Inst. Tech., 1967, M.Mgmt. Sci., 1970; m. Mary Jane Lewis, Sept. 18, 1954; children—Jonathan Lewis, Christopher Alan, Valerie Anne. Designer, Newport News Shipbldg. & Dry Dock Co. (Va.), 1959-60; air-conditioning and refrigeration engr. York div., Borg-Warner Corp., York, Pa., 1960-63; project engr. Worthington Corp., Harrison, N.J., 1963-65; asst. chief engr., 1965-67; mgr. engring. Gamon meter div., 1967-69; v.p. engring. Gamon-Calmet Industries, Inc., subsidiary Studebaker-Worthington Corp., Florence, Ky., 1969-71, pres., 1971-73, also dir.; pres. Rucker-Shaffer div. Rucker Co., Houston, 1973—. Chmn. environmental control com. Borough New Providence, N.J., 1968-69. Served with AUS, 1953-55. Registered profl. engr., Pa. Mem. Am. Mgmt. Assn., Am. Soc. M.E., Am. Water Works Assn., Tau Beta Pi. Club: Anderson Hills Tennis (Cinn.). Patentee in field. Home: 218 Renoir St Houston TX 77024 Office: 520 Niels Esperson Bldg Houston TX 77002

MUNME, HENRY THEODORE, JR., dentist, naval officer; b. New Orleans, Sept. 22, 1921; s. Henry Theodore and Juanita Eleanore (Augustin) M.; D.D.S., Loyola U. South, New Orleans, 1945; m. Evelyn Rose Jordan, Dec. 26, 1946. Commd. ensign U.S. Navy, 1943-45, advanced through grades to capt., 1959; asst. dental officer Naval Tng. Center, Bainbridge, Md., 1945-47; pvt. practice dentistry, New Orleans, 1947-49; prosthodontist VA Hosp., New Orleans, 1949-50; sr. dental officer in U.S.S. Arcadia, 1960-61, in U.S.S. Grand Canyon, 1961-62; asst. dental officer Naval Air Sta., Pensacola, Fla., 1962-66; staff dental officer Naval Tng. Center, Kenitra, Morocco, 1966-68; asst. officer-in-charge Dental Detachment, Marine Corps Recruit Dept., Parris Island, S.C., 1968-71, officer-in-charge, 1971-72; dist. dental officer 8th Naval Dist., also sr. dental officer Naval Support Activity, New Orleans, 1972—. Mem. Am. Dental Assn., Assn. Mil. Surgeons U.S., S.A.R., S.C.V., Psi Omega. Republican. Roman Catholic. K.C.; mem. Order of Alhambra. Home: 3641 Rue Colette New Orleans LA 70114

MUNO, RICHARD CARL, museum ofcl.; b. Arapaho, Okla., July 2, 1939; s. Randolph and Julie Josephine (Jelinek) M.; certificate comml. art Okla. State U., 1959; m. Norma Faye Simpson, Oct. 14, 1960; children—Iris Amanda, Will Randolph. Preparator, Thomas Gilcrease Inst. Am. Art, Tulsa, 1960-64; curator Nat. Cowboy Hall of Fame and Western Heritage Center, Oklahoma City, 1965-69, art dir., 1970—. Sculptor Western art; lectr. art and lost wax process of casting. Trustee Nat. Acad. Western Art. Home: 6300 E Danforth Edmond OK 73034 Office: 1700 NE 63d St Oklahoma City OK 73111

MUNOZ-MORALES, LORENZO, banker; b. Bayamon, P.R., May 14, 1916; s. Carmelo Munoz and Aurelia Morales; B.S., U. P.R., 1942; m. Iris Miriam Franco, Apr. 5, 1941; children—Lorenzo, Miriam Rosa. Various engring. positions, 1942-57; dir. bus. housing coops. Coop. Devel. Adminstrn., 1957-60; asso. dir. P.R. Program of Housing for Families of Low and Moderate Incomes, 1960-61; asso. dir. P.R. Urban Renewal and Housing Corp., 1961-62; pres. Housing Bank of P.R., 1962-69; v.p. Banco de San Juan, Santurce, 1969—, mem. exec. com., 1969-74; dir. Coop. Bank of P.R., 1962-68; hon. adviser Nat. Housing Bank of Dominican Republic, 1962—. Mem. Bankers Assn. P.R. (pres. pub. relations com. 1972-73), Home Builders Assn., Financial Analyst Assn., Gen. Contractors Assn. Democrat. Roman Catholic. Rotarian (pres. 1967-68). Home: 189 Caobas Hyde Park Rio Piedras PR 00927 Office: 1205 Ponce de Leon Av Santurce PR 00936

MUNROE, CLARK CAMERON, banker; b. Cherry Tree, Pa., Oct. 27, 1925; s. Thomas William and Alice Imogene (Cameron) M.; B.S., Tex. A and M. U., 1950; grad. Southwestern Grad. Sch. of Banking, So. Meth. U., 1971; m. Virginia L. Findley, July 28, 1956; children—Michael Cameron, Martha Elizabeth. Dist. supt., sr. engr. Southwestern Bell Telephone Co., Dallas, 1954-62; dir. personnel Tex. A. and M. U., College Station, 1962-67; dir. indsl. relations Albritton Engring. Corp., Bryan, Tex., 1967-69, also dir., 1967-69; sr. v.p. City Nat. Bank, Bryan, 1969-73, also dir.; pres., chmn. bd. Guaranty Nat. Bank and Trust Co., Corpus Christi, Tex., 1973—. Vice chmn. City Planning Commn., Bryan, 1968—; chmn. City Housing Commn., Bryan, 1968—; chmn. United Fund, 1968-69; committeeman Sam Houston Area Council, Boy Scouts Am., 1969—, dist. com., 1966-68. Bd. dirs. Brazos County Indsl. Found., Crestview Home for the Retired. Served with USNR, 1943-46; AUS, 1950-54. Decorated D.S.M., Bronze Star with oak leaf cluster, Purple Heart. Mem. Assn. of U.S. Army, C. of C. (dir. 1965-68). Presbyn. (elder 1968—). Author: A History of the Second Infantry Division in Korea, 1952. Home: 6358 St Andrew St Corpus Christi TX 78413 Office: PO Box 749 Corpus Christi TX 78403

MUNROE, JAMES DOUGLAS, furniture mfg. co. exec.; b. Morristown, Tenn., Aug. 3, 1943; s. Percy Raymond and Katherine (Premny) M.; student U. Tenn., 1961-62; B.S., Carson Newman Coll., 1965; m. Sharon Lee Hux, Mar. 23, 1968; 1 dau., Ashlee Paige. With Modern Upholstered Chair Co., Morristown, 1965—, personnel dir., treas., 1965-69, credit mgr., treas., 1969-72, v.p., treas., chmn. exec. bd., 1972—. Home: Route 6 Echo Hills Morristown TN 37814 Office: PO Box 250 Morristown TN 37814

MUNSON, G. KIBBY, lawyer; b. Rochester, N.Y., May 15, 1893; s. George W. and Lena L. (Kibby) M; A.B., U. Rochester, 1914; LL.B. George Washington U., 1924; m. Grace L. Bulloch, Jan. 4, 1919; 1 dau., Marion Elizabeth (Mrs. William H. Webb, Jr.). Sec. to Rep. A. D. Sanders, 1917-27; engaged in active law practice, 1928—; spl. examiner in so-called sabotage cases before Mixed Claims Commn., U.S. and Germany (Black Tom and Kingsland fire cases), 1929-30; dep. asst. atty. gen. of Ga. to represent Ga. Pub. Service Commn. 1953-54; mem. firm Bird & Tansill, Washington. Served in USNRF, 7 mos. active duty, World War I. Mem. Am. Bar Assn., Bar Assn. D.C., Am. Judicature Soc., Internat. Platform Assn., Smithsonian Assos., Order of Coif, Phi Delta Phi, Delta Upsilon. Republican. Presbyn. Club: Columbia Country (Chevy Chase, Md.). Author legal and tech. articles. Home: 7500 Meadow Lane Chevy Chase MD 20015 Office: 1140 Connecticut Av NW Washington DC 20036

MUNSON, VERNON ARDLAND, wholesale seed co. exec.; b. Howard Lake, Minn., Mar. 13, 1918; s. Albert Wilhelm and Alice (Peterson) M.; grad. Cokato High Sch., 1935; m. Lenora Julia Gabbert, June 18, 1942; children—Vernell Lynnette, Jan. Owner retail store, Howard Lake, Minn., 1945-50; territory mgr. Northrup, King & Co., Mpls., 1951-55, sales promotion mgr., 1955-59, dist. sales mgr., 1959-70, v.p., 1970—. Served to sgt. AUS, 1942-45. Home: 1010 Cardinal Lane Richardson TX 75080 Office: 725 S Central Expressway Richardson TX 75080

MUNTNER, MICHAEL, govt. ofcl.; b. Bklyn., Nov. 11, 1940; s. Irving and Josephine (Birnbaum) M.; B.S., Poly. Inst. Bklyn., 1962, Ph.D. (fellow 1966), 1968; M.S., U. Pa., 1963; m. Judith Feldman, Aug. 24, 1963; children—Amy Laurel, Joshua Barry, Paul Matthew. Mem. tech. staff Bell Telephone Labs., Holmdel, N.J., 1962-66; cons. to Office Sec. Def., Inst. Def. Analyses, Arlington, Va., 1967-70; chief, system engring. div. Def. Communications Agy., Reston, Va., 1970-72; dir. advanced planning and research div. Automated Data and Telecommunications Service, Gen. Services Adminstrn., Washington, 1972—. Mem. I.E.E.E. (chmn. information theory group, Washington 1972—), Sigma Xi, Tau Beta Pi, Eta Kappa Nu. Home: 4 Park Overlook Ct Bethesda MD 20034 Office: 1121 Vermont Av NW Washington DC 20405

MUNYER, EDWARD ARNOLD, mus. ofcl., educator; b. Chgo., May 8, 1936; s. George T. and Martha V. (Carlson) M.; B.S. in Edn., Ill. State U., 1958, M.S., 1962; postgrad. Northwestern U., 1959-60, Ind. State U., 1965-68; m. Janet E. Tinette, Sept. 17, 1960; children—Robert, Richard, Cheryl. Tchr. pub. schs., Chgo., Elgin and Minonk, Ill., 1958-63; instr. biology Ill. State U., Normal, 1963-64; curator zoology Ill. State Mus., Springfield, 1964-67; asso. prof. sci. Vincennes (Ind.) U., 1967-70; coordinator edn. Fla. State Mus., U. Fla., Gainesville, 1970—. Dir. Vincennes Univ. Mus., 1968-70. Bd. dirs. Alachua County (Fla.) Children's Mus., 1973—. Recipient Mayor's Youth Found. award, Chgo., 1954; Gen. Robert E. Wood Citizenship award, 1958. Mem. Am. Assn. Mus., Natural Sci. for Youth Found., Wilson Ornithol. Soc., Gamma Theta Upsilon, Phi Delta Kappa. Lutheran. Editor Fla. State Mus. Newsletter, 1972—. Contbr. articles to various publs. Home: 4324 NW 31st Terrace Gainesville FL 32605 Office: Fla State Mus Gainesville FL 32601

MURAD, JOHN LOUIS, educator; b. Tyler, Tex., Dec. 15, 1932; s. Louis George and Ruby (Sawyer) M.; B.A., Austin Coll., 1956; M.S., North Tex. State U., 1958; Ph.D., Tex. A. and M. U., 1965; m. Mary Nell Deal, Aug. 15, 1958; children—John Nichols, Philip Louis, David Clay, Richard Andrew. Instr. biology Stephen F. Austin State U. at Nacogdoches, 1959-61, Tex. A. and M. U., College Station, 1961-65; mem. faculty La. Tech. U., Ruston, 1965—, asso. prof. zoology, 1967-70, prof., 1970—, research dir. Coll. Life Scis., 1971—. Served with M.C., AUS, 1953-55: Korea. U. Tex. research fellow, Galveston, 1958-59; NSF travel grantee, 1972; NATO regional sci. participant, Germany, 1972. Mem. A.A.A.S., Am. Inst. Biol. Scis., La., N.Y. acads. sci., Helminthological Soc. Washington, Soc. Nematologists, European Soc. Nematology, Am. Soc. Testing Materials, Am. Assn. U. Profs., Sigma Xi. Presbyn. (elder). Kiwanian, Mason (Shriner). Author: Laboratory Exercises in Zoology, 1967; The Laboratory in Biology, 1968; Zoology, 1971. Contbr. articles to profl. jours. Home: 1202 Robinette Dr Ruston LA 71270

MURBACH, EARL WESLEY, chemist; b. Almira, Wash., Oct. 10, 1922; s. Jack and Mary (Thompson) M.; B.Ch.E., Gonzaga U., 1943; M.Ch.E., Wash. State U., 1949, Ph.D., 1952; m. Genevieve Hollandsworth, June 10, 1948; children—Nancy, Jack. Chemist, Phillips Petroleum Co., Idaho Falls, Ida., 1954-56; chemist Atomics Internat., Canoga Park, Cal., 1956-57, supr., 1957-70; mgr. process devel. Allied Gulf Nuclear Services, Barnwell, S.C., 1970—. Served with USNR, 1943-46. Mem. Am. Chem. Soc., Sigma Xi, Alpha Chi Sigma, Phi Lambda Upsilon. Patentee preparation of uranium carbide. Home: 877 Sycamore Dr Aiken SC 29801 Office: Box 847 Barnwell SC 29812

MURCHISON, DAVID CLAUDIUS, lawyer; b. N.Y.C., Aug. 19, 1923; s. Claudius Temple and Constance (Waterman) M.; student U. N.C., 1942-43; A.A., George Washington U., 1947, J.D. with honors, 1949; m. June Margaret Guilfoyle, Dec. 19, 1946; children—David Roderick, Brian Cameron, Courtney Virginia, Bradley Duncan, Stacy Constance. Admitted to D.C. bar, 1949; with Dorr, Hand and Dawson, N.Y.C., 1949-50; mem. firm Howrey Simon, Baker & Murchison; legal asst. under sec. of army, 1949-51; counsel motor vehicle r.r. equipment, textile, aircraft and ordnance and shipbldg. divs., NPA, 1951-52; asso. gen. counsel Small Def. Plants Adminstrn., 1952-53; legal adviser, asst. to chmn. FTC, 1953-55. Served with AUS, 1943-45. Mem. N.Y., Am. (chmn. com. internat. restrictive bus. practices, sect. antitrust law 1954-55, sect. adminstrv. law), Fed. bar assns., Bar Assn. D.C., Phi Delta Phi, Order of the Coif. Republican. Episcopalian. Clubs: Metropolitan (Washington); Chevy Chase (Md.). Home: 5417 Blackstone Rd Westmoreland Hills MD 20016 Office: 1730 Pennsylvania Av NW Washington DC 20006

MURCHISON, JOHN TAYNTON, educator; b. Ft. Niagara, N.Y., Feb. 7, 1906; s. William Gaither and Lydia (Taynton) M.; A.B., U. Neb., 1927; M.A., U. Tex., 1930, Ph.D., 1933; m. C. Eleanor Carr, Aug. 25, 1932; children—John Taynton, Eleanor Susan (Mrs. Richard T. Fiala), William G. III, Mary Carolyn (Mrs. Roger M. Weed). Prof., head dept. chemistry North Tex. Agrl. Coll., Arlington, 1933-41; prof., head dept. chemistry U. Tex., Arlington, 1946-67, asst. dean sci., 1967-71, prof. chemistry, 1971—. Council pres. Girl Scouts Am., Arlington, 1948. Served as lt. col. Ordnance Dept., AUS, 1942-46. Fellow A.A.A.S., Tex. Acad. Sci., mem. Am. Chem. Soc., Res. Officers Assn., Ret. Officers Assn., Sigma Xi, Phi Lambda Upsilon, Alpha Chi Sigma. Presbyn. (deacon, elder, trustee). Author: Notes in General Chemistry, 1957, rev. edit., 1960. Home: 3207 Glasgow Terrace Arlington TX 76015

MURCHISON, JOSEPH DANIEL, archi.ect; b. Henryetta, Okla., Dec. 3, 1924; s. Monroe and Pearl May (Brendel) M.; B.Arch., Ark. U., 1952; m. Winifred Irene Lamb, Mar. 31, 1945; Draftsman, Robert E. Hucker architect, Amarillo, Tex., 1952-54; job capt. Hucker Parge, Amarillo, 1954-60; asso. John P. Work, Amarillo, 1960-64; partner Rittonberry Murchison Alexander, Amarillo, 1964-67; prin. J.D. Murchison, Amarillo, 1967-68; architect, City of Austin, 1968-69, asst. head dept. architecture, 1969—. Served with USNR, 1943-45. Mem. Constrn. Specifications Inst. (pres. 1971-72), A.I.A. (pres. 1967-68). Mason. Home: 2411 Emlglen St Austin TX 78704 Office: PO Box 1088 Austin TX 78767

MURDICK, OLIN JOHN, clergyman, ednl. assn. adminstr.; b. Dewitt, Mich., Apr. 29, 1917; s. Lester Amos and Laura Lucille (Wells) M.; B.A. in Edn., U. Mich., 1938; M.A., 1949; edn. specialist, Mich. State U., 1972. Ordained priest Roman Catholic Ch., 1948; priest Diocese of Saginaw, Mich., 1948—; supt. edn. Diocese of Saginaw, 1962-72; sec. Edn. U.S. Catholic Conf., Washington, 1972—. Mem. Nat. Catholic Ednl. Assn. Home: 4001 14th St NE Washington DC 20017 Office: 1312 Massachusetts Av NW Washington DC 20005

MURDOCK, ROBERT ALDERMAN, hist. assn. adminstr., b. Cleve., June 12, 1939; s. Robert Wilson and Alice Genevieve (Alderman) M.; student Kenyon Coll., 1957-61; B.S., U. San Francisco, 1964; M.A., San Francisco State Coll., 1968; postgrad., U. Va., 1968—; m. Deborah Dale Harrah, Sept. 15, 1962; children—Angus Alexander, Lydia Dale. Exec. dir. Assn. for Preservation of Va. Antiquities, Richmond, 1970—. Served with Intelligence Corps, AUS, 1961-64. Mem. Assn. Preservation Tech., Soc. Archtl. History. Home: Lee High Columbia VA 23038 Office: 2705 Park Av Richmond VA 23221

MURDOCK, ROBERT MEAD, mus. curator; b. N.Y.C., Dec. 18, 1941; s. Robert Davidson and Elizabeth (Mead) M.; B.A., Trinity Coll., 1963; M.A., Yale, 1965; m. Ellen Rebecca Olson, Apr. 22, 1967; children—Alison Mead, Anne Davidson. Ford Found. intern Walker Art Center, Mpls., 1965-67; mus. asst. Albright-Knox Art Gallery, Buffalo, summer 1963; curator, 1967-70; curator contemporary art Dallas Mus. Fine Arts, 1970—. Mem. Delta Kappa Epsilon. Home:

5318 Drane Dr Dallas TX 75209 Office: Dallas Museum Fine Arts Fair Park Dallas TX 75226

MURFF, CLARENCE YUALPA, JR., educator; b. Ft. Worth, Mar. 26, 1918; s. Clarence Yualpa and Evalyn (Rector) M.; student Tex. Christian U., 1935-36; D.D.S., Baylor U., 1940; m. Eldred Ferguson Wells, Jan. 17, 1945; children—Bruce Wells, Joclyn Dianne. Gen. practice dentistry, Seminole, Tex., 1940-42, Ft. Worth, 1945-47; served with USNR, 1942-45; commd. lt. comdr. U.S. Navy, 1948, advanced through grades to capt., 1955; instr. U.S. Naval Dental Technicians Sch., San Diego, 1948-50, officer-in-charge, Bainbridge, Md., 1951-54, San Diego, 1956-62, ret., 1964; prof. operative dentistry and dental anatomy Baylor Coll. Dentistry, Dallas, 1964. Fellow Am. Coll. Dentists; mem. Am., Tex., Dallas County Dental Assns., Delta Sigma Delta, Omicron Kappa Upsilon (pres.). Presbyn. (elder) Home: 9728 Lanshire Dr Dallas TX 75238

MURILLO, HERMELINDA AGUIRRE GAMBOA (MRS. JERRY MURILLO), educator; b. Laredo, Tex.; d. Alfredo and Francisca (Aguirre) Gamboa; B.A., S.W. Tex. State U., 1940, M.A., 1941, M.Ed., 1952; postgrad. U. Tex., 1965, Tex. A. and I. U., 1969-70; m. Jerry Murillo, June 2, 1941 (dec. Mar. 1968); children—Mary Elizabeth (Mrs. Miguel Flores), Gerard T., Virginia Ann, Xavier Steve, Phillip Fausto, Margaret Helen. Tchr. elementary sch. Laredo Ind. Sch. Dist., 1940-42, 44-50, 52-60, jr. high sch., 1965-68; supr. Migrant Presch. and Remedial, 1968—; tchr. Ursuline Acad., Laredo, 1960-65, San Marcos Elementary Sch., 1942-43, 51-52. Active Cub Scouts, Cancer Soc. Mem. Tex. State, Classroom tchrs. assns., Tex. Assn. Supervision and Curriculum Devel., Am. Assn. U. Women (pres. 1967-69), Laredo Hist. Soc. (pres. 1964-67), Nat. Council for Social Studies, Assn. for Childhood Edn., Internat. Reading Assn., Alpha Chi, Pi Gamma Mu. Roman Catholic (mem. Altar Soc.). Club: Womens City. Home: 1401 Mier St Laredo TX 78040

MURPHEY, MILLEDGE, educator; b. Augusta, Ga., Dec. 15, 1912; s. Milledge and Sarah Elizabeth (Pilcher) M.; B.S.A., U. Fla., 1935; Ph.D., Okla. State U., 1953; m. Grace Kathleen McLellan, Oct. 23, 1937; children—Milledge III, Edwinna (Mrs. Verley J. Spivey), Jeannine. Asst. state supr. U.S. Dept. Agr., Gainesville, Fla., 1935-37; entomologist, asst. dir. Ga. Dept. Entomology, 1937-42; state supr. U.S. Dept. Agr., Monticello, Fla., 1946-47; prof. entomology U. Fla., Gainesville, 1947—. Dist. chmn. North Fla. council Boy Scouts Am., 1963-65. Named Prof. of Year, Alpha Zeta, 1956. Served with inf. AUS, 1942-46: ETO. Mem. Ga. (past pres.), Fla. (past pres.), Am. entomol. socs., Fla. Beekeepers Assn., Sigma Xi, Phi Kappa Phi, Gamma Sigma Delta, Alpha Zeta, Alpha Phi Omega, Phi Sigma. Presbyn. (deacon). Club: Gainesville Sailing. Contbr. articles to profl. jours. Home: 725 NW 18th Terrace Gainesville TX 32603

MURPHEY, ROBERT STAFFORD, pharm. co. exec.; b. Littleton, N.C., Oct. 29, 1921; s. Henry Edwin and Mary Lillian (Sharp) M.; B.S., U. Richmond, 1942; M.S., U. Va., 1947, Ph.D., 1949; m. Mary Rebick, Jan. 25, 1946; children—Robert Stafford, Earl Malcolm. Control chemist Allied Chem. & Dye Corp., Hopewell, Va., 1942-45; research chemist Reynolds Metals Co., Richmond, Va., 1945-46; with A.H. Robins Co., Richmond, 1948—, dir. sci. devel., 1966—, asst. v.p., 1967-73, v.p., 1973—. Mem. Am. Chem. Soc., N.Y. Acad. Scis., Va. Acad. Sci., A.A.A.S., Navy League, Sigma Xi, Alpha Chi Sigma. Republican. Presbyn. Club: Willow Oaks Country. Patentee in field. Home: 2300 Chancellor Rd Richmond VA 23235 Office: 1407 Cummings Dr Richmond VA 23220

MURPHREE, MARY JUNE, newspaper editor; b. Calhoun City, Miss.; d. Stanley Thomas and June Elizabeth (Byars) Murphree; B.S. in L.S., Miss. State Coll. for Women, 1952. Reporter, Monitor-Herald, Calhoun City, 1952-55, mgr., 1955-65, editor, 1965—. Publicity chmn. Calhoun County Cancer Soc., Tb Assn., A.R.C., March of Dimes, 1952—; sec. bd. Calhoun City Library, 1959—; chmn. bd. trustees Dixie Regional Library, 1960-61, 63-64, 69; chmn. bd. Calhoun County Library, 1968—. Mem. Calhoun County Delegation to State Democratic Conv., 1955—; sec. Calhoun County Dem. Conv., 1955-59, 63-67; mem. Calhoun City Dem. Exec. Com., 1961—, sec.-treas., 1969—. Bd. dirs. Calhoun County Citizens' Council. Recipient citation D.A.V. Calhoun County chpt. for outstanding service to county and state, 1967. Colonette on hon. staff Miss. Gov., 1964-68, col., 1972-76. Mem. Miss. Press Women, Nat. Fedn. Press Women, Calhoun City C. of C. and Devel. Council, D.A.R., Miss. Library Assn., Murphree Geneol. Assn., North Miss. News Assn. Methodist. Clubs: New Century (Calhoun City), Pine Hills Country of Calhoun County. Home: 204 S Main St Calhoun City MS 38916 Office: 200 S Main St Calhoun City MS 38916

MURPHY, ANDREW PHILLIP, JR., lawyer; b. Swampscott, Mass., Sept. 27, 1922; s. Andrew Philip and Irene Mary (O'Connell) M.; A.B., Harvard, 1943; LL.B., Boston U., 1949; m. Ann Marie O'Hagen, Feb. 13, 1954; children—Sean Francis, Andrew Philip, Chrystal Ann, James Byrne, Paul Clarke. Admitted to Mass. bar, 1949. D.C. bar, 1957; practiced in Lynn, Mass., 1949-50; with Econ. Stablzn. Agy., 1951-53, Office Chief Counsel, WSB, 1951, counsel R.R. and Airline Wage Bd., 1952, alternate mem., counsel Nat. Enforcement Commn., 1953; indsl. relations adv. Office Chief Ordnance, U.S. Army, 1954; labor relations dir. Nat. Assn. Home Builders, 1954-60; pvt. law practice, 1960—. Alternate mem. Constrn. Industry Joint Conf., 1960-61; sec.-treas. U.S. Expn. Sci. and Industry, 1960—; alternate mem. Constrn. Industry Stblzn. Com., Washington, 1971—. Served as lt. (j.g.) USNR. Mem. Fed. Bar Assn. (treas. D.C. chpt. 1952-53, 2d v.p. 1953-54, nat. council 1954-59), U.S. C. of C. (labor relations com. 1955-59). Clubs: Harvard (N.Y.C.); Metropolitan (Washington); Belle Haven Country (Alexandria); Annapolis (Md.) Yacht; Farmington Hunt (Va.); Gibson Island (Md.), Gibson Island Yacht Squadron. Editor in chief Fed. Bar Jour., 1952-59; co-editor Research and Development Procurement, 1958. Home: 1815 Edgehille Dr Alexandria VA 22307 Office: 1133 15th St NW Washington DC 20005 also 40 Court St Boston MA 02109

MURPHY, CHARLES FRANKLIN, educator; b. Des Moines, Dec. 13, 1933; s. Hickman Charles and Greta (Hanmer) M.; B.S., Ia. State U., 1956, Ph.D., 1961; M.S., Purdue U., 1957; m. Carol Elva Parker, Nov. 18, 1961; 1 son, Charles Reid. With N.C. Sate U., 1960—, asso. prof. dept. crop sci., 1967—, vice-chmn. faculty, 1972. Democratic Party precinct chmn., 1970—, vice-chmn. del. to county, dist., state Dem. convs., 1970, 1972. Recipient Progressive Farmer Man of the Year in Service to N.C. Agr. award, 1967; named Outstanding Young Alumnus, Ia. State U., 1968. Mem. Am. Soc. Agronomy, A.A.A.S., Sigma Xi, Alpha Zeta, Delta Upsilon. Home: 820 Richmond St Raleigh NC 27609

MURPHY, CHARLES HAYWOOD, JR., oil co. exec., investor; b. El Dorado, Ark., Mar. 6, 1920; s. Charles Haywood and Bertie (Wilson) M.; student pub. schs., El Dorado and pvt. tutors; LL.D., U. Ark., 1966; m. Johnie Walker, Oct. 14, 1939; children—Michael Walker, Martha Wilson, Charles Haywood III, Robert Madison. Ind. oil producer, 1939-50; pres. Murphy Oil Corp., El Dorado, 1950-72, chmn. bd., chief exec. officer, 1972—; dir. 1st Tenn. Nat. Corp., 1st Nat. Bank El Dorado. Mem. Ark. Bd. Higher Edn. Bd. dirs. Oschner Found. Hosp., New Orleans; trustee Hendrix Coll.; bd. adminstrs. Tulane U. Served with AUS, World War II. Mem. Am. Petroleum Inst. (exec. com., dir.), Nat. Petroleum Council. Home: Calion Rd El Dorado AR 71730 Office: Murphy Bldg 200 E Jefferson Av El Dorado AR 71730

MURPHY, CHARLES JOSEPH, ins. broker; b. N.Y.C., June 17, 1921; s. Francis Joseph and Eva (Smith) M.; student Gen. Motors Inst., 1937-40; B.S., McNeese State U., 1973; m. M. Patricia Farrell, July 24, 1948; children—Kathleen, Clare, Frank, Daniel, Maureen, Michael, Thomas, Veronica, Christopher, Madeline. Cons. indsl. engr., Ill., Ark., La., 1952-72; economic cons., Lake Charles, La., 1973—; ins. broker, Lake Charles, La., 1972—. Served with AUS, 1943-46; PTO. Decorated Purple Heart medal. Mem. La. Engring. Soc., Am. Soc. Metals, Intrument Soc. Am., K. of C. (grand knight 1967-68, dist. dep. 1971-73). Clubs: Rotary, Optomist. Home: 1306 Louisiana Av Lake Charles LA 70601

MURPHY, CLIFFORD ELYMAN, educator; b. Blocher, Ind., Apr. 2, 1912; s. Thomas H. and Viola N. (Gobin) M.; B.A., Hanover Coll., 1936; M.S., U. Ill., 1948; Ph.D., U. Okla., 1962; m. Norma Maurine Hoock, July 27, 1940; children—Marian (Mrs. Leo W. Newland), Margaret. Tchr. pub. schs., Angola, Ind., 1936-38, Andrews, Ind., 1938-39, Whiteland, Ind., 1939-41, South Bend, Ind., 1941-46; instr. U. Ill., Urbana, 1947-48; mem. faculty Tex. Christian U., Ft. Worth, 1948—, prof. biology, 1962—. Cons. Environmental Protection Agy., Dallas, 1972-73. Adv. bd. Ft. Worth Conservation Council, Ft. Worth, 1969-73. Served to lt. comdr. USNR. Environmental Protection Agy. grantee, 1969-71, Tex. Electric Service Co. grantee, 1970-72; So. Council Univs. fellow, 1955-56. Fellow Tex. Acad. Sci. (v.p. 1964-65); mem. World Mariculture Soc., Am. Fisheries Soc., Am. Assn. Limnology and Oceanography, North Tex. Biol. Soc. (pres. 1965-66), Sigma Xi, Delta Epsilon, Phi Sigma, Phi Gamma Delta. Home: 5836 Waltham Av Fort Worth TX 76133

MURPHY, FREDERICK AUGUSTUS, virologist; b. N.Y.C., June 14, 1934; s. Frederick A. and Louise A. (Knizak) M.; B.S., Cornell U., 1957, D.V.M., 1959; Ph.D. (USPHS Postdoctoral fellow 1961-64), U. Cal. at Davis, 1964; postgrad. (Hon. fellow), Australian Nat. U., 1971-72; m. Irene May Warwas, July 2, 1960; children—Frederick III, William, John, Terence. Chief viropathology br. Center for Disease Control, Atlanta, 1964—. Cons. in viral diseases, WHO, 1968—, FAO, 1971—, Pan Am. Health Orgn., 1971—; cons. lunar sample study program NASA, 1968-72. Served to capt. AUS, 1959-61; served to comdr. USPHS, 1964-68. Mem. Internat. Com. Taxonomy of Viruses (vice chmn. subcom. 1971—), Am. Com. Arthropod-Borne Viruses, Am. Soc. Microbiology, Am. Soc. Tropical Medicine, Am. Assn. Immunologists, Electron Microscopy Soc. Am. Editorial bd. Intervirology, 1972—. Contbr. articles to various publs. Home: 2373 Briarcrest Trail NE Atlanta GA 30345 Office: Center for Disease Control Atlanta GA 30333

MURPHY, FREDERICK BRUNSON, dentist; b. Iredelle, Tex., Feb. 19, 1923; s. Frederick Brunson and Mary Annie (Cox) M.; student Auburn U., 1948-49; D.M.D., U. Ala., 1953; m. Cenus Corine Owen, Dec. 27, 1954; children—Frederick Brunson, Cenus Annie, Michele Madge. Pvt. practice dentistry, Tallassee, Ala., 1953—. Sec.-treas., dir. MMR Corp., Tallassee, 1971—; pres., dir. First Fed. Savs. & Loan Assn. Tallassee, 1962—. Finance and dist. chmn. Creek Nation dist. Boy Scouts Am., 1967-71; commr. Tallassee Housing Authority, 1967—. Vice pres., bd. dirs. Better Bus. Devel. Corp., 1968—; chmn. bd. dirs. Greater Ala. Tourist Centers, 1972—; bd. dirs. Ala. Theme Parks, 1973—. Served with C.E., AUS, 1942-46; CBI. Baptist (chmn. bd. deacons 1967-68). Mem. A.A.A.S., Am., Ala. dental assns., 2d Dist. Dental Soc., Jr. C. of C. (pres. 1955-56), Alpha Gamma Rho, Alpha Epsilon Delta, Psi Omega. Rotarian (pres. 1960-61), Mason (Shriner). Home: Box 637 Noble Rd Tallassee AL 36078 Office: Box 637 James St Tallassee AL 36078

MURPHY, GEORGE EDWARD, hosp. adminstr.; b. Conneaut, O., Dec. 17, 1910; s. Patrick Joseph and Grace Adell (Hill) M.; grad. hosp. adminstrn. program U.S. Army-Baylor U., 1951; m. Edna Marie Macht, Dec. 20, 1940; children—Judith Ann (Mrs. James R. Gibbs), David Arthur. Commd. 1st lt. Med. Adminstrv. Corps, U.S. Army, 1942, advanced through grades to col. Med. Service Corps, 1959; various adminstrv. assignments in U.S. Army hosps., 1931-44; exec. officer U.S. Army Hosp., Ft. Chaffee, Ark., 1944-45; dir. personnel Stark Gen. Hosp., Charleston, S.C., 1945; exec. officer 317th Sta. Hosp., Wiesbaden, Germany, 1946-47, med. sect. hdqrs. U.S. Forces in Austria, 1947-49, U.S. Army Hosp., Ft. Campbell, Ky., 1949-50; mgmt. officer, dir. personnel U.S. Army Hosp., Ft. Jackson, S.C., 1951-53; insp. gen. Valley Forge Gen. Hosp., Phoenixville, Pa., 1954-57; exec. officer U.S. Army Med. Group, Korea, 1957, med. sec. Hdqrs. 8th U.S. Army, Korea, 1957-58; exec. officer Gen. Leonard Wood Army Hosp., Ft. Leonard Wood, Mo., 1958-66; adminstr. Middlesboro (Ky.) Appalachian Regional Hosp., 1966—. Bd. dirs. Southeastern Ky. Regional Health Demonstration. Decorated Legion of Merit. Mem. Am. Coll. Hosp. Adminstrs., Ky. Hosp. Assn. Home: 208 Greenwood Rd Middlesboro KY 40965 Office: PO Box 340 Middlesboro KY 40965

MURPHY, KATHRYN MARGUERITE, archivist; b. Brockton, Mass.; d. Thomas Francis and Helena (Fortier) Murphy; A.B. in History, George Washington U., 1935, M.A., 1939; M.L.S., Catholic U., 1950, postgrad., 1966. With Nat. Archives and Records Service, Washington, 1940—, supervisory archivist Central Research br., 1958-62, archivist, 1962—. Lectr. colls., socs. in U.S., 1950—. Founder, pres. Am. Fedn. Govt. Employees, 1965—. Recipient commendation Okla. Civil War Centennial Commn., 1965; named hon. citizen Oklahoma City, Mayor, 1963. Mem. A.L.A., Soc. Am. Archivists (joing com. hosp. libraries 1965—); Phi Alpha Theta (hon.). Home: 1500 Massachusetts Av NW Washington DC 20005 Office: 7th and Pennsylvania Avs NW Washington DC 20408

MURPHY, MARY MARTHA, clin. psychologist; b. Peru, Ind., Oct. 14, 1909; d, Roscoe E. and June (Pence) Murphy; B.S., Northwestern U., 1930; M.A., U. Chgo., 1938, Ph.D., 1952; m. Leonard C. Lund, May 18, 1959 (dec. Mar. 1967). Tchr. remedial reading Hammond (Ind.) pub. schs., 1930-42; clin. psychologist Manteno (Ill.) State Hosp., 1945-51, So. Wis. Tng. Sch., Union Grove, 1952-53, VA Center, Bath, N.Y., 1954; chief psychologist State Colony, Woodbine, N.J., 1955-58, Kent-Sussex Mental Hygiene Clincs, Georgetown and Dover, Del., 1958-60, Southside area Mental Hygiene Clinic, Petersburg, Va., 1960-61; psychol. cons. Regional Tng. Center; mem. adv. com. U. Ala. Med. Center, Birmingham; instr. Richmond Profl. Inst. Coll. William and Mary, 1960-61; research psychologist S.E. La. Hosp., Mandeville, 1962-65; cons. St. Tammany Guidance Center, Covington, La., 1962-65; pvt. practice remedial reading and psychol. services, 1963—; chief psychologist dept. pediatrics Child Devel. Clinic, Sch. Medicine, U. Miss. Med. Center, Jackson, 1965—, asst. prof. dept. pediatrics, 1966—, mem. grad. edn. faculty, 1968—; asso. in psychology U. Miss., Oxford, 1967—. Fellow Am. Assn. Mental Deficiency; mem. A.A.A.S., Am., Miss., So. psychol. assns., Soc. Pediatric Psychology, Bus. and Profl. Women's Club (1st v.p. 1971-74), N.Y. Acad. Scis., D.A.R. Mem. Disciples of Christ Ch. Mem. Order of Eastern Star. Contbr. research studies to profl. jours. Home: 536 Woodbury Rd Jackson MS 39206 Office: Dept Pediatrics U Miss Med Center 2500 N State St Jackson MS 39216

MURPHY, RICHARD ALAN, educator; b. Twin Falls, Ida., July 4, 1938; s. Albert M. and S. Elizabeth (McClain) M.; A.B. cum laude, Harvard, 1960; Ph.D., Columbia, 1964; m. Genevieve M. Johnson, Dec. 16, 1962; children—Hayley McClain, Wendy Louisa Marshall. Postdoctoral fellow Max-Planck Inst. for Physiology, Heidelberg, Germany, 1964-66; research asso. U. Mich. Med. Sch., Ann Arbor, 1966-68; asst. prof. physiology U. Va. Sch. Medicine, 1968-72, asso. prof., 1972—. Recipient NIH Career Devel. award, 1972—; NIH fellow, 1960-64, 64-66. Mem. Am. Physiol. Soc., Biophys. Soc., A.A.A.S., Sigma Xi. Home: Turkey Run Box 262-b Keswick VA 22947 Office: Dept Physiology U Va Sch Medicine Charlottesville VA 22901

MURPHY, THOMAS S., broadcasting exec. Pres. KTRK-TV, Houston. Address: PO Box 12 Houston TX 77001*

MURPHY, WILLIAM PARRY, JR., med. corp. exec.; b. Boston, Nov. 11, 1923; s. William Parry and Harriet (Adams) M.; B.A., Harvard, 1946; M.D., U. Ill., Sch. Medicine, 1947; postgrad. Mass. Inst. Tech., 1947-48; m. Barbara Eastham, Feb. 11, 1943; children—Mary Bronwyn, Christine Clare (Mrs. John Haddon), Kathleen Ann; m. 2d, Beverly Patterson, Aug. 6, 1973. Intern, St. Francis Hosp., 1948-49; instr. Harvard Med. Sch., Boston, 1949-51; chief engr. Fenwal Labs., Framingham, Mass., 1949, 54; research fellow medicine Peter Bent Brigham Hosp., Boston, 1949-51, asst., 1953-55; with Lab. Biol. Control, NIH, Bethesda, 1951-53; research asso. medicine Harvard Med. Sch., 1953-55; dir. research Dade Reagents, Miami, Fla., 1955-57; research asst. Miami Heart Inst., 1956-68; pres. Cordis Corp., Miami and Roden, The Netherlands, 1957—, Cordis Dow Corp., Miami, 1970—. Tech. cons. John Elliott Meml. Blood Bank, Miami, 1955—; research asso. prof. biophysics, chmn. div. Med. Sch., U. Miami, 1958-70; dir. Norland Corp., Ft. Atkinson, Wis., 1972—. Served with USPHS, 1951-53. Recipient Award of Merit, Am. Roentgen Ray Soc., 1948. Mem. I.E.E.E. (sr.), Fla., Dade County med. assns., A.M.A., Am. Soc. Artificial Internal Orgns., Am. Assn. Blood Banks, A.A.A.S. Patentee in field. Home: PO Box 756 Miami FL 33133 Office: 125 NE 40th St Miami FL 33137

MURRAH, ALFRED PAUL, judge; b. Johnston County, Okla., Oct. 27, 1904; s. George Washington and Nora (Simmons) M.; LL.B., U. Okla., 1927; LL.D., Oklahoma City U., 1954; m. Agnes Milam, June 29, 1930; children—Ann, Paul, Sue. Admitted to Okla. bar, 1928; judge U.S. Dist. Ct., 1937-40; became judge U.S. Circuit Ct. of Appeals 10th Jud. Circuit, 1940, now sr. judge, dir. Fed. Jud. Center, Washington. Trustee, So. Meth. U. Recipient Distinguished Service citation U. Okla., 1954; Hattom W. Summers award, 1954. Mem. Am., Okla. bar assns., Order of Coif, Lambda Chi, Phi Alpha Delta. Methodist. Mason (32 deg.). Address: Fed Bldg Oklahoma City OK 73101

MURRAH, PAUL EDWARD, oil and gas co. exec.; b. Brady, Tex., May 17, 1933; s. Elihu and Clara (Schaefer) M.; B.B.A., U. Tulsa, 1961; M.L.A., So. Methodist U., 1973. Sec.-treas. Ormand Industries, Dallas, 1962-66; asst. controller Unitron div. Electric Machinery Corp., Garland, Tex., 1966-68; treas. Summit Energy, Dallas, 1968—; dir. Donnell Drilling Co., Dallas; gen. partner FLM Land and Devel. Co., Dallas. Served with AUS, 1954-56. Mem. Petroleum Accountants Soc. Author: Guide to Better Business Letters, 1967. Home: 7813 Royal Lane Dallas TX 75230 Office: 1925 Mercantile Dallas Bldg Dallas TX 75201

MURRAH, WILLIAM FITZHUGH, lawyer; b. Brookhaven, Miss., Nov. 6, 1889; s. William Belton and Beulah (Fitzhugh) M.; A.B., Millsaps Coll., 1908, LL.D., 1959; M.A., Vanderbilt U., 1909, LL.B., 1912, J.D., 1969; m. Corinne Falls, Apr. 3, 1918; children—William Fitzhugh, Mary Fargason (Mrs. John J. Fitzmaurice), Corinne Falls (Mrs. Paul Preston Wilson). Admitted to Tenn. bar, 1912; asso. firm Fitzhugh & Biggs (later Fitzhugh, Murrah & Fitzhugh), Memphis, 1912-50; practiced in Memphis, 1950—; head trust and title guaranty depts. Fidelity Bank and Trust Co., 1925-29. Pres. Memphis Council Americanism, 1944-51; 1st v.p., dir. Memphis Pub. Library, 1954-70, pres., 1970—; pres. Memphis Community Council, 1946-48; pres. Memphis Community Chest, 1948-50. Bd. dirs. Shelby United Neighbors, 1959; trustee, v.p. Mid-So. Found., 1952. Served as capt. U.S. Army, 1917-19. Mem. Bar Assn. Tenn. (v.p. 1960-61), Am., Memphis, Shelby County (pres. 1957-58) bar assns., Am. Judicature Soc., C. of C. (dir. 1915), Am. Legion (post comdr. 1925), Mil. Order World Wars (chpt. comdr. 1944), Vanderbilt Law Alumni (v.p.), Alumni Millsaps Coll. (dir.), Kappa Alpha, Phi Delta Phi, Sigma Upsilon. Methodist (pres. bd. trustees). Address: 8830 Hwy 72 Germantown TN 38138

MURRAY, DAPHNE NEVILLE WOOD (MRS. ROBERT NELSON MURRAY), civic worker; b. Houston, July 22, 1940; d. Robert Whitney and Elizabeth (Neville) Wood; student Finch Coll., 1959-60; m. Robert Nelson Murray, Sept. 10, 1960; children—R. Nelson, Palmer N., Daphne C. Chmn. Jr. League Well Baby Clinic, Hermann Hosp., 1967-69, mem. adv. bd., 1967-71; asst. chmn. Jr. League Ednl. and Community Research Com., 1969-70; active various community drives. Trustee Mus. Fine Arts, Houston, Houston Ballet Found., Alley Theater. Episcopalian. Home: 3455 Ella Lee St Houston TX 77027

MURRAY, FRANK STEPHEN, psychologist, educator; b. Roanoke, Va., Oct. 22, 1931; s. Monseur Stephen and Mary Elizabeth (Joseph) M.; B.S., Coll. William and Mary, 1959; A.M., Washington U., St. Louis, 1962; Ph.D., U. Ky., 1966; m. Lynda Crawford Beran, Feb. 3, 1968; children—Stephanie Angela, Frank Stephen, Rebecca Alison, Jeremy Joseph. Teaching asst. Washington U., St. Louis, 1959-60; research asst. Central Inst. for Deaf, St. Louis, 1960-62; research asst. NIH-gerontology br., Balt., 1962-63; instr. U. Ky., 1963-66, asst. prof. Evening Sch., 1966-68; asst. prof. Eastern Ky. U., Richmond, 1966-68; asst. prof. Randolph-Macon Womens Coll., Lynchburg, Va., 1968-70, asso. prof., 1970—. Cons. Edn. and Research Found., Lynchburg; participant Summer Insts., U. Mich., 1967, Mass. Inst. Tech., 1970. Served with USAF, 1952-56. Mem. Am. Psychol. Assn., So. Soc. Philosophy and Psychology, Am. Assn. U. Profs., A.A.A.S., Am. Statis. Assn., Am. Psychology-Law Assn., Va. Acad. Sci. Contbr. articles profl. jours. Home: 235 S Princeton Circle Lynchburg VA 24503 Office: Box 283 Randolph-Macon Womans Coll Lynchburg VA 24504

MURRAY, GEORGE MOSLEY, bishop; b. Balt., Apr. 12, 1919; s. Gerard Archibald and Emma (Eareckson) M.; B.S., U. Ala., 1940, LL.D., 1956; B.D., Va. Theol. Sem., 1948, D.D., 1954; D.D., U. of South, 1954; L.H.D., St. Bernard Coll., 1968; m. Elizabeth Garthwaite Malcolm, Mar. 20, 1944; children—George Malcolm, William Gerard, Sarah Duncan. With Gen. Electric Contracts Corp., Charlotte, N.C., 1940-42; ordained to ministry Episcopal Ch., 1948; chaplain U. Ala., 1948-53; suffragan bishop Episcopal Diocese Ala., 1953-59, bishop coadjutor, 1959-68, bishop Ala., 1969—, Central Gulf Coast, 1971—. Mem. exec. council Episcopal Ch., 1963-70, pres. 4th province, 1971—. Bd. regents U. of South, 1959-65, 71—. Served to lt. USNR, World War II. Recipient Algernon Sydney Sullivan award U. Ala., 1953. Mem. Kappa Alpha, Omicron Delta Kappa, Beta

Gamma Sigma. Home: 558 Cumberland Rd E Mobile AL 36608 Office: PO Box 8395 Mobile AL 36608

MURRAY, GROVER ELMER, univ. pres.; b. Maiden, N.C., Oct. 26, 1916; s. Grover Elmer and Lucy (Lore) M.; B.S., U. N.C., 1937; M.S., La. State U., 1939, Ph.D., 1942; m. Nancy Beatrice Setzer, June 21, 1941; children—Martha, Barbara Elizabeth. Research geologist La. Geol. Survey, 1939-41; geologist Magnolia Petroleum Co., Jackson, Miss., 1941-48; prof. dept. geology La. State U., 1948-55, chmn. dept., 1950-53, Boyd prof. geology, 1955-66, v.p., dean acad. affairs, 1963-65, v.p. acad. affairs La. State U. System, 1965-66; pres. Tex. Tech U., Lubbock, 1966—, pres. Tex. Tech U. Sch. Medicine, 1969—. Vis. lectr. U. Tex., 1958; mem. Internat. Commn. on Stratigraphy; mem. Am. Stratigraphic Commn., 1957-63; vice chmn., sec. Am. Commn. Stratigraphic Nomenclature, 1960-62; mem. U.S. Nat. Com. on Geology, 1963-68, chmn., 1964-68; parttime cons. geologist, 1948—; dir. NSF project basic geologic studies in Northeastern Mexico, 1958-61; mem. marine resources adv. com. U.S. Dept. Interior, 1967-69; del. Internat. Geol. Congresses, 1956, 60, 64, 68, 72; del. Internat. Com. on History Geol. Scis., Yerevan, USSR, 1967. Bd. dirs. S.W. Center for Advanced Studies, 1966-69 Internat. Center for Arid and Semi-Arid Land Studies, United Health Founds., 1966-70, Nat. Sci. Bd., 1968—, Royal Resources Exploration, Inc., Western Information Network Assn., 1967—, WHO, 1966-70. Recipient Distinguished Alumnus award U. N.C., 1971. Fellow Geol. Soc. Am. (chmn. symposium on sedimentary vols. in Coastal Plain, U.S. and Mexico, 1951, program chmn. New Orleans Meeting 1955, councillor 1961-64, chmn. ann. meeting 1967, asso. editor 1963-68), World Acad. Art and Sci.; mem. Am. Assn. Petroleum Geologists (chmn. com. geol. names and nomenclature 1952-54, editor 1959-63, pres. 1964-65, chmn. medal awards com. 1968-69, hon. mem. 1970) Soc. Econ. Paleontologists and Mineralogists (editor Jour. Paleontology 1951-54, pres. 1963-64), Am. Geol. Inst., Paleontol. Soc., Orgn. Tropical Studies (dir. 1966-69), Gulf Univs. Research Corp. (dir. 1964-69, pres. 1966, chmn. bd. 1966-67, mem. exec. com. 1965-69), Nat. Assn. Geology Tchrs., Am. Arbitration Assn. (nat. panel arbitrators), Am. Soc. Oceanography, Australian Petroleum Exploration Assn., Soc. Exploration Geophysicists, Am. Inst. Profl. Geologists, Antarctican Soc., Am. Geophys. Union, Paleontol. Research Inst., Geol. and Mining Soc., Natural Fibers and Food Protein Com. Tex., La Sociedad Mexicana de Cactologia, Cactus and Succelent Soc. Am., Norsk Geologisk Forening (life), Associacion Mexicana de Geologos Petroleros, Sociedad Geologica Mexicana, Sigma Xi, Sigma Gamma Epsilon, Omicron Delta Kappa. Author: Geology of Atlantic and Gulf Coastal Province of North America, 1961. Contbr. articles to ednl. and sci. jours. Home: 2909 19th St Lubbock TX 79410

MURRAY, JAMES EDWARD, lawyer; b. Bancroft, Ia., June 12, 1932; s. William A. and Elizabeth M. (McDonald) M.; B.A. cum laude, Notre Dame U., 1955, J.D. cum laude, 1956; m. Mary McNerney, Oct. 1, 1960; children—Kathleen M., Kerry E., William A., Susan A. Law clk. chief Judge Luther M. Swygert, Dist. Ct. No. Dist. Ind., 1956-57; asso. firm Hogan & Hartson, 1960-67, partner, 1967; v.p., gen. counsel Fed. Nat. Mortgage Assn., Washington, 1970-72, sr. v.p., gen. counsel, 1972—. Served with JAG Corps, AUS, 1957-60. Mem. Am., Ia., D.C., Fed. bar assns., Soc. Hosp. Atty.'s, Am. Judicature Soc. Home: 4706 Ft Sumner Dr Washington DC 20016 Office: Fed Nat Mortgage Assn 1133 15th St NW Washington DC 20005

MURRAY, JAMES MILTON, cons. mgmt. and industry; b. Binghamton, N.Y., Aug. 12, 1925; s. Morris F. and Mary (Petrany) M.; B.S., Am. U., 1957, M.S., 1959; m. Annelle K. Kitchen, Apr. 16, 1955. Marketing staff Remington Rand, Washington, 1952-58; cons. Beckman Instruments, Washington, 1958-60; founder Murray Asso. Inc. mgmt. and indsl. cons., Washington, 1960—. Mem. regional export expansion council Internat. Exec. Service Corps, 1946-49. Served to 1st lt. C.E., AUS, 1946-49. Mem. I.E.E.E., Assn. Computing Machinery, Am. Mgmt. Assn., Jaycees, Nat. Space Club (co-founder 1958, pres. 1968-69, bd. govs. 1973-74). Clubs: Congressional, University. Home: 1511 26th St Washington DC 20007 Office: 1625 I St Washington DC 20007

MURRAY, JOSEPH BUFORD, geologist; b. Birmingham, Ala., July 29, 1933; s. Samuel Arthur and Gladys Katherine (Crabtree) M.; B.A., U. Chattanooga, 1955; M.S., U. Tenn., 1960; Ph.D., Case Western Res. U., 1971; children from previous marriage—James Byron, Joseph Hayward. Cartographic engring. aide TVA, Chattanooga, 1955; tchr. Hamilton (Tenn.) County schs., 1955-56; asst. prof. geology and geography Grove City (Pa.) Coll., 1960-66; chief geologist, earth and water div. Ga. Dept. Natural Resources, 1969—. Sigma Xi grantee, 1968. Served as officer AUS, 1956-58. Mem. Geol. Soc. Am. (Penrose research grantee 1968), Soc. Econ. Paleontologists and Mineralogists, Ga. Geol. Soc. (treas. 1971-73). Home: 5555 Roswell Rd NE Apt D13 Atlanta GA 30342 Office: 19 Hunter St SW Atlanta GA 30334

MURRAY, JOSEPH JAMES, JR., educator, zoologist; b. Lexington, Va., Mar. 13, 1930; s. Joseph James and Jane Dickson (Vardell) M.; B.S., Davidson (N.C.) Coll., 1951; B.A., Oxford (Eng.) U., 1954, M.A., 1957, D.Phil., 1962; m. Elizabeth Hick son, Aug. 24, 1957; children—Joseph James III, Alison Joan, William Lister. Instr. biology Washington and Lee U., 1956-58; mem. faculty U. Va., 1962—, prof. biology, 1973—; co-dir. Mountain Lake Biol. Sta., 1964—. Pres. Va. Wilderness Com., 1970. Served with AUS, 1955-56. Rhodes scholar, 1951. Mem. Am. Soc. Naturalists, Am. Soc. Ichthyologists and Herpetologists, Soc. Study Evolution, Am. Genetics Soc. Club: Leander (Henley- on-Thames, Eng.). Author: Genetic Diversity and Natural Selec tion, 1973. Office: Dept Biology U Va Charlottesville VA 22903

MURRAY, MENTON JOSEPH, state legislator, lawyer; b. Dayton, O., Oct. 25, 1907; s. James Joseph and Katherine M. (Menton) M.; student Rice U., 1925-28; LL.B., U. Tex., 1931; m. Betty Marie Nosler, Dec. 27, 1938; children—Menton, Jr., Betty Marie (Mrs. Harold Patton Smith). Mng. editor Rice Thresher, Houston, 1927-28; issue editor Daily Texan, U. Tex., Austin, 1930-31; admitted to Tex. bar, 1931; since practiced in Harlingen; mem. firm McCullough, Murray & McCullough, 1957—; mem. Tex. Ho. of Reps., 1949—, dean, 1963—. Judge Municipal Ct. Harlingen, Justice of Peace, 1938-42. Chmn. Community Chest, Harlingen, 1949-50 U.S.O. Drive, Harlingen, 1943-44. County chmn. Dem. Exec. Com., Cameron County, Tex., 1946-48. Bd. dirs. U. Tex. Ex-Students Assn., Harlingen, 1947-49. Served with USNR, 1944-46. Mem. Cameron County Bar Assn. (pres. 1952-53), State Bar Tex. (committeeman 1973-74), Am. Legion. K.C. (state advocate 1940), Lion (pres. 1941). Club: Texas (pres. 1930-31) (Austin). Home: 1022 E Pierce St Harlingen TX 78550 Office: 320 E Van Buren St Harlingen TX 78550

MURRAY, RICHARD GEORGE, educator; b. Omaha, Jan. 24, 1934; s. George Roy and Margaret Leona (Ormsby) M.; B.S., So. Meth. U., 1959; M.S., U. Mo. at Rolla, 1962; Ph.D. (Pan Am. Petroleum fellow), Okla. State U., 1970; m. Nancy Lou Rhoads, Aug. 3, 1957; children—Justin Roy, George Edwin. Co-op engr. Convair Aircraft, Fort Worth, 1955-59; asst. prof. mech. engring. U. Mo. at Rolla, 1959-64; asst. prof. Western Mich. U., Kalamazoo, 1964-65; adviser mech. engring. edn. Tech. Coll., Ibadan, Nigeria, 1965-68; asso. prof., head dept. mech. power tech. Okla. State U. at Stillwater, 1970—. Pres. (v.p. alternate years), Murray Devel. Co., Camdenton, Mo., 1959—; cons. mech. equipment, engine and aircraft failure, legal firms and ins. cos. Served with AUS, 1953-55; Korea. NSF scholar, summer 1969; NSF-Am. Soc. Engring. Edn. fellow, summer 1973. Registered profl. engr., Okla. Mem. Soc. Automotive Engrs. (vice chmn. edn. 1973), Am. Soc. Engring. Edn., Sigma Xi, Kappa Mu Epsilon, Psi Tau Sigma. Author: Instructors Guide-Course in Applied Heat for 2d Year Mechanical and Electrical Students, 1968; A Student Text in Small Engines Laboratory, 1968. Contbr. articles to profl. jours. Patentee hydrogen fueled engine. Home: PO Box 398 Perkins OK 74059 Office: Sch Technology Oklahoma State U Stillwater OK 74074

MURRAY, ROBERT JAMES, architect; b. Dallas, Jan. 20, 1939; s. James Ralph and Geneva (Tindall) M.; student Arlington State Jr. Coll., 1957-59; B.Arch., U. Tex. at Austin, 1963, postgrad., 1965; m. Elizabeth Lynn McDonald, Mar. 1, 1969; children—Christine Kimberly, Scott Alexander. Draftsman, Woodward, Cape & Partners, Dallas, 1962-65, 66-67; project architect Fisher-Spillman Architects, Dallas, 1967-60; asso., land planner, architect Envirodynamics, Inc., Dallas, 1969-73; partner, dir. Travers/Johnson Architects, Dallas, 1972—. Mem. 500, Inc., fund raising for arts, Dallas, 1970—; active United Fund. Mem. Illuminating Engring. Soc. (affiliate), Dallas Inst. Architects. A.I.A., Tex. Soc. Architects. Clubs: Dallas Sports Car, Sports Car Clubs of Am. Project architect 1800 acre land planning project based on Greenbelt concept, Greenbriar, Oklahoma City, 1972-73. Home: 10836 Meadowcliff Dr Dallas TX 75238 Office: 8204 Elmbrook Dr Suite 198 Dallas TX 75247

MURRAY, WILLIAM DAVID, assn. exec.; b. Rocky Mount, N.C., Sept. 9, 1908; A.B., Duke 1931; m. Carolyn Kirby, 1930; children—Joy (Mrs. R. C. Whitman), Marilyn (Mrs. W. L. Donigan), Carol (Mrs. Marshal Happer). Coach, prin., dean boys Winston-Salem (N.C.) Children's Home, 1931-40, asst. supt., 1933-40; coach U. Del., 1940-51, dir. div. student health, phys. edn., athletics, 1945-51; football coach Duke, 1951-66; exec. dir. Am. Football Coaches Assn., 1966—. Pres. Middle Atlantic States Collegiate Athletic Conf., 1947-49, chmn. football com., 1945-47; mem. exec. council Eastern Coll. Athletic Conf., 1947-50; bd. dirs. Football Hall Fame, Named Coach of Year, Atlantic Coast Conf., 1952, 54, 60-62. Mem. Am. Football Coaches Assn. (dir. 1954-62, pres. 1962—, Amos Alonzo Stagg award 1972), Fellowship Christian Athletes (dir. 1963—, v.p. 1964-65, pres. 1967-69), Eastern Intercollegiate Football Assn. (exec. com.). Home: 3610 Hathaway Rd Durham NC 27707

MURRELL, ARTHUR VAN, assn. exec.; b. Weatherford, Tex., Sept. 6, 1929; s. William Trevor and Lota Idell (Young) M.; B.A., Tex. Christian U., 1953, B.D., 1956, M.Th., 1962; M.A. (scholar 1969-71), Vanderbilt U., 1971, Ph.D., 1972; m. R. June Coker, Dec. 23, 1949; 1 dau., Lisa Ann. Circulation mgr., reporter Riverside Jour., Ft. Worth, 1947-50; dir. YMCA, Ft. Worth, 1950-53; dir. pub. relations Tb Soc. Ft. Worth, 1953-56; ordained minister Christian Ch., 1956; student minister 1st Christian Ch., Moran, Tex., 1953-56; minister 1st Christian Ch., Henderson, Tex., 1956-59; sr. minister Ridglea Christian Ch., Ft. Worth, 1959-65; minister Central Christian Ch., Murfreesboro, Tenn., 1965-69; student minister 1st Christian Ch., Carthage, Tenn., 1969-72; regional dir. Nat. Conf. Christians and Jews, Memphis, 1972—. Adj. prof. Am. church history Memphis Theol. Sem., 1974—. Chaplain USNR. Mem. Naval Res. Assn., Tex. Christian U. Assn., Disciples of Christ Hist. Soc. Club: Cross Cut. Home: 5573 Forsyth Dr Memphis TN 38118 Office: Suite 516 Falls Bldg Memphis TN 38103

MURRELL, LEONARD RICHARD, educator; b. Stamford Centre, Ont., Can., June 17, 1933; s. James Graham and Dorothy Emma Caroline (Nightingale) M.; B.Sc., McMaster U., 1957, M.Sc., 1958; Ph.D., U. Minn., 1964; m. Marie Annette Davey, Jan. 4, 1968. Came to U.S., 1959. Instr. anatomy U. Minn., 1964-65, asst. prof., 1966-67; asst. prof. U. Tenn. Med. Units, Memphis, 1967-68, asso. prof., 1968—. Bd. dirs. Goodwill Homes for Children, 1971—, v.p., 1972, 73. Research fellow Am. Diabetes Assn., 1964-65. Mem. Tissue Culture Assn. (sec. 1970—), Am. Assn. Anatomists, Am. Diabetes Assn., Am. Assn. U. Profs., N.Y. Acad. Scis., A.A.A.S., Sigma Xi. Asst. editor In Vitro, 1970—. Contbr. articles to profl. jours. Research cell and tissue culture. Home: 1560 Galveston St Memphis TN 38114

MURROW, WAYNE LEE, educator; b. Alva, Okla., Jan. 23, 1935; s. Everett Emet and Stella (McGlothlin) M.; B.A., Bethany Nazarene Coll., 1956; student Northwestern State U., summers, 1954-55; M. Teaching in Lang. Arts, Central State U., 1968; Ph.D., Okla. U., 1972; m. Nila Arlene West, Jan. 19, 1968; children—Sherri, Randal, Cynthia, Jeffrey. Ordained to ministry, Ch. Nazarene, 1963; pastor Ch. of the Nazarene, Tex. and Okla., 1956-61; asso. minister Ch. of the Nazarene, Oklahoma City, 1961-70; teacher, dept. head Choctaw (Okla.) Pub. Schs., 1962-68; with Bethany Nazarene Coll., 1968—, asst. prof., 1968-72, asso. prof., 1972-74, prof., 1974—, grad. coordinator, 1971—. Mem. Okla. Edn. Assn., Central State Speech Communication Assn., Speech Communication Assn. Home: 2100 Flamingo St Bethany OK 73008 Office: Bethany Nazarene Coll Bethany OK 93008

MUSCHLITZ, EARLE EUGENE, JR., educator; b. Palmerton, Pa., Apr. 23, 1921; s. Earle Eugene and Ferne Estelle (Altemose) M.; B.S., Pa. State U., 1941, M.S., 1942, Ph.D., 1947; m. Barbara Pfahler, Sept. 17, 1953; children—Robert Earle, Karl William. Instr. Cornell U., Ithaca, N.Y., 1947-51; mem. faculty U. Fla., Gainesville, 1951—, prof. chemistry, 1958—, chmn. dept., 1973—. Cons. NIH, 1962-66. NSF sr. postdoctoral fellow, Harvard, 1963, U. Cal. at Berkeley, 1964; vis. fellow Joint Inst. for Lab. Astrophysics, U. Colo., 1968. Mem. Am. Soc. Mass. Spectrometry, Am. Chem. Soc., A.A.A.S., Am. Assn. U. Profs., Sigma Xi. Fellow Am. Phys. Soc., Am. Inst. Chemists. Home: 4850 NW 20th Pl Gainesville FL 32601

MUSE, MCGILLIVRAY, lawyer; b. Bridgeport, Tex., Apr. 26, 1909; s. Robert V. and Helen (Bailey) M.; A.B., Daniel Baker Coll., 1928; LL.B., U. Tex., 1931; m. Leona McKie, Nov. 9, 1935; 1 son, Marshall McKie (dec.). Admitted to Tex. bar, 1931; asso. with Judge R. E. Lee, in practice of law, Brownwood, Tex., 1931-34; mem. firm McCartney, McCartney & Muse, Brownwood, 1934-36; practiced in Brownwood, 1936-38, Dallas, 1945—; asso. firm Locke, Locke, Dyer & Purnell, Dallas, 1938-45; land owner in Limestone and Brown Counties, Tex., Atoka County, Okla. Pres. Daniel Baker Ex-Students Assn., 1932-33; bd. dirs. Brownwood C. of C., 1936-38, Dallas Big Bros., 1945-49. Mem. Am., Dallas bar assns., State Bar Tex., Beta Theta Pi. Presbyn. (elder). Mason (K.T.). Democrat. Lion. Club: Lancer. Author: Rights of Afterborn Children under Wills (12 Tex. bar jours). Home: 4400 Fairfax Dallas TX 75205 Office: 1st Nat Bank Bldg Dallas TX 75202

MUSGRAVE, RONALD LOUIS, civil engr.; b. Henderson, Ky., Aug. 1, 1945; s. Ernest Earl and Mildred Meade (Broadley) M.; B.S. in Civil Engring., U. Ky., 1968; m. Helen Bernice Stoney, Aug. 21, 1965; 1 son, Paul Martin. Resident engr. Ky. Dept. Hwys., Owensboro, 1968-72; city engr. City of Henderson, 1972-73; supt. constrn. Pace Inc., Henderson, 1973—, also dir. Instr. Henderson br. U. Ky., 1973—. Registered profl. engr., Ky. Mem. Am. Pub. Works Assn., Ky., Nat. socs. profl. engrs. Home: 2709 Flintlock Dr Henderson KY 42420 Office: PO Box 716 Henderson KY 42420

MUSGRAVE, STORY, astronaut; b. Boston, Aug. 19, 1935; B.S. in Statistics, Syracuse U., 1958; M.B.A., U. Cal. at Los Angeles, 1959; B.A. in Chemistry, Marietta Coll., 1960; M.D., Columbia, 1964; M.S. in Biophysics, U. Ky., 1966; m. Patricia Marguertie Van Kirk; children—Lorelei Lisa, Bradley Scott, Holly Kay, Christopher Todd, Jeffrey Paul. Surg. intern U. Ky. Med. Center, Lexington, 1964-65, U.S. Air Force postdoctoral fellow aerospace physiology and medicine, Nat. Heart Inst. postdoctoral fellow, 1965-67; part-time resident gen. surgery Denver Gen. Hosp., 1967—; part-time instr. dept. physiology and biophysics U. Ky. Med. Coll., 1967—; scientist-astronaut NASA, Houston, 1967—. Served with USMC, 1953-56. Mem. Aerospace Med. Assn., Aircraft Owners and Pilots Assn., Air Force Assn., A.A.A.S., Am. Inst. Aeros. and Astronautics, A.M.A., Flying Physicians Assn., Nat. Aeros. Assn., Nat. Aerospace Edn. Council, Nat. Geog. Soc., Soaring Soc. Am., U.S. Parachute Assn. Office: NASA Houston TX 77058

MUSIC, MARVIN E., oil distbg. co. exec.; b. Prestonsburg, Ky., Sept. 21, 1914; s. Sam. K. and Nora (Davis) M.; student Pikeville Jr. Coll., 1934-36; m. Florence Martin, Nov. 11, 1937; 1 son, Marvin E. Sch. tchr., Johnson County, Ky., 1937-39; asst. to county judge, Floyd County, Prestonsburg, 1939-40; service sta. operator, Prestonsburg, 1940-41; gen. foreman Curtiss Wright Corp., Columbus, O., 1942-45; pres. Marvin Music Distbr., Inc., Prestonsburg, 1946—, East Ky. Explosives, Inc., Prestonsburg; dir. 1st Nat. Bank, Prestonsburg. Mem. Ky. Park Bd., 1960-63. Chmn. Ky. Trotting Commn.; chmn. facilities com. Region 11 Mental Health; pres. Floyd County Hall of Fame, 1961-62, now dir. Bd. dirs. State YMCA, Ky. Ind. Coll. Found., adv. bd. Prestonsburg Community Coll. Named to Floyd County Hall of Fame, 1959; recipient Silver Beaver award Boy Scouts Am., 1961. Mem. Ky. (dir. 1968—), Prestonsburg (pres.) chambers commerce. Presbyn. Mason, Kiwanian (finance chmn. Ky. and Tenn. dist. 1960, gov. Ky.-Tenn. dist. 1964). Home: N Lake Dr Prestonsburg KY 41653 Office: PO Box 470 Prestonsburg KY 41653

MUSICK, FRED GRAY, lawyer; b. Winston-Salem, N.C., May 3, 1921; s. Jesse James and Beulah (Thompson) M.; A.B., Milligan Coll., 1943; LL.B., J.D., U. Tenn., 1953; m. Dorothy Jayne Wilcox, Aug. 15, 1942; 1 dau., Kathie Jane. Admitted to Tenn. bar, 1954; asso. law firm Jenkins & Jenkins, Attys., Knoxville, Tenn., 1955-60, partner, 1960—. Mem. Knox County Bd. Edn., 1972—; mem. Knox County Juvenile Ct. Adv. Bd. Trustee Johnson Bible Coll. Served with AUS, 1943-46. Mem. Am., Tenn., Knoxville bar assns., V.F.W. Republican. Mem. Christian Ch. Club: Elks. Home: 201 Sarvis Dr Knoxville TN 37920 Office: 623 Market St Knoxville TN 37901

MUSSER, A. WENDELL, physician; b. Herrick, Ill., Dec. 15, 1930; s. Purl Rhodell and Bertha (Stoneburner) M.; B.S., Purdue U., 1952; M.D., Ind. U., 1956; m. Mary Ann Lininger, Dec. 27, 1953; children—Jeri, Suzanne, Anastasia Clydia, Grant Wendell. Intern Gary (Ind.) Meth. Hosp., 1956-57; resident Ind. U., Indpls., 1957-61; chief lab. service VA Hosp., Durham, N.C., 1963-70; asst. chief med. dir. for planning and evaluation VA, Washington, 1970-74; chief of staff VA Hosp., Lexington, Ky., 1974—. Asso. prof. pathology Duke, Durham, 1963-70; prof. George Washington U., Washington, 1971—. Served with AUS, 1961-63. Dipomate Am. Bd. Pathology. Fellow Am. Coll. Pathologists; mem. A.A.A.S., Am. Assn. U. Profs., A.M.A., Am. Soc. Clin. Pathologists (dep. commr. 1968—), Internat. Acad. Pathology, Am. Assn. Comprehensive Health Planning (adviser to dirs. 1973—). Contbr. to books and jours. Home: 2036 Van List Way Lexington KY 40502

MUSSETTER, JAMES FRED, C.P.A.; b. Shawnee, Okla., Feb. 13, 1916; s. Charles Fred and Naomi (Eslick) M.; B.S. with distinction Tex. Christian U., 1948; m. Anna Marie Tucker, Dec. 24, 1956; children—Cynthia (Mrs. Stephen F. Keuneke), James Fred, David Oliver. Accountant W.A. Trotti & Co., C.P.A.'s, Ft. Worth, Tex., 1948-49; controller Dixie Chrome Products, Irving, Tex., 1949-51; exec. v.p. Southwest Investment Co., Grand Prairie, Tex., 1951-55; asst. to pres. J.B. Klein, Inc., Oklahoma City, Okla., 1955-59; pvt. practice C.P.A., Paris, Tex., 1960—; part-time instr. Paris Jr. Coll.; cons. Hosp. Acctg. and Finance; Medicare-Medicaid. Del. Tex. State Democratic Convs., 1952, 64, 68, 72; pres. Lamar Grassroots Democrats, 1972-73. Served with AUS, 1940-44. Mem. Am. Legion (comdr. 1945-46, adjutant, 1946-47, finance officer 1971-73). Democrat. Mem. Disciples of Christ Ch. Mason. Clubs: Kiwanis (pres. 1953), Optimist. Home: 2390 Crescent Dr Paris TX 75460 Office: PO Box 937 Paris TX 75460

MUSTIN, ALLISON KEITH, broadcasting corp. exec., b. Pleasanton, Tex., Mar. 9, 1941; s. Henry Keith and Lou Gene (O'Neil) M.; B.B.A., U. Tex., 1965; m. Sheila Mary Steele, May 24, 1969; children—Richard, Joseph, Allison Ann. Operations, promotion staff S.W. Republic Corp., Austin, Tex., 1964-67; with Tex. Broadcasting Corp., Austin, 1967-73; dir. sales devel. TV sta. KTBC-TV, dir. Times Mirror Co., Austin, 1973—. Cons. marketing, advt., and pub. relations, 1967—. Pres. Camp Fire Council Am., Boy Scouts Am., Austin, 1965-67. Bd. dirs. Nat. Found. March of Dimes, Austin, 1968—, Am. Cancer Soc., Austin, 1969-70, United Fund, Austin, 1971—, YMCA, Austin, 1971-72. Recipient Distinguished Service award Austin Advt. Club, 1969. Mem. Am. Advt. Fedn. (dir. 1973), U. Tex. Ex Students Assn., Phi Kappa Tau. Club: Advertising (dir. 1969-73; v.p. 1973) (Austin). Home: 2508 Lehigh Dr Austin TX 78723 Office: 119 E 10th St Austin TX 78701

MUT, STUART CREIGHTON, oil co. exec.; b. Dallas, July 27, 1924; s. Sidney Joseph and Eva (O'Connor) M.; B.S. in Elec. Engring., Rice U., 1947, M.S. in Elec. Engring., 1948; m. Mary Margaret Kampe, June 14, 1947; m. Stuart Creighton II, Stephen R., David L., Margaret E., Alan D. Asst. physicist Atlantic Refining Co. (merged with Richfield Oil Corp. to become Atlantic Richfield Co. 1966), 1948-49, adminstrv. asst., 1949-51, asso. physicist, 1951-53, sr. physicist, 1953-55, group supr., 1955-57, dir. exploration sect. research and devel., 1957-61, mgr. engring. div., 1961-63, mgr. Eastern region, Dallas, 1963—, v.p., 1966—. Served with USNR, 1944-46. Mem. Am. Petroleum Inst., Soc. Exploration Geophysicists, Dallas Geophys. Soc., European Assn. Exploration Geophysicists, Am. Inst. Mining, Metall. and Petroleum Engrs. - Soc. Petroleum Engrs. Club: Dallas Petroleum. Home: 4818 Heatherbrook St Dallas TX 75234 Office: PO Box 2819 Dallas TX 75221

MUTCHLER, CALVIN KENDAL, hydraulic engr., govt. ofcl.; b. Oceola, O., Jan. 25, 1926; s. Jesse Cleveland and Bessie Dell (Cox) M.; B. Agrl.Engring., Ohio State U., 1951, M.S., 1952; Ph.D., U. Minn., 1970; m. Margaret N. Hopper, June 9, 1951; children—Sue E., Beth E., Jan E., Leigh A., Don K., Kathryn L. Instr. U. Conn., Storrs, 1952-53; tech. man B.F. Goodrich Co., Akron, O., 1953-54; agrl. engr. Agr. Research Service, U.S. Dept. Agr., Starkville, Miss., 1954-58, St. Paul, 1958-60, Morris, Minn., 1960-72; hydraulic engr., Oxford, Miss., 1972—. Served with AUS, 1944-46. Mem. Am. Soc. Agrl. Engring., Soil Conservation Soc. Am., Alpha Zeta. Mason. Home: 216 Carol Lane Oxford MS 38655 Office: U S Dept Agriculture Sedimentation Laboratory Oxford MS 38655

MYERS, ALLEN GARVER, III, air force officer; b. Ft. Sam Houston, Tex., Dec. 16, 1932; s. Allen Garver and Sylvia Elenor (Flowers) M.; B.S. in Aero. Engring., Auburn U., 1955; M.S. in Aerospace Engring., Okla. U., 1962; postgrad. USAF Test Pilot Sch., 1963, Air Command and Staff Coll., 1966-67, Indsl. Coll. Armed Forces, 1968, Nat. War Coll., 1973-74; m. Miriam Maguire, Aug. 6, 1955; children—Allen Garver, John Gregory, David Grant. Commd. 2d lt. USAF, 1956, advanced through grades to col., 1972, test engr. Gen. Dynamics Corp., Ft. Worth, 1955, pilot, adminstrv. officer 1957-60, chief spl. activities div. fgn. tech. div., Wright Patterson AFB, O., 1962-63, chief flight test operations, test pilot aero. systems div., 1964-65, asst. squadron operations officer 20th Helicopter Squadron, Vietnam, 1965-66, squadron comdr., dep. group comdr. USAF Acad., Colorado Springs, Colo., 1967-70, weapons systems staff officer Office Sec. Air Force Legislative Liaison, Hdqrs. USAF, Washington, 1970-73. Counselor, Boy Scouts Am., Colorado Springs, Alexandria, Va., 1967—. Decorated D.F.C., Air Medal with sixteen oak leaf clusters, Commendation medal with one oak leaf cluster; recipient Outstanding Wrestling award Southeastern Conf., 1955. Registered profl. engr., Ala. Mem. Soc. Exptl. Test Pilots, Quiet Birdmen, Am. Legion, Daedlians, Sigma Pi. K.C. (3 deg.), Elk. Pioneer in devel. over water drone recovery procedures, parachute serial recovery procedure by helicopter; test pilot. Home: 4326 Gramercy Circle Alexandria VA 22309 Office: Box 98 Nat War Coll Fort McNair Washington DC 22319

MYERS, BOBBY LOUIS, financial cons. co. exec.; b. Victoria, Tex., June 10, 1935; s. Louis and Darris Bernice (Simpson) M.; B.S. in Elec. Engring., Walla Walla Coll., 1960; postgrad. U. Ala., 1963-66; m. Elizabeth Ann Ashley, June 8, 1959; children—Serena Bernice, Darren Louis. Sr. research engr. aerospace engring. research Gen. Electric Co., 1960-64, Beckman Instruments, Huntsville, Ala., 1964-65, Lockheed Corp., 1965-67; life underwriter Mass. Mut. Life Ins. Co. Huntsville, 1967-68; pres. Financial Counselors, Inc., Huntsville, 1968—; gen. agt. Columbus Life Ins. Co., Huntsville, 1968—. Served with AUS, 1954-56. Mem. Huntsville Assn. Life Underwriters, Huntsville-Tenn. Valley Gen. Agts. and Mgrs. Assn. (v.p. 1973-74), Sertoma Club (dir. local chpt. 1972—). Home: 401 Westburg Av SW Huntsville AL 35801 Office: 208 Bob Wallace Av SW Huntsville AL 35801

MYERS, CARROLL BRUCE, educator; b. Asheville, N.C., Sept. 6, 1943; s. Carroll Lincoln and Hazel (Varner) M.; B.A., Berea Coll., 1965; M.A., U. Ky., 1967, Ph.D., 1970; m. Linda Joyce Shafer, July 23, 1965; children—James Bruce, Joseph Carroll. Asst. prof. math. Austin Peay State U., 1970-73, asso. prof., 1973—. Coach Babe Ruth Baseball, 1971—; coach Jr. Pro Basketball, 1972—. NSF trainee, 1965-69. Mem. Math. Assn. Am., Nat. Council Tchrs. of Math., Tenn. Edn. Assn., Tenn. Math. Teachers Assn. Club: U.S. Chess Fedn. Home: 407 E Coy Circle Clarksville TN 37040 Office: Box 4567 Austin Peay State U Clarksville TN 37040

MYERS, DANIEL BENTON, mfg. co. exec.; b.Jackson, Miss., July 19, 1925; s. Ellis Lawrence and Emma Kate (Ainsworth) M.; student Hinds Jr. Coll., 1946-48; B.S., Miss. State U., 1951; m. Clara Dean Purvis, Apr. 23, 1943; children—Daniel Benton, James Michael, Joseph Ellis, Kathy Susan. Dir. program mgmt. Thiokol Chem. Corp., Huntsville, Ala., 1951-63, Brunswick, Ga., 1963-65; mgr. operations SPACO, Inc., Huntsville, 1965-67; mgr. engring. Vickers Inc. div. Sperry Rand, Jackson, 1968-72; mgr. Aztec Industries, Jackson, 1972—. Served with USNR, 1943-45. Registered profl. engr., Ala., Miss. Mem. C. of C. Mason. Home: Route 2 Box 55 Pelahatchie MS 39145 Office: Box 67 Plain MS 39218

MYERS, DON ARDEN, hosp. adminstr.; b. Findlay, O., Sept. 11, 1928; s. Lehr Ira and Lucille (Lance) M.; B.S., Toledo U., 1956; M.S., Northwestern U., 1958; D. Pharmacy, U. Mich., 1967; m. Dortha Jean Wilson, July 30, 1956; children—Don Arden, Dianna Kay. Adminstrv. researcher Maury County Hosp., Columbia, Tenn., 1957-58, asst. adminstr., 1958-61; asst. adminstr. Glynn-Brunswick Meml. Hosp., Brunswick, Ga., 1961—. Served with Hosp. Corps, USNR, 1948-52. Fellow Am. Coll. Hosp. Adminstrs.; mem. Am., Ga. hosp. assns., Am., Ga., Glynn County (pres. 1966-67) pharm. assns., Am., Ga., Southeastern socs. hosp. pharmacists, Ga. Acad. Preceptors in Pharmacy, Am. Bd. Diplomates in Pharmacy, S.E. Hosp. Council (pres. 1972-73), Kappa Psi, Alpha Delta Mu. Presbyn. Lion (pres. 1968-69). Home: 4323 6th St East Beach St Simons Island GA 31522 Office: Box 1518 Glynn Brunswick Meml Hosp Brunswick GA 31520

MYERS, EDNA MILDRED, supt. schs.; b. Quinlan, Okla., Jan. 26, 1908; d. Charles P. and Laura (Duncan) Mock; A.B., Northwestern State Coll., Alva, Okla., 1949; M.Ed., Phillips U., Enid, Okla., 1953; postgrad. U. Colo., Okla. A. and M. Coll.; m. Ralph C. Myers, July 29, 1933. Tchr. pub. schs. (including rural area) 28 years; county supt. of schs. Woodward County, Okla., 1953-73. Pres. county supt. dept. N.W. Dist. Okla. Edn. Assn., 1953-54, Audio-visual coordinator for 4-H Club camps, Carnegie Library Reading Programs, hosp. and adult edn., ch. schs. Organized Woodward County Future Tchrs. Club, Northwestern Okla. Pioneer Women, also Woodward County (Okla.) Tchrs. State dir. Okla. Heart Assn.; pres. Woodward County Tb Assn.; sec., dir. Mental Health Assn., 1962—; state rep. Spl. Unit on Aging; chmn. Survey for State Okla. Services to the Retarded; dir. N.W. Okla. Guidance Center, 1970—; pres. local br. Am. Cancer Soc.; treas. Woodward County Salvation Army; v.p. N.W. Okla. Regional Tb and Respiratory Disease Assn. Recipient Outstanding 4-H Leader award, 1951. Mem. N.E.A. (life), Am. Assn. of Sch. Adminstrs. (state membership chmn.), C. of C., Woodward Bus. and Profl. Women's Civic Club (past pres.), Dist. Five County Officers' Assn. (pres. 1960—), N.W. Vocational Rehab. Dept. (exec. bd.), Kappa Kappa Iota (past pres. Alpha Chi chpt.). Methodist. Mem. Rebekah, Royal Neighbor. Club: Toastmistress (pres. Woodward). Home: 512 16th St Box 907 Woodward OK 73801

MYERS, EDWIN NELSON, electronic engr.; b. Sayre, Pa., Jan. 26, 1924; s. Everett Harding and Edith (Lane) M.; B.S., Okla. State U., 1956; M.S., Mass. Inst. Tech., 1961; m. Marian Louise Engler, Aug. 29, 1944; children—Metta Lou, Mari Anne. Commd. 2d lt. USAAF, 1944, advanced through grades to lt. col., 1963; with Continental Weather Wing, 1946-54, asst. chief systems engr. Sage P.O. Air Research and Devel. Command, N.Y.C., 1956-59, research and devel. program mgr. Radar Techniques and Lasers, Pentagon, 1961-65; ret., 1965; staff asst. electronic devices and lasers Office Dir. of Def. Research and Engring., Office Sec. Def., 1965-70, staff asst. to asst. dir. electronics and phys. scis., 1971-72, staff specialist electronic scis., 1972—. Mem. I.E.E.E., Am. Radio Relay League, Mil. Affiliate Radio System, Sigma Xi, Phi Kappa Phi, Eta Kappa Nu, Pi Mu Epsilon. Home: 1010 Priscilla Lane Alexandria VA 22308 Office: Sec of Defense Washington DC 20301

MYERS, EUGENE EKANDER, art adminstr.; b. Grand Forks, N.D., May 5, 1914; s. John Q. and Hattye Jane (Ekander) M.; B.S. in Edn., U. N.D., 1936, M.S. in Edn., 1938; postgrad. U. Ore., summer 1937; M.A., Northwestern U., 1940; M.A., Columbia, 1947; advanced mgmt. program Harvard, 1953; certificate Cambridge (Eng.) U., 1958; postgrad. U. Md., 1958-61, Oxford (Eng.) U., 1964; diploma various mil. schs. Student asst. U. N.D., 1935-36, instr. summer sessions 1936, 37, asst., 1936-37; instr. N.D. Tchrs. Coll., 1938-40, Tchrs. Coll., Columbia, 1940-41; prof. U. Vt., summer 1941, 42; commd. 1st lt. USAAF, 1942, advanced through grades to col., 1951; dir. personnel plans and tng. Hdqrs. Air Force Systems Command, Washington, 1959-60, dir. personnel research and longrange plans, 1960-62, head dept. internat. relations Air War Coll., Air U., Maxwell AFB, Ala., 1962-63, dir. curriculum, dean, 1963-65, dir. res. affairs Hdqrs. Air Res. Personnel Center, Denver, 1965-66; dean Corcoran Sch. Art, Washington, 1966-69; v.p. Corcoran Gallery Art, Washington, 1970-72; art cons., vis. art dir., Palm Beach, Fla. and Washington, 1972—. Bd. dirs. World Arts Found., Columbia Sch. Art, Assos. Artists Equity. Mem. Nat. Soc. Study Communication (hon.), Speech Assn. Am., U. N.D. Alumni Assn. (pres. Washington 1959), Mil. Classics Soc., Co. Mil. Historians, St. Andrews Soc., Clan Donnachaidh (Perthshire), Mil. Order of Carabao, Order of Lafayette (dir.), Mil. Order World Wars, Delta Omicron Epsilon, Lambda Chi Alpha, Delta Phi Delta, Phi Delta Kappa, Phi Alpha Theta. Presbyn. Lion. Clubs: Curzon House (London, Eng.); Union (hon.) (Manchester, Eng.); Army and Navy, Army and Navy Country, Nat. Aviation, George Town, City Tavern, Harvard Business School (Washington); Metropolitan, Salmagundi, Wings, Explorers (N.Y.C.); Minneapolis; Beach, Sailfish of Fla. (Palm Beach, Fla.). Author: (with Paul E. Barr) Creative Lettering, 1938; (with others) The Subject Fields in General Education, 1939; Applied Psychology, 1940. Contbr. articles and reports in mags. and profl. publs. Address: 3320 Volta Pl NW Washington DC 20007 also 1 Royal Palm Way Palm Beach FL 33480

MYERS, GEORGE ANDERSON, JR., tobacco co. exec.; b. Danville, Va., June 1, 1912; s. George Anderson and Evelyn (Smith) M.; student Coll. William and Mary, 1930-31; m. Ethel Sue Boaz, June 24, 1959; stepchildren—Suzanne (Mrs. John L. Pettengill), Harry Kent Swanson III. Partner, Planters Warehouse, Danville, also Myers Warehouse, Chadbourn, N.C., 1937-42; floor mgr. Acrees Warehouse, Danville, Va., 1946-49; sec.-treas., sales supr. Danville Tobacco Market, 1949-50; pres. Neals Tobacco Co., Danville, 1951—, Danville Warehouse Co., Inc., 1966—; v.p. Neals Warehouse, Inc., Danville, 1951—; sec.-treas. United Enterprises and Developers, Inc., Danville, 1964—. Vice chmn. City Beautiful Com., Danville, 1965—; v.p., chmn. award com. Keep Va. Beautiful, 1968—; founder, pres., chmn. Nat. Tobacco-Textile Mus., Danville, 1971—. Served with Finance Corps, AUS, 1942-46. Recipient Man of Year award Kiwanis Club, 1973. Mem. Va. (chmn. agr. com. 1970-74), Danville (dir. 1952-56) chambers commerce, Danville Tobacco Assn. (v.p., dir. 1951-73, pres. 1974—), Piedmont Flue Cured Warehousemen's Assn. (founder, pres. 1972-74), Danville Hist. Soc. (v.p. 1972-73), Kappa Alpha. Methodist (chmn. bd. stewards 1971-73). Mason (32 deg., Shriner), Elk. Club: Danville Golf. Home: 432 Southland Dr Danville VA 24541 Office: 2395 Riverside Dr Danville VA 24541

MYERS, HOMER SAMUEL, synthetic fiber co. exec.; b. Salina, Kan., Feb. 20, 1916; s. Clarence Benton and Maude Mary (Booth) M.; student Kan. Wesleyan U., 1934-35; B.S., Kan. State U., 1942, M.S., 1942; m. Carol Demaree, May 30, 1966; children—Booth R., Gertrude (Mrs. Doug Hadden), Mary E. (Mrs. Jerry Martin), Homer Samuel, Jr. Sr. research staff Campbell Taggart Research Corp., Kansas City, Mo., 1942-43; mem. staff radiation lab. Mass. Inst. Tech., Cambridge, 1943-45; founder, dir., treas. Tracerlab., Inc., Boston, 1945-46, exec. v.p., dir. marketing, 1954-62; group leader Engring. Research Inst., U. Mich., Ann Arbor, 1946-48; founder, dir., pres. Radioactive Products, Inc., Detroit, 1948-54; v.p. operations Spindletop Research, Inc., Lexington, Ky., 1962-65; chmn., treas. Solvex Corp., Louisville, 1965—; pres., dir. Fibrex Corp., Humacao, P.R., 1967—. Cons., mem. adv. com. isotope and radiation devel. U.S. AEC, 1957-63, mem. labor-mgmt. adv. com., 1960-63. Mem. A.A.A.S., Phi Kappa Phi, Gamma Sigma Delta. Clubs: Pendennis (Louisville); Capitol Hill (Washington); Club Nautico De San Juan (P.R.). Patentee in field. Home: 800 S 4th St Louisville KY 40203 Office: PO Box 208 Humacao PR 00661

MYERS, IRA LEE, physician, state ofcl.; b. Monrovia, Ala., Feb. 9, 1924; s. Ira Willie and Azalea (Cobbs) M.; B.S., Howard Coll., 1945; M.D., U. Ala., 1949; M.P.H., Harvard, 1953; m. Dorothy Will Foust, Sept. 4, 1943; children—Martha Crystal, Ira Grady, Stephen Allen, Joanna Lynn. Intern, USPHS Hosp., Seattle, 1949-50; practice medicine, specializing in epidiomology, USPHS, 1950-55; adminstrv. officer Ala. Dept. Pub. Health, Montgomery, 1955-63, state health officer, Montgomery, 1963—; asst. prof. preventive medicine U. Ala. Med. Coll., Birmingham, 1958—. Sec. Ala. Bd. Med. Examiners, Montgomery, 1962—; chmn. Ala. Water Improvement Commn., Montgomery, 1963—; mem. govs. com. to White Ho. Conf. on Aging, Washington, 1960-61. Served to sr. surgeon USPHS, 1949-55. Diplomate Am. Bd. Preventive Medicine. Mem. Ala. (pres. 1963), Am. pub. health assns., Am. Assn. Pub. Health Physicians (pres. 1970), Ala. Thoracic Soc. (pres. 1960), Ala. Hosp. Assn., (hon.), Assn. Sanitarians (hon.), A.M.A., Med. Assn. Ala., Am. Acad. Gen. Practice. Baptist (deacon, trustee). Home: 925 Green Forest Dr Montgomery AL 36109 Office: 501 Dexter Av Montgomery AL 36104

MYERS, JAMES CLARK, advt. exec.; b. Chgo., Aug. 26, 1941; s. Herbert George and Lenore Levi (Goldberg) M.; B.A., Washington U., St. Louis, 1964; m. Judy Schnitzer, Feb. 9, 1964; children—Jeffrey Stephan, Jeremy H. Account exec. Nahas, Blumberg, Zelikow Advt. Agy., Houston, 1967-69; mgr. spl. events Houston Post, Houston, 1969-73; pres. Motivators, Inc., pub. relations, Houston, 1972—. Vice chmn. Internat. Sci. and Engring. Fair Council, Washington, 1972-73; dir. Sci. Engring. Fair Houston, 1969-73, Spring Art Festival, 1969-73. Mem. Houston C. of C., Pub. Relations Soc. Am. (accredited), Jewish Community Council. Jewish religion. Home: 7014 Pyron Way Houston TX 77036 Office: PO Box 42555 Houston TX 77042

MYERS, JAMES FRANCIS, safety systems mfg. co. exec.; b. Plattsburg, Mo., Dec. 2, 1913; s. Frank Marion and Margaret (Glenn) M.; B.S. in Bus. Adminstrn., Mo. Wesleyan Coll., Cameron, 1935; m. Marjorie Anderson, Oct. 27, 1939; 1 son, James Lee. From oil field product trainee to v.p., gen. mgr. Black, Sivalls & Bryson, Inc. (name now B.S. & B. Safety Systems, Inc.), Tulsa. Served with USNR. Mem. Am. Inst. Chem. Engrs., Am. Petroleum Inst. (mem. mfrs. subcom.), Tulsa C. of C. Club: Petroleum (Tulsa). Patentee in field testing of valves with reverse buckling disc installed at valve inlet. Contbr. tech. papers to profl. jours.; lectr. on application of safety devices to pressure systems. Home: 4870 E 68th St Apt 233 Tulsa OK 74136 Office: 7455 E 46th St Tulsa OK 74145

MYERS, KENNETH MORTON, state senator; b. Miami, Fla., Mar. 11, 1933; s. Stanley C. and Martha (Scheinberg) M.; A.B., U. N.C., 1954; LL.B., U. Fla., 1957. Admitted to Fla. bar, 1957; practiced in Miami, 1957—; mem. Fla. Ho. of Reps., 1965-69; mem. Fla. State Senate, 1969—, chmn. ways and means subcom., chmn. health and rehab. services com., vice chmn. criminal justice com. Bd. dirs. Dade County Children's Psychiat. Center, Am. Assn. Comprehensive Health Planning. Mem. Am., Dade County bar assns., Dade County Jr. Bar Assn., Miami-Dade C. of C. Home: 2451 Brickell Av Miami FL 33129 Office: 1428 Brickell Av Miami FL 33131

MYERS, LAWRENCE, agrl. economist, mayor; b. Humboldt, Ia., July 14, 1898; s. George A. and Mary (Barrett) M.; B.S., U. Minn., 1922, postgrad., 1923-27; M.S., Ia. State Coll., 1923; m. Anne Cornelia Henkel, July 15, 1924; children—Margaret Mary (Mrs. James J. Rast), Dorothy Helen (Mrs. James G. Sampas). Instr. agrl. econs. U. Minn., St. Paul, 1925-27; economist Bur. Agr. Econs., U.S. Dept. Agr., Washington, 1927-33; economist, div. dir.. A.A.A., Washington, 1933-39; div. dir. CCC, Washington, 1939-46; dir. textiles and raw materials UNNRA, Washington, 1946; asst. to sec. agr., Washington, 1946; dir. sugar div. U.S. Dept. Agr., Washington, 1947-63; chmn. bd. Nat. Molasses Corp., Washington, 1963-68; Washington rep. C. Brewer & Affiliates, 1968-71; econ. cons., 1972—. Chmn. Internat. Sugar Council, 1955. Served with U.S. Army, 1918. Recipient certificate of merit Dept. Agr., 3 times, Distinguished Service award, 1955. Republican. Clubs: Cosmos (Washington); Potomac (Md.) Hunt. Home: 5530 Friendship Blvd Chevy Chase MD 20015 Office: 1001 Connecticut Av NW Washington DC 20036

MYERS, MELVIL BERT, physician; b. New Orleans, Sept. 12, 1928; s. Melvil B. and Mildred Annette (Bauer) M.; student U. N.C., 1945-47; M.D., Tulane U., 1951; m. Joel Grossman, Dec. 18, 1954; children—Brad, Melanie, Eve. Intern Touro Infirmary, New Orleans, 1951-52, resident, surgery, 1952-55; practice medicine specializing in surgery, New Orleans, 1957-71; staff physician VA Hosp., New Orleans, 1971—; asso. prof. surgery La. State U. Sch. Medicine, 1971—. Served with USPHS, 1955-57. Diplomate Am. Bd. Surgery. Mem. So. Surg. Assn., Plastic Surgery Research Council, A.C.S., Southeastern Surg. Contress, N.Y. Acad. Sci. Contbr. articles to profl. jours. Home: 21 Newcomb Blvd New Orleans LA 70118 Office: 1601 Perdido St New Orleans LA 70146

MYERS, PAUL FREDRICK, govt. ofcl.; b. Turtle Creek, Pa., Dec. 17, 1916; s. Joseph A. and Elizabeth (Reinkemeyer) M.; B.A. magna cum laude, U. Ala., 1941; postgrad. Am. U., 1946-48;; m. Alice Christine Fuls, Nov. 24, 1941; children—David, Christine. Chemist, E. I. du Pont de Nemours, Memphis, 1941-44; statistician, VA, Dept. Navy, U.S. Bur. Census, 1946-62; chief fgn. demographic analysis div. U.S. Bur. Census, Washington, 1962—. Served with AUS, 1943-46. Mem. Population Assn. Am., Internat. Union for Sci. Study Population, Am. Sociol. Assn., Am. Statis. Assn. Author: (with W. Parker Mauldin) The Population of the Federal Republic of Germany and West Berlin, 1952; (with Arthur A. Campbell) The Population of Yugoslavia, 1954. Home: 12811 Crisfield Rd Silver Spring MD 20906 Office: 2400 M St NW Washington DC 20230

MYERS, RANDOLPH PETER, architect; b. Atlanta, Nov. 1, 1941; s. Alfred Leon and Janette Dorothea (Morris) M.; B.Arch., Tex. A. and M. U., 1965; m. Gerry Lynn Golden, Aug. 30, 1964; children—Richard Scott, Deborah Ruth, Kenneth Andrew. Architect, Rucker and Chamlee, Architects, Temple, Tex., 1965-66, Pratt, Box and Henderson, Architects, Dallas, 1966-67, Woodward, Cape and Partners, architects, 1967-70, Marvin E. Beck and Assos., 1970-72; architect Bldg. Services dept. City of Dallas, 1972—. Cons. to Tex. Hosp. Supply Corp., Dallas, 1972—. Mem. A.I.A., Tex. Soc. Architects. Prin. works: Empire Gardens South Office Bldg., 1969, Regal Gardens Office Complex, 1971, Royal Gardens Office Bldg., 1971, Stanley Supply Co. Office and Warehouse, 1971, Greenwood Inn (all Dallas). Home: 6812 St Anne St Dallas TX 75240 Office: 1500 W Mockingbird Lane Dallas TX 75235

MYERS, WILBUR JAY, mech. engr.; b. Bay City, Tex., Jan. 24, 1932; s. Oliver Allen and Wilma Ann (Hanna) M.; B.S., U. Ark., 1960; M.S., U. Tulsa, 1970; m. Olive Ann Munday, Aug. 31, 1958; children—Nancy, Karen, Robert, David. Cons., Planning Research Corp., Los Angeles, 1962-64; sr. design engr. N.Am. Rockwell Corp., Tulsa, 1964-71; pres. Century Devel. Co., Inc., Bentonville, Ark., 1971-73; chief engr., mgr. quality control Hoyt Corp., Rogers, Ark., 1973—. Mem. Bentonville Planning Commn., 1973—. Served with AUS, 1954-56. Registered profl. engr., Ark., Okla. Presbyn. Club: Early Ford V8. Home: 1607 Robinhood Rd Bentonville AR 72712 Office: 1203 N 6th St Rogers AR 72756

MYERS, WILLIAM HUNTER, ret. oceanographer; b. Cumberland, Md., June 28, 1922; s. Hunter Lee and Helen (Merrbaugh) M.; B.S., U. Md., 1943, M.S., 1948, postgrad., 1948-51. Oceanographer, U.S. Naval Oceanographic Office, Washington, 1951-60; oceanographer Nat. Oceanographic Data Center, Washington, 1961-62, dir. quality control div., 1962-67, dir. devel. div., 1968-72. Served with AUS, 1944-46. Home: 313 E St NE Washington DC 20002

MYNETT, JACK WILLIAM, corp. exec.; b. Council Bluffs, Ia., Aug. 7, 1924; s. Charles William and Edna (Burke) M.; B.B.A., So. Methodist U., 1949, M.B.A., 1951; m. Jo Nell Stubblefield, Mar. 1, 1946; children—Judy Lynne, Charles William II. Dir. personnel Hartford Ins. Group, Dallas, 1951-63; v.p. planning, devel. and gen. services Gulf Ins. Group, Dallas, 1963-68; sr. v.p., dir. UCC Financial Corp., 1968-72; resident mgr. Boyden Assos., Inc., 1972-73; pres. Jack W. Mynett & Assos., 1973—. Active various community drives. Trustee, Amigos de las Ams., 1971—. Served with AUS, 1942-46. Mem. Adminstrv. Mgmt. Soc. (Diamond Merit award 1967, Mem. of Year Dallas chpt. 1965, internat. v.p.-treas. 1967-68, chpt. pres. 1964-65), Dallas Mgmt. Assn. (pres. 1963-64), Dallas Personnel Assn. (pres. 1963-64), So. Methodist U. Bus. Sch. Alumni Assn. (pres. 1957), Dallas C. of C. (pres., life mem. club 1965-66, Triple Life mem. 1962, 63, 67). Address: 4308 Alta Vista Lane Dallas TX 75229

MYRBERG, ARTHUR AUGUST, JR., educator; b. Chicago Heights, Ill., June 28, 1933; s. Arthur August and Helen Katherine (Stelle) M.; A.B., Ripon Coll., 1954; M.S., U. Ill., 1958; Ph.D., U. Cal. at Los Angeles, 1961; m. Sue Smith, Nov. 24, 1973; children by previous marriage—Arthur August III, Beverly Priscilla. Research asst. Ill. Natural History Survey, Champaign-Urbana, 1957; mem. faculty U. Miami (Fla.), 1964—, asso. prof. Sch. Marine and Atmospheric Sci., 1967-72, prof., 1972—. Mem. Khoury League, 1967—. Served to 1st lt., inf. AUS, 1954-57. NIH postdoctoral fellow Max Planck Inst Behavioral Physiology, Seewiesen, Germany, 1961-64. Mem. Animal Behavior Soc., Am. Soc. Ichthyologists and Herpetologists, Am. Soc. Zoologists, Ecol. Soc. Am., Am. Inst. Biol. Scis., N.Y. Acad. Scis. Contbr. profl. jours. Asst. editor Bull. Marine Sci., 1964—. Home: 6001 SW 65th Av Miami FL 33143

NAAMANI, ISRAEL TARKOW, educator; b. Zhitomir, Russia, Nov. 3, 1912; s. Peter and Sarah (Sheriff) T.; Ph.B., Marquette U., 1935; postgrad. U. Chgo., 1937, 39; M.A., Ind. U., 1943, Ph.D., 1945; m. Zehava Rabitcher, June 30, 1940; children—Roanete (Mrs. E.A. Goldman), Aviv. Naturalized U.S. citizen, 1937. Mem. faculty U. Louisville, 1949—, prof. polit. sci., 1964—, chmn. dept., 1971—. Vice pres. Nat. Council Jewish Edn., N.Y.C., 1958-60. Fellow Middle East Studies Assn., Middle East Inst.; mem. Nat. Assn. Profs. Hebrew in Am. Instns. Higher Learning (pres. 1962-64). Author: Nefilm Bamaaran (in Hebrew), 1968; Israel; A Profile, 1972; other books. Co-editor: Israel Through the Eyes of its Leaders, 1971; editor: Hebrew Abstracts. Contbg. editor Ency. Judaica, 1971. Contbr. articles to profl. jours. Home: 2804 Lime Kiln Lane Louisville KY 40222

NABHOLZ, ROBERT DANIEL, contractor; b. Conway, Ark., Mar. 16, 1924; s. Emil A. and Mary Ann (Strack) N.; student State Coll. Ark., 1946-48, U. Okla., 1947-48; m. Barbara J. Harpe, June 13, 1949; children—Susan, Robert, David, Nancy, Tim, John. Founder, pres. Nabholz Constrn. Co., Conway, 1949—; founder, sec.-treas. Nabholz Supply Co., 1952—; sec., treas. NABCO Inc., 1959—; v.p. Conark Builders, Conway, 1961—; dir. First Nat. Bank, Conway, 1961—. Pres. Ark. Basin Assn., 1966-68; vice-chmn. Conway Devel. Corp., 1970-72. Served with AUS, 1943-46; ETO. Mem. Am. Inst. Constructors, Conway C. of C. (pres. 1962), Diocesan Council Cath. Men. Roman Catholic. Kiwanian. Home: Route 4 Conway AR 72032 Office: 610 Garland St Conway AR 72032

NABLE, RAYMOND DANIEL, dentist; b. Orlando, Fla., Apr. 21, 1934; s. Gustavus Raymond and Oradell Matilda (Raybon) N.; student U. Fla., 1952-54; D.D.S., Emory U., 1958; m. Mary Ann Austin, Apr. 8, 1961; children—Raymond Daniel, Richard Austin. Pvt. practice dentistry, Atlanta, 1961—; asst. prof. operative dentistry Emory U. Sch. Dentistry, 1962-73; staff Ben Massell Dental Clinic, 1961—, mem. adv. bd., 1965—. Active High Mus. Art. Served with USNR, 1958-61. Mem. Am. Dental Assn., Am. Soc. Preventive Dentistry, Acad. Gen. Dentistry, No. Dist. Ga. Dental Assn., Atlanta C. of C., Delta Sigma Delta. Methodist (steward 1964—). Club: Buckhead Mens Garden (Atlanta). Home: 472 Glencastle Dr NW Atlanta GA 30327 Office: 2970 Peachtree Rd NE Atlanta GA 30305

NACOL, CHARLES SAMUEL, merchant; b. Eunice, La., Apr. 14, 1912; s. Saleem Joseph and Regina (Gabriel) N.; LL.B., U. Tex., Austin, 1933; m. Ida Mae Crouchet, Mar. 15, 1941; children—Charlotte Nacol (Mrs. Charles M. Freeman), Habeeb M. Owner, operator Charles S. Nacol Jewelry Co., Port Arthur, Tex., 1938—; organizer, chmn. bd. Sabine Nat. Bank, Port Arthur, 1956; organizer Port Arthur Savs. and Loan, 1956, chmn. bd., 1965-69; dir. Mcht.'s Bank, Republic Tex. Savs. Active social, civic and polit. activities in community. Vice chmn. bd., pres. Port Arthur Improvement Assn.; mem. bd. Salvation Army, YMCA, Tulsa Christian Coll. Mem. Retail Mchts. Assn., C. of C. Mem. Greek Orthodox Ch. (pres. congregation 1965-66). Democrat. Mason (Shriner). Home: 4700 Lakeshore Dr Port Arthur TX 77640 Office: 3703 Twin City Hwy Port Arthur TX 77640

NADEL, MICHAEL, editor; b. Glasgow, Scotland, Feb. 20, 1901; s. Lazar David and Etta (Gillies) N.; student Coll. City N.Y., 1921-24; m. Frances Muchnick, Mar. 4, 1932; 1 dau., Heidi (Mrs. Ellis Stanley Kempner). Naturalized citizen, 1928. Corporate sec. East Coast Shipyards, Inc., N.Y.C., 1947-55; asst. exec. dir. The Wilderness Soc., Washington, 1955-71, corporate sec., 1964-72, spl. cons., 1971—, editor The Living Wilderness, 1964-71, editor emeritus, 1971—. Mem. adv. com. fish and game N.Y. State Commr. Conservation, 1945-49; v.p., dir. N.Y. State Conservation Council, 1944-55; dir. Natural Resources Council Am., Washington, 1971; pres. Chesapeake and Ohio Canal Assn., Washington, 1967-68; chmn. steering com. Rock Creek Park, Washington, 1963-66; trustee Friends of Forest Preserve, N.Y. State, 1944-55; v.p., dir. Mineral. Soc. D.C., 1966-69, 71; mem. profl. working com. U.S.A.-U.S.S.R. Environmental Program Cooperation, 1973. Mem. library com. Hudson Guild, N.Y.C., 1923. Recipient certificate of merit for exceptional service to conservation, 1953. Mem. Wilderness Soc. (life mem.), Constitutional Council for Forest Preserve (bd. advisers 1974—), Southwestern Assn. Indian Affairs, Md. Acad. Scis. (hon.), Thoreau Soc., Audubon Naturalist Soc., Izaak Walton League Am. (chpt. 1st v.p. 1956-57), Mus. Am. Indian, Smithsonian Assos. Club: Potomac Appalachian Trail (Washington). Author: Scenic, Historic and Natural Sites in Origins of American Conservation, 1966; Revision of Parks and Wilderness in America's Natural Resources, 1967; Eight Biographies for Leaders in American Conservation, 1971; also numerous editorials and articles on environmental matters. Assisted in legislation resulting in Wilderness Act of 1964. Home: 4427 N Pershing Dr Arlington VA 22203 Office: 1901 Pennsylvania Av NW Washington DC 20006

NADER, JEANETTE HELEN BALAGIA, home economist; b. Austin, Tex., Mar. 13, 1927; d. Tofie and Bertha (Johns) Balagia; B.B.A., U. Tex., 1946; m. Nesib Nader, Dec. 27, 1949; children—William, Michael, Linda, Rene. Accountant, Gem Jewelry Co., Austin, 1946-49, 1st. Nat. Bank, Shreveport, La., 1949-52; home economist, Shreveport, 1949—. Mem. Am. Legion Auxiliary, Am. Bar Assn. Auxiliary, U. Tex. Alumni Assn. Republican. Episcopalian. Clubs: Lebanon, Phoenician (Shreveport). Home and Office: 245 Wedgewood Dr Shreveport LA 71105

NADER, NESIB, lawyer; b. Shreveport, La., Aug. 14, 1916; s. Ike A. and Mamie (Monsour) N.; B.A., La. State U., 1940; law student Loyola U., 1947-48. Centenary Coll., 1950-53; m. Jeanette Balagia, Dec. 27, 1949; children—Billy Glenn, Michael Wayne, Linda, Rene. Admitted to La. bar, 1953, since in pvt. practice at Shreveport; asst. atty. gen. State La., 1960—. Mem. Gov.'s staff, 1956—. Vice chmn., adv. council Shreveport Youth Opportunity Center, Shreveport, 1967—. Bd. dirs. Caddo Democratic Assn. Served from pvt. to staff sgt. AUS, 1941-45. PTO. Decorated Bronze Star medal. Mem. Am., La., Shreveport bar assns., Am. Legion (post judge adv. 1961-62, mem. nat. com. membership and post activities, district comdr. 4th dist. La. 1966-67, mem. nat. counter-subversive activities com., chmn. sch. awards 4th dist.), D.A.V., V.F.W., So. Fedn. Syrian-Lebanon-Am. Clubs (pres., del. Nat. Fedn.), Forty and Eight Soc. Episcopalian. Clubs: Optimist, Phoenician (pres. 1960-61), Louisiana (v.p. 1957). Home: 245 Wedgewood St Shreveport LA 71105 Office: Giddens Lane Bldg Shreveport LA 71105

NAESS, MICHAEL RAGNAR, corporate exec.; b. Edenbridge, Kent, Eng., June 18, 1939; s. Erling Dekke and Eleanore Frances (Clowes) N.; came to U.S., 1940, naturalized, 1950; B.A., Amherst Coll., 1961; M.B.A., Harvard, 1969; m. Katrin Julia Singer, June 8, 1968; children—Stephanie Katrin, Michelle Francesca, Jeremy Michael. Exec. v.p. Naess Shipping Co., Inc., N.Y.C., 1961-67; v.p. corp. devel. Southdown, Inc., Houston, 1969-70; exec. v.p., dir. Zapata Corp., Houston, 1970—; chmn. Zapata Naess Shipping Co., Ltd., Bermuda, 1970-73, Boone County Coal Corp., Huntington, W. Va., 1970-71, Zapata Bulk Transport, Inc., N.Y., 1972—, Zapata Agrl. Corp., Fresno, Cal., 1972—; dir. Fannin Bank, Houston, Zapata Constructors, Houston. Served from ensign to lt. (j.g.) USNR, 1962-65. Mem. Am. Bur. Shipping. Republican. Clubs: Forest, Coronado, Criterion (Houston). Home: 347 Westminster Dr Houston TX 77024 Office: 2000 Southwest Tower Houston TX 77002

NAFZIGER, JAMES ALBERT RICHMOND, assn. adminstr., lawyer; b. Mpls., Sept. 24, 1940; s. Ralph Otto and Charlotte Monona (Hamilton) N.; B.A., U. Wis., Madison, 1962, M.A., 1969; J.D., Harvard, 1967. Research asst. Dept. Resource Devel. State Wis., Madison, 1962; law clk. to chief judge U.S. Dist. Ct., Milw., 1967-69; admitted to Wis. bar, 1967; exec. sec. Assn. Student Internat. Law Socs., Washington, 1969-70; fellow Am. Soc. Internat. Law, Washington, 1969-70, adminstrv. dir., 1970—. Lectr. Cath. U. Am. Sch. Law, Washington, 1970—. Served to 1st lt. AUS, 1962-64. Mem. Am., Wis. bar assns., Washington Fgn. Law Soc. (v.p. 1973—), Conf. Secs., Am. Council Learned Socs., Am. Soc. Internat. Law (rapporteur com. on student and profl. devel. 1970—), Assn. Student Internat. Law Socs. (adv. bd. 1972—), Phi Beta Kappa, Phi Kappa Phi, Theta Delta Chi. Note and comment editor Harvard Internat. Law Jour., 1966-67. Contbr. articles profl. jours. Home: 524 Queen St Alexandria VA 22314 Office: 2223 Massachusetts Av NW Washington DC 20008

NAGEL, FRITZ JOHN, chem. co. exec.; b. Bremen, Germany, Oct. 20, 1919; s. Friederick Ludolph and Dorothy Frances (Lane) N.; came to U.S., 1921, naturalized, 1939; B.S. (Matthew J. Carney scholar) in Chem. Engring., U. Notre Dame, 1941, M.S. in Organic Chemistry, 1942; postgrad. Carnegie-Mellon U., 1943; m. Elizabeth Ruth Allison, June 12, 1953; children—Marc Fritz, Alison Lane, Frank Royse. Teaching asst. U. Notre Dame, 1939-42; research engr. Westinghouse Electric Corp., Pitts., 1943-48; materials engr. Gen. Electric Co., Coshocton, O., 1950-55; dir. devel. Polymer Corp., Reading, Pa., 1956-68; dir. comml. devel. Chapman Chem. Co., Memphis, 1970-73, v.p., 1973—; v.p. Quantex Corp., Memphis, 1973—, also dir. Mem. Indsl. Research Inst., Am. Chem. Soc. Republican. Episcopalian. Patentee in field. Home: 1264 E Massey Rd Memphis TN 38138 Office: 412 E Brooks Rd Memphis TN 38109

NAGEL, ROBERT HAMILTON, orgn. exec.; b. N.Y.C., Apr. 19, 1918; s. William C. and Christine (Hamilton) N.; B.S. in Civil Engring., Cornell U., 1939; M.S. in Civil Engring., U. Tenn., 1941; m. Ruth Lyman Davis, Nov. 25, 1939; children—Virginia (Mrs. David A. Culver), Robert D., Cynthia H. (Mrs. John P. Kelly). Engr. TVA, Knoxville, Tenn., 1939-43; asst. prof. civil engring. U. Tenn., Knoxville, 1943-44; bridge engr. So. Ry. Co., Knoxville, 1944-46; sec., treas., editor Tau Beta Pi Assn., Knoxville, 1947—; sec., treas. Internat. Assn. Torch Clubs, Knoxville, 1968—. Registered profl. engr., Tenn. Fellow A.A.A.S., Am. Soc. C.E.; mem. Nat., Tenn. socs. profl. engrs., Tech. Soc. Knoxville, Newcomen Soc. N.Am., Chi Epsilon, Alpha Kappa Mu. Home: 4406 Sunset Rd Knoxville TN 37914 Office: Box 8840 Univ Sta Knoxville TN 37916

NAGLEE, DAVID INGERSOLL, educator, clergyman; b. Somers Point, N.J., Sept. 15, 1930; s. Jacob Hann and Dorcas (Ingersoll) N.; B.A., Houghton Coll., 1953; postgrad. Temple Sch. Theology, 1956-58; B.D., Crozer Theol. Sem., 1959; M.A., Temple U., 1963, Ph.D., 1966; m. Elfriede Elsa Kurz, Sept. 6, 1952; children—David Stephen, Joanna Jane, Deborah Ruth, Miriam Louise, Joy Ann. Ordained to ministry Meth. Ch., 1959; pastor chs., Ellicottville, N.Y., 1953-56, Bridgeton, N.J., 1956-58, Port Norris, N.J., 1958-62, Bridgeton, 1962-64, Millville, N.J., 1964-66; sr. minister of preaching United Congl. Christian Ch., LaGrange, Ga., 1973-74; asst. prof. religion and philosophy LaGrange Coll., 1966-67, asso. prof., 1967-71, Flora Glenn Candler prof. religion and philosophy, 1971-73, prof., 1973—, chmn. faculty, 1972-73, pres. faculty, 1973-75. Lectr. in religion and Bible Southeastern Jurisdiction United Meth. Ch., 1969, 72; automotive cons., technician Norris Racing Co., LaGrange, Ga., 1971-73; musician, cellist Columbus (Ga.) Symphony Orch., 1969-74. Dir. tutorial program for needy children, LaGrange, 1967-68; mem. Human Relations Council, LaGrange, 1966-71; adviser Maidee Smith Nursery, LaGrange, 1966-71. Served with USNR, 1948-49. Mem. Pi Gamma Mu. Mason. Author: The History of the Methodist Church at Port Norris, New Jersey, 1962; The Hauls of Holy Ivy, 1973. Composer: Hymn of Church Renewal, 1969; A Lenten Hymn, 1970; Contemporary Pilates, 1970; Man Come of Age, 1970. Contbr. news articles to newspapers. Home: 804 Piney Woods Dr LaGrange GA 30240

NAGLER, BENEDICT, physician; b. Czermowitz, Austria, Mar. 14, 1900; s. Samuel Oswald and Charlotte Josephine (Schorr) N.; M.D., U. Hamburg, 1925; m. Hilde Laub, Oct. 20, 1927; children—Ralph Lewis, Eva. (Mrs. Barron M. Hirsch). Came to U.S. 1935, naturalized, 1941. Intern, resident neurology, psychiatry, internal medicine, Hamburg and Berlin, 1924-31; practice medicine, specializing in psychiatry and neurology, Berlin, 1931-33, Tunis, N. Africa, 1934, Newark, 1935-43; chief Neurology-Psychiatry Service VA Hosp., Richmond, Va., 1946-53; chief neurology div. Psychiatry and Neurology Service VA, Washington, 1953-57; supt. Lynchburg Tng. Sch. and Hosp., 1957-73; asst. prof. psychiatry and neurology Med. Coll. Va., 1946-67; asso. prof. clin. neurology Georgetown U., 1953-57, professorial lectr., 1957-67; lectr. dept. neurology and psychiatry U. Va., 1957-67; cons. Nat. Inst. Neurol. Diseases and Stroke. Bd. dirs. Partridge Schs. and Rehab. Center, Devel. Council Sweet Briar (Va.) Coll.; trustee Woodrow Wilson Rehab. Found. Served to maj. M.C., AUS, 1943-46. Recipient Nat. Brotherhood award Lynchburg chpt. Nat. Conf. Christians and Jews, 1970. Diplomate Am. Bd. Psychiatry and Neurology (asso. examiner 1953-66). Fellow Am. Psychiat. Assn. (del. 1968-71; Gold Achievement award 1962), Am. Epilepsy Soc. (past councillor), So. Psychiat. Assn. (life), Am. Acad. Neurology (past councillor, past chmn. com. on problems mental retardation), Am. Assn. on Mental Deficiency (past councillor, past chmn. com. internat. activities, past chmn. Mid-Eastern region); mem. A.M.A. (life), Va. Med. Soc. (life), Lynchburg Acad. Medicine, Va. Neuropsychiat. Soc. (past chmn. com. mental retardation), L'Alliance Francaise de Lynchburg (dir.), Mil. Order World Wars (past comdr. Lynchburg chpt.), So. Electroencephalographic Soc. (past pres.), Fedn. Am. Scientists, Assn. for Research Nervous and Mental Diseases, Am. Assn. Med. Supts. of Pub. Mental Hosps. (past councillor), Am. Acad. Mental Retardation (past pres.), Am. Med. EEG Soc., (asso. editor Clin. Electroencephalography 1968—), Internat. Assn. Sci., Study Mental Deficiency (past councillor, chmn. finance com.). Translator: (from German to English) Cerebral Function in Infancy and Childhood, 1963. Cons. editor: Am. Jour. Mental Deficiency, 1961-71; mem. editorial bd. Staff Am. Psychiat. Assn. Publ., 1964-67. Home: 2424 Tate Springs Rd Lynchburg VA 24501 Office: 2404 Langhorne Rd Lynchburg VA 24501

NAHAI, LOTFOLLAH, mining engr.; b. Teheran, Iran, Dec. 12, 1911; s. Jon and Khatoun N.; B.S. in Mining Engring., London U., 1935, B.S. in Mining Geology, 1936; M.S. in Bus. Adminstrn., George Washington U., 1965; diploma, Indsl. Coll. Armed Forces, 1965; m. Gisela H. Deist, Oct. 9, 1948; children—Elaine Kay, Lawrence John. Came to U.S., 1944, naturalized, 1945. Mining engr. Dept. Mines, Govt. Iran, Teheran, 1938-42; asst. sect. engr. Consortiumk Kampsox, Iran, 1942-43; regional engr. War Dept., U.S. Mil. Govt., Wiesbaden, Germany, 1946-48; phys. scientist U.S. Bur. Mines, Washington, 1949-70, spl. asst. for internat. activities to dir. U.S. Bur. Mines, 1970—. Treas. troop Boy Scouts Am., Falls Church, Va., 1970-72. Served with AUS, 1945-46. Mem. Am. Inst. Mining, Metall. and Petroleum Engrs. Contbr. articles to profl. jours. Home: 3145 Valley Lane Falls Church VA 22044 Office: Dept of Interior 18th and E Sts NW Washington DC 20240

NAHIKIAN, HOWARD MOVESS, educator; b. Asheville, N.C., June 9, 1910; s. Howard Movess and Alice (Campbell) N.; A.B., U. N.C., 1933, M.A., 1934, Ph.D., 1939; m. Nancy Blanton, Mar. 22, 1936; children—Dorothy (Mrs. John Michael Spainhour), Sarah (Mrs. E. Vincent Rountree). Instr. N.C. State U., Raleigh, 1935-39, asst. prof., 1939-42, asso. prof., 1946-53, prof. math., 1953—. Served to lt. comdr. USNR, 1942-45. Mem. Am. Math. Assn., N.C. Acad. Sci., Sigma Xi, Phi Kappa Phi. Author: A Modern Algebra For Biologists, 1964; Topics in Modern Mathematics, 1966. Home: 3116 Leonard St Raleigh NC 27607

NAHM, CHARLES SAMUEL, ins. co. exec.; b. Bowling Green, Ky., June 3, 1909; s. Charles Simon and Fannie Blanche (Hellman) N.; grad. Odgen Coll. Prep Sch., Bowling Green, 1926; B.A., U. Ky., 1931; m. Mary Anderson, Nov. 20, 1946; children—Charles D., Harris P. Pres. Nahm, Turner, Vaughan & Landrum, Inc., Louisville, 1970—, dir., 1970—. Vice pres. Banner Transfer Co., Louisville, 1939-73; dir. Ky. Motor Transport Assn., Louisville, 1972-73. Mem. Lloyd's Ky. Agts. Assn. (pres. 1941-60). Mason (Shriner), Elk. Clubs; Midland Trail Golf, Standard Country (Louisville). Home: 3742 Deep Dale Lane Louisville KY 40207 Office: 29th Floor First Nat Tower Louisville KY 40202

NAHSER, CLIFFORD ALBERT, architect; b. Tampa, Fla., Aug. 7, 1927; s. C. Albert and Anna Lee (Bateman) N.; B.S., Ga. Inst. Tech., 1951, B.Arch., 1952; m. Marianne Wade, Mar. 22, 1952; children—Clifford Wade, Neil Craig. Architect, Francis P. Smith, A.I.A., Atlanta, 1957-61; sch. architect Atlanta Pub. Schs., 1961—; also cons. Dir. S.E. Council Ednl. Facilities Planners, 1971—, sec.-treas., 1972-73; dir. Aquatic Environmental Specialists, Inc., Atlanta. Served with USNR, 1945-47. Mem. A.I.A. (nat. com. on architecture for edn.). Optimist (charter; v.p. 1959-60, pres. 1960-61, dir. 1961-62). Home: 11145 Houze Rd Roswell GA 30075 Office: 224 Central Av Atlanta GA 30303

NAHSER, PHILIP JOSEPH, elec. mfg. co. exec., elec. engr.; b. Atlanta, Jan. 31, 1931; s. Clifford Albert and Anna Lee (Bateman) N.; B.S. in Physics, Ga. Inst. Tech., 1958; m. Mary Jane Hall, June 16, 1956; children—Sally Ruth, Philip, Anna Lee. Devel. engr. Western Electric Co., Inc., Burlington, N.C., 1958-66; pres. P.J. Nahser Co., Inc., Burlington, 1967—. Cons. Triangle Biomed., Inc., 1967-69. Served to sgt. USAF, 1951-55. Mem. I.E.E.E., Electronics Reps. Assn., Aircraft Owners and Pilots Assn., Alamance County C. of C. Clubs: Am. Bus. (treas. 1966), Burlington-Graham Engrs. (dir. 1972—), Alamance Wildlife, Alamance Ski. Patentee in field. Home: 3131 Forestdale Dr Burlington NC 27215 Office: PO Box 432 Burlington NC 27215

NAIDORF, CARROL PHILIP, physician; b. N.Y.C., May 1, 1904; s. Zelig and Sarah (Breslau) N.; student Syracuse U., 1921-23; M.D., Syracuse U. Upstate Med. Center, 1927; m. Rose Mann, Apr. 19, 1931. Intern, Bronx (N.Y.) Hosp., 1927-28, resident, 1928-29; practice med., Bklyn., 1927-42, specializing in radiology, 1946—; radiologist Halloran VA Hosp., S.I., N.Y., 1949-50; chief radiologist Gen. Hosp., Ft. Hamilton, N.Y., 1948-62; chief grade radiologist U.S. VA Out Patient Clinic, Bklyn., 1953-68, cons., 1968—; asso. vis. radiation therapist Downstate Med. Center, 1949—; clinician Chest Clinic, N.Y.C. Dept. Health, 1955-65; cons. 1st U.S. Army, 1951-52. Treas. Bklyn. Dr.'s Symphony Orch., 1954-56. Served to col. AUS, 1942-46. Mem. A.M.A., Am. Coll. Radiology, InterAm. Coll. Radiology, N.Y. State, Kings County (pres. 1963-66) radiol. socs., Radiol. Soc. N. Am., N.Y. State, Kings County med. socs., Alumni Assn. Bronx Hosp., Assn. Mil. Surgeons U.S., L.I. Early Fliers, Silver Wings Frat., Phi Delta Epsilon. Mason. Contbr. articles to profl. jours. Address: 9700 E Bay Harbor Dr Bay Harbor Island Miami Beach FL 33154

NAIL, CLYDE RAYMOND, coll. adminstr.; b. Miguel, Tex., Jan. 17, 1910; s. Archie B. and Carrie L. (Desmuke) N.; B.S., Southwest Tex. State Coll., 1931; M.Ed., U. Tex., 1950; LL.D., Howard Payne Coll., 1956; m. Frances Belle Dowdy, Jan. 31, 1932; 1 son, Gerald C. Prin. Christoval (Tex.) pub. schs., 1931-37, supt., 1937-41; supr. vocational classes S.W. Tex. State Coll., San Marcos, 1941-42; asst. chief vocational and rehab. div. San Antonio Regional Office of Vets. Adminstrn., 1945-49; dir. evening div. San Antonio Coll., 1949-56, v.p., dean, 1956-61; v.p. San Antonio Union Jr. Coll., 1961-71, v.p. emeritus, 1971—. Spl. cons. for developing instns. Am. Assn. Jr. Colls., 1968-69. Mem. State Adv. Com. on Manpower Devel. and Tng., 1962; mem. Tex. Senate Adv. Com. for Vocational-Tech. Edn., 1969-70; pres. San Antonio Council Presidents, 1968-69. Trustee Buckner's Bapt. Benevolences, Dallas, 1949—, Bapt. Meml. Hosp., San Antonio, 1951-63. Served to lt. comdr. USNR, 1942-45. Mem. Tex. Pub. Jr. Coll. Assn. (pres. 1963), Assn. Tex. Colls. and Univs. (mem. commn. on standards 1956-62), So. Assn. Colls. and Schs. (mem. com. 1963-68). Mason (32 degree, Shriner) (master 1940-41), Lion (dist. gov. 1967-68; pres. 1963-64; dep. dist. govt. 1966-67). Club: Knife and Fork (pres. 1970-71) (San Antonio). Home: 6701 Blanco St San Antonio TX 78216 Office: San Antonio Union Jr Coll San Antonio TX 78212

NAIL, LOWELL THOMAS, banker; b. Rosedale, Okla., Nov. 22, 1913; s. Eli Thomas and Vera Lucretia (Dawson) N.; student accounting Hills Bus. Coll., 1935; m. Eulalie Ann Reid, Sept. 19, 1948; children—Cathy Marie, Paul Reid, Karen Ann. Bookkeeper First State Bank, Butler, Okla., 1936-39; teller First Nat. Bank, Guthrie, Okla., 1939-42; teller Security State Bank, Weatherford, Okla., 1946-50; head bookkeeper, head teller Roswell (N.M.) State Bank, 1950-52; cashier Rosedale State Bank, Kansas City, Kan., 1952-53; asst. cashier, loan teller First State Bank & Trust Co., Oklahoma City, 1953-55, First Nat. Bank, Yale, Okla., 1955-61; cashier, loan teller Security State Bank, Weatherford, Okla., 1961—. Mem. bd. city commrs., Yale, Okla., 1958-61. Served with USNR, 1942-45. Mem. Weatherford C. of C. Republican. Baptist. (dir. Sunday Sch. 1963-64). Mason. Home: 816 N Caddo St Weatherford OK 73096 Office: PO Box 71 Weatherford OK 73096

NAISMITH, JAMES SHERMAN, civil engr.; b. Lawrence, Kan., May 7, 1913; s. James and Maude Evelyn (Sherman) N.; B.S., U. Kan., 1933; m. Frances Pomeroy, Aug. 8, 1933 (dec. Jan. 1968); children—Frances Anne (Mrs. M.K. Boatright), James Pomeroy, Ian Alan; m. 2d, Katharine Wareham Holmes, Apr. 19, 1969. With Standard Oil of Ind., Lawrence, 1933-35; engr. Myers & Noyes, Cons. Engrs., Dallas and Corpus Christi, Tex., 1935-43, Corpus Christi, 1946-47; engr. Lee Aikin Constrn. Co., Corpus Christi, 1947-49; v.p. Blucher & Naismith, Inc., Cons. Engrs., Corpus Christi, 1949-60, pres., 1960-69; pres. Naismith Engrs., Inc., Corpus Christi, 1969—. Mem. Tex. Bd. Registration for Profl. Engrs., 1965-69. City councilman Corpus Christi, 1953-55. Served to lt. USNR, 1943-46. Recipient Engr. of Year award, 1966. Fellow Am. Soc. C.E.; mem. Nat., Tex. socs. profl. engrs. Home: 625 Ralston St Corpus Christi TX 78404 Office: 109 N Chaparral St Corpus Christi TX 78401

NAIZER, KENNETH CARL, elec. engr.; b. Port Arthur, Tex., Oct. 2, 1946; s. William Joseph and Mary Alice (Zurovetz) N.; B.S., Lamar U., 1968, postgrad., 1972-73. Elec. engr., Texaco, Port Arthur, 1972—. Served as 2d lt. USMCR, 1968-72. Decorated Air medal with seven oak leaf clusters; Vietnamese Cross of Gallantry. Mem. Tex. Soc. Profl. Engrs., I.E.E.E., Am. Radio Relay League. Club: Port Arthur Amateur Radio. Home: 519 13th St Nederland TX 77627 Office: Texaco Box 712 Port Arthur TX 77640

NAKANO, JIRO, pharmacologist, cardiologist; b. Hidaka-cho, Japan, Jan. 21, 1925; s. Kijiro and Kame (Kashihara) N.; M.D., Kobe Med. Coll., 1949, Ph.D., 1959; m. Lillian Misao Gima, Nov. 19, 1953; children—Serene K., Ruthi N. Came to U.S., 1950, naturalized, 1963. Intern St. Francis Hosp., Honolulu, 1950-52; resident Jersey City Med. Center, 1952-56; asst. in med. research fellow Columbia, N.Y.C., 1956-58; asst. prof. in medicine St. Louis U., 1958-61; prof. pharmacology U. Okla., Oklahoma City, 1962—, asso. prof. medicine,

1962—. N.J. Heart Assn. fellow; A.E. Bennett fellow; USPHS grantee; Navy grantee; Okla. Heart Assn. grantee. Mem. Am. Physiol. Soc., Am. Soc. Pharmacol. Exptl. Therapy, N.Y. Acad. Sci., A.A.A.S., Soc. Exptl. Biol. Medicine (S.W. sect. sec.-treas. 1972), Central Soc. Clin. Research., Am. Fedn. Clin. Research, Okla. Heart Assn. (vice chmn. research 1971-72). Contbr. chpts. to monographs, also articles to sci. jours. Home: 4905 NW 58th St Oklahoma City OK 73122

NAKARAI, TOYOZO WADA, educator; b. Kyoto, Japan, May 16, 1898; s. Tosui and Wakae (Harada) N.; A.B., Kokugakuin U., Tokyo, 1920; A.B., Butler U., 1924, A.M., 1925; Ph.D. (fellow Sch. Religion), U. Mich., 1930, also post-doctorate studies; grad. student Nippon U., Tokyo, U. Chgo., Hebrew Union Coll., N.Y. U.; m. Frances Aileen Yorn, June 22, 1933; children—Charles Frederick Toyozo, Frederick Leroy. Came to U.S., 1923, naturalized, 1953. Instr. Tokyo Fourth High Sch., Sei Gakuin Mission Sch., Matsumiya Lang. Sch., Tokyo, 1920-23; instr. Coll. of Missions, Indpls., 1923-25; instr. Semitics, Butler U., Indpls., 1927-28, asst. prof., 1928-29, asso. prof., 1929-31, prof., head dept. Semitics, 1931-65, prof. emeritus, 1965—; vis. prof. Emmanuel Sch. Religion, 1965-67, prof., head dept. semitics, 1965-71, hon. prof. Old Testament, 1971—; profl. appointee Am. Sch. Oriental Research, Jerusalem, 1947-48, hon. asso., 1962-63; alumni lectureship Ky. Christian Coll., 1956, T. H. Johnson Meml. lectr. Manhattan Bible Coll., 1957; lectr. Sch. Ministry, Milligan Coll., 1957, 66; vis. prof. Tainan Theol. Coll., Formosa, 1963. Mem. Gov.'s Abraham Lincoln Commn. to Orient, 1960. Mem. Jerusalem Exam. Com. recipient Baxter Found. award, medal and scroll Internat. Order B'rith Abraham, Nat. Assn. Profs. Hebrew; J. I. Holcomb prize Butler U.; citation and scroll Histadrut Ivrit. Mem. Am. Assn. U. Profs., Am. Oriental Soc., Am. Sch. Oriental Research (chmn. cast investigation com. 1941-42), Am. Acad. Religion, Internat. Platform Assn., Soc. Sci. Study Religion, Soc. Bibl. Lit. (v.p. Midwest br. 1949-51, pres. 1951-52), Nat. Assn. Profs. Hebrew (pres. 1956-58), Israel Exploration Soc., Nippon Kyuyaku Gakkai, World Union Jewish Studies, Eta Beta Rho, Phi Kappa Phi, Theta Phi, Author: A Study of the Kokinshu, 1931, Biblical Hebrew, 1951; (with others) To Do and To Teach, 1953; Shin Tosa Nikki, 1962; An Elder's Public Prayers, 1968. Asso. editor: Hebrew Abstracts; editorial com. Jour. Hebraic Studies; adv. mem. Marquis Biog. Library Soc. Home: Route 4 PO Box 240 Elizabethton TN 37643 Office: Drawer Q Milligan College TN 37682

NAMAN, WILFORD WOLFIE, lawyer; b. Waco, Tex., Mar. 6, 1887; s. Jacob I. and Fannie (Cohen) N.; student Baylor U., 1903-05; A.B., Yale, 1908; grad. student N.Y. U., 1909-10; m. Isidora Levy, Feb. 12, 1923; 1 son, Jay I. Admitted to Tex. bar, 1911, since practiced in Waco; mem. firm Naman, Howell, Smith & Chase, attys., 1917—, now sr. partner; spl. judge 19th Dist. Ct., McLennan County, 1917; lectr. law Baylor U., 1948-50. Chmn. bd. KWTX Broadcasting Co., 1953-64. Chmn. Family Counseling and Child Welfare Com.; trustee Waco Community Chest; pres. McLennan County Assn. for Blind, 1946-49, Waco Legal Aid Clinic; dir. United Charities, Pub. Library; mem. Parks and Recreation Bd. of Waco. Vice pres. Bolton Found. Served from pvt. to 1st lt., F.A., U.S. Army, 1917-19. Fellow Am. Bar Found., Southwestern Legal Found., Am. Coll. Probate Counsel, Am. Coll. Trial Lawyers, Tex. Bar Found.; mem. Internat. Assn. Inst. Counsel, Nat. Planning Assn. (nat. council 1957—), State Bar of Tex. (chmn. bd. dirs. 1952-53), C. of C. (dir. 1939), McLennan County Bar Assn. (pres. 1935), Baylor U. Ex-Students Assn. (pres. 1938), Am. Judicature Soc. Home: 3805 Castle Dr Waco TX 76710 Office: 1st Nat Bldg Waco TX 76701

NAMKOONG, GENE, geneticist, educator; b. N.Y.C., Jan. 25, 1934; s. David Yum and Joen (Wooh) N.; B.S., State U. N.Y. Coll. Forestry, 1958, M.S., 1958; Ph.D. (NSF fellow), N.C. State U., 1963; m. Carol Ann Rosenkrance, Aug. 18, 1956; children—Barbara Jean, Gene David, Melanie Ann. Research forester U.S. Forest Service, Gulfport, Miss., 1958-59, geneticist, Raleigh, N.C., 1963—; asst. prof. genetics N.C. State U., Raleigh, 1963-65, asso. prof., 1965-70, prof., 1970—. Cons. genetics research Va. Poly. Inst., B.C. Forest Service, 1972-73; vis. prof. U. Chgo., 1968. Bd. dirs. Rich Park Low Income Housing Corp., treas., 1967-68, pres. 1970-71. Named Pioneering Research Sci. on Population Genetics U.S. Forest Service, 1971. Recipient Sci. Achievement award Internat. Union Forest Research Orgns., 1972; E. L. Demmon Research award, 1963. Mem. A.A.A.S., Genetics Soc. Am., Biometric So., Evolution Soc., Am. Naturalist, Soc. Am. Foresters, Internat. Union Forest Research Orgns. (chmn. working parties 1967), Sigma Xi, Gamma Sigma Delta, Phi Kappa Phi. Author: Foundations of Quantitative Forest Genetics, 1972. Co-editor: Silvae Genetica, 1972—. Contbr. articles on genetics to sci. publs. Home: 811 Beaver Dam Rd Raleigh NC 27607

NAMROW, ARNOLD, psychoanalyst; b. N.Y.C., Aug. 1, 1924; s. Samuel and Mary (Blecker) N.; student U. Fla., 1940-41; A.B., Washington U. (St. Louis), 1943, M.D., 1947; m. Lillian Coe, Dec. 2, 1950; children—James, Andrew, Laurel, David. Intern, St. Elizabeths Hosp., Washington, 1947-48; resident Perry Point (Md.) VA Hosp., 1948-49, VA Mental Hygiene Clinic, Washington, 1949-51; practice medicine specializing in psychiatry and psychoanalysis, Washington, 1953—; mem. staff Georgetown U., Sibley hosps., Washington; clin. asso. prof. psychiatry Georgetown U., 1968—; instr. Washington Psychoanalytic Inst., 1969—; cons. Glen Dale Tb Hosp., Hebrew Home for Aged, Jewish Social Service Agy. Served with USNR, 1943-45, 51-53. Diplomate Am. Bd. Psychiatry and Neurology. Fellow Am. Psychiat. Assn.; mem. Am. Psychoanalytic Assn., Washington Psychiat. Soc., D.C. Med. Soc., Am. Acad. Psychoanalysis. Home: 6406 E Halbert Rd Bethesda MD 20034 Office: 4501 Connecticut Av NW Washington DC 20008

NANCARROW, WARREN GEORGE, cons. engr.; b. Texarkana, Tex., Aug. 10, 1923; s. Frank Henry and Dorothy Christine (Taylor) N.; B.S. in Petroleum Engring., Tex. A. and M. U., 1947; m. Hilda Cullom Harkness, Apr. 19, 1947; children—Margie (Mrs. Willis Cronkhite), Mindy (Mrs. Samuel Taggard), Mark, Matthew. Engr., Amoco Oil, Vivian, La., 1947-54; engr. DeGolyer and MacNaughton, Dallas, 1954—, sr. v.p., mgr. internat. operations, 1970—; dir. Comtech Computing Co., Dallas. Mem. Am. Petroleum Inst., Am. Inst. Mining Engrs., Nomads (v.p. 1962—). Club: Glen Lakes Golf (Dallas). Contbr. articles to trade jours. Home: 3200 Caruth Dallas TX 75225 Office: One Energy Square Dallas TX 75206

NANCE, C. FRANK, sales engr.; b. Hanson, Ky., July 12, 1920; s. Willis M. and Willie (Crabtree) N.; B.S. in Elec. Engring., U. Ariz., 1943; postgrad. Bowden Coll., 1943, Mass. Inst. Tech., 1943-44; m. Jean Everett, Aug. 28, 1943; children—John, Kenneth, Dave. With Westinghouse Electric Corp., 1946-63, sales asst., Pitts., 1946-47, sales engr., St. Louis, 1947-48, El Paso, Tex., 1948-63; sales engr. Triangle Electric Supply Co., El Paso, 1963—. Served to lt. (j.g.) USNR, 1943-46. Named Salesman of Year, Sales Marketing Execs., 1966, 69. Mem. I.E.E.E., Theta Tau. Methodist (chmn. bd. stewards 1960-63). Mason. Club: Optimist (pres. 1960) (El Paso). Home: 2700 Pierce Av El Paso TX 79930 Office: 3815 Durazno St El Paso TX 79988

NANCE, FRANCIS CARTER, educator, surgeon; b. Manila, P.I., Jan. 1, 1932; s. Dana Wilson and Anna Carter (Boatner) N.; grad. Phillips Acad., 1949; student Vanderbilt U., 1949-52; M.D., U. Tenn., 1959, M.S. in Physiology, 1959; m. Patricia Lee Terry, Feb. 14, 1959; children—Ellen, Michael, Catherine, John. Intern U. Chgo. Clinics, 1959-60; resident in surgery U. Pa., 1960-65; instr. La. State U. Sch. Medicine, New Orleans, 1965-67, asst. prof., 1967-70, asso. prof., surgery, 1970-73, prof. surgery and physiology, 1973—. USPHS fellow; NIH research grantee. Diplomate Am. Bd. Surgery. Fellow A.C.S.; mem. Soc. U. Surgeons, So. Surg. Assn., Am. Gastroenterol. Assn., Sco. for Surgery Alimentary Tract, Am. Assn. for Surgery Trauma, Am. Burn Assn. Contbr. articles in field gastoenterologic surgery to med. jours. Home: 142 Country Club Dr New Orleans LA 70124

NANCE, HOMER EUGENE, bus. machine mfg. co. exec.; b. Chadbourn, N.C., Sept. 16, 1925; s. Nathan H. and Nora (Brown) N.; B.S., Wake Forest U., 1951; M.A., E. Carolina U., 1959; m. Frances E. Jeffers, June 29, 1973; children—Neva Carol, Tina Lynn. Sales rep. regional sales mgr., gen. sales mgr., v.p. sales Universal Bus. Machines, Inc., Columbia, S.C., 1959-63; product sales mgr. Fairchild Davidson div. Fairchild Camera & Instrument Corp., Comack, L.I., N.Y., 1963-64, distbr. sales mgr., 1964-66; pres., chmn. Universal Bus. Machines, Inc., Columbia, 1966—, dir., 1966—, also treas. Served with USNR, 1943-46. Mem. Sigma Pi, Alpha Kappa Psi. Baptist. Mason. Home: 1307 Tanglewood Apts Hunt Club Rd Columbia SC 29206 Office: PO Box 6616 13457 Percival Rd Columbia SC 29260

NANCE, JOHN WESLEY, physician; b. Greensboro, N.C., Dec. 19, 1920; s. Lindsey Edgar and Bessie Ann (Boone) N.; student Elon Coll., 1937-38; B.S., Wake Forest Coll., 1941; M.D., Bowman Gray Med. Sch., 1948; m. Doris Augusta Warner, Sept. 1, 1945; children—Susan, Deborah, Jean, John, William. Intern N.C. Bapt. Hosp., 1949, Pa. Hosp., Phila., 1949-51, individual practice medicine, Clinton, N.C., 1951—. Served with USAAF, 1941-45. Decorated D.F.C. with 1 cluster, 4 air medals. Diplomate Am. Bd. Family Practice. Mem. Sampson County Med. Soc., N.C. Acad. Family Practice, Bowman Gray Med. Sch. Alumni Council (pres. 1972). Address: 403 Fairview St Clinton NC 28328

NANCE, JOSEPH TURNER, lawyer; b. Clarksville, Tex., Apr. 12, 1917; s. Kelce Turner and Mary Hettie (Bryarly) N.; B.B.A., So. Methodist U., 1950, J.D., 1953; m. Margrette Zuleika Grubbs, Aug. 23, 1945; children—John Joseph, Mary Carolyn. Service and inspection mgr. S.W. regional office Sears, Roebuck & Co., 1941-52; admitted to Tex. bar, 1953; practiced in Dallas, 1953—; asso. firm Jenkens, Anson, Spradley & Gilchrist, 1953-60, partner, 1960-67; v.p. law TCO Industries Inc., Dallas, 1967-70; v.p., gen. counsel Europe Holiday Inns Internat., 1970-73; atty. First Internat. Bancshares, Inc., Dallas, 1973—; v.p., asso. gen. counsel Holiday Inns, Inc., 1970-73; v.p. Holiday Inns Italiana, also dir. various Holiday Inns, 1970-73; dir., v.p. Hosps., Inc., 1957-61; sec. Dallas Realty Co., 1959-70; v.p. Northlake Corp., 1960-66; asst. sec. Kirby Petroleum Co., 1960-67; v.p. Henderson County Trading Co., 1962-67; asst. sec. El Paso-Venezuela Co., 1966-67, Caribbean Finance Co., 1965-67. Vis. leader grad. seminar in ethics and law So. Methodist U., 1962-67, admissions counselor Sch. Law, 1969— Govt. appeal agt. local bd. SSS, 1960-70; active various community drives; treas. Mus. Achievement Found., 1966-70; pres. Norrell Found., 1948; mem. adv. council Community Chest Trust Fund, 1969—. Bd. visitors So. Methodist U. Sch. Law, 1966-69; bd. dirs. Hillcrest Estates Assn. Served as 2d lt. USAAF, 1945-46. Mem. Am., Dallas (chmn. by-laws com. 1969-70) bar assns., State Bar Tex., Southwestern Legal Found., Dallas Chamber Music Soc., Dallas C. of C., So. Methodist U. Law Alumni Assn. (dir. 1966-69), Phi Alpha Delta, Alpha Sigma Lambda. Republican. Methodist (ofcl. bd. 1965-68). Kiwanian. Clubs: Northwood, Lancer's; Chateau Sainte-Anne (Brussels, Belgium). Editor: Southwestern Law Jour., 1953, hon. editor, 1954—. Home: 11525 E Ricks Circle Dallas TX 75230 Office: 1039 First Nat Bank Bldg Dallas TX 75284

NANCE, MARGRETTE ZULEIKA GRUBBS (MRS. JOSEPH TURNER NANCE), educator, writer, civic worker; b. Dallas, Sept. 24, 1917; d. Ernest and Carolyn (Roberts) Grubbs; B.S., U. Tex., 1942; M.F.A., So. Meth. U., 1969; m. Joseph Turner Nance, Aug. 23, 1945; children—John Joseph, Mary Carolyn. Writer, dir., broadcaster Greek Round-Up, 1940-42; tchr. Allen Jr. High Sch., Austin, Tex., 1943-44; speech tutor U. Tex., 1944-45; speech instr. So. Meth. U., 1946-47; substitute tchr. Dallas Ind. Sch. Dist., 1955-69; actor role Mrs. Stevenson, Sorry Wrong Number, So. Meth. U., KERA-TV, 1962, author tv script univ. tv workshop. Dallas, Panhellenic Assn., KRLD-TV, 1954, 55; writer columns various newspapers, Dallas, 1963-67. Team capt. United Fund, 1969; vol. specialist A.R.C., 1969; season ticket sales com. mem. Dallas Symphony Orch. League, 1966-68, membership com., 1968-70; mem. woman's com. Dallas Theater Center, 1967-70, 72-73; mem. Soc. Prevention Cruelty to Abandoned and Neglected Children, 1966—, Dallas Summer Musicals Guild, 1967—, Dallas Mus. Fine Arts, 1966—; dir. Spl. Care Sch. Handicapped Children, 1965-66; mem. Preston Hollow P.T.A., 1955-56; exec. v.p. George B. Dealey P.T.A., 1961-62; mem. com. Benjamin Franklin P.T.A., 1962-63. Dir. Hillcrest Estates Assn., 1960-62. Mem. Dallas Council World Affairs, Tex. Ex-Students Assn. (4th v.p. 1960-61), Tex. State Assn. City Panhellenics (sec. 1957-58), Colony of Sch. of Arts Am. Assn. U. Women, Club Internat. Chateau Sainte Anne, Brussels Delta Zeta, Pi Lambda Theta. Republican. Methodist. Clubs: Northwood, Lancers (charter), Mothers' So. Meth. U. (4th v.p., rep. 1968-70), Dallas Lawyer Wives, Tex. Fine Arts Soc., Dallas Federation of Womens (historian 1968-69, chmn. fine arts dept. 1969-70), Austin (Tex.) Womans; Am. Womans (Brussels). Address: 11525 E Ricks Circle Dallas TX 75230

NANCE, PAUL KINT, coll. exec.; b. Perkins Okla., Nov. 20, 1917; s. Wilson Earl and Bertha (Kint) N.; student U. Okla., 1934-37, M.A., 1956; student Oklahoma City U., 1942-43; A.B., Okla. Bapt. U., 1945; postgrad. Columbia. summer 1948; m. Helen Pearl Lee, June 10, 1938; children—Joseph Earl, Paula Nelamari. Accountant Okla. Gas & Electric Co., 1938-43; bus. mgr. Okla. Bapt. U., 1944-48, treas., comptroller, 1949-55, financial v.p., 1956-62, v.p. univ., 1962-63; specialist coll. bus. administrn. U.S. Office Edn., 1963, acting chief bus. adminstrn. sect., 1964—, sect. chief fiscal and adminstrv. group, higher edn. studies br. 1966; v.p., treas. Furman U., 1964; bus. mgr., asst. sec. treas. bd. dirs. Gallaudet Coll., Washington, 1967—. Drive chmn. United Fund, 1960; pres. bd. Camp Fire Girls Am., 1961-62. Precinct chmn. Dem. party, 1957-60. Bd. dirs. B. B. McKinney Music Research Found. Mem. Okla. So., Central assns. coll. and univ. bus. officers, Nat. Assn. Ednl. Buyers, Nat. Fedn. Coll and U. Bus. Officers Assns. (pres. 1950), Washington C. of C., Beta Gamma Sigma. Baptist (pres. Men's Brotherhood 1960, deacon). Rotarian (pres. 1962, program chmn. 1973). Co-author: Guide to College Business Management, 1964; Business Management in Selected Colleges and Universities, 1965; College and University Business Administration, 1968. Contbr. articles profl. jours. Home: 6907 Churchhill Rd McLean VA 22101 Office: Gallaudet Coll 7th at Florida Av NE Washington DC 20002

NANDEDKAR, ARVINDKUMAR NARHARI, educator, biochemist, clin. chemist; b. Nagpur, Maharashtra, India, Apr. 8, 1937; s. Narhari Sheshrao and Ramabai Narhari (Shahdani) N.; B.Sc., Govt. Sci. Coll., Nagpur, India, 1959; M.Sc., Nagpur (India) U., 1961; Ph.D., V. Patel Chest Inst. Delhi (India) U. 1966; m. Meena Ganesh Soman, June 7, 1964; children—Lalit Gauri, Maithili. Came to U.S., 1966. Jr. research fellow Ministry Edn., Govt. India, New Delhi, 1961-65; research asst. Indian Council Med. Research, New Delhi, 1965-66; asst. research officer Indian Council Med. Research, New Delhi, 1966; postdoctoral research asso. NIH grantee at dept. chemistry Georgetown U., Washington, 1966-68; postdoctoral research asso.-instr. AEC grantee at Howard U. and Dept. Biochemistry Howard U. Coll. Medicine, Washington, 1968-71, asst. prof. dept. biochemistry, 1971—, asst. dir. Preliminary Acad. Reinforcement Program, 1972-73. Fellow Am. Inst. Chemists; mem. Am. Chem. Soc., A.A.A.S., Soc. Biol. Chemists, India (life), Am. Assn. U. Profs., Am. Assn. Clin. Scientists, Sigma Xi. Home: 717 N Garfield St Arlington VA 22201 Office: Howard University Coll Medicine 5th and W Sts NW Washington DC 20001

NANES, ALLAN SAMUEL, govt. ofcl.; b. Bklyn., May 3, 1921; s. Philip and Belle (Hillman) N.; A.B. summa cum laude, Brown U., 1941; A.M., Harvard, 1947, Ph.D., 1949; m. Alice Kutzin, May 11, 1964; children—Erika Rachel, Bruce Preston. With State Dept., Office Intelligence Research, 1949-50; mem. faculty Hofstra Coll., 1950-51 instr. polit. sci. Bklyn. Coll., 1951-54 with Dept. Def., Office Internat. Security Affairs, 1965-66; with Legislative Reference Service, Library of Congress, Washington, 1955-65, specialist internat. devel., 1966—; editorial cons. Everyman's Internat. Ency. Served with USAAF, 1943-45; PTO, CBI. Mem. Soc. for Internat. Devel., Phi Beta Kappa. Contbr. to Current History, 1957-64, 67, 69; New Internat. Year Book, 1957-65; Standard Reference Ency. Year Book, 1969—. Home: 13004 Autumn Dr Silver Spring MD 20904 Office: Library of Congress Washington DC 20540

NANNES, CASPAR HAROLD, journalist, author; b. Fall River, Mass., May 15, 1906; s. Max and Minnie (Silverstein) N.; A.B., Rutgers U., 1931, A.M., 1932, Litt.D., 1966; Ph.D., U. Pa., 1948. Instr. English dept. Rutgers U., 1931-35, 38-42, U. Ill., 1935-38; with Washington Evening Star, 1943-68, gen. reporter, 1943-48, religious news editor, 1949-68, tennis editor, 1946-68. Recipient Religious Heritage award, 1963, Reynolds award, 1964. Fellow Religious Pub. Relations Council (2 awards); mem. Religious Newswriters Assn. (pres. 1956-58), Lawn Tennis Writers Assn. Am. (mem. bd. govs. 1951), Middle Atlantic Lawn Tennis Assn. (mem. exec. com.), Modern Lang. Assn., Phi Beta Kappa. Clubs: Rutgers (pres. 1943), National Press, Edgemoor (Washington). Author: Politics in the American Drama, 1960; National Presbyterian Church and Center, A History, 1969; (play) Cavalcade '76, 1974; also numerous mag. articles nat. publs. Home: 4200 Cathedral Av NW Washington DC 20016

NANNEY, ALLAN DOUGLAS, constrn. co. exec.; b. Lincolnton, Ga., Oct. 22, 1918; s. Add Douglas and Marie (Stribling) N.; student U. N.C., 1935-37, King's Coll., 1937-38; m. Elizabeth Dellinger, Nov. 15, 1947; children—Allan Douglas, Jr., John Edward. Accountant, bus. mgr. Loftis Constrn. Co., Charlotte, N.C., 1938-42; sr. accountant E. B. Taylor, C.P.A., Charlotte, 1942-46; sec., treas. Dickerson, Inc., Monroe, N.C., 1946—, Contractors & Materials, Inc., Monroe, 1960—; v.p. Comml. Products, Inc., Monroe, 1952—. C.P.A., N.C. Mem. N.C. Assn. C.P.A.'s, Am. Inst. C.P.A.'s. Methodist. Mason (Shriner). Home: 6014 Preston Lane Charlotte NC 28211 Office: Box 400 Monroe NC 28110

NAPIER, HENDLEY VARNER, lawyer; b. Macon, Ga., Feb. 1, 1919; s. Hendley Varner, Jr. and Viola (Ross) N.; student Ga. Sch. Tech., 1937-38; A.B., Mercer U., 1941, J.D., 1943; m. Delores Ward, Jan. 21, 1956; 1 dau., Hannah Lee. Admitted to Ga. bar, 1943, since practiced in Macon; mem. firm Martin, Snow, Grant & Napier, 1943—. Pres., dir. St. Paul Apts., Inc. Mem. Macon Bar Assn. (pres. 1962, 63), Macon (dir. 1946), Macon Jr. (pres. 1946) chambers commerce, Kappa Alpha. Episcopalian. Moose. Club: Exchange of Bibb County (pres.). Home: 1515 Briarcliff Rd Macon GA 31201 Office: Home Fed Bldg Macon GA 31201

NARANJO, DANIEL ALBERTO, lawyer; b. San Antonio, Aug. 16, 1939; s. Joe Abel and Alice (Morales) N.; B.A., U. Tex., Austin, 1962, J.D., 1963; m. Monica Rachel Oldenbourg, June 28, 1968; 1 dau., Cecilia Miriam. Admitted to Tex. bar, 1967; mem. firm Nicholas and Barrera, San Antonio, 1967—. Mem. Camp Fire Girls, Inc., San Antonio, 1969, v.p., 1970, pres., 1971, bd. dirs., 1973—; bd. dirs. Drug Abuse Central, San Antonio, 1973—. Bd. dirs. Childrens' Learning Center, Inc., San Antonio. Served to capt. USAF, 1967. Mem. Am. Bar Assn., Tex. Jr. Bar (state dir. 1972-73), San Antonio Jr. Bar (v.p. 1970-71 bd. dirs. 1972-74), Cath. Lawyer's Guild (v.p. 1971, pres. 1972), Bus. and Econ. Soc., Intern-Am. Bar Assn., Delta Theta Phi. Home: 731 Patricia San Antonio TX 78216 Office: 424 E Nueva San Antonio TX 78205

NASAR, SYED ABU, educator; b. Gorakhpur, India, Dec. 25, 1932; s. Syed M. and Syeda (Begum) Yusuf; B.Sc., Agra U., 1951; B.Sc. in Elec. Engring., Dacca U., 1955; M.S., Tex. A. and M. U., 1957; Ph.D., U. Cal. at Berkeley, 1963; m. Sara Samad, Sept. 3, 1961; children—Naheed, Sajida. Asso. prof. Gonzaga U., Spokane, Wash., 1966-68; asso. prof. U. Ky., Lexington, 1968-70, prof. elec. engring., 1970—. Cons. Sci. Research Lab. Ford Motor Co., Dearborn, Mich. Brit. Council visitor Imperial Coll., London. NSF research grantee. Mem. I.E.E.E. (sr. mem.; chmn. sub-com. on generalized machine theory), Inst. Elec. Engrs. (London), Sigma Xi, Eta Kappa Nu. Author: Electromagnetic Energy Conversion Devices and Systems, 1970. Home: 1522 Lakewood Ct Lexington KY 40502

NASH, CHARLES HENRY, physician; b. Union Parish, La., Mar. 14, 1934; s. Joseph Carl and Sally Odessa (Elkins) N.; B.A., La. Tech. U., 1958; M.D., La. State U., 1960; m. Patsy Rougon Foster, July 22, 1956; children—Joseph Craig, Regina Kaye. Intern, T.E. Schumpert Meml. Hosp., Shreveport, La., 1960-61; practice medicine specializing in family practice; partner Family Clinic, 1961-71; v.p. Family Clinic, Inc., 1970—; pres. staff Physicians and Surgeons Hosp.; city physician, Shreveport. Mem. Caddo Bossier Council Alcoholics Anonymous Assn. Mem. Am., La. acads. gen. practice, La. Fourth Dist., Shreveport med. socs., Shreveport C. of C., Internat. Fire Chiefs Assn. (asso.). Home: 245 Pierremont Rd Shreveport LA 71102 Office: 838 Margaret Pl Shreveport LA 71101

NASH, CLINTON BROOKS, educator; b. Gunnison, Miss., Jan. 3, 1918; s. Robert Patrick and Lillian (Williams) N.; B.S., U. Tenn., 1950, M.S., 1952, Ph.D., 1955; m. Rose Shaljian, July 11, 1946; children—Kathleen (Mrs. William T. Wood). Pharmacologist, Mead Johnson Co., Evansville, Ind., 1954-55, sr. pharmacologist, 1956-57, groupleader, 1957-58; asst. prof. pharmacology, U. Tenn. Med. Coll., Memphis, 1958-60, asso. prof. pharmacology, 1960-65, prof. pharmacology, 1965—. Cons. to FDA, Webcon Co. Served as pilot, 1st lt. USAF, 1942-46; ETO. Decorated Air Force Medal, D.F.C. Research fellow U. Tenn., 1950-52; USPHS research grantee; Am. Found. Pharm. Edn. fellow, 1950-52. Mem. Am. Soc. Pharmacology and Exptl. Therapeutics, Soc. Toxicology, Am. Heart Assn., Soc. Exptl. Biol. and Medicine, N.Y. Acad. Sci., Internat. Soc. Biochem. Pharmacology, Japanese Circulation Soc. Author: Pharmacology Rev., 1971. Home: 5344 Timmons Av Memphis TN 38117

NASH, EDITH ROSENFELS (MRS. PHILLEO NASH), educator; b. Oak Park, Ill., July 12, 1913; d. Irwin S. and Helen (Zuckerman) Rosenfels; student Vassar Coll., 1930-31; A.B., U. Chgo., 1934, postgrad., 1934-35; m. Philleo Nash, Nov. 2, 1935; children—Margaret Helen (Mrs. Eric C. Kast), Sally. Field worker in anthropology U. Chgo., Mescalero Indian Reservation, N.M. and Klamath Indian Reservation, Ore., 1935-36; research Library of Congress, Washington, 1942, O.W.I., Bur. Overseas Intelligence, Washington, 1943-44; asst. dir. Georgetown Day Sch., Washington, 1945-51, dir., 1961—. Bd. dirs. Woodley House, Washington, 1966-68. Mem. Assn. Ind. Schs. Greater Washington (sec.-treas. 1968-70), Am. Assn. Sex Educators and Counselors (v.p. 1972—). Home: 540 N St SW Washington DC 20024 Office: 4530 MacArthur Blvd Washington DC 20007

NASH, HENRY WARREN, educator; b. Tampa, Fla., Sept. 19, 1927; s. Leslie Dikeman and Mildred (Johnson) N.; B.S., U. Fla., 1951, M.B.A., 1951, Ph.D. (Loveman's Merchandising fellow), U. Ala., 1965; m. Frances Lora Venters, Aug. 20, 1950; children—Warren Leslie, Richard Dale. Grad. asst. U. Fla., 1950-51, Ind. U., 1951-53; salesman Field Enterprises, Inc., Chgo., 1953; asso. prof. bus. and econs. Miss. Coll., Clinton, 1953-57, faculty Miss. State U., Mississippi State, 1957—, prof., head dept. marketing, 1966—. Partner, Southland Cons. Assos., Starkville, Miss., 1968—. Bd. dirs., pres. Govt. Employees Credit Union, Starkville. Served with USNR, 1945-46. Mem. Sales and Marketing Execs. (internat. chmn. educators com. 1969-71), Miss. Retail Mchts. Assn. (dir.), Am., So. marketing assns., Am. Acad. Advt., So. Econs. Assn., Pi Sigma Epsilon (nat. educator v.p. 1967-69) (nat. pres. 1969-71), Alpha Kappa Psi, Omicron Delta Kappa, Beta Gamma Sigma. Kiwanian (treas. Starkville 1969-70, v.p. 1973—). Author: (with others) Principles of Marketing, 1961. Home: 8 Forest Hill Dr Starkville MS 39759 Office: PO Drawer N Mississippi State MS 39762

NASH, HUGH OWEN, JR., elec. engr.; b. Savannah, Ga., Sept. 6, 1944; s. Hugh Owen and Ruo (Beebe) N.; B.S. in Elec. Engring., Vanderbilt U.; m. Dorothy Potter, Dec. 30, 1966; children—Catherine Taylor, Hugh Owen. Elec. engr. Union Camp Corp., Savannah, 1967-68, Savannah Electric & Power Co., 1968-70; pres. Nash Engring. Co., Savannah, 1970—. Registered profl engr., Ga., S.C. Mem. I.E.E.E., Nat. Elec. Contractors Assn., Ga. Soc. Profl. Engrs., Savannah C. of C., Better Bus. Bur., Beta Theta Pi. Clubs: Savannah Yacht, Savannah Quarterback, Oglethorpe. Home: 160 Hopecrest Av Savannah GA 31406 Office: 513 E Congress Savannah GA 31401

NASH, MARY BURT (MRS. WILLIAM NASH), lawyer; b. Little Rock, June 17, 1912; d. William Burt and Orriette (Morris) Brooks; B.S., Northwestern U., 1931; M.A., U. Ia., 1932; LL.B., Ark. Law Sch., 1934; m. William Nash, Jan. 7, 1937; children—David William, Morris Brooks. Admitted to Ark. bar, 1934; referee Pulaski County Juvenile Ct., 1956—. Vice chmn. Comm. on Crime and Law Enforcement, Ark. Trustee So. State Coll., Magnolia, Ark., 1952-63, sec. bd. trustees, 1961-63. Recipient Alumni award Little Rock U., 1952; Alumni Merit award Northwestern U., 1963; named Woman of Yr. Ark., 1964. Mem. Am. Bar Assn., Nat. Panhellenic Conf. (sec. 1959-61, chmn. 1961-63). Nat Council Juvenile Ct. Judges, Nat., Ark. (pres. 1966-68) assns. women lawyers, Nat. Assn. Women Deans and Counselors, Am. Assn. U. Women (legislative program com. 1955-61, past state pres.), Inter-fraternity Research and Adv. Council (trustee 1961-63), Daus. Am. Colonists (past state regent), D.A.R., Dames Ct. Honor (past state pres.), P.E.O., Altrusa, Delta Kappa Gamma, Alpha Xi Delta (past nat. pres.; nat. council 1951-71). Presbyn. Home: 410 Fairfax Av Little Rock AR 72205 Office: Juvenile Court Juvenile Adminstrn Center 3201 W Roosevelt Rd Little Rock AR 72204

NASH, MICHAUX, JR., banker; b. Dallas, Aug. 20, 1933; s. Michaux and Joel (Waggoner) N.; B.B.A., So. Methodist U., 1956, postgrad. Southwestern Grad. Sch. Banking; postgrad. Harvard, Sch. Bank Pub. Relations and Marketing, Northwestern U.; m. Margaret Eileen Ruebel, Oct. 19, 1956; children—Michaux III, Paige Eileen, Noble, Joel. With Empire State Bank (merged with Nat. Bank of Commerce, 1967), Dallas, 1958—, exec. v.p., 1967—, also dir.; dir. United Fidelity Life Ins. Co., Dallas. Mem. Zoning Commn., University Park, Tex., 1962-68; chmn. commerce and industry div. United Fund Dr., 1965-69; bd. dirs. Hope Cottage-Childrens Bur. 1960-69, treas., 1963-65, pres. 1967-68; bd. dirs. Dallas Zoo, 1964-67, Community Council, Dallas, Childrens Med. Center, Dallas Natural Sci. Assn., Tex. Com. on Natural Resources, Tex. United Community Services, Tex. United Funds; bd. mgmt. Park Cities-North Dallas YMCA, 1962-70, pres., 1967-68. Served to capt. USAF. Mem. Ind. Bankers Assn. Am., Sigma Alpha Epsilon (pres. 1965). Democrat. Episcopalian. Clubs: Terpsichorean, Lancers, Koon Kreek; Dallas Athletic, Sportsmen's of Dallas (pres. adv. com.), Dallas Gun, Dallas Country, Idlewild, Tex. Game Fishing, Ferndale Hunting and Fishing, Dallas Tornado Soccer, Dallas Woods and Waters (exec. v.p. 1967, pres. 1968). Home: 4400 McFarlin Blvd Dallas TX 75205 Office: 1525 Elm St Dallas TX 75201

NASH, PHILLEO, cons. anthropologist, assn. exec.; b. Wisconsin Rapids, Wis., Oct. 25, 1909; s. Guy and Florence Belle (Philleo) N.; A.B., U. Wis., 1932; Ph.D., U. Chgo., 1937; m. Edith Rosenfels, Nov. 2, 1935; children—Maggie Kast, Sally. Lectr. anthropology U. Toronto, 1937-41; mgr. Biron Cranberry Co., 1941-42, pres., 1946—; spl. asst. to dir. White House liaison O.W.I., 1942-46; spl. asst. The White House, 1946-52; adminstrv. asst. President of U.S., 1952-53; lt. gov. Wis., 1959-61; asst. to Asst. Sec. Pub. Land Mgmt., Dept. Interior, Washington, 1961, U.S. commr. Indian affairs Dept. Interior, 1961-66; research asso. Smithsonian Instn., Washington, 1968-70; treas. Am. Anthrop. Assn., 1968-70; adj. prof. anthropology Am. U., 1971-73, prof., 1973—. Spl. cons. sec. war, 1943. Chmn. Dem. Party Wis., 1955-57. Mem. Soc. Applied Anthropology (pres. 1970-71). Club: Cosmos (Washington). Home: 540 N St SW Washington DC 20024

NASH, RICHARD JAMES, banker; b. Detroit, Aug. 8, 1930; s. Ernest John and Edna (Unverdros) N.; student Fla. So. Coll., 1949-50, La. State U., 1957-60; m. Jayne Kerr, May 11, 1951; children—Richard J., Kerin Jayne, Margaret Ann. Cashier Bank of Zephyr Hills (Fla.), 1953-61; exec. v.p. Citizens Bank, Frostproof, Fla., 1961-73, pres., 1973—, also dir. Chmn. Frostproof Zoning Bd. Appeals, 1965—. Chmn. trustees Polk Jr. Coll., Winter Haven, Fla., 1970-71; trustee Lake Wales (Fla.) Hosp. Served with AUS, 1946-48. Mem. Frostproof C. of C. (pres.) Mason. Home: 311 3d St Frostproof FL 33843 Office: 7 Wall St Frostproof FL 33843

NASH, ROBERT MCLEAN, distillery co. exec.; b. Louisville, Nov. 1, 1925; s. McLean and Margaret Edith (Hegewald) N.; B.A., U. Louisville, 1949; m. Ida Thompson, Aug. 18, 1950; children—Louise and Margaret (twins), Katherine. Vice pres., marketing dir. Glenmore Distilleries Co., Louisville, 1954—, also dir.; dir. Old South Life Ins. Co. Served to 1st lt. F.A. AUS, 1944-46. Clubs: Louisville Country, River Valley, Pendennis (Louisville). Home: Covered Bridge Rd Prospect KY 40059 Office: Citizens Plaza Louisville KY 40202

NASH, ROBERT THORNTON, elec. engr., educator; b. Columbus, O., Sept. 20, 1929; s. Simeon and Myrtle (Thornton) N.; B.S. in Physics, Ohio State U., 1952, M.S. in Elec. Engring., 1955, Ph.D. in Elec. Engring., 1961; m. Frances Josephine Smith, Mar. 19, 1960; children—Whitney, Suzanne, Adrienne. Asst. prof. elec. engring. Ohio State U., Columbus, 1961-64, asso. prof., 1964-66; asso. prof. elec. engring. Vanderbilt U., Nashville, 1966—. Registered profl. engr., Tenn. Mem. I.E.E.E., Operations Research Soc. Am., Soc. for History Technology. Home: 201 Mockingbird Rd Nashville TN 37205

NATCHER, WILLIAM HUSTON, congressman; b. Bowling Green, Ky., Sept. 11, 1909; s. J. M. and Blanche (Hays) N.; A.B., Western Ky. State Coll., Bowling Green, 1930; LL.B., Ohio State U., 1933; m. Virginia Reardon, June 17, 1937; children—Celeste, Louise. Admitted to Ky. bar, 1934, pvt. practice, Bowling Green, 1934—. Fed. conciliation commr. Western Dist. Ky., 1936-37; atty. Warren Co., 1937-49; commonwealth atty., 8th Jud. Dist., 1952-53; elected to 83d Congress (to fill unexpired term of Garrett L. Withers), 1953; mem. 84th to 93d Congresses, 2d Ky. Dist. Served as lt. USNR, 1942-45. Mem. Bowling Green Bar Assn. (pres.), Am. Legion, 40 and 8. Democrat. Odd Fellow, Kiwanian. Home: 638 E Main St Bowling Green KY 42101 Office: 414 E 10th St Bowling Green KY 42101

NATHAN, DANIEL EVERETT, physician, surgeon; b. Tifton, Ga., May 8, 1916; s. Max and Edith (Lease) N.; B.S., U. Ga., 1936, M.D., 1940; m. Muriel Halprin, Jan. 24, 1942; children—David Harris, Sherrie Halprin. Intern St. Elizabeth Hosp., Elizabeth, N.J., 1940-41, City Hosp., N.Y.C., 1941-42, resident, 1945; pvt. practice medicine and surgery, Ft. Valley, Ga., 1946—; chief staff Peach County Hosp., 1962, 71-72; dir. Citizens Bank of Fort Valley; pres. Westview Devel. Corp. Lt. Col. Staff Gov. Ernest Vandiver of State of Ga., 1959, 62, lt. col. staff Carl Sandres, 1963-67; vice pres., dir., Ft. Valley Med. Nursing Home, 1967—. Co-ordinating com., Fort Valley; mem. Continental Air Command Res. Forces Policy Council, Surgeon Gen. Air Res. Forces Med. Adv. Council. Bd. dirs. Fedn. Jewish Charities Macon and Middle Ga., 1948-58. Med. adviser Local Draft Bd. 115, Ft. Valley, 1948; citizen's adv. council Robins AFB, Ga., 1963-67. Served from 1st lt. to maj. USAAC, 1942-45. Decorated Air medal, Soldier's medal. Mem. C. of C., Peach Belt, 6th Dist. med. socs., Med. Assn. Ga., Am., So. Aerospace med. assns., Assn. Mil. Surgeons, Ga. Heart Assn. (mem. profl. edn. com. 1961-66, Am. Cancer Soc., Am., (dir.-at-large), So. Cal., Middle Ga. (pres. 1973—) camelia socs., Air-Medics Med. Aviation Assn., Ga. Alumni Soc., Am. Legion, Alpha Epsilon Pi, Phi Delta Epsilon, Jewish religion (dir. temple). Mason (Shriner). Club: Pine Needles Country. Home: 501 Westview Dr Fort Valley GA 31030 Office: 401 Park Av Fort Valley GA 31030

NATHAN, NORMAN, educator; b. Bklyn., Nov. 19, 1915; s. Michael and Fannie (Levine) N.; B.A., N.Y. U., 1936, M.A., 1938, Ph.D., 1947; m. Frieda Agin, July 21, 1940; children—Linda (Mrs. Richard Kuzmack), Michele, Lois Anne. Instr., City Coll. N.Y., 1946-49; lectr. Rutgers U., 1947-49; prof. Utica Coll., Syracuse U., 1949-68; prof. English, Fla. Atlantic U., Boca Raton, 1968—. Vis. prof. Coll. Virgin Islands, 1965-66. Mem. Modern Lang. Assn. Am., Nat. Council Tchrs. English, Am. Assn. U. Profs., Shakespeare Assn. Am. Author: Though Nigh Remain, 1959; Judging Poetry, 1961; The Right Word, 1962; Writing Sentences, 1964; Short Stories, 1969. Contbr. articles to profl. jours. Home: 1189 SW Tamarind Way Boca Raton FL 33432

NATIONS, JOHN DREWRY, wholesale firm exec.; b. Fayette County, Ga., June 1, 1918; s. James Andrew and Birdie Elizabeth (Edmondson) N.; student Ga. Tech., 1935-37; m. Nancy Johnson, Sept. 21, 1940; children—Michael T., Nancy (Mrs. Clifford Ray Davis), Andrew H. Salesman Pye-Barker Supply Co., Atlanta, 1937-43; partner Cotton Gin, Turin, Ga., 1946-48; pres., chmn. bd. Bearings and Drives, Inc., indsl. distbn. firm, Macon, Ga., 1948—. Mem. nat. distbr. adv. councils Dayco Mfg. Co., 1966, 70, Diamond Chain Co., 1970, 73. Served to 1st lt. pilot, USAF, 1943-45. Mem. Bearing Specialists Assn., Power Transmission Distbrs. Assn., C. of C. Methodist (finance chmn. 1960-66, chmn. ofcl. bd. 1962-65). Kiwanian, Elk. Club: Idle Hour Golf and Country (Macon, Ga.). Home: 4416 Old Club Rd Macon GA 31204 Office: 607 Lower Poplar St Macon GA 31208

NAUMAN, ROBERT VINCENT, educator; b. East Stroudsburg, Pa., Dec. 6, 1923; s. Carl Arnold and Bernice Irene (Zacharias) N.; B.S., Duke, 1944; Ph.D., U. Cal. at Berkeley, 1947; m. Jean Marie Hudgeson, Aug. 29, 1955; children—Andrea Carol, Marcus Alan, Stephen Brian, Suzanne Marie. Research asso. Cornell U., Ithaca, N.Y., 1947-52; asst. prof. U. Ark., Fayetteville, 1952-53; mem. faculty La. State U., Baton Rouge, 1953—, prof. phys. chemistry, 1963—, pres. faculty senate, 1972-73, 74-75. Vis. prof. Santa Maria U., Valparaiso, Chile, 1966-67, U. Chile, Santiago, 1971-72. Served with USMCR, 1943-44. Recipient Fulbright-Hayes grant, 1966-67; Outstanding Undergrad. Tchr. award Standard Oil Co., 1969. Mem. Am. Chem. Soc., Am. Phys. Soc., A.A.A.S., Sigma Xi (chpt. pres. 1970-71), Phi Beta Kappa, Omicron Delta Kappa, Phi Lambda Upsilon, Pi Mu Epsilon, Phi Eta Sigma. Republican. Methodist. Home: 864 Diron Circle Baton Rouge LA 70810

NAUMER, HELMUTH JACOB, museum exec.; b. Santa Fe, May 7, 1934; s. Helmuth and Tomee (Reuter) N.; B.A., U. N.M., 1958; postgrad. U. Minn., 1959; m. Carolyn Lou Palmer, Oct. 9, 1966; children—Karina Anne, Helmuth Karl, Kyrsten Anne, Tanya. Marina mgr. Yellowstone Nat. Park Co., Lake, Wyo., 1958; gen. mgr. Twining Ski Corp., Taos Ski Valley, Taos, N.M., 1959; archaeologist in charge Town Creek Indian Mound, N.C. Dept. Archives and History, Raleigh, 1959-60; dir. Charlotte (N.C.) Childrens Nature Mus., 1960-62; exec. dir. Ft. Worth Mus. Sci. and History, 1962—. Faculty mem. Nat. Trust Hist. Preservation; pres. Naumer Mus. Cons., Ft. Worth, 1963—. Pres., Tarrant County United Fund Execs., 1966; mem. exec. bd. Regional Sci. Fair, 1962-67; mem. mus. panels Nat. Endowment for Humanities, Nat. Endowment for Arts. Recipient Elsie M.B. Naumburg award, 1968. Mem. Am. Assn. Youth Museums (pres. 1967-68), Tex. Mus. Assn. (pres. 1964, 66, 69-70), Am. Assn. Museums (mem. governing council), Internat. Council Museums, Mountain-Plains Mus. Conf. (chmn. 1970). Republican. Contbr. articles to profl. jours., books. Home: 6355 Waverly Way Fort Worth TX 76116 Office: 1501 Montgomery St Fort Worth TX 76107

NAVE, JOHN THOMAS, city ofcl.; b. Mountain City, Tenn., Sept. 18, 1921; s. Luther Garfield and Sarah Elizabeth (Dyer) N.; student E. Tenn. State U., 1940-42, B.S., 1947; student U. Tenn., 1942-43; M.S., N.C. State Coll., 1953; m. Ella Erminie McKnight, Mar. 17, 1951; children—Thomas Bradford, Kathy Lynn, Deborah Ann. Tchr. N.C. Pub. Schs., 1955-56; chief pilot Abney Mills, Greenwood, S.C., 1956—; mayor, Greenwood, S.C., 1967-71. Active Boy Scouts Am., P.T.A. County chmn. Republican party, 1964-67, city chmn., 1962-64. Served to lt. col. USAF, 1943-46, 47-55; PTO. Decorated Air medal. Named So. Aristocrat, So. Airways, 1963. Mem. Aircraft Owners and Pilots Assn., Am. Legion, C. of C. (com. chmn. 1963-64). Presbyn. (deacon 1959—). Lion. Clubs: Metropolitan Dinner (Greenwood, S.C.); Terpsichorean Dance (Greenwood); Carillon Ball, Inc. (Columbia). Home: 606 Brooklane Dr Greenwood SC 29646

NAVIA, JUAN MARCELO, educator; b. Havana, Cuba, Jan. 16, 1927; s. Juan and Hortensia (de la Campa) N.; B.S., Mass. Inst. Tech., 1950, M.S., 1951, Ph.D., 1965; m. Josefina Bonich, Aug. 20, 1950; children—Carlos, Juan, Ana, Betty. Came to U.S., 1961, naturalized, 1970. Tech. dir. Cuba Industrial Comml., Havana, 1951-53; dir. labs. FIM de Nutricion, Havana, 1953-57; asst. dir. Instituto Cubano de Investigaciones Technologicas, Havana, 1957-61; asso. prof. Vilanova U., Havana, 1955-57; research asso. Mass. Inst. Tech., Cambridge, 1961-65, asso. prof., asst. dir. tng. program in oral sci., 1965-69; sr. scientist Inst. Dental Research, U. Ala., Birmingham, 1969—, prof. dentistry, 1969—, prof. comparative medicine, 1969—, asso. prof. biochemistry, 1969—. Cons. Nat. Inst. Dental Research, 1971-73, Nat. Acad. Scis., 1973; mem. research and edn. com. VA, Birmingham, 1973—. Recipient San Esteban Conde de Canoga award Acad. Sci. Havana, 1955. Fellow Royal Soc. Health; mem. A.A.A.S., Am. Chem. Soc., Inst. Food Technologists, Internat. Assn. Dental Research (chpt. sec. 1972—), N.Y. Acad. Scis., Soc. for Environmental Geochemistry and Health, Am. Inst. Nutrition, Am. Soc. Microbiology. Author, editor: Experimental Models in Oral Biology, 1975. Contbr. numerous articles to profl. jours. Home: 629 Lexington Rd Birmingham AL 35216 Office: U Ala Inst Dental Research Univ Sta Birmingham AL 35294

NAVRATIL, ROBERT NORMAN, lawyer; b. N.Y.C., Dec. 27, 1928; s. John Reginald and Ida (Weissman) N.; B.A. cum laude, Maryville Coll., 1954; J.D. (scholarship grantee), U. Chgo. Law Sch., 1957; m. Nancy Jane Naylor, July 10, 1955; children—Rebecca Carol, Joseph Naylor, Angela Jane. Instr. polit. sci. Maryville, (Tenn.) Coll., 1957-58; admitted to Tenn. bar, 1958; since practiced in Maryville, Tenn., 1958—; mem. firms Bird & Navratil, 1958-65, Bird, Navratil & Ballard, 1966-72, Bird, Navratil, Ballard & Tate, 1973—. Pres. Blount County United Fund, 1966-67; pres. Blount County Boys Club, 1964-68; mem. Blount County Indsl. Devel. Bd., 1972; chmn. Blount County Democratic party, 1960-66. Vice pres., bd. dirs. Maryville Coll. Alumni Assn. Served with USAF, 1947-50. Mem. Tenn. (del. Ho. of Dels.), Blount County (pres. 1963-64) bar assns., Blount County C. of C. (treas. 1971, v.p. 1972, pres. 1973), Pi Kappa Delta (Alpha chpt.). Presbyn. (elder 1963—). Club: Optimist (pres. Maryville 1962-63). Home: 2038 Eckles Dr Maryville TN 37801 Office: 100 N Court St Maryville TN 37801

NAY, MARY SPENCER, artist, educator; b. Crestwood, Ky., May 13, 1913; d. Ben Franklin and Edna (Stringer) Nay; A.B., U. Louisville, 1941, M.A., 1960; student Art Center Assn. Sch., 1933-40; summer study Internat. Sch. Art, Mexico, 1946; m. Lou Block, Mar. 17, 1951; children—Malu Nay, Fayette. Fed. art project mural Louisville Pub. Library, 1934; N.Y.A. supr. art project, 1938-40; instr. Art Center Assoc. Sch., 1941-59; art prof. U. Louisville, 1959—; one-man show Ruth White Gallery, 1963; retrospective show, U. Louisville, 1967; represented in permanent collections Evansville Mus., J.B. Speed Art Mus., Ohio U., Athens, O., Ky. State Fair Exposition Center, Ashland Oil Co. and others. Dir. Children's Free Art Classes, 1951-55. Sec. bd. Jr. Art Gallery, 1950-55. Bd. dirs. Ky. Arts and Crafts Guild. Recipient bronze medal for contbn. to the arts from IBM, 1939; 4 annual purchase awards Ky. State Fair, 1954, 58, 60, 65, and others. Mem. Am. Assn. U. Profs., J.B. Speed Art Mus., Art Center Assn., Provincetown Art Assn. Democrat. Episcopalian. Club: Arts. Home: 207 S Galt Av Louisville KY 40206

NAYAR, JAI KRISHEN, entomologist; b. Kisumu, East Africa, Jan. 3, 1933 (came to U.S. 1958, naturalized 1968); s. Kishen Parshad and Harbans (Khosla) N.; B.S. with Honors, U. Delhi, India, 1954, M.S., 1956; Ph.D., U. Ill., 1961; m. Gisela Kathe Dora Hoelscher, Oct. 30, 1964; children—Veena, Karen, Gisela. Research asst. Indian Agrl. Research Inst., Delhi, 1956-58; NRC Can. post-doctoral fellow U. Man., Winnipeg, 1961-63; entomologist Fla. Med. Entomology Lab., Vero Beach, Fla., 1963—. Mem. Entomol. Soc. Am., Sigma Xi. Home: 2601 19th Pl Vero Beach FL 32960 Office: PO Box 520 Vero Beach FL 32960

NAYLOR, AUBREY WILLARD, educator; b. Union City, Tenn., Feb. 5, 1915; s. Harry Joseph and Clara Mae (Isbell) N.; B.S., U. Chgo., 1937, M.S., 1938, Ph.D., 1940; m. Frances Valentine Lloyd, Dec. 26, 1940; children—Virginia Dawson, Edith Margaret (Mrs. Jeffrey Ford Eastman). Mem. staff bur. plant industry U.S. Dept. Agr., Chgo., 1938-40; instr. U. Chgo., 1940-44, U.S. Naval Radio, Chgo., 1942-44; instr. botany Northwestern U., 1944-45; asst. prof. botany U. Wash., Seattle, 1946-47; asst. prof. botany Yale, 1947-52; asso. prof. botany Duke, Durham, N.C., 1952-59, prof., 1959-72, James B. Duke prof., 1972—. Cons. biology div. Oak Ridge Nat. Lab., 1957-58; cons. NSF, 1960-61, 62-63, program dir. metabolic biology, 1961-62; cons. Research Triangle Inst., N.C., 1968—, biology div. TVA, 1969—; mem. summer faculties U. N.C., Chapel Hill, 1960-61, U. N.C., Greensboro, 1964-65, Bennett Coll., Greensboro, 1964; vis. prof. botany U. Bristol (Eng.), 1958-59. NRC fellow, 1945-46; NSF sr. fellow, 1958-59, grantee, 1956—; Herman Frasch Found. grantee, 1957-72. Fellow A.A.A.S.; mem. Am. Soc. Plant Physiologists (life mem.; sec. 1953-55, v.p. 1956, pres. 1961, chmn. bd. trustees 1962—), Am. Inst. Biol. Scis., Am. Cell Biology Soc., Bot. Soc. Am. (life), Biochem. Soc., Soc. Exptl. Biologists, Scandinavian, Japanese socs. plant physiologists, N.C. Acad. Scis., Sigma Xi. Club: Cosmos (Washington). Contbr. articles, chpts. to profl. lit. Home: 2430 Wrightwood Av Durham NC 27705 Office: Dept Botany Duke U Durham NC 27706

NAYLOR, PLEAS COLEMAN, JR., realtor; b. Clareville, Tex., Nov. 22, 1914; s. Pleas Coleman and Beulah (Pettus) N.; student U. Tex., 1934-36, LL.D. (hon.), 1969; m. Lorraine Stakes, 1936 (div. Apr. 1960); children—Ruth (Mrs. Charles Schraedley), Ellen Ferne (Mrs. Ron L. Mooney), Patty (Mrs. Don Martin), Chester Slimp III; m. 2d, Ellen Watson, Apr. 14, 1962. Office mgr. Comml. Credit Corp., San Antonio, 1936-46; pres., owner Naylor Realty, Inc., San Antonio, 1946—; faculty mem. St. Mary's U., San Antonio, 1965-69. Dir. Northside State Bank, San Antonio, 1965-69. Dir. Northside State Bank, San Antonio. Mem. San Antonio City Council, 1971-73; campaign chmn. Alamo council Camp Fire Girls, 1971, council adviser, 1971-73. Chmn. Bexar County Democratic Com. for Election Preston Smith for Gov. Tex., 1970. Trustee S.W. Research Inst., 1970-72; bd. dirs. Taxpayers League Bexar County, 1962-64. Served with AUS, 1943-45. Named San Antonio Realtor of Yr., 1958; Tex. Realtor of Yr., 1968. Mem. Nat. (dir. 1973, regional v.p. Tex. and La. 1969), Tex. (bd. dirs.; pres. 1967) assns. relators, San Antonio Bd. Realtors (pres. 1950; dir. 1951-66), Soc. Indsl. Realtors, Nat. Inst. Real Estate Brokers (comml. and investment div.), Nat. Inst. Farm and Land Brokers, Nat. Inst. Real Estate Mgmt., Internat. Real Estate Fedn., San Antonio C. of C. (dir. 1971-73). Mason (32 deg., Shriner). Home: 327 Clubhill Dr San Antonio TX 78228 Office: 8062 Vantage Dr San Antonio TX 78230

NAZARETIAN, ANGELINE, educator; b. Fairfield, Ala., Apr. 29, 1928; d. O. Jeane and Alice (Yarchak) Nazaretian; B.S., Ala. Coll., 1950; M.A., U. Ala., 1958, also postgrad. Tchr. girls' phys. edn., sci. Graysville (Ala) Jr. High Sch., 1951-55; dir. girls' phys. edn. McAdory High Sch., McCalla, Ala., 1955-58; dir. health, phys. edn. Athens (Ala.) Coll., 1958—. First aid, water safety chmn. Limestone County chpt. A.R.C., Athens, 1958—; active Girl Scouts Am.; organizer, 1st pres. Athens Humane Soc., Athens Beautification Program. Bd. dirs. Ala. Heart Assn.; chmn. Limestone County chpt. A.R.C. Recipient Honor award Ala. Assn. Health, Phys. Edn., 1968; named Alumnus of Year Ala. Coll., 1968, Community Leader Am., 1968. Mem.

Jefferson County Tchrs. Assn., Am., Ala., Jefferson County assns. health phys. edn. and recreation, Ala. Edn. Assn., N.E.A., Jefferson County Classroom Tchrs. Assn., Am. Camping Assn., Am. Assn. U. Women (charter treas. Athens), Am. Assn. U. Profs., Athens Bus. and Profl. Women, So., Nat. assns. phys. edn. coll. Women, Delta Kappa Gamma. Pi Delta Epsilon, Kappa Delta Pi, Kappa Delta Kappa, Delta Psi Omega, Pi Tau Chi, Zeta Tau Alpha (chpt. founder). Presbyn. Mem. Order Eastern Star. Club: Athens Country. Home: 212 N Beaty St Athens AL 35611

NAZARIO, LUIS ADAM, dentist; b. Sabana Grande, P.R., Sept. 25, 1909; s. Antero and Ramona N.; B.A., Inter Am. U., 1930; M.Th., Evang. Sem. P.R., 1934; M.S.W., Tulane U., 1943; D.D.S., Loyola U., New Orleans, 1946; m. Rosaline Rodriguez Alonso, Oct. 27, 1936; children—Yolanda N. (Mrs. Ronald Goldman), Nilda N. (Mrs. Bob Brown). Pvt. practice dentistry, Santurce, P.R., 1947—. Pres., founder Health Coop. P.R., 1960-65, Retirement City P.R., 1963-73; pres. bd. trustees Evang. Hosp. Assn. P.R., 1955-73; bd. dirs. Geriatric Commn. P.R., 1966—; pres., founder Club Sebaneno P.R., 1953-60; pres. Gideons Internat. Assn. P.R., 1965-68, Assn. Elderly Persons of P.R., Inc., 1972-73; v.p. Council Chs. P.R., 1968-73. Served with AUS, 1943-44. Fellow Internat. Acad. Law and Sci.; mem. Coll. Dentists P.R., Am., Ohio dental assns. Presbyn. (elder 1955—). Mason (32 deg., Shriner); mem. Order Eastern Star (Grand rep. 1970—). Author: Principles of Dental Health, 1960; My Student Life in New Orleans, 1971; What is Masonry?, 1974. Contbr. articles to dental and cultural mags. Home: 168 Amatista St Golden Gate Guaynabo PR 00657 Office: (mailing) Box 6244 Loiza Sta Santurce PR 00914

NEAL, BILLY JAMES, city ofcl.; b. Hemphill, Tex., May 14, 1935; s. Arvie and Luciet (Williams) N.; grad. high sch.; m. Opal Sue Beard, Dec. 20, 1955; children—William Keith, Kristie Karen, Cindy Carol. Patrolman police force, Nederland, Tex., 1957-60, chief police, 1960—. Vice pres. Jefferson County Law Enforcement Council, 1971. Recipient Distinguished Citizen award Bus. and Profl. Women's Club, 1971; Outstanding Law Enforcement award Sabine Chiefs Assn., 1966. Mem. Jefferson County Sheriff's Posse. Club: Optimist (bd. dirs. 1965-70; pres. 1970-71) (Nederland). Home: 1407 22d St Nederland TX 77627 Office: 1400 Boston St Nederland TX 77627

NEAL, BOB WALLACE, sportscaster; b. Morristown, Tenn., Nov. 14, 1942; s. Carr Wallace and Margaret Lee (Susong) N.; B.S. in Journalism, No. Ill. U., 1964; postgrad. U. Mich., 1965-67; m. Melody Sandra Music, Feb. 23, 1963; children—Robert, David. Announcer, sportscaster sta. WLBK, DeKalb, Ill., 1961-64, sta. WKZO-TV, Kalamazoo, Mich., 1964-66; news editor sta. WKNR, Detroit, 1966-67; news dir. radio sta. WQXI, Atlanta, 1967-69, news and sports dir. WQXI TV, 1969—. Mem. lecturing staff Oglethorpe U., Atlanta. Mem. Nat. Assn. Sportswriters and Sportscasters, Ga. Assn. Newscasters (dir. 1972—), Alumni Assn. No. Ill. U. (regional dir. 1969—), Sigma Delta Chi (pres. Atlanta chpt. 1972-73). Methodist. Club: Atlanta Press. Home: 2223 Meadowvale Dr NE Atlanta GA 30345 Office: 1611 W Peachtree St NE Atlanta GA 30309

NEAL, DARWINA LEE, landscape architect; b. Mansfield, Pa., Mar. 31, 1942; d. Darwin Leonard and Ina Belle (Cook) N.; B.S. in Landscape Architecture, Pa. State U., 1965; postgrad. Cath. U., 1968-70. Landscape architect Nat. Capital Parks, Nat. Park Service, Washington, 1965—. Mem. adv. bd. to landscape architect assistant program George Washington U., 1973—. Mem. Citizen's Assn. Georgetown. Judge, Am. Assn. Nurserymen Landscape Awards program, 1971, 72, 73. Registered landscape architect, Md. Mem. Am. Soc. Landscape Architects (chairperson task force women 1972-74, coordinator steering com. women 1974-75, mem. task force nat. growth 1973-74, pres. Potomac chpt. 1974-75), Nat. Recreation and Park Assn., Pa. State U. Alumni Assn. (trustee D.C. area 1972-74, sec. 1972-73). Contbr. articles to profl. jours. Home: 2511 Q St NW Washington DC 20007 Office: 1100 Ohio Dr SW Washington DC 20242

NEAL, EUGENE PRESTON, petroleum geologist; b. St. Louis, Aug. 20, 1903; s. James Preston and Etta (Wrightsman) N.; Elec. Engr., Rice U.; B.S. in Geology, U. Tulsa, 1940; children—James Stanley, Eugene Wrightsman. Chief draftsman, office engr. Shell Oil Co., Tulsa, 1924-36; regional geologist, landman Tidewater Oil Co., Tulsa, 1937-51; chief geologist Toklan Oil Corp., Tulsa, 1952-55; v.p., chief geologist Kirby Prodn. Co., Tulsa, 1956-64; cons. geologist, real estate exec., 1965-68; chief geologist Viking Petroleum Inc., Tulsa, 1969—; cons. discovery new oil and gas res. Served to 2d lt. AUS. Mem. Am. Assn. Petroleum Geologists, Tulsa, Oklahoma City geol. Socs. Club: Petroleum (Tulsa). Home: 4114 E 42d St Tulsa OK 74135 Office: Suite 806 2805 E Skelly Dr Tulsa OK 74105

NEAL, FRANCES POTTER, librarian; b. Strong, Ark., Oct. 27, 1905; d. Finis and Lucy Letitia (Richardson) Potter; B.S. in Edn., U. Ark., 1945; M.A., U. Denver, 1949; m. Karl Neal, Apr. 25, 1931. Tchr. pub. schs., El Dorado, Ark., 1924-31; librarian Warren (Ark.) Elementary Sch., 1941-47; circulation librarian, reference librarian Ark. Library Commn., 1947-51, exec. sec., state librarian, 1952—. Councilor Ark. Library Assn. to A.L.A., 1951—. Recipient Progressive Farmer Woman of Year, Dem. award. 1957. Mem. A.L.A., Ark. (pres. 1950), Southwestern (dir. 1962—, pres. 1964-66, program chmn. biennial conf. 1964) library assns., Am. Assn. U. Women. Bus. and Profl. Women's Club (2d v.p. Little Rock 1956, Pfeifer Cup 1957), Kappa Delta Pi, Delta Kappa Gamma. Home: 108 Brown St Little Rock AR 72205

NEAL, GEORGE WILLIAM, investment co. exec.; b. Danville, Va., Mar. 19, 1935; s. Ernest Linwood and Kathleen (Fulton) N.; B.S. in Mech. Engring., Va. Poly. Inst., 1958; m. Jane Goodson Flynn, June 7, 1957 (div. Feb. 1968); children—George William II, James Linwood; m. 2d, Minnie Lois Yarbrough, Aug. 16, 1971. With U.S. Army Missile Command, 1960-61, NASA-Marshall Space Flight Center, 1961-65; partner Mason-Neal Enterprises, Huntsville, Ala., 1965-66; owner Neal Enterprises, Huntsville, 1967—; pres., dir. Financial Counselors, Inc., Huntsville, 1968; pres. Neal, Riser & Phillips, Inc., Huntsville, 1968—. Served with AUS, 1958-60. Register profl. engr., Ala. Democrat. Methodist. Clubs: Sports Car Am.; Burningtree Country (Decatur, Ala.); Valley Hill (Huntsville). Home: 1404 Monterrey Dr Huntsville AL 35801 Office: 208 Bob Wallace Av Huntsville AL 35801

NEAL, JAMES ARCHER, lawyer; b. Winston-Salem, N.C., Feb. 20, 1932; s. William Henry and Jeannette (Archer) N.; B.S., Davidson Coll., 1954; LL.B., U. N.C., 1964. Asst. to treas. Davidson (N.C.) Coll., 1955-57; supr. Security Life and Trust Co., Winston-Salem, 1957-61; admitted to N.C. bar, 1964; asst. solicitor Municipal Ct. Winston-Salem, 1964-68; gen. practice Winston-Salem, 1964—. Mem. Am., N.C., Forsyth County bar assns., Pi Kappa Phi, Phi Mu Alpha. Democrat. Presbyn. Club: Winston-Salem Bachelors (pres. 1970). Home: 611 Gunston Ct Winston-Salem NC 27106 Office: Wachovia Bldg Winston-Salem NC 27101

NEAL, JAMES EDWARD, hosp. adminstr.; b. Ooltewah, Tenn., Jan. 10, 1928; s. James Franklin and Arlzie (Parris) N.; B.S. in Commerce, U. Louisville, 1965; M. Hosp. Adminstrn., Med. Coll. Va., 1967; m. Birdie Summerhill, Jan. 8, 1928; children—Karen Sue, Teresa Ann, Edith Annette, James Edward, Jr. Asst. adminstr. High Plains Bapt. Hosp., Amarillo, Tex., 1967-69; adminstr. Berea (Ky.) Hosp., Inc., 1969-71; pres. Wilbarger Gen. Hosp., Vernon, Tex., 1971-73; pres. Mission Hill Meml. Hosp., Shawnee, Okla., 1973—. Bd. dirs. Madison County Mental Health, Richmond, Ky., 1969-71, mem. mental retardation bd., 1969-71. Served with C.E., AUS, 1946-48. Named Ky. Col. Mem. Am. Coll. Hosp. Adminstrs., Am. Coll. Nursing Home Adminstrs. Mason, Rotarian. Home: Box 428 Route 5 Shawnee OK 74801 Office: 1900 Gordon Cooper Dr Shawnee OK 74801

NEAL, JAMES WOODWARD, editor, actor; b. Lometa, Tex., Feb. 7, 1931; s. Roy Edwin and Iva Rue (Woodward) N.; B.A., N.Tex. State Coll., 1956; m. Patricia Ann Dulin, Apr. 17, 1954. Amusements editor Denton (Tex.) Record-Chronicle, 1954-60; Sunday and wire editor Ft. Worth Press, 1960—; actor Tex. Gridiron Show, 1957—, Casa Manana Theater, Ft. Worth, including Guys and Dolls, Lil Abner, Desert Song, Annie Get Your Gun, West Side Story, Fiddler on the Roof, others. Asst. instr. Denton (Tex.) Jr. Optimist Judo Club, 1959-60. Served with USNR, 1949-53. Mem. Actors Equity Assn., Sigma Delta Chi. Home: 5225 Camp Bowie Fort Worth TX 76108 Office: 507 Jones St Fort Worth TX 76101

NEAL, JOHN HILL, textile sales advt. exec.; b. Greensboro, N.C., Feb. 2, 1923; s. William Watt and Lucy (Vance) N.; B.A., U. N.C., 1943; m. Henriette Strickland Manget, Nov. 27, 1946; children—Henriette M., Lucette H., Frederick M. Founder, partner Hege, Middleton & Neal, advt. agy., Greensboro, N.C., 1949-57, pres., 1957-60; sales mgr., dir. advt. and pub. relations Stedman Corp., Asheboro, N.C., 1960, now sr. v.p. marketing. Pres. Tb Assn., 1956-58. Bd. dirs. Children's Home Soc. of N.C., N.C. chpt. Nat. Repertory Theatre. Served with AUS, 1942-45, 51-52. Decorated Purple Heart, Bronze Star. Mem. Pi Kappa Alpha, Delta Sigma Pi. Episcopalian. Clubs: Charlotte City, Asheboro Country. Home: 1110 Rockbridge Rd Asheboro NC 27203 Office: Stedman Corp Asheboro NC 27203

NEAL, JOHN YOUNG, utility co. exec.; b. Williamson, W.Va., June 5, 1930; s. James Young and Mary Frances (Mason) N.; B.C.E., Va. Mil. Inst., 1953; postgrad. Morris Harvey Coll.; m. Clara Miles Shumadine, Feb. 8, 1969; children—Elizabeth Mason, John Young. Staff engr. Columbia Gas System, Charleston, W.Va., 1953-54, 55-60; supt. gas distbn. Va. Electric & Power Co., Norfolk, 1960-64, supt. gas dept., Hampton, 1964-69, supt. gas operations, Norfolk, 1969—. Lectr. Southeastern Gas Assn., So. Safety Assn., Continental Army Command, Va. Electric & Power Co. Served to 1st lt. C.E. AUS, 1954-55. Registered profl. engr., Va., W.Va. Mem. Am. Gas Assn. Rotarian. Home: 1221 Buckingham Av Norfolk VA 23508 Office: Box 329 Norfolk VA 23508

NEAL, MARCUS PINSON, JR., physician, educator; b. Columbia, Mo., Apr. 22, 1927; s. Marcus Pinson and Mathilde (Evers) N.; A.B., U. Mo., 1949, B.S. in Medicine, 1951; M.D., U. Tenn., 1953; m. Gail S. Fallon, May 27, 1961; children—Sandra G., Marcus Pinson III, Ruth Catherine. Intern Medical College Virginia Hospitals, Richmond, 1953-54; resident in radiology. U. Wis. Hosps., Madison, 1954-57, mem. staff, 1957-63; practice medicine, specializing in radiology, Madison, 1957-63; instr. dept. radiology U. Wis. Sch. Medicine, 1957-59, asst. prof., 1959-63; asso. prof. radiology Med. Coll. Va., Richmond, 1963-66, prof., 1966—, dir. postgrad. courses dept. radiology, 1964-73, chmn. div. radiodiagnosis, 1965-68; asst. dean Sch. Med. Coll. Va. Commonwealth U., 1968-71, interim dean, 1971, asst. v.p. for health scis., 1971-73, dir. continuing med. edn., 1969-73, dir. Grad. Med. Edn., 1969-72, provost, 1973—; radiologist Central Wis. Colony, Madison, 1959-63; cons. radiologist VA Hosp., Madison, 1961-63, Wis. Diagnostic Center, Madison, 1961-63, USAF, Truax Field, Madison, 1962-63, McGuire VA Hosp., Richmond, Va., 1963—. Pres. Va. Council Health and Med. Care, 1971—. Served with USNR, 1945-47. Diplomate Am. Bd. Radiology. Fellow Am. Coll. Radiology; mem. Assn. U. Radiologists, Am., So. med. assns., Radiol. Soc. N.Am., Va. Med. Soc., Va., Richmond radiol. socs., Richmond Acad. Medicine, Brit. Inst. Radiology, Am. Roentgen Ray Soc., Phi Beta Pi. Presbyn. Home: 2822 E Weyburn Rd Richmond VA 23235

NEAL, MARY JULIA, educator, author; b. Auburn, Ky., Aug. 15, 1905; d. Presley Taylor and Nettie Lou (Pace) Neal; student Bethel Womans Coll., 1923-25; B.S., Western Ky. U., 1931, M.A., 1933; postgrad. U. Mich., 1943-45, U. Denver, summer 1965, Syracuse U., summer 1967. Instr. English, Western Ky. U., Bowling Green, 1934-41, dir. Ky. Library and Mus., 1964-72; dean of residence Kingswood-Cranbrook, Bloomfield Hills, Mich., 1944-46; asso. prof. English, Florence (Ala.) State Coll., 1946-64. Mem. South Atlantic Modern Lang. Assn., Assn. Am. Archivists, Am. Studies, Internat. Manuscript Soc., Sigma Tau Delta, Chi Delta Phi. Author: Shakers By their Fruits, 1947; The Journal of Eldress Nancy, 1963; (with others) The Shaker Image, 1974. Home: 1523 Park St Bowling Green KY 42101

NEAL, MAYNARD CONARD, transp. co. exec.; b. Birmingham, Ala., June 30, 1926; s. Robert Alva and Emma Lula (Tankersley) N.; grad. high sch.; student Internat. Corr. Schs., 1952; certificate Brickell Inst., 1959; m. Lydia Louise Kinard, Dec. 1, 1946; children—Sherelle (Mrs. Fred Funderburg Jr.), Helen Lynette, Forest Deane, Maynard Carrson. Purchasing agt. Wood Chev. Co., Birmingham, 1942-50; gen. mgr. Kinard Trucking Co., Tupelo, Miss., 1950-65, also sec., treas., 1962-65; traffic mgr. Emerson Electric Co., Tupelo, 1965—. Served to sgt. AUS, 1944-46; PTO. Mem. Northeast Miss. Traffic Club (dir. 1957). Mason. Home: Route 4 Box 260 Tupelo MS 38801 Office: 1015 S Green St Tupelo MS 38801

NEAL, OLLIE LEE, office products co. exec.; b. Louisville, Apr. 1, 1933; s. Ollie Lee and Ruth Allen (Wills) N.; student U. Ky., 1950-52; m. Ruby Jean Wiglesworth, Oct. 23, 1955; children—Myrlena, Ronald, Randall, Kathryn. With U.S. Postal Service, Lexington, Ky., 1955-58; with Office Products div. IBM, Lexington, Ky., 1958—, div. traffic mgr., 1968—. Served with USMCR, 1952-55; Korea. Mem. So. Motor Carrier Conf. Home: Rural Route 5 Vince Rd Nicholsville KY 40356 Office: IBM Corporation New Circle Rd Lexington KY 40505

NEAL, PHIL HUDSON, JR., mfg. exec.; b. Birmingham, Ala., Nov. 17, 1926; s. Phil Hudson and Amy (Gross) N.; A.B., Duke, 1950; M.B.A., Harvard, 1952; m. Sarah Swift Britton, Sept. 19, 1959; children—Amy Brannon, Phil Hudson III, Samuel Abney Britton. Investment analyst 1st Nat. Bank, Birmingham, Ala., 1952-55; procedures analyst Gen. Electric Co., Hendersonville, N.C., 1955-58; with Ala. By-Products Corp., Birmingham, 1958—, asst. mgr. nitrogen sales, 1962-63, mgr. indsl. nitrogen sales, 1963-68, asst. treas., 1964-68, treas., 1968—; dir. Smokeless Fuel Co., Birmingham. Trustee Advent Episcopal Day Sch., 1967—, pres., 1968—; bd. dirs. Advent Episcopal Assn. for Edn.; trustee Ala. Found. for Hearing and Speech, 1967—, v.p., 1968-69, pres., 1969-71. Served with USNR, 1945-46. Mem. Phi Beta Kappa, Sigma Nu, Phi Eta Sigma. Episcopalian. Rotarian. Clubs: Birmingham Country, The Club, Harvard (v.p. 1971—). Home: 3336 Hermitage Rd Birmingham AL 35223 Office: PO Box 10246 Birmingham AL 35202

NEAL, ROBERT ALLAN, toxicologist; b. Casper, Wyo., Apr. 21, 1928; s. William Alfred and Myrtle Lillian (Baker) N.; B.S., U. Denver, 1949; Ph.D., Vanderbilt U., 1963; m. Patricia Taylor, July 5, 1958; children—Paul Allan, Julie Ann, Stacey Lynn. USPHS postdoctoral fellow U. Chgo., 1963-64; asst. prof. biochemistry Vanderbilt U., Nashville, 1964-69, asso. prof. biochemistry, 1969—. Mem. food protection com. Nat. Acad. Sci., 1971—; mem. toxicology study sect. NIH, 1972—. Served with USAF, 1951-59. NIH research grantee, 1963—. Mem. A.A.A.S., Soc. Toxicology, Am. Inst. Nutrition, Am. Assn. Biol. Chemists, Am. Soc. Pharmacol. and Exptl. Therapeutics, Sigma Xi. Home: 229 Leonard Av Nashville TN 37209

NEAL, VERNON, lawyer, state senator; b. Byrdstown, Tenn., Oct. 10, 1931; s. Levi Percen and Mary Delia (Cope) N.; B.S., Tenn. Tech. U., 1952; J.D., U. Tenn., 1956; m. Mona Joyce Mahan, Feb. 16, 1958; children—Belinda Sue, Jeffrey Dale, Melissa Gail. Admitted to Tenn. bar; practiced in Cookeville, Tenn., 1957—; city atty., Algood, Tenn., 1958-64; mem. Tenn. Ho. of Reps., 1962-66, Tenn. Senate, 1966—. Bd. dirs. Bapt. Student Union, Tenn. Tech. U., Vocational Tng. Sch., Cookeville. Mem. Am., Tenn., Putnam County bar assns., Phi Delta Phi. Home: 1008 Oaklawn Dr Cookeville TN 38501 Office: First Nat Bank Bldg Cookeville TN 38501

NEAL, WILLIAM HARRY, JR., utility co. exec.; b. St. Louis, May 29, 1925; s. William Harry and Mabel (Rieder) N.; B.S. in Indsl. Marketing, U. Evansville, 1948; m. Ferry Anne Hall, Dec. 20, 1947; children—Diane (Mrs. James N. Bacus), David, Karen. With Western Ky. Gas Co., Owensboro, 1949—, indsl. engr., Owensboro, 1956-60, dir. indsl. devel., 1960-62, v.p. indsl. devel., 1962-66, pres., mem. bd., 1966—. Chmn. bd. dirs. Wesken Corp., Owensboro, Ky., 1966; v.p. Bus. Devel. Corp. Ky., Louisville, treas. Mem. bd. Jr. Achievement, Owensboro, Owensboro-Daviess County Progress, Inc., Family Y, Owensboro, United Way, Owensboro; mem. Ky.-Tenn. advt. bd. Liberty Mut. Ins. Cos., Louisville; chmn. Ky. Indsl. Devel. Finance Authority, Frankfort. Trustee Brescia Coll., Owensboro; chmn. Ky. Ind. Coll. Found., Louisville; pres., bd. dirs. Owensboro-Daviess County Indsl. Found. Served with USNR, 1943-46. Recipient Liberty Bell award Daviess County Bar Assn., 1971. Mem. Ky. C. of C. (mem. bd.), So. Gas Assn. (chmn. adv. council), Asso. Industries Ky. (chmn.). Democrat. Presbyn. Mason (Shriner). Home: 408 Magnolia Dr Owensboro KY 42301 Office: 311 W 7th St Owensboro KY 42301

NEALE, RONALD JOSEPH, indsl. engr.; b. Detroit, May 11, 1933; s. Cecil H. and Elfrieda (Eckert) N.; B. Indsl. Engring., U. Fla., 1958; postgrad. U. Miami (Fla.), 1969-70, Ga. Tech. U., 1972; m. Mary Jane Weyand, June 16, 1969; children—Jenifer Elise, Nancy Ruth. Draftsman Lockheed Aircraft Co., Marietta, Ga., 1955-56; with Fla. Power & Light Co., Miami, 1958—, sr. methods analyst, 1970-72, supr. projects and standards, 1972—. Served with USMCR, 1950-52. Registered profl. engr., Fla. Mem. Edison Electric Inst., Nat. Microfilm Assn., Am. Inst. Indsl. Engrs. (treas. 1962). Lion (sec. 1973). Home: 12835 NW 1st Ave Miami FL 33168 Office: PO Box 3100 Miami FL 33101

NEDIMYER, JOHN ADRIAN, ins. and mut. funds exec.; b. Flinton, Pa., Mar. 30, 1920; s. Rudolph J. and Mary S. (Gill) N.; grad. high sch.; m. Nadja U. Karachewski, Nov. 16, 1946; 1 dau., Lynn M. With Pa. Funds Corp., 1953-63; with Waddell & Reed, Inc., Washington, 1963—, resident v.p., 1968—. Served with AUS, 1942-46. Club: Washington Gas Light. Home: 3826 Bosworth Ct Fairfax VA 22030 Office: 7900 Westpark Dr McLean VA 22101

NEEDHAM, VIRGIL DWAIN, lawyer; b. Austin, Tex., Sept. 22, 1938; s. Virgil and Janie (Plunkett) N.; B.S., U. Tulsa, 1959, LL.B., 1962; grad. Nat. Coll. Juvenile Justice Nat. Drug Edn. Sch., 1973; m. Linda Kay Bush, July 9, 1962; children—David, Gwen, Scot. Supr. medicare unit Travelers Ins. Co., Salt Lake City, 1962-69; owner, operator Sonic Drive-In Restaurant, Arkadephia, Ark., 1969-72: admitted to Okla. bar, 1962, Ark. bar, 1971; practiced in Arkadelphia, 1971—; juvenile referee, dir. Youth Services Bur., Arkadelphia, 1971—; lectr. juvenile law Ark. Coll. Juvenile Justice, 1972, Henderson State Coll., 1972-73. Asst. scout leader Boy Scouts Am., 1961-62, leader Webelos, 1969-70, dist. commr., 1970 (awards); sec., treas. Little League Baseball, 1972—; pres. Clark County (Ark.) Baseball League, 1971. Chmn. bd. dirs. Clark County Attention Home, 1971—; bd. dirs. United Way, 1972—. Mem. Okla., Ark. bar assns., Arkadelphia Jr. C. of C. (pres. 1969-70, named Outstanding Jaycee 1970, Distinguished Service award 1972), Ark. Jr. C. of C. (v.p. 1970-71), Theta Xi. Mason. Home: 207 N 27th St Arkadelphia AR 71923 Office: 404 Clay St Arkadelphia AR 71923

NEEDLEMAN, MORRISS HAMILTON, sch. adminstr.; b. Bklyn., July 2, 1907; s. Samuel and Dora (Pargament) N.; B.A., Coll. City N.Y., 1931, M.S. in Edn., 1939; m. Jeanette Platzer, Jan. 31, 1932; children—Martin Robert, Rhoda (Mrs. Samuel Frazer), Richard Bruce, Jeffrey L. Tchr. pub. schs., N.Y.C., 1936-57, asst. prin. elementary, jr. high schs., 1957-70, prin. Pub. Sch. 206, Bklyn., 1970—; coordinator adult edn. reading program, adj. asso. prof. reading Bklyn. Coll., 1960—; supr. adult edn., basic reading skills improvement program, adj. asso. prof. reading Queen's Coll., Flushing, N.Y., 1965—, coordinator written expression program Coll. City N.Y., 1966-67. Dir. Facts on Dial, N.Y.C., 1951-53, Ednl. Research Assn., Bklyn., Ednl. Aids Assn., Bklyn., Growth: A Program in Remedial Edn., Bklyn.; cons. editor Barnes & Noble Inc., N.Y.C., 1939-47. Mem. Am. Assn. Sch. Adminstrs., Assn. for Supervision and Curriculum Devel., Internat. Reading Assn., Nat. Assn. Pub. Continuing and Adult Edn., Nat. Council Tchrs. English, N.Y. Soc. for Exptl. Study Edn., N.Y. English Council, N.Y.C. Elementary Sch. Prins. Assn., Council Suprs. and Adminstrs. N.Y.C. Author: (with William Bradley Otis) An Outline-History of English Literature, vol. I to Dryden, 1936, vol. II, since Milton, 1938; also published as one vol. A Survey-History of English Literature, 1938; (with William Bradley Otis) A Refutation of Mr. Lionel Trilling, 1943; (with Bartholow V. Crawford, Alexander C. Kern) American Literature, 1945; A Manual of Pronunciation, 1949; (with Abraham B. Perkel) Biology for All, 1950; (ghostwriter) Control High Blood Pressure and Live Longer, 1952; Handbook for Practical Composition, 1968; Basic Reading-Spelling Communication Vocabulary (Levels 1-10), 1972, Teachers' Manual, 1972. Editor various publs. Contbr. to profl. jours. Home: 2367 E 18th St Brooklyn NY 11229 also Lake Clarke Gardens 2991 S Garden Dr Lake Worth FL 33460

NEEDLES, ROBERT JOHNSON, physician; b. Atlantic, Ia., Mar. 31, 1903; s. Charles Wesley and Estelle (Murray) N.; Ph.G., State U. Ia., 1924, M.D., 1930; m. Helen Irene Swartz, Apr. 18, 1930; children—Eleanor Jane (Mrs. Leroy West Chapin), Susan Irene (Mrs. Glenn A. Schlecht). Intern Henry Ford Hosp., Detroit, 1930-31, asst. in pathology, 1931-32, asso. pathologist, 1934-35, asso. physician div. cardiorespiratory diseases, 1935-39; pathologist, asst. med. dir. Cia Ford do Brasil, Boa Vista, Para, Brazil, 1932-34; pvt. practice, St. Petersburg, Fla., 1939-42, 46—. Founding mem. Citizens Charter Group, St. Petersburg, Fla., 1948—. Served from capt. to lt. col. M.C., USAAF, 1942-46. Diplomate in cardiovascular disease Am. Bd. Internal Medicine. Fellow A.C.P., Am. Coll. Cardiology, Am. Soc. Clin. Pathologists; mem. Am. Heart Assn. (fellow council clin. cardiology), Assn. Am. Physicians and Surgeons (del. from Fla.), Am. Diabetes Assn., Am. Rheumatism Assn., Am., Fla. (pres. 1956-57) socs. internal medicine, Alpha Omega Alpha. Republican. Author: (with Edith Stoney) A Coronary Primer, 1958; Your Heart and Common Sense, 1964, 2d edit., 1973; also papers in field, essays various non-med. jours. Home: 1227 14th Av N St Petersburg FL 33705

NEEL, JACK FAGG, city ofcl.; b. Bluefield, W.Va., Apr. 19, 1930; s. Milton Fagg and Arie (Robey) N.; B.S. in Civil Engring., Va. Poly. Inst., 1952, M.S. in San. Engring., 1956; m. Kathryn Strother Hale, July 22, 1950; children—Deborah, Kathryn, Joanne, Linda, Elizabeth. Asst. maintenance engr. Washington Suburban San. Commn., Hyattsville, Md., 1954-55; teaching fellow Va. Poly. Inst., Blacksburg, 1955-56; design engr. M. H. Connell and Assos., Miami, Fla., 1956-57; mgr. Town of Tazewell (Va.), 1957-59, City of Roxboro (N.C.), 1959-67. City of Albemarle (N.C.), 1967—. Served to 1st lt., arty., AUS, 1952-54. Registered profl. engr., N.C., Va. Mem. Internat. City Mgmt. Assn., N.C. City and County Mgmt. Assn. (pres. 1970-71), Am. Water Works Assn. Lion (dir., v.p., pres. Roxboro, dep. dist. gov.). Address: City Hall Albermarle NC 28001

NEEL, ROBERT GEORGE, meml. park exec.; b. Doe Run, Mo., Mar. 10, 1923; s. Socrates R. and Nina (Vogt) N.; B.A., U. Mo.; m. Annette Yarnell Peter, Nov. 4, 1949; children—Asher, Robin, Nancy, David. Sales rep. H.O. Peet & Co., Kansas City, Mo., 1948-49; pres. Woodlawn Meml. Park, Orlando, Fla., 1949—; dir. Orlando Bank and Trust Co. Pres. Orlando United Appeal, 1962—. Served with AC USNR, 1943-46. Recipient Outstanding Citizen of Orlando award, 1963. Mem. Nat. Assn. Cemeteries (pres.), Orlando C. of C. (pres. 1968), Sales and Marketing Execs. (past pres.) Mason (Shriner), Rotarian (dist. gov.). Contbr. articles to profl. jours. Home: 1415 Country Lane Orlando FL 32804 Office: PO Box 15641 Orlando FL 32808

NEEL, SAMUEL REGESTER, JR., jr. coll. pres.; b. Alderson, W.Va., May 15, 1914; s. Samuel Regester and Blanche (Smith) N.; B.A., Emory and Henry U., 1935; Ph.D., Duke, 1942; m. Adriana Vander Jagt, Aug. 11, 1938 (dec.); children—Helen V. (Mrs. Robert Younskevisius), Samuel Regester III; m. 2d, Eleanor P. Neel, May 17, 1971. Prof., Lambuth Coll., Jackson, Tenn., 1942-44, Fla. State U., Tallahassee, 1948-51, 1952-57; dir. Inter-Church Student Fellowship, Kalamazoo, Mich., 1946-48; founder, pres. Manatee Jr. Coll., Bradenton, Fla., 1957—. Pres. United Fund Manatee County, Bradenton, Fla., 1969-70. Served with AUS, 1944-46, 51-52. Decorated Bronze Star medals (2). Mem. Fla. Assn. Pub. Jr. Colls. (pres. 1961-62), Fla. Assn. Colls. and U. (pres. 1967-68), Omicron Delta Kappa, Phi Delta Kappa, Blue Key. Kiwanian. Author: Personal Development, 1953. Home: 5825 34th St W Bradenton FL 33507

NEEL, WILLIAM STEWART, lawyer; b. Mooresville, N.C., Nov. 25, 1922; s. Samuel Stewart and Bonte (Wiley) N.; A.B., U. N.C. at Chapel Hill, 1943, LL.B., 1949; m. Agnes Preston, June 19, 1947; 1 dau., Frances LaVaun. Admitted to N.C. bar, 1950, since practiced in Mooresville mem. firm Neel and Randall, 1966—; solicitor Recorder's Ct., Mooresville, 1952-62; judge Recorders Ct., 1963-70. Dir., chmn. bd. Carolina First Nat. Bank; dir. Citizens Savs. & Loan Assn., Mooresville Telephone, Inc. Dir., pres. Lowrance Hosp., Inc. Served to lt. (j.g.) USNR, 1943-46. Mem. C. of C. (past pres.). Presbyn. (elder). Elk, Kiwanian (past pres.). Home: 173 Brookfield Circle Mooresville NC 28115 Office: 149 E Iredell Av Mooresville NC 28115

NEELEY, WALTER T., elec. circuit designer; b. Abernathy, Tex., Jan. 25, 1930; s. Troy T. and Elsie E. (Brasher) N.; A.S., Amarillo Coll., 1958; m. Elizabeth Martha Johnson, Dec. 29, 1971. With systems engring. dept. Southwestern Pub. Service Co., Amarillo, Tex., 1951—, sr. engr., 1969—. Tchr. basic electronics and safe boating and seamanship courses. Mem. Randall County Sch. Bd., 1959-61; radio officer USCG Aux., 1971—. Served with USNR, 1948-50. Mem. I.E.E.E., Inst. for Certification Engring. Technicians (sr.). Republican. Clubs: Panhandle Amatuer Radio (pres. 1970), Amarillo Yacht (sec.-treas. 1972). Home: 2902 Memory Lane Amarillo TX 79109 Office: 600 Tyler St Amarillo TX 79105

NEELY, CHARLES LEA, JR., physician: b. Memphis, Aug. 3, 1927; s. Charles Lea and Ruby Perry (Mayes) N.; A.B., Princeton, 1950; M.D., Washington U., St. Louis, 1954; m. Mary Louise Buckingham, Mar. 30, 1957; children—Louise Mayes, Charles Buckingham. Intern, Cornell Service Bellevue Hosp., N.Y.C., 1954-55; resident Barnes Hosp., St. Louis, 1955-57, fellow in hematology, 1957-58; sect. chief med. oncology U. Tenn., Memphis, 1973—; mem. staffs Bapt. Meml., City of Memphis hosps.; prof. medicine U. Tenn., 1971—. Served with USNR, 1945-47. Diplomate Am. Bd. Hematology. Fellow A.C.P.; mem. A.M.A., Am. Soc. Hematology, Am. Fedn. Clin. Research, Sigma Xi. Home: 440 Goodwyn St Memphis TN 38111 Office: 951 Court Av Memphis TN 38103

NEELY, J(AMES) WINSTON, plant breeder; b. Cotton Plant, Ark., Feb. 4, 1906; s. James William and Daisy (Holland) N.; B.S., U. Ark., 1928; Ph.D., Cornell U., 1935; m. Elsie Norris, June 13, 1935 (dec.); 1 son, Eugene Trahin; m. 2d, Betty J. Goodman, Jan. 13, 1973. Asst. in agronomy U. Ark., 1929-30, Cornell U., 1930-35; geneticist U.S. Dept. Agr., 1935-46; plant breeder Stoneville (Miss.) Pedigreed Seed Co., 1946-51; v.p., dir. plant breeding Coker's Pedigreed Seed Co., Hartsville, S.C., 1951-71, cons., 1971—; exec. v.p. S.C. Soybean Assn., 1971-72; adviser Clemson Coll., U.S. Dept. Agr., assns. and orgns.; pres. S.C. Agronomy Soc., 1973-74. Fellow A.A.A.S., Am. Soc. Agr.; mem. Phi Kappa Phi, Sigma Xi. Presbyn. Home: 203 Holly Dr Hartsville SC 29550

NEELY, MATTHEW MANSFIELD, II, educator; b. Fairmont, W.Va., Feb. 11, 1933; s. John Champ and Mary (Faust) N.; B.A., Ohio State U., 1957, M.A., 1961, B.S., 1962, Ph.D., 1967; m. Lahna Rogene Runck, Mar. 9, 1962; 1 son, Matthew Mansfield III. Reporter, Dun & Bradstreet, Inc., Columbus, O., 1957-59; tchr. pub. schs., Columbus, 1962-64; instr. Ohio State U., Columbus, 1967; asst. prof. edn. and philosophy Shepherd Coll., Shepherdstown, W.Va., 1967-70; asso. prof. history Lord Fairfax Coll., Middletown, Va., 1970—. Served with AUS, 1952-55. Decorated Bronze Star; Sigmund Rhee medal for valour (South Korea). Mem. Am. Hist. Assn., Brit., Winchester hist. socs., W.Va. Philos. Soc. (pres.), Va. Social Sci. Assn., Phi Alpha Theta, Tau Kappa Epsilon. Club: Owls (Fairmont). Editor: Jour. W.Va. Philos. Soc., 1968-71. Contbr. articles to profl. jours. Home: PO Box 113 Middletown VA 22645

NEELY, ROBERT ALLEN, physician; b. Temple, Tex., Mar. 1, 1921; s. Jubal A. and Almeida (Fordtran) N.; B.A., U. Tex., 1942, M.D., 1944; postgrad. Washington U., 1951-52; m. Eleanor V. Stein, June 29, 1944; children—Byron D., Warren F. Intern, also resident Hermann Hosp., Houston, 1944-45, 55-57; gen. practice medicine, 1946-51, specializing in ophthalmology, Bellville, Tex., 1955—; trustee, staff mem. Bellville Hosp., Inc. Dir. 1st Nat. Bank of Bellville. Mem. Bellville Ind. Sch. Dist. Sch. Bd., 1948-53; past pres. Bellville Area United Fund; exec. bd. mem. Sam Houston Area council Boy Scouts Am., also mem. Nat. council. Served with USNR, 1943-46, 53-55. Fellow Am. Acad. Ophthalmology and Otolaryngology, A.M.A., Austin-Grimes-Waller Counties (past pres.), Ninth Dist. (past pres.) med. soc., Tex. Med. Assn., Tex. Ophthal. Assn., Houston Ophthal. Soc., Tex. Soc. Opthalmology, Bellville C. of C. Republican. Lutheran. Clubs: Bellville Golf (pres.), Champions Golf, Doctors, Lions (past pres.). Home: 105 E Hacienda Lane Bellville TX 77418 Office: 24 N Bell St Bellville TX 77418

NEELY, STANLEY CARRELL, educator; b. Abilene, Tex., Sept. 11, 1937; s. Auburn Spencer and Mary Maxine (Perry) N.; B.S., So. Meth. U., 1960; Ph.D., Yale, 1965; m. Marilyn Ann Hawkins, June 3, 1959; children—Suzanne Marie, Mary Kathryn. Mem. faculty U. Okla., Norman, 1965—, prof. phys. chemistry, 1965—, mem. exec. com. Coll. Liberal Studies, 1971—, faculty research com., 1971-73. Bd. dirs. U. Okla. Wesley Found., 1966-73. Mem. Chem. Soc., Sigma Xi. Methodist. Home: 4 Bingham Pl Norman OK 73069

NEELY, WOODFIN CARLISLE, textile co. exec.; b. Florence, S.C., June 15, 1910; s. Woodfin Cowan and Florence May (Smoak) N.; B.S. in Commerce, U. S.C., 1931; m. Helen Earle Lee, Aug. 19, 1937; children—Robert Carlisle, Joseph Frederick. Pub. accountant, Columbia, S.C., Greenville, S.C., 1931-37; accountant Clinton Mills, Inc. (S.C.), 1937-41, sec., 1941-70, v.p., treas., 1970—, also dir.; sec., dir. Clinton Mills Sales Corp., N.Y.C., 1948—; accountant Lydia Cotton Mills, Clinton, 1937-48, asst. sec., 1948-62, sec., 1962-64, dir., 1953-64; dir. M.S. Bailey & Son, Clinton, Llanelly Corp., Ft. Washington, Pa., Va. Corp., Clinton, South Land Co., Clinton, Dillard Boland, Jeweler, Inc., Clinton. Mem. Clinton Recreation Commn., 1946-51, Laurens County (S.C.) Bd. Edn., 1951-59, Clinton Planning Commn., 1967-70, Comprehensive Health Planning Com. Upper Savannah Devel. Dist., 1971—; mem. adv. com. Bailey Found., 1951—. Bd. dirs. Clinton Hosp. Dist., 1959—. Mem. Sigma Chi, Delta Sigma Pi. Clubs: Palmetto (Columbia); Lakeside Country (Laurens County); Clinton Cotillion. Home: 303 W Walnut St Clinton SC 29325 Office: 600 Academy St Clinton SC 29325

NEER, HAROLD MAURICE, JR., elec. engr.; b. Oklahoma City, Nov. 17, 1935; s. Harold Maurice and Mary (McAnulty) N.; student N.M. State U., 1954-56; B.S. in Elec. Engring. with high honors U. Ark., 1960; m. Karen Sue Cox, Feb. 11, 1961; children—Dana Kay, David Brent. Civil service coop. trainee White Sands (N.M.) Proving Grounds, 1954-56; electronic engr. research and devel. dept. Phillips Petroleum Co., Bartlesville, Okla., 1960-68; electronic design engr. Applied Automation, Inc., Bartlesville, 1968—. Served with AUS, 1956-58. Mem. I.E.E.E., Tau Beta Pi. Baptist. Patentee digital analog conversion system, peak detector and amplifier circuit, others. Home: 516 Oak Park Rd Bartlesville OK 74003 Office: 216 RB 2 PRC Bartlesville OK 74003

NEES, BERNARD JOSEPH, investment co. exec.; b. East Liverpool, O., Apr. 7, 1908; s. Bernard Martin and Agnes Elizabeth (Snyder) N.; LL.B., George Washington U., 1931; m. Emily Grace Fuller, May 19, 1932; 1 son, Bernard Horace. With Johnston Lemon & Co., Washington, 1929—, partner, 1936—; with Washington Mut. Investors Fund, Inc., Washington, 1952—, pres., 1967—. Mem. adv. bd. Suburban Trust Co., Hyattsville, Md., 1952; dir. Washington Bd. Trade. Mem. Investment Bankers Assn., Nat. Assn. Securities Dealers. Club: University (sec. 1968-72; bd. govs. 1969-72) (Washington). Home: 7007 Chansory Lane Hyattsville MD 20782 Office: Washington Mut Investors Fund Inc Southern Bldg Washington DC 20005

NEESE, C. G., U.S. judge; b. Paris, Tenn., Oct. 3, 1916; s. Charles Gentry and Anna Claire (Nunn) N.; student U. Tenn., 1936; LL.B., Cumberland U., 1937; m. Althea Debord; children—Charles Gelbert III, Gerry Jan. Admitted to Tenn. bar, 1938; practice in Paris and Nashville, 1938-61; exec. asst. gov. Tenn., 1944; adminstrv. asst. Senator Kefauver, 1949-51; U.S. dist. judge Eastern Dist. Tenn., 1961—. Past sec., gen. counsel Capitol Life Ins. Co. Tenn.; past dir. Guaranty Savs. Life Ins. Co. Dir. primary campaigns Senator Kefauver, 1948, 54. A founder, original trustee, 1st pres. Family Clinic, Nashville. Mem. Phi Delta Phi. Democrat. Mason. Home: Greene County TN 37080 Office: US Courthouse Greeneville TN 37080

NEFF, HELEN MARGARET OSTERHOLM, writer, editor; b. Superior, Wis., Oct. 15, 1908; d. Albin N. and Ellen (Julien) Osterholm; student U. Neb., 1925-27, U. Cal., Berkeley, 1929-30; A.B., Washington U., St. Louis, 1933, Rensselaer Poly. Inst.-Tech. Writers' Inst., 1962; m. Carroll Forsyth Neff, Feb. 1, 1930, (div. 1957); children—Charlotte (Mrs. Walter R. Newman), Carroll Forsyth. Sch. reporter Omaha World-Herald, 1923-27; sec. Swedish Vice Consul, Omaha, 1927-29; case worker St. Louis Relief Adminstrn., 1935-36; med. writer dept. surgery Emory U. Sch. Medicine, Atlanta, 1951-55; writer-editor Center for Disease Control USPHS, Atlanta, 1955—, chief, editorial sect. Information Office, 1960—. Bd. dirs., editor newsletter Druid Hills Civic Assn., 1949-70. Fellow Am. Med. Writers Assn. (nat. sec. 1967-70); mem. Am. Pub. Health Assn., A.A.A.S., League Women Voters, Internat. Platform Assn. Methodist. Contbr. articles to profl. jours. Home: 400 Princeton Way NE Atlanta GA 30307 Office: Center for Disease Control Atlanta GA 30333

NEFF, JOHN DAVID, educator, b. Cedar Rapids, Ia., July 30, 1926; s. Howard Edgar and Irene May (Orr) N.; B.N.S., Marquette U., 1946; B.A., Coe Coll., 1949; M.S., Kan. State U., 1951; Ph.D., U. Fla., 1956; m. Mary Frances Muskoff, Sept. 27, 1952. Mem. tech. staff Bell Telephone Labs., N.Y.C., 1952-53; asst. prof. Case Inst. Tech., Cleve., 1956-61; asst. prof. Ga. Inst. Tech., Atlanta, 1961-64, asso. prof., 1964-72, prof. math., 1972—, acting dir. Sch. Math., 1970-72, dir., 1972—. Chief reader Advanced Placement Program in Math. Coll. Entrance Examination Bd., 1968-71, chief examiner, 1971—. Served with USNR, 1943-47. Mem. Am. Math. Soc., Nat. Council Tchrs. Math., Soc. Indsl. and Applied Math., Inst. Math. Statistics, Math. Assn. Am. (sec.-treas. Southeastern sect. 1972—). Home: 1552 Rainier Falls Dr NE Atlanta GA 30329

NEFF, JOHN EARLE, JR., ins. co. exec.; b. Lake Charles, La., July 30, 1924; s. John Earle and Mary Edith (Bergstedt) N.; B.S., U. Tex., 1944, B.B.A., 1946, M.B.A., 1948; student So. Meth. U. Inst. Ins. Marketing, 1957, Life Ins. Agy. Mgmt. Assn., 1959; m. Barbara Louise Davis, Aug. 7, 1948; children—Nancy Louise, Barbara Gretchen, John Earle, III. Mem. home office staff Austin (Tex.) Life Ins. Co., 1950; pres. Am. Savers Life Ins. Co. (merger Am. Founders Life Ins. Co., 1967), San Antonio, 1963-67, sr. v.p., chmn. exec. com., Austin, Tex., 1967-68; pres., mem. bd. Am. Founders Life Ins. Co., Austin, 1968—; dir. Capital Nat. Bank of Austin. Mem. bd. Tex. Life Conv., 1966-72; mem. bd. dirs. Lamar Savs. Assn., Austin, 1961; mem. bd. govs. Internat. Ins. Seminars, Inc., 1970-71; chmn. Ednl. KLRN Channel 9 TV Auction, 1970-71. Pres. Austin High Sch. PTA, 1968-69. Served to lt. (j.g.) USNR, 1944-46. Mem. Tex. Legal Reserve Ofcls. Assn. (pres. 1970-71; mem. bd. 1969-72), Nat. Assn. Life Cos. (mem. bd. 1970-71), Austin Jr. C. of C. (dir. 1952), Travis County Grand Jury Assn., Phi Gamma Delta (trustee 1951—, chmn., 1973—). Episcopalian (sr. warden 1971-72). Lion (dir. 1960-61). Clubs: Headliners, Citadel, Tarry House, Coronet, Admiral's (Austin, Tex.). Home: 1414 Wathen St Austin TX 78703 Office: PO Box 2068 6937 N Interregional St Austin TX 78767

NEFF, LUCINDA BELLE, genealogist; b. Colchester, N.Y.; d. Lewis Bennett and Jennie Lela (Rutherford) Neff; A.B., cum laude, Syracuse U., 1906. Tchr. pub. high schs., Middleburg, N.Y., 1906-08, Rockville Centre, N.Y., 1908-11, Muskogee, Okla., 1911-21; office mgr., law clk. Neff & Neff, Tulsa, 1925-63. Dep. gov. Gen. Soc. Mayflower Descs., 1957—, editor Mayflower Quar., 1961-64, acting sec. gen., 1962, Okla. sec., 1951—, editor Okla. Mayflower Newsletter, 1951—; organizing sec. Elder William Brewster Descs. Soc., 1963; Tulsa parliamentarian D.A.R., 1955-57, Okla. lineage research chmn., 1962-64; organizing pres. Okla. Ct. assts. Nat. Soc. Women Descs. Ancient and Hon. Arty. Co., 1964-65, nat. organizing sec., 1965-68; organizing sec. Oil Capitol unit Nat. Assn. Parliamentarians, 1956-58, pres., 1958-60. Recipient Mayflower cup for improving Mayflower Quar., 1963. Mem. Am. Assn. U. Women, Okla. Hist. Soc., New Eng. Hist. Geneal. Soc., Soc. Genealogists, Colonial Dames, Colonial Clergy, Magna Charta Dames. Research in Eng., Holland on Mayflower passenger, 1961-65. Home: 1316 S Trenton Av Tulsa OK 74120

NEFF, WILLIAM, JR., clergyman; b. Muskogee, Okla., May 22, 1925; s. William and Arnetas (Zink) N.; B.A., U. Tulsa, 1945; B.D., Garrett Bibl. Inst., 1947; m. Margie Fisk, June 19, 1946; children—William, Naomi, Jonathan, David. Ordained to Meth. ministry, 1947; pastor Sheridan Av. Ch., Tulsa, 1947-49, Pilgrim Presbyn. Ch., Vinita, Okla., 1949-55; St. Andrews Presbyn. Ch., Tulsa, 1955—. Chmn. dept. Christian edn., Tulsa Council Chs., radio-TV Tulsa Synod; chaplain Okla. legislature. Dept. Gov. Okla. Mayflower Soc. Mem. Soc. Mayflower Descs. (elder gen.), Descs. Colonial Clergy, Lambda Chi Alpha, Phi Gamma Kappa, Pi Gamma Mu, Pi Kappa Delta. Mason. Home: 10301 S Yale St Tulsa OK 74136 Office: 36th and Yale St Tulsa OK 74135

NEHER, CLARENCE M., chem. co. exec.; b. Twin Falls, Ida., May 14, 1916; s. S.S. and Emma F. (Fike) N.; A.B., Manchester Coll., 1937; M.S., Purdue U., 1937, Ph.D., 1941; m. Eileen Byerly, June 9, 1939; children—James Dean, David M., Mary Janet, Nancy. With Ethyl Corp., 1941—, spl. problems dir., Baton Rouge, 1941-57, dir. comml. devel., 1957-63, v.p., gen. mgr. plastics div., 1964-69, sr. v.p., 1969—, also dir. Mem. Baton Rouge C. of C. (econ. devel. com. 1964), Am. Chem. Soc., Chem. Market Research Assn., Comml. Devel. Assn., Soc. Plastics Industries, Mfg. Chemists Assn. (chmn. plastics com., dir.), Sigma Xi. Methodist. Rotarian. Clubs: Camelot, Baton Rouge Country, City (Baton Rouge); Chemists, Sky (N.Y.C.). Contbr. articles to profl. jours. Patentee in field. Home: 861 Delgado Dr Baton Rouge LA 70808 Office: Ethyl Tower 451 Florida St Baton Rouge LA 70801

NEIGHBORS, RONALD JOE, city mgr.; b. Hominy, Okla., Jan. 4, 1937; s. Joseph Andrew and Ruth Mae (Jordan) N.; student Hardin-Simmons U., 1954-55; B.B.A., Tex. Tech. U., 1958; m. Glenda Cherie Smith, May 18, 1972; children from previous marriage—Norman Bradley, Bryan Devin, Brooks Daron; stepchildren—Krista d'Ann, Mindy Gay. Budget officer City of Lubbock, Tex., 1956-58; asst. city mgr. Snyder, Tex., 1958-60; dir. of finance City of Arlington, Tex., 1960-63; asst. city mgr. Wichita Falls, Tex., 1963-66; city mgr. Carrollton, Tex., 1966-68, Odessa, Tex., 1968—. Bd. dirs. Odessa United Fund, 1968-73. Mem. Odessa C. of C. (dir. 1968—), Tex., West Tex. (pres. 1972), Internat. city mgrs. assns, Tex. Indsl. Devel. Council. Baptist (deacon 1968-71). Rotarian. Clubs: Odessa Exchange (treas. 1973). Home: 1708 Emerald Odessa TX 79761 Office: 411 W 8th Odessa TX 79761

NEIL, HUGH GROSS, instrument mfg. co. exec.; b. Gordonsville, Tenn., Aug. 28, 1920; s. James Benton and Nova Sanders (Dinges) N.; B.A. in Physics, U. Tenn., 1942; postgrad. U. N.C., 1943; m. Mary Elizabeth Euravd, Feb. 17, 1943; children—Hugh Gross, Patricia Jane (Mrs. Laurence Humbert). Physicist, Tenn. Eastman Corp., Oak Ridge, 1943-47; tech. dir. dept. physics U. Tenn., Knoxville, 1947-50, health physicist, 1949-54; with Spl. Instruments Lab., Inc. Knoxville, Tenn., 1948—, pres., 1948—; dir., pres. Spinlab., Inc., Knoxville, 1962—, Fiberlab., Inc., Gastonia, N.C., 1968—; dir. Staulab., Inc., Knoxville, Spinlab, A.G., Zurich, Switzerland. Dir. Civil Def., Knoxville, 1960-64. Mem. Knoxville C. of C. (mem. com. 1968-73), Am. Soc. for Testing Materials, A.A.A.S., Nat. Research Soc., Inter Soc. Color Council, Instrument Soc. Am., Textile Quality Control Assn., Phi Gamma Delta. Episcopalian (mem. vestry 1960-73; bldg. chmn. 1963-65). Club: City (Knoxville). Inventor in field. Home: 2312 Houser Rd Knoxville TN 37919 Office: Spl Instruments Lab Inc 312 W Vine St Knoxville TN 37902 also PO Box 1950 Knoxville TN 37901

NEILL, FLOYD MILTON, bank exec.; b. Gary, Tex., Jan. 18, 1902; s. Joe Darby and Alta (Cleaveland) N.; student grade sch.; m. Birdie Lorene Bearden, Apr. 30, 1926; children—Billie Jo, Charles, Duran Altar, Ruth Leaih, Floyd Ann Minor. Rep. Marshall Prodn. Credit Assn., Marshall, 1936-56; exec. v.p. First State Bank, Lockney, Tex., 1956-62, v.p., 1962; with First State Bank Marlin, Tex., 1962—, chmn. bd., 1962—; chmn. First State Bank, Marlin. Trustee Pine Hill Sch., Pine Hill, Tex., 1940-41. Democrat. Methodist. Mason (Shriner). Home: 425 E Main St Henderson TX 75652 Office: First State Bank 101 Liveoak St Box 720 Marlin TX 76661

NEILL, THOMAS TAYLOR, govt. cons.; b. Washington, Dec. 4, 1903; s. Charles P. and Esther (Waggaman) N.; B.S. in Mech. Engring., Cath. U. Am., 1925; M.S., Mass Inst. Tech., 1926; m. Helen M. Mitchell, June 8, 1929; children—Agnes A., Hugh M. Mech. engr. aircraft engine research lab. Nat. Bur. Standards, Washington, 1926-39; ignition engr. AAC, Dayton, O., 1939-42; asst. to dir. research NACA, Washington, 1942-58; chief research adminstrn. div., office of dir. of advanced research programs, NASA, Washington, 1958-61, chief research and tech. reports div. Office Advanced Research and Tech., 1961-70; cons. Nat. Air and Space Mus. Smithsonian Instn., Washington, 1971—. Mem. Soc. Automotive Engrs. (v.p. aircraft 1953). Author articles in field. Patentee synchronized street traffic control system, 1924, rate of fuel consumption indicator, 1942. Home: 4520 Hawthorne St Washington DC 20016 Office: 900 Jefferson Dr SW Washington DC 20560

NEISTEIN, JOSÉ MENACHE, Brazilian govt. ofcl.; b. São Paulo, Brazil, Oct. 20, 1934; s. Pinhas and Judith (Rosenberg) N.; B.A., U. Sao Paulo, 1955, M.A., 1956; Ph.D. (Austrian Govt. scholar), U. Vienna (Austria), 1962. Lectr. Brazilian studies U. Vienna, 1960-64, Free U. Berlin, Germany, 1964-67; instr. theory drama, aesthetics, philosophy Art. Mus. and Theatre Fedn., Sao Paulo, 1956-59, Nat. U. Paraguay at Asunción, 1968-69; dir. Brazilian Cultural Mission, Brazilian Ministry Fgn. Affairs, Asunción, Paraguay, 1967-69; exec. dir. Brazilian-Am. Cultural Inst., Fgn. Office Brasilia, Washington, 1970—. Mem. Theater Council, Ministry Edn., Rio de Janeiro, Brazil, 1956-59, Drama Critics Assn., São Paulo, 1956-59, Cultural State Commn., São Paulo, 1958-59. Contbg. editor Handbook of Latin Am. Studies, 1972—; contbg. drama critic lit. supplement O Estado de São Paulo, 1954-61. Contbr. articles to mags., newspaper lit. supplements fgn. countries. Home: 818 S 21st St Arlington VA 22202 Office: Fgn Office Brasilia 4201 Connecticut Av NW Washington DC 20008

NELMS, WARREN BOGER, elec. engr.; b. Brooksville, Fla., July 31, 1937; s. Morris O. and Imelda (Boger) N.; B.E.E., U. Fla., 1959; M.B.A., U. Pitts., 1968; m. Patricia D. Flanagan, Sept. 6, 1958; children—David W., Sandra P. Project mgr. Westinghouse Electric Corp., Pitts., 1959-62, 1963-68; quality control engring. sect. leader Martin Co., Orlando, Fla., 1962-63; dist. engr., power systems application engring. Westinghouse Electric Corp., Tampa, Fla., 1968—; tchr. electronics Pinellas County Sci. Center, 1970-71. Named Westinghouse Dist. Engr. of Year, 1972. Registered profl. engr. Mem. Fla. West Coast Power Engring. Soc. (sec.-treas. 1970-71, vice chmn. 1971-72, chmn. 1972-73), I.E.E.E. Methodist (mem. adminstrv. bd. 1971—, mem. ch. choir 1968-71). Club: Lions. Contbr. articles to elec. utility trade mags. Home: 4940 Shore Acres Blvd St Petersburg FL 33703 Office: Westinghouse Electric Corp PO Box 10597 Tampa FL 33609

NELSON, ARNOLD FRANKLIN, clergyman; b. Union, Miss., Jan. 29, 1911; s. Sidney Franklin and Susie (Gordon) N.; student E. Central Jr. Coll., 1930, U. Miss., 1932-34; B.S., U. So. Miss., 1946; B.D., New Orleans Bapt. Theol. Sem., 1949, Th.D., 1952; m. Donnie C. Winstead, June 29, 1935; children—Dorothy Jean, Charlotte Ann. Tchr., coach, prin., pub. schs., Miss., 1934-42; ordained to ministry Bapt. Ch., 1946 student pastor McNeil, Johnston Station and Tylertown, Miss., 1946-52; pastor 1st Bapt. Ch., Thibodaux, La., 1952-61, Calvary Bapt. Ch., Slidell, La., 1961-63; field sec. La. Bapt. Conv., Mansfield, La., 1963—, mem. exec. bd., 1954-62, chmn. state missions com., 1958-62, mem. stewardship commn., 1966—. Bd. dirs. La. Moral and Civic Found. Served with AUS, 1943-46. Mason, Lion. Home: 106 Hope St Mansfield LA 71052

NELSON, BOWEN CRESTON, former mortgage banker; b. Birdsville, Ky., Aug. 19, 1900; s. Carson Marshall and Lavinia (Bowen) N.; LL.B., U. Ky., 1942; m. Hazel Fowler, Oct. 26, 1941; 1 dau., Creston Annette. Admitted to Ky. bar, 1924, Fla. bar, 1930; pvt. practice law Paducah, Ky. 1924-25, Miami, Fla. 1929-33; atty. Keswick Corp. (subsidiary Md. Casualty Co.), Miami, negotiator, field rep. Home Owners Loan Corp., 1933-35; abstractor N.Y. Title and Mortgage Co., Miami, Fla., 1935-37; formed Nelson Mortgage Co., Miami, 1937, inc., 1941, pres., 1941-69, ret.; dir. Smith Ins. Agy., Inc., Peoples Am. Nat. Bank. Mem. Small Bus. Adv. Council Fla. Mem. citizen's com. U. Miami, 1952—. Mem. Miami-Dade County C. of C., Mortgage Bankers' Assn. Greater Miami (pres. 1957-58), Mortgage Bankers Assn. Am. (mem. nat. policy coms., 1957-58, nat. membership com., 1961-69, mem. com. arranging program nat. conv. 1961), Execs. Assn. Greater Miami (rep. of mortgage cos.), Fla. Hist. Assn., Internat. Platform Assn., Sons of Confederacy. Vizcayans Soc. So. Families, Delta Chi. Democrat. Mem. Christian Ch. Clubs: Kiwanis (charter mem. Biscayne Bay chpt.); Coral Gables Country; Century (Coral Gables, Florida). Home: 10255 SW 53rd Av Miami FL 33156

NELSON, DAVID ANDREWS, clergyman; b. Shannon, Miss. Aug. 14, 1926; s. Charles and T. Willie (Grant) N.; student U. Ala., 1946, Samford U., 1949; B.D., So. Bapt. Theol. Sem., 1951, Th.D., 1955; m. Jo Griffin, June 8, 1950; children—David Andrews, Kathryn Brown. Ordained to ministry Bapt. Ch., 1949; pastor Vine St. Bapt. Ch., Louisville, 1949-55, Highland Bapt. Ch., Louisville, 1956-61, 1st Bapt. Ch., Owensboro, Ky., 1961—. Teaching fellow So. Bapt. Theol. Sem., 1951-53. Trustee Ky. So. Coll., 1960-68, Southeastern Bapt. Theol. Sem., 1963-68; pres. Ky. Bapt. Conv., 1965-66; bd. dirs. United Fund, Owensboro Chs. for Better Homes. Served with USAAF, 1944-45. Mem. Alpha Epsilon Delta. Rotarian (pres. 1968-69). Home: 2176 S Stratford Dr Owensboro KY 42301 Office: PO Box 656 Owensboro KY 42301

NELSON, EDWARD SHEFFIELD, utility co. exec.; b. Keevil, Ark., Feb. 23, 1941; s. Robert Ford and Thelma Jo (Mayberry) N.; B.S., State Coll. Ar., 1963; LL.B., Ark. Law Sch., 1966; J.D., U. Ark., 1968; m. Mary Lynn McCastlain, Oct. 12, 1961; children—Cynthia, Lynn, Laura. Mgmt. trainee Ark. La. Gas Co., Little Rock, 1963-64, sales engr., 1964-67, sales coordinator, 1967-69, gen. sales mgr., 1969-71, v.p., gen. sales mgr., 1971-73, pres., dir., 1973—. Mem. N.G., 1957-63. Bd. dirs. Better Bus. Bur. Named Ark.'s Outstanding Young Man, Ark. Jr. C. of C., 1973; One of Am.'s Ten Outstanding Young Men, U.S. Jr. C. of C., 1974. Mem. Am., Ark., Pulaski County bar assns., Ark. (dir.), Little Rock (dir.) chambers commerce, Sales and Marketing Execs. Assn. Democrat. Methodist. Home: 11210 Shenandoah Valley Dr Little Rock AR 72207 Office: 400 E Capitol St Little Rock AR 72201

NELSON, ESTHER MARION, educator; b. Mpls.; d. Victor and Ellen (Martin) Nelson; B.S., U. Ore., 1926; M.A., Columbia, 1929, Ph.D., 1939, postdoctoral research, 1946-48; postgrad. U. Heidelberg, Germany, 1934; postdoctoral Harvard, summers 1940, N.Y. U., 1942. Instr. English, edn. State U. N.Y. Coll. Edn., Oneonta, 1931-43; educator U.S. Naval Operating Base, Guantanamo Bay, Cuba, 1948-50; from asso. prof. to prof. secondary edn. U. Houston, 1950—. Asso., Nat. Survey Edn. Tchrs. U.S., 1931-35; del. Christian Endeavor World Conv., Budapest, Hungary, 1935. Served in WAC, 1943-46. Recipient Internat. certificates of merit Dictionary of Internat. Biography, 1968, 72, Distinguished Achievement awards Two Thousand Women of Achievement, 1969, 70. Mem. Am. Assn. U. Women, Am. Assn. U. Profs., N.E.A., Nat Soc. for Study Edn., Assn. Higher Edn., Tex. State Tchrs. Assn., Acad. Polit. Sci., Nat. Council for Social Studies, Am. Legion, Nat. Audubon Soc., Nat. Wildlife Fedn., Wilderness Soc., Nat. Assn. Smithsonian Instn., Nat. Geog. Soc., Nat. Assn. Drs. in U.S.A., Internat. Platform Assn., Marquis Biog. Library Soc., Internat. Biog. Assn. (life), Nat. Travel Club, Kappa Delta Pi, Pi Lambda Theta, Alpha Lambda Delta, Alpha Sigma Omicron. Republican. Presbyn. Author: Analysis of Content of Student Teaching Courses in State Teachers Colleges, 1939. Editor: FEASC Intelligence Bull., 1944-45. Contbr. to various ednl. publs. Home: 4432 Wheeler St Houston TX 77004

NELSON, FRANK WELLINGTON, hosp. adminstr.; b. Streator, Ill., Aug. 16, 1919; s. Frank William and Anna (Hasenkamper) N.; A.A., LaSalle Peru Oglesby Jr. Coll., 1939; B.S., Ill. Wesleyan U., 1942; D.D.S., St. Louis U., 1945; student Harvard, 1960; m. Helen Agnes Schroeder, Apr. 23, 1944; children—Karen (Mrs. P.D. Hangsleben), Karla Annette. With USPHS, Dept. Health, Edn. and Welfare, 1945—, various positions from intern to chief depts. USPHS hosps., Kirkwood, Mo., Boston, Balt., Atlanta, Lexington, Ky., 1945-67, asst. dir., chief Operations Research Center, USPHS Hosp., San Francisco, 1967-72; dir. USPHS Hosp., Norfolk, Va., 1972—; asst. physiology Emory U., Atlanta, Ga., 1949-52; clin. asso. prosthodontics U. Tenn., Memphis, 1954-58; asso. prof. prosthodontics U. Md., Balt., 1963-66. Mem. Citizens Adv. Council, Marin Coll. Dist., 1970; mem. North Marin Fedn. Home Owners, 1969, Comprehensive Health Planning Council, 1969; dir. Ednl. Panel for Community Congress, 1970. Served with AUS, 1942-44. Fellow Am. Coll. Dentists; mem. Am. Dental Assn., Commd. Officers Assn. (chpt. pres. 1969), Clin. Soc. Pub. Health Service (nat. pres. 1968), Bay Area Armed Forces Dental Study Group (pres. 1969). Home: 1535 Bolling Av Norfolk VA 23508 Office: 6500 Hampton Blvd Norfolk VA 23508

NELSON, GEORGE AGLE, cons. structural engr.; b. Kansas City, Mo., Mar. 29, 1931; s. Gordon Vernon and Myrtle (Agle) N.; B.C.E., Kan. State U., 1953; M.S., 1957; m. Marcia Janyce Bailey, June 22, 1957; children—Jennifer Elaine, Eugene Gordon. Engr. Black & Veatch, Cons. Engrs., Kansas City, Mo., 1957-63; engr. Weitz-Hettelsater Engrs., Kansas City, Mo., 1963-64; engr. Patchen-Mingledorff & Assos., Augusta, Ga., 1965-71; owner George A. Nelson, P.E., Cons. Engr., North Augusta, S.C., 1971—; v.p., dir. Willowwick, Inc., North Augusta, 1970—. Mem. North Augusta Planning and Zoning Commn., 1970—, chmn., 1972-73; dir. Central Savannah River Girl Scout Council, 1972—. Served with USAF, 1953-55. Mem. Am. Soc. Civil Engrs., Nat., Ga. (pres. Augusta chpt. 1973) socs. profl. engrs., Joint Council Engring. and Sci. Socs. (chmn. 1969), Acacia, Sigma Tau. Lutheran. Mason. Home: 802 Springdale Rd North Augusta SC 29841 Office: 506 Georgia Av North Augusta SC 29841

NELSON, HARRY TRACY, lawyer; b. Clayton, Tex., May 30, 1895; s. Henry Calvin and Sudie Lorene (Davis) N.; grad. S.W. Tex. Tchrs. Coll., 1913; LL.B., Jefferson Sch. Law, 1930; m. Carrie Wright Marshall, Oct. 2, 1920; children—Harry Marshall, Virginia Wright. Tchr. pub. schs., Tex., 1914-15; U.S. revenue agt., 1919-20; partner Nelson & Nelson, C.P.A.'s, Dallas, 1926—; dir. Frito Co., Dallas. Counselor in astronomy Boy Scouts Am., 1944-55. Served with U.S. Army, 1917-18. Mem. Tex. Soc. C.P.A.'s (pres. 1937), Am. Bar Assn., Am. Inst. C.P.A.'s, Petroleum Club, Tex. Astron. Soc., Am. Assn. Atty. C.P.A.'s (treas. 1973-74), Chautauqua Literary Soc., Navy League V.F.W., Phi Alpha Chi. Republican. Methodist. Author: Heavens and Earth Declare, 1934; newspaper column Todays Tax Talk, 1936—. Editor: Texas Accountant, 1931-32. Patentee in field. Home: 3545 Southwestern St Dallas TX 75225 Office: 1st Nat Bank Bldg Dallas TX 75202

NELSON, HAZEL FOWLER (MRS. BOWEN CRESTON NELSON), civic worker; b. Mulhall, Okla., May 16, 1905; d. Oscar Frederick and Belle Virginia (Lowe) Fowler; B.A., U. Okla., 1927; postgrad. U. Wis., 1928; m. Bowen Creston Nelson, Oct. 26, 1941; 1 dau., Creston Annette. Tchr. journalism, English, sponsor publs. Chickasha (Okla.) High Sch., 1927-30; reporter Norman (Okla.) Transcript, 1930-37; feature writer Oklahoma City Times, 1937-41; mil. editor Miami (Fla.) Herald, 1942-45; officer Nelson Mortgage Co., Inc., Miami, 1941-69, sec., dir., 1942-69. Mem. bd. Childrens Service Bur., Miami, 1952; pres. Franklin Bush chpt. U. Miami Women's Cancer Assn., 1969. Recipient silver award for assistance through newspaper series Miami's Fgn. War Brides, 1946. Mem. Vizcayans Soc. So. Families, Fla. Hist. Assn., Internat. Platform Assn., Theta Sigma Phi (pres. U. Okla. chpt. 1927, Miami chpt. 1952-53). Democrat. Mem. Christian Ch. Club: Coral Gables Country. Home: 10255 SW 53d Av Miami FL 33156

NELSON, HOWARD COLLINS, civil engr.; b. Milton, Fla., June 4, 1914; s. Erasmus Lenwell and Florie (Brooks) N.; B.C.E., U. Fla., 1946; m. Florence Lucille Finley, May 24, 1936; children—Peggy Lucille (Mrs. James G. Rogers), Jerry Jim and Terry Tim (twins). Resident hydrographer Internat. Boundary Com., USDS, 1937-40; pvt. practice as civil engr., 1946-48; with Soil Conservation Service, U.S. Dept. Agr., 1949—, design engr.-civil. Gainesville, Fla., 1967—. Owner, Ceil's Ceramics, Gainesville, 1968—. Mem. Martin County Planning and Zoning Bd., 1957-58. Served from 2d lt. to maj., arty. AUS, 1941-45, 50-52. Registered profl. engr., Fla. Mem. Am. Soc. C.E., NAOGE (nat. v.p. 1968—, Fla. chpt. pres. 1965—), Am. Soc. Agrl. Engrs. (sect. v.p. 1963-64), V.F.W., Phi Gamma Delta (mem. bd. chpt. advisers 1964—). Clubs: U.S. 441 Square Dance (pres. 1964-65), Swinging Squares Dance (pres. 1968-69). Home: 4118 NW 36th St Gainesville FL 32601 Office: PO Box 1208 Gainesville FL 32601

NELSON, IVORY VANCE, ednl. adminstr.; b. Curtiss, La., June 11, 1934; s. Elijah Henderson and Mable (Tyler) N.; B.S. magna cum laude (T. H. Harris scholar 1959), Grambling Coll., 1959; Ph.D. summa cum laude (Dupont Teaching fellow 1962), U. Kan., Lawrence, 1963; m. Clotiel Riley, Sept. 9, 1960; children—Cherlyn Yvette, Karyn Renee. Tchr. chemistry Grambling (La.) Coll., summer 1961; research chemist Am. Oil Co., summer 1962; mem. dept. chemistry So. U., Baton Rouge, La., 1963-67, chmn. div. natural scis., Shreveport, 1967-68; asst. dean coll. Prairie View (Tex.) A. and M. Coll., 1968-71, v.p. for research and spl. programs, 1971—; Fulbright lectureship Universidad Autonomous de Guadalajara, 1966; vis. prof. Loyola U., New Orleans, 1967; sr. research chemist Union Carbide, 1969; cons. Oak Ridge Asso. Univs., 1969-72. Mem. Houston, Galveston Area Council Goals Study, 1971; mem. adv. com. Tex. Ho. of Reps., 1970. Served to s/sgt. USAF, 1951-55. Mem. A.A.A.S., Am. Assn. Coll. Tchrs., Am. Chem. Soc., Nat. Council U. Research Adminstrs., Phi Beta Kappa, Sigma Xi, Phi Lambda Upsilon, Beta Kappa Chi, Alpha Mu Gamma, Kappa Delta Pi. Contbr. articles scientific jours. Home: PO Box 2599 Prairie View TX 77445

NELSON, JAMES MERRITT, civil engr. b. Mpls., July 25, 1911; s. Merritt Heman and Hannah Esther (Smith) N.; B.C.E., U. Minn., 1933; m. Viola Ruth Williamson, Jan. 24, 1939; children—James Merritt, Stephen C. Surveyman, U.S. Geol. Survey, Minn., 1934, computer, Chattanooga, 1935-35; prin. civil engr. TVA, Knoxville, Tenn., 1935-73. Served from lt. (j.g.) to lt. comdr. USNR, 1943-46. Registered profl. engr., Tenn. Mem. Am. Soc. C.E. Home: 301 Whittington Dr Knoxville TN 37919

NELSON, JOHN PETTIT, lawyer; b. Gulfport, Miss., Aug. 5, 1921; s. John P. and Stella (Foret) N.; student La. State U., 1938-40; B.S., Loyola U., 1947, LL.B., 1950; m. Marie Anna Murphy, June 5, 1946; children—Marie Anna, Jeanne, Cesyle, Stephanie. Admitted to La. bar, 1950; asso. Dodd, Hirsch & Barker, 1950-54; asst. dist. atty. Parish of Orleans, 1953-58; sr. partner Nelson & Nelson, 1958—. Served to capt. AUS, 1940-45. Decorated Silver Star, Bronze Star medal, Purple Heart. Mem. Am., La., New Orleans bar assns., Am. Legion, Nat. Cath. Conf. of Interracial Justice. Home: 2432 Jay St New Orleans LA 70122 Office: Medallion Towers New Orleans LA 70130

NELSON, JOHN RAYMOND, JR., physician; b. Miami, Fla., June 30, 1930; s. John Raymond and Elizabeth (Turnley) N.; B.S., Wake Forest Coll., 1952; M.D., Bowman Gray Sch. Medicine, 1955; m. Gertrude Ann Hunter, June 30, 1956; children—Marilyn, John, Margaret. Intern Bryn Mawr (Pa.) Hosp., 1955-56; resident N.C. Bapt. Hosp., Winston-Salem, 1959-62; practice medicine specializing in internal medicine, Knoxville, Tenn., 1962—; mem. staffs St. Mary's, Fort Sanders hosps. (both Knoxville); asso. prof. clin. medicine U. Tenn., Knoxville, 1963—. Pres. East Tenn. Heart Assn., 1974—. Served to lt. USNR, 1956-59. Diplomate Am. Bd. Internal Medicine. Mem. Am. Soc. Internal Medicine, A.C.P., Knoxville Acad. Medicine (treas. 1970-72, v.p. 1973). Episcopalian. Home: 701 Westborough Rd Knoxville TN 37919 Office: 939 Emerald Av Knoxville TN 37917

NELSON, KENNETH, mfg. co. exec.; b. Diboll, Tex., Apr. 14, 1915; s. Fred Noel and Ora (Doolittle) N.; student Satterwhite Comml. Coll., 1933; m. Virginia Hays, June 4, 1938; children—Carol (Mrs. Melton L. Shaw), Michele (Mrs. Charles Fuller). With Temple Industries Inc., Diboll, Tex., 1932—, v.p., 1962—; v.p. East Tex. Logging Co., Diboll, 1957—. Sec. Diboll Sch. Bd., 1950-63; mem. City Planning and Zoning Commn., 1966—. Mem. Soc. Am. Foresters, Tex. Surveyors Assn. (pres. 1961-62), Tex. Forestry Assn. (dir. 1968-71). Mem. Ch. of Christ. Home: 303 Park St Diboll TX 75941 Office: PO Drawer N Diboll TX 75941

NELSON, LARRY ALAN, educator; b. Omaha, Oct. 28, 1932; s. Rudolph Lawrence and Elizabeth Coleman (Lewis) N.; B.S., Ia. State U., 1954; M.S., Tex. A. and M. U., 1958; Ph.D., N.C. State U., 1961. Research asst. in agronomy Ia. State U., 1954-55, instr. agronomy, 1955-56; research asst. Tex. A. and M. Research Found., 1956-58, N.C. State U., Raleigh, 1958-61; asst. land classification specialist Land Study Bur. U. Hawaii, Honolulu, 1961-64; asst. prof. Inst. Statistics N.C. State U. at Raleigh, 1964-66, asso. prof., 1966-71, prof. statistics, 1971—. Cons. Internat. Soil Fertility Evaluation and Improvement Project, Ministry Tourism Bahamas. Mem. Am. Soc. Agronomy, Soil Sci. Soc. Am., Internat. Biometric Soc. (treas., bus. mgr. 1969—; mng. editor Biometrics 1969—), Sigma Xi, Gamma Sigma Delta (pres. N.C. chpt. 1971-72; Award Merit 1973), Phi Kappa Phi (sec. N.C. chpt. 1972-73). Baptist. Kiwanian (pres. Capital City Club 1972—). Home: 1422 Banbury Rd Raleigh NC 27607

NELSON, LOUIS ROBERT, educator, veterinarian; b. Chgo., Jan. 8, 1930; s. Louis Robert and Emilie (Miehlke) N.; B.S., U. Fla., 1951; D.V.M., Auburn U., 1955; M.S. (NIH fellow), U. Mo., 1970; m. Dorothy Ann Rice, Nov. 24, 1955; 1 dau., Jemelle. Individual practice vet. medicine, large and small animals, Meridian, Miss., 1955-57; owner, operator small animal hosp., Clearwater, Fla., 1957-67; research asso. U. Mo. Sch. Vet. Medicine, 1967-70, asst. prof., 1970-71; dir. Vivarium Coll. Medicine U. South Fla., Tampa, 1971—, asst. prof. pathology Coll. Medicine, 1971—. Served with USAF, 1957-59. Mem. Assn. Lab. Animal Sci., Fla. Vet. Medicine Assn., Am. Assn. Zoo Animal Veterinarians, Alpha Zeta, Phi Zeta. Democrat. Presbyn. (elder 1961). Mason. Home: 5102 Rolling Hill Ct Temple Terrace FL 33617 Office: U S Fla Coll Medicine Tampa FL 33620

NELSON, NEAL STANLEY, govt. ofcl.; b. Chgo., Jan. 1, 1934; s. Stanley F.G. and Evelyn (Doran) N.; student Morgan Park Jr. Coll., 1950-51, U. Ill. at Chgo., 1952-53; D.V.M., U. Ill. at Urbana, 1957; Ph.D., U. Chgo., 1964; m. Margit Antonia David, July 7, 1966; children—Arlane Maria, Tamar Maria. Research asso. dept. pharmacology U. Chgo., 1963-64; NIH, Nat. Cancer Inst. spl. fellow dept. pharmacology U. Milan (Italy), 1965-66; in charge radiation bioeffects studies Nat. Center Radiol. Health, USPHS, Cin., 1966-69; dep. chief toxicologic studies sect., head cellular bioeffects unit Bur. Radiol. Health div. biol. effects USPHS, Falls Church, Va., 1969-70; dep. chief toxicologic studies sect., head cellular bioeffects unit Twinbrook Research Lab., Office Research and Monitoring, Environmental Protection Agy., Falls Church, 1970-73; radiobiologist criteria and standard div. Office Radiation Programs, Environmental Protection Agy., Washington, 1973—. Mem. com. guide for lab. animal facilities and care Nat. Acad. Sci.-NRC, Inst. Lab. Animal Resources, 1965-66, sub. com. cat standards, 1972-73, com. standards for cats, 1973—. Served with USAF, 1957-59. Mem. N.Y. Acad. Scis., A.A.A.S., Am. Vet. Med. Assn., Am. Soc. Lab. Animal Practitioners, Internat. Soc. Biochem. Pharmacology, Conf. Pub. Health Veterinarians, Sigma Xi, Phi Zeta, Lambda Epsilon. Contbr. articles profl. jours. Home: 11011 Saffold Way Reston VA 22090 Office: Environmental Protection Agy 4th & M Sts SW Washington DC 20460

NELSON, PHILIP PAGE, constrn. co. exec.; b. Greensboro, N.C., June 8, 1912; s. Philip and Lily Todd (Woodard) N.; student Coll. William and Mary, 1928-30; B.S. in Civil Engring., Va. Mil. Inst., 1932; m. Bessie Mae White, July 27, 1935; children—William Howard, Leila Lee (Mrs. Jay P. Schwertfeger). Insp., Va. Dept. Hwys., 1932-38; constrn. supt. Williamsburg (Va.) Restoration, Inc., 1938-39, gen. constrn. supt., 1939-41; supt. Doyle & Russell, Norfolk, Va., 1942; constrn. mgr. Walter P. Chrysler, Jr., Warrenton, Va., 1946-47; owner, pres., gen. mgr. Nelson Constrn. Co., 1947-73; pres. Central Concrete Products Inc., 1950—; pres., dir. Fauquier Savs. and Loan Assn., 1960—; mem. adv. dir. Marshall Nat. Bank & Trust Co., 1970—; dir. Sulphur Springs Investment Corp. Chmn. disaster relief com. Fauquier-Rappahannock chpt. A.R.C., 1955-67. Served with USNR, 1942-46. Decorated Bronze Star medal with Combat V. Mem. Am. Soc. C.E., Soc. Am. Mil. Engrs., Sigma Alpha Epsilon. Democrat. Episcopalian. Clubs: Fauquier, Fauquier Springs Country (Warrenton). Address: 194 Culpeper St Warrenton VA 22186

NELSON, RICHARD STANLEY, lawyer; b. Pitts., June 22, 1931; s. Ben and Minna (Blumer) N.; B.A., U. Mich., 1953; LL.B., U. Pitts., 1956; m. Inez Joan Krouse, Oct. 17, 1954; children—David Keith, Gary Robert, Linda Sari, Wendy Barbara. Admitted to Pa. bar, 1956; Ky. bar, 1961; practiced in Pitts., 1956; spl. agt. FBI, U.S. Dept. of Justice, Louisville, Covington, Ky., 1959-61; practiced in Covington, 1961—; judge protem, trial commr. Kenton County Ct., 1964-69; city atty. Ft. Mitchell, 1965—. Adj. asst. prof. law Chase Law Sch., 1973—. Served with AUS, 1956-59. Mem. Am., Ky. (Ho. Dels.), Pa., Kenton County (pres. 1972) bar assns., Am. Arbitration Assn., Soc. Am. Magicians, Soc. Former Spl. Agts. FBI, Am., Ky. trial lawyers assns., Phi Alpha Delta. Democrat. Jewish religion. Home: 135 Thompson Av Fort Mitchell KY 41017 Office: 11 W 6th St Covington KY 41011

NELSON, RICHARD THURLOW, govt. ofcl.; b. Waupaca, Wis., Feb. 23, 1932; s. Reuben Thorwaldt and Gertrude Elizabeth (Mason) N.; student U. Wis., 1950, Northwestern Prep. Sch., 1951; B.S., U.S. Naval Acad., 1955; m. Mary Lucile Delchamps, July 6, 1956; children—Richard T., Robert Frederick, Wayne Stewart. With Delchamps, Inc., Mobile, Ala., 1959-71, asst. to v.p. service operations, 1960-65, dir. service operations, 1965-66, dir. personnel devel., 1966-68, v.p. personnel, 1968-71; adminstrv. asst. to congressman L.A. Bafalis, 1971—. Pres. Children's Dental Clinic, 1967-68. Pres. Greater Gulf State Fair, 1965, Vis. Nurses Assn., 1968; gen. chmn. Am.'s Jr. Miss Pageant, 1967. Mem. Ala. Republican Exec. Com., 1968-71, chmn. 1st. dist. exec. com., 1970-71. Served as aviator USN, 1955-59. Mem. Mobile Jr. (v.p. 1962), Ala. Jr. (Ryan de Graffenreid Meml. award 1966; v.p. 1964) chambers commerce, Am. Soc. Personnel Adminstrs. Methodist (sec. adminstrn. bd. 1963). Home: 9611 Jomar Dr Fairfax VA 22030 Office: 1713 Longworth Bldg Washington DC 20515

NELSON, ROBERT BURWELL, JR., physician, educator; b. Blacksburg, Va., Feb. 6, 1910; s. Robert Burwell and Sallie (Seddon) N.; B.A., U. Va., 1932, M.D., 1936; m. Susanne Richardson Wickes, May 21, 1958; children—Page Mershon, Susan Seddon, Robert Burwell III. Intern surgery Johns Hopkins Hosp., 1936-37; resident obstetrics Garfield Meml. Hosp., Washington 1937-39; resident gynecology N.Y. Postgrad. Hosp. 1939-40; pvt. practice obstetrics and gynecology, Washington, 1946—; sr. attending gynecology Washington Hosp. Center, vice chmn. dept. gynecology, 1959-64, chmn., 1964-69, adminstrv. chmn. dept. obstetrics-gynecology, 1969-70, pres. hosp. med. staff, 1971-72; asso. clin. prof. obstetrics and gynecology George Washington U. Med. Sch., 1965—. Served to col., flight surgeon USAAF, 1940-45; mem. Res. Decorated Bronze Star medal. Diplomate Am. Bd. Obstetrics and Gynecology. Fellow Am. Coll. Obstetrics and Gynecology; mem. A.M.A., Washington Gynecol. Soc. (pres. 1968-69), Med. Arts Soc., Louis Mackall Med.

Soc., Osler Soc., Clinico-Path. Soc. (past pres.), Med. Soc. D.C., Phi Beta Kappa, Alpha Omega Alpha. Episcopalian. Rotarian. Clubs: University (Washington); Chevy Chase (Md.). Author articles in field. Home: 7933 Deepwell Dr Bethesda MD 20014 Office: 916 19th St NW Washington DC 20006

NELSON, ROBERT FREDERICK, educator; b. Chgo., May 26, 1940; s. Gunnard E. and LaVerne (Rice) N.; A.A., Wright Jr. Coll., 1961; B.A. in Chemistry, Northwestern U., 1963; Ph.D. in Analytical Chemistry, U. Kan., 1966; m. Judith E. Elster, Mar. 2, 1972. Asst. prof. dept. chemistry Sacramento State Coll. (Cal.), 1967-71; asso. prof. U. Ida., Moscow, 1971-73, U. Ga., Athens, 1973—. Cons., referee NSF, 1969—. Research Corp. grantee, 1968-69, Am. Chem. Soc. grantee, 1968-70, NSF grantee, 1968-73. Mem. Am. Chem. Soc., Electrochemical Soc. (Eng.), Western Electroanalytical Theoretical Soc. Contbr. profl. jours. Home: 425 Brookwood Dr Athens GA 30601 Office: Dept Chemistry U Ga Athens GA 30601

NELSON, ROBERT STANTON, civil engr.; b. Boston, Feb. 7, 1913; s. William and Hansine (Olson) N.; student Northeastern U., 1934-35, also Internat. Corr. Schs.; m. Muriel Kathryn Jones, Oct. 14, 1939; children—Judith (Mrs. Jon Zubin), Frederick C. With Vt. Dept. Hwys., 1952-60; mgr. Miller-Warden Assos., Balt., 1960-69; chief engr. Penniman & Browne, Balt., 1969-74, Tchr. adult courses U. Md., pvt. seminars for N.J., Md. depts. transp., quality control. Mem. Md. Gov.'s Council on Hiring Handicapped; tng. adviser Md. County Engrs. Assn. Served to 1st lt. AUS, World War II. Mem. Hwy. Research Bd., Am. Soc. C.E. (tng. com.), Nat. Soc. Profl. Engrs. Episcopalian. Mason. Club: Towson (Md.) Golf and Country. Contbr. articles to profl. jours. Home: 139 Woodrose Way Venice FL 33595 Office: Penniman & Browne Falls Rd Baltimore MD 21209

NELSON, ROBERT STUART, physician; b. Atlantic City, Apr. 7, 1911; s. Kent Nelson and Edith (Wills) N.; B.S., U. Minn., 1934, M.D., 1935; m. Mary Agnes Groves, July 11, 1936; children—Mary Sheila (Mrs. Jack Pearson), Patricia W. (Mrs. Scott L. Catlett), Roberta J. Internist, chief gastroenterology sect. dept. medicine M.D. Anderson Hosp. and Tumor Inst., Houston, 1956—; asso. clin. prof. medicine Baylor U. Coll. Medicine, 1961—; prof. medicine gen. faculty U. Tex., 1965—. Served to col., M.C., AUS, 1935-55. Fellow A.C.P.; mem. Am. Gastroent. Assn., A.M.A., Am. Assn. for Cancer Research, Am. Soc. for Gastrointestinal Endoscropy. Contbr. articles to profl. jours. Home: 1400 Hermann Dr Houston TX 77004 Office: 6723 Bertner Blvd Houston TX 77225

NELSON, ROGER LUCIEN JOSEPH, elec. engr.; b. Westbrook, Me., Feb. 22, 1920; s. Walter C. and Lydia F. (Ferron) N.; B.S. in E.E., U. Me., 1949; postgrad. U. Cal. at Los Angeles, 1952-54, U. Ala., 1959-60, U. Fla., 1966-67; m. Dorothy Leslie, Dec. 2, 1944. Mgr., engr. NASA, Kennedy Space Flight Center, Brevard, Fla., 1966—. Served with USAF, 1943-46. Mem. I.E.E.E., Am. Inst. Aeros and Astronautics, Armed Forces Communications Electronics Assn. Home: 3506 Roundtree Dr Cocoa FL 32922 Office: NASA Kennedy Space Flight Center Cape Kennedy Brevard FL 32899

NELSON, ROY CLAYTON, lawyer; b. Grundy, Va., Sept. 28, 1904; s. George Washington and Florence (Charles) N.; A.B., Kings Coll., Bristol, Tenn., 1942; J.D., Cumberland (now Samford) U., 1927; LL.M., McKinley-Roosevelt U., Chgo., 1946; m. Aline Cornett, June 29, 1929. Admitted to Tenn. bar, 1927, since practiced in Elizabeth; admitted to Va. bar, 1931; circuit judge Circuit Ct. 1st Jud. Dist. Tenn., 1966. Owner Roy C. Nelson, Investments: dir. Citizens Bank of Elizabethton. Appeal agt. Carter County Selective Service. Named outstanding male citizen of Carter County, V.F.W., 1972. Mem. Elizabethton C. of C. Mason, Elk (Jester, Shriner), Kiwanian (gov. Ky.-Tenn. dist. internat. 1949). Asso. editor Comml. Law League Jour., 1941-42. Home: 107 E G St Elizabethton TN 37643 Office: Dungan Arcade Bldg Elizabethton TN 37643

NELSON, THOMAS WILLIAM, pub. co. exec.; b. Little Elm, Tex., June 22, 1906; s. James William and Nora (Robertson) N.; student Baylor U., 1924-27; m. Ilvy Jeanne Boulet, June 15, 1930; children—Thomas William, Ward Boulet, Virginia Ruth, David Ray, James Lee. With Gulf Pub. Co., Houston, 1927—, dist. rep., 1930-38, sales mgr., dir., 1938-55, overseas mgr., 1955-57, v.p.-gen. mgr., 1957-68, pres., 1968-73; pres. Gen. Property & Services, Inc., 1973—. Mem. Am. Bus. Press, Am. Petroleum Inst., Assn. Indsl. Advertisers (organizer Houston chpt.), Nat. Oil Equipment Mfrs. and Dels. (past pres., regent), World Trade Assn., Houston Club Men's Forum. Baptist. Mason. Rotarian. Home: 3841 Overbrook St Houston TX 77027 Office: Gen Property Services Inc PO Box 1671 Houston TX 77001

NELSON, WILLIAM ALEXANDER, physician; b. Newport, Tenn., May 28, 1921; s. William Alexander and Ida Bell (Neas) N.; M.D., Emory U., 1945; m. Gloria Elaine Kickliter, Jan. 7, 1946; children—Gloria Elaine, William Alexander. Intern U.S. Marine Hosp., Balt., 1945-46, resident in internal medicine, 1946-48; fellow in medicine Johns Hopkins U. and Med. Sch., Balt., 1948-50; resident in radiology Emory U. Hosp., Atlanta, 1957-60; practice medicine specializing in internal medicine, Knoxville, Tenn., 1950-57, radiology, 1960—; chief of staff East Tenn. Bapt. Hosp., Knoxville, 1973—, chief radiology, dir. dept., 1962—, mem. exec. com., 1961—; mem. staff East Tenn. Children's Hosp., Knoxville, 1964—, U. Tenn. Meml. Research Center and Hosp., Knoxville, 1960—; cons. radiology Valentine Shults Hosp., Newport, 1963—, Oak Ridge Nat. Lab., since 1964—. Dir. Valley Fidelity Bank and Trust Co., Knoxville. Mem. Tenn. Hosp. Licensing Bd., 1956-57. Served with AUS, 1944-45, USPHS, 1945-46. Fellow Am. Coll. Radiology; mem. Knoxville Acad. Medicine (exec. com. 1953-54, ethical relations com., policy, pub. welfare com., regional med. program com. 1965—), Am., Tenn. med. assns., Tenn., East Tenn. (pres. 1969-70), Knoxville radiol. socs., Radiol. Soc. N.Am., Am. Roentgen Ray Soc., Soc. Nuclear Medicine. Club: Cherokee Country (pres. 1968-70) (Knoxville). Contbr. articles to profl. jours. Home: 4265 Holloway Dr Knoxville TN 37919 Office: East Tenn Bapt Hosp Dept Radiology Knoxville TN 37901

NELSON, WILLIAM EUGENE, lawyer; b. Roland, Ia., Sept. 23, 1927; s. Samuel J. and Katherine (Coffey) N.; B.A., State U. Ia., 1950; J.D., Drake U., 1957; m. Sherlee M. Stanford, July 11, 1959; children—Anne Elizabeth, Kristin Stanford, William Coffey, Admitted to D.C. bar, Ia. bar; with Liberty Mut. Ins. Co., 1950-54; atty. U.S. Dept. Justice, 1957-74; partner firm Qualley & Nelson, Washington, 1974—. Served with USNR, 1945-46. Mem. Fed., Am. bar assns., State Bar Ia., Internat. Platform Assn. Order of Coif, Omicron Delta Kappa, Delta Theta Phi. Home: 4422 Ridge St Chevy Chase MD 20015 Office: 1819 H St NW Suite 320 Washington DC 20006

NEMEC, JOSEPH ROBERT, accountant; b. Corpus Christi, Mar. 19, 1943; s. Frederick Joe and Annastazie (Spalek) N.; B.B.A., U. Notre Dame, 1965; postgrad. St. Mary's U., 1966-67; m. Pamela Osterloh, June 15, 1968; 1 dau., Kimberly Ann. Staff accountant Lybrand, Ross Bros. & Montgomery, Houston, 1967-70, Sidney A. Sparks, Alice, Tex., 1970-72; practice certified pub. accounting, Alice, 1972—. Served with USCGR, 1966-73. Mem. Am. Inst. C.P.A.'s, Tex., Corpus Christi socs. certified pub. accountants. Kiwanian (treas. Alice 1971-73, pres. 1973—). Home: 1117 Arcadia St Alice TX 78332 Office: 1328 Roosevelt St Alice TX 78332

NEMUTH, HAROLD ISAAC, physician; b. Norfolk, Va., Mar. 12, 1912; s. Marcus Cohen and Rose (Lasdan) N.; B.A., Columbia, 1934; M.D., Med. Coll. Va., 1939; m. Doreen Graham, Mar. 22, 1947; children—Mark Graham, Karen Lasdan, William Benson. Intern Med. Coll. Va., 1938-39, Knickerbocker, N.Y., 1939-40; Sheltering Arms, Richmond, Va., 1940-41, St. Elizabeth Hosp., Richmond, 1941-42; practice medicine, Richmond, 1947—; asso. in medicine Med. Coll. Va., 1956—, asso. prof. preventive medicine, 1958—, acting chmn. dept. preventive medicine, 1959-62; chief of staff Sheltering Arms Hosp., 1956-57. Served with M.C., USNR, 1942-46. Mem. A.M.A., Med. Soc. Va. (v.p. 1970-71), Richmond Acad. Medicine (v.p. 1970-71), Am. Pub. Health Assn., Assn. Am. Med. Colls., Assn. Tchrs. Preventive Medicine, Pan Am. Med. Assn., Am., Internat. gerontological socs. Jewish religion. Home: 5518 Riverside Dr Richmond VA 23225 Office: 2012 Monument Av Richmond VA 23220

NENTWIG, KLAUS PETER, architect; b. Duisburg, Germany, June 2, 1928; s. Paul and Katharina (Peiler) N.; Vordiplom/Arch. Tech. U. (Braunschweig, Germany), 1952; Dipl. Ingenieur/Arch. Tech. U. (Graz, Austria), 1954; m. June Marion Harkness, Mar. 16, 1957; children—Susanne Adelheid, Michael Talbot. Came to U.S., 1957, naturalized, 1960. Architect, prof. Hanns Dustmann, Duesseldorf, Germany, 1955-57; project architect Knappe & Johnson, Manhasset, N.Y., 1957-59; designer Selmon T. Franklin, Chattanooga, Tenn., 1959-61, asso. architect, 1963-65; project architect, mgr. A.M. Kinney Assos., Cin., 1961-63; pvt. practice architecture, planning, Chattanooga, Tenn., 1965—; instr. Chattanooga City Coll., 1965-67; dir. Wright Systems Internat., 1970—; dir. Chattanooga Choo-Choo Co., 1972—. Chmn. Signal Mountain Planning Commn., 1966—; dir. Chattanooga Area Adult Edn. Council, 1970-72; dir. Consultation on Ch. and Urban Life, 1970-72; pres. Chattanooga Allied Arts Council, 1966-67, v.p. 1965, dir. 1963. Bd. dirs. Chattanooga Opera Assn.; bd. dirs. Cadek Music Conservatory. Served with German Army, 1944-45. Mem. Am. Inst. Architects. Tenn. Soc. Architects (v.p. 1967, dir. 1968), Chattanooga chpt. Am. Inst. Architects (sec.-treas. 1965, v.p. 1966, pres. 1967, dir. 1968, 1973). Home: 311 Signal Mountain Blvd Signal Mountain TN 37377 Office: 300 Professional Bldg Chattanooga TN 37402

NEPVEUX, FELIX JOSEPH IV, cable TV system exec.; b. Jacksonville, Fla., May 19, 1947; s. Felix Joseph and Ethel Seabrook (Trenholm) N.; B.S. in Elec. Engring. with honors, Clemson U., 1969. Mgr., also chief engr. Carolina Cable TV, Inc., Newberry, S.C., 1972-73; asst. mgr. Cable TV of Hartsville, Inc. (S.C.), 1973—. Tech. rep. to bd. dirs. S.C. Cable TV Assn., 1973—. Mem. Newberry Community Players, 1972-73. Served with USNR, 1969-72; Vietnam. Recipient Comdg. Officers Commendation U.S.S. Long Beach; named Distinguished Naval Grad., Navy Officer Candidate Sch., 1969. Republican. Presbyn. Home: Apt E8 Farmington Apts Hartsville SC 29550 Office: Cable TV of Hartsville Box 1045 Hartsville SC 29550

NESBIT, PHYLLIS SCHNEIDER (MRS. PETER N. NESBIT), lawyer; b. New Kirk, Okla., Sept. 21, 1919; d. Vernon Lee and Irma Mae (Biddle) Schneider; B.S. in Chemistry, U. Ala., 1948, LL.B., 1958; m. Peter N. Nesbit, Sept. 14, 1939. Draftsman, Drydock & Shipbldg. Co., Mobile, Ala., 1942-45; tech. sec. B. F. Goodrich Co., Tuscaloosa, Ala., 1949-55; sec. Ala. Bus. Research Council, University, 1955-58; admitted to Ala. bar, 1958; partner firm Wilters, Brantley & Nesbit, Robertsdale, Ala., 1958—; judge Municipal Ct., Daphne, Ala. Sec., Daphne Civic Assn., 1962-71; auditor Joint Legislative Council Ala., 1970-71, treas., 1972-73. Mem. Ala. State Bar, Baldwin County Bar Assn. (pres. 1967-68), Nat. Assn. Women Lawyers, Ala. Women's Lawyers Assn. (pres. 1966-67), Ala. Municipal Judges Assn. (pres. 1970), Am. Judicature Soc., Bus. and Profl. Womens Club (chpt. pres. 1974-75), Gamma Sigma Epsilon. Methodist (steward, sec. 1960-64, sec. treas. 1965—). Mem. Order Eastern Star (worthy matron 1963-64). Home: 411 Church St Daphne AL 36526 Office: Wilters Brantley & Nesbit Box 555 Robertsdale AL 36567

NESBITT, FRANK WILBUR, lawyer; b. Miami, Okla., Dec. 26, 1916; s. Frank Wilbur and Nelle May (Grayson) N.; B.A., Okla. U., 1937; J.D., U. Tex., 1939; m. Delores Marie Shaw, Feb. 4, 1950; children—Mary Nelle (Mrs. Bruce Ralston), Kathleen Marie (Mrs. Dan Smith). Admitted to Tex. bar, 1939; pvt. practice law, Corpus Christi, 1939-40; asst. city atty. Corpus Christi, 1941-42; partner King & Nesbitt, Corpus Christi, 1946-53; partner Wood, Burney, Nesbitt & Ryan, Corpus Christi, 1954—. Served to capt. F.A., AUS, 1942-45. Decorated Bronze Star. Fellow Tex. Bar Found., Am. Coll. Trial Lawyers; mem. Am., Nuces County bar assns., State Bar Tex., Order of Coif, Sigma Nu, Phi Delta Phi. Home: 929 Miramar St Corpus Christi TX 78411 Office: Petroleum Tower Corpus Christi TX 78401

NESMITH, VERA COX, state ofcl.; b. St. Catherines, Ont., Can., Oct. 24, 1917; d. Ernest Henry and Edith (Rogers) Cox; came to U.S., 1921, naturalized, 1941; diploma Losey Secretarial Sch., 1937; certificate Orlando Jr. Coll., 1960; m. J. Vernon NeSmith, Dec. 3, 1966 (dec. Apr. 1974). Staff mem. Losey Secretarial Sch., 1937-38; with Fla. Div. Vocational Rehab., Orlando, also Winter Park, 1938—, dist. sec. to dist. dir., also in charge secs., 1948—, sec. II, DVR, sec. to dir. 1968—. Mem. Am. Assn. Med Assts. (program chmn. nat. conv. 1963, chmn., sec-treas.), Fla. (pres. 1961, del. nat. conv. 1961, 63, program chmn. state conv. 1964, membership chmn.; mem. past pres.'s council, med. Asst. of Year award 1965), Orange County (pres. 1959-61, dir. 1961-64, del. state conv. 1960, 61, rec. sec., Outstanding Mem. of Year award) med. assts. assns., Am. Acad. Med. Adminstrs. (chmn. legislative com.), Nat., Fla. (citation 1964) rehab. assns., Fla. (charter, dir. 1973-75, program chmn. 1972-73), Orlando (charter), Nat. assns. rehab. secs. Methodist. Home: 1912 Weber Av Orlando FL 32803 Office: 934 N Magnolia Av Orlando FL 32801

NETHERCUT, PHILIP EDWIN, assn. exec.; b. Indpls., Apr. 3, 1921; s. William Richard and Ruth Salome (Habbe) N.; B.S., Beloit Coll., 1942; M.S., Lawrence Coll., 1944, Ph.D., 1949; m. Leah Teresa Diehl, Apr. 9, 1949; children—Bruce Philip, Gail Ellen, Anne Louise. With Watervliet Paper Co. (Mich.), 1949-50; research mgr. Scott Paper Co., 1951-56; with T.A.P.P.I., N.Y.C., now Atlanta, 1957—, sec.-treas., 1959-60, exec. sec., 1960—, treas., 1964—. Served to lt. (j.g.) USNR, 1944-46. Recipient Distinguished Service citation Beloit Coll., 1967. Fellow T.A.P.P.I.; mem. Paper Industry Mgmt. Assn., Canadian Pulp and Paper Assn. Tech. Sect., Brit. Paper and Board Makers Assn. Tech. Sect., Australian Pulp and Paper Industry Tech. Assn., Swedish Soc. Pulp and Paper Engrs., French Assn. Technique de l Industrie Papetiere, German Soc. Cellulose and Paper Chemists and Engrs., Finnish Paper Engrs. Assn., Inst. Paper Chemistry Alumni Assn. (chmn. 1960), Council Engring. and Sci. Soc. Secs. (pres. 1968), Phi Beta Kappa, Beta Theta Pi. Conglist. Clubs: Chemists' (N.Y.C.); Scarsdale Town. Home: 9240 Huntcliff Trace NE Atlanta GA 30378 Office: 1 Dunwoody Park Atlanta GA 30341

NETTLES, EUGENE LEROY, lawyer; b. Lake City, S.C., Sept. 15, 1929; s. Leo Clayton and Marian Rosabelle (Rutland) N.; student The Citadel, 1945-47; J.D. cum laude, U.S.C., 1953; m. Beverly Jean Herlong, Mar. 15, 1953; children—Eugene LeRoy, Marian Dawn, Michael Gary. Admitted to S.C. bar, 1952; mem. firm Nettles, Thomy, Floyd & Smith (formerly Nettles & Thomy), Lake City, Pamplico and Surfside Beach (all S.C.), 1953—. Dir. Palmetto Bank & Trust Co., Lake City. Atty. Florence County (S.C.), 1956-60. Mem. S.C. Ho. of Reps., 1955-62; mem. S.C. Hwy. Commn., 1962-69, vice chmn., 1964; mem. S.C. Bd. Juvenile Placement and Aftercare, 1969—, chmn., 1969-71. Vice chmn. bd. dirs. Carolina Acad., Lake City. Served with AUS, 1948-49, 50-51. Named Lake City Young Man of Yr. Mem. Am., S.C., Florence County bar assns., Am., S.C. trial lawyers assns., Am. Legion. Baptist (chmn. bd. deacons 1971-72). Mason, Rotarian. Home: 215 Magnolia Lake City SC 29560 Office: 120 Epps St Lake City SC 29560

NETTLES, JOHN BARNWELL, physician, educator; b. Dover, N.C., May 19, 1922; s. Stephen A. and Estelle (Hendrix) N.; B.S., U. S.C., 1941; M.D., Med. Coll. S.C., 1944; m. Eunice Anita Saugstad, Apr. 28, 1956; children—Eric, Robert, John Barnwell. Intern Garfield Meml. Hosp., Washington, 1944-45; research fellow in pathology Med. Coll. Ga., Augusta 1946-47; resident in obstetrics and gynecology U. Ill. Research and Ednl. Hosps., Chgo., 1947-51; instr. to asst. prof. obstetrics and gynecology U. Ill. Coll. Medicine, Chgo., 1951-57; asst. prof., asso. prof., prof. obstetrics and gynecology U. Ark. Med. Center, Little Rock, 1957-69; dir. grad. edn. Hillcrest Med. Center, Tulsa, 1969-73; prof. U. Okla. Med. Sch., 1969—; mem. Council on Residency Edn. in Obstetrics and Gynecology, 1974—; dir. Tulsa Obs. and Gynecol. Edn. Found., 1969—. Coordinator med. edn. for Nat. Def., Ark., 1961-69. Served as lt. (j.g.) M.C., USNR, 1945-46, as lt., 1953-54. Diplomate Am. Bd. Obstetrics and Gynecology. Fellow Am. Coll. Obstetricians and Gynecologists (dist. sec.-treas., dist. chmn. exec. bd. 1970-73), A.C.S. (bd. govs. 1969-71), Royal Soc. Health; mem. Ark. Obstet. and Gynecol. Soc. (exec. sec. 1959-69), Central Assn. Obstetrics and Gynecology (exec. com. 1966-69, v.p. 1971-72), Internat. Soc. Advancement Humanistic Studies in Gynecology, Assn. Mil. Surgeons U.S., Am., So. (chmn. obstetrics 1973-74) med. assns., Okla., Tulsa County, Chgo. med. socs., Am. Assn. for Maternal and Infant Health, Assn. Am. Med. Colls., Am. Pub. Health Assn., Assn. Hosp. Med. Edn., Assn. Planned Parenthood Physicians, N.Y. Acad. Sci., Soc. for Gynecol. Investigation. A.A.A.S., Am. Soc. for Study Fertility and Sterility, Internat. Soc. Gen. Semantics, Aerospace Med. Assn., So. Gynecol. and Obstet. Soc., Sigma Xi, Phi Rho Sigma; affiliate Royal Soc. Medicine. Lutheran. Research and main publs. on uterine malignancy, kidney biopsy in pregnancy, perinatal morbidity and mortality. Address: Hillcrest Med Center 1120 S Utica St Tulsa OK 74104

NEU, HOWARD MITCHELL, lawyer; b. Chgo., Mar. 22, 1941; s. Maurice A. and Phyllis (Spector) N.; student U. Fla., 1958-61; B.B.A., U. Miami, 1962, J.D., 1968; m. Elinor Sontag, June 18, 1961; children—Carol Deborah, Wendy Joy. C.P.A., Weber, Thompson & Lefcourt, 1962-63, Morgan, Altemus & Barrs, 1963-68; admitted to Fla. bar, 1968; mem. firms William J. Goldworn, Miami, Fla., 1968-69, Goldworn & Neu, Miami, 1969-70, Neu & Hertz, 1971-73; practiced in Miami, 1970-71, 1973—. Asso. judge, North Miami, 1971—. Interim instr. U. Miami Sch. Law, 1969-70; instr. Miami Edn. Consortium, 1971-72. Chmn., Metro-Dade County Library Adv. Bd., 1968-69; chmn. Fla. Library Devel. Council, 1971—. Bd. dirs. Abbey Hosp. C.P.A., Fla. Mem. Am., Fla. insts. C.P.A.'s, North Miami C. of C., Am. Fla., Dade County bar assns., Am. Arbitration Assn., Am. Assn. Atty. C.P.A., U. Miami Alumni Assn. Kiwanian; mem. B'nai B'rith (past pres. Council So. Fla. lodges; exec. com. Anti-Defamation League). Jewish religion (temple choir dir. 1966—). Elk. Club: Tiger Bay Political (Miami). Home: 2180 NE 121st St North Miami FL 33161 Office: 1001 NE 125th St North Miami FL 33161

NEUBAUER, WILLIAM HERMAN, elec. engr.; b. nr. Taylor, Tex., Nov. 6, 1918; s. Benjamin Bernhardt and Henrietta Hanna (Albert) N.; B.S. in Elec. Engring., U. Tex., 1940; m. Lillye Fae Holland, Oct. 24, 1947; children—Nickie Nadine, Nils Nelson. Instrument operator Petty Geophys. Engring. Co., San Antonio, 1940-41; elec. engr. Southwestern Pub. Service Co., Amarillo, Tex., 1946—, chief engr. meters, 1962—. Served to maj. USAAF, 1941-46. Decorated Bronze Star medal. Registered profl. engr., Tex. Mem. Tex. Soc. Profl. Engrs. (chmn. Panhandle chpt. 1952), I.E.E.E. (pres. Panhandle sect. 1963), Univ. Tex. Ex-Students Assn. (dist. councilman 1972—). Republican. Presbyn. (elder 1951—). Lion (pres. 1968-69). Home: 3415 W 10th St Amarillo TX 79106 Office: Box 1261 Amarillo TX 79170

NEUBERGER, JOHN WILLIAM, mathematician; b. Ventura, Ia., Aug. 14, 1934; s. John Mitchell and Pearl Lydia (Ax) N.; B.A., U. Tex., 1954, Ph.D., 1957; m. Barbara Ann Osher, June 7, 1959; children—John Michael, Sandra Ann. Instr., Spl. Inst., U. Tex., 1956-57, Ill. Inst. Tech., 1957-59; asst. prof. U. Tenn., Knoxville, 1959-63; asso. prof. Emory U., Atlanta, 1963-67, prof., 1967—. Mathematician, Mil. Physicis Research Lab., U. Tex., 1955; asso. engr. Convair Corp., Ft. Worth, summer 1956, sr. nuclear engr., summer 1957; mathematician Inst. Air Weapons Research, 1957-59; cons. Union Carbide, Oak Ridge, 1959-65; research cons. N.C. State U., summer 1972; with Inst. for Def. Analyses, summer 1973; vis. prof. math. U. Ky., 1973. Alfred P. Sloan Research fellow, 1967-69. Mem. Am. Math. Soc., Math. Assn. Am. (sect. lectr. 1973-74), Phi Beta Kappa, Sigma Pi Sigma. Contbr. articles to math. jours. Home: 272 Vickers Dr Decatur GA 30030

NEUFELD, C(ORNELIUS) H(ERMAN) HARRY, govt. ofcl.; b. Scottdale, Pa., Apr. 15, 1923; s. Herman and Anna (Neufeld) N.; B.S., Dalhousie U., 1947; Ph.D., U. Notre Dame, 1951; m. Jocelyn Irene Robb, Sept. 24, 1951; children—Alison Carol, Hilary Karen, Christopher Robb. Asst. prof. chemistry Am. U., Washington, 1951-53; with U.S. Dept. Agr., various locations, 1953—, dir. Richard B. Russell Agr. Research Center, Athens, Ga., 1968-72, area dir. So. region, Athens, 1972—. Vis. prof. U. Ariz., Tucson, 1965-66. Bd. dirs. United Way Athens-Clark County, 1970—. Rotarian. Club: Cosmos (Washington). Contbr. article to profl. jours. Home: 135 Gatewood Pl Athens GA 30601 Office: PO Box 5677 Athens GA 30604

NEUHAUS, WILLIAM OSCAR, III, architect, planner, designer; b. Houston, Mar. 16, 1944; s. William Oscar and Betty Palmer (Bosworth) N.; diploma Hill Sch., 1962; B.Arch., Ga. Inst. Tech., 1967; m. Edna Kay Ficklen, Mar. 25, 1965; children—Kimberly Sautelle, Sara Palmer. Prodn. architect CRS Design, Houston, 1968-69; asso. CTA Architects, Houston, 1969-72; prin. Architecture/Planning, Houston, 1972—. Recipient Progressive Architecture Design citation, 1971. Mem. A.I.A., Tex. Soc. Architects. Democrat. Club: Tex. Corinthian Yacht (Baycliff, Tex.). Home: 3266 Locke Lane Houston TX 77019 Office: 1 Chelsea Pl Houston TX 77006

NEUMAN, ROBERT H., lawyer; b. N.Y.C., Oct. 14, 1936; A.B. magna cum laude, Harvard, 1958, LL.B., 1961. Ford Found. fellow, West Africa, 1961-62; admitted to N.Y. State bar, 1962, D.C. bar, 1962; atty. Office Legal Adviser, Dept. State, Washington, 1964-68, asst. legal adviser for Near Eastern and South Asian affairs, 1968-69, asst. legal adviser for politico-mil. and ocean affairs, 1969-70; mem.

firm. Arent, Fox, Kintner, Plotkin & Kahn, Washington. Lectr. internat. law George Washington U., 1966-67; U.S. rep. to UN Conf. on Marine Pollution, 1969. Mem. Am. Soc. Internat. Law, Phi Beta Kappa. Address: 1815 H St NW Washington DC 20006

NEUMAN, SUSAN CATHERINE, pub. relations exec., editor; b. Detroit, Jan. 29, 1942; d. Paul Edmund and Elsie (Goetz) Neuman; A.B. in Am. Civilization, U. Miami, 1964. Reporter, columnist North Dade Hub, 1959-61; reporter, feature writer Miami Herald, 1962-64; reporter, columnist, photographer North Dade Jour., 1964-65; editor, exec. dir. publs. dept. Miami-Dade County C. of C., Miami, Fla., editor Miamian mag., 1965-69; dir. communications Ferendino/Grafton/Pancoast, 1969-70; pres. Susan Neuman, Inc., pub. relations for bus. and industry, 1970—. Editor campus newspaper U. Miami, 1961-62; campus corr. Mademoiselle mag., 1960-64. Recipient various awards. Mem. Am. Assn. U. Women, Advt. Club of Greater Miami (bd. dirs. 1968-70, asso. editor yearbook 1968), Am. Assn. Commerce Publs. (bd. dirs.), Internat. Council Indsl. Editors, Fla. Mag. Assn., Pub. Relations Soc. Am. (accredited), Bus. and Profl. Women's Club (pres. 1973-74), Mag. Pubs. Assn., Theta Sigma Phi (Headliner award 1964, chmn. employment com. 1966, chmn. Date with the Press 1970). Club: Rod and Gun of Miami (sec.-treas. 1971-76). Home: 4080 NW 165th St Miami FL 33054 Office: 12953 NW 7th Av Miami FL 33168

NEUMANN, ANDREW CONRAD, geologist, educator; b. Oak Bluffs, Mass., Dec. 21, 1933; s. Andrew Conrad and Faye Watson (Gilmore) N.; student Queens Coll., 1951-54; B.S. in Geology, Bklyn. Coll., 1955; M.A. in Oceanography, Tex. A. and M. U., 1958; Ph.D. in Geology, Lehigh U., 1963; m. Jane Paula Spaeth, July 7, 1962; children—Jennifer Jane, Christopher Gilmore, Jonathan Hollick. Research asso. Woods Hole (Mass.) Oceanographic Inst., 1958-60; asst. prof. marine geology Lehigh U., Bethlehem, Pa., 1963-65; asst. prof. marine sci. U. Miami, Fla., 1965-69, asso. prof., 1969-72; prof. marine scis. U. N.C. at Chapel Hill, 1972—. Program dir. marine geology and geophysics NSF, Washington, 1969-70. Trustee Bermuda Biol. Sta. for Research, Inc., 1972—. Mem. Geol. Soc. Am., Marine Tech. Soc., Soc. Econ. Paleontologists and Mineralogists, Sigma Xi. Home: 1607 Fountain Ridge Rd Chapel Hill NC 27514

NEUMANN, OTTO, trading stamps and redemption exec.; b. Winnipeg, Man., Can., Jan. 2, 1900; s. Henry and Amanda (Foote) N.; brought to U.S., 1902, naturalized, 1923; student U.S. Army Sch., Coblenz, Germany, 1920-21, U. Tenn., 1961-64; m. Jenny Ann Hartung, Jan. 21, 1923; 1 son, William Ashley; m. 2d, Beatrix L. Moody, Apr. 8, 1957; 1 dau., Colleene A. (Mrs. William A. Wilmoth). With Anaconda Co., Great Falls and Anaconda, Mont., 1917-18, 1939-44; auditor, controller Giesche Spolka Akcyjna, Katowice Poland, Anaconda-Harriman Interests, 1928-39; treas., asst. sec. Electromanganese Corp., Knoxville, Tenn., 1944-56; plant accountant Foote Mineral Co., Knoxville, 1956-58; controller Sea Island Co., Sea Island, Ga., 1959-60; staff accountant Timmons & Co., C.P.A.'s, Knoxville, 1961-65; with Consumers Res. Green Stamp Co., Inc., Knoxville, 1965—, v.p., gen. mgr., 1965—. Bd. dirs. Trading Stamp Inst. Am., 1973-74. Served with AUS, 1919-23. Mem. Nat. Assn. Accountants (emeritus life asso.), V.F.W. (post comdr. 1927). Elk. Home: 908 Cedar Lane Knoxville TN 37912 Office: 111 Patton St Knoxville TN 37917

NEUSTADT, CHARLES ATKING, exhbn. center exec.; b. Columbus, O., Aug. 5, 1935; s. Ben Z. and Ethel A. (Atkin) N.; B.A., Ohio State U., 1957; M.Internat. Mgmt., Am. Grad. Sch. Internat. Mgmt., 1961; m. Sally Ann Abel, Jan. 25, 1973 (div.); children—Kevin, John, Amanda, Steven, Pamela. Air-sea div. mgr. Everett S.S. Corp., Tokyo, Japan, 1961-62; field operations officer CIA, Washington and Germany, 1962-66; internat. marketing mgr. Avery Products Corp., Santa Ana, Cal., 1966-71; dir. State of Ohio Internat. Trade Div., Columbus, 1971-73; dir. internat. devel. Nat. Distbn. Services, Atlanta, 1973-74; pres. Southeastern Fair Corp., Atlanta, 1974—. Mem. U.S. Regional Export Expansion Council, 1971, Gov.'s Adv. Council on Internat. Trade, 1971-72, Exec. Order Ohio Commodores, 1971. Served with AUS, 1957-59. Mem. Internat. Execs. Assn. N.Y.C., Atlanta Arts Alliance, Ga. Internat. Trade Assn., Internat. Assn. Fairs and Expns. Home: 345 Eppington Dr NW Atlanta GA 30327 Office: PO Box 6826 Atlanta GA 30315

NEUSTADT, DAVID HAROLD, physician; b. Evansville, Ind., Dec. 2, 1925; s. Mose and Leah (Epstein) N.; student DePauw U., 1943-44, 46-47; M.D., U. Louisville, 1950; m. Carolyn Jacobson, June 15, 1952; children—Susan Miriam, Jeffrey Bruce, Robert Alan. Intern Morrisania City Hosp., N.Y.C., 1950-51; resident Lenox Hill Hosp., N.Y.C., 1951-52, trainee in rheumatic diseases, 1952-53, resident, 1953-54; practice medicine, specializing in rheumatic diseases, Louisville, 1954—; chief arthritis clinic Louisville Gen. Hosp., 1960—; asst. prof. medicine U. Louisville Sch. Medicine, 1960-67, asso. prof. clin. medicine, 1967—, head sect. rheumatic diseases 1960—; chief dept. medicine Jewish Hosp., Louisville, pres. med. staff, 1966—; cons. in rheumatology VA, 1970—. Former chmn. med. sci. com. Ky. chpt. Arthritis Found. Served with AUS, 1944-46. Fellow Am. Med. Writers Assn.; mem. A.C.P., N.Y. Rheumatism Soc., Ky. (pres. 1956-57), Am. rheumatism assns., A.M.A., A.A.A.S., N.Y. Acad. Scis., Internat. Soc. Internal Medicine. Jewish religion. Mason (32 deg., Shriner). Elk. Author: The Chemistry and Therapy of Collagen Diseases, 1963; (with others) Aspiration and Injection Therapy in Arthritis and Musculoskeletal Disorders, 1972. Editor: Arthritis Abstracts, References Indexes, 1970—. Contbr. numerous articles to profl. jours. Research on rheumatic diseases. Home: 216 Smithfield Rd Louisville KY 40207 Office: Med Towers Louisville KY 40202

NEUSTADT, WALTER, JR., petroleum co. exec.; b. Ardmore, Okla., Mar. 9, 1919; s. Walter and Doris (Westheimer) N.; B.S., Yale, 1940; M.S., Okla. U., 1941; m. Dolores Krasne, Aug. 7, 1951; children—Nancy Kay, Susan Lynn, Kathy Krasne. Geologist, Westheimer-Neustadt Corp., Ardmore, Okla., 1946-60, exec. v.p., 1960-65, pres., 1965—; dir. Dial Financial Corp., Des Moines, Exchange Nat. Bank, Ardmore. Pres., Ardmore United Fund, 1956-57, Ardmore Devel. Authority, 1968; mem. Okla. Dept. Libraries, 1965-69, chmn., 1965-67; v.p. Nat. Jewish Hosp., Denver, 1965—. Bd. regents U. Okla. Served to 1st lt. USAAF, 1942-45. Mem. Am. Assn. Petroleum Geologists, Soc. Econ. Paleontologists and Mineralogists, Ardmore C. of C. (pres. 1966), Sigma Gamma Epsilon, Omicron Delta Kappa. Republican. Jewish religion. Mason (33 deg.). Rotarian. Home: 1805 Stanley St Ardmore OK 73401 Office: Box 788 911 W Broadway Ardmore OK 73401

NEVILLE, CHARLES WILLIS, physician; b. Dalton, Kan., June 9, 1901; s. Charles and Henrietta Isabella (Randall) N.; A.B., Southwestern Coll., 1924; M.D., Vanderbilt U., 1928; m. Edna Mae Hatfield, Dec. 30, 1928; children—Charles Willis, Gordon H. Intern, Hillman Hosp., Birmingham, Ala., 1928-29; gen. practice medicine, Flat Creek, Ala., 1929-45, Birmingham, Ala., 1945—; mem. staff Carraway Meth. Hosp., Birmingham, Bapt. Hosp., Birmingham. Mem. bd. edn., Birmingham, 1964—. Mem. Am. Acad. Gen. Practice (pres. Ala. chpt. 1958), Jefferson County Med. Soc. (pres. 1966). Home: 4269 Overlook Dr Birmingham AL 35222 Office: 2714 31st Av N Birmingham AL 35207

NEVILLE, CHARLES WILLIS, JR., educator; b. Birmingham, Ala., May, 1931; s. Charles Willis and May (Hatfield) N.; B.A., Vanderbilt U., 1953, M.D., 1956; D.M.S., State U. N.Y., 1970; m. Martha Eugenia Wheeler, Mar. 21, 1957; children—Ann Elizabeth, John William, Paul Wheeler, Susan May, Nancy Jean. Intern Vanderbilt Hosp., 1956-57; resident psychiatry McLean Hosp., 1957-59, Beth-Israel Hosp., Boston, 1959-60; teaching fellow psychiatry Harvard Med. Sch., 1959-60; research tng. psychiatry D.M.S. Program, State U. N.Y. at Bklyn., 1962-64; asso. psychiatry Duke U. Med. Center, 1964-65, asst. prof. psychiatry, 1965-70, asso. prof., 1970—, med. dir. Highland Hosp. div. 1965—. Served to capt. AUS 1960-62. Diplomate Am. Bd. Neurology and Psychiatry. Fellow Am. Psychiatric Assn.; mem. Am., N.C. med. assns. A.A.A.S., N.Y. Acad. Sci., N.C. Neuropsychiat. Assn. (sec. 1969-73, v.p. 1973—), Asheville C. of C. Contbr. articles profl. jours. Home: 56 Woodbury Rd Asheville NC 28804

NEVILLE, WILLIAM VINKLEY, JR., lawyer; b. Montgomery, Ala., July 23, 1934; s. William V. and Mildred (Greene) N.; B.S., Ala. Polytech. Inst., 1956; LL.B., U. Va., 1959; m. Anna Sigridur Gisladottir, Apr. 8, 1961; children—William Vinkley, III, Margaret Gudrun. Admitted to Ala. bar, 1959; since practiced in Eufaula, Ala., 1962—. Mem. Ala. Ho. of Reps., 1967-71. Sec., Eufaula Heritage Assn.; treas. Hist. Chattahoochee Commn. Served with USAF, 1959-61. Mem. Phi Kappa Phi, Omicron Delta Kappa, Pi Kappa Alpha. Home: Country Club Rd Eufaula AL 36027 Office: Box 239 Eufaula AL 36027

NEW, JAMES ARTHUR, mech. engr.; b. Tampa, Fla., Dec. 27, 1927; s. Joseph William and Bessie Pearl (Thomas) N.: student Fla. So. Coll., part-time 1959-63; B.S. in Mech. Engring., U. Fla., 1965; m. Peggie Mae Young, June 14, 1948; children—Sharon, Joseph David. Machinist apprentice and machinist Atlantic Coast Line R.R., Tampa and Lakeland, Fla., also Waycross, Ga., 1944-63; fed. insp. locomotives ICC, Southeast U.S.A. and Pitts., 1966; jr. engr. Seaboard Coast Line R.R., Jacksonville, Fla., 1965-67, sr. asst. engr., 1967-70, mech. engr., 1971—. Registered profl. engr., Fla. Mem. Am. Soc. M.E. (chmn. N.E. Fla. sect. 1972-73), Fla. Engring. Soc., Sigma Tau. Democrat. Baptist (deacon 1948-63; supt. Sunday sch. 1953-55; dir. Tng. Union 1954-60; tchr. Sunday sch. 1955-63). Club: Southern and Southwestern R.R. Designed spl. locomotive brake rigging, 1966. Home: 4906 San Clerc Rd Jacksonville FL 32217 Office: 500 Water St Jacksonville FL 32202

NEWBERN, COPELAND DAVIS, food products co. exec.; b. Powells Point, N.C., Aug. 22, 1911; B.S. in Agr., U. Fla., 1933, postgrad., 1936-37; m. Edna Creekmore, Aug. 24, 1935; children—Caroline (Mrs. John Shepard), Nancy. Tchr. vocational agr., coach, Moyock, N.C., 1933-34; operator vocational agr. dept., Hernando County, Brooksville, Fla., 1935; agrl. agt., Hernando and Manatee County, 1938-45; pres., owner Newbern Groves, Inc., 1946—; pres., owner Fancy Fresh Farms, Inc., Tampa, Fla., 1967—; dir. Northside Bank Tampa, Orange Blossom Citrus, Inc., Miami Bank of N. Tampa. Pres. Fla. Agrl. Council, 1973-74. Mem. Stephens Coll. Dads' Com., 1967-69, mem. bd. curators, 1970—; bd. dirs. Poultry Fedn., 1973-74. Mem. Greater Tampa (bd. govs. 1970—), North Tampa chambers commerce, Fla. Fresh Citrus Shippers Assn. (past pres.), United Fresh Fruit and Vegetable Assn. (dir. 1972—). Clubs: Florida (Winter Haven); Tampa Yacht and Country, University (Tampa); Ye Mystic Krewe (Gasparilla). Home: 912 S Himes Av Tampa FL 33609 Office: Newbern Groves Inc PO Box 17237 Tampa FL 33612

NEWBERRY, JAMES RAYMOND, chem. co. engr.; b. Forest Grove, Ore., Dec. 31, 1911; s. James Thomas and Melissa Jane (Dunsmoor) N.; B.S. in Chem. Engring., Ore. State Coll., 1934; m. Judith Ann Klaindorf, Feb. 15, 1947 (div. Aug. 73); 1 son, Mark Newberry; m. 2d, Mary Evelyn Underwood, Oct. 13, 1973. Research engr. Olin Chem. Co., Niagara Falls, N.Y., 1947-50, sect. leader research dept., 1953-68, devel. specialist, Charleston, Tenn., 1970—; mgr. product devel. Am. Chem. and Refining Co., Waterbury, Conn., 1969-70. Served to lt. comdr. USNR, 1943-46. Registered profl. engr., Tenn. Mem. Am. Chem. Soc., Electrochem. Soc., Am. Inst. Chem. Engrs., Reserve Officers of the Naval Services (chpt. pres. 1949), Chi Phi. Unitarian. Patentee in field. Contbr. articles to profl. jours. Home: 1965 Chambliss Ave Cleveland TN 37311 Office: Olin Technical Center Charleston TN 37310

NEWBOLT, LAWRENCE EDWARD, civil engr.; b. Shidler, Okla., Sept. 23, 1939; s. Clarence Dave and Helen (Ferguson) N.; B.S. in Civil Engring., Lamar State Coll. Tech., 1962; M.E. in Civil Engring., Tex. A. and M. U., 1970; m. Patsy Anne Smith, Aug. 26, 1961; children—Christine Renee, Elizabeth Anne. Project engr. U.S. C.E., Galveston, Tex., 1962-73, Dallas, 1973—. Registered profl. engr., Tex. Methodist. Office: 1411 Commerce St Dallas TX 75202

NEWBY, DONALD ORVILLE, clergyman; b. Douthat, Okla., Aug. 13, 1925; s. William Walter and Lottie Mae (Handy) N.; Asso. Sci., Mo. So. Coll., 1945; B.A., Drury Coll., 1947; postgrad, U. Chgo., 1947-50, Union Theol. Sem., 1961, Kan. State Coll., 1966-67; m. Maybelle Miller Reid, Dec. 18, 1948; children—Donna (Mrs. Frank Takacs), Ellen (Mrs. David Arnsmeyer), Daniel, Timothy, Peter. Ordained to ministry Christian Ch., 1950; dir. youth work Mo. Council Chs., Springfield, 1950-52; asso. exec. dir. youth work Nat. Council Chs., Chgo., 1952-56, exec. dir. youth work, N.Y.C., 1956-61; mem. cons. staff for youth work and Christian edn. All Africa Conf. of Chs., Kitwe, Zambia, 1961-63; asso. exec. World Council Christian Edn., Geneva, Switzerland, 1964-66; exec. minister Tulsa Met. Ministry, 1967—. Guest lectr. McCormick Theol. Sem., Chgo., 1954-55, Princeton Theol. Sem., 1959-60, U. Tulsa, 1972-73. Recipient Distinguished Alumni award Drury Coll., 1961. Mem. Nat. Assn. Ecumenical Staffs, World Assn. Christian Communicators, C. of C. Kiwanian. Contbr. articles to profl. jours. Home: 2304 S Cincinnati Tulsa OK 74114 Office: 222 E 5th St Tulsa OK 74103

NEWBY, HI EASTLAND, physician; b. Del Rio, Tex., Dec. 8, 1929; s. Byron Elvel and Amanda (Eastland) N.; student Schreiner Inst., 1947-48; B.A., Baylor U., 1951, M.D., 1957; postgrad. Sul Ross State U., 1948, 51-52; m. Ona Darlene Northcutt, Apr. 25, 1959; children—Byron Edgar, Hi Eastland. Intern, Bexar County Hosp., Dist., San Antonio, 1957-58; practice family medicine, Del Rio, 1957—; chief staff Val Verde Meml. Hosp., Del Rio, 1968-69; med. cons. Tex. Rehab. Agy., San Antonio area, 1966-73; examining physician, So. Pacific Co., 1959—. Mem. charter commn., City of Del Rio, 1966-67. Mem. Del Rio Ind. Sch. Dist. Bd., 1968-71, pres., 1969-71; pres. San Felipe Del Rio Consol. Ind. Sch. Dist., 1971-72; mem. Val Verde County Sch. Bd., 1972—. Diplomate Am. Bd. Family Practice. Mem. A.M.A., Tex. Med. Assn., Tex. Acad. Gen. Practice (dir. 1966-70), Tex. Acad. Family Physicians (chmn. membership and credential com. 1971-72). Mason (Shriner), Rotarian. Home: 201 Park Av Del Rio TX 78840 Office: 1011 E 7th St PO Box 1549 Del Rio TX 78840

NEWBY, JERRY BOWERS, petroleum geologist, engr.; b. Elk, Kan., Aug. 8, 1890; s. Hiram Warner and Ceoria Alice (Bowers) N.; A.B., U. Okla., 1912; student U. Chgo., 1912-13; m. Edna Cash, May 31, 1922; 1 dau., Mary Margaret (Mrs. Robert Lee Pierce). Geologist Gulf Oil Corp., Tulsa, 1913-17; cons. geologist, Tulsa, 1917-18, Oklahoma City, 1919-24; resident mgr. Petroleum Reclamation Co., Bradford, Pa., 1924-29; cons. geologist, engr., Oklahoma City, 1929—. Served as pvt., F.A., U.S. Army, 1918. Mem. Am. Assn. Petroleum Geologists (a founder, hon. mem.), Inst. Mining, Metall. and Petroleum Engrs., Oklahoma City Geol. Soc. (hon. life mem.; pres. 1935), Am. Inst. Profl. Geologists (charter mem., Ben Parker medalist 1973), Sigma Chi, Gamma Alpha, Sigma Gamma Epsilon. Clubs: Petroleum, Men's Dinner, Engineering. Address: 1816 NW 23d St Oklahoma City OK 73106

NEWBY, JOHN SMITH, structural engr., govt. ofcl.; b. Burkesville, Ky., July 12, 1915; s. William H. and Beulah (Smith) N.; student Lindsey Wilson Coll., 1935-37; B.A., Berea Coll., 1939; B.S., U. Ky., 1947; m. Halliene Ramsey, June 30, 1947; children—John, Deborah, Carl, Hugh. Bridge design engr. State of Cal., Sacramento, 1947-52; bldg. design engr. U.S. Army C.E., Savannah, Ga., 1952-58; gen. engr. U.S. Army Ordnance, Huntsville, Ala., 1958-61; structural engr. Voice of Am., Washington, 1961—. Pres. Tillinghurst Elementary Sch. P.T.A., Columbus, Ga., 1958; mem. Athens (Ala.) council Boy Scouts Am., 1960-61. Served to lt. col. USAAF, 1941-63. Registered profl. engr., Ky. Mem. Am. Soc. C.E., Meterol. Soc., Sigma Pi Sigma, Methodist. Home: 4133 Teton Pl Alexandria VA 22312 Office: 1776 Pennsylvania Av NW Washington DC 20547

NEWCOMB, CLAUDE LETCHER, automotive co. exec.; b. nr. Forest, Va., June 2, 1907; s. James Letcher and Mary Lelia (Wilson) N.; student pub. schs.; m. Hilda Mae Barton, Nov. 24, 1937; 1 son, Wayne E. Founder Lynchburg Battery & Ignition Co., Inc. (Va.), 1930, pres., treas., 1930—; founder, pres. Newcomb Auto Parts, Farmville, Va., 1946—; founder, sec. Newcomb, Inc., Lynchburg, 1971—; dir. Bank Central Va., Lynchburg. Bd. suprs. Bedford County, Va., 1963; chmn. Equalization Bd., Lynchburg, Va., 1970. Methodist. Mason (Shriner), Elk. Lion. Home: 3015 Ravenwood St Lynchburg VA 24503 Office: 406 5th St Lynchburg VA 24505

NEWELL, ALTON SCOTT, JR., mfg. co. exec.; b. Kenedy, Tex., Apr. 1, 1929; s. Alton Scott and Winifred Elizabeth (Jandreau) N.; student Baylor U., 1957-59, Trinity U., 1959, Ariz. State U., 1960; m. Donna Emily Vaughn, June 25, 1960; children—Alton Scott III, Sabra Camille. With Newell Salvage Co., Phoenix, 1959-65; with Newell Mfg. Co., San Antonio, 1965—, exec. v.p., 1973—. Trustee Bapt. Meml. Hosp., San Antonio. Mem. Nat. Assn. Recycling Industries (dir. 1974—). Baptist (deacon 1961-74). Club: Oak Hills Country (San Antonio). Home: 269 Cave Lane San Antonio TX 78209 Office: Newell Mfg Co Box 9132 San Antonio TX 78204

NEWELL, CHARLES VANCE, pub. relations counselor; b. Denver, Jan. 23, 1914; s. Charles Haney and Grace (Vance) N.; B.A., Yale, 1935; m. Laura Bess Lee, Feb. 12, 1956; children—Thomas Lee, Charles H., Mrs. R. L. Baker, Caroline (Mrs. Day), Mary. Mem. editorial staff Houston Chronicle, 1935-50, 55-57; exec. Asso. Gen. Contractors Am., Austin, Tex., 1950-55, Max Jacobs Agy., Houston, 1957-60; partner firm Jacobs-Keeper-Newell, 1960-64; v.p. Keeper-Newell & Assos., 1964-67; pres., owner Vance Newell & Assos., Houston, 1967—; dir. Louis Werner Saw Mill Co., 1968. Served with USAAF, 1942-45. Mem. Pub. Relations Soc. Am., Alpha Sigma Phi, Delta Sigma Phi. Democrat. Presbyn. (elder). Clubs: Houston Press; Yale of Southeastern Texas (past bd. dirs.). Home: 2301 Fountain View Houston TX 77027 Office: 3433 W Alabama Houston TX 77027

NEWELL, HAROLD MOSLEY, constrn. co. exec.; b. nr. Montgomery, Ala., May 6, 1912; s. William Samuel and Carrie Bonham (Mosley) N.; student Ga. Inst. Tech., 1935; B.S., Birmingham So. U., 1936; m. Jimmie Louise Jacks, Dec. 29, 1946; children—Harold Jacks, Edwin Lee. Chemist Swan Chm. Co., Birmingham, Ala., 1936-37; supt. hwy. constrn. Newell Bros., Ala., Miss., S.C., 1938-42; engr. Pan Am. Airways, South Am., 1943-44; co-owner Newell Bros. Constrn. Co., Montgomery, 1945—; pres. Newell Roadbuilders, Inc., Hull, Ala., 1958—. Mem. Ga. Hwy. Contractors Assn., Fla. Roadbuilders, Theta Kappa Nu. Rotarian. Club: Arrowhead Country (Montgomery). Home: RD No 1 Hope Hull AL 36043 Office: Rt 1 U S Hwy 31 Hope Hull AL 36043

NEWELL, JAMES THAXTON, govt. engr.; b. Vernon, Ala., Dec. 31, 1939; s. Ernest Clovis and Welthey (Younghance) N.; A.A.S. with honors DeVry Tech. Inst., 1960; postgrad. Fla. Tech. U., 1968—; m. Sylvia Ellen Thomas, Mar. 9, 1963; children—Karen Lynn, James Thomas, Kelley Elizabeth, Jonathan Michael; m. 2d, Susan Gail Malone, Oct. 9, 1973. Reliability engr. McDonnell Douglas Aircraft Co., St. Louis, Mo., 1960-66; reliability program mgr. Emerson Electric Co., St. Louis, 1966-67; engring mgr. Naval Plant Rep. Office, St. Louis, 1967-68; mgr., also reliability and maintainability engr. Naval Tng. Equipment Center, Orlando, Fla., 1968—. Founder, also dir. AstroCel Research Inst. Registered profl. engr., Mo., Fla. Baptist (Sunday sch. tchr. 1962-63). Home: 575 E Jessup Longwood FL 32750 Office: Naval Training Equipment Center Code 411 Orlando FL 32813

NEWELL, WARDEN JOHN, petroleum sales industry exec.; b. Carthage, Mo., Dec. 11, 1907; s. James Patton and Jessie Maude (Caffee) N.; B.S. magna cum laude, Princeton, 1929; m. Virginia Gentry Bailey, Jan. 27, 1973; children—Laurie, Warden John, Joanna, David, Thomas Van Auken (adopted). Geologist Brit. Govt. and Phillips Petroleum Co., 1929-32; sales exec. Gulf Oil Corp., 1932-38; with Newell Oil Co., Alpine, Tex., 1939—, pres., 1939—. Pres. Sirocco Devel. Corp., Alpine, 1952—; sec., treas. Alpine TV Cable, Inc., 1961—, Red House Ranch, Inc., Alpine, 1971—. Mem. Tex. Good Neighbor Commn., 1961-62, 72-73, Internat. Good Neighbor Council, 1958—; chmn. Nat. Parks Devel. Com., 1970—; Treas. Nat. Found., 1955—. Councilman, Alpine, 1962-63. Recipient award most outstanding service to tourist devel. Gov. Tex., 1969, Award of Distinction Tex. Oil Jobbers Assn., 1970. Mem. Tex. Oil Jobbers Assn. (dir. 1948—; pres. 1963), Alpine C. of C. (pres. 1941-43). Democrat. Episcopalian (Bishops warden 1957). Rotarian (pres. 1945-46). Author pamphlet series Newell-Gulf West Texas Road Logs, 1966. Home: 1000 Loop Rd Alpine TX 79830 Office: Box 390 Alpine TX 79830

NEWFIELD, MAYER ULLMAN, lawyer; b. Birmingham, Ala., Apr. 5, 1905; s. Morris and Leah (Ullman) N.; A.B., Howard Coll., Birmingham, Ala., 1927; postgrad. Harvard Law Sch., 1928-29; LL.B., U. Ala., 1931; m. Bertha Lehman, June 8, 1938; children—Jane, Melanie. Admitted to Ala. bar, 1931, U.S. Supreme Ct. bar, 1941; mem. firm London, Yancey & Brower, Birmingham, 1931-34; supervising atty. Home Owners' Loan Corp., 1934-35; with SEC, 1935-47, successively sr. trial atty., chief proxy unit chief of litigation and enforcement sect., asst. regional adminstr., Atlanta, Washington, Phila., N.Y.C., 1935-47; asst. atty. City of Birmingham, 1948-56; gen. practice Birmingham, 1956—; sec., v.p., dir. N. Ala. Mineral Devel. Co. Pres. Civic Opera Assn., 1964-66; nat. commr. Anti-Defamation League, 1956—; Ala. co-chmn. Nat. Conf. Christians and Jews, 1964—; counsel to firm Sirote, Permutt, Friend & Friedman. Chmn. State of Israel Bonds, 1973-74. Bd. dirs. Anti-Tb Assn. of Jefferson County, 1968—, Leo N. Levi Hosp., Hot Springs, 1968—, Jewish Children's Home, 1968—, Urban League, 1968—; pres. bd. dirs.

Jewish Community Center, 1970-71. Mem. Am., Ala., Birmingham bar assns. Democrat. Jewish religion (v.p. temple 1973—). Mem. B'nai B'rith. Home: 2900 Thornhill Rd Birmingham AL 35213 Office: First Fed Bldg 2030 1st Av N Birmingham AL 35203

NEWMAN, BILL N., real estate pres.; b. Dallas, May 28, 1918; s. Georg Owen and Carolyn Eugene (Harrison) N.; student U. Tex. at Arlington, 1936-38, at Austin, 1938-39; B.B.A., So. Meth. U., 1946; m. Marjorie Ann Stinchcomb, Nov. 8, 1948; 1 dau., Catherine Ann. Mem. faculty U. Tex. at Austin, 1948-49; with Mytinger & Casselberry, Long Beach, Cal., 1952-58, sales tng. mgr., 1956-57, field sales mgr., 1957-58; nat. sales mgr. Security Am. Life Ins. Co., Memphis, 1959-60; pres. Universal Food Industries, Memphis, 1962-64; pres. Pizza Inns of Am. Dallas, 1965-69; pres. Bekland Resources Corp., Dallas, 1968—. Chmn. Dallas County 4-H, 1972-73. Served to maj. AUS, 1942-45: ETO. Mem. Tex. Jr. Horse Show Assn. (pres. 1968). Democrat. Author: Handbook of Successful Sales Meetings, 1960. Home: 7211 Aberdeen St Dallas TX 75230 Office: 8548 NW Plaza Dr Dallas TX 75225

NEWMAN, CHARLES FORREST, lawyer; b. Grenada, Miss., Jan. 15, 1937; s. Wiley Clifford and Lurene (Westbrook) N.; B.A. magna cum laude, Yale, 1959, J.D., 1963; postgrad. (Adenauer fellow) U. Bonn (Germany), 1959-60; m. Jeannette Kay Bailey, May 26, 1973. Admitted to Tenn. bar, 1964; law clk. U.S. Dist. Judge Bailey Brown, Western Dist. Tenn., 1963-64; mem. firm Burch Porter & Johnson, Attys., Memphis, 1965—, partner, 1966—. Bd. dirs. Tenn. Conservation League. Mem. Am., Tenn., Memphis, Shelby County bar assns., Am. Judicature Soc., Am. Assn. Trial Lawyers, Wilderness Soc., Airplane Owners and Pilots Assn., L.Q.C. Lamar Soc., Environmental Action Council, Sierra Club, Phi Beta Kappa. Clubs: Tennessee, Yale. Home: 435 N Highland St Apt 2 Memphis TN 38112 Office: 130 N Court Memphis TN 38103

NEWMAN, DAVID, JR., musician; b. Corsicana, Tex., Feb. 24, 1933; s. David and Louise (Cavanaugh) N.; student pub. schs.; m. Esther Rae Peterson, Nov. 14, 1954; children—Elizabeth (stepdau.), Andre, Cadino, Benji. Performed with T-Bone Walker, Lowell Fulson; with Ray Charles band as tenor and alto saxophonist and flute player, 1954-64; rec. artist Atlantic Records, 1959—; formed own group, 1966—. Albums include: Ray Charles presents David Fat Head Newman, 1959, Straight Ahead, 1960; Fat Head Comes On, 1962; Cannonball presents David Newman and James Clay, 1962; House of David, Double Barrelled Soul, Newman and McDuff, 1968. Home: 2623 Downing Av Dallas TX 75216 Office: care B & B Booking Agy 1674 Broadway New York City NY 10019

NEWMAN, JAMES BLAKEY, physicist, educator; b. Little Rock, Ark., Jan. 10, 1917; s. John William and Mattie Garland (Ayres) N.; B.S. in Elec. Engring. Va. Mil. Inst., 1939; Ph.D., Cornell U., 1951; m. Dorothy Elizabeth Heflin, June 27, 1942; children—Dorothy (Mrs. Ted Harrison Brown), Carol Dell, Harriet Ayres. Instr. physics Va. Mil. Inst., Lexington, 1939-42, asst. prof., 1942-49, asso. prof., 1950-56, prof. physics, 1956—, also chmn. physics dept., 1963-69. Served capt. Signal Corps, AUS, 1942-45. George Catlett Marshall fellow. Mem. Am. Nuclear Soc., Am. Phys. Soc., Am. Assn. Physics Tchrs., Am. Soc. for Engring. Edn., Sigma Xi. Presbyn. Home: 406 Virginia Military Institute Parade Lexington VA 24450

NEWMAN, JAMES EARL, dentist; b. Greenville, Ky., Dec. 14, 1943; s. James Raleigh and Jane Frances (Quisenberry) N.; student Fla. State U., 1961-64; D.D.S., Emory U., 1968; m. Jolene Anne Anderson, Dec. 17, 1966; children—Cynthia Ann, James Earl, Laura Kate. Gen. practice dentistry, Fairfax, S.C., 1968—. Co-owner Ga.-Carolina Seafood, Ltd., Charleston, S.C., 1970—; cons. dentistry Salkahatchie Community Action Council, 1968—; affiliate dentist VA, 1968—; mem. staff Allendale County Hosp., Fairfax, 1968—. Mem. Fairfax Jr. C. of C. (Man of Year 1969-70, treas. 1970-71), Am., Coastal Dist. dental socs., Pi Kappa Phi, Psi Omega. Republican. Baptist. Address: PO Box 518 Fairfax SC 29827

NEWMAN, JOE LINDSEY, educator; b. Stout, Tenn., July 24, 1916; s. Clark Lytle and Eunice Belle (Lindsey) N.; B.S. in Civil Engring. U. Ala., 1953, B.S. in Indsl. Arts Edn., 1955, M.A. in Sch. Adminstrn., 1958; m. Ruby Louise Smith, Sept. 28, 1946; children—Frank Lindsey, Richard Clark, Barry Clayton. Adminstrv. officer, Civilian Conservation Corps, Miss., 1939-42; tchr. phys. edn., coach Florence (Ala.) Central High Sch., 1945-49; tchr. crafts Tuscaloosa, Ala., 1955-56; asst. prof. engring. tech., engring. drawing, indsl. engring. U. Ala., University, 1956—. Cons., Redstone Arsenal, Huntsville, Ala., 1960-62, Ala. Mental Health Bd., Bryce Hosp., Tuscaloosa, 1968—. Served to 1st lt. USAAF, 1942-44. Registered profl. engr. Ala. Mem. Ala., Nat. profl. engring. socs., Delta Chi. Baptist. Home: 36 Southmont Dr Tuscaloosa AL 35401 Office: Dept Engineering Univ Ala University AL 35486

NEWMAN, JOHN EDWARD, oil bus. exec.; b. Okmulgee, Okla., Dec. 30, 1914; s. William Campbell and Lena (Fuhrman) N.; B.S., Columbia, 1936; m. Florence Bell, June 22, 1945; children—John Edward, Nancy Jean. With Gulf Oil Corp., 1936-37, Prince Bros. Drilling Co., 1937, Parker Drilling Co., 1937-38; partner Newman Bros. Drilling Co., 1938—; dir. Straus-Frank Co., San Antonio. Bd. dirs. San Antonio Pub. Service Bd. Mem. exec. bd. San Antonio Zool. Soc. Trustee S.W. Research Found. Served to capt. AUS, 1942-45. Clubs: Oak Hills Country, Argyle. Home: 231 W Lynwood St San Antonio TX 78212 Office: 1432 Milam Bldg San Antonio TX 78205

NEWMAN, JOHN WILBUR, chem. engr.; b. Ashland, Ky., Dec. 11, 1937; s. Clarence Mathew and Theresa (Tate) N.; Chem.E. (univ. scholar) U. Cin., 1961; m. Faye Louise Taylor, June 26, 1960; 1 dau., Karen Lynne. Supr. gas chromatography lab. Ashland Oil & Refining Co. (Ky.), 1961-64, research pilot plant engr., 1964-67, research project evaluator, 1967-69, research chem. engr., 1969-73, sr. research engr., 1973-74, group leader, 1947—. Mem. Am. Inst. Chem. Engrs., Am. Chem. Soc. (membership chmn. 1966-67), Am. Soc. Testing Materials (task group chmn. 1973—), Boyd County Hist. Soc. (pres. 1974), Alpha Chi Sigma. Republican. Episcopalian. Patentee petrochems. Home: 2740 Jackson Av Ashland KY 41101 Office: 1409 Winchester Av Ashland KY 41101

NEWMAN, MILDRED EVELYN HILL (MRS. RUSSELL BLAIR NEWMAN), civic worker; b. McClelland, Ark.; d. Samuel Hillard and Sarah Ada (Jackson) Hill; student Beebe Jr. Coll., 1939-40, Ark. State Tchrs. Coll., 1935-36, 40-41, Draughon's Sch. Bus., 1942-43; m. Russell Blair Newman, Nov. 15, 1947; children—Karen Sue, Sammye Lynn. Tchr. Ark., 1936-42; various bus. positions, 1943-48. Chmn. women's div. United Givers Fund, Florence, Ala., 1960; active Girl Scouts Am., 1958-60, 63-65; chpt. organizer Citizens for Decent Lit., Florence, 1962, sec., 1962-63; publicity chmn. United Council of Ch. Women, Florence, 1963-65; local pres. Woman's Soc. Christian Service, 1959-61, dist. v.p., 1963-65; mem. aux. bd. Richmond Cerebral Palsy Center, pres. aux. bd., 1974-75. Recipient certificate of appreciation Girl Scouts Am., 1965. Bd. dirs. Henrico County chpt. A.R.C. Mem. Mooreland Farms Assn., Vols. of Am., Common Cause, Young Life, Va. Mus., St. Mary's Hosp. Aux., Beta Sigma Phi. Presbyn. (bible study leader women of ch. 1969—). Clubs: Hermitage Country, Ladies Golf Auxiliary, River Road Garden. Home: 8913 Norwick Rd Richmond VA 23229

NEWMAN, PAUL KENNETH, physician; b. Neptune, N.J., May 27, 1932; s. Edward Alston and Beatrice Emma (Burns) N.; B.S., Bucknell U., 1958; M.D., Temple U., 1962; m. Audrey Mae White, June 14, 1952; children—Linda Susan, Deborah Carol, Paul Kenneth. Inter, U.S. Naval Hosp., Jacksonville, Fla., 1962-63; resident anesthesiology U.S. Naval Hosp., Phila., 1963-65; chief anesthesiology U.S. Naval Hosp., Jacksonville, 1965-69; attending anesthesiologist Bapt. Meml. Hosp., Jacksonville, 1969—, med. dir. dept. respiratory therapy, 1969—. Served with USN, 1962-69. Diplomate Am. Bd. Anesthesiologists. Fellow A.C.P., Am. Coll. Anesthesiologists. Home: 2255 Miller Oaks Dr Jacksonville FL 32217 Office: 1453 Louise St Jacksonville FL 32207

NEWMAN, PHILLIP BARBOUR, III, food co. exec.; b. Louisville, May 31, 1932; s. Phillip Barbour and Frances Thompson (Powell) N.; B.E., Yale, 1956, B.S., 1957; m. Eleanor Griffith Tarrant, May 15, 1965; children—Phillip Barbour IV, John. Engr. Westinghouse Electric Corp., Balt., 1960-64; first v.p. mfg. Glenmore Distilleries Co., Louisville, 1964—, dir., 1970—. Dir. Bourbon Cooperage Co. Served with USNR, 1956-60. Mem. Ky. Distillers Assn. (chmn. 1972-73). Clubs: Country, Pendennis (Louisville); Yale (N.Y.C.). Home: 3760 Upper Valley Rd Louisville KY 40207 Office: Citizens Plaza Louisville KY 40202

NEWMAN, SANFORD BERNHART, sci. adminstr.; b. N.Y.C., July 26, 1914; s. Otto and Carrie (Bernhart) N.; B.S., Long Island U., 1936; M.A., George Washington U., 1941; Ph.D., U. Md., 1951; m. Dorothy Krall, Aug. 2, 1942; children—Martha, Carl. Trainee U.S. Patent Office, 1939-41; sci. adminstr. Nat. Bur. of Standards, Washington 1941-70, spl. asst. to the dir. for programs, 1970—. Fellow Royal Microscopical Soc., Wash. Acad. Sci.; mem. Am. Soc. for Testing and Materials, Sigma Xi. Club: Cosmos. Contbr. articles in field to profl. jours. Home: 3508 Woodbine St Chevy Chase MD 20015 Office: Adminstrn Bldg Washington DC 20234

NEWMAN, TEDFORD COX, social work adminstr.; b. Camden, Ark., Jan. 2, 1937; s. Dewey Autry and Lola (Tedford) N.; B.S., So. State U., Ark., 1959; postgrad. U. Tenn., 1960-61; M.S.W., U. Okla., 1963; m. Delma Jean Hicks, Nov. 26, 1959; children—Michael Tedford, Alan William. Dir. social services and homemaker services Econ. Opportunity Agy. Pulaski County, Little Rock, 1966-67; with Ark. State Hosp., Little Rock, 1959-66, 67—, dir. community mental health projects, 1969-71, dir. pub. service careers, 1971-72; dir. planning Ark. Dept. Social and Rehab. Service, 1972—. Cons. social work to pub. agys., instns.; spl. instr. sociology Little Rock U., 1963—. Pres. Ark. Conf. on Social Welfare. Mem. Acad. Certified Social Workers, Nat., Ark. confs. social welfare, Nat. Assn. Social Workers (chpt. treas. 1964—, chpt. vice chmn. 1965—). Nat., Ark. assns. for mental health. Baptist. Lion. Home: 1806 Banny Dr Benton AR 72015 Office: 406 Nat Old Line Bldg Little Rock AR 72201

NEWSOM, ANN JOHNSON DOUGLAS (MRS. L. MACK NEWSOM, JR.), journalist; b. Dallas, Jan. 16, 1934; d. J. Douglas and R. Grace (Dickson) Johnson; B.J. cum laude, U. Tex., 1954, B.F.A. summa cum laude, 1955, M.J., 1956; m. L. Mack Newsom, Jr., Oct. 27, 1956; children—Michael Douglas, Kevin Jackson, Nancy Elizabeth, William Macklemore. Gen. publicity State Fair Tex., 1955; advt. and promotion Newsom's Women's Wear, 1956-57; publicity Auto Market Show, 1961; lab. instr. radio-tv news-writing course U. Tex., 1961-62; local publicist Tex. Boys Choir, 1964-69, nat. publicist, 1967-69; pub. relations dir. Gt. S.W. Boat Show Dallas, 1966-72, Family Fun Show, 1970-71, Horace Ainsworth Co., Dallas; asst. prof. dept. journalism, adviser yearbook and mag. Tex. Christian U., Fort Worth, 1970—. Mem. Assn. Edn. in Journalism, Women in Communications (nat. conv. treas. 1967, nat. pub. relations chmn. 1969-71), Pub. Relations Soc. Am. (accredited), Am. Women in Radio and TV, Delta Delta Delta, Mortar Bd. Alumnae. Baptist. Home: 4237 Shannon Dr Fort Worth TX 76116

NEWSOM, DONZELLE ATLAS, retail co. exec.; b. Funston, Ga., Feb. 22, 1920; s. Daniel Atlas and Katherine Eugenia (Smith) N.; student pub. schs., Tampa, Fla.; m. Beatrice Helen Kovich, June 7, 1941; children—Donzelle Atlas, Crighton Dowd. Store supt. E.S. Levy & Co., Galveston, Tex., 1946-60; v.p. operations and planning Lichtenstein's, Inc., Corpus Christi, Tex., 1960—. Served with USNR, 1943-46. Presbyn. (trustee 1965-70, elder 1964-67). Mason (32 deg.). Home: 421 Ashland Dr Corpus Christi TX 78412 Office: 401 N Chaparral St Corpus Christi TX 78403

NEWSOM, ERLE THORNTON, JR., assn. exec.; b. Camilia, Ga., Dec. 2, 1915; s. Erle Thornton and Ethel (Perry) N.; B.S. in Forestry, U. Ga., 1938; m. Lois LaVerne Bell, Nov. 8, 1941; children—Laurie Ann, Elizabeth Jane. Forester Ga. Forestry Commn., Albany and Baxley, Ga., 1939-41; chief forester So. Pine Lumber Co., Diboll, Tex., 1941-42; land acquisition cruiser Ga. Kraft Co., 1945-47, chief forester, 1947-56, dir. Woodlands, 1956-68; field rep. Ga. Div., Inc., Am. Cancer Soc., 1968-69, state crusade coordinator, 1969-71; asso. dir. Ga. Heart Assn., 1971—. Mem. Ga. Bd. Registration for Foresters, 1957-68, chmn., 1960-62, vice chmn., 1965-68. Mem. steering com. U. Ga. Sch. Forestry; adv. com. N.C. State Sch. Forestry. Served with AUS, 1942-45, ETO. Decorated Presdl. Unit citation. Registered forester, Ga., Ala. Mem. Nat. Soc. Fund Raisers, Ga. Soc. Assn. Execs., Internat. Platform Assn., Soc. Am. Foresters (chmn. Ga. chpt. 1952), Ga. Forestry Assn. (dir., v.p.), Ga. Tree Farm Com. (chmn. 1957-61), Am Pulpwood Assn. Baptist. Elk, Kiwanian. Home: 5249 Fleur De Lis Ct Atlanta GA 30340 Office: 2581 Piedmont Rd Atlanta GA 30309

NEWSOM, ROBERT WESLEY, indsl. engr.; b. Winston-Salem, N.C., Feb. 4, 1920; s. Robert Wesley and Hattie (Carter) N.; B.Indsl. Engring., N.C. State U., 1943; m. Florence Abigail Sharp, Aug. 25, 1945; children—Susie Sharp, Robert Wesley III. Asst. engr. Am. S. African Steamship Lines, N.Y.C., 1943-46; with R.J. Reynolds Tobacco Co., Winston-Salem, 1946-68, chief indsl. engr., 1950-68; dir. indsl. engring. R.J. Reynolds Foods Co., N.Y.C., 1968-70; dir. material and engring. services Lorillard Co., Greensboro, N.C., 1970—, v.p. operations, 1971—; dir. N.W. N.C. Devel. Assn., 1965—. Pres. Goodwill Rehab. Center, 1964. Trustee N.C. Sch. Arts. Served with U.S. Maritime Service, 1943. Fellow Soc. for Advancement Mgmt., Am. Inst. Indsl. Engrs. (pres. 1971-72); mem. Operations Research Soc. Am., Am. Statis. Assn., Soc. for Engring. Edn. Republican. Episcopalian. Rotarian. Home: 901 Fairgreen Rd Greensboro NC 27410 Office: Lorillard Co 2525 E Market St Greensboro NC 27420

NEWSOME, JAMES FREDERICK, surgeon, educator; b. Winton, N.C., Mar. 24, 1923; s. Arthur Telle and Evelyn Montgomery (Matthews) N.; A.B., U. N.C., 1944; M.D., Vanderbilt U., 1949; m. Alice Marie Bryant, Aug. 31, 1956; children—Kathy Bryant, Susan Robin, Elizabeth Cicely. Intern Med. Coll. Va. Hosp., Richmond, 1949-50; resident U. N.C. Sch. Medicine, Chapel Hill, 1952-54, chief resident surgery, 1955-56, instr. gen. surgery, 1956-59, asst. prof., 1959-64, asso. prof., 1964-71, prof. surgery, 1971—. Sec. N.C. Beta Found., 1956-70, pres. 1970—. Served to capt. USAF, 1950-52. Home: Route 5 Box 416 Chapel Hill NC 27514

NEWTON, ADRIAN JEFFERSON, jud. ofcl.; b. nr. Thomasville, N.C., Sept. 30, 1901; s. Jefferson Davis and Martha (Mills) N.; J.D., Wake Forest Coll., 1925; m. Lois Long Spaugh, Aug. 10, 1927; children—Mrs. William H. Wilson, Mrs. Richard L. Sommers, Adrian Jefferson, Thomas Long, Henry Williams. Admitted to N.C. bar, 1925, also U.S. Supreme Ct. bar; city clk., clk. Recorder's Ct., Thomasville, 1920; asst. clk. Superior Ct., Davidson County, 1922-24; practice law, Lexington, N.C., 1926-37; judge Davidson County Ct., 1928-34; gen. counsel N.C. Unemployment Compensation Commn., 1937-41; clk. Supreme Ct. N.C., Raleigh, 1941—; tendered post clk. World Ct., Tokyo, Japan, 1945. Chmn., Lexington chpt. A.R.C., 1928-34, chmn. pub. affairs com. Baptist State Conv. N.C., 1966—; bd. dirs. Wake County chpt.; bd. dirs. Raleigh YMCA, N.C. State U. Named Tar Heel of Week, Raleigh News & Observer, 1954. Mem. N.C., Davidson County, Wake County bar assns., Mayflower Soc., Order of Golden Bough, Wake Forest Alumni Assn. (pres. Wake County chpt. 1942), Omicron Delta Kappa, Kappa Sigma (alumnus adviser), Phi Delta Phi. Baptist (deacon 1938—, chmn. bd. 1942, 56). Kiwanian (pres. Lexington chpt. 1933, pres. Raleigh Scholarship Found. 1949-54). Club: Torch (pres. Raleigh 1946-47). Home: 2506 Beechridge Rd Raleigh NC 27608 Office: Justice Bldg Raleigh NC 27602

NEWTON, DEREK ARNOLD, educator; b. Richmond, Eng., Feb. 18, 1930; s. John and Joan (Garnett) N.; A.B., Wabash Coll., 1952; M.B.A., Harvard, 1962, D.B.A. (Ford Found. fellow 1963-64), 1964; m. Beverly Rowayne Blevins, Dec. 10, 1955. Sales mgr. R.H. Donnelley Corp., Washington, 1954-60; lectr. bus. adminstrn. Harvard Bus. Sch., 1964-70; prof. bus. adminstrn. U. Va., Charlottesville, 1970—. Cons. sales and marketing mgmt. to various corps. Mem. Am. Marketing Assn. Author: Cases in Sales Force Management, 1970; Sales Force Performance and Turnover, 1973. Home: 1934 Blue Ridge Rd Charlottesville VA 22903 Office: PO Box 3607 University of Virginia Charlottesville VA 22903

NEWTON, PHILIP TOWNSEND, chem. co. exec.; b. Miami, Fla., May 6, 1927; s. George David and Eloise F. (Townsend) N.; B.B.A., U. Ga., 1950; m. Patricia Preston, Dec. 20, 1950; children—Philip, Preston, Patrick. Financial mgr. C. A. Trussell Motor Co., Athens, Ga., 1950-53; sec., treas. Townsend Bldrs. Supply, Whiteville, N.C., 1953-57; with Dixie-O'Brien Corp., Brunswick, Ga., 1957—, treas., 1961—, v.p., gen. mgr., 1971—, also dir. Parent Co. and subsidiares; dir. First Nat. Bank Brunswick; Pres. United Community Fund, 1970, dir., 1965-70, mem. exec. com., 1971; trustee YWCA, 1965—; mem. exec. com. Okefenokee council Boy Scouts Am., 1971-72. Mem. Bd. Edn. Glynn County, 1970-74, chmn. finance com., 1970-73, chmn., 1973-74. Served with AUS, 1945-47. Named Boss of Year Nat. Assn. Secs., 1971. Mem. Nat. Paint, Varnish and Lacquer Assn. (chmn. 1970-72; speaker convs.), Nat. Credit Mgmt. Assn. (speaker convs.), Com. 100 (dir.), Brunswick C. of C. (dir.). Baptist (chmn. finance com. 1971). Rotarian (pres. 1973-74). Home: 2812 Wildwood Dr Brunswick GA 31520 Office: PO Box 864 Brunswick GA 31520

NEWTON, ROBERT PARK, JR., engring. co. exec.; b. Jackson, Ga., Oct. 25, 1913; s. Robert Park and Bessie (Powell) N.; B.S. in Chem. Engring., Ga. Inst. Tech., 1935; m. Elizabeth Edwards, Aug. 11, 1936; children—Nancy Elizabeth, Robert Park III, William Aris. Asst. chem. instr. Ga. Inst. Tech., 1936; research chemist Swann & Co., Birmingham, Ala., 1936-39; plant design engr. Naval Stores, Valdosta, Ga., 1940; exec. v.p. Wannamaker Chem. Co., Orangeburg, S.C., 1941-45; pres., treas. Applied Engring. Co., Orangeburg, 1946—; pres., treas. Dixie Laundry, Inc., Columbia, S.C., 1955—; dir. 1st Nat. Bank, Orangeburg. Regional trustee Orangeburg Hosp. Mem. Am. Chem. Soc., S.C. C. of C. (dir.), Phi Delta Theta, Tau Beta Pi, Alpha Chi Sigma. Rotarian. Clubs: Palmetto (Columbia); Orangeburg Country; Wildcat Cliffs Country (Highlands, N.C.). Inventor engring. devices. Home: 1120 Moss Av Orangeburg SC 29115 Office: 1525 Charleston Rd Orangeburg SC 29115

NEWTON, WILLIAM HARRISON, SR., chem. co. exec.; b. Ft. Worth, Jan. 25, 1917; s. Thomas Edward and Mae (Harrison) N.; B.A. in Bus. Adminstrn., Tex. A. and M. U., 1939; m. Barbara Helen West, Jan. 3, 1939; children—William H., Douglas W., Barbara Joan. Terminal mgr. Southwestern Greyhound Lines, Ft. Worth, 1939-43; buyer Gulfport Shipbldg. Corp., Port Arthur, 1945-50; buyer Tex. U.S. Chem. Co., Port Neches, 1950-51, purchasing supr., 1951—. Served to 2d lt. USAAF, 1943-45. Mem. Nat. Assn. Purchasing Agts., Aircraft Owners and Pilot Assn., Internat. Platform Assn., Izaak Walton League Am. (life mem.). Home: 3165 Gardendale Dr Port Neches TX 77651 also Sandy Pines Buna TX Office: PO Box 667 Port Neches TX 77651

NEXSEN, JULIAN JACOBS, lawyer; b. Kingstree, S.C., Apr. 14, 1924; s. William Ivey and Barbara (Jacobs) N.; student The Citadel, 1941-43; B.S. magna cum laude, U. S.C., 1948; LL.B. magna cum laude, 1950; m. Mary Elizabeth McIntosh, Jan. 28, 1948; children—Louise Ivey (Mrs. Heyward Harles Bouknight), Julian Jacobs. Admitted to S.C. bar, 1950; sr. partner firm Nexsen, Pruet, Jacobs & Pollard, attys. at law, Columbia, 1950—. Dir. Am. Sentinel Life Ins. Co., Lawyers Abstract Co. Bd. dirs. Columbia Music Festival Assn. Columbia Philharmonic Orch., 1967-70, A.R.C. Richland-Lexington Counties, chmn. bd. trustees Providence Hosp., Richland County Pub. Library. Served to lt. inf. AUS, 1943-46, capt. AUS, 1950-51. Decorated Silver Star, Bronze Star medal. Mem. Am., S.C., Richland County (exec. com.) bar assns., Phi Beta Kappa. Democrat. Presbyn. (elder 1967; trustee Synod S.C. 1969). Club: Forest Lake Country, Palmetto (both Columbia). Kiwanian (dir. Columbia Club 1967-68, 73—). Home: 2840 Sheffield Rd Columbia SC 29204 Office: 1231 Washington St Columbia SC 29201

NEY, RANDOLPH JEROME, retail co. exec.; b. Fort Smith, Ark., Aug. 27, 1937; s. Jerome Marshall and Ione (Sternberg) N.; grad. Choate Sch., Wallingford, Conn., 1955; B.A., Yale, 1959; m. DiAnn Smith, Jan. 27, 1961; children—Jennifer Diann, Marshall Smith. Mdse. mgr. Kerr's, Inc., Oklahoma City, 1960-61; with Boston Store Dry Goods Co., Fort Smith, Ark., 1962—, v.p., gen. mdse. mgr., 1962-70, exec. v.p., gen. mgr., 1970-73, pres., 1973—, dir., 1962—. Dir. White House, Beaumont, Tex. Bd. dirs. Broadway Theater League, 1967—, Episcopal Sch., 1968—. Served with USAF, 1959-60. Mem. Fort Smith C. of C. (div. pres. 1963-65; dir. 1968-70), Nat. Retail Mchts. Assn. (dir. div. 1969—), Whiffenpoofs, Beta Theta Pi. Clubs: Fort Smith Racquet (dir.), Town. Home: 4701 E Valley Rd Fort Smith AR 72901 Office: 40 Central Mall Fort Smith AR 72901

NIBBELIN, DAVID ALLAN, engring. co. exec.; b. Peoria, Ill., Apr. 28, 1931; s. Clarence John and Muriel (Johnson) N.; B.S., Bradley U., 1953; postgrad. Ohio State U., 1955; m. Sondra Rivera, June 23, 1973; children by previous marriage—Russell Allan, Stuart David, Gina Louise. Commd. 2d lt. USAF, 1954, advanced through grades to capt., 1957; research and devel. engring., navigator, Air Force component and systems devel. for aircraft systems; ret. 1961; design specialist Gen. Dynamics Corp., Ft. Worth, 1961-68; v.p. research and engring. NRT Electronics Inc., Weatherford, Tex., 1968-70; pres., dir. Variable Acoustics Corp., Ft. Worth, 1967—. Instr., Tex. Christian U., Ft.

Worth, 1965-67; cons. acoustical engr., 1967—. Pres., Ft. Worth Opera Chorus, 1966-67. Trustee Tex. Boys Choir. Mem. I.E.E.E., Acoustical Soc. Am., Nat., Tex. socs. profl. engrs., Am. Inst. Physics, Audio Engring. Soc. Presbyn. (elder). Club: Texas Boys Choir Parents (pres. 1964-65). Home: 2345 Mistletoe Blvd Fort Worth TX 76110 Office: 2108 W Vickery Fort Worth TX 76102

NIBLING, BOYD, physician; b. San Angelo, Tex., June 5, 1909; s. George William and Jerre (Harrison) N.; B.S., U. Tex., 1936; M.D., U. Tex. at Galveston, 1937; m. Ollie Ruth Frazier, July 3, 1954; children—Iris Lynne, Edith Ann, Lisa Marie. Intern, Robert B. Green Meml. Hosp., San Antonio, 1937-38; resident W. T. Shannon Meml. Hosp., San Angelo, Tex., 1946-47; individual practice medicine, Beaumont, Tex., 1941-42, 47-49, McCamey, Tex., 1949-65; mem. med. and surg. staff Mexia (Tex.) State Sch., 1965-71; staff physician VA Hosp., Waco, Tex., 1971—. Served with AUS, 1942-46. Decorated Battle Star. Mem. Limestone County (pres. 1969), McLennan County med. socs., Tex., Am. med. assns., Nu Sigma Nu. Lion, Rotarian. Home: 9508 Teresa Circle Waco TX 76710 Office: VA Hosp Memorial Dr Waco TX 76703

NICE, CHARLES MONROE, JR., educator, physician; b. Parsons, Kan., Dec. 21, 1919; s. Charles Monroe and Margaret (McClenahan) N.; A.B., U. Kan., M.D., 1943; M.Sc. in Medicine, U. Colo., 1948; Ph.D., U. Minn., 1951; m. Mary Ellen Cranmer, Dec. 21, 1940; children—Norma Jane (Mrs. Dennis E. Murphy), Pamela, Deborah, Julianne, Charles Monroe III, Thomas, Mary Ellen, Rebecca. Intern Grasslands Hosp., 1943-44; resident in radiology U. Minn. Hosp., 1948-50; mem. faculty U. Minn. Hosp., Mpls., 1951-58; prof. radiology Tulane U. Med. Sch., New Orleans, 1958—, chmn. dept., 1960—; mem. staff Charity Hosp., New Orleans, 1958—. Mem. tng. com. NIH, 1967; mem. NRC, 1969; chmn. tng. adv. com. Bur. Radiol. Health, 1970-72. Served with AUS, 1944-46; PTO. Fellow Am. Coll. Chest Physicians, Am. Coll. Radiologists, Royal Soc. Medicine (London). Author: Roentgen Diagnosis of Abdominal Tumors in Childhood, 1957; Clinical Roentgenology of Collagen Disease, 1966; Differential Diagnosis of Cardiovascular Disease by X-ray, 1966; Cardiovascular Roentgenology; a validated program, 1967. Contbr. numerous articles profl. jours. Home: 508 Millandon St New Orleans LA 70118 Office: 1430 Tulane Av New Orleans LA 70112

NICHOL, H(UGH) GORDON, state ofcl.; b. Nashville, July 20, 1902; s. Henry Gifforn and India Lillian (Brinkley) N.; student Vanderbilt U.; m. Margarite Cathey, June 13, 1964; children—H. Gordon, Marcia (Mrs. David Burns), James Patrick. Mgr., Firestone Stores, Nashville, 1931-36; operator 7th Av. Garage, 1936-40; owner Gordon Nichol Tractor Co., 1940-58; dir. Social Security for Tenn., Nashville, 1958—. Democrat. Mason, Lion, Elk. Home: 5025 Franklin Rd Nashville TN 37220 Office: Cordell Hull Bldg Nashville TN 37219

NICHOLAS, DONALD ADAMS, mus. ofcl.; b. Richmond, Va., May 15, 1941; s. Clifton Adams and Eugenia Doris (Foster) N.; student Ferrum Jr. Coll., 1961-62; B.S., U. Richmond, 1965; m. Carol Ann Thomas, June 5, 1965; 1 dau., Crystal Ann. Accounting trainee Reynolds Metals, Richmond, 1965-66, 67-68; math. tchr. Chesterfield County, Va., 1966-67; accountant Lybrands, Ross Bros. & Montgomery, C.P.A.'s., Richmond, 1968-69; asst. adminstr. Va. Mus. Fine Arts, Richmond, 1969-71, adminstr., 1971—. Mem. Am. Assn. Museums. Home: 11833 Kilrenny Rd Midlothian VA 23113 Office: Blvd and Grove Av Richmond VA 23221

NICHOLAS, PAUL HARTMAN, chem., adhesive products co. exec.; b. Northampton, Pa., Dec. 25, 1918; s. Ezra Fred and Bertha Eliza (Hartman) N.; B.S. in Chemistry, Muhlenberg Coll., 1936-40; m. Louis Bertha Burns, Mar. 2, 1946; children—Holly (Mrs. Joseph Roper), Kathryn, Bruce, Paul, Nancy. Chemist, Lone Star Cement Corp., Nazareth, Pa., 1941-42, Union Paste Co., Boston, 1946-52, lab. dir., 1952-57; lab. group leader Interchem. Corp., Cambridge, Mass., 1958-60; lab. mgr. Upaco Adhesives, Inc., Boston, 1961-67, Upaco-So. Adhesives Corp., Richmond, Va., 1968—. Dir., pres. Woodmont Recreation Assn., Richmond, 1970-71. Served to lt. col. AUS, 1942-46. Roman Catholic. Home: 10317 Jason Rd Richmond VA 23235 Office: 4105 Castlewood Rd Richmond VA 23234

NICHOLLS, GERALD JOSEPH, wholesale trade co. exec.; b. Bobcaygeon, Ont., Can., Sept. 6, 1930; s. James Joseph and Stella May (Carty) N.; came to U.S., 1954, naturalized, 1963; student LaSalle Univ., 1957-59; m. Mary Lesenko, May 12, 1951; 1 dau., Jennifer Lynn (Mrs. Charles Bennet Aycock). Transp. supr. C. & O. Ry., Newport News, Va., 1957-58; mgr. transp. dept. Noland Co., Newport News, 1958—. Served with AUS, 1955-57. Mem. Nat. Indsl. Traffic League, Nat. Defense Transp. Assn., Nat. Assn. Wholesaler Distributors, Delta Nu Alpha. Club: Warwick Yacht. Home: 17 Quillen Terrace Newport News VA Office: 2700 Warwick Blvd Newport News VA 23607

NICHOLS, DONALD EUGENE, mech. engr.; b. Nashville, Aug. 21, 1923; s. William T. and Nannie (Sanders) N.; B.S. in M.E., Tenn. Tech. U., 1949; m. Ama Virginia Foster, Dec. 17, 1949; 1 dau., Barbara Ann. Engring. draftsman I.C. Thomasson & Assos., Inc., cons. engrs., Nashville, 1949-51, design engr., 1951-58, asso., 1958-65, sr. asso., sec.-treas., dir., 1965-71, exec. v.p., 1971-72, pres., 1972—. Mem. Metro Nashville Gas Code Com., 1965-67; mem. engring. adv. com. Engring. Devel. Found., Tenn. Tech. U., 1968-72, chmn., 1972—. Registered profl. engr., Tenn. Mem. Am. Soc. Heating, Refrigerating and Air Conditioning Engrs. (pres. Mid-Tenn. chpt. 1961-62, regional dir. 1969-72), Nat., Tenn. (chmn. fees and salary com. 1958) socs. profl. engrs., Tau Beta Pi. Mem. Christian Ch. (chmn. ch. bd. 1967, ch. elder). Mason (Shriner). Home: 5056 Kingsview Ct Nashville TN 37220 Office: 2120 8th Av S Nashville TN 37204

NICHOLS, FREDERICK ROBERT, banker; b. Daytona Beach, Fla., July 7, 1946; s. Lee and Bertie Elizabeth (Burnett) N.; B.B.A., Baylor U., 1968; m. Emily Dell Maberry, Aug. 18, 1967; children—Melanie Dell, Lynda Joy. Staff accountant Peat, Marwick, Mitchell & Co., Houston, 1968-71; v.p., controller Comml. Nat. Bank, Nacogdoches, Tex., 1971—; pres., dir. Nacogdoches Computer Services, Inc. Dir. Deep East Tex. Estate Council, 1972—. Chmn. Nacogdoches County United Fund drive, 1973-74. Mem. Am. Inst. C.P.A.'s, Am. Assn. Accountants, Tex. Soc. C.P.A.'s, Nacogdoches Jaycees (treas. 1972-73), Nacogdoches County C. of C. (treas. 1973—), Beta Alpha Psi, Beta Gamma Sigma. Baptist (deacon). Home: 2600 Pinecrest St Nacogdoches TX 75961 Office: PO Box 847 Nacogdoches TX 75961

NICHOLS, HAROLD DEAN, mech. engr.; b. Thompson Station, Tenn., Oct. 24, 1934; s. Joe Greer and Martha Virginia (Huff) N.; B.S., Tenn. Tech. U., 1957; m. Diane Boyd, Dec. 18, 1956 (div. 1972); children—Lisa Kim, Karen Dawn; m. 2d, Jacqulyn Jo Beam Weiland, July 21, 1972. Facility engr. Boeing Airplane Co., Patrick AFB, Fla., 1957-58; with Ford Motor Co., Nashville and Tulsa, 1958—, engring. supr., Nashville, 1969-72, mgr. engring., Tulsa, 1972—. Registered profl. engr., Tenn., Okla. Mem. Nat., Okla. socs. profl. engrs. Home: 4913-A S 72d East Av Tulsa OK 74145 Office: 4821 S Sheridan Rd Tulsa OK 74145

NICHOLS, HENRY ELIOT, lawyer, savs. and loan exec.; b. N.Y.C., Jan. 3, 1924; s. William and Elizabeth (Lisse) N.; B.A., Yale, 1946; J.D., U. Va. Law Sch., 1948; m. Frances Griffin Morrison, Aug. 12, 1950; children—Clyde Whitney, Diane Spencer. Admitted to D.C. bar, 1950, U.S. Ct. Appeals, 1952, U.S. Supreme Ct. bar, 1969; law clk. Wellman & Smyth, N.Y.C., 1949-50; asso. Frederick W. Berens, Inc., Washington, 1950-52; practiced in Washington, 1952—; real estate columnist Evening Star-News, Washington, 1966—; pres., gen. counsel Hamilton Fed. Savs. & Loan Assn., Washington, 1971—; pres., gen. counsel Century Financial Corp., Washington, 1971—; dir., mem. exec. com. Columbia Real Estate Title Ins. Co., Washington, 1968—. Del. Pres. Johnson's Conf. on Law and Poverty, 1967; vice chmn. Mayor's AdHoc Com. on Housing Code Problems, 1968-71; commr. City Council Commn. Landlord-Tenant Affairs, 1970-71; vice chmn. Washington Area Realtor's Council, 1970; dir., mem. Exec. com. Downtown Progress, 1970; mem. attys. com. Washington Savs. and Loan League, 1971—; mem. atty.'s com. U.S. League Savs. Assn., 1971—. Bd. dirs. Washington Mental Health Assn., 1973. Served to capt. USAF, 1942-46. Named Realtor of Year Washington Bd. Realtors, 1970. Mem. Am., D.C. bar assns., Am. Judicature Soc., Am. Land Devel. Assn., Internat. Real Estate Fedn., Washington Bd. Realtors, Nat. Assn. Realtors, Met. Washington Bd. Trade, Nat. Assn. Real Estate Editors. Home: One Kittery Ct Bethesda MD 20034 Office: 1122 Connecticut Av NW Washington DC 20036 also 1025 Connecticut Av NW Washington DC 20036

NICHOLS, HORACE ELMO, state justice; b. Elkmont, Ala., July 16, 1912; s. William Henry and Louella (Bates) N.; B. Mus., Columbia, 1933, postgrad., 1938; LL.B., Samford U., 1935; m. Edith Bowers, Oct. 20, 1945; children—Nancy Bates (Mrs. James Lewis Glenn), Carol Elizabeth, Horace Elmo. Admitted to Ga. bar, practiced in Canton, 1938-40, Rome, after 1940; judge superior ct. Rome Jud. Circuit, until 1955; judge Ga. State Ct. Appeals, 1955-66; justice Ga. Supreme Ct., Atlanta, 1966—. Mem. Rome, Ga., Am. bar assns., State Bar Ga. Elk. Club: Coosa Country (Rome). Home: 13 Virginia Circle Rome GA 30161 Office: Judicial Bldg Atlanta GA 30334

NICHOLS, JAMES AUBRY, JR., accountant; b. Ennis, Tex., Aug. 11, 1947; s. James Aubrey and Daisy Elizabeth (Sills) N.; B.B.A. with honors, U. Tex., 1970. C.P.A., Haskins & Sells, C.P.A.'s, Houston, 1970—. Mem. Ex-Students' Assn., U. Tex., 1970. C.P.A., Tex. Mem. Tex. Soc. C.P.A.'s (com. Houston chpt. 1972-73), Am. Inst. C.P.A.'s, Beta Alpha Psi, Beta Gamma Sigma. Episcopalian. Home: 2416 Yorktown Houston TX 77027 Office: 1200 Travis St Houston TX 77002

NICHOLS, JAMES OTIS, aero. engr., educator; b. Huntsville, Ala., Nov. 24, 1929; s. James Andrew Jackson and Emily Viola (Harbin) N.; B.S. in Aero. Engring., U. Ala., 1957, M.S. in Engring., 1959; postgrad. (NSF faculty fellow) Cal. Inst. Tech., 1963-65; Ph.D., U. Ala., 1969; m. Sarah Mae Martin, Dec. 22, 1948; children—Gregory Keith, Pamela, Penni. Instr. U. Ala., Tuscaloosa, 1957-59; engr. Hayes Aircraft Corp., Birmingham, Ala., 1959-60; asso. prof. aerospace engring. Auburn (Ala.) U., 1960—. Cons. Jet Propulsion Lab., Pasadena, Cal., 1966-67. Served with USAF, 1948-52. Registered profl. engr. Ala. NASA ASEE summer faculty fellow, 1973. Mem. Am. Soc. Engring. Edn., Am. Inst. Aeros. and Astronautics, Ala. Acad. Sci., Sigma Xi, Tau Beta Pi, Pi Tau Sigma, Sigma Gamma Tau. Lion. Home: 319 Green St Auburn AL 36830

NICHOLS, JAMES RICHARD, civil engr.; b. Amarillo, Tex., June 29, 1923; s. Marvin Curtis and Ethel N.; B.S. in Civil Engring., Tex. A. & M. U., 1949, M.S. in C.E., 1950; m. Billie Louise Smith, Dec. 24, 1944; children—Judith Ann, James R., Jr., John M. Partner Freese and Nichols Fort Worth, 1950—. Farm operator Chisholm, Tex., 1969—; dir. Continental Nat. Bank, Fort Worth. Bd. dirs. Panther Boys Club, Fort Worth, 1969—. Served with AUS, 1943-46. Registered profl. engr., Tex., Okla., N.M. Mem. Am. Inst. Cons. Engrs., Cons. Engrs. Council, Am. Soc. C.E., Nat. Soc. Profl. Engrs. Methodist. Mason, Rotarian. Clubs: Fort Worth, Colonial Country (Fort Worth). Home: 3729 Arroyo Rd Fort Worth TX 76109 Office: 811 Lamar St Fort Worth TX 76102

NICHOLS, ROBERT BARRY, civil engr.; b. Knoxville, Tenn., Aug. 15, 1911; s. Shade B. and Ethel (Hazelwood) N.; B.S., U. Tenn., 1935; m. Helen Marie Moore, Oct. 18, 1939; children—Barbara (Mrs. Andrew G. Smith, Jr.), Patricia (Mrs. Edward B. Brantly). Various civil engring. positions TVA, 1935—, chief nav. engring. br., div. nav. devel., Knoxville, 1957—. Observer 6th Internat. Tech. Conf. Lighthouses, Washington, 1960. Served to capt. AUS, 1941-45, lt. col. Res. ret. Registered profl. engr., Tenn. Fellow Am. Soc. C.E. (task com. on inland waterways ports and terminal facilities 1969—, mem. task com. econs. and dimensions of inland waterways 1972); mem. Internat. Assn. Nav. Congresses (life), Phi Eta Sigma, Tau Beta Pi. Democrat. Roman Catholic. Club: Holston Hills Country. Home: 5500 Crestwood Dr Knoxville TN 37914 Office: Arnstein Bldg Knoxville TN 37902

NICHOLS, WEEDEN BENJAMIN, property mgmt. exec.; b. Horseheads, N.Y., Aug. 20, 1905; s. C. C. and Minerva (Rockwell) N.; ed. Rochester (N.Y.) Athenaeum, Mechanics Inst. Mgr., Smith-Young Tower, San Antonio, 1929-39, Hoblitzelle Properties, Dallas, 1939-46; mgr. comml. real estate dept. Interstate Circuit Inc., Dallas, 1947-50; v.p., gen. mgr. Republic Nat. Bank Bldg. Co., Dallas, 1950-71. Served as col., inf., AUS, 1940-47. Decorated Legion of Merit, Order Poa Ting. Mem. Nat. (past v.p. S.W.), San Antonio (past pres.), Dallas (past pres.) assns. bldg. owners and mgrs., Variety Clubs Internat., Boat Owners Assn. U.S., U.S. Power Squadron, Reserve Officers Assn., Nat. Assn. Real Estate Bds., Dallas Real Estate Bd. Office: PO Box 12841 St Petersburg FL 33733 Home: Yacht Eden Maximo Moorings Marina St Petersburg FL

NICHOLS, WILLIAM FLYNT, congressman; b. Amory, Miss., Oct. 18, 1916; s. William Francis and Daisey (Williams) N.; B.S. in Agr., Auburn U., 1939, M.S. in Agr., 1941; m. Carolyn Fenderburk, Jan. 30, 1942; children—Memorie, Margaret, Flynt. Pres., Parker Gin Co.; v.p. Parker Fertilizer Co. (both Sylacauga, Ala.); mem. Ala. Ho. of Reps., 1959-62, Ala. Senate, 1963-66; mem. 92d-93d Congresses from 4th Ala. Dist., mem. armed forces com. Mem. Sylacauga Sch. Bd., Bd. govs. Nat. Bd., Bd. govs. Nat. Hall of Fame. Trustee Auburn University, 1968—. Served to capt. AUS, 1942-47. ETO. Decorated Purple Heart, Bronze Star medal. Named Most Outstanding Mem. Ala. Senate, 1965, Man of Year in Agr. Progressive Farmer Mag., 1965. Mem. Am. Legion, V.F.W., D.A.V. Ala. Cattlemens' Assn., U. Auburn Alumni Assn., Ala. Farm Bur., Gamma Sigma Delta, Bluckey, Scabbard and Blade. Dem. Meth. (bd. stewards). Mason. Home: PO Box N Sylacauga AL 35150 Office: House Bldg Washington DC 20515

NICHOLSON, ALFRED OSCAR, banker; b. Shamrock, Tex., Apr. 29, 1906; s. Oscar T. and Mabel (Moore) N.; B.S. in Agrl. Adminstrn., Tex. A. and M. Coll., 1927; M.B.A., U. Tex., 1929; grad. Grad. Sch. Banking, Rutgers U., 1949; m. Sue Nelleen Robertson, Feb. 1930 (div. Apr. 1954); children—Betty Sue (Mrs. Fred A. Alexander), Dorothy Ann (Mrs. Ruel E. Walthall), Margaret Dale (Mrs. W.H. Black, Jr.); m. 2d, Marylea Thomas June 1955. Bank examiner State of Tex., 1929-34, Fed. Reserve Bank of Dallas, 1934-36, Fed. Deposit Ins. Corp., 1936-50; v.p. Merc. Nat. Bank at Dallas, 1950-60; pres. Farmers and Mchts. State Bank. Shamrock, Tex., 1955-68, chmn. bd., 1968—. Served from 1st lt. to lt. col., Finance Corps. AUS, 1941-46; col., ret. Mem. S.A.R. Methodist. Mason (Shriner). Home: 800 S Madden St Shamrock TX 79079 Office: 109 E 2d St Shamrock TX 79079

NICHOLSON, BRADFORD LAMONT, mfg. co. pres.; b. Buenos Aires, Argentina, Aug. 27, 1923; s. Vivian Lamont and Mary Veronica (O'Connor) N.; A.B., Duke U., 1946; m. Elsa Roveda, Mar. 31, 1948; 1 dau., Sharman Louise. Pres., Sepsco, Inc., Atlanta, 1955-68; pres. Gladwin Industries, Atlanta and Oakwood, Ga., 1968—. Served with USAAF, 1943-45. Decorated Air medal. Home: Route 3 Gainesville GA 30501 Office: Box 370A Route 1 Oakwood GA 30566

NICHOLSON, CHARLES PRESTON, farm equipment co. exec.; b. Evergreen, Ala., Apr. 26, 1911; s. Charles Preston and Amanda (Cruze) N.; grad. high sch.; m. Lois Pettit, May 28, 1933; 1 son, Charles P. Laborer, 1934-39; sales mgr. Rome Plow Co., Cedartown, Ga., 1939-42, domestic sales mgr., 1942-49; with Athens Plow Co. (Tenn.), 1949—, mgr. sales, 1950—. Mem. Farm Equipment Mfrs. Assn. (pres. 1968-69). Baptist (trustee, mem. finance com., ins. com., sec. men's class). Mason (Shriner). Home: 207 Forest Av NE Athens TN 37303 Office: PO Box 609 Athens TN 37303

NICHOLSON, HENRY HALE, JR., surgeon; b. Statesville, N.C., June 22, 1922; s. Henry Hale and Haseltine (Miller) N.; B.A., Duke U., 1944, M.D., 1947; m. Freda Lewis Hyams, 1956; children—Henry Hale III, T.D. Miller, J. Christie, Michael Witherspoon, Freda Amanda, William Stuart Cooper. Rotating intern Wis., Gen. Hosp., Madison, 1947-48, Ray Brook State Tb Hosp., Ray Brook, N.Y., 1947; resident surgery Med. Coll. Va., Richmond, 1948-49; fellow gen. surgery Alton Ochsner Med. Found., New Orleans, 1949-51, 53-54, inaugural fellow colon-rectal surgery, 1955-56; chief resident La. Charity Hosp., Tulane U., 1954-55; pvt. practice gen., colon and rectal surgery, Charlotte, N.C., 1956—; dir. colon and rectal clinics Charlotte Meml. Hosp.; mem. surg. staff Presbyn., Mercy hosps. (all Charlotte). Med. asso. dir. Mecklenburg County Red Cross Disaster Com., 1958-61; pres. Mecklenburg County div. Am. Cancer Soc., 1967-69. Served from pvt. to pfc., AUS, 1943-46, 1st lt. to capt., M.C., USAF, 1951-53, col. N.C. Air N.G. M.C. Diplomate Am. Bds. Gen. Surgery, Colon and Rectal Surgery. Fellow A.C.S., Am. Proctol. Soc.; mem. Piedmont Proctologic Soc., Am., N.C., So. med. assns., Southeastern Clin. Soc., Duke U. Alumni Assn. (pres. 1944, 60-65, rep. nat. council 1965-70), Alton Ochsner, Charlotte surg. socs., Aerospace Med. Assn., Flying Drs. Soc. East Africa, Mecklenburg County Med. Soc. (treas., mem. cabinet, pres. 1972), St. Andrews Soc. Carolina, Alpha Tau Omega, Phi Chi, Omicron Delta Kappa. Methodist (bd. stewards). Mason (32 deg.). Clubs: Barclay Downs Swim and Racket (dir. 1961-64), Hazel Creek Trout, Robert Burns Soc. (past pres., Charlotte, N.C.), Maracas (Charlotte), Charlotte Country, Hound Ears (Blowing Rock, N.C.), Carolina-Caribbean (N.C. and V.I.). Home: 635 Manning Dr Charlotte NC 28209 Office: 1012 Kings Dr Charlotte NC 28283

NICHOLSON, HUBERT ALLIE, bank exec.; b. Decherd, Tenn., Nov. 30, 1917; s. Thomas Norman and Bessie (Foster) N.; B.S., U. Tenn., 1940; m. Mary James Lindsey, Apr. 23, 1942; children—Norma (Mrs. Michael Powers), Nancy. Pres. Comml. Nursery Co., Decherd, Tenn., 1953—; with First Nat. Bank, Decherd, 1957—, dir., chmn. bd., 1967—. Vice chmn. Decherd (Tenn.) Housing Authority, 1968—. Mem. support council U. Tenn. Space Inst., Tullahoma, 1968—; trustee Meml. Hosp., Winchester, Tenn., 1965-70. Served with AUS, 1942-46, 51-52. Decorated Bronze Star. Mem. Am., Tenn. (pres. 1954), So. (pres. 1959) assns. nurserymen. Methodist (chmn. bd. trustees 1960). Mason. Home: Decherd TN 37324 Office: Box 487 Decherd TN 37324

NICHOLSON, JAMES HERMAN, II, dentist; b. Dallas, May 25, 1924; s. James Herman and Ruth (Chatfield) N.; student U. Houston, 1946-47; B.A., So. Meth. U., 1955; D.D.S., Baylor U., 1949; m. Melva Milatovich, Jan. 2, 1951; children—James Herman III, Melva, Mary. Pvt. practice dentistry, Dallas, 1959—; instr. Baylor U. Coll. Dentistry, 1959—, instr. gross anatomy and histology, 1959-62. Served from pvt. to 2d lt., inf., 1942-46, to capt., 1949-54. Mem. Am., Tex. dental assns., Flying Dentists Assn., Acad. gen. Dentistry, Assn. Am. Dentists, Dallas County Dental Soc. (mem. pub. relations com. 1973—). Republican. Episcopalian (vestryman 1973-74). Clubs: Lakewood Country, East Dallas Exchange. Home: 7102 Lakewood Blvd Dallas TX 75214 Office: 511 Casa Linda Plaza Dallas TX 75218

NICHOLSON, LUTHER BEAL, electronics co. exec.; b. Sulphur Springs, Tex., Dec. 15, 1921; s. Stephen Edward and Elma (McCracken) N.; B.B.A., So. Meth. U., 1942, postgrad., 1946-47, Tex. U., 1947-48; diploma Southwestern Grad. Sch. Banking, 1967; m. Ruth Wimbish, May 29, 1952; children—Penelope Elizabeth, Stephen David. Controller, Varo, Inc., Garland, Tex., 1946-55, dir., 1947—, v.p. finance, 1955-66, sr. v.p., 1966-67, exec. v.p., 1967-70, pres., 1970-71, chmn. bd., 1971-72, cons. to bd. dirs., 1972—. Gen. mgr. Challenger Lock Co., Los Angeles, 1956-58; dir. Varo Inc. Electrokinetics div., Varo Optical, Inc., Biometrics Instrument Corp., Varo Atlas GmbH, Micropac Industries, Inc., Gt. No. Corp., Garland Bank & Trust Co. Bd. dirs., exec. v.p. Harriett Stanton-Edna Murray Found. Served with AUS, 1942-46. Mem. Financial Execs. Inst. (past pres.), Am. Inst. C.P.A.'s, A.I.M., Am. Mgmt. Assn., N.A.M. Home: 1917 Melody Lane Garland TX 75042 Office: 111 S Garland Av Garland TX 75040

NICHOLSON, NELLIE RUTHRAUFF (MRS. GEORGE A. NICHOLSON), civic worker; b. Circleville, O., Apr. 24, 1884; d. John Mosheim and Sarah Ellen (Morrison) Ruthrauff; A.B., Wittenberg Coll., 1903; postgrad. Baker U., 1908-09; m. George Albert Nicholson, Jan. 30, 1907; children—George Albert, Ruth (Mrs. George Fox Trowbridge), Florence Isabelle (Mrs. Charles Overton Stillwell). Tchr., Ariz., Ill., 1904-06; sec., treas. Kusa, Okla. unit Okmulgee County Council Def., 1917-18; chmn. women's div. liberty loan No. half Okmulgee County, 1917-18; mem. Women's Community Council, Kansas City, Mo., 1921-22; treas. Kansas City Conservatory Music, 1923-24; chmn. women's golf com. Mission Hills Club, Kansas City, 1924-47; bd. dirs. YWCA, Kansas City, 1921-24; dir., sec., v.p., Consumers' League Kansas City, 1923-30; bd. dirs. Women's City Club, Kansas City, 1923-26; vice chmn. Daphne Recreation Bd. Pres., Daphne Republican study Club. Named Ala. Republican Woman of Yr., 1971. Mem. Am. Assn. U. Women (v.p., fellowship chmn.), D.A.R. (chpt. vice regent 1959-61), Kansas City Art Inst., Nat. Soc. Colonial Dames Am., Birmingham Hist. Soc., Birmingham Art Assn., Birmingham Opera Assn., Mobile Hist. Soc., Mobile Art Assn., Mobile Opera Guild, Met. Opera Guild, Mobile Symphony Aux., Eastern Shore Art Assn., Delta Delta Delta. Episcopalian. Clubs: Highland Book, Daphne Women's Study, The Club, Lakewood Golf, Mountain Brook. Home: 1019 O'Neal Rd Daphne AL 36526

NICHOLSON, PAUL J., investment co. rep.; b. Chickasha, Okla., Mar. 2, 1905; s. Oscar Farr and Agnes Loretta (Hill) N.; student Okla. State U., 1923-25, 27-32, Okla. U. 1925-26; B.S. in Architecture, Okla. A. and M. Coll., 1932; m. Dorothy McCue, Aug. 4, 1934;

children—Paul Joseph, Robert William. Asst. to state dir. Fed. Emergency Adminstrn. Pub. Works, Oklahoma City, 1933-37; sales engr. Southwest Airtemp Corp., Oklahoma City, 1937-38; clk. of works bldg. program, coll. architect Okla. A. and M. Coll., Stillwater, 1938-40; mgr. Modern Bldg. Co., Stillwater, 1940; asst. to chief engr. Brown Bellows Columbia, Inc., Corpus Christi, 1940-41; plans and expediting engr. Brown & Root, Inc., Austin, Tex., 1941-42; planning and scheduling engr. Austin Co., Cleve., 1942-43; auditor in charge, Office Comptroller Gen., GAO, Washington, 1943-46; asst. to project mgr. Seaboard Constrn. de Mexico, S.A., Chihuahua, 1945-46; asst. to project mgr. McKenzie Constrn. Co., San Antonio, 1946-47; field engr. Portland Cement Assn., Oklahoma City, 1947-52; mgr. gen. services dept. Western Co., Midland, Tex., 1952-57; sr. rep. Waddell & Reed Inc., Kansas City, Mo., 1957—. Mgr., Midland Savs. Bldg. (Tex.) 1962—, Helmsley-Spear Inc., N.Y.C., 1962—. Registered profl. engr., Okla. Mem. Am. Soc. Profl. Engrs., Systems and Procedures Club Assn. Am., Beta Theta Pi. Kiwanian. Club: Exchange (pres., 1972). Home: 2513 Fannin St Midland TX 79701 Office: 300 West Mall St Midland TX 79701

NICHOLSON, RALPH, former newspaper publisher; b. Green Fork, Ind., Feb. 12, 1899; s. Florence C. and Fannie (David) N.; B.A., Earlham Coll., 1920, LL.D., 1962; M.A., Harvard, 1941; m. Jane Elizabeth Blayney Harvey, Apr. 5, 1926; children—Blayney (Mrs. Allison Hodges Pell, Jr.), Martha (Mrs. Willoughby Brooke Beresford Fox). European corr. Phila. Pub. Ledger, 1920-21; v.p. Editorial Research Assn., N.Y.C., 1923-25; prodn. mgr. N.Y. Evening Post, 1925-27; gen. mgr. Japan Advertiser, also Trans-Pacific Advt. Agy., Tokyo, Japan, 1927-28; prodn. mgr. N.Y. Telegram, 1928-30, asst. bus. mgr. Pitts. Press., 1930; mgr. pub. relations dept. Gen. Motors Corp., 1930-31; gen. mgr. MacFadden Newspapers, N.Y.C., 1932; asst. to pub. N.Y. Daily Mirror, 1932-33; co-owner, gen. mgr., v.p., treas. Tampa (Fla.) Times Co., 1933-41, dir., v.p., 1933-51; owner, pres., pub. New Orleans Item, 1941-49; spl. cons. to sec. Dept Army, 1949-50; 1st dir. Office Pub. Affairs, U.S. High Commr. for Germany, 1949-50; owner, pres., pub. St. Petersburg (Fla.) Ind., 1950-52; pres., pub. Charlotte (N.C.) Observer, 1951-53; owner, pres., pub. Dothan (Ala.) Eagle, 1956-66, Troy (Ala.) Messenger, 1961-66, Brundidge (Ala.) Banner, 1962-66, Chronicle, Pascagoula-Moss Point, Miss., 1963-66. Aide, lt. col. gov.'s staff, Fla., 1941; a.d.c. gov.'s staff, La., 1943; hon. col. Ala. Militia, 1964. Del., Democratic Nat. Conv., 1944. Mem. Am. (chmn. postal com. 1959-64), So. newspaper pubs. assns., Am. Soc. Newspaper Editors, La.-Miss. Press Assn., Newcomen Soc., Nat. Def. Exec. Res., Sigma Delta Chi. Clubs: Harvard (N.Y.C.); Metropolitan, Nat. Press (Washington); Boston (New Orleans). Home: Route 1 Box 221 Tallahassee FL 32301

NICKELL, LAWRENCE RAY, physician; b. Lexington, Ky., Apr. 8, 1925; s. Silas Monroe and Clarinda Ellen (Blair) N.; B.S., U. Ky., 1948; M.D., U. Louisville, 1952; m. Mary Ann Roll, June 18, 1949; children—Kitty Clare, Lawrence Ray, Nannette, Courtney. Intern Baroness Erlanger Hosp., Chattanooga, 1952-53; gen. practice medicine, Owingsville, Ky., 1953-56; resident in radiology U. Tex. Med. Br., Galveston, 1956-59; asso. radiologist Erlanger Hosp., Chattanooga, 1959-62; radiologist St. Joseph Hosp., Lexington, Ky., 1962-63; radiologist Maury County Hosp., Columbia, Tenn., also Lawrence County Hosp., Lawrenceburg, Tenn., 1963—. Instr. radiology U. Ky. Coll. Medicine, 1962-63; dir. Sch. Radiologic Tech. Columbia (Tenn.) State Community Coll., 1973—. Mem. Maury County Tb Assn., 1963—, pres., 1969; mem. regional adv. group Tenn. Mid South Regional Med. Program. Bd. dirs. Tenn. chpt. Am. Cancer Soc., 1964-67. Served as sgt. AUS, World War II; ETO. Decorated Purple Heart with oak leaf cluster. Diplomate Am. Bd. Radiology. Mem. Am. Coll. Radiology, Radiol. Soc. N. Am., A.M.A., Tenn. Radiol. Soc. (pres. 1973), Club: Turtle Point Yacht and Country (Florence, Ala.). Home: 112 Bass Dr Columbia TN 38401 Office: Maury County Hospital Columbia TN 38401

NICKERSON, KENNETH STANFORD, psychologist, educator; b. Dartmouth, N.S., Sept. 11, 1930 (came to U.S. 1953, naturalized 1964); s. Stanford Morton and Ethel H. (Sanborn) N.; B.A., U. Kings Coll., Halifax, N.S., 1951; M.A., Dalhousie U., Halifax, 1952; Ph.D., Duke, 1959; m. Deborah Higgins, June 9, 1954 (div.); m. 2d, Connie Brown, June 7, 1969 (div.); children—Kenneth Scott, Bruce Alan. Psychologist, N.S. Hosp., Dartmouth, 1954, 58-59, S.C. State Hosp., Columbia, 1959-65; partner Gertz, Nickerson & Jones, Columbia, 1961-62; lectr. U. S.C., Columbia, 1960-65; asso. prof. psychology U. N.C., Asheville, 1965-71; prof. psychology Clayton Jr. Coll., Morrow, Ga., 1971; chief psychologist Indian River Community Mental Health Center, 1971-72; prof. psychology and faculty adviser U. North Fla., Jacksonville, 1972—. cons. psychologist Lutheran Ch. in Am., 1961-71, Blue Ridge Community Mental Health Center, 1968-70. Bd. dirs. Mental Health Center, Asheville, N.C., 1967-68, Counseling and Consultation Service, Black Mountain, N.C., 1967-69, Circle Childrens Center, Asheville, 1967-70. Mem. Am., N.E. Fla., Fla., Southeastern psychol. assns., Inst. for Rational Living, Am. Personnel and Guidance Assn., Asso. in Ministry Studies, Sigma Xi. Office: Dept Psychology U North Fla PO Box 17074 Jacksonville FL 32216

NICKEY, LAURANCE NOYES, physician; b. Fort Worth, May 25, 1931; s. Laurance N. and Jennie Maye (Langston) N.; student Vanderbilt U., 1948, Tex. Western Coll., 1948-51; M.D., Baylor U., 1955; m. Ann Collins, Dec. 10, 1955; children—Deborah Ann, Laurance N., Donna Lynn, Stephen Harrison. Intern, Jefferson Davis Hosp., Houston, 1955-56 resident Baylor Med. Sch. Affiliated Hosps., Houston, 1956-58; practice medicine, specializing in pediatrics, El Paso, 1960—; mem. staff Providence Meml., Hotel Dieu, R.E. Thomason hosps. Pediatric cons. N.M. Crippled Childrens Hosp., 1960—. Chmn. El Paso Tb Assn., 1965, El Paso County Child Welfare Unit, 1965-66 pediatrician-in-charge Children's Tb Clinic, El Paso, 1960—. Served to capt. M.C., AUS, 1958-60. Diplomate Am. Bd. Pediatrics. Mem. Am. Acad. Pediatrics, Tex. Pediatric Soc. (v.p. 1971-72), Am., So., Southwestern (pres. 1968-70), Tex. (dist. pres. 1970-71), med. assns., El Paso County Med. Soc. (sec. 1965-66). Presbyn. Contbr. articles to profl. jours. Home: 901 Cincinnati Av El Paso TX 79902 Office: 1515 N Oregon St El Paso TX 79902

NICKS, ROY SULLIVAN, univ. adminstr.; b. Chapel Hill, Tenn., June 30, 1933; s. Richard D. and Cora (Sullivan) N.; student Martin Coll., 1952-53; B.S., Middle Tenn. State U., 1955; M.A., U. Tenn., 1957; Ed.D., Memphis State U., 1969; m. Barbara Jean Love, Jan. 22, 1960; children—Beverly Jean, Richard Matthew. Instr., tng. officer U. Tenn., 1956-57; sr. budget analyst Tenn. Dept. Finance and Adminstrn., Nashville, 1959-60, chief budget div., 1960-61, dep. commr., 1961-63; commr. Tenn. Dept. Welfare, Nashville, 1963-65; asst. to Tenn. Gov., Nashville, 1965-67; asst. to pres. Memphis State U., 1967-70; chancellor U. Tenn. at Nashville, 1970—; v.p. urban and pub. affairs U. Tenn. system, 1973—. Pres. Tenn. Conf. Social Welfare, 1964-65, now bd. dirs.; mem. exec. com., scholarship chmn. Frank G. Clements Found., Inc. Trustee United Givers Fund. Served with AUS, 1957-58. Mem. Am. Pub. Welfare Assn. (pres. 1969-70), Tenn. Edn. Assn., Kappa Delta Pi. Democrat. Methodist. Contbr. articles to profl. jours.

NICKSICK, THEODORE, JR., coll. pres.; b. Slovan, Pa., July 30, 1921; s. Theodore and Mary (Mattick) N.; B.S., Tex. Wesleyan Coll., 1948; M.S., N. Tex. State U., 1951; Ed.D., 1957; m. Bernice Stone, Apr. 21, 1946; children—Jana Cecile, Sarah Suzanne. Instr. edn., psychology N. Tex. State U., 1951-57; asso. dean students Austin (Tex.) Coll., 1958-59; pres. Ranger Jr. Coll., 1959-66, Wharton County (Tex.) Jr. Coll., 1966—. Served with AUS, 1943-46. Mem. Tex. Fine Arts Soc., Tex. Jr. Coll. Tchrs. Assn., Wharton C. of C., Phi Delta Kappa. Lion. Home: 1424 Ladelle Wharton TX 77488

NIEBALL, MARY LOUISE ROY, librarian; b. Odessa, Tex., Feb. 28, 1929; d. Tom and Angela Roy; A.A., Odessa Coll., 1956; B.S., Sul Ross State Coll, Alpine, Tex., 1959; M.L.S., Tex. Woman's U., 1963; post-grad. work Ariz. State U., Tex. Woman's U., Cal. Western U., San Diego; M.A., U.S. Internat. U., 1971; m. Paul R. Nieball, Aug. 19, 1950; children—Paul Jay, Jon Roy. Library clk. Ector County Library, Odessa, Tex., 1944-49; asst. librarian Odessa Coll. Library, 1950-51; librarian Shannon Sch. of Nursing, San Angelo, 1951-52; supr. asst. and audio visual librarian Ector County Library, 1953-58; serials clk. U. Tex. Library Sch., Austin, 1956; cataloguer Sul Ross State Coll. Library, Alpine, Tex., 1959; sch. librarian Sam Houston Elementary Sch., Odessa, 1959-62, Gonzales Elementary Sch., Odessa, 1963-64; asst. librarian Odessa Coll. Library, 1964-67, head librarian Odessa Coll. Library, 1967—; cons. on sch. libraries. Mem. Am. Assn. U. Women, League Women Voters, Odessa C. of C., Am., Southwest, Tex. library assns., Tex State Tchrs. Assn., Ector County Tchrs. Assn., Tex. Jr. Coll. Tchrs. Assn., Permian Hist. Assn., Phi Theta Kappa, Kappa Delta Pi, Sigma Tau Delta, Alpha Delta Kappa. Home: 3733 Dover Dr Odessa TX 79760 Office: PO Box 3752 Odessa TX 79760

NIEDENZU, KURT, educator; b. Fritzlar, Germany, Mar. 12, 1930; s. Kurt Franz and Elsbeth (Friedrich) N.; Ph.D., U. Heidelberg (Germany), 1956; m. Evelyn Schaefer, May 17, 1958; children—Barbara, Kurt Stephan, Philipp, Birgid. Came to U.S., 1957, naturalized, 1960. Instr., U. Heidelberg, 1955; chemist U.S. Army Research Office, Durham, N.C., 1958-68; research adminstr. Wintershall Aktien Gesellschaft, 1968-69; prof. chemistry U. Ky., Lexington, 1969—. Mem. Am. German chem. socs. Author: (with J.W. Dawson) Boron-Nitrogen Chemistry, 1966. Contbr. articles to profl. jours. Home: 724 Haverhill St Lexington KY 40503

NIELSEN, WALTER NASBY, steel co. exec.; b. Racine, Wis., Nov. 29, 1909; s. Christian and Birgitte (Jensen) N.; B.S. in Engring., U. Mich., 1932; m. S. Elizabeth Dillon, Aug. 6, 1936; 1 dau., Brenda Nancy. Trainee, Sloss-Sheffield Steel & Iron Co., Birmingham, Ala., 1933-36; utility engr. Woodward Iron Co., Birmingham, 1936; mgmt. engr. Neville, Brown & Walters, 1937-40; asst. supt., supt. U.S. Pipe & Foundry Co., 1940—. Candidate City Council, Birmingham, 1963; mem. Citizens Adv. com., Birmingham, 1963. Chmn. bd. North Birmingham Day Nursery. Mem. Iron and Steel Engrs., Am. Inst. Mining, Metall. and Petroleum Engrs., Tau Beta Pi. Baptist. Eagle. Home: 663 Idlewild Circle Birmingham AL 35205 Office: 3300 1st Av N Birmingham AL 35201

NIELSON, VEIGH JENSEN, petroleum co. exec.; b. Whitney, Ida., Feb. 1, 1921; s. Waldemar W. and Beatrice (Jensen) N.; B.S., U. Utah, 1942; M.B.A., Harvard, 1947; m. Janet Moyle, Jan. 19, 1949; children—Nadine, Veigh M., Henry M., David M., Janet Ann. Indsl. engr. Geneva Steel Co., Provo, Utah, 1947-49; indsl. relations analyst Arabian Am. Oil Co., 1949-50; employee relations mgr. and asst. to exec. v.p. Trans-Arabian Pipe Line Co., 1950-52; tng. dir. Phillips Chem. Co., Bartlesville, Okla., 1952-54, asst. to research and devel. mgr., 1954-59, adminstrv. div. mgr., research and devel. dept., 1959—. Mem. exec. com., chmn. safety com. Cherokee council Boy Scouts Am., 1967—. Served to lt. USNR, 1942-46. Mem. Ch. of Jesus Christ of Latter-day Saints (1st counselor Tulsa State presidency 1960-69, pres. 1969—, chmn. Okla. region welfare com.). Kiwanian. Home: 2100 Skyline Dr Bartlesville OK 74003 Office: Phillips Petroleum Co Bartlesville OK 74004

NIEMANN, FRED A., lawyer; b. Yoakum, Tex., Aug. 25, 1919; s. Charles Henry and Mary Elizabeth (Kaiser) N.; B.B.A., U. Tex., 1942, LL.B., 1947; m. Virginia Freeman, May 21, 1948; children—Larry, Fred A., James Charles, Linda Lee. Admitted to Tex. bar, 1947, practiced in Yoakum, 1947-50, Austin, 1950—; mem. firm Niemann & Niemann, Austin, 1965. Dir. Tex. State Bank. Austin, Pan Am. Nat. Bank, San Antonio. Mem. Tex. Ho. of Reps., 1948-56, Tex. Budget Bd., 1953-54. Served to 2d lt. USAF, 1942-45. Mem. Tex., Travis County bar assns. Club: Austin. Home: 1704 Windsor Rd Austin TX 78703 Office: 1210 Am Bank Tower Austin TX 78701

NIEMANN, RALPH ARTHUR, govt. scientist: b. Centralia, Ill., Oct. 8, 1919; s. Albert Paul and Essie Myrtle (Whittenburg) N.; A.B. in Math. (Rector scholar), DePauw U., 1941; M.S. in Math., U. Ill., 1942; postgrad. Am. U., 1966-67, Okla. U., 1968-69; grad. Fed. Exec. Inst., 1970; m. Betty Jane Crissman, Apr. 6, 1946 (dec. Nov. 1970); children—Linda (Mrs. Jack Evans), Nancy; m. 2d Joyce Virginia Young, May 6, 1972; stepchildren—William Evans, Diane Evans, Jack Evans, Renne, Larry. Head math. programming br., also chief computation div. Naval Proving Ground, Dahlgren, Va., 1947-57; head computation and exterior ballistics dept., Naval Weapons Lab., Fredericksburg, Va., 1967-68, head engring. dept., 1969-70, asst. tech. dir., 1970-72, head warfare analysis dept., 1972—. Pres. Ferry Farms Swimming Pool, Inc., 1956-70. Served with AUS, 1942-46. Decorated Legion of Merit. Methodist (mem. ofcl. bd. 1966-71, chmn. finance com. 1965-71). Home: 25 Marshall Pl Fredericksburg VA 22401 Office: US Naval Weapons Lab Dahlgren VA 22448

NIERMAN, LEONARDO MENDELEJIS, artist; b. Mexico City, Mexico, Nov. 1, 1932; s. Chanel and Clara (Mendelejis) Nierman; B.S. in Physics and Math., U. Mexico, also degrees in Bus. Adminstrn., Music, and hon. degree, 1960; m. Esther Ptak, Feb. 16, 1957; children—Monica Daniel, Claudia. Exhibited one-man shows Proteo Gallery, 1958, 60, C.D.I. Gallery, 1956, Misrachi Gallery, 1964, Galeria Mer-kup, 1969, Mus. Modern Art, 1972 (all Mexico City), Galeria Sudamericana, N.Y.C., 1958, Hammer Galleries, N.Y.C., 1960, I.F.A. Galleries, Washington, 1959, 62, 65, 68, 71, Edgardo Acosta Gallery, Beverly Hills, Cal., 1961, Art Collectors Gallery, Beverly Hills, 1966, Main St. Gallery, Chgo., 1961, Dol & Richard Gallery, Boston, 1963, Pucker Safrai Gallery, Boston, 1969, El Paso (Tex.) Mus. Art, 1964, 71, Wolfard's Gallery, Rochester, N.Y., 1964, Pub. Library Rockville Centre, N.Y., 1964, Little Gallery, Phila., 1964, 70, Neusteters Gallery Fine Arts, Denver, 1965, Judah L. Magnes Meml. Mus., Berkeley, Cal., 1967, Galerie Katia Granoff, Paris, 1969, Alwin Gallery, London, Eng., 1970, Gallery Modern Art, Scottsdale, Ariz., 1971, Pan Am. Union, Washington, 1972, also mus., galleries, Haifa, Israel, Rome, Italy, Toronto, Ont., Can., Paris, France, Madrid, Spain, 1962—; exhibited group shows in museums in Caracas, Venezuela, 1958, Mexico City, 1958—, Havana, Cuba, 1959; Tokyo, Japan, 1963, Paris, France, 1961, Nagoya, Japan, 1963, Kyoto Japan, 1963, Osaka, Japan, 1963, Bogota, Colombia, 1963, Santiago, Chile, 1963, Buenos Aires, Argentina, 1963, Rio de Janeiro, Brazil, 1963, Costa Rica, 1963, Panama, 1963, Oslo, Norway, 1965, Warsaw, Poland, 1965, Madrid, Spain, 1965, Stockholm, Sweden, 1966, Brussels, Belgium, 1966 (also exhibited Expo 1958), also numerous museums and univs. Eastern and Western U.S. and Can., 1958—; executed murals Sch. Commerce University City, Mexico, 1956, San Francisco, 1965, physics bldg. Princeton, 1969; also executed stained glass windows Mexican temples, 1968-69; represented in permanent collections Mus. Modern Art in Mexico, Atlanta Mus., Mus. Modern Art Haifa, Mus. Fine Arts Boston, Meml. Art Gallery, Rochester, Inst. Fine Arts Mexico, Gallery Modern Art, N.Y.C., Phoenix Mus., Pan Am. Union, Washington, Museo de Ponce (P.R.), Santa Barbara (Cal.) Mus., Mpls. Inst. Art, other mus. and galleries. Recipient 1st prize Mexican Contemporary Art, Art Inst. Mexico, 1964, award Palme D'or Des Beaux Arts exhbn., Monaco, Silver medal Found. Tomasso Campanella, Italy, 1970, Royce medal, 1970. Life fellow Royal Soc. Arts (London). Home: Reforma 16-B San Angel Mexico City Mexico Studio: Nuevo Leon 160-701 Mexico City Mexico

NIERNSEE, FRANK MCHENRY, JR., steel fabricating co. exec.; b. Dillon, S.C., Apr. 4, 1915; s. Frank McHenry and Eleanor (Sprunt) N.; student High Point Coll., 1934-36; Wash. U., 1943-44; m. Imogene Landreth, July 13, 1940; children—Eleanor (Mrs. Robert E. Branard), Jean (Mrs. Coleman L. Arnold). Draftsman Memphis Power & Light Co., 1936-39, Tri-State Iron Works, Memphis, 1939-42, Curtis-Wright Airplane div., St. Louis, Mo., 1942-44; with Tri State Iron Works, Memphis, 1946—, chief engr., 1951-63, sec.-treas., 1963-71, v.p., prodn. mgr., 1971—, also dir. Served with USNR, 1945-46. Registered profl. engr., Tenn. Mem. Nat., Tenn., Memphis socs. profl. engrs., Soc. Am. Mil. Engrs., Memphis Engrs. Club.

NIGBERG, JOSEPH, investment counselor; b. N.Y.C., May 2, 1909; s. Abraham and Luba (Fogel) N.; student U. Ark., 1930-32; D.D.S., N.Y. U., 1937; m. Shirley Jean Scheifer, July 14, 1955. Practice dentistry, Bklyn., 1937-42, Valley Stream, N.Y., 1947-70; with VA, Birmingham Gen. Hosp., Van Nuys, Cal., 1946-47; pres. Joab Realty, N.Y.C., 1954-68, Judah Realty, Atlanta, 1958—; asso. partner Glen Alden Assos., Scranton, Pa., 1964-69; pres. Del Prado Condominium Assn. Served with AUS, 1942-46. Mem. Am. Dental Assn., N.Y. 10th Dist., Nassau dental socs., U.S. Power Squadron. Mason (32 deg.). Clubs: Seamens Neck Yacht, Compass Yacht (N.Y.); Del Prado Men's (pres.), Del Prado Marina and Yacht (Fla.). Home: 18061 Biscayne Blvd North Miami Beach FL 33160

NIGH, GEORGE PATTERSON, lt. gov. of Okla., former gov.; b. McAlester, Okla., June 9, 1927; s. Wilbur Roscoe and Irene (Crockett) N.; student Okla. Eastern A. and M. Coll., 1946-48; B.A., Central State Tchr.'s Coll., Ada, Okla., 1950; m. Donna Faye Skinner, Oct. 14, 1963; children—Mike, Georgeann. Tchr. history and polit. sci. McAlester High Sch., 1951-58; mem. Okla. Ho. of Reps., 1951-59; lt. gov. State of Okla., Oklahoma City, 1959-63, 67—, gov., 1963. Served with USNR, 1945-46. Recipient Distinguished Service awards McAlester Jr. C. of C., 1952, 54, 55. Mem. Am. Legion. Mason (32 deg., Shriner), Lion. Home: 8321 Picnic Lane Oklahoma City OK 73127 Office: State Capitol Bldg Oklahoma City OK 73105

NIHART, FRANKLIN BROOKE, mil. affairs writer, museum dir.; b. Los Angeles, Mar. 16, 1919; s. Claude Eugene and Vera (Brooke) N.; B.A., Occidental Coll., 1940; postgrad. George Washington U., 1953-55, Marine Corps Command and Staff Coll., 1956-57, Dept. State Sr. Seminar in Fgn. Policy, 1963-64; m. Mary Helen Brosius, Feb. 11, 1945; children—Mary Catherine, Virginia Brooke. Commd. 2d lt. USMC, 1940, advanced through grades to col., 1957; various assignments 1940-5l, bn. comdr. 1st Marine Div., Korea, 1951-52, duty hdqrs., Washington, 1953-56, staff Sec. Def. Adv. Com. on Prisoners of War, 1955-56, U.S. naval attache, Rangoon, Burma, 1959-61, regtl. comdr. 1st Marine Div., 1961-63, asst. dep. chief of staff Research and Devel., Washington, 1964-66; ret., 1966; sr. research analyst Georgetown Research Project, Atlantic Research Corp., Washington, 1966-68; staff asso. Hist. Evaluation and Research Orgn., McLean, Va., 1968-69; sr. editor Armed Forces Jour., Washington, 1970-73; dep. dir. Marine Corps Museums, 1973—; editor Fortitudine, 1973—. Pres., gov. Co. Mil. Historians, 1966-69. Past trustee Am. Mil. Inst. Decorated Navy Cross, Bronze Star medal. Mem. Am. Assn. Museums, Am. Assn. State and Local History, Inst. for Strategic Studies (London). Clubs: Army and Navy, Ends-of-the-Earth, Carabao. Contbr. articles to various encys., mil. jours. Editor: Almanac of World Military Power, Harrisburg, 1970. Home: 6208 Kellogg Dr McLean VA 22101 Office: Bldg 198 Navy Yard Washington DC 20374

NIKOLIC, ZIVORAD JEZDIMIR, elec. engr.; b. Sarajevo, Yugoslavia, Apr. 4, 1937; s. Jezdimir M. and Branislava J. (Jovanovic) N.; B.S. in E.E., U. Beograd (Yugoslavia), 1960; M.S. in Elec. Engring., Purdue U., 1963, Ph.D. in Elec. Engring. (NSF research grantee 1962-67), 1967; m. Vaida Mikits, Oct. 7, 1967. Came to U.S., 1961, naturalized, 1968. Research asst. Purdue U., Lafayette, Ind., 1962-63, instr., 1963-67; sr. research geophysicist Esso Prodn. Research Co., Houston, 1967-69, sr. research specialist, 1969-72, research asso., 1972—. Served with Yugoslav Army, 1960-61. Mem. I.E.E.E., Sigma Xi. Home: 2815 Bissonnet Houston TX 77005 Office: PO Box 2189 Houston TX 77001

NIPP, RALPH ELGIN, surgeon; b. Union City, Tenn., Apr. 25, 1943; s. Edward Arie and Winnie Mae (McCullough) N.; A.B., U. Tenn. at Chattanooga, 1964; M.D., U. Tenn., 1967; m. Ann Wright Pickering, Dec. 14, 1963; children—Lynette Michelle, Gregory Ralph, Melinda Suzanne. Intern, Meth. Hosp., Memphis, 1967-68; resident in gen. surgery Erlanger Hosp., Chattanooga, 1969-73. Served as maj. USAF, 1973-75. Home: 3250 Schuler Dr Bossier City LA 71010 Office: Base Hosp Barksdale AFB LA 71110

NISBET, WALTER OLIN, III, investment counseling co. exec.; b. Charlotte, N.C., Mar. 18, 1940; s. Walter Olin and Rebecca Wise (Jones) N.; B.A., Davidson Coll., 1963; M.B.A., Harvard Bus. Sch., 1967; m. Marian Harvey McGowan, Aug. 11, 1962; children—Walter Olin IV, William McGowan. Mgr. syndicate and corporate finance Interstate Securities Corp., Charlotte, 1967-68, v.p., 1968-70, dir., mem. exec. com., 1968-70; pres. Sterling Mgmt. Co., Charlotte, 1970—; dir. Conner Homes Corp., Mineral Research and Devel. Co., Manetta Mills, Comm-Sound, Mt. Mitchell Group Ltd. Active campaigns United Community Services. Served to 1st lt. AUS, 1963-65. Mem. Harvard Bus. Sch. Alumni Assn. (pres. Charlotte chpt. 1971), Episcopal High Sch. Old Boys' Council, Sigma Alpha Epsilon. Republican. Presbyn. Clubs: Charlotte Country, Charlotte City. Home: 4028 Ridgecrest Av Charlotte NC 28211 Office: 230 S Tryon St Charlotte NC 28202

NISSELSON, HAROLD, govt. ofcl.; b. Bklyn., Oct. 27, 1918; s. John and Lillian (Machenberg) N.; B.S., Coll. City N.Y., 1938; postgrad. N.Y. U., 1938-39; m. Gloria Ruth Thackaberry, Apr. 6, 1946; children—Catherine Laura, Jane Elizabeth. Statistician U.S. Bur. Research Census, 1940-63; sr. scientist Operations Research, Inc., Silver Spring, Md., 1963-69, principal scientist, 1969-70; asst. dir. research Nat. Center Ednl. Statistics, U.S. Office Edn., Washington, 1970-73; chief math. and statis. adviser U.S. Bur. Census, 1973—; instr. Grad. Sch., U.S. Dept. Agr., Washington, 1946—. Served with USNR, 1944-46. Recipient Meritorious award U.S. Dept. Commerce, 1954. Fellow A.A.A.S., Am. Statis. Assn.; mem. Inst. Math. Statistics, Washington Statis. Soc. (chmn. methodology sect. 1971-72, v.p. 1972-73, pres. 1973-74). Home: 6122 Beachway Dr Falls Church VA 22041 Office: US Bur Census Washington DC 20233

NISSLER, CHRISTIAN WILLIAM, III, constrn. co. exec.; b. Phila., Aug. 27, 1923; s. Christian William and Anna Haynes (Fitzgerald) N.; B.S., U. Mich., 1949; m. Sara Betty Kelly, May 13, 1961. Estimator Walter L. Couse & Co., Detroit, 1949-59, Dunn Constrn. Co., Birmingham, Ala., 1959-63; v.p., estimator Stuart Constrn. Co., Bay Minette, 1963—. Served with USNR, 1943-46, PTO. Recipient Honorable Mention in Sculpture, Spring Hill Coll., 1966. Fellow Am. Soc. C.E.; mem. Phi Delta Theta. Episcopalian (vestryman 1966-70). Club: Holly Hills Country (pres. 1969) (Bay Minette). Home: Route 2 Chalet Ridge Bay Minette AL 36507 Office: PO Box 570 Bay Minette AL 36507

NITCHOLAS, MONTY CLIFFORD, city ofcl.; b. McKinney, Tex., Dec. 8, 1932; s. Charles Edward and Fayma Lee (Smith) N.; B.A., N. Tex. U., 1955; m. Bettie June Britton, Aug. 27, 1954; children—Monty Kent, Teresa Diane, David Lee, Mark Charles. Accountant, City of Garland, Tex., 1958; accountant Grinnen Mortgage Co., Dallas, 1959-60; dir. finance City of McKinney, Tex., 1961-64; county auditor Collin County, Tex., 1964-67; dir. finance city of Sherman, Tex., 1967—. Active United Fund, Austin Coll. Fund drive. Served to 1st. lt. USAF, 1955-58. Mem. Municipal Finance Officers Assn. (v.p. Tex. chpt.), Jr. C. of C. (pres. 1963). Democrat. Roman Catholic. Clubs: Sherman Noon Optimist (v.p. 1969), Sherman Sports Booster (pres. 1973). Home: 2401 Ridgewood St Sherman TX 75090 Office: PO Box 1106 Sherman TX 75090

NIVEN, HENRY DOWNS, ret. banker; b. Matthews, N.C., Nov. 1, 1908; s. Edward Eugene and Theresa Jane (Downs) N.; student U. of N.C., 1926-27; m. Mary Lou Lowry, Sept. 17, 1931; 1 son, Edward Carl. With The Bank of Commerce, Charlotte, N.C., 1930-32, 37-73, exec. v.p., 1972-73, also dir.; farmer, Matthews, N.C., 1932-35; with WPA, 1935-37. Served with AUS, 1944-46. Presbyn. (elder 1951—). Home: 1146 Andover Rd Charlotte NC 28211

NIVEN, KURT NEUBAUER, art appraiser; b. Vienna, Austria, July 19, 1922; s. Salmon and Julia (Waldmann) Neubauer; ed. Austria; m. Rozalija Prah, Mar. 28, 1964; 1 dau., Dorit. Came to U.S., 1958, naturalized, 1963. Certified appraiser Albert Einstein Coll. Medicine, Bronx, N.Y., 1959-61, buyer constrn. dept., 1959-61; pres. Visual Art and Gallery, Inc., Dallas, 1964—; pres. K. Niven Sales Corp., Dallas, 1974—; appraiser of art World Trade Center, 1974—; collector graphic art. Served with Brit. Army, 1939-45, Israeli Army, 1948-49. Mem. Am. Soc. Appraisers, Tex. Art Assn. Odd Fellow. Home: 6321 Bryan Pkwy Dallas TX 75214 Office: 6333 Gaston Av Dallas TX 75214 also Room 330-1 World Trade Center Dallas TX 75207

NIVEN, MALCOLM P., textile co. exec.; b. Dunedin, Fla., Aug. 15, 1914; s. Percy D. and Janie Elizabeth (McLean) N.; B.S. in Bus. Adminstrn., U. Fla., 1937; postgrad. Harvard Grad. Sch. Bus., 1962; m. Nellie Felicia Booker, Dec. 7, 1941; children—Linda (Mrs. Thomas Tiller, Jr.), Sandra, Malcolm P., Jan (Mrs. Eugene Taylor). Pres., founder Carolina Mfg. Co., Greenville, S.C., 1948—; pres. R.W. Eldridge Co., Charlotte, N.C., 1964—; pres. So. Handkerchief Co., Greenville, 1968—; v.p. Fendrich Industries, Greenville, 1971—; dir., mem. exec. com. Carolina Fed. Savs. & Loan Co., Greenville, 1970—. Bd. dirs. Information Center on Alcoholism and Drugs, Greenville County, 1970—, Boys Club, 1969—, Salvation Army, 1969—, Greenville Symphony Assn., 1969—; trustee Montreat (N.C.)-Anderson Coll., 1968—, Presbyn. Coll., Clinton, S.C., 1967—. Served to lt. col. USAAF, World War II. Mem. Nat. Assn. Tobacco Distbrs., Ret. Officers Assn. Presbyn. (elder, trustee). Rotarian. Clubs: Green Valley Country, Greenville Country, Poinsett; Charlotte City. Home: 8 Meyers Dr Greenville SC 29605 Office: Box 5497 Station B Greenville SC 29606

NIX, JOSEPH NELSON, JR., advt., pub. relations exec.; b. Atlanta, Dec. 18, 1942; s. Joseph Nelson and Era Marguerite (Parks) N.; B.A., U. Ga., 1965, M.A., 1970; postgrad. Yuba Coll., 1968-69. News dir. radio stat. WJJC, Commerce, Ga., 1969-70; corporate pub. relations coordinator Citizens and So. Nat. Bank, Atlanta, 1971; dir. pub. relations Mead Packaging, Atlanta, 1972; account exec., field rep. N.W. Ayer & Son, Inc., Phila., 1973, Richmond, Va., 1973—. Comml. broadcast cons., Atlanta, 1973—. Mem., co. rep. Atlanta Internat. Council, 1972, Ga. Bus. and Industry Assn., Atlanta, also Keep Am. Beautiful, Inc., N.Y.C., Nat. Center for Resource Recovery, Washington, Jr. Achievement, Atlanta, 1971-72; committeeman United Way, Atlanta, 1971. Served to capt. USAF, 1965-69. Mem. Atlanta C. of C. (mem. com. 1972), Pub. Relations Soc. Am., Atlanta Press Club, Ga. Press Assn., Air Force Assn., Ga. Assn. Newscasters, Sigma Delta Chi, De Gamma Kappa. Home: 5716 Marbrett Dr Suite 200 Richmond VA 23225 Office: USARMS Def Gen Supply Center Richmond VA 23297

NIX, WILLIAM EDWARD, architect; b. Grove City, Pa., Apr. 3, 1928; s. William Henry and Edythe Romain (Horsman) N.; student U. Ky., 1953; m. Geraldine Theresa Pursch, Aug. 14, 1953; children—Laura Edythe, William Craig. Draftsman Austin Co., Houston, 1953-54; designer Irving & Hoyt, Houston, 1954-55; partner Koetter, Tharp & Cowell, Houston, 1955-67; owner William E. Nix, Houston, 1967-69, Nix, Spencer, Herolz & Durham, Houston, 1969—. Pres. Houston North Assn., Cypress-Fairbans Ednl. Found., 1974. Served with USNR, 1946-49. Recipient Design award Tex. Soc. Architects-Tex. Assn. Sch. Bds., 1972. Mem. A.I.A., Tex. Soc. Architects, Phi Sigma Kappa. Prin. works include Christian Home for the Aged, Houston, 1971; Evelyn S. Thompson Elementary, Aldine Ind. Sch. Dist., Houston, Teague Intermediate Sch., Aldine Ind. Sch. Dist., Houston, Christ Meml. Luth. Ch., Houston, First Fed. Savs. & Loan Assn., Houston, all 1972. Home: 10702 Elmdale St Houston TX 77070 Office: Nix Spencer Herolz & Durham 2010 N Loop W Houston TX 77018

NIXON, ARLIE JAMES, gas and oil co. exec.; b. Ralston, Okla., May 22, 1914; s. James Gordon and Wella May (Platt) N.; B.S., Okla. State U., 1935; m. Wylie Elizabeth Jones, Apr. 21, 1938 (div. May 1950); children—Cole Jay, Kathleen (Mrs. S. Brent Joyce). Airline capt. Trans World Airlines, N.Y.C., 1939-73; pres. Crystal Gas Co., Jennings, Okla., 1960—, Blackburn Gas Co., Jennings, 1964—, Blackberry Oil Co., Jennings, 1969—. Represented U.S. in several official delegations to Internat. Aviation tech. meetings, also represented Internat. Fedn. Air Line Pilots Assns. at internat. confs. Served to lt. (j.g.) USNR, 1935-39. Mem. Internat. Fedn. Air Line Pilots Assn. (regional v.p. 1972). Democrat. Clubs: Wings (N.Y.C.); Cushing (Okla.) Country. Home: RFD 2 Jennings OK 74038 Office: PO Box 68 Jennings OK 74038

NIXON, CLARENCE HERBERT, banker; b. Nashville, Feb. 19, 1929; s. Clarence Hunt and Ossye (Young) N.; B.A., Vanderbilt U., 1951; postgrad. U. Wis., 1959. With 1st Am. Nat. Bank, Nashville, 1951—, asst. auditor, 1960-68, auditor, 1968—. Served with USNR, 1952-53. Mem. Sigma Nu. Mason (32 deg.). Club: Old Hickory Golf. Home: 4010 Ivy Dr Nashville TN 37216 Office: 326 Union St Nashville TN 37202

NIXON, DAVID ALLEN, retail trade co. exec.; b. Pine Bluff, Ark., Aug. 11, 1921; s. Coy M. and Willie B. (Mason) N.; student State Coll. Ark., 1941-43; B.S., U. Ark., 1948; m. Gloria Matthews, Apr. 11, 1953; children—David Allen, Ruth Van Lear. Dep. sheriff and collector Jefferson County, Ark., 1948-50, sheriff and collector, 1951-54; bank officer Simmons 1st Nat. Bank, 1955-57; v.p. E.C. Barton & Co., Jonesboro, Ark., 1957-67, pres., gen. mgr., 1967—. Dir. Am. Found. Life Ins. Co. Bd. dirs. Craighead County Library. Mem. U.S. Indsl. Council (v.p. 1969-71, pres. 1972-74), Ark. C. of C. (v.p. 1968-71, dir. 1967-72). Democrat. Methodist (trustee 1970-71). Elk. Home: 2905 Mockingbird Lane Jonesboro AR 72401 Office: 241 Union St Jonesboro AR 72401

NIXON, DONALD MERWIN, educator; b. Topeka, Nov. 11, 1935; s. Merwin Edgar and Virginia May (Adams) N.; student Kan. State Tchrs. Coll., 1956-58, U. Denver, 1962-63; B.S. in Agrl. Bus., Colo. State U., 1965, M.S. in Agrl. Marketing, 1966, Ph.D. (Univ. scholar, Pacific Dairy and Poultry Assn. scholar) in Agrl. Marketing, 1969; m. Irene Annette Hollingsworth, Dec. 30, 1962; children—Melodee Annette, Dawnita Renee, Andrew Donald. Instr. poultry marketing Colo. State U. at Ft. Collins, 1967-69; asso. prof. agrl. econs., bus. marketing Tex. A. and I.U. at Kingsville, 1969-70, asso. prof. agrl. econs., 1970—; cons. Experience, Inc., Chgo., 1969—. Mem. Coastal Bend Agr.-Bus. council, 1969—, program com., 1972-73. Mem. Make and Keep Kingsville Beautiful, 1970—; vol. Community Concerts, 1970—. Mem. Inst. Food Technologists, Am. Marketing Assn., Poultry Sci. Assn., Soc. Agrl. Econs., Sigma Xi, Phi Kappa Phi, Gamma Sigma Delta. Methodist (sec., treas. Fellowship Class Sunday Sch. 1969-72; commn. edn. 1973-74, chmn. 1974). Kiwanian (sec. local chpt. 1970-72, 2d v.p. 1972-73, 1st v.p. 1973-74). Contbr. articles to profl. jours. Research in utilizing infra-red photography in citrus forecasting; econ. analysis of feedlot beef using reconstituted Kem Store: econs. of crop ins. as a tool in reducing risks; efficiency of Guatemala in producing bananas. Home: 2114 Colorado St Kingsville TX 78363

NIXON, GWINN HUXLEY, lawyer; b. Augusta, Ga., Jan. 17, 1906; s. Gwinn H. and Eliza Huxley (Scott) N.; B.S., U. Ga., 1926, J.D., 1929; m. Nora Palmer Fortson, Apr. 30, 1930; children—Eleanora N. Hoernle, Sally N. Hand, Gwinn Huxley; m. 2d, Caroline Stavely Fortson, May 14, 1954; children—Nelson Alexander, John Maddox. Admitted to Ga. bar, 1929, since practiced in Augusta; sr. partner Nixon, Yow, Waller & Capers; dir. First R.R. & Banking Co., First Ga. Devel. Corp. Pres. Augusta Citizens Union; co-chmn. Augusta Round Table, Nat. Conf. Christians and Jews; chmn. Com. for Good Govt., 1939-40, Augusta Pub. Forum, 1938-41. Dir. Augusta Library, 1947-73, pres., 1951-54; chmn. bd. trustees Gertrude Herbert Inst. Art.; bd. dirs. Augusta Opera Assn. Served with AUS, 1942-46; lt. col. O.R.C., 1953-66; lt. col. AUS, ret., 1966. Mem. Am., Ga., Augusta (pres.) bar assns., Judge Advocates Assn., U. Ga. Alumni Soc. (v.p. 1940-41), Am. Legion, 40 and 8, Res. Officers Assn., S.R., Phi Kappa Phi, Chi Psi. Democrat. Episcopalian (sr. warden; chancellor Diocese of Georgia, 1972—; lay dep. gen. conv. 1964). Elk, Kiwanian. Clubs: Art (pres. 1932-40; dir.), Augusta Sailing (commodore 1957, dir.), Augusta Country; Pinnacle. Home: 3285 Wheeler Rd Augusta GA 30904 Office: Ga Railroad Bank Bldg Augusta GA 30902

NIXON, JAMES MELVIN, exec. dir. YMCA; b. Norfolk, Va., Dec. 24, 1926; s. James Eley and Ebbie (Bryant) N.; B.S., Morgan State Coll., Balt., 1954; postgrad. Va. State Coll., 1962-64, Springfield (Mass.) Coll., 1961-62; m. Theola Amos, May 28, 1958; 1 son, James Melvin. Program dir. Hunton br. YMCA, Norfolk, 1957-59; youth dir. Effingham St. br. YMCA, Portsmouth, Va., 1959—, exec. dir., 1968—. Vol. probation officer Portsmouth Juvenile and Domestic Relations Dist. Ct., 1973—; mem. Chesapeake Dist. Tidewater council Boy Scouts Am.; pres. Portsmouth Job Tng. Center, 1971-73; mem. Tidewater Area Action for Community Improvement, 1970-72, Portsmouth Ednl. Assistance Council, 1969-71, Portsmouth Big Bros. 1972-74, Tidewater chpt. Fellowship Christian Athletes, 1969-74; v.p. Portsmouth Narcotic Rehab. Center, 1970-72. Served with USAAF, 1946-49. Recipient Ann. Outstanding Citizenship award D.A.V., Portsmouth, 1972. Mem. Assn. Profl. Dirs. (mem. nominating com. Va. chpt. 1972, sec. Va. Chpt. 1972), Nat. Assn. Profl. Dirs., C. of C., Nat. Center Youth Outreach Workers, Omega Psi Phi. Episcopalian (vestry 1972—, register 1972—). Home: 1700 Lansing Av Portsmouth VA 23704 Office: Effingham St Br YMCA 1013 Effingham St Portsmouth VA 23704

NIXON, JOHN WILLIAM, dentist; b. Homeland, Fla., Mar. 2, 1922; s. Will and Veivor (Robinson) N.; student Bethune-Cookman Coll., 1939-42, Fisk U., 1946-47; D.D.S., Meharry Med. Coll., 1951; LL.D. (hon.), Daniel Payne Coll., 1973; m. Ethyl Commons, Apr. 12, 1963; children—John William, Karl Henry, Melba Haley. Practice dentistry, Birmingham, Ala., 1952—; instr. dept. dentistry U. Ala., 1971—. Dir. Citizens Fed. Savings and Loan Assn. Chmn. Concentrated Employment Program, 1968—; mem. Downtown Action Com., 1968—; mem. Operation New Birmingham, 1968—; pres. Ensley Neighborhood Credit Union, 1970—; mem. exec. com. Birmingham Area Manpower Resource Devel. Planning Bd., 1971—; chmn. outreach com. Birmingham chpt. Am. Nat. Red. Cross, 1970-71; pres. United Services Assos., 1971; mem. adv. bd. Mercy Hosp. Bd. dirs. Volunteer Bur., Greater Birmingham; apptd. rep. of pub. Southeastern Regional Manpower Adv. Com., 1971; nat. chmn. nat. pvt. resources adv. com. U.S. Office Econ. Opportunity, 1972. Served with AUS, 1943-45. Mem. Ala. Dental Soc. (pres. 1963-64), Frontiers Internat. (pres. chpt. 1960), Kappa Alpha Psi. Baptist. Mason (Shriner), Elk. Author: (with C. A. Brown) Stepping Stones, 1961, God Smiles on a Troubled City, 1963. Home: RFD 6 Birmingham AL 35217 Office: 1728 20th St Ensley Birmingham AL 35218

NIXON, PAUL ROBERT, agrl. engr.; b. Kijabe, Kenya, June 23, 1924 (parents Am. citizens); s. Harmon Sidney and Clara Evelyn (Ohnmies) N.; B.S., Ia. State U., 1952, M.S. (Alca fellow), 1955; M.S., Stanford, 1966; m. Erma I. Koch, Aug. 12, 1950; 1 son, James Harmon. Asst. Soil conservation officer Kenya Dept. Agr., 1943-45; agrl. engr. U.S. Soil Conservation Service, Riverside, Cal., 1952-54; asso. irrigation researcher Ia. State U., Ames, 1955-56; project leader hydroclimate research U.S. Agr. Dept., Lompoc, Cal., 1956-70, investigations leader water mgmt. research, Fresno, Cal., 1970-71, research microclimate and remote sensing, Weslaco, Tex., 1971—. Served with C.E., AUS, 1945-46. Recipient Outstanding Performance award, 1958, Merit certificate, 1968 (both U.S. Dept. Agr.). Registered profl. engr. Mem. Am. Geophys. Union, Am. Soc. Agrl. Engrs., Am. Soc. C.E., Soil Conservation Soc. Am., Sierra Club (sec. 1973—), Sigma Xi, Gamma Sigma Delta. Lutheran. Rotarian. Contbr. profl. jours. Home: 1202 W 4th St Weslaco TX 78596 Office: PO Box 267 Weslaco TX 78596

NIXON, ROBERT WARREN, journalist; b. Salem, N.J., Feb. 7, 1940; s. Harold Ludlum and Edith Louise (Dickson) N.; B.A., Columbia Union Coll., 1961; M.S., Boston U., 1964; postgrad. Am. U.; m. Ellen Margaret Crofoot, Feb. 2, 1961; children—Brian Malcolm, Lynn Marie. Tchr. Montgomery County (Md.) pub. schs., 1961-62, 65-66; instr. Atlantic Union Coll., South Lancaster, Mass., 1962-65; asst. dir. pub. relations Gen. Conf. Seventh-day Adventists, Washington, 1966-68, asso. editor Liberty Mag., asso. dir. pub. affairs and religious liberty dept., Washington, 1972—; asst. periodical editor So. Pub. Assn., Nashville, 1968-69, head book editor, 1969-71. Mem. So. Pub. Assn. (dir. 1969-72). Asst. editor These Times Mag., 1968-69, book editor, 1970-72. Office: 6840 Eastern Av NW Washington DC 20012

NIXON, WILLIAM LOWELL, indsl. engr.; b. Floydada, Tex., July 11, 1937; s. Leslie Loyd and Velma (Jameson) N.; B.S., in Indsl. Engring., Tex. Tech. U., 1963; postgrad. Okla. Grad. Sch., 1972-73; m. Mary Jo Boen, Sept. 4, 1959; children—William Lowell, Kimberly Jo, Paula Sue, Jeffrey Lynn. Indsl. engr. USAF, Tinker AFB, Okla., 1963-66, mgmt. engring., 1966-73, chief mgmt. engring., 1973—. Registered profl. engr., Okla. Mem. Am. Inst. Indsl. Engring. Baptist. Home: 4700 Newport Dr Del City OK 73115 Office: AFLC XOMTE Tinker AFB OK 73145

NIZER, KATHRYN ANN, social worker; b. New Orleans, May 10, 1927; d. William T. and Imelda (Kenner) Nizer; B.S., U. Southwestern La., 1948; M.S.W., Tulane U., 1952. With La. State Dept. Pub. Welfare, 1947-65, med. social worker, 1963-65; med. social cons. La. State Dept. Pub. Health, New Orleans, 1965—. Bd. dirs. Westbank Assn. Retarded Children. Mem. Nat. Assn. Social Workers, St. Bernard Bus. and Profl. Women's Club (pres.). Roman Catholic. Home: 6408 Music St New Orleans LA 70122 Office: 200 Henry Clay Av New Orleans LA 70118

NOAKES, EDMUND DUPREE, civil engr., architect; b. Chickasha, Okla., Dec. 30, 1932; s. Edmund Perry and Margaret Lee (Dupree) N.; B.S. in Civil Engring., Tex. Tech. U., 1956, B.Arch., 1963, M.S. in Civil Engring., 1971; m. Janet C. Lindley, Mar. 30, 1969; children—Valerie Leigh, Darla Renee and Diana Lynn (twins). Engr., Parkhill, Smith & Cooper, Inc., Lubbock, Tex., 1964-69; engr. and planner Forrest and Cotton, Inc., Dallas, 1969-72; chief civil engring. and planning div. CECI Cons. Engrs., 1972-73; planner Dales Y. Foster, Inc., architects, Dallas, 1973—; pres., chief engr. Urban Cons., Inc., Dallas, 1973—; cons. in engring. Served with C.E., AUS, 1956-63. Registered profl. engr., Tex. Mem. Am. Soc. C.E., Soc. Am. Mil. Engrs., Tex. Soc. Profl. Engrs., A.I.A., Am. Inst. Planners. Contbr. articles to profl. jours. Home: 2230 Stafford Lane Mesquite TX 75149 Office: 800 LTV Tower Dallas TX 75201

NOBLE, CHARLES MACINTOSH, cons. engr.; b. Bushnell, Fla., June 10, 1896; s. Charles McIntosh and Mary Jewell (Taylor) N.; student Columbia, 1930-31; m. Kathryn Schubert, Aug. 21, 1917; children—Charles MacIntosh, Vaux Coffyn (Mrs. William Magnus Jamieson), Kathryn Schubarth Taylor (Mrs. Robert Carter Henry), Mary Ball (Mrs. Starling Loving Hanford). With A.F. Harley, Cons. Engr., also U.S. Engrs., Ala. Hwy. Dept., 1914-21; resident engr. Ky. Hwy. Dept., 1921-23, N.J. Hwy. Dept., 1923-25; engr. Port N.Y. Authority, N.Y.C., 1925-38; spl. hwy. engr. Pa. Turnpike Commn., 1938-41; hwy. engr. C.E., Arlington, Va., 1941-42; state hwy. engr. N.J. Hwy. Dept., 1946-49; chief engr. N.J. Turnpike Authority, 1949-57; dir. Ohio Dept. Hwys., 1957-59; adv. cons. civil engr., 1959—. Mem. adv. council dept. civil engring. Princeton, 1952-62. Registered profl. engr., Fla., Md., N.J., N.Y., Ohio, Pa. Served with USNR, World War I, World War II. Decorated Legion of Merit, Bronze Star; recipient Clemens Herschel prize, 1937, Arthur Wellington prize, 1938, hon. award. N.J. Soc. Profl. Engrs., 1950, Theodore M. Matson award, 1962. Mem. Chi Epsilon. Club: Ponte Vedra (Ponte Vedra Beach, Fla.). Contbr. articles profl. jours.; lectr. in field. Home: 895 Ponte Vedra Blvd Ponte Vedra Beach FL 32082 Office: PO Box 386 Ponte Vedra Beach FL 32082

NOBLE, JOHN WOOD, lawyer; b. Longview, Tex., Nov. 2, 1944; s. William Davis and Garland (Pegues) N.; student So. Methodist U., 1962-64, Centenary Coll., 1964-65; B.S. in Bus., Stephen F. Austin U., 1966; J.D., So. Methodist U., 1969; m. Dinah Lee McCalman, Aug. 21, 1965; 1 dau., Leslie. Admitted to Tex. bar, 1969, since practiced in Tyler; asso. firm Lawrence and Lawrence, 1969-70, partner, 1970—. Bd. dirs., mem. exec. council East Tex. Muscular Dystrophy Assn. Mem. State Bar Tex., State Jr. Bar Tex. (dir. 1972), Smith County Jr. (sec. treas. 1971, v.p. 1972), Smith County (sec. 1973) bar assns., Delta Theta Phi, Pi Kappa Alpha. Republican. Episcopalian. Office: 215 Tyler Bank Bldg Tyler TX 75701

NOBLE, MARVIN JACOB, physician; b. Houston, Feb. 3, 1935; s. Ben Zion and Esther (Littmann) N.; B.S., Tex. A. & M. U., 1957, M.S. in Biochemistry, 1957; M.D., U. Tex. Southwestern Med. Sch., 1961; m. Cyvia Yankuner, June 24, 1962; children—Sharon, Samuel Zion, Tamara. Intern Cleve. Met. Gen. Hosp., Cleve., 1961-62; resident anesthesiology Hosp. U. Pa., Phila., 1962-64; instr. anesthesiology U. Tex. Southwestern Med. Sch., Dallas, 1966-68; pvt. practice medicine specializing in anesthesiology, Dallas, 1968—; asst. clin. prof. anesthesiology U. Tex. Southwestern Med. Sch., Dallas, 1969—. Bd. trustees Hillel Found. Tex. A. and M. U., 1968—. Served with M.C., AUS, 1964-66. NIH Spl. fellow in Pharmacology and Anesthesiology, 1967-68. Diplomate Am. Bd. Anesthesiology. Fellow Am. Coll. Anesthesiologists; mem. A.M.A., Am. Soc. Anesthesiologists, Dallas County Anesthesiology Soc. (sec., treas. 1970-72, pres. 1973-74), Internat. Anesthesia Research Soc., Phi Delta Epsilon. Jewish religion (trustee temple 1968-71). Mem. B'nai B'rith. Home: 5719 Watson Circle Dallas TX 75225 Office: 8210 Walnut Hill Lane Dallas TX 75231

NOBLES, DONALD FRANK, lawyer; b. Palestine, Tex., Mar. 3, 1936; s. Durwood Lee and Goldie Aline (Collier) N.; student U. Tex., 1954, LL.B., 1960; A.B., Ohio U., 1958; postgrad. Ohio State U., 1957-58; m. Barbara Fleischauer, Aug. 24, 1957; children—Virginia, Lillian, James. Admitted to Tex. bar, 1960, since practiced in Austin; research asst. Tex. Research League, 1960-61; asso. firm McGinnis, Lochridge & Kilgore, 1961-65, partner, 1966-69; partner firm Davis & Nobles, 1969-73; individual practice, 1973—; lectr. law U. Tex., Austin, 1968—. Bd. dirs. Travis County (Tex.) Legal Aid and Def. Soc., 1966-68, v.p., 1968; mem. health adv. com. Capital Area Planning Council, Austin, 1971—, chmn., 1973—. Fellow Tex. Bar Found.; mem. Austin Jr. Bar (dir. 1963-68, pres. 1966-67), State Jr. Bar Tex. (dir. 1967-70, chmn. 1968-69), State Bar Tex., Am., Travis County (dir. 1965-68) bar assns., Am. Judicature Soc. Home: 5000 Crestway St Austin TX 78731 Office: City Nat Bank Bldg Austin TX 78701

NOBLES, HERBERT ALTON, nursing home exec.; b. Greenville, N.C., Sept. 29, 1929; s. Martin Luther and Huldah Louise (Albritton) N.; B.S., U. N.C., 1966; m. Peggy Jane Hartman, Sept. 4, 1954; children—Laura, William, John, Hubert. Staff accountant Peat, Marwick, Mitchell & Co., C.P.A.'s, Raleigh, N.C., 1966-69; v.p. and treas. Guardian Corp., Inc., Rocky Mount, N.C., 1969—. Served with USAF, 1951-53. C.P.A., N.C. Mem. N.C. Assn. of C.P.A.'s, Am. Inst. C.P.A.'s. Home: 3504 Hawthorne Rd Rocky Mount NC 27801 Office: Sunset Av West PO Box 4305 Rocky Mount NC 27801

NOBLES, MELVIN ALFRED, chem. engr., educator; b. Abilene, Tex., Dec. 5, 1913; s. Alfred and Gertrude (Edins) N.; B.A. in Math., Abilene Christian Coll., 1938; B.S. in Chem. Engring., Tex. Tech. Coll., 1940; M.S., U. Tex., 1942, Ph.D., 1945; m. Addie Belle Carr, Aug. 21, 1948; children—Melvin Alfred, Meladie Ann. Engr. Corning Glass Works Dev. (N.Y.), 1945-47; research technologist Mobil Oil Co., Dallas, 1948-51; research asso. Southwest Research Inst., San Antonio, 1951-52; prof. mech. engring. Okla. State U., Stillwater, 1955-57; prof. and head petroleum engring. La. Poly. Inst., Ruston,

1957-67; prof. chem. engring. Tenn. Technol. U., Cookeville, 1967—. Registered profl. engr., Okla., La. Mem. Am. Chem. Soc., Am. Inst. Chem. Engrs., Am. Inst. Mining, Metall. and Petroleum Engrs., Am. Arbitrators Assn., Keramos, Sigma Xi, Phi Lambda Upsilon, Tau Beta Pi, Sigma Gamma Upsilon. Contbr. articles to profl. jours. Home: 899 Southgate Cookeville TN 38501

NOBLES, WILLIAM ARTHUR, lawyer; b. Decatur, Tex., Dec. 28, 1931; s. Roger Glen and Kathryn Ruth (Helm) N.; student Decatur Baptist Coll., 1947-48; B.S., Austin Coll., 1952; J.D., So. Methodist U., 1955; m. Ann Elizabeth Renshaw, June 12, 1956; children—Kris, Lisa, John. Admitted to Tex. bar, 1955, practiced in Decatur, 1957—; asso. firm H.G. Woodruff and W.B. Woodruff, 1957-61; mem. firm Morgan and Nobles, 1961-73; sr. partner Nobles and Duncan, 1973—; county atty. Wise County (Tex.), 1961-73; city atty. Decatur, 1960—. Dir. First Nat. Bank of Rhome (Tex.). Pres. Decatur Hosp. Authority, 1967—. Served with AUS, 1955-57. Named Decatur Citizen of Year, 1973. Mem. Am., Tex., Wise County bar assns., Decatur C. of C., Alpha Chi, Phi Alpha Delta. Methodist (trustee 1965—). Lion. Home: 106 Circle Dr Decatur TX 76234 Office: 400 S Trinity Decatur TX 76234

NOBRA, DANIEL JOSEPH, system engr.; b. Bremond, Tex., July 11, 1935; s. Joseph Paul and Verna Marie (Mikolajewski) N.; B. Applied Sci., U. Houston, 1969; m. Phyllis Corrine Foster, July 2, 1960; children—Cynthia Ann, Teresa Jo, Daniel Joseph. Electronic maintenance technician FAA, Houston, 1960-65; field engr., IBM, Houston, 1965-69, asso. systems engr., 1969-71, asso. programmer, 1971-73, asso. systems engr., 1973—. Bd. dirs. Parkview Estates Civic Club, Pasadena, 1971-73. Served with Signal Corps, AUS, 1954-57. Recipient Apollo Achievement award NASA, 1969, Safety award IBM, 1968, Silver award Tex. council K.C., 1973. Democrat. Roman Catholic. K.C. Club: Polish National Alliance. Home: 2101 N Fisher St Pasadena TX 77502 Office: 1322 Space Park Dr Houston TX 77058

NODLAND, STANLEY KENNETH, civil engr.; b. Bklyn., Nov. 2, 1930; s. Karl Johan and Johanna Sofia (Aamot) Nodland; B.S., U. Mo., 1963; m. Connie Andrews, Aug. 17, 1968; children—Stanley Kenneth, Kendra Sue. Joined C.E., U.S. Army, 1948, advanced through grades to lt. col., 1968, ret., 1970; project engr. G.A. Fuller Constrn. Co., Allentown, Pa., 1970-71; profl. engr. streets and hwys. div. Jacksonville (Fla.) Dept. Pub. Works, 1972—. Decorated Legion of Merit with oak leaf cluster. Mem. Am. Pub. Works Assn., Soc. Am. Mil. Engrs., Am. Soc. C.E., Phi Kappa Phi, Tau Beta Phi, Chi Epsilon. Democrat. Methodist. Mason (Shriner). Home: 3501 Townsend Blvd Apt 123 Jacksonville FL 32211 Office: Streets and Highways Div City Hall 220 E Bay St Jacksonville FL 32202

NOEL, JAMES SHERIDAN, aerospace engr.; b. Plainview, Tex., June 18, 1930; s. James Simpson and Georgie Pearl (Maxwell) N.; B.S. (W.S. Mosher Meml. scholar 1950-52), Tex. A. and M. U., 1952, M.S., 1958; C.E., Columbia, 1962; Ph.D., U. Tex., 1965; m. Leona Marie Zaleski, Jan. 10, 1953; children—Sharon, Patricia, Jennifer. Structural engr. Grumman Aerospace Engring. Corp., Bethpage, L.I., N.Y., 1958-62; with U. Tex., Austin, 1962-71; design specialist Rockwell Internat., McGregor, Tex., 1971—. Pres. Hair Beautique, Inc., Waco, Tex., 1968—. Served with AUS, 1952-55; lt. col. Res. Registered profl. engr., Tex., N.Y. Mem. Am. Inst. Aeros. and Astronautics (sect. chmn. 1972—), Am. Soc. M.E., N.Y. Acad. Sci., Res. Officers Assn., Aircraft Owners and Pilots Assn., Sigma Xi, Chi Epsilon. Home: 816 Glasgow St Waco TX 76710 Office: Rockwell Internat Box 548 McGregor TX 76657

NOEL, JOHN ARMSTEAD, sch. supply co. exec.; b. Worthington, Ind., Jan. 4, 1920; s. William Bryan and Lorene (Calvert) N.; B.S. cum laude in Bus. Adminstrn., Butler U., 1941; m. Estelle Pullen, Oct. 3, 1943; children—Estelle (Mrs. Michael Morgan Mockbee, Jr.), John Armstead, Carol Carson; m. 2d Merelee Joplin, Oct. 20, 1967. Cost clk. Gen. Electric Co., Schenectady, 1941-42; jr. accountant Dick D. Quin & Co., Jackson, Miss., 1945-47; v.p., treas. Miss. Sch. Supply Co. and subsidiaries, 1947—, also dir. Mem. exec. com. Scoutmaster Andrew Jackson council Boy Scouts Am., 1953-57. Trustee Magnolia State Found., Missco Retirement Trust. C.P.A., Miss. Mem. Nat. Assn. Accountants, Am. Inst. C.P.A.'s, Miss. Soc. C.P.A.'s. Methodist. Club: Jackson Country. Contbr. articles profl. jours. Home: 242 Ashcot Circle Jackson MS 39211 Office: 4155 Industrial Dr Jackson MS 39205

NOEL, WILLIAM DOUGLAS, gas co. exec.; b. Ft. Worth, May 11, 1914; s. Earnest and Inez (Turnpaugh) N.; student U. Tex., 1935; m. Ellen Witwer, May 24, 1937; children—Sherwood (Mrs. John F. McGuigan), Ellen Melissa (Mrs. W. T. Speller). Chemist, Gulf Oil Co., Breckenridge, Tex., 1935-40; pres. Trebol Oil Co., McCamey, Tex., ind. oil operator, Odessa, Tex., 1940-63; pres. Odessa Natural Gasoline Co., 1947—, Odessa Natural Corp., 1968—; pres. West Tex. Gathering Co., El Paso Products Co.; co-owner, dir. Am. Bank of Commerce, Odessa, Tex. Commerce Bank of Lubbock (Tex.), San Angelo Nat. Bank (Tex.), S.W. Drug Corp., Dallas, First Nat. Bank, San Antonio, Tex. Commerce Bank, Houston. Mem. McCamey (Tex.) Sch. Bd., 1942-49; Mem. Tex. Council Higher Edn.; commr. Tex. Liquor Control Bd., 1961-69; sponsor Jr. League Baseball Team, Odessa Symphony, Permian Hist. Soc., Permian Playhouse, Crippled Childrens Clinic. Bd. dirs. Tex. Technol. Coll. Found.; asso. trustee U.So. Cal. Named Man of Month Southwestern Petroleum News, 1963, Outstanding Man of Odessa, 1963. Mem. Tex. Ind. Gas Producers Assn., Permian Basin Petroleum Assn. U. Tex. Dads' Assn., West Tex. C. of C. (Top West Texan award 1967), Beta Theta Pi. Democrat. Presbyn. Club: President's. Home: Route 1 Box 498 Country Club Estates Odessa TX 79762 Office: PO Box 3986 Odessa TX 79762

NOETZEL, GROVER A(RCHIBALD) J(OSEPH), educator; b. Greenwood, Wis., June 14, 1908; s. August Herman and Coralie Marie (Van Den Bossche) N.; A.B., U. Wis., 1929, Ph.D., 1934; certificate in econs., U. London, 1930, U. Geneva, 1936; fellow Social Sci. Research Council, 1935-36; m. Anna B. Dobbins, June 11, 1953. Instr. econ. U. S.D., 1930-32; instr. econ. U. Wis., 1934-35; economist Nat. Bur. Econ. Research, 1936-37; asst. prof. Temple U., 1937-40, asso. prof., 1940-46; pvt. cons. econ. and investment counselor, Phila. and N.Y.C., 1939-46; prof. econ. U. Miami, 1946-48, dean Sch. Bus. Adminstrn., 1948-61, prof. econs., 1961-72, dean emeritus and prof., 1972—, cons. economist, 1961—. Dir., mem. finance com. bd. Am. Bankers Ins. Co. Fla.; dir. Fla. Nat. Bank at Coral Gables, chmn. investment and finance com. Coral Gables Fed. Savs & Loan Assn.; dir. Security Trust Co., Miami. Bd. dirs. Goodwill Industries, Inc., Med. Service Bur. Miami. Mem. Am. Assn. U. Profs., Am. Finance Assn., Am., So. econ. assns., Econ. Soc. S. Fla. (dir., pres. 1956), Newcomen Soc., Phi Kappa Phi, Alpha Phi Omega, Alpha Delta Sigma, Delta Sigma Pi, Artus, Beta Gamma Sigma. Clubs: Rotary (Miami, Fla.); Coral Gables Country, Rivieria Country, Century (Coral Gables). Author: Recent Theories of Foreign Exchange, 1934; Cooperation Entre L'Universite et Les Milieux Economiques, 1956; Objectives of a Management Center, 1956; Decisions That Affect Profits, 1957; also articles in field. Home: 4990 SW 86th St South Miami FL 33143 Office: Sch Bus Adminstrn U Miami Coral Gables FL 33134

NOLAN, BERNARD HENRY, telephone co. exec.; b. New Orleans, Mar. 4, 1913; s. Thomas B. and Henrietta (Bridault) N.; B.S. in Elec. Engring., Tulane U., 1937; m. Rose Roberts, June 28, 1939; children—Robert, Mary Nolan (Mrs. Joseph Looney), Kathleen R., Jean G. With S. Central Bell Telephone Co., New Orleans, 1955—, engring. mgr., 1967—. Bd. dirs. A.R.C., New Orleans. Mem. I.E.E.E., La. Engring. Soc., C. of C. Mason. Home: 2824 State St New Orleans LA 70118 Office: 1215 Prytania St New Orleans LA 70140

NOLAN, GEORGE JUNIOR, educator; b. Stilwell, Okla., Nov. 3, 1935; s. Fate and Theresa Delier (Shook) N.; B.S., Northeastern State Coll., 1958; M.S., U. Ark., 1961, Ph.D., 1964; m. Phyllis Reddell, Oct. 21, 1955; children—George Reddell, Phyllis Carol, James Allen, Douglas Clayton, Steven Joe. Research chemist Phillips Petroleum Co., Bartlesville, Okla., 1964-68; asso. prof. chemistry Northeastern State Coll., Tahlequah, Okla., 1968-74, prof., 1974—. Mem. United Fund Com., 1972—. Bd. dirs. Tahlequah Hosp. Mem. Am. Chem. Soc., Sigma Xi, Phi Sigma Epsilon. Patentee in field. Home: 281 Hickory Dr Tahlequah OK 74464

NOLAN, JACK DEE, lawyer; b. Port Arthur, Tex., Sept. 1, 1938; s. John Davis and Margurite (Little) N.; B.S. in Math., U. Houston, 1965; J.D., S. Tex. Coll., 1973; m. Marie Compton, Dec. 10, 1961; children—Chris, Greg, Steve. System analyst Shell Oil Co., 1965; analyst Gen. Electric Corp., 1966; mem. tech. staff TRW Systems, 1966-73 (all Houston); admitted to Tex. bar, 1973; mem. firm Jones & Nolan, Houston, 1973—. Mem. Am., Tex. bar assns. Home: 1315 NASA Rd 1 Houston TX 77058 Office: 17200 El Camino Real Suite 3 Houston TX 77058

NOLAN, PAUL, educator; b. Boston, Jan. 31, 1919; s. Joseph J. and Fannie (Bransfield) N.; student U. N.H., 1941; Ph.D., Cath. U. Am., 1950, Ph.D., 1954. Instr. Cath. U. Am., 1953-59, asst. prof., 1959-65, asso. prof., 1965—; guest lectr. Georgetown U., 1956, 62, U. Md., 1957-59. Served to capt. AUS, 1945. Asso. editor Bull. Guild Cath. Psychiatrists, 1957—. Home: 503 A St SE Washington DC 20003 Office: Cath U Am Washington DC 20017

NOLAN, RAYMOND PAUL, physician; b. Tullow, Ireland; s. Stephen John and Elizabeth (O'Brien) N.; came to U.S., 1923, naturalized, 1929; B.S., Columbia, 1948; M.D., N.Y. U., 1951; m. Mildred Geiger, Feb. 11, 1957; children—Robert Paul, Kenneth Joseph. Intern St. Vincent's Hosp., N.Y.C., 1951-52; resident Bellevue Med. Center, N.Y. U., 1952-56; practice medicine, specializing in obstetrics and gynecology, Hollywood, Fla., 1960—; asst. prof. obstetrics and gynecology N.Y. U. Coll. Medicine, 1957-60; attending obstetrician and gynecologist, chief dept. Meml. Hosp., Hollywood, Fla. Served with USAAF, 1943-46. Fellow A.C.S.; mem. Am., Fla., Broward County med. assns., Am. Coll. Obstetricians and Gynecologists, Fla., Broward County obstet. and gynecol. socs. Home: 4911 Madison St Hollywood FL 33021 Office: 3711 Garfield St Hollywood FL 33021

NOLAND, IVESON B., bishop; b. Baton Rouge, Sept. 10, 1916; s. Ives B. and Camille (Reynaud) N.; B.A., La. State U., 1937; B.D., Sewanee U., 1940, D.D., 1952; m. Nell Burden, Feb. 3, 1936; children—Iveson B. III, John Burden, Daniel Woodring. Ordained to ministry Episcopal Ch.; rector, Charlotte, N.C., 1946-50, Lake Charles, La., 1950-52; bishop Episcopal Diocese of La., Baton Rouge, 1952—. Mem. bd. exam. chaplains Diocese of N.C. Served as chaplain AUS, 1942-45; PTO. Mem. Scabbard and Blade, Phi Kappa Phi, Sigma Nu. Home: PO Box 50850 New Orleans LA 70150

NOLAND, JAMES RUSSELL, govt. adminstr.; b. Paris, Ky., Jan. 10, 1924; s. James Russell and Christine (Haley) N.; A.B., Emory U., 1945; M.Div., Yale, 1948; postgrad. Columbia, 1951-52; M.A., N.Y. U., 1954; m. Mary Richerson, Dec. 22, 1945; children—James Russell III, Ellen Gay (Mrs. Robert Vernon), Mary Elise. Coordinator urban ch. dept. Nat. Council Chs., 1953-55; exec. dir. Protestant Charities Houston, 1955-67; asst. to pres. Prairie View A. and M. Coll., 1967-68; research sociologist Houston Bapt. Coll., 1968; asst. to dean U. Houston, 1968—, coordinator Farfel lectures, 1969. Pres., Value Guidance Systems, Inc., 1969—; dir. Tchr. Tng. Inst., U. St. Thomas, 1964—. Active Harris County United Fund, Planned Parenthood, Council on Human Relations (award 1964), A.R.C., Community Planning Assn. Trustee Childers Found. Served with USNR, 1942-46. Recipient Head Start award Houston Community Action Program, 1965; Merit Achievement award Protestant Charities of Houston, 1966; Distinguished Service award Houston Tchrs. Assn., 1968. Fellow Am. Sociol. Soc.; mem. Nat. Assn. Social Welfare, Acad. Certified Social Workers, Am. Bus. Writing Assn. Democrat. Episcopalian. Home: 13303 Havershire Houston TX 77024

NOLAND, ROYCE PAUL, assn. exec.; b. Walla Walla, Wash., Dec. 6, 1928; s. Homer Vernon and Mildred Bessie (Royce) N.; B.A., Whitman Coll., 1951; postgrad. U. Washington, 1951; certificate phys. therapy, Stanford, 1952; m. Annabelle Hall, Mar. 27, 1953; children—Royce Paul, Jr., Richard Mitchell. Staff phys. therapist USPHS Hosp., New Orleans, 1953-54, San Francisco, 1954-57; chief phys. therapist Santa Cruz Med. Center, 1957-61; pvt. practice phys. therapy, Santa Cruz, 1961-68; dir. dept. phys. therapy Dominican Hosp., Santa Cruz, 1967-69; exec. dir. State Council, Cal. chpts. Am. Phys. Therapy Assn., 1965-69, Am. Phys. Therapy Assn., Washington, 1969—. Mem. adv. bd. Goodwill Industries Am., Washington, 1971—; vice chmn. Coalition of Ind. Health Professions, 1973—. Contbr. articles to profl. jours. Home: 4202 Ann Fitz Hugh Dr Annandale VA 22003 Office: 1156 15th St NW Washington DC 20008

NOLEN, JOSEPH MICHAEL, real estate broker; b. Birmingham, Ala., June 27, 1936; s. Joseph Carl and Jean Melissa (Harris) Nolen; B.S., Fla. So. Coll., 1958; m. Georgene Ann Leis Nolen, Sept. 7, 1956; children—Joseph Michael, Michele Ann, Steven Brian. Sports editor, reporter Winter Haven (Fla.) Daily News-Chief, 1953-58; asso. realtor Leis Bros., Realtors, Inc., Winter Haven, 1958-66; pres. Action Agy., Inc., real estate and ins., Winter Haven, 1966-68; sec.-treas. Cypress Gardens Realty & Ins., Inc., Winter Haven, 1968-73, pres., 1973—; sec.-treas. Asso. Agts., Inc., ins. agy., Winter Haven, 1971—; partner L&N Groves, Winter Haven, 1966—, Cinco Partnership, Winter Haven, 1969—; dir. Imperial Properties, Inc., Winter Haven. Chmn., Winter Haven Multiple Listing Service, 1969. Mem. City of Winter Haven Spl. Planning Com., 1969; chmn. City of Winter Haven Planning and Zoning Bd., 1971. Bd. dirs. Citrus Center Boys' Club; bd. dirs., mem. exec. com. Lake Regional United Way, 1973-74. Served with AUS, 1958-59. Named Realtor of Year, Winter Haven Bd. Realtors, 1969; Young Man of Year, Winter Haven Jr. C. of C., 1972. Mem. Winter Haven Area Bd. Realtors (pres. 1971), Winter Haven Area C. of C. (pres. 1972-73), Polk Assn. Ins. Agts. Methodist (chmn. adminstrv. bd. 1971-74). Rotarian (dir. 1969-73, pres. elect 1974—), Mason. Home: 758 Av M SE Winter Haven FL 33880 Office: 290 Cypress Gardens Blvd Winter Haven FL 33880

NOLLEY, EUGENE DAVIS, physician; b. Nokesville, Va., Mar. 4, 1924; s. William Davis and Pearl Zena (Shaffer) N.; B.A., Bridgewater Coll., 1952; M.D., Med. Coll. Va., 1956; m. Doris Kathryn Bowman, Sept. 3, 1949; children—Ronald Eugene, Curtis Bowman, Dana Sue, Phillip Lee, Eric Wayne, Kevin Davis. Intern, Johnston-Willis Hosp., Richmond, Va., 1956-57; practice medicine specializing in family practice, Churchville, Va., 1957—; mem. staff King's Daus. Hosp., Staunton, Va. Mem. Va., County med. socs. Home: PO Box 104 Churchville VA 24421 Office: PO Box 100 Churchville VA 24421

NOLLEY, JOHN ROBERT, JR., ins. co. exec.; b. Richmond, Va., Jan. 6, 1929; s. John Robert and Ceta (Beck) N.; B.A., Va. Mil. Inst., 1952; postgrad. U. Richmond, 1956-59; m. Jeanne Marie Hoff, Mar. 5, 1954; children—John Robert III, Scott W., Catherine B. Asst. sec., asst. dir. advt. and pub. relations Life of Va., Richmond, 1962-64, asst. v.p., 1965-66, 2d v.p., 1966-69; v.p. advt. and pub. relations Richmond Corp., 1969—. Bd. dirs. Better Bus. Bur., Richmond, 1972—, Nat. Tobacco Festival, Inc., 1971—; trustee Collegiate Schs., Richmond, 1972-75, Sheltering Arms Hosp., Richmond, 1969—. Served to lt. USAF, 1952-54. Named Man of Yr., Am. Advt. Fedn., 1969. Mem. Life Ins. Advertisers Assn. (mem. exec. com. 1969-71), Richmond C. of C. (dir. 1973—), Kappa Alpha. Presbyn. Home: 206 Walsing Dr Richmond VA 23229 Office: 914 Capitol St Richmond VA 23219

NONNAN, JAMES ROTHWELL, physician; b. Jackson, Tenn., Dec. 13, 1931; s. James Melton and Martha Jeanette (Williams) N.; B.A., Harding Coll., 1952, M.A., 1953; B.S., Bethel Coll., 1954; M.D., U. Tenn., 1964; m. Willa Anne Thompson, Nov. 19, 1954; children—James Reece, Sally, Debbie, Timothy Scott. Intern USPHS Hosp., New Orleans, 1964-65, resident, 1965-66; resident VA Hosp., Memphis, 1966-68; practice medicine, specializing in internal medicine, Dyersburg, Tenn., 1968—; mem. staff Parkview Hosp., 1968—. Pres. W. Tenn. Heart Assn. 1972-73. Served with USNR, 1955-61. Diplomate Nat. Bd. Med. Examiners. Mem. N.W. Tenn. Acad. Medicine (pres. 1972). A.M.A., So. Med. Assn., Tenn. Med. Assn., Alpha Omega Alpha, Sigma Alpha Epsilon, Phi Chi. Kiwanian, Moose. Home: 719 Wade Hampton St Dyersburg TN 38024 Office: 402 Tickle St Dyersburg TN 38024

NOOE, LOUIS ALBERT, JR., utility co. exec.; b. Pittsboro, N.C., Nov. 22, 1924; s. Louis Albert and Myrtle Hill (Pilkington) N.; B.S. in Elec. Engring., Clemson U., 1948; m. Doris Mille, June 18, 1949; children—Louise, Al. Relay application engr. Duke Power Co., Charlotte, N.C., 1948-52, planning engr., 1952-62, system operations engr., 1962-68, asst. mgr. operations, 1968-73, mgr. operations, 1973—. Served with Signal Corps, AUS, 1943-46. Mem. I.E.E.E., Am. Legion. Methodist (chmn. bd. 1956-57). Democrat. Clubs: Windsor Park, Swim, Racquet. Home: 6209 Barcliff Dr Charlotte NC 28212 Office: 422 S Church St Charlotte NC 28201

NORAN, DAVID KENT, civil engr.; b. Cleve., Aug. 24, 1939; s. John E. and Mabel A. (Schroeder) N.; B.S. in C.E., U. Cin., 1963, M.S., 1965. Asst. city engr. City Ft. Thomas, Ky., 1965-67, city engr.-coordinator, 1967—. Civil engr., surveyor, Ft. Thomas, 1969—; owner Kent Acres Apts. and Devels., Ft. Thomas, 1972—. Vice pres. Ky. City Mgrs. Assn., 1972, Campbell-Kenton Regional Crime Commn., 1972—; pres. No. Ky. Area Planning Council, 1973—. Club: Northern Kentucky Region Antique Automobile (founding pres. 1968-69; dir. 1973) (Cin.). Home: Apt 302 40 Pleasant Av Fort Thomas KY 41075 Office: 130 N Ft Thomas Av Ft Thomas KY 41075

NORCROSS, ALVIN WATT, personnel mgmt. cons.; b. Buffalo, Sept. 21, 1918; s. William Watt and Nettie (Alexander) N.; B.A., Baldwin Wallace Coll., 1940; postgrad. Ohio State U., 1940; M. Pub. Adminstrn., Harvard, 1948; m. Charlotte Anne Guptill, Oct. 23, 1948; children—David Lichty, Nancy Dayna. Employment mgr. Nat. Screw & Mfg. Co., Cleve., 1941-43; personnel officer Dept. Air Force, Washington, 1948-54, spl. asst. to dir. civilian personnel, 1954-58; asst. to dir. personnel Gen. Services Adminstrn., Washington, 1958-59, chief of employment, 1959-61; asst. dir. personnel Treasury Dept., 1961-67; dep. dir. Bur. Inspections, U.S. Civil Service Commn., 1967-73; ret., 1973; cons. AID, 1974—. Del., Fairfax County Fedn. Civic Assns., 1957; pres. Vienna Hills Civic Assn., 1958; mem. personnel com. No. Va. council Girl Scouts U.S.A., 1961-62. Town councilman, Vienna, Va., 1959-65; mem. Vienna Civil Def. Com., 1960-62. Served with USAAF, 1943-46, lt. col. res. Recipient Air Force Superior Performance award, 1957, Treasury Meritorious Service award, 1966, Office of Sec. Treasury Honor award, 1966, others. Mem. Am. Soc. Pub. Adminstrn., Soc. Personnel Adminstrn. (v.p. 1972), Am. Soc. for Tng. and Devel. (past pres. Washington chpt.), Internat. Personnel Mgmt. Assn. (exec. council 1973—). Club: Harvard (Washington). Home and Office: 2038 Carrhill Rd Vienna VA 22180

NORDGREN, RONALD PAUL, research engr.; b. Munising, Mich., Apr. 3, 1936; s. Paul A. and Martha (Busse) N.; B.S.E., U. Mich., 1957, M.S.E. (fellow), 1958; Ph.D., U. Cal. at Berkeley, 1962; m. Joan E. McAfee, Sept. 12, 1959; children—Sonia, Paul. Mathematician, Shell Devel. Co., Houston, 1963-68, staff research engr., 1968-74, on spl. assignment The Hague, Netherland, 1970-71, sr. staff research engr., 1974—. Lectr. mech. engring. Rice U., Houston, 1965-68. Mem. Am. Soc. M.E., Soc. Indsl. and Applied Math., Sigma Xi, Tau Beta Pi. Assoc. editor Jour. Applied Mechanics. 1972—. Patentee in field. Contbr. articles to profl. jours. Home: 14935 Broadgreen Dr Houston TX 77024 Office: PO Box 481 Houston TX 77001

NORDLINGER, GERSON, JR., investor; b. Washington, Feb. 2, 1916; s. Gerson and Camille (Bensinger) N.; B.A., George Washington U., 1935; B.C.S., Benjamin Franklin U., 1939. Head, Navy Dept. Bur. Aeros. Budget, 1946-50; treas. Nordlinger Investment Corp., Washington, 1955—; dir. Washington Real Estate Investment Trust, 1961—; sec. Drico, Inc., 1961—. Chmn., D.C. Arts Commn., 1965-67; v.p. Nat. Symphony Orch. Assn., 1953-59, 70-71, Nat. Ballet, 1966—; pres. Prevention of Blindness Soc., 1960-67; treas. Friendship House, 1951-69; vice chmn. D.C. Recreation Bd., 1960-67. Trustee Washington Performing Arts Soc., Opera Soc. Mem. state com. Republican party, 1952-64. Served to lt. comdr. Supply Corps, USNR, 1941-46; PTO. C.P.A., D.C. Mem. D.C. Inst. C.P.A.'s, Washington Bd. Trade. Jewish religion. Clubs: Army-Navy, Arts, International, 1925 F Street. Home: 3115 Cleveland Av NW Washington DC 20008 Office: 1346 Connecticut Av Washington DC 20036

NORMAN, ALBERT GEORGE, JR., lawyer; b. Birmingham, Ala., May 29, 1929; s. Albert G. and Ila Mae (Carroll) N.; B.A., Auburn U., 1953; LL.B., Emory U., 1958; M.A., U. N.C., 1960; m. Catherine Marshall DeShazo, Sept. 3, 1955; children—Catherine Marshall, Albert George III. Admitted to Ga. bar, 1957; asso. Moise, Post & Gardner, Atlanta, 1958-60, partner, 1960-62; partner Hansell, Post, Brandon & Dorsey, Atlanta, 1962—. Served with USAF, 1946-49. Mem. Am., Ga., Atlanta bar assns. Clubs: Lawyers (Atlanta), Cherokee Town and Country. Home: 3381 Valley Circle NW Atlanta GA 30305 Office: First Nat Bank Bldg Atlanta GA 30303

NORMAN, HENRY ROBERT, cons. civil engr.; b. Carlton, Minn., Aug. 12, 1904; s. August R. and Anna (Ullman) N.; B.S. in Civil Engring., U. Minn., 1927, postgrad., 1930-31; m. Minda B. Rodal, May 21, 1929 (dec. Oct. 1963); children—John, Jerry; m. 2d, Doris J. Yawn, Dec. 22, 1964; stepchildren—Richard, Susan. Served from insp. to prin. engr. Milw., St. Paul and Galveston (Tex.) dist. offices, Upper Miss. Valley div. office, and chief engrs., Washington office C.E. U.S. Army, 1927-50; partner Norman Knappen Tippetts

Engring. Co., Houston, 1950-51; transp. engr. KTA Engring. Co., Rangoon, Burma, 1951-53; cons. civil engr. Brown & Root, Inc., Houston, 1953-69, spl. water cons. City of Houston, 1960-69; asst. dir. Dept. Pub. Works, City of Houston, 1969—. Served to lt. col. AUS, 1942-46. Fellow Am. Soc. C.E.; mem. Am. Geophys. Union, Soc. Am. Mil. Engrs., Nat., Tex. socs. profl. engrs., Am. Ordnance Assn., Houston C. of C. (ports and waterways and water supply com.), Am. Soc. Oceanography (charter), Sigma Nu. Contbr. articles to profl. publs. Home: 2336 McClendon St Houston TX 77025

NORMAN, JOHN ROYCE, dentist; b. Jamestown, Tenn., Oct. 19, 1934; s. Ambrosia and Imogene Catherine (Cruze) N.; B.S., U. Tenn., 1956, D.D.S., 1966; m. Andrea Carole Warren, Aug. 7, 1965; children—Carole Jean, John Andrew, Joseph David. Systems analyst Combustion Engring., Inc., Chattanooga, 1956-61; dentist N.C. Dept. Health, Surry County, 1967; gen. practice dentistry, Athens, Tenn., 1967—; mem. staff Epperson Hosp., Athens. Served with AUS, 1957-58. Mem. Am. Endodontic Soc., Am. Dental Assn., Athens C. of C., 3d Dist., Tenn. dental socs. Lion, Elk. Home: Route 2 Athens TN 37303 Office: 109 Park St Athens TN 37303

NORMAN, RALPH MAYNARD, wholesale trade exec.; b. Knoxville, Tenn., Sept. 28, 1922; s. Harrison Anthony and Tennie Evelyn (Pettiford) N.; student U. Tenn., 1947-48; m. Louise Grace Clark, Oct. 12, 1941; children—Ralph Gorden, Sheila (Mrs. Stephen Caradine). Pres. Norman & Watson Brokerage Co., Inc., Knoxville, 1968—, chmn. bd., 1968—. Served with USAF, 1942-45. Decorated D.F.C., Air medal with three oak leaf clusters. Mem. Knoxville Food Brokers (pres. 1974). Lion (v.p. 1973), Mason (32 degree, Shriner). Home: 3524 Plumwood Rd Knoxville TN 37921 Office: 12 Forest Ct Knoxville TN 37919

NORMAN, RAYMOND LEWIS, JR., mech. engr.; b. Birmingham, Ala., Jan. 31, 1935; s. Raymond Lewis and Gladys Lenere (Belcaer) N.; B.S. in Mech. Engring., Auburn U., 1957; M.S. in Research and Devel. Mgmt., Fla. State U., 1965; postgrad. U. Cal. at Los Angeles, U. Ala., Samson U.; m. Eleanor Faith Thompson, Sept. 26, 1958; children—Raymond Martin, Steven Marion. Estimator Harbert Constrn. Co., Birmingham, 1957; plant engr. Stockham Valves & Fittings, Birmingham, 1958; flight test engr. Hayes Internat., Birmingham, 1958-59; mech. and san. engr. Rader & Assos., St. Petersburg, Fla., 1958-59; pad engr. Pan Am. World Airways, Cape Canaveral, Fla., 1959-61; site engr. Gen. Dynamics, Cape Canaveral, 1962; project engr. NASA, John F. Kennedy Space Center, Fla., 1962—. Instr. Brevard Community Coll., Cocoa, Fla., 1962; asst. Fla. State U., 1965; pres. Bioreef, Inc., Merritt Island, Fla., 1971—. Dir. East Merritt Island Home Owners, 1966-68; mem. Brevard County Recreation Bd., 1968-69. Served with AUS, USNR, 1953-62. Mem. Am. Soc. M.E., Canaveral Council Tech. Socs. (past chmn.), Fla. Sport Fishing Assn., Lambda Chi Alpha. Episcopalian. Mason (Shriner). Editor: First Space Congress, 1962. Contbr. to tech. publs. Home: 1325 Girard Blvd Merritt Island FL 32952 Office: LL-PMO NASA John F Kennedy Space Center FL 32899

NORMAN, SUMMERS A., lawyer; b. Rusk, Tex., Aug. 25, 1905; s. Wyatt T. and Brunette (Summers) N.; LL.B., So. Meth. U., Dallas, 1929; m. Mary Nell Odom, Aug. 25, 1929. Admitted to Tex. bar, 1929; with firms Norman & Norman, 1929, Norman, Stone & Norman, 1937, Norman, Stone, Rounsaville & Hassell, 1948-59, Norman, Rounsaville, Hassell & Spiers, 1950-73, Norman, Hassell, Spiers & Holland, 1973—; v.p., dir. First State Bank, Wells; v.p. Mid-Continent Church Furniture Co.; dir., sec. bd. Gen-Tex Aluminum Products, Inc.; dir. Nichols Industries, Inc., 1st Nat. Bank Jacksonville. Chmn. Tex. Liquor Control Bd., 1947-65; chmn. bd. trustees, dir. Nan Travis Meml. Hosp.; chmn. bd. dirs. Jacksonville Indsl. Found. Served as lt. comdr. USNR, World War II. Fellow Southwestern Legal Found., Tex. State Bar Found.; mem. Am. Judicature Soc., State Bar Tex. (bd. dirs. dist. 2), C. of C. (past pres.), Pi Kappa Alpha. Presbyn. (elder, trustee). Mason (Shriner), Rotarian (past pres.). Clubs: Petroleum (Houston); Austin, (Austin); Dallas Athletic (Dallas); Cherokee Country. Home: 1212 Hillcrest Dr Jacksonville TX 75766 Office: First Nat Bank Bldg Jacksonville TX 75766

NORMENT, HARTWELL TALIAFERRO, pharm. co. exec.; b. Richmond, Va., July 14, 1922; s. Thomas Julien and Mattie Lee (Hudson) N.; student U. Richmond, 1939-40, Va. Commonwealth U., 1946-49; m. Lois Proffitt, June 29, 1946. With Wm. P. Poythress & Co., Inc., Richmond, Va., 1940—, analytical chemist, 1946-56, prodn. mgr., 1956-65, plant mgr., 1965—, corp. sec., 1969—, also dir. Served with AUS, 1942-45. Decorated with Purple Heart with two oak leaf clusters. Mem. Am. Chem. Soc. Home: 202 Hickory Dr Manakin VA 23103 Office: 16 N 22nd St Richmond VA 23261

NORRIS, BERRY EARLE, JR., engring. exec.; b. Wichita Falls, Tex., Nov. 8, 1927; s. Berry E. and Vera (Ferguson) N.; B.S., U. Houston, 1952, B.S., 1953, M.S., 1959; m. Sandra Suzanne Ellis, Apr. 22, 1965; 1 dau., Nathalie. Chemist, Shell Devel. Co., Houston, 1950-52; chem. engr. Houston Research Inst., 1952—, dir., treas., 1963—, pres., 1967—; v.p. operations Gulf So. Research Inst., Baton Rouge, 1968-69, v.p., gen. mgr., 1969-73; v.p. Houston Research Inc., 1973-74; mgr. new venture devel. Merichem Co., Houston, 1974—. Campaign mgr. Republican Senatorial candidate, 1964. Mem. Am. Inst. Chem. Engrs., Nat., Tex. socs. profl. engrs. Rotarian. Patentee in field. Home: 3106 Woodland Ct LaPorte TX 77571 Office: 4150 One Shell Plaza Houston TX 77002

NORRIS, BRUCE ARTHUR, grain mcht.; b. Chgo., Feb. 19, 1924; s. James and Marguerite (Loris) N.; A.B., Yale, 1945. With Norris Grain Co., North Miami, Fla., 1947—, pres., 1952—, chmn. bd., 1956—, Norin Corp., North Miami; pres. Norris Cattle Co., Ocala, Fla.; pres. Detroit Red Wings; dir. Louis Sherry, Inc., C., R.I.&P. Ry., Maple Leaf Mills Ltd., Toronto, Ont. Clubs: Chicago Athletic, Chicago, Tavern, Lake Shore (Chgo.); Onwentsia (Lake Forest, Ill.); Everglades (Palm Beach, Fla.). Home: Jockey Club 11111 Biscayne Blvd Miami FL 33161 Office: 12100 NE 16th Ave North Miami FL 33161

NORRIS, SAMUEL HOLLIS, geologist; b. Glasgow, Ky., June 1, 1932; s. Hollis Franklin and Olga Elizabeth (Lane) N.; B.A., Vanderbilt U., 1954; postgrad., U. Ky., 1957-59; m. Anna Owen, Sept. 4, 1960; children—Steven, Nan, Jan, Timothy, Mary, Amy. Geologist Ky. Geol. Cons., Inc., Lexington, 1959-61; pres. Petroleum Drilling Co., Inc., Greensburg, Ky., 1961-62; sr. oil and gas insp., oil and gas div. Ky. Dept. Mines and Minerals, Glasgow, 1962—; pres. Glasgow Marine, Inc., (Ky.), 1964—; dir. Ky. Connector Corp., Citizens Bank and Trust Co. Councilman, Glasgow, Ky., 1962-68; mem. Glasgow Bd. Adjustments, 1968-73; mem. Draft Bd., 1970—; councilman, Glasgow, 1974—. Served with AUS, 1954-56. Mem. Am. Inst. Profl. Geologists (v.p. Ky. sect. 1974—). Address: Route 2 Glasgow KY 42141

NORTH, ELLSWORTH HOWARD, JR., physician; b. Balt., Feb. 7, 1916; s. Ellsworth Howard and Emma Matilda (Schmidt) N.; B.S., U. Md., 1943, M.D., 1946; m. Doris Virginia Forsyth, Aug. 14, 1937; 1 dau., Barbara (Mrs. Joseph Britt). Intern Johns Hopkins Hosp., Balt., 1946, Bon Secours Hosp., Balt., 1946-47; pvt. practice medicine Elizabeth City, N.C., 1949-61; med. dir. Crucible Steel Corp., Pitts., 1961-70, Hillenbrand Industries, Batesville, Ind., 1970-72; cons. occupational medicine, Nags Head, N.C., 1973—. Town commr. Nags Head, 1973—. Served with AUS, 1943-46, USPHS, 1947-49. Diplomate Am. Bd. Preventive Medicine. Mem. Am. Acad. Occupational Medicine, Indsl. Med. Assn., Am. Indsl. Hygiene Assn., Am. Coll. Preventive Medicine, A.M.A., Royal Soc. Health, The Man Will Never Fly Meml. Soc. Internat. (co-founder 1959). Methodist. Med. columnist, Daily Advance, Elizabeth City, 1959-61. Home and office: Box 138 Nags Head NC 27959

NORTH, HERSCHEL I., ret. state ofcl.; b. Fowlerton, Tex., Nov. 16, 1914; s. Herschel Ira and Lola (Cupples) N.; B.A., Abilene Christian Coll., 1934; M.B.A., U. Tex., Austin, 1939; m. Jane Atkinson, Aug. 3, 1940 (dec. Sept. 1962); 1 dau., Linda; m. 2d, Virginia O. Singleton, Nov. 1, 1966; stepchildren—Danny, Kenny, Larry, Kerry. Tchr. pub. schs., Sweetwater and Munday, Tex., 1934-37; auditor Arthur Anderson and Co., Houston, 1939; pvt. practice pub. accounting, San Angelo, Tex., 1940-41; accountant Lockheed Aircraft, Burbank, Cal., 1941-45; realtor H. I. North Co., San Fernando Valley, Cal., 1945-49; adminstrv. asst. Tex. Dept. Health, Austin, 1950-55, dir. finance 1955-59, asst. adminstr., 1959-64, exec. dir. adminstrn., 1964-65, exec. dir., 1965-69, dep. commr. health for finance, 1969-74. C.P.A., Tex. Mem. Tex. Soc. C.P.A.'s, Tex. Pub. Employees Assn. Lion (sec. San Angelo 1940). Home: 7203 Shoal Creek Austin TX 78757

NORTH, PHILLIP RECORD, investor; b. Ft. Worth, July 6, 1918; s. James Mortimer and Lottie Record (N.); A.B., U. Notre Dame, 1939; m. Janis Mary Harris, July 28, 1944; children—Phillip Kevin, Kerry Lawrence, Mairin Kathleen, Deirdre Aine. Exec. editor, v.p. Fort Worth Star-Telegram, Carter Publs., Inc., 1954-62; dir. Continental Nat. Bank, Ft. Worth, Tandy Corp., Ft. Worth. Vice pres. Ft. Worth Diocese Endowment and Devel. Fund Inc., 1971—; mem. adv. council U. Notre Dame, 1967—. Served to maj. AUS, 1940-46. Roman Catholic. Clubs: Fort Worth, Shady Oaks Country, Rivercrest Country (Ft. Worth). Home and office: 6141 Locke St Fort Worth TX 76116

NORTHCLIFFE, LEE CONRAD, educator; b. Manitowoc, Wis., Mar. 20, 1926; s. Lee Conrad and Emily Frances (Johanek) N.; student Mo. Valley Coll., 1944-45; B.S., U. Wis., 1948, M.S., 1951, Ph.D., 1957; m. Hilda Close, Oct. 9, 1953; children—David Lee, Christopher Close. Instr. Yale, New Haven, 1957-60, asst. prof., 1960-65; asso. prof. Tex. A. & M. U., College Station, 1965-70, prof. physics, 1970—. Bd. dirs. Los Alamos Merson Physics Facility User Group, 1972. Served with USNR, 1944-45. Mem. Am. Phys. Soc., Am. Assn. Physics Tchrs., Am. Assn. U. Profs., Tex. Assn. Coll. Tchrs., N.Y. Acad. Scis. Home: 1115 Ashburn St College Station TX 77840 Office: Cyclotron Inst Tex A & M U College Station TX 77843

NORTHEN, CHARLES SWIFT, III, banker; b. Birmingham, Ala., Jan. 25, 1937; s. Charles Swift and Jennie Hood (Hunt) N.; student Princeton, 1955-57; B.A., Vanderbilt U., 1959, M.A., 1961; m. Margaret Carson Robinson, Dec. 27, 1959 (div. Dec. 1972); children—Margaret Allen, Charles Swift IV, Bryce Robinson. With Birmingham Trust Nat. Bank, 1960-64; mem. staff Exchange Security Bank, Birmingham, 1964—, v.p., sr. trust officer, 1973—; dir. Vulcan Life Ins. Co. Bd. dirs. Indian Springs Sch.; pres. Ala. Found. Hearing and Speech. Mem. Ala. Security Dealers Assn. (treas. 1972—), Vanderbilt U. Alumni Assn. (pres. 1970-71), Atlanta Soc. Financial Analysts. Presbyn. (elder), Clubs: Relay House, Mountain Brook (Birmingham). Home: 1300 S 27th Pl Birmingham AL 35205 Office: Exchange Security Bank PO Box 10247 Birmingham AL 35202

NORTHINGTON, CHARLES WILLIAM, san. engr.; b. Cuba, Ala., July 18, 1920; s. William Reeks and Lois (Roy) N.; B.S. in Chem. Engring., Auburn U., 1950; M.S. in San. Engring., U. N.C. at Chapel Hill, 1960; postgrad. North Tex State U., 1973—; m. Susie Raye Bishop, Sept. 21, 1947; children—Suzan Anita (Mrs. Daniel Dunlap), Charles William, Teresa Franciné. Agrl. chemist Ala. Dept. Agr. food and drug control, Montgomery, 1950-57; san. engr., 1957-62; commd. officer USPHS, 1962, advanced through grades to capt., 1968; dir. Lake Erie water pollution study, 1962-66; chief regional water supply program Dept. Health, Edn. and Welfare region VII, Environmental Protection Agy., region VI, Dallas, 1967-72, regional emergency coordinator Environmental Protection Agy. region VI, Dallas, 1972—. Bd. dirs. Boys Club, Duncanville, 1972-73. Served as sgt. U.S. Army, 1941-45. Registered profl. engr., Ala., Tex. Mem. Am. Legion (comdr. 1961). Home: 940 Whitestone Lane Dallas TX 75232 Office: 1600 Patterson St Dallas TX 75232

NORTHROP, GRANGER HAROLD, orgn. exec.; b. Ithaca, N.Y., Feb. 21, 1936; s. Granger Manning and Leona Clover (Van Tine) N.; B.A., Vanderbilt U., 1958, M.B.A., 1959; m. Charlotte Jean Beasley, June 8, 1957; children—Jennifer, Foster, Susan. With So. Bell Tel.&Tel. Co., 1959-69, traffic mgr., New Orleans, 1960-61, personnel mgr., 1961-63, plant mgr., 1963-65, dist. plant mgr., Lafayette, La., 1965-66, div. plant mgr., 1966-69; pres., chief exec. officer Ida Cason Callaway Found. and Gardens Services, Inc., Pine Mountain, Ga., 1969—. Dir. Internat. Assn. Holiday Inns, Inc.; vice-chmn., mem. exec. com. Discover Am. Travel Orgn., 1973—, also dir. Mem. Ga. Bicentennial Commn., 1972—; mem. at large Chattahoochee council Boys Scouts Am., 1971—; mem. exec. bd. Ga. Gov.'s Council Tourism, 1970—. Mem. adv. bd. Longwood Gardens, Kennett Sq., Pa. Served to 1st lt. AUS, 1959-60. Named Outstanding Young Man Am., U.S. C. of C., 1965. Mem. Young Presidents Orgn., Ga. C. of C. (dir., chmn. travel council 1972). Lion. Home: Kings Gap Rd Pine Mountain GA 31822 Office: Callaway Gardens Pine Mountain GA 31822

NORTHROP, MONROE, lawyer; b. Houston, Jan. 1, 1931; s. Joseph Walter and Mary (Harris) N.; B.B.A., U. Tex., 1953, LL.B., 1954; m. Jane Ann Palmer, Dec. 4, 1970; 1 son, Ronald Viator. Admitted to Tex. bar, 1954, practiced in Houston, 1957—; asst. dist. atty. Harris County, Houston, 1957-59; asst. U.S. atty. So. Dist. Tex., Houston, 1959-61; mem. firm Austin, Darney, Northrop and Garwood, attys., 1968—. Served with Counter Intelligence Corps, AUS, 1955-57. Mem. Am., Tex., Houston bar assns., Am. Judicature Soc., Tex., Houston trial lawyers assns., Lawyers Soc. Houston, Sigma Chi. Republican. Episcopalian. Home: 4722 Waring St Houston TX 77027 Office: 1223 Chamber of Commerce Bldg Houston TX 77002

NORTHRUP, JACK RICHARD, city ofcl.; b. Waverly, N.Y., Apr. 10, 1935; s. Harold and Beatrice (Grant) N.; B.S., Ark. State U., 1964; m. Melba Jean Edwards, May 11, 1957; children—Tanya Kay, Jackie Lynn, Terri Jean. Social worker Ark. Dept. Pub. Welfare, Harrisburg, 1964, dir., Marianna, 1964-65; dir. Urban Renewal, Marianna, 1965-66; exec. dir. Housing and Urban Renewal, Marianna, 1967-72; city coordinator City of Olney, Tex., 1972; exec. dir. Olney Neighborhood Devel. Program, 1972—. Bd. dirs. Tex. Urban Renewal Assn., 1973—. Served with AUS, 1954-58. Mem. Nat., Ark. housing and redevel. ofcls., D.A.V., C. of C. (dir. 1969—), Olney One-Arm Dove Hunters Assn. (founder). Lion (2d v.p. 1969—). Home: 604 W Oak St Olney TX 76374 Office: City Hall Olney TX 76374

NORTON, HUGH STANTON, economist, educator; b. Delta, Colo., Sept. 18, 1921; s. Cecil A. and Olive (Stanton) N.; A.B., George Washington U., 1947, Ph.D., 1956; m. Miriam Jarmon, Dec. 17, 1949; children—Pamela, John. Instr., U. Md., College Park, 1948-54; economist U.S. Dept. Agr., Washington, 1954-57; asso. prof. econs. U. Tenn., Knoxville, 1957-60, prof., 1960-66; prof. econs. U. S.C., Columbia, 1966-68, D.H. Johnson prof. econs., 1968—, chmn. dept. econs., 1971-73. Served with AUS, 1942-45. Mem. Am. Econ. Assn., Nat. Assn. Bus. Economists, Order of Artus. Club: Rockbridge Country (past pres.). Author: Modern Transportation Economics, 1963; Economic Policy, 1966; National Transportation Policy, 1968; Economist, Role in Government Policy Making, 1969; Economist in Business, 1969; World of the Economist, 1973. Home: 3335 Overcreek Rd Columbia SC 29206

NORTON, JOHN OLIN, civil engr.; b. Guntown, Miss., Dec. 12, 1924; s. Olin Stephen and Jonnie Goldsten (Gibson) N.; student Miss. State U., 1942-43, Ohio State U., 1943-44; B.S., Miss. State U., 1949; m. Jean Webb, Feb. 4, 1951; children—Olin Perry, Barbara Anne. Civil engr. Memphis Dist. C.E., 1949-56; with U.S. Army Missile Command, Redstone Arsenal, Ala., 1956—, gen. engr., 1965—. Served with C.E. U.S. Army, 1943-46, 1952-53. Registered profl. engr., Ala. Mem. Am. Soc. C.E. (sect. dir. 1968-70; br. pres. 1971), Soc. Am. Mil. Engrs., Tau Beta Pi. Mem. Christian Ch. Home: 7106 Jones Valley Huntsville AL 35802 Office: US Army Missile Command Redstone Arsenal AL 35809

NORTON, MARVIN LEROY, JR., electronic engr.; b. North Wildwood, N.J., Oct. 27, 1935; s. Marvin Leroy and Elizabeth (Steelman) N.; B.S., Rutgers U., 1957; M.S., Newark Coll. Engring., 1962; M.S., Fla. Inst. Tech., 1968; m. Dorothea Johanna Petermann, June 29, 1958; children—Karl Eric, Jeannette Alyson, Joy Alicia, Brian Edward, Arthur Roy, Gail Elizabeth. Asst. engr. N.J. Bell Telephone Co., Newark, 1957-59 engr. Internat. Tel. & Tel. Fed. Labs., Nutley, N.J., 1959-65; engr. RCA Service Corp. Missile Test Project, Patrick AFB, Fla., 1965-66, analyst, 1966-69, leader, 1969—; pres. N.P. Research Corp., 1970—. Adj. instr. Fla. Inst. Tech. Commr., Boy Scouts Am., 1966-67, committeeman, 1968, leader, 1969. Registered profl. engr., N.J., Fla. Fellow Brit. Interplanetary Soc.; sr. mem. I.E.E.E., Fla. Engring. Soc.; mem. Nat. Soc. Profl. Engrs., Am. Geophys. Union, Marine Tech. Soc. (sect. councilor 1969, sec. 1970-71, vice chmn. 1971-73, chmn. 1973—). Internat. Oceanographic Found. Republican. Lutheran. Home: 990 Sarazen Dr Rockledge FL 32955 Office: Mail unit 811 Patrick AFB FL 32935

NORTON, MERVIN LEE, elec. engr.; b. Birmingham, Ala., May 3, 1927; s. Henry Buford and Bertha Mae (Bendall) N.; B.S. in Elec. Engring., Auburn U., 1950; m. Martha Ann Goodman, May 11, 1950; children—Michael L., David W. Joined U.S. Army, 1944, advanced through grades to lt. col., 1966, ret., 1968; pres. Va. Communications Assos., Vienna, Va., 1974—. Decorated Legions of Merit (2). Named Distinguished Mil. Grad. Auburn U., 1950. Mem. I.E.E.E. (sr.). Home: 10002 McDuff Ct Vienna VA 22180 Office: Vienna VA 22180

NORWINE, ROBERT JACKSON, real estate exec.; b. St. Louis, Mar. 31, 1924; s. Olin Dale and Lucille Alter (Kingsland) N.; student Miami U., 1943-45; B.A., Westminster Coll., 1949; m. Betty Lou Straub, Sept. 14, 1962; children—Kerry (Mrs. James Dunning, Jr.), Kyle (by previous marriage), Dale; stepchildren—Theresa, Gregory. Dir. admissions, baseball coach Westminster Coll., 1949-53; dir. admissions Wesleyan U., 1953-64; dean admissions, dean students, v.p. New Coll., Sarasota, Fla., 1964-74; with Aid Realty Inc., Sarasota, 1974—. Pres. Research Bur., Civic League Sarasota County, 1973—. Bd. dirs. Indsl. Devel. Council Sarasota County, 1970-71, Boys Club Sarasota County, 1972-73, United Appeal of Sarasota County, 1974—. Served with USNR, 1943-46; PTO. Recipient Distinguished Alumnus award Westminster Coll., 1966. Mem. Nat. Assn. Coll. Admissions Counselors (v.p. 1954), Beta Theta Pi. Club: Commodore Bird Key Yacht (Sarasota). Home: 405 Pheasant Way Sarasota FL 33577 Office: 1300 Main St Sarasota FL 33577

NORWOOD, JAMES SPENCER, educator; b. Burleson, Tex., Oct. 2, 1932; s. James Washington and Baird Anna (Gulley) N.; B.S., Tex. Tech U., 1954; M.S., Kan. State U., 1955, Ph.D., 1963; postgrad. U. Ill., 1969-70; m. Ann Elaine Barlow, Dec. 27, 1962; children—James Kent, Kerri Daneen. Instr. Southwest Tex. State U., San Marcos, 1955-56, 58-60; asst. prof. U. Tex., Arlington, 1962-63; mem. faculty East Tex. State U., Commerce, 1963—, prof. biology, 1971—. Adviser to pre-dental students, 1970-73; 1st v.p. Biology Assos., Inc., Commerce, 1969—. Served with AUS, 1956-58. Faculty Research grantee East Tex. State U., 1972-73. Mem. Tex. Acad. Sci., Am. Soc. Animal Sci., Sigma Xi, Kappa Sigma, Phi Delta Kappa. Kiwanian (1st v.p. 1968-69), Mason (worshipful master 1969-70). Author: (with others) The Application of Biological Principles to Man and Society, 1969. Home: Route 1 Campbell TX 75422 Office: Dept Biology East Tex State U Commerce TX 75428

NORWOOD, MALCOLM MARK, educator; b. Drew, Miss., Jan. 21, 1928; d. Orsan Pratt and Eva (Smith) Norwood; B.A., Miss. Coll., 1951, M.Ed., 1959; postgrad. U. N.C., 1951, U. Colo., 1955; M.A., U. Ala., 1962; m. Mary Claire Sugg, Aug. 8, 1954; children—Malcolm Mark, William John, Stephanie. Tech. art Jackson (Miss.) City Schs., 1951-61; faculty U. So. Miss., Hattiesburg, 1956, U. Ala., Tuscaloosa, 1961-62, Miss. Coll., Clinton, 1962; prof. art Delta State Coll., Cleveland, Miss., 1962—, head dept. art, 1965—, chmn. Smith-Patterson Meml. Found., 1973—. Project dir. Cleveland Arts Council, 1970—; mem. ednl. adv. bd. Miss. Arts Council, 1972—. Served with USN, 1946-48. Recipient 1st prize Nat. Oil Painting Exhbn., Jackson, 1963; painting award Holiday Arts Festival, 1969; 1st prize in drawing Edgewater Ann., 1970. Mem. Miss. Art Assn. (v.p. 1954-60), Miss. Edn. Assn. (chmn. art sect. 1954, 65). Lion. Home: 600 Canal Av Cleveland MS 38732

NORWOOD, NORMAN ROBERT, bldg. co. exec.; b. Fayetteville, Ark., Feb. 28, 1942; s. Norman and Maureen (Williams) N.; student Baylor U., 1960-61, U. Houston, 1961-66; m. Andrea Lee Ross, Aug. 25, 1962; children—Lauri Lee, Juli Andrea, Kristi Maureen. With Monarch Homes, Inc., Houston, 1962—, salesman, 1962-63, constrn. supt., 1964-67, salesman, 1967-68, sub-div. mgr., 1968-69, prodn. mgr., v.p., 1969-70, v.p., sales mgr., 1970, exec. v.p., 1970-71, pres., 1971—. Mem. Greater Houston Builders Assn. (mem. com. 1970-71). Baptist (deacon 1966—). Club: Tri-County Optimist (Katy, Tex.). Home: 2203 Saddle Horn Trail Katy TX 77450 Office: 8005 Dunlap St Houston TX 77036

NOSS, THEODORE K(ELCHNER), educator; b. Sendai, Japan, Mar. 9, 1903; s. Christopher and Lura (Boyer) N. (parents Am. citizens); B.A., Princeton, 1925; B.D., Union Theol. Sem., 1929; M.A., U. Chgo., 1934, Ph.D., 1940; m. Mary Elise Heckathorn, Jan. 28, 1948; children—Charles Sumner, John Frederick. Instr., asst. prof. Purdue U., 1935-42; vis. asso. prof. U. Tex., 1948; faculty mem. Hunter Coll., 1948-49, Adelphi Coll., 1949-52; dean of students State U. Maritime Coll., N.Y., 1952-53; edn. specialist USAF, 1953-56; asso. prof., prof., chmn. dept. sociology C.W. Post Coll., L.I. U., Greenvale, N.Y., 1956-71; vis. prof. sociology St. John's U., Jamaica, N.Y., 1971-72; prof. sociology Warren Wilson Coll., Swannanoa, N.C., 1973—. Ednl. cons. Esso Standard Oil Co., 1951-52; econ., personnel specialist Supreme Comdr. for Allied Powers, Tokyo, 1946-47; instr. internat. relations to comdg. officer Naval Res. Officers Sch., N.Y.C., 1956-63; cons. Bur. Naval Personnel, U.S. Navy, 1957-63; staff Nat. War Coll., 1960; lectr. Naval War Coll., 1960-63; vis. prof. sociology Long Beach State Coll., 1962; lectr. Queen's Coll., 1961-62; cons. Morris Coll., Sumter, S.C., Spring 1973. Tech. adv. com. Nassau County Youth Bd., 1966—. Dir. Lane Bryant Nat. Awards, 1968-71. Trustee Westbury Friends Sch., 1957—; trustee Friends Acad., 1961-63. Served from lt. to comdr. USNR, 1942-46, PTO. Mem. Am., Eastern sociol. assns., Nat., N.Y. State councils for social studies, Naval Res. Assn., Nassau County Hist. Assn., Navy League, Alpha Kappa Delta, Pi Gamma Mu. Mem. Soc. of Friends. Club: University (L.I.). Author: Resistance to Social Innovation, 1944. Editor various manuals for U.S. Navy, 1958-62. Address: Warren Wilson Coll Swannanoa NC 28778

NOSTER, MANFORD FREEMAN, elec. engr.; b. Bay City, Tex., Jan. 1, 1912; s. Adolph and Annie Laura (Freeman) N.; B.S. in E.E., Tex. A. and M. U., 1934; m. Anita Elizabeth Cox, Feb. 4, 1939; children—Wayne M., Nita Beth (Mrs. Jay Michael Phythian). With So. Prison Co., San Antonio, 1934-35; insp. U.S. Engrs., Vicksburg, Miss., 1935-37; with S.W. Bell Telephone Co., Houston, 1937—, sr. engr., 1951—. Registered profl. engr., Tex. Mem. Am. Inst. E.E. (sect. chmn. 1948-49). Baptist. Home: 9822 Larston St Houston TX 77055 Office: 3100 S Main St Box 1530 Houston TX 77001

NOTT, ERNEST CLAYTON, JR., hosp. adminstr.; b. Ocala, Fla., Apr. 12, 1924; s. Ernest C. and Hilda (Monroe) N.; B.S., Wake Forest Coll., 1945; M.H.A., Med. Coll. Va., 1957; m. Frances Belle Meggs, June 5, 1949; children—Marsha Leigh, Cynthia Marie, Terri Ann. Personnel dir. Baptist Hosp., Jacksonville, Fla., 1957-58; administrv. asst. Broward Gen. Hosp., Fort Lauderdale, Fla., 1958-60, administr., 1960-62; adminstr. Bapt. Hosp., Miami, Fla., 1962—. Bd. dirs. Blue Cross, Fla., Comprehensive Health Planning Council South Fla., Community Health, Inc. Served from lt. to capt., AUS, 1945-53. Mem. Am. Hosp. Assn., Am. Coll. Hosp. Adminstrs., S. Fla. Hosp. Council (pres. 1965-66), Fla. Hosp. Assn. (pres. 1970-71). Baptist (deacon). Kiwanian. Home: 8454 SW 75th St South Miami FL 33143 Office: 8900 N Kendall Dr Miami FL 33156

NOVAK, ARTHUR FRANCIS, educator; b. Balt., Oct. 25, 1916; s. Frank C. and Anna Barbara (Hulka) N.; B.S., U. Md., 1937; M.S., U. Ala., 1939; Ph.D., Purdue U., 1947; postgrad, Johns Hopkins, 1939-40, U. Louisville, 1941-42, U. So. Cal., 1951-53; m. Mary Frances Miller, May 15, 1947; children—Katrina Marie, Stephen Francis. Supr. fermentation Seagram: Calvert, Louisville, 1940-47; prof. bacteriology and chemistry U. Fla., Gainesville, 1947-51; dir. research Nutrilite Products, Inc., Buena Park, Cal., 1951-54; prof., head dept. food sci and tech., prof. marine sci. La. State U., Baton Rouge, 1954—. Cons in foods and drugs, 1947—; cons. to state and fed. agys., 1949—; Ford Found. adviser oceanography and food sci. to Brazil, 1968-69; prof. physiology U. Sao Paulo (Brazil) Faculty of Medicine; tech. dir. Internat. Shrimp Council, 1967—. Mem. Internat. Tech. Assistance Com., 1960—. Bd. dirs. Boys Clubs So. Cal., pres., 1952-54. Fellow Am. Inst. Chemists; mem. A.A.A.S., Gulf Coast Inst. Food Technologists (pres. 1964-65), Am. Pharm. Assn., Am. Nuclear Soc., Oyster Inst. N.Am., Nat. Fisheries Inst., Nat. Shell Fisheries Assn., Am. Soc. Microbiology, Am. Chem. Soc., Marine Tech. Soc., Shrimp Assn. Ams., Shrimp Breeders and Processors Am. (tech. dir.), Nat. Fisheries Inst., So. Assn. Food and Drug Ofcls., Council Am. Bioanalysts, Am. Soc. for Heating, Air Conditioning and Refrigeration Engrs., Inst. Food Technologists (chmn. constn.) and by laws, also food quality control), Rho Chi, Gamma Sigma Epsilon, Phi Kappa Phi, Gamma Sigma Delta, Pi Tau Sigma, Lambda Tau, Phi Kappa, Omicron Delta Kappa. Author: Microbiology of Shellfish, 1962; Fundamentals of Food Science. Contbr. numerous articles to profl. jours. Patentee in field. Home: 656 College Hill Dr Baton Rouge LA 70808

NOVAK, JAMES RONALD, govt. bldg. ofcl.; b. Cleve., Nov. 29, 1934; s. George Joseph and Lenore (Giel) N.; B.S. in Civil Engring. with honors, Ohio U., 1961; M.S., U. Md., 1965; m. Miriam Watts, June 17, 1956; children—John Mark, Jeri, Laura, Nicole. Civil engr. Engring. Br., Pub. Works, Naval Research Lab., Washington, 1961-67, dep. head, 1966-67; projects engr. Nat. Acad. Scis., Washington, 1967-72; bldg. ofcl. Prince George's Cty., Md., 1972—. Served with USNR, 1952-56. Registered profl. engr., D.C. Mem. Am. Soc. C.E., Nat. Soc. Profl. Engrs., Bldg. Ofcls. and Code Adminstrs. Internat., Nat. Acad. Code Adminstrs., N.Y. Acad. Scis., Tau Beta Pi. Home: 6503 Hillview Ave Alexandria VA 22310 Office: 5012 Rhode Island Ave Hyattsville MD 20781

NOVOSAD, RUDY JAMES, banker; b. Yoakum, Tex., July 6, 1933; s. Rudy John and Anne Elizabeth (Jansky) N.; student Wharton County Jr. Coll., Tex., 1951-53; grad. S.W. Grad. Sch. Banking So. Meth. U., 1970; m. Sarah Elizabeth Davis, May 7, 1955; children—Robin Lea Novosad, Ginger Lynn. New bus. rep. United Gas Corp., Rosenberg, Tex., 1955-56; asst. cashier 1st Nat. Bank, Rosenberg, 1956-63; v.p. 1st Savs. and Loan Assn., Alvin, Tex., 1963-65; exec. v.p. Bayshore Savs Assn., LaPorte, Tex., 1965-66, dir., 1965-66; exec. v.p., dir. Pearland State Bank (Tex.), 1966—, chief exec. officer, 1970—; dir. Massey Judge Constrn. Co., Houston. Foreman, Brazoria County Grand Jury, 1973-74; chmn. vocational, office, edn. program Pearland High Sch., 1969-74. Bd. dirs. Brazoria County Fat Stock and Fair, 1972-73; bd. dirs., treas. Pearland Community Library. Served to cpl. AUS, 1953-54. Recipient Boss of Yr. award, Am. Bus. Womens Assn., 1973-74. Mem. Am. Inst. Banking, Bank Adminstrn. Inst., Pearland Area C. of C. (v.p. 1967-68), Brazoria County Bankers Assn. (v.p. 1970), P.T.A. Rotarian (charter mem.; pres. 1966-67). Clubs: Golf Crest Country (Pearland). Home: 3208 Churchill St Pearland TX 77581 Office: 2301 North Main St Pearland TX 77581

NOWAKOWSKI, MICHAEL FELIX, aerospace engr.; b. Erie, Pa., Feb. 24, 1938; s. Michael J. and Sue K. (Demyan) N.; B.S. in Elec. Engring., Gannon Coll., 1961; postgrad. U. Ala., 1967; m. Sara A. Fink, Oct. 13, 1961; children—Michael J. III, Sue K., Brian S., David S., Sherry L. With NASA Marshall Space Flight Center, Huntsville, Ala., 1961—, chief elec.-electronic parts group, 1969—. Partner, Internat. Cons., Huntsville, 1969—. K.C. Home: 600 Valley View Terrace Huntsville AL 35803 Office: Marshall Space Flight Center Huntsville AL 35812

NOWOTNY, GEORGE EDWARD, JR., geophysicist, former state legislator; b. New Braunfels, Tex., Oct. 18, 1932; s. George E. and Margaret (Voight) N.; B.S., U. Tex., 1955; m. Lura Duff Elliston, Aug. 14, 1954 (div. Aug. 14, 1973); children—Edward Duff, George Edward, III, Addison Dance; m. 2d, Dena L. Dills, Mar. 2, 1974. Geophysicist, Standard Oil Co. N.J., 1955-60; partner Barton & Nowotny, Fort Smith, Ark., 1961-63; cons. oil, gas geologist Nowotny & Co., Fort Smith, 1963—; mem. Ark. Ho. of Reps., 1967-72, minority leader, 1967-72; project dir. test program to help implement legislative improvement State Legislative Leaders Found., 1973—. Area disaster chmn. A.R.C., 1966-67, chmn. exec. bd., 1968; active United Fund; mem. State Health Planning Commn., 1968-72; mem. natural resources com. Interstate Oil Compact Comm., 1968-71. Bd. dirs. Civil Air Patrol; bd. dirs., mem. exec. com. Tulsa Civic Ballet. Del. Republican Nat. Conv., 1972; state coordinator re-election Pres., 1972. Mem. C. of C., Am. Assn. Petroleum Geologists, Soc. Exploration Geophysicists, Am. Assn. Petroleum Landmen, Phi Beta Kappa, Delta Tau Delta. Episcopalian (past mem. ch. exec. com., past sr. warden, past vestryman; past mem. exec. council state diocese, past mem. finance com., past mem. bishop's standing com.). Home: 7226 S Gary Pl Tulsa OK 74136 Office: Suite 142 3005 Skelly Dr Tulsa OK 74136

NOYES, WARD DAVID, physician; b. Schenectady, Aug. 25, 1927; s. Ward and Marion L. (French) N.; B.A., U. Rochester, 1949, M.D., 1953; m. Nancy Adair, Aug. 10, 1973; children (by previous marriage)—Patricia, David, Jeffrey, Katherine. Intern and resident in medicine King County Hosp., Seattle, 1953-56; fellow in hematology U. Wash., Seattle, 1956-59, instr. medicine, 1959-61; asst. prof. medicine U. Fla., Gainesville, 1961-65, asso. prof., 1965-70, prof. medicine, 1970—, head hematology, 1968—. Cons. Gainesville VA Hosp. Served with USAF, 1946-47. S.E. Consortium scholar, 1972-73. Mem. Am. Fedn. Clin. Research, Am., Internat socs. hematology, So. Soc. Clin. Investigation, Assn. Am. Med. Colls., Sierra Club, Alpha Omega Alpha. Mem. United Ch. (moderator 1969-70). Contbr. article to profl. jours. Home: 310 NW 25th St Gainesville FL 32601

NUNLEY, LEONARD JAMES, computer co. exec.; b. St. Louis, Oct. 22, 1933; s. Charles Spurgeon and Margaret Minna (Schmidt) N.; B.E.E., U. Fla., 1955; M.S., So. Meth. U., 1962; m. Lorene Weddington, June 7, 1957; children—Stephen, Angela. Design engr. Convair div. Gen. Dynamics, Ft. Worth, 1955-59; project engr. Nat. Data Processing Corp., Dallas, 1959-61; with Recognition Equipment Inc., Irving, 1961—, now sr. v.p. and chief tech. officer. Mem. I.E.E.E. Methodist. Patentee in field. Home: 3936 Shady Creek Lane Dallas TX 75229 Office: 2701 E Granwyler Rd Irving TX 75060

NUNN, GEORGE VIRGIL, supt. schs.; b. Waverly, Ala., Aug. 14, 1910; s. George Gillis and Susie Lloyal (Allen) N.; B.S., Auburn U., 1932, M.S., 1935; m. Maude Prescott Woodward, Dec. 27, 1938; children—Margaret Ann (Mrs. Thomas Hiram Todd, Jr.), Sheila Lynn (Mrs. Samuel Watson Moss), George Woodward. Tchr., Pickens County Bd. Edn., Gordo, Ala., 1932-34, Fairfield City Bd. Edn., 1934-36; prin. Fairfield Jr. High Sch., 1936-40; supt. Fairfield City Schs., 1946-70; supt. Homewood (Ala.) City Bd. Edn., 1970—. Served to col. AUS, 1940-45. Decorated Bronze Star medal. Mem. N.E.A., Am. Assn. Sch. Adminstrs., Ala. Edn. Assn., C. of C. (pres. 1961-62), Kappa Phi Kappa. Baptist (deacon 1968-69). Rotarian. Home: 333 Fair Oaks Dr Fairfield AL 35064 Office: 7 Hollywood Blvd Homewood AL 35209

NUNN, WALTER MELROSE, JR., educator; b. New Orleans, Sept. 16, 1925; s. Walter Melrose and Leah (Hennessey) N.; B.S. in Elec. Engring., Tulane U., 1950; M.S. in Elec. Engring., Okla. State U., 1952; Ph.D., U. Mich., 1960; M.S. in Physics, U. Ill., Urbana-Champaign, 1969; m. Hortense R. Hillery, Aug. 14, 1949. Instr. in elec. engring. Okla. State U., 1950-52, Rensselaer Polytech. Inst., Troy, N.Y., 1952-54; microwave research engr. Hughes Aircraft Co., Culver City, Cal., 1954-56; asst. prof. elec. engring. U. Minn., Mpls., 1960-63; prof. elec. engring. Tulane U., New Orleans, 1963-67, Fla. Inst. Tech., Melbourne, 1969—. Cons. in antennas and electromagnetic theory Mpls.-Honeywell Co., 1960-63; sci. adviser to Nat. Acad. Sci., Washington, 1964; cons. U.S. Navy Marine Engring. Lab., Annapolis, Md., 1965-66; cons. in electromagnetic theory and microwave techniques Radiation, Inc., Melbourne, Fla., 1971; cons. U.S. Dept. Health, Edn. and Welfare, 1972, Fla. Dept. Health and Rehabilitative Services, 1972. Served with USMCR, 1943-46. Sr. mem. I.E.E.E. (faculty counselor Fla. Inst. Tech. student br. 1970-73; mem. exec. com. Canaveral sect. 1971—, chmn. 1973-74), Tau Beta Pi (life), Eta Kappa Nu. Contbr. articles to profl. jours. Office: Dept Elec Engring Fla Inst Tech Melbourne FL 32901

NUNNERY, FRED LEE, JR., mech. engr.; b. Memphis, Apr. 14, 1929; s. Fred Lee and Lillian Amelia (Cartwright) N.; student U. Tenn. Jr. Coll., 1947-49; B.S. in Mech. Engring., U. Tenn., 1956; m. Audrey Calvin, Sept. 15, 1951; children—Catherine Amealia, Amanda Elizabeth. Chief engr. So. Boiler & Tank Works, Inc., Memphis, 1958-64; with W.R. Grace & Co., Memphis, 1964—, insp. engr., 1972—. Served with USAF, 1951-52. Registered profl. engr., Tenn. Mem. Nat. Assn. Corrosion Engrs., Am. Soc. M.E. Home: 3832 Maritavia St Memphis TN 38127 Office: PO Box 27147 Memphis TN 38127

NUNNERY, MURRY EDWARD, veterinarian; b. Jakin, Ga., Oct. 20, 1928; s. Joe McKinley and Daisy (Everett) N.; student Auburn U., 1945-46; D.V.M., U. Ga., 1950; m. Mildred Mary Proden, June 10, 1950; children—Joe Murry, Robert Merritt, Charles Philip. Practice vet. medicine, Marietta, Ga., 1950-51, Augusta, Ga., 1955—; owner Fleming Animal Hosp., 1955-72, pres., 1972—; area supr. U.S. Dept. of Agr., Augusta, 1953-55; meat and food insp. Ga. Dept. Agr., 1955—. Ex-officio mem. Richmond County Bd. Health, 1958-59; pres. Ga. Bd. Vet. Medicine Examiners, 1966-67, 71-72. Mem. Richmond County Republican exec. com.; mem. Richmond County Bd. Edn., chmn. athletic and recreation com.; founder, past pres. Richmond County Bd. Edn. Served to 1st lt. AUS, 1951-53. Mem. Am., So., Ga. (past pres., dir. 1966-67 Veterinarian of Year 1974), East Ga., Ga.-S.C. vet. med. assns., Am. Animal Hosp. Assn., Am. Vet. Radiology Soc., Augusta Humane Soc., Augusta Kennel Club, Richmond County Businessmen's Assn., Greater Augusta C. of C., Ga. Numis. Assn. (past dir.), Augusta Coin Club, Vet. Radiology Soc., Am. Bus. Club (past pres., dir.), Richmond County Fish and Wild Life Conservation Club, Hephzibah Agrl. Club, U. Ga. Coll. Vet. Medicine Alumni Assn., Ga. Sch. Bds. Assn., Inc., Alpha Psi. Methodist (chmn. adminstrv. bd.). Lion (past pres.), Mason, Moose. Clubs: Toastmasters, South Augusta Exchange, Green Meadows Country. Home: 2144 Kingsley Ct Augusta GA 30906 Office: 2436 Peach Orchard Rd Augusta GA 30906

NUSBAUM, ROBERT COLLIER, lawyer; b. Norfolk, Va., Feb. 23, 1924; s. Virginius Harding and Justine Frances (Lowenberg) N.; student Harvard, 1941-43, 46; LL.B., U. Va., 1948; m. Louise Schloss, Oct. 20, 1946; children—Robert Collier, William Lee. Admitted to Va. bar, 1948, since practiced in Norfolk; asso. firm Allan J. Hofheimer, 1948-52, partner firm Hofheimer, Nusbaum & McPhaul, 1952—. Dir. First Nat. Bank of Norfolk; sec.-treas., dir., mem. exec. com. Maritime Terminals, Inc., 1972—. Bd. dirs. Norfolk Symphony. Med. Center Hosps., Inc.; bd. dirs., 1st v.p. Norfolk Forum; bd. dirs. Norfolk A.R.C., 1954-62. Served with AUS, 1943-45; ETO. Mem. Am., Va. (regional v.p. 1964), Norfolk-Portsmouth bar assns. Jewish religion (pres. congregation 1962-64). Clubs: Harbor, Cavalier Golf and Yacht. Home: 211 Oxford St Norfolk VA 23505 Office: 1010 Plaza One Norfolk VA 23510

NUSS, HENRY III, lawyer; b. Dallas, Mar. 14, 1936; s. Henry and Erna Bertha (Hamm) N.; B.A., Wheaton Coll., 1958; J.D., So. Methodist U., 1961; m. Patricia Ray Peterson, Dec. 23, 1960; children—Melynda Susan, Eric Graham, David Christian. Admitted to Tex. bar, 1961; with Peterson Devel. Co., Corpus Christi, Tex., 1963-65; mem. firm Kleberg, Mobley, Lockett & Weil, Corpus Christi, 1965—, partner, 1970—. Dir. Merc. Nat. Bank, Corpus Christi. Vice chmn. Corpus Christi Park and Recreation Bd., 1965-67; chmn. Corpus Christi Civil Service Bd. and Commn., 1967—. Precinct chmn., del. Rep. State Conv., 1964-65. Chmn. Young Life Com., Corpus Christi, 1972—. Served to capt. AUS, 1961-63. Decorated Army Commendation medal. Mem. Am., Tex., Nueces County bar assns., Christian Legal Soc. (founding dir. 1962). Club: Civitan (dir., v.p. Corpus Christi 1964-68). Home: 225 Bayridge St Corpus Christi TX 78411 Office: Box 2446 Corpus Christi TX 78403

NUSYNOWITZ, MARTIN LAWRENCE, physician; b. N.Y.C., July 21, 1933; s. Morris and Esther Clara (Rechtschaffen) N.; B.A., N.Y. U., 1954; M.D. cum laude, State U. N.Y., 1958; m. Harriet Rubinstein, Aug. 28, 1955; children—Murray Mark, Russell Neil, Leah Rachel. Commd. 2d lt. U.S. Army, 1957, advanced through grades to col., 1973; intern Letterman Gen. Hosp., San Francisco, 1958-59; resident in internal medicine Tripler Gen. Hosp., Honolulu, 1959-62; fellow Walter Reed Army Inst. Research, Washington, 1963-64; fellow in endocrinology U. Cal., San Francisco, 1964-65; chief nuclear medicine and endocrinology Tripler Gen. Hosp., Honolulu, 1962-63; chief nuclear medicine and endocrinology William Beaumont Army Med. Center, El Paso, Tex., 1965—. Cons. in nuclear medicine to surgeon gen. U.S. Army. Bd. dirs. El Paso Diabetes Assn., pres. 1970-72. Hutton grantee A.C.P., 1968. Diplomate Am. Bd. Internal Medicine. Am. Bd. Nuclear Medicine. Fellow A.C.P.; mem. Endocrine Soc., Soc. Nuclear Medicine (mem. edn. com. 1973—). Jewish religion. Contbr. articles to profl. jours. Home: 7351-B Ireland Circle El Paso TX 79930 Office: Box 70014 William Beaumont Army Medical Center El Paso TX 79930

NUTTER, DALE EDWARD, mech. engr.; b. Borger, Tex., July 20, 1935; s. I. Earl and Martha (Crowell) N.; student Rice U., 1954-56; B.S. in M.E., Okla. State U., 1958; m. Mary Lou Chambers, May 12, 1962; children—Mark Edward, Michael Earl. Asso. engr. Douglas Aircraft Co., Santa Monica, Cal., 1958-60; sales engr. Nutter Engring. Co., Tulsa, 1960-63, v.p. sales, 1963-68; v.p. devel. Heat/Fluid Engring. Co., Tulsa, 1968—; dir., mem. tech. com. Fractionation Research Inc., Bartlesville, Okla. Registered profl. engr., Okla., Tex. Mem. Am. Inst. Chem. Engrs., Nat. Petroleum Refiners Assn. (supply men's finance chmn. 1968), Acad. Model Aeros. (contest bd. rep. 1965, soaring adv. com. 1972—). Patentee in field. Home: 2498 E 49th St Tulsa OK 74105 Office: 2230 E 49th St Tulsa OK 74105

NYE, SYLVANUS WILLIAM, physician, educator; b. Buffalo, Mar. 28, 1930; s. Sylvanus Fisher and Winifred Alice (Rooth) N.; A.B., Hamilton Coll., 1952; M.D., U. Rochester, 1957; m. Phyllis Buell, June 16, 1956; children—Victoria, Jennifer. Intern, then resident in pathology N.C. Meml. Hosp., Chapel Hill, 1957-62; practice medicine specializing in pathology; asst. prof. pathology U. N.C. at Chapel Hill, 1965-69, asso. prof. pathology, 1969-71; prof. pathology, chmn. dept. East Carolina U. at Greenville, N.C., 1971—; pathologist Lenoir Meml. Hosp., Kinston, N.C., 1971—. Served to capt. M.C., USAF, 1962-65. Mem. Internat. Acad. Pathology, Am. Coll. Pathologists, A.M.A., Am. Assn. Pathologists and Bacteriologists, Am. Soc. Clin. Pathologists. Home: 700 Rountree St Kinston NC 28501

NYFELER, JOHN VERNON, constrn. mgmt. co. pres., architect; b. Dallas, Dec. 21, 1935; s. George Losee and Ruth (Vernon) N.; B.Arch., U. Tex. at Austin, 1958; postgrad. Grad. Sch. Mgmt. U. Dallas, 1972-73, various others, 1960-71; m. Vernell Sue McBee, Aug. 31, 1956; children—Suzan Elizabeth, James Alan, Lori Ruth. Asso., Herman Blum cons. engrs., Austin, 1958-63; asst. project rep. Grayson Gill Inc. architects and engrs., Dallas 1963-65; partner Woodward Cape & Partners, (city), 1965-70; exec. v.p. Devel. Dynamics, Inc., Dallas, 1970-72, pres., 1973—. Architect, Ala., Ariz., Cal., Colo., Fla., Ill., N.M., N.C., Tex. Mem. Nat. Council Archtl. Registration Bds., A.I.A., Tex. Soc. Architects, Constrn. Specifications Inst., Illuminating Engring. Soc. (bd. mgrs. N. Tex. sect. 1972-73). Home: 308 Countryside Dr Irving TX 75062 Office: 3635 Noble St Dallas TX 75204

NYHEN, E. MACDONALD, govt. ofcl.; b. Brookline, Mass., June 14, 1913; s. Joseph Albert Cameron and Mary Evelyn (MacDonald) N.; student Mass. Inst. Tech., 1932-33; S.B., Harvard, 1936, M.B.A., 1938; grad. Indsl. Coll. Armed Forces, 1958; m. Patricia Jane English, Oct. 23, 1948 (dec. June 1964); children—George English, Patricia Cameron. Engr., tech. staff CBS, N.Y.C., 1938-42; asst. mgr. contract sales Internat. Tel. & Tel. Co., N.Y.C., 1946-50; br. chief Nat. Prodn. Authority, Washington, 1951-53; mem. staff Bus. and Def. Services Adminstrn., Washington, 1953-61, dir. electronics div., 1961-67; adviser communications and electronics div. Bur. Domestic Commerce, Commerce Dept., Washington, 1967-72, sci. and electronics div., 1973—. Served with Signal Corps, AUS, 1941-46; ETO; lt. col. Res. ret. Decorated Bronze Star medal. Mem. I.E.E.E., Am. Inst. Aeros. and Astronautics, Audio Engring. Soc., A.A.A.S., Res. Officers Assn. U.S. Clubs: Harvard (Washington); Mass. Inst. Tech. (Washington). Home: 1637 N Greenbrier St Arlington VA 22205 Office: Bur Domestic Commerce US Dept Commerce Washington DC 20230

NYKAMP, HARRIS, aluminum co. exec.; b. Hamilton, Mich., May 21, 1934; s. Henry K. and Minnie (Terpstra) N.; student Chgo. Tech. Sch., U. Mich., U. Miami; m. Alma Joan Boers, Feb. 22, 1957; children—Diana Lynn, Cindy Lou, Dawn Renee, Thomas Lee. Design engr. Hart & Cooley Mfg. Co., Holland, Mich., 1951-56, asst. prodn. control mgr., 1959-61; mgr. adminstrn. Aluminaire, Inc., Miami, Fla., 1962-68, gen. mgr., 1968—. Served with USNR, 1957-58. Mem. Miami C. of C. Republican. Mem. Christian Reformed Ch. (elder). Home: 14570 English Rd Miami Lakes FL 33014 Office: 1600 NW 165th St Miami FL 33169

OAKES, THOMAS CLAYTON, supt. schs.; b. Groesbeck, Tex., May 13, 1914; s. William M. and Nettie (Sims) O.; A.A., Westminster Jr. Coll., 1932; B.A., S.W. Tex. State U., 1942; M.A., Baylor U., 1950, postgrad. 1956—; m. Bernice W. Slaughter, May 23, 1939; children—James C. Judith L. (Mrs. Richard P. Welch). Tchr. Fairoaks Elementary Sch., Groesbeck, 1934-35, prin., 1935-37; coach, prin. Fairoaks High Sch., Groesbeck, 1937-42, supt., 1943-51; supt. Wortham Pub. Schs., Wortham, Tex., 1951-55. Connally Pub. Schs., Waco, Tex., 1955—. Bd. dirs. McLennan Cancer Soc. Mem. Am., Tex. assns. sch. adminstrs., N.E.A., Tex. Tchrs. Assn. Baptist. Mason, Lion, Rotarian (sec. 1967). Home: 609 Theresa St Waco TX 76705

OAKEY, WILLIAM EDGAR, mech. engr.; b. Plainfield, N.J., Sept. 14, 1918; s. William Edgar and Dorothy Cone (Simonton) O.; student Ill. Inst. Tech., part-time 1937-39; B.S. in Mech. Engring., Antioch Coll., 1945; postgrad. St. Mary's U., 1966; m. Sara Louise McKinney, Mar. 27, 1943; children—Marilyn (Mrs. Floyd C. Lott), William S., Richard W. Plant engr. Morris Bean & Co., Yellow Springs, O., 1945-48; chief engr. A.J. Fish Co., Beloit, Wis., 1948-52; sr. research engr. S.W. Research Inst., San Antonio, 1952—, project mgr., 1963—. Recipient IR 100 award Indsl. Research, Inc., 1971. Registered profl. engr., Ohio, Tex. Mem. Research Soc. Am., Am. Soc. M.E., Am. Soc. Metals. Patentee in field. Home: 118 Sunnycrest Dr San Antonio TX 78228 Office: PO Drawer 28510 San Antonio TX 78284

OAKLAND, THOMAS DAVID, psychologist, educator; b. Kenosha, Wis., Nov. 23, 1939; s. Oscar Tredway and Nancy Harriet (Nygren) O.; B.A., Lawrence Coll., 1962; M.S., Ind. U., 1965, Ph.D., 1967; m. Judy Marie Defferding, June 15, 1963; children—David, Christopher. Tchr. DeKalb (Ill.) Jr. High Sch., 1962-63, Orland Park (Ill.) Elementary Sch., 1963-64; research asso., Ind. U., Bloomington, 1965-67, asst. prof., 1967-72; asso. prof. ednl. psychology U. Tex. at Austin, 1972—. Cons. Southwest Ednl. Devel. Lab., 1967—, Sci. Research Assos., 1969-71, Tex. Edn. Agy., 1973—. Pres. Austin Child Guidance Center, 1972—, Austin Evaluation Center, 1971-72. Mem. Am., Tex. psychol. assns., Am. Ednl. Research Assn., Phi Delta Kappa. Author: Auditory Perception, 1971. Guest editor: Jour. Sch. Psychology. Contbr. articles on ednl. and child psychology to profl. jours. Home: 2905 Dover Place Austin TX 78731

OAKLEY, EDWARD HESTER, oil co. exec.; b. Montgomery, Ala., Sept. 14, 1925; s. Edward Barry and Eloise (Hester) O.; B.S. in Accounting, U. Ala., 1949; m. Lucy Amelia Green, June 16, 1951; children—Philip Earl, Edward Randolph. Ticket clk. Louisville and Nashville R.R., Montgomery, Ala., 1942-43; clk. Cities Service Oil Co., Lake Charles, La., 1949-63, order coordinator, 1963-69, pipeline scheduler, Tulsa, 1969-71, traffic mgr., Lake Charles, 1971—. Served with USAAF, 1943-46. Methodist (mem. bd. 1971—). Club: Traffic (sec. 1953-56) (Lake Charles). Home: 313 Jeannine St Lake Charles LA 70601 Office: Box 1562 Lake Charles LA 70601

OAKLEY, PHILLIP GLENN, broadcasting exec.; b. Austin, Tex., Aug. 2, 1945; s. Amos Ray and Mary Alberta (Fells) O.; student U. Tex. at Austin, 1963-66. Announcer, newsman sta. KTBC, Austin, 1964-66; newsman sta. KNOW, Austin, 1966-67; news editor sta. WFAA, Dallas, 1967-68; news dir. sta. KJOE, Shreveport, La., 1968-71, sta. WJBO, Baton Rouge, 1971—, sta. WBRZ-TV, Baton Rouge, 1973—. Mem. media adv. council Pub. Affairs Research Council La., 1974—. Press sec., adviser to U.S. senator J. Bennett Johnston, Jr., for Democratic primary race for gov., campaign adviser for senate race, 1972. Recipient award for radio reporting Radio-TV News Dirs. Assn., 1971, 2 awards, 1972; Nat. Headliners award for outstanding radio reporting, 1972; DuPont-Columbia award for investigative reporting Columbia Sch. Journalism, 1973. Mem. Radio-TV News Dirs. Assn. (award for investigative reporting), United Press Broadcasters La. (pres. 1973—), A.P. Broadcasters Assn. (dir. 1974), Press Club Baton Rouge (pres. 1974). Home: 8181 Brandon Baton Rouge LA 70809 Office: PO Box 2906 Baton Rouge LA 70821

OAKS, BILLY WAYNE, pub. utility ofcl., b. nr. Calera, Ala., Mar. 8, 1932; s. Chester Allen and Rosa Lee (Collins) L.; B.S. in Elec. Engring., Auburn U., 1958; m. Betty June Rudd, Feb. 25, 1949 (div. Feb. 1964); children—Matthew Rudd, Terri Michele. Announcer Radio Station WFEB, Sylacauga, Ala., 1949-50, also program dir.; sr. engr. Ala. Power Co., Birmingham, 1961-63, dist. supt., 1964—, asst. div. supt., 1970-72, asst. to v.p., 1972-73, mgr. indsl. relations, 1973—. Mem. Cluster Group Miles Coll., Birmingham, 1972. Bd. dirs. Indsl. Health Council, 1972. Served with USNR, 1951-55. Mem. Nat. Mgmt. Assn. (pres. Birmingham div. 1966-67). Baptist. Club: Relay House. Home: 1311 Apple Tree Lane Birmingham AL 35226 Office: 600 N 18th Birmingham AL 35203

OATES, CARL EVERETTE, lawyer; b. Harlingen, Tex., Apr. 8, 1931; s. Joseph William and Grace (Watson) O.; student Schreiner Inst., 1948-49, Tex. A. and I. U., 1949-50; B.S., U.S. Naval Acad., 1955; LL.B., So. Meth. U., 1962; m. Patricia Ann Lund, Dec. 21, 1955; children—Carl Blaisdell, Patricia Lund. Admitted to Tex. bar, 1962; mem. firm Akin, Gump, Strauss Hauer & Feld (and predecessor firm), Dallas, 1962—; dir. Town N. Nat. Bank, Dallas, Dallas/Ft. Worth Airport Nat. Bank. Bd. dirs. Park Cities YMCA, 1973; chmn. adv. council Dallas Health and Sci. Mus., 1972-73. Served as pilot USNR, 1955-59. Mem. Am., Tex., Dallas bar assns., Barristers, N. Dallas C. of C. (dir., exec. com. 1973), Sons of Republic of Tex., Delta Theta Phi. Presbyn. (deacon). Kiwanian, Mason (32 degree). Clubs: Northwood, Dallas, City.

OATES, JAMES BART, real estate devel. co. exec.; b. Brownwood, Tex., June 10, 1945; s. John Bart and Bernadette Margaret (Kane) O.; B.B.A. in Accounting, So. Meth. U., 1967, M.B.A., 1969. Accountant E.P. Thompson, Dallas, 1965-69; audit mgr. Alexander Grant & Co., Dallas, 1969-73; treas. Hill Consol. Corp., Dallas, 1973—; treas. Hilco Mgmt. Corp., Dallas, 1973—, Hill Realty Mortgage, Inc., Dallas, 1973—; sec., treas. Interiors by Jeani, Inc., Dallas, 1973—. C.P.A., Tex. Mem. Am. Inst. C.P.A.'s, Tex. Soc. C.P.A.'s, Beta Alpha Psi, Oak Cliff Jaycees. Home: 5423 Peterson Lane Apt 268 Dallas TX 75240 Office: 558 S Central Expressway Richardson TX 75080

OBENOUR, RICHARD ALEXANDER, physician, educator; b. Knoxville, Tenn., Oct. 4, 1930; s. William Hypes and Helen Hutton (Murrian) O.; B.S., U. Tenn., 1953; M.D., 1955; m. Mary Jean Archer, Dec. 22, 1953; children—Patricia Jean, Richard Alexander, Jane Ann. Intern Knoxville Gen. Hosp., 1955-56; resident Duke U. Med. Center Durham, N.C., 1959-62; practice medicine specializing in pulmonary disease, Knoxville, 1962—; chmn. sect. pulmonary disease U. Tenn. Meml. Hosp., 1964-73, chief staff, 1973—; prof. clin. medicine U. Tenn., Knoxville; dir. Med. Chest Clinic U. Tenn. Meml. Hosp. Served to lt. M.C., USNR, 1956-58. Diplomate Am. Bd. Internal Medicine. Fellow A.C.P., Am. Coll. Chest Physicians, Royal Soc. Health; mem. Am. Soc. Internal Medicine, N.Y. Acad. Scis., Am. Thoracic Soc., Am., East Tenn. (pres. 1967) heart assns., Alpha Omega Alpha. Kiwanian. Club: Cherokee Country. Home: 4039 Alta Vista Way Knoxville TN 37919 Office: 1928 Alcoa Hwy Knoxville TN 37919

OBENSHAIN, DAVID, elec. power engr.; b. Rockford, Ill., Feb. 20, 1943; s. Felix and Ernestine (Stokburger) O.; B.S. in Indsl. Engring., Ga. Inst. Tech., 1966; M.S. in Engring., U. South Fla., 1970; m. Mary Kent Booher, Jan. 8, 1965; children—Elizabeth, Mark David. Distbn. engr. Tampa Electric Co. (Fla.), 1966-72, substation engr., 1972-73; planning engr. Jackson Electric Membership Corp., Jefferson, Ga., 1973—. Mem. Fla. Engring. Soc. (sr.), Ga. Soc. Profl. Engrs., Nat. Soc. Profl. Engrs., I.E.E.E. (Power Engring. Soc.). Clubs: MacDill Sports Car, University of South Fla. Sports Car (Tampa). Home: Route 2 Jefferson GA 30549 Office: 117 Athens St Jefferson Ga 30549

OBENSHAIN, JAMES WARNER, supt. schs.; b. Eagle Rock, Va., July 19, 1916; s. Rufus Z. and Estelle (Honts) O.; B.S., Va. Poly. Inst., 1939; M.Ed., U. Va., 1960; m. Mary G. Makinney, June 23, 1944; 1 dau., Sandra Faye. Tchr. vocational agr. Fincastle (Va.) High Sch., 1941-53, prin., 1953-58; supr. Botetourt County (Va.) high schs., 1958-59, supt., 1959—. Mem. Nat., Va. edn. assns., Nat., Va. assns. sch. adminstrs. Baptist (trustee). Rotarian (pres. Fincastle 1945). Address: PO Box 101 Fincastle VA 24090

OBENSHAIN, RICHARD DUDLEY, lawyer; b. Abingdon, Va., Oct. 31, 1935; s. Samuel Shockley and Josephine Mathews (Dudley) O.; B.A., Bridgewater Coll., 1956; LL.B., N.Y. U., 1959; m. Helen Nottingham Wilkins, July 15, 1961; children—Mark, Anne Scott, Kate. Admitted to Va. bar, 1959, U.S. Supreme Ct. bar, 1968; with firm McGuire, Woods & Battle, Richmond, 1959-69, partner, 1966-69; partner firm Obenshain, Hinnant, Dolbeare & Beale, Richmond, 1970—. Chmn. Young Republican Fedn. Va., 1961-64; del. Rep. Nat. Conv., 1964; candidate for U.S. Ho. of Reps., 1964, for atty. gen. Va., 1969; chmn. Rep. party Va., 1972—; mem. Rep. Nat. Com., 1972—. Chmn., Va. March of Dimes, 1971-73. Bd. visitors Va. Commonwealth U., 1970—. Served with USMCR, 1959-60. Named 1 of Va.'s 5 Outstanding Young Men, Va. Jaycees, 1970. Mem. Am., Va. bar assns., Am. Judicature Soc., Bridgewater Coll. Alumni Assn. (pres. 1971-72), S.R., Phi Delta Phi. Presbyn. (elder 1971—). Mason. Home: 5505 Toddsbury Rd Richmond VA 23226 Office: Va Bldg 1 N 5th St Richmond VA 23219

OBERMAN, ALBERT, physician; b. St. Louis, Feb. 9, 1934; s. Max and Helen (Schryer) O.; A.B., Washington U., St. Louis, 1955, M.D., 1959; M.P.H., U. Mich., 1966; m. Marian Kleg, June 20, 1954; children—Steven, David, Karen. Intern, Jewish Hosp., St. Louis, 1959-60, resident, 1960-62; staff physician heart disease control program USPHS, 1962-65; staff physician sub-com. criteria and methods Am. Heart Assn., Birmingham, Ala., 1966-67; prof. pub. health and epidemiology, asso. prof. medicine U. Ala. Med. Center, Birmingham, 1967—; cons. Naval Aerospace Med. Inst., Pensacola, Fla., 1967—. Fellow A.C.P., Am. Coll. Preventive Medicine, Am. Heart Assn. (council epidemiology 1966—, com. on criteria and methods, nat. study group 1970-72); mem. Am. Fedn. Clin. Research, Am. Pub. Health Assn. Home: 3585 Rockhill Rd Birmingham AL 35223

OBERMAYER, HERMAN JOSEPH, editor, publisher; b. Phila., Sept. 19, 1924; s. Leon J. and Julia (Sinsheimer) O.; student U. Geneva (Switzerland), 1946; A.B. cum laude, Dartmouth, 1948; m. Betty Nan Levy, June 28, 1955; children—Helen Julia, Veronica Levy, Adele Beatrice, Elizabeth Rose. Reporter, L.I. Daily Press, Jamaica, N.Y., 1950-53; classified advt. mgr. New Orleans Item, 1953-55; promotion dir. New Bedford (Mass.) Standard-Times, 1955-57; editor, pub. Long Branch (N.J.) Daily Record, 1957-71, No. Va. Sun, Arlington, 1963—. Bd. dirs. exec. council Boy Scouts Am., Monmouth (N.J.) council, 1958-71, Nat. Capital Council, 1971; bd. dirs. Arlington (Va.) Bicentennial Commn. Long Branch Community Adult Sch., Anti-Defamation League N.J. Regional Adv. Council. Trustee Twin Lights Hist. Mus., Highlands, N.J.; mem. Va. Legislative Alcoholic Beverage Control Study Commn., 1972; bd. dirs., asst. v.p. Monmouth (N.J.) Med. Center, 1958-71. Served with AUS, 1943-46; ETO. Recipient Friends of Scouting award, 1966. Mem. Am. Soc. Newspaper Editors, Am., So. (editorial and labor coms.) newspaper pubs. assns., Fairfax (Va.) C. of C. (mem. sr. council), Sigma Chi, Sigma Delta Chi. Jewish religion. Rotarian. Clubs: Dartmouth (N.Y.C.); National Press (Washington); Ocean Beach (Elberon, N.J.); Contbr. column Editor's Viewpoint to No. Va. Sun, articles to popular, trade mags. Home: 4114 N Ridgeview Rd Arlington VA 22207 Office: 1227 N Ivy St Arlington VA 22210

OBERT, GENE MADALENE SAULSBURY (MRS. PAUL M. OBERT), nurse; b. Oklahoma City; d. Claude and Elizabeth (Young) Saulsbury; R.N., St. Anthony Hosp. Sch. Nursing, 1947; B. Nursing Arts, Okla. U., 1947; m. Paul M. Obert, Apr. 27, 1947; children—Mary (Mrs. James Leita), Jeanne, Paul, Elizabeth, Catherine. Supr. nurses Wesley Hosp., Oklahoma City, 1948; directress nursing McCurdy Hosp., 1948-50; dir. Red River Med. Center Corp., Victoria, Tex., 1968-72. First aid instr. A.R.C., 1958—. Bd. dirs. Fine Arts Assn., Victoria. Republican. Roman Catholic. Mem. Tex. Mem. Profl. Nurses Assn., Victoria-Calhoun-Goliad Tri-County Med. Aux. Club: Victoria Country. Home: 303 Tampa St Victoria TX 77901 also Rockport TX Office: Box 3784 Victoria TX 77901

OBERT, PAUL MICHAEL, physician; b. Apache, Okal., Apr. 25, 1924; s. Joseph M. and Mary (Fitter) O.; B.Sc., Stanford, 1944; M.D., U. Okla., 1947; m. Gene Salisbury, Apr. 27, 1947; children—Mary, Jeanne, Paul, Elizabeth. Catherine. Intern, St. Anthony Hosp., Oklahoma City, 1947-48; practice gen. medicine, Purcell, Okla., 1948-50, resident U. Hosp. Oklahoma City, 1950-52, cancer research fellow, 1951-52; practice medicine, specializing in pathology Victoria, Tex., 1956—; chief staff McCurdy Hosp., Purcell, Okla., 1949-50; asst. prof. pathology U. Okla. Sch. Medicine, Oklahoma City, 1952-56; attending pathologist VA Hosp., Oklahoma City, 1953-56; pathologist-in-chief USPHS Hosp., Galveston, Tex., 1953-56; asst. prof. pathology U. Tex. Sch. Medicine, Galveston, 1954-57; chief pathologist, dir. labs. Citizens Meml., Calhoun County Meml. Victoria, Mauritz, Nightengale hosps., all 1956—; cons. pathologist Matagorda County, Huth Meml., Cuero, Burns, Wagner, Yorktown, Palacious City hosps., 1956—; dir. labs. Meml. Hosp., Beeville, Tex., 1963—; vis. pathologist M.D. Anderson Hosp., 1962—; dir. lab Matagorda Gen. Hosp. and Goliod County Hosp., 1963—, Kleberg Hosp., Kingsville, Tex., 1968—; forensic pathologist South Tex., 1968; bd. dirs. Victoria Med. Center, 1963—, pres., 1969—; bd. dirs. Tex. Rehab. Center, Gonzales, 1970—. Tex. dir. Cancer Soc. Trustee Victoria Edn. Found.; bd. dirs. Victoria Fine Arts Assn. Served with AUS, 1943-46; comdr., USPHS, 1953-56. Diplomate Am. Bd. Pathology. Fellow Coll. Am. Pathologists, Am. Soc. Clin. Pathologists; mem. Am., Tex., Victoria-Calhoun-Coliad County med. assns., Internat. Acad. Pathology, Tex. Assn. Pathologists, N.Y. Acad. Scis., A.A.A.S., Soc. Exptl. Biology and Medicine, Am. Assn. Blood Banks. Roman Catholic. Clubs: Victoria Country, Serra (trustee). Contbr. articles to profl. publs. Home: 303 Tampa Dr Victoria TX 77901 Office: 2602 Houston Hwy Victoria TX 77901

O'BRIEN, EDWARD JOHN, III, tobacco co. exec.; b. Louisville, Mar. 28, 1920; s. Edward John and Mary (Malone) O'B.; B.A., Princeton, 1942; m. Lucy Dickenson Scott, July 30, 1960; children—Edward John IV, Mary Scott. With Edward J. O'Brien Co., Louisville, 1946—, sec., 1955-70, v.p., sec., 1970-72, pres., 1972—. Com. chmn., United Way, 1971; vice chmn. Louisville chpt. A.R.C., 1969-73, chmn., 1973—; civic com. Bellarmine-Ursuline Coll., 1960. Bd. dirs. Internat. Center, U. Louisville. Served to capt., AUS, 1942-46. Mem. Tobacco Assn. U.S. (pres. 1973—), Burley Tobacco Dealers Assn. (pres. 1962-63; dir.), Burley Dark Leaf Tobacco Export Assn. Rotarian. Home: 406 Springwood Lane Louisville KY 40207 Office: 100 N Sixth St Louisville KY 40202

O'BRIEN, JAMES JOSEPH, educator; b. N.Y.C., Aug. 1, 1935; s. Maurice J. and Beatrice (Cudihy) O.; B.S. in Chemistry, Rutgers U., 1957; M.S. in Meteorology (NASA fellow), Tex. A. and M. U., 1964, Ph.D. in Meteorology (NASA fellow), 1966; m. Sheila E. O'Keefe, Nov. 28, 1958; children—Karen, Kevin, Sean, Dealyn, Denis. Chemist E. I. duPont, Wilmington, Del., 1960-62; research scientist Nat. Center for Atmospheric Research, Boulder, Colo., 1966-69; mem. faculty Fla. State U., Tallahassee, 1969—, prof. meteorology and oceanography, since 1972—. Served with USAF, 1958-60. Nat. Center for Atmospheric Research fellow, 1966. Mem. Am. Meteorol. Soc., Am. Geophys. Union, Meteorol. Soc. Japan, Oceanographical Soc. Japan, Royal Meteorol. Soc., Chi Epsilon Pi, Pi Mu Epsilon, Pi Kappa Phi, Sigma Xi, Alpha Chi Rho. Asso. editor: Jour. Phys. Oceanography, 1970—. Contbr. articles to profl. jours. Home: 311 Starmount Dr Tallahassee FL 32303

O'BRIEN, LARRY JOE, educator, cardiovascular physiologist; b. Big Spring, Tex., Sept. 14, 1929; s. George H. and Della V. (Cartwright) O.; B.A., Hardin-Simmons U., 1949; M.A., North Tex. State Coll., 1954; Ph.D., U. Tex. Med. Br., 1957; M.D., Med. Coll. Ga., 1971; m. Edith Yvonne Snyder, Dec. 28, 1953; children—Susan, Caryn, Judith. Instr. to asst. prof. physiology Albany Med. Coll. Union U., 1957-60; chief circulatory physiology sect. Civil Aeromed. Research Inst., Oklahoma City, 1960-62, also asso. prof. research physiology U. Okla. Sch. Medicine; asst. prof. dept. physiology Med. Coll. Ga., 1962-66, asso. prof., 1966-72, acting chmn. dept. physiology, 1971-72, asso. prof. surgery, 1971-72; prof. physiology, chmn. dept. Tex. Tech U. Sch. Medicine, Lubbock, 1972—. Vis. faculty Am. Heart Assn.; chmn. sci. various sessions Fedn. Am. Socs. for Exptl. Biology, Grantee Heart Assn. Albany County, USPHS, Ga. Heart Assn., others. Mem. Am. Physiol. Soc., Soc. for Exptl. Biology and Medicine, N.Y. Acad. Sci., Am. Fedn. Clin. Research, Am., Tex. heart assns., Am. Assn. U. Profs., A.A.A.S., Sigma Xi. Contbr. sci. articles to med. jours. Home: 4520 22d St Lubbock TX 79407

O'BRIEN, ROBERT TATE, constrn. exec.; b. Dothan, Ala., Jan. 14, 1931; s. James Fred and Annie Virginia (Tate) O'B.; extension student U. Ala.; m. Naomi Grace McClenny, Dec. 1, 1950; children—Cynthia Lee, Patti Sue. Salesman, Hudson Office Supply Co., Dothan, 1952-54, Charles Woods Constrn. Co., Dothan, 1954-56; draftsman Meadow Corp., Montgomery, Ala., 1956-58; owner Tate O'Brien Realty Co., Dothan, 1958-63; pres. O'Brien Homes Inc., Dothan, 1963—. Served with USAAF. Mem. Homebuilders Assn. Ala. (exec. com., pres. 1971), Dothan Homebuilders Assn. (pres. 1965, chmn. ednl. trust fund com.), Dothan-Houston County C. of C. (dir.). Methodist. Elk, Kiwanian. Club: Dothan Country (v.p. 1972-73). Home: 1702 Del Rio Terrace Dothan AL 36301 Office: 1509 Montgomery Hwy Dothan AL 36301

O'BRIEN, THOMAS MICHAEL, data processing co. exec.; b. Washington, May 18, 1938; s. John F. and Gertrude E. (Oddutt) O'B.; B.A., U. Pa., 1961; postgrad. Am. U., 1963-68; m. Claire Daphers, June 29, 1963; children—Deirdre, Michele, Catherine. Supr. compute support NCR, Inc., Washington, 1965-67; computer cons. Jonker Corp., Gaithersburg, Md., 1967-68; sr. systems analyst Am. Security & Trust Co., Washington, 1968-69; v.p. Data Power of Washington, 1969—; founder Microamption Systems, Inc., Washington, 1968. Faculty, Temple Sch., Washington, 1956-57. Served with AUS, 1961-64. Mem. Assn. Computing Machinery, Data Processing Mgmt. Assn., Am. Civil Liberties Union, Common Cause, Kappa Sigma. Democrat. Clubs: Washington Print, Philadelphia Print.

OBRIG, ELWOOD MANSFIELD, lawyer; b. Summit, N.J., Sept. 5, 1941; s. Elwood Mansfield and Dorothy (Bergman) O.; grad. Manlius Sch., 1959; A.B., U. Richmond, 1963; J.D., U. Miami (Fla.), 1966; m. Mary Elizabeth Coleman, June 15, 1963; children—Paige Elizabeth, Scott Coleman. Admitted to Fla. bar, 1966; research asst. State Atty.'s Office, Appellate Div., Dade County, Fla., 1965, 66; research asst. State atty. Gen.'s Office, Dade County, 1966; asst. state atty., Dade County, 1966-67; asst. city atty., Ft. Lauderdale, Fla., 1967-72; partner Andrews, Lubbers & Obrig, Profl. Assn., Ft. Lauderdale, 1968-73; individual practice, 1973—. Served with AUS, 1967. Mem. Am., Fla., Broward County bar assns., Phi Delta Phi (past pres.), Phi Kappa Sigma (past v.p.). Republican. Presbyn. Home: 2100 NE 59th Ct Fort Lauderdale FL 33308 Office: 2929 E Commercial Blvd Fort Lauderdale FL 33308

O'BRYAN, MAUD (MRS. GEORGE NELSON RONSTROM), newspaper columnist; b. Sulphur Mine, La., June 28, 1914; d. F. Daniel and Annie Christina (Coldwater) O'Bryan; B.A. in Journalism, La. State U., 1932; m. Dr. George Nelson Ronstrom, Sept. 14, 1939. Daily columnist Times-Picayune, New Orleans, also New Orleans States-Item. Mem. Theta Sigma Phi. Contbr. articles to nat. mags., including Antiques, Am. Antiques, Jour., Hobbies. Home: 524 Esplanade Av New Orleans LA 70116 Office: Times-Picayune New Orleans LA 70140

OCAMPO, ROSELI ISABELITA, biologist; b. Manila, Philippines, Nov. 23, 1937; d. Eliseo and Generosa (Campana) Ocampo; B.Sc., U. Philippines, 1958; M.Sc. (Israel Ministry Fgn. Affairs fellow), Hebrew U. Jerusalem, 1966; Ph.D., Fla. State U., 1973; m. Rodolfo Paus, Oct. 21, 1958 (div. July 1973); children—Maria Roseli, Rodolfo. Research asso. Nat. Inst. Sci. & Tech., Manila, 1958-68; teaching asst. Fla. State U., Tallahassee, 1968-71, lab. technologist, research asso., 1971—. Mem. Am. Inst. Biol. Scis., Bot. Soc. Am., British Physol. Soc., Internat. Phycol. Soc., Phycol. Soc. India, Phycol. Soc. Philippines, Philippine Assn. Advancement Sci., Sigma Xi. Office: Dept Biology Fla State Univ Tallahassee FL 32306

OCASIO-ESTEBAN, RAFAEL, constrn. co. exec.; b. San Juan, P.R., June 12, 1931; s. Perfecto and Carmen (Esteban) Ocasio; B.S.C.E., U. P.R., 1954; m. Angelina Carle, Sept. 4, 1959; children—Rafael A., Esteban L., Maria T., Jorge J. Staff engr. P.R. Planning Bd., 1956-57; with IBEC Housing Co., Inc., Rio Piedras, P.R., 1957-73, chief engr., 1960-67, v.p., gen. mgr. operations, 1967-70, pres., 1970-73; pres. ROE Devel. Corp., 1973—; adv. bd. Banco de Economias. Adv. bd. Salvation Army. Served to 1st lt. AUS, 1954-56. Mem. P.R. Inst. Engrs. and Architects, C. of C. of P.R., San Juan Bd. Realtors, Internat. Recreation Assn., Nat. Assn. Home Builders (bd. dirs. 1968-72), P.R. Home Builders Assn. (pres. 1970-71), Nu Sigma Beta. Club: Exchange. Home: 1833 Acacia St Santa Maria Rio Piedras PR 00927 Office: ROE Devel Corp Pan Am Bldg Hato Rey PR 00917

OCHSNER, ALTON, surgeon; b. Kimball, S.D., May 4, 1896; s. Edward Phillip and Clara (Shontz) O.; A.B., U. of S.D., 1918, hon. D.Sc., 1936; M.D., Washington U., 1920; Sc.D., Brigham Young U., 1961, Loyola U., New Orleans, 1969; Doctor Honoris Causa, Universidad Libre de Nicaragua, 1946; LL.D., Tulane U., 1966, McNeese State U., 1972; m. Isabel Kathryn Lockwood, Sept. 13, 1923 (dec. Apr. 1968); children—Alton, John Lockwood, Mims Gage, Isabel; m. 2d, Jane Kellogg, Feb. 12, 1970. Intern, Barnes Hosp., St. Louis, 1920-21, Augustana Hosp., Chgo., 1921-22; exchange surg. asst., Kantons Hosp., Zurich, Switzerland, 1922-23, Staedtisches Krankenhaus, Frankfurt am Main, 1923-24; visited European and Am. clinics, 1924-25; instr. in surgery, Northwestern U. Med. School, 1925-26; asst. prof. surgery, U. of Wis., 1926-27; prof. surgery and chmn. dept. of surgery, Tulane U., 1927-56, prof. clin. surgery, 1956-61, emeritus prof. surgery, 1961—, William Henderson prof. surgery, 1938-56; dir. sect. on gen. surgery Ochsner Clinic, Found. Hosp., 1942-66, sr. cons. surgery, 1967—, sr. surgeon Touro Infirmary; cons. in surgery Charity Hosp., cons. in thoracic surg. USPHS Hosp., VA Hosp., New Orleans; cons. U.S. Air Force Surgeon. Pres. Cordell Hull Found. for Internat. Edn.; pres. Internat. House, 1962. Decorated Order Vasco Nunez de Balboa, Cruz Eloy-Alfaro, Panama; Order of Al Merito, Republic of Ecuador; recipient Service award A.M.A., 1967; Cunningham Inter-Am. Relations award, 1967; Thomas F. Cunningham award Internat. House of New Orleans, 1968. Mem. com. on growth NRC. Diplomate Am. Bd. Surgery (a founder), Am. Bd. Thoracic Surgery (a founder). Fellow Royal Coll. Surgeons. Ireland (hon.), Royal Coll. Surgeons Eng. (hon.), A.C.S. (past pres., past regent), Am. Surg. Assn., So. Surg. Assn. (past pres.); mem. A.M.A., Am. Assn. Thoracic Surgery (past pres.), Internat. Surg. Soc. (pres. 1963), Soc. Clin. Surgery, Southeastern Surg. Assn. (past pres.), Orleans Parish Med. Assn., Soc. Exptl. Biology and Medicine, So. Med. Assn., Am. Cancer Soc. (dir., past pres.), Am. Acad. Orthopedic Surgs., Internat. Soc. Angiology (past pres.), Interstate Postgrad. Med. Assn. (past pres.), Soc. for Vascular Surg. (past pres.), Academia Mexicana de Cirugia (hon.). Internat. Soc. Surgery (pres.), Pan-Pacific Surg. Assn. (pres.), Delta Sigma Pi, Nu Sigma Nu, Alpha Omega Alpha, Sigma Xi, Omicron Delta Kappa. Phi Delta Theta. Clubs: Boston, New Orleans Country. Writer sect. on diseases of veins, Lewis' System of Surgery, monographs on varicose veins. Editor Internat. Surgical Digest; editor surg. sect. The Cyclopedia of Medicine, Surgery and Specialties; emeritus co-editor of Surgery; asso. editor Lewis Practice of Surgery. Home: 1347 Exposition Blvd New Orleans LA 70118 Office: Ochsner Clinic 1514 Jefferson Hwy New Orleans LA 70121

OCHSNER, JOHN LOCKWOOD, physician; b. Madison, Wis., Feb. 10, 1927; s. Edward Alton and Isabel (Lockwood) O.; M.D., Tulane U., 1952; m. Mary Louise Hannon, Mar. 20, 1954; children—John Lockwood, Joby Hannon, Katherine, Frank Hannon. Intern U. Mich. Hosp., 1952-53, surg. resident, 1953-54; surg. resident Jefferson Davis Hosp., Houston, 1956-59, chief resident, 1959; cardio-vascular resident Tex. Children's Hosp., 1960; surg. staff Baylor Med. Sch., 1960-61; staff Ochsner Clinic, New Orleans, 1961; clin. prof. surgery Tulane U. Sch. Medicine; chmn. dept. surgery Ochsner Clinic and Oschner Found. Hosp.; cons. cardiac surgeon La. Bd. Health; cons. gen. and thoracic surgery USPHS Hosp., New Orleans; cons. cardiovascular surgeon Lafayette (La.) Meml. Hosp.; vis. surgeon E.A. Conway Meml. Hosp. Mem. bd. Jefferson Heart Council, 1961; trustee Am. Coll. Cardiology; counsellor Southeastern Surg. Soc. Served with M.C., USAF, 1954-56. Diplomate Am. Bd. Surgery, Am. Bd. Thoracic Surgery. Fellow A.C.S., Am. Coll. Chest Physicians; mem. Internat. Surg. Soc., Am., So. surg. assns., Internat. Cardiovascular Soc., Am. Assn. Thoracic Surgeons, A.M.A., La., Orleans Parish med. socs., So. Thoracic Surg. Assn., Am. Heart Assn., La. Thoracic Soc., So. Med. Assn., New Orleans Surg. Soc., Soc. for Vascular Surgery, S.E. Surg. Congress, Soc. Thoracic Surgeons, Beta Theta Pi, Nu Sigma Nu. Home: 84 Audubon Blvd New Orleans LA 70118 Office: Ochsner Clinic New Orleans LA 70121

O'CONNELL, ROBERT FRANCIS, educator; b. Athlone, Ireland, Apr. 22, 1933; s. William and Catherine (O'Reilly) O.; B.S., Nat. U. Ireland, 1953; Ph.D., U. Notre Dame, 1962; m. Josephine Buckley, Aug. 3, 1963; children—Adrienne, Fiona, Eimear. Came to U.S., 1958, naturalized, 1969. Research asso. Inst. for Advanced Studies, Dublin, Ireland, 1962-64; mem. faculty La. State U., Baton Rouge, 1964—, prof. physics, 1969—. Recipient Sir J. J. Larmor prize in physics Nat. U. Ireland, 1953; Nat. Acad. Sci. NRC Sr. fellow, 1966-68. Fellow Am. Phys. Soc.; mem. Internat., Am. astron. socs. Home: 522 Bancroft Way Baton Rouge LA 70808

O'CONNELL, STEPHEN CORNELIUS, ret. univ. pres.; b. West Palm Beach, Fla., Jan. 22, 1916; s. Daniel Joseph and Nora (McKenna) O'C; B.S., J.D., U. Fla., 1940, LL.B., Jacksonville U., 1968, Notre Dame, 1969; Ed.D., Biscayne Coll., 1969; hon. degree Fed. U. Brazil, 1973; m. Rita Mavis McTigue, Nov. 6, 1946; children—Rite Denise (Mrs. Herbert Cumbie), Stephen C., Martin Robert, Ann Maureen. Admitted to Fla. bar, 1940, and practiced in Ft. Lauderdale, 1940-55; justice Supreme Ct. of Fla., 1955-67, chief justice, 1967; pres. U. Fla., Gainesville, 1967-73, ret. Dir. Fla. Nat. Banks. Chmn., Jud. Council, 1957-59; atty. Fla. Road Dept., 1953, Racing Commn., 1954; chmn. Fla. Citizenship Clearing House, Fla. Elections Commn. Bd. dirs. Newman Found., UF Found. Served from 2d lt. to maj., USAAF, 1942-46. Recipient Annual Brotherhood award Nat. Conf. Christians and Jews, Man of Year award K.C., 1965; Liberty Bell award 8th Jud. Circuit, 1971; decorated Pro Eclesia et Pontifica medal Pope Paul, 1970. Mem. Am. Bar Assn., Fla. Bar, Phi Delta Phi, Phi Kappa Phi, Alpha Tau Omega. Elk. Home: 3007 Shamrock N Tallahassee FL 32303

O'CONNOR, E. JEROME, architect; b. White Plains, N.Y., Apr. 30, 1891; s. John and Mary (Baldwin) O'C.; B.Arch., Cornell U., 1912. Designer, W. Welles Bosworth, N.Y.C., 1912-15; pvt. practice, N.Y.C., 1920-41; exec. architect J. W. O'Connor, 1926-31; asso. architect Frank H. Hutton, 1935-37; co-ordinating architect Pentagon Bldg., Arlington, Va., 1941-42, field dir. airplane plants, 1942-44; designing architect Chem. Warfare plants, 1944-45; pvt. practice Alexandria, and Washington, 1945—; designer, architect Indsl. Mart, Washington; architect Nat. Grange Hdqrs. Bldg., Washington, Coll. Lab. Sch., Frostburg, Md. Mem. Nat. Council Archtl. Registration Bds. Registered architect, N.Y., N.J., Conn., Md., Va., D.C., Ky. Mem. Washington Bldg. Congress, N.Y. State Assn. Architects, Soc. Pentagon. A.I.A., Am. Standards Com. Indsl. Lighting, Constrn. Specifications Inst., Soc. Archtl. Historians. Club: Cornell. Address: 810 18th St NW Washington DC 20006

O'CONNOR, EDWARD JOSEPH, elec. engr.; b. Callicoon, N.Y., Jan. 28, 1926; s. Michael Patrick and Nellie (McEvoy) O.; A.A., St. Petersburg Jr. Coll., 1946; student U. Va., 1944; B.Indsl. Engring., U. Fla., 1949. Engring. supr. Fla. Power Corp., St. Petersburg, 1949-66; with Engring. Sales Co., Inc., St. Petersburg, 1966—, partner, 1970—. Served with USNR, 1944. Mem. I.E.E.E., Southeastern Electric Exchange, Edison Electric Inst., Kappa Alpha. Clubs: Sertoma (pres., chmn. bd. 1965-66), Sunset Country (St. Petersburg), St. Petersburg Yacht. Home: 1935 11th St N St Petersburg FL 33704 Office: PO Box 11387 St Petersburg Fl 33733

O'CONNOR, EDWIN MORTON, III, lawyer; b. Dallas, June 21, 1929; s. Edwin Morton and Mary Elizabeth (Hackel) O.; student Tulane U., 1946-50; B.A., So. Meth. U., 1951; LL.B., Tex. U., 1957; m. Lilian Weir, Aug. 4, 1954; children—Edwin Morton, IV, John K. Admitted to Tex. bar, 1957; since practiced in Lubbock; mem. firm East & O'Connor, Lubbock, 1966—. Vice pres., dir. O'Connor & Co., Dallas, 1965—. Counsel Lubbock County Republican party, 1959-63. Served to maj. USMCR, 1951-54. Home: 3018 21st St Lubbock TX 79410 Office: 1015 Lubbock Nat Bank Bldg Lubbock TX 79401

O'CONNOR, JEAN SMITH (MRS. GERALD FRANCIS O'CONNOR), author; b. nr. Hamlin, W.Va.; d. Oscar French and Florence (Adkins) Smith; grad. W.Va. Bus. Coll.; m. Gerald Francis O'Connor, Aug. 3, 1929; children—Joan Florence (Mrs. Alfred James Dickerson, Jr.), Peggy Frances (Mrs. Lanny J. Pixley), Geraldine Phyllis (Mrs. Philip James Barrons). Mem. editorial staff Echoes of W.Va., Charleston, 1952-56; v.p., sec.-treas. Line Creek Coal Corp., Charleston, 1962-66. Mem. W.Va. Poetry Soc. (state pres. 1967, 68-69), Nat. League Am. Pen Women (state pres. 1964-66, nat. poetry chmn. 1970-72), Cath. Daus. Am., Huntington Poetry Guild, Poetry Soc. Va. Democrat. Roman Catholic. Author: The Quiet Hills, 1963. Home: Plaza E 4300 N Ocean Blvd Fort Lauderdale FL 33308

O'CONNOR, PATRICK REGAN, physician; b. Louisville, Mar. 5, 1937; s. Patrick John Regan and Blanche (Nageleisen) O'C.; B.A., Vanderbilt U., 1959, M.D., 1962; m. Donna Nelson, Aug. 1, 1959; children—Patrick Regan III, Kelly Nelson. Intern U. Miss. Hosp., 1962-63; resident in ophthalmology U. Louisville, 1963-66, chief resident, 1966, asst. prof. ophthalmology, 1969-71, asso. prof., 1971—; dir. retina service Ky. Lions Eye Research Inst., 1969—; cons. Louisville Gen. Hosp., Children's Hosp., Jewish Hosp., VA Hosp., Irland Army Hosp. Fellow Cornell U., 1968-69. Served to capt. M.C., USAF, 1966-68. Diplomate Am. Bd. Ophthalmology. Mem. Am. Acad. Ophthalmology, Louisville Acad. Ophthalmology, Jefferson County Med. Soc., Ky. Med. Assn., Retina Soc. Am., Soc. Heed Fellows, Am. Coll. Surgs. Republican. Catholic. Club: Louisville Boat. Contbr. articles to med. jours. Home: 1021 Alta Vista Rd Louisville KY 40205 Office: 301 E Walnut St Louisville KY 40202

O'CONNOR, ROBERT DORMAN, JR., hosp. adminstr.; b. Vicksburg, Miss., Oct. 8, 1935; s. Robert Dorman and Rubye Austin (King) O'C.; student Hinds Jr. Coll., 1957-59; B.S., U. So. Miss., 1960, M.S., 1961; m. Barbara Ann Williams, June 5, 1959; children—Kimberly Wynne, Leigh Shannon. Asst. dean student affairs, instr. psychology Holmes Jr. Coll., Goodman, Miss., 1961-64; with div. Rehab., Miss. Dept. Edn., 1964-65; asst. adminstr. Hinds Gen. Hosp., Jackson, Miss., 1965-68; adminstr. Rankin Gen. Hosp., Brandon, Miss., 1968—; asso. Malone & Asso., health planning cons., Jackson. Pres. Miss. Assn. Mental Health, 1972-73. Bd. dirs. Goodwill Industries, Jackson, 1966-69, Cleary Heights Assn., Cleary, Miss., 1970-73, Nat. Assn. Mental Health, 1974—, Vol. Action Council, 1973—, Family Blood Assurance Program, 1972—, United Givers Fund, 1973—. Served with AUS, 1954-57. Mem. Am. Coll. Hosp. Adminstrs., Miss. Hosp. Assn. (bd. govs), Rankin C. of C. (exec. com. 1971—). Mason, Rotarian. Contbr. articles to profl. pubs. Home: Route 5 Box 573 Florence MS 39073 Office: 350 Crossgates Blvd Brandon MS 39042

O'CONNOR, TRELYON WALDO, JR., gen. engr.; b. Clifton Forge, Va., Aug. 16, 1921; s. Trelyon Waldo and Lucy (Greene) O'C.; B.S., Va. Polytech. Inst., 1948; m. Dorothy Marie Rogers, July 6, 1952; children—Cynthia, Alice, Rosemary. Engr. Rural Electrification Adminstrn., U.S. Dept. Agr., Washington, 1948-50; engr. rep. Sears, Roebuck & Co., 1950-51; project engr. U.S. Army Mobility Equipment Research and Devel. Center, Ft. Belvoir, Va., 1953-56, chief Mech. Standards Sect. and Topographic Material Sect., 1956-66, dep. chief power engring. div., 1966-71, dep. chief electro tech. dept., 1971—. Mem. Brookland Estates Civic Assn. Panel mem. Bd. Civil Service Examiners for Scientists and Engrs., Mil. Dist. Washington. Served to capt. USAAF, 1942-46, USAF, 1951-53; lt. col. USAF Reserve. Decorated D.F.C., Air Medal with oak leaf clusters, Commendation medal. Registered profl. engr., Va. Mem. Am. Soc. Agrl. Engrs. (asso.), Va. Tech. Alumni and Student Aid Assns., Am. Contract Bridge League, Am. Standards Assn. (mem. sectional com. B-29 for power transmission chains and sprockets), Nat., Va. (dir. 1973, sec. treas. 1974) socs. profl. engrs., Soc. Am. Mil. Engrs., Res. Officers Assn., Am. Bowling Congress (pres. league 1966-67). Lutheran. Home: 5909 Pratt St Alexandria VA 22310 Office: 314 USA MERDC Fort Belvoir VA 22606

O'CONNOR, WILLIAM CHARLES, apparel co. exec.; b. Bowling Green, Ky., May 1, 1927; s. John S. and Mary (Schneider) O'C.; student Stevens Inst. Tech., 1945-46; B.S. in Accounting, Western Ky. U., 1949; LL.B., Nashville YMCA Evening Law Sch., 1958; m. Mary Margaret Campion, Apr. 7, 1951; children—Marianne, Margaret, Thomas. Staff accountant Osborn & Page, C.P.A.'s, Nashville, 1949-56; with Genesco, Inc., Nashville, 1956—, asst. v.p., 1965—; admitted to Tenn. bar, 1958. Served with USNR, 1945-46. Mem. Am., Tenn. bar assns., Serra Internat. K.C. Home: 117 Groome St Nashville TN 37205 Office: 111 7th Av N Nashville TN 37202

O'DANIEL, H. EDWARD, JR., lawyer; b. Bowling Green, Ky., Mar. 12, 1938; s. Henry Edward and Lucy Marie (Robinson) O'D.; B.S., Xavier U., 1960; J.D., U. Louisville, 1968; m. Margaret Dell Thompson, June 18, 1960; children—Shannon Marie, Patrick Brian. Trainee Kroger Co., Louisville, 1960-61; advt. mgr. Brown & Williamson Tobacco Corp., Louisville, 1963-67, purchasing agt., 1967-70; admitted to Ky. bar, 1969; pvt. practice law, Springfield, Ky., 1970—. Counsel Springfield State Bank, 1970—; city atty., Springfield, 1970—. Bd. dirs. Washington County Assn. Mentally Retarded, 1970—; trustee St. Catherine Jr. Coll., Springfield, 1973—. Served with AUS, 1960-62. Mem. Springfield-Washington C. of C. (dir. 1971—, pres. 1972). Democrat. Roman Catholic. Rotarian. Club: Lincoln Country (pres. 1973) (Springfield). Home: 229 Virginia Av Springfield KY 40069 Office: 108 W Main St Springfield KY 40069

ODDO, PAUL CHARLES, pub. co. exec.; b. Bklyn., Feb. 9, 1915; s. Antonio and Pauline (Signorelli) O.; B.B.A., St. John's U., 1936; M.A., Columbia, 1937; m. Genevieve Grillo, Dec. 7, 1946; children—Paul, Charles, Warren. Tchr. pvt. schs., N.Y.C., 1936-40; with Grolier Soc., Inc., N.Y.C., 1942-58, v.p. sch. and library div., 1950-58; cons. to publishers, 1958-64; pres. Oddo Publishing, Inc., Fayetteville, Ga., 1964—. Served with USNR, 1942-46. Mem. A.L.A., Am. Booksellers Assn., Iota Alpha Sigma. Roman Catholic. Rotarian. Home: Beauregard Blvd Fayetteville GA 30214 Office: Storybook Acres Fayetteville GA 30214

ODELL, ARTHUR GOULD, JR., architect; b. Concord, N.C., Nov. 22, 1913; s. Arthur Gould and Grace (Patterson) O.; student Duke, 1930-31; B.Arch., Cornell U., 1935; student Atelier Debat-Ponsan, Ecole des Beaux Arts, Paris, France, 1935-36; m. Polly Robinson, Nov. 10, 1941 (div. 1950); children—William R., Alexandra; m. 2d, Mary Walker Ehringhaus, Oct. 30, 1951; 1 son, Charles Alexander; stepchildren—Carroll, Michael Ehringhaus. Prin. Odell Assos., Inc., Charlotte, N.C., 1940—; works include pub. schs., Charlotte Auditorium and Coliseum, 1955, Charlotte Pub. Library and Belk's Dept. Store, 1956, Charlotte Meml. Hosp., 1960, St. Andrews Presbyn. Coll. of Laurinburg, N.C., 1960, Whitaker Plant, Reynolds Industries, Winston-Salem, N.C., 1961, Balt. Civic Center, 1962, Burlington Industries Research Center, 1965, also corporate hdqrs., Greensboro, N.C., 1971, Spring Mills Offices, Lancaster, S.C., 1969, Hampton Rds. Coliseum, Hampton, Va., 1970, Charlotte Civic Center, 1973; vis. critic Cornell U. Coll. Architecture, 1955-56. Commr., Charlotte Planning Bd., 1951-53; chmn. Charlotte Bldg. Code Bd. Appeals, 1957, N.C. Bldg. Code Council, 1957-59; mem. N.C. Emergency Resources Planning Com., 1963; chmn. adv. com. Environmental Quality Council Charlotte-Mecklenburg, 1972. Mem. various nat. archtl. award juries. Chmn., Potomac Planning Task Force, Dept. of Interior, 1965-67; pres. Charlotte Community Concert Assn., 1952; pres. trustees Mint Museum Art, Charlotte, 1959-63; mem. council Cornell U., 1960-62, 65; bd. dirs. N.C. Archtl. Found., 1954-64, Central Charlotte Assn., 1959—. Served to lt. col., C.E., AUS, 1941-45. Decorated grand ofcl. Orden del Sol del Peru; recipient of School Exec. design award, 1953, Progressive Architecture citation, 1955, 60, Copper and Brass Research Assn. design award, 1960, McGraw Hill Pub. Co. best plant competition award, 1962, Instns. Mag. award, 1964, and others. Fellow A.I.A. (com. Sch. bldgs. 1955-58, nat. dir. 1959-62, pres. N.C. chpt. 1953-55; award of merit 1954, 57, South Atlantic award of merit 1956, N.C. chpt. award merit 1955, 56, 57, 61, 62, 68, 69, 71, nat. 2d v.p. 1962-63, 1st v.p. 1963-64, pres. 1964-65); hon. mem. nat. archtl. orgns. Peru, Chile, Colombia, Venezuela, Brazil, Can., Philippines, Mexico; mem. Charlotte C. of C. (dir. 1963-64, 66-68, dir. at large 1970), L'Ogive, Scabbard and Blade, Alpha Tau Omega. Methodist. Clubs: Charlotte Country, City (director 1958-61), Quail Hollow Country, Charlotte Athletic (Charlotte); Cabarrus Country (Concord). Home: 2149 Sherwood Av Charlotte NC 28207 Office: 102 W Trade St Charlotte NC 28202

O'DELL, JAMES WALTER, supt. schs.; b. Camden, Ark., Feb. 12, 1927; s. Clyde and Alma (Tate) O'D.; B.A., Henderson State Coll., 1950, M.S. in Edn., 1959; Ed.D., East Coast U., 1972; m. Vivian Tollifson, Nov. 25, 1948; children—Sharon, Elaine, Ginger, Scott. Tchr. pub. schs. Mena, Ark., 1950; prin. Tinsman (Ark.) Sch. Dist., 1951-57; supt. Thornton (Ark.) Sch. Dist., 1957—. Mayor Thornton, 1967—. Scoutmaster De Soto Area Council, 1958—. Served with AUS, 1945-47. Mem. Am. Legion (comdr., 1968—), N.E.A., Ark. Edn. Assn., Am. Assn. Sch. Adminstrs., Phi Delta Kappa. Lion. Address: School St Thornton AR 71766

ODELL, JOAN ELIZABETH, lawyer; b. Jo Davies County, Ill., May 3, 1932; d. Peter Emerson and Olive Isabelle (Bonnet) Odell; A.B. cum laude, U. Miami, 1956, J.D., 1958; children—Dominique Rosalyn, Nicole Laurienne (adopted). Admitted to Fla. bar, 1958, D.C. bar, 1974; trial atty. U.S. SEC, 1959-60; asst. state atty., Dade County, Fla., 1960-64; asst. county atty., Dade County, 1964-70; county atty., Palm Beach County, Fla., 1970-71; regional counsel U.S. Environmental Protection Agy., Region IV, Atlanta, 1971-73; asso. gen. counsel U.S. Environmental Protection Agy., Washington, 1973—. Bd. dirs. Mental Health Assn. Palm Beach County. Named among Outstanding Young Women in Am., 1965. Mem. Fed. Fla., Dade County, Palm Beach County bar assns., Nat. Assn. County Civil Attys. (sec.-treas.), Fla. Assn. County Attys. (dir.), Am. Assn., U. Women. Home: 2539 S Bayshore Dr Miami FL 33133 Office: Waterside Mall 401 M St SW Washington DC 20460

O'DELL, ROGER GENE, biologist, govt. ofcl.; b. Clinchco, Va., May 14, 1936; s. Richard Marvin and Macie Alice (Wilborn) O'D.; student Clinch Valley Coll., 1955-56; B.S., East Tenn. State U., 1959; m. Judith Mason Snead, June 16, 1962; children—Kelly Louise, Dennis Milton. Research biologist FDA, Washington, 1962—. Served with AUS, 1959-62. Mem. Am. Inst. Biol. Scis., A.A.A.S., Assn. Ofcl. Analytical Chemists, Soc. Exptl. Biology and Medicine. Home: 1216 N Taylor Arlington VA 22201 Office: 200 C Washington DC 20204

ODEN, FARRIS COTTRELL, ins. co. exec.; b. Amity, Ark., June 30, 1905; s. Thomas B. and Sarah E. (Walker) O.; student Okla. U., 1927; m. Dorothy McCown, Nov. 5, 1927; children—Bob F., Richard Lee, Jon T., Rebecca Ann (Mrs. Jim Weatherall). Ins. agt. Panhandle Ins. Agy., 1930-51; exec. v.p. Western Nat. Life Ins. Co., Amarillo, Tex., 1952-59, pres., 1960-71, chmn. bd., 1971—; v.p., dir. Southwestern Investment Co., 1944—; dir. Security Fed. Savs. and Loan Assn. Pres., United Fund, 1967; pres. Llano Estacado council Boy Scouts Am., 1962-64; active YMCA. Trustee, McMurray Coll., Abilene, Tex., 1970-71. Mem. C. of C. (bd. dirs.; pres. 1969). Rotarian (pres. 1937-38, dist. gov. 1972-73). Club: Amarillo Country. Home: 2314 Harmony St Amarillo TX 79106 Office: Box 871 205 E 10 St Amarillo TX 79105

ODEN, KENNETH, lawyer; b. Yoakum, Tex., Sept. 5, 1923; s. J.D. and Lena (Upchurch) O.; student Kilgore Jr. Coll., 1941-42, U. Tulsa, 1943, Navarra Coll., 1946; A.B., LL.B., Baylor U., 1950; m. Frances Walker, May 29, 1948; children—Kenneth, Theresa Lynne, Patricia Marie. Admitted to Tex. bar, 1950, since practiced in Alice, Tex.; mem. firm Perkins, Davis, Oden & Warburton, 1960—. Sec.-treas., dir., mem. John G. and Marie Stella Kennedy Meml. Found., 1963—. Served to capt. USAAF, 1944-46; ETO. Decorated Air medal with 5 oak leaf clusters. Mem. Com. on Mexican-Am. Law Relations, Am., Coastal Bend (past pres.) bar assns., State Bar Tex. (past mem. prosecuting grievance com.), Am. Judicature Soc., Tex. Assn. Def. Counsel. Baptist. Home: 1821 Walker St Alice TX 78332 Office: 500 E Main St Alice TX 78332

ODEN, WALDO TALMAGE, JR., lawyer; b. Altus, Okla., May 17, 1929; s. Waldo Talmage and Lily (Clark) O.; B.A., U. Okla., 1950, LL.B., 1952, J.D., 1970; m. Rebecca Jane Hazlitt, Mar. 25, 1951; children—Waldo Talmage III, Timothy Patrick, Amy Germaine, Jonathan Andrew. Admitted to Okla. bar, 1952. U.S. Supreme Ct. bar, 1960; practiced in Altus, 1952—; mem. firm Robinson & Oden, 1952-53, Oden & Oden, 1954-67; mng. partner Oden, Oden & Derryberry, 1967—; asst. atty. Jackson County, 1953-54. Dir. Farmers & Mchts. Bank. Instr. bus. law Altus Coll., 1956-59; instr. criminology Altus AFB, 1958; mem. Okla. Jud. Nominating Commn., 1967-71. Dir. Jackson County Civil Def., 1959-68; chmn. Kicking Bird dist. Boy Scouts Am., 1969—; del. Methodist Jurisdictional Confs., 1964, 66, 68, 70, Methodist Gen. Confs., 1964; 68; sec. exec. com. Methodist Series of Protestant Hour, 1968—; mem. exec. com. W.W. and Rosa Woodworth Estate; pres. U. Okla. Wesley Found., 1947, Okla. Methodist Student Movement, 1948. Campaign chmn. Jackson County Democratic Com., 1954-60. Trustee, Altus Library Bd., 1965-72. Mem. Am., Okla., Jackson County bar assns., Am., Okla. trial lawyers assns., Phi Delta Phi. Methodist (chmn. ofcl. bd. 1960-61. Mason, Rotarian (pres. 1959-60). Mem. staff Okla. Law Rev., 1950-52. Home: 913 E Elm St Altus OK 73521 Office: PO Drawer J 209 N Hudson St Altus OK 73521

ODLAND, LURA M(AE), coll. dean; b. Morgantown, W.Va., Nov. 22, 1921; d. Theodore E. and R. Elizabeth (Aamodt) Odland; B.S., U. R.I., 1943, D.Sc., 1969; M.S., U. Conn., 1945; Ph.D. (fellow 1947-50) U. Wis., 1950. Instr. foods and nutrition U. Conn., 1945; nutritionist com. on food composition, food and nutrition bd., NRC, 1945-47; asst. U. Wis., 1947-50; asso. prof. Mont. State Coll. and Agrl. Expt. Sta., 1950-55; adminstr. State Expt. Stas. div. U.S. Dept. Agr., Washington, 1955-59; dean Coll. Home Econs., U. Tenn., 1959—, dir. home sci. under ICA in India, 1959-62. Rep. of U.S. Dept. Agr. to Internat. Congress of Nutrition, 1957, 1966. Fellow A.A.A.S., Am. Pub. Health Assn.; mem. Am. Inst. Nutrition, Am. Chem. Soc., Am. Home Econs. Assn., Tenn. Edn. Assn., Am. Dietetic Assn., Tenn. Home Econs. Assn. (pres. 1964-66), Inst. Food Technologists, Sigma Xi (chpt. pres. 1965-66), Phi Kappa Phi, Omicron Nu. Author numerous tech. publs. Office: Coll Home Econs U Tenn Knoxville TN 37916

ODOM, FRANK LEE, supt. schs.; b. Granby, Mo., Jan. 3, 1926; s. John Thomas and Florence Annie (Miller) O.; B.S., U. Ark., 1949, M.S., 1953; m. Janice Fern Turner, June 29, 1958; children—David Lee, Dana Arnold, Frances Diane. Math. tchr. Gruver (Tex.) High Sch., 1954-56; supt. schs. Miami (Tex.) Ind. Sch. Dist., 1956-59; high sch. prin. Wellman (Tex.) Ind. Sch. Dist., 1959-66, supt. schs., 1966—. Served with AUS, 1944-45. Decorated Combat Inf. badge. Mem. Am., Tex. assns. sch. adminstrs., Tex. Tchrs. Assn. (pres. Terry County unit), Nat. Assn. Secondary Sch. Prins. Methodist. Lion. Home: PO Box 66 Wellman TX 79378 Office: PO Box 68 Wellman TX 79378

ODOM, FREDERICK MARION, JR., utilities exec.; b. Bastrop, La., Jan. 7, 1910; s. Frederic Marion and Emma Inez (Scogin) O.; A.B., Centenary Coll. La., 1929; student Tulane U., 1929-31; m. Betty Hugh Watkins, Sept. 20, 1941; children—Fred Marion III, Ellen Lacy, Mark Watkins. Stenographer, Supreme Ct. of La., New Orleans, 1931-36; with Pennzoil Co., subsidiaries and predecessor firms, 1936—, beginning as laborer, successively clk., sr. clk., sec. to pres., 1947-57, v.p., 1957—; v.p. Pennzoil Producing Co. subsidiary. Served as radio operator USAAF, World War II, Mem. Kappa Alpha. Baptist. Home: 5959 Creswell Rd Shreveport LA 71106 Office: 1525 Fairfield Av Shreveport LA 71101

ODOM, GUY LEARY, physician; b. New Orleans, May 20, 1911; s. Guy Leroy and Marion (Brown) O.; M.D., Tulane U., 1933; m. Suzanne Price, Aug. 19, 1933 (dec. Nov. 1965); children—Linda (Mrs. Wesley Cook), Carolyn (Mrs. Terry H. Little), Guy Leary; m. 2d, Mataline Nye, Dec. 29, 1968. Intern, resident E.La. State Hosp., Jackson, 1933-37; practice medicine, specializing in neurol. surgery, Montreal, Que., Can., 1937-42, New Orleans, 1942-43, Durham, N.C. 1943—; instr. Montreal Neurol. Inst., 1937-42; asso. in surgery La. State U., 1942-43; faculty Duke U. Med. Sch., 1943—, prof. neurosurgery, 1950—, chmn. dept. 1960—; cons. VA Hosp., Durham; cons. neurosurgery Watts Hosp., Durham, Womack Army Hosp., Ft. Bragg, N.C. Mem. Adv. Bd. Med. Specialists. Diplomate Am. Bd. Neurol. Surgery (sec.-treas. 1964-70, chmn. 1970). Mem. A.M.A., Pan Am. Med. Assn., N.C., Durham-Orange County med. socs., World Fedn. Neurol. Surgery, Am. Acad. Neurol. Surgeons (pres. 1967), Soc. Neurol. Surgeons (pres. 1970), Am. Surg. Assn., So. Neurol. Soc. (pres. 1968), Harvey Cushing Soc. (pres. 1971-72). Home: 2812 Chelsea Circle Durham NC 27707 Office: Duke U Med Center Durham NC 27710

ODOM, MRS. JAMES M. (ELLEN PAYNE ODOM), civic worker; b. Blossburg, Ala., July 5, 1906; d. Turner Ashby and Annie Ellen (Ancell) Payne; A.B. summa cum laude, Judson Coll., 1923-26; M.A., U. Ala., 1931; B.S., Howard Coll., 1932; m. James Malcolm Odom, Aug. 25, 1935. Tchr. French, Spanish, Italian, Judson Coll., 1926-30; U. Ala., 1930-31; head dept. romance langs. Norman Coll., Norman Park, Ga., 1933-35. Chmn. Colquitt County March of Dimes, 1953; sec. Colquitt County Civic Music Assn., 1959-65; mem. adv. bd. Ga. Extension Service, 1957-63; dir. Ga. Tb Assn. (mem. exec. com. 1963-66, sec. 1965-66), Moultrie YMCA; adviser 4-H Club, 1936—, state adviser, 1961-62; pres. Colquitt County Tb Assn., 1961-62. Mem. 2d Congl. dist. Ga. Democratic Exec. Com., 1965-66. Trustee Colquitt-Thomas Regional Library, 1963-71, mem. regional bd., 1964-71. Named Colquitt County Woman of Year, 1961. Mem. Friend of Library, League Women Voters, U.D.C. (Ga. div. v.p. 1968-70, parliamentarian 1970— div. exec. bd. 1948—), Huguenots (nat. corr. sec. 1948-49), D.A.R. Club: Woman's (pres. 1957-58). Research Colquitt County, Ga. A Field Lab. for Study and Experiment in Intergovtl. Relations. Author: A History of the Library of Moultrie, Georgia, 1966. Home: Odomfarms RFD 5 Moultrie GA 31768

ODOM, JOEL MARTIN, dentist; b. Muskogee, Okla., July 1, 1936; s. Martin and Emma (Prater) O.; B.S., Southeastern State U., 1957; D.D.S., U. Tenn., 1960; m. Brenda Tabbytite, Sept. 10, 1969; 1 dau., Francine Melony. Pvt. practice dentistry, Okmulgee, Okla., 1961-72, Tulsa, 1972—. Mem. Am., Okla. dental assns., Tulsa County Dental Soc., Okmulgee C. of C. (past dir.), Tau Kappa Epsilon, Psi Omega. Home: 6102 S Fulton St Tulsa OK 74135 Office: 4720 E 51st St Tulsa OK 74135

ODOM, ROY HARRIS, state ofcl.; b. Alexandria, La., Oct. 14, 1906; s. George Andrew and Mary Alma (Deaton) O.; student La. Tech. Coll., 1925-29, La. State U., 1941; m. Willie Mai Tolar, Oct. 10, 1934; children—Roy H., William McBride, Elsa (Mrs. G. W. West). Tech. reports editor State La., Baton Rouge, 1939-52; program dir. La. Forestry Commn., Baton Rouge, 1952—. Owner Gulf South Advt. Agy., Baton Rouge, 1947—. Vice pres. League Am. Wheelmen, 1970—; pres. Baton Rouge Cycle Club, 1969, 71—. Mem. State Information Reps. (pres. 1971), Advt. Splty. Sales Promotion Assn., Splty. Advt. Assn. Internat., Internat. Assn. Bus. Communicators, Pub. Relations Soc. Am. (accredited 1969—). Mason. Club: Press. Home: 558 Nelson Dr Baton Rouge LA 70808 Office: 5150 Florida St Baton Rouge LA 70815

ODOM, WILLIAM ROSS, ednl. data systems adminstr.; b. Oveida, Fla., Jan. 9, 1935; s. Ray Ross and Mamie Irene (Wynn) O.; B.S., Fla. State U., 1956, M.S., 1957, Ed.D. (Kellogg Jr. Coll. Leadership fellow), 1968; m. Janice Patricia Grosser, June 25, 1960; children—Jennifer, Michael. Prof. marine biology and zoology Broward Jr. Coll., Ft. Lauderdale, Fla., 1963-66; asst. to pres. St. Petersburg (Fla.) Jr. Coll., 1968-71; coordinator Planning, Programing, Budgeting System Devel., div. community colls., Tallahassee, Fla., 1971—. Cons. to state agys. and colls., 1968—. Mem. Suncoast Active Volunteers for Ecology., 1971—, YMCA. Mem. Fla. Assn. Ednl. Data Processing. Democrat. Baptist. Author: (with Jerry Leonard) Accounting Manual for Fla.'s Pub. Jr. Colls., 1968, An Approach to Automating a Cost Analysis System, 1971. Home and Office: 3402 Sharer Rd Tallahasse FL 32203

O'DONNELL, HERBERT, constrn. co. exec.; b. New Orleans, Nov. 10, 1922; s. Herbert and Agnes (O'Brien) O'D.; B.E. in Civil Engring., Tulane U., 1943; postgrad. naval architecture, U. Mich., 1944; m. Elsebeth Lendal, Apr. 12, 1961; 1 son, Michael. Project mgr. Haase Constrn. Co., New Orleans, 1952-64; v.p. Claude Hogan Constrn. Co., New Orleans, 1965-72; pres. Herbert O'Donnell, Inc., New Orleans, 1973—. Vice chmn. New Orleans Lakefront Devel. Com., since 1970-73. Served to lt. comdr. USNR, 1943-46, 50-52. Registered profl. engr., La. Mem. Tau Beta Pi, Omicron Delta Kappa. Club: Southern Yacht (commodore 1972-73). Home: 1228 Arabella St New Orleans LA 70118 Office: 242 Focis St New Orleans LA 70005

O'DONOGHUE, DON HORATIO, orthopaedic surgeon; b. Storm Lake, Ia., Nov. 13, 1901; s. James Horatio and Janet (Fairbairn) O'D.; student Buena Vista Coll., Storm Lake, Ia., 1919-20; B.S., Ia. U., 1923, M.D., 1926; D.S., Morningside Coll., 1944; m. Ragnhild Christensen, Jan. 4, 1928; 1 son, Donald Patrick. Surgery resident Ia. U. Hosps., 1926-27; orthopaedic surgery resident Okla. U. Hosp., 1927-30; gen. practice specializing in orthopaedic surgery, Oklahoma City, 1930—; prof., chmn. emeritus dept. orthopaedic surgery and fractures U. Okla. Med. Sch., chmn. bd. trustees U. Hosp.; chief orthopaedics St. Anthony's Hosp., Vets Hosp.; mem. staff Presbyn., Mercy, Bapt. hosps. Chmn. profl. adv. com. Dept. Pub. Welfare; mem. health and hosp. planning Community Council. Bd. dirs. YMCA; trustee United Fund. Recipient Distinguished Service award U. Okla., 1969, U. Ia., 1971, Wisdom award, 1971; named to Okla. Hall of Fame, 1970. Fellow Internat. Coll. Surgeons, Sicot, A.C.S.; mem. Am. Acad. Orthopaedic Surgeons, Am. Orthopaedic Assn. (pres.), A.M.A., So., Okla. State, Oklahoma County med. socs., Clin. Orthopaedic Soc., Western Surg. Assn., S.W. Surg. Congress, Pan-Pacific Surg. Soc., Mid-Central State Orthopaedic Soc., Am. Assn. for Surgery of Trauma, Am. Trauma Soc., (founding mem.), Am. Orthopaedic Soc. Sports Medicine (founding mem., first pres.). Author: Treatment of Injuries to Athletes, 1962, rev. edit., 1970; also articles in profl. jours. Editorial bd. Orthopaedic Review. Home: 1403 Glenwood Av Oklahoma City OK 73116 Office: 1111 N Lee Oklahoma City OK 73103

ODUM, WILLIAM EUGENE, educator; b. Athens, Ga., Oct. 1, 1942; s. Eugene Pleasants and Martha Ann (Huff) O.; B.S., U. Ga., 1964; Ph.D., Inst. Marine Scis., U. Miami, 1970; m. Maria Elizabeth Bagatta, Nov. 18, 1972. Postdoctoral fellow Inst. Resource Ecology, U. B.C. (Can.), Vancouver, 1970-71; asst. prof. dept. environmental scis. U. Va., Charlottesville, 1971—. Bd. dirs. Piedmont Environmental Council, 1973—. Mem. Inst. Fisheries Research Biologists, Ecol. Soc. Am., Am. Soc. Limnology and Oceanography. Home: 763 Madison Av Charlottesville VA 22903

O'DWYER, THOMAS ALOYSIUS, elec. co. exec.; b. Texarkana, Ark., July 21, 1925; s. Thomas A. and Martha (Ryan) O'D.; B.S. in Engring., Texas A. and M. Coll., 1949; m. Jeanne B. Bird, Aug 2, 1950; children—Ann, Kay, Tom, George, Bill. Engr., Southwestern Gas & Electric Co., Texarkana, 1943-44; estimator Ling Electric (now Ling-Oliver-O'Dwyer Electric, Inc.), Dallas, 1949-51, v.p., 1952-57, pres., 1962-73, chmn. bd., chief exec. officer, 1973—, dir. Richardson Heights Bank. Active Boy Scouts Am.; chmn. trustees Jesuit Prep. Sch., Dallas. Served with USNR, 1944-46. Mem. Tex. Mfrs. Assn., Constrn. Employers Council (past pres.), Young Pres. Orgn. Nat. Elec. Contractors Assn. (past pres., dir. N.E. Texas chpt.). Roman Catholic. K.C. (4 deg.). Club: Aggie (dir., exec. com.). Home: 3843 Shenandoah St Dallas TX 75205 Office: 727 S Central Expressway Richardson TX 75080

OEBEN, RUDOLPH WILHELM, chem. co. engr.; b. Flushing, N.Y., May 27, 1938; s. Anton and Erna Louise (Klein) O.; B.S. in Civil Engring., Duke, 1960; M.S. in San. Engring. (USPHS grantee), U. N.C., 1965; m. Alice Dotson Oeben, June 6, 1961; children—Caroline Ennis, Alison Irene. Devel. engr. Union Carbide Corp., South Charleston, W.Va., 1965-68, dept. head Union Carbide Caribe, Inc., Ponce, P.R., 1968-73, dir. environmental affairs, San Juan, P.R., 1973—. Treas. Guaypao Conservation Assn., 1971—, pres., 1970-71. Bd. dirs. Caribbean Sch. Served to capt. USAF, 1960-63. Registered profl. engr., W.Va. Mem. P.R. Mfrs. Assn. (chmn. environmental com. 1974—), Am. Acad. Environmental Engrs., Water Pollution Control Fedn., Lambda Chi Alpha. Lutheran. Contbr. articles to profl. jours. Home: 1931 Rufino Tamayo Borinquen Gardens Rio Piedras PR 00926 Office: Union Carbide Puerto Rico Banco de Ponce Bldg Hato Rey PR 00918

OEHLER, HERBERT EMIL, author; b. Fredericksburg, Tex., June 11, 1904; s. Adolph Emanuel and Susie Sophia (Heimann) O.; student Draughon's Bus. Coll., San Antonio, 1923-24, LaSalle Extension U., Chgo., 1950-51; m. Golda Walls, Jan. 19, 1933. Teller, First State Bank, Kerrville, Tex., 1924-40; chief purchasing sect. QMC, Camp Hulen, Tex., 1940-42; chief clk, QMC, Camp Hood, Tex., 1942-43; dep. collector Internal Revenue Service, Temple, Tex., 1944; prin. Herbert E. Oehler, C.P.A., Temple, 1944-55; asst. sec. Griggs Equipment Inc., Belton, Tex., 1955-69; writer short stories and articles, 1970—; contbr. short stories to Tex. Freemason, 1972-73; short stories reprinted in Masonic publs., Ore. and Ia., 1973; Contbr. to Hill Country mag. supplement Kerrville Daily Times, 1972-73. Mem. community facilites group Citizen's Adv. Co., Temple, Tex., 1971; chmn. accounting adv. bd. City Temple, 1965-66. Recipient 1st prize for short story in Barclay Lit. Contest, Temple, 1970; 2d prize for short story Abilene (Tex.) Writers Guild, 1973. Mem. Am. Inst. C.P.A.'s, Tex. Soc. C.P.A.'s. Republican. Methodist. Club: Toastmasters (pres. Temple 1964). Mason (K.T.), Lion (sec. Temple 1945-55). Home: 1138 Warbler Dr Kerrville TX 78028

OEHLSCHLAGER, FREDERICK KEITH, physician; b. Kansas City, Mo., Apr. 16, 1911; s. Henry George and Lillie Marie (Kaltenbach) O.; A.A., Kansas City Jr. Coll., 1930; B.S., U. Kan., 1933; M.D., 1935; m. Helen Mae Poulson, May 10, 1935 (dec. 1960); children—Richard, Susan, Robert; m. 2d, Jimmie Nell Lietzow, Mar. 10, 1965; stepchildren—Cynthia, Matthew, Celeste, Colleen. Intern U.S. Marine Hosp., New Orleans, 1935-36; pvt. practice Lees Summit, Mo., 1936, Yale, Okla., 1936-51, Odessa, Tex., 1951—; chief of staff Cushing Meml. Hosp., Okla., 1950-51; mem. staff Med. Center Hosp., Odessa, 1951—, chmn. dept. obstetrics and gynecology, 1962-63, 72-73; sec. Permian Basin Investment Corp.; founder, sec.-treas., med. dir. Permian Basin Life Ins. Co., 1954-63. Med. dir., mem. bd. Permian Basin Planned Parenthood, 1971—. Pres. Permian Playhouse, Inc., Odessa, 1962-64; dir. Permian Basin Ballet Assn., 1968-70, Midland-Odessa Symphony Assn., 1968-71; mayor City of Yale, Okla., 1948-50; chmn. Ector County-City of Odessa, Tex. Dept. Parks and Recreation, 1954-62; chmn. Ector County Child Welfare Bd., 1952-56; dir. Tri-County Group Foster Home Bd., 1951-57, A.R.C., 1954-57; pres. Permian Basin Civic Ballet Assn., 1969-70, Midland-Odessa Symphony Assn., 1969-70. Pres. Payne-Pawnee County Med. Soc. (Okla.), 1944. Mem. Am. Cancer Soc. (dir. 1955, Ector County pres. 1967-68, dist. dir. 1968—), Odessa C. of C., Am., Tex. med. assns., Andrews, Ector and Midland County Med. Soc., Pan-Pacific Surg. Assn., West Tex. Soc. Obstetrics and Gynecology, Am. Soc. Study Fertility, Internat. Fertility Assn., Internat. Soc. Obstetrics and Gynecology, Am. Hemercallis Soc., Am. Iris Soc., Bromeliad Soc., Cymbidium Soc., Indoor Light Gardening Soc., Nat. Chrysanthemum Soc., Am. Begonia Soc., Am. Daffodil Soc., Am. Orchid Soc., Am. Gesneriad Soc., Am. Camilla Soc. Methodist. Mason (Shriner). Clubs: Odessa Country, Rotary (pres. 1963-64), Knife and Fork, Men's Garden (pres. 1970-71). Home: 316 Casa Grande Odessa TX 79760 Office: Sherwood Med Center 42d and Everglade Sts Odessa TX 79762

OETTINGER, ELMER ROSENTHAL, JR., educator, lawyer; b. Wilson, N.C., Nov. 24, 1913; s. Elmer Rosenthal and Pearl (Lichtenstein) O.; A.B. in English, U. N.C., 1934, J.D., 1939, M.A. in Dramatic Arts, 1952, Ph.D. in English, 1966; m. Mary Elizabeth Brown, Sept. 22, 1940; children—Elmer R., Kenneth Brown. Admitted to N.C. bar, 1940; staff Inst. Govt., Chapel Hill, N.C., 1939-41; atty., Wilson, N.C., 1941-42, 46-47; radio commentator WGTM radio sta., Wilson, 1941-42, 46-47; news dir. WNAO radio sta., Raleigh, N.C., 1948-51; instr. English, U. N.C., Chapel Hill, 1952-56, lectr. radio, TV and motion pictures, 1956-60, prof. pub. law and govt., also asst. dir. Inst. Govt., 1960—. Cons. Task Force on Criminal Justice and Pub., 1968-71, White House Conf. on Aging, 1971; mem. Gov.'s Study Commn. on Automobile Ins., 1971—; commr. Nat. Conf. on Uniform State Laws, 1973—. Served to lt. USNR, 1943-45. Mem. Am., N.C. State, N.C. bar assns., Soc. Cinema Studies (nat. sec. 1960-61), Phi Beta Kappa. Editor: Popular Govt. Mag., 1962—. Home: 58 Oakwood Dr Chapel Hill NC 27514

OGDON, DONALD POTTER, psychologist; b. Oak Park, Ill., July 26, 1923; s. Glenn H. and Elizabeth (McDonald) O.; B.S., U. Ill., Urbana, 1949; M.A., U. Tex., 1950; Ph.D., U. Mo., 1955; m. Catherine Hatfield Ogdon, Jan. 15, 1966; children—Glenn Scott, Donald Gregory. Instr. psychologist U. Mo., 1953-54; psychologist Mo. State Sch., Marshall, Mo., 1954-55; asso. prof. William and Mary Coll., Richmond, Va., 1955-63; prof. Old Dominion U., Norfolk, 1963—, also chmn. dept. psychology; dir. dept. psychology Bayberry Hosp., Hampton, Va., 1966—. Served to 2d lt. USAAF, 1945-46. Fellow Soc. Personality Assessment; mem. Va. Psychol. Assn. (past pres.), Am. Psychol. Assn., A.A.A.S., Sigma Xi, Psi Chi. Contbr. articles to psychol. jours. Home: 1323 Sussex Pl Norfolk VA 23508 Office: Old Dominion Univ Norfolk VA 23508

OGILBY, JOHN JOSEPH, citrus processing co. exec.; b. Ft. Lauderdale, Fla., Oct. 24, 1926; s. Thomas and Felicia (Zerman) O.; B.S., U. Fla., 1950; m. Muriel Davies, Aug. 7, 1954; children—Jack, Karen. Accountant, Ernst & Ernst, Atlanta, 1950-56; v.p., treas., dir. Tropicana Products, Inc., Bradenton, Fla., 1956—. Pres., treas. Manatee County Blood Bank, 1962-68. Trustee, treas. St. Stephen's Episcopal Sch. Served with AUS, 1944-46. C.P.A., Fla. Mem. Fla. Inst. C.P.A.'s (pres. Gulf Coast chpt. 1963-64). Presbyn. (elder 1967—). Lion. Club: Country (pres., dir. 1969-70) (Bradenton, Fla.). Home: 403 N 31st St W Bradenton FL 33505 Office: PO Box 338 Bradenton FL 33505

OGLESBEE, DWIGHT CONLAN, geol. engr.; b. Virgil, Kan., Jan. 1, 1929; s. Byrd S. and Thelma (Richard) O.; B.S., U. Kan., 1953; postgrad. U. Tulsa, 1962-63; children—Dwight Byrd, Nelda Irene, Lori Ann. Mgr. tech. services Richards & Oglesbee Oil Co., Sedan, Kan., 1948-49; petroleum engr. Sinclair Oil & Gas Co., Independence, Kan., 1950-51; pvt. cons. engr., Lawrence, Kan., 1951-53; sales engr., mgr. Midland Parts & Bearings Co., Kansas City, Mo., 1953-54; engring. tech. asst. aviation gas turbine div. Westinghouse Electric Corp., Kansas City, Mo., 1954; v.p. Black Widow Uranium, Inc., Three Forks, Mont., 1954-55; pres. Oglesbee Oil Co., Sedan, 1955; with Skelly Oil Co., Sweetwater, Tex., also Tulsa, 1956—, advanced staff prodn. engr., 1965-67, sr. corrosion engr., 1967-73, tech. specialist 1—corrosion, 1973—. Cons. Plator Gra-Louise Can. Ltd., Atikokan, Ont., 1953; cons. geologist, petroleum engr., Sedan, 1954-56. Registered profl. engr., Kan. Mem. Am. Inst. Mining, Metall. and Petroleum Engrs., Am. Assn. Petroleum Geologists, Nat. Assn. Corrosion Engrs. (sect. chmn. 1964, mem. various coms., task groups 1962—, chmn. tech. symposia 1972, 73), Am. Petroleum Inst. (various task groups, coms.). Mem. Ch. of Christ. Mason. Contbr. articles to profl. jours., bulls. Inventor deep groundbed anode assemblages, deep groundbed cathodic protection devices, encapsulation systems and devices platinized niobium anodes. Home: PO Box 707 Tulsa OK 74101 Office: 1437 S Boulder St Tulsa OK 74102

OGLESBY, CLAIRE CRAIG, business exec.; b. Logansport, Ind., Oct. 20, 1917; d. Everard Granville and Clare (Fischer) Delgado; A.B. cum laude, Butler U., 1938; m. Robert Oglesby, Aug. 30, 1958. Translator in Spanish, asst. to mgr. S.Am. div. Eli Lilly & Co., Indpls., 1938-40; reservation and ticket mgr. Trans World Airlines, Indpls., 1940-46; founder, owner, pres., gen. mgr. Travel, Inc., Washington, 1946-61; regional v.p. Fugazy Travel Bur., Inc., 1961-66; owner Oglesby Enterprises, Inc., 1966-69; dir. tour and travel and govt. Southeastern div. Hiltons Hotels Corp., 1969—, cons. in travel to Quota Internat., Inc. Adm. of Am. Airlines. Mem. Nat. Assn. Life Underwriters, Nat. Fedn. Bus. and Profl. Women's Clubs, Chi Omega; ambassador mem. Trans World Airlines. Presbyn. Clubs: Quota (dir.) (Washington, D.C.); Clipper of Pan American World Airlines, Nat. Association Executives of Washington. Author: Beginning Spanish, 1938. Home: 4201 Cathedral Av NW Washington DC 20016 Office: Hilton Hotels Corp Washington DC 20009

OGLESBY, GAYLE ARDEN, geologist, govt. ofcl.; b. McGehee, Ark., Mar. 11, 1925; s. Fay and Meryl (Robinson) O.; student Tulane U., 1946-48; B.S. in Geology, U. Ark., 1950, M.S., 1952; m. Edwina Carnahan, Jan. 31, 1946; children—Julie (Mrs. Jeff Klahorst), Gayle A. Staff geologist Ark. Geol. Survey, Little Rock, 1952-55, Ohio Oil Co., Midland, Tex., 1955-56; wellsite geologist Petrobras Exploracao, Salvador, Brazil, 1957, investigator U.S. Geol. Survey, Kilgore, Tex., 1958-63; investigator-in charge, Victoria, Tex., 1963-65; regional geologist br. mineral classification, New Orleans, 1965-73, chief br. marine evaluation, Washington, 1973—. Served with USNR, 1943-46. Mem. Am. Inst. Profl. Geologists, Am. Assn. Petroleum Geologists, New Orleans Geol. Soc., Sigma Gamma Epsilon. Presbyn. (deacon 1963—). Home: 1908 Baton Dr Vienna VA 22180 Office: US Geological Survey National Center Reston VA 22092

OGLESBY, HENRY RUBE, JR., mfg. co. exec.; b. Warrensburg, Mo., Nov. 23, 1914; s. Henry Rube and Mary Ann (Shouse) O.; B.S., Central Mo. State U., 1935; B.S. in Civil Engring., Ga. Inst. Tech., 1938; m. Ruth Keith, Aug. 6, 1938; children—Robert K., Robin Jane. With Municipal Service Co., Kansas City, Mo., 1946-61, v.p., 1950-61, gen. mgr., 1950-61; self-employed in field of real estate, mergers, cons., Palm Beach, Fla., 1961-70; sec. treas. Airtronics Internat. Corp., Ft. Lauderdale, Fla., 1970-72, chmn. bd., pres., 1972—, also dir. Served with C.E., AUS, 1941-45. Registered profl. engr., Mo., Ill. Fellow Am. Soc. C.E. Mem. Am. Water Works Assn. Home: 130 Sunrise Av Palm Beach FL 33480 Office: PO Box 212 Palm Beach FL 33480

OGLETREE, WILLIAM BEECHER, civil engr.; b. Little Rock, Dec. 8, 1928; s. Lee Scotty and Dora Elizabeth (Cunningham) O.; student North Tex. Agrl. Coll., 1946-48, North Tex. State Coll., 1951; B.S. in Archtl. Engring., U. Tex., Austin, 1954; m. Sharon Kay Jones, Aug. 29, 1953; children—Carrie Kay, Leslie Scott, William Bruce. Engr., Convair Aircraft Co., Ft. Worth, 1951; engr. Tex. Hwy. Dept., Austin, 1952; student employee dept. archtl. engring. U. Tex., Austin, 1953-54, research engr., 1958-59; engr. John Broad, Gen. Contractor, Austin, 1954; cons. engr. Walter P. Moore, Houston, 1954-57; engr. Continental EMSCO, Houston, 1957; owner William B. Ogletree, Cons. Engr., Corpus Christi, Tex., 1959-69; partner Ogletree & Gunn, Engring. Cons., Corpus Christi, 1969—; instr. Del Mar Coll., Corpus Christi, 1960-61, asst. prof., 1961-63. Scuba instr. YMCA, 1962—. Served with USNR, 1948-49, USAF, 1950-51. Mem. Nat., Tex. (past treas. Nueces chpt.) socs. profl. engrs., Am. Soc. C.E. (past pres. Corpus Christi br.), Soc. Am. Mil. Engrs. (past pres. Coastal Band post). Rotarian. Author: (with Turnbow) Energy Absorbing Characteristics of Air Bags, 1958; (with Jones) Air Delivery Sampling Net; (with Giddens) Corrosion Protection of Bare Steel Piles, 1973. Patentee in field. Home: 610 Bradshaw St Corpus Christi TX 78412 Office: 1201 Agnes St Corpus Christi TX 78404

O'GORMAN, JUAN, architect, artist; b. Coyoacan, D.F., Mexico, July 6, 1905; s. Cecil Crawford and Encarnacion (O'Gorman) O'G.; Architect deg., Nat. U. Mexico, 1926; m. Helen Fowler, Aug. 7, 1940; 1 dau., Maria Elena O'Gorman, Aug. 31, 1956. With C. Obregon Santacilia and J. Villagran, architects, 1926-29; pvt. practice architecture, 1929-32; prof. sch. engring. Politechnical Inst., Mexico City, 1932—; vis. critic in architecture Yale, 1967; head dept. architecture Secretariat of Pub. Edn., 1932-35. Works include murals for Mexico City Air Port, Patzcuaro (Mich.) Library, (3 frescos) Castle Chapultepec, (fresco) Banco Internacional S.A., (fresco) Center Social Studies Unidad Independencia (all Mexico City), (mosaic) Hotel Pasada de la Mision, Taxco, Guerrero, Mexico, (mosaic) Santiago, Chile; mosaics for the Library of the University City of Mexico, Secretariat Pub. Works and Communications bldgs., Convention Center Bldg., Hemisfair, 1968. One-man show of easel paintings Palace of Fine Arts, Mexico City, 1950; paintings in permanent exhbn. Modern Mus. Art, N.Y.C., Mus. Modern Art, Mexico City. Recipient E. Sourasky prize for the arts, 1967, Nat. prize for the arts, 1972. Mem. Council of Superior Edn. and Sci. Investigation, Mexican Soc. Architects, Mexican Acad. Arts. Author booklets and mag. articles on art and architecture. Home: Jardin 88 San Angel Inn Mexico 20 DF Mexico Office: Calzada San Jeronimo 162 Mexico 20 DF Mexico

OGRAM, ERNEST WILLIAM, JR., univ. adminstr.; b. Hartford, Conn., June 29, 1928; s. Ernest William and Edith (Sickles) O.; B.A., Am. U., 1950; M.A., U. Conn., 1951; Ph.D., U. Ill., 1957; m. Antonia Santangelo, Dec. 26, 1953; 1 dau., Robbin Van Syckel. Asst. prof. Ga. State U., 1957-59, asso. prof., 1959-63, prof., 1963, dir. Inst. Internat. Bus., 1964—. Chmn. Ga. Partners of the Americas Com., 1968—. Bd. dirs. Atlanta Council for Internat. Visitors, Ga. Internat. Trade Assn., So. Consortium for Internat. Edn. Served to 1st lt. AUS, 1943-46.

Recipient Atlanta C. of C. World Trade award, 1970. Mem. Am. Assn. U. Profs. (pres. Ga. State U. chpt. 1968), Acad. of Internat. Bus. Presbyn. (elder). Editor: Essays in International Business, 1967-69, Jour. of International Business Studies, 1970—. Home: 2670 Northside Dr Atlanta GA 30305

O'HANLON, ISAAC HAWLEY, bus. exec., former state legislator; b. Fayetteville, N.C., Sept. 5, 1911; s. George Adkins and Dora (Hawley) O.; student Wake Forest Coll., 1935; m. Emma Merle Sikes, Sept. 1, 1935; children—William Hawley, Edward Willkings. Clk., RFC, Washington, 1935-44; mgr. Orkin Exterminating Co., Fayetteville, N.C., 1945-55; owner Antex Exterminating Co. Inc., Fayetteville, 1955—; mem. N.C. Ho. of Reps., 1953, 1955, 1963, 1965, 1967. Mem. N.C. State Structural Pest Control Commn., 1955-58, 1967-70. Dist. chmn. Boy Scouts Am., 1955; pres. Cumberland County (N.C.) Infantile Paralysis Assn., 1945-60, Methodist Coll. Found., Fayetteville; pres. Southeastern Speech and Hearing Services of N.C., 1973. Exec. bd. trustees Vardoll Hall Red Springs N.C.; chmn. bd. dirs. Fayetteville YMCA, 1961. Trustee E. Carolina Coll., 1953-59. Mem. (hon.) Fayetteville Ind. Light Infantry. Kiwanian (pres. Fayetteville 1959, lt. gov. 4th div.). Home: 3605 Morgantown Rd Fayetteville NC 28304 Office: 406 Washington Dr Fayetteville NC 28301

O'HARA, GEORGE EDWARD, JR., ins. co. exec.; b. Norfolk, Va., May 26, 1920; s. George Edward and Margaret Eula (Dance) O'H.; student Va. So. Coll., 1948, So. Methodist U., 1950-51, Am. Coll. Life Underwriters, 1963-67; m. Louise Thompson, Apr. 26, 1952. Agt., Life & Casualty Ins. Co., Roanoke, Va., 1946-48; with Shenandoah Life Ins. Co., 1949—, agy. sec., 1956-62, dir. spl. services, 1962-66, dir. promotion and advt., 1966-68, asst. v.p. adminstrn., 1968—. Pres., Roanoke Citizens Assn., 1953-54. Bd. dirs. Roanoke Area Tb and Respiratory Assn., 1967—. Served with USNR, 1942-46. Named Outstanding Nat. Chmn., U.S. Jr. C. of C., 1953, recipient Distinguished Service award Roanoke Jr. C. of C., 1956, C.L.U. Mem. Am. Soc. Chartered Life Underwriters (chpt. dir. 1969-70), Am. Advt. Fedn., Nat. Alliance Businessmen, Life Ins. Advertisers Assn., Advt. Club of Roanoke Valley, Pub. Relations Soc. Am. (chpt. pres. 1970), Roanoke Valley (dir. 1956-57), U.S. Jr. (nat. dir. 1953-54) chambers commerce, Beta Tau. Methodist. Mason (Shriner, Jester), Kiwanian (pres. 1970-71, v.p. local found.). Home: 1605 Wilbur Rd SW Roanoke VA 24015 Office: 2301 Brambleton Av SW Roanoke VA 24015

O'HARA, JAMES DONALD MICHAEL, textile co. exec.; b. Miami, Ariz., Sept. 6, 1936; A.B. (Jefferson Standard scholar), U. N.C., 1959; m. Francina Newkirk Dodd, Jan. 17, 1959; children—Mary, James. News editor The News Jour., Raeford, N. C., 1959-60; news editor WSOC-TV, Charlotte, N.C., 1961-63; pub. relations supr. Duke Power Co., Charlotte, 1964-66; mgr. community relations Collins & Aikman Corp., Charlotte, 1966-74, dir. pub. relations, 1974—. Pub. relations cons. Episcopal Child Care Services N.C., 1967—. Dir. pub. affairs N.C. Rep. exec. com., 1963-64. Mem. Pub. Relations Soc. Am., Internat., South Atlantic councils indsl. editors (pres. 1968-69), Am. Assn. Indsl. Editors (dir. 1968-69), Alpha Phi Omega. Episcopalian. Home: 7024 Foxworth Dr Charlotte NC 28211 Office: 701 McCullough Dr Charlotte NC 28201

O'HARA, JOHN J., lawyer; b. Rocky Mount, N.C., Oct. 1, 1922; Ph.B., Xavier U., 1947; J.D., U. Ky., 1949. Admitted to Ky. bar, 1949; commonwealth atty. 16th Jud. Dist. Ky., Covington, 1958—. Mem. Am., Ky. (pres. 1971-72, bd. govs.), Kenton County (v.p. 1956, pres. 1957) bar assns., Ky. Commonwealth Atty.'s Assn. (pres. 1964-65), Nat. Dist. Attys. Assn. (pres. 1973-74), Phi Alpha Delta. Address: Box 187 Covington KY 41011*

O'HARE, JOHN JOSEPH, research psychologist; b. Boston, Oct. 21, 1925; s. Michael J. and Catherine (Connolly) O'H.; B.S., Boston Coll., 1950; M.A., Cath. U. Am., 1952, Ph.D., 1957. Research psychologist med. research lab. USN, New London, Conn., 1953-59; human factors analyst Internat. Electric Corp., Paramus, N.J., 1959-61; head human factors dept., prin. scientist United Aircraft Corp., East Hartford, Conn., 1961-64; mem. tech. staff MITRE Corp., Arlington, Va., 1964-66; asso. prof. psychology, chmn. dept. Georgetown U., Washington, 1966-71; research psychologist Office of Naval Research 1971—. Served with USNR, 1943-46. Mem. Am., Eastern, D.C. (pres. 1974) psychol. assns., Human Factors Soc. (edn. com. 1969-71), A.A.A.S. Home: 301 G St SW Washington DC 20024

O'HAREN, JAMES FRANCIS, mfg. co. exec.; b. Shenandoah, Pa., July 21, 1930; s. James Francis and Elizabeth Margaret (Sauer) O'H.; B.S. cum laude, Mt. St. Mary's Coll., 1956; postgrad. Law Sch., U. Houston, 1962-63, LaSalle Extension U. Law Sch., 1971—; m. Florence Virginia Civiletto, May 17, 1958. Asst. sec., asst. treas. Tex. Butadiene & Chem. Internat., Ltd., Houston, 1956-59, N.Y.C., 1959-60, European Comml. mgr., Lausanne, Switzerland, 1960-62; controller Maurice Pincoffs Co., Houston, 1963-65; controller Marathon Mfg. Co., Houston, 1965-68, treas., asst. sec., 1966-71, v.p., 1968-71, sec., 1971—; sec., dir. Marathon LeTourneau Co., 1970—, Marathon Internat. Co., 1972—, Marathon LeTourneau Offshore Co., 1970—, R.G. LeTourneau, Inc., 1971—, LeTourneau Offshore, Inc., 1971—; v.p., sec. Marathon Battery Co., 1969—, Bus Funds Inc., 1969—, Marathon Leasing Co., 1970—, Marathon Metallic Bldg. Co., 1970—, Marathon Warehouse Co., 1968—, Marathon Marine Engring. Co., 1974—, others; sec., treas. Marathon Galvanizing Co., 1971—; v.p., asst. sec. Marathon Morco Co., 1968—; v.p. Ericsson Chem. Services, Inc.; sec. Marathon Shipbuilding Co., Marathon LeTourneau Sales & Service Co., Marathon RGL Co., Marathon Steel Co., George Franke Sons Co., Marathon Shipbldg. Co. (U.K.), Marathon Carey McFall Co., Marathon Mischer Co., Handy Venetian Blind Corp., Southmost Supply Co. Served with AUS, 1949-50, 50-52; Korea. Mem. U.S. Lawn Tennis Assn., Financial Execs. Inst., Am. Soc. Corp. Secs. Clubs: Doering Place Civic (v.p. 1971), Petroleum, Houston Racquet, Inwood Forest Country (Houston), Admirals (N.Y.C.). Home: 59 Williamsburg Lane Houston TX 77024 Office: Marathon Bldg 600 Jefferson St Houston TX 77002

O'HEARN, WILLIAM WILSON, judge; b. Memphis, Jan. 14, 1914; s. John Joseph and Mollie (Kehoe) O'H.; LL.B., So. Law U., 1941; m. Mary Ann Turley, Aug. 22, 1950 (dec. June 1972); 1 dau., Mary Ann (Mrs. Thomas W. Sawyer). Admitted to Tenn. bar, 1941; Tenn. asst. dist. atty.-gen. 1946-48; partner O'Hearn and Keathley, Memphis, 1957-61, Doneson, Adams, O'Hearn, Grogan and Edwards, Memphis, 1961-64, Moriarty, Fuqua & O'Hearn, Memphis, 1965-66; judge circuit ct. 15th judicial dist. Tenn., Memphis, 1966—. Pres. Memphis Pub. Affairs Forum, 1961-62; mem. sch. bd. St. Anne Sch., 1967—. Trustee Ave Maria Home for Aged, Memphis, 1957-59. Served to maj. with AUS, 1941-45. Decorated Bronze Star medal. Mem. Am., Tenn., Memphis and Shelby County (bd. dirs. 1957-60, chmn. com. discipline and ethics 1963-64, sponsor judiciary com. 1958-59) bar assns., Reserve Officers Assn. (pres. W.Tenn. chpt. 1949-50), Mil. Order World Wars (treas. 1966-67, judge adv. 1959), Am. Legion (exec. com. Memphis chpt. 1948-49), St. Vincent DePaul Soc. (hon.), Serra Internat. (trustee 1967-68). Roman Catholic. K.C. Home: 4264 Rhodes Av Memphis TN 38111 Office: Courthouse Memphis TN 38113

O'HEERON, MICHAEL KINNEY, physician-urologist; b. Elvins, Mo., Aug. 31, 1908; s. John Kinney and Viola (Neely) O'H.; B.A., Culver-Stockton Coll., 1934; M.D., Washington U., 1935; m. Sharmayne Olson, Oct. 19, 1945; children—Michael Kinney, John Bingham, William Edward, Mark Cummings. Intern St. Louis City Hosp., 1935-36; resident in urology Presbyn. Hosp., Chgo., 1936-40; practice medicine, specializing in urology, Houston, 1940—; clin. prof. urology Baylor U., Houston, 1949-66; chief urology sect. St. Joseph's Hosp., 1947—; cons. urologist Methodist Hosp., Houston, 1947—; sr. asso. urologist Jefferson Davis Hosp., Houston, 1946-62; area cons. in urology VA Hosp. Tex. and La., 1951-65; cons. urologist Brooke Army Hosp., 1955-68. Chmn. urology sect. Internat. Coll. Surgeons meeting, N.Y.C., 1953; chmn sci. exhibits com. South Central sect. Am. Urol. Assn., 1951-67; presented papers and demonstrations internat. meeting Internat. Coll. Surgeons, Sao Paulo, Brazil, 1954; chmn. sci. exhibits com. South Central section Am. Urol Assn., 1951-67. Diplomate Am. Bd. Urology. Fellow A.C.S.; mem. A.M.A., Am. Urol. Assn. (pres. S. Central sect. 1969), So. Med. Assn., Internat. Coll. Surgeons (pres. U.S. sect. 1969), Southwestern Surg. Cong., Tex. Med. Assn., Harris County Med. Soc. Contbr. numerous papers and articles in medicine and urology to tech. jours. Home: 7919 Woodway St Houston TX 77042 Office: St Joseph Profl Bldg Houston TX 77002

OHKI, KENNETH, educator; b. Livingston, Cal., June 13, 1922; s. Zenjiro and Yaye (Watanabe) O.; B.S., U. Cal. at Berkeley, 1949, M.S., 1951, Ph.D., 1963; m. Kiyoko Nakano, Apr. 15, 1945; children—Suzanne (Mrs. James Uyeda), Stephen Ken. Project coordinator U. Cal. at Berkeley, 1950-64; research asst. Cal. Inst. Tech., Pasadena, 1950-53; supr. plant physiology research Internat. Mineral & Chem. Corp., Libertyville, Ill., 1964-67, specialist plant physiology research, 1967-71; asst. prof. U. Ga., Experiment, 1971-73, asso. prof. agronomy, 1973—. Committeeman, charter mem. Boy Scouts Am., El Cerrito, Cal., 1962-64, committeeman, Northbrook, Ill., 1964-66. Served with AUS, 1944-46. Mem. Am. Soc. Plant Physiology, Am. Soc. Agronomy, Crop Sci. Soc. Am., Sigma Xi. Methodist (commr. edn. 1966-67). Kiwanian (environment service com. Griffin, Ga., 1971-72). Research in mineral nutrition and growth and devel. sugar beet, critical nutrient requirements of plants, 1950-64; plant growth regulators, 1964-70; microelement nutrition of crops, 1971-73. Home: 206 Larcom Lane Griffin GA 30223

OHLIGER, GLORIA ANN, pub. information specialist; b. Brownsville, Tex., 1925; d. Frederick and Evangeline (Anzaldua) Ohliger; student George Washington U., 1945-46. Editor women's page Washington Daily News, 1963-70; pub. information specialist Bur. Mint, Dept. Treasury, 1970—. Recipient Spl. Award for Excellence Treas. Dept., 1973. Clubs: Washington Press, Am. Newspaper Women's. Home: 1330 New Hampshire Av NW Washington DC 20036 Office: Bur Mint Dept Treasury Washington DC 20220

OHLMAN, MAURICE KORBE, indsl. engr.; b. Louisville, Nov. 7, 1919; s. Louis Edward and Catherine (Peak) O.; A.A., U. Louisville, 1963; student Bellarmine Coll., Ind. State U., U. Evansville, various times; m. Patricia Josephine McLean, Apr. 7, 1945; children—Rita (Mrs. James B. Martin III), Nancy, Donna. Constrn. sheet metal worker various contractors, Louisville, 1938-41, 46-50; foreman sheet metal work Carrier Air Conditioning, Brisbane, Australia, 1950-53; lab. technician Brown Foreman Distillery, Louisville, 1953-57; quality control tech. Ford Motor Co., Louisville, 1957-59; engr., U.S. Naval Ordnance Plant, Louisville, 1960-66; standards engr. J.I. Case Co., Terre Haute, Ind., 1966-68; indsl. engr. Babcock & Wilcox, Mt. Vernon, Ind., 1968-70; quality control mgr. Amax Aluminum Bldg. Products, Evansville, Ind., 1970-72; supr. indsl. engring. ICI Am., Inc., Charlestown, Ind., 1972—. Served with AUS, 1941-46: PTO. Registered profl. engr. Ky. Mem. Nat., Ind. (pres. 1973) socs. prof. engrs., Am. Inst. Indsl. Engrs. (chmn. profl. relations, 1971, chmn. pub. relations com., 1970), Tri State Council for Engring. and Sci., Nat. Assn. Suggestion Systems (v.p. 1969-70), Am. Legion, D.A.V. (life). Roman Catholic. Home: 7623 Colson Dr Louisville KY 40220 Office: ICI America Indiana Army Ammo Plant Charlestown IN 47111

OHLSON, RUSSELL OTIS, elec. mfg. co. exec.; b. Elizabeth, N.J., June 15, 1928; s. Otto Otis and Eleanor Margaret (Civik) O.; B.S., Wash. State U., 1950; m. Norma Lee McCue, Oct. 6, 1951; 1 son, Stuart Bryan. Elec. engr. Gen. IccCo., Phila., 1950-52; elec. engr. Square D Co., Detroit, 1954-56, engring. supr., 1956-58, mgr. product planning, switchgear, 1958-65, mgr. elec. distbn. systems planning, Lexington, Ky., 1965—. Rep. to Nat. Elec. Mfrs. Assn., 1969—, mem. switchgear exec. com., 1970-73. Mem. adv. com. for elec. dept. Central Ky. Area Vocational Sch., 1970—. Served to 1st lt. Signal Corps, AUS, 1952-54. Registered profl. engr., Mich. Mem. I.E.E.E., Tau Beta Pi, Sigma Tau, Phi Kappa Phi. Contbr. papers to profl. lit. Co-inventor elec. power line warning light, 1950. Home: 704 Haverhill Dr Lexington KY 40503 Office: 1601 Mercer Rd Lexington KY 40505

OHM, JACK ELTON, educator; b. Milw., Sept. 23, 1932; s. Walter C. and Mabel S. (Elton) O.; student U. Wis., Milw., 1950-52; B.S., U. Chgo., 1954; Ph.D., U. Cal. at Berkeley, 1959. NSF postdoctoral fellow Johns Hopkins, 1959-60; asst. prof. U. Wis., Madison, 1960-65; asso. prof. La. State U., Baton Rouge, 1965-69, prof. math., 1969—; vis. prof. Purdue U., 1971-72. Wis. Alumni Research Found. fellow U. Cal. at Berkeley, 1964-65. Mem. Am. Math. Soc., Math. Assn. Am. Office: Math Dept La State U Baton Rouge LA 70803

O'KEEFE, DANIEL FRANCIS, JR., lawyer, assn. exec.; b. Belmont, Mass., July 1, 1936; s. Daniel Francis and Helen (Chamberlin) O.; B.A., U. Va., 1957, LL.B., 1960; M.B.A., Harvard, 1963; m. Sandra McKee Smith, July 27, 1957; children—Vicki Elizabeth, Timothy Jude. Admitted to Va. bar, 1960, D.C. bar, 1961, U.S. Supreme Ct. bar, 1967; atty. U.S. Dept. Justice, Washington, 1960-61; atty. U.S. Dept. Commerce, Washington 1963-65, asst. gen. counsel, 1965-67; mgr. employee relations Allied Chem. Corp., N.Y.C., 1967-68; sec. Proprietary Assn., Washington, 1968-73, v.p., 1969-73; pres. The Food & Drug Law Inst., 1973—. Bd. advisers 1st Nat. Bank Washington, 1969—. Bd. dirs. Am. Cancer Soc., Alexandria, Va., 1966-67, Citizens Commn. on Sci., Law and Food Supply, 1973—; trustee Nat. Coordinating Council on Drug Edn., 1970-72. Recipient Dept. Commerce Silver Medal award, 1966. Mem. Am., Va. bar assns., D.C. Bar, Sigma Chi, Phi Delta Phi. Clubs: University, Harvard Business School, Army-Navy Country. Home: 625 Pulman Pl Alexandria VA 22305 Office: 1200 17th St NW Washington DC 20036

O'KEEFE, MICHAEL HANLEY, lawyer, state senator; b. New Orleans, Dec. 1, 1931; s. Arthur J. and Eleonora (Gordon) O'K.; LL.B., Loyola U., 1955; m. Jean Ann VanGeffen, June 18, 1955; children—Michael H., Erin Elizabeth. Admitted to La. bar, 1955; partner O'Keefe, O'Keefe & Berrigan, 1955—; mem. La. Senate, 1959—, Senate floor leader, 1963-67; pres. pro tem, 1971. Chmn. La. Commn. on Intergovtl. Relations; mem. Council State Govts.; chmn. Goals for La., v.p. Council for Music and Performing Arts, Archdiocesan Commn. on Housing and Community Life; mem. La. Commn. Status of Women; chmn. Gov.'s Com. Correctional Treatment and Rehab.; chmn. adv. com. La. Planning Office. Served from 2d lt. to 1st lt., AUS, 1955-57. Mem. C. of C., Am., La., New Orleans bar assns., Res. Officers Assn., Blue Key (hon.). Roman Catholic. K.C., Kiwanian. Home: 4 Gull St New Orleans LA 70124 Office: Am Bank Bldg New Orleans LA 70130

O'KEEFE, RUFUS EARL, investment co. exec.; b. Colorado City, Tex., Feb. 27, 1901; s. R.C. and Stella (Pond) O'K.; student West Tex. State Tchrs. Coll., 1914-16, Tex. Mil. Coll., 1916-18; m. Saxche Simms, June 24, 1925; children—E. Jay, Nanne (Mrs. O.F. Jones III). Co-founder Panhandle Ins. Agy., 1925, gen. partner, 1925-57; pres., gen. mgr. Southwestern Investment Co., Pampa, Tex., 1930-61, chmn. bd., chief exec. officer, 1961—, pres., 1970—; pres., dir. Western Bldg. & Loan Assn. (name now changed to Security Fed. Savs. & Loan Assn.), Pampa, 1928-45, dir., 1945-72; pres., dir. Western Nat. Life Ins. Co., Amarillo, Tex., 1944-60, chmn. bd., 1960-71, chmn. exec. com., treas., 1971—; chmn. bd. Comml. Ins. Co. (name now Comco Ins. Co.), Amarillo, 1948—. Area chmn. Boys Clubs Am., 1951—; mem. regional exec. bd. Boy Scouts Am., 1956—. Trustee Wayland Coll., Plainview, Tex., 1961-66; bd. dirs. Llano Cemetery Assn., 1957-61; bd. dirs., pres., mem. exec. com. Amarillo (Tex.) Area Found., Inc.; bd. dirs., chmn., mem. exec. com. High Plains Bapt. Hosp., Amarillo, Tex. Recipient Regional Chmns. award Boy Scouts Am., 1959, 60, Silver Antelope award, 1965; named Man of Year Globe-News Pub. Co., 1959. Mem. Am. Indsl. Bankers Assn. (mem. exec. com., dir. 1970-72), Amarillo Credit Assn. (pres. 1957-59), Amarillo C. of C. (pres. 1950). Baptist (deacon 1938—). Rotarian. Home: 2808 Hayden St Amarillo TX 79109 Office: PO Box 871 Amarillo TX 79167

OKELL, GEORGE SHAFFER, SR., lawyer; b. Scranton, Pa., May 29, 1906; s. George Muir and Blanche (Shaffer) O.; LL.B., U. Miami, 1933, J.D., 1967; m. Evelyn Maude Pottymer, Feb. 8, 1926; children—George Shaffer, James Muir, Jean Ann (Mrs. Jake Cooper), Jo Byna. Admitted to Fla. bar, 1933, since practiced law in Miami. Trustee Nat. Children's Cardia Home, 1952—; mem. bd. govs. Moosehaven, home for aged mems. Moose, 1952—. Mem. Fla. Ho. of Reps., 1945-55; city atty., Miami, Fla., 1956-57; atty. Dade County League of Municipalities, 1957-58. Organizer Dade County Young Dem. Club, 1931, pres., 1934-36; pres. Young Dem. Clubs of Fla., 1944-45; nat. parliamentarian, mem. exec. com. Young Dem. Clubs of Am., 1939-40. Recipient plaque, S.E. Optometric Assn. of Fla., 1950. Methodist. Elk (past exalted ruler), Moose (past gov. local lodge, pres. Fla. assn. 1948-50), Lion (pres. Coral Gables 1945-46). Home: 1245 Andalusia Av Coral Gables FL 33134 Office: 108 Valencia Av Coral Gables FL 33134

O'KELLEY, HAROLD ERNEST, mfg. co. exec.; b. Jacksonville, Fla., Mar. 20, 1925; s. Edward Barber and Ida Bessie (Blackwell) O'K.; B.E.E., Auburn U., 1947; M.S. in Engring., U. Fla., 1948; m. Sarah Blanche Adcock, June 5, 1949; children—Sarah (Mrs. J. Preston Silvernail), Ellen B., Shannon K., Harold Ernest. Asso. prof. elec. engring. Auburn (Ala.) U., 1948-57; v.p., gen. mgr. Radiation, Inc., Melbourne, Fla., 1964-68; v.p. programs Harris Intertype Corp., Melbourne, 1968-72, v.p. composition equipment group, 1972-73; pres., chief exec. officer, dir. Datapoint Corp., San Antonio, 1973—. Bd. dirs. Central Fla. council Boy Scouts Am., 1971-72, United Fund, 1971—, Computer Industries Assn., 1973—; bd. govs. Brevard Hosp., Melbourne, 1968-73. Mem. Armed Forces Communications and Electronics Assn., I.E.E.E., Western Electronic Mfrs. Assn., Am. Mgmt. Assn., Tau Beta Pi, Eta Kappa Nu. Club: Civitan (pres. 1954-55). Home: 300 Geneseo Rd San Antonio TX 78209 Office: 9725 Datapoint Dr San Antonio TX 78284

O'KELLEY, WILLIAM CLARK, judge; b. Atlanta, Jan. 2, 1930; s. Ezra Clark and Theo (Johnson) O'K.; A.B., Emory U., 1951, LL.B., 1953; m. Ernestine Allen, Mar. 28, 1953; children—Virginia Leigh, William Clark. Admitted to Ga. bar, 1952, practiced in Atlanta, 1957-59; asst. U.S. atty. No. Dist. Ga., 1959-61; partner law firm O'Kelley, Hopkins & Van Gerpen, Atlanta, 1961-70; U.S. dist. judge No. Dist. Ga., Atlanta, 1970—. Corporate sec., dir. Gwinnett Bank & Trust Co., Norcross, Ga., 1968-70. Mem. exec. com., gen. counsel Republican Party Ga., 1968-70. Served as 1st lt. USAF, 1953-57; capt. Res. Mem. Am., Atlanta, Gwinnett bar assns., Ga. State Bar, Am. Judicature Soc., Gwinnett C. of C. (v.p. 1966), Sigma Chi, Phi Delta Phi, Omicron Delta Kappa. Baptist. Kiwanian (past pres.). Clubs: Atlanta Athletic, Lawyers of Atlanta; Berkeley Hills Golf (Norcross, Ga.); Commerce. Home: 550 Ridgecrest Dr Norcross GA 30071 Office: US District Court Old Post Office Bldg Atlanta GA 30301

OKES, IMOGENE ESTA, govt. ofcl.; b. Terre Haute, Ind.; d. Vernor J. and Ethlyn (Willis) Okes; B.S., Ind. State U., 1944; M.A., Am. U., 1960. Clk., editor, librarian U.S. Fgn. Service, China and Norway, 1945-52; groupworker, pub. relations rep. Internat. Inst., Fresno, Cal., 1955-56; research asso. Spl. Operations Research Office, Am. U., Washington, 1957-61, Inst. for Def. Analyses, Washington, 1962-63; adult edn. specialist U.S. Office Edn., Washington, 1965—. Guest lectr. Fgn. Service Inst., U.S. Dept. State, Washington, 1961-62; instr. Ginling Girls Coll., Nanking, China, 1947; co-chmn. for arrangements nat. meeting Assn. Asian Studies, Washington, 1964. Program chmn. YWCA Internat. Womens Club, Nanking, 1947. Mem. Am. Assn. U. Women (sec., mem. bd. Washington br. 1969-71), Inst. Mgmt. Scis. (editorial bd. Washington chpt. 1970-71), Adult Edn. Assn. (dir. Washington br. 1971-72, pres. 1973-74), Am. Sociol. Assn., Am. Statis. Assn., A.A.A.S., Assn. for Ednl. Data Systems, Am. Ednl. Research Assn., Assn. Instnl. Research, Operations Research Soc. Am., Am. Polit. Sci. Assn., Am. Acad. Polit. and Social Scis., Assn. Asian Studies, Mongolia-Tibet Soc. Author: Psychological Operations-Afghanistan Project PROSYMS, 1961; Effective Communications by Americans with Thai, 1961; Participation in Adult Education, 1969; Initial Report, 1971; Adult Education in the Public Education System, 1974. Home: 5480 Wisconsin Av Chevy Chase MD 20015 Office: US Office Edn Washington DC 20202

OKNER, BENJAMIN ALLEN, economist; b. Chgo., Aug. 24, 1936; s. Hyman and Sylvia (Chertob) O.; B.S., Ill. Inst. Tech., 1957; M.A., U. Mich., 1960, Ph.D., 1965. Asst. study dir. Survey Research Center, U. Mich., 1957-60; fiscal economist Office Tax Analysis, U.S. Treasury Dept., 1961-63; mem. staff Council Econ. Advisers, 1965-66; asst. prof. dept. econs. Ohio State U., 1966-67; sr. fellow Brookings Instn., Washington, 1968—. Mem. Am. Econ. Assn., Nat. Tax Assn. Home: 1761 R St NW Washington DC 20009 Office: 1775 Massachusetts Av NW Washington DC 20036

OKRASKI, HENRY CARL, electronics engr.; b. Utica, N.Y., Jan. 22, 1936; s. Andrew J. and Helen (Dowiak) O.; student Mohawk Valley Tech. Inst., 1953; B.E.E., Clarkson Coll. Tech., 1958; postgrad. Hofstra U., 1964, George Washington U., 1965, N.Y. U., 1969; M.E., U. Fla., 1972; m. Patricia Turner, Feb. 3, 1962; children—Anna Kay, Joseph Anthony, Andrew Edward. Electronic engr. Link Div., Gen. Precision, Inc., Binghamton, N.Y., 1958-62; supervisory gen. engr. U.S. Naval Tng. Equipment Center, Orlando, Fla., 1962—. Registered profl. engr., Fla. Mem. Fla. Engring. Soc., Nat. Soc. Profl. Engrs., Clarkson Coll. Alumni Assn., Human Factors Soc., Operations Research Soc. Am., Pi Kappa Phi, Karma. Democrat. Roman Catholic. Home: 2844 Will-o-th-Green Winter Park FL 32789 Office: Naval Tng Equipment Center Orlando Naval Base Orlando FL 32813

OKUN, DANIEL ALEXANDER, civil engr., educator; b. N.Y.C., June 19, 1917; s. William Howard and Leah (Seligman) O.; B.S. in Civil Engring., Cooper Union, 1937; M.S. in Civil Engring., Cal. Inst. Tech., 1938; Sc.D., Harvard, 1948; m. Elizabeth Griffin, Jan. 14, 1946; children—Michael Griffin, Tema Jon. San. Engr. USPHS Ohio River pollution survey Cin., 1940-42; teaching fellow Harvard, Cambridge, Mass., 1946-48; cons. environmental engr. Malcolm Pirnie Engrs., N.Y.C., 1948-52; asso. prof. U. N.C., Chapel Hill, 1952-55, prof., 1955-73, Kenan prof., 1973—, chmn. dept. environmental scis. and engring., 1955-73. Cons., AID, WHO; dir. WAPORA, Inc., environmental cons. orgn., Washington, 1969—; vis. prof. Tech. U. Delft (Netherlands), 1960-61, U. Coll., London, Eng., 1966-67, 73-74. Mem. citizens adv. com. Chapel Hill City Schs., 1958-62. Bd. dirs. Ackland Meml. Art Mus. of U.N.C., 1973—, Warren Regional Planning Corp., Soul City, N.C., 1971—. Served to maj. AUS, 1942-46. Recipient Thomas Jefferson award, U. N.C., 1973, Catedratico Honorario, Universidad National de Ingerieria, Lima, Peru, 1952; Fulbright-Hays Lectureship award to Eng., 1973-74; NSF Sr. Postdoctoral Research fellow, 1960-61; Spl. Research fellow Fed. Water Pollution Control Adminstr., 1966-67. Registered profl. engr. N.C., N.Y. Mem. Nat. Acad. Engring., Am. Acad. Environmental Engrs. (Gordon Maskew Fair award 1972, pres. 1969-70), Water Pollution Control Fedn. (Harrison Prescott Eddy medal for research 1950, dir.-at-large 1969-72, chmn. research com. 1961-66), Am. Assn. Univ. Profs. (pres. U. N.C. chpt. 1963-64), Sigma Xi (pres. U. N.C. chpt. 1968-69). Club: Chapel Hill Tennis (dir. 1969-72). Author: (with Gordon M. Fair and John C. Geyer) Water and Wastewater Engineering, Vol. I: Water Supply and Wastewater Removal, 1966, Vol. II: Water Purification and Wastewater Treatment and Disposal, 1968, Elements of Water and Wastewater Engineering, 1971. Contbr. articles to profl. jours. Home: 526 Dogwood Dr Chapel Hill NC 27514

OKUN, JACK H., orthodontist; b. N.Y.C., Jan. 30, 1932; s. Louis and Rachel (Ziperstein) O.; B.S., N.Y. U., 1953, D.D.S., 1956; M.S., Northwestern U., 1961; m. Rosalind Yagman, Nov. 18, 1967; children—Louis Brian, Michael Scott. Trombone player, N.Y.C., 1948-56; practice dentistry specializing in orthodontics, North Palm Beach, Fla., 1961—. Guest lectr. orthodontics Palm Beach County Dental Research Clinic, 1968-69. Mem. adv. bd. U. Palm Beach, 1969—. Served as capt. USAF, 1956-58. Recipient short story prize USAF, 1957, Mgmt. Dental Corps, USAF, 1957; Founders Day award N.Y. U., 1956. Mem. Am., Fla. (dental edn. com. 1968-70) dental assns., Atlantic Coast, Palm Beach County (chmn. budget and audit com. 1964-69, chmn. sch. edn. com. 1967-70) dental socs. Phi Beta Kappa, Omicron Kappa Upsilon. Contbr. articles to profl. jours. Home: 110 Dory Rd N North Palm Beach FL 33408 Office: 849 Park Av Lake Park FL 33403

OLANSKY, SIDNEY, physician; b. Boston, Jan. 11, 1914; s. Samuel and Anna (Olans) O.; B.S., N.Y. U., 1934; M.D., Duke, 1940; m. Marian Elizabeth Freehafer, Oct. 13, 1945; children—Leann, Alan, David, Ad. Served to med. dir. Venereal Disease Research Lab., USPHS, Atlanta, 1950-55; asso. prof. dermatology Duke U. Sch. Medicine, 1955-59; prof. medicine Emory U., Atlanta, 1959—; intern Met. Hosp., N.Y.C., 1940-41; resident Duke U. Med. Center, 1946-48; practice medicine, specializing in dermatology, Atlanta, 1959—; mem. staff Emory U., Grady Meml., Henriett Egleston hosps. Served with USPHS, 1940-46. Home: 3275 Majestic Circle Avondale Estate GA 30002 Office: Emory U Clinic Atlanta GA 30322

OLDENBURG, THEODORE RICHARD, dentist, educator; b. Muskegon, Mich., Apr. 8, 1932; s. Theodore and Fredricka Alberta (Noordhof) O.; student Davidson Coll., 1950-53; D.D.S., U. N.C., 1957, M.S. in Pedodontics, 1962; m. Sarah Louise DeWitt, Nov. 7, 1959; children—Richard Lawson, Caroline Louise. Practice dentistry, specializing in pedodontics, 1957—; prof. pedodontics U. N.C., Chapel Hill, 1962—. Served with USAF, 1957-60. United Cerebral Palsy fellow, 1960-62. Diplomate Am. Bd. Pedodontics (examiner 1972—). Mem. Am. Acad. Pedodontics (dir. 1973—, sec.), N.C. Soc. Dentistry for Children, Am. Assn. Pedodontic Diplomates (pres. 1970-71), Southeastern Soc. Pedodontics, Phi Delta Theta, Delta Sigma Delta. Republican. Episcopalian (vestryman 1973—). Club: Chapel Hill Country. Home: 403 Laurel Hill Rd Chapel Hill NC 27514

OLDHAM, ARTHUR SEARS, judge; b. Athens, Ga., Nov. 12, 1906; s. Henry Jackson and Julie (Biship) O.; LL.B., U. Ga., 1926; m. Florrie Phillips, July 15, 1932; 1 son, Henry Nevel. Admitted to Ga. bar. 1926, since practiced in Athens; judge City Ct. Athens, 1940—. Mem. Ga., Western Circuit. Athens bar assns. Methodist. Home: 100 Old Princeton Rd Athens GA 30601 Office: Court House Athens GA 30601

OLDHAM, DOROTHY CLOUDMAN (MRS. ROBERT PRICE OLDHAM), advt. agy. exec.; b. Detroit; d. Philip Horace and Mabel (Rigg) Cloudman; student Albion Coll., Mich.; B.A., U. Mich.; m. Robert Price Oldham, Dec. 20, 1944 (div. 1955); 1 dau., Carol Cloudman. Jewelry ad service mgr. Simons Michelson Advt. Co., Detroit; fashion editor Detroit Free Press; account exec. W. B. Doner & Co., Detroit, 1945-47; owner-pres. Cloudman Oldham Advt., Inc., 1947—; editor Detroit & Suburban Life, 1967-71; dir. pub. relations advt. agy., Miami, 1974—. Chmn., Fashion Careers Lectr. Series, Wayne U., 1965; mem. pub. affairs com. Greater Detroit Bd. Commerce, 1967-72. Chmn., Women Out Working for Romney for Gov., 1966; pres. Republican Bus. and Profl. Women, 1966-67. Mem. Am. Women in Radio and TV, Women in Communications, Fashion Group of Miami, Nat. Home Fashions League (historian 1974—), Zeta Phi Eta. Home: 261 Bal Cross Dr Bal Harbour FL 33154 Office: 7300 Biscayne Blvd Miami FL

OLDS, DURWARD, educator; b. Conneaut, O., Apr. 12, 1921; s. Benjamin Harrison and Sada Hannah (Raudabaugh) O.; D.V.M., Ohio State U., 1943; M.S., U. Ill., 1954, Ph.D. (Am. Vet Med. Assn. research fellow), 1956; m. Gertrude M. Walk, Sept. 21, 1947; children—Beverly (Mrs. Melbourne Cobb), John. Inseminator, Clark County Breeder's Coop., Neillsville, Wis., 1944-46; asst. prof. animal scis. dept. U. Ky., Lexington, 1946-50, asso. prof., 1950-56, prof. animal sci., 1956—. Served as pfc. AUS, 1943. Mem. Am. Vet. Med. Assn., Am. Dairy Sci. Assn., Am. Soc. Animal Sci., A.A.A.S., Sigma Xi, Phi Zeta, Gamma Sigma Delta. Lutheran (ch. pres. 1971). Editorial bd. Jour. Dairy Sci., 1958-65. Contbr. articles to profl. jours. Home: 1605 Elizabeth St Lexington KY 40503

OLDS, LAWRENCE BRUCE, pub. relations exec.; b. Hudson Falls, N.Y., Feb. 22, 1922; s. Carlton Bruce and Ethel (Craig) O.; B.S., St. Lawrence U., 1944; m. Elizabeth Fagg, June 20, 1955; 1 dau., Cynthia Craig. Radio monitor Time mag., N.Y.C., 1944-47; audio editor FM & TV mag., Great Barrington, Mass., 1947-49; sr. illustrator Gen. Electric Co., Pittsfield, Mass., 1949-54; tech. writer McGraw-Hill, N.Y.C., 1955; tech. editor Abex Corp., N.Y.C., 1955-57; account exec. Dudley, Anderson, Nutzy, N.Y.C., 1957-62, Cunningham & Walsh, Inc., N.Y.C., 1962-63; dir. field services Am. Iron & Steel Inst., Washington, 1963-73; pvt. cons., 1973—. Mem. Fairfax County Council of Arts. Served with AUS, 1943. Mem. Pub. Relations Soc. Am., Washington Soc. Assn. Execs., Advt. Club Met. Washington, Woodland Trail Riders, Profl. Indsl. Communicators Assn., Alpha Tau Omega. Presbyn. Home: 5110 Rockwood Pkwy Washington DC 20016

OLDS, LLOYD EDWARD, mfg. co. exec.; b. Oklahoma City, June 10, 1927; s. Frank Foster and Nell (Murphy) O.; student Hills Bus. U., 1964-65; m. Virginia Esther Newton, Apr. 3, 1964; children—Estelle Leona, Lloyd Edward II. Shipping clk. Crane Co., Houston, 1957-58; night shipping foreman Stedman Grocery Wholesale Co., Inc., Beaumont, Tex., 1958-60; parts clk. Ideco, Inc., Beaumont, 1960-62; warehouse foreman Gulf Supply, Beaumont, 1962-63; receiving clk. Norman Plumbing Supply, Oklahoma City, 1963-64, purchasing agt., 1964-68; purchasing agt., traffic mgr. Seiberling Latex Products, Oklahoma City, 1968—. Served with AUS, 1948-56. Democrat. Home: 7020 N Comanche Av Oklahoma City OK 73132 Office: 4500 SE 59th St Oklahoma City OK 73135

OLDS, VIRGINIA ESTHER NEWTON (MRS. LLOYD E. OLDS), social worker, educator; b. Binghamton, N.Y., July 20, 1931; d. G. Leslie and Mable (Yost) Newton; B.S., Greenville Coll., 1959; M.S.W., U. Okla., 1962; m. Lloyd E. Olds, Apr. 3, 1964; 1 son, Lloyd Edward II. Registered nurse Williamsport (Pa.) Hosp., 1953-57, dental surgeon, Williamsport, 1954-57; instr. Lycoming Coll., Williamsport, 1956-57; nurse Greenville (Ill.) Coll., 1957-59, Salvation Army, St. Louis, summers 1958-59, Deaconess Hosp., Oklahoma City, 1959-60, part-time 1960-62, social worker, 1962; social worker, instr. U. Okla. Med. Center, Oklahoma City, 1963-67, social worker, asst. prof., Norman, 1967—; med. social work cons., 1972—. Social work cons. Deaconess Hosp., Oklahoma City, 1967-68. Mem. Nat. Assn. Social Workers (chpt. chmn. 1968-69), Am. Nurses Assn., Okla. Health and Welfare Assn., Nat. Rehab. Assn., Nat. Assn. Social Work, Acad. Certified Social Workers, Council Social Work Edn. Democrat. Methodist. Home: 7020 Comanche St Oklahoma City OK 73132 Office: U Okla Sch Social Work Norman OK 73069

O'LEARY, VIRGINIA KYLE BOOTH (MRS. DANIEL B. O'LEARY), journalist; b. Wash. Jan. 8, 1928; d. Kyle and Helen (Sutton) Booth; student George Washington U., Washington, 1944-46; m. Philip Warren, Jr. (dec.); children—Joseph B., Virginia Kyle, Philip C.S., Timothy P.M., Mary M., Ruth N., Kathleen; m. 2d, Daniel B. O'Leary, Nov. 12, 1967. Reporter, Alexandria (Va.) Gazette, 1943-50, women's editor, religious news editor, asst. city editor, 1961-64; columnist N. Va. Free Press, 1948-49; women's editor, city editor No. Va. Sun., 1964-66; pub. relations dir. Arlington Red Cross, 1966; pub. relations dir. Alexandria Hosp., 1966-67; spl. writer Alexandria (Va.) Gazette, 1969-73, women's editor, 1973—. Dir. Nat. capital area chpt. March of Dimes, 1961-67. Mem. Nat. League Am. Pen Women, No. Va. News Assn., Va. Press Women, Chi Omega. Home: 428 Monticello Blvd Alexandria VA 22305

OLEJAR, PAUL DUNCAN, former univ. adminstr.; b. Hazelton, Pa., Sept. 13, 1906; s. George and Anna (Danco) O.; A.B., Dickinson Coll., 1928; m. Ann Ruth Dillard, Jan. 6, 1933; 1 son, Peter. Dir. edn. W.Va. Conservation Commn., 1936-41; coordinator U.S. Fish and Wildlife Service, 1941-42; chief press and radio Bur. Reclamation, Dept. Interior, 1946-47; editor Plant Industry Sta. AGRI, 1948-51; chmn. spl. reports Agrl. Research Adminstrn., 1951-56; dir. tech. information Edgewood Arsenal, Md., 1959-63; chief, tech. information plans and programs Army Research Office, Washington, 1963-64; chmn. chem. information unit NSF, Washington, 1965-70; dir. drug information program Sch. Pharmacy, U. N.C., Chapel Hill, 1970-73, ret. Served with AUS, 1942-46. Decorated Army Commendation medal. Mem. Am. Soc. Information Sci., Am. Chem. Soc., Drug Information Assn., Ravens Claw, Theta Chi, Omicron Delta Kappa. Methodist. Home: 664 SW Port Malabar Blvd Palm Bay FL 32905

OLENDER, JACK HARVEY, lawyer; b. McKeesport, Pa., Sept. 8, 1935; s. Benjamin and Kate (Harris) O.; A.B. summa cum laude, U. Pitts., 1957, J.D., 1960; LL.M., George Washington U., 1960; m. Lovell V. Ruckman, July 15, 1962. Teaching fellow George Washington U. Law Sch., Washington, 1960-61; admitted to D.C. bar, 1961, Md. bar, 1966; individual practice law, Washington, 1961—; sec., gen. counsel Autocomp, Inc., computers and law, Bethesda, Md., 1966—. Lectr., Southeastern U., Washington, 1965-67. Mem. Am., Md., Montgomery County bar assns., Assn. Plaintiffs' Trial Attys. (pres. 1969-70), Bar. Assn. D.C., Am. Trial Lawyers Assn. (asso. editor Torts 1965—, mem. state com. for D.C. 1970—), Am. Judicature Soc., Md. Trial Lawyers Assn. (v.p. 1973), N.Y. State Assn. Trial Lawyers, Pitts. Inst. Legal Medicine, Am. Arbitration Assn., Scribes, World Peace Through Law, Phi Beta Kappa. Contbr. articles to profl. jours. Office: 1725 K St NW Washington DC 20036 also 8641 Colesville Rd Silver Spring MD 20910

OLER, WESLEY MARION, III, physician; b. N.Y.C., Mar. 8, 1918; s. Wesley Marion, Jr. and Imogene (Rubel) O.; grad. Phillips Andover Acad., 1936; A.B., Yale, 1940; M.D., Columbia, 1943; m. Virginia Carolyn Craemer, Dec. 8, 1951; children—Helen Louise (dec.), Wesley Marion IV, Stephen Scott. Intern, Bellevue Hosp., N.Y.C., 1944, resident, 1948-50; fellow Hosp. U. Pa., 1951; practice medicine, specializing in internal medicine, Washington, 1952—; sr. attending physician, vice chmn. dept. medicine Washington Hosp. Center, 1962-64, v.p. med. bd., 1971-72, trustee, 1973—; clin. prof. medicine Med. Sch., Georgetown U. Founder, pres. Washington Recorder Soc.; bd. dirs. Am. Recorder Soc. Served to maj. M.C., AUS, 1944-47. Fellow A.C.P.; mem. Mensa, Osler Soc. Washington (past pres.), Republican. Episcopalian. Clubs: Metropolitan, Cosmos, Chevy Chase. Contbr. to jours. on old musical instruments. Home: 4800 Van Ness St NW Washington DC 20016 Office: 3301 New Mexico Av NW Washington DC 20016

OLESON, NORMAN LEE, educator; b. Detroit, Aug. 19, 1912; s. Christian Gad and Mathilda Lorenzo (Halvorsen) O.; student Wayne State U., 1930-33; B.S., U. Mich., 1935, M.S., 1937, Ph.D. in Physics, 1940; m. Gabrielle Dorothy Sauve, June 18, 1939; children—Karen, Norman Lee, Richard Paul. Physicist Gen. Electric Co., Nela Park, O., 1946-48; asso. prof. physics Naval Postgrad. Sch., Monterey, Cal., 1948-52, prof., 1952-69; chmn. dept. physics U. South Fla., Tampa, 1969—. Cons. in plasma physics Lawrence Radiation Lab., U. Cal., 1958-67; vis. prof. physics Queen's U., Belfast, No. Ireland, 1955-56; vis. prof. nuclear engring. Mass. Inst. Tech., 1967-68. Served with USCG, 1940-46. Office of Naval Research grantee, 1954-67; AEC grantee, 1958-67, 72—; NSF grantee, 1967-68. Fellow Am. Phys. Soc.; mem. A.A.A.S., Sigma Xi. Contbr. articles in gaseous, electronics and plasma physics to profl. jours. Home: 11003 Carrollwood Dr Tampa FL 33618

OLEWINE, DONALD AUSTIN, educator; b. Harrisburg, Pa., May 4, 1928; s. Forrest Wilbur and Helen Elizabeth (Houser) O.; B.S., Dickinson Coll., 1950; postgrad. U. Md., 1951-53; Ph.D., U. N.C., 1957; m. Barbara Jean Mallard, Aug. 12, 1957; children—Michael Charles, Andrew Forrest, Rebecca Carol. Asst. instr. dept. biology Dickinson Coll., Carlisle, Pa., 1950-51; grad. asst. physiology Sch. Medicine, U. N.C., 1953-57; instr. physiology and biophysics U. Vt., Burlington, 1957-58; physiologist Gerontology sect. Nat. Heart Inst., Balt. City Hosps., 1958-62; asst. prof. biology Bucknell U., 1962-65; mem. faculty Ga. So. Coll., Statesboro, 1965—, asst. prof., 1965-67, asso. prof., 1967-70, acting head dept. biology, 1967-70, prof. biology, 1970—. Served with AUS, 1951-53. Mem. Am. Coll. Sports Medicine, A.A.A.S., Am. Soc. Zoologists, Assn. Southeastern Biologists, Ga. Acad. Sci., Ga. Sci. Tchrs. Assn., Ga. Gerontol. Soc., Gerontol. Soc., Fedn. Am. Socs. for Exptl. Biology, Nat. Assn. Biology Tchrs., N.Y. Acad. Sci., Soc. for Study of Reprodn., Sigma Xi, Phi Sigma. Author: Outline of Physiological Function, 1972. Home: 114 Forest Way Statesboro GA 30458

OLIVE, LOUIS LEO, govt. ofcl.; b. St. Thomas, V.I., July 3, 1933; s. Louis Anthony and Ann Florina (Magras) Olive; student Coll. V.I., 1964-67, U. Vt., 1967-68; B.S. in Mech. Engring., Bridgeport Engring. Inst., 1971; m. Mary Ann Nadeau, Sept. 13, 1969 (dec. Mar. 1972). Field engr. Leverty & Hurley, Bridgeport, Conn., 1970-71; asst. mgr. real estate and holdings Nat. Bank of Westchester, White Plains, N.Y., 1971; asst. dir. utilities and sanitation Govt. of V.I., St. Thomas, 1972-73, project dir., 1973—. Served with USNR, 1951-53. Mem. Nat. Solid Waste Mgmt. Assn. (state dir.), Am. Pub. Works Assn. Home: 48-6 Fredenhoj PO Box 4251 St Thomas VI 00801 Office: PO Box 476 Dept Pub Works St Thomas VI 00801

OLIVER, BENJAMIN HUGHER, JR., telephone co. exec.; b. N.Y.C., Mar. 1, 1907; s. Benjamin Hugher and Margaret W. R. (Zoller) O.; M.E., Stevens Inst. Tech., 1928; student N.Y. U., 1930-31; m. Lillie M. Kuhnle, Nov. 24, 1932; children—Susan L., Mary Jane. With N.Y. Telephone Co., 1928-55, 58-62, v.p. upstate, Albany, 1958-62; asst. v.p. plant operations Am. Tel. & Tel. Co., 1955-58, dir. of govt. communications Long Lines Dept., Am. Tel. & Tel. Co., Washington, 1962-64, v.p. govt. communications Long Lines Dept., 1964-68, v.p. gen. depts. and Long Line dept. govt. communications, 1968—. Mem. internat. communications service com. Nat. Industry Adv. Com., 1962—. Bd. dirs. Council of Nation's Capitol, Girl Scouts U.S.A., Washington. Served from capt. to col., AUS, 1942-45. Mem. Armed Forces Communications and Electronics Assn. (nat. pres. 1958-61, 69—, permanent dir., mem. exec. com.), Am. Legion, Def. Orientation Conf. Assn., I.E.E.E. Clubs: Congressional Country, International, Army and Navy (Washington). Home: 9100 Burning Tree Rd Bethesda MD 20034 Office: 2055 L St NW Washington DC 20036

OLIVER, CHARLES DICKSON, mgmt. cons.; b. Ware Shoals, S.C., Jan. 10, 1909; s. Rueben Spencer and Annie (Dickson) O.; C.E., Cornell U., 1931; postgrad. in bus. adminstrn. U. Cin., 1950; m. Alice Thomas, Oct. 18, 1934 (dec. May 1967); children—Charles Dickson, Jr., James William, Nancy Jane; m. 2d, Anne Jones, Jan. 1, 1969. Salesman, Liberty Mut. Ins. Co., Newark, 1933-35, staff sales, Louisville, 1935-39, mgr., Cin., 1940-43, 46-53, regional mgr., East Orange, N.J., 1953-59, So. div. mgr., v.p., Atlanta, 1959-73; mgmt. cons., Atlanta, 1973—. Bd. dirs. Ga. Insurors' Insolvency Fund, Fla. Ins. Guaranty Fund; trustee Ga. State U. Ednl. Found. Served with USNR, 1943-46. C.P.C.U. Mem. Newcomen Soc. Clubs: Commerce (Atlanta); Pendennis (Louisville); Piedmont (Spartanburg, S.C.); Charlotte (N.C.) City; Commonwealth (Richmond, Va.). Home: 271A Lakemoore Dr NE Atlanta GA 30342

OLIVER, EARL PORTER, physician; b. Lamasco, Ky., Apr. 26, 1918; s. Earl F. and Beatrice B. (Burns) O.; B.S., U. Ky., 1940; M.D., U. Louisville, 1943; m. Margurette C. Fultz, Mar. 20, 1943; 1 dau., Margurette (Mrs. Larry B. Stovall). Intern, Louisville Gen. Hosp., 1943-44; practice medicine Halcomb and Oliver Clinic, Scottsville, Ky., 1946—; mem. staff Allen County War Meml. Hosp., 1952—; med. dir. Selective Service Bd., 1946—; mem. Allen County Health Bd.; adminstr., partner Graves Infirmary, 1946-52. Mem. Ky. Commn. on Aging, 1961—, chmn. 1967-69; mem. Mammoth Cave Comprehensive Health Care Council, 1970-72. Served to maj. M.C., AUS, 1944-46. Diplomate Am. Bd. Family Practice. Mem. A.M.A., Ky., So., Allen County med. assns., Am. Acad. Gen. Practice, Am. Soc. Anesthesiologists, Ky. Corps of Long Riflemen. Mason (Shriner), Rotarian. Home: RR 1 Gallatin Rd Scottsville KY 42164 Office: 217 W Main St Scottsville KY 42164

OLIVER, FOSTER FINLEY, data processing exec.; b. Bluntsville, Ala., Oct. 26, 1916; s. Joseph E. and LeNora P. (Lucas) O.; B.S., Jacksonville State U., 1938; m. Ruth Cobb, June 25, 1940. Computer adminstr. NASA, 1962-68; dir. Gen. Computer Services, Huntsville, Ala., 1968-72; dir. Peoples Bank, Pell City, St. Clair Savs. and Loan Assn. Bd. dirs. Huntsville Econ. Devel. Corp. Mem. Pell City C. of C. (pres. 1956-58). Democrat. Methodist (chmn. ofcl. bd. 1952-62). Home: 7015 Whitesburg Dr Huntsville AL 35802 Office: 807 Madison St Huntsville AL 35801

OLIVER, GEORGE EDWARD, judge; b. Covington, Ga., Sept. 20, 1914; s. Frank Marvin and Flora Eugenia (Carr) O.; grad. McCallie Sch., Chattanooga, 1931; A.B., Presbyn. Coll., 1936; LL.B., U. Ga., 1939; m. Dorothy Cornell, May 31, 1944. Admitted to Ga. bar, 1939, practiced in Savannah until 1959; mem. firms Kennedy & McWhorter, 1939-47, Jenkins & Oliver, 1947-53, Oliver & Smith, 1953-59; recorder Savannah Police Ct., 1954-63; judge County Police Ct., Savannah, 1961-63; judge City Ct. Savannah (now State Ct. Chatham County), 1963-70; judge Superior Ct., Eastern Jud. Circuit Ga., Savannah, 1970—. Trustee 1st Fed. Savs. & Loan Assn., Savannah. Pres. Legal Aid Soc., Savannah, 1953. Mem. adv. bd. local Salvation Army, chmn., 1966. Served to lt. USCGR, 1942-45. Recipient Certificate of Merit for proficiency in lay activities S. Ga. Conf. United Meth. Ch., 1961. Mem. Am. Judicature Soc., Am., Ga., Savannah (v.p. 1953) bar assns., Am. Legion, Coast Guard League, Soc. Colonial Wars, S.R., S.A.R. in Ga. (pres. 1966-67), St. Andrews Soc., U. Ga. Club (pres. 1966-67). Methodist (chmn. ofcl. bd. 1959-60, chmn. bd. dirs. 1960—), Mil. Order World Wars (comdr. 1963). Mason (33 degree, grand master Ga. 1973; Shriner, Jester), Elk. Home: 1705 E Duffy St Savannah GA 31404 Office: Chatham County Courthouse Savannah GA 31401

OLIVER, JAMES CLAUD, chem. engr., state ofcl.; b. Daviston, Ala., Oct. 27, 1905; s. Claud Lee and Janie (Gibson) O.; student Howard Coll., 1924-25; B.S., Auburn U., 1929; m. Kathryn Burnett, Mar. 31, 1931; 1 son, James Claud. Steel chemist U.S. Steel, Birmingham, Ala., 1929-31; testing and inspection engr. Ala. State Hwy. Dept., Montgomery, 1935—. Tchr. engring., mgmt. Auburn U., Montgomery, 1942-43; tchr. chemistry U. Ala. night sch., 1949-52. Registered profl. engr., Ala. Mem. Am. Soc. Testing Materials, Am. Concrete Inst., Am. Assn. State Hwy. Officials (award 1963), Assn. Asphalt Paving Technologists. Home: 2036 Amos Montgomery AL 36107 Office: 11 South Union Montgomery AL 36104

OLIVER, LOUIS CECIL, cotton exchange exec.; b. Galveston, Tex., Jan. 18, 1921; s. Louis Green and Cecil (Barker) O.; ed. pub. schs.; m. Julia Manell Lloyd, Dec. 14, 1940; children—Judith Ann (Mrs. James Alvin Hogan), Nancy Evelyn (Mrs. Charles E. Scott), Ellen Jane (Mrs. James C. Crowder, Jr.). Accountant, Todd Shipyards Corp., Galveston, 1941-44, chief clk. Galveston Cotton Exchange and Bd. of Trade, 1946-64, sec., 1965—; pres. Ford & Oliver Accounting Service, 1966—, Sloane & Oliver Enterprises, 1968—. Chief clk. Galveston Maritime Assn., 1946-63, sec., 1964-68; chief insp. so. delivery points N.Y. Cotton Exchange Inspection Bur., Galveston, 1967—. Served with USNR, 1944-46. Baptist (chmn. bd. 1955-61, chmn. trustees 1957-60, treas. Galveston County Bapt. Assn. 1967—). Mason.

Home: 1031 Yupon Dr La Marque TX 77568 Office: 2102 Av C Galveston TX 77550

OLIVER, L(UCIEN) E., dept. store exec.; b. Union, Ore., Jan. 7, 1906; s. Charles Ervin and Edna E. (Remillard) O.; grad. U. Ida., 1926; m. Nava L. Woodard, July 13, 1929; children—Joyce (Mrs. B. Jorgensen), Carol (Mrs. Robert Price), Gayle (Mrs. R.W. Ide, III), Julie (Mrs. Paul Freudenstein). With J.C. Penney Co., 1925-29; store mgr. Montgomery Ward, 1929-33; pres. Western Industries, Monterey, Cal., 1932-33; joined Sears, Roebuck & Co., 1933, dist. sales mgr., 1937-40, nat. retail mdse. mgr., 1949-52, gen. mgr. N.Y.C. office, 1952-58, v.p., 1958—, dir., 1959—; pres. Henry Rose Stores, Inc. (subsidiary of Sears, Roebuck & Co., liquidated, 1955), 1952-55, chmn. bd., 1954-55; chmn. bd. Colonial Stores, Inc.; dir. Allstate Ins. Co., First Nat. Bank of Atlanta, L. & N. R.R. Co., West Point-Pepperell Co. Chmn. Atlanta Arts Alliance. Mem. C. of C. (dir.), Delta Chi, Eta Mu Pi (hon.), Beta Gamma Sigma (hon.). Clubs: Commerce, Piedmont Driving, Capital City, Peachtree Golf (Atlanta); N.Y. Athletic; International (Chgo.). Home: 2222 Mt Paran Rd NW Atlanta GA 30327 Office: PO Box 4358 Atlanta GA 30302

OLIVER, MARY WILHELMINA, law librarian, educator; b. Cumberland, Md., May 4, 1919; d. John Arlington and Sophia (Lear) Oliver; A.B., Western Md. Coll., 1940; B.S. in Library Sci., Drexel Inst. Tech., 1943; J.D., U. N.C., 1951. Asst. circulation librarian N.J. Coll. Women, 1943-45; asst. in law library U. Va., 1945-47; asst. reference, social sci. librarian Drake U., 1947-49; research asst. Inst. Govt., U. N.C., 1951-52, asst. law librarian, 1952-55, asst. prof. law, law librarian, 1955-59, asso. prof. law, law librarian, 1959—, prof. law and library sci., law librarian, 1969—; admitted to N.C. bar, 1951. Mem. Am. Assn. Law Libraries (pres. 1972-73), Spl. Libraries Assn., Am., N.C. bar assns., Assn. Am. Law Schs., Am. Soc. Legal History, Law Alumni Assn. U. N.C., Inc., Internat. Assn. Law Libraries, Seldon Soc., Order of Coif. Home: Box 733 Chapel Hill NC 27514

OLIVER, PHILIP MANUS, govt. ofcl.; b. Hartford, Conn., July 25, 1920; s. Bernard J. and Blanche (Charron) O.; B.A., George Washington U., 1943; div.; children—Tracie, Janice. Personnel adminstr. U.S. Govt., Washington, 1943-54; with Philco-Ford, Palo Alto, Cal., 1954-69; with Dept. of Labor, Office Sec. of Labor, Washington, 1969—, mgr. orgn. planning, 1972—. Bd. dirs. United Fund, Palo Alto, 1966-69, Hope for Retarded Children, San Jose, Cal., 1967-69. Served to 1st lt. USAAF, 1943-46. Mem. Palo Alto C. of C. (dir. 1967-69). Home: 8140 Lake Park Dr Alexandria VA 22309 Office: 1400 Constitution Av Washington DC 20210

OLIVER, PRISCILLA LOWELL FOOTE (MRS. KEITH OLIVER), civic worker, physician; b. Caldwell, N.J., Dec. 28, 1920; d. Lowell Sanborn and Grace (Allen) Foote; A.B., Vassar Coll., 1941; M.D., U. Rochester, 1945; m. Keith Millner Oliver, Sept. 4, 1948; children—Priscilla Hope, Nancy Allen, Faith Sanborn, Wendy Carol, Susan Millner, Keith Millner. Jr. lab technician Rochester Health Dept., 1941-42; intern Duke, 1945-46, asst. resident, 1946-48; gen. practitioner medicine, Purcellville, Va., 1948-50; clinician Loudoun County Health Dept. Leesburg, Va., 1967—; mem. staff Loudoun Meml. Hosp., Leesburg. Chmn. dept. health Jr. Women's Club, 1955; mem. adv. bd. Loudoun County Guidance Clinic, 1958—; pres. Loudoun County Easter Seal Soc., 1960-72; bd. dirs. Girl Scout Council, Washington, 1966-71; social chmn. vestry Madison Parish, Purcellville, 1969-72; cons. Girl Scouts U.S.A., 1965—, tng. coordinator, 1969—, outdoor trainer, 1971—, day camp dir., 1971-72. Mem. Alpha Omega Alpha. Home: Route 1 Leesburg VA 22075 Office: Loudoun County Health Dept King St Leesburg VA 22075

OLIVER, WILLIAM HAYES, dentist; b. Smithfield, N.C., Oct. 29, 1920; s. Rayford Gaston and Lyda Edna (Holt) O.; student The Citadel, 1937-39; B.S., Wake Forest U., 1941; D.D.S., Emory U., 1949; m. Cora Rena Williams, Oct. 12, 1941; children—William Rayford, Frank Hayes. Gen. practice dentistry, Four Oaks, N.C., 1949-54, Smithfield, 1956—. Adv., N.C. Dental Assts. Assn., 1965—. Commr., Four Oaks, N.C., 1951-54, Smithfield, 1963-67; mem. Smithfield Johnston County Library Planning Bd., 1963-67; mem. Johnston County Bd. Health, 1958—. Mem. Smithfield Dist. Sch. Bd., 1962-65. Served with USAF, 1954-56. Fellow Am. Coll. Dentists; mem. Am., N.C., Johnston County (treas. 1968—) dental socs., Fourth Dist. Dental Soc. (pres. 1965-66), Acad. Gen. Dentistry, Am. Legion, Delta Sigma Delta. Mem. Disciples of Christ Ch. (deacon, elder, trustee, treas. 1965—). Mason (Shriner). Contbr. articles to profl. pubs. Home: 807 Vermont St Smithfield NC 27577 Office: 714 Wilkins St Smithfield NC 27577

OLKIN, ALAN JAY, wholesale beauty supply co. exec.; b. Rockaway Beach, N.Y., Dec. 31, 1940; s. Milton Victor and Josepha Amelia (Goldberg) O.; B.S.E.E., U. Miami, 1963; m. Joan Oppenheim, Nov. 24, 1963; children—Terry Michael, Jeffrey Craig. With Boeing Co., Seattle, Wash. and Huntsville, Ala., 1963-64; research and devel. engr. Systems Engring. Labs., Fort Lauderdale, Fla., 1964-67; v.p., co-founder, dir. Datacraft Corp., 1967-74; pres. Neil Beauty Supply, Inc., 1973—. Mem. Assn. for Computer Machinery. Club: Skylake Optimist (North Miami Beach, Fla.). Home: 19830 NE 19th Av North Miami Beach FL 33162 Office: 350 NE 183d St North Miami Beach FL 33162

OLKINETZKY, SAM, educator; b. N.Y.C., Nov. 22, 1919; s. Isidor and Jennie Shana (Zuckerman) O.; B.A., Bklyn. Coll., 1942; postgrad. N.Y. U., 1946-55; m. Sammie Lee Sturdevant, Dec. 24, 1959; children—Joy Shan, Tova Shana. Asst. prof. art Okla. State U., Stillwater, 1947-57; prof. art and humanities U. Ark., Fayetteville, 1962-63, 66-67; prof. art, dir. Mus. Art, U. Okla., Norman, 1957—. Art cons. Keer-McGee Industries, Inc., Oklahoma City, 1964-65. Mem. adv. bd. visual arts Okla. Arts and Humanities Council, 1974, State of Okla. Art Collection, 1971-74; bd. dirs. Contemporary Arts Found., 1966-70. Served with USAAF, 1942-45; ETO. Mem. Am. Assn. U. Profs., Am. Assn. Museums, Okla. Museums Assn. Home: Route 1 Box 151-B Norman OK 73069

OLNEY, CHARLES BERT, mech. engr.; b. Lyndonville, Vt., Mar. 21, 1915; s. Albert J. and Lydia M. (Branstrom) O.; B.S. in Mech. Engring., U. Ky., 1937; m. Mary P. Asher, Apr. 15, 1939; children—Charles David, Lynn (Mrs. Ed Allen). Br. mgr. Crane Co., Grand Junction, Colo., 1948-57; sales mgr. Ball & Roller Bearing Co., Tampa, 1957-60; mfg. rep. Halstead Mitchell Co., Edwards Engring. Co., Modine Mfg. Co., U.S. AIRCO, Ace Tank & Heater Co., Swaby Pump Co., Rangeaire, Tampa, 1960-65; project engr. Fla. Power Corp., St. Petersburg, 1965—. Instr. comml. air conditioning short course for Nat. Environmental Contractors Assn., U. Fla., 1968-73. Served to capt. AUS, 1941-45. Registered profl. engr., Colo. Mem. Fla. Engring., Soc., Nat. Soc. Profl. Engrs., Am. Soc. Heating, Refrigeration and Air Conditioning Engrs. Republican. Presbyn. Club: Rocky Point Golf (Tampa). Home: 1266 Grenada Av Clearwater FL 33516 Office: PO Box 14042 St Petersburg FL 33733

OLNEY, FRED W., educator; b. Marysville, Mo., Dec. 22, 1912; s. Fred Wheeler and Antoinette (Gobiet) O.; B.S., John Brown U., 1938; B.M.E., Tex. A. and M. U., 1942; M.S., U. Ark., 1958; m. La Verne R. Jones, Dec. 20, 1941; children—Fred Paul, Robert John, Rosann (Mrs. Robert C. Crowder). Engr. Wright Aeronaut. Corp., Cin., 1942-45; prof. John Brown U., 1945—; owner Siloam Engring. Service, Siloam Springs, Ark., 1960-71; cons. engr. bldg. constr., air conditioning; land surveying. Registered profl. engr., Ark.; registered land surveyor, Ark. NSF grantee, 1961, 1962, 1964. Mem. Am. Soc. Engring. Edn., Am. Soc. for Testing and Material, Siloam Springs C. of C. Baptist (trustee 1968-73, deacon 1970-74). Kiwanian. Home: Box 224 Route 4 Siloam Springs AR 72761

OLSEN, ANDREW JEREMY, sch. adminstr.; b. Bklyn., Apr. 6, 1937; s. Owen Kruger and Catherine (Helgesen) O.; B.A., Oglethorpe U., 1960; M.Ed. (NSF fellow), U. Ga., 1965; postgrad. Pa. State U., 1969, Emory U., 1962; m. Barbara Helen Coffey, June 18, 1960; children—Catherine Lynne, Jonathan Scott, Andrew Kruger. Tchr. chemistry and biol. scis. DeKalb Sch. System, Decater, Ga., 1960-64, asst. dir. Fernbank Sci. Center, 1966-71, dir. dept. communications, 1971—; grad. teaching asst. U. Ga., Athens, 1964-65; instr. botany-zoology U. So. Miss., Hattiesburg, 1965-66. Pres. Sci. Services, Inc., Atlanta, 1969—; cons. environmental impact studies, nature trail devel., 1966—. Adv. bd. DeKalb YMCA, 1970—. Recipient pvt. endowment A.A.A.S.-Pa. State U., summer 1970. Mem. Nat. Sch. Pub. Relations Assn. (pres. Ga. chpt. 1973—), DeKalb, Ga. edn. assns., Assn. Edn. Tchrs. Sci., Ga., Nat. sci. tchrs. assns., Environmental Action, Oglethorpe U. Alumni Assn. (bd. dirs. 1970—), Phi Delta Kappa. Elk (state chmn. youth scholarship com. 1973—). Co-author textbook. Home: 1956 Briarmill Rd NE Atlanta GA 30329 Office: Dept Communications DeKalb County Bd Edn Decatur GA 30030

OLSEN, CARL EDWIN, mfr.; b. Clifton, Tex., Aug. 3, 1902; s. Petter and Helene (Fjaestad) O.; B.S., Tex. A. and M. U., 1923; m. Elsie Duncan, Oct. 3, 1923; 1 son, Carl Edwin. Profl. baseball player, 1923-26; pres., gen. mgr., dir. Gearench Mfg. Co., Clifton, 1927—. Registered profl. engr., Tex. Mem. Am. Soc. M.E., Am. Soc. Tool Engrs., Houston Petroleum Club, Nomad. Mason, Lion. Patentee in field. Home: PO Box 1221 Houston TX 77001 Office: PO Box 192 Clifton TX 76634

OLSEN, MARVIN N., aircraft co. exec.; b. Duluth, Minn., Oct. 24, 1907; s. Matt and Sofie (Simonsen) O.; B.S., U. Minn., 1929; M.S., Ia. State U., 1946; postgrad. Cornell U., 1948, Harvard, 1950, Mass. Inst. Tech., 1951; m. Marjorie Wolfe, Dec. 28, 1931; children—Donna (Mrs. John Satterfield), Susan. Prof., Ia. State U., 1941-46; prof. Wells Coll., 1946-51; rocketry research mgr. Reaction Motors, Inc., Denville, N.J., 1951-58; tech. mgr. operations mgr. TRW, Inc. Aerospace, Cape Canaveral, Fla., 1958—; exec. dir. Retro, Inc. Pres., bd. dirs. Community Services Council, United Fund. Mem. Am. Assn. U. Profs., A.A.A.S., Am. Inst. Aeros. and Astronautics (sect. chmn.), Am. Phys. Soc., Mental Health Assn. Home: 577 Capri Rd Cocoa Beach FL 32931 Office: 7001 N Atlantic Av Cape Canaveral FL 32932

OLSHAKER, BENNETT, physician; b. Balt., Oct. 5, 1921; s. Samuel M. and Fannie (Klavan) O.; A.B., George Washington U., 1943, M.D., 1945; m. Thelma A. Abramson, Apr. 10, 1946; children—Mark, Robert, Jonathan. Intern Fordham Hosp., N.Y.C., 1945-46; resident in pediatrics Children's Hosp., Washington, 1948-50, fellow child psychiatry, 1951-53; resident in psychiatry St. Elizabeth's Hosp., Washington, 1953-55; practice medicine specializing in pediatrics, Washington, 1950-55; specializing in psychiatry, 1955—; cons. pediatrics and psychiatry Bur. Material and Child Health; D.C. Dept. Human Resources; asso. clin. prof. child health and devel. George Washington U. Sch. Medicine, 1968—; asso. clin. prof. psychiatry and behavioral scis. George Washington U. Sch. Medicine, 1973—. Served to capt. MC AUS, 1946-48. Diplomate Am. Bd. Pediatrics, Am. Bd. Psychiatry and Neurology. Fellow Am. Acad. Pediatrics, Am. Psychiat. Assn., Am. Acad. Child Psychiatry, Am. Orthopsychiat. Assn. Author: Tommy's Tonsillectomy, 1958; What Shall We Tell the Kids?, 1971. Home: 2900 Ellicott Terrace NW Washington DC 20008 Office: 4435 35th St NW Washington DC 20008

OLSHANSKY, CHARLES, community orgn. adminstr.; b. N.Y.C., Jan. 3, 1913; s. Joseph and Mary (Weinman) O.; grad. Savage Sch. for Phys. Edn., 1935; B.S., Columbia, 1937, M.A., 1938; postgrad. N.Y. Sch. Social Work, 1945-46; m. Belle Rothblatt, Mar. 9, 1940; children—Kenneth, Norman, Edward. Dir. activities Grand St. Settlement, N.Y.C., 1930-41; dir. U.S.O., Newport News, Va., 1941-44, asso. dir., San Juan, P.R., 1944-46; exec. dir. Jewish Community Fedn., also Jewish Community Center, Newport News, 1946—. Bd. dirs. Mental Hygiene Clinic Newport News-Hampton, 1961—, pres., 1965-67. Recipient Grand St. Settlement Alumni award, 1959, Civilian Service award War Dept., 1947. Mem. Va. Conf. Social Work (chmn. com. on aging 1944—), Phi Epsilon Kappa. Club: Torch (Newport News). Author: Manual for Playground Directors, 1939. Home: 169 Yeardley Dr Newport News VA 23601 Office: 2700 Spring Rd Newport News VA 23606

OLSON, BURNEY KATHARINE MCAULEY (MRS. RUSSELL H. OLSON), social worker; b. Holly Springs, Miss.; d. Angus Malcolm and Van Burney (Deaton) McAuley; student Superior State Tchrs. Coll., 1931-32, Miss. Synodical Coll., 1932-33; B.S., U. Minn., 1936; M.D. in Social Work, U. Tenn., 1957; m. Russell Howard Olson, Aug. 9, 1938. Caseworker Children's Bur., Memphis, 1955-56, 57-61; caseworker Hope Cottage, Children's Bur., Dallas, 1961-64, dir. child care services, Dallas, 1964-74, staff supr. Hope Cottage, 1974—. Mem. Nat. Assn. Social Workers, Chi Omega. Presbyn. Home: 10564 Royal Club Lane Dallas TX 75229 Office: 2301 Welborn St Dallas TX 75219

OLSON, EDNA HOWARD (MRS. LAWRENCE CARROLL OLSON), librarian; b. nr. Dawsonville, Ga.; d. William Stevens and Esty (Dooley) Howard; B.C.S., Ga. State U., 1950; M. Librarian, Emory U., 1955; m. Lawrence Carroll Olson, Mar. 4, 1939 (dec. Oct. 1953); children—Lawrence Howard, Wayne Carroll, Edna Margaret. Librarian, Ga. Agrl. Expt. Sta., 1949—. Trustee Flint River Regional Library, Griffin, Ga. Mem. Internat. Assn. Agrl. Librarians and Documentalists, Am., Southeastern, Ga. (sec. 1961-63) library assns., Am. Library Trustees Assn., Delta Mu Delta. Baptist. Home: 733 E College St Griffin GA 30223 Office: Ga Agrl Expt Sta Experiment GA 30212

OLSON, EDWARD STURE, educator; b. Mt. Vernon, N.Y., Nov. 18, 1916; s. Edward and Mathilda (Anderson) O.; B.S. in Textile Chemistry, Clemson U., 1938, M.S. in Textile Chemistry, 1960; m. Mary Lang Gill, July 5, 1941; children—Edward Sture, Mary Lang (Mrs. Thomas Wellington Edwards III), Christopher Gill. Night supt. N.C. Finishing Co., Salisbury, 1938-40; night supt. bleaching, resin finishing Dan River Mills., Schoolfield, Va., 1945-51; chemist for research, devel. Deering Milliken Excelsior Plant, Pendleton, S.C., 1951-59; research asst., instr. Clemson (S.C.) U., 1959-61, asst. prof., 1961-63, asso. prof. textile chemistry, 1963—; pres. Kewaco, Inc., Clemson, 67—; cons. chem. and textile industry, 1962—. Bd. dirs. United Fund, 1967. Served to lt. col. AUS, 1940-46; ETO. Decorated Bronze Star medal. Mem. Am. Assn. Textile Chemists and Colorists (chmn. student awards com. 1965, 72, chmn. Palmetto sect. tech. program, chmn. sect. 1967, councillor 1968-71; chmn. com. flock testing, 1969-70, flammability research rest com. 1969-72; v.p. So. region 1973—), Clemson U. Alumni Assn. (chmn. dist. I, 1963; nat. councilman 1964-67). Presbyn. (supt. Sunday Sch. 1953-56, 67-69; deacon 1969—, elder). Contbr. articles to profl. jours. Patentee in field. Research in fabric flammability, organic solvent processing. Home: PO Box 1467 Clemson SC 29631

OLSON, FRANKLYN C(ARL) W(ESTER), govt. oceanographer; b. Waukegan, Ill., Mar. 15, 1910; s. Carl Gottfrid and Ingeborg Maria (Wester) O.; S.B. in Math., U. Chgo., 1933; Ph.D. in Physics, Ohio State U., 1950; m. Mary Ann Joyner, Apr. 13, 1957; children—Storrs L., Susan (Mrs. Eric Wallace), Terri Jean. Physicist Am. Can Co., Maywood, Ill., 1934-42; research asso. Northwestern U., Evanston, Ill., 1943-46; asst. prof. physics U. Ill., Chgo., 1946-47; research asso. Ohio State U., Put-in-Bay, 1947-50; asso. prof. oceanography Fla. State U., Tallahassee, 1950-57; mem. tech. staff RCA Advanced Mil. Systems Group, Princeton, N.J., 1960-63; head Environmental Scis. Br. U.S. Navy Ship Research and Devel. Lab., Panama City, Fla., 1957-60, 63—. Active Bay County Environmental Council, 1968—. Registered profl. engr., Ill. Mem. Internat. Platform Assn., Marine Tech. Soc., Tallahassee Power Squadron (comdr. 1956-57), Sigma Xi. Author: (with C.O. Ball), Sterilization in Food Technology. Home: Route 3 Box 359A Panama City FL 32401 Office: US Naval Coastal Systems Lab Panama City FL 32401

OLSON, GEORGE ALBERT, lawyer; b. San Antonio, Dec. 31, 1936; s. Marion Alfred and Martha Walthall (Pancoast) O.; B.A., U. Tex., 1958, J.D., 1963; m. Margo Whitt, July 11, 1964; children—Martha Whitt, Minette Whitt, George Pancoast. Admitted to Tex. bar, 1963; practiced in San Antonio, 1963—; mem. firm Olson & Olson, San Antonio, 1963-74, Beckmann, Stanard & Olson, 1974—. Dir. Nat. Bank Ft. Sam Houston, San Antonio. Hon. legal counsel El Patronato, 1972-73; mem. adv. and finance com. Good Govt. League San Antonio, 1970-73; mem. Citizens Com. for Tex. Constnl. Revision Commn., 1973—; del. Tex. State Republican Conv., 1972. Served to lt. Supply Corps USNR, 1958-61. Mem. Am., San Antonio (chmn. legal ethics com. 1968; chmn. entertainment com. 1965; chmn. pub. relations com. 1969-71, chmn. accounting and banking com. 1973-74), San Antonio Jr. (treas. 1964-65, pres. 1965-66), Tex. State bar assns., Am. Judicature Soc., Tex. Folkslore Soc., Order of The Alamo, Delta Tau Delta, Alpha Kappa Psi, Phi Eta Sigma. Republican. Episcopalian. Clubs: San Antonio German, San Antonio Country, Conopus, Blue Wing, Plaza, San Antonio Knife and Fork; Duck's Unlimited.

OLSON, HERBERT THEODORE, JR., profl. assn. exec.; b. Bridgeport, Conn., Feb. 9, 1929; s. Herbert Theodore and Inez (Lindahl) O.; student Heidelberg Coll., 1947-49; A.B., Ohio U., 1951, postgrad., 1951-52; m. E. Victoria Cross, Oct. 29, 1960; 1 dau., Christina Victoria. Asst. to dean of men Ohio U., 1951-52; employment mgr. Union Carbide Corp., Charleston, W.Va., 1952-55, indsl. relations div. head, purchasing agt., Torrance, Cal., 1955-67, mgr. employee relations, coordinator pub. affairs, Chgo., 1967-69, corp. mgr. pub. affairs, N.Y.C., 1969-71; exec. v.p. Am. Assn. Homes for the Aging, Washington, 1971—; mem. long-term care for elderly research rev. and adv. com. U.S. Dept. HEW, 1972—, mem. long-term care rev. grant com., 1972—. Nat. chmn. activities Exploring div. Boy Scouts Am., 1970—, mem.-at-large Nat. council, 1970—, mem. adv. council, exec. bd., 1972—, mem. nat. activities com., 1970—, nat. chmn. Explorer President's Congress, 1971; planning commnr., Torrance, 1962-64, city councilman, 1964-67; U.S. Chamber pub. affairs com. Bi-Partisan Com. for Absentee Voters, 1967-73. Served with AUS, 1947-55. Recipient Silver Beaver award, Boy Scouts Am. 1967. Mem. Nat. Press Club, Am. Soc. Assn. Execs., Gerontol. Soc., Meeting Planners Internat. Mason (Shriner). Clubs: Potomac Valley Country; Explorers (N.Y.C.). Home: 8310 Westmont Terrace Bethesda MD 20034 Office: 374 Nat Press Bldg 14th and F Sts NW Washington DC 20045

OLSON, LYNDON LOWELL, lawyer; b. Waco, Tex., Jan. 22, 1925; s. Ernest A. and Beth (Fuller) O.; LL.B., Baylor U., 1950; m. Frances McLaughlin, Sept. 3, 1944; children—Lynden, Jr., Charles. Admitted to Tex. bar, 1950, since practiced in Waco; city atty., Waco, Tex., 1950-53; partner firm Bryan, Wilson, Olson & Stem, 1953—. Trustee Waco Indsl. Sch. Dist., 1964—; bd. dirs. Brazos River Authority, 1971—. Served with AUS, 1943-46. Mem. Waco-McLennan County Bar Assn. (pres. 1963-64), Waco C. of C. (bd. dirs. 1970—). Mason (Shriner). Home: 3917 N 27th St Waco TX 76710 Office: 823 Washington St Waco TX 76701

OLSON, ORDELL PENDOR, govt. ofcl.; b. Lisbon, N.D., Jan. 4, 1930; s. Jens M. and Clara (Munkeby) O.; B.S., N.D. State U., 1953; postgrad. (Fulbright scholar), U. Oslo, 1953-54; M.S., S.D. State U., 1959; Ph.D., Oregon State U., 1963; m. Marjorie Sauer Ott, June 20, 1959; children—Jennifer, Mark. Faculty, N.D. State U., Fargo, 1954-61, Ore. State U., Corvallis, 1963-64, Monmouth (Ill.) Coll., 1964-69; bd. govs. Fed. Res. System, Washington 1969—. Mem. Am., Midwest econ. assns., Phi Kappa Phi, Kappa Delta Pi. Home: 937 N VanDorn St Alexandria VA 22304 Office: 20th and Constitution Washington DC 20551

OLSON, ROBERT MORRIS, broadcasting exec.; b. Dodge City, Kan., Feb. 9, 1921; s. Ernest Morris and Candace Ambrosia (Mosely) O.; grad. pub. high sch., 1938; m. Nadine Griswold, Jan. 9, 1939; 1 son, Robert Andrew. Announcer, writer, producer radio stas., Dodge City, 1938-40, Longview, Tex., 1940, Hastings, Neb., 1940-41, Kansas City, Mo., 1941-43; newscaster sta. WKY Oklahoma City, 1943-44, announcer, writer, producer, 1946-49, dir. WKY-TV 1949, program dir., 1949-55, operations mgr., 1955-56; operations mgr. sta. WTVT, Tampa, Fla., 1956-58, adminstrv. asst., 1958-67, asst. mgr., 1967—. Chmn. Fla. West Coast Broadcast Skills Bank. Gen. chmn. Citizens Com. on Crime Prevention, 1972—. Bd. dirs. Greater Tampa United Fund, Family Service Assn. Served with AUS, 1944-46. Mem. Greater Tampa C. of C., Nat. (legislative liaison com. 1972—), Fla. (v.p. TV 1973—), assns. broadcasters, Mchts. Assn. Greater Tampa (dir.), Broadcast Pioneers. Kiwanian. Clubs: University; Palma Ceia Golf and Country; Krewe of Venue. Home: 2813 Morrison Av Tampa FL 33609 Office: 3213 J F Kennedy Blvd Tampa FL 33609

OLSON, ROY EDWIN, educator; b. Richmond, Ind., Sept. 13, 1931; s. Roy Edwin and Hester Elizabeth (Nelson) O.; B.S. in Engring., U. Minn., 1953, M.C.E., 1955; Ph.D. in Civil Engring., U. Ill., 1960; m. Corrine Hoisington, Aug. 5, 1967; children—Sandra Lee, Cheryl Ann, Chresten Edwin. Asst. prof. civil engring. U. Ill., Urbana, 1960-62, asso. prof., 1962-66, prof., 1966-70; prof. civil engring. U. Tex., Austin, 1970—. Cons. to industry and U.S. govt. 1st Minn. Surveyors and Engr. Soc. scholar, 1953-54; 1st Am. Soc. for Testing and Materials Soc. fellow, 1960. Mem. Am. Soc. C.E. (Walter L. Huber Research prize 1972), Am. Soc. for Testing and Materials (Hogentogler award 1973), Hwy. Research Bd., Clay Minerals Soc., A.A.A.S., Am. Assn. Engring. Edn. Home: 4302 Far West Blvd Austin TX 78731

OLSON, WILLIAM ANDREAS, lawyer, city ofcl.; b. Waco, Tex., July 1, 1923; s. Ernest A. and Beth (Fuller) O.; LL.B., Baylor U., 1950; m. Virginia Malloy, Feb. 14, 1942; children—Suzanne (Mrs. Larry S. Waldrep), William Andresas, John F., Judy C. Admitted to Tex. bar, 1950; pvt. practice law, Waco, Tex., 1950-58; gen. counsel Tex.

Municipal League, Austin, 1958-63; with firm Vinson, Elkins, Weems & Searls, Houston, 1963-64; pvt. practice law, Austin, Tex., 1964-65; city atty., Houston, 1966—. Mem. adv. bd. Center for Municipal Legal Studies, Southwestern Legal Found., Dallas; mem. Gov.'s Tex. Urban Devel. Commn., 1970—; bd. dirs. Tex. Municipal League. Served with AUS, 1942-46; ETO. Mem. State Bar of Tex. (mem. Tex. constn. com.), Tex. City Attys. Assn. (pres. 1968-69). Home: 9900 Memorial Dr Houston TX 77024 Office: 300 City Hall Bagby St Houston TX 77002

OLSTOWSKI, FRANCISZEK, chem. engr.; b. N.Y.C., Apr. 23, 1927; s. Franciszek and Marguerite (Stewart) O.; A.A., Monmouth Coll., 1950; B.S. in Chem. Engring., Tex. A. and I. U., 1954; m. Rosemary Sole, May 19, 1952; children—Marguerita Antonina, Anna Rosa, Franciszek, Anton, Henryk Alexander. Research and devel. engr. Dow Chem. Co., Freeport, Tex., 1954-56, project leader, 1956-65, sr. research engr., 1965-72, research specialist, 1972—. Lectr. phys. scis. elementary and intermediate schs., Freeport, 1961—. Served with USNR, 1944-46. Fellow Am. Inst. Chemist; mem. Electrochem. Soc. (sec. treas. South Tex. sect. 1963-64, vice chmn. 1964-65, chmn. 1965-67, councillor 1967-70), A.A.A.S., Am. Chem. Soc., N.Y. Acad. Sci. Patentee in synthesis of fluorocarbons, natural graphite products, electrolytic prodn. magnesium metal and polyurethane tech. Home: 912 N Av A Freeport TX 77541 Office: Dow Chemical Co U S A Bldg B 3817 Freeport TX 77541

OLTMAN, FLORINE ALMA, ret. librarian; b. Flatonia, Tex., Nov. 13, 1915; d. Louis B. and Almeda (Scarborough) Oltman; B.A., S.W. Tex. State Tchrs. Coll., 1937; B.S. in Library Sci., U. Denver, 1942. Tchr., librarian high sch., Eagle Lake, Weslaco and Port Neches, Tex., 1937-43; librarian U.S. Naval Air Sta., U.S. Naval Hosp., Pensacola, Fla., 1943-46; cataloger U.S. Air U. Library, Maxwell AFB, 1946-47; librarian USAF Spl. Staff Sch., Craig AFB, 1947-50; reference librarian Air U. Library, Maxwell AFB, 1950-55, librarian Air War Coll., 1955-58; chief bibliog. br. Air U. Library, Maxwell AFB, Ala., 1958-71, chief reference br., 1971-72, chief reader services div., 1972-73, ret. Mem. Am. Assn. U. Women (2d v.p. 1964), Ala. (sec. 1956), Southeastern library assns., Spl. Libraries Assn. (pres. Ala. chpt. 1956, sec. mil. library div. 1954, chmn. mil. library div. 1959-60, 2d v.p. 1961-62, pres. 1970-71), Partners for the Alliance. Methodist. Club: Espanol. Home: 512 W San Antonio St San Marcos TX 78666

OLTMAN, JOHN HAROLD, patent lawyer; b. Grand Rapids, Mich., Nov. 18, 1929; s. Peter Harold and Hazel Evelyn (Kelly) O.; B.S. in Chem. Engring., U. Mich., 1952, J.D., 1957; m. Lita Marilyn Hagen, Aug. 16, 1952; children—David K., Laura G., John K. Admitted to Ill. bar, 1957, Ariz. bar, 1964, Mich. bar, 1965, Fla. bar, 1968; mem. firms Mueller & Aichele (Attys.), Chgo., and Phoenix, 1957-64, Barnes, Kisselle, Raisch & Choate (Attys.), Detroit, 1964-65, Settle, Batchelder & Oltman (Attys.), Detroit, 1965-67, Settle & Oltman (Attys.), Detroit and Ft. Lauderdale, Fla., 1967-72, Oltman and Flynn (Attys.), Ft. Lauderdale, 1972—. Trustee for pvt. trust. Served with USMCR, 1952-54. Mem. Am., Fla., Broward County bar assns., Am. Patent Law Assn., Am. Judicature Soc., Fla. Engring. Soc., I.E.E.E., Phi Eta Sigma, Tau Beta Pi. Kiwanian (dir. Ft. Lauderdale Club 1972—; chmn. Key Club com. 1970—). Home: 2130 NE 55th St Fort Lauderdale FL 33308 Office: 915 Middle River Dr Fort Lauderdale FL 33304

OLTMAN, RUTH MARIE, educator, psychologist; b. Cleve.; d. Rudolph Carl and Ida (Schroeder) Oltman; A.B., Oberlin Coll., 1934; M.A., Western Res. U., 1951, Ph.D., 1961. Contact rep. VA, Cleve., 1946-51 adminstrv. asst. (personnel) Navy Finance Center, Cleve., 1951-55; counselor, psychologist Vocational Guidance and Rehab. Services, Cleve., 1955-62; dean of women Baldwin-Wallace Coll., Berea, O., 1962-69; asst. dir. program-Higher Edn. Am. Assn. U. Women, Washington, 1969—. Lectr. in psychology Cleve. Coll. of Western Res. U., 1952-53, Baldwin-Wallace Co., 1962. Served as lt. WAVES, 1942-46. Mem. Am. Psychol. Assn., Nat. Assn. Deans Women, Am. Personnel and Guidance Assn., Nat. Council Adminstrv. Women in Edn., Zonta, Phi Delta Gamma. Methodist. Home: 3760 Persimmon Circle Fairfax VA 22030 Office: 2401 Virginia Av NW Washington DC 20037

O'MALLEY, WILLIAM JOSEPH, JR., social worker; b. Scranton, Pa., July 7, 1934; s. William J. and Catherine (Culkin) O'M.; B.S., U. Scranton, 1956; M.S.W., Fordham U., 1958; m. Margaret Cleveland, Dec. 28, 1957; children—William Joseph III, Suzanne, Miriam, Richard, Lynne, Mark Scott. Caseworker, Lackawanna County Instn. Dist., Div. Child Welfare, Scranton, Pa., 1958-59; clin. social worker VA Hosp., Wilkes Barre, Pa., 1959-63; commd. ensign USPHS, USN, 1963, advanced through grades to comdr., 1967, dir. social services Spalding Rehab. Hosp., Denver, 1968-69, with Lexington (Ky.) Fed. Correctional Instn. (formerly Clin. Research Center), Nat. Inst. Mental Health, 1969-74, dir. community programs, 1974—, dep. chief Excelsior House, 1972-74; chief edn. and tng. sects., 1972—. Mem. Nat. Assn. Social Workers, Commd. Officers Assn. USPHS. Address: 312 Hillsboro Av Lexington KY 40505

OMRAN, ABDEL RAHIM, educator, epidemiologist; b. Cairo, Egypt, Mar. 29, 1925; s. Omran and Khadiga O. (Saad) O.; M.D., Cairo U., 1952, D.P.H., 1954; M.P.H., Columbia, 1956, Dr.P.H., 1959; postgrad. Trudeau Sch. Tb, Saranac Lake, N.Y., 1959; m. Khairia Y. Fawzy, Sept. 13, 1952; children—Mohamed, Eman, Hanan. Came to U.S., 1963. Lectr., Cairo U., 1959-63; research scientist, also clin. asso. prof. N.Y. U., 1963-66; asso. prof. U. N.C., Chapel Hill, 1966-71, prof. epidemiology, 1971—, also dir. WHO Internat. Reference Center for Human Reprodn., U. N.C., 1971—. Asso. dir. Carolina Population Center, 1969—; coordinator WHO health and fertility studies, 1969—; mem. UN Mission to Egypt, 1972—; cons. Ford Found. in India, 1969—. Recipient Medal of Sci. Achievement, Govt. of Egypt, 1955—. Fellow Royal Soc. Health, Am. Pub. Health Assn. (life); mem. Am. Population Assn., Egyptian Med. Assn., Internat. Epidemiol. Assn., Delta Omega. Author: Theory of Epidemiologic Transition, 1971; The Health Theme in Family Planning, 1971. Editor: Egypt: Population Problems and Prospects, 1973; Community Medicine in Developing Countries: Theory and Practice, 1974. Contbr. articles to sci. jours., chpts. to books. Home: 304 Granville St Chapel Hill NC 27514 Office: 407 Pittsboro St Chapel Hill NC 27514

O'NEAL, ELLIS HUGH, mech. engr.; b. Webster, Ia., Jan. 25, 1925; s. Hugh Corwin and Emily Rachel (Ellis) O.; B.M.E. with high honors, U. Fla., 1949; m. Harriet Elizabeth Brush, Nov. 25, 1945; children—Daniel, Kathy, Robin. Test engr. Gen. Electric Co., 1949-50; student engr. Fla. Power & Light Co., Miami, 1950-51, engr., 1951-59, project mgr., 1967-74, asst. chief engr., power plant engring., 1974—. Pres., Kendall Homeowners, Inc., 1967-73. Served with USAF, 1943-44. Decorated Air medal with three oak leaf clusters. Registered profl. engr., Fla. Mem. Am. Soc. M.E., Nat. Soc. Profl. Engrs., Fla. Engring. Soc., Am. Nuclear Soc. Home: 8701 SW 82d Ct Miami FL 33143 Office: Box 3100 Miami Fl 33101

O'NEAL, HUBERT RONALD, research chemist; b. Rotan, Tex., Apr. 27, 1937; s. Albert Jasper and Orpha Rowena (Lyons) O.; B.S. in Chemistry, Tex. Tech U., 1959; M.S. in Chemistry, North Tex. State U., 1964, Ph.D. in Chemistry, 1967; m. Lorraine Helen Oestereich, June 4, 1960; children—Dink Albert, Clark Jasper. Chemist, Sherwin-Williams Co. Tex., Garland, 1959-61; research chemist W.R. Grace & Co., Research Center, Clarksville, Md., 1967-68; research supr. Petro-Tex Chem. Corp., Houston, 1968—. Served with AUS, 1961-62. Mem. Am. Chem. Soc., Sigma Xi. Lutheran. Contbr. articles to profl. jours. Home: 11202 Pecan Creek Dr Houston TX 77043 Office: PO Box 2584 Houston TX 77001

O'NEAL, JOHN BENJAMIN, JR., educator; b. Macon, Ga., Oct. 15, 1934; s. John Benjamin and Ellen (Boyd) O.; B.E.E., Ga. Inst. Tech., 1957; M.E.E., U. S.C., 1960; Ph.D., U. Fla., 1963; m. Mary Neyle Savage, Feb. 7, 1960; children—Edward Shannon, Eve Chaplin. With So. Bell Tel. & Tel. Co., Columbia, S.C., 1952-57; engr. electronic communications Martin Co., Orlando, Fla., 1959-60; engr. electronic communications Bell Telephone Labs., Murray Hill, N.J., 1963-67; prof. elec. engring. N.C. State U., Raleigh, 1967—. Cons. for IBM, Research Triangle Inst. Served with AUS, 1957-58. Mem. I.E.E.E., Am. Assn. Engring. Edn. Contbr. articles in field to profl. jours. Home: 4516 Pamlico Dr Raleigh NC 27609

O'NEAL, JOHN MILTON, JR., producer, dir., writer; b. Mound City, Ill., Sept. 25, 1940; s. John Milton and Rosetta Selena (Crenshaw) O.; B.A., So. Ill. U., 1962; m. Marilyn Norton, June 10, 1972. Producer, dir. Free So. Theater, New Orleans, 1963—. Field sec. Student Non-violent Coordinating Com., Atlanta, 1962-65; field program dir. Com. for Racial Justice United Ch. Christ, N.Y.C., 1966-68; So. regional cons. Gen. Conv. Spl. Program Episcopal Ch., N.Y.C., 1966—. Mem. Alpha Phi Alpha. Writer (plays) Where is the Blood of your Fathers?, 1972; The Hurricane Season, 1973; also essays and poems, 1963—. Office:

O'NEAL, KIRKMAN, steel co. exec.; b. Florence, Ala., June 17, 1890; s. Emmet and Elizabeth (Kirkman) O'N.; student State Tchrs. Coll., Florence, 1905-09; B.S., U.S. Naval Acad., 1909-13; m. Elizabeth Paramore, Oct. 9, 1917; children—Emmett, Elizabeth (Mrs. David H. White). Commd. ensign U.S. Navy, 1913, resigned, 1913, recalled to serve as lt. (s.g.), 1917-19; prodn. engr. Chickasaw Shipbldg. Co., 1919-20, Ingalls Iron Works Co., 1920-21; founder, pres. O'Neal Steel, Inc., Birmingham, Ala., 1921—, now chmn. bd., Ga., Tenn., Fla. and Miss.; chmn. bd. O'Neal Steel, Inc., Del.; dir. Indsl. Paint Co. Bd. dirs. finance com. local chpt. A.R.C.; bd. dirs. Birmingham Civic Symphony, Jr. Achievement of Am.; chmn. bd. dirs. The Kirkman and Elizabeth O'Neal Found. Mem. U.S., Ala., Birmingham chambers commerce, Nat. Assn. Aluminum Distbrs., Am. Warehouse Assn., S. Structural Steel Bd. of Trade, Ala. Hist. Soc., Conf. Bd., N.A.M., Newcomen Soc. N.Am. Presbyn. Clubs: Relay House, Mountain Brook Country, Birmingham Country, Redstone, The Club. Home: 2500 Mountain Brook Pkwy Birmingham AL 35223 Office: 745 N 41st St Birmingham AL 35202

O'NEAL, ROBERT PALMER, marine corps officer; b. Tonapah, Nev., Sept. 20, 1912; s. Robert McWilliam and Aimee (Ford) O'N.; A.B., Occidental Coll., 1935, M.A., 1936; m. Nancy Monroe, June 10, 1935; children—Robert M., Nancy B. (Mrs. Thomas Arthur), Patricia M. (Mrs. Marvin Colyer), Peggy F. (Mrs. Ray Perry). Eastern sales mgr. Monroe Chem. Co., Manchester, Conn., 1937-41; insp. naval aircraft, engines Pratt & Whitney Aircraft Corp., East Hartford, Conn., 1941-43; joined USMC, 1944, advanced through grades to lt. col.; aircraft maintenance officer, Japan, 1958-59; material and aircraft maintenance officer, Cherry Point, N.C., 1959-62; mem. Atlantic Task Force Team, 1962-64; coordinator weapons demonstration SEATO reps., Kadena AFB, Okinawa, 1964, coordinator movements 1st Marine Jet Squadron in combat, South Viet Nam, 1965; prodn. officer Japan Aircraft Corp., Ltd., Atsugi, Japan, 1967-69; aircraft maintenance officer, Chu Lai, Viet Nam, 1969-70; Staff AWSS aircraft maintenance officer, Norfolk, Va., 1971—. Recipient Adm. Coates Outstanding award, 1966. Fellow Internat. Biog. Assn.; mem. Am. Chem. Soc., A.A.A.S., Soc. Am. Mil. Engrs., Am. Ordnance Assn., Engrs. Joint Council Inc., Am. Inst. Aeros. and Astronautics, Internat. Platform Assn., N.C. Acad. Scis., Am. Mgmt. Assn., Optimists Internat., Delta Upsilon. Address: Route 1 Morehead City NC 28557

O'NEAL, SAPIRO DELBRIDGE, supt. schs.; b. Middlesex, N.C., Dec. 7, 1920; s. A. D. and Rebecca (Narron) O'N.; B.A., Atlantic Christian Coll., 1946; M.A., E. Carolina U., 1952; m. Pauline Elizabeth Lewis, Aug. 5, 1941; children—Delbridge S., Emily E. Tchr., asst. prin. Wendell (N.C.) High Sch., 1946-48; prin. Union High Sch., Engelhard High Sch., N.C., 1948-53, Central High Sch., Elizabeth City, N.C., 1953-59, Plymouth (N.C.) High Sch., 1959-61; supt. Washington County Schs., Plymouth, 1961—. Sec. Tidewater Athletic Conf., 1955. Served with AUS, 1943-46. Mem. N.C. Edn. Assn. (past local pres.), N.E.A., Am. Assn. Sch. Adminstrs., Albermarle Sch. Masters Club (past pres.). Baptist (deacon). Rotarian (past pres.), Kiwanian. Club: Ruritan (Elizabeth City, N.C.). Home: 112 Crescent Dr Plymouth NC 27962 Office: PO Box 747 Courthouse Adam St Plymouth NC 27962

O'NEAL, WILLIAM BERNARD, lawyer; b. Covington, Ky., Oct. 18, 1913; s. William Bernard and Nancy (Callahan) O'N.; LL.B., U. Cin., 1937, J.D.; m. Jacqueline Ewan Wood, Dec. 27, 1942; 1 son, William Bernard III. Admitted to Ohio bar, 1937, Ky. bar, 1938; practice law, Cin., Covington, 1937-39; asso. Matthews & Matthews, Cin., 1939-42; enforcement atty. U.S. Govt., Cin., 1946-47; mem. firm Kilcoyne, O'Neal, Meier & Varnau, and predecessor firm, Cin.; sec. Putman Candies, Inc., Cin.; dir., sec., treas. Strathmore Press, Inc., Cin.; dir. Motch, Inc., Covington. Prosecutor, Covington, 1952-55; city solicitor, Covington, 1958-62; judge Covington Municipal Ct., 1965—. Trustee Baker Hunt Found. Served to maj. USMCR, 1942-46. Mem. Marine Corps Res. Officers Assn., Christopher Gist (charter mem.), Ky. hist. socs., Ohio, Ky. Cin., Kenton County (pres. 1958) bar assns. Phi Delta Theta, Phi Delta Phi. Democrat. Episcopalian (vestryman). Clubs: University, Bankers (Cin.), Ft. Mitchell (Ky.) Country, Standard. Home: 2606 Eastern Av Covington KY 41014 Office: Central Trust Tower Cincinnati OH 45202

O'NEALL, ALBERT ELLIS, cons. civil engr.; b. Waynesville, O., Dec. 2, 1908; s. William Elias and Eva Irma (Ellis) O.'N.; student Antioch Coll., 1927-31; B.C.E., U. Fla., 1935; m. Margaret Jean Young, Nov. 27, 1937; children—John Stoakes, Marjorie Ann (Mrs. Hermon K. Herrin, Jr.). Engaged in surveying and engring. bus. prior to 1938; jr. engr. Naval Air Sta., Pensacola, Fla., 1938-40; engr. Smith & Gillespie, Jacksonville, Fla., 1940-41, 46-52, U.S. Engr. Dept., Jacksonville, 1941-43; engr. (owner) A.E. O'Neall Assos., Orlando, Fla., 1952-72, A. E. O'Neall Assos. div. Reynolds, Smith & Hills, Orlando, 1972—; pres. A.E. O'Neall Assos., Inc., 1961-72; v.p. Reynolds, Smith & Hills, Architects-Engrs.-Planners, Inc., 1972—. Trustee W.E. O'Neall Trust, Irma E. O'Neall Trust, Albert E. O'Neall Trust. Served with USNR, 1943-46. Named Engr. of Yr., 1964; recipient Fla. Engring. Soc. Distinguished Service award, 1971. Mem. Fla. Engring. Soc. (pres. 1964-65), Nat. Soc. Profl. Engrs. (dir. 1967-71), Am. Water Works Assn., Am. Pub. Works Assn., Fla. Pollution Control Assn., Am. Acad. Environmental Engrs., Royal Soc. Health, Am. Legion. Republican. Kiwanian (pres. North Orlando Club 1956, lt. gov. 1963). Home: 1111 Bryn Mawr St Orlando FL 32804 Office: 2626 Edgewater Dr Orlando FL 32804

O'NEILL, JAMES EDWARD, govt. ofcl.; b. Renovo, Pa., Feb. 2, 1929; s. Michael Francis and Dolores (Walsh) O'N.; A.B., U. Detroit, 1952, M.A., 1954; Ph.D., U. Chgo., 1961; m. Dorothy Joan Collings, Aug. 29, 1953; children—Cathleen Joan, Colleen Marie, Michael John, Kevin James, Patrick Bernard. Instr. U. Notre Dame, 1957-60, asst. prof. history, 1960-63; specialist Library of Congress, 1963-65; asso. prof. history, Loyola U., Chgo., 1965-69; dir. Franklin D. Roosevelt Library, Nat. Archives and Records Service, Hyde Park, N.Y., 1969-71; spl. asst. to Archivist of U.S., Washington, 1971, dep. archivist of U.S., The Nat. Archives, Washington, 1972—; mem. adv. bd. U.S. Army Mil. History Research Collection, 1973—. Mem. Am. Hist. Assn., Soc. Am. Archivists, U.S. Commn. on Mil. History. Roman Catholic. Contbr. articles to profl. hist., archival jours. Home: 8500 Varsity Ct Annandale VA 22003 Office: Nat Archives and Records Service Room 111 8th & Pennsylvania Av NW Washington DC 20408

O'NEILL, JOHN JOSEPH, elec. engr.; b. Bklyn., Dec. 4, 1930; s. John Joseph and Mary Elizabeth (Feeney) O'N.; B.E.E., N.Y. U., 1957; m. Kathleen Louise Bowmen, Sept. 20, 1952; children—Michael Sanford, Carolyn Jean, Janet Christine. Engr., Sperry Gyroscope Corp., Great Neck, N.Y., 1958-61; groupleader Airborne Instruments Labs., Melville, N.Y., 1961-67; asso. dir. communications Bunker Ramo Corp., Silver Spring, Md., 1967-69; asso. dept. head Mitre Corp., McLean, Va., 1969—; mem. staff Nat. Acad. Engring., Washington, 1970-71. Mem. cable television adv. com. FCC, 1972—. Served with USCG, 1951-54. Mem. I.E.E.E. (mem. com. 1956—). Contbr. articles to various publs. Home: 2613 Lemontree Lane Vienna VA 22180 Office: Westgate Research Park McLean VA 22101

O'NEILL, JOSEPH IGNATIUS, JR., oil co. exec.; b. Phila., Oct. 1, 1914; s. Joseph Ignatius and Helen Marie (Byrne) O'N.; B.S., in Commerce, U. Notre Dame, 1937, also postgrad.; postgrad. in law Temple U., 1937-39; m. Catherine C. Cummings, Nov. 26, 1940 (dec. July 1970); children—Helen (Mrs. Charles Schwab), Joseph Ignatius, Kevin Patrick, Michael Timothy; m. 2d, Mary Eaton Porter, Mar. 5, 1971. Clk., F.I. duPont & Co., Phila., 1938-39; clk. and spl. agt. Home Ins. Co. of N.Y., N.Y.C. and Atlanta, 1939-42; spl. agt. and supr. FBI, San Francisco and Los Angeles, 1942-46; sales mgr. Van Waters & Rogers, Inc., Los Angeles, 1946-48; owner O'Neill Co., oil operations and investments, Midland, Tex., 1948—; dir. Comml. Bank & Trust Co., Midland. Trustee, U. Notre Dame; bd. govs. Midland Meml. Hosp. Found., 1954-72, pres., 1953. Recipient Silver Goalposts, Sports Illustrated mag., 1961. Mem. Ind. Petroleum Assn. Am. (dir. 1966-68), Permian Basin Petroleum Assn. (1st pres. 1962), U. Notre Dame Alumni Assn. (pres. 1953-67, dir. 1958-72). Home: 22 Oaklawn Park Midland TX 79701 Office: 410 W Ohio St Midland TX 79701

O'NEILL, PAUL HENRY, govt. ofcl.; b. St. Louis, Dec. 4, 1935; s. John Paul and Gaynald (Irvin) O'N.; A.B., Fresno State Coll., 1960; postgrad. Claremont Coll., 1960-61, George Washington U., 1962-65; M.P.A. (Nat. Inst. Pub. Affairs fellow), Ind. U., 1965; m. Nancy J. Wolfe, Sept. 4, 1955; children—Patricia, Margaret, Julie, Paul. Office engr. Kinkaid & King, Anchorage, 1955; site engr. Morrison Knudsen, 1956-57; computer systems analyst VA, Washington, 1961-65; budget examiner Bur. Budget, Washington, 1967-70; chief, human resources programs div. Office of Mgmt. and Budget, 1970, asst. dir. Exec. Office of Pres., 1970-73, asso. dir., 1973—. Chmn. health-welfare coms. Fairfax Fedn. Civic Assns. Mem. Am. Econ. Assn. Home: 5522 Kings Park Dr Springfield VA 22151 Office: Office Mgmt and Budget Washington DC 20503

ONSAGER, LARS, educator; b. Oslo, Norway, Nov. 27, 1903; s. Erling and Ingrid (Kirkeby) O.; Ch.E., Norges tekniske hoiskole, Trondheim, Norway, 1925, Dr. Technicae (hon.), 1960; student Eidgenossische Technische Hochschule, Zurich, Switzerland, 1925 and 1926-28; Ph.D., Yale, 1935; D.S., Harvard, 1954; D.Sc., Brown U., 1962; Rensselaer Polytech. Inst., 1962; U. Chgo., 1968; Dr. der Naturwissenschaften, Rheinisch-West-faehlisch Technische Hochschule, Aachen; m. Margarete Arledter, Sept. 7, 1933; children—Erling Frederick, Inger (Mrs. Kenneth R. Oldham), Hans Tanberg, Christian Carl. Came to U.S., 1928, naturalized, 1945. Asso. chemistry, Johns Hopkins, 1928; instr. chemistry, Brown U., 1928-33; Sterling Fellow, Yale, 1933-34, asst. prof. chemistry, 1934-40, asso. prof., 1940-45. J. Willard Gibbs prof. theoretical chemistry, 1945-72; Distinguished Univ. Prof. Conter Theoretical Studies U. Miami (Fla.), 1972—. Fulbright scholar, United Kingdom, Cambridge, 1951, vis. prof. Rockefeller U., 1967; Gaussprof. U. Gottingen (Germany), 1968; Lorentz prof., Leiden, 1970. Recipient Rumford medal, 1953, Lorentz medal, 1958; G.N. Lewis medal 1962; John G. Kirkwood medal, 1962; Willard Gibbs medal, 1962; T.W. Richards medal, 1964; Debye award, 1965; Belfer award, 1966; Nobel prize in chemistry, 1968; Nat. Sci. medal, 1968. Fellow A.A.A.S., Am. Physical Soc., N.Y. Acad.; mem. Am. Philos. Soc., Royal Norwegian, Royal Swedish acads. scis., Norwegian Acad. Tech. Scis., Sci. Soc. Uppsala, Am. Chem. Soc., Conn. Acad., Nat. Acad., Norwegian Chem. Soc. (hon.), Barsen Soc. (hon.), Norwegian Acad. Sci. in Oslo, Am. Acad. Arts and Scis., Neurosci. Assos., Sigma Xi. Contbr. articles to sci. jours. Home: 4851 Biltmore Dr Coral Gables FL 33141

OOTEN, HOMER ANDREW, univ. adminstr.; b. Oakdale, Tenn., Aug. 30, 1942; s. Clarence Esco and Viola (Hamby) O.; B.S., Tenn. Technol. U., 1963; postgrad. Fla. Inst. Tech., 1966; M.S. Fla. State U., 1969, D.B.A. (Univ. fellow), 1973; m. Pamelia Frances McKinney, June 23, 1961; children—Cynthia Darlene, Terry Bryan. Design engr. DuPont Co., Chattanooga, 1963-64, supr., 1964, project coordinator, 1964-66; project engr., altitude chamber test condr. Bendix Corp., Kennedy Space Center, Fla., 1966-67; aerospace systems analysis engr. Boeing Co., Cocoa Beach, Fla., 1967-69; Univ. fellow Fla. State U., Tallahassee, 1969-70, dir. phys. planning, 1970-72, dir. bus. services, 1972—, asst. prof. mgmt., 1973—. Cons. engring. Belefant Assos., Cocoa Beach, Utility Contractors, Titusville, Fla., 1969, Benda Assos., Tallahassee, 1969—. Mem. Young Republican Club, Chattanooga, 1964. Chmn. Fla. State U. United Way Drive, 1973. Registered profl. engr., Fla. Mem. I.E.E.E. (sec. 1969), Soc. Coll., Univ. Planners, Fla. Engring. Soc. (sec. 1973), Nat. Soc. Profl. Engrs., Nat. Assn. Coll. Aux. Services, Nat. Assn. Coll. and U. Bus. Officers, Tau Beta Pi, Kappa Mu Epsilon, Eta Kappa Nu, Sigma Iota Epsilon (past pres.), Beta Gamma Sigma, Phi Kappa Phi. Republican. Presbyn. (deacon 1965). Home: Route 3 Box 564-E Centerville Rd Tallahassee FL 32303 Office: 201 Diffenbaugh Fla State U Tallahassee FL 32306

OPDYKE, JOHN BENJAMIN, civil engr.; b. Weehawken, N.J., Sept. 22, 1909; s. William John and Daisie Longfellow (Higgins) O.; B.S. in Civil Engring., Newark Coll. Engring., 1930, C.E., 1932; m. Marian Eloise George, Dec. 10, 1938; children—Janet, Pieter John, Steven, Kay. Instr. Newark Coll. Engring., 1934-37; asst. supervising engr. Lago Oil & Transporting Co., Ltd., Aruba, Netherlands Antilles, 1937-65, supervising engr. maintenance projects U. Fla., Gainesville, 1965—. Active Boy Scouts Am., Gainesville, 1965—; dir. Historic Gainesville, mem. Alachua County (Fla.) Hist. Commn., 1971—. Recipient Citizenship award Am. Legion, Dept. Panama, 1955; named Hon. Scoutmaster, Netherlands Boy Scouts, 1944; Ambassador of Goodwill, Govt. Aruba, 1965. Registered profl. engr., N.J., Fla. Mem. Am. Assn. U. Profs., Am. Soc. C.E., Am. Soc. E.E.,

Soc. Am. Mil. Engrs., Marine Tech. Soc., Nat. Hist. Soc., Amateur Fencers League Am., Alachua County (pres. 1971-73) hist. socs., U. Fla. Fencers (faculty sponsor), Smithsonian Assos. Republican. Episcopalian (vestryman, lay reader). Home: 1760 NW 14th Av Gainesville FL 32605

OPPENHEIMER, CARL HENRY, marine ecologist, microbiologist; b. Los Angeles, Nov. 13, 1921; s. Carl Henry and Marie Vivian (Hess) O.; B.A., U. So. Cal., 1947, M.A., 1949; Ph.D., Scripps Instn. Oceanography of U. Cal., 1951; Fulbright fellow U. Oslo, 1952-53; m. Dorothy Ann Paul, Mar. 1, 1971; children by previous marriage—Douglas Lee, John Carl, Donna (Mrs. Ray Wiley). Asst. marine biologist Scripps Instn. Oceanography, 1951-55; sr. research scientist Pan Am. Petroleum Corp. Research Center, 1955-57; research scientist, lectr. U. Tex., 1957-61; asso. prof. Inst. Marine Sci. of U. Miami, 1961-64; dir., prof. Oceanographic Inst. of Fla. State U., 1964-66, chmn. dept. oceanography, 1966-69, dir. Marine Lab., 1966-71; dir. U. Tex. Marine Sci. Inst., 1971-73, prof., 1971—. U.S. rep. eco-scis. panel NATO, 1971-73, chem. panel, 1973; mem. Tex. Senate Interim Coastal Zone Study Com., 1971-72, environmental sci. panel NSF, 1969-72, Pres.'s Oil Pollution Panel, Santa Barbara, Cal., 1969-70, environmental quality com. Coastal Bend Council Govts., Corpus Christi, Tex., 1972—; environmental quality advisor So. Interstate Nuclear Bd., 1972. Served with USNR, 1941-45. Mem. Am. Soc. Microbiologists, Soc. Limnology and Oceanography, Soc. Gen. Microbiology, Geochem. Soc., Sigma Xi. Symposium on Marine Microbiology, 1963; transl. Fundamentals Geomicogiology, 1963; Marine Biology II, 1966; Marine Biology IV, 1968. Contbr. articles to profl. jours. Home: 300 White St Port Aransas TX 78373 Office: University of Texas Marine Science Institute Port Aransas TX 78373

OPPENHEIMER, JESSE HALFF, lawyer; b. San Antonio, Jan. 4, 1919; s. Jesse D. and Lillie (Halff) O.; student U. Tex., 1935-37; B.A. with honors, U. Ariz., 1939; J.D. cum laude, Harvard, 1942; m. Susan Julia Rosenthal, July 18, 1946; children—Jesse David, Jean Louise, Barbara Sue. Admitted to Tex. bar, 1946; mem. firm Oppenheimer, Rosenthal, Kelleher & Wheatley, Inc. San Antonio. Former mem. bd. United Fund, Downtown Assn. San Antonio; mem. Steering Com. Met. San Antonio Urban Coalition, 1968-69. Past bd. dirs. Coll.-Community Creative Arts Center, Our Lady of Lake Coll., San Antonio, Symphony Soc. San Antonio, Santa Rosa Children's Hosp., Children's Service Bur., Ursuline Acad. San Antonio; past trustee Robert B. Green Hosp., San Antonio, v.p., trustee Marion Koogler McNay Art Inst., trustee San Antonio, St. Mary's Hall, Jesse H. and Susan R. Oppenheimer Found., Tex. Hosp. Council. Served to lt. col. AUS, 1942-46. Home: 400 Mandalay Dr East San Antonio TX 78212 Office: Suite 620 711 Navarro St San Antonio TX 78205

OPPERT, JOHNNY GARY, basketball coach; b. Dothan, Ala., Sept. 28, 1937; s. George Louis and Annie Mary (Dempsey) O.; A.B., Samford U., 1959; M.S., Troy State U., 1966; m. Carol Clemmons, Dec. 27, 1962; children—Anna Paige, John Gary. Coach football, basketball and baseball Wicksburg High Sch., Newton, Ala., 1959; player profl. baseball Los Angeles Dodger farm system, 1959-62; coach football, basketball and track Girard Jr. High Sch., Dothan, 1963-65; coach basketball, athletic dir. George C. Wallace Jr. Coll., Dothan, 1965—. Named High Sch. Coach of Yr., 1962; High Sch. All-Star Basketball Coach, 1963; Coll. Conf. Coach of Yr., 1971-72, 72-73, 73-74; recipient Silver Glove award, 1962. Baptist (deacon 1968—; chmn. recreation com. 1968-73; mem. pulpit com. 1973). Home: 1705 Adrian St Dothan AL 36301

ORCHARD, JAMES MADISON, hotel exec.; b. Chgo., May 6, 1919; s. Francis M. and Amy (Hunter) O.; student Hill Sch., Pottstown, Pa., 1937-39; B.A., Wesleyan U., 1943, M.A., 1947; m. Bette M. Pohle, Nov. 23, 1942; children—Virginia (Mrs. Chi Ming Tan), Barbara. Program mgr. Sta. WJAR-TV, Providence, 1948-49, Sta. KOTV, Tulsa, 1949-50; account exec. Paramount TV Prodns., N.Y.C., 1950-52, CBS-TV Films, N.Y.C., 1952-56, Sta. WABC-TV, N.Y.C., 1956-58, Lux Brill Films, N.Y.C., 1960-63; prodn. mgr. CBS Network, N.Y.C., 1958-63; marketing mgr. Grumman Aerospace Co., Bethpage, N.Y., 1963-70; mgr. Howard Johnson's Motor Lodge, Islamorada, Fla., 1971-73, Key Largo, Fla., 1973—. Served to lt. USNR, 1942-46. Address: PO Box 1169 Key Largo FL 33037

ORCUTT, THOMAS WILLIAM, physician; b. Wichita Falls, Tex., Jan. 11, 1943; s. William Hall and Helen Valerie (Peters) O.; B.A., DePauw U., 1964; M.D., Vanderbilt U., 1968; m. Betty Ann Swisher, Feb. 8, 1964; children—Tracy Ann, Kristin Dianne. Resident in surgery, Vanderbilt Hosp., Nashville, 1968-73; practice medicine, specializing in burn surgery, U.S. Army Inst. Surg. Research, San Antonio, 1973—. Am. Cancer Soc. fellow, 1971. Home: 12415 Los Campos St San Antonio TX 78233 Office: Brooke Army Medical Center San Antonio TX 78234

ORD, JOHN ALLYN, govt. adminstr.; b. West Elizabeth, Pa., Mar. 9, 1912; s. Edward Young and Ethel Dale (Thompson) O.; B.S. in Physics, Carnegie Inst. Tech., 1934, M.S., 1935, D.Sc. in Physics and Math., 1939; m. Sarah Louise Isler, Dec. 18, 1937; children—Priscilla Ann, Jean Sanders (Mrs. Leigh E. Doptis). Teaching fellow physics Carnegie Inst. Tech., Pitts., 1934-37, instr. physics, 1937-38; asst. prof. physics N.D. State U., Fargo, 1938-40; mgr. advanced concepts Systems Tech. Center Philco Corp., Arlington, Va., 1965-66; chief scientist U.S. Army Fgn. Sci. and Tech. Center, Charlottesville, Va., 1966-68, dep. dir., 1968—. Served to col., Signal Corps, AUS, 1940-65. Decorated Legion of Merit with oak leaf cluster. Carnegie Inst. Tech. grantee, 1934-37. Mem. Scabbard and Blade, Sigma Xi, Tau Beta Pi. Episcopalian. Mason. Home: 3006 Colonial Dr Charlottesville VA 22901 Office: 200-7th St NE Charlottesville VA 22901

O'REILLY, DON, columnist, sportscaster; b. Attleboro, Mass., May 1, 1913; s. Dennis C. and Helen L. (Barden) O'R.; student pub. schs.; m. Edith L. Macomber, July 9, 1938; 1 son, Howard. Owner, Eagle Press, Plainville, Mass., 1930-35; reporter, photographer Attleboro (Mass.) Sun, 1935-40, New London (Conn.) Day, 1940-42; reporter Washington Post, 1945-47; editor, pub. Speed Age mag., Washington, 1947-53; dir. News Bur., Nat. Assn. for Stock Car Racing, 1954-56; syndicated columnist Inside Auto Racing, Fla., also editor Auto News Syndicate, 1956-59, Atlanta, Detroit, 1959—; broadcaster auto races NBC Radio Network Monitor, Northeastern, Southeastern U.S., 1956-59; dir. pub. relations Atlanta Internat. Raceway, 1959-64; broadcaster syndicated radio program Inside Auto Racing, 1963-65; mgr. automotive div. Dynamics Films, Inc. of N.Y.C., Atlanta, Detroit, 1964-69; broadcaster motor sports Mutual Radio Network, 1970—. Served with USCGR, 1942-45. Mem. Nat., Detroit, Indianapolis, Atlanta press clubs, Nat. Press Photographers Assn., Automotive Old Timers, Indpls. Motor Speedway Oldtimers Assn., Nat. Sportscasters and Sportswriters Assn., Ga. Assn. Broadcasters, Am. Auto Racing Writers and Broadcasters Assn. (v.p.), Internat. Motor Press Assn., Nat. Motorsport Press Assn. (1st Pl. Broadcasting award 1965, 72). Republican. Methodist. Home: 4586 Roswell Rd Atlanta GA 30342 Office: Auto News Syndicate PO Box 6431 Marietta GA 30062

ORENTLICHER, HERMAN ISRAEL, lawyer, assn. exec., educator; b. Brockton, Mass., Oct. 26, 1910; s. George Harry and Yetta (Eiferman) O.; A.B., Harvard, 1933, J.D., 1936; m. Jeanette Adah Levin, July 3, 1938; children—John, Kay, George, David, Diane. Admitted to Mass. bar, D.C. bar, U.S. Supreme Ct. bar, practiced in Boston, 1936-37; counsel, chief briefs and opinions sect. U.S. Housing Authority, Washington, 1938-43, asst., acting gen. counsel HHFA, Washington, 1944-48; mem. faculty Nat. Law Center and Law Sch., George Washington U., Washington, 1949-60, prof., 1956-60; asso. sec., counsel Am. Assn. U. Profs., Washington, 1960-69, asso. gen. sec., counsel, 1969—; prof. law Emory U. Sch. Law, 1972—. Vis. prof. Boston Coll. Law Sch., 1967-68; adj. prof. Va. Poly. Inst. and State U. Grad. Sch. Edn., 1972; cons. in field; ex.-officio mem. Edn. Commn. of States, 1966-67. Mem. Phi Beta Kappa, Phi Delta Phi. Jewish religion (trustee, chmn. religious com.). Author: Tools of the National Housing Agency, 1944. Editor: (with William T. Fryer) Casebook, Legal Method and Legal System, 1968. Home: 3223-I Buford Hwy NE Atlanta GA 30329 Office: Emory U Sch Law Atlanta GA 30322

ORGAN, (AVIS) JOYCE CULPEPPER (MRS. RALEIGH RALPH ORGAN), librarian; b. Floresville, Tex., Apr. 6, 1912; d. Darius Ivan and Elfie May (Spencer) Culpepper; student Our Lady of the Lake Coll., San Antonio, 1956-57; m. Raleigh Ralph Organ, June 9, 1938. With Lackland AFB Library System, San Antonio, 1950—, librarian Officer Tng. Sch. Library, 1959—. Mem. Bexar County, Cath. library assns., Tex. Watercolor Soc., San Antonio Art League, River Art Group, San Antonio Conservation Soc., Nat. Audubon Soc., Wilderness Soc., Nat. Parks and Conservation Soc., Nat. Forests Soc., Air Force Assn., Smithsonian Instn. Editor, writer, compiler River Art Group bull., 1955-68. Home: 518 E Mayfield Blvd San Antonio TX 78214 Office: Forbes Hall Medina Annex Lackland AFB San Antonio TX 78214

ORILLION, ALFRED GREGORY, engring. supr.; b. Crowley, La., Sept. 4, 1928; s. George Gregory and Elida (Jeanis) O.; B.S. in Mech. Engring., U. S.W. La., 1953; postgrad. U. Ala., 1962-65; m. Elizabeth Anne Roberts, May 5, 1954; children—Nannette, Matthew, Lise, Roxanne. Trainee Gen. Electric Corp., Schenectady, 1953-54; project engr., Idaho Falls, Ida., 1954-56, Cin., 1956-60, prin. engr., Cin., 1960-61; engring. supr., NASA, Huntsville, Ala., 1961—. Partner, Orillion Estate Enterprises, Crowley, La., 1971—, corp. dir., 1972—. Sub chmn, Local Govt. Study Commn., Huntsville, 1972-73. Bd. dirs. Huntsville Bd. Adjustments, 1967-70, Huntsville Planning Bd., 1964-68, Huntsville Civil Def. Bd., 1964-68. Served with USMCR, 1946-48. Recipient Certificate of Award for Saturn I NASA, 1965. Registered profl. engr., Ala. Mem. La. Engring. Soc. (v.p. student chpt. 1952-53), Am. Inst. Aeros. and Astronautics, Nat. Soc. Profl. Engrs., Am. Nuclear Soc., Launch Vehicle and Missle Tech. Commn., Kappa Mu Epsilon, Tau Beta Pi (pres. chpt. 1952-53). Roman Catholic. Rotarian. Contbr. articles to profl. jours. Patentee in field. Research in aircraft nuclear propulsion, nuclear reactor, shields and propulaions, 1961-63; in Saturn/Apollo advanced space vehicle Systems 1963—. Home: 1201 E Cleermont Circle Huntsville AL 35804 Office: PD-TUG M MSFC AL 35812

ORLEANS, LEO A., govt. ofcl.; b. Russia, June 13, 1924; s. Anton J. and Susan (Agranovich) O. Came to U.S., 1939, naturalized, 1944; B.A., U. So. Cal., 1950; postgrad. in demography, econs., polit. sci. George Washington and Am. Univs., 1951-55; m. Helen Ruth Willis, Aug. 20, 1949; children—Nina, David. Sr. research analyst Library of Congress, Washington, 1951-65, China research specialist, 1966—, cons. NSF; asso. study dir. Office Econ. & Manpower Studies, NSF, Washington, 1965-66. Served with USAAF, 1943-46; PTO. Mem. Assn. for Asian Studies, Population Assn. Am., Internat. Population Union, Soc. Internat. Devel. Author: Professional Manpower and Education in Communist China, 1961; Every Fifth Child: The Population of China, 1972. Contbr. articles to profl. jours. Home: 5301 Brinkley Rd SE Washington DC 20031 Office: Library of Congress Washington DC 20540

ORMES, ROBERT VERNER, editor; b. N.Y.C., Sept. 10, 1921; s. Ferguson Reddie and Mabrie (Verner) O.; A.B., Wabash Coll., 1943; postgrad. Columbia U.; m. Mary Ann Otto, Sept. 2, 1950; children—Julia C., Carolyn V., Margaret F. Instr. English, math. and contemporary civilization Wabash Coll., Crawfordsville, Ind., 1947-49; tech. writer, Cushing & Nevell, N.Y.C., 1954; editorial asst. Science, jour. of A.A.A.S., Washington, 1954-57, asst. editor, 1957-60, mng. editor, 1961—. Served to lt. (j.g.), USNR, 1943-46. Mem. A.A.A.S., Council Biology Editors, Beta Theta Pi, Phi Beta Kappa. Democrat. Home: 2810 Central Av Alexandria VA 22302 Office: 1515 Massachusetts Av NW Washington DC 20005

ORMES, WALTER MASON, JR., educator; b. Ronceverte, W.Va., Mar. 28, 1918; s. Walter Mason and Eulalia (Bower) O.; B.S., Sch. Pharmacy, Med. Coll. Va., 1939; D.D.S., Med. Coll. Va., 1947; m. Elizabeth Ashton Harrison, Feb. 14, 1942; children—Anne Harrison (Mrs. Charles Edward Beal, Jr.), Ashton Harrison, Linda Elizabeth (Mrs. Dennis O'Bryon). Pharmacist, Richmond, Va., 1939-42; pvt. practice dentistry, Richmond, 1947-48; commd. 1st lt. U.S. Army Dental Corps, 1948, advanced through ranks to col., 1967, ret., 1969; asso. prof. Sch. Dentistry, Va. Commonwealth U., 1969—. Decorated Legion of Merit. Fellow Am. Coll. Dentists; mem. Am., Va. dental assns., Richmond Dental Soc., Va. Soc. Periodontists, Am. Acad. Periodontology, Assn. U.S. Army, Retired Officers Assn., Am. Assn. Dental Schs., Kappa Psi, Psi Omega, Omicron Kappa Upsilon, Sigma Zeta, Alpha Sigma Chi. Home: 2701 Walhala Dr Richmond VA 23235

ORMSTON, ALFRED JOSEPH, III, electric utility co. exec.; b. Scranton, Pa., Sept. 2, 1917; s. Alfred Joseph and Gertrude (Hendricks) O.; B.S. in Mech. Engring., U. Fla., 1939; m. Mary M. Murphy, June 26, 1948; children—Mary Lynn, Jean. Cadet engr. steam stas. Fla. Power Corp., St. Petersburg, 1940-41, jr. engr., 1946-50, turbine engr., 1950-51, mech. engr., 1951-55, chief mech. engr., 1955-64, v.p. power, 1964-73, v.p., asst. to sr. v.p., 1973—. Dir. Glanville Mortgage Co., St. Petersburg, Fla., 1973—. Mem. Pinellas County Services Study Commn., 1974. Bd. dirs. Com. of 100 of Pinellas County, Inc., 1972-73, Cath. Social Services of St. Petersburg Diocese, 1972—. Served to lt. comdr. USNR, 1941-46. Registered profl. engr., Fla. Mem. Am. Soc. M.E. (sr., mem. com. 1968—), Edison Electric Inst. (chmn. com. 1965-67), Nat. Soc. Profl. Engrs., Fla. Engring. Soc. (pres. Pinellas chpt. 1971-72), St. Petersburg Area C. of C. (bd. govs. 1973—). Home: 1221 43d Av N St Petersburg FL 33703 Office: Box 14042 St Petersburg FL 33733

ORNISH, EDWIN PAUL, dentist; b. Dallas, Jan. 17, 1925; s. Louis and Hannah (Hoffman) O.; student So. Meth. U., 1941-43; D.D.S., Baylor U., 1946; m. Natalie Gene Moskowitz, Nov. 6, 1949; children—Laurel Ann, Dean Michael, Steven Andrew, Kathy April. Practice dentistry, Dallas, 1949—; pres. Natwin Co. Dallas, 1959—. Prof. oral diagnosis Baylor Dental Coll. Served to capt. Dental Corps, USAAF, 1946-48. Mem. Am., Tex. dental assns., Am., Tex. acads. gen. dentistry, Am., Tex. socs. dentistry for children, Dallas County Dental Soc., Alpha Omega (pres. 1946). Mason. Contbr. articles to profl. jours. Home: 7146 Currin Dr Dallas TX 75230 Office: 6031 Sherry Lane Dallas TX 75225

O'ROURKE, JACQUELYN WARREN (MRS. T. NELSON O'ROURKE), pub. relations exec.; b. Gettysburg, Pa., Sept. 28, 1937; d. Elmer Willard and Gladys (Palmer) Warren; B.A., U. Miami, 1958; postgrad. Am. Inst. Pub. Relations, Chgo., 1970; m. T. Nelson O'Rourke, Mar. 17, 1973. Sales rep., asst. prodn. McMurray Printing Co., Miami, Fla., 1958-59; publicity asst. Fla. Power & Light Co., Miami, 1960-62, publicity rep., 1963-72, employee communicating supr., 1973; mng. editor Sunshine Service News, 1966-69, editor, 1970-73; founder firm Jacque O'Rourke Pub. Relations, Daytona Beach, Fla., 1973—. Recipient Best Feature Story award Fla. Mag. Assn., 1966, Best Picture Story award, 1967, Gen. Excellence award for an internal mag., 1966, 67, 70, 71; Gold Quill award Am. Assn. Indsl. Editors, 1970. Mem. Am. Women in Radio and TV, Women in Communications, Inc. (pres. Miami chpt. 1967-68; co-chmn. nat. conv. 1971), Alpha Sigma Epsilon, Delta Delta Delta. Office: 625-13 N Halifax Av Daytona Beach FL 32018

O'ROURKE, JOHN CASSUS, pump co. exec.; b. Oklahoma City, Jan. 4, 1928; s. John Edward and Anna Isabella (Fischer) O'R.; student Draughn's Bus. Coll., 1947; Asso. Diesel Tech., Okla. State U., 1953; m. Jeanne Carroll Thornton, Nov. 14, 1945; children—Kathryn Janelle, Theresa Mischelle, John Kevin. Plant engr. Reda Pump Co., Bartlesville, Okla., 1953-56, chief engr. plant prodn. and research and devel., 1956-69, mgr. engring., 1969—; v.p. engring., 1972—. Mem. Washington County Citizens Adv. Com., 1968-69, chmn., 1969. Served with USNR, 1945-46. Mem. Bartlesville Engrs. Club, (dir. 1968), Bartlesville C. of C. Republican. Roman Catholic. Elk. Clubs: Hillcrest Country, Toastmasters (adminstrv. v.p. 1966-67) (Bartlesville). Patentee in field. Home: 4956 Amherst St Bartlesville OK 74003 Office: 509 W Hensley St Bartlesville OK 74003

ORR, FRANK HOWARD, III, architect; b. Jasper, Ala., Sept. 4, 1932; s. Frank Howard and Lola Ruth (Lynch) O.; student U. Md., Tripoli, Libya Extension Center, 1956-57; B.S. in Applied Art, Auburn U., 1961; spl. studies U. Tenn., Knoxville, 1967; m. Nancy Gayle Gentry, Apr. 13, 1957; children—Mark Daniel, Steven Gentry, Karen Diann, Amy Ruth. Project mgr. Edwin A. Keeble Assos., Inc. Architects/Engrs., Nashville, 1962-70; asso. architect Bianculli and Tyler, Inc., Architects, Chattanooga, 1970; prin. Frank Orr Architects, Nashville, 1970—. Lectr. on architecture O'More Sch. Design, Franklin, Tenn. Mem. Historic Belmont, Inc., Nashville, 1972—. Adv. bd. for archtl. and bldg. constrn. engring. tech. Nashville State Tech. Inst. Bd. trust Am. Bapt. Theo. Sem., Nashville, also mem. So. Bapt. Ccmmn. Served with USAF, 1954-58. Mem. A.I.A. (corporate mem.; dir. local chpt. 1971—; mem. nat. environmental edn. com. 1973—), Theta Chi, Scarab. So. Baptist (deacon 1968—). Club: Seven Hills Swimming and Tennis (Nashville). Home: 1708 Stokes Lane Nashville TN 37215 Office: 3324 West End Av Nashville TN 37203

ORR, JAMES FITZGERALD, ret. banker; b. Webb City, Mo., July 19, 1905; s. Charles Thomas and Grace (FitzGerald) O.; grad. B.S. in Mining Engring., Mo. Sch. Mines, 1930; m. Pearl Miller, Nov. 7, 1930; 1 dau., Judith Ann (Mrs. Jerry L. Ford). Engr., LeFlure County Gas and Electric Co., Poteau, Okla., 1930-64, dir., 1935-64, dir. athletic mining and smelting, 1937-64, v.p. athletic mining and smelting, 1950-62, pres., 1962-64, ret., 1964; dir. Central Nat. Bank, Poteau, 1933-74, First Nat. Bank, Ft. Smith, Ark., 1963-74. Mason, Rotarian (pres. 1935-36). Home: 901 N Witte St Poteau OK 74953

ORR, JAMES MILTON, dentist; b. Memphis, Tex., May 20, 1918; s. Milton Newton and Nannie Adalee (Vallance) O.; student Tex. Tech U., 1935-37; D.D.S., U. Tex., 1941; m. Elizabeth Hook, Nov. 22, 1941; children—Lynda (Mrs. Carol Joe Davis), Jane (Mrs. Tommy Glenn Thomas), Ann (Mrs. Lynn McLain). Instr. U. Tex. Dental Sch., 1941-45; practice dentistry, Wellington, Tex., 1945—; mem. staff Ollingsworth Gen. Hosp., Wellington. Dir. Wellington State Bank; sec. See More, Inc. Served to maj. USAF, 1953-55. Mem. Am. Dental Assn., Tex., Panhandle Dist. dental socs., Acad. Gen. Dentistry, Southwest Prosthetic Soc., Omicron Kappa Upsilon. Mason (32 deg.), Rotarian (pres. 1959), Kiwanian (pres. 1950). Home: 1700 Dalhart St Wellington TX 79095 Office: 916 West Av Wellington TX 79095

ORR, MARK TAYLOR, educator; b. Mt. Croghan, S.C., Apr. 20, 1914; s. Oliver H. and Jennie (Taylor) O.; student Mars Hill Coll., 1932-34; A.B., U. N.C., 1937, Ph.D., 1954; postgrad. U. Va., 1944, U. Mich., 1945; m. Katherine Wilkinson, Mar. 16, 1944; children—Karen Lee, Mark Taylor. Asst. dir. So. Council on Internat. Relations, Chapel Hill, N.C., 1937-41; instr. U. Tampa, 1941-42; chief edn. div. Gen. Hdqrs. Allied Powers, Tokyo, Japan, 1946-49; instr. U. N.C., 1949-51; coordinator Internat. Studies and Programs, asso. prof. U. S.Fla., Tampa, 1966—. Served with USAAF, 1941-46, to col. USAF, 1951-66. Mem. Japan Soc., Am. Polit. Sci. Assn., Am. Fgn. Service Officers Assn., Air Force Assn., Internat. Studies Assn., Assn. for Asian Studies, Nat. Assn. Fgn. Student Affairs. Author: (with Robert McAllen) Education in Japan, 1947. Editor: The South and World Affairs, 1937-41. Home: 2807 Samara Dr Tampa FL 33618

ORR, ROBERT LEE, clergyman; b. Jone's Mill, Tenn., Aug. 17, 1913; s. Robert Leslie and Lillie Elizabeth (Freeman) O.; A.B., Union U., Jackson, Tenn., 1937; D.D., 1949; Th.M., Southwestern Theol. Sem., Ft. Worth, 1941; m. Sally Linnington Fulghum, Sept. 21, 1936; 1 son, Robert Len. Ordained to ministry Baptist Ch., 1933; pastor chs. in Okla., 1937-41, Miss., 1941-43; pastor Browsville (Tenn.) Baptist Ch., 1943-50, First Bapt. Ch., Dyersburg, Tenn., 1950—. Mem. exec. com. Tenn. Bapt. Conv., 1946—. Chmn. campaigns A.R.C., Dyersburg, 1955. Trustee Union U. (chmn. steering com. to re-locate coll. campus 1971-73), Southwestern Theol. Sem., Bapt. Meml. Hosp. (chmn. bd. 1961-73), Recipient citation Freedoms Found., 1971; Distinguished Alumnus award Union U., 1972. Mem. Alumni Assn. Union U. (pres. 1967-68). Mason, Rotarian. Home: 200 Oak St Dyersburg TN 38024 Office: First Baptist Ch Dyersburg TN 38024

ORR, WILLIAM NEWTON, dentist; b. Memphis, Tex., Dec. 18, 1908; s. Milton Newton and Nannie (Vallance) O.; D.D.S., U. Tex., 1930; m. Leila Mae Brashear, Oct. 15, 1931; children—William Reed, Robert Lee. Practice dentistry, Shamrock, Tex., 1930-32, Littlefield, Tex., 1932-67; dir. Houston Dental Pub. Health, 1968—. Dist. chmn. Boy Scouts Am., 1935-47. Trustee Littlefield Ind. Sch., 1937-49. Named Littlefield Citizen of Year. C. of C., 1965. Fellow Am. Coll. Dentists, Tex. Dental Assn.; mem. Tex. State Assn. (v.p. 1960-61), S. Plains Dental Soc. (pres. 1945), Littlefield C. of C. (trustee 1961-68), U. Tex. Coll. Dentistry Alumni (pres. 1968). Methodist (finance chmn. 1945-54). Mason, Rotarian (pres. 1966). Home: 10118 Hollyspring St Houston TX 77042 Office: 1115 N McGregor St Houston TX 77000

ORTH, DAVID NELSON, educator, physician; b. East Orange, N.J., Mar. 5, 1933; s. John Joseph and Marjorie Adelaide (Wauters) O.; Sc.B. in Chemistry, Brown U., 1954; M.D., Vanderbilt U., 1962; m. Ann Odell Stewart, Aug. 4, 1956; children—John Randall, Jennifer Stewart, Julie Thomas. Intern, Osler Med. Service Johns Hopkins Hosp., Balt., 1962-63, resident, 1963-65; USPHS postdoctoral fellow in clin. endocrinology and metabolism Vanderbilt U., 1965-68, asst. prof. medicine, 1967-72, asso. prof. medicine, 1972—, co-dir. endocrinology research and tng. program, 1968—, dir. Cancer

Research & Tng. Center, 1972—. Cons. Nashville VA Hosp., St. Thomas Hosp., Nashville; investigator Howard Hughes Med. Inst., Miami, Fla. Bd. dirs. Nashville-Davidson County chpt. Am. Cancer Soc. Served to lt. (j.g.), USNR, 1954-57. Recipient Borden award, 1962. John & Mary R. Markle scholar, 1968-73; Mosby scholar, 1962. Mem. A.A.A.S., Am. Fedn. for Clin. Research, Endocrine Soc., So. Soc. for Clin. Investigation, Internat. Soc. for Chronobiology, Nat. Pituitary Agy. (med. adv. bd. 1971), Internat. Endocrine Soc. (central com. 1973—), Alpha Omega Alpha, Sigma Xi, Alpha Delta Phi. Episcopalian. Editorial bd. Jour. Clin. Endocrinology and Metabolism, 1971—. Contbr. articles on endocrinology to profl. jours. Home: 114 Taggart Av Nashville TN 37205 Office: Vanderbilt U Medical Center Nashville TN 37232

ORTH, DONALD JOSEPH, govt. ofcl.; b. Fond du Lac, Wis., July 26, 1925; s. Joseph Peter and Julia Theresa (Shaw) Orth; B.S., U. Wis., 1952, postgrad., 1953; postgrad. U. Colo., 1954, George Washington U., 1963-64; m. Martha Camille Beggs, Dec. 21, 1966; children—LaDonna Marie (Mrs. David Thomas O'Loughlin), Mary Ellen (Mrs. James T. Kent). Cartographer, U.S. Geol. Survey, Denver, 1953-59, geographer, Washington, 1959-73, chief geog. names sect., 1961-73; mem. U.S. Bd. on Geog. Names, U.S. Dept. Interior, Washington, 1973—, exec. sec., 1973—. Commn. mem. Place Name Survey of U.S., 1969—, Pan Am. Inst. Geography and History, 1973—; mem. Internat. Commn. Onomastic Scis., 1972—; professorial lectr. George Washington U., Washington, 1967—. Mem. Arlington County (Va.) Independence Bicentennial Commn., 1972—. Bd. dirs. Arlington Hist. Museum. Served with USNR, 1942-46. Mem. Am. Name Soc. (pres. 1972), Assn. Am. Geographers, Am. Congress of Surveying and Mapping, Arctic Inst. N.Am., Am. Polar Soc., Va. Archaeol. Soc., Soc. for History of Discoveries. Club: Explorers (N.Y.C.). Author: Aux Arcs and Tuckers Terror, 1973; Dictionary of Alaska Place Names, 1967; Place Names and Computers, 1970; Words, Thought, and Landscape, 1972. Home: 212 N Emerson St Arlington VA 22203 Office: Nat Center Reston VA 22092

ORTON, EDWARD WHITFIELD, geologist, educator; b. Monroe, N.C., July 4, 1922; s. Charles Whitfield and Minnie (Storck) O.; student Dickinson Coll., 1946-48; B.S. in Geology, U. Okla., 1950; M.S. in Geology, La. State U., 1952; postgrad. U. Cal. at Berkeley, 1963, U. Tex., 1965, 67, 68, Tex. A. and M., 1970, U. Wyo., 1970; m. Pearl Drumwright, Dec. 21, 1954; children—Charles Edward, Robert Whitfield. Research geologist La. Wildlife and Fisheries Commn., 1954-56; asst. prof. U. Southwestern La., Lafayette, 1957; asst. prof. geology La. Poly. Inst., Ruston, 1957-61; prof. geology Odessa (Tex.) Coll., 1961—, chmn. dept. geology, 1966—. Mem. Geol. Soc. Am., Am. Assn. Petroleum Geologists, Odessa Meteoritic Soc., Sigma Gamma Epsilon. Episcopalian. Home: 3101 Eastover Dr Odessa TX 79762

ORTON, GEORGE WANDELL, educator, former air force officer; b. Slaughters, Ky., Oct. 31, 1919; s. Cecil T. and Jennie (Brooks) O.; B.S., U. Ky., 1943; M.S., Carnegie Mellon U., 1948; Ph.D., Ohio State U., 1961; m. Kathryn Lane Morrison, July 24, 1943; children—Joe Brooks, John Michael. Commd. 2d lt. USAAF, 1943, advanced through grades to col. USAF, 1969; combat pilot, 1943-45; sect. chief metal research, 1948-52, asst. dir. mfg. tech., 1952-55, br. chief materials handling systems, 1955-59; mem. faculty USAF Acad., Colorado Springs, Colo., 1961-66, mil. adviser, Philippines, 1966-68, dir. USAF mfg. tech. div., Wright Patterson AFB, 1968-69; ret., 1969; prof. engring. U. Puerto Rico, Mayaguez, 1969—. Adviser Philippines Armed Forces; chmn. Puerto Rican Environmental Pollution Abatement Seminar, 1970—. Decorated D.F.C; recipient Am. Soc. for Handling Materials award, 1959. NSF grantee, 1964-65. Mem. Am. Soc. for Metals, Am. Soc. for Engring. Edn., Nat. Wildlife Soc., Sigma Xi, Phi Lambda Upsilon, Sigma Gamma Epsilon. Mason. Office: Ingenieria General Recinto Universidad Mayaguez Mayaguez PR 00708

ORVIS, ELMER PAUL, engring. mgr.; b. Cleve., Mar. 26, 1923; s. Harvey Willard and Helen Louise (Gerlach) O.; student Westminster Coll., Pa., 1942-43; B.E.E. cum laude, Fenn Coll., 1949; m. Laverne Elsie Ross, Feb. 14, 1948; children—Robert, Ronald, Richard, Barbara. Devel. engr. Leece Neville Co., Cleve., 1949-56; sect. engr. Lear-Siegler, Inc., Elyria, O., 1956-62; dir. engring. Gen. Industries Co., Elyria, 1962-70; mgr. engring. Franklin Electric Co., Inc. (formerly owned by Singer Co.), Jacksonville, Ark., 1971—; lectr. elec. engring. Fenn Coll., Cleve., 1950-56. Mem. adv. com. S.W. Tech. Inst., 1973—. Served with Signal Corps, AUS, 1943-46. Mem. I.E.E.E., Am. Legion, Tau Beta Pi. Home: 4308 Hazelwood Rd North Little Rock AR 72116 Office: PO Box 887 Jacksonville AR 72076

ORY, ROBERT LOUIS, biochemist; b. New Orleans, Nov. 26, 1925; s. Alfred A. and Louise (Gendron) O.; B.S., Loyola U., New Orleans, 1948; M.S., U. Detroit, 1950; Ph.D., Tex. A. and M. U., 1954; m. Mary Elizabeth Hobley, Dec. 27, 1948 (div. Feb. 1957); children—Barbara Ann, Mary Catherine. With U.S. Dept. Agr., 1954-68, 69—, head protein properties investigations, oilseed and food lab., New Orleans, 1969—; Fulbright research scholar Poly. Inst. Denmark, Lyngby, 1968-69; lectr. Mem. Am. Chem. Soc. (pres. La. sect. 1967-68), A.A.A.S., Sci. Research Soc. Am., Am. Soc. Plant Physiologists, Am. Oil Chemists Soc., Am. Peanut Research Edn. Assn., Union of Holy Name Socs. New Orleans (dist. v.p. 1957-58), Men's Holy Name Soc. Parish Ch. (past pres., Outstanding Man of Year 1958), Sigma Xi. Served with USMCR, 1944-46. Contbg. author: Annual Review of Plant Physiology, 1966, Biochemical Preparations, 1963, Symposium: Seed Proteins, 1973; also contbr. papers to profl. jours. Home: 3547 Roger Williams St New Orleans LA 70119 Office: PO Box 19687 New Orleans LA 70179

OSBORN, GLENN RICHARD, audio engr.; b. Los Angeles, Oct. 25, 1928; s. Glenn Litz and Nellie (Hoffman) O.; B.S. in Audio Engring., U. Hollywood, 1949; m. Joye Elise Hughes, Feb. 15, 1963; children—Eric William, John Howard. Head transmission engr., 1352 Motion Picture Squadron, Hollywood, 1953-60; head, sound dept., Sandia Corp., Albuquerque, 1960-65, supr. sound dept. A-V Corp., Manned Spacecraft Center, Houston, 1965—. Served with AUS, 1950-52. Mem. Audio Engring. Soc., Acoustical Soc. Am., Soc. Motion Picture and TV Engrs. Home: 2117 Willow Wisp Dr Seabrook TX 77586 Office: 2518 N Boulevard Houston TX 77001

OSBORN, MALCOLM EVERETT, ins. co. exec.; b. Bangor, Me., Apr. 29, 1928; s. Lester Everett and Helen (Clark) O.; B.A., U. Me., 1952; postgrad. Harvard, 1952-54; J.D., Boston U., 1956, LL.M., in Taxation, 1961; m. Claire A. Franks, Aug. 30, 1953; children—Beverly, Lester, Malcolm, Jr., Ernest. Admitted to bars Me., 1956, Mass., 1956, N.C., 1965, U.S. Dist. Ct. Mass., Middle Dist., U.S. Tax Ct., U.S. Ct. Claims, I.R.S. Ct.; atty. tax counsel State Mut. Life Assurance Co. Am., Worcester, Mass., 1956-64; asst. gen. counsel Pan-Am. Life Ins. Co., New Orleans, 1964; 2d v.p., tax counsel Integon Corp., and other Integon group cos., Winston-Salem, N.C., 1964-72, v.p., tax counsel, 1972—. Adj. prof. U. N.C., Greensboro, 1968—; lectr. N.Y. U. Annual Inst. on Fed. Taxation, 1973. Bd. dirs., atty. Winston-Salem Swim Club, Inc., 1967—; bd. dirs. Integon Found., Inc., Christian Fellowship Home; trustee N.C. Council Econ. Edn. Mem. Worcester County, Forsyth County, N.C., Fed., Internat., Am. bar assns., Assn. Life Ins. Counsel, Am. Assn. U. Profs., Phi Eta Kappa. Mason. Home: 3639 Kirklees Rd Winston-Salem NC 27104 Office: 420 N Spruce St Winston-Salem NC 27102

OSBORNE, CHARLES EDWARD, chem. co. scientist; b. Mt. Croghan, S.C., Aug. 5, 1929; s. Edward Ruffin and Emeline Gladys (Denham) O.; B.S. in Chemistry, U. N.C., 1951; M.S. in Chemistry, U. Me., 1953; Ph.D., Northwestern U., 1956; m. Columbine Vera Amici, Aug. 6, 1955; children—Christine Megan, Gregory Evan. Chemist Eastman Kodak Co., Rochester, N.Y., 1951-52, Tenn. Eastman Co., Kingsport, 1956-59, sr. chemist, 1959-63, 64-71. devel. asso., 1971—. Mem. A.A.A.S., Am. Chem. Soc., Phi Beta Kappa, Sigma Xi, Phi Kappa Phi, Phi Lambda Upsilon, Episcopalian (vestryman 1968-71, 73—, lay reader 1971—). Patentee in field. Contbr. articles to profl. jours. Home: 1540 Belmeade Dr Kingsport TN 37664 Office: Tennessee Eastman Company Kingsport TN 37662

OSBORNE, COLIN PORTER, JR., dentist; b. Aberdeen, N.C., Jan. 15, 1921; s. Colin Porter and Marguerite Jessie (Brasington) O.; student Guilford Coll., 1938-41; D.D.S., Atlanta-So. Dental Sch., 1944; m. Frances Elizabeth Collins, Oct. 20, 1945; children—Colin Porter III, Pamela Jane, Rebecca Leigh, Margaret Elizabeth. Practice dentistry, Fayetteville, N.C., 1947, Lumberton, N.C., 1947—; chief dental services Robeson County Meml. Hosp.; cons. community colls. dept. N.C. Dept. Edn., 1966-70. Bd. dirs. N.C. Symphony Soc., 1949-54, Community Concert Assn., 1949—, Dental Found. N.C., 1960-73, YMCA, Lumberton, 1960-66. Served with AUS, 1943-44, USNR, 1944-45, USMCR, 1945-46. Recipient Medal Daus. Am. Revolution, 1967; named Outstanding Ch. Clk., 1972. Fellow Am. Coll. Dentists; mem. Am. Dental Assn., N.C., 4th Dist., Southeastern dental socs., Fedn. Dentaire Internat., Am. Soc. Dentistry for Children, Nat. Rehab. Assn., Flying Dentist Assn., Robeson Choral Soc., Robeson Baptist Assn. (clk. 1971—), Delta Sigma Delta (nat. chmn. 1967-68). Democrat. Baptist (deacon). Kiwanian (past pres.). Club: Music of Lumberton (pres. 1957). Home: 2405 Rowland Av Lumberton NC 28358 Office: Rowland Av at 27th St Lumberton NC 28358

OSBORNE, EARL T., judge; b. Benton, Ky., July 10, 1920; s. Willie C. and Dovie (Bradford) O.; LL.B., U. Ky., 1950; m. Helen Cooper, Nov. 17, 1942; children—William P., Thomas L., Phyllis J., Deborah J. Admitted Ky. bar, 1950; practiced in Benton, Ky. 1950-56; circuit judge 42d Jud. Dist. Ky., Benton, 1956-66; judge Court of Appeals of Ky. 1967—. Served with USAAF, 1940-46; ETO. Decorated air medal. Mem. Am., Ky. bar assns., V.F.W., Am. Legion. Democrat. Methodist. Contbr. to profl. jours. Lectr. on Constitution of Ky. Home: Route 1 Gilbertsville KY 42044 Office: Court of Appeals Capitol Bldg Frankfort KY 40601

OSBORNE, FRANKLIN TALMAGE, chem. engr.; b. Pewee Valley, Ky., Dec. 1, 1939; s. Lewis Talmage and Geneva Love (Measle) O.; B.S., Tex. A. & M. U., 1961; Ph.D., N.C. State U., 1969; m. Bernice Faye Darland, Sept. 2, 1961; children—Donna Marie, David Lee. Research engr. Chemstrand Research Center, Durham, N.C., 1964-66, sr. engr., 1968-70, sr. research specialist, 1970-71; sr. group leader Monsanto Co., Pensacola, Fla., 1971—. Served to 1st. lt. AUS, 1962-64. NASA fellow, 1966-68. Mem. Am. Inst. Chem. Engrs., T.A.P.P.I., Sigma Xi, Tau Beta Pi. Baptist. Contbr. articles to profl. jours. Home: 413 Andrew Jackson Trail Gulf Breeze FL 32561 Office: Monsanto Co PO Box 12830 Pensacola FL 32575

OSBORNE, HARRY ALBERT, JR., banker; b. Winston-Salem, N.C., Mar. 23, 1936; s. Harry Albert and Louise (Kimbrough) O.; B.S., N.C. State U., 1958; M.B.A., U. N.C., 1962; m. Gladys Ann Rozier, June 8, 1963; 1 dau., Caroline Louise. Mgmt. trainee Wachovia Bank, Winston-Salem, 1962-63, br. mgr., lending officer loan adminstrn. officer, marketing officer, Goldsboro, N.C., 1963-67, v.p. corporate accounts dept., Winston-Salem, 1967-72, v.p. retail loan adminstrn. dept., 1972—. Mem. admissions and budget com. United Fund, 1965-67; treas. Wayne County Heart Fund, 1966-67. Served as 1st lt. Signal Corps, AUS, 1958-60. Decorated Army Commendation medal. Lutheran (asst. treas. 1969-71). Mason, Elk. Home: 570 Westoak Trail Winston-Salem NC 27104 Office: PO Box 3099 Winston-Salem NC 27102

OSBORNE, JOHN ARTHUR, accountant, univ. business officer; b. Denver, Feb. 7, 1931; s. Harold Humphrey and Erma (Allison) O.; A.A., Coffeyville (Kan.) Jr. Coll., 1954; B.S. with honors, U. Tulsa, 1956, law student, 1956-58; short course (scholarship student) U. Omaha, 1962. Accountant Pan. Am. Petroleum Corp., 1956-57; sr. accountant Frazer & Torbet, C.P.A., Tulsa, 1957-61; asst. sec.-treas. U. Tulsa, 1961—, comptroller, 1968—. Gen. chmn. Southwest Bus. Equipment Show of Tulsa, 1965; mem. planning com. Tulsa Conf. Accountants, 1965—, mayor's system study com., Tulsa, 1967. Served with USAF, 1951-52. C.P.A., Okla., 1959. Recipient Scholarship key Delta Sigma Pi, 1956; Gold medal award Okla. Soc. C.P.A.'s, 1956; certificate of merit Coll. Bus. Administrn., U. Tulsa, 1956, Merit award, Tulsa chapter Systems and Procedures Assn., 1967; named One of Outstanding Young Men in Am., 1966. Mem. Central Assn. Coll. and Univ. Bus. Officers (exec. com. 1963-64), Okla. Assn. Coll. and Univ. Bus. Officers (sec. treas. 1973-74), Assn. Coll. and Univ. Auditors, Am. Inst. C.P.A.'s, Okla., Tulsa socs. C.P.A.'s, U. Tulsa Alumni Assn. (treas. 1960-70), Systems and Procedures Assn. (treas. Tulsa chpt. 1962-64, pres. 1965-66), Nat. Assn. Accountants (chpt. bd. dirs. 1971—, chpt. v.p. 1973-74), Am. Accounting Assn., Coll. and U. Personnel Assn., Assn. Ednl. Data Systems, Photographic Soc. Am., Phi Gamma Kappa (treas.), Alpha Kappa Psi (charter mem. U. Tulsa chpt.). Episcopalian (asso. vestry). Club: University (incorporator, sec.-treas. 1963-69). Home: PO Box 4614 Tulsa OK 74104 Office: 600 S College St Tulsa OK 74104

OSBORNE, JOHN CLARK, educator; b. Independence, Va., June 24, 1918; s. Preston and Ruth A. (Cox) O.; B.S., Va. Poly. Inst., 1939; M.S. (fellow), U. Me., 1941; D.V.M., Duke, 1949; postgrad. Bowman Gray Sch. Medicine, 1967-69; m. Hortense F. Bond, Mar. 8, 1947; children—Linda (Mrs. Gerald Cassell), John Clark, Phylliss, Gregory, Diane, Barbara. Research prof. N.C. State Coll. at Raleigh, 1949-62; prof. vet. sci., research vet. pathologist Va. Poly. Inst. at Blacksburg, 1962—. Dept. chmn. United Fund, Blacksburg, 1969-70. Served to capt. U.S. Army, 1942-46. Postdoctoral fellow Nat. Heart Inst., 1960-61, NIH, 1967-69. Mem. Am., Va., S.W. Va. vet. med. assns., N.C. Vet. Research Found. (founder 1957), So. Animal Disease Research Workers (pres. 1957), Conf. Research Workers in N.Am. Vet. Nutritionists, Sigma Xi. Democrat. Methodist (bd. ofcls.). Mason (K.T.), Toastmaster. Clubs: University, Hokie (Blacksburg). Contbr. numerous articles to profl. jours. Home: 1002 Willard Dr Blacksburg VA 24060

OSBURN, JOHN DUNCAN, electrical products mfg. co. engr.; b. Paris, Tex., Jan. 31, 1940; s. Irvin Fischer and Mary (McMillan) O.; B.S., U. Tex., 1964. Research engr. Electromechanics Co., Austin, Tex., 1965, 67-69; gen. mgr. White Electromagnetics Inc., Rockville, Md., 1969-70; electromagnetic compatibility engr. Tracor Inc., Austin, 1971—. Served with AUS, 1965-67. Recipient Commendation medal for engring. Joint Services. Mem. I.E.E.E. Patentee in field. Home: 1811 Rogge Ln Austin TX 78723 Office: 6500 Tracor Ln Austin TX 78721

O'SHELL, VINCENT JOSEPH, orthodontist; b. Beaumont, Tex., May 10, 1927; s. Michael Vincent and Grace (Canizaro) O'S.; student Loyola U. of South, 1944-45, 46-47; B.S., Baylor U., 1949; D.D.S., U. Tex., 1953; M.S., U. Mo., 1954; m. Aphrodite Barbatis, June 28, 1954; children—Cynthia Graceann, Doria Maria, Michael Vincent. Practice orthodontics, Beaumont, 1954—. Served with U.S. Mcht. Marine, 1945-46; PTO. Mem. Am. Assn. Orthodontists, Tex. Tweed Orthodontic Soc., Tex. Soc. Dentistry for Children, Sabine Dist. Dental Soc., Beta Beta Beta, Xi Psi Phi. Republican. Roman Catholic. K.C. Home: 160 E Caldwood St Beaumont TX 77707 Office: 3325 Calder St Beaumont TX 77706

O'STEEN, CLAYTON ELWIN, hosp. adminstr.; b. Lakeland, Fla., Oct. 8, 1939; s. Clayton and Josephine Louise (Winn) O'S.; grad. Grady Meml. Hosp. Sch. X-Ray Tech., 1958; student U. Fla., 1959-61; B.S., Fla. So Coll., 1966; M.H.A., Med. Coll. Va., 1968; m. Helen Carol Sineath, Sept. 9, 1961; children—Jolene, Heather. Radiol. technologist Lakeland Gen. Hosp., 1961-66; spl. adminstrv. asst. Richmond (Va.) Meml. Hosp., 1968; adminstrv. asst. Columbia (S.C.) Hosp., 1968-69; adminstr. Jackson Hosp., Marianna, Fla., 1969—. Mem. licensed practical nurse adv. bd. Chipola Jr. Coll., 1970; active Am. Cancer Soc. Bd. dirs. Jackson County Guidance Center, 1969-70, v.p., 1971; bd. dirs. N.W. Fla. Mental Health Center, 1970-71; sec. N.W. Fla. Hosp. Council, 1971-72, bd. dirs., 1970-71, pres., 1972-75; Fla. rep. Southeastern Hosp. Conf., 1973-75. Mem. Am., Fla. (mem. pub. relations council, trustee) hosp. assns., Delta Sigma Phi. Elk, Rotarian. Home: 407 Russ St Marianna FL 32446 Office: 3d Av Marianna FL 32446

O'STEEN, WENDALL KEITH, educator; b. Meigs, Ga., July 3, 1928; s. Wellna Hubert and Lillian (Powell) O.; B.A., Emory U., 1948, M.S., 1950; Ph.D., Duke, 1958; m. Mildred Virginia Reichert, Nov. 22, 1951; children—Lisa Diane, Kerry Keith. Instr. biology Emory U., Atlanta, 1948-50; asst. prof. biology Wofford Coll., Spartanburg, S.C., 1951-53; from instr. to prof. U. Tex. Med. Sch., 1958-68; prof. neurosci. Med. Sch. Emory U., Atlanta, 1968—. Research neurophysiologist U.S. Army Res. Walter Reed Hosp., Washington, 1968-73. Served with AUS, 1953-55. Recipient SAMA Outstanding Prof. award, 1967; Outstanding Prof. award Emory U., 1972. Mem. Am. Assn. Anatomists, Endocrine Soc., Soc. for Neurosci., So. Soc. Anatomists (councilor 1971-73). Contbr. articles to sci. jours. Home: 1745 Angelique Dr Decatur GA 30033 Office: Dept Anatomy Emory U Atlanta GA 30322

OSTEEN, WILLIAM LINDSAY, govt. ofcl., lawyer; b. Greensboro, N.C.; s. John Luke and Ruth (Tatum) O.; A.B., Guilford Coll.; LL.B., U. N.C. at Chapel Hill; m. Joanne Snow; children—William Lindsay, John Snow, Robert Bennett. Admitted to N.C. bar; practice law, Greensboro, 1958-69; mem. firm Booth, Osteen, Adams; U.S. dist. atty. for middle N.C., Greensboro, 1969—. Mem. N.C. Ho. Reps., 1960-62, minority leader, 1960-62. Home: 2322 N Elm St Greensboro NC 27406 Office: District Attorney's Office Greensboro NC 27402

OSTER, RICHARD CHARLES, dentist; b. New Orleans, Jan. 20, 1922; s. Fred and Alvina Lenore (Waldmann) O.; student Valparaiso U., 1938-40; D.D.S., Loyola U., 1943; m. Lois Marie Wyneken, Feb. 5, 1944; children—Jean (Mrs. Walter Kretzmann), Barbara Ellen. Practice dentistry, New Orleans, 1946—. Cons. Aetna Ins. Co., New Orleans, 1969-72; vis. lect. La. State U. Dental Sch., 1969-72; dentist Bethlehem Orphan Home, 1947—, New Orleans Saints profl. football team, 1968—. Sec. Vicksburg (Miss.) Luth. Hosp., 1951-53; chmn. St. John Luth. Sch. Bd., 1947-65. Bd. dirs. New Orleans chpt. Am. Leukemia Soc., Luth. High Sch.; trustee, mem. exec. com. Valparaiso U. Served to capt. Dental Corps, AUS, 1943-46; PTO. Named Toastmaster of Year, Toastmasters Club, 1954; recipient Appreciation award Optimist Club, 1966, Alumni Distinguished Service award Valparaiso U., 1970. Mem. Am., La. dental assns., New Orleans Dental Soc. (v.p. 1963), Delta Sigma Delta. Democrat. Lutheran (pres. St. John 1967-68). Clubs: Toastmasters (pres. 1953), Country (New Orleans). Home: 1224 Seville Dr New Orleans LA 70122 Office: 4219 Magnolia St New Orleans LA 70115

OSTERHAUS, LEO BENEDICT, educator; b. Fargo, N.D., Jan. 19, 1920; s. Bernard and Carolyn (Wiltz) O.; B.S., Kan. State U., 1942; M.S., Trinity U., 1961; Ph.D., U. Tex., 1966; m. Edna Reichie, Mar. 9, 1943; children—Susan (Mrs. Thomas O. Baldwin), Annette R. Commd. 2nd lt. U.S. Army, 1943, advanced through grades to lt. col., 1964; with Philippine Command Hdqrs., Manila, 1946-48; stationed Heidelberg, Germany, 1954-57; with Brook Army Med. Center, Med. Field Service Sch., Ft. Sam Houston, 1959-64; ret. 1964; asst. prof. hosp. adminstrn. Baylor U., San Antonio, 1959-64; teaching, adminstrv. asst. U. Tex. at Austin, 1964-66; asso. prof. bus. adminstrn. St. Edwards U., Austin, 1966-69, dir., dean. Holy Cross Coll., 1969-70, dean Center Bus. Adminstrn., 1970—. Vis. prof. mgmt. U. Tex., 1966—, U. Md. European div., 1972-73. Cons. to industry and hosps. Recipient Gilbreth Mgmt. award U. Tex., 1966. Mem. Am. Mgmt. Assn., Acad. Mgmt., S.W. Social Sci. Assn., Austin Personnel Assn., Am. Accounting Assn., Sigma Epsilon. Contbr. articles to profl. jours. Home: 8307 Tecumseh Dr Austin TX 78753

OSTERHOUDT, CHARLES HARDENBERGH, lawyer; b. Kingston, N.Y., Jan. 4, 1937; s. Ross Kenneth and Margaret Elizabeth (Hardenbergh) O.; B.A. in History, U. Va., 1958; LL.B., 1960; m. Beverley Ann Pearce, Sept. 2, 1961; children—Katrina Marie, Karen Elizabeth. Admitted to Va. bar; asso. firm C.R. Langhammer, Roanoke, 1961-62, self-employed, 1963-64; partner firm Langhammer & Osterhoudt, Roanoke, 1965-69; asso. firm Hunter, Fox & Trabue, Roanoke, 1970-71, partner, 1971—. Mem. Salem-Roanoke County Civic Center Com., 1968-71; mem. Roanoke Valley Council Community Services, 1968-71; mem. 5th Plan Dist. Com., 1968-71. Mem. Roanoke County Bd. Suprs., 1968-71, vice chmn., 1968, chmn., 1969-70; chmn. Roanoke County Republican Com., 1972—; escheator, Roanoke County, 1973—. Bd. dirs. Roanoke Valley Heart Fund and Assn., T.A.P., 1968-71. Served to lt. Ordinance Corps, AUS, 1960-61. Named Outstanding Young Men Am., 1972; recipient Law Enforcement Service award Roanoke County, 1972. Mem. Am., Roanoke bar assns., Va. State Bar, Delta Upsilon. Episcopalian (vestryman 1963-65). Elk. Lion. Home: 7217 Lamarre Dr Roanoke VA 24019 Office: PO Box 534 Roanoke VA 24003

OSTERMILLER, RONALD DANIEL, JR., chem. engr.; b. Sterling, Colo., Dec. 18, 1938; s. Ronald Daniel and Argyle Viola (Horton) O.; B.S. in Chem. Engring., U. Colo., 1961; m. Marian Jane Brehm, Dec. 20, 1959 (div. Feb. 1968); 1 dau., Susan Annette. Mem. prodn. supervision staff Monsanto Co. chem. mfrs., Cin., 1961-62, process design staff, Columbia, Tenn., 1962-65, project mgmt. staff, Soda Springs, Ida., 1965-66; mem. process design staff Union Carbide Corp., Houston, 1966-68; sr. process design engr. Pace Co., Cons., Engrs., Houston, Baton Rouge, 1968-70; founded Chem-Tran, Inc., Cons., Engrs., Houston, Baton Rouge, 1970, exec. v.p., dir., 1970—; dir. Nuclear Cons., Inc., Houston. Served with USMCR, 1957-64. Registered profl. engr., Ida., Tex., La., Ala. Mem. Houston Engr. and Sci. Soc., Nat., Tex. socs. profl. engrs., Aircraft Owners and Pilots

Assn., Nat. Pilots Assn. Home: 2634 Yorktown St Houston TX 77027 Office: Chem Tran Inc 701 N Post Oak Rd Houston TX 77024

OSTHAGEN, CLARENCE HILMANN, mgmt. and indsl. cons.; b. North Bergen, N.J., Apr. 9, 1911; s. Hilmann Marius and Elise (Ulricksen) O.; student Cooper Inst. Tech., 1920-25; B.S. in Engring., U. Ky., 1930; grad. student Columbia, 1930-31, George Washington U., 1934-37. Asst. to spl. rep. Allis-Chalmers Mfg. Co., 1920-25; indsl. engr. Henry L. Doherty Co., 1930-31; cons. engr., 1931-33; dep. adminstr. pub. utilities, also exec. asst. div. bus. coop. NRA, 1933-36; successively acting and asst. dir. project control. dir. adminstrv. operations, asst. dir. personnel, dir. employee mgmt. Fed. Works Agy., 1936-42, mgmt. engr., 1946-48; dep. asst. sec. (mgmt.) Dept. Air Force, 1948-50; acting under sec., also asst. sec. U.S. Dept. Commerce, 1950-53; prin. mgmt. cons. Rogers, Slade & Hill, N.Y.C., 1953-56; v.p., exec. dir. Tidewater Va. Devel. Council, Norfolk, 1956-63; dir. mechanization div. Office Asst. Postmaster Gen., 1963-64; commr. Community Facilities Adminstrn., Housing and Home Finance Agy., 1964-66; dir. space and mechanization requirements Office of Asst. Postmaster Gen., 1966-69, spl. asst. to asst. postmaster gen. operations, U.S. Postal Service, 1969-71; now mgmt. and indsl. cons. Served to col. USAAF, World War II; col. Res. Decorated Legion of Merit, Commendation ribbon with 2 oak leaf clusters; recipient Exceptional Civilian Service decoration Dept. Air Force, 1950; Exceptional Service award Dept. Commerce, 1952; Meritorious Honor award P.O. Dept., 1968; Service award U.S. Postal Service, 1971; Centennial medallion, named Distinguished Alumni, named to Hall of Distinguised Alumni, U. Ky. Licensed profl. engr., N.J., Va., D.C., N.Y. Mem. Soc. Advancement Mgmt., Am. Soc. Pub. Adminstrn., Soc. Am. Mil. Engrs., Am. Inst. Indsl. Engrs., Nat., N.J. socs. profl. engrs., Am. Indsl. Devel. Council, Pub. Personnel Assn., Soc. Personnel Adminstrn., Air Force Assn., U. Ky. Alumni Assn., Nat. Sojourners, Order DeMolay, Rotary Internat., Sigma Chi, Omicron Delta Kappa. Mason (Shriner). Clubs: Virginia; Norfolk (Va.) Yacht and Country. Author mgmt. articles. Home: 1332 Eye St NW Washington DC 20005 also 302 Teaneck Rd Ridgefield Park NJ 07660

OSTROFF, AARON JOEL, aero. engr., b. Fall River, Mass., Oct. 2, 1939; s. Sydney and Ruth (Taylor) O.; B.S., Northeastern U., 1962; M.S. in Elec. Engring., George Washington U., 1971; m. Gloria Spivak, Sept. 5, 1965; 1 son, Stuart Alan. Aerospace engr. NASA Langley Research Center, Hampton, Va., 1962—. Recipient Group Achievement award Nat. Aeros. and Space Adminstrn., 1965, Certificate of Outstanding Performance, 1972, 73, Spl. Achievement award, 1973 (both Langley Research Center). Mem. I.E.E.E. Jewish religion (dir. temple 1971-73, sec. 1973—, pres. Men's Club 1972-73). Elk. Patentee star image motion compensator. Home: 560 Viking Dr Newport News VA 23602 Office: M S 494 Langley Research Center Hampton VA 23665

OSWALD, EDWARD ODELL, biochemist, educator; b. Newberry, S.C., Jan. 9, 1940; s. Odell Armond and Andrena (Thomasson) O.; B.S. in Chemistry, Newberry Coll., 1961; M.S., Wake Forest U., Ph.D. (NIH fellow), U. N.C., 1966; m. Margaret Ann Epting, Aug. 6, 1961; children—Bryan Edward, Angelia Ann. Dir. Clin. chemistry Palms of Pasadena Hosp., St. Petersburg, Fla., 1967-68; research chemist Nat. Inst. Environmental Health Scis. Research, Triangle Park, N.C., 1968-74; supervisory research chemist Nat. Environmental Research Center, Environmental Protection Agy., Research Triangle Park, 1974—; adj. asst. prof. biochemistry U. N.C., Chapel Hill, 1968—, also adj. asst. prof. medicinal chemistry, 1970—. NIH postdoctoral fellow, 1966. Mem. Am. Chem. Soc., A.A.A.S., Am. Assn. Clin. Chemists, Am. Oil Chemist Soc., Sigma Xi. Home: 39 Circle Dr Chapel Hill NC 27514 Office: Pesticides and Toxic Substances Effects Lab Chemistry Br Research Triangle Park NC 27711

OTHERSEN, HENRY BIEMANN, JR., physician, educator; b. Charleston, S.C., Aug. 26, 1930; s. Henry and Lyvia Albertine (Smith) O.; B.S., Coll. Charleston, 1950; M.D., Med. Coll. S.C., 1953; m. Janelle Lester, Apr. 4, 1959; children—Megan, Mandy, Margaret, Henry Biemann III. Intern Phila. Gen. Hosp., 1953-54; postgrad. U. Pa., 1956-57; resident gen. surgery Med. Coll. S.C., Charleston, 1957-62, Ohio State U. and Columbus Children's Hosp., 1962-64; research fellow Harvard and Mass. Gen. Hosp., Boston, 1964-65; asst. prof. pediatric surgery Med. U. S.C., Charleston, 1965-68, asso. prof., 1968-72, prof., 1972—, chief pediatric surgery, 1972—; cons. St. Francis Hosp., 1968—, Roper Hosp., 1968—. Bd. dirs. S.C. div. Am. Cancer Soc. Served with USNR, 1954-56: Korea. Diplomate Am. Bd. Surgery, Am. Bd. Thoracic Surgery. Fellow A.C.S., Am. Acad. Pediatrics; mem. Am. Pediatric Surg. Assn., Am. Trauma Soc., Alpha Omega Alpha. Contbr. articles to profl. jours. Club: James Island Yacht. Research in oncology and esophageal problems in children. Home: 891 White Point Blvd Charleston SC 29412 Office: 80 Barre St Charleston SC 29401

OTIS, JOHN JAMES, civil engr.; B. Syracuse, N.Y., Aug. 5, 1922; s. John Joseph and Anna (Dey) O.; B.Chem. Engring. cum laude, Syracuse U., 1943, M.B.A., 1950, postgrad., 1951-55; m. Dorothy E. Fuller, June 21, 1958; children—Mary Eileen, John Leon. With Gen. Motors Corp., Syracuse, 1951-61, process control engr., 1958-59, process engr., 1960-61; engring. writer Gen. Electric Co., Syracuse, 1961-63; asso. research engr. Boeing Co., Huntsville, Ala., 1963-65; asso. mem. staff Planning Research Corp., Huntsville, 1965-67; prin. engr. Brown Engring. div. Teledyne Corp., Huntsville, 1967-69; configuration control engr. Gen. Elec. Co., Phila., 1969; mech. engr. Drever Co., Beth Ayres, Pa., 1970-71; civil engr. Army Corps Engrs., Mobile, Ala., 1971—. Dir. Dexacon Corp., Somerdale, N.J. Served with USNR, 1944-46: PTO. Registered profl. engr., Ala. Mem. Am. Inst. Indsl. Engrs. (past v.p.), Am. Inst. Chem. Engrs., Tau Beta Pi, Phi Kappa Tau, Alpha Chi Sigma. Home: 1584 Andover Blvd Mobile AL 36609 Office: USAED Fed Office Bldg 109 St Joseph St Mobile AL 32602

OTIS, WILLIAM LYNAN, JR., lumber co. exec.; b. Columbia, S.C., Jan. 1, 1940; s. William Lynan and Nancy (Crouther) O.; B.S. in Econs., U. S.C., 1963; m. Alice VanYeverin Hopkins, July 29, 1966; children—William Lynan III, Thomas Porcher. Exec. v.p. Columbia Lumber & Mfg. Co., Inc., Columbia, S.C., 1963-69, pres., 1969—; dir. Home Fed. Savs. & Loan Assn. Chmn. adv. bd. Providence Hosp., 1971—; bd. dirs. Columbia Hist. Mus., 1967-70, Columbia Town Theater, 1968-71. Mem. Archtl. Woodwook Inst. Internat. (pres. 1971-72), So. Woodwork Assn. (pres. 1967-69), Carolina Lumber and Bldg. Material Dealers Assn. (dir. 1960-69). Clubs: Forest Lake Country, Palmetto, Pine Tree Hunt (Columbia). Home: 4535 Devereaux Rd Columbia SC 29205 Office: 500 Hampton St Columbia SC 29202

O'TOOLE, CHRISTOPHER JOHN, clergyman; b. Alpena, Mich., Oct. 1, 1906; s. Christopher and Margaret (McGrarry) O'T.; A.B., U. Notre Dame, 1929; LL.D., 1959; Ph.B., U. Louvain. 1939; M.A., Cath. U. Am., 1942, Ph.D., 1944; LL.D., U. Portland, 1951, St. Edwards U., 1960. Ordained priest Roman Catholic Ch., 1933; instr. philosophy dept. St. Edwards U., 1933-34, U. Notre Dame, 1934-36; master of novices, Dartmouth, Mass., 1936-38; superior Holy Cross Sem., Notre Dame, Ind., 1940; Holy Cross Coll., 1941-45; asst. provincial Ind. Province, 1945-50; supr. gen. congregation Holy Cross, Rome, Italy, 1950-62; superior Dist. of South, Austin, Tex., 1963-68; provincial superior So. Province, Congregation of Holy Cross, 1968—; pres. Priests of Holy Cross, Dist. of Tex., Inc., Austin, 1963. Decorated knight Grand Cross Equestrian Order Holy Sepulchre. Mem. Nat. Cath. Philos. Assn. Contbr. articles to profl. jours. Home: 812 Audubon St New Orleans LA 70118

OTT, JULIAN A., motel and restaurant owner; b. nr. Orangeburg, S.C., Apr. 13, 1921; s. Ben Tillman and Florence (Myers) O.; student U. S.C., 1940-42; B.S., Clemson U., 1944; m. Mary Braswell, Apr. 6, 1947; children—Julian A., Rembert M., Timothy C., Melinda K. Farm owner, operator, 1946-60; pres. Julian A. Ott & Assos., Inc., operators Holiday Inns at Dunn, Elizabeth City and Smithfield, N.C., Rock Hill, Summerton and Santee, S.C., Turbeyville, S.C., Walterboro, S.C., Georgetown, S.C., Pocotaligo, S.C.; pres. Motel Assos., Inc., Investors Realty, Inc., CROW Assos., Inc., OWS & Assos., Inc., Santee Motor Inns, Inc., So. Motels, Inc., Waterboro Inns, Inc. v.p. SOW, Inc., ROW, Inc. Served with USNR, 1943-46. Mem. V.F.W., Am. Legion. Kiwanian, Elk. Club: Orangeburg Country. Home: Route 5 Box 10 Orangeburg SC 29115 Office: 178 Middlenton Orangeburg SC 29115

OTT, THOMAS OLIVER, JR., textile engr.; b. Columbia, S.C., 1905; s. Thomas Oliver and Eliza deChiosel (Dickson) O.; B.S. in Textile Engring., Ga. Inst. Tech.; m. Marian Swindell, Mar. 30, 1930; children—Judith Bryan (Mrs. Carl Schuler), Elisa Dickson (Mrs. William Tunno), Thomas Oliver III. Trainee, then indsl. engr. Rayon div. E.I. duPont de Nemours Co., Old Hickory, Tenn., 1928-31; asst. to supt. Merita Mills, Columbus, Ga.; supt. Jordan Mills, Columbus; head new product devel. Callaway Mills, LaGrange, Ga.; so. editor Textile World, Greenville, S.C., 1941-45; asst. head textile engring. dept. J.E. Sirrene & Co., Mill Engrs., 1945-48; head textile engring. dept. Lockwood Greene Engineers, Spartanburg, N.C., N.Y.C.; operator cons. firm, Spartanburg, 1962—. Mem. econ. com. Latin Am. UN. Registered profl. engr. Mem. Am. Soc. M.E., Nat., S.C. socs. profl. engrs., Quality Control Soc., So. Textile Assn., Materials Handling Soc. Episcopalian. Rotarian, Kiwanian. Contbr. articles to profl. jours. Patentee textile plant equipment and systems. Home: 202 South Park Dr Spartanburg SC 29302 Office: PO Box 5476 Spartanburg SC 29301

OTTLEY, JOHN KING, JR., pub. relations exec.; b. Atlanta, Oct. 8, 1931; s. John King and Mary Henton (Harvey) O.; A.B., Davidson Coll., 1953; M.S., Columbia, 1954; m. Margaret Randolph Meriwether, June 22, 1966; 1 son, James Meriwether. Editorial trainee Charlotte Observer, 1958-59, reporter, 1959-60; reporter, Marietta (Ga.) Daily Jour., 1960-62, mng. editor, 1962-63; pub. relations mgr. So. Services, Inc., Atlanta, 1963-68; pub. relations account exec. Bell & Stanton, Inc., Atlanta, 1968—. Mem. adv. com. A.R.C., Atlanta, 1964—. Bd. dirs. Atlanta Mental Health Assn., Consumer Credit Counseling Service. Served with AUS, 1954-58. Mem. Pub. Relations Soc. Am., Ga. Conservancy, Appalachian Trail Conf., Ducks Unlimited, Reserve Officers Assn., Sigma Delta Chi. Clubs: Atlanta Press, Capital City (Atlanta). Home: 932 Glenbrook Dr NW Atlanta GA 30318 Office: 2016 Peachtree Center Bldg Atlanta GA 30303

OTTLEY, WILLIAM HENRY, assn. exec.; b. N.Y.C., Mar. 7, 1929; s. James Henry and Margaret (Deeble) O.; grad. magna cum laude, Culver Mil. Acad., 1946; B.A., Yale, 1950; Certificate Georgetown U. Sch. Fng. Service, 1952. Asst. dir. pub. relations Thomas A. Edison, Inc., West Orange, N.J., 1954-56; exec. v.p. Career Publs., Inc., N.Y.C., 1956-60; dir. spl. exhibits N.Y. World's Fair Corp., N.Y.C., 1960-65; exec. dir. Nat. Pilots Assn., Washington, 1967—. Dir. Careers, Inc., N.Y.C., 1962-68, Nat. Aeros. Assn., Washington, 1967—, West Indies Devel. Co., N.Y.C., 1962—; dir., pres. Admiral Aviation Corp., Hazlet, N.J., 1961-69; U.S. Del. Fedn. Aeronautique Internationale, Paris, 1967—; mem. Dept. Transp. Flight Information Adv. Com., 1967—; spl. advisor Civil Aeros. Bd., 1970-72. Chmn. Nat. Sport Aviation Council, 1969—. Served with AUS, 1950-51; served to 1st lt. USAF, 1951-53. Mem. U.S. Parachute Assn. (nat. dir. 1966—; v.p. 1972—), Soc. of the Cin. (life). Episcopalian. Clubs: Racquet and Tennis (N.Y.C.); National Aviation (Washington). Editor: Wall Street 20th Century, 1959, NPA News, 1967—. Contbr. articles to various aviation and sporting publs. Home: 2627 Woodley Pl NW Washington DC 20008 Office: 806 15th St NW Washington DC 20005

OTTO, DONALD WAYNE, accountant; b. El Campo, Tex., Dec. 30, 1944; s. Elo E. and Isabel (Martinets) O.; B.B.A., U. Houston, 1969; m. Priscilla J. Dyer, Dec. 27, 1970. Staff accountant Harris Kerr Forster & Co., Houston, 1969-70; tax accountant Arthur Andersen & Co., Houston, 1970—. Served with AUS, 1963. C.P.A., Tex. Mem. Am. Inst. C.P.A.'s, Tex. Soc. C.P.A.'s. Home: 12423 Carriage Hill Houston TX 77077 Office: 910 Travis Suite 1700 Houston TX 77002

OTTS, LEE MACMILLAN, lawyer; b. Greensboro, Ala., May 21, 1922; s. Archie McEachin and Elizabeth (MacMillan) O.; A.B., U. Ala., 1943, LL.B., 1948; m. Mary Frances Byrd, Sept. 4, 1948; children—Harriett Byrd, Martha Frances, Elizabeth McEachin, Mary Lee. Admitted to Ala. bar, 1949; since practiced in Brewton, 1949—. Dir. First Nat. Bank, Brewton, Judge Inferior Ct., Escambia County, Brewton, 1951-53; Escambia County solicitor, 1953—, atty., 1960—. Mem. Ala. Regional Planning Com., 1968—. Mem. Brewton City Bd. Edn., 1961—, pres., 1967—; pres. City Housing Authority, 1966-73; first v.p. Ala. Assn. Sch. Bds. Served to capt., inf. AUS, 1943-46; ETO. Decorated Bronze Star medal, Purple Heart with oak leaf cluster. Mem. Ala. State Bar, Escambia County Bar Assn. (past pres.), C. of C., Am. Legion (past adj.), Phi Gamma Delta (past pres.), Phi Alpha Delta. Presbyn. (elder 1959—, clk of session 1965—). Rotarian (past pres. Brewton). Home: 1515 Poplar St Brewton AL 36426 Office: Jernigan Arcade Brewton AL 36426

OTWELL, RONNIE RAY, theatre, printing exec.; b. Carrollton, Ga., Aug. 13, 1929; s. William Clyde and Hazel (Helton) O.; student Ga. Inst. Tech., 1946-49; m. Mary Crawford Adams, Oct. 25, 1956; children—Ronnie Ray, Hazel Teresa, Timothy Lewis, Daniel Clyde. Mgr., Bremen Theatre (Ga.), 1950; dir. publicity, advt. Martin Theatres, Columbus, Ga., 1950-63; v.p., dir. Martin Theaters of Ga., Inc., 1963—, Martin Theatres of Ala., Inc., 1963—, dir. Martin Theatres of Columbus, Inc., 1963—, pres., dir. Columbus Prodns., Inc., 1966—. Mem. Nat. Assn. Theatre Owners Am., Nat. Assn. Theatres Owners Ga., Columbus C. of C., Columbus Mus. Arts and Crafts, Assn. U.S. Army. Methodist. Club: Columbus Country. Home: 2102 Garrard St Columbus GA 31906 Office: 1308 Broadway St Columbus GA 31902

OUALLINE, JUDD HAMNER, oil co. exec.; b. Conroe, Tex., Oct. 24, 1920; s. Ellis Augustus and Annie May (Hamner) O.; B.A., U. Tex., 1942, postgrad., 1946-47; m. Cynthia Shell Snell, Sept. 12, 1966; children—Judd Hamner, Catherine, Jennifer. Sr., div. staff geologist Stanolind Oil & Gas Co., Houston, 1947-52; dist. and div. geologist Skelly Oil Co., Houston, 1952-62, dist. exploration mgr., 1962-65, mgr. exploration dept., Tulsa, 1965-69, v.p. exploration and prodn. dept., 1969—; v.p., dir. Skelly Internat. Oil Co.; exec. v.p., dir. Skelly Oil Can., Ltd.; exec. v.p. Skelly Mozambique; v.p. Skelly Oil Co. Libya, Skelly Oil Co. of Gt. Britain, Ltd. Served to 1st lt. USAAF, 1943-46. Mem. Am. Petroleum Inst. (gen. com., div. 1968-73), Ind. Petroleum Assn. Am., Am. Assn. Petroleum Geologists, Soc. Exploration Geophysicists, Am. Inst. Mining, Metall. and Petroleum Engrs., Tulsa C. of C. (community devel. div. council 1970), Sigma Gamma Epsilon, Phi Sigma, Lambda Chi Alpha. Methodist (steward 1965-70). Home: 3732 S Utica St Tulsa OK 74105 Office: 1437 S Boulder St Tulsa OK 74102

OUGHTERSON, WILLIAM ALEXANDER, lawyer; b. Nashville, Nov. 3, 1926; s. T.T. and Sarah (Sheppard) O.; student The Citadel, 1943-44, U. Miami, Coral Gables, Fla., 1944-45; B.A., LL.B., U. Fla., 1950; m. Leila Seay, July 13, 1949; children—William Scott, Lisa. Admitted to Fla. bar, 1950; practiced in Stuart, Fla., 1950—; mem. firm Oughterson, Oughterson & Prewitt, Stuart, 1950—; juvenile counselor Martin County, Fla., 1951-59, pros. atty., 1961-72. Trustee, Lawyer's Title Guaranty Fund, 19th Jud. Circuit, 1969—. Pres. Martin County Tb and Health Assn., 1956-57; disaster chmn. Martin County A.R.C., 1958, bd. dirs., 1957-62, chmn. bd., 1961-62. Served with USNR, 1944. Recipient Distinguished Service award Stuart Jr. C. of C., 1959. Mem. Martin County Bar Assn. (past pres.), Stuart C. of C. (chmn. membership drive 1961). Presbyn. (elder). Kiwanian (past officer Stuart; gov. Fla. dist. 1969). Home: 305 Pelican Dr Stuart FL 33494 Office: PO Drawer 86 Stuart FL 33494

OUREDNIK, RUDOLPH FRANK, wholesale trade co. exec.; b. N.Y.C., May 4, 1911; s. Gottlieb Frank and Marie (Pechek) O.; student Sch. Commerce N.Y. U., 1929-30; m. Dorathy Andrews, Dec. 22, 1935; children—Rudolph Frank, Theodore, Marie (Mrs. LeBaron Scarlett). With Noland Co., various locations, 1930—, exec. v.p., Newport News, Va., 1968-70, pres., 1970—; also dir.; dir., pres. Noland Credit Co., Newport News. Chmn. Human Relations Council, 1968-69. Bd. dirs. United Fund, 1968-69, Noland Found., 1968—; trustee Am. Inst. U., Washington, 1966-69. Served to lt. col., C.E., AUS, 1942-46. Mem. So. Wholesalers Assn. (pres. 1968-69), Am. Supply Assn. (v.p. 1973), Peninsula C. of C. (dir. 1970-73). Mason (Shriner). Clubs: James River Country, Huntington. Home: 15 Hilton Terrace Newport News VA 23607 Office: 2700 Warwick Blvd Newport News VA 23607

OUSLEY, LARRY JAMES, clergyman; b. Knoxville, Tenn., May 30, 1948; s. Ralph Lea and Evelyn Louise (Holloway) O.; B.S., U. Tenn., 1970; M. Div., Emory U., 1973; m. Helen Estelle Lewis, June 12, 1971. Programmer, instr. Computing Center, U. Tenn., Knoxville, 1967-70; instr. computer sci. Emory U., Atlanta, 1970-71; ordained to ministry United Methodist Ch., 1971; minister music and youth Canton United Meth. Ch., Canton, Ga., 1971-72; chaplain United Meth. Children's Home, Decatur, Ga., 1972-73; pastor Immanuel United Meth. Ch., Mentor, Tenn., 1973—. Recipient Tenn. P.T.A. scholarship, Alcoa Found. scholarship, Eastern Star scholarship, Dean's scholarship, United Meth. grant. Mem. Assn. Computing Machinery, Fellowship for Planning Ministry. Democrat. Home: Mentor TN 37808 Office: Mentor TN 37808

OUTLAND, RODERICK HENDERSON, educator; b. Hamlin, Ky., Oct. 30, 1922; s. Joel David and Katye Pearl (Barrow) O.; B.S., Murray State U., 1947; M.A., Vanderbilt U., 1949, Ph.D., 1953; m. Frances May Fournet, Nov. 23, 1960. Instr. biology Gettysburg (Pa.) Coll., 1949-50; asst. prof. Northwestern State U., Natchitoches, La., 1953-55; asst. prof. Loyola at New Orleans, 1955-57; prof. Northwestern State U., Natchitoches, 1957—. Mem. St. Mary's Sch. Bd., Natchitoches, 1965-67. Served with USNR, 1943-46. Mem. Am. Bot. Soc., Assn. Southeastern Biologists, La. Acad. Scis., Sigma Xi, Beta Beta Beta, Ph Kappa Phi. Home: 533 Whitfield Dr Natchitoches LA 71457

OUTTEN, JOSEPH FENDALL, dentist; b. Lynchburg, Va., Aug. 19, 1928; s. Clarence Fendall and Mary Jane (Wolf) O.; B.S., Va. Poly. Inst., 1949; postgrad. U. Richmond, 1949-50; D.D.S., Med. Coll. Va., 1954; m. Mildred Lacey Wright, Aug. 2, 1952; children—Joseph Fendall, Mary Cornelia, Samuel Wright, Thomas Hobson. Individual practice dentistry, Greenville, S.C., 1956—; pres. Hosa, Inc., Greenville, 1966—; sec.-treas. Composite Enterprises, Greenville, 1958-72; chmn. Dental dept. Greenville County Hosp. System. Mem. exec. council Officer Econ. Opportunity, 1968—, treas., 1971—. Bd. dirs. United Fund, Greenville, YMCA, Greenville. Served to capt. USAF, 1954-56. Recipient Service to Youth award YMCA, 1971. Mem. Dental Assos. of Greenville (sec.-treas. 1971-72), Am., S.C. dental assns., Am. Soc. Dentistry for Children, Southeastern Acad. Prosthetics, Greenville County Dental Assn. (pres. 1966-67), Piedmont Assn. (dir. 1968-69), Am. Legion, Theta Chi, Psi Omega. Mason. Clubs: American Business, Greenville Country (Greenville); Port Royal Country (Hilton Head, S.C.); Caroline Caribean Corp. (Banner Elk, N.C). Home: 130 Rockingham St Greenville SC 29607 Office: 10 Sevier St Greenville SC 29604

OUTTEN, L(ORA) M(ILTON), educator; b. Pocomoke City, Md., Aug. 17, 1913; s. L. P. and D. Elizabeth (Blades) O.; A.B., Western Md. Coll., 1934, M.A., 1937; M.S., Cornell University, 1950, Ph.D., 1956; postgrad. Ind. U., 1959, Harvard, 1961, Oxford (Eng.) U., 1967, Cambridge (Eng.) U., 1968, 71, Birmingham (Eng.) U., 1971, U. Cal., 1969-73. Lab. asst. Western Md. Coll., 1933-34, 1936-37; tchr. pub. schs., Worcester County, Md., 1934-36, Ridgeway, Va., 1940-41, Buckingham, Md., 1943-44, Chincoteague, Va., 1944-46; instr. Mars Hill Coll., 1946-48, asst. prof., 1948-52, asso. prof., 1952-56, prof. biology, 1956—, also head dept. biology, 1967-71, chair for ecological research, 1971—. Fellow A.A.A.S.; mem. Am. Soc. Naturalists, Am. Soc. Zoologists, Am. Soc. Ichtyologists and Herpetologists, Ecol. Soc. Am., Soc. Systematic Zoology, Genetics Soc. Am., Soc. Limnology and Oceanography, N.C. Acad. Sci., Assn. Southeastern Biologists, Am. Inst. Biol. Scis., Internat. Soc. Limnology, Freshwater Biol. Assn. (Gt. Britain), Am. Fisheries Soc., Animal Behavior Soc., Am. Micros. Soc., Am. Nature Study Soc., Assn. for Tropical Biology, Gulf and Caribbean Fisheries Inst., Assn. for Edn. Tchrs. in Sci., Nat., N.C. edn. assns., Sigma Xi, Beta Beta Beta. Baptist (deacon). Research in field. Contbr. articles to profl. jours. Home: Marshall Rd Box 722-C Mars Hill NC 28754

OVELMAN, ROBERT MAXWELL, cons.; b. Hagerstown, Md., Mar. 9, 1930; s. Robert George and Gay (Frye) O.; A.A., Hagerstown Jr. Coll., 1950; B.S., Va. Poly. Inst., 1953, M.S., 1954; m. Mary Lynn Morini. Chief designer Morton W. Noble, Arhcitect, Washington, 1957-60; architect Am. Airlines, N.Y.C., 1960-63; chief of specifications U.S. P.O. Dept., Washington, 1963-65; sr. architect Eastern Airlines, N.Y.C., 1965-68; dir. facilities Allegheny Airlines, Washington, 1968-74; cons. Ralph M. Parsons Co., Washington, 1974—. Mem. Bldg. Code Appeals Bd., Alexandria, Va., 1963-67, Bldg. Site Selection Com., Leesburg, Va., 1963. Served with USAF, 1955-57. Recipient Archtl. Student award So. Brick and Tile, 1952; Best House Design in Va. award Am. Home Mag., 1959; FAME award Eastern Airlines, 1968. Mem. Soc. Am. Registered Architects, Tau Sigma Delta. Home: 113 Thornton Ct Culpeper VA 22701 Office: 1000 16th St Washington DC

OVERBECK, EDWARD MICHAEL, chem. engr.; b. Dallas, Sept. 29, 1921; s. Clarence E. and Hallie (Vaughn) O.; B.S., Tex. A. and M. U., 1942; m. Evely Jackson Darley, Aug. 4, 1967; children—Douglas Darley, Michael Darley, Douglas, Lesley Michael Franz. Chief draftsman Olin Industries, Inc., Houston, 1947-51; project engr.

Baroid div. Nat. Lead Co., Houston, 1951-54; pres. Stubbs, Overbeck & Assos., Inc., Houston, 1954—. Com. chmn. Sam Houston council Boy Scouts Am., 1958-59; mgr. Little League Baseball, 1958-64. Served to capt. Chem. Warfare Service, AUS, 1942-45; ETO. Decorated Purple Heart, Bronze Star medal with oak leaf cluster. Registered profl. engr., Tex. Mem. Am. Inst. Chem. Engrs., Nat. Soc. Profl. Engrs. Home: 6450 Burgoyne St Houston TX 77027 Office: 3950 Braxton St Houston TX 77042

OVERBEY, WILLIAM HUTCHINGS, JR., judge; b. Lynchburg, Va., Apr. 11, 1939; s. William Hutchings and Anne Callen (Woodson) O.; B.A., U. Va., 1961, LL.B., 1964; m. Josephine Wheatley, Dec. 16, 1961; children—Martha Burks, Stuart Wheatley. Admitted to Va. bar, 1964; mem. firm Overbey & Overbey, Rustburg, 1964—; judge Campbell County Ct., Rustburg, Va., 1972—. Dir. Fidelity Nat. Bank. Leader local Boy Scouts Am., 1973—; chmn. A.R.C., 1968. Bd. dirs. Va. YMCA, 1970—. Mem. Va. State Bar, Va. Assn. Judges (exec. com. 1972—), C. of C. (pres. 1969). Lion (pres. 1968). Home and office: Box 38 Rustburg VA 24588

OVERBY, GEORGE ROBERT, univ. pres.; b. Jacksonville, Fla., July 21, 1923; s. Taylor Earl and Virginia (Hewitt) O.; B.A., Fla. State U., 1951, Ph.D., 1966; M.Ed., U. Fla., 1959, S.Ed., 1963. Tchr., Lake Forest Hills Elementary Sch., 1956-59, Ribault Secondary Sch., 1961-64; prin. Jacksonville Christian Schs., 1959-61; asso. prof. Slippery Rock (Pa.) State Coll., 1966-68; asso. prof. Youngstown (O.) State U., 1968-71; prof., chmn. dept. edn. Shelton Coll., Cape Canaveral, Fla., 1971-74; pres. Freedom U., 1974—. Cons pvt., pub. edn., 1958—. Pres. bd. trustees Christian Enterprises, Inc., 1962-66; pres. bd. dirs. Christian Warriors for Christian Edn., Inc., 1972—; nat. bd. citizens for Decent Lit.; adv. bd. Am. Security Council. Served as aviator USNR, 1943-46. Fellow Intercontinental Biog. Assn. (life); mem. William Holmes McGuffey Hist. Soc., Am. Assn. Higher Ed. (life, charter), N.E.A. (life), Am. Assn. U. Profs., Assn. Childhood Edn. Internat., Nat. Council for Social Studies, U. profs. for Acad. Order (charter), Christian Educators Assn. of S.E., Am. Assn. Christian Schs., Soc. Study Edn., Kappa Delta Pi (life), Phi Delta Kappa (life). Home: PO Drawer C Cape Canaveral FL 32920

OVERCASH, ANNIE JUANITA ROBERTS (MRS. H. HURSHEL OVERCASH), ednl. adminstr.; b. LaGrange, Ga., July 10, 1934; d. Olin Alvin and Annie Kate (Underwood) Roberts; certificate in secretarial sci., LaGrange Coll., 1957; m. H. Hurshel Overcash, Mar. 22, 1953; 1 son, Daryl Hurshel. Exec. sec. to dir. indsl. relations Callaway Mills Co., LaGrange, 1957-60; sec. to acad. dean LaGrange Coll., 1960-63, asso. registrar, 1963-66, acting registrar, 1966-68, registrar, 1968—. Mem. Am., Ga. assns. collegiate registrars and admissions officers. Baptist. Home: Pyne Rd LaGrange GA 30240

OVERHOLT, BERGEIN FREDERICK, physician; b. Battle Creek, Mich., July 4, 1937; s. Bergein M. and Alice Genevieve (Stein) O.; M.D., U. Tenn., 1961; M.S., U. Mich., 1967; m. Evelyn Shafer, Dec. 20, 1958; children—Jonathan Scott, Suzanne. Intern U. Mich., Ann Arbor, 1961-62, resident, 1962-65; chief resident internal medicine, USPHS fellow gastroenterology, 1965-67; fellow gastroenterology N.Y. Hosp.-Cornell Med. Center, 1967-69; practice medicine specializing in gastroenterology, Knoxville, Tenn., 1969—; mem. staff St. Mary's Meml. Hosp., East Tenn. Bapt. Hosp., U. Tenn. Meml. and Research Hosp., Ft. Sanders Presbyn. Hosp. Mem. Knoxville Sch. Bd., 1972—, developer pub. edn. program on drug abuse, 1971—; mem. Knox County Study Commn. on Govt. Revision, 1973-74. Served with USPHS, 1965-67. Recipient Pub. Service award Jaycees, 1971, named Man of Year, 1972. Diplomate Am. Bd. Internal Medicine (gastroenterology). Fellow A.C.P.; mem. A.M.A., So. Med. Assn., Am. Gastroent. Assn., Am. Soc. Internal Medicine, Am. Soc. Gastrointestinal Endoscopy (bd. gov. 1971—). Presbyn. Kiwanian. Primary investigator and developer of flexible fiberoptic colonoscope. Contbr. profl. jours. Home: 937 Carrington St Knoxville TN 37919 Office: 801 W Cumberland St Knoxville TN 37902

OVERHOLT, ROBERT MARION, physician; b. Battle Creek, Mich., June 27, 1938; s. Bergein Marion and Alice (Stein) O.; M.D., U. Tenn., 1962; m. Carole Elizabeth Campbell, Mar. 24, 1962; children—Samuel Mark, John Patrick. Intern Phila. Gen. Hosp., 1962-63; resident internal medicine Univ. Hosp., Ann Arbor, Mich., 1963-66; allergy fellow, U. Mich., 1968-70; practice medicine specializing in allergy, Knoxville; mem. staff St. Mary's Meml. Hosp., Ft. Sanders Presbyn. Hosp., East Tenn. Bapt. Hosp., East Tenn. Children's Hosp. Served with AUS, 1966-68. Diplomate Am. Bd. Internal Medicine. Mem. A.M.A., Tenn. Med. Assn., Knoxville Acad. Medicine. Home: 601 Kempton Rd Knoxville TN 37919 Office: 717 W Cumberland St Knoxville TN 37902

OVERMAN, FRANCES ELIZABETH HENSON, writer, civic worker; b. Eddyville, Ky.; d. John Napoleon and Ida Belle (Koon) Henson; student Union U., 1930-32; A.B., Murray State U., 1937; postgrad. Northwestern U., 1940, U. Wis., 1941, 44; m. Ralph Theodore Overman, June 30, 1945 (dic Jan. 1968); children—Ralph Theodore, Ann Frances. Tchr. elementary schs., Ballard County, Ky., secondary schs., LaCenter, Cadiz, Maysville, and Benton, Ky., 1937-44; tchr. Oak Ridge Schs., 1944-45, 57-59; free lance wirter; contbr. to Fact and Fiction, Internat. (Oak Ridge). Active Cub Scouts, Brownies; adviser Y-Teens; active Oak Ridge Civic Music Assn., Oak Ridge Community Playhouse, Oak Ridge Community Art Center. Recipient Community Service award, 1972; other awards. Fellow Intercontinental Biog. Assn.; mem. Internat. Platform Assn., League Women Voters, Centro Studi E Scombi Internazionali (internat. com. fine arts 1970-71), Internat. Acad. Leonardo Da Vinci, Tau Kappa Alpha. Contbr. articles to profl. jours. Address: 109 Pelham Rd Oak Ridge TN 37830

OVERMYER, ROBERT FRANKLYN, astronaut; b. Lorain, O., July 14, 1936; s. Rolandus and Margaret (Fabian) O.; B.S. in Physics, Baldwin Wallace Coll., 1958; M.S. in Aeros., U.S. Naval Postgrad. Sch., 1964; m. Katherine Ellen Jones, Oct. 17, 1959; children—Carolyn Marie, Patricia Ann, Robert Rolandus. Commd. 2d. lt. USMC, 1958, advanced through grades to lt. col., 1972; completed aerospace research pilot sch. Edwards AFB, 1966; astronaut with Manned Orbiting Lab., 1966-69, NASA Manned Spacecraft Center, Houston, 1969—. Recipient Alumni Merit award Baldwin Wallace Coll., 1967. Mem. Soc. Exptl. Test Pilots (asso.), Sigma Xi. Home: 18510 Pt Lookout St Houston TX 77058 Office: NASA Manned Spacecraft Center Houston TX 77058

OVERSTREET, BONARO WILKINSON, author, lectr.; b. Geyserville, Cal., Oct. 30, 1902; d. Edward and Margaret Elizabeth (Bonar) Wilkinson; A.B., U. Cal., 1925, tchr.'s certificate, 1926; m. Harry Allen Overstreet, Aug. 23, 1932. Research asso. Am. Assn. Adult Edn., 1939-40; instr. adult edn. Claremont Co., Cal., summer, 1940, Mills Coll., Cal., summer, 1941, U. Mich. Extension Service, 1945-46, 49, U. Cal., extension div., 1948. Mem. Am. Assn. for Adult Edn., Sigma Delta Pi, Phi Beta Kappa, Theta Sigma Phi. Clubs: Nat. Press, International (Washington). Author: (books) Poetic Way of Release, 1931; Footsteps on the Earth, 1934; Search for a Self, 1938; Brave Enough for Life, 1941; (with H. A. Overstreet) Town Meeting Comes to Town, 1938; Leaders for Adult Education (Am. Assn. Adult Edn.), 1940; American Reasons, 1943; Courage for Crisis, 1943; Freedom's People, 1945; How to Think About Ourselves, 1948; Understanding Fear: in Ourselves and Others, 1951; The Mind Alive (with H. A. Overstreet), 1954; Hands Laid Upon the Wind, 1956; The Mind Goes Forth 1956; (with H.A. Overstreet) What We Must Know About Communism, 1958, The War Called Peace: Krushchev's Communism, 1961, The Iron Curtain, 1963, The Strange Tactics of Extremism, 1964, The FBI in Our Open Society, 1969. Contbr. to jours. Home: 3409 Fiddler's Green Falls Church VA 22044

OVERSTREET, JESSE ROBERT, JR., lawyer; b. nr. Halifax, Va., May 14, 1924; s. Jesse Robert and Grace Belle (Crenshaw) O.; student U. Va., 1947-48; LL.B., U. Richmond, 1953; m. Harriette Elizabeth Sutherlin, Dec. 23, 1948; children—Mary Marshall, Robert Sutherlin. Admitted to Va. bar, 1952; individual practice law, Clarksville, 1952—; substitute judge Mecklenburg County, 1970—; dir. Fidelity Nat. Bank, Clarksville. Mayor, Clarksville, 1954-56; del. Va. Republican Conv., 1973. Trustee Dixie Youth Baseball Park, 1964-72. Served 3 tours active duty USN; designated naval aviator, 1944; ret. as lt. comdr. Mem. Mecklenburg County (pres. 1964), Va. bar assns., Va. State Bar, Va. Trial Lawyers Assn., V.F.W. Methodist. Comml. pilot. Home and office: PO Box 145 Clarksville VA 23927

OVERSTREET, LUEL PIERCE, veterinarian; b. Merimac, Ky., Jan. 2, 1938; s. Luel W. and Viola (Brown) O.; B.S., Eastern Ky. U., 1960; D.V.M., Auburn U., 1964; m. Mary Lynn Myers, Sept. 2, 1962; children—Luel Kevin, Lacy Kent. Owner Henderson (Ky.) Animal Clinic, 1964—; owner Bluegrass Standardbred Farm, Henderson, 1968—; instr. animal husbandry U. Ky. Northwest Center, 1960—. Recipient Eastern Ky. U. Agr. award, 1959; Davis award Auburn U., 1964. Democrat. Baptist. Mason (Shriner), Lion (v.p. 1970). Home: Route 2 Box 172 Henderson KY 42420 Office: 1640 S Green St Henderson KY 42420

OVERSTREET, N.W., JR., lawyer; b. Jackson, Miss., Nov. 14, 1913; ed. Millsaps Coll.; LL.B., U. Miss., 1936. Admitted to Miss. bar, 1936; mem. firm Overstreet & Kuykendall, Jackson. Served with AUS, 1940-45; col. Res. ret. Fellow Am., Miss. (pres. 1963-65) bar founds.; mem. Am., Hinds County (pres. 1954-55) bar assns., Miss. State Bar (pres. 1967-68). Office: 829 Deposit Guaranty Bldg Jackson MS 39205

OVERTON, HELEN PARKER (MRS. SAMUEL WATKINS OVERTON), civic worker; b. Memphis, Dec. 30, 1920; d. William and Pearl (Pinkston) Parker; m. Samuel Watkins Overton, Sept. 3, 1952; children—Helen Parker, Napoleon Hill. Exec. sec. Memphis State U., 1941-43, Chgo. and So. Air Lines, 1943-46, Memphis Bd. Edn., 1948-50; dir. women's program Sta. WHBQ-TV, Memphis, 1950-52. Pres., Beethoven Club, 1960-66, 72—; mem. Tenn. Arts Commn., 1967-74, chmn., 1967-69; pres. Mid-South Opera Guild, 1966—; dir. auditions Mid-South region Met. Opera, 1961-71, mem. nat. council, 1961—. Bd. dirs. Memphis Acad. Arts, Memphis Opera Theatre, Arts Appreciation. Mem. Sigma Alpha Iota, Alpha Gamma Delta. Club: Memphis Country. Home: 5476 Collingwood Cove Memphis TN 38117

OVERTON, JOSEPH ALLEN, JR., mining exec.; b. Parkersburg, W.Va., Apr. 17, 1921; s. Joseph Allen and Edith (Wharton) O.; LL.B., Washington & Lee U., 1946, J.D., 1970; m. Bette Crosswhite, May 15, 1943; children—Joseph Allen III, Rebecca A., Mallory E. Admitted to W.Va. bar, 1947; mem. firm Handlan, Overton & Earley, Parkersburg, 1949-54; spl. asst. to gen. counsel Dept. Commerce, 1955-56, dep. gen. counsel, 1956-59; mem. U.S. Tariff Commn., 1959-62, vice chmn., 1959-60; adminstrv. v.p. Am. Mining Congress, Washington, 1962, exec. v.p., 1963-71, pres., 1972—, pub. Mining Congress Jour., 1963—. Mem. W.Va. Legislature, 1948-50; exec. dir. W.Va. Republican Exec. Com., 1951-54; spl. asst. to chmn. Nat. Citizens for Eisenhower, 1954-55. Served from pvt. to 1st lt. USAAF, 1941-46. Mem. Am., W.Va., Fed. bar assns., Am. Legion, 40 and 8, Phi Kappa Psi. Episcopalian. Elk. Home: 4677 N Dittmar Rd Arlington VA 22207 Office: Ring Bldg 18th St NW Washington DC 20036

OVERTON, NELSON TILGHMAN, judge; b. Newport News, Va., Feb. 7, 1928; s. Nelson Chilcoat and Lucile (Tilghman) O.; B.A., Va. Mil. Inst., 1949; LL.B., U. Va., 1952; m. Margaret Lee Payne, June 18, 1952; children—Nancy Chilcoat, Waverly Nelson, Margaret Lee. Admitted to Va. bar, 1952, practiced in Hampton, 1952-53, 55-64; judge 8th Jud. Circuit of Va., Hampton, 1964—. Served from 2d lt. inf. to 1st lt. Judge Advocates Gens. Corps, AUS, 1953-55. Mem. Va., Hampton bar assns., Order of Coif, Raven Soc., Kappa Alpha, Phi Delta Phi. Methodist. Home: 102 Congress Av Hampton VA 23369 Office: Circuit Ct Hampton VA 23369

OVERTON, STANLEY D., savs. and loan assn. exec.; b. Dickson, Tenn., May 2, 1928; s. Dallas Stanley and Ova (Dixon) O.; student Fall's Bus. Coll., 1948-49, Internat. Accountants Soc., 1950-52; grad. Savs. and Loan Sch., Ind. U., 1961-63; m. Betty Jo Womble, Aug. 31, 1948; children—Stanley D., James Stanton. With Fidelity Fed. Savs. & Loan Assn., Nashville, 1950—, exec. v.p., 1963-67, pres., 1967—, also dir. Bd. dirs. local A.R.C., YMCA; mem. devel. council Peabody Coll. and U. Tenn. Served with USNR, 1946-48. Mem. U.S. (dir.), Tenn. (past bd. dirs., pres. 1969-70) savs. and loan league, Am. Savs. and Loan Inst. (past pres. Nashville), Nashville Area C. of C. (bd. govs.). Mason (32 deg., Shriner), Kiwanian. Clubs: Hillwood Country (bd. dirs.), City (bd. dirs., pres. 1969-70) (Nashville). Home: 5908 Long Meadow Rd Nashville TN 37205 Office: 401 Union St Nashville TN 37219

OVUNC, BULENT AHMET, civil engr., educator; b. Samsun, Turkey, Oct. 14, 1927; s. Mithat Ahmet And Zehra Fatma (Tahir) O.; M.Sc., Tech. U. Istanbul, Turkey, 1954, Ph.D., 1963; m. Bercis Zaralioglu, June 27, 1957; 1 dau., Ayse. Came to U.S., 1967. Instr. Tech. U. Instanbul, Turkey, 1954-59, asst. prof. mechanics and structures, 1960-65; acad. research asst. U. B.C., Can. 1965-67; asso. prof. U. Southwestern La., Lafayette, 1967-70, prof., 1970—. Cons. on structural designs to various firms. Served to lt. Turkish Air Force, 1959-60. French govt. grantee, 1956, Orgn. Econ. Coop. and Devel. grantee, 1963-64, U. Southwestern La. Found. grantee, 1968, NSF grantee, 1970, 72, Halliburton grantee, 1972. Mem. Am. Soc. M.E., Am. Soc. C.E., Am. Concrete Inst., Internat. Assn. Bridges and Structural Engrng., Assn. Profl. Engrs. B.C., Sigma Xi. Contbr. articles on structural engrng. to profl. publs. Home: 358 Orangewood Dr Lafayette LA 70501

OWEN, AUSTIN EVERETT, III, lawyer; b. Norfolk, Va., July 21, 1924; s. Richard Clement and Judith (Berkley) O.; student Coll. William & Mary, Norfolk, Va., 1941-43, N.C. State Coll., 1943-44, U. Ky., 1944; J.D., U. Richmond, 1950; m. Edythe Virginia Dalton, July 22, 1950; children—Judith Claiborne, Elizabeth Dalton, Martha Berkley, Austin Everett IV. Admitted to Va. bar, 1950; asst. sec. Va. Alcoholic Beverage Control Bd., 1950-52; asst. U.S. Atty., Eastern Dist. Va., 1952-54; mem. firm Kellam & Kellam attys. at law, Norfolk, 1954-60; partner Owen, Guy, Rhodes & Betz, Virginia Beach, Va., 1961—. Pres. and dir. Commonwealth Bldg. Co., Virginia Beach, 1963-68, Virginia Beach Service Center, Inc., 1971-73; commr. in chancery Circuit Ct., City of Virginia Beach, 1970—; dir. Bank of Va.-Tidewater, Virginia Beach; gen. counsel Tidewater Assn. Homebuilders, Norfolk, Va., 1964-67. Bd. dirs. Virginia Beach Tennis Patrons Assn., 1967-68, Health, Welfare, Recreation planning council, 1970—, United Community Fund, 1971—. Mem. Am., Va., Va. State, Norfolk-Portsmouth, Virginia Beach (pres. 1967) bar assns., Va. Trial Lawyers Assn., Delta Theta Phi. Democrat. Episcopalian (vestryman). Club: Princess Anne Country. Home: 3204 Sunnybrook Lane Virginia Beach VA 23452 Office: 281 Independence Blvd Virginia Beach VA 23462

OWEN, BEN, lawyer, state legislator; b. Columbus, Miss., July 12, 1921; s. Frank C. and Mary (Askew) O.; B.A., U. Miss., 1942, LL.B., 1947; married; children—Lydia, Frank, Marsha, David, Judith. Admitted to Miss. bar, 1947, since practiced in Columbus; mem. Miss. Ho. of Reps., 1964-72. Served with AUS, 1942-46. Home: 2000 S 9th St Columbus MS 39701 Office: 2d Av N Columbus MS 39701

OWEN, DELBERT GENE, elec. engr.; b. Red Boiling Springs, Tenn., Mar. 23, 1936; s. Thomas Lee and Ruth (Carver) O.; B.S. in E.E., Tenn. Tech. U., 1962; m. Peggy J. Ferrell, Apr. 6, 1957; children—Cindy Jo, Lisa Paulette. With DuPont, Aiken, S.C., 1962—, sr. supr. power distbn., 1970-73, area engr. elec. and instrument dept. 1973—. Precinct treas. Republican party, Aiken, 1970. Served with USNR, 1954-58. Mem. I.E.E.E. (sec. 1962—). Mem. Ch. of Christ. Home: 104 Clifton St Aiken SC 29801 Office: DuPont Savannah River Plant Aiken SC 29801

OWEN, KENNETH DALE, orthodontist; b. Charlotte, N.C., May 9, 1938; s. Olin Watson and Ruth (Watlington) O.; B.S., Davidson Coll., 1959; D.D.S., U. N.C., 1963, M.Sc. in Orthodontics, 1967; m. Lura Aven Carnes, Feb. 14, 1958; children—Kenneth Dale, Aven Anna. Individual practice orthodontics, Charlotte, 1966—. Asst. clin. prof. U. N.C. Sch. Dentistry, 1969-72. Bd. dirs. N.C. Dental Found., 1973-74, exec. com., 1974. Served with Dental Corps, AUS, 1963-65. Mem. Am. Dental Assn., Am. Assn. Orthodontists, So. Soc. Orthodontists, N.C. Orthodontic Soc., N.C. (Jour. dist. editor 67-69; del. 1969-71), 2d Dist. (sec.-treas. 1971-74), Charlotte (chmn. various coms.) dental socs., U. N.C. Orthodontic Alumni Assn. (sec.-treas. 1971, pres. elect 1973-74), Orthovista Orthodontic Study Group (pres. 1968; treas. 1972), Delta Sigma Delta (past pres. N.C. grad. chpt.), Omicron Kappa Upsilon, Alpha Epsilon Delta. Methodist (steward 1968-69, adminstrn. bd. 1969-71, 74-75). Home: 3724 Pomfret Lane Charlotte NC 28211 Office: 1201 E Morehead St Charlotte NC 28204

OWEN, MARTIN FREDERICK, mining co. exec.; b. Houston, June 26, 1932; s. William Frank and May Elizabeth (Spraull) O.; B.B.A., U. Tex., 1958, LL.B., 1959; m. Nancy Harwell, Aug. 30, 1957; children—Scott, Melissa, Steven. With Humble Oil & Refining Co., Houston, 1959-66; v.p. land and legal affairs Duval Corp., Houston, 1966—. Served with USMCR, 1952-54. Mem. Internat., Am., Tex. bar assns. Home: 6503 Fawnwood St Spring TX 77373 Office: 900 SW Tower St Houston TX 77002

OWEN, REMOND A., broadcasting co. exec.; b. Lynchburg, Va., Jan. 9, 1926; s. William A. and Nellie (Abbott) O.; B.S., Va. Poly. Inst.; m. Mili Rothman, Sept. 9, 1973; children by previous marriage—Kerry S. Urbanski, Betty Seery, Raymond S., Robert D. With radio sta. WLEE, Richmond, Va., 1951-56; mgr. radio sta. KVOA, Tucson, 1956-58; mgr., v.p. radio sta. KCEE, Tucson, 1958-67; v.p. Hearst Radio Inc. WAPA, San Juan, P.R., 1967—. Recipient Man of Year award Exchange Clubs San Juan, 1973. Lion, Rotarian. Home: 14 Yardley Place Santurce PR Office: Box 4563 San Juan PR 00905

OWEN, RIPLEY PENDLETON, hosp. adminstr.; b. Lynchburg, Va., Mar. 27, 1936; s. William L. and Ester M. (Miller) O.; student U. Va., 1957-58, U. Wis., 1959-60, Internat. Accountants Soc., 1967-68, Trinity U., 1972-73; m. C. Jean Hardwick, Dec. 24, 1960; 1 dau., Patricia Hardwick. Indsl. engr. Babcock & Wilcox Co., 1956-60; prodn. engr. Reactive Metals, Inc., 1961-62; quality control mgr., dir. personnel Daystrom div. Schlumberger, 1963-66; adminstr. South Boston (Va.) Gen. Hosp., 1966—, treas., 1968—. Pres. Halifax County Mental Health Assn., 1969-70. Bd. dirs. Danville Area Clinic for Mental Health, 1968—, v.p., 1971-72. Served with USMCR, 1954-55. Recipient citation Halifax County Mental Health Assn., 1970. Mem. Am., Va. hosp. assns. Lion. Home: Route 2 Box 721 Halifax VA 24558 Office: N Main St South Boston VA 24592

OWEN, WILLIAM HUNTER, cons. san. engr.; b. Mt. Pleasant, Tenn., Aug. 21, 1923; s. Park Hanner and Mary Nell (Skillern) O.; B.E., Vanderbilt U., 1944; M.S., Harvard, 1950; m. Deliann Tolliver, Apr. 9, 1949; 1 dau., Stephanie (Mrs. Thomas Carter Gerity). San. engr. Tenn. Dept. Pub. Health, Nashville, 1945-58; asso. Barge, Waggoner, Sumner & Cannon, Engrs. and Planners, Nashville, 1959—. Mem. adv. council Tenn. Water Resources Center, Knoxville, 1968—; mem. Mid-Cumberland Comprehensive Health Planning Council, 1970—. Reigstered profl. engr., Tenn., Ky. Mem. Am. Acad. Environmental Engrs., Nat. Soc. Profl. Engrs., Am. Water Works Assn. (Fuller award 1963), Water Pollution Control Fedn. (Arthur Sidney Bedell award 1964), Alpha Tau Omega. Presbyn. Clubs: Harvard, Hillwood Country (Nashville). Home: 1205 Canterbury Dr Nashville TN 37205 Office: 404 James Robertson Pkwy Nashville TN 37219

OWEN, WILLIAM KENDRICK, physician; b. Little Rock, July 28, 1910; s. William Crook and Corinne Erwin (Kendrick) O.; A.B. Sci., Duke, 1931; M.D., Vanderbilt Med. Sch., 1936; m. Myra Killebrew Williams, Mar. 28, 1938; 1 dau., Earline. Intern Nashville Gen. Hosp., 1936-37; intern surgery St. Vincent Hosp., Birmingham, Ala., 1937-38; gen. practice medicine, South Pittsburg, Tenn., 1938-40, Pulaski, Tenn., 1940—; chief staff Giles County Hosp., Pulaski, 1962-63, 72-73. Dir. Union Bank, Pulaski; mem. Tenn. Bd. Med. Examiners, Nashville, 1965-73, pres., 1971. Named Citizen of Year, V.F.W., 1972; Boss of Year, Bus. and Profl. Women's Club, 1972. Mem. A.M.A., Tenn. Med. Assn., Giles County Med. Soc. Methodist (bd. stewards 1973). Mason. Club: Exchange (Pulaski). Home: 500 W Madison St Pulaski TN 38478 Office: 304 E Jefferson St Pulaski TN 38478

OWENS, ARTHUR MELBOURNE, physician; b. Ocean Falls, B.C., Can., Sept. 13, 1926; s. Roscoe Wheeler and Marie (Stickle) O.; A.B., Pacific Union Coll., 1951; M.D., Loma Linda U., 1955; m. Luthea Eleonore Estey, Aug. 9, 1953; children—Geoffrey, Cynthia, Gregory, Douglas. Intern, Portland (Ore.) Adventist Hosp., 1955-56; med. officer USPHS, D.C., Mont., Ore., 1956-59; med. missionary, Nigeria, 1959-70; pvt. practice medicine, Dunlap, Tenn., 1970—. Diplomate Nat. Bd. Med. Examiners. Licentiate Med. Council Can.; mem. Chattanooga & Hamilton County Med. Soc., Tenn., Am., So. Med. assns. Republican. Mem. Seventh-day Adventist Ch. (elder 1955—). Home: PO Box 176 Dunlap TN 37327 Office: Dunlap Med Clinic Inc Dunlap TN 37327

OWENS, DOUGLAS WAYNE, congressman; b. Panguitch, Utah, May 2, 1937; s. Joseph and Ruth (Dodds) O.; J.D., U. Utah, 1964; m. Marlene Wessel, Aug. 18, 1961; children—Elizabeth, Douglas, Sara, Stephen, Teddy. Admitted to Utah bar, 1965, practiced in Salt Lake City, 1965-68; state asst. to Senator Frank E. Moss of Utah, 1965-69, adminstrv. asst., Washington, 1971-72; mem. 93d Congress from 2d Dist. Utah; Western states coordinator presdl. campaign Robert Kennedy, 1968; adminstrv. asst. to majority leader Senator Edward M. Kennedy of Mass., 1969-71. Dir campaign, 1956; chmn. Garfield County com. Granger for Senate campaign, staff Rampton for Senator, 1962; asst. to chmn. Utah Dem. Campaign, 1956; del. Utah Dem. Conv., 1964, 66, 68; del. Dem. Nat. Conv., 1968. Home: 3243 Highland Lane Fairfax VA 22030 Office: Room 222 Cannon House Office Bldg Washington DC 20515

OWENS, EMMETT LESLIE, civil engr.; b. Palatka, Fla., Feb. 29, 1928; d. Charles Leslie and Lillie Leanora (Evans) O.; B.C.E., U. Fla., 1949; m. Linda Warren, May 10, 1962; children—Richard, Patrick, Lynn, Kara. Hydraulic engr. Bur. of Reclamation, Durango, Colo., 1949-51; engr. Fla. Dept. Transp., Tallahassee, 1953—, state traffic operations engr., 1971—. Served to lt., arty. AUS, 1951-53. Registered profl. engr., Fla. Mem. Nat. Soc. Profl. Engrs., Inst. Traffic Engrs., Fla. Engring. Soc. Mason, Elk. Home: 501 Plantation Rd Tallahassee FL 32303 Office: Haydon Burns Bldg Suwannee St Tallahassee FL 32302

OWENS, MILTON ANTHONY, city ofcl.; b. Portsmouth, Va., Jan. 16, 1906; s. Leonard Joseph and Mattie Temperance (Collins) O.; B.S., Va. Poly. Inst., 1931; m. Anne Virginia Adcock, May 25, 1933; children—Antoinette (Mrs. John S. Ashworth), Elaine (Mrs. William R. Rowe). Salesman, Proctor & Gamble, Balt., 1931-32; profl. football player, Paterson, N.J., 1933; purchasing agt., auditor Fed. Project, Portsmouth, Va., 1934; dep. sheriff City of Portsmouth, 1934-50, sheriff, 1954—; salesman Schlitz Beer, Portsmouth, 1950-54. Pres., Cath. Child and Family Service, 1969-71. Bd. dirs. Maryview Hosp.; pres. adv. bd. Salvation Army, 1965-67. Named Sportsmouthman of Year, Portsmouth Sports Club, 1966. Mem. Va. Sheriff's Assn. (pres. 1962-63). Roman Catholic. Lion (pres. 1966-67), Elk. Club: Ports Sports (pres. Portsmouth 1965-66). Home: 201-A Effingham St Portsmouth VA 23704 Office: 701 Crawford St Portsmouth VA 23705

OWENS, RICHARD C., librarian; b. Kennedy, Ala., Jan. 14, 1928; s. Walter Lurid and Connie Elizabeth (Dollar) O.; B.S., U. Ala., 1952. Librarian, Camp Chaffee, Ark., 1952-53, Aberdeen Proving Grounds, Md., 1953-54; hosp. librarian Ft. McClellan, Ala., 1954-55; post librarian, 1955-58; base librarian Columbus AFB, Miss., 1958—. Named Civilian of Year, SAC, Air Force Assn., 1964; recipient Superior Performance awards Civil Service, 1961, 64, 69. Mem. Am. (mem. civil service com. armed forces br. 1967-69), Miss. (chmn. spl. librarians sect. 1972—) library assns. Home: Route 2 Box 19 Kennedy AL 35574 Office: Base Library Columbus AFB MS 39701

OWENS, ROBERT GUY, health sci. adminstr.; b. Florence, S.C., Jan. 23, 1922; s. Colie Whittington and Eva Louvinia (Isgett) O.; B.S., N.C. State U., 1950; A.M., Columbia, 1951, Ph.D., 1955; m. Helen Evelyn Johnson, Aug. 14, 1954; children—Sheryl, Holly, Diane, Linda. Research scientist Boyce Thompson Inst., Yonkers, N.Y., 1950-61, program dir. microbial chemistry, 1962-66; chief chemistry sect., dep. officer in charge pesticides research lab. Dept. Health, Edn. and Welfare, Perrine, Fla., 1966-67; chief cell biology br. Nat. Inst. Environmental Health Sci., Research Triangle Park, N.C., 1967-72, health sci. adminstr., 1972—. Cons., Norwich Pharmacal Co. (N.Y.), 1956-60; adj. prof. phytopathology N.C. State U. at Raleigh, 1967-72. Served with AUS, 1943-46, USAAF, 1944-45: ETO, CBI. Mem. Am. Phytopath. Soc., Am. Chem. Soc., Sigma Xi. Asso. editor Phytopathology, 1968-70. Contbr. articles to profl. jours. Home: 4800 Connell Dr Raleigh NC 27612 Office: PO Box 12233 Research Triangle Park NC 27709

OWENS, WILLIAM H., mining co. exec.; b. Denton, Tex., Aug. 16, 1893; s. James Madison and Jesse (McCutcheon) O.; student Schs., Hamilton Coll. Law, 1915; m. Elizabeth Sherburne, June 23, 1938; children—Virginia (Mrs. E.C. Meyer), Jeanne (Mrs. William Holcomb), William H. Pres. W. H. Owens Co., Tulsa, also Mexico, 1932—, Carribean Petroleum Co., Tulsa, also Panama, 1958—, Rosario Mining Co., Mexico, 1954—, Continental Mining Co., Mexico, 1955, Panama Exploration Co., 1936—, Western Hemisphere Trading Corp., 1947-59; v.p. Esterex de Mexico, 1945—; dir. all cos.; also dir. Cia-Hidro-Electrica del Amacuzac, S.A., Mexico; pres., chmn. bd. Casa FabMex, S.A., Distribuidora Diamonor, S.A. Home: 1705 E 36th St Tulsa OK 74105 Office: Av San Juan de Letran 21-911 Mexico City Mexico

OWINGS, ADDISON DAVIS, educator; b. Hattiesburg, Miss., Feb. 8, 1936; s. Addison Davis and Elizabeth (Steadman) O.; student Hinds Jr. Coll., 1953-55; B.S., Miss. State Coll., 1957; M.S., Miss. State U., 1962, Ph.D., 1966; m. Janice Kay Grace, Feb. 28, 1964; children—Allen Davis, Don Frazier. Asst. agronomist Miss. Agrl. Expt. Sta., Stoneville, 1957-59; instr. dept. agr. Southeastern La. U., 1963-64, asst. prof., 1964-67, asso. prof., 1967-70, prof., 1970—, head dept., 1967—. Presbyn. (Sunday sch. teacher 1958—, supt. 1969—, deacon 1965-73, elder 1973—). Home: Route 4 Box 158F Hammond LA 70410

OWINGS, WILLIAM JENNINGS BRYAN, ret. physician, surgeon; b. nr. Ashland, Ala., Feb. 25, 1908; s. Thomas Harvey and Josephine (Morris) O.; A.B., U. Ala., 1929, B.S., 1930; M.D., Tulane U., New Orleans, 1932; postgrad. Vanderbilt U., 1936; m. Lena Mae Thompson, Sept. 17, 1930; children—Clyde Lacy, William Orange, Joseph Lee, John and Alice (dec.), Thomas Gene and Linda Kay (twins). Health officer Lamar Co., Ala., 1934-36; asso. USPHS, Hot Springs, Ark., 1940; dir. Bibb. Co. Venereal Disease Clinic, 1940-47, Bibb Co. Pediatric Clinic, 1940-47, Bibb Co. Prenatal Clinic, 1940-47; gen. practice medicine, Brent, Ala., 1936-63; owner, dir. Owings Clinic, 1940-63; sec. staff Bibb County Hosp., Centreville, Ala., 1959-60, v.p., 1962-63. Local surgeon Ill. Central Gulf R.R., Ill. Central Hosp. Assn. Chmn. Bibb County Bd. Health, 1940-63, Bibb County Board Censors, 1937—; med. adviser local bd. Selective Service System, 1941-72; bd. dirs. East End Meml. Hosp., Birmingham, 1944-47; exec. bd. Black Warrior council Boy Scouts Am., 1943-63, v.p., 1946-50. Recipient Selective Service System medal, Wisdom award, 1972. Fellow Am. Inst. Chemists, (life), Royal Soc. Health (life), Am. Geriatric Soc., Am. Acad. Family Physicians (charter); mem. Ala. Acad. Gen. Practice (pres. 1959, chmn. bd. dirs. 1960), Am., So. (asso. councillor 1959-60, life mem.), Ala. (councillor 1941—) med. assns., Black Belt Med. Assn. (pres. 1953), Aero-Med. Assn., Am. Pub. Health Assn., Am. Acad. Gen. Practice (pres. elect 1958, pres. Ala. chpt. 1959-60), Mo. Pacific Hosp. Assn., Bibb County Med. Soc. (past pres.), Soc. (pres.), Phi Chi, Sigma Phi Epsilon. Baptist (deacon), Woodman World (council Comdr.), Mason (32 deg., Shriner), Elk. Clubs: Tuscaloosa Amateur Radio, Ala. Amateur, Civitan. Amateur radio operator. Home: PO Drawer A Brent AL 35034

OWSLEY, ALVIN MANSFIELD, JR., lawyer; b. Dallas, Feb. 9, 1926; s. Alvin Mansfield and Lucy (Ball) O.; A.B., Princeton, 1949; LL.B., U. Tex., 1952; m. Barbara Ann Robinson, June 23, 1950; children—Michael M., Carol R., Steven A. Admitted to Tex. bar, 1952, since practiced in Houston. Dir. Ball Corp., Comml. State Bank. Bd. govs. Acad. Comparative Trial Practice; trustee Alvin and Lucy Owsley Found. Served with F.A., AUS, 1944-46. Mem. Am., Tex., Houston bar assns., Phi Delta Phi, Order of Coif. Presbyn. Clubs: Houston Country, Tejas, Athletic of Houston. Home: 65 Briar Hollow Lane Houston TX 77027 Office: 3000 One Shell Plaza Houston TX 77002

OXENREIDER, WILLIAM EARL, civil engr.; b. Portage, Pa., June 23, 1934; s. Earl Snyder and Mary Pearl (McNally) O.; B.C.E., Cath. U. Am., 1956; m. Mary Elizabeth Harper, Oct. 18, 1958; children—Teresa, Margaret, Deborah, Julia. Design engr. N. Am. Avaition, Inc., Columbus, O., 1956-57; bridge engr. Michael Baker, Inc., Charleston, W.Va., 1957-58, Blauvelt Engring. Co., Richmond, Va., 1958-66; chief structural engr. Am. Engrs., Richmond, 1966—. Registered profl. engr., Va., Fla., N.C. Mem. Am. Soc. C.E., Nat. Soc. Profl. Engrs., West End Jr. C. of C. K.C. Home: 7708 Yolanda Rd Richmond VA 23229 Office: 6002 W Broad St Richmond VA 23230

OXFORD, HUBERT III, lawyer; b. Beaumont, Tex., Sept. 25, 1938; s. Hubert Burton and Virginia Mary (Cunningham) O.; B.S. in Mech. Engring., Tex. A. and M. Coll., 1960; LL.B., U. Tex., 1963; m. Mary Francelia Crittenden, Feb. 25, 1967; children—Mary Francelia, Hubert IV, Mary Cunningham. Admitted to Tex. bar, 1963; briefing clk. to U.S. dist. judge Eastern Dist. Tex., 1966; asst. dist. atty. Jefferson County, Beaumont, Tex., 1967; U.S. commr. Eastern Dist. Tex., Beaumont, 1968-70; mem. firm Benckenstein, McNicolas, Ball, Oxford, Radford, & Johnson, 1967—; city atty. for cities of Nome, China and Lumberton (all Tex.). Bd. dirs. YMCA, Beaumont Red Cross, Beaumont Assn. Mental Health. Served to capt. USAF, 1963-66; Vietnam. Named Outstanding Young Lawyer Jefferson County, 1972. Mem. Tex. Assn. Def. Lawyers, Maritime Law Assn. U.S., Am. Assn. Average Adjusters, State Jr. Bar Tex. (dir. 1969-71, sec. treas. 1971, v.p. 1972), Phi Delta Theta, Tau Beta Pi, Phi Kappa Phi, Phi Delta Phi. Rotarian. Home: 2477 Long St Beaumont TX 77702 Office: 605 San Jacinto Bldg Beaumont TX 77704

OXLEY, MATTHEW WALKER, JR., mfg. co. exec.; b. Birmingham, Ala., Oct. 10, 1923; s. Matthew W. and Marguerite (Elliott) O.; grad. high sch.; m. Lu Ann Mosley, Dec. 27, 1961; children—Matthew, Kim, Trent, Robinson. Asst. mgr. Griffin Garment Co. (Ga.), 1951-54; plant mgr. Hazlehurst Mfg. Co., Vidalia, Ga., 1954-59; pres., gen. mgr. Rosebud Mfg. Co., Vidalia, 1959—; dir. Crimson Crest Enterprises, Inc., Vidalia, Ga., Crimson Crest Enterprises of Fla., Inc., Cross City, Fla. Mem. Vidalia Bd. Edn., 1968-73. Served with USNR, 1942-46. Democrat. Methodist (mem. finance com. 1966-73), Moose, Elk, Kiwanian (pres. Vidalia 1959-60). Club: Vidalia (Ga.) Country. Home: 606 W 4th St Vidalia GA 30474 Office: 108 Dixon St Midalia GA 30474

OYLER, EUGENE JOSEPH, journalist; b. Seattle, Feb 5, 1925; s. Joseph Eugene and Clara (Fox) O.; B.S., E. Tenn. State Coll., 1950; m. Betty Newsom, July 1, 1950; children—Eric Eugene, David Newsom. Sports writer, gen. reporter Press Chronicle, Johnson City, Tenn., 1947-53; telegraph editor Daily Jour., Tupelo, Miss., 1953-56; copyreader News and Courier, Charleston, S.C., 1956, Sunday editor, 1956-57, asst. news editor, 1957-58, asst. city editor, 1958-59, sr. asst. city editor, 1959-61, chief copy editor, 1961-67, exec. women's editor, 1967-68; exec. editor Standard and Review, Aiken, S.C., 1968-72; with Charleston Evening Post, 1972—; exec. editor Aiken Standard, 1968—. Mem. S.C. Asso. Press News Council (pres. 1970-72). Served with AUS, 1941-45. Home: 21 24th St Isle of Palms SC 29451 Office: 134 Columbus St Charleston SC 29451

OZELL, ALAN MUNCI, constrn. co. exec.; b. Izmir, Turkey, Aug. 26, 1917 (came to U.S. 1939, naturalized 1951); s. Cevat M. and Kadriye C. (Sakir) O.; B.S. in Civil Engring., Robert Coll., Istanbul, Turkey, 1939; M.S., U. Ill. at Urbana, 1941, Ph.D., 1944; m. Flo Nell Morris, July 11, 1945; children—Phillip, Camille, Tony, Timothy. Research asso. U. Ill. at Urbana, 1944-46; asso. prof. U. Okla., 1949-54; prof. U. Fla., 1954-61; cons. engr., Ankara, Turkey, 1946-49, Sarasota, Fla., 1961-65; with Mason & Hanger, Jacksonville, Fla., 1966-71; structural engr. Wilson & Asso., Jacksonville, 1971-72; now with firm Ozell, Baker, McGhin; & Padgett, Orange Park, Fla. Registered profl. engr., Fla., Ky., Tenn., La., Miss., Okla. Fellow Am. Soc. C.E.; mem. Am. Concrete Inst., Prestressed Concrete Inst., Welding Research Council. Contbr. articles to nat. and internat. jours. Home: 2446 La Mesa Dr Jacksonville FL 32217 Office: Ozell Baker McGhin & Padgett 2131 Kingsley Av Orange Park FL 32073

OZSVATH, ISTVAN, educator; b. Kolesd, Hungary, Sept. 10, 1928; s. Istvan and Julianna (Benedek) O.; M.S., U. Budapest, 1951; Ph.D., U. Hamburg (Germany), 1960; m. Zsuzsanna Abonyi, June 1, 1950; children—Kathleen, Peter. Came to U.S., 1962, naturalized, 1969. Research asso. Konkoly Observatory, Budapest, 1951-56; Research Soc. fellow Hamburg Observatory, 1957-62; mem. faculty U. Tex. at Dallas, 1962—, asso. prof. math., 1962-67, prof., 1967—. Home: 414 Fall Creek Rd Richardson TX 75080 Office: Dept Math Univ Texas Dallas TX 75230

PACE, CAROLINA JOLLIFF (MRS. JOHN MCIVER PACE), book co. exec.; b. Dallas, Apr. 12, 1938; d. Lindsay Gafford and Carolina (Juden) Jolliff; student Holton-Arms Jr. Coll., 1956-57; B.A. in Comparative Lit., So. Meth. U., 1960; m. John McIver Pace, Oct. 7, 1961. Fashion cons., lectr. Nancy Taylor Sch., Dallas, 1959-61; promotional adv., dir. season ticket sales Dallas Theatre Center, 1960-61; exec. sec. Dallas Book and Author Luncheon, 1959-63; promotional and instnl. cons. Henry Regnery-Reilly & Lee Pub. Co., Chgo., 1962-65; pub. trade rep. various cos., institutional rep. Don R. Phillips Co., Southeastern area, 1965-67; Southwestern rep. Ednl. Reading Service, Inc.-Troll Assos., Mahwah, N.J., 1967-72; v.p., dir. multimedia div. Melton Book Co., Dallas, 1972—. Mem. Womens Nat. Book Assn., D.A.R., Dallas Civic Opera Assn., Dallas Art Assn., Alpha Delta Pi. Presbyn. Club: Cotillion. Home: 4524 Lorraine Av Dallas TX 75205 Office: 111 Leslie St Dallas TX 75207

PACE, CHARLES MILLS, lawyer; b. Spartanburg, S.C., May 19, 1911; s. Otis Leroy and Amanda (Blackwood) P.; B.S., Clemson U., 1932; LL.B., U. S.C., 1935, J.D., 1969, Ph.D., 1970; m. June Cannington, July 23, 1966. Admitted to S.C. bar, 1935, practiced in Spartanburg, S.C., 1935-36, 71—; probate judge, Spartanburg, S.C., 1939-42; judge Superior County Ct., Spartanburg County, 1947-71. Mem. S.C. Ho. of Reps., 1937-38; mem. citizens com. Spartanburg County Council, 1963-66. Served from 2d lt. to maj. AUS, 1942-46; col. Res. ret. Mem. Am., S.C. (pres. county judges assn. div. 1969-70) bar assns., Pace Soc. Am. (1st v.p. 1963-68), Phi Delta Phi, Omicron Delta Kappa, Pi Kappa Alpha. Clubs: Spartanburg Country, Piedmont, Elks. Home: 1166 Woodburn Rd Spartanburg SC 29302 Office: 180 Library St PO Box 2413 Spartanburg SC 29302

PACE, WILL DENT, lawyer; b. Dallas, Nov. 20, 1925; s. William Dent and Azile (Fox) P.; J.D., U. Tex., 1950; m. Patricia Nicklow Pace, Sept. 4, 1948 (div. June 1972); children—Georganne (Mrs. Bobby Ray Epperson), Priscilla; m. 2d, Priscilla Pratt, July 7, 1972. Admitted to Tex. bar, 1950; practice law, Tyler, 1950—; spl. county judge of Smith County, Tyler, 1958-59. Served with USNR, World War II. Mem. State Bar Tex., Am., Tex. trial lawyers assns., Christian Legal Soc. Rotarian, Mason (32 deg., Shriner, dist. dep. grand master 1967-68). Home: 3404 Cameron St Tyler TX 75701 Office: Fair Foundation Bldg Tyler TX 75701

PACHECO, ANTONIO, optometrist; b. San Juan, P.R., Dec. 10, 1923; s. Sixto and Marta (Lafont) P.; O.D., Pa. State Coll. Optometry, 1951; m. Marta Ortiz, Dec. 30, 1947; children—Marta, Maria, Antonio, Rosa. Pvt. practice optometry, Santurce, P.R., 1951—; pres. Bd. Examiners of Optometrists P.R., 1965-67; optometric cons. Div. Mother and Child Dept. Health, 1960-61. Served with AUS, 1943-46. Fellow Am. Acad. Optometry; mem. Coll. Optometrists of P.R. (hon. life, pres. 1967-68), Am. Optometric Assn., Am. Acad. Optometry (pres. P.R. chpt. 1971), Am. Legion (post comdr. 1960-63), Optometric Hist. Soc. U.S.A., Ateneo Puertorriqueno, Phi Theta Epsilon. Elk. Club: Casino de Puerto Rico. Author: Visual Defects and Optometric Manpower in Puerto Rico, 1971; Legal and Historical Development of the Boards of Examiners of Optometrists of Puerto Rico 1898-1970, the 136th Years of Legal Optometric Life of the Pacheco Family, 1973. Home: 16 L St Villa Caparra PR 00619 Office: PO Box 10223 Santurce PR 00908

PACIFICI, JAMES GRADY, chemist; b. Savannah, Ga., May 20, 1939; s. Joseph and Ione (Rachels) P.; B.S., U. Ga., 1962, Ph.D., 1966; m. Mary Frances Kenny, Jan. 14, 1959; children—Phyllis Anne, Elizabeth Ione, Theresa Margaret, Angela Rose. Research chemist Tenn. Eastman Co. div. Eastman Kodak Co., Kingsport, Tenn., 1967-68, sr. research chemist, 1968—. NSF Postdoctoral fellow, 1966-67. Mem. Am. Chem. Soc., Chem. Soc. London, Sigma Xi. Moose. Club: Porsche Club of Am. Contbr. articles to sci. jours. Patentee chem. compositions. Home: Route 16 Kingsport TN 37663 Office: Research Labs Tenn Eastman Co Kingsport TN 37660

PACK, JAMES FERGUSON, savs. and loan exec.; b. Knoxville, Tenn., Dec. 25, 1933; s. Ben A. and Edna (Baldwin) P.; B.S., U. Tenn., 1960, LL.B., 1960; m. Joyce L. Thomas, Nov. 14, 1958; children—Lynn Allison, James Thomas. Accountant, Arthur Andersen & Co., C.P.A.'S, Atlanta, 1960-61; admitted to Tenn. bar, 1960; accountant Decatur Fed. Savs. & Loan Assn. (Ga), 1962-64, v.p., 1964-66; exec. v.p. Gwinnett Fed. Savs. & Loan Assn., Lawrenceville, Ga., 1967-70, pres., 1970—, also dir. Trustee Hi Hope Sch. for Mentally Retarded. Served with USNR, 1951-55. Mem. Lawrenceville C. of C. Lion. Home: Suwanee Rd Lawrenceville GA 30245 Office: PO Box 112 Lawrenceville GA 30245

PACKARD, FRED MALLERY, nat. park service ofcl.; b. Rutherford, N.J., Apr. 2, 1913; s. Elden Lord and Pauline (Mallery) P.; B.A., Harvard U., 1936; M.A., U. Colo., 1942; m. Jean N. Roberts, June 9, 1951; 1 dau., Jean Elden. Exec. sec. Nat. Parks Assn., Washington, 1951-58; dir. Fairfax County (Va.) Park Authority and No. Va. Regional Park Authority, 1958-62; recreation specialist Bur. Land Mgmt., U.S. Dept. Interior, Washington, 1962-64; internat. specialist Nat. Park Service, U.S. Dept. Interior, Washington, 1964—; sec. Internat. Commn. on Nat. Parks, Internat. Union for Conservation Nature and Natural Resources, 1958-71. Served with USNR, 1942-46. Research fellow U. Colo., 1941-42. Mem. Defenders of Wildlife (dir. 1946—). Club: Cosmos (Washington). Home: 4058 Elizabeth Lane Fairfax VA 22030 Office: Div Internat Affairs Nat Park Service U S Dept Interior Washington DC 20240

PACKARD, MARJEAN PHILLIPS (MRS. CHARLES A. PACKARD), ret. sch. adminstr.; b. New Vienna, O.; d. Harley M. and Nancy Ann (Johnson) Phillips; student Miami U., 1920-22; B.S., Wilmington (O.) Coll., 1944; M.Ed., U. Miami, 1954; m. Charles A. Packard, Sept. 7, 1927; 1 son, Charles Edgar. Tchr. Cin. pub. schs., 1922-27; saleswoman William Ruggles Real Estate, Evanston, Ill., 1936-38; tchr. Pine Crest Prep. Sch., Ft. Lauderdale, Fla., 1939-51; prin. Pine Crest Elementary Sch., 1951-73. Pres. Broward County Panhellenic, 1947-48. Mem. bd. Broward County council Girl Scouts. Bd. dirs. Pine Crest Prep. Sch. Named Hon. Alumna, Pine Crest Sch., Citizen of Month Fort Lauderdale C. of C., 1973, bldg. on Pine Crest Sch. Campus named Marjean Packard Learning Center, 1973. Mem. Ft. Lauderdale Hist. Soc., P.E.O. (pres. chpt. X 1947-48), Nat., Fla. depts. elementary sch. prins., Internat. Platform Assn., Ft. Lauderdale Symphony Soc. (dir.), Mus. Arts, Friends Library, So. Assn. Colls. and Schs. (chmn. Fla. affiliation com.), Am. Assn. U. Women (corr. sec. Ft. Lauderdale chpt.), Freedoms Found. at Valley Forge (ednl. v.p. Broward County chpt.), Delta Kappa Gamma (pres. Xi chpt. 1959-62, state pres., chmn. courtesy internat. conv. 1960, S.E. regional dir. internat. bd.; state achievement award), Sigma Kappa. Presbyn. (deacon, trustee). Clubs: Zonta (pres. Fort Lauderdale), Lauderdale Yacht. Contbr. to Jour. of Fla. Edn., Nat. Elementary Prins. Letter. Home: 124 Isle of Venice Box 2105 Fort Lauderdale FL 33301 Office: 1501 NE 62d St Fort Lauderdale FL 33308

PACKARD, MERLIN WADSWORTH, librarian; b. Portland, Me., April 10, 1929; s. James Roy and Mary Esther (Wadsworth) P.; grad. Phillips Acad., Andover, Mass. 1946; B.A., Haverford Coll., 1950; postgrad. U. Munich, 1956-57, Columbia, 1960-64. Research analyst U.S. Dept. Def., Germany, 1950-56; with Dumbarton Oaks Research Library, Washington, 1964—, asst. to librarian, 1964-67, librarian, 1967—. Mem. corp. Haverford Coll. Mem. Am. Hist. Assn., A.L.A., Mediaeval Acad. Am., Am. Assn. U. Profs. Episcopalian. Office: 1616 44th St NW Washington DC 20007

PACKMAN, PAUL FREDERICK, educator; b. Bklyn., July 30, 1938; s. Hy and Lee (Silverman) P.; B.M.E., Cooper Union Coll., 1959; M.S., Syracuse U., 1962, Ph.D., 1964; m. Sandra J. Weingarten, Apr. 15, 1962; children—Jeff L., Jill L. Sr. scientist Lockheed Aircraft Research Labs., Marietta, Ga., 1964-68; sr. fellow Air Force Material Labs. USAF-Nat. Acad. Scis., Dayton, O., 1972-73; prof., dir. div. material scis. and metallurgy Vanderbilt U., Nashville, 1973—; dir. Facts Inc., Consulting Service; prin. cons. failure analysis, non-destructive testing and quality control; staff cons. U.S. Air Force Materials Lab., Air Force Systems. Command. Mem. nat. materials adv. bd. U.S.-Japan Welding Sci. Coop. Exchange Program, 1973; mem. U.S.-Great Britain Tech. Coop. Program, 1973. Mem. Am. Soc. Metallurgy (pres. Mid Tenn. chpt. 1973), Am. Soc. Metals (dir. materials testing and quality control div. 1968-73), Am. Soc. Testing and Materials, Am. Welding Soc., Am. Inst. M.E., Am. Soc. for Nondestructive Testing. Contbr. tech. publs. failure, fracture, non-destructive inspection to tech. jours. Home: 404 W Meade Dr Nashville TN 37205 Office: Box 3245 Sta B Vanderbilt U Nashville TN 37235

PACKO, JOSEPH JOHN, industrialist; b. Toledo, Mar. 9, 1925; s. Joseph Steve and Mary (Toth) P.; spl. student John Carroll U., U. N.C., 1943-44; B.S. in Physics, Math., Bus. Adminstrn., Bowling Green State U., 1948; Dr. Sc., Southeastern Mass. U., 1969; m. Bette Throne, July 10, 1948; children—Jo Anne, Mark. With J.J. Packo Industries, Ft. Lauderdale, Fla., 1953; pres. J.J. Packo Mortgage Corp., 1954-69, Packo Enterprises 1955—, South Fla. Asphalt Co., 1956-65; pres., chmn. Am. Dynamics Internat., Inc. 1969—. Mem. Trade Mission, West Berlin, 1965. Bd. dirs. Fla. chpt. Nat. Soc. Prevention Blindness, Holy Cross Hosp., A.R.C.; bd. dirs. Nova U. Alumnae Assn., v.p. 1966—; bd. dirs. Bowling Green State U. Alumnae Assn., 1972—. Served with USNR, 1943-45. Mem. Opera Guild Ft. Lauderdale, Young Presidents Orgn. (vice-chmn., sec.-treas. Fla. chpt. 1961—), Am. Mgmt. Assn., A.A.A.S., Asphalt Inst., Nat. Bd. Realtors, Nat. Mortgage Brokers Assn., Navy League, Sigma Chi. Patentee in field. Home: 28 Pelican Isle Fort Lauderdale FL 33301

PACOFSKY, EDWARD ANTHONY, chemist; b. Latrobe, Pa., Feb. 19, 1930; s. Albert William and Anna Cecelia (Hricik) P.; B.S., St. Vincent Coll., 1952; M.S., W.Va. U., 1957, Ph.D., 1960; m. Dolores Tushak, Dec. 28, 1957; children—Gregory, Gretchen. Instr. W.Va. U., Morgantown, 1957-60; sr. research chemist E.I. du Pont de Nemours & Co., Kinston, N.C., 1960—. Mem. Lenoir County (N.C.) Drug Action Com., 1970—. Served with AUS, 1953-55. Recipient grant U.S. Army, 1957-58, NSF, 1959-60. Mem. Am. Chem. Soc., Sigma Xi, Delta Epsilon Sigma, Phi Lambda Upsilon. Democrat. Roman Catholic. Contbr. articles to profl. Home: 2300 Rouse Rd Kinston NC 28501 Office: PO Box 800 Kinston NC 28501

PADDISON, RICHARD MILTON, neurologist; b. Rochester, N.Y., Aug. 20, 1919; s. Osborn Howard and Ruby (Rapp) P.; A.B., Duke, 1943, M.D., 1945; m. Josephine Butler Bowles, Dec. 18, 1943 (div. Aug. 1966); children—Richard Milton, Alice Jeannette, David Robert, Patricia Louise, Eileen Ruth, Wendy Anne; m. 2d, Vera Gay Davis, Nov. 20, 1966; children—Stephen Matthew, Diane Bell. Intern Duke Hosp., Durham, N.C., 1945-46; ward officer VA Hosp., Augusta, Ga., 1948; instr. neurology and neuro-anatomy U. Ga. Sch. Medicine, Augusta, 1948-49; resident neurology Jefferson Med. Coll., Phila., 1949-51; fellow psychiatry Pa. Hosp., Phila., 1951-52, fellow Psychiatry Inst., 1952-53; chief neuropsychiatric service Burlington County Hosp., Mt. Holly, N.J., 1953-54; attending psychiatrist Camden County Mental Hosp., Blackwood, N.J., 1953-54; asst. prof. neurology La. State U. Sch. Medicine, New Orleans, 1954-56, asso. prof., 1956-59, prof., 1959—, head dept. neurology, 1965—; vis. physician Charity Hosp. of La., New Orleans, 1954-55, sr. vis. physician, 1955—, chief electroencephalographic lab., 1968—; attending staff Hotel Dieu, Mercy Hosp.; chief electroencephalographic lab. So. Bapt. Hosp., 1956—; cons. neurologist State Colony and Tng. Sch., Pineville, La., 1954—, Crippled Children's Hosp., New Orleans, 1955—, Cerebral Palsy Center, 1955-57. Spl. cons. in neurol. scis. to surgeon gen. USPHS, 1966-70. Served from lt. to capt., M.C., AUS, 1946-48. Diplomate Am. Bd. Psychiatry and Neurology. Fellow A.C.P., Am. Psychiat. Assn., Am. Acad. Neurology, Am. Acad. Cerebral Palsy; mem. A.M.A., Orleans Parish, La. med. socs., N.Y. Acad. Scis., Assn. for Research in Nervous and Mental Disease, So. Electroencephalographic Soc. (pres. 1962-63), Soc. Clin. Neurologists (pres. 1969). Democrat. Home: 5435 Bellaire Dr New Orleans LA 70124 Office: 1542 Tulane Av New Orleans LA 70112

PADDOCK, ARNOLD DAVID, electronic co. exec.; b. Boston, Feb. 4, 1942; s. Max and Shirley (Goldstein) P.; B.S., Rensselaer Poly. Inst., 1963; Ph.D., U. Denver, 1969; m. Janis Kahn, Aug. 21, 1946; 1 son, Michael. Research physicist Polaroid Corp., Cambridge, Mass., 1964-68; metallurgist Motorola Corp., Phoenix, 1968; mem. tech. staff Tex. Instruments, Inc., Dallas, 1969-73, mgr. worldwide assembly tech., 1973—. Mem. Electrochem. Soc., Metall. Soc., Am. Inst. M.E. (asst. treas., electronics materials com. 1972—). Mem. editorial bd. Jours. Electronic Materials. Home: 3952 Candlenut Lane Dallas TX 75234 Office: MS 17 PO Box 5012 Texas Instruments Dallas TX 75222

PADDOCK, AUSTIN JOSEPH, business exec.; b. Washington Court House, O., July 18, 1908; s. Leon A. and Nellie (Hare) P.; B.S. in Civil Engring., U. Mich., 1929; m. Janet Nevin, Aug. 3, 1934 (dec. Aug. 1964); children—Larry C. and Linda M. (twins), Jane M.; m. 2d, JoAnn Rourke, May 1966; 1 dau., Jennifer-Jo. With Am. Bridge div. U.S. Steel Corp., 1929-56, successively timekeeper erecting dept., draftsman engring., dept., rate clk. indsl. engring. dept., asst. to Elmira (N.Y.) plant mgr., mgr. Elmira plant, mgr. Gary (Ind.) plant, v.p. mfg. operations, v.p. contracting 1929-56, pres., 1956-61, adminstrv. v.p. fabrication and manufacture U.S. Steel Corp., 1961-69; chmn. bd. Blount Bros. Corp., B.F. Shaw Co., Blount Bros. Enterprises, Inc., Interstate Inns, Inc., Paramount Equipment Rental & Sales, Inc., Global Erectors, Inc., Scotchcraft Windows, Inc., Ind. Bridge Co., Inc.; dir. Anti-Pollution Systems, Inc., Pyrobath, Inc., U.C., Inc., Pitts.-Des Moines Steel Co. Council dir., v.p., mem. regional exec. com. Boy Scouts Am. Dir. bldg. research adv. bd. Nat. Acad. Sci. Trustee Huntingdon Coll., Montgomery. Mem. U.S. C. of C. (dir. constrn. affairs com.), N.A.M. (dir.), Nat. Alliance Businessmen (adv. bd.), Men. of Montgomery. Clubs: Duquesne, Longue Vue Country (Pitts.), Montgomery Country; The Club (Birmingham, Ala.). Home: Route 1 Box 56C Pike Road AL 36064 Office: Box 949 Montgomery AL 36102

PADDOCK, CAROLINE, librarian; b. Roswell, N.M., d. Ernest Arthur and Winifred (Waughop) Paddock; A.B., Tex. Woman's Coll., Ft. Worth, 1928; B.S. in L.S., U. Denver, 1937; M.L.S., U. Cal. at Berkeley, 1954. Gen. asst. Library Assn. of Portland, Ore., 1937-43; service club librarian, chief camp librarian Army Library Service, Ore., Washington, 1943-46; regional librarian, sub-command librarian Overseas Library Service, Germany, 1946-47; engring. and forestry librarian, sci-tech. librarian, coordinator readers' services La. Tech. U., Ruston, 1948—. Mem. violin sect. Ruston Civic Symphony Orch. Mem. Am., La., Southwestern library assns., Am. Assn. U. Profs. (sec.-treas. local chpt. 1963-65), La. Tchrs. Assn., Spl. Libraries Assn. (sec.-treas. La. chpt. 1966-68), Delta Kappa Gamma. Methodist. Home: PO Box 4702 Tech Station Ruston LA 71270 Office: Prescott Meml Library La Tech U Ruston LA 71271

PADGETT, WILLIAM JOWAYNE, educator; b. Walhalla, S.C., May 15, 1943; s. Joe Jasper and Edith (Abercrombie) P.; B.S., Clemson U., 1966, M.S., 1968; Ph.D., Va. Poly. Inst. and State U., 1971; m. Helen Faye Swayngham, July 3, 1965; 1 dau., Carla Suzanne. Asst. prof. math. and statistics U. S.C., 1971-73, asso. prof., 1973—. Dept. Health, Edn. and Welfare Tng. grantee, 1970-71; U. S.C. Research grantee summer 1972. Mem. Inst. Math. Statistics, Am. Statist. Assn. (sec.-treas. S.C. chpt. 1973), Sigma Xi, Phi Kappa Phi. Author: Random Intergral Equations with Applications to Stochastic Systems, 1971. Contbr. articles to tech. jours. Home: 261 Chartwell Rd Columbia SC 29210 Office: Dept Math and Computer Sci U SC Columbia SC 29208

PADHYE, ARVIND ANANT, microbiologist; b. Poona, Maharashtra, India, May 1, 1932; s. Anant Govind and Laxmibai (Anant) P.; B.Sc., S.P. Coll., Poona, 1955; B.Sc., U. Poona, 1956, M.Sc., 1957, Ph.D., 1966; m. Sudha Gajanan Wadadekar, May 30, 1964; children—Kedar, Sudhir. Asst. research officer Indian Council Med. Research fellow, Poona, 1960-64; sr. sci. officer Hindustan Antibiotics Ltd., Pimpri, Poona, 1964-67; postdoctoral fellow dept. med. bacteriology U. Alta., Edmonton, 1967-68, lectr. bacteriology, 1968—; asst. mycologist Provincial Lab. Pub. Health, Edmonton, 1969—; vis. scientist Center for Disease Control, Atlanta, 1972—. Mem. Internat. Soc. for Human and Animal Mycology, Med. Mycol. Soc. of Americas, Am. Mycob. Soc., Am. Soc. Microbiology. Contbr. articles to profl. jours. Address: Mycology Sect Lab Div Center for Disease Control Atlanta GA 30333

PADRICK, COMER WOODWARD, JR., lawyer; b. Atlanta, Nov. 18, 1926; s. Comer Woodward and Doris (Harper) P.; A.B., Emory U., 1950, LL.B., 1953; m. Dorothy Rebecca South, June 7, 1953; children—Comer Woodward III, Martin Lydell, Tara Jeanne. Admitted to Ga. bar, 1952; mem. editoral bd. The Harrison Co., Atlanta, 1950-52; asso. atty. Sutherland, Asbill & Brennan, Atlanta, 1952-53; Jones, Williams, Dorsey & Kane, Atlanta 1956-59; asso. atty. Hansell, Post, Brandon & Dorsey, Atlanta, 1959-62, partner, 1962—; guest lectr. real estate law. Partner Peachtree Corner, Land Investors Assos., Winchester Apts. East. Mem. Dekalb Bd. Realtors. Active Atlanta Symphony Guild, Atlanta Legal Aid Soc. Served as 1st lt. with AUS, 1953-55. Recipient Medallion Inst. Continuing Legal Edn. in Ga. Mem. Am., Ga., Atlanta bar assns., Am., Atlanta mortgage Bankers assns., Old War Horse Lawyers, Am. Judicature Soc., Atlanta Real Estate Bd., Home Builders Assn. Met. Atlanta, Am. Bus. Law Assn., Emory U. Alumni Council, Internat. Platform Assn., Phi Beta Kappa, Omicron Delta Kappa, Pi Sigma Alpha, Phi Delta Phi. Episcopalian (vestryman). Clubs: Druid Hills Goff; Cherokee Towne and Country; Atlanta City, Lawyers (Atlanta); Civitan. Home: 3999 Beechwood Dr NW Atlanta GA 30327 Office: First National Bank Tower Atlanta GA 30303

PADULA, RICHARD THOMAS, physician, educator; b. Phila., Apr. 10, 1935; s. William V. and Marie T. (Musi) P.; B.S., Ursinus Coll., 1957; M.D., Jefferson Med. Coll., 1961; m. Marta C. Meo, Dec. 26, 1959; children—Marta Anne, Richard W., Thomas J., Robert J., William V. III. Intern Phila. Gen. Hosp., 1961-62; resident surgery Jefferson Med. Coll. Hosp., Phila., 1962-66; practice medicine, specializing in surgery, Phila., 1966-71, Galveston, Tex., 1971—; mem. staff Thomas Jefferson U. Hosp., Phila., U. Tex. Med. Br. Hosps., Galveston; instr. surgery Jefferson Med. Coll., Phila., 1966-67, asso., 1967-68, asst. prof., 1968-69, asso. prof., 1969-71; asso. prof. surgery and thoracic surgery U. Tex. Med. Br., Galveston, 1971-73, prof. surgery and thoracic surgery, chief thoracic surg. service, 1973—. Heart Assn. Southeastern Pa. fellow, 1962-63; Am. Cancer Soc. fellow, 1963-64. Fellow A.C.S.; mem. Assn. for Acad. Surgery, Am. Assn. Thoracic Surgery, Soc. Univ. Surgeons, Soc. for Vascular Surgery, Soc. Thoracic Surgeons, Am. Heart Assn., A.M.A. Home: 20 Adler Circle Galveston TX 77550

PAESSLER, ALFRED H(ENRY), govt. ofcl.; b. Brenham, Tex., Apr. 6, 1916; s. Arno Oscar and Henriette (Schomburg) P.; B.Ch.E., U. Tex., 1939; m. Mildred Binebrink, Nov. 25, 1944; children—Sandra I., Karen M. Supt. water and sewage treatment City of Austin, Tex., 1939-44; exec. sec. State Water Control Bd., Commonwealth of Va., Richmond, Va., 1946—; instr. U. Tex., 1942-44, Va. Commonwealth U., 1966—. Mem. Engring. Com. Ohio River Valley Water Sanitation Commn., 1953—, chmn., 1956-58. Served with USNR, 1944-46. Recipient Conservationist of Year award, 1968. Mem. Water Pollution Control Fedn. (Sidney Bedell award 1971), Am. Pub. Health Assn., Water Resources Assn., Am. Water Works Assn., Assn. State and Interstate Water Pollution Control Adminstrs. (sec. treas. 1968-71, v.p. 1971-72, pres. 1972-73), Assn. Bds. of Certification Operating Personnel in Water and Wastewater Utilities (sec. treas. 1972—), Interstate Conf. on Environment (chmn. 1972-73). Roman Cath. Home: 7904 Dogwood Rd Richmond VA 23229 Office: PO Box 11143 Richmond VA 23230

PAFFORD, RAY WILSON, finance, ranching; b. Justin, Tex., Apr. 30, 1900; s. Walter Fulkerson and Dora Ellen (Wilson) P.; student So. Meth. U., 1918-19, U. Tex., 1919-20; m. Alma Leona Perkins, May 13, 1922; 1 dau., Peggy Ellen (Mrs. Charles D. Johnson). With Acme Brick Co., Ft. Worth, 1921-59, ret., 1959; adminstr. Campbell Meml. Hosp., Weatherford, Tex., 1960-73. Dir. First Nat. Bank, Weatherford. Capt. Parker County Sheriffs Posse, 1955; pres. Parker County United Fund, 1966. Mem. engr. adv. found. U. Tex., 1955. Fellow Am. Ceramic Soc. (pres. 1954-55). Mason (32 deg., Shriner) (master 1932-33). Home: Route 1 Box 64 Weatherford TX 76086 Office: 213 S Houston St Weatherford TX 76086

PAFFORD, WILLIAM NELSON, educator; b. Camden, Tenn., May 21, 1929; s. Robert Preston and Martha P.; B.S., George Peabody Coll., 1957, M.A., 1958, Ed.S., 1963; Ed.D., U. Ky., 1967; m. Mary Jo Hargis, May 20, 1950; children—William Randall, Stanton Lee. Instr. biology Montgomery Bell Acad., Nashville, 1958-63; asst. prof. biology Radford (Va.) Coll., 1963-65; coordinator student teaching U. Ky., 1965-67; prof. sci. edn. East Tenn. State U., 1967—. Served with AUS, 1952-54. Haggin fellow, 1965. Mem. Nat. Sci. Tchrs. Assn., Tenn. Acad. Sci., Tenn., East Tenn. edn. assns., Phi Delta Kappa. Contbr. articles to sci. jours. Home: 3 White Oak Ct Johnson City TN 37601

PAGAN, RAYMOND, fgn. service officer; b. San Juan, P.R., May 23, 1914; A.B., Tufts U., 1937; spl. certificate German lang. and area study U. Pitts., 1944; LL.B., Am. Extension Sch. Law, 1959; spl. certificate in econ. devel. SAIS Johns Hopkins, 1960; m. Theresa Grace DeCarlo, Aug. 27, 1942; children—Daniel Leverett, Virginia Grace, Roxane Ruth. With Alexander Smith & Co., 1939-42; German publs. officer U.S. War Dept., 1945-47; dep. chief publs. div., chief publs. div. High Commr. of Germany, Wiesbaden, 1947-49; entered fgn. service U.S. State Dept., 1949, asst. editor Die Neue Zeitung, Berlin, Germany, 1949-53; information officer Am. embassy, Cairo, Egypt, 1953-54, information specialist USIA, Washington, 1954-55, information officer FOA, ICA, Saigon, Vietnam, 1955-57, communications media officer ICA, Am. embassy, Beirut, Lebanon, 1959-60, asst. program officer, Kabul, Afghanistan, 1960-62, Afghan desk officer AID, 1962-67, program officer population, Washington, 1967—. Served with M.I., AUS, 1942-45. Office: care Agy for Internat Devel Dept of State Washington DC 20523

PAGAN, VICTOR JUAN, med. service exec.; b. San Juan, P.R., Oct. 9, 1922; s. Ricardo F. and Juanita (Fortiz) P.; B.S., U. P.R., 1947; M.D., Temple Med. Sch., 1951; m. Margot Ortiz Colon, May 24, 1942; children—Victor Juan, Myrna M. With Umbo Med. Service, Caparra Heights, P.R., 1951—, dir., 1962—; owner, operator UMBO Comml. Center, Rio Piedras, P.R., 1962—. Served to capt. AUS, 1941-46. Mem. Am. Legion, P.R. Med. Assn. (treas. 1969-70). Lion (pres. 1960-61), Mason (Shriner). Club: Yaucano (San Juan, P.R.). Home: 176 Violeta St Rio Piedras PR 00927 Office: Box V Caparra Heights PR 00922

PAGANINI, OTTO VICTOR, state ofcl.; b. Pitts., Sept. 15, 1911; s. Victor and Irene (Marcon) P.; B.S. in Petroleum Engring., U. Pitts., 1940; m. Mildred Wheeler, June 21, 1938; children—Jane Irene (Mrs. Thayer Draper, Jr.), Lee Ann (Mrs. Thomas J. Cullins). San. engr. Hidalgo County (Tex.), 1946-48; with Tex. State Health Dept., 1948—, chief engr. air pollution control services, Austin, 1956—, engr. Tex. Air Control Bd., 1973—. Served to san. engr. dir. USPHS, 1942-46; Res. Recipient Thanks badge local council Girl Scouts Am., 1960. Registered profl. engr., Tex. Diplomate Am. Acad. San. Engrs., Am. Indsl. Hygiene Bd. Mem. Air Pollution Control Assn., Nat., Tex. socs. profl. engrs., Am. Conf. Govtl. Hygienists (mem. air pollution com. 1963—), Am. Indsl. Hygiene Assn., Tex. Pub. Health Assn., Houston C. of C. (pub. health com. 1946-52). Mason. Contbr. articles to publs. Home: 6104 Shoalwood Av Austin TX 78757 Office: 8520 Shoalcreek Av Austin TX 78756

PAGE, DAVID P., editor, clergyman; b. Galway, Ireland, June 10, 1932; s. Thomas and Mary (Robinson) P.; came to U.S., 1958, naturalized, 1963; M.A., Cath. U. Am., 1962. Ordained priest Roman Catholic Ch., 1958; exec. editor Fla. Cath. Press, Inc., Orlando, 1965—. Pres. Orlando dist. Priest's Senate, 1969-70, 71-72. Mem. Fla. Fedn. Priests' Councils (pres. 1971-72). Home: PO Box 1868 Orlando FL 32802 Office: PO Box 3551 Orlando FL 32802

PAGE, HARRY ROBERT, educator; b. Milw., Mar. 22, 1915; s. Harry Allen and Lydia (Rosendahl) P.; A.B., Mich. State U., 1941; postgrad. U.S. Army Command and Staff Coll., 1945-46, Indsl. Coll. of Armed Forces, 1958-59; M.B.A., Harvard, 1950; Ph.D., Am. U., 1966; m. Jeanne Tompkins, Apr. 1, 1945; children—Patricia Jeanne, Margaret Berenice. From 2d lt. to lt. col. U.S. Army, 1941-46, from lt. col. to col. USAF, 1946-61; exec. officer logistics directorate U.S. Joint Chiefs of Staff, Washington, 1959-61; asst. prof. bus. adminstrn. George Washington U., Washington, 1961-65, asso. prof., chmn. dept., 1965-69, prof., chmn. dept., 1969—. Cons., Advanced Study Program, Brookings Instn., Washington, 1966—; chmn. task group edn. and tng. Commn. Govt. Procurement, 1971-72. Bd. dirs., treas. Council of Chs. of Greater Washington, 1963-68. Decorated Air medal, Purple Heart, Legion of Merit. Mem. Acad. of Mgmt., Am. Assn. U. Profs., Harvard Bus. Sch. Assn., Air Force Assn., Nat. Parks Assn. (trustee), Alpha Phi Omega, Lambda Chi Alpha, Alpha Kappa Psi. Pi Sigma Alpha. Conglist. Author Church Budget Development, 1964; An Analysis of the Defense Procurement Program Decision-Making Process, 1966; co-author: Federal Contributions to Management, 1971. Home: 3612 N Glebe Rd Arlington VA 22207 Office: 710 21st St NW Washington DC 20006

PAGE, HENRIETTA MARIA, librarian; b. Queens County, L.I., N.Y., Dec. 6, 1900; d. William C. and Maria (Weinig) Wutz; student Queens Coll., Columbia, Drake Bus. Coll., Am. Inst. of Banking; m. Henry N. Page, Nov. 5, 1923 (dec.); children—Lois Ann (Mrs. Wendell E. Bennett), Natalie (Mrs. John F. Krause). With Guaranty Trust Co., 1921-23, 1927-33; research dept. Nat. Rep. Com., Washington, 1940-43. Office of Sec. of State, 1943-48; reporter, U.S. Delegation, UN, London, 1946; mil. intelligence research analyst, editor of publs. Air Def. Command, Ent AFB, Colorado Springs, 1949-56; organized Denver div. tech. library The Martin Co., 1956, organized research div., 1956; devel. div. AVCO, Corp., Wilmington, Mass., 1956, chief tech. library for corp., 1956-61; documentation engr. Itek Labs., Lexington, Mass., 1961-63; head library div. U.S. Naval Underwater Weapons Research and Engring. Sta., 1961-65; cons. Providence Pub. Library, 1965-66, Roger Williams Coll., 1965-68; library cons. Foxboro Co. (Mass.), 1967-70. Mem. Spl. Libraries Assn., Nat. Aeronautics Assn. Club: Pilot. Author: World Resources: The Fertile Crescent; The Moslem World; Treatise on Filing; (tng. manual) How to Do Research; Planning the New Library. Address: 747 Sommer Av NE Aiken SC 29801

PAGE, JACK CULBERTSON, cons. co. exec.; b. Evanston, Ill., May 8, 1925; s. Philip P. and Alleyne (McCabe) P.; B.S., Mass. Inst. Tech., 1948; m. Imogene Spoerri, Nov. 21, 1951; children—Katherine H., Carter H., Philip J. Purchasing agt. Ekco Products Co., Wheeling, Ill., 1948-54; sales rep. Morris Paper Mills div. Fed. Paper Bd. Co., Montvale, N.J., 1954-56; v.p. Speed-Fam. Corp., Skokie, Ill., 1956-60; pres. Prodn. Lapping Co., Pasadena, Cal., 1960-61; v.p. Booz, Allen & Hamilton, Inc., Dallas, 1961-72; pres. Jack C. Page Inc., 1972—. Trustee Village of Riverwoods, Ill., 1965-66. Pres. Evanston Jr. C. of C., 1951-52; bd. dirs. Dallas Civic Opera; mem. corp. vis. com. for med. dept. Mass. Inst. Tech. Served with USNR, 1944-46. Clubs: Mass. Inst. Tech. (past pres. Dallas), Northwood, Dallas, Dallas Petroleum, Tavern, Tres Vidas. Home: 4508 Hockaday Dr Dallas TX 75229 Office: 2001 Bryan Tower Dallas TX 75201

PAGE, JESSE BORING, educator; b. Loachapoka, Ala., Dec. 6, 1906; s. Robert Seldon and Lois (James) P.; B.S., Ala. Poly. Inst., 1927. M.S., 1929; m. Frances Whatley, Apr. 1, 1930; children—Frances Anne, Rebecca Jane. Teaching fellowship Ala. Poly. Inst., 1927-28; dir. athletics Langdale (Ala.) High Sch., 1928-29; prin. Smiths Station (Ala.) Consol. High Sch., 1929—. Active Smiths chpt. A.R.C., 1954—. Served from 1st lt. to capt., inf., AUS, 1942-45. Mem. N.E.A., Ala. Edn. Assn., Nat., Ala. (pres. 4th dist. 1964-65) assns. secondary sch. prins., Lee County Tchrs. Assn. (pres. 1934-36, dir. 1958—), Internat. Platform Assn., Kappa Delta Pi. Democrat. Methodist (ofcl. bd.). Club: Ruritan (Smiths, Ala.). Home: Smiths AL 36877

PAGE, MALCOLM IRVING, med. educator; b. Lavonia, Mich., Apr. 28, 1930; s. Christopher and Beatrice Ilene (Badder) P.; A.B., Wayne U., 1952; M.D., U. Chgo., 1956; m. Madge Ozburn, Jan. 10, 1959; 1 son, Malcolm Irving. Intern, Boston City Hosp., 1956-57; resident Mary Imogene Bassett Hosp., Cooperstown, N.Y., 1959-62; practice medicine, specializing in internal medicine, infectious disease, Chgo., 1963-65, Cooperstown, 1965-72, Augusta, Ga., 1972—; asst. prof. medicine U. Chgo., 1963-65; physician-in-chief Mary Imogene Bassett Hosp., also asso. clin. prof. medicine Columbia U., N.Y.C., 1965-72; prof. medicine Med. Coll. Ga., Augusta, 1972—. Served with USPHS, 1957-63. Fellow A.C.P. Home: 3435 Interlachen Rd Augusta GA 30907

PAGE, NORWOOD RUFUS, ednl. adminstr.; b. Lake View, S.C., May 10, 1919; s. Forrest Daniel and Sarah Agnes (Jordan) P.; B.S., Clemson Coll., 1939; M.S., N.C. State U., 1941; Ph.D., U. Ga., 1959; m. Evelyn Lucile Warner, July 8, 1949; children—Russell, Mary, Forrest, Peter. Asst. chemist fertilizer dept. Clemson (S.C.) U., 1941, asst. prof. chemistry, 1946-47, asso. agronomist, prof. agronomy and soils, 1947-60, prof. agronomy and soils, 1960-65, head, soil chemistry dept., 1965—. Served with USAAF, 1941-46. Mem. Am. Soc. Agronomy, Soil Sci. Soc. Am., Sigma Xi, Phi Kappa Phi, Alpha Chi Sigma, Gamma Sigma Delta. Baptist. Rotarian. Asso. editor soils Agronomy Jour., 1972-74; contbr. articles to tech. lit. Home: 106 Calhoun St Clemson SC 29631

PAGE, RAYMOND FRANKLIN, broadcasting co. exec.; b. Malvern, Ark., July 16, 1925; s. Raymond Foster and Stella Irene (Coston) P.; grad. high sch.; m. Helen Louise Hulett, Sept. 23, 1944; 1 dau., Patti Lea. Announcer, KGHI-KLRA, Little Rock, 1940-43; program dir. KWEM, West Memphis, Ark., 1946; announcer KWKH Radio, Shreveport, La., 1947-57, chief announcer, 1950-57, program dir., 1957-69, operations dir., 1969—, emcee La. Hayride, 1948-59; with Sound City Rec. Corp., Shreveport, 1970—, v.p., 1971—. Served with Signal Corps, AUS, 1944-45. Office: Box 1130 Shreveport LA 71120

PAGE, RICHARD MICHAEL, food distbn. exec., oil pollution control exec.; b. New Orleans, Sept. 8, 1910; s. Alfred F. and Eda (Richardson) P.; B.A. in Math., Tulane U., 1935; m. Nellie C. Curtis, Apr. 23, 1938; children—Richard Michael, Elizabeth C. With William B. Reily Co., Inc., New Orleans, 1935-42; prof. math. Tulane U., New Orleans, 1946-47; founder, pres. Arrow Food Distbrs., Inc., New Orleans, 1947—, chmn., 1973—, also dir.; founder, treas., dir. Jefferson Cold Storage, New Orleans, 1953-72; pres., dir. Frozen Food Forum, Atlanta, 1954—; treas., dir. Asso. Cold Storage, Baton Rouge, 1957-72, pres., 1972—; reorganized New Orleans Shrimp Co., 1956, dir., exec. com., 1956-68; dir., pres. Sterling Foods, Inc., Universal Operations, Inc., Atlanta; chmn., dir. Oil Mop Inc., New Orleans, 1969—; dir. New Orleans Frosted Foods Creole Sales Co., Econo Meat Mart, Inc., New Orleans. Served from 2d lt. to capt. USAAF, 1942-46. Named to Royal Order Zerocrats Nat. Frozen Food Assn., 1957. Mem. Nat. (past pres.), Southwestern (founder, 1st pres.) frozen food assns., Nat. Assn. Wholesalers (trustee), Tulane U. Alumni Assn. (past pres., past mem. exec. com.), Phi Beta Kappa, Alpha Tau Omega. Clubs: Tulane T. (past pres.), New Orleans Athletic, Southern Yacht (New Orleans). Episcopalian (past sr. warden, chmn. sch. bd.). Home: 40 Hawk St New Orleans LA 70124 Office: 145 Robert E Lee Blvd New Orleans LA 70124

PAGE, TALMADGE DAWSON, assn. exec.; b. St. Pauls, N.C., Jan. 3, 1926; s. John Thomas and Della S. (Scarborough) P.; A.B. in Bus. Adminstrn., Duke, 1950; student C. of C. Inst., U. Ga., 1968, 69, 70, 71; m. Geraldine Branch, Dec. 31, 1950; children—Debra Kay, Talmadge Dawson. Chief insp. Retail Credit Co., Atlanta, 1950-67; exec. sec. C. of C., Rockingham, N.C., 1967—. Served with USNR, 1944-46. Mem. N.C. Retail Assn. Execs. (dir.). Methodist. Home: 913 Ann St Rockingham NC 28379 Office: PO Box 86 Rockingham NC 28379

PAGE, MISS TONY, publisher, editor; b. Moscow, Ida., July 11, 1910; d. Clarence Mills and Ruby Ethyl (Slee) Edgett; ed. by tutors, grad. Mrs. Williams' Prep. Sch. for Young Ladies, Fort Worth, 1926; m. Holland Page, Jr., Mar. 1947 (div. June 1954). With Flight Mag., Dallas, 1940-45; aviation editor The Valley Times, San Fernando, Cal., 1945-47; writer Cross Country News, Austin, 1947-52, owner, 1952; owner Cross Country News, Ft. Worth, 1954—. Named Woman of the Year in Aviation, Woman's Aero. Assn., 1960, hon. chief Sycamore tribe Okla. Aeros. Commn., 1971; recipient James J. Strebig Meml. Trophy award Aviation Space Writers, 1962; Merit Certificate award Sherman Fairchild Internat. Air Safety Writing award, 1962, 63, 64, 65; Amelia Earhart Medal award Medal of Month Club, 1965. Mem. Aviation/Space Writers Assn., Nat. Aero. Assn., Hump Pilots Assn. (hon.), Women's Nat. Aero. Assn., The Whirly-Girls, Ninety Nines, Inc., Fort Worth Press Club. Club: OX-5 (hon. mem.). Author: Personal Please (poetry), 1957. Home: PO Box 9661 Fort Worth TX 76107 Office: Meacham Field Fort Worth TX 76106

PAGE, WILLIAM SPLANE, radio exec.; b. Detroit, Aug. 16, 1917; s. Blinn Stevens and Carlotta (Splane) P.; student Coll. de St. Germain-en-Laye, France, 1932-33; A.B., Cornell U., Ithaca, N.Y., 1940; m. Marie Sugg, June 26, 1943; children—William Splane, Mary Gayle (Mrs. Robert Grayson Shorkey). Civilian employee USAF, Washington and Trinidad, 1941-43; news editor radio stat. WKNS, Kinston, N.C., 1947-48; pres., gen. mgr. radio stat. WFTC, Kinston, 1949-54; pres. Farmers Broadcasting Service, WELS, Kinston, 1954—; pres. radio stat. WGOL, 1958-69; sec., dir. N.C. TV., Inc., WITN-TV, 1954—. Mem. Kinston Recreation Commn., 1954-59, Kinston Redevel. Commn., 1961—, chmn., 1963—, N.C. Good Neighbor Council, 1966-68; pres. Lamp, Inc., 1965-69. Alderman city of Kinston, 1954-59. Bd. dirs. Broadcasting Found. N.C., Greene Lamp, 1965-71. Served to lt. USNR, 1943-46. Recipient distinguished service award Kinston Jr. C. of C., 1949. Mem. N.C. Assn. Broadcasters (pres. 1955), Kinston Amateur Radio Soc. (pres. 1970), Kinston C. of C., (pres. 1953-54), Sigma Delta Chi (life mem.), Kappa Sigma. Episcopalian (sr. warden 1960-61, 68-70, lay dep. gen. conv. 1961, 64, 67, 69, 70, diocesan council 1961-63, 65-67, 71—, chmn. mutual responsibility commn. 1966—, vol. missionary Liberia, Siera Leone, Congo, 1968, Solomon Islands, 1965, New Hebrides Islands, 1965, 69, 70). Elk, Rotarian (pres. 1960-61). Home: PO Box 871 1306 Perry Park Dr Kinston NC 28501 Office: 1312 W Vernon Av Kinston NC 28501

PAGE, WILLIS, condr.; b. Rochester, N.Y.; grad. with distinction Eastman Sch. Music, Rochester. With Boston Symphony Orch.; prin. bass Boston Pops; condr. Cecilia Soc. of Boston; organizer, condr. New Orchestral Soc. of Boston (name now Boston Festival Orch.); music dir.-condr. Nashville Symphony Orch., 8 years; asso. condr. Buffalo Philharmonic; condr. Yomiuri Nippon Symphony, Tokyo, Japan, 1962-63; prof. conducting Eastman Sch. Music, 1967-69; prof. conducting, dir. orchestral activities Drake U., Des Moines, 1969-71; condr. Des Moines Symphony, 1969-71, Jacksonville (Fla.) Symphony Orch., 1971—. Guest condr. with Boston Pops, Toronto, Rochester Civic, Eastman-Rochester, Denver, Muncie, Kol Israel orchs.; condr. all-state orchs. of N.Y., Ia., Ky., Tenn., Fla., also regional festivals. Ford Found. European travel award, 1967. Address: 46 W Duval St Jacksonville FL 32202

PAIGE, JOHN LOUIS, JR., city ofcl.; b. Washington, Apr. 28, 1930; s. John Louis and Helen Carnelia (Johnson) P.; B.S. in Civil Engring., Howard U., 1958; m. Beatrice Marie Bailey, Sept. 6, 1958; children—Janice Carnelia, Bryan Elwin. Civil engr. U.S. Bur. Reclamation, Ephrata, Wash., 1958-59; civil engr. D.C. Dept. Hwys. and Traffic, Washington, 1959—. Served with AUS, 1948-52. Fellow Am. Soc. C.E., mem. Nat., D.C. socs. profl. engrs., Am. Concrete Inst., Nat. Tech. Assn. Republican. Home: 5214 11th St NE Washington DC 20011 Office: 415 12th St NW Washington DC 20004

PAIGE, LESTER EVANS, JR., city ofcl.; b. Texline, Tex., Dec. 19, 1928; s. Lester Evans and Verna Mattie (Quinby) Paige; B.Arch., Tex. Technol. U., 1958; m. Edna Ellen Wright, Sept. 19, 1959; 1 son, Eric Kevin. Asst. bldg. ofcl. City of Amarillo (Tex.), 1958-61, bldg. ofcl., 1961-71; bldg. ofcl. City of Fort Worth, 1971—. Adviser, Tex. Dept. Community Affairs on Edn. for Insps. and Bldg. Codes, 1973—; mem. housing com. City of Ft. Worth, 1972—. Mem. bd. appeals Dallas-Ft. Worth Regional Airport, 1972—; mem. archtl. edn. rev. com. Tarrant County Jr. Coll., 1973. Served with USAF, 1946-53. Mem. Internat. Conf. Bldg. Ofcls. (chpt. pres. 1964-66, Tex. v.p. 1974—), A.I.A. (asso.), N. Central Tex. Council Govts. (mem. code rev. com. 1971—), N. Tex. Municipal Insps. Assn. (pres. 1972), Bldg. Ofcls. Assn. Tex. Methodist (chmn. adminstrv. bd. 1974). Mason. Home: 3800 Clayton Rd W Fort Worth TX 76116 Office: 1000 Throckmorton St Fort Worth TX 76102

PAINE, NEIL REUBEN, educator; b. Houston, Nov. 23, 1934; s. Reuben Henry and Agnes Irene (O'Neil) Paine: B.A., Rice U., 1957; M.B.A., U.Tex., 1959, Ph.D., 1961. Asst. prof. mgmt. sci. U. Houston, 1961-64, asso. prof., 1964-70, prof., 1970—. Mem. Am. Inst. Decision Scis., Am. Statis. Assn., Phi Beta Kappa, Beta Gamma Sigma. Contbr. articles to profl. jours. Home: 5072 Navarro Apt D Houston TX 77027

PAINE, THOMAS FITE, JR., physician, educator; b. Aberdeen, Miss., Feb. 13, 1918; s. Thomas Fite and Mary Alice (Therrell) P.; B.A., Vanderbilt U., 1939, M.D., 1942; m. Grace Hillman Benedict, July 26, 1941; children—Thomas Fite III, George Carter, Anne Benedict, Grace Barrett. Intern, U. Rochester Strong Meml. Hosp., 1942-43; chief dept. bacteriology Mass. Gen. Hosp., asso. medicine Harvard Med. Sch., Boston, 1950-53; asso. prof. internal medicine and bacteriology U. Mich., 1953-54; prof. medicine, chmn. dept. microbiology U. Ala., 1954-61; prof. medicine Vanderbilt U., chief med. service Nashville Gen. Hosp., 1961—; research fellow Harvard Thorndike Lab. at Boston City Hosp., 1946-48, Mass. Gen. Hosp., 1948-49, dept. biochemistry Cambridge U. (Eng.), 1949-50. Served to capt. MC, AUS, 1943-46. Diplomate Am. Bd. Internal Medicine. Mem. A.C.P., Am. Acad. Microbiology, Infectious Disease Soc. Am., Soc. for Exptl. Biology and Medicine, Sigma Xi, Alpha Omega Alpha. Contbr. articles to profl. pubs. Home: 4308 Iroquois Av Nashville TN 37205

PAINTER, FLOYD EUGENE, archaeologist, editor; b. Granite City, Ill., May 17, 1920; s. William D. and Bessie Florence (Andrews) P.; ed. pub. schs.; m. Katherine Weston Sewell, Dec. 25, 1942; children—Floyd Sewell, Pamela Kay, Deborah Roxanne. Formerly cave explorer, mountain climber, rodeo rider, constrn. worker, fruit picker, laborer archaeol. projects in Mexico; sailor, soldier also successively advt. salesman, store clk., aircraft mechanic, shipyard machinist, 1946-48; archaeologist Norfolk (Va.) Mus. Arts and Scis., 1955-69; editor assn. jour. Chesopiean Archeol. Jour., Norfolk, 1965—. Tchr. archaeol. subjects adult edn. classes Old Dominion U., Norfolk, 1971—; vol. lectr. archaeol. topics to ch. schs., scientific orgns. and civic orgns. Served with USNR, 1941-46, AUS, 1948-55. Mem. Archeol. Soc. Va. (pres. 1958-60, asso. editor jour. 1956-63), Soc. Am. Archaelogy, Chesopiean Archeol. Assn. (pres. 1963-65), Southeastern Archaeol. Conf., Conf. on Historic Site Archaeology. Asso. editor Anthropol. Jour. Can., 1965—; asst. editor Popular Archaeology, 1973—; editor C'Bola, 1974—. Contbr. articles to archeol. jours. Address: 7507 Pennington Rd Norfolk VA 23505

PAINTER, WILLIAM CALVIN, JR., engr., city ofcl.; b. Atlanta, Feb. 23, 1917; s. William Calvin and Ruby (Anchors) P.; B.S. in Indsl. Mgmt., Ga. Inst. Tech., 1938; m. Betty Claire Farmer, May 3, 1946; children—Betsy (Mrs. Haynes Roberts), Susan, Sally. With engring. dept. South-Eastern Underwriters Assn., Atlanta, 1938—, field engr., 1939-48, sr. field engr., 1949-52, staff engrs., 1953-62, div. engr., 1963-66, asst. chief engr., 1967-71, asst. chief engr. ins. services office, Southeastern regional office, 1972—. Mem. Ga. adv. com. on factory-built housing. City commr., Decatur, Ga., 1962—, mayor protem, 1968, 73. Served from 2d lt. to capt. Q.M.C., AUS, 1941-46; now col. Res. Decorated Legion of Merit. Registered profl. engr., Ga. Mem. Ga. Municipal Assn. (dist. pres. 1969—), Ins. Inst. Am. (asso.), Res. Officer Assn. U.S. (pres. Atlanta q.m. chpt.), Mil. Order World Wars, Am. Legion, Am. Logistics Assn., Assn. U.S. Army, DeKalb County C. of C., Hon. Order Blue Goose, Pi Delta Epsilon, Phi Sigma Kappa. Baptist (deacon). Mason, Rotarian. Home: 217 Westchester Dr Decatur GA 30030 Office: 1577 Northeast Freeway NE Atlanta GA 30329

PAIR, HENRY TAZWELL, JR., banker; b. Atlanta, Mar. 30, 1928; s. Henry Tazwell and Dorris (Turner) P.; B.B.A., Ga. State U., 1961; m. Carolyn Holbrook, Aug. 19, 1950; children—Julie Lynn, Vann Henry. Mem. staff Citizens and So. Nat. Bank, Atlanta, 1946-68; v.p. Bank of Cumming, 1968—. Served with AUS, 1953-55. Mem. Forsyth County C. of C. (membership chmn. 1971-72), V.F.W. Baptist (chmn. deacons and finance com. 1958-62). Mason (32 deg.), Kiwanian (pres. 1970-71). Home: PO Box 35 Cumming GA 30130 Office: PO Box 267 Cumming GA 30130

PAJON, EDUARDO RODRIGUEZ, lawyer; b. Ciego de Avila, Camaguey, Cuba, Nov. 22, 1917; s. Francisco Rodriguez Ubals and Maria Luisa Pajon; J.D., U. Havana (Cuba), 1941, U. Miami, 1964; m. Olga M. Fernandez, Jan. 31, 1942 (div. Apr. 1973); children—Olga (Mrs. Ignacio G. del Valle), Eduardo R.; m. 2d, Maribel Maxwell, Dec. 1973. Came to U.S., 1959, naturalized, 1965. Admitted to Fla. bar, 1965; partner firm Helio R. Ecay, Havana, 1941-59, Salley, Barns, Pajon & Immer (now Salley, Barnes, Pajon & Primm), Miami, 1967—; head legal dept., sec. Cuban subsidiaries The Cuban Am. Sugar Co. (name changed to N.Am. Sugar Industries, Inc. 1960), N.Y.C., 1952-60; sec., counsel Talisman Sugar Corp., Miami, 1965-72; v.p., dir. Fla. Sugar Corp., Belle Glade, 1960-62, Sunshine Farms, Inc., South Bay, Fla., 1960-72; dir. The Americas Bank, Miami. Mem. adv. bd. Fla. Meml. Coll., Miami, 1970—, endowment com. U. Miami, 1969—. Mem. Am., InterAm., Fla., Dade County bar assns. Republican. Roman Catholic. Clubs: Miami, LaGorce Country Surf (Miami Beach); Ocean Reef (Key Largo, Fla.); Jockey (North Miami, Fla.); American, Big Five, Bankers (Miami). Home: 5690 SW 84th Terrace Miami FL 33143 Office: Suite 700 100 Biscayne Blvd Miami FL 33132

PALLAS, WILLIAM CHARLES, gynecologist, obstetrician; b. Jamestown, N.Y., Feb. 24, 1920; s. Chris and Magdaline (Plakas) P.; B.A., U. Rochester, 1942; M.D., L.I. Coll. Medicine, 1944; M.S. Obstetrics and Gynecology, U. Colo., 1950; m. Katherine Rigas, Aug. 29, 1951; 1 son, Christopher. Intern, Queen of Angels Hosp., Los Angeles, 1944-45; resident surgery Fordham Hosp., N.Y.C., 1946; resident obstetrics and gynecology U. Colo., 1947-49; asst. instr., instr. dept. obstetrics and gynecology, U. Colo. Sch. Medicine, 1949-50; asst. prof. dept. obstetrics and gynecology U. Ark. Sch. Medicine, 1950-52; asst. prof. dept. anatomy Georgetown U. Sch. Medicine, 1954; med. dir., attending staff, former owner, operator Woman's Hosp.; owner, operator Woman's Clinic; pres., dir. Hosp. Realty Co., Inc.; courtesy staff Baroness Erlanger Hosp. Pres., dir. McCallie Realty Co., Inc., Athens TV Cable Co. Inc., McMinnville TV Cable Co., Harriman TV Cable Co., Rockwood TV Cable Co., Etowah TV Cable Co., Sparta TV Cable Co., Lookout Realty Co., Inc.; builder, owner comml. properties including Downtowner Motor Inn, Met. Life Ins. Co. and Burroughs; dir. Hosp. Affiliates, Inc., Western Empire Financial, Industry Fund Am., Mar-Search, Inc. Mem. med. adv. bd. Bio-Dynamics, Inc. Served as lt. M.C., USNR, 1945-46, in U.S.S. Hercules; lt. to lt. comdr., 1952-54, chief obstetrics Portsmouth Naval Hosp. Diplomate Am. Bd. Obstetrics and Gynecology. Fellow A.C.S., Am. Coll. Obstetrics and Gynecology, Southeastern Surg. Congress, Internat. Coll. Surgeons, Am. Coll. Abdominal Surgeons; mem. C. of C., Am., Tenn. med. assns., Chattanooga and Hamilton County Med. Soc., N.Y. Acad. Scis., Royal Soc. Medicine (affiliate). Clubs: Lookout Mountain Golf, Signal Mountain Golf and Country. Author: Handbook of Obstetrics and Gynecology, 1949. Home: 10 Folts Circle Chattanooga TN 37415 Office: 859 McCallie Av Chattanooga TN 37403

PALLOT, RICHARD ALLEN, banker, lawyer; b. Miami, Fla., July 30, 1930; s. Moses M. and Julia (Marshall) P.; B.A., U. Fla., 1952, LL.B., 1956; m. Rosalind Brown Wedeles, Aug. 19, 1955; children—Joseph Wedeles, Melissa Aden. Admitted to Fla. bar, 1956, Fed. bar, 1956; practice, Dade County, Fla., 1956—; partner Pallot, Stern, Proby & Adkins, 1957—; chmn. bd., pres., chief exec. officer Internat. Bank, Miami, 1969—; lectr. Fla. uniform comml. code, Fla. mechanics lein law, aspects of investment—corp. convertible debentures. Chmn. Fla. State Bd. Bus. Regulation. Trustee Opera Guild. Served to 1st lt. AUS, 1952-54. Mem. Am., Fla., Dade County bar assns., Am., Fla., Dade County bankers assns., Young Pres.'s Orgn., Fla. Council 100, Pi Lambda Phi, Phi Alpha Delta. Clubs: Kings Bay Yacht, Country, Symphony; Standard, Bankers (Miami). Home: 12095 SW 63d Av Miami FL 33156 Office: Internat Bank Bldg Miami FL 33135

PALLOT, WILLIAM LOUIS, lawyer, banker; b. Springfield, Mass., Nov. 9, 1912; s. Moses and Julia (Marshall) P.; LL.B., Cumberland U., 1939; m. Alberta Marie Tanenbaum, Dec. 25, 1939; children—Philip Roger, Barbara Stanli, Scott Marshall. Admitted to Fla. bar, 1940; practiced in Miami, 1940—; sr. partner firm Pallot, Stern, Proby & Adkins and predecessor, 1948—; chmn. Miami Nat. Bank, 1959-63; pres. Inter Nat. Bank of Miami, 1963-68, chmn. bd., 1968—; dir. NVF Corp., Wilmington, Del., Wilson Bros. Co., N.Y.C., Birdsboro Corp. (Pa.), DWG Corp., N.Y.C., Nat. Propane Corp., N.Y.C., Pa. Engr. Corp., New Castle, Sharon Steel Corp., Youngstown, O., Southeastern Pub. Service Corp., N.Y.C., No. Engring. Co., Detroit, Lectromelt Corp., Pitts., Barrington Industries, Inc., N.Y.C. Pres. Bd. Internat. Trade Greater Miami, 1971-72; pres. Internat. Center Greater Miami, 1972—. Mem. Pres.'s Regional Export Expansion Council, 1971—. Judge Municipal Ct., Coral Gables, Fla., 1948-52; city atty., Miami and North Miami, Fla., 1955-59; chmn. Pub. Works Authority, Miami, 1948-58; chmn. Miami Parking Authority, 1951-58; vice chmn. Planning Adv. Bd., Met. Dade County (Fla.), 1961-65; mem. Miami Beach Charter Bd., 1966—; mem. exec. com. Met. Miami Municipal Bd., 1953-55, Dade County Charter Bd., 1955-57; dir. Greater Miami Crime Commn., 1963-68; chmn. Fla. regional bd. Anti Defamation League, 1965-67; chmn. Dade County Criminal Justice Coordinating Council, 1972—. Trustee, Dade County United Fund, 1965—, mem. exec. com., 1969—, chmn. agy. operations com., 1969-70, treas., 1971; mem. citizens adv. bd. Fla. Meml. Coll., Miami, Biscayne Coll. for Men, Miami. Served with USNR 1942-46. Recipient Shield of Israel award, State of Israel, 1971; Sertoma Internat. Freedom award, 1972. Mem. Am., Fla. bankers assns., Am., Dade County bar assns., Fla. Bar, Am. Inst. Banking, Greater Miami Clearing House Assn. (pres. 1966), A.I.M. (pres.'s council), Hombres de Empresa. Mason (Shriner, 32 deg.); mem. B'nai B'rith. Clubs: Progress, Standard, Palm Bay (Miami); Tiger Bay; Cuban-Am. Sertoma (v.p.) (Coral Gables); Propeller (v.p.). Home: 2300 Sunset Dr Sunset Island III Miami Beach FL 33140 Office: 627 SW 27th Av Miami FL 33135

PALMER, CHARLES EARL, ednl. adminstr.; b. Wiggins, S.C., Dec. 18, 1919; s. William David and Theodosia (Yarborough) P.; diploma Rice Bus. Coll., Charleston, S.C., 1937; student LaSalle Extension U., Chgo., 1941, U. Minn., 1944, The Citadel, 1949; D.C.S., Fort Lauderdale U., 1967; m. Rebecca Maull Palmer, Sept. 30, 1950; children—Barbara Faye, Charles Earl, John Clifford, Sarah Rebecca. Asst. to chief clk. Koppers Co., Charleston, S.C., 1937-41; post exchange mgr. Charleston Port of Embarkation, 1941-42; treasury rep. Orient region. Northwest Airlines St. Paul, 1947-49; owner Norfolk Coll., 1953-58, chmn. bd. trustees, 1958-60; pres. Palmer Coll., Charleston, 1949-72, pres. emeritus, 1972—; asso. exec. dir. for adminstrn. State Bd. Tech. and Comprehensive Edn., Columbia, S.C., 1972-73, exec. dir., 1973—; individual practice C.P.A., 1952—. Commr. accrediting commn. Assn Ind. Colls. and Schs., Washington, 1961-65, chmn., 1964-65. Chmn. bd. trustees Ga.-Carolina Found., Inc., 1966—. Served to capt. USAAF, 1942-47. C.P.A., S.C. Mem. S.C. Assn. C.P.A.'s, Am. Inst. C.P.A.'s, S.C. Assn. Bus. Colls. (past pres.), Southeastern Bus. Coll. Assn. (past pres.), Assn. Ind. Colls. and Schs. (past pres.), Am. Assn. Jr. Colls. (mem. commn. legislation 1967-72), Charleston Trident C. of C. (dir. 1964-67). Rotarian (past pres., dist. gov. 1967-68). Co-author College Accounting Theory and Practice, 1963, 2d edit., 1968; Cost Accounting Theory and Practice, 1965, 2d edit., 1971; College Accounting Intermediate/Advanced, 1966; College Accounting for Secretaries, 1970. Contbr. articles to profl. publs. Home: Route 7 Box 270 Lexington SC 29072

PALMER, CHARLES ROBERT, oil well drilling contractor; b. Gorman, Tex., Dec. 15, 1934; s. John Derwin and Alene Elizabeth (Moorman) P.; B.S., So. Meth. U., 1957, M.S., 1966; m. Rebecca Sparks, Feb. 14, 1954; children—Shelley, John. With Rowan Cos., Inc., 1953—, chmn.; chief exec. officer, 1972—; pres. Rowan Internat., Inc., Houston, 1969—; officer, dir. various subsidiaries; dir. West Loop Nat. Bank, Houston. Committeeman Boy Scouts Am., 1967—. Registered profl. engr., Tex., La. Mem. Am. Soc. M.E., Am. Petroleum Inst., Internat. Assn. Drilling Contractors, Tex. Mid Continent Oil and Gas Assn. Clubs: Petroleum, Ramada, River Oak County, Lakewood Yacht (Houston). Home: 13115 Highwood Houston TX 77024 Office: 1900 Post Oak Tower Bldg 5051 Westheimer St Houston TX 77027

PALMER, FRANK CONRAD, govt. ofcl.; b. Richmond, Va., June 17, 1918; s. Frank Conrad and Daisy Bell (Jones) P.; student George Washington U., 1947-48, U. Md., 1954-57, Northwestern U., 1958; m. Helen Arnson, Oct. 26, 1936; 1 son, Walter Joseph. With Arlington (Va.) Police Dept., 1940-53, comdg. officer traffic safety div., 1947-53; dir. traffic safety Dept. Navy, Washington, 1953-60; chief, traffic safety USPHS, Washington, 1960-64; chief traffic safety Office Econ. Opportunity, 1964-69; safety security officer Manpower Adminstrn. Dept. Labor, Washington, 1969—. Dir. Driver Improvement Clinic, Arlington, Va., 1960-74, City of Fairfax, Va., 1970-74. Served with USMC, 1943-46. Mem. Nat. Safety Mgmt. Soc. Mason. Clubs: Aqua Land Yacht (Newburg, Md.); Land Mark Yacht (Alexandria, Va.); Nat. Potomac Yacht (commodore 1973) (Washington). Home: 6000 N 28th St Arlington VA 22207 Office: 601 D St NW Washington DC 20213

PALMER, GEORGE, jewelry co. exec.; b. N.Y.C., Feb. 4, 1918; s. Harry and Rose (Gross) P.; B.S., Coll. City N.Y., 1938, M.S., U. Minn., 1939, Ph.D., 1943; M.S. in Metall. Engring., U. Tenn., 1966; m. Alice Katherine Herbst, Dec. 31, 1939; children—Alexandra Georgia (Mrs. Allen Rosen), Kenneth Howard. Jr. soil surveyor U.S. Dept. Agr., Lincoln, Neb., 1940-41; research chemist TVA, U. Tenn., 1942-44, 46-48; v.p. Alexander Herbst & Co., Knoxville, Tenn., 1948-66; pres. G & A Palmer Co., Knoxville, 1966—, Materials Applications, Inc., welding and metall. cons. Metall. cons. in failure analysis. Served with AUS, 1944-46. Mem. Am. Soc. for Metals, Am. Inst. Mining and Metall. Engrs., N.Y. Acad. Scis., Sigma Xi. Contbr. articles to profl. jours. Home: 5519 Westover Dr Knoxville TN 37919 Office: 619 N Broadway Knoxville TN 37917

PALMER, GEORGE JOSEPH, JR., govt. ofcl.; b. New Orleans, Nov. 27, 1929; s. George Joseph and Juliette (Wehrmann) P.; B.B.A., Tulane U., 1952; postgrad. La. State U., 1954-55; Ph.D., Purdue U., 1958; m. Yolanda Manautou, Dec. 30, 1952; children—George Joseph III, Daphne. Asst. prof. indsl. psychology Tulane U., 1958-61; prof. indsl. psychology La. State U., 1961-62; research dir. Tex. Christian U., 1962-64; research scientist Human Scis. Research, McLean, Va., 1964-66, Century Research Corp., Arlington, Va., 1966-68; chief div. profl. manpower U.S. Dept. Transp., Nat. Hwy. Safety Bur., Washington, 1968-70, manpower program officer Nat. Hwy. Traffic Safety Adminstrn., 1970—. Cons. to utilities firm, 1962, Fasson Products, 1964, Nat. Hwy. Safety Bur., 1968, Diebold Asso., 1968. Served with USNR, 1952-54. Mem. Am. Psychol. Assn., A.A.A.S., Am. Statis. Assn., Internat. Union Psychol. Scis., Psychometric Soc., Sigma Xi. Home: 11205 Bellmont Dr Fairfax VA 22030 Office: Nat Hwy Traffic Safety Adminstrn Dept Transp 400 7th St SW Washington DC 20590

PALMER, GROVER ADDISON, JR., optometrist; b. Lexington, N.C., Aug. 9, 1925; s. Grover Addison and Sarah Myrle (Younts) P.; A.B., Lenoir Rhyne Coll., 1947; D. Optometry, So. Coll. Optometry, 1949; m. Edna Vernelle Gilliam, June 19, 1954; 1 dau., Kaye Vernelle. Pvt. practice optometry, Salisbury, N.C., 1950—. Mem. bd. aldermen Town of Spencer (N.C.), 1951-71; chmn. Rowan County Democratic party, 1972-74. Bd. dirs. Rowan County United Fund, 1973-74. Served with USNR, 1943-46; lt. comdr. Res. ret. Recipient Distinguished Service award Spencer Jr. C. of C., 1954. Mem. Salisbury-Rowan C. of C., Salisbury-Rowan Mchts. Assn. (sec. 1969-70, treas. 1970-71), Am. Optometric Assn., N.C. State (pres. elect 1973-74), Tri-County (pres. 1961) optometric socs. Rotarian (pres. 1971-72). Home: 420 Windsor Dr Salisbury NC 28144 Office: 119 N Church St Salisbury NC 28144

PALMER, HUBERT BERNARD, dentist, ret. air force officer; b. San Antonio, Sept. 6, 1912; s. Hubert Victor and Rosemary (Garvey) P.; student St. Mary's U., 1931-34; D.D.S., Baylor U., 1938; postgrad. George Washington U., 1946-47, U. Md., 1950-53; m. Elizabeth Harriet McAlary, Aug. 16, 1945; children—Hubert Bernard II, Robert Leldon. Commd. 1st lt. USAAF, 1938, advanced through grades to col. USAF, 1971; chief dept. dental research U.S. Army, 1946-50; chief dept. exptl. dentistry, USAF, 1953-54, chief research dentistry div. 1954-56; command dental surgeon, 1958-59, 63-65, 65-68; dental staff officer, 1959-62, dir. dental services, 1968-71; dir. Eastside Dental Clinic San Antonio Met. Health Dist., 1972—; clin. asst. prof. U. Tex. Dental Sch., San Antonio, 1973—. Decorated Legion of Merit, Commendation medal First Oak Leaf Cluster. Fellow A.A.A.S.; mem. Am. Dental Assn., Internat. Assn. Dental Research, Soc. Gen. Microbiology, Am. Soc. Microbiology, Omicron Kappa Upsilon. Contbr. articles to profl. jours. Research reduction decalcification tooth enamel. Home: 6115 Forest Timber San Antonio TX 78240 Office: 210 N Rio Grande San Antonio TX 78202

PALMER, JACK SIDNEY, govt. researcher; b. Lubbock, Tex., Jan. 10, 1926; s. Henry Brewer and Rena (Key) P.; D.V.M., Tex. A. and M. U., 1946; M.P.H., U. Cal. at Berkeley, 1954; m. Lila Bertie Beard, Nov. 22, 1947; children—Jack Coleman, Scott Brewer, Grant Beard, Deanie Dee, Jo Beth. Vet. cons. UNRRA, Washington, 1946-47; practice vet. medicine, Sinton and Crystal City, Tex., 1947-49; dir. Vet. Pub. Health Utah, Salt Lake City, 1954-58; biol. sci. adminstr. Dugway Proving Ground, Utah, 1958-62; dir. VSR, Agrl. Research Service, U.S. Dept. Agrl., Kerrville, Tex., 1962—. Served with AUS, 1950-52; USPHS, 1957. Mem. Am. Tex. vet. med. assns., Am. Coll. Vet. Toxicologists. Democrat. Methodist. Mason (Shriner), Kiwanian (dir.). Contbr. articles to profl. publs. Home: 600 Overhill Dr Kerrville TX 78028 Office: PO Box 311 Kerrville TX 78028

PALMER, JESSE CLOWER, civil engr.; b. Cairo, Ga., Sept. 14, 1914; s. Clarence Eugene and Bessie Merle (Adams) P.; grad. structural engring. Internat. Corr. Schs., 1962; m. Audrey Vonceil Nunez, Jan. 7, 1939 (div. Apr. 1971); children—Jesse Clower, George N., William E., Patricia; m. 2d, Rebecca Doggett, Sept. 16, 1973. With Robert & Co., Atlanta, 1953-55, John J. Harte Co., Atlanta, 1955-57, Waldermor S. Nelson, New Orleans, 1957-58, E. M. Watkins, Tallahassee, 1958-59; pres. Apalachee Engrs. & Land Surveyors, Inc., Tallahassee, 1959—; also Leon County surveyor Leon County, Fla., 1969—. Served to 2d lt. AUS. Registered profl. engr., Fla., Ga., Ala. Mem. Fla. Engring. Soc., Fla. Soc. Profl. Land Surveyors, Nat. Soc. Profl. Engrs., Am. Congress Surveying and Mapping. Elk. Clubs: Havana (Fla.) Golf and Country, Winewood Country (Tallahassee). Designer main spillway and dispersion shoes Fontana Dam, N.C., 1943. Home: 2000 N Meridian Rd Tallahassee FL 32303 Office: PO Box 3163 Tallahassee FL 32303

PALMER, JOHN DERWIN, ret. govt. ofcl.; b. Desdemona, Tex., July 2, 1909; s. John Robert and Edna (Sporer) P.; grad. John Tarleton Coll., 1929; student U. Tex., 1930-31; B.S., Sul Ross State Coll., 1935; M.A., Hardin-Simmons U., 1938; Ph.D., Universdad Inter-Americana (Mexico), 1962; m. Alene Moorman, May 10, 1930; children—Charles Robert, John Truett. Tchr., prin. various high schs., Canyon, Tex., Rochester, Tex., Goree, Tex., 1929-39; adminstrv. officer Social Security Administrn., Amarillo, Tex., 1939-40, Lufkin, Tex., 1940-41, Lubbock, Tex., 1941-43, Austin, Tex., 1941-72, Alexandria, La., 1943-44, New Orleans, 1946-50, Dallas, 1950-53, Waco, Tex., 1953-72; now self-employed in pub. relations; mgr. dist. office, San Antonio, 1953-66; asst. regional dir. information Dept. Health, Edn. and Welfare, Dallas; cons. Social Security to Republic of Costa Rica, Panama, Columbia, Peru, Chile, Guatemala, El Salvador, Nicaragua, Honduras, 1967-69. Pres. Bexar County chpt. Tex. Social Welfare Assn., 1956; mem. adv. bd. Community Services Div., St. Mary's U., 1955-66, cons. vocational counseling Div. Guidance and Placement, 1956-66; dir. Bexar County Tb Assn., 1957; mem. El Patronato, Universidad National de Mexico, 1960-67; C.S. Liaison officer to Instituto Mexicano del Seguro Socia., 1961-66; mem. adv. bd. Universidad Interamericana Saltillo, Coah, Mexico, 1962—; mem. exec. com. Tex.-Peru Partners in Alliance, 1964. Bd. dirs. Mexican Bapt. Children's Home; trustee Instituto Estudios IberoAmericanos, Saltillo, Mexico. Served with AUS, 1944-46. Recipient Boss of Year award, Nat. Secs. Assn., 1960; pres.'s award Lions Internat., 1968, 69. Mem. San Antonio Council Presidents (pres. 1956), South Tex. Personnel and Guidance Assn. (pres. 1956), Nat. Ojce Mgmt. Assn. (pres. San Antonio chpt. 1955), Tex. Personnel and Mgmt. Assn., Am. Personnel and Guidance Assn., Nat. Vocational Guidance Assn. (profl. mem.), Council Internat. Relations (dir. 1957), San Antonio C. of C. (mem. com. 700 1960, mem. fgn. relations com. 1960-66), Hardin-Simmons Alumni Assn. (pres. 1959). Baptist (deacon, bd. tchr. Sunday sch.). Mason (past worshipful master, 32 deg., Shriner), Lion (past pres., dep. dist. gov.-at-large; gov. dist. 2-A2, 1963-64, internat. counsellor). Club: Press (Dallas). Author: El Seguro Social En Los Estados Unidos De America; Seguridad Social. Producer Spanish series Su Seguro Social. Home: 8416 Hunnicut Rd Dallas TX 75228

PALMER, LAUCHLEN SECORD, psychiatrist; b. Cleve., Nov. 1, 1908; s. Sterne Royal and Abigail (Secord) P.; student Washington and Lee U., 1927-30; M.D., U. Rochester, 1934; m. Catharine Mary Fleming, Sept. 1, 1934. Intern, Highland Hosp., Rochester, N.Y., 1934-35; psychiatrist N.Y. Dept. Mental Hygiene, 1935-68; dir. Chemung County Dept. Mental Health, 1958-63; individual practice psychiatry, Elmira, N.Y., 1958-64; dir. day treatment center VA Hosp., Miami, Fla., 1964-70; individual practice psychiatry; Lake Worth, Fla., 1970—. Asso. prof. psychiatry N.Y. State Med. U., 1952-58; clin. instr. psychiatry U. Miami Sch. Medicine, Miami, 1964-70; lectr. in field. Served with USNR, 1942-46. Diplomate Am. Bd. Psychiatry. Fellow Acad. Psychosomatic Medicine. A.C.P., Am. Psychiat. Assn.; mem. Am. Soc. Clin. Hypnosis, A.M.A. Asso. editor Acad. Psychosomatic Jour., 1961-69. Home: 8133 Pine Tree Lane West Palm Beach FL 33406 Office: 1710 4th Av N Lake Worth FL 33460

PALMER, OREN ALSTON, JR., sales co. exec.; b. Fairfax, S.C., Dec. 22, 1922; s. Oren Alston and Lilly Mae (Way) P.; B.Elec. Engring., N.C. State U., 1948; m. Dorothy Maxine Rodgers, Feb. 1, 1945; children—Carole (Mrs. James Edward Glover), Lexia (Mrs. James Ross Churchill). Asso. engr. Va. Electric & Power Co., Richmond, 1948-58; sales engr. Jake Rudisill Assos., Charlotte, N.C., 1958-64; pres. Powertronics, Inc., Thomasville, N.C., 1964—, chmn. bd., 1972—; dir. Oren Enterprises, Inc., Thomasville. Served with USAAF, 1943-45. Mem. I.E.E.E. Presbyn. (deacon 1952-56, elder 1956-58). Elk. Clubs: Pinebrook Country (Winston-Salem, N.C.); Country of South Carolina (Florence). Home: 1459 Denton Rd Thomasville NC 27360 Office: 409 Fisher Ferry Thomasville NC 27360

PALMER, OWEN THACKARA, JR., lawyer; b. Gulfport, Miss., July 15, 1920; s. Owen Thackara and Lula (Barksdale) P.; B.A., U. Miss., 1942, LL.B., 1947; m. Joanne Melton, Apr. 5, 1947; children—Jan Barksdale, Wawice Eugenia. Admitted to Miss. bar 1947; with firm Eaton & Cottrell, Gulfport, Miss., 1947-48; individual practice law, Gulfport, 1948-64; sr. partner, Palmer & Stewart, Gulfport, 1965-73, Palmer, Stewart & Gaines, 1973—. Asst. sec.-treas., Miss. Valley Petroleum Corp., Mississippi City, 1964-69; instr. Am. history U. Miss., 1947. Disaster, chmn., Gulfport chpt. A.R.C., 1949-51; coach, Gulfport Recreation dept., 1954-68. City pros. atty., asst. city atty., Gulfport, 1953-69; atty. Gulfport Municipal Separate Sch. Dist., 1957—. Dir., past pres. Gulfport-Harrison County Library, 1954-68; bd. dirs., 1st v.p., mem. exec. com. Miss. Safety Council, 1971—; past pres. Gulfport Little Theatre. Served with USNR. Mem. Miss. State Bar (chmn. traffic ct. com. 1962—), Am. (rep. State Miss. on adv. com. to traffic ct. com. 1966—), Harrison County (past pres.) bar assns., Am. Trial Lawyers Assn., Am. Judicature Assn., Delta Kappa Epsilon, Phi Delta Phi. Episcopalian. Rotarian. Club: Gulfport Yacht (past commodore). Home: 1308 E Beach St Gulfport MS 39501 Office: 2209 14th St Gulfport MS 39501

PALMER, PHILIP ISHAM, lawyer; b. Chgo., Sept. 12, 1904; s. Frank Austin and Sara Jeanette (Magner) P.; student Northwestern U., 1924, U. Chgo., 1926-27; LL.B., Jefferson Sch. Law, 1930; m. Charline Bolen, Apr. 5, 1924; children—Philip Isham, Stephanie (Mrs Robert H. Connell). Admitted to Tex. bar, 1930; mem. firm Winfrey & Lane, 1931-34, Harris & Palmer, 1934-46; individual practice, Dallas, 1947-48; partner Palmer & Rochelle, 1949-60, Palmer & Palmer, 1960-65, Palmer, Green, Palmer & Burke, 1965-66, Palmer, Palmer & Burke, 1966-71, Palmer, Palmer & Coffee, 1971— (all Dallas). Mem. Am., Dallas bar assns., State Bar Tex. Episcopalian. Home: 5909 McCommas St Dallas TX 75206 Office: 2130 First Nat Bank Bldg Dallas TX 75202

PALMER, RALPH THOMAS, clergyman, educator; b. San Diego, Mar. 18, 1926; s. Olaf Gideon and Dorothy (Decker) P.; B.A., Tex. Christian U., 1948, B.D., 1950; M.S. in Pub. Health, Yale, 1952; postgrad. Duke, 1956-57; D.Ministry, Phillips U., 1973; m. Mary Maxine Jones, Aug. 30, 1948; children—Angella Marie, Carol Celeste. Ordained to ministry, 1947; pastor Cumberland Av. Christian Ch., Waco, Tex., 1947-50; spl. investigator New Haven Pub. Health Dept., 1950-51; research microbiologist Yale Med. Sch., 1951-52; with United Christian Missionary Soc., Indpls., 1952-70, missionary to Japan, 1952-57, exec. sec., 1957-70; dean Coll. of Missions, Indpls., 1957-70; sr. pastor 1st Christian Ch., Pampa, Tex., 1971—. Bd. dirs. High Plains area of the Christian Ch., Japan Internat. Christian U. Bd. dirs. Suicide Prevention and Crisis Intervention of Pampa. Served with USNR, 1944-45. Mem. Tex. Archeol. Soc., Internat. Psychoanalytic Assn., Am. Pub. Health Assn., Am. Mgmt. Assn., Midwest Assn. Marriage Counselors, Am. Psychol. Assn., Pampa C. of C. Club: Knife and Fork (Pampa). Author: Framboesia (Yaws) in Jamaica, West Indies, 1952; Marriage Enrichment in a Christian Context, 1973; co-author chpt. Minister's Own Mental Health, 1961. Contbr. articles on pub. health, missions, psychology to profl. publs. Home: 2404 Camanche Trail Pampa TX 79065 Office: First Christian Church 18th at Nelson Sts Pampa TX 79065

PALMER, RICHARD EUGENE, editor; b. Watertown, N.Y., July 7, 1920; s. Howard Welch and Pauline (Coulthart) P.; student Wesleyan U., Middletown, Conn., 1938-41; A.B., U. Mo., 1947; m. Elizabeth Winfield Lee, May 6, 1950; children—Melissa Lee, James Howard. Sports editor Portchester (N.Y.) Daily Item, 1941-42; news editor Daily Free Press, Kinston, N.C., 1947-48; editor Mid-York Weekly, Hamilton, N.Y., 1948-51; editor News-Herald, Willoughby, O., 1953-60; with State-Times and Morning Advocate, Baton Rouge, 1960—, asso. editor, 1965—, prodn. mgr., 1963—. Mem. adv. com. Research Inst., Am. Newspaper Publishers Assn., Easton, Pa., 1971—. Bd. mgrs. YMCA, Baton Rouge, 1966—, Salvation Army, Baton Rouge, 1965-71; bd. dirs. Baton Rouge C. of C., 1973—; trustee Newspaper Prodn. and Research Center, Oklahoma City, 1966—, chmn. Newspaper Computer Users Group, 1968—. Served to capt. AUS, 1942-46, 51-52. Mem. So. Newspaper Publishers Assn. (chmn. prodn. methods and labor com. 1970-71), So. Prodn. Program (bd. dirs. 1965—), Sigma Delta Chi. Mason. Home: 12363 E Millburn St Baton Rouge LA 70815 Office: 525 Lafayette St Baton Rouge LA 70821

PALMER, SIDNEY J(EWELL), television producer, condr.; b. Houston, Nov. 18, 1928; s. Jewell S. and Lizzette M. (Shilling) P.; grad. Houston Conservatory Music, 1940; B. Mus., U. Tex., 1947, Mus.M., 1949; postgrad. (fellow) Juilliard Sch. Music, 1947-48, Berkshire Music Center, Tanglewood/Lenox, Mass., 1947-49; m. Lanny Sullivan, Aug. 19, 1967; children—Margaret Ann, Mary Elizabeth. Concert pianist, composer, condr., opera stage dir., 1947—; radio dir., producer, various locations 1945-58; producer KARK-TV, Little Rock, 1952-60; exec. producer, prodn. supr. WIS-TV, Columbia, S.C., 1960-73; exec. producer pub. television and ednl. services S.C. Ednl. Television Network, Columbia, 1973—. Condr., New Braunfels (Tex.) Symphony Orch., 1947-48, Houston Symphonette, 1949-51, Ark. State Symphony, 1950-54, Hot Springs (Ark.) Lyric Theatre, 1951-59, Little Rock Philharmonic, 1955-58; artistic dir. Columbia Lyric Theatre, Columbia, 1960-70; artist-in-residence Columbia Coll., 1972—; head, theory and composition depts. Houston Conservatory Music, 1949-50; condr., lectr. U. Ark. Grad. Center, 1954-56. Nat. sec. Television Program Conf., 1973—. Bd. dirs. Russell George Found. Recipient mus. composition awards, including Harold J. Abrams award, 1950, Tex. Composers' Contest award, 1949, several Nat. Fedn. Music Clubs award, Los Angeles Internat. competition, 1955, Mid-South competition, 1958; Broadcast Media awards San Francisco State Coll., 1969, 70. Author: Color Television Manual, 1962. Home: 3101 Barnes Spring Rd Columbia SC 29204 Office: 2712 Millwood Av Columbia SC 29205

PALMER, WILLIAM FISHER, educator; b. Thomasville, N.C., July 9, 1934; s. Jacob Alexander and Etna Terress (Little) P.; A.B., Catawba Coll., 1956; M.Ed., U. N.C., 1959, Ph.D., 1964; postgrad. N.Y. U., 1971-72; m. Anne Hannah Johnson, Aug. 26, 1967; 1 son, Richard Alexander. Tchr. math. and physics High Point (N.C.) Sr. High Sch., 1956-58, 59-60; research asst. U. N.C., Chapel Hill, 1960-62; cons. math. N.C. Dept. Pub. Instr., Raleigh, 1962-64; asst. prof. math. Mercer U., Macon, Ga., 1964-67, asso. prof., 1967-73, prof., 1973, dir. NSF summer insts., 1965-67, 71; vis. prof. edn. N.Y. U., N.Y.C., 1971-72; prof., chmn. dept. edn. Catawba Coll., Salisbury, N.C., 1973—. Cons. Office Econ. Opportunity and U.S. Office Edn., 1967-70. Mem. Nat. Council Tchrs. Math., Nat. Sci. Tchrs. Assn., Am. Ednl. Research Assn., N.C. Assn. Educators, Catawba Coll. Alumni Assn. (dir. 1965—), Phi Delta Kappa. Presbyn. Author: (with Eugene D. Nichols) Modern Geometry, 1968, Holt Geometry, 1974. Home: 304 North Park Dr Salisbury NC 28144

PALMER, WILLIAM MARVIN, mag. exec.; b. Neosho, Mo., July 13, 1918; s. Charles William and Etta Muriel (Martin) P.; LL.B., Atlanta Law Sch., 1950; postgrad. U. Ga., 1956; m. Harriette Caldwell, Dec. 23, 1941; children—William Marvin, Harriette Louise (Mrs. David D. Spires), James C., Emily Ann, Charles H. Admitted to Ga. bar, 1951; graphic arts specialist Tucker Wayne & Co., Advt., Atlanta, 1948-51; advt. and pub. relations dir. Ga. Press Assn., Atlanta, 1960-62; advt. and promotion Huntsville Daily Times, 1957-60, Kansas City (Mo.) Star, 1963-67; editor Electronics Digest div. Tandy Corp., Ft. Worth, 1967—, editor Radio Shack Intercom, 1967—, publs. mgr. Radio Shack div., 1974—. Served to 1st lt., Signal Corps, AUS, USAF, 1939-45, 51-53. Decorated Air medal with silver cluster. Mem. Am. Bar Assn., Internat. Assn. Bus. Communicators, Antique Wireless Assn., Canadian Vintage Wireless Assn., Ft. Worth Press Club. Republican. Mem. Reorganized Ch. of Jesus Christ of Latter-day Saints. Author: Great Men in Electronics, 1970. Home: 7325 Bursey Rd Smithfield TX 76080 Office: 2617 W 7th St Fort Worth TX 76107

PALMORE, JOHN STANLEY, JR., judge; b. Ancon, C.Z., Aug. 6, 1917; s. John Stanley and Antoinette (Gonzalez) P.; student Western Ky. State Coll., 1934-36; LL.B. cum laude, U. Louisville, 1939; student Harvard Grad. Sch. Bus. Adminstrn., 1942-43; m. Eleanor Gertrude Anderson, July 31, 1938; 1 son, John W. Admitted to Ky. bar, 1938; asso. firm King & Flournoy, Henderson, Ky., 1939-42; chief legal br. Jeffersonville (Ind.) Q.M. Depot, 1946-47; partner firm Hunt & Palmore, Henderson, 1947-52, Palmore & Mitchell, Henderson, 1956-59; pvt. practice, 1952-56; Commonwealth's atty. 5th Jud. Dist. Ky., 1955-59; city atty. Henderson, 1954-55; pros. atty. Henderson, 1949-53; city atty. Sebree, Ky., 1954-59; judge Ct. Appeals Ky., 1959—, chief justice, 1966, 73—. Served to lt., Supply Corps, USNR, 1942-46, 51-52. Mem. Ky. Bar Assn. Democrat. Episcopalian. Home: Henderson KY 42420 Office: State Capitol Frankfort KY 40601

PALMQUIST, EMIL EUGENE, ret. govt. ofcl.; b. Otisco, Minn., Aug. 20, 1908; s. Axel G. and Hilma (Palm) P.; B.A., Gustavus Adolphus Coll., 1930; M.D., Northwestern U., 1937; M.P.H., U. Mich., 1942; m. Ingrid J. Ostrom, June 6, 1936; children—Kristin (Mrs. Walter Anton), Linda (Mrs. William M. Mason), Paula (Mrs. Norman Knoll), John. Intern Swedish Hosp., Seattle, 1936-37; practice gen. medicine, Seattle, 1937-38; pub. health officer, Yakima County, Clark County, Whitman County, Olympia Health Dist., Washington, 1938-44; dir. pub. health Seattle, King County, 1944-51; commd. surgeon USPHS, 1950, advanced through grades to asst. surgeon gen., 1970; chief health mission Point Four in Iran, 1951-53, asst. chief div. Internat. Health, USPHS, Washington, 1953-55; clin. prof. pub. health U. Cal. at Berkeley, also dir. pub. health, Berkeley, 1955-57; chief gen. health services USPHS, San Francisco, 1957-61; region III health dir. USPHS, Dept. Health, Edn. and Welfare, Charlottesville, Va., 1961-70, region IV health dir., Atlanta, 1970-72, ret.; asst. clin. prof. pub. health U. Wash., 1947-51; lectr. Sch. Nursing, U. Wash., 1944-48, U. Cal. at Berkeley, 1957-61; vis. lectr. U. Tehran Med. Sch., Iran, 1951-53; teaching mission U.S. Dept. State to Ministry Health, Iran, 1950. Recipient Surgeon Gen.'s medal for meritorious service, 1964. Diplomate Am. Bd. Preventive Medicine. Fellow Am. Pub. Health Assn. (chmn. health officer's sect. 1959), Am. Coll. Preventive Medicine, Assn. Tchrs. Preventive Medicine; mem. A.M.A., Albemarle County Med. Soc., Phi Chi, Delta Omega. Contbr. articles on health adminstrn. to profl. jours. Home: 5381 Fairfield Way Fort Myers FL 33901

PALMROS, ERIC KELVIN, accountant; b. Syracuse, N.Y., May 23, 1908; s. Alexander and Helen Frances (Snow) P.; student Tex. Christian U., 1947; m. Gladys Lucille Hedley, Aug. 25, 1930 (dec. Sept. 1966); children—Eric Kelvin, Alexander; m. 2d, Frances Hollis Tillery, Jan. 20, 1973. Investment banker and broker, N.Y.C., 1928-41; accountant, auditor, 1941-43; auditor, chief cashier Montgomery Ward, 1943-45; bus. mgr. J.M. & O.P. Leonard, 1945-50; pub. accountant, Fort Worth, 1950—; officer, dir., owner several corps. and ventures; pres., T.O.L. Oil Co., 1950—, S.W. Investment & Devel. Co., 1964—. C.P.A., Tex. Mem. Nat. Assn. Accountants (chpt. pres. 1948-49), Am. Inst. C.P.A.'s, Am. Accounting Assn., Stuart Cameron McLeod Soc., Tex. Soc. C.P.A.'s (Ft. Worth chpt.). Episcopalian. Mason (32 deg., Shriner). Office: 1102 Oil and Gas Bldg Fort Worth TX 76102

PALS, CLARENCE HERMAN, assn. exec.; b. Meservey, Ia., July 10, 1907; s. Herman K. and Mintie (Rozeboom) P.; student Ia. State Tchrs. Coll., 1925; D.V.M., Ia. State U., 1932; m. Florence C. Cogswell, June 30, 1931; children—Calvan Herman, Helen Ruth (Mrs. William F. Kingsbury). Practice gen. vet. medicine, Thornton, Ia., 1932; with meat inspection div. U.S. Dept. Agr., Chgo., 1932-34, Washington, 1944-65, dir. U.S. Meat Inspection Service, 1960-65; cons. meat-packing industry, 1966—; exec. v.p. Nat. Assn. Fed. Veterinarians, Washington, 1969—. Mem. Ednl. Commn. for Fgn. Vet. Grads., 1971—. Past chmn. Alexandria (Va.) dist. Boy Scouts Am., chmn. Alexandria dist. Eagle Bds. Rev., 1960—. Recipient Silver Beaver award Boy Scouts Am., 1957, Superior Service award U.S. Dept. Agr., 1955; named to Academie Veterinaire de France, 1964. Mem. World Assn. Vet. Food Hygienists (v.p. 1955-60, pres. 1960-67), Am. Vet. Med. Assn., U.S. Animal Health Assn., Orgn. Profl. Employees U.S. Dept. Agr., Nat. Assn. Fed. Veterinarians, Farm House frat., Phi Zeta. Methodist (lay leader). Mason (32 deg.). Editor The Fed. Veterinarian, 1968—. Home: 2338 S Ode St Arlington VA 22202 Office: National Association of Federal Veterinarians 1522 K St NW Washington DC 20005

PAMPE, WILLIAM RILEY, educator; b. Parkersburg, Ill., Dec. 5, 1923; s. Carl Ernst and Zella Marie (Carrico) P.; A.B., U. Ill., 1947, M.S., 1948; Ph.D. (Shell Oil Co. fellow), U. Neb., 1966; m. Jewell Doris Pruitt, Apr. 15, 1949; children—Allen James, Eugene David. Exploration geologist Pure Oil Co., Ardmore, Okla., 1948-50, dist. geologist, 1950-58, staff geologist, 1958-60, evaluation geologist, 1960-61; asst. prof. geology dept. Lamar U., Beaumont, Tex., 1966-69, asso. prof., 1969—. Served with AUS, 1943-46. Decorated Bronze Star medal. Mem. Paleontol. Soc., Nat. Assn. Geology Tchrs., Tex. Assn. Coll. Tchrs., Tex. Acad. Sci., Soc. Econ. Paleontologists Mineralogists. Mason. Home: 1020 Howell St Beaumont TX 77706 Office: Geology Dept Lamar U Beaumont TX 77710

PAN, CHAI-FU, educator; b. Loshon, Szechwan, China, Sept. 8, 1936; s. I-chen and Shao-tseng (Shih) P.; B.S., Nat. Taiwan U., 1955; Ph.D., U. Kan., 1966; m. Maria Shih, Aug. 18, 1962; children—Lawrence Shou-pung, Mariette Shou-jung. Came to U.S., 1960. Asso. prof. phys. chemistry Ala. State U., Montgomery, 1966-71, prof., 1971—. Fellow Am. Inst. Chemists; mem. Am. Chem. Soc., A.A.A.S., Phi Lambda Upsilon. Home: 2420 Wentworth Dr Montgomery AL 36106

PAN, POH-HSI, geophysicist; b. Hangchow, China, July 15, 1922; s. Mien and Lin (Ling) P.; came to U.S., 1957, naturalized, 1972; B.S. in Mech. Engring., Chekiang U. (China), 1944; M.S. (fellow), Colo. Sch. Mines, 1963; Ph.D. (fellow), Rice U., 1969; m. Yi-Yin Pao, Oct. 30, 1955; children—Wanda, Golden. Seismic and gravity party chief Chinese Petroleum Corp., Taiwan, 1954-59, chief geophysicist, 1959-60; sr. geophysicist Mobil Oil Corp., Dallas, 1963—. Vis. prof. Chengkung U., Taiwan, 1958-60. Mem. Soc. Exploration Geophysicists, Sigma Xi. Home: 12119 Cox Lane Dallas TX 75234 Office: PO Box 900 Dallas TX 75221

PANAK, JOHN JESSE, research engr.; b. Hayden, Colo., Mar. 14, 1937; s. John and Alta May (Beezley) P.; B.S. in Civil Engring., U. Colo., 1958; M.S. in Civil Engring., U. Tex., 1968; m. Carolyn Ann Konz, Aug. 30, 1958; children—Mary, Jeffrey, David, Kathy. Jr. civil engr. Cal. Div. Hwys., Bishop, 1958-61; engr. III, Tex. Hwy. Dept., Austin, 1961-65, supervising design engr. IV, 1972—, research engr. asso. IV U. Tex. Center for Hwy. Research, Austin, 1965-72. Cons. prin. Austin Research Engrs., Inc., 1967-73. Registered profl. engr., Tex. Mem. Am. Soc. C.E., Tex. Soc. Profl. Engrs., Am. Concrete Inst., Sigma Xi, Chi Epsilon. Home: 6008 Shoal Creek Austin TX 78757

Office: Tex Hwy Dept Bridge Div 11th and Brazos Sts Austin TX 78701

PANETTA, CHARLES ANTHONY, educator; b. Albany, N.Y., Sept. 12, 1932; s. Dominic and Mary (Morealle) P.; B.S., Manhattan Coll., 1954; Ph.D., Rensselaer Poly. Inst., 1960; m. Alicia Petruska, Aug. 22, 1959; children—Lawrence Michael, John Carl. Sr. chemist Bristol Labs., Syracuse, 1960-64, project supr., 1964-65; research asso. Mass. Inst. Tech., Boston, 1965-67; prof. chemistry U. Miss., University, 1967—. Grantee Research Corp., 1968-70, NIH, 1968-72, NSF, 1968—. Mem. Am. Chem. Soc., Sigma Xi. Patentee antibiotic versapen. Home: 218 Colonial Rd Oxford MS 38655 Office: Dept Chemistry U Miss University MS 38677

PANGLE, CURTIS GLEN, constrn. engr.; b. Gorman, Tex., Oct. 12, 1929; s. Jobie N. and Neacy E. (Burleson) P.; B.S.C.E., U. Ark., 1959; m. Anita Gonzalez, Oct. 14, 1951; children—Carolyn J., Curtis A., Mark A., Margaret Ruth. Operating engr. contractors, 1948-52, with Ozark Dam Contractors, Bull Shoals, Ark., 1948-50, Kaiser Constrn. Co., Mill City, Ore., 1950-51, Guy H. James Constrn. Co., Oklahoma City, 1951, Falcon (Tex.) Dam Constrn. Co., 1951-52; dist. engr. Ark. Hwy. Dept., Harrison, 1959—. Served with USMCR, 1952-54. Registered profl. engr., Ark. Mem. Nat., Ark. socs. profl. engrs. Elk. Home: 514 N Liberty St Harrison AR 72601 Office: PO Box 610 Harrison AR 72601

PANKEY, FRANK LAWSON, ch. assn. ofcl.; b. Pamplin, Va., Jan. 29, 1925; s. Everette Leonard and Anne Powell (Hunt) P.; B.A., U. Richmond, 1948, D.D., 1971; M.Div., So. Bapt. Theol. Sem., 1951; postgrad. Adult Edn. Inst. Ind. U., 1965, Presbyn. Sch. Christian Edn., 1969; m. Mary Alpha Rudasill, Aug. 19, 1950; children—David, Thomas, Susan, Elizabeth. Ordained to ministry So. Bapt. Ch., 1951; pastor Chesterfield and Skinquarter Chs., Moseley, Va., 1951-54; pastor Azalea Bapt. Ch., Norfolk, Va., 1955-64; asso. sec. tng. union dept. Va. Bapt. Gen. Bd., Richmond, 1965-67, acting sec., 1968-69; sec. dept. teaching and tng. Va. Bapt. Gen. Bd., 1970—. Dir. Sch. Christian Edn., Norfolk, 1958-62; pres. Norfolk Bapt. Pastors Conf., 1960-61. Mem. Va. Bapt. Religious Edn. Assn., U. Richmond Alumni Assn. (pres. luncheon 1958), Va. Alumni Group of So. Bapt. Theol. Sem. (sec. 1962), Va. Bapt. Hist. Soc. Home: 2916 Vesper Rd Richmond VA 23225 Office: PO Box 8568 Richmond VA 23226

PANKEY, GEORGE ATKINSON, educator, physician; b. Shreveport, La., Aug. 11, 1933; s. George Edward and Annabel (Atkinson) P.; student La. Poly. Inst., 1950-51; B.S., Tulane U., 1954, M.D., 1957; M.S., U. Minn., 1961; m. Patricia Ann Carreras, Sept. 22, 1972; children—Susan Margaret, Stephen Charles, Laura Atkinson. Intern, U. Minn. Hosps., 1957-58, resident internal medicine, 1958-60, Mpls. VA Hosp., Mpls. Gen. Hosp., 1960-61; practice medicine, New Orleans, 1961—; partner Ochsner Clinic, New Orleans, 1968—; asst. vis. physician Charity Hosp. La., New Orleans, 1961-62, vis. physician, 1962—; cons. infectious diseases Ochsner Clinic and Found. Hosp., New Orleans, 1963—; instr. dept. medicine Div. Infectious Diseases Tulane U. Sch. Medicine, New Orleans, 1961-63, clin. instr., 1963-65; clin. asst. prof. medicine, 1965-68, clin. asso. prof., 1968-73, clin. prof., 1973—; clin. asso. prof. dept. oral diagnosis, medicine, radiology La. State U. Sch. Dentistry, New Orleans, 1970—. Dir. Century Nat. Bank, New Orleans. Pres. New Orleans Young Republican Club, 1969-71. Adv. bd. Angie Nall Sch. Hosp., Beaumont, Tex.; trustee Nall Found. for Children, Beaumont. Recipient certificate merit Am. Acad. Gen. Practice, 1969, 70; certificate of award So. Med. Assn., 1970. Diplomate Am. Bd. Internal Medicine. Fellow A.C.P., Am. Coll. Preventive Medicine; mem. A.A.A.S., Am. Assn. Contamination Control (chpt. pres. 1968-70), Am. Fedn. Clin. Research, Am. Heart Assn., Am., So. med. assns., Am. Soc. Internal Medicine (del. ann. meeting 1971-72), Am. Soc. Microbiology, Am. Thoracic Soc., Am. Venereal Disease Assn., La. Heart Assn., La. Soc. Internal Medicine (pres. 1972-73), La. Med. Soc., La. Thoracic Soc. (chmn. program com. 1968), Musser Burch Soc., Orleans Parish Med. Soc., N.Y. Acad. Scis., Pan Am. Med. Assn. (diplomate mem. sect. internal medicine 1971), Internat. Oceanographic Found., Am. Mus. Natural Hist., Smithsonian Instn. Mason (32 deg., Shriner). Author: A Manual of Antimicrobial Therapy, 1969. Contbr. numerous articles to profl. jours. Bd. editors Patient Care, 1969—. Home: 4019 Alberta St Metairie LA 70001 Office: Ochsner Clinic 1514 Jefferson Hwy New Orleans LA 70121

PANKEY, GEORGE EDWARD, educator; b. Charlotte Court House, Va., Dec. 2, 1903; s. John Wesley and Cora Smith (Daniel) P.; B.A., U. Richmond, 1926; M.A., U. N.C., 1927; m. Annabel Atkinson, Mar. 6, 1931; 1 son, George Atkinson. Mem. faculty Ogden Coll. and Western Ky. State Tchrs. Coll., 1927-28, La. Poly. Inst., 1928-43; with land dept. Gulf Oil Corp., 1944-46; currently in research work. Mem. Huguenot Soc., S.A.R., Sigma Tau Delta. Baptist. Mason. Author: John Pankey of Manakin Town, Virginia and His Descendants, Vol. I, 1969, Vol. II, 1972; co-author: Five Thousand Useful Words, 1936. Address: PO Box 84 Ruston LA 71270

PANKEY, GEORGE STEPHEN, dentist; b. Durham, N.C., Dec. 3, 1922; s. Edwin Wilburn and Julia (Bender) P.; A.B., U. N.C., 1948; D.D.S., Emory U., 1954; m. Christina R. Curry, Jan. 17, 1959 (div. Feb. 1967); children—Julia Gay, Crista Merry; m. 2d, Diane Joy Flaim, Oct. 14, 1967; adopted children—Laura Jean, Julia Ann, George Stephen. Practice dentistry, Winter Garden, Fla., 1954-58, North Miami Beach, Fla., 1958-59, St. Cloud, Fla., 1959—; dir. Fla. United Investment, Inc. Served with AUS, 1943-46; ETO. Mem. Am. Dental Assn., Fla. State, Central Dist. dental socs., V.F.W., St. Cloud C. of C. (pres. 1961-62), Sigma Chi. Republican. Episcopalian. Mason (worshipful master 1965, Shriner), Rotarian (pres. 1962-63). Home: Pine Lake Estates St Cloud FL 32769 Office: 1216 10th St St Cloud FL 32769

PANKRATZ, HOWARD JOHN, petroleum co. exec.; b. Bristol, Conn., Mar. 10, 1913; s. Wilhelm and Amelia (Potz) P.; B.S. in Civil Engring., U. Kan., 1935; m. Dorothea Sanders, May 29, 1938; children—Howard John, Mary (Mrs. Micheal Nichols). Asst. instr. U. Kan., 1934-35; with H.H. Staley, Topeka, 1936; with Phillips Petroleum Co., Bartlesville, Okla., 1936—, various positions in design, constrn. petroleum, petrochem., plastic, rubber, fertilizer and fiber plants, U.S. and abroad, 1954-60, sr. project mgr., 1963—. Registered profl. engr., Okla. Mem. Am. Soc. M.E., Tau Beta Pi, Sigma Tau. Republican. Lutheran. Kiwanian, Elk. Patentee in field. Home: 3424 Willowood Dr Bartlesville OK 74003 Office: Phillips Petroleum Phillips Bldg Bartlesville OK 74004

PANNELL, CHARLES ADAM, SR., judge; b. Eton, Ga., June 19, 1911; s. Thomas Asbury, Sr. and Ila Catherine (Allen) P.; student Young Harris Coll., 1928-30, Mercer U. Law Sch., 1930-31, 35-36; LL.B., U. Ga., 1937; m. Ruth Ann Loughridge, Dec. 24, 1939; children—Charles Adam, James L., William A. Admitted to Ga. bar, 1937; tchr. history and math. pub. schs. Murray County (Ga.), 1931-35; practiced law, Chatsworth, Ga., 1937-63, city atty., 1942-50, county atty. Murray County, 1944-50, 58-60; judge Ga. Ct. Appeals, Atlanta, 1963—. Mayor, Eton, Ga., 1933-35; mem. Ga. Ho. of Reps., 1939-46, 48-50, 60-62; mem. Ga. Senate, 1946-48, 58-60, 63, floor leader, 1963; mem. Ga. Pardon and Parole Bd., 1950-55, chmn., 1953-55. Mem. Cherokee Bar Assn. (pres. 1958), Young Harris Coll. Alumni Assn. (pres. 1970-72), Sigma Delta Kappa. Democrat. Methodist. Mason (Shriner), Odd Fellow, Lion (pres. Chatsworth 1960). Club: Atlanta Athletic. Home: 433 Chateau Dr Atlanta GA 30305 Office: 420 Capitol Square Atlanta GA 30324

PANNIER, ROBERT ANDREW, JR., assn. exec.; b. Pitts., Sept. 15, 1942; s. Robert Andrew and Dorothy Elisabeth (Whyte) P.; B.S., U. Pitts., 1962; postgrad. Cornell U., 1962-65; m. Nancy Lynn Gibbs, Feb. 5, 1965; children—Sarah Whyte, Hope Stratton. Asst. prof. philosophy U. Tenn., Knoxville, 1965-67, Elmira (N.Y.) Coll., 1967-70; cons., dir. devel. Ross MacAskill Assos., Washington, 1971-72; exec. dir. Nat. Inst. Real Estate, McLean, Va., 1972—. Research grantee Coll. Center of Finger Lakes, 1968-69. Mem. Nat. Inst. of Real Estate (v.p. 1971—, dir. 1971—), Am. Assn. U. Profs., Assn. for Symbolic Logic, Va. Assn. Realtors, No. Va. Bd. Realtors, Common Cause. Contbr. articles to various publs. Home: 1215 N Dinwiddie St Arlington VA 22205 Office: 6825 Redmond Dr McLean VA 22101

PANTON, RONALD LEE, educator; b. Neodesha, Kan., Feb. 14, 1933; s. Charles Wilson and Catheryne Mae (McDowell) P.; A.B. in Math., Wichita State U., 1956, B.S. in Engring., 1956; M.S., U. Wis., 1962; Ph.D., U. Cal. at Berkeley, 1966; m. Ruth Elaine Gulbrandsen, Aug. 6, 1960; children—William, Theodore, Henry. Engr., N. Am. Aviation, Los Angeles, 1956-58; asst. prof. Okla. State U., Stillwater, 1966-69, asso. prof., 1969-71; asso. prof. dept. mech. engring. U. Tex., Austin, 1971—. Served to 1st lt. USAF, 1958-60. Recipient several govt. research grants. Registered profl. engr., Tex. Mem. Am. Soc. M.E., Am. Inst. Aero. Scis., Combustion Inst., Am. Assn. U. Profs., Sigma Xi. Contbr. articles to profl. jours. Home: 5901 Overlook St Austin TX 78731

PANYAN, MARION VEENEMAN (MRS. STEVE WILLIAM PANYAN JR.), psychologist; b. Louisville, Jan. 8, 1943; d. Gerald Leo and Margaret (Stoll) Veeneman; student Nazareth Coll., Louisville, 1960-61, Loretto Jr. Coll., 1961-64; B.A., Webster Coll., 1965; M.A., So. Ill. U., 1968; m. Steve William Panyan, Sept. 9, 1967; 1 son, Eric Steve. Hosp. improvement program grantee State Home and Tng. Sch., Wheatridge, Colo., 1968, psychologist, 1968-70; cons. Wessex Regional Hosp. Bd., Winchester, Eng., 1972; chief psychologist Lubbock State Sch. (Tex.), 1972—. grantee, 1968. Mem. Am. Psychol. Assn., Am. Assn. Mental Deficiency, Lubbock Assn. Psychologists. Clubs: Texas Tech Women's (Lubbock), Lubbock Tennis Assn. Home: 2213 16th St Lubbock TX 79401 Office: Dept Psychology Lubbock State Sch North University and Loop 289 Lubbock TX 79417

PAPKA, RAYMOND EDWARD, educator; b. Thermopolis, Wyo., July 11, 1945; s. Alvin Francis and Catherine Lucille (Van Epps) P.; B.S., U. Wyo., 1967; Ph.D., Tulane U., 1971; m. Pamela E. Peyton, Feb. 2, 1964; children—Ouita Kristi, Paige Amber. Teaching asst. dept. anatomy Tulane U., New Orleans, 1967-69, research fellow, 1970-71; instr. dept. anatomy, also researcher lab. neurobiology U. P.R., San Juan, 1969-70; asst. prof. dept. anatomy U. Ky., Lexington, 1971—. NIH trainee, 1967-71; research fellow NSF, 1966-67. Mem. Am. Assn. Anatomists, So. Soc. Anatomists, A.A.A.S., Sigma Xi, Alpha Epsilon Delta. Democrat. Roman Catholic. Home: 206 State St Lexington KY 40503

PAPPAS, GUS JOHN, county ofcl.; b. Savannah, Ga., June 11, 1918; s. John and Calliope (Vatsios) P.; B.S., U. Ill., 1956; M.Engring. Adminstrn., George Washington U., 1959; m. Kathryn Mildred Avgerinos, Dec. 28, 1941; children—James, Mary Ellen, William. Elec. estimator Byck Electric Co., Savannah, 1937-40; commd. capt. U.S. Army, 1945; advanced through grades to col. U.S. Air Force, 1963; ret., 1969; with 118th F.A. Regt., 1940-42; officer C.E., 1942-48; civil engr. U.S. Air Force, 1948-69; cons. engr. Vollmer Assos., Washington, 1969-70; housing coordinator Met. Planning Commn., Savannah, Ga., 1970-73; asst. county engr. Chatham County, Ga., 1973—. Pres. bd. dirs. Savannah (Ga.) Housing and Devel. Corp., 1970-71. Dist. commr. Coastal Empire council Boy Scouts Am., 1971—. Mem. adv. bd. Salvation Army. Decorated Legion of Merit, Meritorious Service medal, Army Commendation medal, Air Force Commendation ribbon; recipient Distinctive Service award. Soc. Am. Mil. Engrs., 1967. Registered profl. engr., Vt. Fellow Am. Soc. C.E.; mem. Soc. Am. Mil. Engrs. (pres. chpt. 1961-62, 67-68), Am. Pub. Works Assn., Inst. Municipal Engring., Air Force Assn., Ret. Officers Assn., Ga. Water and Pollution Control Assn., Am. Legion. Mem. Greek Orthodox Ch. Lion. Home: 203 Devonshire Rd Savannah GA 31404 Office: 127 Abercorn St Savannah GA 31401

PAPPAS, LEONA MAUDE, journalist; b. Toledo, Nov. 11, 1921; d. George Avey and Alice J. (Link) Watson; grad. high sch.; m. Christo John Pappas, Feb. 12, 1943 (separated); 1 son, Christo John. With hosp. x-ray lab. Kelly AFB, 1942-44; lab. asst., mil. troop assignments Fort Sam Houston, Tex., 1944-45; editorial reporter Express News Corp. (formerly Express Pub. Co.), San Antonio, 1946—. Mem. Execs. Secs., Inc. (pres. 1965), Am. Women in Radio and TV, Women in Communications. Home: 1414 W Hollywood St San Antonio TX 78201 Office: Av E and 3d St San Antonio TX 78297

PAPPAS, STEVE GEORGE, newspaper editor; b. Charlotte, N.C., Apr. 5, 1921; s. George T. and Jenny (Belios) P.; student La. State U., 1939-42; m. Katharine Kalas, June 12, 1947; 1 son, George. With news, sports depts. Charlotte News, 1945-50; with Daytona Beach (Fla.) News-Jour. Corp., 1950—; mng. editor Daytona Beach News-Jour., 1956—. Pres. Daytona Beach (Fla.) Symphony Soc., 1966-68. Served with USAAF, 1942-45. Mem. A.P. Assn. Fla. (pres. 1964-65). Democrat. Author weekly newspaper column, Purely Personal. Home: 548 N Halifax Dr Ormond Beach FL 32074 Office: 901 6th St Daytona Beach FL 32015

PAPPER, EMANUEL MARTIN, univ. adminstr., anesthesiologist; b. N.Y.C., July 12, 1915; s. Max and Lillian (Weitzner) P.; A.B., Columbia, 1935; M.D., N.Y.U., 1938; Dr. Med. (hon.), Univ. Uppsala (Sweden), 1964, U. Turin (Italy), 1969; m. Julia Fisher, Dec. 21, 1939; children—Barbara Ellen, Richard Nelson. Fellow medicine N.Y.U., 1938-39, fellow physiology, 1940, instr. anesthesiology, 1942-46, asst. prof., 1946-49, asso. prof., 1949; intern Bellevue Hosp., 1939-40, resident anesthesiology, 1940-42; prof. anesthesiology, chmn. dept. Columbia, also dir. anesthesiology service Presbyn. Hosp., 1949-69; dir. anesthesiology, vis. anesthesiologst Francis Delafield Hosp., 1951-69; v.p. med. affairs, dean, prof. anesthesiology, U. Miami, 1969—. Cons. div. med. scis. NRC, 1954-69, Huntington (N.Y.) Hosp., 1949-69; nat. cons. surgeon gen. USAF, 1963-70; mem. surgery study sect. NIH, 1958-62; civilian cons. First Army, USN; prin. cons. Nat. Inst. Gen. Med. Scis., 1965-66, chmn. project com. gen. med. research program, 1966-70; mem. nat. heart council NIH, 1962-66; hon. cons. Royal Prince Alfred Hosp., Sydney Australia; trustee Cedars of Lebanon, Mt. Sinai hosps. (both Miami). Served from 1st lt. to maj., M.C., AUS, 1942-46; chief anesthesiology sect. Torney, Dibble and Walter Reed hosps. Diplomate Am. Bd. Anesthesiology (dir. 1956-65, pres. 1964-65). Fellow Faculty Anesthesiologists Royal Coll. Surgeons, Royal Soc. Medicine; mem. N.Y. Acad. Medicine (1st pres. sect. anesthesiology), Am. Soc. Anesthesiologists (pres. 1967-68), N.Y. State Soc. Anesthesiologists (past pres.), NRC (chmn. com. anesthesia 1962-67), Am. Coll. Anesthesiologists, Am. Soc. Pharmacology and Exptl. Therapeutics, A.M.A., N.Y. Acad. Scis., N.Y. Co. Med. Soc., Am., N.Y. socs. anesthesiologists, A.A.A.S., Am. Assn. Thoracic Surgery, Harvey Soc., Am. Soc. Clin. Investigation, Am. Thoracic Soc., Assn. U. Anesthetists (co-founder, 1st pres.), Pan Am. Med. Assn., Assn. Anaesthetists Gt. Britain and Ireland (corr.), Swedish (hon.), Finnish (hon.), Israeli (hon.), Australian (hon.), N.Y. State (hon.), D.C. (hon.) socs. anesthesiologists, Halsted Soc., Phi Beta Kappa, Sigma Xi, Alpha Omega Alpha. Author sci. papers pub. in various med. jours., 6 textbooks. Home: 200 Ocean Lane Dr Key Biscayne FL 33149 Office: PO Box 520875 Biscayne Annex Miami FL 33152

PAPUCHIS, CHARLES JOHN, govt. ofcl.; b. Peabody, Mass., Dec. 22, 1925; s. John and Stella (Delivorias) P.; B.S. in Mech. Engring., Northeastern U., 1950; M.S., George Washington U., 1963; m. Stella Karapiperis, Jan. 15, 1950; children—John, Gary. Test engr., engr. Research & Devel. Labs., Ft. Belvoir, Va., 1950-55; asst. project engr. amphibians Bur. Ships, Washington, 1956-58; project engr. amphibians Naval Ship Systems Command, Navy Dept., Washington, 1958-68, dep. asst. project mgr., 1968-71, asst. project mgr., 1971—. Decorated Bronze Star medal. Registered profl. engr., Vt. Mem. Am. Ordnance Assn., Assn. Sr. Engrs. Naval Ship Systems Command, Order of Am. Hellenic Edn. Progressive Assn. Greek Orthodox (pres., trustee). Home: 4 Saddlebrook Ct Silver Spring MD 20906 Office: Naval Ship Systems Command Washington DC 20362

PARADIES, GILBERT ERNST, civil engr.; b. St. Louis, Nov. 21, 1936; s. Herman John and Ida (Ehlers) P.; B.S., U. Pa., 1958; m. Phyllis Ann Furch, June 17, 1961; 1 dau., Kimberly. Sr. process engr. E.I. duPont de Nemours & Co., Inc., Old Hickory, Tenn., 1962-68; asst. resident engr. Anheuser-Busch, Inc., Jacksonville, Fla., 1968—. Cons. engr. Served with Civil Engr. Corps, USNR, 1958-62; now comdr. Res. Recipient Scheu Meml. trophy North Fla. Cruising Club, 1972. Registered profl. engr., Fla. Mem. Am. Inst. Plant Engrs., Master Brewers Assn. Am., Sigma Alpha Epsilon. Republican. Lutheran. Club: North Fla. Cruising (commodore 1974) (Jacksonville). Home: 1230 Carlotte Rd Jacksonville FL 32211 Office: 111 Busch Dr Jacksonville FL 32218

PARADY, WILLIAM HAROLD, ednl. assn. exec.; b. Waterbury, Conn., May 8, 1919; s. William Oliver and Frances (Campbell) P.; B.S., U. Ga., 1940; M.S., U. Fla., 1951; m. Eloise Deas, Sept. 11, 1943. Area supr., farm mechanics specialist Fla. Dept. Edn., Tallahassee, 1947-51; zone mgr., bus. mgmt. mgr. Fla. Ford Tractor Co., Jacksonville, 1952-64; exec. v.p. Growers Equipment Co., Miami, Fla., 1964; owner, mgr. Parady Ford Tractor Co., Griffin, Ga., 1965-66; coordinator, exec. dir. Am. Assn. for Vocational Instructional Materials Agrl. Engring., U. Ga., Athens, 1967—. Served to maj. AUS, 1940-46. Decorated Croix de Guerre, Bronze Star medal. Mem. Am. Soc. Agrl. Engrs. (Fla. sect. chmn. 1964-65, Ga. sect. chmn. 1972-73), Am. Vocational Assn., Am. Soc. Engring. Edn., Phi Kappa Phi, Gamma Sigma Delta. Mem. Christian Ch. (chmn. bd. 1970-73). Rotarian. Author and co-author several textbooks. Contbr. articles to profl. jours. Home: 293 Cedar Creek Dr Athens GA 30601 Office: Am Assn Vocational Instructional Materials Agrl Engring Center U Ga Athens GA 30602

PARCHER, JAMES VERNON, educator; b. Drumright, Okla., July 21, 1920; s. James Augustus and Pearl (Sharp) P.; B.S., Okla. State U., 1941, M.S., 1948; M.A., Harvard, 1967; Ph.D., U. Ark., 1968; m. Martha Hoff Ruckman, Aug. 7, 1943; children—Carol Susan (Mrs. Daniel Homan), James Robert, David Loris, Dee Ellen, Kay Elaine. Maintenance engr. Remington Arms Co., Kings Mills, O., 1941-42; instr. Okla. State U., Stillwater, 1947-48, asst. prof., 1948-54, asso. prof., 1954-67, prof., 1967—, head Sch. Civil Engring., 1969—. Cons. in soil mechanics and founds., 1952—. Served with C.E., AUS, 1942-46, 50-52. Mem. Am. Soc. C.E., Am. Soc. Engring. Edn., Nat., Okla. socs. profl. engrs., Internat. Soc. of Soil Mechanics and Found. Engring., Sigma Xi, Phi Kappa Phi, Sigma Tau, Chi Epsilon. Author: (with R. E. Means) Physical Properties of Soils, 1962; (with R. E. Means) Soil Mechanics and Foundations, 1968. Home: 1024 W Knapp St Stillwater OK 74074

PAREDES, HELEN JEAN, utility co. exec.; b. Detroit, Aug. 9, 1919; d. Celestino P. and Honora (Waters) Paredes; B.A. in Econs., Berea Coll., 1941. Service rep. Mich. Bell & Telegraph Co., Detroit, 1941-42; service rep. So. Bell Tel. & Tel. Co., Miami, Fla., 1942-46, coach, 1946-47, unit supr., 1947-56, recruiting supr., 1956-65, employee relations supr., 1965—. Mem. Task Group on Rent control for Civil Def.; mem., com. chmn. Fla. Gov.'s Status of Women Commn. Mem. Bus. and Profl. Womens Club (state pres. 1963-64, chpt. pres. 1956-57, dist. dir. 1960-61), Personnel Assn. Greater Miami (sec. 1960-61), Am. Personnel and Guidance Assn., Am. Soc. Personnel Adminstrn., Miami C. of C. Address: PO Box 1471 Miami FL 33132

PARHAM, CLARENCE WILLIAM, III, food co. exec.; b. West Palm Beach, Fla., Dec. 20, 1933; s. Clarence William, Jr. and Lucille (Schroeder) P.; B.S. in Chem. Engring., U. Fla., 1960; postgrad., U. Dallas, 1970—; m. Emily Ann Durrance, July 2, 1960; children—Laurie Ann, Clarence William IV, Heather Lynn. Wage-job study engr. Proctor & Gamble, Macon, Ga., 1960-62; with Superior Foods, Inc., Dallas, 1962—, exec. v.p., 1971—, also dir. Served with AUS, 1956-58. Mem. Sigma Iota Epsilon. Presbyn. Toastmaster (adminstrv. v.p. 1972). Home: 2909 Coronado St Irving TX 75062 Office: 9001 Chancellor Row Dallas TX 75247

PARHAM, DONALD ALBERT, educator; b. Atoka, Okla., Apr. 3, 1930; s. Carl Albert and Louella (Mason) P.; student Eastern State Coll., Okla., 1948-50; B.S., Southeastern Okla. State Coll., 1952; M.S., Okla. State U., 1955; Ed.D., George Peabody Coll., 1959; m. Kay Baker, Dec. 26, 1954; children—David William, Brent Donald, Warren Gene. Asst. prof. phys. edn. So. Ark. State Coll., 1956-59; prof., chmn. dept. phys. edn., baseball coach Southeastern Okla. State Coll., Durant, 1959—, dir. athletics, 1970—. Chmn. Durant City Planning Commn., 1964—. Served with AUS 1952-54. Lion (past pres.). Home: 1221 Dixon St Durant OK 74701

PARHAM, GUY HENRY, JR., ret. educator; b. Knoxville, Tenn., Oct. 4, 1913; s. Guy Henry and Rose (Morrison) P.; B.S., U. Cin., 1939; m. Dorothy Duggan, Oct. 11, 1939; 1 son, Guy Henry III. Faculty, U. Tenn., Knoxville, 1941-43, 46—, prof., 1947-74; individual practice architecture, Fla., Tenn., 1945-46; lectr. safe boating Coast Guard Aux.; pres. Par-D Navigational Co., Knoxville, 1965—. Served with USAAF, 1943-45. Mem. U.S. Naval Inst., Inst. Navigation, Sigma Phi Epsilon, Omicron Delta Kappa. Author: Celestial Navigation, 1964; Oceanic Navigation, 1965; Map and Chart Reading, 1966; Star Identification, 1966; Advanced Celestial Navigation, 1967; Graphical Analysis of Navigation, 1969. Designer navigational computers. Home: 241 Hawthorne Av Knoxville TN 37920 Office: PO Box 2012 Knoxville TN 37901

PARHAM, ROY LEE, JR., environmental engr.; b. Tampa, Fla., Oct. 15, 1926; s. Roy Lee and Arta (Hendricks) P.; B.C.E., U. Fla., 1950; m. Mary Jane Blair, Dec. 22, 1951; children—Janet Irene, Susan Lee, Bonnie Josephine. Design engr. TVA, Knoxville, Tenn., 1950-51; asst. san. engr. N.Y. State Dept. Health, Albany, 1951-54; san. engr.

Hillsborough County Health Dept., Tampa, 1954-55; chief san. engr. Watson & Co., Tampa, 1955-66; chief design engr. Coastal Engring. Co., Brooksville, Fla., 1966; dir. Environmental Engr. Div., Hillsborough County Health Dept., Tampa, Fla., 1966-72; head san. dept. Diaz, Seckinger & Assos., Inc., Tampa, 1972-73; chief engr. Tomasino & Assos., Inc., Temple Terrace, Fla., 1973—. Served with AUS, 1945-46. Mem. Am. Soc. C.E., Am. Acad. Environmental Engrs., Sigma Tau. Home: 2112 W Hiawatha St Tampa FL 33604 Office: 234 Bullard Pkwy Temple Terrace FL 33617

PARHAM, RUBY INEZ M. (MRS. JEWELL A. PARHAM), educator, lodge exec.; b. Tamaha, Okla., Nov. 4, 1914; d. Ola T. and Bursha Bell (Culver) Myers; B.S. in Edn., Northeastern State Coll., 1940, M. Teaching, 1955; m. Rufus K. McCollum, Dec. 31, 1937 (dec. Oct. 1966); m. 2d, Jewell A. Parham, June 10, 1973; stepchildren—Bill, Ann (Mrs. Jim Garrett), Donal, Garry. Tchr. rural schs., Haskell County, Stigler, Okla., 1934-38, Adair County, Stillwell, Okla., 1946-50, Cherokee County, Tahlequah, Okla., 1939-46, 50-66; tchr. Westville (Okla.) Jr. High Sch., 1966-68, Westville High Sch., 1968—. Mem. Nat., Okla. edn. assns., Am. Legion Aux., Cherokee County 4-H Club Leaders (sec. 1964-66), Night Circle Womens Missionary Union (sec., 1965-66, pres., chmn. circle), Northeastern State Coll. Alumni Assn. (life), Kappa Kappa Iota (royal high lady Tahlequah 1953-55, exec. bd. Zeta conclave), Delta Kappa Gamma. Republican. Baptist (asso. supt., sec. beginners dept. Sunday sch., supt. various depts.). Rebekah (noble grand 1959-60, jr. noble grand 1960-61, lodge dep. 1961-63). Home: 215 S College St Tahlequah OK 74464 Office: Westville High Sch Westville OK 74965

PARHAM, WILLIAM HAROLD, assn. exec.; b. Jacksonville, Fla., June 5, 1924; s. J.R. and Elizabeth (Rhodes) P.; student U. Fla., 1946-48; A.B., John B. Stetson U., 1949; grad. Armed Forces Information Sch., 1951; D.Health Adminstrn. (hon.), U. Fla., 1974; m. Mary L. Copeland, Sept. 8, 1950; children—Mary, William Harold. Supr. pub. relations Fla. Med. Assn., Inc., Jacksonville, 1949-53, asso. mng. dir., 1953-58, exec. dir., 1958-69, exec. v.p., 1969—; exec. v.p. Fla. Med. Found., Inc., 1958—, INUTCODES, Inc., 1966—; pres. FLAMEDCO, Inc., Jacksonville, 1972—; chmn. bd. Harlan-Med, Inc., 1972—; sec.-treas. Alpendorf, Linville, N.C., 1973—; profl. assn. cons. Harlan Inc. Fla., 1973—; dir. Southeast First Bank Jacksonville. Sec., Fla. Gov.'s Citizens Med. Com. Health, 1958-58, Gov.'s Steering Com. Health, 1967-70. Bd. dirs. Fla. Regional Med. Program, Inc., 1968-71, sec., 1968-71, treas., 1971. Served with AUS, 1943-46, 51-52. Mem. Am. Assn. Med. Soc. Execs. (pres. 1968-69), Profl. Conv. Mgmt. Assn. (dir. 1968-71), So. Med. Assn. (asso.), A.M.A. (affiliate), Am., Fla. socs. assn. execs., Ye Mystic Revellers. Methodist. Clubs: Fla. Yacht; University (Jacksonville). Home: 3946 McGirts Blvd Jacksonville FL 32210 Office: Fla Med Assn PO Box 2411 Jacksonville FL 32202

PARIS, CHARLES HENRY, physician; b. Memphis, Jan. 20, 1942; s. Charles Henry and Volla (Deen) Paris; B.S., Middle Tenn. State U., 1963; M.D., U. Tenn., 1967; m. Martha Virginia Hill, Dec. 11, 1965; children—Charles Henry III, Stephen Guy and Elizabeth Leigh (twins). Intern City of Memphis Hosps., 1967-68, resident internal medicine and gastroenterology, 1970-73; practice medicine, specializing in internal medicine and gastroenterology, Ft. Smith, Ark., 1973—; mem. staff St. Edward Mercy Hosp., Sparks Regional Med. Center. Served as lt. M.C., USNR, 1968-70. Home: 7709 Camelot Circle Fort Smith AR 72901 Office: Cooper Clinic Waldron Rd Ellsworth Fort Smith AR 72901

PARIS, THOMAS LEE, govt. ofcl.; b. Macon, Ga., July 2, 1938; s. Cleo Eugene and Ena Louise (Barfield) P.; B. Indsl. Mgmt., Auburn U., 1960; m. Thelma Ollene Davidson, Nov. 24, 1960. Engr., Army Missile Command, Redstone Arsenal, Ala., 1963-68; Pershing engr. research, devel. and testing SAFEGUARD System Command, Huntsville, Ala., 1968-69, chief resident office SAFEGUARD System Evaluation Agy., Huntsville, 1969—. Served with AUS, 1961-63. Decorated Army Commendation medal. Registered profl. engr., Ala. Baptist. Home: 712 Esslinger Rd SE Huntsville AL 35802 Office: SAFEGUARD System Command PO Box 1500 Huntsville AL 35807

PARIS, VINARD LEVAINE, sightseeing co. exec.; b. Alamosa, Colo., Oct. 31, 1910; s. Lewis Absolom and Lydia (Couchman) P.; J.D., George Washington U., 1939; m. Ollie Mae Ivey, Oct. 12, 1940; children—Robert Lewis, John Walter. Founder, pres. White House Sightseeing Corp., Washington, 1947—; pres. Am. Sightseeing Internat., Washington, 1964-65, dir., 1958—. Mem. Washington Bd. Trade, 1947—. Mem. Washington Conv. and Visitors Bur., 1947—. Served with AC, AUS, 1942-45. Mason (Shriner, Jester). Clubs: Capitol Yacht (rear commodore 1972-74) (Washington); Kena Yacht (dir. 1970-73, commodore 1970-71) (Alexandria, Va.). Home: 629 Eye St SW Washington DC 20024 Office: White House Sightseeing Corp 519 6th St NW Washington DC 20001

PARIS, WILLIAM ANDREW, physician; b. Chattanooga, Mar. 20, 1924; s. Charles Thomas and Mary Ellen (O'Gravey) P.; student U. Chattanooga, 1944-45; B.S., U. Tenn., 1950, M.D., 1954; m. Frances Catherine McIsaac, June 2, 1951; children—William Andrew, Cathy, Chuck, Mary Ellen, Chris, Michael, John, David, Stephen. Intern, St. Joseph Infirmary, Atlanta, 1955-56; gen. practice medicine, Atlanta, 1955, Memphis, 1956, Lake Providence, La.,'1957—; mem. staff East Carroll Hosp., chief staff, 1967, 71; pub. health cons., 1960-71; chmn. East Carroll Parish Cancer Soc. Coach, Dixie Youth Baseball, 1960; pres. St. Patrick's Sch. Bd., 1971-72. Served with AUS, 1947-49. Fellow Am. Acad. Family Practice, Royal Soc. Health; mem. La. Acad. Gen. Practice, Assn. Am. Physicians and Surgeons, Soc. Bariatrics, Soc. Acupuncture. Roman Catholic (council 1969—). K.C. Club: Quarterback (v.p. 1967-69) (Lake Providence). Home: Briarfield Terrace Lake Providence LA 71254 Office: 224 N Hood St Lake Providence LA 71254

PARISH, NORMAN RAY, animal physiologist; b. Brady, Tex., Mar. 6, 1931; s. Henry E. and Edna M. (Hubbard) P.; B.S., Tex. A. and M. U., 1954; M.S., U Tenn., 1958; m. Seba A. Sutliff, June 8, 1957 children—Michelle, Elisabeth. Asso. prof. physiology of reprodn. U. Tenn., Oak Ridge, 1958-61; animal physiologist King Ranch, Inc., Kingsville, Tex., 1962—. Mem. governing bd. Agrl. Research Inst., 1972—. Mem. Am. Soc. Animal Sci., Costal Bend Agr. Bus. Council (v.p. 1968-69), Kleberg County C. of C. (chmn. agrl. com. 1971-72). Republican. Episcopalian. Kiwanian. Home: 1620 Santa Maria Kingsville TX 78363 Office: King Ranch Inc Kingsville TX 78363

PARISH, OVERTON L., JR., lawyer; b. Ballinger, Tex., Sept. 14, 1924; s. Overton L. and Lillie E. (Murphy) P.; LL.B., U. Tex., 1949; m. Martha Jo Reese, Oct. 31, 1942; children—Pamela Jo (Mrs. Wendell Underwood), Overton L., III. Admitted to Tex. bar, 1949; mem. firm Hathaway & Parish, Attys., Ballinger, Tex., 1949-53; atty. Runnels County Abstract Co., Ballinger, 1949-53, Runnels County, 1955—; pvt. practice law, Ballinger, Tex., 1954—. Dir. First Nat. Bank, Ballinger, Telephone Industries, Inc., Ballinger. Bd. dirs. Ballinger Meml. Hosp.; trustee Ballinger Ind. Sch. Dist., 1952-53. Served with AUS, 1943-45. Fellow Am. Coll. Probate Counsel; mem. State Bar Tex., U.S. Supreme Ct. Bar, V.F.W. Democrat. Methodist. Rotarian. Home: 802 Murrell St Ballinger TX 76821 Office: 704 Park Av Ballinger TX 76821

PARISH, RICHARD LEE, educator; b. Kansas City, Mo., May 31, 1945; s. Charles Lee and Ruth (Dunnan) P.; student Akron U., 1965, Kent State U., 1966; B.S., U. Mo., 1967, M.S., 1968, Ph.D., 1970; m. Patricia Ann Erickson, June 2, 1968; children—Christie Lynn, Kerry Ann. Design and testing engr. Hesston Corp. (Kan.), 1967; asso. prof. agrl. engring. U. Ark., Fayetteville, 1969—. Asst. scoutmaster Boy Scouts Am., 1970-73. NSF fellow, 1967-69. Registered profl. engr., Ark. Mem. Am. Soc. Agrl. Engrs., Soc. Automotive Engrs., Am. Soc. Engring. Edn. Home: 1602 Wedington Dr Fayetteville AR 72701

PARK, EDWARD TAISOO, educator; b. Milyang, Korea, July 9, 1929; s. Sang Hum and Bong Jo (Lee) P.; came to U.S., 1960, naturalized, 1972; B.S., Pusan (Korea) U., 1952, M.S., 1957; Ph.D., U. Wash., 1965; m. Julie Youngae Kwon, Mar. 30, 1958; 1 son, Andrew. Instr., Pusan (Korea) U., 1952-60; research asso. U. Wash., Seattle, 1965-66; asst. prof. U. Md., College Park, 1966-67; scientist Woods Hole (Mass.) Oceanographic Instn., 1967-69; asst. prof. dept. marine scis. Tex. A. and M. U., Galveston, 1969-73, asso. prof., 1973—. ICA fellow, 1958-59; NSF grantee, 1967, 68, 69, 70, 71—. Mem. Am. Soc. Zoologists, Ecol. Soc. Am., Am. Soc. Limnology and Oceanography, Marine Biol. Assn. U.K. Home: 2919 Pine St Galveston TX 77550

PARK, FRANCIS DE RONALD, civil engr.; b. Clarksville, Ark., Oct. 9, 1909; s. Merit Samual and Gladys Earl (Clark) P.; B.S., U. Ill., 1933; m. Helen Elisabeth Gates, July 8, 1933; 1 dau., Melinda Jane (Mrs. L.M. Burnett). With U.S. Army C.E., TVA, Tenn., Miss., Ark., White Rivers projects, 1933-46; asso. with John M. Rice, Pitts., 1947-48; water control engr., Dade County, Fla., 1949-60, chief engr. met. area pub. works, 1960-64, dir. water-control and coastal engring. met. area pub. works, 1964—. Bd. dirs. Fla. Shore and Beach Preservation, pres., 1971-72; adv. com. U. Fla. Coastal Engring. Labs., 1973—. Recipient Certificate of Appreciation, Am. Soc. C.E., 1957. Registered profl. engr., Fla., Pa. Fellow Am. Soc. C.E., Fla. Engring. Soc. (engr. of year award 1972); mem. Soc. Am. Mil. Engrs., Nat. Soc. Profl. Engrs., Am. Pub. Works Assn., Soil and Crop Sci. Soc. Fla. Democrat. Methodist. Home: 4141 Raynolds Av Miami FL 33133 Office: Dade County Pub Works Dept Engring Div Justice Bldg 1351 NW 12th St Miami FL 33125

PARK, HARRY NIEL, banker; b. Pulaski, Tenn., Nov. 12, 1934; s. Claude Reed and Hazel Allen (Gregory) P.; student Mercer U., 1958-62, NABAC Sch., U. Wis., 1964-67, N.Y. State Bankers Assn. Banking Sch., U.S. Mil. Acad., 1970; m. Lucy Mary Willis, June 18, 1955; children—Sherry Leigh, Harry Niel, April Leah. Vice pres. 1st Nat. Bank & Trust Co., Macon, Ga., 1957-73; pres. 1st Nat. Bank Thomasville, Ga., 1973—. Served with USNR, 1953-57. Mem. Greater Macon C. of C. (chmn. recreation com. 1973), Am. Legion. Methodist (treas. 1968-73). Kiwanian, Moose. Home: Cardinal Ridge Rd Thomasville GA 31792 Office: PO Box 200 Thomasville GA 31792

PARK, HARRY RAY, educator; b. Columbus, Ga., Aug. 12, 1921; s. Harry Lee and Annie (Seay) P.; B.S. in Econs., Trinity U., 1953; M.A. in Econs., U. Cal. at Berkeley, 1956; postgrad. N.Y.U., 1960—; m. Juanita Martin, Feb. 10, 1943 (div. 1965); children—Harry Ray, Alton Lee; m. 2d, Jean M. Masterson, Mar. 2, 1965; children—Melissa Lorien, Steven Craig. Served to maj. U.S. Air Force, 1940-57, ret.; air transport pilot, USAF, 1942-48; dir. adminstrn., Frankfurt, Germany, 1948-49; staff dir. adminstrn., San Antonio, 1949-51, dir. personnel, 1951-53; asst. dir. operations and tng., Cal., 1953-55; staff dir. operations and tng., Iceland, 1956-57; asso. prof., asst. dept. chmn. aerospace sci. N.Y.U., N.Y.C., 1959-62; supr. tng. div. Job Orientation in Neighborhoods, N.Y.C., 1963-67; asso. dir. Mgmt. Center, Inst. for Bus. and Community Devel., also asst. prof. U. Richmond (Va.), 1967-73; tng. dir. Control Systems div. Robertshaw Controls Co., Richmond, 1973—. Lectr. mgmt. Hofstra U., L.I., N.Y., 1963-64. Mem. Am. Econ. Assn., Am. Personnel and Guidance Assn., Am. Assn. U. Profs., Am. Mgmt. Assn., Am. Soc. Tng. and Devel., Am. Civil Liberties Union, Am. Humanist Assn. Home: 7617 Marilea Rd Richmond VA 23225

PARK, HELEN ELISABETH GATES (MRS. F.D. RONALD PARK), civic worker; b. Tuscola, Ill., Dec. 29, 1909; d. Ross Williams and Ursie (Thayer) Gates; B.S., U. Ill., 1955; M.Ed., U. Miami, Coral Gables, Fla. 1966; m. F.D. Ronald Park, July 8, 1933; 1 dau., Melinda Jane (Mrs. L.M. Burnett). Tchr. Phinney Sch., Tuscola, Ill., 1929-31, 32-34, Comargo (Ill.) Sch., 1931-33, Conlan Sch., Coral Gables, 1959-61; reading specialist Ponce de Leon Jr. High Sch., Coral Gables, 1961-73. Pres. Miami League Women Voters, 1952-53. Founder Dade Reading Found., Miami, Fla., 1962, bd. dirs., 1962—. Mem. N.E.A., Fla. Edn. Assn., Am. Assn. U. Women, Dade County Classroom Tchrs. Assn., D.A.R., Internat., Fla. State, Dade County reading assns., Hort. Study Soc. Fla. (dir.), Am. Bus. Women's Assn. Democrat. Methodist. Home: 4141 Raynolds Av Miami FL 33133 Office: 5001 Augusto Av Coral Gables FL 33146

PARK, ISABELLE SPRINGER (MRS. DAVID EUGENE PARK), club woman; b. El Paso, Tex., Nov. 9, 1895; d. Thomas Hanson and Mary Louise (Rogers) Springer; certificate Ethical Culture Sch., N.Y.C., 1915; m. William J. Millard, June 9, 1917; children—William J., Mrs. Elizabeth Malley; m. 2d, David Eugene Park, Sept. 26, 1931; 1 son, David Eugene. Vice pres., sec. Am. Woman's Club, Buenos Aires, Argentina, 1932-36, v.p., Bogota, Colombia, 1937-38; charter mem. Campo Allegro Library, Caracas, Venezuela, 1939; pres. Am. unit Venezuela Red Cross, Caracas, 1940-42; mem. woman's com. Nat. Found. Poliomyelitis, N.Y.C., 1948-49; mem. bd. Harris County unit Am. Cancer Soc., Houston, 1958-62, sec.; mem. bd. Pan Am. Round Table, Houston, 1959-60; asso. state dir. Pan-Am. Round Tables Tex. Mem. Am. Inst. Mining, Metall. and Petroleum Engrs. Women's Aux. (dir. 1946-52, v.p.), D.A.R. (mem. chpt. bd. 1962-65), Daus. Republic Tex. Home: 1800 N Stanton St El Paso TX 79902

PARK, LELAND MADISON, coll. librarian; b. Alexandria, La., Oct. 21, 1941; s. Arthur Harris and Jane Rebecca (Leland) P.; student McCallie Sch., 1957-59; A.B., Davidson Coll., 1963; M.L.S., Emory U., 1964; postgrad. Simmons Coll., 1968; Adv. M. in L.S., Fla. State U., 1973, Ph.D., 1974. Reference librarian Pub. Library of Charlotte and Mecklenburg County (N.C.), 1964-65; head of reference and student personnel Davidson (N.C.) Coll. Library, 1967-70, asst. dir., 1970—. Vis. lectr. Emory U., summer, 1972; temporary instr. Fla. State U., 1973. Library cons. Mem. Wake County (N.C.) Citizens for Better Libraries; sec. com. library affairs Piedmont U. Center, 1969-70, chmn., 1970-72. Served to capt. AUS, 1965-67; now capt. Res. Mem. Am., Southeastern, N.C., Metrolina (pres. 1969-71), Mecklenburg County (treas. 1969-70) library assns., Soc. of Cin., S.A.R., Davidson Coll., McCallie Sch. alumni assns., Mil. Order World Wars, Jr. C. of C. (chmn. library com. 1965-67), Res. Officers Assn., Sons of Confederate Vets., Beta Phi Mu, Sigma Nu (chpt. alumni comdr. 1967—). Democrat. Episcopalian. Home: 418A Concord Rd PO Box 2201 Davidson NC 28036

PARK, ROBERT BENTON, lawyer; b. Hayward, Okla., Nov. 21, 1924; s. Charles Avery and Talley (Lord) P.; LL.B., Okla. U., 1949; m. Virginia Guest, July 24, 1948; children—Charles Weldon, Jane Alice. Admitted to Okla. bar, 1949, since practiced in Chickasha. Dir. 1st Nat. Bank & Trust Co., First Fed. Savs. & Loan Assn. Spl. justice Ct. Criminal Appeals; spl. commr. Supreme Ct. Bd. dirs. Jane Brooks Sch. for Deaf, Ambucs; bd. regents Okla. Coll. for Women (now Okla. Coll. Liberal Arts); pres. Sooner Council Girl Scouts Am. Served with USNR, 1942-46. Fellow Am. Coll. Probate Counsel; mem. Am., Okla. (v.p. 1974, bd. govs.) bar assns., Am. Judicature Soc., Chickasha C. of C. (dir.), Delta Theta Phi. Home: 6 Circle Dr Chickasha OK 73018 Office: 118 N 4th St Chickasha OK 73018

PARK, SEI-YOUNG, economist; b. Seoul, Korea, July 17, 1923; s. Chang Hyun and Yong In (Shin) P.; B.A., Chosun Christian U., Seoul, Korea, 1950; M.P.A., Harvard, 1955; m. Heisook Hong, Mar. 1, 1951; children—Eunhei Grace, Mihei Frances, Kihong Samuel, Jahei Virginia. Came to U.S., 1954. Sec. to Pres. Syngman Rhee, Republic of Korea, 1950-54; economist Internat. Bank for Reconstruction and Devel., Washington, 1958—. Founding mem. Korean Student YMCA Fedn., 1947—. Bd. dirs. Am. Korean Found., Inc., N.Y.C. Served with Republic of Korea Army, 1950-51. Decorated Bronze Star medal (U.S.). Mem. Am. Econ. Assn. Home: 6030 Sherborn Lane Springfield VA 22152 Office: 1818 H St NW Washington DC 20433

PARK, TRACY SAMUEL, JR., oil co. exec.; b. Beaumont, Tex., Feb. 19, 1922; s. Tracy Samuel and Nelda Mabel (Imhoff) P.; B.S. in Mech. Engring., Rice U., 1943; postgrad U.S. Naval Acad., 1943, U. Houston, 1968; certificate Mgmt. Inst., Northwestern U., 1960; certificate advanced mgmt. program, Harvard, 1966; m. Eila Mallard, Nov. 7, 1946; children—Tracy Samuel, Lawton, John, Ella. Engr., Tenn. Gas Transmission Co., Houston, 1949-52, sr. mech. engr., 1952-57, asst. gen. supt. operations, 1957-62, dir. research, 1967-68; dep. dir. AID, Thailand, 1962-64, dir., 1964-66; v.p., dir. S.E. Asia operations Tenneco Oil Co., Thailand and Indonesia, 1966-67; v.p. Tenneco Inc., Houston, 1968—. Mem. Inst. Internat. Edn.; pres. Vols. for Internat. Tech. Assistance. Served to lt. USNR, 1943-46; PTO. Decorated Purple Heart. Mem. Houston Engring. Sci. Soc., Am. Soc. M.E., Mus. Fine Arts, Rice U. Alumni Assn., Harvard Bus. Club of Houston. Clubs: Houston Racquet, Royal Bangkok, Sports. Patentee heat exchanger apparatus. Home: 728 Ourlane Circle Houston TX 77024 Office: Tenneco Bldg 1010 Milam St Houston TX 77002

PARKER, ALTON BROOKS, JR., pub. relations exec.; b. San Antonio, Sept. 30, 1930; s. Alton Brooks and Hazel Florence (Lyons) P.; B.A., U. of South, Sewanee, 1957; postgrad. U. Tenn., Nashville, 1960-61; m. Anne Smith, July 30, 1959; children—Carrie, Malissa, Christopher, Alexander. With Ellis Shapiro Agy., San Antonio, 1955-56; research asst. U. of South, 1956-57; pub. relations supr. So. Bell Telephone Co., 1958-60; account exec. Robert H. Horsley Assos., 1960-63; v.p., dir. Buford Lewis Co., 1963-68; dir. Tenn. Health Careers Program, Nashville, 1968-73; chief communications-edn. Tenn. Midsouth Regional Med. Program Vanderbilt U., 1973—; pub. relations cons. Nashville Symphony Assn., 1968; guest lectr. U. Tenn. Coll. Communications, Knoxville. Chmn. Met. Clean Up Week, Nashville, 1968. Vice pres. Tenn. Hosp. Edn. and Research Found., Inc.; bd. dirs. Jr. Bd. Printing Industry Nashville, Goodwill Industries of Middle Tenn. Served with USNR, 1951-53. Recipient grant Nat. Urban Coalition, 1972. Mem. Pub. Relations Soc. Am. (dist. chmn. 1969-70, nat. membership chmn. 1970—, nat. chmn.'s citation 1970, pres. Mid-Tenn. chpt. 1967), Nashville Area C. of C., Nashville Advt. Fedn. Club: Nashville City. Home: 217 Lauderdale Rd Nashville TN 37205 Office: 1100 Baker Bldg Nashville TN 37203

PARKER, ARCHIE DAVID, JR., state ofcl.; b. West Monroe, La., Aug. 23, 1929; s. Archie David and Ethel (Crowell) P.; B.A., Northeast La. U., 1956, M.A., 1969; student U. Ark., 1951-53; C.S.W., La. State U., 1959; m. Virginia Mayan Rhodes, Aug. 31, 1954; children—Daniel, Mark, Barbara. Probation officer, Monroe, La., 1959-62; dist. supr. probation Monroe dist. State of La., 1962-70, correctional instn. supt., Baker, La., 1970—. Pres. Parker-Bergeron Distbg. Co., Monroe, 1963-66. Northeast La. U. dir. Students for Morrison, Barnham for Gov., 1955. Served with AUS, 1945-48, 1953-55. Recipient Northeast La. Alumni Assn. President's Service award, 1969; named Optimist of Yr., Greater Monroe chpt., 1970. Mem. Nat. Assn. Social Workers, Nat. Council on Crime and Delinquency, Nat. Council Juvenile Ct. Judges, Nat. Assn. Correctional Supts., La. Conf. Juvenile Correctional Workers, La. Conf. Social Workers (dir. 1969), Northeast La. U. Alumni Assn. (1st v.p. 1967-68). Episcopalian. Mason (Shriner). Optimist (state bldg. chmn. 1972, pres. Tigertown chpt. 1973). Home: 178 Croydon Av Baton Rouge LA 70806 Office: PO Box 116 Baker LA 70714

PARKER, BOYD ARTIS, JR., container co. exec.; b. Salisbury, N.C., May 11, 1927; s. Boyd Artis and Katie Lovena (Alexander) P.; student Clemson Coll., 1943; A.B., Catawba Coll., 1949; m. Martha Naomi Butler, June 6, 1947; children—Karyn Parker (Mrs. William B. Chandler). Recreation dir. Kiwanis Club, Haw River, N.C., 1949-53; plant mgr. Old Dominion Box Co., Burlington, N.C., 1953-62; with Mid State Paper Box Co., Asheboro, N.C., 1962—, v.p., 1968—, also dir.; dir. Caraway Packaging High Point, N.C., Paragon Packaging, Atlanta. Mem. Randolph County Jury Commn., 1967—, Asheboro Housing Authority, 1967—. Pres. Asheboro Meml. Found., 1970—, Served with USNR, 1943-45. Kiwanian. Home: 1027 Westmont Dr Asheboro NC 27203 Office: 277 N Park St Asheboro NC 27203

PARKER, BRUCE COVELL, educator; b. Rockingham, Vt., June 20, 1933; s. Alvin Dexter and Florence Sophia (Covell) P.; B.S., Tufts U., 1955; M.S., Yale, 1957; Ph.D., U. Tex. at Austin, 1960; m. Christine Dora Mary Rush, July 24, 1961; children—Susan Jane, Thomas Harold. Asst. prof. botany U. Cal. at Los Angeles, 1961-65; asso. prof. botany Washington U., St. Louis, 1965-69; prof. botany Va. Poly. Inst., Blacksburg, 1969—. NSF fellow Univ. Coll., London, Eng., 1960-61. Recipient Darbaker prize in Phycology Bot. Soc. Am., 1970. Mem. Phycol. Soc. Am. (pres. 1970, keeper of archives 1972—). Discovered B vitamins in rainwater; research in conducting tissues in giant seaweeds. Home: 841 Hutcheson Dr Blacksburg VA 24060

PARKER, BURTON J., assn. exec.; b. Worthington, Minn., Dec. 19, 1921; s. William McKune and Anna Lois (Graves) P.; student Hamline U., 1940-43; B.A., Emory U., 1949, postgrad., 1949-53; m. Frances Lucille Bennett, Apr. 11, 1945; 1 dau., Dayna Lee. Residence sec. YMCA, Atlanta, 1946-49; exec. sec. Bay View br. YMCA, Milw., 1949-55; met. program and camping sec. YMCA, Richmond, Va., 1955-60, exec. sec. Med. Coll. br., Richmond, 1960-63; gen. dir. YMCA, Jackson, Tenn., 1963—. Del. Nat. Council YMCAs, 1966-69. Vice pres. Mental Health Assn., Jackson, 1965-67; pres. Am. Field Service, Jackson, 1972—. Served with USAAF, 1943-46. Mem. N. Am. Assn. Youth Work Secs. (sec. 1956-59), Va. and Tenn. Assn. Profl. Dirs. (pres. 1960-62, 69-71), Am. Camping Assn. (pres. Va. chpt. 1957-60). Presbyn. Rotarian. Office: YMCA PO Box 3264 Jackson TN 38301

PARKER, CHARLES SCOTT, oilwell servicing co. exec.; b. San Antonio, Aug. 27, 1935; s. Horatio Maxwell and Francis Page (Venable) P.; B.S. in Petroleum Engring., U. Tex., 1958; m. Barbara

Joan Dresslar, Aug. 31, 1956; children—Jeffrey Scott, Gregory Maxwell. Area engr. Texaco, Inc., various locations, Tex., 1958-62; partner Poynor & Parker, Cons. Engrs., Liberty, Tex., 1962-65; v.p., gen. mgr. Bertman Well Service Co., Liberty, 1965-71; v.p. operations Bertman Gas & Oil Corp., Goodale Bertman & Co., Inc., Liberty, 1969-71; partner, v.p., sec., treas. Adkins-Parker Well Service, Inc., Liberty, 1971-72; owner-pres. Parker Well Service, Inc., Liberty, 1973—. Sec. Liberty (Tex.) Zoning and Planning Commn., 1969—; chmn. Liberty Bd. Equalization, 1971. Served to 1st lt. C.E., AUS, 1959-60. Registered profl. engr., Tex. Mem. Liberty C. of C. (dir. 1969—), Am. Inst. Petroleum Engrs., Gulf Coast Assn. Oilwell Servicing Contractors (chmn. 1968-69), Order Alamo. Methodist (bd. stewards 1969-72). Rotarian (dir. 1972). Club: Megnolia Ridge Country (pres. 1969-72) (Liberty, Tex.). Home: 2415 Hollywood St Liberty TX 77575 Office: PO Box 407 Liberty TX 77575

PARKER, CLEOFUS VARREN, JR., educator; b. Houston, Dec. 20, 1937; s. Cleofus Varren and Mabel Joella (Barnes) P.; student Rice U., 1955-59; B.A., Sam Houston State U., 1961, M.S., 1962; Ph.D., U. Tex. at Austin, 1969; m. Doris Marie Young, May 27, 1961; children—John David, Kevin Glenn. Instr. physics Sam Houston State U., Huntsville, Tex., 1962-63; project leader, research scientist Tex. Nuclear Div., Nuclear Chgo., Austin, 1963-69; dept. head, prof. physics Angelo State U., San Angelo, Tex., 1969—. Mem. Am. Assn. Physics Tchrs., Sigma Xi, Sigma Pi Sigma. Baptist. Home: 2802 Briargrove Lane San Angelo TX 76901

PARKER, CLIFFORD DALE, clergyman; b. Miami, Tex., Apr. 30, 1926; s. Franklin Spencer and Minnie Alice (Maddox) P.; B.A., Phillips U., 1950; M.Div., Tex. Christian U., 1955, D. Ministry, 1973; m. Molita Elsie Kennedy, July 27, 1947; children—Paul Rodney, Linda Carol. Ordained to ministry Christian Ch., 1950; minister First Christian Ch., Spearman, Tex., 1950-52, Bethany Christian Ch., Lubbock, 1955-59, 59-62, N. Amarillo Christian Ch., Amarillo, Tex., 1962-67; sr. minister First Christian Ch., Rowlett, Tex., 1969—. Youth dir., dists. 1, 2 and 3, Tex. Christian Chs., 1955-62, dir. adult work, dists. 1 and 3, 1962-65, pres. dist. 3, 1960-61; dir. Dallas Area Assn. Christian Chs., 1970-73. Pres. Palo Duro Civic Assn., Amarillo, 1967-68. Served with AUS, 1945-46. Lion, Kiwanian. Home: 4210 Main St Rowlett TX 75088 Office: 3910 Main St Rowlett TX 75088

PARKER, COLVIN, ret.; b. Oberlin, Kan., Feb. 22, 1899; s. Lester Morris and Ella Josephine (Colvin) P.; A.B., John B. Stetson U., 1921, LL.B., 1919; m. Ruth Louise Bleech, Dec. 25, 1920; children—Wendell Colvin, Mary Marion (Mrs. Charles Amos Holt), Ruth Jean (Mrs. Roderick Colquitt Davis), Frances Pelton (Mrs. George Erskin Lomax). Admitted to Fla. bar, 1919; practice law, St. Cloud, 1922-28; city atty. City of St. Cloud, 1923-25; tchr. high sch., Milton, Fla., 1929-31; ry. mail clk., 1931-65. Sponsor mem. South Fla. Mus.-Bishop Planetarium, Bradenton, Fla., 1971—. City commr. City of St. Cloud, 1925-28, mayor, 1926-28; Republican candidate for Fla. Ho. of Reps., 1926; county chmn. Rep. Party Osceola County, 1925-28; mem. state Rep. Central Com., 1926-28. Served with U.S. Army, 1918-19, 1st lt., inf. AUS, 1941-43. Methodist (elder 1948-60). Mason (32 degree, K.T.). Home: 5405 Ortega Farms Blvd Jacksonville FL 32210

PARKER, DONALD LEON, educator; b. Dexter, Tex., Oct. 12, 1935; s. Jesse Raymond and Gladys (Ring) P.; B.A., N. Tex. State U., 1957, M.S., 1962; postgrad. Tex. A. and M. U., 1964-68, Ph.D., 1968; m. Doris Marie Dickerman, Nov. 4, 1955; children—Michael, Thomas, David, Catherine, Karen, Susan. Instr. physics N. Tex. State U., 1962-64; asst. prof. Lamar State U., 1967-68; vis. asst. prof. Tex. Tech. U., 1968-70; asst. prof. physics St. Mary's U., San Antonio, 1970-73, chmn. dept., 1971-73; asst. prof. Tex. A. and M. U., 1973—; sr. engr. Jet Propulsion Lab., summer 1970. Served with Armed Forces, 1958-61. Robert A. Welch Found. grantee, Tex. Natural Resources Found. grantee for research projects. Mem. Am. Assn. Physics Tchrs. (Tex. sect.), Sigma Xi. Home: 1104 Goode College Station TX 77840

PARKER, EDGAR TURNER, electronic engr.; b. Rossville, Ga., Dec. 29, 1938; s. Edgar Elliott and Ora (Turner) P.; B.S.E.E., U. Tenn., 1962; Ps.D., Coll. Divine Metaphysics, 1971; M.S.E.E., Fla. State Christian Coll., 1972; m. Lula Mae Clift, Apr. 12, 1963; children—Edgar Turner, Fredrick Boyd. Engring. trainee U.S. Army Ballistic Missile Agy., Redstone Arsenal, Ala., 1958-60; engring. trainee NASA, George Catlett Marshall Space Flight Center, Huntsville, Ala., 1960-62, aerospace technologist, 1962-67; with U.S. Army, 1967-73; electronic engr. Missile Comd., Redstone Arsenal, 1967-68, Materiel Comd. Hdqrs., Washington, 1968-70, Computer Systems Comd. Hdqrs., Fort Belvoir, Va., 1970-73; engr. U.S. Naval Coastal Systems Lab., Panama City, Fla., 1973—. Certified Fallout Shelter Analyst; Registered Profl. Engr., Ala. Mem. Eta Kappa Nu, Tau Beta Pi. Mem. Free Will Baptist Ch. (Sunday sch. supt. 1969-70, deacon, trustee, clk. 1970-71). Home: 6104 Boat Race Rd Route 2 Box 202 Panama City FL 32401 Office: Navy Base Bldg 110 Vernon Av Panama City FL 32401

PARKER, FLOYD LEE, banker; b. Rolla, Ark., Oct. 11, 1934; s. Felix Dempsey and Nora Bell (Goodman) P.; student Henderson State Coll.; grad. Sch. Banking South, La. State U., 1964; m. Joyce Beason, June 2, 1956; children—Kyle Beason (dec.), Kristi Lee, Kara Suzanne. With Malvern (Ark.) Nat. Bank, 1953—, now exec. v.p. Pres. Malvern Boys Club, 1961-62, Malvern Little League, 1963-65; co-chmn. Hot Spring County Library Bd., 1970-72; chmn. adv. bd. Ouachita Vocational Tech. Sch., Malvern. Bd. dirs. West Central Ark. Econ. Devel. Dist., 1969-72, chmn. comprehensive planning com., 1970—; bd. dirs. Ouachita Area council Boy Scouts Am., 1970-71. Recipient Hot Spring County Leadership award Malvern C. of C., 1969, Leadership award Ark. Community Devel. Program, 1969. Mem. Ark. Bankers Assn. (chmn. com. 1971-72, pres. jr. bankers sect. 1966-67), Malvern C. of C. (pres. 1969, mem. com. 1969—). Mem. Assembly of God. Kiwanian (pres. 1967—). Home: 1214 Brownwood St Malvern AR 72104 Office: Main and Page Sts Malvern AR 72104

PARKER, GILBERT NORMAN, bank exec.; b. Kaatspan, N.Y., Oct. 19, 1902; s. Abram V. and Sarah (Marshall) P.; student, Hamilton Coll., 1922-23, Columbia, 1925-27, Columbia Grad. Sch. Bus., 1952-53; m. Marjorie Anne Marshall, Nov. 30, 1930; children—Anne, William. Accountant Alaska Airlines, Anchorage, 1927-43; sec., treas. Alaska Airlines, N.Y.C., 1943-46; chmn. bd. Nat. Bank Sarasota, Fla., 1958-72, sr. chmn. bd., 1972—, pres., 1966-69; chmn. bd. Nat. Bank Gulf Gate, Sarasota, 1963-72, pres., 1966-72, sr. chmn. bd., 1972—; 1st regional v.p. S.W. Fla. Banks, Inc., Ft. Myers, 1973—. Vice chmn. Sarasota County Pub. Housing Authority, 1959-69; chmn. Sarasota County Pub. Hosp. Bd., 1963-68, vice chmn., 1967; mem. Sarasota County Pub. Hosp. Bd., 1971-72. Mem. C. of C., U.S. Coast Guard Aux., U.S. Power Squadron. Clubs: Yacht, Field (Sarasota). Home: 894 Freeling Dr Sarasota FL 33581 Office: Nat Bank Sarasota PO Box 5427 Sarasota FL 33579

PARKER, HAROLD TALBOT, educator; b. Cin., Dec. 26, 1907; s. Samuel Chester and Lucile (Jones) P.; Ph.B., U. Chgo., 1928, Ph.D., 1934; postgrad. Cornell U., 1929-30. Instr. history Duke, Durham, N.C., 1939-42, asst. prof., 1945-50, asso. prof., 1950-57, prof., 1957—. Served with USAAF, 1942-45. Mem. French Hist. Studies (pres. 1957), Am. Assn. U. Profs. (pres. Duke chpt. 1939, 60), Phi Beta Kappa (pres. Duke chpt. 1961). Episcopalian. Author: The Cult of Antiquity and the French Revolutionaries, 1937; Three Napoleonic Battles, 1943. Editor: (with Richard Herr) Ideas in History, 1965. Home: 1005 Demerius St Durham NC 27701

PARKER, HARRY JOHN, educator, psychologist; b. Sioux City, Ia., Jan. 18, 1923; A.B., Elmhurst Coll., 1947; M.A., Northwestern U., 1953, Ph.D., 1956, postgrad., 1958; postgrad. Roosevelt U., 1957-58. Counselor, Northwestern U. Counseling Center, Chgo., 1952-56, counseling psychologist, 1956-59, asst. dir., 1957-58, dir., 1958-59; pvt. practice counseling psychologist, Chgo., 1956-59, Okla., 1959-69; prof. edn. U. Okla., 1959-69; dir. manpower planning, regional med. program and Sch. Health Related Professions U. Okla. Med. Center, Oklahoma City, 1967-69, prof. preventive medicine and pub. health, 1966-69, prof. human ecology, 1969; asso. dean Sch. Allied Health Scis., U. Tex. Health Sci. Center, Dallas, 1969—, prof. phys. medicine and rehab., 1969, prof. psychiatry, 1969—, prof. rehab. sci., 1972. Served with AUS, 1943-46. Licensed psychologist, Okla., Tex. Mem. Am., Southwestern, Dallas, Tex. psychol. assns., Am. Soc. Allied Health Professions, Sigma Xi, Phi Delta Phi. Contbr. articles to profl. jours. Home: 3439 Salisbury Dr Dallas TX 75229 Office: U Tex Health Sci Center 5323 Harry Hines Blvd Dallas TX 75235

PARKER, JAMES ROSS, food co. exec.; b. Balt., Jan. 18, 1930; s. Thaddeus Cornelius and Catherine Marie (Ross) P.; B.S. in Commerce, The Citadel, 1952; m. Barbara June Wilson, Aug. 30, 1953;children—Karen, Jeffrey, Thaddeus. With Pepsi-Cola Bottling Co., Tampa, Fla., 1954—, asst. sales mgr., 1958-59, sales mgr., 1959-60, v.p. sales, 1960-61, pres., 1961—; v.p. sec., dir. Pinellas Bottling Co., St. Petersburg, Fla., 1965—; sec., dir. Service Leasing Co., 1971—; pres. P-S Enterprises, Inc., 1968—; dir. Exchange Bank Temple Terrace, Exchange Bank Tampa. Vice pres. Heart Assn., 1968; mem. Taxi Cab Commn., City of Tampa, 1969; mem. exec. com. U. So. Fla. Found., 1970-71. Bd. dirs., chmn. trust com. Jesuit High Sch. Found., 1968—, Holy Name Acad. Found., 1970—; trustee U. Community Hosp., St. Joseph Hosp. Found. Served to 1st lt. AUS, 1952-55. Mem. Tampa C. of C. (bd. govs. 1969-71), Tampa Chamber (mem. com. 1971), Pres.'s Round Table, Nat. Pepsi-Cola Bottlers Assn. (pres. 1973, chmn. com. 1970-71), Young Pres.'s Orgn. Home: 2821 Parkland Blvd Tampa FL 33609 Office: PO Box 17175 Tampa FL 33612

PARKER, JERALD DWAIN, educator; b. Ardmore, Okla., Feb. 24, 1930; s. Leslie and Gertrude (Burch) P.; B.S., Okla. State U., 1955; M.S., 1957; Ph.D., Purdue U., 1961; m. Verna Lee Hastings, Aug. 11, 1952; children—Ann, Leslie, Frank, Tom. Mem. faculty Okla. State U., Stillwater, 1955—, prof. mech. engring., 1966—. Cons. Served with AUS, 1948-52. Mem. Am. Soc. M.E., Pi Tau Sigma. Mem. Ch. of Christ (elder). Author: (with J.H. Boggs, E.F. Blick) Introduction to Fluid Mechanics and Heat Transfer, 1969. Home: Route 1 Stillwater OK 74074

PARKER, JOHN ALBERT, city and regional planner; b. Kentville, N.S., Can., Mar. 27, 1909; s. Percy Nesbitt and Mary Kathleen (Smith) P.; student U. B.C., 1926-27; S.B. in Architecture, Mass. Inst. Tech., 1932, M.Arch., 1934, M. City and Regional Planning, 1946; m. Jane Elizabeth Curtis, Aug. 27, 1932; children—John Curtis, Robert Curtis. Naturalized, 1938. Worked in archtl. offices N.Y.C., Boston, 1932-35; dir. Lowthorpe Sch. Landscape Architecture, 1936-45; head div. planning R.I. Sch. Design, 1945-46; community planner TVA, 1946; head dept. city and regional planning U. N.C., Chapel Hill, 1946-74, research prof. Inst. Research Social Sci., 1946-66. Cons. on planning edn. to Central Mortgage and Housing Corp., Ottawa, Ont., Can., 1949, AID, Chile, 1962, C. Am., 1963; cons. Nat. Capital Planning Commn., 1964, Office of Gov., 1964, Md. Nat. Capital Parks and Planning Commn., 1965. Mem. Chapel Hill Town Planning Bd. 1947-50; vice chmn. State Capital Planning Commn., 1963-65; chmn. fellowship adv. bd. Dept. Housing and Urban Devel., 1968-69. Mem. Am. Inst. Planners (gov. 1953-55, chmn. membership com. 1954-55), A.I.A. (hon. mem. N.C. chpt.), Am. Soc. Planning Ofcls. (dir. 1961-64), Deutsche Akademie fur Statebau and Landesplanung. Sigma Nu. Author: Utilizing University Resources in the Education of Planners-Planning, 1948; A Permanent State Planning Board for North Carolina, 1949; Planning Education in Canada, 1950; The University as an Aid to Local Planning, 1952; co-author: Strategy for Development, 1964. Editor: Urban Research in the South, 1955. Contbr. Urban Growth Dynamics, Roles of the Planner in Urban Development, 1962. Project director Soviet Theory and Practice in City and Regional Planning, 1952-54; Postgrad. Planning Edn. in Chile, 1962. Home: 219 Ransom St Chapel Hill NC 27514

PARKER, JOHN WILLIAM, educator; b. Murfreesboro, N.C., Oct. 16, 1909; s. John Reuben and Brownie G. (Parker) P.; student Wake Forest Coll., 1926-27; B.A. in Edn., U. N.C., 1930, M.A. in Dramatic Art, 1936; m. Darice Lee Jackson, June 14, 1936; 1 son, Scott Jackson. Tchr., Four Oaks (N.C.) High Sch., 1930-31, High Point (N.C.) High Sch., 1931-34; prof. dramatic art U. N.C., Chapel Hill, 1934—; asso. dir. bus. mgr. Carolina Playmakers, 1936-70; dir. Bur. Community Drama, 1946—, Jr. Playmakers, 1938—. Adviser on outdoor drama, 1939; exec. sec. Carolina Dramatic Assn., 1936-70; gen. mgr. Lost Colony, Manteo, N.C., 1948-50; gen. mgr.-dir. Highland Call. Fayetteville, N.C., 1939-40; mem. Historic Murfreesboro Commn., 1968—. Bd. dirs. Meml. Recreation Forest of Eastern N.C. Served to capt. USAAF, 1942-46. Mem. ANTA, Am. Ednl. Theatre Assn., Roanoke Island Hist. Assn., Inst. Outdoor Drama (dir.), Southeastern Theatre Conf. (past exec. sec.). Club: Faculty. Author: (plays) Sleep on Lemuel, 1932; Itching Heel, 1937. Editor: Caroline Stage 1936-40; Adventures in Playmaking, 1968. Home: 1 Brierbridge Lane Chapel Hill NC 27514

PARKER, JOSEPH MAYON, editor; b. Washington, N.C., Oct. 11, 1931; s. James Mayon and Mildred (Poe) P.; student Davidson Coll., 1949-51; B.A., U. N.C., 1953; postgrad. Carnegie Inst. Tech., 1955; m. Lauretta Owen Dyer, Mar. 23, 1957; children—Katherine Suzanne, Joseph Wilbur, James Dyer (dec.). Sec., mgr. comml. printing div. Parker Bros., Inc., Ahoskie, N.C., 1955—, mng. editor, 1961—, chief editorialist, 1963—, gen. mgr., 1971; pres. Roanoke Valley Pub. Co., Inc., 1971; dir. Tar Heel Bank & Trust Co. First Congl. Dist. chmn. Young Democrats, 1966-68. Treas., Chowan Graphic Arts Found. Bd. dirs. Ahoskie Projects, N.C. Civil Liberties Union. Served with AUS, 1953-55. Mem. Eastern N.C. Press Assn. (past pres.), N.C. Press Assn. (dir.), Sigma Phi Epsilon, Pi Sigma Alpha. Methodist. Rotarian. Home: 310 Colony Av Ahoskie NC 27910 Office: 117-19 McGlohon St Ahoskie NC 27910

PARKER, JOSEPHUS DERWARD, limestone co. exec.; b. Elm City, N.C., Nov. 16, 1906; s. Josephus and Elizabeth (Edwards) P.; A.B., U. South, 1928; postgrad. Tulane U., 1928-29, U. N.C., 1929-30, Wake Forest Med. Coll., 1930-31; m. Mary Wright, Jan. 15, 1934 (dec. Dec. 1937); children—Mary Wright (Mrs. Mallory A. Pittman, Jr.), Josephus Derward; m. 2d, Helen Hodges Hackney, Jan. 24, 1940; children—Thomas Hackney, Alton Person, Derward Hodges, Sarah Helen. Founder, chmn. bd. J. D. Parker & Sons, Inc., Elm City, N.C., 1955—, Parker Tree Farms, Inc., 1956—; founder, pres. Invader, Inc., 1961-63; pres., dir. Brady Lumber Co., Inc., 1957-62; v.p., dir. Atlantic Limestone, Inc., Elm City, 1970—; owner, operator Parker Airport, Eagle Springs, N.C., 1940-62. Served to capt. USAAF, 1944-47. Episcopalian. Moose, Lion. Club: Wilson (N.C.) Country. Address: PO Box 405 Elm City NC 27822

PARKER, JULIUS FREDERICK, JR., lawyer; b. Tallahassee, June 24, 1937; s. Julius Frederick and Katy (Gold) P.; student Va. Mil. Inst., 1955-57, Duke, 1957-59; B.A., Fla. State U., 1960; J.D., U. Fla., 1962; m. Marie Estelle Giddings, Aug. 13, 1960; children—Jennifer Marie, Julius Frederick III, Kelly Kathryn. Admitted to Fla. bar, 1963; atty. Madigan, Parker, Gatlin, Truett & Swedmark, Tallahassee, 1963—, partner, 1967—. Chmn. bd. Hammons Asphalt Paving, Inc., 1966—; gen. counsel, dir. Barnett Bank North, 1969—; dir. Seminole Asphalt Refining, Inc., Barnett Bank of Tallahassee. Mem. Fla. Bd. Regents, 1968—; pres. LeMoyne Art Found., 1965-66; mem. Fla. State U. Found., 1969—. Mem. Phi Delta Phi, Phi Kappa Phi. Home: 100 Bellac St Tallahassee FL 32303 Office: 318 N Monroe St Tallahassee FL 32302

PARKER, LEE BRYAN, JR., physician; b. Dermott, Ark., May 10, 1929; s. Lee Bryan and Viola Lee (Rogers) P.; B.S., U. Ark., 1950, M.D., 1954; m. Beverly Edith Brosell, Dec. 23, 1951; children—Susan Leigh, Elizabeth Ann, Steven Lee, Edith Lynn. Intern Crawford Long Hosp., Atlanta, 1954-55; pvt. practice gen. medicine, Dermott, Ark., 1957-59, McGehee, Ark., 1959-67, Fayetteville, Ark., 1967—; mem. staff Washington County Hosp., City Hosp. Dir. dept. continuing edn. Sch. Medicine U. Ark., 1970—; mem. adv. bd. Ark. Regional Med. Program, 1966-70. Served with USAF, 1955-57. Recipient Distinguished Service award McGehee Jr. C. of C., Mem. Ark. Med. Soc. (2d. v.p. 1971-72), Ark. Acad. Gen. Practice (dir. 1961-67). Home: 1138 Glenn Lane Fayetteville AR 72701 Office: 241 W Spring St Fayetteville AR 72701

PARKER, MALCOLM PATTERSON, museum ofcl.; b. Bethpage, Tenn., Aug. 29, 1909; s. James Milton and Ida (Hanna) P.; student U. Middle Tenn., summers 1929-31; m. La Una Durham, July 8, 1937. Mgr. A. and P. food store, Scottsville, Ky., 1937-40, Gallatin, Tenn., 1946-51; mgr. Kroger food store, Nashville, 1953-63; with Nashville Parthenon, 1964—, mus. dir., 1964—. Lectr. coll. groups, women's clubs. Served with USNR, 1943-45. Democrat. Methodist. Home: 2209 Fernwood St Nashville TN 37216 Offie: Centennial Park West End Nashville TN 37203

PARKER, MARY ANN GARDNER (MRS. MILTON LAWRENCE PARKER), city ofcl., civic worker; b. Waco, Tex., Nov. 4, 1916; d. Leslie Breckenridge and Netten (Wilkes) Gardner; student U. Colo., 1934-36, U. Tex., 1937-38; m. Milton Lawrence Parker, May 11, 1939; children—F. Gardner, Madeleine Leslie. Personnel clk. N. Am. Aviation, Waco, Tex., 1943-44; clk., tech. research dept. Tex. Co., N.Y.C., 1944; v.p. Andrews-Parker, Inc., Bryan, Tex., 1958-65; asso. mem. W. M. Sparks, Realtor Co., Bryan, 1963— v.p. M. L. Parker, Inc., 1965—. Sec. Boys' Clubs of Bryan, 1962—; pres. South Tex. Area council Boys' Clubs Am., 1963-64; sec. Bryan Coll. Sta. Real Estate Bd., 1963—; chmn. City of Bryan Parks and Recreation Bd., 1963-65; ann. chmn. Brazos County Clothing Drive; chmn. Tex. Gov.'s Brazos County Com. on Aging, 1965—; organizer, pres. Girls Club Brazos County, 1968-70; vice chmn. Brazos County com. on alcoholism, 1964—; city commr. Bryan (Tex.), 1969-71; mem. bldg. com. Brazos County Ind. Sch. Dist., 1969-71. Bd. dirs. Greater Bryan United Fund, Brazos County Community Council. Mem. Jr. League Waco, U. Tex. Brazos Valley Ex-Student Assn. (pres.), Woman's Civic League Bryan (sec.), Brazos County Council Social Agys., Kappa Kappa Gamma. Roman Catholic. Home: 810 N Rosemary Dr Bryan TX 77801 Office: 4301 Texas Av Bryan TX 77801

PARKER, MARY EVELYN (MRS. W. BRYANT PARKER), state ofcl.; b. Fullerton, La., Nov. 8, 1920; d. Racia E. and Addie (Graham) Dickerson; B.A., Northwestern State Coll., 1941; Dipl. Social Welfare, La. State U., 1943; m. W. Bryant Parker, Oct. 30, 1954 (dec. May 1965); children—Mary Bryant, Ann Graham. Social worker La. Dept. Pub. Welfare, Baton Rouge, 1941-42, chmn. State Bd. Pub. Welfare, 1950-51, commr. pub. welfare, 1956-63; personnel adminstr. U.S. War Dept., Camp Claiborne, La., 1943-47; editor Oakdale (La.) Jour., 1947-48; exec. dir. La. Dept. Commerce and Industry, Baton Rouge, 1948-52; with Mut. of N.Y., 1952-56; commnr. adminstrn. State La., Baton Rouge, 1964-67; treas. State La., 1968—. Chmn. White House Conf. on Children and Youth, 1960; pres. La. Conf. Social Welfare, 1959-61. Nat. Democratic committeewoman, 1948-52. Bd. dirs. Woman's Hosp., Baton Rouge. Baptist. Home: 2768 McCarroll Dr Baton Rouge LA 70809 Office: State Capitol Baton Rouge LA 70804

PARKER, NEWTON BELMONT, economist; b. N.Y.C., Feb. 26, 1907; s. William Belmont and Helen Louise (Newton) P.; grad. Roxbury Latin Sch., 1925; A.B in English cum laude, Harvard, 1930, M.A. in Latin Am. History, 1944, M.A. in Econs., 1946; m. Cary Millholland, Feb. 6, 1954. Tchr. prep. schs., Mass., N.Y., Ariz., 1930-42; economist U.S. Treasury Dept., Washington, 1946-47; economist Internat. Bank Reconstrn. and Devel., Washington, 1947-67, Paraguay, 1952-55, Honduras, 1956-59, Guatemala, 1963-64; economist Inter-Am. Devel. Bank, Washington, 1967-68; editor-researcher Am. U., Washington, 1969—. Mem. Am. Econ. Assn., Assn. Evolutionary Econs., City Tavern Assn. Home: 4870 Reservoir Rd NW Washington DC 20007

PARKER, ORION GLENN, educator; b. Whiteville, Tenn., July 5, 1930; s. Orion and Floice Edna (Vincent) P.; student Memphis State U., 1948-50, 71; B.S., U. Tenn., 1957, M.S., 1964; m. Mary Autrey Armour, Nov. 7, 1957; children—Bernadette Camille, Keith Jerome. Instrument engr. ARO, Inc., Tullahoma, Tenn., 1957-58; engr. Brown Engring. Co. and NASA, Huntsville, Ala., 1958-63; project engr., dept. head Brown Engring. Co., Huntsville, 1964-69; asso. prof., head instrumentation tech. dept. State Tech. Inst. at Memphis, 1969—. Served with USNR, 1951-55. Registered profl. engr., Tenn. Mem. Am. Soc. Engring. Edn., Instrument Soc. Am. (pres. Memphis 1973-74), Tenn., West Tenn. edn. assns., Tenn. Tech. Edn. Council, Am. Vocational Assn., Chi Beta Phi, Tau Beta Phi, Eta Kappa Nu. Republican. Baptist. Moose. Home: 3779 Voltaire Av Memphis TN 38128

PARKER, ROBERT ALLAN RIDLEY, astronaut; b. N.Y.C., Dec. 14, 1936; s. Allan Elwood and Alice (Heywood) P.; A.B., Amherst Coll., 1958; Ph.D., Cal. Inst. Tech., 1962; m. Joan Audrey Capers, June 14, 1958;children—Kimberly Ellen, Brian David Capers. NSF postdoctoral fellow U. Wis., 1962-63, asst. prof., then asso. prof. astronomy, 1963—; astronaut Manned Spacecraft Center, NASA, 1967—. Mem. Am., Royal astron. socs., Phi Beta Kappa, Sigma Xi. Home: 311 Cedar Lane Seabrook TX 77586 Office: Code CB NASA-MSC Houston TX 77058

PARKER, SIDNEY ARCH, elec. engr.; b. Austin, Tex., Mar. 3, 1929; s. Sidney L. and Adelaide (Lane) P.; B.S. in Elec. Engring., Tex. A. and M. U., 1955; m. Jo E. Snider, Dec. 19, 1953; 1 son, Robert Keith. Project engr. Tex. A. and M. Research Found., Tex. A. and M. U., 1954-55; project engr. Bryant Mfg. Co., div. Carrier Corp., 1955-59; mgr. research and devel. for air conditioning compressors Lennox Industries, Inc., Ft. Worth, 1959—. Cons. engr. field of refrigeration. Served with USNR. Mem. Nat. Soc. Profl. Engrs., I.E.E.E., Am. Soc. Heating, Refrigerating and Air Conditioning Engrs. Contbr. articles in field of refrigeration to profl. jours. Patentee in field of refrigeration in U.S. and fgn. countries, in field bldg. constrn. in U.S. Home: 5820 Diamond Oaks Dr S Fort Worth TX 76117 Office: Hwy 121 at Maxine St PO Box 1839 Fort Worth TX 76101

PARKER, SIDNEY GLENN, research chemist; b. Campbell, Tex., Jan. 21, 1925; s. Sidney and Elizabeth (Ingle) P.; B.S., E. Tex. State U., 1946; Ph.D. (univ. fellow), U. Tex., 1951; m. Bette Joyce Davis, Nov. 9, 1968; 1 son, Charles Covey. Research chemist Mobil Oil, Dallas, 1951-53, E.I. du Pont de Nemours & Co., Inc., Aiken, S.C., 1953-57, Tex. Instruments, Dallas, 1957—. USN grantee, 1947-49; U.S. Army grantee, 1949-50; E.I. duPont fellow, 1950-51. Fellow Am. Inst. Chemists; mem. Am. Chem. Soc., Electrochem. Soc., Am. Crystal Growth Assn., Sigma Xi, Phi Lambda Upsilon. Baptist (deacon; tchr. bible class, 1960—). Contbr. articles to profl. jours. Patentee in field. Home: 6550 Highgate Dallas TX 75214 Office: PO Box 5936 Dallas TX 75222

PARKER, WALLACE O'NEIL, pub. co. exec.; b. Silverdale, N.C., Oct. 4, 1931; s. Robert E. Lee and Essie Marie (Holland) P.; B.S., N.C. State Coll., 1959; postgrad. N.C. State U., 1959-60; m. Annie Fay Morton, Oct. 14, 1955; children—Neil, Donna Lynn, Suzanne Leigh. Dir. information and pub. relations N.C. Farm Bur. Fedn., Raleigh, 1960-62; research planner div. community planning N.C. Dept. Conservation and Devel., Raleigh, 1962-65; research dir. Jacksonville (Fla.) Area C. of C., 1965-72; research and marketing dir. Fla. Times-Union/Jacksonville Jour., Fla. Pub. Co., Jacksonville, 1972—. Pres. Arlington br. YMCA, 1973—; founder Jacksonville Area Research Assn., 1966, pres., 1966-68. Bd. dirs. Metro YMCA. Served with AUS, 1952-54. Mem. Am. C. of C. Researchers Assn. (pres. 1971-72), Fla. Crown Council C. of C. (pres. 1967-68). Methodist (pres. men's club 1967-68, chmn. council on ministries 1972-73). Clubs: River, Deerwood (Jacksonville). Home: 3750 Gurley Rd Jacksonville FL 32211 Office: 1 Riverside Av Jacksonville FL 32202

PARKER, WILLIAM DALE, pub. relations exec.; b. Portsmouth, Va., Apr. 13, 1925; s. Otis Drurie and Eva Estelle (Dempsey) P.; student Coll. William and Mary, 1946; grad. Indsl. Engr., Internat. Corr. Schs., 1956; student U. Del., 1959-60, Cal. Western U. 1961-62, U. Cal., 1964; D.Sc., Jame Balmes U., Saltillio, Mex., 1968; Ph.D., Fla. Inst., 1971; m. Frances Ross Jennings, Feb. 2, 1946 (dec.); children—Frances Lea, Elizabeth Dale, Kim Carolyn Jane, Penny Jo Ann, Jacquelyn Susan; m. 2d, Boots Lee Farthing, 1968. Engr., Gen. Motors Corp., Wilmington, Del., 1949-59, asst. dir. salaried personnel pub. relations, 1959-61; engr., lectr. Gen. Dynamics/Astronautics, San Diego, 1961-64; dir. Internat. Inst. Human Relations, La Jolla, Cal., 1964—; aerospace scientist, mgmt. specialist Gemini and Expts. Program Office, Manned Spacecraft Center, NASA, Houston, 1964-67, program specialist Apollo application program, Cape Kennedy, Fla., 1967-69; family and marriage counselor, Titusville, Fla., 1967-69; pres. Service Corps of Retired Execs., 1969-72; chmn. bd. Multiple Services, Inc., Titusville 1969—; dir. franchising Spangler Television, N.Y.C., 1969-73; v.p. Travel Internat., Inc., Titusville, 1970-73. Founder Monroe Park Civil Def. Orgn., 1951; mem. Wilmington council Boy Scouts Am., 1953-55; chmn. Varions Agy. Fund, 1954-60; co-chmn. Del. Dept. Civil Def. TV Shows, 1956-57; mem. Middle Atlantic States Conf. Correction, 1956-60; chmn. Del., Md., Pa. Tri-State Hosp. Com., 1957-58; mem. Wilmington Inner-City Study Commn., 1957-60; chmn. Del. Civil Def. Evacuation Commn., 1958-59, Del. Hwy. Safety Campaign, 1959-60; active P.T.A.; faculty adviser Mensa Coll. Bd. dirs. Boys and Girls Aid Soc. San Diego, 1962-64, Salvation Army. Served with USCGR, World War II. Named Del. Outstanding Young Man of Year, U.S., Wilmington, Jr. chambers commerce, 1957; recipient Silver award Del. Vol. Bur., 1957; ann. awards VA. Jr. Achievement Inc., 1959; speech award U.S. Jr. C. of C., 1960; Gemini award NASA, 1967; Internat. Distinguished Service to Humanity award 1969, Internat. Humanitarian award, 1971, Keys to City, Wilmington, Del., 1959, 61, 72, Titusville, Fla., 1970, Miami, 1973, named Hon. Sheriff of Portsmouth, Va., 1973. Mem. Wilmington Jr. C. of C., Antique Automobile Club Am., Am. Legion (life), Wilmington Indsl. Mgmt. Club, Mensa Internat., Am. Inst. Indsl. Engrs., Monroe Park Civic Assn. (pres. 1952-53), Vols. Speakers Bur. (San Diego), Internat. Platform Assn., Fraternal Order Police, Authors Guild, Authors League Am. Mason, Elk. Clubs: Royal Oak Country, Mexican, S.Am. Turf. Author: Philosophy of Genius; American Values, Solutions to Family and Marriage Problems, Gutless America, 1973. Columnist, Sentinal Newspaper 1963-64, Campers Illustrated Mag., 1964-65, Star Adv., 1968, INSIGHT, 1969-72, Challenge, 1970—. Home: PO Box 1441 Titusville FL 32780

PARKER, WILLIAM WRIGHT, real estate broker; b. Brunswick, Ga., May 7, 1919; s. William Hyde and May Elizabeth (Wright) P.; B.S., U. Ga., 1941; m. Mary Jean Bright, Jan. 17, 1942; children—Mary J. (Mrs. R. Neal Boswell), Katharine (Mrs. Michael J. Green), William Wright, Leila, Harry, Teresa, Joseph. With Parker Realty Co., Brunswick, Ga., 1941—, pres., 1972—; with Parker-Kaufman Ins. Co., Brunswick, 1957—, v.p., 1972—; dir. Am. Nat. Bank of Brunswick. City commr. City of Brunswick, 1966-70; chmn. Brunswick-Glynn County Joint Planning Commn., 1962-70. Recipient Young Man of Year award Brunswick Jr. C. of C., 1952, Realtor of Year award Brunswick-Glynn County Bd. Realtors, 1960. Served with USAAF, 1942-45; ETO. Mem. Am. Inst. Real Estate Appraisers, Soc. Real Estate Appraisers, Ga. Assn. Realtors, Nat. Assn. Realtors (dir. 1972—), Brunswick-Glynn County Bd. Realtors (pres. 1948), Brunswick-Blynn County C. of C. (pres. 1951-52). Roman Catholic. K.C., Elk, Rotarian (pres. 1959-60). Clubs: Brunswick-Glynn County Yacht; Escorts Social (pres. 1973-74). Home: 303 Union St Brunswick GA 31520 Office: 513 Gloucester GA 31520

PARKINS, REYNELL MONSELL, educator, clergyman; b. Colon, Panama, Sept. 1, 1917; s. George W. and Esther (Barrett) P.; B.A., N.Y. U., 1948; J.D., N.Y. U., 1950; M.Div., Episcopal Sem. Va., 1964. Ordained priest Episcopal Ch., 1964; priest St. Martin's Episcopal Ch., Corpus Christi, Tex., 1964-69; prof. law and sociology of architecture U. Tex., Austin, 1969—. Del., World Council Chs., Sweden, 1968; cons. Central Atlanta Progress, 1973—. Pres., chmn. bd. Community Devel. Corp., Austin, 1970-73. Served with AUS, 1943-46. Danforth asso., 1971. Recipient pub. service award N.A.A.C.P., 1972. Author: History of Clarksville, 1969. Home: 3400 Toro Canyon Austin TX 78746

PARKINSON, JOHN DEE, psychiatrist; b. Riceville, Tenn., Nov. 7, 1936; s. Hugh Frank and Lissa (Vineyard) P.; student Tenn. Tech U., 1955-58, U. Tenn., 1962. Intern, Edgewater Hosp., Chgo., 1963-64; resident psychiatry Mental Health Inst., Cherokee, Ia., 1966-67, U. Ala., 1967-69; practice medicine specializing in psychiatry, Coakeville, Tenn., 1969-71, Cleveland, Tenn., 1971—; mem. staff Bradley Meml. Hosp., Cleveland, chief emergency dept., 1971—; psychiatrist Cleveland-Bradley County Mental Health Center, 1974—; in charge emergency med. tech. program Cleveland State Community Coll., 1972-73. Fellow Royal Soc. Health (Eng.); mem. Am. Coll. Emergency Physicians, Tenn. (mem. com. emergency services 1972-73), Bradley County med. socs., So. Med. Assn. Home: 1840 Hillcrest Dr Cleveland TN 37311 Office: Bradley Memorial Hospital Cleveland TN 37311

PARKS, EVELYN AUGUSTA, trade assn. exec.; b. Pitts., Jan. 6, 1927; d. Ralph E. Wagner and Evelyn E. (Gettings) Gaudian; student Pa. State U., 1947-50, Ikeda U. Fine Art, Japan, 1953, 54, U. Nuremberg (Germany) Art, 1960-61, Inst. Orgn. Mgmt., Syracuse U., 1969; m. Robert H. Parks, Aug. 8, 1946 (div. Mar. 1963); children—Diane Renee, Martin Hill. With Nat. Assn. Cemeteries, Arlington, Va., 1961-73, writer, asst. editor trade jour., office mgr., 1965-73, exec. asst. to exec. v.p., 1968-73; exec. asst. v.p. Nat. Assn. Indsl. Parks, 1973—. Mem. Fairfax Hunt, English Speaking Union, Hist. Soc. Fairfax County, Navy League U.S., S.C. Soc., Internat. Platform Assn., Ladies Oriental Shrine, Beta Sigma Phi. Episcopalian. Club: Arts (Washington). Home: 1240 Providence Terrace McLean VA 22101 Office: 1800 N Kent St Arlington VA 22209

PARKS, JEANUS BURRELL, JR., educator, orgn. exec.; b. Washington, Apr. 20, 1929; s. Jeanus B. and Ellen (Wilson) P.; student Howard U., 1947-50, LL.B., 1955; LL.M., Columbia, 1960; m. Jeanne Fields, Apr. 1, 1961; 1 son, John Brian. Admitted to D.C. bar, 1956; gen. practice, Washington, 1956-59; trial atty. Housing and Home Finance Agy., 1959-59; asst. prof. law Howard U. Sch. Law, 1960-63, asso. prof., 1963-66, prof. law, 1966—; exec. dir. Neighborhood Legal Services Program, 1968-69; exec. dir. United Planning Orgn., 1969-74, also sec. bd. trustees. Chmn. bd. dirs. Dist. Communications, Inc., 1973—. Founder mem., dir. United Community Nat. Bank, 1963-65. Mem. Community Police Alert Council, 1967, S.E. Neighbors; mem. nat. adv. bd. Legal Research and Services for Elderly; mem. nat. rev. com. regional Med. Programs Service, Dept. Health, Edn. and Welfare, 1962-63; mem. Bi-Centennial Commn. for D.C.; mem. Mayor's Adv. Com. Narcotics Addiction, Prevention and Rehab., Mayor's Econ. Devel. Com.; mem. Model Cities Commn. Trustee Family and Child Services, 1967-69; bd. dirs. Negro Community Council, Episcopal Center for Children, Nat. Assn. Community Devel., Met. Washington Urban Coalition; bd. organizers Nat. Conf. Black Lawyers. Served with AUS, 1950-52. Fellow Internat. Acad. Law and Sci.; mem. Am. Judicature Soc., Am., Fed. (mem. council community affairs, dir.), Inter-Am. (sr.), Nat., Washington bar assns., Am. Acad. Polit. and Social Sci., Am. Assn. U. Profs., Nat. Lawyers Club (founder mem.), Sigma Delta Tau, Alpha Phi Omega, Phi Alpha Delta. Contbr. articles to profl. jours. Home: 3347 Bangor St SE Washington DC 20020 Office: School of Law Howard University Washington DC 20001

PARKS, ROBERT HALL, petroleum engr.; b. Tulsa, June 27, 1924; s. Edgar Horace and Besse Mae (Henry) P.; B.S. in Petroleum Engring., Tulsa U., 1948; postgrad. Houston U. Law Sch., 1951-56; m. Claralynn Tripp, Oct. 17, 1953; children—Robert Hall, Melanie Kathleen. Petroleum engr. Sunray Oil Corp., Tex., Okla., 1948-51; chief petroleum reservoir engr. Tex. Gulf Producing Co., Houston, 1951-59; petroleum cons., asst. trust officer 1st Nat. Bank Tulsa, 1959-62; sr. analytical engr. Sinclair Oil Co. and Atlantic-Richfield Corp., Tulsa, 1962—. Served with AUS, 1943-46. Registered profl. engr., Tex., Okla. Mem. Soc. Petroleum Engrs., Toastmasters Internat., Kappa Alpha. Methodist. Mason (32 deg.). Home: 5166 E 36th Tulsa OK 74135 Office: Box 521 Tulsa OK 74119

PARKS, SAM LAWS, coll. adminstr.; b. Dover, Tenn., Jan. 9, 1916; s. Samuel Hume and Mary (Laws) P.; sci. diploma Athens Coll., 1950, B.S. in Bus. Adminstrn., 1950; postgrad. Peabody Coll., 1944-47, U. Ky., 1954-57; m. Esten Perry, Sept. 3, 1938; children—Barbara Lane (Mrs. Martin D. Jahn), Linda Ellen (Mrs. John R. Bourne). Accountant, asst. office mgr., order distbr. clk. Internat. Harvester Co., Chattanooga, Knoxville, Tenn. and Nashville, 1940-44; pub. accountant, dir. sales and advt. J. B. Cook Auto Machine Co., Nashville, 1944-47; tchr. accounting, bus. adminstrn., econs. Falls Bus. Coll., Nashville, 1947; bursar Athens (Ala.) Coll., 1948-51, tchr. Sch. Commerce, 1951; office, credit mgr. Quaker Oats Co., Decatur, Ala., 1951-54; bus. mgr.-treas. treas. bd. trustees Union Coll., Barbourville, Ky., 1954-57, 67-71, v.p., treas., 1971—; bus. mgr.-treas. Scarritt Coll., Nashville 1957-67. Dir., treas. Nashville Asbury Fed. Credit Union. Bd. dirs. Heart Fund, Barbourville, 1955-57, Easter Seals, Barbourville, 1955-57, Cumberland council Boy Scouts Am., 1955—. Mem. Nat. Assn. Accountants (v.p., dir.), N.E.A., Ky. Coll., Knox County C. of C. (pres., dir.), Alt. Acad. Sci., Delta Nu Omega, Tau Delta Tau. Methodist (pres. adminstrn. bd.). Mason, Kiwanian (dir.). Club: Methodist Mens (pres.) (Barbourville). Author: Manual for Purchasing Colleges and Universities, 1955. Home: 112 College Park Dr Barbourville KY 40906

PARKS, SUZANNE LOWRY (MRS. PHILLIP HADDON PARKS), educator; b. Columbus, O., Feb. 29, 1936; d. Frank Carson and Mable (Brown) Lowry; B.S., Emory U., 1958, M.S., U. Md., 1959; m. Phillip Haddon Parks, July 20, 1963; children—Jennifer, Kristin, Gregory. Staff nurse Emory U. Hosp., Atlanta, 1958; instr. psychiat. nursing U. Va. Sch. Nursing, Charlottesville, 1959-60, asst. prof., 1960-61; instr. U. N.C., Chapel Hill, 1961-62, asst. prof., 1962-63; instr. med.-surg. nursing Rex Hosp. Sch. Nursing, Raleigh, N.C., 1963; asst. prof., dir. div. psychiat. nursing Duke Sch. Nursing, Durham, N.C., 1964-66, clin. specialist psychiat. nursing, 1966-67; clin. instr. psychiatry Emory U. Sch. Medicine, 1968-73, crisis intervention therapist, 1968-71; asst. prof. Coll. Nursing Clemson U., 1973—. Recipient Outstanding Faculty Mem. award U. N.C. grad. class nursing, 1963. Mem. Mental Health Assn., Am., S.C. nurses assns., Nat., S.C. leagues for nursing, Sigma Theta Tau. Home: 106 A Dove Circle Clemson SC 29631

PARKS, VINCENT JOSEPH, educator; b. Chgo., May 5, 1928; s. Joseph and Nora (Carr) P.; Asso.Sci., Lewis Coll. Sci. and Tech., 1948; B.S. in Mech. Engring., Ill. Inst. Tech., 1953; M.Civil Engring., Cath. U. Am., 1963, Ph.D., 1968; m. Julia Catherine Pyles, Feb. 12, 1955; children—Sean Patrick, Michael, David, Nora, Joseph, Gregory, Lawrence. Electronics engr. Andrew Corp., Orland Park, Ill., 1953-55; research engr. Armour Research Found., Chgo., 1955-61; research asso. Cath. U. Am., Washington, 1961-65, asst. prof., 1965-68, asso. prof., 1968-73, prof. civil and mech. engring., 1973—. Bd. dirs. 1309, Inc. Seigal scholar, 1949; NRC resident research asso., 1971-72. Mem. Soc. Exptl. Stress Analysis (dir. 1970-71), Am. Assn. U. Profs., Sigma Xi, Sigma Phi Epsilon. Roman Catholic. Author: (with A.J. Durelli) Moire Analysis of Strain, 1970. Home: 1240 Kearny St NE Washington DC 20017 Office: Civil and Mech Engring Cath U Washington DC 20017

PARMLEY, LOREN FRANCIS, JR., physician, army officer; b. El Paso, Tex., Sept. 19, 1921; s. Loren Francis and Hope (Bartholomew) P.; B.A., U. Va., 1941, M.D., 1943; m. Dorothy Louise Turner, Apr. 4, 1942; children—Richard Turner, Robert James, Kathryn Louise. Intern Med. Coll. Va., Richmond, 1944; commd. 1st lt. M.C., U.S. Army, 1944, advanced through grades to col., 1962; resident medicine Brooke Gen. Hosp., San Antonio, 1947-48; resident, asst. prof. mil. sci., tactics U. Wis. Med. Sch., 1949-51; asst. army attache U.S. Embassy, India, 1954-56; resident in cardiology Walter Reed Gen. Hosp., Washington, 1956-57; chief cardiology Letterman Gen. Hosp., San Francisco, 1957-63, chief dept. medicine, 1962-63; chief dept. medicine Walter Reed Gen. Hosp., Washington, 1965-68; clin. asso. prof. medicine Georgetown U., 1967-68; asst. dean, prof. medicine Med. U. S.C.; dir. med. edn. Spartanburg (S.C.) Gen. Hosp., 1968—; clin. prof. medicine Med. Coll. Ga. Cons. in field of medicine U.S. Army, Europe, 1963-65; Surgeon Gen., 1966-68; lectr. medicine U. Cal. Sch. Medicine, San Francisco, 1958-62. Decorated Legion of Merit. Diplomate internal medicine and cardovascular disease Am. Bd. Internal Medicine. Fellow A.C.P., Council Clin. Cardiology, Am. Coll. Chest Physicians, Am. Coll. Cardiology (gov. for S.C.), Am. Heart Assn.; mem. A.M.A., So. Med. Assn., Sigma Phi Epsilon, Phi Chi. Contbr. chpts. to textbooks. Address: 232 Beechwood Dr Spartanburg SC 29302

PARNELL, DAVID RUSSELL, retail co. exec.; b. Parkton, N.C., Nov. 16, 1925; s. John Quincy and Clelia (Britt) P.; B.S., Wake Forest U., 1949; m. Barbara Johnson, June 11, 1948; children—David Russell, Anne, Timothy. With J.Q. Parnell, Inc., Parkton, 1949—, mgr., exec. v.p., 1952—; mgr. Parnell Oil Co., 1954—, pres., 1961—; dir. First Union Nat. Bank, St. Pauls, N.C. Mem. Robeson County Indsl. Devel. Commn., 1964—, chmn., 1968; mem. N.C. State Hwy. Commn., 1969—, chmn secondary roads com., 1969-73. Democratic precinct chmn., Parkton, 1964-70. Served with AUS, 1945-46. Baptist. (treas. 1950—, deacon 1951—, chmn. bd. deacons 1961-70). Club: Parkton Ruritan (pres. 1954). Home: PO Box 190 Parkton NC 28371 Office: Parkton NC 28371

PARR, CHARLES HENRY, III, bldg. and devel. co. exec.; b. N.Y.C., Oct. 3, 1921; s. Henry and Babette (Brumbach) P.; B.A., U. Ill., 1942; student N.Y. Trade Sch., 1945, Cooper Union, 1946; m. Madeline R. Mahoney, May 10, 1952; children—Charles Henry, Robert Joseph, Tyana Marie, John Christopher, William David. Buyer, R.H. Macy & Co., N.Y.C., 1946-48; head women's wear div. Mandel Bros., Chgo., 1949-51; marketing dir. Eldon Mfg. Co., Los Angeles, 1952-55; chmn. bd., chief exec. officer Coleman-Parr, Inc., Beverly Hills, Cal., 1956-66; chmn. bd. Asso. Marketing Cons., Inc., Beverly Hills, 1963-66; pres. U.S. Devel. & Land Co., Beverly Hills, 1963-64, Eichler Corp., San Francisco, 1966-67, U.S. Home Townelife, Sarasota, Fla., 1972—; sr. v.p., dir. 1st Devel. Corp. Am., Sarasota, 1967-72; pres. Exhibit Homes div. Century II Corp., Sarasota, 1972—. Guest lectr. U. Cal. at Los Angeles, 1963-64, San Fernando State Coll., Los Angeles, 1964, New Coll., Sarasota, 1968; mem. marketing council Life mag., N.Y.C., 1960-62; cons. McGraw-Hill, N.Y.C., F.W. Dodge Co., N.Y.C., FHA, 1963-66; mem. spl. adv. panel Cal. Real Estate Commn., 1962—. Finance chmn. Sarasota Republican Com., 1968. Bd. dirs. Crippled Childrens Hosp., 1951-66. Served with AUS, 1942-44. Recipient Kennedy award B'nai B'rith, 1964; certificate of appreciation Cal. Real Estate Commn., 1961; Nat. Marketing Oscar award Profl. Builder Mag., 1959; Internat. award O'Keefe & Merritt TV Comml. Networks, 1962; Best Advt. award Fla. Dept. Commerce, 1972. Mem. Nat. Home Builders Assn. (Marketing award 1961), Urban Land Inst., Am. Mgmt. Assn., Internat. Advt. Assn., Nat. Assn. Housing and Redevel. Commn., A.I.M. Republican. Roman Catholic. Mason (32 deg., Shriner). Author: Physical Properties of Phenalic Resins, 1953; Marketing and Merchandising Your Homes, 1961. Contbr. editor Family Housing Conf., Look Mag., 1959; editor Expanding Markets column World Media and Markets mag. Home: 3215 Pine Valley Dr Sarasota FL 33580 Office: First Fed Bldg Sarasota FL 33578

PARRILL, I. BENJAMIN, mens apparel co. exec.; b. N.Y.C., 1917; grad. Columbia U., 1937. Chmn., pres. Miller Bros. Industries, Inc., Dallas; chmn. Adam Hats, Inc., Tex. Miller Products, Inc., Wood Garment Mfg. Co.; pres., dir. Adam Hat Stores; v.p., dir. Tex. Miller Hat Corp., Miller Bros. Hat Sales Corp., Men's Hats, Inc. Home: 3601 Turtle Creek Blvd Dallas TX 75219 Office: 2700 Canton St Dallas TX 75226

PARRIS, STANFORD E., congressman; b. Champaign, Ill., Sept. 9, 1929; B.S., U. Del., 1950; J.D., George Washington U., 1958; m. Jane McCullough, Dec. 22, 1951; children—Michael, Ann, Susan. Pres., Woodbridge Chrysler-Plymouth Corp. and Flying Circus Aerodrome; comml. pilot, active in antique aircraft orgns.; formerly partner in law firm Swazze, Parris, Tydings & Bryan; mem. 93d Congress from 8th dist. Va.; former dir. Bank of Va., Fairfax. Mem. Fairfax County Bd. Suprs., 1964-67; mem. Va. Ho. of Dels., 1969-72; chmn. Joint Senate-House Republican Caucus in 1972 Gen. Assembly. Bd. dirs. Fairfax County YMCA; former trustee George Mason Coll. Served with USAF, Korean War. Decorated D.F.C. with oak leaf cluster, Air medal with clusters, Purple Heart, U.S. and Korean Presdl. citations. Mem. Am., Va., Fairfax County C. of C., Am. Legion, Delta Theta Phi. Republican. Rotarian. Office: 509 Cannon House Office Bldg Washington DC 20515

PARRISH, CHARLES OWEN, realtor; b. Louisburg, N.C., May 12, 1925; s. John Henry and Carmelite Elizabeth (Bourgeous) P.; B.S. in Bus., John B. Stetson U., 1949; m. Edith Lawson Hall, July 23, 1949; children—Pamela Ann, Charlotte Edith. With Leedy & Co., Inc., Birmingham, 1949—, pres., chief exec. officer, 1957—, also dir.; dir. 1st Fed. Savs. & Loan, Birmingham. Instr. appraisal courses U. Ala., 1968—. Served with AUS, 1943-45; ETO. Decorated Silver Star, Purple Heart with oak leaf cluster. Named Realtor of Year Birmingham, 1970. Mem. Am. Soc. Real Estate Counselors, Birmingham C. of C., Am. Inst. Real Estate Appraisers (pres. Ala. chpt. 1971), Birmingham Bd. Realtors (pres. 1970), Am. Right of Way Assn. (pres. Ala. chpt. 1971, internat. dir. 1973), Nat. Assn. Realtors (nat. dir. 1971), Ala. Assn. Realtors (dir. 1973). Club: Exchange (Birmingham). Home: 3041 Ryecroft Rd Birmingham AL 35223 Office: 2131 3d Av N Birmingham AL 35203

PARRISH, EDWARD, lawyer; b. Adel, Ga., Nov. 21, 1911; s. C. E. and Nona (Rountree) P.; grad. Young Harris (Ga.) Coll., 1930; m. Jeannette Crane. Admitted to Ga. bar, 1931, since practiced in Adel; county atty. Cook County, Ga., 1938-42; city atty. City of Adel, Ga., 1940-42, 46—, also city atty. Sparks, Ga.; solicitor-gen. Alapaha Jud. Circuit, 1949—. Dir. Cook-Berrien Service Corp., Cook County Fed. Savs. & Loan Assn., Adel. Served with AUS, 1942-45. Mem. Am. Legion, V.F.W., Woodmen of the World. Lion. Home: 201 E 8th St Adel GA 31620 Office: Sowega Bldg and County Ct House Adel GA 31620

PARRISH, FRANK JENNINGS, frozen foods co. exec.; b. Manassas, Va., Dec. 29, 1923; s. Edgar Goodloe and Alverda (Jennings) P.; student Va. Poly. Inst., 1942-43; m. Lorene Lomax, Feb. 11, 1944; children—Edgar Lee, Julia Lorene. Mng. partner Manassas Frozen Foods, 1946—; pres., mgr. Certified Food Buyers Service, Inc., 1953—; pres. First Nat. Acceptance Co., 1966—; v.p. Manassas Ice & Fuel Co. Mem. bus. adminstrn. adv. com. No. Va. Community Coll. Served to maj. USAAF, 1943-46; CBI; brig. gen. Res. Decorated Air medal. Mem. Nat. Inst. Locker and Freezer Provisioners Am. (past pres.; Industry Leadership award 1968), Va. Frozen Foods Assn. (past pres., dir.), Hump Pilots Assn. Methodist (chmn. bd. trustees 1958-66). Kiwanian, Moose. Home: 9107 Park Av Manassas VA 22110 Office: 450 W Broad St Falls Church VA 22045 also 9416 Main St Manassas VA 22110 also 1500 Little Creek Rd Norfolk VA 23518

PARRISH, JEMIMA BUCHANAN (MRS. A. LEONARD PARRISH), artist, poet; b. Jasper, Ala.; d. John H. and Anne (Tubb) Buchanan; student pub. schs.; m. A. Leonard Parrish, Aug. 17, 1926; 1 son, David Buchanan. Exhibited in group shows at Birmingham

(Ala.) Art Mus., Buchanan Hall Gallery, Samford U. (Birmingham), Atlanta Art Assn., Fine Arts Center (Lynchburg, Va.), Dayton (O.) Art Inst., Emerson Mus. Art (Syracuse, N.Y.), Miami (Fla.) Mus. Modern Art, Smithsonian Instn., Norton Gallery (West Palm Beach, Fla.), Des Moines, Denver Art Mus., Municipal Art Gallery, Los Angeles; represented in permanent collections at Jackson, Miss., Ashville, N.C., Birmingham, Knoxville, Tenn. Mem. Nat. League Am. Pen Women (Ala. art chmn. 1968-70, 72-74), Acad. Am. Poets, Ala. Writers Conclave, Ala. Art League, Ala. Poetry Soc. Club: Quill. Author: New American Poetry, 1945; Testament of Faith, 1942. Home: 1426 24th St N Birmingham AL 35234

PARRISH, ROBERT ALTON, pediatric surgeon; b. Augusta, Ga., Sept. 9, 1930; s. Robert Alton and Thelma Elizabeth (Roney) P.; A.B., Mercer U., 1951; M.S., U. Ga., 1953; M.D., Med. Coll. Ga., 1956; m. Dorothy Ann Burdashaw, Aug. 21, 1954; children—Joyce Ann, Cynthia Ann. Intern Bapt. Meml. Hosp., Memphis, 1956-57; resident surgery U. Tenn., Memphis, 1957-62; practice gen. surgery, Augusta, Ga., 1962-64; instr. surgery Med. Coll. Ga., Augusta, 1962-64, asst. prof., 1964-67, asso. prof., 1967-70, prof., 1970-72, chief sect. pediatric surgery, dept. surgery, 1972—; cons. Univ. Hosp., Augusta, VA Hosp., Augusta, Meml. Hosp., Savannah, Macon (Ga.) Hosp., Ft. Gordon (Ga.) Gen. Hosp. Recipient Outstanding Tchr. of Year award Med. Found. Ga., 1966, Excellence in Teaching award Med. Coll. Ga., 1966, 69. USPHS-Nat. Cancer Inst. research fellow, 1957-58, Am. Cancer Soc. clin. fellow, 1960-61, NIH clin. fellow, 1961-62. Diplomate Am. Bd. Surgery. Fellow A.C.S.; mem. Am. Acad. Pediatrics, So. Surg. Assn., Am. Assn. Surgery of Trauma, Soc. for Surgery Alimentary Tract, Southeastern Surg. Congress, Ga. Surg. Soc., Richmond County Med. Soc., Gamma Sigma Epsilon, Phi Sigma, Alpha Epsilon Delta, Alpha Omega Alpha. Home: 2902 Mayfair Rd Augusta GA 30904 Office: Div Pediatric Surgery Med Coll Ga Augusta GA 30902

PARRISH, SAMUEL RAY, JR., oil co. exec.; b. Dallas, Oct. 17, 1930; s. Samuel Ray and Franke (Longbotham) P.; B.B.A., U. Tex., 1952; m. Kathleen Howell, Dec. 6, 1952; children—James Marvin, Timothy John, Kimberly Eileen, Thomas Samuel. Field clk. Sun Oil Co., Snyder, Tex., 1952-59, auditor, Dallas, 1959-69, supervising auditor, 1969-70, mgr. S.W. auditing, 1970—. C.P.A., Tex. Mem. Am. Inst. C.P.A.'s, Tex., Dallas. socs. C.P.A.'s, Inst. Internal Auditors (pres. Dallas 1970-71), Petroleum Accountants Soc. Dallas (pres. 1973-74), Tex. Midcontinent Oil and Gas Assn., Pi Kappa Alpha. Mason. Home: 9451 Dartridge Dr Dallas TX 75238 Office: PO Box 2880 Dallas TX 75221

PARSLEY, BRANTLEY HAMILTON, librarian; b. Balt., Oct. 15, 1927; s. Clarence Elroy and Florence Sally (Barnes) P.; A.A., Balt. Jr. Coll., 1950; B.A., U. Md., 1952; B.D., New Orleans Bapt. Theol. Sem., 1955, M.R.E., 1958; M.Librarianship, Emory U., 1965; m. Loyce Marie Franklin, Apr. 18, 1951; children—Linda Marie, Brantley Hamilton. Ordained to ministry Baptist Ch., 1956; pastor Calvary Bapt. Ch., Albany, Ore., 1955-57; library asst. New Orleans Pub. Library, 1958-61; supt. night circulation and stacks Theology Library, Emory U., 1961-65; dir. library Campbellsville (Ky.) Coll., 1965—. Bd. dirs. Taylor County Community Concerts. Recipient Sch. award Am. Legion, 1947. Mem. Am., Southeastern, Ky. (chmn. coll. and research sect. 1970-71, sec. treas. edn. sect. 1972-73) library assns., Council Ind. Ky. Colls. (chmn. 1970—), Taylor County Hist. Soc. (bd. dirs. 1970), Taylor County Bapt. Assn. (bd. dirs. 1968-70), Taylor County Bapt. Sunday Sch. Assn. (supt. 1968-70). Home: 114 Longview Dr Campbellsville KY 42718

PARSLEY, ROBERT HORACE, lawyer; b. Erwin, Tenn., Apr. 9, 1923; s. Millard Fillmore and Daisy (Garland) P.; student East Tenn. State U., 1941-43, U. Tenn., 1946-47; LL.B., U. Va., 1949; m. Georganna Alice Strake, Apr. 11, 1953; children—Robert, Sharon, Brian, Sandra, Sally, David, John, Daniel, Jana. Admitted to Tex. bar, 1949; asso. Baker, Botts, Andrews & Parish, Houston, 1949-53; asso. Butler, Binion, Rice, Cook & Knapp, Houston, 1953-57, partner, 1957—. Dir. J.M. West Tex. Corp.; v.p., dir. Autotronic Systems, Inc.; instr. law U. Va., Charlottesville, 1949, U. Houston, 1949-50, Tex. So. U., Houston, 1952-53. Bd. dirs. S.W. Law Inst., Strake Jesuit Coll. Prep.; mem. Tex. Bd. Mental Health and Mental Retardation; trustee West Found. Served to 1st lt. USAAF, 1943-46. Mem. Am., Tex., Houston bar assns., Alpha Tau Omega, Phi Delta Phi. Rotarian. Clubs: Houston, Houston Country. Home: 5219 Shady River St Houston TX 77027

PARSLEY, RONALD LEE, educator; b. Madison, Wis., July 14, 1937; s. Palo and Gertrude Elida (Heidel) P.; A.B., U. Cal. at Los Angeles, 1960; M.S., U. Cin., 1963, Ph.D., 1969; m. Nancy Joan Johnson, Aug. 18, 1962 (div. Sept. 1973); children—Rodney Alexander, Andrew Arthur. Asst. prof. geology Tulane U., New Orleans, 1966-70, asso. prof. geology, chmn. dept. geology, 1970—. NASA grantee for study of Marine 6 and 7 photos of Mars, 1970-71. Mem. A.A.A.S., Paleontol. Research Inst., Paleontol. Soc., Sierra Club, Sigma Xi. Research and publs. in invertebrate paleontology, paleobiology of primitive Echinodermata. Home: 1314 Audubon St New Orleans LA 70118

PARSONS, DAVID LARRY, dentist; b. Charleston, W.Va., Apr. 3, 1943; s. Clarence Eugene and Ocie Mae (Hill) P.; student Duke U., 1961-63, Morris Harvey Coll., 1963-65; D.D.S., B.S. in Chemistry (Pfeiffer research fellow 1966-69), U. N.C., 1969; m. Carolyn Olivia Hackney, Aug. 31, 1963; children—Mary Ann, Christine Ruth, Charles David. Pvt. practice dentistry, Greensboro, N.C., 1969-71, Salisbury, N.C., 1972—, dentist David L. Parsons, D.D.S., Greensboro, 1971—; v.p. Triventures, Inc., Greensboro, 1970-72. Bd. dirs. Francisco Place Assn. Recipient Physics Achievement award Morris Harvey Coll., 1963-64. Mem. Nat., N.C., Guilford, Rowan County dental socs., Kappa Sigma, Psi Omega. Club: Epicureans (membership chmn. 1970-71) (Greensboro, N.C.). Home: 2511-A Patriot Way Greensboro NC 27408 Office: 203 S Main St Randleman NC 27317

PARSONS, EDWIN DAVIS, chemist; b. Amarillo, Tex., Jan. 6, 1914; s. Robert Johnston and Cora Belle (Wilkins) P.; B.S., Tex. Technol. Coll., 1937; M.S., U. Tex., 1939; m. Eva Wayne Duggan, Mar. 22, 1946; children—Pamela Kay, Paul Davis. Chemist U.S. Geol. Survey, Roswell, N.M., 1939-41; instr. chemistry Tex. Coll. Arts and Industries at Kingsville, 1941-42, asst. prof., 1945-46; sr. chemist U.S. Naval Lab., Houston, 1942-45; research engr. Humble Oil & Refining Co., Houston, 1946-47; research chemist Phillips Petroleum Co., Bartlesville, Okla., 1947-54, group leader, 1955—. Mem. Am. Water Works Assn., Nat. Assn. Corrosion Engrs. (chmn. com. on control of corrosion of oil field equipment 1968—). Presbyn. Home: 2810 Redhawe Ct Bartlesville OK 74003 Office: Phillips Petroleum Co Bartlesville OK 74004

PARSONS, FLOYD W., supt. schs.; b. Andice, Tex., Oct. 16, 1909; s. William Culberson and Ida A. (Davis) P.; B.A., U. Tex., 1935, M.A., 1945; m. Christina Fowler, Dec. 25, 1932; children—Lou Anne (Mrs. William Raymond Smoot), Floyd W., Paul. High sch. prin., tchr., coach Johnson City (Tex.) Pub. Schs., 1932-33; elementary prin., tchr. Orangedale (Tex.) Common Sch. Dist., 1933-36; supt. schs., Calallen, Tex., 1936-46, Bishop, Tex., 1946-52, Beeville, Tex., 1952-56, Big Spring, Tex., 1956-61, Little Rock Sch. Dist., 1961—. Instr. dept. sociology U. Tex., summer 1945; instr. Hardin-Simmons U., summer 1959; participant Columbia Workshop, summer 1958. Trustee Ark. State Tchrs. Retirement System; bd. dirs. Salvation Army, YMCA, United Fund, Pulaski County Assn. Mental Health, Boy Scouts Am. Mem. N.E.A. (life), Tex. Tchrs. Assn. (life), Tex. (life), Ark. (life) congresses parents and tchrs., Ark. Edn. Assn., Econ. Edn. Bd., Am. Assn. Sch. Adminstrs. (pres. 1972-73, exec. com.), Assn. for Advancement of Internat. Edn. (exec. sec.), Council of Ednl. Facility Planners, Horace Mann League U.S. (dir.), C. of C. (bd.), Phi Delta Kappa, Alpha Kappa Delta. Kiwanian (past pres. Little Rock). Home: 31 Nob View Circle Little Rock AR 72205 Office: W Markham and Izard Sts Little Rock AR 72201

PARSONS, GREGG BURNS, pharm. mfg. co. exec.; b. Fairfield, Ala., Apr. 11, 1927; s. Frank Enos and Marguerite (Pitman) P.; student U. Miss., 1944; Auburn U., 1944, N.C. State U., 1944, U. Ala., 1947, 49; m. Gloria Ann Self, Sept. 24, 1947; children—Gregg Burns, William Richard, Dee Self. With Johnson & Johnson, Birmingham, Ala., also Miami, Fla., 1949-52, R.L. Zeigler, Inc., Bessemer, Ala., 1952-58; self employed in drug brokerage, Birmingham, 1958-62; pres. Whorton Pharmacal Co., Inc., Fairfield, Ala., 1964—, chmn. bd., 1970—. Mem. med. adv. bd. City of Fairfield, 1970—. Served with AUS, 1944-47. Methodist (finance chmn. 1967—). Kiwanian. Home: 716 Sherwood Rd Fairfield AL 35064 Office: 4202 Gary Av Fairfield AL 35064

PARSONS, JOE MAX, educator; b. nr. Lexington, Tenn., June 20, 1915; s. Cleff and Myrtle (White) P.; student U. Tenn. Jr. Coll., 1935-36, Union U., 1937-39, Syracuse U., 1942-44; B.S., George Peabody Coll. for Tchrs., 1947, M.A., 1948; m. Elizabeth Davis, Mar. 22, 1947. Tchr., sch. prin. Henderson County (Tenn.) pub. schs., 1936-42; instr. math. George Peabody Coll. for Tchrs., 1948, U. Tenn., 1948-52; chief instr. Tenn. Radio Service Sch., Knoxville, 1951-52; dean, head dept. math. Asheville-Biltmore Coll., 1952-63, dean of students, head dept. math., 1963-68, dean men, 1967-69; dean men, asso. prof. U. N.C., Asheville, 1969—. Bd. dirs. Humane Soc., Asheville, Buncombe County (N.C.) Dept. Pub. Welfare. Served to sgt. AUS, 1942-46. Mem. N.C. Coll. Conf., N.C. Edn. Assn. (v.p. div. higher edn. 1959—), Kappa Phi Kappa, Phi Delta Kappa. Democrat. Baptist. Lion. Clubs: School Masters of Western N.C. (pres. 1962), Asheville Executives, Asheville City. Home: 110 Stuyvesant Rd Asheville NC 28803

PARSONS, LARRY JIM, accountant; b. San Francisco, Nov. 2, 1929; s. Laurence E. and June (Mattson) P.; B.S., U. Tenn., 1952; student Weber Jr. Coll., 1947-49; m. Wanda Carolyn Swope, Apr. 25, 1953;children—Priscilla M., Laura L., Juliette. With Ernst & Ernst, C.P.A.'s, 1957—, asst. mgr., Albuquerque, 1957-61, mgr., N.Y.C., 1961-63, Dallas, 1963—, partner, 1966—. Served with AUS, 1950-51. C.P.A. Tenn., N.Y., Tex., N.M., La., N.C. Mem. Am. Inst. C.P.A.'s, Tex. (dir.), N.Y. socs. C.P.A.'s, Dallas Chpt. C.P.A.'s (dir.), Dallas Civic Opera Assn. (dir.). Kiwanian. Home: 6818 Velasco St Dallas TX 75214 Office: LTV Tower 1600 Pacific St Dallas TX 75201

PARSONS, PRESTON DUANE, clergyman; b. Arapahoe, N.C., Sept. 8, 1920; s. Leonard Clifton and Rumah Derah (Salters) P.; B.A., Atlantic Christian Coll., 1942; B.D., Vanderbilt U., 1945; M.Div., 1973; postgrad., U. N.C., Chapel Hill, 1955-59; m. Nina Ray Wilcox, July 19, 1942; children—Celia Ray (Mrs. Paul Mark O'Briant), Preston Duane. Ordained to ministry Christian Ch., 1942; minister Wendell Christian Ch., (N.C.), 1953-59; prof. psychology E. Carolina U., Greenville, N.C., 1960-63; prof. sociology Meredith Coll., Raleigh, N.C., 1963-65; minister Front St. Christian Ch., Burlington, N.C., 1965-74, Highland Park Christian Ch., New Bern, N.C., 1974—. Gen. dir., counselor Psychol. Services and Counseling Center, Burlington, 1971-74; chaplain Burlington squadron Civil Air Patrol, 1969-74. Mem. exec. bd. Alamance Community Action Program, 1966-72, pres., 1967-68; mem. Community Council Alamance County, 1967-74; mem. Com. for Sch. Bonds Issue, Alamance County and Burlington, 1973. Served with USNR, 1945-47, 50-53. Decorated Purple Heart. Mem. Federated Ministerial Assn. Alamance County (pres. 1973-74), Christian Ch. N.C. (gen. bd. 1970-73), Am. Sociol. Assn., Mil. Chaplains Assn., So. Sociol. Soc., Am. Assn. U. Profs. Club: Optimist (Burlington, past pres.). Home: 5108 Pinetree Rd New Bern NC 28560 Office: Highland Park Chrisian Ch New Bern NC 28560

PARSONS, RHEY BOYD, educator; b. Mayfield, Ky., Dec. 22, 1892; s. Jacob Fisher and Althea Willie (Hooker) P.; B.S., U. Chgo., 1917, M.A., 1923, Ph.D., 1935. Tchr. math., prin. elementary and high schs., Ky., Tex., 1913-23; prof. edn. Baylor Coll., 1923-26; asso. prof. edn. U. Tenn., 1926-33; asso. prof. edn., supt. demonstration sch. Fla. State Coll., 1935-38; prof. edn., dept. chmn. Central YMCA Coll., Chgo., 1939-45; civilian employee, br. chief Mil. Govt., Germany, 1945-46; prof. edn. Aurora Coll., 1946-48; prof. edn. Murray (Ky.) State U., 1948-63, prof. emeritus, 1963—. Fellow A.A.A.S.; mem. Phi Delta Kappa, Kappa Delta Pi, others. Mason. Home: 1013 Payne St Murray KY 42071

PARTEE, WOODIE AUGUSTUS, JR., banker, lawyer; b. Washington, Ga., Oct. 3, 1921; s. Woodie Augustus and Edna (Chafin) P.; A.B., U. Ga., 1943; postgrad. Fletcher Sch. Law and Diplomacy, 1949-50; J.D., George Washington U., 1962; LL.M. in Taxation, Georgetown U., 1966. With Riggs Nat. Bank, Washington, 1951—, v.p. credit, 1970—; law clk. to Judge Marvin Jones U.S. Ct. Claims, 1962-63; admitted to D.C. bar, 1963. Served with Transp. Corps, AUS, 1945-49. Mem. Am., Fed. bar assns., Bar Assn. D.C., Robert Morris Assos., Order of Coif, Blue Key, Sphinx, Phi Beta Kappa, Phi Kappa Phi, Omicron Delta Kappa, Phi Eta Sigma, Phi Delta Phi, Sigma Chi. Club: Nat. Lawyers. Home: 2480 16th St NW Washington DC 20009 Office: 1503 Pennsylvania Av NW Washington DC 20005

PARTENZA, MYRNA REAMS (MRS. CHRIS A. PARTENZA), librarian; b. Vero Beach, Fla., Jan. 16, 1937; d. James Manley and Helen M. (Elliott) Reams; A.B., Fla. So. Coll., 1958; M.Ed., Fla. Atlantic U., 1968; m. Chris A. Partenza, Sept. 13, 1956; 1 son, James Christopher. Tchr., librarian Brandon High Sch., Tampa, Fla., 1958-60; librarian, speech tchr. Coral City Jr. High Sch., Miami, 1960-61; librarian Palm Beach County Summer Elementary library program, summers 1963-65; librarian, tchr. Spanish and English, Forest Hill High Sch., West Palm Beach, Fla., 1961-67; charter librarian Palm Beach Atlantic Coll., West Palm Beach, 1968—. Chmn. Palm Beach County Library Specifications Com., 1964-67. Mem. Am. Assn. Higher Edn., Am. Assn. U. Women, Am., Fla., Palm Beach County library assns. Home: 1705 S Lakeside Dr Lake Worth FL 33460 Office: 1101 S Olive Av West Palm Beach FL 33401

PARTRIDGE, LLOYD DONALD, educator; b. Cortland, N.Y., Dec. 18, 1922; s. Bert James and Marian (Rice) P.; B.S., U. Mich., 1948, M.S., 1949, Ph.D., 1953; m. Jean Marie Rutledge, Aug. 6, 1944; children—Lloyd Donald, David Lee, Gayle Ann (Mrs. Roy Kneller). Instr., U. Mich., Ann Arbor, 1953-56; asst. prof. Yale, 1956-62; asso. prof. neurophysiology U. Tenn., Memphis, 1962-70, prof., 1970—. Served with AUS, 1944-46. Contbr. chpts. to books, articles to profl. jours. Home: 3061 Dumbarton Memphis TN 38128

PARVIN, MILLARD GYE, fishery exec., advt. co. exec.; b. Corinth, Miss., Sept. 28, 1920; s. Fred Gye and Callie Lane (Bratton) P.; student Biggersville Sch., 1926-33; m. Mary Ruth Loyd, Nov. 17, 1956; children—Barbara Gail (Mrs. Terrell Hatfield), Sherry Lynn. With Miss. div. King & Stanley Co., Inc., Corinth, 1946—, operations mgr., 1950—; partner Springwater Fish Farms, 1969—; lectr., cons. catfish farming, 1965—. Scoutmaster Boy Scouts Am., 1957—. Bd. dirs. N.E. Miss. Shrine Clown Assn. Served with USMC, 1944-46. Decorated Purple Heart. Mem. Am. Legion, V.F.W., Catfish Farmers Am., Miss. Catfish Assn. (dir. 1968-69), Miss. Electric Sign Assn. Baptist. Mason (32 deg.). Clubs: Saddle (pres. 1964-67) (Corinth, Miss.); Boosters (Glen, Miss.). Inventor catfish brooder and automated catfish feeder, paint stripper. Home: Route 1 Glen MS 38846 Office: 119 W Linden St Corinth MS 38834

PASCHAL, GEORGE HUGH, JR., historian; b. San Antonio, Aug. 22, 1925; s. George Hugh and Mary Louise (Steele) P.; B.A., Trinity U., 1947, M.A., 1956; Ph.D., La. State U., 1967; m. Olive Adelaide Hill, Aug. 1, 1959. Tchr. Am. history San Antonio high schs., 1957-59; instr. Am. history Trinity U., San Antonio 1962-72. Found. for Blind fellow, 1959-62. Mem. Bexar County Hist. Assn. (pres. 1966-67), Phi Alpha Theta. Author: One Hundred Years of Challenge and Change, a History of the Presbyterian Church in Texas, 1967. Home: 214 Primera Dr San Antonio TX 78212

PASCHAL, JERRY DREW, ednl. adminstr.; b. Wewoka, Okla., Apr. 12, 1931; s. Arthur Gordon and Edna (Drew) P.; B.S., High Point Coll., 1956; M.S., U. N.C., 1959, advanced supts. certificate, 1962; Ph.D., Duke, 1971; m. Patricia Kornegay, July 4, 1954; children—Arthur Gordon, Joan Dee. Indsl. engr. Anvil Brand, High Point, N.C., 1956-57; tchr., prin., asst. supt. Jr. Order Children's Home, Lexington, N.C., 1957-59; prin., Eanes Elementary Sch., Lexington, N.C., 1959-60, Chadbourn (N.C.) Union Sch., 1960-61, Charles B. Aycock High Sch., Pikeville, N.C., 1961-64; asst. supt. Goldsboro (N.C.) City Schs., 1965-66, supt., 1966-72; asso. to vice chancellor Fort-Bragg-Pope AFB campus Fayetteville State U., 1972-73; supt. Columbus County Schs., Whiteville, N.C., 1973—. Pres., Pioneer Athletic Conf., 1962-63; mem. evaluation teams So. Assn. Coll. and Schs., 1962-69. Chmn. in edn. United Forces, 1967-68; mem. dist. exec. com. Tuscorora council Boy Scouts Am., 1968-70; mem. state com. Urban Studies Adv. Council, 1970—; mem. Commn. on Religion and Race, 1971—; mem. Mayor's Com. to Recognize Handicapped, 1969—. Bd. dirs. Wayne County Mental Health Assn., Wayne Sheltered Workshop, Boys' Club, Recreation and Parks Commn., Wayne Action Group for Econ. Solvency. Served with AUS, 1954-56. Mem. N.E.A., Am. Assn. Sch. Adminstrs., N.C. Assn. Educators (state dir. 1970-72), Nat. Council State Edn. Assns. (state pres. polit. action com. edn. 1970-72), Nat. Consortium for Humanizing Edn., Nat. Secondary Sch. Prins. Assn., Schoolmaster's Club (pres. 1961-62), Phi Delta Kappa, Kappa Delta Pi. Methodist (dir. 1964-65). Home: 503 Washington St Whiteville NC 28472

PASCHAL, LLOYD ETHERIDGE, JR., aerospace engr.; b. Atlanta, June 20, 1920; s. Lloyd Etheridge and Lottie Juanita (Garrett) P.; B.E.E., Ga. Inst. Tech., 1947; m. Josephine Ruth McKay, Aug. 2, 1952 (dec. Feb. 1967); children—Charlotte Ruth, Mildred Ann, William Etheridge; m. 2d, Carol Goss Roberts; Apr. 24, 1971; stepsons—Mayrel Dean Roberts, David Warren Roberts. Design engr. J.B. McCrary Engring. Corp., Atlanta, 1947-50; design engr. C.E., Savannah, Ga., 1950-58; aerospace instrumentation research and design engr. Army Ballistic Missile Agy., Huntsville, Ala., 1958-60, supervisory aerospace engr. for Saturn space vehicle stages, 1960-66, div. staff engr. Vehicle Elec. Systems Integration Div., 1966-69, supervisory engr. Electro-Chem. Power Sect., NASA, George C. Marshall Space Flight Center, 1969—. Served with AUS, 1942-45; ETO. Recipient Sustained Superior Performance award, 1955, Outstanding Performance rating, 1967, NASA Group Achievement award, 1972, Marshall Space Flight Center Dirs. commendation, 1971. Registered profl. engr., Ga. Mem. I.E.E.E., Ga. Inst. Tech. Alumni Assn. Methodist (adminstrv. bd., finance commn.). Club: Huntsville Georgia Tech. Home: 2108 Colice Rd SE Huntsville AL 35801 Office: NASA George C Marshall Space Flight Center ECIZ Marshall Space Flight Center AL 35812

PASCHALL, H. FRANKLIN, clergyman; b. Hazel, Ky., May 12, 1922; s. Cletus T. and Eva (Jones) P.; B.A., Union U., 1944; B.D., So. Baptist Sem., 1949, Th.D., 1951; m. Olga B. Bailey, June 4, 1944; children—Pam (Mrs. John Freeman), Sandra. Ordained to ministry Bapt. Ch., 1941; pastor Hazel Bapt. Ch., 1941-51, 1st Bapt. Ch., Bowling Green, Ky., 1951-56, 1st Bapt. Ch., Nashville, 1956—. Pres. So. Bapt. Conv., 1966-68, mem. exec. com., mem. Tenn. exec. com., 1964—. Author: The Gospel for an Exploding World, 1967. Home: Bear Rd Nashville TN 37215

PASCHALL, J(OSHUA) E(RNEST), lawyer, state legislator; b. nr. Black Creek, N.C., Aug. 9, 1896; s. Joshua Walter and Sallie (Poole) P.; student U. N.C., 1917; A.B., Atlantic Christian Coll., 1918, LL.D., 1961; LL.B., Am. U., Los Angeles, 1926; m. Claire Hodges, Dec. 18, 1919; children—Julia Daly (Mrs. Charles W. Mauze), James E. With Branch Banking & Trust Co., Wilson, N.C., 1919—, asst. cashier, 1933-43, dir., 1943—, cashier, 1943-52, v.p. 1942-52, pres., 1952-64; dir. Wilson Savs. & Loan Assn., pres., 1944—; mem. N.C. Ho. of Reps., 1964-72; engaged in law practice, Wilson, 1964—. Mem. Banking Commn. N.C., 1961-65. Vice chmn., bd. trustees, mem. exec. com., chmn. finance com. Atlantic Christian Coll.; bd. dirs. Coastal Plain Planning and Devel., assn. pres., 1965-66. Served with USNRF, 1918-19. Mem. Am., N.C., Wilson County bar assns., C. of C. (pres. 1945), Am. Legion (post comdr. 1935-36). Mem. Christian Ch. (ofcl. bd., trustee). Elk, Moose, Rotarian. Club: Wilson. Home: 1718 Wilshire Blvd Wilson NC 27893 Office: 113 E Nash St Wilson NC 27893

PASEWALK, HERBERT MACDONALD, ins. co. exec.; b. Mpls., Dec. 19, 1910; s. Herbert R. and Bertha S. (MacDonald) P.; B.C.S., Benjamin Franklin U., 1934, M.C.S., 1935; m. Mary Elisabeth Jester, Aug. 17, 1937. Night supt. Emergency Hosp., Washington, 1931-33; accountant Clyde B. Stovall & Co., 1934-36; property mgr. Mt. Vernon Mortgage Corp., 1936-42; pres., dir. Firemen's Ins. Co. of Washington, 1946—. also chmn. bd.; exec. v.p., sec., dir. Howard & Hoffman, Inc., 1946—, Home Casualty and Surety Co., 1960—; dir. Howard & Hoffman Life Assos., Inc. Mem. Washington Bd. Trade. Served from 2d lt. to capt. USAF, 1942-45, now maj. res. Decorated Bronze Star medal. Mem. D.C. Assn. Ins. Agts. (past pres.), Air Force Assn., Order Blue Goose, Newcomen Soc. N.Am., Chevy Chase Citizens Assn., Benjamin Franklin U. Alumni Assn. (Distinguished Alumnus award 1971). Clubs: Nat. Press, Reciprocity (past pres.), Touchdown, University (Washington). Home: 6943 33d St NW Washington DC 20015 Office: 303 7th St NW Washington DC 20004

PASEWARK, WILLIAM ROBERT, educator; b. Mt. Vernon, N.Y., Sept. 9, 1924; s. William Robert and Barbara Elisabeth (Hermann) P.; B.S., N.Y. U., 1949, M.A., 1950, Ph.D., 1956; m. M. Jean McHarg, Mar. 17, 1956; children—William Robert, Lisabeth Jean, Jan Alison, Carolyn Ann, Scott Graham, Susan Gayle. Instr., N.Y. U., N.Y.C., 1949-51; asso. prof. Meredith Coll., Raleigh, N.C., 1951-52; asst. prof. Mich. State U., Lansing, 1952-56; prof. bus. edn. Tex. Tech U., Lubbock, 1956—. Mem. Lubbock Office Edn. Adv. Com., 1972—;

field reader, research div. U.S. Office Edn., 1966-70; cons., lectr. office mgmt. and ednl. systems to numerous businesses and ednl. orgns., 1954—. Mem. adv. com. Lubbock Opportunities Industrialization Center, 1972—; mem. troop com. Boy Scouts Am.; pres. Mackenzie Jr. High Sch. P.T.A., 1972, Coronado High Sch. P.T.A., 1973; chmn. Lubbock City-County Child Welfare Bd., 1973-74. Served with USMCR, 1943-46. Named Bus. Tchr. of Year, State of Tex., 1973. Mem. Nat., Mountain-Plains, Tex. bus. edn assns., Nat. Assn. Bus. Tchr. Edn., Am. Vocational Assn., Tex. State Tchrs. Assn., Nat. Assn. Tchr. Edn. for Bus. and Office Edn., Lubbock C. of C., Pi Omega Pi, Kappa Phi Kappa, Phi Delta Kappa, Delta Pi Epsilon, Alpha Kappa Psi. Methodist (supt. ch. sch. 1973-74). Lion. Club: Lubbock Country. Author: Clerical Office Procedures, 5th edit., 1973; other books, monographs, bulls. Editor: The American Business Education Yearbook, 1953; (monograph) Teaching Typewriting Through Television, 1956. Home: 4403 W 11th St Lubbock TX 79416

PASKUSZ, GERHARD FREDERICK, univ. dean; b. Vienna, Austria, Jan. 21, 1922; s. Erwin J. and Rosa K. (Mraz) Paskus; came to U.S., 1938, naturalized, 1943; B.S., U. Cal. at Los Angeles, 1949, Ph.D., 1961; m. Susan Melford, Mar. 20, 1943; 1 dau., Sherry (Mrs. James Ellingwood). Asso. in engring., dept. engring. U. Cal. at Los Angeles, 1952-60, research specialist biotech., 1960-61; mem. faculty Cullen Coll. Engring., U. Houston, 1961—, prof. engring., 1968—, asso. dean engring., 1968—. Bd. dirs. Student Competitions Relevant Engring., Inc., 1971—. Served with AUS, 1943-46. Recipient Good Teaching award U. Cal. at Los Angeles, 1957. Mem. I.E.E.E., Am. Philatelic Soc., Am. Assn. U. Profs., Am. Soc. Engring. Edn., Assn. for Computing Machinery, Sigma Xi, Eta Kappa Nu, Tau Beta Pi, Phi Delta Kappa. Author: Linear Circuit Analysis, 1964. Home: 850 Kuhlman St Houston TX 77024

PASS, BOBBY CLIFTON, educator; b. Cleveland, Ala., Nov. 4, 1931; s. Rufus Clifton and Alma Antionette (Payne) P.; student Snead Jr. Coll., 1949-50; B.S., Auburn U., 1952, M.S., 1960; Ph.D. (Alumni fellow), Clemson U., 1962; m. Ann Rutherford, Aug. 17, 1953; 1 son, Kevin Clifton. Salesman, U.S. Pipe & Foundry Co., Birmingham, Ala., 1955-57; research asst. Auburn (Ala.) U., 1958-60, Clemson (S.C.) U., 1960-62; asst. prof. U. Ky. at Lexington, 1962-67, asso. prof., 1967-68, asso. prof., chmn. dept. entomology, 1968-70, prof., chmn. dept. entomology, 1971—. Cons. Peace Corps, 1968. Served with AUS, 1953-55. Mem. Internat. Orgn. Biol. Programs, Entomol. Soc. Am., A.A.A.S., Ky. Acad. Sci., S.C. Entomol. Soc., Sigma Xi, Phi Kappa Phi, Gamma Sigma Delta. Contbr. articles to profl. jours. Home: 103 Tartan Dr Lexington KY 40503 Office: Dept Entomology U Ky Lexington KY 40506

PASSMAN, OTTO ERNEST, congressman; b. nr. Franklinton, La., June 27, 1900; s. Ed. and Pheriby (Carrier) P.; grad. Comml. Bus. Coll.; m. Willie Bateman. Owner, Passman Equipment Co., Passman Investment Co., Monroe, La. Mem. 80th-93d Congresses from 5th La. Dist. Commd. lt. USN, 1942; material and procurement officer until 1944. Past state comdr. Am. Vets. World War II, Inc. Mem. Am. Legion. Democrat. Baptist. Mason (33 deg., Shriner, K.T., Scottish Rite, Red Cross of Constantine). Home: 120 Walnut St Monroe LA 71201 Office: House Office Bldg Washington DC 20515

PASTERNAK, MICHAEL WILLIAM, banker; b. Bklyn., May 11, 1941; s. Harry Abraham and Helen (Katz) P.; student U. Tex., 1961-64; B.S., L.I. U., 1964; postgrad. Baruch Grad. Sch., Coll. City N.Y., 1965-67; m. Terry F. Ladin, June 25, 1966; children—Scott Robert, Kevin Isaac. With Mfrs. Hanover Trust Co., N.Y.C., 1965-67, Fed. Deposit Ins. Corp., N.Y.C., 1967-69, Financial Ventures, Houston, 1969-71; pres. Orange Bank (Tex.), 1971—. Mem. ACTION-A, commitment to improve Orange, 1973—. Mem. Tex. Mfrs. Assn. (treas.), Orange C. of C. (dir.). Rotarian. Home: 2500 Country Club Orange TX 77630 Office: PO Box 969 Orange TX 77630

PASTRICK, HAROLD LEE, aerospace engr.; b. Ambridge, Pa., June 28, 1936; s. Samuel and Mary (Makara) P.; B.S., Carnegie-Mellon U., 1958; postgrad. Rutgers U., 1959-61, Coll. City N.Y., 1961-63, Mass. Inst. Tech., summers 1961-63, U. Ala., 1964-66, 68-73; M.S., Stanford, 1967, Engr., 1972; m. Vivienne Lee Heinricher, June 3, 1961; children—Tracy Lee, Gregory Harold, Michael Joseph Samuel. Metall. engr. aid J&L Steel Corp., Aliquippa, Pa., 1955-56; asst. designer Am. Bridge div. U.S. Steel Corp., Ambridge, Pa., 1957; elec. engr. Nav. and Flight aids avionics U.S. Army Signal Research and Devel. Labs., Ft. Monmouth, N.J., 1958-63; project engr. inertial systems Missile Research and Devel. Labs., Redstone Arsenal, Ala., 1963-64, tech. dir. Army Inertial Center, 1964-66; aerospace engr. inertial guidance, 1967-71, research aerospace engr. missile guidance and control system analysis, 1972—. Lectr. Sch. Sci. and Engring., U. Ala., Huntsville, 1967—; cons. to various Dept. Def. Labs., 1965—. Served with Signal Corps, AUS, 1958-59. Registered profl. engr., Ala. Mem. Ala. Acad. Sci., Am. Inst. Aeros. and Astronautics, I.E.E.E. (charter program chmn. 1972-73, vice-chmn. 1974-75), Inst. Nav., Soc. for Computer Simulation, Scabbard and Blade. Mem. Greek Orthodox Ch. (pres. 1967, 73). Mason. Club: Greenwhyce (Huntsville, Ala.). Contbr. articles in field to profl. jours. Home: 4017 Dotson Dr Huntsville AL 35802 Office: US Army Missile Command Attention AMSMI-RGN Redstone Arsenal AL 35809

PATE, MARGERY, banker; b. Ft. Gaines, Ga., July 19, 1922; d. James Travis and Amy Estelle (Craft) Pate; grad. high sch. Clk., Baker County Bank, Newton, Ga., 1943-49, cashier, 1949-50; utility clk. First Nat. Bank & Trust Co., Macon, Ga., 1950-60; asst. cashier Ga. Bank & Trust Co., Macon, 1960-63, asst. v.p., from 1963, now v.p., asst. trust officer. Treas., Aid for Leukemia Stricken Children Am., Macon, 1960—; mem. service com. 7th div. Ga. Easter Seal Soc. Mem. Am. Inst. Banking, Nat. Assn. Bank Audit and Control (dir., 1962-63), Nat. Assn. Bank Women. Club: Quota (trustee 1961-65, treas., dir. 1963-65) (Macon). Home: 3089 Highpoint Dr Macon GA 31204 Office: 515 Mulberry St Macon GA 31202

PATE, WALLACE FENNELL, real estate developer; b. Greenville, S.C., Jan. 23, 1933; s. William Wilson and Alethea (Fennell) P.; student Davidson Coll., 1951-52, Furman U., 1952-53; B.B.A., U. Ga., 1955; m. Stella Hutchison Law, Aug. 21, 1953 (div. 1971); children—Stella Law, Wallace Fennell, Dorothy Parker, Alethea Beckham, John McDonald; m. 2d, Lucille Margaret Vanderbilt, Feb. 18, 1971. Vice pres. Wunda Weve Carpet Co., Greenville, 1957-59; pres. Litchfield Realty Co., Georgetown, S.C., 1959-63, Wallace-Pate Real Estate, Inc., Georgetown, 1959—; pres. DeBordieu Corp., Georgetown, 1969—; co-owner Holiday Inn., Georgetown, 1967-72; owner Nautica Marine Center, Georgetown, 1967-69. Chmn., Georgetown Housing Authority, 1968-69. Served to 2d lt. AUS, 1957-58. Mem. Nat. Assn. Real Estate Bds., Winyah Indigo Soc., C. of C. (dir. 1969-70), Ducks Unltd., Sigma Alpha Epsilon. Club: DeBordieu Colony (pres., dir.). Address: Arcadia Plantation Georgetown SC 29440

PATE, WILLIAM WILSON, mfr.; b. Bennettsville, S.C., Aug. 17, 1900; s. William Walter and Willie (McElwee) P.; student Clemson Coll., 1918-19; m. Althea Fennell, Nov. 20, 1928; children—William Wilson, Wallace Fennell. Vice pres. McAlister, Smith & Pate, Greenville, S.C., 1930-42, Convenience, Inc., also Star Cross, Inc., Greenville, 1942-48; pres. Belrug Mills, also Wunda Weve Carpet Co., Greenville, 1946-63, Patewood Corp., 1964—, Byrd Furniture Co., Inc., 1964-74. Campaign chmn. Greater Greenville Community Chest, 1945-46. Trustee Greenville County Hosp., 1953-59. Mem. S.C. Ins. Commn. Served with USN, World War I. Mem. Greenville C. of C. (pres.). Methodist (chmn. ofcl. bd.). Kiwanian (dir.). Clubs: Greenville Country (gov.), Green Valley Country (dir., charter mem.) (Greenville, S.C.); Biltmore (N.C.) Forest Country. Home: Route 10 Patewood Dr Greenville SC 29607 Office: Northwood Indsl Park Greenville SC 29602

PATILLO, LEONARD SYLVESTA, assn. exec.; b. Paducah, Ky., Jan. 25, 1923; s. Prentice Sylvester and Mallie Louise (Hill) P.; certificate Paducah Jr. Coll., 1942; m. Mary Kathryn Kindred, Jan. 15, 1943; children—Patricia (Mrs. Robert Estes), Dennis Lynn. Reporter, photographer Paducah Sun Democrat, 1942-43, 45-46; editor, publicity dir. Houston C. of C., 1946-52, mgr. publs. dept., 1954-59, bus. mgr., 1959-70, gen. mgr., 1970-72, exec. v.p., gen. mgr., 1972—; dir. pub. relations Tex. Mfrs. Assn., 1952-54. Instr. Inst. Orgn. Mgmt., 1973-74. Exec. v.p. Greater Houston Community Found., 1971-74; dir. Korea-Tex. Trade Promotion Council, 1973-74, Houston Port Bur., 1969-75. Bd. dirs. Tex. Soc. Prevention Blindness, 1963-70. Served to 1st lt. USAAF, 1942-45. Decorated Purple Heart with oak leaf cluster. Mem. Am. C. of C. Execs. (v.p. profl. programs 1972-74), Am. Assn. Commerce Publs. (pres. 1965-66), C. of C. U.S. (mem. community and urban affairs com. 1973—), C. of C. Mgrs. and Secs. Assn. S. Tex. (pres. 1968-69), Houston Jr. C. of C. (hon.), So. Assn. C. of C. Execs. (sec.-treas. 1974-75). Rotarian. Clubs: Houston, Advertising (dir. 1956). Contbr. articles to profl. jours. Home: 5402 Rutherglenn St Houston TX 77035 Office: PO Box 53600 Houston TX 77052

PATMAN, WRIGHT, congressman; b. nr. Hughes Springs, Tex., Aug. 6, 1893; s. John and Emma (Spurlin) P.; LL.B., Cumberland U., 1916; m. Merle Connor, Feb. 14, 1919; children—Connor Wright, James Harold, William Neff. Cotton farmer, Tex., 1913-14; admitted to Tex. bar, 1916; practiced in Hughes Springs; asst. county atty. Cass County, Tex., 1916-17; dist. atty. 5th Jud. Dist., Tex., 1924-29; mem. 71st-93d congresses from 1st Tex. Dist. Mem. Tex. Ho. of Reps., 1921-24. Served with U.S. Army, 1917-19. Mem. Am. Legion, D.A.V. Democrat. Baptist. Mason (32 deg.). Club: Texas (pres. Washington). Home: 1205 Main St Texarkana TX 75501 also 500 23d St Washington DC 20037

PATO, MANUAL GONZALEZ, univ. athletic dir.; b. Ponce, P.R., 1913; B.S., La. State U., 1935, postgrad., 1935-37; m. 1941; 2 children. Tchr. pub. schs., P.R., from 1937; supt. community edn. Govt. of P.R., San Juan; faculty dept. phys. edn. Catholic U. P.R., Ponce, 1954—, dir. athletics and recreation, 1966—. Lectr., track and field coach P.R. nat. teams to World Olympics, Pan Am. games, Caribbean and C.Am. games, Iberian Am. games. Active Future Farmers Am., 4-H clubs, Boy Scouts Am., YNCA. Recipient awards for contbns. to youth of P.R. through phys. edn., sports and recreation from civic and ednl. orgns. Mem. P.R. (tech. com.), Caribbean and C.Am. (tech. com.) track and field fedns. Author textbooks on phys. edn., sports and recreation. Office: Catholic University of PR Ponce PR 00731

PATON, DAVID, physician; b. Balt., Aug. 16, 1930; s. Richard Townley and Helen (Meserve) P.; grad. Hill Sch., 1948; A.B. with honors, Princeton, 1952; M.D., Johns Hopkins, 1956; m. Jane Youngblood, Feb. 28, 1969; children—David Townley, Garrison Franke. Intern Cornell U. Med. Center, N.Y.C., 1956-57; resident Wilmer Inst., Johns Hopkins Hosp., Balt., 1959-64; asst. prof. Johns Hopkins Sch. Medicine, 1964-68, asso. prof., 1968-70; prof., chmn. dept. ophthalmology Baylor Coll. Medicine, Houston, 1970—; chief of service, ophthalmology Methodist Hosp., Houston; USPHS clin. asso. Nat. Inst. Neurol. Diseases and Blindness, 1957-59; founder Eye Bank Jordan, 1963. Vice-pres. William C. Conner Found.; mem. med. bd. Iran Found.; mem. dean's com. VA Hosp., Houston. Decorated officer third order of kingdom of Jordan. Diplomate Am. Bd. Ophthalmology. Fellow Am. Acad. Ophthalmology and Otolaryngology (asso. sec., chmn. ophthalmology basic and clin. sci. course), A.C.S. (gov. 1972-73); mem. Am. Soc. Order St. John (asst. hospitaller). Club: University (Houston). Contbr. numerous articles to profl. jours. Home: 5621 Bayou Glen Houston TX 77027 Office: Baylor College of Medicine Dept of Ophthalmology Texas Medical Center Houston TX 77025

PATRICK, JERRY HAMILTON, cosmetic co. exec.; b. Charlotte, N.C., Oct. 22, 1940; s. Earle Wilmore and Mary Evelyn (Jeter) P.; B.S., N.C. State U., 1963; m. Marion Lea Morris, Dec. 29, 1962; children—Kimberlea Marion, Jerry Hamilton, Sherri Morris. Personnel trainee Burlington Industries, Wake Forest, N.C., 1963-64; asst. personnel mgr., Raeford, 1964-65, asst. to div. personnel dir., Halifax, Va., 1965, personnel mgr., Raeford, N.C., 1965-66, Clarksville, Va., 1966-68; personnel mgr. Almay Cosmetics, Apex, N.C., 1968—; mem. retirement com. Schieffelin & Co., N.Y.C., 1971—. Town Commr., Apex, N.C., 1971—; chmn. United Fund, 1971; mem. Triangle J Council Govt., 1972—. Mem. Apex Jr. C. of C. (1st. v.p. projects 1969-70), Apex C. of C. (dir. 1968-71), Apex Civitan, Raleigh Wake Personnel Assn., Sigma Alpha Epsilon. Republican. Methodist (chmn. edn. 1970-72, v.p. council ministries 1970-71). Home: 3413 Wembley Ct Raleigh NC 27607 Office: Box 748 Almay Cosmetics Apex NC 27502

PATRICK, WALTER, lawyer; b. Harrodsburg, Ky., May 20, 1926; s. William L. and Martha (Shepherd) P.; J.D., U. Ky., 1951; m. Nancy Shinnick, Dec. 2, 1951; children—Tandy Carol, William Lewis. Admitted to Ky. bar, 1951, since practiced in Lawrenceburg; city atty., Lawrenceburg, 1952-72; circuit judge 53d Jud. Dist., 1972—. Dir. Anderson Nat. Bank. Served to 1st lt., inf. AUS, 1944-46; PTO. Mem Am. Legion (comdr. 1954-55), C. of C. (pres. 1958-62), Phi Sigma Kappa, Phi Delta Phi. Democrat. Mem. Christian Ch. Rotarian (pres. 1957-58). Home: Route 2 Lawrenceburg KY 40342 Office: Gordon Bldg Lawrenceburg KY 40342

PATRICK, WILLIAM TILDEN, JR., dentist; b. Hampton, Va., Nov. 4, 1906; s. William Tilden and Sally Miller (West) P.; student U. Richmond, 1927-28; D.D.S., Emory U., 1933; m. Faith Crawford, Aug. 26, 1935. Practice of gen. dentistry and dental surgery, Hampton, 1933—; mem. staff Dixie Hosp. Mem. Peninsula Dental Soc., Peninsula C. of C., Nat. Hist. Soc., Phi Gamma Delta, Phi Omega. Mason (32 deg., Shriner), Lion. Clubs: James River Country, Hampton Yacht, Huntington. Home: 1324 Chesapeake Av Hampton VA 23661 Office: 152 Chesterfield Rd Hampton VA 23661

PATT, YALE NANCE, educator; b. Medford, Mass., June 29, 1939; s. Abraham Walter and Sarah Clara (Tankel) P.; B.S., Northeastern U., 1962; M.S. (Tau Beta Pi fellow), Stanford, 1963, Ph.D., 1966; m. Carol Ann Weinstock, Sept. 4, 1966. Asst. prof. elec. engring. Cornell U., Ithaca, N.Y., 1966-67; asso. prof. computer sci. N.C. State U., Raleigh, 1969—. Lectr. Duke U., 1968; cons. Research Triangle Inst., Durham, N.C., 1973—, Frankford Arsenal, U.S. Army, 1973—; chmn. 5th Ann. Southeastern Symposium on Systems Theory, 1973; mem. steering com. 3d Internat. Symposium on Computer and Information Scis., 1969. Served to capt. AUS, 1967-69. Mem. Sigma Xi, Tau Beta Pi, Eta Kappa Nu. Contb. articles to profl. jours. Home: 617 Kirby St Raleigh NC 27606

PATTEN, BERNARD CLARENCE, educator; b. N.Y.C., Jan. 28, 1931; s. Bernard Clarence and Margaret Juliana (Paller) P.; A.B., Cornell U., 1952; M.S., Rutgers U., 1954; M.A., U. Mich., 1957; Ph.D., Rutgers U., 1959; m. Marie Ann DeLattre, Sept. 5, 1953; 1 dau., Karen Marie. Asso. marine scientist Va. Inst. Marine Sci., Gloucester Point, Va., also asst. prof. marine sci. Coll. William and Mary, Williamsburg, Va., 1959-63; ecologist Oak Ridge Nat. Lab., also asso. prof. botany U. Tenn., Knoxville, 1963-68; prof. zoology U. Ga., Athens, 1968—; founder, pres. Ecology Simulations, Inc., Athens, 1971—. Vis. prof. Colo. State U., U. Okla., Mich. State U., Utah State U., U. Mich.; lectr. numerous U.S. univs.; cons. to govt. and business. Served with Chem. Corps, AUS, 1954-56. Grantee Office Naval Research, 1963-64, NSF, 1972-73, Smithsonian Instn., 1972-73. Fellow A.A.A.S.; mem. Ecol. Soc. Am., Am. Soc. Naturalist, Am. Soc. Limnologists and Oceanographers, Soc. Gen. Systems Research, Simulation Councils, Inc., Am. Inst. Biol. Scis., Audubon Soc., Ga. Conservancy, Sierra Club, Zero Population Growth, Sigma Xi. Editor: Systems Analysis and Simulation in Ecology series, 1971—. Editorial bd. Jour. Theoretical Biology, 1967—, Simulation, 1973—. Contbr. articles to profl. jours. Home: 177 Chinquapin Way Athens GA 30601

PATTEN, IRA EUNICE BARRETT (MRS. GERLAND PAUL PATTEN), real estate and investment co. exec.; b. Greenville, Miss.; d. Ernest Arthur and Kittie Winfield (Walker) Barrett; student U. Ark., 1923, Nat. U. Mexico, 1960; m. Gerland Paul Patten, June 10, 1927; children—Gerald William (dec.), Yvonne Claire (Mrs. Yvonne Claire Law). With Western Union, 1924-27, HOLC, 1934-37; clk. U.S. Employment Security, 1942; head central files OPA, 1942-43; with U.S. C.E., 1943-60, cost accountant clk., 1943-60; sec.-treas., dir. Gerland P. Patten & Co., Little Rock, 1965—; sec.-treas. Garland P. Patten Devel. Corp., 1972—. Pres. Ladies Aux. of St. Vincents Infirmary, Little Rock, 1969-70, also vol.; treas. Girls Tng. Sch. Aux., Little Rock, 1965. Mem. Bookfellows (v.p. 1969-70, pres. 1971-73), Little Rock Musical Coterie, Ark. Assn. for Mental Health, Gaines House Aux. Methodist (treas. Womans Soc. Christian service, 1961-67, pres. 1972-73). Clubs: Fine Arts, Little Rock. Home: 8 Sunset Circle Little Rock AR 72207 Office: Nat Investors Life Bldg Little Rock AR 72201

PATTEN, WORCESTER ALLEN BRYAN, banker; b. Chattanooga, Sept. 25, 1940; s. Zeboim Cartter and Elizabeth Nelson (Bryan) P.; A.B., Cornell U., 1962; m. Kathleen Pound Caldwell, June 3, 1967; 1 dau., Kathleen Cartter. With Hamilton Nat. Bank, Chattanooga, 1965—, investment mgmt. officer, 1969—, v.p., 1971. Treas. Chattanooga Art Assn., 1970—. Bd. dirs. Community Services Greater Chattanooga, 1973; bd. dirs. Travellers Aid Soc., 1968—, 1st v.p., 1971-73. Served to 1st lt., inf. AUS, 1962-64. Mem. Inst. Chartered Financial Analysts, Financial Analysts Fedn., Chi Phi. Home: Penley Dr Lookout Mountain TN 37350 Office: 701 Market St Chattanooga TN 37350

PATTEN, ZEBOIM CARTTER, state senator, banker; b. Chattanooga, Feb. 2, 1903; s. Z.C. and Sarah (Key) P.; grad. Asheville Sch. for Boys, 1921; B.S., Cornell U., 1925; D.C.L., U. of South, 1962; m. Elizabeth Bryan, Aug. 19, 1931; children—Sarah (Mrs. Philip Haines Gwynn), Emma (Mrs. Beverly Allen Casey, Jr.), Zeboim Cartter III and W. A. Bryan (twins). Asst. treas. to v.p. Vol. State Life Ins. Co., 1928-39, now dir.; dir. Hamilton Nat. Bank; chmn. bd. First Fed. Savs. & Loan Assn. of Chattanooga. Mem. Tenn. Ho. of Reps., 1958-60, Tenn. Senate, 1961—. Mem. Tenn. Hist. Commn. Trustee U. Chattanooga; chmn. bd. Bonny Oaks Sch. Served to lt. USCGR, 1942-44. Recipient Distinguished Service award Kiwanis Club, 1969; named Tenn. Conservationist of Year, 1970. Mem. Chattanooga Hist. Assn. (pres. 1949; treas. 1949-56). Episcopalian. Author: A Tennessee Chronicle, 1953; Signal Mountain and Walden's Ridge, 1962; So Firm a Foundation, 1968. Home: 406 N Palisades Dr Signal Mountain TN 37377 Office: 33 Patten Pkwy Chattanooga TN 37402

PATTEN, ZEBOIM CARTTER, III, investment adviser; b. Chattanooga, Tenn., Sept. 25, 1940; s. Z. Cartter and Elizabeth Nelson (Bryan) P.; grad. Baylor Sch., Chattanooga, 1958; A.B., Princeton, 1962; m. Betty Lee Weigel, Oct. 7, 1965; children—Ashlee Bryan, Bethany Weigel. Investment analyst Vol. State Life Co., Chattanooga, 1962-68, asst. sec., 1968-70; treas., dir. Patten Investment Co., Chattanooga, 1970—; co-founder, pres., dir. North River Nursery Co., 1972—; dir. Chattanooga Choo Co., Chattanooga Cable TV Co. Mem. Inst. Chartered Financial Analysts, Atlanta Soc. Financial Analysts, Chattanooga Nurseryman's Assn. (pres. 1973-74), Chattanooga Area Hist. Assn. (pres. 1966-68). Clubs: Chattanooga City Farmers (pres. 1968), Fairyland. Home: Ashland Farm Route 8 Chattanooga TN 37409 Office: 33 Patten Pkwy Chattanooga TN 37402

PATTERSON, ANDY JAMES, educator, composer; b. Gordon, Tex., Feb. 20, 1929; s. Andrew Ebenezer and Ida Kate (Fulferi) P.; B.A. in Music, Tex. Christian U., 1948, Mus.M., 1951; Mus.D., Fla. State U., 1969; m. Beverly Jane Shaw, Jan. 25, 1963; children—Andy James, Michael. Adminstrv. asst. to dean fine arts, instr. music Tex. Christian U., Ft. Worth, 1948-51, 53-56; grad. asst. music Fla. State U., Tallahassee, 1956-58; asst. prof. music Fla. A and M U., 1967-68; asst. prof. music Ga. Tchrs. Coll., Statesboro, 1958-59; mem. faculty Hardin-Simmons U., Abilene, Tex., 1959—, asso. prof. music, 1959-69, prof., 1969—, chmn. dept. theory and composition, 1959—, also chmn. grad. studies in music. Served with AUS, 1951-53. Andy J. Patterson award named in his honor Theta Lambda chpt. Phi Mu Alpha-Sinfonia at Hardin-Simmons U.; recipient 1st place award orchestral composition Tex. Composers League Competition Contest, 1969. Mem. Am. Soc. U. Composers, Am. Music Center, Inc., Am. Assn. U. profs. (chpt. pres. 1964-66), Nat. Assn. Coll. Wind and Percussion Instrs., Southeastern Composers League, Pi Kappa Lambda, Phi Mu Alpha-Sinfonia (province gov. 1962-66). Composer large works for orchestra, sonatas, songs and choral works, piano and organ works, concerti for various instruments, others. Home: 1642 Swenson St Abilene TX 79603

PATTERSON, ARCHIBALD OSCAR, civil engr.; b. Monroe, Ga., Dec. 26, 1908; s. Archibald Oscar and Katharine (Hensler) P.; B.S., Ga. Inst. Tech. 1929; m. Gwendolyn Maybelle Theiling, Sept. 2, 1933; children—Katharine Maybelle, James Archibald. Civil engr. Interstate Commerce Comm., Washington, 1929-30; hydraulic engr. U.S. Geol. Survey, Augusta, Me., 1930-32, Charleston, W.Va., 1932-35, Chattanooga, 1935, Lebanon, Tenn., 1936-37, Fayetteville, Tenn., 1937-38, Chattanooga, 1938-41, Knoxville, Tenn., 1942-47; dist. engr. Fla. dist., surface water br., Ocala, 1947-64; dir. div. water resources Fla. Bd. Conservation, Tallahassee, 1964-67; dir. Fla. Water Resources Research Center, prof. environmental engring. U. Fla., Gainesville, 1967-70; cons. engr., 1970—. Recipient Meritorious Service award U.S. Dept. Interior, 1965. Fellow Am. Soc. C.E. (past pres. Fla. sect.). Presbyn. Mason. Home and office: 1444 SE 8th St Ocala FL 32670

PATTERSON, BENNETT BURR, lawyer; b. McCrory, Ark., Aug. 14, 1899; s. Marshall H. and Ethel E. (Lippman) P.; B.A., Hendrix Coll., 1918; postgrad. U. Ark., 1918; LL.B., Georgetown U., 1922; m. June Barbarin, Aug. 13, 1940; children—Sandra (Mrs. L.C. Woods), Kathleen June (Mrs. Wayne Merek). Admitted to Tex. bar, 1922, D.C. bar, 1922, U.S. Supreme Ct. bar, 1951; mem. firm Patterson, McDaniel & Boyd, and predecessor, Houston, 1922-48, sr. partner, 1948—. Prof. Houston Sch. Law, 1926-34; spl. lectr. Rice U., 1956-57, U. Houston, 1957, 45-66. Bd. dirs. Houston Sch. for Deaf Children. Served with U.S. Army, 1918-19. Recipient 1st award Am. Acad. Pub. Affairs Los Angeles, 1956. Mem. Am., Tex. bar assns., Am. Judicature Soc., C. of C. Episcopalian. Mason (33 deg., Shriner). Clubs: Sertoma (past pres.) (Houston); Sagewood Country. Author: The Forgotten Ninth Amendment, 1955. Office: Houston 1st Savs Bldg 711 Fannin St Houston TX 77002

PATTERSON, CARL NORRIS, surgeon; b. Perryville, Md., June 19, 1918; s. Lee Austin and Mildred (Jackson) P.; B.S., Franklin and Marshall Coll., 1941; M.D., U. Md., 1944; m. Ruth Elizabeth Dissinger, Dec. 27, 1943; children—Patrice Elaine, Lee Austin II, Carl Norris. Intern, resident Mercy Hosp., Balt., 1944-46; mem. otolaryngology staff U.S. Naval Hosp., Phila., 1946-47; practice medicine specializing in otolaryngology, Durham, 1947—; physician and surgeon McPherson Hosp., Durham, N.C., 1947—; attending staff Watts Hosp., Durham, 1950—, VA Hosp., Durham, 1965—; asst. clin. prof. Duke Med. Center, 1965—; cons. otolaryngology Dorothea Dix Hosp., Raleigh, 1970—, Murdock Hosp., Umstead Hosp.; clin. cons. surgery (otolaryngology) N.C. Meml. Hosp.; cons. staff Lincoln Hosp. Chmn. bd. Tng. Center for Hearing Impaired Children, Durham, 1969—. Served to lt. (j.g.) M.C., USNR, 1946-47. Diplomate Am. Bd. Otolaryngology. Fellow Am. Acad. Ophthalmology and Otolaryngology, Am. Laryngol., Rhinol. and Otologic Soc. (v.p. So. sect. 1976), A.C.S., Am. Acad. Facial Plastic and Reconstructive Surgery (sec. 1969-74, pres. elect 1975); mem. Am. Council Otolaryngology (com. on health manpower), A.M.A., So. Med. Assn., N.C., Durham-Orange County med. socs., N.C. Eye, Ear, Nose and Throat Soc. (pres. 1965), Lambda Chi Alpha. Episcopalian (vestryman 1958-61, 62-65, 69-72). Mason, Kiwanian. Club: Hope Valley Country (bd. govs., v.p. 1960) (Durham). Contbr. articles to med. jours. Home: 3930 Plymouth Rd Durham NC 27707 Office: 1110 W Main St Durham NC 27701

PATTERSON, CECIL JR., accountant; b. Hattiesburg, Miss., Aug. 13, 1944; s. Cecil and Marguerite Elizabeth (Lott) P.; student U. Syracuse, 1963-64; B.S. (Standard Oil of Ky. scholar), U. So. Miss., 1969; postgrad. U. North Fla., 1972—; m. Lorraine A. Cwalinski, May 30, 1964; 1 dau., Courtney Ayn. Sr. accountant Peat, Marwick, Mitchell, C.P.A.'s, Houston, 1969-71; accountant Jno. H. Swisher & Son, Inc., cigar mfrs., Jacksonville, Fla., 1971—. Served with USAF, 1963-67. C.P.A., Tex. Mem. Am., Fla. insts. C.P.A.'s, Alpha Epsilon Alpha, Phi Kappa Phi. Roman Catholic. Home: 7255 Floral Ridge Dr Jacksonville FL 32211 Office: PO Box 2230 Jacksonville FL 32203

PATTERSON, DONIS DEAN, clergyman; b. Holmesville, O., Apr. 27, 1930; s. Raymond J. and Louella (Glasgow) P.; B.Sc., Ohio State U., 1952, postgrad., 1960-61; postgrad. Harvard Div. Sch., 1956, Coll. Preachers, 1959, Inst. Advanced Pastoral studies, 1960, U.S. Army Command and Gen. Staff Coll., 1973; S.T.B., Episcopal Theol. Sch., 1957, M.Div., 1971; m. JoAnne Nida, Dec. 22, 1951; children—Christopher Nida, Andrew Joseph. Ordained to ministry Episcopal Ch., 1957; asst. Ch. Holy Nativity, South Weymouth, Mass., 1954-55, All Saints' Ch., Chelmsford, Mass., 1955-57; rector St. Andrew's Ch., Washington Court House, O., 1957-63; rector St. Mark's Episcopal Ch., Venice, Fla., 1963-70, headmaster Day Sch., 1963-70; rector All Saints Episcopal Ch., Winter Park, Fla., 1970—. Chmn. armed forces div. So. Ohio Diocese Episcopal Ch., 1958-63; moblzn. designee chief chaplains Dept. Army, 1959—; chmn. div. evangelism Episcopal Diocese of South Fla., 1964-68, mem. exec. bd., 1964, 1965-69, chmn. div. Christian living, 1968-69, chmn. div. Christian edn., 1969-70; mem. diocesan bd. Episcopal Diocese of S.W. Fla., 1969-70, Central Fla., 1972-74, co-chmn. program commn., 1972-73, chmn. deacon tng. program, 1972—; mem. Orlando Deanery Council, 1970—; chmn. armed forces div. Episcopal Diocese of Central Fla., 1970—; sponsor Nat. Evangelism Conf., S.E., 1973; field rep. Anglican Fellowship of Prayer, 1970—, chmn. 15th ann. meeting, 1973. Dist. chmn. Boy Scouts Am., 1960-63, instnl. rep., 1957-72, commr., 1958-60; chmn. clergy div. United Appeal, 1970-71. Bd. dirs., commr. Venice Housing Authority, 1966-70; bd. dirs. Sarasota (Fla.)-Manatee Guidance Center 1968-70, Share-A-Home of Am.; trustee Fla. Episcopal Coll., 1970-72; bd. dirs. Newman Centers in Fla., 1972—. Served with AUS, 1952-54; Korea; lt. col. Res. Recipient 5 George Washington medals Freedoms Found. Valley Forge, 1965-71. Mem. Soc. Colonial Wars, S.A.R. (state chaplain Ohio 1960-62), Mil. Order World Wars (chaplain) Am. Legion (chaplain), Res. Officers Assn., Fayette Ministerial Assn. (pres. 1965-67), Venice Area Ministerial Assn. 1967-70), Chaplain Res. Officers Assn., Mil. Chaplains Assn., Lambda Chi Alpha. Rotarian (pres. 1966-67). Club: Venice Yacht (fleet chaplain). Contbr. articles to various publs. Home: 210 Trismen Terrace Winter Park FL 32789 Office: 338 E Lyman Av Winter Park FL 32789

PATTERSON, DWIGHT F(LEMING), banker; b. Lanford, S.C., Nov. 19, 1907; s. William L. and Janie F. (Fleming) P.; A.B., Wofford Coll., 1929, LL.D., 1959; diploma Grad. Sch. Banking Rutgers U., 1940; m. Mary Smith, June 18, 1935; children—Dwight F., Lawrence Leon, Drayton Smith. Asst. cashier Palmetto Bank, Laurens, S.C., 1931-36, cashier, 1936-46, exec. v.p., dir., 1946-52, pres., 1952—, chmn. bd.; dir. Laurens Indsl. Devel. Corp., Laurens Holding Co., Investors Nat. Life Ins. Co., Inc., Palmetto Spinning Corp., Laurens. Trustee Laurens City Schs., 1947-53, Laurens Co. Library, Laurens Sch. Dist. 55, 1963—; sec. bd. trustees Columbia (S.C.) Coll., 1948-50; sec. bd. trustees Wofford Coll., 1948-68, chmn. bd., 1948-58, trustee 1968—; mem. exec. council Methodist Coll. Found. S.C.; mem. bd. edn. Upper S.C. Conf. Methodist Ch., 1944-48. Mem. Ind. Bankers Assn. Am. (exec. council 1956—), S.C. Bankers Assn. (pres. 1955-56), Blue Key, Phi Beta Kappa, Pi Kappa Phi. Methodist (steward). Kiwanian (past pres.). Club: Piedmont (Spartanburg S.C.). Contbr. articles on current banking to trade mags. Home: 701 W Main St Laurens SC 29360 Office: Pub Sq Laurens SC 29360

PATTERSON, EARL EDGAR, mfg. co. exec.; b. Oklahoma City, Apr. 14, 1923; s. Earl and Bessie Elmira (Threadkel) P.; B.Chem.Engring., Okla. U., 1944, M.Chem.Engring., 1947; Sc.D., Mass. Inst. Tech., 1950; m. Jean May, Nov. 17, 1956; children—Patricia Ann, Robert Earl. Chem. engr. E.I. duPont de Nemours & Co., Newport, Del., 1950-54; with Reynolds Metals Co., Richmond, Va., 1954—, exec. asst. to exec. v.p., 1964-70, gen. dir. metals research div., 1971-72, spl. asst. to exec. v.p., 1972—; dir. Reynolds Research Corp., Richmond. Chmn. Chesterfield County Republican Com., 1960-66; vice chmn. Richmond Rep. Com., 1969—. Served with USNR, 1944-46; PTO. Mem. Am. Chem. Soc., Am. Inst. Chem. Engrs., Am. Soc. for Metals, Sigma Xi, Mem. Disciples of Christ. Home: 8318 Whitewood Rd Richmond VA 23235 Office: Reynolds Metals Co 5th and Cary Richmond VA 23261

PATTERSON, GEORGE ELLIOTT, JR., lawyer; b. East Orange, N.J., Oct. 24, 1916; s. George Elliott and Beatrice (Fair) P.; A.B., Dartmouth, 1939; LL.B., Cornell U., 1942; m. Maxine Webb, May 11, 1944; children—Caroline A. (Mrs. John M. Brumbaugh), Kathleen Fair. Admitted to Fla. bar, 1947; gen. practice law, Miami, Fla., 1947—. Bd. dirs., sec. Dade County Citizens Safety Council, 1964-68. Served with AUS, 1942-46. Mem. Am., Fla., Dade County bar assns., Miami-Dade County C. of C. (pres. marine council 1962-64), Phi Delta Phi, Chi Phi. Club: Coral Reef Yacht (commodore 1968-69). Home: 8285 SW 54th Av Miami FL 33143 Office: NE Airlines Bldg 150 SE 2d Av Miami FL 33131

PATTERSON, JACKSON TAYLOR, ednl. adminstr.; b. Clarksville, Ark., Apr. 29, 1915; s. William N. and Clara (Burt) P.; student Coll. of Ozarks, 1934-35; grad. Draughon's Bus. Coll., 1937; D.Bus. Adminstrn. (hon.), 1970; m. Lucile Sanders, Dec. 24, 1937; children—Jack T., Clara Ann. Accountant, Allis Chalmers Mfg. Co., Dallas, 1937-41; N.Am. Aviation Co., Dallas, 1942-43; treas., bus. mgr. Coll. of Ozarks, Clarksville, 1943—. Chmn., Horsehead Water Users Assn. Johnson County; chmn. comprehensive health planning com. W. Central Ark. Planning and Devel. Dist. Pres. bd. trustees Clarksville Hosp.; mem. exec. bd. Westark council Boy Scouts Am. Mem. Nat., So. assns. coll. and univ. bus. officers, Clarksville C. of C. Democrat. Presbyn. (elder, pres. bd. trustees). Mason (32 deg), Rotarian. Home: Route 3 Box 107 Clarksville AR 72830

PATTERSON, JAMES NATHANIEL, JR., gen. contractor exec.; b. Wichita Falls, Tex., Mar. 10, 1927; s. James Nathaniel and Hal (Godley) P.; B.S., Tex. A. and M. U., 1948; postgrad. Mass. Inst. Tech., 1950; m. Lila Thrace Mathews, July 22, 1950; children—Debra Alice, James N. III, Jana Stone. Engr. Thos. S. Byrne, Inc., 1948-58, v.p., 1958-62, pres., 1962—, chmn. bd., 1973—. Served with AUS, 1951-53. Mem. Assn. Gen. Contractors Am. (pres. Ft. Worth chpt. 1964-65), N. Tex. Contractors Assn. (1st v.p. 1973, pres. 1974). Home: 1724 Aztec Fort Worth TX 76112 Office: Electric Service Bldg Fort Worth TX 76102

PATTERSON, JOHN MELVIN, physician; b. Nettleton, Miss., Dec. 16, 1925; s. John Lee and Melva (Black) P.; B.S., U. Miss., 1950; M.D., Jefferson Med. Sch., 1954; m. Maxine McDaniel, Aug. 24, 1952; children—Bettye Claire, Mary Lise, Patti Ann. Intern, Bapt. Meml. Hosp., Memphis, 1954-55; gen. practice medicine, Pontotoc, Miss., 1955—; mem. staff Pontotoc Community Hosp. Trustee Traceway Manor, Tupelo, Miss., Pontotoc Community Hosp. Served with USNR, 1944-47. Mem. Miss., N.E. Miss. med. socs., A.M.A., Am. Acad. Gen. Practice. Methodist (trustee) Lion. Home: 404 E Oxford St Pontotoc MS 38863 Office: 113 Washington St Pontotoc MS 38863

PATTERSON, MANFORD KENNETH, JR., found. exec.; b. Muskogee, Okla., Aug. 20, 1926; s. Manford Kenneth and SaraLou (Patton) P.; B.S., U. Okla., 1953, M.S., 1954; Ph.D., Vanderbilt U., 1961; m. Nancy Beverly Wilson, Aug. 21, 1953; 1 dau., Shelley Lynne. Sr. research chemist Samuel Roberts Noble Found., Ardmore, Okla., 1961-66, head nutrition sect., biomed. div., 1966-73, dir. biomed. div., 1973—, v.p. found., 1973—. Mem. Gov.'s Com. to Combat Cancer in Okla., 1973—. Served with USNR, 1944-46. Mem. Tissue Culture Assn. (treas. 1971—), Am. Soc. Biol. Chemists, Am. Assn. Cancer Research, (pres. elect Southwest sect. 1973). Kiwanian (sec. 1971-73, dir. 1965-69). Editor: (with P.F. Kruse, Jr.) Tissue Culture-Methods and Applications, 1973. Asst. editor In Vitro, Jour. Tissue Culture Assn., 1971—. Home: 313 Campbell Ardmore OK 73401 Office: Route 1 Ardmore OK 73401

PATTERSON, MILDRED L(UCRETIA), judge; b. Guthrie, Okla., July 30, 1912; d. Columbus W. and Lydia K. (Cash) Patterson; student Okla. City Coll. Law, 1941-45. Legal sec., bookkeeper, underwriter, 1931-51; admitted to Okla. bar, 1945; head law book dept. Co-Op. Pub. Co., Guthrie, 1951-54; asst. editor Ofcl. Session Laws of Okla., 1951, editor, 1953, 55, 57, 59, 61; asst. editor New Ins. Laws of Okla., 1951; county judge Logan County, Guthrie, 1955-69, asso. dist. judge, 1969—. Pres. bd. dirs. Guthrie Community Chest Fund, 1957-58; asso. mem. Gov.'s Com. on Furtherance of Employment for Physically Handicapped, 1957, 58—; mem. Pres.'s Com. on Handicapped; dir. Okla. Mental Health Assn. Trustee I.O.A. Ranch for Boys, Perkins, Okla.; mem. nat. council U.S.O. Mem. Okla. Council Juvenile Ct. Judges (sec.-treas. 1963-65), Am. Legion Aux., Nat. Council Juvenile Ct. Judges, Okla. Juvenile Officers Assn., Bus. and Profl. Women's Club (past pres.), Am. Life Assn. (dir.), Okla. Assn. Women Lawyers (state sec. 1948), Okla. County Officers Assn. (dist. pres.), Iota Tau Tau. Mem. Christian Ch. Mem. Order Eastern Star, Daus. of Nile. Home: 215 N Elm St Guthrie OK 73044 Office: Ct House Guthrie OK 73044

PATTERSON, PAUL STOYLE, advt. exec.; b. Mt. Vernon, O., July 1, 1904; s. James John and Mary Anna (Stoyle) P.; student Western Res. U., 1923, 25-26, U. Pitts., 1930; m. Susan Clark, Dec. 29, 1939;children—Virginia Ann (Mrs. Jesse Callahan Jr.), Jan Judge, James Reynolds. Advt. mgr. zone 5, Nat. Dairy Products Co., Pitts., 1942-53; dir. advt. Fla. Citrus Commn., Lakeland, 1953-57; v.p. Liller, Neal, Battle & Lindsey, Inc., Atlanta, 1957-69; advt. and promotion cons., 1969—. Mem. Active Voters Ga. (v.p. 1968), Brotherhood of New Hope, Atlanta (sec. 1967-68, v.p. 1969). Unitarian-Universalist (sec. 1959-60). Home and office: 496 Bryn Mawr Lane Atlanta GA 30327

PATTERSON, RONALD BRINTON, tobacco co. exec.; b. Wichita, Kan., Apr. 20, 1941; s. Charles Odell and Bonnie Muriel (Houser) P.; A.B., Hastings Coll., 1963; Ph.D., U. Neb., 1970; m. Carolyn Sue Routh, July 7, 1971; children—Phillip Brinton, Melissa Dale. Research chemist, research dept. Lorillard div. Loews Theatres, Inc., Greensboro, N.C., 1969-72, with product devel. dept., 1972—, supr. product devel., 1973—. Mem. Am. Chem. Soc., Greensboro Jr. C. of C., Greensboro Oratorio Soc. Republican. Methodist. Home: 2302 Lakeshore Dr Greensboro NC 27407 Office: 420 English St Greensboro NC 27420

PATTERSON, SANSON CORNELIUS, credit bur. exec.; b. McKeesport, Pa., Sept. 7, 1909; s. William Elmore and Lois Margaret (Close) P.; ed. pub. schs.; m. Mary Elizabeth Stroud, July 19, 1945; children—James Lane, Michael Anthony. Mgr., Beneficial Finance Co. Pa., Cal., Ore., Colo., 1930-40; mgr. Morr Loan Co., Pueblo, Colo., 1940-42; asst. credit mgr. May Co., Denver, 1942-43; credit mgr. Neustetter Co., Denver, 1943-50; gen. credit mgr. Winkelman Bros. Apparel, Inc., Detroit, 1950-58, J.C. Penney Co., N.Y.C., 1958-67; pres., chief exec. officer Nat. Found. Consumer Credit, Inc., Washington, 1967-69, also trustee; owner, pres. Credit Bur. New Haven, Conn., Inc., 1967-70; retail credit cons. 03-P-M Assos., 1969-70; pres. Credit Services Internat., Inc., 1971—. Mem. adv. com. to spl. com. Nat. Conf. Commrs. on Uniform State Laws, 1964-67; chmn. spl. study group industry and labor on Non-Profit Commn. Debt Counseling Service, 1965-67; cons., truth in lending div. Fed. Res. Bd., Washington, 1968—. Mem. Nat. Retail Mchts. Assn. (bd. dirs. 1962-64, dir., chmn. credit mgmt. div. 1962-64), Detroit Retail Credit Men's Assn. (pres. 1953-54, dir. 1954-58), Asso. Credit Burs. Episcopalian. Mason (Shriner). Clubs: Houston, Warwick, Plaza (Houston); International (Washington). Contbr. articles in field to trade mags. Home: 831 Soboda Ct Houston TX 77024 Office: 6767 Southwest Freeway Houston TX 77036

PATTERSON, WILLIAM H., univ. pres.; b. Charleston, S.C., April 10, 1913; s. William H. and Leacadia (Dawson) P.; A.B., U. S.C., 1934, M.A., 1949, Ph.D., 1952; summer student Columbia, U. Wis.; H.H.D., Francis Marion Coll., 1973; m. Frances Rhude Meetze, May 29, 1942 (div. Oct. 1970); m. 2d, Mary Alice Copeland, July 6, 1971. Draftsman FCA, 1934-37; topog. draftsman S.C. Hwy. Dept., 1937-40; archtl. engr. C.E., War Dept., 1940-43; instr. U. S.C., 1943-47, asst. prof. 1947-50, asst. to pres., 1950-52, dean adminstrn., bus. mgr. 1952-61, dean univ., 1961-66, sr. v.p., 1966-68, provost regional campuses, 1967-72, sec. bd. trustees, 1964—, provost, 1968-74, pres., 1974—. Mem. Am., So., S.C. hist. assns., S.C. Soc. Engrs., Soc. History Tchr., Newcomen Soc. Eng. Episcopalian. Home: President's House Columbia SC 29208

PATTERSON, WILLIAM VAUGHAN, educator; b. Oklahoma City, Dec. 3, 1947; s. Elmer William and Elizabeth Ann (Vaughan) P.; B.F.A., U. Okla., 1970; M.F.A., U. Utah, 1972; m. Jane Harriet Richards, June 23, 1973. Mem. box office staff Pioneer Meml. Theatre, U. Utah, Salt Lake City, 1970-71, promotion asst., 1971-72; instr. drama, supr. departmental publicity and pub. relations U. Tex., Austin, 1972-74. Served with AUS, 1970. Mem. Am. Theatre Assn., Univ. and Coll. Theatre Assn., S.W. Theatre Conf., Assn. Coll. and Univ. Concert Mgrs., Phi Kappa Phi, Phi Eta Sigma, Alpha Psi Omega.

PATTESON, ALAN GUY, JR., radio sta. exec. operator, gin co. exec.; b. Jonesboro, Ark., Nov. 14, 1928; s. Alan Guy and Katherine Patricia (Carter) P.; B.S. in Agr., U. Mo., 1950; m. Carol Ann Busch, July 23, 1952; children—Christian, Lucia, Ellen, Guy, Dick. Partner, co-owner, operator Patteson Gin Co., Trumann, Ark., 1950—; co-owner, partner Patteson Bros. Farms, Trumann, 1950—; co-owner, partner, operator radio sta. KBTM AM-FM, Jonesboro, Ark., 1958—; dir. Merc. Bank, Jonesboro, 1968—; treas. Citizens Fed. Savs. & Loan, Jonesboro, 1964—. Chmn. bd. Ark. Council Human Relations, 1969-71; bd. dirs. Nat. Conf. Christians and Jews, Ark. Arts Center, chmn. bd., 1973; chmn. Ark. Library Trustees, 1972; treas. Eastern Ark. council Boy Scouts Am., 1960-67; chmn. Jonesboro Library Bd., 1961-70; trustee Ark. Library Commn. Ark. committeeman Republican party, 1970-72. Recipient Silver Beaver award Eastern Ark. Area council Boy Scouts Am., 1971, Liberty Bell award Craighead Bar Assn., 1972. Mem. Am. Library Trustee Assn. (dir. 1971—), Jonesboro C. of C. (pres. 1965), Northeast Ark. Childhood Devel. Assn. (pres. 1966-68), Agrl. Council Ark. (mem. bd. 1954-65), Inst. Politics (dir. 1971-73). Roman Catholic (chmn. parish edn. bd. 1965-67). Rotarian (pres. 1970-71). Home: 2801 Harrisburg Rd Jonesboro AR 72401 Office: 603 Madison St Jonesboro AR 72401

PATTESON, JOSEPH DRURY, JR., educator; b. Oklahoma City, Dec. 14, 1933; s. Joseph Drury and Verna June (Montooth) P.; student Baylor U., 1951, Okla. Bapt. U., 1952-54; B.A., Wheaton Coll., 1955; B.D., Southwestern Bapt. Theol. Sem., 1960, Th.D., 1965; M.A., U. Chgo., 1969; Dual fellow, asst. Rice U., 1962-63; m. Ida Mae Norris, June 14, 1958; children—Leah Renee, Jennifer Elyse. Jr. partner Patteson & Patteson, Homebuilders, Oklahoma City, 1957-69; part-time instr. philosophy and theology Judson Coll., Elgin, Ill., 1967; asso. prof. philosophy and religion Carson-Newman Coll., Jefferson City, Tenn., 1969—. Mem. Am. Acad. Religion, Am. Assn. U. Profs., Am. Soc. Christian Ethics, Phi Sigma Tau. Democrat. Episcopalian. Home: Box 65 Mill Springs Rd New Market TN 37820 Office: Box 2012 Carson Newman Coll Jefferson City TN 37760

PATTISHALL, FRANKLIN DAVID, orthodontist; b. Burlington, N.C., Mar. 6, 1936; s. William Thomas and Bessie (Vincent) P.; student Elon Coll., 1954-57; D.D.S., U. N.C., 1961, M.S., 1969; m. Bennia Jo Carpenter, Dec. 19, 1959; children—Laura, Franklin David, Jane, Melissa. Pvt. practice dentistry, Morganton, N.C., 1963-67; pvt. practice orthodontics, Charlotte, N.C., 1969—. Bd. dirs. Mecklenburg Cancer Soc. Served to lt. Dental Corps, USNR, 1961-63. Mem. Am. Dental Assn., Am. Assn. Orthodontists, So. Soc. Orthodontists, 2d Dist. N.C. Dental Soc. (exec. com.), Psi Omega. Episcopalian. Club: Civitan (pres. Charlotte 1974—). Home: 2300 Queens Rd E Charlotte NC 28207 Office: 2301 Rama Rd Charlotte NC 28212

PATTISON, DAVID JOHN, govt. ofcl.; b. Hartford, Conn., May 4, 1937; s. William and Ruth (Anderson) P.; B.A., Am. U., 1959, J.D., 1961, M.A., 1965; m. Joyce Adams, June 13, 1959; children—Scott, Stuart, Sharon, Dwight. Corr. Fla. New Service, Washington, 1958-61; editor-reporter Bur. Nat. Affairs, Inc., Washington, 1961-63; asso. gen. counsel Nat. Assn. Life Underwriters, Washington, 1963-69; dir. liaison Office of Emergency Preparedness, Exec. Office of Pres., Washington, 1969-71, asst. to dir. for congl. and pub. affairs, 1971-73, dir. house liaison Dept. Housing and Urban Devel., 1973—. Mem. Fairfax County (Va.) Sch. Bd., 1968-73, Fairfax County Juvenile Crime Study Commn., 1969. Republican candidate for Va. Ho. of Dels., 1967. Mem. Am., Va. bar assns. Home: 3501 Prosperity Av Fairfax VA 22030 Office: Dept Housing and Urban Development Washington DC 20410

PATTON, ALMEDA JANE VANDIKE, librarian; b. Elberon, Ia., May 17, 1914; d. Frank Allen and Clara Marie (Tarvestad) VanDike; student Culver Stockton Coll., U. Ia., 1931-36, B.S., Fla. State U., 1957, M.S., 1967; m. John Henry Patton, Feb. 20, 1937 (div.); children—Jon, Judith (Mrs. John Lotas), Joanna. Librarian, Springfield (Fla.) Elementary Sch., 1956-57, Bay County Pub. Library, Panama City, Fla., 1957—; dir. N.W. Regional Library System, Panama City, 1960—. Mem. Fla. Right-to-Read Adv. Council. Work-study grantee Fla. State Library, 1965-66. Mem. Am. Assn. U. Women (edn. chmn. 1961-66), Am., Southeastern, Fla. (mem. standards com. 1969—) library assns., Aubudon Assn. (program chmn. 1971-72), Panama Art Assn. (program chmn. 1972), C. of C. (chmn. human resource com. 1974), World Future Soc. Clubs: Woman's (chmn. edn. com. 1962-66), Country (Panama City). Home: 1613 Dewitt St Panama City FL 32401 Office: 25 W Government St Panama City FL 32401

PATTON, CHARLES CLIFFORD, ednl. adminstr.; b. Cushing, Okla., July 10, 1936; s. Johnnie Bud and Velma Mae (Wells) P.; B.S. in Petroleum Engring., U. Okla., postgrad. (Humble Oil fellow), 1960-61; Ph.D. (Am. Chem. Soc., Sinclair fellows), U. Tex., 1963. Exploitation engr. Shell Oil Co., Lafayette, La., 1959-60; sr. research petroleum engr. Monsanto Co., Texas City, Tex., 1963-64; research scientist Continental Oil Co., Ponca City, Okla., 1964-67, research group leader, 1967-69; staff engr. Hudson's Bay Oil & Gas Co., Calgary, Alta., Can., 1969-70; asso. prof., dir. Sch. Petroleum and Geol. Engring., U. Okla., Norman, 1970—, Eric P. Halliburton Distinguished Prof., 1972—. Adviser Jr. Achievement, Calgary, 1970; Ponca City mgr. Henry Bellmon for U.S. Senate, 1968. Served with USAF, 1960. NSF grantee, 1972. Registered profl. engr. Mem. Nat. Assn. Corrosion Engrs. (vice chmn. North Central Okla. sect. 1968-69), Soc. Petroleum Engrs. (dir. No. Okla. sect. 1968-69), Am. Inst. Mining, Metall. and Petroleum Engrs., Okla. Soc. Profl. Engrs., Sigma Xi, Tau Beta Pi, Sigma Tau, Omicron Delta Kappa, Pi Epsilon

Tau. Author: Practical Oilfield Water Technology, 1971. Home: 848 Cardinal Creek Blvd Norman OK 73069

PATTON, RAYMOND JAMES, supt. schs.; b. Harrison, Ark., Jan. 23, 1919; s. Walter G. and Fufa Belle (Pennington) P.; B.S., Central State Coll., Edmond, Okla., 1946; M.S., Okla. State U., 1950; m. Elsie Mae Morris, Mar. 8, 1939; children—James Edward, Billy Ray. Prin. high sch., Stroud, Okla., 1943-58; supt. schs., Shidler, Okla., 1958-61, Meeker, Okla., 1961-68, Chandler, Okla., 1968—. Served with AUS, 1944-45. Mem. Chandler C. of C., Am. Legion, Okla. Edn. Assn., N.E.A., Am., Okla. assns. sch. adminstrs., Okla. Sch. Bus. Ofcls. Lion. Home: 203 Moorman Dr Chandler OK 74834 Office: 15 Steele Av Chandler OK 74834

PATTON, ROBERT WILLIAM, judge; b. Wilmington, N.C., Feb. 6, 1911; s. Robert Evan and Ellinora (O'Keef) P.; student Duke, 1928-30; LL.B., U. Fla., 1933. Admitted to Fla. bar, 1933; practiced in St. Petersburg and Tampa, Fla., 1933-64; judge 13th Jud. Circuit of Fla., 1965—; asst. atty., Hillsborough County, Fla., 1959-63, county atty., 1964. Mem. Am., Tampa-Hillsborough County bar assns., Fla. Bar. Kiwanian. Home: 2904 Angeles St Tampa FL 33609 Office: Hillsborough County Ct House Tampa FL 33601

PATTON, ROGER DALE, banker; b. Olive Hill, Ky., June 16, 1933; s. Lon and Lula (King) P.; student Morehead U., 1954-57; m. Jenny Jo Tackett, Dec. 21, 1956; 1 son, Roger Michael. Lab. technician Gen. Refractories Co., Olive Hill, Ky., 1954-57; cashier Peoples Bank, Olive Hill, 1958-72, v.p., 1972-74, pres., 1974—. Served with USAF, 1951-54. Mason. Home: Grefco Heights Olive Hill KY 41164 Office: Main St Olive Hill KY 41164

PATTON, VINCENT DION, state ofcl.; b. Pikesville, Tenn., Nov. 7, 1920; s. John A. and Sarah (Swafford) P.; B.Chem. Engring., U. Fla., 1949; M.S. in San. Engring., U. N.C., 1958; m. Sarah Bowyer, Sept. 2, 1950. Chem. engr. Fla. Citrus Commn., Lakeland, 1949-51, Hawkridge Metals Co., Boston, 1955-56; san. engr. Fla. Bd. Health, Jacksonville, 1956-62, dir. div. indsl. wastes, 1962-68; dir. Fla. Air and Water Pollution Control Commn., 1968-69; exec. dir. Fla. Air and Water Pollution Control Dept., 1969-71; exec. dir. Fla. Pollution Control Dept., 1971-73; dir. environmental services div. Watson & Co., Tampa, Fla., 1973—. Sec. Fla. Air Pollution Control Commn. Served with AUS, 1942-45. Mem. Am. (chmn. Fla. sect.), Fla. planning and civic assns., Fla. Pollution Control Assn. (pres. 1969), Air Pollution Control Assn. (chmn. 1968), Delta Omega. Democrat. Episcopalian. Contbr. articles to profl. jours. Home: 3901 Tudor Ct Tampa FL 33614 Office: 3010 Azeele St Tampa FL 33609

PAUL, E(LL) GRADY, JR., lawyer; b. Montgomery, Ala., Oct. 7, 1918; s. E. Grady and Mamie (Blackburn) P.; student U. Richmond, 1939-41; LL.B., U. Va., 1948. Admitted to Va. bar, 1948; with Income and Estate Tax Dept., Internal Revenue Service, Richmond, Va., 1948-52; practiced in Richmond, 1952—; mem. firm Lane, Paul & Rudd, 1952-65. Served with USAAF, 1941-45. Decorated Silver Star, Purple Heart, Air medal. Mem. Am., Va. (past chmn. bd. govs.) bar assns., Va. State Bar, Theta Chi, Delta Theta Chi. Contbr. articles to profl. jours. Home: 300 E Franklin St Richmond VA 23220 Office: 830 E Main St Richmond VA 23219

PAUL, GWENDOLYN HOPE (MRS. JAMES EDWARD PAUL), civic worker; b. nr. Forest City, N.C., July 7, 1933; d. Leonard T. and Cleo (Vassey) Hope; B.S., Limestone Coll., 1955; M.Ed., U. Ga., 1970; m. Sherman Ray Ellington, June 14, 1957 (div. Nov. 1967); children—Stephen Ray, Alice Lynn, Carol Ann; m. 2d, James Edward Paul, May 17, 1968. Tchr. phys. edn. Gastonia (N.C.) City Schs., 1955-57; tchr. Cherokee County Schs., Gaffney, S.C., 1957-59, Forest Park (Ga.) Sr. High Sch., 1960-66; tchr. safety edn. U. Ga., Athens, 1966-67; DeKalb Jr. Coll., Decatur, Ga., 1966-67; counselor Huie Elementary Sch., Forest Park, Ga., 1966-71; counselor Pebblebrook High Sch., Mableton, Ga., 1971—. Chmn. Cystic Fibrosis Dr., Clayton Co., Ga., 1961—; leader Girl Scouts of Am., 1951-53; pres. Terrell Mill Estate Garden Club, 1973, 2d v.p., 1974; organizer, social chmn. Terrell Mill-Old Mill Trace Homeowners Assn., 1974. Named Woman of Yr., Forest Park, 1961. Mem. N.E.A., Ga., Clayton County Edn. assns., Ga. Sch. Counselor Assn., Am. Personnel and Guidance Assn., Ga. Drivers Edn. Assn. (treas. 1966-67), Chi Beta Phi, Alpha Delta, Beta Sigma Phi (pres. 1962-66). Democrat. Baptist. Home: 1410 Glenwood Ct SE Marietta GA 30060

PAUL, HOMER, banker; b. Claremore, Okla., Sept. 14, 1932; s. Homer and Helen (Lafferty) P.; B.A., U. Okla., 1954, LL.B., 1959; m. Carol Ann Engleman, Aug. 23, 1958; children—Charles William, Lela Carol, Jamie Helen, Jennifer Jean. With Liberty Nat. Bank & Trust Co., Oklahoma City, 1959—, with trust dept., 1959-66, corr. dept., 1966-68, bus. devel. dept., 1968-69, v.p. comml. loan dept., 1969—. Bd. dirs. Okla. Mental Health Council. Served to lt. col. USMCR, 1954-56. Methodist (mem. ofcl. bd.). Home: 2905 Arrowhead Dr Edmond OK 73034 Office: PO Box 25848 Oklahoma City OK 73125

PAUL, LYNN EDWIN, physicist; b. Huntington, Ind., Oct. 9, 1926; s. Charles Maxwell and Merle (Thomas) P.; B.S. Physics, Purdue U., 1951; M.Physics, U. Mich., 1957; m. Phyllis Ann Young, June 20, 1952; children—Mary Dolores, Philip Charles. Research asso. electron tube lab. U. Mich., Ann Arbor, 1953-62, research asso. univ., 1964-65; asso. research physicist Conductron Corp., Ann Arobr, 1962-64; sr. project engr. Bendix Electro Optics Co., Ann Arbor, 1965-69; sr. engr. electron devices div. Varo Corp., Garland, Tex., 1969—; dean Ind. No. U., Gas City, 1964-66. Served with USNR, 1945-46. Mem. I.E.E.E., Full Gospel Businessmen, Sigma Pi Sigma. Episcopalian. Mason, Elk, Kiwanian. Author paper. Home: 4250 Creekdale St Dallas TX 75229 Office: 2203 Walnut St Garland TX 65040

PAUL, RAPHAEL NATHAN, pediatric cardiologist; b. Dayton, O., Oct. 15, 1915; s. Philip and Ethel (Cole) P.; B.S., U. Dayton, 1937; M.D., U. Cin., 1941; m. Jeannine Smid, July 14, 1960; children—Deanna Shainberg, Thomas; stepchildren—Alan, Roslyn, Robert. Intern Cin. Gen. Hosp., 1941-42, Kings County Hosp., Bklyn., 1942-43; asst. in pediatrics Johns Hopkins Hosp., Balt., 1946-47; resident pediatrics Children's Hosp., Phila., 1947-48; practice medicine, specializing in pediatric cardiology, Memphis, 1948—; active staff Le Bonheur Children's Hosp., Memphis, 1952—, chief staff, 1969-71, chief cardiovascular lab., 1956—; cons. pediatric cardiology St. Joseph's Hosp., Meth. Hosp., Bapt. Hosp.; attending staff John Gaston Hosp.; asst. prof. pediatrics U. Tenn., Memphis, 1951—. Served to capt. USAAF, 1942-46. Recipient Man of Year award Am. Physicians Fellowship, 1973. Diplomate Am. Bd. Pediatrics. Fellow Am. Acad. Pediatrics, Am. Coll. Cardiology (gov. 1957-60), Am. Coll. Chest Physicians; mem. A.M.A., Tenn. Med. Assn., Memphis and Shelby County Med. Soc., Tenn., Memphis pediatric socs., Am., Memphis (pres. 1952-53) heart assns., Pan Am. Med. Assn., Am. Physicians Fellowship (trustee 1972—), Royal Soc. Health (Eng.), Internat. Coll. Pediatrics, Sigma Xi. Home: 5660 Rich Rd Memphis TN 38117 Office: 848 Adams St Memphis TN 38103

PAUL, ROBERT, lawyer; b. N.Y.C., Nov. 22, 1931; s. Gregory and Sonia (Rijock) P.; B.A., N.Y. U., 1953; J.D., Columbia, 1958; m. Arlene Naar, Feb. 2, 1953; children—Peter Franklin, Gina. Admitted to Fla. bar, 1958, N.Y. bar, 1959; partner Paul, Landy, Beiley & Bartel, Miami, 1964—, Morrison, Paul, Stillman & Beiley, N.Y.C., 1970—, Landy, Paul, Morrison & White, London, Eng., 1974—; counsel, chmn. bd. dirs. Republic Nat. Bank Miami, 1968—; dir. Prime Equities, Inc., Clifton, N.J., Amcourt Systems, Inc., Miami. Mem. Am., N.Y., Fla., Inter-Am. bar assns. Home: 700 Alhambra Circle Coral Gables FL 33134 Office: 150 SE 3d Av Miami FL 33131

PAULK, JOHN ROBERT, govt. ofcl.; environmental educator; b. West Frankfort, Ill., Feb. 6, 1938; s. James Joseph and Mabel (Hollenbeck) P.; B.A., So. Ill. U., 1963, M.S., 1967; m. Marilyn Weaver, July 14, 1957; children—Lynn Ann, Angela Lee. Tchr. Grant City Consol. Schs., Carbondale, Ill., 1963-65; instr., grad. asst. So. Ill. U., Carbondale, 1965-66; supr. edn. sect. TVA-Land Between the Lakes, Golden Pond, Ky., 1966—; vis. asst. prof. Murray State U.; chmn. Ky. environmental edn. adv. council Ky. State Dept. Edn.; cons. Nat. Environmental Edn. Devel. Nat. Park Service, 1968-69. Served with USMCR, 1956-58. Mem. Conservation Edn. Assn. (dir. 1973—), Assn. Interpretive Naturalists, Nat. Sci. for Youth Found., Nat. Audubon Soc. Home: 1218 Dogwood St Murray KY 42071 Office: Operations Office Education Sect TVA Land Between the Lakes Lake Between the Lakes Golden Pond KY 42071

PAULSON, FRANK OSCAR, cons. engr.; b. Clinton, Ia., Jan. 16, 1899; s. Carl and Hulda (Anderson) P.; B. S. in Mech. Engring., Ia. State U., 1924; m. Susan Imogene Dean, Dec. 11, 1924; children—Loree Alan Dean, Linda Elaine (Mrs. Chester Quillian Reeves). Asst. mech. engr. Atlantic Gulf & Pacific Co., N.Y.C., 1924-41; mech. engr. Norfolk Dredging Co. (Va.), 1941-45, Gahagan Dredging Corp., N.Y.C., Tampa, Fla., 1945-51; cons. engr. domestic and fgn. marine and dredging industry, Charleston, S.C., 1951—; pres. Paulson Engr. Services, Inc., 1951—, Paulson Dean Industries, 1967—, Woodward Paulson Engrs., 1966—. Mem. Am. Soc. Naval Engrs., Soc. Am. Mil. Engrs., Soc. Naval Architects and Marine Engrs., S.C. Soc. Profl. Engrs., Marine Tech. Soc. Methodist. Designer, inventor numerous machines for marine industry, hydraulic dredges for fgn. and domestic corps. Home: 308 Parkwood Estates Dr Charleston SC 29407 Office: Rice Mill Bldg Municipal Marina Charleston SC 29401

PAULSON, OSCAR LAWRENCE, JR., educator; b. El Dorado, Ark., Oct. 2, 1930; s. Oscar Lawrence and Cecelia (Kremer) P.; student Spring Hill Coll., 1948-50; B.S., Miss. State Coll., 1954; M.S., 1955; Ph.D. (Pan Am. Petroleum Found. fellow), La. State U., 1960; m. Linda Wicht, June 1, 1968; 1 son, Derek Lindley. Instr., Miss. State Coll., 1955; with United Geophys. Co., Starkville, Miss., 1955; instr. La. State U., Baton Rouge, 1959-60; research geologist La. Geol. Survey, Baton Rouge, 1960-61; petroleum geologist Gulf Coast Venture, Shreveport, La., 1961-64; ind. geologist, Yazoo City, Miss., 1964-66; asst. prof. geology U. So. Miss., Hattiesburg, 1966-68, asso. prof., 1968—, chmn. dept., 1973—. Cons. petroleum and environmental affairs; dir. Miss. portion, land use study of coastal zone Gulf U. Research Corp., 1968-69; prin. investigator several research projects. Served with inf. AUS, 1951-52. Grantee NSF, 1968-69, Office Water Resources Research, 1972-73, U. So. Miss. Faculty Research, 1968-71. Mem. Am. Assn. Petroleum Geologists, Am. Inst. Profl. Geologists, Miss. Acad. Sci. (chmn. geology and civil engring. sect. 1969-70), Miss. Geol. Soc., Sigma Xi, Phi Kappa Phi. Roman Catholic. Club: Civitan (lt. gov. 1973-74). Contbr. articles to profl. jours. Home: 230 Maplewood Dr Hattiesburg MS 39401 Office: Box 174 Southern Station Hattiesburg MS 39401

PAVEY, GEORGE MADISON, JR., mfg. co. exec.; b. Dallas, Feb. 7, 1919; s. George Madison and Emma Dot (Arnold) P.; B.S., So. Meth. U., 1959; M.A., U. Tex., 1940; postgrad., 1941; m. Eloise Hazel Braatz, Dec. 12, 1942; children—George Madison III (dec.), Frederick Arnold (dec.), Trudy Kathryn, David Saxon, Elizabeth Ann. Engr., RCA, Indpls., 1941-43; research engr. Nat. Geophys. Co., Dallas, 1943-46; partner Marine Instrument Co., Dallas, 1946-50; pres. Marine Seismic Surveys, Dallas, 1950-53; partner Seismic Engring. Co., Dallas, 1958-65, chmn. bd., 1970—; pres. Whitehall Electronics Co., Dallas, 1965-70; pres. Seismic Explorations Internat., (city Dallas, 1970—; dir.) Whitehall Corp., Dallas. Bd. dirs. Dallas Acad. Mem. European Assn. Exploration Geophysicists, Soc. Exploration Geophysicists, I.E.E.E., Dallas Geophys. Soc. Clubs: Dallas Country; Houston Petroleum; Lakewood Country (Dallas). Patentee in field. Home: 7022 Alexander Dr Dallas TX 75214 Office: 1133 Empire Central Dallas TX 75247

PAWEL, RICHARD E., metallurgist; b. Glens Falls, N.Y., Mar. 12, 1932; s. George W. and Thelma (Thomas) P.; B.S., U. Tenn., 1953, M.S., 1954, Ph.D., 1956; m. Teresa Y. Gravette, Oct. 1, 1955; children—Steven J., Janet E. Research asst. U. Tenn., Knoxville, 1953-56; metallurgist, nuclear div. Union Carbide Corp., Oak Ridge Nat. Lab., Oak Ridge, 1959—. Served as 1st lt. USAF, 1957-59. Mem. Am. Soc. for Metals, Electrochem. Soc., Sigma Xi, Tau Beta Pi. Contbr. articles to profl. jours. Home: 107 Davis Lane Oak Ridge TN 37830 Office: Oak Ridge Nat Lab Oak Ridge TN 37830

PAWSON, DAVID LEO, mus. ofcl.; b. Napier, New Zealand, Oct. 5, 1938; s. Leslie Albert and Mary Alice (Wildermoth) P.; B.Sc., Victoria U., Wellington, New Zealand, 1960, M.Sc., 1961, Ph.D., 1964; m. Mary Tobin, Dec. 8, 1962. Came to U.S., 1964. Demonstrator zoology dept. Victoria U., 1960-62, teaching fellow, 1962-63, lectr., 1963-64; asso. curator marine invertebrates Smithsonian Instn., Washington, 1964-65, supr. div. echinoderms, 1965-71; chmn. dept. invertebrate zoology, 1971—; adj. lectr. George Washington U., Washington, 1966—; adj. asso. prof. U. Miami (Fla.). Mem. Soc. Systematic Zoology, Soc. Bibliog. Natural History, New Zealand Marine Scis. Soc., Royal Soc. New Zealand, Sigma Xi. Home: 1905 Memory Ct Vienna VA 22180 Office: Smithsonian Instn Washington DC 20560

PAXTON, FAY MURRAY, club woman; b. Fairview, Kan., May 23, 1889; d. Jacob M. and Friendly (Sewell) Murray; student Central Bus. Coll.; m. James C. Paxton, May 23, 1934 (dec. 1955). Tchr. shorthand and typing Centeral Bus. Coll., Kansas City, Mo., 1912-15; stenographer, bookkeeper, Bartlett Bros. Land & Loan Co., St. Joseph, 1915-20; stenographer, bookkeeper Quapaw Baths, Hot Springs, Ark., 1925-26, asst. mgr., 1928-34; pvt. sec. to Col. John R. Fordyce, Hot Springs, 1927; apt. house owner, Hot Springs, 1936—. Pres. Hot Springs Bus. and Profl. Women's Club, 1934; grey lady Army and Navy Hosp., 1947; mem. state exec. bd. Order Rainbow Girls, 1940-45, state mother adviser, 1945-46; helped organize Hot Springs Shrine Club Aux., 1949, pres., 1955-56; pres. Thinkers' Club, 1962-64; chpt. corr. sec. Phi Sigma Alpha, 1966; pres. Hot Springs Salvation Army Aux., 1968-70. Mem. Order Eastern Star (worthy matron 1943, 52). Home: 602 Quapaw Av Hot Springs AR 71901

PAXTON, TOMAS ADOLPH, textile machinery co. exec.; b. Paducah, Ky., Nov. 12, 1915; s. William Perce and Flora Josephine (Dicke) P.; student Purdue U., 1934-35, U. Tex., 1936-37; B.A. with honors, Harvard, 1945; m. Carolyn Elizabeth Carney, Sept. 26, 1940; children—William Perce II, Tomas Adolph. With So. Textile Machinery Co., Paducah, 1937—, mgr. sales and service dept., 1938-40, v.p., 1941-44, exec. v.p., 1946-53, pres., 1953—; pres., dir. P-S Enterprises, Paducah; dir. Citizens Bank & Trust Co., Paducah Newspapers, Inc., Western Ky. Gas Co., Computer Services (all Paducah, Ky.). Former chmn. Paducah Jr. Coll. Found.; mem. Paducah-McCracken County Devel. Council, State Econ. Devel. Commn.; mem. St. Louis Dist. Export Council, 1972—. Trustee Ky. Ind. Coll. Found. Served with USNR, Mem. Paducah Art Guild, Sigma Chi. Home: Friedman Lane Paducah KY 42001 Office: PO Box 1015 Paducah KY 42001

PAYNE, BOBBIE LEE, oil co. exec.; b. Tulsa, Dec. 31, 1937; s. Harry Claude and Mabel Hazel (Woolsey) P.; B.S. in Petroleum Engring., U. Tulsa, 1960; J.D., U. Oklahoma City, 1967; m. Delores Kay Walton, Apr. 22, 1961; children—Angela, Andrew. Petroleum area research sr. engr. Union Oil Co. Cal., Oklahoma City, 1960-68; asst. to v.p. Amarillo (Tex.) Oil Co., 1968—, v.p., 1969—; dir. Amarillo Exploration, Inc. Mem. Randall County Republican Exec. Com., 1970—. Served with AUS, 1961. Registered profl. engr., Okla., Tex. Mem. Am., Okla., Tex. bar assns., Ind. Petroleum Assn. Am. (dir.), Panhandle Producers and Royalty Owners Assn. (dir., mem. exec. com. 1970—), Am. Assn. Mining, Metall. and Petroleum Engrs., Am. Petroleum Inst., Alpha Tau Omega. Republican. Baptist. Home: 6119 Calumet St Amarillo TX 79106 Office: PO Box 151 Amarillo TX 79105

PAYNE, BOBBY RAY, service co. exec.; b. Grandfield, Okla., June 21, 1928; s. Courtney Ray and Mildred Alvina (Gilger) P.; student Trinity U., 1947-48, U. Corpus Christi, 1954-55; m. Connie Jo Roper, Mar. 15, 1949; children—Deborah Dee, Julie Dianne, Robert Courtney. Mud engr. Milwhite Mud Sales, New Iberia, La., 1956-58; chief engr. Mission Mud Co., Corpus Christi, Tex., 1959-61; gen. mgr. Eaglebar Mud Co., Robstown, Tex., 1961-63; pres. Mud Separators, Inc., Robstown, 1963-71, Payne & Harris Mfg., Robstown, 1969-71; operations mgr. drilling controls div. Milchem., Inc., Houston, 1971—. Served with USMC, 1945-47; PTO. Baptist. Club: National Aero. Address: 7222 Jetty Lane Houston TX 77072

PAYNE, CHARLES WILLIAM, pub. relations cons.; b. Providence, Ky., Jan. 31, 1911; s. John Gammon and Beulah M. (Boyd) P.; student U. Evansville, 1928-29; B.A., Wittenberg U., 1932; postgrad. Northwestern U., 1947-49; m. Vera Mae Hierstein, Feb. 26, 1933; children—Marjorie L. (Mrs. George J. Kopp, dec.), Gammon W. Newsphoto editor AP, Washington, 1939-43; central div. mgr. Acme-N.E.A., Chgo., 1946-52; central div. newspicture mgr. UPI, Chgo., 1952-53; mgr., v.p. Selvage & Lee, Inc., Chgo., 1954-67; spl. asst. to gen. mgr. Ins. Information Inst., 1967, mgr. Washington govt. relations, 1967-74, cons., 1974—; pres. Payne & Assos., pub. relations cons., 1974—. Pres. Mt. Prospect Park Dist., 1955-59, 1961-67, commr., 1955-60, 61-67. Chmn. C.H.O., Inc., charitable corp., 1969-71, co-treas., 1972; founder Navy Fleet Home Town News Center, Navy Journalist Sch. Served with USNR, 1943-46. Recipient George Washington Honor medal Freedoms Found. at Valley Forge. Mem. Pub. Relations Soc. Am., Nat. Press Club, Chgo. Press Club, Chgo. Press Photographers Assn., Sigma Delta Chi, Phi Gamma Delta. Mason (32 deg.). Home: 536 Marshall Rd SW Vienna VA 22180 Office: National Press Bldg Washington DC 20004

PAYNE, FRED RAY, educator; b. Mayfield, Ky., Jan. 26, 1931; s. Joe L. and Bonnie (Vincent) P.; B.S., U. Ky., 1952; M.S., Pa. State U., 1964, Ph.D., 1966; m. Marilyn Maassen, Oct. 12, 1957; children—John Paul, Kevin Ray, Joel Fredrick. Commd. 2d lt. USAF, 1952, advanced through grades to capt., 1958, ret., 1966; research asso., asst. prof. Pa. State U., 1966-67; design specialist in internal aerodynamics Convair, Ft. Worth, 1968-69; asst. prof. aero. engring. U. Tex., Arlington, 1969-70, asso. prof., 1970—. Chess instr. Dan Danciger Jewish Community Center, Ft. Worth, 1972—. Mem. Am. Phys. Soc., Am. Geophys. Union, Am. Soc. M.E., Am. Inst. Aeronautics and Astronautics, Soc. Rheology, Soc. Sigma Xi, Sigma Pi Sigma, Phi Kappa Phi, Sigma Gamma Tau, Tau Beta Pi. Republican. Clubs: University of Texas at Arlington Chess; Greater Fort Worth Chess (youth dir. 1972—). Editor The Pawn Shop, 1972—, Texas Knights, 1973—. Contbr. articles to profl. jours. Home: 4467 Chedlea Av Fort Worth TX 76133 Office: 306 Engr U Texas Arlington TX 76010

PAYNE, HERSHEL RAYMOND, lawyer; b. Ft. Worth, July 30, 1938; s. Alford Raymond and Melba Elizabeth (Thomson) P.; B.S., Tex. Christian U., 1959; J.D., So. Meth. U., 1962; Sir William Trower scholar Lincoln's Inn, London, Eng., 1963-64; m. Sally Jayne Landers, Aug. 10, 1957; children—Andrea Lynn, Hershel Richard. Admitted to Law Soc. Gt. Britian, 1962; Tex. bar, 1962, U.S. Dist. Ct. bar, 1963; called to bar Lincoln's Inn, 1962; spl. counsel Trower, Steel and Keeling, London, Eng., 1962-64; partner firm Hudson, Keltner, Smith and Cunningham, Ft. Worth, 1963—. Adj. prof. Tex. Christian U., 1964-68; dir. Landers Machine Co., Ft. Worth, AGC Industries, Inc., Ft. Worth, Capital Systems Corp., Huron, S.D., Republic Alumimum Corp., Olney, Tex. Chmn., Ft. Worth Zoning Commn., 1970—. Bd. dirs. Ft. Worth Opera Assn., Ft. Worth Civic Music Assn. Mem. Sigma Alpha Epsilon, Delta Theta Phi. Mason (Shriner). Clubs: Rivercrest Country, Fort Worth, Shady Oaks Country Steeplechase. Editor Southwestern Law Jour., 1961-62; contbr. articles to legal jours. Home: 2416 Winton Terrace E Fort Worth TX 76102 Office: Continental Life Bldg Fort Worth TX 76102

PAYNE, LELIA EMILY CLEMENT (MRS. ALBERT S. PAYNE), librarian; b. Ga., Oct. 10, 1920; d. William M. and Leona L. (Davis) Clement; student Maryville Coll., 1937-38; A.B., Shorter Coll., 1958; M.L.S., Emory U., 1963, Diploma for Advanced Study in Librarianship, 1970; m. Albert S. Payne, Aug. 4, 1940; children—LeAnn (Mrs. Robert A. Strom), William Lawsha, English tchr. Model Sch., 1958-59; children and young people's librarian Tri-County Regional Library, 1959-64, acting dir., 1964, dir., 1965—. Instr. Rome Off-Campus Center, U. Ga. System, 1965-70. Mem. Stay and See Ga. Com., 1969; mem. steering com. Civic Center, 1971—. Health Edn. Welfare Insts. grantee, 1968-69. Mem. Internat. Platform Assn., Am. Assn. U. Women, S.E., Ga. (govtl. relations chmn. 1970-71, 72-73) library assns., Ga. Assn. Educators, Floyd County Assn. Educators, Bus. and Profl. Women's Club, Farm Bur. (program com. 1969-70), Atlanta Hist. Soc., Rome Area C. of C. (ednl. com. 1968-71, dir.). Home: Larkwood Dr Rome GA 30161 Office: 606 W 1st St Rome GA 30161

PAYNE, LEO WILLIAM, ins. co. exec.; b. Houston, Okla., Aug. 25, 1934; s. Ted A. and Dora (Sinnett) P.; student Alvin Jr. Coll., 1955-57, Lee Coll., 1957; A.A., U. Houston, 1960; m. Joyce Marie Thurman, Sept. 15, 1952; children—Diane Lee, Leo William, Kenneth Joseph. Gen. agt. Nat. Western Life Ins. Co., 1964-67; pres. Pamco Corp., League City, Tex., 1959-67; gen. agt. Nat. Travelers Life Co., Houston, from 1968—; now pres., chmn. bd. Am. Travelers Life Ins. Co.; pres., dir. Am. Travelers Corp., Travelers Printing Corp., Am. Travelers Finance Corp.; dir. Tool Rentals, Inc. Named Man of Month, Nat. Western Life, 1965, Salesman of Year, Nat. Travelers Life, 1969. Mem. Nat. Assn. Life Underwriters. Elk, Eagle (v.p.). Club: Presidents. Home: 2001 Mariner Way Dickinson TX 77539 Office: 8330 Broadway Houston TX 77017

PAYNE, MARY LIBBY BICKERSTAFF (MRS. BOBBY RAY PAYNE), state ofcl.; b. Gulfport, Miss., Mar. 27, 1932; d. Reece O. and Emily A. (Cook) Bickerstaff; student Miss. State Coll. Women,

1950-52; B.A. cum laude, U. Miss., 1954, LL.B., 1955; m. Bobby Ray Payne, Dec. 20, 1955; children—Reece Allen, Glenn Russell. Admitted to Miss. bar, 1955; partner Bickerstaff & Bickerstaff, Gulfport, 1955-57; employee Guaranty Title Co., Jackson, 1957; asso. Henley, Jones & Henley, Jackson, 1958-61; free-lance research and brief writing, 1962-63; individual law practice, Brandon, 1963-68; exec. sec. Miss. Judiciary Commn., 1968-70; chief research and drafting div., ho. mgmt. com. Miss. Ho. of Reps., 1970-72; asst. atty. gen. Miss., 1972—. Instr. bus. law Miss. Coll., Clinton, 1956-57; v.p., dir. First Finance Corp. of Rankin County, 1964-68; legislative draftsman Miss. Ho. of Reps., 1964-68. Chmn. Pearl-McLaurin Water Investigative Com., 1967; counsel Rankin County Christian Action Com., 1968. Mem. steering com. Rankin County campaign United Drys, 1966. Mem. Miss. State Bar (co-chmn. lawyers placement com. 1965, mem. bd. bar commrs. 1965-67, 71-72, Rankin County Bar Assn. (sec. 1965, v.p. 1966-67, pres. 1968), Am. Judicature Soc., Scribes, Am. Assn. U. Women (chpt. legislative chmn. 1956), P.T.A. (sec. Pearl-McLaurin 1966, parliamentarian 1967, pres. 1968, 69), Miss. Congress Parents and Tchrs. (dir. 1972-73). Home: 3617 Wilcox Dr Pearl MS 39208 Office: Gartin Justice Bldg Jackson MS 39205

PAYNE, MELVIN MONROE, sci. and ednl. exec.; b. Washington, May 23, 1911; s. Julian R. and Jeanette V. (Perry) P.; student Nat. U., 1929-30; LL.B., Southeastern U., 1939; D.Sc., S.D. Sch. Mines and Tech., 1962, Ia. Wesleyan Guild, 1969; LL.D., U. Miami, 1973; m. Ethel B. McDonnell, Sept. 1, 1938; children—Melvin Monroe (dec.), Frances, Nancy Jeanette. With N.Y. Sun, 1927; asst. to sec. Ry. Accounting Officers Assn., 1930-32; with Nat. Geog. Soc., Washington, 1932—, pres., chief exec. officer, from 1967, also trustee; admitted to D.C. bar, 1941. Adv. dir. Riggs Nat. Bank; dir. Equitable Savs. and Loan Assn., Inc., Ethyl Corp., Potomac Electric Power Corp., Govt. Employees Ins. Co., Govt. Employees Life Ins. Co., Govt. Employees Corp., Criterion Life Ins. Co., Washington Mut. Investors Fund, Govt. Employees Financial Corp. Council mem. adv. bd. sec. interior Nat. Park System. Trustee, v.p. U.S. Capitol Hist. Soc., Internat. Oceanographic Found.; bd. dirs. Am. Inst. Nautical Archaeology. Mem. Am. Bar Assn., Am. Assn. Geographers, A.A.A.S. Clubs: Alfalfa, Metropolitan, Cosmos (Washington); Chevy Chase (Md.); Burning Tree (Bethesda, Md.). Home: 8821 Burdette Rd Bethesda MD 20034 Office: 1145 17th St NW Washington DC 20036

PAYNE, VIRON ERNEST, SR., research co. exec.; b. Corsicanna, Tex., Aug. 14, 1918; s. William Rufus and Aletha (Hocker) P.; B.S., Tex. A. and M. U., 1941; postgrad. U. Ala., 1962-63; m. Willodean Davis, Aug. 11, 1957; children—William E., Barry D., Viron Ernest. TV technician RCA, Hollywood, Cal., 1948-49; self-employed as mfr. TV antennas, Los Angeles, 1949-50; field engr. with USAF, Philco Corp., Guam, Korea and U.S.A., 1950-54; project engr. John I. Thompson's Co., Key West, Fla., 1954-55; project engr. Naval Ordnance Unit, Key West, 1955-56, chief analysis div., 1956-62; electronic engr. Future Missile Systems div., Redstone Arsenal, Ala., 1962-63; aerospace mgr., tech. staff to dir. tech. support Kennedy Space Center, Fla., 1963-69; pres. Viron E. Payne & Co., Inc., Merritt Island, Fla., 1955—; dir. Spaceport Flyers, Inc., Merritt Island, 1964-69. Served to 1st lt. USAF, 1941-48. Mem. I.E.E.E., Mensa. Republican. Mem. Ch. of Christ. Patentee in field. Address: 200 Juniper Av Merritt Island FL 32952

PAYNE, WILLIAM MARCUS, profl. assn. exec.; b. Clyde, Kan., Jan. 13, 1930; s. Mose Francis and Julia Esther (Gram) P.; student Kan. State U., 1951-53, U. Houston, 1964-66, Tex. Christian U., 1970-73; m. Jo Ann Hudson, June 12, 1953; children—Marc, Julie, Greg, Jim, Bruce. With Tri County Refrigeration, Manhattan, Kan., 1950-53, Dick's Standard Service, Clay Center, Kan., 1953-55, Firestone Tire and Rubber Co., Salina, Kan., 1955-57; mgr. Stein's Men's Clothing, Wichita, Kan., Tulsa, Odessa, Tex., Natchez, Miss., 1957-64; mgr. Crane County (Tex.) C. of C., 1964-71; exec. v.p. Littlefield (Tex.) C. of C. and Agr. 1971—. Player agt. Crane County Little League, 1964-66, v.p., 1967-71; chmn. parents com. Crane County 4-H Club, 1967-68; chmn. local draft bd. 121, 1971; pres. Pee Wee Baseball, Crane, Tex., 1965-71; pres. Littlefield Little League, 1972—. Served with USN, 1947-50. Named Lion of Yr., Crane (Tex.) Noon Lions Club, 1965. Mem. Perman Basin C. of C. Mgrs. Assn. (pres. 1971), C. of C. Execs. Assn. (bd. dirs. 1966), South Plains Assn. C. of C. Execs. (originating mem. 1972, pres. 1973), Internat. Parks Hwy. US 385-85 Assn. (sec.-treas. 1965-66, Tex. div. pres. 1970—). Mason, Lion (sec. Littlefield 1972-73, dist. cabinet sec. 1973-74). Compiled, published It's Not All Glory, 1966. Home: 201 E 15th St Littlefield TX 79339 Office: Box 507 City Hall Littlefield TX 79339

PEABODY, BREWSTER EARL, librarian; b. Plymouth, Mich., Oct. 18, 1934; s. Brewster Eldred and Emily Caroline (Weinmann) P.; B.A., U. Mich., 1956, M.A. in L.S., 1957, M.A. in History, 1958. Serials librarian U. Del., Newark, 1959-62; asst. librarian So. Ill. U., Edwardsville, 1962-66; library dir. Old Dominion U., Norfolk, Va., 1966—. Served with AUS, 1958-59. Mem. Am., Va., Southeastern library assns., Va. Hist. Soc., Light Rwy. Transport League. Rotarian. Home: 702 Redgate St Norfolk VA 23507 Office: Hampton at 48th St Norfolk VA 23508

PEACE, FREDERICK ELWYNN, clergyman; b. Dundas, Va., Jan. 29, 1914; s. Renza Elwynn and Rebecca (Hawthorne) P.; B.A., Lynchburg Coll., 1937; postgrad. Union Theol. Sem., 1937-38; B.D., Yale, 1940; m. Nelvia Lee Phillips, Mar. 18, 1941; children—Marjorie (Mrs. D. Jeffrey Lenn), Frederick Elwynn, Robert, Thomas. Ordained minister Christian Ch. 1937; minister 1st Christian Ch., Covington, Va., 1940-43, Bowling Green, O., 1943-48, Charleston, W.Va., 1958-68, Lafayette, Ind., 1948-58, Norfolk, Va., 1968—. Pres., South Tidewater Dist. Christian Ch., 1974—. Chmn. religion sect. United Fund, Charleston, 1966-68; pres. P.T.A., Charleston, 1966-68; adviser Lamb Charitable Trust, Charleston, 1965-68. Mem. Alpha Psi Omega. Democrat. Kiwanian (dir. 1965-68). Clubs: Theophilus (Norfolk). Home: 7404 Colony Point Rd Norfolk VA 23505 Office: 1600 Colonial Av Norfolk VA 23517

PEACE, WILLIAM KITTRELL, librarian; b. Rusk, Tex., Mar. 25, 1925; s. George Wesley and LaVada May (Meltabarger) P.; B.A., Tex. Christian U., 1950; M.Ed., U. Tex., 1960; M.S. in Library Sci. (grad. fellow 1966-67), La. State U., 1964; certificate county and regional librarianship Rutgers U., 1954. Library asst. Fort Worth Pub. Library, 1948-49, U. Tex. Library, Austin, 1950-53; asst. legislative ref. librarian Tex. State Library, Austin, 1952-53, extension librarian, 1953-55, asst. state librarian, 1955-60, 1962-66, acting state librarian, 1960-62; librarian Lee Coll., Baytown, Tex., 1967—. Cons. Pub. Library Insts., Tex. State Library, 1954-66, library services Tex. Dept. Corrections for coll. programs, 1969-71. Served with USNR, 1943-46. Mem. Baytown C. of C., Tex. Library Assn. (dist. chmn. 1969), Am. Assn. U. Profs. (chpt. pres. 1968-69), Tex. Jr. Coll. Tchrs. Assn. (chpt. pres. 1969-71 sect. chmn. 1970). Author: History of the Texas State Library With Emphasis on the Period, 1930-59, 1959. Home: Box 356 Mount Belvieu TX 77580 Office: Box 818 Lee Dr Baytown TX 77520

PEACHEY, RUTH (MRS. ROD G. HAPPEL), physician; b. Springs, Pa., Jan. 2, 1925; d. Shem and Salome (Bender) Peachey; B.S., Eastern Mennonite Coll., 1950; M.D., Hahnemann Med. Coll., 1954; M.S. in Psychiatry, Temple U., 1962; m. Dr. Nejat A. Aydin, Dec. 24, 1960 (div. 1963); m. 2d, Rod G. Happel, Dec. 25, 1965. Intern Bridgeport (Conn.) Hosp., 1954-55; practice medicine Grantsville, Md., 1955-58; asst. resident psychiatry N.Y. Hosp., White Plains, N.Y., 1959, Temple U. Med. Center, Phila., 1960-62; practice medicine, Passaic, N.J., part-time 1959-61, Levittown, Pa., 1961-62; research fellow in psychiatry, Eastern Pa. Psychiat. Ins., 1962-63, research asso., 1963-64; instr. psychiatry, Temple U. Med. Center, 1962-64, sr. research scientist, 1964-70; lectr.; research asst. prof. psychiatry, mem. sect. social and community psychiatry Hahnemann Med. Coll., Phila., 1964-70; psychiatrist Div. Mental Health for State Alaska, in charge Mental Health Clinic, Juneau, 1966; active staff Meyersdale (Pa.) Community Hosp., 1955-58, courtesy staff, 1959-70; co-owner, co-mgr. Caribe Adventure Inn, Sanibel Island, Fla. Gen. Practitioner's grant Nat. Inst. Mental Health, 1960-64. Diplomate Nat. Bd. Med. Examiners. Mem. A.A.A.S., World, Am. med. assns., Pa., Phila. County med. socs., Phila. Psychiat. Soc., Population Assn. Am., A.M.A., Am., Pa., Phila. (dir., chmn. com. pub. relations) acads. gen. practice, Med. Women's Internat. Assn., Am. Med. Women's Assn. (chmn. membership com.). Contbr. articles, papers in field. Home: 2669 Gulf Dr Sanibel Island FL 33957

PEACOCK, J(OHN) TALMER, educator; b. Madison, Ga., Aug. 5, 1931; s. John Talmer and Lucille (Finney) P.; B.S., Maryville Coll., 1953; M.S. (Univ. scholar), U. Ala., 1955; Ph.D. (Univ. fellow), U. Tex., 1963; m. Darline Sue Collard, Aug. 28, 1957; children—John Talmer, Sonja Sue. Instr. biology Tex. A. and I. U., Kingsville, 1955-60, faculty, 1962—, prof., 1966—, chmn. dept., 1968—; research asso. plant ecology U. Tex., Austin, 1961-62. Mem. A.A.A.S., Am. Inst. Biol. Scis., Ecol. Soc. Am., Bot. Soc. Am., Nat. Assn. Biology Tchrs., Nat. Sci. Tchrs. Assn., Sigma Xi. Home: 923 W Alice St Kingsville TX 78363

PEAK, PAUL REED, JR., coast guard officer; b. Denver, Mar. 19, 1923; s. Paul Reed and Verl (Nicol) P.; student Tex. Mil. Coll., 1940-41; B.S. in Engring., U.S. Coast Guard Acad., 1944; postgrad. U.S. Naval Postgrad. Sch., 1948-49; M.S. in Physics, Ohio State U., 1951; m. Jane W. Worley, June 8, 1944; children—Roger W., Lucy N., Martha H. Commd. ensign U.S. Coast Guard, 1944, advanced through grades to capt., 1966; asso. prof. U.S. Coast Guard Acad., New London, Conn., 1957-61; chief readiness br. Coast Guard Dist. Staff, San Francisco, 1961-64; comdg. officer USCGC Winnebago, Honolulu, 1964-66; chief mil. liaison br. Office of Sec. of Transp., Washington, 1967-69; regional emergency transp. rep. U.S. Dept. Transp., San Francisco, 1969-71; chief inspection staff 8th Coast Guard Dist., New Orleans, 1971-72, chief staff, 1972—. Committeeman Boy Scouts Am., 1962—; leader Mariner Girl Scouts 1969-71; exec. sec. New Eng. Coll. Rifle League, 1960-61. Mem. Health Physics Soc., Nat. Sci. Tchrs. Assn., Nat. Def. Transp. Assn., U.S. Naval Inst., Sigma Pi Sigma. Unitarian (mem. bd. 1958-60, 72-74). Clubs: Commonwealth, (San Francisco); Propeller, New Orleans Athletic, Southern Yacht, Internat. House, Traffic (New Orleans). Home: 13204 Delta Ct New Orleans LA 70128 Office: 8th Coast Guard Dist Custom House New Orleans LA 70130

PEARCE, CHARLES WELLINGTON, surgeon; b. Ballinger, Tex., Nov. 2, 1927; s. Francis Marion and Fannie (Brown) P.; student Rice U., 1945-46, 48-49, U. Tex., 1948; M.D., Cornell U., 1953; m. Dorothy Andree DeLorenzo, Apr. 2, 1955; children—Charles Wellington, Andrew F., Margaret E., John Y. III. Intern, resident N.Y. Hosp.-Cornell U. Med. Center, N.Y.C., 1953-55, 56-60; resident Baylor U. Affiliated Hosps., 1955-56, Charity Hosp., New Orleans, 1960-61; practice medicine specializing in cardiovascular and thoracic surgery, New Orleans, 1961—; mem. staff Touro Infirmary, So. Bapt. Hosp., Hotel Dieu, Mercy Hosp., Sara Mayo Hosp., West Jefferson Hosp., Methodist Hosp., East Jefferson Hosp., all New Orleans; mem. faculty Tulane U., New Orleans, 1960—, asso. prof. surgery, 1966-69, head sect. cardiovascular and thoracic surgery, 1967-69, asso. prof. clin. surgery, 1969—; vis. surgeon Charity Hosp., New Orleans, 1961—; cons. surgery Huey P. Long Charity Hosp., Pineville, La., 1961—, Lallie Kem Charity Hosp., Independence, La., 1961—, VA Hosp., Alexandria, La., 1961—, Keesler Air Force Hosp., Biloxi, Miss., 1967—; cons. cardiac sect. crippled children program La. Dept. Health. Served with AUS, 1946-48. Diplomate Am. Bd. Surgery, Bd. Thoracic Surgery. Fellow A.C.S., Am. Coll. Chest Physicians, Am. Coll. Cardiology; mem. Am. Assn. Thoracic Surgery, Soc. for Vascular Surgery, Am. Heart Assn. (established investigator 1962-65), Soc. Thoracic Surgeons, Internat. Cardiovascular Soc., Internat. Surg. Soc., So. Med. Assn., Orleans Parish, La. med. socs., La., New Orleans surg. socs., La. Heart Assn., New Orleans Postgrad. Med. Assembly, Soc. Mayflower Descs., S.A.R., New Orleans Opera House Assn., New Orleans Spring Fiesta Assn., Fgn. Relations Assn., La. Landmark Soc., New Orleans Mus. Art, New Orleans Area C. of C., Internat. House, R Assn. Rice U., Phi Chi, Alpha Omega Alpha. Republican. Presbyn. Contbr. articles to profl. jours. Home: 6145 St Charles Av New Orleans LA 70118 Office: 1070 St Charles Av New Orleans LA 70130

PEARCE, DOROTHY ANDREE DE LORENZO, civic worker; b. N.Y.C., Mar. 22, 1927; d. Andrew John and Margaret (Robilotti) De Lorenzo; B.A., Barnard Coll., 1947; m. Charles W. Pearce, Apr. 2, 1955; children—Charles W., Andrew Francis, Margaret Elizabeth, John Y. III. Research asst. cardiac catherization lab. Bellevue Hosp., 1948-50, Cornell Med. Coll., 1950-55; exec. research librarian Shell Chem. Co., 1955-57. Thrift shop rep. Soc. N.Y. Hosp. Women's Aux., 1959-60; bd. govs. New Orleans Opera House Assn. Women's Guild, 1965-73, social hostess, 1966-71, historian, 1969—; chmn. uptown subscription com., 1967-69, mem. children's concerts com., 1964-66; mem. tour com. New Orleans Springs Fiesta Assn., 1966-67; mem. opera orientation com. New Orleans Opera House Assn., 1964-72, registrar, hostess, 1965; active New Orleans Symphony Previews, 1968—; mem. fund raising com. De Paul Hosp. Women's Aux., 1968—; vol. Crippled Children's Hosp. Guild, 1965-66; mem. La. Council for Performing Arts, 1967—; mem. Gallier Hall Women's Com., 1967; mem. bd. Community Concerts Assn., New Orleans; mem. fund raising com. Hotel Dieu Women's Aux., 1968—. Bd. dirs. Mercy Hosp. Women's Aux., 1965-72, pres., 1970; bd. dirs. Sara Mayo Hosp. Guild, 1964—, chmn. hospitality com., 1967-72; bd. dirs. Orleans Parish Med. Soc. Women's Aux., 1969-71, chmn. A.M.A. edn. and research fund com., 1969-71; bd. dirs. Vis. Nurses Assn. Mem. New Orleans Garden Soc. (chmn. Christmas decorations 1969-70), Fgn. Relations Assn., Am. Assn. U. Women, La. Landmark Soc. Republican. Roman Catholic. Club: New Orleans Country. Home: 6145 St Charles Av New Orleans LA 70118

PEARCE, EDWIN MCKIGNEY, JR., lawyer; b. Atlanta, Apr. 25, 1908; s. Edwin McKigney and Ella (Pope) P.; student U. Va., 1925-26; LL.B., Emory U., 1931; m. Joanne Snelson, May 1, 1949; children—Anne, Virginia, Catherine, Edwin McKigney III. Admitted to Ga. bar, 1931, since practiced in Atlanta; partner firm Poole, Pearce & Cooper; regional price atty. Southeastern region OPA, 1944-45, regional price exec., 1946-47; lectr. law Emory U., 1941—. Dir., mem. exec. com. Ga. Life & Health Ins. Co., Ga. Investors, Inc., L.L. Antle & Co., Inc.; dir., trustee WRC Smith Pub. Co. Mem. Atlanta C. of C., Am. (mem. council, chmn. sect. labor relations), Ga. bar assns., Bryan Honor Soc., Sigma Alpha Epsilon, Phi Delta Phi. Baptist. Elk, Optimist, Clubs: Atlanta Athletic, Country, Commerce (Atlanta). Home: 1475 W Paces Ferry Rd NW Atlanta GA 30327 Office: National Bank of Ga Bldg Atlanta GA 30303

PEARCE, GEORGE ERNEST, chem. co. exec.; b. Ocean Grove, N.J., Feb. 11, 1920; s. George Estell and Mae (Bowne) P.; B.S., Rutgers U., 1942; M.S. (Ethyl fellow), U. Tulsa, 1944; m. Dorothy Kate Lawrence, July 3, 1948; children—Pamela (Mrs. Howard Reese), Lawrence George. Estimator, M.W. Kellogg Co., N.Y.C., 1941-43; research fellow U. Tulsa, 1943-44; design engr. Sharples Chem. Co., Wyandotte, Mich., 1944-49; chief engr. Glyco Products Co., Williamsport, Pa., 1949-56; chief engr. Harchem div. Union Camp Corp., Belleville, N.J., 1956-60, mgr. research and devel., Savannah, Ga., 1960—; v.p., dir. Jersey Industries, Bernardsville, N.J., 1967—. Registered profl. engr., Mich. Mem. Am. Chem. Soc., Am. Inst. Chem. Engrs., Am. Oil Chemists Soc., A.A.A.S. Home: 2 Spanish Moss Ct Savannah GA 31406 Office: Harchem Division Union Camp Corp Savannah GA 31400

PEARCE, HOMER LEWIS, JR., elec. engr.; b. Sterling City, Tex., Mar. 7, 1913; s. Homer Lewis and Anna (Brown) P.; B.S., Tex. A. and M. U., 1936; m. Mary Ellen Fry, Dec. 3, 1945; 1 son, Homer Lewis III. Engr., W.Tex. Utilities Co., 1937-41, 46-50; elec. engr. H.N. Roberts & Assos., Lubbock, Tex., 1950-51; lead electronics system engr. Chance Vought Aircraft Co., Dallas, 1952-60; elec. engr. U.S. Army C.E., Abilene, Tex., 1960-61; elec. engr. USAF, Dyess AFB, Tex., 1961—. Pvt. cons. elec. engr. Served to maj. USAF, 1941-46, 51; lt. col. Res., 1960-69. Registered profl. engr., Tex. Mem. Nat., Tex. socs. profl. engrs., I.E.E.E. (sec.-treas., vice chmn. W.Central Tex. 1946-48), Soc. Am. Mil. Engrs., Res. Officers Assn. U.S. Methodist. Home: 2134 Elmwood Dr Abilene TX 79605 Office: 96 CSG DEE Bldg 8006 Dyess AFB TX 79607

PEARCE, MARY MCCALLUM (MRS. CLARENCE A. PEARCE), artist; b. Hesperia, Mich., Feb. 17, 1906; d. Archibald and Mabel (McNeil) McCallum; A.B., Oberlin Coll., 1927; student John Huntington Inst., 1929-34, Cleve. Inst. Art, 1935-37, 54, Dayton Art Inst., 1946-49; m. Clarence A. Pearce, June 30, 1928; children—Mary Martha (Mrs. William B. Robinson), Thomas McCallum. One man shows at Cleve. Women's City Club, 1959, 69, Cleve. Orch., 1967, Cleve. Playhouse Gallery, 1968, 71; exhibited in group shows at Oberlin Art Mus., Akron Art Inst., Grand Rapids (Mich.) Art Gallery, Dayton (O.) Art Inst., Smithsonian Inst., Birmingham Mus. of Art, Am. Watercolor Soc., Cleve. Mus. Art, many others: represented in pvt. collections: tchr. art, supr. pub. schs., Mayfield Heights, O., 1927-28, Maple Heights, O., 1928-30, Chagrin Falls, O., 1938-39. Named best woman artist Ohio Watercolor Soc., 1955; recipient Bush Meml. award Columbus Gallery Fine Arts, 1962; nat. 1st prize, drawing Nat. League Am. Penwomen, 1966, 68; Littlehouse award Ala. Watercolor Soc., 1967; Wolfe award Columbus Gallery Fine Arts, 1971; Merit award Longboat Key Art Center, 1973. Mem. Nat. League Am. Pen Women (treas. 1962), Am. (asso.), Ala. Watercolor Soc. Republican. Conglist. Home: 5400 Ocean Blvd Sarasota FL 33581

PEARCE, WILLIS SCOTT, elec. engr.; b. Millry, Ala., June 12, 1942; s. Arthur Woods and Lillie Mae (Toomey) P.; B.E.E., Auburn U., 1965; student Jones County Jr. Coll., 1960-62; postgrad. U. Ala. at Birmingham, 1972—; m. Carrie Anna Millard, Sept. 27, 1969; 1 son, Jefferson Scott. Asst. engr. So. Services, Inc., Birmingham, 1965, project engr., 1969—; sr. electronics engr. Philco-Ford Co., NASA Manned Spacecraft Center, Houston, 1967-69. Served with AUS, 1965-67. Registered profl. engr., Fla., Ala. Mem. Nat. Mgmt. Assn., I.E.E.E. Baptist. Home: 638 Winwood Dr Birmingham AL 35226 Office: PO Box 2625 Birmingham AL 35202

PEARL, MAURICE ALLEN, physician; b. Bklyn., Dec. 16, 1931; s. William Joseph and Rae (Weinblatt) P.; B.S., Tulane U., 1953, M.D., 1956; m. Rochelle Schreckinger, July 13, 1957; children—Michael, David, Richard. Intern, Mt. Sinai Hosp., N.Y.C., 1956-57; trainee Nat. Heart Inst., Tulane U., 1957-58, research fellow dept. medicine, 1961-63; resident internal medicine Charity Hosp. La., 1958-59; practice medicine specializing in internal medicine and nephrology, New Orleans, 1964—; mem. active staff So. Bapt. Hosp., 1970—, vice. chmn. sect. medicine, 1971—; mem. courtesy staff Touro Infirmary, 1964—; vis. physician Charity Hosp., 1961—; cons. renal diseases USPHS Hosp., New Orleans, 1961—; instr. dept. pathology Tulane U., 1957-58, dept. medicine, 1959-63, asst. prof. medicine, 1963-71, asso. clin. prof. medicine, 1971—. Trustee, chmn. med. adv. bd. Kidney Found. La. Served with USNR, 1959-61. Recipient Undergrad. award for med. research Borden Co., 1956. Diplomate Am. Bd. Internal Medicine. Fellow A.C.P.; mem. Am. Fedn. Clin. Research, A.M.A., Am. Soc. Internal Medicine, Am. Soc. Nephrology, Am., La. (dir. 1968-71) heart assns., La. State, Orleans Parish med. socs., La. Soc. Internal Medicine (pres. 1971-72), New Orleans Acad. Internal Medicine, New Orleans Kidney Soc. (pres. 1969-71), Alpha Omega Alpha. Contbr. articles to profl. jours. Home: 6309 Gladys St Metairie LA 70003 Office: 4303 Magnolia St New Orleans LA 70115

PEARMAN, JEAN RICHARDSON, educator; b. Cherry, Neb., July 15, 1915; s. William Francis and Ruth Gertrude (Richardson) P.; A.B., Neb. State Coll., 1938; M.A., U. Neb., 1945; Ph.D., U. Minn., 1959; m. Alberta Valier Stevenson, July 15, 1941; children—Allen Lee, Sandra (Mrs. Paul Lillis), Marlene Ann, Patricia Valier. Social worker Neb. Pub. Assistance, Lincoln, 1939-41; supt. pub. schs., Ashby, Chester and Liberty, Neb., 1943-46; social worker VA, Des Moines, 1946-47; asst. prof. dept. econs. and sociology No. Mich. U., Marquette, 1947-51, asso. prof., 1951-59, prof., 1959-64, head dept., 1961-64; prof. social welfare Fla. State U., Tallahassee, 1964—, head dept. social welfare, 1964-69. Mem. Exec. com. Leon County chpt. A.R.C., 1967—. Mem. adv. bd. Upward Bound, Fla. Agrl. and Mech. U., 1968-73; adv. bd. social work curriculum Fla. Tech. U., 1970-72. Mem. Acad. Certified Social Workers, Am. Assn. U. Profs., Am. Fedn. Tchrs., Am. Econ. Assn., Nat. Conf. on Social Welfare, Am. Acad. Polit. and Social Sci. Major author; Social Services in the School, 1955; author: Social Science and Social Work, 1973. Contbr. articles to profl. jours. Home: 1330 Sharon Rd Tallahassee FL 32303

PEARSALL, DAVID MIDDLETON, chem. engr.; b. Rocky Mount, N.C., Mar. 22, 1937; s. Leon Moulton and Middleton (Trammell) P.; B.S., Davidson Coll., 1959; B.S. in Chem. Engring., Ga. Inst. Tech., 1961; m. Sally Heltzel, Sept. 7, 1963; children—Sally Ellen, Susan Middleton. Project engr. Internat. Paper Co., Mobile, Ala., 1962-67, sr. project engr., 1967-70, asst. pulp mill supt., 1970—. Served with AUS, 1961. Registered profl. engr., Ala. Mem. T.A.P.P.I., Am. Inst. Chem. Engrs., Mobile Jaycees (project chmn. 1970-71). Presbyn. (deacon 1969-72). Club: University of South Alabama Tip-Off (Mobile) (dir. 1971—). Home: 474 Pine Ct Mobile AL 36608 Office: Box 2448 Mobile AL 36601

PEARSALL, SAMUEL HAFF, diversified co. exec.; b. Guthrie, Ky., July 17, 1923; s. Samuel Haff and Claire (Miller) P.; B.E., Vanderbilt U., 1948, M.S., 1958; m. Isabelle Ikard, July 20, 1946; children—Samuel Haff III, Susan Claire, Sallie Mai, Timothy Hudson. Research and devel. staff WSM, Inc., Nashville, 1946-55; asso. prof. elec. engring. Vanderbilt U., 1955-63; v.p. R.W. Benson & Assos. Inc., Nashville, 1963-71, sec. of bd., 1963—; v.p. Bonitron, Inc., Nashville,

1965-71, sec. of bd., 1965-71; v.p. engring. Cutters Exchange, Nashville, 1971—; v.p., gen. mgr. Cutters Electronics Internat., 1971—. Mem. I.E.E.E. (sr. mem., chmn. Nashville sect. 1968), Sigma Xi. Mem. Christian Ch. (bd. dirs. 1968—). Patentee electronic instrumentation. Home: 118 Spring Valley Rd Donelson TN 37214 Office: 706 19th Av N Nashville TN 37203

PEARSON, BETSY DECELLE (MRS. WELTON DENNIS PEARSON), educator; b. Geromont, Liege, Belgium; d. Leon Gabriel and Camille Mignolet (Francois) DeCelle; student Sisters of Cross, Liege, Ecole Superieure de Demoiselles, Liege, Bus. Scis., Liege, Institut d'Education Physique, Liege; intern in re-edn. St. Laurent Mil. Hosp., 1943-44; M.Ed., U. Tenn., 1968; m. Welton Dennis Pearson, Apr. 24, 1946; 1 dau., Elisabeth Leone. Came to U.S., 1948, naturalized, 1964. Moniteur, Institut d'Education Physique, Liege, 1940-41, prof., 1942-43; asso. prof. Institut des Scis. Sociales, Liege, 1942-45; collaborator Laboratoire de Biometrie Experimentale, Liege, 1942-45, Sorbonne, 1962, N.D.E.A. Inst., 1965; now head lang. dept. Chattanooga High Sch. Vol. tchr. Talented Youth Program and Frey Inst.; mem. Opera Assn.; active Community Concerts, Heart Assn., United Fund, A.R.C.; treas. Newcomers Club. 1949; founder L'Amicale Francaise. Chattanooga, 1952. Served with Army of Liberation, 1940-45. Decorated Medaille de la Resistance (Belgium). Mieux Doues scholar, Liege, 3 years. Mem. Internat. Platform Assn., N.E.A., Am. Assn. Tchrs. French (pres. Tenn. 1967-68), Am. Assn. U. Women. Clubs: Music (dir. 1958-59), Metropolitan. Home: 938 McCallie Av Chattanooga TN 37403

PEARSON, ELBERT LEE, utility co. exec.; b. Cleveland, Tenn., Nov. 18, 1912; s. Gale and Hattie Louvenia (Campbell) P.; B.S. in E.E., Ga. Inst. Tech., 1935; m. Edna Irene Hooper, July 8, 1937; 1 dau., Pamela Lee. Engr., Tenn. Electric Power Co., Cleveland, 1935-39, Ga. Power Co., Atlanta, 1939; chief engr. Cleveland Electric System (Tenn.), 1939-43; with TVA, Chattanooga, 1943—, asst. br. chief, 1964-70, asst. to dir. power marketing, 1970—. Dir. Civilian Def., Bradley County, Tenn., 1941-43. Mem. I.E.E.E. (sr.), Phi Kappa Phi. Presbyn. (deacon). Home: 625 Melville Av Chattanooga TN 37412 Office: TVA Power Bldg Chattanooga TN 37401

PEARSON, GROSVENOR BENJAMIN, psychiatrist; b. Pitts., July 6, 1907; s. Eugene Oscar and Blanche (Righter) P.; B.S., U. Pitts., 1930, M.D., 1932. Intern, Med. Center, Pitts., 1932-33; resident Boston Psychopathic Hosp., 1933-36; practice medicine, specializing in psychiatry, Foxboro, Mass., 1936-42, Pitts., 1942-62, St. Petersburg, Fla., 1962—; dir. Western Psychiat. Inst. and Clinic, Pitts., 1942-49; psychiatrist Mental Health Clinic, VA Outpatient Service, St. Petersburg, 1962—; asso. prof. psychiatry U. Pitts. Med. Sch., 1942-62; clin. asso. prof. dept. psychiatry Coll. Medicine, U. South Fla., Tampa, 1973—. Diplomate Am. Bd. Psychiatry and Neurology, Am. Bd. Clinic Hypnosis. Fellow (life) Am. Psychiat. Assn., Am. Soc. for Psychical Research, A.A.A.S.; mem. A.M.A., Am. Psychopath. Assn. (life), Western Pa. Soc. Clin. Hypnosis (hon.), Parapsychol. Assn. (asso. mem.), Order Ky. Cols., Nu Sigma Nu. Republican. Episcopalian. Club: Bath (St. Petersburg). Home: 10355 Paradise Blvd Treasure Island FL 33706 Office: Fed Bldg St Petersburg FL 33701

PEARSON, NELS R., judge; b. Chgo., May 8, 1934; s. Ragnar H. and Svea (Lilygren) P.; B.B.A., U. Miami, 1955, J.D., 1961; m. Patricia J. Thompson, Dec. 26, 1956; children—Wesley David, Darryl Thomas. Admitted to Fla. bar, 1961; spl. asst. atty. gen. Fla., 1961; city prosecutor, Fort Lauderdale, Fla., 1961-64, judge, 1964-67; judge of indsl. claims Fla. Indsl. Commn., Fort Lauderdale, 1967-68; judge Ct. Record, Broward County, Fort Lauderdale, 1968-73; practice law, Ft. Lauderdale, 1973—. Bd. dirs. Broward County Lions Eye Found. Served with AUS, 1956-58. Mem. Delta Theta Phi. Mason. Club: Lions (pres. 1970-71). Address: 3929 N Andrews Av Fort Lauderdale FL 33309

PEARSON, ORRIN WALTER, dentist; b. Mpls., Nov. 7, 1917; s. Gustav Walter and Esther Marie (Bogren) P.; D.D.S., U. Minn., 1943; m. Mildred Mae Knox, Jan. 5, 1946; children—David Orrin, Marsha Elizabeth. Pvt. practice dentistry, Mpls., 1946-47; staff dentist VA Hosp., St. Cloud, Minn., 1947-51, Oklahoma City, 1951-64, asst. chief dental service, 1964-71, acting chief dental service, 1971-74; instr. dental surgery U. Okla. Sch. Medicine, 1961-66, asst. clin. prof. dental surgery, 1966—, instr. dental anatomy and morphology Coll. Dentistry, 1973—. Asst. scoutmaster, counselor Last Frontier council Boy Scouts Am., 1958-61; active Oklahoma City Symphony Soc. Opera Guild. Bd. dirs. VA Hosp. Fed. Credit Union, 1957-66. Served with USNR, 1943-46; PTO. Mem. Am. Dental Assn. Republican. Baptist. Mason. Home: 4928 N Pate Av Oklahoma City OK 73112 Office: 921 NE 13th St Oklahoma City OK 73104

PEARSON, WELTON DENNIS, prosthodontist; b. Jackson, Tenn., Oct. 20, 1906; s. Nedham B. and Elizabeth (Reid) P.; D.D.S., U. Tenn., 1936; postgrad. U. Pa., Ohio U., U. Mich., Tufts Coll., Northwestern U. Dental Sch., U. Ala. Sch. Dentistry, Marquette U. Sch. Dentistry; m. Betsy DeCelle, Apr. 24, 1946; 1 dau., Elisabeth Leone. Intern, M.C. Hosp., 1936-37; pvt. practice dentistry, Jackson, 1934-41, Chattanooga, 1947—; dir., mem. med. adv. bd. Chattanooga-Hamilton County Speech and Hearing Center; mem. staff Baroness Erlanger Hosp., 1949—; prosthodontist Siskin Rehab. Center for Physically Handicapped. Clinician nat. and internat. meetings; mem. regional cleft palate team Tenn. Health Dept. Served from 1st lt. to lt. col. Dental Corps, AUS, 1942-47; ETO. Elected to Wisdom Hall of Fame, 1972. Diplomate Am. Bd. Prosthodontics. Mem. Fedn. Dentaire Internationale; Am. Coll. Prosthodontists, Am. Dental Assn., Tenn., 3d Dist. dental socs., Am. Denture Soc., So. Acad. Oral Surgery, Am. Soc. Dentistry Children, Royal Soc. Health London, Found. for Dental Research, Nat. Rehab. Assn., Assn. Mil. Surgeons U.S., Chgo. Dental Soc., Delta Sigma Delta. Presbyn. (elder). Mason. Contbr. articles in field. Prosthetics abstract editor Jour. of Tenn. Dental Assn. Address: 938 McCallie Av Chattanooga TN 37403

PEAVY, JAMES EVERETT, JR., state ofcl.; b. Lufkin, Tex., Jan. 21, 1911; s. James Everett and Mamie (McClendon) P.; student Baylor U., 1927-30, M.D., 1935; M.P.H., Harvard, 1955; m. Frieda M. McNeal, July 28, 1936; children—Diane (Mrs. Cox), Janet Marie (Mrs. Prouse). Dir. health unit, Sweetwater, Tex., 1946-47; med. field cons. Tex. Dept. Health, 1947-55, dir. communicable disease div., 1955-59; commr. health Tex. Dept. Health, Austin, 1959—; lectr. Sch. Pub. Health, Houston. Adviser, U.S. delegation to 22d World Health Assembly, Boston, 1969. Served with M.C., AUS, 1942-46; PTO. Recipient Arthur G. McCormack award Am. Assn. Pub. Health Physicians. Diplomate Am. Bd. Preventive Medicine. Mem. A.M.A., Tex. Med. Assn., Am., Tex. pub. health assns., Am. Assn. Pub. Health Physicians, State and Territorial Health Officers (past pres.). Mason (Shriner), Rotarian. Contbr. articles to med. jours. Home: 11908 Oak Trail Austin TX 78753 Office: 1100 W 49th St Austin TX 78756

PECK, HOWARD WAYNE, retirement center exec.; b. Hagerstown, Md., Sept. 16, 1926; s. Felix Brevard and Annie James (Little) P.; student Elmhurst Coll., 1944-45; B.A., Catawba Coll., 1947; B.D., Eden Theol. Sem., 1951; postgrad. Boston U., 1960-61; m. Shirley Ann Ackerman. Sept. 11, 1954; children—Donald Wayne, Kathlyn Ann. Ordained to ministry United Ch. of Christ, 1951; pastor St. John's Evang. and Ref. Ch., Mickleys, Pa., 1953-56, Belfast (Pa.) Evang. and Reform Ch., 1956-62, First United Ch. of Christ, Orlando Fla., 1962-66; exec. dir. Uplands Retirement Center, Pleasant Hill, Tenn., 1966—. Mem. United Ch. of Christ Outreach Commn. of Ala., Tenn., Southeast conf. commn. on instns., council health and welfare services, com. standards health and welfare agys., bd. deacons congregation. Mem. Pleasant Hill Planning Commn., 1966—. Mem. Am., Tenn. (pres. 1970—) assns. homes for aging, Am., Tenn. nursing home assns. Home: PO Box 151 Yonside Pleasant Hill TN 38578 Office: Uplands Retirement Center Pleasant Hill TN 38578

PECK, JOSEPH COSGROVE, physician; b. Haverstraw, N.Y., Aug. 29, 1920; s. Joseph Cosgrove and Sophie Elizabeth (Lipinski) P.; B.S. in Chemistry, John B. Stetson U., 1949; M.D., Temple U. Med. Sch., 1953; m. Mary Bell Goode, Sept. 29, 1945; children—Susan (Mrs. Wyatt Bowman), Linda, Stephen. Intern, Temple U. Hosp., Phila., 1953-54; pvt. practice medicine, Galax, Va., 1954—; mem. staff Galax Gen. Hosp., bd. dirs., 1958—, chief staff, 1967, 72, med. dir. coronary care unit, 1970—; mem. staff Waddell Hosp., Galax. Served with AUS, 1942-46. Mem. Am., Va. acads. gen. practice, S.W. Va. Med. Soc., Va. Med. Soc., A.M.A. Elk. Home: Williams St Galax VA 24333 Office: 400 W Center St Galax VA 24333

PECK, T. T., JR., physician, oil investor; b. Poteau, Okla., Sept. 21, 1923; s. T.T. and Bonnie Louise (Patterson) P.; student Rice U., 1941-43; M.D., Baylor U., 1947-50; m. Ruby Rose Corley, Mar. 27, 1948; children—Larry Temple, Terry Rose. Intern, U.S. Naval Hosp., Pensacola, Fla., 1950-51; gen. practice medicine, Baytown, Tex., 1951-58; practice medicine, specializing med. hypnosis and psychosomatic medicine, 1958-62; NIH grantee, resident psychosomatic medicine, 1962; now in practice, Centerville, Tex.; chief staff Leon County Hosp., Buffalo, Tex. Adviser, Nat. Trainers Assn.; lectr. Pres. Birthdays, Inc.; city and county health officer. Pres., Leon County Devel. Corp.; participant 2d Congress Mental Health, Chgo., 1964. Served as lt. (j.g.), USNR, 1944-46: PTO; as lt. M.C., USNR: Korean War. Mem. Am. Soc. Clin. Hypnosis (life), A.M.A., Tex., Harris County med. assns., Am. Acad. Gen. Practice, Tex. Municipal League, Internat. Traders Assn., Oil and Gas Soc., Acad. Psychosomatic Medicine, Soc. Psychophysiol. Medicine, Brazos County Med. Soc., Royal Soc. Health (London, Eng.), Psychophysiol. Research Assn., Am. Acad. Family Physicians (charter), Internat.-Pan Am. Med. Soc., Phi Beta Phi. Republican. Active in research with LSD-25, mescaline, psilocybin; study of Indians in Mexico using sacred mushrooms; co-inventor Lee Traction Shield; mem. Internat. Symposium on LSD-25 and Psychiatry, Princeton, 1959. Home: Camp NaJaha Box 278 Centerville TX 75833 Office: Centerville Med Center Centerville TX 75833

PECK, WILLIAM EDWIN, elec. engr.; b. Jamestown, N.Y., Jan. 8, 1936; s. George C. and Ethel (Waite) P.; B.S. in E.E., U. Buffalo, 1957; postgrad. U. Ariz., 1959; M.S. in E.E., U. Santa Clara, 1965; m. Shirley Straight, June 15, 1953; children—Ronald, Cindy. Design engr. IBM, San Jose, Cal., 1960-65, project mgr., 1965-68, sr. engr., Boca Raton, Fla., 1968-70, program mgr., 1970-72, mgr. tech. operations, 1972-73; mgr. systems and applied programming, 1974—. Served with USAF, 1957-60. Mem. I.E.E.E., U. Buffalo Engring. Alumni Assn. Baptist (trustee). Home: 1098 W Royal Palm Rd Boca Raton FL 33432 Office: 2000 N 51st St Boca Raton FL 33432

PECKHAM, JOHN CECIL, pathologist; b. Enid, Okla., Nov. 6, 1934; s. John A. and Mary Frances (Harris) P.; D.V.M., Okla. State U., 1958; M.S., Ia. State U., 1961; Ph.D. (USPHS fellow), Wash. State U., 1967; m. Marcia J. Ditzler, May 31, 1958 (div. Apr. 1973); children—John Marc, Richard Anthony, Wallace James, Joseph David; m. 2d, Elizabeth Newell McLaughlin Brown, Sept. 19, 1973. Instr. vet. pathology Ia. State U., Ames, 1958-61; asst. prof. Wash. State U., Pullman, 1963-65; pathologist Pitman Moore div. Dow Chem. Co., Indpls., 1965-67; asso. prof. U. Ga., Tifton, 1967-72; head pathology sect. So. Research Inst., Birmingham, Ala., 1972—. Lectr. Abraham Baldwin Agrl. Coll., Tifton, 1967-69; cons. So. Research Inst., 1971-72; vis. asso. prof. U. Ala. at Birmingham, 1972—; cons. U. Ga. at Tifton, 1973. Active drug edn. programs, Tifton and Adel, Ga. Diplomate Am. Coll. Vet. Pathologists. Mem. Am. Vet. Med. Assn. Mem. Parents Without Partners (treas. 1973). Toastmaster (pres. 1974). Home: 4420 5th Av S Apt 3 Birmingham AL 35222 Office: So Research Inst 2000 9th Av S Birmingham AL 35205

PECKHAM, MORSE, educator; b. Yonkers, N.Y., Aug. 17, 1914; s. Ray Morse and Edith (Roake) P.; B.A., U. Rochester, 1935; M.A., Princeton, 1938, Ph.D., 1947. Asst. prof. The Citadel, Charleston, S.C., 1938-41; instr. Rutgers U., New Brunswick, N.J., 1947-48, asst. prof., 1948-49, U. Pa., Phila., 1949-52, asso. prof., 1952-60, prof. English lit., 1960-67, dir. Inst. Humanistic Studies for Execs., 1953-54, dir. U. Pa. Press, 1953-55; distinguished prof. English and comparative lit. U. S.C., Columbia, 1967—. Served to lt. AUS, also USAAF, 1941-45. Decorated Bronze Star medal. Mem. Modern Lang. Assn., Soc. Archtl. Historians. Author: Charles Darwin's The Origin of Species: A Variorum Text, 1959; Humanistic Education for Business Executives, 1960; (with Seymour Chatman) Word, Meaning Poem, 1961; Beyond the Tragic Vision, 1962; Man's Rage for Chaos, 1965; Romanticism, 1965; Art and Pornography, 1969; The Triumph of Romanticism, 1970; Swinburne: Poems and Ballads and Atalanta in Calydon, 1970; Victorian Revolutionaries, 1970. Home: 6478 Bridgewood Rd Columbia SC 29206

PECKHAM, RUFUS WHEELER, JR., lawyer; b. N.Y.C., Jan. 25, 1928; s. Rufus Wheeler and Virginia (Selden) P.; B.S., Am. U., 1953; LL.B., Washington Coll. Law, 1957. Dep. clk. D.C. Municipal Ct., 1954-57; admitted to D.C. bar, 1958; Washington rep. Wine Inst., 1957-60; pvt. practice law, Washington, 1961-72; spl. partner Shipley Ackerman Stein & Kaps, Washington, 1966-72. Mem. D.C. Alcoholic Beverage Control Bd., 1970-72; asst. dir. field activities Distilled Spirits Council U.S., Inc., 1973—. Mem. D.C. Republican Com., 1955-70, sec., 1968-70; field coordinator Republican Nat. Com., Washington, 1960-61. Served with USMC, 1946-48. Recipient Outstanding Service award D.C. Chief Police, 1969. Mem. Am., D.C. bar assns., Internat. Assn. Chiefs of Police, S.A.R., Alpha Tau Omega, Delta Theta Phi. Episcopalian. Clubs: Metropolitan, International of Washington (hon.). Home: 2501 Q St NW Washington DC 20007 Office: 1300 Pennsylvania Bldg 425 13th St NW Washington DC 20004

PEDEN, JAMES ALTON, JR., lawyer; b. Gainesville, Fla., Apr. 24, 1944; s. James Alton and Frances Merle (Wilson) P.; B.A. summa cum laude, U. Miss., 1966, J.D. (Ford Found. Law fellow), 1970; postgrad. (Fulbright scholar) U. Bristol (Eng.), 1966-67. Admitted to Miss., 1970; partner firm Stennett, Wilkinson & Ward, Jackson, Miss., 1970—; staff asst. to Miss. lt. gov., 1972; reading clk. Miss. Senate, 1972. Staff asst. to Senator John C. Stennis, 1964, 65; asst. publicity dir. William Winter's campaign for Gov. Miss., 1967; mem. Hinds County Democratic Exec. Com., 1972—. Fellow Inst. Politics Miss., 1971-72. Mem. Am., Hinds Co., Jackson Jr. (sec. 1973-74) bar assns., Miss. State Bar (dir. Young lawyers sect. 1973-74), Miss. Hist. Soc., Beta Theta Pi, Omicron Delta Kappa, Phi Delta Phi, Phi Kappa Phi, Phi Eta Sigma, Phi Alpha Theta, Pi Sigma Alpha, Eta Sigma Phi. Baptist. Contbr. articles to legal jours. Home: 507 Merigold Dr Jackson MS 39204 Office: Suite 600 Barnett Bldg PO Box 22627 Jackson MS 39205

PEDEN, PHIL, judge; b. Ft. Worth, Sept. 14, 1916; s. Robert Franklin and Laura (Phillips) P.; A.B., Rice U., 1938; postgrad. Law Sch., George Washington U., 1940-42; m. Lois Lee Qualtrough, Apr. 20, 1941; children—Phil, Scott. Spl. agt. FBI, 1942-47; admitted to Tex. bar, 1946; practiced law, Houston, 1947-51; judge County Ct. at Law, Houston, 1951-57, Civil Dist. Ct., Houston, 1957-67; asso. justice Tex. 1st Ct. Civil Appeals, Houston, 1967—. Mem. Tex. Jud. Qualifications Commn. Mem. State Bar Tex. (past mem. exec. bd. jud. sect.), Soc. Former FBI Agts. (past chmn. Houston), Assn. Rice Alumni (past pres.), Phi Delta Phi. Episcopalian (past sr. warden). Home: 3727 Albans Rd Houston TX 77005 Office: Civil Courts Bldg Houston TX 77002

PEDEN, ROBERT F., JR., lawyer; b. Ft. Worth, July 26, 1911; s. Robert F. and Laura (Phillips) P.; LL.B., Cumberland U., 1933; m. Virginia LeTulle, May 25, 1939. Admitted to Tex. bar, 1934; practice law, Bay City, 1934—; city atty., Bay City, 1935-38, 65—; atty. Matagorda County, Tex., 1939-46, 50-54. Bd. dirs. Bay City Library Assn. Mem. State Bar Tex., Am., Matagorda (pres. 1961-62, v.p. 1967-68) bar assns., Am. Judicature Soc., Bay City C. of C. (dir. 1968-69), Lambda Chi Alpha. Democrat. Presbyn. (clk. session 1969-71). Rotarian (v.p. 1968-69, pres. 1969-70). Club: Knife and Fork (dir. 1968-69, pres. 1970-71). Home: 1916 Austin St Bay City TX 77414 Office: 1212 7th St PO Box 1245 Bay City TX 77414

PEEK, HAROLD FRED, constrn. co. exec.; b. Dallas, Feb. 6, 1939; s. Fred Nash and Ella Rae (Hugghins) P.; student Baylor U., 1957-58; B.B.A., So. Meth. U., 1961; m. Sarah Ann Eaker, Jan. 18, 1963; children—Melissa Ann, Harold Fred. Vice pres. constrn. Peek Enterprises, Inc., Dallas, 1961-65, exec. v.p. 1965-68, pres., chief exec. officer, 1969—; dir. BJSS, INC. Mem. Bldg. Code Bd. adjustment, plumbing Code Bd. Adjustment, Richardson, Tex., 1967-71. Active, United Fund, So. Meth. U. Sustentation Fund. Served with USAF, 1961-67. Mem. Home and Apartment Builders Assn. Met. Dallas (pres. 1971), Tex. Assn. Builders (bd. dirs.), Nat. Assn. Home Builders (bd. dirs.). Baptist. Clubs: Northwood, Mustang, Dervish, Salesmanship (all Dallas). Home: 3611 Villanova Dr Dallas TX 75225 Office: PO Box 12146 Dallas TX 75225

PEEK, WILLIAM L., JR., lawyer; b. nr. Texarkana, Ark., Jan. 27, 1929; s. William L. and Bertha Mae (Watkins) P.; diploma Texarkana Jr. Coll., 1949; LL.B., Baylor U., 1954; m. Joy Dale Armstrong, Mar. 2, 1951; children—Michael Dale, Michele, Marcie Lynn. Admitted to Tex. bar, 1954, Ark. bar, 1965; asst. city atty. Waco, Tex., 1956-60; mem. firm Wheeler, Watkins, Hubbard & Patton, Texarkana, Tex., 1960-63; partner Hubbard, Patton, Peek, Haltom & Roberts, Texarkana, 1963—. Served with AUS, 1954-56. Mem. Am., Texarkana, Bowie County, N.E. Tex., Tex. State Jr., Tex. (chmn. grievance com. 1973-74), bar assns., Internat. Soc. Barristers, Am. Bd. Trial Advs., Tex. Assn. Def. Counsel, Baylor U., Baylor U. Law (dir.) alumni assns. Baptist. Kiwanian. Home: 1 Knightsbridge Pl Texarkana TX 75501 Office: PO Box 1928 Texarkana TX 75501

PEEL, ELBERT SIDNEY, JR., judge; b. Williamston, N.C., Feb. 14, 1922; s. Elbert Sidney and Fannie (Manning) P.; student Va. Episcopal Sch., 1939-40; A.B., U. N.C., 1943, LL.B., 1949; m. Lucia Claire Hutchinson, Feb. 2, 1957; children—Lucia Claire, Sarah Margaret, Sydney Eldridge, Elizabeth Chase. Admitted to N.C. bar, 1949; mem. firm Peel & Peel, Williamston, 1949-63; resident judge 2d jud. dist. N.C., Williamston, 1963—. Chmn. Martin County (N.C.) Hosp. Com., 1960-63. Mem. N.C. Senate, 1959-61; mem. N.C. Ho. of Reps., 1961-63. Served to lt. (j.g.) USNR, 1943-46; served to capt. AUS, 1951-53. Mem. Williamston Jr. C. of C. (pres. 1955), Phi Beta Kappa, Zeta Psi. Democrat. Mem. Christian Ch. Kiwanian (pres. 1962). Home: 906 School Dr Williamston NC 27892 Office: Martin County Courthouse Williamston NC 27892

PEELER, HERMAN RAY, textile co. exec.; b. Salisbury, N.C., Dec. 13, 1926; s. Paul A. and Mittie Frances (Shoe) P.; student Catawba Coll., 1943-44; m. Ermine Alberta Williams, Oct. 1, 1950; children—Irving Ray, Jeffrey Paul, Kim Leigh. Credit mgr. Norman's Furniture, Salisbury, N.C., 1952-56, mgr., 1957-63, gen. mgr. furniture div., Salisbury and Lumberton, N.C., 1959-63, sec., 1964—; asst. treas., credit mgr. Norman's Custom Draperies, 1956-61; sec.-treas. R.W. Norman Co., Inc., drapery and bed spread mfg., Salisbury, 1968—, dir., 1955—. Active bus. div. United Fund, 1962. Mem. Salisbury Spencer Furniture Dealers Assn. (pres. 1959). Lutheran (ch. council 1957-60). Home: 1221 Forestdale Dr Salisbury NC 28144 Office: 225-227 N Main St Salisbury NC 28144

PEELER, RAY DOSS, JR., lawyer; b. Bonham, Tex., May 4, 1929; s. Ray Doss and Opal (Porter) P.; B.A. with high honors, U. Tex., 1948, LL.B., 1951; children—William Bryan, Maribel Porter. Admitted to Tex. bar, 1951; practiced law, Bonham, 1953—, dist. and county atty., Fannin County, 1960-61; pres. Fannin Nat. Bank, Windom, Tex., 1963-70, chmn. bd., 1970—; chmn. bd. 1st Nat. Bank, Bonham, Fannin Properties, Inc., Bonham Mfg. Co. Del. Democratic Nat. Conv., 1960. Trustee S.B. Allen Meml. Hosp., Bonham, Wesley Found., East Tex. State U., Commerce. Served to capt. USAF, 1951-53. Mem. State Bar Tex., Am. Bar Assn., State Jr. Bar Tex. (v.p. 1959-60), Phi Beta Kappa, Phi Gamma Delta, Phi Alpha Delta. Mem. Christian Ch. Home: 400 W 5th St Bonham TX 75418 Office: Peeler Bldg Bonham TX 75418

PEEPLES, JERRY WAYNE, holding co. exec.; b. Wellington, Tex., Dec. 21, 1939; s. Denzil Burgess and Ester Pearl (Smith) P.; B.B.A., North Tex. State U., 1965; m. Linda Lee Farbsten, Jan. 26, 1962; children—Teresa, Philip. Sr. accountant Haskins & Sells, C.P.A.'s, Dallas, 1965-68; exec. v.p., dir. Troy Post Corp., Dallas, 1968—; treas. Post Co., Phoenix, 1969—; sec., treas., dir. Ammest Group, Inc., Dallas, 1972—. Dir. Aquatronics, Inc., Dallas, 1968—. Served with USNR, 1956-60. Mem. Am. Inst. C.P.A.'s, Tex. Soc. C.P.A.'s, Beta Alpha Psi. Episcopalian (vestryman, treas. 1965). Club: Tres Vidas en la Playa (Acapulco, Mexico). Home: 12107 Dixfield Dr Dallas TX 75218 Office: 311 S Akard St Dallas TX 75202

PEET, RICHARD CLAYTON, lawyer, research co. exec.; b. N.Y.C., Aug. 24, 1928; s. Charles Francis and Florence L. (Isaacs) P.; J.D., Tulane U., 1953; m. Barbara Jean McClure, Mar. 17, 1956; children—Victoria Clementine, Alexandra Constance, Elizabeth Erica, Clarissa Barbara. Admitted to La. bar, 1955, also DC bar; law clk. Melvin M. Belli, San Francisco, 1954; The Cal. Co., Standard Oil of Cal., 1955; atty. appellate sect. Lands Div., Dept. Justice, Washington, 1956; asst. to dep. gen. counsel Dept. Commerce, 1957; mem. Rep. policy com. U.S. Senate, 1958, office of minority leader William F. Knowland, 1958; asso. counsel anti-trust subcom. House Judiciary Com., 1959-62; asso. minority counsel House Pub. Works Com., 1969-74; pres. Citizens for Hwy. Safety, 1974—; gen. practice law, Washington, 1962—; with Richard Clayton Peet & Assos., 1972—; pres., dir. Lincoln Research Center, 1965—. Served with AUS, 1946-47. Mem. Am., Inter-Am. bar assns., Internat. Inst. Space Law, Internat. Astronautical Fedn., Phi Delta Phi, Pi Kappa Alpha. Republican. Clubs: National Space, Tulane Alumni of Washington. Author: Goals for a Constructive Opposition 1966; Challenge of the

Seventies, 1967; Parties and Democracy, 1972. Composer song: Stand Up For America (recipient George Washington medal Freedom's Found. 1971), 1971. Patentee reclosable carton. Home: 824 Whann Av McLean VA 22101 Office: 1629 K St NW Washington DC

PEEVY, GEORGE HARRY, constrn. co. exec.; b. Dyer, Ark., Nov. 4, 1933; s. Robert Calvin and Sue May (Mason) P.; asso. sci. Ark. Poly. Coll., 1953; B.S., U. Ark., 1955; m. Wanda Lee Shields, June 19, 1954; children—Harry Mitchell, Gregg Robert, Laura Lisa. With Ark. State Highway Dept., Little Rock, Ark., 1959-64; owner Peevy Constrn. Co., Inc., Tulsa, 1964—. Served with C.E. Corps, USNR, 1956-59. Registered profl. engr., Okla. Mem. Okla., Nat. socs. profl. engrs. Baptist (deacon 1970—). Home: 2137 S Fulton Tulsa OK 74114 Office: PO Box 15689 Tulsa OK 74115

PEGG, PHILLIP OLIVER, dairy marketing coop. exec.; b. Bayard, Neb., Aug. 24, 1929; s. Harley Thomas and Gretna Lois (Gray) P.; B.S., Am. U., 1956, M.B.A., 1958; student U. Neb., 1947-49; m. Ursula Anna M. Frank, July 26, 1954; children—Linda Marie, Phillip Oliver. With U.S. Steel Corp., Fairless, Pa., 1957-61, cost analyst, 1960, methods analyst, 1961; systems cons. CBS, N.Y.C., 1961-63; systems cons. Fawcett Publs., Louisville, 1963-66, mgr. systems design and data processing Fawcett Printing, 1966-69; asst. v.p. data processing Life of Ky. Ins. Co., Louisville, 1969-70; mgr. data processing Dairymen Inc., Louisville, 1970—. Served to 1st lt. USMCR, 1950-54. Mem. Assn. Systems Mgmt. (pres., dir. 1966-67), Data Processing Mgmt. Assn., English Speaking Union. Home: 11106 Ridge Rd Anchorage KY 40223 Office: 200 W Broadway Louisville KY 40202

PEITHMAN, RUSSELL IRVIN, musuem dir.; b. Irvington, Ill., July 21, 1930; s. Irvin Milton and Leona (Hendricks) P.; B.A., So. Ill. U., 1956, M.A., 1961; m. Lois Jean Bauernfeind, Aug. 25, 1956; 1 dau., Lynn Victoria. Mus. asst. Univ. Mus., So. Ill. U., 1944-51, mus. research asst., 1954-56, mus. preparator, 1956-59, curator of exhibits, instr., 1959-63; dir. Charlotte (N.C.) Nature Mus., 1963—; mus. cons. museums and founds. Pres. South Piedmont Sci. Fair, 1969—; mem. citizens adv. con. WTVI. Served with USAF, 1951-54. Recipient Natural Sci. for Youth Found. Elsie M.B. Naumberg award for excellence in museums, 1972. Mem. Am. Assn. Youth Museums (pres. 1966-67, 74-75, dir. 1967—), N.C. Museums Council (pres. 1965-67), Am. Assn. Health and Med. Museums (dir. 1972—), Am. Assn. Museums, Theta Xi, Alpha Phi Omega. Home: 4932 Currituck Dr Charlotte NC 28210 Office: 1658 Sterling Rd Charlotte NC 28209

PELL, ALLISON HODGES, cotton mcht.; b. Richmond, Va., Feb. 25, 1901; s. Edward Leigh and Lucy (Hardison) P.; student U. N.C., 1917-19; m. Ellyn Dortch Gorham, Feb. 7, 1923; children—Allison Hodges, Ellyn Gorham (Mrs. James T. Tanner), Edward Leigh III. Asso. Bradshaw-Roberson Cotton Co., Greensboro, 1919-25; partner McIver & Pell, 1925-43; pres. Pell Cotton Co., 1943—, Pell Devel. Corp. (all Charlotte). Mem. N.Y., Memphis cotton exchanges; mem. cotton adv. com. Sec. Agr., 1955. Past chmn. bd. trustees Charlotte Country Day Sch. Mem. Atlantic Cotton Assn. (past pres.), Am. Cotton Shippers Assn. (past pres.). Methodist (trustee). Clubs: Charlotte Country, Charlotte City. Home: 2001 Carmel Rd Charlotte NC 28201 Office: 1221 Hawthorne Lane Charlotte NC 28211

PELTIER, HARVEY, lawyer; B.A., LL.B., La. State U.; m. May Ayo; children—5 children. Admitted to La. bar; practice law, Thibodaux, La.; pres., dir. Citizens Bank and Trust Co., Thibodaux; chmn. bd., dir. Bay Drilling Corp., Cane Machinery & Engring. Co.; former dir. Nat. Am. Bank of New Orleans; also engaged in oil, sugar, real estate bus., farming, breeding and racing thoroughbred horses. Vice pres. La. Bd. Edn. Mem. La. Ho. of Reps., 1924-30, La. Senate, 1930-40. Bd. suprs. La. State U., 1930-40; bd. regents Loyola U., New Orleans. Address: 101 St Louis St PO Box 647 Thibodaux LA 70301

PELTIER, JAMES ROBERT, dentist; b. New Orleans, Sept. 15, 1930; s. Harvey Andrew and May (Ayo) P.; B.S., La. State U., 1950; D.D.S., Loyola U., New Orleans, 1954; m. Benita Ann Armstrong., Aug. 10, 1952; children—Jeanne Ellen, Robert James, David Charles. Intern Duke Hosp., 1956-57; resident Charity Hosp., New Orleans, 1957-59; practice oral surgery, Thibodaux, La., 1959—; chief dept. oral surgery St. Joseph Hosp., Thibodaux, La., 1959—; mem. courtesy staff Terrebone Gen. Hosp., Houma, La., 1959—; mem. courtesy staff St. Ann Gen. Hosp., Raceland, La., 1967—, La. State U. Div. Oral Surgery Charity Hosp. La., 1967—. Dir. Bay Drilling Corp.; pres. Boat Rentals, Inc., Caminada Corp.; v.p. Cane Machinery and Engring Co. Sec.-treas. Lefourche Assn. for Retarded Children, 1963—; rep. La. State U. Athletic Council, 1966-69, bd. suprs., 1972—; served S.S. Hope, Ceylon, 1968. Served to capt. USAF, 1954-56. Mem. Internat., Am., S.E. socs. oral surgeons, La. State U. Alumni Assn. (pres. 1965), Thibodaux C. of C. (pres. 1971-72), V.F.W. (outstanding citizen's award 1970), Omicron Delta Kappa. Rotarian (past pres.). Home: Route 1 Box 570-A Thibodaux LA 70301 Office: 100 E 5th St Thibodaux LA 70301

PEMMARAJU, NARASIMHA RAO, research scientist; b. Rajahmundry, India, Dec. 20, 1928; s. Rama Rao and Lakshmi N. (Kondepudi) P.; B.S., Andhra U., 1948, M.S., 1950; Ph.D., Calcutta U., 1954; m. Suvarna Rani, June 26, 1953; children—Uma, Ramakrishna, Sankar. Came to U.S., 1958. Research asso. Indian Inst. Sci., Bangalore, 1955-56; sci. officer Nat. Chem. Lab., Poina, India, 1956-58; research asso. S.W., Found. for Research and Edn., San Antonio, 1958-61, chief, organic chemistry sect., 1961-65, head, organic chemistry dept., 1965-67, asso. found. scientist, 1967—. Research prof. chemistry St. Mary's U., San Antonio, 1960—. Fulbright grantee, fellow U. Rochester, 1954-55. Fellow Chem. Soc. London; mem. Am. Chem. Soc. Lion. Contbr. articles to profl. lit. Home: 4307 Westberry San Antonio TX 78228 Office: 8848 Commerce San Antonio TX 78284

PENA, FRANCISCO INOCENTE, physician; b. McAllen, Tex., Dec. 28, 1937; s. Abel N. and Josefa (Lopez) P.; B.A., U. Tex., 1960; M.D., U. Tex., 1962; m. Aurora Guerra, July 14, 1963; children—Maritza, Francisco I., Danellie. Intern, Martin Army Hosp., Fort Benning, Ga., 1962-63; gen. practice medicine with J.H. Trevino and Rafael Garza, McAllen, Tex., 1965—; mem. staff and sec., treas. staff McAllen (Tex.) Hosp., 1968-69. Dir., organizer Met. Nat. Bank, McAllen, Tex., 1970-72, Pub. Relations Bd., McAllen, Tex., 1971. Served with AUS, 1962-65. Decorated Air medal with four oak leaf clusters, Bronze Star medal, Purple Heart. Mem. McAllen C. of C., Cath. War Vets., V.F.W., Am. Legion. Mason, Kiwanian. Home: 512 S McColl St McAllen TX 78501 Office: 714 S Main St McAllen TX 78501

PENCE, FERN MCCOMB, state ofcl.; b. Fort Wayne, Ind., Oct. 27, 1908; d. Hubert James and Addie (Schorr) McComb; A.B., Ind. U., 1930; M.A. (Comonwealth fellow), U. Chgo., 1945; m. Robert G. Pence, Feb. 3, 1933 (div. Dec. 1941). Supr. pub. assistance cons. Ind. Dept. Pub. Welfare, Indpls., 1943-46; dir. social services St. Joseph County Dept. Pub. Welfare, South Bend, Ind., 1946-49, Cleve. Rehab. Center, 1952-56; exec. dir. Children's Day Care Assn., Fort Wayne, 1949-52; dir. welfare Am. Joint Distbn. Com., Casablanca, Morocco, 1956-58; supr. pub. assistance field staff Fla. Dept. Pub. Welfare, Jacksonville, 1959-61, fed. govt. program dir. to organize and direct U.S. Cuban refugee assistance program in Dade County, Miami, Fla., 1961-62, welfare program supr. for pub. assistance field service and Cuban refugee assistance program, Jacksonville, 1962-69; Fla. supr. sub-professionals, vols. Cuban Refugee Services, Jacksonville, 1970-73; asst. chief Bur. Adult Services, Fla. Div. Family Services, 1973—. Pub. assistance cons. Greater Boston Health and Welfare Survey, 1948-49; cons., condr. insts. Child Welfare League Am., 1949-55; Nat. Soc. for Crippled Children speaker Nat. Conf. Social Work, 1951—; condr. grad. insts., pub. welfare adminstrn. Western Res. U. Sch. Applied Social Scis., Cleve., 1949-50, faculty med. social work dept., 1955; sec.-treas. Fla. Council on Aging, 1963-64, sec., 1967-69, 70—; trustee, 1969-70; citation for outstanding service, 1972. Recipient Scroll of Friendship, City of Miami, 1962. Mem. Nat. Assn. Social Workers, Acad. Certified Social Workers, Internat., Nat. confs. social work, Theta Sigma Phi, Phi Mu. Democrat. Episcopalian. Home: 479 Tabor Dr S Jacksonville FL 32216 Office: PO Box 2050 Jacksonville FL 32203

PENCE, SAMUEL ALLEN, JR., chem. engr.; b. Angola, Ind., Mar. 22, 1921; s. Samuel Allen and Loa Ermina (Wines) P.; B.S., Purdue U., 1942; grad. U.S. Army Command and Gen. Staff Coll., 1969; m. Elizabeth Rose Field, Feb. 14, 1948; children—Carole Louise, Alen Arthur. Research engr. Universal Atlas Cement Co. div. U.S. Steel Corp., Gary, Ind., 1949-53, sect. leader, 1954-55; sr. devel. engr. Schlumberger Well Services, Houston, 1955-64; sr. research chemist Dowell div. Dow Chem. Co., Tulsa, 1964-72, research specialist, 1972—. Served to maj. F.A., AUS, 1943-47. Registered profl. engr., Okla. Mem. Am. Chem. Soc., Soc. Petroleum Engrs., Okla., Nat. socs. profl. engrs., Order of the Ring, Tau Kappa Epsilon. Mason. Patentee chems. Home: 2820 E 36th Pl Tulsa OK 74105 Office: Dowell Div Dow Chem Co Co PO Box 21 Tulsa OK 74102

PENDER, POLLARD EUGENE, retail exec.; b. Montgomery, La., Feb. 5, 1931; s. Ralph L. and Annie Marie (Carter) P.; student Northwestern State Coll., Natchitoches, La., 1948-50, Centenary Coll., 1950-51; m. Vera Lynelle George, May 4, 1950; children—J. Scott, Gary W. Sec.-treas., Pak-A-Sak Service Stores, Inc., Shreveport, La., 1950-71; controller, The Southland Corp., Dallas, 1971—; dir. United Mercantile Bank, Shreveport; pres. Penro Mobile Homes, Inc., Bossier City, La., 1967—; v.p. So. Research Co., Shreveport, 1972—; sec.-treas. Highland Lakes Furniture Center, Inc., Marble Falls, Tex., 1971—. C.P.A., La., Tex. Mem. Better Bus. Bur., Ark.-La.-Tex. Airmens Assn. (pres. 1967-69), La., Tex. socs. C.P.A.'s, Am. Inst. C.P.A.'s. Democrat. Episcopalian. Mason. Home: 303 Stonebridge Dr Richardson TX 75080 Office: 2828 N Haskell Av Dallas TX 75204

PENDERGRASS, FRANKLIN LEE, ednl. adminstr.; b. Rutherford County, nr. Rutherford, N.C., July 27, 1928; s. Fred Lee and Viola Lillie (Briscoe) P.; A.A., Gardner Webb Jr. Coll., 1950; A.B., Catawba Coll., 1953; M.A., Appalachian State U., 1960; postgrad. East Carolina U., 1960-63, U. N.C., 1963-65; m. Jean Carolyn Hames, Sept. 15, 1950; children—Steven Lee, George Robert. Tchr. city schs., Marion, N.C., 1953-59; prin. Manning Elementary Sch., Roanoke Rapids, N.C., 1959-65, Bailey (N.C.) High Sch., 1965-66; supt. Currituck County (N.C.) Schs., 1966-73; prin. Catawba (N.C.) Elementary Sch., 1973—. Served with USN, 1946-47. Mem. N.E.A., N.C. Assn. Educators, Am. Assn. Sch. Adminstrs. Lion. Home: PO Box 448 Catawba NC 28609 Office: Catawba Elementary School Catawba NC 28609

PENDLETON, ROGER LEE, civil engr.; b. Carmel, Me., Mar. 2, 1923; s. Raymond Fowles and Lulu Myrtle (Miller) P.; B.S., U. Me., 1949; grad. U.S. Army Command and Gen. Staff Coll., 1969; student Air War Coll., 1972-74, Army War Coll., 1973—; postgrad. Va. Poly. Inst. and State U. Extension at Reston, 1972—; m. Velda Laverne Brown, Nov. 24, 1956; 1 dau., Patricia Lee. Resident engr. Ill. Hwy. Dept., Ottawa, 1949-51; base civil engr. USAF, Loring AFB, Me., 1953-55; project engr. Def. Nuclear Agy., Kansas City, Mo., 1955-56; civil engr. cons. Directorate C.E., Hdqrs. USAF, Washington, 1956-67; chief civil engr. Def. Communications Agy., Def. Communications Engring. Center, Reston, Va., 1967—. Bd. dirs. Police and Firemans Assistance Found. Va., Richmond, 1969-73. Served with inf. AUS, 1943-45, 51-52; col. Res. Registered profl. engr., Ky., Vt., Va. Fellow Am. Soc. C.E.; mem. Res. Officers Assn. (chmn. Va. legislative com. 1973-74), U. Me. Alumni Assn. (pres. Washington area 1966-67), Va. (pres. 1969-70), Nat. (nat. dir. 1970-72) socs. profl. engrs., Va. Assn. Professions (treas. 1973). Republican. Mason (Jester, 32 deg., Shriner, Sojourner), Kiwanian (pres. Springfield Club 1971-72). Club: University Maine M. Home: 8909 Cromwell Dr Springfield VA 22151 Office: 1860 Wiehle Av Reston VA 22090

PENG, TAI-CHAN, pharmacologist, educator; b. Vietry, Vietnam, Feb. 28, 1928; s. Tong and Che (Hong) P.; B.Med.Sci., U. Geneva Sch. Medicine, 1956, M.D., 1959; m. Li-Hia Tchong, May 14, 1955; children—Shu-Ming, Huey Lin. Came to U.S., 1959, naturalized, 1971. Intern Hartford (Conn.) City Hosp., 1960; research fellow pharmacology Harvard, 1961-63; research asso. pathophysiology U. Geneva (Switzerland), 1963-64; resident U. Hosp. Geneva, 1964-65; instr. pharmacology Harvard, 1965; mem. faculty U. N.C. Med. Sch., Chapel Hill, 1965—, asst. prof., 1968-72, asso. prof., 1972—. Mem. Endocrine Soc., A.A.A.S., Am. Soc. Pharmacology and Exptl. Therapeutics, Sigma Xi. Mem. rev. panel drug interactions project Am. Pharm. Assn., 1971-75. Contbr. articles to profl. jours. Home: Box 651 Old Lystra Rd Chapel Hill NC 27514 Office: Dept Pharmacology School Medicine Univ North Carolina Chapel Hill NC 27514

PENN, THOMAS JEFFERSON, surgeon; b. Georgetown, Ky., May 25, 1923; s. L. Tandy and Dewey (Swinford) P.; A.B., U. Ky., 1945; M.D., U. Louisville, 1946; m. Kathleen Little, Dec. 1, 1956; children—Albert Tandy, Thomas J. III, William Robert. Intern, Good Samaritan Hosp., Lexington, Ky., 1947-48; pvt. practice Medicine, Nicholasville, 1948-51; resident surgery St. Joseph's Hosp., Lexington, 1953-56; pvt. practice medicine, specializing in surgery Grundy (Va.) Hosp., 1956-62; mem. surg. staff Somerset (Ky.) Hosp., 1964; chief surgery Grundy (Va.) Hosp., 1964—. Chmn. bd. March of Dimes, 1961; devel. council U. Ky., 1973—. Served with AUS, 1943-46; as capt. M.C., 1951-53. Diplomate Am. Bd. Surgery. Fellow A.C.S. Southeastern Surg. Congress; mem. A.M.A., Va., Buchanan-Dickinson County med. socs., U. Ky. Alumni Assn. (dir. 1973—). Methodist (dir.). Rotarian. Home: Grundy VA 24614 Office: Grundy Hosp Grundy VA 24614

PENNINGTON, BROOKS, state senator, seed co. exec.; b. Pennington, Ga., Oct. 21, 1925; s. Brooks Maddox and Lucile (Braswell) P.; student N. Ga. Mil. Coll., 1942-43; B.S., U. Ga., 1949; m. Jacquelyn C. Pennington, Aug. 14, 1953; children—Brooks III, Penny, Robert, Dan. Pres., Pennington Grain & Seed, Inc., Madison, Ga., 1950—; v.p. Piedmont Acid Delinting, Inc., Winder, Ga., 1960—; dir. Cotton Hybrid Research, Inc., Winder; mem. Ga. Senate, 1963—, chmn. agr. com. 1963—. Chmn. Morgan County Hosp. Authority, 1958-62; past chmn. Morgan County Bd. Commrs. bd. dirs. Agri-Bus. Council Ga., 1965—. Mem. Ga. Ho. of Reps., 1962-63, exec. com. Ga. Democratic party, 1963—. Served with USAAF, 1943-49. Mem. Ga. Seedsmen's Assn. (past pres.), So. Field Seed Council (past pres.), N.Ga. Coll. Alumni Assn. (pres. 1970-72). V.F.W. Methodist. Club: Morgan County Touch-Down (pres. 1955—). Address: PO Box 290 Madison GA 30650

PENNINGTON, WILLIAM L., oil producer, operator; b. Erick, Okla., Apr. 2, 1923; s. William L. and Ona (McClinton) P.; B.S., U. Okla., 1949; m. Georgia Armstrong, Dec. 23, 1942; children—Paula Lynn, Patricia Anne, Denise. Geologist, Frank Wood, Wichita Falls, Tex., 1949-53, chief geologist, 1953-55; sr. geologist Texaco Inc., Wichita Falls, 1955-57; ind. cons. geologist, Wichita Falls, 1957-63; oil producer, operator, Wichita Falls, 1963—; pres. W. L. Pennington, Inc., 1964—, Brook Plaza, Inc., 1967—, Helix Oil Inc., 1967—; sole gen. partner Penpar Ltd., 1969— (all Wichita Falls). Served with AUS, 1946-47. Mem. Am. Assn. Petroleum Geologists, Am. Inst. Profl. Geologists, North Tex. Oil and Gas Assn., Tex. Ind. Producers and Royalty Owners Assn., Am. Inst. Mining, Metall. and Petroleum Engrs., Ind. Producers Assn. Am. (dir.), U. Okla. Alumni Assn., Sigma Gamma Epsilon. Clubs: Wichita, Wichita Falls Country, Lancers. Home: 4201 Cedar Elm Wichita Falls TX 76308 Office: Oil and Gas Bldg Wichita Falls TX 76301

PEPPER, CLAUDE DENSON, congressman; b. Dudleyville, Ala., Sept. 8, 1900; s. Joseph Wheeler and Lena (Talbot) P.; A.B., U. Ala., 1921; J.D., Harvard, 1924; LL.D., McMaster U., 1941, U. Toronto, U. Ala., 1942, Rollins Coll., 1944; m. Irene Mildred Webster, Dec. 29, 1936. Instr. law U. Ark., 1924-25; admitted to Ala. bar, 1924, Fla. bar, 1925; practice law, Perry, Fla.; mem. Fla. Ho. Reps., 1929; practice law, Tallahassee, 1930; mem. Fla. Bd. Pub. Welfare, 1931-32, Fla. Bd. Law Examiners, 1933; mem. U.S. Senate from Fla., 1936-51, mem. coms. on small bus. and fgn. relations, on mil. affairs, small bus., reorgn. of congress, chmn. com. on inter-oceanic canals, Middle East sub-com. of senate fgn. relations com., 12 yrs.; mem. 88th-89th Congresses 3d Dist. Fla., 90th-92d congresses 11th Dist. Fla., 93d Congress 14th Dist. Fla., mem. house rules, house internal security coms., chmn. house select com. on crime. Officer, dir. Washington Fed. Savs. & Loan Assn. Chmn., Fla. delegation Democratic Nat. Conv., 1940-44, del., 1948, 52, 56, 60, 64, 68. Served with Armed Forces, 1918. Recipient Albert Lasker Pub. Service award, 1967. Mem. Internat., Inter-Am., Am., Fla. (exec. com.), Tallahassee, Miami Beach, Coral Gables, Dade County bar assns., Bar Assn. City N.Y., Am. Legion, 40 and 8, Vets. World War I, Blue Key, Gold Key. Phi Beta Kappa, Omicron Delta Kappa, Phi Alpha Delta, Sigma Upsilon, Kappa Alpha. Baptist. Elk, Mason (Shriner), Moose, Kiwanian, Woodman of World. Clubs: Harvard (Washington, Miami); Jefferson Island, Army and Navy (Washington); Coral Gables Country; Miami Shores Country; La Gorce Country (Miami Beach); Columbia Country (Chevy Chase, Md.); Burning Tree (Bethesda, Md.). Contbr. to periodicals. Home: 2121 North Bay Shore Dr Miami FL 33137 also 402 Wilson Av Tallahassee FL 32303 also 4210 Cathedral Av NW Washington DC 20016 Office: 1701 Meridian Av Miami Beach FL 33139 also Cannon House Office Bldg Washington DC 20515

PEPPER, JACK WILSON, civil engr.; b. Yazoo City, Miss., Jan. 12, 1918; s. Jack Horton and Evie Louise (McRaven) P.; B.S. in Civil Engring., Miss. State U., 1939; m. Dorothy Heidel Luse, Mar. 23, 1946; 1 son, Jack Douglas. Hydraulic engr. U.S. Geol. Survey, Ocala, Fla., 1939-41; owner Pepper Engring. Co., Yazoo City, Miss., 1946-56; state water engr. Miss. Bd. Water Commrs., Jackson, 1956—. Mem. adv. com. Coll. Engring., Miss. State U., 1969-73. Mem. Miss. Air and Water Pollution Control Commn., 1966—; chmn. So. Environmental Resources Conf., Council State Govts., 1972-73; mem. exec. com. Interstate Conf. Water Problems, Council State Govts., 1969—, 1st vice chmn., 1973—. Served to maj. AUS, 1941-46. Registered profl. engr., Miss., Ark., La. Fellow Am. Soc. C.E. (pres. Miss. sect. 1971-72); mem. Nat. Soc. Profl. Engrs., Miss. Engring. Soc. (pres. 1973-74). Home: Route 1 Benton MS 39039 Office: 416 N State St Jackson MS 39201

PERCY, WALKER, author; b. Birmingham, Ala., May 28, 1916; s. Leroy Pratt and Martha Susan (Phinizy) P.; B.A., U. N.C., 1937; M.D., Columbia, 1941; m. Mary Bernice Townsend, Nov. 7, 1946; children—Mary Pratt, Ann Boyd. Intern Bellevue Hosp., N.Y.C., 1942; author, 1943—. Recipient Nat. Inst. Arts and Letters award, 1967. Fellow Am. Acad. Arts and Scis.; mem. Nat. Inst. Arts and Letters. Roman Catholic. Author: The Moviegoer (Nat. Book award 1962), 1961; The Last Gentleman, 1966; Love in the Ruins, 1972. Contbr. philos., critical and med. essays to jours. and mags. Address: Old Landing Rd Covington LA 70433

PERDUE, CLYDE HOLLAND, lawyer; b. Redwood, Va., Oct. 15, 1902; s. Jesse L. and Nannie (Holland) P.; student Coll. William and Mary., 1921-23; LL.B., U. Va., 1927; m. Helen Shelburne, Nov. 6, 1943; children—Emma Shelburne (Mrs. William M. Parcell), Nannie Holland (Mrs. Hansford B. Leake), Helen Randolph, Clyde Holland. Admitted to Va. bar, 1926; practiced in Rocky Mount, 1927—; mem. firm Clyde, Holland & Perdue, 1927—. Dir. Peoples Nat. Bank, Rocky Mount. U.S. magistrate, 1963—. Trustee Franklin Meml. Hosp., Rocky Mount. Home: 222 Diamond Av Rocky Mount VA 24151 Office: 106 N Main St Perdue-Montgomery Bldg Rocky Mount VA 24151

PERDUE, MAX WENDELL, utility exec.; b. Cullman, Ala., Oct. 9, 1933; s. Cottie D. and Dovie (Calvert) P.; B.S. in Elec. Engring., U. Ala., 1961; m. Mar Emma Gray, Mar. 11, 1956; children—Lynn, Karen. With Ala. Power Co., various locations, 1961—, dist. supt., Jasper, Ala., 1969, dist. mgr., 1969—. Vice chmn. Walker County chpt. A.R.C., 1972—; chmn. pacemaker div. Walker County chpt. United Appeal, 1969-70, campaign chmn., 1971; chmn. Explorer com. Mountain dist. Black Warrior council Boy Scouts Am., 1970; chmn. adv. com. Walker County State Trade Sch., 1973. Served with USNR, 1953-57. Registered profl. engr., Ala. Mem. Jasper Area C. of C. (dir.), I.E.E.E., Nat. Mgmt. Assn. (pres. 1968-69). Home: 303 Cherokee Circle Jasper AL 35501 Office: 1814 3d Av Jasper AL 35501

PERDUE, NATHANIEL WILLIAM, state ofcl.; b. Petersburg, Va., Dec. 24, 1929; s. Nathaniel Grover and Elva Gladys (Jackson) P.; B.S. in Social Sci., Va. Commonwealth U., 1953; m. Jacquelin H. Reese, Aug. 24, 1957; children—Amy Anne, Samuel Scott, Lisa Carol. Tchr., recreation dir. Southampton Correctional Farm, Capron, Va., 1955-59; probation and parole officer Dist. 7, Petersburg, Va., 1959-62; probation and parole supr. Probation and Parole Bd., Richmond, Va., 1962, tng. supr., 1962-71, exec. sec., 1971—. Mem. Va. Probation and Parole Bd., 1974—. Served with AUS, 1953-55. Mem. Assn. Paroling Authorities, Nat. Council Crime and Delinquency, Am., So. States correctional assns. Methodist. Home: PO Box 816 Chester VA 23831 Office: 6767 Forest Hill Av Richmond VA 23225

PEREIRA, FRANCISCO FELIBERTO, clergyman; b. Iguara Las Villas, Cuba, Mar. 9, 1938; s. Francisco S. and Hermenegilda (Navarro) P.; B.A., Sem. Theology, Placeta, Cuba, 1960; m. Jacqueline Rosales, Mar. 31, 1961; children—Joel, Ruth. Came to U.S., 1969. Ordained to ministry Christian Ch. (Disciples Christ), 1970; minister Asociacion Evangelica de Cuba, Central Lugareno, 1960-69, 2d Christian Ch., San Benito, Tex., 1970—, dir. radio program La Hora Cristiana, 1973—. Youth counselor Hispanic

Christian Ch. Tex., 1971-74; staff chaplain Dolly Vinsant Meml. Hosp., San Benito, 1972—; columnist Christian Courier newspaper, Fort Worth, 1973—; ad hoc adviser Hispanic Ministry Indpls., 1973—. Mem. Latin Am. com., Rio Grande Valley, 1970—. Trustee Hispanic Am. Inst. Austin (Tex.), Mem. San Benito Ministerial Alliance (pres. 1971-72), Hispanic Ministers Disciples Christ U.S.A. (treas., state pres. 1972-74). Address: 335 Corral St San Benito TX 78596

PERESS, MAURICE, symphony condr.; b. N.Y.C., Mar. 18, 1930; s. Haskell Ben Ezra and Elka (Tygier) P.; B.A., N.Y. U., 1951; postgrad. Mannes Coll. Music, N.Y. U. Grad. Sch. Musicology; m. Gloria Vando, July 2, 1955; children—Lorca Miriam, Paul Avram, Anika Tygier. Asst. condr. Mannes Coll. Music, 1957-60; music dir. N.Y. U., 1958-61; asst. condr. New York Philharmonic, 1961-62; music dir. Corpus Christi (Tex.) Symphony, 1961—; music dir. Joffrey Ballet, 1966, Austin Symphony, 1970-72; dir. Bur. Indian Affairs pilot project Communication through Music, 1968; faculty N.Y. U., 1957-61, Queens Coll., 1969-70, U. Tex., 1970—. Host for NET TV Series Backstage with the Austin Symphony, 1970-71; Mus. Dir. Revival of Candide, 1971; condr. world premier Mass (Leonard Bernstein) for Inaugural J.F. Kennedy Center, Washington, 1972. Served with U.S. Army, 1953-55. Recipient Beethoven medal from German Consul Gen., 1969; named Arts Council Artist of Year, 1969. Millicent James fellow N.Y. U., 1955, Mannes Coll. scholar, 1955-57. Mem. A.S.C.A.P. Jewish religion. Pub. orchestrations: Monteverdi, Tocatta and Ritornelli from Orfeo; Bernstein, West Side Story Overture; Ellington, Black Brown and Beige Suite. Author: Some Music Lessons for American Indian Youngsters, 1968. Contbr. articles to profl. jours. Home: 145 Atlantic St Corpus Christi TX 78404 Office: PO Box 495 Corpus Christi TX 78402

PEREZ, EUGENE REYES, surgeon; b. San Juan Bautista, Cal., Jan. 6, 1908; s. Frederick P. and Christina E. (Rozas) P.; A.B., U. Cal. 1931; M.D., C.M., McGill U., Montreal, Que., Can., 1936; m. Evelyn E. Peterson, May 28, 1937; children—Teresa Dolores (Mrs. Albert Balz), Camila Ines (Mrs. Thomas Baumgartner). Postgrad. surg. tng. U. Cal. Hosp., San Francisco, 1936-37, 40-41; Letterman Gen. Hosp., San Francisco, 1938-40, Royal Victoria Hosp., McGill U., 1937-38; asst. chief resident surgeon U. Cal. Hosp., 1945-46; pvt. and indsl. surgery practice, San Jose, Cal., 1946-60; clin. instr. in surgery Stanford Sch. Medicine, 1958-60; dir. med. edn. and research Washington County Hosp., Hagerstown, Md., 1960-61; dir. med. edn. Williamsport (Pa.) Hosp., 1961-62; asst. supt., dir. profl. services and edn. Meadowbrook Hosp., L.I., 1962-63; med. dir. Rossmoor Leisure World Clinic, Walnut Creek, Cal., 1964-66; med. dir. Petersburg (Va.) Gen. Hosp., 1966-67; dir. Va. Regional Med. Program, also asst. prof. med. edn., Med. Coll. Va., 1967—. Vice pres. Va. League Nursing, 1970-72. Served as lt. col., M.C., AUS, 1941-45. Fellow A.C.S. (past pres. No. Cal. chpt.); mem. A.M.A., Pan Am. Med. Soc. (state dir.), A.A.A.S., Am. Assn. for History of Medicine, San Jose Surg. Soc. (pres. 1956-57), Am. Hosp. Assn., Assn. Am. Med. Colls., Assn. Hosp. Dirs. Med. Edn., Am. Soc. Abdominal Surgery, Va. Med. Soc., Richmond Acad. Med. Club: Bull and Bear. Office: VA Regional Med Program 700 E Main St Richmond VA 23219

PEREZ, VIRGINIA MAYERS (MRS. MARIO J. PEREZ), home economist; b. Loredo, Tex., Oct. 1, 1944; d. Pablo and Bertha Hilda (Vidaurri) Mayers; B.S., Tex. Woman's U., 1967; postgrad. Tex. A. and M. U., 1970, Tex. Tech. U., 1973, Tex. A. and I., Laredo, 1974; m. Mario J. Perez, Aug. 29, 1964; 1 dau., Melissa. Asst. home demonstration agt. Tex. Agrl. Extension Service, Hidalgo County, 1967-68, asso. home demonstration agt., Cameron County, 1969-71, Webb County, Laredo, Tex., 1971—; extension agt. Expanded Nutrition Program, Webb County; mem. Equal Employment Opportunity adv. com. Mem. Lower Rio Grande Valley Consumer Com., 1967-71. Mem. Am. Assn. U. Women, Nat. Assn. Extension Home Economists, Am., Tex. home econs. assns., County Home Demonstration Agts. Assn. Tex., Tex. State Nutrition Council, Tex. Farm Bur. Assn. Roman Catholic. Home: 2710 Laredo St Laredo TX 78040 Office: 2000 San Jorge St Laredo TX 78040

PEREZ PIMENTEL, PEDRO, justice P.R. Supreme Ct.; b. Vieques, P.R., Apr. 1, 1904; s. Dionisio Perez Valles and Natividad Pimentel; LL.B., U. P.R., 1927; m. Margarita; children—Pedro Angel, Maria Margarita. Admitted to P.R. bar, 1927, practiced in Humacao, 1927-42; legal advisor of treas. of P.R., 1942-45; dist. judge, Guayama, P.R., 1945, Humacao, 1945-49, San Juan, 1949-52; asso. justice Supreme Ct. P.R., 1952-73, chief justice, 1973—. Mem. Bar Assn. P.R. Rotarian. Home: Calle Martin Travieso 1512 Santurce PR 00911 Office: Supreme Ct San Juan PR 00936

PEREZ-SOTO, ARMANDO, physician; b. Utuado, P.R., Feb. 12, 1936; s. Eduardo and Luisa (Soto) Perez-Ayala; B.S. cum laude, U. P.R., 1957. M.D., 1961; m. Ana L. Zabala, July 2, 1960; children—Armando L., Maria del Pilar, Roberto. Intern, Univ. Hosp., Rio Piedras, P.R., 1962; practice medicine specializing in internal medicine, Arecibo, P.R., 1966—. Served to capt. AUS, 1962-66. Mem. A.M.A., U. P.R. Med. Grads. Assn. Home: 54 Andres Garcia St Arecibo PR 00612 Office: 107 Hernandez Huertas St Arecibo PR 00612

PERKINS, ABNER LAVERNE, hwy. engr., land surveyor; b. Cairo, Ga., May 20, 1937; s. Thomas Abner and Mildred (Strickland) P.; student U. Okla., 1955-57, U. Ky., 1957; m. Inez Janet Worley, Mar. 1, 1959; children—Derwood Laverne, Melody Renee. Worker, mgr. Curry Furniture & Funeral Home, Chandler, Okla., 1953-55; worker Primrose Funeral Home, Norman, Okla., 1955-57; with Ky. Dept. Hwys., Lexington, 1957—, civil engr. asst., 1967, asst. dist. engr. for planning, 1967—. Recipient certificate of service award Ky. Dept. Hwys., 1967, 72. Registered profl. engr., Ky. Mem. Nat., Ky. socs. profl. engrs. Mem. Ch. of God. Designer, builder Ch. of God, Lexington, 1964. Home: 107 Sutton Pl Lexington KY 40504 Office: 763 New Circle Rd Lexington KY 40504

PERKINS, CARL D., legislator; b. Hindman, Ky., Oct. 15, 1912; s. J.E. and Dora (Calhoun) P.; grad. Jefferson Sch. Law, Louisville, 1935; m. Verna Johnson; 1 son, Christopher. Practice of law, Hindman, Ky., 1935; commonwealth atty. 31st Jud. Dist., 1939; mem. Ky. Gen. Assembly from 99th Dist., 1940; Knott County atty., 1941-48; counsel Dept. Hwys., Frankfort, Ky., 1948; mem. 81st to 93d congresses 7th dist. of Ky., chmn. house com. on edn. and labor, 1967—. Served with AUS, World War II: ETO; participated in battles No. France, Battle of the Bulge, Rhineland, Central Europe. Democrat. Home: Hindman KY 48122 Office: Rayburn Bldg Washington DC 20013

PERKINS, CARRYE E., metals treating co. exec.; b. Corrigan, Tex., Nov. 11, 1911; s. Clarence Moore and Josie (McGill) P.; ed. pub. schs.; m. Bertha Mae Anthony, Feb. 15, 1948; children—Patsy (Mrs. Walter Stierhoff, Jr.), Carrye L., Claudia, Carl, Betty (Mrs. Merlin Vollman), Bernice (Mrs. James Permenter), James Arnold. Gen. foreman N. Am. Aviation Corp., Dallas, 1941-46; mgr. Houston Heat Treating Co., 1947-48; supr. ClecoAir Tools, Houston, 1948-51; v.p. Superior Heat Treating Co., Fort Worth, 1951-58; founding pres. Perzy Heat Treat Inc., Arlington, Tex., 1959—. Mem. Am. Soc. Metals (chmn. 1958-59), Tex. Mfg. Assn. (chmn. Mid-Cities chpt.). Home: 718 McKay Dr Arlington TX 76010 Office: PO Box 1347 2900 Randol Mill Rd Arlington TX 76010

PERKINS, DANIEL WOOD, govt. ofcl.; b. Capps, Fla., Oct. 21, 1945; s. Fred M. and Bruce (Ingram) P.; B.S., Fla. State U., 1971; m. Janice Kitchem, June 22, 1968. Tchr. South Daytona (Fla.) elementary sch., 1972—; asst. therapeutic group leader Fla. div. Youth Service, Daytona Beach, Fla., 1968-69, asst. supt., 1969-71, supt., 1971—; cons. N.H. Youth Devel. Center. Mem. Fla. Community Service Assn., Internat. Halfway House Assn., Chi Delta Tau. Home: 1047 Madison Av Daytona Beach FL 32014 Office: 1047 Madison Av Daytona Beach FL 32014

PERKINS, DOUGLAS NELSON, accountant; b. Littlefield, Tex., Dec. 16, 1935; s. Jeff Adair and Mattie (Brown) P.; B.B.A., Tex. Tech U., 1957; m. Jackye Lynn Hill, Feb. 17, 1956; children—Dana L., Kimberly D., Sharla K. Jr. accountant Arthur Young & Co., Tulsa, 1957-58, sr., accountant, 1959-60; internal auditor Gunn Bros., Inc., Amarillo, Tex., 1961-63; partner Leon L. Hoyt & Co., pub. accountants, Amarillo, 1963—. C.P.A., Tex. Mem. Am. Inst. C.P.A.'s Tex. Soc. Pub. Accountants (dir. 1972—, chpt. pres. 1973—), Sigma Nu. Methodist. Home: 7104 Elmhurst St Amarillo TX 77106 Office: Box 2211 Amarillo TX 79105

PERKINS, FRANK OVERTON, biologist; b. Fork Union, Va., Feb. 14, 1938; s. Frank Otie and Mary Ella (Hughes) P.; B.A., U. Va., 1960; M.S., Fla. State U., 1962, Ph.D., 1966; m. Alma Vivian Smith, June 15, 1961. Asso. marine scientist Va. Inst. Marine Sci., Gloucester Point, 1966-69, sr. marine scientist, head dept. microbiology-pathology, 1969—. Research grantee NASA, 1969-72, NSF, 1971—. Mem. Mycol. Soc. Am., Soc. Protozoologists, Electron Microscopy Soc. Am., Assn. Southeastern Biologists, Am. Soc. Cell Biology. Contbr. articles to profl. jours. Home: PO Box 162 Gloucester Point VA 23062 Office: Va Inst Marine Sci Gloucester Point VA 23062

PERKINS, HARRY GILMER, JR., city ofcl.; b. Tampa, Fla., Aug. 17, 1934; s. Harry G. and Barbara (Smith) P.; B.S., Auburn U., 1957; M.A., U. Ga., 1970; m. Sue M. Latimer; children—Donna Anne, Harry Gilmer III, Ashley, Stephen. Asst. dir. State Ga. Motor Vehicles Dept., Atlanta, 1964-67; systems analyst RCA, Atlanta, 1967-69; city mgr. City of Tifton (Ga.), 1971—. Sec. County Health Bd., 1971—; chmn. Coastal Plain Econ. Opportunity Adminstrn., Tift County, 1971—; mem. Airport Authority Tift County, 1971—. Served to capt. USAF, 1958-64. Mem. Internat. City Mgrs. Assn., Am. Soc. Pub. Adminstrn., Ga. Peace Officers Assn., Res. Officers Assn., C. of C. (dir. 1971—), Ga. City/County Mgrs. Assn. Methodist. Mason (Shriner), Rotarian, Elk. Author: (with Robert T. Golembienski) Cases in Public Management, 1973. Home: 608 Azalea Dr Tifton GA 31794 Office: City Hall Box 229 Tifton GA 31794

PERKINS, MARCUS FRANKLIN, foam plastics mfg. exec.; b. Macon, Mo., Oct. 26, 1909; s. Walter Wingford and Anna (Reynolds) P.; student Ft. Lewis Coll., 1927-28, U. Utah, 1929-30; B.S., U. Okla., 1932; m. Oma Nicholson, Aug. 19, 1960; children—Delano, Gary, Douglas. Tchr. high sch., Colo., 1934-39; rancher, Dove Creek, Colo., 1934-60; operator El Rey Hotel, San Diego, 1947-61, Rogette Motel, Dove Creek, 1951-60; mfr. foam plastics, Fort Worth, 1958—. Mem. Sch. Bd., Dove Creek, 1940-52. Mem. Delta Sigma Phi. Patentee in amusement field. Home: 7320 Coronet St Fort Worth TX 76118 Office: 205 S Sylvania St Fort Worth TX 76111

PERKINS, MARGARET NELSON KAYE (MRS. WILLIAM ROBERTSON PERKINS, JR.), artist-painter; b. Topeka, Sept. 7, 1904; d. James Philip and Frances (Nelson) de Bevers Kay; student art, Florence, Italy, 1922-24; grad. N.Y. Sch. Fine and Applied Art, 1927; spl. student Randolph-Macon Woman's Coll., 1946-48; m. William Robertson Perkins, Jr., Oct. 1, 1938; 1 dau., Sarah Frances. One-man shows Lynchburg Art Club, 1961, Myrtle Beach, S.C., 1967; 2-man show Randolph-Macon Woman's Coll., 1948; exhibited in group shows Va. Mus. Fine Arts, Nat. Biennial Am. League Am. Pen Women, others. Recipient 1st prize Lynchburg Civic Art, 1949, 55, Va. Fed. Women's Clubs, 1955-58, Va. Biennial Nat. League Am. Pen Women, 1963. Mem. D.A.R., Archeol. Inst. Am., Assn. for Preservation Va. Antiquities, Historic Lynchburg Found., L'Alliance Francaise de Lynchburg, N.E. Hist Geneal. Soc., Am. Pen Women (v.p. Lynchburg br. 1966-67). Club: Garden of Virginia, Lynchburg Art. Illustrated booklet Christmas in Colonial Virginia, 1957. Home: 3116 Rivermont Av Lynchburg VA 24503

PERKINS, PERCY HAROLD, JR., architect; b. Metter, Ga., Sept. 8, 1905; s. Percy Harold and Bertha Mae (Warwick) P.; student Ga. Sch. Tech., 1923-27; grad. The Infantry Sch., 1932, Command and Gen. Staff Sch., 1942, Gemological Inst. Am., 1966; m. Mary L. Martin, Nov. 5, 1933 (dec. June 1962); m. 2d, Estelle B. Bennett, Jan. 25, 1963; 1 stepson., James Gordon Bennett. Archtl. draftsman, 1927-41, Atlanta, 1941-46; asso. architect Barili & Humphreys, Atlanta, 1946-51; architect Percy H. Perkins Jr. & Assos., Atlanta, 1951—. Gemologist, 1966—; lectr. gems and gemology. Served from 2d lt. to col., USAR, 1927-65; Col. Res. (ret.). Aide-de-camp Gov.'s staff, 1971—. Decorated Bronze Star medal, Purple Heart; Czechoslovakia War Cross. Mem. Ga. Mineral Soc., Ga. Gem Soc., Res. Officers Assn. (past pres. Greater Atlanta chpt.), Atlanta Hist. Soc., Atlanta Art Assn., Fulton County Grand Jurors Assn., Am. Legion, A.I.A. (past dir. Ga. chpt.), Ga. Archtl. and Engring. Soc., Am. Gem Soc. (asso.), Ret. Officers Assn. (life), 16th Armored Div. Assn. (life), 760th Tank Bn. Assn., Men's Garden Club, Atlanta and Buckhead, Scabbard and Blade, Pi Kappa Alpha. Presbyn. (elder). Mason (Shriner, 32 deg.), Kiwanian. Former newspaper columnist. Home: 5450 Peachtree-Dunwoody Rd NE Atlanta GA 30342 Office: 3110 Maple Dr NE Atlanta GA 30305

PERKINS, RICHARD BURLE, real estate broker; b. Rockville, Ind., July 1, 1923; s. Walter Mac and Olevia Maude (Vinson) P.; student Ball State U., 1941-42, Oberlin Coll., 1944-45, U. Mich., 1946; B.A., DePauw U., 1947; m. Mariam Catherine Jamail, Aug. 1, 1959; children—Richard Burle II, Mele Angelique. Territory mgr. P & G Edible Oils, Tex., La., Okla., 1947-53; dist. mgr. Southwest U.S. DCA Food Industries, spl. flours, mixes and machinery, Houston, Tex., 1953-62; pres. Gold Seal Donuts, Houston, 1962-63; div. mgr. Nat. Oats Co., Houston, 1963-68; mgr. apt. mng. systems Office Services, Inc., Houston, 1970—; owner Dick Perkins Co., realtor, Houston, 1970—; registered securities rep. Waddel & Reed, Houston, 1970-71; gen. mgr. Seven-Up Bottling Corp., Houston, 1969. Chmn. orgn. and extension com. Sunset dist. Boy Scouts Am., 1970; com. chmn. Cub Scout Pack 855, 1968—; coach, sponsor Spring Branch Little League Baseball, 1967—. Served with USMC, 1942-46. Mem. Pi Sigma Alpha. Club: Memorial Plaza Civic (pres. 1968) (Houston). Home: 5915 Havenwoods Dr Houston TX 77066 Office: 5302 Lawn Arbor Dr Houston TX 77066 also 13027 Champions Dr Suite C Houston TX 77069

PERKINS, WILLIAM ALLAN, JR., lawyer; b. Charlottesville, Va., Dec. 19, 1925; s. William Allan and Hazelhurst (Bolton) P.; student Duke, 1943-44; LL.B., U. Va., 1949; m. Ann Patterson, Jan. 28, 1950; children—Allan, Ann, Howell, Channing. Admitted to Va. bar, 1949; mem. firm McGuire, Woods & Battle, and predecessor firms, Charlottesville, 1949—. Mem. Albemarle County Planning Commn., 1960-70. Bd. dirs., mem. Miller bd. trustees Perry Found., 1955—. Served to 2d lt. USMCR, 1943-46; capt. Res. ret. Mem. Am. Judicature Soc., Am., Va. State (chmn. domestic relations com. 1971-72) bar assns., Va. State Bar, Va. Trial Lawyers Assn. (pres. 1964-65), Charlottesville-Albemarle Bar Assn. (pres. 1972-73), Va. Conf. Bar Execs. (v.p. 1973-74). Elk, Rotarian. Clubs: Red-Land (pres. 1973-74), Farmington Country, Farmington Hunt, Greencroft (Charlottesville). Home: 23 Farmington Dr Charlottesville VA 22901 Office: McGuire Woods & Battle Court Square Bldg Charlottesville VA 22902

PERLEY, MARTIN MOSES, county ofcl., clergyman; b. Phila., Oct. 11, 1910; s. Benjamin and Tillie (Goren) Perelmuter; B.A., McGill U., 1930; M.H.L., Hebrew Union Coll., 1934, D.D. (hon.), 1959; m. Maie E. Clements, July 11, 1938. Rabbi, 1934; rabbi, Melbourne, Australia, 1934-36; dir. Hillel Found., U. Ill., Champaign-Urbana, 1937-38, Ind. U., Bloomington, 1938-41; rabbi B'rith Sholom, Louisville, 1946-68; exec. dir. Louisville and Jefferson County Human Relations Commn., 1968—. Chmn. Louisville Area Council on Religion and Race, 1964-66; vice chmn. Louisville-Jefferson County Community Action Commn., 1966-68. Served to maj. Chaplain Corps, AUS, 1943-46. Decorated Bronze Star medal. Recipient Outstanding Kentuckian award Louisville Defender, 1966. Mem. Central Conf. Am. Rabbis (mem. exec. bd. 1948-50, chmn. projects for Israel com. 1961-66), Louisville Bd. Rabbis (chmn. 1967-68). Home: 507 Country Lane Louisville KY 40207 Office: 400 S 6th St Louisville KY 40203

PERLIK, CHARLES ANDREW, JR., trade union ofcl.; b. Pitts., Nov. 13, 1923; s. Charles Andrew and Theresa (Kraft) P.; B.S. in Journalism, Northwestern U., 1949, M.S., 1950; m. Marion Virginia Ford, Jan. 3, 1948; children—Paul, Lesley, Stephen. Newsman, U.P., Pitts., Chgo., 1946-48; reporter Buffalo Evening News, 1950-52; internat. rep. Am. Newspaper Guild (now The Newspaper Guild 1971—), Buffalo, 1952-55, sec.-treas., Washington, 1955-69, pres., 1969—. Sec.-treas. Mellett Fund for Free and Responsible Press, 1967—. Served to 1st lt. USAAF, 1943-46. Mem. Sigma Delta Chi. Home: 2407 Barbour Rd Falls Church VA 22043 Office: care The Newspaper Guild 1125 15th St NW Washington DC 20005

PERLMAN, MATTHEW S., lawyer; b. Washington, Aug. 30, 1936; A.B. magna cum laude, Brown U., 1957; LL.B., magna cum laude, Harvard, 1960. Admitted to D.C. bar, 1960, Md. bar, 1960, U.S. Supreme Ct. bar, 1964, U.S. Ct. Claims bar, 1965; atty. Office Gen. Counsel, Dept. Air Force, 1960-65; mem. Armed Services Bd. Contract Appeals, 1965-67; gen. counsel President's Commn. on Postal Orgn., 1967; asst. gen. counsel Dept. Transp., 1967-69; mem. firm Arent, Fox, Kintner, Plotkin & Kahn, Washington. Mem. Am. (chmn. contract adjustment bd. com. pub. contract law sect. 1970—), Fed. (chmn. govt. contracts com. 1971-74) bar assns., Phi Beta Kappa. Editor: Harvard Law Rev., 1959-60. Office: Federal Bar Bldg Washington DC 20006

PERLMUTTER, LEONARD LEON, playwright; b. N.Y.C., Mar. 23, 1912; s. Harry and Dora (Orgel) P.; student Columbia, 1928-31; B.A., U. Rochester, 1932; postgrad. U. Vienna Med. Sch., 1932-35; M.A., U. Miami, 1971, postgrad., 1971—; m. Mary Elizabeth Watters, June 3, 1950. Salesman, Pearl Mfg. Co., Bklyn., 1935-41; indsl. engr. Dept. Army, 1941-46, Dept. Navy, 1946-70; writer plays, including The Conquests of Helen, prod. Tamarac (Fla.) Workshop, 1972, The Inheritance, prod. Tamarac Workshop, 1973. Pres. Tamarac Workshop for Performing Arts, 1972-73. Sam Shubert Playwrighting fellow, 1970-71. Registered profl. engr., D.C. Mem. Am. Theatre Assn., Dramatists Guild, Epsilon Tau Lambda. Patentee in field. Home: 5610 NW 49th Terrace Fort Lauderdale FL 33313

PERMENTER, ROY ARCH, supt. schs.; b. Joaquin, Tex., Jan. 15, 1913; s. James Archie and Mary (Childress) P.; B.S., Stephen F. Austin U., 1933; M.Ed., U. Houston, 1947; postgrad. U. Tex., U. Houston, 1960-65; m. Marianella Matlock, Aug. 18, 1935; 1 son, James Roy (dec.). Prin. high sch., Garrison, Tex., 1933-37; coach high sch., Chester, Tex., 1937-39; prin., coach high sch., Anahuac, 1939-42; prin. elementary sch., Beaumont, Tex., 1945-49; asst. supt. schs. South Park Schs., Beaumont, 1949-63; supt. schs. South Park Ind. Sch. Dist., Beaumont, 1963—, bus. mgr., 1951-60. Cons. ednl. adminstrn. Mem. N.E.A., Tex. Tchrs. Assn., Am., Tex. assns. sch. adminstrs., Jefferson County Adminstrs. Assn. Mason, Lion (pres. 1951-54). Home: 476 Longmeadow Beaumont TX 77707 Office: 1025 Woodrow St Beaumont TX 77706

PERREN, JOHN THOMAS, lawyer; b. nr. Villa Rica, Ga., Apr 22, 1932; s. Grady Bannister and Lilla (Newman) P.; LL.B., Atlanta Law Sch., 1951; m. Mildred Louise Byram, July 7, 1951; children—Lajuana Denise, Gale Renee, Marion John Thomas, Melanie Dee. Bookkeeper, Continental Ins. Co., Atlanta, 1948-52; claims adjuster Fidelity & Casualty Co. N.Y., Columbia, S.C., 1952-55; admitted to Ga. bar, 1951; gen. practice law, Dallas, 1955—; asst. solicitor gen. Tallapoosa Jud. Circuit, 1959-67, dist. atty., 1967—. Mem. Paulding County Bd. Edn. 1956-60. Named Young Man of the Year Paulding County, 1964. Mem. Am. Bar Assn., State Bar Ga. Baptist. Democrat. Mason (Shriner, K.T.). Home: 310 S Hardee St Dallas GA 30132 Office: Courthouse Dallas GA 30132

PERRIN, DONALD EMILIEN, social worker; b. New Orleans, July 14, 1932; s. Donald Stephen and Rose-Aimee (Fittere) P.; B.A., Tulane U., 1959, M.S.W., 1962; m. Nancy Ruth Hunley, Aug. 11, 1962; 1 dau., Vivienne Michelle. Family counselor Family & Childrens Services, Beaumont, Tex., 1962-64; exec. dir. Family Service Agy. Washington County, Md. Inc., Hagerstown, 1964-71; exec. dir. Florence Crittenton Services, Charlotte, N.C., 1971-72; exec. dir. Family Counselling Service of East Baton Rouge Parish, Baton Rouge, 1972—. Pres. Washington County Mental Health Assn., 1966; dir. Washington County Community Action Council, 1967-71; mem. health adv. bd. Mental Health Adv. Com., 1967-71. Served with USAF, 1953-57. Mem. Nat. Assn. Social Workers. Kiwanian. Address: 1155 Aurora Pl Baton Rouge LA 70806

PERRIN, EDWARD PATTERSON, lawyer; b. Spartanburg, S.C., Sept. 19, 1925; s. Lewis Wardlaw and Elizabeth (Patterson) P.; B.S., U. Va., 1948; J.D., U. S.C., 1950; m. Anne Porcher Zeigler, Apr. 7, 1951; children—Anne T., Sallie E., Edward Patterson. Admitted to S.C. bar, 1950; partner Perrin, Perrin & Mann, Spartanburg, 1951—; a founder, dir. Spartanburg Bank & Trust Co., 1963—, chmn. bd., 1970-72; dir. First State Savs. & Loan Assn., Moreland Chem. Co., Inc., Fiske-Carter Constrn. Co. (all Spartanburg). Gen. chmn. United Fund Campaign Spartanburg County, 1964, pres., 1967; pres. Spartanburg County Tb Assn., 1962; vice chmn. Mountainview Nursing Home, 1963-64. City atty. City of Spartanburg, 1959-60; trustee, vice chmn. bd. Spartanburg Sch. Dist. 7, 1966—. Served with USAAF, 1944-45. Named Young Man of Year, Spartanburg Jr. C. of C., 1958; recipient Distinguished Eagle award Boy Scouts Am., 1971. Presbyn. (elder 1966—, commr. to gen. assembly 1971, moderator Enoree Presbytery 1972). Rotarian (local pres. 1972-73). Club: Spectator. Home: 1111 Woodburn Rd Spartanburg SC 29301 Office: PO Box 1655 Spartanburg SC 29301

PERRITT, R. T., clergyman; b. Winnsboro, Tex., May 20, 1926; s. James Hogg and Clara (White) P.; A.A., Jacksonville (Tex.) Coll., 1948; B.D., Bible Bapt. Sem., Arlington, Tex., 1958; Th.M., Okla. Missionary Bapt. Inst. and Sem., 1960, Th.D., 1961; m. Betty Ruth Powell, Nov. 23, 1944; children—Robert Lynn, John Mark, Ruth Ann, James Lance. Ordained to ministry Bapt. Ch., 1945; pastor Calvary Missionary Bapt. Ch., Sherman, Tex., 1949-51, Liberty Missionary Bapt. Ch., Ft. Worth, 1951-56, Cavanaugh Missionary Bapt. Ch., Fort Smith, Ark., 1956-59, 5th St. Missionary Bapt. Ch., Marlow, Okla., 1959—; dean Okla. Missionary Bapt. Inst. and Sem., 1961-63, pres., 1963—; asst. moderator Bapt. Gen. Assembly Okla., 1970-72, moderator, 1973—. With Farm Security Adminstrn., Dallas, 1945-46. Pres., Cavanaugh Baseball Club, 1957-59. Served with U.S. Maritime Service and Mcht. Marine, 1944-45. Named Community Leader Am., 1969. Mem. Am. Bapt. Assn. (v.p., chmn. missionary com. 1966—). Democrat. Lion. Author: The Natural and the Spiritual, 1960; Kindling Fires for Church Growth, 1965; Mastery in Sorrow, 1969; also numerous religious tng. course quars. Home: 610 W Kiowa St Marlow OK 73055 Office: 415 W Cherokee St Marlow OK 73055 also 9th and Caddo Sts Marlow OK 73055

PERROT, JOHN DAVID, elec. products co. exec.; b. Saginaw, Mich., Dec. 1, 1934 ; s. David Lewis and Mary (Resseguie) P.; B.S., U. Miami (Fla.), 1960; M.S., Fla. Inst. Tech., 1969; m. Ethel M. Hasse, July 20, 1957; children—Mary Jane, Kimberly Sue, Deborah Lynn. Designer elec. and hydraulic system Jackson & Church Co., AuGres, Mich., 1952-59, v.p., 1968—; design engr., mem. Minuteman launch team Boeing Co., Cape Kennedy, Fla., 1960-63; launch complex operations mgr. Gen. Electric Co., Kennedy Space Center, Fla., 1963-68; pres. Jackson & Church Electronics Co., Melbourne, Fla., 1968—; v.p. Harbor City Office Supply, 1963—, Platinum Coast Industries, Inc., 1965—. Councilman, Satellite Beach, Fla., 1972-73; chmn. Satellite Beach Bd. Adjustment, 1972—. Registered profl. engr., Fla., Mich. Mem. Fla. Engring. Soc. (sr. mem.), Nat. Soc. Profl. Engrs., Instrumentation Soc. Am. Mason (Shriner), Elk. Club: Eau Gallie (Fla.) Yacht. Contbr. articles to profl. pubs. Home: 650 Cinnamon Dr Satellite Beach FL 32937 Office: 436 S Neiman Av Melbourne FL 32901

PERRY, ANTHONY JOHN, cons. engr.; b. Boston, Sept. 7, 1905; s. Anthony A. and Ellen M. (Connors) P.; A.B., Boston Coll., 1926; S.B., Mass. Inst. Tech., 1929. Civil and elec. engr. Bur. Reclamation, Dept. of Interior, specializing in design and constrn. hydro-electric power and high tension transmission, 1930-65. Cons. engr. electric generation and transmission; spl. assignment Point 4 program, Iran, Lebanon and Italy, 1952, ICA, Cambodia, 1958; cons. govts., Brazil, 1964, Republic Korea, 1966, Bolivia, 1967-68, Argentina, 1972-73, U.S. State Dept., UN, AEC. Registered profl. engr., Colo., D.C. Fellow Am. Soc. C.E. (life); mem. Nat. Soc. Profl. Engrs., Am. Def. Preparedness Assn. Democrat. Roman Catholic. K.C. Address: 4000 Massachusetts Av NW Washington DC 20016

PERRY, CHARLES EDWARD, univ. pres.; b. Holden, W. Va., July 25, 1937; s. Lester and Ethel (White) P.; student Marshall U., 1956; B.A., Bowling Green State U., 1958, B.S., 1959, M.A., 1964, L.H.D., 1970; postgrad. U. Mich., 1964-67; LL.B., Bethune-Cookman Coll., 1969; m. Betty Eleanor Laird, Sept. 17, 1960; children—Thomas Edward, Lynnette Eleanor. Tchr., coach East Detroit (Mich.) pub. schs., 1959; admissions counselor Bowling Green State U., 1959-61, dir. admissions, 1961-64, dir. devel., asst. to pres., 1964-67; spl. asst. to gov. for ednl. affairs, Tallahassee, 1967-68; vice chancellor State U. System Fla., Tallahassee, 1968-69; pres. Fla. Internat. U., Miami, 1969—. Chmn., Gov.'s Ednl. Adv. Council, 1967—, Council for Jr. Coll. Affairs, 1968-69; mem. Select Council on Post High Sch. Edn., So. Regional Edn. Bd., Southeastern Ednl. Lab., Fla. Edn. Council; mem. Fla. Commn. on Latin Am. Affairs, 1969—, Nat. Com. on Utilization of Ednl. TV, 1968—, Nat. Com. for Support of Pub. Schs., Council of 100 Edn. Com., 1968—; mem. U.S. Commn. to UNESCO, 1970—; mem. UN World Edn. Commn. Mem. Fla. Am. Revolution Bicentennial Commn. Served with AUS, 1960, 61-62. Recipient Outstanding Young Man award U.S. Jr. C. of C., 1965, 66, Spl. Appreciation award for Outstanding Contbns. to State of Fla., 1968; named one of America's 10 Outstanding Young Men, 1971; named Outstanding Young Man of Bowling Green, 1966. Mem. Am. Assn. for Higher Edn., Am. Assn. State Colls. and Univs. (com. on internat. programs), Young Presidents Orgn., Internat. Assn. U. Presidents, Assn. Urban Univs., Assn. Upper Level Colls. and Univs., Ohio Soc. N.Y., Fla., Greater Miami chambers commerce, Pi Sigma Alpha, Alpha Kappa Delta, Phi Delta Kappa, Sigma Nu. Methodist. Kiwanian. Author: (with Cliff Boutelle) The Inauguration of a College President, 1964; (with others) Profile of an Administrator, 1965. Contbg. editor The State University-Creator or Conformist, 1965; exec. editor Education in Florida: Perspective for Tomorrow, 1967. Contbr. articles to profl. jours. Home: 1142 S Greenway Dr Coral Gables FL 33134 Office: Fla Internat Univ Tamiami Trail Miami FL 33144

PERRY, CHARLES LEWIS, educator; b. Culver, Ind., Dec. 9, 1933; s. Leujay Joseph and Bertha Elizabeth (Lebold) P.; B.A., Ind. U., 1955; Ph.D., U. Cal. at Berkeley, 1965; m. Carolyn Sue Calhoun, Oct. 24, 1964; 1 son, Bradford J. Research asso. Kitt Peak Nat. Obs., Tucson, 1963-65, Mt. Stromlo Obs., Canberra, Australia, 1965-66; asst. prof. dept. physics La. State U., Baton Rouge, 1966-71, asso. prof., 1971—. Lick Obs. fellow in astronomy, 1959-61; NSF research grantee, 1967-72. Mem. Am. Astron. Soc., Royal Astron. Soc. Eng., Astron. Soc. Pacific, Internat. Astron. Union. Home: 442 Raintree Rd Baton Rouge LA 70810

PERRY, CHARLES RANDOLPH, elec. engr.; b. Paris, Tenn., May 6, 1943; s. William Baxter and Mary Ruth (Hurt) P.; student Murray State U., 1961-62; B.S., U. Tenn., 1967; m. Jane Lou Brown, Aug. 28, 1967; children—Elizabeth, Jennifer. Chief engr. elec. dept. Paris (Tenn.) Bd. Pub. Utilities, 1967—. Tchr. electronics Grove High Sch., Paris, 1967-68. Registered profl. engr., Tenn. Mem. I.E.E.E. Home: 203 Jean St Paris TN 38242 Office: Box 460 Paris TN 38242

PERRY, GEORGE WILLIAM, lawyer; b. St. Louis, May 28, 1924; s. Clarence A. and Helen (Smith) P.; student Westminster Coll., Fulton, Mo., 1942-43; A.B., Washington U. St. Louis, 1949, J.D., 1950; m. Bertha Drake Scott, Nov. 22, 1950; children—George William Jr., Anne Scott. Admitted to Mo. bar, 1950, Tex. bar, 1964; mem. firm Alexander & Robertson, St. Louis, 1954-59; asst. to pres. Res. Life Ins. Co., Dallas, 1959-68; mem. firm Hartt & Perry, Inc., Dallas, 1968—, sec.-treas., 1970—. Pres. Tex. Safety Assn., 1969-71; mem. Gov.'s Traffic Safety Com., Gov.'s Study Com. Reorganization Tex. Traffic Cts., 1971-72. Served with USNR, 1943-46, Mem. Am., Tex., Dallas, St. Louis bar assns., Charter Property and Casualty Underwriters (pres. S.W. chpt. 1970), Data Processing Mgmt. Assn., Beta Theta Pi, Phi Delta Pi. Club: Nooday (St. Louis). Home: 4128 McFarlin St Dallas TX 75205 Office: Fidelity Union Life Bldg Dallas TX 75201

PERRY, J(AMES) LEE, lawyer; b. Atlanta, Aug. 3, 1935; s. Eddie Willis and Dorothy (Burk) P.; B.S., Ga. Inst. Tech., 1957; LL.B., Emory U., 1962; m. Carol Ann Brendel, July 28, 1962; children—Kevin Andrew (dec.), Steven Brian, Bruce Burke, Colin Brendan, William Conor. Draftsman, Ga. Power Co., Atlanta, 1958-59; admitted to Ga. bar, 1961; law asst. to justice Supreme Ct. Ga., Atlanta, 1962-64; practiced in Atlanta, 1964-67; mem. firms Latimer & Allen, Latimer, Haddon & Stanfield, 1964-67; asso. atty. Bd. Edn. Atlanta, 1964-67; asst. atty. gen. State of Ga., Atlanta, 1968-74; atty. constrn. div. Ga. State Financing and Investment Commn., 1974—. Instr., Atlanta Pub. Schs., 1967. Served with AUS, 1957. Mem. Am., Ga. bar assns., Theta Chi, Phi Delta Phi. Methodist. Club: River Bend Gun. Home: 245 Glencourtney Dr Atlanta GA 30328 Office: 207 Trinity-Washington Bldg Atlanta GA 30334

PERRY, JOHN, educator; b. Kingston, N.Y., Nov. 12, 1937; s. Al John and Effie (Walton) P.; B.S., Syracuse U., 1960, M.A., 1964; Ph.D., So. Ill. U., 1971; postgrad. U. Rochester (N.Y.), Oxford (Eng.) U., summer 1964, Breadloaf Sch. English Middlebury Coll., summer 1965. Tchr. Paul V. Moore Central Sch., Central Square, N.Y., 1960-61, Olympia High Sch., Greece, N.Y., 1961-62, Newark (N.Y.) High Sch., 1963-66; spl. doctoral asst. So. Ill. U., Carbondale, 1967-68; asst. prof. English and drama Coll. Ida., Caldwell, 1969-70; head dept. speech and drama, chmn. div. fine arts Blue Mountain (Miss.) Coll., 1972-74; vis. lectr. drama Hiram Scott Coll., Scottsbluff, Neb., summers 1969-70; mem. Phila. Writers Conf., 1973-74. Am. Heritage grantee, 1967-68; Nat. Def. Edn. Act grantee, 1965; Lissfelt Meml. scholar, 1972. Contbr. articles to profl. jours, mags. Office: Box 126 Blue Mountain Coll Blue Mountain MS 38610

PERRY, JOHN KARL, constrn. engr., govt. ofcl.; b. Bridgeport, W. Va., Feb. 9, 1923; s. Hollis Cole and Esther Marie (Cornwell) P.; B.S., John Brown U., 1948; M.S., Okla. A.& M. U., 1952; m. Ruth Evelyn Newell, Nov. 26, 1949; children—John Carl, Jean Kaye. Bridge engr. Ore. Hwy. Dept., Eugene, 1952-55; chief and bridge engr. U.S. Govt., Juneau, Fairbanks and Ft. Greely, Alaska, Auburn, Wash., Corvallis, Ore., Cin., Durham, N.C., 1955—, also constrn. engr. and facilities officer. Served with AUS, 1943-46. Registered profl. engr., Ore., Ohio, N.C. Mem. Profl. Engrs. N.C., Nat. Soc. Prof. Engrs., Soc. Am. Mil. Engrs., Am. Soc. M.E., Am. Soc. C.E. Home: 5112 Sourwood Rd Durham NC 27704

PERRY, JOHN STEPHEN, air force officer; b. Lynbrook, N.Y., Oct. 18, 1931; s. Stephen Augustine and Phyllis Mary (Brown) P.; B.S. magna cum laude in Math., Queens Coll., 1953; B.S. in Meteorology, U. Wash., 1954, M.S., 1960, Ph.D., 1966; grad. Air Command and Staff Coll., 1964, Air War Coll., 1971; m. Olive Barbara Jones, Sept. 15, 1953; children—Stephen Kenneth, Robert John. Commd. lt. USAF, 1953, advanced through grades to col., 1973; weather officer, Korea, 1954-55; briefing officer, Barksdale, La., 1955-58; systems analyst, Offutt AFB, Neb., 1960-63; staff officer Air Weather Service, Scott AFB, ILL., 1966-70; program mgr. Advanced Research Projects Agy., Arlington, Va., 1971—. Chmn. interdepartmental subcom. on computers in atmospheric scis., 1973. Decorated Air Force Commendation medal. Mem. Am. Meteorol. Soc., Am. Assn. Watch and Clock Collectors, Phi Beta Kappa, Sigma Xi. Contbr. to publs. in field. Home: 6205 Tally Ho Lane Alexandria VA 22307 Office: ARPA/IPT 1400 Wilson Blvd Arlington VA 22209

PERRY, REEVES BALDWIN, educator; b. Greenville, Tex., Feb. 12, 1935; s. Walter and Ella Ferguson (Lynch) P.; B.S., East Tex. State U., 1954; M.S., North Tex. State U., 1956; Ph.D., U. Tex., 1966; m. Marilyn Grace Kothmann, June 27, 1964; children—Bruce Reeves, Brenda Ella. Research chemist Texaco, Inc., Bellaire, Tex., 1956-59, 65-66; asst. prof. chemistry S.W. Tex. State U., San Marcos, 1966-69, asso. prof., 1969—. Mem. Am. chem. Soc., Tex. Acad. Sci., Tex. Assn. Coll. Tchrs., Sigma Xi, Alpha Chi Sigma. Author: (with Robert G. Lowman and Billy J. Yager) Introductory Experimental Chemistry, 1973. Home: 104 Panorama St San Marcos TX 78666

PERRY, ROBERT E., lawyer; b. Rienzi, Miss., June 16, 1916; B.Sc., U. Miss., 1937, J.D., 1939. Admitted to Miss. bar, 1939; mem. firm Perry, Phillips, Crockett & Morrison, Jackson, Miss. Chmn., Miss. Law Inst., 1951. Served to lt. USNR, 1943-46. Fellow Miss. Bar Found.; mem. Am., Hinds County, Jackson Jr. (pres. 1952-53) bar assns., Miss. State Bar, Miss. Oil and Gas Lawyers Assn., Am. Judicature Soc., Estate Planning Council, Phi Delta Phi. Address: Deposit Guaranty Nat Bank Bldg Jackson MS 39205

PERRY, ROBERT NATHAN, salesman, horse breeder; b. Suffolk, Va., Aug. 5, 1933; s. J. Starkie and Virginia S. (Samuels) P.; grad. high sch.; m. Faye Carter, May 25, 1958; 1 dau., Deborah Faye. Owner, operator Perry Texaco Sta., Suffolk, 1954-60; foreman F. Perry Lumber Co., Suffolk, 1960-71; salesman, collector BelAire Chevrolet Corp., 1971—; breeder standard breed horses, Suffolk. Mem. U.S. Trotting Assn., U.S. Horsebreeding Assn. Mem. Christian Ch. (mem. bd. deacons 1970-74, v.p. Eastern Va. laymens fellowship 1974-75), Moose. Clubs: Travelers Protective, Liberty Spring Ruritan (pres. 1972) (Suffolk). Home: Rural Route 1 Box 315 Suffolk VA 23434 Office: 1038 W Washington St Suffolk VA 23434

PERRY, ROTRAUD MEZGER (MRS. JOHN WILSON PERRY), lawyer; b. Berlin, Germany, Aug. 29, 1927; d. Fritz and Luise (Scheuerle) Mezger; A.B., Bryn Mawr Coll., 1948; L.B., U. Mich., 1952; m. John Wilson Perry, Sept. 9, 1950; children—Erik David, Julia Louise, Kathleen Anne, Duncan Gerrit, Ellen Eva. Accessioner, Library of Congress, 1947, translator German Aero. Collection, 1948, asst. librarian, 1949, acting head Am.-Brit. Exchange, 1949, European Exchange Specialist, 1950; admitted to D.C. bar, 1954, Md. bar, 1974; admiralty lawyer for Mil. Sea Transp. Service of Navy Dept., 1955-56; gen. practice Washington, 1957—. Mem. Criminal Justice Act Com. Mem. Am. Soc. Internat. Law, Bar Assn. D.C., Am. Judicature Soc., Assn. Plaintiff's Trial Attys., Fgn. Law Soc., Women's Bar Assn. D.C. Lutheran. Clubs: Bryn Mawr of Washington, Air Force Officers' Wives. Home: 5407 Ridgefield Rd Springfield MD 20016 Office: 5272 River Rd Washington DC 20016

PERRY, RUSSELL H., ins. exec.; b. Cornell, Ill., Nov. 8, 1908; s. Walter O. and Mabel (Hilton) P.; student N.Y. U., 1937; J.D. cum laude, Bklyn. Law Sch., 1940; m. Phoebe Sherwood, June 2, 1956. Clk., Chgo. Fire & Marine Ins. Co., 1925-32; underwriter Republic Ins. Co., N.Y.C., 1934-38, charge eastern dept. underwriting, 1939-42, asst. to v.p., 1942-43, spl. agt. for L.I. and Westchester, 1934-44, mgr. eastern dept., 1945-47, resident sec., 1947-49, v.p., 1949-59, exec. v.p., 1959-60; pres., dir. Republic-Vanguard, Blue Ridge Ins. Cos., 1961-72, chmn. bd., chief exec. officer, 1972—; pres., dir. First Trans-Carribbean Corp., Republic-Vanguard Ins. Co. Ill.; chmn. Republic-Vanguard Life Ins. Co., Vanguard Underwriters Ins. Co., Republic Underwriters; pres., dir. Republic Financial Services, Inc., 1961-71, chmn. bd., pres., 1971-72, chmn. bd., chief exec. officer, 1972—; trustee Murray Mortgage Investors; dir. Allied Finance Co., Indsl. Life Ins. Co. Dir. Ins. Information Inst., N.Y.C. Bd. dirs. Greater Crime Commn.; bd. dirs., chmn. Dallas Council on World Affairs; chmn. exec. com. Dallas Postal Customers Council; Co-chmn. big gifts div. United Way Dallas County; dir. Greater Dallas Planning Council; mem. Dallas Citizens Council, Citizens Coordinating Com. Dallas County; mem. council Boy Scouts Am.; mem. Dallas Bapt. Council Devel. Bd.; adv. bd. Salvation Army, Dallas. Chmn. Dallas Community Chest; bd. dirs., vice chmn. Dallas County unit Am. Cancer Soc., Texas Research League, Tex. Safety Assn.; trustee Dallas Alliance Minority Enterprise, Tex. Bur. Econ. Understanding, Inc.; bd. dirs. KERA-TV, Dallas. Mem. C. of C. N.Y., Philonomic Soc., Am., N.Y., Dallas bar assns., State Bar Tex., Tex. Good Roads Assn. (chmn.), Newcomen Soc. N.Am., U.S. (pub. affairs subcom.), Dallas (chmn. central hwy. com.), N.Y., East Tex. (pres.) chambers commerce, Delta Theta Phi. Clubs: Lawyers of N.Y.; New York University; Insurance, Knife and Fork, Dallas Petroleum, Dallas Country, Rotary, Lancers (Dallas); Austin. Home: 4505 N Versailles Av Dallas TX 75205 Office: 2727 Turtle Creek Blvd Dallas TX 75219

PERSON, HARRY WILLIAM, mfg. co. exec.; b. Gallatin, Tenn., Apr. 21, 1925; s. Harry William and Prudie Winchester (Hitchcock) P.; student George Peabody Coll., 1948-50; B.S., U. Tenn., 1952. Chief time clk. Yale & Towne Mfg. Co., Gallatin, 1952-55; accountant Tenn. Prodn. & Chem. Corp., Nashville, 1955-58; comptroller Gallatin Aluminum Prods. Co., Inc., 1958—. Chmn. Sumner County Arts Council, 1967—; pres. Gallatin Community Theatre, 1965—. Served with USNR, World War II. Mem. Am. Legion, U. Tenn. Alumni Assn. (pres. 1965-66), Jr. C. of C. (sec. 1954-55), Delta Sigma Pi, Sigma Chi. Presbyn. (deacon). Kiwanian. Home: 519 S Water St Gallatin TN 37066 Office: Maple St Gallatin TN 37066

PERSONS, BENJAMIN STEPHEN, cons. engr.; b. Macon, Ga., Mar. 3, 1923; s. Ben. S. and Mary (Scandrett) P.; B.C.E., Ga. Tech. Inst., 1949; grad. advanced course Engr. Sch., Ft. Belvoir, Va., 1950; m. Frances Neisler, Dec. 29, 1946; children—Donna Maria, Benjamin Stephen, Robert Scandrett. Civil engr. with Charles Lee, San Francisco, 1950; engr., personnel mgr., asst. to exec. partner Dames & Moore, cons. engrs., San Francisco, Los Angeles, Chgo., 1950-54, partner, Atlanta, 1954—, mem. exec. com., 1961-62; dir. Coleman, Meadows, Pate Drug Co., Fairburn Rd., Inc. Engring. cons. Army Corps Engrs.; mem. Ga. gov.'s staff. Served from 2d lt. to capt., Engring. Corps., AUS, World War II; sr. san. engr. USPHS Res. Decorated Silver Star, Bronze Star. Fellow Am. Soc. C.E. (dir. Ga. sect.); mem. Geol. Soc. Am., Cons. Engrs. Council (dir. 1958), Cons. Engrs. Assn. Ga. (pres. 1959), Am. Soc. C.E. (dir. Ga. sect.). Presbyn. (ruling elder 1952—). Author: Laterite, Genesis, Location, Use, 1970. Contbr. articles on civil engring. and related topics to profl. jours. Home: 1110 Mt Vernon Hwy NW Atlanta GA 30327 Office: 455 E Paces Ferry Dr NE Atlanta GA 30305

PERSONS, JO ROBERT, univ. adminstr.; b. Montgomery, Ala., Apr. 24, 1917; s. Jo Robert and Georgia Freeman (Garrett) P.; student U. Cal. at Los Angeles, 1937-38; B.B.A., Tulane U., 1939; m. Ellen Constance Martin, July 31, 1944; children—Jo Robert III, Ellen (Mrs. Lee Bourland), Charles Martin. With Haskins & Sells, New Orleans, 1939-41; tax supr. Peat, Marwick, Mitchell Co., New Orleans, 1951; comptroller, asst. to div. mgr. Champion Papers, Houston, 1951-58; v.p. Champion Cellouse S.A., San Paulo, Brazil, 1958-62; spl. asst. Champion Papers/Montag Div., Atlanta, 1962-67; dir. corporate planning Southland Papers, Lufkin, Tex., 1967-68; comptroller Rice U., Houston, 1968—. Served with AUS, 1941; with USNR, 1941-46, to lt. comdr., 1951-52. C.P.A., Tex., La. Mem. Am. Inst. C.P.A.'s, Tex., La. socs. C.P.A.'s, Nat. Assn. Coll. and Univ. Bus. Officers, So. Univ. Bus. Officers, Phi Delta Theta. Rotarian (pres. Student's Ednl. Fund Inc. 1973-74, chmn. Houston endowment com. 1973-74). Home; 6 W 11th Pl Houston TX 77005

PERUSSINA, MARY ANN, librarian; b. Galveston, Tex., May 2, 1927; d. George John and Julia Marie (Curran) Perussina; B.S. in Secondary Edn., U. Tex., 1949; M.L.S., Tex. Woman's U., 1966. Tchr., Galveston Ind. Sch. Dist., 1949-53, Dept. Army, Orleans, France, 1953-54; tchr. Temple (Tex.) Ind. Sch. Dist., 1954-57, librarian, 1957-67; dir. library services Galveston Coll., 1967—. Mem. Am. Assn. U. Women, Tex. Library Assn. (pres. jr. coll. library sect. 1972-73) Tex. Jr. Coll. Tchrs. Assn. (pres. library sect. 1972-73), Galveston Hist. Found., Galveston Art League. Home: Fort Crockett Apts Galveston TX 77550 Office: 4015 Av Q Galveston TX 77550

PESEK, LEON FRANCIS, lawyer; b. Yoakum, Tex., Sept. 17, 1928; s. Emil Phillip and Annie (Benys) P.; LL.B., St. Marys U., 1951; m. Shirley Hutchins, June 26, 1954; children—Leon Francis, Phillip A., Catherine, Michael J. Admitted to Tex. bar, 1951; practiced in Texarkana, 1952—; county atty. Lavaca County, 1954-58; asst. atty. gen. Tex., 1958-62; partner Raffaelli, Keeney & Pesek, 1962-67; city atty., Texarkana, 1967-71, Hitt & Pesek, 1971—; gen. counsel Cath. Women Fraternal of Tex. Served to 1st lt., Judge Adv. Gen. Corps. AUS, 1952-54. Mem. State Bar of Texas. Rotarian. Home: 1311 Canadian St Texarkana TX 75501 Office: 2605 Texas Blvd Texarkana TX 75501

PESTANA, CARLOS, physician, med. educator; b. Tacoronte, Tenerife, Canary Islands, Spain, June 10, 1936; s. Francisco and Blanca (Suarez) P.; B.S., Nat. U. Mex., 1952, M.D., 1959; Ph.D. in Surgery, U. Minn., 1965; m. Myrna Lorena Serrato, Aug. 25, 1966; children—Becky Elizabeth, George Byron. Came to U.S., 1968, naturalized, 1973. Intern, St. Mary of Nazareth Hosp., Chgo., 1959-60; resident Mayo Clinic, Rochester, Minn., 1961-65; surgeon Hosp. 20 de Noviembre Mexico City, also asst. prof. surgery Nat. U. Mexico, 1966-67; asst. prof. surgery U. Tex. Med. Sch. at San Antonio, 1968-70, asso. prof., 1970—, asso. dean for acad. devel., 1971-73, asso. dean for student affairs, 1973—; chief gen. surgery service Audie Murphy VA Hosp., San Antonio, 1973—. Recipient Edward John Noble Found. award, 1965, Piper Prof. award Minnie Stevens Piper Founds., 1972. Mem. Assn. Acad. Surgery, A.M.A., A.C.S., N.Y. Acad. Scis., Tex., Bexar County med. socs., Western, San Antonio surg. socs., Soc. for Surgery Alimentary Trace, Assn. Am. Med. Colls., Priestley Soc., Sigma Xi. Home: 10123 N Manton San Antonio TX 78213 Office: 7703 Floyd Curl Dr San Antonio TX 78229

PETER, EMMETT BLACKSHEAR, JR., writer, editor; b. Leesburg, Fla., Nov. 19, 1919; s. Emmett Blackshear and Mary Ellen (Brown) P.; student Emory U., 1938-39, Stetson U., 1940-41; m. Marjorie Brown, June 10, 1944; children—Marcia (Mrs. B. Murray Tucker, Jr.), Melanie (Mrs. Lee A. Poole), Emmett III. Editor, pub. Eustis (Fla.) Lake Region, 1941-42; editor Leesburg Comml., 1946-47; reporter Tampa (Fla.) Tribune, 1947-50, Sunday editor, 1950-54; editor Daily Comml., Leesburg, 1955-60, editorial page dir., 1961-63; asso. editor Lakeland (Fla.) Ledger, 1964-68; chief editorial writer, editorial page editor Orlando Sentinel Star, 1969—. Owner, Peter Citrus Groves, Leesburg; founder, dir. Channel 24 pub. tv, Orlando, 1969—. Asso. editor Quill, Chgo., 1960-65. Mem. Fla. Bd. Forestry, 1959-66, v.p., 1963-65; mem. nat. adv. com. to sec. agr., 1965-69. Served with USAAF, 1942-45. Recipient Nat. Headliner and Sigma Delta Chi awards for pub. service, 1960; Brotherhood citation Nat. Conf. Christians and Jews, 1964. Mem. Fla. Soc. Editors (charter, pres. 1963-64), Sigma Delta Chi (pres. Central Fla. profl. chpt. 1960-61), Phi Delta Theta. Democrat. Methodist. Contbr. to The New Republic. Home: 320 Lakeview Apt 106 Orlando FL 32802 Office: PO Box 2833 Orlando FL 32802

PETER, JOHN EDWARD, architect; b. Oklahoma City, Dec. 23, 1934; s. Maurice Lyle and Claribel (Oldfield) P.; B.Arch., Okla. State U., 1958; m. Judith Louise Rice, Jan. 26, 1957; children—David Mark, Kevin Andrew, Anita Deborah. Chief draftsman Bignell-Fischer, Oklahoma City, 1961-62, ind. practice John E. Peter & Assos., Oklahoma City, 1962-67, Woodward, Okla., 1968—. Mem. diocese com. on architecture Episcopal Diocese Okla., 1964—, com.

on clergy replacement; mem. bd. advisers Goodwill Industries Okla., 1964-68, Mayor's Com. for Hire Handicapped Oklahoma City, 1964-68; dist. commr. Boiling Springs dist. Boy Scouts Am., 1970, v.p. Gt. Salt Plains council; pres. Woodward Elks Rodeo, 1970-72. chmn. precinct, 1971-73. Pres. bd. Okla. N.W. Guidance Center, Okla. N.W., Inc. Registered profl. architect, Okla., Kan., Tex. Mem. Constrn. Specifications Inst., A.I.A., Mooreland C. of C., Laymen Inc., Woodward Cattlemen's Assn., Woodward C. of C. Episcopalian (lay reader, treas. 1969-72). Lion, Elk. Clubs: Woodward Dance, Young Men's Skyhawk Flying. Home: 911 35th St Woodward OK 73801 Office: 1009 1/2 Main St Woodward OK 73801

PETER, LILY, plantation operator, writer; b. Marvell, Ark.; d. William Oliver and Florence (Mobrey) Peter; B.S., Memphis State U., 1927; M.A., Vanderbilt U., 1938; postgrad. U. Chgo., 1930, Columbia, 1935-36; L.H.D., Moravian Coll., Bethlehem, Pa., 1965. Owner, operator plantations, Marvell and Ratio, Ark., writer poetry, feature articles pub. in S.W. Quar., Delta Rev., Cyclo Flame, Etude, Am. Weave, others; mem. staff S.W. Writers Conf., Corpus Christi, Tex., 1954—, sponsor Ark. Writers' Conf. Chmn., Poetry Day in Ark., 1953—; chmn., sponsor music Ark. Territorial Sesquicentennial, 1969. Bd. dirs. Ark. Arts Festival, Little Rock, Grand Prairie Festival Arts, Ark. Festival of Arts, 1971; chmn. bd. Phillips County Community Center, 1969-71. Hon. trustee Moravian Music Found. Recipient Moramus award Friends of Moravian Music, 1964; Distinguished Alumni award Vanderbilt U., 1964; named Poet Laureate Ark., 1971; Democrat Woman of Year, 1971. Mem. D.A.R., (hon. state regent), Nat. League Am. Pen Women, Ark. Authors and Composers Soc., Poets' Roundtable Ark., poetry socs. of Tenn., Tex., Ga., Met. Opera Assn. (mem. nat. council), Cotton Ginners Assn. (dir. 1971-74), Sigma Alpha Iota. (hon.). Democrat. Methodist. Clubs: Pacaha (Helena, Ark.); Woman's City (Little Rock). Author: The Green Linen of Summer, 1964; The Great Riding, 1966; The Sea Dream of the Mississippi, 1973. Home: Route 2 Box 69 Marvell AR 72366

PETERS, HENRY JOHN, JR., baseball exec.; b. St. Louis, Sept. 16, 1924; s. Henry John and Estelle (Biehl) P.; student Rubicam Bus. Coll., 1946; m. Dorothy Kleimeier, Nov. 21, 1950; children—Steven John, Sharon Joyce. Asst. farm dir. St. Louis Browns Baseball Club, 1949-53; gen. mgr. Burlington (Ia.) Baseball Club, 1954; farm dir. Kansas City Athletics, 1955-60, asst. gen. mgr., farm dir., 1962-65, gen. mgr., 1965-66; farm dir. Cin. Reds, 1961; farm dir. Cleve. Indians, 1966, v.p., dir. player personnel, 1967—; pres. Nat. Assn. Profl. Baseball Leagues, 1971—. Served with AUS, 1943-46. Lutheran. Elk. Home: 6577 Sahara Dr Seminole FL 33542 Office: 225 4th St S St Petersburg FL 33731

PETERS, WILLIAM LEE, educator; b. Leavenworth, Kan., June 27, 1939; s. Raymond L. and Mildred V. (Evans) P.; B.A., U. Kan., 1960; M.A., U. Utah, 1962, Ph.D., 1966; m. Janice Goldthwaite, May 14, 1966; 1 dau., Rae Ellen. Asso. prof. entomology Fla. A. and M. U., Tallahassee, 1967—; adj. asso. prof. Fla. State U., Tallahassee, 1967—; researvh asso. Fla., Dept. Agr., Gainesville, 1968—; coordinator U.S. Dept. Agr. Fla. A. and M. U., Tallahassee, 1970—; prof. entomology U. Fla., Gainesville, 1970—. Prin. investigator grants from Coop. State Research Service, U.S. Dept. Agr., NSF, Nat. Geog. Soc., U.S. Forest Service, Sigma Xi, others. Mem. Entomol. Soc. Am., Soc. Systematic Zoology, other orgns. Editor: (with J.G. Peters) Proc. First Internat. Conf. on Ephemeroptera, 1970. Research and publs. on taxonomy and ecology of Ephemeroptera. Home: 1803 Chuli Nene Tallahassee FL 32301

PETERSEN, DONALD JAMES, state ofcl.; b. N.Y.C., May 10, 1929; s. H. Clark and Anna (Fiorella) P.; student Wofford Coll., 1954-58, A.B. in Psychology, 1970; m. Thalia LaMona Ham, Mar. 27, 1954; children—Timothy S., Tamara A., Donald James III, Thalia LaMona. Med. service rep. A.H. Robins Co., Inc. Columbia, S.C., 1958-71; cons. on health facilities S.C. Bd. Health, Columbia, 1971-72; Southwest rep. Hosp. Bur., 1972—. Mem. steering coms. Stop Polio Campaign, Columbia 1963-64, Anti-Tetanus Program, Columbia, 1964-65; pres. Satchelford Road Sch. P.T.A., 1964; coach and asst. coach Forest Baseball League, Columbia, 1965-69; asst. scoutmaster Congaree council Boy Scouts Am., 1969-70. Served with USN, 1946-51. Recipient Community Service award Stop Polio Campaign, 1963, 64. Mem. Palmetto Sertoma (pres. 1967-68), Sertoma Internat. (dist. gov. 1968-69, Distinguished Gov. award 1968). Methodist (mem. ch. bd.). Club: Gold Honor (pres. 1967). Home: 4661 Norwood Rd Columbia SC 29206

PETERSEN, JAMES JOLLY, entomologist; b. Salt Lake City, Oct. 12, 1938; s. Ervin A. and Lula Mae (Jolly) P.; B.S., U. Utah, 1961, M.S., 1963, Ph.D., 1966; m. Virginia Lee Barnes, Mar. 15, 1942; children—Bryan James, Carrie Ann. Research entomologist Gulf Coast Mosquito Research Lab., Agrl. Research Service, U.S. Dept. Agr., Lake Charles, La., 1966—. Scoutmaster Boy Scouts Am., 1971—. Bd. dirs. Little League Baseball, 1972—, mgr., 1967—. Research fellow U. Utah, 1963-64, NSF, summer 1963, NIH, 1964-66. Mem. Entomology Soc. Am., Am., La. mosquito control assns., La. Entomology Soc., Sigma Xi. Mem. Ch. of Jesus Christ of Latter-day Saints (elder). Contbr. articles to profl. jours. Home: 1008 Cherry Hill St Lake Charles LA 70601 Office: Av J Chennault Lake Charles LA 70601

PETERSON, CARTER CALHOUN, broadcasting co. exec.; b. Ailey, Ga., Sept. 29, 1912; s. Thomas Alexander and Stella Edieth (Carter) P.; B.A., U. Ga., 1934, J.D., LL.B., 1936; m. Ann Elizabeth Hogan, June 3, 1955; 1 dau., Stella Carter. Admitted to Ga. bar, 1936; practiced in Montgomery and Fulton Counties (Ga.), 1936-41; with Ga. SSS, 1941-42; pres., owner radio sta. WCCP, Dixie Broadcasting Co. (now WBYG-Space Broadcasting, Inc.), Savannah, Ga., 1946—; dir. Ailey Mfg. Co., 1958—; v.p., dir. Metter Mfg. Co., 1954-60. Asst. sec. Ga. Senate, 1933-38; mayor of Ailey, 1936-39. Served to lt. USNR, 1942-46. Mem. Ga. Bar Assn., S.R., Am. Legion, St. Andrews Soc., Blue Key, Delta Tau Delta, Sigma Delta Chi. Democrat. Episcopalian. Mason. Club: Gridiron (Washington). Home: 5507 Waters Dr Savannah GA 31406 Office: PO Box 943 Savannah GA 31401

PETERSON, CHARLES BASCOM, JR., banker; b. Dallas, Nov. 27, 1913; s. Charles Bascom and Lida (Skillern) P.; grad. Rutgers U. Grad. Sch. Banking, 1952; student Inst. Mgmt., So. Methodist U., Nat. Indsl. Conf. Bd. Exec. Seminars; m. Helen Fair, Apr. 12, 1936; children—Sue Fair, Ann. With Tex. Bank & Trust Co., 1931-61, pres., 1958-61; exec. v.p. Republic Nat. Bank of Dallas, 1961—, also chmn. trust com.; dir. Frito Co., dir., mem. investment com., mem. exec. com. Employers Casualty Co., Sammon Enterprises, Inc. Instr. grad. courses Am. Inst. Banking. Mem. adv. bd. Salvation Army, also chmn. long range planning com.; v.p. Boys' Club Dallas; Chmn. membership and fund campaign Dallas A.R.C., 1959; active Dallas Community Chest. Trustee Freeman Meml. Clinic, Tex. Research Found.; trustee, pres. bd., mem. exec. com., mem. finance com. Meth. Hosp.; bd. dirs. Children's Med. Center; exec. bd. Circle Ten council Boy Scouts Am. Club: Preston Trail Golf (dir.). Home: 5114 Royal Crest Dr Dallas TX 75229 Office: Republic Nat Bank of Dallas PO Box 5961 Dallas TX 75222

PETERSON, CHARLES CARTER, hwy. engr.; b. Panama City, Fla., Jan. 11, 1938; s. Charles Emory and Vashti (Carter) P.; B.Civil Engring., U. Fla., 1970, M.Civil Engring., 1973; m. Joyce Lanton, Dec. 29, 1959; children—Carlena Io, Teresa Paulette. With Fla. Rd. Dept., 1958-69, project engr., Jacksonville, 1965-69; with Fla. Dept. Transp., 1970—, profl. engr. estimates sect., Tallahassee, 1971-73, state preliminary estimates engr., 1973—. Named chevalier Order DeMolay, 1955. Registered profl. engr., Fla. Mem. Am. Soc. C.E., Inst. Traffic Engrs. Democrat. Baptist. Home: Route 14 Box 362 Tallahassee FL 32304 Office: 605 Suwannee St Tallahassee FL 32304

PETERSON, CLARENCE ANTON, JR., clergyman; b. Denver, Sept. 15, 1943; s. Clarence Anton and Margaret (Reynolds) P.; student Anderson Coll. & Theol. Sem., 1961-64, Warner Pacific Coll., 1964-65, Cal. State Coll. at Long Beach, 1965-66; m. Graciela Echeverria, June 13, 1969. Ordained to ministry, Ch. of God, 1971; minister youth and music South Bay Ch., Torrance, Cal., 1965-67, Glendale (Cal.) Ch. God, 1967-70; asso. pastor First Ch. God, Wichita, Kan., 1970-72; sr. minister South Park Community Ch., Tulsa, 1973—; traveled nationwide in presentation of choral workshops for chs., 1961—. Spokesman Bay Area council on Drug Abuse, State Cal., 1967; coordinator Wichita "Hotline", 1971, El Dorado, Kan., 1972; chmn. Lawndale (Cal.) Christmas Pageant, 1966; pres. Wichita Opportunity and Recreation Center, 1970-72. Mem. Am. Choral Dirs. Assn., West Coast Fellowship of Ch. Youth (pres. 1968), Bay Area (pres. 1959), So. Cal. (pres. 1965) youth assns. Home: 9706 E 33d St Tulsa OK 74145 Office: 10811 E 41st St Tulsa OK 74145

PETERSON, DONALD LEROY, dentist; b. Columbus, Kan., Dec. 6, 1908; s. Fred William and Myrtle Inez (Arnold) P.; D.D.S., Loyola U., New Orleans, 1932; m. Mary Alma Bishop, Aug. 21, 1951; 1 son, Donald Leroy. Practice gen. dentistry, New Orleans, 1932—; mem. vis. staff Charity Hosp. La., New Orleans, 1932—, sr. vis. surgeon, 1945-61, mem. bd. adminstrs., 1956-72, vice chmn., 1956-60, 64—, dental cons., 1961—; dental cons. Eye, Ear, Nose and Throat Hosp., 1947—, So. Bapt. Hosp., 1958—; instr. dept. physiology and chemistry Loyola U., 1933-34; asso. clin. prof. dept. oral surgery Dental Sch., La. State U., 1969—. Chmn. dental div. Greater New Orleans area chpt. A.R.C., 1950-51; mem. Greater New Orleans Cancer Assn., 1960—, pres., 1966-68. Sec. bd. dirs. Health Edn. Authority La., 1968—. Fellow Am. Coll. Dentists; mem. Am., La., New Orleans (dir. 1950-54; v.p. 1950), dental assns., Orleans Parish Med. Soc. (asso.), Kells Odontological Soc., New Orleans, U.S. power squadrons, Blue Key, Grand Isle Tarpon Rodeo (pres. 1956; dir. 1957-72), Psi Omega, Omega Kappa Upsilon. Roman Catholic. Clubs: Pendennis, Southern Yacht, New Orleans Big Game Fishing (New Orleans); Talley-Ho. Home: 1616 Mirabeau Av New Orleans LA 70122 Office: 711 Maison Blanche Bldg New Orleans LA 70112

PETERSON, EDWARD ADRIAN, lawyer; b. St. Louis, May 19, 1941; s. Adrian Juus and Virginia (Hamlin) P.; B.S. in Bus. Adminstrn., Washington U., St. Louis, 1963; LL.B., So. Meth. U., 1966; m. Catherine Younghouse, Dec. 17, 1960; children—Kristen Kathryn, Kendra Lynn. Admitted to Tex. bar, 1966; instr. bus. law and accounting Midwestern U., Wichita Falls, Tex., 1966-67; mem. firm Schenk & Westbrooks, Asso., Wichita Falls, 1966-67, Newman, Moore & Peterson, Dallas, 1967-72, Moore, Peterson & Bach, Dallas, 1972-73, Moore, Peterson, Bauer & Williams, Dallas, 1973—. Mem. State Bar Tex., Am. Bar Assn., Sigma Alpha Epsilon, Phi Alpha Delta. Lutheran (bd. edn. 1970—). Clubs: The Lancer's, 2001 (Dallas). Home: 9527 Mossridge Dallas TX 75238 Office: Suite 3930 2001 Bryan Tower Dallas TX 75201

PETERSON, FRANCIS DALE, petroleum co. exec.; b. Beaumont, Tex., Dec. 25, 1915; s. Albin Eugene and Mabel (Nelson) P.; B.S. in Elec. Engring., U. Tex., 1950; m. Mae Beth Thompson, Jan. 9, 1943; children—Betsy (Mrs. James R. Mabry), Judy Lynne, Jill Jane. Field engr. IBM Corp., Austin, Tex., 1950-56; methods analyst Chance Vought Aircraft Corp., Dallas, 1956-60; mgr. data processing Champlin Petroleum Co., Enid, Okla., 1960—. Vol. Worker Enid chpt. United Fund, 1965—. Served with AUS, 1941-45. Decorated Legion of Merit. Mem. Tau Beta Pi, Eta Kappa Nu. Republican. Methodist (trustee). Lion, K.P. Home: 2010 Live Oaks St Enid OK 73701 Office: 318 W Cherokee St Enid OK 73701

PETERSON, NEWTON CURTIS, JR., landscape architect; b. Lakeland, Fla., Aug. 23, 1922; s. Newton Curtis and Caroline Ellen (Smith) P.; student George Washington U., 1941-42, Fla. So. Coll., 1950-53; m. Ethel Lucille Schultz, Apr. 8, 1944; children—Newton Curtis III, Peter Karl. Foreman, Peterson's Nurseries, Lakeland, Fla., 1945-47, landscape supt., 1947—, landscape designer, 1948-53, landscape architect, 1953—, gen. mgr., 1954—, partner, 1958—. Ornamental horticulture rep. Agrl. Adv. Council, Fla. Dept. Agr., 1961—, sec.-treas. council, 1966-70; chmn., 1970—; mem. plant industry tech. com. Div. Plant Industry Fla., 1961—; nursery industry rep. Fla. Agrl. Tax Council, 1962—; pres., 1967-70; mem. Ornamental Horticulture DARE Com. Polk County, 1965—, Spreading Decline Ways and Means Com., 1966-68; mem. horticulture adv. com. Polk County Vocational Tech. Sch. Mem. Polk County Dem. exec. com., chmn. campaign com.; mem. Fla. Senate, 1972—. Bd. dirs. Polk County Assn. Retarded Children, 1963, v.p., 1971-72; bd. dirs. Agribus. Inst. Fla., 1971-72, Fla. Sheriff's Girls Villa, 1972—; sec.-treas. Fla. Clergy Econ. Edn. Conf., 1967-68; exec. committeeman Fla. Community Devel. Coordinating Council, 1967-68; mem. Lakeland Beautification Bd., 1965-68; cubmaster Boy Scouts Am., 1964-66; pres. Lakeland Conv. Bur., 1965-66; mem. horticulture adv. com. Polk Jr. Coll., 1964—. Served with USCGR, 1942-45. Named Fla. Nurseryman of Year, recipient Odenkirk Trophy, 1961. Mem. Am. Assn. Nurseryman, So. Nurseryman's Assn., Fla. Nurseryman and Growers Assn. (past pres.), Sigma Nu. Democrat. Baptist. Home: 1504 Warren Av Lakeland FL 33803 Office: 225 New Auburndale Rd Lakeland FL 33801 also PO Box 180 2034 S Combee Rd Eaton Park FL 33840

PETERSON, PAUL HAROLD, editor; b. Fairbury, Ill., Nov. 16, 1941; s. Harold Emanuel and Doreen (Christenson) P.; B.A., U. Louisville, 1963. News editor Shively (Ky.) Newsweek, 1958-60; title examiner, asst. to pres. Lincoln Fed. Savs., Louisville, 1962; editor Cardinal Newspaper, Louisville, 1962-63; editor employee and dealer publs. Standard Oil Co., Louisville, 1963-68, advt. specialist, 1968—; sales mgr. Apple Valley Resort, Lake Cumberland, Ky., 1973—. Publicity dir. Miss Ky. Pageant; dir. Belknap Theatre; mem. pub. relations com. Ky. Derby Festival, 1972. Mem. Ky. Indsl. Editors (v.p. 1968), Internat. Editors (dir. internat. affairs 1968), Am. Council Indsl. Editors, Audubon Soc., Kentuckiana, Delta Upsilon Alumni Club (pres. 1966), Phi Delta Epsilon, Pi Sigma Alpha, Omicron Delta Kappa. Author: Standard Oil: Yesterday, Today and Tomorrow, 1967. Home: 1837 Mary Catherine Dr Louisville KY 40216 Office: PO Box 1446 Louisville KY 40201

PETERSON, RUBY KETTLES (MRS. ARTHUR G. PETERSON), lawyer; b. Dalton, Ga., Mar. 20, 1910; d. Van F. and Lola (Harris) Kettles; student Ga. State Coll. Women; diploma in accountancy Internat. Accounts Soc., Inc., 1944; LL.B., Woodrow Wilson Coll. Law, 1947; postgrad. Benjamin Franklin Sch. Accountancy, U. Ga. Evening Sch.; m. Arthur G. Peterson, Feb. 1, 1953. Tchr. county elementary schs., 1928-36; admitted to Ga. bar, 1947, U.S. Supreme Ct. bar; with Internal Revenue Service, Washington, 1949—, spl. asst. to head rev. div. Chief Counsel's Office, 1956-59, staff asst. to chief counsel, 1959-61, chief corp. tax br., joint com. div., 1961-65; tech. asst. to chief counsel, 1965-69, Regional Counsel's Office, Jacksonville, Fla., 1969—. Treas. DeBary Arts and Crafts Club; parliamentarian DeBary Garden Club. Recipient Certificate of award Dept. Treasury, 1966, Superior Performance award, 1968, Albert Gallatin award, 1970; spl. Achievement award Internal Revenue Service, 1970. Mem. Am. Soc. Women Accountants (organizer D.C. chpt., 1950), Am., Ga., Fed., Whitfield County (first woman mem.) bar assns., Ga. Assn. Women Lawyers, Fla. Fedn. Garden Clubs (horticulture chmn. dist. IV), Internat. Ikebana Club, Ikebana Ikenabo Club. Home: 16 Madera Rd De Bary FL 32713

PETERSON, SHAILER, univ. adminstr.; b. Albert Lea, Minn., Oct. 12, 1908; s. P. Augustus and Annie Christine (Olsen) P.; B.A., U. Ore., 1930, M.A., 1933; Ph.D. in Ednl. Psychology, U. Minn., 1943; m. Ella Cleone Devereaux, Nov. 1, 1935; 1 son, Devereaux Shailer. Chmn. sci. dept. Lebanon (Ore.) High Sch., 1933-35; instr., U. Ore., 1935-36, U. Minn., 1936-43; asso. prof. S.D. State Coll., 1944; asst. prof. U. Chgo., 1945-47; dir. ednl. measurements Council Dental Edn., Am. Dental Assn., Chgo., 1947-48, sec., 1948-61, asst. sec. ednl. affairs Am. Dental Assn., 1959-61; prof. dentistry, dean U. Tenn. Coll. Dentistry, Memphis, 1961-69; asso. dean, prof. U. Tex. Dental Sch., San Antonio, 1969—, prof. dental br., Houston, 1969-71. Clin. asso. prof., guest lectr. Loyola U. Dental Sch., Chgo.; mem. dental tng. com. Nat. Instr. Dental Research; hon. mem. expert com. aux. dental personnel WHO; spl. cons. USPHS; cons. So. Regional Edn. Bd., Am. Dental Assn.; cons. to evaluation com. dental dept. Tenn. Pub. Health Dept.; chmn. com. dental student utilization USPHS. Fellow Internat., Am. (hon.) colls. dentists, A.A.A.S.; mem. R.D. and M. Deans' Odontological Soc. (hon.), Psychometric Soc., Memphis (hon.), Chgo. (hon.), N.C. (hon.), W. Va. (hon.), San Antonio Dist. (hon.) dental socs., N.E.A., Am. Psychol. Assn., Am. (asso.), Tenn. dental assns., Am. Statis. Assn., Am. Dental Hygienists Assn. (hon.), Am. Assn. Dental Examiners (hon.), Am. Ednl. Research Assn., Am. Pub. Health Assn., Am. Acad. Dental Medicine (hon.), Am. Acad. Gen. Dentistry (hon.), Am. Med. Coll. Assn., Internat. Assn. Dental Research, Am. Amateur Relay League, Quarter Century Wireless Assn., Sociedad Odontological Dominicana (hon.), San Antonio C. of C., Sigma Xi, Pi Mu Epsilon, Delta Sigma Delta (hon. life), Phi Delta Kappa, Omicron Kappa Upsilon. Club: Top of Hundred (Memphis). Author: How Well Are Indian Children Educated, 1945. Editor: Clinical Dental Hygiene, 1963, 4th edit., 1972; The Dentist and His Assistant, 1961, 3d edit., 1972; A Comprehensive Review for Dental Hygienists, 1965, 3d edit., 1974; Review and Test Manual for Dental Assistants, 1967; Things to Know Before You Go For An Interview, 1974. Home: 5511 Keystone Dr San Antonio TX 78229

PETERSON, VERNON LEROY, ednl. adminstr.; b. LaJunta, Colo., July 27, 1925; s. William Peter and Florence (Griffin) P.; B.A., Northwestern State Coll., 1949; M.Ed., Phillips U., 1951; Ed.D., Ohio Christian Coll., 1967; m. Katherine Virginia Simpson, July 31, 1946; children—Vernon Wayne, Gary Lynn, Sheryl Sue. Tchr., Woodward (Okla) Jr. High Sch., 1949-52; prin. high sch., Sharon, Okla., 1952-53; supt. schs., Fargo, Okla., 1953-61, Keyes, Okla., 1961-69, North Enid Pub. Schs., Enid, Okla., 1969—. Mem. Okla. Commn. for Ednl. Advancement. Served with USNR, 1943-46. Mem. Okla. Edn. Assn., N.E.A., Am. Okla. assns. sch. adminstrs., Okla. Assn. Sch. Bus. Ofcls. Lion (bd. dirs. 1970-72). Home: 3114 N Lincoln St Enid OK 73701 Office: Route 6 Enid OK 73701

PETTINGER, WILLIAM A., physician; b. Cumberland, Ia., May 26, 1932; s. Adolph and Virginia (Lauhoff) P.; B.S., Creighton U., 1954, M.S., 1957, M.D., 1959; m. Margaret Carney, Aug. 12, 1961; children—Maria, Thomas, Elise, Will. Intern, Med. Center, Jersey City, 1959-60, asst. resident, 1960-61; clin. investigator exptl. therapeutics, attending physician Nat. Heart Inst., Bethesda, Md., 1961-63; sr. asst. resident Yale U. Grace-New Haven Hosp., 1963-64; postdoctoral fellow, instr. medicine and pharmacology Vanderbilt U. Sch. Medicine, Nashville, 1964-66, asst. prof., 1966-67; asso. dept. clin. pharmacology Hoffmann-LaRoche, Inc., Nutley, N.J., 1967-71, chief sect. cardiovascular pharmacology, 1969-71, research dir. clin. pharmacology unit Newark City Hosp., 1967-71; asso. prof. medicine N.J. Coll. Medicine, Jersey City; asso. prof. pharmacology and medicine Southwestern Med. Sch., U. Tex., Dallas, 1971-74, prof., 1974—, dir. clin. pharmacology, 1971—. Mem. med. adv. bd. council high blood pressure research Am. Heart Assn. Served with USPHS, 1961-63. Recipient Burroughs Wellcome Scholar award, 1974. Diplomate Am. Bd. Med. Examiners, Am. Bd. Internal Medicine. Fellow A.C.P., Am. Coll. Cardiology; mem. Am. Fedn. Clin. Research, Am. Soc. Pharmacology and Exptl. Therapeutics, Am., N.Y. acads. scis., Am. Soc. Clin. Pharmacology (dir.), So. Soc. Clin. Investigation. Contbr. articles to profl. jours. Home: 15432 Spring Creek Rd Dallas TX 75240 Office: 5323 Harry Hines Blvd Dallas TX 75235

PETTIS, ELIZABETH E. WADE (MRS. IRVING MCFARLAND PETTIS), health agy. exec.; b. Nappanee, Ind., Dec. 16, 1902; d. Raymond J. and Ella L. (Yarian) Wade; A.B., DePauw U., 1924; M.A., U. Chgo., 1926; postgrad. Northwestern U., 1928; m. Irving McFarland Pettis, Jan 28, 1933; children—Janet Louise (Mrs. Hunter Mason Morris), Robert Irving, Alan Wade. Caseworker, Family Welfare Assn., Evanston, Ill., 1926-28; dir. religious edn. 1st Methodist Ch., Evanston, 1928-29; exec. Family Welfare Assn., Evanston, 1930-32; chief social worker McLennan County Rehab. Center for Children and Adults, Waco, Tex., 1961-68; exec. dir. McLennan County Rehab. Center, Waco, 1968—. Vice pres. Waco Traffic Commn., 1951-52; mem. Citizens Charter Commn. Waco, 1957-70. Bd. dirs. Waco Council for Social Welfare, 1952-59, United Charities Waco, 1949-50, Waco Assn. Retarded Children, 1968-69. Mem. Nat. Assn. Social Workers, Acad. Certified Social Workers, Nat. Conf. Social Work, Nat. Easter Seal Execs. Assn., Am. Assn. U. Women, League Women Voters (state bd. 2d v.p. 1961-62), Alpha Chi Omega. Home: 1539 Western Oaks Dr Waco TX 76710

PETTUS, REGINALD HOFFMAN, legislator, lawyer; b. Keysville, Va., June 11, 1920; s. George Overton and Bertha (Hanmer) P.; J.D., Washington and Lee U., 1948; m. Anne Howard Early, Oct. 7, 1947; children—Pamela Kent, Regina Hanmer, Anne Tompkins, Thomas Richardson Randolph. Admitted to Va. bar, 1949, since practiced in Southside; pros. atty. Charlotte County (Va.), 1955-63; asso. county judge, 1963-69; mem. Va. Ho. of Reps., 1969-72. Chmn. bd. State Bank, Keysville; mem. Va. Airports Authority, 1959; commr. of accounts, 1963—. Served with USAAF, 1942-45. ETO. Mem. Va. Bar Assn. (mem. council 1964-70). Democrat. Baptist. Address: Keysville VA 23947

PETTY, CHARLES SUTHERLAND, pathologist; b. Lewistown, Mont., Apr. 16, 1920; s. Charles Frederic and Mae (Reichert) P.; B.S., U. Wash., 1941, M.S., 1946; M.D., Harvard, 1950; m. Lois Muriel Swenson, Dec. 14, 1957; children—Heather Ann, Charles Sutherland II; children by previous marriage—Daniel S., Carol L. Intern, Mary Imogene Bassett Hosp., Coopertown, N.Y., 1950-52; resident pathology Peter Bent Brigham Hosp., Children's Med. Center, New Eng. Deaconess Hosp., Boston, 1952-55; instr. pathology La. State U.

Sch. Medicine, 1955-56, asst. prof., 1956-58; asst. med. examiner State of Md., 1958-67; asst. prof. forensic pathology U. Md. Sch. Medicine, 1958-64, asso. prof., 1964-67; lectr., then asso. Johns Hopkins U. Sch. Hygiene and Pub. Health, 1959-67; dir. Balt. Regional A.R.C. Blood Program, 1959-67; prof. forensic pathology Ind. U. Sch. Medicine, Indpls., 1967-69; dir. lab. Ind. Commn. on Forensic Scis., 1967-69; chief med. examiner Dallas County, 1969—; prof. forensic scis., pathology U. Tex. Southwestern Med. Sch., Dallas, 1969—; also dir. Southeastern Inst. Forensic Scis., 1969—. Served from ensign to lt. comdr. USNR, 1941-45. Fellow Coll. Am. Pathologists, Am. Soc. Clin. Pathologists, A.C.P., Am. Acad. Forensic Scis. (pres. 1967-68); mem. Sci. Research Soc. Am., Sigma Xi. Episcopalian. Home: 3964 Goodfellow Dr Dallas TX 75229 Office: 5230 Medical Center Dr Dallas TX 75235

PETTY, GEORGE RONALD, hosp. adminstr.; b. N.Y.C., Mar. 6, 1917; s. George Beecher and Nellie Hannah (Gage) P.; grad. high sch.; m. Barbara Ann Vos, May 15, 1940 (div.); 1 son, Ron Jackson; m. 2d, Judith Ann MacDonald, July 18, 1969; children—Scott MacDonald, Janet Kay. Radio operator Press Wireless, Inc., N.Y.C., 1939-41, comml. mgr., 1941-42; asst. mgr. broadcasting div. Raytheon Mfg. Co., N.Y.C., 1945-46; tech. secretariat Internat. Air Transport Assn., Montreal, 1949-51; asst. dir. Me. Civil Def. Agy., Augusta, 1951-56; exec. dir. Me. Osteo. Assn., 1956-62; adminstr. Waterville (Me.) Osteo. Hosp., 1962-73; mng. dir. Circus Hall of Fame, Sarasota, Fla., 1973—. Pres., Health Council of Me., 1961-62; dir. Waterville Hosp. Council, 1969-73, Regional Health Agy. Kennebec Valley, 1966—. Served with AUS, 1936-38, 42-45. Decorated Bronze Star medal. Mem. Me. Hosp. Assn., Me. Osteo. Hosp. Assn. (pres. 1970-71). Me. Osteo. Assn. Rotarian (pres. 1971-72). Home: care Sun N Fun Box 297J Sarasota FL 33577 Office: 6255 N Tamiami Trail Sarasota FL 33578

PETTY, JOHN, JR., dir. univ. art gallery; b. Montcoal, W.Va., Oct. 4, 1938; s. John Leroy and Georgia (Hanson) P.; B.A., Bob Jones U., 1962; student U. Ariz., 1962-66; m. Evelyn Jane Ralston, May 31, 1961; children—Michelle, Mark, Michael, Matthew. Exhibited one-man shows Old Pueblo Artists Gallery, Tucson, 1965, Gallery G, Wichita, Kan., 1967, Bob Jones U., 1968, David, David, Inc., Phila., 1968, Auslew Gallery, Norfolk, Va., 1969; curator U. Ariz. Art Gallery, 1962-66; acting dir., curator Wichita Art Museum, 1966-67; dir. Washington County Museum of Fine Arts, Hagerstown, Md., 1967-70; dir. Art Gallery Bob Jones U., 1970—; condr. art seminars and art study courses. Founding dir., trustee Potomac Symphony Orch. Mem. Internat. Inst. Conservation Mus. Objects, Am. Appraisers Assn., Inst. Conservation Mus. Objects Am. Group, Am. Assn. Museums. Baptist. Home: 1049 E Perry Rd Greenville SC 29609 Office: Art Gallery Bob Jones U Greenville SC 29614

PETTY, OLIVE SCOTT, geophys. engr.; b. Olive, Tex., Apr. 15, 1895; s. Van Alvin and Mary Cordelia (Dabney) P.; student Ga. Inst. Tech., 1913-14; B.S. in Civil Engring., U. Tex., 1917, C.E., 1920; m. Mary Edwina Harris, July 19, 1921; 1 son, Scott. Adj. prof. civil engring. U. Tex., 1920-23; structural engr. R.O. Jameson, Dallas, 1923-25; pres. Petty Geophys. Engring. Co., San Antonio, 1925-52, chmn. bd., 1952-73; pres. Petty Geophys. Co., San Antonio, 1944-52, chmn. bd., 1952-73, cons., 1973—; pres. Petty Labs., Inc., San Antonio, 1932-52, chmn. bd., 1952-73; chmn. bd. Petty Geophys. Engring. Co. de Mex. S.A. de C.V., 1950-73; partner Petty Ranch Co., 1968—; also ranching, minerals, timber and investment interests. Sponsor San Antonio Symphony Soc.; patron San Antonio Art Inst.; mem. exec. com., founding mem. chancellor's council U. Tex. Served to 1st lt. engrs. U.S. Army, 1917-18; AEF in France. Recipient Distinguished Engring Grad. award U. Tex., 1962. Registered profl. engr., Tex. Fellow Tex. Acad. Sci. (hon. life); mem. San Antonio Livestock Assn. (life), Texas-Mid-Continent Oil and Gas Assn. (dir.), Am. Soc. C.E. (hon. life), Am. Inst. Mining, Metall. and Petroleum Engrs., Am. Assn. Petroleum Geologists, A.A.A.S., Am. Geophys. Union, Houston Geophys. Soc., S. Tex. Geol. Soc., Soc. Am. Mil. Engrs., Soc. Exptl. Geophysicists (hon. life and founding mem.), Newcomen Soc., Soc. 1st Div., 1st Officers Tng. Camp Assn., Tex., Tex. Heritage Found., Nat. Rifle Assn. (life), Tex. Soc. Profl. Engrs., Ind. Petroleum Assn. Am., Profl. Engrs. in Industry, Ex-Students' Assn. U. Tex. (life), Dads' Assn. U. Tex. (life), Tex. Sheep and Goat Raisers Assn., Tex. and Southwestern Cattle Raisers Assn., Nat. Wool Growers Assn., Am. Farm Bur., Nat. Wildlife Fedn., Chi Epsilon (hon. life), Theta Xi, Tau Beta Pi. Baptist. Clubs: San Antonio Country, Argyle, St. Anthony (San Antonio). Patentee geophys. instruments, exploration methods. Home: 101 E Kings Hwy San Antonio TX 78212 Office: Travis Park West Bldg San Antonio TX 78205

PETTY, SCOTT, JR., engring. co. exec.; b. San Antonio, Apr. 10, 1937; s. Olive Scott and Edwina (Harris) P.; B.S., U. Tex., 1960, M.S., 1961; m. Marie Louise James, June 10, 1959; children—Joan Louise, Susan Harris, Scott James. Asst. to pres. Petty Geophys. Engring. Co., San Antonio, 1961-63, v.p. 1963-65, dir., 1958-73, pres., 1967-73, also pres. and dir. subsidiaries, 1967-73; pres. Petty Labs., Inc., 1965-67; exec. v.p. Petty-Ray Geophys., Inc., San Antonio, 1973—. Served to lt. AUS, 1959-60. Registered profl. engr., Tex., La. Mem. Tex. Soc. Profl. Engrs., Soc. Exploration Geophysicists, Am. Assn. Petroleum Geologists, Am. Inst. Mining, Metall. and Petroleum Engrs., Soc. Am. Mil. Engrs., Phi Gamma Delta, Sigma Gamma Epsilon, Tau Beta Pi. Home: 202 Lajara Blvd San Antonio TX 78209 Office: PO Drawer 2061 San Antonio TX 78297

PETTY, VAN ALVIN, JR., exploration geologist; b. San Antonio, Aug. 18, 1914; s. Van Alvin and Estelle Edna (George) P.; B.S. in Geology, U. Tex., 1940, M.A., 1941; m. Maxine Inez Lambert, June 21, 1935; children—Patricia Estelle (Mrs. Allan Raymond Zinsmeyer, Jr.), Christine Sharon (Mrs. Chauncey Wightman Pa), Maxine Mary (Mrs. John Wesley Kenny). Asst. seismologist Petty Geophys. Engring. Co., San Antonio, 1940-41, v.p., 1942-55, dir., 1942-72; geologist Navarro Oil Co., Shreveport, La., 1941-42, Union Product Co., Houston, 1942; ind. exploration geologist, San Antonio, 1955—. Mem. Am. Assn. Petroleum Geologists, Soc. Exploration Geophysicist, South Tex. Geol. Soc., Sci. Research Soc. Am., Am. Geol. Inst., San Antonio Petroleum Club, Petroleum Club of Houston; Sigma Xi, Sigma Gamma Epsilon. Episcopalian. Home: 7502 N Vandiver St San Antonio TX 78209 Office: 7502 N Vandiver St San Antonio TX 78209

PETTYJOHN, CHARLES STEPHENS, realtor; b. Denver, Aug. 30, 1910; s. Don C. and Myrtle (Stephens) P.; student Wis. Sch. Mines, 1929-33; B.S., Mich. Tech. Inst., 1934, postgrad. 1935; Petroleum Engr., Purdue U., 1937; postgrad. U. Chgo., 1940; m. Margaret A. Nekervis, July 26, 1937; children—Charles S. and Robert B. (twins). Research, inspection engr. Socony Vacuum Oil Co., East Chicago, Ill., 1936-47; engr., gen. mgmt. Standard Vacuum Petroleum, Mij, Palembang, Sumatera, 1947-58; sales finance Driggers Realty, Mount Dora, Fla., 1959-67; owner, realtor Asso. Realty Services, Mount Dora and Leesburg, Fla., 1967—. Commr. Planning and Zoning, Lake County, Fla., 1969—, chmn., 1971—; sec. Sun Coast Clinic, Largo, Fla. Trustee Waterman Meml. Hosp., Eustis, Fla. Named Realtor of Year Lake County, 1970, 72. Mem. Nat. Assn. Real Estate Bds., Nat. Inst. Real Estate Brokers, Lake County, Leesburg bds. realtors, Mt. Dora C. of C. (pres. 1970). Kiwanian (past pres., lt. gov.-elect). Home: Box 103 Fairview Point Tavares FL 32778 Office: 237 Eustis-Mt Dora Hwy 19A Mount Dora FL 32757

PEURIFOY, PAUL GARLAND, judge; b. Wortham, Tex., Aug. 9, 1906; s. Roy G. and Laura Pearl (Burton) P.; student U. Tex., 1923-26, So. Meth. U., 1926-27; m. Mary Jo Mouzon, Sept. 24, 1929; m. 2d, Audrey Posey, May 1, 1970. Admitted to Tex. bar, 1927; practiced in Dallas, 1941-42, 47-48; mem. firm Davis, Synnott & Hatchell, Dallas, 1927-29, Church, Read & Bane, Dallas, 1929-31, Hardy & Peurifoy, Dallas, 1931-36; asst. dist. atty. Dallas (Tex.) County, 1937-41, presiding judge, 1958-59, 63-64; chmn. juvenile bd., 1957-58, 60-62; atty. OPA, 1945-47; judge County Ct. at Law 1, Dallas, 1948-52; dist. judge 95th Dist. Ct., Dallas, 1953-72; presiding judge 1st Adminstrv. Dist. Tex., 1973—. Guest lectr. govt. So. Meth. U., 1948-51. Bd. dirs. Dallas Big Bros., 1947-53. Served with USAAF, 1943-45; MTO. Mem. Am., Dallas bar assns., State Bar Tex. Democrat. Methodist. Mason (32 deg., Shriner). Clubs: Dallas Athletic, Down-Town. Home: 11306 Hillcrest Rd Dallas TX 75230 Office: Court House Dallas TX 75202

PEVLER, HERMAN H., r.r. exec.; b. Waynetown, Ind., Apr. 20, 1903; s. Chris and Bertha (Hoover) P.; B.S. in Civil Engring., Purdue, 1927; m. Roma H. Haines, June 6, 1931. Asst. engring. corps Pa. R.R., Phila., 1937, asst. supr. track Atlantic and Middle divs., 1927-29, supr. track Balt., Atlantic and Phila. divs., 1929-35, div. engr. St. Louis, Ft. Wayne and Pitts. divs., 1935-37, div. engr. gen. office, Phila., 1937-39, supt. Logansport div., 1939-40, supt. freight transp. Eastern region, Phila., 1940-42, supt. Phila. term. div., 1942, gen. supt. Eastern Pa. div., 1942-46, gen. mgr. Western region, Chgo., gen. mgr. Central region, Pitts., 1946-48, v.p. N.Y. zone, 1948-51, v.p. Western region, Chgo., 1951-55, v.p., regional mgr. Northwestern region, 1955-59, officer, dir. subsidiary cos., pres. Wabash R.R., 1959-63; officer, dir. subsidiary cos., pres. Norfolk & Western Ry., 1963-70, chmn., 1970-73; dir. Dominion Bankshares Corp., Roanoke, First Nat. Exchange Bank of Va., A.E. Staley Mfg. Co., Decatur, Ill., Community Hosp. of Roanoke Valley Inc. Trustee Va. Found. Ind. Coll.; bd. visitors Va. Mil. Inst. Clubs: Shenandoah, Roanoke Country (Roanoke, Va.); Crystal Downs Country (Frankfurt, Mich.); Bogey (St. Louis); Royal Palm Yacht and Country (Boca Raton, Fla.). Home: 15 Cardinal Rd SW Roanoke VA 24014 Office: Suite 126-127 Hotel Roanoke 19 N Jefferson St Roanoke VA 24006

PFAFF, WILLIAM SIEVERS, JR., newspaper exec.; b. New Orleans, July 5, 1919; s. William S. and Irene (Krummel) P.; student Soule Bus. Coll., 1936-40, Am. Acad. Art, 1947; m. Audrey M. Knecht, Dec. 26, 1942; 1 dau., Karol Ann. Advt. artist, copy writer Times-Picayune Pub. Corp., New Orleans, 1946-60, promotion mgr., 1960—, v.p., 1969—. Instr., Loyola U., New Orleans, 1966. Served with USAAF, 1942-45. Mem. Internat. Newspaper Promotion Assn. (pres. So. region 1964, Bronze award 1966), Advt. Club New Orleans (past dir.), Am. Marketing Assn. (past chpt. v.p.). Home: 3640 Post Oak Dr New Orleans LA 70114 Office: 3800 Howard Av New Orleans LA 70140

PFEIL, WALTER JAMES MALONEY, ins. co. exec.; b. Buffalo, Sept. 20, 1945; s. Walter Fred and Mildred Agness (Maloney) P.; academia OAS, Quito, Ecuador, 1962; A.B. magna cum laude (George Catlin fellow, Nat. Def. Edn. Act fellow), Union Coll., Schenectady, 1968; M.A., U. Fla., 1969; m. Jane Elizabeth Hagans, Dec. 28, 1968; 1 dau., Jennifer Jane. Mgr., Walter F. Pfeil Wholesale Lumber Co., Williamsville, N.Y., 1964-65; chief liaison officer minority enterprise small bus. investment cos. Small Bus. Adminstrn., Dept. Commerce, Washington, 1969-70; research analyst Prudential Ins. Co. Am., Jacksonville, Fla., 1971-74, sr. research analyst, 1974—. Pres., Help Them Learn Fund, Williamsville, N.Y., 1962-68. Mem. Am. Econ. Assn., U. Fla., Union Coll. alumni assns., Phi Beta Kappa, Beta Gamma Sigma, Phi Kappa Phi, Psi Upsilon. Republican. Episcopalian. Author: newspaper column Fire Facts, Clarence, N.Y., 1964-66. Home: 931 Neptune Lane Neptune Beach FL 32233 Office: Planning and Analysis div South Central Home Office Prudential Ins Co Jacksonville FL 32207

PFOUTS, RALPH WILLIAM, educator; b. Atchison, Kan., Sept. 9, 1920; s. Ralph Ulysses and Alice (Oldham) P.; B.A., U. Kan., 1942, M.A., 1947; Ph.D., U. N.C., 1952; m. Jane Hoyer, Jan. 31, 1945; children—James William, Susan Jane, Thomas Robert, Elizabeth Ann. Research asst., instr. econs. U. Kan., 1946-47, U. N.C., Chapel Hill, 1947-50, lectr. 1950-52, asso. prof., 1952-58, prof., 1958—, chmn. grad. studies dept. econs. Sch. Bus. Adminstrn., 1957-62, chmn. dept. econs., 1962-68. Social Sci. Research Council fellow U. Cambridge, 1953-54; Ford Found. faculty research fellow, 1962-63. Served as deck officer USNR antisubmarine duty, 1943-46. Mem. Am., N.C. (pres. 1951-52) statis. assns., Am., So. (pres. 1965-66) econ. assns., Population Assn. Am., Econometric Soc., A.A.A.S., Phi Beta Kappa, Pi Sigma Alpha, Alpha Kappa Psi, Omicron Delta Epsilon. Author: Elementary Economics: A Mathematical Approach, 1972. Editor So. Econ. Jour., 1955—. Editor, contbr. Techniques of Urban Economic Analysis, 1960, Essays in Economics and Econometrics, 1960. Mem. editorial bd. Metroeconomica, 1961—, Atlantic Econ. Jour., 1973—. Contbr. articles profl. jours. Home: 502 Ransom St Chapel Hill NC 27514

PHARR, MARSHALL ALVIN, city ofcl.; b. Lubbock, Tex., Apr. 11, 1931; s. Homer Lee and Mabel (Chapman) P.; B.B.A., Tex. Technol. Coll., 1954, postgrad., 1957-58; postgrad. Wayland Baptist Coll., 1964-65; m. Edith Ann Standifer, June 17, 1955; children—Terri Annette, Mark Standifer, Denise Marie, Angela Kay. Mgr., Lubbock, Club, Inc., 1953-54; adminstrv. asst. City of Lubbock, 1957-59; city mgr. Andrews, Tex., 1959-64, Plainview, Tex., 1964—. Vice chmn. Haynes dist. Boy Scouts Am., 1965-67, chmn., 1967—, v.p. Southplains council; v.p. loyalty fund bd. Tex. Technol. Coll., 1960-64; mem. Wayland Law Enforcement Adv. Council, 1971—, Plainview Indsl. Contacts Team, 1972. Bd. dirs. Andrews Indsl. Found., 1962-64, Plainview Indsl. Found. Served to lt. USNR, 1955-57. Mem. Internat., Tex., (dir. 1965-66, 71—), Panhandle (pres.). West Tex. city mgrs. assns., Tex. Municipal League (dist. sec.), Plainview C. of C. (chmn. civic com.), Phi Delta Theta. Democrat. Methodist (pres. Methodist Men 1965-66, steward 1960-64, ch. sch. supt. 1961-64, chmn. finance campaign 1963-64). Mason, Rotarian (pres. Plainview and Andrews, dir.). Home: 2801 W 17th St Plainview TX 79072 Office: Box 520 Plainview TX 79072

PHELPS, ASHTON, newspaper exec., lawyer; b. New Orleans, Dec. 30, 1913; s. Esmond and Harriott K. (Barnwell) P.; grad. Woodberry Forest Sch., 1931; A.B., Tulane U., 1935, LL.B., 1937; student U. Mich. Law Sch., summer 1936; m. Jane C. George, Nov. 21, 1939; 1 son, Ashton. Admitted to La. bar, 1937, since practiced in New Orleans; mem. firm Phelps, Dunbar, Marks, Claverie & Sims, 1946-67; pres., pub. The Times-Picayune Pub. Corp., New Orleans, 1967—, also dir. Mem. bd. Christian edn. Presbyn. Ch. U.S., 1958-61, also mem. com. wills and bequests; pres. bd. New Orleans Community Health Assn., 1945-49, Howard Meml. Library Assn., 1950—; chmn. adv. bd. Female Orphan Soc. New Orleans, 1946-59; bd. visitors Tulane U., 1953-55, v.p. bd. adminstrs., 1955-72, adv. adminstr., 1972—; trustee Mountain Retreat Assn., 1958-67; bd. dirs. New Orleans Pub. Library, 1948-62, New Orleans YMCA, 1954—, New Orleans chpt. A.R.C., 1954-60. Oschner Found. Hosp. Mem. Bd. of Liquidation City Debt, Sewerage and Water Board. Served from ensign to lt. (s.g.). USNR, 1942-45. Mem. Am. (spl. com. anti trust sect. on revision rules FTC), La., New Orleans bar assns., Assn. Bar City N.Y., Am. Law Inst., Am. Newspaper Pubs. Assn. (dir.), Order of Coif, Phi Beta Kappa, Delta Tau Delta, Phi Delta Phi, Omicron Delta Kappa. Clubs: Boston, Louisiana, New Orleans Country; City (Baton Rouge). Presbyn. (elder, trustee). Home: 1457 State St New Orleans LA 70118 Office: 3800 Howard Av New Orleans LA 70140

PHELPS, C. PAUL, state ofcl.; b. Baton Rouge, Nov. 8, 1932; s. C. Paul and Auril Carmen (Williams) P.; student U. of South, 1950-52; B.A., La. State U., 1957, M.S.W., 1963; m. Betty Halbert, Aug. 27, 1955; children—Andrea Diane, Cynthia Ann. With East Baton Rouge Parish Family Ct., 1957-67, chief probation officer, 1964-67; with La. Dept. Corrections, Baton Rouge, 1967—, asst. dir., 1967—. Served with USAF, 1953-55; capt. Res. ret. Mem. Nat. Council on Crime and Delinquency, Am. Correctional Assn., Kappa Sigma. Mason. Home: 8833 Bayside St Baton Rouge LA 70806 Office: PO Box 44304 Capitol Station Baton Rouge LA 70804

PHELPS, FLORENCE LOUISE HARLLEE (MRS. JOHN C. PHELPS, JR.), social worker; b. Dallas; d. Norman Washington and Florence (Coleman) Harllee; A.B., Howard U., 1925; M.S.W., Atlanta U., 1949; M.Ed., N. Tex. State U., 1958; postgrad. summers, 1954, 64, U. Ill., 1959, So. Meth. U., 1963; m. John C. Phelps, Jr.; children—Norma Belle (Mrs. George Barratt), Lucy Pearl (Mrs. Albert Simeon Patterson). Social worker City County Dept. Pub. Welfare, Dallas, 1936-41; sch. social worker Dallas Ind. Sch. Dist., 1941-71; asst. prof. U. Tex. Grad. Sch. Social Work at Arlington, 1971-72. Instr., acting dir. Wiley Coll. Extension Sch., Dallas, 1955; cons. spl. case and adoptions Hope Cottage, Children's Bur., summer 1961. Mem. Goals for Dallas Task Force, 1968-69; chmn., Community Round Table on Social, Health and Welfare Problems, 1962-64. Bd. dirs. Dallas Opportunities Industrialization Center, Vis. Nurses Assn., 1970-73, CEMA-Financial Corp., 1968-72. Mem. Nat. Assn. Social Workers, Acad. Certified Social Workers, Vis. Tchrs. Assn. Tex., Tex. United Community Service (dir. 1970-73), League Women Voters, Dallas Health Planning Council, Internat. Platform Assn., Alpha Kappa Alpha. Home: 2804 Magna Vista Dr Dallas TX 75216

PHELPS, JACK, educator; b. Guymon, Okla., Feb. 15, 1926; s. Ewing W. and Nettie Amelia (Foreman) P.; B.S., Panhandle A. and M. Coll., 1948; M.A., Western State Coll., Gunnison, Colo., 1954; Ed.D., Okla. State U., 1963; m. Mary Glenna Hale, May 28, 1946; children—Jacqueline Kaye, Judith Lee, Janet Sue, Jon Clayton. Tchr., coach pub. schs., Griggs, Okla., 1948-52, Turpin, Okla., 1952-53; tchr., coach, Baker, Okla., 1953-61, adminstr., 1958-61; faculty math. dept. Southwestern State Coll., Weatherford, Okla., 1963-66; chmn. math. dept. Northwestern State Coll., Alva, 1966—. Cons. Okla. Dept. Edn., 1967-68. Precinct ofcl. Democratic party, Alva, 1973—. Served with USAAF, 1943-45. NSF, grantee, 1961-62. Mem. Nat. Council Tchrs. Math., Math. Assn. Am., Okla. Edn. Assn., Okla. Acad. Sci., Alva C. of C. Author: Elementary Mathematics-Theory and Practice, 1970. Home: 1440 Young St Alva OK 73717

PHELPS, JONATHAN BAILEY, JR., synthetic fibers co. exec.; b. Texarkana, Tex., June 17, 1916; s. Jonathan Bailey and Patty (Holman) P.; student Hendrix Coll., 1932-34; B.S. in Chem. Engring., U. Tex., 1936, M.S., 1938; m. Roberta Otting, Jan 28, 1939; 1 son, Bailey Preston. Devel. engr. Lion Oil Co., El Dorado, Ark., 1938-41; process supt. Phillips Petroleum Co., Borger, Tex., 1941-46; asst. div. mgr. Celanese Corp., Corpus Christi, Tex., 1946-59; exec. v.p. Fiber Industries, Inc., Charlotte, NC., 1959-73, pres., 1973—, also dir.; pres., dir. FII Trading Co., Charlotte, Fiber Industries Internat., Charlotte; dir. Milhaven Fibers, Ltd. (Canada). Mem. Gov.'s Council for Econ. Devel., 1967-72; dist. chmn. Boy Scouts Am., 1963-66. Bd. dirs. Jr. Achievement; bd. advisers Gardner Webb Coll., Central Piedmont Community Coll. Mem. Am. Inst. Chem. Engrs. Republican. Presbyn. (elder 1965-68). Rotarian, Kiwanian. Home: 125 Great Oak Lane Matthews NC 28105 Office: PO Box 10038 Charlotte NC 28201

PHELPS, RICHARD ARTHUR, diversified industry exec.; b. Pittsfield, Mass., Aug. 5, 1928; s. Harley Proctor and Beatrice (Nichols) P.; B.S., Purdue U., 1951; M.S., Mich. State U., 1955, 56, Ph.D., 1959; m. Carolyn Acola, May 19, 1961; 1 son, Gary Richard. Asst. dir. research and edn. Nat. Cottonseed Producers Assn., Dallas and Memphis, 1958-65; asst. tech. dir. oil mills and feeds Anderson Clayton & Co., Houston, 1965-69, dir. tech. information services, 1969—. Served with AUS, 1951-53. Mem. Am. Chem. Soc., Poultry Sci. Assn., Am. Dairy Sci. Assn., Am. Soc. Animal Sci., Am. Oil Chemists Soc., Am. Soc. Farm Mgrs. and Rural Appraisers, Am. Peanut Research and Edn. Assn., Nat. Cottonseed Producers Assn. (chmn. 1969-71), Soybean Research Council, Council for Agrl. Sci. and Tech., Houston Power Squadron, Sigma Xi. Home: 14 Old Hickory Dr Conroe TX 77301 Office: PO Box 2538 Houston TX 77001

PHIFER, JOSEPH RUTLEDGE, dentist; b. Houston, Sept., 30, 1935; s. James Judson and Mamie Allien (Baskett) P.; B.A., U. St. Thomas, 1957; D.D.S., U. Tex., 1963. Pvt. practice dentistry, Houston, 1963—; pres. J. Rutledge Phifer, D.D.S., Inc., Houston, 1970—. Mem. Am., Tex. dental assns., Houston Dist. Dental Soc., Delta Sigma Delta. Episcopalian. Home: 111 W Hambrick Houston TX 77037 Office: 4501 Airline Dr Houston TX 77022

PHILIPSON, ALBERT, lawyer; b. Ossining, N.Y., Feb. 23, 1910; s. Henry and Rose (Arnson) P.; A.B., Columbia, 1931; LL.B., 1933; m. Edna Gumenick, Apr. 3, 1938; children—Romlee J. (Mrs. Allan J. Weinstein), Lorrin G. (Mrs. Kenneth Rosenbaum). Admitted to N.Y. bar, 1933, D.C. bar, 1944, U.S. Supreme Ct., 1946; with FCA, 1934-35; pvt. practice law. Westchester County, N.Y., 1936-41, Washington, 1946—. Vice pres., Calvert Homes, Inc., Chesapeake Ranch Club, Inc., Chesapeake Ranch Water Co., 1960—. Officer, trustee Nat. Found. for Research in Medicine, Albert and Edna Philipson Found. Served to maj. Q.M.C., AUS, 1942-46. Decorated Legion of Merit. Mem. Bar Assn. D.C. (chmn. corp. law com. 1953-57, 63-67), Fed., Am. bar assns., Beta Sigma Ro. Democrat. Jewish religion. Contbr. articles to law jours. Home: 3731 Fessenden St NW Washington DC 20016 Office: 1775 K St NW Washington DC 20006

PHILLEO, ROBERT EUGENE, govt. ofcl.; b. Spokane, Wash., Aug. 21, 1923; s. Archibald Marvin and Helen Mar (Slater) P.; B.S. in Civil Engring., Carnegie Inst. Tech., 1946; m. Margaret Guthrie, Apr. 3, 1948; children—Diane, Barbara, Margaret, Paul. Research engr. Portland Cement Assn., Chgo., 1946-58; chief concrete branch Office Chief Engrs., Directorate of Civil Works, Washington, 1958—. Lectr. Northwestern U., 1951-57; cons. concrete materials and constrn., 1967—. Pres., Broyhill Crest Citizens Assn., Annandale, Va., 1966. Served with AUS, 1943-46. Mem. Am. Concrete Inst. (pres. 1973), Am. Soc. Testing and Materials (com. chmn. 1957-73), Hwy. Research Bd. (com. chmn. 1957-72), Joint Internat. Commn. Statis. Control of Concrete Quality. Author: (with J.J. Waddell) Concrete Construction Handbook, 1968. Asso. editor: Cement and Concrete Research, an internat. jour., 1970-73. Home: 7420 Annanwood Court

Annandale VA 22003 Office: Office Chief Engineers Attention DAEN-CWE-C Washington DC 20314

PHILLEY, JOHN CALVIN, educator, geologist; b. Indianola, Miss., Oct. 17, 1935; s. J.W. and Mary Elizabeth (Farrar) P.; B.S., Millsaps Coll., 1957; M.S., U. Tenn., 1959, Ph.D., 1971; m. Betty Lou Davis, Aug. 22, 1959; children—John Davis, Marsha Leigh, Melissa Louise. Instr. geology Morehead (Ky.) State U., 1960-64, asst. prof., 1964-69, asso. prof., 1969-73, prof., 1973—. Geologist, U.S. Geol. Survey, 1967—. Mem. Geol. Soc. Am., Am. Assn. Petroleum Geologists, Nat. Assn. Geology Tchrs., Geol. Soc. Ky. (v.p. 1970), Sigma Xi, Phi Kappa Phi, Sigma Gamma Epsilon. Kiwanian (lt. gov. 1973-74). Author: Laboratory Manual for College Physical Science, 1963. Home: 1001 Knapp Av Morehead KY 40351

PHILLIPS, A(NDREW) CRAIG, ednl. adminstr.; b. Greensboro, N.C., Nov. 1, 1922; A.B., U. N.C., 1943, M.A., 1946, Ed.D. in Sch. Adminstrn., 1956; m. 1943; 4 children. Tchr., asst. supt. Winston-Salem (N.C.) City Schs., 1946-55, supt. schs., 1957-62; supt. Charlotte-Mecklenburg (N.C.) Schs., 1962-67; adminstrv. v.p. Richardson Found., 1967-68; supt. pub. instrn. State of N.C., Raleigh, 1969—. Mem. steering com. N.C. Gov.'s Com. To Study N.C. Pub. Sch. System, 1967-68; mem. So. Regional Edn. Bd.; mem. Council Chief State Sch. Officers, 1969—. Bd. visitors Duke Div. Sch. Mem. N.E.A., N.C. Assn. Edn., Am. Assn. Sch. Adminstrs. (exec. com. 1971—), Nat. Acad. Sch. Execs. (dir. 1969), So. Assn. Colls. and Schs. (trustee). Home: 2200 Barfield Ct Raleigh NC 27612 Office: State Dept Public Instruction State Capitol Raleigh NC 27602

PHILLIPS, A(USTAVE) P(AUL), JR., advt., public relations and travel agy. exec.; b. Atlanta, May 30, 1903; s. A. P. and Kate (Faith) P.; student Washington and Lee U., 1920; B.S., U. Ala., 1925; m. Medda Euphemia Highleyman, May 5, 1926. Pres., owner A. P. Phillips Co., Orlando, Fla., 1925—, Phillips Internat. Travel Hdqrs., Orlando and Jacksonville, 1967—; editor, pub. Forward Orlando, 1926-37, Orlandoan, 1926-42. Del. Democratic Nat. Conv., 1928, 32, 36. Served as maj. USAAF, 1942-46; now lt. col. Res. ret.; dep. dir. information Res. Forces, Scott, AFB, Ill., 1960-63. Decorated 10 battle stars, Bronze Star, 2 Presdl. Citations, Air Medal; donor Advt. Achievement awards to Fla. univs. and colls. Mem. Fla. State (mil. affairs com. 1964—), Orlando (founder, pres. 1927), U.S. (v.p., dir. 1926-32), Internat. (senator) jr. chambers commerce, Internat. Pub. Relations Assn. (del. world congress 1958, 61, 64, 67), Am. Soc. Travel Agts., Pub. Relations Soc. Am. (nat. dir. 1956-57, dist. v.p. 1956, So. area dir. 1958, assembly del. for Fla. 1960-63, assembly del. N.-Central Fla. chpt. 1963-67, Fla. pres. 1955, S.E. dist. chmn. 1963-64), World Marketers, Advt. Fedn. Am. (dist. gov. 1950), Advt. Club Orlando (pres. 1949), Orlando Area Advt. Club (pres. sr. council 1966-68), Res. Officers Assn. (dept. pres. 1951, mem. nat. air force affairs com. 1952—), Mil. Order World Wars (regional comdr. 1956-60, mem. gen. staff at large 1960-67, comdr. Central Fla. 1955), Orlando Area C. of C. (mil. affairs com. 1968—), Am. Legion (comdr. post 1948, vice chmn. nat. pub. relations com. 1955-56), 40 and 8, Newcomen. Soc. N.Am., Fla. Pub. Relations Assn. (chmn. pub. relations ednl. standards com. 1966-67, trustee 1973—), D.A.V., V.F.W., Air Force Assn. (v.p. 1962-66), Interallied Confedn. Res. Officers, Ret. Officers Assn., Order Lafayette, S.C.V., Alpha Delta Sigma. Methodist. Elk, Mason (Shriner). Clubs: University (Winter Park and Jacksonville, Fla.); Country, Citrus (Orlando); River, Skal (Jacksonville, Fla.). Author: Spirits of the Free, 1957; Communications, A Matter of Survival, 1958; Action-A Blueprint for Freedom, 1960; The Rightful Challenge of Public Relations, 1964; Our Heritage Under God, 1965; Our Heritage and the Challenge of Life, 1966; Our Future, A Reflection of the Past, 1970; Our Heritage, Men of Good Faith, 1971; Our Precious Heritage, These Things We Hold Most Dear, 1971; The Blessings of Freedom, 1972; The Story of America, A Continuous One!, 1974. Home: 1354 Ivanhoe Blvd S Orlando FL 32804 Office: 1045 Legion Pl Orlando FL 32801 also 220 W Monroe St Jacksonville FL 32202

PHILLIPS, CECIL RANDOLPH, JR., assn. exec.; b. Birmingham, Ala., July 30, 1933; s. Cecil Randolph and Alberta (Smith) P.; B.S., Ga. Inst. Tech., 1955, M.S., 1960; postgrad. Fed. Inst. Tech., Zurich, Switzerland, 1955-56; m. Sara Lee Kirby, Aug. 25, 1956; children—Taylor Cy, Leslie Hope, Daniel Lee. Tech. editor advt., sales promotion dept. Gen. Electric Co., Schnectady, 1956-58; project leader Operations Research, Inc., Silver Spring, Md., 1960-62, asst. tech. dir., Atlanta, 1962-63; exec. v.p. Mgmt. Sci. Atlanta, Inc., 1963-67; mgr. Kurt Salmon Assos., Inc., Atlanta, 1967-73, v.p., 1974; exec. dir. Ga. Conservancy, 1974—, also trustee. Active Boy Scouts Am. Mem. Assn. for Systems Mgmt., Inst. Mgmt. Consultants, ANAK Soc., Am. Prodn. and Inventory Control Soc., Sierra Club, Save America's Vital Environment, Friends of the River, Nat. Wildlife Fedn., Ga. Canoeing Assn., Nat. Audubon Soc., Omicron Delta Kappa, Alpha Tau Omega, Alpha Pi Mu. Club: Sagamore Community (trustee). Author: (with Joseph J. Moder) Project Management With CPM and PERT, 1964, 2d edit., 1970. Contbr. articles to profl. jours. Home: 1711 Timberland Rd NE Atlanta GA 30345 Office: 3376 Peachtree Road NE Suite 402 Atlanta GA 30326

PHILLIPS, CECIL VERNON, elec. engr.; b. Hutchinson, Kan., Nov. 24, 1914; s. Charles Ezra and Ina (Boone) P.; student Hutchinson Jr. Coll., 1933-35; B.S. in Elec. Engring., Kan. State U., 1939; m. Mary Elizabeth Nolder, July 2, 1939; children—Inabelle Marlene (Mrs. John R. Wright), Roger Vernon. Div. engr. Kan. Power & Light Co., Hiawatha, 1939-43; utility engr. State Commn. Revenue and Taxation, Topeka, 1943-50; electronic engr. telephone div. Rural Electrification Adminstrn., Washington, 1950-52; elec. engr. USAF, Washington, 1952—. Instr. engring. sci., mgmt. war tng. program U. Kan., 1942-43. Scoutmaster, Sunflower council Boy Scouts Am., 1946-47. Recipient Outstanding Performance award Dept. Air Force, 1968. Mem. Nat., Kan. socs. profl. engrs., Am. Legion, Soc. Am. Mil. Engrs., Kappa Eta Kappa. Presbyn. (deacon 1954-57, ruling elder 1964-67). Home: 2001 Columbia Pike 306 Arlington VA 22204 Office: Hdqrs USAF (AFPRE) Washington DC 20330

PHILLIPS, CHARLES GAYLE, oil field equipment co. exec.; b. Greenville, Tex., June 12, 1931; s. Charles Herbert and Jessie Mae (Bradshaw) P.; B.S., Tex. A. and M. U., 1953; m. Ann Judice, Nov. 24, 1956; children—Stephanie (Mrs. George Dekerlegand, Jr.), Gayle, Matt, Paula. Petroleum engr. Texaco, Inc., South Tex. area, 1955-58; sales engr. Axelson, Inc., Marrero, La., 1958-60, dist. mgr., Lafayette, La., 1960-67, area sales mgr., Houston, 1967, mgr. engring., Longview, Tex., 1967-68, v.p. marketing and engring., 1968-69, pres., 1969—, also dir.; dir. USI Venezolana, S.A., Burtonwood, S.A., UIS Can. Ltd. Bd. dirs. Good Shepherd Hosp., Longview. Served with C.E., AUS, 1953-55. Mem. Soc. Petroleum Engrs., Am. Inst. Mining, Metall. and Petroleum Engrs., Petroleum Equipment Suppliers Assn. Episcopalian. Club: Deep East Texas A. and M. (Longview). Home: 4 Lindsey Lane Longview TX 75601 Office: PO Box 2427 Longview TX 75601

PHILLIPS, DORIS JEAN STURGIS (MRS. CAREY W. PHILLIPS, JR.), physician; b. Birmingham, Ala.; d. Franklin and Bethel (Crow) Sturgis; A.B., Samford U., 1946; M.D., Med. Coll. Ala., 1950; postgrad. Washington U., St. Louis, 1952-54; m. Carey W. Phillips Jr., Sept. 14, 1951; children—Anne Sturgis, Paula Beth, Jean Carey. Intern, Univ. Hosp., Birmingham, 1950-51; resident St. Louis Children's Hosp.; practice medicine specializing in pediatric allergy, Birmingham; mem. staff Children's Hosp., Birmingham; asso. clin. prof. pediatrics Med. Coll. Ala., Birmingham, 1954—. Mem. Women's Aux. Birmingham Symphony, Arlington Hist. Soc., A.M.A., Ala., Jefferson County med. socs., So. Med. Assn., Am. Acad. Pediatrics, Am. Coll. Allergists, Am. Acad. Allergy, Jefferson County Pediatric Soc., Med. Progress Assembly, D.A.R., Delta Zeta. Home: 2930 Carlisle Rd Birmingham AL 35213 Office: 942 S 18th St Birmingham AL 35205

PHILLIPS, ERNEST FRANKLIN, mayor; b. Fork Mountain, Tenn., Oct. 25, 1940; s. Lonas and Eva (Jones) P.; B.S. in Bus. Adminstrn., Tenn. Tech. U., 1963; m. Anne Slater, Apr. 1, 1967; children—Theresa Eileen, Ernest Franklin, Lonas Denton. Sales rep. Pomona Pipe Products Corp., Greensboro, N.C., 1965-67; owner Phillips Coal Co., Oliver Springs Tenn., 1967—; mayor Oliver Springs, 1973—. Mem. Oliver Springs Jr. C. of C. (dir.). Home: Route 3 Spring St Oliver Springs TN 37840 Office: PO Box 303 Oliver Springs TN 37840

PHILLIPS, FRANCES MARIE, univ. ofcl.; b. Hale Center, Tex., Nov. 8, 1918; d. Clyde C. and Ada (Stutzman) Phillips; B.A., West Tex. State Coll., 1940, M.A., 1946; Ph.D. (Univ. fellow), U. N.M., 1956; postgrad. (Fulbright scholar), U. London, 1954-55. Tchr. pub. schs. Channing, Miami, Tex., Palisade, Colo., Tucumcari, N.M., 1940-46; supr. State Tchrs. Coll. Campus High Sch., Wayne, Neb., 1947-51; instr. U. Md. Overseas Program, Eng., 1955; grad. asst. U. N.M., 1955-56; asst., asso. prof. history Sul Ross State Coll., Alpine, Tex., 1956-60, prof. history, dean grad. div., 1962-71; asst. prof. Mankato (Minn.) State Coll., 1960-62; dir. baccalaureate programs coordinating bd. Tex. Coll. and Univ. System, Austin, 1971—. Mem. Tex. Bd. Examiners for Tchr. Edn., 1972—; mem. Tex. Adv. Council for Ednl. Personnel Devel., 1972—; chmn. bd. Wesley Found., Carlsbad Dist., 1962-66; v.p. Assn. Tex. Grad. Schs., 1967-69, pres., 1969-70. Mem. Am. Assn. U. Women, Am. Hist. Assn., Orgn. Am. Historians, N.M. Hist. Soc., N.E.A., Tex. Assn. Coll. Tchrs., Tex. Tchrs. Assn., Alpha Chi, Phi Kappa Phi, Phi Alpha Theta, Delta Gamma Kappa. Democrat. Methodist (mem. N.M. Conf. Bd. Edn., ch. ofcl. bd.). Research in Anglo-American relations, 1954-56, 1962. Home: 8700 Millway Dr Austin TX 78758 Office: Box 12788 Capitol Station Austin TX 78711

PHILLIPS, GLYN RONALD, judge; b. nr. Clintwood, Va., Jan. 9, 1923; s. Robert A. and Rachel (Kiser) P.; A.B., Lincoln Meml U., 1946, LL.D., 1973; student Carson Newman Coll., 1943, Northwestern U., 1944; LL.B., U. Va., 1948; postgrad. U. Nev., 1969; grad. Am. Acad. Jud. Edn., U. Ala., 1972, U. Colo., 1973; m. Rita Lambert, Oct. 7, 1950; children—Deborah Lee, Jennifer Lynn, Glyn Ronald. Admitted to Va. bar, 1948, practiced in Clintwood, 1948-56; atty. for Commonwealth of Va., 1956-60; judge 27th Jud. Circuit, Clintwood, 1967—. Vice pres. Wise (Va.) Appalachian Regional Hosp., 1968—, Cumberland Bank and Trust Co., Clintwood, 1972—. Mem. Va. Ho. of Dels., 1952-56; chmn. Dickenson County Democratic party, 1952-56. Bd. dirs. Johnston Meml. Hosp., Abingdon, Va. Served as lt. USNR, 1943-46: PTO. Mem. Am., Va. bar assns., Council on Ministries (chmn. 1969—). Methodist. Kiwanian (lt. gov. 1964). Address: Box 598 Clintwood VA 25228

PHILLIPS, GRACE BRIGGS, research center exec.; b. Mobile, Ala., Apr. 15, 1923; d. Grace Briggs and Annie Captoliz (Decell) P.; B.S., U. Md., 1954; Ph.D. (Founders Day award), N.Y.U., 1964; m. Clemmie Louise Butts, Dec. 29, 1951; children—Lee Briggs, Mary Louise, Robert Briggs. Asst. dir. indsl. health and safety Ft. Detrick (Md.), 194—66; with USPHS, Houston, 1966-67; dir. biol. safety and control Becton, Dickinson, Balt., 1967-69, dir. Research Center, Raleigh, N.C., 1969—; cons. NASA, USPHS. Served with Chem. Corps, AUS, 1943-46. Sec. Army Research and Study fellow, 1969. Fellow Am. Pub. Health Assn., Am. Acad. Microbiology; mem. Am. Assn. for Contamination Control (pres.). Author: Microbial Contamination Control Facilities, 1969. Contbr. articles to profl. jours. Home: Route 6 Springdale Estates Raleigh NC 27612 Office: PO Box 12016 Triangle Park NC 27709

PHILLIPS, HARMON, newspaper editor; b. Bellmont, Ill., Oct. 12, 1903; s. Charles R. and Minnie (Blair) P.; grad. high sch.; m. Lora Hutchinson, 1925; 1 son, Charles Robert. Reporter, Tulsa Tribune, 1927-37, city editor, 1937-44, mng. editor, 1944—, now exec. editor. Home: 119 S Indianapolis St Tulsa OK 74112 Office: 315 S Boulder Av Tulsa OK 74103

PHILLIPS, HARRY, judge; b. Watertown, Tenn., July 28, 1909; s. Norman Cates and Bernice (Neal) P.; A.B., Cumberland U., 1932, LL.B., 1933, LL.D., 1951; m. Virginia Major, Nov. 26, 1936; children—Harriet (Mrs. Robert E. Scott), Rachel (Mrs. Sidney E. Eagles, Jr.), Caroline (Mrs. Robert M. Ligon), Martha. Admitted to Tenn. bar, 1933; practiced in Watertown, 1933-37; mem. firm Phillips, Gullett & Steele and predecessor, Nashville, 1950-63; asst. atty. gen., Tenn., 1937-43, 46-50; exec. sec. Tenn. Code Commn., 1953-63; judge U.S. Ct. Appeals, 6th Circuit, 1963-69, chief judge, 1969—. Mem. Tenn. Legislature, 1935-37. Served to lt. comdr. JAG, USNR, 1943-46. Recipient award merit Bar Assn. Tenn., 1960. Mem. S.A.R., Order Coif (hon.), Sigma Alpha Epsilon. Baptist. Clubs: University (Cin.); Cumberland, Exchange. Author: Phillips Family History, 1935; Phillips Prichard on Wills and Administration of Estates, 1955; (with others) History of Wilson County, Tennessee, 1962. Home: 2809 Wimbledon Rd Nashville TN 37215 Office: US Ct House Nashville TN 37203 also US Ct House Cincinnati OH 45202

PHILLIPS, JEAN M. MAHONY (MRS. PAYTON GRAY PHILLIPS), psychologist, educator; b. Portland, Me., Oct. 8, 1927; d. Daniel Patrick and Ethel (Stevens) Mahony; B.A., U. Okla., 1957; Ed.M., Boston U., 1962, Ed.D., 1964; m. Payton Gray Phillips, Jan. 27, 1945 (div. 1966); 1 son, Patrick Gray. Elementary sch. tchr., East Stoneham, Me., 1946-47; therapist Okla. Speech and Hearing Clinic, Oklahoma City, 1956; elementary tchr., Natrona County, Wyo., 1957-58; psychometrist Wyo. Dept. Edn., 1958; spl. edn. tchr. jr. high and high sch., Corcoran, Cal., 1958-60; lectr. psychology U. Alaska, College, 1960-61; asst. then asso. prof. psychology No. Mich. U., Marquette, 1964-70, dir. counseling center, 1965-70; staff psychologist, then sr. psychologist, dept. psychol. services Prince George's County Bd. Edn., Upper Marlboro, Md.; trainee, then trainer Nat. Drug Edn. Program for State of Md.; pvt. practice; tng. program South Shore Guidance Center, Quincy, Mass., 1962-63; diagnostic cons. Upper Peninsula Child Guidance Center, Cath. Social Services Cuban program, K.I. Sawyer AFB, Gwinn, Mich., Vocational Rehab. Office, county probate ct., pub. schs.; cons. Loudon County (Va.) Sch. System, U.S. Office of Edn. Pres. Community Social Services Orgn.; mem. Zone 3 Health Planning Council-Mental Health Com.; mem. adv. council to Probate Ct.; mem. adv. com. on women in services Dept. Def., 1971-73; supr. psychol. services Prince George's County (Md.) Bd. Edn., 1973—; field reader Bur. Edn. for Handicapped, U.S. Office of Edn. Nat. Def. Edn. Act. fellow, 1961-64. Mem. A.A.A.S., Am. Assn. Mental Deficiency, Am. Psychol. Assn., Council Exceptional Children (past sec.-treas. Kings County, Cal.); Phi Beta Kappa, Alpha Lambda Delta, Kappa Delta Pi, Pi Lambda Theta. Episcopalian. Home: 6423 Carriage Dr Alexandria VA 22310 Office: Instructional Services Bldg Bd Edn Upper Marlboro MD 20870

PHILLIPS, JOEL PATRICK, JR., citrus coop. exec.; b. nr. Orlando, Fla., Aug. 23, 1921; s. Joel Patrick and Grace (Horrop) P.; student Maryville Coll., 1940-42, Nat. U. Mexico, 1951, Rollins Coll., 1950; m. Elizabeth A. Bryant, Sept. 1942; children—Robert Patrick, John H., Barbara Grace. Pilot, Fla. Airways, Orlando, 1946-48; citrus grower and trucking, Winter Park Fla., 1949-57; pub. relations, asst. mgr. Plymouth (Fla.) Citrus Growers Assn., 1957-62, exec. v.p., dir., gen. mgr., 1962—; v.p., dir. Plymouth Citrus Products Coop.; dir. The State Bank of Apopka, Grower's Loan & Guarantee, Seold-Sweet Growers, Inc. Pres. Central Fla. council Boy Scouts Am., 1962—, Orange County chpt. Am. Cancer Soc., 1958—; mem. nat. adv. council Small Bus. Adminstrn. Del. Republican Nat. Conv., 1960, 64. Served with USAAF, 1944-46. Home: 2233 Howard Dr Winter Park FL 32789 Office: Plymouth FL 32768

PHILLIPS, JOHN TAYLOR, judge; b. Greenville, S.C., Aug. 20, 1921; s. Walter Dixon and Mattie Sue (Taylor) P.; student Glenville State Coll., 1949-52; J.D., Mercer U., 1955; m. Elizabeth Parrish, Dec. 18, 1954; children—John Allen, Mary Susan, Linda Lea, Julia Taylor. Salesman, Brown & Williamson Tobacco Corp., Miami, Fla., 1941-47; W. Va. sales mgr. Penick & Ford Ltd., 1947-49; salesman Dan Williams Brokerage, Charleston, W.Va., 1949-50; admitted to Ga. bar, 1954; judge State Ct. Bibb County, 1964—; dir. trial practice and proc. Mercer U. Law Sch., 1968—. Bd. dirs. Bibb County Heart Fund; bd. dirs. United Cerebral Palsy, nat. v.p. Mem. Ga. Ho. of Reps., 1959-63, Ga. Senate, 1963-64. Served with USMC, 1942-45, 50-51. Decorated Purple Heart. Mem. Am., Ga., Macon bar assns. Methodist. Lion. Home: 1735 Winston Dr Macon GA 31206 Office: Courthouse Macon GA 31201

PHILLIPS, JOSEPH ROBINSON, psychiatrist; b. Clarksville, Tenn., Dec. 28, 1931; s. Fletcher P. and Elizabeth (New) P.; B.S., Tenn. A. and I. U., 1954, M.S., 1956; postgrad. U. Neb., 1955-56; M.D., Meharry Med. Coll., 1963; m. Sarah L. Wesley, May 31, 1956; children—Joseph Robinson II, De Natalie Christine, Vincent Wesley, De Lanie Maria. Acting chmn., instr. dept. biology Clark Coll., 1956-58; asst. prof. dept. anatomy Meharry Med. Coll., Nashville, 1959-68, instr. dept. psychiatry, 1968, asst. prof., 1970-73, asso. prof., 1973—, asso. grad. faculty in anatomy, 1969—; intern Hubbard Hosp., Nashville, 1963-64, resident, 1965-68; practice medicine specializing in psychiatry, Nashville, 1963—; cons. psychiatrist Nat. Inst. Mental Health, Matthew Walker Neighborhood Health Center; mem. adv. bd. Am. Sickle Cell Found. Bd. dirs. Big Bros. Agy. Am. Mem. Am., Tenn. psychiat. assns., Nat., So., Vol. State med. assns., R.F. Boyd Med. Soc., Nashville Acad. Medicine, Tenn. Med. Assn., Beta Kappa Chi, Omega Psi Phi. Home: 6512 Cornwall Dr Nashville TN 37205 Office: 1916 Patterson St Nashville TN 37203

PHILLIPS, MARCELLA LINDEMAN (MRS. JAMES F. PHILLIPS), physicist; b. Cumberland, Ia., Jan. 15, 1901; d. Frank and Marie (Marley) Lindeman; grad. Highland Park Coll., 1917; B.A., State U. Ia., 1921, M.S., 1922; m. James F. Phillips, June 27, 1927; children—Laura Marley, Frederica Lindeman (Mrs. Ulric Henry Weil). Asst. physicist State U. Ia., 1919-22; instr. Hunter Coll., N.Y.C., 1924-25; physicist Gen. Electric Co., Nela Park Lab., Cleve., 1925-27, Thomas and Hochwait Lab., Dayton, O., 1930-31; prof. physics Adamson U., Manila, Philippines, 1937-39; physicist Carnegie Inst., 1940-42, Nat. Bur. Standards, Washington, 1942-51, Mass. Inst. Tech., 1951-53, cons. physicist, 1953—, also cos. including Am. Car & Foundry Industries, Electro-Physics Lab., Columbia, Md., Internat. Tel. & Tel., Comite Consultativ Internat.-Radio, Union Radio Sci. Internat., 1953—. Mem. Am. Phys. Soc., Am. Geophys. Union, Washington Philos. Soc., Acoustical Soc. Am., Washington Acad. Sci., I.E.E.E. (chmn. wave propagation com. 1956-62), Sigma Xi, Contbr. profl. publs. Address: 2510 Virginia Av NW Washington DC 20037

PHILLIPS, ORIE LEON, judge; b. nr. Viola, Ill., Nov. 20, 1885; s. Edward and Susan (Thompson) P.; student Knox Coll. 1904-05; J.D., U. Mich., 1908, LL.D., 1935 E.D., Colo. Sch. Mines, 1940; LL.D., U. Denver, 1951, Colo. Coll., 1951, Knox Coll., 1955, Trinity Coll., 1955; m. Helen Mercedes Bissell, June 21, 1910 (dec. Feb. 1968). Admitted to N.M. bar, 1909, Fed. bar, 1912; practiced in Raton, N.M., 1910-23; asst. dist. atty. 8th Dist., N.M., 1912-16; majority leader N.M. Senate, 1923; U.S. Dist. judge, N.M., 1923-29; U.S. Circuit judge, 1929—; chief judge U.S. 10th Circuit, 1941-56. Vis. prof. law Northwestern U., 1936-37, U. Mich., 1939; commencement address Freedoms Found., 1951; council chmn. of Survey of Legal Profession of Am. Bar Assn. 1947-60. Recipient medal, citation Am. Bar Assn., 1950. Mem. Am., Colo., N.M. bar assns. Author: Conduct of Judges. Home: 1785 Gulf Shore Blvd N Naples FL 33940 Office: PO Box 2210 Denver CO 30201

PHILLIPS, PAUL WALLER, JR., mag. editor; b. Salisbury, Md., Nov. 27, 1927; s. Paul Waller and Helen (Wilhelm) P.; A.B. in Journalism, U. S.C., 1953; m. Joan Kay Coleman, Apr. 28, 1956; 1 dau., Kathryn Helen. Reporter U.P.I., Columbia, S.C., 1953-57, bur. mgr., Birmingham, Ala., 1957-63; with Columbia Newspapers Inc., (S.C.), 1963-72, editor 1970-72; editor Trends mag. publ. S.C. State Devel. Bd., Columbia, 1972—, also pub. information specialist. Served with AUS, 1946-48. Mem. Sigma Delta Chi. Episcopalian. Club: Richland Sertoma (hon.). Died Mar. 10, 1974. Home: 21 Garden Springs Rd Columbia SC 29209

PHILLIPS, RAYMOND MCDONALD, former govt. ofcl.; b. Sylacuga, Ala., July 24, 1908; s. Bela Aterbide and Bessie Mae (McDonald) P.; B.S. in Elec. Engring., U. Ala., 1930; m. Patricia Margaret Lettice, June 27, 1942; children—Martha Mae, Margaret Ann, Sally Foster, Raymond McDonald. With Gen. Electric Co., 1930-31, Curtis Publ. Co., 1931-34; commd. lt. U.S. Army Res., 1930, advanced through grades to col., 1953; engr. Civilian Conservation Corp., 1935-38, engr., Eng., France, Germany, 1942-46; civilian engr., chief army engrs., Washington, 1941-42, 46-55; ret. 1960; civilian engr. U.S. P.O. Dept., Washington, 1955-71. Asst. to prof. physics U. Ala., Tuscaloosa, 1928-29, asst. to prof. elec. engring., 1929-30; rep. NRC, Washington, 1947—. Decorated Bronze Star medal (U.S.); Croix De Guerre with Star of Vermeil (France). Registered profl. engr., Ga. Mem. Nat., Va. socs. profl. engrs., U. Ala. Alumni Assn., Tau Beta Pi, Pi Mu Epsilon, Chi Beta Phi, Alpha Sigma Phi (past pres., sec.). Methodist. Club: Mt. Vernon Yacht (mem. organizing com. 1955, past dir., rec. sec.) (Alexandria, Va.). Home: 2710 S Inge St Arlington VA 22202

PHILLIPS, RICHARD DAWSON, judge; b. Jesup, Ga., May 2, 1938; s. Richard Denham and Rosalie (Dawson) P.; student Ga. So. Coll., 1957-60; LL.B., U. Ga., 1963; m. Hilda Jane Terry, Dec. 5, 1964; 1 dau., Jennifer Jane. Admitted to Ga. bar, 1962, practice in Ludowici, 1963—; judge state ct. Long County, Ludowici, 1965—. Dir. Exchange Bank, Ludowici, 1968—. Mem. Coastal Area Planning and Devel. Commn., 1968—. Mem. Long County Health Bd.; vice chmn. Long County Hosp. Authority, 1972—. Mem. Long County Jr. C. of C. (dir. 1971-72, v.p. 1972-73), Long County C. of C. (dir.), Am., Ga. bar assns., Assn. Trial Lawyers Am., Ga. Trial Lawyers Assn., Ga., Atlantic Jud. Circuit (pres. 1971-72), Phi Kappa Phi, Phi Alpha

Delta (pres. 1960-61). Democrat. Methodist (adminstrv. bd. 1969—). Home and office: PO Box 66 Ludowici GA 31316

PHILLIPS, ROBERT JAMES, chem. mfg. co. exec.; b. Mart, Tex., Aug. 25, 1922; s. William B. and Katie (Barrow) P.; B.S. in Chem. Engring., U. Tex., 1948; m. Mary Jo Bass, Dec. 27, 1944; children—Andrew Bass, Robert James II. Chem. engr. Humble Oil & Refining Co., Baytown, Tex., 1948-52; editorial dir. Gulf Pub. Co., Houston, 1952-53; with Howe-Baker Engrs., Inc., Tyler, Tex., 1955-70, v.p., 1955-60, pres., 1960-69, chmn. bd., 1970, dir., 1957-70; pres. Internat. Technovation, Inc., 1970-71; pres., chmn. bd. Amtech, Inc., 1971—; dir. Tyler Bank & Trust Co.; exec. v.p., dir. Tyler Savs. & Loan Assn. Bd. dirs. Nat. Youth Found., 1961, United Community Fund, Salvation Army. Served to capt., USAAF, World War II. Mem. Am. Chem. Soc., Tex. Soc. Profl. Engrs., Am. Inst. Chem. Engrs., E. African Wild Life Soc., Tex. Council Higher Edn. Methodist (mem. ofcl. bd.). Mason (32 deg.). Clubs: Union League Chicago; Adventurers; Shikar-Safari, The Explorers, Houston, Willow Brook Country. Home: 2107 Parkway Pl Tyler TX 75701 Office: 1909 S Broadway Tyler TX 75701

PHILLIPS, SHERMAN ALFRED, educator; b. Hope, N.M., Mar. 30, 1919; s. Soloman Alfred and Vida (Young) P.; B.S., La. State U., 1949, M.S., 1956; m. Jane Heyd, Feb. 1949 (div.); children—Sherman Alfred, Wayne, Robert. Asso. prof. La. State U., St. Joseph, 1949-55, asso. prof., Winnsboro, 1956—, supt. exptl. station, 1956—. Mem. Am. Soc. Agronomy, La. Soc. Agronomy, La. Plant Food Inst. Lion. Home: Route 5 Box 244 Winnsboro LA 71295

PHILLIPS, SILAS BENT, JR., utilities exec.; b. Portland, Ore., Feb. 3, 1915; s. Silas Bent and May (Stevenson) P.; B.S., Harvard, 1937; m. Frances May Rau, Jan. 17, 1943; children—Dabney Carr, Elizabeth May, Jane Rowland, William Stevenson. Dist. mgr. West Tex. Utilities Co., Marfa, 1953-57, adminstrv. asst., Abilene, 1957-60, v.p., 1960-64, pres., dir., also chief exec. officer, 1964-65; pres., dir. Central & S.W. Corp., Wilmington, Del., 1965—; pres., dir. CSR Services, Inc., Dallas, 1969—. Served from pvt. to maj. USAAF, 1941-46. Home: 4711 N Lindhurst Dallas TX 75229 Office: 300 Delaware Av Wilmington DE 19899 also 2828 One Main Pl Dallas TX 75250

PHILLIPS, WALTER RAY, lawyer, educator; b. Democrat, N.C., Mar. 19, 1932; s. Walter Yancey and Bonnie (Wilson) P.; A.B., U. N.C., 1954; LL.B., Emory U., 1957, LL.M., 1962, J.D., 1970; postgrad. Yale, 1965-66; m. Patricia Ann Jones, Aug. 28, 1954; children—Bonnie Ann, Rebecca Lee. Admitted to Ga. bar, 1957, Fla. bar, 1958, Tex. bar, 1969, to U.S. Supreme Ct. bar; with firm Jones, Adams, Paine & Foster, West Palm Beach, Fla., 1957-58; law clk. to chief judge U.S. Dist. Co., Atlanta, 1958-59; with firm Powell, Goldstein, Frazer & Murphy, Atlanta, 1959-60; bankruptcy judge U.S. Cts., Atlanta, 1960-64; prof. law U. N.D., 1964-65; teaching fellow Yale, 1965-66; prof. law Fla. State U., 1966-68; prof. law Tex. Tech. U., Lubbock, 1968-71; Distinguished Vis. prof. law Baylor U., 1971; atty. Commn. on Bankruptcy Laws of U.S., Washington, 1971-72, dep. dir., adminstrv. officer, 1972-73; prof. Sch. Law, U. Ga., 1973—, also chmn. grad. studies; reporter Gov.'s Legislation for Ga., 1973—. Vice pres., dir. Killearn Estates, Inc. Bd. dirs. Lubbock Day Nurseries, 1969, pres., 1970-71. Served with USAF, 1950. Mem. Am. (mem. consumer bankruptcy com. 1973—), Fed., Fla., Tex., Lubbock, Ga. (publs. com.) bar assns., Am. Judicature Soc., Phi Alpha Delta (chief tribune). Presbyn. Club: Belvedere Optimist of Decatur (dir. 1960-61). Author: Florida Law and Practice, 1960; Encyclopedia of Georgia Law, 1962; Seminar for Newly Appointed Referees in Bankruptcy, 1964; (with James William Moore) Debtors' and Creditors' Rights, Cases and Material, 1966; The Law of Debtor Relief, 1969, 2d edit., 1972; Rule 6, Moore's Federal Practice, 1969. Home: Red Fox Run Route 3 Athens GA 30601

PHILLIPS, WAYNE A., supt. schs.; b. Marshall, Ark., Oct. 15, 1905; s. William Pinkney and Ara (LaVina) P.; student Tech. Coll. Russellville (Ark.), 1930; A.B., Northeastern State Coll., Okla., 1937; M.A., U. Okla., 1950; m. Eileen B. Billington, Dec. 29, 1929; 1 dau., Wanda Elaine. Tchr. elementary schs. Searcy County, Ark., 1924-29, Haskell County, 1929-44; supt. high sch. Onapa, 1944-46, Maud, Okla., 1946-57; supt. Webbers Falls (Okla.) High Sch., 1957-71; supt. schs. Muskogee (Okla.) County, 1971—. Bd. dirs. Okla. Heart Assn., 1965-71, Am. Heart Assn., 1965-71; instl. rep. Webbers Falls council Boy Scouts Am., 1970-71. Bd. dirs. County Cancer Assn., 1957. Hon. farmer Future Farmers Am. Mem. Okla. (treas. 1971—), Muskogee County (pres. 1964-65) edn. assns., Am., Okla. assns. sch. adminstrs, Ruritan Club (charter). Baptist. Mason (32 degree, Shriner). Home: 105 N Main St Webbers Falls OK 74470 Office: Court House Muskogee OK 74401

PHILLIPS, WESLEY FLETCHER, physician; b. Asheboro, N.C., Mar. 7, 1937; s. William Roy and Hannah Dorothy (Schendel) P.; A.A., So. Pilgrim Coll., 1956; A.B., Greenville Coll., 1958; M.D., Bowman Gray Sch. Medicine, 1962; m. Patsy Darlyne Stamey, June 22, 1957; children—Pamela Michelle, Brian Keith, Dawn Rene. Intern U.S. Army Madigan Gen. Hosp., 1962-63; flight surgeon U.S. Army Hosp., Teheran, Iran, 1964-66; practice gen. medicine, Walkerson, N.C., 1966-68, Kernersville, N.C., 1968—; aviation med. examiner, 1967—; mem. staff Forsyth Meml. Hosp. Dir. Northwestern Bank of Kernersville. Bd. dirs. Unified Wesleyan Coll.; mem. dist. bd. adminstrn. N.C. Dist. Wesleyan Ch.; trustee Kernersville Wesleyan Acad. Served with USNR, 1963-64, U.S. Army, 1964. Diplomate Am. Bd. Family Practice. Mem. A.M.A., N.C., Forsyth County med. assns., Am. Acad. Family Practice, Kernersville C. of C. Methodist. Home: 104 Saddlewood Dr Kernersville NC 27284 Office: Box 727 Kernersville NC 27284

PHILLIPS, WILLIAM EARL, physician; b. Amory, Miss., July 16, 1939; s. Will J. and Lula (Dabbs) P.; student U. Miss., 1957-60, U. Vienna, Austria, 1958, Millsaps Coll., 1959, Tulane U., 1960-61; M.D., U. Tenn., 1964; M.P.H., U. Cal. at Los Angeles, 1967. Intern, City of Memphis Hosps., 1964-65; pub. health physician Memphis and Shelby County Health Dept., 1965, dir. Tb control, dir. chronic disease control, 1967-72, dir. disease detection, 1972—; asst. prof. U. Tenn. Coll. Medicine, 1972—. Mem. chest disease task force Tenn. Comprehensive Health Planning Council; mem. program com., bd. dirs. Community Action Agy. Memphis-Shelby County; mem. community service com., bd. dirs. Memphis Heart Assn.; mem. Memphis Area Council on Nutrition; program cons., bd. dirs. Planned Parenthood of Memphis, 1969—; adv. com. Memphis & Shelby County Medicare; Bd. dirs., program com. Memphis Tb and Health Assn. Recipient Community Service awards Memphis Area Council on Alcoholism, 1969, Memphis Heart Assn., 1972. Mem. A.M.A., So. Med. Assn., Tenn., Memphis and Shelby County med. socs., Am. Pub. Health Assn., Assn. State and Territorial Dirs. and Coordinators Research, Assn. Tchrs. Preventive Medicine, Am. Assn. Pub. Health Physicians, Memphis Heart Assn. (dir.), Soc. for Advanced Med. Systems, Phi Chi. Contbr. articles to profl. jours. Home: 1139 Stage Av Memphis TN 38127 Office: 814 Jefferson Av Memphis TN 38105

PHILLIPS, WILLIAM HENRY, civil engr.; b. Lexington, Ky., July 21, 1945; s. Jack Cornelius and Martha (West) P.; B.S., U. Ky., 1967, M.S., 1968; m. Misha Andrea Williams, July 5, 1969. Civil engr. Ky. Bur. Hwys., Frankfort, 1967-69, 72—. Served with USMCR, 1969-72; Vietnam. Registered profl. engr., Ky. Mem. Ky. Assn. Hwy. Engrs., Ky. Soc. Profl. Engrs., Chi Epsilon, Tau Beta Pi. Home: 3821 Walhampton Dr Lexington KY 40503 Office: Daley Av Frankfort KY 40601

PHILLIPS, WILLIAM MILLER, editor; b. Pitts., Nov. 21, 1920; s. William Shannon and Elva (Miller) P.; B.S., U. Pitts., 1942; M.S., Columbia U., 1950; m. Marjorie I. Higgins, Oct. 20, 1944; children—Stacie M., William S., Shannon H. Editor, reporter Lake Charles (La.) Am. Press, 1948, Jamestown N.Y. Post Jour., 1949, Pitts. Post Gazette, 1949, St. Petersburg (Fla.) Times, 1950, Tampa (Fla.) Tribune, 1950, Miami Herald, 1951-65, also feature editor, Sunday editor, 1958-65; mng. editor Tallahassee Democrat, 1965—. Instr. U. Miami, 1960-65. Served with USNR, 1941-45: PTO. Mem. Fla. Soc. Newspaper Editors, Fla. Press Assn., A.P. Mng. Editors Assn., Sigma Delta Chi, Delta Tau Delta. Elk, Rotarian. Home: 3206 Brookforest Rd Tallahassee FL 32303 Office: 277 N Magolia Dr Tallahassee FL 32302

PHILLIPS, WILLIS PAUL, dentist; b. Hale Center, Tex., Oct. 7, 1927; s. Clyde C. and Ada Erma (Stutzman) P.; B.S., Tex. Tech. Coll., 1947; postgrad. Tex. A. and M., 1948, Wayland Coll., 1962, West Tex. State U., 1963; D.D.S., Baylor U., 1967; m. Grace Holden, Apr. 6, 1950; children—Charles Vincent, Barbara Camille, Brenda Karen. Instr., Knox County Vocational Sch., Munday, Tex., 1948-50, Hale County Vocational Sch., Plainview, Tex., 1950-53; owner, operator dairy and farm, Hale Center, Tex., 1953-63; instr. Baylor U. Coll. Dentistry, Dallas, summer 1967; pvt. practice dentistry, Weatherford, Tex., 1967—; sec., dir. Preston Park Gas Coop., Hale Center, 1961-63. Mem. Planning and Zoning Bd., City of Weatherford, 1969—. Mem. Am., Tex. dental assns., Fort Worth Dist. Dental Soc., Am. Soc. Dentistry for Children. Methodist (lay leader 1968-71). Mason, Rotarian (bd. dirs. 1969-71, pres. 1970). Patentee in field. Home: 603 Hilltop Dr Weatherford TX 76086 Office: 200 E Rentz St Weatherford TX 76086

PHILPOTT, ALBERT LEE, legislator, lawyer; b. Philpott, Va., July 29, 1919; s. John E. and Gertrude (Prillaman) P.; B.A., U. Richmond, 1941, LL.B., 1947; m. Katherine Spencer, Aug. 7, 1941; children—Judy (Mrs. Philip Steward Marstiller), Albert Lee. Admitted to Va. bar, 1947; practiced in Bassett, 1947-52, 58—; partner firm Philpott & McGhee, Bassett, 1958—; commonwealth's atty. Henry County (Va.), 1952-57; mem. Va. Ho. of Dels., 1958—. Dir. 1st Nat. Bank, Bassett, Va. Bd. dirs. Patrick Henry Mental Health Clinic, Martinsville, Va. Served with USAAF, 1941-45. Mem. Am., Va., Martinsville, Henry County bar assns., Am. Legion, Lambda Chi Alpha. K.P., Moose, Elk. Home: Route 4 Bassett VA 24055 Office: Main St Bassett VA 24055

PHILPOTT, CHARLES WILLIAM, educator; b. Canadian, Tex., Jan. 29, 1932; s. George Arthur and Reba (Johnson) P.; B.A. in Biology, Tex. Technol. Coll., 1957, M.S., 1958; Ph.D., Tulane U., 1962; postdoctorate Harvard, 1962-64; m. Loralee I. Lewis, June 2, 1960; children—Charles A., Pamela B. Mem. faculty dept. biology Rice U., Houston, 1964—, asso. prof., 1966-70, prof., 1970—, also headmaster Baker Residential Coll., 1967-73. Served with AUS, 1954-56. Recipient Brown outstanding teaching award Rice U., 1970, spl. service award Baker Coll., 1973; Danforth asso., 1966—. Mem. Tex. Soc. Electron Microscopy (pres. 1965), Am. Soc. Cell Biology, Am. Soc. Zoologists, N.Y. Acad. Scis. Home: 2323 Gramercy St Houston TX 77025 Office: 6100 S Main St Houston TX 77001

PHINNEY, CARL LAWRENCE, lawyer; b. Marble Falls, Tex., Oct. 22, 1904; s. C. D. and Lillie (Shugart) P.; student U. Tex., 1921-27; m. Louise Snow, Aug. 17, 1928; children—Louise Snow (Mrs. Josef Caldwell), Carl Lawrence. Admitted to Tex. bar, 1931; practiced in Dallas, 1931—; sr. partner firm Phinney, Hallman, Pulley & Coke, Dallas, 1939—. Mem. Tex. N.G., 1925-61, maj. gen. comdg. 36th Inf. Div., 1953-61. Decorated Silver Star, Legion of Merit (U.S.); Italian Cross of Officer cavalier Order of Sts. Maurizio and Lazzara. Mem. Mil. Order World Wars, Am., Tex., Dallas bar assns., Soc. Mayflower Descs., N.G. Assn. (past v.p.). Democrat. Methodist. Mason (33 deg., Shriner). Home: 4204 Shenandoah Av Dallas TX 75205 Office: First Nat Bank Bldg Dallas TX 75202

PHIPPS, BENJAMIN KIMBALL, II, lawyer; b. Boston, Jan. 16, 1933; s. Benjamin Kimball and Bertha Elizabeth (Forsyth) P.; B.S. in Commerce, U. Va., 1955, LL.B., 1958; m. Phyllis Jarrett Anderson, Jan. 10, 1962; children—Lisa Jarrett, Christina Caroline. Admitted to Fla. bar, 1964; editor Municipal Code Corp., Tallahassee, 1964-65; practice law, Tallahassee, 1965—. Chmn. Historic Tallahassee Preservation Bd., 1970—; pres. Fla. Heritage Found., 1967. Counsel tax com. Fla. Ho. of Reps., 1966-70, counsel to speaker, 1972—. Trustee Maclay Sch. Served to capt., airborne arty. AUS, 1958-64. Mem. Am., Tallahassee, bar assns., Jefferson Soc., Sigma Alpha Epsilon, Phi Alpha Delta, Phi Delta Epsilon. Clubs: Cosmos, Exchange, Tiger Bay (dir.) (Tallahassee). Contbr. articles in field. Home: Jubilee Thomasville Rd Tallahassee FL 32303 Office: PO Box 1351 Tallahassee FL 32302

PICCIONE, JOSEPH JAMES, lawyers, artist; b. Lafayette, La., July 23, 1916; s. Sam and Mary (Mangiapane) P.; B.A., U. Southwestern La., 1937; LL.B., Tulane U., 1940, J.D., 1969; m. Wilma Kirkland, Dec. 17, 1946; children—Juanita, Jo Ann, Sylvia Beth, Cheryl Ann, James Kirk. Admitted to La. bar, 1940, since practiced law, Lafayette; partner Peter C. Piccione and Charles N. Wooten, 1952-71, sr. mem. Piccione, Piccione & Wooten, 1966-72. Exhibited paintings in one-man show at First Nat. Bank, Lafayette, 1973. Mem. Parish Mental Health Assn., pres. 1963-64; chmn. March of Dimes, 1956; chmn. Easter Seal sale, 1958; pres. Tb Assn., 1950-59; chmn. Crippled Children and Adults Assn., 1955-56; mem., acting chmn. Lafayette Capitol Improvement Com., 1965-70; mem. Cardinal Newman Forum, U. Southwestern La., chmn., 1965-67. Pres. bd. Cardinal Newman Found., U. Southwestern La., Lafayette, 1967-69. Served to capt. AUS, 1942-46. Recipient Medal Honor Am. Legion, 1935. Mem. Nat., La. trial attys. assns., Lafayette Parish (pres. 1958-59), 15th Jud. Dist. (pres. 1960-61), La. State (bd. govs. 1972-74, com. local bar assns.) bar assns., Am., La. trial lawyers assns., Judicature Soc., Internat. Platform Assn., Order Coif. Kiwanian (pres. 1953, Outstanding Kiwanian of Year 1973). Club: Knife and Fork (pres. 1950). Bd. editors Tulane Law Review. Home: 2030 W St Mary Blvd Lafayette LA 70501 Office: 115 E Main St Lafayette LA 70501

PICKARD, JOSEPH ALLEN, supt. schs.; b. Tazewell, Ga., June 23, 1913; s. William Edwin and Clara E. (Hogg) P.; A.B., Mercer U., 1935; M.S., U. Ga., 1941; postgrad. Columbia U., U. Va., Auburn U., U. Ala. Elementary tchr. Edison, Ga., 1932-34, high sch. tchr., athletic coach, prin., 1935-36, supt., 1937-42; supt., Damascus, Ga., 1936-37; prin. jr. high sch., Lynchburg, Va., 1946-53, dir. instrn., 1953-57; supt. schs., Selma, Ala., 1957—. Dir., Am. Educators Ins. Co. Pres. United Community Services, 1967. Bd. dirs. Dallas County Scholarship Found., 1963—. Served with USAAF, 1942-46. Mem. Ala., Nat. edn. assns., Am. Assn. Sch. Adminstrs., Blue Key, Kappa Alpha, Phi Delta Kappa. Methodist. Home: 2019 Broad St Selma AL 36701 Office: PO Box F Selma AL 36701

PICKELL, CHARLES NORMAN, clergyman; b. Haddonfield, N.J., Dec. 18, 1927; s. William Norman and Ada Marie (Kelley) P.; B.A., Juniata Coll., 1949; B.D., Western Theol. Sem., Pitts., 1952; Th.M., Pitts.-Xenia Theol. Sem., 1957; postgrad. Harvard Div. Sch., 1959-60, Andover-Newton Theol. Sch., 1961-62; D.D., Sterling Coll., 1964; M.Div., Pitts. Theol. Sem., 1971; m. Christina L. Frazer, Mar. 11, 1972; children—Rachel Grace, Stuart Charles, Arthur John. Ordained to ministry Presbyn. Ch. U.S.A., 1952; pastor Chelsea Presbyn. Ch., Atlantic City, 1952-55, 1st Presbyn. Ch., Monongahela, Pa., 1955-57, United Presbyn. Ch., Newton, Mass., 1957-63, Wallace Meml. United Presbyn. Ch., Hyattsville, Md., 1963-70, Vienna (Va.) Presbyn. Ch., 1970—. Moderator, Presbytery of Boston, 1959, Synod of New Eng., 1960; chmn. ministerial relations Presbytery of Boston, 1961-63, chmn. nat. missions, 1962-63, chmn. evangelism Presbytery of Washington City, 1964-66, vice moderator, 1969, asst. stated clk., 1971; mem. Nat. Capital Union Presbytery, 1972—; guest lectr. practical theology Gordon Div. Sch., Wenham, Mass., 1958-63, trustee, 1959-70. Incorporator, bd. dirs. Gordon-Conwell Theol. Sem., Hamilton, Mass., 1968-70; trustee Gordon Coll., Wenham, 1959—, chmn. acad. affairs, 1965—; trustee Westminster Coll., New Wilmington, Pa., 1957-61. Mem. Presbyn. Hist. Soc., Am. Soc. Ch. History, Fairfax County Council of Chs., Vienna-Oakton Ministerial Assn. Author: Preaching to Meet Men's Needs, 1958; Colossians, A Study Manual, 1965; Works Count Too!, 1966; The Presbyterians, 1972. Editor, contbr.; Presbyterianism in New England, The Story of a Mission, 1962. Contbr. articles to religious publs., God.'s Minute, 1971. Office: Box 351 Vienna VA 22180 Home: 237 Church Park St NE Vienna VA 22180

PICKENS, CURTIS EDWARD, agr. co. exec.; b. Little Rock, July 28, 1931; s. Dallas and Hellen Irene (Birdsong) P.; B.S., Fla. So. Coll., 1957; m. Patricia Ellen Braymaire, Oct. 2, 1960; children—Kathey, Steven. Pres. Winter Garden KOA Inc., 1970—; pres. Citrus Grower Mgmt. Inc., Windermere, Fla., 1969—; pres. Winter Garden Travel Center, Inc., 1972—; gen. mgr. Brevard Groves, Inc.; dir. West Orange Indsl. Park. Mem. Windermere Town Council, 1969-70. Bd. dirs. YMCA; trustee Endgewood Boys Ranch, 1971—. Served with USNR, 1950-54. Recipient Outstanding Service award Fla. So. Coll., 1966. Mem. Fla. KOA Campground Owners Assn. (past pres., dir.). Rotarian (pres. 1969-70). Home: 618 Buller St Windermere FL 32786 Office: 279 Hwy 50 Winter Garden FL 32787

PICKENS, WILLIAM EDWARD, architect; b. Austin, Tex., July 2, 1941; s. Jack Hayden and Ella (Salge) P.; B.Arch., U. Tex., 1965; m. Dagmar Dow Dunn, Jan. 23, 1965; 1 son, William Shannon. Archtl. apprentice R.G. Roessner, Austin, 1965-67; with Perkins & Will, architects, Washington, 1969-71; pres. Civil Systems, Inc., and team architecture, Alexandria, Va., 1971—. Mem. Alexandria Bd. Trade. Trustee Barker Found., Waashington. Served with AUS, 1967-69. Decorated Army Commendation medal. Mem. Sphinx, Sigma Alpha Epsilon. Episcopalian. Important works include: Am. Hort. Soc. Hdqrs., Mt. Vernon, Va., Wildlife Preserve, Largo, Md. Home: 807 Arcturus on the Potomac Alexandria VA 22308 Office: 110 S Pitt St Alexandria VA 22314

PICKETT, OWEN BRADFORD, legislator, lawyer; b. Richmond, Va., Aug. 31, 1930; s. Robert L. and Mary J. (Southworth) P.; B.S., Va. Poly. Inst., 1952; LL.B., U. Richmond, 1955; postgrad. U. Va., 1958-59; m. Sybil Catherine Kelly, Dec. 19, 1952; children—Laura Catherine, Karen Theresa, Mary Bradford. Admitted to Va. bar, 1955, D.C. bar, 1961; practiced in Richmond, 1955-56, Virginia Beach, 1965—; practice pub. accounting, Richmond, 1956-58; asst. to v.p., treas. Tex. Utilities Co., Dallas, 1958-60; gen. counsel Gallant, Inc., Washington, 1960-63; controller Kettler Bros., Inc., Washington, 1964-65; mem. Va. Ho. Dels., 1972—. Chmn. Virginia Beach City Democratic Com., 1967-71; mem. Dem. State Central Com. Va., 1968—; mem. Hampton Rds. Area Com., 1969-70. C.P.A., Va. Mem. Am., Va., D.C., Virginia Beach bar assns., Va. Trial Lawyers Assn., Am. Inst. C.P.A.'s. Rotarian, Lion, Moose. Club: Ruritan (Princess Anne). Home: 321 Apasus Trail Virginia Beach VA 23452 Office: 2859 Virginia Beach Blvd Virginia Beach VA 23452

PICKHOLTZ, RAYMOND LEE, educator; b. N.Y.C., Apr. 12, 1932; s. Isadore and Rose (Turkish) P.; B.S. in Elec. Engring., Coll. City N.Y., 1954, M.S. in Elec. Engring., 1958; Ph.D., Poly. Inst. Bklyn., 1965; m. Eda Rebecca Mittler, June 30, 1958; children—Robin, Andrew, Julie. Research engr., RCA Labs., Princeton, N.J., 1954-57, ITT Labs., Nutley, N.J., 1957-61; asso. prof. elec. engring. Poly. Inst. Bklyn., 1961-71; prof. George Washington U., Washington, 1972—. Cons., IBM, Fairchild Industries, Tech. Service Corp., Touche-Ross, and others. Recipient Research award RCA Labs., 1954; NSF grantee, 1967-68, 72-75, NASA grantee, 1966-71. Mem. Am. Assn. U. Profs., I.E.E.E. (sr.; exec. com. 1957—), Sigma Xi, Eta Kappa Nu. Contbr. articles to profl. jours. Patentee communications electronics. Asso. editor I.E.E.E. Transactions, 1971—. Home: 3613 Glenbrook Rd Fairfax VA 22030 Office: Dept Engineering and Applied Science George Washington Univ Washington DC 20006

PICKLE, CECYL LAMAR, lawyer; b. Jacksonville, Fla., June 8, 1925; s. Henry A. and Amanda (Houston) P.; student Fla. So. Coll., 1946-48; LL.B., U. Fla., 1951; m. Margot Reinburg, June 23, 1951; children—Jean Carol, Bruce Henry. Admitted to Fla. bar, 1951; claims adjuster U.S. Fidelity and Guaranty Co., Miami, Fla., 1951-53; practiced in Miami, 1953—; asso. firm Fowler, White, Gillen, Yancey and Humkey, 1953-55, Knight, Underwood, Peters, Hoeveler and Pickle, 1955—. Trustee, adv. council Bapt. Hosp., Miami, 1962-66. Served with USAAF, 1944-45. Mem. Fla. Bar (vice chmn. continuing legal edn. 1971), Am., Dade County bar assns., Internat. Assn. Ins. Counsel, Dade County Defense Bar (dir. 1965-66, 70, treas. 1971, pres. elect 1972), Phi Alpha Delta, Lambda Chi Alpha. Democrat, Baptist. Clubs: Coral Gables Country, Kiwanis (pres. 1965). Contbr. articles profl. jours. Home: 3401 Toledo St Coral Gables FL 33134 Office: Ingraham Bldg Miami FL 33131

PICKLE, J. J., congressman; b. Roscoe, Tex., Oct. 11, 1913; s. J. B. and Mary P.; B.A., U. Tex.; children—Peggy (Mrs. James Norris), Richard McCarroll and Graham McCarroll. Area dir. Nat. Youth Adminstrn., 1938-41; co-organizer Sta. KVET, Austin, Tex.; pub. relations and advt. bus.; dir. Tex. Democratic Exec. Com., 1957-60; mem. Tex. Employment Commn., 1961-63; mem. 88th-93d congresses 10th Dist. Tex. Served with USNR, World War II. Home: 3900 Watson Pl Washington DC 20016 Office: Cannon House Office Bldg Washington DC 20515

PICKRAL, GEORGE MONROE, JR., educator; b. Gretna, Va., Jan. 2, 1922; s. George Monroe and Ann Elizabeth (Gay) P.; B.S., Va. Mil. Inst., 1943; M.S., Miami U., Oxford, O., 1950; Ph.D., U. Cin., 1953; m. Edna Moore McCormick, Mar. 10, 1945; children—James, Thomas, Robert, Janet (Mrs. James C. Ruoff), Elizabeth. Instr. chemistry Va. Mil. Inst., Lexington, 1946-49, prof., 1952—. Scoutmaster Stonewall Jackson council Boy Scouts Am., 1961-65. Mem. Lexington Planning Commn., 1964-70, vice chmn., 1969. Served to lt. USMCR, 1943-46. Mem. Am. Chem. Soc., Sigma Xi, Phi

Lambda Upsion. Presbyn. Kiwanian. Home: 501 Brooke Lane Lexington VA 24450 Office: Dept Chemistry Virginia Military Inst Lexington VA 24450

PICKRELL, THOMAS RICHARD, petroleum co. exec.; b. Jermyn, Tex., Dec. 30, 1926; s. Mont Bolt and Martha Alice (Dodson) P.; B.B.A., N. Tex. State U., 1951, M.B.A., 1952; postgrad. Ohio State U., 1954-55, Ind. U., 1967; m. Earline Bowen, Sept. 9, 1950; children—Thomas Wayne, Michael Bowen, Kent Richard, Paul Keith. Accountant, Hunt Oil Co., Dallas, 1952-54; instr. Ohio State U., 1954-55; internal auditor Continental Oil Co., Ponca City, Okla., 1955-61, dir. coordinating and planning, 1961-62, mgr. accounting, Houston, 1965-67, asst. controller, Ponca City, 1967—; asst. prof. Okla. State U., 1962-63; controller Douglas Oil Co., Los Angeles, 1963-65. Sr. lectr. U. So. Cal., 1964-65. Bd. dirs. Kay Guidance Clinic Found, Ponca City, Ponca City YMCA. Served with AUS, 1945-46; ETO. Mem. Financial Execs. Inst. (dir., pres.), Am. Inst. C.P.A.'s, Am. Accounting Assn., C. of C., Am. Petroleum Inst. (accounting research com. 1965—), Beta Gamma Sigma, Beta Alpha Psi. Presbyn. Rotarian. Home: 2205 Meadowbrook St Ponca City OK 74601 Office: Box 1267 Ponca City OK 74601

PICO, ALBERTO A., nat. guard officer; b. Coamo, P.R., Aug. 23, 1918; s. Carlos and Eulalia (Leon) P.; student La. State U.; B.A., U. P.R.; m. Mignon Valls, May 9, 1942; 1 dau., Mignon (Mrs. Walter Vivaldi). Served to capt. AUS, 1940-45; to maj., 1950-53; to maj. gen. Res., ret. 1972. Decorated Bronze Star, Legion of Merit, Combat Infantryman's badge; Mil. Cross Antonio Marino (Colombia). Mem. N.G. Assn. U.S., P.R. N.G. (adj. gen. for P.R. 1969—), U.S. Custom Assn., Armor Assn. U.S., Assn. U.S. Army, Nat. Customs Service Assn., Phi Eta Mu. Clubs: Casino (Coamo); San Juan Yacht; Deportivo de Ponce, Ponce Yacht and Fishing; P.R. Nat. Guard Officers. Address: Santa Anastacia St Cupey El Vigia Rio Piedras PR

PICOU, LEON ADAM, JR., lawyer; b. Garyville, La., Oct. 3, 1912; s. Leon Adam and Mary (Tufant) P.; B.A., Southwestern State U., Lafayette, La., 1936; J.D., La. State U., 1951; m. Orel Palmer, July 17, 1937; children—Saundra (Mrs. W. Lee Overton), Cynthia (Mrs. Stanley Excel Branton). High sch. tchr., Destrehan, La., 1936-40; dir. pub. welfare, Lafourche Parish, La., 1940-41; asst. mgr. Wesco Paints Inc., Good Hope, La., 1941-42; La. state parole and probation officer, 1942-44, 45-48; admitted to La. bar, 1951, since practiced in St. Francisville. Dist. atty. 20th Jud. Dist. Ct. La., 1972—. Served with M.C., AUS, 1944-45. Mem. La. Municipal Assn. City Attys. (pres.), Holy Name Soc. (past pres.), Gamma Eta Gamma. Roman Catholic (chmn. cemetery com.). Lion. Home and office: Ferdinand St St Francisville LA 70775

PIEPER, SAMUEL JOHN LOUIS, JR., dir. health center; b. Beeville, Tex., Oct. 14, 1931; s. Samuel John Louis and Beulah S.N. (Pullin) P.; student Rice U., 1948-51; M.D. cum laude, Baylor U., 1955; m. Joan Bruce Woods, July 14, 1962; children—Wanda Lynne, Melanie Ruth, Cheryl Yvonne, Karen Lee, John Samuel, David Bernard. Intern Meth. Hosp., Houston, 1955-56; resident neurology Baylor U. Hosp., 1958-61, psychiatry Northwestern U., Evanston, Ill., 1966-68, fellow, 1968-69; instr. neurology Baylor U. Coll. Medicine, Houston, 1961-64; dir. med. and neurol. service Big Spring (Tex.) State Hosp., 1964-66; med. dir. Regional Mental Health Center, Oak Ridge, 1969—. Mem. med. adv. bd. Mid-East Tenn. Area, Tenn. Mid-South Regional Med. Program, 1971-73, med. adv. bd. Oak Ridge Nat. Epilepsy Found., 1973. Served with USPHS, 1956-58. Diplomate Am. Bd. Psychiatry and Neurology. Mem. Am. Acad. Neurology, A.M.A., Am. Psychiat. Assn., Commd. Officers Assn. USPHS, Alpha Omega Alpha. Home: PO Box 484 Oak Ridge TN 37830 Office: 315 Rutgers Av Suite 108 Oak Ridge TN 37830

PIERAS, JAIME, JR., Republican nat. committeeman, lawyer; b. San Juan, P.R., May 19, 1924; s. Jaime and Ines (Lopez-Cepero) P.; B.A., Catholic U. Am., 1945; LL.B., Georgetown U., 1948; m. Elsie Castaner, June 6, 1953; children—Awilda Ines, Jaime Roberto. Asso. Luis E. Dubon Law Office, 1949-52, Hartzell, Fernandez & Novas Law Office, 1953-59; partner Pieras & Torryella, 1959—. Gen. counsel P.R. Tourism Bur., 1953. Mem. finance com. San Juan Electoral Campaign, 1960, chmn., 1964; alternate del. Rep. Nat. Conv., 1964, del., 1968, del., chmn. delegation, 1972; chmn. finance com. Statehood Rep. Party, P.R.; mem. polit. action com.; Rep. nat. committeeman, 1968—; pres. P.R. Rep. Nat. Com., 1972; mem. U.S. mission adv. com., 1972, Inter-Am. adv. Council, 1972-73. Served with AUS, 1946-47. Mem. Am., Fed., P.R. bar assns., Cath. U. Am. Alumni Assn., Georgetown U. Alumni Assn., C. of C., K.C., Rotarian. Club: San Juan Country. Home: 1 Washington Av Condado San Juan PR 00907 Office: P O Box 507 Hato Rey PR 00919

PIERCE, CLEVELAND CARROLL, banker; b. Opp, Ala., Jan. 3, 1921; s. Grover Cleveland and Georgia B. (Carroll) P.; student Marion Inst., 1935-39; La. State U. Sch. Banking, 1960-62; m. Kathryn Eloise Mathews, Dec. 9, 1939; children—Caroline (Mrs. Roger F. Etheridge), Louise (Mrs. Rowayne Harper), Rebecca (Mrs. Ronald McLeod), George C. With First Nat. Bank Opp, 1939—, asst. cashier, 1945-49, v.p., cashier, 1949-64, pres., dir., 1964—. Treas. City of Opp Bd. Edn., 1971—, Covington County Bd. Edn., 1971—. Trustee Mizell Meml. Hosp., Opp, 1968—; bd. dirs. Opp Hist. Soc., Covington County Mental Health Assn., Covington County Econ. Devel. Bd. Served with Transport Service, AUS, 1943-46; ETO. Mem. Ala., Am., Independent bankers assns. Methodist (trustee ch.). Mason (Shriner). Clubs: Civitan (dir. 1969-70), Country (Opp). Home: 204 E Ida Av Opp AL 36467 Office: PO Drawer A Opp AL 36467

PIERCE, CLIFFORD DAVIS, JR., lawyer; b. Memphis, Sept. 9, 1934; s. Clifford Davis and Isabelle (Curran) P.; B.A., Yale, 1956; LL.B., U. Va., 1961; m. Margaret Trumbull, Apr. 16, 1966. Admitted to Tenn. bar, 1961; partner law firm Pierce, Rice, Bratcher & Pierce, Memphis, 1961—; mem. Tenn. Ho. of Reps., 1963-65; asst. city atty., Memphis, 1964—. Bd. dirs. Tenn. Mental Health Assn., 1962-66; chmn. Civic Research Com., Inc., 1966—. Served to lt. (j.g.), USNR, 1956-58. Mem. Am., Memphis, Shelby County bar assns., State Bar Tenn., Beta Theta Pi, Phi Alpha Delta. Democrat. Episcopalian. Home: 684 Center Dr Memphis TN 38112 Office: First Am Bank Bldg Memphis TN 38103

PIERCE, EARL BOYD, lawyer; b. Fort Gibson, Okla., Jan. 29, 1904; s. James M. and Nancy (Anderson) P.; LL.B., U. Okla., 1928; m. Ruth Clark, Aug. 26, 1923; 1 dau., Norma Jo (Mrs. Harry M. Shytles, Jr.). Admitted to Okla. bar, 1928, since practiced in Muskogee; asst. county atty. Muskogee County, 1931-33; state legal adviser NRA., 1933-34, litigation atty., Chgo., 1934-35; atty. Dept. Interior, 1935-36, Dept. Justice, Washington, 1936-37; prodn. specialist, expeditor Task Force Materiel, Ordnance Dept., U.S. Army, 1942-44; Cherokee tribal atty., 1948-62, gen. counsel Cherokee Nation, 1963—. Bd. dirs. Five Civilized Tribes Mus., Cherokee Found., Hall of Fame for Famous Am. Indians. Mem. Am., Okla. bar assns., Okla. Hist. Soc. (dir.), Am. Trial Lawyers Assn., Cherokee Hist. Soc. Methodist. Mason (32 deg., Shriner). Club: Muskogee Country. Spearheaded successful judgements in favor of Cherokee Nation for treaty violations. Home: 1003 S Terrace Muskogee OK 74401 Office: PO Box 498 Fort Gibson OK 74434 also 1026 17th St NW Washington DC 20036

PIERCE, ELLA JANET, educator; b. Colerain, N.C., d. Franklin and Anastasia (Garrett) Pierce; A.B., Meredith Coll., 1921; B.M.T., So. Baptist Theol. Sem., 1923; postgrad. Columbia, 1929, Harvard, summer 1937, 38; M.A., Cornell U., 1933, Ph.D., 1936. Mem. faculty Mars Hill Coll., 1925-65, chmn. dept. English, 1938-65; chmn. dept. English, Chowan Coll., Murfreesboro, N.C., 1965—. Instr., Blue Mountain Coll., Miss., 1939, Wake Forest and Meredith, summer, 1936-37; counselor Y.W.A., 1926-29, dean women, 1930-36; counselor Vols. for Christ, 1936-65; faculty adviser Baptist Student Union, 1945-63, chmn. Honor Point System, 1937-40, chmn. library com. 1945-65. Mem. Nat. Council Tchrs. English (membership chmn. eastern div.), Murfreesboro Hist. Assn., Kappa Nu Sigma, Delta Kappa Gamma (v.p. Gamma chpt., chmn. scholarship, program com.). Home: 14 Liberty St Murfreesboro NC 27855

PIERCE, GEORGE CHESTER, communications co. exec.; b. Alexandria, Va., May 16, 1930; s. Chester Gaver and Jeanette (Cochran) P.; B.S. in Econ. and Engring., Mass. Inst. Tech., 1952; m. Lois Marie Bowden, Feb. 2, 1952; children—Rebecca (Mrs. Michael E. Bradley), Arnold, Stephen. Controller, Chesapeake Instrument Corp., Shadyside, Md., 1954-55; asst. to dir. EM div. Atlantic Research Corp., Alexandria, 1952-54, asst. dir., 1955-62, dir. Teleproducts div., 1962-64; chmn. bd., chief exec. officer, treas. Pulse Communications, Inc., Falls Church, Va., 1964—; dir. Geotronics, Inc., Sci. Communication, Inc., Alexandria Amusement Corp. Mem. Washington Bd. Trade. Club: Mass. Inst. Tech. Alumni (sec. 1970-71) (Washington). Home: 3245 Rio Dr Falls Church VA 22041 Office: 5714 Columbia Pike Falls Church VA 22041

PIERCE, GEORGE FOSTER, JR., architect; b. Dallas, June 22, 1919; s. George Foster and Hallie Louise (Crutchfield) P.; student So. Meth. U., 1937-39; B.A., Rice U., 1942, B.Arch., 1943; diplome d'architecture, Ecoles d'Art Americaines, Ecole des Beaux-Arts, 1958; m. Betty Jean Reistle, Oct. 17, 1942; children—Ann Louise (Mrs. Robert G. Arnett), George Foster III, Nancy Reistle. Pvt. practice architecture, Houston, 1946—; sr. partner G. Pierce, Goodwin & Flanagan; instr. archtl. design Rice U., 1945, preceptor in sch. architecture, 1962-67; projects include 8 bldgs. Rice U. Campus; So. Meth. U. Student Center; 3 bldgs. Tex. A. and M. U. Campus; Houston Mus. Natural Sci. and Planetarium; Exxon Center Complex Houston; Tex. Tech U. biology bldg.; Houston Intercontinental Airport; S.W. Bell Telephone Co. hdqrs. office bldg.; Petroleum Club of Houston, U. Houston Student Center and Center for Continuing Edn.; 500 bed teaching hosp. U. Tex. Med. Sch., Galveston; Two Houston Center office bldg. Mem. exec. bd. Sam Houston area council Boy Scouts Am.; past pres., chmn. bd. trustees Contemporary Arts Mus., Houston; pres., trustee Tex. Archtl. Found.; trustee Houston Mus. Natural Sci.; trustee, mem. exec. bd. Rice Center for Community Design and Research. Served as ensign USNR, World War II. Recipient Outstanding Young Texan award Jr. C. of C., 1954; also numerous nat., state, local archtl. awards for design. Fellow A.I.A. (past nat. chmn. com. on aesthetics, com. chpt. affairs, nat. com. on design), Sociedad de Architectos Mexicanos (hon.); mem. Tex. Soc. Architects (past pres., v.p., sec. treas.), Houston Jr. C. of C. (past officer, dir.), Kappa Alpha. Methodist. Clubs: Houston Country, Petroleum (Houston). Home: 5211 Green Tree Houston TX 77027 Office: PO Box 13319 Houston TX 77019

PIERCE, HARRY BROOKE, beverage co. exec.; b. Trion, Ga., Feb. 12, 1922; s. Harry Lewis and Vennie Mae (Greenwood) P.; B.S. in Edn., U. Ga., 1943; M.A., George Peabody Coll., 1959; m. Juanita Burkett, July 25, 1948; children—Cheryl Ann, Susan Lanier. Athletic dir., coach Summerville (Ga.) High Sch., 1946-50, Gordon Lee High Sch., Chickamauga, Ga., 1950-59; supt. Chickamauga City Schs., 1959-66; pres., co-owner Royal Crown Bottling Co., Chattanooga, 1966—, also dir. Served to capt. USMCR, 1943-46. Decorated Purple Heart. Mem. V.F.W. Democrat. Baptist (deacon). Lion, Mason. Club: Chickamauga Fly & Bait Casting (pres.). Home: 4416 Lilac Lane Chattanooga TN 37411 Office: 201 Broad St Chattanooga TN 37402

PIERCE, JAMES CLARENCE, physician, educator; b. Huron, S.D., Aug. 5, 1929; s. Henry Montreville and Carrie Bernice (Matson) P.; B.A., Carleton Coll., 1951; M.D., Harvard, 1955; M.S. (USPHS fellow), U. Minn., 1963, Ph.D. (USPHS fellow), 1966; m. Carol Sue Wilson, Apr. 6, 1967; children—Henry McDonald, Richard Matson, Elizabeth Gail. Intern Peter Bent Brigham Hosp., Boston, 1955-56, resident, 1956-57; resident U. Minn., 1959-66; practice medicine specializing in gen. surgery, Richmond, Va., 1966—; mem. faculty Med. Coll. Va., Richmond, 1966—, asso. prof. surgery, 1969-72, prof., 1972—. Cons., McGuire VA Hosp., 1966—. Served with M.C., USAF, 1957-59. Royal Soc. Medicine (Eng.) traveling fellow, 1971. Diplomate Am. Bd. Surgery. Fellow A.C.S.; mem. Soc. Univ. Surgeons, Am. Fedn. Clin. Research, Am. Soc. Exptl. Pathology, Transplantation Soc. Contbr. articles to profl. jours. Research with transplantation of kidneys. Home: 4518 Newport Dr Richmond VA 23227 Office: Med Coll Va Station Box 95 Richmond VA 23298

PIERCE, KENNETH RAY, educator; b. Snyder, Tex., May 21, 1934; s. Clois Vernon and Ellen (Goolsby) P.; D.V.M., Tex. A. and M. U., 1957, M.S., 1962, Ph.D. (NSF fellow), 1965; m. Anne Stasney, Aug. 31, 1956; children—Cynthia Cae, Melaney Rae. Instr. vet. anatomy Tex. A. and M. U., College Station, 1957-59, asst. prof., 1961-65, asso. prof., 1965-69, prof., 1969—, chief, sect. vet. clin. pathology, 1967—; pvt. vet. practice San Angelo (Tex.) Vet. Hosp., 1959-61. Cons., sect. exptl. animals M.D. Anderson Tumor Inst. and Hosp., Houston, 1971—. Diplomate Am. Coll. Vet. Pathologists. Mem. Am. Soc. Vet. Clin. Pathologists, Internat. Acad. Pathology, Am., Tex. vet. med. assns., Sigma Xi, Phi Kappa Phi, Phi Zeta, Gamma Sigma Delta. Presbyn. (deacon, elder). Co-editor Vet. Pathology jour., 1971—. Home: 1500 Laura Lane College Station TX 77840 Office: Dept Veterinary Pathology Texas A and M Univ College Station TX 77843

PIERCE, LAWRENCE H., govt. ofcl., accountant; b. Peoria, Ill., July 13, 1936; s. Homer L. and Mabel (Kent) P.; B.A., Am. U., 1960, M.B.A., 1966; m. Arlene Tarlow, Apr. 16, 1959; 1 dau., Pitzy. Auditor Haskins & Sells Co., Washington, 1962-64; br. accountant SEC, Washington, 1964-68; mgr. financial analysis Liberty Equity Corp., Washington, 1968-69; sr. accounting analyst bd. govs. Fed. Res. System, Washington, 1969—. Instr., Strayer Coll., Washington, 1966—; lectr. No. Va. Community Coll., Alexandria, 1972—. Music dir. Bethel United Ch., Arlington, Va., 1963-68; tenor soloist Adas Israel Congregation, Washington, 1961-69. Served with AUS, 1958-61. C.P.A., D.C. Mem. Am. Inst. C.P.A.'s, Washington Soc. Investment Analysts, Tau Kappa Epsilon, Phi Mu Alpha. Home: 6622 Goldsboro Rd Falls Church VA 22042 Office: Fed Res System Washington DC 20551

PIERCE, LEE COMPTON, religious assn. exec., clergyman; b. El Reno, Okla., Oct. 23, 1915; s. Luther Alexander and Faye (Compton) P.; B.A., Tex. Christian U., 1938, B.D., 1947, D.D. (hon.), 1954; m. Fotula John Boozalis, Sept. 1, 1936; children—Kenneth Lee, Michael John, Melinda Sue (Mrs. James Ballard). Ordained to ministry Christian Ch., 1936; minister First Christian Ch., Lancaster, Tex., 1937-38, Magnolia Park Christian Ch., Houston, 1939-41, First Christian Ch., Baytown, Tex., 1941-43, 46-49, Jackson, Miss., 1949-54, Tyler, Tex., 1954-56; dir. ch. relations Tex. Christian U., Ft. Worth, 1956-62; minister First Christian Ch., Norman, Okla., 1962-65; v.p. Lexington (Ky.) Theol. Sem., 1965—. Bd. dirs. Community Chest, Jackson, Miss., 1949. Served as chaplain AUS, 1943-46. Mason (Shriner). Home: 2121 Nicholasville Rd Lexington KY 40503 Office: 631 South Limeston Lexington KY 40508

PIERCE, THOMAS FLOYD, retail trade exec.; b. Bartlett, Tex., Feb. 2, 1916; s. Floyd Nunez and Ellen Gertrude (Wood); student U. Tex., 1934-38; m. Iris Eilers, Mar. 20, 1947; 1 son, Thomas Eilers (dec.). Partner, F.N. Pierce & Co., cotton mchts., Taylor, Tex., 1945-52; pres. Delta Constrn. Co., Taylor, 1952-64; partner Williamson County Equipment Co., Inc., retail farm equipment, automobiles, Taylor, 1943-73, chmn. bd., 1973—; dir. City Nat. Bank, Taylor. Mem. Sch. Bd., Taylor, 1964-70. Served with AC, USNR, 1942-45. Decorated D.F.C., Air medal. Presbyn. Home: 117 E 6th St Taylor TX 76574 Office: 1426 N Main St Taylor TX 76574

PIERCE, VIRGINIA ALLEN (MRS. KENDRICK E. PIERCE), banker; b. Monticello, Ark.; d. Andrew Emmett and Florence (Grisham) Allen; student Atlanta Bus. Coll., 1927; m. Kendrick E. Pierce, Nov. 8, 1936 (dec. Aug. 1960); children—William Allen, Jackson E. With Union Bank & Trust Co., Monticello, 1942—, asst. cashier 1945-58, v.p., 1958—. Chmn., Drew County Savs. Bonds, 1960-65; active various civic and philanthropic orgns. Mem. Nat. Assn. Bank Women, Drew County Hist. Soc., P.E.O. Presbyn. (elder). Home: 220 W Union St Monticello AR 71655 Office: PO Box 270 Monticello AR 71655

PIERCE, WILLIAM FRANKLIN, dentist; b. Dyersburg, Tenn., July 1, 1936; s. William Franklin and Alma Louise (Switzer) P.; B.A., Vanderbilt U., 1958; D.D.S., U. Tenn., 1962; m. Mary Lucile Whelchel, Dec. 27, 1961; children—William Franklin IV, David Jordan, Mark Thomas. Extern, Tenn. Pub. Health, 1962; practice of dentistry, Dyersburg, Tenn., 1965—; mem. staff Parkview Hosp., 1965—. Vice pres. Community Concerts, 1969-71; vice chmn. Dyer County Bd. Edn., 1970—; chmn. Dyer County Sch. Bd., 1972, vice chmn., 1973; pres. Dyer County Easter Seal, 1965-68. Served with USNR, 1962-65. Mem. Tenn. Council Dental Health, 7th Dist. Dental Soc. (sec., treas. 1970—), Dyersburg Jr. C. of C. (v.p. 1967-68), Am. Acad. Dentistry (sec.-treas. Tenn. chpt.), Pierre Fauchard Acad. Kiwanian (bd. dirs.), Moose. Club: Dyersburg Country. Home: 2124 Morning Rd Dyersburg TN 38024 Office: 520 East Parkview St Dyersburg TN 38024

PIERMARINI, GASPER JOHN, chemist; b. Leominister, Mass., Apr. 26, 1933; s. Ester Gasperino and Venerina Eugenia (Casassa) P.; A.B., Boston U., 1955; M.S., Am. U., 1962, Ph.D., 1971; m. Elfriede Erna Geyer, Dec. 31, 1960; children—Andrea Lucia, Gabriele Cornelia. Research phys. chemist Nat. Bur. Standards, Washington, 1959—. Cons. high pressure physics, high pressure crystallography to govt., industry and ednl. instns., U.S. and abroad. Served with AUS, 1956-58. Recipient Spl. Achievement award Dept. Commerce, 1973. Mem. Am. Chem. Soc., Am. Crystallographic Assn., A.A.A.S. Research with high pressure diamond-anvil optical cells for various research applications. Contbr. profl. jours. Home: 1202 Colonial Rd McLean VA 22101 Office: National Bureau Standards Washington DC 20234

PIERRE, DALLAS, dentist; b. Charenton, La., June 9, 1933; s. Russell and Eva (Larry) P.; B.S., Prairie View A. and M. Coll., 1955; M.S., Tex. So. U., 1963; D.D.S., U. Tex., 1968; m. Carol Ann Yates, Aug. 27, 1960; 1 son, James Darian. Gen. practice dentistry, Lufkin, Tex., 1968—; dir. Nat. Security Bank, Tyler, Tex. Pres., Pub. Relations Orgn. for Community Laity Improvement, Lufkin, 1970—; chmn. adv. com. Manpower, Edn. and Tng. Center, Lufkin, 1971—. Bd. dirs. East Tex. Boy Scout Found., Angelina County Heart Fund, Lufkin Sheltered Workshop and Opportunity Center. Served with USAF, 1956-60. Mem. Nat. Platform Assn., U. Tex., Tex. Dental Br. alumni assns., Citizens C. of C. (bd. dirs. 1969—); Eastex Med. Dental Pharm. Assn. (pres. 1971—), Phi Beta Sigma. Baptist (deacon 1970—). Home: 106 McMullen St Lufkin TX 75901 Office: 809 Kurth Dr PO Box 1236 Lufkin TX 75901

PIKE, JESSE MILLER, retail drugstore chain exec.; b. High Point, N.C., June 2, 1919; s. Joseph William and Sally Leora (Miller) P.; B.S. in Pharmacy, U. N.C. at Chapel Hill, 1940; M.S., Western Res. U., 1941; m. Dorothy Brock Duckett, Feb. 22, 1942; children—Jesse Miller, Lourene (Mrs. Paul Dewey Thaxton). Pres. Pearl Drug Co., Concord, N.C., 1941-44; chief pharmacist VA Hosp., 1946-48; profl. service rep. E.R. Squibb & Sons, 1948-54; founder Pike's Drug Stroes, brs. Concord, Charlotte, N.C., Harrisburg, N.C., Kannapolis, N.C., Locust, N.C., 1955, now chmn. bd.; dir. N.C. Mut. Wholesale Drug Co.; mem. adv. panel Smith-Kline-Rench Lab. Mem. N.C. Bd. Pharmacy, 1968-73. Bd. dirs. N.C. Pharmacy Research Found. Served with USNR, 1944-46. Recipient A.H. Robins Bowl of Hygeia award, 1966, Blanton award, 1970, DeMolay Legion of Merit, 1970, Distinguished Service award U. N.C., 1971; named Schering Corp. Pharmacy Family of Year, 1968. Mem. Concord C. of C. and Mchts. Assn. (dir. 1961—), Cabarrus County Indsl. Devel. Corp. (dir. 1961—), N.C. Mchts. Assn., Nat. Assn. Retail Druggists (v.p., exec. com.), Kappa Psi (dir. housing corp.). Rotarian, Mason (Shriner). Contbr. articles to profl. jours. Home: 136 Beverly Dr Concord NC 28025 Office: 863 Church St North Concord NC 28025

PIKE, KENNETH JEROME, mfg. co. exec.; b. Evansville, Ind., Feb. 23, 1937; s. Alexander Herman and Paulene Mildred (Ingram) P.; student U. Evansville, 1959-61; B.S. in Civil Engring., Purdue U., 1965; m. Marilyn Jane Adcock, June 1, 1957; children—Rebecca, Emily. Office engr., Perini Corp., Uniontown, Ky., 1966-68; field engr. Portland Cement Assn., Evansville, 1968-70; plant mgr. Precision Prestressed Products, Henderson, Ky., 1970-71, Constrn. Products Corp., 1971-72; sales mgr. Featherlite Precast, Lexington, Ky., 1972—. Served with AUS, 1955-56, 61-62. Registered profl. engr. Ind., Ky. Mem. Am. Soc. C.E. (pres. 1969-70), Nat. Soc. Profl. Engrs., (v.p. 1970-71). Home: 3252 Cornwall Dr Lexington KY 40505 Office: PO Box 5436 Lexington KY 40505

PIKE, ROBERT MERRETT, microbiologist; b. Hiram, Me., Apr. 5, 1906; s. John Bennett and Cora (Hubbard) P.; A.B., Brown U., 1928, M.A., 1930, Ph.D., 1932; m. Mary Brownell, June 17, 1932; children—Elizabeth (Mrs. Joe L. Dunlap), Mary Lu (Mrs. Ellery W. Sinclair), Robert B. Bacteriologist, Bassett Hosp. and Otsego County Labs., Cooperstown, N.Y., 1932-43; prof. microbiology U. Tex. Southwestern Med. Sch., Dallas, 1943—. Diplomate Am. Bd. Microbiology. Fellow Am. Acad. Microbiology; mem. Am. Soc. Microbiology, Am. Assn. Immunologists, Sigma Xi, Alpha Delta Phi. Research in med. bacteriology and immunology. Contbr. articles in field to profl. jours. Home: 5815 Elderwood Dr Dallas TX 75230 Office: 5323 Harry Hines Blvd Dallas TX 75235

PIKER, EVE SANDERS (MRS. HERBERT M. PIKER), editor, bus. exec.; b. Frankfort, Ind., Nov. 2, 1918; d. Fred and Mamye A. (Gwin) Sanders; student Franklin Coll.; m. James H. Heaney, Aug. 30, 1941 (killed in action 1942); 1 son, James Alfred; m. 2d, Herbert M. Piker, Oct. 30, 1970. Editor, Hendricks County Republican newspaper, Danville, Ind., 1942-46; continuity dir. radio sta. WIBC, Indpls., 1946-47, WTHI, Terre Haute, Ind., 1947-49; account asst.

Newman, Lynde & Asso. Advt. Agy., 1949-64, corp. sec., 1960-64; editor, bus. mgr. Jacksonville Mag., Jacksonville (Fla.) Area C. of C., 1964-71; editor The Review, Jacksonville Episcopal High Sch., 1972—. Active Camp Fire Girls; sec. Civic Round Table of Jacksonville, 1967—. Trustee Episcopal Child Day Care Centers; bd. dirs. Vol. Jacksonville, Inc., 1974—. Mem. Am. Assn. Commerce Publs. (past pres.), Nat. League Am. Pen Women, Fla. Pub. Relations Assn. (pres.), Gamma Alpha Chi (hon.). Episcopalian. Mem. Order Eastern Star. Home: Ca'd'Oro Villa Apt 112 5039 Timuguana Rd Jacksonville FL 32210

PILAND, VOLLIE MATHIS, architect; b. Dallas, Dec. 13, 1927; s. Vollie Mathis and Margaret Ann (Stroheeker) P.; student Kan. State U., 1944; B.Arch., Okla. State U., 1951; m. Mary Lou Osborne, Apr. 25, 1948; children—Cynthia Ann (Mrs. Tom Ezell), Sheralee (Mrs. Larry Turner), Deborah Jean, Robert Bruce. Design engr. Phillips Petroleum Co., Bartlesville, Okla., 1952-57; partner Butz-Piland & Assos., architects, Bartlesville, 1957-65; proprietor V.M. Piland Assos., Tulsa, 1965—; lectr. in field. Cons. to several univs. Committeeman Cherokee Indian Nation council Boy Scouts Am., 1954-70. Served with USAF, 1944-46. Decorated Bronze Star medal. Recipient All-Electric Bldg. award Okla. Pub. Service Co., 1966, Outstanding All-Electric Project award Nat. Elect. Contractors Assn., 1966. Registered architect, 46 states. Mem. Nat. Council Archtl. Registration Bds., Am. Inst. Hosp. Cons., Pan Am. Med. Assn., Internat. Platform Assn., Tulsa World Trade Assn., Met. Tulsa C. of C. Baptist (deacon 1950—). Kiwanian. Home: 3749 South Braden Tulsa OK 74135 Office: PO Box 4828 Tulsa OK 74104

PILCHER, BENJAMIN LEE, educator; b. Corpus Christi, Feb. 25, 1938; s. John Fuller and Maurine (Rogers) P.; B.S., Tex. Tech. Coll., 1961, M.S., 1963; Ph.D., U. N.M., 1969; m. Melissa Jane Payne, June 5, 1965; 1 son, Walter Fuller. Instr. U. Tex. at Arlington, 1963-66; asso. prof. botany McMurry Coll, Abilene, Tex., 1969—, head dept., 1969-73. Mem. environmental health com. County Health Adv. Bd. Exec. bd. Abilene Zool. Soc. Mem. A.A.A.S., Bot. Soc. Am., Am. Inst. Biol. Scis., Cactus and Succulent Soc. Club: West Texas Camera (pres. 1970-72). Home: 3526 S 20th St Abilene TX 79605

PILCHER, JAMES BROWNIE, lawyer; b. Shreveport, La., May 19, 1929; s. James Reese and Mattie (Brown) P.; B.A., La. State U., 1952; J.D. summa cum laude, John Marshall U., 1955; postgrad. Emory U.; m. Frances M. Pettit, Jan. 28, 1951; children—Lydia, Martha, Bradley. Admitted to Ga. bar, 1955, since practiced in Atlanta; legal counsel to speaker Ho. Reps., Ga., 1961-64; asso. city atty., Atlanta, 1965-70. Prof. law, John Marshall U., 1955-59; pres. Brentwood Enterprises, Inc., Trans-Atlanta Investment Corp. Mem. Ga. Democratic Exec. Com., 1962-66, pres. Active Voters, 1966-69; chmn. Fulton County Dem. Com., 1969-71. Bd. dirs. Whitehead Meml. Boys Club, Atlanta Assn. UN; trustee Vanguard Housing Corp. Served with USNR, 1946-48. Named Outstanding Young Man of Atlanta in Community Affairs, 1962, Ga. 1963. Mem. Am., Ga., Atlanta bar assns., Trial Lawyers Am. Assn., Atlanta Jaycees (pres. 1961-62). Baptist. Kiwanian. Club: Young Democratic of Fulton County (Atlanta) (pres. 1964-65, Ga. 1965-66). Home: 434 Brentwood Dr NE Atlanta GA 30315 Office: Profl Bldg 1799 Lakewood Terrace SE Atlanta GA 30315

PILKEY, ORRIN H., educator; b. N.Y.C., Sept. 19, 1934; s. Orrin H. and Elizabeth (Street) P.; B.S., Wash. State U., 1957; M.S., Mont. State U., 1959; Ph.D., Fla. State U., 1962; m. Sharlene M. Greenaa, Dec. 29, 1956; children—Charles, Linda, Diane, Keith, Kerry. Research asso. U. Ga. Marine Inst., Sapelo Island, 1962-65; asso. prof. geology Duke, 1965-72, prof., 1972—. Active shoreline conservation. Editor: (with D.J. Swift and D.B. Duane) Shelf Sediment Transport, 1972. Contbr. articles to profl. jours. Home: Route 4 Box 426 Hillsborough NC 27278 Office: Dept Geology Duke Univ Durham NC 27708

PINARDI, NORMAN JOSEPH, banker; b. N.Y.C., June 16, 1936; s. Marco and Adelle (Anselmi) P.; B.S., U. Fla., 1958; m. Bobby Jo Kight, June 8, 1957; children—Theresa Lynn, Robert Anthony. Dir. information Fla. Alcoholic Rehab. Program, Avon Park, 1961-65; dir. pub. relations Manatee County Com. of 100, Bradenton, Fla., 1965-67; v.p. pub. relations Inter City Nat. Bank, Bradenton, 1967-73, sr. v.p., 1973—, also v.p. affiliate Bayshore State Bank, Bradenton, 1970-73, dir., 1972-73. Tchr. bank pub. relations Bank Adminstrn. Inst., 1970. Dir. pub. relations Manatee County LeRoy Collins for Senate Campaign. Publicity vol. United Fund, 1967. Bd. dirs. DeSoto Boys Club, Bradenton, 1967-70, United Fund, Bradenton, 1967—. Served with USAF, 1958-61. Mem. Manatee County C. of C., Pub. Relations Soc. Am. (pres. Central and N. Fla. chpt. 1974), Fla. Pub. Relations Assn. (pres. Ringling chpt. 1969). Rotarian. Club: Bradenton Country. Home: 5812 9th Av Dr W Bradenton FL 33505 Office: PO Box 771 Bradenton FL 33507

PINCKNEY, JOHN ADAMS, ret. bishop; b. Mt. Pleasant, S.C., Mar. 8, 1905; s. Francis Douglas and Mary Lee (Adams) P.; student Coll. Charleston, 1925-26, DuBose Meml. Sch., 1926-28; B.D., U. of South, 1931, D.D., 1964; m. Hilda W. Emerson, Oct. 8, 1931; children—Hilda Emerson (Mrs. William C. Ross), John Adams, Francis Douglas. Ordained to ministry Episcopal Ch., 1931; minister Diocese of S.C., 1931-37, Ch. of Holy Cross, Tryon, N.C., 1937-39; rector St. Paul's Ch., Charleston, S.C., 1939-41; minister Holy Trinity Ch., Clemson, also chaplain Episcopal students Clemson Coll., 1941-48; rector St. James' Ch., Greenville, 1948-59; archdeacon Diocese of Upper S.C., 1959-63, bishop, 1963-72. Dir. youth confs. Kanuga Confs., Hendersonville, N.C., 1932-42, dir. confs. program, 1942-50; sec. Diocese of Upper S.C., also sec. Diocesan Exec. Council, 1954-63; dep. to Gen. Convs. and Provincial Synods. Mem. Newcomen Soc. Home: 307 Harrow Dr Columbia SC 29210 Office: PO Box 1789 Columbia SC 29202

PINCKNEY, ROBERT HOWE, optometrist; b. Charleston, S.C., Sept. 18, 1920; s. Edward Hall and Hattie Vernon (Whitaker) P.; B.S., Coll. Charleston, 1943; O.D., No. Ill. Coll. Optometry, 1951; m. Kathleen Ethridge Weldon, Dec. 28, 1948; children—Kay, Ellen, Bobby, Ed. Practice optometry, Jackson—McDonough, Ga., 1951—. Chmn. Butts County chpt. Nat. Found. State chmn. Ga. Optometric Assn. Vocational Guidance Com., Ins. Com. Served with AUS, 1943-46. Mem. 4th Dist. Optometric Soc. (trustee 1957, pres. 1960), Butts County Jaycees (pres. 1954-55). Methodist (chmn. official bd. Jackson unit 1965-66). Kiwanian (pres. 1961, chmn. youth services 1966-73). Home: 379 West Av Jackson GA 30233 Office: 336 East Third St Jackson GA 30233

PINCUS, GEORGE, educator; b. Havana, Cuba, July 5, 1935; s. Max and Ana (Slutzkaya) P.; student U. Havana, 1953-56; B.Civil Engring. with honors, Ga. Inst. Tech., 1959, M.S., 1959; Ph.D., Cornell U., 1963; M.B.A., U. Houston, 1974; m. Dora Dzubquevich, June 8, 1958; children—Cynthia Judith, David Nathan, Karen Joy. Came to U.S., 1957, naturalized, 1966. Asst. prof. structural engring. U. Ky., Lexington, 1963-66, asso. prof. civil engring., 1966-69; prof. civil engring. U. Houston, 1969—, also dir. structural mechanics lab., 1972—. Chief party grad. engring. program AID, Rio de Janeiro, Brazil, also prof. Fed. U., Rio de Janeiro, 1967-68; cons. in field. Registered profl. engr., Ky., Tex., Fla. Mem. Am. Soc. C.E. (recipient D.V. Terrell award 1965), Am. Soc. Engring. Edn., Am. Concrete Inst., Phi Kappa Phi. Contbr. articles to profl. jours. Home: 9722 Checkerboard St Houston TX 77035 Office: U Houston Houston TX 77004

PINCUS, JOSEPH, educator; b. N.Y.C., Apr. 17, 1919; s. Samuel and Lillian (Sirotkin) P.; B.S.S., Coll. City N.Y., 1941; M.A., Am. U., 1947, Ph.D., 1953; m. Ethel Frances London, July 6, 1952; children—Terri Ellen, Salley Nella, Robert Alan. Internat. economist Latin Am. studies project U.S. Tariff Commn., Washington, 1946-47, 61-62; economist, fgn. affairs analyst Div. Research Am. Republics Dept. State, Washington, 1949-58; tariff adviser ICA, USOM/Honduras, 1958-60, rep. with Continental Allied Co. to study indsl. devel., 1961; program officer, then econ. adviser AID, Costa Rica, 1962-64, acting dir. mission, 1964, econ. adviser, pvt. enterprise adviser Am. embassy, Paraguay, 1964-66, acting econ. officer, 1967, pvt. enterprise devel. officer, El Salvador, 1967-69, acting program officer, 1968, loan economist, 1968-69; dir. research Brokers Internat. Ltd., Miami, Fla., 1972-73; adj. prof. econs. Fla. Internat. U., Embry-Riddle Aero. U. Mem. Am. Fgn. Service Assn., Latin Am. Studies Assn., Soc. Internat. Devel., Acad. for Internat. Bus., Carribean Studies Assn., Omicron Delta Epsilon, Beta Gamma Sigma. Adv. bd. Comite Para El Desarrollo De Recursos Humanos. Contbr. numerous articles to profl. jours. Home: 14525 SW 85th St Miami FL 33143 Office: 1612 Ponce de Leon Blvd Coral Gables FL 33144

PINEAU, ROGER, mus. ofcl.; b. Chgo., Nov. 17, 1915; s. Auguste G. and Olga Constance (Erickson) P.; A.A., Flint (Mich.) Jr. Coll., 1940; B.A., U. Mich., 1942; grad. U.S. Naval Lang. Sch., 1943; J.D., George Washington U., 1954; m. Maxine Jessie Good, Nov. 4, 1942; children—Suzanne Lisette (Mrs. James Dulcan), Julienne Louise, Anthony Auguste, Antoinette Elizabeth. Asst. to S.E. Morrison for 10 vols. History of United States Naval Operations in World War II, 1947-57; Far east intelligence officer Dept. State, 1957-61, social sci. officer, 1961-65; editor Smithsonian Instn., Washington, 1965-72; dir. Navy Meml. Mus., Washington, 1972—. Served with USNR, 1942-50; now capt. Res. Author: (with R. Sherrod) A Picture History of the Pacific War, 1952; (with M. Fuchida, M. Okumiya, C.H. Kawakami) Midway, The Battle that Doomed Japan, 1955; (with R. Inoguchi, T. Nakajima) The Divine Wind, 1958; (with T. Hara, F. Saito) Japanese Destroyer Captain, 1961; (with M. Ito, A. Kuroda) The End of the Imperial Japanese Navy, 1962. Editor: The Japan Expedition, M.C. Perry's personal diary, 1968. Author various Smithsonian exhibit catalogs. Contbr. articles to profl. pubs. Home: 9403 Holland Av Bethesda MD 20014 Office: Navy Meml Museum Washington Navy Yard SE Washington DC 20374

PINKARD, LUTHER DWIGHT, civil engr.; b. Milltown, Ala., Feb. 23, 1927; s. Royal and Ezza (Stevens) P.; B.S., Auburn U., 1950; postgrad. U. Tenn., 1966-72; m. Laura Elizabeth Trantham, Oct. 31, 1952; children—Robert, Susan, David, John, Roy. Materials engr. U.S. Bur. Reclamation, Lindsay, Cal., 1950; jr. engr. Tenn. Coal & Iron Co., Birmingham, Ala., 1951-52; asst. plant engr. Am. Bitumuls & Asphalt Co., Mobile, Ala., 1952-53; constrn. engr. Intrusion-Prepakt, Inc., Cleve., 1953-55; asst. dir. engring. So. Sash Sales & Supply Co., Sheffield, Ala., 1955-61; engr. TVA, Muscle Shoals, Ala., Knoxville, Tenn., 1961—. Served with USAAF, 1945-47. Mem. Nat. (chpt. pres. 1965), Tenn. socs. profl. engrs., Profl. Engrs. in Govt. (state vice chmn.), Lambda Chi Alpha, Phi Kappa Phi, Chi Epsilon. Home: 9029 Carlton Circle Route 34 Knoxville TN 37922 Office: 100 Fidelity Bldg Knoxville TN 37902

PINKETT, HAROLD THOMAS, archivist; b. Salisbury, Md., Apr. 7, 1914; s. Levin Wilson and Leah Catherine (Richardson) P.; A.B., Morgan Coll., 1935; A.M., U. Pa., 1938; postgrad. Columbia, 1939-40; Ph.D., Am. U., 1953; m. Lucille Cannady, Apr. 24, 1943. Tchr. high sch., Balt., 1936-37; prof. history Livingstone Coll., Salisbury, N.C., 1938-39, 41-42; mem. staff and supervisory archivist Nat. Archives, Washington, 1942-71, chief natural resources br., 1971—. Lectr. Am. history and archival adminstrn. Howard U., Washington, 1970—. Bd. dirs. Forest History Soc.; trustee U.S. Capitol Hist. Soc. Served with AUS, 1943-46; ETO, CBI. Fellow Council on Library Resources, 1972-73; recipient Commendable Service awards Nat. Archives, 1964, 70. Fellow Soc. Am. Archivists (editor Am. Archivist 1968-71); mem. Agrl. History Soc. (exec. com. 1972—), Am. Hist. Assn., Orgn. Am. Historians. Author: Gifford Pinchot, Private and Public Forester, 1970. Co-editor Northeast News neighborhood jour., Washington, 1962-69. Contbr. to profl. jours. Home: 5741 27th St NW Washington DC 20015 Office: National Archives Bldg Washington DC 20408

PINKNEY, CHARLES COATSWORTH, landscape architect; b. Denver, Jan. 14, 1906; s. Fred Coatsworth and Jessie (Gallagher) P.; B.S. in Horticulture, Colo. Agrl. Coll., 1927, B.S. in Entomology, 1927; M.Landscape Architecture, Harvard, 1934, Charles Elliott traveling fellow, 1934-35; m. Evelyn Robinson, Nov. 17, 1934; children—Patti Lynn (Mrs. Bert Walter Schulle), Mary Elizabeth (Mrs. Halley Orin Bradford), Fred. Landscape architect, Boston, 1936-39; city planner City of Austin (Tex.), 1941-42; pvt. practice landscape architecture, Austin, 1940—. Lectr. landscape architecture to various garden clubs, Austin; lectr., panelist local gardening schs.; mem. Com. for License Registration of Landscape Architects in Tex., 1967-69; cons. Heritage Soc. Austin, 1955—. Mem. Am., Tex. socs. landscape architects, Alpha Zeta, Alpha Gamma Rho. Presbyn. (deacon 1950—). Club: Harvard (Austin). Address: 5424 Shoal Creek Blvd Austin TX 78756

PINNELL, RAYMOND A., JR., archtl. engr.; b. Wichita Falls, Tex., July 5, 1925; s. Raymond A. and Anna (Carter) P.; B.S., U. Tex. at Austin, 1950; m. Mary Waller, Mar. 23, 1947; children—Gary R., M. Angela. Jr. engr. R. Marvin Shipman Cons. Engrs., San Antonio, 1950-53; exec. v.p. Lift Slab Group & Research Co., Texstar Corp., 1953-55, pres., 1955-60; partner Freigenspan & Pinnell, cons. engrs., San Antonio, 1960—; pres. Prestressing Industries, 1958-60. Served with USNR, 1943-46. Recipient award of merit for outstanding engring. achievement for design of Palacio Del Rio Hotel, 1968. Mem. Nat., Tex. socs. profl. engrs., Am. Concrete Inst. Club: Alamo Heights Optimist (past treas.) (San Antonio). Prin. engring. designs include Tower of the Americas, San Antonio, 1968. Office: 335 W Sunset St San Antonio TX 78209

PINSON, ANNA DOTSON (MRS. BLAKE PINSON), business exec.; b. Phelps, Ky., June 7, 1914; d. Paris W. and Allie (Dotson); student Pikeville Coll., 1932-34; B.S., Eastern State Coll., Richmond, Ky., 1936; M.A., Morehead U.; M.S., U. Louisville; Ph.D., Fla. State U.; m. Blake Pinson, June 7, 1936 (dec. June 1971); children—Larry Blake, Robert D. Tchr., Pike County (Ky.) Schs., 1936-40, sch. supr., 1940-43; office mgr. Pinson Motor Freight Co., Pikeville, also Huntington, W.Va., 1943-47; notary pub., 1947—; mgr., buyer Style Shop, Pikeville, 1947-50; mgr. Pinson Hotel; real estate broker Pinson Realty Co., 1950—; founder, mgr. Ann Pinson Interiors; pres. Pinson Ins. Agy., 1958—; v.p. L & P Contracting Co., Pikeville, 1955—; regional chmn. Heritage Life Ins. Co.; exec. v.p. Letcher Mfg. Co. Chmn., Small Bus. Service Center, 1965—; mem. Pikeville Library Bd., 1966—; mem. coms. on tourist promotion, edn., pub. relations, civic affairs Pikeville, 1963—; mem. Gov.'s Conf. on Edn., Louisville, 1956, Meth. Hosp. Guild, 1965—, Mental Health Assn., 1965—; active local P.T.A., band boosters assn., 1954—; mem. Children's Hosp., Louisville, 1963—; chmn. Model City neighborhood adv. council. Mem. Nat. Real Estate Bd. (mem. Women's Council), Am., Ky. hotel assns., Ky., Pikeville chambers commerce, Pikeville Coll. Alumni Assn. (pres. 1969—), Nat. Appraisers Assn. (charter mem.), Pikeville hist. socs., Internat. Platform Assn., Am. Assn. U. Women (publicity chmn.). Club: Pikeville Woman's. Home: 405 2d St Pikeville KY 41501 Office: Pinson Hotel Pike Av Pikeville KY 41501

PIPBERGER, HUBERT VINCENT, physician, educator; b. Camberg, Germany, May 29, 1920; s. Johannes and Elizabeth (Weyrich) P.; B.A., Deutsches Kolleg, Bad Godesberg, Germany, 1938; M.D., Rheinische Friedrich Wilhelms U., Bonn, Germany, 1951; m. Hanna Agnes Zulauf, Apr. 30, 1955. Came to U.S., 1955, naturalized, 1960. Chief clin. electrophysiology lab. Zurich (Switzerland) Univ. Hosp., 1953-55; chief VA Research Center for Cardiovascular Data Processing, Washington, 1957—. Mem. faculty Georgetown U., Washington, 1959-71, asso. prof. medicine, 1965-71; prof. clin. engring. and medicine George Washington U., Washington, 1971—. Recipient William S. Middleton award VA, 1961. Fellow Am. Coll. Cardiology; mem. Am. Heart Assn. (chmn. com. electrocardiography 1972—). Club: Shannondale Community (Charlestown, W.Va.). Editor. bd. Circulation, 1967-72, Jour. Electrocardiology, 1967—; asso. editor Methods of Information in Medicine, 1965—. Home: 3900 A Watson Pl NW Washington DC 20016 Office: VA Hosp 50 Irving St NW Washington DC 20422

PIPER, GLEN LEO, educator; b. Cottonwood, Ariz., June 28, 1939; s. William M. and Ina E. (Speer) P.; B.A., Northwestern State Coll., Alva, Okla., 1962, M.Teaching, 1970; postgrad. Okla. State U., 1972; m. Donna Rae Schupbach, June 7, 1963; children—Troy, Ty, Trina. Tchr. high sch. Enid, Okla., 1963, Hugo, Colo., 1964-66, Medicine Lodge, Kan., 1966-67, Kowa, Kan., 1967-70; instr. accounting, coach baseball and basketball No. Okla. Coll., Tonkawa, 1970—. Named All State Athlete State Kan., 1957, Nat. All Am. Athlete 1957; Coach of Year by Conf. Coaches, 1963-65, Tchr. of Year by Local Assn. Kan., 1968. Mem. Fellowship Christian Athletes, Jr. C. of C. (pres. 1965), N.E.A., Okla. Edn. Assn., Okla. Accounting Assn., Nat. Jr. Coll. Athletic Assn. Coaches Assn. Home: 1605 E Tonkawa St Tonkawa OK 74653 Office: Dept Accounting Northern Okla Coll Tonkawa OK 74653

PIPER, ROY HERBERT, banker; b. Elgin, Ill., June 17, 1927; s. David Roy and Cleora Stuart (Greene) P.; B.A. with honors, U. Ill., 1949; postgrad. U. N.C., 1950-51, Stonier Grad. Sch. Banking, 1967; M.B.A., Augusta Coll., 1974; m. Betty Eidson, Aug. 25, 1950; children—Phyllis, Catherine, David, Joseph. Secondary sch. tchr. Rutherford County, N.C., 1949-53; v.p. Ga. Railroad Bank & Trust Co., Augusta, Ga., 1953—. Instr. Am. Inst. Banking, 1961-70. Chmn. nat. essay contest Am. Soc. Personnel Adminstrn., 1968; mem. study com. Bd. Commrs. Richmond County, Ga., 1969; chmn. Merit System Commn., Richmond County, 1972—. Mem. Am. Soc. Personnel Adminstrn., Personnel Assn. Central Savannah River Area, Phi Alpha Theta. Home: 189 Myrtle Dr Augusta GA 30904 Office: 699 Broad St Augusta GA 30902

PIPES, CHARLES JEFFERSON, JR., educator; b. Terrell, Tex., Dec. 24, 1917; s. Charles Jefferson and Rose Leah (Yates) P.; B.A., U. Okla., 1940, M.A., 1948, Ph.D., 1950; m. Dorothy Mae Daugherty, Dec. 28, 1939; children—Janice (Mrs. James McKinney), Larry Neil. Instr. math. U. Okla., Norman, 1946-50; mem. faculty So. Meth. U., Dallas, 1950—, asso. prof., 1953-58, prof., 1958—. Served with USNR, 1943-46. Mem. Math. Assn. Am. (gov. 1971-74), Am. Math. Soc., Am. Assn. U. Profs., A.A.A.S., Phi Beta Kappa, Sigma Xi. Home: 3104 Purdue St Dallas TX 75225

PIPKIN, JOHN B., II, banker; b. Greensboro, N.C., Feb. 8, 1935; s. Willis Benton and Ruth (Pringle) P.; B.A., Va. Mil. Inst., 1957; M.B.A., U. Va., 1961; student Stonier grad. sch. Banking, Rutgers U., 1968; m. Anne Hunter Baker, Nov. 1, 1958; children—Anne Hunter, Ruth Pringle. With N.C. Nat. Bank, 1961—, v.p., mgr. credit dept., 1963-69, v.p., dir. credit adminstrn. and services, 1969-71, v.p., sr. comml. loan officer, 1971-73, sr. v.p., sr. comml. loan officer, 1973—; dir. Knob Creek Morganton, Inc. Trustee, St. James (Md.) Sch. Served with AUS, 1957-59. Mem. Nat. Assn. Accountants (Nat. Pub. Relations award 1969, dir. chpt.), Robert Morris Assos. (bd. govs. Carolina-Va. chpt. 1972—), Piedmont Credit Club, N.C. Motor Carriers Assn. (accounting council). Clubs: Charlotte City, Charlotte Country. Contbg. editor The Bankers Handbook, 1966. Home: 316 Lockley Dr Charlotte NC 28207 Office: 200 S Tryon St Charlotte NC 28201

PIPKIN, MICHAEL BRUCE, librarian; b. Mena, Ark., Oct. 3, 1934; s. Compere Allen and Leyland (Chambers) P.; student Peabody Conservatory of Music, 1956-68; B.A., U. Md., 1961; M.L.S., U. N.C., 1952; m. Betty J. Jordan, Aug. 21, 1960; children—Michael, David, Christopher, Thomas. Librarian I, Free Library of Phila., 1962-64; base librarian Olmsted AFB, Pa., 1964-67; librarian City of Hampton (Va.), 1967-73; regional librarian USIA, 1973—. Served with AUS, 1953-56. Mem. Am., Va., S.E. library assns., Va. Jr. Member's Round Table (chmn. 1969-70), Armed Forces Librarians Sect. (chmn. devel. com. 1965-66; library adminstrn. div. small libraries publ. com. 1973-75), Hampton Hist. Soc. (v.p. 1969-71), Archaeol. Soc. Va. (v.p. 1967-68). Home: 9701 St Andrews Dr Fairfax VA 22030 Office: USIS Bangkok Thailand APO San Francisco CA 96346

PIPPEN, JOSEPH FRANKLIN, ins. co. exec.; b. Richmond, Va., Mar. 14, 1925; s. Icha Linwood and Margaret (Childress) P.; grad. Smithdeal Bus. Coll., 1946; m. Selma Browne Seay, July 5, 1944; children—Joseph Franklin, Bruce S. Clk., U.S. Govt., 1946-47; debit agt. Life of Va., Richmond, 1948-53, asso. mgr., Miami, Fla., 1953-54; with Atlantic Life Ins. Co. (merged with Southwestern Life Ins. Co. 1961), Richmond, 1954—, v.p. in charge combination div., 1961—, now v.p. Southwestern Life Ins. Co.; sr. v.p., dir. Southwestern Gen. Life Ins. Co., Dallas, 1970-73, pres., dir., 1973—. Served with USMCR, 1943-45, 50-51. Republican. Methodist. Home: 7123 Briarmeadow St Dallas TX 75230 Office: PO Box 799 Dallas TX 78421

PIPPIN, WARREN FLOYD, electronics co. exec.; b. Mulberry, Kan., Feb. 26, 1919; s. Arnold Golden and Nellie (Walthour) P.; B.S., Colo. State U., 1941; M.S., Okla. State U., 1958, Ph.D., 1968; M.Ed., Our Lady Lake Coll., 1973; m. Belle Dixson Porter, Dec. 8, 1942; children—Virginia, Warren, Donald. Served with AUS, 1942-46, quarantine insp. U.S. Dept. Agr., Nogales, Ariz., 1946-48, San Antonio, 1948-52; commd. capt. USAF, 1952, advanced through grades to lt. col., 1968; med. entomologist Army biol. lab., Ft. Detrick, Md., 1952-54; med. chief Entomology br. Ramey AFB, P.R., 1954-56; med. entomologist Air Force Inst. Tech., Okla. State U., Stillwater, 1956-58; chief, entomology br. Air Force Med. Service Sch., Gunter AFB, Ala., 1958-61; chief entomology br. 5th Epidemiological Flight, Japan, 1961-63, Philippine Islands, 1963-64; asst. chief, entomology br., epidemiological lab. Aerospace Med. Div., Lackland AFB, Tex., 1964-68, ret., research entomologist, 1968-71; cons. Southwest Research Inst., 1969-71; prin. scientist Lockheed Electronics Co., Inc. Mem. Entomol. Soc. Am., Am. Mosquito Control Assn., Nat. Sojourners, Sci. Research Soc. Am., Sigma Xi, Phi Sigma, Alpha Zeta, Beta Beta Beta, Phi Kappa Phi. Republican, Presbyn. Mason (Shriner).

Home: 16201 El Camino Real 12-A Houston TX 77058 Office: Lockheed Co Aerospace Systems Div C-17 16811 El Camino Real Houston TX 77058

PIRANIO, ANTHONY F., owner investment co.; b. Dallas, Dec. 15, 1918; s. Joseph T. and Lena (LaRoca) P.; certificate real estate So. Meth. U., 1962; m. Katherine Angelo, Nov. 27, 1946; children—Lynn Rose, Dana Louise, Gina Frances. Owner, operator A.F. Piranio Investments, Dallas, 1946—, A.F. Piranio Constrn. Co., Dallas, 1948—; sr. partner Piranio & Piranio Investments, Dallas, 1950—, Dal-Tex Builders, Inc., Dallas, 1955-57; co-owner PiLi Farms, Van Zandt County (Tex.), 1962—, P & L Cattle Co., 1969—. Cons. real estate, 1948—. Served with AUS, 1941-45; PTO. Home: 6705 Braeburn Dr Dallas TX 75214

PIRKLE, DAVID EUGENE, mech. engr.; b. Atlanta, Aug. 8, 1927; s. David Ambrose and Eugenia (Bragg) P.; B.S., Ga. Inst. Tech., 1952; m. Mildred Ransie Edgens, Jan. 31, 1959. Mech. engr. Lockheed Aircraft Co., Marietta, Ga., 1952-59; individual engring. practice, Atlanta, 1959-63, 70—; mech. engr. Atlanta Army Depot, Forest Park, Ga., 1963-70. Recipient award Lockheed Mgmt. Club, 1954; award for outstanding performance in engring. Dept. Army, 1966, 69. Registered profl. engr., Ga. Address: 2203 Polar Rock Pl SW Atlanta GA 30315

PIRTLE, GEORGE WILLIAM, geologist; b. Cecelia, Ky., Nov. 1, 1902; s. Thomas Louis and Laura (Shipley) P.; B.S., U. Ky., 1924, M.S., 1925; m. El Freda Taylor, July 16, 1928; 1 son, George William. Geologist, Ky. Geol. Survey, 1924-25; cons. geologist, partner Hudnall & Pirtle, Tyler, Tex., 1925-69; petroleum cons. Pirtle & Townsend, Inc., 1970—; dir. Peoples Nat. Bank, Gibraltar Life Ins. Co. Trustee Tyler Jr. Coll. Dir. South Central Region Boy Scouts Am., mem. nat. exec. bd. Recipient Silver Beaver, Silver Antelope, Silver Buffalo awards Boy Scouts Am.; named Tyler's Outstanding Citizen, 1962. Mem. Tex. Acad. Sci., Tyler C. of C. (past dir.), Geol. Soc. Am., Am. Assn. Petroleum Geologists, Mich. Acad. Sci., Am. Inst. Mining, Metall. and Petroleum Engrs., Sigma Xi, Omicron Delta Kappa. Methodist. Home: 115 E 2d St Tyler TX 75701 Office: 610 People Bank Bldg Tyler TX 75701

PIRTLE, IVYL LEORA FLEMING (MRS. J. MAX PIRTLE), educator, librarian; b. nr. Ottumwa, Ia., Jan. 11, 1906; d. Barton Earl and Lillie (Roberts) Fleming; student Ia. State Coll., 1931; B.A., U. Fla., 1944; M.A., Fla. State U., 1951; m. J. Max Pirtle, Sept. 17, 1938. Tchr. elementary schs., Ia., 1924-39; tchr. Grace Stern Pvt. Sch., Miami Beach, Fla., 1939-40; tchr. elementary schs., Indiantown, 1940-43; tchr. primary grades, Stuart, 1943-50; demonstration tchr. Fla. State U., Tallahassee, summer 1949; tchr. Palmetto Sch., West Palm Beach, 1950-55; supr. elementary edn. Palm Beach County, 1955-65, dir. library services, 1965-70. Mem. Fla. steering com. Nat. Def. Edn. Act, 1958-68. Trustee Jr. Mus. Palm Beach County, 1960-63. Recipient Certificate of Appreciation Fla. Dept. Edn., 1969. Mem. Assn. Childhood Edn. Internat. (br. pres. 1953-55, primary edn. com. 1954-56), Fla. Assn. Sch. Librarians (area chmn. 1959-62), N.E.A., Fla. Edn. Assn. (state chmn. dept. suprs. 1959-60, dept. suprs. citation 1968), Assn. Supervision and Curriculum Devel., Delta Kappa Gamma (chpt. pres. 1955-59), Kappa Delta Pi, Phi Kappa Phi. Club: Zonta. Contbr. articles profl. jours. Home: 340 Nottingham Blvd West Palm Beach FL 33405

PISTOR, CHARLES HERMAN, traffic cons.; b. St. Louis, Aug. 23, 1901; s. Charles F. and Augusta (Reh) P.; LL.B., Benton Coll., 1925, LL.M., 1926; student Washington U., 1927-28; m. Virginia Grace Brown, Jan. 18, 1929; children—Charles Herman, Walter Brown, Virginia Reh. Stenographer, clk. Mobile & Ohio R.R., St. Louis, 1918-24; commerce clk., chief rate clk. M.-K.-T. R.R., 1924-28; with T. & P. Ry., 1928-67, successively clk., chief clk., asst. gen. freight agt., gen. freight agt., asst. freight traffic mgr., freight traffic mgr., 1928-53, gen. freight traffic mgr., 1953-60; asst. v.p. marketing, 1960-67; cons. Western Traffic Cons., Dallas, 1967—. Life mem. Jr. C. of C. of St. Louis, former dir. Mem. Am. Soc. Traffic and Transp., Nat. Freight Traffic Assn., Assn. ICC Practitioners, Dallas Knights of the Round Table (pres. 1945), Transp. Club of Dallas. Presbyn. (elder). Club: Dallas Athletic. Address: 7038 Currin Dr Dallas TX 75230

PITCHER, GRIFFITH FONTAINE, lawyer; b. Balt., Nov. 1, 1937; s. William Henry and Virginia Griffith (Stein) P.; grad. Gilman Sch., 1956; A.B., Johns Hopkins U., 1960; LL.B., U. Va., 1963; m. Virginia Kyle Badham, June 27, 1959; children—Virginia T., Lawrence B., William T.B., Margaret W. Admitted to Ala. bar, 1963, Fla. bar, 1971; asso. firm Bradley, Arant, Rose & White, Birmingham, Ala., 1963-71; mem. firm van den Berg, Gay, Burke & Dyer, Orlando, Fla., 1971—. Pres. Bessemer Plaza Hotel Corp. (Ala.), 1966-67; dir. Bessemer Coal, Iron and Land Co., 1964-71, Blount Springs Investment Co., 1964-71. Mem. Am., Ala., Fla. bar assns., Soc. Cincinnati, S.R., Soc. 1812, Desc. Lords of Md. Manors, Soc. Colonial Wars, Beaux Arts Krewe, St. Andrew Soc. (vice chancellor 1971), Ala. Aquarium Soc. (v.p. 1970), Order of Coif, Delta Phi (pres. Xi chpt. 1959-60). Republican. Episcopalian. Clubs: Mountain Brook (Birmingham); Emerald Valley Resort (Pinson, Ala.); Citrus (Orlando, Fla.). Editorial bd. Va. Law Rev., 1961-63. Home: 440 Henkel Circle Winter Park FL 32789 Office: 16 S Magnolia Av Orlando FL 32802

PITCHFORD, ARMIN CLOYST, chemist; b. nr. Mountain Home, Ark., May 12, 1922; s. Fred Lee and Tera May (Wilson) P.; B.S., U. Ark., 1947, postgrad., 1947-48; student State Coll. Ark., 1940-41; m. Willie Allyn Coger, Mar. 25, 1944; children—Larry Alan, Armin Charles. With Phillips Petroleum Co., various locations, 1948-56, 59—, chemist, Bartlesville, 1952-56, project mgr., 1959—; propellant devel. chemist Rocketdyne, Waco, Tex., 1956-58. Active Boy Scouts Am. Precinct chmn. Democratic party, 1971-72. Served with AUS, 1943-45. Decorated Combat Infantryman Badge. Mem. Am. Chem. Soc. Baptist. Patentee in field. Home: 4912 SE Princeton Dr Bartlesville OK 74003 Office: Phillips Petroleum Co Research Center 83-E Bartlesville OK 74004

PITCHFORD, HARRIET DAY, librarian; b. Canton, Miss.; d. Sterling G. and Lidie (Hunnicutt) Pitchford; B.S., Miss. So. U., 1935; M.A., George Peabody Coll., 1959; postgrad. Columbia, summers 1961, 64, 66. Tchr. elementary sch., Miss., 1935-41; librarian Main Post Library, Camp Van Dorn, Miss., 1941-43, Camp Roberts, Cal., 1943-47, Camp Zama, Japan, 1947-49, Ft. Benning, Ga., 1949—, assigned Vietnam, 1970-71. Mem. Am. Assn. U. Women, UN Assn. of Am. Club: Altrusa (pres. 1967-68) (Columbus, Ga.,). Home: 115 Matheson Rd Columbus GA 31903 Office: PO Box 1972 Ft Benning GA 31905

PITCOCK, LOUIS, JR., oil and gas co. exec.; b. Fort Worth, Tex.; s. Louis and Medora (Shepherd) P.; student N. Tex. State U., 1941-43, Dallas Coll. So. Methodist U., 1947; B.A., Southwestern U. Tex., 1949; postgrad. North Tex. State U., 1973; m. Mary Ellen McFarlane, June 29, 1949; children—Ellen Shepherd (Mrs. Charles F. Morris), Louis III, Thomas Carl. With Pitcock Bros., concrete, Graham, Tex., 1949-56, Pitcock Drilling Co., oil well drilling, 1956-67; sec.-treas. Pitcock, Inc., oil and gas prodn., 1967—, v.p., 1969—. Pres. Graham area United Fund, 1965-66. Del., Tex. Democratic Convs., 1960—, precinct committeeman, 1958—, chmn. Young County Dem. Exec. Com., 1974—. Bd. regents Midwestern U., 1968-74, acting chmn., 1970-71; trustee Graham Pub. Library, chmn., 1966—; bd. dirs. Graham area Day Care Center, v.p., 1970—; mem. adv. bd. Tex. Library System, 1972—. Served with USAAF, 1943-46; CBI. Mem. North Tex., West Tex. oil and gas assns., Graham C. of C. (v.p. 1956-57, 69-70), Phi Delta Theta. Methodist (vice-chmn. central Tex. conf. bd. lay activities 1955-63, dist. bd. trustees 1956—). Rotarian (pres. 1955-56, sec. 1953-55). Home: 813 Elm St Graham TX 76046 Office: PO Box 747 Graham TX 76046

PITT, WOODROW WILSON, JR., chem. engr.; b. Rocky Mount, N.C., Aug. 14, 1935; s. Woodrow Wilson and Stella Marie (Whitley) P.; B.S., U. S.C., 1957; M.S., U. Tenn., 1966, Ph.D., 1969; m. Katherine Ann Morton, Jan. 1, 1958; children—Deborah Ann, Abigail Marie, Katherine Elizabeth. Devel. engr. Oak Ridge (Tenn.) Nat. Lab., 1960-70, sr. engr., group leader, 1970—. Bd. dirs. Clinch Valley council Campfire Girls, 1972—. Served as lt. (j.g.) USNR, 1957-60; comdr. Res. AEC fellow in nuclear sci. engring., 1966-67. Registered profl. engr., Tenn. Mem. Am. Inst. Chem. Engrs., Nat. Soc. Profl. Engrs., A.A.A.S., Sigma Xi, Tau Beta Pi. Methodist. Patentee in field; contbr. articles to profl. jours. Home: 254 Iroquois Rd Oak Ridge TN 37830 Office: Bldg 4500-N ORNL PO Box X Oak Ridge TN 37830

PITTMAN, BLAND PARK, land planner; b. Hugo, Okla., Sept. 4, 1938; s. Bland and Ernestine (Park) P.; B.S., La. State U., 1963, postgrad., 1963-64; m. Sandra Lee Sample, Nov. 27, 1959; children—Bland Brooks, Hunter Lee. Grad. tchr. landscape architecture La. State U., 1963-64; planning specialist Kellogg Research Center U. Okla., 1964-67; landscape architect Phillips, Proctor, Bowers & Assos., Land Planners and Landscape Architects, Dallas, 1967-73; dir. land planning Day, Davies & Poe - Poe & Assos., Planners, Engrs. and Architects, Tulsa, 1973—. Recipient Nat. Design Competition Blue Seal award, 1962; Oklahoma City Urban Renewal Design award, 1963. Mem. Am. Soc. Landscape Architects. Rotarian. Home: 512 Meadowood Broken Arrow OK 74012 Office: 5800 E Skelly Dr Tulsa OK 74135

PITTMAN, CHALMERS VAN ANGLEN, geophysicist; b. Trenton, N.J., July 25, 1904; s. Raymond Hill and Evanna Catherine (Van Anglen) P.; B.S., Haverford Coll., 1925; m. Margaret Ellen Hallett, Aug. 10, 1929; 1 dau., Janet McLellan. Geophysicist Geophys. Research Corp., Houston, 1927-30, Geophys. Service, Inc., Dallas, 1930-42; exec. v.p., chmn. bd. Geochem. Surveys, Dallas, 1942—. Bd. mgrs., Haverford Coll. Mem. Am. Assn. Petroleum Geologists, Soc. Exploration Geophysicists, Dallas Petroleum Club, S.A.R., Soc. Colonial Wars, Hereditary Order Descs. Colonial Govs., Corp. Haverford Coll., Nat. Huguenot Soc., Soc. Descs. Colonial Clergy. Mem. Soc. of Friends. Club: Dallas Country. Home: 3909 Miramar Av Dallas TX 75205 Office: 2505 Turtle Creek Blvd Dallas TX 75219

PITTMAN, CLARENCE WALLACE, aerospace co. exec.; b. Covington, Ky., Sept. 5, 1929; s. Frederick Huffman and Elizabeth John (Chapman) P.; B.Sc. summa cum laude, Ohio State U., 1958, M.Sc., 1958; postgrad. U. Cal. at Los Angeles, 1960-61; m. Annmarie Rogers, May 30, 1963; 1 son, Anthony Rogers. Engr., Space Tech. Labs., Los Angeles, 1958-62; sect. head Aerospace Corp., Los Angeles, 1962-65; project mgr., operation mgr. TRW Systems Group, Houston, 1965—; dir. Nassau Bay Nat. Bank, Houston. Chmn. housing com. Houston Council Human Relations, 1967-68; chmn. aerospace industries United Fund Appeal, 1969. Chmn. bd. dirs. Urban Affairs Corp., Houston, 1971-73. Served with USAF, 1950-54. Recipient Pub. Service award NASA, 1969, Presdl. Freedom medal, 1970. Mem. Am. Inst. Aeros. and Astronautics, I.E.E.E., Tau Beta Pi, Clear Lake C. of C., Sigma Xi, Eta Kappa Nu, Pi Mu Epsilon. Democrat. Mem. United Ch. of Christ (pres. 1969-70). Clubs: Houston; Bay Area Racket (Houston). Home: 615 Baronridge Dr Seabrook TX 77586 Office: Space Park Dr Houston TX 77058

PITTMAN, ISHAM WATSON, mfg. co. exec.; b. Turbeville, S.C., Feb. 19, 1913; s. Isham Watson and Alice Newell (Turbeville) P.; student Stokes Bus. Coll., Charleston, S.C., 1930; m. Katherine Mathis, Mar. 27, 1936; children—Katrina, John. Salesman Nat. Cash Register Co., Charleston, S.C., 1930-32, Nat. Life and Accident Ins. Co., Atlanta, 1933-36, Minn. Mining and Mfg. Co., 1937-48, Wm. and Harvey Rowland, Atlanta, 1948-53; pres., gen. mgr. Joint and Clutch Service, Charlotte, N.C., 1953-57; salesman William and Harvey Rowland of Ga., Inc., mfg. power transmission components for heavy duty trucks and equipment, Atlanta, 1949-68, asst. v.p., gen. mgr., 1968—. Baptist (pres. men's Bible class 1968, deacon). Mason. Clubs: Automotive Booster (pres. 1948), Druid Hills Golf (Atlanta). Home: 301 Heaton Park Dr Decatur GA 30030 Office: PO Box 43386 Atlanta GA 30336

PITTMAN, JAMES ALLEN, JR., univ. dean, physician; b. Orlando, Fla., Apr. 12, 1927; s. James Allen and Jean C. (Garretson) P.; B.S., Davidson Coll., 1948; M.D., Harvard, 1952; m. Constance Ming-Chung Shen, Feb. 19, 1955; children—James Clinton, John Merrill. Intern, asst. resident medicine Mass. Gen. Hosp., Boston, 1952-54; teaching fellow medicine Harvard, 1953-54; clin. asso. NIH, Bethesda, Md., 1954-56; instr. medicine George Washington U., 1955-56; chief resident medicine U. Ala. Med. Center, Birmingham, 1956-58, instr. medicine, 1956-59, asst. prof., 1959-62, asso. prof., 1962-64, prof. medicine, 1964-71, dir. endocrinology and metabolism div., 1962-71, co-chmn. dept. medicine, 1969-71, also asso. prof. physiology and biophysics, 1966-71; asst. chief med. dir. research and edn. in medicine U.S. Vets. Adminstrn., 1971-73; prof. medicine Georgetown U. Med. Sch., Washington, 1971-73; dean U. Ala. Sch. Medicine, 1973—. Mem. pharmacology, endcrinology fellowships rev. commn. NIH, 1967-68. Fellow A.C.P. (life); mem. Endocrine Soc., Am. Thyroid Assn., N.Y. Acad. Scis. (life), Soc. Nuclear Medicine, Am. Diabetes Assn., Am. Chem. Soc., Wilson Ornithol. Club, Am. Ornithologists Union, Am. Fedn. Clin. Research (pres. So. sect., mem. nat. council 1962-66), So. Soc. Clin. Investigation, Phi Beta Kappa, Alpha Omega Alpha, Omicron Delta Kappa. Author: Diagnosis and Treatment of Thyroid Diseases, 1963. Contbr. articles in field to profl. jours. Home: 5 Ridge Dr Birmingham AL 35213

PITTMAN, MALCOLM GALUSHA, JR., ins. co. exec.; b. Chgo., Aug. 25, 1924; s. Malcolm Galusha and Helen (Cottingham) P.; student Miami U., Oxford, O., 1943-44, Oberlin Coll., 1944-45; A.B., Central Meth. Coll., 1945; m. Norma June Matthews, Oct. 31, 1947; children—Malcolm Galusha III, Russell Warren III. Sr. underwriter Bus. Mens Assurance Co., Kansas City, 1946-51, Bankers Life Co., Des Moines, 1951-54; mgr. health underwriting Gulf Life Ins. Co., Jacksonville, Fla., 1954-61; underwriting v.p. Kennesaw Life & Accident Ins. Co., Atlanta, 1961-63; v.p., sec. Ga. Life & Health Ins. Co., Atlanta, 1961—. Mem. Mensa, Sertoma Internat. (life). Home: 3655 Woodstream Circle NE Atlanta GA 30319 Office: 66 Luckie St NW Atlanta GA 30303

PITTMAN, ROBERT HERBERT, ednl. adminstr.; b. Alexandria, La., Mar. 22, 1915; s. Jackson Boyd and Lillie (Davis) P.; student U. Wis., 1938; A.B., Northwestern State Coll. La., 1938; M.Ed., La. State U., 1949; Ed.D., U. Miss., 1961; m. Kathleen Higdon, July 17, 1950; children—Martha Joe, Kathleen Ann, Susan Elizabeth, Sharon Evelyn. Tchr. Rapides Parish Sch. Bd., Lecompte, La., 1938-42; tchr., coach LaSalle Parish Sch. Bd., Urania, La., 1942-48; vis. tchr. Jena, La., 1948-49; prin. Cameron Parish Sch. Bd., Grand Chenier, La., 1949-57; prof., head elementary edn., dir. ednl. research and services McNeese State Coll., Lake Charles, La., 1957-70, v.p., 1970-72; dir. Ednl. Cons. Assos., 1972—. Cons. sch. dists. and colls., Hurricane Audrey and Carla Disaster Studies; adminstr., coordinator Cameron Parish Police Jury for Hurricane Audrey Disaster, 1957-58. Mem. La. Tchrs. Assn., Nat. Acad. Sci., Assn. Supervision and Curriculum Devel., Assn. Student Tchrs., Phi Delta Kappa, Kappa Delta Pi. Baptist. Mason (Shriner). Author: (with others) The Social and Psychological Consequences of a Natural Disaster, 1963. Home: 314 University Dr Lake Charles LA 70601

PITTS, FRED, cons. elec. engr., artist; b. Alexander City, Ala., Sept. 19, 1934; s. Mathew Otis and Irene (Tate) P.; B.E.E., U. Fla., 1958; postgrad. Corcoran Sch. Art, 1963-69; m. Marjorie Elizabeth McInnis, Nov. 6, 1965; 1 dau., Samantha. Asso. engr. Westinghouse Electric Corp., Pitts., also Balt., 1958-62; project engr. Booz, Allen & Hamilton, Inc., consultants, Bethesda, Md., 1962-69, 72—; pvt. cons. collaborations in art and technology, Washington, 1969-72. Mem. faculty Corcoran Sch. Art, Washington, 1972—, Nat. Park Service, Glen Echo (Md.) Creative Workshop, 1972—; faculty Smithsonian Inst., Washington, 1973—, exhbns. cons., 1970—; executed with Juan Downey, electronic scupture, Tel Aviv Museum; collaborations in exhbns. for Bklyn. Mus., Corcoran Gallery, Everson Mus. and comml. galleries. Mem. Neighborhood Arts Council, D.C. Commn. on Arts, 1972—. Served with AUS, 1954-56. Registered profl. engr., D.C. Research and devel. in heliography for printing large images on canvas, 1969. Patentee microwave radar devices. Home: 2636 Woodley Pl NW Washington DC 20008 Office: 4733 Bethesda Av Bethesda MD 20014

PITTS, LLOYD FRANK, oil co. exec.; b. Wesson, Miss., Oct. 7, 1910; s. John L. and Addie Mae (Sandifer) P.; student Copiah-Lincoln Jr. Coll., 1925-31, Northwestern U., 1932; m. Mary Martha McCann, Dec. 28, 1935; children—Lloyd F. (dec.), Linda (Mrs. William A. Custard). With Nu-Enamel Corp., 1931-48, pres., dir., 1939-48; pres., dir. Nu-Enamel Internat., 1947-48; owner Pitts Oil Co., Dallas, 1948—; v.p., dir. Star Oil Co., Dallas, 1946-60; pres., dir. Longhorn Prodn. Co., Dallas, 1960—; chmn. bd., chief exec. officer Exploration Surveys Inc., Dallas, 1961—, pres., 1967-71, dir., 1957-71; pres., dir. Computer Systems Corp., Dallas; 1967-70. Pres., Park Cities Rotary Club Found., Inc., 1967-68; mem. Baylor U. Devel. Council, Waco, 1966—, Golden Gate Sem. Devel. Council, Mill Valley, Cal., 1966—. Bd. dirs. Dallas Civic Opera, 1970—, v.p., 1972—. Mem. Am. Assn. Petroleum Landmen, Ind. Petroleum Assn. Am., Tex. Mid-Continent Oil and Gas Assn., Tex. Ind. Producers and Royalty Owners Assn. Baptist (deacon). Clubs: Park Cities Roatry (pres. 1966-67, dir.), Dallas Petroleum, Dallas, Brookhollow Golf, Preston Trails Golf. Home: 4938 DeLoache St Dallas TX 75220 Office: Meadows Bldg Dallas TX 75206

PIXLEY, JOHN SHERMAN, research co. exec.; b. Detroit, Aug. 24, 1929; s. Rex Arthur and Louise (Sherman) P.; B.A., U. Va., 1951; postgrad. Pa. State U., 1958-59; m. Peggy Marie Payne, Oct. 16, 1949; children—John Sherman, Steven, Lou Ann. Asst. cashier Old Dominion Bank, Arlington, Va., 1953-56; tech. dir. John I. Thompson & Co., research and engring. firm, Bellefonte, Pa., 1956-65; co-founder, exec. v.p. Potomac Research, Inc., Baileys Crossroads, Va., 1965—. Mem. Fairfax County Republican Com., Annandale, Va., 1964-72; mem. finance com. for U.S. Rep. Joel T. Broyhill, Republican, Va., 1970-72. Served to 1st lt. AUS, 1952-53; maj. Res. ret. Decorated Army Commendation medal. Mem. I.E.E.E., Sleepy Hollow Woods Civic Assn. (v.p., pres. 1969-71). Presbyn. Club: Quantico (Va.) Flying (charter mem.). Home: 3711 Sleepy Hollow Rd Falls Church VA 22041 Office: 7655 Old Springhouse Rd Westgate Research Park McLean VA 22101

PLANAS, JUAN ENRIQUE, engring. co. exec.; b. Havana, Cuba, July 5, 1940; s. Juan I. and Leonor (Martinez) P.; B.S. in Civil Engring., U. Miami, 1963; m. Sylvia Novo, Sept. 15, 1962; children—Sylvia M., Juan E., Luis I., Lourdes M., Jorge M. Jr. engr. Connell Assos., Miami, Fla., 1962-64; engr. Meekins Prestress, Hallandale, Fla., 1964-66; sr. engr. Ross Assos., Miami, 1966-67; pres., cons. engr. Planas & Franyie Engrs., Inc., Miami, 1967—; pres. Cauto Investment Corp., PFE Enterprises, Inc., Profl. and Constrn. Mgmt. Co., PCM Constrn. Corp.; dir. PFE Mortgage Services, Inc., Bravo & Assos., architects, Inc. Part-time tchr. U. Miami, 1963-64, Broward Jr. Coll., Ft. Lauderdale, Fla., 1965-66; mem. Cons. Engrs. Council. Mem. transp. adv. com. Dade County (Fla.). Bd. dirs. Bethany Residence. Registered profl. engr., Fla. Mem. Nat. Soc. Profl. Engrs., Am. Soc. C.E., Am. Concrete Inst., Constrn. Specifications Inst., Agrupacion Catolica Universitaria, Asociacion Interamericana de Hombres de Empresa, Coral Gables C. of C. Fla. Engring. Soc., Fla. Inst. Cons. Engrs. Kiwanian. Home: 3300 SW 17th St Miami FL 33145 Office: 1825 Coral Way Miami FL 33145

PLANT, RICHARD, dentist; b. Madison, Fla., July 12, 1924; s. Clarence Mosley and Francis Marie (Garbutt) P.; B.S., U. Fla., 1949; D.M.D. U. Louisville, 1953; m. Renna Mae Pickens, Aug. 26, 1954; children—Rachel and Rebecca (twins). Intern, Fla. State Hosp., Chattahoochee, 1953-54; practice dentistry, Darlington, S.C., 1955-59, Tallahassee, 1962—; asst. dir. Fla. Instl. Dental Service, 1960-62; sr. dental staff Tallahassee Meml. Hosp. Cons. Fed. Correctional Inst.; Gideon dental missionary to Mexico. Pres., Big Bend Tb and Respiratory Disease Assn., 1968-71. Served with USAAF, 1943-45. Mem. Am. Dental Assn. Methodist (asst. dist. lay leader 1967-72). Elk. Club: Toastmasters. Home: 3061 Carlow Circle Tallahassee FL 32303 Office: 1901 Miccosuke Rd Tallahassee FL 32303

PLATT, ALLAN, metals co. exec.; b. Bayonne, N.J., Aug. 24, 1925; s. David and Jane (Shilkoff) P.; student Williamsport Jr. Coll., 1944, Bayonne Jr. Coll., 1946; B.M.E., Clarkson Coll. Tech., 1950; m. Ann Heryla, Aug. 2, 1958; children—Carlton Jay, Douglas Glenn. Insp. engr. Picatinny Arsenal, Dover, N.J., 1950-56, chief, quality assurance spl. munitions, 1956-59, mgr. ballistic missile and warhead sects. Army Munitions Command, 1959-64; dep. project mgr. guided missile system Army Missile Command, Redstone Arsenal, Ala., 1964-71, chief engring. div., 1971-72; plant mgr. Fed. Copper and Aluminum Co., 1972—. Served with USAAF, 1943-45; with AUS, 1951-52. Recipient Meritorious Civilian Service award Dept. Army; Sr. Exec. award Army Missile Command. Profl. engr., Ala. Mem. Soc. Mfg. Engrs. Home: 8016 Craigmont Rd Huntsville AL 35802

PLATT, LOIS IRENE, physician; b. Oil City, Pa., May 23, 1908; d. Hugh Ashley and Myrtle (Dolby) Platt; A.B., Goucher Coll., 1931; M.D., U. Md., 1946. Tchr. pub. schs., Baltimore County, Md., 1931-42; intern, resident Garfield Meml. Hosp., 1946-47; cancer trainee Nat. Cancer Inst., NIH, 1947-49; practice medicine specializing in pathology, Washington, 1949—; clin. instr. pathology George Washington U., 1949-54, asst. prof., 1954-66, asso. prof., 1966—; prof. biology Gallaudet Coll., 1966—; cytologist Cancer Clinic, 1949—; cons. VA; dir. dept. pathology Sch. Cytotech., George Washington U. Hosp., 1963-73, emeritus, 1973—; dir. Employment and Counseling Service of No. Va., 1959-64. Trustee D.C. div. Am.

Cancer Soc. Recipient Appreciation award Am. Cancer Soc.; Nat. Divisional award Am. Cancer Soc., 1972, St. George medal D.C. div., 1972. Mem. A.M.A., Am. Med. Women's Assn., Am. Soc. Cytology, A.A.A.S., N.Y. Acad. Scis., Smithsonian Instn. Assos. Episcopalian. Club: Soroptimist of Arlington (Va.). Contbr. articles to profl. pubs. Home: 3500 Perry St Fairfax VA 22030 Office: Sch Medicine and Health Scis 2300 Eye St NW Washington DC 20037

PLATTER, ALLEN ANDREW, educator; b. Houston, Dec. 9, 1921; s. George William and Leila (Martin) P.; B.F.A., U. Houston, 1947, M.L., 1948, Ed.D., 1961; m. Paula Leone Peterson, Sept 6, 1952; children—Candice Lee, Lance Lane. Instr., asst. prof. architecture U. Houston, 1947-52; instr. art Brazosport Sch. System, Freeport, Tex., 1954-61; asst. prof. art Colo. State Coll., Greeley, 1962-66; asst. prof. edn. Southeastern State Coll., Durant, Okla., 1966-67, chmn. dept. art, 1967—, prof., 1967—. Exhibited in group shows at Houston Mus. Fine Arts, Dallas Mus. Fine Arts, U. Houston, Colo. Coll., Colo. State Coll., So. Colo. State Coll., Central State Coll. (Edmond, Okla.), Southeastern State Coll. (Durant, Okla.). Served with inf., AUS, 1942-45. Decorated Bronze Star medal. Mem. Okla. Edn. Assn., Nat. Art Edn. Assn., Durant, C. of C., Phi Kappa Phi, Phi Delta Kappa, Kappa Delta Pi. Episcopalian (sr. warden 1970-72). Rotarian (sec. 1967-68, v.p. 1973-74, pres. 1974-75. Club: Durant Country. Home: Briarwood Mead OK 73449

PLATZ, ADOLPH AUGUST, food co. exec.; b. Jersey City, Aug. 28, 1920; s. Leopold and Olga (Gietz) P.; B.S., N.Y. U., 1943, M.B.A., 1954, C.P.A., 1947; m. Anna L. Erlemann, Sept. 20, 1952; children—Frederick, Valerie, Stephanie, Irene. With Guaranty Trust Co., N.Y.C., 1937-40; ins. accountant Gen. Cover Underwriters Assn., 1940-42; auditor Ernst & Ernst, 1942-43, 45-52; chief accountant to asst. treas., then controller, treas. Eskimo Pie Corp., Richmond, Va., 1952-69, v.p., treas., 1969—, also dir. Treas. bd. Ridgetop Recreation Assn., 1956-63, pres. assn., 1964-65. Served as warrant officer finance dept. Signal Corps, AUS, 1943-45. Mem. Am. Inst. C.P.A.'s, Nat. Accountants Assn., Systems and Proc. Assn., Financial Exec. Inst. Home: 513 Gardiner Rd Richmond VA 23229 Office: 530 E Main St Richmond VA 23212

PLAYER, THELMA B., librarian; b. Owosso, Mich.; d. Walter B. and Grace (Willoughby) Player; B.A., Western Mich., U., 1954. Reference asst. USAF Aero. Chart & Information Center, Washington, 1954-57; reference librarian U.S. Navy Hydrographic Office, Suitland, Md., 1957-58; asst. librarian, 1958-59; tech. library br. head U.S. Navy Spl. Project Office, Washington, 1959-68, Strategic Systems Project Office, 1969—. Mem. Spl. Libraries Assn., Am. Soc. for Information Sci., D.C. Library Assn., Am. Assn. U. Women, Internat. Platform Assn., English-Speaking Union. Episcopalian. Home: 2025 38th St SE Washington DC 20020 Office: Dept Navy Washington DC 20376

PLEASANTS, JOHN EDWARD, oral surgeon, educator; b. Aberdeen, N.C., Dec. 17, 1916; s. Charles E. and Evelyn (Harrington) P.; student Presbyn. Jr. Coll., 1934-35; D.D.S., Emory U., 1939; postgrad. U. Tex., 1952-55; m. Anne Arrasmith, Dec. 26, 1941; 1 dau., Mary Evelyn Smith. Practice dentistry, Chapel Hill, N.C., 1939-42; commd. 1st lt. U.S. Army, 1942, advanced through grades to col., 1963; ret., 1965; oral surgeon U.S. Army Hosp. Ship Francis Y. Slanger, Atlantic, W.W. II; div. dental surgeon, Korean war; dir. dental edn., intern and residency tng. Ireland Army Hosp., Fort Knox, Ky.; asso. prof. surgery U. Tex., 1965-68, prof., 1968—. Cons. oral surgery VA Hosp., USPHS, surgeon gen. U.S. Army. Decorated Bronze Star medal. Diplomate Am. Bd. Oral Surgery. Fellow Am. Coll. Dentists; mem. Am., Tex., Houston Dist. dental assns., Houston (sec.-treas.), Am. socs. oral surgeons, Omicron Kappa Upsilon, Xi Psi Phi. Contbr. articles in field to profl. jours. Home: 4003 Martinshire St Houston TX 77025 Office: U Tex Houston TX 77025

PLEASANTS, WILLIAM SHEPARD, advt. co. exec., author; b. New Orleans, Apr. 2, 1898; s. George Joseph and Elizabeth (Toulmin) P.; m. Wilhelmina Woodville, Oct. 1, 1926; 1 son, William Shepard. Vice pres. Reese Advt. Agy., 1924-26; asst. advt. mgr. New Orleans Item, 1926-35, advt. mgr., 1935-44, advt.-bus. mgr., 1951-54; v.p., gen. mgr. Walker Saussy Advt. Agy., New Orleans, 1944-51; v.p., copy chief Bauerlein Advt. Agy., New Orleans, 1954—. Served to 2d lt. AUS, World War I. Named Advt. Man of Year New Orleans, 1965. Mem. Advt. Club New Orleans (hon. life). Author: The Stingaree Murders, 1932. Home: 71 Versailles Blvd New Orleans LA 70125 Office: Hibernia Bank Bldg New Orleans LA 70112

PLENTL, WILLARD GATHINGS, state ofcl.; b. Houston, Mar. 22, 1919; s. Adolph Hugo and Alliene (Gathings) P.; student U. Wichita, 1954, U. So. Cal., 1955, Air Force Command and Staff Sch., 1958; m. Gloria Belle Jones, Jan. 10, 1942; children—Willard Gathings, Joy Van (Mrs. Michael S. Hensley), John Patrick. Served with AUS, 1940-42; commd. 2d lt. USAF, 1943, advanced through grades to lt. col., 1960, ret., 1962; asst. dir. Va. Div. Aeros., Richmond, 1962-64, dir., 1964—. Mem. Pres.' Adv. Commn. Aviation. Decorated D.F.C., Air medal with clusters. Recipient Meritorious Service awards FAA, 1965, Air Craft Owners and Pilots Assn., 1967; Distinguished Service award Flight Safety Found., 1968. Mem. Nat. Assn. State Aviation Ofcls. (past pres.), Air Force Assn. (past pres. Richmond chpt.). Mason (32 deg., Shriner), Rotarian. Home: 401 Kramer Dr Highland Springs VA 23075 Office: 4508 S Laburnum Av Richmond VA 23231

PLETCHER, ELDON LEE, editorial cartoonist; b. Goshen, Ind., Sept. 10, 1922; s. Arthur and Dora (Cripe) P.; student Chgo. Acad. Fine Arts, 1940-41, John Herron Art Sch., Indpls., 1946-47; m. Barbara Jeanne Jones, Jan. 29, 1948; children—Thomas Lee, Ellen Irene. Editorial cartoonist Sioux City (Ia.) Jour., 1949-66, New Orleans Times-Picayune, 1966—. Represented permanent collections Syracuse U., So. Miss. U., Wichita State U., State Hist. Soc. Mo. Served with AUS, 1943-46. Recipient Christopher award, 1951; ten awards Freedoms Found. Mem. Assn. Am. Editorial Cartoonists. Presbyn. Home: 3435 Pittari Place New Orleans LA 70114 Office: 3800 Howard Av New Orleans LA 70140

PLITT, WALTER EDWARD III, shipping co. exec.; b. Houston, Feb. 22, 1941; s. Walter Edward and Corrine Elizabeth (Sweitzer) P.; grad. Southwestern Bus. Coll., 1965; m. Jean Ann Pearson, Apr. 15, 1964; children—Walter Edward IV, Sharon Lynn. With Plitt & Co., Brownsville, Tex., 1960-61; mgr. Brownsville Equipment & Contracting Co., 1961—; mgr. Arroyo Fertilizier & Storage, Harlingen, 1965—. Curator, developer conventional museum Confederate Air Force, 1968-74. Mem. Harlingen Jr. C. of C. (dir. 1966 sec. 1967-68). Democrat. Club: Valley Sportsman (v.p. 1967) (Harlingen, Tex.). Home: 107 Country Club Estates Brownsville TX 78520 Office; Southside Av Port of Brownsville TX 78520

PLOSSL, GEORGE WILLIAM, mgmt. cons.; b. Bklyn., July 3, 1918; s. George Wilfred and Irene Margaret (McGarvey) P.; A.B., Columbia, 1939, B.S. in Mech. Engring., 1940, M.S. in Mech. Engring., 1942; m. Marion Louise Hagen, May 24, 1942; 1 son, Keith Robin. Materials mgr. Stanley Tools, New Britain, Conn., 1961-64; plant mgr. Stanley Steel Strapping Systems, New Britain, 1964-68; pres. G.W. Plossl & Co., mgmt. counseling, Decatur, Ga., 1968—. Instr. Columbia Sch. Engring., 1941-42; prof. Western New Eng. Coll., Springfield, Mass., 1956-61. Mem. Pub. Service Study Com., West Springfield, 1960. Corporator New Britain Gen. Hosp., 1967-68. Served to lt. USNR, 1942-46. Mem. Am. Prodn. and Inventory Control Soc. (mem. adv. planning council 1965—, chmn. certification council 1971—). Mason. Club: Fairington Country (Decatur, Ga.). Author: (with O.W. Wight) Production & Inventory Control, Principles & Techniques, 1967; Manufacturing Control; Last Frontier for Profits, 1973. Editor APICS Bibliography, 1968; chpt. editor APICS Handbook, 1970. Contbr. articles to profl. jours. Patentee oil refinery processing equipment. Home: 103 Willowick Dr Decatur GA 30032 Office: PO Box 32490 Decatur GA 30032

PLOTKIN, STEVEN ROBERT, lawyer; b. New Orleans, Apr. 19, 1936; s. Sam and Sarah Regina (Jacobs) P.; B.A., Tulane U., 1956, LL.B., 1959; grad. Southwestern U. Pros. Atty. Sch., 1963; m. Lynn Tobie Gertler, July 15, 1965; children—Louis Lowell, Scott Randall, Rachel Melissa. Admitted to La. bar, 1959, U.S. Supreme Ct. bar, 1967; practiced in New Orleans, 1959—; asst. dist. atty. Parish Orleans, 1962-64. Vice chmn. S.E. Council La. Lung Assn.; mem. La. Bicentennial Commn., New Orleans Music and Drama Found., Vols. of the Shelter. Bd. dirs. La. Tb and Respiratory Disease Assn., Am. Lung Assn., 1974—; bd. dirs. Zionist Orgn. Am., v.p. Southwest region, also New Orleans dist.; bd. govs. Jewish Community Center; bd. advisers New Orleans br. State of Israel Bonds; bd. dirs. Jewish Welfare Fedn., also mem. community relations com. Served with AUS, 1953-55. Mem. Am., La., Civil, Greater New Orleans (past pres.) trial lawyers assn., Am., La. bar assns., New Orleans Criminal Bar Assn., Internat. Acad. Law Sci., La. Soc. du Droit, Nat. Hall Fame (charter mem. New Orleans chpt.). La. Hist. Assn., New Orleans C. of C., Fgn. Relations Assn. New Orleans, Fraternal Order Police, Nat. Police Hall Fame, Genesis (pres.) Mason (Shriner). Home: 5524 Jacquelyn Ct New Orleans LA 70124 Office: Baronne Bldg New Orleans LA 70112

PLOTNICK, BARRY REYMAN, realtor, pub. relations cons.; b. Stamford, Conn., Feb. 15, 1937; s. Bernard and Selma Jean (Reyman) P.; student U. Va., 1959; m. Virginia Murray Leonard, Feb. 14, 1970; 1 dau., Brooke Barney. Radio broadcaster, 1957-61; founder Records for Recollectors, Stamford, 1963; sec.-treas., dir. finance and devel. Edn., Inc., Charlottesville, Va., 1972—; owner Rey Barry Assos., Charlottesville, 1972—. Publisher, editor Central Va. Mag., 1964-66; columnist, edn. writer The Daily Progress, Charlottesville newspaper, 1966-71; TV producer U. Va., 1973—; asso. Whitt & Co., Realtors, 1974—; vis. lectr. U. Va. Sch. Continuing Edn., 1970—. Pres., Charlottesville-Albermarle Mental Health Assn., 1972—. Bd. dirs. Central Va. Child Devel. Assn., Central Va. Civil Liberties Union, New Sch., Charlottesville. Recipient Meritorious Service award Civil Air Patrol, 1967. Mem. Edn. Writers Assn., Council for Basic Edn., Asso. Press Mng. Editors Assn., Chesapeake Bay Found., Mensa. Office: PO Box 312 Charlottesville VA 22902

PLOUGH, FRANCIS AZZO, savs. and loan pres.; b. New Orleans, Aug. 27, 1923; s. Azzo Joseph and Pauline Carolyn (Steckler) P.; A.B., Tulane, 1948; postgrad. La. State U., 1957; m. Helen Margaret Stich, June 18, 1949; children—Carolyn M., Joanne Frances, Gerald F. Asst. cashier La. Bank & Trust Co., 1953-55, Nat. Bank Commerce, New Orleans, 1955-56; v.p. Investors Homestead Assn., New Orleans, 1956-57, pres., 1957—. Mem. pres.'s adv. council Jesuit High Sch., 1970-72, career adv. com. Tulane U. Grad. Sch. Bus. Adminstrn., 1972-73; active United Fund, Crippled Childrens Hosp., House of Good Shepherd, Girl Scouts, Heart Fund, St. Elizabeth's Hosp. Mem. Bd. Commrs. City Park, 1968—. Served with USNR, 1942-46. Mem. C. of C., Nat. League Insured Savs. Assns. (state gov. 1960-61), La. (exec. com. 1962-64), New Orleans (pres. 1963) savs. and loan leagues, S. Clairborne Av. Bus. Men's Club. Clubs: New Orleans Country, Windsor, Ambassador, Azalea, Essex, Athletic. Home: 2418 Joseph St New Orleans LA 70115 Office: 1119 Tulane Av New Orleans LA 70112

PLUMMER, A. Q., accountant; b. Moran, Tex., Dec. 23, 1921; s. John W. and Mittie (Gill) P.; B.B.A., U. Tex., 1947; m. Betty F. Cantrell, June 4, 1949; children—John Cantrell, Jim Mcclung, Betsy Beal. Accountant, The Tex. Co., Houston, 1947-55; tax accountant Tex. Gulf Producing Co., Houston, 1956-60, chief accountant, 1960-65, Libyan Am. Oil Co., Houston, 1960-65; sec.-treas. Barbers Hill Salt Water Co., Houston, 1960-65; pvt. practice C.P.A., Brenham, Tex., 1965—. Instr. accounting S. Tex. Coll., 1956-57; mem. Washington County Bluebonnet Trials Com., treas., 1961; mem. S.W. Houston Cub Scout pack Boy Scouts Am., Brazos Valley Estate Council. Bd. dirs. Bohne Hosp.; trustee St. Jude Hosp. Served with USAAF, 1943-45. C.P.A., Tex. Mem. Tex. Exec. Inst. (sec., treas. Houston), Tex. Soc. C.P.A.'s Washington County C. of C. Methodist (steward, auditor, sec. stewardship and finance commn.). Lion (sec.). Home: Plum Hill Brenham TX 77833 Office: 201 W Main St Brenham TX 77833

PLUMMER, BENJAMIN FRANK, educator; b. Burlington Junction, Mo., Feb. 29, 1936; s. Marvin Ray and LouElla (Maier) P.; B.S., Ia. State U., 1958; Ph.D., Ohio State U., 1962; m. Gail Masterman, Mar. 25, 1961; children—Scott, Douglas, Suzanne, Jeffrey. Asst. instr. Ohio State U., Columbus, 1961; asst. prof. chemistry S.D. State U., 1962-66; asso. prof. Trinity U. at San Antonio, 1968-74, prof., 1974—. Postdoctoral asso. Ga. Inst. Tech., 1962. R.A. Welch Found. grantee, 1968—. Mem. Am. Chem. Soc., A.A.A.S., Am. Assn. U. Profs., Sigma Xi. Author: Selected Principles of Organic Chemistry. Home: 734 Susie Ct San Antonio TX 78216

PLUNK, JOEL ALLEN, accountant; b. Hedley, Tex., June 20, 1926; s. William Crawford and Josie Wilson (Fain) P.; B.B.A., West Tex. State U., 1949, postgrad., 1949-50; m. Vera Ann Sledge, Dec. 23, 1950; children—Steven Craig, Martha Lou. Exec. tng. program treasury dept. Shell Oil Co., Midland, Tex., Hobbs, N.M., New Orleans, 1953-56; treas., dir. Lefors Petroleum Co., Inc., Pampa, Tex., 1957-66; partner Brown & Plunk, C.P.A.'s, Pampa, 1967; practice individual accounting, Pampa, Tex., 1968—; sec., treas. Texstar Exploration, Inc., 1969—, gen. mgr., 1972—, dir., 1969-73. Served with AUS, 1944-46, 50-51. Mem. Am. Inst. C.P.A.'s, Tex. Soc. C.P.A.'s, West Tex. State U. Ex-Students Assn. (dir., treas. Top of Tex. chpt.), Am. Legion (past post comdr.). Club: Pampa Country. Home: 1330 Hamilton St Pampa TX 79065 Office: Box 2022 Pampa TX 79065

POAGE, HERMAN CLIFTON, JR., accountant; b. Plainview, Tex., Oct. 27, 1935; s. Herman Clifton and Wanda E. (Hewett) P.; B.B.A., Tex. Tech. U., 1961; m. Wanda Sue Guerry, June 2, 1961. Staff accountant Bollinger, Segars & Burk, Lubbock, Tex., 1960-62; bus. mgr. Leaseway-S.W., Inc., Lubbock, 1962-67; staff accountant Ernst & Ernst, Lubbock, 1967-71; controller, Omega-Alpha, Inc., Dallas, 1971-74; controller Sammons Enterprises, Inc., Dallas, 1974—. Served with AUS, 1954-56. C.P.A., Tex. Mem. Am. Inst. C.P.A.'s, Tex. Soc. C.P.A.'s, Phi Kappa Alpha. Home: 8347 Southwestern Dallas TX 75206 Office: PO Box 5235 403 S Akard Dallas TX 75222

POAGE, WILLIAM ROBERT, congressman; b. Waco, Tex., Dec. 28, 1899; s. William Alan and Helen Wheeler (Conger) P.; A.B., Baylor U., 1921, LL.B., 1924, LL.D., 1968; L.H.D., Mary Hardin-Baylor, 1973; student U. of Tex., summer 1919, U. Colo., summer 1923; m. Frances Cotton, Feb. 14, 1938. Farmer Throckmorton County, Tex., 1920-22; instr. geology Baylor U., 1922-24, instr. law, 1924-28; admitted to Tex. bar, 1924, since practiced in Waco; mem. firm Poage & Neff, 1928-35; mem. 75th to 92d Congress, 11th Tex. Dist., chmn. com. on agr. Am. del. to Inter-Parliamentary Union, Cairo, 1947—. Served as apprentice seaman USNRF, 1918. Mem. Am. Legion. Democrat. Universalist. Mason. Home: 600 Edgewood Av Waco TX 76708 Office: Rayburn Office Bldg Washington DC 20515

POCHMANN, RUTH FOUTS (MRS. HENRY POCHMANN), author, civic worker; b. Nacogdoches, Tex., Mar. 20, 1903; d. Wilbur Courtland and Lela (Roquemore) Fouts; student So. Meth. U., 1920-23; B.A., Stephen F. Austin State U., 1925; M.A., Columbia, 1927; postgrad. U. Wis. at Madison, 1958-59; m. Henry August Pochman, Sept. 11, 1928; 1 dau., Virginia Ruth (Mrs. Theodore P. Weis). Tchr., Nacogdoches High Sch., 1923-24; asst. prof. Stephen F. Austin State U., Nacogdoches, 1924, 25, 27, 28; substitute asst. prof. La. State U., Baton Rouge, 1929, English dept. U. Miss. at Oxford, 1930-31, Miss. State U., Starkville, 1932-35; tchr. English grammar U.S. Air Force Inst., 1941-43. Lectr. in field conservation; also on dollmaking in our social history. State sec.-treas. Wis. Fedn. Garden Clubs, 1942-43; mem. West Side Garden Club, Madison, 1939-71, Madison Dist. Garden Clubs, 1939—, chmn. conservation and landscape architecture, 1944-69; mem. Pines Garden Club, Nacogdoches, 1971—; mem. Nacogdoches City Council, 1972. Recipient 1st Distinguished Citizen award for unique contbn. to appreciation rural living Waushara Co. Electric, 1968. Mem. Wis. Press Women, Wis. Regional Writers Assn., Madison Area Writers Workshop, Am. Pen Women, Wis., Miss., E. Tex. hist. assns., Audubon Soc., Alpha Delta Pi, Alpha Chi. Republican. Methodist. Author: Some Early Texas Families, a genealogy, 1942; Triple Ridge Farm (non-fiction) (Hull award for hert, interest Nat. Fedn. Garden Clubs 1971; cash prize and 1st pl. contests Council Wis. Writers and Wis. Press Women 1968; cash prize and 2d pl. nat. contest Am. Pen Women 1969; selected as 1 of 67 new books for Ambassador's List 1968), 1968. Home: 524 Inwood Lane Nacogdoches TX 75961

POE, EDGAR ALLEN, newspaperman; b. Jasper, Ala., Feb. 12, 1906; s. Thomas W. and Dora (Gunter) P.; m. Frances Margaret Harwood, Nov. 16, 1929; children—Edgar Allen, Thomas Lea. Reporter, Birmingham (Ala.) News, 1928-30; mem. staff New Orleans Times-Picayune, 1930—, war corr. Pacific, World War II, Washington corr., 1947—. Mem. House and Senate Press Galleries. Recipient commendation U.S. Navy, 1945. Mem. White House Corr. Assn. (pres. 1972-73), Washington Overseas Writers (treas. 1961—), Sigma Delta Chi (past pres. Washington profl. chpt.) Club: Gridiron (pres. 1971-72) (Washington). Home: 2615 S Lynn St Arlington VA 22202 Office: Nat Press Bldg Washington DC 20004

POE, JAMES DANIEL, assn. exec.; b. Cisco, Tex., Nov. 17, 1932; s. Andrew C. and Madeline F. (Hooker) P.; student Cisco Jr. Coll., 1954-55, Bethany Nazarene Coll., 1955-56; B.S., Hardin Simmons U., 1965; postgrad. Tex. Tech U., 1965-66; m. Anna Ruth McCrary, Mar. 11, 1951; children—Jane (Mrs. John P. Jackson), Laura, James Hugh, William. Ordained to ministry Ch. of the Nazarene, 1959; minister Ch. of the Nazarene, Colorado City, Tex., 1956-58, Littlefield, Tex., 1958-62; program dir. YMCA, Abilene, Tex., 1964-65, Midland Tex., 1965-68, camping exec., San Antonio, Tex., 1968-69, exec. dir., Jonesboro, Ark., 1969—. Bd. dirs. United Way Jonesboro, 1969—. Served with USN, 1950-53; Korea. Mem. Assn. Profl. Dirs. YMCA's U.S., Am. Camping Assn., Adult Edn. Assn., Am. Forestry Assn. Lion (dir. 1971-73). Home: 1300 Holly St Jonesboro AR 72401 Office: 1421 W Nettleton St Jonesboro AR 72401

POE, JAMES EDWARD, lawyer; b. Garfield, Ark., Feb. 21, 1935; s. Louis L. and Maude (Banta) P.; B.A., U. Tulsa, 1957, LL.B. cum laude, 1959; m. Virginia Gattis, Oct. 29, 1960; children—Jon Mark, Emily Diane, Edward Adrian. Admitted to Okla. bar, 1959; also fed. ct. bars; practice law, Tulsa, 1959—. Atty., adviser Okla. bd. govs. Registered Dentists of Okla., 1964—; atty. mem. City-County Appeal Bd., 1969-70; mem. Tulsa County Excise Bd., 1971—. Active Cub Scouts Am. Precinct chmn., dir. Republican Zone Com., 1964-71. Recipient Vernon Law Book Co. award for scholarship, 1959, also other scholarship awards. Mem. Okla. (del. 1969-70, mem. med.-legal relations com. 1970—), Tulsa County (sec. 1971) bar assns., Toastmasters Internat., Cum Laude Soc., Delta Theta Phi, Pi Gamma Mu, Phi Alpha Theta, Phi Gamma Kappa. Home: 5808 E 63d St Tulsa OK 74136 Office: Pythian Bldg Tulsa OK 74103

POE, WILLIAM EDWARD, lawyer; b. South Hill, Va., Dec. 18, 1923; s. William Dowd and Douglas (Thornton) P.; B.S., Wake Forest U., 1947; J.D., Harvard, 1950; m. Mary Warren, Aug. 26, 1948; children—William Edward, Stephen D., Kenneth W., Richard S., Michael D., Anne L. Admitted to N.C. bar, 1950; asst. dir. U. N.C. Inst. Govt., Chapel Hill, 1950-52; partner Grier, Parker, Poe, Thompson, Bernstein, Gage & Preston, Charlotte, N.C., 1952—. Mem. Charlotte-Mecklenburg Bd. Edn., 1964—, chmn., 1966—; pres., N.C. Sch. Bds. Assn., 1969-71; pres. elect So. Region Sch. Bds. Assn.; bd. dirs. Charlotte Christian Rehab. Center. Trustee, Wake Forest U., N.C. Bapt. Children's Homes. Served with USAAF, 1943-46. Decorated Air medal. Mem. Am., N.C. bar assns., Charlotte C. of C. (bd. dirs.). Baptist. Democrat. Rotarian (bd. dirs.). Co-author: Motor Vehicle Law in N.C., 1952. Home: 2101 Coniston Pl Charlotte NC 28207 Office: Law Bldg Charlotte NC 28202

POFF, RICHARD H(ARDING), justice; b. Radford, Va., Oct. 19, 1923; s. Beecher David and Irene Louise (Nunley) P.; student Roanoke Coll., Salem, Va., 1943-43, LL.D., 1969; LL.B., U. Va., 1948; m. Jo Ann Ragan Topper, June 24, 1945; children—Rebecca Topper, Thomas R., Richard Harding. Admitted to Va. bar, 1947; mem. 83d-92d Congresses, 6th Cong. Dist. Va.; chmn. House Republican Task Force on Crime, asso. justice Supreme Ct. Va., 1972—. Vice chmn. Nat. Com. Reform Fed. Criminal Laws. Named Outstanding Young Man 1954, Va. Jr. C. of C. Served with USAAF, 1943-45. Decorated D.F.C., Air medal. Mem. Am., Va. bar assns., C. of C. (pres.), V.F.W., Am. Legion. United Comml. Travellers Am., Grounding Club Am., Sigma Nu Phi. Mason, Moose. Club: Radford Lions. Home: 2910 W Brigstock Rd Midlothian VA 23113 Office: Supreme Ct Bldg Richmond VA

POFF, WILLIAM BEVERLY, lawyer; b. nr. Radford, Va., Aug. 23, 1932; s. John William and Pansy Louise (Booze) P.; B.S., Va. Tech. U., 1952; LL.B. summa cum laude, Washington and Lee U., 1955; m. Magdalen Barbara Andrews, Dec. 28, 1957. Admitted to Va. bar, 1955; asso. mem. firm Woods, Rogers, Muse, Walker & Thornton and predecessor firm, Roanoke, Va., 1959-62, partner, 1963—. Pres., Sister City Com., 1964—; chmn. Roanoke Bicentennial Commn., 1972—. Mem. Va. Bd. Edn., 1971-75; chmn. 6th Dist. Rep. party, 1970—, Roanoke City Rep. party, 1970-72; mem. central com. and exec. com. Va. Rep. party, 1970—; campaign chmn. Dalton for Lt. Gov., 1973. Bd. dir. YMCA, Jr. Achievement. Served to lt. JAG Corps, AUS, 1956-59. Named Roanoke's Outstanding Young Man, Roanoke Jr. C. of C., 1969, one of five Outstanding Young Men of Va., Va. Jr. C. of C., 1969; recipient Civil Merit medal Republic Korea, 1970. Mem. Va. Trial Lawyers Assn. (gov. 1966—, pres. 1971-72), Am., Va., Roanoke (dir. 1968-70) bar assns., Internat. Soc. Barristers. Unitarian. Editorial bd. Va. Lawyers Practice Handbook, 1966.

Home: 2231 Woodcliff Rd SE Roanoke VA 24014 Office: 105 Franklin Rd SW Roanoke VA 24004

POGUE, FORREST CARLISLE, historian; b. Eddyville, Ky., Sept. 17, 1912; s. Forrest Carlisle and Frances (Carter) P.; A.B., Murray State Coll., 1931, LL.D., 1970; M.A., U. Ky., 1932; Ph.D., Clark U., 1939; Am. Exchange fellow, Inst. des Hautes Etudes Internationales, U. Paris (France), 1937-38; Litt. D., Washington and Lee U., 1970; m. Christine Brown, Sept. 4, 1954. Instr. Western Ky. State Coll., 1933; from instr. to asso. prof. Murray (Ky.) State Coll., 1933-42, prof. history, 1954-56; mem. hist. sect. U.S. Forces, ETO, 1944-46; with Office Chief Mil. History, Dept. Army, 1946-52; operations research analyst Operations Research Office, Johns Hopkins, Heidelberg, Germany, 1952-54; dir. George C. Marshall Research Center, Arlington, Va., 1956-64, George C. Marshall Research Library, 1964-74, Dwight D. Eisenhower Inst. Hist. Studies, Smithsonian Instn., Washington, 1974—; exec. dir. George C. Marshall Research Found., 1964-74, mem. adv. com., 1974—; Mary Moody Northen vis. prof. history Va. Mil. Inst., 1972. Mem. adv. com. Dir. Naval History, Dept. Navy; past chmn. Am. Com. History World War II; mem. adv. com. publ. Eisenhower papers Johns Hopkins, publ. Roosevelt and Fgn. Relations series Roosevelt Library. Regent Omar N. Bradley Found. Served with AUS, 1942-45; ETO. Decorated Bronze Star; Croix de Guerre (France); recipient Distinguished Alumnus award Murray State Coll., 1964; Distinguished Alumnus Centennial award U. Ky., 1965. Mem. Am., So. hist. assns., Orgn. Am. Historians, N.E.A., Am. Polit. Sci. Assn., Oral History Assn. (past pres.), Am. Mil. Inst. (pres.), Am. Legion. Democrat. Presbyn. Author: The Supreme Command, 1954; George C. Marshall: Education of a General, vol. 1, 1963; George C. Marshall: Ordeal and Hope, 1939-42, vol. 2, 1966; George C. Marshall: Organizer of Victory, 1943-45, vol. 3, 1973. Co-author: The Meaning of Yalta, 1956. Contbr. to Command Decisions, 1960, Total War and Cold War, 1962, D-Day: The Normandy Invasion in Retrospect, 1971, Soldiers and Statesmen, 1973. Address: 1111 Army-Navy Dr Arlington VA 22202

POGUE, WILLIAM REID, astronaut; b. Okemah, Okla., Jan. 23, 1930; s. Alex W. and Margaret (McDow) P.; B.S. in Secondary Edn., Okla. Bapt. U., 1951; M.S. in Math., Okla. State U., 1960; m. Helen Juanita Dittmar, Oct. 26, 1952; children—William Richard, Layna Sue, Thomas Reid. Commd. 2d lt., USAF, 1952, advanced through grades to col., 1973; combat fighter pilot, Korea, 1953; gunnery instr., Luke AFB, Ariz., 1954; mem. acrobatic team USAF Thunderbirds, Luke AFB and Nellis AFB, Nev., 1955-57; asst. prof. math. USAF Acad., 1960-63; exchange Test pilot Brit. Royal Aircraft Establishment, Ministry Aviation, Farnborough, Eng., 1964-65; instr. USAF Aerospace Research Pilots Sch., Edwards AFB, Cal., 1965-66; astronaut NASA, Manned Spacecraft Center, Houston, 1966—, pilot 3d Manned Skylab Mission, 1973-74. Decorated Air medal with oak leaf cluster; D.S.M., Air Force Commendation medal; Distinguished Service medal NASA. Mem. Soc. Exptl. Test Pilots, Sigma Xi, Pi Mu Epsilon. Home: 306 Lakeshore Dr Seabrook TX 77586 Office: Code (CB) NASA-Johnson Spacecraft Center Houston TX 77058

POIRIER, JACQUES CHARLES, educator; b. Mehun sur Yevre, France, Jan. 3, 1927; s. Anthony Joseph and Renee Berthe (Potier) P.; came to U.S., 1927; Ph.B., U. Chgo., 1947, S.B., 1948, S.M., 1950, Ph.D., 1952; m. Marsha London, June 22, 1951; children—Marc Raymond, Charles Joseph, Julia Eve. NSF postdoctoral fellow, Yale, New Haven, 1952-53; Corning Glass Works Found. postdoctoral fellow U. Cal. at Berkeley, 1953-55; asst. prof. chemistry Duke, 1955-60, asso. prof., 1960-67, prof., 1967—. Vis. asso. prof. Ind. U., Bloomington, 1961; cons. Union Carbide, Charleston, W.Va., 1955-57. Served with USNR, 1944-45. Alfred Sloan fellow, 1959-63; research grantee Research Corp., 1964, NSF grantee, 1967-69, Army Research Office-Durham grantee, 1970-71, NIH grantee, 1970—. Mem. Am. Chem. Soc., Am. Phys. Soc., Phi Beta Kappa, Sigma Xi. Home: 210 W Lavender Av Durham NC 27704

POLAN, CARL EDWIN, educator; b. Blandville, W.Va., Sept. 14, 1931; s. Willie Davisson and Flossie Iona (Trent) P.; B.S., W.Va. U., 1953, M.S., 1960; Ph.D., N.C. State U. at Raleigh, 1964; m. Ann Lee Underwood, June 8, 1956; children—Mark Edwin, Gregory Carl, Leanne, David Louis. Herd mgr., instr. agr. Potomac State Coll., Keyser, W.Va., 1956-58; dairy extension agt. W.Va. U., 1960; research asso. U. Minn., St. Paul, 1963-65; mem. faculty Va. Poly. Inst. and State U., Blacksburg, 1965—, asso. prof. animal nutrition, 1969-73, prof., 1973—. Served with AUS, 1953-55. Mem. Am. Dairy Sci. Assn., Am. Inst. Nutrition, Sigma Xi, Gamma Sigma Delta. Home: 1202 Westover Dr Blacksburg VA 24060

POLK, MALCOLM BENNY, educator; b. Chgo., Feb. 2, 1938; s. Andrew and Irene (Walton) Mosley; B.S., U. Ill., 1960; Ph.D., U. Pa., 1964. Organic chemist E.I. duPont Co., Wilmington, Del., 1965-67, chemist, tech. rep., 1968-72; asso. prof. chemistry Prairie View (Tex.) Coll., 1967-68; asso. prof. chemistry Atlanta (Ga.) U., 1973—, also dir. indsl. chemistry program. Mem. Am. Inst. Chemists, Am. Chem. Soc., Phi Lambda Upsilon. Patentee in field. Home: 1717 Central Villa Dr SW Atlanta GA 30311 Office: 223 Chestnut St SW Atlanta GA 30314

POLK, WALTER BRASHEAR, chem. engr.; b. Vicksburgh, Miss., Dec. 9, 1920; s. Walter Howe and Mary (Brashear) P.; student Ark. A. and M. Coll., 1940-42; B.S. in Chem. Engring., Okla. State U., 1944; m. Martha Nelle Burton, May 27, 1949; 1 dau., Ann. Chemist, process engr., mech. design engr., Borger Refinery, Phillips Petroleum Co., Borger, Tex., 1945-50, chemist, process engr., Plains Plant, Borger, 1950-55, supr. process engring and maintenance, 1955-64, process design and cons. engring. div., Bartlesville, Okla., 1964-70, cons., environment control engr., 1970—. Instr., Frank Phillips Coll., Borger, 1957-63, coordinator and process cons. for design, constrn. N.V. Petrochim, London, Eng., 1965-66, Antwerp, Belgium, 1966-68. Registered profl. engr., Okla., Tex. Mem. Am. Chem. Soc., Am. Inst. Chem. Engrs. (founder Tex. Panhandle sect.), Sigma Tau, Phi Lambda Upsilon, Kappa Sigma Kappa, Blue Key. Club: American (Antwerp). Presbyn. (deacon, elder). Patentee in field. Home: 6025 SE Cornell Dr Bartlesville OK 74003 Office: Phillips Petroleum Co Bartlesville OK 74004

POLLAK, EDWARD, constrn. co. exec.; b. Houston, Dec. 3, 1916; s. Edward and Rose M. (Cohen) P.; student Rice U., 1933-37; m. Lillian B. Wiesenthal, June 30, 1940; children—Stephanie (Mrs. Allan Maierson), Fredell H. (Mrs. Lon Bergstrom). Engr., Harry L. Edwards Drilling Co., Houston, 1937-42; asst. project engr. U.S. C.E., Galveston, 1942-43; equipment mgr., asst. sec.-treas. Tellepsen Constrn. Co., Houston 1943—; v.p. Whitelak, Inc., Houston, 1962—. Mem. Soc. Automotive Engrs. Home: 3602 Aberdeen Way Houston TX 77025 Office: PO Box 2536 Houston TX 77001

POLLARD, BILLY MOORE, dentist; b. Gates, Tenn., Nov. 9, 1926; s. William Thomas and Alma Norma (Chisholm) P.; student Union U., 1946-48; D.D.S., U. Tenn., 1951; m. Mary Jean Riddle, June 6, 1948; children—Michael Thomas, Jean Michelle. Pvt. practice dentistry, Jackson, Tenn., 1953—. Cons. U. Tenn. Coll. Dentistry, Dept. Oral Diagnosis, Dean in Curricular Affairs, 1971; asso. prof., chmn. dept. dental hygiene Med. Coll. Ga., Augusta, also asso. prof. periodontics. Commr. Jackson Housing Authority, 1971—; chmn. annual loyalty program L. G. Noel Meml. Found., 1971-72. Served with USNR, 1945-46, 51-53. Mem. Pierre Fauchard Acad., Acad. Gen. Dentistry, Am. Soc. Preventive Dentistry, Am., Tenn (trustee 1970-73) dental assns., So. Acad. Oral Surgery, Seventh Dist. Dental Soc. (pres.-elect 1972-73), Jackson Dental Study Club, Delta Sigma Delta, Alpha Tau Omega. Methodist. Mason, Kiwanian. Address: Dept of Dental Hygiene Medical College of Georgia Augusta GA 30902

POLLARD, JOSEPH PAGE, govt. ofcl.; b. Minor, Va., Sept. 15, 1913; s. Joseph Lawrence and Page (Hoskins) P.; B.S., Coll. William and Mary, 1935; M.D., U. Va., 1939; m. Mary Ruth Walker, Nov. 28, 1941 (dec.); children—Ann Page (Mrs. Brian A. Pumphrey), Joseph Lawrence, Mary Kathryn; m. 2d, Marietta Klee Warner, Oct. 9, 1970. Intern Charity Hosp. La., New Orleans and Gallinger Municipal Hosp., Washington, 1939-40; resident Alexandria (Va.) Gen. Hosp., 1941-41; commd. lt. (j.g.) USN, 1941, advanced through grades to capt., 1968; head aviation med. research, 1958-68; dir. astronautical medicine, 1960-67; dir. research div., 1964-67; asst. chief bur. medicine and surgery for research and mil. med. spltys. Navy Dept., 1967-68; ret., 1968; dir. biol. and med. scis. Office Naval Research, Arlington, Va., 1968—. Navy mem. aerospace med. panel, adv. group on aerospace research and devel. NATO, 1960—; mem. research adv. group FAA, 1960-67. Recipient Theodore C. Lyster award Aerospace Med. Assn., 1972. Diplomate Am. Bd. Preventive Medicine. Fellow Aerospace Med. Assn., Am. Coll. Preventive Medicine; mem. Internat. Acad. Aviation and Space Medicine, Acad. Medicine Washington. Club: Cosmos (Washington). Contbr. articles to profl. jours. Home: 3540 N 36th Rd Arlington VA 22207 Office: Office Naval Research 800 N Quincy St Arlington VA 22217

POLLARD, OVERTON PRICE, lawyer; b. Ashland, Va., Mar. 26, 1933; s. James Madison and Anne Elizabeth (Hutchinson) P.; A.B., Washington and Lee U., 1954, LL.B., 1957; m. Anne Aloysia Meyer, Oct. 1, 1960; children—Mary Overton, William Price, John Spotswood, Anne Kusterer, Charles Meyer. Admitted to Va. bar, 1962; claims supr. Travelers Ins. Co., Richmond, Va., 1964-67; asst. atty. gen. Va., 1967-68, 70-71; spl. asst. Va. Supreme Ct., 1968-70; practiced law, Richmond, 1971—. Exec. dir. Pub. Defender Commn.; dir. J.M. Pollard & Sons, Inc.; state cons., Nat. Legal Aid and Defender Assn. Served with USN, 1957-59. Mem. Am., Va. bar assns., Am., Va. trial lawyers assns., Nat. Assn. Criminal Def. Lawyers, Va. Jr. C. of C. Democrat. Lion, Civitan. Club: Bull and Bear. Home: 7726 Sweetbriar Rd Richmond VA 23229 Office: 1001 E Main St Richmond VA 23229

POLLARD, STEWART MACLAINE LAURENS, assn. exec.; b. Lyman, Me., May 31, 1922; s. Ralph John and Millwee (Westmoreland) P.; student Bowdoin Coll., 1945-46; m. Margret Russell, Dec. 8, 1946; children—Carol Le, Bruce Edward. Joined U.S. Army as pvt., 1939, advanced through grades to capt., 1959; ret., 1970; mem. Nat. Sojourners, Alexandria, Va., 1956—, nat. sec.-treas., 1974—, also editor. Mem. Waldoborough (Me.) Hist. Soc., 1971—; state chmn. Medal of Honor Grove, Freedoms Found., Valley Forge, Pa., 1972—. Decorated Silver Star, Purple Heart. Recipient Honor medal Freedoms Found., 1973-74. Mem. Nat. Assn. Uniformed Forces (life), Am. Legion, S.A.R., Knox Meml. Assn. (life), Pearl Harbor Survivors Assn. (life), Res. Officers Assn., Heroes of 76 (nat. adj. 1970—), Va. Craftsman (hon.), Matrons and Patrons Assn. Germany (life), Philalethes Soc. Republican. Conglist. Mason (33 deg., K.T.). Author: Tied to Masonic Apron Strings, 1968; Proudly Serving The Cause of Patriotism, 1973. Home: 4600 Duke St Alexandria VA 22304 Office: 4600 Duke St Suite 300 Alexandria VA 22304

POLLARD, THOMAS BROWN, JR., lawyer; b. Nashville, July 24, 1933; s. Thomas B. and Hilda (Jolley) P.; A.B., U. S.C., 1954, LL.B., 1959; m. Patricia Jean Hough, June 8, 1954; 1 dau., Suzanne Lee. Admitted to S.C. bar, 1959; asso. mem. firm Cooper, Gary, Nersen & Pruet, Columbia, S.C., 1959-64, partner, 1964—(name changed to Nexsen, Pruet, Jacobs & Pollard, 1973). Served with USNR, 1954-56. Mem. Am., S.C., Richland County bar assns., Nat. Rifle Assn., Lambda Chi Alpha, Phi Delta Phi. Methodist. Clubs: Palmetto, Summit, Spring Valley, Ferrari of America. Home: 5903 Lakeshore Dr Columbia SC 29206 Office: 1231 Washington St Columbia SC 29201

POLLIN, ABE, builder; b. Phila., Dec. 3, 1923; s. Morris and Jennie (Sack) P.; student U. Md., 1941-44; B.A., George Washington U., 1945; m. Irene S. Kerchek, May 27, 1945; children—Robert Norman, James Edward. Engaged in home bldg. bus., 1945—; pres. Abe Pollin, Inc., Balt., 1962—; pres. Balt. Bullets Basketball Club, Inc., 1964—; dir. County Fed. Savs. & Loan Assn., Rockville, Md. Bd. dirs. United Jewish Appeal, Nat. Jewish Hosp., Jewish Community Center; bd. dirs., mem. adv. com. John F. Kennedy Cultural Center. Mem. Nat. Assn. Home Builders, Asso. Builders and Contractors Md., Washington Bd. Trade. Jewish religion. Home: 2 Goldsboro Ct Bethesda MD 20034 Office: 6101 16th St Washington DC 20011

POLLOCK, WILLIAM JOHN, JR., retail store owner; b. Hammond, Ind., July 2, 1918; s. William John and Annie Coronius (Addison) P.; student elec. engring. U. Tenn., 1937-41; m. Deszmer Lee Crane, Dec. 27, 1953; children—James William, Anna Deszmer. Elec. instr. Tenn. Eastman Co., Oak Ridge, 1943-45; owner Pollock Wired Music System, Oak Ridge, 1944-51; partner Music Box, Oak Ridge, 1950-56, owner, 1956—. Mem. Oak Ridge C. of C., I.E.E.E., Am. Inst. Elec. Engrs. (pres., 1950-51), Kappa Sigma. Rotarian. Club: 43. Home: 104 Maple Lane Oak Ridge TN 37830 Office: 131 Broadway Oak Ridge TN 37830

PONCE, HUMBERTO EDUARDO, archtl. and urban designer; b. Guadalajara, Jalisco, Mexico, Sept. 29, 1929; s. Joaquin Ponce and Carmen Adame; student Escuela de Arquitectura, U. Guadalajara, 1948-54; student regional planning, Nat. U. Mexico, 1964; m. Aurora Rabago, Dec. 23, 1963; children—Eduardo-Humberto, Gabriela. Designer, Arquitectos A. en P., Guadalajara, 1955-60; urban designer Guadalajara City Council, 1960-63; urban and regional planner State Jalisco Pub. Works Dept., 1964-70; bldg. mgr. COPOSA (Constructora Popular, S.A.), Guadalajara, 1970-72; tech. dir. Indeco Jalisco, fed. housing, Guadalajara, 1972—; dir. Sch. Fine Arts, U. Guadalajara, 1959-62, dir. Sch. Architecture, 1963-71; city planner Ciudad Primavera (New Town), 1971—; founder Seprin A. en P., environmental design, 1972—, tech. cons. nat. programs Indeco Mexico, 1974—. Sec. Com. Fed. Electoral Jalisco, 1957-58; founder Centro de Estudios Politices, Econs. y Sociales del PRI (CEPES), 1958—. Trustee U. Femenina de Guadalajara, 1960—; bd. dirs. Am. Sch. Guadalajara, 1972-74. Mem. Arquitectos Colegiados de Jalisco, Colegio Nac. de Arquitectos, Soc. Mexicana de Planificacion, Soc. Mexicana de Arquitectos Urbanistas, Assn. de Colonos y Propiatarios de Ciudad Primavera, Gran Fraternidad Universal. Club: Deportivo Guadalajara. Author: Armaduras Tri-Axiales para Cubiertas Alternadas, 1955; Apuntes Sobre las Teorias del la Arquitectura, 1960; Guadalajara, 1969; La E Kiplanistica un Nuevo Congecto de Diseno Integral, 1974. Home: 1581 Ruben Dario Guadalajara Jalisco ZP 6 Guadalajara Mexico Office: 2623 Planeta Guadalajara Jalisco ZP 5 Guadalajara Mexico

PONDER, NORMAN ALARIC, real estate exec.; b. Sherman, Tex., Sept. 13, 1938; s. Hugh Arnold and Maud Leo (Cox) P.; Asso. Sci., Arlington State Coll., 1959, student, 1956-60; B.S., U. Tex., 1962, Petroleum Engr., 1960-62; postgrad. Central Pilgrim Coll., 1964-65, Okla. State U., 1965-66; postgrad. real estate N.Y. U., 1968-70; grad. Exec. Devel. Program, Cornell U., 1970; m. Charlotte Marie White, Jan. 29, 1960; children—Nancy Anne, Susan Diane, Karen Marie. Grad. trainee Cities Service Oil Co., Bartlesville, Okla., 1962-63, buyer purchasing div., 1963-66, asst. real estate coordinator, Tulsa, 1967-68; real estate analyst Cities Service Co., N.Y.C., 1968-70, mgr. real estate projects, 1970-71, mgr. real estate operating properties, 1972-73; pres., dir. Sixty Wall Tower, Inc., N.Y.C., 1971-73; v.p. dir. Cities Service Realty, Inc., 1969-73; v.p., dir. Citgo Atlanta, Inc., 1970-73, Ft. Wayne Bank Bldg., Inc., 1970-73, Cities Service Tulsa, Inc., 1970-73, Chesebrough Bldg. Co., 1969-73, Holgate Devel. Corp., 1970-73; mgr. Carlton Shopping Center Co., Dallas, 1973—. Treas., United Fund, Bartlesville, Okla., 1966-67; mem. Real Estate Bd. N.Y., 1971—. Del. to Republican Precinct County and State Convs. party, 1966. Recipient Presdl. award of honor, Certificate of Merit, Bartlesville Jr. C. of C., 1964. Mem. U.S. Power Squadron, (N.J.), N.Y. C. of C., Bldg. Owners and Mgrs. Assn. of N.Y., Commerce and Industry Assn. N.Y., Downtown Owners Com., Nat. Assn. Real Estate Bds., Am. Mgmt. Assn. Club: Corinthian Sailing. Home: 9229 Raeford Dr Dallas TX 75231 Office: One Turtle Creek Village Dallas TX 75219

PONDER, WILLIAM GRAHAM, publisher; b. Rutledge, Ga., Nov. 5, 1923; s. Paul Holloway and Mary (Graham) P.; student Emory U., 1943-44; B.S., Clemson U., 1948; postgrad. U. Ga., 1949; m. Adelaide Douglas Wallace, Apr. 24, 1948; children—Anne, Mary Graham, Adelaide Douglas, William Graham. Pub., The Madisonian, Madison, Ga., 1957—; pres. Madisonian Pub. Co., Inc.; sec.-treas., dir. Madison Investment Co., dir., sec.-treas. Greater Ga. Printers, Inc., 1969—; dir. Hardman & Stuckey Travel Investments, Inc., 1970—, Bank of Rutledge, 1972—. Mem. City and County Planning Commns., 1960-62; mem. bldg. com. Ga. Press Found. Mem. City Council, Madison, 1958-62. Pres. Mental Health Assn.; chmn. bd. Morgan County Hosp. Authority. Served with USNR, 1944-47. Mem. Ga. Press Assn. (pres. 1965-66, com. chmn.), Atlanta Press Club (charter mem.), Sigma Nu, Sigma Delta Chi. Kiwanian (pres. 1970). Episcopalian. Home: 782 S Main St Madison GA 30650 Office: 131 E Jefferson St PO Box 191 Madison GA 30650

PONS, VICTOR MANUEL, JR., sec. state P.R., lawyer; b. Rio Piedras, P.R., Apr. 5, 1935; s. Victor Manuel and Carolina (Nunez) P.; diploma Hill Sch., 1952; student Swarthmore Coll., 1952-54; B.A. magna cum laude, U. P.R., 1956, LL.B. magna cum laude, 1959; m. Carmen Luisa Rexach, Feb. 26, 1960; children—Carolina Sofia, Carmen Luisa, Victor Manuel, Juan Antonio. Admitted to P.R. bar, 1959, since practiced in San Juan, P.R.; asso. firm Fiddler, Gonzalez & Rodriguez, 1959-62, partner, 1963-72; sec. State P.R., 1973—. Ad honorem instr. U. P.R. Sch. Dentistry. Mem. Council on Higher Edn. P.R., 1966-71. Mem. Am., Inter-Am. bar assns., Colegio de Abogados de P.R., P.R. C. of C. (dir. 1971—). Home: GPO Box P San Juan PR 00936 Office: Dept State San Juan PR 00936

POOL, JOHN CHARLES, banker; b. nr. Jasper, Tex., Feb. 15, 1940; s. Charles Cade and Lillie Ruth (Rainey) P.; B.B.A., U. Tex.; postgrad. Southwestern Grad. Sch. Banking, Dallas; m. Janet Gayle Messer, Feb. 20, 1964; 1 dau., Kendell. Exec. tng. program First Security Nat. Bank, Beaumont, Tex., 1964-65; vice chmn. bd. First State Bank, Jasper, Tex., 1971—. Served with AUS, 1966-69. Mem. Jasper C. of C., Jasper Jaycees (v.p., past state dir.), Beta Theta Pi. Lion (past treas.). Home: 1307 Northwood Dr Jasper TX 75951 Office: PO Box 640 Jasper TX 75951

POOLE, GEORGE GRAHAM, JR., real estate and loan exec.; b. Mullins, S.C., June 1, 1925; s. George Graham and Sarah Ally (Haltiwanger) P.; student Clemson Coll., 1942-43; m. Ruby Elizabeth Brant, July 1, 1946; children—Elizabeth Anne, George Martin. With George G. Poole Real Estate and Loans, Mullins, 1946—, owner-mgr., 1953—; dir. Davis Nat. Bank, Mullins. Mem. Marion County Bd. Commrs., 1959—; chmn. Mullins Pub. Housing Authority, 1968—; co-founder, chief Mullins Community Fire Dept., 1951; county rep. Clemson U. Iptay, 1965—, dist. dir., 1971—, sec.-treas., 1972—. Bd. dirs. Ind. Consumer Finance Assn. S.C. Served with C.E., AUS, 1943-46. Mem. Mullins C. of C. (pres. 1962-64), Am. Legion (vice comdr. 1948-49), V.F.W. Home: Poole Dr Mullins SC 29574 Office: 125 W Wine St Mullins SC 29574

POOLE, PIERRE PATILLO, physician; b. Cross Anchor, S.C., Sept. 8, 1917; s. Mack Collier and Kate (Holcombe) P.; B.S., John B. Stetson U., 1936; M.D., Duke U., 1940; postgrad. (Rockefeller fellow) Tulane Sch. Medicine, New Orleans, 1946-47; m. Elizabeth Porcher Gignilliat, Mar. 22, 1946; children—William Pierre, John Gignilliat. Rotating intern, Charity Hosp., New Orleans, 1940-41, resident medicine, 1941-42; instr. medicine Tulane Sch. Medicine, 1946-47; pvt. practice medicine, specializing in internal medicine and cardiology, Rocky Mount, N.C., 1947-50, Brownsville, Tex., 1950—; mem. staff, electrocardiographer Mercy Hosp., Brownsville, Tex., chief dept. medicine, 1951-54, 56-57, 60-72, pres. staff, 1952; cons. internal medicine USPHS, Brownsville, 1960-73. Served to maj. AUS, 1942-46. Diplomate Am. Bd. Internal Medicine. Fellow Am. Coll. Chest Physicians, A.C.P.; mem. Am., Tex., heart assns., A.M.A., Cameron Willacy County Med. Soc. (pres. 1958), Am., Tex. socs. internal medicine, Tex. Acad. Internal Medicine, Am. Legion. Presbyn. Home: 205 Calle Jacaranda Brownsville TX 78520 Office: 44 E Levee St Brownsville TX 78520

POOLE, REID, musician; b. Toccoa, Ga., July 20, 1919; s. David Young and Jane Ann (Means) P.; B.A., U. Chgo., 1946, M.A., 1947; m. Doris Jane Wilson, Apr. 4, 1942; children—Christopher Howard, Deborah Doris. Instr. music Roosevelt U., 1947-49; mem. faculty U. Fla., 1949—. Asst. dir. bands, 1949-58, dir. bands, 1958-61, prof., chmn. dept. music, 1961—. Former treas. Fla. Arts Council. Served with AUS, 1941-45. Mem. Fla. Music Educators Assn. (past pres.), Assn. Coll. and Concert Mgrs. (bd. dirs., v.p.). Club: Torch. Editor: Fla. Music Dirs. Mag., 1965-71; mus. compositions and arrangements used by sch. and coll. bands. Home: 3706 SW 6th Pl Gainesville FL 32601

POOLE, RICHARD WILLIAM, educator; b. Oklahoma City, Dec. 4, 1927; s. William Robert and Lois (Spicer) P.; B.S., U. Okla., 1951, M.B.A., 1952; Ph.D., Okla. State U., 1960; m. Bertha Lynn Mehr, July 28, 1950; children—Richard William, Laura Lynne, Mark Stephen. Research analyst Okla. Gas & Electric Co., Oklahoma City, 1952-54; mgr. Sci. and Mfg. Devel. dept. Oklahoma City C. of C., 1954-57; asst. to pres. Frontiers of Sci. Found., 1955; mgr. Office of James E. Webb, Washington, 1957-58; instr. econs., asst. prof., asso. prof., prof., Okla. State U., 1960-65, dean Coll. of Bus., 1965-72, v.p. univ. relations and devel., 1972—. Cons. NASA, Midwest Research Inst. Mem. Gov's. gen. adv. com., tech. com. Statis. Standards, 1964—; mem. adv. exec. com. Nat. Govs. Conf., 1965. Bd. dirs. Stillwater Indsl. Found., 1967—, Stillwater YMCA, 1966. Mid-Continent Research and Devel. Council, 1965—, chmn., 1969; bd. dirs. Okla. Council on Econ. Edn., 1965—, mem. exec. council, 1965—. Served from pvt. to 2d lt., AUS, 1946-48. Mem. Am., So.

econ. assns., Okla. (dir. 1965—), Stillwater (dir. 1965—, pres. 1968) chambers commerce, Regional Sci. Assn., Am. Assn. Collegiate Schs. Bus. (bd. dirs. 1971-72), Southwestern Econ. Assn. (pres. 1968), Midwest Econ. Assn., Res. Officers Assn., Southwestern Bus. Adminstrn. Assn. (pres. 1972), Phi Eta Sigma, Beta Gamma Sigma, Pi Gamma Mu, Phi Kappa Phi, Omicron Delta Kappa. Lion. Contbr. articles to profl. jours. Home: 124 Georgia Av Stillwater OK 74074

POOLE, THOMAS CARL, JR., mfg. co. exec.; b. Leeds, Ala., Feb. 19, 1921; s. Thomas Carl and Grace (King) P.; B.S., Auburn U., 1948; postgrad. Coll. Advanced Traffic of Chgo. at Jacksonville State U., 1950-51; m. Mary Louise Miller, Oct. 7, 1960; children—Thomas Carl III, John Preston. Mgr. Traffic and shipping planning Dresser Mfg. div. Dresser Industries, Anniston, Ala., 1949—. Traffic cons. various firms, 1960—. Served with USAF, 1943. Mem. N.E. Ala. Traffic and Transp. Club (gov. 1960), Phi Kappa Tau. Home: Route 5 Box 567 Anniston AL 36201 Office: W 23d St Anniston AL 36201

POOLE, WILLIAM DANIEL, editor; b. Statesville, N.C., Nov. 3, 1932; s. William Oscar and Edna (Brewer) P.; B.A., Wake Forest Coll., 1955; m. Erika Kiene, Oct. 18, 1958. Reporter, Norfolk (Va.) Virginian-Pilot, 1955-57; reporter Washington Evening Star, 1957-61, real estate editor, 1961-71, features editor, 1971—. Recipient News Writing award Va. Press Assn., 1956, Real Estate Sect. award Nat. Assn. Home Builders, 1963, 69, Feature Writing award Nat. Assn. Real Estate Bds., 1965, 67, 69, Consumer Oriented Articles award Nat. Assn. Real Estate Editors, 1970. Mem. Nat. Assn. Real Estate Editors (dir. 1966-67, sec. 1968, treas. 1969, pres. 1971), White House Corrs. Assn., Newspaper Comics Council (mem. exec. com.), Nat. Press Club, Am. Assn. Sunday and Feature Editors, Omicron Delta Kappa, Sigma Phi Epsilon. Home: Watergate East Washington DC 20037 Office: 225 Virginia Av SE Washington DC 20003

POOLER, FRANCIS, JR., meterologist; b. Waltham, Mass., Mar. 30, 1926; s. Francis and Constance (Palmer) P.; B.S., Mass. Inst. Tech., 1949; Ph.D., Pa. State U., 1972; m. Barbara Giles, Dec. 27, 1952; children—Charles F., Margaret R., Betsy, Randall. Meteorologist, U.S. Weather Bur., Buffalo and Washington, 1950-55; research meteorologist USPHS and EPA, Cin., 1955-69, Research Triangle Park, N.C., 1969—. Pres., Greater Newtown (O.) Civic League, 1960-61. Served with USNR, 1944-46. Mem. Am. Meteorol. Soc., Am. Geophys. Union. Home: 2131 Meares Rd Chapel Hill NC 27514 Office: National Environmental Research Center EPA Research Triangle Park NC 27711

POOR, RICHARD LONGSTREET, utilities exec.; b. Summit, N.J., Dec. 28, 1910; s. Charles Longstreet and Mary L. (Austin) P.; B.S., U.S. Naval Acad., 1933; m. Margaret Key English, July 12, 1934 (div. July 1940); children—Richard Longstreet, Austin E.; m. 2d, Elizabeth Louise Snavely, July 1942 (div. July 1962); 1 son, Earl S.; m. 3d, Elizabeth Maurey Salvesen, Oct. 17, 1963; stepchildren—Tina S., Jan S. Electric field supt. Beach Electric Co., Newark, 1946-48; electric insp. Fla. Power & Light Co., Miami, 1948-49, electric constrn. supt., 1949-50, asst. distbn. supr., 1950-52, comml. supr., 1952-53, asst. mgr. comml., 1953-55, asst. purchasing agt., 1955-60, asst. to v.p. operating, 1960—. Served with AC, U.S. Army, 1933-34; from ensign to comdr. USN, 1934-46. Decorated D.F.C. and Gold star, Air medal. Registered profl. engr., N.J., Fla. Mem. I.E.E.E., Nat. Soc. Profl. Engrs., Fla. Engring. Soc., Soc. Am. Mil. Engrs., Miami Beach C. of C. (zoning, bldg. com. 1953-54), Navy League, Greater Miami Aviation Assn. (edn. com. 1966—), Fla. Air Pilots Assn. Episcopalian. Rotarian. Club: Florida Aero (Miami). Home: 9011 N Bayshore Dr Miami FL 33138 Office: 4200 Flagler St Miami FL 33134

POORE, THOMAS WASHINGTON, city ofcl.; b. Jonas Ridge, N.C., Feb. 25, 1912; s. Joseph L. and Cora E. (Keller) P.; student Crossnore Comml. Sch., 1932-33; m. Pauline Maynard, Dec. 22, 1934 (div. Apr. 1949); children—Karen (Mrs. Hugh Bridge, Joyce (Mrs. Donald R. Brown), Susie, Fred Cubitt; m. 2d, Ruth Branch Reep, May 22, 1959; stepchildren—Dallas, Samuel C. With various constrn. cos., 1939-49; city employee City of Morganton (N.C.), 1949—, supt. Sanitation Dept., 1951—. Mem. Regional Health Council, 1973-74, Regional Solid Waste Commn., 1973—. Chmn. fund-raising Oxford, orphange and home, 1971-74. Mem. Am. Pub. Works Assn. (N.C. dir. 1970-73, chpt. v.p. san. div. 1974). Baptist (asso. Sunday sch. supt. 1961-65, pres. brotherhood 1959-63). Mason (32 deg.); mem. Order Eastern Star. Home: 507 Mull St Morganton NC 28655 Office: PO Drawer 430 Morganton NC 28655

POPE, ANDREW JACKSON (JACK), JR., judge; b. Abilene, Tex., Apr. 18, 1913; s. A.J. and Ruth (Taylor) P.; B.A., Abilene Christian Coll., 1934; LL.B., U. Tex., 1937; m. Allene Nichols, June 11, 1938; children—A.J. III, Walter Allen. Admitted to Tex. bar, 1937; began practice of law in Corpus Christi, Tex., 1937, mem. firm Pope & Pope, 1937-44, Cannon, Pittman & Pope, 1946; judge Dist. Ct., 94th Jud. Dist., 1946-50; justice Ct. Civil Appeals, 4th Jud. Dist., San Antonio, 1950-65; asso. justice Supreme Ct. Tex., Austin, 1965—. Chmn. Tex. Judicial Sect., 1962. Pres. San Antonio YMCA, 1957. Served with USNR, 1944-46. Recipient Silver Beaver award Boy Scouts Am. Mem. Am. Judicature Soc., Am., Nueces County (pres. 1947), San Antonio, Travis County bar assns., State Bar Tex., Order of Coif, Phi Delta Phi. Mem. Ch. of Christ. K.P. (grand chancellor Tex. 1948). Contbr. articles to profl. jours. Office: Supreme Ct Bldg Capitol Sta Box 12248 Austin TX 78711

POPE, BENJAMIN JAMES, aluminum co. exec.; b. Richmond, Va., May 7, 1929; s. Benjamin James and Rena May (Taylor) P.; student Memphis State U., 1947-48; B.J., U. Mo., 1951; m. Rosanne Mary Stiles, Aug. 18, 1951; 1 dau., Rena Blanche. Reporter, editor Richmond Times-Dispatch, 1951-58, asst. press relations mgr. Owens-Ill., Toledo, 1958-61; mem. staff news bur. Goodyear Tire, Akron, 1961-65; div. pub. relations mgr. Reynolds Metals Co., Richmond, 1965—. Bd. dirs. Keep Va. Beautiful, 1967. Served with USMCR, 1946-47. Mem. Pub. Relations Soc. Am. (dir. 1974), Kappa Alpha. Home: 1201 Essex Av Richmond VA 23229 Office: Reynolds Metal Co 6601 W Broad St Rd Richmond VA 23218

POPE, FRANK STARR, JR., lawyer; b. Dallas, June 26, 1927; s. Frank Starr and Klyda Kathleen (Dyer) P.; B.B.A., U. Tex., 1950, LL.B., 1952. Admitted to Tex. bar, 1952; asso. mem. firm Frazer & Torbet, C.P.A.'s, Houston, 1952-53; asso. Kleberg, Mobley, Lockett & Weil, Corpus Christi, Tex., 1953-61, partner, 1961—; dir. B.D. Holt Co. Pres., Am. Cancer Soc., Nueces County, 1962, Corpus Christi Assn. Congregations, 1967, Community Devl., Corp. Corpus Christi, 1971, Corpus Christi Mus. 1969, Nat. Conf. Christians and Jews, Corpus Christi, 1972, Coastal Bend Christian Service Assn., 1972. Appeal agt., local bd. Selective Service Systems, 1964-71, mem. bd., 1971—; del. Tex. Dem. Conv., 1972. Served with USNR, 1945-46. Fellow Am. Coll. Probate Counsel; mem. Nueces County (pres. elect), Tex., Am. bar assns., Am. Judicature Soc., Phi Eta Sigma, Phi Delta Theta. Episcopalian. Home: 901 N Carancahua St Corpus Christi TX 78401 Office: PO Box 2446 Corpus Christi TX 78403

POPE, JAMES ARTHUR, III, educator, mgmt. scientist; b. East Orange, N.J., Nov. 15, 1942; s. James Arthur and Eleanor (McElheney) P.; B.A., Coll. Wooster, 1964; M.A., Northwestern U., 1966; postgrad. U. N.C. at Chapel Hill, 1966-67, 72-74; m. Nell Eleanor Volc, Sept. 10, 1965; children—Jennifer Angela, James Andrew. Instr. Guilford Coll. Greensboro, N.C., 1965-67; logistician Lackland AFB, San Antonio, 1967-70; statistician Lowry AFB, Denver, 1970-72; instr. mgmt. Guilford Coll., Greensboro, N.C., 1974—. Hon. instr. U. Colo., Denver, 1970-72. Dir. research Barnwell for Congress Com., 6th Dist. N.C.; 1966. Mem. Am., So. econ. assns. Home: 3906 Sedgegrove Rd Greensboro NC 27407

POPE, LARRY JACOB, librarian; b. Cin., Feb. 26, 1937; s. Jesse B. and Estelle M. (Moneyhon) P.; A.B., U. Ky., 1959, M.S., 1961; m. Genevieve Scott Johnston, July 10, 1965. Librarian, serials cataloger main library U. Ky., Lexington, 1961-64, head circulation librarian, 1964-66; asst. periodicals librarian Eastern Ky. U., Richmond, 1966-67, chief periodicals librarian, 1967—. Mem. Am., Southeastern Ky. library assns., Tech. Service Librarians (Ohio Valley group), Theatre Guild Soc. Am. Home: 112 Buckwood Dr Richmond KY 40475 Office: Crabbe Library Eastern Kentucky University Richmond KY 40475

POPE, MICHAEL THOR, educator; b. Exeter, Eng., Apr. 14, 1933; s. Hector Maurice and Edith Mary (Hewett) P.; B.A., Oxford U., 1954, M.A., 1958, D.Phil., 1957; m. Ann Mavis Potter, July 12, 1957; children—Gregory, Lucy. Came to U.S., 1962. Chemist, Laporte Chems., Luton, Eng., 1959-62; mem. faculty Georgetown U., Washington, 1962—, asso. prof., 1967-73, prof., 1973—. Postdoctoral fellow Boston U., 1957-59; Petroleum Research Fund internat. award fellow, vis. prof. Tech. U. Vienna, Austria, 1970-71. Research grantee NSF, Petroleum Research Fund, Army Research Office, Air Force Office Sci. Research. Mem. Am. Chem. Soc., Chem. Soc. London, Sigma Xi. Contbr. articles to profl. jours. Office: Dept Chemistry Georgetown Univ Washington DC 20007

POPE, THOMAS HARRINGTON, lawyer; b. Kinard, S.C., July 28, 1913; s. Thomas H. and Marie (Gary) P.; A.B., The Citadel, 1935; LL.B., U. S.C., 1938; LL.D., Newberry Coll., 1969; grad. Command and Gen. Staff Coll., 1951; m. Mary Waties Lumpkin, Jan. 3, 1940; children—Mary Waties (Mrs. R.H. Kennedy, Jr.), Thomas Harrington III, Gary Tusten. Admitted to S.C. bar, 1938, also U.S. Supreme Ct.; practice in Newberry, 1938—; spl. circuit judge Richland and Lexington counties, 1955-56; dir. Citizens and So. Nat. Bank S.C., Standard Savs. and Loan Assn., Am. Sentinel Life Ins. Co. Mem. S.C. Ports Authority, 1957-65, Jud. Council S.C., 1957—, S.C. Archives Commn., 1965—. S.C. Tricentennial Commn.; mem. adv. bd. Nat. Trust for Historic preservation, 1967-73; chmn. Newberry County Sesqui-Centennial Commn., 1939. Mem. S.C. Ho. of Reps. from Newberry County, 1936-40, 45-50, speaker, 1949-50; chmn. S.C. Democratic Party, 1958-60; del. at large Dem. Nat. Conv., 1956, 60; pres. S.C. Dem. Conv., 1958, 62. Trustee, also chmn. S.C. Found. Ind. Colls., Newberry Coll., U. of South, 1965-69; bd. visitors The Citadel, 1939-40, 46. Served to lt. col. AUS, 1941-45; ETO; brig. gen. S.C.N.G. ret. Fellow Am. Coll. Trial Lawyers; mem. Am., S.C. (pres. 1964, chmn. exec. com. 1956-58), Newberry County (pres. 1951) bar assns., Am. Law Inst., Am. Judicature Soc., Nat. Assn. R.R. Trial Counsel, Am., So. hist. assns., S.C., Newberry County (pres. 1966) hist. socs., Phi Beta Kappa, Omicron Delta Kappa, Phi Delta Phi, Alpha Tau Omega. Episcopalian (sr. warden 1963-65). Mason (grand master S.C. 1958-60; Albert Gallatin Mackey medal Grand Lodge S.C. 1965, Henry Price medal Grand Lodge Mass. 1960). Clubs: Newberry Country; Spring Valley Country, Palmetto, Pine Tree Hunt (Columbia, S.C.); Army-Navy (Washington). Author: The History of Newberry County, South Carolina, 1973. Home: 1700 Boundary St Newberry SC 29108 Office: 1201 Boyce St Newberry SC 29108

POPE, WILLIAM BAKER, pub. relations cons.; b. Atlanta, Feb. 15, 1933; s. Arthur Bozeman and Juliette (Murray) P.; B.B.A., Emory U., 1955; m. Sarah Harper Anderson, Apr. 28, 1966; children—Juliette Rogers, Andrew Porter. Reporter, Dallas Morning News, 1957-59; state news editor Atlanta Constn., 1959-62; news editor Bahamas Ministry Finance and Tourism, Nassau, Hill & Knowlton, Inc., N.Y., 1963-66; self-employed as publicist and pub. relations cons., Atlanta, 1966—; pres. Attitude Research and Cons., Inc. Served with AUS, 1955-57. Mem. Pub. Relations Soc. Am., Am. Acad. Polit. and Social Sci., Alpha Tau Omega. Club: Doghouse (Nassau). Home: 1016 Farmington Lane NE Atlanta GA 30319 Office: PO Box 18787 Atlanta GA 30326

POPE, WILLIAM ROBERT, lawyer, ex-state rep.; b. Mt. Mourne, N.C., Feb. 24, 1918; s. James Robert and Mary (Kelly) P.; grad. Brevard Jr. Coll., 1938; B.S., Davidson Coll., 1940; LL.B., U. N.C., 1948; m. Ina Amelia Barber, Sept. 16, 1946; children—William Robert, James Shuford, Charles Vance, Elizabeth Barber, Deborah, Caroline Amelia. Admitted to N.C. bar, 1948; pvt. practice, Mooresville, 1948—; judge Mooresville Recorder's Ct. 1952-63; gen. counsel Crescent Electric Membership Corp. Dir. Cornelius Devel. Co., Inc.; pres. Braco, Inc.; bd. mgrs. Northwestern Bank. Mem. N.C. House of Reps., 1951-52, 63-64. Chmn. adv. com. Iredell County Govtl. Complex. Mem. Lowrance Hosp., Inc.; bd. regents Barium Springs Home for Children. Served to lt. USNR, 1940-46. Decorated D.F.C. Mem. Am., N.C., Iredell County bar assns., Phi Delta Phi. Democrat. Presbyn. Mason, Elk, Rotarian. Home: US 21 Mooresville NC 28115 Office: PO Box 27 Mooresville NC 28115

POPEJOY, LEE TARENCE, II, physician; b. Ada, Okla., June 17, 1935; s. Lee Tarence and Vivienne (Flowers) P.; student Tex. A. and M. Coll., 1953-54; B.S., Centenary Coll., 1957; M.D., La. State U., 1961; m. Edith Louise Griggs, Dec. 2, 1973; children by previous marriage—Lauralee, Caroline Vivienne, Lee Tarence III, Augusta Susannah. Research asst. dept. anatomy La. State U., 1958-61; intern William Beaumont Army Hosp., El Paso, Tex., 1961-62; practice medicine specializing in gen. medicine, Jasper, Tex., 1964—. Vice pres. Hardy Hancock Hosp., Jasper, 1966—; pres. Mechanized Services Am., 1964—. Bd. dirs. M.E. Dickerson Hosp. Served to capt. M.C., AUS, 1961-64. Mem. Am., So., Tex. med. assns., Jasper, Newton County Med. Soc. (pres. 1974), Jasper C. of C. Presbyn. (elder). Rotarian. Contbr.: The Squirrel Monkey, 1969. Home: Bevilport Jasper TX 75951 Office: 1001 Dickerson Dr Jasper TX 75951

POPENOE, HUGH LLYWELYN, educator; b. Tela, Honduras, Aug. 28, 1929 (parents Am. citizens); s. Frederick Wilson and Dorothy (Hughes) P.; B.S., U. Cal. at Davis, 1951; Ph.D., U. Fla., 1960. Mem. faculty U. Fla., Gainesville, 1960—, dir. Center for Tropical Agr., 1965—, dir. internat. agr. programs, 1966—, prof. soils, geography, agronomy and botany, 1971—, also dir. state univ. system sea grant program. Research adviser Latin Am. program Nat. Com. on Econ. Devel., 1963-64; cons. Fgn. Area Fellowship program, N.Y., 1969-72. Bd. dirs. Gulf Univs. Research Consortium, 1970—; trustee Latin Am. Scholarship Program Am. Univs., Cambridge, 1971; chmn. trustees Escuela Agricola Panamaericana, Honduras, 1971—. Served with C.E., AUS, 1952-54. Grantee Rockefeller Found., NSF, Ford Found., NIH, AEC. Fellow A.A.A.S., Am. Geog. Soc., Internat. Soils Sci. Soc., Am. Soc. Agronomy, mem. Gulf Univs. Research Consortium (dir. 1970), Sigma Xi, Gamma Sigma Delta, Alpha Zeta. Gamma Theta Upsilon. Asso. editor Jour. Agronomic Edn., 1971-73. Home: Box 13533 Gainesville FL 32611

POPOVIC, VOJIN, educator; b. Belgrade, Yugoslavia, Sept. 18, 1922; s. Pavle and Bojana (Pavlovic) P.; Ph.D., U. Belgrade, 1951; m. Pava Javanovic, Oct. 2, 1948; 1 son, Ray. Came to U.S., 1957, naturalized, 1967. Chmn. dept. physiology Belgrade U., 1955; research asso. Lab. Physiology, Paris, France, 1956; vis. prof. U. Rochester (N.Y.), 1957, NRC Can., Ottawa, Ont., 1958-59; asso. prof. U. Houston, 1960-61; asso. prof. physiology Med. Sch. Emory U., Atlanta, 1961-65, prof., 1965—. Recipient Career Devel. award NIH, 1962-72. Mem. Soc. Exptl. Biology and Medicine (pres. 1970-72), Am. Physiol. Soc., Soc. Cryobiology, Aerospace Med. Assn. Contbr. articles to profl. jours. Research in hypothermia and depressed metabolism. Home: 2342 Street de Ville NE Atlanta GA 30329

POPPENDIECK, ROBERT, govt. ofcl.; b. Carlstadt, N.J., Aug. 21, 1908; s. William and Etta (Prehn) P.; student Springfield (Mass.) Coll., 1926-28; A.B., Montclair (N.J.) State Tchrs. Coll., 1931; M.A., Tchrs. Coll., Columbia, 1934; Ed.D., Rutgers U., 1954; m. Gertrude Atkinson Pell, Aug. 19, 1934; children—Carol Ann, Gertrude Annsley (Mrs. Banks G. Prevatt), Janet Elizabeth (Mrs. John R. Kernodle, Jr.). Tchr. English, jr. high sch., Garwood, N.J., 1931-35; sec. YMCA, Mercer County, Trenton, 1935-37; tchr. English Jonathan Dayton Regional High Sch., Springfield, 1937-42, dept. head, 1938-42; personnel mgr. U.S. Hammered Piston Ring Co., Inc., Stirling, 1942-48; lectr. edn. Rutgers U., New Brunswick, 1948-54, asso. prof., 1954-58, dir. adminstrv. services Sch. Edn., 1954-58; specialist for tchr. edn. U.S. Office Edn., Washington, 1958—, acting chief tchr. edn. and devel. programs sect., 1962-63; dir. programs br. Tchr. Corps, 1966-68, dir. field services Bur. Ednl. Personnel Devel., 1968—. Cons., Ednl. Testing Service, Princeton, N.J., 1957; dir. adult sch. Jonathan Dayton Regional High Sch. Dist., 1957-58. Mem. East Hanover Twp. Bd. Edn., 1933-35; mem. Springfield Civil Def. Unit, 1942-45. Trustee, Albright Coll. Recipient Distinguished Alumni award Rutgers U. Sch. Edn., 1963. Mem. N.J. Personnel and Guidance Assn. (hon. life), Assn. Higher Edn., Assn. Field Services in Tchr. Edn., N.E.A. (life), Nat. Commn. Tchr. Edn. and Profl. Standards (liaison cons.), Phi Delta Kappa. United Methodist. Contbr. articles to profl. jours. and bulls. Home: 3112 Circle Hill Rd Alexandria VA 22305 Office: US Office Edn Washington DC 20202

PORTER, AUBREY L., lawyer; b. Mt. Pleasant, Tex., July 6, 1898; s. R. J. and Lavenia (Hall) P.; student E. Tex. Tchr's Coll., 1917-21; LL.B., Kent Coll. Law, Chgo., 1925; m. Hazel Harvey, Jan. 2, 1927; 1 son, Robert M. Admitted to Fla. bar, 1926, Circuit Ct., 1926, Fed. Ct., 1932, pros. atty. Wakulla Co., Fla., 1926-32; county judge, 1932-57; gen. law practice, 1957—; tree farming. Mem. Wakulla County Welfare Assn. Past chmn. adv. com. Tallahassee Jr. Coll. Mem. Am. Legion, 40 and 8, Fla. Bar, 2d Jud. Circuit Bar Assn. (past pres.), Wakulla County C. of C. (past pres.). Democrat. Methodist (ofcl. bd. mem., past chmn.). Mason; mem. Order Eastern Star. Address: Crawfordville FL 32327

PORTER, DUNCAN MACNAIR, botanist; b. Kelseyville, Cal., Apr. 20, 1937; s. James Duncan MacNair and Dorothy (Swender) P.; student Ventura Coll., 1955-57; A.B., Stanford, 1959, A.M., 1961; Ph.D., Harvard, 1967; m. Sarah Josephine Holyoke, Sept. 14, 1966; 1 son, Charles Holyoke. Postdoctoral asst. Cal. Acad. Scis., San Francisco, 1966-67; asst. prof. dept. biology U. San Francisco, 1967-68; curator Flora Panama, Mo. Bot. Garden, St. Louis, 1968-72; editor-in-chief Flora N. Am. Project, Smithsonian Instn., Washington, 1972-73; asso. program dir. for systematic biology NSF, Washington, 1973—; asst. prof. dept. botany Washington U., St. Louis, 1968-70, adjunct asst. prof. dept. biology, 1970-73. Served with USAF, 1961. NSF fellow, 1965, grantee, 1969-72. Mem. Am. Inst. Biol. Scis., Am. Soc. Plant Taxonomists (sec.), Assn. Tropical Biology, Bot. Soc. Am. (sec.-treas. systematics sect.), Cal. Bot. Soc., Ecol. Soc. Am., Internat. Assn. Plant Taxonomy, Internat. Orgn. Plant Biosystematists, New Eng. Bot. Club, Sigma Xi. Mem. edit. bd. Wasmann Jour. Biology, 1966-67, Annals Mo. Bot. Garden, 1968-72, Madrono, 1970—. Author: (with Ira L. Wiggins) Flora of the Galapagos Islands, 1971. Home: 141 S Columbus St Arlington VA 22204 Office: Systematic Biology Program NSF Washington DC 20550

PORTER, GARLAND BURNS, editor, pub.; b. Dabney, N.C., June 3, 1897; s. William and Letitia (Cockerham) P.; A.B., U. N.C., 1922, M.A., 1923; m. Polly Wolff, June 22, 1925 (dec. Apr. 1941); children—Polly Jean (Mrs. V. Hugo Sewell), Garland Burns, David Darlington; m. 2d, Ruth Vail Selby, 1945 (div. Feb. 1951); 1 son, Joseph M. V.; m. 3d, Margaret McFarland, Feb. 1954; stepchildren—William Wyman, Margaret Tracy. Reporter, Atlanta Constitution, 1922; reporter-city editor Winston-Salem (N.C.) Jour., 1923-25; nat. advt. mgr. Atlanta Georgian, 1927-39; So. mgr. Hearst Advt. Service, 1934-40; mgr. N.C. News Bur., Raleigh, 1942-43; editor-gen. mgr. So. Advt. & Pub. Atlanta, 1949-64; editor, pub. So. Markets/Media, Atlanta, 1965-71; founder Porter Pub. Co., 1942; pub. So. Plastics Mag., 1945-46. Pres. N.C. Soc., Atlanta, 1930. Served to 2d lt. USMCR, 1918. Mem. So. Newspaper Pubs. Assn., Am. Advt. Fedn., Nat. Press Club, Sigma Delta Chi, Delta Tau Delta, Sigma Upsilon, Club: Poor Richard (Phila.). Contbr. articles to popular mags. Home: 69 Mobile Av NE Atlanta GA 30305

PORTER, GRANVILLE DWIGHT, elec. engr.; b. Ashtabula, Ohio, June 23, 1916; s. Jesse Wheeler and Lina (Dwight) P.; B.S.E.E., U. Miami, 1960; M.A., U. Okla., 1973; m. Mary Jane Dicken, Apr. 19, 1943; children—Jane Shirley, Alma LaDue (Mrs. Richard Marshall Winfield III) (dec. Aug. 1970), Paul Dwight, Phyllis Elizabeth. Pvt. practice cons. engring., 1950-55 engr. Dade County, Fla., 1955-58 cons. engr., Miami, Fla., 1958-60; electronics engr. U.S. Navy, Washington, 1960-64; frequency engr. U.S. European Command, Paris, France, 1964-67; elec. engr. NASA, Marshall Space Flight Center, Ala., 1967—; cons. engr. Commnr. N.E. France dist. Boy Scouts Am., 1964-66. Served with USN, 1937-41. Registered profl. engr., Fla., Ala., D.C. Mem. A.A.A.S., I.E.E.E., Soc. Am. Mil. Engrs. Mason (32 deg., Shriner). Home: Yacht Sea Mint 1114 Ferry St NE Decatur AL 35601 Office: A & PS-FAC-EM Marshall Space Flight Center AL 35812

PORTER, JAMES TINSLEY, textile co. exec.; b. Atlanta, Jan. 15, 1922; s. John Russell and Augusta (Tinsley) P.; B.S. in Chem. Engring., Ga. Inst. Tech., 1943, B.S. in Textile Engring., 1948; m. Catherine Tift, Dec. 7, 1944; children—Catherine, Pattie, James Tinsley, Thomas, Russell. Pres., Porter Carpet Mills, Inc., Cartersville, Ga., 1946—; v.p. Piedmont Cotton Mills, East Point, 1946—. Trustee Westminster Schs., Atlanta. Served to lt. USNR, 1943-45. Mem. Young Pres.'s Orgn. Presbyn. (elder 1958-64, 66—). Rotarian. Clubs: Piedmont Driving, Capital City, Peachtree Racket, University Yacht (all Atlanta); Union League (Chgo.). Home: 295 W Wesley Rd NW Atlanta GA 30305 Office: PO Box 688 Cartersville GA 30120

PORTER, JOSEPH ALEXANDER, clergyman; b. Talladega, Ala., Mar. 29, 1922; s. George Joshua and Cora (Yester) P.; student Emory U., 1940-43; B.A., Vanderbilt U., 1945; B.D., Yale, 1948; m. Lillian C. Kane, June 14, 1947; children—Joseph David, Thomas Alexander. Instr., Jr. Coll. Commerce, New Haven, 1946-48; ordained to ministry Meth. Ch., 1948 asso. dir. W.Va. U., Wesley Found., dir. U. Mich., Wesley Found., 1949-51; pastor 1st Congl. Ch., Marion, Mass., 1951-54; dean students State N.C. State Coll., exec. dir. United Campus Ministry, Mich. State U., 1956-62; campus minister U. N.H.,

1962-63; pastor 1st Congl. Ch. Ledyard, Conn., 1963-66, Congl. Ch., Tavares, Fla., 1967—. Moderator, N.E. Assn. Fla. Conf. United Ch. of Christ. Bd. dirs. Lake County Boys Ranch; mem. Council on Aging N. Fla. Chaplain, Exchange Club, East Lansing, Mich., 1961-62. Chmn. renewal and outreach com. Fla. Conf. United Ch. Christ, chmn. mission council N. Central area, 1974—; mem. Fla. Council Chs. Commn. on Christian Life and Mission. Mem. Tavares C. of C. (dir.). Kiwanian (chmn. Key Club com.). Address: 122 St Clair Abrams Av Tavares FL 32778

PORTER, ULWIN DONALD, credit agy. exec.; b. La Plata, Mo., Sept. 18, 1904; s. Orrin Malcolm and Eva Susie (Perrin) P.; B.B.A., U. Colo., 1928; m. Ida Lee Wallace, Nov. 4, 1933; 1 son, Donald Raymond. Accountant, Price Waterhouse & Co., Kansas City, Mo., and St. Louis, 1928-38, Houston, 1938-41; treas. Levy Bros. Dry Goods Co., Houston, 1942-52; accountant Peat, Marwick, Mitchell & Co., Houston, 1952-69; treas. Asso. Credit Services, Inc., Houston, 1969—. C.P.A., Tex., Mo. Mem. Am. Inst. C.P.A.'s, Financial Execs. Inst., Alpha Sigma Phi, Beta Alpha Psi, Delta Sigma Pi. Presbyn. Home: 2247 Goldsmith St Houston TX 77025 Office: 2309 Fannin Houston TX 77002

PORTER, WILLIAM LUTHER, lawyer, financial exec.; b. Washington, May 23, 1918; s. James A. and Anna (Foster) P.; B.S., Am. U., 1949, LL.B., 1954, J.D., 1968; m. Mae C. Hill, June 27, 1942. Accountant, auditor Smith & Davis, Washington, 1945-47; sr. partner Porter, Adams & Cramer, Washington, 1947-48; agt. Internal Revenue Service, Washington, 1948-59; sr. accountant M.B. Hariton & Co., Washington, 1959-66; commr. D.C. Pub. Service Commn., Washington, 1966-70; treas. Center for Community Change, Washington, 1970-72; prof. accounting Washington Tech. Inst., 1970-71; partner Lucas, Tucker & Co. C.P.A.s, Washington, 1971—. Financial adviser Jamaica Pub. Utilities Commn., Kingston, Jamaica, 1971—; cons. Potomac Electric Power Co., 1973—; v.p., gen. counsel Marine Services Ltd., 1973—. Chmn. Southwest Neighborhood Assembly, Washington, 1968-70; mem. D.C. Mayor's Econ. Devel. Com.; vice chmn. D.C. Bd. Higher Edn.; bd. dirs. Washington Home Rule Com. Inc., Interracial Council Bus. Opportunity; bd. dirs. D.C. chpt. A.R.C. treas. Greater Washington Ednl. Telecommunications Assn. Mem. Democratic Central Com., 1964-66. Served with AUS, 1943-44. C.P.A., D.C. Mem. Am., D.C. (sec.) insts. C.P.A.'s, Washington Bar Assn., Am. Assn. U. Profs., Assn. Practicing C.P.A.'s, Urban League, Nat. Assn. Regulatory Utility Commrs., Internat. Platform Assn., Met. Washington Bd. Trade, Nat. Assn. State Bds. Accounting, Brookings Instn., Omega Psi Phi. Clubs: Pigskin; Prince Georges Country; Constant Spring Golf (Kingston, Jamaica). Home: 907 6th St SW Washington DC 20024 Office: 907 6th St SW Washington DC 20024

PORTERFIELD, ALSON GERALD, civil engr.; b. Nathan, Ark., July 17, 1935; s. Otis Herman and Rossie Lee (Cline) P.; B.S., Tex. A. and M. Coll., 1960; m. Martha Jeanette Wilson, Oct. 29, 1955; children—Phillip Wilson, Arnold Jayson, Tamara Jean. Engr., Tex. Hwy. Dept., Paris, 1960-63, Worth Constrn. Co., Ft. Worth, 1963-65, R.S. Woodruff & Assos., cons. engrs., Ft. Worth, 1965-67, Prescon Corp., prestressed steel fabricators Corpus Christi, 1967-72; city engr. City of Weatherford (Tex.), 1972-74, dir. pub. works, 1974—. Mem. Dallas-Ft. Worth Met. Hwys. Com., 1972—. Served to 1st lt. AUS, 1962-63. Mem. Am. Soc. C.E., Tex. Municipal League, Am. Pub. Works Assn., Inst. for Municipal Engrs. Mason, Rotarian; mem. Order Eastern Star. Home: 1103 N Elm St Weatherford TX 76086 Office: 119 Palo Pinto St Weatherford TX 76086

PORTERFIELD, AUSTIN LARIMORE, sociologist, educator; b. Salem, Ark., Oct. 16, 1896; s. John and Mary Emily (Rodman) P.; A.B., Oklahoma City U., 1923; B.D., Phillips U., 1926; A.M., Drake U., 1924; Ph.D., Duke, 1936; m. Rose Ella McCollum, Mar. 14, 1917 (dec. Oct. 1966); children—Frances Marie (Mrs. Clayton B. Willis), Vernon Eltinge, Rosella (Mrs. W. J. Chastant); m. 2d, Irene Shepherd Cox, Dec. 17, 1968. Ordained to ministry Christian Ch.; pastor, Okmulgee, Okla., 1927-28; chmn. dept. sociology Southeastern State Coll., Durant, Okla., 1928-37, Tex. Christian U., 1937-67; prof. sociology U. of Americas, Mexico City, 1967-68; vis. tchr. sociology Duke Summer Schs., 1938, 39, 42; vrs. Distinguished prof. sociology Memphis State U., 1972-73. Research cons. Ft. Worth Fed. Housing Authority, 1939; mem. exec. com. Ft. Worth Council Social Agys., 1939-44. Bd. dirs. Leo Potishman Found., 1946; trustee Jarvis Christian Coll. Mem. Nat. Probation and Parole Assn., Am. (exec. com. 1946-47), Southwestern (pres. 1948) sociol. socs., Southwestern Social Sci. Assn. Author: Creative Factors in Scientific Research, 1941; Youth in Trouble, 1946; Crime, Suicide, and Social Well-Being in Your State and City, 1948; Mid-Century Crime in Our Culture, 1954; Wait the Withering Rain, 1953; Mirror, Mirror: On Seeing Yourself in Books, 1957; Marriage and Family Living as Self-Other Fulfilment, 1962; Cultures of Violence; The Tragic Man in Society, 1965; Mirror for Adjustment, 1967; The Now Generation, 1971. Collaborator: The Urban South, 1955. Editor Jour. Health and Human Behavior, 1960—. Contbr. articles to sociol. Jours. Address: 3825 Carolyn Rd Fort Worth TX 76109

PORTMAN, JOHN CALVIN, JR., architect; b. Walhalla, S.C., Dec. 4, 1924; student U.S. Naval Acad.; B.S. in Architecture, Ga. Inst. Tech., 1950; m. Joann Newton; 6 children. Formerly with Ketchum, Gina & Sharp, H. M. Heatly, Asso. Architects, N.Y. and Atlanta, also with 2 Atlanta archtl. firms, until 1953; opened own office, Atlanta, 1953; partner Edwards & Portman, Architects, Atlanta 1956-68; prin. John Portman & Assos., 1968—. Chmn. Atlanta Mdse. Mart; pres. Portman Properties; partner Peachtree Center Devel., Atlanta, Embarcadero Center, San Francisco; dir. C. & S. Nat. Bank, Atlanta. Bd. visitors Emory U., 1964. Trustee Atlanta Arts Alliance; sponsor Atlanta Symphony. Served with USNR, World War II. Recipient Southland Investment Corp. award, 1963; Ivan Allen award N. Ga. chpt. A.I.A., 1964; Annual award Ga. chpt. Pub. Relations Soc. Am., 1967; named Outstanding Young Man of Yr., Ga. Jr. C. of C., 1959. Registered architect, Ga. Mem. A.I.A. (chmn. profl. practice com. Ga. chpt. 1956), Architects and Engrs. Inst. (dir. 1960-61). Prin. works include: Regency Hyatt House (hotel), Atlanta Mdse. Mart, Atlanta Decorative Arts Center, Peachtree Center Office Bldg., Greenbriar Shopping Center, Peachtree Center South Bldg., Atlanta Gas Light Tower, Trailways Bus Terminal and Parking Decks (all Atlanta), Dana Fine Arts Bldg. at Agnes Scott Coll. (Decatur), Regency Hyatt House (O'Hare), Security Pacific Bank Bldg. (San Francisco), Blue Cross Bldg. (Chattanooga), Hyatt Regency (San Francisco). Home: 5195 Northside Dr NW Atlanta GA 30305 Office: 1900 Peachtree Center South Bldg Atlanta GA 30303

PORTNOY, WILLIAM MANOS, educator; b. Chgo., Oct. 28, 1930; s. Joseph and Bella (Saltzman) P.; B.S., U. Ill., 1952, M.S., 1952, Ph.D., 1959; m. Alice Catherine Walker, Sept. 9, 1956; children—Catherine Ann, Michael Benjamin. Mem. tech. staff Hughes Aircraft Co., Newport Beach, Cal., 1959-61, Tex. Instruments, Inc., Dallas, 1961-67; mem. faculty Tex. Tech U., Lubbock, 1967—, prof. biomed. engring., 1973, prof. elec. engring., 1972—. Adj. asso. prof. Baylor Coll. Medicine and Inst. Health Services Research, Houston, 1969—; resident cons. Hughes Research Labs., Malibu, Cal., 1972. Bd. dirs. Am. Heart Assn., Lubbock County, 1972—. Nat. Heart Inst. postdoctoral trainee, 1969; NASA sr. postdoctoral resident research asso., Manned Spacecraft Center, Houston, 1968. Fellow Soc. Advanced Med. Systems; mem. I.E.E.E. (sr.), A.A.A.S., Am. Phys. Soc., Assn. Advancement Med. Instrumentation, Sigma Xi. Contbr. articles to profl. jours. Patentee in field. Office: Dept Electrical Engring Tex Tech Univ Lubbock TX 79409

POSEY, ABBIE RAYMOND, clergyman; b. Hereford, Tex., Nov. 13, 1908; s. Ellis B. and Luella Ivy (Fuqua) P.; B.A., Hardin Simmons U., 1942; Th.M., Southwestern Bapt. Theol. Sem., 1945, 52; m. Leau Ada Bowen, Aug. 1, 1928; children—Ellis B., Barbara Rae (Mrs. Ronnie Gandy). Cashier, First Nat. Bank, Hereford, Tex., 1937-39 ordained to ministry Bapt. Ch., 1939; pastor 1st Bapt. Chs., Chillicothe, Tex., 1945-48, Hamlin, Tex., 1948-51, Temple, Okla., 1952-54, Bapt. Temple Ch., Big Spring, Tex., 1954-62, Richland Heights Bapt. Ch., Richland, Wash., 1963-65, 1st Bapt. Ch., Sweet Home, Ore., 1965-68, Immanuel Bapt. Ch., Abilene, Tex., 1968-74; ret., 1974—. Author: The New Testament Baptising Ones, 1966; Victory Over the Adversaries, 1972. Address: 1004 NW Av I Seminole TX 79360

POSEY, WILLIAM THOMAS, rancher; b. Tehuacana, Tex., Apr. 19, 1910; s. Jonathan Reed and Bertha Mae (Bounds) P.; A.A., Westminster Jr. Coll., 1929; student Allan Coll., 1929-30, Tex. A. and M. U., 1931-32; m. Julia Lelon Robbins, Dec. 25, 1932; children—Patsy Jean (Mrs. Bailey Earl Wheeless), Richard Thomas. Prin., Brandon Pub. Schs., Hill County, Tex., 1930-31; county agrl. agt. Extension Service, Tex. A. and M. U., Gilmer, 1934-35, Emory, 1935-38, Clarksville, 1938-41, Fort Stockton, 1941-66; rancher, Fort Stockton, 1967—. Mem. Sch. Bd., Emory Independent Sch. Dist., Rains County, Tex., 1936-38; livestock insp. Intermediate Credit Bank. Recipient award County Agts. Assn., 1949. Mem. County Agts. Assn. (bd. dirs. 1955-56), Tex. Southwestern Cattlemen Assn., Am. Soc. Animal Sci., Tex. Beef Cattle Assn., Sigma Alpha Epsilon. Democrat. Methodist (chmn. bd. 1963-64). Mason, Kiwanian, Lion. Home: 105 S Rio St Box 1703 Stockton TX 79735 Office: Box 1015 Van Horn TX 29855

POSEY, WILLIAM THOMAS, mfg. co. exec.; b. Duncan, Okla., Nov. 23, 1915; s. Raymond L. and Lillian (Parker) P.; B.S. in Elec. Engring., Tex. Technol. Coll., 1943; m. Dorothy I. Nare, Feb. 6, 1944; children—Faith (Mrs. Everett R. Andrus), William Thomas, David Tyler, Mark Alan. Engring. supr. Gen. Electric Co., Schenectady and Buffalo, 1943-54; v.p., chief engr. Gordos Corp., Bloomfield, N.J., 1954-68; owner Hermetic Switch, Inc., Chickasha, 1968—. Registered profl. engr., N.Y., N.J., Okla. Mem. C. of C. Club: Touchdown. Patentee reed switch operations. Home: Rural Route 1 Box 79 Chickasha OK 73018 Office: Box 1325 Chickasha OK 73018

POSS, WOODROW WILSON, dentist; b. Strathmore, Va., Nov. 19, 1916; s. Burton Wilner and Lillie Walker (Jacobs) P.; B.S., U. Va., 1940; postgrad. U. Richmond, 1945-46; D.D.S., Med. Coll. Va., 1950; m. Vivienne McCay Morrissette, Aug. 7, 1943. Quarterman, Newport News Shipbuilding and Dry Dock Co. (Va.), 1940-45; practice gen. dentistry, Gordonsville, 1950—. Chmn. Gordonsville Troop com. Boy Scouts Am., 1952-67. Mem. Orange County Sch. Bd., 1964-65. Fellow Va. Dental Assn. (dental edn. com. 1966-74, com. chmn., 1970—), Internat. Coll. Dentists; mem. No. Va. Dental Soc. (past pres.), Gordonsville Bus. Men's Assn. (pres. 1952-53), Gordonsville C. of C. (pres. 1969-70). Presbyn. (trustee 1968—, clk. of session 1968—). Mason, Rotarian (pres. 1963-64). Clubs: Greene Hills Country, Woodberry Forest Golf. Home: PO Box 486 Gordonsville VA 22942 Office: P O Box 486 Gordonsville VA 22942

POST, ALLEN, lawyer; b. Newnan, Ga., Dec. 3, 1906; s. William Glenn and Rosa Kate (Muse) P.; A.B. summa cum laude, U. Ga., 1927; B.A. with first honors in Jurisprudence (Rhodes scholar), Oxford U., 1929, B.C.L., 1930, M.A., 1933, Ph.D.; m. Mary Chastaine Cook, Dec. 27, 1934; 1 son, Allen. Admitted to Ga. bar, 1930; spl. atty. gen. Ga., 1933, 1935; asst. atty. gen. assigned Ga. Pub. Service Commn., 1934; partner Moise, Post & Gardner, Atlanta, 1942-61, specializing in bus. and corp. law; partner Hansell, Post, Brandon & Dorsey, 1962—; dir., mem. exec. com. Atlanta Gas Light Co.; dir. First Nat. Bank Atlanta, First Nat. Holding Corp., Thomaston Mills, Am. Cast Iron Pipe Co.; dir., mem. exec. com. Retail Credit Co.; dir. numerous other corps.; also lectr., writer on legal subjects. Chmn. Navy Day, Atlanta, 1937-39; pres. Atlanta Estate Planning Council, 1960; trustee W.N. Banks Found., Howell Fund. Mem. State Democratic Exec. Com., mem. com. to rewrite election laws and revise primary rules of Ga., 1956; Dem. presdl. elector. Mem. Govs. staff; mem. State Com. to Revise Income Tax Laws of Ga., 1956; mem. Ga. Income Tax Study Commn. Served as lt. comdr., USNR World War II. Fellow Am. Coll. Trial Lawyers, Am. Coll. Probate Counsel; mem. Atlanta (exec. com., pres. 1956), Am., Ga. bar assns., Am. Judicature Soc., Atlanta Claims Assn., S.A.R., Navy League, Res. Officers Naval Services (1st pres. Atlanta chpt.), Mil. Order World Wars, Am. Legion (comdr.), Am. Assn. Rhodes Scholars, Sphinx, Phi Beta Kappa, Phi Kappa Phi, Phi Delta Phi, Kappa Alpha. Methodist (chmn. adminstrv. bd., trustee). Clubs: Rotary, Capital City, Piedmont Driving, Lawyers (Atlanta); Old War Horse Lawyers (pres. 1962); Commerce. Home: 620 Peachtree Battle Av NW Atlanta GA 30327 Office: 1st Nat Bank Tower Atlanta GA 30303

POST, CLEMENS, vehicle leasing co. exec., b. N.Y.C., July 23, 1918; s. Harry and Clara (Alter) P.; m. Mildred Rubin, Apr. 18, 1943; children—Peter, Jane. Gen. mgr. used trailer div., A.V.P. Highway Trailer Co., Chgo., 1959-62; v.p. operations Berman Leasing Co., Pottstown, Pa., 1962-67; v.p. Avis Truck Div., Garden City, N.Y., 1969-72; pres. Pepsi Co Truck Rental, Inc., Tulsa, 1972—. Pres. Civic Assn., Westbury, N.Y., 1960-63; com. mem. adv. council for occupational edn. N.Y.C. Bd. Edn., 1971-72. Served to capt. Signal Corps, AUS, 1941-46. Mason. Home: 3427 E 75th St Tulsa OK 74145 Office: 1925 N Sheridan St Tulsa OK 74151

POSTELL, WILLIAM DOSITE, librarian, educator; b. Plaquemine, La., Oct. 5, 1908; s. William Dazelle and Frances Clementine (Kleinpeter) P.; B.S., La. State U., 1930, M.S., 1932, B.S. in L.S., 1933; m. May Belle Andries, Aug. 11, 1937; children—Philip, Mary (Mrs. Joseph Davis), John, William Dosite, David. Asst. librarian Sabine Parish Library, Many, La., 1933-34; librarian Mansfield (La.) Pub. Schs., 1934-38; med. librarian, prof. med. bibliography La. State U. Sch. Medicine, New Orleans, 1938-59, Tulane U. Sch. Medicine, New Orleans, 1959—. Instr. various univs. and hosps. Pres., Pocket Parks Inc., New Orleans, 1971. Pres. Our Lady of Lourdes Sch. Bd., New Orleans, 1971-72. Served With USCGR, 1944-45. Recipient certificate of merit City of New Orleans, 1952, Marcia C. Noyes award Med. Library Assn., 1958. Mem. La. Tchrs. Assn. (pres. sect. 1934-35), La. (pres. 1950, Essee M. Culver awards 1972), Med. (pres. 1952-53) library assns., La. Hist. Assn., Am. Assn. History Medicine. Author: Introduction of Medical Bibliography 1951; Health of Slaves on Southern Plantations, 1951; Applied Medical Bibliography for Students, 1955; Classification for Med. Literature, 2d edit., 1973. Editor: Libraries of New Orleans, 1945. Editor bull. Med. Library Assn., 1945-49. Home: 1930 General Pershing St New Orleans LA 70115

POSTON, ERNEST EUGENE, coll. pres., clergyman; b. Chesnee, S.C., July 14, 1918; s. Summie A. and Minnie (Conner) P.; A.A., Gardner-Webb Coll., 1941-43; B.A., Wake Forest Coll., 1944; B.D., So. Bapt. Theol. Sem., 1947, Th.M., 1948, Th.D., 1950; m. Dorothy Elizabeth Jenkins, Jan. 28, 1939; children—Robert Stephen, Gloria Jean, Elizabeth Ann. Ordained to ministry Bapt. Ch., 1943; pastor Wise and Rock Springs chs. in Tar River Assn. N.C., 1943-44, Monterey, Swallowfield, Elk Lick and Dallasburg chs., Ky., 1944-50, Wallace (N.C.) Ch. 1951-57, First Ch., Jonesboro, Ga., 1958-59; head dept. religion Gardner-Webb Coll., Boiling Springs, 1959-61, pres., 1961—. Dir. Union Trust Co., Boiling Springs, Cleveland Savs. and Loan Assn., Shelby, N.C. Pres. N.C. Bapt. Pastor's Conf., 1956-57; moderator Wilmington (N.C.) Bapt. Assn. Chs. Del. White House Conf. on Children and Youth; active Boy Scouts Am. Mem. Democratic Nat. Com. Bd. dirs., v.p. N.C. Conf. Social Service; sec. N.C. Found. Ch. Related Colls. Recipient Alumnus of Year award Gardner-Webb Coll. Alumni Assn., 1967. Mem. Am. Assn. U. Profs., Soc. Bibl. Lit. and Exegesis. Mason, Rotarian. Clubs: Exchange (Jonesboro, Ga.); Lions (Boiling Springs). Home: Box 792 Boiling Springs NC 28017

POSTON, JERRY LEE, hwy. engr.; b. Walters, Okla., July 23, 1936; s. Harry and Ruby (Cowan) P.; B.C.E., U. Okla., 1959; m. Janice Marie Hanes, Sept. 4, 1956; 1 dau., Janice Lee. Hwy. engr. Ala. div. U.S. Bur. Pub. Rds., Montgomery, 1961-69, project engr., Kuwait, Kuwait, 1969-71; hwy. engr. Fed. Hwy. Adminstrn., Washington, 1971—. Served with AUS, 1960; maj. Res. Mem. Okla., Ala. socs. profl. engrs., Delta Upsilon. Baptist (deacon). Home: 6108 Sherborn Lane Springfield VA 22152 Office: 400 7th St SW Washington DC 20590

POSTON, TALMADGE CHESLEY, banker; b. Valley Mills, Tex., Jan. 10, 1915; s. Dewitt T. and Molly Odell (Jones) P.; student Tarleton State Coll., 1934-35; m. Kathryn Velma Biggs, Oct. 12, 1936; children—Molly Alicia (Mrs. Alfred J. Berry), James T. Owner, Poston Feed Mill, Stephenville, Tex., 1940—; with Stephenville State Bank, 1947—, v.p., 1962—. Lion. Club: Tejas Country. Home: 1065 W Frey St Stephenville TX 76401 Office: 1020 N Graham St PO Box 146 Stephenville TX 76401

POTEAT, WILLIAM HARDMAN, educator; b. Kaifeng, Honan, China, Apr. 19, 1919; s. Edwin McNeill and Wilda (Hardman) P.; student Mars Hill Jr. Coll., 1936-37; A.B., Oberlin Coll., 1941; B.D., Yale Div. Sch., 1944; Ph.D., Duke, 1951; m. Marian Kelley, Sept. 8, 1943; children—Anne Carlyle, Susan Colquitt, Edwin McNeill III. Asso. sec. YMCA, U.N.C., 1944-46, acting sec., 1946-47, instr. dept. philosophy, 1947-50, asst. prof., 1950-54, asso. prof., 1954-57; Quin prof. philos. theology and Christian criticism Episcopal Theology Sem. of S.W., 1957-60; asso. prof. Christianity and culture Duke, 1960-66, prof., 1966-69, prof. religion and culture, 1969-71, prof. religion and comparative studies, 1971—, chmn. dept., 1972—. Vis. prof. Stanford U., 1970, U. Tex., 1971. Cons. spl. com. liberal studies Am. Assn. Colls., 1967; mem. Nat. Humanities Faculty, 1969—; mem. devel. bd. Lenoir Rhyne Coll., 1968—; mem. council grad. studies Danforth Found., 1967—; cons., lectr. World Student Christian Fedn., 1953-56; cons. research and devel. Gov. Terry Sanford, 1961-64; chmn. central com. Nat. Council for Religion and Higher Edn., 1954-55. Distinguished Humanities scholar Haverford (Pa.) Coll., 1969. Mem. Am. Philos. Assn., Am. Acad. Polit. and Social Sci., So. Soc. for Philos. and Psychology, Phi Beta Kappa. Democrat. Episcopalian. Contbr. articles in field to profl. jours. Co-editor, contbg. author Intellect and Hope: Essays in the Thought of Michael Polanyi, 1968. Home: 621 Greenwood Rd Chapel Hill NC 27514

POTEET, MARK DEE, oil co. exec.; b. Olive, Mo., Sept. 16, 1920; s. G. W. and Nora U. (Salsman) P.; student Mo. U., 1937, Drury Coll., 1937-38, Draughons Bus. Coll., 1938-39; B.B.A., S.W. Mo. State U., 1954; m. Marjorie Elizabeth Potts, Jan. 31, 1939; children—James M., Cheryl (Mrs. Guy W. Stephenson), David W. Trainee Ajax & Interstate Pipe Line Co., Springfield, Mo., 1941-43, supt. materials, Springfield, Mo., Tulsa, Okla., 1946-54; coordinator employee devel. Cities Service Petroleum Co., Bartlesville, Okla., 1954-61; mgr. employee and pub. relations Skelly Oil Co., Tulsa, Okla., 1961-73, adminstrv. v.p., 1972—; pres., dir. Vanply, Inc., Vanply of Liberia; mem. policy com. Chemplex Co.; dir. Hawkeye Chem. Co., Vancouver Plywood Co., Inc. Mem. vis. com. Sch. Bus., U. Okla., 1968—. Chmn. Republican Dist. Com., 1960, precinct vice-chmn., 1970. Bd. dirs., pres. Skelly Oil Co. Found., 1970-73; trustee Hillcrest Hosp., Tulsa, 1973—. Served with USMCR, 1943-46. Mem. Pub. Relations Soc. Am. (dir. 1965—). N.A.M. (mem. pub. affairs com. 1966—), Petroleum Club Tulsa (dir.), U.S. C. of C. (mem. pub. affairs com. 1965). Clubs: Hurricane (dir. 1963), Tulsa Country (Tulsa). Home: 2149 S Fulton Pl Tulsa OK 74114 Office: 1437 S Boulder St Tulsa OK 74102

POTTER, ANDREW ELWIN, chemist; b. St. Petersburg, Fla., Nov. 29, 1926; s. Andrew E. and Lucille (Frisbie) P.; B.S., U. Fla., 1948; Ph.D., U. Wis., 1953; postgrad. U. Coll., London, 1960; m. Shirley Marie Barrett, July 7, 1952; children—Andrew Elwin III, Lloyd B., Thomas N. Research scientist NACA, Lewis Flight Propulsion Lab., Cleve., 1953-58; head combustion fundamentals sect. NASA, Lewis Research Center, Cleve., 1958-64, chief elec. energy sources br., 1964-68, staff scientist space physics div. NASA Johnson Space Center, Houston, 1968-70, chief applied physics br., 1970—, mem. atmospheres subcom. space sci. steering com., 1960-70. Served with USNR, 1944-45. Recipient jr. achievement award Cleve. Tech. Socs., 1962. Mem. Am. Chem. Soc., Am. Geophys. Union, Combustion Inst., Cosmos Club, Sigma Xi, Delta Tau Delta. Research on flame quenching, devel. thin-film solar cells, planetary atmospheres, static electricity in spacecraft, earth observations from spacecraft. Home: 1018 Woodbank Dr Seabrook TX 77586 Office: NASA Johnson Space Center Houston TX 77058

POTTER, GORDON COOPER, civil engr.; b. Denver, Mar. 14, 1920; s. Cecil William and Sibley (Deshayes) P.; B.S. cum laude, U. Colo., 1943; postgrad. U. Chgo., 1944; m. Marilyn Elizabeth Oldland, June 25, 1949; children—Charles Edward, Anne Louise. Bridge designer Crocker & Ryan, Cons., Denver, 1946-49; with Exxon Co. U.S.A., Denver, Billings, Seattle, Houston, 1949—, tech. adviser, Houston, 1961—. Served with USAAF, 1943-46. Registered profl. engr., Colo. Mem. Tau Beta Pi. Presbyn. Home: 13502 Appletree St Houston TX 77024 Office: Exxon Bldg Houston TX 77001

POTTER, RICHARD RALPH, electronic engr.; b. Lawrence, Kan., May 9, 1926; s. Earl and Geraldine (Hull) P.; B.S. in Elec. Engring. (Summerfield scholar), U. Kan., 1948, M.S., 1950; m. Doris Dean Edmiston, Feb. 21, 1950; 1 dau., Alexandra Amy. Jr. electronic engr. U.S. Naval Weapons Lab., Dahlgren, Va., 1949-50, electronic scientist, 1951-55, supervisory gen. engr., 1956-59, supervisory research electronic engr., 1959-64, asst. dir. Weapons Devel. and Evaluation Lab., 1965-68, research asso., 1969—. Served with USNR, 1945-46. Mem. I.E.E.E., Am. Ordnance Assn., Fed. Profl. Assn., Sigma Xi, Tau Beta Pi, Sigma Tau, Pi Mu Epsilon, Phi Delta Theta. Home: Route 2 Box 371 J King George VA 22485 Office: US Naval Weapons Lab Dahlgren VA 22448

POTTER, ROBERT ELLIS, librarian; b. Knoxville, Tenn., Mar. 16, 1937; s. Pollye Jack and Violet Belle (Walker) P.; B.S., U. Tenn., 1961; postgrad. U. So. Cal. at Los Angeles, 1963-64; m. Rosemary Byrd Lee, Dec. 28, 1963; children—Robert Ellis II, and Kenyon David (twins). Student asst. U. Tenn. Libraries, 1959-61; copyreader The Knoxville News-Sentinel, 1961-62; library asst. U. Tenn. Libraries, 1962-63; library aide Los Angeles County Library System, El Monte, Cal., 1963-65; reference librarian, bus. and sci. collection City of Hialeah Library div. Hialeah John F. Kennedy Library (Fla.), 1966-73, head librarian bus., sci. and tech. dept., 1973—. Counselor, Trail Blazer's Camps, Inc., N.Y.C., 1958; chaplain's asst. U.S. Army Res., 1959-64. Mem. Mus. Sci. and Planetarium, Miami, Fairchild Tropical Garden, Miami. Served with AUS, 1959. Mem. Am., Southeastern, Fla., Dade County (pres. 1970-71) library assns., Internat Platform Assn., U. Tenn. Century Club, U. Tenn. Alumni Annual Giving Program, U. Tenn. Alumni Assn. (bd. govs. Greater Miami chpt.), Hist. Assn. So. Fla., East Tenn. Hist. Soc., Sigma Delta Chi. Mem. United Ch. of Christ (mem. county mission council, mem. ch. council, chmn. ch. music com.). Editor newsletter Dade County Library Assn., 1971—, bull. SORT, A.L.A., 1971—. Contbr. articles to profl. jours. Home: 258 W 46th St Hialeah FL 33012 Office: 190 W 49th St Hialeah FL 33012

POTTER, THEODORE, JR., art gallery dir.; b. Springhill, Kan., Dec. 6, 1932; s. Theodore and Blanche Ruth (Harris) P.; B.A., Baker U., 1954; postgrad. fine arts U. Kan., 1958-59, U. Cal., 1960; M.F.A., Cal. Coll. Arts and Crafts, 1961; m. Barbara Ann Palmer, June 18, 1968; 1 dau., Kelly Palmer. Dir. Shelby Galleries, Sausalito, Cal., 1966; art dir. Glide Found., San Francisco, 1966-67; dir. Gallery Contemporary Art, Winston-Salem, N.C., 1967—. Cons. N.C. Arts Council, Inc., 1971—, visual arts div. Nat. Endowment for Arts, 1971—; mem. adv. council N.C. Art Soc., 1970—. Served with AUS, 1957-58. Rotarian. One-man exhbns. at Vanderbilt U., Salem Coll., Davidson Coll., others. Home: 2149 Country Club Rd Winston-Salem NC 27104 Office: Gallery of Contemporary Art 500 S Main St Winston-Salem NC 27101

POTTINGER, J. STANLEY, lawyer, govt. ofcl.; B.A. with honors in Govt., Harvard, 1962, LL.B., 1965; m. Gloria Jean Anderson; children—Paul, Kathryn, Matthew. Admitted to Cal. bar, 1965; asso. firm Broad, Khourie and Schulz, San Francisco, 1965-69; atty. Western region Dept. Health, Edn. and Welfare, San Francisco, 1969-70, dir. Office for Civil Rights, also asst. to sec. for civil rights, 1970-73; asst. atty. gen. civil rights div. Dept. Justice, 1973—. Past pres. Richmond Dist. Community Council, San Francisco. Past mem. bd. dirs. Lighthouse for Blind, San Francisco. Contbr. articles to profl. jours. Home: 7112 Laverock Lane Bethesda MD 20034 Office: Dept Justice Washington DC 20530

POTTS, BENJAMIN FRANKLIN, JR., wood products co. exec.; b. Louisville, Oct. 28, 1920; s. Benjamin Franklin and Theresa Jane (Everard) P.; student U. Louisville, 1945; m. Elvina Catherine Stottman, Jan. 24, 1942; children—Marilyn (Mrs. Harold Silverman), Joan (Mrs. Kenneth Danner), Kathleen (Mrs. Patrick Welsh), Steven, John, Mark. Engring. draftsman E.I. DuPont Co., Charlestown, Inc., 1940-42; draftsman, estimator sales Kister Lumber Co., Louisville, 1945-62; v.p. sales Anderson Wood Products Co., Louisville, 1962—. Mem. scholarship Fund com. Catherine Spalding Coll., 1968-72. Served with USAAF, 1942-45. Decorated Air medal with 2 oak leaf clusters, 3 Bronze Stars. Roman Catholic. K.C. Clubs: Kenwood Optimist, Iroquois Civic, South Park Country (Louisville). Home: 920 Southview Rd Louisville KY 40214 Office: 1381 Beech St Louisville KY 40211

POTTS, DONALD CULLEN, stock broker; b. Dallas, Sept. 2, 1938; s. Cullen Floyd and Marie Elizabeth (Clayton) P.; B.B.A., N. Tex. State U., 1963; postgrad. So. Meth. U., 1963-64; m. Sara Sue Stone, Oct. 4, 1958; children—Kristi Dawn, Donald Cullen II. Instl. salesman Merill Lynch, Pierce, Fenner & Smith, Inc., 1964-69; v.p., dir. instl. sales Walston & Co., Dallas, 1969-73; v.p., br. mgr. Jesup & Lamont, Inc., Dallas, 1973—. Dir. Lakewood Bank & Trust Co. Active Dallas Metropolitan Ballet Guild. Mem. Ins. Inst. Am., 500, Inc. (mem. exec. 1968-71), Iota Nu Sigma (pres. 1961-63). Mason (Shriner). Club: Optimist (pres. 1966) (Dallas). Home: 6920 Joyce Way Dallas TX 75225 Office: Suite 414 211 N Ervay St Dallas TX 75201

POTTS, JOHN GARY, ret. dentist; b. Salisbury, Md., Sept. 4, 1899; s. Reginald Harrell and Annie Christian (Moore) P.; student Randolph Macon Coll., 1917-20; D.D.S., Med. Coll. Va., 1924; m. Virginia Carter Tyree, June 19, 1929; children—Nancy Duval (Mrs. Jack Preston Weikel), Anne Elizabeth (Mrs. Edward Alan Heady). Pvt. practice dentistry, Lynchburg, Va., 1924-74. Mem. Bedford County Sch. Bd., 1948-62; mem. Va. Sch. Bd. Assn., pres., 1957-58. Mem. Am. Va., dental assns., Lynchburg (pres.), Piedmont (pres.) dental assns., Kappa Alpha Order, Psi Omega. Methodist (chrm. bd. 1953-54). Kiwanian. Club: Ruritan. Home: Westbury Apts 5001 Boonsboro Rd Lynchburg VA 24503

POU, JOHN WILLIAM, banker; b. Elmwood, N.C., July 8, 1917; s. William Clarence and Mary (Arey) P.; B.S. (Danforth fellow 1937) N.C. State Coll., 1938; M.S., U. Wis., 1947; Ph.D., Cornell U., 1951; Nat. 4-H fellow U.S. Dept. Agr., 1941; m. Margaretha Brinn Craig, May 2, 1942; children—John William, Constance Craig; m. 2d, Emily Hotchkiss Quinn, Oct. 6, 1973. Asst. county agt. Iredell County, Statesville, N.C., 1938-41; dairy extension specialist N.C. State Coll., 1946, head animal industry dept., 1953-58, also mem. faculty senate; extension dairyman U. Md., College Park, 1947-50, head dairy dept., 1951-53; dir. Ariz. Agrl. Extension, U. Ariz., 1958-61; v.p., mgr. agrl. dept. Wachovia Bank & Trust Co., Greenville, N.C., 1962-66, v.p., head Greenville offices, 1966-68, v.p. marketing N.E. div., 1968—. Dir. N.C. YMCA; coach Nat. Champion 4-H Dairy Cattle Judging team, 1950; mem. Ariz. Gov.'s Civil Def. Council, 1960-61; pres. Coastal Plains Planning and Devel. Commn., 1964-65, N.C. 4-H Devel. Fund, Inc., 1964, 65, Pitt County United Fund, 1965-66; dir. N.C. Home Econs. Found., Inc., 1964-65; mem. bd. dirs. 4-H Club Found. Served from 2d lt. to maj., AUS, 1942-45, PTO; lt. col. Res. Mem. Am. Dairy Sci. Assn. (chmn. type com., chmn. So. div. 1958-59), Western States Extension Dirs. (chmn. 1958-59), N.C. Bankers Assn. (chmn. agrl. com. 1963-64), Greenville C. of C. (pres. 1969), Assn. Agrl. Bankers (pres. 1970), Blue Key, Alpha Zeta, Phi Kappa Phi. Baptist. Kiwanian (chmn. agrl. and conservation com., N.C. 4-H Honor (4-H alumni award Iredell County, 1954), Rotarian (pres. Greenville 1970). Home: 1108 Greenville Blvd Greenville NC 27834 Office: Wachovia Bank & Trust Co Greenville NC 27834

POU, RAFAEL, mfg. co. exec.; b. Ponce, P.R., Dec. 6, 1916; s. Joaquin and Julia (Vives) P.; student Xavier U., Cin., 1936-38; m. Aida Rivas, July 25, 1941; children—Rafael, Pilar, Aida Elena, Maria de Los Angeles, Candido. With Nat. City Bank, Ponce, 1934-41, Sears Roebuck Co., Ponce, 1941-45; accountant Nat. City Bank; mgr. Sears Roebuck & Co.; gen. mgr. Ponce Candy Corp., Ponce Salt Industries. Named Mfr. of Year P.R. Mfrs. Assn., 1972. Mem. Am. Candy Technologists, Nat. Confectioner Assn., mfgrs. assns. and others. Clubs: Deportivo, Nautico. Home: Torres and Roosevelt Sts Ponce PR 00731 Office: Ponce Candy Industries PO Box 1749 Ponce PR 00731

POULOS, RALEIGH ANEST, shopping center exec.; b. Galveston, Tex., Aug. 8, 1922; s. Anastasio Pete and Christine (Kalaboukidou) P.; student pub. schs.; m. Martha Panagos, Oct. 19, 1968. Mgr. D. Masus & Sons, Monroe La., 1945-52; gen. mgr. Palais Royal, specialty stores, Houston, 1952-67; gen. mgr., partner Town and Country Village, Houston, 1967—; partner Moody, Moody, Poulos, 1974—. Commr. Housing Authority, Monroe, 1950-52. Mem. bd. devel. YMCA, Houston, 1963-67. Served with AUS, 1942-45. Mem. Tex. Retail Fedn., C. of C. Mem. Greek Orthodox Ch. Home: 359 North Post Oak Lane Apt 328 Houston TX 77024 Office: Town and Country Village Houston TX 77024

POUNCY, MITCHELL LOUIS, librarian; b. Palestine, Tex., Apr. 3, 1930; s. Dee and Detroit (Denman) P.; A.B., Prairie View A and M. Coll., 1951; M.S. in Library Sci., Atlanta U., 1955; certificate La. Poly. U., 1970. With library So. U., Baton Rouge, 1955—, circulation librarian, 1961-65, catalog librarian, 1965—. Mem. Vis. Com. for Evaluation 3 High Schs. La., 1958-62. Mem. Community Assn. for Advancement of Sch. Children. Served as sgt. USMCR, 1952-54. Mem. A.L.A. Baptist. Office: Box 10031 So Br PO Baton Rouge LA 70813

POUND, WINSDON NORWOOD MONTRESSEUR, ednl. adminstr.; b. Lynchburg, Va., Aug. 25, 1922; s. James Malcolm and Mary Whitemenzes (DeForrest) P.; A.B., Lynchburg Coll., 1950; postgrad. Longwood Coll., 1950-52; M.Ed., U. Va., 1955; postgrad. Radford Coll., Va. Poly. Inst., State U. Va.; m. Madeline Elizabeth Spencer, June 4, 1949; children—Charles Winsdon, Carolyn Elizabeth. Teaching prin. West End. Sch., Lunenburg County, Va., 1950-53; prin. Burkeville Elementary Sch., Nottoway County, 1953-56; prin. Dublin Elementary Sch., Pulaski County, 1956—. Pres., Mountain Empire Tb and Respiratory Disease Assn., 1970. Bd. dir. Salvation Army. Served with AUS, 1943-46. Mem. Nat., Va. (dist. pres. 1970-71, bd. dirs. 1970-71), Pulaski County (pres. 1963-65), Nottoway (pres. 1955-56), Lunenburg County (v.p. 1952-53) edn. assns., Va. Congress Parents and Tchrs. (hon. life mem.), Phi Delta Kappa, Kappa Delta Pi. Episcopalian. Clubs: Lions (chmn. sight saving com. 1956-63), Ruritan (mem. edn. com.) (Dublin, Va.). Home: Route 2 Box 65 Pulaski VA 24301 Office: PO Box 1106 Dublin VA 24084

POUNDS, HASKIN RICHARD, state ofcl.; b. Augusta, Ark., July 9, 1933; s. Ralph and Ruby (New) P.; B.S., Henderson State Coll., 1954; M.Ed., U. Ark., 1959, Ed.D., 1963; 1 dau., Roxanne. Tchr., Alma (Ark.) High Sch., 1957-58; prin. Paris (Ark.) Elementary Sch., 1958-60; supt. schs., Scranton, Ark., 1960-61; asst. prof. edn. U. Ark., 1963-65; asst. prof. edn. U. Ga., 1965-68, asst. vice chancellor Univ. System of Ga., Atlanta, 1968—. Served with AUS, 1954-56. Mem. Ga., Nat. edn. assns., Am. Assn. Sch. Adminstrs., Phi Delta Kappa. Rotarian, Lion. Author: Organizing, Supervising and Administering the Elementary School, 1969. Home: 1587 Creekford Way Stone Mountain GA 30083 Office: Bd Regents 244 Washington St SW Atlanta GA 30334

POUNDS, JAMES ARTHUR, cons. engr.; b. Pletcher, Ala., Nov. 25, 1920; s. Isham Frank and Minnie J. (Crane) P.; A.A., Pensacola Jr. Coll., 1961; student U. Md., 1951, U. Ala., 1953-55, U. Chgo., 1961-63.; m. Angela D. Rossetti, Feb. 9, 1950; 1 dau., Jeanette Angela. Lab. mgr. A.W. Williams Co., Mobile, Ala., 1954-55; supt. Sanitation div. City of Pensacola, Fla., 1956-63; gen. mgr. Econ. Utilities Corp., Orlando, 1963-64; supt. water div. City of Pensacola, 1964-68; city engr., dir. pub. works City of Auburn, Ala., from 1968; now owner, pres. Pounds & Assos., Inc., cons. engrs., Atlanta; partner James A. Taylor, Assos., Inc., Cons. Engrs., Tucker, Ga. Tchr. mil. sci. and tactics U. Me., 1949-51. Radiol. def. officer Escambia County (Fla.) Civil Def., 1957-67; bd. dirs. City Employees Credit Union, Pensacola, 1967. Served to capt. C.E., AUS, 1942-53. Decorated Bronze Star medal. Registered profl. engr., Ala., Miss., Ga., Me. Mem. Nat., Ala. socs. profl. engrs., Am. Pub. Works Assn., Am. Water Works Assn. (trustee), Fla. Water and Waste Water Operators Assn. (regional dir., mem. bd. examiners 1959-67), Fla. Engrs. Soc. Methodist. Home: PO Box 28634 Atlanta GA 30328 Office: 1021 Northside Dr NW Atlanta GA 30318

POV, EMILY HOTCHKISS, educator; b. Pitts.; d. Leonard B. and Thelma (Jennings) Hotchkiss; B.S., Ga. State Coll. for Women, 1948; M.S., U. Wis., 1962, Ph.D., 1964; m. Robert Earl, Aug. 25, 1955 (div. June 1958); 1 son, David Michael; m. 2d, John William Pov, Oct. 6, 1973. Extension home economist U. Ga., Athens, 1955-56, U. Ariz., Tucson, 1956-61; fellow U. Wis.-Madison, 1961-63; asso. prof. edn. N.C. State U., Raleigh, 1964-67, prof. edn. and state leader tng., 1967-71; dean Sch. Home Econs. U. Ga., 1971—. Mem. Adult Edn. Assn. of U.S., Ga. Adult Edn. Assn., Ga. Nutrition Council, Am., Ga. home econs. assns., So. Assn. Home Econs. Adminstrs., Assn. Adminstrs. Home Econs. (exec. bd.), Phi Upsilon Omicron, Omicron Nu, Delta Kappa Gamma. Author: (with E.J. Boone, E.H. Quinn) Curriculum Development In Adult Basic Education, 1967. Cons. editor Adult Edn. Jour. Home: 350 Ashton Dr Athens GA 30601

POVEY, THOMAS GEORGE, office systems co. exec.; b. Norristown, Pa., Dec. 27, 1920; s. Thomas and Blanche (Groff) P.; B.S., Temple U., 1948; m. Bettina O. Houghton, June 2, 1945; children—Bettina C., Denise E. With Sperry-Remington div. Sperry Rand Corp., Phila., also Newark, N.Y.C., 1948—, eastern regional gen. sales mgr., 1960-63, nat. gen. sales mgr., N.Y.C., 1966-67, dir. marketing, Marietta, O., 1968-71, v.p. marketing, 1972-73, v.p. fed. govt. marketing, Washington, 1973—. Lectr. Newark High Sch., 1954-56, Belleville (N.J.) High Sch., 1956-58, Fairleigh Dickinson Coll., Paterson, N.J., 1957-58, Pace Coll., N.Y.C., 1965—, Georgetown U., 1974—, ednl. TV, N.Y.C., 1965—. Dir. Community Fund, Essex Fells, N.J., 1967. Served as 1st lt. with USAF, 1942-45. Decorated Air medal; named Remington Dartnell Salesman of Year, 1950. Mem. Internat. Platform Assn., Pi Delta Epsilon (pres. 1948). Republican. Methodist. Clubs: Washington Athletic. Home: 227 Cape St John Rd Annapolis MD 21401 Office: 2233 Wisconsin Av NW Washington DC 20007

POWELL, ABNER RILEY, JR., lawyer; b. Andalusia, Ala., Mar. 21, 1916; s. Abner Riley and Gertrude (Deer) P.; LL.B., U. Ala., 1937; m. Jean Smith, June 8, 1937; children—Patricia (Mrs. Lomax Cassady), Annette (Mrs. C. Ward Hall, Jr.), Abner Riley III. Admitted to Ala. bar, 1937, since practiced in Andalusia; sr. partner Powell & Sikes, 1966—. Mem. Ala. Bar Commrs., 1942-43. Register Circuit Ct., 1938-66. Served with USNR, 1944-45. Mem. Am., Ala., Covington County (pres. 1961) bar assns., Ala. Def. Lawyers Assn. (dir. 1964-67), Phi Alpha Delta, Sigma Nu. Baptist (former deacon). Home: 122 Thames St Andalusia AL 36420 Office: 102 N Cotton St Andalusia AL 36420

POWELL, ANICE CARPENTER (MRS. ROBERT WAINWRIGHT POWELL), librarian; b. Moorhead, Miss., Dec. 2, 1928; d. Horace Aubrey and Celeste (Brian) Carpenter; student Sunflower Jr. Coll., 1945-47, Miss. State Coll. Women, 1947-48; B.S., Delta State Coll., 1961, M.L.S., 1973; m. Robert Wainwright Powell, July 19, 1948; children—Penelope Elizabeth, Deborah Alma. Librarian, Sunflower (Miss.) Pub. Library, 1958-61; instr. English, Isola (Miss.) High Sch., 1961-62; coordinator Sunflower County Library, 1962—. Mem. adv. council State Instl. Library Services, 1967-71; participant Inst. Library Service to Disadvantaged, U. S.Fla., summer 1971. Chmn. Miss. Heart Assn., Sunflower, 1963-73; chmn. library category Sunflower County Merit Program, 1973. Mem. Miss. Library Assn. (sect. chmn. 1965, treas. 1970, fed. relations coordinator 1973), Am., Southeastern library assns., Kappa Delta Pi. Methodist. Home: Box 387 Sunflower MS 38778 Office: Box 428 Sunflower MS 38778

POWELL, CHARLES KENNETH, lawyer, Republican nat. committeeman from S.C.; b. Greenwood, S.C., Aug. 11, 1939; s. Charles Willis and Gladys (Ouzts) P.; B.S. in Indsl. Mgmt., Clemson U.; LL.B., U. S.C., 1964; m. Edna Durant. Admitted to S.C. bar, 1964; practiced law, 1964-69; sr. partner Powell & Smith (and predecessor firms), Columbia, S.C., 1969—. Past legal counsel Young Ams. for Freedom. Mem. S.C. Gov.'s Conf. on Youth. Organizer, adviser S.C. Teenage Republicans; adviser Richland County Teenage Reps., 1968-69; chmn., Richland County Rep. Com., 1970, S.C. Rep. Com., 1971—; chmn. credentials com. S.C. Rep. Conv., 1970; mem. S.C. Rep. Election Law Study Com., 1970; mem. Nat. Rep. Com., 1971—. Bd. dirs. Richland County br. Am. Cancer Soc. Mem. S.C. Bar Assn., Sons Confederate Vets., Clemson U. Nat. Alumni Council, Blue Key. Baptist (past pres. men's brotherhood, past Sunday Sch. tchr.). Mason (3d deg.). Club: Exchange (sec.). Home: 138 Cardiff St Columbia SC 29209 Office: 3012 Devine St Columbia SC 29205*

POWELL, CHILTON, bishop Protestant Episcopal Diocese Okla. Address: PO Box 1098 Oklahoma City OK 73101*

POWELL, EDWARD CLEVELAND, mfg. co. exec.; b. Spartanburg, S.C., Feb. 8, 1932; s. Ralph Carleton and Caro Virginia (Cleveland) P.; B.A., U. Va., 1954; m. Laura S. Russell, Apr. 12, 1958; children—Edward, Robert, Benjamin, Ralph Carleton. Account exec. Ted Bates & Co., N.Y.C., 1957-62, Reach McClinton & Co., N.Y.C., 1962-66; v.p. marketing Conwood Corp., Memphis, 1966—, also dir. Served to 1st lt. U.S. Army, 1955-57. Mem. Am. Mgmt. Assn., Am. Marketing Assn., Chi Psi. Episcopalian. Club: University. Home: 4220 Montrose Dr Memphis TN 38117 Office: 701 N Main St Memphis TN 38107

POWELL, EDWARD LEWIS, JR., dentist; b. Cumberland, Md., Nov. 24, 1941; s. Edward Lewis and Edith Redwood (Christian) P.; student Tulane U., 1961-62; B.A., U. Tex., 1965; D.D.S., Baylor U., 1969, M.S.D., 1971; m. Billie Sue Henna, June 15, 1963; children—Edward Lewis III, Catherine Christian. Practice dentistry, specializing in periodontics, San Antonio, 1971-73, Austin, 1973—; periodontal cons. Childrens Med. Center, Dallas, Denton (Tex.) State Sch. Recipient Merritt-Parks award in periodontology, clinic awards from Dallas Midwinter Clinics, Tex. Dental Assn., 1969-72; clinic award Chgo. Midwinter Clinic, 1972. Mem. Am., Tex. dental assns., Austin Dist. Dental Soc., Am. Acad. Periodontology, S.W. Soc. Periodontology, Kappa Sigma, Delta Sigma Delta. Contbr. articles to profl. jours. Home: 3930 Balcones Dr Austin TX 78703 Office: 310 Medical Park Tower Austin TX 78705

POWELL, ELIZABETH BALAS (MRS. NORBORNE BERKELEY POWELL), physician, educator; b. McKeesport, Pa., Oct. 22, 1914; d. Paul Steven and Lillian (Krisson) Balas; B.S., U. Pitts., 1936; M.D., Duke, 1938; m. Norborne Berkeley Powell, Dec. 18, 1939; children—Norborne Berkeley, Barbara Key. Intern Duke Hosp., Durham, N.C., 1938-39; resident Charity Hosp. of La., New Orleans, 1939-41; practice medicine, specializing in pathology, Houston, 1942—; pathologist Jefferson Hosp., Bapt. Hosp., Birmingham, Ala., 1942, Meml. Hosp., Houston, 1942-45; instr., asst. prof. pathology Baylor U. Sch. Medicine, 1945-71, asso. prof., 1971—. Diplomate in pathologic anatomy and clin. pathology Am. Bd. Pathology. Mem. Am., Tex. med. assns., Am. Soc. Cytology, Tex. Soc. Pathologists, Harris County Med. Soc., Alpha Omega Alpha. Presbyn. Contbr. articles to med. jours. Home: 2410 Avalon Pl Houston TX 77019

POWELL, EPPIE CHARLES, physician; b. Holly Springs, N.C., June 10, 1910; s. Eppie Clifton and Annie (Knight) P.; B.S., U. N.C., 1931; M.D., U. Pa., 1935; postgrad. Columbia, N.Y.U., U. Tenn.; m. Eleanor Laura Bizzell, July 1, 1936; children—Eleanor Patricia, Charles Thomas. Intern Park View Hosp., Rocky Mountain, N.C., 1935-36; pvt. practice medicine Rocky Mountain, 1937-40, Goldsboro, 1946-70, mem. cons. staff, 1970—; chief staff Wayne County Meml. Hosp., 1952-54, chief obstetrics, 1955-70; chmn. dept. sci. Wayne Community Coll., Goldsboro, 1970—. Mem. Carolina Charter Tercentenary Commn.; mem. joint com. allied health edn. N.C. Bd. Higher Edn. Served from capt. to col. M.C., AUS, 1940-45, Decorated Bronze Star medal. Fellow Am. Coll. Obstetricians and Gynecologists; mem. Confederate Stamp Alliance, Nat. Guard Assn. U.S., Am. Ordnance Assn. (dir. Carolina post), Wayne County Hist. Soc. (dir.), A.A.A.S., Coastal Plains Obstet.-Gynecol. Soc., Assn. Mil. Surgs. U.S., Goldsboro Area Broadcasters, Nat. Sci. Tchrs. Assn., Nat. League Nursing, Citizens Band Radio Club N.C. Presbyn. (elder). Clubs: Goldsboro Country, Croda (pres.), Walnut Creek Country (bd. dirs.). Home: Walnut Creek Estates Goldsboro NC 27530 Office: Wayne Community Coll Goldsboro NC 27530

POWELL, FRANK JOSEPH, mech. engr.; b. Wilkes-Barre, Pa., Feb. 18, 1923; s. Frank Joseph and Mary Gertrude (Smolok) Poulitch; B.S., Bucknell U., 1949; M.S., U. Md., 1954; m. Anne Roberta Herstek, June 18, 1949; children—James Thomas, Frank Joseph. With Nat. Bur. Standards, Washington, 1959—, asst. chief mech. engr., 1964-69, chief mech. engr., 1969—. Instr. mech. engring. George Washington U., Washington, 1954-57. Served with AUS, 1943-45; PTO. Dept. Commerce sci. and tech. fellow, 1968-69; recipient Sustained Superior Performance award Bur. Standards, 1968, Superior Accomplishment award, 1973. Mem. Am. Soc. Heating, Air-Conditioning and Refrigerating Engrs., Am. Soc. for Testing and Materials, Am. Nat. Standards Inst., Internat. Inst. Refrigeration, Internat. Bldg. Research Inst., Georgetown Civic Assn. K.C. Contbr. to profl. jours. Home: 9919 Mayfield Dr Bethesda MD 20034 Office: National Bureau Standards Washington DC 20234

POWELL, JAMES ORMOND, editor; b. Andalusia, Ala., Oct. 24, 1919; s. Abner Riley and Gertrude (Deer) P.; B.A., U. Fla., 1942; m. Ruth Hogan, June 27, 1951; children—James Ormond, Lee Riley. Reporter, Ala. Jour., Montgomery, 1940; reporter, state capitol corr. Tampa (Fla.) Tribune, 1946-54; state capitol corr. Miami (Fla.) Herald, 1955; adminstrv. asst. Senator George Smathers, Washington, 1955-56; editorial writer, asso. editor Tampa Tribune, 1956-59; editor editorial page Ark. Gazette, Little Rock, 1959-73, editorial dir., 1973—. Chmn. media group tour to People's Republic of China, China-Am. Relations Soc., 1973. Exec. com. Gov.'s Council Human Resources, 1967-70; pres. Community Concert Assn. Little Rock, 1968; bd. dirs. Ark. Opera Assn., 1961-63. Served with AUS, 1941-45. Recipient Mrs. David Terry award Little Rock Council on Human Relations, 1971. Mem. Am. Soc. Newspaper Editors, Nat. Conf. Editorial Writers, Nat. Conf. Christians and Jews (dir. Ark. council 1964-65, recipient nat. editorial writing award 1969), Nat. Com. Support of Pub. Schs., Sigma Delta Chi (chpt. v.p. 1965), Sigma Nu. Democrat. Baptist. Home: 311 Schoolwood Lane Little Rock AR 72207 Office: Ark Gazette 112 W 3d St Little Rock AR 72201

POWELL, JOHN ROLFE, accountant; b. Birmingham, Ala., Mar. 23, 1915; s. Bolling Raines and Marie (Arnold) P.; B.Accounts, Wheeler Bus. Coll., Birmingham, 1933; grad. LaSalle Extension U., 1936; m. Sarah Randolph Lacy, Apr. 15, 1939; children—Sarah Lacy (Mrs. Howard Peter Pudner, Jr.), Medora Braxton (Mrs. Dale Laverne Fahnestock), Marie Bolling, John Rolfe. Pub. accountant John Rolfe Powell, Montgomery, Ala., 1941—. Dir. Starke Bros. Realty Co., Inc. Chmn. budget and finance com. Montgomery Child Care Council, 1967-69. C.P.A., Ala. Mem. Ala. Soc. C.P.A.'s (chpt. pres. 1961-62), Ala. Assn. Pub. Accountants (chpt. pres. 1954), Nat. Assn. Accountants (chpt. pres. 1967-68), Am. Inst. C.P.A.'s. Episcopalian. Rotarian. Home: 1345 Glen Gratten Av Montgomery AL 36111 Office: 507 Executive Bldg Montgomery AL 36104

POWELL, LESLIE CHARLES, JR., educator; b. Beaumont, Tex., Dec. 13, 1927; s. Leslie Charles and Tillie Bee (Wallace) P.; B.S., So. Meth. U., 1948; M.D., Johns Hopkins, 1952; m. Carol Estelle Coggins, June 11, 1952; children—Jeffrey Johns, Randall Gardner, Daniel Charles, Gerard Paul. Intern, then resident U. Tex. at Galveston, 1952-55; instr. obstetrics and gynecology, 1957-59, asst. prof., 1959-63, asso. prof., 1963-68, prof., 1968—. Cons., Richmond State Sch., 1969-74. Pres. Am. Cancer Soc., Galveston County, 1972-73. Served with M.C., AUS, 1955-57. Recipient Hannah award Tex. Assn. Obstetrics and Gynecology, 1955. Research grantee cervical cancer screening HEW, 1967-71. Diplomate Am. Bd. Obstetrics and Gynecology Mem. Alpha Tau Omega, Phi Beta Pi. Contbr. articles to profl. jours. Home: 24 Cedar Law St S Galveston TX 77550 Office: 800 Av B U Tex Med Sch Galveston TX 77550

POWELL, LEWIS FRANKLIN, JR., asso. justice U.S. Supreme Ct.; b. Suffolk, Va., Sept. 19, 1907; s. Lewis Franklin and Mary Lewis (Gwathmey) P.; B.S., Washington and Lee U., 1929, LL.B., 1931, LL.D., 1960; LL.M., Harvard, 1932; LL.D., Hampden Sydney Coll., 1959, Coll. William and Mary, 1965, U. Fla., 1965, U. Richmond, 1970, U. S.C., 1972; m. Josephine Rucker, May 2, 1936; children—Josephine (Mrs. Richard S. Smith), Ann Pendleton (Mrs. Basil T. Carmody), Mary Lewis Gwathmey (Mrs. Christopher J. Sumner), Lewis Franklin, III. Admitted to Va. bar, 1931, U.S. Supreme Ct. bar, 1937; since practiced law in Richmond; partner in firm, Hunton, Williams, Gay, Powell and Gibson, 1937-71; asso. justice, U.S. Supreme Ct., 1971—. Chmn. spl. Charter Commn. for City of Richmond (prepared new city charter, approved in spl. election Nov. 1947); mem. Nat. Commn. Enforcement and Adminstrn. Justice, 1965-67; mem. Blue Ribbon Def. Panel to study Def. Dept., 1969-70. Chmn. Richmond Pub. Sch. Bd., 1952-61; mem. Va. Bd. Edn., 1962-69, pres., 1968-69; mem. Va. Library Bd., 1954-64. Trustee Washington and Lee U.; chmn. bd. trustees Colonial Williamsburg Found. Served from lt. to col. USAAF, 1942-46, 33 months overseas; now col. Res. ret. Decorated Legion of Merit, Bronze Star (U.S.); Croix de Guerre with palms (France).; hon. bencher Lincoln's Inn. Fellow Am. Bar Found. (pres. 1969-71), Am. Coll. Trial Lawyers (pres. 1969-70); mem. Am. (gov., pres. 1964-65), Va., Richmond (pres. 1947-48) bar assns., Bar Assn. City N.Y., Nat. Legal Aid and Defender Assn. (v.p. 1964-65), Am. Law Inst., Soc. Cin., Sons Colonial Wars, Phi Beta Kappa, Phi Delta Phi, Omicron Delta Kappa, Phi Kappa Sigma. Presbyn. Clubs: Alfalfa, Country of Va., Commonwealth; Century, University (N.Y.C.). Home: 1238 Rothesay Rd Richmond VA 23221 Office: US Supreme Ct Washington DC 20543

POWELL, LOUISE HILL CONKEY (MRS. W. ROYCE POWELL), researcher; b. Kansas City, Mo.; d. George Lissant and Louise Eugenia (Hill) Conkey; student spl. courses U. Grenoble (France), 1935-36; A.A., George Washington U., 1941, B.A., 1943, M.A., 1946; postgrad. Wilson Tchrs. Coll., 1944, George Washington U., 1945-46; m. W. Royce Powell, Mar. 24, 1934 (dec. Apr. 1961); children—Lissante Hill (Mrs. Francis LoBianco), Julienne (Mrs. James Perry Johnson), Katherine Evelyn (Mrs. James Edward Crawley). Various positions, 1930-36; research asst. dept. physiology George Washington U. Med. Sch., 1939-53, asst. to chmn. physiology dept., 1953-55; research and adminstrv. asst. to various physicians, George Washington U. Med. Sch., also Columbia, 1953-65; adminstrv. asst. dept. pharmacology Georgetown U. Med. Sch., Washington, 1966-67; asst. to editor Navy mag. of Navy League U.S., Washington, 1968—. Publicity chmn. Georgetown Hosp. Ladies Bd., 1963-65, 68—. Precinct chmn. Republican Party, 1952; rec. sec. D.C. League Rep. Women, 1961-63; adminstrv. asst. to chmn. Inaugural Concert Com., Rep. Party, Washington, 1969, rep. vol. White House Spl. Projects, 1969-70. Mem. Magna Charta Dames, Nat. Trust Historic Preservation, Smithsonian Assos., Colonial Dames Am., Colonial Dames Md., Daus. Brit. Empire in U.S.A., U.S. Naval Inst., World Affairs Forum, Preservation of Historic Georgetown Found., Kenmore Assn., Inc., Descs. Lords of Md. Manors, Md. Hist. Soc., Prince Georges' County Hist. Soc., Pilgrims St. Mary's, Jamestowne Soc., Sigma Xi. Clubs: Nat. Travel, Washington, Diplomatic and Counselor Officers Ret. Home: Volta House 3434 Volta Pl NW Washington DC 20007 Office: Navy League of US 818 18th St Washington DC 20006

POWELL, MINA JO, hotel exec.; b. Gainesville, Fla., Apr. 11, 1928; d. Caleb Allen and Josie Mae (Roberts) Powell; B.S. in Pub. Adminstrn., Fla. State U., 1950, M.S.W. (Mental Health scholar), 1963; postgrad. U. Houston, 1953-54. Med. sec. Prudential, Houston, 1958-59; pub. assistance social caseworker Pub. Welfare, Houston, 1959-61; psychiat. social worker N.E. Fla. State Hosp., Macclenney, 1963-64; with Holiday Inn, Thomasville, Ga., 1963—, dir., 1963—, pres., 1967—. Mem. research and resource com. Fla. State U., 1973-74, mem. com. to study intercollegiate athletic program, 1974. Vol. aux. Archbold Hosp., Thomasville, 1968-74. Sec. Thomas County Republican Com., 1970-74; v.p. Thomas County Fedn. Republican Women, 1974—. Bd. dirs. Fla. State U. Seminole Boosters. Mem. Fla. Hotel Motel Assn. (mem. com. 1962), Fla. State U. Alumni Assn., Thomasville Restaurant Assn. (sec. 1974). Methodist. Club: Seminole (chmn. 1966-74) (Thomasville). Address: PO Box 1055 Holiday Inn Thomasville GA 31792

POWELL, NORBORNE BERKELEY, urologist; b. Montgomery, Ala., July 24, 1914; s. Floyd Berkeley and Eloise (Sadler) P.; M.D., Baylor U., 1938; m. Elizabeth Mary Balas, Dec. 18, 1939; children—Norborne Berkeley, Barbara Key. Intern, Duke Hosp., Durham, N.C., 1938-39, Charity Hosp., New Orleans, 1939-40; resident Tulane Service Charity Hosp., 1940-42; pvt. practice urology, Houston, 1942—; mem. staff Ben Taub Gen. Hosp.; Staff Twelve Oaks Hosp., Houston, chief of staff, 1974. Clin. prof. urology Baylor Coll. Medicine, 1965—. Trustee Baylor Med. Found., 1945-55. Diplomate Am. Bd. Urology. Fellow A.C.S., Internat. Coll. Surgeons; mem. Mexican (corr.), Am. (Sci. Exhbn. 1st prize 1951) urol. assns., Houston Urol. Soc. (pres., 1955). Club: River Oaks Country (Houston). Contbr. articles to profl. jours. Home: 2410 Avalon Pl Houston TX 77019 Office: 4126 Southwest Freeway Houston TX 77027

POWELL, ROY JAMES, ednl. adminstr.; b. Miami, Fla., Feb. 18, 1934; s. Ernest Everett and Edna Lodessa (Hand) P.; B.Ed., U. Miami, 1966; M.Ed., Fla. Atlantic U., 1967; Ph.D., U. Miami, 1971. Broadcast engr. radio station WRUF, Gainesville, Fla., 1958-59; communications technician City Miami, Fla., 1959-60; electronics tech. Eastern Airlines, Miami, 1960-64; sci. instr. Youth Manpower Tng. Program, 1964; curriculum writer Dade County Pub. Schs., 1965; electronics instr. Miami Sr. High Sch., 1965-66; researcher Dade County Pub. Schs., 1966-67; grad. asst. tchr. corps tng. program U. Miami, Coral Gables, 1967-68; research asso., dir. bus. affairs Fla. Migratory Child Survey Center, 1968-69; chmn. Dept. Elec. Engring. Techs., Miami-Dade Jr. Community Coll., 1969—. Engring cons. Gemini Marine Research, Hialeah, Fla., 1965; sound cons. Ferendino Grafton Spillis Candela, Architects, Engrs. and Planners, Inc., Miami, 1971-73; audio cons. pvt. indvls., Miami, Fla., 1963. Served with USAF, 1952-56. Mem. Am. Tech. Edn. Assn., Am. Soc. Engring. Edn., Fla. Assn. Community Colls., Med. Electronics and Data Soc., I.E.E.E., Phi Delta Kappa. Author: Electronics Instructor's Guides, 1965. Editor and contributor Radio and Television Servicing Instructor's Guide and Electricity Instructor's Guide, 1965. Contbr. to Migrant Children in Florida, 1969. Home: 850 Palm Springs Mile Hialeah FL 33012

POWELL, RUSSELL HENRY, librarian; b. Windber, Pa., July 29, 1943; s. James Raymond and Judith Beatrice (Russell) P.; B.A., Juniata Coll., 1965; M.L.S., U. Pitts., 1966; m. Beverly Jean Ambrose, Aug. 25, 1965; children—Deborah Louise, Kimberly Jean. Sci. librarian Juniata Coll., Hunt, Pa., 1966-68; engring. librarian U. Ky., Lexington, 1968—, instr. Coll. Library Sci., 1970—. Mem. A.L.A., Spl. Libraries Assn., Am. Soc. Engring. Edn. (vice chmn. sect. 1969-71), Soc. for Preservation and Encouragement Barber Shop Quartet Singing Am. Home: 973 Stonewall Rd Lexington KY 40504

POWELL, THOMAS EDWARD, JR., biol. supply co. exec.; b. Warrenton, N.C., July 6, 1899; s. Thomas Edward and Clara (Bobbitt) P.; A.B., Elon Coll., 1919, Sc.D.(hon.), 1968; M.A., U. N.C., 1923; Ph.D., Duke, 1930; m. Maude Sharpe, July 22, 1922 (dec. Sept. 1944); children—Sophia Maude (Mrs. A. E. Wolfe), Thomas Edward III, James Bobbitt, John Sharpe; m. 2d, Annabelle Council, Aug. 31, 1945; children—William Council, Joseph Eugene, Samuel Christopher, Annabelle Council. Instr. Elon (N.C.) Coll., 1919-21, asst. prof., 1921-27, prof., head dept. geology and biology, 1927-32; pres. Carolina Biol. Supply Co., Burlington, N.C., 1932—; dir. Wachovia Bank and Trust Co., Burlington, 1960-70. Mem. Alamance County Bd. Edn., 1934-61, N.C. Citizens Com. for Better Schs., 1957-59; pres. N.C. Sch. Bd. Assn., 1943-45. Bd. dirs. Va. Mil. Inst. Research Labs., 1963-69. Served to lt. U.S. Army, 1918. Named Alumnus of Year, Elon Coll., 1964; Paul Revere Patriot of Commonwealth Mass., 1965. Mem. A.A.A.S., Newcomen Soc., Soc. Protozoologists, Am. Inst. Biol. Scis., Assn. Scientists and Industrialists, Burlington-Alamance County C. of C. (dir. 1965-67). Methodist. Mason. Research primarily concerned with the life history and control of Lasioderma serricorne, the tobacco beetle. Address: 2400 York Rd Burlington NC 27215

POWELL, WILBUR LLOYD, accountant; b. Marquez, Tex., Mar. 14, 1912; s. Albert Lloyd and Mattie (McLean) P.; student Tex. A. and I. U., 1931-34; m. Virginia Jeroline Moore, June 30, 1934; 1 dau., Jennye Lou (Mrs. Frank L. Cannon, Jr.). Accountant, Benson & Co., 1938-41, Benson, Powell & Sparks, 1941-44, Benson & Powell, 1944-48, Benson, Powell & Morrison, 1948-55, W.L. Powell C.P.A., 1955-67, Powell & Donald, C.P.A.'s, Alice, Tex., 1967-71; prin. W.L. Powell C.P.A., 1971—. Auditor, Jim Wells County, Tex., 1945—. Mem. Am. Inst. C.P.A.'s, Tex. Soc. C.P.A.'s. Baptist. Home: 1900 Alta Vista Alice TX 78332 Office: 62 N Cameron Alice TX 78332

POWELL, WILLIAM EDWARD, III, food scientist; b. Leroy, Ala., Mar. 29, 1944; s. William Edward, Jr. and Ina Cornelia (Etheredge) P.; B.S., Auburn U., 1966, Ph.D., 1970; m. Elizabeth Crawford, Sept. 9, 1967. Asst. prof. dept. animal sci. Auburn (Ala.) U., 1969-70, specialist in food sci. Coop. Extension Service, 1970—, v.p. Student Body, 1965-66. First v.p. Nat. Red Angus Assn., 1971—. Recipient Sigma Xi award for outstanding research, 1971; named Outstanding Grad., Sch. Agr., 1966. Pres. Danforth Summer Fellowship, 1965, Nat. Def. Edn. Act fellow. Mem. Am. Soc. Animal Sci., Am. Meat Sci. Assn., Sigma Xi, Phi Kappa Phi, Alpha Gamma Rho, Gamma Delta Zeta, Omicron Delta Kappa, Phi Eta Sigma. Methodist. Home: 409 Flame Ct Mobile AL 36608

POWER, WALTER H., sch. adminstr.; b. Salyersville, Ky., July 24, 1925; s. William Holt and Lona (Patrick) P.; B.A., Eastern Ky. U., 1954, postgrad., 1954-56; M.A., Morehead State U., 1956; m. Thelma Hackworth, Jan. 18, 1952; children—Leona Alice, Patricia Ann. Tchr. Magoffin County (Ky.) Schs., 1943-51; prin. Camargo High Sch., Mt. Sterling, Ky., 1951-55, McKee (Ky.) High Sch., 1959-63; supt. Gallatin County (Ky.) Schs., 1963-67; chmn. sch. facilities survey team Ky. State Dept. Edn., 1967-69; prin. Briar Hill Sch., Lexington, Ky., 1969—. Chmn. Magoffin County Republican Exec. Com., 1949-53; mem. Fayette County Republican Exec. Com., 1972—; active Wilderness Trail council Boy Scouts Am., 1955-58. Served with USNR, 1944-45. Recipient Eastern Ky. State U. Ednl. Leadership award, 1967; Morehead State U. Distinguished Alumni award, 1968. Mem. Ky. Assn. Secondary Sch. Prins. (chmn. 1954-55), Am. Assn. Sch. Adminstrs., Internat. Platform Assn., Phi Delta Kappa. Republican. So. Baptist. Mason, Kiwanian (pres. Jackson County br. 1961-62, v.p. Mt. Sterling br. 1957-58, sec. Salyersville br. 1948-49), Lion (pres. Boonesboro br. 1953-54, sec. Warsaw br. 1964-65). Club: Ky. Mountain. Author: A Procedure for Conducting School Facilities Surveys, 1969. Home: 625 Buckingham Lane Lexington KY 40503 Office: Route 4 Lexington KY 40505

POWER, WALTER ROBERT, JR., geologist; b. Seattle, Nov. 7, 1924; s. Walter Robert and Marie Elizabeth (Madden) P.; B.S., U. Wash., 1949; Ph.D., Johns Hopkins U., 1959; m. Martha Ann Thompson, June 18, 1960; children—John Robert, Joseph Patrick. Geologist, U.S. Geol. Survey, Spokane, and Boston, 1950-54; asst. prof. geology U. Ga., Athens, 1957-60; chief geologist Ga. Marble Co., Tate, 1960-64; prof. Ga. State U., Atlanta, 1960—. Cons. geologist indsl. minerals. Served with AUS, 1943-45. Fellow Geol. Soc. Am.; mem. Am. Inst. Mining Engrs., Soc. Econ. Geologists, A.A.A.S. Home: 4188 Liffey Lane Decatur GA 30034 Office: Dept Geology Ga State Univ Atlanta GA 30303

POWERS, DONALD ELROY, lawyer, judge; b. Tryon, Okla., Nov. 17, 1919; s. Floyd L. and Ethel L. (Barclay) P.; B.S., Central State Coll., Edmond, Okla., 1941; LL.B., U. Okla., 1948; m. Mary H. Mayes, Oct. 17, 1942; children—Donald ElRoy, James Edward. Admitted to Okla. bar, 1948; atty. Lincoln County, Chandler, Okla., 1949-50; sec. to Congressman Tom Steed, Washington, 1952-54; dist. judge 23d Jud. Dist., Chandler, 1955—. Pres., Will Rogers council Boy Scouts Am., 1962-64. Chmn. bd. trustees Central State Coll. Alumni Found., 1965-66. Served to lt. USAAF, 1942-45; capt. Okla. N.G., 1950-52; Korea. Decorated D.F.C., Air medal with four oak leaf clusters; recipient Silver Beaver award Boy Scouts Am., 1961. Mem. Am., Okla. bar assns., Am. Judicature Soc., Nat. Assn. State Trial Judges, Okla. Jud. Conf. (pres. 1966), Central State Coll. Alumni Assn. (pres. 1967). Methodist. Lion, Mason; mem. Order Eastern Star. Home: 323 W 6th St Chandler OK 74834 Office: Court House Chandler OK 74834

POWERS, GEORGIA M., state senator; b. Springfield, Ky., Oct. 29, 1923; d. Ben and Frances (Walker) Montgomery; ed. Louisville Municipal Coll., 1940-42; m. James L. Powers; 1 son from previous marriage, William F. Supr. IBM Data Processing div. U.S. Census Bur., 1959-62; asst. hosp. adminstr., Louisville, 1966; mem. Ky. State Senate, 1968—. Mem. Gov.'s Adv. Council on Mental Retardation, 1967-68. Dist. chmn. Jefferson County Democratic Exec. Com., 1964-66; chmn. Blume for Congress campaign, 1966; del. Dem. Nat. Conv., 1968. Bd. dirs. Louisville area chpt. A.R.C., 1970-72. Recipient Kennedy-King Meritorious award Ky. Young Dems., 1968; Achievement award Zion Bapt. Ch., 1968; certificate of appreciation Ky. Sch. Bds. Assn., 1968. Mem. So. Christian Leadership Conf., N.A.A.C.P., Urban League. Presbyn. Address: 733 Cecil Av Louisville KY 40211

POWERS, L. B., mining engr.; b. Frakes, Ky., July 18, 1932; s. Julius and Nona (Lambdin) P.; B.S., U. Ky., 1956. Asst. engr. Blue Diamond Coal Co., Knoxville, Tenn., 1957-65, mining engr., 1965-66, chief engr., 1966-67, 73—, asst. to the pres., 1969-72; gen. supt. Scotia Coal Co., 1967-68. Mem. Adv. com. Appalachian Resources Project, U. Tenn., 1973. Bd. dirs. So. Appalachian Sci. and Engring. Fair, 1971—. Served to lt. Signal Corps, AUS, 1956-57. Registered profl. engr., Ky., Tenn. Mem. Ky. Mining Inst., Ky. Coal Assn. (dir. 1969-72), Hazard Coal Operators Assn. (dir. 1969-72), Tau Kappa Epsilon. Republican. Baptist. Home: PO Box 10927 8039 Kingston Pike NW Knoxville TN 37919 Office: PO Box 10008 Knoxville TN 37919

POWERS, LEON GANO, chief of police; b. Itasca, Tex., Jan. 19, 1926; s. George and Birtamae (Burnett) P.; student FBI Nat. Acad., 1962; m. Maydel Curry, Sept. 12, 1946; children—Freddie, Jack. Patrolman, City of Irving (Tex.), 1956-57, Sgt., 1957-58, asst. chief, 1958-68; chief police City of Greenville (Tex.) 1968—. Vis. instr. East Tex. State U., Commers, 1968. Served with USMC, 1944-46. Decorated Presdl. Citation; recipient Meritorious Service citation Am. Legion, 1970. Mem. Tex. Police Assn. (mem. exec. com. 1970-71), FBI Nat. Acad. North Tex. (pres. 1963), Tex. (sec., treas. 1971), North Tex. (pres. 1971) police chiefs. Mem. Ch. of Christ (elder 1971—). Kiwanian (bd. dirs. 1960, 70-71; 1st v.p. 1961). Home: 617 Deer Dr Greenville TX 75401 Office: 2800 Washington St Greenville TX 75401

POWERS, ORMUND DEVERE, newspaper editor; b. Concordia, Kan., Sept. 26, 1914; s. Edward Ray and Clara (Peterson) P.; student U. Fla., 1932-34; m. Barbara Ann Griffin; children—Richard DeVere, James N., Leslie H., Amanda Lee. With Orlando (Fla.) Sentinel-Star, 1934—, now polit. editor. Episcopalian. Mason, Elk, Rotarian. Home: 1134 Western Way Orlando FL 32804 Office: 633 N Orange Way Orlando FL 32804

POWERS, VERNON EUGENE, editor; b. Lamar, S.C., May 16, 1915; s. Evan and Mary (McLendon) P.; student Newberry Coll., 1935-36; 1 dau., Virginia (Mrs. Wayne Haley). Sports editor Whiteville (N.C.) News Reporter, 1946—; sports corr. Raleigh (N.C.) News and Observer, 1948, Fayetteville (N.C.) Observer, 1950; radio-TV corr. Wilmington, Raleigh and Florence, S.C., 1962. Sportswriter, Wilmington (N.C.) Morning Star, 1944—. Publicist, Waccamaw Athletic Assn., 1958-73, Three Rivers Athletic Assn., 1973—, East Waccamaw Conf., 1973—; sports publicist Southeastern Community Coll., 1970—. Recipient 1st place award N.C. Press Assn., 1970. Mem. Nat., N.C. press assns. Clubs: Dixie Youth Baseball (Whiteville), Wolfpack (N.C. State U.). Donor Jiggs Powers Athletic scholarship to Southeastern Community Coll. Home: Box 11 Brunswick NC 28424 Office: Box 472 Whiteville NC 28472

POYDASHEFF, ROBERT STEPHEN, army officer; b. N.Y.C., Feb. 13, 1930; s. Stephen Alexander and Pauline (Miller) P.; A.B., Citadel, 1954; M.B.A., Boston U., 1967; J.D., Tulane, 1957; grad. Command and Gen. Staff Coll., 1968-69; m. Anastasia Catherine Latto, Aug. 29, 1954; children—Catherine Alexandra, Robert Stephen. Commd. 2d lt. U.S. Army, 1955, advanced through grades to lt. col., 1969; asst. judge advocate, Berlin, 1964-67; chief civil law and staff judge advocate, Vietnam, 1967-68; chief civilian personnel law Office Judge Advocate Gen., Washington, 1970-73; legislative counsel Office Sec. Army, Washington, 1973—. Lectr., Am. U., 1960-63; U. Md., 1965-69. Pres., Riverside P.T.A., 1970-72, W. Whitman P.T.A., 1971; chmn. Mt. Vernon Council Civic Assns., 1973—. Decorated Legion of Merit with oak leaf cluster, Bronze Star; knight comdr. Order St. Dennis; recipient Outstanding Service award P.T.A. Mt. Vernon, 1971, Service certificate Boy Scouts Am., 1970. Mem. Am., S.C., Fed. bar assns., Phi Delta Phi. Mason (Shriner). Club: Army Navy (gov. Washington 1971—). Episcopalian. Served successfully as chief counsel to several high ranking officers involved in My Lai Case. Home: 8303 Bound Brook Lane Alexandria VA 22309 Office: Office Sec Army General Dept Army Washington DC 20310

POYNOR, KENNETH J., realtor; b. Chelsea, Okla., July 3, 1916; s. James Madison and Nova K. (Aldridge) P.; B.S., Okla. State U., 1937; m. Dorothy O. Smith, May 24, 1937. With U.S. Dept. Agr., Stillwater, Okla., 1938-43; tchr. vocational agr. Noble, Okla., 1943-44, Altus, Okla., 1944-45; owner, operator Ken Poynor Agy. real estate and ins., Norman, Okla., 1951—. Owner, operator farms and ranches. Mem. Okla. Ho. of Reps., 1958-62. Named Norman Realtor of Year, 1969. Mem. Okla. Realtors (state chmn. legislative com. 1965-73, agrl. research and edn. com. 1965-73), Norman Bd. Realtors (pres. 1960-71), C. of C., Okla. U. Alumni Assn. (life). Mason (Shriner, 32 deg.), Kiwanian. Club: Twin Lakes Country. Home: 1306 Melrose Dr Norman OK 73069 Office: 708 W Main St Norman OK 73069

POYNTER, NELSON, editor, pub.; b. Sullivan, Ind., Dec. 15, 1903; s. Paul and Alice (Wilkey) P.; A.B., Ind. U., 1924, A.M., Yale, 1927; Litt.D., Stetson U., 1962, Fla. State U., 1970; m. Henrietta Malkiel, Aug. 8, 1942 (dec. 1968); m. 2d, Marion Knauss, May 4, 1970. Reporter Scripps-Howard, Washington, 1923; news editor Japan Times, Tokyo, 1924; bus. mgr. Washington Daily News; editor Ohio Scripps-Howard, 1935-37; owner St. Petersburg (Fla.) Times, 1938—; chmn. bd. Times Pub. Co., 1968—; owner Evening Ind., 1962—; chmn. bd. Congl. Quarterly Publs., also Editorial Research Reports, Washington. Served as dep. dir. COI-OWI, 1941-44. Mem. Am. Soc. Newspaper Editors, Am. Newspaper Pubs. Assn., Phi Gamma Delta, Sigma Delta Chi (nat. hon. pres. 1970). Clubs: National Press, Metropolitan (Washington); Yacht, Bath (St. Petersburg). Author: Post War Jobs, 1945. Contbr. to Freedom of Press: Interpretations of Journalism. Office: Times PO Box 1121 St Petersburg FL 33731 also 1735 K St NW Washington DC 20006

PRADO, FRED TIMMINS, artist; b. Monterrey N.L., Mexico, Sept. 26, 1907; s. Herman Timmins and Jesusita (Morales) T.; brought to U.S., 1908; student artist Jose Arpa, 1928-31; m. Carmen Valdez, Dec. 17, 1933; 1 dau., Mary Evelyn (Mrs. Ralph Tibiletti). With art dept. San Antonio Light newspaper, 1927—, chief artist, head editorial art dept., 1946-72. Mem. Coppini Acad. Fine Arts, Witte Mus. San Antonio, San Antonio Art League. Home: 6903 Dorothy Louise Dr San Antonio TX 78229

PRADOS, JOHN WILLIAM, univ. adminstr.; b. Spring Hill, Tenn., Oct. 12, 1929; s. Gustave Oliver and Elizabeth (Branham) P.; B.S. in Chem. Engring., U. Miss., 1951; M.S., U. Tenn., 1954, Ph.D., 1957; m. Ruth Lynn Baird, Sept. 2, 1951; children—Elizabeth, Laura, Anne. Mem. faculty dept. chem. engring. U. Tenn. at Knoxville, 1953—, asso. prof., 1959-64, prof., 1964—, asso. dean engring., 1969-71, dean admissions and records, 1971-73, acting chancellor, 1973, v.p. acad. affairs, 1973—. Cons. Oak Ridge Nat. Lab., 1957—. Served with USAF, 1951-53. Recipient Alumni Outstanding Tchr. award U. Tenn., 1967; Ford Found. faculty resident grantee, 1965-66. Fellow Am. Inst. Chemists; mem. Am. Chem. Soc., Am. Inst. Chem. Engrs., Am. Soc. Engring. Edn., Sigma Xi, Tau Beta Pi, Omicron Delta Kappa, Phi Kappa Phi, Phi Eta Sigma, Alpha Tau Omega. Roman Catholic. Contbr. articles to profl. jours. Home: 7021 Stagecoach Trail Knoxville TN 37921 Office: U Tenn Knoxville TN 37916

PRANGE, ARTHUR JERGEN, JR., educator; b. Grand Rapids, Mich., Sept. 19, 1926; s. Arthur Jergen and Martha (Elliott) P.; B.S., U. Mich., 1947, M.D., 1950; m. Sarah Elizabeth Bowen, Feb. 4, 1950; children—Christine Anne, Martha Louise, Laura Beth, David Elliott. Intern Wayne County Gen. Hosp., Eloise, Mich., 1950-51; resident anesthesiology Detroit Receiving Hosp., 1951-52; resident psychiatry U. N.C. Meml. Hosp., Chapel Hill, 1954-57; mem. faculty dept. psychiatry Med. Sch., U. N.C. at Chapel Hill, 1957—, asso. prof., 1964-68, prof., 1968—, also asso. dir. div., 1966-69, dir. research, devel., 1970—; vis. scientist Med. Research Council, Epson, Surrey, Eng., 1968-69. Mem. clin. projects research rev. com. Dept. Health, Edn. and Welfare and Nat. Inst. Mental Health, 1972—. Served to lt. M.C., USNR, 1953-54. Nat. Inst. Mental Health grantee, 1961—, career scientist award grantee, 1969—. Diplomate Am. Bd. Psychiatry and Neurology. Fellow Am. Psychiat. Assn., Am. Coll. Neuropsychopharmacology; mem. Royal Coll. Psychiatrists (London), Internat. Soc. Psychoneuroendocrinology. Home: 1804 Rolling St Chapel Hill NC 27514

PRASIL, ANTONE GEORGE, pub. utility exec.; b. Friendship, Wis., Aug. 24, 1922; s. Anton Mike and Anna (Burian) P.; B.S., U. Wis., 1946; B.S. in Chem. Engring., Harvard, 1968; m. Helen Ethel Smith, July 27, 1945; children—Antone George, Jr., Edward Joseph, Peggy Ann, Richard Alan, James Rupert. Dist. engr. Wis. Pub. Service, Oshkosh, 1946-51, staff engr., 1951-58; engr. So. Union Gas, Dallas, 1958-60, chief engr., 1960-67, v.p., chief engr., 1967-72, v.p., mgr. operations, 1972-73, sr. v.p. operations, 1973—; chief engr. Southern Union Gathering Co., 1967—. Dir. So. Union Energy, So. Union Internat., Asso. Pipelines. Mem. Council Boy Scouts Am., 1958-64, Camp Fire Girls U.S., 1959-62. Served with USNR, 1943-45. Registered profl. engr., Wis., Tex., Okla., Ariz., N.M., Colo. Mem. Am. Soc. Mech. Engrs., Am. Inst. Chem. Engrs., Nat. Assn. Corrosion Engrs. (pres. N. Tex. chpt. 1959-63), Profl. Engrs. Soc., Petroleum Engrs., N.E. Tex. Measurement Soc., Am. Gas. Assn., So. Gas Assn., Alpha Chi Sigma. Home: 10042 Coppedge St Dallas TX 75229 Office: Fidelity Union Tower Dallas TX 75201

PRASSEL, ALLEN WILLIAM, wholesale lumberman; b. New Orleans, Jan. 13, 1922; s. Bruno William and Lucille (Allen) P.; student Hinds Jr. Coll., 1940-41, Colo. State U., 1941-42, Pasadena City Coll., 1942, Stanford U., 1942-43; m. June Steagall, July 17, 1947 (div. 1954); children—Allen William, Suzanne; m. 2d, Peggy Buckley, Aug. 11, 1962; children—Tana Lyn, Bryan William. Owner, Prassel Co., Leesville, La., 1946-55; pres. Prassel Lumber Co., Inc., Jackson, Miss., 1957—, Prassel Furniture & Boxwoods, Co., Jackson, 1960—, Prassel Enterprises, Inc., Jackson, 1961—, Prassel Internat., Jackson, 1972—, Prassel Trading Co., Jackson, 1973—; owner A-D Ranch, Raymond, Miss., 1966—. Served to 2d lt. AUS, 1941-45. Baptist. Address: 120 Avian Lane Apts PO Box 8305 Battlefield Station Jackson MS 39204

PRATER, JESSE WALLACE, dentist; b. Ocala, Fla., Mar. 23, 1932; s. Jesse A. and Helen (Jones) P.; D.M.D., U. Louisville, 1962; m. Bettye Beam, June 15, 1952; children—Jesse W., Suzanne Beam. Practice dentistry, Tampa, Fla., 1962—. Pres., Stat Inc., 1969—, TRI ARC Prodns., 1970—(both Tampa). Lectr. dental practice mgmt. and tech. dentistry. Faculty adviser Fla. Coll. Med. and Dental Assts.; cons. Fla. Dept. Health and Rehabilitative Services, Fla. Cripple Children's Soc. Served with AUS, 1953-55. Fellow Royal Soc. Health; mem. Lauritzen (chmn. 1968-69), Hillsboro County dental research groups, Am. Soc. Preventive Dentistry (v.p. Fla. chpt. 1972-73, pres. Fla. chpt. 1973-74), Fedn. Dentaire Internationale, Am. Dental Assn., Fla. W. Coast Dental Soc., Am. Acad. Dental Practice Adminstrn., Hillsboro County Dental Soc., Pierre Fauchard Acad., So. Acad. Clin. Nutrition (charter), Am. Equilibration Soc., Internat. Platform Assn., Nat. Rifle Assn., Psi Omega, Alpha Epsilon Delta. Mason (32 deg., Shriner). Club: Sertoma. Author: Book Ways to Better Days in Your Practice, 1970. Cons. editor Dental Mgmt. mag. Home: 12101 Lake Carroll Dr Tampa FL 33618 Office: 2630 W Water Av Tampa FL 33614

PRATT, EDWARD TAYLOR, JR., hotel co. exec.; b. Joplin, Mo., Aug. 12, 1923; s. Edward Taylor and Etner (Peek) P.; grad. high sch.; m. Billie Ruth Skelton, Aug. 27, 1941; children—Carolyn Sue (Mrs. Charles E. Hickey), Diana L. (Mrs. Richard Heisler), Edward Taylor, III, Sharon R. Mng. partner Pratt & Co., Dallas, developing Holiday Inns in Tex., Mexico and C. Am., 1960—, Prattco, Inc., operating co. for Holiday Inns, 1969—. Chmn. Mineral Wells (Tex.) Planning-Zoning Commn., 1967—. Chmn. bd. Bristol Hosp., Dallas, 1962—. Served with AUS, 1942-46. Mem. C. of C. (dir. 1962-69). Republican. Home: 908 Lakeview Dr Mineral Wells TX 76067 Office: Brazos Shopping Center PO Box 939 Mineral Wells TX 76067

PRATT, JOHN HELM, judge; b. Portsmouth, N.H., Nov. 17, 1910; s. Harold Boswell and Marguerite (Rockwell) P.; A.B. cum laude, Harvard, 1930, LL.B., 1934; m. Bernice G. Safford, Oct. 25, 1938; children—Clare, Lucinda (Mrs. Daniel D. Pearlman), John Helm, Patricia, Mary. Admitted D.C. bar, 1934, since practiced in Washington; partner firm Morris, Pearce, Gardner & Pratt, 1954-68; asst. counsel Boys Club Greater Washington, 1948-68; U.S. district judge, Washington, 1968—. Chmn. Montgomery County (Md.) Housing Authority, 1950-53. Chmn. bd. trustees D.C. Legal Aid Agy., 1967-68. Served to capt. USMCR, 1942-46; PTO. Decorated Bronze Star medal, Purple Heart; recipient Army citation for civilian service in field prosthetics, 1948. Mem. Am. Bar Assn. (ho dels. 1963-64), Am. Bar Found., Bar Assn. D.C. (pres. 1963-64), Harvard Law Sch. Assn. (pres. Washington 1952-53), Asso. Harvard Clubs (pres. 1952-53), Marine. Res. Corps Officers Assn. (judge adv. gen. 1961-68). Democrat. Roman Cath. Clubs: Barristers (pres. 1959), Lawyers, Harvard (pres. 1949-51) (Washington); Chevy Chase; Metropolitan. Home: 4119 Rosemary St Chevy Chase MD 20015 Office: US Courthouse Washington DC 20001

PRAY, HAROLD LYNN, educator; b. Bellville, Tex., Sept. 7, 1938; s. Olen Hamer and Maggie Mirtle (Shockley) P.; B.S. with honors, State Coll. Ark., 1964; M.S. (Dept. Health Edn. and Welfare fellow), U. Tenn., 1966; Ph.D. (AEC fellow), 1972; m. Myrna Rea Ott, June 19, 1958; children—Kevin Harold, Kenton Lynn. Instr. physics dept. State Coll. Ark., Conway, 1966-68, asso. prof., 1970—. Served with USNR, 1956-60. Mem. A.A.A.S., Am. Assn. Physics Tchrs., Alpha Chi, Sigma Pi Sigma. Home: Route 2 Box 518 Conway AR 72032

PREEG, ERNEST HENRY, fgn. service officer; b. Englewood, N.J., July 5, 1934; s. Ernest Winfield and Claudia Teresa (Casper) P.; B.S., N.Y. State Maritime Coll., 1956; M.A., New Sch. for Social Research, 1961, Ph.D., 1964; m. Florence Leicester Tate, May 12, 1962. Served from 3d officer to chief officer U.S. Mcht. Marine, 1956-61, resigned, 1961; lectr. econs. Bklyn. Coll., 1962-63; fgn. service officer State Dept., 1963—, economist Office of Trade, 1963-65; mem. U.S. delegation to Kennedy Round of Trade Negotiations, 1965-67, econ. officer, London, Eng., 1968-69, mem. planning and coordination staff, Washington, 1969—. Fgn. Affairs fellow Council on Fgn. Relations, 1967-68; guest scholar Brookings Instn., 1967-68; mem. internat. staff Nat. Planning Assn., 1972-73. Mem. Am. Econ. Assn., Am. Fgn. Service Assn. Author: Traders and Diplomats, 1970; Economic Blocs and U.S. Foreign Policy, 1973—. Contbr. articles to profl. jours. Home: 420 N Irving St Arlington VA 22201 Office: Room 7336 Dept State Washington DC 20520

PREISS, LESTER LOUIS, III, elec. engr.; b. Miami, Sept. 22, 1943; s. Lester L. and Evelyn (Hamon) P., Jr.; B.S. in Elec. Engring., U. Fla., 1967; postgrad. West Coast U., 1970-72; m. Emelia Anne Rosario, Aug. 27, 1965; children—Elizabeth Elaine, Collette Dawn. Test engr. Ga. Power Co., Atlanta, 1972-74, test engr., Macon (Ga.) div., 1974—. Served to capt., systems command USAF, 1968-72. Decorated Air Force Commendation medal. Mem. I.E.E.E. Methodist. Home: 1152 Darlington St Macon GA 31204 Office: Ga Power Co 960 Key St Macon GA 31204

PREJEAN, JOE DAVID, physiologist; b. Pampa, Tex., Feb. 9, 1940; s. Joseph Carlyle and Blanche (Groves) P.; A.A., Tyler Jr. Coll., 1960; student U. Tex., 1960-62; B.S., Stephen F. Austin State Coll., 1963; M.A., E. Tex. State U., 1965; Ph.D., Tex. A. and M. U., 1969; children—Michael David, K'Anne. Grad. asst. E. Tex. State U., Commerce, 1963-65; research asst. Baylor U. Med. Center, Dallas, 1965; grad. asst. Tex. A. and M. U., College Station, 1965-69, fellow, 1969; research biologist So. Research Inst., Birmingham, Ala., 1969-71, sr. biologist, 1971—, head chem. carcinogenesis sect., 1972—. Bd. dirs. Jefferson County unit Am. Cancer Soc. Mem. Sigma Xi. Presbyn. Club: Chace Lake Country (Birmingham). Home: 2708 Acton Rd Birmingham AL 35243 Office: 2000 9th Av Birmingham AL 35205

PRELL, IRVING NORMAN, radio sta. exec.; b. St. Louis, Dec. 6, 1925; s. David and Lillian (Besser) P.; student U. Mo., 1943, Stanford, 1944, Harvard, 1946; m. Beatrice E. Eisenberg, June 9, 1946; children—Roxanne (Mrs. Michael Statsmann), Robert Asher. Asst. mgr. KYAK, Yakima, Wash., 1947-52; sales mgr. KGA, Spokane, 1952-53; salesman KHQ-TV, Spokane, 1953-54, KXLY Radio-TV, Spokane, 1954-56; sales mgr. KELP-TV, El Paso, Tex., 1957-58, KTSM Radio, El Paso, 1958-69; mgr. KROD, El Paso, 1969—. Served with inf. AUS, 1944-46. Decorated Purple Heart. Mem. El Paso Advt. Club (pres. 1969), Nat. Conf. Christian and Jews. Jewish religion (pres. temple men's club 1970). Mem. B'nai Brith (sec.-treas. 1959). Home: 317 Windrose St El Paso TX 79912 Office: 2201 Wyoming St El Paso TX 79903

PREMACK, IRWIN JOSEPH, marketing research co. exec.; b. Chgo., June 2, 1927; s. Hyman Abraham and Bertha (Friedman) P.; B.S. in Psychology, Roosevelt U., 1948; m. Audrey Twersky, Dec. 19, 1948; children—Steven, Richard. Dist. mgr. Dumont Corp., Chgo., 1953-55; dir. marketing Hotpoint Corp., Chgo., 1955-57; v.p. Kritzer Air Conditioning Co., Chgo., 1957-59, Fgn. Automobile Marketing Corp., Chgo., 1959-60; pres. Premack & Assos. Inc., St. Petersburg, Fla., 1960—. Columnist Miami Rev.-Bergida Enterprises, 1971—; lectr. TV program Channel 13, Tampa, Fla., Channel 10, Miami, Channel 4, Miami, also producer 11 TV spls., 1971-74. Served with AUS, 1945. Recipient Marketing Man Year, Hotpoint Corp., 1956, Sales Man Year award Philco Corp., 1952; subject of 3 TV spls., 1973. Mem. Am. Assn. Polit. Consultants, Am. Marketing Assn. (charter mem.), St. Petersburg (dir. marketing com.), Orlando (mem. environmental resources com.) chambers commerce. Republican (cons. Nat. Com.). Jewish religion. Club: Tiger Bay (Miami). Home: 717 Pruitt Dr Madeira Beach FL 33708 Office: 6727 1st Av S St Petersburg FL 33707

PRENDERGAST, THOMAS AIDEN, mfg. exec.; b. N.Y.C., Dec. 10, 1933; s. Thomas Aiden and Margaret (Dalton) P.; B.S., Fordham U., 1955; postgrad. U. Tex., 1957-60; m. Mary Alice Peinado, Aug. 4, 1956; children—Laura Ann, Elizabeth Jane. Accountant, Hurdman & Cranstoun, C.P.A.'s, N.Y.C., 1955; auditor El Paso (Tex.) Pub. Schs., 1957-61; C.P.A., El Paso, 1958-61; v.p. finance, dir. Farah Mfg. Co., Inc., El Paso, 1961-71; chmn. bd. Billy The Kid, Inc., El Paso, 1971—. Trustee El Paso Community Coll. Served to 2d lt. AUS, 1955-57. Home: 4252 Park Hill El Paso TX 79902 Office: 100 S Cotton El Paso TX 79988

PRENSNER, STEVEN, educator; b. Passaic, N.J.; s. Stephen and Susana (Nacsa) P.; grad. Newark State Normal, 1934; B.S., Sam Houston State Tchrs. Coll., 1938; M.Ed., U. Houston, 1950, Ed.D., 1971; m. Selma Ida Berger, July 4, 1936; children—Douglas S., Gary L., Steven R. Tchr. shop, drawing pub. schs., Brazoria and Galveston counties, 1934-48; prin. high schs., Friends Wood, 1948-54, Pearland, Tex., 1954-66; supt. Pearland Schs., 1966-68; research asst. U. Houston, 1968-72. Active Boy Scouts Am., Eagle Scout, 1935. Mem. Nat., Tex. assns. secondary sch. prins., Tex. Tchrs. Assn., Am. Soc. Tool Engrs., Am. Assn. Sch. Adminstrs., Kappa Delta Pi, Phi Delta Kappa. Methodist. Rotarian (charter), Lion. Died Nov. 18, 1972. Home: Box 503 Pearland TX 77581

PRESCOTT, JOHN S., JR., newspaper exec.; b. Cleve., grad. Williams Coll.; m. Robin Balch; 4 children. With classified and retail advt. dept. Balt. Sun Newspapers, 1950-55; gen. mgr. Macomb Publ. Co., Detroit, 1955-62; with Knight Newspapers, 1962-71; asst. to pub. Detroit Free Press, 1962-66; asst. to pub. Miami (Fla.) Herald, 1966-67; asst. gen. mgr. Charlotte (N.C.) Observer, 1967-68, gen. mgr., 1968-70; v.p., gen. mgr. Phila. Newspapers, Inc., pubs. Phila. Inquirer, Phila. News, 1970-72; pres. Washington Post, 1972—. Served with USNR, 1945-46. Office: 1150 15th St NW Washington DC 20005

PRESLEY, W. DEWEY, banker; b. Wills Point, Tex., May 26, 1918; s. Dewey and Myrtle (Threatt) P.; B.A., Baylor U., 1939; m. Virginia Shepperd, Nov. 22, 1940; children—Charlotte, Suzanne, Rachel. With Magnolia Oil Co. and Magnolia Pipe Line Co., 1939-42; spl. agt. FBI, 1942-52; with First Nat. Bank, Dallas, 1952—, sr. v.p., 1960-63, chmn. bd., mem. and chmn. exec. com., dir., 1963—, also pres.; dir. Southeastern Drilling, Inc. Bd. dirs. Baptist Found. Tex. C.P.A., Tex. Mem. Am. Inst. C.P.A.'s, Tex., Dallas socs. C.P.A.'s. Baptist. Home: 7715 Bryn Mawr Dr Dallas TX 75225 Office: 1401 Main St Dallas TX 75202

PRESSEY, RUSSELL, plant physiologist; b. Pine River, Man., Can., Sept. 5, 1935; s. Michael and Jeanne (Toporowsky) Prysiazniuk; B.S., U. Man., 1958, M.S., 1960; Ph.D., Ia. State U., 1962; m. Barbara Jo Goshorn, June 1, 1962; children—Edward Walter, Andrew Michael, Joseph Gerald. Came to U.S., 1959, naturalized, 1966. Chemist, Gen. Mills, Inc., Mpls., 1962-64; chemist Agrl. Research Service, U.S. Dept. Agr., East Grand Forks, Minn., 1964-69, Athens, Ga., 1969—. Mem. Am. Chem. Soc., Am. Soc. Plant Physiologists. Contbr. articles to profl. jours. Home: 410 Greencrest Dr Athens GA 30601 Office: PO Box 5677 Athens GA 30601

PRESTIDGE, JERRY ELMO, petroleum engr.; b. Earlsboro, Okla., Dec. 19, 1929; s. Marion Thomas and Lillie (Lemons) P.; A.A., Wharton Jr. Coll., 1953; B.S., Tex. A. and I. U., 1956; m. Mary Beth Anderson, Dec. 19, 1953; children—Jerry, Leigh Ellen, Terri Elizabeth. Gas engr. Texaco, Snyder, Tex., 1956-57; gas engr. Superior Oil Co., Alleyton, Tex., 1957-68, sr. design engr., 1970-71; mgr. process gas devel., Union Tex. Petroleum, Houston, 1969-73 mgr. E. Tex. processing plant Tex. Oil and Gas Corp., 1973-74; supt. E. Tex. dist. Westland Oil Devel. Corp., 1974—; cons., 1971—. Served with USMCR, 1948-49, 51-52. Registered profl. engr., Tex. Mem. Houston, Permian Basin gas men. Rotarian. Address: 1604 Glenrose Longview TX 75601

PRESTON, ARNETT CARL, architect; b. Big Spring, Tex., Nov. 1, 1934; s. Arnett Carey and Docia Faye (Terrell) P.; grad. Howard County Jr. Coll., 1954; B.Arch., Tex. Technol. Coll., 1959; m. Claudie Delle Carpenter, June 2, 1959; children—Randal Wayne, Russell Dean. Draftsman, Atchison, Kloverstrom, Saul & Atchison, architects, Denver, 1960-63, Urban C. Weidner, Jr., architect, Santa Fe, 1963-65, Boone & Pope, architects and engrs., Abilene, Tex., 1965-69; partner Cozby & Preston, architects, Abilene, 1969—. Mem. A.I.A. (chpt. pres. 1974), Constrn. Specifications Inst. (chpt. pres. 1972-73). Baptist. Club: Optimist (pres. 1972-73) (Abilene). Home: 1537 Yorktown Dr Abilene TX 79603 Office: 302 N Willis St Abilene TX 79603

PRESTON, FRANK BROCKENBROUGH, JR., bank exec.; b. Buenos Aires, Argentina, June 3, 1927; s. Frank Brockenbrough and Margaret Erwin (Jones) P.; B.A. in Internat. Relations, Yale, 1951; J.D., U. Va. Law Sch., 1956; grad. Stonier Grad. Sch. Banking, 1966; m. Pauline Widen, Mar. 31, 1951; children—Frank Brockenbrough III, Helen Margaret. With U.S. Govt., 1951-53; exec. trainee First Nat. Bank Boston, 1956-57, apoderado, Havanna, Cuba, 1957-60; asst. v.p., comml. loan officer First Nat. Bank Tampa, 1961-63, v.p., comml. loan officer, 1963-68; pres., dir. Ellis Nat. Bank Tampa, 1968-71; pres., dir. Barnett Bank of Tampa, 1971—. Dir. Bennett, Wallace, Welch & Green Ins., Inc., St. Petersburg, Fla., 1968—. Vice chmn. Tampa Port Authority, 1970-72, treas., 1969-70; mem. Com. of 100, 1969—. Trustee St. John's Parish Day Sch., 1967—; bd. dirs. Easter Seal Soc. Crippled Children & Adults Hillsborough County, 1963—, pres., 1969; bd. dirs. Am. Cancer Soc. Hillsborough County, 1964—, campaign chmn., 1966—. Served with U.S. Maritime Service, 1945-47. Mem. Chi Phi, Phi Alpha Delta. Republican. Episcopalian (treas., vestryman 1971—). Toastmaster (past pres.), Krewe of Venus (dir. 1966—), Rotarian. Clubs: Tampa Yacht and Country (Tampa, Fla.); Republican Mens (dir. 1970—), Palma Ceia Golf and Country, University (Tampa). Home: 5020 The Riviera St Tampa FL 33609 Office: 1000 N Ashley Dr Tampa FL 33601

PRESTON, JOHN RONALD, mus. exec.; b. Seminole, Okla., Nov. 20, 1932; s. Ray S. and Lorena (Blanton) P.; B.S., Okla. State U., 1955; M.S., U. Ark., 1961; m. Sara R. Huggins, Nov. 25, 1952; children—Teresa R., Ron, Lora, Aaron. Curator, Fort Worth Mus. Sci. and Natural History, 1959-66; dir. Mid Fairfield County Mus., Westport, Conn., 1966-67; asst. dir. U. Ark. Mus., Fayetteville, 1967-69; dir. Mus. Sci. and Natural History, Little Rock, 1969—, dir. mus. spl. activity and ednl. programs. Mem. Am. Assn. Museums, Ark. Mus. Assn. (pres.), Soc. Am. Mammals, Nat. Audubon Soc. Home: 7914 W 29th St Little Rock AR 72204 Office: MacArthur Park Little Rock AR 72203

PRESTON, LOYCE ELAINE, educator; b. Texarkana, Ark., Feb. 25, 1929; d. Harvey Martin and Florence (Whitlock) Preston; student Texarkana Jr. Coll., 1946-47; B.S., Henderson State Tchrs. Coll., 1950; certificate in social work La. State U., 1952; M.S.W., Columbia U., 1956. Tchr. pub. schs., Dierks, Ark., 1950-51; child welfare worker Ark. Dept. Pub. Welfare, Clark and Hot Spring counties, 1951-56, child welfare cons., 1956-58; casework dir. Ruth Sch. Girls, Burien, Wash., 1958-60; asst. prof. spl. edn. La. Poly. Inst., Ruston, 1960-63; asst. prof. Northwestern State Coll., Shreveport, La., 1963-73; asst. prof. La. State U., Shreveport, 1973—. Chpt. sec. La. Assn. Mental Health, 1965-67, Gov's. adv. council, 1967-70; mem. Mayor's Com. for Community Improvement, 1972—. Mem. Am. Assn. Univ. Women (dir. Shreveport br. 1963-69), Acad. Cert. Social Workers, Nat. Assn. Social Workers (del. 1964-65, pres. N. La. chpt., state-wide com. 1968-69), La Conf. Social Welfare, La. Fedn. Council Exceptional Children (pres. 1970-71), La. Tchrs. Assn. Home: 602 Pickwick Pl Shreveport LA 71108 Office: 8515 Youree Dr Shreveport LA 71105

PRESTON, ROBERT ANDREWS, ednl. adminstr.; b. Richmond, Va., June 6, 1931; s. Joseph Martin and Mary Edyth (Andrews) P.; A.B., Belmont Abbey Coll., 1953; M.A., Cath. U. Am., 1958, Ph.D., 1960; m. Helen Solari, Sept. 6, 1958; children—Kathryn, Robert, Mary Frances, Margaret Helen, James Martin. Lectr. philosophy Cath. U. Am., 1959-60; asst. prof. philosophy John Carroll U., 1960-63, St. Louis U., 1963-66; asso. prof. Bellarmine Coll., Louisville, 1966-67, chmn. dept. philosophy, 1967-68, acad. dean, 1968—, v.p. acad. affairs, 1969—. Served with AUS, 1953-55. Mem. Am. Assn. U. Profs., Am. Assn. Acad. Deans, Nat. Cath. Edn. Assn., Assn. Am. Colls., So. Assn. Acad. Deans, English Speaking Union (dir. Ky. chpt. 1969—). Home: 1869 Douglass Blvd Louisville KY 40205

PRESTON, WILL MANIER, lawyer, banker; b. Nashville, May 27, 1904; s. Robert Hatton and Dayse (High) P.; LL.B., Vanderbilt U., 1925; m. Eunice Lannom, Dec. 29, 1926; 1 dau. Dolores Clyntelle (Mrs. William H. Fields). Admitted to Tenn. bar, 1925, Fla. bar, 1926; practice in Miami, 1926—; mem. firm Scott, McCarthy, Preston & Steel, 1943-65; gen. counsel Everglades Nat. Park Assn., 1947; counsel Scott. McCarthy, Steel, Hector & Davis, 1965—. Chmn. bd., dir. Dade Nat. Bank, Miami, 1956-69; dir. Fla. Power and Light Co., Wackenhut Corp. Charter mem., past pres., dir. Orange Bowl Com. Mem. Am., Dade County (past pres.) bar assns., Fla. Bar. Lion (past pres. Miami), Kiwanian (past pres. Miami). Home: 710 Lake Rd Miami FL 33137 Office: First Nat Bank Bldg Miami FL 33131

PRESTON, WILLIAM ARNOLD, savs. and loan exec.; b. Henderson, Tex., Dec. 14, 1917; s. Edward Massenburg and Opal (Arnold) P.; grad. high sch.; m. Nancy Johnson, Mar. 14, 1942; children—Charles W., Edward A. With Henderson Fed. Savs. & Loan Assn., 1940—, pres., 1958—. Dir. Cherokee Water Co., 1956—. Mem. Henderson Vol. Fire Dept., 1937. Mem. Middle Sabine Nav. Dist., 1960—. Bd. dirs. Henderson Meml. Hosp., 1964—, now treas. Served with USAF, 1941-45, 51-53. Mem. C. of C. Kiwanian. Home: 822 Laylon Av Henderson TX 75652 Office: Box 1029 Henderson TX 75652

PREVATT, RUBERT WALDEMAR, educator; b. Seville, Fla., May 15, 1925; s. Wallie A. and Elizabeth M. (Frierson) P.; B.S., U. Fla., 1948, M.S., 1951, Ph.D., 1959; m. Edna Harmon, Sept. 12, 1953; children—Suzanne Kay, Carol Anne. Soil technologist, U. Fla., Gainesville, 1948-51, asst. in horticulture, 1956-59; soil chemist, asst. prodn. mgr. Dr. P. Phillips Co., Orlando, Fla., 1951-54; indsl. agronomist, supr. research Internat. Mineral and Chem. Corp., Mulberry, Fla., 1959-70; prof. citrus Fla. So. Coll., Lakeland, 1971—. Cons. Fla. flower growers and citrus growers; nat. lectr. on rose culture. Chmn. City of Lakeland Beautification Bd., 1969. Bd. dirs. Lakeland Council Camp Fire Girls, 1962. Mem. Am. Soc. Agronomy, Am. Soc. Hort. Sci., Fla. Hort. Soc., Soils and Crops Soc. Fla., Fla. Agrl. Research Inst., Am. Rose Soc. (dist. dir. 1971), Sigma Chi, Alpha Zeta. Methodist. Toastmaster. Home: 2705 Collins Av Lakeland FL 33803 Office: Fla Southern College Lakeland FL 33802

PREWITT, TOM ORIN, JR., social worker; b. Jackson, Miss., Aug. 13, 1934; s. Tom Orin and Lois (Minor) P.; B.A., Millsaps Coll., 1956; M.S.W., Fla. State U., 1959; m. Patricia Morgan, June 30, 1956; children—Tom Orin III, Susan M. With Miss. Dept. Pub. Welfare, Jackson, 1957—, now dir. field services. Mem. Miss. Conf. Social Welfare (past pres.). Home: 705 Tanglewood St Clinton MS 39056 Office: PO Box 4321 Foudren Sta Jackson MS 39216

PREWITT, VERLON WAYNE, garment co. exec.; b. Ravenna, Ky., Oct. 17, 1935; s. William Roscoe and Elizabeth Belle (Hughes) P.; B.S., Eastern Ky. U., 1963, postgrad., 1968-69; m. Patricia Lee Tucker, Nov. 23, 1956; children—Christopher Wayne, William Gregory. Switchman, Louisville and Nashville R.R., Ravenna, Ky., 1957-64; plant engr. Carhartt, Inc., Irvine, Ky., 1964-69, plant mgr., 1969—. Scoutmaster Blue Grass council Boy Scouts Am., 1969—. Mem. Estill County Bd. Edn., 1969—. Mem. Am. Inst. Indsl. Engrs., Res. Officers Assn., Estill County C. of C. (pres. 1967-69). Club: Estill County Golf (dir. 1970—). Home: 117 Francis St Irvine KY 40336 Office: Box 88 Irvine KY 40336

PREYER, L. RICHARDSON, congressman; b. Greensboro, N.C., Jan. 11, 1919; s. William Y. and Mary Norris (Richardson) P.; grad. Woodberry Forest Sch.; A.B., Princeton, 1941; LL.B., Harvard, 1949; m. Emily Irving Harris, May 11, 1946; children—L. Richardson, Mary Norris, Britt Armfield, Jane Bethel, Emily Harris. Admitted to N.C. bar; mem. firm Preyer & Bynum, Greensboro, 1950-56; city judge, Greensboro, 1953-56; N.C. superior ct. judge, 1956-61; U.S. dist. judge 18th Dist. N.C., 1961-63; engaged in N.C. gubernatorial campaign, 1963-64; sr. v.p., trust officer N.C. Nat. Bank, Greensboro, 1964-66, exec., 1966-68; mem. 91st-93d Congresses from 6th Dist. N.C. Dir. Reins. Corp. N.Y., Piedmont So. Life Ins. Co., Richardson Corp. Trustee St. Andrews Coll., Woodberry Forest Sch.; bd. visitors Wake Forest Sch. Law. Served with USNR, World War II. Decorated Bronze Star medal; named Greensboro's Outstanding Young Man, U.S. Jr. C. of C., 1954, Outstanding Leader, Inter-Club Council, 1968. Mem. Newcomen Soc. Democrat. Home: 605 Sunset Dr Greensboro NC 27408 Office: Longworth House Office Bldg Washington DC 20515

PRICE, BENJAMIN ALVIN, III, banker; b. Baton Rouge, Sept. 5, 1938; s. Benjamin Alvin and Lucy (Hill) P.; B.Journalism, U. Mo. at Columbia, 1961; postgrad. Northwestern U., 1966; m. Margaret White, Oct. 4, 1964; children—Christopher White. Dir. advt. La. Nat. Bank, Baton Rouge, 1962-71; v.p., dir. marketing Union Nat. Bank, Little Rock, 1971-73, Central Bank, Monroe, La., 1973—. Chmn. publicity and programs Sales Marketing Exec. Assn., Little Rock, 1972. Bd. dirs. Ark. Festival Arts, 1972-73. Recipient presdl. outstanding achievement certificate Baton Rouge Jr. C. of C., 1964. Mem. Monroe Advt. Club, Bank Marketing Assn., Kappa Sigma. Methodist. Club: Bayou Desiard Country (Monroe). Home: 2018 Valencia St Monroe LA 71201 Office: 300 DeSiard St Monroe LA 71201

PRICE, BOYCE POSTON, assn. exec.; b. Montreal, Que., Can., June 1, 1914 (parents Am. citizens); s. Chester Boyce and Louise (Poston) P.; B.A., Dartmouth, 1936; postgrad. Yale, 1936-38; m. Elizabeth Boalt Williams, Dec. 20, 1941; children—Marion (Mrs. Allen Chandler Moore, Jr.), William Chester. Indsl. designer Russel Wright Assos., N.Y.C., 1938-41; asst. to editorial dei. Time, Inc., N.Y.C., 1946-49; asso. editor Archtl. Forum, N.Y.C., 1950-52; account exec. Wildrick & Miller, advt., N.Y.C., 1952-56; v.p. McCann Erickson, advt., N.Y.C., 1956-65; pres. Wood Marketing, Inc., Washington, 1965-68; exec. v.p. Am. Wood Council, Washington, 1968—. Served with C.E., AUS, 1941-46. Decorated Legion of Merit. Mem. Am. Soc. Assn. Execs., Theta Chi. Episcopalian. Clubs: Association Executives (Washington); West River Sailing (Galesville, Md.). Home: 3127 O St Washington DC 20007 Office: 1619 Massachusetts Av NW Washington DC 20036

PRICE, C. JACK, hosp. dist. adminstr.; student Wingate Jr. Coll., 1938-39, 46-47; B.A., Catawba Coll., 1949; grad. hosp. adminstrn. course Meml. Mission Hosp., Asheville, N.C., 1951. Office mgr. Southeastern div. R.B. Tyler Constrn. Co., Monroe, N.C., until 1943; asst. adminstr. Meml. Mission Hosp., 1951-55; adminstr. Stanly County Hosp., Albemarle, N.C., 1955-62; asso. adminstr. Dallas County Hosp. Dist., Dallas, 1962-63, adminstr., 1963—. Vice pres. Dallas Hosp. Council, 1966, pres., 1967; mem. hosp. adv. com. North Central Tex. Council Govts., 1968-71; clin. prof. preventive medicine and pub. health U. Tex. Southwestern Med. Sch., 1963—, mem. med. faculty council, 1968—; mem. adv. hosp. council Tex. Dept. Health, 1965-70; cons. manpower div. USPHS, 1970-71; mem. Dallas County Spl. Drug Abuse Study Com.; mem., spl. cons. neurology program-project A com. Nat. Inst. Neurol. Diseases and Stroke, NIH, 1969—; mem. membership body Dallas County Health Planning Council, 1971—. Active numerous civic orgns. Bd. dirs. Vis. Nurse Assn., Dallas Area Respiratory Health Assn., Dallas Council on Alcoholism, 1968-71. Served with AUS, 1943-46. Fellow Am. Coll. Hosp. Adminstrs.; mem. Royal Soc. Health (London), Am. (com. on rehab. 1966-68), Tex. (trustee 1968-71, v.p. 1970-71, pres.-elect 1971-72, pres. 1972-73) hosp. assns., Dallas C. of C. (pub. health com. 1968-71). Methodist (past steward). Rotarian (past treas. Dallas). Club: Press (Dallas). Office: Dallas County Hospital District 5201 Harry Hines Blvd Dallas TX 75235

PRICE, CHARLES EUGENE, educator; b. Apalachicola, Fla., Mar. 13, 1924; s. Charles P. and Lela (Joseph) P.; B.A., Johnson C. Smith, 1946; M.A., Howard U., 1949; LL.B., Am. Sch. Law, 1951: J.D., John Marshall Law Sch., 1967; postgrad. Johns Hopkins, 1951-52, Boston U., 1956; m. Lennie Florence Bryant, Nov. 25, 1946; 1 son, Charles Eugene (dec.). Tchr. high sch., Ga., 1947-48, Fla., 1948-49; asst. prof. history and polit. sci. Butler Coll., 1950-52, dean, 1952-53; asso. prof., dean Fla. Meml. Coll., 1953-55; field sec. N.A.A.C.P., 1955-57; asst. prof. Livingstone Coll., 1957-59; asso. prof. polit. sci. Morris Brown Coll., Atlanta, 1960—, asst. dean, 1967-71. Mem. Dekalb Republican Exec. Com., 1964-68; mem. Fulton Rep. Exec. Com., 1972—, ho. dist. chmn., 1972—. Bd. dirs., treas. Dekalb Econ. Opportunity Authority, 1965-70. Recipient Sincere Leadership award N.A.A.C.P., 1966, Albert award DeKalb N.A.A.C.P., 1965. Mem. Am. Polit. Sci. Assn., Assn. Social Sci. Tchrs., N.A.A.C.P. (pres. Dekalb chpt. 1964-68), Am., Nat., Atlanta, Gate City bar assns., State Bar Ga., Alpha Kappa Mu, Sigma Rho Sigma, Alpha Phi Alpha. Home: 1480 Austin Rd Atlanta GA 30331

PRICE, CHARLES RILEY, advt. agcy. exec.; b. Asheville, N.C., Aug. 13, 1941; s. Charles R. and Duane (Thomas) P.; A.B., U. N.C., 1963; m. Charlene Haynes, Sept. 29, 1963; children—Charla Duane, Charles Riley III. Advt. salesman Asheville Citizen-Times, 1963-65; advt. specialist Olin Matheson Chem. Corp., 1965-67; pres. Price/McNabb Advt. Agcy., Asheville, N.C., 1967—. Prof. advt., marketing, Western Carolina U., Cullowhee, 1968-69. Bd. dirs. Handi-Skills Workshop. Served with AUS, 1965. Mem. Asheville Sales Marketing Execs., Asheville Jr. C. of C., Sigma Delta Chi. Clubs: Asheville Country (gov.), Asheville City (gov.). Baptist. Home: 2 Deerview Lane Asheville NC 28804 Office: Northwestern Bank Bldg Asheville NC 28801

PRICE, EDGAR HILLEARY, JR., citrus processing co. exec., ex-state senator; b. Jacksonville, Fla., Jan. 1, 1918; s. Edgar Hilleary and Mary (Phillips) P.; student U. Fla., 1937-38; m. Elise Ingram, May 24, 1947; 1 son, Jerald Steven. Gen. mgr. Terra Ceia Bay Farms, Inc., Palmetto, Fla., 1945-49; mgr. Fla. Gladiolus Growers Assn., Bradenton, 1949-55; exec. v.p. Tropicana Products, Inc., Bradenton, Fla., 1955-73, also dir.; dir. Indsl. Glass Co., Inc.; dir. First Nat. Bank of Bradenton, Fla., Fla. Power and Light Co., Gen. Telephone Co. Fla., 1st Fed. Savs. and Loan Assn. Manatee; mem. Fla. Senate, 1958-66. Adv. com. Fla. Citrus Mut.; dir. Fla. Citrus Expn., 1958—; chmn. Fla. Citrus Commn.; bus. and agrl. cons. Gov. of Fla., 1971—. Del. Democratic Nat. Conv., 1958-62. Mem. gov.'s com. employment of physically handicapped, 1960; chmn. bd. trustees Manatee County Sch. Dist., 1956-57; chmn. Bradenton Housing Authority, 1951-57, commr., 1951—; bd. dirs. Salvation Army, Bradenton, 1954—; regional chmn. Crusade for Freedom, 1952-53; active A.R.C., Manatee County Crippled Childrens Soc., Boys Club, Blood Bank; commr. Census of 12th Jud. Circuit, 1957; mem. Fla. Bd. Control, 1957-58; mem. Fla. Plant Bd., 1957-58; chmn. Gov.'s Freeze Damage Survey Team, 1957-58; commr. Manatee County Indsl. Commn., 1956. Trustee Univ. S. Fla. Found., Fla. Investment Trust. Served from pvt. to sgt., M.C., AUS, 1941-43, to 1st lt. USAAF, 1943-45. Decorated Air medal with 4 oak leaf clusters; named outstanding freshman senator Fla. Legislature, 1959; recipient Distinguished Service award U.S. Jr. C. of C., 1949; Fla. Man of Yr. in Agr. Progressive Farmer mag., 1961; Good Govt. award Jr. C. of C., 1961; Allen Morris award most valuable mem. Fla. legislature, 1965; St. Petersburg Times award for most outstanding senator, 1965. Mem. Fla. (dir. 1956—, pres. 1970-71, chmn. roads and bridges com. 1953-54, finance com. 1954-55, new bldg. com. 1955-56), Bradenton (dir.), Bradenton Jr. (past v.p.), Manatee County (pres. 1968) chambers of commerce, Com. of 100 (vice chmn.), Fla. State Fair Assn. (dir.), Future Farmers, Fla. Hort. Soc. (pres. 1967-68), Fla. Fruit and Vegetable Assn. (dir. 1968), N.A.M. (dir. 1971-73). Baptist (deacon, tchr. Sunday sch.). Kiwanian (past pres. Bradenton). Home: 3009 Riverview Blvd W Bradenton FL 33505 Office: 9th St and 13th Av W Brandenton FL 33505

PRICE, EUGENIA, author; b. Charleston, W.Va., June 22, 1916; d. Walter Wesley and Ann (Davidson) Price; student Ohio U., 1933-35, Northwestern U., 1935-38, D.Litt. (hon.), Alderson-Broaddus Coll., 1967. Scriptwriter NBC, Chgo., 1939-41, CBS, Chgo., 1942-44; owner Eugenia Price Prodns., Chgo., 1944-49; writer, dir. radio drama Unshackled Chgo., 1950-56; cons., speaker radio and TV workshops. Eugenia Price collection formed in her honor Mugar Library, Boston U., 1967. Mem. Coastal Ga. Hist. Soc. Author: Discoveries, 1953; The Burden is Light, 1954; Early Will I Seek Thee, 1956; Woman to Woman, 1958; Beloved World, 1961; The Beloved Invader, 1965; The Wider Place, 1966; Make Love Your Aim, 1967; Just As I Am, 1968; New Moon Rising, 1969; Lighthouse, 1971; many others. Home: Frederica Saint Simons Island GA 31522

PRICE, GEORGE RAYMOND, JR., architect; b. Greenwood, S.C., Nov. 30, 1925; s. George Raymond and Edyth Marion (Prince) P.; Student Whaley Sch. Art, 1945; B.S. in Architecture, Clemson U., 1950; children by previous marriage—James Frank, George Raymond III, Scarlett Marie, Gina Lisa; m. 2d, Jonnie Jo Ann Barton, Nov. 19, 1966; 1 dau., Nicole Renee. Architect J.B. Urquhart, Columbia, S.C., 1950-52, W.S. Stork, Columbia, 1952-54, Lyles, Bissett, Carlisle & Wolff, Columbia, 1954-57, Maynard Pearlstine, Columbia, 1961-63, Reid Hearn & Assos., Columbia, 1962-63; supt. George R. Price, Gen. Contractor, Columbia, 1957-60; asso. Califf, Geiger & Price, Columbia, 1963-65; chief architect Jones & Fellers, Augusta, Ga., 1965-68; owner George R. Price & Assos., Aiken, S.C., also Augusta, 1968—. Partner George R. Price Constrn. Co., Columbia, 1950-62. Mem. dist. com. Boy Scouts Am., 1963; mem. Friends of Library, Aiken, S.C., 1968—, Historic Augusta, Inc., 1970—; bd. dirs., mem. exec. com. Augusta Opera Assn., 1969—; pres. Carolina Opera Guild, 1970-71; treas. Aiken Civic Ballet, 1970-71, bd. dirs., 1971—; founder Greater Aiken Arts Council, 1971, v.p., 1972. Served with inf. AUS, 1944-46; ETO. Decorated Combat Inf. medal, Purple Heart; recipient Scouters award, 1957, Order of Arrow, 1957, Scouting Wood Badge, 1959, Scouters Keys (3). Mem. A.I.A., Constrn. Specifications Inst. (pres. 1971), Guild for Religious Architecture, Internat. Platform Assn., Les Amis DuVin, Columbia Mus. Art, Rose Hill Art Center, Council on Aging. C. of C. Greater Augusta, Alston Wilkes Soc., Richmond County Hist. Soc., V.F.W., D.A.V. Republican. Roman Catholic. K.C. Clubs: Sertoma (charter mem. Aiken, C-back award, Gem award both 1972, life mem.), Aiken Quadrille, Fermata Swim and Tennis (Aiken); Augusta Country, (Augusta); Green Boundary; Lettermens (Clemson U); Sand Hills. Co-inventor brick laying aide. Home: 455 Sumter St Aiken SC 29801 also 107 Macartan St Augusta GA 30902 also 140 Newberry St Aiken SC 29801

PRICE, JAMES LESTER, utility co. exec.; b. Many, La., May 8, 1919; s. Wiley Norman and Maude (Pate) P.; B.S., La. Tech. U., 1940; m. Frances Virginia Bays, Aug. 11, 1940; children—Margaret (Mrs. Sammy Jay Tinsley), James Lester, Susan (Mrs. Herbert Vicory), Donna Rebecca. With Ark. Power & Light Co., Pine Bluff, 1940—, transmission design supr., 1967-71, mgr. transmission and constrn., 1971—. Served with USNR, 1942-46; capt. Res. ret. Registered profl. engr., Ark. Mem. Nat. Soc. Profl. Engrs., I.E.E.E. (sr.). Baptist. Home: 1712 W 37th St Pine Bluff AR 71601 Office: 6th and Pine Sts Pine Bluff AR 71601

PRICE, JAMES TRAVIS, lawyer, city ofcl.; b. Springfield, Tenn., Dec. 20, 1920; s. Belah Edward and Lora Ione (O'Brien) P.; A.A., George Washington U., 1950, LL.B., 1954; m. Martha Lois Driscoll, Jan. 1, 1943; children—Steven O'Brien, Emily Susan, Laura Wiley, Robert Andrew. Clerical worker First Nat. Bank, Clarksville, Tenn., 1939-41; civilian personnel position classifier VA, Washington, 1945-46; classifier Office of Sec. Navy, Washington, 1946; adminstrv. officer Judge Adv. Gen. of Navy, 1946-54; admitted to D.C. bar, Tenn. bar, 1954; since practiced in Springfield; mayor, Springfield, 1959—. Pres. Mid Cumberland Council Govts. and Devel. Dist., 1970; chmn. Mid-Cumberland Emergency Med. Services Adv. Com., 1972-73. Active Boy Scouts Am., United Givers Fund, and others. Bd. dirs. Mid-Cumberland Comprehensive Health Planning Council. Served to 1st lt. M.C., AUS, 1942-45. Named Tenn. Mayor of Yr., Tenn. Municipal League, 1966. Mem. Am., Tenn., Robertson County bar assns., Tenn. Municipal League (bd. dirs. 1965-71, pres. 1966-67), Am. Pub. Power Assn. (legal com.). Methodist (bd. stewards 1957—), Mason (32 deg. Shriner), Lion. Home: 318 Garner St Springfield TN 37172 Office: 121 5th Av W Springfield TN 37172

PRICE, JIMMY RAY, banker; b. Dublin, Tex., Sept. 26, 1937; s. William Paul and Effie (Ovela) P.; B.B.A., Tex. Tech. U., 1963; postgrad. Am. Inst. Banking, 1965, U. Okla., 1970, So. Meth. U. Sch. Banking, 1972-73; m. Judith Rae Dennis, Aug. 24, 1957; children—Amy Gwyn, Elizabeth Ann. With First Nat. Bank, Sweetwater, Tex., 1954-59; with First Nat. Bank, Lubbock 1959—, asst. cashier, 1964-66, asst. v.p., 1966-68, v.p., 1968—. Pres. Lubbock Assn. Credit Mgmt., 1968; instr. Am. Inst. Banking, 1969-72; guest speaker Tex. Tech. U., 1964-73. Vice chmn. comml. div. United Fund, Lubbock, 1968; chmn. bd. dirs. Lubbock Urban Renewal Agy., 1969—. Bd. dirs. YMCA, Lubbock, 1969, Goodwill Industries, 1969. Named Kiwanian of Yr. Lubbock Kiwanis Club, 1964; Top Ranch Boss, YMCA, Lubbock, 1969; recipient Distinguished Service award Lubbock Jr. C. of C., 1969. Mem. C. of C. (chmn. task force 1970), Phi Kappa Phi, Phi Alpha Kappa, Beta Gamma Sigma. Baptist (deacon 1970, chmn. deacons 1972-73). Kiwanian (bd. dirs. 1964-68, pres. 1967). Home: 3501 78th Dr Lubbock TX 79413 Office: P O Box 1241 Lubbock TX 79408

PRICE, JOHN PRESSLEY, pharmacist; b. Louisville, Apr. 17, 1921; s. John Frank and Nannie Lou (Herndon) P.; student U. N.C., 1944-46; B.S., Mercer So. Coll. Pharmacy, 1951; m. Virginia Marie Mason, Aug. 17, 1946; children—Gloria, Jackie, Mason. Owner, Price Pharmacy, Chickamauga, Ga., 1955-64; pres., Price Pharmacy, Inc., Trenton, Ga., 1961—; pres. Price Ringgold Drug, Inc., Ringgold, 1963—; owner Creekland Stock Farm, Chickamauga; dir. Am. Consumers, Inc. supr. Coosa River Soil and Water Conservation Dist. Mem. Walker County (Ga.) Planning Commn., 1968—; mem. City Council, Chickamauga, Ga., 1963-68. Served with USN, 1940-46. Mem. Am., Ga. pharm. assns., Nat. Assn. Retail Druggists, Sigma Nu. Baptist (trustee 1957, chmn. bd. trustees). Address: Route 4 Chickamauga GA 30707

PRICE, J(OHN) WILLIAM, paper co. exec.; b. Quebec, Que., Can., June 23, 1927; s. John Herbert and Lorna (Macdougall) P.; student U. N.B., 1945-47, Bishops U., 1947-48; m. Helen Julia Stevenson, Jan. 15, 1954; children—Diana, John, David. Came to U.S., 1952. Asst. forestry engr. Powell River Paper Co., Vancouver, B.C., Can., 1948-50; adminstrv. asst. Bowaters Nfld. Pulp & Paper Co., 1950-52; serviceman Bowater Paper Co., N.Y.C., 1952, service mgr., 1953-54, salesman, 1954-55, dist. sales mgr., 1956-58, v.p. N. Am. sales, 1959-64; v.p., dir. Perkins Goodwin Co., Inc., N.Y.C., 1964—, chmn. bd., 1970—; dir. Southland Paper Mills, Inc. Clubs: Canadian (N.Y.C.); Winged Foot Golf (Mamaroneek, N.Y.); Preston Trail, Brookhollow (Dallas). Home: 5423 Meaders Lane Dallas TX 75229 Office: 10400 N Central Expressway Dallas TX 75231

PRICE, LARRY EUGENE, educator; b. Little Rock, Aug. 16, 1934; s. Lew J. and Marcia (Stark) P.; A.A., Little Rock Jr. Coll., 1953; B.S.E.E., U. Ark., 1959, M.B.A., 1961, Ph.D. in Finance, 1966; m. Barbara Ann Parke, June 3, 1956; children—Jane Elizabeth, Carol Lynn, Steven Russell. Electronics engr. missile div. Bendix Aviation Corp., Mishawaka, Ind., 1956-58; instr. gen. bus. U. Ark., Fayetteville, 1960-63; asst. prof. sch. bus., Ga. So. Coll., Statesboro, 1963-67, asso. prof., 1968-71, prof., also chmn. finance and law dept., 1971—. Mem. Regional Export Expansion Council, 1967—. Mem. Am., So. econ. assns., Am., So. finance assns., Am. Assn. U. Profs., Am. Radio Relay League (dir. 1972—, dir. found. 1973—), Beta Gamma Sigma, Omicron Delta Epsilon. Episcopalian. Club: Forest Heights Country. Home: 222 S Edgewood Dr Statesboro GA 30458

PRICE, LEE GEORGE, govt. ofcl.; b. Washington, Sept. 1, 1940; s. David George and Katharine (Blake) P.; student Washington and Lee U., 1959-60; A.A., George Washington U., 1961, A.B. in Govt., 1963; postgrad. Am. U., 1963-65; m. Janice Anne Kennard, Oct. 26, 1961; 1 dau., Deborah Lee. Clk. typist, student asst. various fed. govt. agys., Washington, 1959-63; adminstrv. asst. First Nat. Bank, Washington, 1964-66; mgmt. intern Internal Revenue Service, Washington, 1966; program analyst Office Comptroller of the Navy, Washington, 1967—. Mem. Am. Soc. Mil. Comptrollers, Am. Soc. Pub. Adminstrn., Fed. Govt. Accountants Assn. Methodist (chmn. finance com.). Home: 2315 Ashboro Dr Chevy Chase MD 20015 Office: The Pentagon Washington DC 20350

PRICE, MADISON RANKIN, dentist; b. Aiken, S.C., Dec. 29, 1933; s. Bruce Hays and Eva (Rankin) P.; B.A., U. Richmond, 1955; D.D.S., Med. Coll. Va., 1959; m. Dorothy Lee Stiff, Aug. 25, 1956; children—Robert Bruce, Thomas Madison, Leslie Britton. Research fellow Nat. Inst. Health, Richmond, Va., 1957-58; analytical chemist Naval Weapons Sta., Yorktown, Va., 1955-56; practice dentistry, Newport News, Va., 1961—. Asst. clin. prof. pedodontics Va. Commonwealth U.-Med. Coll. Va. Sch. Dentistry, Richmond, 1970—. Served to capt. Dental Corps, USAF, 1959-61. Fellow Acad. Gen. Dentistry; mem. Am., Va. State (exec. council 1971—), Peninsula (pres. 1967-68) dental assns., Va. Acad. Gen. Dentistry (pres. 1973-74), Am. Soc. Dentistry for Children (exec. council Va. chpt. 1968—, pres. Va. chpt. 1972-73), Fedn. Dentaire Internationale, Omicron Kappa Upsilon, Sigma Zeta, Delta Sigma Delta, Sigma Phi Epsilon. Baptist (deacon). Home: 50 Settlers Rd Newport News VA 23606 Office: 367 Denbigh Blvd Newport News VA 23602

PRICE, MARK A., dentist; b. Bernice, La., Nov. 13, 1924; s. Mark A., Jr. and Mary (Moore) P.; student La. Tech. U., 1948; D.D.S., Emory U., 1956; m. Margie Nell Allen, June 7, 1946; children—Mary, John Marcus. Practice dentistry, specializing in orthodontics, Monroe, La., 1956—. Served with USNR, 1943-46. Mem. Am. Assn. Orthodontists, Southwestern Soc. Orthodontists (sec.-treas., pres. elect), Am. (del.), La. (1st v.p., speaker ho. of dels.), Fifth Dist. (past pres.) dental assns. Rotarian. Home: 3801 Deborah Dr Monroe LA 71201 Office: 1212 Stubbs Av Monroe LA 71201

PRICE, ORVILLE OLIVER, math. statistician; b.Greenbrier, Ark., Apr. 7, 1907; s. William and Emma (Webb) P.; B.S., State Coll. Ark., 1931; postgrad Am. U., 1948-51; m. Alice Elizabeth Love, Dec. 17, 1945; children—Barbara (Mrs. John R. Bridgeman), Orville O. Math instr., dean of boys Idabel (Okla.) High Sch., 1931-35; statistician U.S. VA, Washington, 1935-62; chief sampling staff Internal Revenue Service, U.S. Treasury Dept., 1962-67, cons. Office of Compliance, 1968-69; pvt. cons. math. statistics, 1969—. Served with AUS, 1943-44. Mem. Am. Statis. Assn., Am. Soc. Quality Control. Contbr. articles to profl. jours. Address: 2270 NW 21st Av Gainesville FL 32605

PRICE, REGINALD CARRIER, engr.-econ.; b. Rio, Wis., May 17, 1911; s. Charles Nicholas and Emily Augusta (Carrier) P.; B.S. in C.E., U. Wis., 1935, C.E., 1946; student U. Minn., 1936; M.A., Am. U., Washington, 1943; student Columbia, 1945; m. Esther Louise King, July 14, 1937; children—Lee Nicholas, Margaret Louise, Laurie Jean. Instrumentman, Greendale project Resettlement Adminstrn., 1935-36; dist. san. engr. Wis. State Bd. Health, 1936-39; asst. survey analyst flood control Dept. Agr., 1939-41; hydraulic engr. Nat. Resources Planning Bd., 1941-43; econ. analyst Fed. Power Commn., 1943; asst. prof. coll. engring. N.Y. U., 1943-46; engring. economist bur. reclamation Dept. Interior, 1946-47, spl. asst., asst. sec. Dept. Interior, 1947-50, dir. Div. Water and Power, 1950-53; sr. officer Bur. Flood Control and Water Resources Devel., UN Econ. Commn. Asia and Far East, Thailand, 1954-57; deputy asst., dir. program and econ. policy ICA, Korea, 1957-60; loan officer Devel. Loan Fund, Washington, 1960-61; deputy dir. Cal. Dept. Water Resources, 1961-66; asst. commr. planning Fed. Quality Adminstrn., Washington, 1967-68; water resources adviser Mekong Basin Plan Report, Bangkok, Thailand, 1968-72; water resources adviser, water planning div. Environmental Protection Agy., Washington, 1972—;

U.S. observer inter-Am. conf. on conservation renewable natural resources, Denver, 1948; U.S. del. UN sci. conf. on conservation, utilization resources, Lake Success, N.Y., 1949; U.S. del. UN Conf. Water Resources Devel., 1957, 66, 68. Mem. Am. Friends Service Com., 1950—; asst. clk. Pacific Yearly Meeting (Friends), 1966-67. Bd. dirs. Potomac Coop. Fedn., Washington, 1948-52, pres., 1949-51; bd. trustees United Community Services, Washington, 1952-54. Recipient Dir.'s award Cal. Dept. Water Resources, 1966. Licensed profl. engr., Wis. Mem. Am. Soc. C.E., Am. Econ. Assn., Nat. Planning Assn., World Affairs Council (Sacramento pres. 1965-66), UN Assn. (sacramento v.p. 1965-66), N.Y. Acad. Sci., Soc. Internat. Devel., Tau Beta Pi, Alpha Tau Sigma, Chi Epsilon. Club: Royal Bangkok Sports. Co-author: Proposed Practices for Economic Analysis of River Basin Projects, 1950; Plan for Development, Sacramento-San Joaquin Delta, 1965; Report on Indicative Basin Plan for Lower Mekong River, 1970. Contbr. articles profl. publs. Home: 7702 Holiday Terrace Bethesda MD 20034

PRICE, ROBERT CARMEL, cons. engrs.; b. Hawkins County, Tenn., Dec. 17, 1901; s. Clyde A. and Annie Melinda (Heck) P.; student Ga. Inst. Tech., 1931-33; grad. civil engring. Internat. Corr. Schs., 1936; m. Selma Warren, May 25, 1932 (dec.); 1 dau., Janet (Mrs. Lance Folsom); m. 2d, Christine Gamble, Aug. 17, 1968. Jr. engr. mapping div. U.S. Geol. Service, Copper Hill, Tenn., 1933-34; asst. engr. for planning TVA, Murphy, N.C., 1934-36; hydraulic engr. P.R. Reconstrn. Adminstrn., Adjuntas, P.R., 1936-40; resident constrn. engr. Harza Engring. Co., Moncks Corner, S.C., 1940-42; hydraulic engr. Fed. Power Commn., Atlanta, 1943-45, head planning engr. Water Resources Authority, San Juan, P.R., 1945-48, engr.-in-charge regional office, Atlanta, 1948-51, regional engr., 1951-71; Mem. Cons. Cons. engr., Atlanta, 1971—. bd. UN, 1955-71, U.S. Congree on Large Dams, 1958—. Registered profl. engr., Ga. Fellow Am. Soc. C. Presbyn. Mason. Home: 2887 Osborne Rd NE Atlanta GA 30319

PRICE, ROBERT CARMEL, cons. engr.; b. Hawkins County, Tenn., Dec. 17, 1901; s. Clyde A. and Annie Melinda (Heck) P.; student Ga. Inst. Tech., 1931-33; grad. civil engring. Internat. Corr. Schs., 1936; m. Selma Warren, May 25, 1932 (dec.); 1 dau., Janet (Mrs. Lance Folsom); m. 2d, Christine Gamble, Aug. 17, 1968. Jr. engr. mapping div. U.S. Geol. Service, Copper Hill, Tenn., 1933-34; asst. engr. for planning TVA, Murphy, N.C., 1934-36; hydraulic engr. P.R. Reconstrn. Adminstrn., Adjuntas, P.R., 1936-40; resident constrn. engr. Harza Engring. Co., Moncks Corner, S.C., 1940-42; hydraulic engr. Fed. Power Commn., Atlanta, 1943-45, head planning engr. Water Resources Authority, San Juan, P.R., 1945-48, engr.-in-charge regional office, Atlanta, 1948-51, regional engr., 1951-71; cons. engr., Atlanta, 1971—. Mem. cons. bd. UN, 1955-71, U.S. Congress on Large Dams, 1958—. Registered profl. engr., Ga. Fellow Am. Soc. C.E. Presbyn. Mason. Home: 2887 Osborne Rd NE Atlanta GA 30319

PRICE, ROBERT CARROLL, found. exec.; b. Alderson, W.Va., Aug. 1, 1927; s. Edgar Silas and Mabel Gladys (Wilson) P.; B.A., W.Va. U., 1950; M.A., U. Richmond, 1951; certificate speech therapy U. Va., 1952; certificate reading Weiss Reading Inst., 1954; m. Betty Jean Griesenauer, June 13, 1954; children—Paul Edgar, Blake William. Speech therapist Richmond (Va.) pub. schs., 1950-52; dir. Richmond Speech and Hearing Center, 1952-54; owner Indsl. Psychol. Cons., 1952-54; acting exec. dir. div. field services, dir. speech and hearing Va. Soc. Crippled Children and Adults, Roanoke, 1954-60, interim exec. dir., 1960-61, exec. dir., 1961-64; owner Profl. Services, Roanoke, 1964—; exec. v.p. Reading Reform Found., Roanoke, 1967—. Mem. Pres.'s Com. on Employment of Handicapped, 1961-63. Served with USNR, 1945-46. Recipient nat. award for contbns. to Am. edn., S.A.R., 1966. Mem. Internat. Reading Assn., Va. Speech and Hearing Assn. (charter), Council for Basic Edn., Roanoke C. of C. (mem. edn. com. 1961-62). Kiwanian (local pres. 1970-71). Club: Botetourt Country (Fincastle, Va.). Author publs. in field. Home: 542 Elden Av Roanoke VA 24019 Office: 5720 Williamson Rd Roanoke VA 24012

PRICE, ROBERT DALE, congressman; b. Reading, Kan., Sept, 7, 1927; s. Ben F. and Gladys (Watson) P.; B.S., Okla. State U., 1951; m. Martha Ann White, Dec. 29, 1951; children—Robert Grant, Benjamin Carl, Janice Ann. Rancher, Pampa, Tex., 1955-66; mem. 90th-92d congresses from the 18th Tex. Dist., mem. 93d congress from 13th Tex. Dist.; mem. House Agrl. Com., Armed Services Com. Mem. bd. dirs. devel. bd. Wayland Bapt. Coll., Plainview, Tex. Served to 1st lt. USAF, 1951-55. Decorated Air medal. Mem. Top O'Texas Rodeo Assn. (hon., dir.), West Tex. C. of C., USAF Assn., Tex. and Southwestern Cattle Raisers Assn., Panhandle Producers and Royalty Owners Assn., Congl. Underwater Explorers Club, Okla. State U. Alumni Assn., V.F.W., Am. Legion, Sigma Alpha Epsilon. Republican. Baptist. Mason, Kiwanian (past pres. chpt.). Club: 90th (past pres.). Home: 2135 Charles St Pampa TX 79065 Office: Cannon Office Bldg Washington DC 20510

PRICE, ROBERT EBEN, lawyer; b. Waco, Tex., Jan. 13, 1931; s. Robert Eben and Mary Hamilton (Barnett) P.; B.A., So. Meth. U., 1952, J.D., 1954, LL.M., 1972; m. Ann Hodges, June 4, 1954; children—Eben, Mary, Ann, Emily. Admitted to Tex. bar, 1954; Howell, Johnson, Mizell, Taylor, Price & Corrigan, Dallas. Lectr. law So. Methodist U., Dallas, 1973—. Trustee St. Michael and All Angels Found. Served with Judge Adv. Gen. Corps, USAF, 1954-56; now lt. col. Res. Mem. Phi Alpha Delta, Phi Eta Sigma, Phi Delta Theta. Episcopalian. Home: 4300 Arcady Av Dallas TX 75205 Office: 2700 Republic Bank Tower Dallas TX 75201

PRICE, WALTER LEE, lawyer; b. Johnson City, Tenn., Mar. 14, 1914; s. Samuel Walter and Nannie Lee (Ratclift) P.; student Milligan Coll., 1931-33; J.D., U. Tenn., 1936; m. Esda Masters, Sept. 25, 1939. Admitted to Tenn. bar, 1936; partner Price & Price, Johnson City, 1936-40; spl. agt. FBI, Washington, 1940-45; partner Price & Price, Johnson City, 1945-59, Bryant, Price, Brandt & Jordan, Johnson City, 1959—; sec., dir. Johnson City Foundry and Machine Works, Inc., 1968—. Mem. Tenn. Higher Edn. Commn., 1973—. City atty., Johnson City, 1948-52, law dir., 1956-66. Bd. dirs. People-to-People of Johnson City, Tenn., Inc.; pres., bd. dirs. Christian Home for Aged, Inc., Johnson City, 1963-72. Mem. Am., Washington County (pres. 1948-49) bar assns., Bar Assn. Tenn., Assn. Trial Lawyers Am., Tenn. Trial Lawyers Assn., Law-Sci. Acad. Am., Am. Arbitration Assn., Kappa Sigma. Fellow Am. Coll. Probate Counsel. Republican. Mem. Christian Ch. (chmn. bd. elders). Elk, Rotarian (pres. 1973-74). Home: 2017 Sherwood Dr Johnson City TN 37601 Office: 200 W Fairview Av Johnson City TN 37601

PRICE, WILLIAM ERNEST, ret. educator; b. Macon, Ga., Oct. 31, 1903; s. David and Emma (Bowden) P.; A.B., Morris Coll., 1926; postgrad. Dickinson Law Sch., 1927-29, Atlanta Sch. Social Work, 1935-36, Ohio State U., 1950-56; M.A., Hampton Inst., 1944; Pd.D., Morris Coll., Sumter, S.C., 1965; m. Ada Lee Olive, Aug. 22, 1935. Prin., Cordele (Ga.) Bd. Edn., 1930-35, Jefferson County, Bartow, Ga., 1935-38, Dawson, Ga., 1938-40, Louisville (Ga.) Acad. Sch., 1940-72. Vis. prof. social studies Savannah State Coll., summer sch., 1946-49. City chmn. A.R.C., polio, cancer, and heart funds; chmn. survey com. on bldg. facilities Jefferson County Sch. System; chmn. County Clean Up Campaign. Mem. exec. com. Community Welfare; bd. dirs. Interracial Devel. Corp.; chmn. exec. com. Community Beautification Program, 1950-55; city chmn. Pub. Relations Program; lt. col., a.d.c. on Ga. gov.'s staff. Mem. Nat. Tchrs. Assn., Jefferson County Prins. Council (pres.), Ga. (trustee, dir., past regional dir.), Jefferson County (chmn. exec. com.) tchrs. and edn. assns., Louisville C. of C. (exec. bd.). Baptist (chmn. bldg. program, chmn. bd. deacons). Mason (33 deg., chmn. bldg. fund). Club: Lakeview Country (chmn. bldg. fund). Home: 3155 Imperial Dr Macon GA 31201 Office: Jefferson County High Sch PO Box 128 Louisville GA 30434

PRICKETT, JOHN SAMUEL, JR., ret. state ofcl.; b. nr. Bowdon, Ga., Jan. 26, 1910; s. John Sanford and Iula Permela (Hearn) P.; B.S., U. Ga., 1938, M.S., 1940; postgrad. N.Y. U., 1950; m. Burnell Faye Wright, June 20, 1931; children—John Sanford III, Betty Carole (Mrs. Robert J. Taggart), Lanny Asbury, Rebecca Nan (Mrs. Marshall Miller). Tchr., prin. Ga. schs., 1931-42; counselor vocational rehab. Ga. Dept. Edn., Atlanta, 1942-44, dist. supr., 1944-51, asst. dir., 1951-64, dir., 1964-67, asst. state supt. schs., 1967-72. Pres., State Dept. Edn. Credit Union, 1961-64; mem. Joint Commn. on Correctional Manpower and Tng., 1967; adv. bd. Mental Retardation Inst., U. N.C., Butner, 1967—; mem. adv. com. to rehab. counseling program Fla. State U., 1967-72, U. Ga., 1970-72; mem. Manpower Adv. Council Coastal Plains Area, 1968. Pres., Ga. Tb Assn., 1964-65, mem. bd., 1957-74; mem. adult vocational adv. bd. United Cerebral Assn., N.Y., 1952-63; mem. bd. Goodwill Industries Atlanta, Inc., 1968—, co-chmn. Gov.'s Com. for Arthritis, 1969-70. Trustee Atlanta Community Services for the Blind, 1967-73. Recipient Distinguished Service award Ga. Rehab. Assn., 1961. Mem. Nat. (nat. membership chmn. 1966-67, mem. bd. 1967—, pres. 1973-74), Ga. (pres. 1959-60) rehab. assns., U. Ga. Alumni Assn. (pres. DeKalb County chpt. 1962), Kappa Phi Kappa. Methodist (chmn. ofcl. bd. 1962-64). Home: 1162 Berkeley Rd Avondale Estates GA 30002

PRIDDY, ASHLEY HORNE, oil and gas co. exec.; b. Wichita Falls, Tex., Apr. 1, 1922; s. Walter Mason and Swannanoa (Horne) P.; student Rice U., 1939-41; B.B.A., U. Tex., 1949, B.S. in Petroleum Engring., 1949; m. Kathryn Amsler, Dec. 30, 1947; children—Hervey, Betty, Ann. With Sabine Royalty Corp., Dallas, 1949—, petroleum engr., 1949-55, v.p., 1958-68, pres., chief exec. officer, 1968—. Mem. council Town of Highland Park, (Tex.), 1966-70; mayor, Highland Park, 1970—. Bd. trustees Hockaday Sch., Dallas, Engring. Sch. Found. U. Tex. Served to lt. USNR, 1943-46; PTO. Mem. Beta Theta Pi, Tau Beta Pi, Pi Tau Sigma. Clubs: Dallas Petroleum; Dallas Country, Brook Hollow Golf (Dallas). Home: 4222 Arcady Av Dallas TX 75205 Office: Mercantile Bank Bldg Dallas TX 75201

PRIEBE, LOUIS VICTOR, assn. exec.; b. Enid, Okla., Nov. 11, 1941; s. Victor Hugo and Helen (Morell) P.; B.A. in Journalism, U. Okla., 1964; m. Florence Ann McClain, June 25, 1966. Pub. relations asst. Atlanta Gas & Light Co., 1966-68; with Ins. Information Inst., 1968-72, mgr. New Orleans dist., 1968-70, asst. mgr. relations, Washington, 1970-72; Washington pub. relations rep. Carl Byoir & Assos., 1972-74; dir. pub. relations dept. Am. Automobile Assn., Falls Church, Va., 1974—. Mem. La. Gov.'s Hurricane Task Force, 1970; arrangements chmn. 10th Ann. Dixie Pub. Relations Conf., 1967. Served to lt. AUS, 1964-66. Recipient Spl. Resolution Appreciation New Orleans Ins. Exchange, 1971. Mem. U.S. Senate Press Secs. Assns., Pub. Relations Soc. Am. (asso., Silver Anvil award 1969, dir.), Tex., Okla. State socs. Washington, Govt. Information Orgn., Smithsonian Assos., Beta Theta Pi. Presbyn. Clubs: Capitol Hill, Country of Fairfax (Va.); Nat. Press. Washington editor Pub. Relations News. Home: 5946 Queenston St Springfield VA 22152 Office: 8111 Gatehouse Rd Falls Church VA 22042

PRIESMEYER, ANDREW FRED, banker; b. Taylor, Tex., June 25, 1900; s. Henry and Henrietta (Tieman) P.; student Nixon Clay Coll., 1920; m. Winnette A. Abbott, Mar. 16, 1940. Employed in grocery bus., 1918-20, 21-23; with First Taylor Nat. Bank (Tex.), 1923—, sr. v.p., 1970—. Mem. Sons of Harman, C. of C. Lutheran. Mason. Club: Taylor Country (sec. 1934-37). Home: 1720 McLain St Taylor TX 76574 Office: PO Box 1009 Taylor TX 76574

PRIESTER, FRANCIS ALLEN, elec. engr.; b. Augusta, Ga., July 6, 1924; s. Wyman Jesse and Bessie Bell (Corley) P.; Jr. Coll. certificate, Middle Ga. Coll., 1947; B.E.E., Ga. Inst. Tech., 1949; m. Hazel Maxine Linnville, Apr. 22, 1950; children—Allen, Judy. Jr. engr. Gulf Power Co., Pensacola, Fla., 1949-51; elec. engr. U.S. Navy Mine Def. Lab., Panama City, Fla., 1951-60; elec. engr. inertial guidance and control lab. U.S. Army Missile Command, Redstone Arsenal, Ala., 1960-70, br. chief land combat maintenance engring. div., 1970—. Served with USNR, 1943-46. Registered profl. engr., Ala. Mem. Nat. Soc. Profl. Engrs., I.E.E.E. (past chmn. Huntsville chpt.), Am. Ordnance Assn., Assn. U.S. Army. Presbyn. (elder). Home: 3410 Euclid Circle Huntsville AL 35810 Office: AMSMI-NLP Redstone Arsenal AL 35809

PRIGMORE, CHARLES SAMUEL, educator; b. Lodge, Tenn., Mar. 21, 1919; s. Charles H. and Mary Lou (Raulston) P.; A.B., U. Chattanooga, 1939; M.S., U. Wis., 1947, Ph.D., 1961; m. Shirley Melaine Buuck, June 7, 1947; 1 son, Philip Brand. Social caseworker Children's Service Soc., Milw., 1947-48; social worker Wis. Sch. for Boys, Waukesha, 1948-51; supr. tng. Wis. Bur. Probation and Parole, Madison, 1951-56; supt. Tenn. Vocational Tng. Sch. for Boys, Nashville, 1956-59; asso. prof. La. State U., 1959-64; ednl. cons. Council Social Work Edn., N.Y., 1962-64; exec. dir. Joint Commn. Correctional Manpower & Tng., Washington, 1964-67; prof. Sch. Social Work, U. Ala., 1967—, chmn. com. on Korean relationships; Fulbright lectr., Iran, 1972-73; part-time cons. with four research projects, 1959-65; part-time tchr. U. Md., 1965-67; frequent lectr. and workshop leader. Chmn. Ala. Citizens Environmental Action, 1971-72, Tuscaloosa Council Environmental Quality, 1970-72. Served to 2d lt. USAAF, 1940-45. Decorated Air medal with oak leaf cluster. Recipient Conservation award Woodmen of the World, 1971. Mem. Acad. Certified Social Workers, Am. Correctional Assn., Am. Assn. U. Profs., Am. Soc. Criminology, Am. Sociol. Assn., Council Social Work Edn., Nat. Assn. Social Workers, Nat. Council Crime and Delinquency, Royal Soc. Health, Tuscaloosa C. of C., Tuscaloosa Civitan Club, Alpha Kappa Delta, Beta Beta Beta. Author: Textbook on Social Problems, 1971. Editor 2 books. Contbr. articles in field to profl. jours. Home: Box 1935 University AL 35486

PRIM, WILLIS GERALD, banker; b. Ridgeway, Tex., May 6, 1905; s. George Stevenson and Verna Mae (Stewart) P.; student E.Tex. State Coll., Commerce, 1921-23; m. Doris Robinson, Dec. 16, 1944; children—Mary Kathrine (Mrs. P. F. Bradley), Alice (Mrs. Don W. Bradley), Ruth Ann (Mrs. Charles Britton). With Ridgeway State Bank, 1924-27; dir., chief exec. officer Sulphur Springs (Tex.) State Bank, 1927—; dir. Sulphur Springs Loan & Bldg. Assn. Treas., Hopkins County Crippled Childrens Assn., Hopkins County Rural Progress Club. Presbyn. (elder). K.P., Rotarian. Club: Sulphur Springs Country (dir., past pres.). Home: 505 Jefferson St Sulphur Springs TX 75482 Office: 100 W Jefferson St Sulphur Springs TX 75482

PRINCE, JAMES REX, optometrist; b. Canton, O., Dec. 8, 1929; s. John Ashford and Glenna (Bowman) P.; A.B., Tufts U., 1952; O.D. cum laude, Mass. Coll. Optometry, 1957; m. Sylvia Mary Churchill, Sept. 15, 1956; children—John C., Susan M., Marjorie A., Mary E., Thomas E. Asso. mem. firm M.W. Reithmiller, Richmond, Va., 1957-61; sole practice optometry, Kilmarnock, Va., 1961—; clin. examiner Va. Optometric Center, Richmond, 1962—; mem. Va. Bd. Examiners Optometry, 1973—. Institutional rep. troop Robert E. Lee council Boy Scouts Am., 1964-67. Bd. dirs. Kilmarnock Pub. Library, 1967-70; trustee Christ Ch. Found., Irvington, Va., 1972—. Served to lt. (j.g.) USNR, 1952-54; Europe. Fellow Am. Acad. Optometry (lectr. 1968-70), Va. Acad. Optometry; mem. Va. Optometric Assn. (pres. 1970-71), So. Council Optometry (pres.). Episcopalian. Mason, Rotarian. Club: Indian Creek Y & C (Brydton, Va.). Home: Walnut Rd Kilmarnock VA 22482 Office: Gravitt Med Center Kilmarnock VA 22482

PRINCE, JULIAN DAY, supt. schs.; b. Greenwood, Miss., Mar. 5, 1927; s. Julian Day and Lois (Jones) P.; B.S., Millsaps Coll., 1949; M.Ed., Emory U., 1953; m. LaVerne Carnell Baker, Jan. 22, 1949; children—Joanne, Julian, John, David. Tchr., McComb (Miss.) High Sch., 1949-52, prin. 1953-59; asst. supt. McComb Pub. Schs., 1959-60, supt., 1965—; supt. Corinth (Miss.) Pub. Schs., 1960-65; pres. Edn. Systems Devel. Corp., 1968—; mgr. manpower div. Miss. Research and Devel. Corp., 1969-70. Scoutmaster, Yocona Area council Boy Scouts Am., 1963-67; chmn. Community Fund Drive, Corinth, 1963-64, McComb, 1971-73; chmn. Miss. Council Pub. Sch. Systems, 1973; mem. Miss. Commn. on Hosp. Care, 1963—. Served with AUS, 1945-47; PTO. Ford Found. fellow, 1952-53. Mem. Am., Miss. assns. sch. adminstrs., Miss. Edn. Assn., Millsaps Coll. Alumni Assn. (dir. 1961—), Lambda Chi Alhpa. Methodist (ch. steward 1957—). Lion. Home: 647 Louisiana Av McComb MS 39648

PRINE, GORDON MADISON, agronomist; b. Valdosta, Ga., Feb. 16, 1928; s. Surry G. and Mattie Lou (Cothron) P.; student S. Ga. Coll., 1945-46, Abraham Baldwin Agrl. Coll., 1950; B.S., U. Ga., 1952, M.S., 1954; Ph.D., Ohio State U., 1957; m. Mary Alzenia Wells, Apr. 23, 1957; children—Jeffrey Gordon, Leslie Lynn. Asst. agronomist Ga. Coastal Plain Expt. Sta., Tifton, 1954-55; asst. agronomist Fla. Agrl. Expt. Sta., Gainesville, 1958-65, asso. agronomist, 1965—. Vis. scientist Internat. Maize and Wheat Improvement Center, El Batan, Mexico, 1972; cons. maize and sorghum prodn. problems Guyana and El Salvador. Served with USAF, 1946-49. Mem. Am. Soc. Agronomy, Crop Sci. Soc. Am., Assn. So. Agrl. Workers, Soil and Crop Sci. Soc. Fla., Sigma Xi, Gamma Sigma Delta, Phi Kappa Phi. Democrat. Baptist. Contbr. articles to profl. jours. Home: 923 NW 36th Dr Gainesville FL 32605 Office: 314 Newell Hall U Fla Gainesville FL 32611

PRINGLE, BURT EVINS, graphic artist; b. Savannah, Ga., Feb. 11, 1929; s. Coleman M. and Clara (Brown) P.; student Chatham Acad., 1943; m. Ursula Renate Häusermann, Sept. 7, 1954; children—Burt E. Jr., Jorg F. Display and advt. mgr. Lourie's, Columbia, S.C., 1950-52; display mgr. Haltwanger's, Columbia, 1950-52; display dir. Burke's, Nashville, 1955-56; display and advt. dir. Rosenblum's, Jacksonville, Fla., 1956—; designer several postage stamps, 1966—. Artist, custodian Gator Bowl Hall Fame, Jacksonville, 1962—. Served with AUS, 1952-55. Recipient 15 honorariums philatelic designs, UN, 1966—, 2 Gold medals, 1 Bronze medal Display World Internat., 1957, 58, 2d place award Soc. De L'Exposition Universelle, World's Fair, Brussels, Belgium, 1958. Mem. Jacksonville C. of C. (pres. retail display, advt. com. 1958, 59), Jacksonville Art Dirs. Club (past pres.), Am. Fedn. Arts, St. Augustine Art Assn., Jacksonville Art Mus. One man show philatelic design Norton Gallery, West Palm Beach, Fla., 1968; designer Migratory Bird Treaty commemorative stamp, 1966; V.I. 50th Anniversary air mail post card, 1967, and others. Home: 7028 Altama Rd Jacksonville FL 32216 Office: 204 W Adams St Jacksonville FL 32202

PRITCHARD, JOHN HAYES, architect; b. Indpls., May 5, 1905; s. John M. and Leona Dell (Hayes) P.; B.S. in Architecture, Ga. Sch. Tech., 1930; m. Charlie Lowe, June 10, 1930; 1 son, John Hayes. Archtl. designer, draftsman, Beaumont, Tex., 1928-34; designer rural farm communities U.S. Govt., Austin, 1934-36; asso. bd. govs. Fed. Res. System, Washington, 1937; chief architect Nat. Youth Adminstrn., Washington, 1938-40, so. regional dir., Memphis, 1940-42; pvt. practice architecture, Tunica, Miss., 1946—; asso. Pritchard & Nickles, architects and engrs., Tunica, 1951—. Mem. archtl. adv. council Miss. State U. Alderman, Town Bd., Tunica, Miss. Exec. com. Boy Scouts Am., 1947—, chmn. dist. com., 1948-59, mem. nat. council 1952—, mem. nominating com. Delta Area council Silver Beaver award, 1957. Served as maj., AUS, 1943-46. Decorated Bronze Star medal. Registered architect Miss., Tenn., Tex., Ark. Fellow A.I.A. (pres. Miss. chpt. 1950-51, mem. nominating com.; mem. nat. jud. bd., nat. inquiry com.; nat. bd. examiners 1955-56; regional dir. Gulf States region; Miss. chmn. legislative com. 1963); mem. Miss. Archtl. Assn., Soc. Friends Tewkesbury Abbey (life), Soc. Archtl. Historians (Delta council coms., health com. ednl. policy com.) North Miss., Miss. archeol. assns., V.F.W., 40 and 8, Am. Legion, Sigma Phi Epsilon. Episcopalian (vestryman, sr. warden). Rotarian (pres. 1950-51). Address: PO Box 236 Tunica MS 38676

PRITCHETT, JOHN RAY, grain and milling co. exec.; b. Coalgate, Okla., Feb. 7, 1910; s. B. Frank and Cora Lela (Brandon) P.; student Okla. Bapt. U., 1930-31, East Central State U., 1931; m. Lucile Coffey, Apr. 16, 1933 (dec. Oct. 1969); children—Linda Lucile (Mrs. Dane Everton), Pricilla Ray (Mrs. Jess Wayne Sammann). Div. head salesman H. J. Heinz Co., 1933-45; gen. sales mgr. Harvest Queen Mill, 1945-50; pres., chmn. bd. N.M. Mill and Elevator Co., Clovis, 1950—; pres. Golden West Seed Co., 1957—. City councilman, Plainview, Tex., 1948—. Trustee High Plains Research Found. Mem. N.M. (past pres., dir.), So. (pres. 1970; mem. exec. com. 1973) seedmens assns., C. of C. (pres. 1947). Baptist. Home: 1405 W 11th St Plainview TX 79072 Office: 1000 Wheeler St Texico NM 88101 also 301 Curry St Clovis NM 88135

PRIVETT, REX, state govt. ofcl.; rancher; b. Maramec, Okla., May 28, 1924; s. Arnold Loyde and Muriel (Hauser) P.; B.A., Okla. State U., 1949; m. Patricia Ann Nichols, Aug. 8, 1947 children—Deborah Ann (Mrs. James R. Fletcher), Rex Nichols, Patricia Michelle. Rancher, Maramec, Okla., 1949—; mem. Okla. Ho. of Reps., 1957—, vice chmn. State Personnel Com., 1959-61, chmn. County, State and Fed. Govt. Com., 1961-63, speaker pro tempore, 1963-67, speaker Ho. Reps., 1967-73; corp. commr. State of Oka., 1973—. Mem. exec. com. Nat. Conf. State Legislative Leaders, 1969—; mem. exec. com. Council State Govt., 1969—, v.p., 1970; mem. exec. com. Nat. Legislative Council, 1969—, So. Conf. Council State Govts., 1969—. Committeeman Boy Scouts Am., 1965—, council mem. at large Will Rogers Council, 1967—; hon. mem. Pawnee Indian Tribe, 1967—. Mem. bd. dirs. Bi-State Mental Health Found. Mem. Ambassadors Corps. Served with AUS, 1943-46; PTO. Recipient Gold Watch, Pawnee C. of C., 1967. Mem. Pawnee County Cattlemen's Assn. (pres. 1953-57), Kappa Sigma (treas. 1946-49). Democrat. Methodist (chmn. ofcl. bd. 1954-55; lay speaker 1955—). Home: Route 1 Maramec OK 74045 Office: Speaker's Office Okla State Capitol Oklahoma City OK 73105

PROCTOR, FRANK DANA, army officer; b. Galveston, Tex., Feb. 18, 1927; s. William James and Bertha Susana (Graham) P.; B.B.A. cum laude, U. Houston, 1959; M.Pub. Adminstrn., Am. U., 1969; m. Helen Ruth McCartney Holt White, Mar. 30, 1946; children—Gary Dana, Holly Lynn, Dana Joy. Joined U.S. Army as pvt., 1945, advanced through grades to col., 1968; instr. Rice U., Houston, 1957-61; adviser Guatemala Mil. Acad., 1962-65; bn. comdr. U.S. Army, Korea, 1966-67; dir. command and control Automatic Data Processing, Hdqrs. Dept. Army, Washington, 1969—. Decorated Bronze Star medal. Joint Service Commendation medal, Army Commendation medal. Mem. Assn. for Computing Machinery, Data Processing Mgmt. Assn. (mem. exec. panel of datamation 1972—). Mason. Home: 4700 Eaton Pl Alexandria VA 22310 Office: MF-735-B The Pentagon Washington DC 20310

PROCTOR, FRANK ELDEN, clergyman; b. Tillamook, Ore., May 17, 1942; s. Donald Clifford and Beryl Lee (Kight) P.; B.Th., N.W. Christian Coll., 1964; M.Div. (Robert B. Pulse Meml. scholar), Christian Theol. Sem., 1969; M.Mus., Butler U., 1970; m. Enola Eileen Knisley, Jan. 24, 1970. Ordained to ministry Christian Ch., 1964; minister youth and music Kern Park Christian Ch., Portland, Ore., 1964-66; music asst. Northwood Christian Ch., Indpls., 1967-71; minister edn. and music Oak Cliff Christian Ch., Dallas, 1971—. Chmn. Christian edn. dept. Dallas Area Assn. Christian Chs., 1971-73; chmn. steering com. Tex. Assn. Christian Chs. Educators, 1973-74; mem. Portland (Ore.) Symphonic Choir, 1964-66, Symphonic Choir, Indpls., 1969-70. Bd. dirs. N. Tex. Christian Communication Commn., 1971—. Eli Lilly grantee, 1968, 69, 70. Home: 2905 W Pentagon Pkwy Apt 205 Dallas TX 75233 Office: 1222 W Kiest Blvd Dallas TX 75224

PROCTOR, JESSE VIRGIL, mech. engr.; b. LaGrange, Ky., Aug. 31, 1905; s. Richard and Leah (Tharp) P.; B.S., U. Ky., 1930; postgrad. Princeton and Mass. Inst. Tech., 1944; m. Elizabeth Hazlitt Hanson, Mar 28, 1932; children—James Virgil, Eleanor Hanson (Mrs. Alfred E. Coleman). Field engr. Ky-W.Va. Gas Co., 1930-35; engr. charge constrn. U. Ky., 1935-42; mech. disign engr. Wilson, Bell & Watkins, 1942-44; pres. Proctor-Ingels & Assos., Inc., Lexington, Ky., 1946—; dir. J.J. Tuttle & Assos., Inc.; pres. P.I.S.W., Inc. Served with USAAF, 1944-46; PTO. Recipient Medal of Freedom, Gen. Curtis E. LeMay, 1946. Mem. Cons. Engrs. Council Ky. (past pres.), Nat. Cons. Engrs. Council (dir. 1965). Episcopalian. Home: 210 Shady Lane Lexington KY 40503 Office: 915 Limestone St Lexington KY 40503

PROCTOR, MELVIN P(ORCH), constrn. co. exec.; b. Cisco, Tex., Aug. 8, 1928; s. Jess and Ina (Leveridge) P.; student Cisco Jr. Coll., 1945, 47, U. Houston, 1949-51; m. Rita B. Henderson, Apr. 28, 1950; children—Stephen Jeffrey, Donna Rae, Linda Diane, Gwen Ann. Salesman, Able Supply Co., Houston, 1950-56; v.p. Thorpe Insulation Co., 1956-60; v.p. J.T. Thorpe Co., constrn., 1960—; dir., sec.-treas. Thorpe Insulation Co., Corpus Christi, Tex., 1966—; dir., sec. Thorpe Realty Co., Houston, 1963-69. Active Boy Scouts Am. Served with AUS, 1946-47. Mem. Thermal Insulation Soc. (bd. dirs. 1959-61). Republican. Clubs: Glenbrook Valley Civic (bd. dirs. 1970-72), Golfcrest Country (Houston). Home: 7515 Rockhill St Houston TX 77017 Office: 6833 Kirbyville St Houston TX 77033

PROELSS, HENNING FREDRICK, chemist; b. Kaufbeuren, West Germany, June 30, 1939; s. Albert and Frieda (Wolfinger) P.; B.S. in Chemistry, Munich (Germany) Inst. Tech., 1961, M.S. in Analytical Chemistry, 1964, Ph.D. in Phys. Chemistry, 1967; m. Eleanor Payne, Apr. 19, 1969; 1 dau., Rachel Erika. Came to U.S., 1967. Research asso. Tech. U. Munich, 1966-67; USPHS grantee City Univ. N.Y., 1967-68; postdoctoral fellow clin. chemistry Baptist Med. Centers, Birmingham, 1968-69, chief div. clin. chemistry and toxicology, 1970—. Cons. in field. Fellow Am. Inst. Chemists; mem. Am. Chem. Soc., Am. Assn. Clin. Chemists. Home: 2365 Garland Dr Birmingham AL 35216 Office: 701 Princeton Av Birmingham AL 35211

PROFFITT, JOHN ROSCOE, JR., textile co. exec.; b. Tifton, Ga., July 31, 1924; s. John R. and Floreid (Adams) P.; B.A., Emory U., 1944, M.A., 1948, Ph.D., 1950; m. Sybil Joyce Harrison, Mar. 13, 1948; children—John Roscoe III, William Terrell. Research chemist E.I. du Pont de Nemours, Waynesboro, Va., 1950-55, research supr., 1955-59; pres., dir. Proffitt Masters, Dalton, Ga., 1956—; exec. v.p., dir. Proffitt Textile Co., 1959—; treas., dir. Proffitt Sales Assn., Inc., 1971—; dir. Hardwick Bank and Trust Co., Dalton. Vice chmn. Bd. Edn., City of Dalton, 1961—; chmn. City of Dalton-Whitfield County Merger Commn., 1969-70; chmn. Whitfield County Bd. Tax Equalization. Bd. dirs. Jr. Achievement, Dalton, Big Bros., Dalton; bd. visitors Emory U. Served with AUS, 1944-56. Mem. Am. Chem. Soc., A.A.A.S., Am. Assn. Textile Chemists and Colourists, Sigma Xi, Phi Beta Kappa, Chi Phi. Democrat. Baptist. Club: Dalton Golf and Country. Patentee in field. Home: 1022 E Lakeshore Dr Dalton GA 30720 Office: Box 729 Dalton GA 30720

PROMISEL, NATHAN E., govt. ofcl.; b. Malden, Mass., June 20, 1908; s. Solomon and Lyna (Samwick) P.; B.S., Mass. Inst. Tech., 1929, M.S., 1930; postgrad. Yale, 1932-33; m. Evelyn Sarah Davidoff, May 17, 1931; children—David Mark, Larry Jay. Research chemist, asst. tech. dir. Internat. Silver Co., Meriden, Conn., 1930-40; cons., Boston, 1940-41; head materials br., chief materials scientist, bur. aeros. Dept. Navy, Washington, 1941-59, dir. materials div., chief material scientist Bur. Naval Weapons, 1959-66; materials adminstr. U.S. Navy, 1966; exec. dir. Nat. Materials Adv. Bd., Nat. Acad. Sci., Washington, 1966-73, cons., 1973—. Cons. to NATO, OECD; lectr. numerous colls. and univs. Mem. adv. coms. U. Pa., Lehigh U., Navy Labs. Recipient Superior Accomplishment award Dept. Navy, 1953, 59; Burgess award, 1961. Fellow Brit. Inst. Metallurgy, Am. Soc. Metals (pres. 1971); mem. Fedn. Materials Soc. (pres. 1973), Am. Soc. Testing and Materials (hon), Soc. Automotive Engrs. (chmn. materials div.), Am. Inst. Mining, Metall. and Petroleum Engrs., Soc. Adv. Materials and Process Engrs., Brit. Metall. Soc. Contbr. articles to profl. jours., chpts. to tech. books. Patentee in electrochem. field. Home: 12519 Davan Dr Silver Spring MD 20904

PROPST, MARGARET GRAYBEAL (MRS. GILES BLACKBURN PROPST), home economist; b. Roan Mountain, Tenn., Aug. 12, 1914; d. Cicero Robert and Florence Victoria (Calhoun) Graybeal; B.S., East Tenn. State Coll. (name changed to East Tenn. State U.), 1937, M.A., 1959; m. Giles Blackburn Propst, Jan. 1, 1942; 1 dau., Katherine (Mrs. Basil Newton Wolfe, Jr.). Tchr., Cloudland High Sch., Carter County Bd. Edn., Roan Mountain, 1937-40, 46-60; home supr. U.S. Dept. Agr., Farm Security Adminstrn., Rutledge, Tenn., 1940-41; extension agt. Agrl. Extension Service, U. Tenn., Greenville, 1960—. Adviser Greenville-Greene County Vocational Sch., 1973—. Asso. dir. Greene County Fair, Greeneville, Tenn., 1963—, Appalachian Dist. Fair, Gray, Tenn., 1965—; mem. adv. welfare com. Greene County, Greeneville, 1967—. Bd. dirs. Roby Fitzgerald Sr. Citizens Center, 1973—. Mem. Am., Southwest Va., Tenn. (dist. membership chmn. 1973—), East Tenn. home econs. assns., Nat. Assn. Extension Home Economists (Distinguished Service award 1971), Greeneville C. of C. (mem. agr. com. 1961—), Epsilon Sigma Phi. Home: PO Box 745 Greeneville TN 37743 Office: County Courthouse Greeneville TN 37743

PROSCHAN, FRANK, educator; b. N.Y.C., Apr. 7, 1921; s. Israel and Rose (Gelman) Proschansky; B.S., Coll. City N.Y., 1941; M.S., George Washington U., 1948; Ph.D., Stanford, 1959; m. Edna Mae Greene, Mar. 22, 1952; children—Virginia Susan, Michael Arthur. Statistician Nat. Bur. Standards, Washington, 1941-52, Sylvania Electric Products, Waltham, Mass., 1952-56, Mountain View, Cal., 1956-60, Boeing Co., Seattle, 1960-70; prof. dept. statistics Fla. State U., Tallahassee, 1970—. Cons. in field. Fellow Am. Statis. Assn., Inst. Math. Statistics; mem. Internat. Statis. Inst. Author: (with Wiley) Mathematical Theory of Reliability, 1965; Statistical Theory of Reliability: Probability Models, 1974. Editor: Reliability and Biometry, 1974. Home: 2325 W Pensacola St #211 Tallahassee FL 32304

PROSKY, LEON, biochemist; b. N.Y.C., Aug. 2, 1933; s. Myer and Beckie (Prosk) P.; B.S., Bklyn. Coll., 1954; M.S., Rutgers U., 1955, Ph.D., 1958; m. Heather Dee Dubin, Apr. 29, 1973. Teaching fellow Rutgers U., New Brunswick, N.J., 1955-58; fellow pharmacology Washington U. Sch. Medicine, St. Louis, 1960-62; research asso., dept. biochemistry Albert Einstein Coll. Medicine, Bronx, N.Y., 1963-65; supervisory research biochemist, div. nutrition FDA, Washington, 1965-73, chief proteins, amino acids and carbohydrate sect., 1973—. Served as 1st lt. Med. Service Corps, AUS, 1958-60. Fellow Am. Inst. Chemists, A.A.A.S.; mem. N.Y. Acad. Scis., Soc. Exptl. Biology and Medicine, Am. Chem. Soc., Sigma Xi. Jewish religion. Contbr. articles to profl. jours. Home: 9521 Cherry Oak Ct Burke VA 22015 Office: 200 C St SW Washington DC 20204

PROSS, LESTER FRED, educator, artist; b. Bristol, Conn., Aug. 14, 1924; s. Harry Lester and Adelia Norris (Visscher) P.; B.A., Oberlin Coll., 1945, M.A., 1946; student Ohio U., summer 1952, Skowhegan Sch. Painting and Sculpture, 1953, Am. U. in Cairo, 1968; m. Mary Louise Caldwell, June 24, 1950; children—David Randall, Mark Alan, Susan Laurel. With Berea (Ky.) Coll., 1946—, prof., chmn. art dept., 1950—; Fulbright lectr. art U. Panjab, Lahore, Pakistan, 1957-58; vis. asso. prof. art Union Coll., Ky., 1961; vis. prof. art Am. U. in Cairo, UAR, 1967-68; exhibited in one-man shows at U. Ky., 1954, Morehead State U., 1973, Somerset and Paducah Community Coll., 1973; exhibited in group shows at Louisville Art Center anns., 1950-64, Midstates exhbns., 1963-64, Face of Ky., 1968-70, Appalachian Corridors travelling shows, 1970-71, Ky. Bicentennial, 1974; also occasional exhbn. judge, cons./lectr. Mem. bd. Central Ky. Civil Liberties Union, 1968—. Bd. dirs. Doris Ulmann Found.; chmn. adv. bd. Appalachian Mus., Berea Coll. Fulbright grantee to Pakistan, 1957-58; Haskell Travelling fellow, Oberlin Coll., 1957-58. Mem. Ky. Art Edn. Assn. (pres. 1955), Ky. Guild Artists and Craftsmen (pres. 1961-63), Coll. Art Assn. Am., Asia Soc., Assn. Asian Studies, Phi Kappa Phi. Democrat. Mem. Ch. of Christ. Home: 1287 College Sta Berea KY 40403

PROSSER, MICHAEL HUBERT, educator; b. Indpls., Mar. 29, 1936; s. Marshall H. and Clydia C. (O'Dea) P.; B.A., Ball State U., 1958, M.A., 1960; Ph.D., U. Ill., 1964; m. Carol Hogle, Nov. 27, 1958; children—Michelle Ann, Leo Michael, Louis Mark. Tchr. Latin and speech Urbana (Ill.) Jr. High Sch., 1960-63; asst. prof. speech State U. N.Y. at Buffalo, 1963-69; vis. lectr. Queens Coll., summers 1966-67; asso. prof. Ind. U., 1969-72; vis. asso. prof. Cal. State Coll. at Hayward, 1971; prof., chmn. dept. speech communication U. Va., 1972—; vis. prof. Meml. U. Nfld., spring 1972. Chmn. internat. communication devel. council Midwest Univs. Consortium for Internat. Activities, 1971-72; del. internat. confs., Germany, 1958, 59, 68, Eng., 1968, Can., 1970, 73. Mem. Speech Communication Assn. (chmn. commn. for internat./intercultural communication 1971—), Internat. Communication Assn., Soc. Cross Cultural Research, Speech Assn. Eastern States (editor Today's Speech 1968-70), N.Y. State Speech Assn. (exec. sec. 1964-68). Editor: An Ethic for Survival: Adlai Stevenson Speaks on International Affairs, 1936-65, 1969; Readings in Classical Rhetoric, 1969; Sow the Wind, Reap the Whirlwind: Heads of State Address the United Nations, 2 vols., 1970; Intercommunication Among Nations and Peoples, 1973; Readings in Medieval Rhetoric, 1973. Home: 2816 Northfields Rd Charlottesville VA 22903

PROSSER, MOORMAN PAUL, psychiatrist; b. Kansas City, Mo., Apr. 10, 1910; s. Albert Percy and Elizabeth (Moorman) P.; A.A., Kansas City Jr. Coll., 1929; A.B., Western Res. U., 1931; B.S. in Med. Sci., U. Okla., M.D., 1935; m. Margaret Elizabeth Hoy, Sept. 23, 1937; children—Margaret Elizabeth (Mrs. James Douglas Rippeto), Carol Ann (Mrs. Gary Don Magness), Dorothy Lorraine (Mrs. Jeremiah J. Keller), Mary Louise (Mrs. Silvio Flaim), Alice Pauline (Mrs. Eugene A. Litteken). Intern, Santa Rosa Hosp., San Antonio, 1935; resident St. Elizabeth Hosp., Washington, 1936-37, Washington Life Adjustment Center and Child Guidance Clinic, 1936-37, Army Sch. Mil. Neuropsychiatry, A.C.P., 1942; physician Central State Hosp., Norman, Okla., 1938-45, clin. dir., 1946-47; practice psychiatry, neurology Oklahoma City, 1948—; mem. staff Bapt. Med. Center, St. Anthony, Drs., Gen., Mercy, Bone and Joint, Univ. and Crippled Children's hosps.; mem. faculty U. Okla. Sch. Medicine, Oklahoma City, 1938—, asso. prof., 1946-55, clin. prof. nervous, mental diseases, psychiatry, neurology, behavioral scis., 1955—. Pres., Oklahoma City Neuropsychiat. Clinic, 1962—; psychiat. cons. Okla. Dept. Vocational Rehab. Bd. dirs. Okla. Psychiat. Found., Coyne Campbell Hosp. Served to lt. col. M.C., AUS, 1941-45. Diplomate Am. Bd. Psychiatry and Neurology. Fellow Am. Psychiat. Assn., A.M.A., A.C.P.; mem. Okla. Med. Assn., Okla. County, Elizabeths Hosp. med. socs., Midwest Psychiat. Assn. Home: 6902 Avondale Dr Oklahoma City OK 73116 Office: 437 Pasteur Med Bldg Oklahoma City OK 73103

PROTHRO, GEORGE WILLIAM, physician; b. Wesson, Ark., Dec. 29, 1920; s. Henry Bussey and Norma (Baker) P.; student Eastern N.M.U., 1938-40; B.S., U.N.M., 1942; M.D., Washington U. Med. Sch., 1945; M.P.H., Univ. of North Carolina, 1967; m. Anna Margaret Lark, Sept. 25, 1943; children—George Lark, Karen Ann. Intern Lincoln Gen. Hosp., Lincoln, Neb., 1945-46; pvt. practice pediatrics, Clovis, N.M., 1948-64; dist. health officer N.M. Dept. Pub. Health, Dist. 10, 1965-68; dir. Tulsa City-County Health Dept., 1968—; clin. asst. prof. U. Okla. Coll. Medicine and Health. Served as lt. (j.g.), M.C., USNR, 1946-47. Fellow Am. Pub. Health Assn., Am. Sch. Health Assn.; mem. A.M.A., Okla. Med. Soc., Tulsa County Med. Soc., Phi Kappa Phi, Phi Sigma, Kappa Mu Epsilon, Delta Omega. Methodist. Rotarian. Home: 5424 S 76th E Av Tulsa OK 74145 Office: 4616 E 15th St Tulsa OK 74145

PRUETT, HASKELL, educator; b. Mingus, Tex., June 16, 1897; s. Ozie D. and Minerva (Small) P.; B.S., Peabody Coll., 1926, M.A., 1930, Ph.D., 1933; M.S., U. Okla., 1930; m. Agnes Murray, July 28, 1920; children—Mildred, Dresslar. Sch. tchr., Greer County, Okla., 1917-20; county supt. schs., Greer County, 1920-23; state rural sch. supr. State Okla., 1923-26; dir. sch. bldgs. and transp. Okla. Dept. Edn., 1926-35; bus. mgr. Okla. State U., 1935-36, prof. edn. 1936-48, head dept. photography, 1948—. Pres., Old Greer County Museum and Hall of Fame, 1972—. Mem. Photog. Soc. Am., Profl. Photogs. Am., Phi Kappa Delta, Kappa Delta Pi. Baptist. Mason (32 deg.). Author articles on edn. and photography. Home: 155 S Redwood Dr Stillwater OK 74074

PRUETT, JEFFERSON WILLIAM, JR., soft drink co. exec.; b. Atlanta, Aug. 15, 1930; s. Jefferson W. and Marguerite (Smith) P.; B.F.A., U. Ga., 1952; m. Nancy Hart, June 7, 1958; children—Jefferson William III, Benjamin Hart. Indsl. editor Lockheed Aircraft Corp., Marietta, Ga., 1954-56; v.p. Conway Publs., Inc., Atlanta, 1956-59; dir. press relations Coca-Cola Co., Atlanta, 1959-63, mgr. pub. relations dept., 1963—, asst. v.p., 1971-73, v.p. pub. relations, 1973—. Served with AUS, 1952-54. Mem. Pub. Relations Soc. Am., Ga. Press Assn. Clubs: Atlanta Press, Commerce. Home: 2070 Chrysler Dr Atlanta GA 30345 Office: 310 North Av NW Atlanta GA 30313

PRUNTY, MICHAEL NEAL, dentist; b. Jenkins, Ky., June 17, 1934; s. Marshall Erlo and Geneieve Carmel (Cordray) P.; B.A., U. Ky., 1957; D.D.S., Med. Coll. Va., 1962, M.S., 1968; m. Nancy Carroll Stapleton, Jan. 13, 1957; children—Michael Neal, Genevieve, Mark. Dir. children's clinic, instr. dept. periodontics Med. Coll. Va., 1964-66; practice dentistry, specializing in orthodontics, Lexington, Ky., 1968—. Mem. Lexington Bd. Health, 1970—. Mem. Young Republican Com. Served to capt. Dental Corps, AUS, 1962-64. Mem. Am., Ky. dental assns., So. Soc. Orthodontics, Am. Assn. Orthodontics, Kappa Alpha. Rotarian (chmn. entertainment com. 1970). Club: Pyramid. Home: 361 Queensway St Lexington KY 40502 Office: 540 E Main St Lexington KY 40508

PRYCE, EDWARD LYONS, landscape architect; b. Lake Charles, La., May 26, 1914; s. George Samuel and Dora Cook (Raymond) P.; B.S. in Agr., Tuskegee Inst., 1937; B. Landscape Architecture, Ohio State U., 1948; M.S., U. Cal. at Berkeley, 1953; m. Woodia Bernice Smith, Nov. 2, 1940; children—Marilyn (Mrs. George X. Nichols), Joellen Grace. Landscape gardener, Los Angeles, 1937-39; landscape architect Los Angeles City Park Dept., 1939-41, Def. Industries, Columbus, O., 1941-45, State Ohio, Columbus, 1945-48; pvt. practice as landscape architect, Tuskegee Institute, Ala., 1948—; mem. faculty Tuskegee Inst., Ala., 1948—, prof., 1969—; dir. Tuskegee Fed. Savs. and Loan Assn. Model cities commr., Tuskegee, 1969-72; commr. Tuskegee City Planning Commn., 1969-72; adv. bd. Ala. State Hist. Commn., 1965—. Mem. Am. Soc. Landscape Architects (sec.-treas. Ala. sect. 1973—). Works include master plans for Tuskegee Inst., Tex. Coll., St. Augustine's Coll. Address: PO Box 246 Tuskegee Institute AL 36088

PRYOR, WILLIAM LEE, educator; b. Lakeland, Fla., Oct. 29, 1926; s. Dahl and Lottie Mae (Merchant) P.; A.B., Fla. So. Coll., 1949; M.A., Fla. State U., 1950, Ph.D., 1959; postgrad. U. N.C., 1952-53; pvt. art study with Florence Wilde; pvt. voice study with Colin O'More and Anna Kaskas. Asst. prof. English, dir. drama Bridgewater Coll., 1950-52; vis. instr. English Fla. So. Coll., MacDill Army Air Base, summer 1951; grad. teaching fellow humanities Fla. State U., 1953-55, 57-58; instr. English, U. Houston, 1955-59, asst. prof., 1959-62, asso. prof., 1962-71, prof., 1971—, asso. editor Forum, 1967, editor, 1967—; vis. instr. English, Tex. So. U., 1961-63; vis. instr. humanities, govt. U. Tex. Dental Br., 1962-63; lectr. The Women's Inst., Houston, 1967-72; lectr. humanities series Jewish Community Center, 1972-73; originator, moderator weekly television and radio program The Arts in Houston on KUHT-TV and KUHF-FM, 1956-57, 58-63. Bd. dirs. Houston Shakespeare Soc., 1964-67; bd. dirs., program annotator Houston Chamber Orch. Soc., 1964—; bd. dirs., program annotator Music Guild, Houston, 1960-67, v.p., 1963-67, adv. bd. 1967-70; bd. dirs. Contemporary Music Soc., Houston, 1958-63; mem.-at-large bd. dirs. Houston Grand Opera Guild, 1966-67; mem. repertory com. Houston Grand Opera Assn., 1967-70; bd. dirs. Houston Grand Opera, 1970—; mem. cultural adv. com. Jewish Community Center, 1960-66; bd. dirs. Houston Friends Pub. Library, 1962-67, 73—, 1st v.p., 1963-67; adv. mem. cultural affairs com. Houston C. of C., 1972—. Mem. Coll. English Assn., Modern Langs. Assn., L'Alliance Francaise, English-Speaking Union, Alumni Assn. Fla. State U., Am. Assn. U. Profs., S. Central Modern Lang. Assn., Coll. Conf. Tchrs. English, Phi Beta (patron), Phi Mu Alpha Sinfonia, Alpha Psi Omega, Pi Kappa Alpha, Sigma Tau Delta, Tau Kappa Alpha, Phi Kappa Phi. Episcopalian. Contbg. author: National Poetry Anthology, 1952; Panorama das Literaturas das Americas, 4 vols., 1958-60. Home: 2625 Arbuckle St Houston TX 77005 Office: 3801 Cullen Blvd Houston TX 77004

PTACEK, CHARLES FRANK, paint corp. exec.; b. Chgo., Feb. 12, 1940; s. Charles William and Rose (Chroust) P.; student Ga. State U., 1956-60; m. Sharon Kathleen Jackson; children—Charles Frank, Kimberly Rose, Michael Davey, Tammy Zee. With Precision Paint Corp., Atlanta, 1961—, v.p., 1962-65, exec. v.p., 1965-68, pres., chmn. bd., 1968—. Mem. Aircraft Owners and Pilots Assn. Club: Cherokee Town and Country. Home: 1555 Spalding Dr NE Atlanta GA 30338 Office: 5275 Peachtree Industrial Blvd Atlanta GA 30341

PUCCI, GERARD RICHARD, lawyer, mech. engr.; b. N.Y.C., Aug. 7, 1924; s. Santo and Mary (Principe) P.; B.S. in Mech. Engring., Va. Poly. Inst., 1944; J.D., George Washington U., 1949; m. Ruth Motz, July 20, 1955. Admitted to Fla. bar, 1949; patent engr. RCA, 1946-48; tool designer Douglas Aircraft Corp., 1950-51; patent atty. U.S. Navy Ordnance Test Sta., 1951-52; staff analyst, N.Am. Aviation, 1952-54; pvt. practice as atty. and engr., 1954—. Prof. aerospace dept. Miami-Dade Jr. Coll.-South Campus, 1966—. Chmn. Planning Bd. Coral Gables, Fla., 1959-63, mem. Zoning Bd., 1959-63; mem. dist. advancement com. Boy Scouts Am., S. Fla., 1967-70. Served as lt. (j.g.) USNR, 1944-46. Registered profl. engr., Fla. Recipient Old Guard award Am. Soc. M.E., 1944; George Washington award Freedoms Found. Valley Forge, 1963. Mem. Nat. Soc. Profl. Engrs., Fla. Engring. Soc., Tau Beta Pi, Pi Tau Sigma. Rotarian (sec., dir. S.W. Miami 1960). K.C. (4 deg.). Roman Catholic. Producer, Speaker own radio program on Am. Govt., Miami, 1962-65. Author: (textbook) Aviation Law-Fundamental Cases, 1970, 2d edit., 1974. Home: 35 Menores Av Coral Gables FL 33134 Office: 250 Bird Rd Coral Gables FL 33146

PUCKETT, JAMES DEAN, obstetrician, gynecologist; b. East Chicago, Ind., Jan. 23, 1943; s. Hosea Vermont and Gertrude Frances (Jessup) P.; B.S., Wake Forest Coll., 1964; M.D., Bowman Gray Sch. Medicine, 1968; m. Judith Delores Alexander, Oct. 20, 1971. Intern Greenville (S.C.) Gen. Hosp., 1968-69, resident, 1969-71, 73—. Served with AUS, 1971-73. Jr. fellow Am. Coll. Obstetricians and Gynecologists; mem. A.M.A. (student), Gamma Sigma Epsilon, Alpha Epsilon Delta. Republican. Methodist. Home: 200 Bromsgrove Dr Greenville SC 29609

PUCKETT, JAMES RICHARD, metal products co. exec.; b. Anderson, Ind., Aug. 2, 1929; s. Jefferson Thomas and Wilma Inez (Funkhouser) P.; student U. Evansville, 1947-48; m. Patricia Ann Thornton, Aug. 30, 1949; children—Gary Michael, Neal Allen. Zone mgr. Airtex Products, Inc., Fairfield, Ill., 1951-62; regional mgr. A.P. Parts Corp., Toledo, 1962-67; sales mgr. Inca Metal Products Corp., Carrollton, Tex., 1967—; dir. Cisco Material Handling, Inc., Dallas. Swimming commr. Richardson Sports, Inc. (Tex.), 1966-67. Served with AUS, 1950-51. Mem. Automotive Warehouse Distbrs. Assn. (material handling com. 1972-73). Elk. Club: Braniff Internat. (Dallas). Home: 1614 Juniper St Lewisville TX 75067 Office: PO Box 897 Lewisville TX 75067

PUCKETT, RUBY PARKER (MRS. LARRY WILLARD PUCKETT), dietitian; b. Dora, Ala., Nov. 26, 1932; d. John Franklin and Ethel Victoria (Short) Parker; B.S., Auburn U., 1954; postgrad. U. Fla., 1970—; m. Larry Willard Puckett, July 2, 1955; children—Laurel Lynn, Hollie Kristina. Intern in dietetics Henry Ford Hosp., Detroit, 1955; staff dietitian VA Hosp., Houston, 1955-56; dietitian Matty Hersee Hosp., Meridian, Miss., 1957-58; asst. dir. dietetics U. Miss., Jackson, 1960-61; dir. dietetics Fort Sanders Presbyn. Hosp., Knoxville, Tenn., 1961-63, Waterman Meml. Hosp., Eustis, Fla., 1963-68, J. Hillis Miller Health Center, U. Fla., Gainesville, 1968—. Preceptor, coordinator corr. course for food service suprs. Am. Dietetic Assn., 1965-70; guest lectr. Santa Fe Jr. Coll., 1970-72, U. Fla., 1971-72; tchr. mgmt. systems and philosophies to dietetic interns; mem. adv. com. Fla. State Dept. Edn., 1966-67, Santa Fe Jr. Coll., 1968-69; pres. Field Agy. Nutrition Service, Gainesville, 1970-71; mem. White House Conf. Food, Nutrition and Health, 1969; mem. faculty Fla. Conf. Food Nutrition Health, 1970. Named Outstanding Dietitian Fla., 1972. Fellow Royal Soc. Health; mem. Am. Fla., Gainesville (pres. 1970) dietetic assns., (chmn. AHA-ADA com. 1971), Dietetic Internship Council, Fla. Dietetic Assn. (exec. bd. 1965—, sec. 1968, pres. 1973), Hosp. Instl. Edn. Food Service Soc. (founder Fla. chpt. 1965), Southeastern Hosp. Conf. Dietitians (nominating com. 1969, sec. 1974), Am. Soc. Hosp. Food Service Adminstrs., Nat. Nutrition Soc. (charter), Pi Lambda Theta, Kappa Delta Pi. Republican. Mem. Ch. Jesus Christ of Latter Day Saints. Club: Pilot (pres. 1967). Author: (with others) Diet Manual Shands Teaching Hospital, 1971; Study Guide for Food Service Supervisors, 1972, 2d edit., 1974; Basic Guide to Nutrition and Diet, 1974; Modification Manual Preceptors Guide for Food Service Supervisors, 1974. Contbr. articles to profl. jours. Home: 3806 SW 4th Pl Gainesville FL 32601 Office: Box 770 J Hillis Miller Health Center Gainesville FL 32601

PUCKETT, RUSSELL ELWOOD, elec. engr.; b. Ewing, Ky., Mar. 28, 1929; s. Ben and Nettie (Peach) P.; B.S., U. Ky., 1956, M.S., 1959; m. Dorothy C. Hoskins, Aug. 10, 1949; children—Malcolm Wayne, Stanley Allen, Janet Arlene, Owen Keith, Michael Edwin. Engr. U.S. Dept. Def., 1956-57; asst. prof. elec. engring. U. Ky., Lexington, 1957-66, research asso., 1967-68, asso. dir. office research Coll. Engring., 1968—, asso. prof. engring. tech., 1970—, chmn. div. engring. tech., 1972—; sr. research engr. Tex. Instruments, Versailles, Ky., 1966-67; pres., chmn. bd. REPCO, Inc. Cons. expert witness in patent infringement, trade secret lawsuits; mem. nat. com. electronic research Hwy. Research Bd. of Nat. Acad. Scis., 1964-70. Served with USAAF, 1946-49, with USAF, 1951-54. Registered profl. engr., Ky. Mem. I.E.E.E. (sr. mem., treas. Lexington sect. 1962-65, chmn. sect. 1969-70), Am. Soc. Engring. Edn., Nat., Ky. (dir. Bluegrass chpt. 1971-73, sec. 1973-75) socs. profl. engrs. Eta Kappa Nu, Tau Beta Pi, Phi Gamma Delta. Mason (32 deg., Shriner), Kiwanian. Patentee in field. Author: (with H. A. Romanowitz) Introduction to Electronics, 1968. Home: 1012 Lane Allen Rd Lexington KY 40504 Office: Anderson Hall U Ky Lexington KY 40506

PUGH, HAROLD EUGENE, lawyer; b. Altavista, Va., May 11, 1937; s. Abner F. and Annie M. (Gibson) P.; student Mars Hill Coll., 1959; B.S., U. Richmond, 1963; LL.B., U. Va., 1966. Admitted to Va. bar, 1966; partner firm Arthur, Harvey, Pugh & Eller, Altavista, 1966—. Pros. atty., Altavista, 1967—; town atty. Town of Hurt (Va.), 1974—, chmn. planning commn., 1972—. Mem. Am., Va., Lynchburg bar assns., Alpha Soc. Rotarian (past pres., dir.). Baptist. Home: Route 1 Box 293 Hurt VA 24563 Office: 513 Main St Altavista VA 24517

PUGH, JOHN BALDWIN, timber constrn. co. exec.; b. Berwyn, Ill., May 29, 1928; s. Cloyd Long and Marion Elizabeth (Baldwin) P.; B.S. in Agrl. Engring., Ia. State U., 1951; m. Jane Novak, Oct. 11, 1952; children—Carrie Ann, D. Edmund. Sales rep. Weyerhaeuser Co., Pitts., 1955-62, dist. sales mgr. Southeast U.S., Tampa, Fla., 1962-65; pres. Engineered Timber Sales, Inc., Tampa, 1965—. Registered profl. engr., Fla., Pa. Mem. Am. Inst. Timber Constrn., Forest Products Research Soc., Asso. Builders and Contractors. Rotarian (pres. 1974-75). Address: 3016 Graham Lane Tampa FL 33618

PUGH, MOFFETT LEONARD, geophysicist; b. Oreville, O., Feb. 16, 1916; s. John Paul and Elva (Cain) P.; B.S., Aero. Engr., La. State U., 1939; postgrad. Centenary Coll., 1954; m. Doris Robbins, Oct. 18, 1942; 1 son, John Thomas. Petroleum engr. trainee Pugh-Dekalb Co., Centralia, Ill., 1939-41; geophysicist Ark. Natural Gas Co., Shreveport, La., 1945-53; chief geophysicist Ark. La. Gas Co., Shreveport, 1953-70; chief geophysicist Amarex, Inc., Oklahoma City, 1970—. Dir. Caddo and Bossier parishes, dir. area II, Civil Def., 1954-61. Served with Ordnance Corps, AUS, 1941-46. Registered profl. engr., La. Mem. Soc. Exploration Geophysicists, Geophys. Soc. Oklahoma City, Nat. Soc. Profl. Engrs., Internat. Platform Assn. Club: Shreveport Petroleum. Designer spl. target abuttement to speed up testing and recovery of armorpiercing ammunition, 1942. Home: 4625 NW 34th St Oklahoma City OK 73122 Office: Amarex Inc Suite 200 200 N Harvey St Oklahoma City OK 73102

PULLEN, JOHN THOMAS, JR., mech. engr.; b. Covington, Tenn., Nov. 18, 1903; s. John Thomas and Thersa (Miller) P.; archtl. engring. degree U. Ill., 1926; m. Martha Frances Gragg, Aug. 21, 1928; children—Martha Jane (Mrs. Eugene Edward Tibbs), John Thomas III. Field engr. Gauger-Korsmo Constrn. Co., Memphis 1926-28; resident engr.; designer W. F. Schulz, architect-engr., 1928-32; engr. charge bank protection party Corps Engrs., U.S. Army, 1932-38; staff engr. Firestone Tire & Rubber Co., Memphis, 1938-48; mech. engr. T. J. O'Brien Engring. Co., 1948-54; owner firm John T. Pullen, cons. engr., Memphis, 1954—. Air raid warden, 1941-46. Registered profl. engr., Tenn., Mo., Ark., Miss. Mem. Am. Soc. Heating, Refrigerating and Air-Conditioning Engrs., Nat. Soc. Profl. Engrs., Engrs. Club Memphis. Democrat. Methodist. Mason. Club: Big Ten. Home: 3764 Gragg Av Memphis TN 38108 Office: Falls Bldg Memphis TN 38103

PULLEN, THOMAS MARION, educator; b. Elmodel, Ga., June 17, 1919; s. Tom Metts and Mamie Lee (Rooks) P.; B.S., U. Ga., 1940, M.Ed., 1958, Ph.D., 1963; m. Miriam Burge Sproull, Sept. 14, 1940; 1 son, Thomas Marion. Tchr. pubs. schs. Jenkins County, Ga., 1940-44, Bartow County, Ga., 1950-58; asst. prof. biology U. Miss., University, 1963-65, asso. prof., 1965-66, prof., 1966—. Served with AUS, 1944-46; PTO. NSF grantee, 1966, 69. Mem. Internat. Assn. Plant Taxonomy, Am. Soc. Plant Taxonomists, Am. Inst. Biol. Scis., A.A.A.S., Bot. Soc. Am., Assn. Southeastern Biologists, Ga., Miss. acads. scis. Asso. editor Jour. Miss. Acad. Sci., 1970—. Home: 103 Glen Eagle Rd Oxford MS 38655 Office: Dept Biology Univ Miss University MS 38677

PULS, WAYNE ELVIN, banker; b. Pueblo, Colo., Dec. 12, 1923; s. Fred William and Nora Malinda (Pulliam) P.; student U. Idaho, 1943, Central Coll., Fayette, Mo., 1944-45; B.A., U. Michigan, 1947; m. Sally Russell Robbins, Aug. 7, 1971; 1 dau., Susan Elaine. With Gen. Motors Acceptance Corp., several Fla. cities, 1948-60, mgr. br., Ft. Lauderdale, 1956-60; v.p., comml. loan officer First Nat. Bank, Orlando, 1960-65; pres. Central Nat. Bank, Jacksonville, 1965-67; sr. v.p. Barnett First Nat. Bank, Winter Park, 1967-71; pres., dir. Barnett Bank of Orlando, 1971; pres., dir. Barnett Bank Ft. Lauderdale (Fla.), 1971—; Trustee, Las Olas Gen. Hosp., Ft. Lauderdale; chmn. adv. bd. Salvation Army, Ft. Lauderdale; bd. dirs., mem. exec. com. Broward County chpt. A.R.C. Served with USNR, 1942-46. Mem. Ft. Lauderdale C. of C., Navy League (bd. dirs. 1970—). Clubs: Winter Park Racquet; Coral Ridge Country, Inverrary Racquet, Tennis, Tower, Rotary (Ft. Lauderdale). Home: 5309 Buttonwood Ct Fort Lauderdale FL 33313 Office: 15 E Broward Blvd Fort Lauderdale FL 33302

PUMPHREY, NORMAN DEAN, state ofcl.; b. Sheridan, Ark., Feb. 19, 1932; s. Winfred and Ruby (Walker) P.; student U. Ark., 1950-51; m. Bobbye Jean Winbury, Sept. 9, 1951; children—Norman D., Gregory C., David L. Rodman, Ark. State Hwy. Dept. (part-time), 1946-50, instrument man, 1951-55; engr. asst. Short & Brownlee Constrn. Co., 1955-56; with Ark. State Hwy. Dept., Little Rock, 1957—, instrument man, 1957-59, acting resident engr., 1959-61, sr. resident engr., 1961-69, asst. constrn. engr., 1969—. Adviser constrn. tech. curriculum Southwest Inst. Tech., Camden, Ark., 1968-70. Mem. Ark. (Southwest chpt. pres. 1962-63 Outstanding Engr. award 1969), Nat. socs. profl. engrs., Ark. Assn. Registered Land Surveyors, Am. Congress Surveying Mapping. Baptist. Home: 5720 Chaucer Lane Little Rock AR 72209 Office: PO Box 2261 Little Rock AR 72209

PUPPA, HENRY GEORGE, mgmt. cons.; b. N.Y.C., Jan. 9, 1919; s. Henry and Marie (Woltron) P.; B.B.A., Coll. City N.Y., 1939; M.S., Columbia, 1940, postgrad., 1940-41; m. Jean Virginia White, May 2, 1942; children—Henry G., Janet G., William S., Robert J., Anne M. Teaching fellow, tutor in econs. Coll. City N.Y., 1939-41; chief progress and requirements br. U.S. Navy Bur. Ordnance, Washington, 1946-51; budget examiner U.S. Bur. Budget, Washington, 1951-61; various positions with Office Asst. Sec. Def., Washington, 1961-67; dir. program and policy planning Gen. Services Adminstrn., Washington, 1967-72; cons. Stanford Research Inst., Washington, 1972—. Professorial lectr. statistics Am. U., Washington, 1946-56, 62-63. Pres., Help for Retarded Children, Washington, 1952-53. Served from ensign to lt. comdr. USNR, 1941-46. Mem. Am. Statis. Assn., Operations Research Soc. Am., Washington Operations Research Council, Beta Gamma Sigma. Episcopalian. Home: 4608 Albemarle St NW Washington DC 20016 Office: 1611 N Kent St Rosslyn Plaza Arlington VA 22209

PURCELL, THOMAS HECTOR, JR., aerospace engr.; b. Hope Mills, N.C., Sept. 11, 1920; s. Thomas Hector and Mabel Conrad (Pate) P.; B.Aero.Engring. with honors, N.C. State U., 1943; M.S.Aero. Engring., U. Mich., 1947; m. Mary Barbara Stevens, June 15, 1945; children—Barbara Katherine, Archie Thomas. Aerodynamicist, Fairchild Aircraft, Hagerstown, Md., 1948-50; chief design engr. Prewitt Aircraft, Clifton Heights, Pa., 1950-54; chief mech. engr. Missile and Electronics div. ESB Inc., Raleigh, N.C., 1966-72; mgr. Corporate Engring. and Devel. Co., 1972—; pres. Flight Dynamics, Inc., Raleigh, 1956—. Served with USAAF, 1943-48. Registered profl. engr., N.C. Mem. Exptl. Aircraft Assn. (charter, regional rep.), Nat. Assn. Sport Aircraft Designers. Presbyn. (elder, past ch. treas. and chmn. bd. deacons). Pioneer flyer manned flexwing aircraft off water, 1962; designer, builder, flyer Flightsail VII, amphibian, 1971; patentee aerospace designs. Home: 2709 Everett Av Raleigh NC 27607 Office: PO Box 5070 Raleigh NC 27607

PURCELL, WALTER LAMBUTH, financial mgmt. cons. firm exec.; b. Shady Dale, Ga., Mar. 26, 1922; s. William Edgar and Lillie (Neese) P.; A.A., Reinhardt Coll., 1941; B.S. in Math., Piedmont Coll., 1943, B.A. in Social Sci., 1943; LL.B., Emory U., Atlanta Law Sch., 1959; LL.M., Atlanta Law Sch., 1963; m. Dorothy Lanette Dimsdale, Jan. 17, 1947; children—Dorothy Cheryl (Mrs. Michael Perry Adams) and Melvyn Kenneth (twins). Dist. reporting and service mgr., also bus. cons., Dun & Bradstreet, Inc., 1947-62; dir. Dept. Community Services DeKalb County, Atlanta, 1962-64; pres. Purcell Cons. Assos., Inc., Decatur, Ga., 1964—. Lectr. various colls., univs.; instr. seminars; mem. faculty Grad. Sch. Arts and Scis., Emory U., Atlanta, 1965—; chmn. bd. Exec. Edn., Inc., Decatur, 1966—. Div. chmn. DeKalb unit Am. Cancer Soc., 1965—; mem. budget com. Atlanta Met. United Way, 1966—; bd. dirs. Met. area A.R.C., DeKalb County Heart Council, S.E. Region YMCA, Ga. Heart Assn., Atlanta Assn. Retarded Children; trustee Ga. Hemophilia Assn.; pres. DeKalb Community Council, 1963-67; regional v.p. Inst. Mgmt. Cons. Named DeKalb County Citizen of Year, civitans of DeKalb County, 1964. Mem. So. Finance Assn., Atlanta Soc. Financial Analysts, Pub. Relations Soc. Am., Ga. Pub. Relations Soc., Assn. Mgmt. Cons., Am. Pub. Health Assn., Ga. Hosp. Assn., So. Assn. Inst. Psychol. Services, Am. Recreation Soc., Ga. Recreation and Park Soc., Ga. Library Assn., Ga. Gerontology Soc., Assn. Mgmt. Cons. (trustee), DeKalb County C. of C. (dir.), Delta Theta Phi. Methodist (pres. bd. trustees 1959—). Clubs: Atlanta Press, Kiwanis (Ga. dist. com. chmn. 1964-67), Toastmasters International (chpt. pres. 1952-53), Decatur Executive, Druid Hills Golf. Home: 1526 Rainier Falls Dr NE Atlanta GA 30329 Office: First Nat Bank Bldg Decatur GA 30030

PURDIE, DOUGLAS HAIG, ednl. adminstr.; b. Harrison, N.J., Oct. 27, 1916; s. William James and Charlottee (Taylor) P.; B.S., Ga. Evening Coll., Atlanta, 1941; postgrad. U. Hawaii, 1944; M.Ed., Emory U., 1949; postgrad. U. Ga., 1956; m. Frances Ethelyn Boswell, June 23, 1939; children—Ethelyn (Mrs. Robert Browning), Laura Joyce. Tchr., counselor Russell High Sch., East Point, Ga., 1941-52; vis. tchr. Fulton County (Ga.) Sch. System, 1952-55; counselor Hapeville (Ga.) High Sch., 1955-65, prin., 1965-70; adminstrn. asst. to dep. supt. Fulton County Sch. System, Hapeville, 1970-73, dir. counseling services, 1973—. Mem. Ga. Counseling and Testing Adv. Bd., 1961-63. Vol. worker Atlanta Area council Boy Scouts Am., 1945-65, Atlanta YMCA, 1945—; chmn. pensions bd. Fulton County Tchrs. Retirement Bd., 1960-73. Bd. dirs. Annewaakee Found., Little Red School House for Exceptional Children. Served with USNR, 1943-45. Mem. Nat., Ga. edn. assns., Fulton County Tchrs. Assn., Ga. Assn. Sch. Counselors (pres. 1957), Audubon Soc. Presbyn. (elder 1948-72). Home: 4495 Danforth Rd SW Atlanta GA 30331 Office: 580 College St Hapeville GA 30354

PURDUE, JACK OLEN, educator; b. McLoud, Okla., Mar. 2, 1913; s. Roy A.E. and Ethel V. (Miller) P.; B.S., Okla. Bapt. U., 1934; postgrad. Okla. State U., 1934-35, Princeton, 1944-45; M.S., U. Okla., 1939; Ph.D., 1948; m. Caryl Iris Goodson, June 19, 1941; children—James Richard, Helen Caryl, Eugene Olen. With Champlin Refining Co., Oklahoma City, 1935-38; mem. faculty Okla. Bapt. U., Shawnee, 1938—, prof. chemistry,, 1950—, Distinguished Service prof., 1964, chmn. div. natural scis., 1968—. Precinct chmn. Democratic party, Shawnee, 1968-72, del. State Conv., 1968, 72. Served to lt. comdr. USNR, 1943-46: PTO. NSF grantee, Dept. Interior grantee, 1956-64. Mem. Am. Chem. Soc. (councilor 1971-74), A.A.A.S., Am. Assn. U. Profs., Sigma Xi. Lion. Research desalination of water. Home: 2000 N Market St Shawnee OK 74801

PURDY, ALTON BURTON, elec. engr.; b. Bassett, Va., May 8, 1918; s. William King and Alma Bertha (Reynolds) P.; student Nat. Bus. Coll., 1938; B.S., Tex. A. and M. U., 1949; m. Mary Frances Board, Oct. 9, 1954; children—Mary Alicia, Richard Alton. Staff engr. Appalachian Power Co., Roanoke, Va., 1950—. Served to 2d lt. USAAF, 1941-46. Registered profl. engr., Va. Mem. I.E.E.E. (exec. com.), Nat. Assn. Corrosion Engrs. (chmn. corrosion coordinating com.), Tau Beta Pi. Home: 5729 Brahma Rd SW Roanoke VA 24018 Office: 40 Franklin Rd Roanoke VA 24009

PURDY, HAROLD JOHN, clergyman; b. Newcomerston, O., June 14, 1914; s. Earle Edson and Mabel (Wilson) P.; student Alderson-Broadus Coll., 1932-34, Salem Coll., 1934-36, A.B., 1946; D.D., So. Bapt. Theol. Sem., 1942, B.D.; postgrad. Oxford (Eng.) U., 1965; m. Virginia Elisabeth Burdette, Apr. 23, 1935. Ordained to ministry Bapt. Ch., 1935; pastor 1st Ch., Madison W. Va., 1935-39, Northview Ch., Clarksburg, W. Va., 1933-35; asso. pastor Deer Park Ch., Louisville, 1939-41; pastor 1st Ch., Madisonville, Ky., 1941-46, 1st Ch., Bowling Green, Ky., 1946-50, Belmont Heights Ch., Nashville, 1950-64, 1st Bapt. Ch., Madisonville, Ky., 1964—. Trustee Bapt. Sunday Sch. Bd.; exec. bd. Ky. Bapt. Conv., 1964-73, mem. hosp. commn., 1964-73; mem. exec. com. So. Bapt. Conv., 1966-73; pres. Tenn. Bapt. Conv., 1963, mem. ednl. commn., 1951-56, mem. exec. bd., 1960; moderator Nashville Bapt. Assn., 1962-63. Trustee Tenn. Bapt. Children's Home, 1951-63, Belmont Coll., 1953-64. Mem. com. alcohol studies State Tenn., 1952. Kiwanian. Contbr. ch. periodicals. Home: Greenville Pike Madisonville KY 42431 Office: 1st Baptist Ch 246 N Main St Madisonville KY 42431

PURI, OM PARKASH, physicist, educator; b. Sialkot, India, Apr. 27, 1935; s. Des Raj and Budh Wanti (Kohli) P.; B.A., Punjab U., 1956; M.S., Sagar U., 1958, Ph.D., 1960; m. Nancy Rogers, June 13, 1964; children—Krishan, Ravi. Postdoctoral research fellow U. Notre Dame, 1960-61; prof., chmn. dept. physics Clark Coll., Atlanta, 1961—. Cons. numerous colls. Trustee, Clark Coll. Recipient Distinguished Tchrs. award So. Assn. Meth. Colls., 1972. Author: Concepts in Physical Science; Experiments in Physical Science. Contbr. articles to profl. jours. Home: 1087 Norwich Circle NE Atlanta GA 30324

PURKEY, WILLIAM WATSON, educator; b. Shenandoah, Va., Aug. 22, 1929; s. William Watson and Elizabeth (Reynolds) Shenk; B.S., U. Va., 1957, M.Ed., 1958, D.Ed., 1964; m. Imogene Ellen Hedrick, Mary 8, 1951; children—William Watson, Cynthia Ann. Tchr. pub. schs., Chatham, N.J., 1958-61; mem. faculty U. Fla., Gainesville, 1964—, asso. prof. edn., 1967-70, prof., 1970—. Coordinator Fla. area, Common Cause, 1972—. Served with USAF, 1951-55. Named Nat. P.T.A. Mem. of Month, 1972. Mem. Am. Psychol. Assn., Am. Ednl. Research Assn. Author: Self Concept and School Achievement, 1971; Helping Relationships, 1972. Home: 2032 NW 24th St Gainesville FL 32601

PURKS, WILLIAM KENDRICK, physician; b. Greensboro, Ga., Sept. 1, 1905; s. James Harris and Lulie Carswell (Kinman) P.; B.S. cum laude, Emory U., 1926, M.D. with honor, 1929; m. Mary Helen Kemper, June 22, 1935; children—William Kendrick (dec.), Robert K. Intern, Grady Hosp., Atlanta, 1929-30; med. resident, 1929-30; asst. med. resident Peter Brent Brigham Hosp., Boston, 1931-34; practice medicine specializing in internal medicine, Vicksburg, Miss., 1934—; chief staff Vicksburg Hosp., 1962—, chief med. service, 1934—, pres. bd. dirs., 1962—; instr. medicine U. Miss. Med. Sch., 1956—. Mem. Vicksburg Sch. Bd., 1945-60, pres., 1955-60. Bd. dirs. YMCA, Vicksburg, pres., 1969-70; bd. dirs. Vicksburg Hosp. Med. Found., pres. 1962—. Diplomate Am. Bd. Internal Medicine. Fellow A.C.P. (gov. 1960-66); mem. Am., So., Miss. med. assns., West Miss. Med. Soc., Am. Fedn. Clin . Research, Am. Coll. Chest Physicians, Am. (bd. dirs. 1954-60), Miss. (pres. 1953) heart assns., Chi Phi, Phi Beta Kappa, Alpha Kappa Kappa. Kiwanian (pres. 1938). Contbr. articles to profl. pubs. Home: 1400 Baum St Vicksburg MS 39180 Office: 3311 Frontage Rd Vicksburg MS 39180

PURRINGTON, ROBERT DANIEL, educator; b. Alamosa, Colo., Apr. 11, 1936; s. Robert George and Edith Brooke (Manley) P.; B.S., Tex. A. and M. U., 1958, M.S., 1963, Ph.D., 1966; postgrad. U. Cal. at Berkeley, 1959-60; m. Ethel Loraine Smith, Sept. 12, 1959; children—Jacqueline Brooke, Stephen Daniel, Jennifer Anne, Christopher Wilson. Research asso. Tex. A. and M. Research Found., College Station, 1964-66; asst. prof. physics Tulane U., New Orleans, 1966-70, prof., 1970—. Research participant Oak Ridge Nat. Lab., 1968. Served to 2d lt. AUS, 1958-59. Woodrow Wilson fellow, 1958; NSF summer fellow, 1960; NASA trainee, 1961-64. Mem. Am. Phys. Soc., Nat. Audubon Soc., La. Ornithol. Soc. (pres. 1969-71), Sierra Club, Wilderness Soc., Sigma Xi, Phi Kappa Phi, Sigma Pi Sigma. Contbr. articles to profl. jours. Home: 4700 Bissonet Dr Metairie LA 70003 Office: Dept Physics Tulane Univ New Orleans LA 70118

PURSELL, WALTER LEE, petroleum co. exec.; b. Alva, Okla., Dec. 13, 1910; s. Loran A. and Lois (Walton) P.; B.S. in Elec. Engring., Okla. A. and M. Coll., 1936, M.S. in Chemistry and Mech. Engring., 1937; postgrad. in mgmt. Kan. U., 1943-44, So. Meth. U., 1960; m. Edith Luceille Vogelman, June 14, 1940; children—Gerald Kent, Karen Sue. With Skelly Oil Co. Refinery, 1937—, chief process engr., 1945-50, chief engr., 1950-61, refinery mgr., 1961-64, spl. rep. engring. and constrn. dept., 1964-68, project mgr. project devel. dept., 1968—. Committeeman, Cub, Boy Scouts Am., El Dorado, 1957-60; safety chmn. P.T.A., El Dorado, 1960; mem. Kan. Gov.'s Emergency Resources Planning Com., 1962. Bd. dirs. Augusta-El Dorado Water Assn., Ark-Walnut River Basin Assn., Ark. Basin Devel. Assn. in Kan.; trustee Allen Meml. Hosp. Registered profl. engr., Kan., Okla. Mem. Am. Petroleum Inst., Soc. Automotive Engrs., Nat. Assn. Corrosion Engrs., Nat. Petroleum Refiners Assn., El Dorado C. of C. (dir. 1961-65), Phi Kappa Phi, Phi Lambda Upsilon, Sigma Tau. Methodist (steward). Rotarian. Club: El Dorado Country. Contbr. articles to profl. jours. Address: PO Box 1650 Tulsa OK 74102

PURVIS, EDNA O'SHIELDS (MRS. JOHN WILLIAM PURVIS), bank exec.; b. nr. Tupelo, Miss., Sept. 27, 1916; d. Bolivar and Julia Budde (Epting) O'Shields; student Jr. Coll., Lee County, Miss., 1933-34; m. John William Purvis, Jan. 17, 1959. With First Nat. Bank, Mobile, Ala., 1942—, security officer, 1970—. Mem. Nat. Assn. Bank Women. Baptist Clubs: International Trade, Bienville (Mobile). Home: 1 Camilla St Mobile AL 36606 Office: First Nat Bank Mobile AL 36601

PURVIS, JOHN TAYLOR, neurol. surgeon; b. Morristown, Tenn., Feb. 4, 1929; s. Robert Averette and Katherine (Taylor) P.; student Carson-Newman Coll., 1948-49, U. Tenn., 1946-48, 50; M.D., U. Tenn., 1953; m. Patricia Ann Lane, Sept. 24, 1971; 1 son, Robert Henson; children (by previous marriage)—Katherine (Mrs. Alfred D. Sharp III), Elizabeth Harrison (Mrs. Gene Grace), John Taylor, Allyn Hunter, David Chilton. Intern, McGill U. Royal Victoria Hosp., Montreal, Que., Can., 1953-54; resident gen. surgery, neurol. surgery U. Va. Hosp., Charlottesville, 1956-60; commd. 1st lt. M.C., USAF, 1953, advanced through grades to maj., 1963; chief dept. neurol. surgery USAF Hosp., Wright-Patterson AFB, O., 1961-65; chief dept. neurol. surgery USAF Hosp., Clark Air Base, P.I., 1965-66; ret., 1966; pvt. practice medicine specializing in neurol. surgery, Birmingham, Ala., 1966-67, Richmond, Va., 1967-68, Knoxville, Tenn., 1968—; asst. prof. neurol. surgery U. Ala. Med. Center, 1966—; attending neurosurgeon St. Mary's Meml., Ft. Sanders Presbyn., E. Tenn. Baptist, E. Tenn. Childrens hosps. Clin. asso. prof. neurol. surgery U. Tenn., Knoxville. Diplomate Am. Bd. Neurol. Surgery. Fellow A.C.S.; mem. Am., Tenn. med. assns., Knoxville Acad. Medicine, Congress Neurol. Surgeons, So. Neurosurgical Soc., Am. Assn. Neurol.

Surgeons, Assn. Air Force Mil. Surgeons, Phi Gamma Delta, Phi Ki. Methodist. Elk. Contbr. chpt. to book; papers to profl. jours. Home: Route 2 Smith Rd Concord TN 37720 Office: Ft Sanders Profl Bldg Knoxville TN 37916

PURYEAR, ELMER LEE, educator; b. nr. Raleigh, N.C., Aug. 20, 1920; s. Rufus A. and Chloe (Strickland) P.; B.A. summa cum laude, Wake Forest U., 1943; M.A., U. N.C., 1947, Ph.D., 1954; m. Lois Bradley, Feb. 3, 1944; children—Paul, Leigh. Instr. history Wake Forest U., 1947-52; asst. prof. history W.Va. U., 1954-56; asso. prof. history Coll. of Charleston (S.C.), 1956-59, prof., 1959-62; prof. history, polit. sci. Greensboro (N.C.) Coll., 1962-71, dean, 1963-71; Graham A. Barden prof. govt. Campbell Coll., 1971—. Served with USNR, 1943-46; ETO. Mem. N.C. Hist. Soc. (sec., treas. 1965-69, pres. 1971-72), Am., So. hist. assns., So. Polit. Sci. Assn. Rotarian. Author: (with others) Orange County, 1752-1952, 1953; Democratic Party Dissension in North Carolina, 1928-36, 1962. Contbr. articles to profl. jours. Home: 4013 Groometown Rd Greensboro NC 27407

PUSTER, FRANCES GARNETT (MRS. J. GREGG PUSTER), travel agy. exec.; b. Canon City, Colo., July 14, 1911; d. William Lacy and Persis (Briskey) Garnett; degree Rome Bus. Coll., 1930; student Internat. Corr. Schs., 1943; degree Am. Inst. Banking, 1955; student N.Y. Inst. Photography, 1959; m. J. Gregg Puster, July 10, 1972. Bookkeeper, Nat. City Bank, Rome, Ga., 1932-38, teller, 1939-47, head teller, 1948-59, head collection dept., 1960-68; owner-mgr. World Travel Agy., Rome, 1950—. Mem. Rome Symphony Orch., treas. 1950-56. Mem. Nat. Audubon Soc., Nat. Freelance Photographers Assn., Rome C. of C., Internat. Platform Assn., Photog. Soc. Am. Episcopalian. Office: World Travel Agy 430 Broad St PO Box 1393 Rome GA 30161

PUTMAN, WILLIAM BENJAMIN, III, lawyer; b. Springdale, Ark., Aug. 23, 1923; s. William Benjamin and Maxine (Corbin) P.; B.A., U. Ark., 1947, J.D. with High Honors, 1953; m. Barbara Elizabeth Johnson, June 5, 1951; 1 son, William Benjamin IV. With Stanolind Oil & Gas Co., 1948-51; practice law, admitted to Ark. bar, 1953; mem. firm Putman, Davis & Bassett, Fayetteville, 1953—. Lectr. in law U. Ark. Sch. Law, 1956—, pres. Ark. Law Sch. Found., 1966—; spl. justice Supreme Ct. of Ark., 1968, 70, 71; mem. Ark. Bd. Law Examiners, 1959-64; mem. Ark. Supreme Ct. Com. on Jury Instrns., 1962—. Chmn., Washington County Democratic Central Com., 1957-61; mem. Washington County Bd. Election Commrs., 1957-61. Bd. dirs. Ark. Bar Found. Served with AUS, 1943-46. Decorated Purple Heart. Fellow Internat. Soc. Barristers; mem. Am., Ark. (spl. award 1966), Washington County bar assns., Am. Judicature Soc., Medico Legal Soc. London, Phi Alpha Delta, Omicron Delta Kappa, Sigma Alpha Epsilon. Editor, Ark. Law Rev., 1953. Home: 122 W Meadow St Fayetteville AR 72701 Office: 19 E Mountain St Fayetteville AR 72701

PUTNAM, FREDERICK WARREN, JR., bishop; b. Red Wing, Minn., June 17, 1917; s. Frederick W. and Margaret (Bunting) P.; B.A., U. Minn., 1939; M.Div., Seabury-Western Theol. Sem., 1942, D.D., 1963; postgrad. student, State U. Ia., 1946-47; m. Helen Kathryn Prouse, Sept. 24, 1942; children—James Douglas, John Frederick, Andrew Warren. Ordained deacon, priest Episcopal Ch., 1942; pastor in Windom and Worthington, Minn., 1942-43, Iowa City, 1943-47, Evanston, Ill., 1947-59, Wichita, Kan., 1960-63; Episcopalian chaplain State U. Ia., 1943-47; suffragan bishop Episcopal Diocese Okal., 1963—. Cons. Oklahoma City Community Relation Commn., 1966-70. Pres. Okla. Conf. Religion and Race, 1963-67; v.p. Greater Oklahoma City Council Chs., 1966-67; nat. chaplain Brotherhood of St. Andrew, 1967—, mem. brotherhood legion, 1972—; priest asso. Order Holy Cross, 1942—; exec. com. Conf. Diocesan Execs., 1969—, pres., 1972—; mem. Okla. Commn. United Ministries in Higher Edn., 1970—, pres., 1973—. Founder, pres. Oklahoma City Met. Alliance for Safer City, 1972—. Trustee Seabury-Western Theol. Sem., 1959-65, Episcopal Theol. Sem. Southwest, 1966-69, St. Simeon's Episcopal Home, 1963—, St. Crispins Episcopal Conf. Center, 1963—, Casady Sch., 1963—, Holland Hall Sch., 1963—, Episcopal Soc. Cultural and Racial Unity, 1967-70; trustee Neighborhood Services Orgn., treas., 1969; founder, 1st pres. Friends of Wichita Pub. Library, 1962. Recipient Distinguished Service award Evanston Jr. C. of C., 1952. Fellow Coll. Preachers; mem. Inst. Pastoral Care, Acad. Religion and Mental Health, Am. Civil Liberties Union, Asso. Parishes (pres. 1960-64), Overseas Mission Soc., Assn. Am. Indian Affairs, Photog. Soc. Am., Am. Com. for KEEP (v.p. 1961—), Assn. Clin. Pastoral Edn., Religious Pub. Relations Council, Wilderness Soc., Ch. Soc. Coll. Work, Nat. Cathedral Assn., Okla. Camera Club, Nat. Wildlife Assn., Nat. Audubon Soc., Center Study Dem. Instns., Nat. Citizens Com. for Broadcasting, Am. Acad. Polit. and Social Sci., World Future Soc., Clergy Assn. Diocese Okla., U. Minn. Alumni Assn., Nat. Geog. Soc., Phi Kappa Psi. Club: Admirals. Author articles. Editor, pub. Shareres mag., 1957-63. Home: 1704 Camden Way Oklahoma City OK 73116 Office: Box 1296 Oklahoma City OK 73101

PUTNAM, WILLIAM THOMAS, state ofcl.; b. Florence, S.C., July 30, 1926; s. Bluford Hugh and Lucy (Self) P.; B.S., U. S.C., 1948; m. Elizabeth Burch Harrell, July 14, 1951; children—William Thomas, Susan Elizabeth. Field auditor S.C. Tax Commn., Columbia, 1948-53, chief clk. income div., 1953-57, individual supr., 1957-61, dir. data processing div., 1961-66, asst. state auditor, 1966—. Served with USAAF, 1945-46. Baptist (deacon). Home: 109 Chartwell Rd Columbia SC 29210 Office: Wade Hampton Bldg Senate St Columbia SC 29202

PUTNEY, BLAKE FUQUA, coll. dean; b. Farmville, Va., July 16, 1923; s. Samuel Waverly and Annie Randolph (Vaughan) P.; B.S., Med. Coll. Va., 1947; Ph.D. (Samuel W. Melendy fellow) U. Minn., 1952; m. Marie-Louise Flinker, Sept. 2, 1950; children—Blake Fuqua, Thomas Randolph, Barbara Marie. Mem. faculty Rutgers U. Coll. Pharmacy, 1952-67, asst. prof., 1952-58, asso. prof., 1958-67; prof. pharmacy, chmn. dept. Med. U. S.C., Charleston, 1967—, asst. dean Coll. Pharmacy, 1970—. Mem. blue ribbon com. Nat. Assn. Bds. Pharmacy, 1969—. Trustee, Franke Home, Charleston, 1969-72. Served with AUS, 1943-46. Mem. Am. Pharm. Assn., Sigma Xi, Rho Chi, Kappa Psi. Lutheran (pres. council). Home: 479 Wade Hampton Dr Charleston SC 29412 Office: 80 Barre St Charleston SC 29401

PUTNEY, CHARLES WALKER, elec. engr.; b. Staunton, Va., June 10, 1936; s. Charles Walker and Louise (Gathright) P.; B.S., Va. Mil. Inst., 1957; M.S., San Jose State Coll., 1968; m. Karen Marie Albright, Jan. 12, 1957; children—Wainscott, Pamela, Sarah. Maintenance test engr. U.S. Steel, Munhall, Pa., 1957-60; test and evaluation engr. Polaris Fire Control and Guidance, Gen. Electric, Pittsfield, Mass., 1960-63; dynamics engr. Lockheed Missiles & Space Co., Sunnyvale, Cal., 1963-66; sr. hybrid computer simulation engr. Martin Marietta, Orlando, Fla., 1968—; dir. Silvercrest Furnishings, Inc., Orlando. Served to 2d lt. USAF, 1957-58. Mem. I.E.E.E. Republican. Baptist. Home: 2233 Via Tuscany Winter Park FL 32789 Office: MP-171 Martin Marietta Orlando FL 32802

PUTNEY, ROBERT BRADFORD, indsl. engr.; b. Adams, Neb., June 15, 1914; s. Charles Robert and Helen Juliete (Cook) P.; student U. Neb., 1932-34; B. Indsl. Engring., Ga. Tech. Coll., 1951; m. Virginia Harris Kelly, Sept. 10, 1949; 1 dau., Margaret. Journeyman toolmaker, 1938-42; machine designer Chattanooga Box & Lumber Co., 1951-53; cons. engr., Fred Salmon & Assos., Chattanooga, 1953-54; engr. E.T. Barwick Mills, Inc., LaFayette, Ga., 1954-55; chief engr. Chattanooga Box & Lumber Co., 1955-61; corp. engr. E.T. Barwick Industries, Chamblee, Ga., 1961—, Pres., Fortune Grammar P.T.A., Lafayette, 1965-66, Kensington Community Club, 1965-67. Mem. Walker, Catoosa and Dade County Devel. Assos., 1966-68, Coosa Valley Area Planning and Devel. Commn., 1967-74. Bd. dirs. Kensington Water Assn., 1967-73, v.p., 1968-69, pres. 1969-71. Served with USNR, 1942-45. Registered profl. engr., Tenn., Ga. Mem. Profl. Engrs. Club, Personnel Club, Soc. Advancement Mgmt. Republican. Methodist. Lion, Rotarian, Elk. Home: Route 1 Kensington GA 30727 Office: PO Box 441 LaFayette GA 30728

PUYEAR, DONALD EMPSON, coll. pres.; b. Cape Girardeau, Mo., Aug. 21, 1932; s. Hugh Gates and Isabel (Brewer) P.; B.S., U. Mo. Sch. Mines and Metallurgy, 1954, M.S., 1958; Ph.D., Va. Poly. Inst., 1965; m. JoAnn Hindman, Sept. 7, 1957; children—Elizabeth, Kenneth, Sarah, Amy. Engr. duPont Co., Wilmington, Del., 1954-55; asst. prof. chem. engring. Va. Poly. Inst., Blacksburg, 1958-64; prof. engring., dir. Dabney S. Lancaster Community Coll., Clifton Forge, Va., 1964-67, pres., 1967-69; pres. Va. Highlands Community Coll., Abingdon, 1969-73; pres. Central Va. Community Coll., Lynchburg, 1974—. Various dist. and council offices Boy Scouts Am., 1958—; mem. Mt. Rogers Citizens Devel. Corp., 1970—. Mem. Clifton Forge Sch. Bd., 1967-69. Bd. dirs. Washington County United Fund, 1970—, Va. Highlands Festival, Inc., 1970-72. Served to lt., C.E., AUS, 1955-57. Recipient Silver Beaver award Boy Scouts Am., 1973. Mem. Washington County C. of C. (dir. 1971—), Sigma Xi, Alpha Chi Sigma, Tau Beta Pi, Phi Delta Kappa. Methodist. Rotarian. Home: Route 2 Altavista VA 24517 Office: PO Box 4098 Fort Hill Sta Lynchburg VA 24502

PUZAR, VINCENT DOMINIC, realtor, mgmt. cons.; b. Grand Rapids, Mich., Mar. 30, 1928; s. Vincent Alexander and Anna Marion (Bajorinas) P.; Asso. Sci., Grand Rapids Jr. Coll., 1947; student U. Central Mich., 1957-58, U. Mich., 1959-62; m. Joan Eileen Thompson, Apr. 4, 1959; children—Barbara Jean, Brad Kendall, Nancy Ellen, Laurie Anne. Analyst, researcher Dow Chem. Co., Midland, Mich., 1949-56; owner Accordion Inst., Midland, 1956-59; owner Midland Real Estate Exchange, 1959-62; v.p. comml. sales and devel. Brantley Assos., Realtors, St. Petersburg, Fla., 1963-67; pres. Vince Puzar Assos., realtors, Action Mgmt., Inc., Action Properties, Inc., St. Petersburg, 1967—. Nat. and state judge classical accordion competitions; computer cons. Realtron Corp., Detroit, 1972—; dir. Gulf Beach-Seminole Bd. Realtors, 1969—, pres., 1971; mem. St. Petersburg Bd. Realtors, Clearwater Bd. Realtors. Alternate del. Mich. Republican Conv., 1962. Mem. finance com. Little Ears, Inc., St. Petersburg. Recipient citation for articles on real estate exchanging Internat. Traders Club, 1964; named Realtor of Year, Gulf Beach-Seminole Bd. Realtors, 1971. Mem. Nat., Fla. assns. realtors, Nat., Fla. assns. mortgage brokers, Nat. Musicians Union. Elk. Author: A Computerized Bookkeeping System-Plan A, 1973. Composer: Rhapsodie Dramatique, 1958. Patentee in chem. engring. field. Home: 520 59th Av St Petersburg Beach FL 33706 Office: 5905 Gulf Blvd St Petersburg Beach FL 33706

PYE, PERRY GLENN, oil co. exec.; b. Leesville, La., May 6, 1913; s. Perry Gouldsby and Grace Estelle (Martin) P.; student La. Coll., 1930-32; B.B.A., U. Tex., 1934; postgrad. La. State U., 1948, U. Houston, 1950; m. Frances Mildred Kemp, June 3, 1931; 1 son, Perry Gregory. Financial v.p. Manabi Exploration Co., Houston, 1953-55; treas. Claud B. Hamill Oil Co., Houston, 1955—. Treas. Autumn Oaks Civic Club, 1973. Trustee The Hamill Found. Served 1st lt. Q.M.C., AUS, 1943-44. C.P.A., Tex., La. Mem. Am. Inst. C.P.A.'s, Tex. Soc. C.P.A.'s, Tax Execs. Inst. (pres. 1959). Baptist (deacon 1965). Club: Houston. Home: 10826 St Mary's Lane Houston TX 77024 Office: 2306 First City Nat Bank Bldg Houston TX 77002

PYLE, JOHNNIE AUGUSTUS, insulation co. exec.; b. Crockett, Tex., Oct. 16, 1914; s. Otis Augustus and Mary Bell (Richardson) P.; student pub. schs.; m. Iola McKnight, Dec. 1, 1945; children—Billy G., Shirley (Mrs. Lewis Watts, Jr.), Bobbie (Mrs. Edward Schiller), Linda. Warehouseman, B & B Engring & Supply Co., Houston, 1945-46, purchasing agt., 1947-55, mgr. purchasing, 1956-70; v.p. B & B Insulation, Inc., Houston, 1971—. Served with USNR, 1945. Eagle. Home: 2006 Chaparrel St Houston TX 77043 Office: 6250 W Park St Houston TX 77027

PYLE, RICHARD ALDEN, lawyer; b. Eufaula, Okla., Apr. 16, 1931; s. Luther Alden and Margaret Catherine (Turner) P.; B. A., Central State U., 1964; LL.B., U. Okla., 1966; m. Forrest Marjorie Busha, Aug. 23, 1952; children—Traci Lou, Trent Alden. Admitted to Okla. bar, 1966; practiced in Eufaula, 1966-69; U.S. atty. for Eastern Dist. Okla., Muskogee, 1969—. Served with AUS, 1950, 52. Mem. McIntosh County (pres. 1970), Muskogee County, Fed. bar assns., Delta Theta Phi. Republican. Home: 206 Broadway St Eufaula OK 74432 Office: 333 Fed Bldg Muskogee OK 74401

QUADE, DANA, educator; b. Cardston, Alta., Can., Jan. 11, 1935; s. Edward Schaumberg and Sylvia (Anthony) Q. (parents Am. citizens); B.A., U. Cal. at Los Angeles, 1955; Ph.D., U. N.C., 1960; m. Erna Adriana Goetz, Aug. 18, 1962; children—Jonny, Christopher, Ingrid. Mem. commd. corps USPHS, Atlanta, 1960-61, Washington, 1961-62; asst. prof. dept. biostatistics U. N.C., 1962-65, asso. prof., 1965-70, prof., 1970—. Recipient NIH Career Devel. award, 1968-73. Fellow Am. Statis. Assn.; mem. Inst. Math. Statistics, Biometric Soc. Lutheran. Home: Markham Dr Chapel Hill NC 27541

QUALLS, ROBERT L., coll. adminstr.; b. Burnsville, Miss., Nov. 6, 1933; s. Wes E. and Letha (Parker) Q.; B.S., Miss. State U., 1954, M.S., 1958; postgrad. La. State U., 1959-61; LL.D., Whitworth Coll., Brookhaven, Miss., 1974; m. Mildred Daphne Ward, Nov. 5, 1966. Prof., chmn. div. econs. and bus. Belhaven Coll., Jackson, Miss., 1962-66, asst. to pres., 1965-66; asst. prof. finance Miss. State U., State College, 1967-69; sr. v.p. Bank of Miss., Tupelo, 1969-74; v.p. Wesleyan Coll., Macon, Ga., 1974—; cons. First Fed. Savs. & Loan Assn., Jackson, 1963-68, dir. marketing, 1968-69; marketing cons. Ill. Central Industries, Chgo., 1964. Mem. faculty, Thesis examiner Stonier Grad. Sch. Banking, Rutgers U., 1973—; mem. faculty Miss. Sch. Banking, U. Miss., 1973—. Chmn. community service and continuing edn. com. Tupelo Community Devel. Found., 1972-73. Mem. Miss. 4-H adv. council, 1969; active Boy Scouts Am. Served to lt. AUS, 1954-56. Found. for Econ. Edn. fellow, 1964; Ford Found. faculty research fellow, 1963-64. Mem. Am. Bankers Assn. (marketing planning and research com. 1972-73), Bus. and Profl. Group of Am. (dir. 1969), Newcomen Soc., Blue Key, Omicron Delta Kappa, Delta Sigma Pi, Sigma Phi Epsilon. Rotarian. Contbr. articles to profl. jours. Home: 140 Tyrone Blvd Macon GA 31204

QUANDT, WILLIAM BAUER, govt. ofcl., polit. scientist; b. Los Angeles, Nov. 23, 1941; s. William Carl and Dorothy Elaine (Bauer) Q.; B.A., Stanford, 1963; Ph.D. (Social Sci. Research Council fellow), Mass. Inst. Tech., 1968; m. Anna Spitzer, June 21, 1964. Mem. social sci. research staff Rand Corp., Santa Monica, Cal., 1968-72; instr. polit. sci. U. Cal. at Los Angeles, 1969, 71; fgn. policy analyst on staff Nat. Security Council, Washington, 1972-74; asso. prof. polit. sci. U. Pa., 1974—. Internat. Affairs fellow Council on Fgn. Relations, 1972-73. Mem. Am. Polit. Sci. Assn., Middle East Studies Assn., Middle East Inst., Phi Beta Kappa. Author: Revolution and Political Leadership: Algeria, 1954-68, 1969; The Politics of Palestinian Nationalism, 1973. Home: 1250 4th St Washington DC 20024 Office: National Security Council Staff Washington DC 20506

QUARLES, GILFORD GODFREY, govt. ofcl.; b. Charlottesville, Va., Dec. 24, 1909; s. Charles H. and Carolynn (Payne) Q.; B.S. in Elec. Engring., U. Va., 1930, M.S. in Physics, 1933, Ph.D. in Physics, 1934; m. Mary Ethel Kase, Mar. 24, 1934 (div.) m. 2d, Betty Jane Haugh, Sept. 2, 1961. Tchr. physics Mercer U., 1934-35, U. Ala., 1935-41, Furman U., 1941-44; research asso. Harvard, 1944-45; prof. engring. research Pa. State U., 1945-58, dir. Ordnance Research Lab., 1952-58; tech. cons. comdg. gen. Army Ballistic Missile Agy., 1956-58; chief scientist Army Ordnance Missile Command, 1958-59, C.E., U.S. Army, 1959-60; dir. long range mil. planning Bendix Corp., 1960-61; chief sci. adviser C.E., U.S. Army, 1961—. Mem. Am. Phys. Soc., I.E.E.E., A.A.A.S., Assn. U.S. Army, Am. Soc. Engring. Edn., Sigma Xi, Theta Tau, Tau Beta Pi. Author: Elementary Photography, 1948; also articles electro-optics, acoustics, vibrations, space tech. Home: 1913 Earldale Ct Alexandria VA 22306 Office: Office Chief of Engrs Washington DC 20314

QUARM, JOAN HELANA PHELAN, educator, critic; b. Bristol, Eng.; d. Samuel George and Mary (O'Phelan) Phelan; B.A. Edn., Portsmouth Coll., U. Reading (Eng.), 1940; M.A., San Francisco State Coll., 1966; m. Thomas Quarm, 1949 (div. 1964); children—Susanna Rosemary Summ (Mrs. Terry Gardner), Michael, Robin, Christopher, Nicholas. Came to U.S., 1946, naturalized, 1948. Tchr., A.S. Neill's, Summerhill, Eng., Lisbon, Portugal, 1943, with Brit. Council, Peru, 1949-51, Cerro de Pasco Co., Central Africa, 1956; faculty U. Tex., El Paso, 1958—, asst. prof. English, 1967—; drama and music critic El Paso Herald-Post, 1962—. Co-founder The Theatre, El Paso, 1962, Festival Theatre, 1964, dir., 1965—. Recipient personal grant to found a bilingual theatre in El Paso from Nat. Found. Arts and Humanities and Tex. Fine Arts Commn., 1969; Nat. Critics' Inst. fellow O'Neill Meml. Theatre Conf., 1973. Mem. Actors Equity Assn., Am. Assn. U. Profs., Nat. Soc. Arts and Letters, Tex. Womens Press Assn. Home: 1520 Upson Av El Paso TX 79902

QUARTANA, JOSEPH JOHN, cons. engr.; b. New Orleans, June 9, 1923; s. John and Ida (Passalaqua) Q.; student Tulane U., 1943; B.M.E., La. State U., 1947; m. Roma Burris, Nov. 12, 1949; children—Donna (Mrs. Lawrence Joseph Moeller), Lawrence Joseph. Constrn. engr. E. I. du Pont de Nemours, Tex., Del., Tenn., 1947-53; mech., elec. supr. deLaureal & Moses, New Orleans, 1953-56; prin. Quartana & Assos., Metairie, La., 1956—; prof. architecture Tulane U., part-time 1960—. Served with USNR, 1942-46. Mem. Am. Inst. Aeros. and Astronautics, Am. Soc. Heating, Refrigerating and Air Conditioning Engrs., Cons. Engrs. Council. Author: Chart-o-Book, 1961. Home: 235 Hollywood Dr Metairie LA 70005 Office: 3813 Division St Metairie LA 70002

QUATTLEBAUM, WALTER EMMETT, JR., telephone co. exec.; b. Midville, Ga., Dec. 22, 1922; s. Walter Emmett and Eva (Bagley) Q.; student Murrey Vocational Sch., 1941, U. Hawaii, 1943; m. Dorothy Evelyn Clewis, Oct. 22, 1946; children—Walter Emmett III, Amalia Ann. Former owner Fla. Telephone Exchange, Sneads, 1948—, Cottondale, 1954—, Grand Ridge, 1954—, Bonifay, 1955—, Westville, 1957—, Seagrove Beach, 1958—; past pres., chmn. bd. dirs. Tri-County Telephone Co., Bonifay; v.p., dir. Seminole Telephone Co., Donalsonville, Ga.; now investment analyst. City councilman, Sneads, 1950-52, pres. City Council, 1953. Served with AUS, 1944-46. Mem. Fla. Telephone Assn. (dir.), Telephone Pioneers Am. Methodist. Address: Bonifay FL 32425

QUATTLEBAUM, WILLIAM CASPER, dentist; b. Cullman, Ala., Aug. 19, 1924; s. Samuel Oscar and Lillie Cordelia (Hines) Q.; A.A., St. Bernard Coll., 1947; D.M.D., U. Ala., 1952; m. Virginia Ruth Houston, Nov. 16, 1946; children—Kenneth Wesley, Jane Lori, Samuel Oscar. Pvt. practice dentistry, Birmingham, Ala., 1952—. Served with AUS, 1943-45. Mem. Am. (del. 1959-68), Ala. dental assns., 3d Dist. Dental Soc. (v.p. 1960, pres. 1961). Baptist. (deacon 1956—, pres. trustees 1964—). Kiwanian (sec. 1955). Home: 2077-B Vestavia Park Ct Birmingham AL 35216 Office: 1729 1/2 3d Av N Birmingham AL 35203

QUEHL, THOMAS MALCOLM, physician; b. Ft. Thomas, Ky., Apr. 3, 1929; s. Thomas Henry and Nan Louise (Dulaney) Q.; B.S., La. State U., 1952; M.D. with honors, Tulane U., 1956; m. Barbara Jean Leitner, Sept. 5, 1955; children—Thomas John, Malcom Marcus, Nancy Lynn, Sarah Elizabeth, George Joseph. Intern, Mound Park Hosp., St. Petersburg, Fla., practice medicine, St. Petersburg, 1956—; dir. Para Med. Enterprises, Inc., St. Petersburg, 1960—. Speaker on drugs and alcohol abuse on TV, radio, also to various groups. Dir. Bur. Alcoholic Rehab., State Fla., 1970-74. Trustee Gulf Med. Service Corp. Profit Sharing Plan for Employees. Served with AUS, 1946-49. Recipient City of St. Petersburg Outstanding Civic award, 1971-73. Mem. Fla. Acad. Family Physicians (dir. 1967-70, 70-71, pres. elect 1972, chmn. bd. dirs. 1974), A.M.A., So. Med. Assn., Am. Acad. Family Physicians. Clubs: Lakewood Country, Exchange. Contbr. articles on drugs and alcohol abuse to profl. jours. Home: 1501 Alhambra Way S St Petersburg FL 33705 Office: 5039 Central Av St Petersburg FL 33710

QUENG, JOSEPH T., allergist; b. Fukien, China, Sept. 20, 1933; M.D. (cum laude), U. Santo Tomas, Philippines, 1958; m. Theresa P. Chan. Rotating intern, Kings County Hosp. Center, Bklyn., 1958-59; resident in pediatrics Beth-El Hosp., Bklyn., 1959-60; asst. in pediatrics Baylor U. Coll. Medicine, Houston, 1960-64, resident in pediatrics, 1960-62, fellow in pediatric allergy, 1962-64, clin. asst. prof. pediatrics, 1969—; asst. prof. pediatrics Far Eastern U. Inst. Medicine, Manila, Philippines, 1965-67; clin. asso. prof. allergy, U. Tex. Grad. Sch. Bio-Med. Scis., Houston, 1970—; chief, pediatric allergy clinic Children's Med. Center, Quezon City, Philippines, 1964-67; St. Luke's Hosp., Quezon City, 1966-67; St. Joseph's Hosp., Houston, 1969—; now practice medicine specializing in allergies, Houston; mem. staff Tex. Children's Hosp., Hermann Hosp., Bayshore Gen. Hosp.; cons. in allergy Rosewood Gen. Hosp. Lectr. on allergies. Recipient Mead Johnson Travel grant Am. Coll. Allergists, 1963. Diplomate Am. Bd. Pediatrics, Am. Bd. Allergy and Immunology. Fellow Am. Acad. Allergy, Am. Coll. Allergists, Am. Assn. Certified Allergists, Am. Acad. Pediatrics; mem. Internat. Corr. Soc. Allergists, Philippines Pediatrics Soc, A.M.A., Tex. Med. Assn., Harris County Med. Soc., So. Med. Assn., Tex. Pediatric Soc., A.A.A.S., Sigma Xi. Office: McGovern Allergy Clin 6969 Brompton St Houston TX 77025

QUESENBERRY, CHARLES PRICE, statistician; educator, b. Dugspur, Va., Apr. 13, 1931; s. Fuster and Mary (Marshall) Q.; student Randolph-Macon Coll., 1953-54; B.S., Va. Poly. Inst., 1957, M.S., 1958, Ph.D., 1960; m. Lessia Odell Willis, Mar. 28, 1953; children—Karen Lynn, Charles Price, Thomas Lee, Mary Ann. Asst. prof. math. Mont. State U., 1960-63, asso. prof., 1963-66; prof. statistics dept. N.C. State U., 1966—; cons. Becton, Dickenson Research Labs., 1970—; research statistician Battelle Meml. Inst., summer 1962; cons. Mont. Fish and Game Dept., 1960-66. Served with USMCR, 1950-53. Decorated Silver Star, Purple Heart. NASA Research grantee, 1964-66. Fellow Am. Statis. Assn.; mem. Biometric Soc., Inst. Math. Statistics, Sigma Xi, Phi Kappa Phi, Pi Mu Epsilon. Conglist. Contbr. numerous articles to profl. jours. Home: 224 Northbrook Dr Raleigh NC 27607

QUESENBERRY, WILLIAM FITZHUGH, food broker; b. Jacksonville, Fla., Dec. 3, 1922; s. William Fitzhugh and Caroline (Kittrell) Q.; B.A., U. of South, 1943; m. Mary Belle Gardner, Apr. 13, 1946; 1 dau., Mary Belle (Mrs. Robert McIntyre). With Quesenberry & Catlin, Miami, Fla., 1946—, salesman, 1946-49, partner, 1949-53, sr. partner, 1953—. Bd. dirs. Muscular Dystrophy Soc. Fla.; trustee U. of South; bd. advisors Fla. Meml. Coll. Served to lt. comdr. USNR, 1943-46. Mem. Miami (pres. 1951-52), Nat. (dir. 1966-67) food brokers assns., Fla. Frozen Food Assn. (dir.), Hist. Soc. Fla., Traffic Club of Greater Miami (v.p. 1951-52), Phi Gamma Delta. Episcopalian (sr. warden 1970-71). Kiwanian (pres. Miami 1972-73). Clubs: Riviera Country, Coral Gables Country, Two Hundred of Greater Miami. Home: 4102 Monserrate St Coral Gables FL 33146 Office: 735 NW 22d Av Miami FL 33135

QUICKSALL, JAMES LOUIS, distbg. co. exec.; b. Waco, Tex., Dec. 21, 1894; s. James Louis and Maidie (Bolton) O.; A.B., Baylor U., 1916; m. Carlyn Trautwein, June 20, 1921 (dec. Jan. 1945); m. 2d, Ettie Claire Jolley, Nov. 28, 1946. Salesman, asst. mgr. Swift & Co., Amarillo, Tex., 1919-25; partner Westmoreland Co., 1925-30; pres. Quicksall-Pryor Co., Inc., Lubbock, Tex., 1925—; dir. First Fed. Savs. & Loan Assn. Lubbock. Mem. A.C. Electronics div. Gen. Motors Distbrs. Council, 1964. Pres., bd. dirs. Symphony Orch. Served to 1st lt. AUS, 1917-19. Mem. Tex., Lubbock (past pres.) chambers commerce, Automotive Wholesalers Assn. Tex. (past pres., dir.), Nat. Assn. Automotive Service Industry Assn. (dir.), Nat., Tex. trade assns., Am. Legion. Baptist. Mason (32 deg., Shriner), Rotarian. Home: Apt 1107 Altura Apts Lubbock TX 79405 Office: PO Box 1946 Lubbock TX 79408

QUIGGINS, KENNETH LAVERNE, optometrist; b. Gibson County, Ind., June 23, 1914; s. William H. and Nannie M. (McAtee) Q.; D.Optometry, No. Ill. Coll. Optometry, 1940; m. Louise Clark Drum, Dec. 11, 1949 (dec.); children—Alice, William Preston; m. 2d, Mary Mathis Rucker, Mar. 3, 1972. Practice optometry, Charlotte, N.C., 1940-41, Greenville, 1946—. Mem. N.C. State Bd. Examiners in Optometry, 1947-57. Served with AUS, 1942-46. Mem. N.C. State Optometric Soc., Am. Optometric Assn., Am. Optometric Found. Democrat. Mem. Disciples of Christ Ch. Mason (Shriner), Moose, Elk. Clubs: Civitan (Civitan of Year 1961-62, pres. 1960-61). Home: 1708 Rosewood Dr Greenville NC 27834 Office: 116 W 5th St Greenville NC 27834

QUILLEN, FORD C., lawyer; b. Gate City, Va., Sept. 21, 1938; s. Cecil D. and Louise (Carter) Q.; B.S., U. Tenn., 1961, LL.B., 1966; m. Gail Burdette, Dec. 18, 1961; children—Madri, Carter, Lenoir. Admitted to Va. bar, 1966; individual practice law, Gate City, 1966—. Mem. Va. State Legislature, 1970—, chmn. Age of Majority Study Com., 1972—; mem. Va. Legislative and Audit Rev. Commn., Legislative Process Commn., Va. Housing Commn. Served with AUS, 1961-63. Mem. Va., Scott County bar assns. Address: Box 337 Gate City VA 24251

QUILLEN, HOWARD EUGENE, dentist; b. nr. Gate City, Va., July 16, 1920; s. Hobart McKinley and Cora Mae (Vermillion) Q.; B.A., Emory and Henry Coll., 1950; postgrad. E. Tenn. State U., 1951, 57-58; D.D.S., Med. Coll. Va., 1962; m. Grace Jacqueline Broadwater, Dec. 31, 1949; children—Jacqueline Ann, Howard Eugene. Coach, Washington County Sch. Bd., 1948-50, Scott County Sch. Bd., 1950-53, Tazewell County Sch. Bd., 1953-57; pvt. practice dentistry, Gate City, Va., 1962—. Mem. gen. adv. com. Scott County Vocational Center, 1973—. Served with AUS, 1942-46. Recipient Deleware Valley Outstanding Student award Med. Coll. Va. Dental Sch., 1962. Mem. Am. Hist. Soc., Am., Va. State (mem. ethics com. 1971-72) dental assns., Smithsonian Assos., Am. Legion, Am. Heritage Soc., Nat. Hist. Soc., A.A.A.S., V.F.W. Republican. Methodist (mem. finance com. 1971—). Rotarian. Home and Office: PO Box 482 Gate City VA 24251

QUILLEN, JAMES H(ENRY), congressman; b. Wayland, Va., Jan. 11, 1916; s. John A. and Hannah (Chapman) Q.; ed. high sch.; LL.D. (hon.), Steed Coll. Tech., Johnson City, Tenn., 1963; m. Cecile Cox, Aug. 9, 1952. With Kingsport Press, 1934-35, Kingsport Times, 1935-36; founder, pub. Kingsport Mirror, 1936-39; founder, pub. Johnson City Times, 1939-44, converted to daily, 1940; founder, owner, pres. (inactive) Kingsport Devel. Co., Model City Investment Corp., Kingsport Devel. Co. Ins., Inc., Kingsport Devel. Co. Real Estate-Loans, Inc., Kingsport Devel. Co. Gen. Contractors, Inc.; chmn. bd. Johnson City Ins. Agy., Inc., Wofford Bros., Inc., Johnson City; dir. Kingsport Nat. Bank; mem. Tenn. Ho. of Reps., 1954-62, legislative council, 1957-59, 61; mem. 88th-93d Congresses 1st Tenn. Dist., mem. house rules com., 1965—, house com. standards of ofcl. conduct. Bd. dirs. Sullivan County Tb Assn., past state dir.; past dir. Kingsport chpt. A.R.C. Served to lt. USNR, 1942-46. Recipient Young Man of Yr. award Johnson City Jr. C. of C., 1942. Mem. Kingsport Real Estate Bd. (dir., past pres.), Am. Legion, V.F.W., C. of C. Republican. Methodist. Lion. Clubs: Ridgefield Country (Kingsport); Capitol Hill (Washington). Home: 1601 Fairidge Pl Kingsport TN 37664 Office: Cannon Bldg Washington DC 20515

QUILLIAM, WILLIAM REED, JR., lawyer, educator; b. Beaumont, Tex., Jan. 21, 1929; s. William Reed and Gladys (Harned) Q.; B.A., U. Tex. at Austin, 1949, B.B.A., 1951, J.D., 1953; LL.M., Harvard, 1969; m. Myrna Corinne Simmons, June 6, 1953; children—Mary Corinne, Kathryn Harned, William Reed III. Admitted to Tex. bar, 1953; asst. prof. Tex. Tech. U., 1955-56, prof. law, 1969—, acting asso. dean, 1973—; trust officer Am. State Bank, 1959-60; pvt. practice law, Lubbock, Tex., 1956-58, 60-68; pres. Lubbock Lands, Inc., 1966—. Mem. Tex. Ho. Reps., 1961-69. Named Outstanding First-Term House Mem., U.P.I. poll, 1961, Outstanding prof. Tex. Tech. U., 1971. Served as lt. (j.g.) USNR, 1953-55; now lt. comdr. Res. Mem. State Bar Tex., State Jr. Bar Tex. (dir. 1957-59), Theta Xi, Phi Alpha Delta. Presbyn. Club: Lubbock. Home: 5703 Geneva St Lubbock TX 79413 Office: Sch Law Tex Tech U Lubbock TX 79409

QUILLIAN, WILLIAM FLETCHER, JR., coll. pres.; b. Nashville, Apr. 13, 1913; s. William Fletcher (D.D.) and Nonie (Acree) Q.; A.B., Emory U., 1935, Litt.D., 1959; B.D., Yale, 1938, Ph.D. (Day fellow, Rosenwald fellow), 1943; postgrad. U. Edinburgh (Scotland), 1938-39, U. Basel (Switzerland), 1939; LL.D., Ohio Wesleyan U., 1952, Randolph-Macon Coll., 1967; m. Margaret Hannah Weigle, June 15, 1940; children—William Fletcher III, Anne Acree, Katherine, Robert. Student asst. Stamford (Conn.) Presbyn. Ch., 1936-38; del. to gen. com. World Student Christian Fedn., Bievres, France, 1938; discussion leader World Conf. Christian Youth, Amsterdam, Holland, 1939; pastor Claredon (Vt.) Community Ch., summer 1940; ordained to ministry Methodist Ch., 1942; asst. prof. philosophy Gettysburg (Pa.) Coll., 1941-43, prof., 1943-45; prof. philosophy Ohio Wesleyan U., 1945-52; pres. Randolph Macon Woman's Coll., Lynchburg, Va., 1952—. Tchr., Garrett Bibl. Inst., summer 1951. Mem. univ. senate Methodist Ch., 1952-72. Bd. dirs. Lynchburg Gen. Hosp. Mem. Va. Found. Ind. Colls. (pres. 1958-61), Assn. Va. Colls. (past pres.), So. Univ. Conf. (pres. 1967-68), So. Assn. Colls. Women (pres. 1956), Am. Philos. Assn., Nat. Council Religion Higher Edn. (central com. 1945-48, chmn. 1947-48), Nat. Assn. Bibl. Instrs., Am. Assn. U. Profs., Phi Beta Kappa, Omicron Delta Kappa, Alpha Tau Omega. Author: The Moral Theory of Evolutionary Naturalism, 1945; Evolution and Moral Theory in America; Evolutionary Thought in America, 1950. Contbr. articles to philos. and religious jours. Home: 2460 Rivermont Av Lynchburg VA 24503

QUIMBY, FREEMAN HENRY, physiologist; b. Battle Creek, Mich., June 11, 1915; s. Lyle Edward and Chloe (Eisenhood) Q.; B.A., Andrews U., 1938; M.S., Northwestern U., 1941; postgrad. Mich. State U., 1940; Ph.D., U. Md., 1947; m. Juanita Lenore Artress, Nov. 10, 1949; children—Kelvin, David, Carole. Mgr., Penny-a-dish cafeteria, Battle Creek, 1935-36; prof. biology Columbia Union Coll., 1941-48; head physiology br. Office Naval Research, San Francisco, 1948-56, chief scientist, 1956-59; chief research analysis Army Research Office, Arlington, Va., 1959-60; chief exobiology br. NASA, Washington, 1960-66; specialist life scis. Library of Congress, Washington, 1966—. Cons. Operations Research Office, U.S. Army. Mem. Fedn. Am. Soc. Exptl. Biology, A.A.A.S., Am. Phys. Soc., Wildlife Fedn., Wilderness Soc., Am. Acad. Polit. Social Scis., Sigma Xi. Author: Search for Extraterrestrial Life, 1963, The Participation of Federal Agencies in International Scientific Programs, 1967; Medical Experimentation on Human Beings, 1968; The State of Technology in Nonlethal Guns, 1968; Chemical and Biological Weapons, 1969; Flouridation: A Modern Paradox in Science and Public Policy, 1970; The Politics of Global Health, 1971. Contbr. articles to profl. jours. Home: 3926 Rickover Rd Silver Spring MD 20902 Office: Library of Congress Washington DC 20540

QUIMBY, GEORGE FRANCIS, computer design engr.; b. Ft. Sam Houston, Tex., Oct. 27, 1936; s. George and Mildred (Miller) Q.; student St. Mary's U., 1954-56; B.E.E., U. Tex., 1959; M.S., So. Methodist U., 1969; m. Anna Marie Krenek, Dec. 28, 1959; children—Stephen, Michael, David. Design engr. Philco Corp., Phila., 1959-62; design engr. Tex. Instruments Inc., Dallas, 1962-63, project engr., 1963-67, engring. mgr., Austin, Tex., 1967—. Pres., bd. dirs. Balcones Little League. Mem. I.E.E.E. Roman Catholic. Home: 4002 Greenmountain Lane Austin TX 78759 Office: 12501 Research St Austin TX 78767

QUINN, CORBETT LATIMER, physician, mayor; b. nr. Pink Hill, N.C., Oct. 6, 1926; s. Corbett L. and Ina (Turner) Q.; B.A., U. N.C., 1949, certificate in medicine, 1951; M.D., U. Md., 1953; m. Ruth Arlene Montgomery, May 26, 1953; children—Corbett Latimer, Risa Teresa. Rotating intern Mercy Hosp., Balt., 1953-54, resident, 1954-55; gen. practice medicine, Magnolia, N.C., 1955—; pres., chief staff Duplin Gen. Hosp., 1955—; N.C. State Surgeon, 1973—; mayor, Magnolia, 1961—. Dir. Br. Banking & Trust Co., Warsaw, N.C. Mem. med. com. for driver evaluation N.C. Dept. Motor Vehicles, 1964—; mem. med. adv. com. James Sprint Inst., 1966—; rep. to Duplin County Cystic Fibrosis Soc., 1968—; civil def. dir., Magnolia, 1958—; surgeon 30th Inf. div. N.C. Army N.G., 1971—. Mem. Magnolia Town Bd. Commrs., 1957-61, mem. adv. com. on mental health, 1969—. Chmn. Duplin County Republican Party, 1970—. Chmn. Magnolia Community Meml. Found. Served with AUS, World War II. Diplomate Am. Bd. Family Practice. Mem. Am. Acad. Gen. Practice, Am. Geriatric Soc., A.M.A., So. Med. Assn., N.C., Duplin County (past pres.) med. socs., Duplin County Tb Assn. (past pres.), Duplin County Cancer Soc. (dir.) Address: Railroad St PO Box 128 Magnolia NC 28453

QUINN, JAMES LEE, savs. and loan assn. exec.; b. Greenwood, Miss., July 23, 1938; s. Jesse Joseph and Mary Lois (Kent) Q.; B.S., Miss. State U., 1960; m. Danice Brewer, June 5, 1958; 1 son, James Michael. With 1st Fed. Savs. & Loan Assn., Greenwood, Miss., 1965-72, loan officer, 1965-68, mng. officer, 1968-72; exec. v.p. Magnolia Fed. Savs. & Loan Assn., Jackson, Miss., 1972—; v.p. dir. Capitol Agy., ins., 1973—; sec.-treas., dir. Americana Corp., land devel., 1974—. Chmn. advance gifts div. United Givers Fund, 1971; chmn. orgn. and extension com. Delta Area council Boy Scout Am., 1967-69. Mem. Greenwood Zoning Bd., 1972. Served to 1st lt. USAF, 1960-63. Mem. Am. Inst. Real Estate Appraisers (residential), Greenwood Leflore C. of C. (dir., 1971-72), Miss. Savs. and Loan League (pres., 1973), Nat. Soc. Controllers and Financial Officers Savs. Instns., Financial Controller Soc. Miss., Soc. Real Estate Appraisers (asso.), Greenwood and Jackson real estate bds., Miss. State U. Alumni Assn. (sec.-treas. 1971-72), Loyalty Found. Miss. State U., Coll. Bus. Alumni Assn., Pi Kappa Alpha. Roman Catholic. Kiwanian (pres.). Home: 5356 Canton Heights Dr Jackson MS 39211 Office: 200 N Congress St Jackson MS 39205

QUINN, JAMES WADE, JR., food co. exec.; b. Osceola, Ark., June 9, 1936; s. James Wade and Jean (Fisher) Q.; student Memphis State U., 1954-57; m. Edris Johanna Gooch, Apr. 18, 1964; children—James Wade III, James Gooch, Patience Kay. Asst. mgr. Food Center Tenn., Memphis, 1957-58, Weingarten's, Memphis, 1959; mgr., owner Time Saver, Inc., Memphis, 1959-64, Pic'n'Sac, West Memphis, 1963-69, Jr. Food Stores, 1965—; pres. Quinn Wholesale Co. (name changed to J. Wade Quinn Inc.), Jonesboro, Ark., 1969—, Sunshine Laundry, 1973—; dist. mgr. Brevoni Hosiery, 1970—. Mem. Jonesboro Bd. Adjustments, 1968-70. Methodist. Lion, Elk. Club: Jonesboro Country. Home: 2515 S Culberhouse Rd Jonesboro AR 72401 Office: 2515 S Culberhouse Rd Jonesboro AR 72401

QUINN, JOHN R., archbishop; b. Riverside, Cal., Mar. 28, 1929; s. Ralph J. and Elizabeth (Carroll) Q.; Ph.B., Gregorian U., Rome, 1950, S.T.B., 1952, S.T.L., 1954. Ordained priest Roman Cath. Ch., 1953; asst. priest St. George Ch., Ontario, Cal., 1954-55; prof. theology Immaculate Heart Sem., San Diego, 1955-62, vice rector, 1960-62; rector St. Francis Coll. Sem., El Cajon, Cal., 1962-64, Immaculate Heart Sem., 1964-68; aux. bishop, vicar gen., San Diego, 1967-72; bishop, Oklahoma City, 1972-73; archbishop Oklahoma City, 1973—; provost U. San Diego, 1968-72. Mem. Cath. Theol. Soc. Am., Canon Law Soc. Am., Am. Cath. Hist. Soc. Address: 1521 N Hudson Oklahoma OK 73103

QUINN, OLIN BYRON, banker; b. Long Leaf, La., Sept. 30, 1917; s. Willie W. and Elizabeth (Alexander) Q.; B.S., La. State U., 1949, M.S., 1951; m. Hazel Hogan, Dec. 21, 1941; children—Laura E., Julianne I. Research staff La. State U. 1951-52; asst. treas. Fed. Intermediate Credit Bank, 1952-59; treas., sr. v.p. Fed. Land Bank of New Orleans, 1959-68, pres., 1968—. Served to lt. USNR, 1941-46. Democrat. Methodist. Kiwanian (dir.). Home: 308 Crystal St New Orleans LA 70124 Office: PO Box 50590 New Orleans LA 70150

QUINTANA, RONALD PRESTON, educator; b. New Orleans, Feb. 23, 1936; s. Robert Roig and Clara (Schneider) Q.; B.S., Loyola U., New Orleans, 1956; M.S., U. Wis.-Madison, 1958, Ph.D. in Pharm. Chemistry, 1961; m. Alma Marie Fuxan, Sept. 7, 1957; children—Ronald Preston, Mary Catherine. Instr. dept. medicinal chemistry Coll. Pharmacy U. Tenn. Med. Units, 1960-61, asst. prof., 1961-65, asso. prof., vice-chmn. dept., 1965-67, prof., vice-chmn., 1967-71, distinguished service prof., vice-chmn., 1971—, prof. dept. periodontics, Coll. Dentistry, 1972-74; del. U.S. Pharmacopeial Conv., 1970—. Mem. Acad. Pharm. Scis., Am. Chem. Soc., Am. Pharm. Assn., The Chem. Soc., Sigma Xi, Alpha Sigma Nu, Phi Lambda Upsilon, Rho Chi. Roman Catholic. Co-editor, contbr. Surface Chemistry and Dental Integuments, 1973. Contbr. articles to profl. jours. Home: 1591 Old Mill Rd Germantown TN 38138 Office: 26 S Dunlap St Memphis TN 38163

QUIROZ, RODERICK SOTELO, meteorologist; b. Ajo, Ariz., Nov. 6, 1923; s. Francisco Quiroz and Rosa Sotelo; student U. Ariz., 1942-43, U. Cal. at Berkeley, 1943-44; B.A., U. Cal. at Los Angeles, 1950; M.S., U. Md., 1970. Research meteorologist U.S. Air Force, 1950-66; research meteorologist Nat. Meteorol. Center, Washington, 1966—. Lectr. Von Karman Inst. for Fluid Dynamics, Brussells, Belgium, 1970; mem. U.S. Standard Atmospheric Com., 1961-74. Served with USAF, 1943-48. Recipient Civilian Meritorious Service award Dept. Def., 1960, 68. Mem. Am. Geophys. Union, Am. Meteorol. Soc. (chmn. com. on atmospheric problems of aerospace vehicles 1968-72). Editor: Meteorological Investigation of the Upper Atmosphere, 1968. Home: 1021 Arlington Blvd Arlington VA 22209 Office: Nat Meteorol Center 5200 Auth Rd Washington DC 20023

QUIST, ARVIN SIGVARD, chemist; b. Blair, Neb., Nov. 15, 1933; s. Alfred S. and Clara F. (Anderson) Q.; B.S., Dana Coll., 1954; M.S., U. Neb., 1957, Ph.D., 1959; m. Doris Anne Grocock, June 9, 1957; children—Erik, Brian, Mark. Research asso. U. Pitts., 1959-60; instr. U. Neb., at Lincoln, 1960-61; mem. research staff Oak Ridge Nat. Lab., 1961—. Mem. environmental quality adv. bd., Oak Ridge, 1970—, chmn., 1970-73. Vis. asso. U. Karlsruhe (West Germany), 1967-68. Mem. Am. Chem. Soc. Contbr. articles to profl. jours. Home: 104 Neville Lake Oak Ridge TN 37830 Office: Oak Ridge Nat Lab PO Box X Oak Ridge TN 37830

RABINOVITCH, BERNARD, educator; b. London, Eng., Nov. 4, 1922; s. Philip and Netta (Goldberg) R.; B.Sc. with honors, London U., 1943; Ph.D., Cambridge (Eng.) U., 1948; m. Annette M. Baron, June 10, 1951; children—Karen, Miriam, Rebecca. Came to U.S., 1948, naturalized, 1960. Eli Lilly fellow Harvard, 1948-49; asst. prof. Ill. Inst. Tech., Chgo., 1949-55, U. Chgo., 1955-60; prof. biophysics U. Okla. at Oklahoma City, 1967—; prin. scientist United Tech. Center, Sunnyvale, Cal., 1963-65. Cons. research in ophthalmology U. Okla. Health Scis. Center, Okla. Eye Inst. NIH spl. fellow Stanford, 1965. Mem. A.A.A.S., Assn. Research in Vision and Ophthalmology, Am. Chem. Soc., Am. Soc. Photochemistry and Photobiology. Contbr. articles to profl. jours. Home: 2230 Ravenwood Lane Norman OK 73069

RABORN, MICHAEL STEVEN, data processing co. exec.; b. Blythe, Cal., June 7, 1944; s. James Jesse and Mary Catherine (Wilkerson) R.; B.B.A., U. Tex., 1967; m. Mary Ann Raborn. Auditor Lybrand, Ross Bros., Houston, 1967; controller Tex. Industries, Inc., Houston, 1968-70; v.p. finance United Horticulture, Orlando, Fla., 1972; owner OWP Data Processing, Inc., Orlando, 1972—. Freelance photographer. C.P.A., Tex. Mem. Tex. Soc. C.P.A.'s, Nat. Assn. C.P.A.'s. Home: 423 Oak Haven Altamonte Springs FL 32701 Office: 202 ak St Sanford FL 32771

RABOURN, WARREN JOSEPH, JR., chemist; b. Indpls., Nov. 12, 1921; s. Warren Joseph and Mary Olive (Rothenbush) R.; B.S., Purdue U., 1949, M.S., 1950, Ph.D., 1953; m. Hazel Lucille Laird, June 2, 1965; 1 son, Warren Jeffrey. Instr. U. Pitts., 1953-54; postdoctoral fellow, asst. prof. Purdue U., 1954-57; chemist Upjohn Co., LaPorte, Tex., 1963—. Bd. dirs. Houston YMCA. Served with USNR, 1940-45. Decorated Purple Heart. Mem. Am. Chem. Soc., A.A.A.S., Am. Inst. Chemists, Am. Legion (comdr. 1959-60), Sigma Xi. Unitarian. Eagle. Contbr. articles jours. Home: 1202 E Princeton Lane Deer Park TX 77536 Office: PO Box 685 LaPorte TX 77571

RACHFORD, HENRY HERBERT, JR., educator; b. El Dorado, Ark., June 14, 1925; s. Henry Herbert and Helene Elise (Akin) R.; B.S. in Chem. Engring., Rice U., 1945, M.A. in Chemistry, 1947; Sc.D. in Chem. Engring., Mass. Inst. Tech., 1950; m. Josephine Hiett, Apr. 27, 1957; children—Susan Elise, Laurie Ann. Research asso. Humble Oil & Refining Co. (now div. of Exxon), Houston, 1949-64; prof. math. and math. scis. Rice U., Houston, 1964—; pres. Douglas, Dupont, Rachford, Inc., cons., Houston, 1969—. Mem. Am. Math. Soc., Soc. for Indsl. and Applied Math., Am. Inst. Chem. Engrs., Soc. Petroleum Engrs., Inst. Mining, Metall. and Petroleum Engrs. Home: 6150 Chevy Chase St Houston TX 77027

RACHMEL, LEO, educator; b. N.Y.C., Aug. 31, 1919; s. Jack and Sarah (Winter) R.; B.B.A., Coll. City N.Y., 1940; M.S., U. Richmond, 1964; Ed.D., U. Sarasota, 1972; m. Carolyn Hentschel Miller, June 12, 1943; children—Lee Winter, Sandra Rae (Mrs. David Ellis Evans). Commd. 2d lt. U.S. Army, 1942, advanced through grades to lt. col., 1961; asst. prof. N.C. State U., 1949-53; instr. U.S. Army Logistics Mgmt. Center, Fort Lee, Va., 1962-67, logistics research analyst, 1967-69, chmn. research, devel., test and evaluation dept., 1969-71, dir. intern tng., 1971—; asst. prof. Sch. Bus. Adminstrn. Va. State Coll., Petersburg, 1966-74, asso. prof., 1974—. Instr. econs. Richard Bland Coll., Petersburg, Va., 1965-66, Coll. William and Mary, Williamsburg, Va., 1965-68; chmn. combined fed. campaign U.S. Army Logistics Mgmt. Center, Ft. Lee, Va., 1971. Mem. Nat. Def. Exec. Res. Office Pres. U.S., 1972. Bd. dirs. Tri-Cities YMCA, 1973—, Southside Va. Mental Health Assn., 1966—. Decorated Army Commendation medal with oak leaf cluster, Bronze Star medal. Recipient Outstanding Performance award U.S. Civil Service, 1967. Fellow Soc. Logistics Engrs. (chmn. nat. edn. com. 1966-68); mem. Am. Assn. U. Profs., Am., So. econs. assns., Amateur Athletic Union U.S. (bd. mgrs. Va. assn. 1960-62), Va. Bus. Edn. Assn., Am. Contract Bridge League. Home: 2123 Armistead Av Petersburg VA 23803 Office: Bus Adminstrn Dept Sch Bus Adminstrn Va State Coll Petersburg VA 23803

RADCLIFF, ALAN LAWRENCE, civic worker, ret. air equipment mfr. exec.; b. N.Y.C., May 27, 1920; s. Benjamin and Mollie (Kirman) Rachleff; B.A., Cornell U., 1941, M.A., 1942; postgrad. marketing Pace Coll., 1951-52; m. Barbara B. Brown, June 1, 1958; children—Jonathan Bruce, Bennett James. Vice pres. Teweles-Radcliff, Inc., advt., N.Y.C., 1947-49; advt. mgr. Hygrade Food Products, Inc., Newark, 1949-51; dir. marketing Duane Jones Co., N.Y.C., 1951-53; marketing cons. Alan Radcliff Co., 1953-55; eastern regional dir., mem. founding group Top Value Enterprises, Inc., Dayton, O., 1955-57; pres. Air Guide Corp., Miami, Fla., 1957-70; now civic leader, Miami area. Chmn. Citizens' Bd. U. Miami; founder, pres. Friends of Theatre U. Miami. Chmn. bd. trustees Players Repertory Theatre, Miami; chmn., exec. producer Omni-Theatre Festival Greater Miami; bd. dirs. Friends of Art Lowe Art Mus.; v.p. bd. govs. Mus. Sci. Served with USAAF, 1943-47. Recipient Fla. Gov.'s award Fine Arts, 1974; named Outstanding Citizen Dade County, 1973-74. Mem. Merchandising Execs. Club N.Y. (past pres.), Am. Antique Automobile Assn., Alpha Psi Omega, Jewish religion. Clubs: The Viscayans, Two Hundred (Miami). Author: Adventures of a Vintage Car Collector. Contbr. articles to profl. jours. Home: 3341 Poinciana Dr Coconut Grove FL 33133

RADCLIFFE, HAROLD, cons. engr.; b. New Bedford, Mass., Apr. 5, 1919; s. James and Emma (Moss) R.; B.S., Mass. Inst. Tech., 1941; m. Alice Isherwood, Oct. 4, 1941; 1 dau., Alyson. Sr. engr. Tuscarora Oil Co. Ltd., Harrisburg, Pa., 1946-53; sr. staff engr. Glace & Glace, Inc., Harrisburg, 1953-57; exec. v.p. Glace Engring. Corp., St. Petersburg, Fla., 1957-63, pres., 1963-68; pres. Glace & Radcliffe, Inc., St. Petersburg, 1968—. Chmn. zoning commn. Town of North Redington Beach, 1972—. Served to maj. AUS, 1941-46. Registered profl. engr. Fla., Pa., Conn., La. Mem. Am. Pub. Works Assn., Nat. Soc. Profl. Engrs., Fla. Engring. Soc. (chpt. treas. 1969), Fla. Pollution Control Assn., Air Pollution Control Assn. Episcopalian. Home: 401 Bath Club Blvd S North Redington Beach FL 33708 Office: 6727 1st Av S St Petersburg FL 33707

RADDON, HENRY ELIJAH, JR., hotel exec.; b. Laurel, Miss., Aug. 28, 1929; s. Henry Elijah and Carrie (Nelson) R.; A.S., Marion Mil. Inst., 1949; student Western Res. U., 1949-50; B.S., Miss. State Coll., 1951. Asst. mgr. J.C. Penney Co., Columbus and Brookhaven, Miss., 1952-59; innkeeper Holiday Inn., McComb, Miss., 1960-73; pres. Pike Investments, Inc. holding co. for Holiday Inn, McComb, 1971—. Served to 2d lt. inf. AUS, 1951-53. Recipient Top 8—awards Holiday Inn, 1962, 70. Mem. A.I.M. (pres.'s council), Miss. Innkeepers Assn. (dir.), S.W. Miss. Art Assn. (pres.). Episcopalian (warden). Home: Lawrence St Summit MS 39666 Office: Holiday Inn Delaware Av McComb MS 39648

RADER, LLOYD EDWIN, state ofcl.; b. Bridgeport, Okla., Aug. 30, 1906; s. Otis Zimmerman and Bedia Sarah (Boston) R.; student Southwestern State Coll., 1924-26; LL.B., Oklahoma City U., 1956; m. Ruth Schreiner, Sept. 30, 1930; 1 son, Lloyd Edwin. Asst. sec. Bldg. and Loan, also in ins., real estate, Weatherford, Okla., 1925-31; county relief dir. Custer County, Okla., 1932-33; chief auditor sales tax div. Tax Commn., Oklahoma City, 1933-35, dir. gen. enforcement div., 1935-39; in hardware, lumber, implement, constrn. bus., also ranching, Okla., 1939-51; dir. pub. welfare Okla., Oklahoma City, 1951—. Mem. Exec. Council State Welfare Dirs., 1953—; sec. Okla. Capitol Improvement Authority, 1959—; mem. adv. bd. Children's Convalescent Hosp., Bethany, Okla., 1959—; mem. Okla. Mental Health Planning Commn., 1965—; mem. Pres.'s Panel on Mental Retardation, 1966—. Elected to Okla. Hall Fame, 1966. Mem. Am. Pub. Welfare Assn. (treas. 1965-67), Okla. Health and Welfare Assn., State Welfare Dirs. and Commrs. Assn., Nat. Assn. Tng. Schs. Democrat. Mem. Disciples of Christ. Ch. Mason. Home: 6413 N Harvard Av Oklahoma City OK 73132

RADFORD, GARLAND, banker; b. Monroe, Ga., May 30, 1907; s. John Robert and Mary Eugenia (Brown) R.; B.B.A., Emory U., 1929; m. Vera Waller Kamper, Sept. 9, 1930; children—Vera (Mrs. Edmund W. Hughes), Mary (Mrs. Donald B. Hawkins), Nancy (Mrs. John P. Kokko), Garland Radford. Jr. accountant Joel Hunter & Co., Atlanta, 1929-31; with Standard Brands, Inc., Atlanta, 1931-33, Birmingham, Ala., 1933-34, 46-52, Cleve., 1934-43, N.Y.C., 1943-46; exec. v.p., dir. Nat. Bank, Monroe, 1952-63, pres., trust officer, 1963—; dir. Monroe Walton Co., Citizens & So. Fiduciary Stock Fund, Inc. Chmn., City of Monroe Housing Authority, 1969—. Trustee, chmn. bd. Walton County Hosp. Mem. Am., Ga. bankers assns., Walton County C. of C. (dir.), Phi Delta Theta. Democrat. Methodist (trustee). Kiwanian. Club: Monroe Golf and Country. Home: 146 Pine Crest Dr Monroe GA 30655 Office: 100 N Broad St Monroe GA 30655

RADIGAN, CHARLES MCDONNELL, lawyer; b. Washington, Nov. 21, 1938; s. Charles M. and Virginia Alice (McDonnell) R.; A.B., Dartmouth, 1960; LL.B., U. Va., 1964; m. Elizabeth Sargent Knox, June 15, 1963; children—Katherine Knox, Joseph McDonnell. Admitted to Va. bar, 1964; mem. firm Adams, Porter, Radigan and Mays, Arlington, 1968—; substitute judge Arlington Gen. Dist. Ct., Arlington, Va. Mem. Adv. Bd. Clarendon Bank and Trust Co., Fairfax, Va., 1971—. Chmn. operating com. Washington Regional Blood Center, A.R.C., 1971—; chmn. blood program Arlington County Red Cross, 1968—. Served to 2d lt., AUS, 1960-61. Mem. Arlington C. of C. (mem. com. exec. 1972—), Am., Va. State (mem. council 1973-74), Arlington bar assns., Va. Trial Lawyers Assn., Newcomen Soc. in N. Am. Roman Catholic. Clubs: Washington Golf and Country (dir. 1972—). Home: 4650 N 35th St Arlington VA 22207 Office: 1415 N Courthouse Rd Arlington VA 22201

RADIN, ARTHUR, physician; b. Pitts., Jan. 6, 1916; s. David and Rose (Harris) R.; B.S., U. Pitts., 1941; M.D., U. Miami, 1957; m. Elizabeth A. Barnishin, Jan. 12, 1941; children—Patricia (Mrs. Milton J. Wallace), Dorothy, Rebecca. Intern, Mt. Sinai Hosp., Miami Beach, Fla., 1957-58; pvt. practice medicine, Hialeah, Fla., 1958-59; owner Century Med. Offices, Miami, 1959—; med. dir. Wilson Nat. Life Ins. Co., 1963—; mem. staff Bapt. Hosp., Miami, Am. Hosp., Miami; personnel physician Dade County, 1963-67. Dir. Nat. Properties, Inc., Biscayne Bank, Miami. Mem. adv. bd. Dade County Pub. Health. Served with AUS, 1941-46. Decorated Purple Heart. Mem. A.M.A., So., Fla., Dade County med. socs., Century Alumni U. Miami, Phi Delta Epsilon. Home: 5825 SW 82d Av Rd Miami FL 33143 Office: 7890 Coral Way Miami FL 33155

RADOFF, LEONARD IRVING, librarian; b. Houston, Jan. 9, 1927; s. Morris and Jennie (Goldberg) R.; B.A. (Hoenthal scholar 1948) Rice U., 1949; M.L.S., U. Tex., 1965; m. Lisel Ruth Ephraim, July 25, 1953; 1 dau., Lesley. Tchr., Houston Ind. Sch. Dist., 1949-53; silk screen operator Rustproof Sign & Metal Co., 1953-59; tchr. Aldine (Tex.) Ind. Sch. Dist., 1959-61, sch. librarian, 1961-63; asst. to dir. Grad. Sch. Library Sci., U. Tex., 1963-64; pub. service librarian Abilene Pub. Library, 1964-65; dir. Pasadena Pub. Library, 1966-70; chief br. services Houston Pub. Library, 1971—. Vice pres. Pasadena South Houston Neighborhood Centers Assn., 1970; pres. Houston Great Books Council, 1970-72. Served with USNR, 1945-46. Nat. Def. Edn. Act scholar, 1960. Mem. Am., Southwestern, Tex. (dist. vice chmn. 1969-70, dist. chmn. 1970-71) library assns. Home: 2302 Colquitt St Houston TX 77006 Office: 3102 Center St Houston TX 77007

RADY, JOSEPH JAMES, civil engr.; b. N.Y.C., Oct. 4, 1899; s. Jacob J. and Rose (Swarz) R.; C.E., Cornell U., 1921; m. Bettye M. Clark, June 9, 1928. Owner, Joe J. Rady & Co., Ft. Worth, 1924—, now pres., chmn. bd. Rady & Assos., cons. engrs. Bd. dirs. Panther Boys Club. Served with U.S. Army Engrs., World War I. Named Engr. of Year Ft. Worth, Tex. Soc. Profl. Engrs., 1957. Fellow Am. Soc. C.E. (hon., pres. Tex. sect. 1964), Am. Water Assn., Nat. Soc. Profl. Engrs., Chi Epsilon, Tau Beta Pi. Rotarian. Clubs: Fort Worth, Colonial Country (dir.) (Fort Worth). Home: 2626 Simondale Dr Fort Worth TX 76109 Office: Continental Life Bldg Fort Worth TX 76102

RADZEWICZ, PAUL ANTHONY, oil co. exec.; b. nr. Hudson County, N.J., Apr. 7, 1925; s. Anthony Radzewicz and Helen (Lewicki) R.; grad. Fort Trumble Maritime Acad., 1944; student Millsaps Coll., 1950-51; LL.B., Jackson Sch. Law, 1951; m. Ethel Odel Cole, Sept. 15, 1949; children—Gene Anthony, Maureen Ethel. Instr. nav. machinery USN, Pearl Harbor, Honolulu, Hawaii, 1941-43; organizing sec., chief engr. internat. S.S. Line, Long Beach, Cal., 1947-49; pres. Starboard Oil Co., Jackson, Miss., 1949—; pres. Anthony's Yachts Co., Jackson, 1968—. Served with U.S. Maritime Service, 1943-46; PTO. Mem. Am. Petroleum Inst. (pres. Miss. chpt. 1968), Jackson Power Squadrons, Ind. Petroleum Assn. Am., Internat. Oil Scouts Assn., Marine Engrs. Benefit Assn., Internat. Assn. Petroleum Landmen, Miss. Landmen's Assn. Clubs: Gulfport (Miss.) Yacht; Patio (Jackson), Jackson Yacht, Jackson Country Capital City-Petroleum. Home: 1802 Eastover Dr Jackson MS 39211 Office: Deposit Guaranty Nat Bank Bldg 200 E Capitol St Jackson MS 39201

RAFFA, FREDERICK ANTHONY, economist; b. Liberty, N.Y., Feb. 19, 1944; s. Anthony and Julia Vera (Segar) R.; B.S., Fla. State U., 1965, M.B.A., 1966, Ph.D., 1969; m. Jean Alyda Benedict, June 15, 1964; children—Juliette Louise, Matthew Benedict. Instr. dept. econs. Fla. State U., Tallahassee, 1967-69; asst. prof. dept. econs. Fla. Tech. U., Orlando, 1969-74, asso. prof., 1974—. State dir. Fla. Clergy Econ. Edn. Council, 1969—; cons. E. Central Fla. Regional Planning Council, Dept. Health, Edn. and Welfare, Project RETRO. Recipient Distinction in Teaching award Fla. State U., 1969. NSF Summer Trainee fellow, 1968. Mem. Am., So. econs. assns., Omicron Delta Epsilon, Delta Sigma Pi. Episcopalian. Author: (with R.E. Hicks, W.J. Klages) Economics: Myth, Method or Madness, 1971. Home: 2901 Lolissa Lane Maitland FL 32751 Office: Dept Econs Fla Tech U Orlando FL 32816

RAGSDALE, SILAS BAGGETT, pub. co. dir.; b. Brownwood, Tex., Sept. 15, 1896; s. Paul Carter Calhoun and Maggie (Baggett) R.; B.A., U. Tex., 1918; m. Sadie Marie Jones, Apr. 4, 1923; children—Silas Baggett, Joan Marie (Mrs. Pat M. Baskin). Reporter, Brownwood Bull., 1915; city editor Galveston (Tex.) News, 1918-19, news editor, 1919-23, mng. editor, 1923-43; sec., dir. News Pub. Co., Galveston, Tex., 1923-43, dir., 1961-63; mng. editor Galveston Tribune, 1926-43, Oil Weekly, Houston, 1920-21, 44-47, Petroleum Refiner, Houston, 1947-54; editorial dir. Hydrocarbon Processing (formerly Petroleum Refiner), 1955-66; ret., 1966; dir. Gulf Pub. Co., Houston, 1955—. Mem. Nat. council YMCA, 1935-38; life mem. adv. council U. Tex. Sch. Communication, 1950—. Mem. U. Tex. Ex-Students Assn. (life), S.A.R., Sons Republic Tex., Delta Tau Delta, Sigma Delta Chi. Presbyn. Mason (32 deg., Shriner), Rotarian (past pres. Houston R club). Home: Apt 711 4718 Hallmark St Houston TX 77027

RAHENKAMP, ROBERT ARTHUR, data processing co. exec.; b. Pitts., Nov. 9, 1928; s. Arthur Paul and Margaret Blanchard (Cooley) R.; B.S. in Elec. Engring., U. Pitts., 1950; postgrad., Ohio State U., 1962, 63, Exec. Devel. Program, IBM Mgmt. Sch., 1970; m. Barbara Elizabeth Illig, June 23, 1951; children—Karen Lee, Paul Robert, Craig Arthur. With IBM, 1950—, customer engr., Pitts., 1950-53, planning and devel. data processing systems, Poughkeepsie, N.Y., 1953-57, with office products div., Lexington, Ky., 1957—, mgr. word processing strategies and planning, 1972—. Instrumental in establishing Spindletop Research Inst., Lexington, 1961; mem. Fayette County Parks and Recreation Bd., 1968-72. Served to 1st lt., AUS, 1951-53. Recipient invention awards IBM, 1967, 70. Mem. I.E.E.E., Eta Kappa Nu, Phi Eta Sigma. Republican. Presbyn. (deacon, elder). Club: Lexington Country. Patentee in field. Home: 1108 The Lane Lexington KY 40504 Office: IBM Corp New Circle Rd Lexington KY 40507

RAILSBACK, BERNICE HICKMAN (MRS. JAMES ERNEST RAILSBACK), educator; b. Mountain Home, Ark.; d. Charles Isaac and America Maria (Lewis) Hickman; student Mountain Home Coll., 1927, 29, Ark. State Coll., summers 1930-31; B.S., Tex. Tech. Coll., 1941, M.S., 1951; m. James Ernest Railsback, June 9, 1932; children—Norman Leighton, Charles Hickman, Phyllis Elaine (Mrs. George A. Carlton). Tchr. pub. schs., Buford, Ark., 1927-28; tchr., girls coach Salem (Ark.) pub. schs., 1929-32, McClung Sch., Slaton, Tex., 1933-34; tchr. Hodges Sch., Levelland, Tex., 1939-41; tchr. jr. high sch. math. and reading Levelland Pub. Schs., 1947-54, dir. elementary edn., 1954-70, cons., 1970—. Mem. study com. tchr. certification Tex. Edn. Agy. Bd. dirs. Hockley County div. Am. Heart Assn., v.p. Tex. affiliate; bd. dirs. Tex. Com. for Pub. Edn. Recipient poetry award S. Plains Writers Assn., 1964, 65; named Woman of Year, Levelland C. of C., 1969. Mem. Assn. Supervision and Curriculum Devel. (Tex. rep. nat. bd. 1962-67, state pres. 1966-67, 69-70), Tex., W.Tex. (regional pres. 1966-67) assns. for supervision and curriculum devel., Tex. Assn. Instrnl. Suprs. (state pres. 1959-60), Am. Assn. U. Women, Tex. Congress Parents and Tchrs. (life), Internat. Platform Assn., Poetry Soc. Tex., S. Plains Writers Assn., Tex. Assn. for Improvement of Reading, Internat. Reading Assn., Tex. Assn. Edn. Young Children (dir.), Marigolds, Delta Kappa Gamma. Mem. Order Eastern Star (past worthy matron). Clubs: Matrons Study, Levelland Music. Contbr. to various publs. Home: 707 17th St PO Box 156 Levelland TX 79336

RAILSBACK, LUTHER JAMES, instnl. adminstr.; b. Marlin, Tex., Feb. 8, 1943; s. Arvil William and Lola Lee (Williams) R.; B.B.A., N. Tex. State U., 1965; m. Carolyn Ann McClinton, Jan. 21, 1967. Accountant Arthur Young & Co., Houston, 1965-70, Durst, Wood & Ingram, Bryan, Tex., 1970-71; head finance and accounting dept. Meth. Home Found., Waco, Tex., 1971-73; asst. adminstr. fiscal affairs Meth. Home, Waco, 1973—; pvt. accounting practice; farmer, rancher. Served with AUS, 1971. Home: 1217 Lawrence St Waco TX 76710 Office: 1111 Herring St Waco TX 76708

RAINER, LAMAR SIDNEY, JR., banker; b. Troy, Ala., Jan. 19, 1925; s. Lamar Sidney and Violet (Dantzier) R.; student U. Vt., 1944; B.A.A., Auburn U., 1949; m. Helen Joyce Braswell, Oct. 21, 1950; children—Beverly Lynn, Lamar Sidney III. Advt. sales promotion Sears, Roebuck & Co., Columbus, Ga. and Tuscaloosa, Ala., 1950; with Gen. Ins. Co., Elba, Ala., 1951-54; home office mgr. claims and underwriting dept. Nat. Security Ins. Co., Elba, 1955-59; pres. Emergency Aid Ins. Co., Elba, 1959-62; organizer Peoples Bank, Elba, 1963, chmn., pres., 1964—; organizer, dir. 1st Fed. Savings & Loan Assn., Enterprise, Ala. City councilman, Elba, Ala., 1956-60; bd. dirs., mem. finance com. Ala. Council on the Arts and Humanities, 1968—; mem. exec. bd. S.E. Ala. Council, Boy Scouts Am., Dothan, Ala., 1964-67. Treas., bd. dirs. Indsl. Bd. City of Elba, 1962—; chmn. bd. dirs. Water Works and Electric Bd., City of Elba, 1956-60, 63—; charter mem. Citizens Conf. on Ala. State Cts., 1966—, sec.-treas., 1969—; chmn. Elba Hosp. Assn., 1965-70; organizer, dir. Elba Little Theatre. Served with USAAF, 1943-45. Mem. V.F.W., Am. Legion, Elba C. of C., Phi Kappa Phi. Democrat. Methodist. Home: 579 E Davis St Elba AL 36323 Office: 304 Simmons St Elba AL 36323

RAINES, EDWARD E., machine mfg. co. exec.; b. Hugo, Okla., Nov. 7, 1911; s. Edgar Lee and Dovie Ophelia (Johnson) R.; student Amarillo Jr. Coll., 1944-46, Tex. A. and M. Coll., summers 1945-46; m. Willie Marie Sattawhite, Feb. 21, 1932; children—Robert Clark, Terry Edward. Machinist apprentice Weddington Repair Shop, Hugo, 1926-33; with Hugo Furniture Co., 1933-41; tchr. machinist classes, 1941-42; ship coordinator Consol. Steel Corp., Orange, Tex., 1942-44; tchr. machine shop Amarillo High Sch., 1944-47; machine shop supt. Graham-Hoeme Plow Co., Amarillo, 1947-50; tradesman, supr. machinist trade, 1951-62; pres. Raines Machine Products, Inc., Ft. Worth, 1962—. Baptist. Mason. Patentee in field. Home: 3901 Bonnie Dr Fort Worth TX 76116 Office: 3959 Vickery Blvd Fort Worth TX 76107

RAINES, ERNEST RUDOLPH, supr. schs.; b. Breaks, Va., Apr. 30, 1921; s. Joseph and Dana (Sutherland) R.; B.A., Berea Coll., 1948; postgrad. William and Mary Coll., summer 1961; M.A., E. Tenn. State U., 1970; m. Shirley Estep, Aug. 3, 1945; children—Ernest Gary, James Howard, David Gregory, Lisa Carol. Tchr. high sch., Buchanan County Schs., Grundy, Va., 1948-55, prin. elementary sch., 1955-63, elementary supr., 1963-64, gen. supt., 1964-73, dir. instrn., 1973, acting supt., 1973—. Chmn. com. for evaluation and planning, 1968—. Cub scoutmaster, 1955-57. Treas., Buchanan County Democratic Com., 1963-65; mem. Buchanan County Planning Commn., 1967-70; dir., coordinator Transp. Services for Civil Def. Buchanan County, 1967—. Served as staff sgt. USAAF, 1942-45. Decorated Purple Heart. Mem. Nat., Va., Buchanan (pres. 1954-56, chmn. profl. standards com. 1956-64) edn. assns., C. of C., Va. Assn. Supervision and Curriculum Devel., S.W. Regional Sch. Suprs. (program chmn. 1968-69), P.T.A. (life). Home: Breaks VA 24607 Office: Buchanan County School Board Grundy VA 24614

RAINEY, CLAUDE GLADWIN, hosp. adminstr.; b. Enloe, Tex., Apr. 21, 1923; s. Claude C. and Pauline (Whitlock) R.; student Pub. Health and Adminstrv. Medicine, Columbia, 1961-62; m. Peggy Ballard, July 27, 1947; children—Kathy Suzanne, David Claude, Mark Jeffery, Joel Allen, Peggy Jan, Susan Elise. Med. adminstr., officer VA Dept. Medicine and Surgery, Temple, Tex., 1946-51, Muskogee, Okla., 1951-56; med. adminstr. Fite Clinic, Lakeland Med. Center, Muskogee, 1956-59; hosp. adminstr. M.-K.-T. R.R. Employees Hosp. Assn., Denison, Tex., 1959-62, also sec., treas., trustee; hosp. adminstr., cons. Denison Hosp. Authority, Meml. Hosp., 1962-66; adminstr. Seton Hosp., Austin, Tex., after 1966; now exec. v.p. Ft. Worth Osteo. Hosp. Pres. Am. Cancer Soc., North Grayson County, 1960-66, dir. Tex., 1961—. Served with USNR, 1942-46. Fellow Am. Coll. Hosp. Adminstrs.; mem. Am., Tex. hosp. assns. Home: 1725 Preston Hollow Ct Arlington TX 76012 Office: 1000 Montgomery St Fort Worth TX 76107

RAINS, ALBERT, banker, lawyer; b. DeKalb County, Ala., Mar. 11, 1902; ed. pub. schs., student Snead Sem., State Tchrs. Coll., U. Ala.; LL.D., Jacksonville U.; m. Allison Blair, Dec. 29, 1939. Admitted to Ala. bar, 1928, mem. firm Rains & Rains, Gadsden, Ala.; chmn. bd. 1st City Nat. Bank, Gadsden; dep. sol. Etowah County, Ala., 1930-35; city atty. Gadsden, 1935-44; mem. Ho. of Reps., Ala. legislature, 1942-44; mem. 79th to 87th Congresses, 5th Ala. Dist., mem. 88th U.S. Congress at large; chmn. housing sub-com.; mem. banking and currency com., joint com. def. prodn.; now committeeman from Ala. nat. Democratic party. Home: 221 Alpine View Gadsden AL 35901 Office: 1st City Nat Bank Bldg Gadsden AL 35901

RAINS, GEORGE PAUL, utility co. exec.; b. Williamsburg, Ky., Dec. 16, 1940; s. John and Hattie (Jones) R.; student Cumberland Coll., 1958-59; B.C.E., U. Ky., 1963; m. Jo Eileen Patrick, Nov. 12, 1965; children—Paula Faye, Stephen J. Resident engr. Ky. Hwy. Dept., 1963-65; chief engr. T.C. Young Constrn. Co., Williamsburg, 1965-67; gen. mgr. Corbin (Ky.) Utilities Commn., 1968—, dir., 1967—. Mem. Corbin C. of C. (dir. indsl. devel. 1970-71). Mason. Home: 1219 Reasor St Corbin KY 40701 Office: 901 S Main St Corbin KY 40701

RAINS, L. CRAIG, advt. exec.; b. Little Rock, Mar. 4, 1940; s. James Filmore and Aepha Irene (DeGood) R.; B.S. in Bus. Adminstrn., U. Ark., 1963; student Harvard Bus. Sch., 1969; m. Judith Bell, Apr. 13, 1963; children—Brent Powell, Michael Craig, Margaret Ellen. Account exec. Cranford/Johnson and Assos., Little Rock, 1965-69; dir. INSEARCH, Little Rock, 1969-72, Area Market Research Assos., 1969-72; pres. Starshine Group, 1972; dir. marketing Cranford/Johnson/Hunt, 1969-72; prin. Mangan/Rains/Ginnavenl Assos., Little Rock, 1972—; lectr. comml. design U. Ark. at Little Rock, 1971-72. Mem. Am. Advt. Fedn. advanced mgmt. seminar planning com., Harvard Bus. Sch., 1969-70. Mem. edn. com. Model Cities Program, 1969-71; Justice of Peace, Big Rock Twp., Pulaski County, Ark., 1966—. Bd. dirs. West Little Rock YMCA, 1973—. Served to capt. AUS, 1963-65. Recipient George Washington Honor medal, Freedom's Found., 1965. Mem. Little Rock Jr. C. of C., Ark. Advt. Fedn., (dir. 1968-74, sec. 1974—), Pub. Relations Soc. Am., Am. Marketing Assn., The Travel Research Assn., Ozark Soc., U. Ark. Alumni Assn. (dir. 1965—), Sierra Club, Wilderness Soc., Nat. Wildlife Soc. Alpha Kappa Psi, Sigma Chi (pres. 1961-62). Episcopalian (vestryman 1970-73). Home: 4905 Crestwood Little Rock AR 72207 Office: Gaines Pl 3 St at Gaines Little Rock AR 72201

RAIT, ROBERT ALEXANDER, petroleum co. exec.; b. Lincoln, Neb., Mar. 10, 1911; s. Alexander Hamilton and Ida (Hoffman) R.; B.S. in Civil Engring., U. Neb., 1933; m. Sybil Frances Smith, June 11, 1939; children—Rosemary (Mrs. David Sykes), Patricia (Mrs. Gary Middleton). With Exxon Co. U.S.A., Corpus Christi, Tex., 1944—, tech. adviser design, constrn. gas facilities, 1973—. Registered profl engr., Tex. Fellow Am. Soc. C.E. (pres. Houston br. 1956, past chmn. exec. com. pipeline div.); mem. Tex., Nat. socs. profl. engrs., Am. Inst. Mining Engrs., Pi Mu Epsilon. Home: 702 Monette St Corpus Christi TX 78412 Office: Wilson Tower 520 N Caranchua Corpus Christi TX 78401

RAKENTINE, LLOYD WILLIAM, comptroller; b. E. Rutherford, N.J., Jan. 26, 1915; s. William and Sarah (Niebling) R.; student Internat. Corr. Schs., 1946-47, Dallas Night Sch., 1951-55; m. Viola Ethel Varga, Sept. 11, 1942; 1 child, G. Ilona. Salesman, Crucible Steel Co. Am., N.Y.C., 1931-46; with purchasing dept. Celanese Corp. Am., N.Y.C., 1946-50; asst. sec.-treas., comptroller Tears Engrs. Inc., Dallas, 1950—; dir., comptroller Hunnicut Corp., 1958—; sec.-treas. Ford, Bacon & Davis Tex., Inc., 1966—; asst. sec.-treas. Ford, Bacon & Davis Utah, Inc., Salt Lake City, 1972—. Served with USAAF, 1942-45. Mem. Nat. Assn. Accountants, Am. Legion. Methodist. Republican. Home: 6624 Hialeah Dr Dallas TX 75214 Office: 2908 National Dr Garland TX 75040

RAKESTRAW, BRYAN LAVERN, banker; b. Snyder, Okla., Dec. 5, 1910; s. Elias Vern and Ella Adella (Fry) R.; A.B., U. Okla., 1933; LL.B., 1939; LL.M., Georgetown U., 1949; grad. Okla. Bankers Assn. Intermediate Sch. Banking, 1968; m. Arthur Lory Morris, Jan. 19, 1942; children—Ella Kay (Mrs. Richard T. Yery), Don William, Lee Franklin. Asst. collector Internal Revenue Service, Okla., 1939-40; admitted to Okla. bar, 1940; commd. 1st lt. U.S. Army, 1940, advanced through grades to col., 1951; with Judge Adv. Gen.'s Dept., Washington, 1946-51, staff judge adv. Tng. Command, Tactical Air Command, U.S. Air Force in Europe, 1961-65; ret., 1966; v.p. Fidelity Bank, Nat. Assn., 1966—. Pres., Langley AFB Youth Assn., 1960; pres. Wildewood Devel. Assn., 1968; pres. United Cerebral Palsy of Greater Oklahoma City, Inc., 1970-72. Decorated Legion of Merit with oak leaf cluster; recipient award United Cerebral Palsy Assn., Oklahoma City, 1969. Mem. Am., Okla., Oklahoma County bar assns., Methodist. Mason (Shriner, 32 deg.). Club: Whitehall. Contbr. articles to profl. publs. Home: 5717 N Everest St Oklahoma City OK 73111 Office: Fidelity Bank NA Robert S Kerr and Robinson Sts Oklahoma City OK 73102

RALEY, JOHN WESLEY, JR., lawyer; b. Bartlesville, Okla., May 23, 1932; s. John Wesley and Helen (Thames) R.; A.B., Okla. Bapt. U., 1954; J.D., U. Okla., 1959; m. Mary Layne Perry, Dec. 20, 1958; children—John Wesley III, Robert Thames. Admitted to Okla. bar, 1959; practice law, Oklahoma City, 1959-69, Ponca City, Okla., 1969—; asst. U.S. atty. Western dist. Okla., Oklahoma City, 1961-69; mem. firm. Northcutt, Northcutt, Ellifrit, Raley and Gardner, Ponca City, Okla., 1969—. Drive chmn., pres. United Fund, 1971-72; mem. exec. council Boy Scouts Am., 1970-73. Bd. dirs. United Fund Ponca City, Ponca City YMCA; trustee Okla. Bapt. U., Shawnee, Okla. Served to comdr. USNR, 1952-56. Recipient George Washington Honor medal Freedoms Found., 1972. Mem. Am. (state chmn. Law Day 1972-73), Okla bar assns., Ponca City C. of C. (dir.), Pioneer Hist. Assn. (pres. 1973-74), Okla. Assn. Def. Counsel, Res. Officers Assn. (state v.p. for Navy 1974—), Am. Legion, Navy League (pres. Ponca City 1971-74), Naval Res. Assn., V.F.W., Phi Alpha Delta, Omicron Delta Kappa. Democrat. Baptist (deacon). Mason, Kiwanian (pres. 1973). Home: 2312 Woodthrush Rd Ponca City OK 74601 Office: Security Bank Bldg Ponca City OK 74601

RALL, LLOYD LOUIS, civil engr.; b. Galesville, Wis., Dec. 7, 1916; s. Louis A. and Anna L. (Kienzle) R.; student Gale Coll., Galesville, Wis., 1934-36; B.S. in Civil Engring., U. Wis., 1940; m. Mary M. Moller, July 12, 1952; children—Lauris, David, Christopher, Jonathan. Commd. 2d lt. U.S. Army C.E., 1940, advanced through grades to col., 1955; asst. dist. engr., Seattle, 1952-54; dir. def. mapping and charting, Washington, 1969-72; ret., 1972; civil engr., Alexandria, Va., 1972—. Prof. mil. sci. U. Mo., Rolla, 1957-60. Decorated Legion of Merit with oak leaf cluster, Bronze Star medal. Registered Profl. engr., Wis. Mem. Am. Congress on Surveying and Mapping. Home: 301 Cloverway Alexandria VA 22314

RALLS, RAWLEIGH HAZEN, educator, cons.; b. Oklahoma City, Dec. 12, 1932; s. Rawleigh Hazen and Rosemary Thelma (Sprigg) R.; B.S., U.S. Mil. Acad., 1955; M.S., U.S. Naval Postgrad. Sch., 1964; D.B.A., George Washington U., 1971; m. Anne Byram Singer, June 7, 1955; children—Elizabeth Anne, Devon Anne, Rawleigh Hazen IV. Commd. 2d lt. arty. U.S. Army, 1955, advanced through grades to maj., 1965; various assignments, 1955-66, chief arty. systems group Office Army Chief of Staff, Washington, 1966-67, prof. operations research U.S. Army Mgmt. Sch., Fort Belvoir, Va., 1967-68; asso. prof. quantitative mgmt. sci., also coordinator statistics Coll. Bus. Adminstrn., U. Ark., Fayetteville, 1968—. Gen. partner Edn. & Research Assos., Alexandria, Va., 1968; pvt. cons. mgmt. and decision sci., Fayetteville, 1969—; pres. Edn. and Research Assos., Inc., 1970—. Trustee Whitney Scholarship Fund. Fellow A.A.A.S.; mem. Operations Research Soc. Am., Am. Econ. Assn., Am. Inst. for Decision Sci., Mensa. Episcopalian. Home: 412 Assembly Dr Fayetteville AR 72701

RALPH, JAMES WALKER, otolaryngologist; b. Washington, Nov. 16, 1936; s. Henry deForest and Dorothy (Walker) R.; A.B., Stanford, 1958; M.D., Duke, 1962; m. Marilyn Jean King, July 3, 1958 (separated); children—Elizabeth, Philip, Randolph. Intern Letterman Gen. Hosp., San Francisco, 1963; resident otolaryngology Manhattan Eye and Ear Hosp., N.Y.C., 1967-70; pvt. practice otolaryngology and related plastic surgery, Englewood, N.J., after 1970; mem. staffs Englewood (N.J.) Hosp., Manhattan Eye & Ear Hosp., N.Y.C., South Bergen Hosp., Hasbrouck Heights, N.J.; now staff Sampson County Hosp., Clinton, N.C. Nat. del. Young Republican Nat. Fedn., 1969—; mem. exec. bd. N.J. Conservative Union, 1971—. Served as flight surgeon/paratrooper AUS, 1963-66; lt. comdr. USNR, 1970—. Decorated Silver Star, D.F.C., Bronze Star, Army Commendation medal. Air medal (11), Purple Heart; Vietnamese Gallantry cross (3). Mem. Aerospace Med. Assn., Assn. U.S. Army, Am. Coll. Sports Medicine, Bergen County Med. Soc., Res. Officers Assn., V.F.W., Am. Legion, Navy League, Nat. Wildlife Fedn., U.S. Naval Inst. Presbyn. Office: Sampson County Hosp Clinton NC

RALSTON, CARL CONRAD, constrn. co. exec.; b. Owensboro, Ky., Nov. 1, 1927; s. Carl C. and Elizabeth (Little) R.; Asso. B.B.A., Ky. Bus. Coll., 1949; B.A., Ky. Wesleyan Coll., 1956; m. Gerrie Henning, May 28, 1947; 1 dau., Pamela Kay. Pub. accountant, 1956; chief accountant, estimator Mills & Jones Inc., 1957-60, project mgr., 1960-65; v.p. Mills & Jones Constrn. Co., St. Petersburg, Fla., 1965—. Pres., Cross Bayou Little League, Seminole, Fla., 1959-61; treas. Seminole Lake Civic Assn., Seminole, 1959-62. Trustee Southeastern Ironworkers' Health and Welfare Fund. Served with USAAF, 1945-47. Mem. Am. Mgmt. Assn., Assn. Gen. Contractors (chpt. dir. 1969-70), Am. Inst. Constructors. Clubs: Seminole Lake Country (gov. 1964-67, chmn. bd. 1967-68); Bardmoor Country. Home: 8499 Pelican Lane Seminole FL 33540 Office: 400 23d St S St Petersburg FL 33731

RAMIREZ, MARIO EFRAIN, physician; b. Roma, Tex., Apr. 3, 1926; s. Efren Manuel and Carmen (Hinojosa) R.; student U. Tex., 1942-45; M.D., U. Tenn., 1948; m. Sarah B. Aycock, Nov. 25, 1949; children—Mario, Patricia Anne, Norman Michael, Jaime Eduardo, Roberto Luis. Intern, Shreveport (La.) Charity Hosp., 1948-49, resident, 1949-50; gen. practice medicine, Roma, Tex., 1950—; health officer Starr County, 1952-69; owner, med. dir. Manuel Ramirez Meml. Hosp., Roma, 1958—. Vice chmn. S. Tex. Devel. Council, 1971—; chmn. Tri-County Bd., Community Action Council, 1971—. Judge Starr County, 1969—. Served to capt. USAF, 1955-57; Japan. Recipient spl. citation for work done during Hurricane Beulah from surgeon gen. 1967; citation Tex. Acad. Gen. Practice, 1953. Diplomate Am. Bd. Family Practice. Mem. A.M.A., Tex. (Distinguished Service award 1972), Hidalgo-Starr County med. assns., Am., Tex. (v.p. 1972-73) acads. family practice, C. of C., K.C., Rotarian, Lion. Built pvt. hosp. to serve Roma area, 1958. Address: Box 188 Roma TX 78584

RAMIREZ, RAFAEL ROBERTO, cons. water resources engr.; b. Arecibo, P.R., June 7, 1900; s. Rafael and Vicenta (Espino) R.; student U. P.R., Mayaguez, 1920-21; grad. Cornell U., 1924; m. 2d, Juanin Perez, June 30, 1965. Former asst. exec. dir. P.R. Water Resources Authority, Santurce; cons. engr. P.R. Water Resources Authority, San Juan, 1965-70, ret. Cons. engr. Centrais Electricas, Sao Paulo Brazil, 1968-72. Bd. dirs. P.R. Communications Authority, 1930-73. Recipient resolution for 45 years extraordinary service in Water Resources Authority, P.R. Senate, 1972. Address: GPO Box 2145 San Juan PR 00936

RAMOS YORDAN, LUIS ERNESTO, physician, P.R. legislator; b. Ponce, P.R., Feb. 2, 1915; s. Federico Ramos Antonini and Felícita (Yordan) R.; B.S., Lincoln U., 1941; M.D., Nat. U. Mexico, 1947; M.P.H., Columbia, 1954; m. Lenabelle Smith, Mar. 13, 1943; children—Harry Luis, Lysa Lee. Prof. pub. health U. P.R. Coll. Pharmacy, 1948-50; med. dir. Arroyo City Hosp., 1949-51, Arecibo Dist. Hosp., 1951-53; pres., hosp. dir. Ramos-Yordan, Inc., 1957—; pres. Lenabelle & Burhans Lab., Inc., 1957-70, Ramos & Smith Realty, Inc., 1964—; cons. indsl. medicine and safety P.R. Ho. of Reps., 1967-68. Cons. indsl. medicine and occupational health P.R. Dept. Labor, 1955-56, P.R. Dept. Health, 1958-59; v.p. Internat. Congress Indsl. Accidents, Brussels, Belgium, 1958; bd. dirs. Internat. Congress for Study Better Living and Working Conditions, Cannes, France, 1956; mem. permanent com. occupational medicine Internat. Congress Occupational Med Assn., Vienna, Austria, 1968. Mem. and Popular Democratic Party floor leader, 1969-71, speaker Ho. of Reps., 1972; Mem. ad-hoc adv. group Commonwealth Status P.R., 1973—. Served from capt. to maj., M.C., AUS, 1956-58. Mem. Indsl. Med. Assn., P.R. Med. Assn. Roman Catholic. Home: 40 SO and De Diego Av La Riviera PR 00921 Office: PO Box 10847 Caparra Heights Station PR 00922

RAMPP, DONALD LOUIS, speech pathologist; b. Meramac, Okla., Feb. 10, 1935; s. Harold Anthony and Faye Alma (Gentry) R.; B.A., Northeastern State Coll., 1957; M.A., Ohio State U., 1958; Ph.D., U. Okla., 1967; m. Nancy Nell Tarkington, Sept. 22, 1959; children—Robin, Randy. Speech pathologist Tulsa Pub. Schs., 1958; asst. prof., supr. clin. practice Northeastern State Coll., 1958-62; research asso. U. Okla. Med. Center, 1964-66; chief speech pathology and audiology U. Tenn. Med. Units, 1966-69; coordinator med. services dept. speech pathology and audiology Memphis State U., 1969—; cons. otolaryngology and maxillofacial surgery U. Tenn., 1971-73, cons. craniofacial anomalies center, 1972-73, lectr. orthodontics, 1971-73; head dept. audiology and speech pathology La. State U. Med. Center, New Orleans, 1973—. Mem. Am. Speech and Hearing Assn., Tenn. Speech and Hearing Assn. Editor of Jour. Tenn. Speech and Hearing Assn., 1971-73. Contbr. chpts. in textbooks. Home: 1100 Florida Av New Orleans LA 70119

RAMPTON, FRANCIS ROBERT, orthodontist; b. Mason City, Ia., Sept. 29, 1919; s. Frank Cyras and Effie (Van Note) R.; student Mason City Jr. Coll., 1937-39; B.A., State U. Ia., 1941, D.D.S., 1946, M.S., 1949; m. Esther Marie Kehl, Mar. 22, 1942 (div. 1966); children—Linda Kehl, Steven Robert, Nancy Ellen, Frank Cyrus. Pvt. practice gen. dentistry Manly, Ia., 1946-48, orthodontics Jacksonville, Fla., 1952—. Pres. Ramco Mining, Inc., Cia. Minera Rosario Ltd. First v.p. Camp Fire Girls, 1955-56; bd. dirs. Jacksonville Opera and Choral Soc., 1960-61, dental div. United Fund, Jacksonville, 1972. Served with AUS, 1943-44; with USAF, 1950-52, lt. col. Res. Mem. Fla. Dental Soc. (del. exec. council 1963-65), Am. Assn. Orthodontists, Am. Dental Assn., Fla. Orthodontic Soc., Fedn. Dentaire Internat. Office: 3958 Oak St Jacksonville FL 32205

RAMSAUR, EDMUND ADAMS, communications exec.; b. Greenville, S.C., Apr. 9, 1925; s. Claud and Dorcas (Lott) R.; student Davidson Coll., 1942-43, U. S.C., 1946-47; B.A., U. Va., 1949; m. Dorothy Ann Peace, Sept. 4, 1947; children—Edmund Adams, Etca Ann. Research analyst U.S. Def. Dept., Washington, 1949-52; polit. reporter Greenville News, Washington, 1952-54; Columbia, S.C., 1954-55, state editor, Greenville, 1955-58, asso. editor, 1959-66; v.p., asst. pub. Greenville News-Piedmont Co., 1966-68, dir., asso. pub., gen. mgr., 1968-73, exec. v.p., 1968-73, pres., co-pub., 1973—; v.p. Multimedia, Inc., Greenville, 1968-73, pres., 1973—, dir., 1968—; dir. Bankers Trust of S.C. Vice pres. United Fund, Greenville County, 1967; commr. S.C. Dept. Parks, Recreation and Tourism, 1967—. Chmn. bd. dirs. Red Shield Boys Club, 1964; trustee Greenville County Found., 1970—, chmn., 1973. Served with USNR, 1943-46. Mem. So. Newspaper Pub. Assn., S.C. Press Assn., Greater Greenville C. of C. (pres. 1966), Sigma Delta Chi, Sigma Alpha Epsilon. Presbyn. Clubs: Greenville Country, Nat. Press, Poinsett. Home: 1 Rockingham Rd Greenville SC 29607 Office: Box 1688 Greenville SC 29601

RAMSAY, WILLIAM MCDOWELL, educator; b. Huntsville, Tex., Aug. 3, 1922; s. Charles Sumner and Catherine (McKay) R.; B.A., Southwestern at Memphis, 1946; B.D., Union Theol. Sem., Richmond, Va., 1949; Ph.D., U. Edinburgh (Scotland), 1954; postgrad. Union Theol. Sem., N.Y.C., 1966-67, Columbia, 1966-67; m. DeVere Maxwell, Apr. 27, 1954; children—William McDowell, John Alston. Ordained to ministry Presbyn. Ch., 1950; pastor Houston and Lebanon Presbyn. chs., Knoxville, Tenn., 1950-54, Forest Hills Presbyn. Ch., Paducah, Ky., 1954-59; editor, asso. dir. dept. adult edn. Bd. Christian Edn. Presbyn. Ch. U.S., Richmond, 1959-69; prof. philosophy King Coll., Bristol, Tenn., 1969—. Mem. Abingdon Presbytery, 1969—. Served with AUS, 1943-46. Author: The Christ of the Earliest Christians, 1959; The Meaning of Jesus Christ, 1964; (with John Leith) The Church, a Believing Fellowship, 1965; Cycles and Renewal, 1969. Contbr. articles to religious jours. Address: 416 MockingBird Rd Bristol TN 37620

RAMSDALE, DAN JERRY, acoustical scientist; b. El Paso, Tex., Dec. 12, 1942; s. Bryan William and Helen Harrel (Winters) R.; B.S., U. Tex., El Paso, 1964; Ph.D. (NASA fellow), Kan. State U., 1969; m. Portia Elizabeth Rissler, June 14, 1969; 1 dau., Jerry Elizabeth. Dir. acoustic research, govt. contracting activities GUS Mfg., Inc., El Paso, 1968-74; research physicist Acoustics div. Naval Research Lab., Washington, 1974—. Prof. math. El Paso Community Coll., 1971-74; cons. in acoustics. Mem. Am. Geophys. Union, Am. Meteorol. Soc., Acoustical Soc. Am. (reviewer), Brit. Acoustical Soc., Am. Inst. Physics. Mason. Contbr. articles to profl. jours. Home: 3860 Fairfax Sq Fairfax VA 22030 Office: Naval Research Lab 4555 Overlook Av Washington DC 20375

RAMSEY, DERO SAUNDERS, physiologist, educator; b. Starkville, Miss., June 17, 1928; s. George Bancroft and Louise (Saunders) R.; B.S., Miss. State U., 1950, M.S., 1953; Ph.D., U. Wis., 1957; m. Margaret Adelaide Arnold, Oct. 1, 1950; children—Lawrence, Dero. Asst. prof. physiology Miss. State U., State Coll., 1956-60, asso. prof., 1960-68, prof., 1968—. Served to lt. AUS, 1951-52; col. Res. Decorated Bronze Star, Purple Heart. Mem. A.A.A.S., Am. Dairy Sci. Assn., Gamma Sigma Delta, Sigma Xi. Presbyn. (elder 1967—). Home: Route 5 Box 6 Starkville MS 39759 Office: Drawer DD Mississippi State University Mississippi State MS 39762

RAMSEY, GEORGE EDWARD III, lawyer; b. Washington, Apr. 7, 1939; s. George Edward, Jr. and Winifred (Barrons) R.; B.B.A., U. Tex., 1962, LL.B., 1965; m. Mary Jo Peterson, Sept. 2, 1961; children—George Edward IV, Catherine Peterson, Charlotte Scaife. Admitted to Tex. bar, 1965; law clk. U.S. Dist. Ct., Eastern Dist. Tex., Tyler, 1965-66; partner firm Watkins, Ledbetter, Hayden & Ramsey, Austin, Tex., 1967—. Trustee McDonogh Sch. Mem. Am., Austin Jr. (dir. 1970-72, treas. 1972-73) bar assns., State Bar Tex., Young Men's Bus. League Austin (dir. 1969-71), Phi Alpha Delta, Phi Kappa Psi. Presbyn. (deacon 1969-71). Club: West Austin Optimist. Author: Commercial Collections Manual, 1972. Home: 2603 Escondido Cove Austin TX 78703 Office: City National Bank Bldg Austin TX 78701

RAMSEY, JAMES PRESTON, transp. co. exec.; b. Valdese, N.C., Aug. 26, 1936; s. Robert Preston and Letha Louise (Cooper) R.; grad. high sch.; m. Priscilla Brawley, June 30, 1956; children—Bobby, Kimberly. Quality control. exec. Gen. Electric Co., Hickory, N.C., 1955-61; radio sales-announcer WSVM, Valdese, 1961-63; with Crestline Furniture Co., Inc., Valdese, 1963—, traffic mgr., 1970—. Precinct chmn. Republican party, Drexel, N.C., 1966—. Mem. So. Furniture Mfg. Assn. (dir. 1972—). Home: PO Box 601 Drexel NC 28619 Office: PO Box 40 Valdese NC 28690

RAMSEY, JERRY WARREN, chemist; b. Springfield, Ill., June 30, 1932; s. Herman Eugene and Eleanor (Luttrell) R.; student U. Ill., 1950-51; B.A., Ill. Coll., 1956; M.S., A. and M. Coll. Tex., 1958; m. Elizabeth Joanne Huffman, Nov. 27, 1952; children—Katherine Julia, Warren Howard, Ellen Marie. Instr., Tex. Western Coll., El Paso, 1958-59, Pa. State U., Pottsville, 1959-62, Pottsville Gen. Hosp., 1961-62; chemist Anthracite Research Center, U.S. Bur. Mines, Schuylkill Haven, Pa., 1962-64, research chemist, 1964-65, research chemist Laramie (Wyo.) Petroleum Research Center, 1965-67, program mgr. Office of Dir. Petroleum Research, Washington, 1967-70, asst. to the chief div. Shale Oil, 1970—; mem. program analysis subcom. Dept. Interior Oil Shale Task Force, 1972-73; mem. AEC Oil Shale Task Force, 1974; mem. Project Independence-1980 Energy Strategy Analysis Task Force, 1973-74; mem. oil shale sub panel com. energy research and devel. grants Fed. Council Sci. and Tech., 1972. Chmn. troop com. Nat. Capital Area council Boy Scouts Am., 1970-73, asst. scoutmaster, 1973—. Served with C.E., AUS, 1952-54. Elected to Order of the Arrow, Boy Scouts Am.; recipient Certificate of Commendation for outstanding service Dept. Interior, 1973. Mem. Am. Chem. Soc., Washington Soc. Ill. Coll. (past pres.), Ill. Coll. Alumni Assn. (past trustee), Sigma Xi, Phi Alpha. Methodist (chmn. council on ministries 1972-74). Contbr. articles to profl. jours. Home: 7718 Ontario Rd Gainesville VA 22065 Office: US Bur Mines Washington DC 20240

RAMSEY, JETTIE CECIL, county ofcl.; b. Daytona Beach, Fla., Aug. 31, 1925; s. Joseph James and Nonnie (Mann) R.; B.B.A., Massey Coll., 1955; postgrad. Fla. Jr. Coll., 1968, 73, Ga. U., 1972, Fla. Technol. U., 1972; m. Pauline Cordelia Thaden, May 9, 1942; children—Wilson Lujack, Joseph Cecil (dec.), Pauline Diana (dec.). Engr., Duval Engring. & Constrn. Co., Jacksonville, Fla., 1946-66; with Office of Sheriff, Duval County, Fla., 1966—, warden Duval County Prison, 1969-71, rehab. officer, 1971-73, supt. jails, 1973—. Mem. Duval County Exec. Com., 1958—; vice-comdr. Jacksonville Police Res., 1968—; troop scoutmaster Boy Scouts Am., 1962-64. Served with USNR, 1943-46. Mem. V.F.W., Correctional Officers Assn., Fla. Peace Officers Assn., Fraternal Order Police. Democrat. Mason (32 deg., Shriner). Mem. Order Eastern Star (worthy patron 1960). Home: 1039 Hood Av Jacksonville FL 32205 Office: 400 E Bay St Jacksonville FL 32201

RAMSEY, OTTO BRYANT, educator; b. Sparta, Tenn., Feb. 7, 1909; s. George Washington and Arabelle (Watson) R.; A.B., Howard U., 1931; M.A., Columbia, 1940, Deans scholar Tchrs. Coll., spring 1945; postgrad. Nat. U. Mexico, summer 1947; Spanish Cultural Inst. exchange scholar U. Madrid (Spain), 1951-52; Ph.D. in Spanish, Universidad Interamericana, Saltillo, Mexico, 1966. Instr., dir. remedial reading clinic Xavier U., New Orleans, 1945-47; asst. prof. Spanish, Tex. So. U., Houston, 1948-51, asso. prof. Spanish, 1952-70, prof., 1970—, head dept. fgn. langs. and lits., 1970-73. Bd. dirs. La Universidad Interamericana de Saltillo, Coahuila, Mexico, 1969—, Inst. Hispanic Culture, Houston, 1970-72. Mem. Am. Assn. U. Profs., Am. Assn. Tchrs. Spanish and Portuguese, La Sociedad Nacional Hispanica, Sigma Delta Pi. Author: The Development of Reading Rate and Comprehension in Spanish; A Simplified Spanish Guide; Revised Edition, Parts 1, 2, 3, 1972. Home: 3134 Southmore Blvd Houston TX 77004

RAMSEY, RALPH HEYWARD, JR., lawyer; b. Wedgefield, S.C., Apr. 7, 1900; s. Ralph Heyward and Una Elizabeth (Wells) R.; B.S., U. S.C., 1921, M.A., 1923, LL.B., 1924; m. Mary Dick Alford, Aug. 27, 1926; children—Mary Ann, Ralph Heyward III, Gayle Edward, Sarah Martha. Admitted to S.C. bar, 1924, N.C. bar, 1926; mem. firm Purdy & Ramsey, Sumter, S.C., 1924-26; practice of law, Hendersonville, N.C., 1926, Brevard, N.C., 1926—; sr. mem. firm Ramsey, Hill, Smart & Ramsey and predecessor firm, 1961—. Mayor, Town of Brevard, 1931-33, city atty., 1933-53; county atty. Transylvania County, N.C., 1939-60, 64-72; state senator 32d dist. of N.C., 1935-37; dir., sec. Keystone Camp, Inc., Golf Club Estates, Inc., Round Hill Estates, Inc.; asst. sec. Sapphire Valley Devel. Corp., Connestee Falls Devel. Corp.; sec.-treas., dir. Evergreen Devel. Co. Mem. N.C. Sch. Commn., 1941-43, Commn. on Solicitorial and Jud. Dists., 1945-47, N.C. Gen. Statues Commn., 1946-49; N.C. Med. Care Commn., 1953-56; Western N.C. Regional Planning Commn., 1956-61. Trustee, past chmn. Transylvania Community Hosp.; trustee Mars Hill Coll., 1962-66, 68-71, vice chmn., 1965-66, chmn., 1970-71; chmn. Lyday Meml. Hosp., Brevard, 1933-40. Mem. C. of C. (dir.), Am. Legion, Brevard Music Found. (mem. bd. trustees 1947-60). Am., 29th Jud. Dist. (pres. 1945), Transylvania County, N.C. bar assns., N.C. State Bar (council 1962—, chmn. grievance com. 1968-71, 1st v.p. 1972-73, pres. 1973-74), Am. Judicature Soc., Internat. Platform Assn., Pi Kappa Phi. Democrat. Baptist. Clubs: Kiwanis (sec. 1928-30, pres. 1930, dir. 1931-48, lt. gov. N.C. Dist. 1965), Lake Toxaway Country, Sapphire Valley Golf. Author: (booklet) Economic and Social Survey of Sumter County, 1923; (articles) Indians of Sumter County, The Old Village of Manchester. Home: High Meadows Route 4 Box 196 Brevard NC 28712 Office: Legal Bldg Brevard NC 28712

RAMSEY, ROGER ALAN, solid waste mgmt. co. exec.; b. Houston, June 25, 1938; s. Theo Adolph and Madeline Esther (Anderson) R.; B.S. cum laude, Tex. Christian U., 1960; m. Gayle Etta Garbs, Jan. 27, 1957; children—Roger Craig, Christopher Alan, Carrie Gayle, Curtis Theo. Tax mgr. Arthur Andersen & Co., Houston, 1960-69; v.p., dir. ARS, Inc., 1969, dir., 1969—; v.p. finance Browning-Ferris Industries, Inc., Houston, 1969—; dir. Fannin Group, Inc., Environmental Equipment Corp. Trustee Tex. Benevolent Found. Mem. Am. Inst. C.P.A.'s, Tex. Soc. C.P.A.'s, Houston Chpt. C.P.A.'s, Financial Execs. Inst., Sigma Alpha Epsilon, Beta Gamma Sigma. Methodist. Clubs: Houston Yacht, Plaza, Racquet. Home: 380 Blalock Houston TX 77024 Office: Fannin Bank Bldg Houston TX 77025

RAMSEY, SALLY ANN SEITZ, state ofcl.; b. Columbus, O., Feb. 15, 1931; d. Albert Blazier and Mildred (Dodson) Seitz; B.A., Ohio State U., 1952, M.A., 1955, postgrad. 1963-66; postgrad. St. Mary Coll., Xavier, Kan., 1962; m. Edward Lewis Ramsey, Apr. 11, 1953 (div. Aug. 1962); children—Edward Lewis, Sylvia Ann. Research engr., then sr. research engr. N.Am. Aviation, Inc., Columbus, O. and Downey, Cal., 1962-67; legislative intern State of Ohio, 1964-65; research and information officer Ohio Dept. Urban Affairs, Columbus, 1967-68; adminstrv. specialist Ohio Dept. Devel., Columbus, 1968; asso. planner Div. State Planning, Fla. Dept. Adminstrn., Tallahassee, 1968—. Gray Lady, A.R.C., 1961-62; den mother Cub Scouts Am., 1964-65. Congl. campaign cons., 1966. Mem. Am. Polit. Sci. Assn., Am. Soc. Pub. Adminstrn., Kappa Kappa Gamma, Pi Sigma Alpha. Home: PO Box 3643 Tallahassee FL 32303 Office: 660 Apalachee Pkwy Tallahassee FL 32301

RANA, SHER J., economist, govt. ofcl.; b. Lahore, India, Dec. 14, 1931; s. Khairati Lal and Kaushalya (Devi) R.; B.A., Punjab U., Solan, India, 1952; M.A., Am. U., 1959. Came to U.S., 1955, naturalized, 1961. Adminstrv. asst. Office Chief Minister and Gov. Punjab, 1949-52; asst. to signal engring. mem. Ry. Bd. India, New Delhi, 1952-53; adminstrv. asst. WHO, 1953-55; instr. Dept. State Fgn. Service Inst., Washington, 1957; instr. U. Alaska, 1959-60; asst. prof. econs. U. P.R. Grad. Dept. Econs., 1960-61; asso. prof. econs. and finance Nichols Coll., Dudley, Mass., 1961-62; bus. economist, spl. research and projects Nat. Income Div. Office Bus. Econs. Dept. Commerce, Washington, 1962-63; research scientist, fgn. areas studies div. Am. U., Washington, 1963; asso. prof. econs. E. Carolina

U., Greenville, 1963-66; economist office sec. treasury, Washington, 1966-67; economist AID-Dept. State, Washington, 1967-71, econ. adviser, 1973—; regional econ. adviser UN Econ. Commn. for Asia and Far East, Bangkok, Thailand, 1971-72. Mem. Am. Polit. Sci. Assn., Am., So. econ. assns., Am. Assn. U. Profs., Soc. Internat. Devel. Contbr. to U.S. Army Handbooks on India, Iran. Home: PO Box 9434 Rosslyn Sta Arlington VA 22209

RANCK, NATHAN HOOVER, mgmt. cons.; b. Bellevue, Pa., May 3, 1913; s. James Marsh and Lou Alice (Hoover) R.; student U. Tex., 1934-36; B.S., U. Md., 1952; m. Noralee Castle, May 6, 1938; 1 son, Kendall Castle. Commd. 2d lt. U.S. Army Air Force, 1938, advanced through grades to lt. col., 1944; wing operations officer, China; exec. for res. forces legislation Hdqrs. USAF; dep. comdr. Iceland Air Def. Force; ret., 1958; mgr. airline sales Borg Warner Corp., Bedford, O., 1958-60; supt. plannet-pert sect. Pan Am. World Airways, Air Force Eastern Test Range, Cape Canaveral, Fla., 1960-65; mgr. support control systems Trans World Airlines, Kennedy Space Center, Fla., 1965—; sr. engring. planning specialist Xerox Corp., Rochester, N.Y., 1969—. Cons. mgmt., lectr., 1969—; corporate planner, treas. Energy Systems, Inc., Melbourne, Fla., 1970-71, pres., dir., treas., 1971-72. Loaned exec. Brevard County (Fla.) United Fund, 1968; mem. Pres.'s Nat. Def. Exec. Res., 1959—. Decorated D.F.C., Air medal, Bronze Star medal. Sr. mem. Am. Inst. Indsl. Engrs. Originator Vis-a-Plan mgmt. control technique. Address: 401 Orlando Blvd Indialantic FL 32903

RANDALL, ALAN H., lawyer; b. N.Y.C., Mar. 6, 1934; s. George A. and Betty A. Randall; B.A., Columbia, 1954, LL.B., 1956; m. Marlene Tamby Yurick, July 17, 1956; children—Gavin B., Kerry M. Admitted to N.Y. bar, 1956, P.R. bar, 1968; law clk. to judge Eastern Dist. Pa., 1956-57; atty., adviser internat., econ. affairs div. Office Legal Adviser, Dept. State, 1957-58; supr. atty. 2d region NLRB, N.Y.C., 1959-66, asst. regional atty. region 24, P.R., 1966-68; partner firm O'Neill & Borges, Hato Rey, P.R., 1968—; lectr. seminars in field. Pres. Assn. Labor Relations Practitioners for P.R. and V.I., 1968-69; mem. commn. to draft rules and regulations for V.I. Dept. Labor, 1969; mem. com. to rev. rules of U.S. Dist. Ct. for P.R., 1971—; mem. com. inter-profl. relations Colegio de Abogados de P.R., 1971-72. Mem. Am., Fed. (pres. P.R. chpt. 1972-73, chmn. spl. com. to study fed. employee profl. assns. 1973—) bar assns. Contbr. legal jours. Office: 10th Floor Chase Manhattan Bank Bldg Hato Rey PR 00918

RANDALL, HOWARD MORGAN, JR., educator; b. Rockville Center, N.Y., May 5, 1936; s. Howard Morgan and Caroline (MacIntosh) R.; B.S., U. R.I., 1958; Ph.D. (NIH fellow 1960-65), U. Rochester Sch. Medicine, 1965; m. Evelyn Ann Wittmann, July 28, 1962; 1 dau., Barbara Ann. Instr. La. State U. Med. Center, New Orleans, 1965-68, asst. prof., 1968-71, asso. prof. physiology, 1971—. USPHS grantee, 1968—. Mem. Am. Physiol. Soc., A.A.A.S., Biophys. Soc., La. Heart Assn. (mem. sr. research and fellowship com., med. student fellowship com.), Sigma Xi, Phi Kappa Phi, Phi Sigma. Club: Beach (New Orleans). Contbr. articles on metabolic and functional interrelationships in normal and stressed kidney to sci. jours. Home: 1620 Charlton Dr New Orleans LA 70122 Office: 1100 Florida Av New Orleans LA 70119

RANDALL, J. MALCOM, hosp. adminstr.; b. East St. Louis, Ill., Aug. 9, 1916; A.B., McKendree Coll., Lebanon, Ill., 1939; postgrad. U. Minn., 1950; M. Hosp. Adminstrn., St. Louis U., 1956; grad. Exec. Devel. Program, U. Chgo., 1957; postgrad. U. Wis., 1963, Milw. Inst. Tech., 1964. Asst. to athletic dir. McKendree Coll., 1939; supr. So. Ill. dist. WPA, 1939-42; adminstrv. officer br. office VA, St. Louis, 1946-49; asst. area dir. spl. services St. Louis Med. Area office VA, 1949-53; adminstrv. analyst Office Controller, Dept. Medicine and Surgery, Washington, 1953; spl. asst. to dir., chief spl. services VA Hosp., St. Louis, 1953-56; asst. dir. VA Hosp., Spokane, Wash., 1956-57; asst. dir. VA Research Hosp., Chgo., 1957-58, VA Hosp., Indpls., 1958-60, VA Center, Wood, Wis., 1960-64; dir. VA Hosp., Miles City, Mont., 1964-66, VA Hosp., Gainesville, Fla., 1966—; asso. prof. health and hosp. adminstrn. U. Fla., 1966—, mem. pres.'s community-campus council, mem. council J. Hillis Miller Health Center, 1966—, mem. adminstrv. council, 1966—; preceptor dept. health care adminstrn. George Washington U., 1968—. Chmn. Nat. Com. to Assess Ednl. Capacity of VA System; pres. N. Central Fla. Health Planning Council; chmn. Nat. Panel to Select Career VA Employees for Placement in Grad. Programs in Health Care Adminstrns.; mem. adv. group hosp. dirs. to Chief Med. Dir., VA; dep. chmn. Naval Res. Mgmt. Study Group, 1970; mem. nat. adv. coms. nation computer policies and applications, nationwide cost reduction program, mgmt. improvement program VA; chmn. bd. Inter-Agy. Bd., U.S. Civil Service Examiners Fla. Chmn. Alachua County Employment Opportunities Council. Bd. dirs. United Fund Gainesville and Alachua County, North Central Fla. Regional Planning Council; mem. Fla. adv. group Fla. Regional Med. Program; mem. Fla. Health Planning Council, Community Health Adv. Council; bd. dirs. Center Vol. Action. Served with USN, 1942-46; capt. Res. Fellow Am. Coll. Hosp. Adminstrs. (mem. council regents); mem. Am., Fla. (chmn. council edn.) hosp. assns., assn. Am. Med. Colls., Res. Officers Assn., Naval Res. Assn., Navy League (chmn. Gainesville council), Fed. Ofcls. Assn., Am. Legion. Rotarian. Contbr. articles in field to profl. jours. Office: VA Hosp Archer Rd Gainesville FL 32601

RANDALL, JAMES BENNETT, JR., coll. athletic dir.; b. Mobile, Ala., Oct. 23, 1923; s. James Bennett and Grace Evelyn (Dewey) R.; B.E., Tulane U., 1948; M.S., M.A., U. So. Miss., 1957; m. Barbara Bailey, Sept. 13, 1946; children—Sandra, Robin, James, Scott, Sharman, Stacy, Stephanie. Coach Pascagoula (Miss.) Schs., 1948-51; athletic dir., football coach Miss. Delta Jr. Coll., 1951—, also ins. salesman Dixie Nat. Life Ins. Co. Served with USNR, 1943-46. Named jr. coll. coach of year Miss. Jr. Colls. Assn., 1972, 73. Home: Route 1 Indianola MS 38751 Office: Mississippi Delta Junior College Moorhead MS 38761

RANDALL, WILLIAM MADISON, educator; b. Belleville, Mich., Aug. 16, 1899; s. Will M. and Emma Adele (Henry) R.; A.B., U. Mich., 1921, A.M., 1924; Ph.D. summa cum laude, Hartford Theol. Sem., 1929; Litt.D. (hon.), U. N.C., 1971; travelling fellow Gen. Edn. Bd., 1935, Am. Assn. Learned Socs. (Middle East), 1938; m. Myldred Randolph Cady, June 21, 1924; children—William David, Duncan Peter; m. 2d, Mary Johnson McGee, 1954. Asso. prof. library sci. U. Chgo., 1929, prof., 1931, asst. dean of students, 1938; v.p. Snead & Co., Orange, Va., 1946; dir. libraries, student affairs U. Ga., 1947; capt. U.S. Maritime Service; acad. dean U.S. Mcht. Marine Acad. 1948-51; dean Wilmington (N.C.) Coll., (name changed to U.N.C. at Wilmington 1969), 1951-58, pres., 1958-68, pres. emeritus, prof. modern langs., 1968—. Pres. Wilmington chpt. N.C. Symphony Soc., 1957-60. Mng. editor Library Quarterly, 1931-42; cons. Carnegie Corp. of N.Y., 1929-32; active in ednl. survey work, Gen. Edn. Bd., Meth. Bd. Edn., N. Central Assn., 1929-39; dir. Nat. Conf. Christians and Jews; chmn. county chpt. Nat. Found. Infantile Paralysis. Mem. legislative com. So. Assn. Jr. Colls.; sec.-treas. N.C. Jr. Coll. Athletic Conf., 1955-63. Mem. commn. sent to reorganize Vatican library, Carnegie Endowment for Internat. Peace, 1928. Served to lt. col. USAAF, 1942-45, with War Dept. Intelligence, stationed Cairo, Egypt, Casablanca, Morocco. Mem. N.C. State Community Coll. Com. 1952. Mem. A.L.A., N.E.A., Phi Sigma. Democrat. Episcopalian. Clubs: Rotary, Executives. Author: The College Library, 1932; (with F. L. D. Goodrich) Principles of College Library Administration, 1935; Acquisition and Cataloging of Library Materials, 1941. Home: 4622 Mocking Bird Lane Wilmington NC 28401

RANDELL, M. T., stage legislator; b. Ft. Myers, Fla., Nov. 15, 1924; B.S.F., U. Fla., 1950; m. Mary Elizabeth Bunnell; children—Elizabeth, Wallace Frank, Laura Fair. Mem. Fla. Ho. of Reps., 1964—. Dir. Am. Bank Ft. Myers. Bd. dirs. Lee County Assn. Retarded Children, YMCA. Served with AC, AUS, World War II. Mem. Am. Ordnance Soc., Audubon Soc., Farm Bur., C. of C. Mason (32 deg.), Kiwanian, Woodmen of World. Episcopalian (vestryman, past jr. warden). Home: 1453 Lynwood Av Fort Myers FL 33901 Office: PO Box 1668 Fort Myers FL 33902

RANDOLPH, FREDERIC MEGAN, shoe retailing exec.; b. Evanston, Ill., Feb. 17, 1933; s. John Francis and Annabel J. (Megan) R.; student San Antonio Bus. Coll., 1950-51; B.A., Trinity U., 1953; retail seminars Kent State U., 1967-68; m. Peggy Jean Dalhover, Jan. 4, 1972; children—Jack, Terry, James; children from previous marriage—Deborah Ann, Melissa Anne. Vice pres. Nobil Shoe Stores, Akron, O., 1957-69; pres. Beck Shoe Stores, N.Y.C., 1969-71; pres. Louis Ostrov Shoe Co., retail shoe chain, Barberton, O., 1971-73, also dir.; now dir. retail orgns. Caribbean Bata Shoe Co., Santurce, P.R. Named Humanitarian of the Year Jewish War Vets., Bronx, N.Y., 1970. Mem. Two-Ten Assos. (v.p. 1963-73). Roman Catholic. Address: Victoria Plaza Apt 17A Candina 10 Santurce PR 00907

RANDOLPH, HENRY ENGLAND, educator; b. Sparta, Tenn., May 21, 1935; s. John Thomas and Mary Louise (England) R.; B.S. in Dairy Sci., Tenn. Poly. Inst., 1957; M.S. in Dairy Tech., Ohio State U., 1959, Ph.D., 1962; m. Bette Rose Davis, Dec. 25, 1954; children—Kenneth E., David T., Marsha H., Beth A. Instr., also research asso. dept. dairy tech. Ohio State U., Columbus, 1959-62; asst. prof., also extension specialist in dairy tech. U. Ky., Lexington, 1963-67; asso. prof. dept. animal sci. Tex. A. and M. U., College Station, 1967-73, prof. food sci., 1973—. Cons. to dairy and food processing cos. Mem. Internat. Assn. Milk, Food and Environmental Sanitarians, Inst. Food Technologists, Am. Dairy Sci. Assn., Dallas-Fort Worth Dairy Soc. (hon.; recipient Charles Galyen award 1972), Tex. A. and M. Dairy Sci. Club. Contbr. articles on milk and milk products to sci. jours. Home: 3610 Sweet Briar St Bryan TX 77801 Office: Dairy Section Texas A and M University College Station TX 77843

RANDOLPH, ROBERT MANICE, edn. and cons. firm exec.; b. N.Y.C., July 31, 1934; s. Robert S. and Peggy (Price) R.; B.B.A., U. Okla., 1956; M.B.A., Northwestern U., 1959; m. Valerie Jean Vandaveer, Oct. 20, 1956; children—Tamera M., Teresa M., Robin V. Dist. mgr. Gen. Am. Transp. Corp., Tulsa, 1959-61, asst. gen. mgr. container div., Chgo., 1961-65; asst. to exec. v.p. Joy Mfg. Co., Pitts., 1965-66; div. planning mgr. Marbon div. Borg-Warner Corp., Parkersburgh, W.Va., 1966-68, group planning mgr., 1968-69; founder, pres., dir., also chief exec. officer Planagement Inc., Northbrook, Ill. 1969-72, Tulsa, 1972—; dir. Internat. Speakers Network Inc., Elgin, Ill. Faculty YMCA Coll., Chgo., 1969-71. Bd. dirs. Chgo. chpt. Cystic Fibrosis, 1971-72. Served as lt. j.g. USNR, 1956-58. Mem. Am. Mgmt. Assn. (speaker 1968—, chmn. programs 1968), Am. Marketing Assn., Beta Gamma Sigma, Delta Sigma Pi, Delta Tau Delta. Contbr. articles to profl. jours. Home: 6921 S Delaware Pl Tulsa OK 74136 Office: Planagement Inc 823 S Detroit St Tulsa OK 74120

RANDOLPH, THOMAS ALEXANDER, supr. schs.; b. Elk Horn, W.Va., Mar. 25, 1908; s. John Peter and Rose Ella (Butler) R.; B.S. in Edn., Bluefield State Tchrs. Coll., 1932; M.Ed., U. Va., 1969; m. Lauramer Autherine Williams, June 12, 1946; 1 son, Thomas Alexander. Tchr., Henry County, Va., 1932-33, elementary supr. Henry County Schs., Martinsville, Va., 1933—. Mem. Drug Use and Abuse Workshop, Radford Coll., 1970, 71. Chmn., Algonquian dist. Boy Scouts Am., 1960. Mem. Assn. for Supervision and Curriculum Devel., Va., dist. and local edn. assns. Home: PO Box 672 Fieldale VA 24089 Office: PO Box 511 Martinsville VA 24112

RANDQUIST, BOBBY WAYNE, sch. supt.; b. Cordell, Okla., Sept. 11, 1928; s. Carl Martin and Gladys Marie (Brown) R.; B.S., S.W. State Coll., Weatherford, Okla., 1951; M.Ed., U. Okla., 1957, Ed.D., 1970; m. Ruby Nell Crouch, Dec. 31, 1949; children—Robert Martin, Kathryn Annette. Prin., Davenport (Okla.) High Sch., 1960-62; supt. Oney Pub. Schs., Albert, Okla., 1962-64, Carnegie (Okla.) Pub. Schs., 1968—; asst. supt. Anadarko (Okla.) Pub. Sch., 1964-68. Cons. Indian Edn. Workshops, 1969—, Indian Edn. Curriculum Materials, 1969—. Mem. bd. Anadarko City Library, 1966-68. Served with AUS, 1946-47; PTO. Mem. N.E.A., Okla. Edn. Assn., Am. Assn. Sch. Adminstrs., Caddo County Tchrs. Assn. (pres. 1967-68). Baptist (tng. union dir. 1964-66). Rotarian (pres. 1970-71). Home: 26 Carol St Carnegie OK 73015 Office: Box 159 Carnegie OK 73015

RANGE, ROBERT LOUIS, electric co. exec.; b. Cuero, Tex., May 20, 1933; s. Louis Henry and Laura May (Mills) R.; B.B.A., S.W. Tex. State U., 1957; m. Laurie Lorraine Creel, Nov. 1, 1957; children—Robin Lynne, Robert Lee. Asst. sec. Central and S.W. Corp., Wilmington, Del., 1969—, asst. treas., 1969—, asst. to pres., 1970—; treas. CSR Services, Inc., Dallas, 1969—, v.p., 1972—. Served with AUS, 1953-55. C.P.A., Tex. Mem. Am. Inst. C.P.A.'s, Tex. Soc. C.P.A.'s Home: 9635 Crestedge St Dallas TX 75238 Office: 2828 One Main Pl Dallas TX 75250

RANGEL, DAVID MEDINA, lawyer; b. San Luis Potosi, Mex., Oct. 27, 1919; s. Antonio Rangel Ruiz de Esparza and Anastasia Medina Nunez; Lawyer, Nat. U. Mexico, 1943, D. in Law, 1951; m. Consuelo Ortiz, June 1, 1950; children—David, Carlos, Horacio, Alfredo, Monica, Luis Xavier. Admitted to Mexican bar, 1945; mem. firm Basham, Ringe & Correa, Mexico City, 1942—. Prof. adminstrv. law Iberoamericana U. Mexico, 1965—. Recipient Gt. Cross of Forensic Order of Honor, Mexican Bar and Nat. Lawyers Assn., 1971. Founder Mem. Mexican Assn. Indsl. Property Agts. (pres. 1966—), Inst. Pub. Adminstrn., Internat. Assn. for Protection of Indsl. Property (sec. Mexican group 1964-74); mem. Mexican Bar, Mexican Acad. Internat. Law, Inter-Am. Bar Assn., World Peace Through Law Center, Mexican Acad. Processal and Criminal Law, Interam. Assn. Indsl. Property (hon.), Bolivian Assn. Indsl. Property (corr.), Colombian Assn. Indsl. Property (corr.), League Internat. contre la Concurrence Deloyale (corr.). Author: Copyright and its Legal Protection in Mexico, 1944; Trademarks and its Compulsory Legende, 1958; Mexican Trademark Treatise, 1960; (with others) The Regime of the Industrial Property and the Economic Integration of the ALALC, 1969, World Patent Litigation, 1967, International Encyclopaedia of Comparative Law, 1974. Contbr. to publs. in field. Home: 251 Allende St Mexico City 16 Mexico Office: 123 Liverpool St Mexico City 6 Mexico

RANGEL-GUERRA, JORGE, univ. adminstr.; b. Monterrey, Mexico, Nov. 8, 1926; s. Enrique Rangel and Dolores Guerra DeRangel Estrella; Doctorate, Universidad de Nuevo Leon, 1951; m. Rosa Margarita Luna de Rangel, Feb. 13, 1956; children—Jorge, David, Dolores, Carlos. Dir., Del Museo Regional De N.L., Monterrey, Mexico, 1956-74; dir. arte ac, dir. D.F. La Facultad de filosofia y Letras JefeDel Opto Extension Universitaria, Monterrey, 1974—; dir. faculty of philosphy, psychology and letters Universidad de Nuevo Leon Ciudad Universitaria, Monterrey, 1969-71. Home: 114 Amazonas Pte Monterrey NL Mexico Office: Torre De La Rectoria-Ciudad Universitaria Monterrey NL Mexico

RANGRA, AVINASH KUMAR, educator; b. Hariana, Panjab, India, Mar. 30, 1939; s. Kundan Lall and (Rampyari) R.; grad. H.N. Coll., India, 1956; B.Sc. with honors, Panjab U., 1959, M.Sc. with honors, 1960; Ph.D., Okla. State U., 1967; m. Anju Tara, Oct. 8, 1969; 1 son, Amit Kumar. Came to U.S., 1962, naturalized, 1973. Lectr. in chemistry H.N. Coll., Hariana, India, 1960-62; teaching asst. Okla. State U., Stillwater, 1962-63, 66-67, research asst., 1963-66; asst. prof. chemistry Sul Ross State U., Alpine, Tex., 1967-70, asso. prof. chemistry, 1970—, fgn. student adviser, 1970—. Mem. Am. Chem. Soc., Internat. Platform Assn., Am. Inst. Chemists, A.A.A.S., Tex. Inst. Chemists (mem. students awards com. 1971-72), Sigma Xi, Phi Lambda Upsilon. Lion. Contbr. articles to profl. jours. Home: 502 June St Alpine TX 79830

RANKEN, HOWARD BENEDICT, real estate exec.; b. Troy, N.Y., Sept. 14, 1898; s. William Hugh and Alma Florence (Eichholz) R.; student Rensselaer Poly. Inst., 1914-18; m. Edith May Manning, Mar. 5, 1920; children—Howard Benedict, William Allison, Doris Eleanor (Mrs. George M. Angleton). Design and devel. engr. Glesn Falls (N.Y.) Machine Works, 1919-21, 1922-24; civil engr. W.C. Bliss, Miami, 1921-22, 1924-26; structural engr. M.H. Treadwell Co., N.Y.C., 1926-27; maintenance engr. Bklyn. Edison Co., 1927-28, The Tex. Co., Port Arthur, 1928-29; devel. engr. Smoot Engring. Co., N.Y.C., 1929-31; supervising engr., also asst. state supr. N.J. Geodetic Survey, Newark, 1933-40; marine devel. engr. Lidgerwood Mfg. Co., Elizabeth, N.J., 1941; ordnance engr. U.S. War Dept., N.Y.C., 1942-43; cons. engr. Cranford, N.J., 1944-45; cons. engr., also realtor, New Smyrna Beach, Fla., 1945—. Councilman, City of Edgewater (Fla.), 1954-55. Served with U.S. Army, 1918-19. Named Realtor of Year, S.E. Volusia County, 1972. Mem. Am. Soc. Mech. Engrs., Am. Ordnance Assn., Soc. Am. Mil. Engrs., S.A.R., Am. Legion, New Smyrna Beach Bd. Realtors (pres. 1949-54, treas. 1966—). Democrat. Episcopalian. Rotarian. Home: Ranken Dr PO Box 202 Edgewater FL 32032 Office: 310 Canal St New Smyrna Beach FL 32069

RANKIN, EDWARD LEE, JR., textile co. exec.; b. Chattanooga, May 12, 1919; s. Edward Lee and Gladys (Narramore) R.; A.B. in Journalism, U. N.C., 1940; m. Frances Wallace, June 12, 1948; children—Jane Elizabeth, Ann Wallace, Edward Lee III. Reporter, Salisbury (N.C.) Post, 1940-41, Raleigh (N.C.) News & Observer, 1941; night editor A.P., Charlotte, N.C., Columbia, S.C., 1946; dir. pub. relations State Hwy. & Pub. Works Commn., Raleigh, 1946-47; press sec. U.S. Sen. William B. Umstead, Washington, 1947-48; pub. relations exec. Burlington Mills, Greensboro, N.C., 1948-53; pvt. sec. to Gov. N.C., Raleigh, 1953-59; v.p. John Harden Assos., pub. relations firm, Raleigh, 1960-65; dir. State Dept. Adminstrn., Raleigh, 1965-67; exec. v.p. N.C. Citizens Assn., 1967-71; dir. pub. relations Cannon Mills Co., Kannapolis, N.C., 1972—, v.p., 1973—. Served to lt. USNR, 1941-46; U.S.S. LST 355 (comdg. officer), and 356, N.Africa, Sicily, Salerno, Normandy. Named Tar Heel of Week, News & Observer, Raleigh, 1959. Mem. Pub. Relations Soc. Am. Democrat. Presbyn. Clubs: Sphinx, Watauga, Cabarrus Country. Home: 524 Windsor Pl NE Concord NC 28025 Office: Cannon Mills Co Kannapolis NC 28081

RANKIN, HENRY HOLLIS, JR., lawyer; b. Mission, Tex., Jan. 11, 1915; s. Henry Hollis and Iva (Adams) R.; A.A., Edinburg Jr. Coll., 1933; LL.B., U. Tex. at Austin, 1936; m. Ann Lucille Chesnutt, July 24, 1939; children—Henry Hollis III, Robert Carlton, Deborah Ann (Mrs. Gary Paul Wagner). Admitted to Tex. bar, 1936; gen. practice law, Edinburg, Tex., 1936-58; partner firm Rankin, Kern & Martinez, McAllen, Tex., 1958—; judge Hidalgo County Ct. at Law, 1951-53. Mem. Tex. Hist. Commn., 1969—. Trustee Mission Ind. Sch. Dist., 1963-69. Bd. dirs. Tex. Hist. Found., 1969-71. Mem. Am., Hidalgo County (dir. 1973), Tex. bar assns., S.A.R., Phi Theta Kappa, Theta Xi. Democrat. Methodist. Club: McAllen Country. Home: 900 E Cedar St McAllen TX 78501 Office: 804 Pecan Av McAllen TX 78501

RANKIN, J(AMES) M(ATTHEW), wheat farmer; b. Rockdale, Tex., Oct. 19, 1892; s. Jackson M. and Sarah Alice (Mayfield) R.; student U. Tex., U. Grenoble (France); B.A., Tex. Tech. Coll., 1929, M.A., 1932; m. Maude E. Benton, May 12, 1920; children—Jean M., Joe D. (twins). Pub. Sch. adminstr., 1914-38; supt. Ralls (Tex.) pub. schs., 1931-38; editor, pub. Slaton Statonite, 1938-41; staff columnist Ralls Banner and Lorenzo Tribune, 1941—; farm mgr., Ralls 1941—; judge Crosby County, 1950-54. Sec.-treas. Crosby County chpt. A.R.C., 1950—. Bd. dirs. Plains Cotton Growers; Crosby County rep. Boll Weevil Control. Mem. Selective Service Bd. Served 1st div., U.S. Army, World War I. Decorated Purple Heart, Silver Star. Mem. Am. Legion. Baptist. Mason (32 deg.), Rotarian (past pres. Ralls). Address: Sect Nine Farms Box 190 Ralls TX 79357

RANKIN, JOE DAVID, coop. exec.; b. Ralls, Tex., May 8, 1929; s. James Matthew and Maude (Benton) R.; B.A., Tex. Technol. U., 1951; m. Emily Elizabeth Brasfield, Aug. 22, 1954; children—Joe David, Robin, James Matthew II. Dir., Plains Coop. Oil Mill, Lubbock, Tex., 1964—, pres., 1970—; dir. Farmer Coop. Compress. Served with USAF, 1951-54. Mem. Plains Cotton Coop. Marketing Assn. (dir.), Tex. Farmers Union (dir.). Rotarian. Home: Box 190 Ralls TX 79357 Office: 2901 Av A Lubbock TX 79404

RANKIN, MARY MARGARET, banker; b. Forestburg, Tex., Sept. 20, 1921; d. Oscar Dennis and Margaret Leon (Martin) Perryman; certificate Am. Inst. Banking, 1972; m. James Audrey Rankin, Jan. 31, 1939; children—Margaret Sharon (Mrs. McCown), Mary Kathryn (Mrs. Gordon L. Collins), James Gary, Patricia Elaine (Mrs. Kenneth Peterson). Sec. to comdg. officer U.S. Army Glider Sch., Lamesa, Tex., 1942, Dawson County War Bd., U.S. Dept. Agr., Lamesa, fall 1942-43, 44; office mgr., full-charge bookkeeper, advt. dept. MiniMax Feed & Elevator Co., Lamesa, 1945-48; reporter Denton Record-Chronicle, Denton, Tex., 1957-59; charter women's editor Lewisville (Tex.) Leader, 1960-62; with Lewisville (Tex.) Nat. Bank, 1963—, pub. relations rep., 1963-67, asst. cashier, 1967-70, asst. v.p., 1970-72, v.p., 1972—. Charter v.p. Lewisville unit Am. Cancer Soc., 1969-70, pres., 1970-71. Mem. bd. Cross Timbers council Girl Scouts U.S.A., Tex., 1964-69, Denton County chpt. Am. Cancer Soc., 1969—; co-founder Lewisville Community Library; co-founder Lewisville YMCA, 1972, now bd. dirs. Named Outstanding Woman of Yr. Bus. and Profl. Women's Club, Lewisville, 1967-68; Lewisville Boss of Yr. Office Edn. Assn. Club, Vocational Ednl. Assn., Lewisville High Sch., 1970-71. Mem. Nat. Assn. Bank Women, Bank Marketing Assn. (North Tex. chpt.), Lewisville's Resume Club (charter; pres. 1967-68), Lewisville Band Club (charter), Athletic Booster Club (charter), Beta Sigma Phi (charter; pres. Lambda Epsilon chpt. 1948). Democrat. Methodist (mem. ofcl. bd. 1959-60; pres. Women's Soc. Christian Service 1959-60). Address: 332 South Shore Pl Lewisville TX 75067 Office: 250 Stemmons Expressway Lewisville TX 75067

RANNIGER, KLAUS, radiologist, educator; b. Ahrensburg, Germany, July 4, 1926; s. Walter E. and Elisabeth M. (Wachholz) R.; M.D., U. Keil (Germany), 1952; student radiology U. Chgo., 1955-58; m. Renate Hartwich, Apr. 20, 1963; children—Monica A., Claudia U. Came to U.S., 1955, naturalized, 1964. Instr. U. Chgo., 1958-60, asst. prof., 1960-64, asso. prof., 1964-68, prof., 1968-72; prof. radiology Med. Coll. Va., Richmond, 1972—. Mem. Research Soc. N.Am., A.M.A., N.Y. Acad. Sci., Internat. Radiol. Sci., Sigma Xi. Home: 8104 River Rd Richmond VA 23229

RANSOM, HARRY HUNTT, former univ. chancellor; b. Galveston, Tex., Nov. 22, 1908; s. Harry Huntt and Marion Goodwin (Cunningham) R.; A.B. U. of South, 1928; A.M., Yale, 1930, Ph.D., 1938; student Harvard, 1929-30; Litt.D., U. of South, 1958, U. N.D., 1970, U. Dallas, 1971; LL.D., Baylor U., 1958, Trinity U., 1963, Tex. Christian U., 1963; L.H.D., Austin Coll., 1966, So. Meth. U., 1972; D.Eng., Colo. Sch. Mines, 1972; m. Hazel Louise Harrod, Aug. 11, 1951. Instr. English and journalism State Tchrs. Coll., Valley City, N.D., 1930-32, 33-34; instr. English and history Colo. State Coll., 1934-35; instr. English, U. Tex. at Austin, 1935-38, asst. prof., 1938-42, asso. prof., 1946-47, prof., 1947—, asst. dean Grad. Sch., 1951-53, asso. dean, 1953-54, dean Coll. Arts and Scis., 1954-57, v.p., provost, 1957-60, pres., 1960-61, chancellor U. Tex. System, 1961-71, chancellor emeritus, 1971—. Dir. Southwestern Bell Telephone Co., 1967—. Trustee Carnegie Found. for Advancement of Teaching, 1962-71; past mem. Commn. on Colls. and Univs. of the So. Assn. Past chmn. hist. commn. Internat. Copyright League; past mem. Commn. on White House Fellows, Pres.'s Commn. on Patent System, Nat. Adv. Commn. on Libraries, Nat. Adv. Council for Edn. in Health Professions; mem., pres. Internat. Commn. for Library Devel., 1965-68, mem. com. on profl. sch. and world affairs, 1965-67; mem. permanent com. Oliver Wendell Holmes Devise, 1964-72, Nat. Com. on Accrediting Bd. Commrs., 1966-70; mem. commn. on acad. affairs Am. Council Edn., 1966-70. Served to maj. USAAF, 1942-46. Decorated Legion of Merit. Fellow Tex. Hist. Assn.; mem. Modern Lang. Assn., Grolier Club, Tex. Philos. Soc., Tex. Inst. Letters, Phi Beta Kappa, Kappa Sigma. Episcopalian. Author: Bibliography of English Copyright History, 1948; Notes of a Texas Book Collector, 1950; The First Copyright Statute, 1955. Editor: (With J. Frank Dobie and M. C. Boatright) Texas Folklore Publications, XIV, XV, XVI, XVII. Asso editor Tex. Folklore Soc., 1938-41, Southwest Hist. Quarterly, 1952-56; English Copyright Cases, 1660-1775, 1956. Editor Texas Quarterly, 1958—. Home: 1610 Watchill Rd Austin TX 78703

RAO, SRINIVASA VASNDEVA, physician; b. Mysore, India, Oct. 16, 1935; s. Vasudeva and Radha Bai (Achar) Murthy; M.D., Med. Coll. Mysore, India, 1960; m. Shantha Rayan, Sept. 18, 1970; 1 son, Ganesh. Intern Bergen Pines Hosp., Paramus, N.J., 1962-63; resident U. So. Cal. Sch. Medicine, Los Angeles, 1964-66; practice medicine specializing in chest disease, Edmonton, Can.; asst. prof. medicine U. Alberta, Edmonton, Can., 1968-72, also cons. physician chest disease, Univ. Hosp., Edmonton, 1968-72; chief chest disease sect. VA Hosp., Temple, Tex., 1972—. Fellow Royal Coll. Physicians of Can.; mem. Canadian Med. Assn. Contbr. articles on clin. pulmonary physiology to med. jours. Home: 3320 Thornton Lane Temple TX 76501 Office: VA Hospital Temple TX 76501

RAPER, CHARLES ALBERT, cement co. exec.; b. Charleston, W.Va., Aug. 18, 1926; s. Kenneth B. and Louise (Williams) R.; student Okla. State U., 1945; B.S., U. Ill., 1949; m. Margaret Ann Weers, Dec. 26, 1947; children—Kathleen, Josephine, Charles. Sales mgr. Meyer Furnace Co., Peoria, Ill., 1949-54; v.p. marketing Master Consol., Inc., Dayton, O., 1954-61; mgmt. cons. McKinsey & Co., Inc., Chgo., 1961-67; v.p. marketing Gen. Portland Cement Co., Dallas, 1967-69, pres., 1969—, also dir. Charter mem. Sales Execs. Group, Peoria, 1954. Coordinator, Tomorrow's Am. Citizens Today Program, Dallas, 1969-71. Chmn. bd. dirs. Dallas C. of C.; bd. dirs. Portland Cement Assn.; vice chmn., devel. bd. U. Tex. at Dallas; mem. exec. bd. Circle Ten council Boy Scouts Am. Served with USNR, 1944-46. Mem. Phi Gamma Delta. Methodist. Clubs: Northwood, Dallas, Dallas Gun, (Dallas). Home: 7029 Gateridge Dr Dallas TX 75240 Office: PO Box 324 Republic Nat Bank Tower Dallas TX 75221

RAPETTI, VINCENT ANTHONY, librarian; b. Floral Park, N.Y., Jan. 26, 1926; s. James Vincent and Lucille Florence (Antonacchio) R.; A.B., Rollins Coll., 1950; M.A. in L.S., U. Mich., 1952, A.M. in History, 1952. Librarian, Soc. of the Four Arts, Palm Beach, Fla., 1952-57; adminstrn. asst. tech. services and extension Orlando (Fla.) Pub. Library, 1957-61; head cataloger, dept. dir. library system Nassau, N.Y., 1961-63; chief librarian LTV/Service Tech. Corp., J.F. Kennedy Space Center, Fla., 1964-71, v.p. profl. services div., project mgr., chief librarian New World Services, Inc., 1971—. Served with USAAF, 1944-46. Home: 817 Glen Arden Way Altamonte Springs FL 32701 Office: J F Kennedy Space Center Library Kennedy Space Center FL 32899

RAPOPORT, BERNARD, ins. co. exec.; b. San Antonio, July 17, 1917; s. David and Riva (Feldman) R.; B.A., U. Tex., 1939; m. Audre Jean Newman, Feb. 15, 1942; 1 son, Ronald B. Partner Art's Jewelry Store, Waco, Tex., 1944-48; gen. agt. Pioneer Am. Life Ins. Co., Fort Worth, 1950-51; agy. dir. Am. Income Ins. Co., Indpls., 1951-54; exec. v.p., dir. Am. Income Life Ins. Co., Indpls., 1954-59, pres., dir., Waco, 1960—; pres., dir. Income Investment Corp., Waco, 1960—; dir. Citizens Nat. Bank, Waco. Mem. White House Conf. on Aging; mem. Com. for Pub. Justice, N.Y.C., 1971—; sponsor Inst. Am. Democracy, Washington, 1968—; sec.-treas. Action Coalition Tex., 1971—; mem. John F. Kennedy Meml. Commn., Austin, Tex., 1970—; regional mem. Tex. Assn. Developing Colls., United Negro Coll. Fund Campaign. Mem. finance council Democratic Nat. Com., 1971—. Bd. dirs., founder Center for Study Democratic Instns., Santa Barbara, Cal., Digestive Disease Found., Bethesda, Md.; dir. adv. council Social Work Found. U. Tex., Austin; trustee Paul Quinn Coll., Waco. Mem. Tex. Intercollegiate Student Assn. (dir. 1971—). Jewish religion. Home: 2332 Wendy Lane Waco TX 76710 Office: 1200 Wooded Acres Waco TX 76707

RAPPELET, ALBERT OTTO, contractor; b. New Orleans, Sept. 18, 1918; s. Rene S. and Evelina (Terrebonne) R.; grad. high sch.; m. Velvina Vegas, June 10, 1950; children—Charles, Geraldine, Sharon, Rene; m. 2d, Michelle Bitoun; 1 son, Albert Otto. Pres., La. Constrn. & Material Co., Inc., Galliano, 1943—; owner Creole Kitchen, Boutte, La., 1945—, Home Ins. Agy., Galliano, 1956—, Larose Lumber Co. (La.), 1967—, Marshland Constrn. and Materials Co., Cut Off, La.; mem. La. Ho. of Reps., 1968-72. Organizer, Internat. Found. for Exceptional Children, 1960, chmn. bd., 1960-63; pres., chmn. bd. Greater Lafourche Port Commn., 1960—. Mem. La. Senate, 1948-52, 56-64. Recipient awards including Nicholls Alumni Fedn. award, 1969. Mem. La. Bldg. Material Dealers Assn., State Contractors Assn. Democrat. Methodist. Lion. Club: Young Men's Business (South Lafourche). Address: PO Drawer R Larose LA 70373

RARDIN, WILLIAM GLEN, state ofcl.; b. Ravenswood, W.Va., Apr. 26, 1905; s. William DeWitt and Amy (Cox) R.; A.B., Lynchburg Coll., 1929; postgrad. U. Ill., 1933; m. Nell Mae Jack, Apr. 3, 1936. History tchr., dir. athletics, coach Randolph-Macon Acad., Bedford, Va., 1929-33; dir. athletics, asso. prof. phys. edn., coach Lynchburg (Va.) Coll., 1933-41; claims rep. div. war vets. claims Va. Dept. Law, Roanoke, 1945-51, asst. dir., 1951—. Treas., Roanoke Valley Enterprises, Inc., 1965—; counselor Am. Legion Boys State of Va., Inc., 1946-52, asst. dir., 1953-54, dir. 1955—, mem. dept. Boys State com., 1948-53. Bd. dirs. Roanoke County Fair. Served with USNR, 1943-45. Recipient Hobbs Achievement award Lynchburg Coll., 1958, Citizenship award Am. Legion, Va., 1956. Mem. Am. Legion (hon. life mem.), V.F.W., D.A.V., Nat. Service Officers. Mason. Club: Roanoke Country. Home: 2751 Richelieu Av Roanoke VA 24014 Office: 211 W Campbell Av SW Roanoke VA 24012

RARICK, JOHN R., congressman; b. Waterford, Ind., Jan. 29, 1924; student Ball State Tchrs. Coll., 1942, 44-45, La. State U., 1943-44; J.D., Tulane U., 1949; m. Marguerite Pierce; three children. Admitted to La. bar, 1949; judge 20th Jud. Dist. La., 1961-66; mem. 90th-93d Congresses 6th Dist. La. Served with AUS, World War II; ETO. Decorated Bronze Star medal, Purple Heart. Mem. D.A.V., V.F.W., Am. Legion. Democrat. Mason (32 deg., Shriner, K.T.); mem. Order Eastern Star. Office: 1525 Longworth House Office Bldg Washington DC 20515

RAS, FLORENCE ANN, educator; b. Chgo.; d. Andrew C. and Frances (Lechart) Ras; B.A., Barat Coll.; M.A., Northwestern U., 1962; M.Ed., Fla. Atlantic U., 1968. Tchr., Ft. Lauderdale (Fla.) Oral Sch., 1958—, asst. dir., 1962-64, dir., 1964—. Instr., Confraternity of Christian Doctrine, 1963-64; tchr. deaf children, West Palm Beach, Fla., 1961. Leader, Girl Scouts U.S.A., Chgo., 1946-47; vol. worker A.R.C., Chgo., 1948-49; chmn. speech reading classes for adults, Broward County, Fla., 1966; mem. adv. com. for workshops and facilities State Dept. Edn. Div. Vocational Rehab., 1967-68. Bd. dirs., adviser Young Deaf Adult Club, Ft. Lauderdale, 1967-68. Mem. Alexander Graham Bell Assn., Conv. Am. Instrs. of Deaf, Am., Fla. Broward County (dir. 1965-67, pres. bd. 1967-68) speech and hearing assns., N.E.A., Barat Coll., Northwestern U. alumni assns. Home: 3124 NE 42d Ct Fort Lauderdale FL 33308 Office: 3100 SW 8th Av Fort Lauderdale FL 33315

RASBERRY, CHARLES LOREL, broadcasting co. exec.; b. Brookland, Ark., Sept. 14, 1934; s. Roy H. and Nellie (Shockney) R.; B.S., Ark. State U., 1956; M. TV, U. Ill., 1961. Announcer, newsman sta. KDRS, Paragould, Ark., 1953-56; newsman, sta. WILL and WILL-TV, Urbana, Ill., 1960-61; dir. broadcasting Ark. State U., Jonesboro, 1961—, dir. closed-circuit TV system, 1967—; gen. mgr. radio sta. KASU, Jonesboro, 1961—. Dir. Ark. State U. Indian Sports Network, 1961—, chmn. div. radio-TV, 1969—. Served with USNR, 1956-60. Mem. Nat. Assn. Profl. Broadcasting Edn., Nat. Assn. Ednl. Broadcasters (bd. dirs.), Kappa Tau Alpha, Pi Gamma Mu, Kappa Kappa Psi, Sigma Delta Chi. Methodist. Home: 208 Pekin St Jonesboro AR 72401 Office: Radio-TV Bldg Ark State Univ Jonesboro AR 72401

RASBERRY, W(ILLIAM) C(LINTON), corp. exec.; b. Tupelo, Miss., Aug. 31, 1906; s. William Dixon and Gertrude (Bass) R.; student Miss. A. and M. Coll., 1924-27; B.A., Southwestern U. at Memphis, 1928; postgrad. YMCA, 1929; m. Helen Robinson, Jan. 9, 1936; children—Doris Gayden, William Clinton. Dir. phys. edn., coach Southwestern U., 1929-30; asst. coffee purchasing agt. Maury-Cole Co., Memphis, 1931-33; mgr. Monogram Coffee Co., Shreveport, La., 1933-35; pres. Shreveport Horse & Mule Co., 1933-35; bus. mgmt. and real estate devel., 1935-42; v.p., mgr. Forest Park Cemetery, Inc., Shreveport, 1942-44, pres., 1946—; pres. Brookwood Corp., La. Monument Co., Forest Park Cemetery West, Inc., Allen Monument Co., Westport Devel. Corp.; partner Rasberry & Rasberry Real Estate Investment, 1959—, Crow & Rasberry Timber Lands; pres. Rasberry Timber Lands & Investments; chmn. bd., pres. First Nat. Bank, Niceville, Fla.; v.p. Agora Corp.; dir. Comml. Nat. Bank, Dixie Seed & Feed. Dir. Indsl. Devel. Com., 1962—; an owner Capt. Shreve Hotel, Shreveport; dir. 1st Bank Crestview (Fla.), chmn., dir. Holiday in Dixie, 1957-58; dir. Pub. Appeals Review Council, 1955-58; vice chmn., dir. 1st Nat. Bank, Niceville, Fla.; pres. Shreveport Beautification Found., 1957-58, Norwela council Boy Scouts Am., 1956-58, YMCA bd., 1957-69. Pres., La. State Fair Assn., 1966-67; v.p. Caddo Parish Sch. Bd., 1958-59, pres., 1959-60; pres. Pub. Affairs Research Council, 1967-70; mem. Fla. Council of 100. Served with USNR, 1944-46. Recipient Brotherhood citation Nat. Conf. Christians and Jews, 1969; named Mr. Shreveport. Mem. Nat. (past pres.), So. (past pres.), La. (past pres.) assns. cemeteries, C. of C. (dir. 1957, pres. 1961), U.S. C. of C. (policy com. 1965-70, dir.), Am. Legion (past post comdr.), English Speaking Union. Kiwanian. Clubs: Shreveport Country, Shreveport (dir. 1959—). Home: 820 Slattery Blvd Shreveport LA 71104 Office: PO Box 1764 Shreveport LA 71166

RASCHKE, RICHARD REINHOLD, spacecraft co. engr.; b. Troy, N.Y., Apr. 15, 1924; s. Reinhold Richard and Lina (Bailer) R.; student Union Coll., 1944-45; B.Elec. Engring., Rensselaer Poly. Inst., 1948; postgrad. Union Coll., 1957-60; m. Mary Elaine Danielson, July 28, 1951; children—Erica Lynn, Richard Edward, Karen Ellen, Kristine Ann. With Gen. Electric Co., 1942—, engr., Schenectady, 1942-43, 51-63, lab. asst. Gen. Engring. Lab., 1942-43, test engr., Pittsfield, Mass., also Syracuse, N.Y., 1948-51, devel. engr. aeros. and ordnance systems dept., 1951-56, microwave engr. Advanced Tech. Lab., 1956-63, electronic simulation engr. Apollo and Ground Systems Dept., Daytona Beach, Fla., 1964—. Served with USNR, 1943-45. Mem. I.E.E.E., Eta Kappa Nu. Episcopalian. Researcher on scale model antennas and computer analysis of antennas. Home: 103 University Circle Ormond Beach FL 32074 Office: Box 2500 Mason Ave Daytona Beach FL 32015

RASH, ALAN VANCE, lawyer; b. Fallbrook, Cal., Dec. 10, 1931; s. Glenn and Clara Beatrice (Chambers) R.; B.A., Tex. Western Coll., 1953; J.D., Tex. U. at Austin, 1960; m. Joy Ann Shinaut, May 26, 1956; children—Stephen W., Richard G., Paul M. Admitted to Tex. bar, 1960, since practiced in El Paso; mem. firm Diamond, Rash, Leslie and Smith, 1960—. Atty., Tex. Republican Party, 1972; chmn. El Paso County Rep. Party, 1963-65, 69-70; mem. bd. equalization City of El Paso; mem. Electoral Coll., 1972. Served with AUS, 1953-55. Mem. Am., Tex., El Paso bar assns., Comml. Law League. Methodist. Mason, Kiwanian. Home: 9137 McFall St El Paso TX 79925 Office: 1208 Southwest Center El Paso TX 79901

RASKIN, MARCUS G., inst. exec.; A.B., U. Chgo., 1954, J.D., 1957. Legislative asst. to 12 congressmen, 1958; disarmament adviser to Pres. Kennedy; mem. spl. staff Nat. Security Council; co-founder, co-dir. Inst. for Policy Studies, Washington, 1963—. Trustee, Antioch Coll., 1965-71. Author: (with Bernard Fall) The Viet-Nam Reader, 1965; (with Arthur Waskow) Limits of Defense; After Twenty Years; Being and Doing, 1971; Washington Plans an Agressive War; Notes on the Old System, 1974. Gen. editor: Ency. of Social Reconstrn. Office: Inst for Policy Studies 1520 New Hampshire Av NW Washington DC 20036

RASMUSSEN, GEORGE LEWIS, JR., auditor; b. Dallas, Feb. 23, 1926; s. George Lewis and Regina (Keller) R.; B.B.A., So. Meth. U., 1950; m. Corinne Rudy, Aug. 29, 1947; children—Carol, Anne. Internal revenue agt., Dallas, 1950-56; with John B. Reid & Co., 1956-57; sr. auditor U.S. Dept. Agriculture, Dallas, 1957-59, head group, 1960-61; asst. dir. regional audit Fed. Nat. Mortgage Assn., Dallas, 1962-69; area audit mgr. FHA, Dallas, 1969-70; asst. regional insp. gen. U.S. Dept. Housing and Urban Devel., Fort Worth, 1970—. Served with USAAF, 1944-46. C.P.A., Tex. Mem. Dallas, Tex. socs. c.p.a.'s, Fed. Govts. Accountants Assn., Fed. Bus. Assn. Mem. Christian Ch. (chmn. curriculum com. 1972-73, chmn. world outreach dept. 1973—). Home: 1725 Crowberry Dr Dallas TX 75228 Office: 819 Taylor St Fort Worth TX 75102

RASMUSSEN, MAURICE LEE, educator; b. Coon Rapids, Ia., June 2, 1935; s. Carl Verner and Rose Carolyn (Hochstrasser) R.; B.S., Ore. State U., 1957, M.S., 1959; Ph.D., Stanford, 1964; m. Barbara Anne Connors, June 24, 1961; children—Eric Lee, Matthew Scott. Research engr. NASA, Moffett Field, Cal., 1958-59; asst. prof. Stanford (Cal.) U., 1964-67; prof. aerospace engring. U. Okla., Norman, 1967—. Recipient Okla. Regents award for outstanding teaching, 1971. Mem. Am. Inst. Aeros. and Astronautics (sec. central Okla. 1968-69, pres. 1970-71), Am. Phys. Soc. Contbr. articles to sci. and tech. jours. Home: 1325 Brookhaven Blvd Norman OK 73069 Office: 865 Asp St Norman OK 73069

RASMUSSEN, WAYNE DAVID, govt. ofcl.; b. Ryegate, Mont., Feb. 5, 1915; s. Anton and Ethel (Bassett) R.; student Eastern Mont. State Coll., 1932-33; B.A., U. Mont., 1937; M.A., George Washington U., 1939, Ph.D., 1950; m. Marion Hollingworth Fowler, Dec. 27, 1939; children—Paul Wayne, Karen Ellen, Linda Marion. Records mgmt. U.S. Dept. Agr., Washington, 1937-40, agrl. historian, 1940—, chief agrl. history br., 1961—, lectr. Grad. Sch., 1950—. Lectr. U. Md., 1963—. Served with AUS, 1943-46. Mem. Agrl. History Soc. (exec. sec. 1952-62, 65—; pres. 1965), Am. Hist. Assn., Orgn. Am. Historians, Econ. History Soc. Club: Cosmos (Washington). Author: History of the Emergency Farm Labor Supply Program, 1943-47, 1951; Readings in the History of American Agriculture, 1960; (with others) Century of Service, The First 100 Years of the United States Department of Agriculture, 1963; (with Gladys L. Baker) United States Department of Agriculture, 1972. Home: 3907 Ridge Rd Annandale VA 22003 Office: US Dept Agr Washington DC 20250

RASOR, MAC ROY, pub. relations exec.; b. Austin, Tex., Nov. 11, 1918; s. Roy Jonathon and Mattie (Chapman) R.; B.J., U. Tex., 1941; m. Reba Claire Graham, Dec. 24, 1946; children—John Graham, Daniel Lee, Nancy Claire. Reporter, sports editor, editor Austin Dispatch, 1936, 38-39; amusements editor Austin Statesman, 1940-41; reporter Ft. Worth Press, 1941; newswriter-editor, state capital bur. A.P., 1945-55; pub. relations cons., Austin, 1955-61; v.p. Bus. Research Corp. Tex., Austin, 1956-61; exec. sec. Texas Legal Res. Ofcls. Assn., 1955-61; dir. pub. relations Southwestern Life Ins. Co. Dallas, 1961-63, 2d v.p., pub. relations dir., 1963-67; v.p. for pub. relations, 1967—; vis. instr. journalism U. Tex., 1956. Dir. pub. relations Tex. Democratic Presdl. campaigns, 1956, 60. Served with USMCR, 1941-45; PTO; to maj. Res. Mem. U. Tex. Journalism Ex-Students Assn. (past pres.), Pub. Relations Soc. Am. (past pres. N. Tex. chpt.), Dallas Advt. League, Life Ins. Advertisers Assn., Life Ins. Pub. Relations Council, Sigma Delta Chi (past state pres.). Mem. Christian Ch. (deacon). Clubs: Dallas Press, Dallas Advertising. Home: 5650 Meadow Crest Dr Dallas TX 75230 Office: 1807 Ross Av Dallas TX 75201

RASSMAN, EMIL CHARLES, lawyer; b. Indpls., July 27, 1919; s. Fred Wolf and Helen (Leming) R.; A.B., Washington and Lee U., 1941; LL.B., U. Tex., 1947; m. Annie de Montel, Jan. 31, 1943; children—Laura Helen (Mrs. Edward E. Bates, Jr.), James Neal. Admitted to Tex. bar, 1947; practiced in Midland, 1948—; mem. firm Rassman, Gunter & Boldrick. Dir. Comml. Bank & Trust Co., Midland. Mem. Tex. Civil Jud. Council, 1958-61. Campaign chmn., pres. Midland County United Fund, 1956-57; chmn. Midland County chpt. A.R.C., 1971-73. Chmn. bd. executors Permian Basin Petroleum Museum, Library and Hall of Fame, 1973—; trustee Midland Ind. Sch. Dist., 1958-61, Stratford Coll., Danville, Va., 1967-74; chmn. bd. regents State Sr. Colls. Tex., 1967-69. Served to capt. AUS, 1941-46. Fellow Am. Coll. Trial Lawyers, Internat. Acad. Trial Lawyers, Am. Coll. Probate Counsel, Tex. Bar Found., Am. Bar Found.; mem. Midland County Bar Assn. (pres. 1960), State Bar Tex. (dir. 1972—), West Tex. (pres. 1973-74), Tex. (pres. 1973-74) chambers commerce, Phi Delta Phi. Episcopalian. Mason (32 deg., Shriner). Contbr. articles to profl. jours. Home: 2805 Lockheed Dr Midland TX 79701 Office: 400 Midland Tower Bldg Midland TX 79701

RATCLIFF, APPLETON BONDS, JR., civil engr.; b. St. Joseph, La., May 15, 1910; s. Appleton Bonds and Annie (Muir) R.; grad. pub. schs., corr. schs.; m. Mildred Burford, Mar. 4, 1933; 1 dau., Carol (Mrs. Don Ray Beard). Constrn. worker U.S. C.E., Natchez, Miss., 1930-33; surveyor, mapper U.S. Geol. Survey, Washington, 1933-35; with La. Dept. Hwys., 1935—, draftsman, 1935-39, asst. chief engr., 1939-71, dir., 1967-69, chief engr., 1971—. Recipient State La. Dept. Civil Service Certificates for Outstanding Service Rating, 1963-65, 1967. Registered profl. engr., La.; registered land surveyor, La. Mem. La. Hwy. Engring. Assn., Am. Pub. Works Assn., Am. Assn. State Hwy. and Transp. Ofcls. (v.p. 1972-73, standing com. 1970—), Am. Soc. C.E. Methodist. Mason (32 deg.). Club: Briarwood Country. Home: 1224 Lee Dr Baton Rouge LA 70708 Office: PO Box 44245 Capitol Station Baton Rouge LA 70804

RATHLE, PIERRE, educator; b. Cairo, Egypt, July 3, 1926; s. Andre And Mathilde (Boulad) R.; student Coll. de la Ste. Famille, 1933-46, Mass. Inst. Tech., 1958-59; Lic. de Scis., U. Paris, 1954, D. Molecular Physics, 1965; m. Raymonde Michel, Dec. 12, 1958; children—Joyce, Yves, Jean, Frank. Came to U.S., 1969. Publicity mgr. Cifarm Labs., 1954-60; chief nuclear magnetic resonance labs. Roussel Labs., Romainville, France, 1960-69; prof. phys. chemistry Nicholls State U., Thibodaux, La., 1969—. NSF grantee, 1970, Nicholls Found. grantee, 1973. Mem. Am. Chem. Soc., A.A.A.S. Research in quantum chemistry, molecular structure. Home: 1302 Menard St Thibodaux LA 70301

RATLIFF, BARTON WADE, oil well drilling contractor; b. Drew, Miss., Dec. 2, 1925; s. Albert Wade and Ruth (Bullock) R.; student U. Miss., 1946-47; B.S., U. Okla., 1950; postgrad. U. Pitts., 1961, Tulsa U., 1967; m. Leah Frances Britton, Nov. 8, 1963; children—Carla, John, Alison, Brian, Lee, Barton, Margaret. With Skelly Oil Co., 1950-68, asst. prodn. mgr., Tulsa, 1961-63, dist. prodn. engr. Okla. dist., 1963-67, mgr. joint prodn. operations, 1967-68; pres., owner Ratliff Drilling Co., Duncan, Okla., 1968—. Served with USAAF, 1943-45. Mem. Internat. Assn. Oilwell Drilling Contractors (dir.), Soc. Petroleum Engrs., Am. Petroleum Inst., U.S., Duncan chambers commerce. Presbyn. (deacon). Elk. Home: 305 W Hickory St Duncan OK 73533 Office: 1510 W Main St Duncan OK 73533

RATLIFF, BOBBY HAROLD, coal mining co. exec.; b. Harman, Va., Jan. 19, 1944; s. Carvel Edward and Beuna (Stiltner) R.; B.S. in Bus. Adminstrn., East Tenn. State U., 1965; m. Rita Sue Farmer, Dec. 20, 1964; children—Bobby Harold, Richard Brandon. Prodn. mgr. Black Diamond Coal Corp., Grundy, Va., 1957-65; pres., gen. mgr. Belibe Coal Corp., Grundy, 1966—; corporate dir. Internat. Coal Sales, Inc., Grundy, Belibe Coal Corp; partner Grundy Sports Center. Active Grundy Parent Tchrs. Group; exec. dir. Boy Scout Troop, 1970. Mem. Ind. Coal Operator's Assn., Am. Fedn. Small Bus. Mem.

Ch. of Christ (deacon 1968). Home: 120 Russell Hill Grundy VA 24614 Office: Box 875 Grundy VA 24614

RATLIFF, DALE HENDRICK, educator; b. Hollywood, Fla., Mar. 30, 1928; s. Baylor Barker and Arda Laura (Hedrick) R.; B.A., Centre Coll., 1949; M.Div., Louisville Presbyn. Sem., 1953, Th.M., 1958, D.Min., 1974; D.D., Am. Div. Sch., 1950; m. Henrietta L. Nemeroff, June 9, 1951; children—Todd H., Robin D., Scott H., Hale H. Dir., Prot. Service Bur., 1956-62, Pastoral Counseling Service, 1962—, Am. Assn. Religious Therapists, 1960—; prof. marriage and family Broward Coll., 1965—; breeder Paso Fino horses. Bd. dirs. Am. Assn. Religious Therapists Ednl. Found. Sigma Chi scholar, 1948. Mem. Am. Assn. Religious Therapists, Am. Assn. Pastoral Counselors, Am. Assn. Marriage and Family Counselors, Am. Assn. Univ. Profs., Half-Paso Assn. (dir.). Club: Kiwanis (Miami). Author: Challenge of Christ, 1955; Sexual Psychopathologies, 1974. Home: 5800 SW 130th Av Fort Lauderdale FL 33314 Office: 13733 NW 7th Av Miami FL 33168

RATLIFF, JAMES EDWIN, dentist; b. Kingston, W.Va., Jan. 22, 1941; s. Hertaux and Lily Marie (Potter) R.; B.A., U. Louisville, 1962, D.M.D., 1966; m. Shirley Ellen Hamlin, Jan. 26, 1962; children—Tametha Lee, James Edwin II, Michael Todd, Mellie Elizabeth. Pvt. practice dentistry, Salyersville, Ky., 1969—. Served with AUS, 1966-69. Decorated Army Commendation medal. Mem. Am., Ky., Ky. Mountain dental assns., Delta Sigma Delta. Home: 1 Cardinal Ct Salyersville KY 41465 Office: Med Clinic Salyersville KY 41465

RATLIFF, JOHN WALTER, coal co. exec.; b. Wolfpit, Ky., Jan. 17, 1924; s. Roy Thomas and Olba (Raitliff) R.; student pub. schs.; m. Flora Jean Stiltner, Dec. 29, 1948; children—John Walter, Alecia Jean. With Harmon Coal Co.; owner Marrowbone Coal Co. (Ky.), 1943-54; owner Black Diamond Coal Co., Inc., Grundy, Va., 1954-67; owner Ratliff Farms, 1968—, BeLibe Coal Co.; v.p. Internat. Coal Co.; exec. dir. Grundy Nat. Bank. Served with AUS, 1942-43. Ky. col. Mem. U.S. C. of C., A.I.M. Home: Route 1 Box 136 Tazewell VA 24651

RATTAN, GARLAND WARD, supt. schs.; b. Lamesa, Tex., June 15, 1933; s. Andy Ward and Vernie Pearl (Scott) R.; B.S., West Tex. State U., 1954, M.Ed., 1962; m. Shirley Jim Porter, Dec. 17, 1953; children—David Ward, Christopher Jerome. Tchr., asst. coach, prin. high sch., Matador, Tex., 1955-56, Boys Ranch, 1956-62; supt. schs., Boys Ranch Ind. Sch. Dist., Cal Farley's Boys Ranch, Boys Ranch, Tex., 1962—. Recipient Distinguished Service award Tex. Vocational Agr. Tchrs. Assn., 1965. Mem. Tex. Tchrs. Assn., N.E.A., Am., Tex. Assns. sch. adminstrs., Fellowship Christian Athletes, Red Red Rose, Phi Delta Kappa. Baptist. Mason, Lion; mem. Order Eastern Star. Address: Boys Ranch TX 79010

RAUCH, JEANNE GIRARD (MRS. MARSHALL ARTHUR RAUCH), textile mill exec.; b. Gastonia, N.C., Sept. 15, 1923; d. Frank Henry and Ida Sadie (Paradies) Goldberg; student Duke, 1940-41; B.S., Syracuse U., 1944; m. Marshall Arthur Rauch, May 18, 1946; children—Ingrid, Marc, Peter, Stephanie, John. With Pyramid Mills, Bessemer City, N.C., 1959—, v.p., 1963—, also dir. Sec. Rauch Found., Inc., 1965-72. Bd. dirs., United Fund, Gaston, 1970, 71, 72; mem. county bd., Girl Scouts, 1950; arts commr. N.C. Museum Art, 1973—. Occupational adv. bd. Gaston Coll., 1971-73; bd. visitors Sacred Heart Coll., 1971-72. Mem. Sisterhood Hadassah (pres. 1954-57), Little Theater (1st sec. 1949, 50), Gaston Art Guild (1st pres. 1963, 65), Sir Walter Cabinet (v.p. 1969), Alpha Epsilon Phi, Alpha Epsilon Rho. Democrat. Home: 1121 Scotch Dr Gastonia NC 28052 Office: Box 755 Bessemer City NC 28016

RAUCH, MARSHALL ARTHUR, textile co. exec.; b. N.Y.C., Feb. 2, 1923; s. Nathan A. and Tillie (Wohl) R.; student Duke, 1940-43; m. Jeanne Girard, 1946; children—John, Ingrid, Marc, Peter, Stephanie. Chmn. bd., treas., dir. Rauch Industries, Inc., Gastonia, N.C., Pyramid Mills Co., Inc., Bessemer City, N.C., 1954—, Pyramid Dye Corp., Bessemer City, 1956—, Homeside Yarn, Inc., Bessemer City, 1960—, Nile Star, Inc., Woodmere, N.Y., 1961—, Gastonia Dyeing Corp. (N.C.), 1968—; treas., dir. E.P. Press, Inc., Gastonia, 1965—; dir. Sedgefield Realty Corp., Gastonia, Majestic Ins. Financing Corp., Gastonia, Advance Investment Fund, N.Y.C.; mgr. Narco Molding Co., Bessemer City. Chmn. Gaston Jewish Welfare Fund, 1958-62, 68-70; 1st v.p. N.C. Assn. Jewish Men, 1966; mem. nat. council Am. Jewish Joint Distbn. Com., 1968-70; mem. Gov.'s Good Neighbor Council, 1963—; chmn. Gastonia Human Relations Com., 1964-67; chmn. N.C. Com. on Population and Family, 1968—; mem. N.C. Jail Study Commn., 1968; pres. Asso. Industries, 1964-65; chmn. Employ the Handicapped Com., 1964-65; mem. N.C. Citizens Com. for Dental Health, 1968; sr. adviser Gastonia Boys Club, 1947-63; mem. cons. commn. Pioneer council Girl Scouts U.S.A., 1968-69; pres. Gaston County YMCA, 1972. Mayor pro tem City of Gastonia, 1952-54, 61-63, mem. city council, 1952-54, 61-65; mem. N.C. State Senate, 1967-73. Bd. dirs., treas. Rauch Found.; bd. dirs. N.C. United Jewish Appeal Cabinet, 1968-70, Gaston Skills, 1964-66, Salvation Army Boys Club, 1963—, United Fund, 1963-67, Gaston Boys Club, 1964—, Carolina Amateur Athletics Union, 1951-53, Gaston Mus. Natural History, 1963-64, Holy Angels Nursery, Belmont, N.C., 1960—, Planned Parenthood and World Population, N.Y.C., 1968-69, Gaston Community Action, 1966, Gaston-Cleveland Tb Assn., 1968; bd. govs. N.C. Jewish Home for the Aged, 1968-70; mem. adv. council N.C. Com. for Children and Youth, 1968-69; bd. dirs. Gastonia YMCA, 1959-62, 67-69, v.p., 1968-70; v.p., bd. dirs. Community Concert Assn., 1960-61; mem. top mgmt. adv. com. Gaston County Indsl. Mgmt. Club, 1963-65; bd. advisers Gardner Webb Coll., 1969-70; trustee U. N.C., 1969-70; mem. adv. com. N.C. Vocational Textile Sch., 1970-71. Served with AUS, World War II; ETO. Decorated Combat Infantry Badge; recipient Nat. Recreation citation Nat. Recreation Assn., 1965; Brotherhood award Nat. Council Christians and Jews, 1969; named Man of Yr., Gastonia Jaycees, 1957, Gastonia Jr. Women's Club, 1964, Gaston County chpt. Omega Psi Phi, 1966, N.C. Health Dept., 1968, Gastonia Red Shield Boys Club, 1970. Mem. Duke Alumni Assn. (pres. Gaston chpt. 1961-62). Jewish religion (pres. temple 1962-64, tchr. Sunday sch. 1951-56). Mem. B'nai B'rith. Home: 1121 Scotch Dr Gastonia NC 28052

RAUF, MUHAMMED ABDUL, educator; b. Abusir, Gharbien, Egypt, Dec. 27, 1917; s. Muhammad Abdul-Razek and Hanem (Abdul-Rauf) Abdul-Rauf; Aliyah, Al-Azhar U., Cairo, 1942, Alimayah, 1944; B.A., Cambridge U., Eng., 1954, M.A., 1958; Ph.D., London U., 1963; m. Buthaynah Ayad, Aug. 15, 1946; children—Feisal, Aisha, Ali, Salwa, Muhammed Ayman. Came to U.S., 1965. Mem. faculty Al-Azhar U., Cairo, 1945—; founder Islamic Inst., Kuwait, 1947-49; mem. sociology faculty Al-Azhar U., Cairo, 1954-55; founder, prin. Muslim Coll. of Malaya, 1955-64, head dept. Islamic studies U. Malaya, 1958-64; dir. Islamic missions dept. Al-Azhar U., 1964-65; dir. Islamic Center, N.Y.C., 1965-71, Islamic Center of Washington, 1971—. Del. of World Muslim Congress on UN Non-Govtl. Orgns., 1959—. External examiner U. Malaya, 1970—. Trustee Islamic Center of N.Y. Decorated Johan Mangku Negara (Malaysia). Mem. Am. Oriental Soc., Middle East Studies Assn. N.Y., Middle East Inst. Washington. Author: Brief History of Islam, 1964; Life and Teachings of the Prophet Muhammad, 1964; Islamic Religious Knowledge, 1965; Malay: Description and Impressions, 1965; A Manual of Marriage on Islam, 1972; Sacred Texts of Islam, 1973; Arabic For English Speaking Students, 1973. Address: 2551 Massachusetts Av NW Washington DC 20008

RAULERSON, JOHN DERIEUX, JR., indsl. engring. and tng. cons.; b. Bartow, Fla., July 24, 1921; s. John Derieux and Thelma Francis (Poe) R.; B.S. in Chem. Engring.; Ga. Sch. Tech., 1943; M.S. in Engring., U. South Fla., 1970; m. Anne Gladney Widerquist, Aug. 27, 1954; stepchildren—Richard Eyman, John Eyman; children—Janet, Joanne. Sr. Engr. IMC Corp., Bartow, 1946-49; pres. Lakeland (Fla.) Engring. Assos., 1954-58; v.p. Frank M. Murphy Corp., Bartow, 1958-63; indsl. engring. and tng. cons., Bartow, 1964—. Dir. econ. devel. Bartow C. of C., 1972-73. Served to capt., AUS, 1943-46. Mem. Am. Inst. Indsl. Engrs., Fla. Indsl. Devel. Council. Author: (with Martin R. Wong) A Guide To Systematic Instructional Design, 1974. Home: 1230 First Av Bartow FL 33830 Office: PO Box 570 Bartow FL 33830

RAULT, JOSEPH MATTHEW, JR., petroleum co. exec.; b. New Orleans, Feb. 24, 1926; s. Joseph M. and Calista (Morgan) R.; student Georgetown U., 1948; B.S., Mass. Inst. Tech., 1948; LL.B., Tulane U., 1950; children—Katherine delaVergne, Joseph Matthew III. Pres. Joseph M. Rault, Jr., Inc., New Orleans, 1959—. Rault Petroleum Corp., New Orleans, 1962—, Continental Rigs Internat., S.A. of Panama, 1960—, Rault Petroleum Corp. Venezuela, 1963—, The Lamplighter Club, Inc., 1967—, Lake Hillsdale Estates, Inc., 1970—, Domed Stadium Hotel, Inc., 1972—, Lake Hillsdale Holiday Inn, Inc., 1973—; dir. Constructora Otlla, S.A. of Mex. Exec. chmn. Internat. Relations Com., City New Orleans, 1964-66; gen. chmn. U.S. Savs. Bond 25th Anniversary, New Orleans, 1966; mem. Miss. River Pkwy Commn., 1965-68. Chmn. bd. New Orleans R.R. Terminal; bd. regents Loyola U., New Orleans. Served to lt. USNR, 1943-46. Mem. La. Soc. for Promotion of Music and Performing Arts. Address: 1111 Gravier St New Orleans LA 70112

RAUTH, GLEN EUGENE, agrl. engr.; b. Boonville, Ind., Nov. 19, 1928; s. Louis F. and Nora (Bierbaum) R.; B.S., Purdue U., 1950; m. Betty J. Higgins, Jan. 20, 1951; children—Carol Ann, Jane Virginia, Gene Alan. Prodn. mgr. farming Flavor Pict Coop., Delray Beach, Fla., 1951-62; chief engr. FMC Corp., Ocoee, Fla., 1962-69; asst. dir. grove operations citrus prodn. Foods div. Coca Cola Co., Auburndale, Fla., 1969—. Bd. dirs. Central Fla. Lions Sight Clinic. Served with AUS, 1952-54. Mem. Am. Soc. Agrl. Engrs., Fla. Hort. Soc., Citrus Industry Harvesting Com. (exec. com. 1969-71), Alpha Zeta. Presbyn. (elder 1959-71). Rotarian. Patentee in field. Home: 519 S Lake Florence St Winter Haven FL 33880 Office: PO Box 247 Auburndale FL 33823

RAUTH, LOUIS FREDRICK, agr. co. pres.; b. Boonville, Ind., Nov. 14, 1900; s. John George and Barbara (Roth) R.; student Ohio State U., 1919; m. Nora Emma Bierbaum, Aug. 28, 1927; children—Glen E., Robert G., Ruth (Mrs. Donal S. Rusk), Marie (Mrs. Lewis W. Currier, Jr.). Partner, Rauth Bros., Boonville, 1918-34, owner, 1934—; developer Vine Ripe Tomato Industry, 1952—; pres. Flavor Pict Co-Op, Delray Beach, Fla., Flavor Pict, Inc., Delray Beach, both 1967—. U. Fla. appointee Dare Com., Share Com., 1967-71. Named So. Ind. Bean King Ind. Farmers Guide, 1952, Palm Beach County Family of Year, 1963; recipient Efficiency award vegetable crops Nat. Ford Farm, 1963; Atmos clock Sec. Agr., 1973. Mem. Fla. Fruit and Vegetable Assn. (vice chmn. competition and marketing com. 1965—), Fla. Tomato Com. (chmn. 1959-68). Mem. United Ch. of Christ (trustee). Pioneer work in home freezer, 1938. Home: 314 NW 7th St Delray Beach FL 33444 Office: PO Box 1810 Delray Beach FL 33444

RAVENEL, HENRY, JR., banker; b. Washington, Jan. 7, 1934; s. Henry and Nancie Turner (Benoist) R.; A.B., Dartmouth, 1956; m. Alicia Moran, Sept. 16, 1961; children—Nancie C., James G. With Riggs Nat. Bank, Washington, 1958—, asst. v.p., 1967-71, v.p., 1971—. Treas., Boys Club, Met. Police Washington, 1970—; asst. treas. Washington Nat. Monument Assn., 1972—, Corcoran Gallery Art, 1973—. Served with AUS, 1956-58. Mem. Confrerie de Chevaliers du Tastevin. Clubs: Chevy Chase, Metropolitan. Office: 1503 Pennsylvania Av Washington DC 20013

RAVESON, BETTY RICH (MRS. SHERMAN H. RAVESON), columnist; b. Schenectady, June 16, 1913; d. Edwin L. and Florence (Nutree) Rich; A.B., Columbia, 1934; m. Sherman H. Raveson, Apr. 26, 1932. Eastchester editor Herald Statesman, Yonkers, N.Y., 1940-42; night bur. mgr. U.P. Assn., Albany, 1942-43; Delray editor, columnist Palm Beach (Fla.) Illustrated, 1959-62; columnist Palm Beach Daily News, Delray Beach News-Jour., 1962-69, Boynton Beach News-Jour., 1966-69, Franklin (N.C.) Press, 1967—; feature writer Palm Beach Life mag., 1962-69, TV commentator, 1964—, exec. editor Palm Beach Voice, 1969-70; editor, v.p. Mountain Living mag., 1970—. Pub. relations dir. Delray Beach Playhouse, 1959-61. Mem. N.C. Press Assn., Bus. and Profl. Women's Club. Presbyn. Clubs: Fla. Women's Press; Fla. Gold Coast Press (Outstanding Achievement award 1963) (Delray Beach); Quills (Palm Beach); Atlanta Press. Home: Wayah Valley Rd Franklin NC 28734 Office: PO Box 290 Franklin NC 28734

RAVESON, SHERMAN HAROLD, artist; b. New Haven, June 11, 1907; A.B., LL.B., Cumberland U. Art editor, Vanity Fair mag., 1929-34, Life mag., 1935, Esquire mag., 1936; with Pettingell & Fenton, 1937-41; v.p., art dir. Sterling Advt. Agy., N.Y.C., 1951-55; one-man shows Assn. Am. Artists, 1941, Grand Central Art Gallery, N.Y.C., 1955, 56, Carriage House Studios, Phila., 1956; works represented in collections numerous racetracks, U.S. Pres., advt. dir. Mountain Living mag., 1970—. Editor: Classified Boating Directory of Fla. East-West Coast, 1967-70, Palm Beach Shopping Guide to Worth Av., 1967-70. Home: Wayah Valley Rd Franklin NC 28734

RAWITSCHER, JACK JOSEPH, lawyer; b. Williston, N.D., May 11, 1932; s. Alec and Minnie (Cersonsky) R.; B.A., U. Wis., 1955; LL.B., U. Tex., 1957; m. Sydney Greenblatt, Aug. 12, 1964; children—Karey Lea, Michael Steven. Admitted to Tex. bar, 1957; asst. dist. atty. Harris County (Tex.), 1957-60; asso. atty. firm Dixie & Schulman, Houston, 1960-68; partner firm Smith, Schulman & Rawitscher & Cordray, Houston, 1968—. Mem. faculty Nat. Coll. Criminal Def. Lawyers and Pub. Defenders, 1972-73; clin. prof. law Bates Coll. Law, U. Houston, 1972—; guest participant in law programs television and radio stas. KTRH, KILT, KENR. Served with AUS, 1957-63. Recipient Outstanding Service award Midtown Kiwanis of Houston, 1971. Mem. Harris County Criminal Lawyers Assn. (dir.), Tex. Criminal Def. Lawyers Assn. (dir., recipient commendation 1972-73), Bill of Rights Found., Anti-Defamation League (dir.), State Bar Tex. (past chmn. grievance com. sect. 8), Tex., Houston (past chmn. criminal law sect.) bar assns. Jewish religion (bd. trustees temple 1971-73). Kiwanian (pres. 1973-74). Home: 5603 Darnell St Houston TX 77035 Office: 806 Main St Houston TX 77002

RAWL, PAUL THOMAS, supt. schs.; b. Gaston, S.C., Nov. 10, 1938; s. Otis and Carrie Nea (Bodie) R.; A.B., U. S.C., 1959, M.A., 1966, postgrad. 1971—; m. Lynda Robinson, Sept. 10, 1960; children—Paul Thomas, Stanley Lewis. Coach, tchr. high sch., Aiken, S.C., 1960, Salem, S.C., 1960-61, North High Sch., Hopkins, S.C., 1961-65; sch. adminstr. Lower Richland High Sch., Hopkins, 1965-68; prin., dist. supt. Lexington (S.C.) High Sch., 1968—. Capt., United Fund, Lexington, 1970-71; mem. Lexington-Richland Drug Abuse Council; mem. tech. adv. group Columbia Area Transp. Study, 1968-71. Bd. dirs. S.C. Tb. Assn. Named outstanding young educator Lexington Jr. C. of C., 1970. Mem. Nat., S.C. (life mem., publs. com. 1968-71), Lexington County, Richland County (chmn. publicity com. 1966-67) edn. assns., Am. Assn. Sch. Adminstrs., Secondary Prins. Assn., Lexington County Supts. (chmn. 1969-71), Lexington C. of C. (dir. 1969-71, chmn. edn. com. 1969-71), Elementary Secondary Edn. Act Adminstrs. (audit com. 1969-70), Vietnam Prisoners of War. Lion (dir. 1969-71). Home: 618 N Lake Dr Lexington SC 29072 Office: PO Box 218 Lexington SC 29072

RAWLEY, JAMES WILLIAM, ret. oil co. exec.; b. Palestine, Tex., Apr. 26, 1911; s. Walter Fleming and Mable Dean (Hallett) R.; grad. advanced mgmt. program Harvard, 1956; m. Carolyn Johnson, Feb. 7, 1937; 1 dau., Sarah Nan. With Seaboard Oil Co., Dallas, 1933-58, v.p., mgr. div., 1955-58, v.p., mgr. domestic div., 1958; asst. gen. mgr. domestic producing div. Texas Co. Houston, 1958-69; mgr. domestic producing div. Texaco, Tulsa, 1959-61, mgr. div., New Orleans, 1962-67, gen. mgr. Eastern U.S., Houston, 1967-71, v.p. S.E. region, New Orleans, 1971-74. Mem. Mid-Continent Oil and Gas Assn. (bd. dirs. 1960-72), Am. Petroleum Inst., Am. Assn. Petroleum Landmen. Home: 428 Seawind St Austin TX 78746

RAWLEY, PARKER HALLETT, investment co. exec.; b. Palestine, Tex., June 22, 1913; s. Walter Fleming and Mabel Dean (Hallett) R.; student Nixon Bus. Coll., 1933-34; m. Ann Marie Bachert, Nov. 14, 1936; 1 son, Paul Hallett. Salesman, Liggett-Meyers Tobacco Co., Galveston, Tex., 1934-36; S.W. div. mgr. Johnson & Johnson, surg. supplies, Dallas, 1936-53; regional sales mgr. Hazel Bishop Cosmetics, Dallas, 1954-65; owner retail drug stores, San Antonio, 1954-55, Dallas, 1955-65; pres. Redson Sales, Inc., Dallas, 1965—, Preston Forest Investment Co., Dallas, 1965—; dir. N. Dallas Bank & Trust Co. Active United Fund, Heart Assn. Mem. Drug Travelers State of Tex., Houston Drug Travelers (v.p. 1945-46), Dallas Sales Execs. Club. Republican. Episcopalian. Clubs: Brookhaven Country (Dallas). Home: 4325 Forest Bend Dallas TX 75234 Office: 5925 Forest Lane Dallas TX 75230

RAWLINGS, JOHN OREN, statistician, educator; b. Archer, Neb., July 26, 1932; s. Cecil Curtis and Mildred Louise (Suck) R.; B.S., U. Neb., 1953, M.S., 1957; Ph.D., N.C. State Coll., 1960; m. Mary Jane Reichardt, Aug. 17, 1952; children—Gweneth Marie, Bradley John, Kalen Louise. Geneticist, U.S. Dept. Agr., Raleigh, N.C., 1959-60; statistician N.C. State U., Raleigh, 1960-61, asst. prof. dept. statistics, 1961-63, asso. prof., 1963-68, prof., 1968—. Vis. prof. U. Reading (Eng.), 1967-68. Served with AUS, 1953-55. Mem. Am. Soc. Agronomy, Crop Sci. Soc. Am., Biometrics Soc., Sigma Xi (research award 1964, v.p. N.C. State U. chpt. 1971-72), Alpha Zeta, Gamma Sigma Delta (sec. treas. 1965-67), Phi Kappa Phi (pres. 1973-74). Contbr. articles on quantitative genetics to research publs. Home: 626 Stacy St Raleigh NC 27607 Office: Statistics Dept North Carolina State Univ Raleigh NC 27607

RAWLS, J. LEWIS, JR., lawyer, peanut oil co. exec.; b. Suffolk, Va., Dec. 7, 1923; s. J. Lewis and Azzie (Gatling) R.; student Va. Mil. Inst., 1942-43, Duke, 1943-44; LL.B., U. Va., 1950; m. Mary Helen Macklin, Oct. 4, 1947; children—John Lewis III, Rebecca Macklin (Mrs. Habel), Frank Macklin. Admitted to Va. bar, 1950; gen. counsel Taylor Cos., 1952-57; individual law practice, Suffolk, 1950-52, 57-63; partner Rawls & Bagnell, Suffolk, 1963—; mem. Va. Ho. of Dels., 1962-70. Pres., chief exec. Suffolk Oil Mill, Inc., 1969—; dir., sec.-treas. Old Dominion Investors Trust, Suffolk, 1967—; dir. Tidewater Group, Norfolk, Va.; mem. Suffolk bd. Va. Nat. Bank; chmn. bd. Atlantic Nat. Life Assurance Co. Pres., March of Dimes, Suffolk, 1951-52. Served with USNR, 1945-46. Mem. Am., Va. bar assns. Mason, Elk, Rotarian. Home: 603 Dumville Av Suffolk VA 23434 Office: PO Box 1458 Suffolk VA 23434

RAWLS, OSCAR GREISON, city engr.; b. Climax, Ga., July 8, 1913; s. John Greison and Lelia Alice (Smallwood) R.; B.S., Clemson U., 1935; M.S., U. Mich., 1964; m. Carolina Florence DeMontigne, July 16, 1936; 1 dau., Carolina DeMontigne (Mrs. Rudolph P. Bergfeld III). Civil engr. T.V.A., Knoxville and Savannah, Tenn., 1935-36; various positions to chief of project planning Jacksonville (Fla.) dist. U.S. Army Corps of Engrs., 1936-70; city engr. City of Jacksonville, 1970—. Mem. bd. advisers Goodwill Industries; pres. Fla. Shore and Beach Preservation Assn. Served to lt. col. AUS, 1942-46; ETO. Recipient medal for outstanding civilian service Dept. of Def., 1970. Mem. Soc. Am. Mil. Engrs. (past pres. Jacksonville), Blue Key, Tau Beta Pi. Episcopalian. Home: 1357 Tiber Av Jacksonville FL 32207 Office: City Hall Jacksonville FL 32207

RAWLS, WALTER CECIL, JR., scientist, lawyer, bus. exec.; b. Richmond, Va., Sept. 13, 1928; s. Walter Cecil and Ella (Freeman) R.; A.B., U. Mo., 1951; J.D., Washington U., St. Louis, 1958; m. Sheila Daphne Kirsch; children—James David, Richard Wayne. Agt. for France, Am. Trust Life Ins. Co., Wichita Falls, Tex., 1953-54; admitted to Fla. bar, 1958, since practiced in Jacksonville; mem. firm Ragland, Kurz, Toole, 1958, Marks, Gray, Yates, Conroy, Gibbs, 1959; pvt. practice, 1960-63, 1969—; partner Thomas & Rawls, 1963-67, Ogier, Stubbs & Rawls, 1967-69, RAWB & Co.; pres. Biomagnetics Internat., Inc.; treas., dir. Ga.-Fla. Oil Co.; dir. F.I.D. Internat., Internat. Film Corp., Capitol Res. Ltd. Mem. adv. council Washington U. Law Sch., St. Louis. Served with AUS, 1951-53. Mem. Internat., Am., Jacksonville bar assns., Fla. Bar, Am. Soc. Internat. Law, Am. Judicature Soc., Am. Legion, S.A.R., Sons Confederate Vets., English Speaking Union, Am. Trial Lawyers Assn., Am. Arbitration Assn. (arbitrator), Internat. Platform Assn., Am. Philatelic Soc., Com. of 100, Jacksonville C. of C., Phi Delta Theta, Delta Theta Phi. Republican. Conglist. Clubs: Capitol Hill (Washington); Republican, Metropolitan Dinner (officer, mem. orgn. com.) (Jacksonville, Fla.). Co-author: Magnetism and its Effects on the Living System. Home: 6962 Almours Pl Jacksonville FL 32217 Office: Fla Nat Bank Jacksonville FL 32202

RAWSON, RULON WELLS, physician; b. Idaho Falls, Ida., Sept. 28, 1908; s. Wilford Woodruff and Eugena (Lefgren) R.; student Weber Coll., 1926-27, U. Utah, 1930-32; M.B., Northwestern U., 1937, M.D., 1938; m. Jane Young, Aug. 21, 1940; children—James R.Y., Elizabeth Jane, Daniel Y. Research fellow Harvard Med. Sch., 1938-42, instr. and Henry P. Walcott fellow clin. medicine, 1942-45, asso. med., 1945-47, asst. prof. med., 1947-48; asst. physician Mass. Gen. Hosp., 1946-47, asso. physician med., 1947-48; asso. prof. medicine Cornell U. Med. Coll., 1948-51, prof., 1951-67; attending physician Meml. Hosp., N.Y.C., 1948-68, chmn. dept. of medicine, 1958-68; chief dept. medicine Meml. Sloan-Kettering Cancer Center, 1958-67, vis. scientist, 1967—; prof. medicine, dean, v.p. N.J. Coll. Medicine and Dentistry, 1967-72; v.p. edn. and program devel. M.D. Anderson Hosp. U. Tex., Houston, 1972—; dir. extramural programs

U. Tex. System Cancer Center, 1972—. Mem. adv. com. med. uses of isotopes AEC, 1959-69; mem. com. on personnel for research Am. Cancer Soc., 1958-63, chmn. 1959-63; mem. adv. com. sr. clin. traineeship program Dept. Health, Edn. and Welfare, 1962-68; mem. adv. council on Health Manpower, 1967-71. Mem. exec. bd. Hutchinson River Council Boy Scouts Am., 1961-72, v.p., 1963-72, chmn. Pelham dist., 1961-63, also mem. Nat. council. Recipient award, Am. Goiter Assn., 1959, Centennial award Northwestern U., 1959, Distinguished Eagle Scout award Boy Scouts Am., 1969. Fellow N.Y. Acad. Med.; mem. A.C.P., A.M.A., Am. Physiol. Soc., A.A.A.S., Am. Goiter Assn. (council 1950-53, pres. 1955-56), Endocrine Soc. (pres. 1966-67); chmn. publs. com. 1957-63, Am. Assn. Cancer Research, Am. Soc. Clin. Investigation, N.Y. State Med. Soc., Harvey Soc. (sec. 1955-58), Assn. Am. Physicians. Clubs: Harvard (Boston and N.Y.C.). Author sci. papers, chpts. in texts on physiology and diseases of the thyroid and endocrinology of cancer. Home: 1600 Holcombe Blvd Houston TX 77025 Office: MD Anderson Hosp and Tumor Inst 6723 Bertner Av Houston TX 77025

RAY, CHARLES ALBERT, accountant; b. Ft. Worth, Dec. 26, 1935; s. Joseph Berry and Hattie (Kitchell) R.; B.B.A., N. Tex. State U., 1957; M.B.A., U. Houston, 1963; m. Patsy Grimes, Sept. 8, 1956; children—Bruce Edwin, Charles Keith. Jr. accountant Tenn. Gas Transmission Co., Houston, 1957-60; field agt. Internal Revenue Service, Houston and Ft. Worth, 1960-64; tax sr. Alexander Grant & Co., C.P.A.'s, Dallas, 1964-65; instr. accounting U. Tex., Arlington, 1965-67; accountant C.A. Ray, C.P.A., Arlington, 1966-70; partner Ray, Long & Co. C.P.A., 1970-71; prin. Charles A. Ray C.P.A., 1971-72, 73—; partner Ray, Hoyle, Kiblinger & Co., 1972-73. Active Boy Scouts Am. Bd. dirs. YMCA, Arlington, 1970-73, treas., 1971, 72. Mem. Tex. Soc. C.P.A.'s (dir. Ft. Worth chpt. 1971-73, sec. 1973-74), Am. Inst. C.P.A.'s. Rotarian. Baptist. Home: 2618 Brentwood Circle Arlington TX 76010 Office: 600 E Abram Arlington TX 76010

RAY, CHARLES TOLMAN, research co. exec.; b. Madill, Okla., Oct. 9, 1932; s. Otto and Isabell Slena (Tolman) R.; B.B.A. with distinction, U. Okla., 1954; J.D. cum laude, U. Houston, 1965; m. Martha Kay Malone, Oct. 7, 1956; children—Stephen William, Kevin Charles. Jr. Accountant U. Okla., Norman, 1952-54; tax accountant Humble Oil & Refining Co., Houston, 1954, tax accountant and tax atty., 1958-65; mgr. taxes Sunray DX Oil Co., Tulsa, Okla., Sun Oil Co., Dallas, 1965-71; v.p. finance and adminstrn. The Resource Sciences Corp., Tulsa, 1971—. Active Boy Scouts Am. Served to capt., USAF, 1954-58. C.P.A., Tex., Okla. Mem. Am. Bar Assn. Am. Inst. C.P.A.s, Okla. Soc. C.P.A.s, Petroleum Club of Tulsa. Mem. Christian Ch. (deacon). Home: 6701 S Atlanta Av Tulsa OK 74136 Office: 321 S Boston St Tulsa OK 74103

RAY, DONALD JETER, lawyer; b. Nashville, Apr. 9, 1943; s. Jeter Seehorn and Reva Juanita (Proffitt) R.; B.A., U. Tenn., 1965, J.D., 1968; m. Harriet Smith, Sept. 10, 1966; children—Donald Jeffrey, Elizabeth Lane. Admitted to Tenn. bar, 1968, since practiced in Tullahoma; mem. firm Haynes, Hull and Ray, 1968—. Mem. exec. com., atty. Multi-County Mental Health Center, 1972—; bd. dirs. Coffee County Mental Health Assn., 1973—. Mem. Middle Tenn. Young Lawyers Conf. (v.p., 1970-71), Coffee County Bar Assn. (v.p. 1973—). Club: Tullahoma Optimist (v.p. 1969-71). Home: 213 Crestwood Dr Tullahoma TN 37388 Office: 214 N Atlantic St Tullahoma TN 37388

RAY, H(OSEA) M(ANFRED), U.S. atty.; b. Rienzi, Miss., Aug. 9, 1924; s. Thomas Henry and Isabelle (Dunlap) R.; LL.B., U. Miss., 1949, J.D., 1968; m. Merle Burt, Nov. 28, 1953; children—Howard Manfred, Mark Andrew. Admitted to Miss. bar, 1949; practiced law, Corinth, 1949-61; pros. atty. Alcorn County, Miss., 1956-57, 58-61; U.S. atty. No. Dist. Miss., Oxford, 1961—. Treas., dir. Corinth Machinery Co., Am. Sawmill Machinery Co., Corinth, 1957-58. Chmn. Corinth Alcorn County Airport Bd., 1959-61. Mem. Miss. Ho. of Reps., 1948-51, author Miss. Workmens' Compensation Act, 1948. Mem. Atty. Gen.'s Adv. Com. of U.S. Attys., 1973—, chmn. legislation and ct. rules subcom., 1973—. Served with USAAF, 1943-45, with USAF, 1951-53. Recipient Young Man of Distinguished Service award Corinth Jr. C. of C., 1958. Mem. Miss. State Bar, Am., Fed. bar assns., Delta Sigma Pi, Sigma Chi. Democrat. Presbyn. Mason, Kiwanian (lt. gov., dir. Miss., La., W. Tenn. dist. 955). Home: 104 Colonial Rd Oxford MS 38655 Office: Fed Bldg W Jackson Av Oxford MS 38655

RAY, JACK LEROY, banker; b. Gadsden, Ala., Jan. 1, 1928; s. John L. and Mary Lou (Allday) R.; student Tenn. Mil. Inst., 1945; A.B., Duke, 1949; m. Lugenia Morgan, Feb. 17, 1949; children—John Richard, Harold Daniel, William Allen. Salesman, Dowd Press, Charlotte, N.C., 1949-50, Mut. Life Ins. Co. of N.Y., Protective Life, 1950-54; pres. Ray Constrn. Co., Gadsden, 1954—; pres., chmn. bd. 1st State Bank, Altoona, Ala., 1959—; vice chmn. bd., dir. Exchange Bank, Attalla, Ala.; pres., dir. Gadsden Corp., Attalla Trust Co. Mem. Am., Ala., Ind. bankers assns., Home Builders Assn. Etowah County (pres. 1957), Beta Theta Pi. Baptist. Lion (pres. Gadsden 1958-59). Home: 2917 Scenic Hwy Gadsden AL 35901 Office: 1st State Bank Altoona AL 35952

RAY, JAMES RICHARD, constrn. co. exec.; b. Haynesville, La., Nov. 23, 1937; s. James Elbert and Jewell Loraine (Skelton) R.; B.B.A., Lamar State U., 1960; m. Frances Pauline Overstreet, Aug. 6, 1960; children—Sonja Pauline, Jimmie Sharlene. Accounting supr. Jefferson Chem. Co., Inc., Houston, 1966-70; chief accountant US Homes of Tex., Houston, 1970-71; v.p. finance Northwood Homes, Inc., Dallas, 1971—. Served with AUS, 1960-62. C.P.A., Tex. Mem. Ch. of Christ. Home: 2312 Valleywood St Carrollton TX 75006 Office: 211 N Ervay St Suite 1004 Dallas TX 75201

RAY, MOSES ALEXANDER, dentist; b. Clinton, N.C., Sept. 25, 1920; s. Moses and Carrie Estelle (Beamon) R.; B.S., Shaw U., 1941; D.D.S., Howard U., 1945; m. Helen Bettina Jones, June 15, 1944; children—Shelia Anne, Ernest Alexander. Pvt. practice dentistry, Tarboro, N.C., 1946—; mem. staff Edgecombe Gen. Hosp., Tarboro. Pres., founder Panola Heights Housing Devel. Corp., Inc., 1970—; dir. Nash Edgecombe Econ. Devel. Corp., Tarboro Edgecombe Econ. Devel. Corp. Pres., East Tarboro Citizen's League, 1965—; councilman, Tarboro, 1967—; mem. N.C. Gov.'s Council Occupational Health, 1968-71. Trustee Edgecombe Econ. Devel. Corp. Served with USAF, 1951-53. Mem. N.C. Dental Soc., Am. Dental Assn., Omega Psi Phi. Democrat. Baptist. Mason. Home: 704 Panola St Tarboro NC 27886 Office: 409 Panola St Tarboro NC 27886

RAY, ROBERT SIDNEY, physician; b. Noonday, Tex., July 1, 1922; s. Lewis Edwin and Nellie (Armstrong) R.; certificate graduation, Tyler Jr. Coll., 1941; student U. Tex., 1941-42; B.A., U. Colo., 1948; M.D., U. Tex. at Galveston, 1954; m. Nancy Frances Waits, Apr. 21, 1945; children—Robert Sidney, Sally Louise, Gregory Francis. Intern, Brackenridge Hosp., Austin, 1954-55; resident in radiology Bexar County Hosp., San Antonio, 1969-71; practice gen. medicine, Seguin, Tex., 1956-69; staff radiologist Guadalupe Valley Hosp., Seguin, 1972—. Pres., sec. MedSur, Inc., Seguin, 1959-69; sec. Placid Heights, Inc., Seguin, 1966—. Chmn., Seguin Home Rule Charter Commn., 1971. Mem. Seguin Ind. Sch. Dist., 1966-72. Served with USNR, 1942-45. Mem. A.M.A., Guadalupe County, Tex. med. assns., Alamo, Tex., Am. acads. family practice, Seguin-Guadalupe County C. of C. (1st v.p. 1965). Home: 702 E College St Seguin TX 78155 Office: 702 E College St Seguin TX 78155

RAY, WILLIAM BROWN, newspaper editor; b. Louisville, Miss., May 17, 1926; s. Emmette Nathan and Ruby (Clark) R.; B.S., Miss. State U., 1950; m. Mary Elizabeth Wall, Sept. 21, 1952; children—William Michael, David Emmette, Sylvia Denise. Sports editor, advt. mgr. Winston County Jour., Louisville, Miss., 1950-51; sports editor Meridian (Miss.) Star, 1951-52; sports editor Daily Corinthian, Corinth, Miss., 1952-53; sports editor, photographer Vicksburg (Miss.) Evening Post, 1953—. Served with USNR, World War II. Decorated Purple Heart medal; named Miss. Sportswriter Year, 1973; recipient numerous awards writing and photography. Mem. Cotton States Baseball Sports Writers (pres. 1951), Big Eight Sportswriters Assn. (pres. 1958, 73), Football Writers Assn. Am., Nat. Sportswriters-Sportscasters Assn., Sigma Delta Chi. Home: 922 Polk St Vicksburg MS 39180 Office: 920 South St Vicksburg MS 39180

RAYNES, OATHER EDMUND, educator; b. Commerce, Tex., Apr. 4, 1910; s. William Franklin and Daisy (Jackson) R.; B.A., E. Tex. U., 1935, M.A., 1941; postgrad. Tex. U., 1940, N. Tex. U., 1950-52; m. Susan Alice Cargile, June 7, 1955. Tchr., Sulphur Bluff (Tex.) High Sch., 1933-36, Union Grove High Sch., Gladewater, Tex., 1936-43; tchr. pub. schs., Dallas, 1943-69; sr. counselor Woodrow Wilson High Sch., Dallas, 1969-71; facilitator Dallas Tchr. Edn. Center and Personnel Devel., Dallas, 1971—. Del. World Conf. for Teaching Profession, 1971; life mem. P.T.A. Named Outstanding Educator, E. Tex. U., 1971, Dallas Pub. Schs. Mem. N.E.A. (life, del. 1958-72), Nat., Dallas (pres. 1956-57) councils tchrs. English, Nat., Tex. (pres. 1960-62), Dallas speech assns., Tex. Tchrs. Assn. (pres. dist. 1969-70), Tex. (pres. 1970-71), Dallas (pres. 1964-66) classroom tchrs. assns., Phi Delta Kappa. Club: Optimist (Dallas). Home: 6530 Anita St Dallas TX 75214 Office: 2218 Bryan St Dallas TX 75201

RAYNOR, LEIGHTON ALFRED, JR., optometrist; b. Raleigh, N.C., Aug. 26, 1924; s. Leighton Alfred and Ella (Carpenter) R.; B.S., Presbyn. Coll., 1945; Optometry Dr., So. Coll. Optometry, 1947; m. Hortense Bridgers, Dec. 22, 1948; children—Leighton Alvin, David Shelton, Leigh Annette. Practice optometry, Apex, N.C., 1948—. Cons. vision Lufkin Rule Co., Apex, 1968—. Vol. Apex Fire Dept., 1950—. Bd. dirs. Apex Area Centennial Commn. Named Young Man of Year, Apex Jr. C. of C., 1957. Mem. Am., N.C. Optometric assns., N.C. Optometric Soc. (pres. Eastern dist. 1950), Omega Delta. Methodist (trustee, adminstrv. bd.). Mason, Lion; mem. Order Eastern Star. Club: McGregor Downs Country (Cary, N.C.). Home: 603 Hunter St Apex NC 27502 Office: 203 E Chatham St Apex NC 27502

RAYNOR, STANLEY, govt. ofcl.; b. N.Y.C., Apr. 5, 1924; s. Morris and Fan (Spinner) R.; student Bklyn. Coll., 1941-43, Columbia, 1943-44; D.D.S., N.Y. U., 1948; m. Muriel Goldstein, July 3, 1948; children—Gene Seth, Jill Lesley, Elise Mara. With USPHS, Bur. Prisons, 1948—, dental officer Fed. Correctional Inst., Ashland, Ky., 1948—, dental officer Fed. Reformatory, Chillicothe, O., 1952-56, sr. dental officer Fed. Penitentiary, Lewisburg, Pa., 1956-64, chief dental services, dental dir. Bur. Prisons, Washington, 1964—, ed. Health Services Newsletter, 1961—. Served with USNR, 1941-46. Recipient Meritorious Service medal USPHS, 1969. Mem. Am. Dental Assn., Commd. Officers Assn. USPHS, Clin. Soc. USPHS, Alpha Omega. Contbr. articles to dental jours. Established Central Dental Lab. for tng. dental technicians. Home: 7420 Leahy Rd New Carrollton MD 20784 Office: Bureau of Prisons US Public Health Service 101 Indiana Av Washington DC 20537

RAYNSFORD, ROBERT WAYNE, economist; b. Neptune, N.J., July 13, 1935; s. Robert Wayne and Maud Marshall (Mason) R.; B.A. in History (Tyng scholar), Williams Coll., 1957; M.A. in Econs., Harvard, 1963, Ph.D., 1966; m. Irmela Ellen Erdmut Reichelt, Apr. 23, 1964; 1 son, Anthony Wayne. Economist, Metallgesellschaft AC, Frankfurt Main, West Germany, 1963-66; economist Econ. Devel. Adminstrn., Commerce Dept., Washington, 1966-68; economist Office Mgmt. and Budget, 1968-72, asst. chief statis. policy div., 1972—. Served with USAF, 1957-60. Woodrow Wilson fellow, 1960. Mem. Am. Econ. Assn., Am. Statis. Assn., Phi Beta Kappa, Delta Psi. Contbr. articles profl. jours. Home: 3850 Tunlaw Rd Washington DC 20007 Office: Statistical Policy Div US Office Mgmt and Budget New Executive Office Bldg Room 10208 Washington DC 20503

RAZZANO, MICHAEL RICHARD, dentist; b. Patchogue, N.Y., Sept. 11, 1939; s. Vincent M. and Mary F. (Fedumn) R.; B.S., U. Fla., 1962; D.D.S., U. Md., 1966; m. Georgia L. Hodges, Sept. 7, 1962; children—Lisa, Michael, Vincent. Pvt. practice dentistry, Ocala, Fla., 1969—; mem. staff, cons. Monroe Meml. Hosp., Ocala. Chmn., Walk for Mankind, Fla. Jr. C. of C., 1970; mem. Marion County Gov.'s Adv. Com., 1971-74; regional coordinator Project Concern, 1970—. Served with USPHS, 1966-69. Recipient Harry E. Kelsey award, Harry B. Schwartz award U. Md., 1966. Mem. Am., Fla. dental assns., Marion County Dental Soc., Royal Soc. Health, Jr. C. of C. (Tommy Thompson award 1971, pres. 1971—), C. of C., Psi Omega, Omicron Kappa Upsilon. Elk. Contbr. articles to profl. pubs. Home: 4818 SE 17th Place Ocala FL 32670 Office: 1301 SW 1st Av Ocala FL 32670

REA, JOHN EDWARD, JR., engring. firm exec.; b. Los Angeles, Mar. 17, 1917; s. John Edward and Catherine (Wagner) R.; B.S. in Civil Engring., U. N.M., 1941; m. Reva Alka, Sept. 7, 1940; children—Nancy Lee (Mrs. D. Lee Jacobs), John Edward III, Thomas H. Hydraulics engr. U.S. Bur. Reclamation, Oklahoma City, 1941-42, 46-47; stress and liason engr. Douglas Aircraft Co., Oklahoma City, 1942-44; engr. Phillips & Stong Engring. Co., Oklahoma City, 1947-48; partner, engr. Rea Engring. Co., Oklahoma City, 1948-62; pres. Rea Engring. & Assos., Inc., Oklahoma City, 1962-73, chmn. bd., chief exec. officer, 1973—; pres. Rea Bignell, Fischer & Moore, architects, engrs., 1969—; dir. Southwestern Bank & Trust Co., Oklahoma City. Mem. exec. bd. Last Frontier council Boy Scouts Am., 1969-74. Served to lt. (j.g.) USNR, 1944-46. Registered profl. engr., Okla. Mem. Cons. Engrs. Council Okla. (pres. 1966), Pub. Works Council Okla. (pres. 1965), Nat., Okla. socs. profl. engrs., Am. Pub. Works Assn., Am. Water Works Assn., Kappa Sigma. Republican. Episcopalian. Rotarian (South Oklahoma City pres. 1963). Home: 2201 Alderham St Oklahoma City OK 73160 Office: 1133 SW 74th St Oklahoma City OK 73139

REA, JOHN WILLIAM, sch. supt.; b. Randolph, Miss., Apr. 24, 1909; s. James Thomas and Modena (Gardner) R.; B.S., Ark. State U., 1949; M.Ed., U. Miss., 1951; m. Zola Lucille Beshears, Jan. 11, 1937; children—Patricia (Mrs. Joe Ray Price), William L. Prin., Center Elementary Sch., Wynne, Ark., 1941-48, McCrory (Ark.) High Sch., 1948-55, Crawfordsville (Ark.) High Sch., 1955-56; supt. Gosnell Sch., Blytheville, Ark., 1956—. State chmn. Impacted Area Schs. Information Service, 1969—, area chmn. region 6, 1970—. Mem. Ark Edn. Assn., Am., Ark. assns. sch. administrs., Nat. Sch. Bd. Assn. Methodist. Mason (Shriner); mem. Order Eastern Star; Kiwanian (bd. dirs.). Home: 600 Hwy 181 Blytheville AR 72315

READ, A. LOUIS, broadcasting exec.; b. New Orleans Oct. 12, 1914; A.B., Loyola U., 1937; m. Nathalie Doris Owings; children—Michael Owings, Susan Louise (Mrs. E. Douglas Johnson, Jr.), Carolyn Mary (Mrs. Edward Simmons), Stephen Louis. Mem. sales staff Blue Plate Foods, 1937-38; comml. mgr. radio sta. WWL, 1938-41, 45-47; advt. dir. Wembley, Inc., 1947-48; gen. mgr. WABB, Mobile, Ala., 1948-49; commr. mgr. WDSU, WDSU-TV, New Orleans, 1949-65, pres., 1965-72; pres. WDSU-TV, Cosmos Broadcasting La., Inc., 1973—; vice chmn. bd., dir. Royal St. Corp.; v.p., treas. Interchange Realty Co., Inc., operators Oakwood Shopping Center; v.p. Royal St. Investment Corp.; exec. v.p., dir. Starwood Land Corp., Aspen, Colo.; dir. Bank New Orleans. Chmn. NBC-TV Affiliates, 1963-67; chmn. bd. TV Stations, Inc., 1968-69; dir. TV Bur. Advt., 1958-62, chmn., 1961; mem. exec. com. U.S. Broadcasters for UN; chmn. S. Atlantic dist. Broadcast Pioneers Campaign Fund. Mem. Nat. Adv. Council on Supplemental Centers and Services, 1968-70; mem. com. on communications U.S. Catholic Conf., 1968; sr. v.p. Met. Area Com. New Orleans, mem. exec. com., 1967—; mem. task force on transp. Goals for La. program; mem. policy and information com. Council for Better La.; mem. community action and crime prevention com. La. Commn. Law Enforcement and Adminstrn. Criminal Justice. Charter mem. Goals Found. Met. New Orleans; past trustee Greater New Orleans Area United Fund, gen. campaign chmn., 1969; mem. exec. com. New Orleans Tourist and Convention Commn.; bd. dirs. Better Bus. Bur., Met. New Orleans Safety Council, Internat. Trade Mart, Internat. House, Christopher Homes, Catholic Human Relations Commn., Internat. Radio and TV Found.; mem. adv. council Loyola Coll. Bus. Adminstrn.; bd. govs. Tulane Med. Center; mem. adv. council U. Notre Dame Coll. Bus. Adminstrn.; bd. lay regents Xavier U., New Orleans, 1959-69; trustee St. Mary's Dominican Coll., 1965-71. Served as lt. comdr. USNR, World War II. Named La. Broadcaster of Yr. La. Assn. Broadcasters, 1968; recipient F. Edward Hebert award as outstanding alumnus Jesuit High Sch., 1968. Mem. Navy League, Nat. Assn. Broadcasters (chmn. TV bd. 1971-72, chmn. TV information com., chmn. bd. Radio Advt. Bur.), Soc. TV Pioneers. Office: 520 Royal St New Orleans LA 70130

READ, EMERSON BRACKETT, real estate broker, ins. agt.; b. Dobbs Ferry, N.Y., Aug. 9, 1925; s. Thomas C. and Helen E. (Emerson) R.; student U. Pitts., 1944, Coll. Charleston, 1946; B.S. in Civil Engring., The Citadel, 1950; m. Doris E. Boyd, Dec. 2, 1950 (dec. 1973); children—Anne Standish, Elizabeth Emerson, Susan Lee, Emerson Brackett; m. 2d, Patricia Davenport, Jan. 26, 1974. Propr., Read & Read, realtors, Charleston, S.C., 1947-50, 65—; salesman Carleton Dooley, realtors, Miami, Fla., 1950-54, gen. sales mgr., 1954-55, sales exec. v.p., 1955-56; sales sr. asso. Keyes Co., Miami, 1956-61, exec. v.p., gen. sales mgr., 1961-65. Lectr. real estate exchanging and taxation U. S.C. Realtors Inst. Served with USAAF, 1943-45. Mem. Am. Legion, Charleston Real Estate Bd. (pres. 1972), Nat. Assn. Real Estate Bds., Charleston Bd. Ins. Underwriters, Nat. Assn. Ind. Fee Appraisers (sr. mem.), S.A.R., S.C.V., Huegenot Soc. Episcopalian (past vestryman). Kiwanian. Club: Carolina Yacht (Charleston). Home: 19 King St Charleston SC 29401 Office: 37 Broad St Charleston SC 29401

READ, FOY ELLIS, city ofcl.; b. Laurel, Miss., Mar. 20, 1922; s. Artis Guilbert and Lotchie Ola (Hendry) R.; student U. Tenn., 1943-44; m. Blanche Virginia Scaife, Oct. 5, 1942; children—Suzanne Joy (Mrs. David Henry Sherrill), Ronald Keith. With Bur. Streets, Bridges and Drainage, Memphis Div. Pub. Works, 1945—, head bur., 1972—. Chmn. bd. trustees Sky Lake, Memphis, 1966—; founder Sky Lake Civic Club, 1963, pres., 1963-65. Served to maj., USAAF, World War II; Korea. Decorated Air Medal with 3 clusters. Mem. Am. Pub. Works Assn., Memphis Engrs. Club. Baptist. Home: 2827 Dumbarton Dr Memphis TN 38127 Office: Div Pub Works City Hall N Main St Memphis TN 38127

READ, RALSTON BAKER, JR., microbiologist; b. Rehoboth, Mass., Mar. 31, 1926; s. Ralston Baker and Ida Josephine (Horton) R.; student U. Me., 1943-44; A.B., Brown U., 1946; M.S., U. N.H., 1949; Ph.D. (Lotta Crabtree fellow), U. Mass., 1956; m. Helen E. Murdock, June 11, 1949; children—Judith (Mrs. Lawrence Bell), Ralston Baker, Steven Edward. Master, St. Andrews Sch., Barrington, R.I., 1946-47; instr. Westbrook Jr. Coll., Portland, Me., 1947-48; microbiologist St. Luke's Hosp., New Bedford, Mass., 1949-50; asst. prof. U. Mass., Amherst, 1956-60; microbiologist USPHS, Phoenix, 1950-52, asst. chief food microbiology, Cin., 1960-69, chief, 1969-71, dep. dir. div. microbiology FDA, Washington, 1971—. Pres., P.T.A., Sunderland, Mass., 1957-58. Served with USNR, 1944-46. Mem. A.A.A.S., Am. Soc. Microbiology, Am. Dairy Sci. Assn., Internat. Assn. Milk, Food and Environmental Sanitarians, Sigma Xi. Editorial bd: Jour. Milk and Food Tech., 1970—. Contbr. articles to profl. jours. Patentee method for prodn. vaccines. Home: 10402 Hunt Country Lane Vienna VA 22180 Office: 200 C St SW Washington DC 70002

READ, WILLIAM GEORGE, univ. adminstr.; b. Stratton, Colo., Apr. 13, 1921; s. George Wayne and Laura (Frankamp) R.; B.S., Fort Hays State Coll., Kan., 1943, M.S., 1948; Ph.D., U. Kan., 1956; m. Maxa Anne Rorabaugh, Jan. 23, 1948. Mem. faculty physics dept. Murray (Ky.) State U., 1949-70, asst. prof., 1949-52, asso. prof., 1952-56, prof., 1956-70, chmn. dept., 1959-70, v.p. acad. affairs, dean faculties, 1970—. Mem. Ky. Sci. and Tech. Adv. Council, 1961—; mem. Gov.'s Commn. on Sci. subcom. on status nuclear sci. edn. and engring. in Ky., 1963-64; mem. Ky. Adv. Com. on Optometry, 1964-71. Served to lt. USAAF, 1943-46. Mem. Am. Assn. Physics Tchrs. (asso. counselor Ky.), Am. Council Higher Edn., A.A.A.S., Ky. Acad. Sci. (dir.), Am. Physics Soc., Sigma Xi, Phi Kappa Phi, Delta Epsilon. Contbr. to profl. jours. Home: 1620 Sunset Dr Murray KY 42071

REAGAN, GEORGE WILLIAM, constrn. co. exec.; b. Knoxville, Tenn., Sept. 10, 1898; s. Fletcher L. and Nancy Maleta (Roberts) R.; B.S., U. Tenn., 1920; m. Mary Alice Hackney, Sept. 27, 1945; children—Barbara (Mrs. Frank M. Carter, Jr.), William H., Mary (Mrs. Fred McMurray). Estimator, J.M. Dunn & Son, gen. contractors, Knoxville, 1922-25; v.p. V.L. Nicholson Co., gen. contractors, Knoxville, Tenn., 1925-33; v.p. Kennedy & Reagan Co., gen. contractors, Miami, Fla., 1933-34; pres. George W. Reagan Co., gen. contractors, Knoxville, 1934-71, chmn. bd., 1971—. Pres. Knoxville Citizens Group, 1957-64, 70-71. Served with USNR, 1918, as Seabee co. comdr. USNR, 1943-45; PTO. Mem. Associated Gen. Contractors (nat. dir. 1967-69, pres. Tenn. br. 1961-63; recipient Scroll award 1971). Clubs: Knoxville Civitan (pres. 1954-55), Cherokee Country, Holston Hills Golf and Country, Deane Hills, Century. Writer, narrator Story of Bible, radio sta. WNOX, Knoxville, 1964—. Home: 5107 Shady Dell Trail Knoxville TN 37914 Office: 1700 Grainger St Knoxville TN 37901

REAGAN, MARION ALLEN, JR., gas co. exec.; b. Waco, Tex., July 20, 1926; s. Marion Allen and Jessie May (Rogers) R.; student Tex. A. and M. Coll., 1943-44; B.A. in Geology, U. Tex., 1950, postgrad., 1950-51; m. Martha Edna Riley, Sept. 4, 1948; children—Deborah Ellen, Berkley Allen. Geologist Standard Oil Co. Tex., Houston, 1951-52; successively geologist, asst. chief geologist, asst. to gen. mgr., mgr. planning and marketing. Dow Chem. Co., Houston, 1952-65, mgr. evaluation, then mgr. hydrocarbons, Midland, Mich., 1965-69; sr. v.p. Houston Natural Gas Corp., 1969—; pres. Houston Pipeline

Co., Valley Pipelines, Inc., Valley Gas Transmission, Inc., Intratex Gas Co., HNG Petrochems., Inc., HNG Fossil Fuels Co.; v.p., dir. Oasis Pipeline Co., Zeigler Coal Co.; dir. HNG Oil Co., Interstate Natural Gas Co., Mid La. Gas Co. Mem. Geol. Found. Adv. Council U. Tex. at Austin. Served with USNR, 1944-46. Mem. Natural Gas Men Houston, Am. Petroleum Inst., Am. Inst. M.E., Am. Assn. Petroleum Geologists, Lambda Chi Alpha. Methodist (adminstrv. bd.). Clubs: Ramada, Lakeside Country, Midland. Home: 238 Gessner St Houston TX 77024 Office: 1200 Travis St Houston TX 77002

REAGAN, RAWLEIGH TERRELL, constrn. co. exec.; b. Charleston, S.C., May 2, 1942; s. Royce Jennings and Ruby Pauline (Smith) R.; B.A., Baylor U., 1963; B.S., U. Tex., 1966. Vice pres. R.J. Reagan Co., Inc., Waco, Tex., 1960—; project engr. R.M.K.-B.R.J., Manila, Philippines, 1966-69; pres. Stahr & Gregory, Inc., Temple, Tex., 1969—; pres. Republic Roofing Corp., Austin, Tex., 1970—, Air Systems Engring., 1972—; v.p. Holley Reagan Constrn. Co., Waco, Barnhart Supply Co., Austin, Multi-Bilt Corp., Waco. Pres. bd. dirs. Temple Civic Theatre. Recipient Cost Reduction award Dept. Navy, 1969; named Outstanding Civitan, 1971. Mem. Am. Inst. Physics, Am. Math. Assn., Am. Soc. M.E., Am. Soc. Archtl. Engrs., Am. Soc. C.E. Republican. Mem. Ch. of Christ. Lion. Author movie script The Hit Men, 1974. Home: 1300 N 11th Temple TX 76501 Office: Box 186 Temple TX 76501

REAMES, JAMES MITCHELL, univ. librarian; b. Rembert, S.C., Aug. 31, 1920; s. James Alex and Carrie (James) R.; B.A., Furman U., 1941; B.L.S., U. N.C., 1942; M.L.S., U. Mich., 1954; m. Mary Beall Hall, July 24, 1948; 1 son, James Alan. Reference librarian Clemson U., 1946-52; asso. librarian, asso. prof. Northwestern State U. La., 1952-58; dir. U. S.C. Undergrad. Library, 1958-66, asso. dir. libraries, 1966-70; dir. James A. Rogers Library, prof. Francis Marion Coll., Florence, S.C., 1970—. Mem. evaluation com. So. Assn. Colls., 1962—; cons. library devel. Warren Wilson Coll., Erskine Coll., Lander Coll. Dir., mem. exec. com. Alston Wilkes Soc., 1968-73; mem. Gov.'s Mansion and Lace House Commn., 1970-71; bd. govs. Christian Action Council, 1968-72. Trustee Claflin Coll. Served with USNR, 1942-46. Mem. S.C. (pres. 1949, 70-71), Southeastern library assns., Am. Assn. U. Profs. Democrat. Methodist (del. S.C. ann. conf. 1974, mem. adminstrv. bd. 1971—). Contbr. articles to ednl., religious periodicals. Home: 1905 Marsh Av Florence SC 29501

REAMEY, HERBERT KIRKLAND, JR., aluminum co. exec.; b. Newport, Ark., July 26, 1924; s. Herbert Kirkland and Mildred May (Jordan) R.; student U. Utah, 1943; B.S. in Mech. Engring., U. Ark., 1949; postgrad. U. Pitts., 1950-51; m. Dorothy Jane Thompson, May 19, 1944; children—Herbert Kirkland III, John H., Elizabeth (Mrs. Richard B. Thompson). Mech. engr. Westinghouse Electric Co., Pitts., 1949-52; with Reynolds Metals Co., various locations, 1952—, prodn. supt., Listerhill, Ala., 1969-70, plant mgr., Jones Mills, Ark., 1970-74, plant mgr., Listerhill, 1974—; dir. Asso. Industries Ala., Central Bank Ala., Florence. Vice pres. Ouachita Area council Boy Scouts Am., 1971-73; chmn. bldg. com. YMCA, Florence, Ala., 1970. Mem. Sch. Bd., Arkadelphia, Ark., 1959-69, pres., 1967-69. Served with AUS, 1943-46. Bd. dirs. Garland County Community Coll., Hot Springs, Ark., 1973—. Registered prof. engr. Ala. Mem. Am. Soc. Mech. Engrs., Am. Inst. Mining and Metall. Engrs., Tau Beta Pi, Pi Mu Epsilon. Methodist. Rotarian. Recipient Merit Patent award Reynolds, 1963. Home: 313 Nottingham Rd Florence AL 35630 Office: PO Box 191 Sheffield AL

REAMS, WILLIAM DINWIDDIE, JR., judge; b. Culpeper, Va., Apr. 24, 1929; s. William Dinwiddie and Flora (Hudson) R.; student U. Md., 1948-49; B.A., U. Va., 1955, LL.B., 1958; m. Nancy Jane Walker, Aug. 6, 1955; children—William D. III, Laura Daniel, Gilbert Walker. Admitted to Va. bar, 1958; commonwealth atty. Culpeper County, Culpeper, 1958-68; judge Culpeper County Ct., 1968-70; judge Juvenile and Domestic Relations Dist. Ct., 1973—. Served with USMC, 1950-52. Mem. Culpeper Bar Assn. (pres. 1968-73), Va. State Bar. Mason, Kiwanian (dir. 1969—). Home: RFD 1 Box 464 Culpeper VA 22701 Office: W Davis St Culpeper VA 22701

REAP, CHARLES AUGUSTUS, JR., dentist; b. Albemarle, N.C., Nov. 24, 1931; s. Charles Augustus and Mildred (Bostian) R.; student Duke, 1948-51, Catawba Coll., 1953-54; D.D.S., U. N.C. Sch. Dentistry, 1958; m. Betty Efird Taylor, May 6, 1956; children—Ellen, Cynthia, Linda, Charles, III, Hunter. Clin. instr. U. N.C., Chapel Hill, 1958-59; pvt. practice dentistry, Chapel Hill, 1958—; clinician various dental groups, 1964—. Pres. bd. dirs. YMCA; bd. dirs. N.C. Cancer Soc. Served with USAF, 1951-53. Named City Father of Year, Chapel Hill C. of C., 1968. Mem. Orange-Durham (pres. 1969), 3d Dist. N.C. (v.p. 1971, sec. 1973-74) dental socs., Jr. C. of C. (pres. 1967-68). Methodist (mem. ofcl. bd. 1962-65). Rotarian (treas. 1970-71, sec. 1971-72). Club: Civitan (v.p. 1963-64) (Chapel Hill). Author: Handbook for Dental Secretaries, Assistants and Hygienists, 1973. Contbr. articles to profl. jours. Home: 2305 Honeysuckle Rd Chapel Hill NC 27514 Office: 861 Willow Dr Chapel Hill NC 27514

REASONOVER, WILLIAM SUMTER, coll. pub. relations ofcl.; b. Camden, S.C., July 22, 1927; s. Marvin M. and Olive Z. (Rhame) R.; B.S. in Agrl. Econs., Clemson U., 1947. Dir. pub. relations Farmers Mut. Exchange, Durham, N.C., 1947-48; nat. advt. mgr. The Robesonian, Lumberton, N.C., 1949-57; dir. community and pub. relations Alaska Meth. U., Anchorage, 1957-58; dir. pub. relations Pfeiffer Coll., Misenheimer, N.C., 1958—. Sec. Richfield Park Com., 1971—. Bd. dirs. Stanley County Community Concert Assn. Mem. Albemarle-Stanley County C. of C. (v.p., dir. 1967—), Charlotte Pub. Relations Soc. (dir. 1966—), Coll. News Seminar Carolinas (pres. 1964; dir. 1968—) Am. Alumni Council, N.C. Civitan Youth Leadership Conf. (chmn. bd. govs. 1965-67), Pub. Relations Soc. Am., Am. Coll. Pub. Relations Soc. Methodist (lay speaker 1960—; mem. commn. communications 1968—, chmn. com. conf. jour. Western N.C. conf. 1973). Club: Civitan (Richfield N.C.). Editor: Pfeiffer College Bull., 1960—. Contbr. articles to newspapers, mags. Home: 2 James Apartment Misenheimer NC 28109 Office: Drawer D Pfeiffer Coll Misenheimer NC 28109

REAVES, LEE, TV sta. exec.; b. Warren, Ark., Dec. 10, 1909; s. B.A. and Ellie (Martin) R.; A.B., Ark. A. and M. Coll., 1934; M.S., U. Ark., 1947; m. Glenda Pittman, Feb. 21, 1942; children—Glenda Anne (Mrs. Robert W. Downs, III), Robin Lee (Mrs. J.F. Hawkins, Jr.). Instr., Sch. for Blind, Little Rock, 1931-33; tchr. pub. schs., Warren, 1934-36; supt. schs., Hermitage, Ark., 1936-51; adminstr. Bradley County Meml. Hosp., Warren, 1951-53; part owner, operator Radio Sta. KWRF, Warren, 1953-59; v.p. Ark. A. and M. Coll., Monticello, 1959-63; dir. Ark. Ednl. TV Commn., Conway, 1963—. Mem. Ark. Senate, 1939-55, sec. senate, 1961—; chmn. Bradley County Democratic Com., 1945-49; mem. Ark. State Dem. Com., 1947-55. Mem. War Meml. Stadium Commn., 1948-63; chmn. Warren Planning Bd., 1957-59; mem. Warren Sch. Bd., 1953-59, Bradley County Sch. Bd., 1957-59. Mem. Warren C. of C. (dir. 1954-59, pres. 1956-58). Methodist (vice chmn. bd. stewards). Rotarian (v.p. Warren 1951-59). Author: Rule Book for the Arkansas Senate, 1943. Home: Hillman and Mitchell Sts Conway AR 72032 Office: 350 S Donaghy St Conway AR 72032

REAVIS, WILLARD, architect; b. Locker, Tex., Apr. 13, 1920; s. Francis Marion and Lucy (Harris) R.; B.Arch., U. Tex. at Austin, 1950; m. Sarah Ann Ferguson, June 1, 1946; children—Carl Brett, Jenny. With Reavis & Assos., Arlington, Tex., 1952-56, Preston Geren, architects and engrs., Fort Worth, 1956-63, Hueppelsheuser & White, architects and engrs., Fort Worth, 1963-67, Lawrence D. White, architects and engrs., Fort Worth, 1967-71; owner Reavis Assos., architects, Arlington, Tex., 1971—. Art instr. Arlington summer culture program, 1952-56. Served to capt., AUS, 1941-46, as capt., C.E., 1951-52. Decorated Bronze Star medal, Combat Infantryman's badge. Recipient 1st award Gateway to Mexico Lower Rio Grande Valley C. of C., 1950. Registered architect, Tex., Miss. Mem. Tex. Soc. Architects, A.I.A., Arlington C. of C. (sec.-treas. 1954), Arlington Art Assn. (pres. bd. 1956). Methodist (chmn. edn. commn. 1963, sec. ch. bd. 1965). Works include Tarrant County Conv. Center, 1965. Home: 1115 Lynda Lane Arlington TX 76013 Office: 1231 Colorado Lane Arlington TX 76013

REBH, GEORGE ANTHONY, army officer; b. Detroit, Sept. 14, 1921; s. Anthony George and Myra Sophie (Manica) R.; B.S., U.S. Mil. Acad., 1943; B.A. (Rhodes scholar), Oxford U., 1950, M.A., 1954; grad. Command and Gen. Staff Coll., 1957, Indsl. Coll. Armed Forces, 1962; m. Jeanne Garner, Apr. 26, 1947; children—George Leonard, Richard Garner. Commd. 2d lt. U.S. Army, 1943, advanced through grades to maj. gen., 1973; chief of staff 7th Army Support Command, 1963-64; dep. chief of staff 7th Army, 1964-65; dist. engr. Tulsa Engr. Dist., 1965-67; dep. div. engr. Huntsville Engr. Div., 1967-68; dep. brigade comdr. 18th Engr. Brigade, 1969; chief force devel. plans div. Pentagon, 1970; dep. dir. mil. constrn. Office Chief of Engrs., also asst. to chief of engrs. for NASA support, 1970—, also dir. postal constrn., 1970—; dir. mil. constrn. for Dept. Def. Agys., C.E., 1973—. Decorated Legion of Merit (2), Bronze Star medal, Air medal (3). Registered profl. engr., Okla. Mem. Assn. Am. Rhodes Scholars, Soc. Am. Mil. Engrs., Assn. U.S. Army. Home: 1600 S Joyce St Arlington VA 22202 Office: Forrestal Bldg 1000 Independence Av Washington DC 20315

REBSAMEN, RAYMOND H., corp. exec.; b. Lancaster, Tex., Apr. 8, 1898; s. William Frederick and Edna Mae (Miller) R.; student U. Ark. (Distinguished Alumnus citation 1960), LL.D. (hon.); Litt.D. (hon.), Subiaco Coll.; C.P.A., Am. Inst. Accountants; m. Martha Jane Dickinson; children—Ruth Elizabeth (Mrs. Roland R. Remmel), Frederick Raymond. Organizer, chmn. Rebsamen Cos., Inc., Little Rock; chmn. Rebsamen Fund, Little Rock; dir. Ark. La. Gas Co., Shreveport, Dillard Dept. Stores, Little Rock; chmn. bd. Fed. Res. Bank, St. Louis, 1963-66. Served as pvt. U.S. Army, 1918; lt. col. Ordnance Corps, AUS, 1942-45. Mem. Sigma Alpha Epsilon. Presbyn. Mason (33 deg.). Clubs: Little Rock Country; University, Racquet (St. Louis); Hunt and Polo, Memphis Country (Memphis). Home: 2500 N Jackson St Little Rock AR 72207 Office: Tower Bldg Little Rock AR 72201

RECHHOLTZ, ROBERT AUGUST, business cons.; b. N.Y.C., Mar. 29, 1937; s. August Bruno and Frances (Wirth) R.; B.S., U. N.C., 1958; m. Caroline Morton Osborne, May 2, 1959; children—Laurie, Jennifer, Kristen. Marketing asst. Procter & Gamble Co., Cin., 1958-59, asst. copy supr., 1959-60; account supr. Bradham & Co., Greensboro, 1960-61; v.p. marketing, dir. R.J. Reynolds Tobacco Co., 1961-72; v.p. Young & Rublcam, Inc., 1972-73; bus. cons., 1973—; dir. Westfall Prodns., ABC. Dir. Assn. Nat. Advertisers, Am. Advt. Fedn. Bd. dirs. Winston-Salem YMCA. Served with AUS, 1958, 61-62. Mem. Phi Beta Kappa. Republican. Episcopalian. Clubs: Winston-Salem Tennis, Forsyth Country (Winston-Salem). Home: 110 Sherwood Forest Rd Winston-Salem NC 27104 Office: Westfall Prodns 521 Fifth Av New York City NY 10017

RECKLESS, JOHN BRIAN, physician; b. Walsall, Eng., Aug. 12, 1929; s. Norman Vivian and Doris Lily (Lancaster) R.; student Queen Mary's Sch., Walsall, 1941-48; M.D., U. Birmingham (Eng.), 1954; m. Lieselotte Klose, Aug. 31, 1958; children—Brian, Monica. Came to U.S., 1958, naturalized, 1964. Intern Birmingham Gen. Hosp.; resident psychiatry Duke U. Med. Center, Durham, N.C., 1958-61, prof. psychiatry, 1961-73; pvt. practice medicine, specializing in psychiatry John Reckless Clinic, Durham, 1973—. Med. adviser U.S. Dept. Health, Edn. and Welfare. Served to maj. M.C., Brit. Royal Army, 1955-58. Fellow Am. Psychiat. Assn., A.C.P., Am. Acad. Psychosomatic Medicine. Home: 2437 Tryon St Durham NC 27705 Office: 5504 Durham-Chapel Hill Blvd Durham NC 27707

RECORD, JAMES RALPH, county ofcl.; b. New Market, Ala., Dec. 27, 1918; s. John Raymond and Lillie Belle (Fisk) R.; student U. Ala., 1960-62; B.S., Cramwell U., 1963; m. Lillian Aho, June 15, 1946 (dec. Feb. 1963); children—Carole Denise, James. Partner, Huntsville (Ala.) Accounting Services, 1958—; owner Record Pub. Co., Huntsville, 1958—. Past vice chmn. Ala. Dept. Pensions and Security, 1958-72. Mem. adv. bd. Ala. Civil Def. Dept., 1959, League Women Voters; bd. dirs. Ala. Tb Sanitorium, Friends of Library. Mem. Ala. Senate, 1961-62; chmn. bd. county commrs. Madison County, 1962—. Served with USAAF, 1942-46. Mem. Huntsville C. of C. (dir.), V.F.W., Am. Legion, Ala. Hist. Soc. (pres.), Madison County Farm Bur., Ala. Assn. County Commrs. (pres.). Baptist. Woodmen of World, Elk. Home: 9107 Hogan Dr Huntsville AL 35802 Office: Courthouse Huntsville AL 35804

RECORD, PHILLIP JULIUS, newspaper editor; b. Fort Worth, Jan. 12, 1929; s. Phillip Cross and Frances (McElwee) R.; B.A. in Journalism, U. Notre Dame, 1950; m. Patricia Ann Edwards, Sept. 29, 1954; children—Phillip Christopher, Gregory Edwards, Timothy James. Gen. reporter Lubbock (Tex.) Avalanche Jour., 1950-54; copy editor, reporter Fort Worth Star-Telegram, 1954-67, asst. city editor, 1967-68, city editor, evening edit., 1968—. Free-lance mag. writer. Mem. Fort Worth-Tarrant County (Tex.) Civil Def. Policy and Adv. Com.; troop committeeman Boy Scouts Am. Bd. dirs. Fort Worth Opera Assn., Catholic Social Services. Served with inf. AUS, 1950-52. Recipient 17 journalism awards for writing, photography and headline writing. Mem. Press Club of Fort Worth (past v.p.), Sigma Delta Chi (dir., pres. local chpt.). Democrat. Roman Catholic. Home: 5533 Wheaton Dr Fort Worth TX 76133 Office: 400 W 7th St Fort Worth TX 76102

RECORDS, JOHN WILLIAMS, physician; b. Kansas City, Mo., Feb. 10, 1911; s. William Claude and Mabelle Frances (Covey) R.; student Kansas City Jr. Coll., 1928-29, U. Mo., 1929-31; M.D., Washington U., St. Louis, 1936; m. Eleanor Allen Jeffrey, Feb. 24, 1933; children—George Jeffrey, Susan (Mrs. C.J. Harrison), Nancy (Mrs. K.A. Poush), Ellen (Mrs. D.D. Morgan), John Williams III. Intern, St. Luke's Hosp., St. Louis, 1936-37, resident in obstetrics, gynecology, 1937-39; practice medicine specializing in obstetrics, gynecology, Oklahoma City, 1939—; obstetrician, gynecologist Oklahoma City Clinic, 1939—; faculty U. Okla. Sch. Medicine, Oklahoma City, 1939—; clin. prof. obstetrics, gynecology, 1958—; mem. Univ. Hosp. and Health Scis. Center, 1939—; staff Presbyn. Hosp., Oklahoma City, 1939—, chmn. dept. obstetrics, gynecology, 1946—, also bd. dirs. Served to lt. col. M.C., AUS, 1940-46. Diplomate Am. Bd. Obstetrics and Gynecology. Fellow A.C.S., Am. Coll. Obstetrics and Gynecology; mem. Am., Okla. med. socs., So. Obstet. and Gynecol. Soc. (pres. 1973), Sigma Nu Alumni Assn. Oklahoma City, Phi Beta Pi. Republican. Presbyn. (ruling elder). Club: Oklahoma City Golf and Country. Editorial bd. So. Med. Jours., 1970—. Contbr. articles to profl. jours. Home: 6800 N Country Club Dr Oklahoma City OK 73116 Office: 301 NW 12th St Oklahoma City OK 73103

RECTOR, NORMAN KENNETH, cons. engr.; b. Newkirk, Okla., Oct. 14, 1902; s. Ira Clifford and Daisey (Farmer) R.; student Okla. State U., 1921-24; m. Mary Josephine Johnson, Nov. 24, 1927. Draftsman, Okla. State Hwy. Dept., 1925-26, Marland Oil Co., 1926-27, Oklahoma City Engring. Dept., 1927-28, jr. engr. Forrest E. Gilmore Co., Tulsa, 1928-30; design engr. Petroleum Engring., Inc., Tulsa, 1930-34; plant supt. Gregg-Tex Gasoline Co., Longview, Tex., 1934-36; with Petroleum Engring., Inc., 1936-51; ind. cons. engr., Houston, 1951-52, Tulsa, 1952—. Registered profl. engr., Okla., Tex. Mem. Engrs. Soc. Tulsa, Patentee in field. Home: 1905 E 36th St Tulsa OK 74105 Office: Mayo Bldg 420 S Main St Tulsa OK 74103

RECTOR, ROBERT ROSS, seismic exploration co. ofcl.; b. Pocatello, Ida., May 29, 1940; s. Roscoe Garnet and Constance Roberta (Bassett) R.; Asso. Electronic Tech., DeVry Tech. Inst., 1962; B.S. in Elec. Engring., La. Poly. Inst., 1967; m. Marjorie Aiken, July 6, 1963; children—Kimberly Karole, Stephanie Suzanne. Elec. engr. Western Geophys. Co. Am., Houston, 1967-68, computer programmer hardware interfacing, 1968-71, supr. nav. operations, 1971, gen. mgr. mfg. facility, Galveston, Tex., 1971—. Served with AUS, 1958-60. Mem. I.E.E.E., Assn. Computing Machinery, Kappa Sigma. Home: 926 Shorewood Dr Seabrook TX 77586 Office: PO Box 3340 Galveston TX 77550

RECTOR, WILLIAM LEE, physician; b. Shawnee, Okla., Nov. 30, 1919; s. William Lee and Mary Elizabeth (Reese) R.; B.S., Okla. State U., 1940; M.D., Okla. U., 1943; m. N. Jane Fielder, May 3, 1943; children—Nancy Jane, Lee Anne. Intern, Ia. Lutheran Hosp., Des Moines, 1944-45; resident Scott and White Clinic, Temple, Tex., 1947-50; practice medicine specializing in internal medicine, Med. and Surg. Clinic, Wichita Falls, Tex., 1950—; cons. internal medicine Wichita Falls, State Hosp., 1951—. Mem. regional health adv. com. Health, Edn. and Welfare, 1970-73; mem. census adv. com. on privacy and confidentiality U.S. Dept. Commerce, 1972—. Chmn. Tex. Republican Task Force Human Rights Responsibilities, 1967—, chmn. Rep. State Conv., 1970, mem. state exec. com., 1964—; del. Rep. Nat. Conv., 1968, 72. Trustee, chmn. bd. Community Center Mental Health-Mental Retardation. Served to capt. M.C., AUS, 1945-47. Recipient award for pub. service Altrusa Club, 1963. Mem. A.C.P., A.M.A., Tex., Wichita County (pres. 1964) med. assns. Baptist. Home: 4021 Taft St Wichita Falls TX 76308 Office: 1518 10th St Wichita Falls TX 76301

REDDICK, THOMAS LEONARD, educator; b. Springfield, Mo., Apr. 29, 1938; s. Leonard L. and Josephine L. (Campbell) R.; A.B., Drury Coll., 1960; M.Ed., U. Mo., 1963; Ph.D., U. Miss., 1967; m. Donna Mae Montgomery, Apr. 20, 1962; children—Kurt Erich, Karissa Jadonna. Tchr. Central Sr. High Sch. and Med. Center for Fed. Prisoners, Springfield, Mo., 1961-65; ednl. research analyst U. Miss., University, 1965-67; spl. asst. to asso. commr. U.S. Office Edn., Washington, 1967-68; mem. faculty Tenn. Technol. U., Cookeville, 1968—, asso. prof. profl. edn. 1970—. Cons. various sch. systems, 1968—; cons. expert U.S. Office Edn., 1968-69. Mem. Am. Assn. Sch. Adminstrs., Am., Mid-South (dir.) ednl. research assns., N.E.A., Tenn. Edn. Assn., Phi Delta Kappa, Kappa Delta Pi, Phi Alpha Theta, Pi Gamma Mu, Sigma Delta Pi, Phi Kappa Phi. Episcopalian. Author: (with Edell M. Hearn) Simulated Behavioral Teaching Situations, 1971. Contbr. articles to profl. jours. Home: 1235 E 9th St Cookeville TN 38501

REDDICK, W(ALKER) HOMER, social worker; b. River Junction, Fla., Mar. 26, 1922; s. Walker H. and Lillian (Anderson) R.; B.S., Fla. State U., 1951, M.S.W., 1957; m. Anne Elizabeth Hardwick, Sept. 7, 1947; children—Walker Homer, Andy Hardwick (dec.). Chief juvenile probation officer Muscogee County Juvenile Ct., Columbus, Ga., 1952-53; sr. child welfare worker Floyd County Dept. Pub. Welfare, Rome, Ga., 1955-56; chief social worker Montgomery County Dept. Pub. Health, Montgomery, Ala., 1957-59; dir. social services Ala. Bapt. Childrens Home, Troy, 1959-64; casework supr. Youth Devel. Center, Milledgeville, Ga., 1964-71; dir. Family Counseling Center, Macon, Ga., 1972—. Mem. Ala. State Adv. Com. on Children and Youth, 1961-64. Served with AUS, 1940-43. Fellow Royal Soc. Health; mem. Nat. Assn. Social Workers, Acad. Certified Social Workers. So. Bapt. Social Service Assn. Baptist. Mason. Contbr. articles to profl. jours. Address: PO Box 21 Milledgeville GA 31061

REDETZKI, HELMUT MAX, educator, physician; b. Memel, Lithuania, Sept. 23, 1921; s. Emil and Hedwig (Preising) R.; student U. Freiburg (Germany) Sch. Medicine, 1941-43, U. Koenigsberg (Germany) Sch. Medicine, 1943-44, U. Graz (Austria) Sch. Medicine, 1944; M.D., U. Hamburg (Germany), 1948; m. Joyce Ehman, Mar. 15, 1957. Came to U.S., 1956, naturalized, 1961. Intern, U. Hamburg, 1947-48, research asso. in biochemistry, 1948-52; resident St. Georg Hosp., Hamburg, 1952-56; McLaughlin Found. postdoctoral research fellow U. Tex. Med. Br., Galveston, 1956-59, instr., 1959-60, asst. prof., 1960-61; asso. prof. La. State U. Med. Sch., New Orleans, 1961-66, prof., 1966-68; prof., head dept. pharmacology and therapeutics La. State U. Sch. Medicine, Shreveport, 1968—. Cons. in clin. pharmacology VA Hosp., Shreveport, 1969—, acting asso. chief staff for research and edn., 1970-72; vis. physician Confederate Meml. Hosp., Shreveport, 1968—. Recipient Deneke medal City of Hamburg, 1955. NIH grantee in cancer research and alcoholism, 1960-69. Fellow A.C.P.; mem. Am. Soc. Pharmacology and Exptl. Therapeutics, Soc. Exptl. Biology and Medicine, Am. Heart Assn., La. Med. Soc., Am. Soc. Clin. Pharmacology and Therapeutics, Am. Acad. Clin. Toxicology (chmn. alcohol studies com. 1971), Sigma Xi. Contbr. articles to med. jours. U.S. and abroad. Home: 643 Monrovia St Shreveport LA 71106 Office: PO Box 3932 Shreveport LA 71130

REDFERN, JOHN JOSEPH, III, petroleum co. exec.; b. Oklahoma City, Jan. 9, 1939; s. John Joseph, Jr. and Rosalind (Kapps) R.; B.A. in Math., U. Tex., 1961, M.B.A., 1964; m. Doris Jean Purcell, Jan. 25, 1963; children—Mary Randall, John Joseph IV. Financial analyst Redfern Devel. Corp., Midland, Tex., 1964; security analyst trust dept. investment sect. Ft. Worth Nat. Bank, 1964-66; sec., treas., dir. Flag-Redfern Oil Co., Midland, 1966—; sec., dir. Pennant-Puma Oils, Ltd., 1973—. Mem. Houston Soc. Financial Analysts, Phi Gamma Delta. Home: 2506 Sinclair St Midland TX 79701 Office: PO Box 23 410 Wall Towers West Bldg Midland TX 79701

REDIKER, JOHN MICHAEL, lawyer; b. N.Y.C., Feb. 20, 1942; s. Norris and Lorol Roden (Bowron) R.; A.B. magna cum laude, Princeton, 1964; J.D., Harvard, 1967; m. Susan Elizabeth Walter, Oct. 11, 1969. Admitted to Ala. bar, 1967; asso., Cabaniss, Johnston, Gardner & Clark, attys. at law, 1967-69; partner, Ritchie & Rediker, attys. at law, Birmingham, Ala., 1970—; sec., dir. Dixon Powdermaker Furniture Co., Jacksonville, Fla., 1967—; dir. Rucker Industries, Inc. Lectr. Law U. Ala. Law Sch., 1969—. Bd. dirs. Birmingham Jr. C. of C. Found., Positive Maturity, Inc., Community Service Council, Central Ala. chpt. Nat. Multiple Sclerosis Soc.

Served with AUS, 1963. Mem. Am., Birmingham bar assns., Ala. State Bar, Birmingham Jr. C. of C. (dir. 1967-69). Clubs: Mountain Brook, Downtown (Birmingham); Princeton (N.Y.C.). Home: 3400 N Woodridge Rd Birmingham AL 35223 Office: First National-Southern Natural Bldg Birmingham AL 35203

REDMAN, JAMES LUTHER, lawyer, state legislator; b. Plant City, Fla., Jan. 19, 1932; s. James William and Madeline (Miller) R.; B.S.B., U. Fla., 1953, LL.B., 1958; m. Ruby Jean Barker, Aug. 9, 1957; children—Susan, Pamela, Jeanne. Admitted to Fla. bar, 1958, since practiced in Plant City; partner Trinkle, Trinkle & Redman, 1960-63, Trinkle, Redman, Clawson & Peavyhouse, 1965-73, Trinkle, Redman, Clawson, Alley & Swanson, 1974—; asso. city judge Plant City, 1960-65; mem. Fla. Ho. of Reps., 1966—. Mem. Hillsborough County Democratic Exec. Com., 1962-66; mem., sec. Hillsborough County Fair, 1965; active United Fund. Chmn. bd. dirs. S. Fla. Bapt. Hosp. Served with USAAF, 1954-55. Mem. Am., Hillsborough County bar assns., Plant City C. of C. Baptist. Home: Keen Rd Plant City FL 33566 Office: 306 W Reynolds St Plant City FL 33566

REDMAN, MANVILLE, lawyer; b. Oklahoma City, Aug. 17, 1925; s. Manville R. and Minnie (Lasby) R.; B.A., U. Okla., 1947, LL.B., 1949; m. Deanna K. Porter, Dec. 25, 1962; children—Tamara J., Sharon M., John N., Jennifer K. Admitted to Okla. bar, 1949; practiced in Lawton, 1950, 57—; asst. county atty. Comanche County, 1951-53, county atty., 1953-57; partner Newcombe, Redman & Doolin, 1963—. Mem. Okla. Ho. of Reps., 1960-62. Pres. Lawton Camp Fire Girls; chmn. adv. bd. Salvation Army, 1960. Served with AUS, 1943-47; col. Res. Named Outstanding Young Man of Lawton, 1955. Mem. Okla., Comanche County bar assns., Lawton Jr. C. of C. (pres. 1954), Phi Alpha Delta, Phi Gamma Delta. Methodist. Kiwanian (pres. 1958). Home: 325 N 35th St Lawton OK 73501 Office: Security Bank Bldg Lawton OK 73501

REDMOND, JOHN, JR., environmental engr.; b. Grove Hill, Ala., Nov. 7, 1918; s. John and Sibyl (Calhoun) R.; B.C.E., Ala. Poly. Inst., 1940; M.P.H., U. Minn., 1950; grad. U.S. Army Command and Gen. Staff Coll., 1958; m. Sara Lee Davis, June 7, 1941; children—John III, Dianna (Mrs. Andrew Poynter). San. engr. Ala. Health Dept., 1940-42; commd. 2d lt. Med. Service Corps, U.S. Army, 1943, advanced through grades to col., 1966; assigned hdqrs. 7th Army, 1958-61, hdqrs. 6th Army, 1961-66; chief environmental engring. Office Surgeon Gen., Dept. Army, also asst. chief Med. Service Corps, 1966-70; chmn. environmental pollution control com. Def. Dept., 1969-70; ret., 1970; profl. asso. Nat. Acad. Scis., Washington, 1970—. Decorated Army Commendation medal, Joint Service Commendation medal, Legion Merit. Diplomate Am. Acad. Environmental Engring. Fellow Am. Soc. C.E., Fed. Water Quality Assn., Royal Soc. Health; mem. Am. Water Works Assn., N.Y. Acad. Scis., Nat. Soc. Profl. Engrs., Air Pollution Control Assn., Soc. Am. Mil. Engrs., Conf. Fed. Environmental Engrs., Chi Epsilon. Home: 6202 Nethercombe Ct McLean VA 22101 Office: Nat Acad Scis 2101 Constitution Av Washington DC 20418

REDMOND, JOHN LYNN, geologist; b. Maple Creek, Sask., Can., Sept. 19, 1930; s. Henry Lynn and Adeline Henrietta (Woodin) R.; B.S. in Geology, U. Tulsa, 1953; M.S. in Geology, Stanford, 1962; Ph.D., U. Ore., 1966; m. Mary Katherine Concannon, Sept. 15, 1962; children—Michael John, Marc James. Geologist, Ohio Oil Co., Casper, Calgary, Bismarck, Dawson City, 1953-56, 58-60, Oasis Oil Co., Libya, 1956-58; instr. geology U. Ore., Eugene, 1965; geologist McCreary-Koretsky, engrs., San Francisco, 1961-62, Tex. Petroleum Co., Bogota, Colombia, 1966-72; sr. staff geologist Texaco Inc., Miami, Fla., 1972—. Recipient Tulsa Geol. Soc. award, 1953. Fellow Geol. Soc. Am.; mem. Am., Canadian socs. petroleum geologists, Miami Geol. Soc. Mem. Christian Ch. Club: Canadian of Colombia (pres. 1970). Editor: Colombian Geol. Soc. Guidebook, 1969. Office: Box 3300 Coral Gables FL 33134

REE, WILLIAM OSCAR, govt. ofcl.; b. South Milwaukee, Wis., Mar. 13, 1913; s. Magnus and Theresa Josephine (Larson) R.; B.S. in Civil Engring., U. Wis., 1935; postgrad. Okla. State U., 1955-57; m. Mary Elizabeth James, Jan. 24, 1948; 1 son, William Oscar. With U.S. Dept. Agr., 1935—, draftsman Soil Conservation Service, La Crosse, Wis., 1935-37, hydraulic engr., Spartanburg, S.C., 1937-41, research leader Agrl. Research Service, Stillwater, Okla., 1941—. Served with USNR, 1942-46. Registered profl. engr., Okla. Mem. Am. Soc. C.E., Am. Soc. Agrl. Engrs., Am. Geophys. Union, Internat. Assn. for Hydraulic Research, Soil Conservation Soc. Am. Toastmaster. Home: Box 96 Stillwater OK 74074 Office: Box 551 Stillwater OK 74074

REECE, CLAUDE JEFFERSON, JR., cons. engr.; b. Waynesville, N.C., Mar. 20, 1936; s. Claude Jefferson and Nora (Massie) R.; A.S., Oak Ridge Mil. Inst., 1955; B.S.E.E., Clemson U., 1957; m. Judith Mary Wasgatt, May 14, 1960; children—Caroline Judith, Charles Jefferson. Elec. engr. Champion Papers, Canton, N.C., 1957-58, Champion Internat., 1960-72, now cons.; prin. Jeff Reece Engrs., Waynesville, 1967-73; pres. successor firm Reece, Noland & McElrath, Inc., 1973—. Chmn. Waynesville Townlift Commn. Mem. exec. com. Waynesville Dist. Mission Soc. Served to capt. USAF, 1958-60. Registered profl. engr., N.C., Ga., Fla. Mem. I.E.E.E. (past chmn. Western N.C. sect. 1964-65, sr. mem.), Nat. Soc. Profl. Engrs., N.C. Soc. Engrs. (pres. Western chpt., state bd. govs.), Profl. Engrs. in Pvt. Practice, Instrument Soc. Am. (sr. mem.), Illuminating Engring., Haywood County Elec. League (sec.), Soc. Methodist (trustee, lay reader chmn. bd., vice chmn. dist. council ministries). Mason (Shriner), Rotarian. Clubs: Asheville Downtown City, Mountain Valley Golf (pres., dir. past sec.-treas). Home: 204 Grimball Dr Hazelwood NC 28738 Office: Box 540 Waynesville NC 28786

REECE, ERROL KEMP, securities co. exec.; b. Jonesville, N.C., Sept. 12, 1922; s. John Edgar and Clyde (Holcomb) R.; B.S., Wake Forest U., 1943; m. Mildred Frances Hayworth, May 8, 1953; children—Anne Clyde, Errol Kemp. Vice pres., resident mgr. Interstate Securities Corp., Greensboro, N.C., 1964—. Vice pres. Y Mens Club, 1947-48; Hi Y adviser, 1948-49; scoutmaster Boy Scouts Am.; mem. N.C. Civil War Round Table, 1963—; pres. Greensboro Sports Council. Vice pres. bd. dirs. Jr. C. of C.; bd. dirs. Guilford County Tb. Assn. Served with USNR, 1943-46. Recipient Internat. Sales Producers award, 1954. Mem. Investment Bankers Assn., Nat. Securities Traders Assn., Newcomen Soc., Am. Legion (past adj.). Methodist. Mason (32 deg., Shriner), Kiwanian (pres.). Clubs: Greensboro Country, Cedarbrook Country, Red Shield Boys (dir.), Guilford Wildlife (dir.); Wake Forest U. Deacon (pres.). Home: 1816 St Andrews Rd Greensboro NC 27408 Office: 119 N Elm St Greensboro NC 27401

REECE, JOE WILSON, educator; b. Elin, N.C., Mar. 1, 1935; s. Thad Marshall and Anita (Hobson) R.; B.Nuclear Engring., N.C. State U., 1957, M.S., 1961; Ph.D., U. Fla., 1963; m. Nancy Lee Fletcher, Aug. 25, 1955; children—James Thad, Joel Wade. Instr. engring. mechanics N.C. State U. at Raleigh, 1958-61; asst. prof. mech. engring. Auburn (Ala.) U., 1963-67, asso. prof., 1967—. Cons. E.I. DuPont de Nemours, Inc., Wilmington, Del., 1965-72; cons. Combustion Engring., Inc., Chattanooga, 1972—, U.S. Army Missile Command, 1972—. Campus Drive chmn. Auburn United Fund, 1969, chmn. bd., 1971. Named Distinguished Classroom Tchr. N.C. State U. Sch. Engring., 1961; named Outstanding Faculty Member Auburn U. Sch. Engring., 1965, 73. Registered profl. engr., Ala. Mem. Am. Soc. Engring. Edn. (chmn. mechanics div. S.E. sect. 1972, v.p., also program chmn. S.E. sect. 1973), Auburn Civitan Club (v.p. 1967, pres. 1968), Ala. Acad. Sci., Scabbard and Blade, Sigma Xi, Phi Kappa Phi, Tau Beta Pi, Phi Eta Sigma, Sigma Pi Sigma, Theta Tau, Pi Tau Sigma. Methodist (lay leader 1967, chmn. trustees ch. 1972). Clubs: Dixie Sailing (Montgomery, Ala.), Saugahatchee Country (Auburn). Home: 242 Conrey Dr Auburn AL 36830

REECE, MONROE FRANKLIN, govt. ofcl.; b. Carnegie, Okla., Aug. 27, 1926; s. M. F. and Lucile (Kimbrough) R.; B.S., Okla. State U., 1949; M.S., Okla. U., 1966; m. Jan Harman, Aug. 2, 1952; children—Karen, Nancy. Sanitarian Payne County (Okla.) Health Dept., Stillwater, 1949-54; milk control supr. Tulsa City-County Health Dept., 1954-63, chief environmental health div., 1963-72, asst. dir., 1972. Mem. Okla. Bd. Registration for Profl. Sanitarians. Served with AUS, 1946-47. Mem. Internat. Assn. Milk and Food Sanitarians, Nat. Assn. Sanitarians, Am. Pub. Health Assn. Lion. Home: 5628 S 77th E Av Tulsa OK 74145 Office: 4616 E 15th St Tulsa OK 74112

REED, CARL EUGENE, ednl. adminstr.; b. Amity, Me., Feb. 28, 1913; s. Hubert John and Nellie (Vail) R.; B.S., Ricker Classical Inst., Colby Coll., 1935; M.Ed., Boston U., 1951; Ed.D., U. Houston, 1955; m. Eleanor Eldora Shaw, July 9, 1934; children—Terence John, Sandra Darling. Prin., Somerset Acad., Athens, Me., 1935-38, Island Falls (Me.) High Sch., 1938-41; tchr. Bangor (Me.) High Sch., 1941-43; tchr. sci. Winchester (Mass.) High Sch., 1946-51; princ. Kinkaid (Tex.) High Sch., 1951-64; headmaster Bolles Sch., Jacksonville, Fla., 1964—. Served with AUS, 1943-46; lt. col. Res. Mem. Fla. Council Ind. Schs. (pres. 1971—), Jacksonville C. of C. (com. of 100, 1968—), Phi Delta Kappa. Republican. Conglist. Rotarian. Clubs: St. Johns Dinner, University (Jacksonville). Editor: Disaster Control, 1962-63. Home: 7378 San Jose Blvd Jacksonville FL 32217 Office: 7400 San Jose Blvd Jacksonville FL 32217

REED, CHESTER RAY, archtl. engr.; b. Ponca City, Okla., Jan. 30, 1931; s. Paul Emery and Eva Cecelia (Eaton) R.; Asso. Sci., No. Okla. Jr. Coll., 1951; B.Archtl. Engring., Okla. State U., 1954; m. Ethel Cylvesta Adams, Mar. 15, 1957; children—Thomas Paul, Clayborn Ray. Engr.-in-tng. Roof Structures, Inc., St. Louis, 1954-55; engr.-in-tng. to profl. engr. Mullen & Powell Cons. Structural Engrs., Dallas, 1955-60; prin. C.R. Reed, structural engr., Dallas, 1960-69; pres. Chester R. Reed, Inc., 1969—. Pres. Probe Test Systems, Inc., Dallas, 1970—. Cons. structural engring. Pres. United Fund, Heart Fund. Registered profl. engr., Tex., Okla. Mem. Tex. Soc. Profl. Engrs., Am. Concrete Inst., Nat. Fedn. Independence Bus., Dallas, North Dallas chambers commerce, Sigma Tau, Chi Epsilon, Phi Kappa Phi. Mem. Christian Ch. (deacon 1957—). Club: Royal Oaks Country. Principal works: Dallas Cowboy Football Stadium roof, Irving, Tex., 1971, 4th Nat. Bank Bldg., Tulsa, 1971, Preston Tower Apts., Dallas, 1963, others. Home: 4501 Arcady Av Dallas TX 75205 Office: 3511 Cedar Springs Rd Dallas TX 75219

REED, DANIEL JOHN, govt. ofcl.; b. Springfield, Ill., July 19, 1922; s. John Patrick and Laurine Anne (Burger) R.; B.S., St. Louis U., 1947, M.A., 1948; Ph.D., U. Chgo., 1958; m. Helen M. DeMars, May 15, 1945; six children. Instr., St. Louis U., 1947-49; instr. U. Detroit, 1950-53, dir. libraries, 1953-59; asst. chief manuscript div. Library of Congress, Washington, 1959-65; historian Nat. Portrait Gallery, 1965-68; asso. dir. Nat. Adv. Commn. on Libraries, 1967; asst. archivist for presdl. libraries Nat Archives, GSA, 1968—. Mem. adv. bd. Archives Am. Art, 1967-73, Am. History and Life, 1970—. Served with USCGR, 1942-45. Mem. Am. Hist. Assn., Am. Assn. for State and Local History (mem. council, sec. 1972—), Soc. Am. Archivists, Orgn. Am. Historians. Author: Portraits of Presidents, 1968. Home: 130 N Jackson St Arlington VA 22201 Office: Office Presidential Libraries Room 104 Nat Archives Bldg Washington DC 20408

REED, DAVID BENSON, bishop; b. Tulsa, Feb. 16, 1927; s. Paul Spencer and Bonnie Francis (Taylor) R.; B.A., Harvard, 1948; M.Div., Va. Theol. Sem., 1951, D.D. (hon.), 1964; D.D. (hon.), U. of South; m. Susan Riggs, Oct. 30, 1954; children—Mary, Jennifer, Sarah, Katherine. Ordained priest Episcopal Ch.; missionary priest, Colombia, 1951-58; asst. to dir. overseas dept. Nat. Council Episcopal Ch., 1958-61; vicar St. Matthews Ch., Rapid City, S.D., 1961-63; consecrated bishop; bishop of Colombia, 1964-72, of Equador, 1964-70; bishop coadjutor Diocese of Ky., 1972-73; bishop of Ky., 1974—. Pres. Anglican Council Latin Am., 1969-71. Trustee U. of South, 1971-74; bd. dirs. Louisville Children's Hosp. Served with USNR, 1945-46. Home: 320 Blankenbaker Lane Louisville KY 40207 Office: 2 421 S 2d St Louisville KY 40202

REED, ERBIE LOYD, dentist; b. Chesterfield, Tenn., Oct. 11, 1920; s. Erbie Lester and Mary Velt (Blankenship) R.; student Memphis State U., 1946; D.D.S., U. Tenn., 1949; m. Marcille Duke, Dec. 12, 1942; children—Linda Faye (Mrs. Frank McCalla), Mark Loyd, Kevin Duke. Mgr., Reed's Saw Mill, 1936-41; farmer, Chesterfield, 1936-41; postmaster, Chesterfield, 1941-42; owner, operator Reed's Grocery & Gen. Store, Chesterfield, 1941-42; pvt. practice dentistry, Millington, Tenn., 1949—. Mem. Millington Recreation Com., 1950-56; mem. Millington Housing Authority, 1960-68; sec. Millington Biracial Com., 1967—; sec. Millington Bd. Zoning Appeals, 1953—. Bd. dirs. Millington Community Fund, 1970—. Served with USNR, 1942-45. Mem. Pierre Fauchard Dental Acad., Am., Tenn. dental assns., Memphis Dental Soc., Millington C. of C. (pres. 1970-71). Baptist (treas. 1951—). Lion, Rotarian. Home: 4890 2d Av Millington TN 38053 Office: 4770 Easley St Millington TN 38053

REED, FORREST FRANCIS, book co. exec.; b. Fulton, Miss., Sept. 11, 1897; s. Charles Nathaniel and Alma (Gregory) R.; LL.B., Andrew Jackson U., 1940; m. Katherine Mueller, Dec. 17, 1925; children—John Martin, Martha (Mrs. M. Thomas Collins, Jr.). Mgr., Ark. Book Co., 1930-35; organizer, pres. Tenn. Book Co., Nashville, 1935-65; owner Reed & Co., pubs., Nashville, 1965—. Pres. Tenn. Conv. Christian Chs., 1957. Bd. dirs. Coll. of Bible, 1954-60, Disciples of Christ, Hist. Soc., 1952—, chmn. bd., 1962-66, endowed the soc.'s Forrest F. Reed Lectures, 1965. Mem. Am. Booksellers Assn., Tenn. Edn. Assn., A.L.A., Tenn. Hist. Soc., U.S. C. of C., S.A.R., Tenn. Businessmen's Assn. (pres. 1961). Club: Civitan (local pres. 1951). Home: 732 Myhr Dr Nashville TN 37221 Office: Wilson-Bates Bldg Nashville TN 37215

REED, GEORGE JOSEPH, govt. ofcl.; b. Haigler, Neb., May 31, 1914; s. Edwin W. and Cleo (Randall) R.; A.B., Pasadena Coll., 1938, LL.D., 1953 Eastern Nazarene Coll., 1957; postgrad. U. So. Cal., 1948; m. Lois C. Goetze, Oct. 10, 1938; 1 son, George C. Probation officer Los Angeles County (Cal.), 1938-43; field rep. Cal. Youth Authority, Sacramento, 1946-49; dep. dir. Minn. Youth Correction Dept., 1948-53, chief div. delinquency prevention and parole, 1949-53; mem. U.S. Bd. Parole, 1953-65, chmn. bd., 1957-61; chief Parole and Probation of Nev., Carson City, 1965-67; dir. Lane County Juvenile Dept., Eugene, Ore., 1968-69; chmn. U.S. Bd. Parole, Washington, 1969—. Adminstr. Interstate Compact Nev., 1965-67; mem. Commn. Model Code for Administering State Correctional System, 1966—. Served with USNR, 1942-46. Fellow Am. Soc. Criminology, Am. Acad. Criminology; mem. Nat. Parole Council (chmn. 1960-64), Nat. Council Crime and Delinquency (trustee, mem. profl. council 1950—), Am. Congress Corrections, Am. Law Inst. (mem. model criminal code com. 1958—). Club: Nat. Exchange (com. chmn. 1959—). Contbr. chpts. to textbooks, articles to profl. publs. Home: 4201 Cathedral Av NW Washington DC 20016 Office: 101 Indiana Av NW Washington DC 20001

REED, GUY DEAN, osteo. physician; b. Kirksville, Mo., Nov. 4, 1922; s. Arthur Guy and Lena (Murphy) R.; student Wentworth Mil. Acad., 1939-41, Tulane U., 1942-43, Okla. State U., 1941-42, 45-46; D.O., Kansas City Coll. of Osteopathy and Surgery, 1949; m. Elizabeth Marguerite Matheson, Oct. 20, 1957. Intern Okla. Osteo. Hosp., Tulsa, 1949-50; practice osteo. medicine specializing in surgery, New Lexington O., 1950-55, Newark, O., 1955-57, Tulsa, 1957—, Owasso, Okla., 1958—; mem. staff Okla. Osteo. Hosp. Pres., chmn. bd. Owasso Devel. Corp., Sheridan Village Med. Clinic, Tulsa, Willow Dale Mobile Home addition, Owasso, Owasso Coin Op Car Wash, Utotem Grocery Store, Broken Arrow, Okla., Rally Dodge Co., Tulsa, Mingo Valley Shopping Center, Inc., Owasso; chmn. bd. Clover Leaf Shopping Center, Inc., Tulsa, Rally Chrysler-Plymouth, Muskogee, Okla. Served with M.C., AUS, 1942-45. Decorated Silver Star medal, Bronze Star medal with oak leaf cluster, Purple Heart. Mem. Am. Coll. Gen. Practitioners in Osteopathy and Surgery, Am., Okla., Ohio, Tulsa Dist. osteo. assns., Tulsa, Owasso (pres. 1959-60) chambers commerce. Mason, Lion. Home: 6775 S Atlanta Av Tulsa OK 74136 Office: 6109 E Admiral Pl Tulsa OK 74115

REED, JOHN KENNETH, entomologist, educator; b. Cadiz, O., Oct. 13, 1915; s. Harry C. and Sarah E. (Smiley) R.; B.S., Ohio U., 1942; M.S., Ia. State U., 1947, Ph.D., 1954; m. Mary V. Heldman, Feb. 26, 1946; children—Ruth Elizabeth, Carol Ann. Asso. prof. entomology and zoology Clemson (S.C.) U., 1950-59, prof., 1959-71; prof. biology, head dept. The Citadel, Charleston, S.C., 1971—. Served with AUS, 1942-46. Mem. A.A.A.S., Entomol. Soc. Am., S.C. Acad. Sci. Address: The Citadel Charleston SC 29409

REED, LAWRENCE FRANKLIN, diversified industry exec.; b. Toledo, June 17, 1908; s. Edward and Mae (Carpenter) R.; student U. Toledo, 1926-29; M.B.A., U. Mich., 1931; m. Geraldine Mary Lightfoot, Mar. 30, 1926; children—Lauren Edward, Gerald Lee. Asst. gen. mdse. mgr. Lamson's Dept. Store, Toledo, 1931-42; price exec. OPA, Toledo, 1942-45, OPS, 1950-52; gen. mdse. mgr. Owens Ill., Inc., Toledo, 1950-59, mgr. corporate marketing, 1960-72, marketing cons., 1972—. Asso. prof. marketing U. Toledo, 1946-50; marketing and research cons. Toledo C. of C., 1946-50. Mem. Am. Marketing Assn. (chpt. pres. 1949-50, chpt. dir. 1950-52), Alpha Kappa Psi, Phi Kappa Psi. Mason (32 deg., Shriner), Elk. Address: 75 Hickory Lane Imperial Terrace Tavares FL 32778

REED, MURRAY O., judge; b. Fulton, Miss., Jan. 27, 1899; s. Charles Nathaniel and Alma (Gregory) R.; student Ark. Law Sch.; m. Ellen Vineyard, Apr. 23, 1922; 1 dau., Meralen (Mrs. David A. Ruffin). Admitted to Ark. bar, 1920, practiced in Little Rock, 1921-56; mem. Ark. Ho. of Reps., 1930-32; dep. pros. atty. 6th jud. dist., 1934, 42, 46; asst. bank commr. Ark., 1937-41; chancery judge 2d Div., 1st Chancery Dist. Ark., 1948-49; gen. counsel Ark. Hwy Commn., 1949-52; municipal judge City of Little Rock, 1955-56; judge Chancery Ct. 1st Div., 1st Chancery Circuit Ark., 1957—. Pres., Jud. Council Ark., 1969-70. Pres. Little Rock Bd. Edn., 1940-41. Mem. Am., Ark., Pulaski County bar assns., Am. Judicature Soc. Democrat. Mem. Christian Ch. Kiwanian. Home: 4920 Lakeview Rd North Little Rock AR 72116 Office: Office Court House Little Rock AR 72201

REED, O.M., dentist; b. Belfield, N.D., Nov. 17, 1920; s. George Allison and Edna Reid (Kane) R.; B.A., U. Cal., Berkeley, 1943; D.D.S., U. Cal., San Francisco, 1949; m. Evelyn Campbell, June 25, 1945; 1 son, Mark Allison. Practice dentistry, San Antonio, 1950—; dental research asso. S.W. Found. for Research and Edn., San Antonio, 1962—; cons. Migrant Workers Dental Health Edn., 1969. Served to 1st lt. USAAF, 1942-45. Decorated Air Medal with 5 oak leaf clusters, D.F.C. Nat. Inst. Dental Research grantee, 1965-74. Fellow Am. Coll. Dentists; mem. Am. Assn. Anatomists, Internat. Assn. Dental Research, Am., Tex., San Antonio Dist. (pres.) dental assns., Psi Omega. Contbr. articles profl. jours. Home: 302 Cardinal St San Antonio TX 78209 Office: 1017 Shook Av San Antonio TX 78212

REED, PHILIP LANIER, elec. products co. exec., elec. engr.; b. Montgomery, W.Va., Apr. 8, 1941; s. Archie Lanier and Pauline Pearl (Meador) R.; B.S. in Elec. Engring., Va. Poly. Inst., 1964; m. Janice Lee Ellison, June 15, 1963; 1 son, Richard Lee. Materials engr. poly sci. div. Lytton Systems, Inc., 1964-66, design engr., 1967-69, devel. engr., 1969-70, sales mgr. internat. accounts, 1970—. Mem. I.E.E.E., Blacksburg Jr. C. of C. (external v.p. 1966-67, internal v.p. 1971-72). Presbyn. (deacon 1972—, treas. 1973—). Office: 1213 N Main St Blacksburg VA 24060

REED, RICHARD JAY, physician; b. Gilmer, Tex., June 23, 1928; s. Earnest Wayne and Laura Leone (Childress) R.; student U. Tex., 1945-48; M.D., Tulane U., 1952; m. Peggy Jane Bivins, Nov. 21, 1953; children—Lauralee, Richard Jay, James Robert. Intern, Parkland Hosp., Dallas, 1952-53; fellow dept. pathology Tulane U. Sch. Medicine, 1957-60; practice medicine, specializing in pathology, 1961—; pathologist Warren Med. Research Found. Tulsa, 1970-71; faculty dept. pathology Tulane U. Sch. Medicine, New Orleans, 1957-70, prof. pathology, 1970—; mem. staff Charity Hosp., New Orleans; cons. USPHS Hosp., New Orleans, Ochsner Found. Hosp., New Orleans. Served with USAF, 1955-57. Diplomate Am. Bd. Pathology. Mem. Am. Soc. Clin. Pathologists (mem. council on anatomic pathology, and com. on continuing edn. 1970—). Home: 12 Versailles St New Orleans LA 70125 Office: 1430 Tulane Av New Orleans LA 70112

REED, ROBERT WENDELL, elec. engr.; b. Caroleen, N.C., Sept. 10, 1925; s. Martin Robert and Viola Mae (McDaniel) R.; B.E.E., N.C. State U., 1951; m. Montrose Katherine Beam, Dec. 23, 1948; children—Robert Russell, Allyson Wendella. With So. Bell Telephone Co., Charlotte, N.C., 1946-48, 51—, jr. engr., 1951-55, engr., 1955-66, project engr., 1966-68, supervising engr., 1968-72, equipment engr., 1972—; on loan Western Electric Co. to assist Def. Communications Agy., S. Vietnam, 1966-67. Served with USNR, 1943-45. Registered profl. engr., N.C. Licensee amateur radio, radiotelephone. Home: 426 Boyce Rd Charlotte NC 28211 Office: PO Box 240 Charlotte NC 28201

REED, STANLEY FOSTER, editor and pub.; b. Bogota, N.J., Sept. 28, 1917; s. Morton H. and Beryl (Turner) R.; student George Washington U., 1939-40, Johns Hopkins, 1940-41; m. Stella Swingle, Sept. 28, 1940; children—Nancie, Beryl Ann, Alexandra. With Bethlehem Steel Corp., Balt., 1940-41; cons. engr., 1942-44; founder, pres. Reed Research, Inc., Washington, 1945-62; pres. Reed Research Inst. Creative Studies, Washington, 1951—; founder, chmn. LogEtronics, Inc., Washington, 1955; founder, pres. Tech. Audit Corp., Washington, 1962; editor, pub. Mergers & Acquisitions, The Jour. Corp. Venture, 1965; dir. Internat. Travel Advisors, Inc., T-K

Internat., Inc., Hayden Pub. Co.; lectr. Union Theol. Sem., Prescott Coll., George Washington U., U. Pa., Pa. State U., U. Colo., Am. U., Claremont Coll., Cambridge Inst., Japan. Registered profl. engr., D.C. Mem. Soc. Naval Architects and Marine Engrs., I.E.E.E., Am. Econ. Assn., Soc. Internat. Devel., Aspen Inst. Humanistic Studies (vice chmn. Aspen East). Clubs: N.Y. Yacht; International. Contbr. articles to jours. and mags. in books. Patentee in field. Home: 1621 Brookside Rd McLean VA 22101 Office: Box 36 McLean VA 22101

REED, THOMAS BEAVERS, JR., banker; b. Iaeger, W.Va., Apr. 5, 1918; s. Thomas Beavers and Lexye Linda (Clifton) R.; student LaSalle Extension U., 1936-39; m. Grace E. Gullatt, June 1, 1940 (dec.); children—Linda (Mrs. John R. McNally), Dianne (Mrs. Neil V. Spillane), Vikki (Mrs. Robert K. Hayden), Thomas Beavers III, David; m. 2d, Carmen Kellam. Asst. treas. Comml. Credit Corp., Charleston, W.Va., 1939-44, Macon, Ga., 1945-53; mgr. finance Gen. Acceptance Corp., Atlanta, 1953-55; sr. v.p. Pan Am. Bank, Miami, Fla., 1954-59; v.p. Walter Heller Co., Chgo., 1959-60, also asst. to pres.; sr. v.p. Union Trust Nat. Bank, St. Petersburg, Fla., 1960—. Tchr. consumer lending Am. Inst. Banking, 1955-58, mem. com. Boy Scouts Am., 1960—; v.p. No. Fla. Eye Bank, 1970-71, pres. 1971-72. Bd. dirs. Fla. Lions Found. for Blind. Served with AUS, 1945. Mem. C. of C. (gov.), Consumer Bankers Assn. (bd. govs.), Am. Bankers Assn. (mem. adv. bd.), Fla. Bankers Assn. (chmn. credit div. 1970-71; chmn. installment credit com. 1969-70), Group IV Installment Bankers Assn., Am. Legion, 40 and 8. Lion (dist. gov. 1969-70, pres. 1965-66; chmn. council govs. Fla. 1969-70; chmn. adv. council Bur. for Blind Services 1971-72), Mason. Clubs: Commerce, Lake Seminole Country (St. Petersburg). Address: 2349 Woodlawn Circle E St Petersburg FL 33704 Office: Central Av at 9th St St Petersburg FL 33701

REED, TRUMAN PERKINS, JR., educator, performing arts dir.; b. Oil City, Pa., Oct. 7, 1938; s. Truman Perkins and Isabelle (Robinson) R.; grad. Deerfield Acad., 1957; B.S. with honors, Columbia Coll., 1961; M.A., Penn. State U., 1963; 1 dau., Heather. Theatre tech. dir. Penn. State U., 1963-69; prodn. dir. Pensacola Jr. Coll., Fla., 1969—, also theatrical set designer. Dir. Cold Turkey Drug Edn. program, Escambia and Santa Rosa counties, Fla., 1971. Mem. Am. Theatre Assn., Speech Communication Assn., Internat. Alliance Theatrical Stage Employees. Episcopalian. Author: Anne Frank: A Child Gone By, 1973. Home: 4130 Kingsberry Dr Pensacola FL 32504 Office: 1000 College Blvd Pensacola FL 32504

REEDER, HAROLD LEE, social worker; b. Asheboro, N.C., Aug. 15, 1940; s. James Walter and Mozelle (Williams) R.; B.A., High Point Coll., 1961; M.S.W., U. N.C., 1965; m. Linda Louise Hartley, June 20, 1965. Caseworker, Rowan County Dept. Social Services, Salisbury, N.C., 1961-63; social work supr. Mecklenburg County Dept. Social Services, Charlotte, N.C., 1965-71; chief social worker Randolph Clinic, Charlotte, 1971-73; pvt. practice family therapy, 1973—. Mem. Charlotte Police Community Council, 1967-69; mem. steering com. Big Bros. Orgn. of Charlotte, 1970-71. Bd. dirs. Alexander Children's Center, 1970-73. Mem. Nat. Assn. Social Workers (rec. sec. 1967-69), N.C. Social Service Assn. (vice chmn. chpt. 1970-71). Home: 709 Shopton Ct Fayetteville NC 28303 Office: 509 Owen Dr Fayetteville NC 28304

REEDER, JAMES ARTHUR, lawyer; b. Baton Rouge, June 29, 1933; s. James Brown and Grace (Britt) R.; B.A., Washington and Lee U., 1955; postgrad. So. Meth. U., 1957-58; LL.B., U. Tex., 1960, La. State U., 1961; m. Leone Guthrie, Dec. 30, 1958; children—Mary Virginia, James Arthur, Elizabeth Colby. Admitted to La. bar, 1961, since practiced in Shreveport; asso. firm Pugh & Schober, 1961, Booth, Lockard, Jack, Pleasant & LeSage, 1961-64, partner, 1964-73; mng. partner, gen. counsel KOKA Broadcasting Co., 1973—. Participant Nat. Security Forum, Air War Coll., 1971. Active United Fund, Boy Scouts Am.; bd. dirs. Goodwill Industries, pres., 1972; pres. Holiday-in-Dixie, 1969. Served with AUS, 1955-57. Named Shreveport's Outstanding Young Man of Year, 1968; La. Outstanding Young Man of Year, 1968; La. Outstanding Young Lawyer of Year, La. Bar Assn., 1969. Mem. Am. (exec. council young lawyers sect. 1965-66, dir. young lawyers), La., Shreveport bar assns., State Bar Tex., La. State Jr. Bar (chmn. 1965-66), So. Meth. U. Alumni Assn. (past pres. Shreveport). Roman Catholic. Home: 419 Janie Lane Shreveport LA 71106 Office: PO Box 1550 Shreveport LA 71120

REES, PHILIP ADRIAN, librarian; b. Manitowoc, Wis., Oct. 19, 1931; s. Thomas Hugh and Winifred Agnes (Flatman) R.; B.A., Denison U., 1954; M.S. in L.S., Case Western Res. U., 1955; m. Margaret Louise Stamm, May 23, 1970. Reference librarian Union Coll., Schenectady, 1955-58; librarian Museum of City of N.Y., N.Y.C., 1959-62; readers' services librarian Sarah Lawrence Coll., Bronxville, N.Y., 1962-68; art librarian U. N.C., Chapel Hill, 1968—. Mem. Soc. Archtl. Historians, Victorian Soc. Am., Nat. Trust for Historic Preservation. Episcopalian. Home: Box 423 Chapel Hill NC 27514 Office: Ackland Art Center U NC Chapel Hill NC 27514

REESE, ADDISON H(ARDCASTLE), banker; b. Baltimore County, Md., Dec. 28, 1908; s. Gordon Lippencott and Edith Octavia (Ford) R.; grad. Marston's U. Sch., Riderwood, Md., 1926; student John Hopkins, 1926-29; LL.D., U. N.C., 1968; m. Gertrude Craig, Apr. 22, 1936. Asst. nat. bank examiner Treasury Dept., 1932-36, nat. bank examiner, 1936-40; v.p., dir. Nicodemus Nat. Bank, Hagerstown, Md., 1941-47; pres., chmn. bd. County Trust Co. of Md., Balt., 1947-51; exec. v.p. Am. Trust Co., Charlotte, N.C., 1951-54, pres. 1954-60; pres., dir. N.C. Nat. Bank, 1960-67, chmn. bd., 1967-73, dir., chmn. finance com., 1973—; dir. Ruddick Corp., Speizman Industries. Chmn., Found. U. N.C. Bd. dirs. Mercy Hosp., N.C. Citizens Assn., N.C. Textile Found.; chmn. bd. trustees U. N.C. at Charlotte. Served from lt. to maj. USAF, 1942-45. Mem. Assn. Res. City Bankers (hon. life mem., dir., past pres.), Alpha Delta Phi. Episcopalian. Clubs: Charlotte Country, Quail Hollow Country, City (Charlotte); Sankaty Head Golf (Nantucket); Elkridge (Balt.). Home: 441 Eastover Rd Charlotte NC 28207 Office: Box 120 Charlotte NC 28201

REESE, DAVID MOSLEY, art museum ofcl.; b. Newnan, Ga., Oct. 9, 1915; s. James Joseph and Nanny Elizabeth (Kimble) R.; certificate High Mus. Sch. Art, Atlanta, 1937; student Art Students League, N.Y.C., 1938-39; certificate Fashion Acad., 1939; student Fla. State U., summer 1954; m. Elsie Jean Boyd, July 25, 1947; children—Karen (Mrs. Bill Dale), Valerie Jean, Leslie Kimble. Instr. figure drawing Fashion Acad., N.Y.C., 1939-40; dir. advt. O'Connor, Atlanta, 1945; instr. advt. design, figure drawing, painting High Mus. Sch. Art, Atlanta, 1946-53; dir. Telfair Art Sch., Savannah, Ga., 1953-58, Telfair Acad. Arts and Scis., Savannah, 1958-64; exec. dir. Loch Haven Art Center, Inc., Orlando, Fla., 1964—. Served with USAAF, 1940-45. Recipient Carnegie grant, 1951, McDowell Colony fellowship, 1960. Mem. Am. Assn. Museums, Southeastern Museums Conf., Fla. Craftsmen, Fla. Art Museum Dirs., Fla. Arts Council (dir. 1965). Home: 1540 Bonnie Burn Circle Winter Park FL 32789 Office: 2416 N Mills Av Orlando FL 32803

REESE, HOMER SCALES, city ofcl., rancher; b. Allen, Okla., Dec. 16, 1895; s. Samual P. and Henryetta (Floyd) R.; student Southeastern State Coll., Durant, Okla., 1913-17; B.A., U. Okla., 1922, M.A., 1929; m. Edna Lyday, June 19, 1920; children—Harry B., Homer C. Tchr. pub. schs., Ozark, Okla., 1920-23; high sch. prin., Mangum, Okla., 1926-33; supt. schs., Mangum, 1933-37; high sch. prin., Heavener, Okla., 1937-41, supt. schs., 1947-55; rancher, Heavener and Le Flore, Okla., 1947—; city mgr., Heavener, 1966—. Served with U.S. Army, World War I, AUS, World War II. Decorated Bronze Star, Legion of Merit (U.S.); Silver Star, Croix de Guerre (France); Cross of Czechoslovakia. Named Man of the Year Heavener, Okla., 1972. Mem. Nat., Okla. edn. assns., Okla. Sch. Adminstrs., C. of C., Res. Officers Assn. Mem. Christian Ch. Mason, Lion.

REESE, JAY SHIREMAN, physician; b. Martinsville, Ind., Apr. 28, 1937; s. Jay Dean and Frances (Shireman) R.; grad. Culver Mil. Acad., 1954; B.A., DePauw U., 1959; M.D., Ind. U., 1961; m. Laura Ann Record, Aug. 23, 1958 (div. Aug. 1972); children—Ann Elizabeth, Jacqueline Sue, Suzanne Jane. Intern, Marion County Gen. Hosp., Indpls., 1961-62; pvt. practice medicine specializing in family practice, indsl. medicine, Martinsville, 1962-68; gen. practice medicine Bond Clinic, Winter Haven, Fla., 1969-72; practice medicine Temple Terrace Profl. Assn., Tampa, Fla., 1972—; med. dir. Exec. Health Services Inc., Lakeland, Fla., 1972—; mem. staff Winter Haven Hosp., 1969-72, Univ. Community Hosp., Tampa, 1972—; chief med. staff Morgan County Meml. Hosp., Martinsville, 1967, sec. med. staff, 1963-66. Bd. dirs. Tampa Area Council on Alcoholism, Gulf Coast Multiple Sclerosis Soc. Served with M.C., USNR, 1968-69. Mem. Am., Fla., Hillsborough County, Ind. (pres. 7th dist. 1966, chmn. sect. on gen. practice 1967-68) med. assns., Am., Fla. acads. family physicians, Assn. Am. Physicians and Surgeons, Jr. Chamber Internat. (senator 1968—, charter mem. Fla. senate 1970, sec.-treas. 1973—). Club: Jaycees (Fla. internat. dir. 1971-72, Fla. adminstrv. nat. dir. 1970-71, Fla. dist. v.p. 1969, Ind. regional nat. dir. 1967-68, Ind. v.p. 1966-67, pres. Martinsville chpt. 1964-66). Lion (med. adviser Cancer Control Fund of Ind. 1965-68, 3d v.p. Temple Terrace 1973—). Address: Temple Terrace Profl Assn 5202 Busch Blvd Tampa FL 33617

REESE, JESSE TIMOTHY, JR., real estate, ins. co. exec.; b. Columbia, S.C., Jan. 16, 1913; s. Jesse Timothy and Mary Hill (Mobley) R.; B.A., The Citadel, 1934; m. Aimee Gibbes Urquhart, Oct. 14, 1936; children—Aimee (Mrs. John D. Kornegay), Judith (Mrs. John Nye), Jesse Timothy, III, Mary (Mrs. Richard N. Burnside). With Jesse T. Reese, Inc., Columbia, S.C., 1934—, pres., 1967—; dir. Palmetto Wholesale, Columbia, 1950—, Calhoun Life, Columbia, 1950—, Palmetto Metal Products, Columbia, 1953—, Consol. Ins. Co., Columbia, 1954—. Pres. Columbia Real Estate Bd., 1950-51. Chmn. Bd. Assessors, 1946-50; chmn. Election Commn., Richland County, 1950-59; mem. city council, 1968—. Served with AUS, 1941-46; ETO. Mem. Nat. Assn. Real Estate Bds., Assn. Citadel Men (life), Hugenot Soc. (life). Democrat. Episcopalian. Mason (Shriner). Clubs: Forest Lake, Spring Valley (Columbia). Home: 2803 Canterbury St Columbia SC 29204 Office: 1319 Pickens St Columbia SC 29202

REESE, JIMMY MALCOLM, savs. and loan exec., mayor; b. Columbus, Ga., July 31, 1928; s. Clyde Bowden and Ora (Webb) R.; student Auburn U., 1945-46; grad. U. N.C. Southeastern Inst. for Orgn. Execs., 1957, U. Ind. Grad. Sch. for Savs. and Loan, 1960; m. Ann Stewart, Aug. 9, 1949; children—Joseph Bowden, James Malcolm. Head teller Columbus Bank & Trust Co., 1947-53; exec. sec., treas., mng. officer, dir. Fitzgerald Fed. Savs. & Loan Assn. (Ga.), 1953-60; mng. officer, dir. Security Fed. Savs. & Loan Assn., Perry, Ga., 1960—, pres., 1962—; mayor city Perry, 1970—. Pres., dir. Ben Hill Enterprises, Inc., Fitzgerald, 1958—; dir. Houston Halls, Inc., Houston Lake Devel., Inc., Fed. Home Loan Bank Atlanta, Secura Corp., Equity Mortgage Corp. Vice pres. Central Ga. council Boy Scouts Am. Pres., dir. Perry Club Council; mem. Fitzgerald Planning and Zoning Commn., 1956-60, Perry Municipal Planning Commn., Fitzgerald, 1958-59. Named One of Ga.'s 5 Outstanding Young Men, Ga. Jr. C. of C., 1960, Outstanding Young Man, Perry Jr. C. of C., 1960. Mem. U.S. (dir.), Ga. (dir. 1956-61, pres. 1961) savs. and loan leagues, Am. Savs. and Loan Inst. (gov. 1963-64), Soc. Savs. and Loan Controllers, Perry C. of C. (pres. 1963-67-68), Soc. Real Estate Appraisers. Kiwanian, Elk. Home: 1417 Baker St Perry GA 31069 Office: 916 Main St Perry GA 31069

REESE, KENNETH LEE, elec. engr.; b. Carbon, Tex., Dec. 12, 1937; s. Travis and Sadie Rae (Crosby) R.; student Arlington State Coll., 1956-57, Ranger Coll., 1958-60; B.S. in Elec. Engring., Texas A. and M. U., 1967; m. Sandra Jane Curtis, July 6, 1957; children—Barry Lee, Whitney Elaine. Staff engr. John Denison Co., College Station, Tex., 1966-67; asso. elec. engr. Tex. Electric Service Co., Odessa, 1967-68, supr. distbn. engring., 1968-69, supr. distbn. dispatch and service depts., 1970-72, supr. transmission div. maintenance operations and constrn., 1970-72, supt. Eastland Transmission div. 1972—. Vol. staff and team dir. United Fund, Odessa, 1968-72. Bd. dirs. Boy Scouts Am., Odessa Blue and Gold Council, 1970-71. Served with AUS, 1960-63. Recipient Distinguished Service award Tex. A. and M. Former Students, 1966, Meml. Student Center, 1967. Registered profl. engr., Tex. Mem. Tex. Soc. Profl. Engrs. (young engr. of year Permian Basin chpt. 1969, publicity chmn. and ethics chmn. Permain chpt., 1967—, pubs. com. 1971, edn. com. 1972—), I.E.E.E. (sec.-treas. Permian chpt. 1971-72, v.p. 1972, hospitality chmn. 1970-71, sec.-treas. Abilene chpt. 1973—). Home: 517 S Walnut St Eastland TX 76448 Office: PO Box 351 Eastland TX 76448

REESE, LYMON CLIFTON, coll. dean; b. Murfreesboro, Ark., Apr. 27, 1917; s. Samuel Wesley and Nancy Elizabeth (Daniels) R.; B.S., U. Tex., Austin, 1949, M.S., 1950; Ph.D. (Gen. Edn. Bd. Cal. fellow, NSF fellow), U. Cal. at Berkeley, 1955; m. Eva Lee Jett, May 28, 1948; children—Sally (Mrs. Michael Melant), John, Nancy. Rodman, Internat. Boundary Commn., San Benito, Tex., 1939-41; layout engr. E.I. DuPont Co. de Nemours & Co., Inc., Pryor, Okla., Childersburg, Ala., 1941-42; surveyor U.S. Naval Constrn. Bns., Aleutian Islands, Okinawa, 1942-45; field engr. Asso. Contractors & Engrs., Houston, 1945; draftsman Phillips Petroleum Co., Austin, 1946-48; research engr. U. Tex., Austin, 1948-50; asst. prof. civil engring. Miss. State Coll., State College, 1950-51, 53-55; asst. prof. U. Tex., Austin, 1955-57; asso. prof., 1957-64, prof., 1964—, chmn. dept., 1965-72, asso. dean engring. for program planning, 1972—. Cons. Shell Oil Co., Shell Devel. Co., 1955-65, Dames & Moore, Cranford, N.J., 1970—, McClelland Engrs., Houston, 1970—; Taylor prof. engring. Tex. U., 1972—. Served with USNR, 1942-45. Recipient Thomas Middlebrooks award Am. Soc. Engrs., 1958. Registered profl. engr., Tex. Fellow Am. Soc. C.E.; mem. Am. Soc. Engring. Edn., Nat. Soc. Profl. Engrs., Am. Soc. Testing Materials, Sigma Xi, Tau Beta Pi, Chi Epsilon, Phi Kappa Phi. Baptist (deacon). Rotarian. Contbr. articles to profl. jours. Home: 4602 Laurel Canyon Austin TX 78731 Office: Dept Civil Engring U Tex Austin TX 78712

REESE, PAUL MICHAEL, II, air freight and charter service exec.; b. New Orleans, Feb. 17, 1942; s. Paul Michael and Cathryn (Carter) R.; student La. State U., New Orleans, 1961, Tulane U., 1962-64; m. Elizabeth Saunders, Apr. 23, 1965; 1 son, Paul Michael III. With Gulf Oil Corp., New Orleans, 1964-69; owner Newton Printing Co., New Orleans, 1969-71; part owner, v.p., chmn. bd. Vanguard Airways, New Orleans, 1971—; diver, free lance under water photographer; Luger editor Guns and Ammo Mag., Los Angeles, 1970—; pres. Franklin Models, Ltd.; v.p. Benjamin Franklin Galleries, Ltd.; spl. assignments editor Nat. Diver Mag., Am. Blade Mag.; dir. photog. research Sea Research Soc. S.C. Served with USMCR, 1960-68. Author: U.S. Trials/1900 Luger, 1970; Collectors Guide to Luger Values. Contbg. editor Oceans mag. Designer Chael III Diver's Companion Knife. Home: 3619 State St Dr New Orleans LA 70125 Office: PO Box 52364 New Orleans LA 70152

REESE, ROBERT JOHN, constrn. engr.; b. Clements, Kan., Aug. 10, 1922; s. John M. and Amelia Guilda (Tschepel) R.; student Kan. State U., 1940-42; B.S. in Civil Engring., U. Okla., 1950; m. Billie Jo Gooch, Sept. 3, 1948; children—James Robert, Patricia Ann, Susan Elizabeth. With U.S. Bur. Reclamation, Denver, 1950-51, Superior, Neb., 1953-54; with Ideal Cement Co., Ada, Okla., 1954-55, 57-65, 70—, Denver, 1955-57, 67-70, Seattle, 1965-67. Cons. engr., land surveyor, 1962—. Served to lt. USNR, 1943-46, 51-52. Registered profl. engr., Okla. Mason. Club: Athletic O (U. Okla.). Home: Route 4 Box 118 Ada OK 74820 Office: PO Box 398 Ada OK 74820

REESE, THOMAS DEAL, indsl. distbn. co. exec.; b. Nacogdoches, Tex., Sept. 25, 1913; s. James Early and Laura (King) R.; student Stephen Austin State U., 1931-33, U. Tex. at Austin, 1935-36; m. Virginia Elizabeth Jackson, Apr. 9, 1938; children—Thomas D., J. Mark, Jamie Elizabeth. With Gulf Consol. Service, Inc. (Gulf Supply Co., Inc., Nunn Electric Supply Corp., Bay Supply Co., Inc., Reichardt Electric Co., Inc., Island Supply Co., Inc.), Houston, 1947—, v.p., 1971-73, sr. v.p., 1973—, also dir. Mem. adv. council indsl. distbn. Tex. A. and M. U., Houston, 1970—. Episcopalian (mem. exec. bd.; dep. Gen. Conv., 1961, 64, 67, 70, 73). Clubs: Houston, Champions Golf (Houston). Home: 29 Colony East-Champions Houston TX 77069 Office: 7220 N Loop East Houston TX 77028

REESE, WEIMAN HERMAN, geophs. co. exec.; b. Lake Charles, La., Aug. 16, 1921; s. John Ira and Alma (Jessen) R.; student McNeese Jr. Coll., 1939-41; B.S., La. State U., 1943; m. Dorothy Meyer, Sept. 11, 1945; children—Cheryl (Mrs. Richard Nordin), Randy (Mrs. J.M. Duhon), Vicki (Mrs. James Mayfield), Edward. With Nat. Geophys. Co., Dallas, 1943-47, Geophys. Assos., Houston, 1947-55; v.p. McCollum Exploration (merged into Ray Geophys. 1959, then Mandrel Industries 1960), Houston, 1955-59; v.p. Mandrel Industries, Houston, 1960—. Served to lt. (j.g.) USNR, 1944-46. Mem. Soc. Exploration Geophysicists, Houston Geophys. Soc. Clubs: Houston; Explorers (N.Y.C.). Address: 584 Trianon St Houston TX 77024

REEVE, JAMES KEY, museum curator; b. Lewistown, Mont., Sept. 24, 1925; s. John Rumsey and Isabelle (Key) R.; B.A., U. Tulsa, 1950; M.A., N.Y. U., 1954; postgrad. U. London Courtauld Inst., 1961-63. Lectr. Toledo Mus. Art, 1954-58; curator Univ. Art Gallery, asst. prof. art history U. Notre Dame, 1958-61; curator Anglo-Am. Art Mus., asst. prof. La. State U., 1963-67; curator Am. art Toledo Mus. Art, 1967-71; curator Philbrook Art Center, Tulsa, 1972-74; lectr. USIS, Am. Embassy, London, 1962-63. Mem. Mayor's Spl. Com. on Archtl. Preservation, Toledo, 1968-71. Served with USCGR, 1943-46. Mem. Coll. Art Assn. Am., Soc. Archtl. Historians, Nat. Trust for Historic Preservation, Am. Assn. Museums, Lambda Chi Alpha. Home: 3103 S Cincinnati St Tulsa OK 74105

REEVE, RAYMOND TOWNER, broadcasting co. exec.; b. Niagra Falls, N.Y., Apr. 25, 1901; s. Amos Gillette and Adilade (Campbell) R.; student Dartmouth, 1919-23; m. Marguerite Pierce, Sept. 20, 1941; children—Margot Towner, Sarah Michelle (Mrs. Wayne Underhill), Raymond Towner. Salesman, Oneida Ltd., 1923-31; announcer Radio Sta. KGMB, Honolulu, 1931-35, Radio Sta. KJBS, San Francisco, 1935-37, Teleflash Inc., N.Y.C., Balt. and Washington, 1937-39; sports dir. Capitol Broadcasting Co., Inc., Raleigh, N.C., 1939—; night mgr., sports dir. WRAL TV, 1956-71. Served with USNR, 1918-19. Named Hall of Fame N.C. Sports, 1967. Hall of Fame, Assn. Broadcasters, 1971. Home: 1607 Canterbury Rd Raleigh NC 27608 Office: PO Box 12000 Raleigh NC 27605

REEVES, BENJAMIN FRANKLIN, govt. ofcl.; b. Bowling Green, Ky., May 7, 1922; s. Ben Peden and Marguerite (Harvison) R.; A.B. in Journalism, U. Ky., 1949, postgrad. in Polit. Sci., 1951; m. Mavis Andree Mann, Sept. 15, 1956; 1 dau., Andree Elizabeth. Instr. journalism Richmond Profl. Inst. Coll. William and Mary, Richmond, Va., 1949-50; reporter Evansville (Ind.) Press, 1951; reporter Courier-Jour., Louisville, 1952-59, asst. mng. editor, 1959-61, mng. editor, 1961-65; Washington corr. Louisville Courier-Jour. and Louisville Times, 1965-66; asst. to chmn. House Com. on Edn. and Labor, 1967—. Intership to study Congress. Am. Polit. Sci. Assn., Washington, 1953-54. Served with USNR, 1942-46. Mem. Am. Polit. Sci. Assn., Phi Beta Kappa. Unitarian. Home: 5601 Wood Way Washington DC 20016 Office: Rayburn House Office Bldg Washington DC 20515

REEVES, CHARLES MERCER, JR., finance co. exec.; b. Sanford, N.C., Feb. 14, 1919; s. Charles Mercer and Suzanne Easten (Purvis) R.; B.S. in Bus. Adminstrn., U. N.C., 1940; m. Sarah Frances Crosby, Oct. 12, 1940; children—Charles Mercer III, David Crosby, Suzanne (Mrs. James Marion Parrott IV), John Mercer II. Pres., chmn. bd. Safeway Suburban Lines, Inc., Sanford, Dunn, Reidsville, N.C., 1946-49; pres. 1st Provident Co., Inc., Sanford, 1949—, Brown's Auto Supply Co., Sanford, 1959-69; pres., chmn. bd. Atlantic & Western Ry., Sanford, 1968—; dir. Carolina Bank, Roberts Co., Sanford, Steel and Pipe Corp., Sanford, S.C. Nat. Bank Corp., Columbia; pres., chmn. So. Provident Life Ins. Co., Phoenix. Partner, Rich Mountain Assos., Boone, N.C., Cape Lookout Assos., Morehead City, N.C. Mem. N.C. Banking Commn., 1954-61, 69—. Mem. N.C. Higher Bd. Edn., 1961-62; dist. exec. com. Boy Scouts Am., 1964—. Commr., Lee County, 1953-55. Served with AC USNR, World War II. Mem. Beta Theta Pi. Methodist. Rotarian. Home: Reeves Ridge Farm Sanford NC 27330 Office: 132 S Moore St Sanford NC 27330

REEVES, DONA RAE BATTY (MRS. EDWARD B. REEVES), educator; b. Kansas City, Mo., Mar. 9, 1932; d. Claude A. and Alma (Deines) Batty; B.A. U. Tex., Austin, 1953, M.A., 1955, Ph.D., 1963; Fulbright scholar, Johannes Gutenberg U. (Germany), 1955-56; postgrad. U. Cal. at Berkeley, 1957-58; m. Edward B. Reeves, Mar. 29, 1958. Teaching asst. U. Tex. at Austin, 1953-55, 58-61, U. Cal. at Berkeley, 1957-58; instr. S.W. Tex. State U., San Marcos, 1961-63, asst. prof., 1963-65, asso. prof., 1965-69, prof., 1969—, chmn. modern lang. dept., 1967-71. Bd. advisers S.W. Ednl. Devel. Lab., 1966-70. Summer Seminar grantee in Germany from West German Govt., 1964. Mem. Modern Lang. Assn., Am. Assn. Tchrs. German (mem. nat. exec. council 1971-73, pres. Tex. chpt. 1964-65, regional dir. Nat. High Sch. German Contest 1964-72), South Central Modern Lang. Assn., Am. Assn. U. Profs. (chpt. pres.), Am. Council on Teaching Fgn. Langs., Tex. Fgn. Lang. Assn. (v.p. 1972, pres. 1973), Assn. Lang. Lab. Dirs., Tex. Assn. Coll. Tchrs. (chpt. pres. 1973-74), Tex. State Tchrs. Assn. U. Tex. Ex-Student Assn. (life). Delta Phi Alpha. Home: Route 1 Box 239A Buda TX 78610 Office: Modern Lang Dept SW Tex State U San Marcos TX 78666

REEVES, GLENN WILLARD, educator; b. Munday, Tex., Aug. 20, 1925; s. James Ely and Elizabeth (Perry) R.; B.Elec. Engring., Ga. Inst. Tech., 1946; B.D., So. Baptist Theol. Sem., 1949, Th.M., 1957, Th.D., 1963; m. Frances Elizabeth Smith, July 23, 1949; children—Glenn Willard, Samuel Ray. Tchr. Buckner Children's Home, Dallas, 1949-50; ordained to ministry Bapt. Ch., 1949; student pastorate New Washington (Ind.) Bapt. Ch., 1956-59; dir. religious activities Cumberland Coll., Williamsburg, Ky., 1963-65, prof., head dept. religion, 1964—, also chmn. div. religion, bib. langs. and philosophy. Scoutmaster, Blue Grass council Boy Scouts Am., 1965-66. Served with USNR, 1943-46, 51-55. Mem. Soc. Bibl. Lit., Am. Acad. Religion. Home: PO Box 429 Williamsburg KY 40769 Office: PO Box 520 Cumberland College Sta Williamsburg KY 40769

REEVES, HUBERT LISBON, economist; b. Little Rock, Sept. 30, 1904; s. Alfred Randolph and Jency (Hubert) R.; B.A., Morehouse Coll., 1924; postgrad. Northwestern U., 1926-28; M.A., Am. U., 1950; postgrad. N.Y. U., 1950-51; m. Stella Elizabeth Jones, Sept. 3, 1938. Economist, War Manpower Commn., Washington, 1942-45, U.S. Dept. Labor, Washington and N.Y.C., 1947-54; asso. internat. labor specialist U.S. Dept. Labor, Washington, 1955, economist, 1956-62, manpower devel. specialist, 1962-64, manpower research analyst, 1964-67; lectr. econs. Savannah State Coll., 1968-72; econ. cons. Sociometrics, Inc., Silver Spring, Md., 1971—. Bd. dirs. Bethle-Community Center. Recipient Superior Performance award Dept. Labor, 1966. Mem. Am. Econ. Assn., Internat. Assn. Personnel in Employment Security, Alpha Phi Alpha. Conglist. Club: Pigskin (Washington). Contbr. articles to profl. jours. Home: 901 E 32d St Savannah GA 31401

REEVES, JAMES BLANCHETTE, microbiologist, educator; b. Beaumont, Tex., Jan. 24, 1924; s. Clinton A. and Blanche (Weber) R.; student Tex. A. and M. U., 1941-42; B.S., La. State U., 1948, M.S., 1949; Ph.D. (NIH grantee), U. Tex., Austin, 1964; m. Jeanne Buckner Patton, June 4, 1947; children—James Patton, Jeanne Clinton. Lab. dir. regional labs. Tex. Dept. Health, San Angelo, El Paso, 1949-55; asst. prof. U. Tex., El Paso, 1955-61, asso. prof., 1961-63, prof. biol. scis., 1964—, head dept. biol. scis., 1961-69, coordinator health related programs, 1970—. Pres., Bios Co., El Paso, 1964-70. Bd. dirs. El Paso Epilepsy Assn. Served with AUS, 1943-45. Fellow A.A.A.S.; mem. Am. Soc. Microbiology (local chmn. Tri-State Fall Meeting 1972), Sigma Xi, Sigma Chi, Phi Beta Pi. Editor: Laboratory Manual for General Biology, 1966-70. Home: 312 Sundown Pl El Paso TX 79912

REEVES, JAMES JERAULD, lawyer; b. Troy, Ala., Oct. 11, 1938; s. David Chester and Goldie Elaine (Jerauld) R.; student Pensacola Jr. Coll., Fla. State U.; LL.B., Stetson U., 1962; m. Lelia Frances Weaver, Apr. 10, 1963; children—Carl Michelle, James Jerauld, Rachel Suzanne. Admitted to Fla. bar; partner firm Hopkins, Hahn & Reeves, Pensacola, Fla., 1962-64, Hahn, Reeves & Shimek, Pensacola, 1964-69, Hahn & Reeves, Pensacola, 1969-70, Hahn, Reeves, Barfield & King, Pensacola, 1970—; chmn. bd. So. Fed. Savs. and Loan, Pensacola. Chmn. Pensacola Downtown Devel. Bd. Mem. Fla. Ho. of Reps., 1966-72. Bd. dirs. Pensacola Zool. Soc., Children's Home Soc. Fla.; bd. govs. Fiesta Five Flags, Pensacola Sports Assn. Served with USMCR. Recipient Distinguished Service award for outstanding young man Escambia County, Pensacola Jr. C. of C., 1966-67. Mem. Am., Fla. bar assns., Am. Trial Lawyers Assn., Soc. Bar 1st Jud. Circuit, Navy League (dir.). Democrat. Presbyn. Toastmaster. Home: 2300 Osceola Pensacola FL 32501 Office: 98 E Garden St Pensacola FL 32501

REEVES, JAMES WILLARD, univ. dean; b. Covington, La., Oct. 31, 1931; s. Leon R. and Julia (Sirmon) R.; B.S., La. State U., 1952, M.S., 1959; Ph.D., U. Ariz., 1970; m. Clara Ruby Robicheaux, Aug. 30, 1958; children—Karen Tracy, Christine Suzanne. Engr., Chance Vought Aircraft Co., Dallas, 1952-53; design engr. La. Dept. Pub. Works, Baton Rouge, 1956-57; chief engr. George Covert & Assos., cons. engrs., Baton Rouge, 1957-59; asso. prof. civil engring. U. Southwestern La., Lafayette, 1959-71, dean Coll. Engring., 1971—. Vice chmn. adv. com. La. Coastal Commn., 1970—. Served to lt. USNR, 1953-56. Recipient Halliburton Edn. Found. award for excellence in teaching, 1971. NSF Faculty fellow, 1967-68. Registered profl. engr., La. Mem. Am. Soc. C.E. (faculty adviser 1965-67), Am. Soc. Engring. Edn., La. Engring. Soc., Sigma Xi. Club: Lafayette Organic Gardening. Author: The Evaluation of Silicones for Use With Concretes, 1966; Design of Thick Walled Cylindrical Pressure Vessels, 1966; Nonlinear Analysis of Axisymmetric Circular Plates, 1970. Home: 212 Montgomery Dr Lafayette LA 70501

REEVES, MARVIN COKE, business exec.; b. Mt. Airy, N.C., Dec. 29, 1911; s. Marvin Coke and Sarah Myrtle (Spaugh) R.; B.A., Westminster Coll., 1933; m. Lynne Elizabeth Martin, June 16, 1951 (div. 1972); children—Marvin Coke III, Mary Lynne, Sarah Elizabeth, Virginia Louise. Civil engr. So. Mapping & Engring. Co., Greensboro, N.C., 1941-44; partner Western Wood Products Co., Houston, 1947-50; pres. Bentex Pharm. Co., Houston, 1950-71; v.p. pharm. group ICN Pharms., Pasadena, Cal., 1971-73; owner Reeves of Tex., 1973—; pres. Reeves Mining Inc., Reeves Minerals Inc., Clear Creek Gold Mines, Inc., 1973—; chmn. bd. Aseptics, Inc., Houston, 1973—; partner Mayan Minerals, Ltd., Honduras. Served to lt. USNR, 1944-47. Mem. Mensa, Phi Delta Theta. Home: 8438 Bluegate Rd Houston TX 77025 Office: Suite 870 2600 Southwest Freeway Houston TX 77006

REEVES, RICHMOND JOEL, accountant; b. Buckner, Ark., Oct. 29, 1945; s. Richmond Curtis and Mary Ruth (Eddy) R.; B.B.A., So. State Coll., Magnolia, Ark., 1967; m. Carlotta Jane Fly, June 2, 1967; children—Matthew Curtis, Michael Benjamin. With Shell Oil Co., New Orleans, 1967; sr. accountant Thomas & Thomas, C.P.A.'s, Texarkana, Ark., 1968-70; accounts mgr. Markham & Wilf, C.P.A.'s, Texarkana, Tex., 1970—. Owner cattle ranch, Buckner. Named Outstanding Young Man, 1973. C.P.A., Tex., Ark. Mem. Texarkana Jr. C. of C. Baptist. Home: Route 7 Box 593-R Texarkana AR 75501 Office: 201 College Dr Texarkana TX 75501

REEVES, WILLIAM AUBREY, supt. schs.; b. Haskell, Tex., June 26, 1914; s. Wyatt Wylie and Annie (Easterling) R.; B.A., Howard Payne Coll., 1935; M.A., Tex. A. and I. U., 1951; postgrad. U. Tex., 1952-56; m. Wilma Carole Miller, Aug. 16, 1938; children—Patsy (Mrs. W. Bruce Reaves), Linda, William Miller. Secondary sci. tchr., coach, prin. Holding Inst., Laredo, Tex., 1935-42; tchr., prin., coach Woodsboro (Tex.) Ind. Sch. Dist., 1942-44, 47-51, supt. schs., 1951—. Inst. Devel. Ednl. Activities fellow, 1969. Mem. Nat. Edn. Assn., Am. Tex. assns. sch. adminstrs., Tex. Tchrs. Assn. Baptist. Lion (pres. 1956). Home: 708 Johnson St Woodsboro TX 78393 Office: 704 Locke St Woodsboro TX 78393

REGAN, JAMES DALE, geneticist; b. Lancaster, O., May 23, 1931; s. Francis Joseph and Beulah Constance (Dale) R.; B.S., Ohio U., 1953; M.S., U. Miami, 1959; Ph.D., U. Hawaii, 1964; m. Christa Maria Hohnhausen, Apr. 27, 1955; children—Jessica Ute, Jeffrey William. NIH postdoctoral fellow biology div. Oak Ridge Nat. Lab., 1964-66, sr. investigator, 1966—, also group leader med. and molecular genetics group; vis. lectr. human genetics U. Tenn., 1967-71. Served with AUS, 1953-55. Mem. Am. Assn. Cancer Research, Am. Soc. Human Genetics, Biophys. Soc., N.Y. Acad. Scis. Contbr. articles profl. jours. Home: 119 Cooper Circle Oak Ridge TN 37830 Office: Biology Division Oak Ridge National Laboratory Oak Ridge TN 37830

REGAN, TERRY MALCOLM, environmental engr.; b. Lexington, Ky., Mar. 18, 1935; s. Herman Daniel and Gladys Mae (Butler) R.; B.S. in Civil Engring., U. Ky., 1957; m. Phyllis Jean McCann, Dec. 21, 1957; children—Kathleen Dawn, Kelly Anne, Kevin McCann. Design and resident engr. Howard K. Bell, cons. engrs., Lexington, 1957-61; civil engr., asst. dir. Dept. Water Pollution Control, City of Lexington, 1962-70, acting dir., 1970—; pres. T.M. Regan, Inc., water quality control services, Lexington, 1970—. Instr., cons. environmental tng. courses for colls. and govt. agys. Mem. Ky. Bd. Certification for Water and Sewage, 1968—, chmn., 1968-71. Trustee Woodland Trust Fund. Served to capt. Inf., AUS, 1957, 61-62. Recipient C.E. Alumni award U. Ky. Coll. Engring., 1969. Registered profl. engr., Ky. Mem. Nat., Ky. (mem. registration com.; recipient Outstanding Young Engr. award 1971; pres. Bluegrass chpt. 1972) socs. profl. engrs., Water Pollution Control Fedn. (recipient William D. Hatfield award 1968, chmn. certification study com. 1971—, bd. control 1973—), Am. Pub. Works Assn. (pres. Ky. chpt. 1968-69), Ky.-Tenn. Water Pollution Control Assn. (chmn. Ky.-Tenn. 1970-71), Am. Water Works Assn., Assn. Bds. Certification (mem. exec. com.), Inst. Municipal Engrs., Inst. Solid Wastes, Ky. Hist. Soc., U. Ky. Alumni Assn., Delta Tau Delta. Mem. Christian Ch. (trustee, elder 1971—). Home: 400 Chinoe Rd Lexington KY 40502 Office: 377 Waller Av Lexington KY 40504

REGGIA, FRANK, elec. engr.; b. Northumberland, Pa., Oct. 30, 1921; s. Nicola and Rachela (DiPhillips) R.; student George Washington U., 1949-53, U. Md., 1955-58; B.S. in E.E. cum laude, Bucknell U., 1970, M.S. in E.E., 1971; m. Betty Jo Patterson, Jan. 14, 1945; children—James Allen, Daniel Lee. Electronic scientist Nat. Bur. Standards, Washington, 1945-54; research electronic engr. (microwaves) Harry Diamond Labs., Dept. Army, Washington, 1954—. Cons. microwave devel. labs. Def. Dept., 1960-74. Pres., Chevy Chase (Md.) Coquelin Run Citizens Assn., 1960-61; scoutmaster Bethesda-Chevy Chase council Boy Scouts Am., 1962-70. Served with USNR, 1940-45; CBI, PTO. Decorated Purple Heart. Named Engr. of Year, Washington Soc. Engrs., 1953; recipient Superior Accomplishment awards Dept. Army, 1959, Commerce Dept., 1954; Dept. Army study fellow U. Md., 1956-57, Bucknell U., 1969-70. Fellow I.E.E.E., Washington Acad. Sci., A.A.A.S.; mem. Soc. Preservation Barbershop Quartet Singing in Am., Am. Legion (dir. 1970-73), V.F.W., Nat. Rifle Assn., Tau Beta Pi. Methodist (trustee). Clubs: Military Officers (Washington); Shenandoah Country (Berryville, Va.). Patentee in microwave acoustics and ferrites. Contbr. articles, tech. reports to profl. jours. Home: 6207 Kirby Rd Bethesda MD 20034 Office: Dept Army Connecticut Av and Van Ness St Washington DC 20438

REGGIE, EDMUND MICHAEL, lawyer, judge; b. Crowley, La., July 19, 1926; s. Fred and Victoria (Andraous) R.; B.A., Southwestern La. Inst., 1946; J.D., Tulane U., 1949; m. Doris Anne Boustany, June 17, 1951; children—Edmund Michael, Victoria Anne, Denis Andrew, Gregory F., Mariam, Raymond. Admitted La. bar, 1949; asso. Denis T. Canan, Crowley, 1949-50; judge, City Ct. of Crowley, 1950—. Sec., dir. Huval Baking Co., Inc., 1954—; v.p., dir. Western Investment Corp., 1954—, Frany Holding Corp., 1953—; chmn. bd. Acadia Savs. & Loan Assn., 1957; vice chmn. bd. La. Bank & Trust Co.; dir., mem. exec. com. City Savs. Bank and Trust Co., DeRidder, La.; dir. Plant Industries, Inc. Specialist to Lebanon, Syria, Jordan, Egypt, Saudi Arabia, for U.S. Dept. State, 1961. Commr. Pub. Welfare of La. until 1965; mem. La. State Mineral Bd., 1964-66. La. chmn. Nat. Library Week, 1964; chmn. Chief Justice's com. La. Spl. Cts. Study. Del. Dem. Nat. Conv., 1956, 60, 64, 68; Dem. presdl. elector La., 1960; mem. Dem. state Central Com., 1956-60. Mem. bldg. com. Internat. Rice Festival, 1957, pres., 1960; chmn. Acadia Parish Polio Fund, 1953, 54, Acadia Paish A.R.C., 1953; pres. St. Vincent de Paul Conf., 1953; counsellor Boy Scouts Am.; exec. dir. La. Commn. Extension and Continuing Edn., 1967—; mem. Pub. Affairs Research Council; mem. La. Council for Music and Performing Arts; mem. La. Council Govtl. Reorgn., La. Conf. Children and Youth Com.; exec. com. La. delegation to Pres.'s White House Conf. Children and Youth. Bd. dirs. S.W. La. Rehab. Center, Nat. Rehab. Assn., Crowley Mental Health Assn., La. Conf. Social Welfare; trustee Williston-Northampton Sch., Notre Dame Sem., New Orleans, St. Joseph Sem. Coll., Covington, La. Named La.'s Distinguished Dem., Young Dems. La., 1963; Cardinal Newman award for S.W. La., 1963. Pres. Cardinal Newman Found. Mem. Nat. Assn. Municipal Ct. Judges, Am. Pub. Welfare Assn., Am., La., Acadia Parish (sec. 1955-56) bar assns., Am. Judicature Soc., La. Conf. Juvenile Correctional Workers, Nat. Council Juvenile Ct. Judges, La. City Judges Assn. (pres. 1971-73), La Societe du Droit Civile, Am. Trial Lawyers Assn., Am. Pub. Welfare Assn., Crowley Mental Health Assn., Nat. Rehab. Assn., Acadia Assn. Retarded Children, Crowley C. of C., Am. Acad. Polit. and Social Sci., N. Am. Judges Assn. Roman Catholic. K.C. (4 deg.). Clubs: Town, Kiwanis (dir. 1950-53, v.p. 1950-54), Bayou Bend Country; Nat. Capitol Democratic, Federal City. Home: 400 W Northern Av Crowley LA 70526 Office: Reggie Bldg Crowley LA 70526

REGULSKI, LEE, comml. constrn. designer; b. Bklyn., Nov. 19, 1926; s. Leo Theodore and Margaret (Jurasko) R.; student St. Bonaventure Coll., 1944-45, U. Ky., 1945; B.C.E., Cornell U., 1949; m. Janice Steele, Apr. 15, 1951; children—Susan, Kurt, Doris, Mark. Engring. asst. Harrisburg Gas Co. (Pa.), 1949-51; constrn. engr. E.I. DuPont de Nemours & Co., Inc., Kinston, N.C., LaPorte, Tex., 1951-54; constrn. mgr. Caldwell & Cook, Rochester, N.Y., 1954-62; v.p. constrn. Rutenberg Homes, Clearwater, Fla., 1962-68; pres. United Mfg. Corp., Clearwater, 1968; self-employed engr., designer, bldr., developer, design and constrn. comml. structures, Clearwater, 1968—. Chmn. secondary schs. com. Pinellas County for Cornell U., 1973—. Served with AUS, 1945-46. Registered profl. engr., Fla.; certified gen. contractor, Fla. Mem. Nat. Soc. Profl. Engrs., Am. Soc. C.E. (pres. Rochester chpt. 1960-61), Cornell Alumni Assn. (pres. Pinellas County 1973-74). Kiwanian. Home: 1045 Chinaberry Rd Clearwater FL 33516 Office: 1045 Chinaberry Rd Clearwater FL 33516

REHM, GERALD STETSON, bus. exec., city ofcl.; b. W. Palm Beach, Fla., Mar. 10, 1927; s. Fred G. and Rose (Delfoe) R.; B.S., U.S. Merchant Marine Acad., 1948; postgrad. Hofstra Coll., 1950-56; m. Frances M. Smeja, Nov. 7, 1948; children—Gregory, Pamela, Scott. Deck officer Waterman S.S. Corp., N.Y.C., 1948-50; planning exec. Sperry Rand Corp., Great Neck, N.Y. and Clearwater, Fla., 1950-66; comptroller Bruce Taylor, Inc., Realtor-Insuror, Clearwater, 1967-69; organizer, pres. Experience Unlimited, Inc., Clearwater, 1969-74; exec. dir. Eckerd Found., 1971—; v.p., gen. mgr. Screens Unltd., 1971—; also mayor city Dunedin, Fla., 1966-71. Co-founder Dunedin Youth Festival; mem. Pinellas area council Boy Scouts Am. Mem. Alumni Assn. U.S. Merchant Marine Acad. (past nat. officer), Bd. Realtors. Republican. Roman Catholic (lay leader). Kiwanian (pres. 1962). Founder Caladesi Island State Park, Pinellas County, Fla., 1965-67. Home: 2228 Webb Av Dunedin FL 33528 Office: PO Box 4689 Clearwater FL 33518

REHNQUIST, WILLIAM HUBBS, U.S. Supreme Ct. justice; b. Milw., Oct. 1, 1924; s. William Benjamin and Margery (Peck) R.; B.A., M.A., Stanford, 1948, LL.B., 1952; M.A., Harvard, 1949; m. Natalie Cornell, Aug. 29, 1953; children—James, Janet, Nancy. Admitted to Ariz. bar; law clk. to former justice Robert H. Jackson, U.S. Supreme Ct., 1952-53; with firm Evans, Kitchel & Jenckes, Phoenix, 1953-55; mem. firm Ragan & Rehnquist, Phoenix, 1956-57; partner firm Cunningham, Carson & Messenger, Phoenix, 1957-60; partner firm Powers & Rehnquist, Phoenix, 1960-69; asst. atty.-gen. office of legal counsel Dept. of Justice, Washington, 1969-72; asso. justice U.S. Supreme Ct., 1972—. Mem. Nat. Conf. Commrs. Uniform State Laws, 1963-69. Served with USAAF, 1943-46; NATOUSA. Mem. Fed., Am. Maricopa (Ariz.) County bar assns., State Bar Ariz., Phi Beta Kappa, Order of Coif, Phi Delta Phi. Lutheran. Contbr. articles law jours., nat. mags. Office: US Supreme Ct Washington DC 20543

REHRER, MERVIN, lawyer; b. Pine Grove, Pa., Mar. 16, 1913; s. Ottis and Cora R. (Zerbey) R.; A.B., Gettysburg (Pa.) Coll., 1939; postgrad. Dickinson Law Sch., Carlisle, Pa., 1940-41; J.D., Stetson Law Sch., DeLand, Fla., 1948; m. Catherine E. Swanson, Feb. 11, 1956; children—Marcia Jo Davis, James C., Laurie Diane. Visitor, Pa. Dept. Pub. Welfare, 1939-40; clk.-supr. U.S. Air Force, Middletown, Pa. and Newark, 1941-45; audit clk. Internal Revenue Service, Phila., 1949-51; auditor Army Ordnance, Phila., 1951-52; admitted to Fla. bar, 1948; practiced in Avon Park, 1953-57, 73—; city atty., Avon Park, 1953-57; judge Highlands County, Sebring, Fla., 1957-73. Founder, trustee Youth Care, Inc. Mem. Am., Fla. bar assns., Fla. County Judges Assn., Nat., Fla. councils juvenile ct. judges. Lutheran (trustee). Rotarian, Elk. Home: 219 E Camphor St Avon Park FL 33825 Office: 120 S Anoka Av Avon Park FL 33825

REICH, DONALD (ROCKY) LAMAR, radio exec.; b. Double Springs, Ala., Apr. 2, 1936; s. Curtis C. and Rilla (Justice) R.; B.S., U. So. Miss., 1959; m. JoAnn Campbell, June 29, 1957; children—Roxanne, Karla Ann, Donald Lamar. Salesman WKRG radio, Mobile, 1959-62, WBSR, Pensacola, Fla., 1962; with WUNI radio, Mobile, 1962—, gen. mgr., 1966—, v.p., 1972—. Pres., Cottage Hill Athletic Assn., 1973—; mem. adv. council Ala. Hist. Commn., 1973—. Mem. Sales and Marketing Execs. Internat. Mobile Area C. of C., Ala. Broadcasters Assn. (dir. 1967—). Baptist. Home: 5820 Mal Dr Mobile AL 36609 Office: 1257 Springhill Av Mobile AL 36604

REICHERT, WALTER STEWART, lab. technician; b. Louisville, Aug. 8, 1929; s. Sauter Frank and Alice (Buschmann) R.; student U. Louisville, 1947-50; m. Ella Carolyn Ross, Feb. 9, 1952; children—Walter Stewart, Carolyn Jean, Paul Frank, David Lawrence. Lab. technician E.I. du Pont Co., Louisville, 1950—; mem. Ky. State Senate, 1966—. Mem. Ky. Ho. of Reps., 1964-66. Served with USAF, 1950-53. Mem. Engrs. and Architects Soc. Louisville, Amvets. Republican. Home: 4909 E Manslick Rd Louisville KY 40219 Office: Box 1378 Camp Ground Rd Louisville KY 40201

REID, JAMES CUTLER, biochemist; b. Akron, O., Apr. 17, 1918; s. Lloyd George and Louise (Cutler) R.; B.S., U. Pa., 1939; M.S., Pa. State U., 1940; Ph.D., U. Cal. at Berkeley, 1944. Instr. chemistry Bowling Green State U., 1940-42; mem. staff Radiation Lab., U. Cal. at Berkeley, 1946-49, research asso. dept. chemistry, 1944-46; mem. research staff Nat. Cancer Inst., NIH, Bethesda, Md., 1949—. Mem. chemistry panel Interagy. Bd. Examiners, U.S. Civil Service Commn., 1967—. Fellow A.A.A.S.; mem. Am. Chem. Soc., Am. Soc. Biol. Chemists, Phi Beta Kappa, Sigma Xi. Author: (with Melvin Calvin and others) Isotopic Carbon, 1949; (with David Greenberg and others) Amino Acids and Proteins, 1951. Home: 4 Wyoming Ct Washington DC 20016 Office: Bldg 10 NIH Bethesda MD 20014

REID, JOHN CLIFTON, cons. mech. engr.; b. Fredericksburg, Va., May 2, 1932; s. Purcell Timberlake and Anne Louise (Patterson) R.; student George Washington U., 1953-55; B.S. in Mech. Engring., Va. Poly Inst., 1959; m. Ann Louise Downer, Feb. 14, 1953; children—Karen Lynn, Gretchen Dianne, Ashley Ann, Kevin Daniel. Asso., Wiley & Wilson, cons. engrs., Richmond, Va., 1959-69; v.p. Hankins & Anderson, cons. engrs., Richmond, also Boston, 1969—. Served with AUS, 1952-55. Registered profl. engr., Va., N.C., Mass., N.Y., D.C., Md., R.I. Mem. Am. Soc. M.E., Am. Soc. Heating, Refrigerating and Air Conditioning Engrs., Nat. Soc. Profl. Engrs., Va. Assn. Profls., Am. Numis. Assn., Pi Tau Sigma, Tau Beta Pi. Methodist. Home: 8208 Chipplegate Dr Richmond VA 23227 Office: 2117 N Hamilton St Richmond VA 23230

REID, KENNETH BROOKS, educator, mathematician, educator; b. Jacksonville, Fla., Mar. 2, 1943; s. Kenneth Brooks and Gwendolyn Wilson (Ware) R.; B.A., U. Cal. at Berkeley, 1964; M.A., U. Ill., 1966, Ph.D., 1968; m. Marion Margaret Taylor, Sept. 3, 1966; 1 dau., Kathryn Margaret. Asst. prof. math. La. State U., Baton Rouge, 1968-73, asso. prof., 1973—. Research grantee NSF, 1971. Mem. Am. Math. Soc., Soc. Indsl. and Applied Math., Math. Assn. Am. Contbr. articles to profl. jours. Home: 1818 Blouin Av Baton Rouge LA 70808

REID, LESLIE WOODS, fruit co. exec.; b. Detroit, May 19, 1913; s. Richard John and Violet Wilhemina (White) R.; student U.S. Army Officer's Candidate Sch., 1954, Lakeland Bus. Inst., 1960; m. Margaret Ann Branam, June 6, 1952; children—Leslie Scott, Rhonda Frances, Mary Anna, Amy Lea. Commd. 2d lt. U.S. Army, 1944, advanced through grades to maj., 1952; q.m. Ft. Bragg, N.C., 1949-50; I Corps, Korea, 1950-52; A.J. Sch., Ft. Benjamin Harrison, Ind., 1953-54; SETAF-Italy, 1954-57; ret., 1957; office mgr. Coca-Cola Bottling Co., Lakeland, Fla., 1960-62; office mgr. Hardee Mfg. Co., Plant City, Fla., 1962-64; treas., dir. Carter Fruit Co., Lakeland, Fla., 1964—; dir. Carter Groves, Inc., Carter Realty Co., C & C Mgmt. Co. Mem. Am. Legion. Elk. Home: Villa 170 Imperial Southgate Lakeland FL 33803 Office: 201 1/2 E Lemon St PO Box 884 Lakeland FL 33802

REID, MARK KERNAN, clergyman, author; b. Sheridan, Ark., Dec. 28, 1936; s. Sidney J. and Laura Mae (Davenport) R.; B.A., Little Rock U., 1965; M.Div., Lexington Theol. Sem., 1968, postgrad., 1973-74; postgrad. U. Ark., 1971-72; m. Evelyn Lonita Hibbard, Oct. 20, 1963; children—Mark Erik, Jason Kyle. Ordained to ministry Christian Ch., 1968; pastor Fox Creek Ch., Lawrenceburg, Ky., 1966-68, First Christian Ch., Berryville, Ark., 1968-69, First Christian Ch., Fayetteville, 1969-73, Woodland Christian Ch., Lexington, Ky., 1973—. Mem. various ecumenical, ecclesiastical, ednl. bds. and commns. Bd. dirs. Econ. Opportunity Agy., Fayetteville, United Campus Ministry, Fayetteville. Recipient various awards of appreciation from social action groups. Office: 530 E High St Lexington KY 40508

REID, MILES ALVIN, sch. prin.; b. West Point, Va., Oct. 23, 1931; s. William Ensley and Cecelia Olymphia (Whiting) R.; B.A., Morgan State Coll., Balt., 1953; M.A., Hampton (Va.) Inst., 1968; postgrad. Va. State Coll., 1958-63, U. Va., 1969-70, Va. Commonwealth U., 1970-71; m. Alice Lee, Aug. 14, 1966; 1 dau., Alicia Mia. Social studies tchr. Central High Sch., King and Queen, Va., 1957-64; prin. King and Queen Elementary Sch., Shanghai, Va., 1964-72. Mem. West Point Bi-Racial Com., 1969—, West Point and Vicinity Community Action Group, 1971—. Mem. West Point Bd. Zoning

Appeals, 1971—; mem. King William County Dem. Com., 1967—. Bd. dirs. West Point Area Improvement Assn., vice chmn., 1970-71; bd. dirs. West Point Centennial Corp., 1970. Mem. King William County Lit. Union (program chmn. 1970), Nat., Va. (pres.-elect dept. elementary sch. prins. dist. C, 1971), King and Queen edn. assns., N.A.A.C.P. Baptist (gen. supt. ch. sch. 1964—, mem. Pamunkey Bapt. Assn. and Ch. Sch. Conv., instr. Bapt. Gen. Conv. Va. Inst. 1964—). Home: 216 16th St West Point VA 23181 Office: Hamilton-Holmes Elementary Sch King William VA 23086

REID, RALPH W(ALDO) E(MERSON), mgmt. cons.; b. Phila., July 5, 1915; s. Ralph Waldo Emerson and Alice Myrtle (Stuart) R.; student Temple U., 1932-34; B.S., Northwestern U., 1936; M.A., U. Hawaii, 1938; Ph.D., Harvard, 1949; m. Ruth Bull, Dec. 7, 1946; 1 son, Robert. Asst. to v.p. Northwestern U., 1938-40; chief municipal govt. br., spl. asst. govt. sect. Supreme Comdr. Allied Powers, 1946-47; spl. asst. under sec. army, 1948-49; chief Far Eastern affairs div. Office Occupied Areas, chief econs. div. Office Civil Affairs and Mil. Govt., Dept. Army, 1950-53; asst. to dir. Bur. Budget, 1953-55, asst. dir., 1955-61; resident mgr. A. T. Kearney & Co., 1961—. Mem. planning bd. NSC, 1954-61. Served from ensign to comdr. USNR, 1941-46. Decorated Dept. Navy Commendation Ribbon; recipient Dept. Army Exceptional Civilian Service award. Mem. Am. Oriental Soc., Am. Polit. Sci. Assn., C. of C. U.S. (com. govt. operations and expenditures, com. improvement fed. budget, adv. task force financing state and local govts.), Inst. Mgmt. Cons. Clubs: Union League (Chgo.); Capitol Hill, Cosmos (Washington). Home: 412 Monticello Blvd Alexandria VA 22305 Office: 1725 K St NW Washington DC 20006

REIFF, JOHN CECIL, elec. engr.; b. Muskogee, Okla., Oct. 5, 1921; s. Cecil K. and Dorothy (McCloud) R.; B.S., Okla. U., 1947; M.S., Okla. A. and M. Coll., 1950; m. Marjorie Louise Jenry, May 8, 1943; 1 son, John Cecil. Instr. elec. engring. dept. U. N.M., 1947-51; research, devel. engr. missile systems Western Electric Co.-Bell Telephone Labs., 1951-54; research and devel. engr. White Sands Missile Range, N.M., 1954-68, supervisory missile systems engr., 1968—; pres. CJC Enterprises, Inc. Instl. rep. Cub Scouts Montgomery dist. Boy Scouts Am., 1955-58. Served with F.A., AUS, 1943-46, to capt., 1951-54; now col. Res. Registered profl. engr., Tex. Mem. I.E.E.E., Tex. Soc. Profl. Engrs., Phi Delta Theta. Baptist. Home: 9809 Gschwind St El Paso TX 79924 Office: SSEA Bldg 1400 White Sands Missile Range NM 88002

REIFF, WILLIAM HENRY, physician; b. Muskogee, Okla., July 24, 1918; s. Cecil K. and Dorothy Ellen (McCloud) R.; B.S., U. Okla., 1939, M.D., 1941; m. Maxine Ruth Hoffer, Feb. 20, 1942; children—William C., Kaethe M. (Mrs. Daniel F. Stella), Patricia A. (Mrs. John F. Moore). Intern, U. Mich. Hosp., 1941-42, asst. resident internal medicine, 1945-46, resident, 1946-48; practice medicine specializing in internal medicine, Oklahoma City, 1948—; mem. staff St. Anthony, Bapt. Meml., Deaconess hosps.; asst. prof. internal medicine U. Okla. Regent Oral Roberts U., Tulsa. Served with AUS, World War II. Decorated Bronze Star medal, Combat Med. badge, French Croix de Guerre with palm; recipient Pfizer Co. award for civil def., 1964. Diplomate Am. Bd. Internal Medicine. Fellow A.C.P.; mem. Soc. Nuclear Medicine, A.M.A., Okla. Med. Assn., Oklahoma County Med. Soc., Phi Chi, Phi Delta Theta. Home: 2505 NW 42d St Oklahoma City OK 73112 Office: 3015 NW 59th St Oklahoma City OK 73112

REILLY, CHARLES AUSTIN, petroleum co. physicist; b. Summerside, P.E.I., Can., May 18, 1916; s. Austin and Agnes Flora (Pillman) R.; B.Sc., Dalhousie U., 1939, M.Sc., 1940; A.M., Harvard, 1946, Ph.D., 1950; m. Helen Frances Warner, Dec. 19, 1942. Came to U.S., 1951, naturalized, 1957. Research physicist Research Council Can., Halifax, N.S., 1940-42; asst. prof. chemistry Dalhousie U., Halifax, 1949-51; physicist Shell Devel. Co., Emeryville, Cal., 1951-72, Houston, 1972—. Served to lt. Royal Canadian Navy, 1943-45. Fellow Am. Phys. Soc., Am. Inst. Chemists; mem. Am. Chem. Soc., Sigma Xi. Club: Sugar Creek Country. Contbr. articles to sci. jours. Home: 2622 Country Club Blvd Sugar Land TX 77478 Office: 3737 Bellaire Blvd Houston TX 77025

REILLY, EDWARD JOSEPH, govt. ofcl., author; b. N.Y.C., Oct. 13, 1920; s. Anthony Joseph and Theresa May (Clancy) R.; A.B., Rutgers U., 1947; M.A., N.Y. U., 1955; m. Olga Antuck, Jan. 28, 1950; 1 dau., Nina Marie. News and spl. events staff NBC, N.Y.C., 1941-42; govt. relations adviser Arabian-Am. Oil Co., Dhahran, Saudi Arabia, 1947-48; univ. relations counsel Ivy Lee & T.J. Ross, Public Relations, N.Y.C., 1948-51; dir. tech. liaison Army Engrs., Washington, Cal., N.Y., 1951-61; dir. information Army Transp., N.Y.C., 1961-62; pub. relations counsel Internal Revenue Service, N.Y.C., 1962-69, information specialist field service, Washington, 1969—. Organizer Am. Legion Jersey Boys State, Rutgers U., 1947. Trustee D.A.V. Hosp. Fund N.J. Served with USMCR, 1942-45; PTO. Decorated Bronze Star, Purple Heart. Mem. D.A.V., Am. Legion, Am. Mil. Engrs., Rutgers Alumni, Pub. Relations Soc., Zeta Psi. Contbr. articles to profl. jours. Home: 1842 Foxstone Dr Vienna VA 22180 Office: Nat Office Internal Revenue Service 1111 Constitution Av NW Washington DC 20224

REILLY, JOSEPH FRANCIS, pharmacologist; b. Waucoma, Ia., May 14, 1915; s. Joseph F. and Grace M. (Lynch) R.; B.A., U. Ill., 1937; M.A., Harvard, 1939; Ph.D., U. Chgo., 1947; m. Joan M. Cowie, Oct. 16, 1948; children—Joseph, Joan, John, Elizabeth, Andrew. Chemist chem. research dept. Armour & Co., Chgo., 1939-43; research asso. antimalarial program U. Chgo., 1943-46; pharmacologist Army Chem. Center, Md., 1947-48; research fellow Cornell U. Med. Coll., N.Y.C., 1948-49, instr. pharmacology, 1949-52, asst. prof., 1953-54; asst. prof. psychiatry and pharmacology, also pharmacologist Payne-Whitney Clinic of N.Y. Hosp. and Cornell Med. Center, 1954-62; chief pharmacodynamics sect. FDA, Washington, 1962-70, chief drug bioanalysis br., 1970—. Cons. Council on Pharmacy and Chemistry of A.M.A., 1956, Council on Drugs, 1966; collaborator U.S. Pharmacopeia, 1970-73. Mem. Am. Soc. Pharmacology and Exptl. Therapeutics, Soc. Toxicology, Harvey Soc., Soc. Exptl. Biology and Medicine (sec.-treas. N.Y. area, 1954-59), Research Soc. Am., Sigma Xi, Gamma Alpha, Tau Kappa Epsilon. Contbr. articles to profl. jours. Home: 9623 Alta Vista Terrace Bethesda MD 20014 Office: 200 C St SW Washington DC 20204

REILLY, TERRENCE EDWARD, banker; b. Providence, Sept. 5, 1920; s. Michael and Flora (DePine) R.; B.S., Bryant Coll., 1948; grad. U. Va. Sch. Consumer Banking, 1965; m. Virginia Mary Durham, Jan. 8, 1949; children—Katherine A., Terrence M., Stephen V., Thomas J., J. Kevin. Office mgr. Comml. Credit Corp., Providence, 1948-53; times sales rep. Indsl. Nat. Bank, Providence, 1953-57; asst. cashier Broward Nat. Bank, Ft. Lauderdale, Fla., 1957-58; v.p. Coral Ridge Nat. Bank, Ft. Lauderdale, 1958-73; pres. Broward Nat. Bank Plantation (Fla.), 1973—. Tchr. Am. Inst. Banking, 1965. Served to maj. USAAF, 1942-46. Rotarian. Home: 529 SW 10th Av Fort Lauderdale FL 33312 Office: 8200 W Broward Blvd Plantation FL 33314

REIMOLD, ROBERT JAMES, ecologist; b. Greenville, Pa., Nov. 15, 1941; s. Frank Ellis and Frances Lyle (Rickard) R.; B.A., Thiel Coll., 1963; M.A., U. Del., 1965, Ph.D., 1968; m. Mardith Harriet Osborne, June 15, 1963; children—Reid Elizabeth, Rae Katherine. Research asst. U. Del., 1966-68; postdoctoral fellow U. Ga., Sapelo Island, 1968-69, research asso. Marine Inst., 1969—, adj. asst. prof. dept. zoology, 1970—. Vis. prof. Fairleigh Dickinson U.; Coastal Zone ecol. cons.; prin. investigator research grants from AEC, NSF, Environmental Protection Agy., U.S. Army C.E., pvt. industry. Mem. Nat. Park Service Earth Resources Commn., 1970—, Ga. State Hwy. Dept. Planning Bd., 1971—, Ga. Gov.'s Sci. Adv. Council, 1972—. Mem. Soc. Am. Mil. Engrs., Am. Fisheries Soc., Am. Soc. Limnology and Oceanography, A.A.A.S., Am. Inst. Biol. Scis., Ecol. Soc. Am., Sigma Xi. Mason. Editor: Ecology of Halophytes, 1973. Contbr. articles profl. jours. Home: 3 Shell Hammock Dr Sapelo Island GA 31327 Office: Marine Inst Sapelo Island GA 31327

REINFURT, DONALD WILLIAM, statistician; b. Wilkes-Barre, Pa., Aug. 30, 1938; s. Frederick William and Catherine Margarite (Partridge) R.; B.S., State U. N.Y., Albany, 1960; M.A., State U. N.Y., Buffalo, 1963; Ph.D., N.C. State U., 1970; m. Mary Karen Hillix, June 19, 1965; children—Kristin Elizabeth, David William. Tchr. math. State U. N.Y., Buffalo, 1960-63; statistician U. N.C. Hwy. Safety Research Center, Chapel Hill, 1968—. USPHS trainee in biostatistics, 1963-68. Mem. Am. Statis. Assn., Signum Laudis, Kappa Mu Epsilon. Baptist. Contbr. articles profl. jours. Home: 403 Highview Dr Chapel Hill NC 27514 Office: Hwy Safety Research Center U NC Chapel Hill NC 27514

REINHARD, ERWIN ARTHUR, educator; b. Poth, Tex., Jan. 29, 1931; s. Erwin John and Agnes Pauline (Miculka) R.; student St. Marys U., 1952-53; B.S. (Schlumberger scholar), U. Tex., Austin, 1956, M.S. (Tex. Found. fellow), 1959, Ph.D. (NSF fellow, W. Alton Jones fellow), 1968; postgrad. U. Pitts., 1959-62; m. Irene Cecilia Salzman, Aug. 11, 1951; children—Nicolette (Mrs. Alan C. Cunningham), Lisa, Francis, Erwin, Tracie, Katherine. Nuclear research scientist Westinghouse Electric Corp., Bettis Atomic Power Lab., West Mifflin, Pa., 1959-63; prof. elec. engring. U. Ala., University, 1963—. Cons., Army Missile Command, Huntsville, Ala., NASA, Huntsville. Pres. Elementary P.T.A., 1963-66; active Warrior council Boy Scouts Am., 1968-70. Served with AUS, 1950-52. Mem. Am. Soc. Engring. Edn. (named Outstanding Elec. Engring. Instr. 1971), I.E.E.E., Soc. Indsl. and Applied Math., Eta Kappa Nu, Tau Beta Pi. Democrat. Roman Catholic. Kiwanian. Author: Basic Electric Circuits for Engineers, 1967; Basic Electronics for Engineers and Scientists, 1972. Contbr. articles profl. jours. Home: 276 Woodland Hills Tuscaloosa AL 35401 Office: PO Box 6169 University AL 35486

REINHEIMER, ROBERT, JR., architect; b. Mercury, Tex., Aug. 8, 1917; s. Robert and Frances Curry (Bell) R.; Asso.Sci., Tarleton State Coll., Stephenville, Tex., 1936; m. Dalma Louise Rawls, July 23, 1938; children—Patricia (Mrs. Donald D. McKinney), Frances (Mrs. Eric R. Steinhauser). Draftsman, Stanley Brown, architect, Marshall, Tex., 1937-38; draftsman, designer Bayard Witt, architect, Texarkana, Tex., 1939-40, 42-43; bldg. insp. Pub. Housing Adminstrn., Texarkana, 1941; prin. Reinheimer & Cox, Texarkana, 1944—. Chmn., Bd. Appeals Texarkana, 1959-62; mem. Bd. Adjustment Texarkana, 1970—. Mem. A.I.A. (citations for 4 bldg. designs pres. N.E. Tex. chpt. 1961-62), Tex. Soc. Architects (citation as chmn. profl. devel. com. 1969-71, v.p. 1967). Mem. Ch. of Christ. Rotarian. Clubs: Texarkana Country; Millwood Country (Ashdown, Ark.). Archtl. works include design Little River Meml. Hosp. (pub. in Archtl. Record 1959). Home: 1115 Canadian St Texarkana TX 75501 Office: 601 Pine St Texarkana TX 75501

REINIG, WILLIAM CHARLES, physicist; b. N.Y.C., June 5, 1924; s. William C.C. and Alice (Schuster) R.; B.Mech. Engring., Bklyn. Poly. Inst., 1945; postgrad. Columbia, 1949-51; m. Marion Borgstrom, Nov. 29, 1949; children—James W., Christine. Health physicist Gen. Electric Co., Richland, Wash., 1946-48, Brookhaven Nat. Lab., Upton, L.I., N.Y., 1948-51; sr. research supr. E.I. duPont de Nemours & Co., Aiken, S.C., 1951—. Chmn., Aiken County (S.C.) Pollution Commn., 1966-69; chmn. Central Savannah River Sci. Fair Assn., 1967; chmn. North Augusta-Jackson (S.C.) Sch. Bd., 1969—. Served with USNR, 1945-46. Diplomate Am. Bd. Health Physics (sec. treas. 1968-74, chmn. 1974—). Mem. Health Physics Soc. (sec. 1964-66), Am. Nuclear Soc., Am. Acad. Indsl. Hygiene, S.C. Acad. Sci., Nat. Council Radiation Protection (chmn. sci. com.). Editor: Environmental Surveillance in Vicinity of Nuclear Facilities, 1970. Home: 1014 Stanton Dr North Augusta SC 29841 Office: Savannah River Lab Aiken SC 29801

REINING, PRISCILLA ALDEN COPELAND (MRS. CONRAD C. REINING), anthropologist; b. Chgo., Mar. 11, 1923; d. Kenneth Bayard and Elsie (Weser) Copeland; A.B., U. Chgo., 1945, M.A., 1949, Ph.D., 1967; m. Conrad (Copeland) Reining, June 26, 1944; children—Robert Cushman, Anne Elizabeth, Conrad Copeland. Fellow, East African Inst. Social Research, Kampala, Uganda, 1951-55; lectr. U. Minn., Mpls., 1956-59, Howard U., Washington, D.C., 1960-65; research asso. Cath. U. Am., Washington, 1966-68, 70—; coordinator Center for Study of Man, Smithsonian Instn., Washington, 1968-70. Cons., lectr. Peace Corps, 1961-63; cons. livestock appraisal mission to Tanzania, Internat. Bank for Reconstrn. and Devel., 1972, AID, 1973. NSF grantee, 1967. Fellow African Studies Assn., Am. Anthrop. Assn., Washington, East African acads. scis.; mem. Internat. African Inst., A.A.A.S., Sigma Xi. Episcopalian. Editor, contbr. Kinship Studies in the Morgan Centennial Year, 1972. Contbr. articles to profl. jours. Home: 3601 Rittenhouse St NW Washington DC 20015 Office: Dept Anthropology Cath U Am Washington DC 20017

REISKIND, JONATHAN, educator; b. S.I., N.Y., May 27, 1940; s. Maxwell I. and Helen A. (Bunzleman) R.; A.B. cum laude, Amherst Coll., 1962; A.M., Harvard, 1965, Ph.D. in Biology, 1968; m. Julia Anne Barth, Feb. 12, 1966; children—Julia Alexandra, Michael Hay. Asst. prof. zoology U. Fla. at Gainesville, 1967-72, asso. prof. zoology, 1972—; research asso. Fla. State Collection of Arthropods, 1968—. Mem. A.A.A.S., Assn. Tropical Biology, Soc. for Study Evolution, Soc. Systematic Zoology, Am., Brit. archeol. socs., Cambridge Entomol. Soc., Wilderness Soc., Am. Fedn. Tchrs., Fla. Defenders Environment, Zero Population Growth, Am. Civil Liberties Union, Sigma Xi. Contbr. articles to profl. jours. Home: 213 SW 41st St Gainesville FL 32607

REISLER, DONALD LAURENCE, data processing cons. firm exec.; b. Bklyn., May 28, 1941; s. Samuel and Sylvia (Rassas) R.; A.B., Rutgers U., 1963; M.S., Yale, 1965, Ph.D., 1967; m. JoAnn Fenton, April 12, 1964; 1 dau., Kimberly Marla. Sr. analyst Research Analysis Corp., McLean, Va., 1967-70; dir. information systems Lambda Corp., Arlington, Va., 1970-73; pres. DBS Corp., Arlington, 1973—. Home: 360 Glyndon St NE Vienna VA 22180 Office: 1515 Wilson Blvd Arlington VA 22209

REISTLE, CARL ERNEST, JR., petroleum engr.; b. Denver, June 26, 1901; s. Carl E. and Leonara I. (McMaster) R.; B.S., U. Okla., 1922; student Harvard Sch. Bus. Adminstrn., 1948; D.Sc., U. Tulsa, 1966; m. Mattie A. Muldrow, June 23, 1922; children—Bette Jean (Mrs. Geo. F. Pierce), Mattie Ann, (Mrs. James Tracy Clark), Nancy L. (Mrs. Wilson Hayes Holliday), Carl Ernest III. Petroleum chemist U.S. Bur. Mines, 1922-29, petroleum engr., 1929-33; chmn. East Tex. Engring. Assn., 1933-36; with Humble Oil & Refining Co., 1933-66, successively engr. in charge, chief petroleum engr., gen. supt. prodn., mgr. prodn. dept., dir. mgr. prodn. dept., dir. charge prodn. dept., 1951-55, v.p. charge prodn. dept., 1955-57, exec. v.p., 1957-61, pres., 1961-63, chmn. bd. and chief exec. officer, 1963-66, cons., 1966—; chmn. bd. Olinkraft, Inc.; dir. Eltra Corp., Reed Tool Co. Trustee Houston Mus. Natural Sci. Recipient Anthony Lucas medal, 1958; Engr. of Year award Nat. Soc. Profl. Engrs., 1966. Mem. Mining and Metall. Soc. Am., Am. Petroleum Inst. (dir.), Am. Inst. Mining and Metall. Engrs. (pres. 1956), Sigma Xi, Tau Beta Pi, Sigma Tau, Alpha Chi Sigma. Clubs: Petroleum, Ramada, River Oaks Country, Anglers of N.Y. Contbr. tech. articles to profl. jours. Home: 3196 Chevy Chase Houston TX 77019 Office: 2605 Humble Bldg Houston TX 77002

REISTRUP, JEANNE MOSS (MRS. JAMES REISTRUP), interior designer; b. Glasgow, Mo., Aug. 11, 1905; d. Samuel and Jennie (Easley) Moss; student U. Ill., 1923-27; study in Europe, 1931; m. James Reistrup, July 23, 1931 (dec.); children—Paul H., John V. Head bur. interior decorating Davidson Bros., Sioux City, Ia., 1928-31; owner firm Jeanne Moss Reistrup Interiors, 1933—; tchr. interior decorating YWCA, Catholic U.; also lectr. Active United Givers, Symphony fund drs. and civic work. Recipient Woman of Achievement award, Sioux City, Ia., 1946. Fellow Am. Inst. Interior Designers (chmn. nat. conf. 1953, exhibit Nat. Housing Center 1959; mem. nat. by-laws com., nat. nominating com.; chmn. bd. govs., corr. sec. D.C. chpt.; mem. nat. nominating com. for govs.; chmn. chpt. relations D.C., chmn. lecture com. D.C. chpt. 1971-74); mem. Ia. State Soc. (v.p. 1963-65), Pan Am. Liaison Com. Women's Orgns. (corr. sec. 1959-60), P.E.O., Delta Zeta. Clubs: Fortnightly (past pres.), Morningside Coll. Faculty Women's (past pres.). Author articles in field. Home: 3701 Connecticut Av NW Washington DC 20008

REITER, EUGENE ANTHONY, banker; b. Chgo., Jan. 17, 1922; s. John Frederick and Barbara (Servais) R.; student Collegiate Bus. Coll., N.Y.C., 1947-49, Sch. Banking, Hofstra U., 1952; m. Gina Victoria Catanese, June 10, 1946; children—Eugene Anthony, Charles, John. Mgr. auto loan dept. Franklin Nat. Bank, Rockville Centre, N.Y., 1954-57; asst. v.p. Nat. Bank of Long Beach (N.Y.), 1957-59; v.p. 1st Va. Bank, Falls Church, Va., 1964—. Served with USNR, 1943-46. Mem. Consumer Bankers Assn. Club: St. Johns Bridge (McLean, Va.). Home: 1714 Linwood Place McLean VA 22101 Office: 6400 Arlington Blvd Falls Church VA 22042

REITER, RUSSEL JOSEPH, med. educator; b. St. Cloud, Minn., Sept. 22, 1936; s. Bernard William and Bernice Philomena (Friedman) R.; B.S., St. John's U., Collegeville, Minn., 1959; M.S., Wake Forest Coll., Bowman-Gray Sch. Medicine, 1961, Ph.D., 1964; m. Linda Gay Deweese, June 20, 1962; children—David Russel, Michael Kendrick. Asst. prof., then asso. prof. anatomy U. Rochester, 1966-71; mem. faculty U. Tex. Med. Sch., San Antonio, 1971—, prof. anatomy, 1973—. Served with AUS, 1964-66. Recipient Career Devel. award USPHS, 1969-71, 72-75. Mem. Endocrine Soc., Internat. Soc. Neuroendocrinology, Am. Assn. Anatomists, A.A.A.S., Am. Soc. Zoologists, Am. Physiol. Soc., Soc. Study Reprodn., Internat. Soc. Research in Biol. Reprodn., Pan Am. Assn. Anatomists, Internat. Soc. Chromobiology, Sigma Xi. Editor: Jour. Neuroendocrinology. Inventor stereotoxic hypophysectomizer. Home: 146 Garrapata St San Antonio TX 78232

REITZ, HERMAN J., educator; b. Belle Plaine, Kan., July 5, 1916; s. Thomas Max and Flora Mae (Powers) R.; B.S., Kan. State Coll., 1939, M.S., Ohio State U., 1940, Ph.D., 1949; m. Alice C. Benton, Feb. 21, 1945; children—Elizabeth, Max. Mem. faculty U. Fla. Agrl. Expt. Sta. at Lake Alfred, 1946—, prof. hort. sci., 1950—, dir. agrl. research Citrus Expt. Sta., 1956—. Served as lt. (j.g.) USNR, 1942-45. Fellow A.A.A.S., Am. Soc. Hort. Sci. (exec. com. 1968-70; Gourley medal 1948); mem. Internat. Soc. Citriculture (dir. 1971—, pres. 1974—). Contbr. numerous articles profl. jours. Home: PO Box 1293 Lake Alfred FL 33850

REITZER, LORENE IDA, banker; b. Hondo, Tex., Oct. 4, 1914; d. Lee Henry and Katherine Barbara (Leinweber) Hardt; student Draughons Bus. Coll., 1941, Am. Tech. Soc., 1946; certificate Am. Inst. Banking Sch., 1971; m. Joel V. Reitzer, Nov. 2, 1938; children—Paulete (Mrs. Melvin Brownfield), Joel V. Asst. chief clk. Kelly AFB, San Antonio, 1941-43; with Highland Park State Bank, San Antonio, 1952—, sec., customer's services, 1952-67, sr. sec., asst. trust dept., 1967-69, asst. trust officer, 1969-73, asst. cashier, trust officer, 1973—. Mem. Am. Inst. Banking (sec. 1967-68), Nat. Assn. Bank Women, S.E. Bus. and Profl. Women (v.p.). Mem. Nazarene Ch. (bd. mem. 1955-72, sec. ch. 1954-67, 70-72; tchr. Sunday sch. 1950-72). Home: PO Box 10002 San Antonio TX 78210 Office: PO Box 10250 San Antonio TX 78210

RELPH, ROSS, civil engr.; b. Minco, Okla., Jan. 24, 1921; s. Tom and Geneva (Ross) R.; student U. Kan., 1939-41; m. Kaye Horner, June 19, 1947; children—Gene Ellen, Rosalind Kaye, Mary Eleda. Partner, sec.-treas. Lowrie-Relph-McNett & Assos., Oklahoma City, 1960—; dir. City Nat. Bank and Trust Co., Oklahoma City. Chmn. Oklahoma City Street Adv. Commn., 1965-66. Served with AUS, 1942-45. Registered profl. engr., Okla., N.M., Kan. Mem. Am. Soc. C.E., Nat., Okla. socs. profl. engrs., Oklahoma City C. of C., Capitol Hill C. of C. Home: 8401 Lakehurst Dr Oklahoma City OK 73120 Office: City National Bank Tower 200 N Robinson Oklahoma City OK 73102

REMEIN, QUENTIN ROBERT, govt. ofcl.; b. Rochester, N.Y., Sept. 5, 1919; s. Harry J. and Florence (Noland) R.; A.B., Calvin Coll., Grand Rapids, Mich., 1945; postgrad. U. Mich., 1946, Am. U., 1948-49; m. Harriet A. Kuipers, Apr. 3, 1944; children—Quentin Robert, Kathryn H., Teresa F. Statistician, venereal disease div. USPHS, Washington, 1946-54, chief statistician chronic disease program, 1954-57, asso. chief operational research, chronic disease program, 1957-62, chief program planning and evaluation Nat. Center for Chronic Disease Control, 1962-69; spl. asst. for planning and program coordination Dept. Health, Edn. and Welfare, Washington, 1969-72, dir. program operations analysis Office Asst. Sec., 1972-73, asso. dir. for program devel. Nat. Center for Health Statistics, 1973—. Served to 2d lt. AUS, 1941-44; PTO. Decorated Purple Heart; recipient Superior Service award Dept. HEW. Mem. Am. Statis. Assn., N.Y., Acad. Scis., Washington Christian Sch. Soc., Am. Acad. Health Adminstrn. Mem. Christian Reformed Ch. (elder). Contbr. articles on pub. health and chronic diseases to sci. jours. Home: 18 Wynkoop Ct Bethesda MD 20034 Office: Nat Center for Health Statistics Dept Health Edn and Welfare 5600 Fishers Lane Rockville MD 20852

REMER, DONALD SHERWOOD, chem. co. engr.; b. Detroit, Feb. 16, 1943; s. Nathan and Frieda Harriet (Stoner) R.; B.S., U. Mich., 1965; M.S. (NSF grantee), Cal. Inst. Tech., 1966, Ph.D., 1970; m. Louise Anita Collen, Dec. 21, 1969; 1 dau., Tanya Elissa. Tchr., Cal. Inst. Tech., Pasadena, 1969; tech. service engr. Exxon Chem. Co., Baton Rouge, La., 1970-71, div. coordinator, 1972, startup process engr., 1972—. Mgr. Red Cross Shelter, 1971—; chem. industry liaison with minority high sch. students, 1971—; field rep. United Givers, 1971; Atlantic Richfield grantee, 1968; Cal. State grantee, 1969. Chmn. Caltech. Alumni Fund drive in La., 1973-74. Recipient Pres.'s Council on Phys. Fitness Jogging award, 1973. Registered profl. engr., La. Mem. Am. Inst. Chem. Engrs. (Nat. Pub. Relations award 1972), Am. Inst. Chemists, Am. Chem. Soc., Nat. Soc. Profl. Engrs., Sigma Xi, Phi Kappa Phi, Phi Lambda Upsilon. Contbr. articles to profl. jours. Home: 686 Monet Baton Rouge LA 70806 Office: Exxon Chem Co Baton Rouge LA 70821

REMES, LURA DUFF ELLISTON, civic worker, poet; b. Ft. Worth, July 20, 1933; d. Fred Addison and Lura Duff (Elliston) M.; student Duke, 1951-52, U. Tex., 1952-54; m. George Edward Nowotny, Jr., Aug. 14, 1954 (div. Aug. 14, 1973); children—Edward Duff, George Edward III, Addison Dance, m. 2d, Eugene Marriott Remes, Apr. 13, 1974; 1 son, Mark Randall. Bd. dirs. Sebastian County Mental Health Assn., 1963-69, Ark. Assn. Mental Health 1966-72; gov. Western Ark. Counciling and Guidance Center, 1969-74; dir. Spark's Hosp. Guild, 1964-70, pres., 1973-74; dir. Community Concert Assn., 1968—; pres. Ft. Smith Affiliation of the Arts, 1968; co-chmn. arts festivals, 1964, 65, 70; leadership cons. Nat. Assn. Retarded Children, 1968-69; mem. Retardation Com. State Health Planning, 1968-69; mem. Sebastian County Youth Services Commn., 1973-74; mem. Comprehensive Health Planning Council, 1969-74; del. Nat. Symposium on Alternatives to Incarceration of Youth, 1974. Republican committeewoman 3d Congl. Dist., 1962-64, 68-70; charter mem. County Rep. Women, 1961—; co-chmn. Rep. United Campaign, 1962; sec. Rep. State Conv., 1968; justice of peace, 1973-74. Trustee Old Fort Museum, 1968-74, pres., 1971-72; trustee St. John's Sch. for Children with Learning Disabilities, 1971-74; mem. adv. bd. St. Edward's Mercy Hosp., 1967-69; bd. govs. Sebastian County Juvenile Detention Center, 1974. Recipient first place award, Ark. Arts Festival, 1968; named one of outstanding young women of Am., 1966. Mem. Jr. League Ft. Smith, D.A.R., Delta Delta Delta. Episcopalian (pres. ch. women 1961-62). Author: New Look Trio, 1970. Founder, designer Ft. Smith Children's Museumobile, 1965; author vol. art enrichment program Ft. Smith Pub. Schs., 1969; design concept mini parks City of Ft. Smith, 1972. Home: 2 River Ridge Rd Little Rock AR 72204

REMINGTON, CHARLES EMMETT, assn. exec.; b. Meridian, Ida., Feb. 12, 1905; s. Guy Amos and Josephine Patterson (Hill) R.; student U. Ida., 1923-27; B.S., Ore. State U., 1929; m. Cleda Raynor, May 29, 1930; children—Richard, Delbert. Engr., Ida. Hwy. Dept., Boise, 1931-35; with U.S. Forest Ser., 1935-61, asst. regional engr., Portland, Ore., 1954-59, regional engr., Denver, 1960-61; chief engr. Bur. Land Mgmt., Interior Dept., Washington, 1961-67; treas. Washington Soc. Engrs., 1969—. Served to lt. col. AUS, 1940-46; 51-54. Decorated Legion Merit; recipient Distinguished Service award Interior Dept., 1968. Mem. Am. Soc. C.E., Soc. Am. Mil. Engrs., Soc. Am. Foresters, Am. Congress Surveying and Mapping. Democrat. Methodist. Mason, Acacian. Home: 2005 Columbia Pike Arlington VA 22204

RENAZCO, ANTONIO JOSE, Nicaraguan diplomat; b. Managua, Nicaragua, Oct. 9, 1926; s. Antonio Jose and Esmeralda (Guerrero) R.; E.E., Worcester Poly. Inst., 1951. With engring. dept. Buffalo Forge Co., 1951-52; chief engr. Technomat CA, Caracas, Venezuela, 1952-62; chief engr. air conditioning dept. Creole Petroleum Corp., Caracas, 1962-65; consul gen. of Nicaragua in New Orleans, 1965-69, in Houston, 1969—. Treas. New Orleans Consular Corps. Decorated Order of Malta; named Hon. Citizen Jackson, Miss. and New Orleans, 1967. Mem. Am. Soc. Heating, Refrigerating and Air Conditioning Engrs., Inst. Hispanic Culture (treas.), Theta Chi. Clubs: New Orleans Country, Plimsoll, Playboy (New Orleans). Home: 11315 Valley Spring Dr Houston TX 77043 Office: 5633 Richmond Av Suite 203 Houston TX 77027

RENEAU, DELBRIDGE WILSON, feed mfg. co. exec.; b. Seguin, Tex., Feb. 16, 1911; s. Everett Roy and Kittie C. (Davenport) R.; grad. high sch.; m. Ruth Nickell, Feb. 9, 1934; children—Nelda Jean, Vernon Hahn. Partner Reneau Bros. Poultry and Egg Co., Seguin, Tex., 1934-70; v.p. Holly Farms Poultry Industries, Seguin, Tex., 1970-72, dir. Field rep. Tex. Dept. Agr., 1972—; mem. Tex. Egg Marketing Bd., 1957—. Served with AUS, 1944. Named Seguin Man of Year C. of C., 1951. Mem. Tex. (dir. 1951-66), Seguin (pres. 1951) Chambers Commerce, San Antonio Mfg. Assn. (dir., v.p. 1967-71), Tex. Poultry Fedn. (dir. 1967-70), Tex. Broiler Council (pres. 1969). Mem. Assembly of God Ch. (deacon 1968). Mason (Shriner), Lion. Home: 1306 Keller Lane Seguin TX 78155 Office: 506 John H Reagan Bldg Austin TX 78711

RENICK, RALPH APPERSON, journalist; b. N.Y.C., Aug. 9, 1928; s. Ralph Apperson and Rosalie (Dwyer) R.; A.B., U. Miami (Fla.), 1949; m. Elizabeth Jane Henry, June 5, 1949 (dec. July 1964); children—Patricia, Kathryn, Ralph A., Susan, Pamela, Michele. News dir. TV Sta. WTVJ, Miami, 1950-58, v.p. for news, 1958—; v.p. Wometco Enterprises, Miami, 1959—; instr. TV news reporting U. Miami, 1952-58. Chmn. Dade County Library Devel. Council; mem. Fla. Library Devel. Council. Regional bd. govs. Nat. Conf. Christians and Jews; trustee Barry Coll.; trustee, bd. dirs. United Fund Dade County; bd. dirs. Boystown of Fla. Recipient Radio-TV Mirror award, 1967. Mem. Radio Television News Dirs. Assn. (nat. pres. 1958-59), Nat. Press Club, Radio-TV Corrs. Assn., Nat. News Council, A.P. Broadcasters Assn. (dir.), Miami-Dade C. of C., Iron Arrow, Sigma Delta Chi, (chpt. pres. 1958-59), Kiwanian. Home: 14040 NW 3d Av Miami FL 33168 Office: 316 N Miami Av Miami FL 33130

RENNINGER, FREDERICK AUGUST, geologist, assn. exec.; b. N.Y.C., Nov. 8, 1936; s. Frederick A. and Ada (Hadler) R.; B.S., Rensselaer Poly. Inst., 1958; postgrad. George Washington U., 1960-61; m. Anne Marie Hoffmann, June 25, 1960; children—David Frederick, Helen Rachel, Daniel Howard. Asst. mgr. Upstate Loan Co., Kingston, N.Y., 1958-59; technician Mt. Alto VA Hosp., Washington, 1959; v.p. operations Nat. Crushed Stone Assn., Washington, 1959—; geology cons. Registered engr., Vt.; certified profl. geologist. Mem. Am. Soc. for Testing and Materials, Am. Inst. Mining, Metall. and Petroleum Engrs., Am. Inst. Profl. Geologists, Transp. Research Bd., Air Pollution Control Assn., Washington Soc. Assn. Execs., Zeta Psi. Presbyn. (deacon, elder). Contbr. articles in field to profl. jours. Home: 6806 Lynbrook Dr Springfield VA 22150 Office: 1415 Elliot Pl NW Washington DC 20007

RENOLL, ELMO SMITH, agrl. engr., educator; b. Glen Rock, Pa., Jan. 25, 1922; s. Paul K. and Mazie C. (Smith) R.; B.S., Auburn U., 1947; M.S., Ia. State U., 1949; m. Margaret W. Waid, Sept. 15, 1945; children—Lynn A., Jean L. Engr., U.S. Dept. Agr., Auburn, Ala., 1945-47, Ames, Ia., 1947-49; asst. prof. agrl. engring. Auburn (Ala.) U., 1949-52, asso. prof., 1952-72, prof., 1972—. Engr. New Holland Machine Co., New Holland, Pa., 1952. Bd. dirs. Chattahoochee council Boy Scouts Am. Served with AUS, 1942-45. Decorated Purple Heart. Recipient Silver Beaver award Nat. Boy Scouts Am., 1966. Mem. Am. Soc. Agrl. Engrs., Am. Soc. Engring. Educators, A.A.A.S., Alpha Zeta, Gamma Sigma Delta. Contbr. articles on agrl. engring. to profl. jours. Home: 939 S Gay St Auburn AL 36830 Office: Dept Agricultural Engineering Auburn University Auburn AL 36830

RENSCH, EDWARD, JR., hosp. adminstr.; b. East St. Louis, Ill., Aug. 16, 1927; s. Edward L. and Dorothy (Munson) R.; B.S., St. Louis U., 1955; M.H.A., Washington U., 1957; m. Marjorie Jill Maisel, June 6, 1956; children—Allison Maria, Todd Edward. Adminstrv. resident VA Hosp., Houston, 1956-57; adminstr. Crete (Neb.) Municipal Hosp., 1957-59, Wabash Gen. Hosp., Mt. Carmel, Ill., 1959-62; asst. supt. New Castle (Ind.) State Hosp., 1962-66; asst. adminstr. St. Vincent Infirmary, Little Rock, 1965-68; dir. health planning program State of Ark., Little Rock, 1968-70; asso. coordinator Ark. Regional Med. Program, Little Rock, 1970—; also adminstr. Central Ark. Radiotherapy Inst. Served with USNR, 1945-49, 51-52. Mem. Am., Ark. hosp. assns., Am. Coll. Hosp. Adminstrs., Nat. Assn. Accountants. Presbyn. Rotarian. Home: 9716 Overby Ct Little Rock AR 72205 Office: Markham & University Sts Little Rock AR 72204

RENSHAW, JOHN CHARLES, TV exec.; b. Pitts., Oct. 22, 1928; s. David E. and Alice (Glover) R.; student Carnegie Inst. Tech., 1945-46; B.S. in Journalism, So. Meth. U., 1950, B.A. in Speech, 1950; m. Nita Faye Payne, Aug. 19, 1961; 1 son, John Charles. Writer, dir. WFAA-TV, Dallas, 1951-53; program dir. KRBC-TV, Abilene, Tex., 1953-54; program dir., v.p. KSLA-TV, Shreveport, La., 1954—. Founder, pres. Gas Light Players, Shreveport, 1959; conductor, dir. Shreveport Savoyards, 1963—; asso. amusements critic Shreveport Jour., 1960—. Bd. dirs. Caddo-Bossier chpt. A.R.C. Mem. C. of C. (cultural affairs com.), TV Programming Conf. (past pres.), Gilbert and Sullivan Soc. Shreveport and N.Y., D'Oyly Carte Opera Trust, Sigma Delta Chi. Republican. Episcopalian. Home: 464 Irving Bluff E Shreveport LA 71107 Office: Box 4812 KSLA-TV Shreveport LA 71104

RENTENBACH, THOMAS JOSEPH, contractor; b. Hancock, Mich., Mar. 30, 1911; s. Thomas Michael and Margaret Helen (O'Neill) R.; B.S., Mich. Tech. U., Houghton, 1932, C.E., 1933; m. La Reine Brelsford, Oct. 10, 1936; children—Thomas Michael, La Reine (Mrs. Kenneth James Fedor), William Brelsford, Robert Patrick. With U.S. Army C.E., St. Paul, Conchas Dam, N.M., Little Rock dist. offices, 1933-40; engr., sr. engr. spl. engring. div. Panama Canal, 1941-42; founder Rentenbach Engring. Co., Knoxville, Tenn., 1946, gen. mgr., 1946-56, pres., 1956-71, chmn. bd., chief exec. officer, 1971—; dir. Hamilton Nat. Bank, Home Fed. Savs. & Loan Assn. Gen. chmn. United Fund Drive, 1969; chmn. steering com. Knoxville Center City Task Force, 1973. Pres. United Way of Greater Knoxville, 1972; trustee Mich. Tech. U. Devel. Fund; mem. lay adv. bd. St. Marys Hosp. Served from 1st lt. to maj., C.E., AUS, 1942-46. Decorated Army Commendation medal. Fellow Am. Soc. C.E.; mem. Nat. Soc. Profl. Engrs. (pres. Knoxville chpt. 1959), Asso. Gen. Contractors Am. (pres. Tenn. br. 1970), Greater Knoxville C. of C. (dir. 1967-69), Tau Beta Pi (nat. exec. council). Elk. Clubs: Cherokee Country, City (Knoxville). Home: 6611 Ridge Rock Lane Knoxville TN 37919 Office: 2400 Sutherland Av PO Box 11087 Knoxville TN 37919

REPASS, FRED GREENE, oral surgeon; b. Richlands, Va., Sept. 2, 1903; s. James Albert and Jennie Belle (Greene) R.; student U. Richmond, 1923-24; D.D.S., Med. Coll. Va., 1928; M.S., Northwestern U., 1938; m. Hazel Gaye Wiles, Aug. 3, 1933; children—Fred Greene, James Albert, John Scott, Thomas Hurt. Instr. dept. oral surgery Med. Coll. Va. Dental Sch., 1928-30; gen. practice dentistry, Bedford, Va., 1930-37, specializing in oral surgery, Roanoke, Va., 1938—; mem. staff Roanoke Meml. Hosp., Community Hosp. Roanoke Valley; cons. oral surgery VA Hosp., Roanoke, 1938—. Served from lt. (j.g.) to lt. USNR, 1930-38. Mem. Am. (life), Va. (life) dental assns., Piedmont, Roanoke dental socs., Am. (life), Southeastern, Va. socs. oral surgeons, Theta Chi, Psi Omega, Omicron Kappa Upsilon. Republican. Methodist. Clubs: Roanoke Country; Hickory Lake. Contbr. articles profl. jours. Home: 1936 Tucker Lane Salem VA 24153 Office: Med Ars Bldg Roanoke VA 24011

RESINGER, HAROLD EUGENE, pathologist; b. Kittanning, Pa., Dec. 18, 1924; s. William Gibson and Mamie Orvetta (Trudgen) R.; student Muskingum Coll., 1943-44; B.A., U. N.D., 1950, B.S., 1952; M.D., U. Neb., 1954; m. Greta Ann Thomas, Nov. 14, 1954; children—James Timothy, John Michael, Paul Jeffrey, David Patrick, Jack Dean, Kelly René, Nancy Diane. Intern, Neb. Meth. Hosp., Omaha, 1954-55; resident Mercy Hosp., Des Moines, 1955-59; practice medicine specializing in pathology, Des Moines, 1959-62, Lexington, Ky., 1962—; chief pathologist Good Samaritan Hosp., Lexington, Ky., 1962—; pres. Clin. Pathology Labs., Lexington, 1968-70; chmn. bd. Internat. Clin. Labs., Inc., Nashville, 1970—; pres. Internat. Clin. Labs. of Ky., Inc., Lexington, 1970—. Dir. Home Fed. Savs. & Loan Assn., Versailles, Ky., v.p., 1973—; dir. Central Bank & Trust Co., Lexington. Vis. asso. prof. clin. pathology U. Ky., 1962—. Bd. dirs. Am. Pathology Found., 1969—, pres., 1972-73. Served with AUS, 1943-46. Fellow Coll. Am. Pathologists, Am. Soc. Clin. Pathologists; mem. Ky. Soc. Pathologists (dir. 1966—, pres. 1967), Ky. Assn. Blood Banks (pres. 1973). Methodist. Home: 240 Rose Hill Versailles KY 40383 Office: 1800 S Limestone St Lexington KY 40503

RESNIK, FRANK EDWARD, tobacco co. exec.; b. Pleasant Unity, Pa., Oct. 14, 1928; s. Vincent and Augusta (Mauser) R.; B.S. in Chemistry, St. Vincent's, Latrobe, Pa., 1952; M.S., U. Richmond, 1955; m. Elizabeth Patterson, June 21, 1952; children—David A., Mary Ann, Anne Margaret. With Philip Morris, Inc., Richmond, Va., 1952—, tech. asst. to research mgr., 1960-62, sr. chemist devel. div., 1962, mgr. analytical services div., 1962-67, dir. comml. devel. tobacco, N.Y.C., 1967-69, dir. comml. devel. tobacco and gum, 1969-71, dir. devel., Richmond, 1971-72, dir. research center operations, 1972—. Mem. St. Edward's Sch. Bd., Richmond, 1972—. Bd. visitors Benedictine High Sch. Served with AUS, 1946-48, 51. Mem. Am. Chem. Soc., A.A.A.S., N.Y. Acad. Sci. Clubs: Salisbury Country (Midlothian, Va.); Downtown (Richmond). Contbr. articles to profl. publs. Patentee in field. Home: 2911 Queenswood Rd Midlothian VA 23113 Office: 4201 Commerce Rd Richmond VA 23234

RESO, ANTHONY, geologist; b. London, Eng., Aug. 10, 1934; s. Harry and Marion (Gerth) R.; came to U.S., 1940, naturalized, 1952; A.B., Columbia Coll., N.Y.C., 1954; M.A., Columbia U., 1955; postgrad. U. Cin., 1956-57; Ph.D. (fellow) Rice U., 1960; postgrad. Grad. Sch. Bus. U. Houston, 1964-68. Instr. geology Queens Coll., Flushing, N.Y., 1954; geologist Atlantic Richfield Corp., Midland, Tex., 1955-56; asst. prof. geology and curator invertebrate paleontology Pratt Mus., Amherst (Mass.) Coll., 1959-62; staff research geologist Tenneco Oil Co., Houston, 1962—. Lectr. U. Houston, 1962-65, mem. bd. advisers Gulf Univs. Research Corp., Galveston, Tex., 1967—, chmn., 1968-69. Mem. Houston Apt. Assn., 1970—; dir. Stewardship Properties, Houston. Recipient research grants Am. Assn. Petroleum Geologists, 1958, 59, Geol. Soc. Am., 1958, Eastman Fund, 1962; NSF fellow, 1959. Fellow Geol. Soc. Am., A.A.A.S.; mem. Am. Assn. Petroleum Geologists (life); Paleontol. Soc., Soc. Econ. Paleontologists and Mineralogists, Paleontol. Research Instn., Internat. Paleontol. Union, Am. Soc. Oceanography, Houston Geol. Soc. (v.p. 1973-74), Houston Symphony Soc., Sigma Xi, Sigma Gamma Epsilon, Beta Theta Pi. Episcopalian. Club: Shadyside Tennis. Contbr. profl. jours. Home: 1801 Huldy Houston TX 77019 Office: PO Box 2511 Houston TX 77001

RESOR, ROBERT REUBEN, assn. exec.; b. N.Y.C., May 1, 1921; s. Reuben Perry and Jeannette (Hummerstone) R.; B.S., Harvard, 1943; m. Julie Houstoun Harper, July 31, 1948; children—Randolph Richardson, Holly Amanda, Roberta Elizabeth, Hope Margaret. Reporter Voice of Am., Washington, 1946-47; mem. staff various pub. relations firms, N.Y.C., 1947-49; with Bozell & Jacobs, Inc., N.Y.C., 1949-68, sr. v.p., 1961-62, adminstrv. v.p., 1963-66, exec. v.p., 1966-68; spl. asst. labor Assn. Am. Railroads, Washington, 1968-70; dir. office of information services Occupational Safety and Health Adminstrn., U.S. Dept. of Labor, 1971; v.p. marketing Creative Systems, Inc., Washington, 1972-73; exec. dir. Office Free TV, Nat. Assn. Broadcasters, 1973—. Served to 1st lt. USAAF, 1943-46. Decorated Air medal (Army). Mem. Pub. Relations Soc. Am. (mem. com. on standards of profl. practice 1966-68). Episcopalian. Clubs: Harvard (N.Y.C. and Washington); Nat. Press (Washington), Congl. Country (Bethesda, Md.). Author: The Communications Challenges in the Decade of the 60's, 1962. Contbg. editor Trusts and Estates mag., 1962-67. Home: 7307 Burdette Ct Bethesda MD 20034

RESSLER, PARKE E(DWARD), lawyer, accountant; b. Lancaster, Pa., Aug. 21, 1916; s. Parke H. and Sadie (Weiser) R.; B.S., U. Pa., 1947; B.B.A., Baylor U., 1947, LL.B., 1952, J.D., 1969; M.B.A., U. Houston, 1949; m. Margaret B. Tucker, June 3, 1944; children—Nancy Parke, Margaret Anne. Agt. Internal Revenue Service, 1947-50; part time instr. Baylor U., 1950-65; admitted to Tex. bar, 1952, since practiced in Waco; asso. firm Edwin P. Horner. Mem. Am. Inst. C.P.A.'s, Tex. Soc. C.P.A.'s, Am., Tex., McLennan County bar assns., Am. Assn. Atty.-C.P.A.'s, Phi Alpha Delta, Delta Sigma Pi. Mem. Christian Ch. Rotarian. Clubs: Ridgewood Country, Hedonia, Ridgewood Yacht, Baylor Bear. Home: 2209 Arroyo Rd Waco TX 76710 Office: 3201 Franklin Av Waco TX 76710

RETAN, J. WALDEN, physician; b. Syracuse, N.Y., Oct. 30, 1930; s. H. Walden and Dorothy Eleanor (Brooks) R.; student Hamilton Coll., 1948-50, Mass. Inst. Tech., 1950-51; M.D., State U. N.Y., Syracuse, 1957; m. Carol D. Maynard, Feb. 22, 1955; children—Christopher, Nancy, Brian. Intern, Peter Bent Brigham Hosp., Boston, 1957-58, research fellow Cardiorenal Lab., 1958-61; dir. renal div. Wayne State U. Coll. Medicine, Detroit, 1961-63; mem. renal div. U. Ala. Med. Center, Birmingham, 1963-66, mem. pediatric renal div., 1967—; practice medicine specializing in internal medicine & renal diseases, Birmingham, 1967—; mem. staff Baptist Med. Center (Montclair), St. Vincents, Children's, Brookwood hosps.; dir. med. div. Freedom House, Birmingham, 1970-73; dir. med. service Southside Free Clinic and Switchboard, Birmingham, 1973—; pres., med. dir. Narcotic Addiction Treatment Program, Inc., Birmingham, 1972—. Served with USAF, 1951-53. Mem. Alpha Omega Alpha. Home: 3105 Warrington Rd Birmingham AL 35223 Office: 1701 9th Av S Birmingham AL 35205

REUCROFT, PHILIP JOHN, educator; b. Leeds, Eng., Mar. 29, 1935; s. Leonard and Ellen (Foster) R.; B.Sc., A.R.C.S., Imperial Coll., U. London, 1956, Ph.D., D.I.C., 1959; m. Sheila Anne Powers, May 20, 1961; children—Lisa Marie, Miles Alan, Noel Edward. Came to U.S., 1961, naturalized, 1972. Postdoctoral fellow NRC Can., 1959-61; with Franklin Inst. Research Labs., Phila., 1961-69, lab. mgr., 1966-69; asso. prof. materials sci. U. Ky., Lexington, 1969—, Ashland Oil Found. prof., 1970—. Cons., Franklin Inst., Plasti-Pole, Inc., law firm Stoll, Keenon, Park. Mem. Am. Chem. Soc., Am. Phys. Soc., Faraday Soc., Materials Research Soc. Contbr. articles, revs. to scholarly jours. Home: 3513 Lannette Lane Lexington KY 40503

REUDELHUBER, FRANK OTTO, petroleum engring co. exec.; b. Toledo, Jan. 18, 1924; s. George Gildemus and Caroline Elizabeth (Lupfer) R.; B.S., U. Okla., 1948; m. Mary Doris Rountree, Feb. 9, 1950; children—Daniel, Timothy, Margaret. Field engr. Atlantic Refining Co., 1947, 51; mgr. reservoir fluid dept. Core Labs., Dallas, 1951-56, mgr. Francorelab, S.A., Paris, 1959-65, mgr. research and tech. service, 1965-68, asst. to pres., 1968—. Mem. exec. com. Boy Scouts Am., 1970-71. Served with AUS, 1943-46. Decorated Bronze Star medal, Purple Heart with oak leaf cluster. Mem. Am. Inst. Mining, Metall. and Petroleum Engrs. (chmn. L. C. Uren award com. 1971-72). Club: Oak Cliff Country (Dallas). Contbr. articles to profl. jours. Home: 2026 Matagorda St Dallas TX 75232 Office: PO Box 10185 Dallas TX 75207

REUS-FROYLAN, FRANCISCO, bishop; b. San Juan, P.R., Apr. 14, 1919; s. Esteban and Carmen (Froylan) Reus; B.A., U. P.R., 1946, postgrad., 1954; L.Th., DuBose Sem., 1942; S.T.D., Gen. Theol. Sem., 1965; D.D., U. of South, 1968; S.T.D., Interam. U. P.R., 1969; m. Mary Doreen, Apr. 21, 1945; children—Pamela, Sandra, Carolyn. Ordained deacon Episcopal Ch., 1942, priest, 1943, bishop, 1964; curate St. John's Cathedral, 1942-43, rector, dean 1954-64; curate St. Andrews Ch., 1943-44; rector St. Mark's, Ponce, P.R., 1944-45; rector Atonement Ch., Ponce, 1945-48; tchr., chaplain St. Just Sch., 1948-54; bishop, Santurce, P.R., 1964—. Vice pres. P.R. council Boy Scouts Am., 1954-70. Bd. dirs. Episcopal Cathedral Sch., 1954-64, Instituto Sicologico of P.R.; chmn. bd. St. Luke's Episcopal Hosp.; bd. dirs. local A.R.C., 1967-70; bd. dirs. Puerto Rican Migrant Workers; trustee Good Samaritan Found.; chmn. bd. trustees Sem. of Caribbean; mem. exec. council Episcopal Ch., 1970—. Home: Ashford Av 1313 Santurce PR 00908 Office: Box C Saint Just PR 00750

REUTHER, JAMES RICHARD, optometrist; b. Starksville, Miss., Dec. 13, 1907; s. William Franklin and Alma (Johnson) R.; D. Optometry, No. Ill. Coll. of Optometry, 1939; m. Ruth Elizabeth Huffaker, Jan. 26, 1941; 1 dau., Alma Grace. Pvt. practice optometry, Gainesville, Tex., 1940-57; dr. in charge Mast Optical Co., Wichita Falls, Tex., 1958—. Past program dir., sec., treas. Gainesville Community Circus; past nat. chmn. Circus Fans Photography Conv. Served from pvt. to pfc., Med. Service Corps, AUS, 1944-46. Mem. Circus Fans Assn. Baptist. Mason (Shriner, K.T.), mem. Order Eastern Star. Club: Lions. Amateur Magician; chalk artist. Home: 4450 Phillips Dr Wichita Falls TX 76308 Office: 822 Indiana Av Wichita Falls TX 76301

REVELL, WALTER JONES, physician; b. Louisville, Ga., Aug. 10, 1916; s. Samuel Thompson Regrave and Lettie (Jones) R.; B.S., U. Ga., 1937; M.D., U. Md., 1941; m. Jean Eleanor Hunt, Jan. 3, 1948; children—Walter Jones, Jean Hunt, William Samuel, Harry Duff. Intern, U. Md. Hosp., Balt., 1941-42, City Hosp. of Balt., 1947; gen. practice medicine, Louisville, 1946—; mem. staff Jefferson Hosp., Louisville, 1946—. Chmn. Jefferson County Bd. Health, 1950—. Mem. Louisville City Council, 1960—, also mayor pro-tem., 1966—. Served with USNR, 1942-46. Diplomate Am. Bd. Family Practice. Mem. A.M.A., Ga., 10th Dist., Jefferson County med. assns., Nu Sigma Nu. Democrat. Presbyn. (elder). Mason, Kiwanian. Home: 815 Walnut St Louisville GA 30434 Office: 107 W 8th St Louisville GA 30434

REVELS, BERNICE GLADYS HARDY (MRS. P.B. REVELS), civic worker, churchwoman; b. Indpls., May 18, 1908; d. George C. and Daisy (Dunmire) Hardy; student Fla. State U., 1927-29; m. P. Burton Revels, June 20, 1929; children—Joan (Mrs. John F. Gaines), P. Burton. Mem. Palatka (Fla.) Beautification Com., 1965—, Palatka Planning Bd., 1967—; active A.R.C., 1950—; mem. state ednl. com.

Am. Cancer Soc., 1967—; pres. Women's Soc. Christian Service, Palatka, 1942-44, 58-59; mem. ofcl. bd. St. James United Meth. Ch., Palatka, 1958-59, sec. spiritual growth and service, 1967—, supt. jr. dept. ch. sch., 1956—; sec. Gainesville dist. Woman's Soc. Meth. Ch., 1955-59; chmn. nominating com. DeLand dist., 1960-64, v.p., 1964-65. Club: Palatka Women's (social chmn. 1938-40). Home: 1703 Laurel St Palatka FL 32077

REVELS, PERCY BURTON, judge; b. McCra, Fla., Dec. 16, 1901; s. William R. and Alice (Tyre) R.; student U. Fla., 1923-27; LL.B., Southeastern U., 1944; LL.D., Bethune-Cookman Coll., 1966; m. Bernice Hardy, June 20, 1929; children—Joan Dell (Mrs. John F. Gaines), Percy Burton. Admitted to Fla. bar, 1930, U.S. Supreme Ct. bar, 1944; practiced law in Palatka, Fla., 1930-51; atty. Putnam County (Fla.), 1933-51; judge 7th Jud. Circuit Fla., Palatka, 1951—. Dean Fla. Meth. Sch. of Christian Mission, 1970-72; del. Internat. Conf. United Meth. Ch., 1971, mem. legislative com. Christian Social Concerns, 1971, vice-chmn. div. Gen. Welfare, 1972, mem. Fla. Conf. Council. Exec. sec. Young Democratic Club Fla., 1939-40, pres., 1941, county del. state exec. com., 1940-48. Trustee, rec. sec., mem. exec. com. Bethune-Cookman Coll. Served to capt. USMCR, 1942-44. Recipient Good Govt. award Palatka Jr. C. of C., 1961; named Citizen of Year, Alpha Phi Alpha, 1965. Mem. Am. (nat. com. to draft model jud. legislation), Fla., Putnam County bar assns., Am. Judicature Soc., Putnam County Hist. Soc., Am. Camellia Soc., Nat. Assn. State Trial Judges (Fla. del. 1967, nat. com. 1968-69), Am. Legion (comdr. post), Putnam County C. of C., Phi Kappa Tau. Methodist. Vice-chmn. editorial staff Trial Judge's Jour., 1963—. Contbr. articles to profl. jours. Home: 1800 Laurel St Palatka FL 32077 Office: Courthouse Palatka FL 32077

REY, WILLIAM KENNETH, educator; b. N.Y.C., Aug. 11, 1925; s. William and Frances Sophia (Sauer) R.; B.S. in Aero. Engring., U. Ala., 1946, M.S. in Civil Engring., 1949; postgrad. U. Ariz., 1961; m. Ruth Jeanette Vickery, Nov. 27, 1946; children—Jeanette (Mrs. Felix Edward Todd), William Kenneth. Instr. math. U. Ala., University, 1946-47, instr. engring. mechanics, 1947-49, asst. prof. engring. mechanics, 1949-52, asso. prof. aero. engring., 1952-58, prof. aero. engring., 1958-60, prof. aerospace engring., 1960—, acting head dept., 1972, dir. high sch. relations, 1970—; cons. research NACA, NASA, Army and Air Force depts. Active Choctaw dist. Boy Scouts Am., dist. Explorer chmn., 1969-73. Recipient Dist. Scouter award Boy Scouts Am., 1970. Mem. Am. Inst. Aeros. and Astronautics, Am. Soc. Engring. Edn., Air Force Assn., Theta Tau (grand regent, nat. pres. 1963-66, grand marshal 1968-72), Tau Beta Pi, Omicron Delta Kappa, Sigma Gamma Tau, Pi Mu Epsilon. Baptist (deacon). Kiwanian (bd. dirs. Tuscaloosa, Ala., 1969—, 2d v.p. 1973—). Club: University (bd. govs. Tuscaloosa 1970-74). Contbr. NACA and NASA reports, revs., lab manual. Home: 77 Woodland Hills Tuscaloosa AL 35401

REYNOLDS, CHARLES MCKINELY, JR., banker; b. Thomasville, Ga., Jan. 11, 1937; s. Charles McKinley and Johnnie (Hadley) R.; student Morehouse Coll., 1954-56; mortuary sci. certificate Wayne State U., 1962; postgrad. Atlanta U., 1965-66; m. Estella Mary Henry, Aug. 19, 1956; children—Eric Charles, Gregory Preston. Tchr. Southside Jr. High Sch., Albany, Ga., 1962-65; nat. bank examiner U.S. Treasury Dept., Atlanta, 1965-71; exec. v.p. Citizens Trust Co., 1971, pres., 1971—; treas. Pathways, Inc.; exec. sec. Temporary Devel. Agy., Albany, Ga., 1963-65, Atlanta Leadership Inst., 1966-67. Asst. commr. Central dist. Boy Scouts Am., Atlanta, 1969—; mem. Atlanta Coalition on Current Community Affairs; mem. housing task force Gov.'s Goals for Ga. Program; mem. Met. Rapid Transit Authority Commn.; pres. West Manor PTA, Atlanta, 1968-69. Bd. dirs. A.R.C., Atlanta Model Cities Housing Devel. Corp., Butler St. YMCA, United Appeal. Served with USAF, 1956-60. Mem. Ga., Albany (v.p. 1965—) tchr. and edn. assns., Social Sci. Work Study Group (pres. 1964-65), Atlanta C. of C. (housing and redevel. com.), Nat. Bus. League, Alpha Phi Alpha, Epsilon Nu Delta, Gamma Omicron Lambda (chpt. asst. sec. 1964-65). Clubs: Criterion (sec. 1963-65), Morehouse College Alumni. Home: 1525 New Hope Rd SW Atlanta GA 30331 Office: 175 Houston St NE Atlanta GA 30303

REYNOLDS, DAVID PARHAM, metal products mfg. exec.; b. Bristol, Tenn., June 16, 1915; s. Richard Samuel and Julia Louise (Parham) R.; grad. Lawrenceville Sch.; student Princeton, 1938; m. Margaret Harrison, Mar. 25, 1944; children—Margaret Allis, Julia Parham, Dorothy Harrison. With Reynolds Metals Co., 1937—, salesman, asst. mgr. aircraft parts, 1937-44, asst. v.p., 1944-46, v.p., 1946-57, exec. v.p., 1958—, gen. mgr., 1969—; dir. Reynolds Metals Co., United Va. Bank, Reynolds Aluminum Sales Co., Reynolds Internat., Inc., Reynolds Aluminum Co. Can., Eskimo Pie Corp., Reynolds Jamaica Mines, Ltd. Mem. Prime Aluminum Products Industry Adv. Com., Fed. Govt., 1951—. Trustee Lawrenceville Sch., Foxcroft Sch. Presbyn. Home: 8905 Tresco Rd Richmond VA 23229 Office: 6601 Broad St Rd Richmond VA 23261

REYNOLDS, FRANK RUSSELL, physician; b. Wilmington, N.C., 1920; M.D., U. Pa., 1944. Intern Med. Coll. Va. Hosp., Richmond, 1944-45; resident in pediatrics Childrens Hosp., Phila., 1945-46, asst. chief resident, 1949-50; resident in pediatrics James Walker Meml. Hosp., Wilmington, 1948-49, now vis. staff; practice medicine specializing in pediatrics, Wilmington; staff pediatrician Babies Hosp., Wrightsville Sound, N.C., Community Hosp., Wilmington. Served to capt. M.C., AUS, 1947-48. Diplomate Am. Bd. Pediatrics. Mem. A.M.A., Am. Acad. Pediatrics (dist. chmn.), N.C. Med. Soc. (pres. 1974-75). Office: 1613 Dock St Wilmington NC 28401

REYNOLDS, HERBERT HAL, univ. adminstr.; b. Frankston, Tex., Mar. 20, 1930; s. Herbert Joseph and Avanell (Taylor) R.; B.S., Trinity U., 1952, M.S., Baylor U., 1958, Ph.D., 1961; m. Joy Myrla Copeland, June 17, 1950; children—Kevin Hal, Kent Andrew, Rhonda Sheryl. Commd. 2d lt. U.S. Air Force, 1948, advanced through grades to col., 1966; retired, 1968; personnel officer, 1948-54, mem. adv. group to Japanese Air Self Def. Force, 1954-56, asst. prof. air sci. Baylor U., 1956-59, grad. fellow Baylor U., 1959-61, chief comparative psychology Aero. Med. Lab., Holloman AFB, N.M., 1961-65, dir. research and dep. dir. Aero. Med. Lab., 1965-68, interim. dir. Air Force Human Resources Lab., Brooks AFB, Tex., 1968; prof. psychology, exec. v.p., provost Baylor U., Waco, Tex., 1969—. Mem. A.A.A.S., Am. Assn. U. Profs., Am., N.M., Tex. psychol. assns., Sigma Xi. Contbr. articles in field to profl. jours. Office: Baylor U Waco TX 76703

REYNOLDS, HOWARD MAXWELL, jr. coll. athletic dir.; b. Mt. Sterling, Ky., Nov. 21, 1931; s. Emmett Tipton and Nancy Clarice (Thompson) R.; B.A., U. Ky., 1958, M.A., 1961, Ed.D., 1969; m. Wanita Joyce Hart, July 14, 1966; children—Howard Maxwell, Tanya Renee. Tchr.-coach Mt. Sterling High Sch., 1958-60, 63-66, Bellvue (Ky.) High Sch., 1961-63; asst. prin., dir. athletics Bunnell (Fla.) High Sch., 1966-67; research asst. U. Ky., Lexington, 1967-69; dir. athletics Palm Beach Jr. Coll., Lake Worth, Fla., 1969—. Served with USNR, 1952-54. Recipient Outstanding Young Educator award Jr. C. of C., 1966. Mem. Nat. Assn. Collegiate Dirs. Athletics, Am., Fla. assns. health, edn. and welfare, Am. Legion. Lion. Home: 3112 Merion Terrace Lake Worth FL 33460

REYNOLDS, JAMES LOUIS, physician; b. New Orleans, July 10, 1928; s. Lloyd Edward and Irma Catherine B. (Seiler) R.; B.S., Tulane U., 1950, M.D., 1953; m. Mary Elizabeth Fontaine, June 8, 1955; children—Mary Elizabeth, Mary Catherine, James L., Mary Clothilde. Intern, resident Children's Hosp. Med. Center, Boston; resident Charity Hosp., New Orleans; individual practice medicine specializing in pediatrics and pediatric cardiology, Baton Rouge, 1960-62; pediatric cardiologist Tulane U. Med. Sch., 1962-71, also asso. prof. pediatrics and surgery; individual practice pediatric cardiology, New Orleans, 1971—; dir. cardiac catheterization and angiography lab. So. Bapt. Hosp. New Orleans, 1971—. Served to capt., USAF, 1955-57. Fellow Am. Acad. Pediatrics, Am. Coll. Cardiology, Am. Heart Assn.; mem. New Orleans Pediatric Soc. (pres.-elect), La. Heart Assn. (pres. 1972-73), So. Soc. Pediatric Research, Southeastern Pediatric Cardiology Soc. Research in field. Home: 496 Audubon St New Orleans LA 70118 Office: 4440 Magnolia St New Orleans LA 70115

REYNOLDS, JIMMY, state ofcl.; b. Malakoff, Tex., Sept. 16, 1939; s. Walter and Julia Irvin (Pelham) R.; B.S. in Agrl. Engring., Tex. Tech. U., 1963; m. Erma Campbell, Apr. 25, 1964; children—Pamela Kay, Polly Kathleen. Hydraulic engr. Interior Dept., Houston, 1963-65; civil engr. U.S. Dept. Agr., Amarillo, Tex., 1965-66; with Tex. Dept. Agr., insp., Eustace, Tex., 1969—; owner Reynolds Merc. Co., Eustace, Tex., 1966—; engring. cons., Eustace, 1966—. Mem. P.T.A., 1966—; sponsor Circle 10 council Boy Scouts Am., 1969—. Mayor, Eustace, 1974—. Trustee Eustace Sch. Bd., 1967-71; fire chief, Eustace, 1969-71, fire marshal, 1971. Bd. dirs. Am. Cancer Soc. Mem. Am. Soc. C.E., Am. Soc. Agrl. Engrs. Address: PO Box 98 Eustace TX 75124

REYNOLDS, JOHN ARCHIBALD SEABROOK, dentist; b. Lenoir, N.C., Feb. 16, 1933; s. Archibald Seabrook and Eva Mae (Craven) R.; student The Citadel, 1951-54; D.D.S., U. N.C., 1958; m. Jeanne Kathleen Fleming, July 5, 1958; children—Kathleen Fleming, Mary McLeod, Patricia Lynn. Pvt. practice dentistry, Charlotte, N.C., 1960—. Instr. dental interne program Charlotte Meml. Hosp., 1960—; cons. dental asst. program Community Coll., Charlotte, since 1962. Adviser, Explorer Scouts, 1968. Served with Dental Corps, USNR, 1958-60; now comdr. Res. Mem. Am. Dental Assn., N.C. (chmn. ethics com. 1971-72), 2d Dist., Charlotte dental socs., Citadel Alumni Assn., Res. Officers Assn. U.S., Naval Res. Assn., Omicron Kappa Upsilon, Xi Psi Phi. Episcopalian (vestryman 1964-67, lay reader 1958-73). Clubs: Myers Park Country, Lake Norman Yacht, Optimist. Home: 3022 Ferncliff Rd Charlotte NC 28211 Office: 1944 Brunswick Av Charlotte NC 28207

REYNOLDS, LESLIE B(OUSH), JR., physician; b. Lakeland, Fla., Aug. 16, 1923; s. Leslie Boush and Verna (Powell) R.; B.S., Randolph-Macon Coll., 1949 M.S., Ga. Inst. Tech., 1951; Ph.D., Med. Coll. S.C., 1941; M.D., Northwestern U., 1966; m. Alma Carter, Oct. 24, 1947; children—Alma Mary, Margaret Mary. Engr., E.I. du Pont de Nemours & Co., Inc., Kinston, N.C., 1951-53, group leader, 1954-55, lab. supr., 1956-57; asst. prof. physiology Northwestern U. Med. Sch., Chgo., 1961-64, research asso. medicine, 1964-66; intern St. Joseph Hosp., Chgo., 1966-67; practice medicine specializing in pulmonary disease, Memphis, 1968—; mem. staff City of Memphis Hosp., Bapt. Hosp.; asst. prof. medicine U. Tenn., 1967-71, asso. prof. medicine, 1971—, asso. prof. physiology and biophysics, 1967—, acting chmn. dept. physiology and biophysics, 1968-69. Served with USNR, 1942-46. Mem. Am. Physiol. Soc., A.M.A., Am. Thoracic Soc., Am. Coll. Chest Physicians, Aerospace Med. Assn., A.A.A.S., Sigma Xi, Phi Lambda Upsilon. Research in respiratory reflexes, treatment of respiratory diseases. Home: 1601 Old Hickory Rd Memphis TN 38116 Office: 951 Court St Memphis TN 38163

REYNOLDS, MERRILL SHELBY, bank dir.; b. Milton, W.Va., Dec. 21, 1919; s. Shelby Jackson and Mary Ellen (Nichoels) R.; student pub. schs.; m. Leah Katherine Baroff, June 15, 1941; children—Diane (Mrs. Ronnie Dallas Tury), Pamela (Mrs. Daniel Raymond Hair), Kerry Shawn. Glass designer Dunbar Glass Corp. (W.Va.), 1937-41; chem. insp. Union Carbide, South Charleston, W.Va., 1941-55; co-owner Dari Delite, Clearwater, Fla., 1955-57; salesman Tarpon Chevrolet, Tarpon Springs, Fla., 1956-66; pres. Caladesi Auto Sales & Service Co., Inc., Dunedin, Fla., 1966—; v.p. You Ren Kor, Inc., auto rental and leasing; dir. Caladesi Nat. Bank, Dunedin. Mem. Greater Dunedin C. of C. (pres. 1972-73, financial adviser 1973-74), Automobile Dealers Assn., chaine de Rotisseurs. Mason (Shriner), Elk, Rotarian (dir.). Home: 2788 County Rd 70 Quesa Ranch Palm Harbor FL 33563 Office: 553 Causeway Blvd Dunedin FL 33528

REYNOLDS, PORTER GRAVES, landscape architect; b. Lewisville, N.C., Nov. 19, 1912; s. Lamb Archibald and Bessie (Binkley) R.; B.S., U. Fla., 1934; m. Margaret Patricia McManus, Apr. 7, 1967; stepchildren—Colleen (Mrs. Dominic Grosso), Michael K. Myers. Dir. parks and recreation City of Fort Lauderdale (Fla.), 1939-52; pvt. practice landscape architecture, Ft. Lauderdale, 1952—. Mem. Ft. Lauderdale Planning and Zoning Bd., 1953-55; mayor-commr. City of Ft. Lauderdale, 1955-57, mem. city commn., 1957-59. Mem. Am. Soc. Landscape Architects. Republican. Methodist. Elk, Rotarian. Home: 1921 NE 43d St Fort Lauderdale FL 33308 Office: 1041 NE 10th Av Fort Lauderdale FL 33304

REYNOLDS, RANDALL O., state legislator, dentist; b. nr. Chatham, Va., Oct. 19, 1907; s. Booker J. and Rowena (Mahan) R.; student U. Richmond, 1925-26; D.D.S., Med. Coll. Va. Sch. Dentistry, 1930; m. Billie Jean Wheeler, 1963; children—Elizabeth, Mary, Jean; 1 dau. (by previous marriage), Jane Rowe (Mrs. John B. Murray). Practice dentistry, Chatham, 1930—; mem. Va. Ho. of Dels., 1956—. Pres. Planters Bank & Trust Co., 1948-52, 72—, dir., 1938—; pres. Rex Motor Co., Inc., 1956—; pres. Gretna Finance Services, Inc., 1971—. Mayor, Chatham, 1948-50; mem. council Town of Chatham, 1938-48. Trustee Hargrave Mil. Acad., 1945—, sec. bd., 1950—. Mem. Am. Dental Assn., Va., Piedmont dental socs., Pierre Fauchard Dental Hon. Soc., Farm Bur., Farmers Union, Psi Omega. Baptist. Mason, Lion (past local pres.). Club: Cedars Country. Home: Peach St Chatham VA 24531 Office: Main St Chatham VA 24531

REYNOLDS, RICHARD CLYDE, physician, educator; b. Saugerties, N.Y., Sept. 2, 1929; s. Thomas Watson and Myrtle (Myer) R.; B.S., Rutgers U., 1949; M.D., Johns Hopkins, 1953; m. Mary Jane Beck, July 7, 1954; children—Karen Sue, Stephanie Ann, Wayne Thomas. Intern, Johns Hopkins Hosp., Balt., 1953-54, resident, 1954-55, fellow in medicine, 1957-59; practice medicine specializing in internal medicine, Frederick, Md., 1959-68; asso. prof. medicine U. Fla., Gainesville, 1968-71, prof. medicine, prof. community health and family medicine, 1971—, asst. dean Coll. Medicine, 1970—. Served to sr. asst. surgeon USPHS, 1955-57. Diplomate Am. Bd. Internal Medicine. Fellow A.C.P.; mem. A.M.A., Am. Acad. Family Practice. Home: 2015 NW 26th St Gainesville FL 32601

REYNOLDS, RICHARD S., JR., bus. exec.; b. Winston-Salem, N.C., May 27, 1908; s. Richard S. and Louise (Parham) R.; student Davidson Coll.; B.S., U. Pa., 1930; m. Virginia Sargeant; children—Richard S. III, Sargeant (dec.). Mem. N.Y. Stock Exchange, 1930—; partner banking co. Reynolds & Co., N.Y.C., 1930; asst. to pres. Reynolds Metals Co., Richmond, Va., 1938, treas., 1938-48, v.p., 1944-48, pres., 1948-63, chmn. bd., chief exec. officer, 1963-71, chmn. bd., pres., 1971—; chmn. bd. Robertshaw Controls Co., 1955—, chmn. exec. com., 1957-59, chmn., 1959—; chmn. bd. Canadian Reynolds Metals Co., Ltd.; dir. Mfrs. Hanover Trust Co., British Aluminium Ltd., Central Nat. Bank of Richmond, Manicouagan Power Co., Que., Can., Lawyers Title Ins. Corp., Richmond, Richmond Corp. Mem. Aluminum Assn. (past pres.), Richmond C. of C. (past pres.). Presbyn. Clubs: Brook, New York Yacht (N.Y.C.); Metropolitan (Washington); Country of Va., Commonwealth (Richmond); Farmington Country; Deep Run Hunt; Bucks (London, Eng.). Home: 4509 Sulgrave Rd Richmond VA 23221 Office: Richmond VA 23261

REYNOLDS, VIRGIL HOMER, JR., hydroelec. power plant supt.; b. Sheffield, Ala., Jan. 17, 1925; s. Virgil Homer and Heelon Aleen (Sharp) R.; B.A., Auburn U., 1950; m. W. Glenn Austin, Apr. 15, 1951. Elec. engr. TVA, Wilson Dam, Ala., 1950-69, Fontana Dam and Hiwassee Dam, N.C., 1969-72, power plant supt., Hiwassee Dam, 1972—. Served with AUS, 1943-46; ETO. Registered profl. engr., Ala. Democrat. Presbyn. (ruling elder, clk. of session). Lion. Home: 805 Valley River Av Murphy NC 28906 Office: Route 4 Suit NC 28906

REYNOLDS, WILLIAM JENSEN, ch. musician, hymnologist, composer; b. Atlantic, Ia., Apr. 2, 1920; s. George Washington and Ethel (Horn) R.; student Okla. Baptist U., 1937-39; A.B., Southwest Mo. State Coll., 1942; M.S.M., Southwestern Bapt. Theol. Sem., 1945; M.M., North Tex. State U., 1946; Ed.D., George Peabody Coll. Tchrs. 1961; m. Mary Lou Robertson, July 6, 1947; children—Timothy Jensen, Kirk Mallory. Minister of music First Bapt. Ch., Ardmore, Okla., 1946-47; minister of music First Bapt. Ch., Oklahoma City, 1947-55; music editor Ch. Music dept. Bapt. Sunday Sch. Bd., Nashville, 1955-62, dir. editorial services, 1962-67, supr. music publs., 1967-71, head ch. music dept., 1971—, music dir. So. Bapt. Conv., Houston, 1958, Phila., 1972, Portland, Ore., 1973, Dallas, 1974; music dir. Bapt. World Alliance, Rio de Janeiro, 1960; choral dir., Miami Beach, 1965; music dir. Bapt. World Youth Conf., Toronto, 1958, Beirut, 1963, Berne, 1968; mem. hymnal com. Baptist Hymnal, 1956; chmn. hymnal com., gen. editor Baptist Hymnal, 1975; composer: Ichthus, 1971; Reaching People, 1973; Share His Word, 1973; numerous choral anthems, hymn tunes, songs, etc. Recipient B.B. McKinney Found. award, 1960; W. Hines Sims Achievement award, 1971; North Tex. State U. Sch. Music Alumni citation, 1972. Mem. Hymn Soc. Am. (exec. com. 1960—), Ch. Music Pubs. Assn. (v.p. 1973—), Am. Soc. Composers, Authors and Publs., Nat. Acad. Rec. Arts and Scis., Gospel Music Assn., So. Bapt. Ch. Music Conf. Mason. Author: A Survey of Christian Hymnody, 1963; Hymns of our Faith, 1964; Christ and the Carols, 1967. Home: 2817 White Oak Dr Nashville TN 37215 Office: 127 9th Av N Nashville TN 37234

REYNOLDS, WILLIAM ROGER, educator, geologist; b. Chgo., Dec. 27, 1929; s. Francis Eugene and Vida L. (White) R.; B.S. in Geology, U. Wis., 1958; M.S., Fla. State U., 1963, Ph.D., 1966; m. Miriam Janet Leddy, Apr. 7, 1956; children—William F., Susan Marie, Cindi Carol, Timothy Edward, Andrew Philip. Geologist sr. grade Amoco Prodn. Co., New Orleans, 1966-68; prof. geology, geol. engr. U. Miss., 1968—, also research geologist Engring. Exptl. Sta. and Inst. Mineral Resources. Active Boy Scouts Am., Oxford Civic Youth League. Served with USAF, 1951-56. Mem. Am. Assn. Petroleum Geologists, Soc. Econ. Paleontologists and Mineralogists, Clay Minerals Soc. (charter), Sigma Xi. Home: 1415 Jefferson St Oxford MS 38655 Office: Dept Geology Univ Miss University MS 38677

RHEA, CLAUDE HIRAM, JR., educator; b. Carrollton, Mo., Oct. 26, 1927; s. Claude H. Cecil Virginia (Walden) R.; A.B. in History, William Jewell Coll., 1950; postgrad. U. Mo., 1950-51; B.Music Edn., Fla. State U., 1953, M.Music Edn., 1954, Ed.D., 1958; m. Carolyn Priscilla Turnage, Aug. 26, 1951; children—Claude Hiram III, Charles Randall, Margaret Elizabeth. Prof. music, also dean Sch. Ch. Music New Orleans/Baptist Theol. Sem., 1954-63; prof. music, also adminstrv. v.p. Houston Bapt. Coll., 1963-67; cons. in music Fgn. Mission Bd. of So. Baptist Conv., Richmond, Va., 1967-69; dean Sch. Music Samford U., Birmingham, Ala., 1969—; ordained to ministry Bapt. Ch. Bd. dirs. Birmingham Civic Ballet, Learning Labs., Inc., Multi-Leasco, Inc., Civic Opera, Birmingham Symphony, Children's Theater, Allan-Bryan Ednl. Found. Served as chaplain's asst., AUS, 1945-47. Recipient Citation of Achievement, William Jewell Coll., 1961, Citation, City of Houston, 1965. Mem. Am. Assn. U. Adminstrs., Phi Eta Sigma, Phi Kappa Phi, Beta Beta Beta, Phi Mu Alpha Sinfonia, Pi Kappa Lambda. Kiwanian. Author: A Child's Life in Song, 1964; Claude Rhea's Favorite Gospel Songs, 1966; The Lottie Moon Cookbook, 1969. Record Albums: Sacred Masterpieces, 1957; Majestic Themes, 1960; The Radiance of Christmas, 1962. Home: 3701 River Oaks Lane Birmingham AL 35223

RHEA, KARL BYINGTON, physician; b. Somerville, Tenn., Feb. 2, 1931; s. Howard Matthew and Wilhelmina (Litterer) R.; student Southwestern U., 1949-51, Memphis State U., 1951; M.D., U. Tenn., 1954; m. Mary Elizabeth Borum, June 11, 1959; children—Karl Byington, Robert Howard, William Scott. Intern, Confederate Meml. Hosp., Shreveport, La., 1954-55; with Tenn. Pub. Health Service, 1955-56; resident surgery Kennedy VA Hosp., Memphis, 1958-59; practice gen. medicine, Somerville, 1959—; adminstr. Morris Clinic and Hosp., Somerville, county med. examiner, Fayette County, 1961—, county coroner, 1961—. Former mem. Fayette County Democratic Exec. Com. Bd. dirs. Fayette Acad. Served with USPHS, 1956-58. Diplomate Am. Bd. Family Practice. Mem. W. Tenn. Consol. Med. Assembly, A.M.A., Am. Acad. Gen. Practice, Am. Assn. Physicians and Surgeons, Phi Chi, Kappa Sigma. Democrat. Presbyn. (chmn. bd. deacons). Club: Somerville Country. Home: Oak Rd Somerville TN 38068 Office: 138 Market St Somerville TN 38068

RHEAY, MARY LOUISE, librarian; b. Montgomery, Ala., Mar. 8, 1920; d. Ross Smith and Maria (Cunningham) Rheay; A.B., Ala. Coll., 1940; A.B. in L.S., Emory U., 1941, M.L.S., 1959. Library asst. Atlanta Pub. Library, 1941-42, supr. sch. work, 1942-53, asst. head, 1953-56, head children's dept., 1956-63, asst. dir., 1963—; part-time instr. Ga. State Coll., 1960-69, Emory U. Library Sch., 1960-68. Named Atlanta Woman of Year in Professions, 1962. Mem. Am. (mem. Newberry and Caldecott award com. children's services div. 1962), Southeastern (acting chmn. sch. and children's sect. 1963-64, chmn. pub. library sect. 1968-69), Ga. (chmn. children's and young people's sect. 1949-51, 1st v.p., pres. 1973—), Met. Atlanta (pres. 1964-65) library assns., Zonta Internat. (sec. 1969-70, v.p. 1971, 72), Delta Kappa Gamma (pres. chpt. 1966-68). Home: 4555 Meadow Valley Dr Atlanta GA 30342 Office: 126 Carnegie Way NE Atlanta GA 30303

RHEE, KHEE-CHOON, food scientist; b. Seoul, Korea, June 25, 1938; s. Lin-Mook and Ki-Nam (Song) R.; B.S. in Agrl. Chemistry, Seoul Nat. U., 1961, M.S., 1964; Ph.D. in Food Sci., Mich. State U., 1969; m. Ki-Soon Choi, Apr. 24, 1964; children—Vincent Inho, Raymond Moonho. Came to U.S., 1963. Research asst. Mich. State U., East Lansing, 1966-69; research fellow Brown U., Providence, 1969-70; research fellow Tex. A. and M. U., College Station, 1970—, asst. research chemist, 1971—. Served with Republic of Korea Army,

1959. Mem. Am. Assn. Cereal Chemists, Am. Chem. Soc., Am. Dairy Sci. Assn., Am. Peanut Research and Edn. Assn., Inst. Food Technologists, Korean Scientists and Engrs. Assn. in Am. (pres. Tex. A. and M. U. sect. 1973—), Sigma Xi (Grad. Research award 1969), Phi Tau Sigma. Contbr. articles to sci. jours. Developer aqueous process for prodn. protein products and oil from peanuts. Home: 2203 Oak Grove Lane Bryan TX 77801 Office: Food Protein Research and Devel Center Tex A and M U College Station TX 77843

RHEIN, FRANCIS BAYARD, clergyman; b. Phila., Jan. 5, 1915; s. John Henry Wallace and Elizabeth (Kane) R.; B.S., U. Va., 1938; M.Div., Va. Theol. Sem., 1942, S.T.M., 1971; m. Jane Alice Foster, Sept. 12, 1942; children—Patricia (Mrs. Robert Turner), Eliz (Mrs. Terence Collins), Peter, Jane. Ordained to ministry Episcopal Ch., 1942; rector St. James Ch., Montrose, Va., 1942-43, St. John's Ch., Warsaw, Va., 1946-48, Emmanuel Ch., Newport, R.I., 1948-50, Christ Ch., Millwood, Va., 1950-54, St. Peter's Ch., Phila., 1954-56; asso. prof. Bibl. lit and philosophy Madison Coll., 1956-66; rector Emmanuel Ch., Harrisonburg, Va., 1956-66; rector, Trinity Ch., Upperville, Va., 1966—. Prof. history Foxcroft Sch., 1966-69. Served with USNR, 1943-46; PTO. Episcopalian. Mason. Author: An Analytical Approach to the New Testament, 1966; A Simplified Approach to the New Testament, 1968. Home and office: Box 127 Upperville VA 22176

RHEM, DURWARD DUDLEY, pub. co. exec.; b. Florence, S.C., Aug. 22, 1927; s. Durward Dudley and Muriel (Williams) R.; B.A., Coll. William and Mary, 1952; m. Jane Patricia Odom, July 9, 1955; children—Durward Dudley IV, Patricia Anne, Jennifer Leah. Mgr. publs. Radiation, Inc., Melbourne, Fla., 1954-61; v.p. Soroban Engring., Palm Bay, Fla., 1961-68; pres. Brevard Graphics, Inc., Palm Bay, 1961—, Ednl. Sound Systems, Inc., Melbourne, 1972—. Bd. dirs. Jr. Achievement. Served with M.C., AUS, 1945-47. Mem. Brevard County Printers Assn. (pres.), Am. Mgmt. Assn., Civitan. Mason. Clubs: YMCA Century, Eau Gallie Yacht. Home: 311 Palm Ct Indialantic FL 32901 Office: 829 New Haven Av Melbourne FL 32901

RHEM, SAMUEL DUNN, III, physician; b. Memphis, Aug. 28, 1937; s. Samuel Dunn and Mary (Nolan) R.; M.D., U. Tenn., 1961; J.D., South Tex. Coll. Law, 1971; m. Sharon Jenkins, Feb. 9, 1963; children—Samuel Dunn IV, Marcus. Intern, St. Thomas, Vanderbilt hosps., Nashville; practice medicine specializing in legal medicine, Pasadena, Tex., 1963—; chief staff Southmore Hosp. Fellow Acad. Clin. and Exptl. Hypnosis; mem. Harris County Med. Soc. (sec. S.E. br.), Am., So. (mem. postgrad. assembly) Tex. med. assns., Am. Acad. Family Practice, Am. Acad. Legal Medicine. Home: 2204 Perez St Pasadena TX 77502 Office: 906 E Southmore St Pasadena TX 77502

RHINEHART, FORREST H., dentist; b. Iowa County, Ia., Oct. 4, 1901; s. Homer Hampton and Mary Elizabeth (Bever) R.; D.D.S., U. Neb., 1926; m. Hope Hanson, Feb. 15, 1925; children—Marjorie Lee (Mrs. Harold H. Kemp), Donald Forrest. Practice gen. dentistry, Benkelman and Grand Island, Neb., 1926-42, Tulsa, 1946—. Served with AUS, 1942-46. Mem. Am., Okla. State, Tulsa dental assns., Xi Psi Phi. Episcopalian. Mason (32 deg.), Elk. Home: 235 N Yukon St Tulsa OK 74127 Office: Pythian Bldg Tulsa OK 74103

RHOAD, WILLIAM OTTERBEIN, clergyman; b. Pinegrove, Pa., Aug. 17, 1903; s. Hiram F. and Annie (Houser) R.; B.A., Lebannon Valley Coll., 1925; student Bonebrake Theol. Sem., 1925-26; Th.B., Princeton Theol. Sem., 1928; Th.M., Westminster Theol. Sem., 1944; Th.D., Central U., 1940; m. Myrtle Iva Dymond, Nov. 23, 1931; children—Priscilla, William Otterbein, John Calvin, Rebecca. Ordained ministry Presbyn. Ch., 1931; minister Kensington and Freetown Chs., P.E.I., Can., 1931-41, Ashfield and Ripley Chs., Ont., Can., 1941-49, Maryland Av. Ch., Balt., 1949-54, McDowell (Va.) Ch., 1954-61, Cedar Creek, Cedar Cliff, Mt. Hope chs., 1961-66, Keysville (Va.), Briery (Va.), Meherrin (Va.) Presbyn. chs., 1968—. Moderator Presbytery P.E.I., 1936, clk., 1937-41; moderator Maitland Presbytery, 1944, Huron-Maitland, 1947, Lexington 1957. Home: J St Keysville VA 23947 Office: Box 16 Keysville VA 23947

RHOADES, EDD DARREL, govt. engr.; b. Geronimo, Okla., May 26, 1919; s. Jacob Lee and Ada (Bull) R.; A.S., Cameron Coll., 1939; B.S., Okla. State U., 1942, M.S., 1951, postgrad. 1964-66; m. Erma Rae Embry, Aug. 28, 1946; children—Edd Darrel, Lynda, John. Ordnance engr. U.S. War Dept., 1942-44; agrl. engr. U.S. Soil Conservation Service, Sulpher, Okla., 1946-52; civil engr. U.S. Navy, McAlester, Okla., 1952-57; research agrl. engr. Agrl. Research Service, U.S. Dept. Agr., Chickasha, Okla., 1957—. Teaching fellow Okla. State U., 1949-50. Active local civic affairs, Chickasha. Served to lt. (j.g.) USNR, 1944-46. Mem. Soil Conservation Soc. Am., Am. Soc. Agrl. Engrs. Contbr. articles to profl. pubs. Home: 2400 S 12th St Chickasha OK 73018 Office: PO Box 400 Chickasha OK 73018

RHOADES, EVERETT RONALD, physician; b. Lawton, Okla, Oct. 24, 1931; s. Lee Joseph and Dorothy Apasha (Rowell) R.; student Lafayette Coll., 1949-52; M.D., U. Okla., 1956; m. Bernadine Herwona Toyebo, Sept. 28, 1953; children—Lee Charles, Melanie Cheryl, Melinda Sue, Dorothy Alison, Lisa Patricia. Intern, Gorgas Hosp., Ancon, C.Z.; resident U. Okla. Med. Center, Oklahoma City, 1957-61; chief infectious disease Wilford Hall USAF, Hosp., 1961-66; asst. prof. medicine and microbiology U. Okla. Med. Center, 1966-67, asso. prof., 1967-71, prof., 1972—, chief infectious disease, 1967—. Cons. U. Saigon Med. Sch., Okla. Tb Sanatarium; adv. council NIH, 1972—. Mem. Kiowa Tribal Bus. Com., 1967-70, vice chmn. tribe, 1973—; mem. Inter Tribal Land Use Com., 1967-70. Served to maj. USAF, 1957-66. Recipient fellowship John Hay Whitney Found., 1952, outstanding achievement award VA, 1958, 59. Markle scholar, 1967-72. Mem. Nat. Congress Am. Indians, Assn. Am. Indian Physicians (founder 1971 pres. 1971-72), Nat. Council Minority Bus. Enterprise, Assn. Am. Indian Affairs (bd. dirs. 1970—), Kiowa Ton Kon Gaut Soc., Phi Beta Kappa, Alpha Omega Alpha, Sigma Xi. Contbr. articles to profl. jours. Home: 1808 Dorchester Dr Oklahoma City OK 73120 Office: 921 NE 13th St Oklahoma City OK 73104

RHOADES, RICHARD GARDNER, govt. ofcl.; b. Northampton, Mass., Aug. 15, 1938; s. Lawrence Duncan and Marion (Hollister) R.; B.Chem. Engring., Rensselaer Poly. Inst., 1960, Ph.D. (NSF fellow), 1963; m. Martha Dale Turner, July 29, 1967; children—Lawren Michelle, Anna Elizabeth. Jr. research engr. Eastman Kodak Co., Rochester, N.Y., 1960; research engr. U.S. Army Missile Command, Redstone Arsenal, Ala., 1965-69, program mgr., 1969-73, lab. dir., 1973—. Adj. asst. prof. U. Ala., Huntsville, 1964-69. Served from 1st lt. to capt. AUS, 1963-65. Mem. Am. Inst. Chem. Engrs., Sigma Xi, Tau Beta Pi, Phi Lambda Upsilon. Club: Huntsville Ski. Contbr. articles to tech. lit. Home: 3604 Lookout Dr Huntsville AL 35801 Office: AMSMI-RK Bldg 7120 USAMICOM Redstone Arsenal AL 35809

RHODE, CHARLES MARTIN, surgeon, educator; b. Balt., Oct. 22, 1915; s. Edward and Carrie (Urban) R.; A.B., Johns Hopkins, 1936; M.D., U. Md., 1940; m. Clara Belle Puryear, Sept. 28, 1946; children—Charles Martin, Margaret Puryear, Anne Loraine. Intern, Univ. Hosp., Balt., 1940-42; resident in surgery Hosp. U. Pa., 1948-49, VA Hosp., Perry Point, Md., 1949-54; practice surgery specializing in gen. hand surgery, Augusta, Ga., 1962—; chief surg. service VA Hosp., Augusta, 1954-62, asso. chief staff for research, chief hand surgery sect., 1962—; asso. prof. surgery Med. Coll. Ga., Augusta, 1956—. Bd. dirs. Comprehensive Counselor on Alcohol and Drug Abuse, Augusta, 1971—. Served with USNR, 1944-46. Diplomate Am. Bd. Surgery. Recipient Superior Performance award VA Hosp., Augusta, 1969. Fellow A.C.S.; mem. A.M.A., Richmond County Med. Soc., Med. Assn. Ga., Southeastern Surg. Congress, Am. Fedn. for Clin. Research, Assn. VA Surgeons. Contbr. articles to profl. publs. Address: VA Hosp Augusta GA 30904

RHODES, ALLAN RAY, automotive dealer; b. Owensboro, Ky., July 1, 1923; s. Charles Ray and Iva (Smith) R.; B.S., Ind. U., 1947; m. Nettie Sweeney, Nov. 18, 1948; children—Allan Ray, Robert Todd. Sales rep. Procter & Gamble, 1947-48; gen. mgr. Owensboro Lincoln-Mercury, 1948-59; pres. Allan Rhodes, Inc., Paducah, Ky., 1959—; organizer Tower Nat. Bank, Lima, O.; dir. Citizens Bank & Trust Co., Paducah. Bd. dirs. Greater Paducah Indsl. Devel. Served with AUS, 1942-46, 51-52. Named outstanding dealer for Ky., Time Mag., 1971. Mem. Paducah Dealers Assn. (pres. 1970-72), Ky. Auto Dealer Assn. (pres. 1970-72), Ky. Civil War Roundtable, Paducah C. of C. (pres. 1971). Home: 3653 Forest Circle Paducah KY 42001 Office: 937 Jefferson St Paducah KY 42001

RHODES, ARVIN LOYE, lawyer; b. Hugo, Okla., June 6, 1932; s. William Jennings and Fannie (Forbus) R.; B.A., Abilene Christian Coll., 1957; J.D., U. Tex. at Austin, 1960; m. Nancy Ann Fanson, Mar. 28, 1957; children—Edward, Christiana, Nancy, Sherrie. Admitted to Tex. bar, 1960, since practiced in Abilene; partner Rhodes & Doscher, Abilene; dir. various corps., including Ind. Am. Life Ins. Co., Austin, Tex., Gibson's Discount Center, Dallas; pres. Rhodes Oil Co., Trey Oil Co., Christi Co. Inc. (all Abilene). Lectr. Abilene Christian Coll., 1968—. Pres. Abilene chpt. Nat. Muscular Dystrophy Assn., 1962. Vice pres. Young Democrats Tex., 1959; campaign mgr. Senator Loyd Bentsen, W.Tex. area, 1971. Bd. dirs. Crowley's Ridge Coll., Paragould, Ark., Abilene Zool. Assn. Served with USNR, 1950-54. Decorated Purple Heart. Mem. Am., Tex., Abilene bar assns., Am., Tex. trial lawyers assns., Am., Tex. def. lawyers assns. Democrat. Home: Route 6 Box 132 Abilene TX 79604 Office: Citizens Bank Abilene TX 79604

RHODES, CLARENCE ALBERT, JR., elec. engr.; b. Winston-Salem, N.C., May 10, 1924; s. Clarence Albert and Evy Bell (Johnston) R.; B.S., Va. Poly. Inst., 1949; postgrad. Wake Forest U., 1968-69; m. Peggy Rose Reid, Apr. 11, 1953; children—William Edward, Sarah Weatherington, Ann Taylor, Elizabeth Shepherd. Elec. engr., asso. partner Lashmit, James, Brown & Pollock, architects and engrs., Winston-Salem, 1949-63; cons. elec. engr. C.A. Rhodes, Jr., Winston-Salem, 1963—; cons. engr. Housing Authority Winston-Salem, Old Salem, Inc., Winston-Salem Found. Instr. radiol. monitoring Civil Def. Tng. Program, 1965. Served with AUS 1943-46. Registered profl. engr., N.C., S.C. Mem. A.A.A.S., Tau Beta Pi, Eta Kappa Nu. Methodist. Kiwanian. Home: 1780 Robinhood Rd Winston-Salem NC 27104 Office: Wachovia Bldg Winston-Salem NC 27101

RHODES, DONALD HENRY, lawyer, state legislator; b. Norfolk, Va., Mar. 17, 1933; s. Early Clemons and Ivy Mae (Harris) R.; B.S. in Edn., U. Va., 1955, LL.B., 1961; postgrad. Pa. State U., 1955-56; m. Anna Margaret Young, June 13, 1959; children—Donald Henry, Chester Clemons. Admitted to Va. bar, 1961; dir. field services and summer rehab. center Va. Soc. Crippled Children and Adults, 1956-58, bd. dirs. Va. Beach, 1958—; asst. city atty. Norfolk (Va.), 1961-62; asso. Kellam & Kellam, attys., Virginia Beach, Va., 1962-66, partner, 1967-68; partner Owen, Guy, Rhodes & Betz, Virginia Beach, 1969—. Pres. Thalia Civic League Virginia Beach, 1967. Mem. Virginia Beach City Council, 1970-73, mayor, 1970-72; mem. Va. Ho. of Dels., 1973—. Bd. dirs. Tidewater Mental Health Assn. Virginia Beach, 1965—; mem. exec. bd. Tidewater council Boy Scouts Am. Mem. Men's Democratic Club Virginia Beach. Mem. Va., Virginia Beach, Norfolk-Portsmouth bar assns., Va. State Bar, Delta Theta Phi, Phi Kappa Psi, Clubs: Y.M.C.A. Men's Princess Anne Ruritan, Virginia Beach Sertoma (v.p. 1964-67, pres. 1967-68), Cavalier Golf and Yacht. Home: 621 Heron Point Circle Virginia Beach VA 23452 Office: 281 Independence Blvd Virginia Beach VA 23462

RHODES, DONALD ROBERT, elec. engr., educator; b. Detroit, Dec. 31, 1923; s. Donald Eber and Edna Mae (Fulmer) R.; B.E.E., Ohio State U., 1945, M.Sc., 1948, Ph.D., 1953; m. Martha Ellen Peterson, Mar. 17, 1945; children—Joyce (Mrs. Alvah R. Holbert), Jane (Mrs. J. David Waller, Jr.), Roger Charles, Diane. Research asso. Ohio State U., Columbus, 1945-54; research engr. Cornell Aero Lab., Buffalo, 1954-57; head basic research dept., Radiation, Inc., Orlando, Fla., 1957-61; sr. scientist, Melbourne, Fla., 1961-66; prof. elec. engring. N.C. State U., Raleigh, 1966—. Pres. Central Fla. Symphony Orchestra, Winter Park, 1961-62, also co-founder. Fellow I.E.E.E. (John T. Bolljahn award 1963, mem. adminstrv. com. group on antennas and propagation 1965-73, pres. 1969), A.A.A.S.; mem. Am. Phys. Soc., Sigma Xi, Theta Tau, Eta Kappa Nu, Sigma Pi Sigma. Presbyn. (deacon 1959-61). Author: Introduction to Monopulse, 1959, Synthesis of Planar Antenna Sources, 1974. Home: 5616 Winthrop Dr Raleigh NC 27612 Office: PO Box 5275 Raleigh NC 27607

RHODES, EDWIN FRANKLIN, mfg. co. exec.; b. Mishawaka, Ind., Oct. 24, 1919; s. Edward R. and Edna (Arnold) R.; B.S., N.C. State U., 1940; m. Helen Hickman, Sept. 29, 1952; children—Charles, Mary Lisa, Christopher, Thomas, Cynthia, Priscilla, Eric, Stephanie. Installationist engr. Otis Elevator Co., 1940-41; tchr. pub. schs., Mishawaka, 1941-42, engr., tool engr., spl. project engr., specialist, purchasing agt. Dodge Mfg. Co. div. Reliance Electric, Mishawaka, 1942-58, mgr. purchases, 1958-69; mgr. operations controls Baldor Electric Co., Fort Smith, Ark., St. Louis and Columbus, Miss., 1969—; dir. N.Am. Foundry; mng. dir. Southwestern Die Casting. Mem. C. of C. Methodist. Mason (32 deg., Shriner). Home: 4112 S 35th St Fort Smith AR 72901 Office: Baldor Electric Co Fort Smith AR 72901

RHODES, ERIC FOSTER, editor, pub.; b. Luray, Va., Feb. 5, 1927; s. Wallace Keith and Bertha (Foster) R.; A.A., George Washington U., 1949, A.B., 1950, M.A., 1952, Ed.D., 1967; m. Barbara Ellen Henson, Oct. 19, 1946; children—Roxanne Jane, Laurel Lee; m. 2d, Lorraine Endresen, July 29, 1972. Tchr. high sch., Arlington, Va., 1950-52; counselor Washington Lee High Sch., Arlington, 1952-53, dir. publs., 1953-54, chmn. dept. English, 1954-55; exec. sec. Arlington Edn. Assn., 1952-53, Montgomery County (Md.) Edn. Assn., 1955-57; lectr. edn. George Washington U., 1955-60; salary cons. N.E.A., Washington, 1957-58, asst. dir. membership div., 1958-60, dir. N.Y. regional office, N.Y.C., 1960-64; ednl. cons. Ednl. Research Services, White Plains, N.Y., 1964-65; pres. Ednl. Service Bur., Inc., Arlington, 1965-72, chmn. bd., 1972—; pres. EFR Corp., 1972—. Cons. Va. Dept. Community Colls., 1965—; lectr. edn. Frostburg (Md.) State Coll., 1967; vice chancellor Va. Community Coll. System, 1970-71. Mem. Civil Rights Commn., Franklin Twp., N.J., 1962-64; mem. Franklin Twp. Bd. Edn., 1964-65; mem. adv. bd. Keep Am. Beautiful, 1964—, nat. chmn., 1968. Served with AUS, 1945-47. Mem. Am. Assn. Sch. Adminstrs., N.E.A., Edn. Press Assn., Phi Delta Kappa (chpt. pres. 1959-60), Fed. Schoolmens Club, N.Y. Schoolmasters Club. Lion. Author: Negotiating Salaries. Editor: Adminstrv. Leadership, Salary and Merit. Home: 6631 Wakefield Dr Alexandria VA 22307 Office: 610 Madison St Alexandria VA 22314

RHODES, LYNWOOD MARK, writer, photographer; b. Gonzales, Tex., May 28, 1931; s. Demosthenes and Hildeen (Barrow) R.; B.A. in History, U. Tex., 1952, B.A. in English, 1952, M.A. in Am. Econ. History, 1953. Exec. asst. Office of Gov., Austin, Tex., 1952-63; exec. v.p. Byers Oil Co., Austin, 1963; free lance mag. writer, photographer, Austin, 1963—. Travel cons. Am. Express Co., Neiman-Marcus Co., Dallas, 1963. Recipient Kodak Photo Exhibition award, 1969, George Hedman Meml. award Scandinavian Airlines System, 1970, certificate of Excellence in Travel Journalism Pacific Area Travel Assn., 1972; decorated Papal Cross Honor (Jerusalem), 1965. Mem. Soc. Am. Travel Writers, Soc. Mag. Writers, Phi Alpha Theta, Delta Sigma Phi. Home: 1122 Colorado St Austin TX 78701 Office: PO Box 2141 Austin TX 78767

RHODES, ROBERT GRANT, petroleum co. exec.; b. Caney, Kan., Mar. 23, 1917; s. Charles William and Stella Susan (Toner) R.; B.S., U. Tex., 1939; m. Nellie Foldine Martin, Aug. 20, 1942; children—Cheryl Susan, Mary Rebecca, Robert William. With Phillips Petroleum Co., 1939—, mgr. fertilizer and plastics plant, Pasadena, Tex., 1952-58, mgr. petrochem. div. mfg. dept., 1963-69, alternate mem. operating com., 1965, mgr. operations chem. and refining, 1969-72, gen. mgr. rubber chems., 1972—; prodn. mgr. Phillips Chem. Co., Bartlesville, Okla., 1958-63; dir. Phosphate Chem. Inc. Mem. adv. bd. Salvation Army, Pasadena, 1952-58; mem. Civil Def. Commn., Houston; indsl. adviser U. Tex., 1966—; pres. Nat. Little League Baseball, 1971, Am. Little League Baseball, 1972. Registered profl. engr., Okla. Mem. Nat., Okla. socs. profl. engrs., Am. Inst. Chem. Engrs., Nat. Petroleum Refiners Assn. (mem. mfg. com. 1971), Ind. Petroleum Producers Am. (asso.), Bartlesville Ambassador C. of C. Presbyn. (deacon). Rotarian. Club: Governors. Home: 1721 Cherokee Pl Bartlesville OK 74003 Office: Phillips Petroleum Co Bartlesville OK 74003

RIANO, MANUEL, physician; b. Havana, Cuba, Sept. 5, 1913; s. Agapito and Maria J. (Jauma) R.; M.D., U. Havana, 1942; postgrad. U. Miami, Fla., 1963; m. Belen Dobal, June 1931; 1 son, Manuel J. Came to U.S., 1962. Intern, U. Havana Sch. Medicine, Univ. Hosp., 1942-43; resident Municipal Emergency Hosp., Havana, 1943-46; gen. practice medicine, Havana, 1942-62; head div. hosps. and pub. health services Ministry Pub. Health, Havana, 1948-50; med. dir. Saturnino Lora Gen. Hosp., Santiago de Cuba, Oriente, 1949-50; supt. Nat. Mental Hosp., Mazorra, Havana, 1950-52; internal medicine cons. Out-Patient Clinic, Ministry Pub. Health, Service of Hygiene and Pub. Health, 1946-48; mem. psychiat. staff Wichita Falls (Tex.) State Hosp., 1964—; asst. prof. parasitology and tropical diseases U. Havana Sch. Medicine, 1940-42, instr., 1942-44. Gen. inspection pub. health services Ministry Pub. Health, Havana, 1952-60. Mem. exec. bd. Nat. Coll. Medicine, Havana, 1944-48, 54-60, Havana Coll. Medicine, 1942-44. Mem. Am. Assn. Hosps., A.M.A., Tex. Med. Assn., Wichita County Med. Soc., Centauro (hon. pres.). Address: Box 300 Wichita Falls TX 76307

RICARDS, HAROLD ANDREW, JR., oil co. exec.; b. Balt., June 21, 1917; s. Harold A. and Annette (Simpson) R.; B.E. in Chem. Engring., Johns Hopkins, 1939; M.S. in Chem. Engring., Mass. Inst. Tech., 1941; postgrad. U. Cal. at Berkeley, 1964; m. Eleanor Mae Connor, Dec. 25, 1943; children—Andrea Lee, Nancy Ellette. Unit head research div. Standard Oil Devel. Co., Linden, N.J., 1941-48; sect. mgr. process div. Esso Research & Engring. Co., Linden, 1948-56, mgr. distbn. and engring. research Esso Standard Oil, N.Y.C., 1957-60, asst. mgr. marketing econs., 1960; mgr. planning and evaluation Humble Oil & Refining Co., Houston, 1961-68, adminstrv. mgr. central region, Memphis, 1968, sales mgr. central region, 1969—. Lectr., Pa. State U., 1952-57. Served with USAAF, World War II; ETO. Mem. Am. Quarter Horse Assn., Civil War Round Tables, Sigma Xi, Kappa Sigma, Omicron Delta Kappa, Pi Delta Epsilon. Contbr. articles to profl. jours. Patentee in field. Home: 1228 Brookfield Rd Memphis TN 38117 Office: PO Box 367 Memphis TN 38101

RICE, ATWOOD LUMBERD, JR., marine supply co. exec.; b. New Orleans, Apr. 30, 1918; s. Atwood Lumberd and Carrie Moore (Hayward) R.; student Loyola U. South, 1936-37; m. Nancy Barrier Stubblefield, Dec. 22, 1945; children—Atwood L., III, John Barrier. With Hibernia Nat. Bank, New Orleans, 1935-41; co-founder, partner Byrne & Rice Supply Co., New Orleans, 1946-60, pres. Byrne, Rice & Turner, Inc., 1960—, pres. La. Air Pollution Controls div.; 1969—; v.p. Rio Hondo Oil & Devel. Corp. La., 1960-71; sec., 1965-71. Pres. Orleans Neighborhood Centers, 1949-50; pres. New Orleans Sportsmen's League, 1970; mem. Met. Area Com., Council for a Better La., Pub. Affairs Research Council; pres. Valencia, Inc., 1971—. Bd. dirs. Cancer Assn. Greater New Orleans, Children's Bur. New Orleans. Served to capt. AUS, 1941-45; ETO. Decorated Bronze Star. Mem. La. (co-founder, pres. 1948-49), New Orleans (co-founder, pres. 1939-41) junior chambers commerce, S.R. (pres. 1965-67), Mil. Order Fgn. Wars (comdr. La. 1964-66), Soc. 1812 (dir. La. chpt.), Soc. Colonial Wars (gov. La. 1972-73). Episcopalian (treas. ch. 1968-72, chmn. Young Life New Orleans 1969-71). Clubs: Louisiana, New Orleans Country, Pendennis, Pickwick (New Orleans); Lake Shore (Slidell, La.); Avoca Duck (Morgan City, La.). Home: 1220 Philip St New Orleans LA 70130 Office: 1150 Camp St New Orleans LA 70130

RICE, CHARLES OLIVER, banker; b. Shreveport, La., May 9, 1933; s. Ollie Charles and Linna (Hart) R.; A.A., Allen Mil. Acad., 1954; B.B.A., U. Houston, 1956; certificate, Southwestern Grad. Sch. Banking So. Meth. U., 1967; m. Farolyn Ivey Shaw, Dec. 6, 1958 (div. Oct. 1967); 1 son, Charles O.; m. 2d, Micaela Garibay, Oct. 9, 1970. With Tex. Commerce Bank, Houston, 1956-73, asst. cashier, 1961-63, asst. v.p., 1963-65, v.p., 1965-73; v.p. corr. banking Nat. Bank Tulsa, 1973—. Served with AUS, 1967. Mem. Tulsa C. of C., Mus. Fine Arts. Methodist. Address: 1212 E 26th Pl Tulsa OK 74114

RICE, CLARENCE W., sch. dist. ofcl.; b. New Braunfels, Tex., July 20, 1906; s. Charles Willard and Mathilda (Dannheim) R.; B.A., S.W. Tex. State Tchrs. Coll., 1929; M.A., U. Tex., 1937; postgrad. law, St. Mary's U., San Antonio, 1951; m. Melba Alves, Aug. 21, 1929 (dec. Dec. 1960); children—Shirley (Mrs. Lester C. Hahn), Kim A.; m. 2d, Edythe B. Porter, Sept. 15, 1962. Tchr. English, New Braunfels Sr. High Sch., 1926-31, head social studies, 1931-46; county judge Comal County, Tex., 1947-67; attendance investigator Austin (Tex.) Ind. Sch. Dist., 1967—; real estate broker. Served as 1st lt. USAAF, 1943-45. Recipient Silver Beaver award Boy Scouts Am., 1953. Mem. S. Tex. County Judges and Commrs. Assn. (pres.), Texas Safety Assn. (hon. dir.), Nat., Tex. assns. county ofcls. Elk, Lion. Address: 4006 Edgerock Dr Austin TX 78731

RICE, DAVID FLEMING, state ofcl.; b. Hawkinsville, Ga., Aug. 30, 1907; s. Alexander John and Janie (Fleming) R.; B.S. in Civil Engring., Ga. Inst. Tech., 1929; m. Erlyne Lanier, July 22, 1934; children—David Lanier, Robert Fleming; m. 2d, Anagene P. Bartram, Jan. 29, 1966. Dept. head Sears Roebuck & Co., Atlanta, 1929-37;

owner, operator Ellen Rice Restaurant, 1937-48, Town House Restaurant, 1948-54; apt. builder; officer various corps. Mem. Ga. Bd. Edn., Atlanta, 1961—, vice chmn., 1970—; bd. regents Univ. System Ga., Atlanta, 1954-61. Mem. Am. Assn. Sch. Adminstrs. (mem. mission to study edn. in Soviet Union 1969—), Am. Vocational Assn., N.E.A., Ga. Edn. Assn., Navy League U.S., Atlanta Restaurant Assn. (pres. 1945-46, 52), Internat. Platform Assn., Nat. Assn. State Bds. Edn. (v.p. 1966-67, 67-68), Pi Delta Epsilon, Sigma Nu. Episcopalian. Clubs: Rotary, Atlanta Athletic. Address: 1175 W Conway Rd NW Atlanta GA 30327

RICE, DOWNEY, lawyer; b. Washington, Apr. 13, 1913; s. Fred J. and Agnes (Downey) R.; J.D. Cath. U., 1935, LL.M., 1936; m. Ellen Cushing Smith, Oct. 12, 1937; children—Michael Downey, Ellen Sue (Mrs. William C. Potter, Jr.). Admitted to D.C. bar, 1935; spl. agt. FBI, 1936-45; gen. practice Washington, 1945—; spl. counsel to U.S. Atty., Washington, 1948; asso. counsel to com. investigate organized crime U.S. Senate, 1950-51, spl. counsel to preparedness com., 1952, chief counsel to commerce com., 1953; spl. counsel to anti-trust and monopoly sub-com. judiciary com., 1957, cons. to govt. operations com. McClellan rackets com., 1961; counsel to com. investigation adminstrn. of justice Pa. Legislature, 1973. Mem. Washington Criminal Justice Assn. (bd. mem.), Soc. Former Spl. Agts. FBI, Am. Bar Assn., Am. Judicature Soc. Roman Catholic. Clubs: University, Nat. Press, Washington Athletic. Home: 3244 Aberfoyle Pl NW Washington DC 20015 Office: 1744 R St NW Washington DC 20009

RICE, FIDELIS, clergyman; b. Berwick, Me., Dec. 8, 1908; s. Patrick J. and Elizabeth A. (Burns) R.; student Holy Cross Sem., 1924-28. Ordained priest Roman Cath. Ch., 1936; priest Roman Cath. chs., Jamaica, N.Y., 1937-38, Rome, Italy, 1939-41, Scranton, Pa., 1941-44, Balt., 1944-53, West Springfield, Mass., from 1953; founder-producer weekly internat. radio program Hour of the Crucified, Crossroads; now retreat master Our Lady of Fla. monastery, North Palm Beach, Fla.; producer weekly radio program This Mixed World. Mem. Cath. Broadcasters Assn., Cath. Homiletic Soc. Home: 1300 US Hwy 1 North Palm Beach FL 33408

RICE, HOMER CRANSTON, univ. athletic adminstr.; b. Bellevue, Ky., Feb. 20, 1927; s. S.C. and Nancy Grace (Wilson) R.; A.B., Center Coll., Danville, Ky.; B.S., also M.Ed., Eastern Ky. State U.; m. Phyllis Wardrup, Aug. 12; children—Nancy Kathryn, Phyllis Wardrup, Angela. Coach Spring City (Tenn.) High Sch., 1952-53, Highland High Sch., Ft. Thomas, Ky., 1954-61; head offensive football coach U. Ky., 1962-65, U. Okla., 1966; head football coach U. Cin., 1967-68; dir. athletics U. N.C., 1969—; lectr. in field. Mem. TV com. Nat. Collegiate Athletic Assn.; panel coordinator Nat. Assn. Coll. Dirs. Athletics, Denver, 1973; pres. Triangle chpt. Nat. Football Found. and Hall of Fame. Bd. dirs. YMCA, Centre Coll. Alumni. Served with Armed Forces, World War II. Named Ky. Col., Hon. Tex. Citizen. Methodist (lay speaker; mem. adminstrv. bd.). Author: How to Organize Football Practice, 1962; The Explosive Short-T, 1963; Homer Rice on Triple Option Football, 1973. Contbr. articles to athletic jours. Home: 349 Tenney Circle Chapel Hill NC 27514

RICE, JACK VAUGHAN, hotel exec.; b. Lexington, Miss., Nov. 19, 1937; s. James Watford and Grace Wirt (Vaughan) R.; B.B.A., U. Miss., 1959. Mem. marketing research staff Plough, Inc., Memphis, 1960-62; exec. asst. to pres. Holiday Inns, Inc., Memphis, 1962-70, exec. asst. to vice chmn. bd., 1970—; dir. Medicenters Am., Inc., Memphis, Alodex Corp., Memphis, Manor Care, Inc., Silver Spring, Md., Wallace E. Johnson Enterprises, Memphis, Med. Devel. Services, Inc., Memphis. Trustee Sam Houston Meml. Hosp., Houston, Wallace E. Johnson-E.B. McCool Found., Memphis. Served with AUS, 1960. Mem. Sigma Chi. Club: University. Home: 4952 Devonshire St Memphis TN 38117 Office: 3742 Lamar St Memphis TN 38118

RICE, LAURENCE BLISS, computer scientist; b. Urbana, Ill., Apr. 21, 1935; s. Herbert Orvil and Cynthia (Corrie) R.; B.S., U. Ill., 1957; M.S., Clemson Coll., 1959; Ph.D., U. Va., 1962; m. Barbara Louise Slyder, June 17, 1963; children—Cynthia Louise, Catherine Barbara, Cory Laurence. With RCA, Patrick AFB, 1957-73, project engr. advanced analysis, 1965-70, mgr. reentry physics advanced range instrumentation ships, 1970-72; computer software systems analyst, mgr. safeguard perimeter acquisition radar group Sci. Applications Inc., Huntsville, Ala., 1973—. Adj. prof. Fla. Inst. Tech., 1962-70. Mem. Quality Edn. Brevard County (Fla.) Commn., 1968-69. Bd. dirs. Home Owners Snug Harbor. Named Ky. col. Mem. I.E.E.E., Toastmasters Internat. (pres. 1970-71). Sigma Xi. Home: 308 Flemington Rd Huntsville AL 35802 Office: 2109 W Clinton Av Huntsville AL 35805

RICE, PAUL WINSTON, city mgr.; b. Huntsville, Mo., Aug. 31, 1917; s. Asa Isaac and Lola Elizabeth (Chrane) R.; student Bethany Nazarene Coll., 1935-38; B.S., Okla. U., 1948; postgrad. Yale, 1948-49; m. Dorothy Jean Graves, Sept. 4, 1948; children—Larry Steven, Brenda Gayle. Traffic engr. of Tulsa, 1949-52; traffic engr. of Evansville, Ind., 1952-56; dir. traffic engring. Corpus Christi, Tex., 1956-64; city mgr., Bethany, Okla., 1964—; tchr. transp. Bethany Nazarene Coll., 1965, 68. Bd. dirs. Bethany Mus. and Hist. Soc., Bethany Child Guidance Center, Okla.; chmn. bd. dirs. Municipal Retirement Fund. Served to 2d lt., C.E., USAAF, 1943-46. Selected as Most Useful Citizen Bethany C. of C., 1967; recipient Outstanding Alumnus award Bethany Nazarene Coll., 1964. Registered profl. engr., Okla., Ind., Tex. Mem. Internat. City Mgmt. Assn., Inst. Traffic Engrs., City Mgrs. Assn. Okla. (dir., past pres.), Internat. City Mgmt. Assn. (v.p. Mountain Plains region 1973-74). Kiwanian. Contbr. articles profl. jours. Originator Yield Right of Way sign. Home: 2012 Alexander Lane Bethany OK 73008

RICE, THEODORE ROOSEVELT, biologist, govt. ofcl.; b. Staffordsville, Ky., Jan. 19, 1919; s. Isaac Grant and Della (Caudall) R.; A.B., Berea Coll., 1941; M.A., Harvard, 1947, Ph.D., 1949; m. Frankie Gaines Mantooth, Dec. 27, 1941; children—Theodore Roger, Gregory Keith, Philip Scott. Fishery research biologist, asst. dir. radiobiol. research Bur. Comml. Fisheries, Beaufort, N.C., 1949-60, chief radiobiol. program, 1960-63, dir. radiobiol. lab., 1963-68; dir. Atlantic Esturine Fisheries Center, Nat. Marine Fisheries Service, Beaufort, 1968—. Adj. prof. zoology dept. N.C. State U., Raleigh, 1963—. Served to maj. AUS, 1942-46. Recipient Nat. Oceanic Atmospheric Adminstrn. Sci. and Achievement award, 1972. Mem. Am. Soc. Limnology and Oceanography, Ecol. Soc. Am., Health Physics Soc., Am. Nuclear Soc., Gulf and Caribbean Fish Inst., Assn. Southeastern Biologists, Am. Water Resources Assn., Atlantic Estuarine Research Soc., Nat. Shellfisheries, Assn. Home: 115 Holly Lane Morehead City NC 28557

RICE, WILLIAM THOMAS, railroad exec.; b. Hague, Va., June 13, 1912; s. John and Elizabeth Conway (Snow) R.; B.S. in Civil Engring., Va. Poly. Inst., 1934; LL.D. (hon.), Stetson U., 1959; m. Jaqueline Johnston, Sept. 14, 1935; children—John Thomas, Jacqueline Norma. With Pa. R.R., 1934-42; joined Richmond, Fredericksburg & Potomac R.R. Co., 1946, pres., dir., 1955-57; pres., dir., exec. com. Atlantic Coast Line R.R. Co., 1957-67; pres., chief exec. officer Seaboard Coast Line R.R. Co., 1967-70, chmn. bd., chief exec. officer, 1970-72, chmn. bd., 1972—; chmn. bd., chief exec. officer Seabord Coast Line Industries, Inc., 1970—, also dir., mem. exec. com.; chmn. bd. Louisville & Nashville R.R. Co.; dir. subsidiary and affiliated lines and stas.; dir. Alico Land Devel. Co.; dir. Chem. Bank N.Y. Trust Co., Graniteville Co., First & Mchts. Nat. Bank of Richmond, Fla. Nat. Bank of Jacksonville, Home Ins. Co., Borden Co., Ethyl Corp., Commonwealth Nat. Gas Co. Richmond. Trustee P.E. Theol. Sem. Va., Alexandria. Served from 1st lt. to lt. col. AUS, 1942-46. Decorated Legion of Merit with 2 oak leaf clusters. Mem. Assn. Southeastern R.R.'s, Va. Poly. Inst. Alumni Assn., Transp. Assn. Am., Nat. Def. Transp. Assn. (life), Nat. Freight Traffic Assn., Newcomen Soc., Omicron Delta Kappa, Tau Beta Pi. Episcopalian. Clubs: Augusta (Ga.) Nat.; Sky, Union League (N.Y.C.); Metropolitan (Washington); Country of Va., Commonwealth (Richmond, Va.); River, Timuquana Country (Jacksonville, Fla.); Rotary. Home: 8739 Riverside Dr Richmond VA 23225 Office: 3600 W Broad St Richmond VA 23230 also 500 Water St Jacksonville FL 32202

RICE, WILLIAM VAUGHN, JR., air force officer; b. Hiawassee, Ga., Dec. 5, 1926; s. William Vaughn and Anne Julia (O'Quinn) R.; B.S., U.S. Mil. Acad., 1949; M.B.A., USAF Inst. Tech., 1958; Ph.D., La. State U., 1974; m. Claire L. Mikulin, Aug. 24, 1950; children—Michael D., William Vaughn III, Tamara Anne. Commd. 2d lt. USAF, 1949, advanced through grades to lt. col., 1967; air crew mem. SAC, 1950-57; ednl. adviser Republic of Korea Air Acad., Seoul, 1958-59; asst. prof. aerospace studies La. State U., 1960-66; sr. instr. Acad. Instr. Sch., Air U., Montgomery, Ala., 1967-68, chief, labor-mgmt. relations div., 1969-75; instr. econs. Troy State U. Adult Edn. Program, 1966-75; asst. prof. econs. and mgmt. U. Houston at Clear Lake City, Tex., 1975—. Mem. Am., So. econ. assns., Am. Assn. U. Profs., Air Force Assn., Omicron Delta Epsilon. Mason. Author: Introduction to Air Force Labor Relations, Vol. I, 1971. Contbr. articles to profl. jours. Office: U Houston Clear Lake City TX

RICH, ARNOLD RAY, holding co. exec.; b. Scotsville, Ky., Mar. 26, 1942; s. Clyde Arnold and Selma Mae (Wade) R.; student Bowling Green Coll. Commerce, 1962-63; B.S. in Accounting, Western Ky. U., 1965; m. Carol Joann Smith, Oct. 21, 1967; 1 son, John David. Staff accountant Humphery Robinson, accounting firm, Louisville, 1965-68; sec., also controller Am. Pyramid Cos., Inc., Louisville, 1968—; dir. TSI, Inc., Louisville, asst. sec., 1969—; dir. Western Pioneer Life Ins. Co., Louisville, asst. sec., 1971—; v.p., also asst. sec. Independence Nat. Corp., Columbus, O., 1972—; sec., dir. Am. Holding Corp., Louisville, Am. Consol. Corp., Louisville. Mem. Ky. Efficiency Task Force, 1967. Served with AUS, 1959-62. C.P.A., Ky. Mem. Am. Inst. C.P.A.'s, Ky. Soc. C.P.A.'s, Delta Sigma Pi. Baptist. Home: 613 Rymer Way Louisville KY 40223 Office: 4211 Norbourne Blvd Louisville KY 40207

RICH, ARTHUR DOUGLAS, lawyer; b. Mattapan, Mass., Jan. 15, 1915; s. Arthur Warren and Matilda J. (McNeill) R.; A.B., U. Buffalo, 1938; LL.B., Harvard, 1940; m. Dora Jackson, Aug. 25, 1944; children—Arthur W., Kay Carol. Admitted to S.C. bar, 1946; practiced in Spartanburg, S.C., 1946-52, Aiken, S.C., 1952—; mem. firm Lybrand, Rich, Cain & Simons, 1955—. Pres., Richco, Inc., Aiken, 1958—; v.p. Gabs Alinement, Inc., Aiken, 1971—; owner Rich Plaza Shopping Center, Aiken, 1968—; dir. United Fabricators, Inc., Jackson, S.C. Vice pres. Ga.-Carolina council Boy Scouts Am., 1971—. Served to 1st lt. AUS, 1941-45. Recipient Silver Beaver award Boy Scouts Am., 1973. Mason (Shriner), Kiwanian. Club: Pinnacle. Author: Handbook of Income Tax for S.C., 1952-66. Home: 1114 Evans Rd Aiken SC 29801 Office: Palmetto Fed Bldg Aiken SC 29801

RICH, FRANK HART, mcht.; b. Washington, Apr. 13, 1921; s. Herbert J. and Rosa (Frank) R.; B.S., Lehigh U., 1942; postgrad. Harvard, 1943; m. Anadel Seidman, Mar. 15, 1959; children—Frank Hart, Polly Alice, Elizabeth Hart, Ned Swope, Abby Dee. Customer service mgr. The Hecht Co., Washington, 1946-49; v.p. Rich's Shoe Stores, Washington, 1949-56, pres., 1956—. Lectr., Am. U., 1957-58; pres. Metro-Washington Urban Coalition, 1969-71, bd. dirs., 1971-72; mem. urban renewal council, D.C., 1959-66; mem. D.C. Health and Welfare Council, 1958-65; mem. Mayor's Econ. Devel. Com., 1970-73; mem. Human Rights Commn., Washington, 1971—; chmn. Mayor's Adv. Com. on Narcotics, 1971—. Bd. dirs. Washington Area Council on Alcoholism, 1965-71, United Planning Orgn., Washington, 1972; trustee United Givers Fund, Washington, 1955-57. Served from pvt. to maj., AUS, 1942-46, CBI; served as lt. col. USAF, 1951-53. Decorated Bronze Star medal. Mem. Chevy Chase Center Mchts. Assn. (pres. 1957-60), Nat. Shoe Retailers Assn. (dir., pres. 1971-73), Washington Bd. Trade. Jewish religion. Rotarian (Community Service award 1972). Club: Nat. Press (Washington). Home: 5001 38th St NW Washington DC 20016 Office: 1321 F St NW Washington DC 20004

RICH, GILES SUTHERLAND, judge; b. Rochester, N.Y., May 30, 1904; s. Giles Willard and Sarah Thompson (Sutherland) R.; S.B., Harvard, 1926; LL.B., Columbia, 1929; m. Gertrude Verity Braun, Jan. 10, 1931 (dec.); 1 dau., Verity Sutherland (Mrs. Alan D. Grinnell); m. 2d, Helen Gill Field, Oct. 10, 1953. Admitted to N.Y. bar, 1929; registered to practice U.S. Patent Office, 1934; practice law, N.Y.C., 1929-56, specializing patent and trademark law; partner Williams, Rich & Morse, 1937-52, Churchill, Rich, Weymouth & Engel, 1952-56; asso. judge U.S. Ct. Customs and Patent Appeals, 1956—; lectr. patent law Columbia, 1942-56, N.Y. Law Sch., 1952; adj. prof. Georgetown U. Law School, 1963-69. Recipient Jefferson medal, N.J. Patent Law Assn., 1955; Kettering award Patent, Trademark and Copyright Inst. George Washington U., 1963; Freedman Found. award Am. Inst. Chemists, 1967; Founders Day award George Washington U. Patent and Trademark Inst., 1970; Eli Whitney award Conn. Patent Law Assn., 1972. Mem. Assn. Bar City N.Y., Am. Bar Assn., Am., N.Y. (pres. 1950-51) patent law assns., Nat. Lawyers Club (hon.). Clubs: Harvard, Cosmos (Washington). Author articles in field. Home: 4949 Linnean Av NW Washington DC 20008 Office: US Court Customs and Patent Appeals Washington DC 20439

RICH, HARRY LOUIS, physicist; b. N.Y.C., Apr. 30, 1917; s. Meyer and Anna (Nemser) R.; B.A., Bklyn. Coll., 1939; student George Washington U., 1940-45, U. Md., 1946-52; m. Irene Silverman, July 3, 1941; children—Michelle Jo (Mrs. Lawrence White), Margo. Cons. U.S. Naval Ship Research and Devel. Center, Washington, 1941-74, naval sci. adviser, Korea, 1971-72, fleet support liaison, 1972-74. Mem. U.S. delegation Internat. Standards Orgn., 1964—; mem. Internat. Electrotech. Commn., 1964—; Navy rep. tech. adv. group Information Center on Shock and Vibration, Dept. Def., 1957—. Recipient Meritorious Civilian Service award Navy Dept., 1958, 73, Superior Civilian Service award, 1963. Fellow Inst. Environmental Scis. (pres. Nat. Capitol chpt. 1968-70), Soc. Exptl. Stress Analysis, Acoustical Soc. Am., Soc. Naval Architects and Marine Engrs. Patentee shock spectrum recorder. Address: 6765 Brigadoon Dr Bethesda MD 20034

RICH, HELEN WALL (MRS. ARTHUR L. RICH), educator; b. Chester, S.C., May 4, 1912; d. George Addison and Georgia (Hardin) Wall; student Queen's Coll., 1930-32; B.S. summa cum laude, Catawba Coll., 1934 diploma in piano Juilliard Sch. Music, 1938; diplomas Christiansen Choral Sch., 1950, 51; m. Arthur Lowndes Rich, July 26, 1934; children—Arthur Lowndes, Ruth Anne. Instr. music Catawba Coll.; Salisbury, N.C., 1934-43; organist Mercer U., Macon, Ga., 1944-50, asst. prof. music, 1950—; organ recitalist throughout Southeast; v.p. Tudor Apts., Atlanta, 1960-68; sec.-treas. Richelieu Apts., Macon, 1955-68, Mem. Federated Music Clubs (chmn. scholarship contest), Ga. Piano Tchrs. Guild, Nat. Assn. Schs. Music (asso.), Am. Coll. and U. Concert Mgrs. Assn. (asso.), Cardinal Key Soc. Mercer U. (hon.), Delta Omicron. Club: Morning Music (dir.) (Macon). Home: 369 Condler Dr Macon GA 31204

RICH, JOHN MARTIN, educator; b. Tuscaloosa, Ala., Dec. 14, 1931; s. E.M. and Bertha R. (Rose) R.; B.A., U. Ala., 1954, M.A., 1955; Ph.D., Ohio State U., 1958. Asst. prof. edn. U. Tenn., Martin, 1958-60; asso. prof. State U. N.Y. Campus Sch., Oneonta, 1960-61; asst. prof. edn. Ia. State U., 1961-65, asso. prof., 1965-66; asso. prof. founds. edn. U. Ky., 1966-69; prof., chmn. dept. cultural founds. edn. U. Tex., Austin, 1969—. Mem. N. Central (pres. 1966-67), Ohio Valley (pres. 1967-68), Nat. (archivist 1964—, exec. bd. 1967-68, sec.-treas. 1968-70) philosophy edn. socs., Am. Ednl. Studies Assn. (exec. council 1972-75). Author: Readings in the Philosophy of Education, 1966, 2d edit., 1972; Education and Human Values, 1968; Humanistic Foundations of Education, 1971; Conflict and Decision, 1972. Co-editor Educational Studies, 1970—. Contbr. articles to profl. jours. Home: 1801 Lavaca St 8M Austin TX 78701

RICH, LINVIL GENE, educator; b. Pana, Ill., Mar. 10, 1921; s. Orville Cadel and Lillian Murle (Watkins) R.; B.S., Va. Poly. Inst., 1947, M.S., 1948, Ph.D., 1951; m. Peggy Jane Burton, June 17, 1944; children—Linvil Burton, Graham Watkins. Asso. prof. san. engring. Va. Poly. Inst., 1951-55; with USPHS, Bolivia, 1955-56; prof. san. engring. Ill. Inst. Tech., Chgo., 1956-61; dean engring. Clemson (S.C.) U., 1961-72, prof. environmental systems engring., 1972—. Spl. cons. USPHS, Dept. Interior, Environmental Protection Agy. Served with AUS, 1942-46. Diplomate Environmental Engring. Intersoc. Bd. Fellow Am. Soc. C.E.; mem. Sigma Xi, Chi Epsilon, Tau Beta Pi, Phi Sigma, Phi Lambda Upsilon, Phi Kappa Phi. Author: Unit Operations of Sanitary Engineering, 1961; Unit Processes of Sanitary Engineering, 1963; Environmental Systems Engineering, 1973. Contbr. articles to profl. jours. Home: PO Box 1185 Clemson SC 29631

RICHARD, JOHN BENARD, librarian; b. Gulfport, Miss., Nov. 2, 1932; s. John Jesse and Helen Lucille (Schott) R.; student Perkinston Jr. Coll., 1950-52; B.S., Miss. So. Coll., 1954; M.S. in Library Sci., La. State U., 1959; m. Sandra E. Davis Mosley, Dec. 19, 1970; children—Brian Davis Mosley, John Blake, Elizabeth. Preparations librarian La. State U., Baton Rouge, 1959-60; head librarian La. State U., Alexandria, 1960—. Chmn. La. Coll. Conf. Library Sect., 1967-68; exec. dir. La. Nat. Library Week Program, 1968; mem. La. Bd. Library Examiners. Bd. dirs. Central La. Art Assn., Kent Plantation House, Inc., Rapides Art Council. Served with AUS, 1954-57. Mem. Am. (rep. 1970-72), La. (pres. 1969-70), Southwestern library assns., Conf. Academic Library Adminstrs. La. (chmn. 1967), Beta Phi Mu. Roman Catholic. Rotarian (pres. 1962). Contbr. articles to profl. jours. Home: PO Box 364 Lecompte LA 71346 Office: La State U Alexandria LA 71301

RICHARD, OSCAR GABRIEL III, ednl. adminstr.; b. Sunshine, La., Dec. 7, 1921; s. Oscar Gabriel and Abigail (Callaghan) R.; B.A., La. State U., 1942; m. Billie Ruth Gathright, Sept. 20, 1947; children—Kathleen (Mrs. Byron D. Magbee III), Donna, Linda, Kelly, Reed. Dir. publs. La. State U., 1949-65, dir. publs., asso. dir. pub. relations, 1963-64, dir. information services, 1965—, dir. Anglo-Am. Art Museum, 1965—, adminstr. Rural Life Museum, 1972—; designer, Anglo-Am. Pelican Press, Gretna, La. Mem. United Givers Pub. Relations Council, Baton Rouge, 1973. Bd. dirs. Pollard Estates Civic Assn. Served with USAAF, 1942-45. Mem. Am. Coll. Pub. Relations Assn. (past dir.), La. State Information Reps., Am. Legion. Designer La. State U. Centennial Medallion, 1960; author La. State U. Centennial Theme; designer, co-editor La. State U.—The First Hundred Years, 1959; designer Seal of La. State U. Home: 5866 Hibiscus Dr Baton Rouge LA 70808 Office: 244 Thomas Boyd Hall La State U Baton Rouge LA 70803

RICHARDS, CLYDE RICH, govt. ofcl.; b. Paris, Ida., June 9, 1921; s. Clyde Randall and Myrtle (Rich) R.; B.S., Utah State U., 1943; M.S., Cornell U., 1949, Ph.D., 1950; postgrad. U. Cal. at Davis, 1966-67; m. Carrol Maughan, July 18, 1946; children—Russell, Keith, Debra. Grad. asst. Cornell U., 1946-50; lectr. animal breeding Superior Sch. Agr., Athens, Greece, 1950-51; asst. prof., asso. prof. U. Del., 1951-61; prin. animal nutritionist Coop. State Research Service, Dept. Agr., Washington, 1961—, dep. asst. adminstr., 1971-72. Served with USNR, 1943-46. Mem. Am. Inst. Nutrition, Am. Dairy Sci. Assn., Am. Soc. Animal Sci., A.A.A.S., Sigma Xi. Mem. Ch. of Jesus Christ of Latter-day Saints. Home: 6409 Adelphi Rd Hyattsville MD 20782 Office: Coop State Research Service Dept Agr Washington DC 20250

RICHARDS, FREDERICK WILLIAM, sch. adminstr., ret. Air Force officer; b. Green Camp. O., Mar. 28, 1919; s. Charles H. and Jennie (Logsden) R.; B.S., U. Md., 1959; M.S.A., George Washington U., 1974; m. Lola E. Barcus, Mar. 2, 1947; children—Keith Monzell, David Michael, Dana Scott. Enlisted as pvt. USAAF, 1942, advanced through grades to col. USAF, 1965; mil. asst. to dept. asst. sec. of Air Force for financial mgmt., Washington, 1968-71; ret., 1971; dir. accounting and systems Fairfax County (Va.) Pub. Schs., 1971—. Decorated Legion of Merit, D.F.C., Air medal with oak leaf clusters. C.P.A., Ill. Mem. Am. Inst. C.P.A.'s, Ill. Soc. C.P.A.'s, Fed. Govt. Accountants Assn., Assn. Sch. Bus. Ofcls. Address: 8603 Greeley Blvd Springfield VA 22152

RICHARDS, GEORGE LEROY, gas co. exec.; b. El Paso, Tex., July 18, 1926; s. George Eaton and Mamie (Oden) R.; B.S. in Geology, Tex. Coll. Mines and Metallurgy, 1948; m. Ann Carlin, Sept. 3, 1948; children—Julie Ann, Jack Carlin. With Standard Oil Co. Tex., 1948-64; with Coastal States Gas Producing Co., Corpus Christi, Tex., 1964—, v.p., 1969—. Served with USNR, 1944-46. Mem. Am. Assn. Petroleum Geologists, Corpus Christi Geol. Soc. (mem. ho. of dels. 1969-72). Presbyn. Home: Route 4 Box 637 E New Braunfels TX Office: 5 Greenway Plaza East Houston TX 77046

RICHARDS, JAMES WILLIAM, steamship co. exec.; b. Bennettsville, S.C., Dec. 24, 1908; s. Ernest Vincent and Minnie (Pearce) R.; student bus. adminstrn. Tulane U., 1929-31; m. Sylvia Alice Williams, Sept. 4, 1934; 1 dau., Minnie Louise (Mrs. Herbert J. Griener). Accountant, Fed. Land Bank, New Orleans, 1932-33, Weinberger S.S. Corp., New Orleans, 1935-37; with Delta S.S. Lines, New Orleans, 1938-47, 63—, purchasing agt., operations asst., 1938-47, exec. asst., 1963-73, cons. Central Am. sales, 1974—; partner Schofield Trading Co., 1947-57, pres., 1957-62; adv. com. Bank La., New Orleans. Bd. dirs. Internat. House, New Orleans, 1955-57, Seamen's Town House, New Orleans, 1970—, La. Maritime Mus., 1970—. Acting consul, Paraguay, New Orleans, 1970. Clubs: World Trade, Plimsoll, So. Yacht, Propeller (v.p. 1972-73) (New Orleans). Home: 210 Betz Pl Metairle LA 70005 Office: 1700 Internat Trade Mart New Orleans LA 70150

RICHARDS, LLOYD FRANCIS, pub. health ofcl., educator; b. Royal Oak, Mich., Jan. 20, 1908; s. Lyman H. and Emma (King) R.; A.B., Albion Coll., 1931; D.D.S., U. Mich., 1934; M.P.H., U. Cal. at Berkeley, 1949; m. Jane Elizabeth Barringer, Oct. 5, 1945; children—Stephen Lloyd, Pamela Jane. Children's dentist Children's Fund, Detroit, 1934-36; individual practice, Detroit, 1937-43; supr. dental services Oakland (Cal.) pub. schs., 1949-51; pub. health officer div. dental health Cal. Dept. Pub. Health, Berkeley, 1951-52, chief, 1952-67; asso. prof., chmn. dept. dental health Baylor U., Coll. Dentistry, Dallas, 1967-70; also dir. Dallas city dental health program, 1967—. Lectr. U. Cal. Sch. Pub. Health, Berkeley, 1954-67, U. So. Cal. at Los Angeles, 1952-60. Mem health panel Commnunity Council Greater Dallas, 1968—; mem. task force Dallas Agy. on Aging. Served to maj. with Dental Corps, AUS, 1943-47; ETO. Diplomate Am. Bd. Dental Pub. Health. Fellow Am. Coll. Dentists, Am., Tex. (chmn. dental sect. 1968, governing council 1968-71, 73—) pub. health assns., Am. Sch. Health Assn. (governing bd. 1950-57, 60-63, 63-66), A.A.A.S. (v.p., chmn. dental sect. 1965); mem. Am., Cal., Tex., Dallas County dental assns., Am. Assn. Pub. Health Dentists (exec. council 1961-63, 64-67), Cal. sch. Health Assn. (pres. 1957), Assn. State and Territorial Dental Dirs. (pres. 1965-67, hon.), Am. Soc. Dentistry for Children (pres. No. Cal. unit 1958), Tex. Assn. for Services to Children, Dallas C. of C., Sigma Nu, Tau Kappa Omega. Rotarian. Home: 300 W Shore Dr Richardson TX 75080 Office: 3626 N Hall St Suite 720 Dallas TX 75219

RICHARDS, NELSON GLASGOW, physician; b. Orange, N.J., Aug. 15, 1924; s. Nelson and Annette (Glasgow) R.; B.A., U. Va., 1948, M.D., 1952; m. Sara Jean Raudenbush, Sept. 4, 1953; children—Linda (Mrs. Key Clark), Janis G., N. Scott, Karen A., John W. Intern medicine N.Y. Hosp., 1952-53, asst. resident, 1953-55, resident neurology, 1955-57; clin. asso. neurology NIH, 1957-58; mem. neurology staff Cleve. Clinic Found., 1958-69; pvt. practice ltd. to neurology, Roanoke, Va., 1969-73, Richmond, Va., 1973; instr. neurology Georgetown U., 1957-58; clin. asst. prof. neurology U. Va., 1969-73; clin. asso. prof. neurology Med. Coll. Va. Served with Hosp. Corps, USNR, 1944-46. Fellow Am. Acad. Neurology (sec.-treas. 1969-73), A.C.P., Am. Heart Assn.; mem. Soc. Clin. Neurology (pres. 1972-73), Va. Neurol. Soc., Am., So., Eastern EEG socs., Central Neuropsychiat. Assn. Home: 11820 Wakehurst Dr Richmond VA 23235 Office: 1805 Monument Av Richmond VA 23220

RICHARDS, ROBERT DAY, SR., physician; b. Buies Creek, N.C., Feb. 6, 1929; s. George Greer and Ruth (Bass) R.; B.S., Va. Poly. Inst., 1950; M.D., Med. Coll. Va., 1954; m. Narvie Price Adams, Aug. 13, 1949; children—Lora Lea, Robert Day. Intern, Roanoke (Va.) Meml. Hosp., 1954-55; practice medicine specializing in family practice, Wilson, N.C., 1958—; mem. staff Wilson (N.C.) Meml. Hosp. Chmn. Wilson County Bd. Edn., 1969—. Bd. dirs. Wilson County Tech. Inst. Served with USNR, 1955-58. Diplomate Am. Bd. Family Practice. Mem. Am. Acad. Family Physicians, A.M.A., So. Med. Assn., Med. Soc. State N.C., Wilson County Med. Soc. (pres. 1964-65). Home: Route 1 Sims NC 27880 Office: Route 2 Wilson NC 27893

RICHARDS, WARREN NEWTON, supt. edn.; b. Phenix City, Ala., June 12, 1918; s. Warren Newton and Thelma (Turner) R.; B.B.A., U. Ga., 1942; M.Ed., Auburn U., 1961; m. Elyane Dron, July 27, 1946; children—Warren Newton IV, Monique, Elyane, Colette, Nicole. Tchr., Phenix City Bd. Edn., 1950-55, asst. prin., 1955-57, asst. supt. 1957-62; supt. edn. Russell County (Ala.) Bd. Edn., Phenix City, 1962—. Active Russell County A.R.C., United Givers Fund. Served with AUS, 1942-47. Mem. N.E.A., Ala. Edn. Assn. (v.p.), Am., Ala. assns. sch. adminstrs., V.F.W., Am. Legion, Phi Delta Kappa. Methodist. Rotarian. Home: 4002 Lakewood Dr Phenix City AL 36867 Office: PO Box 908 Phenix City AL 36867

RICHARDS, WILLIAM GEORGE, savs. and loan exec.; b. Lockhart, Tex., Feb. 20, 1920; s. Cyrus F. and Gussie (Baldridge) R.; LL.B., U. Tex., 1948; m. Winnifred Adams, Nov. 23, 1940 (dec. May 1969); children—Bettye Ann (Mrs. Rogers), Mark Andrew; m. 2d, Corrie Marsh, Mar. 29, 1972. Admitted to Tex. bar, 1948; practiced law with father, Lockhart, 1948-55; v.p., atty., dir. Lockhart Savs. & Loan Assn., 1948-55; exec. v.p. Benjamin Franklin Savs. & Loan Assn., 1955-64, pres., 1964—, vice-chmn. bd., 1974—; trustee Savs. & Loan Found., Inc., 1957-59. Mem. Tex. Ho. of Reps., 1947-50; mayor of Lockhart, 1954-55. Mem. Nat. League Insured Savs. Assns. (exec. com. 1962-66), Houston C. of C. (dir. 1966, 68-73), Tex. Savs. and Loan League (dir. 1953-63, 63-66; pres. 1967-68), Phi Delta Phi. Democrat. Episcopalian. Club: Houston. Home: 6439 Burgoyne Houston TX 77027 Office: 720 Travis at Rusk Houston TX 77002

RICHARDSON, ALVAH BARTON, ins. co. exec.; b. Pine Bluff, Ark., Feb. 10, 1908; s. Alvah Barton and Martha Viroque (Clark) R.; B. Philosophy, Emory U., 1929; m. Alice Eley McDonald, June 26, 1937; 1 dau., Bonnie Alice (Mrs. Anthony DePinna Armer). Reporter Atlanta Georgian, 1929-36; ed. Newsview mag., Columbia, S.C., 1936; reporter, editor AP, Atlanta, 1937-44; So. rep. Aero. Tng. Soc., Washington, 1945; cons. pub. relations and advt., Atlanta, 1946; dir. pub. relations Life Ins. Co. Ga., Atlanta, 1946-56, v.p., 1956—; also dir. Vice pres. Atlanta Community Chest, 1959, 60, 66, 67; v.p. United Way Atlanta, 1972—. Bd. dirs. Atlanta Community Chest, 1969-71. Recipient Printer's Ink Man of Year in Atlanta silver medal Advt. Fedn. Am., 1959. Mem. Atlanta Advt. Club (bd. dirs. 1954-58), Atlanta Advt. Inst. (chmn., 1956), C. of C. (pub. relations and advt. com., 1969-70), Pub. Relations Soc. Am. (chpt. pres. 1958-59), Life Ins. Advertisers Assn. (pres. 1955-56), Life Insurers Conf. (exec. com. 1966-68), Inst. Life Ins. (pub. relations council 1962—), Sigma Delta Chi, Omicron Delta Kappa, Sigma Upsilon, Pi Delta Epsilon, Sigma Delta Chi, Alpha Delta Sigma. Presbyn. Club: Commerce of Atlanta. Home: 92 26th St NW Atlanta GA 30309 Office: 600 W Peachtree St NW Atlanta GA 30308

RICHARDSON, AMOS HAYNES III, lawyer, assn. exec.; b. Ansonville, N.C., Jan. 14, 1922; s. Amos Haynes and Pattie Florence (McSwain) R.; LL.B., Ark. Law Sch., 1948; postgrad. Rutgers U., 1964; m. Dorothy M. Padgett, Oct. 13, 1951; children—Patti Lea, Robert Preston. Dep. assessor Pulaski County, Ark., 1946; dep. Pulaski Chancery Ct. Clk., 1946-49; admitted to Ark. bar, 1949; field rep. U.S. Brewers Found., 1949-51, dir. voter registration, Little Rock, 1951-65; state dir. Ark. div. U.S. Brewers Assn., Little Rock, 1966—; guest lectr. U. Ark. at Little Rock, 1966—. Served with A.C., AUS, 1942-45 (USAF Res. 1945-48). Mem. Ark., Pulaski County bar assns., Ark. Assn. Assn. Execs., Ark. Press Assn., Ark. Broadcasters Assn., Ark. Law Enforcement Officers Assn., Pub. Relations Soc. Am. (dir. Ark. chpt.), Ark. Advt. Fedn. (dir.), Asso. Industries Ark., Ark. C. of C., Am. Legion. Methodist (adminstrv. bd.). Mason. Club: Arkansas Press (Little Rock). Home: 1200 N Mellon St Little Rock AR 72207 Office: US Brewers Assn 7100 Evergreen Rd Little Rock AR 72207

RICHARDSON, ANNE WORSHAM (MRS. JOHANNES PETER PASZEK), artist, ornithologist; b. Turbeville, S.C., Oct. 22, 1922; d. George Talbert and Jessie (Phillips) Worsham; student pub. and pvt. schs.; m. Marvin Dibble Richardson, Jan, 27, 1942; 1 son, Marvin D.; m. 2d, Johannes Peter Paszek, July 20, 1972. One-man shows at Charleston Mus., Ga. Ornithol. Soc., Berkshire Mus., Turbeville Anne Worsham Richardson Day Exhibit, Gibbes Art Gallery, Columbia Museum Art, Kennedy Galleries, Harbour Town Mus., Hilton Head, S.C., Spartanburg Art Gallery, Sumter Art Gallery, Cal. Mus. Sci. and Industry, 1970, 72, others; exhibited in group shows at Charleston Artist Guild, Telfair Acad., S.C. Artist Guild, Carolina Art State Show, Bob Jones U., Medway Art Festival, others; represented in permanent collections at Albert Leeberg collection, Gibbes Art Gallery, Charleston Mus.; co-owner Birds I View Gallery; bird paintings pub. by Nat. Wildlife Fedn., 1967, 68, 70, 72, 73, 74. Recipient 1st prize Summerville Artist Guild, 1959; 1st prize Coastal Carolina Art Exhibit, Charleston, S.C., 1967; Commendation award Cal. Mus. Sci. and Industry, 1972; Hughes fellow, 1970. Bd. dirs. YWCA, 1965—. Mem. Carolina Art Assn., Charleston Artist Guild (treas. 1953-57, pres. 1968-71, dir. 1962—), Guild S.C. Artists (sec. 1963-64), Am. Ornithol. Union, Wilson Ornithol. Soc., Charleston Natural History Soc. (dir. 1962, 65-66). Nat. Audubon Soc. Clubs: Carolina Bird; Carolina Wren with Yellow Jessamine, 1969. Published Birds from Coastal Gardens, 1967; 16 ltd. edts. Bird Prints. Home: 2391 Furman Dr Drayton on Ashley Charleston SC 29407 Office: Birds I View Gallery 119-A Church St Charleston SC

RICHARDSON, CARL NEWTON, textile co. exec.; b. Honey Grove, Tex., Sept. 18, 1908; s. John Tal and Katie Jo (Newton) R.; student Ga. Inst. Tech., 1926-27; m. Winifred Darsey, Apr. 29, 1932; 1 son, Carl Newton. Vice pres. Rushton Cotton Mills, Griffin, Ga., 1928—. Chmn. Griffin Spalding County Hosp. Authority, 1963—. Trustee Ga. Hosp. Assn. Mem. Ga. Textile Mfrs. Assn. (dir. 1968-72), Ga. Bus. and Industry Assn. (v.p. 1960-68). Baptist. Elk. Home: 1099 Pine Valley Rd Griffin GA 30223 Office: PO Box 97 Griffin GA 30223

RICHARDSON, CARLTON DUQUESNE, financial exec.; b. West Brookfield, Mass., Oct. 5, 1935; s. Milton C. and Charlotte R. (Brooks) R.; B.B.A., U. Mass., 1957; m. Lois Luke, Dec. 23, 1970; children—Christine Dorothy, Carla Duquesne; children by previous marriage—Linda Ann, Craig David. Sr. auditor Arthur Anderson & Co., C.P.A.'s, N.Y.C., 1957-64; audit mgr. Manual Cole & Co., C.P.A.'s, Hartford, Conn., 1964-66; audit supr. C.E., Inc., Windsor, Conn., 1966-67, controller, Chattanooga, 1967-73; v.p. finance C.E. Bldg. Products, Miami, Fla., 1973—; dir. Milton C. Richardson, Inc. Served with Ordnance Corps, AUS, 1961-63. C.P.A., N.J., Tenn. Mem. Am. Inst. C.P.A.'s, N.J., Conn. socs. C.P.A.'s, Financial Execs. Inst. (sec.-treas. 1972-73). Home: 5421 McKinley St Hollywood FL 33021 Office: 1515 NW 167th St Miami FL 33169

RICHARDSON, CLAY VANCE, hosiery mfg. exec.; b. nr. Star, N.C., Dec. 27, 1899; s. John W. and Mary Lou (Parks) R.; student pub. schs.; m. Elsie Presnell Richardson, May 22, 1922 (dec. 1943); children—Emma Louise (Mrs. Jack M. Hartley), Ann Marie (Mrs. C. C. Winstead, Jr.), Joseph E.; m. 3d, Lola Monroe, Dec. 27, 1944; children—Clay Vance, John Monroe. Retail furniture bus., 1924-31; pres. Clayson Knitting Co., Inc., 1931-65, Star Indsl. Corp.; owner, v.p. V. & M. Furniture Mfg. Corp., 1965—. Vice pres. Montgomery Meml. Hosp., Troy, N.C., 1950—, chmn. bd., 1950-65. Mayor Town of Star, N.C., 1963-65. Mem. co-founders club Sch. Medicine, U. N.C., Chapel Hill; mem. adv. bd. N.C. Zool. Soc. Methodist. Rotarian. Address: PO Box 39 Star NC 27356

RICHARDSON, DAVID DURHAM, physician; b. Louisville, Miss., Sept. 6, 1921; s. Elbert Leach and Edna Earl (Triplett) R.; B.S., Miss. State U., 1943; postgrad. Miss. Coll., 1949; M.D., Tulane U., 1953; m. Alma Elizabeth Carl, Aug. 24, 1947; children—David Durham, Beth, Carl Donovan, Richard Laird. Intern, McLeod Infirmary, Florence, S.C., 1953-54; gen. practice medicine, Louisville, Miss., 1954—; chief staff Winston County Community Hosp., Louisville, Miss. Pres., Winston Acad., Louisville, Miss., 1967-70, Lewis Winston Found., 1967-70. Trustee Winston County Community Hosp. and Med. Center; chmn. bd. trustees Winston County Community Hosp. and Nursing Home, 1972—. Served to lt. USNR, 1943-46. Mem. Am. Acad. Gen. Practice, Am. Assn. Physicians and Surgeons, A.M.A., Miss., E. Miss. med. assns., Sigma Chi, Alpha Kappa Kappa. Baptist. Mason. Home: 106 Richardson Rd Louisville MS 39339 Office: 307 W Main St Louisville MS 39339

RICHARDSON, DONALD VALENTINE III, lawyer; b. Florence, S.C., Jan. 14, 1936; s. Donald Valentine and Margaret Roundtree (Deans) R.; B.S. in Bus. Adminstrn., U. S.C., 1958, LL.B., 1960; m. Elizabeth Anne Nelson, June 21, 1958; children—Elizabeth Anne, Katharine Deans, Donald Valentine. Admitted to S.C. bar, 1960; mem. firm Whaley, McCutchen, Blanton & Richardson, 1960-72, Richardson & Plowden, 1973—. State chmn. DRI. Mem. Internat. Assn. Ins. Counsel, S.C., Richland County bars, Am. Bar Assn., S.C. Def. Attys. Assn., Jr. C. of C. (dir.). Clubs: Litchfield Country, Forest Lake Country, Palmetto, Richland Sertoma. Home: 4774 Heath Hill Rd Columbia SC 29206 Office: 1340 Pickens St Columbia SC 29201

RICHARDSON, EARL LEROY, chemist, govt. ofcl.; b. Lebanon, Mo., Mar. 21, 1917; s. Jesse Gaford and Hassie (Lawson) R.; B.S. cum laude, Drury Coll., 1938, M.S., Okla. A. and M. Coll., 1939; Ph.D., Rutgers U., 1948; student N.Y. U., 1939-40; m. Virginia Van Middlesworth, Mar. 21, 1942; 1 son, Kenneth Earl. Control chemist Procter & Gamble Co., Kansas City, Kan., 1939; research chemist Am. Cyanamid Co., Bound Brook, N.J., 1940-42; sr. project chemist Colgate-Palmolive Co., Jersey City, 1942-47, group leader, 1947-50; research dir. Whitehall Labs., Elkhart, Ind., 1951-58, Hammonton, N.J. 1958-66; head technical services for cosmetic chems. Union Carbide Corp., Tarrytown, N.Y., 1967-71; project mgr. div. cosmetics tech. Food and Drug Adminstrn., Washington, 1972—. Mem. Am. Chem. Soc., Am. Pharm. Soc., Soc. Cosmetic Chemists, Assn. Ofcl. Analytical Chemists, A.A.A.S., Acad. Pharm. Scis., Sigma Xi, Phi Lambda Upsilon, Conglist. Author articles profl. jours. Patentee in field. Home: 2309 Cheshire Lane Alexandria VA 22307 Office: 200 C St SW Washington DC 20204

RICHARDSON, EDWIN LELAND, lawyer; b. Magnolia, Ark., Mar. 9, 1904; s. Edwin Sanders and Zenobia (Longino) R.; student George Washington U., 1923-26; J.D., Georgetown U., 1930; m. Olive Maurine Adams, Dec. 31, 1932, 1 dau., Olive Maurine (Mrs. Robert L. Modjeski). Admitted to D.C. bar, 1929, La. bar, 1931; sec. Congressman John N. Sandlin, 1923-31; mem. firm Drew & Richardson, Minden, La., 1931-34; asst. atty gen. La., gen. counsel Dept. Revenue, Baton Rouge, 1934-41; atty. Gov. La., atty. dir. nat. gas conservation, 1943-48; mem. Dale, Richardson & Dale, Baton Rouge and Vidalia, La., 1941-67, Dale, Owen, Richardson, Taylor & Matthews, Baton Rouge, 1968—. Mem. La. Revenue Code Commn., 1946-48; 1st vice chmn. Interstate Oil Compact Commn., 1946-48, mem. legal com., 1947-48, La. rep., 1945-48. Mem. Am., La. (bd. govs. 1938-40, mem. com. draft La. formulary 1952-57) bar assns., Internat. Assn. Ins. Counsel, Assn. Ins. Attys., Internat. Bar Assn., Am. Coll. Trial Lawyers, Phi Delta Phi, Kappa Sigma. Democrat. Methodist. Mason (32 deg., Shriner), Rotarian. Clubs: City (pres. 1970), Baton Rouge Country, Baton Rouge Assembly, Camelot (Baton Rouge); Boston, Plimsoll (New Orleans); Nat. Press (Washington). Author: History of Conservation of Oil and Gas in Louisiana, 1934-48, 1949. Home: 7815 Highland Rd Baton Rouge LA 70808 Office: Reymond Bldg Baton Rouge LA 70801

RICHARDSON, FRANCIS JOSEPH, III, banker; b. New Orleans, Mar. 22, 1943; s. Francis Joseph, Jr. and Stella (Schulze) R.; B.B.A., Tulane U., 1965, postgrad. Law Sch., 1969—; M.B.A., Loyola U., New Orleans, 1970; student Am. Inst. Banking, 1973; m. Carolyn Mary Bienvenu, Apr. 17, 1971. Jr. mech. engr. Boeing Aerospace-Saturn Launch Systems br.-Michoud, New Orleans, 1964-66; computer sci. asst. Computer Datacenter, IBM Corp., New Orleans, 1966-71; investment service officer First Nat. Bank of Commerce, New Orleans, 1971—. Mem. Republican State Central Com. for 1st Rep. Dist., 1969-70; Orleans Parish rep. Mass. Transit Ad Hoc Subcom. Regional Planning Forum 1970. Bd. dirs. Museums Com.-Jeuness D'Orleans and La. Council, Big Bros. of New Orleans. Recipient James C. Kraus award Young Mens Bus. Club, 1968. Mem. Bank Adminstrn. Inst., Am. Inst. Banking, Fgn. Relations Assn., Am. Econ. Assn., Operations Research Soc., Navy League U.S., New Orleans Jr. C. of C. (past dir.), Tulane Assn. Bus. Alumni, New Orleans Geneal. Research Soc., Thackeray Soc. New Orleans (founding dir.), Shakespeare Soc., La. Geneal. and Hist. Soc., La. Hist. Soc., Financial Analysts New Orleans, S.A.R. (treas. La. Soc. 1972-73), Alpha Tau Omega, Phi Delta Phi (treas. Tulane 1970). Clubs: Internat. House, Round Table (2d v.p.), Pendennis (New Orleans). Home: 7832 Burthe St New Orleans LA 70118 Office: 210 Baronne St New Orleans LA 70112

RICHARDSON, HAROLD EDWARD, educator; b. Woodstock, Ky., July 13, 1929; s. Samuel A. and Mary Marcella (Osborne) R.; student U. Ky. Coll. Law, 1949-51; A.B., Eastern Ky. U., 1952, M.A. in Edn., 1954; A.M. in English, U. So. Cal., 1961, Ph.D. in English, 1963; m. Antonia Calvert, Mar. 6, 1953; children—Shawn Edward, Jill Calvert. Instr., Fullerton (Cal.) Jr. Coll., 1956-63; asst. prof. Cal. State U. at Fullerton, 1963; asso. prof. Eastern Ky. U., Richmond, 1963-65, prof. English, 1965-68, chmn. dept., 1965-67; vis. prof. U. So. Cal., summer 1968; prof. English U. Louisville, 1968—; vis. prof. Cal. State U. at Los Angeles, summers 1967, 71. Editorial adviser Prentice Hall; writing cons. Mem. Modern Lang. Assn., Nat. Council Tchrs. English, South Atlantic Modern Lang. Assn., Am. Studies Assn., Ky. Civil War Round Table, Phi Delta Phi. Club: Torch (founding pres. Richmond, Ky. 1965). Author: William Faulkner: The Journey to Self-Discovery, 1969; How to Think and Write, 1971; (with Frederick B. Shroyer) Muse of Fire: Approaches to Poetry, 1971; Cassius Marcellus Clay: Firebrand of Freedom, 1975. Contbr. articles to profl. jours. U.S. and abroad. Home: 1442 Cherokee Rd Louisville KY 40204 Office: Dept of English University of Louisville Louisville KY 40208

RICHARDSON, HAZEL ADAMS, librarian; b. Chireno, Tex., Oct. 28, 1912; d. George Ernest and Mary (Barton) Adams; B.A., U. Tex., 1933, M.A., 1936; B.S. in L.S., La. State U., 1936; m. David Bonner Richardson, June 10, 1944 (div. May 1963); children—George Adams, William Darby. Childrens librarian Tyrrell Pub. Library, Beaumont, Tex., 1936-38, Detroit Pub. Libraries, 1938-42, 44-45, asst. schs. dept., 1958-61; readers adviser Tex. A. and M. U., College Station, 1942-44; asst. adult circulation dept. Redwood City (Cal.) Pub. Library, 1946-48, childrens librarian, 1948-49; head librarian Carnegie Pub. Library, Bryan, Tex., 1961—. Columnist, Bryan Daily Eagle, 1961—. Mem. Tex. Bd. Library Examiners, Brazos County Hist. Survey Com. Mem. Am. Assn. U. Women, Bus. and Profl. Womens Club, D.A.R., Daus. Republic of Tex., Am., Tex. State library assns., Nat. League Am. Pen Women (br. pres. 1966-68), Poetry Soc., U.D.C., Delta Kappa Gamma. Democrat. Episcopalian. Clubs: Womans Civic League (pres. 1963), Womans, Briar Crest Country. Home: 800 S Ennis Bryan TX 77801 Office: Bryan Public Library 201 E 26th St Bryan TX 77801

RICHARDSON, HERSCHEL ELROY, physician; b. Georgetown, Tex., July 3, 1914; s. Herschel Elroy and Mary Anderson (Mann) R.; B.A., Southwestern U. of Tex., 1935; M.D., Vanderbilt Med. Sch., 1939; postgrad. Naval Sch. Aviation Medicine, 1943, Cornell U. Sch. Medicine, 1946-47, U. Pa. Sch. Medicine, 1954-55; m. Suzanne Marie Ahern, Sept. 4, 1943; children—Dennise Marie (Mrs. Richard H. Browne), Mary Jean (Mrs. David A. Glasgow). Commd. lt. (j.g.) USN, 1939, advanced through grades to capt., 1956, ret., 1961; intern U.S. Naval Hosp., San Diego, 1939-40, resident, 1953-54; resident Bellevue Hosp., N.Y.C., 1947; chief medicine U.S. Naval Hosp., Corpus Christi, Tex., 1947-50, U.S. Naval Hosp., Quantico, Va., 1950-51, U.S. Naval Hosp., Yokosuka, Japan, 1951-53, U.S. Naval Hosp., Phila., 1960-61; asst. chief medicine U.S. Naval Hosp. Nat. Naval Med. Center, Bethesda, Md., 1956-60; asso. med. dir. Prudential Ins. Co. Am., Houston, 1962—. Clin. instr. medicine George Washington U. Sch. Medicine, 1957-60; naval guest lecturer Hahnemann Med. Coll., Phila., 1960-61; instr. Maumee Valley Hosp., Toledo, 1961-62, Toledo Hosp., 1961-62. Diplomate Am. Bd. Internal Medicine. Mem. Coll. Physicians Phila., A.C.P., Am., So., Tex. med. assns. Cons. editor Medical Annals of D.C., Washington, 1958-60. Home: 205 Mayerling St Houston TX 77024 Office: 1100 E Holcombe St Houston TX 77025

RICHARDSON, JAMES MILTON, clergyman; b. Sylvester, Ga., Jan. 8, 1913; s. James Milton and Pallie (Stewart) R.; A.B., U. Ga., 1934; B.D., Emory U., 1936, M.A., 1942; postgrad. Va. Theol. Sem., 1938, D.D., 1965; LL.D., John Marshall Law Sch., 1948; D.D., Episcopal Theol. Sem. Ky., 1960, U. South, 1961; m. Eugenia Preston Brooks, June 14, 1940; children—James Milton, Eugenia (Mrs. James R. Nash), Joan Stewart (Mrs. James R. Doty), Preston Brooks. Ordained to ministry Episcopal Ch., 1938; rector St. Timothy's Ch., Atlanta, 1938-40; asst. rector St. Luke's Ch., Atlanta, 1940-43, rector, 1943-52; dean Christ Ch. Cathedral, Houston, 1952-65; bishop Episcopal Diocese Tex., Houston, 1965—. Chmn. bd. trustees St. Stephen's Episcopal Sch., 1965—, Episcopal Theol. Sem. of S.W., 1967—; pres. St. Luke's Episcopal Hosp.; trustee Ch. Pension Fund, Episcopal Radio-TV Found., U. South, Baylor Coll. Medicine. Mem. Blue Key, Phi Beta Kappa, Phi Kappa Phi, Omicron Delta Kappa, Alpha Tau Omega (worthy grand chaplain 1945-52, 56—, nat. pres. 1952-56). Home: 14 Shadowlawn Circle Houston TX 77005 Office: 520 San Jacinto St Houston TX 77002

RICHARDSON, JOHNNY HASKELL, city ofcl.; b. Brownwood, Tex., Nov. 27, 1924; s. Johnny Willis and Annie Laurial (Taylor) R.; B.B.A., Tex. A. and M. U., 1952; m. Sue Wheat, Nov. 24, 1948; children—Denise, Johnny Dean, Micheal, Joy. Oil scout Sinclair Oil & Gas Co., Roswell, N.M. and Midland, Tex., 1952-59; ind. oil man, Midland, 1959-60; oil scout, area mgr. Williams & Lee Oil Co., San Angelo, Tex., 1960-64; dir. finance City of San Angelo, Tex., 1964—. Unit chmn. United Fund, 1968-69; sec.-treas. San Angelo Firemen's Relief and Retirement Fund, 1964—. Served with USAAF, 1943-47. Mem. Municipal Finance Officers Assn. Tex. (pres. 1971-72), Tex. Municipal League (dir.). Baptist (pres. council brotherhoods 1971-72). Club: Civitan (pres. 1958-59 Roswell, N.M.). Home: 2853 A and M San Angelo TX 76901 Office: Box 1751 City Hall San Angelo TX 76901

RICHARDSON, JOSEPH THOMAS, educator; b. Mount Pleasant, Tenn., Oct. 20, 1926; s. Mark Schultz and Lillian (Brown) R.; D.D.S., Middle Tenn. State U., 1947-48; D.D.S., U. Tenn. Coll. Dentistry, 1948-51; M.A. in Teaching, The Citadel, 1972; m. 1950; children—Steve, David; m. 2d, Agnes Bailey Richardson, Jan. 20, 1971; children—Earle, Olivia. Gen. practice dentistry, Columbia,

Tenn., 1954-70; asso. prof. crown and bridge Coll. Dental Medicine, Charleston, S.C., 1970—; mem. dental staff Maury County (Tenn.) Hosp., 1954-70. Resident dentist Tenn. Orphans Home, Spring Hill, Tenn., 1958-70. Mem. Maury County Bd. Health, 1966-70, chmn., 1968-70. Served with U.S. Mcht. Marines, 1945-46; served with USNR, 1952-54. Mem. 6th Dist. Dental Soc. (pres. 1962-63; alternate del. 1970), Am. Legion, Psi Omega. Contbr. articles to profl. jours. Home: 444 Wade Hampton Dr Charleston SC 29412 Office: 80 Barre St Charleston SC 29401

RICHARDSON, KENNETH MILLER, utility co. exec.; b. Manila, Ark., Apr. 5, 1927; s. Albert Lee and Beersheba Rebecca (Miller) R.; grad. in elec. engring. Internat. Corr. Schs., 1963; m. Myra Ann Neely, July 24, 1945; 1 dau., Karen Ann. Engr.'s helper Ark.-Mo. Power Co., Blytheville, Ark., 1948-51, sr. engring. clk., 1951-57, dist. constrn. supt., 1957-64, mgr. Monette (Ark.) area, 1964—; dir. Monette Indsl. Devel. Corp., sec.-treas. 1967—; dir. Ride-A-Rose Engring., Inc., Monette. Sec.-treas. N.E. Ark. Safety Council, 1959, chmn., 1960; active Eastern Ark. council Boy Scouts Am., 1948—, dist. commr., 1963-64, mem. exec. bd., 1960-66, recipient Silver Beaver award, 1960. Served with USNR, 1945-46. Mem. I.E.E.E. Democrat. Baptist (chmn. deacons 1972). Mason, Lion. Home: 301 Ball St Monette AR 72447 Office: 112 Drew St Monette AR 72447

RICHARDSON, KENNETH WAYNE, physician; b. Eustis, Fla., Sept. 10, 1933; s. Ivan Elmer and Annie (Goodson) R.; student Emory U., 1951-54; M.D., U. Miami (Fla.), 1958; m. Betty Jo Minshew, Dec. 26, 1953 (div. Sept. 1972); children—Deborah, Kenneth, Thomas, Mark; m. 2d, Betty Jean Brown Ranew, Oct. 5, 1972. Intern The Med. Center, Columbus, Ga., 1958-59; practice gen. medicine, Apalachicola, Fla., 1959-60, as partner Thompson Clinic, Chattahoochee, Fla., 1960—. Mem. Chattahoochee City Council, 1962-72. Mem. A.M.A., Fla., Pan Handle med. assns. Methodist. Club: Seminole Bass (Chattahoochee). Home: 36 Center St Chattahoochee FL 32324 Office: PO Box 67 Chattahoochee FL 32324

RICHARDSON, MARY ELIZABETH (MRS. HOWARD RICHARDSON), physician; b. Los Angeles, June 3, 1927; d. Edward G. and Eva (Kimbell) Dolch; B.A., U. Cal. at Los Angeles, 1949, M.S., 1952; M.D., Womans Med. Coll. Pa., 1956; m. Howard Lockhart Richardson, 1955. Rotating intern Providence Hosp., Seattle, 1956-57; resident in pathology U. Wash. and Affiliated Hosps., Seattle, 1957-61; spl. resident pathology Washington U. Sch. Medicine, St. Louis, 1961-62, trainee exptl. pathology, 1961-64; asst. pathologist Barnes and Affiliated Hosps., St. Louis, 1962-64; asst. prof. pathology U. Ark. Med. Center, Little Rock, 1964-67; cons. pathologist Maryvale Med. Center, Phoenix, 1967-68; research pathologist, chief electron microscopy Bur. Sci. FDA, Washington, 1968-70; research pathologist, chief electron microscopy Office of Pesticides, Environmental Protection Agy., Washington, 1970—. Diplomate Am. Bd. Pathology. Fellow Am. Soc. Clin. Pathologists; mem. Soc. Pharmacological and Environmental Pathologists, N.Y. Acad. Scis., Internat. Acad. Pathologists, Electron Microscopy Soc. Am., La. Soc. Electron Microscopists, Am. Soc. Nephrology, A.M.A. Sigma Xi. Address: 2000 S Eads St Arlington VA 22202 Office: Registry of Tissue Reaction to Drugs Armed Forces Inst Pathology Washington DC 20306

RICHARDSON, RICHARD JUDSON, educator; b. Poplar Bluff, Mo., Feb. 16, 1935; s. Jewell Judson and Naomi Fern (Watson) R.; B.S., Harding Coll., 1957; certificate (Rotary Internat. fellow) U. Dublin (Ireland), 1958; M.A. (Edgar Stern fellow), Tulane U., 1961, Ph.D., 1967; m. Sammie Sue Cullum, Dec. 29, 1961; children—Jon Mark, Anna Cecile, Ellen Elizabeth. Instr., Tulane U., New Orleans, 1962-64; asst. prof. Western Mich. U., Kalamazoo, 1964-67, asso. prof., 1968-69; vis. asso. prof. U. Hawaii, Honolulu, 1967-68; asso. prof. U. N.C., Chapel Hill, 1969-72, prof. polit. sci., asso. chmn. dept., 1973—; adj. prof. policy scis. Duke, Durham, N.C., 1971—. Cons. to Hawaii Senate, 1968-69, N.C. Gov.'s Com. on Law and Order, 1969-71, Adminstrv. Office of Cts., 1972-73, N.C. finance chmn. Oak Hills Home for Children, 1969; cub scout pack master Occoneechee council Boy Scouts Am., 1972-73; del. Inter-Ch. Council, Chapel Hill, 1973. Del. county conv. Democratic party, 1972. Recipient Tanner award for distinguished teaching U. N.C., 1972. Mem. Am. (Edward S. Corwin award 1967), So. polit. sci. assns. Author: (with Kenneth N. Vines) The Politics of Federal Courts, 1971; (with Darlene Walker) Perspectives on the Criminal Justice System, 1972. Home: 1701 Fountainridge Rd Chapel Hill NC 27514 Office: Dept of Political Science University of North Carolina Chapel Hill NC 27514

RICHARDSON, ROBERT WILLIAMS, JR., architect; b. Montgomery, Ala., Jan. 19, 1917; s. Robert Williams and Lilibel (Williams) R.; student Art Inst. of South, Memphis, 1936-39, N.C. State U., 1950-53; B.Arch., U. Fla., 1955; m. Daisy Adelaide Watkins, Aug. 18, 1940; children—Catherine Gail (Mrs. Clark G. Crozer), Vicki Joan (Mrs. Peter A. Lyon), Robert Williams III. Pvt. practice architecture, Palm Beach, Fla., 1956—; owner Bradley House Hotel, Palm Beach, 1967—; chmn. bd. Richardson Devel. Corp., Palm Beach, 1973—, Nu-Lan Improvement Corp., Palm Beach, 1972—; dir. Lake Dogwood Assos., Inc., Columbia, S.C. Served with Air Transp. Command, World War II. Mem. A.I.A., Fla. Hotel and Motel Assn., Fla. Assn. Architects, Fla. Home Builders Assn., Phi Kappa Phi. Club: Sail Fish (Palm Beach). Home: 111 Bradley Pl Palm Beach FL 33480 Office: 2 Bradley House Arcade Palm Beach FL 33480

RICHARDSON, RUPERT NORVAL, educator; b. nr. Caddo, Tex., Apr. 28, 1891; s. Willie Baker and Nannie (Coon) R.; A.B., Hardin-Simmons U., Abilene, Tex., 1912; Ph.B., U. Chgo., 1914; A.M., U. Tex., 1922, Ph.D., 1928; m. Pauline Mayes, Dec. 28, 1915; 1 son, Rupert Norval. Prin. high sch., Cisco, Tex., 1914-16, Sweetwater, 1916-17; prof. history Hardin-Simmons U., 1917—, dean students, 1926-28, v.p., 1928-38, exec. v.p., 1938-40, acting pres., 1943-45, pres., 1945-53, pres. emeritus, prof., 1953-67, Piper prof., 1963—, Distinguished prof., 1967—; asso. prof., prof. hist. U. Tex. 8 summers, also 1940-41. Mem. So. Bapt. Edn. Commn., 1952-55; mem. Tex. Hist. Survey Com., 1953-67, pres., 1961-63. Served 2d lt. U.S. Army, 1918. Recipient Cultural Achievement in Lit. award West Tex. C. of C., 1967; Ruth Lester award Tex. Hist. Commn., 1972. Fellow Tex. State Hist. Assn. (pres. 1969-70); mem. Am., Miss. Valley hist. assns., Southwestern Social Sci. Assn. (adv. editor 1929-31, pres. 1936-37), Tex. Philos. Soc. (pres. 1962-63). Baptist. Mason. Lion (past pres., dist. gov.). Author: The Comanche Barrier to the South Plains Settlement, 1933; (with C. C. Rister) The Greater Southwest, 1934; Texas: the Lone Star State, 1943; Adventuring with a Purpose, 1952; The Frontier of Northwest Texas, 1963; Colonel Edward M. House: The Texas Years, 1964; Famous Are The Halls: Hardwin-Simmons University as I Have Seen It, 1964; Caddo, Texas: The Biography of a Community, 1966; Along Texas Old Forts Trail, Abilene, 1972. Editor: West Tex. Hist. Assn. Yearbook, 1929—. Contbr. to hist., ednl. publs. Home: 2220 Simmons Av Abilene TX 79601

RICHARDSON, THOMAS PURDIE, elec. engr.; b. Anson County, N.C.; s. Thomas P. and Sally (Wall) R.; B.S., N.C. State U.; m. Mildred Land, July 25, 1930; 1 dau., Mildred Purdie (Mrs. Donald Walker Shuman, Jr.). Engr., Carolina Power & Light Co., Raleigh, N.C., 1928-31; distbn. supt. Tenn. Power Co., Murfreesboro, 1931-34; dist. mgr. Fed. Works Program, Elizabeth City and Charlotte, N.C., 1934-40; mgr. Colonial Mica Corp., Asheville, N.C., 1943-46; owner mgr. Richardson Engring. Service, Asheville, N.C., 1946-60; prvt. cons. engr., Asheville, 1960—. Mem. Roanoke Colony Meml. Assn. (hon.), Nat. Soc. Profl. Engrs., N.C. Profl. Engrs., N.C. Assn. Professions. Address: 320 Montford Av Asheville NC 28801

RICHBURG, WILLIAM E., justice of the peace; b. Talico, Tex., Dec. 29, 1903; s. William Hugh and Winnie Elizabeth (Allen) R.; ed. pub. schs. Tex.; m. Edna Earle Turnipseed, Oct. 6, 1928; children—Mary (Mrs. Cliff Bourland), William Jackson. Dep. clerk Dist. Clerk's Office, Dallas County, Tex., 4 years; justice of the peace Precinct 7, Dallas, 28 years. Recipient citations Law Found., Gov. Tex.; named Outstanding Justice of the Peace in Tex., 1955. Mem. Oak Cliff C. of C. Mason (Shriner), Lion; mem. Blue Lodge. Home: 2511 Wedglea Dallas TX 75211 Office: 410 South Beckley Dallas TX 75203

RICHESON, JAMES PETE, mech. engr.; b. Russellville, Ala., Sept. 29, 1930; s. James G. and Eathel (Hovater) R.; B.S. in Mech. Engring., Auburn U., 1953; B.S. in Bus. Adminstrn., Athens Coll., 1962; m. Julia Ann Lea, July 2, 1961; children—James Jeffrey, Robin Lee, Amy Lynn. Mech. draftsman James B. Clow, Birmingham, Ala., 1951-52; mech. engr. TVA, Chattanooga, 1953-54; supr. engring. Monsanto Co., Decatur, Ala., 1956-70; pres., gen. mgr. Sandek Engring. Inc., Guntersville, Ala., 1970—. Mem. City Council, Trinity, Ala., 1964—; scoutmaster Cub Scouts of Boy Scouts Am., 1972-74. Served with AUS, 1954-56. Registered profl. engr., Ala. Mem. Guntersville C. of C. (chmn. indsl. devel. com. 1974), Am. Legion. Democrat. Baptist. Mason (Shriner). Patentee in field. Home: Route 2 Guntersville AL 35976 Office: PO Box 596 Guntersville AL 35976

RICHTER, CARL ARPAD, food standards and research exec.; b. Budapest, Hungary, Dec. 12, 1917; s. John and Irene (Mathes) R.; came to U.S., 1936, naturalized, 1942; student Trade Sch. for Cooks, Bucharest, Romania, 1931-34, U. Bucharest, 1935-36; m. Frances Regina Brady, Feb. 16, 1943. Chef Casino at Hecules Bad, 1934-35; pvt. chef to wife of Premier of Romania, 1935-36; with Racquet Club, Phila., also Strawbridge & Clothier and Slater System, Phila., 1936-41; with Slater System, Balt., 1946-49; v.p. food standards and research Servomation, Inc., Balt., 1950-72; with food service div. Green Giant Co., Miami, Fla., 1973—; cons. chef; dir. spl. food seminars for chefs and mgrs.; judge culinary art shows; guest speaker. Served with AUS, 1941-45. Recipient silver and gold medal Profl. Inst. Chefs of Am., 1966, gold medal Am. Acad. Chefs. Mem. Epicurean Club Greater Miami, Balt. Culinary Art Assn. (pres. 1964-66), Profl. Inst. Chefs (nat. v.p. 1964-65). Home: 13800 NE 12th Av Miami FL 33161 Office: 7337 NW 37th Av Miami FL 33147

RICHTER, SHERRY (MRS. BERNARD RICHTER), TV broadcaster; b. Hamlet, N.C., Mar. 28; d. Joe and Gladys (Blacker) Levine; student U. N.C., 1946-47, Cath. U., 1949; m. Bernard Richter, Dec. 24, 1950; children—Lloyd, Benjamin. With Lost Colony, 1946; fashion commentator DuMont TV, Washington, 1948-49; in charge children's program WUQW, Charlotte, N.C., 1949—, Sunday Bible program, 1949; program on WSOC-TV, 1957, WB-TV; free-lance programming, Chanels 3 and 9, 1959; program WBTV, 1959—; fashion dir. Autom Fashion Show. Active Mint Mus. of Art, Charlotte Little Theatre, Children's Theatre, Mecklenburg County Girl Scouts. Mem. Am. Women in TV and Radio. Club: Junior Woman's (Charlotte, N.C.). Home: 1030 Huntington Park Charlotte NC 28207 Office: 1 Jefferson Pl Charlotte NC 28207

RICKARD, JOSEPH CONWAY, psychologist, educator; b. Weatherford, Tex., July 16, 1926; s. Joe Smith and Mattie Mae (Wright) R.; A.A., San Angelo Coll., 1948; Ph.D., U. Chgo., 1955; m. Dorothy June Wilson, May 29, 1948; children—Miles, Janis, Robert, Martha, Sarah. Clin. psychologist VA Center, Temple, Tex., 1955-60, chief psychology service, 1960—; individual practice clin. psychology, 1965—. Instr., U. Tex., 1956-59, 60-62, 66-67, Temple Jr. Coll., 1965-66; asso. prof. Mary Hardin-Baylor Coll., 1966—; cons. Bell County Rehab. Center, 1956-61, Temple Sch. System, 1965—, Killeen (Tex.) Sch. System, 1971—. Cubmaster, Heart O'Tex. council Boy Scouts Am., 1959-62, scoutmaster, 1962-65. Bd. dirs. Bell County Soc. for Crippled Children, Bell County Alcoholism Commn. Served with USAAF, 1945-46. Fellow Soc. for Projective Techniques; mem. Am., Southwestern, Tex. (parliamentarian 1973), Central Tex. (pres. 1972) psychol. assns., Bell County Research Soc., Sigma Xi. Home: 3302 Oaklawn Dr Temple TX 76501 Office: VA Center Temple TX 76501

RICKELTON, DAVID, air conditioning co. exec.; b. Glasgow, Scotland, Nov. 8, 1916; s. John and Catherine (Simpson) R.; student Bklyn. Poly. Inst., 1940, Pratt Inst., 1942; m. Virginia Thompson, Nov. 29, 1942 (dec.); children—David Kendall, John Thompson; m. 2d, Geneva Y. Brown, June 19, 1968. Came to U.S., 1923, naturalized, 1929. With Buensod-Stacey Corp. (now Aeronca Inc. Environmental Control Group), Charlotte, N.C., 1940—, successively draftsman, engr., cons., 1940-65, v.p., 1965—. Served from pvt. to lt. AUS, 1942, served to capt., 1944-46. Registered profl. engr., N.C. Mem. Am. Soc. Heating, Refrigeration and Air Conditioning Engrs. (pres.-elect, dir.), Nat. Soc. Profl. Engrs. Mem. Ch. of Christ (elder). Home: 3413 Highview Rd Charlotte NC 28210 Office: PO Box 688 Pineville NC 28134

RICKENBAKER, DUDLEY GENE, lawyer; b. St. Matthews, S.C., Feb. 6, 1941; s. Charlie Dudley and Margaret (Crider) R.; B.S. in Bus. Adminstrn., Univ. S.C., 1963, LL.D., U. S.C. Sch. Law., 1966; m. Mary Kaye Thomas, June 15, 1963; children—Vonda Kaye, Christie Kaye. Admitted to S.C. bar, 1966; asst. U.S. atty. Dist. S.C., Columbia, 1970-71; mem. firm Rogers, Riggs & Rickenbacker, Sumter, S.C., 1971—; Mem. Sumter Com. for Progress; mem. com. to Honor Viet Nam War Vets. State exec. committeeman S.C. Republican Party, 1973—. Served as judge advocate USAF, 1966-70. Mem. Am., S.C., Sumter County bar assns. Mason, Elk. Home: 514 Mattison Av Sumter SC 29150 Office: 104 N Main St Sumter SC 29150

RICKEY, HORACE BUSHNELL, JR., contractor; b. New Orleans, July 2, 1924; s. Horace Bushnell and Marjorie (Bouvier) R.; student Tulane U., 1940-42, 45; B.S. in Civil Engring., U. Wyo., 1947, B.S. in Archtl. Engring., 1948; postgrad. U. Cal. at Los Angeles, 1958; m. Jewel Katherine Seybold, Aug. 15, 1947; children—Sharon, Marjorie, Priscilla Gail. Vice pres., dir. Horace B. Rickey Inc., Lafayette, La., 1948-50, sec.-treas., 1950-67, pres., chmn. bd. dirs., 1967—; pres. S.W. Materials Inc., Lafayette, 1950—, S.W. Homes Real Estate & Ins., Lafayette, 1961-69; v.p., dir. Union Fed. Savs. & Loan Assn., Lafayette, 1958—; sec.-treas. Motor Lodges Lafayette, 1966—; treas. Twp. Developers; dir. Computers for Better Mgmt. Mem. nat. ins. com. Operators Council Howard Johnson, 1968-71. Chief, Lafayette St. Planning Commn., 1964-66; chmn. Lafayette United Gift Fund campaign, 1969-70; mem. adv. bd. Salvation Army, Lafayette, 1966-69; commr. Lafayette Midget Football League, 1963—. Chmn. Republican Parish Municipal Exec. Com., 1954-68, sec. La. Central Com., 1956-61, del. nat. conv., 1956. Bd. dirs. Indsl. Found., Lafayette, U. Southwestern La.; bd. dirs. Lafayette council Girl Scouts U.S.A., 1962-70, v.p. to pres., 1967-70. Served with AUS, 1943-46; ETO. Decorated Combat Inf. Badge. Mem. Lafayette C. of C. (v.p., dir. 1958-61, 69-71), Asso. Gen. Contractors, Am. Soc. C.E., Am. Concrete Inst., Prestressed Concrete Inst. Presbyn. (deacon, elder, commr. gen. assembly). Kiwanian. Clubs: Century (U. Southwestern La.), Lafayette Town House, Lafayette Petroleum. Home: 301 River Dr Lafayette LA 70501 Office: PO Box 3567 Lafayette LA 70501

RICKS, JAMES RALPH, III, physician; b. Oklahoma City, Dec. 29, 1939; s. James Ralph and Evelyn Frances (Murdock) R.; B.S. (Pres.' honor roll) in Pharmacy, Southwestern State Coll., 1963; M.D., Okla. U., 1967; m. Karen Cabaniss, Sept. 7, 1962; children—Robyn Renee, Julie Janae, Kristi Kathleen. Rotating intern Hillcrest Med. Center Hosp., Tulsa, Okla., 1967-68; resident internal medicine Tulsa Med. Edn. Found., 1973—; gen. practice medicine specializing in internal medicine, Watonga, Okla., 1968-73; mem. staff Watonga (Okla.) Municipal Hosp. County Supt. Health, 1971, chmn. coronary care unit; cons. physician Geary Nursing Home, 1970-71, USPHS, 1968-71. Recipient Physicians Recognition award A.M.A., 1968-71. Diplomate Am. Bd. Family Practice. Mem. A.M.A., Am. Acad. Gen. Practice, Am., Okla. pharm. assns., S.A.R., Descs. Colonial Clergy, Okla. Thoracic Soc., Okla. Med. Assn., Blaine County Med. Assn., C. of C., Kappa Psi, Rho Chi. Democrat. Baptist. (deacon 1970—, trustee 1970—). Home: 708 W South Park Blvd Broken Arrow OK 74012

RICKS, JOHNNIE COPELAND (MRS. JOHN PERCY RICKS), librarian; b. Montgomery, Ala., Mar. 19, 1924; d. Robert and Para Lee (Smith) Edwards; B.S., Ala. A. and M. U., 1943; M.L.S., Syracuse U., 1954; advanced certificate (Title II B fellow) U. Pitts., 1971; m. Howard C. Copeland, May 28, 1946, (div. July 1955); 1 dau., Sandra Lee; m. 2d, John Percy Ricks, July 27, 1969; stepchildren—Joyce, John, James, Linda. With Sumter County Tng. Sch., Livingston, Ala., 1943-45; librarian Druid High Sch., Tuscaloosa, Ala., 1945-46, Acad. St. High Sch., Troy, Ala., 1948-51, Hooper City High Sch., Sayreton, Ala., 1951-54, N.Y. Pub. Library, N.Y.C., 1954-55, Ala. A. and M. U., Normal, 1955-57, Ullman High Sch., Birmingham, Ala., 1957-59, Carver High Sch., 1959-65; librarian, dir. library services Theodore Alfred Lawson State Jr. Coll., Birmingham, 1965—, now dir. Learning Resources Center. Recipient certificate merit Dictionary of Internat. Biography, 1969. Mem. A.L.A., Assn. Sch. Librarians (pres. 1964), Ala. Jr. Coll. Library Assn. (sec. 1970, pres. 1974), Ala. Edn. Assn., Beta Phi Mu, Alpha Kappa Alpha. Democrat. Mem. A.M.E. Ch. Home: 1620 Elm St SW Birmingham AL 35211 Office: 3060 Wilson Rd Birmingham AL 35221

RICKS, LEE EDWARD, banker; b. Pleasanton, Tex., June 26, 1904; s. Fletcher Bumpass and Annie Lee (Smith) R.; student U. Tex., 1923-24, Southwestern U., 1924-25; m. Mamie Ware, June 3, 1930; 1 son, Lee Edward. Pres. Ricks Co., Inc., Pleasanton, 1926-49, chmn. Ricks Co., Inc., 1951—; dir. 1st Nat. Bank, Pleasanton. Mem. Pleasanton Sch. Bd., 1945-55, pres., 1955; dir. Nueces Valley Water Dist., 1935-50. Bd. dirs. Mercy Hosp., Jourdanton, Tex., 1960-70. Methodist. Mem. Sigma Chi. Rotarian. Home: 620 W Oaklawn Rd Pleasanton TX 78064 Office: 201 N Main St Pleasanton TX 78064

RICKS, THADDEUS BENTON, pub. relations cons.; b. Tunica, Miss., Aug. 20, 1920; s. Thaddeus Benton and Lou Ollie Belle (Crosthwait) R.; student Baylor U., 1936-39; B.Journalism, U. Mo., 1941; m. Martha Ann Mills, Dec. 29, 1950; 1 dau., Lise. Reporter, copy reader, editor Temple (Tex.) Telegram, 1941, Columbus (Ga.) Enquirer, 1941, Galveston (Tex.) Tribune, 1942, Longview (Tex.) News Jour., 1947-48; Memphis Comml. Appeal, 1948-49; dir. pub. relations and advt. State Fair Tex., 1950-65; cons. pub. relations, Dallas, 1965-69; dir. pub. relations Tex. Industries, Inc., Dallas, 1969-71; project dir. Community Service Bur. Inc., Dallas, 1972-74. Served with USAF, 1942-46. Democrat. Methodist. Home: 5906 E University 101 Dallas TX 75206

RIDDICK, FLOYD MILLARD, parliamentarian; b. Trotville, N.C., July 13, 1908; s. John Bembry and Helen (Blanchard) R.; B.A., Duke, 1931, Ph.D., 1935; M.A., Vanderbilt U., 1932; m. Marguerite Louise Faerber, Feb. 24, 1940; children—Johanne Marjorie (Mrs. William E. Betsch), John Lindsay, Carol Dianne (Mrs. Panos Spiliotakos). Statis. analyst Fed. Govt., 1935-36; instr. polit. sci. Am. U., 1936-39; asso. Congl. Intelligence, Inc., Washington, 1939-43; legislative research dept. law and govt. Columbia, 1942-43; legislative analyst U.S. C. of C., 1943-47; editor Senate sect. Daily Digest of Congl. Record, 1947-51; asst. parliamentarian U.S. Senate, Washington, 1951-64, parliamentarian, 1965—; instr., professorial lectr. George Washington U., 1944-70. Spl. research project and study U. Berlin, Germany, 1937-38. Author: Congressional Procedure, 1941; (with George H. E. Smith) Congress in Action, 1948, 49, 53; U.S. Congress: Organization and Procedure, 1949; (with Charles L. Watkins) Senate Procedure, 1958, 64; Senate Procedure, 1974. Contbr. articles profl. jours. Office: US Capitol Washington DC 20510

RIDDICK, FRANK ADAMS, JR., physician; b. Memphis, June 14, 1929; s. Frank Adams and Falba (Crawford) R.; B.A. cum laude, Vanderbilt U., 1951, M.D., 1954; m. Mary Belle Alston, June 15, 1952; children—Laura Elizabeth, Frank Adams III. Intern, Barnes Hosp., St. Louis, 1954-55, resident medicine, 1957-60; fellow in metabolic diseases Washington U. Sch. Medicine, St. Louis, 1960-61; practice medicine, specializing in internal medicine, New Orleans, 1961—; med. staff Ochsner Clinic, Ochsner Found. Hosp., 1961—, asst. med. dir., 1968-72, asso. dir., 1972—; vis. physician Charity Hosp.; clin. asso. prof. medicine Tulane U. Sch. Medicine. Mem. Am. Bd. Internal Medicine, 1973—. Trustee St. Martin's Protestant Episcopal Sch., Metairie, La., Am. Soc. Internal Medicine Socio-econ. and Research Found., Alton Ochsner Med. Found. Served from 1st lt. to capt., M.C., AUS, 1955-57. Recipient Young Internist award Am. Soc. Internal Medicine, 1969, Teaching award Alton Ochsner Med. Found., 1969. Mead Johnson scholar A.C.P., 1959-60. Fellow Endocrine Soc.; mem. Am. (trustee), La. (past pres.) socs. internal medicine, A.M.A., A.C.P., Am. Diabetes Assn., Phi Beta Kappa, Alpha Omega Alpha, Kappa Sigma, Phi Chi. Episcopalian. Home: 4820 Cleveland Pl Metairie LA 70003 Office: 1514 Jefferson Hwy New Orleans LA 70121

RIDDICK, MAX FORREST, physician; b. Brownsville, Tenn., Jan. 30, 1941; s. Maxie Halbert and Raney (Forrest) R.; student Memphis State U., 1959-62; M.D., U. Tenn., 1966; m. Patricia Morgan, Feb. 2, 1963; children—Max Andrew, Anita Kay. Intern, Tampa (Fla.) Gen. Hosp., 1966-67; orthopedic fellow Campbell Clinic, Memphis, 1970-72; pvt. practice medicine specializing in orthopedic surgery Orthopedic Clinic, Winter Park, Fla., 1973—; mem. staff Fla. Hosp., Orlando, Winter Park Meml. Hosp. Served to capt. USAF, 1968-69. Mason. Club: Exchange North Orange County. Office: 1285 Orange Av Winter Park FL 32789

RIDDICK, WINSTON WADE, cons.; b. Crowley, La., Feb. 11, 1941; s. Herbert Hobson and Elizabeth (Wade) R.; B.A. (T.H. Harris scholar, Joel L. Fletcher fellow), U. Southwestern La., 1962; M.A. (Woodrow Wilson fellow), U. N.C., 1963; Ph.D. (NASA fellow), Columbia, 1973; J.D., La. State U. Law Sch., 1973, m. Patricia Ann Turner, Dec. 25, 1961; 1 son, Winston Wade. Asst. prof. govt., dir. Inst. Govt. Research, La. State U., Baton Rouge, 1966-67; instr. Hunter Coll., N.Y.C., 1965, Rutgers U., New Brunswick, N.J., 1964-65; dir. La. Higher Edn. Facilities Commn., Baton Rouge, 1967-72; exec. asst. Supt. edn. La. Dept. Edn., 1972-73; pvt. cons.

practice, 1973—. Cons. La. Joint Legislative Economy Com., 1966-67, La. Commn. on Extension and Continuing Edn., 1966-67, East Baton Rouge Parish Planning and Zoning Commn., 1969—; election analyst WBRZ-TV, Baton Rouge, 1966-67, ABC, 1964-68, spl. asst. Gov. John J. McKeithen, 1966; sec. Gov's. Efficiency Com., 1966; exec. dir. La. Commn. on Extension and Continuing Edn., 1966; mem. Gov's. Capital Outlay Budget Com., 1969, tech. adviser, 1968. Mem. East Baton Rouge Parish Plan of Govt. Study Com., 1969. Bd. dirs. So. Regional Edn. Bd., Policy Commn., Inst. for Equal Ednl. Opportunity in South, 1968—. Recipient Alumni award U. Southwestern La., 1962. Mem. Assn. Exec. Dirs. Higher Edn. Facilities Commns. (mem. exec. council 1969—, v.p.), Am. Soc. Pub. Adminstrs., Acad. Polit. Sci., Soc. Coll. and Univ. Planning, Am., So. polit. sci. assns., S.W. Social Sci. Assn., Blue Key, Circle K, Sigma Tau Delta, Phi Alpha Theta, Pi Kappa Delta, Pi Lambda Beta. Home: 1563 Oakley Dr Baton Rouge LA 70806 Office: 1563 Oakley St Baton Rouge LA 70806

RIDDLE, DON RAMON, lawyer; b. Abilene, Tex., Dec. 28, 1937; s. Glen Boyce and Pauline (Price) R.; B.A., Baylor U., 1960; J.D., U. Houston, 1966; m. Jenny Lu Brunton, Apr. 27, 1963; children—Stacy Lynn, Todd Arlis. Sports editor Big Spring (Tex.) Daily Herald, 1960; phys. dir. YMCA, Midland, Tex., 1961-63; admitted to Tex. bar, 1966; trial lawyer, Houston, 1966—. Guest lectr. U. Houston Bates Coll. Law, 1970; sec., dir. Phonoscope Corp. Am., Houston, 1972—. Served with USMCR, 1960-61. Mem. Tex. Trial Lawyers Assn. (dir.). Home: 14107 Bonney Brier Houston TX 77069 Office: 711 Fannin Houston TX 77002

RIDDLE, HAROLD JOE, architect; b. Lakeland, Fla., Nov. 4, 1922; s. Wilber Marion and Dora Ethel (Lentz) R.; B.S., Clemson U., 1949; m. Dorothy LaUna Cook, Jan. 20, 1951; children—Edward Neal, Keith Lentz, Celeste Jean. Trainee, J.N. Pease & Co., Charlotte, N.C., 1949-53; asso. William A. Faust, Architect, Myrtle Beach, S.C., 1953-55; partner Faust & Riddle, Myrtle Beach, 1955-57; prin. Harold J. Riddle, Architect, Myrtle Beach, 1957-66; pres. Harold J. Riddle & Assos., Myrtle Beach, 1964-66; pres. Riddle & Wilkes Architects, Inc., Myrtle Beach, 1966—. Mem. Planning and Zoning Commn., Mrytle Beach, 1966—. Served with USAAF, 1942-46. Mem. A.I.A. (pres. 1966, bd. dirs. 1962-67). Presbyn. (deacon). Clubs: Dunes Golf and Beach, Pine Lakes International Country. Architect Coastal Carolina Regional campus, U. S.C., Conway, 1965. Home: Lake Dr Dunes Cove Myrtle Beach SC 29577 Office: PO Box 806 511 Kings Hwy N Myrtle Beach SC 29577

RIDDLE, JAMES DOUGLASS, clergyman; b. Austin, Tex., Oct. 8, 1933; s. Prebble Elmer and Jewel Lee (Nalley) R.; B.A., Southwestern U., 1958; S.T.B., Boston U., 1962, postgrad., 1962-65; m. Marilyn Brown Moore, Sept. 8, 1956; children—Mary Elizabeth, Margaret Allison, Charles Douglass. Dir. youth activities Tex. Christian Rural Overseas Program, Tex. Council Chs., 1954-55; ordained to ministry United Ch. of Christ, 1963; pastor First Meth. Ch., Granger, Tex., 1956-58; pastor Meth. Parish, Biddeford, Me., 1958-62; co-minister First Parish Ch., Lincoln, Mass., 1963-67; minister Community Ch. of Chapel Hill, N.C., 1967—; teaching fellow, lectr. human relations Boston U. Sch. Bus., 1960-64; mem. staff study of structure and mgmt. Mass. Conf., United Ch. of Christ, 1967. Chmn. Clergy Consultation on Problem Pregnancies N.C., 1968-72; mem. exec. bd., chmn. Commn. on Unity N.C. Council Chs., 1968—, mem. commn. on faith and order, 1970-72, mem. gen. bd. Nat. Council Chs., 1969-72; chmn. United Ch. of Christ Commn. on Christian Unity and Ecumenical Study and Service, 1969—, chmn. com. on social action So. Conf., 1968-70; del. Uniting Conf., World Alliance Reformed Chs. and Internat. Congl. Council, Nairobi, Kenya, 1970; mem. United Ch. Christ Council for Christian Social Action, 1971—. Co-chmn. housing com., bd. dirs. Chapel Hill-Carrboro Inter-Ch. Council for Social Service, 1967—; chmn. Assn. Community Agys. Orange County, 1969-72; pres. N.C. Legal Def. Fund, 1969—; sec. Triangle Meml. and Funeral Soc., 1969-71. Del. Democratic State Conv., 1970, 74. Mem. Soc. Sci. Study of Religion, Acad. Religion and Mental Health, Religious Edn. Assn., N.Am. Acad. Ecumenists, Pi Kappa Alpha, Pi Delta Epsilon. Address: Damascus Church Rd Box 336 Chapel Hill NC 27514

RIDDLE, LINDSEY GRANT, broadcasting co. exec.; b. Preston, Mo., Aug. 11, 1910; s. Joseph Grant and Jessie (Lindsey) R.; grad. pub. high sch.; m. Edwina Giles Barthe, Sept. 3, 1951; 1 dau., Martha (Mrs. Gary Bankson). Studio supr. WHB Broadcasting Co., Kansas City, Mo., 1933-46; chief engr. Stephens Broadcasting Service, Inc. (name changed to WDSU Broadcasting Corp., 1950), New Orleans, 1946-48, chief engr., 1949-66, v.p., chief engring. Royal St. Corp., WDSU-TV Inc., New Orleans, 1966—. Mem. tech. adv. com. Delgado Coll., New Orleans, 1970—; chmn. services subcom. La. Industry Adv. Com., 1967—; mem. Lakewood Property Owners Assn. New Orleans, 1961—. Registered profl. engr. La. Mem. Nat. Assn. Broadcasters (tech. com.), Assn. Broadcast Engring. Standards (tech. com.), I.E.E.E. (sr. mem.), Assn. Fedn. Communications Consulting Engrs., Nat. Soc. Profl. Engrs., La. Engring. Soc., Armed Forces Radio Services, Nat. Ry. Hist. Soc., New Orleans Engring. Club, New Orleans C. of C., Young Men's Bus. Club New Orleans, Royal Radio Club (pres.), Delta DX Amateur Radio Club, New Orleans VHF Radio Club, Am. Radio Relay League, Broadcast Pioneers, Old Timers Club. Democrat. Methodist. Contbr. profl. jours. Home: 5646 Bellaire Dr New Orleans LA 70124 Office: 520 Royal St New Orleans LA 70130

RIDER, FRED EUGENE, elec. engr.; b. Hot Springs, Ark., Jan. 2, 1910; s. Charles H. and Pearl (Cook) R.; student pub. schs., Hot Springs; m. Louise Steele Morris, May 26, 1972; 1 son, Keith Bowman. Chief engr. WQAM, Miami, Fla., 1930-39, engr., 1949-56; engr. CBS, N.Y.C., 1940-43, spl. events writer, 1947-48; war corr. CBS, Europe and Pacific, 1943-46 (received Navy commendation); chief engr. WIOD, Miami, 1956—. Free lance writer. Mem. Fla. State Industry Adv. Com. Served with USNR, 1927-30. Mem. I.E.E.E. Mem. Unity Ch. Clubs: Overseas (N.Y.C.); Surf, Palm Bay (Miami). Contbr. articles profl. jours. Home: 1771 N View Dr Sunset 1 Miami Beach FL 33140 Office: PO Box 1177 Miami FL 33138

RIDINGS, G. RAY, radiologist; b. Kennett, Mo., Nov. 22, 1918; s. Gus Hill and Edith Clara (Masters) R.; A.B., Ark. State Coll., 1939; M.D., Vanderbilt U., 1950; m. Mary Ellen White, Dec. 28, 1941; children—Patricia, Sandra. Instr. mil. sci., tactics Ark. State Coll., Jonesboro, 1940-42; intern Vanderbilt Hosp., Nashville, 1950-51, resident, 1951-52, instr. radiology, 1955; resident radiology Univ. Hosp., Ann Arbor, Mich., 1952-54, jr. clin. instr., 1954-55; instr. radiology Vanderbilt U. Med. Sch., 1955; asso. prof. U. Miss. Med. Center, Jackson, 1956-57; prof., head dept. radiology U. Okla. Sch. Medicine, Oklahoma City, 1957-62, cancer coordinator, 1959-62, head dept. radiology Univ. Hosps., 1957-62; prof., head sect. radiation therapy U. Mo. Sch. Medicine, Columbia, 1962-67, cancer coordinator U. Mo. Med. Center, 1965-67; clin. prof. radiology U. Tex. Southwestern Med. Sch., Dallas, 1968-71; acting asst. dean, dir. master planning Tex. Tech. U. Sch. Medicine, Lubbock, 1971; dir. Charles J. Williams Cancer Treatment Center, Bapt. Meml. Hosp., Jacksonville, Fla., 1971—, also chief radiation therapy service; mem. staffs Bapt. Meml., St. Vincent's, Univ., St. Luke's, Meth., Hope Haven Children's hosps. (all Jacksonville); dir. radiation therapy St. Paul Hosp., Dallas, 1967-71. Guest examiner Am. Bd. Radiology, 1963-69; cons. radiation therapy. Bd. dirs. Tex., Fla. divs. Am. Cancer Soc. Served from 2d lt. to maj. F.A., AUS, 1940-46; ETO, PTO. Diplomate Am. Bd. Radiology. Fellow Am. Coll. Radiology; mem. Am. Soc. Therapeutic Radiologists, Am. Assn. Cancer Edn. (charter), Radium Soc., Soc. Nuclear Medicine, Am., Fla. med. assns., Duval County Med. Soc., Mo. Radiol. Soc., Assn. Mo. Tumor Registry Dirs. (exec. sec. 1967), Assn. U. Radiologists, Radiol. Soc. N.Am., A.A.A.S., Assn. for Cancer Teaching, Scabbard and Blade, Sigma Xi, Alpha Omega Alpha, Phi Theta Kappa. Contbr. articles to med. jours. Designer afterloading cervical radium applicator, 1961; organizer computerized tumor registry systems. Home: 4955 River Basin Dr S Jacksonville FL 32207 Office: Bapt Meml Hosp 800 Prudential Dr Jacksonville FL 32207

RIECKEN, WILLIAM EMIL, JR., physician; b. Deleware, O., Feb. 16, 1931; s. William Emil and Alma (Gollner) R.; B.S., Millsaps Coll., 1952; M.D., Tulane U., 1956; M.P.H., U. N.C., 1968; m. Bobbie Jeanenne Pridgen, June 7, 1954; children—Jeanne Lynn, Leigh Ann, William Edward. Intern Miss. Bapt. Hosp., Jackson, 1956-57; health officer Miss. Bd. Health, Attala County, Kosciusko, 1959-67, Leake Co., Carthage, 1959-67; resident in pub. health Miss. Bd. Health, 1968-70; cons. local health services Miss. Bd. Health, Jackson, 1968-70, dir. family planning project, 1969-72, asst. dir. gen. health services, 1970-73, asst. dir. local health services; cons. Assn. State and Territorial Health Officers Health Program Reporting System, 1971—. Med. liaison officer AEC-USPHS Radiol. Network, Miss., 1961-67; cons. preventive medicine Montefort Jones Hosp., Kosciusko, 1959-67. Bd. dirs. Central Miss., Inc., 1965-67. Mem. com. health and safety. Attala County Boy Scouts Am., 1960-65, exec. bd. Andrew Jackson council, Jackson, 1961—, commr. Mataleho dist., 1962-66. Served with USAF, 1957-59; lt. col. Miss. Air N.G. Recipient Walter Reed medal for sr. thesis in preventive med., 1956. Mem. Am., Aerospace med. assns., Central, N. Central (sec. 1964, pres. 1965, sec. 1966, 67) med. socs., Am., Miss. pub. health assns., Am., Miss. (pres. 1973) assns. pub. health physicians, Millsap Coll. Alumni Assn. (v.p. 1965-66), Theta Kappa Psi, Pi Kappa Alpha. Methodist (bd. stewards 1962-67; adminstrv. bd. 1972—; certified lay speaker; Sunday sch. tchr.; asst. choir dir.; Layman of Year 1965; dist. bd. lay activities 1966-67, chmn. commn. missions 1965-67, chmn. evangelism 1973—). Home: 780 Woodhill Dr Jackson MS 39206 Office: Miss Bd Health Jackson MS 39205

RIEDERER, ROBERT EDWARD, physician; b. Rozel, Kan., Sept. 17, 1916; s. John Henry and Blanche Elizabeth (LaBounty) R.; A.B., U. Kan., 1938, M.D., 1942; m. Sarah Josephine Demsey, Oct. 30, 1942; children—Robert Neven, Bruce Fullerton. Intern U. Kan. Hosps., Kansas City, 1942-43; practice medicine specializing in family practice, Olathe, Kan., 1946-61, 68-69; chief profl. tng. VA Central Office, Washington, 1961-62; staff physician Lovelace Clinic, 1962-68; physician, State Sch. Deaf, 1954-61; staff physician Jefferson Health Found., Birmingham, Ala., 1969-73; chief med. cons., disability determination unit Social Security Adminstrn., State of Ala., Birmingham, 1973—; mem. staff St. Mary's Hosp., Kansas City, Mo., Olathe (Kan.) Community Hosp., Bataan Meml. Meth., Presbyn. hosps., Albuquerque, S. Highlands Hosp., Birmingham, Ala. Pres. Bd. Edn., Olathe, Kan., 1957-61. Served to lt. USNR, 1943-46; PTO. Fellow Royal Soc. Health; mem. Am. Acad. Family Practice, So. Med. Assn., Phi Beta Kappa, Alpha Omega Alpha, Delta Tau Delta, Nu Sigma Nu. Clubs: Four Hills (Albuquerque); Green Valley Country (Birmingham, Ala.). Home: 370 Laredo Dr Birmingham AL 35226 Office: 1500 6th Av S Birmingham AL 35205

RIEFENBERG, JOHN ALAN, social worker; b. Omaha, Sept. 30, 1931; s. Elmer August and Cassie Lila (Williams) R.; A.A., Del Mar Jr. Coll., 1952; B.B.A., Tex. Coll. Arts and Industries, 1954; M.S.S.W., U. Tex., 1961; m. Janette Irene Meyer, June 3, 1961; children—Paul Alan, Erica Lynn. Pub. assistance field worker Tex. Dept. Pub. Welfare, Spur, 1957-58; caseworker Children's Services, Corpus Christi, Tex., 1959-60, Family and Children's Services, Shreveport, La., 1961-65; psychiat. social worker Children's Med. Center, Tulsa, 1965-68; pvt. practice counseling, Tulsa, 1966-68; exec. dir. Family Counseling Service, Corpus Christi, 1968-70; chief psychiat. social worker Child Guidance Clinic of Forsyth County, Winston-Salem, N.C., 1970—. Mem. Nat. Assn. Social Workers, Acad. Certified Social Workers, Am. Group Psychotherapy Assn., Am., N.C. assns. marriage and family counselors, Nat. Geog. Soc. Mem. Disciples Christ Ch. Home: 216 Capistrano Dr Winston-Salem NC 27103 Office: 1200 Glade St Winston-Salem NC 27101

RIEHM, CARL LEE, sch. supt.; b. Norfolk, Va., Jan. 23, 1929; s. Andrew Nelse and Nellie (Fitchett) R.; A.B., Citadel, 1952; M.Ed., U. Va., 1957; D.Ed., U. Fla., 1969; m. Barbara Hilton, June 15, 1952; 1 son, Andrew Russell. Tchr., elementary sch. Norfolk, 1953-60, prin., 1960-66; dir. adjustive services Norfolk City Schs., 1967-69; dir. elementary edn. Prince William County, Manassas, Va., 1969-71, asst. supt. for instruction, 1971-74, asso. supt., 1974—. Extension tchr. U. Va., Hampton Roads Center, 1968-69. Served with USNR, 1947-48. Mem. Assn. Supervision and Curriculum Devel., Nat. Soc. Study Edn., Council for Exceptional Children, John Dewey Soc., Internat. Reading Assn., Va. Ednl. Assn., Kappa Delta Pi, Phi Delta Kappa. Methodist. Office: Prince William County Sch Bd Independent Hill Manassas VA 22110

RIEMER, WILLIAM JOHN, govt. ofcl.; b. Los Angeles, Jan. 25, 1924; s. John Leopold and Ada (Neef) R.; B.A., U. Cal. at Berkeley, 1949, M.A., 1953, Ph.D., 1956; m. Lois Carol Stovall, Apr. 27, 1973; children—Elsa, Karl, Emma, Flora. Asst. prof. biology, asso. curator-in-charge Natural Scis. Fla. State Museum U. Fla. at Gainesville, 1955-63; asso. dir. systematic biology program NSF, Washington, 1963-65, planning officer div. biol. and med. scis., 1965—. Served with AUS, 1943-45. Fulbright lectr. U. Tel-Aviv, Israel, 1958-59. Contbg. author Catalogue of American Amphibians and Reptiles, 1962—. Editor: Bulletin Florida State Museum, 1955-63. Research in herpetology. Home: 13919 Mt Pleasant Dr Woodbridge VA 22191 Office: Biol and Med Scis div Nat Sci Found Washington DC 20550

RIES, EDWARD RICHARD, petroleum geologist; b. Freeman, S.D., Sept. 18, 1918; s. August and Mary F. (Graber) R.; student Freeman Jr. Coll., 1937-39; A.B., U. S.D., 1941; M.S., U. Okla., 1943, Ph.D. (Warden-Humble fellow), 1951; postgrad. Harvard, 1946-47; m. Amelia D. Capshaw, Jan. 24, 1948 (div. Oct. 1956); children—Rosemary Melinda, Victoria Elise; m. 2d, Maria Wipfler, June 12, 1964. Asst. geologist Geol. Survey S.D., Vermillion, 1941; geophys. interpreter Robert Ray Inc., Oklahoma City, 1942; jr. geologist Carter Oil Co., Mont., Wyo., 1943-44, geologist Cutbank, Mont., 1944-49; sr. geologist Standard Vacuum Oil Co., India, 1951-53, sr. regional geologist, Indonesia, 1953-59, geol. adviser for Far East and Africa, White Plains, N.Y., 1959-62; geol. adviser Far East, Africa, Oceania, Mobil Petroleum Co., N.Y.C., N.Y., 1962-65; geol. adviser for Europe, Far East, Mobil Oil Corp., N.Y.C., 1965-71, sr. regional explorationist Far East, Dallas, 1971—. Grad. asst., teaching fellow U. Okla., 1941-43, Harvard, 1946-47. Served with AUS, 1944-46. Mem. Am. Assn. Petroleum Geologists, Am. Geol. Inst., A.A.A.S., Nat. Audubon Soc., Nat. Wildlife Fedn., Wilderness Soc., Am. Legion, Sigma Xi, Phi Beta Kappa, Phi Sigma, Sigma Gamma Epsilon. Republican. Mennonite. Club: Harvard (Dallas). Home: 6009 Royal Crest Dr Dallas TX 75230 Office: 8303 Elmbrook Dr Dallas TX 75247

RIESSER, GREGOR HANS, chemist; b. Riga, Latvia, Apr. 13, 1925; s. Hans Eduard and Gilda (von Scherf) R.; came to U.S., 1948, naturalized, 1954; diplome d'Ingenieur Chimiste, Universite de Geneve (Switzerland), 1947; Ph.D., U. Cal. at Berkeley, 1952; m. Joanna Gray, Mar. 1, 1952; children—Cynthia Ann, William Fitzhugh. Chemist, Shell Chem. Co., Donminguez, Cal., 1952-53, research chemist, Houston, 1953-57, group leader indsl. chems. div., 1957-68, research supr., 1968-70, sr. technologist catalyst dept., 1970-72; staff chemist Shell Devel. Co., Houston, 1972—. Mem. Houston council human relations, 1962—, mem. internat. relations com., 1963-64; mem. campaign monitoring com. Common Cause, 1973. Del. Democratic State Conv., 1954—. Mem. Am. Chem. Soc. (chmn. internat. activities com. S.E. sect.), Am. Contract Bridge League (life master), Stella Helvetica, Alliance Francaise de Houston, Houston Mus. Fine Arts, Am. Assn. UN. Unitarian (trustee 1958-59). Contbr. articles to profl. jours. Patentee in field. Home: 13802 Britoak St Houston TX 77024 Office: Shell Devel Co Box 90 Houston TX 77079

RIETH, CHESTER MARTIN, accountant; b. New Orleans, July 29, 1914; s. Anthony and Mary (Price) R.; B.S., Loyola U., 1937; m. Audrey Cecile Melancon, June 21, 1939; children—Marc Chester, Christopher Anthony, Gayvonne Claire, Virginia Louise, Justin Dennis, Kevin Amadeus. Accountant, Barton, Pilie & Sere, New Orleans, 1937-40; auditor State La., 1941; ofcl. City New Orleans, 1942—, asst. sec. bd. liquidation City Debt, 1951-63, sec., 1963—. Vice pres., chmn. prodn. com. New Orleans Opera House Assn., 1957—. K.C. Home: 750 Filmore Av New Orleans LA 70124 Office: 1300 Perdido St New Orleans LA 70112

RIGAU, MARCO ANTONIO, judge; b. Ponce, P.R., Mar. 5, 1919; s. Juan M. and Carmen (Gaztambide) R.; B.A., U. P.R., 1940, LL.B. cum laude, 1942; M.A. in Govt., Harvard, 1947; m. Alice Jimenez, Dec. 16, 1942 (div. Apr. 1968); children—Alma Carmen, Marco Antonio, Maria Alicia; m. 2d, Lucy Torres, Nov. 2, 1968. Admitted to P.R. bar, 1945; asst., atty. gen. P.R., 1947; legislative counsel Legislative Assembly P.R., 1948-49; spl. asst. to gov. P.R., 1949-51, exec. asst., 1951-58; partner firm Rigau, Goldman & Santiago, San Juan, 1959-61; asso. justice Supreme Ct. P.R., 1961—. Mem. adv. bd. Marquis Biograph. Soc. Served to capt., inf., AUS, 1942-45. Decorated Bronze Star medal, Combat Inf. Badge. Mem. P.R. Bar Assn., Am. Judicature Soc., Harvard Alumni Assn., Internat. Law Assn., Am. Soc. Internat. Law. Home: 1309 Magdalena Av Condado San Juan PR 00907 Office: Supreme Court Bldg San Juan PR 00902

RIGBY, WILLIAM LAWSON, ret. sch. supt.; b. Collins, Miss., June 27, 1909; s. William Lawson and Elsa (Watson) R.; B.S., Millsaps Coll., 1932; M.A., Peabody Coll., 1949; m. Mamie Lou Downing, Nov. 24, 1933; children—Clifford L., Wilna (Mrs. T.M. Stewart), Ruth (Mrs. Larry Sappington). Tchr. sci., coach Mendenhall (Miss.) High Sch., 1932-36; supt. Kilmichael (Miss.) Consol. Schs., 1936-41; pres. French Camp Acad., French Camp, Miss., 1941-43; prin. Utica (Miss.) Consol. Sch., 1945-49; prin. Gulfport (Miss.) High Sch., 1949-51, asst. supt., 1951-53, supt., 1953-74. Chmn. adv. council Harrison County Youth Ct., 1957-64; pres. Council Pub. Schs. System, 1965-66; pres. Gulfport area Boy Scouts Am., 1952-53; v.p. Miss. Congress P.T.A., 1960. Mem. Miss. Edn. Assn. (pres. 1967-68), Am., Miss. assns. sch. adminstrs., Gulf Sch. Edn. Assn., White House Confr. Edn. Presbyn. (elder 1942—). Home: 915 2d St Gulfport MS 39501

RIGG, JOHN BROWNLEE, govt. ofcl.; b. Omaha, July 12, 1926; s. James Paul and Ruth Magdeline (Hargleroad) R.; A.B., U. Neb., 1949; m. Shirley Anne Tomlinson, June 9, 1946; children—John Brownlee, Nancy Jane, Elizabeth Anne (Mrs. Hal Maxwell). Self employed, 1950-52, 58-62; with Minerals Engring. Co., 1952-55, Gen. Minerals Corp., 1955-58, Colo. Nat. Bank-Small Bus. Investment Co., 1962-67, Colo. Mining Assn., 1967-69; mem. staff U.S. Dept. Interior, Washington, 1969—, dep. asst. sec. minerals, 1972—. Mem. Colo. Engring. Council, 1966-68, Mining Indsl. Devel. Bd., Western Govs. Mining Adv. Council, 1967-69. Active Colo. Republican party, 1950-69; election commr. City of Denver, 1966. Served with USMCR, 1943-46. Registered profl. engr., Colo. Mem. Am. Inst. Mining Engring., S.A.R. Mason. Club: Capitol Hill. Home: 6523 Deepford St Springfield VA 22150 Office: US Dept Interior Washington DC 20240

RIGGAN, JAMES GORDON, clergyman; b. Raleigh, N.C., Jan. 1, 1914; s. Roy Daniel and Elizabeth (Miller) R.; A.B. cum laude, Davidson Coll., 1939; B.D. (Latta scholar), Union Theol. Sem., 1942; D.D., Eastern Neb. Christian Coll., 1972; m. Louise Alden Wells, May 23, 1942; children—Mary Louise (Mrs. Patrick L. Exley), Elizabeth (Mrs. James F. Free), James Gordon, David Wells, Peggy (Mrs. Richard C. Lenderman), Nancy Carol, Harold Roy. Ordained to ministry Presbyn. Ch., 1942; organizer East Ocean View Presbyn. Ch., Norfolk, Va., 1941, pastor, 1941-49; pastor Bayside Presbyn. Ch., Virginia Beach, Va., 1948; supply pastor Calvary Presbyn. Ch., Norfolk, 1945-49; mission pastor First Presbyn. Ch., Huntington, W.Va., 1949-50; builder Wayne (W.Va.) Ch., 1950; founder, organizer, pastor Enslow Park Presbyn. Ch., Huntington, W.Va., 1949-54; pastor Macon Rd. Presbyn. Ch., 1954-67; pastor East Ocean View Presbyn. Ch., 1967—; moderator Norfolk Presbytery, 1944-45, Kanawha Presbytery, 1951-52; commnr. Gen. Assembly Presbyn. Ch. U.S., 1945, 1952, 1969; chmn. exam. com. Norfolk Presbytery, 1969-71. Served with USNR, World War II. Recipient William Banks Biblical medal, 1939; Tower Room scholar, 1968. Mem. Am. Counselors Soc., Philanthropic Lit. Soc., Eta Sigma Phi, Delta Phi Alpha. Kiwanian. Clubs: Civitan, Variety. Home: 9547 9th Bay St Norfolk VA 23518 Office: 9613 9th Bay St Norfolk VA 23518

RIGGAN, WILSON BUTLER, agrl. economist; b. Waverly, Va., Sept. 15, 1914; s. Jesse Thomas and Ellie (Butler) R.; B.S. with honors, Va. Poly. Inst., 1950; Ph.D., N.C. State U., 1966; m. Edna Irene Downs Joyner, Aug. 8, 1953; children—Wilson Butler, Jesse Edmund. Asst. agrl. economist N.C. State Coll., 1955-57, instr., 1957-58; asst. prof. agrl. econs. and econometrics, grad. prof. U. Fla., 1958-64, supervisory statistician, biometry sect. ecol. research br., div. health effects research Nat. Air Pollution Control Adminstrn., Durham, N.C., 1964-66, chief biometry sect., 1966-67, asst. chief ecol. research br., 1967-71, asst. dir. for research operations, div. health effects research, 1971-73, research coordinator Human Studies Lab., 1973—. Served with U.S. Mcht. Marine, 1942-46. Mem. Am. Farm Econs. Assn., Am. Statis. Assn., Econometric Assn., Am. Econ. Assn., Am. Acad. Polit. and Social Sci., Biometric Assn., Am. Pub. Health Assn., Phi Kappa Phi, Alpha Zeta, Gamma Sigma Delta. Methodist. Home: 3609 Westover Rd Durham NC 27707 Office: Nat Environmental Research Center Environmental Protection Agy Research Triangle Park NC 27711

RIGGINS, ROBERT EARL, radio performer; b. Dallas, Feb. 22, 1935; s. Robert Claude and Blanche Elizabeth (Canada) R.; B.F.A., Tex. Christian U., 1957; m. Doris Ann Soule, Sept. 19, 1958; children—Teresa Ann, Sharon Lynn. Performer, Radio Sta. KJIM, Ft.

Worth, 1957-63, Radio Sta. KTOK, Oklahoma City, 1964—; v.p. programming KTOK Radio, Okla. News Network; program cons. KWBB Radio, Wichita, Kan. Served to lt. Signal Corps, AUS, 1957-58.

RIGGS, CECIL GRAHAM, communications co. exec.; b. Durham, N.C., Aug. 23, 1935; s. Otho Graham and Mildred Louise (Massey) R.; grad. Cleve. Inst. Electronics, 1962; grad. Advanced Mgmt. Program, Harvard, 1973; m. Carolyn Jean Wilson, Oct. 6, 1956; children—Sabrina, Janita. Electronic technician. Automatic Electric Co., 1956-69; v.p. Continental Communications Constrn. Co., Tampa, Fla., 1969-70, pres., 1971-73; pres. Arcata Inst. Can. Ltd., Montreal, 1971—; operating v.p. Arcata Installation Co., Tampa, 1972-73; v.p. Telephone Plant Constrn. Corp., 1972—; pres. Continental Communications Service Corp., Tampa, Fla., 1973—, Concomco Corp., Tampa, 1973—. Asst. dir. Tampa Concentrated Employment Program, 1970—; industry rep. Nat. Alliance Businessmen Program, 1973—. Mem. Ind. Telephone Pioneers Assn. (dir. 1970), Tampa C. of C. Clubs: Tower, Commerce (Tampa); Buckhorn Golf and Country (Brandon, Fla.). Home: 207 Wheeler Rd Seffner FL 33584 Office: PO Box 23727 Tampa FL 33622

RIGGS, KARL A., JR., educator, geologist; b. Thomasville, Ga., Aug. 12, 1929; s. Karl A. and Marjorie Ann (Urquhart) R.; B.S. with honors, Mich. State U., 1951, M.S., 1952; Ph.D., Ia. State U., 1956; m. Patricia Ann Hartrick, June 28, 1952; children—George, Kathryn, Linda. Sr. research technologist Mobil Field Research Lab., Dallas, 1956-59; geologic cons., 1952—; dir. Nortex Oil & Gas Corp., Dallas, 1960-64; asst. prof. Western Mich. U., Kalamazoo, 1966-68; asso. prof. geology Miss. State U., 1968—; cons. Cabot Corp., 1968—; part-time instr. and research asso. Ia. State U., 1952-56. Mem. Starkville (Miss.) Bicentennial Com., 1972—. Dist. chmn. Dallas Republican Party, 1961-62. Bd. dirs. Wesleyan Found., Miss. State U., 1972—, treas., 1973-74. Fellow Am. Inst. Chemists, Geol. Soc. Am.; mem. Soc. Econ. Paleontologists and Mineralogists, Mineral. Soc. Am., Geochem. Soc., Clay Minerals Soc., Am. Geol. Inst., Miss. Acad. Sci., Oktibbeha County C. of C. (chmn. govt. affairs com. 1972-73). Methodist. Kiwanian (dir. Starkville 1962). Author papers, abstracts, reports in field. Home: RFD 5 140 Grandridge Rd Starkville MS 39759 Office: Drawer GG Miss State Univ Mississippi State MS 39762

RIGGS, MYRTLE CRAVER BRADHAM (MRS. LARRY T. RIGGS), motel exec.; b. Newberry, S.C., Mar. 28, 1920; d. William Everett and Myrtle (Ivey) Craver; student Converse Coll., 1936-38, Furman U., Coll. Charleston, 1943-46; m. Richard Bradham, May 27, 1940 (dec. Oct. 1963); 1 dau., Helen (Mrs. Robert Lindley Furnans); m. 2d, Larry T. Riggs, June 26, 1966. Owner, operator Mount Vernon Motel, Charleston, S.C., 1950—; v.p., treas., dir. Superior Motels Inc. Chmn., St. Andrews Playground Commn., 1960—; pres. St. Andrews High Sch. PTA, 1956-58; mem. Gov.'s Com. on Edn., 1958-60; v.p. Charleston Safety Council, 1969; mem. Charleston County Zoning Bd., 1971—; charter mem., pres. Trident chpt. Nat. Multiple Scelerosis, 1971-74. Sec., Club 4 St. Andrews Parish Democratic Com., 1954-64. Bd. dirs. United Fund, Florence Crittendon Home, Progress Found.; vice chmn. bd. commrs. Oak Grove Orphanage; bd. dirs., v.p. Charleston County Cancer Soc.; mem. steering com. Faculty-Alumni Center, Coll. Charleston. Named Charleston Woman of Year, 1958; recipient Hospitality mag. Hall of Fame award, 1969, Distinguished Service award Superior Motels Inc., 1969, 72, Mary Mildred Sullivan award Converse Coll., 1970; Hope Chest award Nat. Multiple Sclerosis Soc., 1973. Mem. Coll. of Charleston Alumni Assn. (v.p. 1968), Converse Coll. Alumnae Council, S.C. (chmn. bd. trustees), (named to Hall of Fame 1971), Nat. (S.C. chmn. Am. Revolution com. 1972—) fedns. women's clubs, Wesley Service Guild (pres.), Soroptimists (gov.), S.C. Hist. Soc., Nat. Trust Soc., Navy League, Preservation Soc., Trident C. of C. of Charleston (women's div. bd.), Alliance Francaise, S.C. Innkeepers Soc., Charleston Innkeeper (pres. 1974—). Methodist (bd. stewards). Home: 1265 Camerton St Charleston SC 29407 also 2826 Marshall Blvd Sullivan's Island SC 29482 Office: Mount Vernon Motel US 17 Charleston SC 29407

RIGGS, ORVAL ELMO, physician; b. Walnut Ridge, Ark., Apr. 18, 1920; s. James Roscoe and Menona Belle (Metheny) R.; A.A., Ark. Tech., 1939-41; B.S., U. Ark., 1951, B.S.M., 1952, M.D., 1953; m. Helen Inez Waldron, Nov. 6, 1942; children—Susan, Tommy, Dianne. Intern St. Louis City Hosp., 1953-54; pvt. practice medicine, Walnut Ridge, Ark., 1954-56; resident gen. surgery U. Ark. Med. Center, 1956-60; pvt. practice medicine, specializing in gen. surgery, Jonesboro, Ark., 1960-66; resident radiology U. Ark. Med. Center, 1966-69; pvt. practice medicine, specializing in surgery, radiology, radiation therapy, Pine Bluff, Ark., 1972-74; fellow thoracic and cardiovascular surgery Baptist Hosp., Memphis, 1974—; instr. radiation therapy Vanderbilt U. Hosp., 1969-70; asst. prof. radiology U. Ark. Med. Center, 1970-72; mem. staff Jefferson Hosp., Pine Bluff, Ark.; courtesy staff U. Ark. Med. Center, Little Rock. Served with USNR, 1941-46. Mem. A.M.A., Ark., So. med. socs., Am. Coll. Surgeons, Am. Coll. Radiology, Southwest Surg. Assn. Home: 1300 N Hughes St Little Rock AR 72207

RIGGS, ROBERT DALE, educator; b. Pocahontas, Ark., June 15, 1932; s. Rosa M. and Grace (Million) R.; B.S.A. with honors, U. Ark., 1954, M.S., 1956; Ph.D., N.C. State Coll., 1958; m. Jennie Lee Willis, June 6, 1954; children—Rebecca, Deborah, Robert Dale, James. Research asst. U. Ark. at Fayetteville, 1954-55, asst. prof., 1958-62, asso. prof., 1962-68, prof. plant nematology, 1968—; research asst. N.C. State Coll., Raleigh, 1955-58. Mem. Am. Phytopath. Soc., Soc. Nematologists, Sigma Xi, Gamma Sigma Delta. Democrat. Baptist (deacon; chmn. diaconate 1972-73). Home: 1840 Woolsey St Fayetteville AR 72701

RIGGS, VIRGINIA LOUISE HOLLOWAY (MRS. ARTHUR J. RIGGS), lectr., clubwoman; b. Conway, Ark.; d. Keith Leaming and Harriett (Bennett) Holloway; B.A., U. Ark.; m. Arthur J. Riggs, Oct. 15, 1942; children—Arthur James, Emily Adele (Mrs. John W. Freeman), Keith Holloway, George Bennett. Editor, Virginia's Kitchen. Park Cities North Dallas News, 1955-60; lectr. cooking, related topics, 1955—, hist. topics, 1960—. Pres., LeBonnet Bleu Garden Club, 1966-68, Seneca Rev. Club, 1967-68, Dallas Browning Club, 1970-72, S'Amuser Club, 1966-67, Jr. Matheon Club, 1971-72. Zone chmn. Am. Cancer Soc., 1966-68; area capt. Carih, 1970. Mem. Kappa Kappa Gamma. Home: 4116 Amherst St Dallas TX 75225

RIGGS, WILLIAM WEBSTER, physician; b. Memphis, May 10, 1934; s. W. Webster and Mary (Norman) R.; B.S., U. Tenn., 1955, M.D., 1958; m. Helen Sands Turner, Dec. 22, 1956; children—Rollin, Russell, Ryan. Intern Bapt. Hosp., Nashville, 1958-59; resident Meth. Hosp., Memphis, 1961-63; chief resident Boston Children's Hosp., 1965; practice medicine specializing in radiology, 1964—; mem. staff City Memphis Hosps., 1964—; dir. radiology Le Bonheur Children's Hosp., Memphis, 1968—; asso. prof. radiology U. Tenn., Memphis, 1966-68. Served to capt. M.C., AUS, 1959-61. Diplomate Am. Bd. Radiology. Mem. Soc. Pediatric Radiology, Sigma Alpha Epsilon, Alpha Epsilon Delta. Home: 7 Belleair Dr Memphis TN 38104 Office: 848 Adams St Memphis TN 38103

RIGGSBEE, JOHN BUNYAN, univ. physician; b. Pittsboro, N.C., Dec. 13, 1920; s. Thomas Vernon and Sarah (Curry) R.; A.B., U. N.C., 1939; M.D., Vanderbilt U., 1943; m. Margaret Alice Seale, June 20, 1941; children—Nancy, Susan (Mrs. Marshall E. Smith), Mark, Edwin. Intern, St. Thomas Hosp., Nashville; instr. anatomy U. N.C., 1946-47; dir. health Ga. Inst. Tech., 1954-70; univ. physician Vanderbilt U., 1970—. Served with M.C., USNR, 1944-46, 51-54. Fellow Am. Coll. Health Assn. Baptist. Home: 3818 Harding Pl Nashville TN 37215

RIGGSBY, DUTCHIE SELLERS (MRS. ERNEST DUWARD RIGGSBY), educator; b. Montgomery, Ala., Oct. 26, 1940; d. Cleveland Malcolm and Marcella (Bedsole) Sellers; B.S., Troy State Coll., 1962, M.S., 1965; tchrs. certificate Auburn U., 1968, Ed.D., 1972; m. Ernest Duward Riggsby, Aug. 25, 1962. Tchr. Montgomery (Ala.) Pub. Schs., 1962-63, Troy (Ala.) City Schs., 1963-67; sci./math. media specialist, ednl. media center Auburn (Ala.) U., 1968-69; vis. prof. U. P.R., summers 1972, 73; dir. Media Services Columbus (Ga.) Coll., 1972—. Asst. dir. Aerospace Edn. Insts., Fort Rucker and Maxwell AFB, Ala., 1964-67. Instr. water safety A.R.C., 1962-69; aerial radiol. monitor Civil Def., Troy, 1966-71. Recipient Star award Nat. Sci. Tchrs. Assn., 1968. Mem. Ala. Acad. Sci. (sect. v.p. 1969-70), Nat. Sci. Tchrs. Assn., Nat. Aerospace Edn. Assn., Nat. Aerospace Edn. Council, Ga. Acad. Sci., Nat. Assn. for Ednl. Communication and Tech., Kappa Delta Pi, Alpha Delta Kappa. Club: Columbus Executives. Home: 2214 Coventry Dr Columbus GA 31904

RIGGSBY, ERNEST DUWARD, educator; b. Nashville, June 12, 1925; s. James Thomas and Anna Pearl (Turner) R.; B.S., Tenn. Poly. Inst., 1948; B.A., George Peabody Coll., 1955, M.A., 1956, Ed.S., 1958, Ed.D., 1964; m. Dutchie Sellers, Aug. 25, 1962. Tech. instr. U.S. Manhattan Engring. Dist., Oak Ridge, 1944-45; with Tenn. Eastman Corp., 1944-45; instr. meteorology USAAF, 1945; instr. sci. and math. U. of South, Sewanee, Tenn., 1955-56; prof. sci. Troy (Ala.) State Coll., 1956-68; prof. sci. edn. Columbus (Ga.) Coll., 1968—; vis. prof. George Peabody Coll., summers 1959-61, Fla. Inst. Tech., summers 1970-73; vis. prof. sci. edn. Auburn U., 1966-68; vis. grad. prof. aerospace sci. U. P.R., 1972-73; coordinator S.E. Ala. Ednl. Media Project, 1966-67. Ednl. cons. in sci. Internat. Paper Co. Spl. Inst., Camden, Ark., 1960. Chmn. aid com. local A.R.C., 1962; radiol. officer Pike County (Ala.) Civil Def. Authority, 1963—; mem. nat. aerospace edn. adv. com. Civil Air Patrol-USAF. Served to col. USAAF, 1944-46. Recipient citation Civil Air Patrol, 1969, 70. Ford scholar, 1963-64; Kettering fellow, 1967-68. Fellow A.A.A.S., Ala. Acad. Sci.; mem. Nat. Aerospace Edn. Council, N.E.A., Nat. Sci. Tchrs. Assn., Miss. Acad. Sci., Nat. Assn. Research Sci. Teaching, Nat. Aerospace Edn. Assn., Kappa Delta Pi, Phi Delta Kappa, Pi Kappa Delta. Contbr. articles to profl. jours. Home: 2214 Coventry Dr Columbus GA 31904

RIGSBY, MARGUERITE LORENE SPIEGLE (MRS. GILBERT L. RIGSBY), librarian; b. Ensley, Ala.; d. Alonzo D. and Lena S. (Higgins) Spiegle; B.S., Auburn U., 1951; postgrad. Peabody Coll., 1965; m. Gilbert L. Rigsby, Apr. 25, 1934; children—Gilbert Lynn, Marguerite Lorene (Mrs. David Gerald Parsons), Charles Owen. Tchr., Cullman County (Ala.) Sch. System, 1931-44, sch. prin., 1944-51; tchr. Cullman City Sch. System, 1952-62; adminstr. Cullman County Pub. Library, 1962—. Bd. dirs. Music Concert Series, 1965-67. Mem. A.L.A. (chmn. publicity pub. libraries div. 1964-65, sec. div. 1967-68, pres. div. 1972-73, chmn. membership com.), Cullman Fedn. Garden Clubs (civic project chmn. 1964-65), Ch. Women United (pres. 1967), Cullman County Hist. Assn. (charter), Ala. Writers Conclave, Delta Kappa Gamma (pres. 1962-64), Alpha Beta Alpha. Mem. Christian Ch. (stewardess 1963-64, sec. bd. 1964-65, dir. youth groups 1947-54, choir dir., 1951-68). Club: Green Earth Garden (pres. 1963-65). Home: 212 12th NE Cullman AL 35055 Office: 200 Clark St Cullman AL 35055

RILEY, BOB COWLEY, lt. gov. of Ark., educator; b. Little Rock, Sept. 18, 1924; s. Columbus Allen and Winnie Mae (Craig) R.; B.A., U. Ark., 1950, M.A., 1951, Ed.D., 1957; m. Claudia Zimmerman, May 26, 1956; 1 dau., Megen. Broker, Freeling Ins. Agy., Little Rock, 1951; instr. Little Rock U., 1951-55; prof. history and polit. sci. Ouachita Baptist U., Arkadelphia, Ark., 1955—, chmn. dir. social sci., 1960—, chmn. dept. polit. sci., 1960—; past solicitor fire and casualty ins. Ark. Ins. Dept.; mem. Ark. Ho. of Reps., 1948-50, parliamentarian, 1969—; lt. gov. State of Ark., Little Rock, 1971—. Cons., Mitchellville Community Devel. Project, 1968. Founder, pres. U. Ark. Young Democrats Club; mem. Arkadelphia City Council, 1960-64, fire commr., mayor, 1965-66; del. Dem. Nat. Conf., 1968. Bd. dirs. Internat. Services for Blind, Nat. Accreditation Council for Agys. Serving Blind and Visually Handicapped. Served with USMCR, 1941-45; PTO. Recipient Distinguished Service award Ark. Municipal League. Mem. Am. Polit. Sci. Assn., Nat. Council Social Studies, Am. Assn. U. Profs., Am. Inst. Parliamentarians, Blinded Vets. Assn. (Nat. Achievement award 1963), D.A.V., Blue Key, Phi Eta Sigma, Phi Alpha Theta, Phi Delta Kappa, Psi Chi, Alpha Phi Omega, Sigma Chi. Baptist. K.P., Eagle, Moose, Rotarian, Knights Korassan. Author: They Never Came Back, 1959; The Party that Almost Was, 1960; The Reorganization of the Arkansas State Legislature, 1969. Home: 1076 Presidents Circle Arkadelphia AR 71293 Office: State Capitol Room 300 Little Rock AR

RILEY, HARRY PAUL, accountant; b. DeQuincy, La., Jan. 10, 1927; s. Thomas Fogg and Lola Marie (Morreau) R.; B.S., U. Omaha, 1963; M.Profl. Accounting, U. Tex., 1968; m. Cloyce Alta Carter, Oct. 5, 1946; children—Rozanne, Paul Alan. Staff accountant Touche Ross and Co., Austin, Tex., 1967-68; controller John Roberts, Inc., Austin, 1968-69; internal auditor Tracor, Inc., Austin, 1969-70; asst. state auditor, Austin, 1970-73; pvt. practice accounting, Austin, 1973—. Served to maj., USAF, 1945-65. C.P.A., Tex. Mem. Nat. Assn. Accountants (dir. 1968-73), Tex. Soc. C.P.A.s (com. chmn. Austin chpt. 1971-73), Am. Inst. C.P.A.s, Phi Kappa Phi. Address: 828 Valley Forge Dr Austin TX 78753

RILEY, JEANNIE C. STEPHENSON (MRS. MITCHELL E. RILEY), vocalist, entertainer; b. Stamford, Tex., Oct. 19, 1945; d. Oscar W. and Nora (Moore) Stephenson; grad. high sch., Anson, Tex.; m. Mitchell E. Riley, Dec. 20, 1963; 1 dau., Kim Michelle. Vocalist, rec. artist popular music; TV appearances include Bob Hope, Hollywood Palace, Joey Bishop, Am. Bandstand, Happening '68, Upbeat, Top of Pops (Eng.) shows. Rec. Harper Valley P.T.A. voted no. 2 single, recipient gold record Rec. Industry Assn. Am., 1968, also recipient gold record for Harper Valley P.T.A. Album, 1968; Harper Valley P.T.A. voted no. 1 Country and Western single Country Music Assn., 1968; voted most promising female vocalist pop field Record World Poll, 1968 and Cash Box Poll, 1968; recipient Gold Cartridge award. Mem. Country Music Assn., Nat. Acad. Rec. Arts and Scis. Address: 806 16th Av S Nashville TN 37203

RILEY, JOHN ROBERT, utility co. exec.; b. Dunn, N.C., July 5, 1913; s. John Manly and Mona (Phillips) R.; grad. in journalism, U. N.C., 1933; m. Neta Lee Townsend, Mar. 10, 1945; children—John Randolph, Lewis Cooper, Neta Vernessa. Reporter, Dunn Dispatch, 1932-33; editor, The Graphic, Nashville, N.C., 1933-37; capital reporter, columnist, Sunday editor The News and Observer, 1937-50; prof. journalism U. N.C., 1950-51, also bd. govs. U. Press and faculty mem. Publs. Bd.; joined Carolina Power & Light Co., Raleigh, N.C., 1951, publicity dir., 1951-63, asst. dir., pub. relations dept., 1963-64, v.p. pub. affairs, 1964—. Pres., Raleigh Concert Music Assn., 1958-60; pres. Wake County Tb Assn., 1958-60. Bd. dirs. U.S. Indsl. Council. Served to maj. USMCR, 1942-46; PTO. Mem. U.S. C. of C. (agrl. com.), N.A.M. (pub. affairs com.). Club: Raleigh Executives (pres. 1961-62). Mem. Christian Ch. (bd. chmn. 1960-61; tchr. Sunday sch. 1946-69; elder). Home: 611 Smedes Pl Raleigh NC 27605 Office: 336 Fayetteville St Raleigh NC 27602

RILEY, JOHN THOMAS, educator; b. Bardstown, Ky., Apr. 2, 1942; s. John Norris and Mary Frances (Jury) R.; B.S., Western Ky. U., 1964; Ph.D., U. Ky., 1968; m. Rita Caroll Hayes, Dec. 23, 1963; children—Sheila Marie, John Paul. Student asso. IBM, Lexington, Ky., summer 1967; asst. prof. chemistry Western Ky. U., Bowling Green, 1968—. NSF grantee Rensselaer Polytech. Inst., summer 1972. Mem. Am. Chem. Soc., Sigma Xi, Kappa Sigma. Democrat. Roman Catholic (ch. treas. 1973—). Author: (with C.M. Wilkerson) An Introduction to Semimicro Qualitative Analysis, 1971. Home: 1511 Woodhurst Dr Bowling Green KY 42101

RILEY, JOSEPH (JOE) PATRICK, ins. co. exec.; b. Charleston, S.C., Apr. 11, 1912; s. Andrew J. and Mary (Oliver) R.; student U. S.C., 1932; LL.D., The Citacel, 1966; m. Helen Schachte, Nov. 1939; children—Joseph P., Suzanne (Mrs. Keith Emge), Mary (Mrs. Chambers), Jane (Mrs. Gerard S. Stelling). Salesman Investor syndicate Co., Charleston, 1933; agt. Life Ins. Co. Va., Charleston, 1934-37; pres. Joseph P. Riley Real Estate & Ins. Co., Charleston, 1937—; pres. Cooper Corp., Charleston, 1954—, East Oak Forest Corp., Charleston, 1948—; dir. First Fed. Savs. & Loan Assn., Charleston; mem. adv. bd. Citizens & So. Nat. Bank of S.C., Charleston, 1945—. Chmn. Charleston Municipal Auditorium Dedication Week, 1968, Charleston Tricentennial Parade Com., 1970, chmn. fund drives United Fund, 1955, Cancer Crusade, 1965; chmn. Azalea Fest., Inc., 1949—; treas. St. Francis Hosp. Devel. Found., 1965—; mem. Charleston Devel. Bd., 1950-70, Citadel Ednl. Found., 1954—, German Friendly Soc., 1935—, Hibernian Soc. Charleston, 1934—, study com. Nat. Naval Mus.; organizer, permanent soc. Mendel Rivers Monument Com., 1971—. Mgr., treas. campaigns Mendel Rivers for Congress, 1939-71. Bd. dirs. S.C. Port Authority, Coll. of Charleston Found., also chmn. fund-raising com.; bd. dirs. Merchants Housing Corp. of Charleston County, A.R.C., Coastal Carolina council Boy Scouts Am., Found. Modern Liquor Regulations and Controls. Recipient Meritorious Pub. Service citation Sec. Navy, 1968, Navy League award, 1966. Mem. Charleston (chmn. urban redevel. com. 1945—), S.C., U.S. (dir. 1954-58) chambers commerce, U.S. Navy League (bd. dirs.), New Eng. Soc., S.C. Soc., Charleston County Navy League (pres.), Charleston Bd. Ins. Underwriters (past pres.), Charleston Bd. Realtors, New Eng. Soc., S.C. Assn. Ins. and Casualty Underwriters, S.C. Bldg. and Loan Assn. (chmn. 9th dist. legls. com.). Lion, K.C. (40). Clubs: Carolina Yacht, Charleston Propeller. Home: 74 Murray Blvd Charleston SC 29401 Office: 13 Broad St Charleston SC 29401

RILEY, JULIUS ELWOOD, hosp. adminstr.; b. Sayre, Okla., Dec. 12, 1918; s. Aubrey Ivan and Mattie May (Davis) R.; B.S. in Edn., U. Okla., 1947, M.Ed., 1954; m. Wanda Marie Inman, July 21, 1940; children—Gary Benton, Peggy Lynne, (Mrs. Larry Gene Girton). Prin. South Side High Sch., Elmer, Okla., 1946-49; supt. schs., 1949-53; supt. schs. Gotebo (Okla.) High Sch., 1953-57; dist. rep. Nat. Educators Life Ins. Co., Fort Worth, 1957; supt. schs. Shattuck, Okla., 1958-60; adminstr. Newman Meml. Hosp., Shattuck, Okla., 1960—. Mem. State Okla. Textbook Commn., 1958-60; mem. Okla. High Sch. Athletic Assn. Bd. Control, 1958-60; mem. govs. adv. bd. Okla. Dept. Pub. Health for Okla. Nursing Homes, 1964-70. Precinct chmn. Democratic Party, Shattuck, Okla., 1960-67. Served with USNR, 1944-46. Mem. Jackson County Sch. Mens Assn. (pres. 1952), Okla. Hosp. Assn. (v.p. 1969-70, pres. 1971-72), Am. Coll. Hosp. Adminstrs., Purchasing Agts. Am. (asso.), Am. Hosp. Assn., Shattuck C. of C. (pres. 1960), Am. Legion, Phi Delta Kappa. Methodist. Mason; mem. Order Eastern Star; Lion. Home: 605 E 7th St Shattuck OK 73858 Office: 919 S Main St Shattuck OK 73858

RILEY, MAX LEROY, oil co. exec.; b. Shamrock, Okla., Apr. 10, 1917; s. Fred Leroy and Mae (McIlroy) R.; B.S., U. Okla., 1940; m. Maxine Koelling, July 3, 1938; 1 son, Max Leroy. Petroleum engr. Anco Gas Corp., Palestine, Tex., 1940-47; chief engr. S.W. Gas Producing Co., Monroe, La., 1947-49, chief engr., asst. mgr., 1949-54, v.p., gen. mgr., 1954-66, exec. v.p., 1966-71, pres., 1971-73, also dir.; v.p. Devon Corp., Oklahoma City, 1973—; pres. Commonwealth Gas Corp., N.Y.C., Monla Gas Co., Inc., Monroe, Carbons Consol., Inc., Monroe, Ouachita Nat. Bank, Monroe, Natural Gas Processors Assn. Mem. natural gas com. Monroe Utilities Commn. Pres., Twin Cities YMCA, 1955-56, chmn. bldg. fund campaign, 1966-67; Monroe area chmn. United Givers Fund Campaign, 1967; mem. biracial com. sch. affairs, 1971. Bd. dirs. YMCA, Monroe, 1957-57, 60-62. Recipient award B'nai B'rith, Monroe, 1958. Mem. Am. Petroleum Inst., Am. Inst. Mining, Metall. and Petroleum Engrs., Monroe C. of C. (v.p. 1965-67, dir. 1956-58, 65-67). Mem. Ch. of Christ (elder 1967—). Home: 1306 Speed Av Monroe LA 72101 Office: 1220 N 18th Monroe LA 72101

RILEY, RAY JOE, agronomist; b. Plainview, Tex., May 11, 1935; s. James Ray and Edna (Davis) R.; student Tex. A. and M. U., 1952-53; B.S. with high honors, Tex. Tech U., 1956, postgrad. 1956-57; m. Jo Eddy Scott, Oct. 7, 1961; children—Kevin Ray, Jodie Ed. Instr. agronomy, registered plant breeder Tex. Tech U., 1957; registered plant breeder Riley Farms, Hart, Tex., 1958-59; registered plant breeder, agronomist Riley Yieldmaster Seed Corp., 1960, exec. v.p., 1961—; v.p., dir. Six R Cattle Co., Bonham, Tex., 1965—; pres., dir. Estacado Industries Inc., Dimmitt, Tex.; partner Four Way Cattle Co. Dir. Running Water Soil and Water Conservation Dist., 1973; pres. bd. trustees Springlake Earth Ind. Sch. Dist., 1974—. Vice-chmn. High Plains Research Found. Served with AUS, 1958. Mem. Plains Cotton Growers Inc. (pres. 1971-74, chmn. bd. 1974—), Tex. Assn. Cotton Producer Orgns. (dir. 1971—), Tex. Certified Seed Producers Inc. (dir. 1966-68), Alpha Zeta, Phi Eta Sigma, Alpha Chi. Democrat. Mem. Ch. of Christ. Author (with Chester C. Jaynes and Coleman Y. Ward) A Laboratory Manual for Freshmen Agronomy Students, 1957. Patentee shelled corn-cottonseed animal feed, 1972. Home: Route 2 Hart TX 79043

RILEY, RICHARD WILSON, lawyer; b. Greenville, S.C., Jan. 2, 1933; s. Edward Patterson and Martha Elizabeth (Dixon) R.; B.A., Furman U., 1954; D.J., U. S.C., 1959; m. Ann Osteen Yarborough, Aug. 23, 1957; children—Richard Wilson, Anne Y., Hubert D., Theodore D. Admitted to S.C. bar, 1960, since practiced in Greenville; partner firm Riley & Riley, 1960; mem. S.C. Ho. Reps., 1963-66, Senate, 1966—, chmn. coms. on aging and jud. reform. Vice pres. S.C. Young Democrats, 1958. Served with USNR, 1954-56. Named Outstanding Young Man of Year, S.C. Jr. C. of C., 1965. Mem. Furman U. Alumni Assn. (pres. 1969-70), Sigma Alpha Epsilon, Phi Delta Phi, Omicron Delta Kappa, Blue Key. Rotarian. Home: 200 Sunset Dr Greenville SC 29605 Office: Box 10084 218 Henrietta St Greenville SC 29603

RILEY, THOMAS NOLAN, chemist, educator; b. Mishawaka, Ind., Dec. 2, 1939; s. James Bertram and Grace Elizabeth (Nolan) R.; B.S. in Pharmacy, U. Ky., 1963; Ph.D. in Medicinal Chemistry, U. Minn., 1969; m. Phyllis Ann Wethington, Nov. 26, 1960; children—Thomas Nolan, Mark Slack. Research trainee Pub. Health Service U. Minn., Mpls., 1967-69; asst. prof. medicinal chemistry U. Miss., University, 1969-72, asso. prof., 1972—, senator, faculty senate, 1972-73. Mem. A.A.A.S., Am. Chem. Soc., Am. Assn. Colls. Pharmacy, Sigma Xi, Rho Chi, Phi Delta Chi (dir. southeastern region 1972—). Home: 400 Vivian St Oxford MS 38655 Office: School of Pharmacy University of Mississippi University MS 38677

RILEY, WILLIAM WHITCOMB, pipe co. exec.; b. Tyler, Tex., May 28, 1932; s. Eugene Benton and Cathelene (Porter) B.; A.A., summa cum laude, Tyler Jr. Coll., 1968; B.B.A., East Tex. U., 1970; m. Mary Kathryn Malone, Mar. 31, 1950; children—Laura Ann, William Benton, Melissa Lynn, Kevin Lee. Store mgr., Butler, Inc., Atlanta, 1951-56; sales rep., Armour and Co., Ft. Worth, 1956-58; dir. transp. distbn. and materials Tyler Pipe Industries, 1958—. Mem. Am. Foundrymen's Soc., Am. Prodn. and Inventory Control Soc., Alpha Chi. Home: 8237 Columbia Dr Tyler TX 75701 Office: PO Box 2027 Tyler TX 75701

RINEHART, EDWIN OLAND, JR., educator, lawyer; b. Findlay, O., May 29, 1943; s. Edwin Oland and Dorothy Lee (Lewis) R.; student U. Notre Dame, 1961-63; B.B.A., So. Meth. U., 1965; M.B.A., U. Tex., 1966, J.D., 1969; m. Jennie Marie Piccola, Oct. 7, 1967; children—Edwin III, Angela Marie, Kathleen Marie. Asso. prof. accounting, law St. Edward's U., Austin, Tex., 1968—; admitted to Tex. bar, 1968; practice law, Austin, 1968—. Mem. adv. bd. Big Bros. Austin, 1971—; mem. Balcones Village Homeowner's Assn., 1971—. Recipient Outstanding Tchr. award St. Edward's U., 1969, 71; named One of Outstanding Educators Am., 1971. C.P.A., Tex. Mem. Am. Bar Assn., Tex. Soc. C.P.A.'s State Bar Tex. Roman Catholic. Club: Balcones Country (Austin). Home: 8812 Balcones Club Dr Austin TX 78759 Office: 512 E Riverside Dr Austin TX 78704

RINGER, LARRY JOEL, educator, statistician; b. Cedar Rapids, Ia., Sept. 24, 1937; s. Joel Burnett and Frances Margaret (Hummer) R.; B.S., Ia. State U., 1959, M.S., 1962; Ph.D., Tex. A. and M. U., 1966; m. Jean Bradley, Nov. 26, 1960; children—Margaret, Michael, Susan. Mem. faculty Inst. Statistics, Tex. A. and M. U., College Station, 1965—, asso. prof. statistics, 1969—; cons. Tex. Transp. Inst., 1971—. Served to 1st lt. AUS, 1961-63. Mem. Am. Statis. Assn., Am. Soc. Quality Control, Tex. Acad. Sci., Sigma Xi, Pi Mu Epsilon, Phi Kappa Phi. Kiwanian (sec. 1972—). Home: 702 Thomas St College Station TX 77840

RINGOLD, ANTHONY FORMAN, lawyer; b. Tulsa, Aug. 6, 1931; s. Murray and Ida (Forman) R.; A.B.,*U. Mich., 1953, LL.B., 1955; M.A., U. Tulsa, 1972; m. Francine Leffler, June 7, 1955; children—Leslie Beth, John Stephen, James Andrew, Suzanne. Admitted to Okla. bar, 1955; practice law, Tulsa, 1957—; mem. Rosenstein, Fist & Ringold, 1965—; sec., dir. CCI Corp., Tulsa, 1958—; Selco, Inc., Tulsa, 1970—. Adj. prof. law U. Tulsa, 1960—. Counsel, bd. dirs. Planned Parenthood Assn. Tulsa, 1963-74. Served with inf. AUS, 1955-57. Mem. Am., Okla., Tulsa County bar assns. Home: 122 E 25th St Tulsa OK 74114 Office: McFarlin Bldg Tulsa OK 74103

RINHART, FLOYD LINCOLN, author; b. Newark, N.J. Sept. 24, 1915; s. William Edward, Sr. and Elizabeth (Nodwell) R.; student Randolph Macon Coll., 1931-33; m. Marion Rebecca Hutchinson, Mar. 3, 1935; children—Joan (Mrs. Bernard N. Johnson), George Robert. With Lindsley Lumber Co., Miami, Fla., 1949-65, sales mgr., 1952-65; author, Melbourne Beach, Fla., 1963—. Cons. Ohio State U., Am. Pioneer Photography, 1973—. Mem. Royal Photog. Soc. (London). Author: American Daguerreian Art, 1967; American Miniature Case Art, 1969; America's Affluent Age, 1971. Contbg. editor New Daguerreian Jour., 1971—. Home: Route 3 Box 340 Melbourne Beach FL 32951

RINHART, MARION HUTCHINSON (MRS. FLOYD LINCOLN RINHART), author; b. Bradley Beach, N.J., Feb. 20, 1916; d. Harry Kelly and Bertha (Gifford) Hutchinson; grad. high sch.; m. Floyd Lincoln Rinhart, Mar. 3, 1935; children—Joan Carol (Mrs. Bernard Johnson), George Robert. Self-employed as author, 1960—; cons. Am. pioneer photography Ohio State U., 1973—. Mem. Photog. Hist. Soc. N.Y., Daguerrean Soc. Author: American Daguerreian Art, 1967; American Miniature Case Art, 1969; America's Affluent Age, 1971. Contbr. editor: The New Daguerreian Journal. Address: Box 340 Route 3 Melbourne Beach FL 32951

RINK, JOHN FELIX, pub. co. exec.; b. Salisbury, N.C., Feb. 7, 1927; s. Hillery Hudson and Carrie (Fleming) R.; B.A., Catawba Coll., 1949; m. Emily Anne Honeycutt, Aug. 14, 1949; children—Jennifer Anne, John Felix. With Post Pub. Co., Salisbury, 1943—, gen. mgr., 1968-70, gen. mgr., 1971—. Active Heart Fund, United Fund. Served with USNR, 1945-46. Named Lion of Year, 1969. Mem. Mid-Atlantic Circulation Mgrs. Assn. (pres. 1967-68), So. Newspaper Pubs. Assn., So. Prodn. Program. Democrat. Methodist. Lion (bd. dirs.), Elk. Home: 203 Maupin Av Salisbury NC 28144 Office: 131 W Innes St Salisbury NC 28144

RINKER, RICHARD NEWTON, clergyman; b. New Britain, Conn., Feb. 17, 1929; s. William Melvin and Helen Dorothy (Dix) R.; B.A., U. Conn., 1952; M.Div., Hartford Theol. Sem., 1955; m. Edna Jane Glidden, Aug. 22, 1953; children—Mark Craig, Cindy Jane, Sharon Jeanne. Pastor Bloomfield Congl. Ch., Pitts., 1955-59; minister of Christian edn. Pa. Conf. Congl. Christian Chs., Milroy, 1959-62, So. Conf. United Ch. Christ, Burlington, N.C., 1962—. Author: East Burlap Parables, 1969. Home: Route 7 Box 46DDD Burlington NC 27215 Office: PO Box 2410 Burlington NC 27215

RIOPELLE, ARTHUR JEAN, psychologist educator; b. Thorp, Wis., Apr. 22, 1920; s. Wilfred G. and Ann Marie (Schroeder) R.; B.S., U. Wis., 1941, M.S., 1948, Ph.D., 1950; m. Mary Jane Astell, May 2, 1942; children—Mary Ann, James, Jean. Asst. prof., asso. prof. Emory U., 1950-57; dir. psychology div. U.S. Army Med. Research Lab., Ft. Knox, Ky., 1957-59; dir. Yerkes Labs. Primate Biology, Orange Park, Fla., 1959-62; dir. Delta Regional Primate Research Center, Tulane U., Covington, La., 1962-72; prof. La. State U., 1972—. Served with AUS, 1942-46. Mem. Am., So. psychol. assns., Am. Physiol. Soc., Soc. for Neurosci., Internat. Primatology Soc., Gerontol. Soc., Am. Inst. for Biol. Sci., A.A.A.S., Am. Assn. Phys. Anthropologists, Sigma Xi. Home: 9710 Highland Rd Baton Rouge LA 70810

RIOUX, ROBERT LESTER, govt. geologist; b. Natick, Mass., June 11, 1927; s. Alphonse Charles and Flore Laura (Delage) R.; B.A., U. N.H., 1953; M.S. (Univ. fellow), U. Ill., 1955, Ph.D., 1958; m. Carmen Joyce Calva, Oct. 18, 1958; children—Carmen Flore, Therese Edith, Jacqueline Elise, Robert Charles, Catherine Marie, Richard Walter. Geologist, U.S. Geol. Survey, Denver, 1955-61, asst. regional geologist, and map editor, 1961-63, asst. chief Br. Mineral Evaluation, Washington, 1963-72, asst. div. chief resource evaluation, Reston, Va., 1972—. Served with USNR, 1945-49. Shell Oil Co. grantee, 1955-56. Recipient Meritorious Service award Dept. Interior, 1968. Fellow Geol. Soc. Am.; mem. Am. Inst. Profl. Geologists (v.p. Va. sect. 1973—), Am. Assn. Petroleum Geologists, (capital dist. rep. 1968-69), Colo. Sci. Soc., Geol. Soc. Washington, Phi Beta Kappa, Phi Kappa Phi. Home: 10112 Ranger Rd Fairfax VA 22030 Office: US Geol Survey Nat Center Reston VA 22030

RIPLEY, KENNETH CLAY, physicist; b. Winchester, Ind., Apr. 17, 1904; s. Giles E. and Harriet L. (Marsh) R.; B.M.E., U. Ark., 1927; M.Sc., U. Pitts., 1932; m. Ellen Kearns, Dec. 28, 1949; 1 dau., Margaret M. Asst. engr. Research Labs., Westinghouse Electric & Mfg. Co., 1927-31; instr. machine design Purdue U., 1935; asst. physicist Naval Research Lab., 1936-39; asst. engr., asso. physicist, physicist, research group Bur. Ships, 1939-49; staff, comdr. Joint Task Force ONE (Operation Crossroads), 1946; sr. physicist (fluid dynamics) sci. sect. Bur. Ships, 1949-60; cons. on roll stblzn. of ships John J. McMullen Assoc., Inc., naval architects, N.Y.C.; self-employed fluid mechanics physicist, inventor, 1960—. Mem. Am. Phys. Soc., Tau Beta Pi. Methodist. Author: (with Dr. O.G. Tietjens) Air Resistance of High-Speed Trains and Inter-urban Cars. Home: 3058 Harrison St NW Washington DC 20015

RIPLEY, S(IDNEY) DILLON, 2D, zoologist, museum dir.; b. N.Y.C., Sept. 20, 1913; s. Louis Arthur and Constance Baillie (Rose) R.; grad. St. Paul's Sch., 1932; B.A., Yale, 1936, M.A., 1961; Ph.D., Harvard, 1943; D.H.L., Marlboro Coll., 1965, Williams Coll., 1972; D.Sc. (hon.), George Washington U., 1966, Catholic U., 1968, U. Md., 1970, U. Cambridge (Eng.), 1974; LL.D., (hon.), Dickinson Coll., 1967, Hofstra U., 1968; m. Mary Moncrieffe Livingston, Aug. 18, 1949; children—Julie Dillon, (Mrs. Robert S. Ridgely), Rosemary Livingston, Sylvia McNeill. Staff, Acad. Natural Sci., Phila., 1936-39; vol. asst. Am. Mus. Natural History of N.Y., 1939-40; teaching asst. Harvard, 1941-42; asst. curator bds. Smithsonian Instn., Washington, 1942, sec., 1964—; lectr., asso. curator Yale, 1946-52, asst. prof., 1949-55, curator, 1952-64, asso. prof. zoology, 1955-61, prof. biology, 1961-64; expdns. to South Pacific, S.E. Asia, India, Nepal; dir. Peabody Mus. Natural History, 1959-64. Dir. Am. Security & Trust Co. Trustee Henry Francis du Pont Winterthur Mus., White Meml. Found.; pres. Internat. Council of Bird Preservation; bd. dirs. U.S. chpt. World Wildlife Fund. Served as civilian with OSS, 1942-45. Decorated Order White Elephant, Freedom medal (Thailand). Fulbright fellow, 1950, Guggenheim fellow, 1954; NSF fellow, 1954; recipient Gold medal N.Y. Zool. Soc., Royal Zool. Soc. Antwerp, Ord Arts et Lettres (France). Fellow A.A.A.S., Nat. Acad. Scis., Am. Ornithologists Union, Zool. Soc. India; mem. Council Fgn. Relations, Am. Naturalists Soc., Brit. Ornithol. Union, French (corr.), Argentine (corr.), S. African, New Zealand, Copper ornithol. socs., Soc. Systematic Zoology, Bombay Natural History Soc., Soc. Study Evolution, Wilson Soc., Internat. Wild Waterfowl Assn., Sigma Xi. Author: Trail of the Money Bird, 1942; Search for the Spiny Babbler, 1952; A Paddling of Ducks, 1957; (with L. Scribner) Ornithological Books in Yale Library; Synopsis Birds Indian and Pakistan, 1961; Land and Wildlife of Tropical Asia, 1964; (with Salim Ali) A Handbook of Indian Birds, 9 vols., 1968—; The Sacred Grove, 1969. Home: 2324 Massachusetts Av NW Washington DC 20008 also Litchfield CT 06759

RIPLEY, THOMAS HUNTINGTON, govt. ofcl.; b. Bennington, Vt., Nov. 18, 1927; s. Robert M. and Sue (Huntington) R.; B.S., Va. Poly. Inst., 1951, Ph.D., 1958; M.S., U. Mass., 1954; m. Anne Cabel Browning, June 16, 1948; children—Elizabeth, James, Constance. Grad. fellow U. Mass., Amherst, 1951-53; leader research project Mass. Div. Fisheries and Game, Marstons Mills, 1953-56; instr. biology Va. Poly. Inst., Blacksburg, 1956-57; leader research project Va. Commn. Game and Inland Fisheries, Blacksburg, 1957-58; with U.S. Forest Service, 1958-69, asst. dir. Southeastern Forest Expt. Sta., Asheville, N.C., 1965-67, asst. to dept. chief, Washington, 1967-69; dir. Forestry, Fisheries and Wildlife div. TVA, Norris, Tenn., 1969—. Adj. prof. Va. Poly. Inst., Blacksburg, 1965—, dept. forestry, U. Tenn., Knoxville, 1970—; mem. curriculum adv. com. Sch. Forestry, U. Fla., Gainesville, 1964—; mem. Pres.'s Recreation Adv. Study Com. on Measurement of Outdoor Recreation, Washington, 1965-68. Served with USNR, 1946-47. Mem. Soc. Am. Foresters, Wildlife Soc., Am. Fisheries Soc., Sigma Xi, Phi Sigma, Xi Sigma Phi, Alpha Zeta, Phi Kappa Phi, Omicron Delta Kappa. Episcopalian. Home: 7134 Cheshire Dr Knoxville TN 37919 Office: TVA Norris TN 37828

RIPPY, WILSON CRUNK, JR., physician; b. Tampa, Fla., Dec. 11, 1926; s. Wilson Crunk and Ollie (Lankford) R.; student Ga. Sch. Tech., 1944-45, Emory U., 1946-48, B.S., 1949, M.D., 1952; m. Betty Joan Cross, Dec. 22, 1951 (div.); children—Douglas Wilson, Alice Joan, Elizabeth Ann. Intern medicine VA Hosp., Atlanta, 1952-53, resident medicine, 1953-54; asst. resident neurology and psychiatry U. Va. Hosp., Charlottesville, 1954-56; resident child psychiatry N.C. Meml. Hosp., Chapel Hill, 1956-57, fellow child psychiatry, 1957-58; clin. dir. Childrens Psychiat. Unit, Murdoch Center, Butner, N.C., 1958-63; gen. practice child psychiatry, Tampa, Fla., 1963—; clin. asst. prof. child psychiatry U. Fla. Coll. Medicine, 1964—; asst. prof child psychiatry Coll. Medicine, U. South Fla., 1972—; staff Tampa Gen. Hosp., 1964—, St. Joseph Hosp., 1965—; dir. child-adolescent psychiat. service St. Elizabeth Hosp., Tampa. cons. Fla. Div. Vocational Rehab., 1966—, Guidance Center of Hillsborough County, 1966—, MacDill Air Force Hosp., 1966—. Bd. dirs. Hillsborough County Mental Health Assn.; profl. adv. com. MacDonald Found., Tampa; bd. dirs. Donald S. Hendrick Found., Tampa. Served with USNR, 1945-46. Diplomate in psychiatry and child psychiatry Am. Bd. Psychiatry and Neurology. Fellow Am. Acad. Child Psychiatry, Am. Orthopsychiat. Assn.; mem. Am., Fla., Hillsborough County med. assns., Am. Psychiat. Assn., N.Y., N.C., Fla. acads. sci., A.A.A.S., Am. Acad. Polit. and Social Sci., Assn. Advancement Psychotherapy, Fla. Psychiat. Soc. Home: 13518 N Florida Av Tampa FL 33612 Office: 13518 N Florida Av Tampa FL 33612

RIPS, SERGE, econ. cons.; b. Minsk, Russia, Feb. 28, 1907; s. Jack and Raissa (Muravin) R.; student Royal Athenaeum and high course polit. and econ. sci., Antwerp, 1921-27. Came to U.S., 1940, naturalized 1944. Asso. with newspaper Neptune and Midi, Belgium, also mgr. ins. co., 1926-40; employed U.S. Govt., O.W.I., Bd. Econ. Warfare, Fgn. Econ. Adminstrn., 1942-45; econ. adviser to Greece, Washington 1946; adviser to Royal Thai Govt., spl. asst. on wartime financial problems to Ministry of Fgn. Affairs of Thailand, 1947-55; spl. asst. to the Pres. of Haiti, 1955; econ. cons. Washington, 1946—. Decorated officer Order Legion of Honor (France); knight comdr. Order of White Elephant (Thailand); knight comdr. Order Sacred Treasure (Japan); knight of Isabel the Cath. (Spain); knight Order of Crown (Italy); officer Order of Crown (Rumania); Order of Jade, Order of Golden Ear (China). Mem. Siam Soc. (Bangkok), Japan-Am. Soc. Club: Internat. of Washington. Home: 2801 New Mexico Av NW Washington DC 20007

RISBY, EDWARD LOUIS, microbiologist, educator; b. Clarksdale, Miss., Sept. 14, 1933; s. Van D. and Eddie Lee (Sargent) R.; B.S., Lane Coll., 1956; M.A., So. Ill. U., 1958; Ph.D. (NSF fellow), Tulane U., 1968; m. Elva Mary, Apr. 23, 1965; children—Emile, Edward, Rita. Asst. prof. biology Lane Coll., Jackson, Tenn., 1958-61, Talladega Coll., Talladega, Ala., 1961-62, So. U., New Orleans, 1962-66; asso. prof. microbiology Meharry Med. Coll., Nashville, Tenn., 1968—, also asst. dean, 1971—, chmn. com. on Instl. Research Advancement, 1972—. Active Civitans Council Boy Scouts Am. Recipient George Henry Penn award Tulane U., 1969, Instl. Research award Meharry Med. Coll., 1968, Brown-Hazen Research award, 1969, Sinsheimer award Mfrs. Hanover Trust Co., 1970. Mem. Am. Soc. Microbiology, Am. Soc. Parasitology, Soc. of Protozoologists, Alpha Phi Alpha. Home: 4023 Hydes Ferry Pike Nashville TN 37218 Office: Meharry Medical College Nashville TN 37208

RISINGER, BURTON RONALD, coll. dean; b. Lillie, La., Apr. 7, 1913; s. George Larkin and Louisa Anne (Burton) R.; A.B. cum laude, La. Poly. Inst., 1935; M.B.A., La. State U., advanced grad. student, 1937-40; m. Beatrice Wade, Dec. 31, 1932; children—Burton Ronald, Vance, Troy. Asst. La. State U., 1935-37; instr., 1937-45; asst. dean Coll. Commerce, 1939-42, purchasing agt., 1942-45; dean Coll. Bus. Adminstrn., La. Tech. U., 1945—, acting bus. mgr., 1947-48; dir. Lincoln Securities Corp., Lincoln Bank & Trust Co.; pres. Ruston Investment Corp. Mem. Beta Alpha Psi, Phi Kappa Phi, Beta Gamma Sigma, Pi Gamma Mu, Omicron Delta Kappa, Delta Sigma Pi, Sigma Iota Epsilon. Democrat. Baptist. Lion. Home: Vienna LA 71270 Office: Box 5796 Tech Station Ruston LA 71270

RISINGER, ROGER IRVIN, electronics engr.; b. Lampasas, Tex., June 8, 1944; s. John Irvin and Lois Alyne (Kirby) R.; B.S. in Elec. Engring., U. Tex. at Arlington, 1967; postgrad. So. Meth. U., 1969—; m. Grady Carol Rhodes, Apr. 5, 1968; 1 son, Eric Layne. Designer electronic systems E-Systems (formerly LTV Electrosystems), Dallas, 1967—, electronic systems engr., 1972—. Baptist. Home: 2526 Cumberland St Mesquite TX 75149 Office: PO Box 6118 Dallas TX 75222

RISKIND, REUBEN SAUL, banker; b. Eagle Pass, Tex., Mar. 28, 1919; s. Michael and Rachel (Edelstein) R.; student U. Tex. at Austin, 1937-41; m. Esther Swirce, July 6, 1941; children—David Herschel, Miriam Judith, Dan Joel. With M. Riskind, Inc., Eagle Pass, 1945—, v.p., 1945—, pres. subsidiaries The 21 Shop, 1964—, Coed Shop, 1967—; dir. 1st Nat. Bank Eagle Pass. Pres. Internat. Fiesta Assn., 1959-60, Maverick Planned Parenthood, 1969-70; chmn. Tri-County OEO, 1964-66, Jewish Welfare Bd., 1966-70, United Jewish Appeal, 1954-71. Bd. dirs. Maverick County United Fund, 1970-71; mem. bd. Eagle Pass Pub. Housing Commn., 1969-70; chmn. Eagle Pass Planning and Zoning Commn., 1969—. Del. Tex. Democratic Conv., 1960. Served with USAAF, 1941-45: CBI. Mem. Maverick County Hist. Soc., Eagle Pass C. of C. (pres. 1962-63), Sigma Alpha Mu. Democrat. Jewish religion. Home: 1919 Olive St Eagle Pass TX 78852 Office: 364 Main St Eagle Pass TX 78852

RISLEY, BURT LEROY, state ofcl.; b. San Antonio, Nov. 26, 1919; s. Clyde H. and Alice (Dillon) R.; B.B.A., U. Tex., 1948, M.B.A., 1949; postgrad. U. Colo., 1949. Supervisory tng. specialist div. extension U. Tex., Austin, 1950-52; field personnel mgr. Southeastern Drilling Co., Dallas, 1952-53; coordinator adult edn. for petroleum industry Odessa Coll., 1953-54; owner investment co., Austin, 1954-64. Mem. Nat. Citizens Adv. Com. on Vocational Rehab., 1966-68; mem. Nat. Adv. Com. on Vocational Rehab., 1970—. Bd. dirs. Tex. Commn. for Blind, Austin, 1958-64. Served with USAAF, 1940-44. Mem. Nat. Rehab. Assn., Am. Assn. Workers for Blind, Ex-Student's Assn. U. Tex., Blinded Vets. Assn. Clubs: Headliners (Austin); St. Anthony (San Antonio). Home: PO Box 12313 Capitol Station Austin TX 78711 Office: 800 City Nat Bank Bldg Austin TX 78701

RITCH, PAUL A., coll. adminstr.; b. Cedartown, Ga., May 19, 1935; s. Joseph Doyle and Dorothy Mae (Davis) R.; grad. in theology, Tenn. Temple Coll., 1960, B.A., 1963; Ed.M., U. Chattanooga, 1969, Ed.D., 1973; m. Joyce Ann Price, Sept. 4, 1970; children by previous marriage—David Allen, Dennis Paul. Data processing specialist Combustion Engring., Inc., Chattanooga, 1958-63; mgr. systems, data processing Modern Carpet Industries, Dalton, Ga., 1963-66; div. head computer sci., mgmt. Chattanooga State Tech. Community Coll., 1966—; cons. Magic Chef, Inc., Hamilton County Health Dept., Cherokee Area council Boy Scouts Am., Met. Council Community Services. Mem. Data Processing Mgmt. Assn. (treas. 1968-69, 69-70; cons. Chattanooga chpt. 1964—, chpt. and regional man of year 1974), Am., Tenn. vocational assns. Club: Sertoma (dir. Chattanooga 1972-73, pres. 1973—, Sertoman of year 1973). Home: 1634 Mary DuPre Dr Chattanooga TN 37421

RITCHEY, DAN ARCHIE, JR., realtor, appraiser, insuror, counselor; b. De Ridder, La., Oct. 7, 1917; s. Dan Archie and Lottie (Donlon) R.; student spl. comml. courses U. Southwestern La., 1936-38; grad. Realtors Inst.; m. Cecilia Kelly, Aug. 31, 1941; children—Christine Cecile, Ronald James, Susan Marie. Real estate clk., Lafayette, La., 1935-40; salesman real estate Mike Donton, Realtor, 1947-56; fee appraiser, counselor, Lafayette, 1954—; owner, operator Dan A. Ritchey, Realtor, Insuror, Lafayette, 1956—. Cons. evaluation in condemnation City of Lafayette, also various attys.; mem. Bishop's Adv. Com. Real Estate Evaluation, Lafayette, 1963—; mem. Lafayette Bd. Adjustment for Zoning, 1963—; organizer, 1st chmn. Lafayette Planning Commn., 1953-57. Dir. Civil Def. for 8 La. parishes, 1961-63. Bd. dirs. Cath. Youth Orgn., Lafayette Pub. Bldgs. Corp., United Givers. Served to maj. inf. AUS, 1940-46; ETO. Decorated Bronze Star medal; named Realtor of Yr., Lafayette Bd. Realtors, 1960. Mem. Nat., La. (past pres.), Lafayette bds. realtors, Nat. Assn. Realtors, La. Realtors Assn. (dir.), Am. Right of Way Assn. (sr.), Nat. Assn. Ind. Fee Appraisers (pres. Lafayette chpt. 1964-65, sr. appraiser, counselor), Am. Soc. Appraisers (sr.), C. of C. (dir.), Mgmt. Inst., La. Nat. Guard Assn. (life, past pres.). Kiwanian (past pres.). Home: 223 Beverly Dr Lafayette LA 70501 Office: 311 W University Av Lafayette LA 70501

RITCHIE, CHARLES WILLIAM, civil engr.; b. Louisville, May 25, 1938; s. William Coleman and Minnie (McCallum) R.; B.C.E., U. Louisville, 1962; m. N. Louise Goad, July 9, 1966; 1 son, Craig Coleman. Design engr. Hazelet & Erdal, cons. engrs., Louisville, 1962-67; chief engring. services Ky. Dept. Mental Health, 1967-74; supr. engring. design unit, engring. services, facilities service br., bur. for adminstrn. and operations Ky. Dept. for Human Resources, Frankfort, 1974—. Mem. West Point (Ky.) Vol. Fire Dept., 1956-66, sec.-treas. 1958-62. Served with AUS, 1968-69. Decorated Bronze Star medal. Mem. Am., Ky. (corr. sec. 1970-72) socs. civil engrs., Nat., Ky. socs. profl. engrs., Am. Soc. Hosp. Engrs., Am. Concrete Inst. Methodist (trustee 1969—). Home: 209 Pin Oak Pl Frankfort KY 40601 Office: PO Box 678 Frankfort KY 40601

RITCHIE, ELISAVIETTA YURIEVNA ARTAMONOFF (MRS. LYELL HALE RITCHIE), author, educator, translator; b. Kansas City, Mo.; d. George Leonidovich and Jessie (Downing) Artamonoff; degre superieur, Sorbonne, Paris, 1951; student Cornell U., 1951-53; B.A., U. Cal. at Berkeley, 1954; m. Lyell Hale Ritchie, July 11, 1953; children—Lyell Kirk, Elspeth Cameron, Alexander George. Pub. relations asst. Bay Area Council & World Trade Center, San Francisco, 1956; publicity campaign Assemblyman John Busterud, San Francisco, 1956-58; translator French, Russian, various govt. agencies, pvt. business, 1960—; grad. teaching fellow lang. dept. Am. U., 1968—; poet-in-residence Fairfax County Schs., 1972, John Eaton Sch., 1973-74. Recipient numerous prizes including Conrad Aiken prize, Reedy prize Poetry Soc. Am., 1973. Author: Readings in French-Speaking World, 1969; Timbot, 1970; Tightening the Circle Over Eel Country, 1974; transl. The Twelve (Aleksandr Blok), 1968; contbr. numerous poems, stories, articles, revs., transls. pub. in various mags. and newspapers, including N.Y. Times, Washington Post, Paris Herald Tribune, Mass. Rev., Denver Post, Denver Quar., Chgo. Tribune, Epoch, New Republic, Christian Sci. Monitor, So. Poetry Rev., others; poems reprinted in The Diamond Anthology, New Generation Poetry, Adam Among the Television Trees, other anthologies. Home: 3207 Macomb St NW Washington DC 20008

RITCHIE, ERIS ALTON, JR., coll. adminstr.; b. Athens, Ala., Apr. 18, 1935; s. Eris Alton and Mary Ethel (Tackett) R.; B.S. cum laude, Abilene Christian Coll., 1957, M.Ed., 1961; m. Annita Hartsell, July 29, 1960; children—Matthew Eris, Robin Annette. Band dir. Trent (Tex.) Pub. Schs., 1957-59, Cisco (Tex.) Pub. Schs., 1959-68; pub. relations dir., band dir. Cisco Jr. Coll., 1968—, one of 15 bands appearing in Macy's Thanksgiving Day Parade, N.Y.C., 1971, 73. Dir. Cisco Jr. Music Festival, 1960—; adjudicator for band and twirling contests, West, Central, N. Tex., 1965—; dir. summer camp clinics for baton twirlers, drum majs., cheerleaders, girls' drill teams, 1960—. Bd. dirs. Cisco Community Chest. Mem. Cisco Jr. C. of C., Cisco C. of C. (pres. 1970-71, Outstanding Young Citizen award 1964, Outstanding Citizen 1968). Mem. Ch. of Christ. Rotarian. Home: 1307 Park Dr Cisco TX 76437

RITCHIE, JERRY CARLYLE, govt. ecologist; b. Richfield, N.C., Dec. 13, 1937; s. Clarence Lee and Bernice (Ballard) R.; B.A., Pfeiffer Coll., 1960; M.S., U. Tenn., 1962; Ph.D., U. Ga., 1967; m. Carole Jean Atanasoff, Sept. 17, 1966; children—Jarryl Brooke, Karen Lynn. Researcher Oak Ridge Nat. Lab., 1962; ecologist U. Ga., Athens, 1967-68; botanist U.S. Dept. Agr. Sedimentation Lab., Oxford, Miss., 1968—. Served with AUS, 1962-64. Mem. Am. Inst. Biol. Scis., Ecol. Soc. Am., British Ecol. Soc., Agronomy Soc. Am., Assn. Southeastern Biologists. Home: 1410 Lawson St Oxford MS 38655 Office: PO Box 30 Oxford MS 38655

RITCHIE, JOE TACKETT, soil scientist; b. Palestine, Tex., June 2, 1937; s. Eris A. and Mary Ethel (Tackett) R.; B.S., Abilene Christian Coll., 1959; M.S., Tex. Tech. U., 1961; Ph.D. in Soil Physics, Ia. State U., 1964; m. Ann Allen, July 11, 1959; children—Joe Allen, Julie Kay. Prin. physicist Tex. Research Found., Renner, 1964-66; soil sci. Agrl. Research Service, U.S. Dept. Agr., Temple, Tex., 1966—. Cons. Tex. Instruments, Inc., NASA Jet Propulsion Lab.; US AID mission in India, 1971. Active Boy Scouts Am., 1969—. Bd. dirs. Abilene Christian Coll., York Coll. Named Outstanding Aggie of Year, Abilene Christian Coll., 1970. Mem. Am. Soc. Agronomy, Soil Sci. Soc. Am., Internat. Soc. Soil Sci., Am. Geophys. Union, Am. Meteorol. Soc., Research Soc. Am., Soil Conservation Soc. Am., Sigma Xi, Gamma Sigma Delta. Home: 3306 Oaklawn Temple TX 76501 Office: PO Box 748 Temple TX 76501

RITCHIE, LYELL HALE, JR., finance co. exec.; b. Chgo., Sept. 28, 1927; s. Lyell Hale and Elspeth (Wolff) R.; A.B. cum laude, Harvard, 1950; m. Elisavietta Artamonoff, July 11, 1953; children—Kirk, Cameron, Alexander. Investment analyst Wells Fargo Bank, San Francisco, 1953-56; investment analyst Dean Witter & Co., San Francisco, 1956-59; sr. v.p. Porter, Internat. Co., Washington, 1960—. Dir. Washington Home Rule Com., 1961-63. Bd. dirs. Jr. Citizens Corps, 1962-71, 12th St. YMCA, 1965-70. Served with AUS, 1950-52. Mem. Washington Soc. Investment Analysts (pres. 1972-73). Club: Seigniory (Can.). Author: National Investment Bank of Ghana, 1962; Tourism Development in Central America, 1965. Home: 3207 Macomb St NW Washington DC 20008 Office: 1776 K St NW Washington DC 20006

RITCHIE, ROBERT BROOKE, lawyer, contracting co. exec.; b. Pitts., July 5, 1918; s. Thomas C. and Elizabeth (Brooke) R.; B.A., Va. Mil. Inst., 1940; LL.B., Blackstone Sch. Law, 1972; m. Irene Gilliam, Mar. 31, 1944; children—Jean Elizabeth, Kathryn Louise, Robert Brooke. Partner, Abbott & Ritchie, gen. contractors, Richmond, Va., 1947-56; owner, mgr. R.B. Ritchie, gen. contractor, Richmond, 1956-62; pres. Contractors, Inc., Richmond, 1962—, Empire Inns, Inc., Richmond, 1966-68, Auctioneers, Inc., 1969—; dir. Va. Preferred Land Ltd., 1970-72; exec. v.p. Va. Telecasters, Inc., Richmond, 1966-69; owner, mgr. Ace Realty Co., Richmond, 1960—; partner Breezewood Motel, Williamston, N.C., 1967-68; chmn. bd. Peoples Bank of Hanover County, Mechanicsville, Va.; admitted to Va. bar, 1973, since practiced in Richmond; partner firm Conner, Hooker & Ritchie, 1973—. Served to lt. col. AUS, 1940-46. Decorated Silver Star medal, Legion of Merit, Bronze Star medal, Purple Heart with oak leaf cluster. Mem. Nat., Va. (dir.) auctioneers assn., Va. Trial Lawyers Assn., Richmond Bd. Realtors. Home: 600 Pagebrooke Dr RFD 2 Richmond VA 23233 Office: 14000 Patterson Av PO Box 4657 Richmond VA 23229

RITCHIE, RUFUS HAYNES, physicist; b. Blue Diamond, Ky., Sept. 24, 1924; s. Rufus and Eula (Haynes) R.; B.S., U. Ky., 1947, M.S., 1949; Ph.D., U. Tenn., 1959; m. Dorothy Estes, Dec. 2, 1944; children—Susan Ritchie Witkowski, David Alan. Instr. physics U. Ky., Lexington, 1948, prof. physics, 1968-69; physicist Oak Ridge Nat. Lab., 1949—; prof. physics U. Tenn., Knoxville, 1968—. Served to 2d lt., USAAF, 1943-46. Fellow Am. Phys. Soc.; mem. Health Physics Soc., Radiation Research Soc., Scientists and Engrs. for Appalachia. Contbr. numerous articles profl. jours. Home: 133 Normandy Rd Oak Ridge TN 37830 Office: Oak Ridge Nat Lab Oak Ridge TN 37830

RITTELMEYER, LOUIS FREDERICK, JR., physician, educator; b. Mobile, Ala., Dec. 23, 1924; s. Louis Frederick and Anita (Delchamps) R.; B.S., Spring Hill Coll., 1945; M.D., Med. Coll. Ala., 1947; m. Patricia Caroline Hamersly, July 9, 1949; children—Michael, James, Frederick, Paul, John, William, Robert, Anita. Intern, Mercy Hosp., Chgo., 1947-48; mem. faculties U. Tenn., 1954-55, U. Miss., 1955-59; v.p. Mead Johnson & Co., Evansville, Ind., 1960-63; resident Georgetown U. Hosp., Washington, 1963-66; asst. prof. Georgetown U. Sch. Medicine, 1966-71, asso. prof., 1971—. Cons. med. services adminstrn. Dept. Health, Edn. and Welfare, 1967—. Served with AUS, 1950-52. Diplomate Am. Bd. Psychiatry and Neurology. Fellow Am. Psychiat. Assn.; mem. Washington Psychiat. Soc. (pres. 1974—). Home: 940 Dead Run Dr McLean VA 22101 Office: 3800 Reservoir Rd Washington DC 20007

RITTENBERG, LEON HIRSCH, JR., lawyer; b. New Orleans, May 17, 1934; s. Leon H. and Katherine (Polack) R.; LL.B., Tulane U., 1959; B.S. in Econs., U. Pa., 1956; m. Cynthia Neuwirth, May 30, 1965; children—Leon Hirsch III, Andrew Philip, Babette. Admitted to La. bar, 1959; practiced in New Orleans, 1959—; partner Polack, Rosenberg & Rittenberg, New Orleans, 1964—. C.P.A., La. Mem. La., New Orleans, Am. bar assns., Am. Judicature Soc., U. Pa. Alumni Club La. (pres. 1964—), U. Pa. Alumni Clubs (nat. exec. com.). Jewish religion (v.p. synagogue). Contbr. articles to profl. jours. Home: 5300 Marcia Av New Orleans LA 70124 Office: Hibernia Bank Bldg New Orleans LA 70112

RITTENBURY, MAX SANFORD, educator, surgeon; b. Bailey, N.C., Dec. 16, 1928; s. Rom S. and Mary Elizabeth (Stanfield) R.; student The Citadel, 1946-49; M.D., Med. Coll. Va., 1953; m. Julia Margaret Brooks, Dec. 20, 1950; children—Margaret Elizabeth, Julia Anne. Intern, U.S. Naval Hosp., Bethesda, Md., 1953-54; resident in surgery Med. Coll. Va., Richmond, 1956-59, 61-62, surg. research fellow, 1959-62, USPHS research fellow, 1960-62, instr., 1962, asst. prof. surgery, 1964-66; asst. prof. surgery Med. Coll. S.C., Charleston, 1966-67, asso. prof. Med. U. S.C., Charleston, 1967-72, prof. surgery, 1972—, project dir. Trauma Center, 1969—, chmn. Univ. Assn. Emergency Med. Services, 1971—, chmn. Computer Center Adv. Com., 1971—; mem. staff Roper Hosp., Charleston. Mem. adv. com. emergency med. services S.C. Bd. Health, 1968-70, chmn. adv. council, 1970-73; program dir. studies asso. rehab. in trauma Social and Rehab. Service of U.S. Dept. Health, Edn. and Welfare, 1969-72; program dir. planning study for central tumor registry S.C. Regional Med. Program, 1968-69. Served as lt. USNR, 1953-56. Spl. research fellow USPHS, 1963-64; USPHS research grantee 1959-68, NIH research grantee 1961-66, 72—. Mem. A.C.S. (chmn. S.C. com. on trauma 1967—), Surg. Biology Club, Soc. for Surgery of Alimentary Tract, Am. Assn. Surgery of Trauma, So. Surgery Assn., Pancreas Club (nat. sec. 1970-73), Reticuloendothelial Soc., Am. Fedn. Clin. Research, Internat. Soc. for Burn Injuries, N.Y. Acad. Scis., A.A.A.S., Soc. Exptl. Biology and Medicine, S.C., Pan-Am., Alaska (hon.) med. assns., A.M.A., Am. Burn Assn., Charleston County Med. Soc., S.C. Surg. Soc. Contbr. articles on trauma and emergency surgery to med. jours., also presentations to profl. meetings. Home: 125 Broad St Charleston SC 29401 Office: Dept of Surgery Medical University of South Carolina Charleston SC 29401

RITTER, JAMES WILLIAM, JR., city ofcl.; b. High Point, N.C., Mar. 22, 1910; s. James William and Maud (Jenkins) R.; student pub. schs.; m. Catherine Luck, Dec. 26, 1939; children—James William III, Ann Robin. Civil engr. Chesapeake & O. Ry., 1929-32, Va. Dept. Hwys., 1935-42, U.S. Engrs., 1942-43, So. Ry., 1943-48; town mgr. Manassas, Va., 1948-51, Marion, Va., 1951-63, Leesburg, Va., 1963—. Mem. Internat. City Mgrs. Assn., C. of C. Baptist. Mason, Kiwanian. Address: Town Hall Leesburg VA 22075

RITTER, ROGERS CHARLES, educator; b. Pleasanton, Neb., Oct. 27, 1929; s. Frederick Julian and Bertha Margaret (Kreitzer) R.; B.S., U. Neb., 1952; Ph.D., U. Tenn., 1961; m. Marlene Marilyn Hill, Aug. 27, 1950; children—James R., William C., Michael G. Instrument engr. Oak Ridge Gaseous Diffusion Plant, 1952-59, Orau fellow Oak Ridge Nat. Lab., 1959-61; prof. physics U. Va., Charlottesville, 1961—. Cons. various hosps.; vis. scientist Acad. Zickenhuis, Leiden, Holland, 1972—. Mem. Am. Phys. Soc., Am. Assn. Phyicists in Medicine, Am. Assn. Physics Tchrs., Am. Assn. U. Profs., A.A.A.S., Internat. Continence Soc., Urodynamics Soc., Sigma Xi, Sigma Tau, Eta Kappa Nu, Delta Upsilon. Inventor urinary drop spectrometer; contbr. articles to sci. lit. Home: 118 Buckingham Rd Charlottesville VA 22903

RITTERMAN, STUART I., speech pathologist, educator; b. Bklyn., May 21, 1937; s. Nathan and Ettie (Fried) R.; B.A., N.Y. U., 1959; postgrad Coll. City N.Y., 1962-64; Ph.D., Case Western Reserve U., 1968; 1 dau. by previous marriage, Moriah. Speech clinician Bklyn. Coll. Clinic, City Univ. N.Y., Bklyn., 1963, Bergan Pines County Hosp., Paramus, N.J., 1963-64; Vocational Rehab. Adminstrn. trainee Cleve, Hearing and Speech Center, 1964-66; speech clinician Benjamin Rose Hosp., Cleve., 1965-66; NIH career investigator trainee Case Western Res. U., Cleve., 1966-68, research asso. in dental edn., 1967-68; asst. prof. dept. communication disorders U. Okla. Med. Center, Oklahoma City, 1968-69, dir. diagnostic services in speech pathology, 1968-69; asst. prof. speech pathology and audiology inst. U. S. Fla., Tampa, 1969-71, asso. prof., 1972—, dir. diagnostic services, 1969-71, acting dir. program in speech pathology and audiology Coll. Social and Behavioral Sci., 1971, dir., 1971—. Cons. in speech pathology Cleve. Soc. for Crippled Children, 1967-68, Dept. Health and Rehab. Services, Fla. Bur. for Crippled Children, Tampa, 1970—, U. Okla. Center, Oklahoma City, 1968-69, Tampa Gen. Hosp., 1970-71, Model Cities, Wolf Diagnostic Center, Tampa, 1970—, Multiphasic Evaluation and Treatment-Community Coordinated Child Care Pilot Clinic, Tampa, 1971. Dept. Dept. Health Edn. and Welfare, grantee, USPHS, 1971, Office Edn., 1971; Fla. Dept. Edn. grantee, 1971. Mem. Am., Fla. speech and hearing assns., Am. (research com. 1972—), S.E. Am. (chmn. speech pathology and audiology sec. 1969—, local arrangements chmn. ann. meeting 1971) assns. on mental deficiency, Southeastern Conf. on Linguistics, Nat. Soc. for Programmed Instrn., Linguistic Soc. Am. Contbr. articles to profl. jours. Home: 803 Bellemeade Circle Temple Terrace FL 33617 Office: U S Fla UNA 29 Tampa FL 33620

RIVENBARK, REMBERT REGINALD, shipbldg. exec.; b. St. Paul, S.C., Sept. 9, 1912; s. Reginald Vernon and Kathleen Frances (Fussell) R.; grad. Goldsboro (N.C.) High Sch.; m. Marie Barbour, July 20, 1932; children—Patricia (Mrs. Dewey H. Pate), Rembert Reginald, Herbert William Barbour. Foreman bottling dept. Coca Cola Bottling Co., New Bern, N.C., 1927-32; with Barbour Boat Works, New Bern, 1932—, successively bookkeeper, office mgr., gen. mgr., v.p., gen. mgr., 1945-57, pres., 1957-71, chmn. bd., 1957—; chmn. bd., pres. Marine Trading Corp., New Bern, 1948—; dir. Ocean Scallops, Inc. Bd. dirs. United Fund. Mem. Am. Boat Builders and Repairers Assn. (pres. 1963), Am. Boat Builders and Engine Mfrs. Assn., N.C. Med. Assn. (hon.), Am. Mgmt. Assn., U.S. C. of C., Am. Ordnance Assn., Crippled Childrens Assn. (life), N.C. Wildlife Assn., N.C. Fisheries Assn. (dir.). Methodist (ofcl. bd., chmn. commn. on stewardship and finance). Mason (Shriner), Elk, Rotarian. Club: East Carolina Yacht (charter). Home: Trent Shores Dr New Bern NC 28560 Office: 522-525 Tryon Palace Dr New Bern NC 28560

RIVERA-EMMANUELLI, RAFAEL LUIS, banker; b. Guayanilla, P.R., Apr. 11, 1933; s. Rafael Rivera and Luisa Maria Emmanuelli; B.B.A., Cath. U. P.R., 1960; postgrad. Sch. Banking U. Wis., 1963, P.R. Sch. Banking, 1972; m. Maria A. Maiz, Dec. 22, 1955; children—Rafael, Naida, Mayra, Roberto. Asst. auditor Arthur Andersen & Co., San Juan, P.R., 1960; with Banco Credito y Ahorro Ponceno, San Juan, 1960-68, asst. comptroller, 1963-68, asst. v.p. trust operations, 1968-69; bank cons. Peat, Marwick, Mitchell & Co., San Juan, 1969; v.p., comptroller Banco Economias, San Juan, 1970-73, sr. v.p., 1973—. Chmn. bd. Internat. Banking Sch., Santurce, P.R., 1973—. Mem. Club Ponce Mus. Art, 1962-65. Served with AUS, 1953-55. Mem. Am. Inst. Banking (pres. 1961-62), Bank Adminstrn. Inst. (pres. 1971-72), Financial Execs. Inst. (treas. 1973-74). P.R. Bankers Assn. (sec. 1973), Phi Sigma Alpha. Clubs: Casino de Puerto Rico (San Juan); Exchange (Rio Piedras). Home: 302 Galvez St Borinquen Gardens Rio Piedras PR 00926 Office: 221 Ponce de Leon San Juan PR 00919

RIVERS, ERNEST W., lawyer; b. Corbin, Ky., July 31, 1923; student Cumberland Coll.; LL.B., U. Ky., 1951. Admitted to Ky. bar, 1951; atty. Ky. Bd. and Dept. Health, 1951-53; 1st asst. U.S. dist. atty., 1962-65; U.S. dist. atty. for Western Dist. Ky., Louisville, 1965-70; mem. firm Melton and Rivers, Paducah, Ky. Mem. Am., Fed., Ky., Louisville, McCracken County bar assns., Phi Delta Phi. Mem. editorial staff Ky. Law Jour., 1949-51. Home: 3520 Marlborough Way Paducah KY 42001 Office: 233 N 7th St PO Box 1407 Avondale Sta Paducah KY 42001

RIVERS, ERSKINE HAROLD, clothing co. exec.; b. Gamble Mines, Ala., Dec. 3, 1921; s. Malcolm Lou and Lois (Wiggins) R.; B.A., Birmingham So. Coll., 1950; postgrad. U. Tenn., 1953-54, U. Va., 1957-58; m. Frieda Lee Bonds, Sept. 21, 1946; 1 son, Erskine Harold. With Dun & Bradstreet, Inc., 1946-61, 61-65, mgr., Birmingham, Ala., 1946-51, Knoxville, Tenn., 1952-57, Washington, 1957-61, Raleigh, N.C., 1961, account exec., Phila., 1961-64, Atlanta, 1964-65; loan rev. officer Small Bus. Adminstrn., Washington, 1961; credit mgr. Sewell Mfg. Co., Bremen, Ga., 1965—, dir., 1966—; cons. Exec. Edn., Inc., Decatur, Ga., 1967—. Trustee Bremen Gen. Hosp. Served with USAAF, 1942-45. Decorated Air medal with oak leaf cluster, Purple Heart with oak leaf cluster. Mem. Nat. Assn. Credit Mgmt., V.F.W., Phi Beta Kappa. Methodist. Rotarian (pres. Bremen 1974-75). Home: 517 Knollwood Dr Bremen GA 30110 Office: 113 Atlantic Av Bremen GA 30110

RIVES, ALBERT GORDON, lawyer; b. Birmingham, Ala., Apr. 12, 1901; s. John R.T. and Mamie Lillian (Gordon) R.; LL.B., U. Ala., 1924; m. Hester Maude Burchfield, May 22, 1926 (dec. Aug. 1963); m. 2d, Margaret Gordon Crawford, Mar. 9, 1968. Asst. dir. athletics U. Ala., 1924; admitted to Ala. bar, 1925, since practiced in Birmingham; sr. partner firm Rives, Peterson, Pettus, Conway & Burge, 1958—. Served to lt. comdr. USNR, World War II. Mem. Am., Ala., Birmingham bar assns., Internat. Assn. Ins. Counsel, Am. Judicature Soc., S.A.R., S.C.V., Ala. Hist. Soc., Phi Alpha Delta, Sigma Chi. Baptist (chmn. bd. trustees). Mason (Shriner). Clubs: Bath and Tennis (Palm Beach, Fla.); Vestavia Country, Relay House, The Club (Birmingham). Home: 3415 Pine Ridge Rd Mountain Brook Birmingham AL 35213 Office: Suite 800 1st Nat-So Natural Bldg Birmingham AL 35203

RIVES, JAMES ALLEN, civil engr.; b. Norfolk, Va., Dec. 16, 1914; s. James Allen and Catherine Holly (Drewry) R.; student Old Dominion U., 1934-36; B.S. in Civil Engring., Va. Poly. Inst., Blacksburg, 1938, M.S. in San. Engring., 1940; m. Ethel Maxine Burks, Sept. 6, 1947; children—James Allen, Frank Burks. Supt. constrn. R.R. Richardson & Assos., Norfolk, 1938-39, 41-42; san. engr. Kellogg Found., Allegan, Mich., 1940; asso. prof. civil and san. engring. Va. Poly. Inst., 1946-51, head dept. san. engring., 1949-51; cons. engr. McGaughy, Marshall & McMillan, Norfolk, 1951—. Past pres. Va. Bd. for Exam. and Certification Architects, Profl. Engrs. and Land Surveyors; past dir. N.E. Zone, Nat. Council State Bds. Engring. Examiners. Mem. Norfolk Democratic Exec. Com., 1966—, Sec., 1969-73, chmn., 1973—; co-chmn. dist. adv. Com. Dems. for Gov. Mills E. Grodwin. Pres. Larchmont-Edgewater Civic League, 1968, Naval Base Little League. Served from ensign to comdr. CEC, USNR, 1942-46. Fellow Am. Soc. C.E. (past pres. Va. sect.); mem. Va. Soc. Profl. Engrs. (past pres., recipient certificate for outstanding service), Va. Water Pollution Control Assn. (past pres.), Am. Pub. Works Assn., Am. Water Works Assn. (Old Dominion citation), Solid Wastes Inst., Chi Epsilon, Alpha Phi Omega. Mem. Legion Honor, Order DeMolay. Kiwanian. Club: Norfolk Yacht and Country. Contbr. articles profl. Jours. Home: 5401 Argall Av Norfolk VA 23508 Office: 220 W Freemason St Norfolk VA 23510

RIVES, RICHARD TAYLOR, judge; b. Montgomery, Ala., Jan. 15, 1895; s. William Henry and Alice Bloodworth (Taylor) R.; student Tulane U., 1911-12; student law in office of Hill, Hill, Whiting and Stern, Montgomery; LL.D., U. of Notre Dame, 1966; m. Jessie Hall Dougherty, July 23, 1918; children—Richard Taylor, Callie Dougherty, Jesse Hall Rives. Admitted to Ala. bar, 1914; practice in Montgomery; judge Fifth Circuit, U.S. Ct. of Appeals, 1951-59, chief judge, 1959-60, judge, 1960-66, sr. U.S. circuit judge, 1966—. Del. Democratic Conv., Chgo., 1940. Served in N.G. Mexican Border, 1915-16, served as 1st lt. Signal Corps, A.E.F., 1918-19. Mem. Montgomery (former pres.), Ala. (pres. 1939), Am. bar assns., Am. Legion, Order of Coif (hon.). Presbyn. Mason. Home: 902 Park Av Montgomery AL 36106 Office: Federal Bldg Montgomery AL 36104

RIVKIND, LEONARD MELVIN, lawyer; b. Phila., Sept. 24, 1926; s. Samuel A. and Mae E. (Polishner) R.; B.B.A., U. Miami, 1950, J.D. magna cum laude, 1954, M.L., 1971; m. Hope E. Tanenbaum, June 20, 1948 (div.); children—Teri, Mark, Brett. Admitted to Fla. bar, 1954, since practiced in Miami Beach; now partner firm Rosen & Rivkind; spl. asst. state atty.; spl. asst. atty. gen. Chmn. adv. com. to combat pornography City of Miami Beach. Served as sgt. AUS, 1945-47. Mem. Miami Beach Bar Assn. (pres. 1966), Omicron Delta Kappa, Nu Beta Epsilon, Tau Epsilon Phi. Mason. Clubs: Massachusetts of Miami (pres. 1965) (Miami Beach); Optimist (pres. 1961-62). Home: 7133 Bay Dr Miami Beach FL 33141 Office: 420 Lincoln Rd Miami Beach FL 33139

RIXSE, CHARLES EVERETT, JR., city ofcl.; b. Little Rock, Sept. 29, 1929; s. Charles E. and Myrtle (Brewer) R.; B.A., U. Ark., 1951; m. Patricia Rawls, May 29, 1948; children—Donna, Sharon, Andra. Reporter, Ark. Democrat, 1953-55, reporter, night city editor Ark. Gazette, 1955-58; mng. editor North Little Rock Times, 1958-60; sales promotion dir., sec. Southland Security Life Ins., 1960-62; mgr. Little Rock Conv. Bur., 1962-65; exec. dir. Hot Springs (Ark.) Conv. Bur., 1965-70; exec. dir. Little Rock City Advt. and Promotion Commn., 1970—, Little Rock Bur. Convs. and Visitors, 1970—, Pulaski Visitors Council, 1970—, Little Rock Conv. Center, 1970—; sec.-treas. Heart of Ark. Travel Assn., 1970—. Served with AUS, 1951-53. Mem. Internat. Assn. Conv. Burs. (dir.), Internat. Assn. Auditorium Mgrs., Am. Soc. Assn. Execs. Home: 12640 Southridge Dr Little Rock AR 72207 Office: 1 Convention Center Plaza Little Rock AR 72203

RIZER, GENE CROMWELL, army officer; b. St. Joseph, Mo., Nov. 1, 1938; s. Myron Stimpson and Virginia Josephine (Vancil) R.; B.S., U. Mo., 1960; M.S., Purdue U., 1966; m. Edna Louise Burnside, May 31, 1960; children—Dawn Michele, Steven Michael. Structural engr. McDonnell Aircraft, St. Louis, 1960-61; commd. 2d lt. U.S. Army Corps. of Engrs., 1961, advanced through grades to maj., 1968; served in Orleans, France, 1961-64, Ft. Lewis, Wash., 1966-67, Ft. Belvoir, Va., 1968-69; served in Vietnam, 1967-68, 70-71; chief rds. and airfields br. U.S. Army Engr. Sch., Ft. Belvoir, 1972—. Decorated Bronze Star with oak leaf cluster (U.S.), Honor Medal 1st Class (Vietnam). Registered profl. engr., Mo. Mem. Am. Soc. C.E., Soc. Am. Mil. Engrs., Assn. U.S. Army, Tau Beta Pi, Chi Epsilon. Home: 7324 Bath St Springfield VA 22150 Office: B Co 2d Bn USAES Ft Belvoir VA 22060

RIZK, JOSEF SALEEM, TV tech. exec.; b. Orlando, Fla., Mar. 24, 1917; s. Saleem K. and Wadeeha (Fatooch) R.; B.E.E., U. Fla., 1940; postgrad. Northwestern U., 1940, Mass. Inst. Tech., 1943; m. Mary V. Rizk, Feb. 8, 1947; 1 dau., Melinda Mary. Chief engr. Gibbs Marine Electronic Lab., Jacksonville, Fla., 1946-47; dir. instns. Inst. Radio and TV, 1947-50; pres. Southeastern Electronics, Inc., 1950-51; tech. dir. sta. WJXT-TV, Jacksonville, 1951—. Cons. U. Fla., 1952-57, Fla. State U., 1952-57. Served from ensign to lt. comdr., 1940-46. Registered profl. engr., Fla. Mem. Fla. Engring. Soc., Nat. Soc. Profl. Engrs., Soc. Am. Mil. Engrs. Home: 3501 Townsend Blvd

Jacksonville FL 32211 Office: 1851 Southampton St Jacksonville FL 32207

RIZK, WADE SALEEM, physician; b. Jacksonville, Fla., Mar. 25, 1903; s. Saleem Kaleel and Wadeeha (Fisher) R.; B.S., Georgetown U., 1927, M.D., 1929; m. Lois Greiner, Nov. 3, 1933; children—Roger Wade, Norman Wade, Katherine Wade. Commd. lt. (j.g.) M.C., U.S. Navy, 1929, advanced through grades to comdr., 1943, ret., 1945; intern U.S. Naval Hosp. Bklyn.. 1929; resident radiology U. Pa., 1945-46, Louisville Gen. Hosp., 1946-47, Bellevue Hosp., N.Y.C., 1947-48; dir. dept. radiology St. Luke's Hosp., Jacksonville, 1950-60; practice medicine, specializing in radiology, Jacksonville, 1960—; mem. staff Univ. Hosp., Meth. Hosp., Bapt. Hosp., Meml. Hosp., all Jacksonville, Broward County Hosp., Starke, Fla., Union County Hosp., Lake Butler, Fla. Dir. Joe Berg Sci. Seminars for High Sch. Students; pres. N.E. Fla. Regional Sci. Fairs, 1967-68. Diplomate Nat. Bd. Med. Examiners, Am. Bd. Radiology. Fellow Am. Coll. Radiology; mem. Fla. Radiology Soc. (pres. 1969-70), Am. Radium Soc., Radiol. Soc. N.Am., A.M.A., Fla., So. med. assns., Fla. Thoracic Soc., Duval County Med. Soc. (pres. 1966-67), A.A.A.S. Kiwanian (pres. 1959). Club: Ortega School Dad's (pres. 1956-57). Contbr. articles to profl. jours. Home: 3861 Ortega Blvd Jacksonville FL 32210 Office: 1471 San Marco Blvd Jacksonville FL 32207

ROACH, JACK WEDDINGTON, oil cons.; b. Guymon, Okla., Apr. 24, 1913; s. Dee and Osie (Hickman) R.; B.S., U. Tex., 1936; m. Betty Lee Cason, Nov. 2, 1940; children—Robert Kiernan, James Michael, David Dee, Thomas Lea. With Phillips Petroleum Co., 1936-46; chief project engr. Stanolind Oil and Gas Co., Tulsa, 1946-49, div. gas supt., Ft. Worth, 1949-52; mgr. operations, refinery div. Kerr-McGee Corp., Oklahoma City, 1952-55, mgr. operations operations div., 1955, v.p., asst. to pres. Deep Rock Oil Co. subsidiary, 1955-56, v.p. refinery tech. services, 1956-59, v.p., asst. to pres, Kerr-McGee Corp., Inc., 1959-60, v.p. personnel, 1960-66, v.p. chems., 1966-68, v.p. hydrocarbon devel., 1968-73; cons. in field, 1973—. Mem. Petroleum Club, Am. Soc. M. E., Am. Chem. Soc., Am. Petroleum Inst., Am. Phi Kappa Psi. Presbyn. Democrat. Lion. Home: 1401 Glenwood St Oklahoma City OK 73116 Office: Kerr-McGee Bldg 133 Robert S Kerr Av Oklahoma City OK 73102

ROACH, LONNIE LEE, JR., biol. mfg. co. exec.; b. Mullens, W.Va., Feb. 3, 1925; s. Lonnie Lee and Macie Flara (Poe) R.; B.S. in Biology, Concord Coll., 1948; postgrad. U. N.C., 1954-55; m. Agnes Jane Holland, Oct. 15, 1947; 1 dau., Jane (Mrs. James Walton Lineberger). Plant mgr. biol. prodn. Sylvania Co., Milburn, N.J., 1956-61; supt. diagnostics-biol. prodn. Lederle Labs., Pearl River, N.Y., 1961-68; pres. biol. prodn. Lee Labs., Inc., Grayson, Ga., 1968—. Served with AUS, 1943-46. Decorated Bronze Star, Silver Star. Mason. Home and office: Route 1 Box 37 Grayson GA 30221

ROACH, MYRON SIDNEY, mobile home mfg. co. exec.; b. DeFuniak Springs, Fla., May 12, 1942; s. Charles Starkey and Elizabeth Dell (Grice) R.; B.S. in Bus. Adminstrn., Fla. State U., 1964, J.D., 1971; m. Barbara Scott Douglass, Sept. 22, 1962; children—Sidney Scott, Christopher Bradley. Staff accountant firm Pace A. Allen, Crestview, Fla., 1964-66; controller, also v.p. Mobile Home Industries, Inc., Tallahassee, Fla., 1968—. Served to 1st lt., AUS, 1966-68. Decorated Bronze Star medal. C.P.A., Fla. Mem. Am., Fla. insts. C.P.A.'s, The Fla. Bar, Tallahassee (dir. 1972), DeFuniak Springs (treas. 1965) Jaycees, Phi Alpha Delta. Home: 1106 Lasswade St Tallahassee FL 32304 Office: 1309 Thomasville Rd Tallahassee FL 32304

ROACH, THOMAS ALBERT, farmer; b. Deport, Tex., Jan. 2, 1918; s. Thomas Abner and Lillie (Gunter) R.; student Freed-Hardeman Coll., 1936-38, E. Tex. State U., 1943-44; m. Ruby Terry Edwards, Nov. 24, 1938; 1 dau., Terry Ann (Mrs. Robert Nim Voelkle). Farmer, rancher, Paris, Tex., 1939—; chmn. bd. Paris Milling Co. Mem. Tex. Soil and Water Conservation Bd. Bd. dirs. Christian Coll. of S.W. Recipient Tex. Bank & Trust Co. Area award, 1959; Hoblitzelle award for contbn. to advancement of rural life, 1964; named hon. Lone Star farmer, 1960. Mem. Paris C. of C. (past dir.). Mem. Ch. of Christ (elder). Lion. Home: 2940 Abbott Lane Paris TX 75460

ROACH, THOMAS GATES, plastic mfr.; b. Houston, Dec. 27, 1924; s. Ben and Florence G. (Burum) R.; B.A., Rice U., 1948; m. Carmen Lee Blagg, June 27, 1972; children by previous marriage—Jana (Mrs. Michael Stockberger), Daryl, Michael. Pres. Florence Roach, Inc., Houston, 1948-51; v.p. Mecca Cable & Service, Inc., Houston, 1954-61; pres. Teledyne Mecca, Inc., Houston, 1961—; dir. Tres Computer Systems (Dallas). Served with USNR, 1942-46, 51-53. Mem. R Assn. Club: Brae Burn Country (Houston). Patentee in field. Home: 3233 Mangum St Houston TX 77018 Office: PO Box 36393 Houston TX 77036

ROACH, WILLIAM LESTER, high sch. prin.; b. Ashland, Miss., Aug. 29, 1911; s. Julius P. and Nannie (Kidd) R.; B.S., George Peabody Tchrs. Coll., 1937; M.S., Miss. State Coll., 1945; M.E., U. Miss., 1953; postgrad. U. Tex., summer 1937, Miss. State U., summer 1970; m. Ethye D. Young, Nov. 21, 1945; children—William Lester, Ruby Nan. Tchr. sci., coach Egypt (Miss.) High Sch., 1937-38, Noxapater (Miss.) High Sch., 1938-41; prin. elementary sch., coach high sch., Carthage, Miss., 1941-42; prin. Columbia (Miss.) Grammer Sch., 1942-46, Brookhaven (Miss.) High Sch., 1946—. Mem. Miss. Accrediting Commn., 1952-58, chmn., 1957-58; chmn. conf. steering com. Big Eight Athletic Conf., 1963—; col. gov.'s staff, 1960-68; mem. Miss. Ednl. Finance Commn., 1972—; mem. supt.'s adv. com. Y-Teens and Hi-Y. Trustee Lincoln County Hosp., 1960—. Recipient Distinguished Profl. Service certificate Nat. Assn. Secondary Sch. Prins., 1957. Mem. Nat., Miss. (chmn. high sch. sect. 1953-54), Brookhaven edn. assns., Big Eight Prins. Orgn, (chmn. 1955-58), Nat. Assn. Secondary Sch. Prins., Miss. Assn. Sch. Adminstrs., Miss. Assn. Secondary Sch. Prins. (chmn. 1957-58), Miss. High Sch. Activities Assn. (sec. dist. 7, 1950—, mem. state council 1966-68, 72—, mem. Miss. exec. com. 1968-72), Henry Boswell Soc. (trustee 1950—. pres. 1954-59), Red Red Rose, Phi Delta Kappa, Kappa Delta Pi. Baptist. Mason (Shriner), Lion (past sec.). Contbr. articles on discipline to profl. jours. Home: 505 Pine Dr Brookhaven MS 39601 Office: High Sch E Monticello St Brookhaven MS 39601

ROACH, WILLIAM RANKIN, accountant; b. San Angelo, Tex., Apr. 28, 1946; s. William Thomas and Christine Helen (Glenn) R.; B.B.A., Tex. Christian U., 1968, M.B.A. (grad. fellow), 1970; m. Bobby Jo Woodside, June 7, 1968. Adminstrv. asso. Sun Oil Co., Dallas, 1970-71, auditor, 1971-74; individual practice C.P.A., Dallas, 1972-74; controller Reamco Inc., 1974—. Treas., Dallas Investment Fund, 1972-74; dir. Mediserve Assos., Inc., Dallas. Recipient certificate of Merit U.S. Jr. C. of C., 1969. Mem. Am. Inst. C.P.A.'s, Tex. Soc. C.P.A.'s, Kappa Sigma. Home: 1013 Broadmoor St Lafayette LA 70501 Office: PO Box 52369 Lafayette LA 70501

ROACHE, BONNARD ERNEST, constrn. co. exec.; b. Pelzer, S.C., Apr. 25, 1931; s. Ernest Augustus and Lillie Mae (Galloway) R.; student Furman U., 1947-48; B.S., Newberry Coll., 1952; postgrad. Clemson U., 1954-57; m. Linda Locke, Dec. 31, 1971. Tchr. sci. Belton (S.C.) High Sch., 1954-55, Anderson (S.C.) Schs., 1955-59; owner Roache Builders and Williamston Constrn. Co., 1957—; dir. So. Bank & Trust Co. Chmn. Williamston Planning and Devel. Bd., 1970—, Williamston Planning Commn., 1971—. Bd. dirs. Williamston Recreation Center. Served with AUS, 1952-54. Mem. Home Builders Assn. Anderson, Carolinas Assn. Mut. Ins. Agts., Anderson Area C. of C. Home: 1211 Dickens Av Williamston SC 29697 Office: 104 Greenville Dr Williamston SC 29697

ROADY, JOE GENTRY, lawyer; b. San Marcos, Tex., July 27, 1935; s. John McKinley and Mildred Augusta (Gentry) R.; student U. Ala., 1953-54; LL.B., U. Tex., 1961; m. Edwina Doris Simmons, Aug. 13, 1971; children—Cheryl, Celia, Melissa, Melinda, Bernard. Admitted to Tex. bar, 1961, U.S. Dist. Ct., 1962, U.S. Supreme Ct. bar, 1969; asso. Fountain, Cox & Gaines, Houston, 1961-68, partner, 1968-69, partner successor firm Cox, Evans, Pakenham & Roady, 1969-73, successor firm Cox, Pakenham & Roady, 1973—. Mem. Mayor's Com. for Houston Police Dept., 1969—, Harris County Drug Abuse Com., 1968—; pres. Crime-Spot, Inc., 1969—. Bd. dirs. Houston Legal Found., 1969-73, exec. com., 1970-72; bd. dirs. Tex. Bill of Rights Found., 1969-71, exec. com., 1970-71. Mem. Am. Bar Assn. (co-chmn. state membership), Tex. (chmn. emergency legal assistance com.), Houston (dir., treas., v.p., pres.) jr. bar assns., Phi Delta Phi, Delta Tau Delta, Republican. Mem. Christian Ch. Club: Houston Athletic. Contbr. articles to legal jours. Home: 7914 Sharpview Houston TX 77036 Office: 2500 Two Shell Plaza Houston TX 77002

ROAF, CLIFTON GEORGE, dentist; b. Pine Bluff, Ark., Feb. 10, 1941; s. Arthur Lee and Charlotte (Boughton) R.; B.S. in Zoology, Mich. State U., 1963; D.D.S., Howard U., 1969; m. Andree Yvonne Layton, July 6, 1963; children—Phoebe, Mary, William, Andrew. Practice dentistry with W.L. Molette, Pine Bluff, 1969—; mem. staff Jefferson Hosp., Pine Bluff, U. Ark. Med. Center, 1971—; dental dir. Jefferson Comprehensive Care Clinic, 1973—. Mem. Pine Bluff Planning Commn., 1971—; mem. Pine Bluff Sch. Bd., 1973—; v.p. Interested Citizens for Voter Registration, 1970—. Mem. Pine Bluff Inter-Faith Council, 1971—; mem. adv. bd. Emergency Sch. Assistance Program, 1971—. Bd. dirs. S.E. Ark. chpt. A.R.C. Mem. Nat., Am. dental assns., Acad. Gen. Dentistry, Ark. Med., Dental and Pharm. Assn., Alpha Phi Alpha. Home: 3 Bonnie Park Dr Pine Bluff AR 71601 Office: 817 S Cherry St Pine Bluff AR 71601

ROANE, CURTIS WOODARD, educator; b. Norfolk, Va., Apr. 19, 1921; s. Lee Adam and Elizabeth Bonney (Evans) R.; B.S., Va. Poly. Inst., 1943, M.S., 1944; Ph.D., U. Minn., 1953; m. Martha Ann Kotila, Sept. 15, 1947; children—Martha Aurora (Mrs. Larry VanBuskirk), Ernest Lee. Asst. prof. Va. Poly. Inst., Blacksburg, 1947-49, asso. prof., 1949-68, prof. plant pathology, 1968—. Mem. various coms. Boy Scouts Am., 1961—, chmn. com. Explorer Post 444, 1968—. Mem. Va. Acad. Sci., A.A.A.S., Am. Phytopath. Soc. (chmn. genetics com. 1970-71), Bot. Soc. Am., Sigma Xi (pres. Va. Poly. Inst. chpt. 1966-67), Phi Sigma, Gamma Sigma Delta. Presbyn. (deacon). Club: Blacksburg Torch (v.p. 1973—). Editorial bd. Phytopathology Jour. 1968-71. Co-breeder corn, barley, oat varieties. Home: 610 Lucas Dr Blacksburg VA 24060

ROANE, PHILIP RANSOM, JR., virologist; b. Balt., Nov. 20, 1927; s. Philip Ransom and Mattie (Brown) R.; B.Sc., Morgan State Coll., 1952; Sc.M., Johns Hopkins, 1960; Ph.D., U. Md., 1970; m. Jean Austin Bennett, July 21, 1962. Asst. in microbiology Johns Hopkins, 1960-64; virologist Microbiol. Assos., Inc., Bethesda, Md., 1964-72, dir. quality control, 1967-72; asst. prof. microbiology Howard U., Washington, 1972—. Served with USAAF, 1946-47. Mem. Am. Assn. Immunologists, Am. Soc. Microbiology, Sigma Xi. Research, publs. in field of virology. Home: 3327 Mt Pleasant St NW Washington DC 20010

ROARK, GARLAND, author; b. Groesbeck, Tex., July 26, 1904; s. James and Mona Lee (Davidson) R.; grad. high sch.; m. Leola Burke, Sept, 14, 1939; children—Sharon Leigh (Mrs. Austin), Wanda Louise (Mrs. James G. Ledbetter). Retail advt., Tex., 1921-46, Chgo., 1929; novelist, 1939—; writer feature hist. articles Houston Chronicle, 1960-64; oil paintings in permanent collection Sam Houston Room, Nacogdoches, Tex. Mem. Tex. Inst. Letters, Colo. Authors League, East Tex. Hist. Assn. Republican. Presbyn. Author: Wake of the Red Witch, 1946; Fair Wind to Java, 1948; Rainbow in the Royals, 1950, Slant of the Wild Wind, 1952; The Wreck of the Running Gale, 1953; Star in the Rigging, 1954; The Outlawed Banner, 1956; The Cruel Cocks, 1957; Tales of the Caribbean, 1959; The Lady and the Deep Blue Sea, 1958; Should the Wind Be Fair, 1960; The Witch of Manga Reva, 1962; The Coin of Contraband, 1964; Bay of Traitors, 1966; Hellfire Jackson, 1966; Angels in Exile, 1967; Drill A Crooked Hole, 1968; (Western novels under pseudonym George Garland) Doubtful Valley, 1951; The Big Dry, 1953; Apache Warpath, 1959; Bugles and Brass, 1964; The Eye of the Needle, 1970; Slow Wind in the West, 1973. Address: 3300 Pearl St Apt 113 Nacogdoches TX 75961

ROBARDS, FRANK BENJAMIN, JR., banker; b. Henderson, N.C., Dec. 11, 1929; s. Frank Benjamin and Alice Milam (Thomas) R.; B.S., The Citadel, 1951; grad. Stonier Grad. Sch. Banking, Rutgers U., 1965; m. Mildred Kenyon Roberts, Sept. 28, 1957; children—Frank Benjamin III, James Roberts, Mary Kenyon. Asst. trust officer, asst. cashier Citizens & So. Nat. Bank, Augusta, Ga., 1955-62; asst. v.p. Citizens Bank & Trust Co., Henderson, 1962-64, v.p., 1964-66; exec. v.p. Rock Hill Nat. Bank (S.C.), 1966-69, pres., 1969—. Bd. dirs. United Fund, YMCA; trustee Catawaba Acad., Inc., York County Library. Served to capt. USAF, 1951-54; Mem. S.C. Bankers Assn. (dir. 1971—), Assn. Citadel Men, Rock Hill C. of C. Club: Country (Rock Hill). Home: 2057 Eakle Dr Rock Hill SC 29730 Office: PO Box 112 Rock Hill SC 29730

ROBB, CHARLES ARLEE, pharm. co. exec.; b. Naylor, Mo., Oct. 17, 1933; s. Charley and Zilpha (Sapp) R.; B.S., U. Mo., 1960, M.A., 1961, Ph.D. in Physiology, 1965; m. Ann Julie Naggs, May 9, 1958; children—Eric Scott, Sarah Beth. Instr. Kirksville (Mo.) Coll. Osteopathy and Surgery, 1965-66; NIH postdoctoral fellow U. Mo. at Columbia, 1966-68; sr. scientist sect. urol. research Alcon Labs., Ft. Worth, 1968-70, sect. product devel., 1970-71, head sect. toxicol. research, 1971-72, dir. dept. tech. services, 1972—. Coach Youth Athletic Program, Ft. Worth, 1968-70, dir., 1971—. Served with USAF, 1954-57. Mem. Pharm. Mfrs. Assn., Sigma Xi, Delta Upsilon. Contbr. articles profl. jours. Home: 3604 Winifred Dr Fort Worth TX 76133 Office: Alcon Labs 6201 S Freeway Fort Worth TX 76101

ROBB, DAVID METHENY, art mus. curator; b. Mnpls., Apr. 12, 1937; s. David Metheny and Jane Elizabeth (Howard) R.; A.B., Princeton, 1959; M.A., Yale, 1967; m. Frances Louise Osborn, Feb. 12, 1965; children—Andrew Osborn, Matthew Howard. Research asst. Nat. Gallery of Art, Washington, 1963; curator collection of Mr. and Mrs. Paul Mellon, Upperville, Va., 1963-65; curatorial intern Walker Art Center, Mpls., 1967-69; curator Kimbell Art Mus., Ft. Worth, 1969—. Served to lt. (j.g.) USNR, 1960-63. Heritage Found. fellow, 1958, Ford Found. fellow, 1967-69. Mem. Coll. Art Assn., Am. Assn. Museums, Naval Res. Assn. Club: Merion Cricket. Contbr. 20th. century sculpture and art of the Congo to Walker Art Center. Editor: Kimbell Art Mus. Catalogue, 1972. Office: Kimbell Art Museum Will Rogers Rd West Fort Worth TX 76107

ROBB, FELIX COMPTON, assn. exec.; b. Birmingham, Ala., Dec. 26, 1914; s. Felix Compton and Ruth (Nicholson) R.; A.B. summa cum laude, Birmingham-So. Coll., 1936; M.A., Vanderbilt U., 1939; student George Peabody Coll., 1939-40; Ed.D., Harvard, 1952; D.Ped., W.Va. Wesleyan Coll., 1968; LL.D., Mercer U., 1968. Tchr. jr. high sch., Irondale, Ala., 1936-37; tchr. Ensley High Sch., Birmingham, 1937-38; instr. English, Birmingham-So. Coll., 1940-42, successively alumni sec., registrar, 1946; asst. to pres. Peabody Coll., 1947-51, acting dir. Library Sch., 1947-48, acting dean coll., 1948-49, asso. prof. higher edn., 1950-53, prof., 1953-66, acting dir. surveys and field services, summer 1951, dean instrn., 1951-61, pres. coll., 1961-66; dir. So Assn. Colls. and Schs., Atlanta, 1966—; coordinator edn. project in Korea, 1956-58. Dir. Carnegie fellowships in teaching, 1950-60, Peabody Bldg. Fund Campaign, 1958; chief staff The Study of Coll. and Univ. Presidency, 1958-60; mem. Tenn. Adv. Council Tchr. Edn. and Certification, 1954-58; case writer Inst. Coll. and Univ. Adminstrs., Harvard, 1955; nat. selection com. Fulbright awards, 1955-57; dir. workshops in TV, ednl. TV program series, Nashville; chmn. gov.'s conf. edn. beyond high sch., 1958; mem. com. specialized personnel Dept. Labor, Tenn. Commn. Human Relations, 1964-66; exec. com. Met. Action Commn., 1965-66; chmn. S.E. Manpower Adv. Com., 1965-68; mem. bd. So. Edn. Reporting Service, 1961-69; pres. So. Council Tchr. Edn., 1956-57; chmn. scholarship com. Presser Found.; mem. Cleve. Conf., Higher Edn. Colloquium, Trustee Longview Found. Served to lt. USNR, 1943-46. Mem. Phi Delta Kappa, Omicron Delta Kappa, Phi Delta Kappa, Kappa Phi Kappa, Pi Gamma Mu, Kappa Alpha, Kappa Delta Pi. Methodist (chm. ch. adminstrv. bd.). Rotarian. Home: 2520 Peachtree Rd NW #216 Atlanta GA 30305 Office: 795 Peachtree St NE Atlanta GA 30308

ROBB, LESTER HARRY, assn. exec.; b. Cin., Dec. 18, 1911; s. Charle F. and Mary (Rigdon) R.; A.B., U. Cin., 1933, M.A., 1935; m. Louise E. Coffey, Oct. 25, 1935; children—Mary Louise (Mrs. Harold V. Tidwell), Pamela (Mrs. Barclay D. Wilson), Charles Lester. Sr. social worker City Cin., 1935-37; dir. Neighborhood Councils for Community Chest and City Cin., 1937-41; exec. sec. Council Community Forces, Chattanooga, 1941-43; exec. sec. Community Chest, Lexington, Ky., 1946-49, Nashville, 1949-54; chief exec. officer United Givers Fund, Nashville, 1954—. Served to lt. USNR, 1943-46. Mem. S.E. Conf. United Funds and Councils (past pres.), Blue Ridge Inst. Community Service Execs. (past pres.), Tenn. Conf. Social Welfare (past pres.), United Community Funds and Councils Am. (bd. dirs. 1962-68). Episcopalian. Rotarian. Home: 308 Walnut Dr Nashville TN 37205 Office: 404 James Robertson Pky Nashville TN 37219

ROBB, ROGER, judge; b. Bellows Falls, Vt., July 7, 1907; s. Charles Henry and Nettie May (George) R.; A.B., Yale, 1928; LL.B., 1931; m. Mary Ernst Cooper, 1932; 1 son, Charles Cooper; m. 2d, Lillian Nordstrom, 1943. Admitted to D.C. bar, 1931; asst. U.S. atty., D.C., 1931-38; practice law, Washington, 1938—; partner Robb, Porter, Kistler & Parkinson, and predecessor firms, 1951-69; judge U.S. Ct. Appeals for D.C., 1969—. Asso. counsel spl. Ho. com. investigate NLRB, 1939-40; counsel AEC Personnel Security Bd., 1954; mem. com. on admissions and grievances U.S. Dist. Ct. for D.C., 1953-69; mem. Commn. on Revision of Fed. Ct. Appellate System, 1973—; spl. hearing officer U.S. Dept. Justice, 1956-58. Trustee Legal Aid Agy. D.C., 1960-68, chmn. bd., 1965-67. Fellow Am. Bar Found., Am. Coll. Trial Lawyers; mem. Am., D.C. (v.p., 1953-54) bar assns., Phi Beta Kappa. Clubs: George Town, Chevy Chase (Washington); Yale (N.Y.C.). Home: 1700 Hoban Rd Washington DC 20007 Office: US Courthouse Washington DC 20001

ROBBERSON, GUY EDWARD, supt. schs.; b. Gainesville, Tex., Feb. 27, 1917; s. John Wesley and Pearl (Hampton) R.; B.S., Central State Coll., Edmond, Okla., 1938; M.Ed., Okla. State U., 1946; postgrad. Okla. U., 1965; m. Zelda M. Combs, June 1, 1941; children—John Howard, James Kent. Tchr. math., sci., Bixby, Okla., 1938-41; supt. schs., Keystone, Okla., 1941-43, Hydro, Okla., 1946-49, Lindsay, Okla., 1949—; prin., sci. tchr., Bixby, 1943-45. State com. mem. North Central Assn. Secondary Schs. and Colls.; mem. Okla. Adv. Bd. for Vocational Edn., 1973—. Vice chmn. Black Beaver council Boy Scouts Am., 1968-72, acting chmn., 1972. Served with USNR, 1945-46. Recipient Most Useful Citizen's award Lindsay, Okla., 1956, Distinguished Former Student's award Central State Coll., 1965, Outstanding Service award P.T.A., 1963. Mem. N.E.A. (life), Okla. Edn. Assn. (dir. 1956-58, 61-63), Am., Okla. (dir. 1960-63) assns. sch. adminstrs., Lindsay C. of C. (dir. 1955-67). Methodist (asso. dist. lay leader). Rotarian (past pres.). Home: 923 W Creek St Lindsay OK 73052 Office: 302 SW 8th St Lindsay OK 73052

ROBBIE, JOSEPH, lawyer, profl. football exec.; b. Sisseton, S.D,, July 7, 1916; s. Joseph and Jennie (Ready) R.; student No. States Tchrs. Coll., Aberdeen, S.D., 1953-58; A.B., U. S.D., 1943, LL.B., 1946; m. Elizabeth Lyle, Dec. 28, 1942; children—Diane, David, Janet (Mrs. John Glode), Joseph Michael, Deborah, Lynn, Timothy, Brian, Danny, Kevin. Admitted to S.D. bar, 1946; practiced in Mitchell, S.D., 1946-51, Mpls., 1953—; regional counsel OPS, 1951-52, regional dir., 1952-53; founder, pres., gen. mgr. Miami Dolphins, Ltd., profl. football team, 1965—. Asst. prof. econs. Dakota Wesleyan U., 1946-48; debate coach, instr. speech Coll. St. Catherine, 1953-54. Nat. v.p. Am. Lebanese Syrian Assn. Charities, 1964—; chmn. Miami Easter Seal campaign, 1969. Trustee Biscayne Coll.; bd. govs., chmn. budget com. St. Jude Children's Research Hosp., Memphis; bd. dirs. Community Relations Bd., Dade County, Fla., Crippled Children's Soc. Miami. Served with USNR, 1941-45. Decorated Bronze Star medal. Mem. Am. Bar Assn., Am. Judicature Soc., Am. Trial Lawyers Assn. K.C. Home: 339 W Elmwood Pl Minneapolis MN 55419 also 1301 NE 100th St Miami Shores FL Office: 904 Cargill Bldg Northstar Center MN 55402 also 330 Biscayne Blvd Miami FL 33132

ROBBINS, DAVID CARTER, data processing cons.; b. Indpls., Dec. 27, 1933; s. Max and Bessie (Auerbach) R.; student Union Coll., 1952-56; A.B. in Econs., U. Miami, 1957; m. Linda Phyllis Sheiness, July 15, 1962; children—Stephen Edwin, Sandra Allaine. Mgr. customer services Fed. Pacific Electric Co., Newark, 1961-66; supr. systems Dichl div. Singer Co., Somerville, N.J., 1966-68; dir. systems and data processing Abex Corp., mfg., Winchester, Va., 1968-69; supr. div. systems Dade div. Am. Hosp. Supply, Miami, Fla., 1969-70; v.p. Systematics, Inc., cons., Miami, 1970-72; pres., also chmn. bd. Interaction Assos., Inc., computer support services, Miami, 1972—. Founder CIC Profls., local soc. and certification program, 1973. Served with USCGR, 1957-60. Mem. Internat. MENSA Soc. (founder N. Central N.J. chpt. 1966, chmn. chpt. 1966-68), Assn. for Systems Mgmt., Progress Club Miami. Author: Systematics on the Frontiers of Creativity, 1970. Editor Mensanity, 1966-70, The Skyline, local data processing jour., 1971—. Home: 4901 SW 87th Ct Miami FL 33165 Office: 777 NW 72d Av Miami FL 33126

ROBBINS, DONALD EUGENE, physicist; b. San Saba, Tex., July 4, 1937; s. Aubrey Lonzo and Nila Lee (Duey) R.; student U. Tex., 1955-56; B.A. in Physics, Tex. Christian U., 1960; postgrad. Rice U., 1964-67; Ph.D. in Physics, U. Houston, 1969; m. Martha Dell Porter, July 28, 1956; children—Gary Don, Philip Mark, Martha Sheree. Nuclear engr. Gen. Dynamics Corp., Ft. Worth, 1955-62; sr. nuclear engr. Ling Temco Vought Co., Dallas, 1962-63; physicist Johnson

Space Center NASA, Houston, 1963—. Lectr. physics San Jacinto Coll., Pasadena, Tex., 1959-60, U. Houston, 1972—. Mem. Am. Geophys. Union, Am. Astron. Soc. Home: 15423 Baybrook Dr Houston TX 77058 Office: TN2 NASA Johnson Space Center Houston TX 77058

ROBBINS, EVELYN WALL (MRS. HOMER ERWIN ROBBINS, JR.), musician; b. Lake City, S.C., Oct. 21, 1914; d. Victor Sterling and Ella Lou (Able) Wall; A.B., Agnes Scott Coll., 1937; m. Homer Erwin Robbins, Jr. Mar. 4, 1950. Asst. voice dept. Agnes Scott Coll., 1937-40; organist, dir. Decatur (Ga.) 1st Bapt. Ch., 1937-40, Meth. Ch., Atlanta, 1940-42; minister music Peachtree Rd. Meth. Ch., Atlanta, 1947-50; organist Larchmont Av. Ch., N.Y.C., 1950, Summerfield Meth. Ch., Port Chester, N.Y., 1951-52, St. John's Meth. Ch., New Rochelle, N.Y., 1952-54; minister music Salem United Ch. of Christ, Allentown, Pa., 1954-67; organist-dir. music St. James Meth. Ch., Atlanta, 1967-71, Druid Hills United Meth. Ch., Atlanta, 1972—; tchr. organ Cedar Crest Coll., Allentown, 1955-58. Mem. Am. Guild Organists (past dean Lehigh Valley chpt.), Meth. Musicians, Atlanta Music Club. Home: 7362 Cardigan Circle NE Atlanta GA 30328

ROBBINS, HARRY COOLIDGE, real estate exec.; b. Blowing Rock, N.C., Jan. 10, 1925; s. Grover Cleveland and Lena (Miller) R.; student Davidson (N.C.) Coll., 1945-46; m. Revalle Byrd, Nov. 20, 1948; children—Wendy Lee, Christopher Brooke, John Kevin, Mark Byrd. Exec. v.p., sec., asst. treas., dir. Carolina Caribbean Corp., Banner Elk, N.C., 1965-70, pres., chief exec. officer, dir., 1970—, chmn. bd., 1971—; pres., chief exec. officer Hound Ears Lodge & Club, Inc., Tweetsie R.R., Inc., Univ. Village, Inc., Carolina Mill & Lumber Co., Inc., Dominican Caribbean Corp. Crusade chmn. Am. Cancer Soc., 1971. Trustee Blowing Rock Hosp.; bd. visitors Davidson Coll., Appalachian State U., Lees McRae Coll. Served with USNR, 1942-45. Clubs: Bal Harbour; Hound Ears (Blowing Rock); Indian Creek Country (Miami); Blowing Rock Country; Carolina Caribbean (Banner Elk). Home: Meadow Lane Blowing Rock NC 28605 also 226 Bal Cross Dr Bal Harbour FL 33154 Office: Box 227 Blowing Rock NC 28605

ROBBINS, JOHN SHUBEL, coop. mgr.; b. Jennings, La., Dec. 14, 1914; s. John Roscoe and Katie Sue (McCraw) R.; B.S., La. Poly. Inst., 1936; m. Ethel L. Evans, Aug. 11, 1939; children—Richard, Patricia Gayle (Mrs. George R. Woods), John Michael. With T.L. James & Co., 1936-37; geol. oil exploration Gulf Research & Devel. Co., 1937-43; mgr. br. office Gen. Gas Corp., Port Gibson, Miss., 1946-47; gen. mgr. Jefferson Davis Elec. Coop., Inc., Jennings, 1947—; sec.-treas. Cajun Elec. Power Coop., Inc., Com. on Power for S.W.; dir. Assn. La. Elec. Coop., Inc.; v.p. Tex-La Elec. Coop., Inc. Active Boy Scouts Am. Served to lt. (j.g.) USNR, 1943-46; PTO. Registered profl. engr., La.; 2d class comml. radio telephone operator. Mem. I.E.E.E., La. Engring. Soc., Nat. Soc. Profl. Engrs., Am. Legion, Vets. Fgn. Wars, Jennings Assn. Commerce (pres. 1965). Baptist. Mason (32 deg., K.T., Shriner); mem. Order Eastern Star, Royal Order of Scotland. Club: Jennings Kiwanis (lt. gov. internat. 1965). Home: 414 4th St Jennings LA 70546 Office: 906 N Lake Arthur Av Jennings LA 70546

ROBBINS, JOSEPH TUDOR, aviation lighting specialist; b. Okmulgee, Okla., Dec. 26, 1921; s. William Lewis and Maurine Edmiston (James) R.; student Rice U., 1940-41; B.S., Okla. State U., 1948; m. Susanna H. Hare, Sept. 8, 1950; children—James K., Mary L. Contract engr., sales rep. Westinghouse Elec. Corp., 1948-55; salesman Crane Co., 1956-60; sales engr. Powers Regulator Co., 1961-62, Dresser Industries, 1963-64; regional aviation specialist Crouse-Hinds Co., Houston, 1965—. Served with AUS, 1943-46. Mem. I.E.E.E., Petroleum Elec. Supply Assn. Presbyn. Home: 12430 Broken Arrow St Houston TX 77024 Office: 6065 Hillcroft St Houston TX 77036

ROBBINS, LAWRENCE J., city ofcl.; b. Lansing, Mich., Dec. 22, 1922; s. J.C. and Eloise (McConnell) R.; B.S., Mich. State U., 1942; m. Betty Ingram, Oct. 16, 1971. Production mgr. Wilcox-Gay Corp., Charlotte, Mich., 1946-57; police officer city Eau Gallie, Fla., 1957-61; city mgr. city Palm Bay, Fla., 1961-67; village mgr. North Palm Beach, Fla., 1967—. Vice pres. Municipal Research Assos., cons., North Palm Beach, Fla., 1971—. Served with USAAF, 1942-45. Mem. Internat. City Mgmt. Assn., Palm Beach County City Mgrs. Assn. (past pres.). Club: North Palm Beach (Fla.) Country. Home: 125 Shore Ct North Palm Beach FL 33408 Office: 501 US 1 North Palm Beach FL 33408

ROBERSON, ADRIAN L., civil engr., constrn. co. exec.; b. Hornbeak, Tenn., June 24, 1916; s. George S. and Minnie (Deane) R.; B.S., U. Tenn., 1941; m. Elaine Miller, June 22, 1946; children—Patricia Elaine, Len David, Margaret Ann. Pres., Roberson Constrn. Co., Columbia, S.C., 1946-74, Indsl. Devel. Corp., Columbia, 1962—, Roberson Internat., Austin, Tex., 1969-74. Cons. constrn. engr. Bd. govs. U. Tenn. Served as lt. col. C.E., AUS, 1941-46. Mem. Asso. Gen. Contractors, Columbia Contractors Assn. (past pres.). Club: Sertoma (past dir.). Died Jan. 28, 1974. Home: 1728 Bannockburn Dr Columbia SC 29206

ROBERSON, CLARENCE ALFRED, coll. chancellor; b. Wall, Tex., July 10, 1929; s. Clarence Alfred and Annie Mae (Bean) R.; B.B.A., Tex. Technol. U., 1950, M.B.A., 1951; m. Shirley Joyce Stevens, May 24, 1957; children—Frank, Philip, Ronald, Carla. Bus. mgr. San Angelo (Tex.) Coll., 1951-54; accountant Legislative Budget Bd., Austin, Tex., 1954-55; dean student Sul Ross (Tex.) State U., 1955-60; bus. mgr. Odessa (Tex.) Coll., 1960-66; vice chancellor Tarrant County Jr. Coll., Ft. Worth, 1966—; cons. jr. coll. adminstrn. Bd. dirs. Tex. Surplus Property Agy., 1953—; chmn. adv. com. coll. finance Coordinating Bd. Tex. Coll. and Univ. System, 1970-73. Mem. budget com. Ft. Worth United Fund, 1970-72. C.P.A., Tex. Mem. Ft. Worth C. of C. (dir. 1970-73). Presbyn. (ruling elder). Club: Ft. Worth Optimist.

ROBERSON, FRED MCRAE, physician; b. Camden, Ark., Apr. 9, 1938; s. Fred Milton and Mary Jane (Gann) R.; B.S., La. Tech. U., 1960; M.D., La. State U., 1964; m. Jo Ellen Talley, July 2, 1960; children—Fred McRae, Jr., Scott Eldred, Mary Catherine. Intern, Confederate Meml. Med. Center, Shreveport, La., 1964-65; practice medicine, specializing in family practice, Vivian, La., 1965, Linden, Tex., 1967—; chief staff Linden Municipal Hosp. Cons., Cass County Family Planning Clinic, 1969—; mem. adviser Cass County Selective Service, 1969—; health officer Cass County, 1970, Linden, 1971—. Served to capt. AUS, 1965-67. Decorated Legion of Merit, Bronze Star, Air Medal with oak leaf cluster. Mem. Linden C. of C. (pres. 1968-69), Cass-Marion Med. Soc. (sec., treas. 1970-71), Tex. (mem. edn. com. 1971—), N.E. Tex. (pres. 1969-72) acads. gen. practice, A.M.A., Am. Acad. Family Physicians, Tex. Med. Assn., Nat. Rifle Assn., Am. Orchid Soc., Kappa Sigma, Phi Chi. Democrat. Baptist. Home: Hwy 59 North Linden TX 75563 Office: PO Box 780 Linden TX 75563

ROBERTS, AARON HOOD, assn. exec.; b. Jacksonville, Fla., Aug. 11, 1928; s. Aaron Knight and Blanche (Dittmar) R.; B.A., U. Fla., 1951, M.A., 1955; Ph.D., U. Wis., 1961; m. Carolyn Gillen, Oct. 11, 1950; children—John Hood, Miles Richard. Instr. dept. English, Centenary Coll. La., Shreveport, 1955-57; instr. U.S. Fla., Tampa, 1961-62, asst. prof., 1962-63; asst. prof. Western Res. U., Cleve., 1963-66; dep. dir. Center for Applied Linguistics, Arlington, Va., 1966—. Exec. sec. adv. com. automatic lang. processing Nat. Acad. Scis.-Nat. Research Council, Washington, 1964-65; cons. RAND Corp., 1967-68, Inst. Def. Analyses, 1967—, NRC, 1970—; mem. adv. panel English teaching U.S. Information Agy., 1969—. Served to lt. inf., AUS, 1946-48, 51-53. Decorated Bronze Star with one oak leaf cluster. Mem. Am. Fedn. Information Processing Socs. (dir.), Am. Dialect Soc. (exec. sec.), Assn. Computational Linguistics (sec. treas.), Linguistic Soc. Am., Mod. Lang. Assn. (Am. sec. internat. com. computational linguistics). Club: Cosmos (Washington). Author: A Statistical Linguistic Analysis of American English, 1965. Editor Newsletter Am. Dialect Soc., 1969—, Newsletter Assn. Computational Linguistics, 1964—; Language and Automation, 1970. Home: 6215 Foxcroft Rd Alexandria VA 22307 Office: 1611 N Kent St Arlington VA 22209

ROBERTS, ALBERT SIDNEY, JR., coll. adminstr.; b. Washington, N.C., Sept. 16, 1935; s. Albert Sidney and Lorena (Jefferson) R.; B.S. in Nuclear Engring., N.C. State U., 1957, Ph.D. (AEC and Ford Found. fellows), 1965; M.S. in Mech. Engring., U. Pitts., 1959; m. Mary Llewellyn Bowers, Sept. 21, 1957; children—Leigh, Sidney, Llewellyn Amanda. Asso. engr. Westinghouse Elec. Corp., Pitts., 1957-60; asst. prof. engring. Old Dominion U., Norfolk, Va., 1965-67, asso. prof., 1967-72, prof., 1972—, asso. dean engring., 1974—; guest scientist Swedish AEC, Studsvik, 1968-69. Cons. to NASA, Langley Research Center, 1966—. Mem. Am. Soc. M.E., Am. Nuclear Soc., Am. Soc. Engring. Edn., Sigma Xi. Club: Torch. Contbr. articles to profl. jours. Home: 5437 Glenhaven Crescent Norfolk VA 23508

ROBERTS, BARON GEORGE, sr. v.p. Liller Neal Battle & Lindsey, Inc. Home: 2170 Street DeVille Atlanta GA 30345 Office: Life of Ga Tower Atlanta GA 30308

ROBERTS, BONNY K., judge; b. Sopchoppy, Fla., Feb. 5, 1907; s. Thomas and Florida (Morrison) R.; LL.B., U. Fla., 1928; LL.D., U. Miami, 1954; m. Mary Newman, Aug. 20, 1937; children—Mary Jane, Thomas Frederick. Admitted to Fla. bar, 1928; practice law, Tallahassee, 1928-49; justice Supreme Ct. Fla., 1949—; chief justice, 1953-54, 61-63, 71-72. Bus. exec., 1928—; past Pres. Capital Lincoln-Mercury Inc., Shoppicenter, Inc.; v.p. Tallahassee Bank & Trust Co., 1948-49; chmn. Jud. Council of Fla.; mem. Fla. Constn. Revision Com., 1966-67. Mem. bd. counselors Fla. Presbyn. Coll. Mem. Fla. Improvement Commn., 1949; U.S. shipping commr. Port of Jacksonville, 1943-45. Pres. Fla. State U. Found.; past pres. Fla. Heritage Found. Served as lt. comdr. USCG, 1942-45. Recipient Juror award Freedoms Found. Valley Forge, 1962; Distinguished Citizen award Stetson Law Coll., 1962. Fellow Am. Bar Found.; mem. Am. (mem. com. internat. jud. cooperation, ofcl. ct. rep. meeting London 1957), Internat., Tallahassee (past pres.), Inter-Am. bar assns., Fla. Bar (past v.p.), Am. Law Inst., Am. Judicature Soc., Newcomen Soc. Eng. in N.Am., Nat. Conf. Chief Justices (dep. chmn. 1972-73), Am. Legion, Soc. Wig and Robe, Alpha Kappa Psi, Blue Key, Gold Key, Phi Alpha Delta, Delta Chi. Mason (Shriner), Elk, Odd Fellow, Kiwanian. Home: Meridian Pl Tallahassee FL 32303 Office: Supreme Ct Florida Tallahassee FL 32304

ROBERTS, BRAMLETT, lawyer; b. Oxford, Miss., May 4, 1907; s. William Isaac and Letitia (Wilson) R.; LL.B., U. Miss., 1930; m. Doris Allen, Aug. 9, 1936; children—Pama Lou (Mrs. Charles S. Pendleton), John Charles. Admitted to Miss. bar, 1930; gen. practice Oxford, 1930—; asst. prof. law U. Miss., parttime, 1946-64. Pros. atty. City of Oxford, 1933-60, atty. City of Oxford 1934-37, 56-60. Served with USNR, 1942-45. Mem. Am. Bar Assn., Miss. State Bar. Baptist. Home: 415 Longest Rd Oxford MS 38655 Office: 115 1/2 N Lamar Oxford MS 38655

ROBERTS, BRUCE DAN, systems engring. exec.; b. Lorain, O., Nov. 22, 1939; s. Dan Norman and Genevieve (Hancock) R.; B.S., St. Lawrence U., 1961; M.Systems Engring., U. Fla., 1966; m. Betsy Bancroft Barratt, Mar. 6, 1965; children—Kenneth Lee, Kathryn Ann; m. 2d, Sandra Walker Constanza, Sept. 30, 1972; children—Randall James, Richard Carl. Analyst, Gen. Electric Co., Syracuse, N.Y., 1961-65, reliability engr., Daytona Beach, Fla., 1965-67, systems engr., 1967-69, mgr. engring. information systems and data processing, Cape Canaveral, Fla., 1969-70, mgr. computer systems engring., 1970-73, mgr. systems analysis, 1973—. Coach, Daytona Beach Cath. Basketball League, 1965-69, 70-71, v.p., 1968; coach Holly Hill Recreation Basketball League, 1972—, Ormond Beach Jr. Major Baseball League, 1973—; mgr. Ormond Beach Little Major Baseball League, 1971—. Mem. I.E.E.E., Operations Research Soc. Am., Phi Beta Kappa, Sigma Pi Sigma, Sigma Chi, Pi Mu Epsilon. Home: 381 Apache Trail Ormond Beach FL 32074 Office: Apollo Park Gen Electric Co PO Box 2500 Daytona Beach FL 32015

ROBERTS, CARLETON WHITMAN, educator; b. Bklyn., Apr. 29, 1921; s. Malcolm and Justine Edwards (Hibbard) R.; B.A., N.Y. U., 1943; M.S., Polytech. Inst. Bklyn., Ph.D., 1949; postdoctoral, U. Ill., 1950, Cornell U. Med. Sch., 1951-53; m. Charlotte June Trombla, Aug. 18, 1956; children—Charlotte Justine, Margaret Elizabeth, Eliza Carleton. Chemist, E. Bilhuber, Inc., drugs, Orange, N.Y., 1943-46; sr. research chemist Colgate-Palmolive Co., Jersey City, N.J., 1950-51; asst. prof. Purdue U., 1953-56; asso. scientist Dow Chem. Co., Midland, Mich., 1956-70; asso. prof. textile chemistry Clemson (S.C.) U., 1970—. Mem. Com. on Textile Functional Finishes, Nat. Acad. Sci.-NRC, 1960—. Fellow N.Y. Acad. Scis., A.A.A.S., Am. Inst. Chemists, Am. Assn. Textile Colorists and Chemists; mem. Am. (nat. chmn. council com. on technician activities 1969—), Brit. chem. socs., Harvey Soc., Ind. Acad. Sci., Sigma Xi, Alpha Chi Sigma, Phi Lambda Upsilon, Zeta Psi. Patents, publs. in field. Home: 102 Brookwood Lane Clemson SC 29613 Office: Sirrine Hall Clemson U Clemson SC 29631

ROBERTS, CHALMERS MCGEAGH, reporter b. Pitts., Nov. 18, 1910; s.; Franklin B. and Lillian B. (McGeagh) R.; A.B., Amherst Coll., 1933, L.H.D., 1963; m. Lois Hall Roberts, Sept. 11, 1941; children—David H., Patricia E., Christopher C. Reporter, Washington Post, 1933-34; reporter A.P., Pitts. bur., 1934-35, Toledo News-Bee, 1936-38, Japan Times, Tokyo, 1938-39; asst. mng. editor Washington Daily News, 1939-41; Sunday editor Washington Times-Herald, 1941; staff OWI, London, Washington, 1941-43; staff Life mag., 1946-47, Washington Star, 1947-49; with Washington Post, 1949—, reporter local and nat. news, 1949-53, fgn. affairs reporter, 1953-59, chief nat. news bur., 1959-65, columnist, 1971—. Served from pvt. to capt., USAAF, 1943-46. Recipient Sigma Delta Chi award, 1953; Washington Newspaper Guild nat. news award, 1954, 60; citation Overseas Press Club, 1955; Washington Newspaper Guild Front Page grand prize, 1957, 60; Raymond Clapper Meml. award, 1957. Mem. Am. Newspaper Guild. State Dept. Corrs. Assn. (pres. 1958-59). Club: The International (Washington). Author: Washington Past and Present, 1950; Can We Meet the Russians Half Way? 1958; First Rough Draft, 1973. Contbr. articles to popular mags. Home: 6699 MacArthur Blvd Washington DC 20016 Office: 1515 L St Washington DC 20005

ROBERTS, CHARLES TRUMAN, govt. ofcl.; b. Winnsboro, Tex., Apr. 26, 1912; s. Charles Luin and Carrie Jane (Turner) R.; B.A., E. Tex. State Tchrs. Coll., 1936; M.A., U. Colo., 1947; postgrad. summers, U. So. Cal., 1948, Columbia, 1951, 52; Ed.D., U. Tex., 1960; m. Connie Virginia Dickens, May 5, 1937; children—Charles Truman II, Connie Debra. Tchr., Muleshoe (Tex.) Elementary Sch., 1930-34; prin. Quitman (Tex.) Elementary Sch., 1934-37; tchr. Texas City Jr. High Sch., 1937-40; prin. Heights Elementary Sch., Texas City, 1940-46; prin. Robstown (Tex.) High Sch., 1946-49; supt. Wellington (Tex.) Schs., 1949-54; teaching fellow U. Tex., 1954-56; dir. planning Tex. Edn. Agy., Austin, 1956-61; specialist planning Office of Edn., Health, Edn. and Welfare, Washington, 1961-64, dir. statis. systems Nat. Center for Edn. Statistics, 1964—; stock broker, Washington, 1969—. Pres., Ednl. Cons., Washington, 1968—, Computer Credit Systems, Washington, 1969—. Mem. Am. Assn. Sch. Adminstrs., Nat. Council Sch. Planners, N.E.A., Washington Met. Bd. Trade, Austin C. of C., Phi Delta Kappa. Home: 8326 Wagon Wheel Rd Alexandria VA 22309 Office: 400 Maryland Av SW Washington DC 20202

ROBERTS, CHARLES WERTH, JR., elec. engr.; b. Augusta, Ga., Mar. 29, 1933; s. Charles Werth and Lucile Lyle (Williams) R.; B.S. in Elec. Engring., Auburn U., 1955; m. Frances Melanie Walthall, Aug. 4, 1955; children—Charles Werth III, Melanie Walthall, Susan, Carol Lynn, Thomas Arthur. Engr., Gen. Electric Co., Schenectady, 1955-56, Pittsfield, Mass., 1956-58; engr. Ala. Power Co., Montgomery, 1958-62, dist. supt., Demopolis, 1962—. Trustee Bryant Whitfield Meml. Hosp., Demopolis. Registered profl. engr., Ala. Mem. Sigma Alpha Epsilon. Episcopalian (jr. warden 1971—). Club: Demopolis Country (pres. 1971—). Home: 1814 Marengo Dr Demopolis AL 36732 Office: Box 819 Demopolis AL 36732

ROBERTS, CHARLES WESLEY, journalist; b. Huntington, W.Va., Dec. 19, 1916; s. Charles Wesley and Bessie Bright (Clack) R.; student Northwestern U., 1935-36; B.A., U. Minn., 1940; m. Mary Stewart, Nov. 10, 1945; children—Judith (Mrs. Richard Getrich), Jill (Mrs. John Boehnert). Reporter, Evanston (Ill.) News-Index, 1934-35, Mpls. Jour., 1936, City News Bur., Chgo., 1940, Chgo. Tribune, 1941, Chgo. Sun, Sun-Times, 1946-50, Chgo. Daily News, 1951; editor Minn. Daily, 1939-40; Chgo. bur. chief Newsweek, 1951-53, asso. editor, N.Y.C., 1953-54, chief White House corr., 1954-69, contbg. editor, Washington, 1969-73; asso. dir. Washington Journalism Center, 1973—. Served to lt. USNR, 1941-45. Recipient Page One award Chgo., 1951, Excellence in Reporting awards Ill. Press Assn., 1935, Pi Delta Epsilon, 1939. Mem. Nat. Press Club, Grey Friars, Phi Delta Theta. Episcopalian. Clubs: Federal City; Kenwood Country (Bethesda). Author: LBJ's Inner Circle, 1965; The Truth About the Assassination, 1967. Contbr. articles to nat. mags. Home: 8400 Fenway Rd Bethesda MD 20034 Office: 2401 Virginia Av NW Washington DC 20037

ROBERTS, CLARA IRENE BROADWAY (MRS. PHILIP CAREY ROBERTS), civic worker; b. Pocahontas, Ark., Dec. 29, 1914; d. Rance Enmand and Olive (Alphin) Broadway; certificate Memphis Tech. Night Sch., 1956; licensed vocational nurse, Memphis Vocational Sch., 1954; m. Philip Carey Roberts, May 23, 1957 (dec. Feb. 1964); children by previous marriage—Clara Lee (Mrs. William David Burnside), Henrietta (Mrs. Wilbur Osburn Davis), Mildred Lucille (Mrs. Walter Eugene Dollahite). Co-owner, Lehman-Roberts Co., Inc., Memphis, 1964—. Sec., Recreation Services for Handicapped, Memphis, 1964-65, mem. exec. bd., 1965-67; treas. Lenna P. Hart circle King's Daus., 1961. Named Vol. of Year, Recreation Services for Handicapped, Inc., 1965, 66. Home: 5452 N Suggs Dr Memphis TN 38117

ROBERTS, CLARENCE RICHARD, educator; b. Cushing, Okla., May 4, 1926; s. Clarence Leo and Elsie Margarete (Morgan) R.; B.S., Okla. State U., 1949, M.S., 1951; Ph.D., Tex. A. and M. U., 1964; m. Twilla Jo Teel, Aug. 24, 1951; children—Sharon, Susan, Gayla, Donna. Asst. county agt. Okla. State U., Jay, 1950-54; extension hort. specialist Kan. State U., Manhattan, 1954-61, extension hort. asso. prof., 1964-67; asso. extension prof. horticulture U. Ky., Lexington, 1968-69, prof., 1969—. Served with AUS, 1944-46; PTO. Mem. Am. Soc. Hort. Sci., Epsilon Sigma Phi, Gamma Sigma Delta. Baptist. Home: 1287 Gainesway Dr Lexington KY 40502 Office: Agr Sci Center Univ Ky Lexington KY 40506

ROBERTS, CLARENCE ZEBEDEE, JR., mgmt. cons.; b. Birmingham, Ala., Mar. 25, 1932; s. C.Z. and Anne (Fason) R.; B.Indsl. Mgmt., Auburn U., 1953; m. Carolyn Crawford, Nov. 7, 1953; children—Stephen, Janice, Leslie, Wesley. With Kurt Salmon Assos., Inc., mgmt. cons., Nashville, 1953—, v.p., 1967—. Mem. Inst. Mgmt. Cons. (founding mem.), Pi Kappa Alpha. Club: Hillwood Country (Nashville). Home: 2519 Ridgewood Dr Nashville TN 37215 Office: 1618 Parkway Towers Nashville TN 37219

ROBERTS, DAVID WILLIAM HARRISON, educator; b. Williamston, S.C., Jan. 25, 1931; s. William Perry and Inez (Tucker) R.; A.A., Anderson Coll., 1950; A.B., Erskine Coll., 1955; postgrad. U. S.C., 1958-59, Furman U., 1960-64. Owner Roberts Theaters, Williamston, 1958—; tchr. supr. Sch. Dist. #1, Anderson, S.C., 1956—; condr. workshops communication and tech. Chmn. March of Dimes, Anderson County, S.C., 1968-74. Exec. committeeman Democratic Party, Williamston, 1964-74; alderman, Williamston, 1973-75. Bd. dirs. United Fund, Anderson County, 1967-69. Mem. Anderson County, S.C., Nat. edn. assns., Nat. Assn. Ednl. Communication and Tech. (nat. dir. 1973-76), Ednl. Tech. and Communications Assn. S.C. (pres. 1970-71). Lion (pres. club 1966-67, zone chmn. 1967-69, dep. dist. gov. 1970, dist. gov. 1970-71). Home: 214 Edgewood St Williamston SC 29697 Office: Hamilton St Williamston SC 29697

ROBERTS, DERRELL CLAYTON, coll. pres.; b. Ocilla, Ga., May 24, 1927; s. William Clayton and Marie (Sandifer) R.; student S. Ga. Coll., 1944-45; B.S., Ga. Tchrs. Coll., 1949; M.A., George Peabody Coll., 1950; Ph.D., U. Ga., 1958; m. Leta Faye Hammond, Aug. 17, 1955; children—Ramona, Marianna, Danalee. Tchr. social sci. Tifton (Ga.) High Sch., 1949-55; instr. history Ga. State Coll., Atlanta, 1957-58; chmn. dept. history Fla. Soc. Coll., Lakeland, 1958-63; chmn. social sci. div. Mobile (Ala.) Coll., 1963-66; dean Kennesaw Jr. Coll., Marietta, Ga., 1966-70; pres. Dalton (Ga.) Jr. Coll., 1970—. Served with AUS, 1946-47. Mem. So. Hist. Assn., Ga., Fla. hist. socs. Democrat. Baptist. Rotarian, Elk. Author: Joseph E. Brown and the Politics of Reconstruction, 1973. Home: 1202 Sherwood Dr Dalton GA 30720

ROBERTS, GENEVA NICHOLS, banker; b. Jena, La., Aug. 16, 1918; d. William Thomas and Julia Azalia (White) Nichols; student Dodd Coll., 1931-33, Am. Inst. Banking, 1966-71; m. Willie Clifton Roberts, Nov. 1, 1940 (div. 1958); 1 dau., Linda Christine. Supr. teller operations Long Point Nat. Bank Houston, 1956-66; mgr. new accounts Internat. Bank, Houston, 1967-69; with Northwest Nat. Bank, Houston, 1969—, mgr. new accounts, also bus. devel., 1969—, asst. v.p., 1972—. Dir. Guardian Engring. Co., Inc. Named Outstanding Woman in Banking, Houston, 1973. Mem. Nat. Assn. Bank Women Am. Inst. Banking (conv. com. chmn. 1971, bd. govs.), Bank Marketing Asso., Bus. and Profl. Women's Club. Club: The Bank

Women's (past pres.) (Houston). Home: 6643 Edloe St Houston TX 77005 Office: 1716 Mangum St Houston TX 77018

ROBERTS, GRIFF HOWARD, JR., financial mgmt. exec.; b. Irvington, Ky., Apr. 4, 1935; s. Griffie Howard and Orelia (Jones) R.; B.S., Western Ky. U., 1965; student Ky. Wesleyan Coll., 1953-55; m. Omeida Louise Fentress, Feb. 23, 1957; children—Kimberly, Kelly, Bryan, Scott. City clk., adminstr. Leitchfield, Ky., 1958-61; dormitory dir. Western Ky. U., Bowling Green, 1961-65; budget officer, personnel asst. Middletown, O., 1965; adminstrv. asst. to city mgr. Middletown, 1965-68; city mgr. Ocala, Fla., 1969-73; sr. v.p., treas. Ocala Fed. Savs. & Loan Assn.; v.p., dir. Central Fla. Financial Services, Inc., 1973—. Mem. bus. mgmt. adv. com. Central Fla. Community Coll., 1972—. Mem. Middletown Civic Assn., 1965-68, 10 yr. Survey Com., 1966-68; v.p. P.T.A. Wildwood Elementary Sch., Middletown, 1967; mem. N. Fla. Council Boy Scouts Am., 1971-72. Served with AUS, 1957. Mem. Fla. City County Mgmt. Assn. (dir. 1973), Fla. League Cities, Marion League Cities (dir. 1972-73), Internat. City Mgmt. Assn., C. of C., Com. 100. Mem. Christian Ch. (elder). Rotarian. Club: Ocala Municipal Golf and Tennis Assn. Home: 1014 SE 13th Av Ocala FL 32670 Office: 406 E Silver Springs Blvd Ocala FL 32670

ROBERTS, HYMAN JACOB, physician; b. Boston, May 29, 1924; s. Benjamin and Eva (Sherman) R.; M.D. cum laude, Tufts U., 1947; m. Carol Antonia Klein, Aug. 9, 1953; children—David Barry, Jonathan Stuart, Mark Elliott, Stephen, Scott F., Pamela Beth. Intern Boston City Hosp., 1947-48, resident, 1948-49; resident Municipal Hosp., Washington, 1949-50; fellow in medicine Lahey Clinic, Boston, 1950-51; instr. in medicine, research fellow Tufts U. Med. Sch., Boston, 1948-49, Georgetown Med. Sch., Washington, 1949-50; pvt. practice medicine, West Palm Beach, Fla., 1955—; mem. cons. staff St. Mary's Hosp., Good Samaritan Hosp.; cons. endocrinology Gables Acad., Broward Acad.; 1st Eugene Dibble ann. lecture Tuskegee Inst., 1967; dir. Palm Beach Inst. for Med. Research. Trustee Am. Physicians Fellowship for Israel Med. Assn. Served from lt. (j.g.) to lt. USNR, 1943-45, 51-54. Recipient Fla.'s Outstanding Young Men award Jr. C. of C., 1959. Diplomate Am. Bd. Internal Medicine. Fellow Am. Coll. Angiology, Royal Soc. Health, Am. Coll. Chest Physicians; mem. Am. Fedn. Clin. Research, Endocrine Soc., Am. Assn. Study Headaches, Am. Soc. Internal Medicine, N.Y. Acad. Scis., A.C.P. (asso. mem.), Am., Fla. heart assns., Am. Diabetes Assn., A.A.A.S., Internat. Assn. for Accident and Traffic Medicine, Am., So., Fla. med. assns., Assn. for Psychophysiol. Study Sleep, Physicians for Automotive Safety, Am. Assn. for Automotive Medicine, Fla. Thoracic Soc., Alpha Omega Alpha. Mem. B'nai B'rith (v.p. 1958-59). Rotarian (charter mem., dir. 1956-58) (West Palm Beach, Fla.). Author: Difficult Diagnosis; A Guide To The Interpretation of Obscure Illness, 1958; The Causes, Ecology and Prevention of Traffic Accidents, 1971; An Inquiry Into the Safety of Vasectomy, 1974, also numerous sci. papers. Home: 6708 Pamela Lane West Palm Beach FL 33405 Office: 300 27th St West Palm Beach FL 33407

ROBERTS, JACK, judge, b. 1910; LL.B., U. Tex. 1933. Admitted to Tex. bar, 1933; now dist. judge Austin, Tex. Address: US Courthouse Austin TX 78701

ROBERTS, JAMES ELTON, banker; b. Terrell, Tex., Nov. 24, 1910; s. Henry Oscar and Ida Olivia (Phillips) R.; B.S., Tex. A. and M. U., 1933, M.S., 1947; m. Virgia L. Wileman, Oct. 4, 1935; 1 son, James Elton. Tchr. vocational agr., Mt. Vernon, Tex., 1933-34, Van, Tex., 1934-37, Denton, Tex., 1937-38; supt. Tex. Agrl. Expt. Sta., 1938-54; farms mgr. farms service dept. Tex. A. and M. U., 1954-68; v.p., dir. 1st Nat. Bank, Bryan, Tex., 1968—. Ford Found. cons. to Dominican Rep., 1962. Drive chmn. College Station United Chest, 1965; pres. Bryan Greater United Fund, 1973. Mem. Bryan—College Station C. of C. (dir. 1947-49, pres. 1974). Mason (32 deg., Shriner). Clubs: Bryan-College Station Knife and Fork (past pres.), Van Lions (past pres.). Home: 840 S Rosemary St Bryan TX 77801 Office: 120 N Main St Bryan TX 77801

ROBERTS, JAMES ERNEST, entomologist; b. Newport, Ark., May 17, 1924; s. James Green and Sarah Anna (Fivecoat) R.; student Ark. State U., 1946-47; B.S.A. (John Rust scholar), U. Ark., 1954, M.S. in Entomology (fellow), 1955; Ph.D., Kan. State U., 1962; m. Lula Pearl Wright, Mar. 3, 1946; children—Sarah (Mrs. Robert Wesley McPherson), James Ernest, Patricia Gail. Instr., asst. vocational agr. Strawberry (Ark.) High Sch., 1947-52; instr. entomology U. Ark. at Fayetteville, 1955-56, extension entomologist, 1965-69; asst. prof. entomology Ga. Expt. Sta. at Experiment, 1956-65; extension specialist entomology Va. Poly. Inst. and State U., Blacksburg, 1969—. Served with USMCR, 1943-46. Mem. Va. Pesticide Assn. (program com. 1972-73), Entomology Soc. Am. (membership com. Eastern br. 1954-73), Am. Legion (vice com. post Blacksburg 1971-72, adj. 1972-73, comdr. 1973-74), Sigma Xi, Gamma Sigma Delta (chmn. awards com. 1972-72), Alpha Zeta, Phi Sigma. Baptist (deacon). Mason, Toastmaster (pres. Blacksburg 1971-72). Contbr. numerous articles to profl. jours. Home: 1007 Kentwood Dr Blacksburg VA 24060

ROBERTS, JAMES GORDON, dairy exec.; b. Lincoln, Neb., July 20, 1909; s. James Russell and Clare (West) R.; A.B., U. Neb., 1932; m. Dolly Wilson Anderson, Sept. 23, 1967; children—Diane Virga (Mrs. Frank Virga), Sheila Rae. Advt. mgr. Roberts Dairy Co., Omaha, 1932-39, exec. v.p., 1939-44, pres., 1944-70, chief exec. officer, 1970—, chmn. bd., 1944—; dir. Omaha Nat. Bank, 1964-72. Chmn Omaha com. Am. industry Nat. Fund for Med. Edn., 1957; mem. Pres. Eisenhower's Citizens Adv. Com. on Fitness of Youth, 1957-61; council mem. at large Boy Scouts Am., 1958; del., treas. Neb. com. White House Conf. on Children and Youth, 1959-60; conferee White House Conf. Food, Nutrition and Health, 1969. Bd. dirs. Douglas County unit Am. Cancer Soc., 1962—, Jr. Achievement, Omaha, 1962—, Omaha-Douglas County A.R.C., 1962-64, YMCA, Omaha, 1958-63, Milk Industry Found., 1960-66, Big Brothers of Omaha, 1961-64; pres.; chmn. bd. dirs. Nat. Boys Football Found., 1948-60, chpt. pres., 1962; adv. bd. Lutheran Hosp., Omaha, 1957-60; bd. regents Coll. St. Mary's, 1966—; trustee Inst. Gen. Semantics, 1958—, Omaha Safety Council, 1958—, Douglas County chpt. Nat. Multiple Sclerosis Soc., 1960-64, Brownell Hall, 1957-65, Met. Coll., Council Bluffs, Ia., 1966—. Recipient numerous awards for civic and youth work. Mem. Neb. Assn. Mental Health, (pres. 1965), Dairy Soc. Internat. (dir. 1957-60), Omaha Zool. Soc. (dir. 1962-69), Nat. Independent Dairies Assn. (exec. com. 1969—), S.A.R. (chpt. pres. 1963-65), U. Neb. Alumni Assn., Phi Epsilon Kappa. Contbr. articles to profl. publs. Home: 161 Flamingo Dr Clearwater FL 33516 Office: Suite 401 7171 Mercy Rd Omaha NE 68106

ROBERTS, JAMES TRAVIS, JR., civil engr.; b. Alpine, Tex., May 11, 1937; s. James Travis and Pauline (Bierschwale) R.; B.S. in Civil Engring., Tex. A. and M. U., 1960; m. Cassandra Lynn Stumberg, Oct. 8, 1960; children—James Travis III, Teresa Ann. Engring. aid Tex. Hwy. Dept., Alpine, 1960-63; engr. asso. design engr. Hunter Assos., Inc., Dallas, 1963—, now v.p. City engr., Carrollton and Rowlett, Tex. Cons. engr. various cities; cons. engr., project engr. Runaway Bay Devel. on Lake Bridgeport, Wise County, Tex., 1966—. Active YMCA. Served to lt. AUS, 1960; now capt. Res. Registered profl. engr., Tex., Okla., La. Mem. Nat., Tex. socs. profl. engr., Fed. Water Pollution Control Fedn., Tex. Water Pollution Control Assn., Soc. Am. Mil. Engrs., Am. Soc. C.E. Presbyn. (elder). Club: Dad (v.p. 1969). Home: 7216 Bucknell Dr Dallas TX 75214 Office: 5630 Yale Blvd Dallas TX 75206

ROBERTS, JOHN CARROLL, SR., civil engr.; b. Frankfort, Ky., Apr. 15, 1934; s. Bowen Henry and Mayme (Burchfield) R.; B.S., U. Ky., 1960; m. Roberta Bow Miller, Apr. 14, 1956; children—Kathryn Miller, John Carroll, Patricia Jane. Sales rep. Atlas Powder Co., Wilmington, Del., 1960-63; chief engr. Geoghegan & Mathis, Inc., Bardstown, Ky., 1963-69, v.p., 1967-69; v.p. Ky. Materials Co., Frankfort, 1963-67, pres., 1972—; pvt. practice civil engring., 1972—, v.p. D B Grugin Oil Co., 1963—; chief engr. Bush Contracting Co., Frankfort, 1969-71, T.C.H. Coal Co., Frankfort, 1969-71. Former chmn. Frankfort Municipal Sewer Bd.; mem. Capital Plaza Authority, 1970—; pres. Elkhorn Elementary PTA, 1969-70. Bd. dirs. Franklin County chpt. A.R.C. Served with USNR, 1955-57. Registered profl. engr., Ky. Mem. Nat., Ky. socs. profl. engrs., Ky. Hist. Soc. (life), U. Ky. Alumni Assn. (life), Am. Soc. C.E., Kappa Sigma. Democrat. Mem. Christian Ch. (deacon). Elk. Club: Frankfort Country (pres. 1966—). Home: Elk. Club: Frankfort Country. Home: 300 Ute Trail Frankfort KY 40601 Office: 326 W Main St Frankfort KY 40610

ROBERTS, JOHN ELGIN, mag. editor; b. Shelby, N.C., Sept. 14, 1926; s. John Ellis and Annie (Spake) R.; diploma Gardner-Webb Jr. Coll., 1947-49; B.A., Furman U., 1951, LL.D., 1972; M.A., George Peabody Coll. Tchrs., 1952; D.Litt., Bapt. Coll. at Charleston, S.C., 1971; m. Helen E. Goodwin, Sept. 8, 1950; children—Wayne, Mark, Glenn, Jonna, Jill, Julie. Tchr. Gastonia (N.C.) City Schs., 1951-54; dir. pub. relations Gerdner-Webb Coll., 1954-60; dir. pub. relations, editor Charity and Children Bapt. Children's Homes of N.C., Thomasville, 1960-65; editor, bus. mgr. The Bapt. Courier, Greenville, S.C., 1966—. Mem. So. Bapt. Editors Conf., So. Bapt. Inter-Agy. Council; bd. advisers New Orleans Bapt. Theol. Sem.; instl. rep. Boy Scouts Am.; mem. Thomasville (N.C.) Bd. Edn., 1963-65. Served with AUS, 1945-46. Mem. So. Bapt. Pub. Relations Assn. (pres. 1956—), Bapt. World Alliance Commn. on Teaching and Tng. Baptist (deacon). Rotarian. Home: 106 Trinity Way Greenville SC 29609 Office: 100 Manly St Greenville SC 29602

ROBERTS, JOHN MELVILLE, educator; b. Toronto, Ont., Can., Feb. 16, 1931; s. Thomas Melville and Florence Genevieve (Sadd) R.; B.A.Sc., U. Toronto, 1953, M.A. Sc., 1954; Ph.D. (Union Carbide and Carbon research fellow), U. Pa., 1960; m. Gwennth Eleanor Leslie, July 13, 1957; children—Karlyn Ann, Marion Jill. Came to U.S., 1959. Metallurgist, Aluminum Labs. Ltd., Kingston, Ont., Can., 1954-56; mem. faculty Rice U., Houston, 1959—, asso. prof. materials sci., 1965-70, prof., 1970—. Guest prof. Max Planck Inst. fur Metallforschung, Inst. fur Physik, Stuttgart, Germany, 1972-73. Guggenheim fellow U. Paris, 1964-65. Mem. Am. Inst. Mining and Metall. Engrs. (chmn. Houston metals sect. 1969), Am. Phys. Soc., Am. Soc. Metals, Am. Inst. Mining, Metall. and Petroleum Engrs., Sigma Xi, Tau Beta Pi. Home: 7614 Windswept Lane Houston TX 77042 Office: Dept Materials Sci Rice Univ Houston TX 77001

ROBERTS, LOUIS DOUGLAS, educator; b. Charleston, S.C., Jan. 27, 1918; s. Louis Wigfall and Evelyn (Douglas) R.; A.B. with honors, Howard Coll., 1938; postgrad. Johns Hopkins, 1938-39; Ph.D., Columbia, 1941; m. Marjorie Lawson, Aug. 29, 1942; 1 dau., Joyce Carol (Mrs. Charles Bennett Heck). Research fellow Cornell U., 1942; research lab. Gen. Elec. Co., Schenectady, 1942-46; nuclear power research and devel. Oak Ridge Nat. Lab., 1946-68, also prof. U. Tenn., 1963-68; prof. physics U. N.C., 1968—. Fulbright and Guggenheim fellow Oxford U., Eng., 1958-59. Fellow Am. Phys. Soc. (chmn. Southeastern sect. 1962-63). Research and publs. on electronics, nuclear physics, solid state physics. Home: Sourwood Circle Chapel Hill NC 27514

ROBERTS, MARCUS LAFAYETTE, JR., ednl. adminstr.; b. Altoona, Ala., Dec. 7, 1926; s. Marcus L. and Meade (Fant) R.; A.B., Jacksonville State U., 1947, B.S., 1947; M.A., U. Ala., 1951; m. Edith Lynn Harper, June 30, 1957; children—Marcus L. III, Melanie Lynn. Pub. sch. tchr. Tuscaloosa, Ala.; chmn. dept. bus. edn. Tuscaloosa Sr. High Sch., 1947-54; prof. edn. U. Ala., University, 1954—, dir. student services, 1960-70, asst. dean Coll. Edn., 1970—, head area of curriculum and instruction Coll. of Edn., 1971-73. Cons. sch. systems Calhoun, Jefferson, Madison, Montgomery, Tuscaloosa counties, Mountain Brook, Ala., 1955—; pres. Ala. Credit Union, U. Ala., 1967. Mem. Nat., Ala. edn. assns., Nat., So., Ala. bus. edn. assns., Kappa Delta Pi, Phi Delta Kappa, Pi Tau Chi. Democrat. Methodist. Club: Tuscaloosa Exchange. Contbr. articles to profl. jours. Home: 204 32d Pl E Tuscaloosa AL 35401 Office: Box R University AL 35486

ROBERTS, MILTON KENDALL, ins. exec.; b. Dallas, Aug. 26, 1936; s. Milton Jennings and Mabel Loraine (Shiflett) R.; B.B.A., U. Tex. at Arlington, 1962; M.B.A., So. Meth. U., 1969; m. Betty Bucher, Aug. 4, 1958 (div. Sept. 1963); children—Leslie, Vicki, Terri, Mike. Tax accountant Peat, Marwick, Mitchell & Co., Dallas, 1962; sr. cost accountant Southwestern Life Ins. Co., Dallas, 1962-64; adminstrv. v.p. Anderson Service Co. auto service contracts, Dallas, 1964-68; chief accountant, asst. v.p. Nat. Western Life Ins. Co., Austin, 1968-72; asst. comptroller Acacia Mut. Life, Washington, 1972—. C.P.A., Tex. Mem. Nat. Assn. Accountants (dir. local chpts. 1969—, dir. communications, 1973-74, dir. spl. activities, 1972-73, dir. communication, 1973-74). Home: 4631 Seminary Rd Alexandria VA 22304 Office: 51 Louisiana St NW Washington DC 20001

ROBERTS, MORTON SPITZ, astronomer; b. N.Y.C., Nov. 5, 1926; B.A., Pomona Coll., 1948; M.S., Cal. Inst. Tech., 1950; Lick Obs. fellow, U. Cal., 1956-57, Ph.D. in Astronomy, 1958. Asst. prof. physics Occidental Coll., 1949-52; physicist underwater ordnance U.S. Naval Ordnance Test Sta., 1952-53; jr. research astronomer U. Cal., 1957-58, NSF fellow, 1958-59, lectr. astronomy, asst. research astronomer Radio Astron. Lab., 1959-60; lectr. astronomy, research asso. obs. Harvard, 1960-64; scientist Nat. Radio Astronomy Obs., Charlottesville, Va., 1964—, asst. dir., 1971-72. Mem. Am. Astron. Soc. (v.p. 1971-72), Royal Astron. Soc. Research in galaxies, galactic structure, radio astronomy. Address: Nat Radio Astronomy Obs Edgemont Rd Charlottesville VA 22901

ROBERTS, NOBLE LAFAYETTE, govt. ofcl., biologist; b. Arkadelphia, Ark., June 10, 1925; s. Newman Lafayette and Emma Inez (McCallum) R.; B.S., Ouchita Bapt. Coll., 1951; M.S., George Peabody Coll., 1962; Ph.D. (teaching fellow), U. So. Miss., 1966; m. Lillian Frances Maxson, Sept. 1, 1951; children—Marian Lynne, Rachel Lee. Farmer, Rohwer, Ark., 1946-48; prin. Desha Central Sch., Rohwer, 1951-52, also coach; owner, mgr. Desha County Farmers Assn., Watson, Ark., 1952-59; tchr. sci. and math. South Bay (Fla.) Jr. High Sch., 1959-61; tchr. biology and chemistry Melbourne (Fla.) High Sch., 1962-63, Brevard Jr. Coll., Cocoa, Fla., 1963-64; prof. biology Campbellsville (Ky.) Coll., 1966-72, also chmn. biology dept.; dir. Louisville and Jefferson County pub. health labs., Louisville, 1973—. City councilman Watson, 1954-59. Served with USCGR, 1943-46. NSF Research grantee, 1967-70. Mem. A.A.A.S., Am. Inst. Biol. Sci., Ky. Acad. Sci. Mason (Shriner), Lion (dist. gov. 1970-71). Home: 1418 Goddard Av Louisville KY 40204 Office: 400 E Gray St Louisville KY 40202

ROBERTS, RAY, congressman; b. nr. McKinney, Tex., Mar. 28, 1913; s. Roy C. and Margaret (Burton) R.; student Tex. A. and M. Coll., 1930-31, North Tex. State Coll., 1931-32, U. Tex., 1933-35; m. Elizabeth Bush, Nov. 12, 1946; 1 dau., Kay (Mrs. Tom Murray II). Mem. staff Speaker Sam Rayburn, U.S. Ho. of Reps., 1940-42; mem. Tex. Senate from 9th Dist., 1955-62; elected 87th Congress to fill unexpired term of Speaker Rayburn, 1962; mem. 88th-93d congresses from 4th Tex. Dist. Served to capt. USNR, World War II. Democrat. Home: 509 Tucker St McKinney TX 75069 Office: 2455 Rayburn House Office Bldg Washington DC 20515

ROBERTS, RICHARD DAVID, broadcasting exec.; b. Quincy, Mass., June 15, 1934; s. Cecil Austin and Helen Catherine (Knebel) R.; B.S., U.S. Naval Acad., 1956; M.B.A., Harvard, 1963; m. Shirley Phyllis Hanson, Aug. 3, 1957; children—Catherine, Helen, Caroline. Research dir. WTAR Radio-TV Corp., Norfolk, Va., 1963-64; research dir. Landmark Communications, Norfolk, 1964-65, asst. to pres., 1965-68, sec., 1967—; v.p. operations, sec., dir. TeleCable Corp., 1968—; dir. 16 TeleCable subsidiaries. Pres. Portsmouth Girls Club, 1970, dir., 1965—. Served with USNR, 1956-61. Presbyn. (elder). Moose, Lion (pres. club 1973, dir. 1966—). Home: 115 Snead Fairway Portsmouth VA 23701 Office: 740 Duke St Norfolk VA 23501

ROBERTS, ROBERT EARL, food service co. exec.; b. Crawfordville, Ga., Sept. 3, 1932; s. Charles Stakley and Lettie (Denny) R.; B.S., U. Ga., 1954; m. Mary Arnold, Sept. 11, 1953; children—David Earl, Mark Arnold, Stuart Elliott. Asst. plant mgr. Kinnett Dairies, Columbus, Ga., 1956-57; creamery mgr. U. Ga., Athens, 1967; mgmt. cons. Am. Dairy Queen Corp., 1965-67, dir. field services, quality control Southeastern div., 1967-68, operations mgr. So. region, Atlanta, 1968-71; dist. mgr. Krystal Co., Atlanta, 1971-73, dir. tng., 1973—. Mem. adv. com. Sch. Bd., Clarke County, Ga., 1967-68. Served to 1st lt. with AUS, 1954-56. Mem. Atlanta Dairy Tech. Soc. (exec. sec. 1966-67), Am. Dairy Sci. Assn. (sect. chmn. 1967), Res. Officers Assn. Army (chpt. v.p. 1965). Baptist (deacon). Kiwanian (pres. 1964). Home: 3612 Prestwick Dr Tucker GA 30084 Office: Krystal Co 701 Cherry St Chattanooga TN 37402

ROBERTS, ROLAND DOUGLAS, JR., architect; b. Tulsa, Jan. 8, 1937; s. Roland Douglas and Cortez (Williamson) R.; B.Arch., Rice U., 1960; postgrad. Okla. U., 1962-63; m. Nancy Ray Carman, June 18, 1966; 1 dau., Lina Charlene. Designer, Grayson Gill, Inc., Dallas, 1961; tchr. U. Tex., Arlington, 1963-64; designer Smith & Warder, Grand Prairie, Tex., 1964-65; architect Leman H. Wilson, Tulsa, 1965-67, Brush, Hutchison & Gwinn, Nashville, 1967-70, owner archtl. firm Roberts & Assos., Nashville, 1970—. Fallout shelter analyst. Served with USAF, 1960-61. W.W. Watking traveling fellow in architecture, recipient Nat. Council Archtl. Registration Bds. certificate. Registered profl. architect, 25 states. Mem. Nashville C. of C., Am. Concrete Inst., A.I.A., Tenn. Soc. Architects, Illumination Engring. Soc., Guild for Religious Architecture, Constrn. Specifications Inst. Club: Torch Internat. Archtl. works include: Highland Hosp., Portland, Tenn., Calvary Bapt. Ch., Winston-Salem, N.C., Buchi Plumbing Co., Nashville, Trevecca Towers for Elderly, Nashville, Ch. of Christ, Belpre, O., Moffitt Rd. Bapt. Ch., Mobile, Ala., Holy Redeemer Cath. Ch., Kissimmee, Fla., and numerous comml. structures. Home: 845 Forest Hills Dr Nashville TN 37220 Office: 2814 Granny White Pike Nashville TN 37204

ROBERTS, ROYSTON MURPHY, educator; b. Sherman, Tex., June 11, 1918; s. Charles Stanly and Leska (Murphy) R.; B.A., Austin Coll., 1940; D.Sc., 1965; M.A., U. Ill., 1941, Ph.D., 1944; m. Phyllis Arlene Benson, Sept. 18, 1943; children—Richard, David, Stanly, Jean Ellen. Research chemist Merck & Co., Inc., 1945-46; research asso. U. Cal. at Los Angeles, 1946-47; asst. prof. chemistry U. Tex., 1947-50, asso. prof., 1951-60, prof., 1961—; cons. Mem. Am. Chem. Soc., Sigma Xi, Alpha Chi Sigma, Phi Kappa Phi, Phi Lambda Upsilon. Presbyn. (elder). Author: Introduction to Modern Experimental Organic Chemistry, 1969, 2d edit., 1974. Contbr. articles profl. jours. Home: 841 E 38th St Austin TX 78705

ROBERTS, THOMAS, research physicist; b. Ft. Smith, Ark., Apr. 27, 1929; s. Thomas Lawrence and Emma Lee (Stanley) R.; A.A., Armstrong Coll., Savannah, Ga., 1953; B.S., U. Ga., 1956, M.S. (Alumni fellow), 1957; postgrad. (Spl. Alumni fellow), 1958; Ph.D., N.C. State U., 1965; m. Alice Anne Harbin, Nov. 14, 1958; children—Lawrence Dewey, Regina Anne; foster child, Marcia Yvette Barber. Instr. physics U. Ga., 1956-57; research physicist U.S. Army Missile Command, Redstone Arsenal, Ala., 1958—; dir. Clark, Roberts and Co., Huntsville, Ala. Instr. physics U. Ala., Huntsville, evenings, 1960-61, Athens (Ala.) Coll., evenings, 1968-69. Served with USAF, 1948-52. Recipient Wheatley Physics award U. Ga., 1956, Sci. and Engring. Achievement award Dept. of Army and Army Missile Command, 1968, Research award U.S. Army, 1970. Mem. Am. Phys. Soc., Am. Rocket Soc., Assn. U.S. Army, Am. Optical Soc., Toastmasters Internat. (exec. lt. gov. dist. 48, 1962-63), Phi Beta Kappa, Sigma Psi, Phi Kappa Phi, Sigma Pi Sigma, Pi Mu Epsilon. Episcopalian. Patents, publs. in field. Home: 2815 Bentley St SE Huntsville AL 35801 Office: US Army Missile Command AMSMI RRP Redstone Arsenal AL 35809

ROBERTS, THOMAS EDWIN, lawyer; b. Lufkin, Tex., Oct. 1, 1928; s. Charles Maury and Mary Lee (McCommon) R.; B.B.A., Tex. Tech. Coll., 1950; M.B.A., So. Meth. U., 1955, J.D., 1962; m. Mary Lee Jones, Apr. 3, 1954; children—Marilynn, Thomas, Karen, Barbara. Accountant, Frye, Gregory & Linsteader, accountants, Dallas, 1951-63; admitted to Tex. bar, 1962; mem. firms Bailey, Steele & Roberts, Dallas, 1963-66, Collie, McSpedden & Roberts, Dallas, 1967—. Dir. Abactor, Inc., Dallas, Bell & Murphy & Assocs., Inc., Dallas, Cowen Bros., Fort Worth, Dallas Weathermatic, Landscape Sprinkler System, Lock-Artic, Reproductions, Ltd., Union Sling Co., (all Dallas). Troop com. mem. and chmn. Circle Ten council Boy Scouts Am., 1968-73, Philmont Scout Ranch trek leader, 1971. Served with AUS, 1946-48. C.P.A., Tex. Mem. State Bar Tex., Am., Dallas bar assns., Tex. Soc. C.P.A.'s. Methodist. Rotarian (pres. Dallas South 1966-67, community service and scholarship chmn. Dallas Redbird, 1967—). Home: 516 McCoy St Irving TX 75062 Office: Collie McSpedden & Roberts Fidelity Union Tower Dallas TX 75201

ROBERTS, VERNELL RAYMOND, dentist; b. Pelham, Ga., May 4, 1920; s. Charles and Indiana (Williams) R.; B.S., Fla. A. & M. U., 1943; D.D.S., Howard U., 1951; m. Arneatha Jones, Mar. 18, 1961; children—Vernell, William, Emmie Denise. Pub. health dentist Va. State Health Dept., Richmond, 1951-56; dental officer D.C. Govt., Washington, 1956—; pvt. practice dentistry, Washington, 1956—. Served with AUS, 1943-45. Mem. Dist. Dental Soc., Nat., Am. dental assns., Robert T. Freeman Dental Soc., Phi Beta Sigma. Club: Century (Washington). Home: 382 N St SW Washington DC 20024 Office: 5503 Georgia Av NW Washington DC 20011

ROBERTS, WARREN AUSTIN, oil co. exec.; b. Pitts., Nov. 28, 1915; s. Warren Austin and Laura H. (Dennis) R.; B.S. in Chem. Engring., Carnegie Inst. Tech., 1937; m. Margaret E. Fry, Mar. 19, 1942; children—Warren Austin, III, Margaret Ann. With Phillips Petroleum Co., 1937—, dist. supt., Hobbs, N.M. and Los Angeles,

1953-60, div. mgr., Oklahoma City, 1960-63, vice chmn. operating com., Bartlesville, Okla., 1963-66, chmn. operating com., 1966-68, v.p. exploration and prodn. dept., 1968-69, sr. v.p., 1969-71, exec. v.p., 1971—, also dir.; dir. Pacific Petroleum Co. Ltd., Westcoast Gas Transmission Ltd. Mem. nat. council, pres. Cherokee area council Boy Scouts Am.; nat. bd. dirs. Camp Fire Girls; chmn. industry liaison com., deep sea drilling project Scripps Inst. Oceanography; mem. Nat. Acad. Sci. panel on drilling technique Project Mohole, 1958-64; mem. Okla. Air Pollution Council, 1967-72. Served from 2d lt. to maj. C.E., USAAF, 1942-46. Registered profl. engr., Okla. Mem. Okla. Petroleum Council (pres. 1965-66; Distinguished achievement award 1962), Am. Petroleum Inst. (chmn. com. pub. affairs), Nat. Soc. Profl. Engrs., Oklahoma City C. of C. (chmn. oil and gas div. 1962, 63), Bartlesville C. of C. (chmn. hwy. com. 1964-68; dir. 1970—). Home: 1208 Swan Dr Bartlesville OK 74003 Office: Phillips Bldg Bartlesville OK 74003

ROBERTS, WILBURN R., religious orgn. exec.; b. Mt. Olive, Miss., Apr. 9, 1910; s. James and Martha (Arender) R.; B.S., U. So. Miss., 1937; m. Nellie Mixon, Feb. 24, 1934; children—Kathleen (Mrs. Klaus B. Striegler), Wilburn R., John Mixon. Supt. schs., Petal, Miss., 1933-40, Silver Creek, Miss., 1940-44; with Miss. Bapt. Conv. Bd., Sc. Bapt. Conv., 1944—, annuity sec. Miss., Jackson, 1958—. Mem. stewardship commn. So. Bapt. Conv., 1967—. Trustee Bapt. Meml. Hosp., Memphis. Baptist (deacon). Mason. Home: 156 S Denver St Jackson MS 39209 Office: Bapt Bldg PO Box 530 Jackson MS 39205

ROBERTS, WILLIAM HENRY, textile co. exec.; b. Winfield, Ala., June 19, 1916; s. Walter Lee and Sarah (Smith) R.; student Internat. Corr. Sch., 1936-40; m. Annie Beth Perry, Oct. 2, 1937; children—Billie Anne (Mrs. Charles Leonard Simpson), Walter Perry. Supr. Ala. Mills Inc., Winfield, Ala., 1938-46, supt., 1946-56, supt. Ala. Mills div. Dan River Mills Inc., 1956-59; plant mgr. Moultrie Textiles div. Moultrie Cotton Mills (Ga.), 1960—. Mem. Winfield City Sch. System, 1951-55. Mason (Shriner). Lion, Kiwanian (dir. 1952). Club: Moultrie Sunset Country. Home: 1340 4th St SW Moultrie GA 31768 Office: PO Box 70 11th St SW Moultrie GA 31768

ROBERTS, WILLIAM JOHN, chem. co. exec.; b. Phila., June 5, 1918; s. William G. and Olive (Schoppe) R.; A.B., U. Pa., 1942, M.S., 1944, Ph.D., 1947; m. Eleanor Florence Kennedy, Oct. 2, 1948; children—John William, Wendy Eleanor. With Pa. Indsl. Chem. Corp., Chester, 1946-57, dir. research, 1955-57; dir. research Summit Research Labs., Celanese Corp., Summit, N.J., 1957-64; v.p., tech. dir. Celanese Fibers Co., Charlotte, N.C., 1965-72; v.p., tech. dir. Fiber div. FMC Corp., Phila., 1973—. Fellow Am. Inst. Chemists; mem. Am. Chem. Soc., Soc. Chem. Industry, Textile Research Inst., Fiber Soc., Sigma Xi, Pi Mu Epsilon. Clubs: Chemists (N.Y.C.); Lake Norman Yacht. Home: 1031 Huntington Park Dr Charlotte NC 28211 Office: 1617 John F Kennedy Blvd Philadelphia PA 19103

ROBERTS, WILLIAM LAWRENCE, mfg. co. exec.; b. Boston, Jan. 20, 1924; s. James Joseph and Mary Margaret (Galvin) R.; student Northeastern U., 1949-51, Rutgers U., 1952-54; LL.B., Blackstone Sch. Law, 1959; m. Josephine Mary DeLeo, July 22, 1945; children—James Joseph, Linda Marie (Mrs. John Hamilton Glover), William Lawrence. With RCA, Camden, N.J., 1951-58, Midwest regional rep., 1955, N.E. regional rep., 1956; sr. mem. tech. staff Thompson Ramo Wooldridge Co., Redondo Beach, Cal., 1958-60, N.E. regional mgr., 1960-61; mgr. marketing Sperry Rand Research Center, Sudbury, Mass., 1961-62; research and devel. marketing mgr. Litton Industries, Beverly Hills, Cal., 1962-65, dir. data systems, div. aero Service Corp., 1965-66; with Collins Radio Co., Dallas, 1966—, venture analyst, 1973—, mgr. sales service div., 1973—. Chmn. cub scouts Fort Stanwix council Boy Scouts Am., 1956-57, asst. dist. commr., 1965-66; pres. Meadowbrook P.T.A., Pennsauken, N.J., 1953-54. Campaign mgr. Kennedy/Johnson, Rome, N.Y., 1960. Served with USNR, 1942-45: PTO. Recipient Citizens award City Utica (N.Y.), 1963. Mem. I.E.E.E. (sr. mem., nat. exec. com. 1960-64), Armed Forces Communications and Electronics Assn. (nat. dir. 1959-67), Author: (with Vernon Poehls) Naval Shipboard Communications Building Block Design Handbook, 1952; Test Agenda and Record of Performance of Shipboard Electronic Systems, 1953. Home: 3021 Princeton Dr Plano TX 75074 Office: Collins Radio M/S 407-131 Richardson TX 75080

ROBERTSHAW, JAMES, lawyer; b. Greenville, Miss., May 19, 1916; s. Frank Newell and Mary (Aldridge) R.; B.S., Miss. State U., 1937; J.D. Harvard, 1940; m. Sylvia Yale Schively, Apr. 28, 1956; children—Mary Nicholson, Sylvia Yale, James, Frank Paxton. Admitted to Miss. bar, 1940; gen. practice, Greenville, 1946—; partner Robertshaw, Merideth & Swank, 1964—. Charter bd. dirs. Washington County Ednl. Found., 1965—. Mem. Miss. Ho. of Reps., 1953-46. Mem. Community Relations Com.; v.p. Greenville Indsl. Found. chmn. Greenville Airport Commn. Served to col. AUS, 1941-46. Decorated Legion of Merit; Croix de Guerre (France). Mem. Am., Washington County (past pres.) bar assns., Miss. State Bar. Episcopalian (jr. warden). Clubs: Greenville Golf and Country, University, Lions (past pres.); Refuge Hunting (dir.). Home: 844 Arnold Av Greenville MS 38701 Office: Woolworth Bldg Greenville MS 38701

ROBERTSON, ADRIAN ANDREW, dentist; b. Moneta, Va., Apr. 16, 1939; s. Dan Field and Elsie (Moles) R.; student Ferrum Jr. Coll., 1958-59, U. Richmond, 1959-61; D.D.S., Va. Commonwealth U., 1965; m. Doris Elizabeth Joyner, July 26, 1964; children—Nicholas Andrew, Jennifer Joy. Pvt. practice dentistry, Newport News, Va., 1967—; dental cons. Patrick Henry Hosp., 1969-72. Counselor, Augsburger Crusade, 1970, Harrington Crusade, 1971. Bd. dirs. Peninsula Youth for Christ, 1971-72; trustee Youth for Christ, 1970—. Served with USNR, 1965-67. Mem. Acad. Gen. Dentistry, Am. Dental Assn., Peninsula Dental Soc., Am. Soc. Dentistry for Children. Baptist (deacon 1969-70, 72—, dir. Sunday sch. 1970-73, chmn. ch. nominating com. 1969, 72, pulpit com. pulpit com. 1970, mem. finance com. 1969-70). Mason, Kiwanian (dir. 1969-71, 73—, Distinguished Service award 1973). Home: 104 Peirsey Pl Newport News VA 23602 Office: 559 Denbigh Blvd Newport News VA 23602

ROBERTSON, ARNOLD LAVERNE, evangelist; b. Ames, Ia., Sept. 10, 1926; s. James Peter and Lida Beatrice (Severson) R.; student Northwestern Bible Coll., 1945, Bob Jones U., 1949, 50; grad. Moody Bible Inst., 1949; B.A., Guilford Coll., 1956; B.D., Southeastern Bapt. Theol. Sem., 1960; m. Mitzi Marie Haymore, June 2, 1951; children—Mark Laverne, James Grant. Evangelist, dir. Youth for Christ, Chgo., also Grand Rapids, Mich., 1944-49; ordained to ministry Baptist Ch., 1950; pastor Lindley Park Bapt. Ch., Greensboro, N.C., 1951-60; evangelist, 1960—; v.p. Trans World Radio, religious radio sta., 1954—; pres. Arnie Robertson Evangelistic Assn., 1960—, also dir.; bd. dirs. Northwoods Youth Crusade, 1962—; pres. N. Am. Bible Inst., Ellison Bay, Wis., 1949-51. Tchr. John Wesley Coll., Greensboro, N.C., 1955. Mem. Pres.'s Com. for Handicapped, 1956. Bd. dirs. Internat. Evangelism, Inc. Mem. So. Bapt. Evangelists, Greensboro C. of C. Home: 2122 New Garden Rd Greensboro NC 27410 Office: PO Box 9461 Greensboro NC 27408

ROBERTSON, BALDWIN, physicist; b. Los Angeles, Sept. 26, 1934; s. Baldwin and Mary (McCaffrey) R.; B.S., Stanford, 1956, M.S., 1957, Ph.D., 1965; m. Ann B.C. Dyer, Apr. 7, 1962; children—Rebecca C., Sarah E., Baldwin V. Research asst. Washington U., St. Louis, 1962-64; instr. Cornell U., 1964-66; physicist Nat. Bur. Standards, Washington, 1966—. Mem. Am. Phys. Soc., Am. Phys. Assn. Home: 6815 Selkirk Dr Bethesda MD 20034 Office: Nat Bur Standards Washington DC 20234

ROBERTSON, BENJAMIN WILLIAM, clergyman, coll. pres.; b. Roanoke, Va., Apr. 6, 1931; s. Clarence and Anna Mary (Holland) R.; B.Th., Va. Sem., 1951; A.B., Va. Union U., 1954; M.Div., Va. Theol. Sem. and Coll., 1957, D.D., 1959; LL.D., Union Bapt. Sem., 1965; m. Dolores Wallace, Mar. 15, 1955; 1 son, Benjamin William. Ordained to ministry Bapt. Ch., 1948; pastor 1st Union Bapt. Ch., Chesterfield, Va., 1952-53, Piney Grove Bapt. Ch., Virginia Beach, 1953-55, Cedar St. Meml. Bapt. Ch. of God, Richmond, Va., 1955—. Tchr. Nat. Progressive Bapt. Congress, 1962—; founder Robertson's Coll., Richmond, 1958, pres. 1958—. Founder Progressive Nat. Bapt. Conv., 1965; preacher radio sta. WLEE, 1961—, radio sta. WANT, 1965—. Bd. dirs. Commonwealth Girl Scouts, Salvation Army Boys Club, East End Community Soc., Inc., Community City League, 1972; trustee Va. Theol. Sem. and Coll., 1956—, Baptist Children Home. Recipient Minister of Year award Richmond's Ushers, 1956; Humanitarian award Richmond Community Hosp., 1972. Mem. St. Luke Benevolence Soc., Alpha Phi Alpha (super pub. service award 1960). Mason (sec. 1959—). Editorial bd. Progressive Nat. Pub. Bd., 1972—. Home: Route 5 Box 312Y Richmond VA 23231 Office: 716-726 N 24th St Richmond VA 22223

ROBERTSON, BERNICE TALMADGE BELL (MRS. RICHARD DALE ROBERTSON), hosp. adminstr.; b. Pittsburg, Tex., Mar. 25, 1920; d. Barney Arthur and Letha Bernice (Gautney) Bell; student Columbia U., 1962-63; m. Richard Dale Robertson, Dec. 23, 1938; children—Sherry (Mrs. Will Edd Grimes), Genie (Mrs. Cecil Boren, Jr.). PBX operator, adminstrv. clk. Desha County Hosp., Dumas Ark., 1952-55, bookkeeper, 1955-56, bookkeeper, adminstrv. asst., 1956-59, adminstr., 1959-65; surveyor, insp. State Health Dept., Little Rock, 1966; adminstr. McGehee Desha County Hosp., McGehee, Ark., 1966—. Sec., McGehee Ecology Commn., 1970—; pres P.T.A., Dumas, 1952-53, Desha County Health Adv. Council, 1969—; mem. area adv. council State Ark. Dept. Edn. Div. Vocational, Tech. and Adult Edn., 1971—; coordinator Candy Stripers, 1967—; treas. Grady Soc. Christian Service, 1958—; mem. publicity com. Ark. Red Cross Blood Program; mem. Area-Wide Comprehensive Health Council; county coordinator Statewide Immunization Program; mem. Com. on Higher Edn. for Health. Bd. dirs. Areawide Health Adv. Council, 1969—. Mem. Women's C. of C. (pres. 1973), Am. Hosp. Assn., Am. Hosp. Financial Assn., Ark. Adminstrs. Forum (sec. 1961-62), Southeast Ark. Hosp. Council (pres. 1961-62, 1969-70, sec. 1971-72), Am. Coll. Hosp. Adminstrs. Methodist. Club: Women's Civic (pres. 1970-71) (McGehee). Home: Jefferson St McGehee AR 71654 Office: Green Meadow Addition McGehee AR 71654

ROBERTSON, BILLY PERKINS, cons.; b. Bangs, Tex., July 23, 1915; s. Nicholas Perkins and Addie May (Schulze) R.; B.S., U. Tex., 1942; postgrad. Northwestern U., 1964; m. Ida Elizabeth Gilliland, Dec. 29, 1943; children—Brian Paul, Elizabeth Jan. Research engr. Westinghouse Electric Corp., Pitts., 1942-47; sales engr. Humble Oil & Refining Co., Houston, 1947-49, mgr. sales engring., 1949-53, supt. spl. products mfg., 1955, dist. mgr., 1956-57, region mgr. gen. office, consumer sales, 1958-65, new products coordinator, 1965-72; now with Bus. Counselors, cons. firm, also Hompark Realty. dir. Humble Leasing Co. Bd. dirs. Bellaire Presbyn. Day Sch.; trustee Brazos Presbyn. Homes. Recipient certificate commendation Am. Soc. M.E., 1957, Council award, 1959. Registered profl. engr., Tex. Mem. Tex. Mfrs. Assn., E. Tex., Houston chambers commerce, Houston Engring. and Sci. Soc. (pres., dir.), Engring. Council Houston (exec. com.), Pi Tau Sigma. Presbyn. (deacon, elder). Contbr. articles to profl. jours. Patentee in field. Home: 5819 Queensloch Houston TX 77035 Office: 5520 Cedar St Bellaire TX 77401

ROBERTSON, CARY, ret. journalist; b. Louisville, Apr. 18, 1902; s. Archibald T. and Ella (Broadus) R.; student Wake Forest Coll., 1920-22, U. Va. 1922-25; Nieman fellow, Harvard, 1945-46; m. Priscilla Smith, May 26, 1934; children—Charlotte, Harry, Cary. With Louisville Courier-Jour., 1925—, reporter, 1925-27, day city editor, 1927, makeup editor, 1928, Sunday editor, 1930-68, book editor, 1968-73; Ky. corr. Newsweek mag. 1950—; lectr. univs. Mem. Orgn. com. Assn. Chamber Music Players, N.Y.C., 1948—. Dir. George Rogers Clark Heritage, Inc. (chmn. 1966); trustee Louisville Chamber Music Soc., pres., 1964, 65. Mem. Am. Assn. Sunday and Feature Editors (v.p. 1964, pres. 1965), Locally Edited Mag. Editors Assn. (chmn. 1950), Anchorage Trails (pres. 1961), Sigma Delta Chi. Club: Owl Creek Country (Anchorage, Ky.). Home: 12627 Osage Rd N Anchorage KY 40223

ROBERTSON, DOUGLAS WELBY, electronic research engr.; b. Crawford, Ga., June 13, 1924; s. William Fletcher and Julia Pope (McWhorter) R.; B.S., Ga. Inst. Tech., 1951, M.S., 1957; m. Martha Lois Gardner, June 4, 1949; children—Donald Bradford, Charles Julian, Carol Janet. Asst. research engr. to research engr. Ga. Inst. Tech., 1951-57, sr. research engr., 1959-62, chief communications div., 1962—; mem. tech. staff ITT Labs., Atlanta, 1957-59; cons. in field. Served with USAAF, 1944-46. Mem. I.E.E.E. (sr.), Acoustical Soc. Am., A.A.A.S., Sigma Xi. Contbr. articles to profl. jours. Patentee in field. Home: 2937 Henderson Rd Tucker GA 30084 Office: Communications Div Ga Inst Tech Atlanta GA 30332

ROBERTSON, FRANK LEWIS, bishop; b. Covington, Ga., Apr. 22, 1917; s. Herman William and Nell (Hutchins) R.; A.B., Emory U., 1940; M.Div., Yale, 1942; postgrad. Columbia; D.D., LaGrange Coll., 1961; L.H.D., Ky. Wesleyan U., 1973; m. LuReese Ann Watson, June 18, 1941; children—Jane (Mrs. Jackson), Frank Lewis. Ordained to ministry United Methodist Ch., as deacon, 1942, elder, 1944; pastor, Baker Village Ch., Columbus, Ga., 1942-47, First Ch., Hawkinsville, Ga., 1947-51, First Ch., Douglas, Ga., 1951-55, St. Luke Ch., Columbus, Ga., 1955-60, Mulberry St. Ch., Macon, Ga., 1964-69, First Ch., Valdosta, Ga., 1969-72; dist. supt. Savannah, Ga., 1960-64; consecrated bishop, 1972; bishop Louisville area, 1972—. Trustee Andrew Coll., Cuthbert, Ga., Epworth-by-the Sea, Ga., Lake Junaluska Assembly, N.C., Ky. Wesleyan Coll., Lindsey Wilson Coll., Ky., Union Coll., Barbourville, Ky. Kiwanian, Rotarian. Home: 800 S 4th St Louisville KY 40203 Office: 1115 S 4th St Louisville KY 40203

ROBERTSON, FRANKLIN LEE, constrn. co. engr.; b. Tigrett, Tenn., Jan. 22, 1934; s. Huey Franklin and Fannie Lee (Harper) R.; student Freed-Hardeman Coll., 1952, U. Tenn., 1961; B.S., in Civil Engring., Tenn. Tech. U., 1964; m. Roberta Lawrence, Sept. 24, 1961; children—Jeffrey Lee, Steven Lawrence. Project mgr., also constrn. engr. Forcum-Lannom Assos., Inc., Dyersburg, Tenn., 1964-69, asst. sec., also dir., 1970—. Served with AUS, 1956-58; ETO. Mem. Tenn. Soc. Profl. Engrs. (pres. W. Tenn. Chpt. 1972-73, state dir. 1973-74). Mem. Ch. of Christ. Home: 2030 Crossgate Rd Dyersburg TN 38024 Office: PO Box 768 Dyersburg TN 38024

ROBERTSON, GEORGE GORDON, educator; anatomist; b. Saint John, N.B., Can., Jan. 30, 1916; s. Elston Roy and Mary Creana (Jones) R.; B.Sc., Acadia U., 1936, B.A., 1937; Ph.D., Yale, 1941; m. Margaret Mason, Feb. 22, 1946; children—George Gordon III, William Don. Came to U.S., 1937, naturalized, 1949. Instr. anatomy La. State U. Med. Sch., 1942-43; mem. faculty Baylor U. Med. Sch., 1943-52, asso. prof. anatomy, 1947-52; prof. anatomy U. Tenn. Med. Units, 1952—, chmn. dept., 1961—. Mem. Am. Assn. Anatomists, Am. Soc. Cell Biology, Teratology Soc., A.A.A.S., Inst. Internat. d'Embryologie, So. Soc. Anatomists (pres. 1968-69), Sigma Xi. Author articles in field. Home: 2087 Hampton Hill Dr Memphis TN 38134

ROBERTSON, IDA ROBERTS (MRS. SAMUEL THOMPSON ROBERTSON), home economist; b. Shawboro, N.C., Mar. 8, 1918; d. James M. and Ida C. (Perkins) Roberts; B.A., East Carolina U., 1939; postgrad. Woman's Coll., U. N.C. (now U. N.C. at Greensboro), 1948, 62; m. Samuel Thompson Robertson, June 30, 1949. Faculty pub. high sch., Kenansville, N.C., 1939-40; home mgmt. supr. county Farmer's Home Adminstrn., Raleigh, N.C., 1940-46; vocational home econs. tchr., high sch., Williamston, N.C., 1946-48; tchr. English high sch., Woodsdale, N.C., 1954-55; asst. dir. Dairy Council Richmond (Va.), 1957-62. Mem. Am. (life), Richmond (v.p. 1958-60, publicity chmn. 1960-62, membership chmn. 1963-66, treas. 1965-67), home econs. assns., Va. (chmn. ways and means com. 1959-61), Richmond home economists in bus., Currituck County Hist. Soc., East Carolina Alumni Assn. (life mem., sec.-treas. Richmond area 1963-70), Richmond Agrl. Grange, Phi Sigma Alpha (pres. 1967-68, named Woman of Year 1968, extension officer, 1971-73, publicity chmn. 1970-71, corr. sec. 1968-71, 73-74). Democrat. Methodist. Home: 5710 W Franklin St Richmond VA 23226

ROBERTSON, JAMES CARTER, JR., elec. mfg. co. exec.; b. River Junction, Fla., Oct. 13, 1934; s. James Carter and Mary Elizabeth (Graves) R.; B.S. in Indsl. Mgmt., Carnegie-Mellon U., 1956; postgrad. U. N.M., 1956-58, Fla. Inst. Tech., 1969-71; m. Joy Auten, June 29, 1957; children—Jull Suzanne, Merry Carole. Instr., Fla. Inst. Tech. Melbourne, 1960-62; sect. head Radiation Inc., Melbourne, 1964-66, dir. reliability and quality, 1966-69, dir. computer services, 1969-70; dir. mfg. operations Harris Controls Co., Melbourne, 1970—. Cons. on prodn. and quality problems, 1970—. Town councilman Indialantic, Fla., 1961-67; police commr., 1963-67; mem. gov.'s. rev. com., 1967. Bd. dirs. Community Services Council. Mem. Am. Soc. for Quality Control, I.E.E.E. Home: 150 Deland Av Indialantic FL 32903 Office: PO Box 430 Melbourne FL 32901

ROBERTSON, JAMES MEBANE, physician; b. Olin, N.C., Aug. 4, 1906; s. William Lee and Augusta (Weisner) R.; B.A., U. N.C., 1928, postgrad., 1929-30; M.D., Temple U. Med. Sch., 1932; m. Ann Jones, Mar. 2, 1934; 1 son, James Mebane, Jr. Intern Hamot Hosp., Erie, Pa., 1932-33; pvt. practice gen. medicine and pediatrics, Harmony, N.C., 1933—; mem. staff Iredell Meml. Hosp., Statesville, N.C. Mayor, Harmony, N.C., 1971—. Mem. A.M.A., Iredell County Med. Soc., Am. Acad. Gen. Practice, Phi Rho Sigma. Democrat. Presbyn. (elder 1945-72). Mason (Shriner), Elk, Moose. Club: City (Statesville, N.C.). Home: 25 N Main St Harmony NC 28634 Office: 10 Union Grove Rd Harmony NC 28634

ROBERTSON, JOHN LOVELL, banker; b. Marietta, O., Aug. 14, 1919; s. Benjamin Harrison and Alice (Lovell) R.; grad. high sch.; m. Geneva P. White, Nov. 9, 1940; children—Susan W., John W. Engaged in cattle ranching, Okla. and Tex., 1938-42, 45-53; with First Nat. Bank and Trust Co., Tulsa, 1953—, exec. v.p., 1961-67, pres., 1967—, chmn. bd., 1974—, also dir.; v.p. Fifth & Boston Corp.; dir. Firstul Mortgage Co., Midwest Finance Co. Mem. Tulsa Clearing House Assn.; dir., treas. Industries for Tulsa; mem. Tulsa Airport Authority; pres. United Fund Drive, Tulsa; mem. sr. adv. council Okla. Cattlemens Assn. Vice pres., dir. St. Francis Hosp. Served with USAAF, 1942-46. Mem. Tulsa C. of C. (1st v.p.). Methodist. Clubs: Tulsa, Southern Hills Country (past pres., dir.) (Tulsa). Home: 7217 S Gary Av Tulsa OK 74136 Office: First Nat Bank & Trust Co Tulsa OK 74193

ROBERTSON, JOHN MARSHALL, JR., natural gas pipeline co. exec.; b. Houston, Sept. 10, 1924; s. John Marshall and Annie Goforth (Toland) R.; B.S., Tex. A. and M. U., 1948; postgrad. Harvard Bus. Sch., 1972; m. Margaret Jean Anderson, June 11, 1948; children—Barbara Jean, John Marshall III, Thomas Allan. Design engr. Parkersburg Rig & Reel Co., Houston, 1948-50; engr. Tenn. Gas Transmission Co., Houston, 1950-61; sales rep., 1961-65; v.p. East Tenn. Natural Gas Co., Knoxville, 1965-67; v.p. Midwestern Gas Transmission Co., Houston, 1967-72, pres., 1972—, also dir. Served with AUS, 1942-46. Mem. Midwest, So. gas assns. Club: Houston, Home: 1210 Riverbend Houston TX 77042 Office: PO Box 2511 Houston TX 77001

ROBERTSON, RICHARD BOYD, govt. ofcl.; b. Richmond, Va., Nov. 14, 1936; s. Walter G. and Annie (Boyd) R.; B.S., Va. Mil. Inst., 1958; Certificate in Hwy. Traffic, Yale, 1961; M. in Regional Planning, U. N.C., 1964; m. Patricia Jean Atkinson, Aug. 29, 1959; children—Elizabeth Bruce, Richard Boyd. With Va. Dept. Hwys., Richmond, 1958-67, hwy. traffic engr., 1964-65, transp. planning engr., 1965-67; exec. dir. Richmond Regional Planning Dist. Commn., 1967-70; dir. Office of Transp. Planning, Div. of State Planning and Community Affairs, Office of the Gov., Commonwealth of Va., 1971; sr. regional planner Appalachian Regional Commn., Washington, 1972—. Fellow Inst. Traffic Engrs.; mem. Am. Inst. Planners, Am. Soc. C.E. Clubs: Va. Mil. Inst., Sportsman's (Richmond). Home: 7725 Canal Ct McLean VA 22101 Office: Appalachian Regional Commn 1666 Connecticut Av NW Washington DC 20008

ROBERTSON, ROBERT LAFON, entomologist, educator; b. Blountsville, Ala., July 20, 1925; s. Herbert Leon and Effie Estelle (Lafon) R.; student Snead Jr. Coll., 1946-47; B.S. in Agrl. Sci., Auburn U., 1950, M.S. in Entomology, 1954; m. Ruth Lenore Farmer, Mar. 13, 1965; 1 dau., Karen Perry. Asst. County Agt. Auburn (Ala.) U., 1950-52, research asst. in entomology, 1952-54, asst. research entomologist, 1954-56; staff entomologist Am. Cyanamid Co., N.Y.C., 1956-58; extension entomologist U. Ga., Athens, 1958-59; extension asst. prof. entomology N.C. State U., Raleigh, 1960-64, asso. prof., 1964-69, prof., 1970—. Cons. Eli Lilly & Co., Boynton Beach, Fla., 1967—. Served with USNR, 1943-46. Grantee in pest mgmt. U.S. Dept. Agr., 1970-71, 71-72. Mem. N.C. Acad. Sci., Pesticide Assn. N.C., Carolinas Golf Course Supts. Assn., Entomol. Soc. Am., N.C. Entomol. Soc. (sec.-treas. 1971-73), Am. Inst. Biol. Sci., Alpha Zeta, Gamma Sigma Delta, Phi Kappa Phi, Sigma Xi. Methodist (Nashville dir. 1967-68, Cary dir. 1968-71). Contbg. editor: The Progressive Farmer, 1970-73, The Flue-Cured Tobacco Farmer, 1965-73, The Peanut Farmer, 1966-73, Virginia-Carolina Peanut News, 1965-73. Contbr. articles to profl. jours. Home: 409 Holly Circle Cary NC 27511 Office: 2309 Gardner Hall North Carolina State University Raleigh NC 27607

ROBERTSON, ROBERT NELSON, civil engr.; b. Bay City, Tex., Nov. 26, 1933; s. John Houston and Madge (Clement) R.; B.S. in Archtl. Engring., U. Tex., 1956, M.S. in Civil Engring., 1961; m. Carol Beth Villarreal, June 7, 1958; children—Marta Elaine, Steven

Michael, Douglas Arthur, Robert Carroll. With Walter Kidde, engrs., S.W., Houston, 1956-57, W. Clark Craig, engrs., Austin, Tex., 1957-58, Tex. Hwy. Dept., Austin, 1958-61; with Lockwood, Andrews & Newnam, Inc., Houston, 1961-73; structural engr. Port of Houston Authority, 1973—. Registered profl. engr., Tex. Mem. Am. Soc. C.E. (chmn. structural com. Tex. sect. 1969), Am. Inst. Steel Constrn., Am. Concrete Inst., Tex. Soc. Profl. Engrs., Phi Eta Sigma, Chi Epsilon. Presbyn. (elder 1969-70). Home: 1420 Richmond St Apt 2046 Houston TX 77006 Office: 1519 Capitol St Houston TX 77001

ROBERTSON, ROLAND BURLSON, JR., physician; b. Taylorsville, Miss., Feb. 17, 1934; s. Roland Burlson and Nellie (Vowell) R.; B.S., U. So. Miss., 1955; M.D., U. Tenn., 1958; m. Anita Jane McKelvey, Apr. 14, 1957; children—Katherine Ann, John David Roland. Intern, John Gaston Hosp., Memphis, 1958-59; gen. practice medicine, Taylorsville, Miss., 1959-61; resident in internal medicine U. Miss. Med. Center, 1963-66; practice medicine, specializing in internal medicine, Meridian, Miss., 1966-67; staff physician VA Hosp., Jackson, Miss., 1967—, asst. chief med. service, 1970—, asso. chief staff for edn., 1973—; asst. prof. medicine U. Miss. Med. Center, 1967—, asst. dean for edn., 1973—. Served with USAF, 1961-63. Mem. Central Med. Soc., Miss. State, Am. med. assns., A.C.P., Miss. (pres. 1971-72), Am. thoracic socs., Jackson Acad. Medicine, Alpha Omega Alpha. Episcopalian (warden 1970-72). Home: 541 Woodson Dr Jackson MS 39206 Office: 1500 E Woodrow Wilson Jackson MS 39216

ROBERTSON, THOMAS JAMES, banker; b. Columbia, S.C., Dec. 16, 1897; s. Edwin W. and Evelyn (Perkins) R.; grad. Hotchkiss Sch., Lakeville, Conn., 1917; A.B., Yale, 1921; m. Mary Martin, Oct. 20, 1923; children—Edwin Wales II, Mary Ravenel; m. 2d, Mary McN. Milling, Aug. 16, 1948. Began with Nat. Loan & Exchange Bank, Columbia, 1921, becoming pres. in 1927; now chmn. bd. First Bankshares of S.C., Columbia; pres. Columbia Real Estate & Trust Co. Served as comdr. U.S. Navy, World War II. Served as ensign Naval Aviation, U.S. Navy, World War I. Mem. Alpha Delta Phi, Scroll and Key (Yale). Presbyn. Clubs: Forest Lake, Palmetto, Pine Tree Hunt. Address: First National Bank Columbia SC 29201

ROBERTSON, THOMAS PASCHE, airline exec.; b. Austin, Tex., Mar. 14, 1915; s. Walter Lee and Gertrude (Pasche) R.; B.B.A., U. Tex., 1938; m. Agness Francis Foster, Mar. 24, 1941; children—Thomas Ross, Sharon Anne (Mrs. Duval F. Moss III). Accountant, Fed. Land Bank of Houston, 1939-42; indsl. relations analyst Lockheed Aircraft Corp., Dallas, 1942-43; statis. analyst Douglas Aircraft Corp., Oklahoma City, 1943-46; with Braniff Airways, Inc., Dallas, 1946—, v.p., 1960—. Mem. Newcomen Soc., Nat. Economists Club, Dallas Economist Club (past pres.), Delta Sigma Pi. Home: 6220 Royalton Dr Dallas TX 75230 Office: PO Box 35001 Dallas TX 75235

ROBERTSON, WILLIAM BERNARD, govt. ofcl.; b. Roanoke, Va., Jan. 31, 1933; s. Irvin W. and Rebecca (Roberts) R.; B.S., Bluefield State Coll., 1954; M.S., Radford Coll., 1965; m. Johnnie Lucille Early, Nov. 6, 1953; children—William Allen, Bernice Victoria. Tchr. pub. schs., Roanoke, Va., 1956-65, elementary supr., 1965-69; spl. asst. to Gov. Va., Richmond, 1970—; moderator Your Community Speaks program WTOY, Roanoke, 1968-69; moderator Valley Views program WRFT-TV, 1968-69. Pres. Southwest Va. Community Devel. Fund, 1968-69; mem. speakers bur. Roanoke Fine Arts Center, 1967-69; mem. Pres.'s Com. on Mental Retardation, 1970—, Pres.'s Adv. Com. Sickle Cell Anemia, 1971, Nat. Motor Vehicle Safety Adv. Com., 1972—. Trustee Roanoke Valley United Fund; bd. dirs. Catholic Family and Childrens Service of Roanoke, Family Service-Travelers Aid, Va. State Mental Health, Juvenile and Domestic Relations Ct., King-Kennedy Found. Mem. Roanoke, Va., Nat. edn. assns., Omega Psi Phi. Roman Catholic. Home: 4800 K Terrace View Apts Blacksburg VA 24060 Office: Gov's Office State Capitol Richmond VA 23219

ROBERTSON, WILLIAM EDWARD, research co. exec.; b. Carteret, N.J., Dec. 15, 1916; s. William E. and Beneva (Roy) R.; B.A., Bucknell U., 1938; m. Dorothy Mary Dunn, Sept. 21, 1940 (div.); children—William E. III, Malcolm B., Douglas A.; m. 2d, Regina E. Gallagher, Nov. 24, 1971. Reporter, editorial writer Courier-News, Plainfield, N.J., 1938-42; asst. to pub. Harpers Mag., N.Y.C., 1946-50; asso. pub. dir. U.S. News & World Report, Washington, 1950-69; chmn. bd. Communications Marketing, Inc., Washington, 1970-72, also dir.; pres. Marketing Concepts, Washington, 1972—, also dir. Served to capt. AUS, 1942-46, 51-52. Mem. Nat. Press Club, Am. Marketing Assn., Am. Assn. Pub. Opinion Researchers, Assn. Indsl. Advertisers, Internat. Newspaper Promotion Assn., Izaak Walton League, Nat. Economists Club, Nat. Assn. Execs. Club, Washington Soc. Assn. Execs. Republican. Episcopalian. Clubs: Washington Golf and Country (Arlington, Va.); National Capitol Gun (Washington). Home: 4005 Featherstone Pl Alexandria VA 22304 Office: 1629 K St NW Washington DC 20006

ROBERTSON, WILLIAM HARRIS PETERMAN, editor; b. New Orleans, July 22, 1920; s. John G.W. and Eleanor (Peterman) R.; B.S., U.S. Naval Acad., 1942; m. Arden Marion Bullock, Sept. 5, 1953; children—Caroline, Zaring, Winter. With Thoroughbred Record, Lexington, Ky., 1952—, mng. editor, 1955-63, editor, 1963—; pres. Record Pub. Co., Lexington, 1964-71, chmn., 1971—. Served with USN, 1942-52. Clubs: Thoroughbred Am., Iroquois Hunt, Spindletop Hall, Ryland Lakes Country. Author: History of Thoroughbred Racing in America, 1964. Home: Briar Hill Pike Route 4 Lexington KY 40505 Office: Thoroughbred Record 904 N Broadway Lexington KY 40505

ROBERTSON, WILLIAM SHORE, lawyer; b. Richmond, Va., June 20, 1939; s. Alexander Cralle and Eugenia Young (Bailey) R.; A.B., Coll. William and Mary, 1961; LL.B., U. Va., 1964; m. Barbara B. Williams, June 26, 1966; 1 son, Stuart Alexander. Admitted to Va. bar, 1964; asso. mem. firm Martin & Alexander, Warrenton, 1966-67, partner, 1967-70; partner Martin, Alexander & Robertson, Warrenton, 1970—. Pres., Va. Museum, Fauquier Chpt., 1968-69. Asst. commonwealth atty. Fauquier County, 1968-73; sec. Warrenton Bd. Zoning Appeals, 1967-70; mem. Highland Sch. Bd., 1972. Bd. dirs. Fauquier County Mental Health Assn., 1970—, Fauquier Hosp. Maternity Clinic, 1971. Served to capt. AUS, 1964-66. Mem. Fauquier County (v.p. 1973), Am. bar assns., Va. State Bar (council 1969-73), Nat. Lawyers Club, Jr. C. of C. (dir. 1969), Lambda Chi Alpha, Omicron Delta Kappa, Phi Alpha Delta. Methodist. Clubs: Fauquier, Fauquier Springs Country (both Warrenton, Va.). Home: 269 Dover Rd Warrenton VA 22186 Office: 12 Culpeper St Warrenton VA 22186

ROBERTSON, WILLIAM THOMAS, SR., farm exec.; b. Greenville, Miss., Oct. 17, 1920; s. Thomas Dotson and Irene (Cooke) R.; B.S., Miss. State Coll., 1943; m. Frances Scott Bostick, June 3, 1943; children—William Thomas, Edna Kirk (Mrs. Henderson Alfred Moore III), Alexander Bostick. Partner, Holly Ridge Planting Co. (Miss.), 1943—, Holly Ridge Ranch, 1951—, Husbandville Plantation Farming Operations, Chatham, Miss., 1958—; pres. Holly Ridge Gin Co., Inc., 1958—, Kan. Plantation, Inc., Inverness, Miss., 1962—; dir. Valley Chem. Co., Yazoo Valley Oil Mill, Inc., Planters Bank & Trust Co., Ruleville, Miss., First Savs. & Loan, Indianola, Miss., Bell, Inc., St. Rest Plantation, Inc. Trustee Cotton, Inc. Served with AUS, World War II. Mem. Miss. Soybean Assn., Miss. Econ. Council, Delta Council, Sunflower County Farm Bur. Methodist (steward), Rotarian. Home: PO Box 95 Holly Ridge MS 38749 Office: PO Box 95 Holly Ridge MS 38749

ROBERTSON, WILLIAM WOODROW, educator; b. Beckville, Tex., Dec. 17, 1917; s. Ivy Guy and Elsie (Speck) R.; B.A., U. Tex., 1941, M.A., 1945, Ph.D., 1955; m. Margaret Merecedes Parkington, Mar. 5, 1950; children—Catherine Ann, James Stephen, Michael Louis. Instr. U. Tex. at Austin, 1944-55, asst. prof., 1955-59, asso. prof., 1959-63, prof. physics, 1963—. Fellow Am. Phys. Soc.; mem. Sigma Xi, Phi Beta Kappa, Sigma Pi Sigma, Phi Lambda Upsilon, Phi Eta Sigma. Contbr. numerous articles profl. jours. Home: 3505 Cherry Lane Austin TX 78703

ROBERTSTAD, GORDON WESLEY, educator; b. Madison, Wis., Sept. 29, 1923; s. John J. and Ingeborg (Hansen) R.; B.S., U. Wis., 1949, M.S., 1951; Ph.D., Colo. State U., 1959; m. Janice Mildred Lowe, Aug. 21, 1948; children—Arnold John, Jane Carol, Nancy Sue, Mary Lynn. Instr. U. Wyo., Laramie, 1949-59, asst. prof., 1959-62, asso. prof., 1962-64; NIH fellow Center for Disease Control, 1964-65; prof., chmn. dept. bacteriology S.D. State U., Brookings, 1964-68; prof. microbiology U. Tex. at El Paso, 1968—. Served with USAAF, 1942-46. Mem. Am. Soc. Microbiology, Internat. Soc. Human and Animal Mycoses, Mycol. Soc. Am., Med. Mycol. Soc. Ams., Inter Varsity Christian Fellowship, Beta Beta Beta, Sigma Xi, Phi Kappa Phi, Gamma Delta Sigma, Farm House Frat. Contbr. articles to sci. jours. Home: 4338 Emory Rd El Paso TX 79922 Office: Dept of Biological Sciences University of Texas at El Paso El Paso TX 79968

ROBESON, EDWARD JOHN III, textile co. exec.; b. Newport News, Va., Jan. 11, 1921; s. Edward John, Jr. and Ruth (Richards) R.; student U. Va., 1939-41; B.S., U.S. Naval Acad., 1944; m. Clara Austin Averett, June 10, 1944; children—Ann Austin Holmes, Edward John IV, Ruth Tinsley, Mastin, Helen, Elizabeth. Commd. ensign U.S. Navy, 1944, advanced to lt., 1945; comdg. officer U.S.S. LST 854, 1944-46; ret., 1947; maintenance foreman E.I. duPont de Nemours & Co., Martinsville, Va., 1950-53; maintenance supr. Monsanto (Chemstrand), Pensacola, Fla., 1953-55; maintenance supt., 1955-58, coordinator process improvement, 1958-59; plant engr. Monsanto, Greenwood, S.C., 1959-65; gen. mgr. George W. Park Seed Co., Greenwood, 1965-67; pres. Carolina div. Schlegel Mfg. Co., Chester, S.C., 1967—. Pres. Greenwood United Fund, 1965; v.p. Chester County Bd. Commerce and Devel. Bd. dirs. Chester County United Fund, Greenwood YMCA, 1964-65; sec. bd. trustees Bryan Coll.; mem. adv. bd. Salvation Army. Mem. Soc. M.E., S.C. (dir.), Greenwood (past dir.) chambers commerce, Alpha Tau Omega, Alpha Kappa Psi. Presbyn. (elder). Rotarian. Home: 119 York St Chester SC 29706 Office: PO Box 190 Chester SC 29706

ROBESON, JAMES LEE, architect; b. Wilmington, N.C., Jan. 9, 1905; s. Ben Arline and Alice (Lee) R.; B.S. in Architecture, Ga. Inst. Tech., 1926; m. Julia McLendon, Nov. 16, 1935; 1 son, James Lee. With Francis L. Abreu, architect, Atlanta, 1929-35; v.p. Abreu & Robeson, architects, Atlanta, 1935-69, pres., 1969—; prin. works include Farmers Market, Atlanta, 1956, Tech. Inf. Sch., Ft. Benning, Ga., 1965, also numerous hosps. Mem. A.I.A., Tau Beta Pi. Mason, Elk, Rotarian. Home: 1329 Sycamore Av Brunswick GA 31520 Office: 135 Walton St NW Atlanta GA 30303

ROBESON, VERNON SCOTT, mech. engr.; b. Tama, Ia., Sept. 1, 1921; s. Scott Carlyle and Blanche Irene (Coe) R.; student Dana Coll., 1940; B.S. in M.E., U. Neb., 1949; postgrad. U. Ala. at Huntsville, 1960-64; m. Nina Mildred Peck, Sept. 27, 1941; children—Vicki Joan (Mrs. Dan Williams Nash), Philip Scott. Engr., Boeing Co., Seattle, 1949-50; chief engr. Kelly Ryan Farm Equipment Co., Blair, Neb., 1952-56; mech. engr. Omaha Dist. C.E., 1956-59; staff specialist, supr. facilities planning staff office Army Ballistic Missile Agy., Redstone Arsenal, Ala., 1959-63, value engring. mgr. Lance Missile System Project Office, 1964-74, engr. in Rocket System Project Office, 1974—. Served with AUS, 1943-46; ETO. Decorated Combat Infantryman's badge; recipient Outstanding Value Engr. award Army Missile Command, 1965; named One of Ten Top Stock Car Drivers, Washington County, Neb., 1956. Registered profl. engr., Ala. Mem. Amateur Radio Relay League, Sigma Tau, Pi Tau Sigma. Baptist. Painter oils and portraits; Neb. State champion model airplane flyer, 1948. Home: 8500 Camille Dr Huntsville AL 35802 Office: Rocket System Project Office Redstone Arsenal AL 35809

ROBEY, HARRY RUSSELL, coll. adminstr.; b. Buena Vista, Va., Sept. 30, 1895; s. William Thomas and Susan (Connor) R.; grad. Dunsmore Coll. Accounting, 1917; Washington and Lee U., 1918; m. Margaret Durham, Sept. 12, 1922. Cashier Kingsport Pulp Corp. (Va.), 1918-19; treas. Farmers & Mchts. Mills, Buena Vista, Va., 1920-22; treas., bus. mgr., partner So. Sem. and Jr. Coll., Buena Vista, Va., 1922—. Mem. Buena Vista City Council, 1934-50; mem. Buena Vista Planning Commn., 1936-50; chmn. Buena Vista United Fund, 1968-72; organizer Buena Vista Health Dept., City Recreation Dept., City Planning Commn. Served with USNR, 1917-19. Episcopalian (mem. exec. council 1970-72). Mason. Clubs: Farmington Country, Shenandoah, Tri-Brook Country. Home: 2656 N Chestnut Av Buena Vista VA 24416 Office: Southern Seminary & Jr Coll Buena Vista VA 24416

ROBEY, KATHLEEN MORAN (MRS. RALPH WEST ROBEY), club woman; b. Boston, Aug. 9, 1909; d. John Joseph and Katherine (Berrigan) Moran; B.A., Trinity Coll., Washington, 1933; m. Ralph West Robey, Jan. 28, 1941. Actress appearing in Pride and Prejudic, Broadway, 1935, Tomorrow is a Holiday, road co., 1935, Death Takes a Holiday, road co., 1936, Left Turn, Broadway, 1936, Come Home to Roost, Boston, 1936; pub. relations N.Y. Fashion Industry, N.Y.C., 1938-43. Mem. Florence Crittenton Home and Hosp., Women's Aux. Salvation Army, Gray Lady, D.C. chpt. A.R.C.; mem. Seton Guild St. Ann's Infant Home. Mem. Internat. Platform Assn., English Speaking Union. Republican (mem. League Rep. Women D.C.). Roman Catholic. Club: City Tavern, Cosmos (Washington); Springdale Hall (Camden, S.C.). Home: 4000 Cathedral Av NW Washington DC 20016

ROBIDEAU, ROBERT GORDON, accountant; b. Rayville, La., Oct. 2, 1933; s. George Gordon and Ida (Mayo) R.; B.S., Miss. State U., 1962; m. Irma Jeanette Robideau, Oct. 20, 1958; children—Michael Gordon, James Richard. Staff accountant Arthur Anderson & Co., 1962-65; partner Walborg, Lockett, Paul & Co., Houston, 1965—, now v.p., sec.-treas. Dir. Goodman-Murray Industries, Inc., Houston, Central Welding Supply Co. Trustee, chmn. finance com. Leukemia Soc. Am., Houston., 1968-69. Served with USMCR, 1953-56. C.P.A., Tex. Mem. Am. Inst. C.P.A.'s, Tex. Soc. C.P.A.'s, Nat. Assn. Accountants, Soc. for Advancement Mgmt., Beta Alpha Psi. Democrat. Baptist (deacon 1956—). Mason. Home: 711 Longview Dr Sugarland TX 77478 Office: 1401 College Av South Houston TX 77578

ROBIE, CARROLL H., JR., physician; b. Danville, Ky., Nov. 21, 1923; s. Carroll H. and Myrtle (Baker) R.; A.B., U. Ky., 1946; M.D., Ohio State U., 1949; m. Barbara Jean Brooks, Sept. 17, 1949; children—Marilyn Baker, David Brooks. Intern, Jefferson Med. Coll. Hosp., Phila., 1949-50; resident Henry Ford Hosp., Detroit, 1952-56; practice medicine specializing in internal medicine, Louisville, 1956—; asst. clin. prof. medicine U. Louisville Sch. Medicine, 1968—; mem. active staff Ky. Baptist, Methodist Evangelical, St. Anthony hosps.; mem. courtesy staff Jewish, St. Joseph, Norton Infirmary hosps. Mem. Ky. Health Facilities Council, 1971—. Served with AUS, 1943-46, USAF, 1951-52. Fellow A.C.P.; mem. A.M.A., Am. Soc. Internal Medicine, Am. Coll. Chest Physicians, Ky. Med. Assn. (v.p. 1971-72), Ky. (pres.-elect), Louisville (pres. 1969) socs internists. Mem. Christian Ch. (deacon 1960-72). Clubs: Optimist, Jefferson, Filson (Louisville). Home: 2556 Seneca Dr Louisville KY 40205 Office: 1169 Eastern Pkwy Louisville KY 40217

ROBIN, VINCENT JOSEPH, III, corp. exec.; b. Larose, La., Mar. 4, 1918; s. Vincent Joseph and Edverine (Savoie) R.; student Internat. Corp. Sch., 1943-45, Internat. Corr. Schs., 1965; Certificate in Mgmt. Tng., La. State U., New Orleans, 1965; m. Erline E. Chaisson, June 1, 1935; children—Joel P., Marian (Mrs. Russell DiMarco), Donald J., Vincent Joseph IV. Owner, exec. pres. Robin Boat Rental Service, Inc., Robin, Inc., Offshore Crewboats, Inc., Erline E., Inc., Marine Taxis, Inc., Marian Ann, Inc., Robin Internat. Marine Towing Corp., Robin Marine Corp., Robin Towing Corp., Robin Realty, Inc., Robin Cresboat Corp., Harvey, La., 1947—; owner, mgr. Triple R Ranch, Foxworth, Miss., 1971—. Mem. New Orleans C. of C., Am. Security Council, A.I.M., Nat. Ocean Industries Assn., Am.-Internat. Charolais Assn., Harvey Canal Indsl. Assn., Propeller Club U.S. Rotarian, K.C. Clubs: Krewe of Bacchus, Krewe of Janus Carnival, Young Man's Business (New Orleans). Home: 797 Marlene Dr Gretna LA 70053 Office: 440 Pailet St PO Box 526 Harvey LA 70058

ROBINETTE, JOHN ZACK, project engr.; b. Pacolet, S.C., Aug. 29, 1925; s. John Zack and Marie (Byars) Robinette; B.S. in Mech. Engring., Clemson A. and M. Coll., 1947; m. Edith Juanita Hames, Dec. 27, 1946; children—John Hames, Russell Conrad. Mgr. Robinette Motor Co., Pacolet, 1947-51; jr. engr. Deering Milliken Service Corp., Spartanburg, S.C., 1951-52, engr., 1954-56; plant engr. Gayley Mill Corp., Marietta, S.C., 1952-54; project engr. Lockwood Greene Engrs., Spartansburg, 1956-64, Fabric Services, Inc., Orangeburg, S.C., 1964-65, Woodside Mills, Inc., Greenville, S.C., 1965—. City engr., Pacolet, 1960-64. Served with USAAF, 1944-45. Registered profl. engr., S.C., Tenn., Ala., Ky. Mem. S.C. Soc. Profl. Engrs., C. of C. Home: 133 Fernbrook Circle Spartanburg SC 29302 Office: 260 S Pleasantburg Dr Greenville SC 29606

ROBINS, C(HARLES) RICHARD, educator, marine scientist; b. Harrisburg, Pa., Nov. 25, 1928; s. Claude R. and Helen (Ayres) R.; A.B., Cornell U., 1950, Ph.D., 1954; postgrad. Stanford Hopkins Marine Sta., 1956; m. Catherine Hale, Sept. 3, 1965; children—Elaine, Robert. Field research for U. Mich. in Mexico, 1949; grad. asst. Cornell u., Ithaca, N.Y., 1950-54, research asso. in oceanography, summer 1952; aquatic biologist N.Y. State Conservation Dept., summers 1950, 51; research asst. prof. U. Miami (Fla.) Marine Lab., 1956-60, asso. prof. U. Miami Inst. Marine Sci., 1960-64, chmn. dept. marine sci. U. Miami, 1961-63, prof. marine sci. Inst. Marine and Atmospheric Scis., 1964—, curator of fishes, 1956—, Maytag prof. ichthyology, 1969—. Served with Chem. Corps, AUS, 1954-56. Jessup scholar Acad. Natural Sci., Phila., summer 1960. Mem. Am. Soc. Ichthyologists and Herpetologists (bd. govs. 1958-62, 64-68, 70-74; v.p. finance, 1964), Nat., Tropical (dir. 1967—) Audubon socs., A.A.A.S., Am. Fish Soc. (asso. editor Trans. 1969—), Am. Inst. Biol. Sci., Am. Inst. Fisheries Research Biologists, Am. Ornithologists Union, Am. Soc. Zoologists, Biol. Soc. Washington, Fla. Acad. Sci., Herpetologists' League, Marine Bilogy Assn. India, Soc. Study Evolution, Soc. Systematic Zoology, Wilson Ornithol. Soc., Sigma Xi, Phi Kappa Phi, Sigma Phi Epsilon. Asst. editor Bull. Marine Sci. Gulf and Caribbean, 1958-61, editor, 1961-62; mem. editorial bds. Copeia, 1963-64, Bull. Marine Sci., 1963—, Tulane Studies in Zoology, 1959—, Studies in Tropical Oceanography U. Miami, 1965—. Contbr. articles to sci. jours. Home: 9190 SW 61st Ct Miami FL 33156 Office: School of Marine and Atmospheric Sciences University of Miami 10 Rickenbacker Causeway Miami FL 33149

ROBINSON, ADELBERT CARL, lawyer; b. Shawnee, Okla., Dec. 13, 1926; s. William H. and Mayme (Forston) R.; student Okla. Baptist U., 1944-47; LL.B., Okla. U., 1950, J.D., 1970; m. Marilyn Ruth Stubbs, Dec. 28, 1963; children—William, James, Schuyler, Donald, David, Nancy, Lauri. Admitted to Okla. bar, 1950; practiced in Muskogee, 1956—; with legal dept. Phillips Petroleum Co., 1950-51; adjuster U.S. Fidelity & Guaranty Co., 1951-54, atty., adjuster-in-charge, 1954-56; partner Fite & Robinson, 1956-62; partner Fite, Robinson & Summers, 1963-70, Robinson & Summers, 1970-72, Robinson, Summers & Locke, 1972—; police judge, 1963-64; municipal judge, 1964-70. Pres., dir. Wall St. Bldg. Corp., 1969—, Three Forks Devel. Corp., 1968—. Chmn. Inter-Organizational Relations Com., 1960-63; chmn. Muskogee County Law Day, 1963; chmn. Muskogee Area Redevel. Authority, 1963; chmn. Muskogee County chpt. Am. Cancer Soc., 1956; chmn. Profl. Cooperation Com., 1965-69. Pres., bd. dirs. Muskogee Community Council; bd. dirs. Muskogee Community Concert Assn., Muskogee Tourist Information Bur., 1964-68; bd. dirs., gen. counsel United Cerebral Palsy Eastern Okla., 1964-68. Served with inf. AUS, 1945-46. Mem. Okla. (chmn. uniform law com., past regional chmn. grievance com.), Muskogee County (pres. 1971, mem. exec. council) bar assns., Okla. Assn. Def. Counsel (dir.), Okla. Assn. Municipal Judges (dir.), Muskogee C. of C., Delta Theta Phi. Methodist. Rotarian (pres. 1971-72). Home: Route 3 Box 141 Muskogee OK 74401 Office: 213 N 3d St P O Box 87 Muskogee OK 74401

ROBINSON, ANDREW ADOLPHUS, ednl. adminstr.; b. Jacksonville, Fla., May 21, 1930; s. Andrew A. and Gladys A. (Vicars) R.; B.S., Fla. A. and M. Coll., 1950; M.A., Columbia U., 1955; Ed.D., 1963; m. Mildred Cooley, Nov. 26, 1957; children—Estella Price, Conchita W. Gen. sci. tchr. James Weldon Johnson Jr. High Sch., Jacksonville, Fla., 1955-57; tchr. biology, chmn. sci. dept. Northwestern Jr.-Sr. High Sch., Jacksonville, 1957-59; coordinator sci. and maths. Duval County, Fla., 1959-64; prin. William M. Raines Sr. High Sch., Jacksonville, 1964-69; dir. inservice training for faculty desegregation Duval County Sch. Bd., 1969-70; asst. dean of faculties U. N. Fla., Jacksonville, 1970-71, asst. dean Coll. Edn., 1971-73, asso. dean, 1973—, chmn. dept. adminstrn. and supervision, 1971—. Mem. state adv. council Title III, Elementary Secondary Edn. Act, 1968—; mem. Fla. Ednl. Research and Devel. Adv. Council, 1969-70; mem. tchr. edn. adv. council Task Førce on Tchr. Edn. Program Approval, 1970; mem. The Fla. com. So. Assn. Colls. and Schs. Commn. on Secondary Schs., 1969-70; commr. Housing Authority of Jacksonville, 1966-69; mem. Mayor's Adv. Panel on Employment, 1968; mem. United Fund. Finance Com., 1968-70, exec. com., 1970—; vice-chmn. Community Relations Commn., 1971-72; co-chmn. Conference Race Relations, 1971—. Served to 2d lt. AUS, 1951-54. Mem. Jacksonville C. of C. (gov. 1972—). Home: 7334 Richardson Rd Jacksonville FL 32209 Office: PO Box 17074 Jacksonville FL 32216

ROBINSON, AUBREY EUGENE, JR., U.S. dist. judge; b. Madison, N.J., Mar. 30, 1922; s. Aubrey Eugene and Mabel (Jackson) R.; B.A., Cornell U., 1943, LL.B., 1947; m. Sara E. Payne, Dec. 31, 1946; children—Paula, Sheryl. Admitted to N.Y. and D.C. bars, 1948; practice with law firms in Washington, 1948-65; asso. judge Juvenile Ct. D.C., 1965-66, U.S. Dist. Ct. for D.C., 1966—. Gen. counsel Am. Council Human Rights, 1953-55, dir., 1955; mem. D.C. Commrs.'s Com. Child Placement Regulations, 1954-62. Mem. D.C. Pub. Welfare Adv. Council, 1963-65; mem. Washington Urban League Adoption Project, 1959; mem. membership steering com. Health and Welfare Council D.C., 1961-66; mem. budget steering com. Health and Welfare Council Nat. Capital Area, 1963-66; mem. exec. com. Interreligious Com. Race Relations, 1966-67; exec. com. bd. dirs. D.C. Citizens for Better Pub. Edn., 1964-66. Trustee United Planning Orgn. D.C., 1963-66, Washington Center Met. Studies, 1967—; bd. dirs. Family and Child Services Washington, 1954-63, v.p., 1958-61; bd. dirs. Family Service Assn. Am., 1958-68, Washington Action for Youth, 1962-64, Barney Neighborhood Settlement House, 1962-64, Eugene and Agnes E. Meyer Found, 1969—, Consortium Univs. Washington Met. Area, 1969—. Mem. Am. (mem. com. cts. and community 1972—, mem. adv. com. judges function 1970-72), Nat., D.C., Washington bar assns., Nat. Conf. Fed. Trial Judges (chmn.-elect 1972), Am. Law Inst. Served with AUS, 1943-46. Home: 1796 Sycamore St NW Washington DC 20012 Office: US Court House Washington DC 20001

ROBINSON, AUBREY GLASS, dentist; b. Montgomery, Ala., Sept. 12, 1923; s. Aubrey Bradley and Rena Leigh (Glass) R.; D.V.M., Auburn U., 1946; grad. student U. Houston, 1957-58; D.D.S., U. Tex., 1962, M.S. in Dentistry, 1964; m. Ann Marie Stinson, June 29, 1950; children—Bruce Aubrey, Craig Stinson, Celia Ann. With Bur. Animal Industry, Mexico, 1946-50; pvt. practice vet. medicine, Ft. Walton Beach, Fla., 1950-57; teaching fellow U. Tex. Dental Br., Houston, 1962-64, asst. prof. pedodontics, 1964-66; pvt. practice pediatric dentistry, Clearwater, Fla., 1966—. Served with AUS, 1943-45. Diplomate Am. Bd. Pedodontics. Mem. Am., Fla. dental assns., West Coast Dental Soc., Am., Fla. Southeastern socs. dentistry for children. Home: 7 Leeward Island Clearwater FL 33515 Office: 430 Pinellas St Clearwater FL 33516

ROBINSON, AUGUST ROBERT, JR., engr., educator; b. San Antonio, Tex., Apr. 24, 1921; s. August R. and Georgia (Carmack) R.; B.S. in Civil Engring., U. Ia., 1947; M.S. in Civil Engring., Colo. State U., 1952; m. Martha Burney, June 16, 1948; 1 dau., Gwen. Hydraulic engr. U.S. Dept. Agr., Ft. Collins, Colo., 1952-63; dir. research center, Twin Falls, Ida., 1963-69, dir. Sedimentation Lab., Oxford, Miss., 1969—; prof. civil engring. U. Miss., Oxford, 1970—. Served with AUS, 1943-46. Mem. Am. Soc. C.E., Am. Soc. Agrl. Engrs., Nat. Soc. Profl. Engrs., Am. Geophys. Union, Internat. Assn. Hydraulic Research, Sigma Xi, Chi Epsilon. Contbr. articles to profl. jours. Home: 301 Murry St Oxford MS 38655 Office: Box 30 Oxford MS 38655

ROBINSON, BETTE GIGUETTE (MRS. STANLEY T. ROBINSON JR.), statistician; b. Pasadena, Cal., Apr. 11, 1922; d. Curtis and Mary T. (Proctor) Giguette; B.A., Marymount Coll., Los Angeles, 1942; student Immaculate Heart Coll., Los Angeles, 1942-43; m. Stanley T. Robinson, Jr., Aug. 20, 1949; children—Curtis B. Postel, Suzanne E., Michael T. Research asst. Bd. Govs. Fed. Res. System, Washington, 1961-66, 72—. Wishing Well chmn. Los Angeles League Crippled Children, 1940-49; decoration chmn. Los Angeles Jr. Guild, 1941-49; AEC hospitality chmn. Sandia Base Women's Club, Albuquerque, 1953-59; sec.-treas., show sec. Albuquerque Rabbit Breeders Assn., 1954-57; sec. Nat. Capitol Rabbit Breeders Assn., 1959-61; sec.-treas. Free State Rabbit Breeders Assn., 1961; active League Women Voters, Fairfax, Va., 1965-69. Clubs: River Bend Golf and Country (chmn. women's golf assn. 1969-71, tournament chmn. women's golf assn. 1971-72) (Great Falls, Va.), McLean (Va.) Women's (safety chmn. 1970-71). Home: 10103 Sanders Ct Great Falls VA 22066

ROBINSON, BRYAN WRIGHT, physician, educator; b. Thomasville, Ga., Dec. 11, 1929; s. Alfred Green and Frances (Wright) R.; B.S., Davidson Coll., 1952; M.D., Emory U., 1956; m. Julia Hill Willingham, Aug. 23, 1953; children—Bryan David, Carol Susan, Stephen Kirk, Margaret Hill. Intern, U. Rochester (N.Y.), 1956-57, asst. resident psychiatry, 1957-58; research asso. neurophysiology NIH, 1958-63; resident, spl. fellow neurology, Stanford, 1963-65; practice medicine, specializing in neurology, Atlanta, 1965-68; chief lab. neurophysiology Yerkes Primate Center Emory U., 1965-68, asst. prof. medicine (neurology), research dir., asso. prof. phys. medicine Sch. Medicine, 1965-68; prof. psychology Fla. State U., Tallahassee, 1968-70; asst. prof. medicine (neurology) U. Fla., 1970—; mem. staff Tallahassee Meml. Hosp.; cons. neurologist Archbold Meml. Hosp., Thomasville, Ga. Dir. Barnett Bank Tallahassee North. Founder, pres. Tallahassee Neurol. Found. Bd. dirs. LeMoyne Art Found., YMCA. Served with USPHS, 1948-63. Mem. Phi Beta Kappa, Kappa Alpha, Omicron Delta Kappa. Regional editor: Physiology and Behavior, 1962—. Contbr. articles to profl. jours. Home: 613 Piedmont Dr Tallahassee FL 32303 Office: 2412 W Plaza Dr Tallahassee FL 32303

ROBINSON, BUEFORD EDDIE, textile exec.; b. Valdese, N.C., Feb. 10, 1929; s. Jeff Logan and Flossie (Coffey) R.; B.A., Lenoir Rhyne Coll., 1956; m. Jewell Deanna Wilson, June 18, 1955; children—Timothy Mark, Donna Marie. Accounting clk. Valdese Mfg. Co., 1956-64, controller, 1964-67, corporate sec., 1967—, sec. co. found. Chmn., United Fund, Valdese, 1967. Mem. Valdese Sch. Bd., 1966—, chmn. bd., 1968-69; chmn. Valdese Parks and Recreation Commn., 1971—. Served with USAF, 1948-52. Mem. Catawba Valley Exec. Club. Baptist (deacon). Rotarian (treas. 1969-70). Home: 600 Carolina St Valdese NC 28690 Office: PO Drawer 10 Valdese NC 28690

ROBINSON, CHARLES DEE, educator; b. Dallas, July 16, 1932; s. Samuel Melton and Marguerite Gentry (Morriss) R.; B.A. summa cum laude Hardin-Simmons U., 1956; M.A., U. Tex., Austin, 1961, Ph.D. (NSF fellow), 1964; m. Clydene Rush, Aug. 29, 1954. Asst. prof. math. Ariz. State U., Tempe, 1964-65; asso. prof. math. U. Miss., Oxford, 1965-68; prof., head dept. math. Hardin-Simmons U., Abilene, Tex., 1968—, chmn. sci. div., 1969—. Served with AUS, 1950-52. Mem. Am. Math. Soc., Math. Assn. Am., A.A.A.S. Lion (dir. club 1971-72). Author: An Introduction to College Algebra, 1959; Concerning Normed Linear Spaces, 1964. Home: 2024 N Willis St Apt 1 Abilene TX 79603

ROBINSON, DONALD LOUIS, govt. ofcl.; b. Ottawa, Ill., Dec. 8, 1936; s. Arthur and Louise (Freebury) R.; B.A., Northwestern U., 1958, M.A., 1959; Ph.D., American U., 1963; m. Sara Moore, Aug. 4, 1962; children—Marshall, Margaret. Adminstrv. asst. to U.S. Rep. Henry S. Reuss, Washington, 1963—; Democratic co-chmn. bi-partisan intern program Ho. of Reps., Washington, 1969-70; Democratic co-chmn. bipartisan intern program Congress of U.S. Washington, 1971—; asso. prof. polit. sci. George Washington U., Washington, 1964—. Mem. Americans for Dem. Action; mem. Am. Civil Liberties Union, co-chmn. nat. speakers bur. Young Citizens for Johnson-Humphrey, 1964. Served to lt. USNR, 1959-62. Mem. Alpha Tau Omega, Phi Mu Alpha, Pi Sigma Alpha, Phi Alpha Theta, Pi Gamma Mu, Alpha Phi Omega. Home: 1817 Kenyon St NW Washington DC 20010 Office: 2186 Rayburn House Office Bldg Washington DC 20515

ROBINSON, EDWIN SIMONS, educator; b. Saginaw, Mich., Apr. 29, 1935; s. Melvin Oliver and Francis Josephine (Simons) R.; B.S. in Geology Math., U. Mich., 1957, M.S. in Geology, 1959; Ph.D. in Geophysics, U. Wis., 1964; m. Valarie Ann Kelch, Feb. 10, 1962; children—Lindsay Harriet, Evan Richard. Oil exploration Socony Mobil de Venesuela, S.Am., 1957; geophys. exploration of Ross Shelf Antarctic, Arctic Inst. N.Am., 1957-58; research Willow Run Research Labs., Mich. Corps Engrs., Ann Arbor, 1958-59; polar research Antarctica, U. Wis., 1959-64; asst. prof. geophysics U. Utah, Salt Lake City, 1964-67; asso. prof. Va. Poly. Inst., Blacksburg, 1967-72, prof. geophysics, 1972—; geophysicist U.S. Geol. Survey, 1967—. Recipient Antarctic Service medal NSF, 1957, 63. Mem. Am. Geophys. Union, Geol. Soc. Am., Soc. Exploration Geophysicists, Glaciol. Soc. Contbr. numerous articles profl. jours. Home: 613 Alleghany St Blacksburg VA 24060

ROBINSON, ENDERS ANTHONY, geophys. cons.; b. Boston, Mar. 18, 1930; s. Edward Arthur and Doris (Goodale) R.; B.S., Mass. Inst. Tech., 1950, M.S., 1952, Ph.D., 1954; m. Eva Arborelius, Sept. 9, 1962 (div. May) children—Anna, Erik Arthur, Karin. Dir. Mass. Inst. Tech. Geophys. Analysis Group, 1952-54; asso. prof. U. Wis., 1958-62; dep. prof. Uppsala (Sweden) U., 1960-64; v.p., dir. Digicon, Inc., Houston, 1965-70; geophys. cons. Tex. Geophys. Co., Houston, 1970—. Served to 2d lt. Ordnance Dept., AUS, 1950-51. Recipient medal Soc. Exploration Geophysicists, 1969. Author: Random Wavelets and Cybernetic Systems, 1962; Statistical Communication and Detection, 1967; Multichannel Time Series Analysis, 1967. Home: 911 Gondola Sugar Land TX 77478 Office: Tex Geophys Co 5400 Memorial Dr Houston TX 77007

ROBINSON, FEROL MACON, univ. ofcl.; b. Jewett, Tex., June 1, 1918; s. Bob and Cloud (Speer) R.; B.S., Sam Houston State U., 1942, M.A., 1947; D.Ed., U. Mo., 1953; m. Mary Creed Engledow, Jan. 27, 1946; children—Pamela, Patricia. Mem. faculty Sam Houston State U., Huntsville, Tex., 1946—, prof., dir. journalism, dir. information, 1953-71, v.p. univ. services, 1971—. Alderman, Huntsville, 1968-72. Served with AUS, 1942-46. Mem. Huntsville C. of C., Sigma Delta Chi, Phi Kappa Delta, Kappa Delta Phi, Pi Kappa Alpha. Methodist (mem. bd. stewards 1960—). Home: 1528 Pin Oak Dr Huntsville TX 77340

ROBINSON, HARRY ENGLISH, brick co. exec.; b. Atlanta, Apr. 25, 1914; s. James Dixon and Emily Alexander (English) R.; A.B., Va. Mil. Inst., 1936; postgrad. Harvard Grad. Sch. Bus. Adminstrn., 1936-37; m. Ermine Dupont Cater, Dec. 14, 1937; children—Harry English, Peyton Cater. Account exec. Clement A. Evans, Courts & Co., 1946-54; exec. v.p. Chattahoochee Brick Co., Atlanta, 1954-57, pres., 1957-70, chmn. bd., 1970—, also dir.; dir. First Nat. Holding Co., First Nat. Bank of Atlanta, Southeastern Capital Corp. Mem. adv. bd. Ga. State Coll. Served to lt. col. AUS, 1940-46. Decorated Army Commendation medal. Mem. Soc. Colonial Wars, Atlanta Hist. Soc., Newcomen Soc. N.Am., Atlanta Arts Alliance. Presbyn. Clubs: Piedmont Driving; Commerce; Capital City; Johns Island; Nine O'Clocks; Homosassa Fishing. Home: 3633 Dumbarton Rd NW Atlanta GA 30327 Office: P O Box 39158 Bolton Sta Atlanta GA 30318

ROBINSON, JACK HARDY, educator; b. Mt. Vernon, N.Y., Mar. 27, 1925; s. Harry J. and Lida M. (Hardy) R.; B.S. in Physics, Yale, 1945; M.A. in Edn., Stanford, 1950; Ed.D. in Sci. Edn., Harvard, 1960; m. Barbara Clare Oak, Dec. 29, 1947; children—Charles Oak, Susan Gray. Instr. physics and surveying Vallejo (Cal.) Jr. Coll., 1948-50; asst. prof. phys. sci. Kan. State U., Manhattan, 1953-60; asso. prof. sci. edn. U. P.R., 1960-62; prof. phys. scis. U. South Fla., Tampa, 1963-71; prof. sci. edn. and astronomy U. South Fla., St. Petersburg, 1971—; cons. Ednl. Testing Service, Princeton, N.J., 1960—, Tampa (Fla.) Commn. Community Relations, 1966-67. Served with USNR, 1943-47, 51-53. NSF faculty fellow, 1962-63. Mem. A.A.A.S., Nat. Sci. Tchrs. Assn. Research archaeo-astronomy, spl. theory relativity. Home: 3507 Nakora Dr Tampa FL 33618 Office: 830 1st St S St Petersburg FL 33701

ROBINSON, JAMES KENNETH, congressman; b. nr. Winchester, Va., May 14, 1916; s. Ray and Ida Helen (Robinson) R.; B.S., Va. Poly. Inst., 1937; m. Kathryn Rankin, Mar. 28, 1946; children—James Kenneth (dec.), Patrick M., Keveney M., Helen Ray, James, J. Kelly, Sallie. Sec.-treas. R & T Packing Co., 1951—; pres. Winchester Apple Growers, 1960; now dir.; dir. Green Chem. Co., Inc., Winchester Cold Storage; mem. 92d-93d congresses from 7th Dist. Va. Mem. Dulles Airport Devel. Commn., 1968—; adviser Va. Poly. Inst. Agr. Coll., 1961—. Mem. Va. Senate, 1965-70. Vice pres., exec. bd. Shenandoah Boy Scouts Am.; bd. dirs. Apple Blossom Festival, Winchester Meml. Hosp. Served to maj. Inf. AUS, World War II. Named Farmer of Year, Progressive Farmer mag., 1964. Mem. Va. Poly. Inst. Alumni Assn. (dir.), Winchester C. of C. (dir.), Am. Legion, Winchester Hist. Soc., Izaak Walton League. Republican. Mem. Soc. of Friends. Rotarian. Moose, Elk. Home: Merrimans Lane Route 4 Winchester VA 22601 Office: House Office Bldg Washington DC 20515

ROBINSON, JEWEL ESELENE PATTERSON, home economist; b. nr. Lott, Tex.; d. Claud W. and Laura (Smith) Patterson; B.S., Mary Hardin Baylor Coll., 1935; M.S., Tex. Tech. Coll., 1963; m. John W. Robinson, Oct. 24, 1941 (div. Jan. 1951); children—James William, Judy Jean (Mrs. Jerry Dan Prothro), Jerry Pat. Tchr. pub. schs., Falls County, 1933-35; home demonstration agt., McCulloch County, 1936-38, Wise County, 1939-41, Dickens County, 1948-49, Hockley County, 1949—; lunch room supr. Montaque County, Tex., 1941-42. Cons. dietetician South Plains Hosp., Levelland, Tex.; mem. Tex. Nutrition Council, 1960—, sec., 1968; mem. adv. bd. South Plains Mus., Levelland. Sec. county Easter Seal Soc., 1970. Recipient Distinguished Service award Nat. Assn. Extension Home Economists, 1971. Mem. Am., Tex. home econs. assns., Home Demonstration Agts. Assn. (dist. dir. 1969-70). Home Demonstration Agts. Assn., Epsilon Sigma Phi. Club: Rose Garden (Levelland). Home: 801 17th St Levelland TX 79336 Office: Court House Annex Levelland TX 79336

ROBINSON, JIM, mayor of Montgomery; b. Columbus, Ga., Aug. 23, 1929; m. Dorothy Wells; children—Donald James, Vickie Lynn. Pres. paper co.; mayor City of Montgomery (Ala.), 1971—. Baptist (deacon, finance com.). Office: Office of Mayor City Hall 127 N Perry St Montgomery AL 36102

ROBINSON, JOHN PAUL, physician; b. Sarepta, La., Dec. 5, 1924; s. Samual Cecil and Valera (Browning) R.; B.S., Centenary Coll., 1948; M.D., La. State U., 1951; m. Edith Haggard, July 13, 1942 (dec.); children—James Lee, Constance Sue (Mrs. Charles Norman Huggs), Carol Ann, Mark Clinton. Intern, Santa Rosa Hosp., San Antonio, 1951-52; resident ophthalmology Confederate Meml. Med. Center, Shreveport, La., 1957-60, now mem. staff; practice medicine, Shreveport, 1953-57, specializing in opthalmology, 1960—; mem. clin. staff La. State U. Med. Sch., Shreveport, 1968—; mem. staff T.E. Schumpert Sanitarium, Highland, P. & S., Drs., Willis Knightin, Bossier Gen. hosps. Pres., Men's Art Guild, Shreveport, 1966-67. Served with USNR, 1943-46. Diplomate Am. Bd. Ophthalmology. Mem. Am., So. med. assns., La. Med. Soc., Ark.-La.-Tex. Ophthalmology and Otolaryngology Soc. (pres. 1964-65), Contact Lens Assn. Opthalmologists, Am. Assn. Physicians and Surgeons, Alpha Kappa Kappa. Episcopalian. Mason. Home: 8302 Spring Lake Dr Shreveport LA 71106 Office: 850 Margaret Pl Shreveport LA 71101

ROBINSON, LEWIS WILLIAM, JR., city ofcl.; b. Dallas, Nov. 29, 1909; s. Lewis William and Mary (Roane) R.; B.S. in Civil Engring., U. Fla., 1933; m. Mary Whitmyer, Aug. 14, 1946; 1 dau., Ann Lucretia. Bldg. insp. City of Coral Gables (Fla.), 1939-42, supt. pub. works, 1946-54, city clk., finance dir., 1954-58, city mgr., 1959—; with C.E., U.S. Army, Trinidad, W.I., 1943-45. Pres. Coral Gables Municipal Credit Union, 1949—. Recipient Good Govt. award Coral Gables Jr. C. of C., 1960, Hendrick award, 1970-71, George K. Zain award, 1972. Mem. Internat., Fla. (pres. 1963-64), Dade County (pres. 1966-67) city mgrs. assns. Mason (Shriner, Jester), Lion. Home: 1228 Av Placetas Coral Gables FL 33146 Office: 405 Biltmore Way Coral Gables FL 33134

ROBINSON, LUTHER DABNEY, psychiatrist; b. Tappahannock, Va., Dec. 22, 1922; s. William Harvey and Fannie (Pollard) R.; B.S., Va. State Coll., 1943; M.D., Meharry Med. Coll., 1946; postgrad. George Washington U., 1959-60; m. Betty Gay Boyd, Mar. 18, 1950; children—Jan Turso, Barry Boyd, Vance Dabney. Intern Mercy Hosp., Phila., 1946-47; asst. physician Lakin (W.Va.) State Hosp., 1947-49; practice gen. medicine, Richmond, Va., 1952-53; resident psychiatry Freedmen's Hosp., Washington, 1953-54, St. Elizabeth's Hosp., Washington, 1954-55; mem. staff St. Elizabeth's Hosp., 1955—, clin. dir., 1964-68, 1st asst. physician, 1968-69, acting supt. hosp., 1969-72, supt. hosp., 1972—; mem. faculty Howard U., Washington, 1956-68, Gallaudet Coll. for Deaf, Washington, 1968—. Mem. profl. adv. com. D.C. Mental Health Assn., 1968—. Served with AUS, 1943-46, to capt. M.C., 1949-52. Recipient Superior Service award Dept. Health, Edn. and Welfare, 1966, Superior Work Performance award St. Elizabeth's Hosp., 1968. Diplomate Am. Bd. Psychiatry and Neurology. Fellow Am. Psychiat. Assn.; mem. A.M.A., Nat. Med. Assn., Med. Soc. St. Elizabeth's (pres. 1965-66), Washington Psychiat. Soc., Internat. Platform Assn. Baptist. Address: Burroughs Cottage St Elizabeths Hosp 2700 Martin Luther King Jr Av SE Washington DC 20032

ROBINSON, MARY LOU (MRS. ALBERT JAMES ROBINSON), lawyer, judge; b. Dodge City, Kan., Aug. 25, 1926; d. Gerald J. and Frances Aynn (Pierce) Strueber; student Amarillo Coll., 1944-46; B.A., U. Tex., 1948, LL.B., 1950; m. Albert James Robinson; children—Rebecca, Diana, Matthew. Admitted Tex. bar., 1950; mem. firm Robinson & Robinson, Amarillo, 1950-55; judge county ct. law, Potter County, Tex., 1955-59, 108th Dist. Ct. 1961-73; asso. justice 7th Ct. Civil Appeals, 1973—. Mem. Amarillo Bar Assn., State Bar Tex. Presbyn. Home: 5302 Berget St Amarillo TX 79106 Office: Potter County Court House Amarillo TX 79101

ROBINSON, PAUL BAINBRIDGE, headmaster; b. Marysville, O., Apr. 16, 1911; s. John Clyde and Charlotte (Bainbridge) R.; B.S., Tenn. Poly. Inst., 1935; M.A., U. So. Miss., 1958; L.H.D. (hon.), Judson Coll., 1967; m. Vera Judd, July 31, 1934; children—Charlotte Ann, John Arnold, Paul Matthew, David Johnson (dec.), Joseph Melvin. Instr., coach Moore County High Sch., Lynchburg, Tenn., 1935-37; instr., coach, dean boys Warren County Central High Sch., McMinnville, Tenn., 1937-42; instr., coach, comdr. cadets Sewanee (Tenn.) Mil. Acad., 1942-40; asso. supr. Gulf Coast Mil. Acad., Mississippi City, Miss., 1948-49; instr., comdt. Marion (Ala.) Mil. Inst., 1949-52, pres., 1959—; supr. U. Mil. Sch., Mobile, 1952-59. Adv. com. higher edn. Ala. Bd. Edn. Mem. Nat. Council Ind. Schs. (So. rep. 1956-58), So. Assn. Ind. Schs. (pres. 1957-58), Ala. Assn. Jr. Colls. (pres. 1962-63, chmn. athletic affairs com.). Assn. Ala. Coll. Adminstrs. (dir. div. higher edn. 1962-63), Assn. Mil. Colls. and Schs. U.S. (pres., exec. com.). Phi Delta Kappa, Presbyn. (elder). Club: Marion Golf. Home: 110 Brown St Marion AL 36756

ROBINSON, RALPH CARLISLE, JR., lawyer; b. Columbia, S.C., Aug. 27, 1935; s. R. Carlisle and Anna Elizabeth (Hiller) R.; B.S., Univ. S.C., 1957, J.D., 1966; m. Sara Elyce Powell, Dec. 2, 1964; children—Ralph C., Heyward Elliot, Sara E. Admitted to S.C. bar, 1966, practiced in Columbia, 1967—; law clk. U.S. Dist. judge Hemphill, Dist. S.C., Columbia, 1966-67; mem. firms Berry, Lightsey, Gibbs & Bowers, 1969-71. Served with USAF, 1957-63. Mem. S.C. State Bar, Fed., Am., S.C., Richland County bar assns., Am. Judicature Soc. Home: 5 Myrtle Court Columbia SC 29205 Office: 1717 Gervais St Columbia SC 29211

ROBINSON, RALPH ROLIN, physician; b. Nashville, Kan., July 7, 1913; s. Walter S. and Mary (Inslee) R.; B.S. in Indsl. Arts, Okla. A and M, 1935; M.D., U. Wash., 1951; m. Mona R. McGraw, Mar. 28, 1953; children—Kim, Mark, Nancy, Ralph Rolin II, Katherine. Engr., Vornado Corp., Stillwater, Okla., 1934-41, Boeing Co., Seattle, 1941-51; intern Okla. U. Hosp. 1951-52, resident 1952-55; practice medicine, specializing in obstetrics and gynecology, Oklahoma City, 1951-55, Middlesboro, Ky., 1955—; asso. prof. U. Okla., 1955. Pres., Creative Ornament Co., Edmond, Okla.; v.p. R.K. Odor Research Co., Oklahoma City. Pres. staff Miners Meml. Hosp., Middlesboro, 1958. Chmn. Safety Com. Okmulgee County, 1956. Fellow A.C.S.; mem. Am. Coll. Obstetrics and Gynecology, Am. Soc. Abdominal Surgery, Phi Kappa Phi. Author: Endocrine Therapy for Gynecology, 1957. Co-inventor Vornado airplane, 1935; inventor controceptor. Home: 322 Englewood Rd Middlesboro KY 40965 Office: 2024 Cumberland Av Middlesboro KY 40965

ROBINSON, RALPH SMYRE, JR., textile co. exec.; b. Charlotte, N.C., June 2, 1935; s. Ralph Smyre and Charlotte Frances (Conant) R.; student Davidson Coll., 1953-54; B.S., U. N.C., 1957; m. Sally McConnell, Aug. 22, 1953; children—Russell McConnell, Leigh Anne, Gregory Lee. Vice-pres., Robinson Mills, Inc., Gastonia, N.C., 1957-70, pres., 1970—; dir. First Union Nat. Bank, treas. Family Counciling Service, 1964-67; pres. Gastonia Community Concert Assn., 1967-68. Bd. dirs. Gaston County United Appeal, 1972—, Salvation Army Boy's Club, 1968-71; trustee The Ralph S. Robinson Found., St. Andrews Presbyn. Coll.; bd. dirs. Presbyn. Home of Charlotte. Mem. Am. Yarn Spinners Assn. (bd. dirs. 1973-75), Combed Yarn Spinners Assn. (bd. dirs. 1966-68), Am. Textile Mfrs. Assn., Nat. Cotton Council, Newcomen Soc., Kappa Sigma, Alpha Kappa Psi. Mason. Club: Gaston County. Home: 2633 Sheffield Dr Gastonia NC 28052 Office: 338 N New Hope Rd Gastonia NC 28052

ROBINSON, REGINALD EDWARD, JR., civil engr.; b. Summerville, S.C., July 29, 1933; s. Reginald Edward and Luren (Knight) R.; C.E., Ga. Inst. Tech., 1957; M.S. in Engring. Adminstrn., So. Meth. U., 1967; m. Nancy Helen Grooms, Aug. 10, 1957; children—Susan Lynn, Kenneth Braden. Coop engring. student Charleston Naval Shipyard (S.C.), 1951-56; test engr. Chance Vought Aircraft Inc., Dallas, 1957-60; test engr. Martin Co., Orlando, Fla., 1960-62; engring. splst. LTV Aerospace Corp., Dallas, 1962—. Served to 2d lt. AUS, 1958. Mem. Tex. Soc. Profl. Engrs. (treas. Mid-Cities chpt. 1968), Soc. Exptl. Stress Analysis (pres. North Tex. sect. 1972-73) Chi Epsilon. Home: 1021 S Gloucester St Irving TX 75062 Office: PO Box 5907 Dallas TX 75222

ROBINSON, ROBERT HOWARD, physician; b. Verda, La., Jan. 21, 1919; s. Robert Lee and Florence (Courtney) R.; B.S., La. State U., 1938, M.D., 1942; m. Marguerite Barbara Boudreaux, July 7, 1943; children—Robert Stanley, Thomas Warren, Mary Katharine. Intern Tri-State Hosp. Shreveport, La., 1942-43; teaching fellow and clin. instr. in dermatology La. State U. Sch. Medicine, 1947-53, 66—; pvt. practice St. Martinville, La., 1945-47; dermatologist, pvt. practice, Lafayette, 1949—; owner, dir., Lafayette Skin and Skin Cancer Clinic, 1957—; cons. physician dermatology Lafayette Meml. San., Our Lady of Lourdes, Lafayette Charity hosps.; dep. comdr. and wing surgeon La. Wing Civil Air Patrol, 1954—. Sr. med. examiner FAA. Served as med. officer AUS, 1943-45. Decorated Purple Heart. Fellow Acad. Internationale of Medicine; mem. A.M.A., Am. Acad. Dermatology, La., Lafayette Parish med. socs., La. State Dermatology Soc., Aero Space Med. Assn., Lafayette C. of C. (chmn. aviation com.), Royal Order of Scotland, Sheriff Flying Squadron (maj., head Lafayette parish 1968—). Episcopalian. Mason (32 deg., K.T., Shriner); mem. Order of Eastern Star. Home: 119 Girard Woods Rd Lafayette LA 70501 Office: 1144C Coolidge St Lafayette LA 70501

ROBINSON, ROBERT LEWIS, assn. exec., editor; b. Richfield Spa, N.Y., Jan. 1, 1915; s. Lewis Henry and Alice Ethel (Fisk) R.; B.S., St. Lawrence U., 1936; M.A., Fletcher Sch. Law and Diplomacy, 1937; postgrad. N.Y. State Tchrs. Coll., 1940-41; m. Anna Marion Weir, July 16, 1940. With U.S. Dept. Commerce, Washington, 1946-48; dir. pub. affairs Am. Psychiat. Assn., Washington, 1948—, editor Psychiat. News, 1966—. Vis. lectr. colls. and univs. Trustee, Woodley House, Washington. Served to capt. AUS, 1941-46. Hon. fellow Am. Psychiat. Assn.; mem. Am. Pub. Health Assn., Nat. Assn. Sci. Writers, A.A.A.S., A.M.A. (affiliate). Club: Cosmos (Washington). Cons. editor Psychiatry and Medical Education, 1952; Training the Psychiatrist to Meet Changing Needs, 1964; other books and jours. Home: 3721 Livingston St NW Washington DC 20015 Office: Am Psychiat Assn 1700 18th St NW Washington DC 20009

ROBINSON, ROBERT WILLIAM, realtor; b. Lancaster, S.C., Dec. 1, 1917; s. Redic Earl and Myrtle (Beckham) R.; B.S. in Textile Chemistry, Clemson Coll., 1938; m. Carolyn J. Crews, May 29, 1938; children—Joan C., Robert W. Partner, E. Robinson Laundry, 1938-41, pres., 1946-51; pres. Robinson Realty Co., Columbia, S.C., 1951—; pres. E. Robinson Laundry & Dry Cleaning Co., Inc., Robinson Realty & Ins. Co., Inc., Robinson Laundry & Cleaners Machinery Co., Inc., 1961—, Robinson Holding Co., Inc., 1961—, E & M, Inc., 1962—; v.p. Robinson, Inc., 1960—, Matco, Inc., 1968—, New Lighthouse Co., Inc., 1970—. Served as capt. USAAF, 1942-46. Baptist. Lion. Club: Summerwood on the Gulf (v.p. 1970—). Home: 4314 Converse St Columbia SC 29206 Office: 2549 Forest Dr Columbia SC 29204

ROBINSON, ROSCOE ROSS, physician, educator; b. Oklahoma City, Aug. 21, 1929; s. Roscoe and Tennie (Ross) R.; B.S., Central State U., Edmond, Okla., 1949; M.D., U. Okla., 1954; m. Ann Allen, Aug. 24, 1952; children—Susan, Brooke. Intern medicine Duke U. Med. Center, Durham, N.C., 1954-55, jr. asst. resident medicine, 1955-56, chief resident, instr. medicine, 1957-58, asso. in medicine, 1960-62, asst. prof. medicine, dir. div. nephrology, 1962-65, asso. prof. medicine, dir. div. nephrology, 1965-69, prof. medicine, dir. div. nephrology, 1969—; Am. Heart Assn. research fellow, vis. fellow dept. medicine Columbia-Presbyn. Med. Center, N.Y.C., 1956-57; chief resident, instr. medicine VA Hosp., Durham, 1957-58, clin. investigator, 1960-62, attending physician, 1962—; cons. nephrology VA Hosp., Fayetteville, N.C., U.S. Naval Hosp., Portsmouth, Va., Research Triangle Inst. (Research Triangle Park, N.C.), 1964—; nat. cons. to Surgeon Gen., USAF, 1970—. Mem. kidney adv. com., N.C. Bd. Health, 1970—, chmn., 1971—; mem. tng. com. B, Nat. Heart and Lung Inst., Bethesda, Md., 1968-70, mem. cardiovascular tng. com., 1970-72; mem. VA Merit Rev. Bd. Nephrology, 1972—; mem. artificial kidney-chronic uremia sci. adv. com. Nat. Inst. Arthritis and Metabolic Digestive Diseases, Bethesda, 1973—. Served to capt. M.C., USAF, 1958-60. Diplomate Nat. Bd. Med. Examiners, Am. Bd. Internal Medicine. Fellow A.C.P.; mem. N.Y. Acad. Scis., Am. Clin. Climatol. Assn., Am. Fedn. Clin. Research (nominating com. So. sect. 1964, councillor 1968-71), Assn. Am. Physicians, European Dialysis and Transplant Assn., Am. (exec. com. renal sect., council circulation 1967-69, exec. com. council on kidney in cardiovascular diseases 1969—, chmn. 1969-71, central com. med. and community program, bd. dirs. 1969-71), N.C. (sr. investigator 1962—, exec. com., bd. dirs. 1971-72) heart assns., Am., So. socs. clin. investigation, Am. Physiol. Soc., Am. Soc. Artificial Internal Organs (councillor 1968-71, publs. com. 1971-72), Am., Internat. (nominating com. 1969, editor Kidney Internat. jour. 1971—, exec. com. 1972—) socs. nephrology, Nat. Kidney Found. (sci. adv. bd. 1970—), Kidney Found. N.C. (chmn. med. adv. com. 1967—), Alpha Omega Alpha. Editorial bd. Archives Internal Medicine, 1970—, Perspectives in Nephrology and Hypertension, 1972—. Contbr. numerous articles to profl. jours. Home: 3929 Nottaway Rd Durham NC 27707 Office: Duke U Med Center Box 3014 Durham NC 27710

ROBINSON, ROY GARLAND, JR., educator; b. Arkansas City, Kan., Mar. 14, 1921; s. Roy Garland and Amelia Christina (Smith) R.; B.S., U. Ariz., 1948; M.S., U. So. Cal., 1954, Ph.D., 1965. Instr. histology U. So. Cal., 1953-58, instr. histology and physiology, 1958-60, chmn., instr. physiology, 1960-65, chmn., asst. prof., 1965-67; asso. prof. biology McNeese State U., Lake Charles, La., 1967-69, prof. zoology, 1969—, predental adviser, 1967—. Served with AUS, 1940-45; ETO. Fellow A.A.A.S.; mem. La. Conf. Edn. and Biol. Scis. (pres. 1973-74), Am. Soc. Mammalogists, La. Acad. Sci., V.F.W. Methodist. Author: (with others) Introduction to Zoology in the Laboratory, 1971. Research in metabolism and histology. Home: 1021 Cherrydale St Lake Charles LA 70601

ROBINSON, SARA KATHARINE MOORE (MRS. DONALD L. ROBINSON), lawyer; b. Chgo.; d. Herbert Jackson and Margaret Emma (Roberts) Moore; B.A., Beloit Coll., 1959, J.D., Columbus Sch. Law, Catholic U. of Am., 1965; m. Donald L. Robinson, Aug. 4, 1962; children—Marshall Jackson, Margaret Moore. Admitted to D.C. bar, 1966; state campaign sec. Wis. Humphrey for Pres. Com., Milw., 1959; exec. sec. Congressman Henry S. Reuss of Wis., Washington, 1960-65; legal asst. Congressman Henry S. Reuss, Wis., Washington, from 1965, now counsel to Congressman Henry S. Reuss. Bus. mgr. St. Stephen's Ch. Enterprises, Inc., Washington, 1969-71; vis. faculty mem. Civil Service Commn. Exec. Seminar Centers, Berkeley, Cal., Kings Pt., N.Y., Oak Ridge, 1973. Bd. dirs. Washington Half-Way Home for Women, Inc., 1967—, Powerhouse, Inc., 1966-71. Mem. Kappa Beta Pi (chpt. dean 1967-69). Episcopalian (jr. warden 1968-69). Home: 1817 Kenyon St NW Washington DC 20010 Office: 2186 Rayburn House Office Bldg Washington DC 20515

ROBINSON, TERRENCE ANDREW, landscape architect; b. Bloomfield, N.J., Sept. 14, 1941; s. Samuel Joseph and Margaret Jane (Conway) R.; B.S., U. Mass., 1963; M.Landscape Arch., Harvard, 1966; m. Suzanne Mertens, Sept. 10, 1966; 1 dau., Amy Baines. Landscape architect Albin Assos., N.Y.C., 1965, Mason & Frey, Cambridge, Mass., 1965-66; project planner V.I. Planning Bd., St. Thomas, 1966-68; prin. Design Collaborative, St. Thomas, 1968—. Instr., Coll. of V.I.; dir. Fish N' Fool Internat. Bd. dirs. V.I. Conservation Soc. Mem. Am. Soc. Landscape Architects, St. Thomas-St. John C. of C. (dir.), Alpha Zeta. Episcopalian. Rotarian. Club: V.I. Yacht. Author: Death, Decision and Design, 1965. Home: PO Box 3979 St Thomas VI 00801 Office: Design Collaborative Sub Base Aux Carrier St Thomas VI 00801

ROBINSON, WAVERLY HALE, crane and rigging co. exec.; b. Richmond, Va., Jan. 2, 1932; s. John Hudson and Elizbeth (Goodman) R.; student U. Va., 1950-52; B.S. in Civil Engring., U. W.Va., 1956; J.D., U. N.C., 1965; m. Janice Evelyn Cossill, May 5, 1973. Civil engr. Nello L. Teer Co., Durham, N.C., 1956-65; co-owner Carolina Crane Corp., Raleigh, N.C., 1966—, also sec.-treas.; co-owner, sec.-treas. Old South Devel. Corp., Raleigh, 1967—; co-owner, pres. Umstead Water Co., Raleigh, 1968—, Carolina Crane & Rigging Corp., Charlotte, N.C., 1968—; co-owner, sec.-treas. Carolina Pile Driving Corp., Raleigh, 1969—, Carolina Rigging & Erection Corp., Raleigh, 1970—; dir., Chesapeake Internat. Corp., Durham; admitted to N.C. bar, 1966; practice law, Raleigh, 1966—. Registered profl. engr., W.Va., N.C. Home: 5513-J Albemarle Rd Charlotte NC 28212 Office: Route 8 Box 114 Raleigh NC 27612

ROBINSON, WAYNE AUSTIN, author; b. Clinton, Okla., Aug. 13, 1937; s. Theodore Ralph and Minnie Elizabeth (Pryor) R.; Th.B., Southwestern Coll., 1959; B.A., Oklahoma City U., 1961; M.Th., So. Meth. U., 1967; m. Sharon Lee Cook, Mar. 30, 1963; children—Laura Beth, Brett, Carol. With Oral Roberts Assn., Tulsa, 1967-71, editor-in-chief publs. (Daily Blessing, Abundant Life, Outreach), 1967-68, v.p. communications, 1968-69, exec. producer Oral Roberts Presents and Contact TV shows, 1969-70, communications cons., 1970-71; v.p. pub. affairs Oral Roberts U., Tulsa, 1971-72; exec. editor Forum House, Atlanta, 1972—. Mem. Direct Mail Advt. Assn. Democrat. Methodist (elder 1968—). Author: What's a Nice Church Like You Doing in a Place Like This?, 1972; I Once Spoke in Tongues, 1973; The Passing of the Night, 1974. Editor The Okla. Meth., 1969-70. Ghostwriter for Oral Roberts. Home: 6309 Connaught Ct Oklahoma City OK 73132

ROBINSON, WILBURN VAUGHN, steel co. exec.; b. Whigham, Ga., Apr. 28, 1934; s. Rufus Hill and Martha Elaine (Vaughn) R.; B.B.A., U. Ga., 1962, M.B.A., 1963; m. Gayle Walden, Dec. 19, 1968; children—Michael, Richard. With Peat, Marwick, Mitchell & Co., Greenville, S.C., 1963-68; asst. dir. for fiscal affairs Spartanburg (S.C.) Gen. Hosp., 1968-69; dir. hosp. implementation Computer Communications Network, Inc., Nashville, 1969-70; with Georgetown (S.C.) Steel Corp., 1971-74, v.p., controller, 1972-74; v.p., controller Korf Industries, Inc., Charlotte, N.C., 1974—. Dir. Trammell Candy Co., Atlanta, 1970-73. Served with AUS, 1955-58. Recipient Haskins and Sells Found. award, 1962. C.P.A., Ga., S.C. Mem. Am. Inst. C.P.A.'s. Methodist. Moose. Home: 3000 Wamath Dr Charlotte NC 28210 Office: PO Box 10876 Charlotte NC 28234

ROBINSON, WOODROW WILSON, supt. schs.; b. Washington County, Va., Apr. 20, 1912; s. Ben Franklin and Bertha Mae (McClelland) R.; B.A., King Coll., 1932, Ed.D. (hon.), 1961; M.A., Duke, summer, 1942; m. Marily Virginia McGhee, Nov. 26, 1942; children—Martha Jean (Mrs. Sylvio Zaidan), Barbara Anne (Mrs. Martin L. Slavin). Tchr. pub. schs., Washington County, Va., 1932-34, prin. high sch., 1934-37; tchr. Tazewell (Va.) High Sch., 1937-38; asst. prin. Marion (Va.) High Sch., 1938-42; prin. Virginia High Sch., Bristol, Va., 1943-45; prin. Radford (Va.) High Sch., also supr. student teaching for Radford Coll., 1945-53; supt. county schs., Floyd County, Va., 1953-56, Shenandoah County, 1957—; mem. summer faculty Radford Coll., 1945-53. Mem. McMath Commn., 1968. Recipient Distinguished Service award Woodstock C. of C., 1968. Mem. N.E.A. (life), Am. Assn. Sch. Adminstrs., Va. Edn. Assn. (dist. pres. 1939-41, 51-55; pres. 1961, treas. 1955-61), Woodstock C. of C. Presbyn. (elder). Rotarian (pres. club 1970), Kiwanian (pres. Radford). Club: Ruritan (pres. 1956). (Floyd). Home: 259 Summit Av Woodstock VA 22664 Office: Court St Woodstock VA 22664

ROBISON, CHARLES BARRETT, environmental health adminstr.; b. Brownsville, Tex., Mar. 8, 1939; s. Calvin Leroy and Elizabeth Ware (Jones) R.; B.S., Stanford, 1962; M.S.E., U. Ala. 1970; m. Susan Ann Manuel, Nov. 23, 1963; children—Amy Suzanne, Barri Lynn. Engr., USPHS, 1962-66; air pollution control engr. Jefferson County Dept. Health, Birmingham, Ala., 1966-70, asst. dir. Bur. Environmental Health, 1970—. Instr., U. Ala., Birmingham, 1970—. Mem. Environmental Improvement Award Selection Com., Birmingham, 1973—. Served to capt. USPHS, 1962-66. Registered profl. engr., Ala. Mem. Ala. Pub. Health Assn., Conf. Local Environmental Health Adminstrs., Air Pollution Control Assn., Phi Delta Theta. Methodist (chmn. Council on Ministries 1972, lay leader 1973). Contbr. articles to profl. jours. Home: 7237 Pine Tree Lane Fairfield AL 35064 Office: 1912 8th Av S Birmingham AL 35203

ROBISON, E. SHAW, JR., educator; b. Oxford, Miss., May 3, 1932; s. Edgar Shaw and Vivienne (Suber) R.; B.A., U. Miss., 1954, M.A., 1960, postgrad., 1967. Mem. faculty Ark. State Coll., Jonesboro, 1960-61, U. Tenn., Martin, 1961-64, Judson Coll., Marion, Ala., 1964-66; mem. faculty Pensacola (Fla.) Jr. Coll., 1967—, asst. prof. speech and theatre, 1969—, dir. theatre, 1967—. Area rep. Fla. Theatre Conf., 1971-72; co-chmn. local arrangements Southeastern Theatre Conf., 1973; bd. dirs. Pensacola Little Theatre, 1969-70, 72-74. Served with AUS, 1955-57. Mem. Sigma Nu, Kappa Kappa Psi, Alpha Psi Omega. Democrat. Presbyn. Moose. Home: 1308 Panferio Dr Pensacola Beach FL 32561

ROBISON, G(EORGE) ALAN, pharmacologist, educator; b. Lethbridge, Alta., Can., Nov. 4, 1934; s. Douglas Charles and Margaret Elizabeth (Barr) R.; came to U.S., 1957; naturalized, 1971; B.Sc., U. Alta., 1957; M.S., Tulane U., 1960, Ph.D., 1962; postgrad. Western Res. U., 1962-63; m. Jill Jeanine Seaman, Mar. 12, 1956; children—James Darcy, Amelia N'Orlean. Research asso. Vanderbilt U., Nashville, 1963-64, instr., 1964-66, asst. prof., 1966-69, asso. prof., 1969-72; prof. pharmacology U. Tex. Med. Sch., Houston, 1972—, dir. pharmacology program, 1972—. Pfizer fellow Clin. Research Inst., Montreal, Que., Can., 1970; investigator Howard Hughes Med. Inst., 1970-72; mem. bd. sci. advisers Nelson Research & Devel. Co., Irvine, Cal., 1972; mem. pharmacology study sect. NIH, 1973; prin. organizer 1st Gordon Research Conf. on Cyclic AMP, Plymouth, N.H., 1970; sci. sec. 1st Internat. Conf. on Cyclic AMP, Milan, Italy, 1971. 2d Internat. Conf., Vancouver, B.C., Can., 1974. Recipient E.L. Woods Meml. prize Can. Found. for Advancement Pharmacy, 1957. Mem. Am. Humanist Assn., Am. Chem. Soc., Am. Soc. for Pharmacology and Exptl. Therapeutics, Endocrine Soc., N.Y. Acad. Sci. Sigma Xi. Author: (with R.W. Butcher, E.W. Sutherland) Cyclic AMP, 1971. Editor: (with P. Greengard) Advances in Cyclic Nucleotide Research, 1972—; mem. editorial bd. Archives of Biochemistry and Biophysics, 1972—. Biochemical Pharmacology, 1973—. Home: 250 Stoney Creek Dr Houston TX 77024

ROBISON, HENRY WELBORN, zoologist, educator; b. Albany, Ga., Mar. 24, 1945; s. Henry Welborn and Margie Francis (Avera) R.; B.S., Ark. State U., 1967, M.S., 1968; Ph.D., Okla. State U., 1971; m. Catherine Davis, June 18, 1966; 1 son, Patrick Henry. Asst. prof. zoology So. Ill. U., Carbondale, 1971; asst. prof. zoology So. State Coll., Magnolia, Ark., 1971-73. Cons. rare and endangered fishes U.S. Forest Service, Bayou Dorcheat Environmental statement, U.S. Corps Engrs. Rare and endangered fishes of U.S. Nat. Forests in Ark. and Okla. grantee, 1972. Mem. Am. Soc. Ichthyologists and Herpetologists, Animal Behavior Soc., Assn. Southwestern Naturalists, Am. Fisheries Soc., Sigma Xi. Baptist. Author: The Fishes of Oklahoma, 1973. Home: PO Box 320 Route 4 Magnolia AR 71753 Office: PO Box 1216 Southern State College Magnolia AR 71753

ROBSON, WILLIAM SION, III, utilities co. exec.; b. LaGrange, Tex., Apr. 16, 1929; s. William Sion II and Frankie L. (Lowry) R.; B.S. in Elec. Engring., Tex. A. and M. U., 1957; children—William Sion, Kenneth Franklin. Student engr. Brazos Electric Power Coop., Inc., Waco, Tex., 1956; asst. elec. design engr., 1957-60, chief dispatcher, 1960-62, asst. supt. operations, 1960, mgr. engring. div., 1960-70, mgr. transmission div., 1970-73; exec. asst., 1973—; owner R.E.S. Co., Waco, Tex., 1973—. Served with USAF, 1950-54. Registered profl. engr., Tex. Mem. I.E.E.E., Tex., Nat. socs. profl. engrs., Amateur Radio Relay League. Mason (Shriner). Home: 7301 Sanger St Apt 114 Waco TX 76710 Office: 2404-12 La Salle Av Waco TX 76706

ROBUCK, JOHN BENTON, power light co. exec.; b. Helena, Tex., May 1, 1907; s. Charles H. and Anna (Daughtrey) R.; student Southwestern U., 1924-26; B.S. in Elec. Engring., U. Tex., 1929; m. Josephine Hurt, June 30, 1930; children—Eva, Marvin Womack, Joel Henry. With Tex. Power & Light Co., 1929-74, successively student engr. Hillsboro, engr., dist. operator, Sherman, electrician, McKinney, asst. div. engr., engr. Dallas, asst. supt. transmission, substa. engr., system engr., adminstrv. asst., 1959-61, asst. chief engr., 1961-68, chief engr., 1968-69, v.p. in charge engring., 1969-72, cons., 1972-74; cons. N.M. Electric Service, 1974—. Registered profl. engr., Tex. Fellow I.E.E.E.; mem. Tex. Soc. Profl. Engrs., Tau Beta Pi, Eta Kappa Nu. Methodist. Mason. Home: 1519 Matagorda Dr Dallas TX 75232

ROCA, RAFAEL ANGEL, ins. exec.; b. Yauco, P.R., Aug. 11, 1928; s. Gaspar G. and Luisa (Natali) R.; B.S. in Econs., Wharton Sch., U. Pa., 1949; student Advanced Multiple Line Underwriting Course, Am. Ins. Group, Newark, N.J., 1950. Sales supr. Caribbean Electric, Inc., P.R., 1949-50; accountant Christopher Columbus Rum Distillery, P.R., 1950; trainee Am. Ins. Co., Newark, 1950-51; casualty underwriter Anglo-Porto Rican Ins. Agys., Inc., San Juan, P.R., 1951-54; asst. sec. Puerto Rican-Am. Ins. Co., San Juan, 1954-58, sec., 1958-60, asst. v.p., 1960, exec. v.p., 1960-61, pres., 1961—, dir., 1954—, mem. exec. com., 1962—, mem. finance com., 1954—; pres. Puerto Rican Reins. Agy., Inc., 1962—, also dir.; chmn. Nat. Life Ins. Co., 1969-71; pres., mem. exec. and finance coms. Preferred Risk Ins. Co., 1968—, also dir.; pres. Puerto Rican-Am. Corp.; v.p. Santa Barbara Corp., 1964-65; dir. Inversiones Future, Inc., Banco Commercial de Mayaqyez, former dir. Albert E. Lee & Son, Inc., Ins. Cos. Am. chmn. J. Walter Thompson Co. Caribbean, 1968—. Mem. adv. ins. bd. Commonwealth P.R., 1964-68; mem. governing bd. Internat. Ins. Seminars, 1967—; mem. exec. com. P.R. Inspection and Rating Bur., 1966—, vice chmn. exec. com., 1971—, chmn. finance com., 1971; mem. P.R. casualty com. Nat. Bur. Casualty Underwriters; chmn. P.R. ins. information com. Ins. Information Inst., 1969—; chmn. adv. com. ins. matters Sec. Treasury P.R., 1972. Mem. exec. bd. P.R. Council Boy Scouts Am., 1973—. Fellow Ins. Inst. P.R. (dir., bd. govs. lectr. Sch. Ins.), Benjamin Franklin Assos.; mem. Ins. Soc. N.Y., Am. Ins. Assn. (chmn. P.R. adv. com. 1965—), Assn. Casualty & Surety Cos. (pres. P.R. adv. com. 1963-64), P.R. Fire and Allied Lines Underwriting Assn. (dir.) Navy League U.S., Young Pres.'s Orgn., Wharton Alumni Group, Bankers Club P.R. Clubs: Cornell (Pa.); Caribe Hilton Swimming and Tennis; Pan Am. Gun. Home: 6 Joffre St Condado Santurce PR 00907 Office: PO Box 112 San Juan PR 00902

ROCH, ROBERT HOOVER, lawyer; b. Jacksonville, Tex., Dec. 10, 1937; s. Lewis Marshall and Gladys Irene (Hoover) R.; B.S. in Commerce, Tex. Christian U., 1958; J.D. cum laude, Baylor U., 1961; Margaret Lynn Lebrand, Apr. 18, 1964; children—Sharon Elaine, Carolyn Diane. Admitted to Tex. bar, 1961. U.S. Dist. Ct., 1962, U.S. Ct. Appeals, 1970, since practiced in Houston; asso. firm Hill, Brown, Kronzer & Abraham, 1961-66; partner firm Fisher, Roch, McLendon & Gallagher, 1966—. Lectr. law S. Tex. Coll. Law, 1966—. Mem. State Bar of Texas (mem. grievance com. 1968-71. chmn. 1970-71), Am., Houston Jr. bar assns., Am. Assn. Trial Lawyers, Tex. Assn. Trial Lawyers, Am. Judicature Soc., Houston Trial Lawyers Assn., Alpha Chi, Delta Tau Delta, Phi Alpha Delta. Methodist (adminstrv. bd. 1969-72). Home: 10807 Pine Bayou Houston TX 77024 Office: 723 Main St Suite 610 Houston TX 77002

ROCHELL, CARLTON CHARLES, librarian; b. Lawrenceburg, Tenn., Nov. 2, 1933; s. William Frank and Mae (Crews) R.; B.S. in Math., George Peabody Coll., 1959; M.S. in L.S., Fla. State U., 1961; m. Rebecca Anne Ridley, Sept. 9, 1961; children—Carlton Charles, Anne Leslie. Reference librarian, spl. asst. to dir. Nashville Pub. Library, 1957-60; dir. Hattiesburg (Miss.)-Forrest County Pub. Library, 1961-63, Pub. Library Anniston and Calhoun County (Ala.), 1963-65, Pub. Library Knoxville and Knox County (Tenn.), 1965-68; Atlanta Pub. Library, 1968—; library service and bldg. cons., 1965—. Mem. exec. bd. Community Action Com., Anniston, 1963-65; mem. Model Cities Tech. Adv. Bd., Atlanta. Served with USNR, 1953-57. Recipient spl. citation City Anniston, 1965. Mem. Am. (standards com.), Tenn. (treas. 1966), Southeastern (pres. pub. library div. 1970), Ala. (past v.p., pres. elect pub. library div. 1965) library assns., Atlanta C. of C. (edn. com.). Democrat. Episcopalian. Home: 248 The Prado NE Atlanta GA 30309 Office: Atlanta Pub Library 126 Carnegie Way NW Atlanta GA 30303

ROCHELLE, RUDOLPH CEDRIC, pub. relations exec.; b. Grow, Tex., Mar. 28, 1932; s. T.D. and Edith Grace (Biddy) R.; student Tex. Tech. U., 1949-50; B.J., U. Tex., 1958; m. Shirley Mae Hamilton, Aug. 10, 1971. Asst. financial editor Dallas Morning News, 1958-64; v.p. Rom Rominger Agy., Dallas, 1964-68; pres. Tierney & Assos., Dallas, 1968—. Served with USN, 1951-55. Mem. Pub. Relations Soc. Am., Nat. Investor Relations Inst., Press. Club of Dallas. Contbr. articles to profl. jours. Home: 3819 One Way Circle Dallas TX 75234 Office: Mercantile Dallas Bldg Dallas TX 75201

ROCK, DAVID MIGUEL, environmental engr.; b. Havana, Cuba, Aug. 9, 1921; s. David Thomas and Olga Maria (Moenck) R.; B.S. in Chem. Engring., Mass. Inst. Tech., 1944, M.S., 1946; m. Cira Ruiz, Jan. 15, 1966; 1 dau., Anne-Marie. Came to U.S., 1962, naturalized, 1968. Teaching asst. Mass. Inst. Tech., Cambridge, 1944-45; process and product control supr. Ind. Consolidadas de Matanzas, Cuba, 1946-53, research mgr., 1953-59, tech. dir., 1959-60; tech. mgr. Rayon Said Ind. Quim., Chile, 1960-62; rayon research leader Am. Enka Co., Enka, N.C., 1962-65, project engr., 1965-70, environmental engr., 1970—, project coordinator Environmental Protection Agy. research and devel. grant, 1968-70. Mem. Am. Inst. Chem. Engrs. (vice chmn. water quality engring. symposium 1971), Am. Chem. Soc., Sigma Xi, Tau Beta Pi, Alpha Chi Sigma. Club: Enka Lake. Home: PO Box 6 Enka NC 28728 Office: Central Engineering Dept American Enka Company Enka NC 28728

ROCK, JEROME IRWIN, dentist; b. Bklyn., Sept. 4, 1928; s. Louis A. and Ethel G. (Resnik) R.; B.A., Bklyn. Coll., 1946-50; D.D.S., N.Y. U., 1955; m. Margaret Felton, July 8, 1956; children—Melanie Ann, Robin Elizabeth. Pvt. practice dentistry, Montego Bay, Jamaica, W.I., 1957-61, Falls Church, Va., 1961—, Middleburg, Va., 1963—. Served to capt. AUS, 1955-57. Mem. Am., N. Va. dental assns., Fairfax County Dental Soc. Clubs: Middleburg Tennis, Orange County Hunt. Home: Box 126 Middleburg VA 22117 Office: Seven Corners Profl Bldg Falls Church VA 22044 also Middleburg VA 22117

ROCKETT, ELEANOR WILSON STINSON (MRS. DON LEE ROCKETT), coll. ofcl.; b. Saline, La.; d. William Lee and Ida (Payton) Stinson; B.S., La. Poly. Inst., 1938, M.S. in Edn., 1969; m. Don Lee Rockett, Oct. 14, 1939 (dec. Jan. 1960); children—Donald Robin, Galen Wilson, Brian Lee. Sec. extension dept. La. Poly. Inst. (now La. Tech. U.), Ruston, 1938-41, sec. student guidance, 1942-43, sec., bus. mgr., 1959-60, asst. registrar, 1960-68, registrar, 1968—; sec. La. State U. Agrl. Extension Service, Baton Rouge, 1941-42; head program clk. Agrl. Stblzn. and Conservation Service, Rayville, La., 1956-59. Mem. Am., So., La. assns. collegiate registrars and admissions officers, Am. Assn. U. Women, Phi Kappa Phi (membership chmn. 1960—), Sigma Kappa (scholarship com. 1965-69). Baptist. Club: Quota (pres. 1973-74) (Ruston). Home: Briarwood Dr Northwood Terrace Ruston LA 71270

ROCOVICH, JOHN GEORGE, JR., lawyer; b. Roanoke, Va., Jan. 19, 1945; s. John George and Flora Elizabeth (Holden) R.; B.S. in Bus. Adminstrn. with honors, Va. Polytech. Inst., 1966; J.D., U. Richmond, 1967; LL.M. in Taxation, N.Y. U., 1968; m. Sue Ellen Butler, Sept. 9, 1967; 1 dau., Elizabeth Holden. Admitted to Va. bar, 1967; individual practice law, Blacksburg, Va., 1967-68; asso. Martin, Hopkins & Lemon, Roanoke, 1968-70, partner, 1970—. Instr., Am. Coll. Life Underwriters, 1973—; lectr. various seminars, colls., law schs. Mem. adv. council Coll. Bus., Va. Polytech. Inst. and State U., 1971—. Bd. dirs. Roanoke Valley Heart Fund. Chmn., Cavespring dist. Democratic party Va., 1971—; treas. 6th Dist. Dem. Com. Va., 1972—. Mem. Am., Va. State, Roanoke bar assns., Va. State Bar, Va. Trial Lawyers Assn., Am. Judicature Soc., Roanoke Estate Planning Council, Phi Delta Phi, Phi Kappa Phi. Rotarian. Home: 3943 Hummingbird Roanoke VA 24018 Office: Box 931 Roanoke VA 24005

RODDY, CLYDE WILBUR, city ofcl.; b. Dayton, Tenn., Aug. 16, 1910; s. Harvey and Maude (Kile) R.; grad. Rhea Central High Sch.; m. Evelyn Clair Little, Nov. 23, 1938; children—Agatha (Mrs. Luther John Maynor), Clyde Ray. Sales mgr. Arnold Z Motor Co., Dayton, Tenn., 1938-42, 50-68; city mgr. City of Dayton, Tenn., 1968—. Served with AUS, 1943-45. Mem. C. of C. (dir. 1969—). Rotarian. Home: Edgewater Rd Dayton TN 37321 Office: First Ave Dayton TN 37321

RODEHAVER, SAMUEL CHARLES, lawyer; b. El Paso, Tex., Apr. 24, 1942; s. Samuel Boyce and Gladys Blanche (Kemp) R.; student Tex. Western Coll., 1960-62; B.A., U. Tex., 1963. L.L.B., 1966; m. Barbara Anne Leland, Aug. 23, 1963; children—Wendy Sue, Teri Lynn. Admitted to Tex. bar, 1966; atty. City Atty's. Office, Lubbock, Tex., 1966-67; partner Wyrick, Rodehaver & Walker, Dallas, 1967—. Bd. dirs. S.E. YMCA. Named an Outstanding Young Man of Am., Pleasant Grove C. of C., 1971. Mem. State Bar of Tex., Dallas County, Lubbock County jr. bar assns., Toastmasters Internat., Kappa Sigma, Phi Alpha Delta. Presbyn. (chmn. bd. deacons 1971, elder 1973). Kiwanian. Home: 11039 Carissa St Dallas TX 75218 Office: 555 Griffin Sq Suite 700 Dallas TX 75202

RODENBERGER, CHARLES ALVARD, educator; b. Muskogee, Okla., Sept. 11, 1926; s. Darcy Owen and Kathryn Martha (Percival) R.; B.S., Okla. State U., 1948; M.S., So. Meth. U., 1959; Ph.D. (NSF fellow), U. Tex., Austin, 1968; m. Molcie Lou Halsell, Sept. 3, 1949; children—Kathryn Sue, Charles Mark. Sr. design engr. Gen. Dynamics, Ft. Worth, 1954-60; prof. aerospace and interdisciplinary engring. Tex. A. and M. U., 1960—. Cons., Gen. Motors Def. Research Labs., S.W. Research Inst., 1967—; v.p., dir. Meiller Research, Inc., College Station, Tex., 1966—. Bd. dirs. A. and M. Wesley Found., 1969—, chmn., 1971—. Served with USAAF, 1945, to 1st lt., USAF, 1951-53. Recipient Faculty Distinguished Achievement award in teaching Tex. A. and M. U., 1962; Halliburton prof. engring., 1966. Asso. fellow Am. Inst. Aeros. and Astronautics; mem. Nat. (nat. dir. 1973), Tex. (state dir. 1970-73, named Engr. of Year Brazos chpt. 1972) socs. profl. engrs. Patentee propellant lined high velocity accelerator, orthopedic shoe constrn. Home: 508 Crescent Dr Bryan TX 77801 Office: Dept Aero Engring Tex A and M U College Station TX 77843

RODESNEY, FRANK, elec. engr.; b. Oklahoma City, Dec. 8, 1921; s. Frank F. and Josephine (Vobornik) R.; B.S. in E.E., U. Okla., 1943; postgrad. indsl. engring. Okla. State U., 1952; m. Louise Brown, July 1, 1944; children—Marilyn (Mrs. Jerry Taylor), Steven, Jeanette, Richard, Paul, Bruce, Doris. Design engr., Okla. Gas & Electric Co., Oklahoma City, 1947-54; with Benham-Blair & Affiliates and predecessor firms, Oklahoma City, 1954—, sr. v.p., 1972—, mem. exec. com., 1973—, also dir. Mem. vis. com. Coll. Engring. U. Okla., 1969-71. Served to 2nd lt., Signal Corps, AUS, 1943-46. Registered profl. engr., Okla. Named to U. Okla. Engring. Hall of Fame, 1971. Sr. mem. I.E.E.E. (chmn. Oklahoma City sect. 1969-70); mem. Illuminating Engring. Soc., Cons. Engrs. Council (pres. 1972-73), Nat., Okla. (pres. 1968-69) socs. profl. engrs., Armed Forces Communications and Electronics Assn., Mil. Order World Wars, Eta Kappa Nu, Okla City C. of C. Clubs: Mens Dinner, Twin Hills Golf and Country, Regency (pres. 1972-73). Home: Route 4 Box 610 Oklahoma City OK 73121 Office: 6323 N Grand Blvd Oklahoma City OK 73118

RODGERS, EARL GILBERT, educator; b. Trenton, Fla., Jan. 21, 1921; s. Thomas Irvin Gilbert and Lillie Mathis (NesSmith) R.; B.S., U. Fla., 1943, M.S., 1949; Ph.D., Ia. State U., 1951; m. Jewell Carolyn O'Steen, May 15, 1943; children—Ronald Gilbert, Patricia (Mrs. David Rigsby). Asst. county agrl. agt. Hardee County, Fla., 1946-47; mem. faculty U. Fla., Gainesville, 1947—, prof. agronomy, 1959—, coordinator resident instrn. and student counselor in agronomy, 1961—. Cons., Eglin AFB, Fla., 1955-57, Buckeye Cellulose Corp., Foley, Fla., 1955-64; vis. asso. prof. Auburn (Ala.) U., 1954. Served to lt. col. USMCR, 1943-46. Rockefeller Found. fellow, 1949-50. Fellow Am. Soc. Agronomy; mem. Weed Sci. Soc. Am. (pres. 1973-74), Crop Sci. Soc. Am., So. Weed Sci. Soc. (pres. 1956), Soil and Crop Sci. Soc. Fla., Fla. Acad. Scis., Gamma Sigma Delta (internat. pres. 1962-64), Sigma Xi, Phi Kappa Phi, Alpha Zeta, Alpga Gamma Rho, Phi Sigma. Baptist (deacon). Editor: Weed Sci. Jour., 1965-71, Weeds Today mag., 1970-71, Weed Sci. newsletter, 1966. Contbr. profl. jours. Home: 611 SW 16th Pl Gainesville FL 32601 Office: Dept Agronomy Univ Florida Gainesville FL 32611

RODGERS, ELLEN DAVIES (MRS. HILLMAN P. RODGERS), club woman, planter, author; b. Brunswick, Tenn., Nov. 13, 1903; d. Gillie M. and Frances Ina (Stewart) Davies; B.S., George Peabody Coll., 1924; M.A., Columbia, 1927; m. Hillman P. Rodgers, Dec. 21, 1932, foster-children—Sarah B. Gandy, Frances Gandy, Elba Gandy, Mary Gandy (Mrs. Burnell D. Hardee). Critic tchr. campus sch., Memphis State U., 1924-26, also prof. early childhood edn.; prof. elementary edn., Evansville (Ind.) Coll., summer, 1926; prin. Arlington High Sch., 1928-29, Lausanne Sch. Girls, 1953; state elementary supr. W. Tenn., 1938-40; mem. Shelby County Bd. Edn., 1961-65; dir. Tenn. Sch. Bds. Assn., 1963-65. First Shelby County (Tenn.) historian, 1965—. Organized Pleasant Hill Cemetery Assn., 1937, pres., 1937—. Del. Dem. Nat. Conv., 1956. Del. Tenn. Constl. Conv., 1953, 59. State exec. vice chmn. Woman's Adv. Council, Civil Def. Organized Zachariah Davies chpt. D.A.R. (organizing regent 1945-46, chpt. regent 1946-48; state regent 1956-59, hon. regent 1959), nat. vice chmn. Am. history month, 1964-67. Named Woman of Year, Memphis Kiwanis Club, 1965; one of 10 women cited by Memphis Comml. Appeal, 1969. Mem. Tenn. Assn. Childhood Edn. (past pres.), Memphis and Shelby County Council Garden Clubs (past pres.), Memphis State U. Alumni Assn. (past pres.), Alumni Assn. Memphis St. U. (life), Daus. Am. Colonists, U. D.C., Children Am. Revolution (state and nat. promotor), Memphis Geneal. Soc. Hermitage Assn., Tenn. Hist. Soc. (v.p. W. Tenn. 1967), Tenn. Poetry Soc., So. Dames Am. (nat. parliamentarian 1965-67), Am. Assn. State and Local History, Nat. Congress P.T.A. (life), Nat. Council State Garden Clubs (life), Tenn. Fedn. Garden Clubs (life mem.; past pres.), YWCA, Internat. Platform Assn., Phi Mu (life mem.; pres. Memphis Kappa Lambda House Corp. 1960, treas. 1961, woman of year award 1966), Beta Sigma Phi (internat. hon. mem.). Episcopalian. Clubs: Brunswick Road Garden (organizing pres. 1965—); Quota (hon. mem.; past pres.) (Memphis); Nineteenth Century. Author (under name Ellen Davies-Rodgers): The Romance of the Episcopal Church in West Tennessee, 1964; The Holy Innocents, 1966; The Casket Case, 1970; Education, Then, Now and Yon, 1971; The Great Book, 1973. Contbr. numerous articles and items to mags. Home: Davies Plantation Brunswick Memphis TN 38128

RODGERS, GORDON ALEXANDER, JR., dentist; b. Anniston, Ala., Oct. 28, 1915; s. Gordon Alexander and Fannie Mamie (Lewis) R.; B.A., Talladega Coll., 1937; D.D.S., Meharry Med. Coll., 1941; m. Agnes Elizabeth Durrah, Feb. 29, 1951; children—Gordon, III, Cheryl, Beverly, Michelle. Pvt. practice dentistry, Anniston, Ala., 1946—. Mem. Anniston City Council, 1969—. Bd. dirs. Choccolocco council Boy Scouts Am., 1969-72, Ala. Mental Health Assn., 1965-71. Served with Dental Corps, AUS, 1941-46. Mem. Nat. Dental Assn., Ala. Dental Soc., Am. Legion, N.A.A.C.P. (br. pres. 1954-55), Omega Psi Phi. Home: 1001 Claxton St Anniston AL 36201 Office: 1616 Cooper St Anniston AL 36201

RODGERS, HENRY LEE, justice Miss. Supreme Ct.; b. Philadelphia, Miss., Apr. 6,, 1903; s. H. H. and Ettie Lee (Brantley) R.; student Miss. Coll., 1920-22, Cumberland U., 1922-24; LL.B., U. Miss., 1927; m. Leola Edwards, May 18, 1929. Admitted to Miss. bar, 1927, practiced in Louisville, until 1951; dist. atty. 5th Dist. Miss., 1946-51; circuit judge 5th Dist. Miss., 1951-61; asso. justice Miss. Supreme Ct., Jackson, 1961—. Mem. Miss. N.G., 1929-35; served with AUS, 1943-44. Mem. Miss. State Bar, S.C.V., Am. Legion, 40 and 8. Methodist. Mason (Shriner). Author articles. Home: 432 N Spring Av Louisville MS 39339 also 751 N President St Jackson MS Office: Supreme Ct Bldg Jackson MS 39205

RODGERS, HILLMAN PHILLIP, planter, paper salesman; b. Lexington, Miss., Nov. 28, 1899; s. William Clay and Sarah Phillip (Eubank) R.; student Freed-Hardeman Coll., 1916-18; m. Frances Ellen Davies, Dec. 21, 1932; foster children—Sarah B. Gandy, Frances Gandy, Eiba Gandy, Mary Gandy (Mrs. Burnell Dwight), Hardee. Salesman, Southland Paper Co. Memphis, 1931-72; mill rep. Crown Zellerbach Corp., also Duro Paper Mfg. Co., 1972—; sales asso. Ike L. Myers Paper Co., 1972—. Mem. Memphis Retail Drug Club, Shelby County Livestock Assn. (past pres.), Shelby County Farm Bur. (dir.), Shelby County Soil Erosion Control Assn. (dir.), Memphis Agrl. Club, S.A.R. (librarian Shelby chpt. Brunswick, Tenn., state and nat. promoter CAR), Sons of Confederacy. Democrat. Episcopalian. Mason (Shriner). Clubs: Holly Hills Country, Colonial Country. Home and Office: Davies Plantation Brunswick TN 38014

RODGERS, JAMES FRANKLIN, dentist; b. Charlotte, N.C., June 11, 1927; s. John Boyce and Ella Graymo (Cornelius) R.; student The Citadel, 1944-45, Duke, 1945-46; B.S., Davidson Coll., 1950; D.D.S., U. N.C., 1956; m. Dorothy Louise Herring, Dec. 27, 1955; 1 son, John Herring. Pvt. practice dentistry, Statesville, N.C., 1956-67; mem. staff N.C. State Bd. Health, Statesville, 1967—. Mem. Statesville City Council, 1974—. Served with USNR, 1945-46. Mem. Am. Dental Assn., N.C. Dental Soc., Delta Sigma Delta. Presbyn. (elder). Rotarian. Home: 412 Ridgeway Av Statesville NC 28677 Office: PO Box 182 Statesville NC 28677

RODGERS, JAMES TURNER, petroleum engr.; b. El Dorado, Ark., Aug. 26, 1934; s. James Turner and Mazie Mabel (Moak) R.; B.S. in Petroleum Engring., La. State U., 1956; M.S. in Petroleum Engring., U. Tex., 1958; m. Claudette Yvonne Moore, Aug. 19, 1955; children—James, Rene, Stacey. Petroleum engr. Gulf Oil Corp., Beaumont, Tex., 1956; petroleum engr. Amoco Prodn. Co., Tex., N.M., Okla., 1961-73, div. engr. engring. mgmt., New Orleans, 1973—. Asst. prof. U. Tex., Austin, 1957-58, Tex. Technol. U., Lubbock, 1958-61. Active various community orgns. Mem. Am. Petroleum Inst., Am. Inst. Mining Engrs., Pi Epsilon Tau, Sigma Nu. Republican. Methodist (adminstrv. bd.). Elk. Contbr. articles to profl. jours. Home: 3670 Mimosa Ct New Orleans LA 70114 Office: PO Box 50879 New Orleans LA 70150

RODGERS, JOSEPH LEE, JR., educator; b. Hugo, Okla., Dec. 19, 1923; s. Joseph Lee and Wilma May (Wickizer) R.; B.S., U. Okla., 1946, M. Regional and City Planning, 1953; m. Mary Joyce Norwood, Apr. 9, 1948; children—Joseph Lee III, Mary Ellen, Robert Norwood, Lawrence Richard. Engr., asst. city mgr., Norman, Okla., 1946-48; planning and engring. cons., 1949—; sr. planner Okla. Center Urban and Regional Studies, Norman, 1951-61, dir., 1961—; chmn. dept. regional and city planning Okla. U., 1961—, prof., 1966—, dir. Undergrad. Urban Studies Program, 1961-72. Sec., Capitol Improvement and Zoning Commn., 1956-57. Served with USNR, 1944-46. Named Outstanding Educator of Am., 1973. Registered profl. engr., Okla. Mem. Am. Soc. Planning Ofcls., Am. Inst. Planners (pres. Ark. Valley chpt. 1967), Okla. Community Planning Assn. (pres. 1956), Okla. Planning Congress, Assn. Collegiate Schs. of Planning (instl. rep.), U.S. Lawn Tennis Assn., Smithsonian Assos. Democrat. Methodist (trustee). Author: Okla. State Capitol Plan, 1954; Okla. Metropolitan Planning Enabling Act, 1957; Okla. Model Housing Code, 1961; New Town Plan: Mannford, Okla., 1961; New Towns for the Ozarks Region, 1968; Cameron College Campus Plan, 1985, 1968; Physical Development Plan-U. of Okla., 1966; Model Planning Doc.-Midwest City, 1970. Contbr. articles profl. jours. Home: 517 Merrywood St Norman OK 73069 Office: 650 Parrington Oval Norman OK 73069

RODGERS, LAWRENCE RODNEY, physician; b. Clovis, N.M., Mar. 9, 1920; s. Samuel Frank and Lillian (O'Connor) R.; B.S., W. Tex. State U., 1940; M.D., U. Tex., 1943. Intern, Phila. Gen. Hosp., 1943-44, resident medicine, 1946-49; asso. internist Tumor Inst., U. Tex. M.D. Anderson Hosp., Houston, 1949—; chmn. dept. medicine Hermann Hosp., Houston, 1966-71; asso. prof. clin. medicine Baylor U., 1949—; prof. clin. medicine U. Tex., 1972—. Bd. dirs. Tex. Med. Found. Served to maj. M.A., AUS, 1944-46. Decorated Bronze Star with oak leaf cluster. Diplomate Am. Bd. internal Medicine. Fellow A.C.P.; mem. A.M.A., Am. Heart Assn., Am., Houston (pres. 1974) socs. internal medicine. Home: 5508 Briar Dr Houston TX 77027 Office: Hermann Profl Bldg Houston TX 77025

RODGERS, ROBERT KAY, bank exec.; b. Cane Hill, Ark., Dec. 21, 1895; s. William F. and Mary Ellen (Reed) R.; Dr. Bus., Coll. Ozarks, 1958; m. Bessie Howard, Nov. 22, 1913; children—Wilma Faye (Mrs. B.T. Blevins), Roberta Kay (Mrs. Ed Pevehouse). Pres., Checkered Transfer and Storage Co., Ft. Smith, Ark., 1935—, Fort Smith Stockyards Co., Inc., 1950—, Rodgers Furniture Co., Ft. Smith, 1947—; pres. First Fed. Savs. and Loan Assn., 1954-67, chmn. bd., 1967—; pres. Modern Meat Processing Co., Inc., 1957-70; dir. First Nat. Bank, Ft. Smith Gas Co., Ark. Okla. Gas. Corp. Bd. dirs. Westark. area council Boy Scouts Am., until 1972, pres., 1946-47; chmn. Community Chest, 1948-49; pres. Sparks Meml. Hosp., 1949-65; bd. dirs. Ark.-Okla. Livestock Show, 1946-71, Ark. Livestock Show. Served from pvt. to sgt., Signal Corps, 1917-18. Recipient Golden Deed award Exchange Club, 1961. Mem. C. of C. (pres. 1941). Democrat. Mason (33 deg.; venerable master Western Ark.; Shriner), Kiwanian. Club: Noon Civic (Ft. Smith). Home: 5601 Park Av Fort Smith AR 72901 Office: First Fed Bldg Fort Smith AR 72901

RODGERS, VERNON LEON, restaurant exec.; b. Hot Springs, Ark., May 18, 1928; s. Oran A. and Hazel N. (Perry) R.; M.E., Little Rock Jr. Coll., 1956; student U. Tex., 1956-57, U. Ark., 1957-58; m. Dorothy Ward, May 18, 1946; children—Tracy Lynn, Lisa Anne. Dist. warehouseman Tex. Eastern Transmission Co., Little Rock, 1953-56; salesman, kitchen designer Dixie Equipment Co., Little Rock, 1960-63; salesman Master Bldg. Co., Cleve., 1963-65; v.p. Minute Man Inc., Little Rock, 1965-73, exec. v.p., 1973-74, pres., 1974—. Served with USAF, 1951-53. Mem. Pulaski County Bus. Men's Assn. Baptist (mem. finance com. 1970-72, bldg. fund com. 1970-71). Home: 6816 Canna Rd Little Rock AR 72209 Office: 7th and Collins St Little Rock AR 72202

RODGERS, WALTER M., lawyer; b. Greenwood, S.C., Mar. 26, 1915; B.S. in Elec. Engring., Clemson U., 1937; J.D., George Washington U., 1947. Admitted to D.C. bar, 1947, U.S. Ct. Customs and Patent Appeals bar, 1949, Ga. bar, 1953, U.S. Supreme Ct. bar, 1965; practiced in Atlanta. Served to maj. USAAF, 1941-45. Registered profl. engr. Mem. Am. (patent, trademark and copywright sect. com. on internat. patent treaties and laws), Atlanta bar assns., State Bar Ga. (chmn. sect. patents, trademarks and copyrights 1969-70), Am. Patent Law Assn., Am. Judicature Soc., Blue Key, Tau Beta Pi. Club: Lawyers (Atlanta). Office: 1918 Gaslight Tower 235 Peachtree St NE Atlanta GA 30303

RODMAN, TASKER NEWTON, physician; b. Newark, Ark., Jan. 13, 1919; s. Thomas Newton and Ethel (McGee) R.; student Ark. Coll., Batesville, 1936, Ark. State Tchrs. Coll., Conway, 1937-39; M.D., U. Ark., 1943; m. Geneva Geraldine Arnold, Feb. 8, 1941; children—Tasker N., II, Lynda, Rita (Mrs. Jerry Lee Hitt). Intern, Mo. Meth. Hosp., St. Joseph, 1943-44; postgrad. in obstetrics and gynecology, Washington U., St. Louis, 1946; practice medicine, Grays Hosp., Newport, Ark., 1946; gen. practice medicine, Leachville, Ark., 1946—; owner Rodman Clinic and Hosp., 1947—. Dir., Leachville State Bank. Participant preceptorship program U. Ark. Med. Sch., 1954—. A founder Little League Baseball, Leachville, 1954, coach, 1954-61; scoutmaster N.E. Ark. council Boy Scouts Am., 1955-58; mem. Leachville Sch. Bd., 1962—, pres., 1966, 72. Served with AUS, 1944-46; ETO. Decorated Bronze Star medal. Recipient Man of Year award Leachville C. of C., 1955. Mem. A.M.A., Am. Acad. Gen. Practice, Ark. Med. Soc., Mississippi County Med. Soc., Leachville P.T.A. (hon. life), Sigma Tau Gamma, Phi Beta Pi. Methodist (trustee). Mason (32 deg.). Club: Big Lake Country (Manila, Ark.). Home and office: PO Box 260 Leachville AR 72438 PO Box 260 Leachville AR 72438

RODNITE, VINCENT JOSEPH, state auditor; b. New Kensington, Pa., June 2, 1942; s. William Andrew and Eleanora Jean (Rutkowski) R.; B.B.A., U. Tex., 1967. Auditor, State of Tex., Austin, 1965—; pub. accountant, Austin, 1970—. C.P.A., Tex. Mem. Am. Inst. C.P.A.'s, Tex. Soc. C.P.A.'s, Am. Motorcycle Assn., Tex. Motorcycle Roadriders Assn. Author poetry under pseudonym Rod Knight. Author: To: The Women in My Life - The Past Six Years, 1972. Home: 7576 Chevy Chase Apt 104 Austin TX 78752 Office: PO Box 1031 Austin TX 78767

RODRICKS, JOSEPH VICTOR, govt. ofcl.; b. Brockton, Mass., Feb. 25, 1938; s. Joseph Anthony and Rose Mary (Popolo) R.; B.S., Mass. Inst. Tech., 1960; Ph.D., U. Md., 1968; postdoctoral scholar U. Cal., 1969-70. Research chemist FDA, Washington, 1965-69, chief biochemistry br., program mgr. mycotoxins and natural toxins, 1971—. Asst. prof. chemistry U. Md. Mem. U.S.-Japan Natural Resources Panel on Toxic Micro-organisms. Dept. Health Edn. and Welfare postdoctoral fellow, 1969-70; Gillette-Harris research fellow, 1963-65. Mem. Am. Chem. Soc., Assn. Ofcl. Analytical Chemistry, A.A.A.S., Sigma Xi. Contbr. articles to profl. jours., chpts. to books. Home: 10312 Calumet St Silver Spring MD 20901 Office: 200 C St SW Washington DC 20204

RODRIGUES, LEO L., educator; b. Thurber, Tex., Sept. 13, 1918; s. Genaro and Jesse (Trevino) R.; B.S., Central State U., Edmond, Okla., 1947; M.S., Okla. U., 1954; postgrad. Okla. State U., 1966—; m. Martha Evelyn Jones, July 7, 1945; children—Marketa Sue (Mrs. Ronald A. Burrow), Lynda Lynne (Mrs. Lyles Trussell). Tchr. pub. schs., Blackwell, Okla., 1949-52; tchr., dept. chmn. Ponca City Sch. System, 1952-64; instr., mus. dir. No. Okla. Coll., Tonkawa, 1964—. Instr. Army Adj. Gen. Sch., 1955-60, Command and Gen. Staff Coll., 1962-66. Block monitor Civil Def., 1964—; charter mem. Okla. Polit. Action Com. for Educators, 1964-70. Served to lt. col., inf. AUS, 1940-45; ETO. Decorated French Croix de Guerre with silver star. Named Ponca City Tchr. of Year, 1963. Fellow Okla. Acad. Sci.; mem. Okla. Mus. Dirs. Assn., Okla. (past pres.), No. Dist. (past pres.) sci. tchrs. assns., Ponca City Tchrs. Assn. (past pres.), Kay County Schoolmasters (past pres.), Okla. Edn. Assn. (pres. dept. higher edn. 1973—). Methodist (chmn. bd. trustees 1963). Mason. Home: 3107 Meadow Lane Ponca City OK 74601 Office: 1220 E Grand St Tonkawa OK 74653

RODRIGUEZ, ALEJANDRO JAVIER, diversified industry exec.; b. Monterrey, N.L., Mexico, Apr. 19, 1939; s. Servando and Enriqueta (Miechielsen) R.; B.S. in Chem. Engring., Universidad de Nuevo Leon, Monterrey, 1960; postgrad. Notre Dame U., 1962; M.B.A., U. Pa., 1964; m. Carmen Bonetti de Rodriguez, Aug. 31, 1961; children—Alejandro, Carmen Teresa, Ivonne, Karla. High sch. prof. chemistry and math., 1957-58; plant operator Fierro Esponja, 1959, research and devel., 1960; procurement mgr. Empresas Industriales, 1960-62; asst. to metall. supt. Hojalata y Lamina, 1964-65, prodn. planning and control mgr., 1965-66, marketing mgr., 1966-69; corporate planning dir. Valores Industriales, Monterrey, 1969—. Tchr. engring. econs. State U., Nuevo Leon, 1964; tchr. adminstrn. grad. level U. N.L., 1965-69; marketing mgmt., 1966-67. Mem. Am. Soc. Metals (v.p.), Am. Marketing Assn., Instituto Mexicano de

Ingenieros Quimicos. Clubs: Futbol Monterrey (pres.), Casino (Monterrey); Casino del Valle (Valle Alto). Home: 439 ote Mississippi Monterrey NL Mexico Office: PO Box 755 Monterrey NL Mexico

RODRIGUEZ, ALMA IRIS, economist; b. San Juan, P.R., June 20, 1930; d. Bernardo and Justa (Ocasio) Rodriguez; B.A. magna cum laude, U. P.R., 1953, M.A., 1960; m. Eugenio Morales, Apr. 29, 1961 (div. Jan. 1963); 1 son, Eugenio B. Tchr. Dept. of Edn., Hato Rey, P.R., 1954-56; asst. economist Econ. Research Div., Legislative Reference Service, San Juan, 1956-57, economist, 1959-60; economist Econ. Research Div., Dept. of the Treasury, San Juan, 1961-62; economist, Econ. Devel. Adminstrn., Santurce, P.R., 1962-67; economist Econ. Research Dept., Santurce, 1967—; analysis studies Curet and Assos., Rio Piedras, P.R., 1967-68; statis. and research work Office of Investigation and Adminstrv. Service, Hato Rey, 1966-67. Bd. dirs. P.R. Devel. Bank Employees Assn. (pres. 1969-70); Fomento Coop., 1971—. Mem. Am. Econ. Assn. Democrat. Roman Catholic. Home: 180 San Lorenzo St Rio Piedras Heights Rio Piedras PR 00926 Office: PO Box 9183 Santurce PR 00908

RODRIGUEZ, EDUARDO ROBERTO, lawyer; b. Edinburg, Tex., Nov. 13, 1943; s. Amador Calvillo and Alicia (Alamia) R.; B.A. in Govt., George Washington U., 1965; J.D., U. Tex., 1968; m. Bonnie Smith, Nov. 26, 1964; children—Michael, Patrick, Melanie. Admitted to Tex. bar, 1968, since practiced in Brownsville; asso. firm Hardy & Sharpe, 1968-71, partner firm Hardy, Sharpe & Rodriguez, 1971—. Tchr. govt. Tex. Southmost Coll. Evening Div., 1969-70; v.p. Cameron County Legal Aid Bd., 1972-73. Pres., St. Vincent De Paul Soc., 1971. Bd. dirs. Driscoll Found. Children's Hosp., Villa Bethany Home for Girls, 1971-72, pres., 1972. Mem. State Bar of Tex., Am. (vice chmn. com. mental health, rights and instn. reform 1973-74), Cameron County (dir.), State Jr. bar assns., Nat. Assn. Def. Lawyers in Criminal Cases, Tex. Criminal Def. Lawyers Assn., Internat. Order of Alhambras. Kiwanian. Home: 24 Poinsettia St Brownsville TX 78520 Office: 1010 E Washington St Brownsville TX 78520

RODRIGUEZ, JUAN GUADALUPE, entomologist, acarologist, educator; b. Espanola, N.M., Dec. 23, 1920; s. Manuel D. and Lugardita (Salazar) R.; B.S., N.M. State U., 1943; M.S., Ohio State U., 1946, Ph.D., 1949; m. Lorraine Ditzler, Apr. 17, 1948; children—Carmen, Teresa, Carla, Rosa. Asst. entomologist U. Ky., Lexington, 1949-55, asso. entomologist, 1955-61, prof. entomology, 1961—; adviser entomology Universidad de San Carlos, Guatemala, 1961; vis. scientist Warsaw U., Poland, 1971. Del. Internat. Congress Entomology, Vienna, Austria, 1960, Moscow, 1968, 1st Internat. Conf. Insects and Diseases of Coffee, San Jose, Costa Rica, 1965; del. 1st Internat. Congress Acarology, Ft. Collins, Colo., 1963, 2d Internat. Congress, Nottingham, Eng., 1967, 3d Internat. Congress, Prague, Czechoslovakia, 1971, 4th Internat. Congress, Saalfelden, Austria, 1974. Bd. dirs. Lexington chpt. Nat. Conf. Christians and Jews. Served with inf. AUS, World War II. Recipient U. Ky. Alumni Assn. award for distinguished research, 1963; Thomas Poe Cooper award for distinguished achievement in research U. Ky. Coll. Agr., 1972. Mem. Am. Inst. Biol. Scis., Ky. Acad. Sci., A.A.A.S., entomol. socs. Can., Ont., Am. (br. sec.-treas. 1963-65; br. com. man-at-large 1968—), Ky. Research Club, Hon. Order Ky. Cols., Sigma Xi, Alpha Tau Alpha, Gamma Alpha, Gamma Sigma Delta. Roman Catholic. Editor: Insect and Mite Nutrition, 1972. Contbr. numerous sci. and tech. publs. Researcher ecology and nutritional physiology of acarina, axenic arthropoda. Home: 1550 Beacon Hill Rd Lexington KY 40504

RODRIGUEZ-HERNANDEZ, JESUS M., hosp. adminstr.; b. Quebradillas, P.R., Apr. 25, 1930; s. Jesus Maria and Maria Luisa (Hernandez) Rodriguez; B.S., U. P.R., 1952; M.S., Columbia, 1957; m. Maria Teresa Estevez, May 1, 1954; children—Jesus M., Maria Teresa. Hosp. adminstr. Humacao (P.R.) Health Center and Hosp., 1954-55; asst. exec. dir. Ponce (P.R.) Dist. Hosp., 1957-58, Arecibo (P.R.) Dist. Hosp., 1958-59, asst. dir. adminstrv. services no. health area Dept. Health, 1959-69; adminstr. San Juan (P.R.) Municipal Hosp., 1969-71, Presbyn. Community Hosp., San Juan, 1971—. Dist. chmn. Boy Scouts Am., 1958-60, A.R.C. campaign, 1960; dist. supr. Cancer Campaign, 1959; mem. Indsl. Com. Arecibo; mem. P.R. Health Com., 1969—; mem. Com. to Study and Establish Universal Health Plan, 1973—. Bd. govs. Girl Scouts Am.; bd. dirs. Nat. Assn. Crippled Children and Adults, Blue Cross of P.R., Employees City of Arecibo; trustee Dept. Health Coop., P.R., 1959-61; pres. finance com. San Antonio Abad Coll., 1972. Served as lt. AUS, 1952-54. Named Exec. of Year, Secs. Assn. San Juan Municipal Hosp., 1970, Presbyn. Community Hosp., San Juan, 1972. Mem. Am. Hosp. Assn. (trustee P.R. chpt. 1960-61), Am. Coll. Hosp. Adminstrs., Royal Soc. Health, Tb Assn., Navy League U.S., Hosp. Adminstrs. Assn. P.R., P.R. Hosp. Assn. (dir.), P.R. Hosp. Adminstr. Assn. (dir.), Chamber of Arecibo (v.p. Key Mem. Yr.), Phi Eta Mu (pres. supreme council 1961). Roman Catholic. K.C., Lion. Clubs: Rotary, Arecibo Country. Home: 559 Independencia St Baldrich Hato Rey PR 00919 Office: Presbyn Hosp 1451 Ashford Av Condado San Juan PR

ROE, THOMAS ANDERSON, bldg. supply co. exec.; b. Greenville, S.C., May 29, 1927; s. Thomas Anderson and Leila (Cunningham) R.; B.S., Furman U., 1948; diploma bus. mgmt. LaSalle Extension U., 1956; m. Bette Verner Bain, Oct. 14, 1950; children—Elizabeth Overton, Thomas Anderson III, Philip Stradley, John Verner. Cancer research asst. Furman U., Greenville, S.C., 1947-48; with Builder Marts of Am., Inc., Greenville, 1948—, asst. mgr., 1948-58, mgr., 1958-61, pres. 1961-69, now chmn. bd., chief exec. officer; chmn. bd. First Piedmont Corp., First Piedmont Bank & Trust Co. Mem. Greenville Civil Def. Council, 1956-60; air insp. Civil Air Patrol, Greenville, 1949-50; pres. Greenville Housing Found., 1971-72; mem. Greenville County Redevel. Authority. Vice chmn. S.C. Republican Party, 1963-64, mem. state budget and orgn. com., 1963-64, mem. party rules and forms com., 1963-64, state finance chmn., 1963-64; mem. Nat. Rep. Finance Com., 1963-64; state committeeman Greenville County Rep. Com., 1962-64; hon. asst. sgt. at arms Rep. Nat. Conv., Chgo., 1960. Bd. dirs. Greenville United Cerebral Palsy, 1959-63; bd. dirs. Greenville chpt. A.R.C.; trustee Christ Ch. Episcopal Sch. Named Greenville Builder of Yr., Greenville Home Builders Assn., 1962 Mem. Nat. Assn. Home Builders, Greenville Home Builders Assn. (dir. 1961-64, v.p. 1962-63), Nat. Lumber and Bldg. Material Dealers Assn. (alt. dir. 1965-66), Carolina (pres. 1965-66), Greenville (past pres.) bldg. material dealers assns., Greenville C. of C. (dir., chmn. legislative com. 1962, pres. 1970). Episcopalian. Clubs: Players (pres. 1951), Sertoma (local pres. 1960-61, Distinguished Service award 1959, Superior Leadership award 1961), Green Valley Country, Altamount dir.), Poinsett. Office: 1600 Daniel Bldg Greenville SC 29602 Home: Altamount Rd Paris Mountain RFD 7 Greenville SC 29609

ROEDER, MARTIN, biologist, educator; b. Long Branch, N.J., Aug. 19, 1925; s. Herbert Julian and Selma (Hurwitz) R.; B.S., Queens Coll., N.Y.C., 1948; M.S., U. N.M., 1951; Ph.D., U. N.C., 1954; m. Rachel Shively Haralson, Aug. 11, 1957; children—Renee, Karl Martin. Grad. asst. U. N.M., 1949-51; U.S. AEC fellow U. N.C., Chapel Hill, 1951-53, asst. prof. chemistry U. N.C., Greensboro, 1954-56, asst. prof., asso. prof. biology, 1956-64; asso. prof. biol. sci. Fla. State U., Tallahassee, 1964—, asst. dean Coll. Arts and Scis., 1966-69, asso. dean, 1969-72, acting dean, 1973—. Precinct chmn. Democratic Party N.C., 1963-64. Served with AUS, 1943-46. Fellow A.A.A.S.; mem. Am. Soc. Zoologists, Soc. Gen. Physiology, Assn. S.E. Biologists, Am. Inst. Biol. Scis., Sigma Xi. Home: 121 Ridgeland Rd Tallahassee FL 32303

ROELING, GERARD HENRY, investment co. exec.; b. New Orleans, July 11, 1939; s. William Henry and Gladys Nathalie (Pavlovich) R.; B.A., U. Mich., 1960, M.B.A., 1961; m. Bette Ann Bichet, Jan. 30, 1960; children—Gerard Patrick, Stewart VanWay, William Jeffrey. Chemist, La. FDA, New Orleans, 1957-59; mem. div. and corp. financial and marketing staff Ford Motor Co., Dearborn, Mich., 1961-66; mem. marketing staff Exxon Corp., Houston, 1966-69; dir. research and planning Asso. Credit Burs., Inc., exec. v.p. Credit Services Internat., Inc., Houston, 1969-72; pres., chmn. bd. Am. Forum Corp., Houston, 1972—. Mem. econ. adv. com. to staff Pres. Nixon, 1970-72. Pres., Brookwood Estates Assn., Livonia, Mich., 1964-66; 1st v.p. Livonia Fedn. Civic Assn., 1965, pres., 1966; chmn. Livonia Civic Affairs Com., 1965; mem. Citizens Adv. Com., 1964-66; mem. Capital Improvement and Long Range Planning Com., 1964-66, Sch. Bd. Adv. Com., 1965-66, United Fund, 1966-67, Houston Advanced Urban Analysis Com., 1968, Meml. Glen Assn., 1968, 69, Inst. Internat. Edn., 1972—. Bd. dirs. Mus. Am. Architecture and Decorative Arts. Mem. Am. Marketing Assn., Nat. Assn. Real Estate Bds., C. of C., Phi Kappa Phi, Alpha Kappa Psi. Home: 11910 Clarendon Lane Houston TX 77024 Office: 6300 Richmond Av Houston TX 77027

ROELSE, ALVIN LEON, elec. engr.; b. Douglas, Okla., May 6, 1936; s. Arthur Alvin and Ruth Amelia (Boepple) R.; B.S. in elec. engring., Okla. State U., 1959; m. Beatrice Cross, May 25, 1958; children—Michael, Gary, Deborah. Lab. asst. Okla. Gas and Electric Co., 1958; project engr. Collins Radio Co., 1959-63; engring. supr. Lockheed Electronics Co., Houston, 1963—. Treas. R.C. Patterson Sch. P.T.A., 1971-72. Recipient Snoopy Pin award NASA/Johnson Space Center, 1970, Apollo 11 Team award, 1969. Mem. Nat. Mgmt. Assn. (bd. dirs. Lockheed Houston chpt., 1965—; recipient Service Achievement award 1973, Pioneer award 1973), I.E.E.E. Research spl. purpose communication and telemetry systems for earth and space applications. Home: 5115 French Creek Houston TX 77017 Office: 16811 El Camino Real Houston TX 77058

ROEMER, JOSEPH SHULTZ, research engr., ret. air force officer; b. Bowling Green, Ky., Aug. 31, 1924; s. Adolph and Ola (Shultz) R.; student Western Ky. State Coll., 1946-47, U. Ky., 1947-48; B.S., U. Ill., 1957. Transmitter engr. Radio Sta. WLBJ, Bowling Green, 1949-51; enlisted as tech. sgt., USAF, 1951, advanced through grades to maj., 1967; chief engring. div. 6936 Communications Security Depot Group, USAF Security Service, San Antonio, 1962-63, chief maintenance USAF Cryptologic Depot, 1963-64; program support officer, dep. for program support Hdqrs. Air Force Eastern Test Range, Patrick AFB, Fla., 1964-67, ret. USAF, 1967; research engr. Boeing Co., 1967-69; sr. elec. engr. facilities maintenance dept. Ingalls Shipbldg. div. Litton Ship Systems, Pascagoula, Miss., 1969—, also mgr. elec. shop, 1970-72, elec. systems dept., 1972—. Served with USNR, 1943-46. Mason. Home: 123 W El Bonito Dr Ocean Springs MS 39564 Office: Pascagoula MS 39567

ROENSCH, EDWARD BURNS, archtl. cons.; b. Waco, Tex., Sept. 6, 1906; s. Max M. and Mamie (Burns) R.; B.A., Rice U., 1926; postgrad. Cornell U., 1927; m. Florence Tuten, Dec. 24, 1968. Engr., Don Hall Constructor, Houston, 1927-28; v.p. Tex. Devel. Corp., 1927-30; pvt. practice architecture, Houston, 1930-48, San Antonio, 1948—; pres. Carpet City. Cons. N.E. Sch. Dist., Atlas Floors, Transam. Devel. Co. Dist. commr. Boy Scouts Am., 1953-54; mem. alumni bd. Rice U., 1966-69. Recipient Silver Beaver award Boy Scouts Am., Houston, 1926. Methodist. Club: Seven Oaks Country San Antonio (pres. 1967-68). Patentee prefabricated concrete panels. Office: 1121 E Hildebrand St San Antonio TX 78201

ROESEL, ALBERT JULIUS, mech. contracting exec.; b. Augusta, Ga., Aug. 12, 1917; s. Albert Julius and Annie Ruth (Stelling) R.; B.S. in E.E., Ga. Inst. Tech., 1938; m. Rosalyn Louise Sulvester, May 3, 1941; children—Albert Julius III, Richard B., Rosalyn (Mrs. Kirk Martin), Christopher J., Paul F., Philip Keith, Gregory. Sec.-treas. Savannah Armature Works (Ga.), 1948-50; pres. Elec. Machinery Co., Inc., Savannah, 1950-57, H.A. Sack Co., Inc., Statesboro, Ga., 1957—. Sec.-treas. Engineered Fiberglass Co., Estill, S.C., 1970—; partner Gen. Equipment Rental Co., Savannah, 1950—; sec.-treas., Elec. Machinery Co., Savannah, 1957-73. Mem. elec. com. Swainsboro (Ga.) Vocational Tech. Sch., 1973—. Charter mem. Statesboro Community Relations Council, 1971—. Mem. Statesboro Elec. Examining Bd., 1972—; chmn. Statesboro and Bulloch County Airport Com., 1971-73. Served to capt. AUS, 1941-46. Mem. Am. Soc. Heating, Air Conditioning and Refrigeration Engrs., I.E.E.E., Am. Assn. Airport Execs., Illuminating Engring. Soc. (asso.), Statesboro and Bulloch County C. of C. (pres. 1973). Rotarian (dir. 1970-71). Home: 103 Nottingham Trail Statesboro GA 30458 Office: Stockyard RD Statesboro GA 30458

ROESLER, ROBERT HARRY, newspaper editor; b. Hammond, La., Oct. 5, 1927; s. Albert N. and Hilda (Schwartz) R.; student Tulane U.; m. Cloe Alferez, May 7, 1955; children—Kim, Bob, Toby. Mem. sports staff Times Picayune, New Orleans, 1949-67, sports editor, 1964—. Served with USNR, World War II, Korean conflict. Mem. Football Writers Am., Basketball Writers Assn., Am. Legion. Club: Press (pres. New Orleans 1959-60, sports writing awards). Home: 6958 Colbert St New Orleans LA 70124 Office: Times Picayune 3800 Howard Av New Orleans LA 70125

ROESSLER, PAUL ALBERT, govt. ofcl.; b. Buckman, N.M., Oct. 8, 1920; s. Joseph H. and Perfecta M. (Torrez) R.; B.S. in Fgn. Service, Georgetown U., 1949, postgrad., 1949-51; postgrad., U. Md., 1965—; m. Ann E. Collier, May 24, 1946; children—Paul, Elizabeth, Richard, Barbara, Mary Frances, Nancy, Timothy, Eric, Christina. Field rep. War Claims Commn., Washington, 1949-51, legislative analyst, 1951-52, Philippine liaison officer, 1952-53; fgn. liaison officer Fgn. Claims Settlement Commn., Washington, 1953-56 asst. attache AEC, Japan, 1957-61, fgn. affairs officer, 1961-63; asso. program dir. NSF, Washington, 1963-65; internat. economist Dept. of Army, Washington, 1965-70, fgn. affairs officer, 1970—. Cons. Am. Indsl. Consultants, Inc., 1961—. Exec. sec. Nat. Delta Phi Epsilon Found., 1967-68. Served with AUS, 1941-46. Mem. Nat. Economists Club, Soc. Govt. Economists, Internat. House of Japan, Soc. Internat. Devel., V.F.W., Am. Legion, D.A.V., Am. Defenders Bataan and Corregidor, Delta Phi Epsilon. Contbr. to American Prisoners of War, 1948. Home: 6731 Greentree Rd Bethesda MD 20034 Office: Dept of Army Pentagon Washington DC 20310

ROETHEL, DAVID ALBERT HILL, surg. assn. ofcl.; b. Milw., Feb. 17, 1926; s. Albert John and Elsie Margaret (Hill) R.; B.S., Marquette U., 1950, M.S., 1952; certificate Oak Ridge Sch. Reactor Tech., 1953; m. Suzanne Harding Berger, Aug. 22, 1953; children—Elizabeth Jane, Susan Margaret. Chem. engr. naval reactors br. AEC., Washington, 1953-57; mgr. profl. relations Am. Chem. Soc., Washington, 1957-72; exec. dir. Nat. Registry in Clin. Chemistry, Washington, 1967-72; exec. dir. Am. Assn. Clin. Chemists, Washington, 1968-70, Am. Orthotic and Prosthetic Assn., Washington, 1973—, Am. Acad. Orthotists and Prosthetists, Washington, 1973—, Am. Bd. Certification in Orthotics and Prosthetics, 1973—. Vice pres. Pensions for Profls., Inc., Washington, 1970-72. Mem. Gov.'s Md. Com. on Sci. Devel., 1969. Served with USAC, 1944-46; CBI. Mem. A.A.A.S., Am. Chem. Soc., Am. Assn. Clin. Chemists, Alpha Chi Sigma, Sigma Gamma Chi, Pi Mu Epsilon. Club: Sports Car Am. (dir. 1964-67, local officer 1960—). Home: 1216 Brantford Av Silver Spring MD 20904 Office: 1440 N St NW Washington DC 20005

ROGALL, EDWARD MYRON, city ofcl.; b. Bklyn., Feb. 20, 1911; s. Benjamin and Rose (Elias) R.; student Coll. City N.Y., 1928-31; m. Pearl N. Goldstein, Sept. 1, 1933; children—Elisabeth (Mrs. Stephen A. Weseley), Stephanie. Partner, Lopin-Rogall Property Mgmt. Co., N.Y.C., 1931-60; pres. Eldorado Hotel Corp., St. Petersburg, Fla., 1954—; chmn. Housing Authority St. Petersburg, 1964—. Treas. Southeastern region Nat. Jewish Welfare Bd., 1969—; pres. Jewish Community Council, St. Petersburg, 1965-67, Jewish Community Center, 1967-69, Gulf Coast Jewish Family Service, Inc., 1973—. Bd. dirs. Nat. Housing Conf., Anthonians. Mem. Nat. Assn. Housing and Redevel. Ofcls., Ceres Union, Phi Epsilon Pi. Clubs: Pasadena Golf (St. Petersburg). Home: 2150 Pelham Rd St Petersburg FL 33710 Office: 325 9th St S St Petersburg FL 33705

ROGERS, ALICE BRADSHAW, pub. relations, advt. exec.; b. Dayton, Tex., Sept. 18, 1911; d. William Benjamin and Mannie Willis (Davis) Bradshaw; student U. Tex., 1927-29, U. Houston, 1953, 59; m. Evert A. Rogers, Aug. 17, 1934, (div. May 1950); children—Jane (Mrs. A. Russel Matthews), Elizabeth (Mrs. Wesley M. Bannister), Nancy Lynn (Mrs. Richard E. Stephanow). Sec., Henry L. Doherty, stocks and bonds, 1930-33, L.E. Norton Real Estate, 1933-34; sec. Fisk Electric Co., 1934-37; sec.-treas. Art Engraving Co., 1939-49, pres., 1949-50; pres. Advt. Arts Bldg. Corp., 1952-54, Houston Tradetypers, 1955-57, Goodwin-Dannenbaum Advt. Agy., 1957; dir., sec.-treas., pres. Art Engraving Co., Inc.; dir., pres. Advt. Arts Bldg. Corp.; v.p., dir., sec.-treas. Houston Advt. Club, Inc.; dir. 10th Dist. Advt. Fedn. Am., 1955—; pub. relations dir. Houston Youth Symphony, 1962; bus. relations dir. Better Bus. Bur., Houston; community club awards dir. Houston Chronicle, 1963-65; now asso. editor, bus. mgr. The Houston Clubber, co-ordinator activities The Houston Club. First v.p. Achievement Rewards Coll. Scientists Found.; dist. chmn. publicity bd. Girl Scouts of Am., 1946-50; mem. publicity com. United Fund, 1952-54; mem. Pin Oak Horse Show advt. program com., Houston Fat Stock Show advt. program com. Mem. C. of C., Am. Advt. Fedn., Houston Soc. Assn. Execs., Houston-Harris County Heritage Soc., Gamma Alpha Chi. Clubs: Advertising (sec.), Press (life) (Houston); Mothers (Zeta Tau Alpha). Home: 4723 Merwin Houston TX 77027 Office: Houston Club Houston Club Bldg Houston TX 77002

ROGERS, ALLAN DARROW, mfg. co. exec.; b. Mt. Kisco, N.Y., June 26, 1928; s. George Franklin and Grace (Allan) R.; B.S. in Elec. Engring., Clarkson Coll. Tech., 1951; m. Florence Elisabeth Browns, Aug. 28, 1951; children—Karen Anne, Robin Lynn. With Morganite, Inc., Long Island City, N.Y., 1953-65, Dunn, N.C., 1965—, v.p. mfg., 1970—, also dir.; dir. Morganite Modmor Inc., Costa Mesa, Cal., Midwest Molding Inc., Gurnee, Ill. Served with U.S. C.E., 1951-53. Mem. Am. Mgmt. Assn., Soc. Plastics Engrs., Am. Powder Metallurgy Inst. Mason. Club: North Ridge Country (Raleigh, N.C.). Home: 4008 Colby Dr Raleigh NC 27609 Office: 401 N Ashe Av Dunn NC 28334

ROGERS, CARROLL PICKINS, JR., mining co. exec.; b. East Flat Rock, N.C., Mar. 30, 1912; s. Carroll Pickens and Susan Mildred (Ershine) R.; B.S., U. N.C., 1933; m. Eleanor Floyd, July 24, 1937; children—Carroll Pickens III, William Z., Eleanor S., Margaret E. With Feldspar Milling Co., Burnsville, N.C., 1933-55, gen. mgr., 1939-55; v.p. Feldpar Corp., Spruce Pine, N.C., 1955-70, pres., 1970—, also dir.; dir. Pacific Tin Consol. Corp., N.Y.C., Northwestern Bank, Spruce Pine. Chmn., Morehead scholarship com. Mitchell County, N.C., 1953. Bd. dirs. Penland (N.C.) Sch. Crafts, Warren Wilson Coll., Swannoa, N.C. Mem. Am. Inst. Mining Engrs., Am. Ceramic Soc., Beta Gamma Sigma, Delta Psi. Clubs: Spruce Pine Country, Asheville City, Mountain City (Asheville, N.C.). Home: 315 Rogers St Spruce Pine NC 28777 Office: Box 99 Spruce Pine NC 28777

ROGERS, CHARLES MCPHERSON ADUSTON, III, banker; b. Mobile, Ala., Nov. 10, 1932; s. Charles McPherson Aduston and Elisabeth (Benson) R.; B.A., Williams Coll., 1954; LL.B., U. Ala., 1959; m. Gail Whitehurst, June 19, 1954; children—Anne Aduston, Charles McPherson Aduston IV, Bradshaw Aduston. Admitted to Ala. bar, 1959; asso. McCorvey Turner Johnstone Adams & May, attys., Mobile, 1959-64, partner, 1964-67; v.p., trust officer Am. Nat. Bank & Trust Co., Mobile, 1967-71, exec. v.p., 1971-72, pres., 1972—, also dir. Hon. consul of Belgium, 1970—; vice chmn. Consular Corps of Mobile, 1971—. Pres. Mobile Symphony and Civic Music Assn., 1966-68. Mem. Ala. Ho. of Reps., 1960-66. Trustee St. Paul's Episcopal Day Sch., Mobile; bd. dirs. Community Chest, Mobile Pub. Library. Served to 1st lt. USAF, 1955-57. Mem. Am., Ala. bar assns., Mobile Area C. of C. (dir. 1969—), Phi Delta Theta, Phi Delta Phi, Omicron Delta Kappa. Episcopalian. Clubs: Athelstan (pres. 1972—) (Mobile); Country of Mobile (Ala.). Home: 4010 Old Shell Rd Mobile AL 36608 Office: 130 St Joseph St Mobile AL 36602

ROGERS, DAVID WILLIAM, SR., ednl. adminstr.; b. Greensboro, N.C., May 29, 1925; s. Archibald Alexander and Mattie Belle (Straughan) R.; A.A., Campbell Coll., 1952; B.A., Wake Forest Coll., 1954; M.Ed., Duke, 1958, Ed.D., 1964; m. Rosa Christine Slaughter, Feb. 19, 1949; children—Joan Marie, Gloria Jean, David William. Elementary sch. tchr., prin., Coswell County, N.C., 1954-57; secondary sch. tchr., 1957-59; asst. prof. Furman U., 1960-61; dir. instrn. Lumberton (N.C.) City Schs., 1961-63; asso. supt. Burke County Schs., Morganton, N.C., 1963-67; asso. supt. Person County Schs., Roxboro, N.C., 1967—. Mem. exec. bd. Cherokee council Boy Scouts Am., 1968—; mem. family life com. N. Central Area Devel. Corp., 1969—; mem. adv. com. Mars Hil Coll., 1967-69; mem. N.C. State Assessment Com., 1973—. Trustee Piedmont Tech. Inst., Roxboro, N.C. Served with USAAF, 1943-46. Mem. N.E.A., Am. Assn. Sch. Adminstrs., N.C. Assn. Educators, Phi Delta Kappa, Kappa Delta Pi. Baptist (ordained pastor 1956). Rotarian. Club: Optimist (Morganton). Home: Route 2 Box 382 Roxboro NC 27573 Office: Box 1078 Roxboro NC 27573

ROGERS, DONALD LEE, trade assn. exec.; b. E. Steubenville, W. Va.; s. Mark Whittaker and Virginia (Campbell) R.; A.B., Miami U., Oxford, O., 1951; J.D., Ohio State U., 1953; m. Helen E. Long, 1960. Admitted to Fed. bar, 1957, Ohio bar, 1953; asst. counsel U.S. Senate Com. on Banking and Currency, Washington, 1953-54, counsel, 1955-58; exec. dir. Assn. Registered Bank Holding Cos., Washington, 1958—. Mem. Am. (banking com.), Fed., Ohio bar assns., Order of Coif. Methodist. Clubs: Capitol Hill, Nat. Press, Exchequer (pres.), City Tavern (Washington). Home: 4200 Massachusetts Av NW Washington DC 20016 Office: 730 15th St NW Washington DC 20005

ROGERS, EDDY JAMES, JR., lawyer; b. Belleville, Ill., Nov. 29, 1940; s. Eddy James and Mildred G. (Johnson) R.; B.A. magna cum laude, Harvard, 1962, J.D. cum laude, 1965; m. Patricia Lee Wall,

Aug. 17, 1963; children—Blakely Ann, Eddy James, Todd Wall, Rachel Ashley. Admitted to Tex. bar, 1965, since practiced in Houston; asso. firm Baker, Botts, Shepherd & Coates, 1965-69; partner firm Woodard, Hall, McCrory, Henry & Primm, 1969—. Served to capt., AUS, 1966-68. Recipient Commendation medal. Mem. Tex., Houston, Houston Jr. bar assns., Phi Beta Kappa. Club: Harvard of Houston (chmn. schs. and scholarship com. 1972—). Editor: Harvard Law Review, 1965. Home: 13826 Myrtlea Dr Houston TX 77024 Office: 350 Esperson Bldg Houston TX 77002

ROGERS, EDWARD ALLEN, surveying engr.; b. Birmigham, Ala., Jan. 25, 1917; s. Alexander Hunter and Julia Magdalene (Hury) R.; student mapping and surveying, Internat. Corr. Schs., 1945, land surveying, U. Ala., 1949; m. Berney Jane McCormack, Nov. 12, 1937; children—Clark McCormack, Edward Allen. Field engr. Ala. Power Co., 1936-59; land surveyor James M. Keel & Assos., Birmingham, 1959; engr. constrn.-inspection Rust Engring. Co., various locations, 1960-65; field engr. and surveyor Birmingham Water Works, 1965—; propr. land surveying bus., 1949—. Served with AUS, 1945-46. Mem. Ala. Profl. Land Surveyors, Birmingham Baptist Brotherhood Assn. (pres. 1957). Baptist (deacon 1950-73). Home: 1310 Columbia Dr Birmingham AL 35226 Office: 2114 1st Av N Birmingham AL 35203

ROGERS, ERNEST P(AUL), lawyer; b. nr. Duluth, Ga., Sept. 10, 1903; s. Raymond Clifford and Ora (Bloodworth) R.; student Darlington Sch., Rome, Ga., 1917-21; LL.B., U. Ga., 1926; m. Mary Weems, June 18, 1932; children—Mary Ann Rogers Hammaker, Ronald Weems, Michael Clayton, Ernest Paul. Admitted to Ga. bar, 1927; atty. legal staff Coca-Cola Co., Atlanta, 1927-35; asso. Harold Hirsch & Marion Smith, Atlanta, 1935-39; mem. firm Kilpatrick, Cody, Rogers, McClatchey & Regenstein, 1939—. Pres., Scripto Pencil Co., 1945-46, dir., mem. exec. com., 1936-73; pres., dir. Laow Investment Co., Inc.; dir. Colonial Stores, Inc. Trustee Darlington Sch.; permanent trustee Atlanta Lawyers Found., Inc. Mem. Am. Judicature Soc., Am., Ga., Atlanta bar assns., Kappa Sigma, Phi Delta Phi. Methodist. Kiwanian. Clubs: Lawyers (past pres.), Piedmont Driving, Capital City, Commerce (Atlanta). Home: 2933 Andrews Dr NW Atlanta GA 30305 Office: Equitable Bldg Atlanta GA 30303

ROGERS, FORD BARKER, JR., aviation co. pres.; b. Kansas City, Mo., May 25, 1921; s. Ford B. and Anna Brock (Showalter) R.; student Fairmont (W.Va.) State Coll., 1939-40; m. Julie Ann Everson, Sept. 16, 1946; children—Ann (Mrs. James B. Stillman, Jr.), Ford Barker III, Steven B., Julie E., John M. and Joan P. (twins). Partner, Showalter Airpark, Winter Park, Fla., 1945-65; pres., Showalter Flying Service, Orlando, 1965—; dir. Sun Bank of East Orlando. Mem. Orlando Orange County Airport Zoning Bd., 1973—. Bd. dirs. Council of Arts and Sci., Orlando, 1969—. Served to capt. USAAF, 1940-45; ETO. Decorated Air medal with 4 oak leaf clusters. Mem. Fla. Aviation Trades Assn. (pres. 1973-74), Nat. Aviation Trades Assn. (dir. 1973-75), C. of C. (bd. dirs.), Central Fla. Devel. Com., Com. 200. Rotarian. Club: Country Orlando. Home: 507 Palmer St Orlando FL 32801 Office: PO Box 20753 Herndon Airport Orlando FL 32814

ROGERS, FRANCIS KING, aviation co. exec.; b. Buffalo, Feb. 19, 1927; s. John M. and Harriet Jane (Savage) Moore; A.A., U. Fla., 1953; m. Connie Kelsheimer, Dec. 27, 1950; children—William, Carolyn, James. Sales engr. Spltys., Inc., Charlottesville, Va., 1953-63; v.p., gen. mgr. Horizon Aviation, Lynchburg, Va., 1963-68; chief exec., gen. mgr. Appliachian Flying Service, Inc., Bloutville, Tenn., 1968—; dir., sec. Tenn. Airmotive, Inc.; dir. Am. Aviation. Served with USAAF, 1944-46. Mem. Aircraft Owners and Pilots Assn. Club: Internat. Exchange. Home: 715 Rambling Rd Johnson City TN 37601 Office: Tri-City Airport Box 366 Bloutville TN 37617

ROGERS, GLENN EDWIN, librarian; b. Ft. Scott, Kan., Oct. 9, 1923; s. Earl Allen and Margaret Lillian (Williams) R.; B.S., John Brown U., 1953; M.Ed., U. Ark., 1955; M.L.S., U. Okla., 1961; m. Vineta M. Pryor, Dec. 8, 1945; children—Russell Gordon, Rita Jean. Dean of men John Brown U., Siloam Springs, Ark., 1953-56, asst. librarian, dir. audio-visual services, 1957-69, librarian, 1959—. Mem. Sunday sch. forum panel Sta. KUOA, Siloam Springs, 1955-66. Bd. dirs. Siloam Springs Pub. Library. Served with AUS, 1943-46; ETO. Mem. Ark. Library Assn. Mem. Ch. of God. Kiwanian (pres. club 1973). Home: Route 4 Box 289 Siloam Springs AR 72761

ROGERS, IDA ADRIAN RICE (MRS. GEORGE P. ROGERS), artist, educator; b. Calico Rock, Ark.; d. Alex and Edna (Cotheran) Adrian; B.A. in Art, Hendrix Coll., 1954; M.A., U. Ark., 1955; postgrad. Leyden U., 1960-61; m. John J. Rice, Apr. 1, 1926 (div. Jan. 1932); children—Sammie L., George J. (dec.), Sue; m. 2d, George P. Rogers, Feb. 26, 1943. Faculty, Little Rock U., 1957—, asst. prof. art, 1958—, chmn. visual arts dept., 1957—. Exhibited in shows at LaScala Gallery, Florence, Italy, 1971, Ark. Art Center, 1971, Ark. Dept. Edn., 1971; portraits represented in pvt. collections; archaeologist throughout Middle East, 1960-66. Tchr. arts, crafts Little Rock Boys Club, 1942—; art chmn. one-man shows Ark. Art Festival, 1962-63. Recipient Medal Merit for service in arts, scis. Centro Studi E Scambi, Rome, 1970. Mem. Am. Artists League N.Y. (state chmn. Am. art week 1959-60), Nat., Ark. (art chmn. 1963) socs. arts and letters, Internat. Platform Assn., Internat. Investigators and Spl. Police, Poets Round Table of Ark., Artists, Authors and Composers Assn., Am. League Pen Women, Delta Kappa Gamma. Author: (poems) Thoughts of the Wanderer, 1971. Home: 2409 W 16th St North Little Rock AR 72114 Office: 33d and University Av Little Rock AR 72204

ROGERS, JAMES GAMBLE, II, archtl. engring. co. exec.; b. Chgo., Jan. 24, 1901; s. John A. and Elizabeth (Baird) R.; student Dartmouth, 1921-24; m. Evelyn Claire Smith, Sept. 28, 1929; children—James Gamble IV, John Hopewell. Established archtl. engring. firm Rogers, Lovelock & Fritz (formerly Jas. Gamble Rogers, II), Winter Park, Fla., 1935—, chmn. bd. trustees R.L.&F. retirement fund, 1961—. Dir. Orlando (Fla.) Fed. Savs., 1964—, Chelynia, Inc., Deland, Fla., 1965—, Republic Service Corp., Orlando, 1970—. Cons. and authority on jail design. Mem. Fla. Assn. Architects, 1935—. Named Architect of the Year, Bldg. Stone Inst., 1963; recipient certificates of appreciation, Sec. Army, 1959, Chief of Engrs., 1959. Mem. Fla. Bd. Architecture 1935-44, pres., 1940-44. Mem. A.I.A. (pres. central chpt. 1938-42, chmn. Fla. regional judiciary com. 1963), Archtl. League N.Y., Soc. Am. Mil. Engrs., Am. Hosp. Assn., Ch. Archtl. Guild Am., Nat. Jail Assn., Orlando Art Assn., Archtl. League N.Y., Hispanic Inst. Presbyn. Club: University (Winter Park). Contbr. articles to profl. jours., popular mags. Executed Fla. Supreme Ct. Bldg., Tallahassee, 1949; county courthouse Orlando, 1958, courthouse Fort Pierce, Fla., 1960; mil. work in U.S. and fgn. countries including launching platforms at Cape Canaveral (Fla.), guidance towers Kennedy Space Center and Antigua Island; hosp. Fla. A and M. Coll., Tallahassee, 1949, hosp. MacDill AFB, Tampa, 1971, student union Stetson U., Deland, 1956; academic bldgs. Fla. State U., Tallahassee, 1959-62, Orlando Jr. Coll., 1954-65, Rollins Coll., Winter Park, 1951-68, addition Hillis Miller Health Center, Gainesville, Bush Sci. Center, Rollins Coll., 1969. Home: 1290 Palmer Av Winter Park FL 32789 Office: 145 Lincoln Av Winter Park FL 32789

ROGERS, JOHN, lawyer; b. Wheatland, Mo., Apr. 4, 1890; s. Pleasant Jasper and Nancy Frances (Dent) R.; LL.B., U. Okla., 1914; LL.D., U. Tulsa, 1958, John Brown U., 1966; L.H.D., Philips U., 1958, So. Meth. U., 1969; m. Hazel M. Beattie, Feb. 19, 1921; 1 son, John. Admitted to Okla. bar, 1914; atty. McMan Oil Co., Tulsa, 1915-17, atty., v.p. McMan Oil & Gas Co., 1919-31; receiver Superior Oil Corp., 1930-33, pres., 1933-35; atty. Chapman & McFarlin Interests, 1930—; dean, sch. law U. Tulsa, 1948-57; dir. Home Fed. Savs. & Loan Assn., 1950-73. Dir. Okla. Med. Research Found., pres., 1947-67; mem. State Regents for Higher Edn., 1941-59, pres., 1958-59; trustee U. Tulsa; regent U. Okla., 1924-31, 40-41; pres. YMCA, 1931-36, Tulsa Council Social Agys., 1941-42, Tulsa Community Chest, 1945; trustee John Brown U.; bd. dirs. Holland Hall Sch., Tulsa, 1959-66. Selected as Man of Yr. in Tulsa, 1945; recipient distinguished service citation U. Okla., 1956. Fellow Am. Bar Found.; mem. Am., Okla. bar assns., Am. Soc. Internat. Law, Am. Judicature Soc., Okla. Hist. Soc., Tulsa C. of C. (pres. 1938), Beta Theta Pi, Phi Delta Phi, Delta Sigma Rho. Mem. Disciples of Christ Ch. Club: Tulsa. Home: 3727 S Xanthus St Tulsa OK 74105 Office: Box 3209 Tulsa OK 74101

ROGERS, JOHN CICERO, JR., ednl. adminstr.; b. Alto, Tex., June 17, 1912; s. John Cicero and Katye Gertrude (Banks) R.; B.A., Stephen F. Austin U., 1932; M.A., U. Tex., 1940; m. Mary Nixon Stephens, June 17, 1937; children—John Stephen, Mary Jean (Mrs. Arnim Vernis Haynes). Tchr., Canton (Tex.) Pub. Schs., 1932-34; tchr., coach Nat. Consol. Schs., Nacogdoches, Tex., 1934-35. Hearne (Tex.) Pub. Schs., 1935-38; tchr., coach, prin., supt. Columbia-Brazoria Schs., West Columbia, Tex., 1938-63; supt. Lamar Consol. Schs., Rosenberg, Tex., 1963—. Mem. Tex. State Textbook Com., 1954; regional chmn. exec. com. Ednl. Service Center, 1970-71; chmn. Tex. Adv. Com. Data Processing, 1972—. Mem. Tex. Tchrs. Assn. (dist. pres. 1954). Methodist. Rotarian, Mason. Home: 1028 Lindsey Dr Rosenberg TX 77471 Office: Sch Adminstrn Bldg Rosenberg TX 77471

ROGERS, JOHN KOEHN, paper co. exec.; b. Appleton, Wis., Sept. 1, 1940; s. Clifford August and Dorothea Louise (Koehn) R.; A.B., Ripon Coll., 1962; M.S., Lawrence U., 1964, Ph.D., 1968; m. Georgina Kay Granberg, June 23, 1966; 1 dau., Emily Martha. With Owens-Ill., Inc., 1967—, environment control and tech. supt., Valdosta, Ga., 1973—. Mem. T.A.P.P.I., Am. Chem. Soc., Research Soc. Am., Phi Beta Kappa. Republican. Episcopalian. Research in devel. non-sulfur pulping process. Home: 205 Sunnymead Dr Valdosta GA 31606 Office: Owens-Illinois Inc Valdosta GA 31601

ROGERS, JOHN RICHARD, lawyer; b. Ashburn, Ga., June 30, 1924; s. Edwin A. and Ella Mae (Evans) R.; LL.D., U. Ga., 1949; m. Reginald Ann Cox, Aug. 6, 1953; children—Sylvia, Dawn, Starr. Admitted to Ga. bar, 1949; gen. practice, Ashburn, 1949—. Pres. Monroe Mall Corp., 1965—; pres. First Fed. Savs. & Loan Assn. of Turner County. Served to 1st lt. AUS, 1944-46. Mem. Turner County C. of C. (pres., past dir.), Am., Tifton Circuit bar assns., Am. Trial Lawyers Assn., Am. Judicature Soc., Phi Eta Sigma, Sigma Chi, Phi Alpha Delta. Home: Madison Av Ashburn GA 31714 Office: Rogers Plaza Ashburn GA 31714

ROGERS, JOHN THOMAS, JR., state ofcl.; b. Cleburne, Tex., Oct. 20, 1927; s. John Thomas and Lonnie (Wilbanks) R.; grad. Gulf Coast Sch. Bus. Adminstrn., 1948, Tex. Hwy. Patrol Tng. Acad., 1951; student U. Tex., 1968-69; B.S. in Police Adminstrn., Sam Houston State U., 1974; m. Juanita Elizabeth Shelley, Dec. 24, 1945; children—Linda Susan. Hwy. patrolman Tex. Dept. Pub. Safety, 1951, stationed in Houston, 1951-57, sgt., Brenham, Tex., 1957-61, dist. radar operator, photographer, police instr., counselor Tex. Dept. Pub. Safety Tng. Acad., 1961, 68-69; sgt. hwy. patrol, Area 2A-11, Hdqrs. Region 2, Houston, 1961—; spl. agt. La. State Police; adviser Washington County Civil Def., 1957-61. Active Merit Badge work Boy Scouts Am., Brenham, 1957-61; mem. Washington County Traffic Safety Commn., 1958-60; safety chmn., mem. exec. com. Brenham P.T.A., 1959-60. Mem. Nat. Rifle Assn., Tex. Police Assn., Tex. Pub. Employees Assn., Conn. Assn. Chiefs of Police (hon.). Mem. Ch. of Christ (past deacon, tchr., supr. Sunday sch. dept.). Mason (past master); Rotarian (dir. Brenham 1960-62). Home: 4515 Briar Hollow Pl Apt 320 Houston TX 77027 Office: 10110 Northwest Freeway PO Drawer D Oak Forest Sta Houston TX 77018

ROGERS, KING WALTER, JR., grocery stores exec.; b. Dyersburg, Tenn., Aug. 19, 1912; s. King Walter and Essie (Martin) R.; B.A., U. Tenn., 1934; postgrad. Harvard Bus. Sch., 1934-36; m. Mildred Hampton Moss, May 23, 1943; children—King Walter III, Robert Moss. Exec., Pennel-Edenton Wholesale Grocery, Dyersburg, 1936-39; with K.W. Rogers & Son, Inc., Dyersburg, 1939—, pres., dir., 1943—; pres. Nehi Bottling Co., Dyersburg, Ardmore Tel. Co. (Tenn.); dir. Holiday Inns, Dyersburg, United Tel. Co., Chapel Hills, Tenn., Crockett Tel. Co., Friendship, Tenn., First Citizens Nat. Bank Dyersburg, First Fed. Savs. & Loan Assn., Dyersburg; pres. Tipton County Utilities Inc., Dyersburg. Chmn., U. Tenn. Devel. Council, 1969-70; mem. Tenn. Planning Commn., 1970; mem. exec. com. Hosp. for Crippled Adults, Memphis, 1961-70. Mem. exec. com. Obion-Forked Deer Basin Authority. Bd. dirs. West Tenn. Area council Boy Scouts Am.; bd. mgrs. Meth. Hosp., Memphis. Served with AUS, 1942-45. Recipient Boy Scouts Silver Beaver award. Mem. Tenn. Retail Mchts. Council (pres. 1967), Nat. Piggly Wiggly Operators Assn. (pres. 1964-65). Methodist (trustee Memphis conf. 1953-56). Rotarian (dist. gov. 1960-61). Home: 950 Troy Av Dyersburg TN 38024 Office: 408 W Court St Dyersburg TN 38024

ROGERS, LEDWITH BERT, banker; b. Jacksonville, Fla., Jan. 13, 1937; s. Winston James and Sara Elizabeth (Bryan) R.; B.A., U. of South, 1962; m. Louise Hay, Jan. 28, 1962; children—Winston James, Katherine Louise, Elizabeth Hay. Adminstrv. asst., operations supr. C.& S. Nat. Bank, Atlanta, 1962-65, operations auditor, 1966-70; v.p., cashier Central Bank of Montgomery (Ala.), 1970—; dir. Winstar, Inc. Served with AUS, 1956-59. Mem. Nat. Assn. Accountants (dir.), Bank Adminstrn. Inst., Montgomery C. of C. Club: Arrowhead Country of Montgomery (dir.). Home: 130 Arrowhead Dr Montgomery AL 36109 Office: 150 Dexter Av Montgomery AL 36101

ROGERS, LEO ABBOTT, physicist; b. Salt Lake City, July 6, 1934; s. Leo R. and Norma (Abbott) R.; B.S. in Metall. Engring. (Kennecott scholar), U. Utah, 1959, Ph.D. (Nat. Def. Edn. Act IV fellow) in Metallurgy, 1962; m. Loralie Bracy, Sept. 12, 1959; children—Keith, Larain, Arlin, Brian. Sr. Metallurgist Corning Glass Works (N.Y.), 1962-63, Lawrence Radiation Lab., Livermore, Cal., 1963-68; sr. physicist El Paso Natural Gas Co., Tex., 1968—. Instr., Elmira (N.Y.) Coll., 1962-63, Stanaslaus State Coll., Cal., 1967-68. Leader, Boy Scouts Am., Livermore, El Paso, 1963— (several leadership, tng. awards). Mem. A.A.A.S., Am. Geophys. Union. Mem. Ch. of Jesus Christ of Latter-day Saints. Contbr. articles to profl. jours. Home: 217 Oleander Way El Paso TX 79922 Office: PO Box 1492 El Paso TX 79978

ROGERS, LON B(ROWN), lawyer; b. Pikeville, Ky., Sept. 5, 1905; s. Fon and Ida (Brown) R.; B.S., U. Ky., 1928, LL.B., 1932; m. Mary Evelyn Walton, Dec. 17, 1938; children—Marylon Walton, Martha Brown, Fon II. Admitted to Ky. bar, 1932; practiced law in Lexington, 1932-38, Pikeville, 1939—; dir. East Ky. Beverage Co., Pikeville, 1950—. Mem. Pikeville City Council, 1951; mem. local bd. SSS, 1958-69; mem. Breaks Interstate Park Commn., Ky.-Va., 1960-68, chmn., 1960-62, 64-66, vice chmn. 1966-68; chmn. Community Services Commn. Pikeville Model Cities, 1969-71; mem. Ky. Arts Commn., 1965-72, Ky. Travel Council, 1967-70, 73—; pres. Ky. Mountain Laurel Festival Assn., 1971-72. Chmn. bd. trustees Presbytery Ebenezer, U.S.A., 1950-71, Pikeville Coll., 1951-72, 73—; sec. bd. trustees Presbytery of Transylvania, 1971—. Bd. Nat. Missions, United Presbyn. Ch. Am., 1954-66; trustee Appalachian Regional Hosps., Inc., 1963-67; trustee Ky. Ind. Coll. Found., 1973—; bd. dirs. Meth. Hosp. of Ky., 1966—. Mem. Ky. C. of C. (regional v.p. 1962-64, 69-74), Ky. Hist. Soc., S.A.R., Sigma Alpha Epsilon, Phi Delta Phi. Republican. Presbyn. (elder). Clubs: Kiwanis (past lt. gov.); Filson, Green Meadow Country, LaFayette, Blue Grass Automobile (pres. 1971-74, dir.). Home: 501 5th St Pikesville KY 41501 Office: PO Box 181 Rogers Bldg Pikeville KY 41501

ROGERS, LORENE LANE (MRS. BURL GORDON ROGERS), univ. adminstr.; b. Prosper, Tex., Apr. 3, 1914; d. Mort M. and Jessie L. (Luster) Lane; B.A., N.Tex. State Coll., 1934; M.A. (Parke, Davis fellow), U. Tex., 1946, Ph.D., 1948; D.Sc., Oakland U., 1972; m. Burl Gordon Rogers, Aug. 23, 1935 (dec. June 1941). Prof. chemistry Sam Houston State Coll., Huntsville, Tex., 1947-49; research scientist Clayton Found. Biochem. Inst. U. Tex., Austin, 1950-64, asst. dir. 1957-64, prof. nutrition, 1962—, asso. dean Grad. Sch., 1964-71, v.p. univ., 1971—, mem. dean's adv. com. grad. fellowship program, 1966-71. Vis. scientist, lectr., cons. NSF, 1959-62; cons. S.W. Research Inst., San Antonio, 1959-62; mem. Grad. Record Exams. Bd., 1972—; adv. com. Internat. Tel. & Tel. Corp. Internat. Fellowship, 1973—. Eli Lilly fellow, 1949-50. Recipient U. Tex. Students Assn. Teaching Excellence award, 1963; Distinguished Alumnus award N. Tex. State U., 1972; Outstanding Woman of Austin award, 1971. Fellow Am. Inst. Chemists; mem. A.A.A.S., Am. Chem. Soc. (sec. 1954-56), Am. Inst. Nutrition, Am. Soc. Human Genetics, Assn. Grad. Schs. (internat. edn. com. 1967-71), Sigma Xi, Phi Kappa Phi, Iota Sigma Pi. Research in hydantoin synthesis, intermediatry metabolism, biochem. and nutritional aspects of alcoholism, mental retardation, congenital malformations. Home: 4 Nob Hill Circle Austin TX 78746 Office: U Tex Austin TX 78712

ROGERS, NELSON KIMBALL, ednl. adminstr.; b. Flushing, N.Y., May 17, 1928; s. Lewis Edward and Marion Ruth (Nelson) R.; student Williams Coll., 1945-46; B.S., U.S. Naval Acad., 1950; M.S., Ga. Inst. Tech., 1956; m. Marian Louise Morris, June 20, 1953; children—Edward Morris, Kimball Amanda, James Madison. Asst. dir. engring. research Pan-Atlantic S.S. Corp., Mobile, Ala., 1956-58; asst. to pres. Sea-Land Service, Inc., Port Newark, N.J., 1958-59, v.p. operations and constrn., Elizabeth Port, N.J., 1959-63; sr. mem. N.K. Rogers & Assos., Cartersville, Ga., mgmt. cons. to transp. industries, 1963—. Asso. prof. indsl. and systems engring. Ga. Inst. Tech., 1965-73, asso. dir. undergrad. studies, 1973—. Served with USNR, 1946-54. Mem. Am. Inst. Indsl. Engrs., Am. Soc. M.E., Am. Soc. Engring. Edn., Soc. Naval Architects and Marine Engrs., T.A.P.P.I. Home: 9 Ridgeview Dr Cartersville GA 30120

ROGERS, OSCAR ALLAN, JR., coll. pres.; b. Natchez, Miss., Sept. 10, 1928; s. Oscar Allan and Maria (Jackson) R.; Sr.; A.B., Tougaloo Coll., 1950; S.T.B., Harvard, 1953, A.M. in Teaching, 1954; Ed.D., U. Ark., 1960; m. Ethel Lee Lewis, Dec. 20, 1950; children—Christopher, Christian, Christoff. Ordained to ministry of Congl.-Christian Ch., 1953, Bapt. Ch., 1954; asst. pastor St. Mark Congl.-Christian Ch., Roxbury, Mass., 1951-54; dean-registrar Natchez Jr. Coll. (Miss.), 1954-56; pres. Ark. Bapt. Coll., Little Rock, 1956-59; dean of students, prof. social sci. edn. Jackson (Miss.) State Coll., 1960—, dean Grad. Sch., 1969—; pastor Asbury Meth. Ch., Bolton, also Kingly Chapel, Edwards, Miss., 1962—. Mem. exec. bd. Little Rock Urban League, 1957-59. Served with USN, 1946-47. Mem. Am. Assn. U. Profs., Alpha Phi Alpha, Phi Delta Kappa, Kappa Delta Pi. Home: 1510 School View Dr Jackson MS 39213

ROGERS, PAUL E., JR., savs. and loan assn. exec.; b. Kerrville, Tex., Apr. 29, 1947; s. Paul E. and Eva M. (Brownfield) R.; B.S., Abilene Christian Coll., 1969; m. Woodye Kaye Yoakum, Dec. 17, 1966; children—Amy M., Gregory P. Staff Auditor Arthur Andersen and Co., Dallas, 1969-71; sr. tax accountant Arthur Young and Co., Dallas, 1971-72; financial controller Dallas Fed. Savs. and Loan Assn., Dallas, 1972—. Active Jr. Achievement. Trustee Christian Services of the S.W. C.P.A., Tex. Mem. Tex. State Soc. C.P.A.s. Am. Inst. of C.P.A.s, Controllers Soc. Savings Institutions. Republican. Mem. Ch. of Christ. Home: 11234 Cactus Lane Dallas TX 75238 Office: 1505 Elm St Dallas TX 75201

ROGERS, PAUL (GRANT), congressman; b. Ocilla, Ga., June 4, 1921; s. Dwight L. and Florence (Roberts) R.; B.A., U. Fla., 1942, J.D., 1948; hon. degrees Albany Med. Coll., N.Y. Med. Coll., George Washington U., U. Miami, U. Md., Fla. Atlantic U., Nova U.; m. Rebecca Bell, Dec. 15, 1962; 1 dau., Rebecca Laing. Admitted to Fla. bar, 1948, U.S. Supreme Ct. bar; mem. 84th-93d congresses, 9th Dist. Fla. Served as maj. F.A., AUS, 1942-45; ETO. Recipient Outstanding Man of Year award West Palm Beach Jaycees, 1953; Distinguished Service award Fla. Jaycees, 1956; John M. Russell Markle Scholars award, 1973. Mem. Fla. bar (bd. govs. jr. sect. 1952-53), Am., Palm Beach County bar assns., Maritime Law Assn., U.S., Phi Delta Phi, Phi Delta Theta. Methodist. Kiwanian. Home: 2800 N Flagler Dr West Palm Beach FL 33407 Office: Rayburn Bldg Washington DC 20515

ROGERS, PAUL MCKENDRY, food broker; b. Morrison, Tenn., Mar. 2, 1906; s. Mack H. and Nancy (Browne) R.; student U. Chattanooga, 1925-27, Tex. Western Coll., 1930; m. Sidney Rice, Nov. 28, 1935; 1 son, Paul McKendry. Office sec. YMCA, El Paso, Tex., 1929-37; salesman Nat. Biscuit Co., El Paso, 1937-51; founder, owner Paul M. Rogers Co., food broker, 1951—, now partner. Mem. Nat., El Paso food brokers assns., C. of C. Methodist. Mason (Shriner, 32 deg.). Club: 20-30 (past pres.) (El Paso). Home: 1817 E Robinson Av El Paso TX 79902 Office: 711 N Walnut St El Paso TX 79903

ROGERS, PETER H., research instn. physicist; b. N.Y.C., Jan. 8, 1945; s. Raphael and Rose (Manasewich) R.; S.B., Mass. Inst. Tech., 1965; Ph.D. (NSF trainee), Brown U., 1970; m. Alice Levenson, Aug. 7, 1966; children—Edward Martin, David Bennett, Leanne Stacey. Research asso. Brown U., Providence, R.I., 1969; research physicist Naval Research Lab., Washington, 1969—; adj. prof. math. Va. Poly. Inst., 1973—. Mem. Acoustical Soc. Am., Sigma Xi. Contbr. articles to profl. jours. Home: 11313 Handlebar Rd Reston VA 22091 Office: Code 8158 Naval Research Laboratory Washington DC 20375

ROGERS, STEARNS WALTER, educator, chemist; b. Alva, Okla., July 28, 1934; s. Grant Stearns and Jennie Florence R.; B.S. in Chemistry, Northwestern State Coll., Alva, 1953-56; Ph.D. in Biochemistry, Okla. State U., 1961; m. Billie Charlene Parker, July 3, 1955; children—Billie Dawnette, Jack Eugene. Mem. faculty Northwestern State Coll., 1961—, prof. chemistry, 1967—, head dept. chemistry, 1973—. Precinct ofcl. Democratic Party, 1967—; coordinator gubernatorial race in county, 1966-70, Congl. race in county, 1964, 66, 68, 70; councilman, Alva, 1974—. Bd. dirs. Northwestern State Found. NSF research grantee. Mem. Am. Chem. Soc., Am. Assn. U. Profs., Okla. Edn. Assn. (treas. 1970-73, del. to state bd. 1968), N.W. Edn. Assn. (sec.-treas. 1962—), Am. Inst. Chemists, Phi Lambda Upsilon (pres. 1960), Alpha Psi Omega. Mem. Christian Ch. (elder 1966-73, chmn. bd. 1965-67, tchr. 1961—). Author articles. Home: 1014 5th St Alva OK 73717

ROGERS, THOMAS EARL, microbiologist; b. Saline, La., Oct. 25, 1933; s. Thomas Cornelius and Addie Mae (Barnhart) R.; B.S., Northwestern State Coll. La., 1957, M.S., 1959; Ph.D., La. State U., 1963; m. Doris Elaine Burr, May 31, 1953; children—Keith, John, Stephen. Instr. animal disease research La. State U., Baton Rouge, 1960-63; asst. prof. microbiology Med. U. S.C., Charleston, 1963-68; dir. clin. microbiology and immunology sects., pathology dept. St. Luke's Episcopal Hosp., Houston, 1968—. Cons. clin. microbiology Med. Clinic Houston, 1972—, Spring Br. Meml. Hosp., Houston, 1971—, Rockglen Gen. Hosp., Houston, 1972—, Lind, Milam & Assos., Houston, 1970—. Mem. Am. Soc. Microbiology, Am. Soc. Clin. Pathologists, Soc. Exptl. Biology and Medicine, Sigma Xi. Home: 2315 Glen Haven St Houston TX 77025 Office: 6720 Bertner St Houston TX 77025

ROGERS, W.D., JR., broadcasting exec., former mayor; b. Waco, Tex.; ed. Baylor U.; m. Edith Tighe; children—Kerry (Mrs. Sam Caddell), Kay (Mrs. Daryl Lowe), Karol. Founder sta. KEYL-TV (now sta. KENS-TV), San Antonio, 1949, operator, 1949-51; founder Tex. Telecasting, Inc., 1951; founder sta. KDUB-TV, Lubbock, Tex., 1952; established West Tex. TV Network, 1956, operator, 1956-61; now pres. Rogers Broadcasting Co., Lubbock, Rogers Capital Corp., Lubbock, Plains Capital Corp., Lubbock; chmn. bd. Champion Life Ins. Co., Dallas, also dir.; mayor, Lubbock, 1966-70. Co-founder, past chmn. bd. TV Bur. Advt., N.Y.C., now chmn. emeritus; founder TV Stas., Inc., N.Y.C. organizer Automatic Program Logging for TV stas. to IBM. Mem. Tex. Council Higher Edn.; mem. adv. bd. Tex. Tourist Devel. Council; past chmn. Lubbock Auditorium-Coliseum and Civic Center, Inc.; past chmn. Citizens Adv. Com. City of Lubbock. Past. bd. dirs. Salvation Army, Lubbock, Tex. United Fund, Lubbock United Fund, Caprock council Girl Scouts Am.; past mem. adv. bd. Lubbock Christian Coll.; past trustee, chmn. pub. relations and devel. com. Meth. Hosp., Lubbock. Decorated Order Republic of Chad; named to Am. Hall of Fame, 1969; recipient Legion of Honor Order DeMolay, Outstanding Community Salesman award, 1970. Mem. Nat. Assn. Broadcasters (founder predecessor TV Assn. Broadcasters; past chmn. bd.), Soc. TV Pioneers (pres. 1957—), Assn. Broadcasting Execs. Tex., Young Pres. Orgn., Lubbock C. of C. (past pres.; past chmn. indsl. and econ. devel. com.), So. Plains Assn. Govts., Tex. Assn. Mayors, Councilmen and Commrs., Sales Execs. Club, Kappa Kappa Psi, Alpha Delta Sigma. Mem. Christian Ch. (deacon). Lion (mem. League for Crippled Children). Address: 1103 8th St Lubbock TX 79401

ROGERS, WEBSTER ALEXANDER, mgmt. systems cons.; b. Richmond, Va., Jan. 8, 1920; s. Hugh Alexander and Emily (Lewis) R.; student U. Florence (Italy), 1945; B.S., Va. Union U., 1948; postgrad. Howard U., 1951-52; m. Louise Leanna Gary, Dec. 17, 1950; children—Webster Alexander, Harold J., Esther L., Thomas M. Tchr. secondary math. Cumberland County (Va.) Sch. Bd., 1948-51; computer systems analyst Nat. Services Adminstrn., Washington, 1952-67; U.S. govt. math. statistician, 1967-70; mgmt. systems cons. U.S. Dept. Health, Edn. and Welfare, Washington, 1970—. Tchr. secondary mathematics Armstrong Adult Ednl. Center, Washington, 1968-71. Neighborhood commr. Boy Scouts Am., Washington, 1960-68; mem. Neighbors, Inc. Served with 92d inf. div. AUS, 1943-46. Decorated Purple Heart. Mem. Am. Math. Soc., Am. Statis. Assn., Municipal Officers Club D.C., Alpha Phi Alpha. Club: Toastmasters International (Washington). Author, editor Medicaid Mgmt. Information System documents. Home: 6223 9th St NW Washington DC 20011 Office: 330 C St SW Washington DC 20201

ROGERS, WILLIAM BRITTON, JR., lawyer; b. Carlsbad, N.M., Sept. 18, 1930; s. William Britton and Mabel (Patrick) R.; grad. N.M. Mil. Inst. 1949; B.A., U. Okla., 1951, LL.B., 1955; m. Joanne Harper, Aug. 30, 1955 (div. Jan. 1959); 1 son, Kevin Patrick. Admitted to Okla. bar, 1957; law clk. to A.P. Murrah, 10th Circuit Ct. Appeals, Oklahoma City, 1957-58; practiced in Oklahoma City, 1958—; mem. firm Ames, Daugherty, Byrun, Black, Ashabramner & Rogers, 1958—. Vice pres., dir. Harden Mortgage Loan Co., Oklahoma City, 1964-66, Western Paving Co., Oklahoma City, 1964-66, Oklahoma City Pub. Market, 1964-66; dir. Central Cenetry Co. of Ill., Chgo., Keller-Williams Furniture Mfg. Co., Oklahoma City, Haggards, Inc., Oklahoma City. Asso. prof. law Oklahoma City U., 1964—. Trustee Rose Hill Burial Park; dir. Sigma Nu Corp. of Okla. Served to 1st lt. USAF, 1955-57. Mem. Am., Okla., N.M. bar assns., Am. Judicature Soc. Democrat. Episcopalian. Home: 7004 N Roff St Oklahoma City OK 73116 Office: 219 Couch Dr Oklahoma City OK 73102

ROGERS, WILLIAM PIERCE, lawyer; b. Norfolk, N.Y., June 23, 1913; s. Harrison Alexander and Myra (Beswick) R.; A.B. Colgate U., 1934; LL.B., Cornell U., 1937; m. Adele Langston, June 27, 1936; children—Dale, Anthony Wood, Jeffrey Langston, Douglas Langston. Mem. editorial bd. Cornell Law Quar., 1935-37; admitted to N.Y. bar, 1937, D.C. bar, 1950; asst. dist. atty., N.Y. County, 1938-42, 46-47; counsel Senate War Investigating Com., 1947, chief counsel, 1947-48; chief counsel Senate Investigations Sub-Com. Exec. Expenditures Com., 1948-50; mem. firm Dwight, Royall, Harris, Koegel & Caskey, N.Y.C. and Washington, 1950-53; dep. atty. gen. U.S., 1953-57, atty. gen., 1957-61; partner firm Royall, Koegel & Rogers, N.Y.C. and Washington, 1961-69; sec. state, 1969-73; partner firm Rogers & Wells, Washington and N.Y.C., 1973—. U.S. rep. 20th Gen. Assembly, UN, 1967, UN Ad Hoc Com. on South Africa, 1967; mem. Pres.'s Commn. Law Enforcement and Adminstrn., 1965-67. Served as lt. comdr. USN, 1942-46. Fellow Am. Bar Found.; mem. Bar Assn. City N.Y., Am., N.Y. State, D.C. bar assns., Am. Law Inst., Order of Coif, Sigma Chi. Clubs: Burning Tree, Country (Bethesda, Md.); Sky, Racquet and Tennis (N.Y.C.); Chevy Chase (Md.) Golf. Home: 7007 Glenbrook Rd Bethesda MD 20014 also 870 UN Plaza New York City NY 10017 Office: 1666 K St NW Washington DC 20006 also 200 Park Av New York City NY 10017

ROGERS, WILMER ALEXANDER, educator, parasitologist; b. Mt. Dora, Fla., Aug. 17, 1933; s. Thomas M. and Maude L. (Gunter) R.; B.S., U. So. Miss., 1958; M.S., Auburn U., 1960, Ph.D., 1967; m. Carole Ann Pierce, Jan. 23, 1961; children—Julie, Natalie, Nancy, Melissa. Dist. fishery biologist Ala. Dept. Conservation, Tuscaloosa, 1960-62; asst. dir. U.S. Bur. Sport Fisheries and Wildlife Warmwater Fisheries Tng. Sch., Marion, Ala., 1962-64; instr. Auburn U., 1964-67, asst. prof., 1967-71, asso. prof., 1971—, leader S.E. Coop. Fish Disease Project, 1968—. Cons. to fish farmers, extension service, TVA, others. Served with USNR, 1951-54. Mem. Am. Fisheries Soc., Am. Soc. Parasitologists, Wildlife Disease Assn., Helminthological Soc. Wash. Contbr. articles to sci. lit. Home: 1212 Sanders Auburn AL 36830

ROGERSON, ASA BENJAMIN, chem. co. exec.; b. Martin County, N.C., Oct. 24, 1939; s. Delmus and Mildred (Manning) R.; B.S., N.C. State U., 1962; M.S., Va. Poly. Inst., 1964—, Ph.D., 1967; m. Betty Wynn, Aug. 29, 1965; children—Anissa, Asa Benjamin. Asst. prof. crop sci. N.C. State U., Raleigh, 1968-70; area supr. agrl. chem. div. Uniroyal, Inc., Raleigh, 1970-72, regional mgr., 1972—. Served with AUS, 1965. Mem. Weed Sci. Soc., Am. Soc. Plant Physiologists, Am. Inst. Biol. Scis., Alpha Gamma Rho Alumni. Home: Rural Route 8 Box 407 Raleigh NC 27612 Office: 2209 Century Dr Raleigh NC 27612

ROGERSON, MILTON HAROLD, pub. relations exec., photographer; b. Washington, N.C., Feb. 4, 1925; s. Simon Elmer and Josephine Julia (Burgess) R.; student East Carolina U., 1945-48; m. Melrose Garden Wilson, June 21, 1947; children—Milton Harold, Teresa Louise. Writer Washington (N.C.) Daily News, 1949-50; free lance writer, also photographer; mng. editor The Sun Jour., New Bern, N.C., 1955-61; publicity dir. Atlantic Christian Coll., Wilson, N.C., 1961—. Served with USAF, 1942-45; ETO. Decorated two Bronze Star medals. Mem. Univ. Photographers Assn. Am. (sec. treas. 1971-73), Profl. Photographers N.C., Am. Coll. Pub. Relations Assn., Sertoma Internat. Wilson (v.p. 1963-65). Home: 808 W Lee St Wilson NC 27893 Office: 600 W Lee St Wilson NC 27893

ROGG, NATHANIEL H., assn. exec.; b. N.Y.C., July 27, 1913; s. H.N. and Nettie (Fihrer) R.; B.A. magna cum laude, N.Y. U., 1934, M.A. with honors in Econs., 1935; postgrad. Brookings Inst., 1937-38; J.D. with honors, George Washington U., 1951; m. Genevieve DeVere, Nov. 14, 1964; children—David N., Katherine, Elizabeth, Daniel, Margaret. Econ. adminstr. Fed. Works Agy., Washington, 1935-42; econ. adviser Nat. Housing Agy., Washington, 1946-47, Housing and Home Financing Agy., Washington, 1947-54; chief economist Nat. Assn. Homebuilders, Washington, 1954—, exec. v.p., 1965—. Vis. prof. econs. Harvard, 1962-63; adj. prof. Am. U., 1965-66; cons. in field. Mem. Nat. Commn. Mortgage Interest Rates, 1968-69. Served to lt. comdr. USNR, 1942-46. Mem. Phi Beta Kappa. Clubs: Cosmos (Washington); Army-Navy Country (Arlington, Va.); Plantation (Hilton Head, S.C.). Home: 1718 Q St NW Washington DC 20009 Office: 1625 L St NW Washington DC 20036

ROHLICH, GERARD ADDISON, educator; b. Bklyn., July 8, 1910; s. Henry Otto and Margaret Loretta (Burns) R.; B.S., Cooper Union, 1934; B.S., U. Wis., 1936, M.S., 1937, Ph.D., 1940; m. Mary Elizabeth Murphy, Sept. 8, 1941; children—Mary Ellen (Mrs. James McNally), Gerard Addison, Thomas H., Karl O., Catherine A., Henry J., Virginia J., John H., Richard J., James W. Engring. asst. City of N.Y., Bklyn., 1929-34; instr. civil engring. Carnegie Inst. Tech., Pitts., 1937-39, 40-41; asst. prof. civil engring. Pa. State U., State College, 1941-42; chief project engr. Esna Corp., Union, N.J., 1944-45; asso. prof. Pa. State U., State College, 1945-46; prof. civil engring. U. Wis., Madison, 1946-72; C.W. Cook prof. environmental engring., prof. pub. affairs U. Tex., Austin, 1972—. Vis. prof. U. Cal. at Berkeley, 1963, U. Helsinki (Finland), 1970; cons. various fed. and state agencies, world health orgns., municipalities and industries; mem. Wis. Natural Resources Bd., 1967-72. Commr., Madison Water Utility, 1968-71. Recipient Harrison Prescott Eddy medal for research Water Pollution Control Fedn., 1955, Benjamin Smith Reynolds award for teaching excellence U. Wis., 1962, Karl E. Hilgard award Am. Soc. C.E., 1972, Wis. Fuller award Am. Water Works Assn., 1969. Diplomate Am. Acad. Environmental Engrs. Fellow Am. Soc. C.E.; mem. Nat. Acad. Engring., Am. Soc. Engring. Edn., Am. Water Works Assn., Water Pollution Control Fedn., Nat. Soc. Profl. Engrs., Sigma Xi. Contbr. profl. jours. Home: 2101 Pecos St Austin TX 78703 Office: Dept Environmental Engineering Univ Texas Austin TX 78712

ROHNE, WAYNE ARLEN, lawyer, mayor; b. Cranfills Gap, Tex., Sept. 8, 1931; s. Paul Bernhart and Alma Bendina (Tergerson) R.; A.A., Clifton Jr. Coll., 1951; A.B., Luther Coll., Ia., 1953; J.D., U. Tex., 1958; m. Jurdiss Marie Colwick, Nov. 7, 1953; children—Bruce Edward, Eric Thomas, Janet Lynne. With Bosque Co., 1953, Am. Airlines, 1953-54; admitted to Tex. bar, 1958; with Crowley, Wright, Miller & Garrett, 1958-67; pvt. practice law, Arlington, Tex., 1967—; partner Rohne & Hoodenpyle. Mem. Pantego (Tex.) Town Council, 1970-71, mayor, 1971—; mem. regional bldg. code com. N. Central Tex. Council Govts. Served with Signal Corps, AUS, 1954-56. Mem. Arlington (pres. 1972-73), Ft. Worth-Tarrant County (dir.), Ft. Worth-Tarrant County Jr. (past officer) bar assns., Phi Alpha Delta. Lutheran (pres. congregation, sec. dist. com. Am. missions). Club: Noon Optimist (pres. 1971). Home: 3310 Peach Tree St Pantego TX 76013 Office: Arlington Bank & Trust Co Bldg Arlington TX 76010

ROHRBACH, PETER THOMAS, author, editor; b. N.Y.C., Feb. 27, 1926; s. James Peter and Kathryn (Foley) R.; A.B. in Philosophy, Cath. U. Am., 1951, M.A. in Edn., 1953; m. Sheila Ann Sheehan, Sept. 21, 1970; 1 dau., Sarah Catherine. Author: Conversation With Christ, 1956; A Gentle Fury, 1959; A Girl and Her Teens, 1959; Bold Encounter, 1960; The Search for Therese, 1961; The Photo Album of Therese, 1962; The Art of Dynamic Preaching, 1965; Journey to Carith, 1966; The Disillusioned, 1968; also mystery short stories and novels under pen name; editor Spiritual Life Mag., Washington, 1966-70; book editor City Mag., Washington, 1970—. Tchr. Georgetown U., Cath. U. Am., other colls., 1956-66. Editorial cons. govt. agys., 1968—. Contbr. articles to mags. and newspapers. Home: 4000 Massachusetts Av NW Washington DC 20016 Office: City Magazine 2100 M St NW Washington DC 20037

ROHRER, JAMES VERNON, ednl. adminstr.; b. Wadsworth, O., Aug. 23, 1928; s. Samuel Dayton and Ella Mae (Rohrer) R.; student Eastern Mennonite Coll., 1946-48, Madison Coll., 1949; B.A., Goshen Coll., 1949; M.Ed., U. Va., 1956; m. Mary June Turner, Aug. 28, 1949; children—Jennifer, James, Jordan, Jane. Tchr., Bergton (Va.) Sch., 1949-52; prin. Broadway (Va.) Elementary Sch., 1952-64; prin. John C. Myers Intermediate Sch., Broadway, 1964-67; supr. instrnl. materials Rockingham County Schs., Harrisonburg, Va., 1967—. Mem. Ch. of Brethren. Home: Route 2 Timberville VA 22853 Office: 120 N Liberty St Harrisonburg VA 22801

ROJAS, CARLOS, educator; b. Barcelona, Spain, Dec. 8, 1928; s. Carlos and Luisa (Vila) R.; M.A., U. Barcelona, 1951; Ph.D., U. Madrid (Spain), 1955; m. Eunice Mitcham, Mar. 19, 1966; 1 son, Carlos. Came to U.S., 1957. Asst. prof. Romance langs. Rollins Coll., Winter Park, Fla., 1957-60; faculty Emory U., Atlanta, 1960—, prof., 1967—. Mem. Modern Langs. Assn., Am. Assn. U. Profs. Recipient Nat. Prize Lit. Spain, 1968; Planeta prize, 1973. Author: El Asesino de Cesar, 1958; Auto de Fe, 1968; Por Què Perdimos La Guerra, 1970; Azana, 1973; Diez Figuras Antes La Guerra Civil, 1973. Home: 1344 Briarwood Dr Atlanta GA 30306

ROJAS-GARCIDUENAS, MANUEL, educator; b. Salamanca, Mexico, Oct. 1, 1925; s. Joel and Victoria (Garciduenas) R.; biologist U. Nat. Mexico, 1952; M.S., U. Minn., 1956; m. Beatriz Herrera, Jan. 15, 1955; children—Beatriz, Cristina, Dora Berta, Manuel. Faculty, Instiuto Tecnologico de Monterrey (Mexico), 1953—, prof. biology, 1970, head dept., 1970—. Vis. summer prof. U. de Caldas, Colombia, 1964, U. El Salvador, San Salvador, 1963. Rockefeller fellow Mexican Govt., 1949-52. Mem. Academia de la Investigacion Cientifica, Weed Sci. Soc. Am., Sociedad Botanica de Mexico, Soc. Latin Am. Fisiol. Vegetal, Sigma Xi. Author: Fisiologia Vegetal Aplicada, 1972. Contbr. profl. jours. Home: 325 Capela Monterrey Nuevo Leon Mexico Office: Dept Biology Inst Tech Monterrey Mexico Mailing address: Apartado Postal 4644 Sucursal de Correos J Monterrey Mexico

ROLEN, CHARLES OREN, educator; b. Eros, La., Sept. 5, 1929; s. Joel Jackson and Margaret (Oglesbee) R.; B.S., Northwestern State U., 1958; M.B.A., La. State U., 1959; Ph.D., U. Ark., 1969; m. Virginia Alice Long, July 8, 1950; children—Charles David, Jonathan Mark, Timothy Derren, Philip Lamar, Joel Anthony. With U.S. Steel Corp., Orange, Tex., 1950-51, 54-55; faculty La. State U., 1958-59; with Arthur Andersen & Co., New Orleans, 1959-60; auditor, tchr. N.E. La. State U., Monroe, 1962-63; faculty U. Ark., Fayetteville, 1963-65; prof., chmn. accounting and data processing Middle Tenn. State U., Murfreesboro, 1965-68, 1969—; faculty Nicholls State Coll., Thibodeaux, La., 1968-69. Served with U.S. Army, 1952-53. Recipient plaque as outstanding bus. grad. Northwestern State U., 1958. C.P.A., Tex. Mem. Am. Inst. C.P.A.'s, Am. Accounting Assn., Nat. Assn. Accountants, Middle Tenn. State U. Accounting Soc. (hon., organizer 1966), Pi Omega Pi, Phi Kappa Phi, Beta Alpha Psi, Delta Mu Delta, Beta Gamma Sigma. Mem. United Pentecostal Ch. Home: 306 Northfield Blvd Murfreesboro TN 37130

ROLEY, ROLF WIGHT, cons. engr.; b. Pana, Ill., Apr. 14, 1918; s. Paul Wight and Eula (Neal) R.; B.S. in Mine Engring., U. Mo., 1940; E.M., 1952; D.Sc., Marlowe U., 1968; Ph.D., Ill. Christian Coll., 1968; m. Mary F. Brown, Aug. 5, 1939; 1 son, Robert D. Gen. engr. Ill. Hwy. Dept., 1934-40; with various mining and constrn. cos., 1940-52; with Reynolds Metals Co., Little Rock, 1952-62; pres. Roley Engrs., Inc., Roley Forensics, Kennesaw, Ga., 1962—. Cons in safety accident studies, forensic sci., 1948—; asso. prof. civil engring. Ga. Inst. Tech., 1962-68. Mem. Ark. Republican Com., 1954-60. Registered profl. engr., Ga., Ill., Wyo. Mem. A.A.A.S., Nat., Ga., Cobb County (dir.) socs. profl. engrs., Nat. Soc. Forensic Consultants, Nat. Fire Protection Assn., U.S., Ga. cons. engrs. councils, Nat. Oceanographic Soc. Club: Explorers (N.Y.C.). Contbr. articles to profl. jours. Home: Marrol House Madison GA 30650 Office: Shiloh Hills Kennesaw GA 30144

ROLF, WILLIAM MATTHEW, banker; b. Covington, Ky., Oct. 25, 1932; s. Henry William and Elsie Cecelia (Farrell) R.; B.A., Xavier U., 1957; m. Mary Janet Heringhaus, Sept. 10, 1960; children—David William, Thomas Edward, Karen Anne. With Covington Trust & Banking Co., 1957—, treas., 1964-68, v.p., 1966-72, sr. v.p., 1972—. Mem. adv. bd. Nat. Inst. Loan Commn. Bd. dirs. North Ky. Amateur Athletic Union, YMCA. Served with AUS, 1953-55. Mem. World War II Vets. of Ludlow. Home: 1579 St Anthony Dr Fort Wright KY 41011 Office: 540 Madison Av Covington KY 41011

ROLFSEN, RICHARD HERMAN, pharmacist; b. Ludlow, Ky., Feb. 4, 1931; s. John Henry and Martina (Santel) R.; student Villa Madonna Coll., 1946-48; B.S., Cin. Coll. Pharmacy, 1952; m. Lois Ann Brinkman, May 16, 1959; children—Nancy Ann, Jill Marie, Richard Joseph. Pharmacist, Orzali Pharmacy, Covington, Ky., 1954-55, owner, 1955-64; mgr. Cherokee Drugs, Independence, Ky., 1964-65, owner, 1965—. Organizer Scottie Drugs, Inc., 1960—, pres. 1966-67. Mem. Fort Wright Civic Club, 1962—. Regional dir. continuing edn. series U. Ky. TV, 1971-74. Served with AUS, 1952-54. Named Duke of Paducah Ky. Mem. No. Ky. (chmn. bd. 1971-72), Ky. (chmn. bd. 1972-73) pharm. assns., Druggist Guild St. James (v.p. 1957-60), Am. Pharm. Assn., Am. Acad. Gen. Practice, Nat. Assn. Retail Druggist, Covington Kenton County Jr. C. of C., Ludlow Vets. Roman Catholic. K.C. Club: Bluegrass Swim (Ft. Wright, Ky.). Home: 21 Augusta St Fort Wright KY 41011 Office: 6439 Taylor Mill St Independence KY 41051

ROLL, WILLIAM GEORGE, JR., parapsychologist; b. Bremen, Germany, July 3, 1926 (parents Am. citizens); s. William George and Gudrun (Agerholm) R.; B.A., U. Cal. at Berkeley, 1949; B.Litt., Oxford U., 1960; m. Muriel Gold, June 22, 1950; children—Lise Renata, Leif Agerholm, William George III. Louis K. Anspacher fellow in parapsychology, parapsychology lab. Duke, 1957-58, research asso., 1958-60, project dir., 1960; project dir. Psychical Research Found., Inc., Durham, N.C., 1961—. Mem. Underground Danish Resistance Forces, 1943-45. Mem. A.A.A.S., Assn. Transpersonal Psychology, Parapsychology Assn. (council 1957-60, 62-65, pres. 1964), Soc. Psychical Research London, Am. Soc. Psychical Research, Oxford U. Soc. Psychical Research (pres. 1952-57). Author: The Poltergeist, 1973. Editor: Jour. Parapsychology, 1958-60, Theta, 1963—, P.A. Proceedings, 1964-71, Research in Parapsychology, 1972—. Contbr. articles to profl. jours. and anthologies. Home: 3509 Rugby Rd Durham NC 27707 Office: Duke Station Durham NC 27706

ROLLER, HERBERT ALFRED, zoologist, chem. co. adviser; b. Magdeburg, Germany, Aug. 2, 1927; s. Alfred H. and Elfriede (Wartner) R.; B.S., Christian Thomasius Schule, Halle, Germany, 1946; Ph.D., U. Gottingen (Germany), 1962; m. Manuela R. Buresch, Dec. 20, 1957. Came to U.S., 1962. Project asso. zoology U. Wis., 1962-65, asst. prof. pharmacology, 1965-66, research asso. zoology, 1966-67, asso. prof., 1967-68; prof. biology Tex. A. and M. U., 1968-74, prof. biochemistry and biophysics, 1974—, dir. Inst. Developmental Biology, 1973—; v.p. research Zoecon Corp., Palo Alto, Cal., 1968-72, sci. adviser, 1972—; mem., research dir. Internat. Centre Insect Physiology and Ecology, Nairobi, Kenya, 1970—. Fellow Tex. Acad. Sci.; mem. Am. Soc. Zoologists, Akadamie der Naturforscher Leopoldina, Am. Inst. Biol. Scis., A.A.A.S., Am. Assn. U. Profs., Entomol. Soc. Am., Sigma Xi. Home: 1000 E 30th St Bryan TX 77801

ROLLINGS, HARRY EVAN, physician; b. Hattiesburg, Miss., July 23, 1920; s. Robert Evan and Emma (Siebe) R.; B.S., U. So. Miss., 1939; med. certificate U. Miss., 1941; M.D., Tulane U., 1943; m. Irma Lee Pittman, Jan. 12, 1945; children—Cynthia, Alane, Pamela, Janet, Ellen, Robert. Intern Phila. Gen. Hosp., 1943-44; resident medicine Tulane U. service Charity Hosp., 1944-46; chief med. resident, 1945-46, instr. medicine Sch. Medicine, 1944-48; staff internist Ochsner Clinic and Ochsner Found. Hosp., Touro Infirmary, 1946-48; practice internal medicine, Savannah, Ga., 1948-51, 53—; chief of staff, trustee Warren A. Candler Hosp., Candler Central Hosp., Candler Telfair Hosps.; chmn. lab. com. Candler Gen. Hosp.; cons. staff St. Josephs Hosp.; courtesy staff Meml. Hosp., all Savannah. Cons. internal medicine USAF Hosp., Hunter AFB, Ga.; sr. med. examiner FAA. Dir. Colony Mortgage Co., Savannah, Helmet Petroleum Co., Denver. Served to capt. AUS, 1951-53; col. M.C., USAF Res. Diplomate Am. Bd. Internal Medicine. Fellow A.C.P., Internat. Coll. Physicians, Am. Coll. Chest Physicians; mem. Med. Assn. Ga., Ga. Med. Soc., Internat., Am. assns. internal medicine, Am. Diabetes Assn., Am. Geriatrics Assn., A.M.A., So. Med. Assn., Internat. Congress Internal Medicine, Aircraft Owners and Pilots Assn., Flying Physicians Assn., Air Force Assn., Am. Heart Assn. Methodist (ofcl. bd.). Clubs: Savannah Yacht, Savannah Golf, Windsor Forest Golf. Contbg. author Communicable Disease, 1948. Contbr. articles to profl. jours. Home: 514 Arlington Rd Savannah GA 31406 Office: 100 E Park Av Savannah GA 31401

ROLLINGS, OLLIE EARL, III, dentist; b. Birmingham, Ala., Apr. 11, 1942; s. Ollie Earl, Jr. and Hazel E. (Huggins) R.; B.S., Auburn U., 1964; D.M.D., U. Ala., 1968; m. Cecilia Jane Brooks, June 20,

1964; children—Robert Brooks, Christy Lillian. Practice dentistry, Cape Coral, Fla., 1968—. Served to lt. USNR, 1968-70. Mem. Am., Fla. dental assns., West Coast Dental Soc., V.F.W., Cape Coral C. of C., Psi Omega, Pi Kappa Alpha. Republican. Baptist (deacon). Club: Tarpon Hunters (Cape Coral). Home: 1625 SE 41st St Cape Coral FL 33904 Office: 4117 Del Prado Pkwy Cape Coral FL 33904

ROLLINS, ALBERT WILLIAMSON, cons. engr.; b. Dallas, July 31, 1930; s. Andrew Peach and Mary (Williamson) R.; B.S. in Civil Engring., Tex. A. and M. Coll., 1951, M.S. in Civil Engring., 1956; m. Martha Ann James, Dec. 28, 1954; children—Elizabeth Ann, Mark Martin. Engring. asst. Tex. Hwy. Dept., Dallas, 1953-55; dir. pub. works City of Arlington (Tex.), 1956-63, city mgr., 1963-67; partner Schrickel, Rollins & Assos., land planners-engrs., Arlington, 1967—. Mem. Gov.'s Energy Crisis Council; chmn. Tex. Mass Transp. Commn. Bd. dirs. Tex. Turnpike Authority. Served as 1st lt. AUS, 1951-53. Registered profl. engr., Tex., La., Okla. Mem. Internat. City Mgmt. Assn., Nat. Soc. Profl. Engrs., Am. Soc. C.E., Am. Water Works Assn., Water Pollution Control Fedn., Sigma Xi, Phi Eta Sigma, Tau Beta Pi, Phi Kappa Phi, Chi Epsilon. Contbr. articles to profl. jours. Home: 3004 Yellowstone Dr Arlington TX 76013 Office: 604 Av H East Arlington TX 76011

ROLLINS, RICHARD ALBERT, coll. dean; b. Phila., Nov. 30, 1927; s. Nathaniel McKinley R.; A.B., Lincoln U., 1952; M. Div., Union Theol. Sem., N.Y.C., 1955; S.T.M., Boston U., 1960; D. Religion, Claremont Sch. Theology, 1969; m. Audrey J. King, Aug. 19, 1960. Instr. Bishop Coll., Dallas, 1955-57, asst. prof. religion, 1957-59, asso. dean adminstrn., dean of men, 1969-70. Cons. to Negro clergy of Los Angeles, 1969-70, Seminarians, Claremont Sch. Theology. Chmn. bd. mgmt. Moorland br., YMCA, 1972—. Mem. Nat. Assn. Coll. Deans, Registrars and Admissions Officers, Acad. Religion, Am. Assn. Learned Socs., Am. Conf. Acad. Deans, Am. Assn. U. Profs., Assn. Am. Colls., Kappa Alpha Psi. Baptist. Home: 630 Woodacre Dr Dallas TX 75241 Office: PO Box 6 3837 Simpson Stuart Rd Dallas TX 75241

ROLSTON, B. FIELDING, indsl. engr.; b. Harrisonburg, Va., Apr. 25, 1941; s. Ben F. and Lelia Y. R.; B.S. in Indsl. Engring., Va. Poly. Inst. and State U., 1964; M.S., Am. U., 1968; m. Joyce Mundy, June 28, 1963; children—Benjamin Clay, Tina Dawn. Indsl. engr. Tenn. Eastman Co., Kingsport, 1964-65, systems analyst, 1968-69, sr. indsl. engr., 1970—; project analyst U.S. Army Data Support Commn., Washington, 1966-67; lectr. in field. Mem. Tenn. Gov.'s Study Group Cost Control, 1971. Publicity chmn. Upper East Tenn. Council Alcoholism and Drug Dependence. Registered profl. engr., Tenn. Mem. Am. Inst. Indsl. Engrs. (past chpt. pres.), East Tenn. Engring. Assns. Council (chmn.), Nat. Soc. Profl. Engrs., Tau Beta Phi, Alpha Pi Mu. Methodist (chmn. finance com.; tchr.). Home: 409 Meadow Lane Kingsport TN 37663

ROMAN, JAMES RUDOLPH, JR., educator; b. Jamestown, N.Y., Feb. 10, 1936; s. James Rudolph and Violet (Nyholm) R.; B.S., Bucknell U., 1957; M.B.A, U. Md., 1960, postgrad. 1960-63; D. Bus. Adminstrn., George Washington U., 1970; m. Nancy Ann Kelley, June 17, 1961. Instr., U. Md., 1959-63, U. Del., 1959-63; instr. George Washington U., 1963-66, asst. prof., 1966-70, asso. prof., 1971—; invest Lectr., mgmt. cons. in traffic, transp. bus. mgmt.; mem. adv. council Small Bus. Adminstrn. Mem. Am. Accounting Assn., Am. Assn. U. Profs., Soc. Advancement Mgmt., Am. Econs. Assn., Assn. Edn. in Internat. Bus., USCG Aux., Chautauqua Power Squadron, Beta Gamma Sigma, Delta Sigma Pi, Tau Kappa Alpha, Delta Nu Alpha. Clubs: Traffic; Tantallon Country; Chautauqua Lake Yacht, Chautauqua Yacht, Ft. Washington Yacht and Tennis, George Washington University. Contbr. to Americana Ency. Ann., also profl. jours. Home: 12201 Holly Bank Dr Tantallon-on-the-Potomac Washington DC 20022 also 209 Gustavus Av Jamestown NY 14701 Office: 710 21st St NW Washington DC 20006

ROMANO-PACHECO, ARTURO, museum ofcl.; b. Ciudad, Mexico, Sept. 29, 1921; s. Samuel and Dolores (Pacheco) Romano; M.D., cum laude, Escuela Nacional de Antropologia e Historia, 1956; m. Carmen Vazquez Galvan, Sept. 11, 1952; children—Lourdes, Patricia, Magdalena. Asst. researcher Instituto Nacional de Antropologia e Historia, 1946-57, chmn. dept. prehistory, 1957-61; chmn. dept. photography Nat. Mus. Anthropology, 1949-52, sec., 1956-59, dir. dept. phys. anthropology, 1964-68, dir., 1961-64, 68-70, adj. dir., 1970-72; tchr. Nat. Sch. Anthropology and History, 1949—. Recipient grants for archaeol. excavations at Tlatilco, Mex. Mem. Soc. Mexicana de Antropologia, Soc. Mexicana de Historia y Filosofia de la Medicina, Soc. de Geografia e Historia de Guatemala, Am. Assn. Phys. Anthropologists, Soc. for Am. Archaeology. Home: 85-4 Eligio Ancona Mexico City 4 Mexico Office: Reforma y Gandhi Mexico City 5 Mexico

ROMANUS, CHARLES FRANKLIN, govt. ofcl.; b. Decatur, Ill., July 6, 1915; s. Charles Henry and Lulu Lucille (Crail) R.; student Blackburn Coll., 1932-34; A.M., U. Ill., 1937; postgrad. La. State U., 1937-41; m. Annie A. Armstrong, Aug. 12, 1940; children—Kathleen (Mrs. David William Smith), Charles Franklin, Charlene Ann. With Office of Chief Mil. History, Dept. Army, Washington, 1945—, chief gen. reference br., 1962—. Served to capt. AUS, 1943-46. Author: Stilwell's Mission to China, 1953; Stilwell's Command Problems, 1956; Time Runs Out in C.B.I., 1959. Home: 9022 Leesburg Pike McLean VA 22101 Office: 2d and R Sts SW Washington DC 20315

ROMEDY, JAMES MICHAEL, broadcaster; b. Jacksonville, Fla., Sept. 4, 1941; s. James Riley and Gladys (Gissendana) R.; E.E., Jacksonville U., 1962; B.B.A., Mercer U., 1973; m. Diane Puckett, Feb. 2, 1969; 1 son, James Andrew. With WJXT-TV, Jacksonville, 1962-64, WJCT-TV, Jacksonville, 1964-65, WCIV-TV, Charleston, S.C., 1965-66; charge air operations WAGA-TV, Atlanta, 1966—. Prodn. coordinator Muscular Dystrophy Assn. Am., 1972-73, Emory U. Community Edn., 1972-73. Group leader Explorer Scouts. Recipient Television Broadcasters awards for commls., 1972. Mem. Television Programming Conf. (dir. 1973). Home: 6355 Memorial Dr Stone Mountain GA 30083 Office: 1551 Briarcliff Rd Atlanta GA 30319

ROMERO BARCELO, CARLOS, mayor, lawyer; b. San Juan, P.R., Sept. 4, 1932; s. Antonio Romero and Josefina Barcelo; grad. Phillips Exeter Acad., Exeter, Mass., 1949; B.A., Yale, 1953; LL.B., U.P.R., 1956; m. Kathleen Donnelly, Jan. 2, 1966; children—Carlos, Andres, Juan Carlos, Melinda. Admitted to P.R. bar, 1956, since practiced in San Juan; asso. firm Rivera Zayas, Rivera Cestero & Rua, 1956-62, partner, 1962-63; mem. firm Segurola, Romero & Toledo, 1963-68; mayor, San Juan, 1968—. Pres., Citizens for Statehood, 1965-67; pres. polit. edn. and evaluation com. Statehood Republican Com.; a founder United Statehooders Group; a founder New Progressive Party, 1967, v.p., 1967, 1st v.p., 1971; mem. exec. com. Nat. League Cities, 1969—, U.S. Conf. Mayors, 1971—. Named Young Man of Yr., Jr. C. of C., 1968. Office: City Hall San Francisco St San Juan PR 00901

ROMERSTEIN, HERBERT, govt. ofcl.; b. N.Y.C., Aug. 19, 1931; s. Philip and Rose (Alpert) R.; student Bklyn. Coll., 1950-51, 54-55; m. Patricia Cole, Oct. 10, 1961; children—Shari, David, Victoria, Rebecca. Cons. to various fed. and state agys., 1954-64; investigator N.Y. State Legislature, 1954-56; investigative cons. Waterfront Commn. N.Y. Harbor, 1962-63; investigator N.Y. State Senate, 1964; investigator com. on un-Am. activities U.S. Ho. of Reps., N.Y.C., 1965-69, investigator com. on internal security, 1969-71, chief investigator (minority staff) com. on internal security, 1971—. Served with AUS, 1952-53. Mem. Am. Numis. Assn., Civil War Token Soc. Jewish religion. Republican. Author: Communism and Your Child, 1962; (monograph) The Communist International Youth and Student Apparatus, 1963; (with Grover Criswell) The Official Guide to Confederate Money and Civil War Tokens, 1971. Office: Cannon House Office Bldg Room 310 Washington DC 20515

RONA, PETER ARNOLD, oceanographer; b. Trenton, N.J., Aug. 17, 1934; s. Gustav G. and Elizabeth (Herzog) R.; A.B., Brown U., 1956; M.S., Yale, 1957, Ph.D. (Dana, Gibbs and Sheffield Sci. Sch. fellows), 1967. Exploration geologist Standard Oil Co. N.J., Southwestern U.S., 1957-59; geophysicist Columbia, Hudson Labs., N.Y.C., 1960-69; sr. research geophysicist Atlantic Oceanographic and Meteorol. Labs., Miami, Fla., 1969—; chief scientist Trans-Atlantic Geotraverse Nat. Oceanic and Atmospheric Adminstrn., 1970—. Cons. to UN in seabed resources, 1970—. Fellow Geol. Soc. Am., Am. Geog. Soc., Explorers Club; mem. Am. Geophys. Union, Soc. Exploration Geophysicists, Acoustical Soc. Am., N.Y. Acad. Scis., Marine Tech. Soc., Am. Assn. Petroleum Geologists, A.A.A.S., Sigma Xi. Contbr. articles to sci. jours. Office: 15 Rickenbacker Causeway Miami FL 33149

RONE, CHARLES RONALD, engring. exec.; b. Sweetwater, Tex., Apr. 24, 1934; s. L.C. and Ima Mae (Nunn) R.; B.S. in Civil Engring., Tex. Tech. U., 1965; A.S., Odessa Jr. Coll., 1962; m. Roberta B. Swartzbaugh, Sept. 4, 1959; children—Rhonda Anne, Robert Charles. Sales rep. Southwestern Portland Cement, Liberal, Kan., 1965-66; soils engr., mgr. soils div., divisional mgr. Ft. Worth office Southwestern Labs., 1966-72; pres. Rone Engring., Inc., Arlington, Tex., 1972—; works include Ft. Worth-Dallas Regional Airport, Ft. Worth Nat. Bank. Served with AUS, 1956-58. Chmn. adv. com. Constrn. Research Center, U. Tex. at Arlington. Registered profl. engr., Tex. Mem. Am. Soc. C.E. (pres.-elect 1973-74, chmn. found. com.), Nat., Tex. socs. profl. engrs., Am. Concrete Inst. (treas. 1971-72), Assn. Engring. Geologists, Nat. Assn. Home Builders, Constrn. Specifications Inst., Builders Assn. Tarrant County (chmn. found. com.). Home: 1104 Circle Lane Bedford TX 76021 Office: 2000 E Randol Mill Arlington TX 76011

RONE, WILLIAM EUGENE, JR., editor; b. Atlanta, Nov. 7, 1926; s. William Eugene and Marguerite (Kellett) R.; A.B., Wofford Coll., 1949; LL.B., U. S.C., 1951; m. Margaret Louise Banks, July 17, 1953; 1 son, James Kellett. With The State, newspaper, Columbia, S.C., 1950—, city editor, 1962-65, asso. editor, 1966-69, editorial page editor, 1969—. S.C. corr. So. Edn. Reporting Service, Nashville, 1962-68; columnist Raleigh (N.C.) News & Observer, Atlanta Jour.-Constn. Organizer, chmn. S.C. Athletic Hall of Fame, Columbia, 1957-61. Served with USNR, 1945-46. Recipient S.C. A.P. award for best reporting in depth, 1962. Mem. Am. Soc. Newspaper Editors, Nat. Conf. Editorial Writers, Kappa Sigma, Phi Delta Phi. Episcopalian. Author: Biography of Max Hirsch, 1956. Home: 726 Fairway Lane Columbia SC 29210 Office: Box 1333 Columbia SC 29202

RONEY, HAROLD NELSON, lawyer; b. Madison College, Tenn., Jan. 17, 1939; s. Harold Brizendine and Elsie Marie (Nelson) R.; B.S., David Lipscomb Coll., Nashville, 1960; J.D., Vanderbilt U., 1963; m. Judith Rose, Feb. 21, 1970. Admitted to Tenn. bar, 1963; individual practice law, McMinnville, Tenn., 1963-70; partner Camp & Roney, McMinnville, 1971—. Dir. Tenn. Metal Fabricating Corp., McMinnville. Dist. commr. Boy Scouts Am., 1972—. Mem. bd. aldermen City of McMinnville, 1964-67, vice mayor, 1967; mem. Tenn. Ho. of Reps., 1960-64. Bd. dirs. Middle Tenn. Christian Found., Sunny Acres Home for Children. Mem. Am., Tenn. (ho. of dels.) bar assns., Tenn. Trial Lawyers Assn. (bd. govs.), Assn. Trial Lawyers Am., Alpha Kappa Psi, Delta Theta Phi. Democrat. Mem. Ch. of Christ (part time minister 1954—). Rotarian. Home: Country Club Dr McMinnville TN 37110 Office: Box 590 McMinnville TN 37110

RONEY, RAYMOND GEORGE, librarian; b. Phila., July 26, 1939; s. Wallace and Rosezell (Harris) R.; B.A., Central State U., Wilberforce, O., 1963; M.L.S., Pratt Inst., 1965; postgrad. Catholic U., 1967—; m. Ruth A. Westgaph, Apr. 4, 1970. Asst. br. librarian Queens Borough Pub. Library, Jamaica, N.Y., 1964-65; supr. reference dept. Howard U. Library, Washington, 1965-66; dir. libraries Nat. League of Cities/U.S. Conf. Mayors, Washington, 1967-70; dir. library Washington Tech. Inst., 1970—. Cons. D.C. Pub. Schs.-Model Schs. Innovative Team, Washington. Mem. S.W. Washington Edn. Community Com., 1969-70; pres. Shepherd Park Citizen's Assn., Washington, 1973—; del. Fedn. Civic Assn., 1973-74, Fedn. Citizens Assn., 1973-74. Recipient Outstanding Achievement award Bright Hope Baptist Ch., Phila., 1963. Mem. Am. Polit. Sci. Assn., Am. Acad. Polit. and Social Sci., Met. Washington Area Urban Studies Libraries, N.E.A., A.L.A., D.C. Library Assn., Spl. Library Assn. Home: 1521 Kalmia Rd NW Washington DC 20012 Office: 4100 Connecticut Av NW Washington DC 20008

ROOD, NATHAN BARNETT, utility co. exec.; b. Odessa, Russia, Sept. 16, 1902 (came to U.S. 1905, naturalized 1920); s. Morris and Paula (Zlatopolski) R.; A.B., Columbia, 1924, LL.B., 1930; postgrad. Harvard, 1925, Mexico City Coll., 1958; m. Roddy Crossman, May 29, 1937; children—Judianne (Mrs. Sydney S. Traum), Ginger (Mrs. Steven B. Jacobs). Admitted to N.Y. bar, 1931, practiced, Peekskill, 1932-42; pres. City Constrn. Co., Miami, Fla., 1946-50, Rood Constrn. Co., 1950—, Atlantic Utilities Corp., 1961-66; pres., dir. North Dade Water Co., 1953-61, North Lauderdale Corp., Miami, 1960—, Atlantic Gas Corp., Miami, 1961-66; v.p., dir. South Broward Water Co., Ft. Lauderdale, Fla., 1953-67; chmn. bd. Great Am. Mgmt. & Research Co. Ltd., 1965-66; pres. U.S. Mgmt. Corp., 1969-70, chief exec. officer, 1970; chmn. bd. Pan Am. Bank Hialeah N.A., 1966—, Constrn. Research, Inc., 1971—, First Internat. Realty Securities Fund Ltd., 1969—; dir. Pan Am. Bancshares, 1969—. Mayor, North Lauderdale, Fla., 1963-69. Mem. citizens bd. U. Miami; adv. bd. Fla. Meml. Coll.; trustee Cedars of Lebanon Hosp.; bd. govs. Miami Jewish Fedn.; mem. nat. exec. bd., past pres. Miami chpt. Am. Jewish Com. Served from capt. to lt. col. AUS, 1942-46; col. Res. Mem. Fla. Water and Sewage Assn. (pres. 1960-63), Archaeol. Soc., Soc. Internat. Devel., Zool. Soc., Inst. Mayan Studies Econ. Soc. Miami. Clubs: Kings Bay Yacht and Country; Calusa Country; Standard; Bankers, Jockey. Home: 2451 Brickell Av Miami FL 33129 Office: 1428 Brickell Av Miami FL 33131

ROOKER, ALBERT ALBIN, state ofcl.; b. Ennis, Tex., May 31, 1924; s. Jesse Clair and Margaret (Jennings) R.; B.S. in Phys. Edn., U. Tex., 1948, M.Ed. 1950; m. Jo Pearl Bass, Nov. 27, 1947; 1 son, Michael Scott. Asst. dir. intramural sports for men U. Tex., Austin, 1948-59, dir. intramural sports for men, 1959-72; exec. dir. Tex. Gov.'s Commn. Phys. Fitness, 1971—. Dir summer camp Camp Son-Ro, 1956-57; owner S.W. Recreation Service, Austin, 1956—. Lifesaving and water safety instr. A.R.C., 1947-63; scoutmaster Circle Ten council Boy Scouts Am., 1940-42. Served to 1st lt. USAAF, 1943-45. Mem. Nat. Intramural Assn. (pres. 1967, cons. 1969—), Am., Tex. assns. health, phys. edn. and recreation, Coll. Phys. Edn. Assn., Hotel Sales Mgrs. Assn., Tex. Soc. Assn. Execs., N.E.A., Omicron Delta Kappa. Methodist. Mason. Home: 2811 W 50th St Austin TX 78731

ROOSEVELT, EDITH KERMIT, journalist; b. N.Y.C., Dec. 19, 1927; d. Archibald Bulloch and Grace (Lockwood) Roosevelt; B.A., Barnard Coll., 1948; m. Alexander Gregory Barmine, Sept. 8, 1948 (div.); 1 dau., Margot. Reporter, feature writer U.P.I., San Francisco, Los Angeles, Washington, 1950-55; feature writer, asso. editor Spadea Syndicate, N.Y.C. 1956-59; reporter, rewrite Newark Star Ledger, 1959-62; syndicated newspaper columnist, Washington, 1962—; Washington corr. for Manchester Union Leader, Vt. Sunday News, St. Alban's Messenger, Conn. Sunday Herald, N.H. Sunday News; lectr. in field. Contbr. to popular mags. Home: 1661 Crescent Pl NW Washington DC 20009

ROOSEVELT, ELLIOTT, JR., oil co. exec.; b. Ft. Worth, July 14, 1936; s. Elliott and Ruth (Googins) R.; grad. Phillips Acad., Andover, Mass., 1954; B.S. in Agr., Colo. State U., 1958; m. Jo Anne McFadden, Jan. 24, 1959; children—Laura, Elliott III, Elizabeth, David. Dist. landman Ambassador Oil Corp., Denver, 1960-64; pres. Gen. Petroleum Corp., Dallas, 1964—, Tex. Interstate Oil and Gas Co., Dallas, 1967-69, Del Mar Petroleum, Inc., Dallas, 1969-71; v.p. Shenandoah Oil Corp., Ft. Worth, 1971—. Served to capt. AUS, 1959. Episcopalian. Office: 1500 Commerce Bldg Fort Worth TX 76102

ROOT, HARLAN DAVID, physician; b. Riders Mills, N.Y., Feb. 16, 1926; s. Franklin Fowler and Alice (Snook) R.; A.B., Cornell, 1950, M.D., 1953; Ph.D. in Surgery, U. Minn., 1961; m. Catherine Bradford Friedrich, June 26, 1953; children—Susan, David, Julie, William. Intern, U. Minn. Hosps., Mpls., 1953-54, resident, 1954-61; practice medicine specializing in gen. thoracic surgery, San Antonio, 1966—; faculty dept. surgery U. Minn. Med. Sch., Mpls., 1961, asst. prof., 1961-66; asso. prof., dept. surgery U. Tex. at San Antonio Med. Sch., 1966-67, prof., 1967—, asst. chmn. dept., 1966—; asso. dir. surgery Ancker Hosp., St. Paul, 1962-66; mem. staff Bexar County, Santa Rosa, San Antonio Chest hosps. Cons., Tex. State Chest Hosp., San Antonio, 1966—. Pres., P.T.A., San Antonio, 1963; mem. Common Cause. Served with USNR, 1945-46. N.Y. Med. Sch. scholar, 1949-53; Am. Cancer Soc. advanced clin. fellow, 1959-61. Diplomate Am. Bd. Surgery, 1961. Fellow A.C.S.; mem. Am. Coll. Chest Physicians, A.M.A., Tex., Bexar County, med. assns., San Antonio, Minn., Mpls., St. Paul, Central, Tex. surg. socs., Soc. Nuclear Medicine, Soc. U. Surgeons, Am. Assn. History Medicine, Am. Assn. Surgery Trauma, Soc. Surgery Alimentary Tract, Sigma Xi, Phi Gamma Delta, Phi Chi, Alpha Epsilon Delta. Contbr. articles to profl. jours. Home: 1115 Grey Oak Dr San Antonio TX 78213 Office: 7703 Floyd Curl Dr San Antonio TX 78284

ROOT, LLOYD WARREN, JR., electronics engr.; b. Appleton, Wis., Sept. 5, 1933; s. Lloyd Warren and Lillian Alice (Hume) R.; B.E.E., U. Dayton, 1956; M.S., U. Ala., 1971; m. Marjorie Ann Sikorski, Nov. 22, 1958; children—Michael, Christopher, Jennifer, Sarah. Electronics engr. So. Asso. Engrs., Huntsville, Ala., 1958-60; chief engr. WAFG-TV, Huntsville, 1960; electronics engr. U.S. Army Missile Command, Redstone Arsenal, Ala., 1960—. Pres., Madison County Tb Assn., 1961-63; scoutmaster Troop 93 Boy Scouts Am., 1961-63, dist. rep., 1964-66; v.p. Madison Pike P.T.A., 1973. Served to 1st lt., AUS, 1956-58. Mem. Nat. Speleological Soc. (life), I.E.E.E. (dir. Huntsville chpt. 1964-66), Electronic Warfare Assn. (pres. Huntsville chpt. 1965-67), Ala. Acad. Scis., Rocket City Astron. Assn., Sigma Pi Sigma. K.C. (4 deg.). Patents, publs. in field. Home: 528 Harolds Dr NW Huntsville AL 35806 Office: AMSMI RER Bldg 5400 Redstone Arsenal AL 35809

ROOT, VERNON METCALF, tech. publs. exec.; b. Balt., Feb. 11, 1923; s. Francis Metcalf and Barbara (Bradley) R.; B.S., Haverford Coll., 1944; Ph.D., Yale, 1950; m. Elspeth Wood Mainland, Dec. 26, 1966; children—Christopher, Carolyn. Instr. philosophy Lehigh U., Bethlehem, Pa., 1950-52; tech. editor Applied Physics Lab., Johns Hopkins U., Silver Spring, Md., 1952-58, supr. edn. and tng., 1958-64, supr. tech. publs., 1964—. Served with USNR, 1944-46. Fellow Soc. Tech. Writers and Pubs. (chpt. chmn. 1955-56, nat. pres. 1960-62); mem. Council Communication Socs. (pres. 1970-71, 72-73), Am. Philos. Assn. Unitarian (trustee 1965-68). Author: (with E. Clarke) Your Future in Technical and Science Writing, 1972. Home: 5100 Saratoga Av Washington DC 20016 Office: 8621 Georgia Av Silver Spring MD 20910

ROOTS, ORBY GENE, architect; b. San Benito, Tex., Mar. 16, 1927; s. Orby T. and Irene E. (Nystrom) R.; student Brownsville Jr. Coll., 1947-48; B.A., Rice U., 1952, B.S. in Architecture, 1953; m. Rilla Jean White, Apr. 19, 1958; 1 dau., Alissa Robin. Draftsman Cocke-Bowman York, Harlingen, Tex., 1953-54, R.L. Vogler, Corpus Christi, Tex., 1954; chief designer Smyth & Smyth, Corpus Christi, 1954-64; owner Orby G. Roots, Architect, Corpus Christi, 1964—; works include Greenwood Br. Pub. Library, Taft Hosp., Weldon Smith Elementary Sch., Greenwood Park and Swimming Pool. Chmn. Corpus Christi Housing Authority, 1971-73. Mem. adv. bd. Carmelite Day Sch. Served with USAAF, 1945-47. Mem. A.I.A. (pres. Corpus Christi chpt. 1970), Tex. Soc. Architects, Constrn. Specifications Inst. (pres. Corpus Christi chpt. 1973), Soc. Am. Mil. Engrs. Club: Southside Rotary (Corpus Christi). Home: 402 Palmetto St Corpus Christi TX 78412 Office: 1806 S Alameda St Corpus Christi TX 78404

ROPER, CLYDE FORREST EUGENE, curator; b. Ipswich, Mass., Oct. 1, 1937; s. Howard Gleason and Louise Calvey (Norcross) R.; B.A., Transylvania U., 1959; M.S., U. Miami (Fla.), 1962, Ph.D., 1967; m. Ingrid Hilde Braunohler Sept. 13, 1958; children—Erik C., Christopher T. Research asst. Inst. Marine Scis., 1964-66; asso. curator div. mollusks Nat. Mus. Natural History, Smithsonian Inst., Washington, 1966-72, curator div. mollusks, 1972—. Adj. asso. prof. U. Miami, 1968—; adj. lectr. George Washington U., Washington, 1968—; external examiner Meml. U. Nfld., Can., 1970-73. Rep., Vienna Hills Civic Assn. to Town of Vienna, Va., 1971-73. Recipient Distinguished Alumni award Transylvania U., Lexington, Ky., 1970; named an Outstanding Young Man of Am., 1971. Internat. Oceanographic Fedn. fellow, 1960-61, U.S. Bur. Comml. Fisheries fellow, 1961-64. Mem. Systematics Assn., Soc. Systematic Zoology, Biol. Soc. Washington, Am. Soc. Limnology and Oceanography, Am. Malacological Union, Council Systematic Malacologists, Marine Biol. Assn. (U.K.). Editorial bd. Malacologia, 1970—, Malacological Rev., 1970—. Contbr. articles to tech. lit. Office: Nat Mus Natural History Div Mollusks Smithsonian Inst Washington DC 20560

ROPER, JOHN LONSDALE, III, shipyard exec.; b. Norfolk, Va., Jan. 19, 1927; s. John Lonsdale and Sarah (Dryfoos) R.; B.S. in Mech. Engring., U. Va., 1949; B.S. in Naval Architectures, Mass. Inst. Tech., 1951; m. Jane Harman Preston, Sept. 29, 1951; children—John Lonsdale IV, Susan S., Sarah P., Jane H., Katherine Hayward. Asst. supt. Norfolk Shipbldg. & Drydock Corp., 1951-67, v.p., asst. treas., asst. gen. mgr., 1967-69, exec. v.p., gen. mgr., 1969-73, pres., gen. mgr., 1973—. also dir.; pres., dir. Maritime Terminals, Inc.; dir. John L. Roper Estate, Inc., Lonsdale Corp., Cruise Internat., Life Fed. Savs. & Loan Assn., Botetourt Corp., United Va. Bank Internat. Mem. president's adv. council Va. Wesleyan Coll. Bd. dirs. Norfolk chpt.

A.R.C., Jr. Achievement, Norfolk Gen. Hosp., Va. Coll. Fund, United Community Fund; trustee Norfolk Acad. Served with USCGR, 1945-46. Mem. Am. Legion (past post comdr.), Norfolk C. of C., Soc. Naval Architects and Marine Engrs. (past sect. chmn.), Sigma Xi. Episcopalian. Clubs: Norfolk Yacht and Country, Norfolk German, Virginia, Harbor (Norfolk), Princess Anne Country (Virginia Beach, Va.); Propeller of U.S. Home: 8005 Blanford Rd Norfolk VA 23505 Office: PO Box 2100 Norfolk VA 23501

ROPER, RAYMOND WARREN, JR., assn. exec.; b. Springfield, Mo., Apr. 26, 1940; s. Raymond Warren and Mary (Hacker) R.; B.A. cum laude Benedictine Coll., 1961; m. Judith Ann Haynes, Jan. 5, 1963; children—Mark Christopher, Sean Gregory, Douglas Warren. Personnel officer Frisco Ry., Springfield, Mo., 1965-69; dept. dir. U.S. Jaycees, Tulsa, Okla., 1969-72, exec. v.p., 1972—. Commnr. Springfield (Mo.) Human Rights Commn., 1969. Trustee, sec.-treas. U.S. Jaycees War Meml. Fund; trustee U.S. Jaycees Found. Served with AUS, 1963. Mem. Am. Soc. Assn. Execs. Rotarian. Home: 227 E 27th St Tulsa OK 74114 Office: PO Box 7 Tulsa OK 74102

ROPPOLO, JOHN WAYNE, hosp. adminstr.; b. Waco, Tex., Apr. 1, 1939; s. Joseph Louis and Lydia (Perry) R.; B.A., Baylor U., 1961; postgrad., Tex. Tech. U., 1961-62; m. Marilyn Frances Royce, Apr. 12, 1964; children—Robin Rene, Joseph William, John Mark, Mary Beth. Pub. relations asst. Baylor U., 1959-61; editorial asst. Tex. Cath., Dallas, 1961; asst. dir. pub. information Tex. Technol. Coll., Lubbock, 1961-62; dir. pub. relations St. Paul Hosp., Dallas, 1963-68, asst. adminstr. pub. relations and devel., 1971-73, v.p. pub. relations and devel., 1973—; adminstrv. asst. for pub. relations and vols. Dallas County Hosp. Dist., Dallas, 1968-71. Clin. asso. prof. hosp. med. care U. Tex. S. W. Med. Sch., 1960-71. Mem. pub. relations adv. com. Dallas Area Tb, 1971, Dallas County Met. United Fund, 1971-72; mem. Dallas Diocesan Bd. Edn., 1972—; v.p. St. Monica Home and Sch. Assn., 1972—. Bd. dirs. Dallas chpt. Am. Heart Assn. Mem. Pub. Relations Soc. Am. (treas., pres. N. Tex. chpt., assemblyman), Tex. Soc. Hosp. Pub. Relations Dirs. (1st pres.), Press Club Dallas, Am., Tex. hosp. assns., Dallas-Ft. Worth Hosp. Jour. Club (chmn.), Dallas Hosp. Council (pub. relations chmn.), Tex. Conf. Cath. Health Facilities (program chmn.), Am. Soc. Hosp. Pub. Relations Dirs., N. Dallas C. of C. (dir.), Sigma Delta Chi. K.C. Club: Dallas Baylor. Home: 3227 Grantwood Dallas TX 75229 Office: 5909 Harry Hines Blvd Dallas TX 75235

RORSCHACH, HAROLD E., lawyer, engr.; b. Parsons, Kan., Mar. 21, 1896; s. Emil and Emma (Roush) R.; student Tulsa U., 1929-32, Okla. Sch. Bus., 1922-24; m. Margaret Hermes, Aug. 25, 1919; children—Robert Louis, Harold E., Richard G. Constrn. and cons. engr., 1916-25; admitted to Okla. bar, 1932, U.S. Supreme Ct. bar, 1935, 9th and 10th Circuit Cts. Appeal, Ct. Claims of U.S., also U.S. Tax Ct., Gen. Accounting Office; pres., dir. Panhandle Producing Co., Ajax Investment Co.; pres., gen. counsel Colonial Royalties Co., sec. Nemaha Investment Corp.; counsel Transwestern Mining Co. Registered profl. engr., Okla. Mem. Am. (life), Okla. bar assns., Nat. Rifle Assn. (endowment mem.), Am. Inst. Mining, Metall. and Petroleum Engrs. (life, legion of honor 1973), Ind. Petroleum Assn. Am., Okla. Ind. Petroleum Assn. (dir., chmn. legislative com.), Mem. Christian Ch. Mason (Shriner). Contbr. articles to engring. and legal publs. Home: 2544 S Norfolk St Tulsa OK 74114 Office: Resource Sciences Center Tulsa OK also 1100 River Oaks Bank & Trust Bldg 2001 Kirby Dr Houston TX also Fisk Bldg Amarillo TX 79102

ROSARIO, IGNACIO R., accountant; b. San Juan, P.R., Oct. 22, 1933; s. Ignacio R. and Eladia (Ramos) R.; B.B.A., U. Tex. at El Paso, 1965; M. Accounting, Tex. Christian U., 1974; m. Maylo Hernandez, June 7, 1960; children—Maylo, Melissa. Sr. accountant Bixler, Carlton & Rister, 1965-68; partner Hollifield, Wise & Rosario, 1968-71; pvt. practice pub. accounting, Ft. Worth, 1971—. Dir. Jackson Sq. Nursing Centers of Tex., Inc. Served with AUS, 1953-61. Mem. Am. Inst. C.P.A.'s, Tex. Soc. C.P.A.'s. Club: Ft. Worth Sertoma (dir. 1971-72). Home: 2804 Las Vegas Trail Fort Worth TX 76116 Office: 1401 Ballinger St Fort Worth TX 76102

ROSBOROUGH, ROBERT FRANKLIN, oil co. exec.; b. Marshall, Tex., Dec. 24, 1904; s. James Craig and Hazel (Bonham) R.; B.S., Tex. A. and M. U., 1926; m. Marie Watson, Aug. 5, 1933; 1 dau., Gail (Mrs. Henri A. Meis, Jr.). Owner, Rosborough & Byrne Ins. Agy., 1929-44; v.p. Marshall Fed. Savings & Loan Assn., 1955-67; owner Rosborough Oil Co., Marshall, Tex., 1952—; dir. Peoples State Bank. Pres., Community Chest, 1949; co-chmn. Bond drive, 1965; mem. Citizens Com., 1965. Trustee Marshall Meml. Hosp. Served to capt. USAAF, 1942-46. Mem. Tex. A. and M. U. Ex-Students Assn. (regional dir. 1956-58). Methodist (steward 1947—). Mason, Rotarian. Club: Marshall Country (pres. 1939). Home: 402 Miller Dr Marshall TX 75670 Office: 505 E Travis St PO Box 356 Marshall TX 75670

ROSE, BEATRICE SCHROEDER (MRS. WILLIAM H. ROSE), harpist; b. Ridgewood, N.J., Nov. 15, 1922; d. Henry Willian and Ida (LeHovey) Schroeder; student Inst. Mus. Art, 1940-41; studied with Lucile Lawrene and Carlos Salzedo; student (scholar) Mannes Coll. Music, 1944; m. William Harrison Rose, Apr. 10, 1954; 1 son, Daniel. Concert and radio debut N.Y. World's Fair, 1939; soloist, Damrosch Music Appreciation Hour Broadcast, 1940, for Duke Windsor's Save the Children Fund Gov. House, Nassau, Bahamas, 1941; asso. harpist Radio City Music Hall Orch., N.Y.C., 1944-50; various radio and solo performances N.Y. area, 1944-51; concert artist, Italy, U.S. and Can., 1952, 53; prin. harpist Houston Symphony, 1953—; harp instr. U. Houston, 1953—; mem. Contemporary Music. Soc., soloist, 1959, 60; soloist Houston Chamber Orch., 1969; founder, dir. Houston Harp Ensemble. Sec. Craigwood Civic Club, 1957. Recipient 1st prize Fed. Music Clubs Contest, 1936; winner N.Y. Hour of Music award, 1945. Mem. Coll. Music Soc., Am. Harp Soc. (charter, pres. Houston chpt. 1966-67), Phi Beta. Author (with Grace Follet) Outline of Six-Year Harp Course for Elementary, Jr. and Sr. High School, 1966. Composer: Enchanted Harp, 1955; also recs. for Houston Symphony, Stokowski, Everest and Capitol records. Home: 1315 Friarcreek Lane Houston TX 77055 Office: care of Houston Symphony Jones Hall Houston TX 77002

ROSE, BENJAMIN LACY, clergyman, educator; b. Fayetteville, N.C., Dec. 12, 1914; s. Charles Grandison and Irene (Lacy) R.; A.B., Davidson Coll., 1935, D.D.; B.D., Union Theol. Sem. in Va., 1938, Th.M., 1950, Th.D., 1955; postgrad. Columbia, Union Theol. Sem., N.Y.C., Princeton Theol. Sem.; D.D., King Coll.; m. Anne Claiborne Thompson, June 23, 1938; children—Anne Claiborne (Mrs. J. Michael Vosler), Margaret Rockwell (Mrs. J. Robert Day), Lucy Atkinson, Benjamin Lacy. Ordained to ministry Presbyn. Ch. in U.S., 1938; pastor in Chinquapin, Bethel, Beulaville, N.C., 1938-41, Central Presbyn. Ch., Bristol, Va., 1946-55, 1st Presbyn. Ch., Wilmington, N.C., 1955-56, Lake Waccamaw (N.C.) Presbyn. Ch., 1969-70; Benjamin Rice Lacy profl. pastoral leadership and homiletics Union Theol. Sem. in Va., Richmond, 1956—, also trustee; in-parish-resident profl. Wrightsville Beach (N.C.) Presbyn. Ch., gen. pastor, Wilmington Presbytery, 1973—. Chmn. Bd. Nat. Ministries, Gen. Assembly Presbyn. Ch. U.S.; moderator 111th Gen. Assembly, So. Presbyn. Ch., 1971-72. Past trustee Peace Coll., Raleigh, N.C., St. Andrews Presbyn. Coll., Laurinburg, N.C. Served with AUS, 1941-46; ETO; col. Res. Decorated Bronze Star medal, Legion of Merit. Mem. Assn. Sem. Profs. in Practical Fields (past sec.-treas.). Author: Confirming Your Call. Editor Questions Column, Presbyn. Survey mag. Office: 25 W Oxford St Wrightsville Beach NC 28480

ROSE, CHARLES ALEX, lawyer; b. Louisville, June 14, 1932; s. Hector Edward and Mary (Shepard) R.; B.A., U. Louisville, 1954, J.D., 1960; m. Patricia Lechleiter, Apr. 24, 1954; children—Marc Alexander, Craig Allen, Lorna Jean, Gordon Curtis. Admitted to Ky. bar, 1960, since practiced in Louisville; mem. firm C. A. Rose, 1960-63, Jones, Ewen, MacKenzie & Peden, 1963-65, Curtis & Rose, 1965—. Served with USAF, 1954-56. Mem. Ky., Louisville, Am. bar assns., Nat. Ry. Hist. Soc. (dir.), Pi Kappa Phi, Phi Alpha Delta, Omicron Delta Kappa. Republican. Episcopalian. Clubs: Wildwood Country; Pendennis. Home: 2728 Riedling Dr Louisville KY 40206 Office: Marion Taylor Bldg Louisville KY 40202

ROSE, CHARLES GRANDISON III, congressman; b. Fayetteville, N.C., Aug. 10, 1939; s. Charles Grandison, Jr. and Anna Frances (Duckworth) R.; A.B., Davidson Coll., 1961; LL.B., U. N.C., 1964; m. Sara Louise Richardson, June 30, 1962; children—Charles Grandison IV, Sara Louise. Admitted to N.C. bar, 1964; chief prosecutor Dist. Ct., 12th Jud. Dist., 1967-70; mem. 93d Congress from 7th N.C. dist. Pres. N.C. Young Democrats, 1968. Presbyn. Home: 2802 Millbrook Rd Fayetteville NC 28302 Office: 1724 Longworth Bldg Washington DC 20515

ROSE, DAVID SHEPHERD, bishop; b. Nashville, Mar. 10, 1913; s. Charles Solon and Amy (Payne) R.; B.A., U. of South, 1936, B.D., 1938, D.D., 1959; D.D., Va. Episcopal Sem., 1959; m. Frances Lewis Luce, Jan. 6, 1947; 1 son, Hill Luce. Ordained to ministry P.E. Ch., 1938; rector in Memphis, 1938-39, Pensacola, Fla., 1939-42; asst. to bishop of Fla., 1946-48; rector, Corpus Christi, Tex., 1948-58; suffragan bishop Diocese of So. Va., 1958-64, bishop coadjutor 1964-71, bishop, 1971—. Trustee Va. Theol. Sem., U. of South, St. Paul's Coll., Lawrenceville, Va. Served to maj., chaplain, AUS, 1943-46. Home: 6603 Caroline St Norfolk VA 23505 Office: 600 Talbot Hall Rd Norfolk VA 23505

ROSE, DONALD FREDERICK, architect; b. Waco. Tex., May 21, 1940; s. Adolf Frederick and Lela Pauline (Crow) R.; B.A. (Hayden scholar), Rice U., 1962, B. Arch., 1963; m. Teresa Diane Belt, June 3, 1967; children—Lloyd Frederick, Jamie Adele. Architect firm Bush and Witt, Waco, 1963-67, firm Thomas E. Stanley, Dallas, 1967-68, firm Jarvis, Putty, Jarvis, Dallas, 1968-71, firm Bush and Dudley, Architects, Engrs., Inc., Waco, 1971—. Served with USAF, 1963-64. Baptist (deacon 1972—). Home: 210 N 30th St Waco TX 76710 Office: 406 Citizens Tower Waco TX 76710

ROSE, JERRY KENT, broadcasting co. exec.; b. Terrell, Tex., July 31, 1941; s. William Flenoy and Jackie Velma (Humphrys) R.; student Paris Jr. Coll., 1960-61, N. Tex. State U., 1963; m. Shirley Jean Rider, Aug. 6, 1967; children—Jeffrey Todd, Trevor Lane. Prodn. asst. Sta. KERA-TV, Dallas, 1963; staff announcer KMAP-FM, Century Broadcasting, Dallas, 1964, KGAF-AM, Gainesville, Tex., 1964; prodn. asst. WFAA-TV, Bele Corp., Dallas, 1965-67; producer, dir. KDTV-TV, Doubleday Broadcasting, Dallas, 1967-70; program mgr. KROD-TV, Doubleday Broadcasting, El Paso, Tex., 1970-73; network operations mgr. KXTX-TV, Christian Broadcasting, Dallas, 1973—. Mem. faculty U. Tex., El Paso, 1973. Mem. broadcast devel. com., licensed minister Assemblies of God. Bd. dirs. Teen Challenge, El Paso, 1972-73, Dallas, 1973. Served with USCGR, 1963-69. Recipient award for comml. campaign, El Paso Advt. League, 1972. Home: 2510 El Cerrito Dallas TX 75228 Office: 3707 Haggar Way Dallas TX 75209

ROSE, JOHN DANIELS, JR., tobacco co. exec.; b. Henderson, N.C., May 14, 1919; s. John Daniels and Frances (Abbitt) R.; student U. N.C., 1937; m. Anne Whitehurst Mills, June 21, 1941; children—John Daniels III, David M., Cindy Claire. Foreman, J.P. Taylor Co., Henderson, 1938, tobacco buyer, 1948-54, br. mgr., 1954-56, dist. purchasing supr., Richmond, Va., 1957-61, v.p., 1959; v.p. Southwestern Tobacco Co., 1960; v.p. Universal Leaf Tobacco Co., Inc., Richmond, 1970-73; dir., 1973—; pres. Rose Gin Supply Co., Henderson, 1966—. Trustee Maria Parham Hosp., Henderson. Served to 1st lt. AUS, 1942-45. Baptist. Club: Henderson Country. Mailing Address: 327 Lakeview Dr Henderson NC 27536 Office: Hamilton St at Broad St Richmond VA 23260 327 Lakeview Dr Henderson NC 27536

ROSE, LEO, wholesale and retail toy distbn. co. exec.; b. Mpls., Mar. 11, 1921; s. Philip L. and Rose (Weisler) R.; student San Antonio Night Bus. Sch., 1938-40; m. Marjorie Ringel, June 3, 1966; children—Kenny, Laurie, Cathy, Julie, Nancy, Stephen. Salesman, Shiner-Sien Paper Co., San Antonio, 1938-42; founder, partner Lachman-Rose Co., Inc., San Antonio, 1946-71; pres. Lachman-Rose Co., subsidiary W.R. Grace & Co., San Antonio, 1971—; v.p. leisure-performance group W.R. Grace Co., pres. toy/hobby/housewares div. Co-owner San Antonio Spurs basketball team. Div. chmn. San Antonio United Fund drive, 1971—, also dir., 1973, 74. Pres. San Antonio Jewish Community Center, 1968-71; gen. co-chmn. Jewish Social Service Fedn. San Antonio, 1972-73, chmn., 1974—; active Nat. Conf. Christians and Jews, Community Guidance Council, Research and Planning Council; trustee Bexar County Hosp. Dist. Employee Pension Trust. Served with USAAF, 1942-45. Decorated Air medal with 4 oak leaf clusters, D.F.C. with 2 oak leaf clusters; recipient Nat. Conf. Christians and Jews Brotherhood award, 1974. Jewish religion (past dir. temple). Kiwanian. Home: 8 Lazy Lane San Antonio TX 78209 Office: 3200 E Houston St San Antonio TX 78295

ROSE, WARREN LEE, investment co. exec.; b. Richmond, Va., Nov. 19, 1939; s. John Herbert and Irma Lee (Reid) R.; student U. Richmond, 1957-60; m. Barbara Marie McDonnell, Mar. 5, 1960; children—Warren Lee, Joseph Lee, Frank Lee, Barbara Marie. With Davenport & Co., mems. N.Y. Stock Exchange, Richmond, Va., 1957-63; mgr. municipal bond dept. Investment Corp. of Va., mems. N.Y. Stock Exchange, Norfolk, 1963—, v.p., sec., dir., 1968—. Mem. Bond Club Va. (dir.), Nocturnal Adoration Soc. (pres. Norfolk chpt.). Roman Catholic. Clubs: St. Pius X Mens (pres.); Virginia (dir.). Home: 1672 Sheppard Av Norfolk VA 23518 Office: 5 Main Plaza E Norfolk VA 23518

ROSE, WESLEY HERMAN, music pub.; b. Chgo., Feb. 11, 1918; s. Fred and Della (Braico) R.; B.S. in Accounting, Walton Sch. Commerce, 1939; m. Margaret Erdelyan, Nov. 16, 1940; 1 dau., Scarlett (Mrs. John Neil Brown). Accountant, Standard Oil of Ind., 1944-45; gen. mgr. Acuff-Rose Pub., Inc., Nashville, 1945-51, partner, 1951—; with Hickory Records, Inc., Nashville, 1953—, pres., 1961—; pres. Fred Rose Music, Inc., Nashville, 1961—, Acuff-Rose Far East, Inc., Nashville, 1966—, Acuff Rose Internat., Inc., Nashville, 1966—, dir. fgn. affiliated firms; v.p., dir. Harry Fox Agy., N.Y.C.; dir. 1st Am. Nat. Bank. Mem. med. bd. Vanderbilt U. Bd. dirs. Country Music Found. Named Country Music Man of Yr., Billboard mag., 1963; Metronome award Mayor Nashville, 1967. Mem. Country Music Assn. (founding mem., dir. 1958—; chmn. bd. 1959, 60, 63, v.p. 1968), A.S.C.A.P. (bd.), Nat. Music Pubs. Assn. (bd.), Nat. Assn. Rec. Arts and Scis. (nat. trustee; pres. 1971-72), Country Music Assn. (dir.), Nashville area C. of C. (gov. 1969—). Club: Friar's. Lion. Home: Belle Harbor Dr Hendersonville TN 37075 Office: 2510 Franklin Rd Nashville TN 37204

ROSE, WILLIAM DAKE, editor, geologist; b. Nashville, Mar. 15, 1928; s. William Dake and Alice Catherine (Arnold) R.; A.B., Vanderbilt U., 1950, M.S., 1953; m. Virginia Joy Owen, Dec. 19, 1952; children—Barbara Ann (Mrs. Stephen Kenneth Downs), Paul James, Mary Alice. Petroleum geologist Gulf Oil Corp., Ft. Worth and Midland, Tex., 1953-56, Ky. Geol. Survey, Henderson, 1956-66; geol. editor Ky. Geol. Survey, Lexington, 1966-70, Okla. Geol. Survey, Norman, 1970—. Served with AUS, 1946-48, 50-52. Fellow Geol. Soc. Am., mem. Am. Inst. Profl. Geologists (v.p. Okla. sect. 1972-73, pres. 1973-74), Assn. Earth Sci. Editors (sec. treas. 1968-71), Am. Assn. Petroleum Geologists. Home: 705 Westridge Terrace Norman OK 73069 Office: 830 Van Vleet Oval Norman OK 73069

ROSEBOOM, EUGENE HOLLOWAY, JR., geologist, govt. ofcl.; b. Columbus, O., Sept. 21, 1926; s. Eugene Holloway and Thelma (Matheny) R.; B.S., Ohio State U., 1949, M.S., 1951; Ph.D., Harvard, 1958; m. Joan Margret Bradley Farrow, Feb. 8, 1958; children—Stephen, Jennifer, Christopher, Adrian. Research geologist U.S. Geol. Survey, Washington, 1959-74, regional geologist, eastern region, Reston, Va., 1974—. Served with USNR, 1944-46. Post-doctoral fellow Carnegie Inst. Washington, 1956-59. Mem. Geol. Soc. Washington (v.p. 1970), Geochem. Soc., Am. Geophys. Union, Am. Mineral. Soc., Soc. Econ. Geologists. Home: 5502 Beech Av Bethesda MD 20014 Office: US Geol Survey Reston VA 22092

ROSELAND, PAUL LUTHER, furniture co. exec., artist; b. Viroqua, Wis., May 11, 1917; s. Luther M. and Alida B. (Anderson) R.; student Augsburg Coll., 1935-37; B.A., U. Minn., 1941; M.F.A., U. So. Cal., 1960; postgrad. U. Mexico, 1937, U. Cal. at Los Angeles, 1959; m. Evelyn Marie Sandberg, Aug. 30, 1942; children—Nancy Lynn, Paul Luther. Exhibited one-man show at Tex. Woman's U., 1962; exhibited two man show at U. So. Cal., 1960; exhibited group shows at Ball State Coll., 1961, Beaumont Art Mus., 1961, S.W. Am. Painting and Sculpture, Okla., 1962; represented in permanent collections at City of Los Angeles, also pvt. collections; regional mgr. Knoll Internat., N.Y.C., 1945-49; mgr. Western states Herman Miller Inc., Zeeland, Mich., 1949-59; asso. prof. art Tex. Womens U., 1961-67; prof. art Tex. Technol. U., Lubbock, 1968-71; mgr. ion div. Am. Desk Mfg. Co., Temple, Tex., 1972—. Vis. prof. design Ohio U., 1967-68. Served from ensign to lt., USNR, 1942-45. Mem. Am. Inst. Interior Designers. Lutheran. Home: 2114 S 5th St Temple TX 76501

ROSEN, IRVING LOUIS, physician; b. New Orleans, Mar. 28, 1928; s. Ulrich and Jeanette Blanche (Cohen) R.; B.S., Tulane U., 1947, M.D., 1949; m. Carol Lise Brenner, Mar. 9, 1957; children—Elizabeth Lynn, Edith Louise. Intern, Touro Infirmary, New Orleans, 1949-50; resident, 1950-54, staff mem., charge electrocardiographic research lab., 1955-62; resident Charity Hosp., New Orleans, 1950-54; practice medicine specializing in internal medicine and cardiology, New Orleans, 1955—; partner Fisher Rabin Med. Center, New Orleans; asst. clin. prof. La. State U. Sch. Medicine. Served to capt., M.C., USAF, 1951-52. USPHS research grantee, 1960-62. Fellow A.C.P., Am. Coll. Chest Physicians, Am. Coll. Cardiology. Jewish religion (trustee temple). Contbr. articles to profl. jours. Home: 500 Audubon St New Orleans LA 70118 Office: 4015 Jefferson Hwy New Orleans LA 70121

ROSEN, JACK, audiologist, speech pathologist; b. N.Y.C., Jan. 18, 1913; s. Louis and Mollie (Pentasky) R.; student City Coll. N.Y., 1930-36; A.B., Stanford U., 1951, M.A., 1953, Ph.D., 1962; m. Nedda N. Eisman, Dec. 1, 1945. Teaching asst. Stanford Counseling and Testing Center, 1951-52; research dir. San Francisco Hearing and Speech Center, 1952-56; dir. audiologic services Cleve. Hearing and Speech Center, 1956-59; asst. prof. Western Res. U., 1956-59; exec. dir. New Orleans Speech and Hearing Center, 1959—. Mem. profl. services bd. Am. Bds. Examiners in Speech Pathology and Audiology; speech and hearing cons. La. div. Vocational Rehab., La. Bd. Health, Delgado Vocational Rehab. Center; chmn. Council on Specific Learning Disabilities, La. Dept. Edn. Bd. dirs. Cottage Sch.; mem. Workshops and Rehab. Facilities Com. Served with USNR, 1943-45. Mem. Am., La. (past pres.) speech and hearing assns., Acoustical Soc. Am., Am. Cleft Palate Assn., A. G. Bell Assn. for Deaf, Gerontol. Soc. Am., Acad. Rehab. Audiology, Council Exceptional Children, La. Assn. Children with Learning Disabilities, New Orleans Neurol. Soc. (pres.), Assn. Service Programs in Communicative Disorders. Research in galvanic skin response audiometry, auditory disorders of Rh children, speech perception of nerve-deafened, and others. Home: 6818 Canal Blvd New Orleans LA 70124 Office: 1636 Toledano St New Orleans LA 70115

ROSEN, KENNETH ALAN, physician; b. Miami Beach, Fla., June 7, 1945; s. Harry and Lillian Betty (Wilensky) R.; student Emory U., 1962-65; M.D., U. Miami, 1969; m. Lynne Frances Galton, Aug. 26, 1967; 1 dau., Danielle Leigh. Intern, City of Memphis Hosps., 1969-70, resident, 1970-72, chief resident dermatology, 1972-73; attending physician dermatology U. Miami Sch. Medicine, Mt. Sinai Hosp., Miami Beach. Mem. Dade County Med. Assn. Home: 7821 SW 103d Pl Miami FL 33156 Office: 8720 N Kendall Dr Miami FL 33156

ROSEN, KENNETH DAVID, realty co. exec.; b. Boston, Mar. 21, 1929; s. Jacob Morris and Miriam (Belson) R.; B.B.A., Boston U., 1952; m. Patricia Heleene Olsen, Oct. 16, 1956; children—Robin, Britt, Jonathan, Nancy, Robert, Miriam. Mgr. sales David Probinsky Co., Realtors, Wildwood, N.J., 1952-54; founded Greater Miami Realty Inc. (Fla.), 1955, pres., 1955—; pres. Kenneth David Properties, Inc., Miami, 1973—, Dade County Properties, Inc., Miami, 1956—, Rosen-Cabasso, Inc., gen. ins., Miami, 1970—. Mem. Miami Mayor's Auditorium Site Selection Com., 1971; mem. Dade County (Fla.) Planning Bd., 1972-73; chmn. apprenticeship adv. com. Fla. Real Estate Commn., 1972-73. Mem. Democratic Party Nat. Conv. Com., 1971-72. Trustee Lands for People. Served with AUS, 1946-47. Mem. Miami Bd. Realtors (realtor of year 1971, pres. 1971-72), S. Fla. Council Real Estate Bds. (chmn. 1971). Jewish religion (trustee temple). Mason (32 deg., Shriner). Home: 4730 Santa Maria St Coral Gables FL 33146 Office: Greater Miami Realty Inc 3746 W Flagler St Miami FL 33134

ROSEN, SEYMOUR MICHAEL, govt. ofcl.; b. N.Y.C.; s. Harry Francis (stepfather) and Sonia (Sarakowska) Dwyer; A.B., Brown U., 1950; M.A., Columbia, 1952, certificate Russian Inst., 1952; m. Elizabeth Henrietta Meyer, June 6, 1950; children—Edith Vivien, Kenneth Adlai, Julie Ann. Research analyst Soviet area U.S. Dept. State, Washington, 1953-56; sr. social sci. research analyst Library of Congress, Washington, 1957-59; specialist in comparative edn. for USSR and Eastern Europe, Office Edn., U.S. Dept. Health, Edn., and Welfare, Washington, 1960—. Vis. lectr. Fgn. Service Inst., U.S. Dept. State, 1963-65, Am. U., 1963, Loyola Coll., Balt., Md., 1963, Mich. State U., 1963, McGill U., Montreal, Que., Can., 1964; chmn. U.S. delegation to study Soviet edn. system, U.S.S.R., 1963. Served with USNR, 1942-46. Mem. Am. Assn. Advancement Slavic Studies, Comparative and Internat. Edn. Soc. Author: Higher Education in the USSR, 1963; Part-time Education in the U.S.S.R.; Evening and

Correspondence Study, 1965; Education and Modernization in the USSR, 1971; also articles. Editor: Soviet Edn., 1968-69. Home: 9801 Culver St Kensington MD 20795 Office: 7th and D St SW Washington DC 20202

ROSENAU, JACK CLAYTON, hydrologist; b. Detroit, Oct. 26, 1919; s. Arthur Henry and Florence (McNally) R.; B.S., Mich. State U., 1949; m. Jean Louise Aitkenhead, Sept. 6, 1945; children—Andrew, Ann (Mrs. Gregg Stanton), James, Robert, David, Steven, Sandra. Geologist, Mich. Geol. Survey, Lansing, 1949-52, 53-54; pub. relations staff Abrams Aerial Survey Co., Lansing, 1952-53; resident geologist Mackinac Bridge, D.B. Steinman, cons. engr., St. Ignace, Mich., 1954-56; hydrologist U.S. Geol. Survey, Trenton, 1956-62, Honolulu, 1962-69, Tallahassee, 1969—. Pres., Rosenau Mokulele Corp., Honolulu, 1968-73. Mem. Aloha Council Boy Scouts Am., 1962-69. Served with USMCR, 1940-45; lt. col. USAF Res. Fellow Geol. Soc. Am., mem. Gen. Aviation Council Hawaii, Nat. Water Well Assn., Internat. Assn. Hydrogeologists. Author: Geology and Ground Water Resources of Salem County, N.J., 1969; The Water Resources of North-Central Oahu, Hawaii, 1971. Home: 1177 Old Ford Dr Tallahassee FL 32301 Office: 903 W Tennessee St Tallahassee FL 32304

ROSENBAUM, DAVID MARK, govt. ofcl.; b. Boston, Feb. 11, 1935; s. Fredrick and Elizabeth (Gelman) R.; Sc.B., Brown U., 1956; M.S., Rensselaer Poly. Inst., 1958; postgrad. Harvard, 1958-60; Ph.D., Brandeis U., 1964; m. Karen Jeanne Smith, Dec. 27, 1964; children—Benjamin Micah, Shoshana Elizabeth. Asst. prof. Boston U., 1964-65; mem. sr. staff Inst. for Def. Analyses, Arlington, Va., 1965-67; expert Office Emergency Preparedness, Washington, 1967-68; asso. prof. Poly. Inst. Bklyn., 1968-69; pres., chmn. bd. Network Analysis Corp., Glen Cove, N.Y., 1968-70; sr. staff mem. Mitre Corp., McLean, Va., 1970-72; asst. dir. Dept. Justice, Washington, 1972-73; cons. AEC, Bethesda, Md., 1973—. Del., Va. Democratic Conv., 1972. Mem. program adv. com. Pub. Utilities Commn., Arlington, Va., 1972-73. Recipient Appreciation certificate Exec. Office Pres., 1968. Asso. editor Networks, an Internat. Jour., 1970. Contbr. articles to profl. jours. Home: 4713 Rock Spring Rd Arlington VA 22207 Office: AEC 7920 Norfolk St Bethesda MD 20545

ROSENBAUM, STANLEY, educator; b. Denver, Oct. 1, 1910; s. Louis and Anna (Block) R.; A.B., Harvard, 1931; M.A., U. Denver, 1932; m. Mildred Ruth Bookholtz, Nov. 27, 1938; children—David, Jonathan, Alvin, Michael. Theatre mgr. partner, Muscle Shoals Theatres (later Rosenbaum Theatres), Florence, Ala., 1932-60; mem. faculty Florence (Ala.) State U., 1961—, asst. prof. English. Pres., Ala. Council Human Relations, Florence, 1963, 64; state co-chmn. Nat. Council Christians and Jews; finance chmn. Tennessee Valley council Boy Scouts Am., 1959-60; pres. Muscle Shoals Diabetic Assn., 1968, Muscle Shoals Area Fine Arts Council, 1970-71; treas. Florence-Lauderdale County Library Bd., 1945—, Muscle Shoals Regional Library Bd., 1947—; co-chmn. Florence Lauderdale County United Fund Drive, 1952; pres. Muscle Shoals Mental Health Assn., 1967, 68. Jewish religion (pres. congregation). Mem. B'nai B'rith (state pres., dist. treas., dist. comptroller). Club: Exchange (past pres.). Home: 117 Riverview Dr Florence AL 35630 Office: Dept English Florence State Univ Florence AL 35630

ROSENBERG, ADOLPH, editor, publisher; b. Albany, Ga., Aug. 14, 1911 Aaron Leon and Anna (Bercovicci) R.; A.B., U. Ga., 1932. Editorial staff Albany Herald, 1931-32, U.S. Daily, Washington, 1932-33, Atlanta Jour., 1934-40, Atlanta Constn., 1941-42; editor So. Israelite, Atlanta, 1940-42, 45—, pub. 1951—; pres. Star Printing Co., 1954—. Served with USAAF, 1942-45. Mem. Am. Jewish Press Assn. (treas., sec., pres. bd. dirs.), Zionist Orgn. Am., Am. Jewish Com., Jewish War Vets., Atlanta Hist. Soc., Ga. Scholastic Press Assn. (pres. 1929), Sigma Delta Chi, Phi Kappa Phi. Deocrat. Mason (32 deg.); mem. B'nai B'rith. Club: Atlanta Press. Home: 1301 Juniper St NE Atlanta GA 30309 Office: 390 Courtland St NE Atlanta GA 30303

ROSENBERG, DENNIS MELVILLE LEO, surgeon; b. Johannesburg, South Africa, Jan. 27, 1921; s. Nathan and Dorothy (Lee) R.; B.Sc. with honors, U. Witwatersrand, South Africa, 1941, M.B., B.Ch., 1945; m. Jeanna Van der Kar, Jan. 1947. Came to U.S., 1946, naturalized, 1953. Intern Johanesburg Gen. Hosp., 1946; resident in surgery Tulane U. Ochsner Found. Hosp., New Orleans, 1947-51; Childrens Hosp., Johannesburg, 1952; asst. thoracic surgeon Biggs Hosp., Ithaca, N.Y., 1953-54; practice medicine, specializing in cardiovascular and thoracic surgery, New Orleans, 1955—; sr. surgeon Touro Infirmary, New Orleans, 1955—, chief dept. cardiovascular and thoracic surgery, 1972—; surgeon East Jefferson Gen. Hosp., Metairie, La., 1970—, chief dept. cardiovascular and thoracic surgery, 1972—; surgeon, chief dept. cardiovascular and thoracic surgery, St. Charles Gen. Hosp., New Orleans, 1972—; sr. vis. surgeon Charity Hosp., New Orleans, 1962—; sr. investigator Touro Research Inst., 1964—. Served with South African M.C., 1940-45. Fellow A.C.S.; mem. Am. Coll. Chest Surgeons, Am. Coll. Cardiology, A.M.A., Am. Heart Assn., Am. Assn. Thoracic Surgery, So. Thoracic Surg. Assn., Internat. Cardiovascular Soc., Am. Thoracic Soc., Soc. Thoracic Surgeons, Soc. Vascular Surgery, Soc. Internationale de Chirugie. Home: 1550 2d St New Orleans LA 70130 Office: 3600 Prytania St New Orleans LA 70115

ROSENBERG, ELIAS WILLIAM, physician, educator; b. Phila., Mar. 11, 1930; s. Jacob Engel and Rose (Grossman) R.; B.S., Franklin and Marshall Coll., 1952; M.D., U. Pa., 1956; m. Evelyn Izenberg, June 1, 1958; children—Larisa, Jessica, Jonathan. Intern, Phila. Gen. Hosp., 1956-57; resident in dermatology Mass. Gen. Hosp., Boston, 1957-59; fellow U. Miami (Fla.), 1959-60; practice medicine specializing in dermatology, Memphis, 1962-67; prof. dermatology U. Tenn. Coll. Medicine, Memphis, 1967—; cons. VA Hosp., Memphis, U.S. Naval Hosp., Memphis, 1962—. Fellow A.C.P.; mem. Soc. Investigative Dermatology, Am. Dermatol. Assn. Home: 6055 Sweetbriar Cove Memphis TN 38138

ROSENBERG, HARRY, elec. engr., govt. ofcl.; b. Fuerth, Germany, Oct. 19, 1928; s. Otto and Lilly (Arnstein) R.; came to U.S., 1940, naturalized, 1946; B.E.E., Cooper Union Sch. Engring., 1951; postgrad. U. Md., 1951-59, George Washington U., 1971-74; m. Daisy Abelson, June 26, 1960. Elec. engr. Navy Dept. Bur. Ships, Washington, 1951-59, strategic systems projects office, 1959-74, electronic engr., 1970—, also supervisory gen. engr. Registered profl. engr., Va., D.C.; mem. I.E.E.E., Soc. Logistic Engrs., Nat. Soc. Profl. Engrs. Home: 1900 S Eads St Arlington VA 22202 Office: Navy Dept Strategic Systems Project Office Washington DC 20390

ROSENBERG, HARRY ZACHERY, research and devel. co. exec.; b. Buffalo, Jan. 13, 1920; s. Harry Zachery and Anna (Fox) R.; B.Indsl. Engring., Rensselaer Poly. Inst., 1940; m. Eleanor White, July 27, 1967; children—Jeffrey Alan, Andrew Bruce, Toby Jean. With Curtis Wright Corp., Buffalo, 1940-42, Am. Aviation Corp., 1942-44, H.Z. Rosenberg & Co., Buffalo, 1946-58; indsl. sales Am. Internat. Tool Corp., 1958-60; pres. Zackery & Assos., Ft. Lauderdale, cons., 1963-65; co-founder Gray Industries, Inc., Ft. Lauderdale, Fla., 1965-73, exec. v.p., 1965-73, also dir. Chmn. aviation com. Buffalo Jr. C. of C., 1951. Vice pres. United Way Broward County, Fla., 1972, S.E. Fedn. Temple Brotherhoods, 1970-72. Active Nixon campaign com., 1968. Mem. alumni adv. com. Rensselaer Poly. Inst.; bd. dirs. Jewish Edn. and Jewish Fedn. Buffalo, 1956; adv. bd. continuing edn. Nova U., Ft. Lauderdale, 1971—; nat. bd. dirs. Nat. Fedn. Temple Brotherhoods, 1973, 74. Served with AUS, 1944-46. Recipient Alumni award Rensselaer Poly. Inst., 1970. Mem. Am. Inst. Indsl. Engrs. (founder Buffalo and Miami chpts.), Rensselaer Alumni Assn. (pres. Buffalo 1947, South Fla. 1970-72). Jewish religion (trustee, officer temple; founder Temple Beth Am, Amherst, N.Y., pres. 1957-58). Mason. Clubs: Westwood Country (Williamsville, N.Y.); Crystal Lago Country (Pompano Beach, Fla.). Home: 1101 Crystal Lake Dr Pompano Beach FL 33060 Office: 3038 E Commercial Blvd Fort Lauderdale FL 33308

ROSENBERGER, HOMER TOPE, historian, personnel tng. cons.; b. Lansdale, Pa., Mar. 23, 1908; s. Daniel Hendricks and Jennie Kulp (Markley) R.; grad. Albright Coll., 1929, LL.D., 1955; M.A., Cornell U., 1930, Ph.D., 1932; m. Gertrude Pauline Richards, July 14, 1934; children—Arley Jane (Mrs. Harry C. Furminger), Lucretia Hazel (Mrs. Patrick Robert Myers). Tchr. history Tidioute (Pa.) High School, 1930-31; tchr. Adult Night School, Lock Haven, Pa., 1933-35; prof. history and govt. Susquehanna U., summer 1933; ednl. research and adminstrn. U.S., Office Edn., 1935-42; supr. tng. U.S. Bur. Prisons, 1942-57; chief tng. br. Bur. Pub. Rds., Dept. Commerce, 1957-65; mem. steering com. Tng. Officers Conf., U.S. Govt., 1947-67, chmn., 1949-50, 55-57, chmn. com. preparation Tng. Specialists' Directory, 1948-49, exhibits com., 1947, 49; mem. com. on tng., mem. subcom. tng. policy and legislation Fed. Personnel Council, 1949-51; trustee Nat. Inst. for Reading Improvement, 1953-54; mem., vice chmn. Pa. Bd. Pvt. Corr. Schs., 1957-72, chmn., 1972—. Mem. adv. com. on career counseling U.S. Dept. Agr. Grad. Sch., 1965-66; cons. mgmt. Inst. Pub. Adminstrn., N.Y.C., 1963-64; cons. personnel mgmt. United Hosps., Newark, 1960-69, Pa. Dept. Hwys., Pa. Civil Service Commn., State N.Y. Dept. Civil Service. Organizer, moderator Rose Hill Seminars, 1963—; study tour govtl. mgmt. recommendations Western Nigeria, Africa, 1963-64. Mem. Pa. Com. on Correctional Staff Tng., 1955-57; mem. exec. com. corrections sect. United Community Services Washington, 1954-55; dir. Bur. Rehab. Nat. Capital Area, 1951—, pres., 1958-61, mem. exec. com., 1967-71; mem. Civilian Conservation Corps Safety Council, 1938-42; organizer Pa. Hist. Junto, 1942, pres. 1942-46, 54-56, exec. com., 1942—, chmn. program com., 1946-49; mem. Pa. Hist. and Mus. Commn., 1972—; editorial bd. Social Studies Tchrs. Adminstrs., 1949-59. Mem. Pa. Hist. Assn. (mem. governing body 1945—, chmn. membership com., 1943-45, chmn. pubs. com., 1946-48, 51-67, chmn. program com., 1947; pres. 1967-69), Pa. German Soc. (dir. 1949—, v.p. 1952-57, chmn. citation com. 1954-56, pres. 1957-69), Pa. Prison Soc. (exec. com. 1949-65, chmn. award com. 1952-64), Howard League Penal Reform (London), Columbia Hist. Soc. Washington (bd. mgrs. 1953—, 1st v.p. 1959-68, chmn. program com. 1959-68, chmn. exec. com. 1959-68, pres. 1968—). Am. Peace Soc. (dir. 1960—, exec. com. 1961-64, chmn. com. publ. monographs 1963-65), Phi Alpha Theta, Alpha Pi Omega, Phi Delta Kappa, Pi Gamma Mu. United Methodist. Club: Cosmos (hist. com.) (Washington). Author: Testing Occupational Training and Experience, 1948; What Should We Expect of Education, 1956; Techniques for Getting Things Done, 7th edit., 1964; Letters from Africa, 1965; The Pennsylvania Germans, 1891-1965, 1966; Adventures and Philosophy of a Pennsylvannia Dutchman, 1971; Man and Modern Society: Philosophical Essays, 1972; The Philadelphia and Erie Railroad: Its Place in American Economic History, 1974; Mountain Folks: Fragments of Central Pennsylvania Lore, 1974. Editor: Pennsylvania's Contributions to the Professions, 1964; Intimate Glimpses of the Pennsylvania Germans, 1965; Pennsylvania's Contributions to Art, 1967; contbg. editor Pa. History mag., 1943—. Contbr. articles to profl. jours. and mags. Author visual edn. and guidance materials, employee tng. courses and occupational tests. Home: 2121 Massachusetts Av NW Washington DC 20008 Office: 1307 New Hampshire Av NW Washingotn DC 20036

ROSENBLATT, PETER RONALD, lawyer; b. N.Y.C., Sept. 4, 1933; s. William and Therese Amalia (Steinhardt) R.; grad. Riverdale Country Day Sch., 1950; B.A., Yale, 1954, J.D., 1957; postgrad. fellow Tel-Aviv U., 1971; m. Naomi Henriette Harris, July 1, 1952; children—Therese Sarah, Daniel Harris, David Steinhardt. Admitted to N.Y. bar, 1959, D.C. bar, 1969; asst. dist. atty. N.Y. County, 1959-62; asso. Stroock & Stroock & Lavan, N.Y.C., 1962-66; dep. asst. gen. counsel AID, Washington, 1966; mem. White House staff, Washington, 1966-68; jud. officer, chmn. bd. contract appeals U.S. Post Office Dept., Washington, 1968-69; v.p., dir. EDP Technology, Inc., Washington, 1969-71; chmn. Internat. Devel. Service, Washington, 1969-71; spl. cons. to Senator Edmund S. Muskie, 1970-72; mem. firm Wolf & Rosenblatt, Washington, 1972—. Sec., mem. exec. com. Coalition for a Democratic Majority, 1973—. Served to 2d lt. Q.M.C., AUS, 1957-58. Mem. D.C. Bar, Assn. Bar City of N.Y., N.Y. County Lawyers Assn., Am. Bar Assn. Jewish religion. Home: 6431 Western Av NW Washington DC 20015 Office: 1001 Connecticut Av NW Washington DC 20036

ROSENBLOOM, ARLAN LEE, physician, educator; b. Milw., Apr. 15, 1934; s. Harris Phillip and Esther (Schneider) R.; B.A., U. Wis., 1955, M.D., 1958; m. Edith Kathleen Peterson, Sept. 14, 1958; children—Eric David, Maliah Jo, Disa Lynn, Harris Phillip. Intern, Los Angeles County Gen. Hosp., 1958-59; resident gen. practice Ventura County (Cal.) Hosp., 1959-60; physician-in-charge Medico Hosp., Kratie, Cambodia, 1960-61; med. officer, Pahang, Malaysia, 1961-62; resident pediatrics U. Wis. Hosps., Madison, 1962-63, 64-65, fellow pediatric endocrinology, 1963-64, 65-66; mem. USPHS, 1966-68; asst. prof. pediatrics U. Fla., Gainesville, 1968-71, asso. prof., 1971-74, prof., 1974—, asso. dir. Clin. Research Center, 1969-74, dir., 1974—, dir. Nat. Found. March of Dimes Birth Defects Center, 1969-73. Pres., dir. Fla. Camp Children and Youth with Diabetes, 1970—; med. dir. Gainesville Youth Clinic, 1972-74; mem. Fla. Family Planning Council, Fla. Com. Children and Youth, 1972—. Mem. Am. Acad. Pediatrics, Am. Fedn. Clin. Research, Am. (com. pub. edn. and detection 1971-73), Fla. (dirs.) diabetes assns., Alachua County Med. Soc. (chmn. sch. health com. 1972—), Endocrine Soc., Lawson Wilkins Pediatric Endocrine Soc., Soc. Pediatric Research. Contbr. numerous articles to profl. jours. Home: 2902 SW 1st Av Gainesville FL 32601

ROSENBLUTH, MORTON, periodontist; b. N.Y.C., Sept. 28, 1924; s. Jacob and Eva (Bigeleissen) R.; B.A., N.Y.U., 1943, grad. program in periodontia, oral medicine, D.D.S., 1946; m. Sylvia Fradin, July 2, 1946; children—Cheryl Bonnie, Hal Glen. Intern Bellevue Hosp. N.Y.C., 1946-47, resident, 1947; individual practice dentistry, N.Y.C., 1947-59; individual practice periodontia North Miami Beach, Fla., 1960—; periodontist Mt. Sinai Hosp., N.Y., Polyclinic Hosp. and Med. Sch. N.Y., Mt. Sinai Hosp., Miami Beach, Fla., Parkway Gen. Hosp.; chief dental dept. North Miami Gen. Hosp.; chmn. periodontia sect. Dade County Research Center. Lectr. throughout U.S.A., Israel, Mexico, Rome, Teheran, Bangkok, Hong Kong, Tokyo, Honolulu, Jamaica, Paris, London, Sicily, Budapest, Berlin, Luxembourg, South Africa, and others; vis. lectr. U. Tenn. Dental Coll., N.Y.U. Dental Coll.; cons. VA Hosp., Miami; mem. adv. bd. U. Fla. Coll. Dentistry; mem. profl. adv. bd. North Dade Childrens Center, Hope Sch. for Mentally Retarded Children; mem. sci. adv. com. United Health Found. Chmn. Dental div. United Fund of Dade County, Combined Jewish Appeal; nat. chmn. Hebrew U. Sch. Dental Medicine; bd. dirs. Health Planning Council S. Fla. Served with AUS, 1943-44; served as capt. USAF, 1951-52. Diplomate Am. Bd. Periodontology. Fellow Am. Coll. Dentists, Internat. Coll. Dentists; mem. Am. Acad. Periodontology, Am., Fla. socs. periodontists, Am. Assn. Hosp. Dental Chiefs, Am. Acad. Dental Medicine, Am. Soc. Advancement Gen. Anesthesia in Dentistry, Am. Dental Assn., Northeastern Soc. Periodontists, Fla. (chmn. council on legislation), Miami, Miami Beach, East Coast (sec.-treas. 1968, pres. 1971-72), North Dade (pres. 1963-64) dental socs., Fedn. Dentaire Internationale, Fla. Acad. Dental Practice Adminstrn., Alpha Omega (pres. 1967-68, internat. regent 1973—). Jewish religion (trustee congregation 1961-64). K.P., Mason, Kiwanian (dir. 1965). Clubs: Nocoma (pres. 1958-60), N.Y.U. Century (local chmn.). Contbr. articles to profl. jours. Home: 2030 NE 197th Terrace North Miami Beach FL 33160 Office: Profl Center 1100 NE 163d St North Miami Beach FL 33162

ROSENFELD, LOUIS, surgeon; b. Nashville, June 18, 1911; s. David and Minnie (Lowenstein) R.; B.A., Vanderbilt U., 1933, M.D., 1936; m. Helen Werthan, Mar. 7, 1949; children—Roger Werthan Cohn (foster son), Robert Louis. Intern Vanderbilt Hosp., 1936-37, asst. resident, resident surgeon, 1939-42; asst. resident surgeon Beth Israel Hosp., Boston, 1937-39; gen. practice surgery, Nashville, 1946—; prof. clin. surgery Vanderbilt Med. Sch., 1963—; cons. surgeon Thayer VA Hosp., 1947—. Pres. Davidson County unit Am. Cancer Soc., 1965—. Served with AUS, 1942-45. Decorated Bronze Star medal. Diplomate Am. Bd. Surgery. Fellow A.C.S.; mem. Nashville Surg. Soc. (past pres.), Nashville Acad. Medicine (pres. 1969), Soc. Univ. Surgeons, So. Surg. Assn., Soc. Head and Neck Surgeons, Southeastern Surg. Congress, So., Tenn. med. assns., A.M.A., H. William Scott Surg. Soc., Vanderbilt Alumni Assn. (past pres.), Alpha Omega Alpha. Contbr. articles to profl. jours. Home: 4434 Tyne Blvd Nashville TN 37215 Office: 1211 21st Av S Nashville TN 37212

ROSENFIELD, SAM JULIUS, shoe retail chain exec.; b. Galveston, Tex., Sept. 15, 1919; s. Joseph Levy and Helen (Gittelsohn) R.; student U. Tex., 1937-40; m. Annette Leff, Oct. 21, 1942; children—Phyllis (Mrs. Phillip Stoup), Joseph Levy, Sandra. With Kruger Jewelry Co., Austin, Tex., 1940-57, supr., 1946-50, v.p., 1950-57; pres. Pay-Less Shoe Stores, Austin, 1957—; pres. 40 other corps.; dir. Bank Austin. Mem. Grand Jury Assn., 1966—; v.p., chmn. fund raising United Jewish Appeal, 1969-70. Bd. dirs. Hillel Found., 1963-67, Travis County Sch. for Blind, Austin, 1970. Chmn. bldg. com. Temple Beth Israel, 1971-72. Mem. Two-Ten Assn., Jewish Chataugua Soc. Democrat. Jewish religion (pres. temple 1961-63). Mem. B'nai B'rith. Home: 3400 Westledge Circle Austin TX 78731 Office: 2835 Real St Austin TX 78722

ROSENTHAL, HAROLD, govt. ofcl.; b. Bklyn., May 25, 1924; s. Samuel and Anne (Weinstein) R.; B.A., George Washington U., 1949; postgrad., Am. U., 1949-52; m. Maye Feuerstein, Jan. 18, 1948; children—Diana Mikel (Mrs. Francis Daniel Purcell, Jr.), Jean Sylvia. Various fed. positions, 1949-66; chief information services div. Information Center, U.S. Office Econ. Opportunity, 1966-69; asst. to dir. statis. reports and analysis staff Office of Asst. Sec. for Adminstrn., U.S. Dept. Housing and Urban Devel., Washington, 1969—. Statis. cons. pvt. firms. Served with AUS, 1943-46. Mem. Am. Statis. Assn. Home: 6130 31st St NW Washington DC 20015 Office: 451 7th St SW Washington DC 20410

ROSENTHAL, JULIAN BERNARD, lawyer, assn. ofcl.; b. N.Y.C., July 4, 1908; s. Alex Sidney and Katherine (Goodman) R.; student Columbia, 1925-26; LL.B., Fordham U., 1929; m. Frances Stone, Nov. 14, 1941; children—Brian, John L. Admitted to N.Y. State bar, 1931, Ga. bar, 1973; practice in N.Y.C.; now of counsel Javits & Javits. Mem. Air Force Assn., 1945—, life mem., 1946—, sec., 1946-59, chmn. bd. dirs., 1959-60, chmn. constn. com., 1946-72, permanent bd. dirs., 1960—, treas. Iron Gate chpt., 1971-72, recipient Man of Year award, 1953. Govt. appeal agt. SSS, 1943-44. Mem. motion picture div. Democratic Nat. Com., 1940. Past nat. sec. Aerospace Edn. Found.; past treas., bd. dirs. Lydia M. Morrison Found.; formerly v.p., treas., bd. dirs. Vanguard Found.; past chmn. bd. Aerospace Edn. Council, N.Y.C. sec., bd. dirs. Herbert I. and Shirley C. Rosenthal Found. Served with USAAF, 1944-45. Mem. Am. Bar Assn., N.Y. County Lawyers Assn., Assn. Bar City N.Y., Fordham U. Alumni Assn. Home: 37 Olde Ivy Sq Atlanta GA 30342 Office: 1345 Av of the Americas New York City NY 10019

ROSIN, MORRIS, mfg. co. exec.; b. San Antonio, Feb. 21, 1924 Berco and Leia (Dupchansky) R.; student Tex. A. and M. U., 1942, St. Mary's U., 1941-45, 47; m. Ethel Rosenberg, Dec. 15, 1965; children—Susan, Charles, Lindsay. Sec.-treas. Bimbi Mfg. Co., 1949-67; pres. Bimbi Shoe Co. div. Athlone Industries, San Antonio, 1970—; v.p. Athlone Industries, Parsippany, N.J., 1967-72; pres. Ardo Pro, San Antonio, 1966-74, Yoakum Bend Corp., San Antonio, 1968—; sec.-treas. R & R Corp., San Antonio, 1970-72. Served with USAAF, 1942-45. Mason (32 deg., Shriner). Home: 6325 B Bandera Dallas TX 75225 Office: PO Box 12625 Dallas TX 75225

ROSS, BARRY, accountant; b. Phila., Aug. 11, 1942; s. Myron L. and Pearl S. (Layton) Rosenbleeth; B.S. in Bus. Adminstrn., U. Fla., 1964; m. Elaine Chausky, June 19, 1965; children—Sheri, Marc. Accountant S.D. Leidesdorf & Co., N.Y.C., 1964-65; sr. accountant Rashba & Pokart, N.Y.C., 1965-66; auditor Ernst & Ernst, Miami, Fla., 1966-68; with Cavanagh Communities Corp., Miami Beach, Fla., 1968-73, chief adminstrv. and financial officer, 1969, then sr. v.p., treas., dir., mem. exec. com.; mng. partner Ross & Bookspan, Miami, 1973—. Instr. U. Miami, 1969—. C.P.A., N.Y., Fla. Mem. Am. Inst. C.P.A.'s, Fla. Inst. C.P.A.'s, N.Y. State Soc. C.P.A.'s, Miami Jr. C. of C., Nat. Assn. Accountants, Alpha Chi Sigma, Beta Alpha Psi, Tau Epsilon Phi. Mason; mem. B'nai B'rith. Clubs: Jockey, Kings Bay (Miami); Ocean Reef (Key Largo, Fla.); Rotonda West (Fla.). Home: 10590 SW 100th St Miami FL 33156 Office: 3050 Biscayne Blvd Miami FL 33137

ROSS, DAN CONNOR, cable TV co. exec.; b. Indpls., Apr. 20, 1923; s. Connor Dan and Anna (Dennison) R.; student Amherst Coll., 1943-44; B.S., Purdue U., 1946, M.S., 1949; postgrad. Columbia, 1952-53, 59; Dr. Engring., Johns Hopkins U., 1964; m. Deen Dunn, Oct. 12, 1945; children—Douglas, Keith, Kenneth, Alan, Glen, Elizabeth. Instr. elec. engring. Purdue U., 1946-51; instr. U.S. Mil. Acad., 1951-53; engr., exec. Fed. Systems div. IBM, Kingston, N.Y., also Gaithersburg, Md., 1953-69; pres. Ross Telecommunications Engring. Corp., Washington, 1969—; pres. CATV Gen. Corp., Washington, 1971—; instr. Johns Hopkins U., 1960-61, 1964-66, cons. engring. faculty, 1966—. Served with AUS, 1943-46, 51-53. Mem. I.E.E.E., A.A.A.S., Soc. Gen. Systems Research. Clubs: Johns Hopkins (Balt.); Army and Navy (Washington). Contbr. articles to tech. jours. Patentee computer input-output systems; computer data transmission systems; air traffic control and nav. systems. Home: 6308 Maiden Lane Bethesda MD 20034 Office: 1750 Pennsylvania Av NW Washington DC 20006

ROSS, DELOY CORNELIUS, food and beverage co. exec.; b. Leesville, La., Mar. 27, 1925; s. William Cornelius and Josey (Chance) R.; grad. high sch.; m. Louise Burna Lenahan, Sept. 23, 1951; 1 son, Richard Deloy. Owner, W. C. Ross & Son, Anacoco, La., 1940-68; pres., mng. dir. Ross Continental Motor Lodge, Leesville, La., 1965—, Continental Services, Inc., Leesville, La., 1967—; pres. Ross Investment Corp., Leesville, La., 1968—; dir. Mchts. & Farmers Bank, Leesville, La. Mem. Fort Polk Community Relations Council, 1965—. Served with USMCR, 1943-45. Decorated Purple Heart (2). Mem. C. of C. Democrat. Baptist. Lion. Home: Box 83 171 Hwy Anacoco LA 71446 Office: Box 1447 Leesville LA 71446

ROSS, ELWOOD, advt. exec.; b. Bklyn., June 14, 1918; s. Louis and Josephine (DeGorter) R.; student N.Y. U., 1936-38; m. Gwendolyn Faye Durant, Jan. 15, 1964; children—Nan, Alan. Salesman, Sparkes Mfg. Co. Ltd., N.Y.C., 1946-49; owner Ross Distbrs., Dallas, 1949-53; salesman Axel Bros. Inc., Jamaica, N.Y., 1953-60; pres. Pyramid Products Inc., Dallas, 1960-64; pres. Product Promotions, Inc., Dallas, 1964—, Ross Agy., Inc., Dallas, 1967—. Sales cons., various cos.; contbg. columnist Lewisville Leader. Dir. information Town of Flower Mound, 1968-71. Served with USAAF, 1942-45. Mem. Dallas C. of C., Dallas Better Bus. Bur., Dallas Advt. League, Nat. Fedn. Ind. Bus., Dallas All Sports Assn. Clubs: Brookhaven Country, Admirals, Sportsmen's of Texas. Home: Route 3 Roanoke TX 76262 Office: Products Promotions Bldg 11338 Emerald St Dallas TX 75229

ROSS, JAMES MILLER, physician; b. Knoxville, Tenn., July 19, 1938; s. Robert Marshall and Alma (Miller) R.; B.S., East Tenn. State U., 1961; M.D., U. Tenn., 1963; m. Johnnie Sue Vest, Sept. 29, 1961; children—Ann Elizabeth, James Miller, Robert Charles. Intern Martin Army Hosp., Ft. Benning, Ga., 1964, Hickory (N.C.) Meml. Hosp., 1965, now staff mem.; gen. practice medicine, Claremont, N.C., 1966—; mem. staff Catawba Meml. Hosp., Hickory, N.C. Dir. Mar-Loc Corp., Claremont, Sun World Broadcasting Co., Orlando, Fla. Mem. Claremont Zoning Bd., 1971—. Bd. dirs. Lov-N-Care Day Care Center, Newton, N.C. Served to capt., M.C., AUS, 1964-65. Diplomate Am. Bd. Family Practice. Mem. A.M.A., N.C., Catawba County med. socs, Alpha Kappa Kappa, Phi Sigma. Republican. Methodist (steward). Club: Catawba Country (Hickory). Home: E Main St Claremont NC 28610 Office: PO Box 508 Claremont NC 28610

ROSS, JOHN JOSEPH, lawyer; b. St. Johns, N.Y., Apr. 6, 1929; s. John J. and Anna Marie (Heatherton) A.; B.S., Va. Mil. Inst., 1951; LL.B., Georgetown U., 1956; m. Marie B. Katch, July 5, 1954; children—Terence P., Brendan S., Maura A., Kara A. Admitted to D.C. bar, 1956; asso. firm Hogan & Hartson, Washington, 1956-64, partner, 1964—. Dir. Jewell Ridge Coal Sales Co., Tazewell, Va., 1965-66. Chmn. P.L.I. Equal Employment Compliance Programs, 1972, 73; chmn. P.L.I. Affirmative Action Workshop, 1973. Served to maj. USMCR, 1951-54. Decorated Navy Cross, Silver Star. Mem. Am. Fed., D.C. bar assns., Am. Judicature Soc., Am. Acad. Polit. Sci., Newcomen Soc. Clubs: Army-Navy, Belle Haven Country, Metropolitan. Author: Special Problems in the Protection of Trade Secrets in Dealing with the Government, 1966. Home: 7021 Marlan Dr Alexandria VA 22307 Office: 815 Connecticut Av NW Washington DC 20006

ROSS, JOHN TURNER, JR., steel co. exec.; b. Riddlesburg, Pa., Feb. 4, 1918; s. John Turner and Mable (Barnett) R.; B.A., Franklin and Marshall Coll., 1940; postgrad. U. Pa., 1940-41; m. Jeannette Scudder, June 7, 1947; children—George Ann, Leslie Jane, Susan Turner, Elizabeth Lee. With observer corps, U.S. Steel Co., Homestead, Pa., 1947-48; pipe sales Bethlehem Steel Co. (Pa.), 1948-51; mgr. tubular sales Edgcomb Steel Co., Phila., 1951-66; exec. v.p. Johnson City Foundry & Machine Works, Inc. (Tenn.), 1966—, also gen. mgr. Bd. dirs. United Fund, Johnson City. Served to capt. USNR. Mem. Am. Soc. Metals, Nat. Foundry Assn., Am. Ordnance Assn., Am. Foundry Soc., Am. Legion, C. of C. (dir. 1968), Blue Key, Phi Kappa Sigma. Republican, Episcopalian. Mason (Shriner), Rotarian, Elk. Club: Johnson City Country. Home: 705 E Holston Av Johnson City TN 37601 Office: 920 W Walnut St Johnson City TN 37601

ROSS, LEDYARD ELREE, orthodontist; b. Stokes, N.C., July 12, 1925; s. Ledyard Elree and Mildred Celia (Dupree) R.; Jr. Accountant, Hardbargers Bus. Coll., 1946; B.S., East Carolina Coll., 1949; D.D.S., Northwestern U., 1953; M.S. in Orthodontics, U. N.C., 1959; m. Elsie Martiel Congleton, Aug. 1, 1964; children—Dennis Paul, Kathryn Lynn, Jody Martiel, Cindy Beth. Gen. practice dentistry, Ayden, N.C., 1953-54, Greenville, N.C., 1954-57; practice orthodontics, Greenville, 1959—; v.p. Jaro Corp., New Bern, N.C., 1966—; sec.-treas. Bill Haddock Chrysler, Plymouth, Dodge, Greenville; dir. Urban Builders, Norfolk, Va., Utility Distbrs., Inc., Richmond, Va. Served with USMCR, 1943-46. Mem. Am. Dental Assn., N.C., 5th Dist., Pitt and Beaufort County dental socs., Am. Assn. Orthodontics, N.C. Orthodontic Soc. (sec.), Eastern N.C. Orthodontic Study Club (pres. 1963-64), Begg Orthodontic Soc. Methodist (dir. 1961-62, 70-72). Mason, Elk, Kiwanian. Home: 217 Churchill Dr Greenville NC 27834 Office: 602 E 10th St Greenville NC 27834

ROSS, MARY LOU HEATON SKINNER, govt. ofcl.; b. Dalhart, Tex., Dec. 22, 1909; d. Roy Henry and Hazel (Conger) Heaton; B.S. in Edn., U. N.D., 1935; M.P.H. in Health Edn., U. Cal. at Berkeley, 1948; m. Howard Edward Skinner, Jan. 9, 1944 (div. Oct. 1948); m. 2d, C. Philip Ross, Feb. 28, 1973. Dietetic intern Grasslands Hosp., 1935-36; dietitian charge therapeutic diets N.Y. Infirmary for Women and Children, 1936-37; health edn. sec. Yonkers (N.Y.) Tb and Health Assn., 1937-38; exec. sec. Newburgh (N.Y.) Tb and Health Assn., 1938-41; field advisor on local work N.Y. State Com. on Tb and Pub. Health, 1941-44; substitute tchr. Tulare County Schs., Cal., 1944-45; cons. Cal. Tb and Health Assn., 1945-46; asso. in pub. health U. Cal. Sch. Pub. Health at Berkeley, 1947-49; health educator div. dental pub. health USPHS, 1949-52, health edn. cons. regions I and II, N.Y.C., 1953-55, Indian health behavior study, 1955-59, health edn. cons. region IV, Atlanta, 1959—. Adv. com. to Nat. Tng. Labs., N.E.A.; adv. com. Atlanta-Regional Lab. Community Leadership Devel., 1966-67. Fellow Am. Pub. Health Assn. (chmn. health edn. sect. So. br. 1966-67, sect. chmn. program com. 1967), Soc. Pub. Health Educators (treas., 1953-55, eligibility com. 1959-61); mem. Adult Edn. Assn. U.S.A., Soc. for Psychol. Study Social Issues, Commd. Officers Assn. USPHS (v.p. 1970, sec. 1969, pres. Atlanta br. 1971), Internat. Union for Health Edn. of Pub., Delta Omega, Pi Lambda Theta, Nu Delta Pi, Pi Beta Phi. Contbr. articles to profl. jours. Office: Dept Health Education and Welfare USPHS 50th 7th St NE Atlanta GA 30323

ROSS, RONALD DUDLEY, editor; b. Fargo, N.D., Apr. 19, 1921; s. Earle Dudley and Ethel (Newbecker) R.; B.S., Ia. State U., 1943; m. Dorothy Ann Klein, Dec. 24, 1943; children—Ronald Dudley Jr., Elizabeth, Karl M. News editor, staff writer Sci. Service, Washington, 1946-49; Washington corr. McGraw-Hill Washington bur. Elec. World, 1949-51; mng. editor Pub. Power, Am. Pub. Power Assn., Washington, 1951-65, editor, 1965—. Served with USNR, 1943-46. Mem. Soc. Nat. Assn. Publs. (pres. 1968-69), Nat. Assn. Sci. Writers (life), Am. Soc. Bus. Press Editors, Sigma Delta Chi. Democrat. Unitarian. Club: Nat. Press. Home: 1201 N Evergreen St Arlington VA 22205 Office: 2600 Virginia Av NW Washington DC 20037

ROSS, THOMAS BERNARD, newspaper corr.; b. N.Y.C., Sept. 2, 1929; s. Henry M. and Evelyn (Timothy) R.; B.A., Yale, 1951; postgrad. (Nieman fellow) Harvard, 1963-64; m. Gunilla Ekstrand, Nov. 2, 1963; children—Maria, Anne, Kristina. Reporter, Internat. News Service, Atlanta 1955-56, Hartford, Conn., 1956-57, Washington, 1957-58; reporter U.P.I., Washington, 1958; reporter Chgo. Sun-Times, Washington, 1958-68, fgn. corr., Beirut, Lebanon, 1968-69, Paris, France, 1969-70, Washington bur. chief, 1970—. Served to lt. (j.g.) USNR, 1951-54. Recipient Marshall Field award, 1961, 71. Roman Catholic. Author: (with David Wise) The U-2 Affair, 1962; The Invisible Government, 1964; The Espionage Establishment, 1967. Home: 2911 P St NW Washington DC 20007 Office: 1717 Pennsylvania Av Washington DC 20006

ROSS, THOMAS LLEWELLYN, cardiologist; b. Pretoria, Ga., Dec. 31, 1907; s. Thomas L. and Helen (Roberts) R.; B.S., Mercer U., 1926; M.D., Emory U., 1930; m. Rachel Johnson, Aug. 29, 1936; children—Susan (Mrs. Jerry Sawyer), Helen (Mrs. Julian Tolbert). Intern, Cin. Gen. Hosp., 1930-31, resident, 1931-33; practice medicine specializing in cardiology, Macon, Ga., 1935-69; chief cardiology Macon Hosp., 1946-69; asso. dir. Ga. Regional Med. Program, Macon, 1969—; mem. staffs Macon, Middle Ga. hosps. Cons. cardiology Dublin U., 1949-69; founder Macon Heart Clinic, 1948, chief clinic, 1948-69. Served to lt. col. M.C., AUS, 1942-46. Recipient Citizenship award Am. Legion, 1959, Award of Merit Am. Heart Assn., 1968. Diplomate Am. Bd. Internal Medicine. Fellow A.C.P. mem. Am. (dir. 1962-68), Ga. (pres. 1952-53, chmn. bd. dirs. 1957-58) heart assns., A.M.A., Med. Assn. Ga. Rotarian (pres. 1965). Home: 944 Nottingham Dr Macon GA 31201 Office: 707 Pine St Macon GA 31201

ROSSBACHER, RICHARD IRWIN, govt. ofcl.; b. Corry, Pa., Apr. 19, 1924; s. Richard Homer and Ila Lenore (Irwin) R.; B.S. cum laude, Allegheny Coll., 1949; M.A., Yale, 1951; postgrad. pub. adminstrn. Okla. U., 1965-68, bus. adminstrn., physics Am. U., 1958-66, Fed. Exec. Inst., 1969; m. Jean Mary Dearing, Nov. 19, 1946; children—Lisa Ann, Amy Jean (Mrs. Timothy Kimmitz), Nancy Dearing. Interior ballistician Naval Proving Ground, Dahlgren, Va., 1952-57; head cartridge actuated devices div. Naval Weapons Lab., Dahlgren, Va., 1957-61, dir. warhead and terminal ballistics lab., 1961-69, head surface warfare dept., engring. dept., warfare analysis dept., asst. tech. dir., 1969—. Lectr. math. Am. U., Washington, 1958-61, professorial lectr., 1961-69; prof. Fed. Exec. Inst., Charlottesville, Va., 1973. Served with USAAF, 1943-46. Mem. A.A.A.S., Am. Math. Soc., Am. Mgmt. Assn., Phi Beta Kappa. Lutheran. Contbr. profl. jours. Home: 1005 Hill Crest Dr Argyle Heights Fredericksburg VA 22401 Office: Naval Weapons Lab Dahlgren VA 22448

ROSSE, WENDELL FRANKLYN, med. educator; b. Sidney, Neb., June 5, 1933; s. James Clyde and Shirley Freda (Nelson) R.; A.B., U. Omaha, 1953; M.S. in Physiology, U. Neb., 1956; M.D. with honors, U. Chgo., 1958; m. Simonne Vernier, July 1, 1959; children—Jennifer, Christopher Douglas, Stephanie Pascale, Philippe Samuel James. Intern, jr. asst. resident Duke Hosp., 1958-60; clin. asso. NIH, 1960-63, sr. investigator, 1964-66; vis. research fellow Postgrad. Med. Sch., London, Eng., 1963-64; faculty Duke Med. Sch., 1964—, asso. prof. immunology, 1970—, chief immunohematology sect., 1971—, prof. medicine, 1972—; chief med. service Durham VA Hosp., 1973—. Co-chmn. Duke Med. Center Blood Bank. Mem. Am. Fedn. Clin. Research, Am. Soc. Hematology, Am. Soc. Clin. Investigation, Sigma Xi, Alpha Omega Alpha (sec.-treas.). Home: Route 7 Box 223 Durham NC 27707

ROSSMASSLER, STEPHEN ATWATER, govt. ofcl.; b. White Plains, N.Y., Jan. 15, 1920; s. Edward Collins and Marjory Garrison (Atwater) R.; B.A., Amherst Coll., 1941; M.S., U. Utah, 1948, Ph.D., 1950; m. Mildred Lang, Jan. 30, 1945; children—Richard Lang, Maxwell Peter. Chemist, E.I. duPont de Nemours & Co., Inc., Wilmington, Del., 1950-62; asst. dir. Office of Critical Tables, Nat. Acad. Scis., Washington, 1963-64; area program mgr. Nat. Bur. Standards, Office Standard Reference Data, Washington, 1964-68, 70—; staff tech. asst. Office Sci. and Tech., Exec. Office of Pres., Washington, 1968-69. Served with AUS, 1944-46. Mem. Am. Chem. Soc., Coblentz Soc., Sigma Xi, Phi Beta Kappa. Contbr. articles to profl. jours. Home: 9403 Kingsley Av Bethesda MD 20014 Office: Nat Bur Standards US Dept Commerce Washington DC 20234

ROSSON, GLENN RICHARD, operations bldg. products exec.; b. Galveston, Tex., Aug. 17, 1937; s. John Raymond and Elsie Lee (Reece) R.; B.B.A., Tex. Tech. U., 1959; m. Edwina Lucile Hart, June 2, 1956; children—Darrell Richard, Alex Mark. Supr., accountant Axelson div. U.S. Industries, Inc., Longview, Tex., 1960-67, controller, 1968; group financial v.p. U.S. Industries, Inc., Dallas, 1969, group chmn. 1969-72, v.p., 1973-74, sr. v.p., 1974—. Mem. Am. Inst. C.P.A.'s, Tex. Soc. C.P.A.'s, Nat. Assn. Accountants (past nat. dir., past pres. E. Tex. chpt.). Club: Dallas Athletic. Home: 11367 Drummond Dr Dallas TX 75228 Office: 1000 Expressway Tower Dallas TX 75206

ROSSON, JOHN WALLACE, elec. engr.; b. Erick, Okla., Jan. 1, 1930; s. Leroy and Rada (Griffin) R.; B.S. in Elec. Engring., Tex. Tech. U., 1951, M.S., 1953; m. Leota Ann Cover, Dec. 25, 1954; children—Donald, Cynthia, Thomas, Larry, Sarah. With Bell Telephone Labs., 1953-73, supr. mech. information systems, Greensboro, N.C., 1965-73; pres. WestOak Industries, Erick, 1973—. Mem. I.E.E.E. Home: Box 1185 Erick OK 73645 Office: 114 N Main St Erick OK 73645

ROSTHAL, ROBERT BERNARD, educator; b. N.Y.C., Oct. 16, 1923; s. James and Antoinette (Limansky) R.; B.A., U. Wis., 1944; diploma Washington and Jefferson Coll., 1944; postgrad. U. Paris, 1948-51, Columbia, 1953-54; M.A., U. Chgo., 1954; Ph.D. (fellow), U. Mich., 1960; m. Marianne Heineberg, Mar. 8, 1952; 1 son, Andrew. Instr. N.Y.U., 1953-54, Bklyn. Coll., 1954-55, U. Mich., 1958-59; vis. lectr. Ohio State U., Columbus, 1959-60; asst. prof. Kenyon Coll., Gambier, O., 1960-61; asst. prof. U. N.C., Greensboro, 1961-64, asso. prof. philosophy, 1965—, head dept. philosophy, 1969—. Committeeman, N.C. Democratic Com., 1970—. Served with AUS, 1943-46; ETO. Decorated Purple Heart. Ford Found. grantee, 1964-65; N.C. research grantee, 1965. Mem. Am. Philos. Assn., Am. Assn. U. Profs., So. Assn. Philosophy and Psychology, Metaphys. Soc. Am., Am. Soc. Aesthetics. Home: 4403 Graham Rd Greensboro NC 27410

ROSZEL, PATRICK ELDON, oil co. exec.; b. Coffeyville, Kan., Apr. 19, 1934; s. R.S. and L. (Braughton) R.; B.S., S.W. Tex. State U., 1957; M.B.A., St. Louis U., 1967; m. Wanna Joan Wright, Feb. 7, 1958; 1 dau., Rebecca Joan. Mem. tech. dept. Sinclair Oil Corp., Wood River, Ill., 1957-65; chem. lab. supr. Olin Mathieson Chem. Corp., Alton, Ill., 1965-68; quality adminstrn. mgr. Atlantic Richfield Co., Houston, 1968—; dir. Terra Mart Investment Corp., Houston. Served with USAF, 1958-61. Mem. Am. Soc. for Testing and Materials, Am. Soc. for Quality Control, Houston C. of C. Club: Noon Optimist. Home: 2215 Harper St Pasadena TX 77502 Office: PO Box 2451 Houston TX 77001

ROTH, JACK, broadcasting co. exec.; b. San Antonio, July 17, 1926; s. Eugene J. and Dorothy (Schaffer) R.; B.S., Trinity U., 1952; m. LaVerne Whitehead, Dec. 14, 1948; children—John, Nancy, Lee, Julie. Pres., Mission Broadcasting Co., San Antonio, 1959—; pres., owner Mission Central Co., stas. KONO and KITY-FM, San Antonio, 1967—, Mission East Co., stas. WWOK and WIGL-FM, Miami, Fla., 1966—; pres. Mission Broadcasting Co., Nev., 1967—, Mission Advt. Co., San Antonio, 1960—, Mission Charlotte Co. (N.C.), sta. WAME, 1968—, Mission Denver Co., sta. KERE, 1971—. Mem. planning bd. San Antonio Coll. Bd. dirs. A.R.C. Served with USNR, 1944-46. Mem. Tex. Assn. Broadcasters (pres. 1963), San Antonio Zool. Soc. (dir.). Home: 136 Cas-Hills St San Antonio TX 78213 Office: PO Box 2338 San Antonio TX 78298

ROTH, RICHARD DICK, market research cons.; b. N.Y.C., June 17, 1936; s. Paul and Margaret (Roth) R.; B.A., U. Miami, 1958; M.A., Fla. State U., 1959; m. Jacqueline M. Rosenthal, June 17, 1958; children—Paul Edward, Scott Martin, Andrea Gale. Econ. cons. Rader & Assos., Miami, Fla., 1959; econ. cons. First Research Corp., Miami, 1959-62, v.p., 1963-66; pres. Continental Research Cons., Inc., Miami, 1966—. Mem. Am. Geographers Assn., Am. Marketing Assn., Assn. Am. Geographers, Urban Land Inst., Bank Marketing Assn., Am. Econ. Assn., Econ. Soc. S. Fla. Club: Optimist. Home: 9043 SW 65th Terrace Miami FL 33143 Office: 7211 SW 62d Av South Miami FL 33143

ROTHMAN, SAM, govt. ofcl.; b. N.Y.C., Feb. 1, 1920; s. Jacob and Sarah (Moveretz) R.; B.S., L.I. U., 1943; M.A., Am. U., 1954, Ph.D., 1959; m. Florence Rosen, Dec. 11, 1944; children—Arlene Linda, Sandra Ruth. Chemist, Nat. Bur. Standards, Washington, 1946-55; research and devel. adminstr. Navy Dept., Washington, 1955—. Adj. prof. Am. U. Served with USAAF, 1943-46. Mem. Am. Chem. Soc., A.A.A.S. Home: 613 Hyde Rd Silver Spring MD 20902 Office: Crystal Plaza 6 Arlington VA 22202

ROTHSCHILD, DAVID, II, textile co. exec.; b. Columbus, Ga., Jan. 10, 1921; s. Irwin Bernard and Aleen Moore (Samuels) R.; B.S. in Commerce, U. Va., 1941; J.D., Yale, 1947; m. Barbara Galeski, Dec. 16, 1949; children—Aleen, David III, Walter Galeski, John Lowenberg. Admitted to Ga. bar, 1948; practice in Columbus, 1948; v.p. sales David Rothschild Co., High Point, N.C., 1949-55, exec. v.p., Columbus, 1956—; dir. 1st Nat. Bank, Columbus; v.p. Eagle Broadcasting Co., Sta. WYEA-TV, Columbus, 1969—; pres. David Realty Co., Columbus, 1962—. Mem. exec. com. Columbus Mus. Arts and Crafts, 1970—. Bd. dirs. Musuogee County Sch. Dist., United Givers. Served to capt. AUS, World War II; ETO. Decorated Bronze Star medal. Mem. Ga. Sch. Bd. Assn. (dir. 3d dist. 1970—), State Bar Ga. Jewish religion. Mason (Shriner), Rotarian. Clubs: Green Island Country, Harmony (Columbus). Home: 2134 Springdale Dr Columbus GA 31906 Office: 500 11th St Columbus GA 31902

ROTHSCHILD, EDWARD A., lawyer; b. Chgo., Mar. 8, 1926; s. Emanuel A. and Mina (Straus) R.; B.S., U. Louisville, 1949; LL.B., Jefferson Sch. Law, 1952; m. Frances Hoffman, Sept. 23, 1954; children—Diane, Peter, Nancy, Edward A. II. Admitted to Ky. bar, 1952; mem. firm Washer, Kaplan, Rothschild, Aberson, Miller & Dodd, Louisville, 1962—; sec. Western Dry Wall Corp., Louisville, 1969—, Eminence Speaker Co.; dir. Southland Electric Co.; prof. fed. estate and gift tax law U. Louisville, part-time 1971—. Bd. dirs. Jewish Hosp. Assn.; pres. Jewish Vocational Service, Louisville, 1970-72. Served with USNR, 1944-46; CBI, PTO. C.P.A., Ky. Mem. Louisville, Ky., Am. bar assns., Ky. Soc. C.P.A.'s. Jewish religion (past dir. temple). Rotarian (pres.). Clubs: Hi Twelve, Standard Country (Louisville). Home: 2218 Wynnewood Circle Louisville KY 40222 Office: ME Taylor Bldg Louisville KY 40202

ROTROFF, ROBERT WILLIAM, banker; b. Tipton, Ind., Apr. 8, 1922; s. Louis Melvin and Mildred (Pangborn) R.; student Ball State U., 1940-42, Tex. A. and M. U., 1942-43; m. Bettie Eileen Maxwell, Apr. 23, 1943; 1 son, Stephen Robert. Mgr. Franklin Security Co., Muncie, Ind., 1945-51; asst. credit mgr. Cleve. Trust Co., 1951-56; asst. cashier Irwin Union Bank & Trust Co., Columbus, Ind., 1956-60; exec. v.p., chief adminstrv. officer Alexandria Nat. Bank (Va.), 1960—. Bd. dirs. Alexandria Hosp. Served with USAAF, 1942-45. Mem. Robert Morris Assos., Alexandria (pres. 1967), Va. chambers commerce. Republican. Methodist. Rotarian. Office: 330 N Washington St Alexandria VA 22313

ROTTMANN, PAUL OTTO, cons. engr.; b. Rottenbach-Thruingia, Germany, Nov. 4, 1896; s. Oskar L. and Adeline (Gruen) R.; degree in elec. engring. Poly. Inst. Ilmenau (Germany), 1921; student Tech. Hochschule Charlottenburg, 1922-23; student Northwestern U., 1927-31; m. Hildur C. Olson, Sept. 25, 1936. Came to U.S., 1923, naturalized, 1929. Draftsman, A.M. Lockett Co., New Orleans, 1923-24, Westinghouse Electric Co., Chgo., 1925; engr. Pub. Service Co. No. Ill., Chgo., 1926-32, R.K. Werner, Ft. Worth, 1933-35; designer Carrier Corp., Chgo., 1936; chief engr. Wyatt C. Hedrick, Ft. Worth, 1939-46; pvt. practice as cons. engr., Shreveport, La., 1946—. Recipient profl. engring. achievement award Engring. and Sci. Council Shreveport, 1969. Mem. Am. Soc. Heating, Refrigerating and Air-Conditioning Engrs., La. Engring. Soc. Mason (Shriner), Rotarian. Home: 456 Albany Av Shreveport LA 71105 Office: 906 Market St Shreveport LA 71101

ROUBEY, LESTER WALTER, clergyman, educator; b. Balt., Feb. 11, 1915; s. Abraham and Sara (Cordish) R.; A.M., Johns Hopkins, 1936, Ph.D., 1938; M.H.L. and Rabbi, Hebrew Union Coll., 1947, D.D. (hon.), 1972; m. Charlotte Helen Stern, June 1, 1947; 1 son, Robert Arthur Stern. Rabbi, 1947; rabbi, Lancaster, Pa., 1947-53, Reading, Pa., 1954-64, East Orange, N.J., 1964-66, Baton Rouge, 1966; adj. prof. religion Franklin and Marshall Coll., Lancaster, 1951-53; asso. prof. Romance langs. Kutztown (Pa.) State Coll., 1961-64; lectr. Romance langs. La. State U., Baton Rouge, 1966-70, asso. prof., 1970—. Mem. civic com., Lancaster, 1950-53; mem. adv. bd. Baton Rouge Gen. Hosp., 1967—, trustee, 1972—; mem. religious com. reading round table Nat. Conf. Christians and Jews; chmn. reading com. Am. Jewish Tercentenary, 1954-55; bd. dirs. A.R.C., 1968—. Mem. Central Conf. Am. Rabbis, Hebrew Union Coll.-Jewish Inst. Religion Alumni Assn. (trustee 1953-56), Am. Assn. Tchrs. French, Am. Assn. Tchrs. Italian, Am. Assn. U. Profs., Modern Lang. Assn., Am. Council Teaching Fgn. Langs., South Central Modern Lang. Assn. (chmn. Italian sect. 1969), Phi Sigma Iota. Mason (32 deg. Shriner), Rotarian. Club: Baton Rouge Country Producer, conductor series of TV worship programs, Lancaster, 1951-53. Office: 3354 Kleinert Av Baton Rouge LA 70806 also Dept Fgn Langs La State U Baton Rouge LA 70803

ROUBY, JASON PIERRE, govt. ofcl.; b. Cleve., June 9, 1923; s. Maurice S. and Pearl E. (Rosenberg) R.; B.A., Western Res. U., 1948; m. Marguerite Schmuck, Feb. 23, 1952; children—Carole (Mrs. Charles Canelli), Christina, David. Reporter, Cleve. Plain Dealer, 1948-49, Jonesboro (Ark.) Evening Sun, 1949-51, Ark. Gazette, Little Rock, 1952-59; asst. to pres. Urban Progress Assn., Little Rock,

1959-62; dept. mgr. Omaha C. of C., 1962-66; exec. dir. Metroplan, Little Rock, 1966—. Cons. met. devel., mass transit. Mem. Little Rock AFB Community Council, 1968—, Gov. Ark. Adv. Council Nat. Transp. Needs, 1972—; steering com. Goals for Central Ark., 1972—. Served with AUS, World War II; ETO. Decorated Bronze Star. Congl. fellow Am. Polit. Sci. Assn., 1956-57. Mem. Nat. Assn. Housing and Redevel. Ofcls., Am. Inst. Planners (affiliate), Internat. City Mgmt. Assn., Am. Transit Assn. Rotarian. Home: 11 McKinley Cirlce Little Rock AR 72207 Office: 100 Main St Little Rock AR 72201

ROUGHTON, RICHARD WELLS, motel exec.; b. Perry, Ga., July 4, 1924; s. Rawlings Howard and Eunice (Wells) R.; grad. high sch.; m. Alice Jewel Tucker, Jan. 10, 1954. Owner, R.W. Roughton Constrn. Co., Perry, 1952-64; prin., owner Capri Motel and Restaurant, Perry, 1966—. Mem. Bd. Appeals City Perry, 1966—. Served with Mcht. Marine, 1943-48, with AUS, 1948-51; Korea. Mem. C. of C. (charter), V.F.W. Club: Perry Country. Home: 1209 Cater Circle Perry GA 31069 Office: Capri Motel Perry GA 31069

ROUND, BETTYE HAMMONS (MRS. THORNTON EDGERLY ROUND), realtor; b. Barberville, Fla.; d. Benjamin Abner and Alice Adella (Ward) Hammons; grad. high sch.; student various courses in real estate, decorating, bus. mgmt.; m. Thornton Edgerly Round, July 27, 1961; 1 dau., Alice Adair Gilbert (Mrs. Darrell D. Brown). Free lance interior designer, Coral Gables, Miami, Fla., 1935-39; agt., Independence Life Ins. Co., Orlando, Fla., 1950-51; broker Homestead Devel. Co., 1952-56; owner real estate broker firm Bettye H. Gilbert, 1956-61; Betty H. Round Realtor, 1961—; owner, Windsor Manor, Inc., Orlando, 1961—; co-owner Lee's Inn, Highlands, N.C., 1961-69. Mem. Vis. Nurses Assn., 1962—; mem. Orlando Day Nursery, 1964-72; mem. women's com. Fla. Symphony Orch., 1964-71. Mem. Orlando Winter Park Bd. Realtors (sec. 1958, pres. women's council 1959-60), Fla. Bd. Realtors (corr. sec. 1958). Democrat. Episcopalian. Clubs: Sorosis, Dubsdread Country, Orlando Country (Orlando). Home: 722 Alameda Dr Orlando FL 32804 Office: 722 Alameda Av Orlando FL 32804

ROUNTREE, AUBREY EUGENE, vending co. exec.; b. Dunbarton, S.C., July 21, 1938; s. Aubrey B. and Minnie (McElveen) R.; B.S., U. S.C., 1961; m. Emily Ida Sprawls, July 13, 1957; children—Dana Ruth, Julie Anne, Gina Claire, Emily Maria, Amy Carol. Mgr., Price Waterhouse & Co., Charlotte, N.C., 1961-67; pres., dir. Food Service, Inc., Columbia, S.C., 1967—. Tchr. accounting Richland Tech. Edn. Center, 1969—. C.P.A., N.C. Mem. Am. Inst. C.P.A.'s, Nat. Assn. Accountants. Baptist. Club: Gamecock (Columbia). Home: 286 Sandhurst Rd Columbia SC 29210 Office: 1238 Arrowwood Rd Columbia SC 29210

ROUNTREE, CHARLES BYRON, broadcasting co. exec.; b. Montgomery, Ala., Aug. 8, 1936; s. William Byron and Lois E. (Ruff) R.; student Huntingdon Coll., 1958. Dist. mgr. Ala. Jour., Montgomery, 1948-53; youth adviser Boy's Club, Montgomery, 1953-54; program/operation mgr. WCOV TV, Montgomery, 1953-58, 62-68; program mgr. WBMG TV, Birmingham, Ala., 1968—. Pres., 17th ann. TV Programming Conf., Louisville, 1972-73. Served with AUS, 1958-62; ETO. Mem. Birmingham Jr. C. of C., Jefferson County Radio and TV Council (pres. 1973—). Home: 419 A Elder Oaks Way Birmingham AL 35209 Office: 2075 Golden Crest Dr Birmingham AL 35209

ROUNTREE, THOMAS JEFFERSON, educator, author; b. Pinckard, Ala., July 22, 1927; s. Nathan Harmon and Hortense (Warren) R.; B.A., Troy State U., 1950; M.A., U. Ala., 1952; Ph.D., Tulane U., 1962; m. Virginia Earle Ward, Aug. 12, 1967. Instr. English, Troy (Ala.) State U., summer 1953, 54, asst. prof., summer 1957; instr. English, East Tex. State U., Commerce, 1956, asst. prof., 1960-61; asst. prof. English, Southeastern La. Coll., Hammond, 1958-60; instr. English, U. Ala., University, 1961-62, asst. prof., 1962-65, asso. prof., 1965-71, dir. creative writing program, 1963-71; prof., chmn. dept. English U. South Ala., 1971—. Guest lectr. creative writing S.D. Fine Arts Conf., Yankton, 1962, 63. Served with USNR, 1945-46, AUS, 1954-56. Recipient Prewitt Semmes, Jr. creative writing awards, 1952, 53, 1st prize Short Story award Birmingham Festival of Arts, 1963; Carnegie scholar, 1953-54. Mem. Modern Lang. Assn. Am., South Atlantic Modern Lang. Assn., Ala. Coll. English Tchrs. Assn., So. Literary Festival, Wordsworth Circle, Rydal Mt. Summer Sch. Assn., Episcopalian. Author: This Mighty Sum of Things: Wordsworth's Theme of Benevolent Necessity, 1965; study guides on The Last of the Mohicans (Cooper), 1965, Emma (Austen), 1967, also articles, short stories, poems. Editor: Critics on Melville, 1972; Critics on Hawthorne, 1972; Critics on Emerson, 1973. Address: Box U-342 U South Ala Mobile AL 36688

ROUSE, JOHN WILSON, JR., educator; b. Kansas City, Mo., Dec. 7, 1937; s. John Wilson and Gail A. (Palmer) R.; B.S., Purdue U., 1959; M.S., U. Kan., 1965, Ph.D., 1968; m. Loretta L. Romines, June 10, 1956; 1 son, Jeffrey Scott. Devel. engr. Bendix Corp., Kansas City, Mo., 1959-64; research coordinator Center Research, Inc., U. Kan., Lawrence, 1964-68; prof. elec. engring., dir. Remote Sensing Center, Tex. A. and M. U., College Station, 1968—. Indsl. cons., 1968—. Active Kan. Jr. C. of C., 1965-68. NASA trainee, 1964. Recipient Bendix Corp. award, 1962. Mem. I.E.E.E. (tech. editor transactions), Internat. Union Radio Sci., Am. Soc. Photogrammetry, Sigma Xi, Eta Kappa U. Contbr. articles to profl. jours. Home: 2100 Briar Oaks St Bryan TX 77801 Office: Remote Sensing Center Tex A and M Univ College Station TX 77843

ROUSE, RAYMOND VICTOR, profl. soccer team coach; b. Swansea, Wales, Mar. 16, 1936. With English League for Crystal Place, 1956-62, Oxford United, 1963-64, Leyton Orient, 1965-66; with Atlanta Chiefs, 1967—, asst. coach, dir. youth devel., 1969-70, head coach, gen. mgr., 1970—. Named to Welsh Nat. Team, 1960, 61. Office: Atlanta Chiefs PO Box 4064 Atlanta GA 30312*

ROUSE, ROY DENNIS, coll. dean; b. Andersonville, Ga., Sept. 20, 1920; s. Joseph B. and Janie (Wicker) R.; student Ga. S.W. Coll., 1937-39; B.S. in Agr., U. Ga., 1942, M.S. in Agr., 1947; Ph.D., Purdue U., 1949; m. Madge Mathis, Mar. 6, 1946; children—David Benjamine, Sharon. Faculty, Auburn (Ala.) U., 1949—, prof. agronomy, 1956-66, asso. dir., asst. dean Sch. Agr. and Agrl. Expt. Sta., 1966-72, dean, dir. Sch. Agr. and Agrl. Expt. Sta., 1972—. Served to capt. USNR, 1942-46; PTO. Mem. Am. Soc. Agronomy, Soil Sci. Soc. Am., Assn. So. Agrl. Expt. Sta. Dirs., Assn. So. Agrl. Workers, Assn. Univs. and Land Grant Colls., Sigma Xi, Phi Kappa Phi, Alpha Zeta, Xi Phi Xi, Gamma Sigma Delta. Presbyn. Lion. Clubs: Aquatic Booster, Men's Camellia, Auburn Outing. Contbr. articles to profl. jours. Home: 827 Salmon Dr Auburn AL 36830

ROUSH, HARRY, dentist; b. Phila., Oct. 1, 1915; s. Louis and Rose (Likoff) R.; B.S., Duke U., 1936; D.D.S., Emory U., 1940; m. Ann Herman, July 4, 1947; children—Alan Loni, Lois Beth. Pvt. practice dentistry, Arlington, Va., 1940—. Mem. Comprehensive Health Planning Council No. Va., 1970-73; adv. council No. Va. Community Coll., 1966-69. Served to lt. comdr. USNR, 1942-46. Mem. Arlington (pres. 1956), No. Va. (pres. 1969) dental socs., Alpha Omega (v.p. 1942). Jewish religion. Lion (pres. N.W. Arlington 1962). Home: 6308 Waterway Dr Falls Church VA 22044 Office: 3801 N Fairfax Dr Arlington VA 22203

ROUSSEL, HERBERT JOSEPH, JR., engring. co. exec.; b. New Orleans, July 13, 1931; s. Herbert Joseph and Dorothy (Moll) R.; B.C.E., Tulane U., 1961, M.C.E., 1964, postgrad., 1964—; m. Joyce Ellen Freeling, Aug. 4, 1956; children—Herbert Joseph III, Karen Elizabeth. Engr., Shell Oil Co., Norco, La., 1961-62, J. Ray McDermott & Co., New Orleans, 1962-64, Avondale Shipyards Inc., New Orleans, 1964, Boeing Co., New Orleans, 1964-65; asso. N.P. Jeffrey, New Orleans, 1965-68; pres. Roussel Engring., Inc., Metairie, La., 1968—; adj. prof. civil engring. Tulane U., 1964—. Served with AUS, 1952-54. Recipient La. Hwy. Engr. Assn. award, 1961; W.F. Thompkin's award Tulane U., 1961, Alumni award, 1969. Mem. Am. Concrete Inst., Am. Soc. C.E., Soc. Tulane Engrs., La. Engring. Soc., Nat. Soc. Profl. Engrs., Am. Soc. for Testing and Materials, Am. Welding Soc., Soc. Petroleum Engrs., Sigma Xi, Tau Beta Pi, Alpha Sigma Lambda. Home: 1901 Cleary Av Metairie LA 70001 Office: 3017 Kingman St Metairie LA 70002

ROUTH, DONALD EUGENE, electronics engr.; b. Mountain View, Mo., Aug. 14, 1936; s. Alvis Clarence and Thelma Jane (Blew) R.; B.S. in Elec. Engring., Washington U., St. Louis, 1960; postgrad. Auburn U., 1966, U. Ala. at Huntsville, 1968-69; m. Wilma Marie Quick, June 10, 1956; children—Marcy, Katherine, Linda. Systems and liaison engr. McDonnell Aircraft Co., St. Louis, 1958-63; sect. chief Astronics Lab., NASA Marshall Space Flight Center, Hunstville, Ala., 1969—. Leadership coordinator Young Life Campaign, Huntsville Area, 1973—. Registered profl. engr., Ala. Mem. Ala. Soc. Profl. Engrs., MARS Assn. Marshall Space Flight Center (pres. 1965), Marshall Space Flight Center Exchange Club (sec. 1970-73). Baptist. Home: 9001 Willow Hills Dr Huntsville AL 35802 Office: S&E-ASTR-R Marshall Space Flight Center Huntsville AL 35812

ROUTH, PORTER (WROE), ch. exec.; b. Lockhart, Tex., July 14, 1911; s. Eugene Coke and Mary M. (Wroe) R.; A.B., Okla. Baptist U., 1934, LL.D., 1951; postgrad. So. Bapt. Theol. Sem., 1937, U. Mo., 1938, George Peabody Coll., 1946-47; m. Ruth Elizabeth Purtle, June 7, 1936; children—Eugene Charles, Elizabeth Ann, Dorothy Kate, Mary Susan, Lelia Ruth. Dir. publicity and instr. polit. sci. Okla. Bapt. U., 1935, dir. univ. press, 1936-37, instr. journalism, editorial staff Shawnee News, 1938-40; asso. sec. Okla. Bapt. Sunday Sch. and Tng. Union Dept., Oklahoma City, 1940-41, sec. Okla. Bapt. Brotherhood and Promotion Dept., 1942-43; sec. dept. survey, statis. and information Bapt. Sunday Sch. Bd., Nashville, 1945-51; exec. sec. of exec. com. So. Bapt. Conv. 1951—; mem. exec. com. Bapt. World Alliance, 1955—, mem. adminstrv. com., 1956—; treas. Conv. Found. Mem. Nat. council Boy Scouts Am.; mem. com. on medicine and religion A.M.A. Mem. So. Bapt. Hist. Soc., Am. Bible Soc. (dir.). Author: My World Too, 1948; Meet the Presidents, 1952; 77,000 Churches, 1964. Editor: Okla. Bapt. Messenger, 1943-45; Quar. Rev., 1945-52. Home: 3426 Hampton Av Nashville TN 37215 Office: 460 James Robertson Pkwy Nashville TN 37219

ROUTT, MELVIN WILLIAM, electronics engr.; b. Tampa, Fla., Oct. 3, 1935; s. John William and Martha Ann (Pozoski) R.; student St. Petersburg (Fla.) Jr. Coll., 1959-60, 63-64, 65-66, 68, Pinelas County Vocational Adult Edn., 1961, 66, 67; m. Margaret Elise Lee, July 16, 1960; children—Katherine Elise, Kristofer Erston. With Routt's Auto Parts, Tampa, 1954, 58, 63, R.T. Joughin & Co., Tampa, 1958, Sperry Microwave and Electronics Co., Clearwater, Fla., 1958-63, 63-71; self-employed, 1971; engring., asst. H.E. Johnson & Assos., Inc., Clearwater, 1971—. Vice pres. Fla. W. Coast Conf. Sports Car Clubs, 1960-61; chmn. Safety Harbor Auditorium study com., 1969-71; mem. Pinellas County Childbirth and Parent Edn. League, 1964-65. Precinct committeeman Pinellas County Republican Exec. Com., 1970-74. Served with USMCR, 1954, USAF, 1954-58. Recipient Distinguished Service award Safety Harbor Jaycees, 1969-70, Key Man award, 1968-69; Presdl. award honor Pinellas Park and Safety Harbor Jaycees, 1966, 71; certificate merit St. Petersburg Jr. Coll., 1968. Mem. Jr. C. of C. Internat. (editor Mentors 1973-74, pub. relations dir. U.S. JCI Senate 1972-73, past exec. dir., editor, sec.-treas., now pres. Fla. JCI Senate), Fla. (orientation and directory chmn. 1971-72, v.p. 1969-71, various dist. offices), Safety Harbor (past pres., other offices) jaycees, Internat. Sports Car Assn. (charter pres. 1959, fgn. sec. 1965, treas. 1964). Author, editor numerous jaycees publs. Home: 50 W Joyce St Safety Harbor FL 33572 Office: 211 S Ewing Av Clearwater FL 33516

ROVIRA, EDWIN JOSEPH, JR., accountant; b. New Orleans, Oct. 5, 1929; s. Edwin Joseph and Bernadette (Webre) R.; B.B.A., Tulane U., 1950; m. Anne Marie Zeringue, May 23, 1953; children—Kyle Anne, Dwayne Edwin, Keith Joseph. Jr. accountant E.J. Rovira, Sr., C.P.A., New Orleans, 1950-53; sr. accountant Malcolm M. Dienes & Co., New Orleans, 1953-54; pvt. practice pub. accounting, Metairie, La., 1956—; treas., dir. Masonry Products Sales, Inc., New Orleans, 1966—. Bd. dirs. Christian Bros. Found., East Jefferson Hosp. Found. Served with USCGR, 1954-56. C.P.A., La. Mem. Am. Inst. C.P.A.'s. La. Soc. C.P.A.'s, Metairie Club Gardens Assn. (dir., pres.). Democrat. Roman Catholic. Club: Metairie Country. Home: 402 Vincent Av Metairie LA 70005 Office: 3212 16th St Metairie LA 70002

ROWAN, CARL THOMAS, journalist; b. Ravenscroft, Tenn., Aug. 11, 1925; s. Thomas David and Johnnie (Bradford) R.; student Tenn. State U., 1942-43, Washburn U., 1943-44; A.B., Oberlin Coll., 1947, D.Litt., 1962; M.A., U. Minn., 1948; D.Litt., Simpson Coll., 1957, Hamline U., 1958, Coll. of Wooster, 1968, Drexel Inst. Tech., 1969; L.H.D., Washburn U., 1964, St. Olaf Coll., 1966, Knoxville Coll., 1966, Talladega Coll., 1965, R.I. Coll., 1970, U. Me., 1971; LL.D., Howard U., 1964, Alfred U., 1964, Temple U., 1964, Atlanta U., 1965, Allegheny Coll., 1966, Colby Coll., 1968, Clark U., 1971, U. Notre Dame, 1973; D.P.A., Morgan State Coll., 1964; m. Vivien L. Murphy, Aug. 2, 1950; children—Barbara, Carl, Goeffrey. Reporter, Mpls.-Tribune, 1948-61; dep. asst. to sec. state, Washington, 1961-63; ambassador to Finland, 1963-64; dir. USIA, 1964-65; syndicated columnist, TV commentator Post-Newsweek Broadcasting Co., Washington, 1965—; dir. D.C. Nat. Bank. Mem. com. of 100 legal def. fund N.A.A.C.P., 1964—, chmn. adv. com. Nat. Com. Against Discrimination in Housing, 1967. Served with USNR, 1943-46. Recipient numerous awards, including Sidney Hillman Found. award, 1952, Am. Teamwork award Nat. Urban League, 1955, Distinguished Achievement award Regents of U. Minn., 1961, Golden Ruler award Phila. Fellowship Commn., 1961, Communications award in Human Relations, Anti-Defamation League of B'nai B'rith, 1964, Distinguished Service award Capital Press Club, 1964, Nat. Brotherhood award Nat. Conf. Christians & Jews, 1964; Elijah P. Lovejoy award, 1968. Mem. Sigma Delta Chi. Author: South of Freedom, 1953; The Pitiful and the Proud, 1956; Go South to Sorrow, 1957; Wait Till Next Year, 1960. Home: 3116 Fessenden St NW Washington DC 20008 Office: 1101 17th St NW Washington DC 20036

ROWE, BONNIE GORDON, music co. exec.; b. Buford, Ga., May 3, 1922; s. Bonnie Gordon and Alma (Poole) R.; student Ga. Evening Coll., 1939-41, U. Wichita, 1948-49, Ga. State Coll., 1949-52; m. Mary Wilburta Shidler; 1 dau., Sharon Lynn; m. 2d, Gloria Lucille Fairfax, Feb. 17, 1962 (div.); 1 dau., Susan Rebecca. Traffic mgr. Bonanza Air Lines, Las Vegas, 1946-48; music tchr. 1948-52; owner Rowe Accordion Distbg. Co., Rowe Accordion Center, Atlanta, 1952-56, Atlanta Music Pub. Co., 1956—, B. Rowe Music Co., Atlanta, 1957—; pres. B. Rowe Enterprises, Inc., 1973—, BCR Corp., 1974—. Served to lt. col. USAAF, World War II; ETO. Decorated Air medals with three oak leaf clusters. Mem. Southeastern Accordion Assn. (past pres.), Nat. Assn. Music Mchts., Atlanta Fedn. Musicians, Travelers Protective Assn., Atlanta C. of C. Res. Officers Assn., Internat. Platform Assn., Gamma Delta Phi. Elk. Club: Dobbins AFB Officers. Composer: Accordionique, 1953, Vivolet, 1956, More and More and More, 1964, Dedication, 1964, All I Really See Is You, 1965, I Love Only You, 1965, Predudio Reminisci, 1969. Home: 5085 Erin Dr Atlanta GA 30331 Office: 2841 Greenbrier Pkwy SW Atlanta GA 30331

ROWE, CHARLES BARKER, lawyer; b. Southampton County, Va., July 29, 1938; s. Charles Henry and Eula Clementine (Barker) R.; B.A., Randolph-Macon Coll., 1959; LL.B. magna cum laude, Washington and Lee U., 1964; m. Nancy Brooke Taylor, Feb. 17, 1968; children—Ashley Brooke, Tazewell Southgate. Tchr. English, Warwick High Sch., Newport News, Va., 1959-61; admitted to Va. bar, 1964; practice in Courtland, 1967—; partner firm Pulley & Rowe, 1971—; judge Courtland Municipal Ct., 1971—; substitute judge Southampton County Ct., 1971-73, Gen. Dist. Ct. Southampton County, 1973—. Pres., Southampton unit Am. Cancer Soc., 1969-70; chmn. Courtland Community Fund, 1971, 73. Trustee Walter Cecil Rawls Library and Museum, Courtland. Served to capt. AUS, 1964-67. Decorated Bronze Star. Mem. Am., Va., Southampton (sec. 1968-73) bar assns., Southampton Hist. Soc., Order of Coif, Phi Beta Kappa, Omicron Delta Kappa. Episcopalian (vestryman, treas.). Clubs: Cypress Cove (Franklin, Va.); Norfolk Yacht and Country. Office: Main St Courtland VA 23837

ROWE, HAROLD CLIFTON, assn. exec.; b. Springfield, Mass., Feb. 28, 1925; s. Harold Clifton and Henrietta (Trunkfield) R.; B.S., Am. Internat. Coll., 1947; postgrad. Springfield Coll., 1947-48, Yale, 1949-55, Mich. State U. Inst. Organizational Mgmt., 1956; children—Chrisse Ann, Harold Clifton III, Suzanne, Gail, Russell. Research dir. Springfield Taxpayers Assn., 1950-52; exec. sec. Brookville (Pa.) C. of C., 1952-54; exec. v.p. Middletown (Conn.) C. of C., 1954-58; sec. commodity div. Nat. Assn. Waste Material Dealers, N.Y.C., 1958-60; sec. membership relations Printing Industries Met. N.Y., N.Y.C.; exec. dir. Environmental Mgmt. Assn., Clearwater, Fla., 1962—. Mem. S.A.R., Am., Fla. (pres. 1973-74) socs. assn. execs., Sigma Alpha Phi. Home: 2429 Fairbanks Dr Clearwater FL 33516 Office: 1710 Drew St Clearwater FL 33515

ROWE, JAMES MELVIN, journalist; b. Nagasaki, Japan, Dec. 17, 1910 (parents Am. Citizens); s. John Hansford and Margaret (Cobb) R.; student Baylor U., Centenary Coll., U. Tex., 1930-34; m. Florence Arlene Womack, Apr. 10, 1950; children—James Melvin (dec.), John Hansford. With country weekly newspapers, Quitman, Tex. and Aransas Pass, Tex., 1937-40; reporter, polit. writer Corpus Christi (Tex.) Caller-Times, 1940-54, editorial writer, 1954-60, chief editorial writer, 1960—. Served to maj. AUS, 1941-46. Decorated Bronze Star medal. Democrat. Baptist. Home: Route 1 Box 990 Ingleside TX 78408 Office: PO Box 9136 Corpus Christi TX 78408

ROWE, LOUIS PAUL, dentist; b. Good Luck, Ky., Nov. 14, 1939; s. Paul Bedford and Vera Lillian (Ford) R.; D.M.D., U. Louisville, 1964; m. Dianna Winifred Boylan, Sept. 21, 1960; children—Louis Paul, Kirk A., Kelly S. Practice dentistry, Louisville, 1964-65, Erlanger, Ky., 1968—. Served with Dental Corps, AUS, 1966-67. Decorated Army Commendation medal. Mem. Am. Dental Assn., Gideons Internat. (pres. No. Ky. 1970—, zone leader Ky. 1970—), Phi Kappa Tau, Psi Omega. Baptist (deacon 1964). Home: 328 Stevenson St Erlanger KY 41018 Office: 24 Commonwealth Av Erlanger KY 41018

ROWE, WALLACE P., physician, govt. ofcl.; b. Balt., Feb. 20, 1926; student Coll. William and Mary, 1943-44, summer 1945; M.D., Johns Hopkins U., 1948; m. 2 children. Student asst. N.Y. State Tb Sanatarium, Ray Brook, 1947; intern N.C. Baptist Hosp., Winston-Salem, 1948-49; research fellow Bowman Gray Sch. Medicine, Wake Forest Coll., 1949; virologist Naval Med. Research Inst., Bethesda, Md., 1949-52; commd. sr. asst. surgeon USPHS, 1952, advanced through grades to med. dir., 1960; investigator Nat. Inst. Allergy and Infectious Diseases, NIH, Bethesda, 1952—, chief oncolytic and oncogenic virus unit virus sect., 1957-68, chief Lab. Viral Diseases, 1968—. Served with USNR, 1945; to lt., M.C., 1949-52. Office: Lab Viral Diseases Nat Inst Allergy and Infectious Diseases NIH Bethesda MD 20014

ROWE, WILLIAM DAVID, govt. ofcl.; b. Orange, N.J., Jan. 7, 1930; s. Milton Harold and Pauline (Straus) R.; B.A., Wesleyan U., Middletown, Conn., 1952; postgrad. U. Pitts., 1954-57; M.B.A., U. Buffalo, 1961; Ph.D., Am. U., 1973; m. M. Jeanette Frease, May 4, 1957; children—William David, Andrew Lynne, Deirdre Anne, Ryan Wesley. Engr., Westinghouse Electric Corp., Pitts., 1952-57, engr., Buffalo, 1957-61; dir. ind. research and devel. Sylvania Electronic Systems, Needham, Mass., 1961-68; head environmental systems dept. Mitre Corp., McLean, Va., 1968-72; dep. asst. adminstr. for radiation programs EPA, Washington, 1972—; dir. Quintex Corp., Falls Church, Va.; pres. Rowe Research Assos., Sudbury, Mass., 1964-68. Lectr. Am. U., Washington, 1971-72. Chmn., Hwy. Commn., Sudbury, 1964-68. Registered profl. engr., Mass. Mem. Sigma Chi. Mason (Shriner), Kiwanian. Patentee in field. Contbr. articles to profl. jours. Home: 6423 Woodville Dr Falls Church VA 22044 Office: EPA Waterside Mall E Washington DC 20460

ROWE, WILLIAM MOYER, JR., elec. engr.; b. Atlanta, Dec. 11, 1927; s. William M. and Ila A. (Poole) R.; B.S. in Physics, Stanford, 1961; E.E., Marquette U., 1966; m. Marcella Queenia, June 23, 1947; children—Charles, William, Paul, Teresa, Ralph. Engr., Dept. Commerce, 1946-57; with Gen. Electric Co., 1957—, sr. devel. engr., St. Petersburg, Fla., 1966—; pres. Maillou Builders Inc., Clearwater, 1972—, Elec. Specialities, Clearwater, 1972—; pvt. cons. practice, 1971—. Active fund raising YMCA. Served with USNR, World War II. E.C. Converse honors scholar, 1960; Gen. Electric scholar, 1959. Registered profl. engr., Fla. Mem. Am. Phys. Soc. Republican. Home: 1723 Winfield Rd N Clearwater FL 33516 Office: 789 Highland Av Largo FL 33540

ROWELL, JOHN THOMAS, psychologist; b. Lloyd, Fla., Mar. 21, 1920; s. Irvin Caleb and Ester Estelle (Rouden) R.; R.N., McLean Hosp. Sch. Nursing, 1942; A.B., U. Mich., 1949; Ph.D., Fla. State U., 1958; m. Mabel Zelma Mason, Aug. 15, 1942; children—James Roger, Douglas Hugh, Martin Allen. Chief psychologist Milledgeville (Ga.) State Hosp., 1951-57; human factors scientist RAND Corp., Santa Monica, Cal., 1957; mgr. anti-submarine warfare programs System Devel. Corp., Falls Church, Va., 1958-69, pres. N.C. Leadership Inst., Inc., 1969-72; v.p. Essex Corp., 1972-74; pres. John Rowell Assos., 1972—. Served with AUS, 1943-46. Mem. Am., Southeastern psychol. assns., Human Factors Soc., A.A.A.S. Author: National Document Handling Systems for Science and Technology,

1967. Home: Three Oaks Farm Route 2 Madison NC 27025 Office: Exec Sq 2720 N Church St Greensboro NC 27405

ROWLETT, RAYMOND, hosp. adminstr.; b. Calvin, Ky., Mar. 1, 1929; s. Dexter Marvin and Millie (Brooks) R.; student Nat. Sch. Bus., 1949-50; Lincoln Meml. U., 1957-58; m. Laura Jean Pursifull, Nov. 17, 1951; 1 son, Brooks Ashley. Stock, salesman Scotts Dept. Store, Pineville, Ky., 1947-49; br. office mgr. Pinnacle Motors, Pineville, Ky., 1953-56; accounts receivable clerk Middlesboro (Ky.) Meml. Hosp., 1956-58; bus.-admissions supr. McDowell (Ky.) Meml. Hosp., 1958-63; asst. patient accounts mgr. U. Ky. Med. Center, Lexington, 1963-65; adminstrv. asst. McDowell Appalachian Regional Hosp., 1965-66; adminstrv. asst. Williamson (W.Va.) Appalachian Regional Hosp., 1966-67, asst. adminstr., 1967-72; acting adminstr. Whitesburg (Ky.) Appalachian Regional Hosp., 1969-70; adminstr. Morgan County Appalachian Regional Hosp., 1972—. Served with AUS, 1951-53. Baptist (Sunday sch. supt. 1959-61). Lion. Address: PO Box 7 West Liberty KY 41472

ROWLEY, GEORGE ARTHUR, JR., ednl. adminstr.; b. Ringwood, Okla., Apr. 18, 1927; s. George Arthur and Beulah Mae (Wimberly) R.; A.B., Northwestern State Coll., 1949; M.A., Phillips U., 1953; Ed.D., Okla. State U., 1967; m. Alice Fern Doll, Dec. 21, 1946; children—Jerry Warren, Kenny Dean, Robert Wayne, Valli Jo. Prin., Freedom (Okla.) High Sch., 1949-51; supt., Crawford, Okla., 1951-56, Coyle, Okla., 1956-62; dir. Oklahoma City Schs. Food Service Div., 1962-63; supt. Perkins (Okla.) Pub. Schs., 1963-66, Blackwell (Okla.) Schs., 1966-73, Edmond (Okla.) Schs., 1973—. Mem. Okla. Commn. on Ednl. Adminstrn., 1971-74. Chmn. ednl. div. United Fund, 1967-69; v.p. Bi-State Mental Health Found., 1969-70. Bd. dirs. Kay County Juvenile Com. Served with USNR, 1945-46. Recipient Grant NSF, 1957; named Boss of the Year Jr. C. of C., 1971. Mem. Am., Okla. (pres. 1971-72) assns. sch. adminstrs., Okla. Edn. Assn., Blackwell C. of C. (dir. 1970-72), Phi Kappa Phi, Phi Delta Kappa. Democrat. Presbyn. (elder 1971-72). Rotarian. Home: 1101 East Dr Edmond OK 73034 Office: 1216 S Rankin St Edmond OK 73034

ROY, FRANCIS CHARLES, elec. co. exec.; b. Iota, La., Nov. 28, 1926; s. Fernan A. and Gussie M. (Matte) R.; B.S. in Elec. Engring., La. State U., 1949; M.S., U. Tex., Austin, 1958; m. Pauline Bertha Dischler, June 4, 1949; children—Mary Monica, Michael Anthony, Richard Regan. Engr., Allis Chalmers Mfg. Co., 1949-51; instr. Jeff Davis Vocational Tech. Sch., Jennings, La., 1951-55; asso. prof. engring. La. Tech. U., 1955-65; engr., exec. v.p. Indsl. Supply Co. La., Inc., Lake Charles, 1965—; computer specialist, program engring. tchr. NSF, summers 1961-62; cons. United Gas Co. research labs., summer 1965. Served with USAAF, 1944-46. Registered profl. engr., La. Sr. mem. I.E.E.E. (past sect. pres.); mem. La. Engring. Soc. (pres. Lake Charles chpt. 1973-74), Tau Beta Pi, Eta Kappa Mu. Home: 216 Park Av Lake Charles LA 70601 Office: PO Box 1663 Lake Charles LA 70601

ROYALL, DAN MURCHISON, JR., retail exec.; b. Corsicana, Tex., Sept. 16, 1931; s. Dan Murchison and Mary Ann (Gentry) R.; grad. Tex. Technol. Coll., 1953; postgrad. Sch. Modern Mdse. and Mgmt., Detroit, 1956; m. Ann Kathleen Lamb, Feb. 1, 1952; children—James Dan, Julie Marie. Pres., Royall Chevrolet Buick Opel & Jeep Co., Malakoff, Tex., 1955-67, dirs., chmn. bd. 1967—; pres., chmn. bd. Citizens State Bank, Malakoff, 1965-71; exec. v.p. Tex. Clay Industries, Malakoff, 1968; pres. Temtex Leisure Vehicles Inc., Dallas, 1970-72. Mem. Malakoff City Council, 1960, Sch. Bd., 1969-72. Served to 1st lt. AUS, 1953-55. Mem. C. of C. (pres. 1958), Aircraft Owners and Pilots Assn. Methodist. Home: Route 1 Star Harbor Malakoff TX 75148 Office: 510 W Royall Blvd PO Box 369 Malakoff TX 75148

ROYALS, EDWIN EARL, educator, chemist; b. Climax, Ga., Jan. 23, 1919; s. Joseph Edwin and Eula (McLendon) R.; A.B., Emory U., 1940, M.S., 1941; Ph.D., U. Wis., 1944; m. Mary Edith Boyette, June 16, 1942; children—Homer Earl, Joseph William, John Lloyd, Mary Edith. Instr. chemistry Ga. Inst. Tech., 1944-46; asst. prof., then asso. prof. Emory U., 1946-62; research asso. Heyden-Newport Chem. Corp., 1962-65; prof., head dept. chemistry Pensacola Jr. Coll., 1965—; cons. to naval stores and terpene industries. Mem. Am. Chem. Soc., A.A.A.S., Delta Tau Delta. Baptist. Kiwanian. Author: Advanced Organic Chemistry, 1954; also articles. Home: 2016 Swan Lane Pensacola FL 32504

ROYALTY, ROBERT MALCOLM, lawyer; b. Danville, Ill., Jan. 7, 1933; s. Gerald Loren and Virginia Ellen (Davis) R.; B.A. summa cum laude, Beloit Coll., 1954; J.D. cum laude, Harvard, 1959; m. Patricia Eileen Ruth Clark, July 16, 1954; children—Virginia Beth, Robert Malcolm, John G., Patricia M., Sarah E. Admitted to Ga. bar, 1964; asso. firm Crowell and Leibman, Chgo., 1959-61; asso. firm Sutherland, Asbill and Brennan, Atlanta, 1962-68, partner, 1968—. Pres. P.T.A., 1971-72. Candidate for Atlanta City Exec. Com., 1965; mem. exec. com. Fulton County Republican Party, 1971—. Bd. dirs. MetroAtlanta Mental Health Assn. Served with AUS, 1954-66. Mem. C. of C. (mem. life quality steering com. 1970-71), Atlanta (sec.-treas. 1970-72, exec. com. 1972-73), Ga., Am. bar assns., Lawyers Club of Atlanta. Episcopalian (mem. vestry 1969—). Clubs: Cherokee Town and Country, Atlanta City. Home: 3512 Old Ivy Lane NE Atlanta GA 30342 Office: 3100 First National Bank Tower Atlanta GA 30303

ROYCE, PHILIP LEE, coll. pub. relations exec.; b. Mount Kisco, N.Y., Aug. 18, 1936; s. Levi Stearns and Esther (Hull) R.; A.A., St. Petersburg Jr. Coll., 1956; B.A., Fla. State U., 1959; B.D., Southeastern Bapt. Theol. Sem., 1964; m. Rosemary Thomas, June 9, 1961; children—Jon Thomas, Karen Elizabeth. Ordained to ministry Bapt. Ch., 1967; minister edn. and youth 1st Bapt. Ch., Crestview, Fla., 1964-67; minister Bapt. Student Union Troy (Ala.) State U., 1967-69; dir. coll. relations Chowan Coll., Murfreesboro, N.C., 1969—. Mem. Bapt. Pub. Relations Assn. (recipient Exceptional Merit award for radio 1973), News Seminar of the Carolinas, Am. Coll. Pub. Relations Assn. (deacon). Home: 209 Holly Hill Rd Murfreesboro NC 27855 Office: Chowan College Murfreesboro NC 27855

ROYCROFT, HOWARD FRANCIS, lawyer; b. Balt., Sept. 9, 1930; s. Howard F. and Bessie (Weaver) R.; B.A., U. Md., 1953; LL.B., Georgetown U., 1958; m. Barbara Lee Seal, Mar. 20, 1954; children—Suzanne Carol, Nancy Lee. Admitted to D.C. bar, 1958, since practiced in Washington; mem. firm Hogan & Hartson, 1958, now partner, mem. exec. com., 1970-73; lectr. Howard U. Sch. Law, 1973-74. Mem. Met. Washington Bd. Trade. Bd. dirs. YMCA Met. Washington. Served to 1st lt. USMC, 1953-55. Mem. Am., Va. State, Fed. Communications bar assns., Bar Assn. D.C., Nat. Broadcasters Club, Barristers, Nat. Acad. TV Arts and Scis., Bryce Mountain Assn. (dir, pres. 1974), Kappa Alpha, Beta Kappa. Republican. Methodist. Clubs: Washington Athletic, Washington Tennis Patrons, Internat. Home: 8703 Eaglebrook Ct Alexandria VA 22308 Office: 815 Connecticut Av Washington DC 20006

ROYER, ROBERT LEWIS, pub. utility co. exec.; b. Louisville, Jan. 2, 1928; s. Carl Brown and Martha Helen (Garrett) R.; B.S. in Elec. Engring., Rose Hulman Inst. Tech., 1949; m. Carol Jean Pierce, June 24, 1950; children—Jenifer, Todd, Douglas. With Louisville Gas & Electric Co., 1949—, v.p. operations, 1969—, also dir. Vice pres. Old Ky. Home council Boy Scouts Am., 1970—. Served with AUS, 1953-55. Mem. I.E.E.E., Power Soc., Theta Xi. Methodist. Club: Optomist Internat. Home: 4014 Norbourne Blvd Louisville KY 40207 Office: PO Box 354 Louisville KY 40201

ROYSTER, GEORGE ERWIN, life ins. co. exec.; b. Statesville, N.C., July 10, 1928; s. Ira Gay and Catherine Margaret (Poesy) R.; B.A., U. Tenn., 1955; m. Joy Angeline Inman, Nov. 23, 1968; 1 dau., Joy Angeline. Asst. v.p. Integon Corp., Winston-Salem, N.C., 1955-68; v.p. Liberty Life Ins. Co., Greenville, S.C., 1968—; pres., dir. LIBCO, Inc., Greenville, 1970; sr. v.p. marketing Am. Found. Life Ins. Co., Little Rock, 1971-74, exec. v.p., 1974—, also dir., mem. exec. com.; dir. Sales Marketing Internat. Pres., bd. dirs. Durham County March Dimes, 1962. Mem. Nat. Assn. Securities Dealers, Nat. Assn. Life Underwriters, C. of C., Sigma Alpha Epsilon. Episcopalian (lay reader 1962). Clubs: Little Rock, Little Rock Racquet, Country of Little Rock. Home: 8 Huntington Rd Little Rock AR 72207 Office: 4th and Ringo Sts Little Rock AR 72203

ROYSTER, WIMBERLY CALVIN, coll. dean; b. Robards, Ky., Jan. 12, 1925; s. Fred R. and Ruth Furman (Denton) R.; B.S., Murray State U., 1946; M.A., U. Ky., 1948, Ph.D., 1952; m. Betty Jo Barnett, July 1, 1950; children—David, Paul. Asst. prof. math. Auburn (Ala.) U., 1952-56; faculty U. Ky., Lexington, 1956—, prof. math., 1963—, chmn. dept., 1963-69, dir. Sch. Math. Scis., 1967-69, dean Coll. Arts and Scis., 1969-72, dean Grad. Sch., coordinator research, 1972—. Mem. Inst. Advanced Study, Princeton, N.J., 1962, NRC, 1972-75. Mem. A.A.A.S., Am. Math. Soc., Math. Assn. Am., Sigma Xi. Rotarian. Home: 133 Vanderbilt Dr Lexington KY 40503

ROZETT, ROBERT, engring. exec.; b. N.Y.C., Mar. 16, 1927; s. William and Emily (Ruzicka) R.; B.S., Columbia, 1946, M.S., 1947; Ph.D., N.C. State U., 1958; m. Jane Ellen Mercer, Oct. 1, 1949; children—Christopher Scott, Amy Irene. Chem. engr. Socony Vacuum Oil Co., Paulsboro, N.J., 1947-51; process engr. Catalytic Constrn. Co., Phila., 1951-54; instr. chem. engring. N.C. State U., also cons. Bur. Ships, pvt. engring. practice, 1954-58; group leader Merck & Co., Danville, Pa., 1958-61; tech. supr. Allied Chem. Co., Morristown, N.J., 1962-63; sect. head Celanese Corp., Summit, N.J., 1963-65; dir. fibers research and devel. lab. Celanese Fibers Co., Charlotte, N.C., 1965-68; tech. dir. Celanese Coatings Co., Louisville, 1968-70; pres. Ecotechnics, Louisville, 1970—. Dir. Maria Center. Mem. Am. Inst. Chem. Engrs. (sect. chmn. 1960), Sigma Xi, Phi Kappa Phi, Phi Lambda Upsilon. Republican. Club: Louisville Boat. Home: 2009 High Ridge Rd Louisville KY 40207

ROZZELL, GEORGE MCALLASTER, JR., mech. contracting co. exec.; b. Little Rock, June 10, 1926; s. George McAllaster and Pauline Lucretia (Craig) R.; B.S., Purdue U., 1946; postgrad. Ohio State U., 1947; m. Alice Margaret Kepner, July 9, 1948; children—Margaret Anne (Mrs. Ben C. Davenport), Susan Alice (Mrs. Harry D. Langley), George McAllaster II, Paula Jean. With Curtiss-Wright Aircraft Co., Columbus, O., 1946-47, E.W. Daniel Plumbing and Heating, North Little Rock, Ark., 1947-55; with Ark. Mech. Contractors, North Little Rock, 1955—, pres., 1969—; pres. AMC, Inc., North Little Rock, R-T Leasing Co., North Little Rock, Ark., Mech. Contractors, North Little Rock, Woodland, Inc., North Little Rock; dir. Twin City Bank, North Little Rock. Chmn. North Little Rock Youth Center, 1965. Chmn. North Little Rock Water Commn., 1970—; vice chmn. North Little Rock Port Authority, 1965-69. Bd. dirs. St. Louis Children's Home, St. Louis. Served with USNR, 1943-46. Registered profl. engr., Ark. Mem. Am. Soc. M.E., Am. Soc. Heating, Refrigerating and Air-Conditioning Engrs. (dir. 1974), Constrn. Specifications Inst., Sigma Chi. Mem. Christian Ch. (trustee 1968-71). Clubs: North Hills Country (North Little Rock); Capitol (Little Rock).

ROZZELL, THOMAS CLIFTON, environmental scientist; b. Gastonia, N.C., Apr. 5, 1937; s. Robert Clifton Hall and Cleo Birdie (Farris) R.; B.S. in Chemistry, Fisk U., 1959; M.S. in Indsl. Hygiene, U. Cin., 1960; Sc.D. in Environmental Health, U. Pitts., 1968; m. Maryann Rebecca Gay, Dec. 27, 1959; children—Liane Gay, Eric Thomas, Jon Thornton. Lab. technician Nat. Carbon Co., Niagara Falls, N.Y., summer 1957; chemist Union Carbide Metals Co., Niagara Falls, summer 1959; radiochemist Taft San. Engring. Center, USPHS, Cin., 1960-65; asst. prof. environmental radiation U. Pitts. Grad. Sch. Pub. Health, 1968-71; environmental scientist Office Naval Research, Arlington, Va., 1971—. Cons. in field. Mem. USPHS Task Force Environmental Health, 1970, pres. USPHS Fed. Credit Union, 1963-65. Bd. dirs. Fairfax County YMCA. Union Carbide Corp. fellow, 1956-59; Gabriel scholar, 1956; Textiles, Inc. scholar, 1955-59; Grad.-AEC spl. fellow, 1959-60; USPHS doctoral study fellow, 1965-66. Recipient Research award Continental Oil Co. Mem. Health Physics Soc. (chmn. subcom. environmental radioactivity 1969-71), Am. Pub. Health Assn., Water Pollution Control Assn., Am. Nat. Standards Inst., Am. Water Works Assn., Am. Chem. Soc., Sigma Xi, Omega Psi Phi. Home: 4307 Ann Fitzhugh Dr Annandale VA 22003 Office: 800 N Quincy St Arlington VA 22217

RUA, MILTON FRANCISCO, lawyer; b. San German, P.R., Dec. 8, 1919; s. Urbano F. and Josefa A. (Gonzalez-Ferrer) R.; B.A. cum laude U. P.R., 1941, LL.B., 1943; m. Marina Cabrer, Mar. 31, 1945; children—Milton J., Jaime L. Admitted to P.R. bar, 1943; legal counsel Dept. Finance of P.R., 1943-46; sr. partner Rivera-Zayas, Rivera-Cestero & Rua, San Juan, P.R., 1950-73; founder Rúa, Mercado & Gonzalez, Hato Rey, P.R., 1973, sr. partner, 1973—; founder Banco Mercantil de P.R., Rio Piedras, 1966, counsellor, 1966—, vice chmn. bd. dirs., 1971—; founder Asso. Ins. Agencies, Inc., San Juan, 1972, counsellor, 1972—; legal counsel Fajardo Fed. Savs. & Loan Assn., Fajardo, P.R., 1972—; pres., dir. Lincoln Financial Mortgagees, Inc., San Juan; bd. dirs. Am. Internat. Life Ins. Co. of P.R., San Juan, Bank-Merc Investment Group, Inc., San Juan, Sports Digest, Inc. Mem. bar exam. com. Supreme Ct. P.R., 1955-56; spl. counsel com. natural resources and beautification P.R. Ho. of Reps., 1967-68; mem. citizens com. nuclear plants Environmental Quality Bd. of P.R., 1972; chmn. Electoral Reform Commn., 1973—. Mem. organizing com. First Latin Am. Biennal Graphic Arts, P.R., 1970. Bd. dirs. Casa el Libro, chmn. 1960-70; bd. dirs. Inst. of Culture of P.R., Students Art League of San Juan, Mus. P.R. Mem. Bar Assn. P.R., Am., Inter-Am. bar assns., Iberoamerican Inst. Aero. Law. Elk. Clubs: Bankers, Casino de Puerto Rico (San Juan); Union League (N.Y.C.). Home: Condominio del Mar 1401 Delcasse St Condado PR 00907 Office: 1 Mercantile Plaza Hato Rey PR 00919

RUBEN, LEONARD, artist, educator, advt. agy. exec.; b. St. Paul, June 3, 1921; s. Theodore and Elizabeth (Hauchman) R.; B.F.A., Pratt Inst., 1952; M.A. in Fine Arts, Columbia, 1961; Ph.D., N.Y.U., 1970; m. Sue Levey, Dec. 23, 1970. Art dir. Young & Rubicam, Inc., N.Y.C., 1955-60; head art group North Advt., N.Y.C., 1960-62; instr. Columbia, 1962-63; v.p., asso. creative dir. J.M. Mathes, Inc., N.Y.C., 1966-68; creative dir. Lake Spiro Shurman, Memphis, 1968-69; pres. Len Ruben & Friends Advt., 1969—; partner, dir. Ruben & Ruben; asst. prof. art N.E. La. U., Monroe, 1969-71; asso. prof. U. Tex., Austin, 1971—. Served to 1st lt. AUS, 1940-46. Recipient numerous awards from Am. TV Commls. Festival, N.Y. Art Dirs., Am. Inst. Graphic Arts, Graphex 70, Art Dirs. and Designers Assn. of New Orleans, Memphis Advt. Club, Memphis Art Dirs. Club, Mid-South Art Dirs. Show, So. Creativity Show, Am. Advt. Fedn., N.Y. Advt. Club, Am. TV and Radio Commls. Festival, others. Mem. Tex. Advt. Profs. Assn. (pres.), Austin Ad Club (dir., Gold medal). Address: 4000 Pete's Path Austin TX 78731

RUBEY, MYRON ROSS, financial exec.; b. Hattiesburg, Miss., Nov. 30, 1910; s. Louis and Ida (Block) R.; B.B.A., U. Balt., 1933; m. Mary R. Rocklin, Mar. 8, 1942; children—Stephen L., Robert F. Pres., Ross Jewelers, Mobile, Ala., 1947-70, Myron R. Rubey & Assos., Mobile, 1970—; dir. Valley Savs. & Loan Assn., Balt., Savs. Bank Reistertown, Md. Head, United Fund, 1948; asso. Mobile Infirmary, 1955-69; adv. bd. March of Dimes, 1964-66; chmn. Am. Jewish Com., 1965-73, Israel-Am. Affairs, 1969—; pres. Welfare Bd., Mobile, 1953-69; mem. Ala. Bd. Edn., 1952. Served to capt. USAAF, 1943-46. Decorated by Gen. Eisenhower for invention of life sav. device for downed flyers, 1944; recipient Service awards David Ben Gurion, 1968, Prime Minister Golda Meir, 1970; named Mobile Press-Register Man of Year, 1954. Mem. Mobile (head 1961), U.S. chambers commerce. Optimist, Rotarian, Mason (Shriner), Kiwanian; mem. B'nai B'rith (pres. 1969-73). Club: Exchange. Home: 216 Berwyn Dr Mobile AL 36608 Office: 1111 Beltline Hwy S Mobile AL 36616

RUBIN, ALVIN BENJAMIN, judge; b. Alexandria, La., Mar. 13, 1920; s. Simon and Frances (Prussack) R.; B.S. in Bus. Adminstrn., La. State U., 1941, LL.B. 1942; m. Janice Ginsberg, Feb. 19, 1946; children—Michael H., David S. Admitted to La. bar, 1942; practiced in Baton Rouge, 1946-66; partner firm Sanders, Miller, Downing, Rubin & Kean, 1946-66; U.S. dist. Judge Eastern Dist. La., New Orleans, 1966—. Vis. lectr. law La. State U. Law Sch., 1946—; lectr. taxation Tulane U. Tax Inst., Ga. Tax Inst., La. State U. Mineral Law Inst.; arbitrator Fed. Mediation and Conciliation Service, 1950-66. Chmn. Baton Rouge Zoning Study Com.; mem. La. Legislative Adminstrv. Procedure Com. Sec. Baton Rouge United Givers Fund, 1954-67; past bd. dirs. Baton Rouge chpt. Girl Scouts U.S.A., Mental Health Guidance Center, Community Chest, Community Services Council, Nat. Assn. Crippled Children and Adults; past adv. bd. local Salvation Army, YWCA, Blundon Orphanage. Served to capt. AUS, 1942-46; ETO. Recipient Golden Deeds award for civic service, 1964, Brotherhood award, 1968. Mem. Am. (chmn. estate and gift tax com. 1964, chmn. sect. bar activities 1963, lawyer referral 1970-72), La. (chmn. sect. trust estates, probate and immovable property law 1961, chmn. labor law sect. 1957, jr. bar sect. 1955) bar assns., Nat. Acad. Arbitrators, Am. Arbitration Assn., La. Law Inst., Order of Coif, Phi Delta Phi, Omicron Delta Kappa. Mason (32 deg.). Author: (with McMahon) Louisiana Pleadings and Judicial Forms Annotated; (with Janice G. Rubin) Louisiana Trust Handbook. Home: 225 Walnut St New Orleans LA 70118 Office: 400 Royal St New Orleans LA 70130

RUBIN, BERNARD, govt. ofcl.; b. Boston, July 1, 1922; s. Morris and Anna (Kaplan) R.; A.B., Harvard, 1944; Ph.D., Ohio State U., 1951; m. Selma Lois Wenesky, June 29, 1952; children—Susan M., Eric R., David H. Research chemist Nat. Bur. Standards, 1951-54; sect. chief USAF Cambridge Research Labs., Bedford, Mass., 1954-66; program mgr. NASA, Washington, 1966—. Served with USNR, 1944-46. Fellow Am. Inst. Chemists; mem. Am. Chem. Soc., Sigma Xi, Phi Lambda Upsilon. Contbr. articles to tech. lit. Patentee in field. Home: 5609 Ridgefield Rd Bethesda MD 20016 Office: 600 Independence Av SW Washington DC 20546

RUBIN, HENRY CARL, state ofcl.; b. Alexandria, La., Aug. 22, 1942; s. Abe and Pauline Doris (Levy) R.; B.S., La. Coll., 1964. Sec., E. Levy & Co., Alexandria, 1964-72; spl. asst. Gov. La., 1972—. Dir. La. Am. Revolution Bicentennial, Alexandria, 1972-73. Served with AUS, 1964-70. Named Outstanding Jaycee, Alexandria, 1965-66, Outstanding 1st Year Jaycee in La., 1965-66, Outstanding Vice Pres. La. Jaycees, 1968-69, Outstanding La. Dir., 1969-70. Mem. La. Alliance, U.S., La. (v.p. 1968-69, pres. 1970-71), Alexandria (pres. 1967-68) jr. chambers commerce, Am. Legion. Mason. Home: PO Box 44343 Baton Rouge LA 70804

RUBIN, LEON C., govt. ofcl.; b. Chgo., June 12, 1914; s. Charles and Sophie (Wilsker) R.; B.S. in Accounting, U. Ill., 1936; m. Lillian Schwartz, Jan. 10, 1943; children—Sherry Ann, Robert Bruce. Field auditor Ill. Dept. Finance, 1936-41; financial analyst SEC, Washington, 1941-51, sr. financial analyst, 1957—, chief financial analyst div. corporate regulation, 1972—; cost accountant Gen. Account Office, 1951-52; bus. accountant Renegotiation Bd., 1952-57, dep. supr., 1955-57. Served with USNR, 1943-45. C.P.A., Ill., Pa. Mem. Am. Inst. Accountants, Pa. Inst. C.P.A.'s, Fed. Govt. Accountants Assn., Washington Soc. Investment Analysts, Beta Alpha Psi. Home: 6801 Renita Lane Bethesda MD 20034 Office: 500 N Capital St NW Washington DC 20549

RUBIN, MARTIN ISRAEL, educator; b. N.Y.C., Nov. 2, 1915; s. Herman and Augusta (Buchbinder) R.; B.S., Coll. City N.Y., 1936; Ph.D., Columbia, 1942; m. Edith Feldbau, May 30, 1942; children—Joanne (Mrs. Ronald Orleans), Richard, Naomi (Mrs. Robert King), Deborah. Fellow Mt. Sinai Hosp., N.Y.C., 1940, Johns Hopkins Med. Sch., Balt., 1941; with Wallace & Tiernan Co., N.J., 1942-46, Schering Corp., 1946-48; prof. biochemistry Georgetown U., 1948—; cons. Nat. Insts. Health, W.H.O., Pan Am. Health Orgn., F.D.A., Nat. Research Council. Recipient Smith, Kline award, Capitol Clin. Chemist award. Mem. Internat. Union Pure and Applied Chemistry, Internat. Fedn. Clin. Chemists (pres.), Am. Bd. Clin. Chemistry (dir.), Am. Assn. Clin. Chemistry (dir. 1965-69), Assn. Clin. Biochemists (hon.), Polish Soc. Lab. Diagnosis. Editor: Clinica Chimica Acta. Contbr. articles profl. jours. Patentee in field. Home: 3218 Pauline Dr Chevy Chase MD 20015 Office: Georgetown University Washington DC 20007

RUBIN, MELVIN LYNNE, physician; b. San Francisco, May 10, 1932; s. Morris and May (Gelman) R.; A.A., U. Cal. at Berkeley, 1951, B.S., 1953, M.D., 1957; M.S., State U. Ia., 1961; m. Lorna Isen, June 21, 1953; children—Jan, Daniel, Michael. Intern, U. Cal. Hosp., San Francisco, 1957-58; resident State U. Ia., 1958-61; asst. prof. surgery U. Fla., Gainesville, 1963-66, asso. prof. ophthalmology, 1966-67, prof., 1967—, chief retina div., 1963—. Chmn., Nat. Ophthalmic Knowledge Assessment Program, 1968—. Mem. Gainesville Assn. Creative Arts, 1967—; co-founder Pro Arte Musica Gainesville, Inc., 1969, pres., 1971-73; co-founder Citizens for Pub. Schs., 1966. Bd. dirs. N. Fla. Eye Bank. Served with USPHS, 1961-63. Recipient Fight for Sight citation, 1970, Gainesville Community Service award, 1971, Merit award Am. Acad. Ophthalmology and Otolaryngology, 1972. Fellow A.C.S., Am. Acad. Ophthalmology and Otolaryngology (asso. sec.); mem. A.M.A., Fla. Med. Assn., Alachua County Med. Soc., A.A.A.S., Retina Soc., Club Jules Gonin, N.Y. Acad. Scis., Pan Am. Assn. Ophthalmology, Ophthalmic Photographers Soc., Sigma Xi, Alpha Omega Alpha. Mem. B'nai B'rith. Author: Studies in Physiological Optics, 1965; Fundamentals of Visual Science, 1968; Optics for Clinicians, 1971; also articles, revs.; asso. editor Survey of Ophthalmology, 1968—, Investigative Ophthalmology, 1967—. Home: 1122 NW 20th Dr Gainesville FL 32605 Office: Box 733 Shands Teaching Hosp Gainesville FL 32610

RUBINOWITZ, ARTHUREA BROWN (MRS. STANLEY HENRY RUBINOWITZ), supt. schs.; b. nr. Mobile, Ala.; d. Arthur Isom and Beatrice (Knight) Brown; student Livingston (Ala.) Coll., 1934-36, Hardin-Simmons U., 1941-42; B.A., Am. U., 1958, M.A., 1960, Ed.D., 1966; m. Stanley Henry Rubinowitz, Aug. 6, 1943; children—Arthur Lee, Ben Brown. Tchr. schs., Ala., Tex., Va., Germany, 1935-60; prin. Fairfax (Va.) Pub. Schs., 1961-68; asst. adminstr., dir. instrn. K-12 Fairfax County Pub. Schs., 1968-70, area supt., 1970—; professorial lectr. Am. U., 1964—, U. Va., 1967—. Cons. Title III Edn. Center. Mem. Nat., Va., Fairfax County (personnel policy and salary coms.) edn. assns., Nat. Council on Measurement Edn., Assn. Supervision and Curriculum Devel., Nat., Va., Fairfax County (pres. 1967-68), elementary prins. assns., Am. Edn. Research Assn. (participant 1967 pre-session), Assn. for Childhood Edn. Internat., Dept. Elementary Sch. Prins., Delta Kappa Gamma, Alpha Delta Kappa. Author articles in field. Home: 6115 Clearbrook Dr Springfield VA 22150 Office: 6402 Franconia Rd Springfield VA 22150

RUBLY, GRANT RUSSELL, ret. mining engr.; b. Cleve., June 7, 1906; s. Carl John and Louise F. (Sump) R.; B.S., Case Inst. Tech., 1928, E.M., 1939; m. Lucille Alyce Pickering, Oct. 5, 1929; children—John Charles, Grant Allen, Elizabeth Anne (Mrs. Charles E. Sills), Carl Andrew, Sharon Eloise (Mrs. William D. Tilley). Mine engr. Miami Copper Co. (Ariz.), 1928-37, chief mine engr., 1937-44; resident engr. Magma Copper Co., Superior, Ariz., 1944-45, San Manuel Copper Corp., Superior, 1945-47; check and right of way engr. Ore. Hwy. Commn., Salem, 1947-48; mining supr. Magnet Cove Barium Corp., Malvern, Ark., 1948-50; engr. Def. Minerals Adminstrn., U.S. Bur. Mines, Campus U. Ariz., Tucson, 1950-51; asst. chief mine engr. Reynolds Mining Corp., Bauxite, Ark., 1951-56, jr. staff engr., 1956-58, sr. staff asst., 1958-71; cons. engr., 1971-74. Fellow A.A.A.S.; mem. Am. Inst. Mining, Metall. and Petroleum Engrs., Sigma Xi, Phi Kappa Tau, Theta Tau. Methodist. Mason (32 deg., K.T.). Contbr. articles to profl. jours. Home: PO Box 154 Malvern AR 72104

RUBOTTOM, DONALD JULIAN, investment banker; b. Tulsa, Sept. 29, 1926; s. George W. and Nellie D. (Core) R.; B.S. in Finance, Okla. State U., 1951; postgrad. mgmt. Tulsa U., 1957-59; m. Wanda Mae Stockton, Apr. 29, 1951; children—Rinda L., Joy L., Donald J., Jill A. Account exec. Harris Upham & Co., Tulsa, 1950-51; v.p. trust dept. First Nat. Bank, Tulsa, 1955-66; exec. v.p., dir. F & M Bank & Trust Co., Tulsa, 1966-68; propr. Rubottom & Assos., Tulsa, 1968—; dir. several corps.; mem. faculty Okla. Sch. Banking, 1972—. Mem. endowment com. Tulsa YMCA; past pres. local PTA; mem. alumni corp. Pi Kappa Alpha. Bd. dirs. John 3:16 Mission, Tulsa. Served with AUS, 1945-46. Mem. Am. Bankers Assn. (past mem. common trust funds com.), Financial Analysts Fedn. (past v.p., dir.), Tulsa Soc. Investment Analysts (past pres.), Okla. Soc. Financial Analysts (past pres.), Inst. Chartered Financial Analysts. Methodist (bd., chmn. commn. evangelism). Rotarian. Clubs: Tulsa; Cedar Ridge Country (Tulsa). Home: 5820 E 58th Pl Tulsa OK 74135 Office: 1920 First Nat Bank Bldg Tulsa OK 74103

RUBY, ROBERT HARLEY, radio sta. personality; b. Des Moines, Apr. 23, 1937; s. Harold Orville and Johanna Christina (Sorenson) R.; B.A. in History, U. Mont., 1959; m. Eunice Alice Goodman, Oct. 13, 1962; children—Matthew Conor, Jo Alice. Singer, N.Y.C., 1960-64; capitol corr. U.P.I., Helena, Mont., 1968; adminstrv. asst. Gov. Forrest Anderson of Mont., 1968-69; host Mornings Are Ruby show WWL Radio Sta., New Orleans, 1969—. Served with USAF, 1961-62. Mem. Am. Fedn. Radio and TV Artists, Broadcast Music Inc., Sigma Nu. Democrat. Home: 3570 Somerset Dr New Orleans LA 70114 Office: 1024 N Rampart St New Orleans LA 70176

RUCH, ROBERT MILTON, obstetrician and gynecologist; b. Chaffee, Mo., Nov. 4, 1923; s. Walter Allwein and Frances H. (Helmkamp) R.; A.B., Princeton, 1943; M.D., U. Pa., 1947; m. Emily Boone, Jan. 26, 1952; children—Emily Boone, Rondi Frances, Robert Milton. Intern Pa. Hosp., 1947-48; resident Barnes Hosp., St. Louis, 1948-49, John Gaston Hosp., Memphis, 1949-50, Barnard Skin and Cancer Hosp., St. Louis, 1950-51; practice medicine, specializing in obstetrics and gynecology, Memphis, 1953—; asso. prof. U. Tenn. Med. Sch., 1966—; chief staff Bapt. Meml. Hosp., 1973. Past pres., now bd. dirs. Memphis and Shelby County chpt. Am. Cancer Soc.; bd. dirs. W. Tenn. Cancer Clinic. Served with USAF, 1951-53. Am. Cancer Soc. fellow, 1951-52. Mem. Memphis and Shelby County Med. Soc., Am. Radium Soc., Am. Coll. Obstetricians and Gynecologists, S. Central (pres. 1967-68), Tenn., Memphis (pres. 1973) obstet. and gyncol. socs., Am. Soc. Study Sterility. Episcopalian. Rotarin. Home: 115 Grove Park Circle Memphis TN 38117 Office: 20 S Dudley St 509-B Memphis TN 38103

RUCH, WALTER ALLWEIN, JR., physician, educator; b. Memphis, Aug. 8, 1930; s. Walter Allwein and Frances Louise (Helmkamp) R.; A.B., Princeton, 1951; M.D., Washington U., 1955; m. Margaret Ann Peet, Aug. 15, 1954; children—Walter Allwein, Charles David. Intern, St. Luke's Hosp., St. Louis, 1955-56; resident in obstetrics and gynecology Barnes Hosp., St. Louis, 1956-60; practice medicine specializing in obstetrics and gynecology, Memphis, 1962—; asst. clin. prof. obstetrics and gynecology U. Tenn. Sch. Medicine, 1968—; chmn. obstetrics and gynecology dept. Bapt. Meml. Hosp., 1973. Bd. dirs. Planned Parenthood World Population, 1968—, mem. nat. med. com., 1969-72. Served to capt. USMCR, 1960-62. Diplomate Am. Bd. Obstetrics and Gynecology. Mem. Am., Tenn. med. assns., Memphis Planned Parenthood Assn. (pres. 1969-72). Episcopalian (vestry 1967-69). Club: University. Home: 4303 Hathaway Lane Memphis TN 38117 Office: 20 S Dudley Memphis TN 38103

RUCKDESCHEL, FREDERIC BRILL, economist; b. Phila., Mar. 7, 1937; s. John Kessler and Anna Elizabeth (Brill) R.; A.B., Earlham Coll., 1959; M.A., Princeton, 1962; Ph.D., U. Pa., 1971; m. Kristin Shackford, Aug. 10, 1963; children—David Brill, Jonathan. Economist, Bd. Govs. Fed. Res. System, Washington, 1963—. Dir. River Park Mutual Homes, Inc., 1970-72, Fed. Res. Bur. Fed. Credit Union, 1972-74. Mem. Washington Soc. Investment Analysts. Home: 1328 4th St SW Washington DC 20024 Office: Fed Res Bd Washington DC 20551

RUCKEL, CHARLES WALTER, JR., banker; b. Pensacola, Fla., Jan. 1, 1927; s. Charles Walter and Marion (Plew) R.; student Davidson (N.C.) Coll., 1944-45, North Ga. Coll., Dahlonega, 1945; diploma Soule Bus. Coll., New Orleans, 1948, Okaloosa-Walton Jr. Coll., Niceville, Fla., 1974; m. Gilda Juliet Meaut, Feb. 9, 1946; children—Charles Walter III, James Plew, Gregory Meaut; m. 2d, Wava Dyer, July 7, 1964; children—Marion Louise, Sharon Joyce; stepchildren—Stephen W., Martin L. Tille. With Valparaiso Bank & Trust Co. (Fla.), 1948—, dir., asst. v.p., 1950-51, pres., chmn. bd., 1955-64, chmn. bd., 1964—; pres., dir. Ruckel Properties, Inc., 1955—; dir. Gulf Power Co., Pensacola, F.W. Means & Co., Chgo. Pres. exec. bd. Gulf Coast council Boy Scouts Am., 1961-62; pres. Okaloosa County Community Chest, 1965-66; lt. col. Civil Air Patrol, Fla. Wing, 1960—. Bd. dirs. Okaloosa Island Authority, 1967-71. Served with USAAF, 1944-47. Named Man of Yr., Niceville-Valparaiso Rotary Club, 1957, 70. Mem. Fla. Bankers Assn., Krewe of Bowlegs. Republican. Rotarian. Clubs: Fort Walton Yacht (Ft. Walton Beach, Fla.); Eglin Golf, Rocky Bayou Country (Niceville). Home: Route 1 Box 176-R Niceville FL 32578 Office: 23 S John Sims Pkwy Valparaiso FL 32580

RUCKER, HAROLD JAMES, lawyer; b. Paducah, Ky., Dec. 8, 1921; s. Morton Val Dean and Birdie (Flora) R.; A.B., U. Ky., 1947, J.D., 1949; m. Robbie Boggess, Mar. 12, 1974; children by previous marriage—Carol Jane, Morton Val Dean, Douglas McCauley, Helen Lynne Louise. Admitted to Ky. bar, 1949, Tex. bar, 1950; mem. staff land dept. Shell Oil Co., Midland, Tex., 1949-50; practiced in Midland, 1950—; mem. firm Perkins, German, Mims & Bell, 1951-54, Perkins & Bezoni, 1955-56, Rucker & Rassman, 1958-60; dir. Brantly Drilling Co., Inc., Huckabay Chevrolet, Inc., West Tex. Enterprises, Inc., Western Equipment Co., Master Rentals, Chancellor Chair Co., Chaparral Cars, Inc., Midland, Black Bear Oil & Gas Corp. (W.Va.), Brantly Internat., Rio de Janeiro, Brazil. Past pres., bd. dirs. Am. Cancer Soc., Midland, 1960-61; mem. Midland YMCA, 1961-68, pres., bd. dirs., 1962-68, chmn. endowment com., 1964-65, chmn. Century Club, 1965-66, pres., bd. dirs. S.W. Area Council, 1962-66, mem. program com., chmn. workshop area council meeting, Dallas, 1963; past bd. dirs. Midland County Child Welfare Unit, 1957-58; pres., bd. dirs. Midland Diagnostic Cancer Clinic, 1961-62; pres. bd. trustees Trinity Sch., Midland; trustee St. Andrew's (Tenn.) Sch., Sch. Bd. of Diocese of N.W. Tex. (Episcopal). Served to 1st lt. AUS, 1942-46. Named Boss of Year, Legal Secs. Assn., Midland, 1963. Mem. Am., Midland County, Ky. bar assns., State Bar Tex., Am. Judicature Soc., Phi Alpha Delta, Sigma Chi. Episcopalian (vestryman). Kiwanian (pres., dir. 1955-57). Clubs: Racquet, Torrero (Midland). Office: First Nat Bank Bldg Midland TX 79701

RUCKER, NORMAN HENRY, physician; b. Washburn, Tenn., Feb. 26, 1918; s. John Thomas and Doris (Clark) R.; M.D., U. Tenn., 1940; postgrad. Columbia, 1949; m. Katharan Gladys Bradley, 1944; children—Patricia (Mrs. Jack Walker), Ann (Mrs. Jesse Lynn), John, Bradley. Intern Knoxville (Tenn.) Gen. Hosp., 1940-41; resident Manhattan St., Columbia Presbyn. Hosp., 1945-48; practice medicine specializing in psychoanalysis, New Orleans, 1949-72, Knoxville, 1972—; mem. staff Charity Hosp.; asst. prof. psychiatry Tulane U., 1949-51; clin. prof. psychiatry La. State U. 1967-72; tng. and supervision analyst New Orleans Psychoanalytic Inst., 1954-72; staff physician St. Mary's Hosp., Knoxville, 1972—; cons. Childrens Bur., VA Hosp. Sec., Green Acres Civic Assn. Bd. dirs. Family Service Soc. Served to maj. AUS, 1942-45. Mem. A.M.A., Am. Psychiat. Assn., Am. Psychoanalytic Assn., Phi Rho Sigma. Democrat. Baptist. Home: 4914 Mountain Crest Dr Knoxville TN 37918 Office: 701 Magdalon St Clarke Towers Knoxville TN 37918

RUCKER, THOMAS NELSON, radiologist; b. Huntington, W.Va., Oct. 13, 1930; s. Erle Taliferro and Pauline Lemon (Boley) R.; B.A., Va. Mil. Inst., 1952; M.D., U. Va., 1956; m. Caroline Bartlett Morton, July 14, 1956; children—Marshall, Thomas Nelson II, Elizabeth, Janet, Margaret. Intern Grady Meml. Hosp., Atlanta, 1956-57; resident U. Va. Hosp., Charlottesville, 1959-62, asst. prof. radiology, 1963-66; with dept. radiology Holston Valley Community Hosp., Kingsport, Tenn., 1966—; program dir. Cleve. Radiol. Soc., Sullivan County Med. Soc. Served with USAF, 1957-59. Am. Cancer Soc. fellow, 1960-61. Mem. Am. Roentgen Ray Soc., Am. Radiol. Soc., Am. Coll. Radiology (alternate counsilor). Elk. Club: Ridgefields Country (Kingsport, Tenn.). Home: 725 Fleetwood Rd Kingsport TN 37660 Office: Holston Valley Community Hosp W Ravine St Kingsport TN 37660

RUCKLE, WILLIAM HENRY, educator, mathematician; b. Neptune, N.J., Oct. 29, 1936; s. Ernest George and Marjorie Elizabeth (Faller) R.; A.B., Lincoln (Pa.) U., 1960; Ph.D., Fla. State U., 1963; m. Cynthia Anne Grill, Aug. 31, 1960; 1 dau., Marjorie Anne. Asso. prof. math. Lehigh U., 1963-69; prof. math. Clemson U., 1969—. Served with USAF, 1955-58. NSF grantee, 1969. Mem. Am. Math. Soc., Soc. Indsl. and Applied Math., Math. Assn. Am., Sigma Xi. Home: Route 1 Seneca SC 29678 Office: Dept Math Sci Clemson Univ Clemson SC 29631

RUDD, GEORGE ELLIS, physician; b. Birmingham, Ala., Apr. 10, 1928; s. George W. and Bessie (Ellis) R.; B.S., U. Ala., 1950; M.D., 1955; m. Patricia Sprague, Oct. 18, 1958; children—Ellis, Julia, Rebecca. Intern, Caraway Methodist Hosp., Birmingham, 1955-56, now staff mem.; gen. practice medicine, Pinson, Ala., 1956—; mem. staff East End Meml. Hosp., Birmingham, also mem. exec. com. 1971—. Mem. adv. bd. Roebuck br. City Nat. Bank, Birmingham, 1970—. Vice pres. P.T.A., Pinson, 1967-68; chmn. Community Com. for Locating Jr. Coll. in Jefferson County, 1965—; mem. Com. for New Pinson Valley High Sch., 1970-71; mem. adv. com. health service Jefferson State Jr. Coll., Birmingham, 1966—; physician, adviser State Tng. Sch. for Girls, Birmingham, 1968—. Mem. Jefferson County Bd. Edn., 1972—. Bd. dirs. Community Service Council, Birmingham, 1969—. Served to lt. (j.g.), M.C., USNR, 1956-59. Named Man of Year, Eastern Area Birmingham C. of C., 1969. Mem. A.M.A., Med. Assn. Ala., Jefferson County Med. Soc. (trustee, pres. 1973-74), Am. (past pres.), Ala. (dir.) acads. gen. practice. Methodist (chmn. com. on stewardship and finance). Clubs: Civitan (Pinson); The Club, Metropolitan Dinner of Greater Birmingham, Pioneer-Diner's, Cumberland Lake Country (Birmingham). Home: 1019 Oak St Pinson AL 35126 Office: N Main St Pinson AL 35126

RUDD, SAMUEL WHEELER, TV broadcasting co. exec.; b. Portsmouth, O., Aug. 12, 1932; s. S. Wheeler and Carrie Pace (Coats) R.; B.S., Xavier U., Cin., 1954; postgrad. U. Louisville, 1959; m. Susan Roberts, July 1, 1972; children—Cynthia, Scott, Pamela, Amy. Collection mgr. Colonial Finance Co., Cin., 1953-55; salesman McGraw Edison Co., Cin., 1955-57; local sales mgr. station WAVE TV, Louisville, 1957—. Guest lectr. U. Louisville Edn. Dept., 1968—. Mayor, Moorland, Ky., 1961-62; Republican precinct capt., 1966-70. Bd. dirs. Ky. Derby Festival Com., 1972—. Mem. Louisville Assn. Mfrs. (rep. 1966-67), Advt. Club Louisville (v.p. 1967-68, 72-73, dir. 1965—). Clubs: Bluegrass Sponsors, Jefferson, Hurstbourne Country. Home: 908 Cannons Lane Louisville KY 40207 Office: 725 S Floyd St Louisville KY 40203

RUDE, JOE CHRISTOPHER, physician; b. Granite, Okla., Oct. 27, 1905; s. Joe Christopher and Ella Nancy (Lowder) R.; B.A., U. Okla., 1926, B.S., 1928, M.D., 1930; m. Eleanor Wallenfels, May 5, 1934; children—Eleanor Jo, Franklin J., Elizabeth Carolyn, Joe Christopher III. Intern Parkland Hosp., Dallas, 1930-31; asst. resident radiology U. Mich., 1933-34; resident radiology N.Y. Hosp. and Cornell Med. Center, 1935-38; Littauer fellow in radiology Harvard, 1938-39; also asst. roentgenologist C.P. Huntington Meml. Hosp., Boston, 1938-39; instr. radiology U. Tex. at Galveston, 1940, chief dept., prof. radiology, 1949-53; instr. Duke, 1941-42; radiologist Brackenridge Hosp., Austin, Tex., 1953—; cons. radiology Bergstrom AFB; nat. cons. to Office Surgeon Gen., 1955-58, Austin State Hosp., 1953—; hon. cons. 2d Air Force Strategic Air Command. Mem. Teletherapy Evaluation Bd., Oak Ridge, 1950-53. In res., AUS, 1930—, col. M.C. ret. Diplomate Am. Bd. Radiology and Nuclear Medicine. Fellow Am. Coll. Radiology (life), Am. Coll. Nuclear Medicine; mem. Aerospace Med. Assn., Radiol. Soc. N.Am. (life), A.M.A., So. Med. Assn. (life), Tex., Travis County med. socs. Home: 4005 Balcones Dr PO Box 5125 Austin TX 78703 Office: 15th St and East Av Austin TX 78767

RUDER, PHILLIP SAUL, musician, educator; b. Chgo., Sept. 21, 1939; s. Leo and Isabell (Bronson) R.; B.A. summa cum laude, Hartt Coll. Music, U. Hartford, 1964, M.A., 1965; m. Ruth Louise Adler, Aug. 5, 1967; 1 son, Eric David. Debut recital Carnegie Hall N.Y.C., 1964; concertmaster New Orleans Philharmonic, 1965-67, Dallas Symphony, 1969—, Santa Fe (N.M.) Opera Orch., 1969—; artist-in-residence N.C. Sch. Arts, 1967-69; mem. Casals Festival Orch., 1968-70; participant Festival of Two Worlds, Spoleto, Italy, 1964, Slzburg Festival, Austria, 1965. Mem. Dallas Chamber Music Soc. (program com. 1969-71). Home: 6441 Joyce Way Dallas TX 75225 Office: Dallas Symphony Orch Dallas TX 75205

RUDNICK, VAUGHN JOSEPH, judge; b. Chgo., May 15, 1932; s. Joseph Anthony and Dorothy (Blaha) R.; A.A., North Park Jr. Coll., 1952; B.A., Augustana Coll., 1954; J.D., U. Miami, 1959; postgrad. Nat. Coll. State Trial Judges, 1968, data processing for justice adminstrs., 1973; m. Bonita Mary Haflett, Apr. 8, 1961; children—Douglas Michael, Keith Joseph. Admitted to Fla. bar, 1959; practiced firm J. Leo Chapman, West Palm Beach, 1959-67; judge Criminal Ct. of Record, Palm Beach County, West Palm Beach, 1967-72; judge Circuit Ct., Palm Beach County, West Palm Beach, 1973—. Adviser to law enforcement planning counsel office Gov.'s Task Force on Narcotics, Dangerous Drugs and Alcohol Abuse, 1969-71. Judge ad litem Municipal Ct., West Palm Beach 1961-66. Served with AUS, 1954-56. Mem. Am., Palm Beach County bar assns., Fla. Bar. Episcopalian. Lion (pres. 1967-68). Office: Palm Beach County Courthouse West Palm Beach FL 33401

RUESTER, RAYMOND JOHN, newspaper editor; b. East St. Louis, Ill., July 5, 1929; s. Herbert L. and Julia Victoria (Campo) R.; student U. Ga., 1952-53, Fla. State U., 1953-54, U. Cin., 1955; m. Janis Juanita Corbett, June 20, 1950; children—Rene Jon, Lenny Vic, Christopher Lee. TV-radio announcer WDBO-TV, WKIS, Orlando, Fla., 1954, 58; radio sports dir., TV weatherman WDBO Radio-TV, Orlando, 1959-61; dir. news and spl. events WFTV, Orlando, 1961-69, v.p., 1965-69; polit. editor Daytona Beach (Fla.) News Jour., 1969—, asso. editor, 1971—. Bd. counselors Bethune-Cookman Coll., Daytona Beach, 1970-71. Served with USMC, 1948-51. Mem. Fla. Assn. Broadcasters, UPI Fla. Broadcasters Assn. (pres. 1962-68), Radio-TV News Dirs. Assn. Home: 210 Jennie Jewel Dr Orlando FL 32806 Office: PO Box 431 Daytona Beach FL 32015

RUFFIN, JAMES STERLING, JR., physician; b. Covington, Tenn., Feb. 24, 1911; s. James Sterling and Mary Caroline (Feezor) R.; M.D., U. Tenn., 1936; m. Kathryn Witherington, Aug. 20, 1940; children—James Sterling III, Patsy Ann (Mrs. Ronald G. Pairamore). Intern, John Gaston Hosp., Memphis, 1936-37, asst. resident medicine, 1937-38; resident physician U. Tenn. Hosp., Knoxville, 1938-41; gen. practice medicine, Covington, 1946—; chief staff Tipton County Meml. Hosp. Vice pres. Tipton County Fed. Savs. & Loan Assn.; dir. Union Savs. Bank. Mem. Tifton County Quarterly Ct., 1956—; mem. Covington Planning Commn., 1957—, chmn., 1965—; historian Tipton County, 1966—; mem. Covington Sch. Bd., 1948-66. Served from 1st lt. to lt. col., M.C., AUS, 1941-46. Mem. Am. Acad. Family Practice, A.M.A., Am. Legion, Mid-South (v.p. 1971), Tenn. med. assns., Tipton County Med. Soc. (pres. 1967—), Kappa Sigma, Theta Kappa Psi. Presbyn. (elder 1969—). Mason (Shriner), Lion. Home: 328 E Liberty Av Covington TN 38019

RUIZ-SURIA, FERNANDO, lawyer; b. Rio Piedras, P.R., May 18, 1916; s. Abelardo and Teresa (Suria) R.; B.A., U. P.R., 1938, LL.B. cum laude, 1940; m. Irma Bosch, Aug. 18, 1946; children—Fernando, Vanessa (Mrs. Eduardo Elejaldl), Ivan, Mimi. Admitted to P.R. bar, 1941; house counsel Shell Co., Ltd., San Juan, P.R., 1942-53; sr. partner Sifre and Ruiz-Suria, San Juan, 1953-67; sr. partner McConnell, Valdes, Kelly, Sifre, Griggs and Ruiz-Suria, San Juan, 1967—. Pres., dir. EMEF Ocean Towers, Inc., San Juan, 1967—; dir., sec. Albert E. Lee & Son, Inc., San Juan, 1965—, Casa Lee Computers, Inc., San Juan, 1972—. Mem. P.R. Jud. Conf., 1973—, P.R. Bd. Bar Examiners. Mem. P.R. Bar Assn., P.R. C. of C. Alpha Phi Sigma. Rotarian (program chmn. 1962), Elk, K.C. Clubs: Racquet, Bankers, Cangrejos Yacht. Home: Penthouse E Ocean Tower Condominium Isla Verde PR 00913 Office: 255 Ponce De Leon Av San Juan PR 00917

RULE, WILLIAM III, physician; b. Knoxville, Tenn., Apr. 30, 1912; s. William and Charlotte (Gunby) R.; B.S., Davidson Coll., 1932, LL.D., 1965; M.D., U. Pa., 1936; m. Effie Hampton Crane, Dec. 31, 1941; children—William IV, Charlotte (Mrs. Stephen White), Elizabeth Hampton, Paul Crane, Barbara Rowland, John Hedden. Intern, Bryn Mawr (Pa.) Hosp., 1936-37; resident Hosp. U. Pa., Phila., 1937-38, Ashland (Pa.) State Hosp., 1938-39; gen. practice medicine, Knoxville, 1939-40, 70—, Belgian Congo, 1940-70; med. missionary Presbyn. Ch. U.S. to Belgian Congo, Republic of Zaire, 1939-70; adminstr. Institut Med. Christian du Kasai, 1955-70; chief emergency dept. St. Mary's Hosp., Knoxville, 1973—. Med. sec. Congo Protestant Council, 1958-61; exec. sec. Congo Protestant Relief Agy., 1960-61; trustee Knoxville area A.R.C., 1971—. Mem. Am. Coll. Emergency Physicians, A.M.A., Am. Soc. Tropical Medicine and Hygiene. Presbyn. (elder). Home: 7120 Cresthill Dr Knoxville TN 37919 Office: St Mary's Hosp Knoxville TN 37917

RUMAGE, NANCY SIMMS (MRS. JOSEPH PAUL RUMAGE), psychologist; b. Chgo., Aug. 15, 1927; d. William Augustus and Sarah (Price) Simms; B.S., Northwestern U., 1948; M.A., U. Neb., 1951; postgrad. Tulane U., 1951-52; m. Joseph Paul Rumage, June 15, 1955; children—Sarah Agnes, Joseph Paul, William Simms. Research asst. Tulane U., Urban Life Research Inst., 1951-52, chief psychologist, children's unit Tulane U. Med. Sch., 1952-56; psychologist Jefferson Parish Sch. Bd., Gretna, La., 1953-63; gen. practice psychology, New Orleans, 1956—; chief psychologist New Orleans Regional Mental Health Center, 1965-68; psychologist Ednl. Research and Treatment Center, 1968—; v.p. Terry Cay Co., Ltd., Nassau, Bahamas, treas. Mem. bd. Orleans Neighborhood Centers, 1963-65. Mem. Am., La. psychol. assns., Midwestern 4 Assn., Southwestern Assn., Soc. Child Devel., Psi Chi. Home: 1754 Robert E Lee Blvd New Orleans LA 70122 Office: 3619 Prytania St New Orleans LA 70115

RUMAGGI, LOUIS JACOB, ret. army officer, cons.; b. Memphis, Dec. 3, 1900; s. Louis and Garnet (Huntsbarger) R.; student Miami U., Oxford, O., 1917-18; B.S., U.S. Mil. Acad., 1922; B.S. in Civil Engring., U. Cal. at Berkeley, 1927; m. Miriam Louise Tuggle, Mar. 30, 1950; 1 dau., Louise Herron (Mrs. Alan Lyndal Reed). Commd. 2d lt. C.E., U.S. Army 1922, advanced through grades to maj. gen., 1953; acting chief engr. Army Forces, S.W. Pacific, 1945-46; engr. 8th U.S. Army, Korea, 1952-53; dep. chief engrs. U.S. Army, 1954-55; chief staff 6th U.S. Army, 1955-57; div. engr. North Central div., Corps Engrs., 1957-59; asso. Tex. Instruments, Inc., 1959-62. Decorated Legion of Merit with oak leaf cluster, D.S.M.; Ulchi medal (Korea). Fellow Am. Soc. C.E.; mem. Mil. Order World Wars, S.A.R., Newcomen Soc. N.Am., Soc. Am. Mil. Engrs., Am. Legion. Mason (Shriner), Rotarian. Club: Army and Navy (Washington). Home: 8639 Edgemere Rd Dallas TX 75225

RUMLEY, JAMES DEWEY, JR., clergyman; b. Burlington, N.C., Dec. 1, 1920; s. James Dewey and Octavia Eula (Wilson) R.; A.B., Elon Coll., 1941; B.D., Lancaster Theol. Sem., 1958; m. Charlotte Grovelin Bridewell, June 6, 1958; children—James Dewey III, Caroline Elizabeth. Ordained to ministry United Ch. Christ, 1958; minister Lincoln Charge United Ch. Christ, Maiden, N.C., 1958-65, South Norfolk United Ch. Christ, Chesapeake, Va., 1965-66, St. Mark's United Ch. Christ, Cressona, Pa., 1966-72, Holiday (Fla.) United Ch. Christ, 1972—. Conf. rep. to dept. evangelism Pa. Council Chs., 1967-68; sec. commn. on evangelism Pa. S.E. Conf. United Ch. Christ, 1967-69; chmn. com. on evangelism Schuylkill Assn. Pa. S.E. Conf., 1967-69, moderator, 1969-71; pres. Schuylkill Assn. Ministerium Pa. S.E. Conf., United Ch. Christ, 1968-70; del. to Gen. Synod United Ch. Christ, 1971-73, del. to North Central Area Council, Fla. Conf. Mem. Blue Mt. chpt. Am. Field Service, 1967-70. Mem. Am. Platform Assn., Lancaster Sem. Alumni Assn. Home: 1703 Forest Hills Dr Holiday FL 33589 Office: 1303 Pine Bough Lane Holiday FL 33589

RUMMEL, EMMETT CLAIR, planning engr.; b. Leander, Tex., Aug. 6, 1918; s. Reinhardt Charles and Lena Leota (Whitton) R.; B.S. in Civil Engring., U. Tex., 1947, M.A. in Physics, 1952; m. Mary Ernestine Jackson, Feb. 26, 1949; children—Louis, James, Leah. With elec. utility dept. City Austin, 1947—, planning engr., 1970—. Served with AUS, 1942-46. Registered profl. engr., Tex. Mem. I.E.E.E., Tex. Soc. Profl. Engrs. Home: 5507 New Haven Ct Austin TX 78765 Office: PO Box 1088 Austin TX 78707

RUMMERFIELD, BENJAMIN FRANKLIN, geophysicist; b. Denver, May 25, 1917; s. Lawrence L. and Helen A. (Roper) R.; Engr. Geology, Colo. Sch. Mines, 1940; grad. Harvard Advanced Mgmt. Program, 1947, Indsl. Coll. Armed Forces, 1963, Aspen Inst. Humanistic Studies, 1958; m. Elizabeth Whitlow, Sept. 15, 1944; children—Ann S., Michael J., Benjamin F., Mary Susan. Asst. mgr. Seismograph Service Corp., Mexico City, Mexico, 1947-50, Caracas, Venezuela, and Colombia, 1945-47; exec. v.p. Century Geophys. Corp., Tulsa, 1950-60, also dir.; pres. GeoData Corp., Tulsa, 1960—, Gulf Coast GeoData, Houston, 1962—; v.p. Saga Oil Ltd., Calgary, Alta., Can., 1971—; dir. Hudsons GeoData, Internat. of London (Eng.), Permian Exploration, Custom Data Services; cons. Petroleos Mexicanos. Bd. dirs. YMCA, Tulsa, 1955—, pres., 1956-59, recipient Outstanding Service award, 1958, 63. Mem. Tulsa Geol. Soc., Colo. Sch. Mines Alumni Assn. (pres. 1953), Asociacion Mexicana de Geologos Petroleos, Am. Assn. Petroleum Geologists, Soc. Exploration Geophysicists (nat. v.p. 1958), Sigma Gamma Epsilon. Clubs: Tulsa, Harvard (Tulsa). Contbr. numerous articles to profl. jours. Home: 6787 Timberlane Dr Tulsa OK 74105 Office: Thompson Bldg Tulsa OK 74103

RUNDE, ELDON JAMES, coll. adminstr.; b. Davenport, Ia., Mar. 16, 1945; s. Eldon Walter and Shirley Katherine (Strane) R.; B.S., Loras Coll., 1967; M.S., State U. N.Y. at Stoney Brook, 1970. Dir. mgmt. information systems Clarke Coll., Dubuque, Ia., 1969-72; coordinator instl. research Furman U., Greenville, S.C., 1972-74, dir. computer center, 1974—. Cons., Nat. Lab. for Higher Edn., Durham, N.C., 1970—, also So. Regional Ednl. Bd., Inst. Higher Edn., Athens, Ga., Concord Coll., Athens, W.Va.; mem. adv. bd. Nat. Center for Higher Edn. Mgmt. Systems, Boulder, Colo., 1970—; mem. coordinating bd. Tex. Coll. and Univ. System, Austin. Mem. Assn. for Computing Machinery. Developer generalized information retrieval systems now used in 600 instns. in U.S. and abroad. Home: 34 Bridgeview Hunt's Bridge and Duncan Rds Greenville SC 29611 Office: Furman Univ Greenville SC 29613

RUNNELS, POLLARD RHODE, III, dentist; b. Terrell, Tex., Mar. 9, 1943; s. Pollard Rhode and Nelle (Boggess) R.; B.A., U. Tex., 1965, D.D.S., 1969; m. Martha Joan Thomas, June 17, 1967; children—Angela Michele, Kelly Elizabeth, Thomas Jason. Pvt. practice dentistry, Terrell, 1969—. Mem. Terrel Airport Adv. Bd., 1972-73; pres., Kaufman County unit Am. Cancer Soc., 1970—, campaign chmn., 1972-73; campaign chmn. Greater Terrell United Fund, 1971, pres., 1972-73. Mem. 4th Dist. Dental Soc., Tex., Am. dental assns., Terrell C. of C. (dir. 1972-73), Psi Omega (chief inquisitor 1966-67). Mem. Christian Ch. (sec. bd. 1970-71). Rotarian. Club: Oak Grove Country (dir. 1972-73). Home: 806 Griffith St Terrell TX 75160 Office: 300 N Catherine St Terrell TX 75160

RUNNINGER, JACK, optometrist; b. Aurora, Ill., July 16, 1923; s. Guy M. and Gladys (Grossman) R.; student (Rector scholar) De Pauw U., 1941-44; Dr. Optometry So. Coll. Optometry, 1948; m. Mary Gibson, July 31, 1945; children—Nancy (Mrs. Joe Watson), Star, Janet. Practice optometry, Rome, Ga., 1948—. Treas. YMCA, 1963-66; pres. Rome Inter Club Council, 1954. Mem. Gov.'s Comprehensive Health Planning Council, 1970-73. Served to 1st lt. (j.g.) USNR, 1943-46. Recipient Distinguished Service in Journalism award Am. Optometric Assn., 1971. Mem. Ga. Optometric Assn. (pres. 1953), So. Council Optometrists (pres. 1961), Am. Acad. Optometry (pres. Ga. chpt. 1962), Rome Jaycees (pres. 1952). Methodist (steward 1949—). Lion (pres. 1957). Club: Rome Exec. (pres. 1959). Author: (with Nick Powers) Junior Samples Jokebook and Favorite Jokes of Mountain Folks in Boogar Hollow, 1971. Editor So. Jour. Optometry, 1973—. Contbr. articles to popular mags. and profl. jours. Home: 1 Pine Valley Rd Rome GA 30161 Office: 206 E Third St Rome GA 30161

RUPP, ADOLPH FREDERICK, basketball coach; b. Halstead, Kan., Sept. 2, 1901; s. Henry and Anna (Lichti) R.; A.B., Kan. U., 1923; M.A., Columbia, 1930; m. Esther Smith, Aug. 29, 1931; 1 son, Adolph Frederick. Head basketball coach U. Ky., Lexington, 1930-73; now ret. Dir. Central Dist. Warehousing Corp., Lexington. Mem. Nat. Basketball Rules Com., 1961—. Chmn., Shrine Crippled Childrens Hosp., 1942—. Named Southeastern Conf. Coach of Yr., 1963-66, 68-72, Nat. Coach of Yr., U.P.I., A.P., 1951, 59, 66; mem. Basketball Hall of Fame, 1968—. Mem. Ky. Hereford Assn. (pres. 1953-69), Nat. Assn. Basketball Coaches (dir. 1961—, pres. 1970-71), Delta Sigma Pi, Omicron Delta Kappa. Mason. Author: Championship Basketball, 1948, 56; Adolph Rupp's Basketball Guidebook. Home: 175 Eastover Dr Lexington KY 40502

RUSH, FRANK WILFORD, JR., business exec.; b. Selma, Ala., Oct. 31, 1938; s. Frank W. and Leila (Hillman) R.; student Jones County Jr. Coll., 1956-58; B.S., Miss. State U., 1964; m. Mary Frances Brown, Aug. 1, 1964; children—Misty Rose, Randy Wilford. With Arthur Andersen & Co., New Orleans and Memphis, 1964-69, sr. accountant, Memphis, 1967-69; treas. Bagwell-Neal div. Macke Co., Baton Rouge, 1969-70; controllor Schulte & Dieckhoff (USA), Inc., Charlotte, N.C., 1970-72; asst. to pres. Carolina Pump & Supply Co., Inc., 1972—. Served with AUS, 1959-62. C.P.A., Miss., Tenn., La. Mem. Am. Inst. C.P.A.'s. Office: PO Box 10514 Charlotte NC 28201

RUSH, JAMES AVERY, JR., oil and gas co. exec.; b. Luxora, Ark., Nov. 22, 1922; s. James Avery and Lois (Chandler) R.; B.A., U. Tex., 1943, LL.B., 1947; m. Dorothy Jane Jenkins, June 9, 1945; children—Dorothy Jo (Mrs. John Mozola), James Avery III, Nancy Chandler, Carol Jane. Admitted to Tex. bar, 1947; mem. firm Baker, Botts, Andrews & Shepherd, Houston, 1947-53; atty. legal dept. Shamrock Oil & Gas Corp., Amarillo, Tex., 1953, asst. gen. counsel, 1957-61, gen. counsel, 1961-62, v.p., 1962-65, exec. v.p., 1965-67; v.p. finance Diamond Shamrock Corp., Cleve., 1967-69, exec. v.p., 1972—; pres. Diamond Shamrock Oil & Gas Co., 1969—. Mem. bd. city devel., Amarillo, 1970—. Bd. dirs. United Way, Amarillo, 1972—, Tex. Children's Home Found., Amarillo, 1973—. Served with USAAF, 1942-45, with USAF, 1950-51. Mem. Amarillo, Tex., Am. bar assns., Tex. Mid-Continent Oil and Gas Assn., Natural Gas Processors Assn., Am. Petroleum Inst., Ind. Petroleum Assn. Am. (mem. exec. com. 1970-73, import policy com. 1968—, natural gas com. 1968—), Panhandle Producers and Royalty Owners Assn. (dir. 1968—), Tex. Mfrs. Assn. (dir. 1972—), Chancellors, Order of Coif, Phi Kappa Psi, Phi Delta Phi. Clubs: Amarillo, Amarillo Country; Union (Cleve.); Petroleum (Houston). Home: 3902 Paramount St Amarillo TX 79109 Office: Diamond Shamrock Oil and Gas Co First Nat Bank Bldg 8th and Tyler Sts PO Box 361 Amarillo TX 79173

RUSH, ROBERT HOWSON, savs. and loan assn. exec.; b. Alexandria, Va., July 23, 1928; s. Kemp Robert and Margaret Evelyn (Lynch) R.; grad. Episcopal High Sch., Alexandria, 1946; B.A., U. Va., 1949; grad. diploma, Am. Savs. and Loan Inst., 1959; m. Mavis J. Crouch, Oct. 13, 1972; children by previous marriage—Robert Thomas, Constance Anne, Stephanie Rena. Vice pres. First Fed. Savs. and Loan Assn., Alexandria, 1951-59; exec. v.p., dir. Fidelity Savs. and Loan Assn., Alexandria, 1959-63; exec. v.p. Republic Savs. and Loan Assn., Washington, 1963-67, United Savs. and Loan Assn., Arlington, Va., 1967—; sec., dir. United Services Corp., Arlington, Mavis' World of Beauty, Fairfax, Va. Treas. Alexandria chpt. Va. Soc. Crippled Children and Adults; pres. Alexandria chpt. Am. Cancer Soc. Treas. Alexandria City Republican Com. Bd. dirs. Alexandria Hosp. Recipient Distinguished Service award Alexandria chpt. U.S. Jr. C. of C., 1962. Mem. Am. Savs. and Loan Inst. (past pres. No. Va. chpt.), Am. Soc. Appraisers (sr.). Kiwanian. Home: 5433 Richenbacher Av Alexandria VA 22304 Office: 3121 Lee Hwy Arlington VA 22201

RUSH, WAYNE FRANKLIN, lawyer; b. Greenwood, S.C., Oct. 4, 1935; s. John Kirksey and Ethel Pauline (Watson) R.; B.S., U. S.C., 1957, LL.B., 1964. Admitted to S.C. bar, 1964; asso. firm Roberts, Jennings & Thomas, Columbia, S.C., 1964-67, partner, 1968-73; partner Callison, Tighe, Nauful & Rush, Columbia, 1973—. Sec., dir. Middleburg, Inc., Columbia. Served with USAF, 1958-61. Mem. Am., S.C. (exec. com. 1970-71), Richland County bar assns., Assn. Trial Lawyers Am., Am. Judicature Soc., S.C. (pres. 1969-70), Columbia (pres. 1966-67) young lawyers, Wig and Robe, Phi Delta Phi, Lambda Chi Alpha. Clubs: Palmetto, Summit (Columbia). Editor: The Transcript, 1967-68. Home: 4427 Blossom St Columbia SC 29205 Office: 1400 Pickens St Columbia SC 29201

RUSHIA, EDWIN LOUIS, physician, educator; b. Lake City, Ia., Sept. 5, 1916; s. Lewis Oscar and Elsie (Welch) R.; B.S., Ia. State Coll., 1938; M.D., N.Y. U., 1942; m. Mary Anna Loughridge, June 20, 1948; children—Edwin Linn, Mary Lynn (Mrs. Al Fowler), Barbara, Robert, Judith. Intern USN Hosp., Bklyn., 1942-43; resident anesthesiology U. Ia. Hosps., 1947-49; prof. anesthesiology, head dept. U. Ark. Sch. Medicine, 1949-51; asso. prof. anesthesiology Med. Coll. Ga., 1951-67; prof. anesthesiology Emory U. Sch. Medicine, 1967-70, U. Va. Sch. Medicine, 1970—. Player flute and piccalo Augusta (Ga.) Civic Symphony, 1964-67; baritone Emory U. Wind Ensemble, 1969-70; baritone, flutist Charlottesville Municipal Band, 1971—. Served with USN, 1942-47. Diplomate Am. Bd. Anesthesiology. Fellow Am. Coll. Anesthesiologists; mem. A.M.A., Va. Soc. Anesthesiology, Internat. Anesthesiology Research Soc. Mason (K.T., Shriner). Home: 228 Carrsbrook Dr Charlottesville VA 22901

RUSHING, BARNIE ELMER, JR., retail co. exec.; b. Plainview, Tex., Oct. 27, 1916; s. Barnie Elmer and Zelma A. (Flake) R.; student Tex. Technol. Coll., 1933-35, U.S. Coast Guard Acad., 1944; m. Dorothy Ann York, Feb. 11, 1939; 1 son, Robert York. With Hemphill-Wells Co., Lubbock, Tex., 1934—, v.p., sec., 1952—. Pres., United Fund, Lubbock, 1959-60, former dir. Tex. United Fund; organizational chmn. Lubbock Council Chs., 1960; chmn. devel. commn. Civic Center, Library. Bd. dirs. Tex. Found. Mental Health and Mental Retardation, 1970—, Tex. Tech. U. Med. Sch. Found., 1970, Tex. Tech U. Found., 1970—; vice chmn. bd. dirs., Textile Research Found., Tex. Tech U., 1969-70; chmn. bd. mgrs. Lubbock County Hosp. Dist., 1969—; trustee, vice-chmn. Tex. Bd. Mental Health and Mental Retardation, 1970—; trustee Spencer A. Wells Found., 1958—, Hemphill-Wells Found., 1963—; bd. dirs. West Tex. Health Planning Systems, Methodist Hosp., Salvation Army. Served with USCG, 1941-45. Recipient Distinguished Salesman's award for community service, 1965. Mem. Retail Mchts. Assn. Tex. (past exec. com.), Nat. Better Bus. Bur. (past gov.), Lubbock Better Bus. Bur. (past pres.), Red Raider Club, Kappa Sigma, Delta Sigma Pi. Mem. Christian Ch. (past chmn. ofcl. bd. 1954, past chmn. bd. elders 1956). Mason (Shriner), Kiwanian. Clubs: Lubbock Country, Lubbock. Home: 4510 W 17th St Lubbock TX 79416 Office: PO Box 981 1212 Av J Lubbock TX 79408

RUSHING, DYKES TAYLOR, state hwy. engr.; b. Elba, Ala., Jan. 27, 1939; s. John and Jessie Lee (Taylor) R.; student U. Ala., 1958-59; B.S., Troy State U., 1962; m. Linda Spurlin, Oct. 22, 1965; children—Will, Taylor, Katie. Engr. asst. State of Ala. Hwy. Dept., Troy, 1958-63, highway design engr. I, 1963-65, hwy. design engr. II, 1965-72, profl. civil engr., 1972—. Served with AUS, 1962-63. Home: 2813 Hickman St Elba AL 36323 Office: State of Alabama Highway Dept Troy AL 36081

RUSHING, JOE BOB, coll. chancellor; b. Zephry, Tex., May 23, 1921; s. Cordie M. and Vallie (Parson) R.; B.A., Howard Payne Coll., 1946; M.A., East Tex. State Coll., 1949; Ph.D., U. Tex., 1952; postdoctoral study U. Mich., 1959; m. Elaine Whitis, Dec. 21, 1946; children—Anita Sherron, Cynthia Ann, Robert Scott. Tchr. sci., adminstr. Levelland (Tex.) High Sch., Mt. Pleasant (Tex.) High Sch., 1946-50; teaching fellow, U. Tex., 1950-52; dir. adult edn. Wharton Jr. Coll., 1952-54; dean grad. div. Howard Payne Coll., 1954-58, adminstrv. v.p., 1956-60; pres. Jr. Coll. of Broward County. Ft. Lauderdale, Fla., 1960-65; pres. Tarrant County Jr. Coll. Dist., Ft. Worth, 1965-69, chancellor, 1969—. Served with AUS, 1942-46. Mem. Pi Sigma Alpha, Phi Delta Kappa, Kappa Delta Pi. Baptist. Home: Ft Worth Nat Bank Bldg Fort Worth TX 76102

RUSHLOW, PHILIP LEO, indsl.-fashion exec.; b. Covington, Ky., Feb. 2, 1929; s. Leo B. and Elinor (Slater) R.; B.A., Wayne State U., 1945; M.A., Mich. State U., 1949; m. Bonnie L. Miller, June 25, 1945; children—Philip Lee, David R. Regional mgr. B.F. Goodrich Co., Detroit, 1949-56; pres. Lansing Gen. Tire Co. (Mich.), 1956-59, Azure Internat. Corp., Lansing, 1959-64; pres., chief exec. officer Fashion Industries, Inc., Miami, Fla., 1964-69, Group Three Advt. Corp., Richelieu Assos., Inc.; chief exec. officer Motivational Marketing Systems, Inc., Miami, Wig Lady, Inc.; v.p. Bonnie Rushlow, Inc., Fort Lauderdale; dir. Mona Lisa Co., N.Y.C., Venture Internat. Corp., Ft. Lauderdale, Fla. Miami. Cons., Nat. Fashion Assn. Contbr. articles to profl. jours. Home: 2823 NE 26th Pl Fort Lauderdale FL 33306 Office: 2485 E Sunrise Blvd Fort Lauderdale FL 33304

RUSHTON, MARY FAY HOPKINS (MRS. LONNIE CONNON RUSHTON), educator; b. Dallas; d. John Raymond and Viola (Shultz) Hopkins; B.A., U. Tex., 1940; M.A. in Counseling Psychology, Tex. A. and I. U., 1964; m. Lonnie Connon Rushton, Oct. 20, 1935; children—Mary Ann (Mrs. Joe A. Hoppe), Nancy Martha (Mrs. Jere P. Parrish). Curator anthropology mus. U. Tex., 1940-42; tchr. pub. schs., Mercedes, Tex., 1954-72, vocational adjustment coordinator Mercedes Schs., 1964-72; psychologist, counselor Rio Grande Habitation Ind. Sch. Dist., Edinburg, Tex., 1972—. Registrar council Girl Scouts Am., 1948-53; mem. Nat. Safety Council, 1955-64; pres. bd. dirs. Mercedes Pub. Library. Mem. D.A.R., Tex. Psychol. Assn., Council Exceptional Children, Colonial Dames, Nat. Soc. Magna Carta Dames, Am. Assn. U. Women, Tex. State Tchrs. Assn., Am. Anthrop. Assn., Phi Theta Kappa. Club: Garden (pres. 1949-50). Home: Box 687 Mission TX 78572

RUSHTON, WILLIAM JAMES, life ins. exec.; b. Birmingham, Ala., July 10, 1900; s. James Franklin and Willis (Roberts) R.; B.S., Washington & Lee U., Lexington, Va., 1921; H.H.D., Southwestern at Memphis, 1959; m. Elizabeth Perry, November 24, 1926; children—William James, III, James. Asst. mgr. Birmingham Ice & Cold Storage Co., 1922-27, v.p., 1927-32, pres. 1932-38, v. chmn. bd., sec., 1938-57; pres. Protective Life Ins. Co., 1937-67, chmn. bd. dirs., 1967—; mem. adv. bd. Investment Co. of Am.; chmn. bd. Franklin Coal Mining Co., 1927-42; dir. First Nat. Bank of Birmingham, Alabama Power Co., Ill. Central Gulf R.R. Served to col., U.S. Army, World War II. Chief, Birmingham Ordnance Dist., U.S. Army, 1946-61. Vice chmn., trustee, So. Research Inst. Pres. Birmingham Boy Scout Council, 1927-30 (dir. 1925-55); mem. nat. citizens com. United Community Campaigns Am., 1961; dir. Birmingham Community Chest, 1937— (pres., 1954), Birmingham Mus. Art; trustee Children's Hosp., Agnes Scott Coll., Decatur, Ga., 1935-45. Mem. Am. Ordnance Assn. (v.p.), Nat. Assn. Ice Indus (dir. 1928—; pres. 1936-37); Nat. Assn. Refrigerated Warehouses (pres. 1933-35; mem. Nat. Code Authority), Am. Warehousemen's Assn. (pres. 1935-36), Life Ins. Assn. of Am. (dir. 1955-61), Health Ins. Assn. Am. (dir. 1964—), Am. Life Conv. (Ala. v.p.), Beta Gamma Sigma, Beta Theta Pi, Omicron Delta Kappa, Delta Sigma Rho. Presbyn. (mem. bd. annuities and relief Presbyn. Ch. in U.S. 1959—). Mason (32 deg., Shriner). Dec. Legion of Merit. Clubs: Rotary (pres. 1952-53), Mountain Brook, Country, Downtown, The Club, Relay House (Birmingham); Chaparal (Dallas). Home: 2848 Balmoral Rd Birmingham AL 35223 Office: Protective Life Ins Co Birmingham AL 35203

RUSKIN, DAN BERNARD, bus. exec.; b. Bklyn., Oct. 5, 1899; s. Harris L. and Anna (Oginz) R.; grad. Eron Coll., 1920; m. Mollie Kaplan, July 12, 1922; children—Charlyne (Mrs. James Meyer), Lloyd L., Andrea (Mrs. Robert C. Magoon). Co-owner Pub. Nat. Investors, 1961— sec.-treas. O and R Co., 1945—; v.p. Rusoro Corp., 1955—; pres. P & P Holding Corp., 1960— (all Greater Miami, Fla.); dir. Community Nat. Bank & Trust Co., Bal Harbour, Fla. Campaign chmn. Greater Miami Jewish Fedn., 1950, pres., 1951-52, hon. pres., 1952; mem. citizens bd. U. Miami, 1959—. Trustee Mt. Sinai Hosp.; 1946-, v.p., 1952-; trustee Temple Israel Greater Miami. Served with USCGR, 1944-45. Mason (Shriner), Elk. Home: 5255 Collins Av Miami Beach FL 33140 Office: 1 Lincoln Rd Miami Beach FL 33139

RUSOFF, LOUIS LEON, educator, dairy nutritionist; b. Newark, Dec. 23, 1910; s. Max and Rachel (Rodin) R.; B.S., Rutgers U., 1931; M.S., Pa. State U., 1932; Ph.D., U. Minn., 1940; certificate Oak Ridge Inst. Nuclear Studies, 1950; m. Sylvia Levin, May 15, 1945; children—Gail (Mrs. Donald Roache), Marsha. Asst. in nutrition U. Fla., 1932-35, mem. faculty, 1935-42, asst. prof., 1938-42; mem. faculty La. State U., Baton Rouge, 1942—, prof., nutritionist, 1950—; dir. La. State U. Regional Sci. Fair, 1954-71. Named Man of Yr., La. B'nai B'rith Assn., 1965. Fellow A.A.A.S., Am. Inst. Chemists; mem. Am. Chem. Soc. (chmn. Baton Rouge 1956; Charles E. Coates award 1965), Am. Dairy Sci. Assn. (pres. So. div. 1972; Borden award 1965, Honors award So. div. 1969), Am. Inst. Nutrition, Sigma Xi (pres. La. State U. chpt. 1958), Phi Kappa Phi (pres. La. State U. chpt. 1965), Gamma Sigma Delta, Omicron Delta Kappa. Contbr. profl. jours. Home: 1704 Myrtledale Av Baton Rouge LA 70808

RUSSELL, CHARLES STEVENS, judge; b. Richmond, Va., Feb. 23, 1926; s. Charles H. and Nita M. (Stevens) R.; B.A., U. Va., 1946, LL.B., 1948; grad. Nat. Coll. State Judiciary, 1973; m. Carolyn Elizabeth Abrams, Mar. 18, 1951; children—Charles Stevens, David Tyler. Admitted to Va. bar, 1949; practiced in Arlington and Fairfax counties, Va., 1951-67; mem. firm Jesse, Phillips, Klinge & Kendrick (name later changed to Phillips, Kendrick, Gearheart & Aylor), Arlington, 1951-57, partner, 1957-67; judge 17th Circuit, Va., 1967—. Dir. Mt. Vernon Nat. Life Ins. Co., Arlington. Counsel, Va. Hwy. Commn., 1957-67. Mem. Arlington County Commn. Precinct Revision, 1962-64, Commn. on Youth Arlington County, 1965-67. Served to lt. comdr. USNR, 1943-46, 49-51. Mem. Am., Va. (exec. com., council 1960-67, ethics com. 1965-67), Arlington County (v.p. 1959-60) bar assns., Raven Soc., Jefferson Soc., Sigma Nu Phi, Sigma Phi Epsilon, Omicron Delta Kappa. Episcopalian (vestryman). Home: 4618 N Dittmar Rd Arlington VA 22207 Office: Arlington County Ct House Arlington VA 22201

RUSSELL, DAN M., JR., U.S. dist. judge; b. Magee, Miss., Mar. 15, 1913; s. Dan M. and Beulah (Watkins) R.; B.A., U. Miss., 1935, LL.B., 1937; m. Dorothy Tudury, Dec. 27, 1942 children—Ronald Truett, Dorothy Dale, Richard Brian. Admitted to Miss. bar, 1937; practiced in Gulfport and Bay St. Louis, Miss.; U.S. judge So. Dist. Miss., Biloxi, 1965—. Dir. So. Savs. & Loan Assn., Gulfport. Chmn. Hancock (Miss.) Civic Action Assn., 1964—. Democratic presdl. elector, 1964; chmn. Hancock County Election Commn., 1959-64. Served to lt. comdr. USNR, 1941-45. Mem. Miss. Hancock County (v.p. 1964-65) bar assns., Hancock County C. of C. (pres. 1946), Scribblers, Tau Kappa Alpha. Rotarian (pres. Bay St. Louis 1946). Home: 321 Main St Bay St Louis MS 39520 Office: US Courthouse Biloxi MS 39533

RUSSELL, DAVID EMERSON, cons. mech. engr.; b. Jacksonville, Fla., Dec. 20, 1922; s. David Herbert and Wilhelmina (Ash) R.; B.Mech. Engring., U. Fla., 1948. Mech. engr. United Fruit Co., N.Y.C., 1948-50, U.S. Army C.E., Jacksonville, 1950-54; v.p. Beiswenger Hoch and Assos., Inc., Jacksonville, 1954-57; owner, operator David E. Russell and Assos., cons. engrs., Jacksonville, 1957—. Chmn. Jacksonville Water Quality Control Bd., 1969-73; mem. Jacksonville Centennial Commn., 1973—. Served to 2d lt. AUS, 1943-46. Registered profl. engr., Fla., Ga. Mem. Am. Soc. M.E. (chmn. N.E. Fla. 1967-68), Nat. Soc. Profl. Engrs., Am. Soc. Heating, Refrigerating and Air Conditioning Engrs., Fla. Engring. Soc. Episcopalian. Club: University (Jacksonville). Contbr. articles to profl. jours. Patentee in field. Home: 1606 King St Jacksonville FL 32204 Office: 110 Riverside Av Jacksonville FL 32202

RUSSELL, DONALD STUART, U.S. circuit judge; b. Lafayette Springs, Miss., Feb. 22, 1906; s. Jesse and Lula (Russell) R.; A.B., U. S.C., 1925, LL.B., 1928, LL.D.; postgrad. U. Mich., 1929; LL.D., Wofford Coll., Lander Coll., The Citadel, U. S.C., Clemson U., C.W. Post, L.I.; m. Virginia Utsey, June 15, 1929; children—Donald, Mildred, Scott, John. Admitted to S.C. bar, 1928, practiced in Spartanburg, 1930-42; asso. firm Nicholls, Wyche & Byrnes, Nicholls,

Wyche & Russell, and Nicholls & Russell, 1930-38; pvt. practice, 1938-42; mem. Price Adjustment Bd., War Dept., Washington, 1942; asst. to dir. econ. stablzn., 1942, asst. to dir. war moblzn., 1943; dep. dir. Office War Mobzn. Reconversion, 1945; asst. sec. state, 1945-47; pres. U. S.C., 1951-57; pvt. law practice, 1957-63; gov. State of S.C., 1963-65; apptd. to U.S. Senate from S.C., 1965; U.S. dist. judge S.C., 1967-71; U.S. circuit judge 4th Jud. Circuit, 1971—. Mem. Wriston Com. Fgn. Service, 1954. Trustee Emory U., Converse Coll., Benedict Coll.; bd. dirs. Christ Sch. Served as maj. AUS, 1944; ETO. Mem. Am. Legion, Phi Beta Kappa. Methodist. Home: 716 Otis Blvd Spartanburg SC 29302 Office: Fed Bldg 205 Magnolia St Spartanburg SC 29301

RUSSELL, EDWIN ROBERTS, research co. chemist; b. Columbia, S.C., June 19, 1913; s. Nathaniel Philip and Mary Elizabeth (Roberts) R.; B.S., Benedict Coll., 1935; M.S., Howard U., 1937; m. Dorothy Eugenia Nance, Aug. 31, 1941; 1 dau., Vivian (Mrs. Benjamin Talmadge Martin). Tchr. Howard U., Washington, 1937-42; asso. chemist, also group leader Metall. Lab., Chgo., 1942-47; chmn. Sci. Div. Allen U., Columbia, S.C., 1947-53; chemist E.I. duPont, Savannah River Lab., Aiken, S.C., 1953—. Cons. Argonne Lab., 1947-50. Mem. Housing Authority, New Ellenton, S.C., 1971. Bd. dirs. Services Council of Aiken County, pres., 1971—. Mem. Am. Chem. Soc. (sec.-treas. Savannah River Sect. 1971—), Men's League (pres. 1949-51), Sigma Xi, Sigma Pi Phi, Beta Kappa Chi. Mem. Meth. Episcopal Ch. (vice chmn. bd. trustees 1958-70). Patentee in field. Contbr. articles to profl. jours. Home: 405 S Boundary St New Ellenton SC 29809 Office: Savannah River Plant Aiken SC 29801

RUSSELL, ERNEST EVERETT, educator; b. Jackson, Miss., Apr. 16, 1923; s. Ernest Ervin and Mildred (Green) R.; B.S., Miss. State U., 1949, M.S., 1955; Ph.D., U. Tenn., 1965; m. Dixie Allison Evans, June 1, 1949; children—Ernest Everett, William Evans, Allison Hardy. Instr. U. Tenn., 1954-55; mem. faculty Miss. State U., 1955—, prof. geology, 1967—; cons. geologist Tenn. Div. Geology. Sec.-treas. Univ. Heights Corp.; pres. Landel Corp. Served as pilot USAAF, 1942-46, USAF, 1951-53. Decorated Air medal with 5 oak leaf clusters, D.F.C. with oak leaf clusters. Fellow Geol. Soc. Am.; mem. Am. Inst. Profl. Geologists, Am. Assn. Petroleum Geologists, Paleontol. Soc. Am., Paleontol. Research Inst., Miss. Acad. Scis. (dir. 1967, pres. 1968), Sigma Xi. Home: Box R Mississippi State MS 39762

RUSSELL, GEORGE FRANKLIN, JR., engring. co. exec.; b. McAlester, Okla., Feb. 11, 1913; s. George Franklin and Edna (Booth) R.; student U. Houston, 1936-39; B.S. in Chem. Engring., U. Okla., 1943, M.Chem. Engring., 1944; m. Ruth Ella Boehm, May 11, 1935; children—Robert Franklin, Carolyn Ruth (Mrs. Robert T. Ortegon). Am. Gas Assn. research fellow U. Okla. at Norman, 1942-43, asst. prof. chem. engring., 1944-45; asso. prof. petroleum engring. La. State U. at Baton Rouge, 1946-47; chem. engr. Standard Oil Co. of La., Baton Rouge, 1945-46; cons. engr. Natural Gas & Gasoline, Houston, 1947-50; pres. Russell Engring. Corp., Houston, 1950—. Registered profl. engr., Tex., Colo. Mem. Soc. Petroleum Engrs., A.A.A.S., Nat. Soc. Profl. Engrs., Sigma Xi, Tau Beta Pi, Sigma Tau, Alpha Chi Sigma. Presbyn. Mason (Shriner). Club: Petroleum of Houston. Contbr. articles tech. lit. Home: 4414 Merwin St Houston TX 77027 Office: Russell Engring Corp 1310 Britmoore Rd Houston TX 77024

RUSSELL, JAMES RICHARD, editor; b. Wingo, Ky., Apr. 21, 1933; s. Voris Boaz and Cleo Patra (Holloway) R.; A.B., Ind. U., 1961; postgrad. U. Ky., 1963-64; m. Diana Ruth Bryant, Aug. 11, 1956; children—James Nathan, Cassandra Ruth. Copy editor Evening Republican, Columbus, Ind., 1961; asst. publs. editor Coop. Extension Service U. Ky., Lexington, 1962-68, chmn. pub. information, 1968-71; farm editor Louisville (Ky.) Courier Jour., 1971—. Served with USNR, 1952-56. Named Ky. col. Mem. Ky. Hist. Assn., Ky. Farm Press and Radio Assn., Newspaper Farm Editors Am. Home: 820 Marengo Dr Middletown KY 40243 Office: 525 W Broadway Louisville KY 40202

RUSSELL, JERRY LEWIS, advt. and pub. relations exec.; b. Little Rock, July 21, 1933; s. Jerry Lewis and Frances (Lieb) R.; B.A. in Journalism, U. Ark., 1958; m. Alice Anne Cason, Feb. 14, 1969; children (by previous marriage)—Jerry L. III, Susan Frances, Leigh Anne, Andrew J. III. Pub. relations dir. Little Rock C. of C., 1958; editor, pub. The Visitor, Little Rock, 1959-60; sec.-mgr. Ark. Press Assn., Little Rock, 1960-61; account exec. Brandon Agy., Little Rock, 1961-65; founder Guide Advt. (now part of River City Enterprises), also River City Pubs., Little Rock 1965-70, 72—; dir. pub. relations services S.M. Brooks Agy., Little Rock, 1970-72. Pres., Pulaski County Young Democrats Club, 1963; mem. Pulaski County Dem. Com., 1966-67. Served with AUS, 1953-56. Mem. Little Rock Advt. Club (pres. 1967-68, sec. 1963-65, 69-71), Pub. Relations Soc. Am. (pres. Ark. chpt. 1974), Rackensack Folklore Soc., Little Big Horn Assos., Ark., Pulaski County hist. socs., Am. Assn. Local and State History, Civil War Round Table Ark. (charter pres. 1964-65), Civil War Round Table Assos. (exec. dir.), Circus Fans Assn. Am., Circus Hist. Soc., Westerners Internat. Home: 9 Lefever Lane Little Rock AR 72207

RUSSELL, JOE DAVID, elec. engr., retail trade exec.; b. Drumright, Okla., Mar. 26, 1920; s. David and Adelaide (Weightman) R.; B.S. in Elec. Engring., U. Okla., 1949, M.E.E., 1950; m. Gloria Gala, Dec. 26, 1959; 1 dau., Maria. Electronic engr. Tinker AFB, Oklahoma City, 1950-55; sr. electronic engr. Melpar, Inc., Falls Church, Va., 1955, Lockheed Electronics Co., Plainfield, N.J., 1955-59; sr. design engr. G.D. Astronautics, San Diego, 1959-65; mgr. design engring. sect. Lockheed Electronics Co., White Sands Missile Range, N.M., 1965-70; owner, mgr. Hydrospray Car Wash, El Paso, Tex., 1968—; owner, mgr. J.D. Russell Co., 1972—; asso. Trans-World Financial Corp., 1974—. Served with AUS, 1942-45. Registered profl. engr., Okla. Mem. I.E.E.E. Home: 4955 Marie Tobin Dr El Paso TX 79924 Office: 9555 Dyer St El Paso TX 79924

RUSSELL, JOHN PATRICK, gas co. exec.; b. New Rochelle, N.Y., Jan. 13, 1929; s. Michael Joseph and Catherine Agnes (McCabe) R.; student Lafayette Coll., 1948-49, student Iona Coll., 1950; m. Joan Moira Bottinelli, July 11, 1953; children—Michael, Susan, Mary, Katherine, Charles. With Pyrofax Gas Corp., subsidiary Tex. Eastern Transmission Corp., 1949—, supr. bulk sales, N.Y.C., 1949-60, sales mgr., N.Y.C., 1960-64, mgr. New Eng. div., West Springfield, Mass., 1964-67, v.p., gen. sales mgr., Houston, 1967-71, exec. v.p., Houston, 1971—. Served with AUS, 1952-54. Mem. Nat. Liquefied Petroleum Gas Assn. (dir. 1971—, chmn. market devel. com. 1972-74), Am. Inst. Mgmt. Home: 13311 Kingsride Lane Houston TX 77024 Office: PO Box 2521 Houston TX 77001

RUSSELL, JOHN TENNYSON, educator; b. Winamac, Ind., June 13, 1924; s. Elvin John and Glenna Viola (Swayzee) R.; A.B., Oberlin Coll., 1949; M.Div., Seabury Western Theol. Sem., 1952; S.T.M., U. of the South, 1965; Ph.D., Ind. U., 1969; postdoctoral student Harvard, 1970. Ordained to ministry Episcopal Ch., 1952; canon, Cathedral Ch. St. Luke, Orlando, Fla., 1955-56; rector Christ the King Ch., Orlando, Fla., 1956-69, also headmaster Christ the King Sch., 1957-69; prof. edn. Pembroke (N.C.) State U., 1969—. Asst., Trinity Ch., Lumberton, 1970-73. Served with AUS, 1943-45. Eli Lilly fellow, 1966-67. Mem. N.E.A., Lumberton Civic Music Assn. (dir. 1973-74), Adult Edn. Assn. U.S., Philosophy of Edn. Soc., Am. Civil Liberties Union, Phi Beta Kappa, Phi Delta Kappa. Republican. Episcopalian. Author: The Episcopal Church and Education, 1966. Home: 1006 N Walnut St Lumberton NC 28358 Office: Box 22 Pembroke State Univ Pembroke NC 28372

RUSSELL, LAO (MRS. WALTER RUSSELL), educator; b. nr. Tring, Eng.; d. Alfred William and Florence (Hills) Cook; naturalized, 1947; ed. pvt. tutors; m. Walter Russell, July 29, 1948. Founder, Walter Russell Found. (now known as U. Sci. and Philosophy), Waynesboro, Va., 1948, pres., 1948-57, dir., 1957—; founded Shrine of Beauty known as Swannanoa Palace and Sculpture Gardens, 1948. Founder Man-Woman Equalization League, 1955, Age of Character Clubs, 1966. Author: Scientific Answer to Human Relations, 1948; God Will Work With You But Not For You, 1955; Love-A Scientific and Living Philosophy of Love and Sex, 1966; Why You Cannot Die! The Continuity of Life-Reincarnation Explained, 1972; (with Walter Russell) Home Study Course in Universal Law, Natural Science and Living Philosophy, 1950, Atomic Suicide, 1957, World Crisis-Its Explanation and Solution, 1958, The One-World Purpose, 1960, An Eternal Message of Light and Love, 1964. Executed statue (with husband) The Christ of the Blue Ridge. Address: Univ Science and Philosophy Swannanoa Waynesboro VA 22980

RUSSELL, LEWIS FRANKLIN, judge; b. Dallas, Apr. 19, 1915; s. John L. and Rebecca (Jones) R.; B.A., So. Methodist U., 1935, LL.B., 1941; postgrad. Columbia Law Sch., 1941; m. Katherine Higginbotham, July 20, 1940; children—Carol, Lewis Franklin, Lee H., Katherine. Admitted to Tex. bar, 1941; atty. U.S. Bd. Tax Appeals, 1942; spl. agt. FBI, 1942-47; practiced in Dallas, 1947-58; judge Juvenile Ct., Dallas County, 1959—. Chmn. Juvenile Bd. Dallas County; lectr. S.W. Legal Found. Bd. dirs. East Dallas YMCA. Mem. Nat. Council Juvenile Ct. Judges (v.p.), Nat. Council Crime and Delinquency (adv. council judges), Tex. Council Adminstrn. of Justice, State Bar Tex., Am., Dallas bar assns. Baptist (chmn. bd. trustees). Mason (Shriner), Lion (dir., pres. 1969-70). Home: 6758 Avalon St Dallas TX 75214 Office: Ct House Dallas TX 75202

RUSSELL, NORMAN H., JR., ednl. adminstr., author; b. Big Stone Gap, Va., Nov. 28, 1921; s. Norman H. and Lois K. (Rhodes) R.; B.S., State Tchrs. Coll., Slippery Rock, Pa., 1946; postgrad. U. Tenn., 1946-47; Ph.D., U. Minn., 1951; m. Arline Borquist, June 26, 1963. Prof., Grinnell Coll., Ia., 1951-59, Ariz. State U., Tempe, 1959-63; vis. prof. Rutgers U., Newark, N.J., 1963-65; prof. Buena Vista Coll., Storm Lake, Ia., 1967-69; dean sch. math. and sci. Central State U., Edmond, Okla., 1965-67, 69—. Served with USAAF, 1942-46. Author: An Introduction to the Plant Kingdom, 1958; Violets of Eastern and Central United States, 1968; Indian Thoughts: The Small Songs of God, 1972. Contbr. sci. articles to research jours. and poetry to lit. jours. Home: 2102 Thrush Circle Edmond OK 73034 Office: School of Mathematics and Science Central State University Edmond OK 73034

RUSSELL, PHEBE GALE (MRS. FRANK M. RUSSELL), broadcasting, TV exec.; b. N.Y.C., Dec. 23, 1910; d. George H. and Marian (Hyde) Gale; grad. high sch.; m. Frank M. Russell, Sept. 25, 1940; children—Gale, Morgan N. Publicity dir. NBC, Washington, 1929-39; v.p. radio sta. WICO, Salisbury, Md., 1958-62; pres. Ellensburg (Wash.) TV Corp., 1961-68, PGR Enterprises, 1962-70; owner TV Cable Cos., Appalachia, Norton, and Big Stone Gap, Va., 1962-71. Mem. women's bd. George Washington U. Hosp. Mem. D.A.R., Mayflower Soc. Huguenot Soc., Internat. Platform Assn., Nepal Soc. U.S., D.C. Women's Golf Assn., Daus. of Cincinnati. Clubs: Congressional Country (Washington); Kenwood Garden (pres. 1962-64). Address: 5101 River Rd Apt 918 Washington DC 20016

RUSSELL, PHILIP KING, physician, mil. officer; b. Syracuse, N.Y., Jan. 26, 1932; s. Richard King and Katherine Adele (Fleisch) R.; A.B., Johns Hopkins, 1954; M.D., U. Rochester, 1958; m. Constance Rice, Aug. 20, 1955; children—Katherine, Ellen, Richard. Intern, N.C. Meml. Hosp., Chapel Hill, 1958-59; resident in medicine U. Hosp., Balt., 1961-63; clin. investigator Pakistan Med. Research Center, U. Md., Lahore, 1963-64; chief virology dept. U.S. Army Med. Component, S.E. Asia, 1965-68; with dept. virus diseases Walter Reed Army Inst. Research, Washington, 1959-61, 64-65, chief virus dept., 1968-73, dir. div. communicable disease and immunology, 1970—. Exec. mem. Am. Com. on Arthropodborne viruses, 1968—, chmn., 1971-74; mem. commn. on virus diseases Armed Forces Epidemiologic Bd., 1969-72; sci. adv. com. on dengue Pan Am. Health Orgn., 1970—, chmn., 1974. Bd. dirs. Gorgas Meml. Inst. Tropical and Preventive Medicine. Diplomate Am. Bd. Internal Medicine. Fellow Am. Acad. Microbiology; mem. Am., Royal socs. tropical medicine and hygiene, Am. Soc. Microbiology, Am. Assn. Immunologists, Infectious Disease Soc. Am., Am. Epidemiology Soc. Contbr. articles to profl. jours. Home: 11909 Coldstream Dr Potomac MD 20854 Office: 6825 16th St NW Washington DC 20012

RUSSELL, RICHARD ANTHONY, computer co. exec.; b. Louisville, Dec. 25, 1923; s. Joseph Francis and Nora (Reedy) R.; E.E., U. Louisville, 1947; m. Nancy Caroline Hudspeth, Feb. 13, 1946; children—Mark Cochran, Nancy Pamela, Christopher Reedy. With IBM, Raleigh, N.C., 1948—, functional mgr. Communication Systems Publ. Center, IBM Raleigh System Devel. Div., 1965—. Owner, Raleigh Rock Shop, 1970—. U.S. rep. Internat. Council for Tech. Communication, London, Eng., 1971; chmn. Internat. Tech. Communication Congress, Tel Aviv, Israel, 1968. Asso. fellow Soc. Tech. Communication (dir. 1963, 64, pres. 1967-68). Home: 1811 Fairley Rd Raleigh NC 27607 Office: PO Box 12275 Research Triangle Park Raleigh NC 27709

RUSSELL, RICHARD ROBERT, physician; b. Dallas, Nov. 19, 1931; s. William Byron and Mattie Bennie (Russell); B.S., So. Meth. U., 1953; M.D., U. Tex., 1956; m. Bertha Joy Liles, Nov. 29, 1957; children—Gina Lori, Lisa Michelle, Brian Keith. Intern, U.S. Naval Hosp., San Diego, 1956-57; practice medicine, specializing in family practice, Mesquite, Tex., 1960—; mem. staff Mesquite Meml. Hosp., chief staff, 1964-66, 72-73, also mem. bd. dirs. Dir. Mesquite State Bank, Town East Savs. & Loan Assn., Aloe Vera Am., Inc. Mem. bd. edn. Mesquite (Tex.) Ind. Sch. Dist., 1971—, now v.p. Trustee, sec. bd. Christian Coll. S.W. Served with USNR, 1956-60. Diplomate Am. Bd. Family Practice. Fellow Am. Acad. Family Physicians (pres. Dallas chpt. 1970-71). Mem. Ch. of Christ (deacon 1970—). Home: 410 Riggs Circle Mesquite TX 75149 Office: 200 W Kearney St Mesquite TX 75149

RUSSELL, WILLARD LORANE, lawyer; b. Hallettsville, Tex., Aug. 14, 1898; s. Henry Hamilton and Annie (Hemphill) R.; B.S., U. Tex., 1924; A.M., Baylor U., 1930; LL.B., South Tex. Sch. Law, 1933; LL.D., Tex. Wesleyan Coll., 1959, Howard Payne Coll., 1965; m. Stella Wolters, Dec. 24, 1928. Supt. pub. schs., Hallettsville, 1925-29; instr. Baylor U., 1930; admitted to Tex. bar, 1933, since practiced in Houston; chmn. bd. Shiner Oil Mill & Mfg. Co. (Tex.); v.p., dir. So. Warehouse Corp.; owner, operator farm and ranch enterprises. Founder, donor Russell Found., religious, edn., charitable trust, 1948. Trustee U. St. Thomas, Houston, Baylor U., Waco, Tex., Baylor Med. Coll., Houston; bd. dirs. Houston St. and Newsboys Club, Lincoln Ednl. Found., N.Y. Mem. State Bar Tex., Am., Houston bar assns., Am. Judicature Soc., Ind. Rice Growers Assn. Baptist. Mason (Shriner), Odd Fellow, Rotarian. Clubs: Farm and Ranch, Torch (Houston); Knife and Fork (dir.). Author: Peace and Power Within, 1951; Invincible Forces, 1959; Belief and Respect, 1961; Belief and Human Worth, 1967; Peace and Power within the Individual and Among Our People, 1970. Contbr. articles to mags. Home: 3412 S Parkwood Dr Houston TX 77021 Office: 4101 San Jacinto St Houston TX 77004

RUSSIAN, FRANCIS X., oil mill exec.; b. Carbondale, Pa., Aug. 19, 1942; s. Frank and Mary Lillian (Skorupa) R.; B.S., Fairleigh Dickinson U., 1967; m. Janice Naomi Henzelmann, Apr. 6, 1963; children—Elizabeth, Frank, Kathryn, Suzanne. Lab. technician Lever Bros., Edgewater, N.J., 1963-67, organic research chemist, 1967-68; mgr. chem. analytical lab. IFF, Union Beach, 1968-72; v.p., gen. mgr. Paks Corp., Junction, Tex., 1972—. Home: 205 W Cedar St Junction TX 76849 Office: Box 325 Junction TX 76849

RUSSIN, NICHOLAS CHARLES, chem. co. adminstr.; b. Butler, Pa., Feb. 6, 1922; s. Nicholas and Rose (Stastka) R.; A.B., Washington and Jefferson Coll., 1943; M.S., Carnegie Inst. Tech., 1949, D.Sc., 1950; m. Marian Marie Dumbaugh, May 24, 1947; children—Thomas N., Nicki Marie, Sarah D. Chemist, Tenn. Eastman Co., Kingsport, 1950-52, sr. chemist, 1952-73, devel. asso., 1973—. Bd. dirs., v.p. Symphony Orch. of Kingsport; bd. dirs. Kingsport Fine Arts Center. Served with USNR, 1943-46; PTO. Fellow Am. Inst. Chemists; mem. Am. Assn. Textile Technologists, Phi Beta Kappa, Sigma Xi. Republican. Presbyn. (ruling elder 1951—). Mason, Eagle. Patentee in polymers. Home: 312 McTeer Dr Kingsport TN 37663 Office: Tennessee Eastman Company Kingsport TN 37662

RUST, GORDON DICKINSON, architect; b. Washington, Oct. 15, 1918; s. Robert Nelson and Joshan (Brown) R.; B.S., Va. Poly. Inst., 1942; m. Lilian Paige Martin, Jan. 2, 1943; children—Josephine (Mrs. Alton Noble Palmer, Jr.), Caroline (Mrs. John Chisman Hanes, Jr.), Gordon Dickinson, James Smith, Laurence Martin. Individual practice architecture, Alexandria, Va., 1948—. Mem. Archtl. Bd. Rev., Alexandria, 1953-62, 70-72, Alexandria Bldg. Code Com., 1965-70, Alexandria Urban Renewal Archtl. Panel, 1970-72. Served with AUS, 1943-46. Fellow Constrn. Surveyors Inst., Internat. Inst. Arts and Letters, Am. Registered Architects (mem. adv. com. 1957); mem. A.I.A., Nat. Trust for Historic Preservation. Club: Alexandria Businessmen's. Home: Little Persimmon Box 43 Rural Route 1 Round Hill VA 22141 Office: Little Persimmon Box 43 Round Hill VA 22141

RUST, RUSSELL NEWTON, paper products co. exec.; b. Lynchburg, Va., Oct. 10, 1925; s. Russell and Elva Louise (Smith) R.; student U. Mo., 1943, Bowling Green State U., 1946-47; B.E.E., Ga. Inst. Tech., 1951; m. Lucy Reola Doss, Sept. 3, 1947; children—Susan, Michael, Nancy, Robin. Engr., Merritt-Chapman & Scott Corp., Pensacola, Fla., 1951-54; staff engr. St. Regis Paper Co., Pensacola, 1955-58, St. Joe Paper Co., 1958-63; project engr. Olin Inc., Monroe, La., 1963-66; project engr. Union Camp Corp., Atlanta, 1966—. Served with AUS, World War II: ETO. Mem. A.I.E.E., T.A.P.P.I. Mason. Club: Exchange. Home: 1821 Galilee Ct Tucker GA 30084 Office: 3420 Whipple St Atlanta GA 30354

RUTH, EARL BAKER, congressman; b. Spencer, N.C., Feb. 7, 1916; s. Earl Monroe and Marion (Baker) R.; A.B., U. N.C., 1938, M.A., 1942, Ph.D., 1955; m. Jane Wiley, Dec. 27, 1938; children—Billie Jane (Mrs. Franklin Foil), Earl Wiley, Marian Ann (Mrs. Joe Reber), Jacqueline Dell (Mrs. Clay Burleson). Tchr., coach Chapel Hill (N.C.) High Sch., 1938-39, Piedmont Jr. High Sch., Charlotte, N.C., 1939-40; with shipping dept. McCrary Mills, Asheboro, N.C., 1940-41; asst. supt. N.C. State Parks, 1941; grad. asst. phys. edn. U. N.C., 1941-42; dir. recreation, King Mountain, N.C., 1945-46; football coach, baseball and basketball coach, athletic dir., chmn. dept. phys. edn., dean students Catawba Coll., Salisbury, N.C., 1946-68; mem. 91st-93d congresses from 8th Dist. N.C. Active local Boy Scouts Am. Mem. city council, Salisbury, also mayor pro tem, 1967-68. Bd. dirs. Salisbury YMCA. Served as lt. USNR, 1942-45. Mem. Am. Legion, V.F.W., Nat. Sportscasters and Sportswriters (past pres. awards program). Republican. Presbyn. (elder). Elk. Club: Civitan. Home: 2601 Woodley Pl Washington DC 20008 Office: 129 Cannon House Office Bldg Washington DC 20515

RUTHERFORD, GORDON HENRY, univ. adminstr.; b. Elkins, W.Va., Aug. 5, 1936; s. Henry Ames and Marjorie Leona (Bennett) R.; B.Arch., Pa. State U., 1959; m. Annella Lundberg, July 18, 1959; children—Gordon B., Carolyn C., Mary A., Stephen H. Cons. architect State of N.C., Raleigh, 1963-70; dir. facilities planning U. N.C., Chapel Hill, 1970—. Served with C.E.C., USNR, 1959-63. Mem. A.I.A., Triangle. Democrat. Episcopalian. Home: 3113 Glenridge Dr Raleigh NC 27604 Office: U NC Chapel Hill NC 27514

RUTLEDGE, DELBERT LEROY, educator; b. Mooreland, Okla., July 20, 1925; s. John Henry and Tena Clementine (Croissant) R.; B.S., U. N.M., 1946; M.S., Okla. State U., 1949, Ed.D., 1958; m. Helen Louise Fithen, June 1, 1947; children—Kristena Lee (Mrs. Vester Marshall, Jr.), John Henry. Asst. prof. physics Central State U., 1948-57; asso. prof. physics Okla. State U., 1957-71, prof., 1971—; asst. and acting program dir. spl. projects program NSF, 1964-65. Served with USNR, 1943-46. Kellogg Found. fellow. Fellow Okla. Acad. Sci.; mem. Nat. Sci. Tchrs. Assn., Am. Assn. Physics Tchrs., Phi Delta Kappa, Sigma Pi Sigma. Home: 1924 E McElroy Rd Stillwater OK 74074

RUTLEDGE, EDWARD PAUL, univ. adminstr.; b. Charleston, S.C., Oct. 22, 1941; s. James Garold and Jeanne Marie (Hymel) R.; B.S., U. Ala., 1967, M.A. (Nat. Def. Edn. Act fellow), 1968; m. Martha Gail Dutton, June 9, 1962; children—Paul, Peter, Joan. Research asso. U. Ala., 1969-72, asso. dir. Center for Bus. and Econ. Research, 1972-73, dir., 1973—. Cons. econs., statistics. Statis. adviser Tuscaloosa Community Council, United Fund, 1972—; mem. Tuscaloosa Community Devel. Action Com., 1972—. Served with AUS, 1961-65. Mem. Beta Gamma Sigma, Omicron Delta Epsilon. Home: 62 Southmont Dr Tuscaloosa AL 35401 Office: PO Box AK University AL 35486

RUTLEDGE, RALPH JENNINGS, JR., dentist; b. San Antonio, July 30, 1937; s. Ralph Jennings and Nonie Virginia (Ewing) R.; A.B., W.Va. U., 1959; D.D.S., 1963; m. Sally Ann Jordan, July 7, 1956; 1 son, Mark. Pvt. practice dentistry, Colonial Heights, Va., 1966—. Mem. Bd. Health Planning Com., 1971—. Mem. Va. Dental Peer Rev. Com. Bd. dirs. Colonial Heights-Chesterfield Cancer Soc. Served with Dental Corps, AUS, 1963-66. Mem. Acad. Gen. Dentistry, Am., Va. dental assns., Southside Va. Dental Soc., Am. Legion, Delta Sigma Delta. Methodist (bd. mem. 1968-70). Mason (32 deg., Shriner), Kiwanian (pres. Colonial Heights 1971-72). Home: 204 Fairmont Dr Colonial Heights VA 23834 Office: 3401 Boulevard St Colonial Heights VA 23834

RUWE, VICTOR WILLIAM, govt. ofcl.; b. Cin., Dec. 28, 1936; s. Victor George and Dorothy Francis (Robertson) R.; B.E.E., Auburn U., 1961; M.S.E., U. Ala., 1968, postgrad., 1968—; m. Billie Jean

McGaughy, Oct. 21, 1961; children—Joseph Victor, Edward Victor. Design engr. Chrysler Corp., Huntsville, Ala., 1962-66; project engr. Gen. Electric Co., Huntsville, 1964-66; research engr. U.S. Army, Huntsville, 1966-71, project engr., mgr., 1971—. Mgmt. cons. Sci. System Internat., Huntsville, 1971—, H & S Engring., 1973—; flight instr. South Huntsville Airport, 1970—; instr. mgmt., bus. dept. Calhoun Jr. Coll., 1973—. Served with USAF, 1961-62. Recipient Sci. and Engring. Achievement awards, 1970, 71. Registered profl. engr., Ala. Mem. Aircraft Owners and Pilots Assn. Home: 6417 Deramus Dr NW Huntsville AL 35806 Office: Redstone Arsenal Huntsville AL 35809

RYAN, CLARENCE FLETCHER, digital systems engr.; b. Eola, Tex., Apr. 23, 1927; s. Clarence F. and Lillian (Killam) R.; student San Angelo Jr. Coll., 1946-48, Internat. Corr. Schs., 1949-52; E.E., Odessa Jr. Coll., 1956; student Nat. Radio Inst., 1957-59; m. Patricia Sue Dantin, Apr. 28, 1966; children—Michael Ray, Steven Curtis, Carla D'awn, Kimberly Ranae. Engr. research and devel. Rotary Engring. Co., Midland, Tex., 1949-59, Ray Geophys. Co. Mandrel Industries, Inc., Houston, 1959-67; v.p., system engr. Geophys. Data Processing Center, Inc., Houston, 1967—. Cons. digital data systems and numerical controls. Served with USNR, 1944-46. Mem. Soc. Exploration Geophysicists, A.A.A.S., Smithsonian Assn. Mason. Home: 4218 Knotty Oaks Trail Houston TX 77045 Office: 5322 Elm St Houston TX 77036

RYAN, DORIS ANN, banker; b. Three Rivers, Que., Can., Dec. 23, 1926; d. Joseph Arthur and Daisy (Cunningham) Fish; grad. pub. schs.; m. John Marshall Ryan, Nov. 6, 1950. With The State Nat. Bank of El Paso (Tex.), 1950—, asst. trust officer, 1967-70, trust officer, 1970—. Mem. El Paso Estate Planning Council, Nat. Assn. Bank Women. Republican. Episcopalian. Club: Soroptimist Club of El Paso. Home: 9909 Fenway Dr El Paso TX 79925 Office: 1 State Nat Plaza El Paso TX 79901

RYAN, RICHARD LEROY, marketing specialist; b. Tulsa, Aug. 24, 1945; s. Arthur Guy and Frances Geneva (Hays) R.; B.S. in Bus. Adminstrn., Tulsa U., 1967; m. Judy Carol Childers, June 4, 1966; 1 dau., Lisa Kathleen. Market analyst marketing staff, head market research T.D. Williamson, Inc., Tulsa, 1969—. Bd. dirs. Family and Childrens Services, Tulsa. Served with Adj. Gen. Corps, AUS, 1967-69. Mem. Am. Marketing Assn. (treas. 1969—). Baptist (tchr. 1964—). Home: 3215 W 40th St Tulsa OK 74107 Office: 2733 S Latimer St Tulsa OK 74107

RYAN, ROBERT FRANK, physician, educator; b. Hoquiam, Wash., June 23, 1922; s. Andrew Boudot and Zylma Fern (Upson) R.; A.B., Stanford, 1944, M.D., 1947; M.S., U. Minn., 1956; m. Marilyn Yvonne Arnoult, Mar. 30, 1964. Intern, Stanford Service City and County Hosp., San Francisco, 1956-57; asst. resident surgery Emergency Hosp., Washington, 1950-51, resident, 1952; fellow gen. surgery Mayo Found., 1953-56; preceptee in plastic surgery Tulane U., New Orleans, La., 1956-58, instr. in surgery, 1956-59, asst. prof. surgery, 1959-63, asso. prof. surgery, 1963-67, prof. surgery, 1967—, chief plastic surgery sect., 1969—. Served with M.C., USN, 1947-50. NIH grantee, 1960-65; Am. Cancer Soc. grantee, 1957-59; recipient Hektoen Gold medal, A.M.A., 1959. Diplomate Am. Bd. Surgery, Am. Bd. Plastic Surgery. Mem. Am., So. med. assns., Am. Assn. Cancer Research, Am. Assn. Plastic Surgeons, Am. Assn. Surg. Trauma, Am. Assn. Cancer Edn., Am., La. surg. assns., Assn. Am. Med. Colls., Am. Burn Assn., Am. Cancer Soc., Am. Soc. Artificial Internal Organs, Soc. Univ. Surgeons, Southeastern Soc. Plastic and Reconstructive Surgeons, Am. Soc. Plastic Surgeons, Internat. Soc. for Burn Injury, Soc. Head and Neck Surgeons, Am. Soc. Aesthetic Plastic Surgery, New Orleans, Alton Ochsner, Oscar Creech surg. socs., La. Heart Assn., Sigma Xi. Home: 1524 7th St New Orleans LA 70115 Office: 1430 Tulane Av New Orleans LA 70112

RYAN, ROBERT JOHN, SR., accountant, govt. ofcl.; b. Champaign, Ill., May 18, 1920; s. Edward Travis and Rose (McAdams) R.; B.S., U. Ill., 1942; m. Mary Leona Conn, Sept. 21, 1943; children—Robert John, Ruth Ann (Mrs. Byron B. Barnes). Sr. accountant Haskins & Sells, C.P.A.'s, Chgo., 1945-46, 49-54, San Francisco, 1954-55; asst. comptroller W. Lewis & Co. Dept. Store, Champaign, Ill., 1946-49; chief accountant Fibreboard Paper Products Corp., San Francisco, 1955-57; supervisory accountant U.S. Gen. Accounting Office, San Francisco, 1957-60, def. div., Washington, 1960-69, asst. dir. audit standards staff div. financial and gen. mgmt. studies, Washington, 1969—. Served with USNR, 1942-45. C.P.A., Ill., Cal. Mem. Am. Inst. C.P.A.'s, Am. Accounting Assn., Fed. Govt. Accountants Assn. Home: 8249 Branch Rd Annandale VA 22003 Office: Room 6025 441 G St NW Washington DC 20548

RYAN, TED LAMAR, mech. engr.; b. Chattanooga, Jan. 6, 1938; s. Luther Erskine and Margaret Blanche (Price) R.; B.S. in Mech. Engring., U. Tenn., 1961; m. Glenda Ilene Carlton, June 16, 1961; children—Andrea, Valerie, Gregory. Designer engr. Douglas Aircraft Co., Santa Monica, Cal., 1961-62, N. Am. Aviation Inc., Downey, Cal., 1962-64; br. mgr. Teledyne Brown Engring. Co., Huntsville, Ala., 1964—. Registered profl. engr., Ala. Mem. Delta Sigma Phi (pres. Omicron chpt. 1960-61). Home: 1505 Wind River Dr Huntsville AL 35802 Office: 300 Sparkman Dr Huntsville AL 35806

RYDMAN, EDWARD J., psychologist, marriage counselor; b. Toledo, Aug. 3, 1916; s. Edward Joseph and Nell (Vail) R.; B.S., Ohio State U., 1938, M.A., 1954, Ph.D., 1965; postgrad. Columbia, 1942-43; m. Jean Storey, Dec. 29, 1939; children—Edward Jay, Nancy Lynn (Mrs. Richard G. Ellis), Suzanne Claire (Mrs. Clark M. Straw), Joan Christine. With YMCA, Cin., 1938-41, Bklyn. and Queens, N.Y., 1941-44, Miami, Fla., 1944-46; minister to youth First Community Ch., Columbus, O., 1946-54; exec. dir. Planned Parenthood of Columbus, also pvt. practice marriage counseling, 1955-59; exec. dir. Planned Parenthood of Dallas, pvt. practice marriage counseling, 1959-67; exec. dir. Am. Assn. Marriage Counselors, Inc., pvt. practice, Dallas, 1967-72; pvt. practice marriage counseling, 1972—. Tchr. marriage and family life edn. Denison U., 1958-59, So. Meth. U., 1966-67, Perkins Sch. Theology, 1968-69; lectr. Meth. Hosp. Sch. Nursing, Dallas, Tex. Womens U. Sch. Nursing; cons. profl. staff Dallas YMCA, USAF Family Life, 1968. Pres., Dallas Council for Family Life Edn.; v.p. Bd. Edn. Grandview Heights, O. Bd. dirs. Ohio-W.Va. area YMCA, Community Action program Office Econ. Opportunity, Dallas, Urban Generation Found. Fellow Am. Assn. Marriage Counselors, Am. Orthopsychiat. Assn.; mem. Am. Psychol. Assn., Am. Sociology Assn., A.A.A.S., Groves Conf. on Marriage and Family, Nat. Council on Family Relations (dir.), Am. Camping Assn. (pres. Central Ohio sect.). Home: 12651 Croydon Circle Dallas TX 75230

RYLANDER, MICHAEL KENT, zoologist, educator; b. Hillsboro, Tex., Dec. 25, 1935; s. Halley Garison and Annabelle (Wildenthal) R.; B.A., N. Tex. State U., 1956, M.S., 1962; Ph.D., Tulane U., 1965; m. Elizabeth Anne Gibson, May 8, 1970; children—Michael Kent, Sharon Allison. Instr. depts. biology and German, N. Tex. State U., 1961-62; instr. biology Tulane, 1964-65; asst. prof. biology Tex. Tech. U., Lubbock, 1965-72, asso. prof., 1972—, adj. prof. anatomy Med. Sch., 1973—, research asso., curator birds Tex. Tech. Mus., 1972—. Mem. scientists adv. com. Environmental Def. Fund, N.Y.C., 1971—. Served with AUS, 1959-61. Mem. Am. Assn. Anatomists, Am. Ornithologists Union, Am. Anthrop. Assn., Royal Anthrop. Soc., Current Anthropology, Big Bend Natural History Assn. (dir. 1967—), Lubbock Audubon Soc. (founder). Editor: Bull. Tex. Ornithol. Soc., 1967—. Contbr. articles to numerous profl. publs. Home: 2818 24th St Lubbock TX 79410 Office: Dept Biology Texas Tech U Lubbock TX 79409

RYLEE, ROBERT TILMAN II, med. device mfg. co. exec.; b. Dallas, Oct. 24, 1930; s. William Jackson and Carolyn Inez (Kusnick) R.; B.A., U. Tex. at Austin, 1956, J.D., 1958; m. Sarah Jane English, Aug. 27, 1956 (div. Aug. 1968); children—Linda Jane, Robert Tilman III. Admitted to Tex. bar, 1957, U.S. Dist. Ct. bar, 1958, U.S. Ct. Appeals bar, 1959, U.S. Supreme Ct. bar, 1962; practiced in Corpus Christi, 1958-69; partner firm Wood, Boykin, Rylee & Wolter, 1965-69; pres., chief exec. officer Wright Mfg. Co., orthopaedic implants and instruments, Memphis, 1968—, also dir.; dir. Acme Engring. Co., Greensboro, N.C. Mem. adv. bd. Salvation Army, 1963-68; bd. dirs. Tex. Youth Guidance Found., Austin, 1964-68, Friends of Pub. Libraries, 1965-68. Served to capt. AUS, 1951-53. Adm., Tex. Navy, 1959; Squire, Tenn., 1966. Mem. Orthopaedic Surg. Mfrs. Assn. (pres. 1970—), Am. Soc. Testing and Materials, Internat. Standards Orgn., Am. Judicature Soc., Am. Bar Assn., State Bar Tex. Clubs: Colonial Country, Summit. Home: 5744 Barfield St Memphis TN 38117 Office: 411 N 3d St Memphis TN 38105

RYON, THOMAS S(HIPLEY), tobacco co. exec.; b. Washington, May 29, 1917; s. Norman Eugene and Mary (Shipley) R.; A.B., Duke, 1938; m. Ruth Elizabeth Green, Apr. 12, 1940; children—Thomas Shipley, David Osmond. Travel and study in Europe and Africa, 1938; real estate and income tax specialist, Washington, 1939; mgr. A.C. Monk Enterprises, 1940-43; accountant A.C. Monk & Co., Inc., Farmville, N.C., 1943-45, asst. sec., 1945-54, sec., 1954—, v.p., 1971—; v.p. Dixon Hamilton Tobacco Suppliers, 1968—; sec., dir. Eastern Tobacco Co.; sr. v.p., dir. First Fed. Savs. & Loan Pitt County, 1972—. Pres. Farmville Tobacco Bd. Trade, 1966-68. Chmn. Farmville com. Boy Scouts Am., 1957-63; dir. Farmville Little League, Farmville Community Chest, Farmville United Fund; vice chmn. Farmville Sch. Bd., 1957, chmn. 1958-63. Mem. N.C. World Trade Assn. (dir.), Farmville C. of C. (dir.). Democrat. Episcopalian. Clubs: Wilson Coin; Farmville Coin, Farmville Country (past sec.-treas.). Home: 1007 Fountain Hwy Farmville NC 27828 Office: West Marlboro Rd Farmville NC 27828

RYWLIN, ARKADI MICHAEL, physician, educator; b. Danzig, July 22, 1923; s. Michael and Bertha (Kossowski) R.; B.A. with distinction Am. U. Beirut, 1946; M.D., U. Geneva, 1949, specialist in pathology, 1952; m. Hava Rywlin, Nov. 7, 1953; 1 son, Daniel. Came to U.S., 1952, naturalized, 1958. Intern Michael Reese Hosp., Chgo., 1952-53, resident, 1953-55; resident U. Geneva, Switzerland, 1949-52; practice medicine, specializing in pathology, 1955—; prof. pathology U. Miami Sch. Medicine, 1971—; dir. dept. pathology and lab. medicine Mt. Sinai Med. Center, Miami Beach, 1966—. Served to capt., M.C., AUS, 1956-58. Diplomate Am. Bd. Pathology. Mem. Am. Soc. Clin. Pathologists, A.M.A., Coll. Am. Pathologists, Am. Soc. Hematology, Internat. Acad. Pathology. Researcher in hematology. Home: 108 W Dilido St Miami Beach FL 33139 Office: 4300 Alton Rd Miami Beach FL 33140

SAAD, MOUNZER AMIN, utility exec.; b. Ain Anoub, Lebanon, Nov. 13, 1942; s. Amin Ali and Wedad (Halabi) S.; B.S. in Elec. Engring., U. S.C., 1967; m. Nabila Fakih, Feb. 18, 1973; 1 dau., Claudia Jenan. Came to U.S., 1963, naturalized, 1970. Jr. engr. S.C. Electric and Gas Co., Columbia, 1967-68, asst. engr., 1968-72, asso. engr., 1972-73, supt. communications, 1973—. Registered profl. engr., S.C. Mem. I.E.E.E. Club: Pine Island. Home: 1324 Chevis St Columbia SC 29205 Office: 300 Main St Columbia SC 29218

SAARINEN, ARTHUR WILLIAM, banker; b. Newberry, Fla., May 16, 1902; s. Ulrick Knut and Naima (Anderson) S.; student U. Fla., 1922-25; m. Elsie Gillespie, July 12, 1925; children—Arthur William, James W. Asst. cashier Bank of Newberry, 1919-22; state bank examiner, Fla., 1926-33; sr. bank examiner Fed. Res. Bank of Atlanta, 1933-43, chief examiner, 1943-45; v.p., dir. Broward Nat. Bank, Ft. Lauderdale, Fla., 1945-54, exec. v.p., dir., 1954-59, pres., dir., 1959-70, chmn. bd., dir., 1970-73; pres., chief exec. officer Broward Bankshares, Inc., 1970-73, now dir.; dir. Ft. Lauderdale Nat. Bank, 1947—, Coral Ridge Nat. Bank, Broward Nat. Bank of Plantation; pres. Lauderdale Lakes Nat. Bank, 1971-72, dir., 1970—; dir. Fed. Res. Bank, Jacksonville, 1963-65. Mem. Downtown Devel. Authority Ft. Lauderdale, 1965-73, chmn., 1969-70; state chmn. Fla. Am. Bankers Assn. for Savs. Bonds, 1964, 65; Broward dist. chmn., v.p. S. Fla. council Boy Scouts Am., 1948-51. Bd. dirs. Blue Shield Fla., 1951—; trustee Ft. Lauderdale U., 1969-74. Recipient Silver Beaver award Boy Scouts Am., 1959; named Citizen of Month Greater Ft. Lauderdale C. of C., 1973. Mem. Delta Chi, Alpha Kappa Psi. Methodist. Club: Lauderdale Yacht (Ft. Lauderdale). Home: 221 E Tropical Way Plantation FL 33314 Office: 25 S Andrews Av Fort Lauderdale FL 33301

SAARINEN, ARTHUR WILLIAM, JR., civil engr.; b. West Palm Beach, Fla., Dec. 9, 1927; s. Arthur William and Elsie (Gillespie) S.; student Ga. Inst. Tech., 1944-45; B.C.E., U. Fla., 1950; m. Mary Jane Emig, June 30, 1950; children—Mary Louise, Linda Jane (div. May 1973); m. Jacqueline René Smith, Mar. 1, 1974. With Fla. Bd. of Health, 1950, Broward County Bd. County Commrs., 1951; staff engr. J.H. Philpott, engrs., 1953-54, v.p., 1954-67, pres., 1967—; exec. Ross, Saarinen, Bolton & Wilder, Inc., Fort Lauderdale, Fla. Cons. to Govt. of Bahama Islands for water supply, 1966-72. Chmn. Broward County Water Resources Adv. Bd., 1964—. Vice pres. Fla. Atlantic U. Found. Mem. exec. council South Fla. council Boy Scouts Am.; hon. trustee Broward Community Coll. Served with AUS, 1946-47. Diplomate Am. Acad. Environmental Engrs. Fellow Am. Soc. C.E.; mem. Fla. Inst. Cons. Engrs. (pres. 1962-63), Am. Cons. Engrs. Council (dir. 1971-72), Am. Water Works Assn., Water Pollution Control Fedn., Sigma Chi. Methodist. Rotarian (pres. chpt. 1964-65). Club: University Fla. Alumni (dist. v.p. 1966). Home: 2797 NE 51st St Fort Lauderdale FL 33308 Office: 2001 NW 62d St Fort Lauderdale FL 33309

SABGHIR, AARON SEYMOUR, economist; b. Bklyn., Apr. 21, 1921; s. Jacob and Mollie (Vernoff) S.; B.S., City Coll. N.Y., 1941; postgrad. Columbia U., 1941-42, Am. U., 1946-48; m. Beatrice Janet Simmons, Aug. 30, 1942; children—Naomi (Mrs. Allen R. Zeiger), David, Judith (Mrs. Ronald A. Zeiger), Jonathan. With Fed. Govt. Career Service, 1942—, successively economist in OPA, chief sampling techniques Bus. Census, U.S. Bur. Census, dir. survey review div. OPS, dir. quality control bus. census U.S. Bur. Census, 1942-55, chief economist bldg. materials and constrn. div. U.S. Dept. Commerce, 1955-68, dir. constrn. and bldg. materials div., 1968—. Dir., bd. dirs. Group Health Assn., Inc., Washington, 1963-65. Mem. Am. Statis. Assn., Soc. Govt Economists. Editor Construction Rev., monthly dept. of commerce publ., 1959-68, 70—. Home: 723 Lowander Lane Silver Spring MD 20901 Office: 14th and Constitution Av Washington DC 20230

SABIS, WILLIAM ROBERT, cons. environmental engr.; b. Syracuse, N.Y., Oct. 7, 1939; s. William Anthony and Helen (Lowe) S.; B.C.E., Syracuse U., 1964, M.S., 1966; m. Elaine Joyce Mt. Pleasant, June 29, 1963; children—Douglas Robert, Donna Lynn, Rebecca Elaine. San. engr. Atlas Chem. Industries, Wilmington, Del., 1966-67; dir., san. engr., water pollution control div. Del. Water and Air Resources Commn., Dover, 1967-68; project mgr. Smith-Davis & Assos. (purchased by Sverdrup and Parcel Cons. Engrs. of St. Louis 1972), Gainesville, Fla., 1968—, sec.-treas., 1971—. Recipient Am. Field Service Fgn. Student scholarship award to Germany, 1956. Mem. Sigma Xi. Home: 5715 NW 4th Pl Gainesville FL 32607 Office: 2512 SW 34th St Gainesville FL 32608

SABISTON, DAVID COSTON, JR., educator, surgeon; b. Onslow County, N.C., Oct. 4, 1924; s. David Coston and Marie (Jackson) S.; B.S., U. N.C., 1943; M.D., Johns Hopkins, 1947; m. Agnes Barden, Sept. 24, 1955; children—Anne Barden, Agnes Foy, Sarah Coston. Successively intern, asst. resident, chief resident surgery Johns Hopkins Hosp., 1947-53; successively asst. prof., asso. prof., prof. surgery Johns Hopkins Med. Sch., 1955-64, Howard Hughes investigator, 1955-60; Fulbright research scholar U. Oxford (Eng.), 1960; research asso. Hosp. Sick Children, U. London (Eng.), 1961; James B. Duke prof. surgery, chmn. dept. Duke Med. Sch., 1964—. Served to capt. M.C., AUS, 1953-55. Recipient Career Research award NIH, 1962-64. Fellow A.C.S.; mem. Soc. Univ. Surgeons (pres. 1968-69), Am., So. surg. assns., Am. Assn. Thoracic Surgery, Soc. Clin. Surgery, Internat. Cardiovascular Surgery, Soc. Vascular Surgery, Halsted Soc., Surg. Biology Club II, Soc. Thoracic Surgery, Soc. Surgery Alimentary Tract, Soc. Thoracic Surgeons Great Britain and Ireland, Phi Beta Kappa, Alpha Omega Alpha. Co-editor: Gibbon's Surgery of the Chest. Editor: Davis-Christopher Textbook of Surgery. Chmn. editorial bd. Annals Surgery, 1974—, Jour. Cardiovascular and Thoracic Surgery, Circulation. Home: 1528 Pinecrest Rd Durham NC 27706

SACHS, LEONARD BERTRAM, lawyer; b. DeLand, Fla., Mar. 26, 1929; s. Benjamin and Sara Rebecca (Weiss) S.; student Coll. William and Mary, 1947-48; LL.B., U. Va., 1958; m. Sarita Rebe, Jan. 4, 1953; children—Jeffry Alden, Jacquelyn Robin, Amy Gwyn. Admitted to Va. bar, 1958, since practiced in Norfolk; law clk. U.S. Dist. Ct., 1958-60; asso. firm Kanter and Kanter, Attys., 1960-63; partner Kanter, Kanter and Sachs, 1963-67; practice law, 1967-70; partner Furniss, Davis and Sachs, Attys., 1970—. Mem. com. on biomed. ethics East Va. Med. Sch., 1973—, mem. med. legal curriculum com., 1974—. Chmn. Community Relations Com. United Jewish Fedn. Norfolk, 1973—. Served with USAF, 1951-55. Mem. Va. Trial Lawyers Assn. (v.p. 1970-73, chmn. legislation and code revision com. 1970-74), Norfolk-Portsmouth, Va. bar assns., Am. Bar Assn., Am. Trial Lawyers Assn., Maritime Law Assn. U.S., Am. Judicature Soc. Jewish religion. Mem. B'nai B'rith (chmn. Va. bd. Anti Defamation League 1971—). Office: 203 Plaza One Bldg Norfolk VA 23510

SACHS, SIDNEY STANLEY, lawyer; b. Washington, Dec. 25, 1916; s. William Michael and Rebecca (Krupsaw) S.; B.A., Am. U., 1937; LL.B., Georgetown U., 1941; m. Betty Kossow, Nov. 20, 1941; children—Ellen Rodin, Susan Goldman, Jane, John. Admitted to D.C. bar, 1942, Md. bar, 1949, also U.S. Supreme Ct.; law clk. to judge U.S. Emergency Ct. Appeals, 1943-45; asst. U.S. atty. D.C., 1945-49; pvt. practice law, Washington and Md., 1949—; instr. Washington Coll. Law, Am. U., 1947-52; mem. bd. Inst. Criminal Law and Procedure, Georgetown U., 1955—. Mem. Jud. Conf. for D.C., 1958-64, 66-72; sec., dir. Capitol Inst. Tech., 1965—. Mem. Washington Sch. Psychiatry, 1973—. Bd. dirs. D.C. Assn. Mental Health, 1964-66; trustee Pub. Defender Service, 1965—; bd. govs. Citizens Communication center. 1967. Fellow Am. Bar Found.; mem. Am. (ho. of dels. 1970—, state del. 1972—), Fed. bar assns., Bar Assn. D.C. (pres. research found. 1959, pres. assn. 1966-67), Am. Civil Liberties Union. Jewish religion. Clubs: Federal City, Burning Tree. Home: 2717 Daniel Rd Chevy Chase MD 20015 Office: 1620 Eye St NW Washington DC 20006

SACHSE, VICTOR A., lawyer; b. Baton Rouge, Sept. 21, 1903; s. Victor A. and Fannye (Bloomenstiel) S.; LL.B., La. State U., 1925; m. Janice Rubenstein, Jan. 2, 1929; children—Victor A. III, Harry R. Admitted to La. bar, 1925; practice law, Baton Rouge; mem. firm Breazeale, Sachse & Wilson; 1st asst. gen. counsel, gen. counsel Surplus Property Adminstrn., 1945-46. Dir. Fidelity Nat. Bank. Chmn. City-Parish Plan Commn., 1947-48; parish atty., East Baton Rouge, 1949-50. Chmn. Air Force Adv. Com. Prisoners War, 1964. Exec. com. Council for Better La., Found. for Better La.; dir. La. State U. Found.; trustee La. Arts and Sci. Center, 1964-67. Served to lt. col., Judge Adv. Gen. Dept., AUS, 1942-45. Decorated Legion of Merit. Fellow Am. Coll. Trial Lawyers; mem. Am., La. (bd. govs. 1957-58), Baton Rouge (pres. 1941-42) bar assns., Am., La. (council) law insts., Mil. Order World Wars, Am. Legion, Am. Jewish Com. (mem.-at-large ho. dels.), Order Coif, Phi Delta Phi. Mason (master 1936). Home: 370 S Lakeshore Dr Baton Rouge LA 70808 Office: Fidelity Bank Bldg Baton Rouge LA 70801

SACK, RONALD LAWRENCE, broadcaster; b. Chgo., Mar. 5, 1934; s. William Hobart and Cecilia Gertrude (Grath) S.; B.A., DePaul U., 1957; m. Barbara Ann Courtney, Aug. 6, 1960; children—Kevin John, Courtney David. Adminstrv. asst. Gulf Oil Corp., Chgo., 1958; dir. advt. and promotion radio sta. WLS, Chgo., 1958-62; dir. advt. and program devel. ABC owned radio stas., N.Y.C., 1962-68; v.p., gen. mgr. radio sta. KXYZ, Houston, 1968—. Treas. Houston Council on Alcoholism. Served with AUS, 1957-63. Mem. Nat., Tex. assns. broadcasters, Houston Advt. Club. Home: 13610 Barryknoll St Houston TX 77024 Office: 1602 Fannin Bank Bldg Houston TX 77025

SACKETT, ARTHUR JOHNSON, civil engr.; b. Ft. George, Fla., May 25, 1884; s. John Warren and Louise (Johnson) S.; student U. Pa., 1905-06; m. Ethel Lee Clancy, Sept. 2, 1907; 1 dau., Virginia Lee; m. 2d, Julia Hopkins, Nov. 5, 1932; 1 dau., Louise (Mrs. Bernard McCray). Asst. engr. on constrn. East River Tunnel for Pa. R.R., 1906-11; asst. engr. on constrn. Catskill Aqueduct, Mason & Hanger Co., 1911-17, chief engr. on constrn. Camp Taylor, 1917, chief engr. of company, 1919-29, pres., 1929-55, also dir.; chmn. bd. Mason & Hanger-Silas, Mason Co., Inc., 1955—. Served as maj. Q.M.C., U.S. Army, 1918-19. Mem. Am. Soc. C.E., Soc. Am. Mil. Engrs. Episcopalian. (jr. warden). Mason (Shriner). Clubs: Engineers, Turf and Field (N.Y.C.); Virginia Country, Commonwealth (Richmond, Va.); Shoreham (L.I.) Country; St. Augustine (Fla.) Golf. Home: Riverview Farm Charles City VA 23030 Office: 437 Madison Av New York City NY 10036

SACKETT, PAUL EDMUNDS, banker; b. Lynchburg, Va., Aug. 29, 1907; s. Henry Mosley and Mina (Otey) S.; B.A., U. Va., 1929, LL.B., 1931; m. Elizabeth Graves, Nov. 4, 1933; children—Paul E., William Graves. Admitted to Va. bar, 1930; practiced in N.Y.C., 1931-32; mem. firms Carter, Ledyard & Milburn, attys., N.Y.C., 1931-32, Williams & Sackett, attys., Lynchburg, Va., 1932-38; sec.-treas. The Lynchburg Trust & Savs. Bank, 1938-48, v.p., 1948-54, pres., 1954-55; sr. v.p., trust officer First Nat. Trust & Savs. Bank (name now changed to United Va. Bank/First Nat.), 1955-61, pres., 1955-61, pres., 1961-72, chmn. bd., 1972—; dir. Ala.-Tenn. Natural Gas Co., First Colony Life Ins. Co., Lynchburg Gas Co., Montague-Betts Co., Inc., WLVA Inc., CapitoLine Investment Services, Inc.; v.p. Va. Hot Springs Inc. Mem. adv. council Lynchburg Coll., 1965—; mem. adv. com. Randolph-Macon Woman's Coll., 1964—. Bd. dirs. Lynchburg Gen.-Marshall Lodge Hosps., Inc. Mem. Va. State Bar Assn., Lynchburg C. of C. (treas. 1950-70). Home: 2003 Link Rd Lynchburg VA 24503 Office: 1010 Main St Lynchburg VA 24504

SACKNER, MARVIN ARTHUR, physician; b. Phila., Feb. 16, 1932; s. Albert and Goldie (Haber) S.; B.S. in Pharmacy, Temple U., 1953; M.D., Jefferson Med. Sch., 1957; m. Ruth Karsch, June 24, 1956; children—Sara, Deborah, Jonathan. Intern Phila. Gen. Hosp.,1957-58; chief div. pulmonary diseases Mt. Sinai Med. Center, Miami Beach, Fla., 1967—, also prof. medicine U. Miami, 1973—; mem. pulmonary diseases adv. com. Nat. Heart and Lung Inst. Mem. Am. Physiol. Soc., A.C.P., Am. Thoracic Soc. Author: Scleroderma, 1967. Contbr. articles to profl. jours. Home: 300 W Rivo Alto Dr Miami Beach FL 33139 Office: 4300 Alton Rd Miami Beach FL 33140

SACONAS, EDWARD SHERMAN, real estate developer, banker; b. Elkhart, Ind., May 7, 1939; s. George and Louise (Tamburine) S.; B.A. summa cum laude, St. Mary's U., San Antonio, 1960; LL.D. cum laude, U. Houston, 1965 Pres., Bayou Vista Land Corp., Hitchcock, Tex., 1963—; dir. Mainland Bank, Texas City, Tex., 1966—, vice chmn., 1969—; dir. Citizens Nat. Bank, Beaumont, Tex., Vidor State Bank; chmn. E. Tex. State Bank, Buna. Mem. Galveston County Seawall Adv. Com., 1968—. Served to lt. AUS. Mem. Hitchcock C. of C. Home: 638 Warsaw Dr Hitchcock TX 77573 Office: PO Box 8 Hitchcock TX 77563

SADIK, MARVIN SHERWOOD, govt. ofcl.; b. Springfield, Mass., June 27, 1932; s. Harry Benjamin and Florence (Askinas) S.; A.B., Harvard, 1954, A.M., 1960. Curator, Mus. Art, Bowdoin Coll., 1961-64, dir., 1964-67; dir. Mus. Art, U. Conn., 1967-69; dir. Nat. Portrait Gallery, Smithsonian Instn., Washington, 1969—. Mem. adv. bd. Archives of Am. Art. Bd. dirs. Com. of Religion and Art in Am. Mem. Colonial Soc. Mass. (corr.). Author: Colonial and Federal Portraits, 1966; Exhibition Catalogues; The Drawings of Hyman Bloom, 1968; The Paintings of Charles Hawthorne, 1968. Mem. editorial bd. Am. Art Jour. Home: 2801 New Mexico Av NW Washington DC 20007 Office: 8th and F St NW Washington DC 20560

SADLER, GUY ALBERT, architect; b. Norfolk, Va., Sept. 6, 1933; s. Robert Dewey and Dorothy Lovisa (Diggs) S.; B.Arch., Va. Poly. Inst., 1960; m. Orpha Ann Quesenberry, Apr. 22, 1961; 1 dau., Pamela. Intern archtl. firms, Washington, 1960-64; architect, Beery & Rio, architects, Annandale, Va., 1964-67; self-employed as architect and land planner, Falls Church, Va., 1967—. Served with USAF, 1951-55. Mem. A.I.A. Methodist. Prin. archtl. works include Adeson Residence, Village Square Townhouse Project, Wheystone Court Townhouse Project, Franconia Village Townhouse Project, Fairfax County, Va., United Methodist Ch., Fredericktown, O. Home: 11301 Fieldstone Lane Reston VA 22091 Office: 803 W Broad St Falls Church VA 22046

SADLER, HOWARD C., lawyer; b. Port Arthur, Tex., July 19, 1924; s. Robert H. and Mary (Branch) S.; student Baylor U., 1943-44, U. Tex., 1947-48; J.D., U. Tex., 1951; m. Michele G. Delbeck, July 6, 1946; children—Robert Jerry, Patricia Beverly. Was admitted to the Texas State bar, 1951; mem. firm Sadler & Sadler, Port Arthur, Tex., 1952—. Former trustee Port Arthur Coll. Active A.R.C. Former pres. bd. trustees St. Mary's Hosp., now gen. counsel, bd. dirs. Served with AUS, 1943-47, 51-52; lt. col. Res.; ret. Decorated Belgium Fourrageres (Belgium); Bronze Star medal, Combat Infantryman's Badge (U.S.). Mem. Am., Jefferson County (pres. 1965-66), Port Arthur bar assns., Tex. Trial Lawyers Assn. (dir. 1963-65), State Bar Tex., Am. Trial Lawyers Assn., Am. Hosp. Assn. (Soc. Hosp. Attys.), Res. Officers Assn. Elk. Club: Port Arthur Town. Home: 4500 Evergreen Dr Port Arthur TX 77640 Office: Box 3466 Sadler Bldg 2300 Memorial Blvd Port Arthur TX 77642

SAEGERT, CLARENCE EMIL, advt. co. exec.; b. Seguin, Tex., July 10, 1919; s. Joe F. and Clara (Haenel) S.; student Tex. Luth. Coll., 1935-36; B.S., ampla cum laude, U. Tex., 1941; m. Evelyn Gartman, July 18, 1939; children—Joel Gartman, Jerry Charles, Claire Louise. Pres., Tex. Mailing & Printing Co., Austin, 1955—, Clarence E. Saegert Pub. Co., Austin, 1963—, H.E. Enterprises, Austin, 1969—; v.p. Decision Dynamics, Inc., Austin, 1963—. Vice pres. Austin Symphony Soc., 1970-72; pres. Austin U.S.O., 1971-72; vice-commodore Austin Aqua Festival, 1968-70; mem. exec. com. Austin Better Bus. Bur. Bd. dirs. Nat. Conf. Christians and Jews, Austin, 1968-70. Served to lt. USNR, 1943-46; PTO. Mem. Austin Advt. Club (pres. 1959-60), Austin C. of C. (v.p., dir., chmn. Austin postal com.). Lutheran (chmn. membership services com. Internat. Laymen's League 1964-66, supt. Bible classes 1968—, dir. Ann. Visitation and Stewardship Effort 1969—). Home: 3300 Kim Lane Austin TX 78705 Office: 703 W 7th St Austin TX 78701

SAENGER, RUDI FRED, govt. ofcl.; b. Berlin, Germany, July 24, 1932; s. Arthur and Olga (Glaser) S.; came to U.S., 1950, naturalized, 1953; B.S., Trinity U., 1959; postgrad. U. Mich., 1967, Mass. Inst. Tech., 1969; m. Inge Gertrud Rusch, Apr. 10, 1963; children—Elisabeth Olga, Katharina Gerda, Alexander Rudi. Instr. mathematics, San Antonio, 1959-60; geodesist Coast and Geodetic Survey, Washington, 1960-61; mathematician Naval Oceanographic Office, Washington, 1961-63; alternate div. dir. Nat. Oceanographic Data Center, Washington, 1963-66; dep. head sci. analysis Naval Air Systems Command, Washington, 1966-70, head sci. computing, 1970—. Served with USAF, 1952-56. Recipient certificate of merit, U.S. Navy, 1966. Mem. Assn. Computing Machinery, Am. Math. Soc., Washington Numismatic Soc. (exec. bd. 1967-70), U.S. Capitol Hist. Soc. (founding mem.). Club: Carderock Springs (Md.). Home: 8126 Lilly Stone Dr Bethesda MD 20034 Office: Naval Air Systems Command Washington DC 20361

SAENZ, NANCY ELIZABETH KING (MRS. MICHAEL SAENZ), civic worker; b. Greenville, Tex., Jan. 28, 1930; d. Henry M. and Vallie (Wheatley) King; A.B. with honors, Tex. Christian U., 1950, B.S. magna cum laude, 1952; postgrad. Hartford Sem. Found., 1952-53; Escuele de Idiomas, 1953; Lexington Theol. Sem., 1953; m. Michael Saenz, July 28, 1950; children—Michael King, Cynthia Elizabeth. Missionary, United Christian Missionary Soc., Indpls., serving in P.R., 1954-65; bd. dirs. Adminstrv. Bd. Christians Chs., P.R., 1950-65; counsellor and tchr. State Christian Youth Fellowship Conf., P.R., 1954-57; chmn. dept. Christian edn. Christian Chs., P.R., 1962-64, sec., 1954-61, state dir., 1963; dept. Christian edn. P.R. Council Chs., 1959-64, sec., 1959-60; sec. and counsellor State Christian Women Fellowship of Christian Chs., P.R., 1955-57, 59-63, dist. chmn., 1968—. Sec., Disciples of Christ Acad. P.T.A., Bayamon, P.R., 1962-63; mem. state com. Home for Aged, United Ch. Women, P.R., 1963; womens com. Ind. State Symphony Soc., 1967—; womens com. Internat. Christian U. Japan, 1962-64, 65—, pres. Indpls. chpt. 1967-68; mem. exec. bd. Indpls. council P.T.A., 1967-70; mem. vocational-tech. adv. council Laredo Ind. Sch. Dist., 1971—; mem. Laredo Mercy Hosp. Aux., 1973—; dist. cons., mem. adminstrv. com. Christian Women's Fellowship in Tex. Bd. dirs. Greater Indpls. Fedn. Chs., 1970-71. Laredo Planned Parenthood Assn., 1972—. Mem. Irvington Union of Clubs (exec. bd. 1966—, 2d v.p. 1968-70), Young Mothers Club Irvington (v.p. 1965, pres. 1967), Marion County Guardian Home Guild (pres. 1968-70), Art Assn. Indpls., Art League, Irvington, Am. Assn. U. Women, Laredo Pan Am. Roundtable, Alpha Chi, Phi Sigma Iota. Clubs: Rotary Anns, Women's College (P.R.); Irvington Womens; Laredo Tuesday Music and Literature (pres. 1973); Women's City. Author: Winds of Change, 1968. Home: P-34 Fort McIntosh Laredo TX 78040

SAFER, JOEL JARRETT, dentist; b. Baton Rouge, Mar. 13, 1940; s. Mike S. and Nina L. (Jarrett) S.; B.S., La. State U., 1962; D.D.S., Loyola U. South, 1966; m. Joy Lee Hodges, Aug. 15, 1964; children—Heidi Elizabeth, Joel Jarrett II. Practice dentistry, Baton Rouge, 1968—; pres. Capitol Steel, Inc., 1969-70, Safer Corp., 1970—. Mem. Baton Rouge Area Com. on Dental Care for Underpriviledged, 1968-72; mem. staff Baton Rouge Gen., Our Lady of Lake hosps. Chmn. dental div. United Givers Fund Campaign, 1972-73. Served with Dental Corps AUS, 1966-68. Mem. Am., La., Tex. dental assns., Royal Soc. Health, Acad. Gen. Dentistry, 6th Dist., East Baton Rouge. Parish dental socs., Baton Rouge C. of C. Republican. Club: Roundtable. Home: 6185 Esplanade St Baton Rouge LA 70806 Office: 900 S Acadian St Baton Rouge LA 70806

SAFFIR, HERBERT SEYMOUR, cons. civil engr.; b. N.Y.C., Mar. 29, 1917; s. A. L. and Gertrude (Samuels) S.; B.S. in Civil Engring. cum laude, Ga. Inst. Tech., 1940; m. Sarah Young, May 9, 1941; children—Richard Young, Barbara Joan. Civil engr. TVA, Chattanooga, 1940, NACA, Langley Field, Va., 1940-41; structural engr. Ebasco Services, N.Y.C., 1941-43, York & Sawyer & Fred Severud, N.Y.C., 1945; engr. Waddell & Hardesty, Cons. Engrs., N.Y.C., 1945-47; asst. county engr. Dade County, Miami, Fla., 1947-59; cons. engr. Herbert S. Saffir, Coral Gables, Fla., 1959—. Adj. lectr. civil engring. Coll. Engring., U. Miami, 1964—; cons. Govt. Bahamas on bldg. codes; cons. on engring. in housing to UN. Served with AUS, 1943-44. Recipient Outstanding Service award Fla. Profl. Engrs., 1954. Registered profl. engr., Fla., N.Y., Tex., P.R., Miss. Fellow Am. Soc. C.E. (sect. past pres.), Fla. Engring. Soc. (award for outstanding tech. achievement 1973); mem. Soc. Am. Mil. Engrs., Am. Concrete Inst., Am. Soc. for Testing Materials, Colegio de Ingenieros P.R., Nat. Panel Arbitrators, Am. Arbitration Assn., C. of C. Miami, Tau Beta Pi. Author: Housing Construction in Hurricane Prone Areas, 1971. Contbr. articles to profl. jours. Home: 4818 Alhambra Circle Coral Gables FL 33146 Office: 123 Madeira Av Coral Gables FL 33134

SAGE, DONALD LEE, electric co. supr.; b. West Palm Beach, Fla., June 24, 1934; s. Alfred George and Virginia Lee (Beazley) S.; B.S. in Indsl. Engring., Va. Poly. Inst. and State U., 1956; postgrad. Wharton Sch. U. Pa., 1970; m. Mary Etta Glenn, Aug. 25, 1956; children—Mary Elizabeth, David Wyatt, Donna Suzanne. Asst. engr. Western Electric Co., Winston-Salem, N.C., 1956-62, devel. engr., 1963-67, dept. chief operations research and systems devel. dept., 1967-71, chief quality systems evaluation, 1971-73, dept. chief statis. quality control and mfg., Richmond, Va., 1973—. Served to 1st lt., Ordance Corp., AUS, 1956-58, Signal Corp., 1961-62. Mem. Jr. C. of C. (dir. 1967), Am. Inst. Indsl. Engrs. (dir. prodn. planning and control div., award for Excellence Region III 1972), Am. Soc. for Quality Control. Baptist (deacon 1972-73). Contbr. articles to profl. jours. Home: 1930 Castlebridge Rd Midlothian VA 23113 Office: 4500 Laburnum Av Richmond VA 23231

SAGE, RUSSELL RICHARD, lawyer; b. Omaha, Aug. 27, 1931; s. James Russell and Claire (Frank) S.; B.S. in Law, U. Minn., 1953, LL.B., 1955; m. Arleta Marie Jons, Feb. 10, 1952; children—Robert Richard, James Russell, Vickie Ann. Admitted to Minn. bar, 1955, D.C. bar, 1962, Va. bar, 1968; atty. ICC, Washington, 1957-62; practice law, Washington, 1962—; mem. firm Turney, Major and Sage, 1963-67, Major, Sage & King, 1968—. Served with AUS, 1955-57. Mem. D.C., Minn., Va. bar assns., Assn. ICC Practitioners, Motor Carrier Lawyers Assn. Democrat. Presbyn. Home: 4807 Manion St Annandale VA 22003 Office: Tavern Square Alexandria VA 22314

SAIN, CHARLES HASKELL, cons. engr.; b. New Market, Ala., Jan. 23, 1923; s. Will Oris and Clayta (Speck) S.; student Lincoln Meml. U., 1940-42; B.C.E. magna cum laude, U. Fla., 1949; m. Marie Myers, Aug. 8, 1942; children—Charles Randolph, Elizabeth Lester, Ann Marie. Project mgr. Moss-Thornton Co., Inc., Texarkana, Tex., 1949-52, chief engr., Leeds, Ala., 1952-54, v.p. 1954-60; gen. mgr. Vecellio & Grogan, Inc. Beckley, W.Va., 1960-64; v.p. A.E. Burgess Co., Inc., Birmingham, Ala., 1964-67; exec. v.p. Peyton & Sain Co., Inc., 1967-74; v.p., dir. Ranger Fuel Corp., Beckley, Golf Center, Inc., Birmingham; owner Charles H. Sain & Assos., civil and structural cons. engrs. Expert witness on constrn. problems. Named Ky. col. Registered profl. engr., W.Va., Ky., Ala., Ark., Tex., Ga., Miss., Tenn., Fla., Okla., Va., N.C., S.C., La. Mem. W.Va. Soc. Profl. Engrs. Am. Soc. C.E. (mem. maintenance com.), Am. Rd. Builders Assn., Asso. Gen. Contractors Am., Soc. Am. Mil. Engrs., Cons. Engrs. Council, Kappa Alpha, Sigma Tau, Tau Beta Pi, Gamma Lambda Sigma. Independent. Mason (Shriner). Clubs: The Club; Green Valley Country. Contbg. author: Civil Engineering Handbook, 1966. Contbr. articles profl. jours. Home: 1320 Badham Dr Birmingham AL 35216 Office: PO Box 5705 Birmingham AL 35209

SAINE, LEONARD WATSON, contractor; b. Acworth, Ga., July 1, 1894; s. James Paty and Elizabeth (Watson) S.; student civil engring. Ga. Sch. Tech., 1911-14; student law U. Mich., 1915; LL.B., Atlanta Law Sch., 1916; m. Mary Ruth Hudson, Apr. 17, 1918; 1 dau., Mary Elizabeth (Mrs. Robert Reynolds). Engr., constrn. supt. J.B. McCrary Co., Atlanta, 1917-27, salesman, sales mgr., dir. Central Foundry Co., N.Y.C., 1927-33, sales engr. Walworth Co., N.Y.C., 1935-40; pres., dir. Saine Co., Inc., gen. contractors, 1942—, owner Leonard W. Saine Registered Dealers, municipal and utility supply co., Orlando. Served with C.E. Corps, USN, 1918-19. Registered profl. engr. Mem. Nat. Soc. Profl. Engrs., Fla. Engring Soc., Beta Theta Pi. Mason. Home: 1555 W Fairbanks Av Winter Park FL 32789 Office: 314 Piedmont St Orlando FL 32806

ST. CLAIR, DAVID EDWARD, petroleum co. exec.; b. Dallas, Oct. 20, 1941; s. Dan W. and Hannah L. (Chambers) St. Cl.; B.B.A., U. Tex., 1963; M.B.A., 1966; m. Jacqueline A. Franz, July 18, 1964; children—David Edward, Todd W. Staff accountant Price Waterhouse & Co., Houston, 1963-64; internal audit Exxon U.S.A., Houston, 1964-68, corporate planning, 1969-70, financial adviser central market region, Memphis, 1970-72; financial analysis div. head Esso Inter-Am., Inc., Coral Gables, Fla., 1972—. C.P.A., Tex., Tenn. Mem. Tex., Tenn. socs. C.P.A.'s., Am. Inst. C.P.A.'s. Republican. Methodist. Lion (treas. 1973—). Home: 8300 SW 150th Dr Miami FL 33158 Office: 396 Alhambra Circle Coral Gables FL 33134

ST. CYR, CAROL RUTH, educator; b. Meriden, Conn., Dec. 25, 1924; d. Donald J. and Margaret (Horan) St. Cyr; B.S., Willimantic State Coll., 1946; M.A., Trinity Coll., 1949; Ph.D., U. Mich., 1955. Elementary tchr., Meriden, 1946-53; research asst. U. Mich., Ann Arbor, 1953-55; vis. prof. U. N.C., summer 1955; asst. prof. George Washington U. Sch. Edn., Washington, 1955-60, asso. prof., 1960-64, prof., 1964—. Ednl. cons. Mem. Am. Assn. U. Women, Am. Assn. U. Profs., Nat. Aerospace Edn. Assn. (bd. dirs. 1967—, pres. 1972—), Assn. for Supervision and Curriculum Devel., A.A.A.S., Pi Lambda Theta. Home: 1701 N Kent St Arlington VA 22209 Office: Sch of Edn George Washington U Washington DC 20006

ST. JOHN, HENRY SEWELL, JR., utility co. exec.; b. Birmingham, Ala., Aug. 18, 1938; s. H. Sewell and Carrie M. (Bond) St. J.; student David Lipscomb Coll., 1956-58, U. Tenn., 1958-59, U. Ala., 1962-64; m. J. Ann Morris, Mar. 9, 1959; children—Sherri Ann, Brian Lee, Teresa Lynn, Cynthia Faye. Engring. aide Ala. Power Co., Enterprise, 1960-62, Birmingham, 1962-66; asst. chief engr. Riviera Utilities, Foley, 1966-71, sec.-treas., gen. mgr., 1971—. Mem. I.E.E.E., South Ala. Power Distbrs. Assn. (chmn. 1973-74), Municipal Electric Utility Assn. Ala. (mem. exec. com., dir. 1971—), South Baldwin C. of C. (pres. 1974). Mem. Ch. of Christ. Rotarian. Home: PO Box 818 Foley AL 36535 Office: PO Box 550 Foley AL 36535

ST. JOHN, JOHN, food co. exec.; b. Battle Creek, Mich., Aug. 8, 1921; s. Raymond Martin and Hazel (Eastman) St. J.; B.A., Mich. State U., 1943; m. Lorraine Margaret McCarthy, Feb. 27, 1943; 1 dau., Shannon Elaine. With Minute Maid Co., and predecessors, 1949-68, financial v.p., 1963-65, pres. 1965-68; v.p. finance and operations Citrus Central, Inc., Orlando, Fla., 1969-70, exec. v.p., 1971—; dir. N.Y. Cotton Exchange, Orlando Bank & Trust Co., Agfoods, Inc., Farm Credit Bd. Columbia (S.C.). Served with USAAF, 1943-46. Episcopalian. Clubs: Winter Park (Fla.) Racquet; Country (Orlando). Home: 910 Pace Av Maitland FL 32751 Office: PO Box 17774 Orlando FL 32810

ST. JOHN, WYLLY FOLK, journalist, author; b. nr. Ehrhardt, S.C., Oct. 20, 1908; d. William Obed and Annie Claire (Mattox) Folk; A.B.J. summa cum laude, U. Ga., 1930; m. Thomas F. St. John, Jan. 1, 1930; 1 dau., Anne (Mrs. Neil D. Pratt). Staff writer Atlanta Jour. and Constn. mag., 1941—; free lance writer. Bd. dirs. Sr. Citizens Council, Walton County, Ga. Named Ga. Author of Year, 1968, Ga. Author of Year in Fiction, 1973; recipient spl. award as Edgar nominee Mystery Writers Am., 1973, 74. Mem. Authors Guild, Mystery Writers Am., Atlanta Press Club, Phi Beta Kappa, Phi Kappa Phi, Theta Sigma Phi (Brenda award for oustanding contbn. to journalism 1970). Clubs: Atlanta Plot, Social Circle Garden. Author: The Secrets of Hidden Creek, 1966; The Secrets Of The Pirate Inn, 1967; The Mystery Of The Gingerbread House, 1968; The Christmas Tree Mystery, 1969; The Mystery Of The Other Girl, 1971; The Ghost Next Door, 1971; Uncle Robert's Secret, 1972; The Secret of the Seven Crows, 1973. Contbr. stories, articles to numerous mags. Home: 198 Dogwood Av Social Circle GA 30279 Office: 72 Marietta St Atlanta GA 30302

ST. PETER, ALPHONSE FRANCIS, gas co. exec.; b. St. Johnsbury, Vt., Nov. 18, 1914; s. A.L. and Francella (Downing) St. P.; B.S., Marquette U., 1951; M.B.A., U. Wis., 1954; m. Margaret E. Whitney, Oct. 6, 1944; children—James W., Frances H. Staff asst. employee relations Mobil Oil Co., Milw., 1939-56; personnel mgr. Kyle Products Plant of Line Material Indsl., Milw., 1956-59; indsl. relations mgr. Delhi-Taylor Oil Corp., Dallas, 1959-63; dir. adminstrv. services So. Union Gas Co., Dallas, 1963-69, v.p. adminstrv. services, 1969—. Instr. Marquette U., 1955-57. Bd. dirs. Dallas Mental Health Assn. Served with USAAF, 1942-46. Mem. Am. Soc. Personnel Adminstrn., Am. Mgmt. Assn., Am., So. gas assns., Dallas Personnel Assn. (past pres.). Presbyn. (elder). Kiwanian (past pres., past lt. gov., dist. chmn.). Home: 5225 Preston Haven Dr Dallas TX 75229 Office: Fidelity Union Tower Dallas TX 75201

SAINZ, JORGE MANUEL, lawyer; b. Saltillo, Mexico, Sept. 11, 1935; s. Banjamin Mario and Maria del Refugio (Sainz) Sainz; B.A., U. Mexico, 1952, LL.B., 1958; postgrad. Ind. State Tchrs. Coll., 1959, So. Meth. U., 1959-60; m. Luz Maria G. Azuela, May 23, 1959; children—Luz Maria, Jorge, Itzel. Admitted to Mexican bar, 1958; clk. Goodrich, Dalton, Little & Riquelme, Mexico City, 1956-58, atty., 1958-66, jr. partner, 1966-71, sr. partner, head tax dept., 1971—. Prof. sociology U. Mexico, 1960-64; tax law Mexican Inst. Fiscal Studies, 1968—. Adviser, Tax Studies Commn., Mexican Employers Assn., 1966-72; mem. Mexican Treasury Dept. Commn. to Elaborate Income Tax Law Regulations, 1973, Pvt. Orgn. Commn. for European Common Market Value Added Tax Study, 1968. Mem. Internat. Fiscal Assn., Mexican Fiscal Law Acad. of Mexican Attys. Assn. Roman Catholic. Club: Mundet Sports (Mexico City). Author: The Joint Venture and its Tax Treatment, 1972; Construed Interest in the Mexican Income Tax Law, 1958. Contbr. articles to profl. jours. Home: Luis Cabrera 9 Ciudad Satelite Estado de Mexico Mexico Office: Paseo de la Reforma 355-20 Piso Mexico 5 DF Mexico

SALA, PEDRO ALFONSO, elec. engr.; b. Mexico City, Mexico, Oct. 30, 1933; s. Pedro and Concepcion (Venzor) S.; B.S., Milw. Sch. Engring., 1959; m. Gerda Brigitte Alisch, Oct. 14, 1967; children—Ricardo, Kristina. With Gen. Electric de Mexico, S.A., Mexico City, 1959—, chief engr., 1964-68, mgr. mfg. and engring., 1968—. Mem. Electronics Mfrs. Chamber Mexico (v.p., 1973), I.E.E.E. Author: Television a Colores, Teoria y Aplicacion, 1967. Home: Lomas de Tarango 250 Mexico 19 DF Mexico Office: Apartado Postal 14-175 Mexico 14 DF Mexico

SALATICH, JOHN SMYTH, physician; b. New Orleans, Nov. 28, 1926; s. Peter B. and Gladys (Malter) S.; B.S. cum laude, Loyola U., New Orleans, 1946; M.D., La. State U., 1950; m. Patricia L. Mattison, Sept. 26, 1959; children—John Smyth, Elizabeth, Allison, Stephanie. Intern Charity Hosp., New Orleans, 1950-51, resident, 1951-54, dir. emergency rooms and satellite clinics; practice medicine, specializing in cardiology and internal medicine, New Orleans, 1954—; dir. EKG dept. Southeastern La. Hosp., Mandeville, La., Plaquemines Parish Hosp., Port Sulphur, La., Lakewood Hosp., Morgan City, La.; asst. prof. clin. medicine La. State U.; mem. staff Touro Infirmary, St. Charles Gen. Hosp., East Jefferson Hosp.; chmn. dept. medicine Hotel Dieu. Bd. dirs. La. Regional Med. Program, 1972. Adv. bd. Bank La. Served to capt. M.C., AUS, 1954-56; Korea. Decorated Medallion of Greek Army. Diplomate Am. Bd. Internal Medicine. Fellow Am. Coll. Chest Physicians, A.C.P., Am. Coll. Emergency Room Physicians; mem. Am., La. (dir.) heart assns., New Orleans Acad. Internal Medicine, La. Thoracic Soc., La. Soc. Internal Medicine, A.M.A., La., Orleans Parish med. socs., Theta Beta, Alpha Sigma Nu, Delta Epsilon Sigma. Clubs: New Orleans Country. Contbr. to profl. and bus. jours. Home: 433 Country Club Dr New Orleans LA 70112 Office: Maison Blanche Bldg New Orleans LA 70112

SALFEN, HAROLD JOSEPH, airline exec.; b. O'Fallon, Mo., Jan. 6, 1920; s. S. J. and Josephine (Sattler) S.; student U. Mo., 1939-42; B.B.A. in Mgmt., Ga. State U., 1956; postgrad. Syracuse U., 1961-62; m. Marjorie McGregor, Sept. 12, 1945; children—Harold M., Ronald P., Terry W., Jack A., Kathy Jo, Marty G. With Delta Air Lines, Atlanta, 1950-62, sales rep., 1950-52, dir. govt. travel, 1952-55, sales promotion mgr., 1955-62; v.p. sales, marketing Central Airlines Corp., Fort Worth, 1962-65; v.p. marketing Ozark Airline, 1966-72; v.p. passenger, cargo sales Braniff Internat. Airlines, Dallas, 1972—. Mem. White House Conf. Edn., 1954-55; pres. Citizens Adv. Council,

Parkway Sch. Bd., Chesterfield, Mo., 1970. Co-chmn. bd. dirs. Ga. chpt. Soc. Crippled Children, 1955-56; bd. dirs. Grad. Sch. Sales Mgmt., Marketing, Syracuse (N.Y.) U., 1971-74; trustee Ga. State Coll., Atlanta. Served with USAAF, 1942-43; ETO. Recipient Father Year award Atlanta Boys Club, 1952; named Man Year, Atlanta Jr. C. of C., 1953, outstanding young man Ga. Jaycees, 1954. Mem. Air Traffic Conf. Am. (past pres.), Res. Officer Assn. (Ga. v.p. 1956, outstanding liaison officer 1971), Kappa Alpha. Club: Brookhaven Country (Dallas). Home: 3841 Whitehall St Dallas TX 75229 Office: PO Box 35001 Dallas TX 75235

SALINAS MARTÍNEZ, ARTURO, lawyer; b. Monterrey, Mexico, Aug. 25, 1924; Bachiller, U. Nuevo León, 1941; Licenciado en Ciencias Juridicas, 1947; Docteur en Droit, U. Paris, 1949; diploma in comparative law Inter-Am. Law Inst., N.Y. U., 1950; Docteur Honoris Causa, U. Bordeaux, France, 1963. Admitted to Mexico bar, 1947; prof. corp. law U. Nuevo León, 1951-63, dean Law Sch. 1961-63, dir. Inst. Comparative Law, 1961-63; prof. corp., comml., tax law and finance, Inst. Tecnológico de Monterrey, 1951-61, 66-70; dean Law Sch., U. de Monterrey, 1970—. Lectr. Nat. U. Mexico, 1959, Inst. Comparative Law, Nat. U. Mexico, 1960, Sch. Law St. Mary's U., San Antonio Tex., 1962. Mem. Colegio de Abogados de Nuevo León, Inter-Am. Bar Assn. Author: Participating Certificates, 1947. Contbr. articles on law to profl. jours. Office: Edificio Chapa 606 Monterrey Nuevo León Mexico

SALINGER, PIERRE EMIL GEORGE, corp. exec., author; b. San Francisco, June 14, 1925; s. Herbert and Jehanne (Bietry) S.; B.S., U. San Francisco, 1947; m. Nancy Brook Joy, June 28, 1957 (div.); children—Marc, Suzanne, Stephen; m. 2d, Nicole Helene Gilmann, June 18, 1965; 1 son, Gregory. Reporter, night city editor San Francisco Chronicle, 1946-55; guest lectr. journalism Mills Coll., 1950-55; West Coast editor, contbg. editor Collier's mag., 1955-56; investigator select com. to investigate improper activities in labor or mgmt. field U.S. Senate, 1957-59; press sec. to U.S. Senator Kennedy, 1959-60, to Pres. Kennedy, 1961-63, to Pres. Johnson, 1963-64; U.S. Senate from Cal., 1964; v.p. Nat. Gen. Corp., 1965; pres. Fox Overseas Corp., 1965—; v.p. internat. affairs Continental Airlines, Inc. and Continental Air Services, Inc. subsidiary, 1965-68; pres. Gramco Devel. Corp., 1968—. Press officer Cal. Stevenson for Pres. campaign, 1952, Richard Graves for Gov. Cal. campaign, 1954. Served with USNR, World War II. Decorated Navy and Marine Corps medal. Club: Nat. Press (Washington). Author: With Kennedy, 1966; On Instructions of My Government, 1971. Home: 14 Avenue du Square Paris 16 France Office: Norfolk House Frederick St PO Box 4883 Nassau Bahamas

SALMON, FINNIS LARRY, lawyer; b. Rome, Ga., Mar. 29, 1938; s. Finnis Cartwright and Bonnie Smith (Caldwell) S.; student Ga. Inst. Tech., 1956-57; B.B.A., U. Ga., 1962, J.D., 1963; m. Sally Frances Meroney, July 23, 1961; children—Stacy Leigh, Finnis Kevin. Admitted to Ga. bar, 1962; with Legal Aid Dept., Athens, Ga., 1962-63; practice law, Rome, 1963-69; asst. solicitor gen., Rome, 1966-69; dist. atty. Rome Judicial Circuit, 1969—. Mem. exec. com. Floyd County Democratic Assn., 1973; pres. Young Democrats of Floyd County, 1967; treas. Young Democrats Ga., 1967; chmn. Ga. delegation Nat. Conv. Young Democrats Am., 1968, Southeastern region dir., 1968-69. Recipient young Democrat of year award Young Democrats of Floyd County, 1968. Mem. Am., Rome bar assns., State Bar Ga. (chmn. criminal law sect. 1973-74), Nat., Ga. (mem. exec. com. 1973) dist. attys. assns., Floyd-Polk County Young Lawyers Sect. (pres. 1973-74), Am. Judicature Soc., Phi Delta Phi, Alpha Tau Omega. Baptist. Home: Route 1 Rome GA 30161 Office: Floyd County Courthouse Rome GA 30161

SALOOM, KALISTE JOSEPH, JR., judge; b. Lafayette, La., May 15, 1918; s. Kaliste and Asma (Boustany) S.; B.A. with high distinction, Southwestern La. Inst., 1939; J.D., Tulane U., 1942; m. Yvonne Adele Nassar, Oct. 19, 1958; children—Kaliste Joseph III, Douglas Leanne, Gregory John. Admitted La. bar, 1942; pvt. practice, 1942—; city atty. Lafayette, 1948-52, city judge, 1953—. Mem. judicial council La. Supreme Court. Chmn. La. Parish Draft Bd. 1950-71; mem. La. Youth Commn., 1958—, chmn., 1970—; mem. com. cts., codes and laws La. Hwy. Safety Commn.; mem. La. Pub. Affairs Research Council. Bd. dirs. S.W. La. Mardi Gras Assn., United Democrates La., 1957-59; trustee Am. Lebanon-Syrian Asso. Charities, 1957-65. Del. White House Conf. on Children and Youth, 1960; invitee 1st Nat. Conf. on Bail and Criminal Justice, Dept. Justice, Washington, 1963; chmn. com. on traffic law revision Jud. Council of La. Supreme Ct. Dir. La. Gulf Coast Oil Expn.; exec. bd. Evangeline area council Boy Scouts Am.; mem. bd. dirs. United Givers Fund; founder Lafayette Area Safety Council, 1961; mem. bd. Lafayette Mental Health Assn.; bd. dirs. Lafayetts Diocese Cath. Youth Orgn. Chief U.S. del. World Congress Christian Bros. Sch. Alumni, Spain, 1964, Can., 1967. Served as spl. agt. CIC, U.S. Army, 1942-45. Recipient Alumni award; U. Southwestern La., 1939, grant-in-aid, Esso Safety Found., Traffic Safety Conf., 1958, award traffic safety program, Am. Bar Assn., 1958, 59, 61, 63, 64; Lafayette Civic Cup award, 1965; named Man of Year, Salvation Army, 1966. Fellow Law-Science Acad. Am.; mem. Am. (lectr. traffic ct. advance seminars, mem. asso. and adv. com., recipient Outstanding Traffic Ct. judge award 1969), Lafayette (pres. 1955-56) bar assns., Am. Judicature Soc., Nat., La. (pres. 1963-64) councils juvenile court judges N.Am. (bd. govs. 1969—), La. City judges assns. (past pres.), La. Law Inst. (adv. com.), Am. Legion (judge adv. La. 1953-56), La. Conf. Social Welfare (dir. 1961), Blue Key, Nat. Inst. Municipal Law Officers, S.W. La. Univ. Alumni Assn. (pres. 1959—), Nat. Council on Crime and Delinquency; Nat. Council Municipal Judges, La. Hist. Soc., Order Coif, Kappa Sigma, Pi Gamma Mu, Pi Kappa Delta, Alpha Phi Omega, Phi Alpha Theta, Phi Kappa Phi. Clubs: Knife and Fork (dir.), Lafayette Town House (dir.), Rotary. Author: Traffic Court Judge's Check List, 1965. Home: 502 Marguerite Blvd Lafayette LA 70501 Office: 211 W Main St Lafayette LA 70501

SALTER, ADELE SARAH BODKER (MRS. ROGER NOBLE SALTER), librarian; b. Ponchatoula, La., Mar. 9, 1915; d. Albert John and Sarah Caroline (Bendix) Bodker; B.A., Newcomb Coll., 1936; B.S. in L.S., La. State U., 1952; m. Roger Noble Salter, Jan. 9, 1971. Tchr., Ponchatoula (La.) High Sch., 1936-39; asst. Ponchatoula br. Tangipahoa Parish Library, 1949-53, librarian Tangipahoa Parish Library, Amite, La., 1953—. Mem. S.W., La. (chmn. pub. library sec. 1961), Am. library assns., Beta Phi Mu. Democrat. Presbyn. Home: Box 236 Ponchatoula LA 70454 Office: Box 578 Amite LA 70422

SALTZMAN, BENJAMIN NATHAN, physician; b. Ansonia, Conn., Apr. 24, 1914; s. Joseph N. and Frances (Levine) S.; A.B., U. Ore., 1935, M.A., 1936, M.D., 1940; m. Ruth Elizabeth Bohan, Dec. 19, 1941; children—Sue Ann, John Joseph, Mark Stephen. Intern Gorgas Hosp., Ancon, C.Z., 1941, resident, 1942; pvt. practice, Mountain Home, Ark., 1946—; mem. staffs Mountain Home, Ark., Boone County Hosp., Harrison, Ark., Marion County Hosp., Yellville, Ark.; chief of staff Baxter Gen. Hosp.; pres. Saltzman-Guenthner Clinic Ltd.; preceptor U. Ark. Sch. Medicine, Little Rock, also asso. clin. prof., 1972—. Mem. Gov.'s Health Council Ark.; mem. rev. com. Community Health Services, Washington, 1965-67; mem. gov.'s Com. on Mental Retardation, Ark., 1962-66, Ark. Comprehensive Health Planning Council, 1967—, Gov.'s Adv. Council Developmental Disabilities, 1970—; bd. dirs. First Ark. Devel. Finance Corp. Baxter County Health Officer, Mountain Home. Pres. Ark. Tb Assn., 1958-63, nat. rep. dir., pres. So. Tb Conf., 1969-70; past pres., dir. Tri-States Assn. for Cripples, 1959-60; pres. bd. Ozark Regional Mental Center, 1970-74; mem. bd. Baxter County Day Service Center. Alderman, Mountain Home City Council, 1947-52. Bd. dirs. Hosp. Crippled Adults, Memphis, 1969—; bd. dirs., regional v.p. Nat. Assn. Retarded Citizens; pres. Ark. div. Am. Cancer Soc., 1970-71, Ark. Assn. Retarded Children, 1971-73. Served from lt. to capt. AUS, 1942-46; lt. col. USAF Res. Named Man of Year, Ark. Conf. Tb Workers, 1960; recipient outstanding award Nat. Tb Assn., 1961. Diplomate Am. Bd. Family Practice. Fellow Am. Acad. Family Physicians; mem. Ark. Acad. Gen. Practice (pres. 1954-55), Ark. Med. Soc. (pres. 1974-75), World, Am. (chmn. council rural health), So. Ark. (treas.), Baxter County (past pres., sec.) med. assns., Am., Ark. thoracic socs., Am., Ark. (outstanding achievement award) pub. health assns., Am. Sch. Health Assn. (com. mem.), Aeromed. Assn., Assn. Mil. Surgeons, Civil Aviation Med. Assn., Ark. Heart Assn. (dir. 1972—), Ark. Gerontol. Soc. (dir. 1971—), Aircraft Owners and Pilots Assn., Nat. Aero. Assn., Nat. (dir.), Ark., Res. Officers Assn., Am. Legion (former comdr.), Flying Physicians Assn. (nat. v.p.), Flying Farmers Assn., Nat. Pilots Assn., Mountain Home C. of C. (pres. 1954-56, 65-67), V.F.W., Sigma Xi. Democrat. Unitarian. Mason (Shriner), Elk (pres. Ark.), Rotarian (dist. gov. 1952-54, pres. Mountain Home, 1959, internat. dir. 1961-63, trustee Internat. Found. 1965-67). Home: Hwy 5 NW Mountain Home AR 72653 Office: 126 W 6th St Mountain Home AR 72653

SALTZMAN, HERMAN, lawyer; b. New Haven, Jan. 29, 1916; s. Joseph N. and Frances (Levin) S.; A.B., U. Fla., 1940; J.D., John B. Stetson U., 1950; m. Irene P. Cameron, Mar. 21, 1946; children—Martin Howard (dec.), Arlene Norma. Enlisted USAAF, 1941, commd., 1942, advanced through grades to lt. col., 1962; served PTO and CBI, 1943-45, Germany and Morocco, 1953-56; former staff judge adv. Moody AFB, Ga.; staff judge adv., Kadena AFB, Okinawa, 1962-63; chief mil. justice div. Amarillo Tech. Tng. Center, Texas, 1963-66; ret., 1966; practice law, Jacksonville, Fla., 1966—. Fellow Internat. Biog. Assn.; mem. Am., Jacksonville bar assns., Trial Lawyers Assn., Fla. Bar, Am. Judicature Soc., Judge Adv. Assn. Mason (Shriner). Home: 2701 Ocean Dr S Jacksonville Beach FL 32250 Office: Saltzman Bldg Jacksonville FL 32202

SALWIN, HAROLD, govt. food technologist; b. Kansas City, Nov. 24, 1915; s. Earl R. and Minnie (Wolf) S.; B.S., U. Chgo., 1941; postgrad. Ill. Inst. Tech., 1946-51; m. Shirley Zelda Minsk, June 20, 1943; children—Arthur Elliott, Barbara Clare. Head food biochemistry lab. Quartermaster Food and Container Inst. for Armed Forces, Chgo., 1958-61), acting chief chemistry and microbiology br., 1961; head decomposition and preservation sect. FDA, Washington, 1961-71, chief Protein and Cereal Products Br., 1971—. Recipient Rohland A. Isker award Research and Devel. Assos. Mil. Food and Packaging Systems, 1962. Fellow Assn. Ofcl. Analytical Chemists (gen. referee 1963-73, sec. subcom. C 1967-73); mem. Am. Chem. Soc., Inst. Food Technologists, Phi Beta Kappa. Contbr. articles to sci. jours. Home: 706 Kerwin Rd Silver Spring MD 20901 Office: 200 C St SW Washington DC 20204

SALWIN, LESTER NATHAN, lawyer, govt. ofcl.; b. Kansas City, Mo., Nov. 18, 1911; s. Earl R. and Minnie (Wolf) S.; student Jr. Coll. Kansas City, 1927-29; A.B. cum laude, U. Ill., 1931, LL.B. cum laude, 1933; m. Lillian Levinson, Jan. 13, 1932; 1 dau., Marjorie Beth. Admitted to Ill. bar, 1933, Mo. bar; practiced in Chgo., 1933-39; adjudicator Social Security Adminstrn., Washington, 1940-42; with OPA, 1942-43; asst. to gen. counsel Smaller War Plants Corp., 1943-44; with ct. rev., research and opinion div. OPA, 1944-45; alien property custodian Office of Gen. Counsel, 1945-46; chief trade laws and spl. asst. for legal affairs Econ. and Sci. sect., SCAP, 1945-52; chief Japan mission U.S. Dept. Justice, Am. Embassy, Tokyo, Japan, 1952-60; with legislative div. U.S. Civil Adminstrn. of Ryuku Islands, 1960-61; spl. asst. Legal Investment div. Office Gen. Counsel, Small Bus. Adminstrn., 1961—; spl. counsel on adminstrv. procedures Nelsen Commn., 1971—. Mem. Atlantic Council of U.S. Mem. Fed., Mo., Ill. bar assns., Acad. Polit. Sci., Acad. Polit. and Social Scis., Nat. Lawyers Club, Phi Beta Kappa, Order of Coif. Author articles in field. Home: 3812 N Nelson St Arlington VA 22207 Office: Imperial Bldg 1441 L St NW Washington DC 20005

SAMAAN, NAGUIB ABDELMALIK, physician; b. Girga, Egypt, Apr. 2, 1925; s. Abdelmalik and Amasil (Hanna) S.; M.B., Ch.B., Alexandria (Egypt) U., 1951, D.M., diploma in Internal Medicine, 1953; Ph.D. in Medicine, U. London (Eng.), 1964; m. Jean Moffatt, Nov. 18, 1961; children—Sarah Ann, Mary Elizabeth, Jane Susan, Catherine Thia, Michael James. Came to U.S., 1964, naturalized, 1969. Rotating intern Alexandria U. Hosp., 1951-52, resident, 1952-54, sr. med. resident, instr., 1954-55; sr. research fellow Chest Inst. Brompton Hosp., London, 1955-56, Neurology Inst., Queen Square, London, 1956; clin. fellow Postgrad. Med. Sch., London, 1957; clin. asst. prof. dept. endocrinology and therapeutics, asst. physician Royal Infirmary, Edinburgh, Scotland, 1957; sr. med. resident North Cambridge Hosps., Cambridge, Eng., 1958-60; staff physician, asst. prof., sr. research fellow Royal Postgrad. Med. Sch., London, 1960-64; research asso., asst. physician and endocrinologist, Case Western Res. U., Cleve., 1964-66; staff physician, asst. prof. dept. internal medicine U. Ia. Hosps., Iowa City, 1966-69; med. staff physician and endocrinologist VA Hosp., Iowa City, 1966-69; chief sect. endocrinology U. Tex. M.D. Anderson Hosp. and Tumor Inst., Houston, 1969—, asso. internist, asso. prof. medicine, 1969-72, internist, prof. medicine, 1972—; asso. prof. medicine and physiology U. Tex. Grad. Sch. Biomed. Scis., Houston, 1969-72, prof., 1972—; prof. internal medicine U. Tex. Med. Sch., Houston, 1971-73, prof., 1973—; cons., attending physician dept. Internal medicine Hermann Hosp., Houston, 1970—. Brit. Med. Research Council grantee, 1962-64, NIH grantee, 1969—, Am. Cancer Soc. grantee, 1971—. Fellow A.C.P.; mem. Brit. Med. Assn., A.M.A., Royal Coll. Physicians (Eng.), Royal Coll. Physicians (Scotland), Am. Endocrine Soc., Am. Fedn. for Clin. Research, Am. Physiol. Soc., Fedn. Am. Socs. for Exptl. Biology, Central Soc. for Clin. Research, Soc. for Gynecologic Investigation, N.Y. Acad. Sci., Harris County Med. Soc., Houston Soc. Internal Medicine, Am., Brit. (sr. research fellow 1960-62) diabetes assns. Club: Nottingham Forest (Houston). Home: 14315 Heatherfield St Houston TX 77024 Office: 6723 Bertner Av Houston TX 77025

SAMAHA, FRANCIS JOSEPH, periodontist; b. Washington, Apr. 16, 1928; s. Toufig Nickolas and Edna (George) S.; D.D.S., Georgetown U., 1951; m. Lili Ann Sheahin, July 4, 1951; children—Jeffrey F., Gary M., Lisa M., Richard G.; m. 2d, Gina A. Rota, Sept. 15, 1973. Commd. 2d lt. USAF, 1950, advanced through grades to col., 1968; intern Fitzsimmons Army Hosp., Denver, 1951-52; assigned Bergstrom AFB, Tex., 1952-56; resident Tufts U., Boston, 1956-58; assigned Ramey AFB, P.R., 1958-61, Andrews AFB, Md., 1961-69, Clark Air Base, Philippines, 1969-70; ret., 1970; practice dentistry, 1970—; asso. prof. periodontics Georgetown U., Washington, 1970-72, U. Md., 1972-73. Cons. to surgeon gen. USAF, 1961-69; nat., internat. lectr. in field. Pres., Holy Name Soc., Bergstrom AFB, 1955-56; coach, mgr. Little League Baseball, Andrews AFB, 1961-64. Bd. dirs. Prince Georges County Boys Club, 1965-67. Decorated Legion of Merit. Fellow Am. Coll. Dentists, Am. Acad. Occlusodontia; mem. Am. Dental Assn., Am. Acad. Oral Medicine, Am. Acad. Periodontology, Am. Acad. Oral Pathology, Greater Washington Soc. Periodontology (sec. 1964-66, pres.-elect 1966-67, pres. 1967-68). Roman Catholic. Home: 1551 Dunterry Pl McLean VA 22101 Office: 6845 Elm St McLean VA 22101

SAMET, PHILIP, physician; b. N.Y.C., Jan. 30, 1922; s. Samuel and Anna (Mattus) S.; B.A., N.Y. U., 1942, M.D., 1947; children—Annetta, Joan (Mrs. Peter Galler), Gerald. Intern Mt. Sinai Hosp., N.Y.C., 1947-48; resident internal medicine Bronx VA Hosp., 1948-50; asst. attending physician Irvington House Followup Cardiac Clinic for Rheumatic Heart Disease, 1947-55; sr. surgeon USPHS Hosp., Bklyn., 1951-53; dir. cardiopulmonary service Mt. Sinai Hosp., Miami Beach, Fla., 1955-64, chief div. cardiology, 1964—; prof. medicine U. Miami. Served with USPHS, 1953-55. Diplomate Am. Bd. Internal Medicine. Fellow A.C.P.; mem. Am. Coll. Cardiology, Am. Coll. Chest Physicians, Am. Heart Assn., Am. Physiol. Soc., Am. Assn. U. Profs., A.M.A., Am. Physicians Fellowship, Inc. for Israel Med. Assn., A.A.A.S., Am. Med. Writers Assn., Am. Soc. Internal Medicine, Nat. Rehab. Assn., Alpha Omega Alpha. Author: Cardiac Pacing, 1973. Mem. editorial staff of Circulation, 1972—, Am. Jour. Cardiology, 1973—. Home: 5951 Alton Rd Miami Beach FL 33140 Office: 4300 Alton Rd Miami Beach FL 33140

SAMFORD, MAURYCE STACY, architect; b. Denison, Tex., Dec. 11, 1922; s. Ocie Lee and Lucy Jane (Willig) S.; student Austin Coll., 1947-49; B.S., U. Houston, 1951; m. Betty June Rich, Oct. 5, 1946; children—Gregory Mark, Jeffrey Dale, Todd Stacy. Architect firm Charles Oliver, Architect, Houston, 1950-51; architect U.S. Corp. of Engrs., Galveston, Tex., 1951-52; architect firm Thomas M. Price, Architect, Galveston, 1963-66; resident architect U. Tex. Med. Br., Galveston, 1952-63, 1966-73; practice architecture, Galveston, 1967-73. Mem. Elementary Study Com. Galveston Indep. Sch. Dist., 1972—. Served with USAF, 1943-46. Mem. Am. Inst. Architects. Baptist (deacon ch. 1957-73). Home: 2506 Pine St Galveston TX 77550 Office: The University of Texas Medical Branch Galveston TX 77550

SAMFORD, THOMAS DRAKE, III, lawyer; b. Opelika, Ala., Mar. 4, 1934; s. Thomas Drake and Aileen (Maxwell) S., Jr.; A.B. magna cum laude, Princeton, 1955; LL.B., U. Ala., 1961; m. Jacqueline Screws, June 7, 1955; children—Thomas Drake IV, Jacquelyn, Robert Maxwell, Richard Drake. Admitted to Ala. bar, 1961, since practiced in Opelika; partner firm Samford & Samford, 1961—. Judge, Recorders Ct., Opelika, 1961—; owner, mng. partner realty, broadcasting, timber and farming operations; lectr., contbr. continuing legal edn. program Ala. State Bar, 1963—. Dir. Diversified Products Corp. Chmn., Opelika Downtown Action Com., 1967—; atty. Auburn U., 1967—, Ala. Wildlife Research Found., 1965—, Auburn Research Found., 1967—, Ala. 4-H Clubs, 1961—. Dir. bd. trustees Opelika Community Chest, 1965-68, pres., 1966-67; bd. dirs. U. Ala. Law Sch. Found., Jr. Achievement Chattahoochee-Lee. Served from 2d lt. to capt. USMCR, 1955-58. Recipient John G. Buchanan prize in politics Princeton, 1955, Farrah Order of Jurisprudence U. Ala., 1958, named one of Outstanding Young men of Ala., Jr. C. of C., 1967. Mem. Opelika C. of C. (pres. 1967), Am., Lee Co. (pres. 1965) bar assns., Ala. State Bar, U. Ala. Nat. Alumni Assn. (pres. 1966-67), Phi Beta Kappa, Alpha Tau Omega, Phi Delta Phi, Omicron Delta Kappa. Presbyn. (chmn. bd. deacons 1965-66). Kiwanian (dir. 1966-67, pres. 1969-70). Editor-in-chief Ala. Law Rev., 1960-61. Home: 805 Ridgewood St Opelika AL 36801 Office: Samford Bldg Av A Opelika AL 36801

SAMLI, A. COSKUN, educator; b. Istanbul, Turkey, July 21, 1931; s. Suleyman Seref and Ayse (Tuncer) S.; came to U.S., 1954; B.A., Istanbul Acad. Comml. Scis., 1953, M.A., 1953; M.B.A., U. Detroit, 1956; Ph.D., Mich. State U., 1962; m. Marqueta Hill, June 18, 1959; 1son, Evan Kaya. Asst. prof. bus. adminstrn. Sacramento State Coll., 1961-65; asso. prof. marketing, asst. dir. bus. research bur. So. Ill. U., Carbondale, 1965-66; asso. prof. marketing, asst. dir. research inst. bus. and econ. U. So. Cal., Los Angeles, 1966-68; prof. bus. adminstrn. Va. Poly. Inst. and State U., Blacksburg, 1968—. Dir. Sacramento Consumers Coop., 1963-65, Nu-Mac Inc., Marion, Ill., 1965-66. Ford Found. fellow, 1963-64; Internat. Bus. Workshop fellow, 1966. Mem. Am., Western, So. econ. assn., Am., So. marketing assns., Gerontological Soc., Beta Gamma Sigma, Alpha Kappa Psi. Contbr. to profl. jours. Home: 1106 Kam Dr Blacksburg VA 24061

SAMMON, PATRICK FRANCIS, business exec.; b. N.Y.C., Feb. 15, 1926; s. Patrick F. and Cecelia (O'Reilly) S.; grad. high sch.; m. Dorothy Laverne Sheffield, Jan. 20, 1945; children—Dorothy Jan, Patrick Thomas, Stacey Teresa. Control tower supr., link instr. So. Airways, Bainbridge, Ga., 1951-61; owner, operator Pat Sammon Ins. & Realty Agy., Colquitt, Ga., 1949—; pres. Pat Sammon Chevrolet Co. Inc., Colquitt; v.p., dir. Peoples Bank, Colquitt; commr., chmn. Housing Authority, of Colquitt 1957-60, exec. dir., 1960-73; mem. Miller County-City of Colquitt Planning Commn., Airport Authority, 1968-73. Adviser, Miller County Hosp., Colquitt, 1967-71; dir. Civil Def. Colquitt-Miller County, 1961-66, Miller County Redevel. Corp., 1965-73, Office Econ. Opportunity, 1966-73. Served with USAAF, 1944-45. Mem. Am. Legion (past comdr.). Mason, Lion. Home: Oak Dr Colquitt GA 31737 Office: 102 1st St Colquitt GA 31737

SAMPLE, NOLAN LEE, petroleum products co. exec.; b. El Dorado, Ark., May 17, 1928; s. William Coy and Georgia Marine (Leavitt) S.; student La. Tech. U., 1945-46; B.S., Centenary Coll., 1953; postgrad. U. Tex., 1953-54; m. Frances Jean Boydstun, May 20, 1950 (dec. 1973); 1 dau., Leslie Jean. Map draftsman Caddo Abstract Co., Shreveport, La., 1949-50; with Pennzoil Co., Shreveport, 1954—, mgr. systems services, 1968—. Adviser Jr. Achievement, 1964-65. Served with USAF, 1946-49. Mem. Assn. Computing Machinery, Alpha Tau Omega. Democrat. Episcopalian. Home: 2014 Shadywood Lane Shreveport LA 71105 Office: PO Box 1407 Shreveport LA 71102

SAMS, ERNEST WILLIAM, mfg. co. exec.; b. Erwin, Tenn., May 2, 1923; s. James Carl and Elizabeth Anne (Daves) S.; B.S., U. Tenn., 1952; m. Colleen Moore, Aug. 8, 1944; children—Jennifer (Mrs. Richard Wayne Hall), James Alexander. Traffic analyst Akers Motor Lines, Gastonia, N.C., 1952-54; traffic mgr. Am. & Efird Mills, Mount Holly, N.C., 1954-56; gen. traffic mgr. Fieldcrest Mills, Inc., Eden, N.C., 1956-73; Duplan Corp., Winston-Salem, N.C., 1973—. State coordinator Nat. Def. Exec. Res. Office Emergency Transp., 1967-73. Served with USNR, 1942-44. Mem. Burlington Traffic Club (pres. 1964), Carpet Rug Inst. (chmn. traffic com. 1967-70), Textile Traffic Mgrs. Conf. (chmn. 1969), So. (bd. govs. 1970-73), N.C. (bd. govs. 1970-73) traffic leagues, Am. Textile Mfrs. Inst., N.C., Ga.-Ala. textile mfrs. assns., Delta Nu Alpha. Lion, Mason. Home: 411 Dogwood Dr Eden NC 27288 Office: PO Box 2898 Winston Salem NC 27288

SAMS, JAMES C., clergyman; b. Cochran, Ga., Feb. 19, 1909; s. Lonnie and Charlotte Sams; B.S., Fla. A. and M. Coll., 1946; m. Cornelia Fleming, Sept. 29, 1930. Ordained to ministry Baptist Ch.; pastor in Jacksonville, Fla. for 32 years; pres. Progressive Bapt. Conv. Fla. for 17 years; 1st v.p. Nat. Bapt. Conv. Am., 1961-67, 70—, pres., 1967-70. Vice chmn. bd. trustees Fla. Meml. Coll.; trustee Edward

Waters Coll. Home: 1724 Jefferson St Jacksonville FL 32209 Office: 954 Kings Rd Jacksonville FL 32204

SAMS, JAMES HAGOOD III, air force officer, civil engr.; b. Greenville, S.C., July 15, 1933; s. James Hagood and Elizabeth (Dargan) S.; B.C.E., Clemson U., 1954; M.S., U. Ill., 1955; postgrad. U. Colo., 1959-70, Ga. Inst. Tech., 1967-68; m. Dorothy Ann Cox, Jan. 31, 1955; children—Cynthia Ann, Candace Dargan, Timothy Hagood. Asso. aircraft engr. Lockheed Aircraft Corp., Marietta, Ga., 1954; research asst. civil engring. dept. U. Ill. at Urbana, 1954-55; engring. div. Boeing Airplane Co., Melborne, Fla., 1957-58; cons. asso. Tanner, Thomas, D'Alli, Heartz & Assos., Melborne Beach, Fla., 1958; design specialist Martin-Marietta Corp., Denver, 1958-64; scientist Lockheed-Ga. Co., Marietta, 1964-71; commd. officer U.S. Air Force, 1954, now maj., civil engr. N.G. bur., Washington, 1971—. Registered profl. engr., Ga., Colo. Mem. Am. Soc. C.E., Air Civil Engrs. Assn., N.G. Assn. U.S., Sigma Xi, Tau Beta Pi, Phi Kappa Phi, Phi Eta Sigma. Episcopalian. Contbr. articles to profl. jours. Home: 8811 Stockton Pkwy Alexandria VA 22308 Office: Civil Engring Div NG Bur Pentagon Washington DC 20310

SAMUELS, SEYMOUR, JR., lawyer; b. Nashville, Oct. 23, 1912; s. Seymour and Maude Stella (Rosenfeld) S.; B.A., Vanderbilt U., 1933, LL.B., J.D., 1935; m. Essie Schoen Wenar, July 7, 1937; children—Seymour III, Charles Wenar. Admitted to Tenn. bar, 1935, admitted to practice before U.S. Supreme Ct., Supreme Ct. Tenn., U.S. Ct. Appeals 6th Circuit, U.S. Dist. Ct. and Trial Cts. Tenn.; practicing atty., 1935-40; partner Samuels & Allen, 1940-42; area rent atty., dep. rent dir. OPA, 1942-43; partner Nashville Bag & Burlap Co., 1946-62; dep. dir. law Met. Govt. of Nashville, 1963-67; with Hooker & Willis, 1967; partner Hooker, Hooker, Willis & Samuels, 1968, Farris, Evans & Evans, 1969-71, Farris, Warfield & Samuels, Nashville, 1972—; lectr. met. govt. Malone Coll. Mem. Met. Traffic and Parking Commn., 1967-70; chmn. Davidson County Dem. Campaign Com., 1968; mem. Met. Govt. Charter Revision Com.; mem. Tenn. Bot. Gardens and Fine Arts Center, Nashville Symphony Assn., The Temple. Served with USNR, 1943-46. Mem. Am., Tenn., Nashville bar assns., Am. Judicature Soc., Nashville Area C. of C., Order of Coif, Artus Club, Phi Beta Kappa. Club: Nashville City. Home: 4225 Harding Rd Nashville TN 37205 Office: 3d National Bank Bldg Nashville TN 37219

SAMUELSON, FRED BINDER, artist, educator; b. Harvey, Ill., Nov. 29, 1925; s. Frederick Gustav and Theresa Marie (Binder) S.; student U. Chgo., 1947-53; B.F.A., Art Inst. Chgo., 1951, M.F.A., 1953; m. Sylvia C. DeBaca, Sept. 22, 1951; children—Fredric Michael, Lisa Maria. Adult edn. Chgo. Park Recreational Program, 1951-53; head lithography dept. Instituto Allende, San Miguel Allende, Guanajuato Mexico, 1955-63, head grad. studies, 1964—; faculty chmn. San Antonio Art Inst., 1963-64; seminars Hill Country Art Found., Ingram, Tex., 1967—; guest lectr. Art Students League, Houston, Art League, Laredo, Tex., Laguna Gloria Art Mus., Austin, Tex.; executed mural for Conv. Center, Hemisfair, 1968. Served with USAAF, 1943-45. Home: 17 Fuentes Apdo 70 San Miguel de Allende Guanajuato Mexico

SANABRIA, ARTURO ENRIQUE, physician; b. San German, P.R., Dec. 12, 1921; s. Nicolas and Ines (Cotis) S.; B.A., Inter-Am. U., 1946; M.D., Jefferson Med. Coll., 1952; m. Ana Teresa Rivera, Dec. 21, 1962; children—Ivelisse, John E.; (by previous marriage)—Vivian, Arturo Enrique. Intern, Arecibo (P.R.) Dist. Hosp., 1952-53; med. dir. Ciales Hosp., 1953-63; practice gen. medicine, Ciales, P.R., 1963—. Med. cons. Selective Service, Ciales, 1969—. Mem. local com. Popular Democratic party, 1960—. Mem. P.R. Med. Assn. Home: Jaguas County Ciales PR 00638 Office: 10 Palmer St Ciales PR 00638

SANBORN, HERBERT JAMES, museum ofcl.; b. Worcester, Mass., Oct. 28, 1907; s. Herbert C. and Grace A. (Thayer) S.; Pulitzer Traveling fellow, Nat. Acad. Design, 1926-29; student Columbia U. Tchrs. Coll., 1930-31, U. Chgo., 1933-35; m. Kathrine Kincaid Blood, June 20, 1934; 1 son, Herbert James. Instr. graphic arts, U. Ia., Iowa City, 1932-33; dir. Davenport Municipal Art Gallery, Davenport Ia., 1934-35, Museum Oglebay Inst. Wheeling. W.Va. 1936-43; exhibits officer Library Congress, Washington, 1946—; works exhibited throughout U.S., 1946—; represented in permanent collections Library Congress, Nat. Collection Fine Arts, Hunterdon County Art Center, Clinton, N.J. Served with USNR, 1943-46. Mem. Print Club Phila., Am. Inst. Graphic Arts, Washington Soc. Printmakers, Hunterdon County Art Assn. Contbr. articles profl. jours. Home: 3541 Forest Dr Alexandria VA 22302 Office: Library Congress 1st and Constitution Av Washington DC 20540

SANCHEZ, JUAN TOMAS, constrn. co. exec.; b. Havana, Cuba, Feb. 2, 1943; s. Julio and Maria Dolores (Sotolongo) S.; B. Sci. and Letters, Instituto del Vedado, 1960; B.S. in Civil Engring., U. Miami, 1971; m. Dora Eugenia Vidal. Nov. 28, 1964; children—Julian Augusto, Juan Thomas. Came to U.S., 1961, naturalized, 1971. Project mgr. J. A. Valls Constrn., Inc., Miami, Fla., 1971-73; project mgr., exec. v.p. Devon Constn. Co., Miami, 1973; asso. Arello, Mendoza & Assos. Inc., Miami, 1974—. Mem. Am. Soc. C.E., Colegio de Ingenieros Civiles de Cuba en el Exilio. Home: 8840 SW 92d Av Miami FL 33156 Office: Suite 1116 Dupont Plaza Center 300 Biscayne Blvd Way Miami FL 33131

SANCHEZ, RAMIRO, banker; b. Nuevo Laredo, Mexico, Sept. 25, 1908; s. Celso Sanchez-Castro and Manuela (Aguirre) S.; brought to U.S., 1912, naturalized, 1938; Dipl. Comml. Banking, Stonier Grad. Sch., Rutgers U., 1954; m. Verena Guerra, Oct. 5, 1930; children—Sylvia (Mrs. Rogelio Salinas), Elva (Mrs. Servando Ramos), Delia (Mrs. Israel Gonzales), Martha (Mrs. Augustine Galvan), Ramiro Sanchez. Exec. v.p. Laredo Nat. Bank (Tex.), 1963-68, pres., 1968—, vice chmn. bd., 1973—; chmn. bd. City Nat. Bank, Laredo. Chmn., Regional Export Expansion Council, Dept. Commerce, 1961—; chmn. Small Bus. Adminstrn., San Antonio, 1965—. Chmn. fund drive A.R.C., 1950—; 1st v.p. Easter Seal Soc. Tex. Treas. City of Laredo, 1970—. Bd. dirs., sec. Boys Club, 1958—. Mem. Laredo C. of C. (past pres.), Nat. Fedn. Ind. Bus. (county chmn.), Winter Garden Bankers Assn. (past pres.). Roman Catholic. Lion. Clubs: French, Knife and Fork (pres.), Order Alhambra (Laredo). Home: 1302 Mier St Laredo TX 78040 Office: 700 San Bernardo Laredo TX 78040

SANCHEZ, ROY, JR., govt. ofcl.; b. Houston, Oct. 24, 1933; s. Roy and Matilde (Trujillo) S.; A.A., Del Mar Coll., 1960; B.S., U. Corpus Christi, 1962; A.A.S. in Data Processing, Del Mar Coll., 1973; m. Elvia Ramirez, Aug. 28, 1955; children—Roy C., Elizabeth, Ronald. Supervisory accountant Kelly AFB, Tex., 1962-65; internal revenue agt. Internal Revenue Service, Houston, 1965—. Instr. adult edn. Del Mar Coll., Corpus Christi, 1972-74. Served with USAF, 1952-56. C.P.A., Tex. Mem. Tex. Soc. C.P.A.s.

SANCHEZ-MEJORADA Y VELASCO, CARLOS, lawyer; b. Mexico City, Mexico, June 18, 1940; s. Carlos Sanchez-Mejorada y Rodriguez and Carmen Velasco Adalid; B.A., Coll. Alexander von Humboldt, 1958; abogado cum laude, Escuela Libre de Derecho, 1964; LL.M., Harvard, 1965; m. Adela Barona Mariscal, Oct. 29, 1965; children—Regina, Paulina, Carlos, Adriana. Admitted to Mexican bar, 1964; asst. legal dept. Banco Internat., S.A., Mexico City, 1961-63; vice consul Mexican Fgn. Service, Mexico City, 1963-68; head Europe, Asia and Africa dept. Mexican Fgn. Affairs Ministry, 1964, head internat. claims dept., 1965-68, legal counsel, 1965-68; partner firms Sanchez-Mejorada Velasco, and predecessor, Mexico City, 1965-74, Hidalgo, Barrera, Siqueiros y Torres Landa, 1974—; semina instr. pub. internat. law Escuela Libre de Derecho, 1966-69. Alternate dir. Banco Internat. de Fometo Urbano, S.A., dir. other corps. Mem. Am. Soc. Internat. Law, Internat. Law Assn., Assn. Mexicana de Derecho Internat., Inter-Am., Internat. bar assns., Barra Mexicana-Colegio de Abogados (dir., asst. treas. 1967-73), lustre y Nacional Colegio de Abogados, Harvard Law Sch. Alumni Assn. Roman Cath. Author article. Home: Fuente de Cleo 37 Tecamachalco Mexico City 10 DF Mexico Office: Sinaloa 153 Mexico City 7 DF Mexico

SANCILIO, LAWRENCE FRANCIS, pharm. co. exec.; b. Bklyn., Dec. 13, 1932; s. Damiano and Rosa (Aloise) S.; B.S. in Pharmacy, St. John's U., 1954; Ph.D. in Pharmacy (Geschickter fellow), Georgetown U., 1960; m. Rose Alice Liffrig, July 30, 1960; children—Susan, Michele, Damian, Diane, Lawrence. Teaching fellow Georgetown U. Sch. Medicine, Washington, 1958-59; research pharmacologist Miles Labs., Inc., Elkhart, Ind., 1960-68; asso. research pharmacologist A.H. Robins Co., Richmond, Va., 1968-71, group mgr., 1971—. Vis. lectr. Med. Coll. of Va., 1970—. Mem. Soc. Exptl. Biology and Medicine, Am. Soc. Pharmacology and Exptl. Therapeutics. Contbr. articles to profl. jours. Home: 8334 Abbey Rd Richmond VA 23235 Office: 1211 Sherwood Ave Richmond VA 23220

SANDERS, AARON PERRY, educator; b. Phoenix, Jan. 12, 1924; s. DeWitt and Ruth (Perry) S.; B.S., Tex. Western Coll., 1950; M.S. (AEC fellow), U. Rochester, 1952; Ph.D., U. N.C., 1964; m. Betty Mae Gelein, Aug. 11, 1944 (div.); children—Merle Anne, Julie Ruth, James DeWitt; m. 2d, Georgia Anne Bullock, Nov. 26, 1972; 1 dau., Kai Marie. Asso. health physicist Brookhaven Nat. Lab., Upton L.I., N.Y., 1951-53; instr. physics, radiol. safety officer N.C. State Coll., 1953; instr. radiology Duke Med. Center, Durham, N.C., 1953-56, dir. radioisotope lab., 1953-65, asso. radiology, 1956-57, asst. prof., 1957-64, asso. prof., 1964-65, asso. prof., dir. div. radiobiology, 1965-70, prof., dir. div. radiobiology, 1971—, also asst. prof. physiology. Cons., N.C. Bd. Health, 1961—. Served with USNR, 1942-45. Fulbright lectr. health physics, Argentina, 1958-59. Diplomate Am. Bd. Health Physics. Mem. A.A.A.S., Am. Phys. Soc., Soc. Exptl. Biology and Medicine, Health Physics Soc., Soc. Nuclear Medicine, Biophys. Soc., Radiation Research Soc., Undersea Med. Soc. Sigma Xi, Sigma Pi Sigma. Contbr. articles to profl. jours. Address: Box 3164 Duke U Med Center Durham NC 27710

SANDERS, ALFRED PERRY, aerospace technologist; b. Indpls., Jan. 2, 1936; s. John A. and Willetta G. (Pagel) S.; A.A., Phoenix Coll., 1962; B.S., Ariz. State U., 1964; m. Alice Lucille Ivey, Apr. 27, 1957; 1 dau., Diane Elaine. Custom monolithic engr. semicondr. div. Motorola, Inc., Phoenix, 1964-65; aerospace technologist NASA Johnson Space Center, Houston, 1965—. Served to 1st lt. USMC, 1956-59. Mem. I.E.E.E., Air Force Assn., Am. Inst. Aeros. and Astronautics, Am. Mgmt. Assn. Research on hydrogen and oxygen prodn. from thermally dissociated water using perm-selective membranes, extraterrestrial consumables prodn. and utilization, oxygen and/or water from lunar or similar soil. Home: 18100 Nassau Bay Dr Houston TX 77058 Office: Johnson Space Center AT2 Houston TX 77058

SANDERS, ALLEN, banker; b. Lawton, Okla., Apr. 16, 1932; s. Quincy A. and Mildred (Graves) S.; A.B. cum laude, Harvard, 1954, M.B.A., 1956; m. Dorothy Ann Mould, Sept. 4, 1954; children—Julia, Christopher. With First Nat. Bank, Dallas, 1956—, asst. v.p., 1961-63, v.p., 1963-67, sr. v.p., 1967—; dir. First Dallas Capital Corp. Instr. Am. Inst. Banking, Southwestern Grad. Sch. Banking. Group chmn. Dallas County United Fund, 1969-73. Democratic precinct chmn., 1964-66. Methodist (past chmn. adminstrv. bd.). Club: Harvard Business School (past pres. Dallas-Ft. Worth). Home: 13517 Far Hills Lane Dallas TX 75240 Office: 1401 Elm St Dallas TX 75222

SANDERS, BOBBY LEE, lawyer; b. Sayre, Okla., Oct. 25, 1939; s. Leslie Loyd and Margarette Katherine (Turner) S.; student W. Tex. State U., 1957-59; B.B.A., U. Tex., 1965, LL.B., 1967; m. Virginia Ann Johnson, May 6, 1961; children—Leslie Kent, Brian Lee. Admitted to Tex. bar, 1967; briefing atty. for Tex. Supreme Ct., Austin, 1967-68; asso. firm Turpin, Smith, Dyer, Harman and Osborn, Midland, Tex., 1968-70, partner, 1970—. Bd. dirs. Midland Found., Inc., v.p., 1969—; bd. dirs. West Tex. Found., Inc. Recipient Chavlier Degree, Order of Demolay, 1958. Mem. State Bar of Tex., Midland County, Jr., Midland County bar bar assns., Phi Alpha Delta. Democrat. Optimist. Home: 802 Elk St Midland TX 79701 Office: PO Box 913 Midland TX 79701

SANDERS, CARL JULIAN, bishop; b. Star, N.C., May 18, 1912; s. Hugh T. and Annie Margaret (Crowell) S.; B.A., Wofford Coll., 1933, D.D., 1973; B.D., Star Candler Sch. Theology, 1936; D.D., Randolph Macon Coll., 1953, Athens Coll., 1973; m. Eleanor Louise Luop, Sept. 28, 1935; children—Lundi S. (Mrs. Mansfield), Eleanor S. (Mrs. Paul Kasler). Ordained to ministry United Methodist Ch.; pastor various chs. Va. Conf.; consecrated bishop, 1972; bishop Birmingham (Ala.) area, 1972—. Formerly pres. Va. Conf. Bd. Evangelism; formerly sec. Jurisdictional Council, Southeastern Jurisdiction; mem. Gen. Bd. Publs., 1956-68, sec., 1960-68; mem. Commn. on Ecumenical Affairs, 1968-72; del. World Meth. Conf., Oslo, London, Denver; now pres. United Meth. Com. on Relief; v.p. Bd. Global Ministries; del. various confs., 1960—. Trustee Emory U., Alaska Meth. U., Carraway Med. Center, Birmingham So. Coll., Athens Coll., Huntingdon Coll., Lake Junaluska Assembly; bd. govs. Wesley Theol. Sem. Home: 2205 Vestavia Dr Birmingham AL 35216 Office: 6 Office Park Circle Suite 301 Birmingham AL 35223

SANDERS, CHARLES ROLAND, JR., textile mills exec.; b. St. Matthews, S.C., Dec. 23, 1926; s. Charles Roland and Annie (Keller) S.; A.B. in Journalism, U. S.C., 1946; m. Frances Earle Halford, Oct. 12, 1956; children—Annie Frances, Charles Roland III, James Gordon Halford. Wire editor, govtl. affairs editor, Columbia Newspapers, Inc. (S.C.), 1946-59, city editor, 1959-62, mng. editor, 1962-65; dir. corporate pub. relations, govtl. affairs Greenwood Mills (S.C.), 1965—. Mem. S.C. Pardon, Probation and Parole Bd., 1968—. Mem. Pub. Relations Soc. Am. Presbyn. Home: 129 N Cedar Dr Greenwood SC 29646 Office: Box 1017 Greenwood Bldg Greenwood SC 29646

SANDERS, FAYE BEVELEY (MRS. JOHN HOLLIS MARTIN), lawyer; b. nr. Brooklet, Ga., Feb. 6, 1934; d. Carroll Eugene and Addie Louise (Prosser) Sanders; student Ga. So. Coll., 1952-54, Woodrow Wilson Coll. Law, 1955-56; m. John Hollis Martin, Feb. 26, 1960; children—Janna, Jenny Lynn. Admitted to Ga. bar, 1956; practiced in Statesboro, Ga., 1956—; partner firm Anderson and Sanders, 1956—. Mem. Ga., Bulloch County (sec.-treas. 1966-73), Ogeechee bar assns., Ga. Assn. Women Lawyers (v.p. 1959-60), Statesboro Bus. and Profl. Womens Club, Statesboro-Bulloch County C. of C., Zeta Tau Alpha. Home: 106 Chelsea Circle Statesboro GA 30458 Office: 8 Siebald St Statesboro GA 30458

SANDERS, HAROLD GLEN, clergyman; b. Aurora, Mo., Aug. 2, 1907; s. Charles T. and Margaret Ellen (Wheeler) S.; A.A., S.W. Bapt. Coll., 1930; A.B., William Jewell Coll., 1932; postgrad. U. Mo., 1932-33; Th.M., So. Bapt. Theol. Sem., 1937, Th.D., 1941; D.D., John B. Stetson U., 1961, Georgetown U., 1963; grad. Am. Mgmt. course, Ch. Exec. Devel. Conf.; m. Mary Lou Myers, Apr. 30, 1936 (dec. Oct. 1950); children—Margaret Ellen, Harold Glen; m. 2d, June Celeste Holloway, Aug. 1, 1952; children—Susan, Ronald. Pastor Pleasant Home Baptist Ch., Spruce, Mo., 1932-35, Bapt. Ch., Christianburg, Ky. and New Liberty Bapt. Ch., Ind., 1936-39, Riverview Bapt. Ch., Cox's Creek, Ky., 1939-41, Norwood Bapt. Ch., Birmingham Ala., 1941-43; pastor First Bapt. Ch., Tallahassee, 1946-61; exec. sec.-treas. Ky. Bapt. Conv., Middletown, Ky., 1961-72. Exec. bd. Fla. Bapt. Conv., 1947-54, pres., 1953-54; chmn. trustees Bapt. Retirement Centers, 1958-61; chmn. stewardship commn. So. Bapt. Conv., 1960-62; pres. United Christian Action, 1958-60. Served as Chaplain USNR, 1943-46; PTO. Recipient citation for achievement William Jewell Coll., 1952; Life Service award S.W. Bapt. Coll., 1962. Mem. Tallahassee, Louisville chambers commerce, So. Bapt. Chaplains Assn. (pres.), Mil. Chaplains Assn. (area v.p.), V.F.W. (nat. chaplain 1956-57), Am. Legion, Order Ky. Cols. Contbr. to various religious periodicals. Home: 5404 Pawnee Trail Louisville KY 40207

SANDERS, HARVEY GIBERT, JR., lawyer; b. McCormick, S.C., Nov. 19, 1936; s. Harvey G. and Sue Lee (Keown) S.; B.S. in Bus. Adminstrn., U. S.C., 1957, LL.B., 1960; m. Barbara Ann Langley, June 10, 1956; children—Suzanne Kaye, Harvey G. III, Barry Langley. Admitted to S.C. bar, 1960; asso. Leatherwood, Walker, Todd & Mann, Greenville, 1960-65, partner, 1966—. Instr., Palmer Bus. Coll., Columbia, S.C., 1958-60; dir. Diran Corp., Greenville. Pres., U. S.C. Law Fedn., 1959; parliamentarian August Rd. Sch. P.T.A., 1964-65; mem. Mayor's All Am. City com., 1965; Mayor's adv. com. on Certified Workable Housing Program, 1970-73; mem. adv. com. Community Service and Continuing Edn. Seminars, 1967; mem. Greenville County Commn. on Alcoholism, 1968-71. Mem. adv. com. U. S.C. Carolina Scholars program, 1974, Greenville TEC Found. Adv. Com., 1974. Mem. Am., S.C. (exec. com. Young Lawyers sect. 1965-66), Greenville County bar assns., Cornerstone Investment Club (pres. 1964, 73), Greenville Young Lawyers Club (v.p. 1965), Greater Greenville Estate Planning Council (v.p. 1974), Greenville Jr. C. of C. (pres. 1966-67, named Outstanding Local Pres. 1966-67), Greater Greenville C. of C. (adv. com., chmn. bus. ethics com. housing com., dir. 1967, v.p. 1972), Greenville Literacy Assn. (pres. 1969-70), Order of Wig and Robe, Greenville Art Museum (dir. 1968), U. S.C. Alumni Assn. (circuit v.p. 1971-72), Phi Alpha Delta. Baptist (Sunday sch. tchr. 1960—, deacon). Clubs: Greenville-Pickens Gamecock (pres. 1965-66); Greenville Touchdown (pres. 1974), Greenville Country. Home: 1414 Parkins Mill Rd Greenville SC 29607 Office: 217 E Coffee St Greenville SC 29602

SANDERS, JAMES LINDELL, aerospace exec.; b. Meridian, Miss., Feb. 10, 1927; s. James Eugene and Margaret (McElroy) S.; B.A., Auburn U., 1948; M.E., Yale, 1951; Ph.D., U. Ala., 1973; m. Elizabeth Ellen Kirk, Dec. 25, 1946; children—Elizabeth Irene, Linda Ellen, Lesa Jane. Atlas propulsion pros. engr. Ramo-Wooldridge, 1957; engring. specialist Chance Vought, 1958-60; asst. to dir. Future Projects Office, MSFC-NASA, 1962, br. chief, 1969—; preliminary design of missiles systems and space vehicles systems Dept. mgr. Brown Engring., Huntsville, Ala., 1965-69. Served with USAAF, 1945-46. Registered profl. engr., Ala. Mem. Am. Astronautical Soc., Tau Beta Pi, Phi Kappa Phi, Gamma Alpha, Scabbard and Blade. Home: 705 Watts Dr SE Huntsville AL 35801 Office: Marshall Space Flight Center AL 35812

SANDERS, JAY WILLIAM, educator; b. Balt., July 26, 1924. s. Jay Will and May Magdalene (Fisher) S.; A.A., Louisburg Jr. Coll., 1948; B.A., U. N.C., 1950; M.A., Columbia, 1951; Ph.D., U. Mo., 1957; postgrad. (NIH fellow) Northwestern U., 1962-64; m. Mary Elizabeth St. John, Aug. 27, 1950; children—Mary Jean, John Jay, Elizabeth Ann. Instr. speech U. Mo., Columbia, 1952-57; asst. prof. speech Trenton State Coll., 1957-59, asso. prof., 1959-62; asst. prof. audiology Vanderbilt U., Nashville, 1964-65, asso. prof., 1965-71, prof. audiology, 1971—, research audiologist Bill Wilkerson Hearing and Speech Center, 1964—. Cons. in indsl. hearing conservation, 1968—. Served as pilot, USNR, 1943-45. Fellow Am. Speech and Hearing Assn.; mem. Tenn. Speech and Hearing Assn. Kiwanian. Asso. editor Jour. Speech and Hearing Research, 1967-70. Contbr. articles to profl. jours. Home: Route 1 Box 325 Old Hickory TN 37138 Office: Vanderbilt University Nashville TN 37232

SANDERS, JOE WILLIAM, state chief justice; b. Pleasant Hill, La., May 31, 1915; s. Oliver Lud and Ozie (Allen) S.; B.A., La. State U., 1935, LL.B., 1938; m. Marie Sistrunk, Oct. 26, 1940. Admitted to La. bar, 1938; pvt. practice, Many, 1938-42, Baton Rouge, 1946-54; judge Family Ct. Parish E. Baton Rouge, 1954-60; asso. justice Supreme Ct. La., 1960-73, chief justice, 1973—. Chmn. E. Baton Rouge Parish Juvenile Commn., 1951-54; chmn. Blue Ridge Tng. Inst. So. Juvenile Ct. Judges, 1957, mem. adv. council judges Nat. Council Crime and Delinquency, 1955—. Mem. La. Ho. of Reps. from Sabine Parish, 1940-44; del. La. Democratic Conv., 1940, Nat. Dem. Conv., 1952. Bd. dirs. Baton Rouge, YMCA 1952-55, 58-61. Served to capt. AUS, 1942-46. Mem. Am., La. bar assns., Am. Judicature Soc., Conf. Chief Justices, Am. Legion, Amvets (past post comdr.), V.F.W., Order of Coif, Am., La. law insts., Phi Kappa Phi, Omicron Delta Kappa, Gamma Eta Gamma, Pi Sigma Alpha, Pi Gamma Mu, Theta Xi. Mason; mem. Woodmen of World. Home: 209 Lover's Lane Dr Baton Rouge LA 70806 Office: Supreme Ct Bldg 301 Loyola Av New Orleans LA 70112

SANDERS, MAJOR SPENCER, SR., state ofcl.; b. Concord, N.C., Oct. 27, 1919; s. Major Herbert and Annie Elizabeth (Murphy) S.; B.S., Tenn. A. and I. State U., 1942; M.S., Agrl. and Tech. U., Greensboro, N.C., 1955; m. Bessie Marjorie Ramsey, Feb. 10, 1942; children—Major Spencer, Clifton Ramsey, Marjorie Kathleen. Asst. dir. Morrison Tng. Sch., Hoffman, N.C., 1942-43; instr. vocational agr. Henderson (N.C.) Inst., 1945-66; supr. agrl. edn. N.C., Dept. Pub. Instrn., Raleigh, 1966-70, area dir. occupational edn., 1970—. Sec. Henderson Citizens League, 1947-49. Bd. dirs. Tri-County Investment Cooperation, 1969. Served with AUS, 1943-44. Recipient longevity service award U.S. Office Edn., 1970, N.C. Assn. Occupational Adminstrs., 1973. Mem. N.E.A., Nat. Suprs. of Agr., N.C. Agrl. Tchrs. Assn. (pres. 1963-66), Nat., N.C. vocational assns., N.C. Assn. Occupational Adminstrs., Vance County Tchrs. Assn. (pres. 1955-57), Agrl. and Tech. State Alumni Assn. (county chmn. 1963-65), Omega Psi Phi. Mason, Elk. Home: PO Box 793 Henderson NC 27536 Office: Dept Public Education Raleigh NC 27602

SANDERS, MELVIN HILL, indsl. engr.; b. Atlanta, Sept. 9, 1928; s. Shelby Lockard and Ada (Hill) S.; student Troy State U., 1948-50; B.S., Auburn U., 1952; m. Mary Lloyd Kelly, Feb. 26, 1954; children—Cheryl Elaine, Cathy Lynn, Ginger Marie. Asst. engr. wage incentives Western Electric Co., Burlington, N.C., 1952-56, indsl. engr., 1956-63, sr. indsl. engr. work measurement program, 1963-68, sr. planning engr. Safeguard Anti-Ballistic Missile project, 1968—, instr. ednl. TV courses, 1968—. Precinct judge, Graham, N.C., 1968. Served with USNR, 1946-47. Registered profl. engr., N.C. Mem. Nat. Soc. Profl. Engrs., Profl. Engrs. N.C., Am. Inst. Indsl. Engrs. (pres. Raleigh chpt. 1966-67, dir. 1968, chmn. standing com. 1962-69, membership chmn. region 3 1968-70), Burlington-Graham Engrs. Club, Telephone Pioneers Am., Delta Sigma Phi. Presbyn. Club: Piedmont Crescent Country. Home: 618 Johnson Av Graham NC 27253 Office: 204 Graham-Hopedale Rd Burlington NC 27215

SANDERS, OLIVER PAUL, educator; b. Caney, Okla., Dec. 26, 1924; s. Ernest Dillon and Effie Anna (Alford) S.; B.A., Southeastern State Coll., 1947; M.S., Okla. State U., 1949, Ph.D., 1956; m. Virginia Lee Frederick, Apr. 1, 1945; children—Stephen Paul, Gina Karin. Asst. prof. Southeastern State Coll., 1949-54; instr. Okla. State U., 1954-56; asso. prof. La. Poly. Inst., 1956-59; prof., chmn. math. dept. Hardin-Simmons U., 1959-62; faculty Appalachian State U., 1962—, chmn. math. dept., 1962-65, dean, 1965-68, vice chancellor for acad. affairs, 1968-74, prof., 1974—. Served with AUS, 1943-46. Mem. Math. Assn. Am. Author: Elementary Mathematics: A Logical Approach, 1963. Home: 203 Eastbrook St Boone NC 28607

SANDERS, RALPH WAID, orgn. exec.; b. Ft. Smith, Ark., Feb. 15, 1937; s. Floyd Hall and Ruth (Cooper) S.; A.A., Ft. Smith Jr. Coll., 1957; B.A., U. Tulsa, 1959; m. Roberta Hood, Apr. 2, 1960; children—Ralph Terrell, Mary Anne, Timothy Waid. Freelance writer, photographer, 1955-56; journalist KOTV News, Tulsa, 1957-60; dir. pub. relations U.S. Jr. C. of C., Tulsa, 1960-63; exec. v.p., chief operating officer World Neighbors, Oklahoma City, 1963—. Mem. Pub. Relations Soc. Am., Am. Mgmt. Assn., Internat. Platform Assn., Sigma Delta Chi. Home: 10821 Greystone St Oklahoma City OK 73120 Office: 5116 N Portland St Oklahoma City OK 73112

SANDERS, ROBERT NORTON, chemist; b. Carlinville, Ill., Feb. 2, 1935; s. Norton Herald and Vera Marie (Metcalfe) S.; B.S., Shurtleff Coll., 1957; M.A., Washington U., St. Louis, 1960; Ph.D., La. State U., 1965; m. Alta Rae Van Deusen, Aug. 16, 1957; children—Patricia Rae, Thomas Norton. Research asst. Shell Oil Co., Wood River, Ill., 1956-57; instr. MacMurray Coll., Jacksonville, Ill., 1959-62; scientist Lockheed Missiles & Space Co., Sunnyvale, Cal., 1962-63; sr. research chemist Ethyl Corp., Baton Rouge, 1965—. Methodist. Home: 13239 Todd St Baton Rouge LA 70815 Office: PO Box 341 Baton Rouge LA 70821

SANDERS, ROBERT VESTER, hosp. adminstr.; b. Birmingham, Ala., Jan. 13, 1927; s. Robert Vester and Lula M. (White) S.; B.S. in Accounting, Samford U., Birmingham, 1949; m. Bettye J. Means, Dec. 27, 1952; children—Rob, Mike, Barre, Joan. Bus. mgr. Norwood Clinic, Birmingham, 1949-56; bus. mgr. Carraway Meyer Rehab. Center, 1953-55; asst. div. accountant Union Supply div. U.S. Steel Co., 1956-57; adminstr. Hill Crest Hosp., Birmingham, 1963—; adj. asst. prof., preceptor Sch. Community and Allied Health Resources, U. Ala. at Birmingham. Chmn. bd. dirs. Community Hosp., Ensley, Birmingham; mem. bd., mem. exec. com., project rev. com., health facility tech. adv. com. Community Health Planning Commn., chmn.; mem. paramed. adv. com. Jefferson State Jr. Coll.; chmn. Mental Health Tech. Com.; mem. Citizens Adv. Com. to Jefferson County Bd. Health; pres. Birmingham Regional Hosp. Council. Pres. Hill Crest Found.; trustee Indsl. Health Council. Served with AUS, 1945-46. Mem. Am. Coll. Hosp. Adminstrs., Assn. Mental Health Adminstrs., Ala. Hosp. Assn. (trustee). Baptist (deacon). Lion, Mason. Office: PO Box 2896 Birmingham AL 35212 Home: 2640 Dolly Ridge Rd Birmingham AL 35243

SANDERS, THOMAS JOSEPH, elec. products co. engr.; b. Indpls., July 10, 1942; s. William Henry and Cecelia Josephine (Rauser) S.; B.S. in Elec. Engring. (Square D scholar), Purdue U., 1964, M.S. in Elec. Engring., (NSF fellow), 1966, Ph.D. (NSF fellow), 1969; m. Judith Ann McDonald, June 6, 1964; children—Deborah Sue, Thomas Joseph. Tchr. engring. Purdue U., W. Lafayette, Ind., 1966-68; elec. engr. Harris Semiconductor Co. (formerly Radiation, Inc.), Melbourne, Fla., 1968-70, sect. leader, 1970—. Mem. Electrochem. Soc., I.E.E.E., Sigma Xi, Phi Kappa Theta, Tau Beta Pi, Eta Kappa Nu. K.C. (sec. 1970-71). Home: 331 Seabreeze Dr Indialantic FL 32903 Office: PO Box 883 Melbourne FL 32901

SANDERS, WILLIAM EVAN, clergyman; b. Natchez, Miss., Dec. 25, 1919; s. Walter Richard and Agnes Mortimer (Jones) S.; B.A., Vanderbilt U., 1942; B.D., U. of South, 1945, D.D., 1959; S.T.M., Union Theol. Sem., 1946; m. Kathryn Cowan Schaffer, June 25, 1951; 4 children. Curate St. Paul's Ch., Chattanooga, 1945-46; asst. St. Mary's Cathedral, Memphis, 1946-48, dean, 1948-62; bishop coadjutor Tenn., Knoxville, 1962—. Address: 908 Bank Knoxville Bldg Knoxville TN 37902*

SANDGROUND, MARK BERNARD, lawyer; b. Boston, June 6, 1932; s. John Henry and Rose (Plotler) S.; B.A., U. Mich., 1952; LL.B., U. Va., 1955; m. Marcia Gurevich, July 20, 1959; children—Mark Bernard, Bruce J. Admitted to Va. bar, 1955, D.C. bar, 1955; trial atty. Dept. Justice, Washington, 1955-56; partner firm Amram, Hahn and Sandground, Washington, 1956—. Pres. La Nicoise, Inc., Le Canard, Inc., Wash. Palm Inc., Park Assos., Inc. Pres. Friends of the Corcoran Art Museum, 1968-71. Vice chmn. Republican Inaugural Com., 1969, 73. Bd. dirs. Psychiat. Inst. Found. Clubs: Nat. Press, Capital Hill, B.F.W. Home: 119 Quay St Alexandria VA Office: 700 Colorado Bldg Washington DC 20005

SANDIFER, MYRON GUY, JR., physician, educator; b. Lowrys, S.C., Sept. 4, 1922; s. Myron Guy and Cornelia (Hope) S.; B.S. cum laude, Davidson Coll., 1943; M.D., Harvard, 1947; m. Jean Waters Cohn, June 30, 1973; children—Ellen, Myron Guy. Intern, Mass. Gen. Hosp., Boston, 1947-48, resident medicine, 1948-49; resident psychiatry Yale, 1949-50, Beth Israel Hosp., Boston, 1952-54; practice medicine, specializing in psychiatry, 1954—; asst. prof. psychiatry U. N.C., Chapel Hill, 1958-66; dir. Research N.C. Dept. Mental Health, 1959-65; prof. psychiatry U. Ky. Coll. Medicine, Lexington, 1966—, asso. dean acad. affairs, 1969—. Served with USNR, 1950-52. Diplomate Am. Bd. Psychiatry. Fellow Am. Psychiat. Assn.; mem. Ky. Psychiat. Assn. (pres. 1970-71), Boylston Med. Soc., Phi Beta Kappa, Omicron Delta Kappa. Kiwanian. Contbr. articles to profl. jours. Home: 4008 Mayflower St Lexington KY 40504

SANDITEN, EDGAR RICHARD, tire co. exec.; b. Okmulgee, Okla., Feb. 1, 1920; s. Herman and Anna (Sanditen) S.; student Western Mil. Acad., 1934-37; B.S. in Bus., Okla. U., 1941; m. Isabel Raffkind, Jan. 26, 1945; children—Linda Caryl, Judith Marie, Ellen Jane, Michael Jay. With Otasco (formerly Okla. Tire & Supply Co.), Tulsa, 1941—, exec. v.p., 1970—; dir. Merc. Nat. Bank, Tulsa, Farmers & Mchts. Bank, Las Cruces, N.M., Western Diversified Industries. Chmn. United Jewish Appeal, Tulsa, 1960; mem. adv. bds. U. Okla. Alumni, 1962—, Y.M.C.A., Tulsa, 1966—; chmn. Tulsa Charity Horse Show, 1969-71; Bd. dirs. Tulsa Opera, 1967—, Civic Ballet, 1960-68 Tulsa Econ. Devel. Commn., St. John's Hosp. Served with USAAF, 1943-46; CBI. Decorated Purple Heart; recipient Alumni Devel. Fund citation U. Okla., 1968. Mem. Tulsa Jr. C. of C. (bd. dirs., mem. material conservation com. 1940-43; honor award 1943), Quarter Century Club Automotive Industry. Jewish religion (pres. temple 1969-71). Clubs: Summit, Meadowbrook Country (Tulsa). Home: 2140 E 30th St Tulsa OK 74114 Office: PO Box 885 Tulsa OK 74102

SANDOLOSKI, SANDY MOISE, lawyer; b. Dallas, Nov. 30, 1921; s. Leo Bill and Cora (Weil) S.; LL.B., So. Meth. U., 1949; m. Bernice Madvine, Mar. 12, 1950; children—Lee Robert, Ellen Rae. Admitted to Tex. bar, 1949; practiced in Dallas, 1949—; mem. firms Weinberg & Sandoloski, 1952-73, Weinberg, Sandoloski & McManus, 1973—. Served with USAF, 1941-45. Mason, Optimist (pres. 1961-62). Home: 7322 Azalea St Dallas TX 75230 Office: 1800 Republic Nat Bank Tower Dallas TX 75201

SANDOZ, GEORGE ELLIS, JR., polit. scientist; b. New Orleans, Feb. 10, 1931; s. George Ellis and Ruby (Odom) S.; B.A., La. State U., 1951, M.A., 1953; Dr. oec. publ., U. Munich (W. Germany), 1965; student U. N.C., summer 1950, Georgetown U., 1952-53, U. Heidelberg, 1956-58; m. Therese Alverne Hubley, May 31, 1957; children—Ellis III, Lisa, Erica, Jonathan. Instr., asst. prof., asso. prof. polit. sci. and philosophy La. Polytech. Inst., Ruston, 1959-67, prof., 1967-68, dir. Center for Comparative Internat. Studies, 1966-68, prof., head dept. polit sci. E. Tex. State U., 1968—. Cons. La. Pilot Project Internat. Edn., 1966-68, Mem. exec. council S.W. Alliance for Latin Am., 1966-68. Served with USMC, 1953-56. Recipient Fulbright Scholar, 1964; Fulbright Achievement Certificate, 1965; H.B. Earhart fellow, 1964. Fellow Germanistic Soc. Am.; mem. Am., So., Southwest (pres. 1974—) polit. sci. assns., Internat. Studies Assn., Am. Soc. for Polit. and Legal Philosophy. Author: Political Apocalypse: A Study of Dostoevsky's Grand Inquisitor, 1971. Contbr. articles in field to profl. jours. Home: PO Box 4315 E T Sta Commerce TX 75428

SANDS, ROBERT KENNETH, lawyer; b. Worcester, Mass., Aug. 25, 1926; s. John M. and Edith (Hammarlund) S.; B.A. with honors in Polit. Sci., Ohio State U., 1949; J.D., Yale, 1952. Admitted to Tex. bar, 1952, U.S. Supreme Ct. bar, 1971; practiced in Dallas, 1952—; asso. firm Leachman, Matthews and Gardere, 1952-54, Matthews, Shelton and Fisher, 1954-55, Matthews, Shelton, Fisher and Budd, 1955-56, Matthews, Fisher, Budd and Stroud, 1956-60; mem. firm Matthews, Fisher, Budd and Sands, 1960-61, Matthews, Payne, Sands and Benners, 1961-67, Matthews, Sands and Tyler, 1967-69, Sands, Tyler Trimble and Jones, 1969-70; pres. Sands, Tyler and Trimble, 1970—. Bd. dirs. Dallas Arts Found., 1973—. Served with USNR, 1944-46. Mem. Am., Tex., Dallas bar assns., Yale Law Sch. Assn. of Dallas (pres. 1966—), Confrerie des Chevaliers du Tastevin, Phi Beta Kappa. Club: Dallas. Home: 2912 Hood Apt A Dallas TX 75219 Office: 2030 Republic National Bank Tower Dallas TX 75201

SANDZA, JOSEPH GERARD, chemist; b. N.Y.C., Feb. 4, 1917; s. Francis and Rose (Campana) S.; B.S., Poly. Inst. Bklyn., 1937; M.S., Fordham U., 1940, Ph.D., 1942; m. Rositalia Torres-Braschi, Jan. 29, 1942 children—Joseph G., Raymond C., Richard W., Walter F., Peter A. Rockefeller Found. research asso. Northwestern U., 1942-44; head dept. penicillin process improvement Lederle Labs., Pearl River, N.Y., 1942-47; sr. devel. chemist Hoffman-LaRoche, Nutley, N.J., 1948; asst. dir. eastern research center Stauffer Chem. Co., Chauncey, N.Y., 1949-63; cons. Econ. Devel. Adminstrn., Commonwealth of P.R., San Juan, 1963-68; pres. Caribtech Tech. Assos. and Caribtec Labs., Inc. (San Juan), 1968—. Prof. chemistry, chmn. div. sci. and tech. World U., San Juan, P.R., 1965—. Mem. Am. Chem. Soc., Am. Inst. Chem. Engrs., Colegio de Quimicos de P.R., Chemists Club, Sigma Xi, Phi Lambda Upsilon. Home: 192 Pajuil St Rio Piedras PR 00926 Office: PO Box 2242 San Juan PR 00936

SANFORD, J(AMES) KENNETH, univ. ofcl.; b. Clyde, N.C., Jan. 23, 1932; s. James Edward and Bernice (Crawford) S.; A.A., Mars Hill Coll., 1952; A.B., U. N.C., 1954, M.A., 1958; m. Alice Pearl Reavis, Sept. 22, 1957; children—Timothy Edward, Scott Vernon, Jeanette LuAnn. Pub. relations officer United Appeal of Asheville and Buncombe County, Asheville, N.C., 1954; reporter, 2d copy editor Winston-Salem Jour. and Sentinel, 1957-59, asst. state editor, 1959-61, news editor, 1961-63, editorial writer, 1963-64; dir. information U. N.C., Charlotte, 1964—. Served with AUS, 1954-56. Mem. Pub. Relations Soc. Am. (accredited), Charlotte Pub. Relations Soc. (treas. 1971, sec. 1972, pres. 1974), Coll. News Assn. of Carolinas (chmn. 1967), Charlotte C. of C. (pub. relations com. 1971, communications action council 1973), Kappa Tau Alpha. Baptist (chmn. bd. asso. deacons 1967). Home: 1216 Braeburn Rd Charlotte NC 28211

SANFORD, JAY PHILIP, physician; b. Madison, Wis., May 27, 1928; s. Joseph Arthur and Arlyn (Carlson) S.; M.D., U. Mich., 1952; m. Lorraine Burklund, Apr. 7, 1950; children—Jeb, Nancy, Sarah, Philip, Catherine. Intern Peter Bent Brigham Hosp., Boston, 1952-53; research fellow Harvard Med. Sch., Boston, 1953-54; resident Duke U. Hosp., Durham, N.C., 1956-57; practice medicine, specializing in internal medicine, Dallas, 1957—; mem. staff Parkland Meml. Hosp., St. Paul Hosp., Presbyn. Hosp. (all Dallas), John Peter Smith Hosp., Ft. Worth. Mem. faculty U. Tex. Southwestern Med. Sch. at Dallas, 1957—, prof. internal medicine, 1965—; chief microbiology lab. Parkland Meml. Hosp., 1957—, pres. med. staff, 1968-69; cons. Dallas VA Hosp., Wilford Hall USAF Hosp., Brooke Gen. Hosp., Ft. Sam Houston. Mem. adv. council Dallas Health & Sci. Mus., 1968—; mem. Gov.'s Commn. Phys. Fitness, 1971—. Bd. dirs. Dallas County chpt. 1965—, med. adviser, 1966—. Served with M.C., AUS, 1954-56. Recipient Certificate of Award, Div. Health Moblzn., USPHS, 1963, 64, Pfizer award for civil def., 1965, Presdl. citation for health moblzn. planning, 1970. Fellow Am. Acad. Microbiology, A.C.P.; mem. Assn. Am. Physicians, Nat. Inst. Allergy and Infectious Diseases (chmn. tng. grant com. 1971), Am. Fedn. Clin. Research (pres. 1968-69), A.A.A.S., Am. Soc. Microbiology, Am. Rheumatism Assn., Central Soc. Clin. Research, Soc. Exptl. Biology and Medicine, Am. Soc. Clin. Investigation, Am. Thoracic Soc., Infectious Disease Assn. Am., Sigma Xi. Contbr. papers to profl. jours. Home: 3516 St John's Dr Dallas TX 75205 Office: 5323 Harry Hines Blvd Dallas TX 75235

SANTELMANN, PAUL WILLIAM, educator; b. Ann Arbor, Mich., Oct. 18, 1926; s. Alfred William and Frances Hazel (Eppens) S.; B.S., U. Md., 1950; M.S., Mich. State U., 1952; Ph.D., Ohio State U., 1954; m. Susanna Porter, Dec. 28, 1950; children—Patricia (Mrs. Philip Millington), Steven, Douglas, Barbara. Asst. prof. agronomy U. Md., 1954-61, asso. prof., 1961-62; asso. prof. agronomy Okla. State U., Stillwater, 1962-65, prof. agronomy, 1965—. Mem. adv. group on pest mgmt. and research Pres.' Council on Environmental Quality, 1971-72; mem. herbicide study group of adv. com. on hazardous materials, Environmental Protection Agy., 1972-73; mem. pest control team Nat. Acad. Scis., 1973—. Served with AUS, 1944-46. Mem. Am. Soc. Agronomy, Soil Sci. Soc. Am., Weed Sci. Soc. Am. (exec. com. 1966-70, sec. 1970-72, editor newsletter, 1972—, named outstanding tchr. 1972), Am. Inst. Biol. Sci., So. Weed Sci. Soc. (v.p. 1973—). Mem. Methodist Ch. (treas. ch. 1967—). Contbr. articles to sci. jours. Home: 1101 Lakeridge Dr Stillwater OK 74074

SANTI, KATHLEEN MARY, physician; b. Washington, Aug. 11, 1941; d. Mark G. and Lucinda Ann (Bolan) Santi; B.S. in Biology, U. Fla., 1963; M.D., Emory U., 1967; m. George Clifford Chappell, Dec. 27, 1969; 1 son, Mark Handley. Rotating intern, then resident obstetrics and gynecology St. Paul's Hosp., Dallas, 1968-69; gen. practice, Palatka, Fla., 1970—; sec.-treas. staff Putnam Meml. Hosp. Mem. Fla. Acad. Family Practice, Fla. Med. Assn., Am. Profl. Practice Assn., Putnam County Med. Soc. (sec.-treas.), Putnam County C. of C., Palatka Jaycees, Pilot Club; hon. mem. Palatka Jr. Women's Club. Home: 1401 S Palm Av Palatka FL 32077 Office: 310 S Palm Av Palatka FL 32077

SAPIENZA, JOHN THOMAS, lawyer; b. South Orange, N.J., Feb. 26, 1913; s. James C. and Rosalie (Giaimo) S.; A.B., Harvard, 1934, LL.B., 1937; m. Virginia H. Gignoux, Feb. 12, 1972; children (by previous marriage)—John Thomas, James K. Admitted to N.Y. bar, 1938, D.C. bar, 1943; law clk., Judge A. Hand. N.Y.C., 1937-38; Justice Stanley Reed, Washington, 1938-39; asso. firm Wright, Gordon, Zachry and Parlin, N.Y.C., 1939-41; asso. firm Covington & Burling, Washington, 1941-43, 46-48, partner, 1949—. Served to lt. comdr. USNR, 1943-46. Mem. Internat., Am., Fed., D.C. bar assns., Am. Law Inst., Confrerie des Chevaliers du Tastevin, Phi Beta Kappa. Clubs: Burning Tree, Metropolitan, Internat. (Washington). Home: Watergate East 2510 Virginia Av NW Washington DC 20037 Office: 888 16th St NW Washington DC 20006

SAPP, ARMISTEAD WRIGHT, JR., lawyer; b. Greensboro, N.C., Feb. 28, 1929; s. Armistead Wright and Dorothy (Greenlaw) S.; student N.Y.U., 1948-50, 1952-64; LL.B., U. N.C., 1957; m. Ada Jane Moore, Mar. 21, 1959; children—Armistead Wright, III, Henry King, William Moore. Admitted to N.C. bar, 1957; partner Sapp & Sapp, Greensboro, N.C., 1957—. Dist. Commr. Boy Scouts Am. Served with USNR, 1950-52. Mem. Internat., Am., N.C., Greensboro Dist. bar assns., Am. Trial Lawyers Assn., Am. Soc. Juvenile Ct. Judges, Am. Soc. Internat. Law, Am. Acad. Polit. and Social Sci., Am. Judicature Soc., Am. Arbitration Assn., U.S. Trademark Assn. (govt. liaison com.), Internat. Platform Assn., Def. Research Assn., Am. Security Council, Am. Legion, N.C. Hist. Assn., The Indignant Brotherhood, Starmount Forest, Greensboro C. of C., Phi Alpha Delta. Presbyn. Lion (bd.). Club: Country of Greensboro. Home: 2417 Berkley Pl Greensboro NC 27403 Office: 219 W Washington St Greensboro NC 27401

SAPP, EDWARD O'NEILL, elec. mfg. co. exec.; b. Louisville, May 6, 1928; s. Raymond Paul and Beulah Lee (Pierce) S.; student Xavier U., Cin., 1946-48; B.A. in Math., U. Louisville, 1956; m. Patricia Delores Albert, Aug. 2, 1950; children—Edward O'Neill, Cheryl Anne, Stephanie Lynne. Sales corr. Tube Turns Inc., Louisville, 1952-55; mfg. engr., systems analyst Gen. Electric Co., Louisville, 1955-66, quality control mgr., 1968—; indsl. engring. mgr., materials mgr. Cabot Piping Systems, Louisville, 1966-68. Served with USN, 1948-52. Named Ky. col. Registered profl. engr., Ky. Mem. Kentuckiana Football Ofcls. Assn., Ky. and Ind. High Sch. Athletic Assn. Roman Catholic. Moose, K.C. Home: 2806 Dell Brooke Av Louisville KY 40220 Office: Appliance Park Louisville KY 40225

SAPP, OSCAR LEMAY III, physician, univ. dean; b. Jacksonville, Fla., Aug. 7, 1925; s. Oscar LeMay and Jessie (Macon) S.; student Guilford Coll., 1942-44, Wake Forest U., 1944; M.D., Bowman Gray Sch. Medicine, 1947; m. Inez Tallie Jones, Apr. 3, 1948; children—Rebecca Leah, Judith Anne, Miriam Elaine. Intern Touro Infirmary, New Orleans, 1948-49; resident in internal medicine Walter Reed Army Hosp., Washington, 1953-56; fellow in gastroenterology N.C. Meml. Hosp., Chapel Hill, 1958-60, now mem. staff; practice medicine, specializing in gastroenterology, 1960—; instr. in medicine U. N.C. Sch. Medicine, Chapel Hill, 1960-62, asst. prof. medicine, 1962-65, asso. prof., 1965-71, prof. medicine, 1971—, asso. dean sch. medicine, 1972—. Served with M.C., AUS, 1951-58. Decorated Bronze Star; named Distinguished Alumnus, Bowman Gray Sch. Medicine, 1972, Father of Year, Chapel Hill C. of C., 1971. Diplomate Am. Bd. Internal Medicine. Fellow A.C.P.; mem. Am. Fedn. Clin. Research, Sigma Xi. Democrat. Baptist. Contbr. articles to profl. jours. Home: 450 Lakeshore Lane Chapel Hill NC 27514

SAPP, PHYLLIS WOODRUFF (MRS. J.D. SAPP), author, lectr.; b. Oklahoma City, Oct. 21, 1908; d. John A. and Maude (Laws) Woodruff; student Oklahoma City U., 1926-27; B.A., Okla. U., 1930; m. J.D. Sapp, June 5, 1930; children—Kathryn (Mrs. Karl Malthaner), John Davis, Phillip Woodruff. Organizer, dir. Oklahoma City's first children's theatre, 1930-35; dir. Okla. City Theatre Guild, 1940-42; jr. high sch. tchr. drama Oklahoma City pub. schs., 1946-49; part-time instr. J.D. Sapp Sch. Real Estate. Recipient $4,000 first prize Zondervan's Christian Fiction Contest, 1957. Mem. Internat. Platform Assn., Nat. Legue Am. Pen Women (br. v.p. 1963-65, pres. local br. 1968-70, nat. 4th v.p. 1970-72, chmn. nat. letters bd. 1972-74, nat. chaplain 1974—), Mortar Bd., Alpha Phi, (Distinguished Alumnus award honor 1972), Pi Kappa Delta. Baptist. Author: Accidental Hero (3-act play), 1949; The Ice Cutter, 1948; Whisper Out of the Dust, 1951; For Such a Time, 1954; The Long Bridge, 1957; God of All the Earth, 1960; Gifts from God, 1962; Small Giant, 1957; Life at Its Best, 1963; Living for Jesus, 1961; Working Together in Our Church, 1963; Lighthouse on the Corner, 1964; Creative Teaching in the Church Sch., 1967; 59 Programs for Pre-Teens, 1969; (juvenile) Who Am I?, 1972; (juvenile) Jeff the Baptist, 1973; Real Estate Workbook, 1973. Contbr. to sch. quarterlies So. Bapt. Sunday Sch. Bd. Address: 7100 S Kentucky St Oklahoma City OK 73159

SAR, MADHABANANDA, veterinarian, endocrinologist; b. Palchakada, India, Dec. 31, 1933; s. Paramananda and Gunjar (Pati) S.; came to U.S., 1961, naturalized, 1970; B. Vet. Sci., Bihar U., 1956; M.S., Mich. State U., 1963, Ph.D., 1968; m. Mohini Pal, Jan. 5, 1957; children—Bibhuti K., Minati K., Prasant K. Vet. asst. surgeon dept. animal husbandry and vet. service, Orissa, India, 1956-59; instr. Orissa Coll., Bhubaneswar Orissa, 1959-61; instr., research asso. dept. pharmacology U. Chgo., 1969-70; research asso. labs. for reproductive biology U. N.C. at Chapel Hill, 1970—. Mem. A.A.A.S., Endocrine Soc., Soc. for Study of Reprodn., Internat. Brain Research Orgn., Sigma Xi, Phi Zeta. Contbr. articles on hormone localization and neuroendocrinology to sci. jours. Home: 2429 Tilghman Circle Chapel Hill NC 27514 Office: 111 Swing Bldg University North Carolina Chapel Hill NC 27514

SARDO, WILLIAM HENRY, JR., trade assn. exec.; b. Washington, July 23, 1912; s. William Henry and Marie Therese (Saffell) S.; student Sch. Internat. Studies, Geneva, Switzerland, 1933; B.S., Georgetown U. Fgn. Service Sch., Washington, 1935; postgrad. Princeton, 1942-43; m. Jeannette Felicia Jarrin, June 10, 1935; 1 dau., Teresa (Mrs. William Clark Baldwin). Asst. to sec., mgr. Nat. Wooden Box Assn., Washington, 1935-37, trade promotion mgr., 1940-42, exec. sec., 1946-49; mng. dir. Standard Packaging Inst., Orlando, Fla., 1937-39; v.p. sales Fungitrol div., Nuodex Products Co., Elizabeth, N.J., 1949-54; exec. v.p. Nat. Wooden Pallet Mfrs. Assn., Washington, 1954—; treas., dir. Suburbia Savs. & Loan Assn., Washington, 1960—; chmn. bd. Chevy Chase Travel, Inc., Bethesda, Md., 1973—. Pres., Springfield Civic Assn., 1959-60. Area chmn. Republican Party, Montgomery County, Md., 1963; chmn. 1st and 13th Precincts Montgomery County, 1953-63. Bd. dirs. Grocery Pallet Council, Chgo., 1973—; bd. govs. Gonzaga Coll. High Sch., Washington, 1973—. Served from ensign to lt. comdr. USNR. Fellow Brit. Inst. Dirs.; mem. Nat. Wood Council Washington (vice chmn. 1960-61, mem. exec. com. 1960-63), Am. Material Handling Soc. (dir. 1963-64), Am. Soc. Assn. Execs. Contbr. articles to various mags.

Home: 5504 Albia Rd Washington DC 20016 Office: 1619 Massachusetts Av NW Washington DC 20036

SARGENT, GORDON ALFRED, educator; b. Winterton, Eng., Apr. 8, 1938; s. Leslie William and Eleanor (Denniss) S.; B.Sc. in Engring., Imperial Coll. London U., 1960, Diploma, 1963, Ph.D., 1964; Asso., Royal Sch. Mines, 1960; m. Amy Therese Skinner, Sept. 17, 1966; children—Andrew, Mark, Maria, Anne, Adrian, Elizabeth. Came to U.S., 1962, naturalized, 1972. Fellow, Mellon Inst., Pitts., 1962-67; prof. engring. U. Ky., Lexington, 1967—. NSF grantee, 1973. Mem. Am. Soc. Metals. Contbr. articles on metallurgy and materials sci. to profl. jours. Office: U Ky Lexington KY

SARON, ROBERT, pharm. distbn. co. pres.; b. Bklyn., May 28, 1923; s. Jacob and Jennie (Stein) S.; B.S., Bklyn. Coll. Pharmacy, 1944; m. Sarah Black, Oct. 3, 1948; children—John Robert, William Kirk. Pharmacist, Webb's City dept. store, St. Petersburg, 1946-47; chief pharmacist Mound Park Hosp., St. Petersburg, Fla., 1948-56; founder, pres. Saron Pharmacal Corp., St. Petersburg, 1957—, Para-med. Enterprises holding co., St. Petersburg, 1968—; dir. Continental Bank Fla. Bd. dirs. Suncoast Heart Assn., St. Petersburg, St. Petersburg Sci. Center. Mem. Nat. Ethical Pharm. Assn., Am. Pharm. Assos., Am. Mgmt. Assn. (pres.'s assn.), Fla., St. Petersburg chambers commerce. Club: Fla. Contract Bridge League (pres. 1963, 70, dir.). Home: 8343 37th Av N St Petersburg FL 33710 Office: PO Box 13547 1640 Central Av St Petersburg FL 33733

SARRIS, CHARLES CHRIS, JR., marketing firm exec.; b. Gulfport, Miss., Dec. 23, 1924; s. Charles Chris and Ruby Eugenia (Wilder) S.; student Utah State U., 1943-44; B.A., Tulane U., 1949; m. Val Haydel, Jan. 15, 1947; children—Charles Chris, John Thomas, Terry Lynn, Robert Alan. Asso., C.H. Stout Co. Inc., 1950-58; owner Chris Sarris & Assos., 1958-70; pres., owner Derbes-Sarris and Assos., New Orleans, 1970—. Served with USMCR, 1943-45. Decorated Silver Star. Mem. Elec. Assn. New Orleans. Home: 523 Walker St New Orleans LA 70124 Office: 628 Papworth Ave Metairie LA 70005

SARRO, THOMAS PETER, lawyer; b. Jamestown, N.Y., Dec. 13, 1929; s. Peter V. and Theodhosia (Temos) S.; B.A., U. Rochester, 1952; LL.B., Georgetown Law Center, 1959; m. Mary Darke, Sept. 15, 1957; children—Kristine, Stephanie, Peter, Thea. Admitted to Va. bar 1961, D.C. bar 1962; practiced law in Washington, 1956-67; mem. firm Adam, Forward and McLean, Washington, 1956-67; partner firm Larson, Taylor & Hinds. Instr. Eastman Kodak Trainee Program, Washington, 1969—. Vice pres. Collingwood Citizen Assn., Va., 1969-70. Bd. dirs. Mt. Vernon Park Assn., Va., 1969-72. Served with AUS, 1952-54. Mem. Am., Va. bar assns., Bar Assn. D.C. (dir. 1972-73, chmn. patent, trademark and copyright 1971-72), Washington Patent Lawyers, Am. Patent Lawyers Assn. Home: 1212 Falster Rd Alexandria VA 22308 Office: 727 23rd St S Arlington VA 22202

SARTAIN, AARON QUINN, educator; b. Gibtown, Tex., Sept. 5, 1905; s. Lee Russell and Iva Jane (Heasley) S.; A.B., So. Meth. U., 1928; MA., 1930; Ph.D., U. Chgo., 1939; m. Thelma Wylie, June 12, 1930; children—Richard Wylie, Margaret Gwen, Barbara Susan. Prin. high sch., Hobbs, N.M., 1931-32; with So. Meth. U., Dallas, 1932—, from instr. to asso. prof. psychology, 1932-46, prof., 1946—, chmn. dept., 1946-52, chmn. dept. personnel adminstrn., 1947-59, prof. indsl. relations, 1959-71, emeritus, 1971—, dir. grad. studies dept. mgmt., 1959-63, dean Sch. Bus. Adminstrn., 1963-68. Mem. Am., S.W. psychol. assns., A.A.A.S., Phi Beta Kappa, Sigma Xi, Beta Gamma Sigma. Methodist. Author: (with W.W. Finlay and W.M. Tate) Human Behavior in Industry, 1954; (with others) Psychology: Understanding Human Behavior, 4th edit., 1973; (with Alton W. Baker) The Supervisor and His Job, 2d edit., 1972. Home: 3924 University Blvd Dallas TX 75205

SARVER, GEORGE LESLIE, electronic engr.; b. Smith Creek, Mich., July 12, 1927; s. Charles Leslie and Helen Beatrice (Lindquist) S.; B.S. in Agr. Edn., Mich. State U., 1951; B.S. in E.E., Air Force Inst. Tech., 1963; postgrad. George Washington U., 1971—; m. Priscilla Jeanne Robinson, Aug. 11, 1951; children—Cynthia J., Christopher C. Commd. 2d lt. USAF, 1951, advanced through grades to lt. col., 1968; ret., 1971; staff engr. Martin Marietta Corp., Denver, 1971-73; electronic engr. Western Union Telegraph Co., McLean, Va., 1973—. Pres., P.T.A., Plattsmouth, Neb., 1960-61. Decorated Legion of Merit. Registered profl. engr., Ohio. Mem. I.E.E.E., Alpha Zeta. Mason.

SASHOFF, STEPHAN P(ENCHEFF), educator; b. Drenovo, Bulgaria, Sept. 22, 1901; s. Pencho and Meta (Detcheva) S.; came to U.S., 1921, naturalized 1930; student Nat. Boys Gimnasium, Gabrovo, Bulgaria, 1915-20; B.S. in E.E., Purdue U., 1925; M.S., U. Pitts., 1929, pre-doctorate student, 1929-31; m. Zilla Bodie, Sept. 2, 1937 (dec. 1953); m. 2d, Elizabeth McCollum, Dec. 24, 1961. Research engr. Westinghouse Electric, Pitts., 1925-31; television research engr. RCA, Camden, N.J., 1931-32; asst. prof. elec. engring. U. Fla., Gainesville, 1932-37, grad. prof. elec. engring. 1951-72, emeritus, 1972—. Served as comdr. USNR, 1941-46. Received commendation from Sec. of Navy, 1945. Registered profl. engr., Fla. Mem. Am. Phys. Soc., Soc. Profl. Elec. Engrs., A.A.A.S., I.E.E.E., Fla. Acad. Sci. Sigma Xi, Sigma Tau. Democrat. Orthodox. Contbr. articles on electron tubes and circuits to profl. jours. Holder of patents and patent disclosures on electron tubes and circuits. Home: Rural Route 1 Box 303 Melrose FL 32666

SASLAW, MILTON SIBLEY, physician; b. Bklyn., May 1, 1911; s. Isidor and Esther (Wallach) S.; B.S., Washington Sq. Coll., N.Y. U., 1931; M.D., N.Y. U. and Bellevue Hosp. Med. Coll., 1934; M.P.H., U. Cal. at Los Angeles, 1967; m. Adeline Sokoloff, Apr. 28, 1937; children—Shari Lenore (Mrs. Esbitt), Gerald Evan. Intern North Hudson Hosp., Weehawken, N.J., 1934-35; pvt. practice internal medicine and cardiology, 1937-40, 46-51; dir. med. research Nat. Children's Cardiac Hosp., Miami, Fla., 1951-64; dir. research and epidemiology Dade County Dept. Pub. Health, Miami, 1965-67, asst. county health dir., 1967-69, dir., 1969—; research asso. prof. dept. microbiology, 1959, 60, clin. asso. prof. dept. preventive medicine Sch. Medicine, U. Miami, 1960-69, clin. prof. dept. epidemiology and pub. health, 1970—; sr. research scientist Grad. Sch. U. Miami, 1965; mem. dental program project com. Nat. Inst. Dental Research, 1965-69; cons. Dept. Health P.R.; spl. cons. USPHS. Pres. Heart Assn. Greater Miami, 1953-54; pres. Fla. Heart Assn., 1957-58; fellow council on Epidemiology, Am. Heart Assn., 1965; mem. Fla. Textbook Com. on Sci., 1964-66; chmn. health div. Welfare Planning Council, 1960-61; dir. Fla. Found. Future Scientists, Nat. Assn. Gifted Children; chmn. platform com. Fla. Cooperating Council on Children and Youth. Served as lt. col. M.C., AUS, World War II. Recipient citations Employ Physically Handicapped Miami C. of C., 1954, Nat. Employ The Physically Handicapped, Pres.'s Com., 1954. Fellow Am. Coll. Chest Physicians, Am. Coll. Cardiology (gov. Fla.), Am. Pub. Health Assn., Royal Soc. Health; mem. Dade County Med. Assn. (mem. pub. health adv. com.), Internat. Assn. for Dental Research Am. Soc. Microbiology. Author numerous Sci. publs. Home: 1420 S Bayshore Dr Miami FL 33131 Office: Dade County Dept Pub Health 1350 NW 14th St Miami FL 33125

SASS, META WHEELER, civic worker; b. Marion, S.C., d. Edward Blue and Meta (Nichols) Wheeler; student St. Mary's Coll., Raleigh, N.C., Converse Coll., 1947; m. Robert T. Snyder, Aug. 16, 1944 (dec. Apr. 1945); m. 2d, Fritz Norton Johnson, June 14, 1947 (div. Feb. 1970); children—Barbara Blue (Mrs. Charles Code Birch), Cherry Wheeler; m. 3d, Herbert Ravnel Sass, Nov. 10, 1972. Sales rep. Stevenson Zimmerman Devel. Corp., Charleston, S.C. Pres., Marion County Mental Health Soc., 1958-59; pres. Pee Dee area Med. Aux., 1955; co-chmn. S.C. Med. Aux. Conv., 1956, publicity chmn., 1957, 4th v.p., 1958-59, 3d v.p., 1960-61; troop leader Pee Dee council Girl Scouts U.S.A., 1962-66; sr. leader Snow Island Soc. Children Am. Revolution, 1968-70; chmn. 6th congl. dist. S.C. Gov.'s Mansion Commn. for restoring and furnishing mansion, 1965—; mem. staff Charleston Mus., 1970—; ways and means chmn. Ft. Sumter chpt. Am. Bus. Women's Assn. Chmn. S.C. Democratic Women's Council, Mullins, 1969-70. Mem. Mullins Garden Council (pres. 1957), Marion County Hist. Soc., D.A.R. Methodist (ch. circle chmn. 1958-70). Home: Atlantic St Charleston SC 29401

SASS, REED, ret. banker; b. Marietta, Okla., Mar. 24, 1908; s. Nathan and Lalla (Reed) S.; student Tex. Christian U., Ft. Worth, 1927-28, U. Mo., 1928-29, Jefferson Sch. Law, 1932; LL.B., North Tex. Sch. Law, 1934; m. Kathryn LaVerne Beck, Feb. 14, 1942; children—Sharon Leigh (Mrs. William L. Feather), Shelley Kay. With Ft. Worth Nat. Bank, 1926-73, successively messenger boy, clk., teller, various positions trust, advt. bus. devel. depts., asst. cashier, asst. v.p., 1926-51, v.p., dir. pub. relations and research dept., 1952-73; lectr. Sch. of Banking of South, La. State U.; lectr., thesis cons., examiner Stonier Grad. Sch. Banking, Rutgers U., S.W. Grad. Sch. Banking, So. Meth. U. Admitted to Tex. bar, 1935. Sec.-treas. Ft. Worth Clearing House Assn., 1958. Dir. Ft. Worth council Camp Fire Girls, 1956-59; trustee Tex. Boys Choir, 1960-73; exec. com. United Fund Tarrant County, 1961-62. Served from 2d to maj. USAAF, 1942-46. Mem. Bank Marketing Assn. (pres. 1959-60), Ft. Worth and Tarrant County Bar Assn., Am. Inst. Banking, Am. Bankers Assn. (chmn. pub. relations com. 1964-67), Ft. Worth C. of C. (bd. dirs. 1962-63), Downtown Ft. Worth Assn. (director 1957-61). Mem. Christian Ch. Club: Steeplechase. Contbr. articles banking publs. Home: 2717 Colonial Pkwy Fort Worth TX 76109

SASSER, DOROTHY PILLEY (MRS. JOHN T. SASSER), educator; b. Pantego, N.C., Aug. 15, 1926; d. Leonard R. and Mattie (Winfield) Pilley; B.S. in Secretarial Adminstrn., Woman's Coll. U. N.C., 1947; postgrad. U. Tenn., 1952; m. John T. Sasser, Dec. 30, 1951 children—Sandra, Sabrina. Co-owner, dir. Myrtle Beach (S.C.) Bus. Coll., 1952; owner Quality Mimeograph Shop, Whiteville, N.C., 1953—; tchr. pub. schs., Clarkton, N.C., 1953-57; tchr. Hallsboro (N.C.) Sch., 1957-59, Elizabethtown (N.C.) Sch., 1959, Alexander Graham Jr. High Sch., Fayetteville, N.C., 1960; chmn. bus. edn. dept. Terry Sanford Sr. High Sch., Fayetteville, 1961—. Mem. N.C. Edn. Assn., N.C., Nat., So. bus. edn. assns., Am. Vocational Assn., Bus. and Profl. Woman (corr. sec. 1958), Delta Kappa Gamma. Democrat. Presbyn. Clubs: Evening Garden (sec. 1957-58), Executives, Merrymakers (Elizabethtown). Home: 906 Emeline Av Fayetteville NC 28303 Office: Fort Bragg Rd Fayetteville NC 28303

SASSER, DOUGLAS REID, coll. adminstr.; b. Ga.; grad. Young Harris Coll., Ky. Wesleyan Coll., Columbia; postgrad. Emory U.; H.H.D., Ky. Wesleyan Coll., 1969; LL.D., Sch. of Ozarks, 1974; m. Trelle Joyner (dec. Nov. 1972); children—Julia Frances, Jennifer Lynn, Douglas Reid; m. 2d, Joanne Cartledge Kitchens, Apr. 19, 1974. Staff mem., dept. English, Ky. Wesleyan Coll., successively asst. to pres., dean students, v.p.; pres. Young Harris (Ga.) Coll., 1966-71; pres. Pfeiffer Coll., Misenheimer, N.C., 1971—. Chmn. regional bd. dirs. Appalachian Adult Basic Edn. Commn.; mem. exec. com. Coll. Coordinating Council, Western N.C. United Methodist Conf.; mem. commn. on ednl. credit Am. Council on Edn. Bd. dirs. Piedmont U. Center. Served with USNR, Korean war. Mem. Council Pvt. Colls. and Univs., Am. Assn. Jr. Colls., N.C. Assn. Ind. Colls. and Univs. (exec. com.), Albemarle-Stanly County C. of C., Phi Theta Kappa (hon. nat.), Alpha Kappa Psi, Phi Delta Sigma, Sigma Nu. Methodist. Rotarian. Clubs: Stanly County Country, Charlotte City. Office: Pfeiffer Coll Misenheimer NC 28109

SASSER, JOHN THOMAS, sch. adminstr.; b. Wilson, N.C., Apr. 6, 1923; s. James Tonkin and Bettie (Howell) S.; A.A., Mars Hill Coll., 1942; B.A., Wake Forest Coll., 1944, M.A., 1948; postgrad. U. N.C., 1950-51; m. Dorothy Pilley, Dec. 30, 1951; children—Sandra, Sabrina. Researcher Library of Congress, 1944; prin. Topsail Pub. Sch., Hampstead, N.C., 1944-47, Leaksville-Spray High Sch., Leaksville, N.C., 1947-51; pres. Myrtle Beach Bus. Coll., 1951-53; prin. Whiteville High Sch., Whiteville, N.C., 1953-59, Elizabethtown (N.C.) pub. schs., 1959-60, Terry Sanford Sr. High Sch., Fayetteville, 1960—. Mem. Nat. Assn. Secondary Sch. Prins., N.C. Prins. Assn., Nat. (life), N.C. (pres. Whiteville unit 1954-55) edn. assns., Horace Mann League Am. Presbyn. Rotarian (pres. 1957-58). Home: 906 Emeline Av Fayetteville NC 28303 Office: Fort Bragg Rd Fayetteville NC 28303

SASSER, TERRY J., real estate and investment exec.; b. Austin, Tex., Dec. 2, 1941; s. Sterling Joseph and Margret (Bryan) S.; student Concordia Luth. Coll., 1963, U. Tex.; grad. Nat. Assn. Mut. Agts. Sch., Oberlin Coll., 1963; m. Jannet Eloise Arbogust, Aug. 30, 1968; children—Jarrett Lamar, Mitchell Landon. With Sterling Sasser & Sons, Austin, 1963—, partner, 1965—, now v.p.; partner Sasser Properties, Austin, 1963—; gen. partner Sterling Investments Ltd., Mariposia Investments Ltd., Comml. Investors Ltd.; pres. Regency Sq. Properties, Inc., Financial Devel. Corp., Austin and Houston; v.p. Walter W. Scarborough Inc., Architects, Houston and Austin; dir. Cumberland Mgmt. Systems, Inc., Nashville and Houston, Cumberland Pub. and Recording Co., Inc., Nashville and Houston, Boma Bldg. Commodore Austin Aqua Festival, 1971, pres., 1972; chmn. bus. div. Cancer drive, Travis County, Tex., 1966; treas. Austin council U.S.O. Precinct chmn. Democratic party, 1966-67. Mem. Ins. Adv. Bd., Nat., Tex. assns. realtors, Nat. Assn. Mut. Ins. Agts., Sales and Marketing Execs. Internat. (blue ribbon com. 1969), Sales and Marketing Execs. Austin (pres. 1969-70), Mgmt. Assn. Austin. Clubs: Downtown Rotary, INS of Austin (founder 1974). Mem. editorial bd. Tex. Real Estate News. Contbr. articles to profl. jours. Home: 4528 Balcones Dr Austin TX 78753 Office: 719 W 6th St Austin TX 78701

SASTRY, BHAMIDIPATY VENKATA RAMA, educator; b. Rayavaram, India, Oct. 21, 1927; s. B.V. and B.S. (Lakshmi) Chandrasekharam; B.Sc. with honors, Andhara (India) U., 1949, M.Sc., 1950, D.Sc., 1956; M.S. (fellow), Emory U. 1959; Ph.D., Vanderbilt U., 1962; m. Annette Marie Kirchner, Dec. 28, 1968; children—William Sekar, Susan Marie. Came to U.S., 1956, naturalized, 1971. Lectr., Andhra U., Waltair, India, 1952-57; research asst., asst. fellow Emory U., Atlanta, 1957-59; mem. faculty Vanderbilt U., Nashville, 1959—, asso. prof. pharmacology, 1965-71, prof., 1971—. Fellow Royal Inst. Chemistry (London), Am. Inst. Chemistry; mem. Am. Soc. Pharmacology and Exptl. Therapeutics, Soc. Exptl. Biology and Medicine, Soc. Toxicology, Am. Soc. Nephrology, A.A.A.S., N.Y. Acad. Sci., Sigma Xi. Contbr. profl. jours. Home: 6412 Wildwood Valley Dr Brentwood TN 37027 Office: Dept Pharmacology Vanderbilt Univ School Medicine Nashville TN 37232

SATTERFIELD, DAVID EDWARD III, congressman; b. Richmond, Va., Dec. 2, 1920; s. David Edward, Jr. and Blanche (Kidd) S.; student U. Richmond, 1939-42; LL.B., U. Va., 1948; m. Anne Elizabeth Powell, Dec. 27, 1943; children—David Edward IV, John Bacon. Admitted to Va. bar, 1948, since practiced in Richmond; partner firm Satterfield, Haw, Anderson, Parkerson & Beazley; asst. U.S. atty. Eastern Dist. Va., 1950-53; councilman, City Richmond, 1954-56; mem. Va. Gen. Assembly from Richmond City, 1960-64; mem. 89th to 93d Congresses from 3d Dist. Va. Past. sec.-treas., dir. Richmond Baseball, Inc., The Virginians, A.A.A. baseball club of Internat. League. Served to lt., pilot, USNR, World War II: PTO; capt. Res. Decorated Purple Heart. Mem. Phi Gamma Delta, Phi Alpha Delta. Democrat. Mason (32 deg., Shriner). Home: 511 St Christopher's Rd Richmond VA 23226 Office: Federal Bldg Richmond VA 23290 also Cannon House Office Bldg Washington DC 20515

SATTERFIELD, ISAAC JOSEPH, chem. co. exec.; b. Salisbury, N.C., Dec. 26, 1929; s. McSwain and Julia (Chatfield) S.; B.S. in Chemistry, U. N.C., 1953; Ph.D. in Organic Chemistry, (Univ. fellow, Jefferson Chem. Co. fellow), U. Tex., 1958; m. Nancy Cunningham, July 26, 1957; children—Joseph, Mary, William, Julia, Carol. Research chemist Humble Oil & Refining Co., Baytown, Tex., 1958-63, sr. research chemist, 1963-66; research specialist Esso Research & Engring. Co., Baytown, 1966-71; account rep. plastics dept. Enjay Chem. Co., Houston, 1971-73; sr. account rep. plastics dept. Exxon Chem. Co., U.S.A., Houston, 1973—. Teaching fellow U. Tex., Austin, 1952-56; lectr. U. Houston, 1970. Mem. vis. com. Lee Coll., Baytown, 1968. Bd. dirs., chmn. bldg. com. Happy Harbor Methodist Home for Aged, LaPort, Tex., 1965-71. Mem. Am. Chem. Soc., Am. Inst. Chem. Engrs., Soc. Plastic Engrs., Alpha Chi Sigma, Phi Lambda Upsilon. Democrat. Episcopalian. Patentee in field. Home: 1504 Harold St Houston TX 77006 Office: Exxon Chemical Company USA Box 3272 Houston TX 77001

SATTERFIELD, JAMES MCSWAIN, govt. ofcl., aerospace engr.; b. Salisbury, N.C., Oct. 14, 1928; s. McSwain and Julia (Chatfield) S.; B.E.E., N.C. State U., 1949, M.E.E., 1963; m. Jacqueline Marie Creef, June 28, 1952; children—James McSwain, Georgielee Creef. Transmission engr. Carolina Tel. & Tel. Co., Tarboro, N.C., 1949-51; asso. engr. Indsl. Research Labs., Balt., 1953-55; engr. Hastings-Raydist, Inc., Hampton, Va., 1955-59; aerospace technologist NASA, 1959—, dep. div. chief, Flight support div. Johnson Space Center, Houston, 1971—. Space communications lectr. Dept. Def. Space Medicine Sch., Patrick AFB, Fla., 1961-62. Served to 1st lt. USAF, 1951-53. Recipient Am. Spirit Honor medal USAF, 1951; Superior Achievement award NASA, 1969, Apollo 7 Operations Team award, 1968, Outstanding Performance award, 1969, Exceptional Service medal, 1973, Apollo 15 TV Team award, 1971. Registered profl. engr., Tex. Mem. Sigma Phi Epsilon, Tau Beta Pi, Eta Kappa Nu., Phi Kappa Phi (hon.). Contbr. articles to profl. lit. Home: 1202 Woodbank Dr Seabrook TX 77586 Office: Johnson Space Center Houston TX 77058

SATTERWHITE, CECIL FRANKLIN, graphic arts co. exec.; b. Richmond, Va., Mar. 11, 1924; s. John Walton and Nettie Ester (Phillips) S.; grad. high sch.; m. Gloria Louise Stanley, Sept. 5, 1949. Supr. printing dept. U.S. Govt., Richmond, Ft. Monroe, Va., 1946-48; salesman, printer Riddick Advt. Co., Richmond, 1948-49; mgr. spl. service dept. Presbyn. Bd. Christian Edn., Richmond, 1949-53; founder Satterwhite Printing Co., Richmond, 1953, pres., 1953—. Field worker Heart Fund drive, 1966—, Arthritis Found., 1973—. Active local, fed. campaign hdqrs., Richmond, 1958—. Served with USNR, 1942-46; PTO, ETO. Recipient 3M Co. Printing Job of Year award, 1971. Mem. Printing Industries Am. (award of achievement 1973), Printing Industries Vas. (Dietz Meml. award 1960, dir.), Richmond Printers Assn., Richmond Club Printing House Craftsmen. Club: Bull and Bear, Richmond. Home: 8200 Gwinnett Rd Richmond VA 23229 Office: Carlton St Richmond VA 23230

SATTERWHITE, THOMAS BRANSCOMB, lawyer, farmer; b. Lexington, Ky., Oct 22, 1910; s. Thomas B. and Nanettte Stuart (Smith) S.; A.B., Swarthmore Coll., 1933; M.A., U. Ky., 1935, LL.B.; m. Barbara Jane Bennett, Oct. 28, 1944; children—Thomas B. III, Ann Bennett. Owner, operator Greenway Farm, Woodford County, Ky., 1946—; pres. Ball and Co., Lexington, 1957-61; dir. Sovereign Industries Inc., WLEX-TV, Inc. Prof. econs. Transylvania Coll. Trustee Shakertown at Pleasant Hill, Inc.; bd. visitors Guilford Coll. Served as lt. USNR, World War II. Mem. Ky. Hist. Soc., Am. Judicature Soc., Am., Ky., Fayette County bar assns., Audubon Soc., Cumberland Falls Preservation Assn. (sec.). Episcopalian, Club: Filson; Idle Hour Country (Lexington, Ky.); Wausaukee (Wis.); Iroquois Hunt, Chevy Chase (Washington). Address: Greenway Farm Versailles KY 40383

SAUCIER, SIDNEY PETER, aerospace engr.; b. Vicksburg, Miss., June 7, 1936; s. Sidney P. and Ophelia (Caston) S.; B.S., Miss. State U., 1959; student U. Ala. at Huntsville, 1959; m. Ann Jasper, July 12, 1958; children—Ann Marie, Patricia Dawn, Sidney John. Aerospace engr. flight systems NASA Marshall Space Flight Center, Ala., 1962—. Dir. Huntsville indsl. expansion com., 1971-72. Mem. Huntsville Air Pollution Control Bd., 1970—, Huntsville City Council, 1972—. Bd. dirs. Huntsville Jaycee Kidney Found., 1971—. Served to lt. USAF, 1959-62. Mem. Miss. State Alumni Assn., U.S. (dir., 1970-71, internat. senator), Ala. (v.p., 1969-70), Huntsville (pres., 1971-72), Jaycees, Huntsville C. of C. (dir., 1971-72), Pi Kappa Alpha. K.C. Home: 6705 Marsh Av Huntsville AL 35806 Office: Marshall Space Flight Center Marshall Space Flight Center AL 35812

SAUCIER, WALTER JOSEPH, educator; b. Moncla, La., Oct. 5, 1921; s. Louis E. and Sidonie (Moncla) S.; B.S., U. Southwestern La., 1942; S.M., U. Chgo., 1947, Ph.D., 1951; m. Helen A. Nobles, May 8, 1943; children—Walter Joseph, Susanne C., Diane H., Janine M., Gerard T., Laurence E., Loraine A. Asst., instr. meteorology U. Chgo., 1946-52; asst. prof. Tex. A. and M. U., 1952-54, asso. prof., 1954-58, prof. meteorology, 1958-60; prof. meteorology U. Okla., 1960-69, chmn. dept., 1965-68, dir. atmospheric research lab., 1960-68; prof. meteorology N.C. State U. at Raleigh, 1969—. Cons. World Book Ency., USAF, U.S. Army, NRC, Nat. Oceanic and Atmospheric Adminstrn.; trustee University Corp. Atmospheric Research, Boulder, Colo., 1967-69. Served to capt. USAAF, 1942-46; col. Res. Fellow A.A.A.S.; mem. Am. Meteorol. Soc. (bd. certified cons. meteorologists 1970—), Am. Geophys. Union, Sigma Xi. Author: Principles of Meteorological Analysis, 1955. Research in atmospheric circulation systems. Home: 2000 Hillock Dr Raleigh NC 27612

SAUER, LESTER MARTIN, banker; b. Michigan City, Ind., Sept. 24, 1920; s. O. Adelbert and Beata (Thieme) S.; B.S., U. Richmond, 1941; certificate in Prodn. Engring., Pa. State Coll., 1942; m. Elsie E. Ellington, Apr. 19, 1947; children—Richard, Mark, Martha. With First & Mchts. Nat. Bank, Richmond, Va., 1942—, asst. cashier, 1955-61, asst. v.p., 1961-66, v.p., 1966-71, sr. v.p., 1971—; mem. faculty Va.-Md. Sch. Bank Mgmt., Charlottesville, 1967—. Pres. Civic Assn., 1966; treas. Luther Meml. Sch., 1966—; pres. Chamberlayne Laburnum Athletic Assn., 1968; dist. dir. Boy Scouts Am., 1968. Bd. dirs. Bethlehem Lutheran Found. Mem. Am. Statis. Assn., Nat.

Financial Analysts Fedn. (v.p.), Inst. Chartered Financial Analysts, Am. Assn. Bus. Economists, Am. Inst. Banking (past pres. Richmond), Richmond Financial Analysts (past pres.). Lutheran. Home: 308 Burnwick Rd Richmond VA 23227 Office: 827 E Main St Richmond VA 23217

SAUFLEY, ZACK CHURCH, banker; b. Stanford, Ky., Aug. 1, 1930; s. Henry Rowan and Jessamine Lee (Church) S.; student Va. Mil. Inst., 1949; B.S., U. Ky., 1955, M.S., 1957; m. Yvonne Yates, Mar. 1, 1953; children—Jessamine, Church, Claire, Carrie, Jennifer. Extension specialist U. Ky., Lexington, 1957-71; dir. Farmers Bank & Capital Trust Co., Frankfort, Ky., 1969—, v.p., 1971—. Mem. Frankfort Bd. Realtors. Bd. dirs., v.p. Frankfort Big Bros., Frankfort Habilation, Inc.; dist. dir. Boy Scouts Am. Served to capt. U.S. Army, 1952-54, 61; col. Res. Mem. Ky. Bankers Assn., Frankfort C. of C. (dir.), Ky. Farm Bur. Mgrs. and Rural Appraisers (v.p. 1966-67), Res. Officers Assn. Presbyn. (deacon). Rotarian. Clubs: Frankfort Country; Lafayette (Lexington). Home: Peaks Mill Rd Frankfort KY 40601 Office: Farmers Bank Plaza Frankfort KY 40601

SAUNDERS, CALVIN DUANE, petroleum prodn. co. exec.; b. Norfolk, Neb., Aug. 31, 1921; s. George Edward and Bertha (Fisher) S.; B.Chem. Engring., U. Okla., 1943; m. Bobbie Louise Curtess, May 16, 1943; children—Barbara (Mrs. William Walter Landholt), Jana (Mrs. Jesse Elmo Vincent). Engr. Halliburton Services div. Halliburton Co., Duncan, Okla., 1946-48, research supr., 1948-59, asst. mgr. chem. research, 1959-71, mgr. research, 1971—. Pres. Okla. U. Research Inst. Vice-pres., bd. dirs. Frontiers of Sci. Found. Okla.; bd. dirs. Mid Continent Environmental Center Assn. Served with AUS, 1943-46. Mem. Am. Petroleum Inst., Soc. Petroleum Engrs. of Am. Inst. Mining, Metall. and Petroleum Engrs. Elk. Contbr. articles to profl. jours. Home: 901 Highland Av Duncan OK 73533 Office: Box 1431 Duncan OK 73533

SAUNDERS, CHARLES BASKERVILLE, JR., govt. ofcl.; b. Boston, Dec. 26, 1928; s. Charles Baskerville and Lucy (Carmichael) S.; grad. St. Marks Sch., 1946; A.B., Princeton, 1950; m. Margaret MacIntire Shafer, Sept. 9, 1950: children—Charles Baskerville III, George Carlton, Margaret Keyser, Lucy Carmichael, John Rolfe. News reporter, polit. columnist Ogdensburg (N.Y.) Jour., 1950-51; edn. reporter Hartford (Conn.) Times, 1951-53; asst. dir. pub. relations Trinity Coll., Hartford, 1953-55; asst. dir. pub. information Princeton, 1955-57; legislative asst. Sen. H. Alexander Smith, 85th Congress, 1957-58; asst. to asst. sec. for legislation U.S. Dept. Health, Edn. and Welfare, 1958-59, adminstrv. asst. to sec., 1959-61, dep. asst. sec. for legislation U.S. Dept. Health, Edn. and Welfare, 1969-71, dep. commr. for external relations U.S. Office of Edn., 1971-73, dep. asst. sec. for edn., 1973—; asst. to pres. The Brookings Instn., 1961-69. Mem. Montgomery County Bd. Edn., 1966-70. Trustee Montgomery Coll., 1969-70. Republican. Presbyn. Club: University Cottage. Author: The Brookings Institution: A Fifty-Year History, 1966; Upgrading The American Police: Education and Training for Better Law Enforcement, 1970. Home: 7622 Winterberry Pl Bethesda MD 20034 Office: 400 Maryland Av SW Washington DC 20003

SAUNDERS, CLAY NEBHUT, lawyer; b. Memphis, Oct. 10, 1939; s. Shirley Nebhut and Irene (Boyd) S.; B.A., Memphis State U., 1961; J.S., U. Tenn., 1964; m. Erma Jean Awalt, Nov. 28, 1964; children—Clay Nebhut, Allyson Lowe. Researcher, writer FBI, Washington, 1961-62; admitted to Tenn. bar, 1964; law clk. U.S. Dist. Judge Marion Boyd, Memphis, 1964-65; asst. dist. atty. gen. 13th Jud. Dist. Tenn., Memphis, 1965-68; mem. firm Pittman, Clay, Morgan, Cole & Gilliland, Memphis, 1968—. Transp. counsel Nat. Cotton Council Am., 1972—. Mem. Phi Delta Phi. Republican. Home: 348 Greenway Rd Memphis TN 38117 Office: 2700 Sterick Bldg Memphis TN 38103

SAUNDERS, DONALD EUGENE, steel co. exec.; b. Enid, Okla., Mar. 14, 1924; s. Russell John and Mabel Henrietta (Anderson) S.; grad. high sch.; m. Phyllis DeMar Barber, Aug. 4, 1946; children—Diane Michele (Mrs. Michael Lynn Haxel), Lynda Dawn (Mrs. Gary Michael Henry). Draftsman, W & W Steel Co., Oklahoma City, 1946-54; with Ceco Corp., Oklahoma City, 1954—, dist. mgr. 1971—. Mem. adv. com. Okla. State U. Tech. Sch., 1974—. Served with USNR, 1942-46. Mem. Am. Concrete Inst. (dir. 1974—), Oklahoma City C. of C. Mason (32 deg.). Home: 3008 Center St Village OK 73120 Office: 7401 N Broadway Oklahoma City OK 73114

SAUNDERS, HAROLD HENRY, govt. ofcl.; b. Phila., Dec. 27, 1930; s. Harold Manuel and Marian (Weihenmayer) S.; A.B. magna cum laude, Princeton, 1952; Ph.D., Yale, 1956; m. Barbara Ann McGarrigle, May 4, 1963 (dec. Oct. 1973); children—Catherine Elizabeth, Mark Harril. Asst. to dean of freshmen Yale, 1955-56; lectr. U.S. history Coll. Gen. Studies, George Washington U., 1959-61, 63-65; with CIA, 1959-61; with Nat. Security Council, White House, Washington, 1961-74, sr. staff mem., 1967-74; dep. asst. sec. state for Near East and South Asian affairs, 1974—. Served to 1st lt. USAF, 1956-59. Mem. Am. Hist. Assn., Phi Beta Kappa. Presbyn. Home: 2119 Great Falls St Falls Church VA 22043 Office: Dept State Washington DC 20515

SAUNDERS, MAURICE MONROE, physicist; b. Pampa, Tex., June 28, 1918; s. James Muse and Margaret Elizabeth (Benton) S.; student Mass. Inst. Tech., 1939-41; B.S. in Physics, St. Mary's U., 1962; m. Florence Tokar, June 28, 1939; children—Reynolds James, Mark Philip, Eileen Cecilia, Patricia Ann. Farmer, Uvalde, Tex., 1946-56; partner House of Photography, Uvalde, 1948-55; mgmt. analyst USAF, Kelly AFB, Tex., 1962-63; physicist USAF Sch. Aerospace Medicine, Brooks AFB, Tex., 1963-68; cons. physicist, investment analyst, San Antonio, 1968—; prodn. supr. electronics div. Insp. Equipment Mfg. Corp., San Antonio, 1973-74. Lectr. on stock market investment and trading techniques, 1969—. Served with AUS, 1943-46. Mem. I.E.E.E., Am. Assn. Physics Tchrs., Nat. Council Math. Tchrs., Math. Assn. Am., Nat. Rifle Assn., Mensa. Address: 102 Lochaven Lane San Antonio TX 78213

SAUNDERS, RALPH L., newspaper bus. exec.; b. Roanoke, Va., Apr. 16, 1933; s. Hammett L. and Lena (Pasley); B.S. in Bus. Adminstrn., Va. Poly. Inst., 1959-3m. Barbara Sanders, Sept. 13, 1958; children—Kevin, Scott, Karen, Steve. Asst. controller Washington Star, 1961-65; bus. mgr. Nashville (Tenn.) Tennessean, 1965—, treas., 1967—. Served with AUS, 1953-55. C.P.A., Tenn. Mem. Am. Inst. C.P.A.'s, Tenn. Soc. C.P.A.'s. Kiwanian. Home: 219 La Vista Dr Nashville TN 37215 Office: 1100 Broadway St Nashville TN 37203

SAVAGE, WILLIAM FREDERICK, govt. ofcl.; b. Anchorage, May 23, 1923; s. Gordon Prescott and Josephine Isabelle (Smith) S.; B.Aero. Engring., Rensselaer Poly. Inst., 1943; M.S. in Aero. Engring., Purdue U., 1949; grad. Oak Ridge Sch. Reactor Tech., 1958, Fed. Exec. Inst., 1968; m. Mary Helen Carter, June 25, 1949; children—Kathleen, William. Aerodynamacisit Convair, Fort Worth, 1944-46; asst. prof. U. Ky. at Lexington, 1946-52; chief engr. Kett Corp., Cin., 1952-55; mgr. Gen. Electric, Cin., 1955-60; dir. corp. office Martin Marietta, Balt., 1961-67; asst. dir. Office Saline Water, Dept. Interior, Washington, 1967—. Registered profl. engr., Ohio. Mem. Am. Soc. M.E., Am. Nuclear Soc., Sigma Xi, Pi Tau Sigma. Methodist. Home: 8025 Garlot Dr Annandale VA 22003 Office: Dept Interior Office Saline Water Washington DC 20240

SAVAGE, WILLIAM WOODROW, educator; b. Onley, Va., Jan. 9, 1914; s. Frank Howard and Florence Elmira (Twyford) S.; A.B., Coll. William and Mary, 1937; M.A., U. Chgo., 1946, Ph.D., 1955; student U. Va., summer 1951; m. Margaret Jane Clarke; children—Earl R., William W. Research editor, div. rural research Fed. Emergency Relief Adminstrn., Richmond, Va., 1935-36; div. mgr. Montgomery Ward & Co., Newport News, Va., 1937-38; statis. worker WPA, Richmond, 1938-39; counselor Va. Consultation Service, Richmond, 1939-42, acting dir., 1942-45; asst. state supr. guidance and consultation services Va. Dept. Edn., 1946-47; dean Longwood Coll., Farmville, Va., 1947-52; project coordinator, asso. dir. Midwest Adminstrn. Center, U. Chgo., 1952-56; dean Coll. Edn., U. S.C., 1956-65, prof. edn., 1965—, curator mus. of edn., 1973—. Mem. visitation and appraisal com. Nat. Council Accreditation Tchr. Edn., 1964-67. Mem. Am. Assn. Sch. Adminstrs. (mem. com. advancement sch. adminstrn., 1955-56), Am. Assn. U. Profs., Phi Delta Kappa. Methodist (ofcl. bd.). Club: Executives (Columbia). Co-author: Readings in American Education, 1963. Author: Interpersonal and Group Relations in Educational Administration, 1968. Editor: Work and Training, monthly Va. Bd. Edn., 1941-47, Administrator's Notebook, monthly Midwest Adminstrn. Center, 1954-56, U. S.C. Edn. Report, 1957—; adv. com. Sch. Rev., 1954-56. Contbr. articles various jours. Home: 6316 Eastshore Rd Columbia SC 29206

SAVELL, LASLEY BERNARD, hosp. exec.; b. Girard, La., Dec. 3, 1934; s. Jesse James and Eunice (McGowan) S.; B.Music, Memphis State U., 1961-66; student Academia Musicale Chiqaua (Italy), 1964, U. Ala., 1970; m. Sara Ann Tanksley, Nov. 21, 1957; 1 dau., Amy Lynn. With Methodist Hosp., Memphis, 1966—, dir. pub. relations, 1967—. Chmn. Memphis Bd. Rev., 1971—. Bd. dirs. Mid-South Eye Bank. Mem. Tenn. Hosp. Assn. (chmn. pub. relations adv. com.). Bass-baritone Memphis Opera Theatre, 1960—. Home: 1582 Whitten Rd Memphis TN 38128 Office: 1265 Union Av Memphis TN 38104

SAVERANCE, CLIFTON R., supt. schs.; b. Bethune, S.C., Sept. 16, 1913; s. Junius Edwin and Beulah I. (Carter) S.; B.S., Clemson U., 1938; M.Ed., U. S.C., 1955; m. Martha Augusta Godbold, June 16, 1939; children—Clifton R., Robert Edwin. Tchr., Williamsburg County Schs., Hemingway, S.C., 1938-42; tchr. Lamar (S.C.) Schs., 1946-50, prin., 1953-57; supt. Hemingway Area Schs., 1957-68, Lamar (S.C.) Schs., 1968—. Served to maj., inf. AUS, 1942-46; PTO; 1950-52. Mem. S.C., Am. assns. sch. adminstrs., S.C., Darlington County, Williamsburg County edn. assns., Internat. Platform Assn., Forty and Eight, Am. Legion, Alpha Tau Alpha. Prsbyn. Mason. Club: Civitan (Lamar). Home: Box 603 Lamar SC 29069

SAVERIANO, GENNARRINO JAMES, pipe fabrication mfg. co. exec.; b. Paterson, N.J., Sept. 28, 1922; s. Joseph and Josephine Aurora (Fuduli) S.; B.S. magna cum laude in Indsl. Mgmt., Fairleigh Dickinson U., 1954; m. Margaret Burge, Apr. 21, 1945; 1 dau., Toni. Asst. dir. marketing Wright Aero. div. Curtiss-Wright, Woodridge, N.J., 1951-62; v.p., dir. operations ITT Def. Communications Div., Nutley, N.J., 1963-72; pres., gen. mgr. ITT Grinnell Indsl. Piping, Inc., Kernersville, N.C., 1973—. Chmn. bd. Recreational and Ednl. Mgmt. Corp.; pres., trustee Childhood Inst. Learning, Wayne, N.J. Served as pilot USAF, 1943-45. Mem. Phi Zeta Kappa, Phi Omega Epsilon. Home: 45 L Vinegar Hill Dr Greensboro NC 27470 Office: PO Box 566 Kernersville NC 27284

SAVINS, JOSEPH GEORGE, chemist; b. Fort Sill, Okla., Aug. 15, 1925; s. George Francis and Herlinda (Chavez) S.; B.S. in Chemistry, Tex. A. and M. U., 1949; m. Jeannette (Hastings), June 24, 1950; children—George, Michael, James, Matthew, Richard, Timothy, Eric. Jr. chemist Magnolia Petroleum Co., Dallas, 1949-52; research chemist Socony Mobil Oil Corp., Dallas, 1952-56, sr. research chemist, 1956-62; research asso. Mobil Research & Devel. Corp., Dallas, 1962—. Asst. editor Transactions Soc. Rheology, 1969—; mem. profl. accrediting com. Tex. Inst. Chemists; vis. lectr. dept. petroleum engring. Stanford, 1972. Served with AUS, 1943-46. Fellow Am. Inst. Chemists, (profl. accredited chemist); mem. Am. Inst. Chem. Engrs., Soc. Rheology, Soc. Natural Philosophy, Tex. Inst. Chemists, Brit. Soc. Rheology, Am. Gas. Assn. (mem. supervising pipeline research com.). Contbr. articles to profl. jours. Patentee in field. Home: 1828 Shady Glen Lane Dallas TX 75232 Office: PO Box 900 Dallas TX 75221

SAVIT, CARL HERTZ, geophysicist; b. N.Y.C., July 19, 1922; B.S. with honors, Cal. Inst. Tech., 1942, M.S., 1943, postgrad. also teaching fellow in advanced math. 1943-44, 46-48; m. 1946; three children. Statis. cons. Long Range Meteorology Project USAF, 1943-44; asso. prof. math. San Fernando Valley (Cal.) State Coll., 1959-60; chief mathematician Western Geophys. Co., Litton Industries, Inc., 1948-60, dir. systems research, 1960-65, v.p. systems research devel. 1965-70, sr. v.p. tech., 1971—; asst. for earth, sea, air scis. to U.S. Pres.'s Sci. Adv.; chmn. Interagy. Com. for Atmospheric Scis., 1970-71; mem. panel On-Site Inspection Unidentified Seismec Events, Disposition of Oil Leasing in the Santa Barbara Channel, Offshore Pollution, U.S. Initiatives in Transp., 1971; mem. com. on Seismology Nat. Acad. Scis.-NRC, 1971—, chmn., 1972—; mem. U.S. nat. com. on tunneling Nat. Acad. Scis.-NRC, 1972—, chmn. subcom. on tech. data and information, 1972—, mem. panel on earthquake prediction, 1973—; dir. Nat. Ocean Industries Assn., vice chmn. bd., 1973—; mem. nat. adv. council Tex. Marine Biomed. Inst., 1973—. Served as 2d lt. USAAF, 1944-46. Fellow Geol. Soc. Am.; mem. Assn. Earth Sci. Editors, European Assn. Exploration Geophysicists, Associacion Mexicana de Geofisicos de Exploracion, Marine Tech. Soc., Am. Petroleum Inst., Soc. Exploration Geophysicists (named Classic Author of Geophysics 1960, editor jour. 1968-69, del. to USSR 1971, pres. 1971-72, chmn. 43d ann. meeting 1973), Am. Mgmt. Assn. (mem. research and devel. council 1974—), Internat. Assn. Geophys. Contractors (pres. 1973—), Sigma Xi. Club: Cosmos. Address: 13626 Tosca Lane Houston TX 77024

SAWYER, FLOYD DANIEL, coll. adminstr.; b. Durham, N.C., Jan. 17, 1929; s. Charles Franklin and Blanche Anne (Wright) S.; B.A., Duke, 1959; postgrad. U. Ky., 1967-70; m. Marion Florence Buttry, June 11, 1950; children—Floyd Daniel, Sharon Kay, Timothy Douglas. Chief accountant Duke, 1959-67; v.p. bus., treas. N.C. Wesleyan Coll., Rocky Mount, 1967—. Active Travel Council. Bd. dirs. United Fund. Served with C.E., AUS, 1952-54. Decorated Army Commendation medal. Mem. Nat. Auditors Coll. and Univ., Coll. and Univ. Personnel Assn., Nat. Assn. Coll. and U. Bus. Officers, So. Assn. Coll. and Univ. Bus. Officers, Ednl. and Instl. Inst., C. of C. (mem. edn. com. 1969-72), mem. task force civic center 1973-74), Nat. Assn. Ednl. Buyers. Methodist (finance chmn. 1970-74). Kiwanian (dir. 1969-74, Distinguished Mem. award 1973). Home: 1200 West Haven Blvd Rocky Mount NC 27801

SAWYER, HENRY VERNON, optometrist; b. Mullins, S.C., Aug. 23, 1918; s. Henry Dozier and Mertie Vera (Wiggins) S.; Dr. Optometry, So. Coll. Optometry, 1951; m. Lucia Gwendolyn Rowell, Dec. 18, 1943; children—Gwen Anne (Mrs. F.P. Owens), Henry V., Linda Gail (Mrs. James T. Hollis), Thomas Allen. Practice optometry, Marion, S.C., 1951—. Councilman, Marion, S.C., 1957—; county chmn. Nat. Found. Infantile Paralysis, 1955-56; dir. United Fund, 1959-66; pres. Marion United Fund. Served to capt. AUS, 1941-46. Named Young Man of Yr., 1954. Fellow Am. Acad. Optometry; mem. S.C., (pres. 1960), Pee Dee (pres. 1954) optometric assns., So. Council Optometrists (pres. elect 1963, pres. 1965), S.C. Recreation Soc., Am. Legion (comdr. local post), V.F.W., C. of C., Farm Bur. Baptist. Lion (pres. chpt. 1970-71). Home: 213 W Mullins St Marion SC 29571 Office: Corner Academy and W Dozier Sts Marion SC 29571

SAWYER, RANDALL ALEXANDER, clergyman; b. St. Joseph, Mo., Mar. 30, 1939; s. Ralph Alexander and Juanita Vadna (Adams) S.; B.A., Tex. Christian U., 1966; M.Div., Brite Div. Sch., 1969; m. Donna Marian Dwyer, July 11, 1964; children—Rodney, Dana. Ordained to ministry Christian Ch., 1968; asso. minister First Christian Ch., Port Arthur, Tex., 1969-71; minister First Christian Ch., Rogers, Ark., 1971—. Mem. Benton County (Ark.) Democratic Com., 1972—. Served with U.S. Army, 1962-64. Mason, Lion. Home: 1211 W Cherry St Rogers AR 72756 Office: 905 S 13th St Rogers AR 72756

SAWYER, WARREN ALLEN, librarian; b. Bay Shore, N.Y., June 22, 1937; s. George John and Thelma (Caldwell) S.; B.S., Hampden-Sydney Coll., 1959; M.S. in Library Sci., U. N.C., 1961; m. Judith Alvord Littlepage, Jan. 25, 1958; children—Anne Louise, Angus Caldwell. Librarian Augusta Mil. Acad., Fort Defiance, Va., 1964-66, Coll. Charleston (S.C.), 1966-68; dir. libraries Med. U. S.C., 1968—, and Coll. Charleston, 1970—. Served with AUS, 1962-64. Mem. Am., Med., S.C., Southeastern library assns., Am. Assn. U. Profs. Home: 27 Gadsden St Charleston SC 29401 Office: 80 Barre St Charleston SC 29401

SAWYERS, JOHN LAZELLE, physician; b. Centerville, Ia., July 26, 1925; s. Francis Lazelle and Almira (Baker) S.; A.B., U. Rochester, 1946; M.D., Johns Hopkins, 1949; m. Julia Edwards, May 25, 1957; children—Charles Lazelle, Al Baker, Julia Edwards. House officer surgery Johns Hopkins Hosp., Balt., 1949-50; asst. resident, resident in surgery Vanderbilt U. Hosp., Nashville, 1953-58; practice medicine specializing in surgery, Nashville, 1958—; surgeon Edwards-Eve Clinic, 1958-60; chief surg. service Nashville Gen. Hosp., 1960—; prof. surgery Vanderbilt U. Bd. dirs. Davidson County unit Am. Cancer Soc. Served from lt. (j.g.) to lt., M.C., USNR, 1950-52. Diplomate Am. Bd. Surgery, Am. Bd. Thoracic Surgery. Fellow A.C.S.; mem. Am. Surg. Assn. Home: 403 Ellendale Dr Nashville TN 37205 Office: Gen Hosp Nashville TN 37210

SAX, NEWTON IRVING, cons. health physicist; b. Albany, N.Y., May 12, 1914; s. Louis and Anna (Mereberg) S.; B.S., Rensselaer Poly. Inst., 1936; m. Paula Birgbenthal, Jan. 11, 1942; children—Susan (Mrs. Arthur Poremba, Jr.), Jana (Mrs. Ira Chip Lupu). Engr., chemist Gen. Electric Co., Schenectady, 1940-52; chemist health and safety lab. AEC, N.Y.C., 1952-55; dir. safety and mgr. chemistry Nuclear Devel. Assn., White Plains, N.Y., 1955-58; dir. radio scis. lab. N.Y. Dept. Health, Albany, 1958-69; pres., dir. Cambridge Tech., Inc., Newton Upper Falls, Mass., 1969-70; cons. occupational health and indsl. pollution, Boca Raton, Fla., 1972—. Adj. prof. bioenvironmental engring. Rensselaer Poly. Inst., Troy, N.Y., 1971-72. USPHS grantee, 1961-68. Fellow Am. Inst. Chemists; mem. Fedn. Am. Scientists, Am. Indsl. Hygiene Assn., Health Physics Soc., Sci. Inst. Pub. Information, Friends of Earth, Royal Soc. Health. Author: Handbook of Dangerous Materials, 1951; Dangerous Properties of Industrial Materials, 1957, 3d edit., 1968. Address: 7 Royal Palm Way Boca Raton FL 33432

SAXBE, WILLIAM B., atty. gen. U.S.; b. Mechanicsburg, O., June 24, 1916; s. Bart Rockwell and Faye Henry (Carey) S.; A.B., Ohio State U., 1940, LL.B., 1948; hon. degrees Central State U., Findlay Coll., Ohio Wesleyan U., Walsh Coll., Capital U., Wilmington Coll.; m. Ardath Louise Kleinhans, Sept. 14, 1940; children—William Bart, Juliet Louise (Mrs. Charles S. Lopeman), Charles Rockwell. Admitted to Ohio bar, 1948; practiced in Mechanicsburg, 1948-55; partner firm Saxbe, Boyd & Prine, 1955-58; mem. Ohio Gen. Assembly, 1947-48, 49-50, majority leader Ho. Reps., 1951-52, speaker, 1953-54; atty. gen., Ohio, 1957-58, 63-68; partner firm Dargusch, Saxbe & Dargusch, 1960-63; mem. U.S. Senate from Ohio, 1969-74; atty. gen. U.S., 1974—. Served with 107th Cav., AUS, 1940-42, USAAF, 1942-45; col. Res. Mem. Am., Ohio bar assns., Am. Judicature Soc., Chi Phi, Phi Delta Phi. Republican. Episcopalian. Mason. Clubs: University, Columbus Athletic, Columbus, Scioto Country (Columbus); Urbana (O.) Country; Burning Tree Country (Bethesda, Md.). Home: Route 2 Mechanicsburg OH 43044 Office: Dept Justice Washington DC 20530

SAXENA, DHIRENDRA SWARUP, engring. testing co. exec.; b. Allahabad, India, June 11, 1940; s. Mahesh Swarup and Omwati (Verma) S.; B.S., U. Allahabad, 1958; B.Tech. (honors), Indian Inst. Tech. (Kharagpur), 1962; M.Engring. in Civil Engring. (NRC Can. grantee 1966-67), Nova Scotia Tech. Coll. (Halifax, Can.), 1968; m. Urmila Saxena, Feb. 4, 1964; children—Anupam, Jayant. Came to U.S., 1969. Civil engr. Heavy Engring. Corp. Ltd., Ranchi, India, 1962-66; soils engr. firm Dames & Moore, Toronto, Ont., Can., 1967-69; sr. soils engr. Internat. Minerals & Chem. Corp., Bartow, Fla., 1969-70; sr. engr. Woodward-ETCO & Assos., Houston, 1970-73; v.p. geotech. engring. operations Harlan Engring. Labs. Inc., Lakeland, Fla., 1973—. Registered profl. engr., Tenn., Tex., Ont. Mem. Am. Soc. C.E. (mem. nat. soil dynamics com. 1972—), Nat. (membership com. 1971-72), Tex. (named outstanding engr. year 1972), socs. profl. engrs., Am. Soc. Mining Engrs., Am. Soc. Testing Materials, Canadian Soc. Civil Engrs., Fla. Engring. Soc. Lion. Home: 2920 Willow Av Lakeland FL 33803 Office: PO Box 2657 Lakeland FL 33803

SAXTON, JAMES CUMMINGS, chem. engr.; b. Pitts., Dec. 5, 1936; s. James Allen and Margaret Mary (Helsol) S.; student Princeton, 1954-57; B.E.S., Johns Hopkins, 1959; Ph.D., U. Cal. at Berkeley, 1966; postgrad. econs. Va. Poly. Inst., 1973—; m. Carolyn Alice Cummings, Aug. 22, 1959; children—Megan Alicia, James Allen III, Jennifer Aine. Supr., Bellcomm, Inc., Washington, 1964-71; dir. engring. Internat. Research & Technol. Corp., Arlington, Va., 1971—. Recipient Achievement award NASA, 1970, Bellcomm, 1970. Fellow Am. Inst. Chemists; mem. Am. Inst. Chem. Engrs., A.A.A.S., D.C. Soc. Profl. Engrs., Common Cause, Am. Civil Liberties Union. Unitarian. Democrat. Home: 11472 Orchard Lane Reston VA 22090 Office: Internat Research and Technology Corp 1501 Wilson Blvd Arlington VA 22209

SAYAS, HERBERT LOUIS II, educator; b. New Orleans, Dec. 5, 1936; s. Herbert Louis and Louise (Berger) S.; B.A., U. S.W. La., 1959; M.A., U. Denver, 1961; postgrad. U. Ind., 1963-65; m. Ann Bentley Wilson, Aug. 17, 1964; 1 son, Herbert Louis III. Asst. prof. dept. speech, theatre State U. N.Y. at Brockport, 1964-65, Benedict Coll., Columbia, 1967-68, So. Univ., Baton Rouge, 1968—. Mem. architecture com. Baton Rouge Civic Theatre, 1972-73. Mem. Common Cause, 1973—. Active Democratic party. Served with AUS, 1961-63. Mem. Children's Theater Conf., Speech Communications Assn., Am. Theatre Assn., U.S. Inst. Theatre Technicians, S.W.

Theatre Conf. Home: 825 Albert Hart Dr Baton Rouge LA 70808 Office: Dept Speech and Theatre So Univ Baton Rouge LA 70813

SAYE, JAMES ANGUS, JR., advt. agcy. exec.; b. Montezuma, Ga., Apr. 4, 1929; s. James A. and Muriel (Heard) S.; B.A., Emory U., 1951; B.A., U. Ga., 1954; m. Geraldyne A. Whitfield, Apr. 18, 1956; children—James A. III, Timothy D. Advt. asst. Atlanta Gas Light Co., 1954-55; account exec. McCann-Erickson, Inc., Houston, 1955-60, Rives-Dyke & Co., Houston, 1960-61, Robinson-Gerrard, Inc., Houston, 1961-66; pres., founder Star Advt. Agy., Houston, 1966—. Publicity chmn. Harris County delegation Tex. Democratic Conv., 1962; precinct chmn. Republican party, Goldwater for Pres., 1964; del. Tex. Rep. Conv., 1972. Served to lt. (j.g.), USNR, 1951-53. Recipient award for best indsl. direct mail campaign, 1968; honor certificate award Freedoms Found., 1972. Mem. Am. Legion, S.C.V. (camp comdr. 1973), Order of Stars and Bars (comdr. Tex. chpt. 1972), Houston Advt. Club (Best Indsl. Ad award 1958), Alpha Delta Sigma, Sigma Chi Alumni Assn. Republican. Baptist. Club: (Houston). Home: 4931 Jason St Houston TX 77035 Office: 3501 W Alabama St Houston TX 77027

SAYEGH, SALEM FATHI, surgeon, educator; b. Mosul, Iraq, May 17, 1921; s. Fathi A. and Amina (Khalil) S.; M.D., Royal Coll. Medicine, Baghdad, Iraq, 1946; postgrad. Tulane U., 1952-55; m. Myrl A. Jagot, Nov. 23, 1958; children—Linda, David, Lisa. Came to U.S., 1952; naturalized, 1960. Intern Royal Teaching Hosp., Baghdad, Iraq, 1946-47; resident Ochsner Found. Hosp., New Orleans, 1952-55; asso. prof. surgery La. State U. Med. Sch., New Orleans, 1968—; mem. staff VA Hosp., New Orleans, 1960—, chief thoracic and cardiovascular surgery sect., 1960—. Served to capt., Iraqi Army, 1947-49. Diplomate Am. Bd. Thoracic Surgery, Am. Bd. Gen. Surgery. Mem. A.C.S., Am. Coll. Chest Physicians, Southeastern Surg. Congress, New Orleans Surg. Soc., Met. Area Rose Soc. (pres. 1969-71, 73—). Research in organ transplantation and cancer. Home: 315 Silver Oak Lane New Orleans LA 70123

SAYLER, HENRY BENTON, state senator; b. Savannah, Ga., Jan. 16, 1921; s. Henry B. and Jessie (Dixon) S.; B.S., U.S. Mil. Acad., 1943; m. Wyline Chapman, Mar. 22, 1947; children—Lee, Alan, Robin, Van. Pres. Security Planning Fla., Inc., St. Petersburg, 1955—; mem. Fla. Senate, 1966—. Dir. Community Banks Fla., Inc., Bank of Seminole, Founders Life Assurance Co. Bd. dirs. YMCA, St. Petersburg. Served to lt. col. USAF, 1943-55. Decorated D.F.C., Air medal with six clusters. Republican. Kiwanian. Home: 220 Rafael Blvd NE St Petersburg FL 33704 Office: 333 31st St N St Petersburg FL 33713

SAYRE, EDWIN MUREL, profl. orgn. exec.; b. Silver City, N.M., Dec. 19, 1915; s. Arthur Nuell and Edna (Yarbro) S.; grad. U.S. Army Command and Gen. Staff Coll., 1950, Armed Forces Staff Coll., 1954, Army War Coll., 1961; m. Betty Jane Mavrico, Sept. 7, 1946. Commd. 2d lt. U.S. Army, 1941, advanced through grades to col., 1950; comdr. 1st bn. 17th Inf., 7th Inf. Div., Korea, 1951-52; operational planner Far East Command, Tokyo, Japan, 1952-54; operational planner Armed Forces Staff Coll., Norfolk, Va., 1955-58; operational planner, mem. staff Gen. Westmoreland, Vietnam, 1964-65; operational planner Joint Chiefs Staff, Pentagon, Washington, 1965-68; ret., 1968; mgr. Breckenridge (Tex.) C. of C., 1968—. Vice pres. Citizens Nat. Bank Breckenridge, 1973—. Sec. Breckenridge Indsl. Found., 1968—. Decorated D.S.C., Silver Star, Legion of Merit with oak leaf cluster, Bronze Star with 3 oak leaf clusters, Air medal, Purple Heart with 2 oak leaf clusters Mem. V.F.W., Am. Legion. Presbyn (elder). Rotarian, Mason. Home: Route 1 Box 225 Breckenridge TX 76024 Office: 112 W Walker St Breckenridge TX 76024

SAYRE, JOHN LESLIE, clergyman, educator; b. Hannibal, Mo., Mar. 28, 1924; s. John Leslie and Clara (Haden) S.; student U. Okla., 1942-43; A.B., Phillips U., 1947; B.D. cum laude, Yale, 1950; M.L.S., U. Tex. at Austin, 1963; postgrad. Union Theol. Sem., 1955; Ph.D., U. Tex. at Austin, 1973; m. Herwanna Lee Harrouff, June 18, 1948; children—Barbara Ann, John Richard, Alan Douglas, Melody Lyn. Ordained to ministry Christian Ch. (Disciples of Christ) 1946; asso. minister Christian chs., Enid, Okla., 1945-47, minister, Stillwater, Okla., 1950-57, Austin, Tex., 1957-62; instr. Phillips U., 1954-55, asso. prof. theol. bibliography, 1962—, sem. librarian, 1962-71, dir. univ. libraries, 1971—; instr. Okla. State U., 1950-57; sometimes lectr. Mem. Am. Theol. Library Assn., Am., Okla., S.W. library assns., Beta Phi Mu, Theta Phi, Phi Kappa Phi. Democrat. Author: A History of Disciples Student Work, 1950; A Manual of Forms for Term Papers and Thesis, 1966; An Index to Festschriften in Religion, 1971; An Illustrated Guide to the Anglo-American Cataloging Rules, 1971; Tools for Theological Research, 1972. Address: Box 2158 University Sta Enid OK 73701

SAYRE, ROBERT DUANE, engring. firm exec.; b. Canton, S.D., Oct. 20, 1928; s. Lawrence Carl and Edith Lydia (Doolittle) S.; B.S. in Civil Engring., S.D. Sch. Mines and Tech., 1950; M. Civil Engring., U. Va., 1952; m. Margaret Estelle Mann, May 1, 1954; children—Robert Duane, David Mann. Area engr. E.I. DuPont de Nemours, Savannah River Project, S.C., 1952-53; chief engring. lab. Corps of Engrs., Washington, 1953-56; materials engr. Parsons, Brinckerhoff, Quade and Douglas, Richmond, Va., 1956-58; chief engr., also corporate sec. Froehling and Robertson, Inc., Richmond, 1958-68; cons. engr., Richmond, 1968-73; pres. Sayre and Sutherland, Cons. Engrs., Richmond, 1973—. Dir. Terra Ins. Ltd. Fellow Am. Soc. C.E.; mem. Va. Soc. Profl. Engrs. (recipient Outstanding Service award 1968, Distinguished Service award 1973; pres. 1972-73), Va. Assn. Professions, Internat. Soc. Soil Mechanics and Found. Engring., Engrs. Club Richmond (pres. 1970). Presbyn. (deacon 1967—). Mason. Home: 6604 W Franklin St Richmond VA 23226 Office: PO Box 9532 5407 Lakeside Ave Richmond VA 23228

SCALES, CLARENCE RAY, lawyer; b. Morton, Miss., Aug. 23, 1922; s. Felix A. and Zola (Dubose) S.; J.D., U. Miss., 1949; m. Lura Evelyn Lee, Aug. 20, 1948; children—Clarence Ray, Linda Evelyn, Philip Lee. Admitted to Miss. bar, 1949; gen. practice law, Jackson, 1949—, sr. mem. firm Scales & Scales, 1956—. Served with AUS, 1942-46. Mem. Am., Hinds County bar assns., Miss. State Bar. Home: 1220 Druid Hills Dr Jackson MS 39206 Office: Deposit Guaranty Bank Bldg Jackson MS 39201

SCALES, JAMES RALPH, univ. pres.; b. Jay, Okla., May 27, 1919; s. John Grover and Kate (Whitley) S.; A.B., Okla. Baptist U., 1939; M.A., U. Okla., 1941, Ph.D., 1949; postgrad. U. Chgo., 1945-47, U. London, 1958; LL.D., Alderson-Broaddus Coll., 1971; Litt.D., No. Mich. U., 1972; m. Elizabeth Ann Randel, August 4, 1944; children—Laura (dec.), Ann Catherine. Reporter, Miami (Okla.) News Record, 1934-35, Shawnee (Okla.) News-Star, 1935-36; instr. Okla. Baptist U., Shawnee, 1940-42, asst. prof., 1946-47, asso. prof., 1947-51, prof. history, govt., 1951-61, v.p., 1950-53, exec. v.p., 1953-61, pres., 1961-65; dean arts and scis. Okla. State U., Stillwater, 1965-67; pres. Wake Forest U., Winston-Salem, N.C., 1967—. Dir. Integon Corp., Home Fed. Savs. & Loan Assn. Mem. Pres.'s Com. Edn. Beyond High Sch., 1957, Okla. Commn. Tchr. Edn. and Certification, 1955-61. Mem. Okla. delegation Democratic Nat. Conv., 1956. Bd. dirs. Pottawatomie County chpt. A.R.C., Winston-Salem Urban Coalition, Goodwill Industries; trustee Presbyn. Hosp., Oklahoma City. Mem. Am. Hist. Assn., Am. Polit. Sci. Assn., Am. Assn. U. Profs., N.E.A., So. Assn. Bapt. Colls. (pres. 1969-70), N.C. Assn. Ind. Colls. (pres. 1968-70), Winston-Salem C. of C. (dir.), Phi Beta Kappa, Omicron Delta Kappa, Phi Eta Sigma, Pi Kappa Delta, Kappa Delta Pi. Baptist (deacon). Rotarian. Address: President's Home Wake Forest U Winston-Salem NC 27109

SCALZI, JOHN BAPTIST, govt. engr.; b. Milford, Mass., Nov. 13, 1915; s. Joseph and Jennie (Verrelli) S.; B.S., Worcester Poly. Inst., 1938; M.S., Mass. Inst. Tech., 1940; Sc.D. (Am. Welding Soc. fellow), 1951; m. Jennie Elizabeth Celozzi, Nov. 11, 1940; children—Joan (Mrs. Peter S. Eisenhut), Rosemary (Mrs. David William Wilson). Field engr. Metcalf and Eddy, Boston, 1938-39; engr. Curtiss-Wright Corp., Buffalo, 1940-45; engr. Nat. Aniline Co., Buffalo, 1945-46; prof. engring. Case Inst. Tech., Cleve., 1946-60; lectr. Western Res. U., Cleve., 1946-60; dir. marketing tech. services U.S. Steel Corp., Pitts., 1960-71; engr. Dept. Housing and Urban Devel., Washington, 1971-73; program mgr. earthquake engring. NSF, Washington, 1973—. Lectr. Carnegie Inst. Tech., 1965-71; cons. engr., Cleve., 1946-60; founder Steel Scaffolding and Shoring Inst. Ohio, 1959. Named Pitts. Businessman of the Week, sta. WTAE, 1968. Mem. Am. Soc. C.E. (nat. dir. 1960, pres. Cleve. sect. 1956, pres. Pitts. sect. 1968), Am. Concrete Inst., Sigma Xi, Chi Epsilon. Author: (with Omer Blodgett) Design of Welded Structural Connections, 1960; (with Boris Bresler and T.Y. Lin) Design of Steel Structures, 1968; (with Walter Podolny and Wayne Teng) Design Fundamentals of Cable Roof Structures, 1968. Contbr. articles to profl. jours. Home: 2111 Jefferson Davis Hwy Arlington VA 22202 Office: 1800 G St NW Washington DC 20550

SCANLAN, WILLIAM ARTHUR, mgm. services co. exec.; b. Tuscumbia, Ala., Aug. 25, 1922; s. William Arthur and Alice (Belser) S.; student George Washington U., 1942-43; B.S., U. Tenn., 1950; m. Frankie Hall Pride, June 15, 1955; children—William Arthur III, Hammond Pride. With Prudential Ins. Co. Am., Asheville, N.C., also Charlotte, N.C., Cin., 1951-61, dist. group mgr., 1954-61; with Synercon Corp. and predecessor firm, Nashville, 1961—, v.p. Blair, Follin, Allen, Walker & Forest Life div., 1964-74, v.p. marketing, 1969—. Mem. C. of C., Sales and Marketing Execs. Club. Methodist. Home: 3636 Estes Rd Nashville TN 37215 Office: 301 Plus Park Blvd Nashville TN 37210

SCARBOROUGH, CLAUDE MOOD, JR., lawyer; b. Columbia, S.C., Dec. 7, 1929; s. Claude M. and Gelene (Stallworth) S.; student U. of South, 1947-49; A.B., U.S.C., 1951, LL.B., 1952; m. Sarah Carpenter, June 30, 1955; children—Sarah Catherine, Elizabeth Ann, Claude M. III, Gelene Bivins. Admitted to S.C. bar, 1952, U.S. Ct. Appeals, 1957; asso. firm Nelson, Mullins & Grier, Columbia, S.C., 1955-61, partner Nelson, Mullins, Grier & Scarborough, 1961—. Spl. hearing officer U.S. Dept. Justice, 1962-68. Trustee Legal Aid Soc. Richland Co., 1960-67, pres., 1960-64; mem. indsl. adv. bd. S.C. Dept. Corrections, 1974—. Served to 1st lt. AUS, 1952-55. Mem. Internat. Assn. Ins. Counsel, Am., S.C. (treas. 1968-72, exec. com. 1972—, chmn. exec. com. 1973, pres.-elect 1974) Richland County bar assns., S.C. State Bar, Am. Judicature Soc., Phi Delta Phi. Episcopalian. (lay reader, vestryman) Clubs: Palmetto, Summit, Forest Lake Country. Home: 1514 Tanglewood Rd Columbia SC 29205 Office: 1321 Bull St Columbia SC 29201

SCARSBROOK, CLARENCE EDWIN, educator; b. Orrville, Ala., Sept. 26, 1915; s. Clarence Eugene and Mattie Evelyn (Bozeman) S.; B.S., Auburn U., 1942; Ph.D., N.C. State U., 1949; m. Mildred Mobley Moore, Feb. 16, 1943; children—Ellen W., Miriam (Mrs. John Saxon). Asso. agronomist La. State U., Baton Rouge, 1949-53; prof. soil chemistry Auburn (Ala.) U., 1953—. Served with AUS, 1942-46. Decorated Bronze Star. Fellow A.A.A.S.; mem. Am. Soc. Agronomy, Sigma Xi, Gamma Sigma Delta (internat. pres. 1968-70), Alpha Zeta. Presbyn. (elder 1958—). Contbr. articles to profl. jours. Home: 426 Hare St Auburn AL 36830

SCARTH, PETER, ednl. cons.; b. Buffalo, Apr. 8, 1932; s. Harry and Priscilla (Wolfe) S.; B.A., U. N.H., 1955, M.Ed., 1960; Ed.D., Boston U., 1966. Tchr. sociology Laconia (N.H.) High Sch., 1958-59; asst. sch. psychologist Portsmouth (N.H.) Sch. Dept., 1960-61, sch. psychologist, 1962-64; dir. guidance Supervisory Union No. 55, Plaistow, N.H., 1961-62; cons. psychologist Tamworth (N.H.) Pub. Sch., 1962-65; instr. U. N.H., Durham, 1963-64; programalyst Action for Boston Community Devel., 1965; exec. asso. Upward Bound project Ednl. Projects, Inc., Washington, 1965-66, dir. migrant and seasonal farm worker project, 1966-68, v.p. for program, 1967-68; pres. Ednl. Systems Corp., Washington, 1968-71, Exec. Systems Corp., Washington, 1968-71, Am. Vocational Research Corp., 1971-72, Fibercraft, Inc., 1957-60; supervisory operations research analyst ACTION, Washington, 1972—. Chmn. sch. drop-out study Seacoast Regional Guidance Council, 1963-65; mem. ad-hoc com. role and function jr. and community colls. U.S. Senate, 1969; co-chmn. com. on Negro in higher edn., 1968. Bd. dirs. Portsmouth Mental Health Clinic, 1962-64. Served with USAF, 1955-57. Mem. Am. Psychol. Assn., Am. Soc. Adlerian Psychology, N.E.A., Am. Personnel and Guidance Assn. (program chmn. New Eng. conv. 1964). Author: Individual Psychology: Its Implications for School Psychology, 1966; Bibliography for Migrant Education Programs, 1967; also articles. Home: 4545 MacArthur Blvd NW Washington DC 20007 Office: 806 Connecticut Av NW Washington DC 20525

SCATES, ALICE YEOMANS, govt. ofcl.; b. Pitts., Jan. 21, 1915; d. William E. and Georgiana L. (Lloyd) Yeomans; B.S., State Tchrs. Coll., Glassboro, N.J., 1936; M.Ed., Duke, 1949; Ed.D., George Washington U., 1963. Elementary sch. tchr., Haddon Heights, N.J., 1937-43; civilian personnel officer Sedalia Army Airfield, Mo., Greenville Army Air Field, S.C., 1944-46; tng. officer VA Center, Dayton, O., 1947-48; research asso., dir. Am. Council on Edn. Staff for Office Naval Research Projects, 1949-53; asst. dir. Nat. Home Study Council, 1954; editor, research asst. Office of Edn., U.S. Dept. Health, Edn. and Welfare, 1955, research analyst and coordinator Coop. Research Program, 1956-64, program planning officer Occupational Research Program, 1965-66, dir. basic research br. secondary edn., 1967-69, program planning and evaluation officer Nat. Center Ednl. Research and Devel., 1969-71, Office of Planning, Budgeting and Evaluation, 1971—. Served to capt. AUS, 1943-46. Fellow A.A.A.S.; mem. Am. Sociol. Assn., Am. Anthrop. Assn., Am. Acad. Polit. and Social Sci., Am. Ednl. Research Assn., Adult Edn. Assn., Kappa Delta Pi, Phi Delta Gamma. Author research reports. Contbr. articles in field to profl. jours. Home: 560 N St SW Washington DC 20024 Office: Office of Planning Budgeting and Evaluation US Office Edn Washington DC 20202

SCHACHTEL, HYMAN JUDAH, rabbi; b. London, Eng., May 24, 1907; s. Bernard and Janie (Spector) S.; came to U.S., 1914, naturalized, 1921; B.A., U. Cin., 1928; B.H. Rabbi, Hebrew Union Coll., 1931; student Columbia Tchrs. Coll., 1933-37; Ed. D., U. Houston, 1948; D.D., Hebrew Union Coll., 1958; D.H.L., Southwestern U., 1955; m. Barbara H. Levin, Oct. 15, 1941; children—Bernard, Ann Mollie. Ordained rabbi, 1931; rabbi West End Synagogue, N.Y.C. 1931-43; chief rabbi Temple Beth Israel, Houston, 1943—; tchr. philosophy U. Houston, 1950-55; lectr. Judaic studies St. Mary's Sem., Houston; lectr. Jewish history U. Houston; adj. prof. religion Inst. Religion, Houston. Pres. Tex. Kallah Rabbis, 1962, Houston Rabbinical Assn., 1960; mem. exec. bd. Central Conf. Am. Rabbis, 1965-67, v.p., sec.-treas. Southwest region, 1966—; chaplain Variety Club, Houston, 1955—, Houston Fire Dept., 1964—; v.p. N.Y. Bd. Rabbis, 1942-43. Pres. Harris County Mental Health Assn., 1960; bd. dirs. Houston Symphony Soc., 1955—, San Jacinto council Girl Scouts U.S.A., 1962—, Houston Heart Assn., 1964—, Houston Crime Commn., 1962-65, Houston-Harris County chpt. A.R.C., 1974—; mem. nat. planning bd., trustee United Fund Harris County, 1965—; bd. overseers Hebrew Union Coll.-Jewish Inst. Religion, 1961-65. Recipient Coronat medal St. Edward's U., Austin, Tex., 1963. Mem. Phi Delta Kappa, Phi Epsilon Pi (hon.). Kiwanian. Author: Real Enjoyment of Living, 1954; The Life You Want to Live, 1956; The Shadowed Valley, 1964; Aspects of Jewish Homiletics, 1964; How to Meet the Challenge of Life and Death, 1974. Home: 2527 Glenhaven St Houston TX 77025 Office: 5600 N Braeswood Houston TX 77035

SCHAEFER, PAUL MACK, builder; b. St. Louis, July 4, 1928; s. Paul O'Neill and Catherine Agnes (McEvilly) S.; A.B., U. Notre Dame, 1950; m. Norah Kathleen Sidow, Aug. 14, 1955; children—Mary, Timothy, Christopher, John, Ann, Michael, Patrick, Justin. Radio newswriter A.P., Louisville, 1950; gen. mgr. Gen. Tire Co., Miami, Fla., 1955-69; asst. to exec. v.p. Deltona Corp., Miami, 1969-70, v.p. adminstrn., 1970—. Mem. program devel. task force United Fund, 1973—; 1st vice chmn. Better Bus. Bur. Bd. dirs. Crime Commn. Greater Miami. Served to 1st lt. USAF, 1951-55. Decorated Air medal with 2 oak leaf clusters. Mem. Execs. Assn. Greater Miami, St. Vincent de Paul Soc., Res. Officers Assn., Vizcayans. Republican. Roman Catholic. Clubs: Serra (sec.), Notre Dame of Greater Miami. Home: 598 NE 56th St Miami FL 33137 Office: 3250 SW 3d Av Miami FL 33129

SCHAETTI, HENRY JOACHIM, petroleum exploration co. exec.; b. Kodaikanal, India, Aug. 10, 1921; s. Henry Martin and Clara (Brunnschweiler) S.; Ph.D., U. Bern (Switzerland), 1949; postgrad. (Rotary Found. fellow) Stanford, 1949-50; m. Rachel Helen Miller, Aug. 23, 1950; children—Margery, Barbara, Susan. Came to U.S., 1952. Geologist, Brit. Am. Oil Co., Calgary, Alta., Can., 1951-52; sect. head Carter Oil Co. Research, Tulsa, 1952-60; geologist Esso Argentina Inc., Buenos Aires, 1961; chief geologist Esso Sahara Inc., Algiers, Algeria, 1961-66; gen. mgr. Esso Exploration Inc., Walton-on-Thames, Eng., 1966-67, Dakar, Senegal, 1967-69, Rabat, Morocco, 1969-70, Kuala Lumpur, Malaysia, 1970-71, v.p., dir., Houston, 1971—. Served with Swiss Army, 1940-49. Mem. Am. Assn. Petroleum Geologists, Am. Geophys. Union, N.Y. Acad. Scis., A.A.A.S., Geol. Soc. London, Swiss Geol. Soc. Home: 13722 Alchester St Houston TX 77024 Office: PO Box 146 Houston TX 77001

SCHAFER, LOTHAR, chemist, educator; b. Dusseldorf, West Germany, May 5, 1939; s. Ernest Rudolf and Sybilla (Nolden) S.; diploma in Chemistry, U. Munich, Germany, 1962, Ph.D. in Chemistry, 1965; m. Gabriele Maria Brand, Apr. 9, 1965; children—Nicole, Nathalie. Came to U.S., 1967. Research asso. Ind. U., 1967-68; asst. prof. dept. chemistry U. Ark., Fayetteville, 1968-72, asso. prof., 1972—. NATO postdoctoral fellow U. Oslo, Norway, 1965-67; Research corp. grantee, 1970, NSF grantee, 1970, Dreyfus Found. grantee, 1971. Mem. Am. Chem. Soc., Chem. Soc. Eng., Am. Assn. Univ. Profs. Contbr. articles on chemistry to sci. jours. Home: 828 Skyline Dr Fayetteville AR 72701

SCHAFFNER, ALVIN WILFORD, state ofcl.; b. Westhoff, Tex., Nov. 9, 1911; s. Gus and Rosa (Mueller) S.; grad. high sch.; m. Isabella Kruse, Dec. 21, 1935. Poultry specialist Uncle Johnny Feed Mills, Houston, 1938-46; pres. Farmbilt Mills, Cuero, Tex. 1946-58, Schaffner Feed, Inc., Cuero, 1958-67; salesman Duckett Motor Co., Cuero, 1967-69; meat inspector Tex. Health Dept., Cuero, 1969—. Served with USMCR, 1943-46. Mem. Tex. Pub. Health Assn., Cuero C. of C., V.F.W. (life mem., dist. comdr. 1971-72, State Dept. instr. 1972-73), 4-H Club (Alumni award 1959, hon. mem.), Am. Legion. Lutheran. Clubs: Cuero County, Cuero Dance. Home: Cuero TX 77954 Office: PO Box 221 Cuero TX 77954

SCHANDLER, AARON MANEY, food store exec.; b. Asheville, N.C., July 10, 1913; s. David Sigmund and Sarah (Salem) S.; B.A., Asheville-Biltmore Coll., 1932; certificate of registered grocer Nat. Grocers Inst., 1940; m. Shirley Lee Senner, Jan. 1, 1942; children—Roberta Faun (Mrs. Joshua Grossman), Trudy Anne, Linda Jeanne (Mrs. Fred Newman). With Schandler's Pickle Barrell, Asheville, N.C., 1940—, pres., 1948—. Vice pres., dir. Mut. Distbg. Co., Asheville, 1955—. Served with AUS, 1940-46; ETO; lt. col. Res. ret. Decorated 3 Battle Stars. Mem. Res. Officers Assn. (pres. West N.C. chpt. 1967), Asheville Jr. C. of C., Gold Nuggett Stock Investment Club (pres. 1966-67). Jewish Religion (bd. dirs. 1964—). Mem. DeMolay Chevaliar (mem. ct. 1935—, scribe 1936-40). Home: 285 Macon Av Asheville NC 28804 Office: 50 Broadway Asheville NC 28807

SCHANGER, WILLIAM THOMAS, journalist; b. N.Y.C., Feb. 21, 1919; s. Jacob Jay and Sylvia (Reh) S.; A.A.S. Coll. City N.Y., 1954, N.Y. U., 1942; m. Edith Apfelroth, Feb. 11, 1954 (dec. Nov. 1959). Promotions dir., asst. advt. dir. Ever Ready Label Corp., N.Y.C. also Belleville, N.J., 1949-58; writer-editor Mil. Med. Supply Agy., Bklyn., 1958-59; information specialist N.Y. Naval Shipyard, 1959-61; editor Statis. Summary U.S. Dept. Agr., Washington, 1964-71, contbg. writer Agrl. Situation, 1970-73, information specialist, editor, 1962—. Mem. Fed. Editors Assn. Patente-designer Plastolier Reversible Plastic Tables. Home: 5601 Seminary Rd Falls Church VA 22041 Office: ERS US Dept Agr Washington DC 20250

SCHARDT, ALOIS WOLFGANG, govt. ofcl.; b. Dresden, Germany, Sept. 15, 1923; s. Alois Jacob and Mary Sophia (Dietrich) S.; student Loyola U., 1941-42; B.S., Cal. Inst. Tech., 1944, Ph.D. magna cum laude, 1951; m. Carla L. Curtis, Apr. 18, 1953; children—James Alois, Bruce Curtis, Mary Martha, Thomas Dorn, Elizabeth Ann. Came to U.S., 1939, naturalized, 1944. Asso. physicist Brookhaven Nat. Lab., Upton, N.Y., 1950-54; staff physicist, Los Alamos Sci. Lab., N.M., 1954-61; chief High Altitude Test Detection, ARPA, Office of Sec. Def., Washington, 1961-63, dep. dir. Nuclear Test Detection, 1963; chief particles and fields NASA Hdq., Washington, 1963-70, dep. dir. physics and astronomy, 1970-73, dir. physics and astronomy, 1973—. Served with AUS, 1944-46. Mem. Am. Phys. Soc., Am. Geophys. Union, Am. Astron. Soc., Fed. Exec. Inst., A.A.A.S., Sigma Xi, Tau Beta Phi. Roman Catholic. Research in nuclear reactions and radio activity. Contbr. articles in field to profl. jours. Home: 926 Woburn Ct McLean VA 22101 Office: 400 Maryland Av Washington DC 20546

SCHARLAU, CHARLES EDWARD, gas co. exec.; b. Chgo., Apr. 24, 1927; s. Charles Edward and Esther (Powell) S.; J.D., U. Ark., 1951; m. Clydene Yi Sloop, Aug. 17, 1960; children—Charles Edward IV, Martha Iva, Caryn Lyn, Robin Rai, Greg Scott. Admitted to Ark. bar, 1951; gen. atty. Ark. Western Gas Co., Fayetteville, 1951-59, asst. sec.-asst. treas., 1959-66, v.p., 1966-67, exec. v.p., 1967-68, pres., 1968—. Mem. State Council on Econ. Edn., 1970-72; mem. State Econ. Expansion Study Commn., 1969—; mem. U. Ark. Devel.

Council, 1969-72; mem. adv. council U. Ark. Bus. Sch., 1970-71. Served with USMCR, 1945-46. Mem. So. Gas Assn., Ark. Bar Assn. (officer mineral law sect. 1967-68), Ark. State (dir. 1970-71), Fayetteville (pres. 1967-68) chambers commerce, U. Ark. Alumni Assn. Methodist (bd. stewards 1970-71). Home: 410 Oliver St Fayetteville AR 72701 Office: 28 E Center St Fayetteville AR 72701

SCHECHTER, DAVID ALAN, lawyer; b. Charlottesville, Va., Oct. 17, 1939; s. Monroe I. and Isabelle (Post) S.; B.A. in Econs., U. Mich., 1959; J.D., 1962; LL.M., N.Y. U., 1963; m. Marilyn Grodsky, Mar. 25, 1959; children—Ira, Ronald. Admitted to bar N.Y., 1963, Ill., 1964, Ky., 1968; with Commerce Clearing House, Chgo., 1963-65, Arthur Andersen and Co., Chgo., 1965-67; tax counsel Brown and Williamson Tobacco Corp., Louisville, 1967—. Lectr., U. Louisville Sch. Law, 1972—, N.Y. U. Inst. on Fed. Taxation, 1973. C.P.A., Ky., Ill. Mem. Ky., Ill. socs. c.p.a.s, Am., N.Y., Ill., Ky. bar assns., Am. Inst. C.P.A.s. Mem. B'nai B'rith. Contbr. articles to profl. jours. Home: 4601 Lynnbrook Dr Louisville KY 40220 Office: 1600 W Hill St Louisville KY 40201

SCHECHTER, ROBERT SAMUEL, educator; b. Houston, Feb. 26, 1929; s. Morris S. and Helen Ruth (Brilling) S.; B.S., Tex. A. and M. U., 1950; Ph.D., U. Minn., 1956; m. Mary Ethel Rosenberg, Feb. 15, 1953; children—Richard Martin, Alan Lawrence, Geoffrey Louis. Mem. faculty U. Tex. at Austin, 1956—, prof. chem. engring., 1961—, chmn. dept., 1970-73. Vis. prof. U. Edinburgh, 1965-66, U. Brussels, 1966. Cons., tech. editor Aztec Pub. Co., Austin, Tex., 1973—. Served with AUS, 1951-53. Mem. Profl. Engrs. Tex., Am. Chem. Soc., Soc. Petroleum Engrs., Am. Inst. Chem. Engrs., Am. Inst. Mining Engrs., Sigma Xi. Author: Variational Method in Engineering, 1967; Optimization: Theory and Practice, 1970. Home: 4700 Ridge Oak Dr Austin TX 78731 Office: Dept Chemical Engineering Univ Texas Austin TX 78712

SCHECTER, GEORGE, scientist; b. Phila., Jan. 14, 1917; s. Abraham and Anna (Tilishevsky) S.; B.S., Temple U., 1947; m. Pearl Grossman, Oct. 18, 1941; children—Ellen L., Peter M. Research adviser, supervisory physicist U.S. Army, Phila., 1941-72; v.p. Technalysis, Inc., Phila., 1949-53; sr. asso. Ketron, Inc., 1972—. Cons., Sandia Corp., AEC. Vice pres. Phila. Gt. Books Council, 1969-70. Mem. Research Soc. Am. (pres. 1958), Am. Phys. Soc., Operations Research Soc. Am., Am. Ordnance Assn. Mason. Author: Information Retrieval, 1967. Patentee in field. Home: 1215 N Ft Myer Dr Arlington VA Office: Suite 1200 1901 N Ft Myer Dr Arlington VA 22209

SCHEEL, NIVARD, univ. adminstr.; b. Balt., Nov. 8, 1925; s. Joseph August and Julianna (Hintenach) S.; A.B., Catholic U. Am., 1949, M.S., 1951, Ph.D., 1961. Instr. dept. physics and chemistry Xaverian Coll., Silver Spring, Md., 1949-54, 58-60, pres., 1960-66; instr. physics parochial high sch., White Plains, N.Y., 1954-56, Louisville, Ky., 1956-58; prin. parochial high sch., Bklyn., 1966-67; adminstr. Cath. U. Am., Washington, 1967—, acting pres., 1968-69, v.p. adminstrn., 1969-70, v.p. student affairs, 1970—. Mem. Nat. Assn. Student Personnel Adminstrs., Am. Assn. Physics Tchrs., Phi Beta Kappa, Sigma Xi. Staff editor New Catholic Ency., 1962. Home: 721 Monroe St NE Washington DC 20017 Office: 625 Michigan Av NE Washington DC 20017

SCHEELE, CARL HARRY, govt. ofcl.; b. Cleve., June 19, 1928; s. Carl August and Frances Jane (Standring) S.; grad. Cleve. Inst. Art, 1952; B.F.A., U. Ill., 1954; M.A. in History, Western Res. U., 1957; m. Joanne Bales Brewer, June 21, 1954; children—Martha Anne, August Kurt. Comml. artist, Cleve., 1946-48; tchr., pub. schs., Cleve., 1957-59; asst. curator div. postal history Smithsonian Instn., Washington, 1959-63, asso. curator, 1963-70, curator in charge div., 1970-71, chmn. dept. applied arts, 1969-74. Served with AUS, 1954-56. Mem. Am. Hist. Soc., Postal History Soc. Ams., Am. Philatelic Congress, Am. Acad. Philately, Am. Philatelic Soc., Soc. Philatelic Ams. Author: A Short History of the Mail Service, 1970; Neither Snow Nor Rain..., 1970; also numerous articles. Home: 2912 N 22d St Arlington VA 22201 Office: 12th & Constitution Av Washington DC 20560

SCHEER, LEO S., Christian Sci. practitioner, former condr., music educator; b. Jersey City, Oct. 2, 1909; s. Jonas Maurice and Amelia (Luft) S.; student San Diego State Coll., 1936-37, Inst. Mus. Art, 1929-30; grad. with honors U.S. Naval Sch. Music, 1931; pvt. study with Pierre Monteux, Arnold Schoenberg, Naoum Blinder; m. Ruth Helen Jenner, Nov. 18, 1934; children—Antoinette Ruth (Mrs. Harry Robert Stowe), David Leon, Rosalind Jenner (Mrs. Godfrey David Carvan John). Tchr. instrumental music San Diego County schs., 1935-45; condr. Fed. Symphony, San Diego, 1938-41; asso. condr. San Diego Symphony, 1940-43; founder, condr. San Diego Youth Symphony, 1944-52; asso. condr. San Diego Civil Light Opera Co., 1944-50; condr. Eagle Rock Civic Symphony, Los Angeles, 1951-52; faculty Los Angeles Conservatory, 1947-52; music dir. Uniao Cultural Brasil-Estados Unidos, Sao Paulo, Brazil, 1953-55; asst. condr. Kansas City Philharmonic, 1955-56; music ednl. dir. Jenkins Music Co., Kansas City, 1956-60; founder, condr. Kansas City Youth Orch., 1958-60; condr. Abilene Philharmonic, 1960-65; condr., artist in residence Hardin-Simmons U., Abilene, Tex., 1963-65; music dir., condr. Lexington (Ky.) Philharmonic, 1965-71; asst. prof. music U. Ky., Lexington, 1965-71; now Christian Sci. practitioner, Louisville. Served with USN, 1931-35. Recipient nat. award for composition Composer's Press, 1944; citizen's award for youth symphony work, San Diego, 1952. Mem. Am. Fedn. Musicians, Nat. Assn. Am. Composers and Condrs., Nat. Soc. Arts and Letters (hon.), Phi Mu Alpha. Christian Scientist. Rotarian. Author: Scheer Violin Method, 3 vols., 1945. Composer: Lament for English horn and piano, 1944. Home: 136 N Peterson Av Apt 2 Louisville KY 40206 Office: 981 Starks Bldg Louisville KY 40202

SCHEIBEL, LEONARD WILLIAM, physician; b. Hays, Kan., Jan. 18, 1938; s. Raymond Philip and Thelma (Bane) S.; B.S., Creighton U., 1960, M.S., 1962; D.Sc. (NIH fellow), Johns Hopkins, 1966; M.D., U. Fla., 1973. Div. biochemist Walter Reed Army Inst. Research, Washington, 1967-70; research asso. dept. pharmacology Sch. Medicine, U. Fla., Gainesville, 1970-73; intern Gorgas Hosp., Balboa Heights, C.Z., 1973-74. Served to capt. AUS, 1967-70. Mem. A.M.A., Am. Soc. Tropical Medicine, Nat. Rifle Assn., Underwater Soc. Am. Clubs: Delaware Underwater Swim (Wilmington); Maryland Waterbugs (Balt.); Barnicle Busters, Skin Diving (Gainesville). Contbr. articles to profl. jours. Home: 0763 Williamson Pl Balboa CZ Office: Gorgas Hosp PO Box 0 Balboa Heights CZ

SCHEIDT, JOHN LUDWIG, utilities co. engr.; b. Phila., Mar. 10, 1933; s. Ludwig and Gussy (Freundorf) S.; B.E.E., U. Fla., 1962; m. Margaret Ellen O'Connor, July 21, 1962; children—Susan Elizabeth, Ann Margaret, Catherine Lynn. With Fla. Power Corp., St. Petersburg, 1962—, mgr. system operations, 1970—. Served with USAF, 1953-57. Registered profl. engr., Fla. Conglist. (trustee ch. 1973—). Rotarian (treas. 1969-70). Home: 6726 12th Ave N St Petersburg FL 33710 Office: PO Box 14042 St Petersburg FL 33733

SCHELEEN, JOSEPH CARL, pub. co. exec.; b. Newark, Aug. 12, 1904; s. Carl Algot and Mathilda (Anderson) S.; B.S. in Journalism, Butler U., 1928; m. Alice DeVol Phillips, Nov. 28, 1931; 1 dau., Sarah (Mrs. Linton E. Kilmon, Jr.). Reporter, Shelbyville (Ind.) Republican, 1928-30, city editor, 1931-36, 1938-40; asst. mgr. Indpls. Better Bus. Bur., 1937; reporter Traffic World, Washington, 1940-48, chief news bur., 1948-51, mng. editor, 1952-53, editorial dir., 1954-55; editor, 1956—; v.p. Traffic Service Corp, Traffic World, 1957—. Mem. adv. com. transp. studies Am. U., Washington, 1955—. Mem. Am. Soc. Traffic and Transp., Delta Nu Alpha, Delta Tau Delta, Sigma Delta Chi. Clubs: Nat. Press., University, Nat. Aviation (Washington). Presbyn. Home: 3211 Old Dominion Blvd Alexandria VA 22305 Office: Washington Bldg Washington DC 20005

SCHELLIN, ERIC PAUL, lawyer; b. N.Y.C., Sept. 30, 1927; s. Paul and Elise (Schulze) S.; A.B., Columbia, 1948, postgrad., 1948-51; J.D., George Washington U., 1956; m. Miss Zbrzezny, June 12, 1954; children—Lisa, Christine, Victoria, Eric Paul, Peter, Katherine, David. Admitted to Washington bar, 1958; sr. partner firm Schellin and Hoffman, 1968—. Chmn. bd. Am. Conf. for Internat. Market Devel., Inc., 1972—; pres. Erdo Group Cos., 1960—; exec. v.p. Nat. Patent Council, 1969—; mem. Nat. Com. Small Bus. Tax Reform, 1971—. Mem. Nat. Small Bus. Assn. (trustee 1970—). Club: Langley. Editor: Patent Trends, 1969—. Home: 6831 Cloisters Dr McLean VA 22101 Office: 1225 19th St NW Washington DC 20036

SCHELLSTEDE, ELOISE JEANNETTE, artist; b. Tulsa, Sept. 11, 1918; d. Delmer Robert and Carrol (Rouse) Rees; B.A., Tulsa U., 1939; m. John E. Schellstede, Nov. 30, 1940 (dec. 1973); children—John Robert, Richard Lee. Owner D.R. Rees & Co. Ins. Agy., Tulsa, 1939—; instr. art, 1939—; exhibited numerous one-man shows including University Club, YMCA, various chs., clubs, 1963—; exhibited group shows including Mayo Hotel, Nat. Bank Tulsa, Merc. Bank & Trust Co., Camelot Inn, Tulsa, Coll. Union, Tahlequah, Okla., Shangri-la Lodge on Grand Lake, Afton, Okla., Kerr Mus., Poteau, Okla.; owner Gallery of Fine Art, Tulsa, 1970—; mem. Gilcrease Mus.; represented in Kerr Mus., Cherokee Archives Mus., Ft. Gibson, Selco Corp collection, other permanent collections. Founder Green Country Art Assn., Green Country Art Found., Green Country Sch. Art. Mem. D.A.R., Okla. Heritage Assn., Tulsa County Hist. Soc., Kappa Delta. Presbyn. Clubs: Soroptomist, Insurance Women of Tulsa. Home: 6254 S Utica St Tulsa OK 74136 Office: Suite 759 Camelot Inn I-44 at Peoria Tulsa OK 74105

SCHEMMER, BENJAMIN FRANKLIN, editor, pub., author; b. Winner, S.D., Apr. 22, 1932; s. Clinton Henry and Minna Mathilda (Heese) S.; grad. Philips Acad., Andover, Mass., 1950; B.S. (Phillipian Prize scholar), U.S. Mil. Acad., 1954; m. Cynthia Blythe Sweatt, Feb. 14, 1955; 1 son, Clinton Howard. Chief customer liaison Mil. Aircraft Systems, Boeing Co., Seattle, 1959-63, mgr. Advanced Systems Planning, Phila., 1963-65; dir. Land Forces Weapons Systems Office Sec. of Def., Washington, 1965-67; editor, pub. Armed Forces Jour., Washington, 1968—. Cons. to Dept. Army on Aviation Studies, 1965. Served to 1st lt. AUS, 1954-57. Fgn. Policy Research Inst. grantee, 1971. Author: The Howard Hughes Affair, 1972; Almanac of Liberty, 1974. Contbr. articles to Look, New Republic, other publs. Home: 11216 South Shore Dr Reston VA 22090 Office: 1710 Connecticutt Av NW Washington DC 20009

SCHENCK, ARTHUR CARL, cons. engr.; b. Phila., July 31, 1910; s. Rev. Dr. A. Clarence and Hattie Olive (Ritter) S.; B.S., U. Ala., 1934; m. Eloise Elena Williams, July 6, 1934; children—Nancy Elizabeth (Mrs. Robert Edward Smith), Jean Gray (Mrs. Richard George Rice). Field and resident engr. Stone & Webster Engring. Corp., 1934, 1936-42; engr. Stone & Webster Engring. Corp., 1934, 1936-42; insp. U.S. C.E., Phila., 1935-36; v.p. Carpenter Constrn. Co., Inc., Norfolk, Va., 1942-63; prin., A. Carl Schenck & Assos., constrn. mgmt. & engring. cons., 1963—. Mem. Bd. Review Real Estate Assessments, 1955—; mem. Va. Airports Authority, 1958—. Mem. Engring. Com. Devel. Council, U. Ala., 1958-62. Exec. council Tidewater chpt. Boy Scouts Am., 1958—. Chmn. DePaul lay adv. bd., 1962—; mem. Citizens Adv. Com. Norfolk, 1965-68; mem. adv. council Norfolk Area Med. Center Authority, 1970—. Mem. Va. Soc. Profl. Engrs., Asso. Gen. Contractors Am. (pres. Va. br. 1962), Builders and Contractors Exchange (dir. 1960-62), Am. Arbitration Assn., Tau Beta Pi, Theta Tau, Chi Beta Phi. Lutheran Clubs: Engineers (Hampton Roads); Kiwanis (pres. 1966), Virginia (Norfolk); Harbor. Home: 5601 Huntington Pl Norfolk VA 23509 Office: PO Box 7097 Norfolk VA 23509

SCHENKER, TILLIE ABRAMSON, librarian; b. Baton Rouge, Nov. 12, 1910; d. Abraham and Matilde (Mendelsohn) Abramson; B.S., La. State U., 1930, B.S. in L.S., 1934; m. Michael Max Schenker, Mar. 31, 1940 (dec. 1953). Field worker circulation dept. La. State Library, 1934-39; asst. librarian E. Baton Rouge Parish Library, 1939-46, librarian, 1947—. Bd. dirs. Community Services Council, 1957-63, Baton Rouge Area Tb Assn., 1960-66, Baton Rouge Guidance Center, 1962-63, Family Counseling Service, 1957-60, Mem. Am., La. (pres. 1962-63), Southwestern library assns., La. Adult Edn. Assn. Jewish religion (bd. dirs. synagogue 1953-65). Club: Baton Rouge Library. Home: 220 Steele Blvd Baton Rouge LA 70806 Office: 700 Laurel St Baton Rouge LA 70802

SCHENKKAN, ROBERT FREDERICK, TV sta. exec.; b. N.Y.C., Mar. 4, 1917; s. Joseph and Flora (Vander Zyl) S.; A.B., U. Va., 1941; postgrad. U. N.C., 1941-42, M.A. in Drama, 1947; m. Jean McKenzie, Aug. 26, 1944; children—Pieter, Dirk, Robert, Gerard. Mgr. WUNC-TV, Chapel Hill, 1954-55; pres., gen. mgr. KLRN-TV, Austin, Tex., 1964—; dir. Communication Center, also prof. radio-TV-film U. Tex., Austin, 1955—. Dir. Tex. Knowledge Network, 1962—; chmn. bd. mgrs. chmn. bd. dirs. Pub. Broadcasting Service, 1973-74; chmn. Nat. Ednl. TV Affiliates Council, 1969. Vice pres. Arts Council Austin, 1969-70; pres. Austin P.T.A., 1970-71; chmn. U. Tex. United Fund Drive, 1968-69. Bd. dirs. Austin Symphony, 1956-57, Austin Ballet Soc., 1958-62, Recordings for the Blind. Served with USNR, 1942-46. Rockefeller Found. grantee, 1941-42; Fulbright grantee, 1969, 72; Ford Found. grantee, 1970. Mem. Nat. Assn. Ednl. Broadcasters (vice chmn. 1968), So. Ednl. Communications Assn. (dir. 1971—, chmn. planning com. 1971—, mem. exec. com. 1971—). Author: (with Kai Jurgensen) Plays of Henrik Ibsen, a translation, 1966. Home: 1804 Robin Hood Trail Austin TX 78703 Office: PO Box 7158 Austin TX 78712

SCHEPPEGRELL, CERIL SOLON, dentist; b. New Orleans, July 29, 1911; s. George Henry and Lily Louise (Wuertz) S.; student Tulane U., 1931, 32, La. State U., 1932-33; D.D.S., Loyola U. of the South, 1939; m. Virginia Mary Kepper, Jan. 27, 1940; children—John Ceril, Elizabeth Mary, June Marie, George William, Virginia Mary, Ann (Mrs. Earl Joseph Parr), Stewart James. Intern, U.S. Marine Hosp., New Orleans, 1939-40; served as lt. comdr. USPHS, 1940-47; pvt. practice dentistry, New Orleans, 1947—. Instr. crown and bridgework Loyola Dental Sch., 1946-47. Chmn. Model Aviation in New Orleans Area, 1958; chmn. Crime Prevention Week in New Orleans, 1959. Fellow Royal Soc. Health; mem. Cath. Alumni Soc. Loyola U. (pres. 1951-61). Clubs: Paul Morphy Chess (mem. bd. govs.), Exchange (pres. 1960-61) (New Orleans); Green Acres Country (Metairie, La.). Home: 2008 Colony Rd Metairie LA 70003 Office: Hibernia Bank Bldg New Orleans LA 70112

SCHEPS, CLARENCE, univ. adminstr.; b. Houston, Jan. 16, 1915; s. Benjamin and Libby (Solman) S.; B.A., Rice Inst., 1935; M.S., Columbia, 1936; Ph.D., La. State U., 1943; m. Mary E. Brown, Aug. 28, 1939; children—Philip, Edward. Instr. accounting La. State U., 1936-41; supr. finance La. Dept. Edn., 1941-46; comptroller U. Miss., 1946-47; exec. asst. to pres. Tulane U., 1947-48, comptroller, 1948-57, v.p., comptroller, 1957-66, exec. v.p., 1966—. Dir. Internat. City Bank New Orleans. Gen. chmn. United Fund Campaign Greater New Orleans, 1958; chmn. New Orleans A.R.C., 1966-68; mem. bd., exec. council Internat. House, New Orleans; pres. Southeastern La. Girl Scout Council, 1962-65. Mem. Orleans Parish Sch. Bd., 1950-56, pres., 1952-55. Mem. Nat. Assn. Coll. and Univ. Bus. Officers (pres. 1965-67), Nat. Fedn. Coll. and Univ. Bus. Officer Assns. (exec. com. 1959, dir. 1952-68), Controller's Inst., So. Assn. Coll. and Univ. Bus. Officers (pres. 1959-60, Sec. 1961-65). Author: Accounting for Colleges and Universities, 1949, rev. edit., 1971. Home: 6321 Freret St New Orleans LA 70118

SCHERER, CLARENCE HENRY, city ofcl.; b. Timber Lake, S.D., Apr. 21, 1926; s. Clement and Anna (Kamperschroer) S.; B.S., St. John's U. (Collegeville, Minn.), 1950; M.S., Trinity U., 1953; m. Eoline G. Jordan, Dec. 2, 1947; children—Andrew, Bonnie (Mrs. Harrel Alcorn), Mary (Mrs. Phillip Risner), Susan (Mrs. Joseph Velasquez), David, Theresa. Chemist, City San Antonio, 1950; dir. research Tex. State Health Dept., Donna, Tex., 1951-52; research scientist U. Tex., Austin, 1953; supt. water supply treatment and reclamation City Amarillo, Tex., 1954—. Owner, cons. water and wastewater Chemlab. Service of Amarillo, 1960—. Vice chmn. environmental com. Panhandle Regional Planning Commn., 1970—; chmn. water quality monitoring com. Canadian River Water Authority, 1969—; vice chmn. Tex. Bd. Water and Waste Water Certification, 1972—; pres. elect Assn. Bds. Certification for Water and Wastewater Utility Operators U.S., 1974—. Served with Paratroops, AUS, 1945-47. Mem. Tex. Water Utilities Assn. (pres.), Water Pollution Control Fedn. (George B. Gascoigne award 1953, 71, William D. Hatfield award 1970), Am. Water Works Assn., Am. Pub. Works Assn. Republican. Roman Catholic. K.C. Author: (with others) Manual for Sewage Plant Operators, 1964; (with others) Manual for Wastewater Operations, 1971. Home: 7202 Applewood St Amarillo TX 79108 Office: PO Box 1971 Amarillo TX 79186

SCHERER, LESTER EUGENE, county govt ofcl.; b. St. Augustine, Fla., Dec. 16, 1937; s. Alvin Whitney and Meta (Price) S.; B.S. in Agr., U. Fla., 1961, M.S., 1963; m. Anne Mason, June 9, 1962; children—Gregory, Scott, Clay. Research asst. U. Fla., Gainsville, 1960-61; research asst. U.S. Dept. Agr., Gainesville, 1961-63; asst. dir. Palm Beach County Mosquito Control Bd., West Palm Beach, Fla., 1963-68; dir. Martin County Mosquito Control, Stuart, 1968—. Tchr. adult edn. courses Martin County, 1969—. Pres. Civitan Club, Stuart, 1970—. Recipient Distinguished Service award Jr. C. of C., 1970. Mem. Am., Fla. Entomol. socs., Am. Mosquito Control Assn., Hyacinth Control Soc., Audubon Soc. Martin County. Home: 1024 E 5th St Stuart FL 33494 Office: 2280 S Dixie Hwy Stuart FL 33494

SCHERER, PAUL CLARENCE, lawyer; b. Evansville, Ind., Mar. 5, 1926; s. Paul Carl and Mildred (Rowe) S.; B.B.A., U. Tex., 1949, LL.B., 1949; m. LaNoe Fenner, July 28, 1949; children—Michael, Leta, Jane. Admitted to Tex. bar, 1948; asso. firm Peareson & Peareson, Richmond, 1949-51; partner firm Peareson, Scherer, Roberts & Slone, Richmond, Tex., 1952—; pres. Peareson Fort Bend Abstract Co. Dir. Sugar Land State Bank (Tex.). Atty., City of Richmond, 1949—. Trustee Lamar Consol. Sch. Dist., 1955—. Served with USAAC, 1944-45. Fellow Am. Coll. Probate Counsel; mem. Mem. Am., Tex., Fort Bend County bar assns., Phi Delta Phi., Am. Legion. Methodist (trustee). Rotarian. Home: 915 Foster St Richmond TX 77469 Office: 210 3d St Richmond TX 77469

SCHERMBECK, CLARENCE EDWARD, govt. ofcl.; b. Leavenworth, Kan., Apr. 22, 1922; s. Edward Fredrick and Helen (White) S.; student Kan. State Coll., 1940-41; B.A., Tex. Christian U., 1948, M.A., 1951; m. Venicia Guajardo, May 20, 1967; children—Barbara Gwynn, James Edward. Tchr. social sci. Crane (Tex.) Pub. Schs., 1951-52; research asst. Kan. Legislative Council, 1952-53; research asso. Inst. Pub. Affairs, U. Tex., 1955-57; with Urban Renewal Adminstrn, Dept. Housing and Urban Devel., Ft. Worth, 1957—, area coordinator Colo., Kan., Okla., Region V, 1967-70, program mgr. Oklahoma City area office, 1970—. Served with USAAF, 1942-45. Mem. Am. Polit. Sci. Assn., Common Cuase, Pi Sigma Alpha. Author: Parking Traffic and Transportation in Texas Cities, 1956; Urban Renewal for Texas, 1957. Contbr. articles profl. jours. Home: 5952 NW 71st St Oklahoma City OK 73132 Office: 301 N Hudson Oklahoma City OK 73102

SCHERTZ, WALTER ARTHUR, city ofcl.; b. Schertz, Tex., Feb. 17, 1920; s. Walter Joseph and Alma Ida (Wuest) S.; student Draughons Bus. Coll., 1936-40; real estate certificate St. Mary's U., 1965; m. Lula Mae Gottschall, June 2, 1953. Water supt., part owner Schertz Water Works, Inc., 1941-63; Councilman City of Schertz, 1958-63; water supt., 1963-65; exec. dir. Urban Renewal Agy., Schertz, 1965—; chmn. bd. Randolph Field Nat. Bank, Universal City, Tex. Sec., Tex. Urban Renewal Assn., 1970-71, Green Valley Devel. Co., Inc., 1964—, Lone Oak Home Builders, Inc., 1968—. Served with USAAF, 1941-46. Mem. V.F.W., C. of C. (dir.). Methodist. Lion. Home: PO Box 386 321 Main St Schertz TX 78154 Office: 507 Main St Schertz TX 78154

SCHEUMANN, MARCUS CARL, lawyer; b. Cin., May 13, 1926; s. Marcus Carl and Freda (Henderson) S.; student U. Cin., 1946-49; B.S. in Commerce, Ohio U., 1961; J.D., Coll. William and Mary, 1971; m. Patricia Speckman, July 1, 1950; children—Marcus Carl, Melissa D., Mary H., Jeffrey G. Admitted to Va. bar, 1971, since practiced law in Hampton; partner firm Montague and Montague, 1971—. Prof. law George Washington Grad. Sch., 1972—. Served with USMCR, 1944-46; served to lt. col., AUS, 1949-68. Decorated Legion of Merit, Bronze Star. Mem. Va. State Bar, Va. State, Am. bar assns., Va. Trial Lawyers Assn., Phi Alpha Delta, Phi Delta Theta. Author: Mechanized and Armor Combat Operations in Vietnam, 1964. Home: 335 Elizabeth Lake Dr Hampton VA 23669 Office: 1 E Queen St PO Box 96 Hampton VA 23669

SCHEVING, LAWRENCE EINAR, educator; b. Hensel, N.D., Oct. 20, 1920; s. Einar L. and Mary (Brown) S.; B.S. in Biology, DePaul U., 1949, M.S. in Zoology, 1950; Ph.D., Loyola U., Chgo., 1957; m. Virginia M. Krumdick, Apr. 6, 1949; children—Lawrence, Mary, John, Gennifer, Patricia (dec.). Mem. faculty Lewis Coll., Lockport, Ill., 1950-57, successively instr., asst. prof., asso. prof. and head dept. biol. sci. 1954, 57; prof. anatomy Chgo. Med. Sch., 1957-67, La. State U. Med. Sch., New Orleans, 1967-70; prof. anatomy U. Ark. Med. Sch., Little Rock, 1970—. Served to capt. AUS, 1940-45. Decorated Bronze Star medal; recipient Research award, Chgo. Med. Sch. Bd. Dirs., 1962; named Prof. Year, Student Council Chgo. Med. Sch., 1964; recipient Golden Apple award student body U. Ark. Med. Sch., 1972; Alexander von Humboldt Found. award, 1973. Mem. Am. Soc. Anatomists, Am. Soc. Zoologists, Internat. Soc. Electro-Myographic

Kinsesiologists, Internat. Soc. Chronobiology (sec.-treas.), So. Assn. Anatomists (councillor), Sigma Xi. Contbr. chpts. to books, articles in field of chronobiology and other biol. areas to profl. jours. Editorial bd. Internat. Jour. Chronobiology, Chronobiologie. Home: 1 Redcoat Lane Little Rock AR 72207

SCHICK, FRANK JOSEPH, III, educator; b. Huntsville, Ala., July 15, 1933; s. Frank Joseph and Grace Lee (Foster) S.; B.A., Auburn U., 1955; M.A., U. Ala., 1965; m. Myra Jean Brock, Feb. 22, 1962; children—Heather, Heidi, Brock. Asst. headmaster Birmingham (Ala.) Univ. Sch., 1956-69; prin. Isidore Newman Sch., New Orleans, 1969-73; counselor Fla. Jr. Coll., Jacksonville, 1973—. Mem. ednl. task force Greater New Orleans Goals Found., 1971-72. Mem. Nat. Assn. Elementary Sch. Prins, Am. Psychol. Assn. (asso.), Phi Mu Alpha. Episcopalain (sr. warden 1968-69). Home: 6813 Gaillardia Rd Jacksonville FL 32211

SCHICK, FRANK L., librarian; b. Vienna, Austria, Feb. 4, 1918 (came to U.S. 1938, naturalized 1943); s. Egon and Anna (Lapper) S.; B.A., Wayne State U., 1946; B.L.S., M.A., U. Chgo., 1948; M.L.S., U. Mich., 1955, Ph.D., 1957; m. Renee Silberfeld, Aug. 9, 1938; children—Thomas Egon, James Benjamin, Ellen Diane. Jr. asst. librarian Wayne State U., Detroit, 1948-54, asst. librarian, 1955-58; lectr. U. Mich., 1951-54, 55-58; asst. to dean Columbia U., N.Y.C., 1954-55; coordinator adult edn. and library statistics, asst. dir. library services br. U.S. Office Edn., Washington, 1958-66, chief library surveys br. Nat. Center for Ednl. Statistics, 1971—; dir., prof. Sch. Library and Information Sci., U. Wis. at Milw., 1966-71; vis. prof. U. N.C., 1962, 64. Rapporteur, UNESCO Conf. on Pub. Statistics, Paris, 1964, pres. UNESCO Conf. on Library Statistics, Paris, 1970; pres. Internat. Library Statistics Conf., The Hague, Netherlands, 1966, Paris, France, 1968, Prague, Czechoslovakia, 1971. Guest lectr. West German library schs., 1967; cons. Israel libraries, 1968; chmn. library statistics com., tech. com. 46, Internat. Orgn. for Standardization, Berlin, 1964-72; sec. library a statistics and standard com. Internat. Fedn. Library Assns., The Hague, 1972—. Served with AUS, 1943-45. Mem. A.L.A. (chmn. library edn. legislation com., statistics coordinating com.; mem. council), Spl. Libraries Assn. (chmn. documentation group Washington chpt. 1971-72), Am. Nat. Standards Inst. (chmn. library statistics subcom. 1966-68, 73—). Author: The Paperbound Book in America, 1958. Editor: Trends in Am. Book Publishing, 1958; The Future of Library Service, 1959; North Am. Library Edn. Directory and Statistics, 1966-68, 69-71; Survey of Spl. Libraries Serving the Fed. Govt., 1968; Directory of Health Scis. Libraries U.S., 1969; Bowker Ann., 1969-74. Contbr. over 100 articles to profl. jours. Home: 2809 Blazer Ct Silver Spring MD 20906 Office: 400 Maryland Av SW Washington DC 20202

SCHIFF, FRANK WILLIAM, economist; b. Greifswald, Germany, July 15, 1921; s. Fritz and Hildegarde (Caro) S.; came to U.S., 1936, naturalized, 1944; A.B., Columbia, 1942, postgrad., 1946-49; m. Erika Deussen, June 11, 1974. Instr. econs. Columbia, 1946-51; with Fed. Res. Bank N.Y., 1951-64; sr. staff economist Pres.'s Council Econ. Advisers, 1964-68; dep. undersec. monetary affairs U.S. Treasury, 1968-69; v.p., chief economist Com. for Econ. Devel., Washington, 1969—. Adviser, Nat. Bank Vietnam, 1955, 57; chief finance div. U.S. AID Mission, Saigon, 1955. Chmn., Downtown Economists Luncheon Group, N.Y.C., 1961-63. Served with AUS, 1943-45; ETO. Decorated Bronze Star. Mem. Council Fgn. Relations, Am. Econ. Assn., Nat. Economists Club (pres. 1973-74), Phi Beta Kappa. Home: 700 New Hampshire Av NW Washington DC 20036 Office: 1000 Connecticut Av NW Washington DC 20036

SCHILLING, EDWIN CARLYLE, JR., lawyer; b. Greensburg, La., Sept. 25, 1921; s. Edwin Carlyle and Myrtle (Holland) S.; J.D., La. State U., 1948; m. Ann LeTard, Feb. 7, 1942; 1 son, Edwin Carlyle III. Admitted to La. bar, 1948, since practiced in Amite; individual practice law, 1948-62; mem. law firm Schilling & Simpson, 1963-73, Schilling, Simpson & Reid, 1974—. Dir. Hammond Bldg. & Loan Assn. (La.); dir., chmn. bd. Advanced Edn., Inc., Baton Rouge. Mem. adv. council La. Moral and Civic Found.; mem. exec. com. La. Bapt. Conv. Trustee La. Coll., Pineville, Pub. Affairs Research Council. Served with AUS, 1943-46. Mem. Am., La., Twenty First Jud. Dist. bar assns., Amite C. of C. (past pres.). Baptist (deacon). Rotarian (past pres.). Home: 305 Cedar St Amite LA 70422 Office: 109 N Bay St Amite LA 70422

SCHILLING, RALPH FRANKLIN, univ. pres.; b. Morris, Okla., July 5, 1921; s. R.F. and Mattie E. (Crume) S.; Ed.D., Tex. Tech. Coll., 1957; M. Ed., Okla. U., 1950; B.A., Oklahoma City U., 1948; m. Mary Katherine Brooks, Jan. 19, 1942; 1 son, Ralph Franklin. Instr., asst. coach Oklahoma City U., 1947-50; high sch. prin., Crosbyton, Tex., 1950-52, Littlefield, Tex., 1952-54; supt. schs., Littlefield, 1954-60; pres. Pan Am. U., Edinburg, Tex., 1960—. Chmn. adv. bd. Littlefield Salvation Army, 1959. Named Littlefield Man of Year, 1958. Mem. N.E.A. (life), Tex. P.T.A. (life), Am. Assn. Sch. Adminstrs., Tex. Tchrs. Assn., Tex. Adminstrs. Assn. Methodist (past chmn. stewards, lay leader). Rotarian (pres. Littlefield 1959-60), Mason (32 deg.). Home: Box 232 Edinburg TX 78539

SCHINDLER, CHARLES ALVIN, educator; b. Boston, Dec. 27, 1924; s. Edward Esau and Esther (Weisman) S.; B.S. in Biology, Rensselaer Poly. Ins., 1950; M.A., U. Tex. at Austin, 1955, Ph.D., 1961; m. Barbara Jean Francois, Jan. 29, 1955; children—Esther M., Susan E., Neal L. Commd. 2d lt. U.S. Air Force, 1951, advanced through grades to maj., 1964; research scientist various armed forces research labs., including Armed Forces Inst. Pathology, Washington, 1961-67, USAF Armament Lab, Elgin AFB, Fla., 1967-68; ret., 1968; asst. prof. dept. microbiology U. Okla., Norman, 1968-72; asst. prof. natural sci. Flagler Coll., St. Augustine, Fla., 1972-73. Cons. Mead Johnson Research Center, 1961-67. Chmn. Cleve. County precinct Democratic party, Norman, Okla., 1973—. Served with USAAF, 1943-46. Charles E. Lewis fellow, 1958; NSF grantee, 1971. Mem. Am. Soc. Microbiologists (exec. sec. Mo. Valley br. 1969-71), Am. Chem. Soc., N.Y. Acad. Scis., Soc. Gen. Microbiology (Gt. Britain), Sigma Xi. Patentee in field. Contbr. profl. jours. Home: 2000 Morgan Dr Norman OK 73069

SCHINNERER, VICTOR OSCAR, ins. co. exec.; b. Wyncote, Pa., Feb. 13, 1906; s. Frederick D. and Sarah (Field) S.; A.B., Pa. State U., 1928; m. Muriel Reid Johnson, Sept. 8, 1934; children—Sally (Mrs. Thomas D. Fant), William Reid, Sandra (Mrs. John J. Younger). Underwriter, spl. agt., ins. analyst Aetna Casualty & Surety Co., Phila., 1928-37, supt. of agts., Washington, 1937-38; formed own firm in 1938, which inc. in 1947 as Victor O. Schinnerer & Co., Inc., (became subsidiary Marsh & McLennon Inc.), now chmn.; sr. v.p., Marsh & McLennon, Inc., 1970—, dir. Nat. Sav. & Trust Co., Washington. Trustee Fed. City Council, 1970—. Bd. assos. Gettysburg Coll., 1965—. Dir. Met. Washington Bd. of Trade, 1954-67, pres., 1958-59, mem. sr. council, 1959—; chmn. Washington Conv. and Visitors Bur., 1962-65, mem. exec. com., 1965—; adv. council Boy Scouts Am., 1963—; pres. D.C. Soc. for Crippled Children, 1962-64; bd. dirs. Washington Heart Assn., 1960-61. Mem. D.C. (past pres.), Nat. (past dir.) assns. ins. agts., Am. Mgmt. Assn., Nat. Assn. Life Underwriters, Newcomen Soc. (mem. Washington com.), Phi Kappa Psi. Clubs: University: Kiwanis (Washington); Columbia Country, Congressional Country, Seaview Country; Ocean Reef Yacht, Card Sound Golf, Key Largo Anglers. Home: 9020 Brickyard Rd Potomac MD 20854 Office: Schinnerer Bldg 5028 Wisconsin Av NW Washington DC 20016

SCHLANT, ROBERT CARL, physician, educator; b. El Paso, Tex., Apr. 16, 1929; B.A., Vanderbilt U., 1948, M.D., 1951. Intern Peter Bent Brigham Hosp., Boston, 1951-52, jr. asst. resident in medicine, 1952-53, sr. asst. resident, 1955-56, asst. in medicine, 1956-58; research fellow in medicine Harvard Med. Sch., 1956-58; asst. prof. medicine Emory U. Sch. Medicine, 1958-62, asso. prof., 1962-66, prof., 1967—. Fellow Am. Coll. Cardiology (gov. Ga.), A.C.P. (exec. com.), Council on Clin. Cardiology, Am., Ga. (dir.) heart assns.; mem. Am. Assn. U. Cardiologists, Am. Fedn. Clin. Research, So. Soc. for Clin. Investigation (mem. subsplty. bd. cardiovascular disease). Home: 3340 E Wood Valley Rd NW Atlanta GA 30327 Office: 69 Butler St SE Atlanta GA 30303

SCHLEGEL, DOROTHY MILDRED BADDERS (MRS. MARVIN W. SCHLEGEL), educator; b. Harford County, Md., July 18, 1910; d. John Joseph and Lucy Alice (Davis) Badders; B.A., Dickinson Coll., 1932; M.A., Coll. William and Mary, 1948; Ph.D., U. N.C., 1954; postgrad. U. Vienna, 1954, Sorbonne, 1955, U. Frankfort, 1954-55, 62; m. Marvin W. Schlegel, Apr. 9, 1941. Tchr. English, Hannah Penn Jr. High Sch., York, Pa., 1932-34; tchr. English, French, Latin, William Penn Sr. High Sch., York, 1934-47; instr. English, St. Helena Extension, Coll. William and Mary, 1948; asst. prof. English and comparative lit. Longwood Coll., Farmville, Va., 1953-57, asso. prof., 1957-63, prof., 1963-66, chmn. freshman English, 1964-66; prof. English, Norfolk State Coll., 1966—. Mem. Internat. Comparative Lit. Assn., Freies Deutches Hochstift, Modern Lang. Assn., South Atlantic Modern Lang. Assn., Coll. English Assn. N.C.-Va. Coll. English Assn., Nat. Council Tchrs. English, Va. Assn. Tchrs. English, Am. Assn. U. Profs., Cabell Soc. (pres. 1969-72), Soc. 18th Century Studies, D.A.R., Mayflower Soc., Phi Beta Kappa, Sigma Alpha Iota. Episcopalian. Author: Shaftesbury and the French Deists, 1956; Writing from Research, 1964; also articles. Home: 476 Linkhorn Dr Virginia Beach VA 23451 Office: Norfolk State Coll Norfolk VA 23504

SCHLEIER, ROBERT GLASS, lawyer; b. Houston, July 17, 1925; s. William Martin and Maud (Glass) S.; J.D., U. Tex. at Austin, 1950; m. Nora Virginia Potts, May 29, 1948; children—Robert G. Jr., William A., Laura Elaine. Admitted to Tex. bar, 1949, La. bar, 1955; atty.-land mgr. Hudson Gas & Oil Corp., Shreveport, 1954-56; gen. counsel Carter-Jones Drilling Co., Inc., Kilgore, 1956-59; partner firm Bean, Ford, Schleier, Allen & Gardner, Kilgore, Tex., 1959—. Mem. exec. bd. East Tex. Area council Boy Scouts Am., 1971—; pres. East Tex. Treatment Center Physically Handicapped, Kilgore, 1964. Bd. regents Tyler (Tex.) State Coll. Served with USNR, 1943-46. Mem. State Bar Tex., State Bar La., Fed. Power, Gregg County (pres. 1972) bar assns., Kilgore C. of C. (pres. 1965), Phi Alpha Delta, Beta Theta Pi. Presbyn. (ruling elder). Rotarian. Home: 404 Hill Terrace Dr Kilgore TX 75662 Office: 115 S Martin St PO Box 1251 Kilgore TX 75662

SCHLESINGER, B. FRANK, architect; b. N.Y.C., Sept. 17, 1925; s. Augustus and Ethel (Brower) S.; student Middlebury Coll., 1946-48; B.S., U. Ill., 1950; B.Arch., Harvard, 1954; m. Draga A. Christy; children—Jeff, Nike, Katherine, Christy, Daniel, (stepson) Francis L. Haley. Draftsman, Hugh Stubbins Assos., 1953-55, Marcel Breuer, 1955-56; practice architecture, Princeton, N.J., 1956-59, Doylestown, Pa., 1959-69, Phila., 1969-71, Washington, 1971—; instr. archtl. design U. Pa., 1957-60; vis. critic Columbia Sch. Architecture, 1962-63; prof. Sch. Architecture U. Md., 1971—. Served with USNR, 1943-46. Arthur Wheelwright fellow in architecture Harvard, 1963; recipient honor awards Phila. chpt. A.I.A., 1960-65, 68, 69, Pa. Soc. Architects, 1960, 61, 63-65, Bronze medal, 1965; Design award Progressive Architecture, Mercer-Jackson Urban Renewal Area, 1966, Genesee Crossroads Plaza, 1967, Fairmount Park Nature Center, 1969, tubular steel framed residence, 1972. Fellow A.I.A. (dir. Phila. chpt. 1970-72); mem. Harvard Grad. Sch. Design Assn. (pres. 1971-73). Address: 2913 Garfield St NW Washington DC 20008

SCHLESINGER, EUGENE RICHARD, economist; b. N.Y.C., Mar. 19, 1925; s. Julius and Rhea (Rogen) S.; A.B., Harvard, 1947, A.M., 1948, Ph.D., 1950; m. Louise Fleur Myers, June 19, 1948 (div. June 1967); children—Louis, Thomas, Kenneth, Kathryn. Economist Fed. Res. Bank N.Y., 1948-52, World Bank, 1952-54; mng. partner Eugene Schlesinger & Co., 1954-59; asst. prof. N.Y. U., 1954-60, asso. prof., 1960-64; chief economist U.S.-P.R. Commn. on Status of P.R., 1964-66; lectr. Econ. Devel. Inst., Internat. Bank of Reconstrn. and Devel., Washington, 1966—. Cons. U.S. Dept. Commerce, Econ. Commn. Latin Am., Fiscal div. UN, Joint Tax program Latin Am. Served to lt. (j.g.) USNR, 1943-46. Recipient Ford Faculty Research fellowship, 1960-61. Mem. Am. Econ. Assn., Am. Finance Assn., Nat. Tax Assn., Soc. Internat. Devel., Phi Beta Kappa. Author: Multiple Exchange Rates and Economic Development, 1952; (with J.H. Adler and E. Olsen) Public Finance and Economic Development, 1952; (with J.H. Adler and E. Van Weslerberg) The Pattern of United States Import Trade, 1952. Home: 2301 E St NW Washington DC 20037 Office: 1818 H St NW Washington DC 20433

SCHLESINGER, JAMES RODNEY, sec. Def.; b. N.Y.C., Feb. 15, 1929; s. Julius and Rhea (Rogen) S.; A.B. summa cum laude, Harvard, 1950, A.M., 1952, Ph.D., 1956; m. Rachel Mellinger, June 19, 1954; children—Cora K., Charles L., Ann R., William F., Emily, Thomas S., Clara, James R. Asst. prof., then asso. prof. U. Va., 1955-63; sr. staff mem. RAND Corp., 1963-67, dir. strategic studies, 1967-69; asst. dir. Bur. of Budget, 1969-71; chmn. U.S. AEC, 1971-73; dir. CIA, 1973; sec. Def., 1973—. cons. in field. Mem. bd. assos. Fgn. Policy Research Inst., U. Pa., 1962-63. Recipient Frederick Sheldon prize fellowship Harvard, 1950-51. Mem. Am. Econ. Assn., Phi Beta Kappa. Republican. Lutheran. Author: The Political Economy of National Security, 1960; Organizational Structures and Planning, 1967. Co-author: Issues in Defense Economics. Asso. editor Jour. Finance, 1964-65. Home: 3601 N 26th St Arlington VA 22207 Office: Pentagon Washington DC 20301

SCHLOM, JEFFREY, educator; b. N.Y.C., June 22, 1942; s. David and Anna (Klein) S.; B.S. (Pres.'s scholar), Ohio State U., 1964; M.S., Adelphi U., 1966; Ph.D., Rutgers U., 1969. Instr., Columbia Coll. Physicians and Surgeons, 1969-71, asst. prof., 1971-73; chmn. breast cancer virus segment Nat. Cancer Inst., NIH, Bethesda, Md., 1973—; asso. prof. George Washington U., Washington, 1973—. Mem. A.A.A.S., Harvey Soc., N.Y. Acad. Scis. Contbr. articles to profl. jours. Home: 5601 Seminary Rd Falls Church VA 22041 Office: Landow Bldg Nat Cancer Inst NIH Bethesda MD 20014

SCHLOSSER, JOSEPH LEO, architect; b. Phila., Aug. 22, 1925; s. John and Teresa Mary (Stuhl) S.; B.S., Ga. Inst. Tech., 1953, B.Arch., 1954; m. Delia Gray Brown, June 14, 1947; children—Teresa, Joe, Jane Marie, Joann. Draftsman, designer Laurence S. Miller, Brunswick, Ga., 1954-61; v.p., architect Miller, Schlosser & Miller, Brunswick, 1961-67; pres., architect Schlosser & Miller, Inc., Brunswick, 1967-72; individual practice, 1972—; dir. Sea Circus, Inc., Jekyll Island, Ga. Pres., Glynn County Heart Assn., 1968-72; mem. Glynn County Bldg. Code Appeals Bd., 1966-72; sec. Brunswick Housing Standards Appeal Bd., 1968-72; div. chmn. United Community Fund, 1972—; adv. com. drafting dept. Brunswick Jr. Coll., 1972—; adv. com. Manpower Tng. Sch., 1973—. Served with USNR, 1943-46. Mem. A.I.A., Constrn. Specifications Inst. Roman Catholic (mem. parish bd. 1973—, chmn. sch. bd. 1964-68). Kiwanian (v.p.). Illustration of architl. work Brunswick Mall pub. in Chain Store Age, 1970. Home: 1027 Lanier Blvd Brunswick GA 31520 Office: Office Park Bldg Brunswick GA 31520

SCHLUETER, EDGAR ALBERT, educator; b. Milw., Sept. 23, 1918; s. Albert Henry and Anna (Gaffrey) S.; student U. Wis. at Milw., 1938-40; B.S., North Tex. State U., 1942; M.S. in Zoology, U. Wis. at Madison, 1949, Ph.D., (Wis. Alumni Research Found. fellow 1957-59), 1962; m. Mary Ann Hodel, Aug. 3, 1957; children—Cynthia, Thomas, Susan. Instr. dept. biol. sci. Mich. State U., East Lansing, 1949-59; asst. prof. dept. biology U. Wis.-Superior, 1959-62; asso. prof. North Tex. State U., Denton, 1968-69, prof. biol. sci., 1969—. Scoutmaster, Longhorn council Boy Scouts Am., 1971—. Served with M.C., AUS, 1944-45. Mem. Am. Soc. Parasitologists, North Tex. Biol. Soc. (permanent sec.), Am. Microscopical Soc., Tex. Acad. Sci., A.A.A.S., Sigma Xi, Gamma Alpha. Home: 1105 Piping Rock Lane Denton TX 76201

SCHLUMP, JOHN ARTHUR, gen. contractor; b. N.Y.C., July 17, 1929; s. John Robert and Anna (Ichnacek) S.; B.S. in C.E., Rensselaer Poly. Inst., 1951; postgrad. Columbia, 1958-59; m. Angela Maria Casciano, Feb. 4, 1956; children—Lynn, Judith, Joan, Jill. Soils engr. Porter, Urquhart, French Morocco, 1952-53; project engr. Daugherty-Tyler-Breslin, Azores, 1956-58; v.p. Pavarini Constrn. Co., Inc., N.Y.C. and San Juan, P.R., 1958—; dir. Concrete Metal Forms, Inc., San Juan, Casa Luchetti, Inc., San Juan. Served with AUS, 1953-55. Mem. Am. Soc. C.E., Phi Kappa. K.C. Clubs: Nautico, Racquet. Home: 54 Kings Court Santurce PR 00911 Office: 1225 Ponce de Leon St Santurce PR 00908

SCHMAEDECKE, WILLIAM LOUIS, lawyer; b. Covington, Ky., June 1, 1936; s. Walter Augustine and Emma Anna (Jansen) S.; A.B., Thomas More Coll., 1956; J.D., Salmon P. Chase Coll. Law, 1962; m. Mary Katherine Nunan, Aug. 12, 1961; children—Sara Marie, Walter Thomas, William Hardin. Insp. FDA, Cin., 1956-57; food technologist Kroger Co., Cin., 1957-63; admitted to Ky. bar, 1963, since practiced law in Covington. Mem. Ky. House of Reps., 1972—. Bd. overseers Thomas More Coll. Mem. Covington-Kenton County Jaycees (pres. 1967-68), Jaycees Internat. (dir. 1970-71), Thomas More Coll. Alumni Assn. (chmn. bd. 1973-74), Am., Ky., Kenton County (sec. 1964-65) bar assns. Home: 67 Thompson Ave Fort Mitchell KY 41017 Office: 401 Pike St Covington KY 41011

SCHMAUS, FRANCIS THEODORE, librarian; b. Lancaster, Pa., Nov. 2, 1919; s. Harold Eugene and Eleanor (Uhlir) S.; A.B., U. Colo., 1950; M.A. in English, U. Denver, 1951, M.A. in L.S., 1953; postgrad. U. Tex., 1954-59; m. Jean Barditzky, Feb. 13, 1955; Faculty, U. Denver, 1950-54; with reference dept. U. Tex. at Austin, 1954-59, engring. librarian, 1959—. Served with AUS, 1941-45. Mason. Author: A Library Reference Manual for Engineering Student, 1963. Home: 4515 Rosedale Av Austin TX 78756

SCHMELZ, GARY WILLIAM, nature center dir.; b. Jersey City, July 24, 1939; s. Henry and Katherine (Tibbatts) S.; B.S., Farleigh Dickinson U., 1961; M.S. in Zoology, U. Del., 1964, Ph.D. (Univ. fellow), 1970; m. Bernice A. Davies, Nov. 4, 1965. Research asso. U. Del., 1970-71; chief aquatic ecologist Deltona Corp., Marco Island, Fla., 1971; naturalist Big Cypress Nature Center, Naples, Fla., 1971-73, dir., 1973—. Instr. Edison Community Coll., 1972—. Served with USNR, 1964-66. Mem. Nat. Wildlife Fedn., A.A.A.S., Nat. Audubon Soc. Home: 1224 Hilltop Dr Naples FL 33940 Office: Route 3 Box 140 Naples FL 33940

SCHMERTMANN, HAROLD, govt. ofcl.; b. N.Y.C., Mar. 28, 1935; s. John and Margaret (Carstens) S.; B.A., Fla. State U., 1961, M.S. in Geography, 1962; m. Gloria Jean Bowen, Dec. 22, 1962; children—Gregory, Kerry. Community planner Fla. Devel. Commn., Tallahassee, 1963-66; city planner St. Petersburg, 1966-67; dir. planning and recreation div. Fla. Devel. Commn., 1967-69, planning mgr. Fla. Dept. Community Affairs, 1969-71, chief, bur. local assitance, 1971—. Served with USAF, 1953-57. Home: 1529 E Indian Head Dr Tallahassee FL 32301 Office: 2571 Executive Center Circle E Tallahassee FL 32301

SCHMERTMANN, JOHN HENRY, educator; b. N.Y.C., Dec. 2, 1928; s. Johannes Conrad and Margaret Anne (Carstens) S.; B.S. in Civil Engring., Mass. Inst. Tech., 1950; M.S. in Civil Engring. Northwestern U., 1954, Ph.D., 1962; postgrad. (NSF fellow), Norwegian Geotech. Inst. 1962-63; m. Pauline Anne Grange, Aug. 11, 1956; children—Carl Paul, Gary Robert, Neil Johan, Joy Anne. Soils engr. Moran Proctor Mueser and Rutledge, N.Y.C., 1951-54; asst. prof. U. Fla., Gainesville, 1956-62, asso. prof. civil engring., 1962-65, prof. civil engring., 1965—. Sabbatical leave Nat. Research Council Can., 1971-72; cons. in field. Served with C.E., AUS, 1954-56. Fellow Am. Soc. C.E. (br. pres. 1970-71; recipient Collingswood prize, 1956, Norman medal 1971), Fla. Engring. Soc. (recipient award for Outstanding Tech. Achievement 1972), Am. Soc. Testing and Materials. Research on soil mechanics and found. engring. Home: 2926 NW 14th Pl Gainesville FL 32605

SCHMIDT, ARTHUR EARL, physician; b. St. Louis, Jan. 1, 1923; s. Arthur Earl and Elsa (Kallmeyer) S.; M.D., Washington U., St. Louis, 1946; m. Norma Jean Saggau, July 6, 1947; children—Robert Eric, Christine Ann, Arthur Earl III, Cindy Lou. Intern, Presbyn. Hosp., Chgo., 1946-47, resident, 1951-53; resident St. Louis County Hosp., Clayton, Mo., 1950-51; fellow in cardiology U. Okla. Hosp., 1953-54; chief med. service Central State Hosp., Norman, Okla., 1954-56; practice medicine specializing in internal medicine and cardiology, Oklahoma City, 1956—; mem. staff Univ., Baptist, Deaconess, St. Anthony, Mercy, VA hosps. (all Oklahoma City); instr. dept. medicine U. Okla. Med. Sch., 1954-63, asst. clin. prof. medicine, 1963-70, asso. clin. prof. medicine, 1970—. Active Okla. Heritage Found., Okla. Mus. Art, Red Ridge, Okla. Art Center. Served to capt., M.C., AUS, 1943-46, 47-50. Mem. A.M.A., A.C.P., Am. Coll. Cardiology, Am. Coll. Chest Physicians, Am. Heart Assn., Okla. Thoracic Soc., Am., Okla. (pres. 1963) socs. internal medicine, Okla., Oklahoma County med. assns. Mason. Club: Quail Creek Golf and Country (Oklahoma City). Home: 11909 Chestnut Ridge Oklahoma City OK 73120 Office: 3141 NW Expressway Oklahoma City OK 73112

SCHMIDT, ERNEST JOHN, boat mfg. co. exec.; b. Rosenberg, Tex., Jan. 1, 1936; s. Ernest J. and Etta (Riley) S.; B.B.A., U. Tex., 1954-55, 58-61; student North Tex. State U., 1957-58; m. Linda A. Wegner, July 19, 1958; children—Kallin Gaye, Steven Owen. Asst. mgr. advt. Magcobar Corp., Dresser, Ind., 1962-65; mgr. advt. Welex Corp., Houston, 1965-66, Tracor Int., Austin, Tex., 1966-67; asst. sales mgr. Glastron Corp., Austin, 1967-69, gen. sales mgr., 1969-73, v.p. sales, 1973—. Sec. Houston chpt. Assn. Indsl. Advertisers, 1965. Mem. Travis County Grand Jury, 1973—. Bd. dirs. Austin Mental Health Assn., 1974—. Served with AUS, 1955-57. Mem. Boating Industry Assn. (shows com.), Sales and Marketing Execs. Assn. Club:

University Hills (pres. 1971) (Austin). Home: 8800 Fairway Hill Austin TX 78759 Office: PO Box 9447 Austin TX 78766

SCHMIDT, HAROLD EUGENE, civil engr., land co. exec.; b. Cedar Rapids, Ia., Oct. 12, 1925; s. Alfons W. and Lillie (Schlegel) S.; B.S., U. Ia., 1949; M.S., Mass. Inst. Tech., 1953; m. Lucy Hermann, Apr. 13, 1957; children—Harold, Sandra. Research, devel. engr. Chgo. Pump Co., 1949-51; engr. A.B. Kononoff, Engrs., Miami, Fla., 1956-58; with Gen. Devel. Corp., Miami, 1958—, v.p. utilities, 1966-67, corporate officer, asst. v.p., 1967-72; pres. Gen. Devel. Utilities, Inc., 1972, v.p. community div., 1973—; dir. Port Charlotte Bank (Fla.). Served to capt. Med. Service Corps, USAF, 1951-56. Mem. Am. Water Works Assn., Water Pollution Control Fedn., Sigma Xi, Chi Epsilon. Home: 641 W 53d St Hialeah FL 33012 Office: 1111 S Bayshore Dr Miami FL 33131

SCHMIDT, RALPH JULIUS, aircraft mfg. co. exec.; b. Los Angeles, Nov. 19, 1921; s. Fred and Emma (Stratman) S.; student U. Cal. at Los Angeles, 1951-52, Tex. Christian U., 1958-59; m. Alva June Sherk, Feb. 28, 1942; children—Paul R., Diane M. (Mrs. Richard Newton), David M. With Menasco Mfg. Co., Fort Worth, 1940—, v.p., gen. mgr. Tex. Div., 1964-73, sr. v.p. operations, 1973—; dir. First State Bank, Bedford, Tex. Served with AUS, 1944-46. Mem. Am. Assn. Tool and Mech. Engrs. (sr. mem.), Air Force Assn., Assn. U.S. Army (v.p.), Am. Hellicopter Assn. Baptist. Home: 7000 Deville St Fort Worth TX 76118 Office: PO Box 7656 Fort Worth TX 76111

SCHMIDT, STEPHEN, museum dir.; b. N.Y.C., Dec. 11, 1925; s. Stephen and Margaret (Szeleznyk) S.; B.A., U. N.M., 1951; m. Carol Elizabeth Ketchum, Sept. 11, 1955; children—Elizabeth Grace, Stephen Bernard, Margaret Helen. Dir. Martin County Museums, Stuart, Fla., 1957-65, Sci. Mus. and Planetarium of Palm Beach County, West Palm Beach, Fla., 1965-67, Fort Concho Preservation and Museum, San Angelo, Tex., 1968—. Cons. dir. Daytona Mus. Arts and Scis., Daytona Beach, Fla., 1967. Pres., Santa Rita P.T.A., San Angelo, 1970-72; mem. adv. bd. Fiesta del Concho, 1973-74. Mem. Tex. Museums Conf. (pres. 1972), Am. Assn. Museums (Mountain Plains exec. mus. bd.). Episcopalian. Rotarian. Home: 717 W Washington Dr San Angelo TX 76901 Office: 213 E Av D San Angelo TX 76901

SCHMIED, RONALD DENNIS, engr., planner; b. Chgo., Aug. 13, 1930; s. Helmuth Walter and Ethel (Ross) S.; B.S., U. Ill., 1954; m. Joan Eileen Lorentzen, Dec. 28, 1955; children—Diana Lee, Lori Ann, Susanne Loren, Joanna Rachel. Civil engr. H. Balke Engrs., Cin., 1954-57; with Harland Bartholomew & Assos., Planners, Engrs., Architects, Memphis, 1957-71, planning dir., 1965-71, asso. partner, 1961-71; v.p. William S. Pollard Cons., Planners, Engrs., Memphis, 1971—. Instr. chemistry St. Bernard's Sch. Nursing, Chgo., 1951; instr. engring. tech., Memphis State U., 1966. Cons. rep. Miss.-Ark.-Tenn. Council Govts., 1967-68; mem. Germantown Design Review Commn. Served with AUS, 1951. Registered profl. engr., Ill., Tenn., Ohio, Ala. Mem. Am. Inst. Planners, Am. Soc. Planning Ofcls., Nat. Acad. Sci., Nat. Soc. Profl. Engrs., Am. Soc. C.E., Am. Soc. Photogrammetry, Nat. Assn. Housing and Redevel. Ofcls., Memphis Area Planners Club (pres. 1969). Club: Germantown Civic. Home: 7605 Ashworth Rd Germantown TN 38138 Office: 60 N 3d St Memphis TN 38103

SCHMITT, CHARLES RUDOLPH, chem. co. scientist; b. Bklyn., Mar. 31, 1920; s. Charles Joseph and Mary Catherine (Gerlinger) S.; B.S., Queens Coll., 1942; m. Alma Jean Peters, Nov. 10, 1945; children—Charles Jeffrey, Katherine Anne. Supr. TNT prodn. Plum Brook Ordnance Works, Sandusky, O., 1942-43; devel. engr. K-25 gaseous diffusion plant nuclear div. Union Carbide Corp., Oak Ridge, 1945-56, devel. chemist y-12 plant, 1956-65, sr. research chemist, 1965-68, devel. supr., 1968—. Cons. Rust Engring. Co. Served with AUS, 1944-45. Recipient Manhattan Dist. Spl. award U.S. War Dept., 1945. Registered profl. engr., Tenn. Mem. Am. Chem. Soc., Tenn. Acad. Sci., Nat., Tenn. socs. profl. engrs., Tenn. Wastewater Assn. Republican. Lutheran (trustee 1960-70). Author: Pyrophoricity, 1973. Contbr. articles to profl. jours. Home: 110 Montana Ave Oak Ridge TN 37830 Office: PO Box P Oak Ridge TN 37830

SCHMITT, GILBERT EUGENE, utility exec.; b. Seguin, Tex., Aug. 27, 1906; s. Lorenz and Mathilde (Glaeser) S.; B.S. in Elec. Engring., U. Tex., 1928; m. Maudine Hampton, Dec. 25, 1930; 1 dau., Patricia Nadine (Mrs. Henry A. Bunting III). Engr. substa. design and constrn. Central Power & Light Co., Corpus Christi, Tex., 1928-32, resident engr., 1929, gen. engr. design and constrn. changes, 1933-38; transmission supt. operations, engring. cons. Lower Colorado River Authority, Austin, Tex., 1939-40, chief engr., 1941-43, asst. gen. mgr., chief engr., 1944-73; cons. energy resources, 1974—. Fellow I.E.E.E. (past v.p.); mem. Tex. Soc. Profl. Engrs. (past pres.), Austin C. of C. (past v.p.), Ramshorn Club, Eta Kappa Nu. Mem. Ch. of Christ. Kiwanian. Home: 2804 Greenlee Dr Austin TX 78703 Office: 2804 Greenlee Dr Austin TX 78703

SCHMITT, HARRISON HAGAN, geologist, astronaut; b. Santa Rita, N.M., July 3, 1935; s. Harrison A. and Ethel (Hagan) S.; B.S., Cal. Inst. Tech., 1957; postgrad. (Fulbright fellow) U. Olso, Norway, 1957-58; Ph.D. (NSF post doctoral fellow), Harvard, 1964. Geologist, U.S. Geol. Survey, 1964-65; astronaut NASA, Houston, 1965—; lunar module pilot Apollo 17, 1972. Address: Lyndon B Johnson Space Center NASA Houston TX 77058

SCHMITT, VINCENT JEROME, realtor; b. N.Y.C., Nov. 29, 1911; s. John F. and Florence R. (Cumiskey) S.; student U. Mich., 1930; m. Margaret C. Reilley, Apr. 22, 1939; children—John, Richard, Alicia. Draftsman, John McMillan Co., N.Y.C., 1934-35; with Pan Am. Refining Corp., Texas City, 1935-47; owner V. J. Schmitt & Co., Texas City, Tex., 1947—; pres. Meml. Properties, Inc., 1967—; dir. Mainland Bank, Texas City. Chmn. Texas City Planning Commn., 1966—. Named Tex. Realtor of the Year, 1961. Mem. Nat. Assn. Real Estate Bds. (dir. 1954, 66-68, 69-71, trustee ins. trust real estate group 1972—), Nat. (regional v.p.), Tex. (pres. 1953-54, chmn. legislative taxation com. 1961, chmn. edn. com. 1967, chmn. mag. com. 1964-66) assns. realtors, Texas City Real Estate Bd. (pres. 1957, 61), Texas City-LaMarque Assn. Ins. Agts. (pres. 1956-57). Texas City (dir. 1962-64), Texas City-LaMarque (dir. 1968-70) chambers commerce. Roman Catholic. K.C. Home: 1121 Mainland Dr Texas City TX 77590 Office: 524 9th St Texas City TX 77590

SCHMITZ, CHARLES EDISON, clergyman; b. Mendota, Ill., July 18, 1919; s. Charles Frances and Lucetta M. (Foulk) S.; student Wheaton Coll., 1936-37, summer 1937, 38, 39; A.B., Wartburg Coll., Waverly, Ia., 1940; B.D., Wartburg Theol. Sem., Dubuque, Ia., 1942; m. Eunice M. Ewy, June 1, 1942; children—Charles Elwood, Jon Lee. Home mission developer and parish pastor Am. Luth. Ch., 1942-65, serving as founding pastor nine parishes including Ascension (Los Angeles), Am. Evang. Luth. Phoenix, others in Prescott, Glendale, Ariz., Scottsdale, Ariz., Portales, N.M.; formerly founder and prin. parochial schs. in Los Angeles and Phoenix; synodical Bible evangelist Am. Luth. Ch., 1965-73; dir. Intermountain Missions, 1948-60; dir. parish mission builder program; pastor Peace Luth. Ch., Palm Bay, Fla., 1973—. Former chmn., bd. mem. Ariz. Christian Conf., Christian Instnl. Ministry, Camelback Girls Residence, Ariz. Alcohol and Narcotics Edn. Assn., Phoenix Council Chs., Evang. Ministers Assn.; pres. Intermountain Conf., 1954-65; vice chmn. Nat. Worship and Ch. Music Commn., 1961-65; chmn. Billy Graham Ariz. Crusade, 1964, Nat. Luth. Social Welfare Conf., 1944—. Mem. Ariz. Conf. Crime and Delinquency Control, 1957-65; referee Maricopa County Juvenile Ct., 1959-61; mem. Gov.'s Com. Marriage and Divorce Problems, 1962-64; chief chaplain Maricopa County Civilian Def., 1961-65. Recipient Distinguished Alumni award Wartburg Coll., 1959. Lion (founding sec. and bd. mem. North Phoenix 1952-65). Co-editor: The ABC's of Life; editor: Body of Christ-Evangelism for the Seventies. Contbg. editor Good News mag., 1965-71. Home: 301 SE Port Malabar Blvd Palm Bay FL 32905

SCHMITZ, TERRY R., accountant; b. Colt, Ark., Aug. 22, 1936; s. Garland L. and Sue (Gilbert) S.; B.B.A., Memphis State U., 1962; children—Lee, John, Morgan. Staff accountant Harris, Kerr, Forster & Co., Memphis, 1962-63, Minor & Moore, C.P.A.'s, Memphis, 1963-65; audit supr. James Talcott, Inc., Atlanta, 1965-66, Ernst & Ernst, Jackson, Miss., 1966-70; individual practice accounting, Jackson, 1970—. Served with USAF, 1954-58. C.P.A., Tenn., Miss. Mem. Am. Soc. C.P.A.'s, Nat. Assn. Accountants, Miss. Art Assn., Memphis Jr. C. of C., Am. Legion, Delta Sigma Pi (life). Home and office: 1255 County Line Rd Jackson MS 39209

SCHNEE, RONALD GENE, research co. exec.; b. Lawton, Okla., Mar. 2, 1942; s. Edwin L. and Opal Janette (Armestead) S.; Asso. Sci., Cameron State Coll., 1962; B.S., Okla. State U., 1964, M.S., 1966, Ed.D., 1970; m. Janet Sharon Henderson, Dec. 28, 1963; children—Ronald Lamar, Krista Renee. Instr., U. Tex. at El Paso, 1968-69; Okla. State U., Stillwater, 1968-69; counselor Stillwater Pub. Schs., 1969-70; research dir. Okla. City Pub. Schs., 1970—. Pres. Evaluative Research Assos., Oklahoma City, 1970—; cons. U.S. Office Edn., 1971-73. Fund raiser, Young Republicans for Nixon, 1971-72; cons. Okla. Crime Commn., 1971-73. Bd. dirs. Lawton YMCA, 1960-62. Served with AUS, 1966-68. Ednl. Research Services fellow, 1969-71. Mem. Research Dirs. Urban Schs., Am. Ednl. Research Assn., Nat. Soc. for the Study Edn., Okla. Edn. Assn. (del. 1973-74), Oklahoma City Jr. C. of C., Phi Delta Kappa, Phi Theta Kappa. Club: Red, Red Rose. Home: 2316 NW 120th St Oklahoma City OK 73120 Office: 900 N Klein St Oklahoma City OK 73106

SCHNEIDER, CALVIN DWAINE, supt. sch.; b. Custer, Okla., Nov. 7, 1931; s. Thomas Raymond and Emma (Hamburger) S.; B.S. in Edn., Southwestern State Cobl., Weatherford, Okla., 1953; M.S. in Ednl. Adminstrn., Okla. U., 1959, profl. diploma ednl. adminstrn., 1971; m. Wanda Fay Motley, Aug. 18, 1956; children—Vickie Ann, Thomas Dwaine, Valinda Kay, Vinita Fay. Tchr., Bradley High Sch., 1955-58; tchr., adminstr., Custer (Okla.) High Sch., 1959-68; supt. Thomas (Okla.) High Sch., 1968—. Farming mgr. R. Schneider Trusts, Custer, 1965—, trustee, 1965—. Served with AUS, 1953-55. Mem. Thomas C. of C. (dir. 1970—), N.E.A., Okla. (mem. 1st del. assembly 1969—), Custer County edn. assns., Okla. Assn. Sch. Adminstrs., Am. Assn. Sch. Adminstrs. Methodist (dist. lay leader Okla. Conf. 1970—). Home: 406 E Roh St Thomas OK 73669 Office: 920 N Main St Thomas High School Thomas OK 73669

SCHNEIDER, DONALD JACOB, hotel exec.; b. Columbus. O., Apr. 24, 1924; s. Herbert Uhlrich and Gladys (Davis) S.; student Jones Bus. Coll., 1953-54, U. Fla., 1954-55; m. Ruth Louise Higginbotham, Sept. 3, 1949; children—Donald Jacob, Patricia Michele, Nancy Ann. Asst. sales mgr. Culligan Soft Water Co., Jacksonville Beach, Fla., 1947-49; with Ponte Vedra Club, Ponte Vedra Beach, Fla., 1949—, asst. mgr. reservations, 1963-66, v.p., mgr., 1966—; dir. Ponte Vedra Corp., Pres., P.T.A. Ponte Vedra-Palm Valley High Sch., 1971; mem. exec. com. Shawnee council Boy Scouts Am., 1962—; mem. adv. com. hotel curriculum Fla. Jr. Coll., 1970—; coach-player Jacksonville Beach Dolphins basketball team, 1953-58, baseball teams, 1963-65. Bd. dirs. Tourist and Conv. Bur., Jacksonville, 1973—. Served with inf. AUS, 1943-46; ETO. Decorated Bronze Star medal (2); Croix de Guerre (France). Mem. Fla. Hotel and Motel Assn. (bd. dir., sec.-treas.), Jacksonville Beach C. of C. (dir. 1970—), Ponte Vedra Men's Golf Assn. Democrat. Baptist. Clubs: Rotary (dir. 1974—), Quarterback (dir. 1973—) (Jacksonville Beach). Home: 194 San Juan Dr Ponte Vedra Beach FL 32082 Office: Ponte Vedra Blvd Ponte Vedra Beach FL 32082

SCHNEIDER, GEORGE THEODORE, physician; b. New Orleans, July 25, 1920; s. George Edmond and Erna Marie (Kraft) S.; B.S., Tulane U., 1941, M.D., 1944; certificate German, U. Heidelberg (Germany), 1937; m. Ann Lejeune, Oct. 9, 1948; children—Lynne, Ann. Intern Touro Infirmary, New Orleans, 1944, resident, 1945-46; chief resident U.S. Naval Dependents' Hosp., Great Lakes, Ill., 1946-48; practice medicine specializing in obstetrics and gynecology, New Orleans, 1949—; mem. staff Ochsner Found., New Orleans, La. Charity Hosp., New Orleans, Sara Mayo Hosp., New Orleans. Asso. chmn. dept. obstetrics and gynecology Ochsner Clinic and Found. Hosp., New Orleans, 1960—; clin. asso. prof. La. State U. Med. Center, New Orleans, 1967—. Pres., Am. Cancer Soc., New Orleans, 1972-74; mem. exec. com. New Orleans Midwinter Sports Assn., 1972-75. Bd. dirs. Dryades Homestead Assn., 1973—. Served to lt., M.C., USNR, 1946-48. Diplomate Am. Bd. Obstetrics and Gynecology. Mem. Obstetrics and Gynecology Soc. El Salvador, Costa Rica, Nicaragua (hon.), New Orleans Obstetrics and Gynecology Soc. (v.p. 1973-74), Am. Fertility Soc. (sec. 1973-75), Family Planning Assn. (dir. 1972—). Clubs: Stratford, Plimsoll, Pendennis, International House, New Orleans Country, New Orleans Lawn Tennis. Contbr. articles to profl. jours. Home: 218 Audubon Blvd New Orleans LA 70118 Office: 1514 Jefferson Hwy New Orleans LA 70121

SCHNEIDER, IRWIN, govt. physicist; b. N.Y.C., Aug. 17, 1932; s. David and Bertha (Felker) S.; B.S., U. Ill., 1954, M.S., 1956; Ph.D., U. Pa., 1963; postgrad. (Lab. Insulation Research fellow) Mass. Inst. Tech., 1963-64, (Nat. Acad. Sci. fellow) Naval Research Lab., 1964-65; m. Harriet Udeleff, Apr. 29, 1959; children—Andrea Lee, Steven Gary. Exptl. physicist U.S. Naval Research Lab., Washington, 1965—. Mem. Am. Phys. Soc., Research Soc. Am., Sigma Xi. Contbr. articles to profl. jours. Home: 2402 Daphne Lane Alexandria VA 22306 Office: Code 6440 Naval Research Lab Washington DC 20375

SCHNEIDER, NATHAN JOSEPH, microbiologist; b. Balt., Feb. 19, 1916; s. Michael and Rebecca (Wolfson) S.; B.S. in Chem. Engring., U. Fla., 1938; M.Sc., 1949; M.P.H., U. Pitts., 1953, Ph.D., 1954; m. Thelma Segal, June 11, 1939; children—Victor S., Michael N. With Fla. Bd. Health, Jacksonville and Miami, 1946—, asst. dir. Bur. Labs., Jacksonville, 1954-57, dir., 1957—. Asst. prof. microbiology U. Fla. at Gainesville, 1954—. Trustee Jacksonville Jewish Center, 1964. Served with AUS, 1941-46. Diplomate Am. Bd. Med. Microbiology. Recipient Phillip R. Edwards award, 1970, Meritorious Service award Fla. Pub. Health Assn., 1971. Fellow Am. Pub. Health Assn. (chmn. 1969-72); mem. Fla. Pub. Health Assn. (pres. 1960, Meritorious Service award 1971), Conf. Pub. Health Lab Dirs. (chmn. 1966-67), Assn. State and Territorial Pub. Health Lab. Dirs. (pres. 1966-68). Contbr. articles to profl. jours. Research in tuluremia, TB, diarrheal diseases, polio, pox viruses, pesticides. Office: PO Box 210 Jacksonville FL 32201

SCHNEIDER, RAYMOND THEODORE, chem. engr.; b. Cin., July 17, 1929; s. Joseph A. and Eleanor (Schaefer) S.; Chem.E., U. Cin., 1952; m. Mary Jovita Diersen, July 5, 1958; children—Rita M., Ruth A., Joseph R., Mary M., Carol M. Chem. engr. U.S. AEC, Fernald, O., 1952-54; process engr. Vulcan-Cin. Inc., 1956-62; project engr. Formica Corp., Cin., 1962-63; sr. process engr. Chem. & Indsl. Corp., Cin., 1963-65; sr. devel. engr. Wellman-Lord Inc., Lakeland, Fla., 1965-69; individual practice as cons. chem. engr., Lakeland, 1970-72; pres. Schneider Engring., Inc., Lakeland, 1972-73; sr. process engr. Davy Power Gas, Inc., Lakeland, 1973—. Bd. dirs. St. Joseph Sch., Lakeland, 1969-72, pres. parents' club, 1969-70. Served with AUS, 1954-56. Registered profl. engr., Fla., Ohio. Mem. Nat. Soc. Profl. Engrs., Fla. Engring. Soc., Am. Inst. Chem. Engrs., Am. Chem. Soc. Rotarian, K.C. Patentee in nitric acid manufacture, sulfur dioxide recovery. Home: 1338 Robinhood Lane N Lakeland FL 33803 Office: Box 2436 Lakeland FL 33803

SCHNEIDER, RICHARD ELMER, oil co. explorationist; b. Cleve., Aug. 15, 1930; s. Elden E. and Thelma (LeBeau) S.; B.S. in Geology, Western Res. U., 1952; m. Barbara Irie, June 9, 1951; 1 son, Richard Stanley. Geophysicist, Petty Geophys. Engring. Co., San Antonio, 1952-56; with Continental Oil Co., 1956—, now sr. staff geophysicist exploration-geophysics, Ponca City, Okla. Cons., Mexican Sulphur Co., 1966-69. Chmn., United Fund, Ponca City, 1968, bd. dirs., 1967—; bd. dirs. A.R.C., Ponca City, 1968—, Ponca City YMCA, 1969—. Recipient awards including Able Toastmaster award, 1969; Distinguished Toastmaster award (1st Oklahoman), 1971; Key Man award, 1972. Mem. Soc. Exploration Geophysicists, Internat. Platform Assn., Pi Kappa Alpha, Kappa Kappa Psi. Presbyn. Elk. Club: Toastmasters International (local pres. 1965, state gov. 1969, 70, dir. 1972). Home: 2115 Garden St Ponca City OK 74601 Office: Conoco-Geophysics Box 1267 Ponca City OK 74601

SCHNEIDER, WILLIAM CHARLES, govt. ofcl.; b. N.Y.C., Dec. 24, 1923; s. Charles J. and Margaret (Stoeffler) S.; B.S., Mass. Inst. Tech., 1949; M.S., U. Va., 1952; postgrad. Catholic U., 1960-65; m. Rose Ann Vasco, Oct. 6, 1964; children—Catherine M., Jeanne M., Robert J., Robert S. Research scientist NACA Langley Research Center, Hampton, Va., 1949-55; asst. br. head Air-to-Air Missiles Bur. Air, Washington, 1955-60; dir. space vehicles USN Bur. Weapons, Washington, 1960-61; dir. space systems Internat. Tel & Tel., Nutley, N.J., 1961-63; dep. dir. Gemini program Office Manned Space Flight NASA Hdqrs., Washington, 1963-65, Mission dir. Gemini program, 1965-66, dir. Apollo applications missions, 1966-67, dep. dir. for missions Apollo program, 1967-68, dir. SKYLAB program, 1968—. Served with USNR, 1942-46. Recipient Exceptional Service medal, also Distinguished Service medal NASA; named Man of Year, Montgomery County, Md., 1970. Mem. Am. Inst. Aeros. and Astronautics. Home: 11801 Clintwood Pl Silver Spring MD 20902 Office: NASA Hdqrs Code ML Washington DC 20546

SCHNELL, ROBERT LEE, forester; b. Lodi, O., July 21, 1916; s. Byron Arthur and Zoe (Williams) S.; B.S. in Forestry, Purdue U., 1939; postgrad. Va. Poly. Inst., 1939-40; m. Marian Nash Nelly, Nov. 29, 1941; children—Robert Lee, Barbara Elaine, Byron Arthur, Beverly Elisabeth. With forestry relations div. TVA, 1940—, calculating machine operator, 1941, forestry aide, Lawrenceburg, Tenn., 1946-49, forester, Norris, Tenn., 1949, staff forester wood harvesting and processing sect. Forest and Wildlife Resources br. Div. Forestry Devel., Norris, 1949—. Served with AUS, 1942-46; PTO. Mem. Soc. Am. Foresters, Forest Products Research Soc. Democrat. Methodist. Home: 70 Pine Rd Norris TN 37828 Office: TVA Forestry Bldg Norris TN 37828

SCHNELLBACHER, EMIL ST. ELMO, govt. ofcl.; b. Quincy, Ill., Dec. 18, 1901; s. Charles Christian and Anna (Beach) S.; A.B., U. Ill., 1923; LL.B., Georgetown U., 1926; m. Mary Elizabeth Holt, Feb. 4, 1926; children—Emil, Margaret Ann, Charles William. Purchasing agt. United Foundry Co., Quincy, 1917-19; asst. librarian Ill. Natural History Survey, Urbana, 1921; real estate listing, Urbana, 1922-23; bus. asst. Bur. Fgn. and Domestic Commerce, Washington, 1924-26, asst. chief comml. intelligence div., 1926-40, chief, 1940-42, chief div. commerce and econ. information, 1942-45. dir. intelligence and services div. Office Internat. Trade, 1946-50, asst. dir., 1950-53, dir. office intelligence and services Bus. Fgn. Commerce, 1953-56, dir. office trade promotion, 1956—, asst. dir. Bur. Internat. Bus. Operations, 1961-63, asst. dir. Bur. Internat. Commerce, 1963—. Mem. ECA Commerce Mission to Europe, 1949, co-chmn. U.S. del. Regional Conf. Trade Promotions, UN Econ. Commn. Asia and Far East, 1951. dep. chmn. U.S. delegation Caribbean Conf. Trade Promotion, 1954. chmn. U.S. Trade Mission, India, 1955, Union of South Africa, 1957; U.S. del. 2d meeting Trade Com. ECAFE, Tokyo, 1956; cons. to fgn. trade Dept. Commerce. Recipient gold medal Dept. Commerce, 1950; Man of Year award World Trade Writers Assn., 1956. Mem. Corda Fratres, Assn. Cosmopolitan Clubs, Scabbard and Blade, Phi Alpha Delta, Delta Phi Epsilon (nat. pres. 1964-68). Roman Catholic. Author: Credit and Payment Terms, 1931; Sources of Foreign Credit Information, 1931; Export and Import Practice (with F.R. Eldridge), 1938; Government and Foreign Trade, 1954. Contbr. articles bus. publs. Home: 4540 Warren St NW Washington DC 20016 Office: Dept Commerce Washington DC 20230

SCHNOOR, RICHARD HARRY, govt. ofcl.; b. N.Y.C., Mar. 14, 1931; s. Harry Henry and Eleanor E. (Speer) S.; student St. Louis U., 1949-50; B. Indsl. Engring., N.Y. U., 1953, M.Indsl. Engring., 1958; m. Mary Jane McAllister, June 13, 1953. Indsl. engr. Aluminum Co. Am., Bridgeport, Conn., 1956-57; sr. indsl. engr. Atomics Internat. div. N. Am. Rockwell Corp., Canoga Park, Cal., 1958-61; prof. indsl. engring. A.F. Inst. Tech., Dayton, O., 1961-64; dep. chief Mgmt. Systems Office, J.F. Kennedy Space Center, NASA, Kennedy Space Center, Fla., 1966-73, chief documentation div., 1974—. Chmn., NASA Exchange Council, 1971-74. Instr. mgmt. courses Brevard Jr. Coll., Cocoa, Fla., 1965-67. Dist. comdr. U.S. Power Squadrons, 1972-73, rear comdr., 1973—; comdr. Cape Canaveral Power Squadron, 1966-67. Served to lt. USAF, 1954-56, maj. Res. Registered profl. engr., Mass. Mem. Am. Inst. Indsl. Engrs. (chpt. pres. 1963-64). Home: 1010 N Fiske Blvd Cocoa FL 32922 Office: John F Kennedy Space Center NASA Documentation Div Kennedy Space Center FL 32899

SCHNURRENBERGER, PAUL ROBERT, educator; b. Youngstown, O., Aug. 19, 1929; s. Gilbert M. and Bernice (Parshall) S.; D.V.M., Ohio State U., 1953; M.P.H., U. Pitts., 1958; m. Marsha K. Blatt, Dec. 28, 1968; children—Jody Lynn, Gregory Paul. Chief pub. health veterinarian Ohio Dept. Health, Columbus, 1956-63; chief pub. health veterinarian Ill. Dept. Health, Springfield, 1963-72, asst. state epidemiologist, 1969-72; prof. pub. health, sch. vet. medicine Auburn (Ala.) U., 1972—. Mem. Ala. Comprehensive Health Planning Council, 1972—. Served with USAF, 1953-55. Mem. Am. (councilor 1965—), Ala. vet. med. assns., U.S. Animal Health Assn., Ala. Pub. Health Assn., Conf. Pub. Health Veterinarian (dir. 1972—), Assn. Tchrs. Vet. Preventive Medicine (dir. 1972—), Wildlife Disease Assn. Editor: Diseases Transmitted from Animals to Man, 1974. Home: 862 Cary Dr Auburn AL 36830 Office: Dept Microbiology Auburn Univ Auburn AL 36830

SCHOBER, MILTON WELSH, lawyer; b. Shreveport, La., Oct. 12, 1927; s. Charles Coleman and Mabel Lee (Welsh) S.; B.S., La. State U., 1948, M.B.A. in Accounting, 1949; lawyers certificate Centenary Coll. La., 1955; m. Mary Beth Fiser, Apr. 14, 1951 (div. Mar. 1966); children—Milton Welsh, Scott Dillon; m. 2d, Susan Ann Meyer, Oct. 12, 1970. Admitted to La. bar, 1955; practice law, Shreveport, 1955-68; asst. dir. div. supervision and regulation Bd. Govs. Fed. Res. System, Washington, 1968-70; gen. counsel Nat. Commn. on Consumer Finance, Washington, 1970-72; practice law, Washington, 1973—. Lectr. Sch. of Banking of the South, 1970-72. Served with AUS, 1946-47. C.P.A., La. Mem. Tax Inst. Ark., La., Tex. (pres. 1964-65), La. Soc. C.P.A.s, La. Bar Assn., Bar Assn. D.C. Contbr. articles to profl. jours. Home: 238 G St SW Washington DC 20024 Office: 1775 K St NW Suite 220 Washington DC 20006

SCHOEN, KENNETH BERNARD, investment banker; b. Louisville, Feb. 2, 1921; s. William Joseph and Virginia (Key) S.; B.A. U. Notre Dame, 1943; postgrad. N.Y. Inst. Finance, 1946; m. Gloria Catignani, Oct. 14, 1944 children—Michael Joseph, Patrick Edward. Vice pres., gen. partner J.C. Bradford & Co., Nashville, 1945-70; v.p. A.G. Edwards & Sons, Inc., 1970—; financial v.p., sec., treas. Aurora Publishers, Inc. Bd. dirs., treas. Cath. Youth Orgn., 1953-70; pres. Nashville Area Council Alcoholism, 1966-68, Project Equality, 1966-70; mem. exec. com. Nashville U.S.O., 1950-69; mem. Nat. Cath. Community Service, 1967—; v.p., dir. Travelers Aid Soc., 1964-71; chmn. Tenn. Alcoholic Beverage Study Commn., 1965-67; state mem. John F. Kennedy Meml. Library Com., 1964-67. Trustee Aquinas Jr. Coll., 1966—, Samaritans Anonymous, 1960-68; chmn. bd. St. Thomas Hosp. Sch. Nursing, 1960-68; mem. bd. Davidson County YMCA, St. Bernard Coll., Cullman, Ala. Served with USCGR, 1943-45. Apptd. Knight of St. Gregory, Pope Paul VI, 1966. Mem. Nat. Nashville (pres. 1955) assns. security dealers, Nat. Council Cath. Men. Roman Catholic. Elk, K.C. (4 deg.). Clubs: Serra (past v.p. internat.), Richland Country, City, Westside Aquatic (pres. 1952-53). Home: 2303 Golf Club Lane Nashville TN 37215 Office: 170 4th Av N Nashville TN 37219

SCHOENFELDT, CHARLES MARTIN, utility exec.; b. Independence, Kan., Feb. 3, 1929; s. Edward Herman and Leora (Charles) S.; B.S., Okla. State U., 1950; postgrad. U. Tulsa, 1954-56; m. Marilyn Jane Cleveland, Sept. 29, 1950; children—Michael C., Patrick C. With Okla. Natural Gas Co., Tulsa, 1950—, asst. to pres., 1969-71, v.p. energy systems and devel., 1971—. Instr. evening div. U. Tulsa, 1956, Okla. Bapt. U., 1962. Mem. Hist. and Ednl. Found. Bd. dirs. West of Main, Tulsa, Devel. Found., Okla. State U., Stillwater, Hurricane Club, U. Tulsa; trustee Children's Med. Center, Tulsa. Served to capt. USAF, 1951-53. Mem. Tulsa C. of C., Am., So. gas assns., Sigma Phi Epsilon. Presbyn. (elder, deacon). Republican. Clubs: Petroleum, Tulsa Country, Exchange (pres. Tulsa 1965-66). Home: 5374 E 21st St Tulsa OK 74114 Office: 624 S Boston St Tulsa OK 74102

SCHOFIELD, CHARLES STIKELEATHER, hotel exec.; b. Florence, S.C., Dec. 21, 1916; s. Robert Pace and Ivey (Stikeleather) S.; grad. high sch.; m. Elizabeth Person Cooke, July 20, 1940; children—Charles Marshall, James Thomas. Vice pres., sec.-treas. Schofield Hardware Co., Inc., Florence, 1933-66; pres., chmn. bd. Carolina Enterprise, Inc., Florence, 1951—; owner Southpark Shopping Center, Florence, 1972—. Dir. People's Bank S.C. Mem. Wofford Coll. Parents Adv. Council. Mem. Florence City Adv. Bd. Served with AUS, 1943-45; PTO. Mem. Am. Legion, V.F.W. Republican. Methodist. Club: Florence Country. Home: 1431 Madison Av Florence SC 29501 Office: PO Box 672 Florence SC 29501

SCHOFIELD, LEMUEL BRADDOCK, II, TV broadcasting exec.; b. Gouverneur, N.Y., Jan. 13, 1935; s. Joseph A. and Mary (Lewis) S.; B.A., U. Pa., 1956; LL.B., U. Pa. Coll. Law, 1959; m. Shirley M. Peck, Oct. 24, 1959; children—Braddock, Jennifer. Admitted to N.Y. State bar, 1959; asst. dist. atty. N.Y. County, 1959-63; sales adminstr. NBC, N.Y.C., 1964-65; gen. counsel Overmyer Communication Co., N.Y.C., 1966-68; gen. counsel, sec. Corinthian Broadcasters Corp., N.Y.C., 1968-71; program dir. KOTV, Tulsa, 1971—. Home: 3950 S Delaware Av Tulsa OK 74105 Office: 302 S Frankfort St Tulsa OK 74120

SCHOGGEN, PHIL, educator; b. Tulsa, Aug. 28, 1923; s. Walter B. and Emma (Alexander) S.; A.B., Park Coll., 1946; M.A., U. Kan., 1951; Ph.D., 1954; m. Maxine F. Spoor, June 28, 1944; children—Leida Beth, Christopher Phil, Ann Louise, Susan Diane. Research asso. Wayne State U., 1954-55; research asso., lectr. U. Kan., 1955-57; asst. prof. to asso. prof. U. Ore., 1957-66; prof., chmn. dept. psychology George Peabody Coll., Nashville, 1966—; psychol. cons. VA. Served to lt. comdr. USNR, 1943-46, 50-51. Fellow Am. Psychol. Assn.; mem. A.A.A.S., Soc. for Research Child Devel., Sigma Xi. Home: 6729 Curreywood Dr Nashville TN 37205

SCHOLL, JOHN WILLIAM, trophy mfg. exec.; b. Louisville, June 4, 1918; s. John Michael and Emma (Pinnick) S.; ed. pub. schs.; m. Mary Fischer, Apr. 11, 1940; 1 son, John Anthony. With John M. Scholl & Son, Engravers, Louisville, 1935-56; owner, pres., designer Scholl Trophies, Inc., Louisville, 1956—. Served with USNR, World War II. Named Ky. col. Mem. Civil Air Patrol, Hon. Order Ky. Cols., Louisville Aero Club. Moose. Club: Owl Creek Country. Home: 304 S Lyndon Lane Louisville KY 40222 Office: Scholl Trophies Inc 3008 Magazine St Louisville KY 40211

SCHOLZ, ARTHUR LEONARD, elec. engr.; b. Greybull, Wyo., Aug. 22, 1923; s. Albert Joseph and Fairy Luverna (Murray) S.; B.S., Mont. State Coll., 1952; m. Ruby Idalee DePew, June 15, 1952; children—Denise Idalee, Thomas Arthur, Michele Diane. Engr., Boeing Co., Seattle, 1952-59, supr., Cocoa Beach, Fla., 1960-63, supr., Huntsville, Ala., 1964-65, mgr. KSC Apollo integration, Kennedy Space Center, Fla., 1966-72, mgr. Lunar Rover Program, 1970-72, mgr. Skylab integration, 1971-73, launch operations program mgr., 1974—. Chmn. Planning and Zoning Bd., Cocoa Beach, 1969-72. Served with AUS, 1943-46. Mem. I.E.E.E. Republican. Presbyn. Oddfellow, Lion. Home: 541 Capri Rd Cocoa Beach FL 32931

SCHONING, ROBERT WHITNEY, govt. ofcl.; b. Seattle, Sept. 29, 1923; s. Nils W. and Olive (Anderson) S.; B.S., U. Wash., 1944, postgrad., 1946-47; m. Barbara McCutcheon, Oct. 4, 1952; children—Randall S., James L., Kerry J., Kip S. Aquatic biologist Ore. Fish Commn., Portland, 1947-52, charge Columbia River investigations, 1952-54, asst. dir. research, 1954-58, dir. research, 1958, asst. state fisheries dir., 1958-60, dir., 1960-71; dep. dir. Nat. Marine Fisheries Service, Nat. Oceanic and Atmospheric Adminstrn., U.S. Dept. of Commerce, Washington, 1971-73, dir., 1973—. Lectr. on fisheries Portland State U., 1970-71. Chmn. Pacific Salmon Inter-Agy. Council, 1963-64; adviser Portland C. of C. recreational resources and environmental standards coms., 1965-71; mem. fishing industry adv. com. U.S. Dept. of State, 1962-71, Ore. Com. Natural Resources, 1960-71; adviser to Am. sect. Internat. North Pacific Fisheries Commn., 1960-71; commr. Internat. Pacific Halibut Commn., 1972—. Mem. Gladstone Sch. Bd., 1961-68, chmn., 1963-64; chmn. for state employees Tri-County United Good Neighbors, 1965-69. Trustee Clackamas County Vector Control Dist., 1967-71, chmn., 1970-71. Served to 2d lt. AUS, 1943-46, to 1st lt., 1950-52. Decorated Bronze Star medal, Army Commendation medal. Mem. Am. Inst. Fisheries Research Biologists, Am. Fisheries Soc., Pacific Fishery Biologists, Izaak Walton League Am., U.S. Handball Assn. (treas. 1950-71). Toastmaster (pres. chpt. 1957-67). Contbr. articles on salmon and Pacific N.W. fishery matters to profl. jours. Home: 6613 Kerns Rd Falls Church VA 22024 Office: National Marine Fisheries Service 3300 Whitehaven St NW Washington DC 20007

SCHORNO, KARL STANLEY, petroleum co. chemist; b. Berkeley, Cal., Nov. 28, 1939; s. Werner Domonic and Margot Ann (Schreier) S.; B.A. in Chemistry, U. Cal., Berkeley, 1962; Ph.D., Okla. State U., 1967, postgrad. fellow, 1967-68; postgrad. U. Kan., 1968-69; m. Karen Sue Baker, May 27, 1966; children—Kistine Sue, Kevin Karl. Sr. research scientist geochemistry br. Phillips Petroleum Co., Bartlesville, Okla., 1969—. Mem. Am. Chem. Soc., N.Y. Acad. Sci., A.A.A.S., Nat. Wildlife Soc., Sigma Xi. Presbyn. (jr. high sch. advisor 1971—). Contbr. articles to profl. jours. Home: 1724 S Osage St Bartlesville OK 74003 Office: 225 RB 1 Bartlesville OK 74003

SCHOTT, JOE LAWRENCE, publisher; b. Castroville, Tex., Oct. 4, 1933; s. Joe F. and Lucille (Tschirhart) S.; B.J., U. Tex., Austin, 1955; m. Barbarajo Woerner, June 17, 1956; children—Robert Joseph, Kathryn Anne. Reporter, San Antonio Light, 1955-63, picture editor, 1963-68, asst. city editor, 1968-70, city editor, 1970-73, asst. mng. editor news, 1973—; co-founder Medina Valley and County News Bull., Castroville, 1958, pub., 1958—. City councilman, Castroville, 1958-59. Served with AUS, 1956-58. Mem. Nat. Newspaper Assn., San Antonio Press Club, Tex. Press Assn., Castroville C. of C. (past mgr.), Sigma Delta Chi. Home: 121 Karm St Castroville TX 78009 Office: Castroville TX 78009

SCHOTTLAND, FREDERIC DOUGLASS, govt. ofcl.; b. N.Y.C., Apr. 2, 1909; s. Benjamin and Eva (Goldman) S.; B.S., U. Pa., 1930; m. Alma Elaine Dorfman, Feb. 18, 1933; children—Donald Bruce, Virginia Gail (Mrs. Robert E. Clentimack). Practice cons. radio engr., N.Y.C. and West Orange, N.J., 1939-59; project engr. RCA Internat., Clark, N.J. and Iran, 1959-61, Northrop Page Communications Engrs., Washington and Ethiopia, 1961-65; regional liaison officer FCC, 1965-73, head engring. sect. hearing div. Broadcast Bur., Washington, 1973—. Registered profl. engr., Md., D.C. Mem. I.E.E.E. (sr.). Contbr. profl. jours. Patentee in field. Home: 4701 Willard Ave Chevy Chase MD 20015 Office: 1919 M St NW Washington DC 20554

SCHRADER, GEORGE FREDERICK, JR., educator, coll. adminstr.; b. Mattoon, Ill., July 21, 1920; s. George Frederick and Ruth E. (McDuffey) S.; student Okla. A. and M. Coll., 1939-41; B.S. in Mech. Engring., U. Ill., 1947, M.S., 1952, Ph.D. in Mech. and Indsl. Engring., 1961; m. Bettie Elizabeth Harvey, Sept. 11, 1943; children—David M., Julie G. Quality control engr. U.S. Time Corp., Abilene, Tex., 1955-56; asst. prof. mech. engring. U. Ill., Urbana, 1947-61; prof. indsl. engring. Okla. State U., Stillwater, 1961-62; head dept. indsl. engring. Kan. State U., Manhattan, 1962-66; dir. indsl. research State of Neb., Lincoln, 1966-69; dir. Transp. Systems Inst., also chmn. dept. indsl. engring. and mgmt. systems Fla. Tech. U., Orlando, 1969—. Chmn., Seminole County Indsl. Devel. Authority, 1971-73. Mem. Casselberry Planning Bd., 1971-72; chmn. Casselberry Zoning Bd., 1971-72. Served with USAAF, 1942-45. Recipient Outstanding Educator award Fla. Tech. U., 1972. Mem. Am. Inst. Indsl. Engrs., Am. Soc. Engring. Educators, Am. Soc. Quality Control, Sigma Xi, Pi Tau Sigma, Alpha Pi Mo, Beta Theta Pi. Club: Sheoah Golf. Author: (with L.E. Doyle) Manufacturing Processes and Materials for Engineers, 1968. Home: 405 Sheoah Blvd Winter Springs FL 32707 Office: Box 25000 Orlando FL 32816

SCHRADER, JOHN WILLIAM, educator; b. Atchison, Kan., Mar. 16, 1944; s. Edwin Carl and Jenna (Tobiason) S.; B.S. in Agronomy (McVey scholar 1962, Blair scholar 1962, Consumers Coop. Assn. scholar 1963, Danforth scholar 1964, Blue Key scholar 1965, Nat. Plant Food Inst. scholar 1965), Kan. State U., 1966; Ph.D. in Crop Sci., Mich. State U., 1970; m. Pamela Ann Vansyoc, Aug. 23, 1969; 1 son, Michael. Grad. research asst., Mich. State U., East Lansing, 1966-70; asst. prof. dept. agronomy N.C. State U., Raleigh, 1970—. Instr. Dale Carnegie Course, 1972—. Vice chmn. bus. div. United Fund, Wake County, N.C., 1972. Mem. Am. Soc. Agronomy (nat. pres. student sect. 1964-65), Weed Sci. Soc. Am., Crop Sci. Soc. Am., Alpha Zeta, Phi Kappa Phi, Gamma Sigma Delta, Blue Key. Methodist (mem. adminstrv. bd., finance com., council ministries). Home: 908 Hemingway Dr Raleigh NC 27609 Office NC State Univ Raleigh NC 27607

SCHRAM, ALFRED CHRISTIAN, educator; b. Brussels, Belgium, Sept. 17, 1930; s. Christian Pierce and Gabrielle (DeVroey) S.; brought to U.S., 1950, naturalized, 1959; B.S. in Chemistry, Bklyn. Poly. Inst., 1954; M.A., U. Tex. at Austin, 1956, Ph.D. (R.B. Hite fellow), 1958; m. Eleanor R. Fletcher, Nov. 30, 1957; children—Gwynnedolyn, Howard. Research biochemist Southwestern Med. Sch. and VA Hosp., Dallas, 1959-65; prof. chemistry W. Tex. State U., Canyon, 1965—, asso. prof., 1965-70, prof., 1970—. Abstractor chem. abstracts Ohio State U., Columbus, 1963—. USPHS grantee, 1963-65; R.A. Welch grantee, 1967-70, 73—. Mem. Am. Chem. Soc., A.M.A. (affiliate mem.), A.A.A.S., Phi Lambda Upsilon, Beta Beta Beta. Presbyn. (past deacon). Contbr. profl. jours. Home: 406 Taylor Lane Canyon TX 79015

SCHRAMM, TEXAS EDWARD, profl. football exec.; b. Los Angeles, June 2, 1920; s. Texas Ernest and Elsa J. (Steinwender) S.; B.A. in Journalism, U. Tex., 1947; m. Martha Anne Snowden, Apr. 15, 1942; children—Mardee Anne, Christi Lee, Kandy Gayle. Sports editor Austin (Tex.) Statesman, 1946-47; publicity dir., gen. mgr. Los Angeles Rams Football Club, 1947-57; asst. dir. sports CBS, 1957-60; v.p., gen. mgr. Dallas Cowboys Football Club, Inc., 1960-66, pres., gen. mgr. 1966—; pres. Tex. Stadium Corp., Dallas Cowboys Enterprises, Inc., Cebe Corp.; dir. Park Cities Bank & Trust Co. Served to capt. USAAF, 1941-45. Home: 9355 Sunny Brook Lane Dallas TX 75220 Office: 6116 N Central Expressway Dallas TX 75206

SCHREIBER, JOSEPH PHILIP, retail sales co. exec.; b. Madison, Wis., Mar. 3, 1917; s. Cecil E. and Harriet Leone (Spoor) S.; B.A., U. Wis., 1940; m. Ruth Helen Lassen, Mar. 9, 1957; 1 son, Barry Alan. Staff auditor Arthur Andersen & Co., Chgo., 1940-42; comptroller, T.C. Esser Co., Milw., 1946-60; v.p., treas., dir. Advance Distbrs. Inc., Advance Publishers, Inc., Adon, Inc., Mid-Fla. Collection Service, Inc., all Orlando, Fla., 1960-72; cons. to pres. Panning Lumber Co., Orlando, Fla., 1972—. Treas. Polit. Action Assn., Central Fla., 1965-66. Served to lt. Supply Corps, USNR, 1943-46; PTO. Mem. Nat. Assn. Accountants. Presbyn. Elk. Clubs: Central Florida Executives, Orlando AFB Officers. Club: Winter Park University. Home: 2123 Chippewa Trail Maitland FL 32751 Office: 5018 Colonial Dr Orlando FL 32808

SCHREINER, RAYMOND LESLIE, JR., state ofcl.; b. Washington, Nov. 7, 1921; s. Raymond Leslie and Helen (Hardy) S.; student U. Md., 1940-41; m. Alice May Gartrell, May 30, 1942; children—Leslie (Mrs. William Bolster), Alice (Mrs. J. Wayne Beachy), Raymond Leslie, Barbara. Announcer, WPID, Petersburg, Va., 1941-42, WHNC, Henderson, N.C. 1946, WBTM, Danville, Va., 1946-50, WHTN, Huntington, W.Va., 1950; program dir. WRNL, Richmond, Va., 1950-62; mgr. WBCI, Williamsburg, Va., 1962-64; news dir. WXEX-TV, Petersburg-Richmond, 1964-66; dir. information Va. Dept. Agr. and Commerce, Richmond, 1966—. Adv. council Office Minority Bus. Affairs Va., 1973—, Green Thumb Va., 1973—. Served with AUS, 1943-46. Mem. So. Assn. Information Officers State Depts. Agr. (pres. 1971-72, sec.-treas. 1973—), Nat. Assn. Farm Broadcasters (asso.), Richmond Pub. Relations Soc., Sigma Delta Chi. Home: 2537 E Tremont Ct Richmond VA 23225 Office: 203 N Governor St Richmond VA 23219

SCHROEDER, GEORGE CHESTER, JR., elec. engr.; b. New Orleans, Oct. 28, 1922; s. George Chester and Dagmar Mathilda (Erickson) S.; student Loyola U. of South Sch. Music, 1941-42; B.S., Tulane U., 1949; m. Carolyn Cutler, June 28, 1945; children—George Chester III, Robert Leonard. Design engr., asso. Louis N. Goodman & Assos., cons. elec. engrs., New Orleans, 1949-55; pres. Schroeder & Assos., cons. elec. engrs., New Orleans, 1955—. Served to maj. USAF, 1942-45; ETO. Decorated Air medal with 2 oak leaf clusters; recipient Lighting awards Illuminating Engring. Soc., 1954, 55, 58, 59, 62, 64, 65, Goddard award, 1966, Guth awards, 1966, 69. Mem. I.E.E.E., Illuminating Engring. Soc., Soc. Tulane Engrs., Cons. Engrs. Council. Lutheran. Home: 6945 Catina St New Orleans LA 70124 Office: 148 W Harrison Av New Orleans LA 70124

SCHROEDER, HERMAN MARCEL, lawyer; b. New Orleans, July 16, 1922; s. Herman A. and Marie (Cauhape) S.; LL.B., Loyola U., 1953; m. Ann Fleming, Nov. 16, 1963. Admitted to La. bar, 1953; partner firm Schroeder, Kuntz & Miranne, and predecessor firm, New Orleans, 1953—. Served to 2d lt. USAAF, World War II. Decorated Air Medal. Mem. La. Trial Lawyers Assn. Democrat. Roman Catholic. Lion. Home: 6127 Perlita St New Orleans LA 70112 Office: Richards Bldg New Orleans LA 70112

SCHROEDER, JUEL PIERRE, educator; b. New England, N.D., Jan. 23, 1920; s. Henry E. and Laura (Mueller) S.; B.S. in Chemistry, U. N.D., 1941; Ph.D. in Chemistry, U. Wis., 1948; postgrad. (Robert A. Welch Found. fellow), U. Tex., 1963-65; m. Dorothy Chynoweth, Nov. 1, 1943. Chemist Monsanto, St. Louis, 1942-43, Springfield, Mass., 1943-46; research chemist Union Carbide, Bloomfield, N.J., 1948-58, asst. dir. research, Bound Brook, N.J., 1958-63; asso. prof. chemistry U. N.C., Greensboro, 1965-68, prof. chemistry, 1968—. Cons. to industry. Fellow A.A.A.S.; mem. Am. Chem. Soc., N.C. Acad. Sci., Am. Assn. U. Profs., Phi Beta Kappa, Sigma Xi, Alpha Tau Omega. Republican. Patentee in plastics. Contbr. articles to profl. jours. Home: 701 Sussex Court Greensboro NC 27410

SCHROEDER, STEPHEN EDWIN, utilities exec.; b. Yorktown, Tex., Aug. 16, 1932; s. Edwin Otto and Ella (Kruse) S.; A.A., Tex. Luth. Coll., 1951; m. Billie Juanell Hutchins, June 14, 1953; children—Stephen Michael, Susan Michelle, Sondra Meliss. Apprentice lineman Central Power & Light Co., Kenedy, Tex., 1953-59, serviceman, Runge, Kenedy, Tex., 1959-62, mgr. Goliad, Berclair, Tex., 1962-69, mgr., Cotulla, Dilley and Millett, Tex., 1969—, conf. leader, 1960-62. Chmn. fund drive Boy Scouts Am., 1964, Girl Scouts, 1973; chmn. nominating com., bd. dirs. Coastal Bend Respiratory Assn., 1969. Bd. dirs. Goliad County Fair Assn. Served with AUS, 1954-56. Recipient pres.'s plaque for outstanding mgr. in marketing program Guadalupe Dist. Central Power & Light Co., 1967, S.Tex. C. of C. plaque for outstanding service, 1967. Mem. Goliad County (dir., past pres.), S. Tex. (dir. 1973-74), Cotulla (pres. 1970-71) chambers commerce. Lutheran (lay reader). Lion (dir. Cotulla 1973-74). Home: 1008 Carizzo St Cotulla TX 78014 Office: 113 Center St Cotulla TX 78014

SCHROEDER, WILLIAM JENNINGS, JR., computer planning exec.; b. New Orleans, Mar. 19, 1930; s. William Jennings and Mary (Bujacic) S.; B.B.A., Loyola U. of South, 1951; M.B.A., Tulane U., 1953; m. Julie Hall, Feb. 14, 1956 (dec.); children—William Timothy, Teresa Colette, Tracy Ann; m. 2d, Beverly Rein, July 31, 1970; 1 son, Alan Conrad. Asst. dept. head tabulating and statis. Esso Standard Oil Co., New Orleans, 1955-59; staff asst. to gen. mgr. New Orleans Retailers Credit Bur., Inc., 1959; sr. systems engr. IBM Corp., New Orleans, 1959-74; dir. planning and devel. Lykes Computing Corp., New Orleans, 1974—. sec.-treas. Coldway Truck Line, Inc. C.P.A., La. Mem. Nat. Assn. Accountants (past pres. New Orleans chpt.), Am. Inst. C.P.A.'s. Home: 6451 Center St New Orleans LA 70124 Office: Plaza Tower 1001 Howard Av New Orleans LA 70113

SCHROETTER, HILDA BLOXTON NOEL (MRS. SAMUEL T. SCHROETTER, JR.), author, educator; b. Lynchburg, Va., Oct. 11, 1917; d. Jesse Cleveland and Hilda (Bloxton) Noel; A.B., Randolph-Macon Woman's Coll., 1938; M.A., U. Va., 1946; m. Samuel T. Schroetter, Jr., June 27, 1944. High sch. tchr., 1938-45; reporter Herald Courier, 1946-47, 50-52; historian Va. World War II History Commn., 1947-50; copy chief WINA Radio, Charlottesville, 1952-54; editor U. Va. Record, 1954-66; mem. adj. faculty Va. Commonwealth U., Richmond. Mem. exec. bd. Women of St. James's Episcopal Ch., chpt. devotional chmn. 1969-70; ch. rep. to Ch. Women United, 1969-70; exec. bd. James Branch Cabell Library Assos.; mem. bd. Historic Richmond Found. Mem. Poetry Soc. Va., Woman's Com. Richmond Symphony. Democrat. Clubs: Woman's, Va. Writer's (exec. bd.). Author: Flowers From St. Francis, 1967; Prayers From the Bible, 1967; Great Thoughts from Knox, 1968; Great Thoughts from Luther, 1968; Great Thoughts from Wesley, 1968; Great Thoughts of Freedom, 1968; Bethune Center Nursery School, 1948. Reviewer book sect. Richmond (Va.) Times-Dispatch, 1949—. Home: 100 W Franklin St Richmond VA 23220

SCHUCK, MARJORIE BRACKENRIDGE MASSEY, publisher, editor; b. Winchester, Va., Oct. 9, 1921; d. Carl Frederick and Margaret Harriet (Parmele) Massey; student U. Minn., 1941-43, New Sch., N.Y.C., 1948, N.Y. U., 1952, 54-55; m. Ernest George Metcalfe, Dec. 2, 1943 (div. Oct. 1949); m. Franz Schuck, Nov. 11, 1953 (dec. Jan. 1958). Mem. editorial bd. St. Petersburg (Fla.) Poetry Assn., 1967-68; co-editor, pub. Poetry Venture Mag., St. Petersburg, Fla., 1968-69, editor, pub., 1969—; founder, owner, pres. Valkyrie Press, Inc., St. Petersburg, 1972—; owner, pres. MS Records, Inc., 1974—, Majorie Schuck Pub., Inc., 1974—; v.p., lectr., chmn. poetry Fla. Suncoast Writers' Confs. Assn. U. South Fla., 1973—; lectr. in field. Corr.-rec. sec. Women's Aux. Hosp. for Spl. Surgery, N.Y.C., 1947-59; active St. Petersburg Mus. Fine Arts (charter), St. Petersburg Sister City Com., St. Petersburg Arts Center Assn.; lectr., mem. Friends of Library St. Petersburg. Bd. dirs., pub. relations chmn. Soc. for Prevention Cruelty to Animals, 1968-71. Mem. Internat. Platform Assn., Com. Small Mag. Editors and Pubs., Coordinating Council Lit. Mags., St. Petersburg C. of C. Acad. Am. Poets, Pi Beta Phi. Democrat. Episcopalian. Author: Speeches and Writings for Cause of Freedom, 1973. Contbr. poetry to profl. jours. Home: 8245 26th Av N St Petersburg FL 33710 Office: 2135-2139 1st Av South St Petersburg FL 33712

SCHUDER, RAYMOND FRANCIS, lawyer; b. Wickford, R.I., Dec. 27, 1926; s. Rollie Milton and Selma (Ball) S.; A.B., Emory U., 1949, J.D., 1951; m. Betty Jo Williams, Apr. 14, 1948; children—Gregg Williams, Glen Arva. Admitted to Ga. bar, 1951; with tax div. trust dept., Trust Co., Ga., Atlanta, 1951-54; asso. firm Wheeler, Robinson & Thurmond, Gainesville, Ga., 1954-59; pvt. law practice, Gainesville, 1959-70; partner firm Schuder & Brown, Gainesville, 1971—. Dir. Lanier Securities, Inc. Municipal ct. judge, Gainesville, 1956-60, 73—; supr. Upper Chattahoochee Soil and Water Conservation Dist., 1973—. Bd. dirs. Charles Thompson Estes Found., Inc., Gainesville. Served to cpl. USMCR, 1944-46. Mem. Am., Gainesville-Northeastern (pres. 1969-70) bar assns., State Bar Ga. (gov. 1966-70), Am. Legion, U.S. Power Squadron (Lake Lanier), V.F.W., Phi Alpha Delta. Methodist. Clubs: Chattahoochee Country, Elks. Home: 2224 Riverside Dr NE Gainesville GA 30501 Office: Lanier Bldg 500 Spring St Gainesville GA 30501

SCHUERENBERG, CHARLES ELBERT, lawyer; b. Sherman, Tex., July 8, 1944; s. Walter Alvin and Lyda (Popplewell) S.; B.B.A., U. Tex. at Arlington, 1966; J.D., Baylor U., 1968; m. Shirley Sue Wallace, June 21, 1969; children—Lori, Denise, Angela. Admitted to Tex. bar, 1968; partner firm Leake, Schuerenberg, & Grimes, Mesquite, Tex., 1968—. Bd. dirs. Mesquite Meml. Hosp. Inc., Mesquite Social Services Inc. Named Boss Year, Mesquite Legal Secs. Assn., 1973. Mem. Mesquite (pres. 1972), Tex., Am. bar assns., Am. Trial Lawyer Assn., Dallas Criminal Bar Assn., Mesquite C. of C. (v.p. 1972), Delta Theta Phi (named one of 8 outstanding mems. U.S. 1967). Elk, Lion. Clubs: Dallas Woods and Waters. Home: Route 1 Box 984M Mesquite TX 75149 Office: PO Box 588 Mesquite TX 75149

SCHUETTE, OSWALD FRANCIS, educator; b. Washington, Aug. 20, 1921; s. Oswald Francis and Mary Patrice (Moran) S.; B.S., Georgetown U., 1943; Ph.D., Yale, 1949; m. Kathryn Cronin, June 7, 1947; children—Patrick, Mary, Elizabeth. Faculty Coll. William and Mary, Williamsburg, Va., 1948-54; staff U.S. Naval Forces, Germany, 1954-58; staff Nat. Acad. Scis., Washington, 1958-60; staff, dir. def. research and engring. Def. Dept., Washington, 1960-63; prof. physics, head dept. U. S.C., Columbia, 1963—. Mem. Greater Columbia Indsl. Devel. Commn., 1966—. Trustee Columbia Mus. of Art. Served to lt., USNR, 1944-46. Mem. S.C. Acad. Sci. (chmn. com. on sci. and govt. 1971—), Am. Phys. Soc., Am. Assn. U. Profs., Sigma Xi. Club: Columbia Torch. Home: 4979 Quail Lane Columbia SC 29206

SCHUG, JOHN CHARLES, educator; b. N.Y.C., Mar. 31, 1936; s. Peter John and Joanna (Triscoli) S.; B. Chem. Engring., Cooper Union, 1957; M.S., U. Ill., 1958, Ph.D., 1960; m. Linette K. Gleason, Feb. 1, 1958; children—Carolyn, Deborah, Steven John. Research chemist Golf Research and Devel. Co., Pitts., 1960-64; asst. prof. chemistry Va. Poly. Inst., Blacksburg, 1964-67, asso. prof., 1967-73, prof. chemistry, 1973—. Cons. Philip Morris Research Center. NSF grantee, 1966-70; NASA grantee, 1968-72. Author: Introductory Quantum Chemistry. Contbr. articles to profl. jours. Home: Route 1 Blacksburg VA 24060 Office: Virginia Polytechnic Institute Blacksburg VA 24061

SCHUL, NORMAN WILLARD, coll. dean; b. nr. New Burlington O., Mar. 3, 1935; s. Willard LeRoy and Katherine (Keyser) S.; B.S., Miami U., Oxford, O., 1956, M.A., 1957; Ph.D., Syracuse U., 1962; m. Marianne Virginia Moffett, Aug. 23, 1958; children—Karl Norman, Kenneth Moffett. Mem. faculty U. N.C., Charlotte, 1967—, asst. prof. geography, Greensboro, 1961-67, chmn. dept. geography, geology, asso. prof. geography, 1967-69, chmn. div. social and behavioral scis., prof. geography, 1969-70, dean Coll. Social and Behavioral Scis., Charlotte, 1970—. Dir. Inst. Urban Studies, U. N.C., Charlotte, 1970—. Mem. Assn. Am. Geographers, Nat. Council Geog. Edn., Assn. Asian Studies, Am. Soc. Planning Ofcls., Am. Assn. U. Profs., Pi Kappa Alpha. Presbyn. Rotarian. Contbr. articles to profl. jours. Home: 410 Lansdowne Rd Charlotte NC 28211

SCHULDT, WALTER JOHN, psychologist, educator; b. Sheboygan, Wis., Dec. 9, 1932; s. Walter J. and Irene (Rickmeier) S.; B.S., U. Wis., 1959; M.A., Mich. State U., 1962, Ph.D., 1964; m. Doris Ann Schuh, Aug. 16, 1958; children—Andrea Jean, Eric John. Teaching asst. U. Wis. at Milw., 1958-59; psychol. trainee VA Hosp., Dearborn, Mich., 1959-60; psychol. trainee VA Hosp., Battle Creek, Mich., 1960-61; intern Child Guidance Clinic, Lansing, Mich., 1961-62; grad. teaching asst. Mich. State U., 1962-63, asst. instr., 1963-64; asst. prof. U. Ark., Fayetteville, 1964-69, dir. Psychol. Clinic, 1967—, asso. prof., 1969—. Served with USAF, 1952-56. Mem. Am., Ark. psychol. assns., Am. Assn. U. Profs. Home: 1523 Hotz Dr Fayetteville AR 72701

SCHULER, CHARLES FRANKLIN, banker; b. Columbus, O., Mar. 4, 1922; s. Virgil Edwin and Ruth Lue (Eckelberry) S.; student Ohio State U., 1940-44, Franklin U., 1948; m. Bertha Neeld, Jan. 3, 1945; children—Charles Franklin, Melanie L. With trust dept. City Nat. Bank, Columbus, O., 1946-54; trust officer Union Nat. Bank, Pitts., 1954-65; v.p., trust officer First Bank & Trust Co., Boca Raton, Fla., 1965—. Served with USNR, 1942-45. Elk. Kiwanian. Home: 1041 NW 6th St Boca Raton FL 33432 Office: 150 E Palmetto Park Rd Boca Raton FL 33432

SCHULER, GEORGE ALBERT, JR., food scientist; b. Altoona, Pa., Sept. 21, 1933; s. George Albert and Elizabeth (Deily) S.; B.S. in Poultry Sci., Pa. State U., 1959; M.S., U. Tenn., 1966; Ph.D. in Food Sci., Va. Poly. Inst. and State U., 1969; m. Barbara Jean Beichler, Jan. 7, 1961; children—Linda Lee, Karen Elizabeth, Beth Ann. Tchr., Madisonville (Tenn.) High Sch., 1964-66; research asst. Va. Poly. Inst. and State U., Blacksburg, 1966-70; extension food scientist U. Ga., Athens, 1970—. Owner, Pa. Poultry Service, Altoona, 1959-61. Served with U.S. Army, 1953-55; Korea. Dept. Commerce sea grantee, 1973. Mem. Catfish Farmers Ga. (exec. sec.), Ga. Poultry Fedn., World Poultry Sci. Soc. (life mem.), Sigma Xi, Phi Sigma. Author various extension booklets including Food Hands and Bacteria, 1971—. Home: 222 Holmes Av Athens GA 30601 Office: Extension Food Sci Dept Coop Extension Service Univ Ga Athens GA 30601

SCHULER, JOHN HAMILTON, electric co. exec.; b. Birmingham, Ala., Oct. 15, 1926; s. Robert Eustace and Doris (Moughon) S.; B.S. in Indls. Mgmt., Auburn U., 1952; m. Elizabeth Locke, Dec. 14, 1954; children—George A. Mattison IV (foster child), Elizabeth Locke, John Hamilton, Robert Eustace II. Cost, indsl. and sales engr. Anderson Electric Corp., Leeds, Alabama, 1950-52, personnel dir., 1952-54, with sales dept., 1954-56, asst. to exec. v.p., 1956-57, v.p. in charge operations, 1957-59, exec. v.p., gen. mgr., 1959-66, pres., 1966-68, chmn. bd., chief exec. officer, treas., 1969—, also dir.; pres. Schuler Investment Co., 1972; chmn. Broad Leaf Industries, Inc.; dir. Altec, Inc., Altec Mfg. Co., 1st Nat. Bank Birmingham, Ala. Bancorp. Pub. mem. U.S. delegation gov. council UN Devel. Program, 1970. Chmn. Ala. Republican Finance Com., 1964-66, 69-70, mem. state exec. com., 1964—; mem. Rep. Nat. Finance Com.; del. Rep. Nat. Conv., 1964, 68; campaign mgr. Nixon-Agnew, Ala., 1968; chmn. Ala. finance com. to Re-elect Pres., 1972. Bd. dirs. Jr. Achievement Jefferson County; met. chmn. Nat. Alliance Businessmen, 1970; pres. Birmingham Symphony Assn., 1967-68, chmn., 1968-70; pres. Ala. Opera Assn.; bd. dirs. Birmingham Urban League, Gorgas Scholarship Found., Regional Export Expansion Council, Children's Hosp., Birmingham; trustee Birmingham Univ. Sch.; bd. visitors U. Ala. Sch. Commerce and Bus.; mem. Pres.'s Devel. Council Samford U. Served with USCG, 1944-46. Mem. Birmingham C. of C. (chmn. aviation com., mem. exec. and policy com.), Asso. Industries Ala. (pres. 1962-63, chmn. 1963-65), N.A.M. (pub. affairs policy com.), Soc. Advancement Mgmt. (adminstrv., council), Nat. Foundry Assn. (adminstrv. council 1964), Elec. Mfrs. Club, Young Pres.' Orgn., Newcomen Soc. N. Am. Episcopalian (vestry, sr. warden). Clubs: Birmingham Country, Mountain Brook, Downtown, The Club, Relay House (Birmingham); Duquesne (Pitts.); Everglades, Bath and Tennis (Palm Beach, Fla.). Home: 2964 Cherokee Rd Birmingham AL 35223 Office: PO Box 455 Leeds AL 35094

SCHULER, THEODORE ANTHONY, civil engr.; b. Louisville, July 1, 1934; s. Henry R. and Virginia (Meisner) S.; B.C.E., U. Lousiville, 1957, M.Engring., 1973; m. Joel Beverly Bader, June 22, 1957; children—Marc, Elizabeth. Design, constrn. engr. Brighton Engring. Co., Frankfort, Ky., 1960-65; design engr. Hensley-Schmidt Inc., Chattanooga, 1965-68, asso. mem., 1969-73, sr. asso. mem., 1973—. Served to lt. (j.g.) USNR, 1957-60. Registered profl. engr., Ky., Tenn.; registered land surveyor, Ky. Mem. Nat., Tenn. socs. profl. engrs., Am. Soc. C.E. Home: 1300 James Blvd Signal Mountain TN 37377 Office: Am Nat Bank Bldg Chattanooga TN 37402

SCHULTZ, BENJAMIN, rabbi; b. Bklyn., Mar. 12, 1906; s. Joseph and Rose (Minskey) S.; B.A., U. Rochester, 1929; M.H.L., Jewish Inst. Religion, 1931; m. Charlotte Elkind, June 6, 1944. Rabbi, 1931; asso. rabbi Temple Ahavath Sholom, Bklyn., 1931-35, rabbi Temple Emanuel, Yonkers, N.Y., 1935-47; nat. exec. dir. Am. Jewish League against Communism, N.Y.C., 1948-60; rabbi Temple Beth Tefilloh, Brunswick, Ga., 1960-62, Temple Beth Israel, Clarksdale, Miss., 1962—. Chmn. N.Y. joint com. against communism, N.Y.C., 1952-60. Recipient Gold medal of Good Citizenship, SAR, 1955. Mem. Coahoma County Ministerial Assn. (pres. 1964—), Central Conf. Am. Rabbis. Mem. B'nai B'rith. Rotarian (pres. 1974). Profl. lectr. on Europe and communism in Miss. Home: 1124 Rose Circle Clarksdale MS 38614 Office: 401 Catalpa St Clarksdale MS 38614

SCHULTZ, DAVID NORMAN, aerospace engr.; b. Canton, O., Feb. 15, 1933; s. Stanley Merrill and Margaret Hilda (Wolfe) S.; B.S., Birmingham So. Coll., 1953; B.E.E., Ga. Inst. Tech., 1957, M.S. in Elec. Engring., 1968; m. Mary Suzanne Tissier, Sept. 19, 1953; children—Thomas M., Melanie M., Lily E. Product engr. Raytheon Corp., Bristol, Tenn., 1957-58; sr. engr. Chrysler Corp., Huntsville, Ala., 1958-62; aerospace engr. NASA Marshall Space Flight Center, Huntsville, 1962—. Served with U.S. Army, 1953-55. Mem. Tau Beta Pi, Eta Kappa Nu. Methodist. Home: 2234 Viscount Dr Huntsville AL 35810 Office: PD-DO-ES MSFC Huntsville AL 35812

SCHULTZ, DONALD O., educator; b. Mount Vernon, N.Y., Oct. 25, 1939; s. Emil Herman and Lilliam (Schalm) S.; B.S., Cal. State U. at Long Beach, 1963; M.Pub. Adminstrn., U. So., Cal., 1967; m. Patricia Gail Omilak, Dec. 27, 1969; 1 son, Donald O. Police officer Orange (Cal.) Police Dept., 1962-67; asst. prof. dept. law enforcement U. Neb., 1968-69; instr. police sci. Broward Community Coll., Fort Lauderdale, 1970—. Republican. Mason (Shriner). Author: (with Loren A. Norton) Police Operational Intelligence, 1968; Special Problems in Law Enforcement, 1971; (with William J. Bopp) A Short History of American Law Enforcement, 1972, Principles of American Law Enforcement and Criminal Justice, 1972; Police Unarmed Defense Tactics, 1973; The Subversive, 1973. Home: 8600 NW 35th St Coral Springs FL 33065

SCHULTZ, EVERETT HOYLE, JR., physician; b. Winston-Salem, N.C., Sept. 13, 1927; s. Everett Hoyle and Etta (Transou) S.; student U. N.C., 1944-45, 1946-48; M.D., Bowman Gray Sch. Medicine, 1952; m. Nancy Mary Jansson, June 24, 1955; children—Susan Carol, Frank Everett, Janet Loesch, Sally Louise. Intern, U. Okla. Hosp., 1952-53; resident N.C. Meml. Hosp., 1955-57, Univ. Okla. Hosp., 1954-55; practiced medicine in Cambridge, Mass., 1957-58; asst. in radiology Mass. Inst. Tech., Cambridge, 1957-58; asst. prof. radiology U. Fla., Gainesville, 1958-61; asso. prof. radiology U. N.C., Chapel Hill, 1961-67; chief radiology St. Anthony's Hosp., St. Petersburg, Fla., 1967—; cons. radiology Watts Hosp., Durham, N.C., 1961-67. Served with USNR, 1945-46. Fellow Am. Coll. Radiology; mem. So. Radiol. Conf. (chmn. 1966), A.A.A.S., A.M.A., Alpha Omega Alpha. Editorial cons. Yearbook of Cancer, 1963—. Home: 1005 Eden Isle Dr St Petersburg FL 33704 Office: St Anthony's Hosp St Petersburg FL 33705

SCHULTZ, FREDERICK JOHN, JR., mech. design engr.; b. Albany, N.Y., Mar. 13, 1942; s. Frederick John and Jennie Frances (Srednicki) S.; B.S. in Mech. Engring. with honors, Clemson Coll., 1962; postgrad. Carrier Air Conditioning Engrs. Design Sch., 1968; m. Mary Emily Parnell, Aug. 29, 1964. Tech. devel. engr. DuPont Inc., Florence, S.C., 1962; distbn. engr. Ala. Power Co., Montgomery, 1966-67; mech. design engr. Maxwell AFB, Ala., 1967-70; sr. mech. design engr. Eglin AFB, Fla., 1970—. Mem. Air Univ. Boiler Plant Operators Licensing Bd., 1970. Active Maxwell AFB United Appeal, 1969, 70. Served to 1st lt. USAF, 1962-66. Recipient Chgo. Tribune Gold Medal award, 1962. Registered profl. engr., Fla. Mem. Am. Soc. M.E., (coll. student paper award 1962, sect. chmn. award 1969-70, group vice chmn. 1968-69, regional devel. com. 1970-72), Am. Soc. Heating, Refrigerating and Air Conditioning Engrs., Nat., Fla. socs. Profl. Engrs. Democrat. Methodist. Home: 660 Golf Course Dr Fort Walton Beach FL 32548 Office: ADTC/DEEE Engineering Design Branch Eglin AFB FL 32542

SCHULTZ, JULIUS, biochemist; b. Rochester, N.Y., May 7, 1914; s. Benjamin and Ann (Duran) S.; student Cornell, 1932-34; B.S., U. Mich., 1936, Ph.D., 1940; postdoctoral studies U. Pa. Sch. Medicine, 1939-46; m. Betty Jane Splane, Oct. 14, 1942. Asst. prof. biochemistry Temple U. Sch. Medicine, 1951-57; asso. prof. Hahnemann Med. Sch., 1957-62, prof., 1962; dir. Papanicolaou Cancer Research Inst. Miami, Fla., 1968-72, presdl. dir., 1972—; adj. prof. U. Miami Med. Sch. Mem. com. on enzymes Nat. Acad. Sci., 1966-70. Fellow A.A.A.S.; mem. Am. (sec. div. biochemistry), English biochem. socs., Am. Chem. Soc. (sec. div. biochemistry), Am. Assn. Cancer Research, Recticulo-Endothialal Soc., Am. Soc. Biol. Chemists, Southeast Cancer Research Assn. (pres. 1973—). Home: 240 W San Marino Dr Miami Beach FL 33139 Office: 1155 NW 14th St Box 6188 Miami FL 33123

SCHULTZ, KENNETH PAUL, investment counselor; b. Foley, Ala., May 20, 1939; s. Gustav H. and Ann Hasseltine (Coaker) S.; B.S., Auburn U., 1961; M.B.A., U. Ala., 1966; m. Nelda Joan Chadwick, Jan. 29, 1966; children—John Chadwick, Heidi Leigh, Christopher Paul. Marketing rep. IBM, Atlanta, 1966-67; trust investment officer 1st Nat. Bank of Atlanta, 1967-74; asst. v.p. Thorndike, Doran, Paine & Lewis, Atlanta, 1974—. Precinct chmn. Republican party, 1972-73. Served with USNR, 1961-64. Mem. Atlanta Jaycees, Atlanta Financial Analysts Soc. (trustee 1973—). Presbyn. Home: 57 Lakeland Dr NW Atlanta GA 30305 Office: 225 Peachtree St NE Suite 1000 Atlanta GA 30303

SCHULTZ, ROBERT BROWN, pathologist; b. Palo Alto, Cal., Sept. 27, 1921; s. Edwin William and Anna Francel (Roberts) S.; A.B., Whitman Coll., 1946; M.A., Stanford, 1948; M.D., Yale, 1952; m. Corinne Marvin, Aug. 7, 1951; children—David Linton, Carolyn Jane. Intern Yale-New Haven Hosp., New Haven, 1952-53, asst. resident, 1953-54; resident in pathology, 1955-56; asst. prof. microbiology U. Minn., Mpls., 1956-57; asst. prof. pathology U. Md., Balt., 1958-60, asso. prof., 1960-67, prof., acting head dept., 1967-70, prof., part-time, 1970-73; practiced medicine specializing in pathology, Ft. Myers, Fla., 1970—. Served with USNR, 1942-46. Recipient Excellence in Teaching award, Student A.M.A., U. Md., 1970; Am. Cancer Soc. research fellow microbiology, 1954-55. Diplomate Am. Bd. Pathology. Mem. N.Y. Acad. Sci., Am. Soc. Clin. Pathology, Internat. Acad. Pathology, Am. Soc. Exptl. Pathology, Coll. Am. Pathologists, Am. Assn. Blood Banks, Am. Geriatric Soc., Sigma Xi. Home: 5563 Winkler Rd Fort Myers FL 33901 Office: PO Drawer 1528 Fort Myers FL 33902

SCHULTZ, RONALD CARL, banker; b. Henderson, Tex., Nov. 15, 1939; s. Carl Milton and Mary Ann (DeGeurin) S.; B.S., Rice U., 1962; M.B.A., U. Tex., 1967; m. JoAnna Murray, June 3, 1961; children—Ronald Carl, William Randall. Investment officer Tex. Tchr. Retirement System, Austin, 1967-68; sr. v.p., investment officer City Nat. Bank of Austin, 1968-73; exec. v.p., investment officer, dir. Tex. State Bank of Austin, 1973—. Cons., Tex. County and Dist. Retirement System, 1972—. Treas. Austin YMCA, 1971, bd. dirs., 1971—; trustee Murray Found., 1965—. Served to capt. USMCR, 1962-65. Mem. Austin Investment Assn. (dir. 1970—, pres. 1972), Austin, San Antonio Soc. Financial Analysts (treas. 1973), Young Men's Bus. League (dir. 1969—), Financial Analyst Fedn., Tex. Ind. Producers and Royalty Owners Assn., Marine Corps Res. Officers Assn., R Assn. Rice Univ. Home: 3105 Scenic St Austin TX 78703 Office: Tex State Bank Bldg Austin TX 78703

SCHULTZ, STUART JAY, market research co. exec.; b. Bklyn., Mar. 21, 1938; s. Jack and Violet (Graff) S.; B.A., Bklyn. Coll., 1959; M.A., New Sch. Social Research, 1961; m. Sharon Glaser, July 7, 1963; children—Lauran Richard, Cheryl Barbara. Dir. marketing research Bobbie Brooks Apparel Mfg. Co., Cleve., 1965-67; asst. v.p. Genesco Corp., Nashville, 1967-73; pres. Market Research & Planning Assos., Nashville, 1973—. Tchr. marketing Fisk U., Nashville, 1968—. Mem. Am. Marketing Assn. Home: 5412 Camelot Rd Brentwood TN 37027 Office: 111 7th Av N Nashville TN 37023

SCHULTZE, HENRY CHRISTIAN, sci. adminstr., bus. exec.; b. Charleston, S.C., Mar. 14, 1915; s. Charles F. and Ethel (Reid) S.; B.S., Coll. Charleston, 1937; Ph.D., U. N.C., 1941; m. Julia Rachel Hunter, Sept. 25, 1940; children—Margaret, Rachel. With research and devel. dept., chems. div. Union Carbide Corp., South Charleston, W. Va., 1941-64, asst. to dir., 1957-58, staff asso., 1958-64, tech. service mgr. Cardinal Chem. Corp., Columbia, S.C., 1964-65; dir. devel. research center S.C. State Devel. Bd., Columbia, 1965-68, mgr. tech. programs, 1968-69; v.p., mgr. eastern operations Chem-Nuclear Systems, Inc., Columbia, 1969—. Cons. in field. Mem. Am. Chem. Soc., Am. Nuclear Soc., Sigma Xi. Patentee in field. Home: 3760 Greenleaf Rd Columbia SC 29206 Office: PO Box 6336 Kittrell Bldg 2711 Middleburg Dr Columbia SC 29260

SCHULZ, HARRY JOHN, lawyer; b. Falls City, Tex., Mar. 27, 1913; s. John G. and Catherine (Sheehy) S.; student St. Mary's U., 1930-32; LL.B., U. Tex., 1935; m. Virginia Swett, Dec. 21, 1938; children—Mary Virginia (Mrs. Jack Johnson), Harriet Ann, Harry J., Betty (Mrs. Edward Schadle), Peggy. Admitted to Tex. bar, 1935; individual practice law, Three Rivers, Tex., 1935—; county atty. Live Oak County, Tex., 1936-40; city atty. Three Rivers, Tex., 1945—. Pres., dir. Schulz Live Stock Co., Three Rivers, 1942-49, Spur S. Farm, Inc., Three Rivers, 1965—; dir. 1st State Bank, Three Rivers. Dir. Nueces River Authority, 1964—. Mem. state exec. com. Democratic party, 1964-66. Trustee Three Rivers Ind. Sch. Dist., 1956—, pres., 1966—; bd. dirs. Coastal Bend Council of Govts., Corpus Christi, Tex. Mem. Am. Bar Assn., Tex. Bar Found., Tex. State Bar, Three Rivers C. of C. Roman Catholic (Papal Knight, Order of St. Gregory). K.C. Rotarian. Home: 101 Hazel St Three Rivers TX 78071 Office: 623 Harborth St Three Rivers TX 78071

SCHULZ, JOHN HAMPSHIRE, paper co. exec.; b. N.Y.C., Apr. 10, 1934; s. Oscar and Eunice Ann (Hampshire) S.; B. Chem. Engring. cum laude, Poly. Inst. Bklyn., 1955; M.S., Inst. Paper Chemistry, 1957, Ph.D., 1961; m. Kathleen Reardon, Jan. 20, 1962; children—Elizabeth, Susan, Thomas. Asst. prof. Western Mich. U., Kalamazoo, 1961-63; tech. dir., also gen. supt. Continental Can Co., Augusta, Ga., 1963—. U.S. rep. to Internat. Standards Orgn., 1967-73. Mem. T.A.P.P.I. (chmn. pulp testing com. 1971-73), Am. Chem. Soc., Am. Assn. U. Profs. Researcher on viscoelastic properties of paper. Home: 603 Regent Road Augusta GA 30904 Office: Continental Can Company Augusta GA 30903

SCHULZ, MICHAEL ANTHONY, JR., civil engr., contractor; b. New Orleans, Dec. 17, 1934; s. Michael Anthony and Hilda (Monnin) S.; B.Sc., La. State U., 1959; m. Ann Miller Hawkins, Aug. 15, 1958; 1 dau., Terri Lynn. Engr., estimator Crawford Corp., Baton Rouge, 1956-57; plant mgr. Tidewood Corp., Baton Rouge, 1957-58; eng., estimator La. Concrete Products, Baton Rouge, 1959-61; dept. head Wilson P. Abraham Constrn. Co., Baton Rouge, 1961-64; constrn. mgr. Odis F. Haymon, Baton Rouge, 1964-67; sec., treas. The Bedford Corp., Baton Rouge, 1967—. Mem. Am. Soc. C.E., La. Engring. Soc., Soc. Am. Mil. Engrs., Alpha Tau Omega. Episcopalian. Club: Baton Rouge Sertoma (v.p.). Designed and constructed Chateau Carre' Apts., New Orleans; Francis Apts., Baton Rouge; Colony House Apts., Baton Rouge. Home: 864 Albert Hart Dr Baton Rouge LA 70808 Office: 871 W Garfield St Baton Rouge LA 70802

SCHUMACHER, SNEAD, cons. engr.; b. Walhalla, S.C., Mar. 8, 1924; s. George D. and Clara (Snead) S.; A.S.T.P., Tex. A. and M. U., 1944; B.S., Clemson Coll., 1947; m. Jimmie Crofford, Apr. 27, 1945; 1 dau., Susan. Constrn. engr., contractor, S.C., Ga., 1947-58; tchr. schs., Walhalla, also Seneca, S.C., 1958-65; civil engr., owner Schumacher Engring. Service & Land Surveyor, Walhalla, 1958—. Mem. S.C. Ho. of Reps., 1965-66, S.C. Senate, 1967-73; mayor pro tempore, Walhalla, 1964, city councilman, 1950-59, 62-64; mem. Oconee County Planning Bd., 1956-65, dir., 1958; mem. S.C. Appalachian Council Govts., 1966-73, S.C. Appalachian Health Council, 1966—; chmn. Oconee County Christmas Seal Campaign, 1964-65. Bd. dirs. Oconee Meml. Hosp., 1967-73; mem. civil engring. and constrn. mgmt. adv. com. Tri-County Tech. Edn. Center, 1969—. Served with AUS, 1942-45. Registered profl. engr., S.C., Ga. Mem. S.C.V., V.F.W. Lutheran. Mason (Shriner), Lion (pres. 1954). Club: Sertoma. Home: 502 N Broad St Walhalla SC 29691 Office: 500 N Broad St Walhalla SC 29691

SCHUMPERT, ROBERT DENNIS, lawyer; b. Newberry, S.C., Oct. 28, 1927; s. Claude C. and Myrtle Roberta (Dennis) S.; student U.S. Coast Guard Acad., 1945-46, Newberry Coll., 1946-49; LL.B., U. S.C., 1951; m. Margaret Ida Hutchinson, Sept. 5, 1951; children—Susan McKeene, Robert Young, Lucia Myrtle, Ida Dennis, Claude Hutchinson. Admitted to S.C. bar, 1951; mem. staff regional attys. OPS, Atlanta, 1951-52; practice law, Newberry, S.C., 1952—.

Dir. Newberry Br. Bankers Trust of S.C. Mem. S.C. Bd. Law Examiners, 1969—. Mem. Gov's. Com. on Crime Prevention and Adminstrn. of Justice, 1967—. Past bd. dirs. Community Chest; trustee Newberry County Meml. Hosp., Counsel, 1955—. Served with USCG, 1945-46. Mem. Omicron Delta Kappa, Phi Delta Phi. Democrat. Lutheran. Lion (pres. club 1960). Clubs: Newberry Cotillion, Newberry Country. Home: 800 Caldwell St Newberry SC 29108 Office: 1201 Boyce St Newberry SC 29108

SCHURIG, RALPH ARTHUR, elec. engr.; b. Morristown, Tenn., July 9, 1939; s. John Eberhard and Anna Louise (Schmidt) S.; B.S., U. Tenn., 1967; m. Judith Elaine McDowell, July 15, 1961; children—Mark Anthony, Todd Andrew. Electronic technician Magnavox Corp., Jefferson City, Tenn., 1958-62; elec. engr. IBM Corp., Huntsville, Ala., 1968—. Served with AUS, 1962-64. Methodist (mem. adminstrv. bd.). Home: 1914 Epworth Dr Huntsville AL 35811 Office: 150 Sparkman Dr Huntsville AL 35807

SCHURMAN, GLENN AUGUST, petroleum exec.; b. Woodland, Wash., Sept. 6, 1922; s. William E. and Ella (Bennett) S.; B.S. in Mech. Engring. cum laude, Wash. State Coll., 1944; M.S. in Mech. Engring., Cal. Inst. Tech., 1947, Ph.D. summa cum laude, 1950; m. Patricia L. Harper, Mar. 4, 1944; children—Valerie Kay, Christy Lynn, D. Lee. With NACA, Cleve., 1944-46, Cal. Inst. Tech. Jet Propulsion Lab., Pasadena, 1946; Standard Oil Co. Cal., 1950-63; with Chevron Oil Co., La. and Tex., 1963-71, asst. gen. mgr. prodn., New Orleans, 1971—. Bd. dirs. Jr. Achievement, Midland, Tex., 1969-71. Mem. Am. Soc. M.E., Am. Inst. M.E., Am. Petroleum Inst., Mid Continental Oil and Gas Assn. Patentee seismic exploration equipment. Author publs. on drilling well control. Home: 4129 Maple Leaf Dr New Orleans LA 70114 Office: 1111 Tulane Av New Orleans LA 70112

SCHWAB, ELMO, lawyer; b. Gonzales, Tex., Jan. 17, 1937; s. Elmo S. and Mary Doris (Reimenschneider) S.; B.A. cum laude, U. Tex. at Austin, 1959, J.D., 1962; m. Claudette Taylor, Sept. 19, 1960; children—Mary Suzanne, Taylor Townsend. Admitted to Tex. bar, 1962, U.S. Supreme Ct., 1968; mem. firm Barker, Lain, Smith & Schwab, Galveston, Tex., 1967—. Dir. Galveston East Beach, Inc. Bd. dirs. Galveston Cultural Arts Council, 1971-73, Friends Rosenberg Library, 1970-72. Mem. Am. Bar Assn., Am. Judicature Soc., Am. Assn. Trial Lawyers, World Peace Through Law Conf., S.A.R., Sons Republic Tex., Sons Confederate Vets. Kiwanian. Home: 2618 Gerol Ct Galveston TX 77550 Office: 2200 Market St Suite 500 Galveston TX 77550

SCHWALENBERG, FRANK ALOYSIUS, ins. co. exec.; b. Newport News, Va., Sept. 14, 1922; s. Frank A. and Clare (Glover) S.; student Newport News Apprentice Sch., 1940-44; m. Mattie Louise Lowe, Apr. 11, 1944; children—Mary Jo (Mrs. Kenneth L. Dawson), Frank C. Apprentice, Newport News Shipbldg. & Dry Dock Co., 1940-44; model maker NASA, Langley AFB, Va., 1944-45; field underwriter Home Life Ins. Co. N.Y., Newport News, 1955—. Chmn. bus. solicitation Peninsula Heart Fund, City of Hampton, Va., 1967-68; mem. Va. Gov.'s Commn. to study health costs. Served with USAAF, 1944-46. Named Man of Year, Peninsula Life Underwriters Assn., 1967, Va. Assn. Life Underwriters, 1973; recipient Nat. Sales Achievement award, 1966-73. Mem. Million Dollar Round Table, Nat. (Nat. Quality award 1956-73), Va. (pres. 1969-70), Peninsula (pres. 1965-66) assns. life underwriters, Peninsula Football Ofcls. Assn. (pres. 1960-61). Clubs: Sertoma (pres. 1968-69) (Hampton); Peninsula Sports (pres. 1971). Home: Cedar Point Crittenden VA 23342 Office: PO Box 541 2600 Washington Av Newport News VA 23607

SCHWARTZ, AARON ROBERT, lawyer, state senator; b. Galveston, Tex., July 17, 1926; s. Joe and Clara (Bulbe) S.; student Tex. A. and M. Coll., 1944-47; LL.B., U. Tex., 1951; m. Marilyn Cohn, July 14, 1951; children—Robert Allen, Richard Austin, John Reed, Thomas Lee. Admitted to Tex. bar, 1951; practiced in Galveston, 1951—; asst. county atty., Galveston, 1951-53; mem. Tex. Ho. of Reps., 1954-58; mem. Tex. Senate, 1959—, pres. pro tem., 1965-66. Vice pres. Harbor Broadcasting Co., Galveston. Chmn. southwestern regional bd. Anti Defamation League of B'nai B'rith, 1961-65, mem. nat. commn. of league, 1966; chmn. Tex. Council Coastal and Marine Affairs. Served with USNR, 1944-46. Recipient awards State of Tex., N.G. Assn. Tex., Tex. Municipal Police Assn., Tex. Council of Retarded Children, Anti Defamation League of B'nai B'rith; Friend of Journalism award Sigma Delta Chi, 1967. Home: 10 S Shore Dr Galveston TX 77550 Office: US National Bank Bldg Galveston TX 77550

SCHWARTZ, ARNOLD EDWARD, univ. dean; b. Rochester, N.Y., Dec. 15, 1935; s. Werner Paul and Josephine Marie (Vernetti) S.; B.S. in Chem. Engring., U. Notre Dame, 1958, M.S. in Civil Engring., 1960; Ph.D. (Ford Found. fellow), Ga. Inst. Tech., 1963; m. Carol Elizabeth Young, June 6, 1959; children—Stephen, Linda, Lisa, Richard, Jeffrey, Melissa. Research engr. Ga. Inst. Tech., Atlanta, 1963; asst. prof. civil engring. Clemson (S.C.) U., 1963-67, asso. prof., head dept. civil engring., 1967-69, dean Grad. Sch., 1969-70, prof. civil engring., dean grad. studies and univ. research, 1970—. Cons. Law Engring. Testing Co., 1961-67. Mem. U.S. Council Grad Schs., Am. Soc. C.E., Sertoma. Sigma Xi, Chi Epsilon. Roman Catholic. Home: 416 Shorecrest Dr Clemson SC 29631

SCHWARTZ, ELMER GEORGE, educator; b. Pitts., July 16, 1927; s. Elmer George and Jennetta Mae (Lemon) S.; B.S., U.S. Merchant Marine Acad., 1950; M.S. in Nuclear Engring., Carnegie Inst. Tech., 1960, Ph.D., 1964; m. Ursula Dellheim, Dec. 10, 1947; children—Robert, Richard, Randall, Russell, Suzanne. Devel. engr. Westinghouse Elec. Corp. Atomic Power Divs., Pitts., 1954-61; prof. engring. U. S.C., Columbia, 1964—. Served with USNR, 1950-52. Researcher on compaction behaviour of metallic and ceramic powders. Home: 4057 Sandwood Dr Columbia SC 29206

SCHWARTZ, HENRY II, lawyer; b. Chattanooga, May 15, 1919; s. Herman Loveman and Willie Frances (Marshall) S.; student U. Miami, 1941; A.B., U. Tenn. at Chattanooga, 1946; J.D., U. Va., 1948; m. Margaret Frances MacMillian, May 26, 1951; 1 dau., Peigi Marshall. Dep. register Hamilton County, Chattanooga, 1939-46; admitted to Tenn., Va. bars, 1948, Tex. bar, 1957; pub. counsel Office Gen. Counsel, CAB, Washington, 1948-50; legal adviser U.S. Tax Ct., Washington, 1950-53, sr. legal adviser, 1953-56; with firm Ramey, Calhoun, Brelsford, Hull & Flock, Tyler, Tex., 1956-59; pvt. practice, Tyler, 1959—. Participant, patron Tyler Civic Theatre. Organizer, charter trustee Endowment Fund of Christ Episcopal Ch., Tyler, vice chmn. bd., 1960-62, hon. trustee, permanent chancellor, 1962—; trustee ex officio Joseph and Helen Davidson Charitable Found., 1967-71. Served to capt. USAAF, 1940-46; lt. col. Res. ret. Mem. Am. (com. on natural resources of taxation sect.), Tex., Va., Smith County bar assns., Am. Judicature Soc., E. Tex. Estate Council (charter mem., sec. 1960-61, dir. 1960-62, 68-71, pres. 1969-70), Southwestern Legal Found., Tyler C. of C., U. Va. (life), U. Tenn. at Chattanooga alumni assns. Episcopalian (vestryman 1959-61, chief usher 1958—, licensed lay reader). Elk. Clubs: Tyler Petroleum; Lookout Mountain (Tenn.) Fairyland. Author: Tax Consequences of the Payment of Substitute Royalties, 1958. Contbr. articles to profl. jours. Home: 608 E 3d St Tyler TX 75701 Office: Tyler Bank & Trust Co Bldg Tyler TX 75701

SCHWARTZ, LARRY H., lawyer; s. Chattanooga, July 29, 1938; s. Samuel and Rose (Rosen) S.; B.S. in Bus. Adminstrn., U. Tenn. at Chattanooga, 1960; J.D., U. Cin., 1963; m. Phyllis Beisly, June 4, 1961; children—Michael Stephen, David Scott, Mark Patrick. Admitted to Ohio bar, 1963, Tex. bar, 1966, Supreme Ct. U.S., 1968; mem. firm Schwartz & Earp, El Paso, 1974—. Pres. Group Against Smog, Pollution (GASP), El Paso, 1973. Bd. dirs. El Paso Legal Assistance Soc. Served to capt. Judge Adv. Gen.'s Corps., AUS, 1964-67. Decorated Army Commendation medal. Mem. Am., Tex., El Paso bar assns., Am., El Paso (pres.), Tex. trial lawyers assns. Jewish religion. Mem. B'nai B'rith. Home: 8508 WH Burges El Paso TX 79925 Office: 932 SW National Bank Bldg El Paso TX 79901

SCHWARTZ, LAWRENCE, govt. ofcl.; b. Bklyn., May 11, 1942; s. Alexander and Marion (Strongin) S.; B.B.A., Baruch Sch., Coll. City N.Y., 1964; M.A., Mich. State U., 1965; postgrad. George Washington U., 1967-68; m. Susan Iris English, Aug. 15, 1964; children—Mark Allan, Ellen Freida. Economist, Center Naval Analyses, Arlington, Va., 1965-67; economist Treasury Dept., Washington, 1967-70, on loan during import surcharge period, 1971, internat. economist-econometrician, 1972—; research program analyst Fed. Res. System, Washington, 1970-72. Mem. faculty Grad. Sch., U.S. Dept. Agr., Washington, 1970—. Recipient certificate Treasury Dept., 1968. Mem. Am. Econ. Assn. Contbr. articles to profl. jours. Home: 13128 Mercury Lane Fairfax VA 22030 Office: US Treasury Dept 14th St and Pennsylvania Av NW Washington DC 20004

SCHWARTZ, LEON M., govt. ofcl.; b. Balt., Apr. 26, 1928; s. Paul H. and Pauline (Shulman) S.; A.B. in Econs. (Alumni scholar), Johns Hopkins, 1950; m. Joan Schinker, July 16, 1953; children—Howard, Richard. Asst. treas. Carpel, Inc., Balt., 1953-60; chief program rev. Goddard Space Flight Center, NASA, Greenbelt, Md., 1960-67; asst. commr. for adminstrn. Office Edn., Dept. Health, Edn. and Welfare, Washington, 1967-71; dep. asst. dir. for program mgmt. NSF, Washington, 1971; asso. dir. for adminstrn. NIH, Washington, 1972—. Served with AUS, 1950-52. Recipient Superior Service award Dept. Health, Edn. and Welfare. C.P.A., Md. Home: 12105 Hitching Post Lane Rockville MD 20852 Office: Nat Insts Health Bethesda MD 20014

SCHWARTZ, RAYMOND LAURENCE, educator; b. N.Y.C., Aug. 16, 1913; s. Frank and Amelia (Shoen) S.; A.B., Cornell U., 1934, M.D., 1937; m. Ruth Ellen Smith, May 21, 1943; children—Raymond, Richard, Ruth, Roberta, Regina, Roger, Rosalyn, Reita. Intern Bellevue Hosp., N.Y.C., 1937-38, resident, 1938-41; med. officer Glenndale Sanatorium, Washington, 1941-43; chief medicine Arlington (Va.) Hosp., 1947-57, chief of staff, 1957-62; clin. prof. medicine Georgetown U. Sch. Medicine, 1948—. Served to maj. M.C., AUS, 1943-46. Fellow A.C.P., Am. Coll. Chest Physicians; mem. Alpha Omega Alpha. Kiwanian. Home: 3231 Juniper Lane Falls Church VA 22044 Office: 1029 N Stuart St Arlington VA 22201

SCHWARTZ, SORELL LEE, pharmacologist, educator; b. Buffalo, Sept. 13, 1937; s. Jacob Maurice and Rosalind (Greenberg) S.; B.S., U. Md., 1959; Ph.D., Med. Coll. Va., 1963; m. Marsha Kohlenstein, June 9, 1963; children—Joanne Beth, Rebecca Lynn. Head, pharmacol. div. Naval Med. Research Inst., Bethesda, Md., 1966-68; asso. prof. pharmacol. Georgetown U. Sch. Medicine, Washington, 1968—. Cons., Fed. Trade Commn., Nat. Inst. Mental Health, Select Com. on Generally Regarded as Safe Substances, Navy Med. Dept. Served to lt. comdr. USNR, 1963-66. Mem. Am. Soc. Pharmacol. and Exptl. Therapeutics, Soc. Toxicology, Reticuloendothelial Soc., A.A.A.S., Sigma Xi. Democrat. Jewish Religion. Mem. B'nai B'rith. Editorial bd. Toxicology Applied Pharmacology, 1972—. Research and publs. in toxicity of tobacco smoke constituents to the lung, systemic defense mechanisms. Home: 11504 Charlton Dr Silver Spring MD 20902 Office: Dept Pharmacology Georgetown University School of Medicine Washington DC 20007

SCHWARTZ, WILLIAM LEWIS, vet. pathologist; b. Columbus, O., Dec. 11, 1931; s. Lewis Glenn and Mildred Opal (Basinger) S.; B.S. in Agr., Ohio State U., 1953, D.V.M., 1957; M.S. in Vet. Pathology, Tex. A. and M., 1970; m. Barbara Ann Custer, June 21, 1953; children—Kimberly Ann, Kay Annette. Practiced vet. medicine, Lancaster, O., 1957-60; dist. veterinarian, also lab. diagnostician Ohio Dept. Agr., Columbus, 1960-64; lab. diagnostician Ga. Coastal Plain Expt. Sta., Tifton, 1964-67; asst. prof. Coll. Vet. Medicine, Tex. A. and M. U., College Station, 1967-70; vet. pathologist Tex. Vet. Med. Diagnostic Lab., College Station, 1970—. Cons. Tex. Specific Pathogen Free Swine Accrediting Agy., 1971—. Mem. Am., Ohio vet. med. assns., Am. Assn. Swine Practitioners, Brazos Valley Vet. Med. Assn., Phi Zeta. Lutheran. Home: 3507 Carter Creek Pkwy Bryan TX 77801 Office: PO Drawer 3040 College Station TX 77840

SCHWARZ, FELIX CONRAD, artist, writer; b. N.Y.C., Apr. 13, 1906; s. Osias L. and Anna (Reifler) S.; First Honors, Corcoran Sch. Art, 1923-26; A.B., George Washington U., 1927, A.M., 1930; Ph.D., Columbia; m. Myrtle Cooper, 1940. Prof. art Mary Washington Coll. (Va.), 1930-34, State U. Minn., 1934-39; research fellow Columbia U., 1939-41, Coll. William and Mary S.S., 1941; feature writer Washington News 1930-32; dir. adult classes in creative writing Community Center, 1932-34; prof. and dir. Sch. Art. Phillaps U., 1944-48; vis. prof. art, Northwestern State Coll., La.; prof., chmn. dept. fine arts Wesleyan Coll., Macon, Ga., 1957-61; prof. art Pembrooke (N.C.) State U., 1961—; prof. fine arts Livingston (Ala.) U., 1966-71; vis. prof. Monticello Coll., Alton, Ill., 1963-65, Parsons Coll., summer 1964, Wis. State U., Superior, 1965-66; lectr. Inst. Lifetime Learning, 1972—. Exhibited paintings throughout country's leading galleries and museums since 1923. Lectr. and painting demonstrator. Fellow Internat. Inst. of Arts and Letters; mem. Soc. Free Lance Writers (pres. 1928-34), Minn. Coll. Art Tchrs. (pres. 1935-39), Okla. Edn. Assn. (chmn. art sect. 1946-47), Enid Artists League (pres.), Nat. Art Edn. Assn., Western Arts Assn., Am. Assn. U. Profs. Contbr. numerous articles to scholarly and popular periodicals. Editor: Advanced Sch. Digest. Columbia, 1939-41. Home: 1500 North Dakota Av NE St Petersburg FL 33703

SCHWARZE, ESTELLA GERALDINE, social work adminstr.; b. New Orleans; d. William J. and Mary (Reynolds) Schwarze; B.S. in Social Sci., Loyola U., New Orleans, 1957, postgrad., 1958-59, 61-62; M.S.W., Tulane U., 1962; postgrad. U. New Orleans, 1973—. With Asso. Cath. Charities, 1946-59; exec. dir. Assn. for Retarded Children, 1956-57; with social service dept. Charity Hosp. of La., New Orleans, 1958—, supr., 1965—. Field work instr. Atlanta U. Grad. Sch. Social Work, 1967—. Cons. social work Treme Neighborhood Improvement Assn.; curriculum cons., organizer, coordinator social studies symposia Rummel High Sch., New Orleans, 1973-74. Founder, charter mem. Irish Channel Action Found., New Orleans, 1964; organizer Parent's Inst., New Orleans, 1962; organizer, originator Projects Aquarius; del. White House Conf. on Children and Youth, 1970, White House Conf. on Aging, 1971; mem. New Orleans Mayor's Task Force Aging; lectr. community medicine La. State U., Tulane U. Mem. adv. bd., cons. health consumer edn. program New Orleans Urban League. Mem. Nat. Assn. Social Workers, (Social Worker of Yr. award S.E. La. chpt. 1965), Am. Pub. Health Assn., Mercy Acad. Alumnae (pres. 1956-58), League Women Voters. Democrat. Home: 915 Jefferson Av New Orleans LA 70115 Office: Social Service Dept Charity Hosp of La 1542 Tulane Av New Orleans LA 70130

SCHWARZSCHILD, RICHARD ISAAC, banker; b. Richmond, Va., July 29, 1912; s. William Harry and Rosa Lee (Held) S.; B.S., U. Pa., 1934; m. Betty Berne, Oct. 26, 1935; children—Ellen Louise (Mrs. Jack M. Kreuter), J. William, Richard J. Training Corps Chase Manhattan Bank, N.Y.C., 1934-35; credit supr. C.I.T. Corp., N.Y.C., 1935-37; with Central Nat. Bank, Richmond, Va., 1937—, cons., 1967; treas. Schwarzschild Bros., Inc., Richmond, 1957—. Treas. Schwarzschild Found., 1956—. Mem. Richmond Sch. Bd., 1970—. Bd. dirs. Lakeside Park, Richmond Jewish Community Council. Mem. Richmond C. of C. (dir. 1954-55). Clubs: Jefferson-Lakeside Country (dir. 1970—), Bull and Bear (Richmond). Home: 5110 Cary St Rd Richmond VA 23226 Office: 219 E Broad St Richmond VA 23261

SCHWEICKART, RUSSELL L., astronaut; b. Neptune, N.J., Oct. 25, 1935; s. George L. Schweickart; B.S. in Aero. Engring., Mass. Inst. Tech., 1956, M.S. in Aeros. and Astronautics, 1963; m. Clare Grantham Whitfield; children—Vicki Louise, Elin Ashley, Russell Brown and Randolph Barton (twins), Diana Croom. Was research scientist Mass. Inst. Tech. Exptl. Astronomy Lab.; now astronaut NASA Johnson Space Center, Houston; lunar Johnson Space on Apollo 9, 1969. Served as pilot USAF, 1956-60, 61, Capt., Mass. Air N.G. Mem. Soc. Exptl. Test Pilots. Office: NASA Manned Spacecraft Center Houston TX 77058

SCHWEITZER, FRANK JACOB, III, hosp. adminstr.; b. Louisville, Feb. 26, 1924; s. Frank Jacob and Nellie (McCullom) S.; student U. Louisville, 1942, Meadows-Draughon Bus. Coll., 1947, Texarkana Coll., 1968-69; m. Plesine Barker, Mar. 13, 1945; children—Betty Jean (Mrs. Robert M. Toups), Marianne, John Franklin. Profl. detailman E.R. Squibb & Sons, Ky., 1948; resident adminstrn. T.J. Samson Community Hosp., Glasgow, Ky., 1948-49; adminstr. Lafayette County Meml. Hosp., Lewisville, Ark., 1949—. Pres., S.W. Ark. Hosp. Dist., 1953. Mem. Ark.'s Hosp. Adv. Council, 1972—. Served with Hosp. Corps, USNR, 1943-46. Mem. Am., Ark. hosps. assns., Am. Coll. Hosp. Adminstrs., Am. Med. Technologists. Home: 311 W 11th St Lewisville AR 71845 Office: 1105 Chestnut St Lewisville AR 71845

SCHWEITZER, PAUL ROBERT, govt. ofcl.; b. Budapest, Hungary, Sept. 17, 1930; s. Ivan and Wanda (Rusz) S.; B.A., Sir George Williams U. (Can.) 1959; M.A., McGill U. (Can.) 1961; m. Agnes Fischer, May 15, 1955; children—John, Alexandra. Came to U.S., 1959, naturalized, 1964. Exec. trainee Canadian Bank Commerce, Montreal, Que., Can., 1957-59; economist Canadian Dept. Labor, Ottawa, Ont., Can., 1959. cons. in econs., Washington, 1960-62; economist Nat. Planning Assn., Washington, 1962-64; economist Fed. Res. System Bd. Govs., Washington, 1964—. Lectr. Howard U., 1962-70. Mem. Am. Econ. Assn. Home: 4309 Van Ness St NW Washington DC 20016 Office: 600 New Hampshire Av Washington DC 20551

SCHWICHTENBERG, ALAN EDWARD, veterinarian, air force officer; b. Washington, July 23, 1931; s. Albert Henry and Lucille Ann (Schumuay) S.; A.A., George Washington U., 1951; B.S., Colo. A. and M. U., 1955; D.V.M., Colo. State U., 1960; M.S. in Pub. Health, U. Mo., 1968; postgrad. Air Command and Staff Coll., Maxwell AFB, Ala., 1972-73; m. Patricia Ann Myers, June 7, 1957; children—Sandra D., Lisa K., Debra L., Linda L., Andrew A. Commd. 1st lt. USAF, 1960, advanced through grades to maj., 1967; base veterinarian, March AFB, Cal., 1960-62, Wiesban AFB, Germany, 1962-66; resident fellow vet. pub. health U. Mo., 1967-69; chief Vet. Services, Kadena AFB, Okinawa, 1969-72; veterinarian Air Force Eastern Test Range, Fla., 1973—. Cons. RCAF Sentry Dog Program in Europe, 1962-66; mem. faculty Grad. Sch., U. Mo., 1968-69. Decorated Meritorious Service medal, Air Force Commendation medal, Nat. Def. medal. Diplomate Am. Bd. Vet. Pub. Health. Fellow Royal Soc. Health (London); mem. Internat. Oceanographic Found. Miami, Am. Vet. Med. Assn., Am. Pub. Health Assn., Sigma Xi. Contbr. articles to profl. jours. Home: 102 Greenwood Dr Panama City FL 32401 Office: PO Box 4824 Patrick Air Force Base FL 32925

SCHWING, CHARLES EDWARD, architect; b. Plaquemine, La., Nov. 21, 1929; s. Calvin Kendrick and Mary Howard (Slack) S.; student La. State U., 1947-51; B.S., Ga. Inst. Tech., 1953, B.Architecture, 1954; 3e Assessit de'Architecture, Ecole Des Beaux-Arts; m. Cynthia Benjamin, June 14, 1952 (div. 1967); children—Calvin Kendick III, Therra Cynthia; m. 2d, Geraldine Fleniken Hofmann, Dec. 27, 1969; 1 stepson, Steven Blake. Field insp. Bodman, Murrell and Smith, Baton Rouge, 1954-55; asso. architect Post & Harelson, Baton Rouge, 1955-59; partner Hughes and Schwing, Baton Rouge, 1959-61; owner Charles E. Schwing, Baton Rouge, 1961-69, Charles E. Schwing & Assos., Baton Rouge, 1969—; dir. Schwing Inc. Mem. A.I.A. (sec. Baton Rouge chpt. 1960-61), La. Architect Assn. (sec.-treas. 1971, v.p. 1972, pres. 1973), C. of C., La. State U. Alumni Fedn., Ga. Tech. Alumni Club, Sigma Alpha Epsilon. Episcopalian. Elk. Clubs: Baton Rouge Country, City. Home: Route 2 Box 380 Baton Rouge LA 70816 Office: 721 Government St Baton Rouge LA 70802

SCIPIO, L(OUIS) ALBERT II, educator; b. Juarez, Mexico, Aug. 22, 1922; s. Louis Albert and Marie Leona (Richardson) S.; B.S. in Architecture, Tuskegee Inst., 1943; B.C.E., U. Minn., 1948, M.S. in Civil Engring., 1950, Ph.D., 1958; m. Katherine Jones, Aug. 15, 1942; children—Louis Albert III, Kathleen, Karen. Archtl. draftsman McKissack & McKissack, 1942-43; instr. archtl. div. Tuskegee Inst., Ala., 1946; structural designer Long & Thorshov, architects, Mpls., 1948-50; teaching fellow in civil engring. U. Minn., Mpls., 1950-52, lectr. aero. engring., 1952-61; Fulbright prof. Faculty of Engring., Cairo (Egypt) U., 1955-56; asso. prof. mechanics Howard U., Washington, 1961-62, prof., 1967-70, univ. prof. space scis., 1970—; prof. phys. sci. U. P.R., Mayaguez, 1962-63; prof. aerospace engring. U. Pitts., 1963-67. Research physicist Hughes Aircraft Co., summer 1955, cons., 1959—; cons. Gen. Mills, Inc., Winzen Research, Inc., Westinghouse Electric Corp., Knowledge Availability Systems Center of NASA, U. Pitts., NSF, NASA. Served to capt. AUS, 1943-46. Recipient D.B. Steinman award for research in structural engring. N.Y. Acad. Scis., 1958. Mem. Washington Acad. Scis. (award 1961), Soc. Natural Philosophy, Internat. Assn. Bridge and Structural Engrs., Am. Inst. Aeros. and Astronautics, Sigma Xi, Phi Beta Kappa, Pi Mu Epsilon, Sigma Pi Sigma, Sigma Gamma Tau, Pi Tau Sigma, Alpha Kappa Mu. Author: Compendium of Aircraft Stress Analysis and Design, 1956; Principles of Continua with Applications, 1966; Structural Design Concepts, 1967; The First Fifty Years: The Building of Fort Benning, 1973. Reviewer for Applied Mechanics Revs., 1961—. Home: 12511 Montclair Dr Silver Spring MD 20904 Office: Grad School Howard U Washington DC 20001

SCISM, MACK, theater exec.; b. Anadarko, Okla., July 26, 1926; s. Delos M. and Grace (Hux) S.; B.S., U. Okla., 1947. Tchr. math. and English, Capitol Hill High Sch., Oklahoma City, 1947-49; founding mem. Mummers Theatre, Inc., Oklahoma City, 1949, producer, dir., 1949—. Bd. dirs., mem. exec. com. Theatre Communications Group, 1961-68. Served with USNR, 1943-45. Ford Found. grantee, 1958. Home: 1130 N E 11th St Oklahoma City OK 73117 Office: 400 W Sheridan Oklahoma City OK 73106

SCKERL, MAX MICHAEL, plant physiologist, chem. co. exec.; b. Watertown, S.D., May 8, 1930; s. Rudolf Edward and Cecilia Marie (Trautner) S.; B.S., S.D. State U., 1961; M.S., N.D. State U., 1963; Ph.D., U. Ark., 1968; m. Jeroldyne Beatrice Rolstad, May 12, 1956; children—Thomas Michael, Carolyn Marie. Plant physiologist Shell Devel. Co., Modesto, Cal., 1968-72; tech. service rep. Shell Chem. Co., Atlanta, 1972-73, tech. support rep., Memphis, 1973—. Troop Com. mem. Atlanta area council Boy Scouts Am., 1972—. Served with AUS, 1953-55. Mem. Weed Sci. Soc. Am., Gamma Sigma Delta, Alpha Zeta. Republican. Roman Catholic. Research in weed sci. Home: 6900 Roxbury Cove Germantown TN 38138 Office: 5575 Popular Av Memphis TN 38117

SCOBEY, ELLIS HURLBUT, geologist; b. Kelso, Wash., Sept. 15, 1911; s. Guy Hurlbut and Bessie Merwin (Barrett) S.; B.A., Cornell Coll., Mt. Vernon, Ia., 1933; B.S., U. Ia., 1935, Ph.D., 1938; m. Dorothy June Wilson, Aug. 5, 1935; children—John, Margaret (Mrs. Jeffry L. Putnam), Michael, Rosaliad. Geologist, Gulf Oil Corp., Mattoon, Ill., 1938-44, Bay Petroleum Corp., Midland, Tex., 1944-47; dist. geologist So. Minerals Corp., Midland, 1947-51; chief geologist Guy Mabee Drilling Co., Midland, 1951-65; chief geologist Mabee Petroleum Corp., Midland, 1965—. Mem. Am. Assn. Petroleum Geologists, Sigma Xi. Home: 2 Chatham Ct Midland TX 79701 Office: 110A Mid America Bldg Midland TX 79701

SCOGGIN, JAMES FRANKLIN, JR., educator; b. Laurel, Miss., Aug. 3, 1921; s. James Franklin and Berenice (Phares) S.; B.S., Miss. State U., 1941; B.S., U.S. Mil. Acad., 1944; M.S., Johns Hopkins, 1951; Ph.D., U. Va., 1957; m. Madeline Eve Lannelle, Mar. 1, 1948; children—Tracy, Beryl, James Franklin III. Commd. 2d lt., U.S. Army, 1944, advanced through grades to col., 1966; ret., 1968; asso. prof. The Citadel, 1968—; cons. U.S. Army Electronics Command, Ft. Monmouth, N.J., 1969—. Recipient Outstanding Teaching award The Citadel, 1971. Mem. Am. Phys. Soc., Am. Meteorol. Soc., I.E.E.E. (chmn. Coastal S.C. sect. 1972), Am. Nuclear Soc., Sigma Xi. Presbyn.

SCOGGINS, JAMES HARVEY, architect; b. Stephens, Ark., Nov. 24, 1929; s. Wisdom Young and Viva Elizabeth (Carpenter) S.; student U. Wichita, 1951-52, (scholar) Instituto Techniloco de Estudiantes Superiores, Monterrey, Mexico, 1953-54; B.Arch., U. Tex., 1957; m. Patricia Ann Elliott, Dec. 20, 1958; children—Mark, Michael. With various architects, West Tex., 1957-60; with firm Douglas R. Grogan, Irving, Tex., 1962-64; partner Grogan Scoggins Assos., Irving, 1964—. Chmn., Irving Fire Zone Com., Irving Joint Planning Group; mem. Irving Traffic Safety Com.; publicity chmn. So. Baptist Conv.; mem. Save Open Space Com., Dallas. Co-chmn. Irving John Tower for Senate campaign, 1968. Trustee, Dallas County Jr. Coll., 1972—. Recipient various awards for archtl. works; named Irving Outstanding Young Man of Year, Irving Jaycees, 1966. Registered architect, Tex. Mem. A.I.A., Tex. Soc. Architects, Soc. Irving Architects (chmn.), Registry Interpreters for Deaf, Tex. Soc. Interpreters for Deaf (pres. 1972), Tex. Baptist Conf. for Deaf, Tex. (citation 1969), Parent-Profl. assns. for deaf, Nat. Sch. Bd. Assn. (Tex. chmn. council community coll. bds.), Assn. Tex. Jr. Coll. Bd. Mems. and Adminstrs. (v.p., pres.). Baptist. Kiwanian (Kiwanian of Year award 1967, Irving Layman of Year award 1970). Prin. works include: Bradenburg Elementary Sch., 1969, Sam Houston Middle Sch., 1974, Irving Civic Center, 1974, Nimitz High Sch., 1972 (all Irving). Home: 1140 S Gloucester St Irving TX 75062 Office: 1711 W Irving Blvd Suite 313 Irving TX 75061

SCOGGINS, ROBERT DERWAYNE, lawyer; b. Little Rock, June 22, 1941; s. Harry DerWayne and Dorothy (Bell) S.; B.B.A., in Accounting and Finance, So. Methodist U., 1962, LL.B., 1966; m. Barbara Macy Frush, June 28, 1961; children—Richard DerWayne, Jocelyn Macy. Admitted to Tex. bar, 1966; staff accountant Boyd, Young, Gano & Stallings, Dallas, 1962-63; mem. corporate legal and financial staff Sammons Enterprises, Inc., Dallas, 1963-67; v.p. Steak & Ale Restaurants of Am., Inc., Dallas, 1967-69; partner Scoggins, Wootton, & Murphree, Dallas, 1969-73; partner Scoggins & Chitty, Dallas, 1974—. Instr. Tex. Christian U., Ft. Worth, 1969-70. C.P.A., Tex. Mem. Am. Bar Assn., State Bar of Tex., Am., Tex. Insts. C.P.A.s. Home: 4508 Belclaire Av Dallas TX 75205 Office: 909 One Main Pl Dallas TX 75250

SCOTT, ALAN, educator; b. Marietta, O., Nov. 21, 1912; s. Isadore and Rebecca Glasser (Shiffman) S.; B.J., U. Mo., 1934, A.B., 1934, M.A. in Journalism, 1938; Ed.D., U. Tex., 1955; m. Sylvia Ruth Shuman, Mar. 27, 1940; children—Anthony Roger, Lizbeth Ann (Mrs. Scott Schleif). With A.P., 1933-35, OWI, San Francisco and N.Y.C., 1942-45; faculty U. Cal. at Berkeley, 1941-42, Mich. State U., 1945-49; faculty U. Tex., 1949—, prof. journalism, 1964—. Exec. dir. Tex. Pub. Relations Assn., 1954-69; Tex. rep. Dudley-Anderson-Yutzy, 1955—. Pub. relations counsel Mayor's Council on Child Devel., 1969—, City of Austin Aqua Festival, 1965—; coordinator pub. relations 10th Internat. Cancer Congress, Houston, 1970. Bd. dirs. Tex. div. Am. Cancer Soc. Pub. Relations Soc. Am. fellow, 1965. Mem. Pub. Relations Soc. Am. (accredited), Tex. Pub. Relations Assn. (pres. 1974—), Assn. for Edn. in Journalism, Kappa Alpha, Sigma Delta Chi, Alpha Delta Sigma, Phi Delta Kappa. Author: Contemporary Public Relations, 1955. Editor Travis County Med. Soc. Jour., 1970—. Home: 7920 Rockwood Lane Austin TX 78758

SCOTT, ANDREW MACKAY, educator; b. Pasadena, Cal., Nov. 27, 1922; s. Andrew MacKay and Ruth (Jarvis) S.; A.B., Dartmouth Coll., 1946; M.A., Harvard, 1949, M.P.A., 1949, Ph.D., 1950; m. Anne Byrd Firor, June 2, 1947; children—Rebecca Jarvis, David MacKay, Donald MacKay. Intelligence officer CIA, Washington, 1949-51; fgn. affairs officer Mutual Security Agy., 1951-54; asst. prof. Dartmouth Coll., Hanover, N.H., 1953-54; asst. prof. internat. politics and Am. fgn. policy Haverford (Pa.) Coll., 1954-58; asso. prof. U. N.C., Chapel Hill, 1958-65, prof., 1965—. Served with USNR, 1943-45. Fulbright fellow Bologna, Italy, 1960-61. Mem. Am. Polit. Sci. Assn. Author: The Anatomy of Communism, 1951; Political Though in America, 1959; (with Earle Wallace) Politics: USA, 4th edit., 1974; (with Raymond Dawson) Readings in the Making of American Foreign Policy, 1965; The Revolution in Statecraft: Informal Penetration, 1965; (with William A. Lucas and Trudi M. Lucas) Simulation and National Development, 1966; (with Margaret Hunt) Congress and Lobbies: Image and Reality, 1966; The Functioning of the International Political System, 1967; Competition in American Politics: An Economic Model, 1970; (with others) Insurgency, 1970. Home: 1028 Highland Woods St Chapel Hill NC 27514

SCOTT, AUGUSTUS BARNETT, surgeon; b. Humboldt, Tenn., Apr. 18, 1934; s. Daniel Joyner and Ruth (Barnett) S.; student Memphis State Coll., 1952-55; M.D., U. Tenn., 1959; m. May Gillespie Tucker, Feb. 14, 1953; children—Sally, David, Carol. Intern U.S. Naval Hosp., Oakland, Cal., 1959-60, resident in surgery, 1962-66; practice surgery Jackson, Tenn., 1970—; mem. staff Jackson-Madison County Gen. Hosp., St. Mary's Hosp., Humboldt, Tenn. Served with USNR, 1959-70. Diplomate Am. Bd. Surgery. Fellow A.C.S.; mem. Tenn. Med. Assn. (v.p. 1972-73). Home: 355 Edenwood St Jackson TN 38301 Office: 686 W Forest St Jackson TN 38301

SCOTT, AUSTIN GROVE, assn. exec.; b. Huffman, Tex., Sept. 5, 1918; s. Austin Russell and Susan Laura (Grove) S.; B.S., Tex. A. and M. Coll., 1940; m. Doris Cornelia Bradburn, Feb. 14, 1946; 1 dau., Suzanne. Probation officer Harris County Probation Dept., Houston, 1941-44, supr. Foster Homes Placement, 1943-44; exec. dir. Dallas Big Bros., Inc., 1944-52; exec. dir. Dallas County Assn. for the Blind, 1952—, sec. trust com., 1966—. Cons. Nat. Industries for the Blind, also bd. dirs.; mem. exec. com. Gen. Council of Workshops for the Blind, sec., 1960-61, v.p., 1967-68, pres., 1968-70. Edn. officer Coast Guard Aux., Dallas, 1973. Bd. dirs. Big Bros. of Dallas, 1962-66. Mem. Am. Assn. Workers for the Blind (plaque 1972), Nat., Tex. rehab. assns., Jr. C. of C. (v.p. 1947-49), Sales and Marketing Execs. Club. Lion. Methodist (chmn. bd. missions 1958-59). Home: 3515 Lakeside Dr Rockwall TX 75087 Office: 3940 Capitol Dallas TX 75204 also PO Box 64420 Dallas TX 75206

SCOTT, CARL MCDONALD, JR., state govt. ofcl.; b. Folkston, Ga., Apr. 20, 1922; s. Carl McDonald and Margaret (Robinson) S.; B.A., Emory U., 1950; postgrad. U. Ga., 1950-51; m. Carolyn Lloyd Schoen, June 28, 1952; children—Carl M., Carol Lynn. Communicable diseases investigator Ga. Dept. Pub. Health, Waycross, 1951-56; asst. dir. Ga. Dept. Entomology, Atlanta, 1956-58; asst. dir. div. entomology Ga. Dept. Agr., 1958-63, dir., 1963—. Chmn. Ga. Structural Pest Control Commn., 1965-67, vice chmn., 1967-73; chmn. Imported Fire Ant Research Workers, 1963; vice chmn. So. Plant Bd., 1970-72, chmn., 1972—. Mem. Leafmore-Creek Park Civic Club, 1957—. Served with USNR, 1942-46. Mem. Ga., Southeastern, Am. entomol. socs., Ga. Beekeepers Assn., Greater Atlanta Structural Pest Control Assn., Ga. Pest Control Assn., Ga. Nurserymen's Assn., Am. Camellia Soc. Club: Leafmore-Creek Park Social (Decatur). Home: 1400 Knollwood Terrace Decatur GA 30033 Office: Capitol Sq Atlanta GA 30334

SCOTT, CHARLES SEALE, physician; b. Middlesboro, Ky., Apr. 26, 1923; s. Charles Sidney and Katherine (Seale) S.; student Lincoln Meml. U., 1941-42, Carson Newman Coll., 1942-43; M.D., U. Ark., 1947; m. Anita G. McWhorter, July 15, 1947; children—Charles Douglas, Carolyn McScott (Mrs. Dale E. Allen). Intern Montefiore Hosp., Pitts., 1947-48; resident John Gaston Hosp., Memphis, 1955-58; practiced medicine in Middlesboro, 1948-52; practice medicine specializing in obstetrics and gynecology, Morristown, Tenn., 1958—; mem. staff Morristown-Hamblen Hosp., v.p., 1966-67, pres., 1967-68, chief obstetrics, 1968-73; mem. staff Doctors Hosp., Jefferson Meml. Hosp. Dir. Citizen Tribune, Morristown, 1967—, Mgmts. Systems, Inc., Knoxville, Tenn., 1966—; pres. Scott-Mueller Inc., Morristown, 1969—, also dir. Mem. exec. com. Hamblen County Cancer Soc., 1960—, bd. dirs., 1969—. Served with USNR, World War II, to capt. USAF, 1952-54. Diplomate Am. Bd. Obstetrics-Gynecology. Fellow Am. Coll. Obstetrics-Gynecology; mem. Tenn. (sec.-treas. 1973—), East Tenn. (pres. 1972-73) obstet.-gynecol. socs., Am. Fertility Soc., Am. Assn. Gynecol. Laproscopists, Ky., Ark., Tenn., Hamblen County (exec. com. 1972—) med. socs. Methodist. Club: Morristown Country. Home: 1219 W 5th N St Morristown TN 37814 Office: 705 McFarland St Morristown TN 37814

SCOTT, DAN DRYDEN, educator; b. Petersburg, Tenn., Apr. 1, 1928; s. Charles Clayton and Mary Lucille (Evans) S.; B.S., Middle Tenn. State U., 1950; student U. South, 1946-49; M.A., George Peabody Coll., 1954, Ph.D., 1963; postgrad. (So. Regional fellow) Harvard, summer 1955; m. Faye Jean Marks, May 26, 1955; children—Margaret Scott, Patrica. Tchr. physics and chemistry Central High Sch., Fayetteville, Tenn., 1952-55; mem. faculty Middle Tenn. State U., Murfreesboro, 1955—, asso. prof. chemistry, 1961-64, prof., 1964—. Guest faculty Peabody Coll., summer 1959; cons. chemist Samsonite Corp., Murfreesboro, Tenn., 1964-69. Served with AUS, 1950-52. Fellow Am. Inst. Chemists; mem. Am. Chem. Soc., A.A.A.S., Southeastern Assn. Advors for Health Professions. Methodist. Author: (with others) Laboratory Manual for Physical Science, 1960, 65. Home: 1806 Diana St Murfreesboro TN 37130 Office: Dept Chemistry Middle Tenn State Univ Murfreesboro TN 37130

SCOTT, DONALD LEE, clergyman; b. Pulaski, Va., Aug. 7, 1929; s. John Preston and Hallie Jewell (Swain) S.; B.A., Lynchburg Coll., 1951; B.D., Lexington Theol. Sem., 1959; M.A., Hartford Sem. Found., 1963; m. Clementeyne Hardy, Aug. 27, 1955; children—Lucinda Lee, Margaret Cardell. Ordained to ministry Christian Ch., 1951; dir. children's work Christian Ch. for Ky., Lexington, 1953-57; minister Christian edn. Woodland Christian Ch., Lexington, 1957-62, Gordon St. Christian Ch., Kinston, N.C., 1963-67; asso. minister First Christian Ch., Richmond, Ky., 1967—. Sec., Ky. Commn. United Ministries in Higher Edn., 1971-72; 2d v.p. Christian Ch. Ky. Bd. dirs. Richmond Opportunity for Wider Tutorial Help, Open Concern, Community Center. Youth chmn. Lexington-Fayette County council on Family Relations. Mem. Madison County Assn. for Retarded Children (dir.), Pi Tau Chi. Kiwanian. Home: Route 7 Deacon Hills Richmond KY 40475 Office: First Christian Ch Main at Lancaster Richmond KY 40475

SCOTT, ELLIS LAVERNE, educator; b. Casey, Ia., June 11, 1915; s. Alexander Catell and Cora (Tilman) S.; B.S. in Edn. summa cum laude, Ohio State U., 1947, Ph.D. in Sociology, 1953; m. Florence Louise Green, Sept. 7, 1950; children—Susan Eileen, Katherine Ellen, Robert Tilman. Teaching asst., research asso. Ohio State U., 1946-53; asst. prof. U. N.M., 1953-56; asso. social scientist Rand Corp., 1957; human factors scientist System Devel. Corp., 1957-64; prof. mgmt. U. Ga., Athens, 1964—. Pres., Center for Study of Automation and Soc., 1969-73; chmn. com. on social implications of automation Internat. Fedn. of Automatic Control, 1972; chmn. automation com. Am. Automatic Control Council, 1970-71, vice chmn., 1972—; mem. Ga. Gov.'s Sci. Adv. Council, 1972—; mem. sci. and mgmt. adv. com. U.S. Army Computer Systems Command, 1972—; participant numerous sci. cons. Pres. Beechwood Hills Community Assn., 1971-72. Served with AUS, 1942-46. Mem. Am. Sociol. Assn. (chmn. sect. applied sociology), Am. Acad. Mgmt., So. Mgmt. Assn., World Future Soc., Phi Kappa Phi, Sigma Iota Epsilon, Alpha Kappa Delta. Co-editor: Automation and Society, 1969; EDP Systems for Public Management, 1968. Contbr. numerous articles to profl. jours. Home: 124 Colonial Dr Athens GA 30601

SCOTT, (FLORRIE) CAROLYNNE BLACKWELL (MRS. KARL LEGRANT SCOTT), editor; b. Birmingham, Ala., Feb. 10, 1937; d. Walter Craig and Florrie (Webb) Blackwell; A.B., Samford U., 1958; m. Karl Legrant Scott, Apr. 18, 1964. Asso. editor Shades Valley Sun, 1958; tchr. Hewitt-Trussville High Sch., 1959-60; reporter women's dept. Birmingham News, 1960-64; fashion editor Birmingham Post-Herald, 1964; asst. editor So. Veterinarian, Birmingham, Ala., 1964, mng. editor, 1965—; editor Blue Cross Wise, Blue Cross-Blue Shield Ala., 1969-70. Publicity dir. Ala. Sesquicentennial, 1969, Birmingham Centennial, 1971-72. Recipient 1st prize in fiction Scope Lit. Competition, Birmingham Festival Arts, 1967; 2d prize Hackney Lit. Competition, Birmingham, 1969, 71; 1st prize Ala. Regional Photog. Competition, 1969. Mem. Birmingham Assn. Indsl. Editors, Ala. Conservancy, Ala. Hist. Assn., Nat. Trust Historic Preservation, St. Clair Hist. Soc. (pres. 1972-74), Zeta Tau Alpha. Episcopalian (v.p. women of ch. 1965-66). Contbg. author: Alabama Prize Stories, 1970. Editorial staff Overture, Birmingham Symphony Orch. mag., 1966. Address: Route 1 Box 241 Springville AL 35146

SCOTT, FRANKLIN ROBERT, physicist, educator; b. Portland, Ore., Aug. 23, 1922; s. Lindyn Douglas and Mabel Gay (Smith) S.; A.B., Reed Coll., 1947; M.S., Ind. U., 1949, Ph.D., 1952; m. Christine Louise Golter, Aug. 10, 1950; children—Barbara Louise, Deborah Joanne, Kenneth Robert. Staff mem. Los Alamos (N.M.) Sci. Lab., 1951-57; research staff, asst. project mgr. Gen. Atomic, San Diego, 1957-67; prof. physics and astronomy U. Tenn., Knoxville, 1967—; on leave to controlled thermonuclear div. AEC, Germantown, Md. Cons., Oak Ridge Nat. Lab., 1967-73; lectr. thermodynamics U. N.M., Los Alamos, 1955-56. Served with AUS, 1943-46. Fellow Am. Phys. Soc.; mem. A.A.A.S., Am. Assn. U. Profs., Sigma Xi. Contbg. editor Internat. Dictionary of Physics and Electronics, 1959. Contbr. articles on physics to profl. jours. Patentee in field. Home: 10530 Cambridge Ct Gaithersburg MD 20760 Office: Controlled Thermonuclear Division AEC Washington DC 20545

SCOTT, GEORGE ARMISTEAD, JR., banker; b. Fredericksburg, Va., Feb. 1, 1915; s. George A. and Nellie (Boatwright) S.; student Hampden-Sydney Coll., 1932-33; certificate Am. Inst. Banking, 1950; m. Lucy Mae Copley, Nov. 4, 1938; 1 dau., Nancy Lee. With Nat. Bank Fredericksburg (Va.), 1933—, v.p., 1952-69, sr. v.p., 1970—, dir., 1945—. Served with N.G. Mem. Va. Bankers Assn. (past mem. com. fed. legislation), Kenmore Assn. (treas. 1956-58, trustee). Kiwanian. Home: 1222 Brent St Fredericksburg VA 22401 Office: 900 Princess Anne St Fredericksburg VA 22401

SCOTT, GEORGE GALLMANN, trucking co. exec.; b. Hattiesburg, Miss., July 8, 1928; s. John Havers and Rebecca Evelyn (Gallmann) S.; B.S., Millsaps Coll., 1949; m. Patsy T. Womack, June 27, 1953; 1 son, George Gallmann. Clk., Spanish Trail Transport, Mobile, Ala., 1949-50, asst. auditor, 1953-55; bookkeeper Met. Engraving & Electrotype Co., Richmond, Va., 1952-53; chief clk Central Truck Lines of Tampa, Fla., Mobile, 1955-56; gen. auditor M.R.&R. Trucking Co., Crestview, Fla., 1956-66, sec.-treas., 1967—. Mem. data processing adv. com. Okaloosa-Walton Jr. Coll., Niceville, Fla., 1965-66, 72-73; mem. Okaloosa County Gen. Adv. Com. for Devel. Vocational Edn., 1973. Served with AUS, 1950-52. Mem. Am. Trucking Assn. (nat. accounting and finance council 1956—), Greater Crestview C. of C. (chmn. bus. ethics com. 1973—), Pi Kappa Alpha. Methodist (choir dir. 1966—, chmn. ofcl. bd. 1971-73). Kiwanian. Home: 244 Seminole Av Crestview FL 32536

SCOTT, JAMES ELWIN, cement mfg. co. exec.; b. Neillsville, Wis., Mar. 2, 1927; s. Jess Walter and Dorothy Helen (Huckstead) S.; B.S. with honors in Civil Engring., U. Wis., 1948, B.Naval Sci., 1948; m. Grace Enid Hoag, Dec. 28, 1950; children—Judith Ann, Linda Jean. Instr. mechanics dept. U. Wis., Madison, 1949; dist. engr. Portland Cement Assn., Chgo., 1950-67; v.p. A. & H. Corp., Chgo., 1968; marketing services mgr. Gen. Portland Inc., Dallas, 1969-71, gen. sales mgr., 1972-74; gen. mgr. N.Tex. operations, v.p. Trinity Concrete Products Co., 1974—. Mem. Citizens Traffic Safety Adv. Bd. Chgo., chmn., 1965. Served to ensign USNR, 1948. Registered profl. engr. Ill., Tex. Mem. Nat., Ill. (pres. Dukane chpt. 1958) socs. profl. engrs., Sales and Marketing Execs., Phi Eta Sigma, Tau Beta Pi. Lutheran (councilman 1967). Clubs: Las Colinas Country, Tanglewood Hills Country, Chaparral. Home: Dallas TX Office: 1545 W Mockingbird Lane Dallas TX 75247

SCOTT, JAMES RANDOLPH, grocery chain exec.; b. Marion, Va., Aug. 17, 1912; s. Samuel Dickey and Emma Elma (Groseclose) S.; grad. Nat. Bus. Coll., Roanoke, Va., 1935; m. Blanche Martha Cook, Sept. 7, 1940; children—James Randolph, John Cameron. Clk., J.D. Bassett Mfg. Co., Bassett, Va., 1936; asst. payroll clk. U.S. Coal & Coke Co., Gary, W.Va., 1936-37; clk. Appalachian Electric Power Co., Welch, W.Va., 1938-41; mgr. Quality Distbg. Co., Norton, Va., 1941-50; gen. ins. agt. Wise Ins. Agy., Inc., Norton, 1950-51; pres., bookkeeper Jackson Coal Co., Inc., Blackwood, Va., 1954-57; sec.-treas. Kennedy's Piggly Wiggly Stores, Inc., Norton, 1957—, also dir. Charter mem. bd. visitors King Coll., Bristol, Tenn., now sec. Served with USAAF, 1944-45. Mem. Am. Legion (comdr. post 1948-49, 58-59). Presbyn. (ruling elder, supt. sch.). Kiwanian (sec. club 1950). Home: 1018 Spruce St Norton VA 24273 Office: 520 Kentucky Av Norton VA 24273

SCOTT, JERRY, judge; b. Nashville, Nov. 11, 1941; B.S., Austin Peay State U., 1962; J.D., Vanderbilt U., 1965; m. Ann Katherine Scott. Admitted to Tenn. bar, 1965, practiced in Waynesboro, 1968-73; mem. firm Keaton, Haggard, Turner and Scott, 1968-73; judge 11th Jud. Circuit, Waynesboro, 1973—. Instr. Columbia (Tenn.) State Community Coll., 1970—, trustee Found., 1971—. Wayne County campaign mgr. for U.S. Senator. Served to capt., Judge Adv. Gen. Dept., USAF, 1965-68. Mem. Am., Fed., Tenn., Decatur-Hickman-Lewis-Perry-Wayne Counties (v.p. 1969-70, sec. treas. 1970-72) bar assns., Assn. Lawyers of Am., Tenn. (v.p. 1972-73), Waynesboro (treas. 1969-70, pres. 1970-71, Distinguished Service award 1971-72) jaycees. Methodist. Moose, Lion (pres. 1971-72). Club: Green River Country. Home: PO Box 431 Waynesboro TN 38485 Office: PO Box 431 Waynesboro TN 38485

SCOTT, JULIUS MAJOR, elec. engr.; b. Sininale, Okla., Apr. 17, 1929; s. Major Theodore and Iola Adeline (Huffman) S.; B.S. in E.E., Hofstra U., 1969; postgrad. U. Houston, 1974—; m. Isabel Henderson Cline, June 7, 1953; children—John, Kenneth, Nancy, Patricia. Engr., Sperry Rand Corp. Great Neck, N.Y., 1952-69; electronic research and devel. engr. Philco-Ford Corp., Houston, 1969—. Owner, Scott Distributorship, Houston, 1956-57. Pres., Woodbury Gardens Civic Assn., Hicksville, N.Y., 1957. Served with AUS, 1946-51. Mem. I.E.E.E. (sec., 1967). Home: 727 Redway Lane Houston TX 77058 Office: 1002 Gemini Av Houston TX 77058

SCOTT, LAWRENCE VERNON, educator; b. Anthony, Kan., Jan. 28, 1917; s. Lawrence Garfield and Mable Grace (Madden) S.; B.A., Phillips U., 1940; M.S., U. Okla., 1947; Sc.D., Johns Hopkins, 1950; m. Elizabeth Buchanan Rowe, Jan. 28, 1945; children—James Robert, Jean Elizabeth, Lawrence Rowe. Asst. prof. bacteriology U. Okla. Coll. Medicine, Oklahoma City, 1950-53, asso. prof., 1953-58, prof. microbiology and immunology, 1958—, chmn. dept., 1961—, prof., chmn. microbiology and immunology Coll. Dentistry, 1972—; cons. St. Anthony Hosp., Oklahoma City, 1957—, VA Hosp., Oklahoma City, 1953—. Served to lt. USNR, 1942-46. Fellow Am. Acad. Microbiology; mem. A.A.A.S., Am. Soc. Microbiology (pres. Missouri Valley br.), S.W. Soc. Exptl. Biology and Medicine, S.W.

Cancer Research Soc., N.Y., Okla. (pres.) acads. scis. Research in viral diseases of man. Home: 4125 NW 61st Terrace Oklahoma City OK 73112

SCOTT, LEONARD WAYNE, lawyer, educator; b. San Marcos, Tex., Nov. 12, 1938; s. Leonard Walter and Bonnie (Hinkle) S.; B.A., S.W. Tex. State Coll., 1961; J.D., U. Tex., 1962; M.A., Baylor U., 1971; postgrad. N.Y. U., summers 1972-73; m. Patricia Louise Pond, Aug. 27, 1960; children—Kelly Lynn, Leonard Wade, Bradford Glenn. Admitted to Tex. bar, 1962; briefing atty. Ct. Criminal Appeals Tex., Austin, 1962-63, Supreme Ct. Tex., 1963-64; asso. mem. firm Sheehy, Cureton, Westbrook, Lovelace & Nielsen, Waco, Tex., 1964-69, partner, 1969-71; lectr. Sch. Law, Baylor U., Waco, 1968-71; asso. prof. law St. Mary's U., San Antonio, 1971—; alternate U.S. commr. Waco div. U.S. Dist. Ct. for Western Tex., 1967-71. Bd. dirs. Campfire Girls, Waco. Mem. Waco-McLennan County (dir., v.p.), Tex. (mem. 11th dist. grievance com. 1969-71, mem. local bar services com.), Am. (mem. ins. and specialization com.), Fed. bar assns., Am. Judicature Soc., Tex. Criminal Def. Attys. Assn. (charter mem.), Am. Assn. Criminal Def. Attys., Co-editor: Tex. Lawyers' Weekly Letter, 1971—. Home: 1016 Mt Rainier St San Antonio TX 78213

SCOTT, NED VAUGHAN, JR., chem. co. exec.; b. Houston, Sept. 28, 1929; s. Ned V. and Sue (Haley) S.; B.S. in Petroleum Engring., U. Tex., 1952; m. Carol Norwood, Sept. 6, 1969. Engr., Standard Oil Co., Houston, 1955-57, Houston Natural Gas Co., 1958-60; pres. Filter Media Co., Houston, 1960—, also dir. Served with USNR, 1952-55. Registered profl. engr., Tex. Mem. Vermiculite Assn. (dir.), Perlite Inst. (dir.), Filtration Soc., Kappa Sigma. Presbyn. Club: Houston Racquet. Home: 12522 Overcup Dr Houston TX 77024 Office: 1616 W Loop S Houston TX 77027

SCOTT, NORMA LINN (MRS. JOHN MITCHELL SCOTT), ret. educator, club woman; b. Wharton, Tex., Oct. 13, 1894; d. John Edward and Elizabeth Frances (Bolton) Linn; student Hollins Coll., 1913-14; B.S. in Edn., U. Tex., 1943, M.A., 1949; m. John Mitchell Scott, July 22, 1914; children—John Linn, Norma Elizabeth (Mrs. John R. Johnson), Lawrence Evans, Virginia Randolph (Mrs. N.B. Dismukes), Patricia Ruth (Mrs. Louis Meade Burton). Tchr. history, govt. and English in high schs. of Tex., 1918-65; with McCallum High Sch. Austin, until 1965, now ret.; asst. dept. govt. U. Tex., 1946-49; prin. Mullin (Tex.) High Sch., 1925-33, Buffalo (Tex.) High Sch., 1945-47; Leon County chmn. Jr. Red Cross, 1943-47; chmn. Buffalo (Tex.) chpt. A.R.C., 1945-46; v.p. YWCA, Austin, 1968-70, pres., 1970-72; active Infantile Paralysis, War Bond, United Fund, Community Chest drives; mem. Travis County and Austin Community Council; mem. Bicentennial Com. Historic Preservation and Hist. Publs. Recipient Kellog Found. scholarship U. Tex., 1944. Mem. Am. Assn. U. Women (br. parliamentarian 1960—; pres. Austin 1962-64). Austin Classroom Tchrs. Assn. (pres. 1958-60), Heritage Soc. Austin, Tex. Geneal. Soc., U.D.C. (state pres. 1968-70, 70-72, chmn. Norma Linn Scott scholarship 1961-75), Tex. Tchrs. Assn. (pres. English sect. dist. X 1956—, mem. ho. dels. 1956—), Austin Ret. Tchrs. Assn. Delta Kappa Gamma (pres. local chpt.), Alpha Epsilon, Gamma Psi. Baptist. Club: Austin Women's (exec. council). Home: 3001 Beverly Rd Austin TX 78703

SCOTT, RALPH ASA, JR., govt. ofcl.; b. Sterling, Ill., July 23, 1930; s. Ralph Asa and Hazel Irene (Llewellyn) S.; B.S., U. Ill., 1952; M.S. (NSF fellow, AEC fellow), U. Okla., 1954; Ph.D. (NSF fellow, AEC fellow, Tex. Acad. Sci. fellow), Tex. A. and M., 1957; m. Kathryn Louise Hartman, Nov. 27, 1959; children—Susan Irene, Craig Philip. Radiochemist, Okla. Research Inst., 1952-53; research plant breeder W. Atlee Burpee Seed Co., Cal., 1954-55; prin. research chemist and dir. waste eval. program Internat. Minerals & Chem. Corp., Fla., 1957-58; research plant physiologist Olin Mathieson Chem. Corp., N.Y., 1958; plant physiologist cotton research center, Crops Res. Div. Agr. Research Service, U.S. Dept. Agr., Phoenix, 1958-61, sr. research plant physiologist Boll Weevil Research Lab., State Coll., Miss., 1961-62; chief chemist U.S. Dept. Defense, U.S. Air Force, N.M., 1962-64; sr. chemist Adv. Test Tech., Joint Chiefs Staff, Desert Test Center, Ft. Douglas, Utah, 1965-66, chief div. chem. Dept. Pub. Health, Washington, 1966-67; dir. aquatic plant control program, Office Chief of Engrs., U.S. Army, Dept. of Def., Washington, 1967-69; chief chem. scientist Office Sec. Def., Dept. of Def. Explosives Safety Bd., Washington, 1969—; cons., 1958—; spl. cons. to Sec. of State, 1969—. Recipient numerous awards. Fellow Am. Inst. Chemists; mem. Am. Chem. Soc., Sigma Xi, Lambda Tau, Phi Sigma. Home: 2819 Elsmore St Fairfax VA 22030 Office: Office Sec Def Explosives Safety Bd Dept Def Washington DC 20314

SCOTT, RANDY JAY, broadcasting co. exec.; b. Dayton, O., Dec. 15, 1941; s. Henry J. and Emily R. (Miller) Herbst; student U. Dayton, 1961, Va. Commonwealth U., 1971-72; m. Alice Lambert, Aug. 12, 1967. Announcer sta. WING, Dayton, 1959-61; asst. program dir. sta. WKEE, Huntington, W.Va., 1961-63, radio sta. WCAW, Charleston, W.Va., 1963-67; program dir. sta. WLEE, Richmond, Va., 1967—, also pub. service dir., 1970—; sports dir. WXEX-TV, Richmond, 1974—. Named TV Movie Screen Personality of Month Sterling mags., 1971. Recipient citation Am. Cancer Soc., 1970. Mason. Home: 730 Pinetta Dr Richmond VA 23235 Office: PO Box 8477 Richmond VA 23229

SCOTT, RICHARD PHILIPPE, librarian; b. Tokyo, Japan, Apr. 6, 1932; s. Ralph Walker and Rose (Ferraris) S.; A.A., Md. State Coll., 1954; B.A. in History, U. Md., 1956; M.S. in L.S., Cath. U. Am., 1958. Asst. librarian Nat. War Coll., Ft. McNair, Washington, 1958-59; asst. libriarian NSF, Washington, 1959-62, cataloging librarian, 1962—. Recipient certificate of commendation NSF, 1964. Mem. A.L.A., Spl. Libraries Assn., Potomac Tech. Processing Librarians (D.C. del. 1972-74, nominating com. 1972-73), Am. Soc. for Information Sci., A.A.A.S., Nat. Hist. Soc. (charter), Nat. Philatelic Soc., NSF Employees' Assn. (v.p. for coop. activities 1970-71), Soc. Philatelic Ams., World of Wine Soc. Home: 860 S Greenbrier St Arlington VA 22204 Office: 1800 G St NW Washington DC 20550

SCOTT, ROBERT CLAUDE, JR., edn. center adminstr.; b. Anderson, S.C., Feb. 16, 1923; s. Robert Claude and Lucy Freeman (Toney) S.; B.A., Furman U., 1949; M.A., George Peabody Coll., 1962; m. Louise Helen Tinsley, Oct. 5, 1946; children—Ronald Charles, Susan Lee. Tchr., coach Anderson County Sch. Dist 4, Pendleton, S.C., 1949-59; adminstrv. asst. Lauren County Sch. Dist., Laurens, S.C., 1959-66; asso. dir. Florence-Darlington Tech. Edn. Center, Florence, S.C., 1966-67, dir. PeeDee Edn., 1967—. Ind. cons. in edn., 1965—. Served with AUS, 1943-46. Decorated Purple Heart, Bronze Star with oak leaf cluster. Mem. Am. Assn. for Sch. Adminstrs., Assn. Suprs. and Curriculum Devel., Nat. Soc. for Study Edn., S.C. Personnel and Guidance Assn., Phi Delta Kappa, Kappa Alpha. Kiwanian. Home: 1430 Fairfax Rd Tarleton W Florence SC 29501 Office: PO Box 829 142-B S Dargan St Florence SC 29501

SCOTT, RONALD FAIRBANKS, state planner; b. South Milwaukee, Wis., May 18, 1915; s. Ronald MacDonald and Viola (Zimmerman) S.; B.S. in Civil Engring., U. Mich., 1938; student Layton Sch. Art, Milw., 1936-37; m. Raiford Cooper, Sept. 10, 1945; children—Lauren Carol, Marian Lee, Beverly Cooper, Perry Alan. Planning engr. City of Superior (Wis.), 1938-42; regional dir. Tenn. Planning Com., Johnson City, 1945-49; dir. planning City of Greensboro (N.C.), 1949-66; regional planning cons. N.C., 1966-69; N.C. state planning officer, 1969-74, N.C. land policy specialist, 1974—; vis. lectr. city planning Inst. of Govt., U.N.C., Chapel Hill, 1955—. Registered profl. engr., Wis., N.C. Mem. Am. Inst. Planners (pres. S.E. chpt. 1963-64), Am. Soc. C.E., Am. Congress on Surveying and Mapping, Am. Soc. Planning Ofcls., N.C. Soc. Engrs., Tau Beta Pi. Unitarian-Universalist. Club: Torch (pres. Greensboro 1962-63). Home: 2108 Dunnhill Dr Raleigh NC 27608 Office: 116 W Jones St Raleigh NC 27603

SCOTT, RUSSELL CECIL, mgmt. cons.; b. Richmond, Va., Aug. 1, 1925; s. Frederic Robert and Elizabeth Barnett (Cecil) Scott; student Princeton, 1943, M.S., 1948; B.M.E., Cornell, 1945; m. Helen McLarin Blackwelder, Mar. 13, 1954; children—Russell Cecil, Helen MacLaren, William Norwood. Asso. engr. applied physics lab. Johns Hopkins U., Silver Spring, Md., 1947-49; with Texaco Experiment, Inc., Richmond, Va., 1949-71, project supr. Ramjets, 1965-71; partner Scott Assos., tech. and mgmt. cons., Richmond, Va., 1971—. Mem. Va. adv. com. on sci., engring. and other specialized manpower SSS, 1961-71, chmn., 1969-71; asso. mem. Va. Marine Resources Commn., 1972—. Trustee Westminster-Presbyn. Homes, Inc., Richmond, 1971—, v.p., 1972-73; trustee Richmond Area Arthritis Found., 1962-69. Served to lt. USNR, 1943-46, 52-54; now comdr. Res. (ret.). Asso. fellow Am. Inst. Aeronautics and Astronautics; mem. Am. Soc. M.E., Soc. Colonial Wars, S.R., U.S. Power Squadron, U.S. Coast Guard Aux., Tau Beta Pi. Presbyn. (elder). Clubs: University Cottage (Princeton U.); Rotunda, Country of Va. (Richmond); Windmill Point (Va.) Yacht; Va. Yacht (Gwynn Island).

SCOTT, VICTOR PINKSTON, steel co. exec., archtl. engr.; b. Sedalia, Mo., Sept. 30, 1932; s. Victor Estes and Virginia Bernice (Pinkston) S.; m. Dorothy Jean Cook, Aug. 21, 1954; children—Stephanie Ann, Victor Sheldon, Stuart Andrew. Design engr. Macomber, Inc., Canton, O., 1959-64, dir. research and devel., 1964-69; exec. v.p., gen. mgr. Owen Joist Corp., Cayce, S.C., 1969—; exec. v.p. Owen Joist of Fla., Starke. Served with arty. AUS, 1954-56. Mem. Am. Soc. Profl. Engrs., Am. Soc. for Testing Materials, Am. Soc. C.E., Am. Soc. for Metals, Exec. Club. Home: 100 Loch Dr Columbia SC 29210 Office: 100 Foster PO Box 3 Cayce SC 29033

SCOTT, WILLARD PHILIP, lawyer; b. Columbus, O., Jan. 8, 1909; s. Wirt Stanley and Mabel Lynne (Rond) S.; A.B. with honors, Ohio State U., 1930; LL.B (Deans Scholar), Columbia, 1933; m. Lucille Westrom, June 27, 1936; children—Robert W., David W., Anne L. Admitted to N.Y. bar, 1934, D.C. bar, 1934, Okla. bar, 1969; partner Oliver & Donnally, N.Y.C., 1938-66; dir. Am. Potash & Chem. Corp., 1951-70; v.p., 1955-68, vice chmn. bd. dirs., 1968—; v.p., gen. counsel Kerr-McGee Corp., 1968-73, v.p. finance, 1973, sr. v.p., 1973—; counsel for bondholders com. in various railroad reorganizations, 1936-54; gen. counsel Savs. Bank Assn. N.Y.; dir. 1st Nat. Bank & Trust Co. Oklahoma City. Mem. bd. of appeals, 1957-68, mayor, Scarsdale, 1955-57, trustee, 1951-55, police commr., 1953-55, acting mayor, 1953-55. Bd. dirs. Oklahoma City Symphony Soc., Okla. Arts and Sci. Found. Fellow Am. Bar Found., Southwestern Legal Found.; mem. Am. Judicature Soc., Internat. Am. (chmn. sect. corp. banking and bus. law 1960-61, chmn. com. corp. laws 1964-70, editor Bus. Lawyer, 1958-59); N.Y., Okla., D.C. bar assns., Am. Law Inst., Assn. Bar City N.Y., Phi Beta Kappa, Phi Kappa Sigma, Phi Delta Phi, Phi Alpha Theta, Pi Sigma Alpha. Republican. Presbyn. (elder). Clubs: Union League, Madison Square Garden (N.Y.C.); Metropolitan (Washington); Oklahoma City Golf and Country, Whitehall, Beacon (Oklahoma City); Scarsdale Golf. Author: various articles on corporate law. Home: 1812 Drury Lane Oklahoma City OK 73116 Office: Kerr-McGee Center Oklahoma City OK 73102

SCOTT, WILLIAM JAMES, elec. engr.; b. Birmingham, Ala., Dec. 29, 1943; s. Legrant Edward and Louise Sophie (Mauk) S.; student Samford U., 1961-62; B.S. in Elec. Engring., U. Ala., 1965, B.S. in Mech. Engring., 1968, postgrad., 1969—; m. Georgia Diane Wall, Aug. 25, 1967; children—William, Tara Diane. Supr. U.S. Steel Corp., Fairfield, Ala., 1965-68; sr. project engr. U.S. Pipe and Foundry Co., Birmingham, Ala., 1968-72; chief elec. engr. Pollution Control Walther, Inc., Birmingham, 1972—. Registered profl. engr., Ala. Mem. I.E.E.E., Delta Chi Alumni Assn. Methodist (chmn. adminstrv. bd. 1973, dir. 1972—). Home: 541 Iroquois Dr Birmingham AL 35214 Office: PO Box 7462A Birmingham AL 35223

SCOTT, WILLIAM LLOYD, senator; b. Williamsburg, Va., July 1, 1915; s. William David and Nora Bell (Ingram) S.; LL.B., George Washington U., 1938, LL.M., 1939; m. Ruth Inez Huffman, Feb. 5, 1940; children—Gail Ann (Mrs. Charles H. Eldred), William Lloyd, Paul Alvin. Admitted to Va. bar; trial atty. Dept. Justice, 1942-60; spl. asst. to solicitor, Dept. Interior, 1960-61; pvt. practice law, Fairfax, Va., 1961-66; mem. 90th to 92d Congresses 8th dist. Va.; mem. U.S. Senate from Va., 1972—. Mem. Va. Republican Central Com., 1964-68; del. Rep. Nat. Conv., 1968, 72. Served with AUS, World War II. Mem. Am., Va., Fairfax County bar assns., Am. Legion, 40 and 8, Sigma Nu Phi (past chancellor). Methodist. Lion, Mason (33 deg., Shriner). Home: 3930 W Ox Rd Fairfax County VA 22030 Office: Dirksen Senate Office Bldg Washington DC 20510

SCOTT, WILLIAM WARREN, physician; b. Little Rock, Mar. 7, 1924; s. Ottis Al and Ruth (Matthews) S.; N.D., U. Ark., 1946; m. Helene Jayne Barre, June 29, 1945; children—Karen, Warren Eric, Timothy. Intern U.S. Naval Hosp., Corpus Christi, Tex.; practice gen. medicine, Pocahantas, Ark.; chief staff Randolph County Meml. Hosp., Pocahantas. Dir. Pocahontas Fed. Savs. & Loan. Founding mem. Pocahontas Planning Commn., 1964—; chapter mem. Randolph United Fund. Mem. City Council Pocahontas, 1969—. Served with USNR, 1943-49. Mem. Ark. Med. Soc., N.E. Ark. Regional Med. Program (charter mem.), Randolph County Med. Soc., C. of C. (pres.). Rotarian, K.C. Club: Arkansas Cadeus (pres.) (Little Rock). Home: 1917 Randolph St Pocahontas AR 72455 Office: 213 W Broadway St Pocahontas AR 72455

SCOTT, WILLODENE ALEXANDER (MRS. RAY DONALD SCOTT), library adminstr.; b. Ethridge, Tenn., Sept. 4, 1922; d. Jesse Cary and Maud (Goff) Alexander; B.A., George Peabody Coll. for Tchrs., 1946, B.S. in Library Sci., 1947, M.A., 1949, postgrad, 1963—; m. Ray Donald Scott, Nov. 27, 1959; 1 dau., Pamela Dean. Librarian Sylvan Park Elementary Sch., Nashville, 1947-51, Waverly Belmont Jr. High Sch., Nashville, 1951-54, Howard High Sch., Nashville, 1954-62, Peabody Demonstration Sch., Nashville, 1962-63, McCann Elementary Sch., Nashville, 1963-66; supr. instructional materials, library div. Metro Nashville-Davidson County Schs., Nashville, 1966-73, dir. instrnl. material and library services, 1973—. Lectr. Peabody Coll. Library Sch., Nashville, summers, 1950-66, 71-72, U. Tenn., Nashville Center, 1970—. Mem. A.L.A., Southeastern (mem. scholarship com. 1968-70), Tenn. Library Assns. (membership chmn. 1955, 64). library assns., Tenn. (pres. library sect. 1954), Met. Nashville edn. assns., N.E.A., Woman's Nat. Book Assn. (charter mem.), D.A.R. (Buffalo River chpt. organizing treas. 1967-69). Baptist. Mem. Order Eastern Star. Club: Nashville Library (pres. 1952-53). Home: 525 Clematis Dr Nashville TN 37205

SCOVILLE, HERBERT, JR., govt. cons.; b. N.Y.C., Mar. 16, 1915; s. Herbert and Orlena (Zabriskie) S.; B.S., Yale, 1937; Ph.D., U. Rochester, 1942; postgrad. U. Cambridge (Eng.), 1937-39; m. Ann Curtiss, June 26, 1937; children—Anthony Church, Thomas Welch, Nicholas Zabriskie, Mary Curtiss. Sr. scientist Los Alamos contract AEC, Washington, 1946-48; tech. dir. armed forces spl. weapons project Dept. Def., Washington, 1948-55; dep. dir. sci. and tech. CIA, Washington, 1955-63; asst. dir. sci. and tech. US Arms Control and Disarmament Agy., Washington, 1963-69; dir. arms control program Carnegie Endowment for Internat. Peace, Washington, 1969-71; cons. arms control program Carnegie Endowment, 1971—, adv. com. nuclear safeguards AEC, 1970—, Arms Control and Disarmament Agy., 1969-73. Chmn. strategic weapons com. Fedn. Am. Scientists, 1970—, chmn. U.S. del., NATO Disarmament Experts Meetings, 1966-68; mem. sci. adv. bd. Air Force, 1955-62; Pres.'s Sci. adv. com. cons., 1957-63; chmn. SALT II Group, Council on Fgn. Relations, 1972-73. Bd. dirs. Pub. Welfare Found., Washington, 1971. Mem. A.A.A.S., Sigma Xi. Clubs: Century (N.Y.C.); Cosmos (Washington). Author: (with R. Osborn) Missile Madness, 1970. Contbr. articles to profl. jours. Address: 6400 Georgetown Pike McLean VA 22101

SCREVEN, J.O., lawyer, bus. exec.; b. Birmingham, Ala., Aug. 11, 1925; s. J.O. and Cecile (Allen) S.; B.S., U. Ala., 1947, LL.B., 1950; LL.M., N.Y. U., 1951; m. Gaynor Anderson, Sept. 15, 1948; children—J.O. III, E.F., J.S. Admitted to Ala. bar; practiced in Birmingham; asso. firm White, Bradley, Arant, All & Rose, 1951-56; gen. atty., sec. Vulcan Materials Co., 1957-68, sec., gen. atty., 1968-72, v.p. law, sec., 1972—. Trustee Birmingham U. Sch. Served with AUS, 1944-46. Mem. U. Ala. Alumni Assn. (past pres. Jefferson County), Phi Delta Theta. Club: Birmingham County. Home: 3568 Riverbend Rd Birmingham AL 35243 Office: PO Box 7497 Birmingham AL 35223

SCRIVNER, FRANK HERMAN, civil engr.; b. Fort Worth, Oct. 12, 1908; s. Arthur James and Helen (Saunders) S.; B.S., U.S. Naval Acad., 1931; m. Bonnie Conlee, Dec. 23, 1938 (dec. Feb. 1966); 1 dau., Suzanne; m. 2d, Beverly Goebel Fabian, Feb. 10, 1973; stepchildren—Barbara, Diane, Carolyn, Catherine. Research engr. Tex. Hwy. Dept., Austin, 1946-55, Nat. Acad. Scis., Ottawa, Ill., 1956-61, Tex. Transp. Inst., College Station, 1961—; project dir. S.J. Buchanan Assos., London, Eng., 1955-56. Served to lt. comdr. USNR, 1941-46. Mem. Nat. Acad. Scis. (chmn. rigid pavement design com. hwy. research bd. 1963-70), Am. Soc. C.E., Sigma Xi. Home: 1929 Wayside Dr Bryan TX 77801 Office: Tex Transp Inst Tex A and M U College Station TX 77843

SCRIVNER, JOE BILL, supt. schs.; b. Wister, Okla., Sept. 15, 1922; s. Fred and Judson (Cheek) S.; B.S., McMurry Coll., 1948; M.A., Hardin-Simmons U., 1953; postgrad. Sul Ross Coll., 1956; m. Eleanor Green, Aug. 15, 1944; children—Joe B., James Thomas. Prin., head athletic coach high sch., Mertzon, Tex., 1948-50; head coach, athletic coach, Rankin, Tex., 1950-54, jr. high sch. prin., 1954-55, became supt. schools, 1955; supt. schs., Goliad, Tex., until 1961, Dumas, Tex., 1961-69, Taylor, Tex., 1969—. Chmn. Rankin Youth Council, 1952-55; adv. council Southwestern Edn. Developmental Labs. Served from pvt. to sgt. USAF, 1941-45. Mem. N.E.A. (area chmn.), Tex. Coaching Assn. (v.p. 1954), Tex. Sch. Adminstrs. Assn. (exec. com.; chmn. dist. 6 1956), Am. Assn. Sch. Adminstrs., Tex. Tchrs. Assn. (dist. chmn. legistlative com.), Univ. Interscholastic League (dist. chmn.), Tex. P.T.A. Scholarship Soc. (chmn.), Panhandle Leaders Assn., (v.p.). Methodist. Rotarian (dir.), Lion (dir.). Home: 1705 Lexington St Taylor TX 76574

SCRUGGS, C. G., editor; b. McGregor, Tex., Nov. 4, 1923; s. John Fleming and Adeline (Hering) S.; B.S., Tex. A. and M. U., 1947; m. Miriam June Wigley, July 5, 1947; children—John Mark, Miriam Jan. Asso. editor Progressive Farmer, Dallas, 1947-61, editor, 1962—, v.p., 1964—, exec. editor, 1972, editorial dir., 1973—; pres. Torado Land & Cattle Co. Pres., Tex. Comml. Agr. Council, 1953-54; sec. 1960—. Mem. Govs. Com. for Agr., 1950; Tex. Animal Health Council, 1955-61; chmn. So. Brucellosis Com., 1956; pres. Tex. Rural Safety Com., 1957-59; mem. farm conf. Nat. Safety Council, 1958-70; chmn. Nat. Brucellosis Com., 1958-59, 71-72; del. World Food Congress, 1963; mem. coordinating bd. Tex. Coll. and U. System, 1965-69; bd. regents Tex. Tech. U., 1971—. Chmn. Joint Senate-House Interim Com. Natural Fibers Tex. Legislature, 1971. Pres., S.W. Animal Health Research Found., 1961-63, trustee, 1961—; bd. govs. Nat. Agrl. Hall of Fame. Served to lt. col. U.S. Army Res. ret. Recipient Southwestern Cattle Raisers award, 1962; Am. Seed Trade Assn. award, 1963; Am. Agrl. Editors Assn. award of honor, 1964; Reuben Brigham award Am. Assn. Agrl. Coll. Editors, 1965; Distinguished Service award Tex. Farm Bur., 1966; Journalistic Achievement award Nat. Plant Food Assn., 1967. Mem. Am. Agrl. Editors Assn. (pres. 1963), Tex. Agrl. Workers Assn., Tex. Assn. Future Farmers Am. (pres. 1940-41), Dallas Agrl. Club (pres. 1951), Nat. Livestock Confedn. Mexico (hon.), Alpha Zeta, Sigma Delta Chi. Office: 820 Shades Creek Pkwy Box 2581 Birmingham AL 35202 also 3612 Noble Av Dallas TX 75204

SCRUGGS, EDWARD NEAL, judge; b. Tuscaloosa, Ala., Jan. 29, 1923; s. Claud D. and Dolly (NeSmith) S.; B.S., U. Ala., 1943, LL.B., 1948; grad. Nat. Coll. State Judiciary, 1971; m. Rebekah Jones, July 2, 1942; children—Edward N., Nancy Ann. Admitted to Ala. bar, 1949; practiced in Guntersville, Ala., 1949-59; circuit judge 27th Jud. Circuit Ala., Guntersville, 1959—. County solicitor, Marshall County, Ala., 1950; county chmn. Marshall County Rural Devel. Assn., 1958-59. Served to capt. AUS, 1943-46. Mem. Marshall County Bar Assn. (past pres.), Ala. Circuit Judges Assn., Kappa Alpha, Phi Delta Phi, Farrah Order Jurisprudence. Methodist. Home: PO Box 543 Guntersville AL 35976 Office: P O Box 543 Guntersville AL 35976

SCRUGGS, RICHARD TURNER, aluminum co. exec.; b. Birmingham, Ala., Apr. 4, 1915; s. Josiah Hubert and Willye (Turner) S.; student Birmingham So. Coll., 1933-34, U. Ala., 1934-36; m. Marilyn Perkins Bade, Sept. 7, 1938; children—Marilyn Craig (Mrs. Charles L. Tucker), Margaret Sarah (Mrs. Jarrel Estes), Richard Turner, John Hubert. Salesman, So. Culvert Co., Birmingham, Ala., 1936-38, v.p., 1938-42; asst. chief aircraft insp. Bechtel-McCone Corp., Birmingham, 1942-46; co-founder Vulcan Metal Products, Inc., Birmingham, 1946, pres., 1956—; pres. Scruggs Investment Co., Inc.; v.p. Ala. Metal Co., Muscle Shoals. Mem. adv. council Salvation Army. Mem. steering com. Lee Assos. Washington and Lee U., Lexington, Va. Recipient Silver Circle award Alpha Tau Omega, 1959, hon. award Washington and Lee U. chpt. Omicron Delta Kappa, 1973. Mem. Screen Mfrs. Assn. (dir.), C. of C., S.A.R., Sales Exec. Club, Newcomen Soc. Methodist (steward). Clubs: Rotary, Birmingham Country, Downtown, The Club. Home: 3524 Victoria Rd Birmingham AL 35223 Office: PO Box 6788 Birmingham AL 35210

SCRUTCHINS, SAMUEL HARVEY, govt. ofcl., auditor; b. Lake City, Fla., July 15, 1945; s. Thomas Baldy and Mary Cable (West) S.; B.S. in Bus. Adminstrn., U. Fla., 1968; m. Marilyn Claire Pankratz, June 22, 1968. Supervisory auditor U.S. Gen. Accounting Office, Dallas, 1969—. Served with AUS, 1966-71. C.P.A., Tex. Mem. Am. Inst. C.P.A.'s, Tex. Soc. C.P.A.'s, Beta Alpha Psi. Unitarian. Home: 420-120 W Park Row Dr Arlington TX 76010 Office: Room 500 1512 Commerce St Dallas TX 75201

SEALE, JOHN THOMAS, lawyer; b. El Dorado, Ark., Jan. 6, 1934; s. Percy and Edna Ruth (Martin) S.; student Phillips U., 1951-52; B.S., La. Poly. Inst., 1959; J.D., Tulane U., 1961; m. Mary Frances Bradshaw, Jan. 2, 1954; children—John Bradshaw, Jay Wesley. Admitted to La. bar, 1961; with land dept. Cal. Oil Co., New Orleans, 1961-64; asso. Lancaster & Baxter, Tallulah, La., 1964; partner Lancaster, Baxter & Seale, Tallulah, 1965—. Asst. dist. atty. 6th Jud. Dist. of La., 1968—. Chmn., Madison Parish Welfare Adv. Bd., 1967—. Mem. Tallulah and Madison Parish Democratic Exec. Coms., 1966—. Trustee Madison Parish Library. Served with USNR, 1952-56. Mem. Madison Parish C. of C. (dir. 1965-68, 70—, pres. 1965-66), Am., La., 6th Jud. Dist (pres. 1966-67) bar assns., Am. Legion (commdr. 1967-69), Phi Delta Phi, Omicron Delta Kappa, Kappa Delta Phi. Home: 209 Virginia St Tallulah LA 71282 Office: PO Box 70 Tallulah LA 71282

SEALE, RICHARD, banker; b. Eunice, La., Jan. 21, 1931; s. Lemuel George and Alma (Fontenot) S.; B.S., Tex. A. and M. U., 1957; m. Julia Ann Stagg, Jan. 26, 1957; children—Richard Mannie, Martha Amanda, Susan Marie. Agrl. rep. First Nat. Bank Edna (Tex.), 1957-59, v.p., 1959-65; v.p., sr. loan officer First Nat. Bank Angleton (Tex.), 1965-66; exec. v.p. First Nat. Bank Crowley (La.), 1966-68, pres., 1968—, also dir. Mem. adv. council Small Bus. Adminstrn., La., 1969-71; chmn. La. Warehouse Commn., 1972—; vice chmn. La. Devel. Authority for Housing Finance, 1972—. Chmn., City of Crowley BiRacial Com. Bd. dirs. Greater Crowley Indsl. Devel. Corp. Served with USNR, 1951-53. Mem. La. Bankers Assn. (legislative com.), Southwestern Clearing House Assn. (pres. 1969—), Greater Crowley C. of C. (ambassador 1969—, pres. 1970-71), Acadia Parish Cattlemen's Assn. Rotarian. Club: Crowley Town (pres. 1971-72, dir.). Home: 529 W 14th St Crowley LA 70526 Office: PO Box 267 Crowley LA 70526

SEALE, ROY Q(UINCY), educator; b. Dallas, Jan 9, 1898; s. William Quincy and Josie (McGlothlin) S.; B.A., So. Meth. U., 1919; M.A., Columbia, 1920; Ph.D., Stanford, 1935; m. Georgie Hudspeth, Dec. 30, 1923; 1 son, George Quincy. Asst. engr. Southwestern Bell Telephone Co., 1920-21, engr., 1921-22; instr. math. dept. So. Meth. U., 1922-24, asst. prof., 1924-31, summer 1933, 34-35, asso. prof. math. 1942-44, prof., 1944-63, emeritus prof., 1963—; now engaged in math. research, mech. invention; asst. in instrn. Stanford, 1931-34; prof. math. and physics, head dept. Del Mar Coll., Corpus Christi, Tex., 1935-42. Mem. Am. Math. Soc., Math. Assn. Am., Am. Assn. U. Profs., A.A.A.S., Tex. Acad. Scis., Alpha Sigma Lambda, Kappa Mu Epsilon, Sigma Alpha Epsilon. Methodist. Mason. Club: Dallas Athletic. Author: Aerial Navigation Sheets, 1941. Inventor oil well testing equipment and airplane engine control devices. Home: 3609 University Blvd Dallas TX 75205

SEALE, THOMAS FREDERICK, ednl. adminstr.; b. Electra, Tex., Dec. 25, 1919; s. James Edgar and Beulah Mae (Hilburn) S.; B.Mus. (fellow in brass), Houston Conservatory Music, 1940; M.Mus., N.Tex. State U., 1941; postgrad., Vanderbilt U., 1946-47; m. Betty Lou Davis, July 14, 1947; children—Dana Lynn, Marsha Kay, James Paul. Trombonist, Houston Symphony Orch., 1936-41; instr. instrumental music Goose Creek Consol. Ind. Sch., Baytown, Tex., 1936-41, supr. pub. sch. music, art, and crafts, 1947—; instr. brass instruments Houston Conservatory Music, 1937-41; instr. music edn. Lee Coll. Baytown, Tex., 1939-41, 49-52. Cons. visual perception. Mem. Baytown Welfare League Bd., 1952-64, pres., 1955-64; active Baytown Community Chest, 1954-55. Served with AUS, 1942-46. Mem. N.E.A., Baytown Edn. Assn., Tex. Tchrs. Assn., Tex. Music Edn. Assn. (pres. suprs.' div. 1958-59), Music Educators Nat. Conf., Am., Tex. choral dirs. assns., Tex. Assn. Sch. Adminstrs. Episcopalian (sr. warden 1953). Elk, Kiwanian. Contbr. articles to profl. jours. Home: 2008 Woodlawn Baytown TX 77520 Office: PO box 30 Baytown TX 77520

SEALY, DESMOND HOLLINSWORTH, govt. ofcl.; b. Trinidad, W.I., Feb. 24, 1924; s. Joseph Nathaniel and Estelle Jestina (Spencer) S.; came to U.S., 1952, naturalized, 1958; B.A. in Econs., Bklyn. Coll., 1959; M.A., U. Chgo., 1960; diploma Dale Carnegie Inst., 1966; m. Beverly Joan Rice, Nov. 25, 1961; children—Desa Joan, Denise Jacquelyn. Econ. analyst Com. for Econ. and Cultural Devel., Chgo., 1962-64; asso. dir. Washington bur. Nat. Urban League, Inc., 1964-66; dir. equal opportunity Bur. Work Programs, Manpower Adminstrn., Labor Dept., Washington, 1966-67, chief div. program and budget planning Manpower Adminstrn., 1967-68, chief div. spl. programs, 1968-69, spl. asst. to dir. Office Tng. and Employment Opportunities, Manpower Adminstrn., 1969—. Panelist White House Conf. Equal Opportunity, 1965, Conf. Tech. Assistance, U.S. Equal Employment Opportunity Commn., 1965; mem. membership and budget com. Nat. Capital Area Health and Welfare Council, 1971. Nat. Urban League fellow, 1965. Mem. Am. Acad. Polit. and Social Sci., Am. Econ. Assn., Washington Urban League. Home: 33d St NW Washington DC 20015 Office: 1741 Rhode Island Av NW Washington DC 20036 Address: PO Box 4886 Washington DC 20008

SEAMAN, ELLSWORTH FRANKLIN, engring., mgmt. cons.; b. Wilmore, Pa., Aug. 25, 1900; s. Emory Samuel and Anna (Dean) S.; student Milw. Sch. Engring., 1918-21, Carnegie Inst. Tech., 1921-22; m. Eva Mae Whitsitt, Aug. 31, 1930; 1 son, Ellsworth F. Jr. With Navy Buships, U.S. Navy, Washington, 1931-62, head standardization br., 1955-62; cons. Gen. Environment Corp., 1965—; cons. engring. and mgmt., Washington, 1963—. Chmn. bd., pres. Profl. Skills Inc., Washington. Recipient Meritorious Civilian Service award U.S. Navy, 1945, Distinguished Civilian Service award, 1961. Registered profl. engr., D.C. Fellow Inst. Environmental Scis., Standards Engrs. Soc. (hon. life); mem. I.E.E.E., Am. Soc. Testing Materials, Indsl. Engring. Soc., Standards Engring. Soc., Am. Ordnance Assn., Internat. Electrothech. Commn. (internat. pres. environmental standards com. 1950-70). Mason, Kiwanian. Patentee in field. Contbr. articles to profl. jours. Home and office: 3113 Westover Dr Washington DC 20020

SEAMAN, JOHN GATES, lawyer; b. Galveston, Tex., Mar. 9, 1919; s. Harry Milton and Bera (Gates) S.; student U. Houston, summers 1938, 39; B.A., U. Tex., 1940, LL.B., 1942; m. Henri Etta Rester, Mar. 7, 1946; children—John G., Stephen H., Sandra Jane. Admitted to Tex. bar, 1942; practiced in Houston, 1946-51, Corpus Christi, Tex., 1951—; mem. firm Neel and Seaman, 1951-65, Keys, Russel, Watson and Seaman, 1965—. Served to lt. USNR, 1942-46. Named adm. Tex. Navy. Mem. State Bar Tex., Am., Nueces County bar assns., Am. Judicature Soc., Am., Corpus Christi assns. petroleum landmen, Navy League, Phi Beta Kappa, Phi Delta Phi, Alpha Tau Omega. Democrat. Episcopalian. Kiwanian. Clubs: Petroleum; Corpus Christi Town. Home: 618 Santa Monica St Corpus Christi TX 78411 Office: Bank and Trust Tower Corpus Christi TX 78401

SEARIGHT, PATRICIA ADELAIDE, radio, TV cons., assn. exec.; b. Rochester, N.Y.; d. William Hammond and Irma (Winters) Searight; B.A., Ohio State U. Program dir. WTOP radio sta. Washington, 1952-63, gen. mgr. information, 1964; radio and TV cons., 1964—; producer, dir. many radio and TV programs; spl. fgn. news corr. French Govt., 1956; v.p. Micro Beads, Inc., 1955-59; sec., dir. Dennis-Inches, Corp., 1955-59; exec. dir. Am. Women in Radio and Television, 1969—. Recipient Kappa Kappa Gamma achievement award. Mem. Am. Women in Radio and TV (program chmn.; corrs. sec.; mem. bd. Washington chpt.; pres. 1958-60, nat. membership chmn. 1962-63, nat. chmn. Industry Information Digest 1963-64, Mid-Eastern v.p. 1964-66), Soc. Am. Travel Writers (treas. 1957-58, v.p. 1958-59), Nat. Acad. TV Arts and Scis., Kappa Kappa Gamma. Episcopalian. Clubs: Soroptimist, Women's Advertising (2d v.p. Washington 1958-59, pres. 1959-60), Washington Press. Home: The Colonnade 2801 New Mexico Av NW Washington DC 20007

SEARS, ERNEST EUGENE, JR., assn. exec.; b. Birmingham, Ala., Dec. 6, 1923; s. Ernest Eugene and Orie Mae (Howard) S.; B.A., U. Ky., 1952, postgrad., 1952; m. Mary Ann Hoyer, Aug. 22, 1964; 1 son, Charles Ernest. Mng. editor Somerset (Ky.) Commonwelath, 1952-53; reporter Muncie (Ind.) Evening Press, 1953-57; pub. relations dir. Portland Cement Assn., Ky. Dist., 1957-66; pub. relations dir. Ky. C. of C., Louisville, also editor, gen. mgr. Ky. Bus. Mag., 1966—. Free-lance writer; pub. relations cons. Served with USNR, 1943-47; PTO. Mem. Ky. Hwy. Users Conf. (exec. committeeman), Am., Ky. assns. C. of C. execs., Ky. Press Assn., Ky. Indsl. Advt. Assn. Mason. Contbr. articles to trade publs. Home: 4424 Westport Rd Louisville KY 40207 Office: 300 W York St Louisville KY 40203

SEARS, JACK WOOD, educator; b. Cordell, Okla., Aug. 12, 1918; s. Lloyd and Pattie Hathaway (Armstrong) S.; B.S., Harding Coll., 1940; M.A., U. Tex., 1942, Ph.D., 1944; m. Mattie Sue Speck, Nov. 25, 1943; children—James David, Pattie Sue, Martha (Mrs. Barry Collins). Instr. dept. zoology U. Tex., Austin, 1944; prof., chmn. dept. biology Harding Coll., Searcy, Ark., 1945—. Pres. Ark. Healing Arts Bd., 1970—; v.p. White County Health Council, 1971—. Bd. dirs. Searcy Vacation Bible Sch. Fellow A.A.A.S.; mem. Ark. Acad. Sci. (editorial bd.), Am. Inst. Biol. Scis., Am. Fisheries Soc., Genetic Soc. Am. Author: Conflict and Harmony in Science and the Bible, 1969. Mem. editorial bd. Twentieth Century Christian Jour. Home: 920 E Market St Searcy AR 72143 Office: Harding Coll Searcy AR 72143

SEARS, MARCIA JANIS MOCKETT (MRS. RALPH W. SEARS), newspaper editor; b. Lincoln, Neb., Aug. 24, 1927; d. Edwin O. and Perdita (Jameson) Mockett;; A.B., U. Neb., 1948; postgrad. U. So. Cal., summers 1949-51; m. Ralph W. Sears, June 19, 1948; children—Steven, Sara Joan, Randall Jane. Tchr., Montevallo (Ala.) High Sch., 1949-50; founder, dir. Meadowlark Nursery Sch., Montevallo, Ala., 1954-61; instr. Spanish, U. Montevallo, 1959-65; v.p. Shelby County Advt. Corp., Calera, Ala., 1959—; v.p., editor Shelby County Reporter, Inc., Columbiana, Ala., 1967—. Chmn. Montevallo Community Chest, 1957-59; pub. relations chmn. Cahaba council Girl Scouts U.S.A., 1965-67. Bd. dirs. Montevallo Library, 1963-72, chmn. bd., 1966-72; sec. Children's Aid Soc., Birmingham, 1973—. Mem. Ala. Press Assn., Am. Assn. U. Women, Bus. and Profl. Womens Club, Mortar Bd., Women in Communications, Psi Chi. Democrat. Presbyn. Home: 596 Ashville Circle N Montevallo AL 35115 Office: PO Box 947 Columbiana AL 35051

SEARS, PAUL GREGORY, chemist, ednl. adminstr.; b. Somerset, Ky., Sept. 5, 1924; s. James Andrew and Dova (Gregory) S.; B.S., U. Ky., 1950, Ph.D., 1953; m. Juanita Reed Crawford, Sept. 22, 1951; 1 dau., Elizabeth. Instr. U. Ky., Lexington, 1953, also research asso., asst. prof. chemistry, 1954-57; research chemist Monsanto Chem. Co., St. Louis, 1957-59; asso. prof. chemistry U. Ky., Lexington, 1959-62, prof., 1962—, spl. asst. to univ. pres., 1970—. Cons. electrochemistry. Trustee, faculty rep. U. Ky., 1969—. Served with USAF, 1942-45. Decorated Air medal with cluster. Mem. Am. Chem. Soc., A.A.A.S., Electrochem. Soc., Ky. Acad. Sci. (pres. 1968), Sigma Xi, Phi Beta Kappa, Omicron Delta. Democrat. Mem. Christian Ch. Contbr. research articles on chemistry to sci. jours. Patentee in field. Home: 3548 Cornwall Dr Lexington KY 40503

SEARS, RALPH WESTGATE, coll. ofcl.; b. Grand Island, Neb., Oct. 8, 1922; s. Mark P. and Alma (Westgate) S.; B.S., U. Neb., 1948; postgrad. U. So. Cal., 1949-51; m. Marcia Mockett, June 19, 1948; children—Steven Ralph, Sara Joan, Randall Jane. Staff announcer KOLN Radio, Lincoln, Neb., 1947-48; dir. radio, asst. prof. speech Ala. Coll., Montevallo, 1948-51; mem. staff Radio KUSC, Los Angeles, summers 1949-51; mem. staff Radio WUOA, Tuscaloosa, Ala., 1951; dir. pub. relations U. Montevallo, 1952—. Pres. Shelby County Advt. Corp., 1959—; owner Radio WBYE, Calera, Ala., 1959—; pub., owner Shelby County Reporter, weekly Columbiana, Ala., 1967—, Childersburg (Ala.) Star, 1972—. City councilman, Montevallo, 1956-72, mayor, 1972—; sec. Shelby Indsl. Devel. Bd., 1956-57. Served with AUS, 1943-45. Mem. Pub. Relations Council Ala. (pres. 1961-62), Ala. Coll. Pub. Relations Soc. (pres. 1958), Am. Coll. Pub. Relations Assn. (dist. dir. 1966-67, dist. chmn.), Assn. Ala. Coll. Adminstrs., pres. (1967-68), C. of C. (pres. 1960-61), Execs. Club Birmingham, Sigma Phi Epsilon, Sigma Gamma Epsilon, Alpha Epsilon Rho. Presbyn. (elder). Clubs: Rotary (pres. 1956-57), University Montevallo Faculty (pres. 1951-52), University Montevallo Golf (pres. 1956-57); Birmingham Press. Home: 596 Asheville Circle Montevallo AL 35115

SEARS, WILLIAM JOHN, aerospace physiologist; b. Oskaloosa, Ia., Apr. 13, 1931; s. Chester Arthur and Mildred Leona Newman; student Ia. Wesleyan Coll., 1948-51; B.S., Ia. State Coll., 1958; M.S., U. So. Cal., 1966, Ph.D., 1968; m. Orpha Mae Fisk, Sept. 9, 1953; children—Michael F., Cheryl A., John L., Patricia L. Served with USAF, 1951-55; comd. 2d lt. USAF, 1958, advanced through grades to lt. col. 1973; aviation physiologist, March AFB, Cal., 1958-61; chief physiol. tng., Carswell AFB, Tex., 1961-64; chief test facilities br. USAF Sch. Aerospace Medicine, Brooks AFB, Tex., 1967-73; aerospace physiologist RAF Inst. Medicine. Cons. NASA. Active Little League, YMCA, 1969-72. Vice pres., bd. dirs. Randolph/Brooks Fed. Credit Union; v.p. Roosevelt High Sch. Booster Club. Recipient 1st Place award in sci. Air Force Assn., 1972, Tech. Achievement award Air Force Systems Command, 1972. Asso. fellow Aerospace Med. Assn. (bd. govs. aerospace physiologist sect.). Mason. Contbr. articles to profl. jours. Home: 309 Driftwind St San Antonio TX 78239

SEATON, EARL ALVA, JR., publisher, editor; b. Swifton, Ark., Sept. 28, 1919; s. Earl Alva and Nora M. (Clark) S.; A.A., Little Rock U., 1947; B.S. in M.E. with honors, U. Ark., 1949; m. Reba Pickard, Dec. 26, 1941; children—Rebecca June, Lynn Earl. Engr., Cities Service Oil Co., Shreveport, La., 1949-54; editor Oil and Gas Equipment, Tulsa, 1954-67, pub., editor Oil, Gas & Petrochem Equipment (name changed 1969), 1967—. Served with USNR, 1941-45. Registered profl. engr., Okla. Mem. Am. Soc. M.E. Unitarian. Home: 4913 E 26th Pl Tulsa OK 74114 Office: PO Box 1260 Tulsa OK 74101

SEATON, WILLIAM RUSSELL, oil co. exec.; b. Ashland, Ky., Jan. 2, 1928; s. Edward William and Virginia (Russell) S.; B.S., Yale, 1949; m. Suzanne Webb, Aug. 9, 1950; children—Katherine Graham, Suzanne Elizabeth, Mildred Webb, Edward William II. Trainee, Ashland Oil, Inc. (Ky.), 1949, trainee personnel dept., 1950, jr. engr. personnel dept., 1950, adminstrv. asst. personnel, 1951-52, asst. ins. mgr., 1953-55, ins. mgr., 1955-60, exec. asst., 1960-67, v.p., 1967, adminstrv. v.p., 1968, dir., 1969—, sr. v.p., chief adminstrv. officer, after 1970, now vice-chmn.; pres., dir. Means & Russell Iron Co., Ashland; dir. Oil Ins. Ltd., Bermuda. Nat. committeeman Ky. Young Republican Party, 1956-60. Mem. Ashland Area C. of C. (chmn. air transp. com. 1965-68), Chi Psi. Episcopalian. Rotarian. Home: 409 Country Club Dr Ashland KY 41101 Office: 1409 Winchester Av Ashland KY 41101

SEAVER, DONALD MACDONALD, univ. ofcl.; b. Johnson City, Tenn., Mar. 16, 1929; s. Wiley Rex and Barbara Jeanette (Fulton) S.; student Richmond U., 1946-47, Appalachian State Tchrs. Coll., 1947-48; A.B. in Journalism, U. N.C., 1957; m. Nancy Rebecca Lee, Sept. 19, 1959; children—Donald Macdonald, Sandra Lee, Debra Jean. Med. writer Charlotte (N.C.) Observer, 1957-63; news dir. Duke U. Med. Center, Durham, N.C., 1964-66, asst. dir. news service Duke U., 1966-70, news dir., 1970—. Dir. N.C. Mental Health Assn., 1960-66, recipient newspaper award, 1960. Bd. dirs. Durham County Golden Age Soc., v.p. 1970-72; bd. dirs. Coordinating Council for Sr. Citizens, Durham County, pres., 1972—. Recipient Med. Press award N.C. Med. Soc., 1960, 61, Green Eyeshade award Sigma Delta Chi, 1960, Albert Lasker Journalism award, 1960. Hist. writer USAF, 1950-54. Mem. Phi Beta Kappa, Theta Chi. Home: 2948 Welcome Dr Durham NC 27705

SEAWRIGHT, MARGARET ELIZABETH ALSOBROOK (MRS. ROBERT M. SEAWRIGHT), psychiat. social worker; b. Rock Springs, Ga., Aug. 3, 1911; d. Daniel C. and Goma (Forrester) Alsobrook; B.S., U. Chattanooga, 1931; M.S., U. Tenn., 1959; m. Robert M. Seawright, July 24, 1936 (dec. Feb. 1956); 1 son, Robert D. With Miss. Bd. of Health, Jackson, 1959—, mental health cons., 1966—. Mem. Nat. Assn. Social Workers, Miss. Conf. Social Welfare, Miss. Pub. Health Assn. Home: 4081 Redwing Av Jackson MS 39216 Office: PO Box 1700 Jackson MS 39205

SEAY, C(HARLES) FRANK, JR., univ. adminstr.; b. Dallas, Dec. 27, 1913; s. Charles Frank and Hazel (Hinckley) S.; B.A. in Physics, U. Tex., 1934; m. Emily Ann Moore, Oct. 5, 1946; children—Charles Frank III, Carolyn Emily. Seismologist, Humble Oil & Refining Co., 1935; demonstration engr. Gen. Motors Corp., 1936; tutor U. Tex. at Austin, 1937, research fellow, 1941, research scientist Def. Research Lab., 1945-52; clk. Magnolia Petroleum Co., Dallas, 1938-40; research scientist Underwater Sound Lab., Harvard, 1941-45; head co. information center Collins Radio Co., Dallas, 1952-58; mgr. tech. information center Tex. Instruments, Inc., Dallas, 1958-61; asst. to pres. Grad. Research Center of S.W., Dallas, 1961-64; asst. to v.p. So. Meth. U., Dallas, 1964-66, dir. govt. relations, 1966-67, asst. to pres., 1967-71, exec. asst. to pres., 1971—. Cons. in acoustics, 1946—. Recipient U.S. Naval Ordnance Devel. award, 1945. Mem. Acoustical Soc. Am., I.E.E.E. (chmn. Dallas sect. I.R.E. 1957-58, dir. S.W. regional conf. 1963), Dallas Council Sci. Socs. (pres. 1961-62), Met. Philos. Soc., Am. Guild Organists, Inst. Noise Control Engring., Phi Beta Kappa, Sigma Xi, Sigma Pi Sigma, Phi Eta Sigma. Presbyn. (deacon 1949—, elder 1956—). Club: Brookhaven Country (Dallas). Home: 6939 Joyce Way Dallas TX 75225

SEAY, MAURICE SHEPARD, mfg. co. exec.; b. Vicksburg, Miss., Oct. 9, 1905; s. Charles B. and Rosa (Mackey) S.; student LaSalle Extension U., 1927-29, Miss. Coll., 1942-44, Alexander Hamilton Inst. Bus., 1952-73; m. Sylvia Roseberry, Dec. 18, 1929 (dec.); children—Maureen S. (Mrs. Richard T. Smart), William H., Donald W., Connie M. (Mrs. Cono Anthony Caranna II); m. 2d, M. Wanna Edward, Jan. 28, 1967. Personnel mgr. Marathon LeTourneau Co., Vicksburg, 1945—. Pres., Junius Ward Johnson Meml. YMCA. Bd. dirs. Miss. Econ. Council. Mem. Am. Soc. Personnel Adminstrn. (past chpt. pres.), Central Miss. Personnel Mgmt. Assn. (past pres.), Miss. Mfrs. Assn. (dir.), Vicksburg Warren County C. of C. (dir.), Indsl. Mgmt. Club (past pres.), Foremans Club (past pres.). Methodist. Clubs: Vicksburg Y's Men's (past pres.), River Town, Optimist (past pres.). Home: 1456 Parkside Dr Vicksburg MS 39180 Office: LeTourneau Rural Sta Vicksburg MS 39180

SEAY, ORUM ELWYN, railroad equipment mfg. co. exec.; b. Teague, Tex., Aug. 19, 1936; s. Orum Lee and Lena Oleta (Bond) S.; B.S. in Mech. Engring., Lamar U. 1958; M.S. in Mech. Engring. (grad. fellow), Tex. A. and M., 1959; postgrad. Oklahoma City U., 1968-69; m. Beverly Jo Die, July 27, 1957; children—Stephen Elwyn, Shana Lynn, Jeffrey Alan. Engr., Halliburton Co., Duncan, Okla., 1959-63, sr. engr., 1963-64, devel. engr., 1964-65, sect. leader, 1965-68, supr., 1968-69; mgr. engring. Freightmaster div. Halliburton Co., Ft. Worth, 1969—. Dir. Halliburton Services Credit Union, 1963-64. Registered profl. engr., Okla., Tex. Mem. Am. Soc. M.E., Okla., Tex. socs. profl. engrs. Baptist. Rotarian. Patentee in oil field and railroad equipment. Home: Route 2 15 Wyche Ct Burleson TX 76028 Office: PO Box 40555 Fort Worth TX 76140

SEAY, WILLIAM GARLAND, bus. systems designer; b. Bardstown, Ky., July 28, 1931; s. Marion Wallace and Louise (Reardon) S.; student U. Louisville, 1952; m. Betty Jean Whelan, June 24, 1953; children—Joseph G., Jeanne Marie, Suzanne, Carol Ann. Systems designer, systems analyst Gen. Electric Co., Louisville, 1956—. Served with Adj. Gen. Corps, U.S. Army, 1951-52. Mem. Data Processing Mgmt. Assn. (v.p. edn. 1963-64, certificate in data processing 1963). Home: 8611 Hudson Lane Louisville KY 40291 Office: Gen Electric Co AP 10-270 Appliance Park KY 40225

SEAY, WILLIAM H., ins. co. exec.; b. 1919; B.B.A., U. Tex., 1941; m. Margie Gurley; children—Bill, Joe, Janie. Partner, Henry, Seay & Black, 1948-57; v.p. Universal Life & Accident Ins. Co., 1958-61, pres., 1961-72, chief exec. officer, 1972—; exec. v.p. Southwestern Life Ins. Co., 1968-69, pres., 1969-73, now chief exec. officer; chmn., chief exec. officer Southwestern Life Corp., Southwestern Gen. Life Ins. Co.; dir. Guardian Savs. & Loan Assn., Dallas, Southwestern Investors Inc. Dir. Tex. Life Conv., Dallas. Chmn. devel. fund Dallas Salvation Army; chmn. gen. campaign Dallas County United Fund. Bd. dirs. Cotton Bowl Council, A.R.C., Tex. Research League, Dallas Health and Sci. Mus., Dallas Zool. Soc., Dallas Citizen's Council; trustee Dallas Community Chest Trust Fund, Southwestern Med. Found., Children's Med. Center, others. Served to capt. AUS, 1942-46. Mem. Am. Life Ins. Assn. (exec. com.), Inst. Life Ins. Presbyn. (elder). Office: PO Box 2699 Dallas TX 75221*

SEAY, WILLIAM JACKSON, educator; b. Birmingham, Ala., Apr. 5, 1930; s. William Berkley and Gladys (Long) S.; B.A. in Indsl. Design, Ala. Poly. Inst., 1956; m. Virginia Andress, Dec. 23, 1951; children—Laura Lee, Brian Brooks. With Atlanta Paper Co. (Ga.), 1956, Robert K. Price Co., Fayetteville, 1957; mem. faculty Ga. Inst. Tech., Atlanta, 1958—, asso. prof. archtl. and indsl. design, 1970—, chmn. dept. design, 1971—, adminstr. plastics short courses dept. continuing edn., 1963—. Dir. Atlanta Dynamics Corp.; v.p. research and devel. Timport, Inc. Indsl. design cons., cons. to 3d Army Tng. Aids Centers, 1965—; panelist Nat. Commn. on Materials Policy. Served with AUS, 1951-53. NSF grantee, 1967-68; recipient Patriotic Civilian Service award. Mem. Soc. Plastics Engrs. (So. region edn. chmn. 1967—, pres. 1968, outstanding service award 1968, chmn. vinyl conf. 1969), World Future Soc. (dir. 1971), Am. Soc. Indsl. Designers, So. Indsl. Designers (sec. 1967), Soc. Plastics Industry (dir. reinforced plastics div.), Auburn Art Guild, Lambda Chi Alpha (v.p. 1955), Tau Sigma Delta. Unitarian-Universalist. Club: Bickers. Home: 330 Woodward Way NW Atlanta GA 30305

SEBASTIAN, REX ARDEN, mfg. co. exec.; b. Robinson, Ill., Sept. 16, 1929; s. Dean and Rhea (Gideon) S.; B.S., Purdue U., 1951; M.B.A., Ind. U., 1952; m. Dorothy Lynne Bryson, Sept. 1, 1951; children—Steven Bryson, Annie Laurie, David Rex, Lisa Gay, Amy Lynne. Prodn. foreman Proctor & Gamble, Cin., 1952; various positions Cummins Engine Co., Inc., Columbus, Ind., 1955-60, mng. dir., Shotts, Lanarkshire, Scotland, 1960-63, v.p. internat., Columbus, 1963-64, London, Eng., 1964-66; v.p. internat. operations Dresser Industries, Inc., Dallas, 1966-71, v.p. operations office of pres., 1971—. Served to lt. Supply Corps, USNR, 1952-55. Mem. Dallas C. of C., Am. Mgmt. Assn., Machinery and Allied Products Inst., Nat. Fgn. Trade Council, Nat. Indsl. Conf. Bd., Sigma Phi Epsilon. Republican. Presbyn. Home: 4526 Dorset Rd Dallas TX 75229 Office: Republic Bank Bldg P O Box 718 Dallas TX 75221

SEBESTA, HENRY ROBERT, mech. engr., educator; b. Rosharon, Tex., Nov. 20, 1938; s. Henry C. and Olga Emma (Ashorn) S.; A.A., Alvin Jr. Coll., 1959; B.S. in Mech. Engring., U. Tex., 1962, M.S. in Mech. Engring., 1964, Ph.D. (Ford Found. fellow), 1966; m. Mary Cecil Mumberson, Aug. 31, 1963; children—David, Robert. Asst. prof. mech. engring. Okla. State U., Stillwater, 1966-69, asso. prof., 1969—. Cons. Sandia Labs., Albuquerque, 1969-71, also research engr., 1969; prin. engr. Bendix Kansas City div., Mo., summers 1970, 71; mech. engr. Kirtland AFB, Albuquerque, summers 1972, 73. Recipient Outstanding Faculty award Am. Soc. Engring. Edn., 1972. Mem. Am. Soc. M.E., Instrumentation Soc. Am., Am. Inst. Aeros. and Astronautics (pres. central Okla. sect. 1969). Home: 1119 Eskridge Pl Stillwater OK 74074

SEBOR, MILOS MARIE, geographer, planner; b. Zbiroh, Czechoslovakia, Sept, 3, 1911; s. Vojtech and Marie (Kopriva) S.; Iur. Dr., Charles U., Prague, 1936; M.A. McGill U. (Can.), 1955; postgrad. La. State U., 1957-58; Ph.D., Polish U., London, 1964; m. Bozena Rutrle, Sept. 3, 1936; 1 dau., Yana de Nepomuk. Came to U.S. 1956, naturalized 1962. With Czechoslovak State Security, 1935-48; head research div., del. to Interpol, Paris, 1946-48; geographer Lutetia Press, Paris, 1948-53; with Canadian Dept. Mines, 1955-56; faculty Spring Hill (Ala.) Coll., 1956-57; asso. prof. geography Tenn. Technol. U., Cookeville, 1958-67; prof. geology Weber State Coll., 1967-68; prof. geography grad. sch. Eastern Ky. U., Richmond, 1968—, dir. planning programs. Sr. planner, Tenn. State Planning Commn., 1962-67; vis. prof. geography U. Miami, 1965; field work on coastal forms and related urban pattern, N.W. Europe, 1966, planning tropical urban communities, Grenada, W.I., summer 1969; research and planning specialist Ky. Program Devel. Office, 1970—. Served to 1st capt. Czechoslovak Gendarmery, 1942-45. Recipient medal Czechoslovak Resistance, 1946; knight Mil. Order St. Lazarus, 1973. Mem. Assn. Am. Geographers, Am. Inst. Planners, Am. Assn. U. Profs., Czechoslovak Soc. Arts and Scis., Am. Austrian Soc., Geol. Soc. Am., Utah Geol. Assn., Am. Legion (Ky. planner-in-charge 1969). Rotarian. Author series of novels in Czech, pub. Rome, 1974. Co-author of new regional div. State of Tenn. into planning regions, 1962-67. Home: Route 7 Stateland Richmond KY 40475

SECREST, EVERETT LEIGH, educator; b. Tioga, Tex., Jan. 5, 1928; s. Walter Everett and Annie Jewell (Holloway) S.; B.S., N. Tex. State U., 1947, M.S., 1948; Ph.D., Mass. Inst. Tech., 1951; m. Bettye Jo Porter, June 4, 1948; children—Robert M., Charles H. Asso. prof. physics N. Tex. State U., 1951-54; chief nuclear physics Convair-Ft. Worth div. Gen. Dynamics, Ft. Worth, 1954-57; asst. mgr. physics and math. Babcock & Wilcox Co., Lynchburg, Va., 1957-59; chief scientist Gen. Dynamics, Ft. Worth, 1959-64; asso. dean engring. U. Okla., 1964-65; grad. dean Tex. Christian U., 1965-68, vice-chancellor for advanced studies and research, 1968-72, pres. TCU Research Found., 1965—, Continental Nat. Bank prof. mgmt. sci., 1972—. Guest lectr. Mass. Inst. Tech., 1972. Bd. dirs. Trinity Valley Sch., Ft. Worth. Mem. Gulf Univs. Research Consortorium (trustee, sec. 1969-71), Oak Ridge Asso. Univs., Met. Philos. Soc. (pres. 1970-71), Assn. Tex. Grad. Schs., Am. Phys. Soc., Am. Nuclear Soc., Am. Soc. Engring. Edn., Soc. Engring. Sci., Nat. Council U. Research Adminstrs., Sigma Xi (pres. Tex. Christian U. br. 1967-68), Alpha Chi (pres. N. Tex. State U. chpt. 1945-46), Sigma Pi Sigma, Pi Mu Epsilon. Contbr. articles to sci. jours. Contbr. papers to profl. soc. meetings. Home: 2415 Wabash Av Fort Worth TX 76109 Office: Tex Christian U Fort Worth TX 76129

SECRIST, PHILIP LEE, ednl. adminstr.; b. Milw., May 4, 1928; s. Harry Paulus and Alice (Shaw) S.; B.S. in Edn., U. Tenn., 1952; M.S., Auburn U., 1955; Ed.D. in Social Sci. and History, U. Ga., 1971; m. Katherine Jane Kimsey, Aug. 20, 1949; children—Phylis (Mrs. Alex McLean), Barbera, James, Scott. Tchr. pub. schs., Atlanta, 1955-61, Marietta, Ga., 1961-68; teaching asst. U. Ga., Athens, 1968-70; asst. prof. history So. Tech. Coll., Marietta, 1970-73; supr. social sci. Cobb County (Ga.) Pub. Schs., 1973-74. Bd. dirs. Kennesaw Mountain Nat. Battlefield Hist. Assn., Cobb County Bi-Centennial Com.; bd. dirs., curator Big Shanty Mus., Kennesaw, Ga., 1973—. Served with USMCR, 1946-48, to lt. AUS, 1952-54. Mem. Ga. Council Social Sci. (pres. 1965-66), Marietta Edn. Assn. (pres. 1964-65), So. Hist. Assn., N.E.A., Nat. Council Social Studies, Atlanta Civil War Round Table. Christian Scientist. Contbr. articles to profl. jours. Home: Frank Kirk Rd Route 1 Kennesaw GA 30144

SEDAM, GLENN JAY, publisher; b. Monongahela, Pa., Aug. 19, 1916; s. Earl Jay and Ica (Baltzell) S.; student Duquesne Sch. Advt. and Journalism, Pitts., 1940-41; m. Dorothy Harriet Gillingham, May 23, 1936; children—Glenn Jay, Tommy Alan, Linda Kay (Mrs. Tom A. McCulloch), Cythia Louise (Mrs. Ted A. Ganczak). Advt. salesman, mgr. Monongahela Daily Republican, 1936-39; advt. salesman McKeesport (Pa.) Daily News, 1939-41, Pitts. Press, 1941-44; advt. dir. Wilmington (N.C.) Post, 1944-45, Clarksburg (W.Va.) Exponent-Telegram, 1945-53; advt. dir., bus mgr. Gadsden (Ala.) Times, 1953-58; pub. Bay City (Tex.) Daily Tribune, 1958—; v.p. So. Newspapers, Inc., Ala., 1957-58. Pres., Matagorda Retarded Children's Council, Bay City, 1960-63; Mem. Tex. Christian U. Adv. Bd., 1965—, Com. 100, 1968—. Bd. dirs. Tex. United Community Services. Recipient Citizen award Gadsden, 1956-57; nominated Fair award as outstanding layman Bay City Ministerial Alliance, 1960. Mem. Etowah County Hist. Soc. (pres. 1956-58), Tex. Press Assn. (pres.), Bay City C. of C. (dir.), Sigma Delta Chi. Mem. Disciples of Christ Ch., (pres. Ala. Christian Men's Fellowship 1955-58, v.p., nat. fellowship 1956-57, pres. 1957-58, pres. Tex. fellowship 1965-66). Home: 2113 Hillcrest Dr Bay City TX 77414 Office: 3013 7th St Bay City TX 77414

SEDBERRY, MARGARET CELESTE MOORE (MRS. MILES E. SEDBERRY), physician; b. Carthage, Tex., Jan. 31, 1925; d. James B. and Maggie (Miller) Moore; B.S., La. State U., 1945; M.D., U. Tex., 1950; m. Miles E. Sedberry, Mar. 9, 1952; children—Lory Lyn, Kirk Miles, Intern Parkland Hosp., Dallas, 1950-51; resident psychiatry U. Tex. Med. Br., Galveston, 1951-54; clin. dir. Austin (Tex.) State Hosp., 1954—. Mem. A.M.A., Tex. Med. Assn., Travis County Med. Soc., Austin Soc. Pub. Adminstrn., Am. Med. Womens Assn., Am., Dist. Br. psychiat. assns., Titus Harris Soc. Home: 3909 Balcones Dr Austin TX 78731 Office: Austin State Hosp Austin TX 78751

SEDLER, ROBERT ALLEN, educator, lawyer; b. Pitts., Sept. 11, 1935; s. Jerome and Esther (Rosenberg) S.; A.B. magna cum laude, U. Pitts., 1956, J.D., 1959; m. Rozanne Friedlander, Jan. 24, 1960; children—Eric, Beth. Admitted to D.C. bar, 1959, Ky. bar, 1968, U.S. Supreme Ct., 1969; asst. dean, asso. prof. law Haile Sellassie I U., Addis Ababa, Ethiopia, 1963-66; asso. prof. law U. Ky., Lexington, 1966-68, prof., 1968—. Asst., also asso. prof. law St. Louis U., 1961-65, instr. Rutgers U., 1959-61; gen counsel Ky. Civil Liberties Union, 1971—. Mem. Am. Bar Assn., Am. Judicature Soc., Am. Assn. U. Profs., Order Coif, Phi Beta Kappa. Author: Conflict of Laws in Ethiopia, 1965; Ethiopian Civil Procedure, 1968. Contbr. profl. jours. Home: 3461 Keithshire Way Lexington KY 40503 Office: Dept Law Univ Ky Lexington KY 40506

SEDWICK, ROBERT CURTIS, educator; b. Pitts., June 27, 1926; s. Hyram Jobe and Annabelle (Silver) S.; B.S., Coast Guard Acad., 1949; M.Engring. Adminstrn., George Washington U., 1960, D.B.A., 1964; m. Elizabeth Angeline King, June 3, 1949; children—Robert Curtis, Elizabeth Ann. Staff engr. Emerson Research Lab., Silver Spring, Md., 1956-57; plant mgr. Polytronics, Inc., Rockville, Md., 1957-58; chief engring. adminstrn. Allis-Chalmers Nuclear Power Dept., Washington, 1958-62; sr. contracts negotiator and adminstr. Johns Hopkins Applied Physics Lab., Silver Spring, Md., 1962-65; dir. Tidewater Center, George Washington U., Hampton, Va., 1965—, prof. bus. adminstrn., 1965—. Dir. Adminstrv. Research Assos., Hampton, Va. Served to lt. USCG, 1949-56. Mem. Am. Econ. Assn., Am. Mgmt. Assn., Soc. for Advancement Mgmt., Presbyn. (deacon, elder). Dir. research, pub. Mortgage Market Survey, Williamsburg, Va., 1966, Econ. Survey, Hampton Waterfront, 1967. Author: Interaction-Interpersonal Relations in Organizations, 1974. Contbr. articles to profl. jours. Home: 505 Carters Grove Ct Hampton VA 23363

SEE, FRANK EDMUND, clergyman; b. Toronto, Ont., Can., June 15, 1919; s. James Edmund and Eva Francis (Freeman) S.; B.A., U. Toronto, also B.D.; D.D., Phillips U.; m. Phyllis M. Moore, July 7, 1945; children—Denton, Robert, Barbara, Debra. Ordained to ministry Christian Ch. (Disciples of Christ), 1944; minister United Ch., Duluth, Minn., 1949-57, First Christian Ch., Casper, Wyo., 1957-65; sr. minister First Christian Ch., Tulsa, 1965—; mem. internat. mission to Japan, 1962; preacher World Assembly Christian Chs., Adelaide, Australia, 1970. Mem. Sem. Council Phillips U., 1964—. Bd. dirs. Disciples of Christ Hist. Soc. Rotarian. Clubs: Southern Hills Country, Tulsa, University (Tulsa). Author: Felling Kind of Temporary, 1968. Contbr. articles to mags., newspapers. Home: 2221 Forest Blvd Tulsa OK 74114 Office: 913 S Boulder St Tulsa OK 74119

SEEDLOCK, ROBERT FRANCIS, engring. and constrn. exec.; b. Newark, Feb. 6, 1913; s. Frank Andrew and Mary Elizabeth (Prosner) S.; student Case Inst. Tech., 1931-33; B.S., U.S. Mil. Acad., 1937; M.S. in Civil Engring., Mass. Inst. Tech., 1940; grad. Armed Forces Staff Coll., 1948, Nat. War Coll., 1958; m. Hortense Orcutt Norton, Sept. 1, 1937; children—Robert Francis, Elizabeth Munsell (Mrs. Norman H. Morrissette), Walter Norton, Mary Marion. Commd. 2d lt. U.S. Army, 1937, advanced through grades to maj. gen., 1963; asst. to dist. engr., Pitts., 1937-39, Tulsa Aircraft Assembly Plant, 1941; regtl. exec. battalion comdr. EUTC, Camp Claiborne, La., 1942; asst. theatre engr., CBI, also comdr. Burma Rd. engrs., and chief engr. Shanghai Base Command, 1943-47; mem. gen. staff U.S. Army, mem. Am. delegation Far Eastern Commn., 1948-49; aide to chief staff U.S. Army, 1949, 54; mem. U.S. del. NATO Ministerial Conf., 1952-53; dep. div. engr. Mediterranean div., 1954-57; mil. asst. to asst. sec. def. pub. affairs, 1958-62; div. engr. Missouri River, Omaha, 1962-63; sr. mem. UN Mil. Armistice Commn., Korea, 1963-64; dir. mil. personnel ODCSPER, Dept. Army, 1964-66; dir. mil. constrn. Office Chief of Engrs., 1966; comdg. gen. U.S. Army Engr. Center and Ft. Belvoir, Va. and comdt.-U.S. Army Engr. Sch. Ft. Belvoir, 1966-68; ret. 1968; pres. Yuba Industries, 1968-69, v.p. Standard Prudential Corp. (merger with Yuba Industries), 1969-70; v.p., dir. Petro-Chme. Devel. Co., Inc., N.Y.C., 1968-70, Petchem Constrn. Co., N.Y.C., 1968-70, Petrochem Isoflow Furnaces, Ltd. (Can.), 1968-70; dir. constrn. and devel. Port Authority of Allegheny County, Pitts., 1970-73; asso. Parsons, Brinckerhoff, Quade & Douglas, N.Y.C., 1973; dep. project dir. Parsons Brinckerhoff-Tudor-Bechtel, Atlanta, 1973—; dir. Yuba Goldfields, Inc., Los Angeles. Bd. dirs. Army and Air Force Exchange and Motion Picture Service, 1964; mem. Miss. River Commn., 1962-63, Bd. Engrs. Rivers and Harbors, 1962-63, Def. Adv. Commn. Edn., 1964; chmn. Mo. Basin Inter-Agy. Com., 1962-63; fed. rep., chmn. Big Blue River Compact Commn., 1962-63; mem. U.S. Com. on Large Dams, 1962—; exec. bd. Nat. Capital Area Council Boy Scouts Am., 1967-68. Decorated Legion of Merit with oak leaf cluster, D.S.M.; chevalier Legion of Honor (France); 1st class, grade A medal army, navy, air force, also spl. breast Order Yun Hui (China). Registered profl. engr. Fellow Am. Soc. C.E.; mem. Soc. Am. Mil. Engrs. (nat. dir.), Assn. U.S. Army, Sigma Xi. Roman Catholic. Rotarian. Clubs: Army-Navy Country (sec. chmn. bd. govs. 1952-54, 61-62) (Arlington, Va.); Massachusetts Institute of Technology (pres. Shanghai 1946); Metropolitan (N.Y.C.); Oglethorpe (Savannah, Ga.); Pike Run Country (Jones Mills, Pa.); Ansley Golf, Atlanta City (Atlanta). Contbr. articles to mil. and engring. jours. Home: 1629 Nottingham Way Atlanta GA 30309 Office: 100 Peachtree St Atlanta GA 30303

SEEGER, C(HARLES) RONALD, geologist, educator; b. Columbus, O., Jan. 31, 1931; s. Karl Elder and Ethel Turney (Jones) S.; B.Sc., Ohio State U., 1953; M.S., George Washington U., 1958; Ph.D., U. Pitts., 1966; m. Barbara Ann Ashley, July 29, 1961; children—Leslie Ethel, Julie Ann. Engring. geologist Photronix, Columbus, O., 1958; operations analyst Inst. for Def. Analyses, The Pentagon, Washington, 1958-60; earth scis. analyst office of naval intelligence Sci. and Tech. Intelligence Center, Washington, 1960-63. Asst. prof. Western Ky. U., Bowling Green, 1968-69, asso. prof., 1969—. Resident research asso. Goddard Space Flight Center, NASA, Greenbelt, Md., 1966-68. Served to lt. (j.g.) USNR, 1953-57. Mem. A.A.A.S., Am. Geophys. Union, Am. Assn. U. Profs. (chpt. pres. 1971-72). Ky. Acad. Sci., Meteoritical Soc., Sigma Xi. Contbr. articles on geology to sci. jours. Home: 2153 Robin Rd Bowling Green KY 42101

SEELIG, JOHN EARL, coll. adminstr.; b. Fredericksburg, Tex., Dec. 11, 1924; s. Charles M. and Katy (Leyendecker) S.; B.S., Hardin-Simmons U., 1946, Dr. Humanities, 1969; M.Religious Edn., Southwestern Baptist Theol. Sem., Fort Worth, 1949; m. Virginia Garrett, Oct. 16, 1947; children—Stephen Clyde, Timothy Garrett. Minister edn. Evans Av. Bapt. Ch., Fort Worth, 1947-49, Birchman Av. Bapt. Ch., Fort Worth, 1950-51, Highland Bapt. Ch., 1951-52. dir. edn. and promotion Dallas Bapt. Assn., 1952-56; minister Travis Av. Bapt. Ch., Fort Worth, 1958-60; asso. tng. union sec. Bapt. Gen. Conv. Tex., 1956-58; asst. to pres. Southwestern Bapt. Theol. Sem., Fort Worth, 1960-73, v.p. adminstrv. affairs, 1973—. Mem. pub. relations adv. com. Bapt. Gen. Conv. of Tex.; loan exec. United Fund. Mem. Pub. Relations Soc. Am., Am. Coll. Pub. Relations Assn. (trustee; mem. nat. publs. com. 1969), Religious Pub. Relations Council (past pres.), Tex. Bapt. Pub. Relations Assn. (past pres.), Bapt. Pub. Relations Assn. (pres. 1969), Fort Worth C. of C. (edn., pub. relations com.), Southwestern Bapt. Theol. Sem. Alumni Assn. (sec. treas. 1960). Baptist (deacon). Lion (dist. gov. 1974—). Clubs: Ridglea Country, Meadowbrook Wranglers, The Fort Worth Breakfast (Fort Worth); Saddle and Sirloin of Kansas City (Mo.). Home: 4441 Stanley Av Fort Worth TX 76115 Office: Box 22000-3e Fort Worth TX 76122

SEES, JAMES EDWIN, electronics and microwave engr., radio astronomer, educator; b. Adair County, Mo., Mar. 23, 1913; s. Irvie and Etta (Miller) S.; B.S. in Physics and Math., N.E. Mo. State Tchrs. Coll., 1933-37; M.S., U. Okla., 1939; postgrad. Cath. U. Am., 1950—; m. Maybelle Evans, Sept. 15, 1940; 1 son, Robert Alan. Chief computer seismograph div. Stanolind Oil & Gas Co., 1940-42; sect. head, radio astronomy br. Naval Research Lab., Washington, 1942-58; asso. prof. elec. engring. U. S.C., 1958—. NASA-Am. Soc. Engring. Edn. faculty fellow U. Houston, 1968, 69. Mem. A.A.A.S., Am. Phys. Soc., Sci. Research Soc. Am., Am. Soc. Engring. Edn., Am. Geophys. Union, Sigma Xi, Sigma Pi Sigma. Home: 1517 Alpine Dr West Columbia SC 29169 Office: Univ SC Columbia SC 29206

SEGAL, LEONARD LOUIS, electronics mfg. co. exec.; b. Phila., May 13, 1928; s. Nathan and Ida (Shusterman) S.; student Nat. Agrl. Coll., Doylestown, Pa., 1947-49; B.S., U. Ga., 1951; postgrad. Emory U., 1957-60; m. Elaine Sherry Gilman, Dec. 25, 1950; children—Jeffrey Bernard, Kenneth Jerome. Tchr. Ridley Twp. High Sch., Ridley Park, Pa., 1954-56, chmn. sci. dept. College Park (Ga.) High Sch., 1957-60; applications engr., field sales mgr. S.E. dist. Electro Tech Inc. (name changed to Brownell Electro Inc.), Hapeville, Ga., 1960—; aircraft insp. Vertol Aircraft div. Boeing Co., Morton, Pa., 1955-57. Lectr. on electronics, religion. Trustee Hebrew Inst. Atlanta, 1963-64. Served with USAF, 1945-47. NSF grantee, 1957-60. Mem. I.E.E.E. (chmn. arrangements regional confs. southeastern textile com. 1968, 70, co-chmn., 1974), Am. Inst. Plant Engrs., Instrument Soc. Am. (sr.). Jewish religion (ednl. dir.). Contbr. articles to profl. jours. Home: 1551 Knob Hill Dr NE Atlanta GA 30329 Office: 3020 Commerce Way Hapeville GA 30354

SEGAL, PAUL MANUEL, municipal govt. ofcl.; b. Jersey City, Jan. 12, 1920; s. David A. and Anna (Feller) S.; B.B.A., Coll. City N.Y., 1948; M.Pub. Adminstrn., N.Y.U., 1949; certificate urban and met. planning Am. U., 1958; m. Shirley R. Klauber, Apr. 4, 1954; children—Charles Lawrence, Brad Marshall. Transp. economist Bur. Pub. Rds., Washington, 1949-58; planning dir. Cecil County, Md., 1959-61; Norwalk, Conn., 1961-65, Plainfield, N.J., 1965-66, Sarasota, Fla., 1966—. Cons. and lectr. in field. Pres., Sarasota County Health Planning Council, 1969; v.p. West Central Fla. Comprehensive Health Planning Council, 1969-71; sec. Sarasota Planning Bd., 1966—. Served with AUS, 1943-45. Mem. Am. Inst. Planners, Am. Soc. Planners, Fla. Planning and Zoning Assn. (v.p. 1969-70), Nat. Assn. Housing and Redevel. Ofcls. Contbr. articles to profl. jours. Home: 722 Siesta Key Circle Sarasota FL 33581 Office: City Hall PO 1058 Sarasota FL 33578

SEGAL, SIMON, real estate exec.; b. Havana, Cuba, Apr. 16, 1941; s. Govsey and Julia (Getzug) S.; brought to U.S., 1955, naturalized, 1970; B.C.E., Cornell U., 1965. Owner, Simon Segal Constrn. Co., Miami Beach, 1971—; pres. Investex Realty Corp., Miami, 1973—. Registered profl. engr., Fla. Mem. Fla. Engring. Soc., Nat. Soc. Profl. Engrs., Am. Soc. C.E. (sec. 1970), Cornell Soc. Engrs., Greater Miami, Cuban Am. (founder, pres. 1971), Internat. (senator) jr. chambers commerce. Home: 208 Meridian Av Miami Beach FL 33139 Office: 343 Ingraham Bldg Miami FL 33131

SEGAL, STANLEY RAYMOND, lawyer; b. Phila., Jan. 20, 1921; s. Phillip P. and Leah V. (Rosenburg) S.; student U. P.R., 1951-54; J.D. magna cum laude, Mercer U., 1957; m. Maria A. Jimenez, May 4, 1946; children—Steven, Arthur. Admitted to Ga. bar, 1956, P.R. bar, 1957; practiced in San Juan, P.R., 1962—; asst. atty. gen. Justice Dept. Tax Litigation Commonwealth P.R., San Juan, 1957-59, dir. office indsl. tax exemption Commonwealth P.R., 1959-62; mem. firm Ramirez, Segal and Latimer, San Juan, 1962—. Dir. Caribbean Leisurewear, Inc., San Juan. Bd. dirs. Commonwealth Consol. Sch., San Juan, 1958-66. Served with USN, 1940-46; PTO. Mem. Am., P.R. bar assns., Comml. Law League, Phi Alpha Delta. Mason (Shriner). Home: 1671 Geranio St San Francisco PR 00926 Office: 208 First Fed Bldg Stop 23 Ponce De Leon Av San Juan PR 00903

SEGALL, BEN ZION, elec. engr.; b. Shavlia, Russia, Apr. 12, 1905; s. Solomon and Deborah Segall; came to U.S., 1906, naturalized, 1912; B.Engring., Tulane U., 1926; m. Ada Joe Frank, Dec. 20, 1928; children—Miriam (Mrs. Leon Weill), Jacqueline (Mrs. Edwin Caplan). With New Orleans Pub. Service Inc., 1926-48, asst. engr. constrn. engring. dept., 1934-43, elec. distbn. engr., 1943-48; exec. v.p., chief engring. Best Electric Co., New Orleans, 1948-52; cons. engr. in elec. hazards, fires, New Orleans, 1928—. Instr., Delgado Trade Sch., V-12 program Tulane. Mem. Southeastern Metermen's Assn. (organizer), Internat. Assn. Elec. Insps. (charter), I.E.E.E., Illuminating Engring. Soc. Cons. editor Elec. Constrn. and Maintenance mag., 1957—. Contbr. articles to profl. jours. Address: 2801 Joseph St New Orleans LA 70115

SEGALL, LEE, broadcasting exec.; b. Dallas, July 18, 1905; s. Simon and Jennie (Sachs) S.; student U. Tex., 1923; m. Mildred Dolores Metzger, Feb. 28, 1929. Mgr. Metzger Dairies, Houston, 1929—; owner Segall & Goodwin Advt. Agy., Houston, 1939—; pres. KIXL and KIXL-FM Radio, Dallas, 1957—; producer-writer various network shows N.Y., 1945—. Creator, owner Dr. I.Q., 1935—, also creator TV version. Cons. to radio, TV stas.; advt. cons. in bus. Radio cons. Eighth service command, War Bond dir., Dallas, 1947—. Dir. Dallas Symphony Orch. Active on civic & pub. service coms.; charter corporate mem. Boys Club Dallas. Tex. rep. broadcasting, voting mem. Am. Heart Assn.; mem. found. com. Tex. Heart Assn. Named Outstanding Broadcaster of 1961, Assn. Broadcasting Execs. Tex. Author: The Wonderful Think-It-Overs; Teasers for Your Think-Tank. Home and office: 3525 Turtle Creek Blvd Dallas TX 75219

SEGARS, KELLY SCOTT, physician, banker; b. Red Bay, Ala., Mar. 11, 1930; s. Dock Scott and Ora Esther (Sims) S.; B.S. in Pharmacy with honors, Auburn U., 1952; M.D. with honors, U. Miss., 1959; m. Martha Ann Thompson, Oct. 3, 1952; children—Kelly Scott, Mark Thompson, Leigh Ann. Intern, USPHS, Norfold, Va., 1959-60; practice medicine, Iuka, Miss., 1960—; pres. Tri-State Savs. and Loan, Iuka, 1963-64; founder, pres. 1st Nat. Bank Iuka, 1964—; chief, med. staff Tishomingo County Hosp., 1968, responsible for constrn. coronary care unit; pres. Horizon Broadcasting, radio stas. WVOM, WTIB, Tuka, Miss., also WDSK, WDLT, Cleveland, Miss., 1970—; dir. various ins., real estate, cattle and farming operations. Chmn. constrn. com. Iuka Airport, 1966-67; chmn. constrn. com. Iuka Municipal Library, 1970; mem. exec. council Yocona area Boy Scouts Am., 1971-. Served to 1st lt. AUS, 1953-55. Col. staff Gov. John Bell Williams. Mem. A.M.A., So., Miss. med. assns., Am., Miss. bankers' assns., Flying Physicians Assn., Internat. Flying Bankers Assn. Methodist (ofcl. bd.). Home: Route 1 Box 165 Iuka MS 38852 Office: 1413 W Quitman St Iuka MS 38852

SEGNER, EDMUND PETER, JR., univ. dean; b. Austin, Tex., Mar. 28, 1928; s. Edmund Peter and Elsie Emily (Grenwelge) S.; B.S. in Civil Engring., U. Tex., 1949, M.S. in Civil Engring., 1952; Ph.D.,

Tex. A. and M. U., 1962; m. Martha Fairfax Smith, Nov. 29, 1952; children—Eddie, John, Nancy, Sandra, Sharon. Engr. United Gas Pipe Line Co., Wichita Falls, Tex., 1949-50; sr. structures engr. Gen. Dynamics Corp., Ft. Worth, 1951-52, 53-54, 56; asso. prof. civil engring. Tex. A. and M. U., College Station, 1954-63; prof. civil engring. U. Okla., Norman, 1963-65; prof. civil engring. U. Ala., Tuscaloosa, 1965—, also asst. dean engring., 1968-71, asso. dean engring., 1971—. Cons. civil engring. Vice pres. Black Warrior council Boy Scouts Am., 1971—. Served to maj., USAF, 1952-53. Mem. Am. Soc. C.E., Am. Soc. Engring. Edn., Nat. Soc. Profl. Engrs., Am. Inst. Steel Constrn., Am. Concrete Inst., Internat. Assn. Bridge and Structural Engrs., Hwy. Research Bd. Contbr. tech. articles on structural engring. to profl. jours. Home: 181 Woodland Hills Tuscaloosa AL 35401

SEGUINE, VIRGINIA MARGERY, librarian; b. Chgo., Feb. 20, 1932; d. Melvin Manee and Frances (Waffle) Seguine; B.A., Bryan Coll., 1954; postgrad. U. Tenn., 1956-57; M.A., Western Mich. U., 1965. Instr., Tenn. State Sch. for Deaf, Knoxville, 1957-58, Ind. State Sch. for Deaf, Indpls., 1958-59, Pennfield Schs., Battle Creek, Mich., 1959-62, Appalachian Bible Inst., Bradley, W.Va., 1962-64; librarian Bryan Coll., Dayton, Tenn., 1964—. Soprano soloist local coll. prodns. Mem. Christian Librarians' Fellowship, A.L.A., Tenn. Library Assn., Christian Bus. and Profl. Women (com. chmn. 1959-62), Delta Kappa Gamma (chpt. pres. 1968—, state 1st v.p. 1971—). Presbyn. (ch. pianist 1964—, Sunday sch. tchr. 1964—). Address: Bryan Coll Dayton TN 37321

SEGURA, MICHAEL GERALD, mental health center adminstr.; b. Abbeville, La., Mar. 30, 1936; s. William A. and Doris (Gooch) S.; B.A., U. Southwestern La., 1958; M.S.W., La. State U., 1960; m. Loretta Guidroz, Nov. 28, 1957; children—Clement, Mark, John, Anne. Exec. dir. Terrebonne Guidance Center, Houma, La., 1960-63, regional coordinator Region VIII, 1963-67, regional mental health adminstr., 1967—; ordained permanent deacon Roman Catholic Ch., 1974. Cons. Lafourche-Terrebonne Council on Alcoholism, 1969—; chmn. Juvenile Detention Center Adv. com., 1969—; coordinator Regional Planning Council for Alcohol Abuse, 1972—. Recipient Profl. of the Year award La. Assn. Mental Health, 1969. Fellow La. Assn. Clin. Social Workers; mem. Acad. Certified Social Workers, Terrebonne Deanery Council, Regional Health Planning Council. Home: 310 Foster Av Houma LA 70360 Office: 500 Legion Av Houma LA 70360

SEGURA, PEARL MARY, librarian, educator; b. Lafayette, La., June 12, 1909; d. Joseph Sidney and Celestine (Gutierrez) Segura; B.A., U. Southwestern La., 1930, postgrad. summer 1932, 42-43, 46-48, 51-52; B.S. in L.S., La. State U., 1941; postgrad. summers, Tulane U., 1931, Columbia, 1939, U. Ill., 1948, U. Houston, 1954. Tchr., librarian Indian Bayou (La.) High Sch., 1930-31; tchr. Maurice (La.) High Sch., 1931-33, tchr., librarian, 1933-41; asst. circulation librarian Stephens Meml. Library U. Southwestern La., Lafayette, 1941-44, acting reference librarian, 1944-46, reference librarian, 1946-62, librarian Jefferson Caffery La. room Dupre Library, 1962—, asso. prof. library sci., 1953—. Mem. Am., Southwestern, La. library assns., Spl. Libraries Assn., Am. Assn. State and Local History, Assn. Coll. and Reference Libraries, Am. Assn. U. Women, Nat. Trust for Historic Preservation, La., Attakapas hist. assns., La. Geneal. and Hist. Soc., La. Folklore Soc., La. Tchrs. Assn., Met. Opera Guild. Lafayette Community Concerts Assn., Lafayette Little Theatre, Lafayette Art Assn., Am. Camellia Soc., La. State U., U. Southwestern La. alumni assns., D.A.R. (1st chpt. vice regent 1968-71, state chmn. U.S.A. bicentennial com. 1967-71, chpt. chmn. 1969—), U.D.C., Cath. Daus. Am., St. Ann's Guild, Am. Iris Soc., S.W. La. Poetry Soc., France Amerique de la Louisiane Acadienne (sec. 1964—), Phi Kappa Phi (pub. relations officer), Beta Phi Mu, Delta Kappa Gamma (pres. chpt. 1947-49), Kappa Kappa Iota (state handbook chmn. 1960-61, pres. Lambda conclave 1957-60). Democrat. Roman Catholic. Author: Acadians in Fact and Fiction: A Classified Bibiliography, 1955. Contbr. articles to profl. jours. Home: 140 S Magnolia St Lafayette LA 70501

SEIBELS, GEORGE R., mayor; b. Cal., July 15, 1913; s. George Goldthwaite and Aileen (Pettit) S.; B.S., U. Va.; m. Norma Graham, 1949; children—George Goldthwaite III, Laura. Councilman, Birmingham, Ala., 1963-67, mayor, 1967—. Served to lt. USNR, World War II. Mem. Birmingham Jr. C. of C. Office: City Hall Bldg Birmingham AL 35203

SEIBERT, SISTER MARY ANGELICE, educator; b. Louisville, Jan. 16, 1922; d. William Karl and Catharine A. (Schmidt) Seibert; B.S. summa cum laude, Ursuline Coll., 1947; M.S., Institutum Divi Thomae, 1950, Ph.D., 1952; Damon Runyon post doctoral fellow St. Louis U., 1953-54. Tchr. Cath. elementary schs., Louisville, 1942-47; instr. chemistry and biology Ursuline Coll., Louisville, 1950, chmn. div. natural scis., 1952-65, dir. coll. relations and devel., 1960-62, acting pres., 1964-65, pres., 1965-68; Fulbright-Hays vis. lectr. U. Coll., Galway, Ireland, 1968-69; vis. prof. biochemistry Smith Coll., 1969-70; prof. chemistry, chmn. div. allied med. scis. Jefferson Community Coll., Louisville, 1970—. Mem. Ky. Acad. Sci., Am. Chem. Soc., A.A.A.S., Internat. Soc. Edn. Health Scis., Assn. Schs. Allied Health Professions, Hastings Center Inst. Soc. Ethics and Life Sci. Sigma Xi. Address: 3105 Lexington Rd Louisville KY 40206

SEIDEMAN, WALTER ELMER, food processing co. exec.; b. West Bend, Wis., Jan. 21, 1933; s. Raymund F. and Clara S. (Gerner) S.; B.S. in Agr., U. Wis., 1959; M.S. in Food Sci., U. Mo., 1962, Ph.D., 1965; m. Cathleen A. Carnito, Sept. 7, 1958; children—Russell, Keith, Bonnie. Food technologist Wilson & Co., Chgo., 1965-71, mgr. research and tech., Oklahoma City, 1973—; asst. to mgr. research and tech. div. Wilson Sinclair Co., Chgo., 1971-72, div. mgr., 1972. Served with USMCR, 1951-54. Mem. Inst. Food Technologists, Poultry Sci. Assn., Sigma Xi. Home: 3116 Thornridge Rd Oklahoma City OK 73120 Office: Wilson & Co Inc 4545 N Lincoln Blvd Oklahoma City OK 73105

SEIFERT, DAVID WALTER, JR., dentist; b. Weldon, N.C., Oct. 9, 1919; s. David Walter and Florence Fairlamb (Rowe) S.; student N.C. State U., 1938; A.B., U. N.C., 1942; D.D.S., Emory U., 1945; m. Flora McDonald, Dec. 1, 1945; children—Flora Stewart (Mrs. Robert Turnage Stewart), Ann Stedman, Caroline Battle. Practice dentistry, Raleigh, N.C., 1947—; dir. Coca-Cola Bottling Works, Manchester, N.H., Coca-Cola Bottling Works of Dover, Del., Inc., Coca-Cola Bottling Works of Salem, N.H., Inc.; dir., sec. Coca-Cola Bottling Works of Henderson, N.C., 1970—; dental cons. N.C. Indsl. Com., 1970—; chmn. Local Bd. for Piloting, 1971; dental chief of staff Rex Hosp., Raleigh, 1958-60. Served with AUS, 1943-44, USNR, 1945-47. Mem. Raleigh Power Squadron, U.S. Power Squadron. Mem. N.C. (mem. ho. of dels. 1970-71), 4th Dist. (pres. 1971—), Raleigh (pres. 1956-57) dental socs., Kappa Alpha, Delta Sigma Delta. Democrat. Episcopalian. (pres. Layman League 1953-54). Clubs: Carolina Country, Sphynx, Raleigh Toastmasters (pres. 1950-51). Patentee Hypodermic syringe. Home: 3708 Shadybrook Dr Raleigh NC Office: 2016 Cameron St Raleigh NC 27605

SEIFERT, LEE ROE, banker; b. Mobile, Ala., Feb. 13, 1917; s. William Ross and Esther (McAuley) S.; student Spring Hill Coll., 1934-36; m. Dorothy Marie Goodman, July 16, 1942; children—Lee R., Gail (Mrs. Matthew J. Dick), William R. With First Nat. Bank of Mobile, 1937—, v.p., 1955-68, sr. v.p., 1968-74, exec. v.p., 1974—; dir. Modern Diversified Industries Inc., Valdosta, Ga. Mem. consulting com. on forestry research Auburn U., 1963—; mem. regional export council Dept. Commerce, 1963—, Nat. Export Expansion Council, 1969—. Bd. dirs. Mobile Port Traffic Bur. Served to 2d lt., AAC, 1942-45. Mem. Internat. Trade Club (pres.), Ala. World Trade Assn. (v.p.), Bankers Assn. Fgn. Trade (past sec.). Nat. Def. Transp. Assn., Mobile Traffic and Transp. Club, Miss. Valley World Trade Assn., Mobile Area C. of C. Episcopalian. Clubs: Internat. House (New Orleans); Propeller of U.S., Mobile Country, Touchdown, Bienville, Three Mystic Socs. (Mobile). Home: 606 E Chelsea Dr Mobile AL 36608 Office: 31 N Royal St PO Box 1467 Mobile AL 36621

SEIFERT, MARTIN WAYNE, herpetologist; b. Chgo., Apr. 26, 1945; s. Martin Markle and Ardis Irene (Kennedy) S.; student Tex. A. and I. Coll., 1964-66; B.S., Midwestern U., 1969, M.S., 1971; m. Christine Ann Hanneman, May 26, 1968; 1 dau., Debbye Lynn. Grad. tchr. Midwestern U., Wichita Falls, Tex., 1969-70; planetarium lectr. Wichita Falls Museum and Art Center, 1968-69; curator herpetology Dallas Museum Natural History, 1971—; prof. biology Eastfield Coll., Mesquite, Tex., 1971—. Mem. Herpetologists League, Brit. Herpetologists Soc., Tex. Acad. Scis., Tex. Herpetologists Soc. (editor 1972—), S.W. Assn. Naturalists, Am. Soc. Ichthyologists and Herpetologists, Soc. for Study of Reptiles and Amphibians. Home: 2335 Santa Cruz St Dallas TX 75227 Office: PO Box 26193 Fair Station Dallas TX 75226

SEIFERT, RAYMOND AUGUST, county ofcl.; b. Rockville, Conn., Dec. 15, 1913; s. August Christian and Matilda (Rostek) S.; B.S., Ga. Inst. Tech., 1939; postgrad. Army Command and Gen. Staff Coll., 1953-54; m. Virginia Truitt Fisher, Sept. 15, 1937; children—Carol (Mrs. Max Bradford Kilbourn), Raymond August, Matilda Ann. Engr., Tenn. Coal, Iron & R.R. Co., Birmingham, 1939-47; commd. 2d lt. C.E., U.S. Army, 1940, advanced through grades to col., 1961; engr., various units, locations, until 1965; engr. insp. gen. Office Chief Engrs., Washington, 1961-63; chief staff Army Tank Automotive Center, Detroit, 1963-65; ret., 1965; dir. pub. works City of Martland (Fla.), 1970-72; dir. utility control office Seminole County, Sanford, Fla., 1972—. Mem. New Eng. Resources Council, 1958-60; pres. Bear Gully Lake Civic Assn., 1963, 73; chmn. Water Adv. Bd. Seminole County, 1971; mem. Fire Standards Bd. Seminole County, Well Drillers Bd. Semiole County. Served with AUS, 1940-46. Decorated Legion of Merit. Registered profl. engr., Ala. Mem. Fla. Engring. Soc. (sr.), Am. Pub. Works Assn., Am. Water Works Assn., Nat. Soc. Profl. Engrs., Permanent Internat. Assn. Nav. Congresses (life), Nat. Sojourners. Baptist. Mason (32 deg.); mem. Order Eastern Star. Home: Route 1 Box 236 Bear Gully Lake Maitland FL 32751 Office: 418 Courthouse Semiole County Sanford FL 32771

SEIGEL, ROBERT KEARNEY, motor lodge exec.; b. Bayonne, N.J., Mar. 16, 1942; s. Max and Margaret (Kearney) S.; student Seton Hall U., 1960-62, Fairleigh Dickinson U., 1962-63; m. Carol Wotanowski, Apr. 20, 1962; children—Scot K., Douglas K., Rodd K. Vice pres., dir. Max Seigel Realty Corp., Clifton, N.J., 1964-68; pres., dir. Continental Inns of Am., Savannah, Ga., 1968—; dir. Savannah Assos., Inc., Hilltop Motor Inn, Inc., Heart Charleston, C.I.A. Motor Lodge, Inc., Interstate Restaurant Supply Corp., Rodd Motel Corp., Savannah Motel, Inc., Scott-Douglas Corp. Clubs: Greater Metropolitan Dinners, Chatham (Savannah); University (Jacksonville, Fla.); Savannah Inn and Country; Shee Farms (Charleston, S.C.); Palmetto Dunes Country (Hilton Head, S.C.); Turf Valley Country (Balt.); XIX (London, Eng.). Home: Route 2 Box 356 Savannah GA 31404 Office: 3710 Ogeechee Rd Savannah GA 31405

SEIGENTHALER, JOHN LAWRENCE, newspaper editor; b. Nashville, July 17, 1927; s. John and Mary (Brew) S.; student Peabody Coll.; Nieman fellow, Harvard; m. Dolores Watson, Jan. 3, 1955; 1 son, John Michael. Staff corr. Nashville Tennessean, 1949-60, editor, 1962—, also pub.; adminstrv. asst. to atty. gen. U.S., 1961; dir. Tennessean Newspapers, Inc. Mem. U.S. Adv. Commn. Information. Bd. dirs. So. Edn. Reporting Service. Mem. Am. Soc. Newspaper Editors, Sigma Delta Chi. Home: Vaughn Rd Nashville TN 37221 Office: 1100 Broadway St Nashville TN 37203

SEINSHELMER, J(OSEPH) F(ELLMAN), JR., ins. exec.; b. Galveston, Tex., Aug. 25, 1913; s. J. F. and Irma (Kraus) S.; grad. Mercersburg Acad., 1932; B.B.A., Tulane U., 1936; m. Jessie Lee Gould, July 19, 1938; children—Joseph Fellman III, Virginia Lee, Robert Louis. Salesman, Seinsheimer Ins. Agy., 1936-41; with Am. Indemnity Group, 1941—, successively agy. mgr., asst. sec., sec., v.p., 1941-51, pres. dir., 1951—; pres., dir. Am. Indemnity Co., Am. Fire & Indemnity Co., Am. Computing Co., Tex. Gen. Indemnity Co., Am. Finance Co., Galveston, U.S. Securities Corp., Am. Indemnity Financial Corp.; dir. Galveston Corp., Cotton Concentration Co., 2217 Bldg., Inc., Tex. Fiberglass Products, Inc., U.S. Nat. Bank, U.S. Nat. Bancshares, Inc. Clubs: Artillery, Galveston. Home: 4809 Woodrow St Galveston TX 77550 Office: 2115 Winnie St Galveston TX 77550

SEITER, EVE VICTORIA CUSHMAN (MRS. KENNETH SEITER), writer, broadcaster, lectr.; b. Richwood, O., June 17, 1906; d. David Clyde and Grace (Watson) Cushman; student Miami U., Oxford, O., 1924-25, Wooster Coll., 1947-57; m. Kenneth David Seiter, Sept. 5, 1925; children—Patricia Jeanne (Mrs. Harry Frederick Burkholder), Richard David. Lectr. lit., civic, religious groups, convs., bus. meetings, libraries broadcaster lit. and religious programs throughout U.S., 1940—, lay preacher; life ins. agt. Prudential of Am., 1944-46. Pub. relations chmn. United Ch. Women of Licking County and South Central Ohio Region, 1949-57; edl. Bible study leader Nat. Presbyn. Women's Convocation, 1958; pres. Zanesville Presbyterial of Presbyn. Ch., 1954-56; ofcl. del. Licking County Council Chs., 1954-58; local spiritual life chmn. Presbyn. Ch., 1963-65; chmn. bd. Knox Library, Westminister Presbyn. Ch., Steubenville, O. Mem. city council Wintersville O., 1962-66; Republican candidate for mayor, Wintersville, 1965. Recipient Appreciation award Kiwanis Clubs, Newark, O., Lorain, O., 1957, Steubenville, O., 1960. Mem. Nat. League Am. Pen Women (2 1st awards 1964, W.Va. sec. 1964-65, chpt. pres. 1970-72), Jekyll Island Arts Assn., Chi Omega. Presbyn. Club: Soroptimist (pres. 1958-59); Wierton Womans (W.Va.); Jekyll Island Garden (chaplain). Contbr. to speech jours., newspapers, mags. Address: 778 S Beachview Dr Jekyll Island GA 31520

SEKADLO, ROGER GEORGE, airport mgr.; b. Two Rivers, Wis., Dec. 14, 1924; s. George Frank and Linda Marie (Arneman) S.; student U. Wis., 1946-48; B.S., Purdue U., 1951; m. Rosalyn Louise Deau, Feb. 28, 1948; children—Steven, Penny, Nancy. Pilot, Purdue Aeros. Corp., West Lafayette, Ind., 1951; mgr. Municipal Airport Authority, Erie, Pa., 1951-57; airport dir. Milwaukee County, Wis., 1957-61; aviation dir. City Fort Worth, 1961-67; exec. dir., mgr. Greensboro-High Point Airport Authority, Greensboro, N.C., 1967—. Instr. airport mgmt. Guilford Tech. Inst., Jamestown, N.C., 1971-72. Served as pilot USAAF, 1943-46. Decorated Bronze Star. Mem. Airport Operators Council Internat. (dir. 1971-75), Am. Assn. Airport Execs. (dir. 1966-69). Lutheran. Elk, Rotarian. Home: 3107 Robinhood Dr Greensboro NC 27408 Office: Box 8113 Greensboro NC 27410

SELAWRY, OLEG SERGEIVITCH, physician, med. adminstr.; b. Freiburg, Germany, Feb. 21, 1924; s. Sergei and Antonina (Stasenkova) S.; E. Letterer Thesis (M.D.), U. Tübingen (Germany), 1948; m. Helena S.T. Pretorius, Apr. 1951; children—Mark, Lubov. Came to U.S., 1954, naturalized, 1961. Intern Children's Hosp., U. Bern (Switzerland), 1949; resident U. Munich (Germany), 1950; research fellow Tb Hosp., Heidelberg, Germany, 1953-55; resident fellow exptl. biology Roswell Park Meml. Inst., Buffalo, 1955-66, also sr. cancer research internist, 1958-66; chief cancer chemotherapy St. Jude's Research Hosp. and dept. medicine U. Tenn. at Memphis, 1966-68; chief med. oncology VA Hosp., Washington, 1968—; mem. operations com., decision network com. Nat. Lung Cancer Program, Nat. Cancer Inst., NIH, Bethesda, Md., 1968—, also coordinator Program, 1973—; instr. medicine State U. N.Y. at Buffalo, 1962-65, asst. research prof., 1965; asso. prof. Med. Units, U. Tenn., 1966-67, asso. prof. pediatrics, 1967; asso. prof. medicine Sch. Medicine, George Washington U., Washington, 1971—. Mem. merit rev. bd. oncology VA System, 1971—. Mem. Am. Assn. Cancer Research, Am. Fedn. Clin. Research, N.Y. Acad. Scis., Am. Soc. Clin. Oncology, Am. Soc. Hematology, Am. Fedn. Clin. Oncologics Socs., Interntat. Assn. Study Lung Cancer. Contbr. articles to profl. jours. Home: 9922 LaDuke Dr Kensington MD 20795 Office: 50 Irving St NW Washington DC 20422 also NIH Bldg 37 6B27 9000 Rockville Pike Bethesda MD 20014

SELBY, DONALD JOSEPH, educator; b. Kansas City, Mo., Feb. 7, 1915; s. Benjamin Wood and Evelyn May (Wharton) S.; A.B., William Jewell Coll., 1946; B.D., Andover Newton Theol. Sch., 1949; Ph.D., Boston U., 1954; m. Clarice Allene Beggs, June 10, 1939; children—Robert Wallace, Donald Lee. Ordained to ministry Congl. Ch., 1948; pastor, Pilgrim Congl. Ch., 1948-56; instr. Boston U. Sch. Theology, 1955-56; asso. prof. dept. religion Catawba Coll., Salisbury, N.C., 1956-61, prof., 1961—, chmn. dept., 1966—. Vis. prof. N.T., Hood Theol. Sem., 1957—. Mem. Soc. Bibl. Lit. and Exegesis, Am. Acad. Religion, Am. Schs. Oriental Research, Soc. for Antiquity and Christianity. Author: Toward the Understanding of St. Paul, 1962; Introduction to the New Testament, 1971. Home: 204 Maupin Av Salisbury NC 28144

SELBY, JOHN HORACE, surgeon; b. Springfield, Mass., Nov. 11, 1919; s. Howard Williams and Ethel (Wagg) S.; A.B., Dartmouth Coll., 1941; M.D., Boston U., 1944; postgrad. U. Pa., 1948; children (by previous marriage) John H., Susan, Sherrill, Lucinda; m. 2d, Carolyn Symes, Feb. 14, 1970. Intern Mary Hitchcock Meml. Hosp., Hanover, N.H., 1944-45; resident New Eng. Deaconess Hosp., 1945-46, Mass. Meml. Hosp., 1949-50, Boston City Hosp., 1950-51 (all Boston), practice medicine, specializing in thoracic surgery, Lubbock, Tex., 1952—; chief thoracic surgery Meth. Hosp., Lubbock; chief of staff St. Mary's Hosp., Lubbock; courtesy staff W. Tex. Hosp., Lubbock, Mercy Hosp., Slaton, Tex.; chief surgery Univ. Hosp.; asso. clin. prof. surgery Tex. Tech. Med. Sch.; trustee, med. dir. All Am. Security Life Ins. Co. Bd. dirs. Tex. Tb Assn., pres., 1967-68; bd. dirs. Lubbock Community Planning Council, 1954-56; chmn. adv. bd. Salvation Army, 1956-57; bd. dirs. Inst. for Internat. Research and Devel. Diplomate Am. Bd. Thoracic Surgery, Am. Bd. Surgery. Fellow A.C.S., Am. Coll. Chest Physicians, Internat. Coll. Surgeons; mem. So. Thoracic Surgery Assn., S.W. Surg. Conf., Am. Thoracic Soc., Tex. Trudeau Soc. (pres. 1959-60), Lubbock-Crosby County Med. Soc., Panhandle S-Plains Med. Soc., Tex. Med. Assn., A.M.A., Am. Cancer Soc. (dir. Tex. div.), S. Plains Heart Assn. (pres. 1957), Lubbock County Tb Assn. (pres. 1959-60). Home: Altura Towers 1617 27th St Lubbock TX 79405 Office: Med-Profl Bldg 3801 19th St Lubbock TX 79410

SELDEN, RAY LEONARD, lawyer; b. Sinclairville, N.Y., Apr. 2, 1894; s. John Harris and Lora (Blackney) S.; LL.B., Hamilton Coll., 1920, J.D., 1930; m. Jeannette Ridgway, Apr. 11, 1914 (dec. 1965); children—Lois (Mrs. Al Brown), John Harris; m. 2d, Rhoda Fay, Sept. 24, 1967. Admitted to Fla. bar, 1920, Ga. bar, 1930, Ind. bar, 1930, U.S. Supreme Ct. bar; practiced in Daytona Beach, Fla., 1920—; mem. firms Selden, Hodgen & Couchman, 1929-36, Selden, Blackney & Williams, Inc., Daytona Beach, Fla., 1945—; pres., atty. Double R Dixie Ranch, Williston, Fla., 1957—, v.p., gen. counsel Fla. Mut. Fire & Marine Ins. Co., 1930—, Fidelity & Surety Co. Fla., Inc., Daytona Beach, 1945—. Dir., v.p. Dick E. Hotchkin Co., Inc., Daytona Beach. Chmn., Fla. Safety Council, Tampa. Chmn., Fla. Congl. Democratic Exec. Com., 1932-40; v.p. Fla. Electoral Coll., 1944-45. Mem. Am., Volusia County bar assns., Fla. Bar (recipient 50-year plaque), Internat. Soc. Tax Consultants, Saddle Horse Assn., Selden Soc. Eng., Epsilon Delta Chi. Democrat. Episcopalian. Elk, Odd Fellow, Moose. Clubs: Optimist (sec. 1952, pres. 1953), Exchange (sec. 1941) (Daytona Beach), University. Home: 800 Main St Daytona Beach FL 32018 Office: Selden Bldg Daytona Beach FL 32018

SELF, GLENDON DANNA, indsl. engr.; b. Waveland, Ark., Jan. 1, 1938; s. Charlie William and Alma (Vinesette) S.; Asso. Sci., Ark. Tech., 1956; B.S., U. Ark., 1958, M.S., 1959; Ph.D., Okla. State U., 1963; m. Sharon Darlene Glenn, June 4, 1960. Statis. quality control engr. Sandia Corp., Albuquerque, 1959-63; project analyst Gen. Dynamics, Ft. Worth, 1963-65; asst. prof. Tex. A. and M. U., College Station, 1965-66, 66-68, asso. prof., 1968-69; research specialist Boeing Co., Renton, Wash., 1966; mem. tech. staff Center for Naval Analyses, Arlington, Va., 1968; mgr. operations research Electronic Data Systems, Dallas, 1969-71, v.p. Dallas, 1971—; adj. prof. math. Tex. Christian U., 1964-65. Cons. in field. Mem. Operations Research Soc. Am., Inst. Mgmt. Sci., Am. Statis. Assn., Am. Soc. for Engring. Edn., Sigma Xi, Tau Beta Pi, Alpha Pi Mu. Baptist. Contbr. articles to profl. jours. Home: 6002 Village Glen Dr Dallas TX 75206 Office: 7171 Forrest Lane Dallas TX 75230

SELF, MARGARET CABELL, author; b. Cin., Feb. 12, 1902; d. Hartwell and Margaret Polk (Logan) Cabell; student Chatham Hall, 1915-17, N.Y. Sch. Applied Design for Women, 1917-19; m. Sydney Baldwin Self, June 11, 1921; children—Sydney Baldwin, Shirley (Mrs. John O. Brotherhood Jr.), Hartwell C., Virginia (Mrs. Harris Bucklin). Portrait artist, 1923-38; author specialty, tech., children's and travel books related to horses, also lectr. relating to subjects; cons. Ecole Equiestre do San Miguel; musician mem. Chamber Orch. of San Miguel. Founder, commandant New Canaan Mounted Troop, Jr. Cavalry Am. Mem. No Friends of Music, Author: Teaching the Young to Ride, 1935; Horses, Their Selection, Care and Handling, 1943; Those Smith Kids, 1945; The Horseman's Encyclopedia, 1945; Ponies on Parade, 1945; Chitter Chat Stories, 1946; A Treasury of Horse Stories, 1946; Riding Simplified, 1948; Horseman's Companion, 1949; Horsemastership, 1953; Irish Adventure, 1954; Pictorial History of the Royal Canadian Mounted Police, 1958; The American Horse Show, 1958; Riding and Hunting Simplified, 1959; Jumping Simplified, 1959; Riding with Mariles, 1960; The How and Why of Horses, 1961; Horses of the World, 1961; Complete Book of Horses and Ponies; Riding Step by Step; The Happy Year; Horses of Today; The Shaggy Little Burro of San Miguel, 1965; The Horseman's Almanac, 1966; Henrietta, 1966; At the Horseshow with Margaret

Cabell Self, 1966; In Ireland with Margaret Cabell Self, 1967; The Morgan Horse in Pictures, 1967; Come Away, 1968; The Quarter Horse in Pictures, 1969; The Young Rider and His First Pony, 1969; Sky Rocket, the Story of a Little Bay Horse, 1970; How to buy the right Horse, 1971; The Hunter in Pictures, 1972. Home: Block Island RI also San Miguel de Allende GTO Mexico

SELF, MELVIN, coll. pres.; b. Bristow, Okla., Nov. 7, 1915; s. John Henry and Dollie (Hill) S.; B.S., Central State Coll., Edmond, Okla., 1938; M.Ed., Phillips U., 1943; Ed.D., Okla. State U., 1953; m. Inez Faye McKinney, Feb. 25, 1939; children—Sondra Jo (Mrs. Jon Plachy), Melva Lee (Mrs. Robert Jones). Tchr. pub. schs., Okla., 1938-60, supt. schs., Deer Creek, 1938-40, Kressdin, 1940-42, Grove, 1946-49, Guthrie, 1949-53, Perry, 1953-60; chmn. edn. dept., dir. tchr. edn. E. Central State Coll., Ada, Okla., 1960-65; pres. Connors State Coll., Warner, 1965—. Served as lt. (j.g.) USNR, 1944-46. Mem. C. of C. Rotarian, Kiwanian, Mason, Odd Fellow. Home and office: Connors State Coll Warner OK 74469

SELIGMAN, MOISE BENJAMIN, JR., paper co. exec.; b. Jacksonville, Tenn., Oct. 8, 1918; s. Moise B. and Lucille (Flynn) S.; B.A., Ouachita Bapt. U., 1941; postgrad. Army Command and Gen. Staff Coll., 1943; m. Mary Elizabeth Strong, Apr. 5, 1942; children—Susan (Mrs. Daniel Fuller), Moise Benjamin III, Mary Elizabeth. Pres., Ark. Paper Co., Little Rock, 1965—; v.p. Consol. Marketing Inc., Shreveport, La., 1969—, also dir.; v.p. Alco-Columbia Paper Co., New Orleans, 1967—, Elms Realty Co., IBI Leasing, Inc., Pappagallo of Little Rock, Inc. mem. adv. council Nekoosa-Edwards Paper Co., 1968—. Mem. Little Rock Tollway Authority, 1968—. Bd. dirs. Met. YMCA, Little Rock. Served to lt. col., AUS, 1941-45; maj. gen. Res. Mem. Res. Officers Assn. (Ark. pres. 1953), Little Rock C. of C. (dir. 1963-70, sec.-treas. 1969). Baptist. Kiwanian (local pres. 1967). Club: Pleasant Valley Country. Home: 1900 Beechwood Av Little Rock AR 72207 Office: 2000 E Roosevelt Rd Little Rock AR 72206

SELIMEYER, RALPH LOUIS, educator; b. Osawatomie, Kan., Sept. 23, 1924; s. Albert George and Ethel Evelyn (Garretts) S.; student Baker U., 1946-48; B.J., U. Mo. at Columbia, 1949; M.A. in Ednl. Adminstrn., U. Mo. at Kansas City, 1949; m. Mildred Lucille Dahlstrom, Sept. 2, 1949; children—Melissa (Mrs. Don Glenn McCoy), Debra, Sheri, Alison. Reporter Independence (Kan.) Daily Reporter, 1952; reporter, photographer, Kansas City (Mo.) Daily Drovers Telegram, 1953-54; sales mgr. Hot Coffee Caterers, Inc., Kansas City, Mo., 1954-57; editor Baldwin (Kan.) Ledger, 1957-60; prof., dir. journalism div. mass communications dept. Tex. Tech., U., Lubbock, 1960—. Dist. officer Boy Scouts Am. Bd. dirs. Caprock council Girl Scouts U.S. Served with USNR, 1942-46, 50-52. Mem. Nat. Profl. Advt. Soc. (nat. pres. 1970-73), Sigma Delta Chi (pres. 1967—). Mason. Author: Professional Approach to Journalistic Photography, 1967, Guide-Book for Preparing and Student Publications, 1973. Editor Photolith Mag., 1973—, Linage Mag., 1970—. Home: 2326 55th St Lubbock TX 79412

SELL, CHARLES GORDON RENNICK, cardiologist; b. India, July 9, 1917; s. Charles Edward and Olive Amy (Nicol) S.; B.A., St. Catharines Coll., Cambridge, 1938; M.B. B.Ch., Kings Coll. Hosp. Med. Sch., 1941; m. Sarah Hamilton, June 2, 1952; children—Charles G., Clive H. Came to U.S., 1949, naturalized, 1955. Intern Kings Coll. Hosp., London, Eng., 1940-41; resident Royal Liverpool (Eng.) Children's Hosp., 1946-49; practice medicine, specializing in cardiology, Nashville, 1954—; fellow Johns Hopkins Hosp., 1949-51; mem. faculty La. State U. Sch. Medicine, 1952-53, Vanderbilt Sch. Medicine, 1954-60; cons. cardiologist VA, Nashville, 1970—. Mem. adv. com. Mended Heart, Inc., 1971—. Served to lt. col. Indian Med. Service, 1941-45. Fulbright travelling fellow, 1949. Fellow Am. Acad. Pediatrics, Am. Coll. Cardiology, Am. Coll Chest Physicians; mem. Royal Coll. Physicians (London), Middle Tenn. Heart Assn. (dir.). Democrat. Episcopalian. Club: Harbor Island Yacht. Home: 3804 Woodlawn Dr Nashville TN 37215 Office: 2501 Hillsboro Rd Nashville TN 37212

SELLARS, HAROLD LEROY, mathematician, petroleum co. exec.; b. Opp, Ala., Mar. 21, 1935; s. Harold Marvin and Charlsie Olivia (Collier) S.; B.S. in Math., U. Ala., 1957, M.A. in Math., 1958; m. Dorothy Frances Wren, Mar. 14, 1959; children—Richard Marvin, Sue Frances, Keith Alan. Physicist Shell Oil Co., Houston, 1958-62, group leader, Houston, 1962-69; mgr. DCS, Houston, 1969-70; mgr. Biles & Assos., Houston, v.p., sec., treas., 1970—. Mem. Am. Inst. Chem. Engrs., Instrument Soc. Am. Home: 2905 Peach St Pasadena TX 77502 Office: Box 26125 Houston TX 77032

SELLARS, ROBERT FREDERICK, elec. engr.; b. Mpls., June 13, 1910; s. Ernest Francis and Drusilla (Johnson) S.; B.S. in Elec. Engring., U.S. Naval Acad., 1934; grad. Submarine Sch., 1939, Guided Missile Sch., 1950, Naval War Coll., 1957; m. Mary Agnes Tongue, June 20, 1936; children—Robert, Marianne (Mrs. Douglas Healea). Enlisted in USN, 1928, commd. ensign, 1934, advanced through grades to capt., 1953; comdr. Naval Ordnance Test Sta., China Lake, Cal., 1955; comdr. officer USS Norton Sound, 1956; dir. naval tests, Cape Canaveral, Fla., 1958; comdr. Submarine Ron 1, 1960; comdr. Naval Weapons Lab., Dahlgren, Va., 1961-64; ret., 1964; staff engr. Martin Marietta Corp., Orlando, Fla., 1964—. Decorated Silver Star (2), Air Force. Recipient appreciation plaque 42 years service Boy Scouts Am., 1964. Asso. fellow Am. Inst. Aero. and Astronautics; mem. Am. Ordnance Assn., I.E.E.E. (sr.), Nav. Inst. Republican. Presbyn. Mason (Shriner), Lion. Club: Rio Pinar Country (Orlando). Home: 2509 Caribbean Ct Orlando FL 32805 Office: Sand Lake Rd Orlando FL 32805

SELLERS, GENE MARION HERRICK (MRS. MATTHEW BACON SELLERS), civic worker; b. Salt Lake City, Nov. 10, 1922; d. Harold Lewis and Marion (Wheelon) Herrick; student Traphagen Sch. Fashion, 1941-42; m. Matthew Bacon Sellers, June 1, 1946; children—Wendy (Mrs. Henry Medford Howell), Tracy. Bd. mem. Friends of Fort Lauderdale (Fla.) Mus. Arts, 1969. Committeewoman Broward County Republican Exec. Com., 1967-73. Mem. Nat. Soc. Daus. Utah Pioneers. Club: Coral Ridge Yacht (Ft. Lauderdale). Home: 3030 NE 40th Ct Fort Lauderdale FL 33308

SELLERS, JACK LEROY, telephone co. exec.; b. Blackwell, Okla., Feb. 18, 1933; s. Charley and Lela Jewell (Wood) S.; B.S., Okla. State U., 1956; m. Maureen Vere Matthews, June 2, 1956; children—Kevin Lamont, Dana Matthew, Michael Kent, Melinda Michelle. Instr. electronics Okla. State U., 1956; with Southwestern Bell Telephone Co., 1956—, staff asst., Oklahoma City, 1956, 1958-59, wire chief, Henryetta, Okla., 1959, plant foreman, Ponca City, Okla., 1960, wire chief, Enid, Okla., 1961-62, dist. engr., Bartlesville, Okla., 1962-63, supervising repair foreman, Tulsa, 1963-64, dist. plant supt., Bartlesville, Okla., 1965-68, personnel devel. supr., Oklahoma City, 1969, mgmt. devel. supr., Oklahoma City, 1970-72, dist. plant mgr., Tulsa, 1973—. Pack chmn. Cub Scouts Am., Bartlesville, 1968; active Boy Scouts Am., 1970—; dir., sec. Bartlesville Fed. Little League Baseball, 1966-68. Served to 1st lt. Signal Corps, AUS, 1956-58. Mem. Bartlesville Engring. Club (dir. 1965-68), Okla. Soc. Profl. Engrs. (chpt. com. chmn. 1965-68), Beta Theta Pi. Mem. Disciples of Christ (deacon 1965-68, elder 1971-72). Toastmaster (v.p. 1966-67). Home: 6781 S 69th East Av Tulsa OK 74133 Office: 8740 E 11th St Tulsa OK 74112

SELLERS, MATTHEW BACON, land developer; b. N.Y.C., Nov. 13, 1919; s. Matthew Bacon and Ethel (Clark) S.; student Lehigh U., 1937-39; B.S., Franklin and Marshall Coll., 1941; m. Gene Herrick, June 1, 1946; children—Wendy (Mrs. H. Medford Howell), Tracy. Dist. and br. mgr. Snow Crop Frozen Foods, Cin., 1946-52; v.p., gen. mgr. Urban Laundry Co., Balt., 1952-55; v.p., sec. Filterite Corp., Balt., 1955-60; land developer Broward and Palm Beach Counties, Fla., 1960—. Pres., Taxpayers League of Broward County, 1968-70; mem. Community Services and Facilities Bd., Ft. Lauderdale, Fla., 1970. Treas., Republican Exec. Com., 1966-67. Bd. dirs. Broward County Heart Assn., 1969-70, Fla. Heart Assn., 1970. Served to comdr. USNR, 1941-45. Mem. Fla. Soc. S.A.R. (pres.), Soc. of Cincinnati, S.R., Soc. Colonial Wars, Washington Family Descs., Navy League U.S., Hon. Order Ky. Cols., Mil. Order of the Crusades, Ams. of Royal Descent, others, Phi Sigma Kappa. Club: Coral Ridge Yacht. Home: 3030 NE 40th Ct Fort Lauderdale FL 33308

SELLS, HARRY GEORGE, lawyer; b. Bellaire, O., Sept. 25, 1922; s. Harold W. and Leeta (Spengler) S.; student Wheeling Coll. Commerce, 1941-42; A.B., U. Pitts., 1949; J.D., George Washington U., 1953; m. Dorothy M. Sells, Sept. 6, 1946; children—Deborah M., David M. (dec.). Admitted to D.C. bar, 1954; law clk. Dow, Lohnes & Albertson, Washington, 1950-54, asso., then jr. partner, 1954-58, partner, 1958-63; partner Sells & Gregory, Counsellors at Law, Washington, 1964—. Officer, dir. Prince William Broadcasting Corp., Manassas, Va., 1957—, Stalcup Furniture Co., Falls Church, Va., 1959—, WQVA, Inc., Quantico, Va., 1961—, WISZ, Inc., Glen Burnie, Md., 1964—; trustee Boston Celtics basketball team; owner Debbie S. Stables. Justice of peace Dranesville Magisterial Dist., Fairfax, Va., 1956-60. Served with AUS, 1942-45, USAAF, 1945-47. Mem. Va. State, D.C. bars, Am., D.C., Fed. Communications bar assns., Falls Church C. of C., Nat., Va., Md., Ohio assns. broadcasters, Chesterbrook Citizens Assn. (past pres.), Delta Theta Phi. Methodist (ofcl. bd. 1954—, trustee). Home: 1453 Laburnum St McLean VA 22101 Office: 2000 L St NW Washington DC 20036

SELLS, JAMES WILLIAM, ret. clergyman; b. Atchison, Kan., June 27, 1897; s. James LeGrande and Clara (Hull) S.; A.B., Millsaps Coll., 1929; LL.D., LaGrange Coll., 1955; D.D., Emory U., 1964; m. Vera Maude Britt, Jan. 13, 1921; 1 dau., Shirley Jeanne (Mrs. J. Robert Adams) (dec.). Ordained to ministry Methodist Ch., 1916; ordained deacon Miss. Ann. Conf., 1927, elder, 1929; supply pastor Taylorsville (Miss.) Meth Ch., 1920-21, Georgetown (Miss.) Meth. Ch., 1921-23; supply pastor Meth. Ch., Pascagoula, Miss., 1925, pastor, 1925-29; pastor Meth. chs., Summit, Miss., 1929-30, Ocean Springs, Miss., 1930-32, Forest, Miss., 1932-36, Hattiesburg, Miss., 1936-40, Crystal Springs, Miss., 1940-44; field sec. Whitworth-Millsaps Coll., 1930; exec. sec. Seashore Meth. Assembly, Biloxi, Miss., 1930-32; producer Meth. series The Protestant Hour, Atlanta, 1945-72, Southeastern Jurisdictional Council, 1945-72; dir. Joint Radio Com., 1945-72; pres. Spiritual Life Publishers, Inc., Atlanta, 1966—, Communicative Arts, Inc., 1970—; rural ch. editor Progressive Farmer, 1944-67, exec. dir. Inst. Communicative Arts, Inc., 1960-69, pres., 1969—; vis. prof. Candler Sch. Theol., Emory U., 1964. Bd. dirs. Protestant Radio and Tv Center, Atlanta, Hinton Rural Life Center, Hayesville, N.C., Paine Coll., Augusta, Ga.; pres. Spiritual Life Research Found. Served with USN, 1917-19. Recipient Rural Minister of the Year award, 1965. Mem. Nat. Meth. Rural Life Conf. (sec. 1947), Miss. Rural Life Council (sec. 1944-45). Author: How God Can Change Your Life; Effective Communication—the Person to Person Process; Partners with the Living Lord, 1974. Home: 457 Burlington Rd NE Atlanta GA 30307 Office: 1380 Oxford Rd NE Atlanta GA 30307

SELOVER, JOHN CHARLES, r.r. exec.; b. Pueblo, Colo., Feb. 13, 1911; s. Alpheus Olin and Mary (Robertson) S.; B.A., U. Kan., 1932; m. Mary Elizabeth Livingston, Nov. 4, 1939; children—Paul Nicholas, Stephanie Lynne (Mrs. Maurice Wilson), Timothy Lee, Andrea Marie (Mrs. Darrel Aldrich), Robin Livingston. With M.P. R.R., 1936—, asst. to v.p. traffic, St. Louis, 1962-63, traffic mgr. Western region, Kansas City, Mo., 1963-68, v.p. Tex. dist., Dallas, 1968—; pres., dir. Mchts. Cold Storage Co., Eagle Ford Land & Indsl. Co.; dir. Abilene & So. Ry., Ft. Worth Belt Ry. Co., Gt. S.W. R.R., Inc., Tex.-N.M. Ry. Co., Weatherford-Mineral Wells & Northwestern Ry. Mem. Transp. Club Dallas. Democrat. Presbyn. Clubs: Dallas City, Dallas Athletic. Home: 5533 Meletio Lane Dallas TX 75230 Office: 505 N Industrial Blvd Dallas TX 75207

SELPH, WILLIAM FRANKLIN, JR., lawyer; b. Laurel, Miss., May 23, 1929; s. William Franklin and Oris (Clegg) S.; B.B.A., U. Miss., 1950, J.D., 1954; m. Ella N. White, Dec. 15, 1950; children—Deborah, William Franklin III. Admitted to Miss. bar, 1954, U.S. Supreme Ct.; with land div. Shell Oil Co., New Orleans and Baton Rouge, 1954-57; mgr. adminstrv. div., The Atlantic Refining Co. (U.S., Can.), Dallas, 1957-62; practiced in Jackson 1962—. Hon. col. Gov.'s staff, Paul B. Johnson, 1964-68, John Bell Williams, 1968-72. Served to capt. Inf., AUS, 1950-52; ETO. Mem. Am., Miss., Hinds County bar assns., Am. Judicature Soc., Jackson C. of C., Am. Assn. Petroleum Landmen, Homebuilders Assn., Sons Confederate Vets., V.F.W., Phi Delta Phi, Omicron Delta Kappa, Pi Kappa Alpha. Episcopalian. Home: 5420 Runnymede Rd Jackson MS 39211 Office: Capitol Towers PO Box 1567 Jackson MS 39205

SEMMER, JOHN RICHARD, physician; b. Nanticoke, Pa., Nov. 7, 1943; s. Frederick Lewis and Betty Romaine (Thomas) S.; B.A., U. of South, 1965; M.D., U. Tenn., 1968; m. Glenna Butler McMahan, Aug. 20, 1966. Intern U. Tenn. Meml. Hosp., Knoxville, 1969-70, resident obstetrics and gynecology, 1970-73; commd. 1st lt. USAF, 1969, advanced to maj., 1973; chief obstetrics and gynecology, Base Hosp., Blytheville AFB, Ark., 1973—. Fellow Am. Coll. Obstetrics and Gynecology (jr.); mem. U. Tenn. Alumni Club, Beta Theta Pi. Methodist. Home: 1608 A South Pine St Blytheville AFB AR 72315 Office: Base Hospital Blytheville AFB AR 72315

SEMTNER, ROY HERMAN, lawyer; b. Oklahoma City, Apr. 13, 1924; s. Otto William and Jennie Bob (Fullbright) S.; A.B., St. Benedicts Coll., 1946; J.D., U. Okla., 1948; m. Patricia Ann Schooling, Dec. 27, 1946; children—Karl Bernard, Christopher Benedict, Nicholas Otto, Roy Herman, Thomas Russell. Admitted to Okla. bar, 1948; pvt. practice law, Oklahoma City, 1948—; asst. county atty., Oklahoma County, 1949-53; municipal judge, Oklahoma City, 1956-58, asst. municipal counselor, 1958-61, municipal counselor, 1961-73. Trustee Oklahoma City Municipal Improvement Authority, 1961-73; bd. dirs. Okla. Safety Council, Municipal Studies Center, S.W. Legal Found. Mem. Okla. (mem. com. legal internship 1968—), Am., (chmn. council local govt. 1973, editor Newsletter 1968-69, adv. bd. to editor The Urban Lawyer 1969—), Oklahoma County (dir. 1968-71) bar assns., Bar ICC, Cath. Lawyers Soc. (v.p. 1960), Oklahoma City Soc. Title Attys. (pres. 1971), Oklahoma City Title Attys. Assn. (pres. 1972), Attys. Title Security Orgn. (trustee 1973—), Okla. Assn. County Attys. (pres. 1952), Okla. Assn. Municipal Attys. (pres. 1963-64), Nat. Inst. Municipal Law Officers (regional v.p. 1966-73, state chmn. 1965-66, chmn. annexation com. 1966-73), Oklahoma City (pres. 1960, dir. 1961), Nat. (dir. 1960) alumni St. Benedicts Coll., Oklahoma Diocesan Confraternity Christian Doctrine (v.p. 1959, pres., dir. 1960), C. of C., Phi Delta Phi. Roman Catholic. K.C. (4 deg., grand knight 1953-55, state sec. 1953-59; state adv. 1959-61, state dep. 1961-63), Lion. Clubs: Gibbons Dinner (pres. 1957), Serra (vice pres. 1959) (Oklahoma City). Home: 324 NW 41st St Oklahoma City OK 73118 Office: 1108 Colcord Bldg Oklahoma City OK 73102

SEN, PRANAB KUMAR, statistician, educator; b. Calcutta, India, Nov. 7, 1937; s. Nagendra Bhusan and Kalyani (Roy) S.; B.S., Calcutta U., India, 1955, M.S., 1957, Ph.D., 1962; m. Gauri Dasgupta, Aug. 3, 1963; children—Devadutta, Aniruddha. Came to U.S., 1964, naturalized, 1968. Lectr. Calcutta U., 1961-64; vis. asst. prof. U. Cal., Berkeley, 1964-65; prof. biostatistics U. N.C., Chapel Hill, 1965—. Recipient Calcutta U. Gold medal, 1957, S.S. Bese Gold medal, 1955. Fellow Inst. Math. Statistics, Am. Statis. Assn. (editorial bd. jour. 1973—). Author (with M.L. Puri) Nonparametric Methods in Multivariate Analysis, 1971. Editorial bd. Jour. Multivariate Analysis, 1971—, Communications in Statistics, 1972—. Contbr. articles on statistics and probability to sci. jours. Home: 512 Colony Woods Dr Chapel Hill NC 27514

SENA, DEAN RICHARD, broker, realtor; b. Rahway, N.J., June 15, 1945; s. Dominic Richard and Dorothy (Parsons) S.; student Miami Dade Jr. Coll., 1964-66; student U. Miami (Fla.), 1966-68; m. Cheryl Joyce Barfield, June 9, 1973. Prin. D.R. Sena, Miami, 1969-73; owner Tropical Printing Co., South Miami, Fla., 1967-69; owner Sena Printing, Miami, 1966—; pres. Sena Enterprises and World Bus. Brokers, Inc., So. Miami, 1969—; real estate salesman Marple Realty, Miami, 1972—. Adviser, cons. social activities Homestead Manor, 1963—. Mem. Am. Marketing Assn., Civitan Club. Club: Coral Gables (Fla.) Country. Inventor navigational plotters and dispensing equipment. Home: 6201 Riviera Dr Coral Gables FL 33143 Office: 8087 S Dixie Hwy 4B South Miami FL 33143

SENKUS, MURRAY, tobacco co. exec., chemist; b. Saskatoon, Sask., Can., Aug. 31, 1914; s. Nicholas and Anne (Waligurski) S.; came to U.S., 1936, naturalized, 1943; student Nutana Collegiate Inst., Sask., 1928-32; B.S. in Chemistry, U. Sask., 1934, M.S., 1936; Ph.D., U. Chgo., 1938; m. Emily Kulcheski, Dec. 31, 1938; children—Neal J., William M., Joanne (Mrs. James Deary), David P. Chemist Commrl. Solvents Corp., Terre Haute, Ind., 1938-46, group leader, 1946-50; dir. research and devel. Daubert Chem. Co., Chgo., 1950-51; dir. chem. research R.J. Reynolds Tobacco Co., Winston-Salem, N.C., 1951-60, asst. dir. research, 1960-64, dir. research, 1964—. Instr. chemistry North Park Coll., Chgo., 1936-38. Mem. N.C. Bd. Sci. and Tech., 1972—. Served as sgt. maj., Canadian Officers Tng. Corps, 1934-36. Mem. A.A.A.S., Am. Chem. Soc., N.Y. Acad. Scis. Kiwanian. Club: Forsyth Country. Contbr. articles on chemistry to sci. jours. Patentee in field. Home: 2516 Country Club Rd Winston-Salem NC 27104 Office: RJ Reynolds Tobacco Co Winston-Salem NC 27102

SENNING, CHARLES EUGENE, mortgage banker; b. Spur, Tex., July 28, 1922; s. Clem Alifare and Adelaide (Finch) S.; B.S., Tex. Tech U., 1944, M.S., 1945; postgrad. Grad. Sch. Banking, So. Meth. U., 1968-70; children—Charles Bain, Thomas Mark, Michael Jan. Co-owner Charles Lee Co., Austin, Tex., 1948-52; co-owner Compere & Senning, Abilene, Tex., 1953-62; mgr. United Improvement & Investing Corp., N.Y.C. and Houston, 1962-65; v.p., mgr. real estate dir. Tex. Commerce Bank, Houston, 1966-72; exec. v.p. Holland Mortgage & Investment Corp., Houston, 1972—. Chmn. Abilene Tax Equalization Bd., 1961. Mem. Soc. Real Estate Appraisers (dir. Houston chpt. 1970-72, pres. West Tex. chpt. 1962-63), Houston C. of C., Soc. Master Brokers Tex. (past pres.), Nat. Assn. Mortgage Bankers. Episcopalian. Mason. Author: Houston Industrial Development: A Pattern for the Future, 1970. Home: s2501 Tanglewide Houston TX 77042 Office: 2701 Kirby Dr Houston TX 77006

SENSING, WILBUR CARSON, JR., steel co. exec.; b. Nashville, July 23, 1929; s.Wilbur Carson and Katherine Lee (Mayo) S.; B.S., Vanderbilt U. Sch. Engring., 1951; m. Lucy Ann Tritschler, Dec. 10, 1960; children—Lillian Lee, Lucy Ann, Wilbur Carson, Benjamin McCreary. Engr. Wilson, Weesner & Wilkinson Co., Nashville, 1951-52, chief engr., 1953-63, sales mgr., 1963-64, exec. v.p. Enco Materials, Inc. div., Nashville, 1964-67, pres., 1967—. Registered profl. engr., Tenn. Mem. Am. Soc. C.E., Tenn. Soc. Profl. Engrs., Sales and Marketing Execs.-Knoxville (dir. 1972, pres. 1973), C. of C. Mem. Christian Ch. (deacon 1971—). Clubs: Nashville City, Knoxville Racquet. Home: 924 Wingate Rd Knoxville TN 37919 Office: 4615 Coster Rd Knoxville TN 37912

SENTER, WILLIAM DONALD, ins., real estate exec.; b. Aspermont, Tex., May 11, 1930; s. Earl E. and Elizabeth (Jordan) S.; B.B.A., Tex. Tech. Coll., 1951; grad. Realtors Inst.; m. Lila Ellexson, May 27, 1950; children—Bill Scott, Steven Earl, Sydney Ann. Salesman South Plains Drug, Inc., Lubbock and Midland, Tex., 1951-53; area mgr. A. H. Robins Co., Midland, 1953-56; partner Wicker-Senter Ins. & Real Estate, Abilene, 1956-62; owner Senter & Senter, Ins. and Real Estate, 1962—; pres. Abilene Leasing Corp., Wicsen, Inc., W.E.B., Inc.; treas. Tom Sports Co.; v.p. Chaparral Homes, Inc.; gen. partner Shoji, Ltd. Mem. gov.'s legislative study com. on multiple use and pollution of all waters in Tex., 1965-67. Named Outstanding Young Man of Abilene, 1962, Boss of Year, 1972. Mem. Assn. Ins. Agts., Abilene Assn. Ins. Agts. (past pres.), Abilene Bd. Realtors (past pres.), Nat. Inst. Real Estate Brokers, Abilene C. of C. Democrat. Mem. Christian Ch. Mason (32 deg., Shriner, K.T.). Clubs: Abilene Country, Exchange, Rotary (Abilene, Tex.). Home: 140 Hedges Abilene TX 79605 Office: 2901 S 1st St Abilene TX 79605

SEOANE, RHODA LOW, artist, author; b. Bklyn.; d. William Gilman and Rhoda (Howe) Low; grad. Chapin Sch., N.Y.C., 1923; m. Consuelo Andrew Seoane, Feb. 12, 1952. Artist; works exhibited Argent Gallery, N.Y.C., 1946—, Lynn Kottler Gallery, N.Y.C., 1967, Arts Club Washington, 1969—. Mem. Colonial Dames Am. Club: York (N.Y.C.) Author: The Whole Armor, 1965; Uttermost East and The Longest War, 1969. Home: Topton NC 28781

SERANT, JOYCE IDELL BIRKELBACH, ins. co. exec.; b. Brenham, Tex.; d. Harry A. and Ruby (Nagel) Birkelbach; student Southwestern U., 1946-47, U. Houston, 1947-48; B.A., U. Tex., 1950; m. William Boris Serant, Dec. 5, 1953 (div. Mar. 1958); 1 son, Michael W. Sec.-treas., dir. Old Nat. Ins. Co., 1950-62; office mgr. Gulf Coast Home Builders, Inc., 1962-64; v.p., sec., dir. Lamar Livestock Ins. Co., 1964-66; v.p., sec., dir. San Jacinto Life Ins. Co., 1966—; dir. Tex. Pet Cemeteries, Inc., So. States Investment Corp. (all Houston). Mem. Alpha Delta Pi. Home: 2051 Winrock St Houston TX 77027 Office: PO Box 66196 Houston TX 77006

SERAPIGLIA, LOUIS ALFRED, JR., trucking co. exec.; b. Louisville, July 30, 1946; s. Louis Alfred and Ruby Emma (Yaeger) S.; B.E.E., U. Louisville, 1969; m. Mary Catherine Jenne, June 6, 1970. Electronics engr. Naval Ordnance Sta., Louisville, 1967-69, 69-71; v.p. C&L Trucking Co., Inc., Louisville, 1971—, also pres., mgr. C&L Services Industries, Louisville. Ky. Col. Mem. I.E.E.E. Democrat. Roman Catholic. Research and design in laser and applications. Home: 2212 Mammoth Way Louisville KY 40299 Office: 733 Grade Lane Louisville KY 40213

SERRANO, ALBERTO CARLOS, physician, educator; b. Buenos Aires, Argentina, Apr. 7, 1931 (came to U.S. 1957, naturalized 1962); s. Alberto P. and Regina (Robredo) S.; B.A., Colegio Mariano Mereno, 1948; M.D., U. Buenos Aires, 1956; m. Maria Nidya Pages, June 15, 1957; children—Marcos Alberto, Henry John, Claudia Ingrid, Christopher William. Resident psychiatry U. Tex. Med. Br., Galveston, 1957-60, resident child psychiatry, 1962-64, research psychiatrist, 1959-62, asst. prof. div. child psychiatry, 1964-66; dir. Community Guidance Center, Bexar County, Tex., 1966—; clin. prof. U. Tex. Med. Sch., San Antonio, 1973—, dir. child psychiatry, 1969—. Served with Argentine Army, 1954. Diplomate in psychiatry and child psychiatry Am. Bd. Psychiatry and Neurology. Fellow Am. Acad. Child Psychiatry, Am. Group Psychotherapy Assn. (dir. 1973-76); mem. A.M.A., Am. Psychiat. Assn., Southwestern (pres. 1969-71) Group Psychotherapy Soc., Soc. Adolescent Psychiatry, Tex. Child Psychiatry Soc. (soc.-treas. 1969-70), Author: (with R. MacGregor et al) Multiple Impact Therapy with Families, 1964. Home: 927 Fabulous St San Antonio TX 78213 Office: 2135 Babcock St San Antonio TX 78229

SERRILL, THEODORE ANDREW, assn. exec.; b. Phila., Apr. 16, 1911; s. John B. and Maty (Lenahan) S.; B.A., Pa. State U., 1932; m. Alice Marguerite Ferner, Oct. 25, 1933; children—Theodore Michael, James Alan. Gen. mgr. Pa. Newspaper Pubs. Assn., Harrisburg, 1950-56; exec. dir. Newspapers Pubs. Assn., Washington, 1956-60; mgr. dept. employee relations Grocery Mfrs. Am., 1960-61; exec. v.p. Nat. Newspaper Assn., Washington, 1961—. Partner, v.p., dir. Brown-Thompson Newspapers, Cambridge Springs, Pa., 1960-72; editor, pub. Publishers' Aux., 1960—. Editor, mem. bd. dirs. Pa. Welfare Forum, 1950-56; pub. mem. U.S. Postal Adv. Council, 1971-73; mem. publs. com. Am. Revolution Bicentennial Commn., 1971—. Bd. dirs. Pa. Soc. Crippled Children. Mem. Newspaper Assn. Mgrs. (past pres.), Nat. Assn. Exec. Club, Washington Trade Assn. Execs., Printing House Craftsmen, Am. Soc. Assn. Execs. (past dir.; chartered exec., Key award), Pub. Relations Soc. Am., Pa. State U. Alumni Assn. (past pres. Central Pa. chpt.), Pa. Soc. Newspaper Editors (founding mem.), Pa. Soc. N.Y., Sigma Delta Chi, Alpha Delta Sigma, Phi Kappa Theta. Clubs: University Torch, Nat. Press (pres. 1974-75) (Washington). Home: 3001 Veazey Terrace NW Washington DC 20008 Office: 491 National Press Bldg Washington DC 20045

SERVANT, EMIL JOHN JR., mining engr., real estate agt.; b. Westland, Pa., Mar. 9, 1914; s. Emil John and Katherine (Gillies) S.; student U. Ala., 1938-40; B.S. in Elec. Engring., U. Pitts., 1942; postgrad. Pa. State Comml. Coll., 1936-38; m. Miriam McConnell, July 25, 1946; children—Linda Lee, Emil John III. Elec. engr. Consolidation Coal Co., Library, Pa., 1946-48; maintenance supt. Truax Traer Coal Co., Kayford, W.Va., 1948-49; asst. gen. mgr. Youngstown Mines Corp., Coalwood, W.Va., 1949-62; pres. Surfside Devel. Co., Surfside Builders, Surfside Beach, S.C., 1962-68, dir., 1968—; owner Surfside Realty Co., Surfside Beach, 1968—. Instr. mechanized mining Pa. State U., University City, 1946-47, W.Va. U., Morgantown, 1948-49. Councilman Surfside Beach, 1966-68, 68-70; chmn. Surfside Beach Zoning and Planning Commn., 1971—; mem. Com. to Incorporate Surfside Beach, 1964; chmn. Surfside Beach Area Republican Party, 1963-65. Bd. dirs. McDowell County Vocational Sch., 1950-54. Served to lt. (s.g.), USNR, 1941-46. Decorated Bronze Star medal. Registered profl. engr., W.Va. Mem. U. Ala., U. Pitts. alumni assns., Surfside Beach Bd. Realtors (sec. 1970, v.p. 1971), Am. Inst. Elec. Engrs., Sigma Tau, Eta Kappa Nu, Phi Eta Sigma. Mason (Shriner). Clubs: Litchfield Country, Winyah Bay Country, Sea Gull Golf, Grand Strand Golfers Assn. Inventor of coal mining equipment. Home: 4th Av N Surfside Beach SC 29577 Office: 213 S Ocean Blvd Surfside Beach SC 29577

SESSIONS, GEORGE PURD, physician; b. Dawson, Ga., July 9, 1931; s. George Purdee and Jessie (Ferguson) S.; student Ga. Southwestern Coll., 1948-50, U. Ga., 1950-51; M.D., Med. Coll. Ga., 1955; m. Martha Ann Hernandez, June 30, 1960; children—William Dean, Neal Bradley, Annette Elaine. Intern, Macon (Ga.) Hosp., 1955-56; resident Charity Hosp., New Orleans, 1958-60; instr. dept. anesthesia Emory U., Atlanta, Ga., 1960-61; chief dept. anesthesiology DeKalb Gen. Hosp., Decatur, Ga., 1961—, Scottish Rite Hosp. for Children, Decatur, 1965—; pres. DeKalb Anesthesia Assos., P.A., 1970—. Served with USPHS, 1956-58. Diplomate Am. Bd. Anesthesiology. Mem. A.M.A., DeKalb County, Ga., So. med. assns., Am., Ga. socs. anesthesiologists, Theta Kappa Psi. Home: 1658 Mason Mill Rd NE Atlanta GA 30329 Office: PO Box 33306 Decatur GA 30033

SESSIONS, MARK WILLIAM, ret. supt. schs.; b. Babcock, Ga., Feb. 14, 1907; s. James Henry and Geta (Johnson) S.; A.B., Mercer U., 1938; M.Ed., U. Ga., 1942; specialist in edn., 1964; m. Jane Lucile Pope, July 29, 1939; children—Cindy (Mrs. Robert Roser), Herman. Prin., Terrell High Sch., Dawson, Ga., 1947-54, Jonesboro (Ga.) High Sch., 1954-56, Waynesboro (Ga.) High Sch., 1956-63, Waynesboro (Ga.) Elementary Sch., 1963-68; supt. Burke County, (Ga.) Schs., Waynesboro, 1969-73; ret., 1973. Mem. Burke County Bd. Health, 1969-72. Mem. N.E.A., Ga. Assn. Sch. Adminstrs. (pres. 1964-65). Ga. Assn. Educators, Ga. Assn. Sch. Supts., Kappa Delta Pi. Methodist (mem. adminstrv. bd). Rotarian. Home: 517 Sunset Dr Waynesboro GA 30830

SESSUMS, THOMAS TERRELL, lawyer, state legislator; b. Daytona Beach, Fla., June 11, 1930; s. Thomas L. and Dorothy (Cornwall) S.; B.A., U. Fla., 1952, LL.B., 1958; LL.D., Fla. So. Coll., 1973; m. Neva Ann Steeves, Aug. 16, 1958; children—Thomas T., Richard H., Sandra Lynn. Admitted to Fla. bar, 1958; asso. Hardee & Ott, Tampa, 1958-60; partner Albritton & Sessums, Tampa, 1961—. Dir. S.E. Bank of Tampa. Mem. Fla. Gov.'s Citizens Com. on Edn., 1972-73; counselor U. Tampa, 1973—; mem. So. Regional Edn. Bd., 1972—. Mem. Fla. Ho. of Reps., 1963—, speaker pro tem, 1968-70, chmn. edn. com., 1970-72, speaker, 1972—. Served to capt. USAF, 1954-56. Mem. Greater Tampa C. of C. (com. 100), Am. Bar Assn., Fla. Bar. Kiwanian. Clubs: Palma Ceia Golf and Country, University. Home: 1113 Dunbar Av Tampa FL 33609 Office: 1st Fed Bldg Tampa FL 33602

SETLIFF, FRANK LAMAR, chemist, educator; b. Lake Charles, La., Sept. 21, 1938; s. Frank Lucky and Anna Vesta (Plummer) S.; B.S. in Chemistry, McNeese State U., 1960; M.S., Tulane U., 1962, Ph.D., 1966; m. Carolyn Lela Carver, Aug. 4, 1962; children—Christopher Lamar, Catherine Claire. Asst. prof. chemistry Little Rock U., 1966-69; asso. prof. U. Ark., Little Rock, 1969-74, prof., 1974—, chmn. chemistry dept., 1973—. Served to 1st. lt., Chem. Corps, 1962-64. U. Faculty Research Fund grantee, 1970, 74. Mem. Am. Chem. Soc., Ark., N.Y. acads. sci., Blue Key, Sigma Xi (research grantee 1970, 73). Contbr. articles on chemistry to sci. jours. Home: 2500 Quebec Dr Little Rock AR 72204

SETO, JANE MEI-CHUN WONG, physician; b. China, May 15, 1927; d. Jee Kwan and Shee (Li) Wong; M.D., Kwang-Hwa Med. Coll., China, 1951; postgrad. Queen's U., Ireland, 1952-57, Tulane U., 1961-63; m. Yeb Jo Seto, Feb. 14, 1958; children—Samuel, Susanna. Intern, Regina (Sask.) Grey Nun's Hosp., 1957-58; resident Providence Hosp., Seattle, 1958-59; phsyician U. Wash. Health Center, 1959-61, Austin (Tex.) State Sch., 1961-62; research asst. M.D. Anderson Hosp., U. Tex., 1964-66; serologist State Bd. Health, New Orleans, 1967-69; instr. medicine Tulane U., 1969-70, research asso. electrosci. and biophysics research group, 1969—. Active Beverly Hill Civic Club (Metairie, La.). Fellow Royal Soc. Health; mem. A.M.A., Am. Pub. Health Assn., Am. Women in Medicine. Contbr. articles to profl. jours. Home: 4824 Purdue St Metairie LA 70003 Office: Tulane University New Orleans LA 70118

SETO, YEB JO, elec. engr., educator; b. China, July 31, 1930; s. Jo Ting and Shee (Chang) S.; came to U.S., 1951, naturalized, 1962; B.S., U. Ida., 1957; M.S., U. Wash., 1960; Ph.D., U. Tex., 1964; m. Jane Mei-Chun Wong, Feb. 14, 1958; children—Samuel K., Susanna L. Research engr. Boeing Airplane Co., Renton, Wash., 1957-60; instr. U. Houston (Tex.), 1960-61, asst. prof., 1964-66; instr. U. Tex., Austin, 1961-63; prof. elec. engring. Tulane U., New Orleans, 1966—, dir. electrosci. and biophysics research group, 1969—. Pres., dir. Applied Research Corp., New Orleans, 1967-71, Sealong, Inc., New Orleans, 1971—. Served with AUS, 1953-55. Recipient NASA-Am. Soc. Engring. Edn. fellowship, 1964, 65. Mem. I.E.E.E., Profl. group on Antenna, Propagation (sect. chmn. 1967—), Sigma Xi, Tau Beta Pi, Eta Kappa Nu. Contbr. sci. articles to profl. jours. Home: 4824 Purdue Dr Metairie LA 70003 Office: Tulane U New Orleans LA 70118

SEVERANCE, FREDERICK DOUGLAS, elec. products mfg. co. exec.; b. Asheville, N.C., Apr. 19, 1927; s. Frederick Duncan and Jane (Fleming) S.; B.S. in Elec. Engring., The Citadel, 1950; postgrad. U. Mich., 1950-51; m. Daphne Aina Johnson, July 26, 1958; children—Alisa, Carl, Sharon, Susan, Craig. Test design engr. Western Electric Co., Burlington, N.C., 1951-54; field engr. Oerlikon Tool & Arms Corp., Asheville, 1954-58; mfrs. rep. Bivins & Caldwell, Inc., High Point, N.C. and Orlando, Fla., 1958-62; organizer BCS Assos. Inc., mfrs. rep., Orlando, 1962-70, Huntsville, Ala., 1970—, v.p., treas., 1962—, br. mgr., 1970—, also trustee profit sharing plan, dir.; dir. So. Bus. Communications, Inc., Orlando. Served with AUS, 1945-48. Mem. I.E.E.E. (past pres.). Republican. Methodist. Club: Yacht (The Citadel). Home: 405 Sherwood Dr SE Huntsville AL 35802 Office: 3322 S Meml Pkwy Huntsville AL 35802

SEVERO, ARMANDO, computer systems cons.; b. Buffalo, June 18, 1935; s. John Anthony and Marietta (Antonelli) S.; B.A. in Math., U. Buffalo, 1957. Research asso. Rensselaer Poly. Inst., 1957-59; coordinator computer systems Nat. Cancer Inst., Washington, 1959-61; computer systems analyst RCA, Washington, 1961-65; computer systems cons. Nat. Bur. Standards, Washington, 1965—. Lectr. Automatic Data Processing. Instr. skiing, Eastern U.S., 1968—; cons. ski programs and activities. Mem. Assn. for Computing Machinery, Eastern Ski Assn. (rep.). Club: Ski of Washington (pres. 1972-73). Home: 1400 S Joyce St B1703 Arlington VA 22202 Office: 933 N Kenmore St Arlington VA 22202

SEVERSON, HARRY LORUN, economist; b. Larchwood, Ia., Feb. 27, 1901; s. Jacob B. and Annie (Johnson) S.; B.S., U. Minn., 1924; M.S., U. Chgo., 1931. Asst. prof. commerce Miss. A. and M. Coll. (now Miss. State U.), Starkville, 1925-26, asso. prof. finance, 1926-30; asst. prof. commerce St. Thomas Coll., St. Paul, 1930-31; acting asst. prof. econs. Ind. U., Bloomington, 1931-32, extension lectr. econs., accounting East Chicago div., 1932-33; asso. prof. econs. U. Omaha, 1935-37; head securities unit FDIC, Washington, 1937-44, asst. chief div. research and statistics, 1944-46; Washington rep. Bankers Trust Co., N.Y.C., 1946-47; cons. economist Municipal Service div. Dun and Bradstreet, N.Y.C., 1947-49; economist HHFA, Washington, 1949-57, OPA, Washington, 1951-52; spl. asst. to asst. dir. OPA, 1952-53; cons. economist, N.Y.C., 1953-64, Mobile, Ala., 1964—. Mem. Am. Econ. Assn., Am. Finance Assn., Lambda Alpha. Author: Severson Projections of Construction Expenditure of State and Local Governments and New Bond Offerings of State and Local Governments, 1957. Contbr. articles to profl. publs. Address: 315 S Monterey St Mobile AL 36604

SEVERY, MERLE EUGEN, editor; b. Los Angeles, Aug. 3, 1922; s. William Carlson and Enid (Severy) Smith; A.B., Columbia, 1942, M.A., 1948, postgrad., 1949-52; m. Teresa Bookholz, 1942 (div. 1951); 1 son, Alan Wayne; m. 2d, Patricia Aman, 1951; children—Randall Carlson, Karen Linwood, Melissa Adams, Leslie Burnett. Asso. editor, trade book div. Prentice-Hall, Inc.; spl. projects editor Doubleday and Co.; sr. editor A.A. Wyn, Inc., 1950-53; mem. editorial staff Nat. Geog. Soc., 1954—, chief Nat. Geog. book service, 1957—. Served with AUS, 1942-46; ETO. Recipient awards Dog Writers' Assn. Am., 1959, Freedoms Found., 1962, Chgo. Book Clinic, 1963, 64, Art Dirs. Club Met. Washington, 1963, 67, 68, 69, 70. Mem. Am. Hist. Assn., Mediaeval Soc. Am., Renaissance Soc. Am., Haukluyt Soc., Am. Inst. Graphic Arts. Club: Nat. Press (Washington). Co-author: Danger is My Destiny, 1955. Editor: Indians of the Americas, 1955; The World in Your Garden, 1957; The National Geographic Book of Dogs, 1958; America's Wonderlands, 1959; Wild Animals of North America, 1960; America's Historylands, 1962; Men, Ships, and the Sea, 1962; Great Adventures with National Geographic, 1963; Song and Garden Birds of North America, 1964; Water, Prey, and Game Birds of North America, 1965; This England, 1966; Everyday Life in Bible Times, 1967; Greece and Rome: Builders of Our World, 1968; The Age of Chivalry, 1969; The Renaissance: Maker of Modern Man, 1970; Vacationland USA, 1970; (with others) American College Dictionary, 1947. Contbr. articles to Nat. Geog. Home: 8814 Chalon Dr Bethesda MD 20034

SEVIER, JAMES, ceramic tile co. exec.; b. Asheville, N.C., Jan 29, 1918; s. Joseph Thomas and Caroline (Rollins) S.; B.S. in Ceramic Engring., N.C. State U., 1941; m. Ilma Claire LaBar, Dec. 11, 1941; children—Christy Noelle (Mrs. Richard Francis Whitfield), James Rollins, Frank LaBar, John Kibler Buchanan. Plant mgr. W.S. George Pottery Co., Cannonsburg, Pa., 1946-48; exec. v.p. So. Potteries, Inc., Erwin, Tenn., 1948-57; v.p. Stylon Corp., Florence, Ala., 1957-68; pres. Mosaic Tile Co., Florence, 1968-70; v.p. DCA Devel. Corp., Florence, 1970-73; v.p., gen. mgr. Florence div. Monarch Tile Mfg., Inc., 1973—. Served to lt. comdr. USNR, 1941-45. Fellow Am. Ceramic Soc.; mem. Nat. Inst. Ceramic Engrs. Kiwanian, Rotarian. Home: 1842 Hermitage Dr Florence AL 35630 Office: 833 Rickwood Rd Florence AL 35630

SEWELL, BARBARA JEAN SCOTT, educator; b. Chrisman, Ill., May 15, 1929; d. R. Otho and Ruth (Morris) Scott; B.S., Ind. State U., 1951; M.A., Western Carolina U., 1967; div.; children—Russell Earl, Barbara Jean. Asst. home adviser Vermillion County Extension, U. Ill., 1951; tchr. vocational home econs. various schs., Ill., 1951-63, Fla., 1963-67; guidance counselor jr. class Manatee High Sch., Brandenton, 1967-69, guidance counselor sr. class, 1969-71; asst. dir.-registrar and admissions Fla. So. Coll., Lakeland, 1970-71; sch. psychologist Community Mental Health, Winter Haven, Fla., 1971-72, Polk County (Fla.) Sch. Bd., Bartow, 1972—. Sec.-treas. Lanehart & Scott Constrn. Co., Lakeland, Fla. Mem. textbook com. Fla. Dept. Edn., 1967-69, chmn. textbook selection com., 1968-69. Recipient awards including certificate of appreciation Fla. Dept. Edn., 1969. Mem. N.E.A., Fla., Manatee County edn. assns., Am., Fla. (mem. state workshop com. 1969-70) personnel and guidance assns., Fla. Sch. Counselors Assn. (mem. research com. 1968-69), Manatee Counselors Assn. (constn. com. mem. 1969), Fla. Assn. Sch. Psychologists, Delta Gamma Alumni. Methodist (mem. Christian vocations com. 1968-70). Home: 1716 Sterling Dr Lakeland FL 33803 Office: Polk County Sch Bd PO Box 391 Bartow FL 33830 also PO Box 1505 Lakeland FL 33801

SEWELL, GRANVILLE CLARK, assn. exec.; b. Lexington, Ky., Oct. 7, 1898; s. James Witt and Elizabeth (Kidd) S.; student Vanderbilt U., 1916-18, Tulane, 1919-20; m. Everall Burdon, June 20, 1925; children—Marianne (Mrs. Warwick Aiken, Jr.), Granville H., John Burdon. Copy chief Chambers Advt. Agy., New Orleans, 1922-33; mgr. Walker Saussy Advt. Agy., New Orleans, 1933-44; pres., owner Sewell Advt. Agy., New Orleans, 1945-65; mgr. Picayune (Miss.) C. of C., 1965-71; mgr. Picayune United Fund, 1971—. Instr. advt. copywriting Tulane U., New Orleans, nights, 1950-53. Chmn. budget com. New Orleans Community Chest, 1955; Served with U.S. Army 1918. Mem. New Orleans Assn. Advt. Agys. (founder 1960, pres. 1960-63). Episcopalian. Mason, Rotarian. Clubs: Orleans Camera, Delta Camera. Home: 1229 Stemwood Dr Picayune MS 39466 Office: So Pearl River County United Fund Picayune MS 39466

SEWELL, HARVEY WELDON, physician; b. Wills Point, Tex., Nov. 10, 1916; s. Julian T. and Ola (Norman) S.; student U. Tex. at Austin, 1933-35; M.D., Baylor U., 1939; m. Charlene Spoonts, Apr. 2, 1942; children—Betty, Anne (Mrs. Clay Johnson), Robert. Intern Parkland Hosp., Dallas, 1939-40, resident surgery, 1940-41; practice medicine, specializing in gen. practice, Belton, Tex., 1941—; health officer Bell County, 1950—. Co-owner Salado (Tex.) Galleries, 1970—. Mem. Belton Sch. Bd., 1961-64. Methodist (steward). Lion (pres.). Home: 402 E 14th St Belton TX 76513 Office: 402 N Main St Belton TX 76513

SEWELL, PAUL GILBERT, edn. adminstr.; b. Jacksonville, Ala., July 17, 1909; s. Raymond Gilbert and Maggie (Bonds) S.; A.A., State Tchrs. Coll., Jacksonville, 1930; B.S. in Indsl. Edn., Ala. Poly. Inst., 1939; postgrad. U. Fla., 1939-41, U. Ga., 1962; m. Margaret Julia Hinds, Aug. 26, 1941; 1 son, Paul Jefferson. Prin. Cedar Springs Consol. Sch., Calhoun County, Ala., 1935-38; instr. indsl. arts and vocational co-op. edn. Thomasville (Ga.) High Sch., 1939-47, dir. vocation, tech. and adult edn. Thomasville and Thomas County Pub. Schs., 1947—. Cons. research on student personnel services. Mem. Tourism Com., Star Student-Star Tch. Com.; mem. City Planning Commn. and Improvement Council, Thomasville, 1966—; cons., committeman Dem. Com., also del.; mem. State Adv. Council on Vocational Edn., Ga. State Council on Goals for Edn. and Intellectual Improvement. Mem. Nat., Ga. trade and indsl. edn. assns., Ga. Tech. Edn. Assn., Ga. (pres. 1960-61), Am. (nat. council local adminstrn. 1965-67) vocational assns., Ga. Assn. Edn., Thomasville Tchrs. Assn., Thomas County C. of C. (edn. com. 1965—), Kappa Delta Pi, Iota Lambda Sigma. Elk, Kiwanian (dir. 1955-62). Club: Glen Arven Country (past dir., pres. 1958-59). Home: 422 Glenwood Dr Thomasville GA 31792 Office: Thomas Area Tech School Hwy 19 at 319 Thomasville GA 31792

SEXTON, OSWELL STANTON, sch. adminstr.; b. Oneida, Tenn., Mar. 21, 1908; s. Caswell and Rachel R. (Cecil) S.; B.S., Tenn. Technol. U., 1937; M.S., U. Tenn., 1951; m. Rema Jeffers, Aug. 17, 1929; children—O. Sibley, Curtis, Donna Kay (Mrs. Robert L. Tallent), Ray Owen, Dwight David, Ella Rachel (Mrs. Danny Williams). Tchr., prin., elementary schs. Scott County, Tenn., 1927-37; coach Robins (Tenn.) High Sch., 1937, prin., 1937-46; edn. supr. Scott County (Tenn.) Schs., 1946; prin. Huntsville (Tenn.) High Sch., 1946-55, Madisonville (Tenn.) High Sch., 1955-64, Cohutta (Ga.) Elementary Sch., 1964-73; instr. Hercules Powder Co., Chattanooga, 1942. Chmn. war fund A.R.C., Scott County, 1943-44; dir. Sabin-Polio Clinic; dir. Monroe County Heart Assn.; chmn. ednl. dept. United Appeal Fund Drive, Whitfield County, 1968. Mem. town council Town Cohutta, Ga., 1969-74. Life mem. N.E.A.; hon. life mem. Tenn. Edn. Assn.; mem. Internat. Platform Assn., Ga. Edn. Assn., Ga. Elementary Principals Assn., Nat. Assn. Secondary Sch. Prins., Monroe County Ednl. Assn. (pres. 1959-60), Whitfield County Adminstrs. Ednl. Assn. (pres. 1968), Phi Delta Kappa. Baptist (deacon). Mason; mem. Order Eastern Star. Clubs: Senior Citizens, Lions (pres. Madisonville 1960); Ruritan (dir.) (Cohutta, Ga.). Home: 3230 US Hwy 411 Madisonville TN 37354

SEXTON, WILSON BENJAMAN, recreational products co. exec.; b. Kansas City, Mo., Nov. 27, 1936; s. John Thomas and Lucy Irene (Wilson) S.; B.B.A., So. Methodist U., 1958, postgrad., 1960-61; m. Marian Laverne Eisenman, Aug. 14, 1957; children—Wilson B., Susan Debra. Accountant Seablue Corp., Dallas, 1956-60, purchasing mgr., advt., sales promotion mgr., 1960-66, v.p., gen. mgr., 1966-72, pres., 1973—, also dir., 1966—. C.P.A., Tex. Mem. Tex. Soc. C.P.A.s, Nat. Swimming Pool Inst. (dir. 1967-70), Kappa Alpha. Methodist (dir. 1966-68, 72-73). Clubs: Willow Bend Polo and Hunt, T Bar M Racquet. Home: 5330 Pebblebrook Dr Dallas TX 75229 Office: 701 Plano Rd Richardson TX 75080

SEYBOLD, WILLIAM DEMPSEY, surgeon, educator; b. Temple, Tex., Feb. 23, 1915; s. Claude Dempsey and Lillian (Cochrane) S.; B.S. in Medicine, U. Tex., 1936, M.D., 1938; M.S. in Surgery, U. Minn. Med. Sch., 1947; m. Frances Rather, May 3, 1940; children—William Rather, Randolph Cochrane, Frances Rather. Intern Barnes Hosp., St. Louis, 1940-41; resident Mayo Found., Rochester, Minn., 1941-44, fellow in surgery, 1946-47; practice medicine, specializing in thoracic surgery, Houston, 1950—; chief surgery St. Luke's Episcopal Hosp., 1956—; chief staff Kelsey-Seybold Clinic, 1972—; clin. prof. surgery Baylor Coll. Medicine, Houston, 1970—. Mem. chancellor's council U. Tex. System; bd. dirs. Kelsey and Leary Found., U. St. Thomas, Nat. Multiple Sclerosis Soc. Served to lt. (j.g.) M.C., USNR, 1944-46. Diplomate Am. Bd. Surgery, Am. Bd. Thoracic Surgery. Mem. A.C.S., A.M.A., Am. Coll. Chest Physicians, Tex. Surg. Soc., Tex. Med. Assn., Am. Assn. Med. Clinics, Am. Assn. Thoracic Surgery, Am. Thoracic Soc., Sigma Xi. Author: (with others) A Synopsis of Clinical Anatomy, 1969. Contbr. articles on surgery to med. jours. Home: 2041 Claremont Lane Houston TX 77019 Office: 6624 Fannin St Houston TX 77025

SEYDEL, JOHN RUTHERFORD, chem. co. exec.; b. Jersey City, May 16, 1918; s. Paul Bernard and Mildred (Woolley) S.; student in chem. engring. Ga. Inst. Tech., 1935-37; m. Jane Reynolds, Dec. 30, 1937; children—Elizabeth (Mrs. John Lewis Morgan), Scott O'Sullivan, Susan (Mrs. Susan Cofer), Mildred Woolley. With Eagle & Phenix Cotton Mills, Columbus, Ga., 1937; with Penn Mut. Life Ins. Co., Atlanta, 1937-38; with Seydel-Woolley & Co., Atlanta, 1938-72, v.p., dir. sales mgr., 1951-61, exec. v.p., 1961, pres., 1962-72; chmn. AZS Corp., 1972—; v.p., dir., mem. exec. com. Mar Gold Margarine Corp., 1948-58; dir. Seydel Cos., Seydel Internat. de Venezuela, S.A., Seydel Internat. de Colombia, S.A. Active fund drives United Appeal. Trustee Seydel-Wooley Found.; trustee Vasser Woolley Found.; trustee AZS Pension Trust. Mem. Internat. Council Textile Slashing Technologists, So. Consortium Internat. Edn., Ga. Bus. and Industry Assn., Sigma Chi. Episcopalian. Rotarian. Clubs:

Piedmont Driving, Commerce (Atlanta). Home: 1027 Peachtree Battle Av NW Atlanta GA 30327 Office: 762 Marietta Blvd NW Atlanta GA 30318

SEYDEL, SCOTT O'SULLIVAN, chem. co. exec.; b. Atlanta, Mar. 29, 1940; s. John Rutherford and Jane (Reynolds) S.; student Ga. Inst. Tech., 1959-62; Textile Engr., U. Ga. Sch. Journalism, 1962-63; student journalism North Tex. State U., 1963; m. Rosina Marie Bairstow, July 2, 1963; children—John Rutherford II, Rosina Marie, Lael Elizabeth, Scott O'Sullivan. With Tex. Textile Mills, Inc., McKinney, 1963-64; personnel dir. 1925 Corp., AZC Corp., Atlanta, 1965, pub. relations dir., 1966, asst. v.p., 1967, asst. exec. v.p., 1968, corporate dir., 1968—, v.p. diversification, dir. internat. activities, 1969-70; pres. Seydel Cos., Atlanta, 1970—; chmn. bd., chief exec. officer SICOL, S.A., Colombia, 1972—; v.p., dir. SIVEN, S.A., Caracas, Venezuela, 1971—, Quimicas de CantroAmerica, 1972—; dir. Seydel Internat. de Colombia, Anilinas Argentinas, Inpal, S.A. Rio de Janeiro, Brazil, M.A., Siturk, Istanbul, Turkey, Iran SEYRAN, Inc., Teheran, SICHEM, Inc., Tapiei, Taiwan; asso. dir. Eastman Chem., Manila, Phillippines. Fellow Am. Assn. Textile Chemists and Colorists; mem. Internat. Council for Textile Technologists (dir. 1957—, sec. 1971—), U.S. C. of C. (exec. res. com., export council), Atlanta Benedicts (v.p. 1972, dir. 1971—), Chi Phi. Rotarian. Club: Piedmont Driving (Atlanta). Contbr. articles to profl. jours. Home: 2600 Woodward Way Atlanta GA 30325 Office: 1401 Ellsworth Industrial Atlanta GA 30325

SEYDELL, MILDRED (MRS. MAX SEYDEL), writer, lectr., traveler; b. Atlanta; d. Vasser and Elizabeth Cobb (Rutherford) Woolley; ed. Washington Sem., Atlanta, The Lucy Cobb Inst., Athens, Ga., and Sorbonne, Paris; m. Paul Bernard Seydel (dec.); children—Paul Vasser, John Rutherford; m. 2d, Max Seydel. Columnist Charleston (W.Va.) Gazette, 1921; rep. Hearst Crime Commn., in Europe, 1926, collecting data for series of articles and interviews; traveled in Belgium and Ireland, 1927, in Balkan States, Hungary, Turkey and Greece, 1929, Sweden, Germany and France, 1931; contributed Talks with Celebrities; made spl. study of liquor regulation in Sweden; traveled through Africa from Capetown to Cairo and into Palestine, 1934; made spl. study of history of diamonds and gold in S. Africa and native customs of Belgian Congo, investigation of activity of Jews in Palestine; adventure in friendship to South Sea Islands, New Zealand and Australia, 1937; Internat. News Service rep. in Germany and Czechoslovakia, 1938, Finland, 1939; corr. U.S. papers; adventures in Europe, 1955, Eng., Wales, 1956; pres. Mildred Seydell Pub. Co. Belgian dir. World Poetry Day. Mem. Ga. Mothers Com.; v.p. Meml. Day Com. Decorated knight Order Leopold (Belgium). Mem. Tape Talk Internat. (pres.), Nat, League Am. Pen Women, Internat. Periodic Press (dir. poetry Belgian sect.), Friends of Emory U. Library (hon.), A.G. Rhodes Home (lhon.), Beta Sigma Phi (hon.). Clubs: Peony Garden (hon.); American Women's (Brussels). Author: Secret Fathers, 1930; Then I Saw North Carolina, 1936; Chins Up, 1939; Come Along to Belgium, 1969. Editor: Poetry Profile of Belgium, 1960. Publisher: Silent Singing (poems); Essays Wise and Otherwise. Mem. adv. bd. Sunshine Mag., Fellowship in Prayer mag. Home: 9530 Scott Rd Route 2 Roswell GA 30075

SEYMOUR, GEORGE AUSTIN, petroleum pipeline co. exec.; b. Westfield, N.J., Mar. 10, 1926; s. Edward Drullard and Ruth (Pierce) S.; B. Mech. Engring., Rensselaer Poly. Inst., 1946; m. Harriet Virginia Harvie, Nov. 29, 1947; children—Ruth, Peter, Harriet, Kathryn. With Mobil Oil Corp. and affiliated cos., various internat. locations, 1947—, mgr. engring. Mobil Pipe Line Co., 1972-73, mgr., Dallas, 1973; v.p., dir. Olympic Pipeline Co., Dallas, 1970-72, 73—, Cook Inlet Pipe Line Co., Dallas, 1970-72, 73—; dir. Wolverine Pipe Line Co., West Shore Pipe Line Co., So. Sask. (Can.) Pipe Line Co., Calgary, Alta. Chmn. sch. bd., Anaco, Venezuela, 1962-64. Dir. Am. Cancer Crusade, 1970-71. Served to lt. USNR, 1944-47, 51-53. Decorated chevalier Order Saharan Merit (France), 1961. Registered profl. engr., Tex. Mem. Am. Petroleum Inst. (U.S. del. to internat. standards orgn. conf. 1970, 72), Am. Numismatic Soc., Orders, Medals Soc. Am., Theta Chi. Republican. Club: Engineers (Dallas). Home: Route 3 Box 348AA Denton TX 76201 Office: PO Box 900 Dallas TX 75221

SEYMOUR, LAWRENCE DARRYL, surgeon, b. Memphis, Feb. 1, 1935; s. Robert Henry and Mary Bell (Jefferson) S.; B.S., Tenn. State U., 1957; M.D., Howard U., 1961; m. Janet A. Arnold, Dec. 27, 1959; children—Lauren Juanita, Eric Lawrence. Intern, City of St. Louis Hosp., 1961-62; resident, 1962-66; instr. urology Boston U., 1966-68; clin. asso. in urology U. Tenn., Memphis, 1969—. Vice pres. Med. Clinics, Inc., Memphis, 1971—. Bd. dirs. Boys' Clubs Memphis, 1969—; trustee Collins Chapel Hosp., Memphis, 1972—. Served to lt. comdr. USNR, 1966-68. Mem. Am., Bluff City med. assns., Alpha Kappa Mu, Beta Kappa Chi, Omega Psi Phi. Mason. Research in urology. Home: 1662 Joanne St Memphis TN 38111 Office: 701 E Mallory St Memphis TN 38106

SEYMOUR, RAYMOND BENEDICT, educator, cons., chem. engr.; b. Boston, July 26, 1912; s. Walter A. and Marie E. (Doherty) S.; B.S., U. N.H., 1933, M.S., 1935; Ph.D., State U. Ia., 1937; postdoctoral Rensselaer Poly. Inst., 1963, U. Utah, 1964; m. Frances B. Horan, Sept. 16, 1936; children—David Ray, Susan (Mrs. Howard Smith), Peter, Phillip Alan. Instr. chemistry U. N.H., 1933-35, U. Ia., 1935-37; research chemist Goodyear Tire & Rubber Co., Akron, O., 1937-39; chief chemist Atlas Mineral Products div. Electric Storage Battery Co., Mertztown, Pa., 1939-41, exec. v.p., gen. mgr., tech. dir., 1949-54, pres., dir., 1954-55; research group leader Monsanto Co., Dayton, O., 1941-45; dir. research, U. Chattanooga, 1945-48; dir. research Johnson & Johnson, New Brunswick, N.J., 1948-49; pres., tech. dir. Loven Chemical of Cal., 1955-58; pres. Corrosion Resistant Products, Inc., 1956-57; pres., chmn. bd. Alcylite Plastics & Chem. Corp., 1958-60. Prof. chemistry, chmn. sci. div. Sul Ross State U., 1959-64; asso. chmn. chemistry dept. U. Houston. 1964-66, coordinator polymer chemistry, 1964—, asso. prof. chemistry, 1964-69, prof., 1969—, asso. dir. research, 1966-68. Cons. edn. AID, U.S. Dept. State, E. Pakistan, 1968. Dir. NSF Inst., 1965. Registered profl. engr., Tex., Ohio. Recipient Western Plastics award, 1960. Fellow A.A.A.S., Am. Inst. Chemists, Tex. Acad. Sci.; mem. Am. Inst. Chem. Engrs., Am. Chem. Soc. (Southeastern Tex. Ann. award 1972), Soc. Plastics Industry, Nat. Assn. Corrosion Engrs., Am. Soc. Oceanography, Am. Assn. U. Profs., Soc. Plastic Engrs., Houston Soc. Scientists and Engrs., Sigma Xi, Alpha Chi Sigma, Gamma Sigma Epsilon. Rotarian. Club: Golfcrest Country (Houston). Author: National Paint Dictionary, 3d edit., 1948; Plastics for Corrosion Resistant Applications; 1955; Hot Organic Coatings, 1959; Introduction to Polymer Chemistry, 1971; General Organic Chemistry, 1971; Experimental Organic Chemistry, 1971; Modern Plastics Technology, 1974; Chemistry and You, 1974; Ann. Plastic Review 1948—; also articles. Patentee in field. Mem. exec. reserves Dept. Def. Home: 4830 Rockwood Dr Houston TX 77004

SHACKELFORD, HARRY CARL, ednl. adminstr.; b. Durham, Ark., Oct. 18, 1905; s. Mondrel Ellington and Sarah Elizabeth (Hobbs) S.; B.S., John Brown Coll., 1929; B.A., Northeastern State Coll., 1950; M.Ed., Phillips U., 1955; m. Reta Pritchard, Feb. 25, 1944; 1 son, James. Tchr. pub. schs., Kan., Okla., 1929-39; supt. schs. Delaware County (Okla.), 1941-44, Laverne, Okla., 1947—. Mem. Okla. Bd. Edn., 1963—. Mem. Okla. Ho. of Reps., 1939-41. Mem. N.W. Okla. Tchrs. Assn. (pres.), Laverne C. of C. Mason, Lion. Home: Box 632 Laverne OK 73848

SHACTER, JOHN, chem. co. exec., cons.; b. Vienna, Austria, Sept. 26, 1921; s. Jacob and Regina (Burstin) S.; came to U.S., 1938, naturalized, 1943; B.S. in Chem. Engring., U. Pa., 1943; m. Kathleen Williams, Mar. 5, 1947; children—Suzanne, Linda, Keith Lundin. Engr., mgr. uranium separation process design Union Carbide Corp., Oak Ridge, 1943-56, project mgr. corporate devel., mgr. planning dept., N.Y.C., 1956-66, dir. AEC combined operations planning, Oak Ridge, 1967-73, exec. asst. to pres., Oak Ridge, 1973—; pres. John Shacter Assos., bus. and tech. cons., Oak Ridge, 1973—. Lectr. grad. bus. and engring. U. Tenn., Harvard, N.Y. U., cons. AEC, Dept. Def. Registered profl. engr., Tenn. Fellow A.A.A.S.; mem. Am. Chem. Soc., Am. Inst. Chem. Engrs. (nat. program com. 1970), Am. Mgmt. Assn. (conf. leader since 1966—), Inst. Mgmt. Scis. Rotarian (dir. 1973-74, chmn. vocational services 1973—). Patentee in field. Home: 107 Westoverlook Dr Oak Ridge TN 37830 also Ten Mile TN 37880 Office: Union Carbide Nuclear Division PO Box Y Oak Ridge TN 37830

SHADID, ERNEST GEORGE, psychiatrist, hosp. adminstr.; b. Elk City, Okla., Dec. 26, 1929; s. George O. and Nerose (Adwon) S.; B.A., U. Okla., 1950, M.D., 1955; m. Joyce N. Cohlmia, Aug. 9, 1953; children—Larry G., David L., Diane L., Gregory E. Intern, St. Francis Hosp., Wichita, Kan., 1955-56; resident psychiatry Menninger Sch. Psychiatry, Topeka, 1956-57; resident psychiatry Central State Griffin Meml. Hosp., Norman, Okla., 1959-61, dir. outpatient dept., 1961-62, clin. dir., 1962-66, asst. supr., 1966—; asst. clin. prof. psychiatry, neurology and behavioral scis. U. Okla. Sch. Medicine, 1968—; cons. psychiatry Okla. State Penitentiary, Okla. Dept. Pub. Welfare. Mem. exec. com. Okla. Council Juvenile Delinquency Planning, 1969; v.p. Okla. Health Planning Agy., 1973; mem. Okla. Mental Health Planning Com., 1963—; mem. St. Joseph Sch. Bd., Norman, Okla., 1964-66; mem., lectr. Nat. Drug Edn. Center Adv. Com., U. Okla., 1970—. Served to capt. USAF, 1957-59. Diplomate Am. Bd. Psychiatry and Neurology. Fellow Am. Psychiat Assn. (pres. Okla. 1969-70), Am. Coll. Psychiatrists; mem. Am. Orthopsychiat. Assn., A.M.A., Mid-Continent Psychiat. Assn., Acad. Religion and Mental Health, Okla. Health and Welfare Assn., Okla. Med. Assn., Cleveland-McClain County Med. Soc. (pres. 1971-72). Rotarian. Home: 2601 Smoking Oak Rd Norman OK 73069 Office: PO Box 151 Norman OK 73069

SHAFER, DAVID ALAN, ednl. adminstr.; b. Alva, Okla., Oct. 17, 1939; s. Carl A. and Anna (Ewing) S.; B.A. in Speech and Sociology, Northwestern State Coll. (Alva), 1962; M.A. in Drama and Corrections, So. Ill. U., 1964; m. Patsy Joyce Gunsaulis, Apr. 20, 1962; children—Dickie Dean, Dirk Alan. Cottage dir. Ia. Tng. Sch. Boys, Eldora, 1964-67; asst. supt. Helena (Okla.) State Sch. Boys, 1967-69, supt., 1969-72; supt. Lloyd E. Rader Children's Diagnostic and Evaluation Center, Sand Springs, Okla., 1972—. Chmn., Sand Springs Drug Awareness Program, 1973—; mem. Okla. Regional Council Juvenile Delinquency, 1970—. Bd. dirs. Eldora Community Theatre, 1964-67. So. Ill. U. fellow, 1962-64. Mem. Helena C. of C. (pres. 1970-71), Western States Conf. Tng. Schs. (pres.), Kappa Delta Pi, Alpha Psi Omega. Mason. Home: Rural Route 3 Box 10A Sand Springs OK 74063 Office: PO Box 399 Sand Springs OK 74063

SHAHUN, LEON, JR., wholesale tobacco co. exec.; b. Memphis, Dec. 12, 1926; s. Leon and Carolena (Strassner) S.; B.A., Va. Mil. Inst., 1949; postgrad. Memphis State U., 1962-65; m. Suzanne G. Beyer, Nov. 22, 1951; children—Leslie, Meryl, Constance, Gregory. With Leon & Leon Cigar Co., Memphis, 1949-69, partner, gen. mgr., 1950-69; chmn. bd., chief exec. officer Samelson-Leon Co., Inc., Memphis, 1969—. Bd. dirs. Liberty Bowl Festival Assn.; trustee Country Day Sch. Served with inf. AUS, 1945-46. Decorated Bronze Star medal. Mem. Nat. Assn. Tobacco Distbrs. (dir. 1960—). Rotarian. Club: Ridgeway Country (Memphis). Home: 5273 Southwood Dr Memphis TN 38117 Office: 160 Cumberland St Memphis TN 38112

SHAIA, HARRY, JR., lawyer; b. Richmond, Va., Aug. 29, 1930; s. Harry and Zackia S.; student U. Va., 1948-50; LL.B., U. Richmond, 1953; m. Margaret Ann Gibrall, Aug. 29, 1959; children—Anthony J., Gregory J., John J., Christopher J., Anne-Marie, Harry J. Admitted to Va. bar, 1953; practiced in Richmond, 1953—; mem. firms Blanton, Lumpkin & Shaia, 1960-70, Blanton, Shaia & Kelly, 1970-72, Shaia, Stout & Markow, 1974—. Served with AUS, 1953-55. Roman Catholic (chmn. ch. councils 1972—). Club: Willow Oaks Country (Richmond). Home: 300 DeSota Dr Richmond VA 23229 Office: 700 Bldg 7th and Main Sts Richmond VA 23219

SHALLOWAY, ARTHUR MELVIN, electronic engr.; b. Atlanta, Mar. 20, 1922; s. David and Jeanne (Gordon) S.; B.S., Ga. Inst. Tech., 1943, M.S., 1951; postgrad. Cornell U., 1953-55; m. Johanna Elfriede Latta, June 12, 1955; children—David Glenn, Heidi Jeanne. Electronic engr. Signal Corps Lab., Red Bank, N.J., 1951-52, Convair Missile div., Pomona, Cal., 1952-53, Westinghouse Tube div., Elmira, N.Y., 1955-56; prin. engr. Stromberg Carlson Electronics div., Rochester, N.Y., 1956-59, Honeywell Inertial Guidance div., St. Petersburg, Fla., 1959-62; electronic engr. Nat. Radio Astronomy Obs., Charlottesville, Va., 1962—. Instr., Cornell U., 1953-54; cons. Max Planck Inst. Radio Astronomie, 1969-71. Served to 1st lt. USAAF, 1943-46. Mem. I.E.E.E., Internat. Union Radio Sci. Patentee in field. Home: 201 Westminster Rd Charlottesville VA 22901 Office: Nat Radio Astronomy Observatory 2015 Ivy Rd Charlottesville VA 22903

SHAMBURGER, (ALICE) PAGE, author; b. Aberdeen, N.C.; d. Frank Dudley and Alice (Page) Shamburger; grad. St. Mary's Sch. and Jr. Coll., 1945, Marjorie Webster Coll., 1947. Roving editor Am. Aviation Mag., 1949-51; script writer radio sta. WHUC, 1951-53; Eastern editor Cross Country News, 1954-67, contbg. editor Air Progress, 1966-74; mem. Woman's Adv. Com. on Aviation, 1964-68; mem. aviation div. N.C. Emergency Transp. Task Force, 1966-67, cons. N.C. Vet. Research Found. Sec. Mid-South Horse Show Assn.; asst. sec. Moore County Hounds. Recipient commendations N.C. Gov., 1967-68, USAF Tactical Command, 1966; Doris Mullen Meml. Scholarship for helicopter tng., 1969, Lady Hay Drummond-Hay award, 1971. Mem. Aviation/Space Writers Assn., 99s-Internat. Orgn. Licensed Woman Pilots, Aircraft Owners and Pilots Assn., Nat. Aero. Assn., Carolina Aero Club, Nat. Pilots Assn., Air Force Hist. Found., Air Force Assn., Am. Aviation Hist. Soc., Wingfoot Lighter-than-air Soc., Antique Airplane Assn., Exptl. Aircraft Assn., Southeastern Aviation Trades Assn., 99's (gov. S.E. sect. and mem. exec. bd. 1969-70, 71, curator mus. 1969—), Univ. Aviation Assn. (dir.), Nat. Intercoll. Flying Assn. (adv. bd.), Whirly-Girl 142. Democrat. Methodist. Author: Tracks Across The Sky, 1964; Classic Monoplanes, 1966; co-author: Command the Horizon, 1968; World War I Aces and Planes, 1968; Summon the Stars (named best non-fiction aviation book 1970 Aviation Space Writers Assn.), 1970; The Curtiss Hawks, 1972. Contbr. articles to profl. publs. Address: 500 Carolina St Aberdeen NC 28315

SHANAHAN, JOHN HARROLD, JR., city planner; b. Rockville Centre, N.Y., Dec. 29, 1941; s. John Harrold and Evelyn Odell (Wood) S.; B.A. (Gibraltar scholar), U. St. Thomas, 1966; M.Arch., Tex. A. and M. U., 1968, M. in Urban and Regional Planning (Community Service fellow), 1970; m. Carol Jeanette Bradshaw, Oct. 7, 1967; children—Erin Elizabeth, Susan Claire, Daniel Patrick. Asst. dir. dept. urban planning Tex. A. and M. U., College Station, 1967-69; staff asst. Office Gov. Tex., Austin, 1969-71; asso. Lifson, Wilson, Ferguson & Winick, mgmt. cons., Houston, 1971-73; partner Shanahan/Wyse Assos., urban planning cons., Houston, 1973—. Lectr. grad. program community planning U. Tex. at Austin, 1970-71; vis. lectr. city planning Rice U., U. Houston, 1971—; mem. State Adv. Com. Urban Edn., 1970-71, state adv. council Dept. Housing and Urban Devel., 1969-71; mem. Mayor's Adv. Com. on Housing, Houston, 1966-67. Bd. dirs., sec. Vols. in Tech. Assistance, Houston, 1971—. Served with USNR, 1962-64. Recipient Econ. award Wall St. Jour., 1966; Outstanding Service award Am. Inst. Planners, 1970, 73. Mem. Am. Inst. Planners, Am. Soc. Planning Ofcls., Am., So. econ. assns., Omicron Delta Epsilon. Roman Catholic. Club: Houston. Home: 4007 Falkirk Lane Houston TX 77025 Office: 2801 S Post Oak Rd Houston TX 77027

SHAND, JULIAN BONHAM, JR., educator; b. Columbia, S.C., Nov. 6, 1937; s. Julian Bonham and Lucy Pride (McDonald) S.; B.S., U. S.C., 1959; Ph.D., U. N.C., 1964; m. Mary Jane Gregg, June 8, 1963; children—Peter, James, Jonathan. Asst. prof. physics U. Ga., 1964-67; prof. physics, chmn. dept. Berry Coll., 1967—, Dana prof. physics, 1968—. Woodrow Wilson fellow, 1959; Nat. Sci. Found. fellow, 1962. Mem. Am. Phys. Soc., Am. Assn. Physics Tchrs., Ga. Acad. Sci., Phi Beta Kappa, Sigma Xi, Kappa Alpha. Episcopalian (jr. warden, vestryman) Contbr. articles profl. jours. Home: 112 Parkway Dr Rome GA 30161 Office: Berry College Mt Berry GA 30149

SHANDS, NED DOUGLASS, JR., lawyer; b. Lufkin, Tex., Jan. 28, 1914; s. Ned Douglass and Olive Lillian (Denman) S.; student Washington and Lee U., 1931; B.A., U. Tex., 1937, LL.B., 1937; m. Mattie Belle Cook, Feb. 19, 1938; children—Ned Douglass III, Carolin (Mrs. Raymond Abney Sanders), Susan (Mrs. Darin L. Simpson). Admitted to Tex. bar, 1937; practice law, Lufkin, 1937—; mem. firms Peavy & Shands, Lufkin; counsel Tex. Power & Light Co., 1939-73, United Gas Co., 1940-73; dir., gen. counsel First Bank and Trust Co., Lufkin, 1937—, Lufkin Telephone Exchange, Inc., 1945—, Lufkin-Conroe Telephone Co., 1970-73. City atty., City of Lufkin, 1939-42. Chmn., Angelina County Democratic Party, 1950-52; mem. Lufkin Ind. Sch. Dist. Bd. Edn., 1950-56, pres., 1953-54. Served with AUS, 1944-45. Mem. State Bar Tex., Angelina Bar Assn. (pres. 1960), Angelina C. of C. (dir. 1949-51), Kappa Sigma. Lion (pres. 1948-49). Home: 1002 Southwood Dr Lufkin TX 75901 Office: 400 H S 1st St Lufkin TX 75901

SHANE, ROBERT SAMUEL, sci. assn. ofcl.; b. Chgo., Dec. 8, 1910; s. Jacob and Selma (Shayne) S.; B.S., U. Chgo., 1930, Ph.D., 1933; m. Jeanne Felice Lazarus, Aug. 21, 1936; children—Stephen, Susan (Mrs. J. Aronson), Jacqueline (Mrs. T. Kirchhoff). Research chemist Nat. Aniline div. Allied Chem. & Dye Corp., 1934-35; chemist Stein-Hall Mfg. Co., 1935-36, Universal Oil Products Co., 1936; tech. dir. Western Adhesives Co., 1937-40; research chemist Gelatin Products Co., 1941-42; plant supt. Amecco Chem., Inc., 1942-43; group leader Bausch & Lomb Optical Co., Rochester, N.Y., 1943-46; owner dry cleaning bus., Rochester, 1946-52; project supr. govt. contract research Wyandotte Chem. Corp. (Mich.), 1952-54; asst. dir. new product devel. Am. Cyanamid Co., Danbury, Conn., 1954-55; mgr. chem. ceramics comml. atomic power dept. Westinghouse Electric Corp., Pitts., 1955-57; nucleonics specialist Bell Aircraft Corp., Buffalo, 1957-58; cons. engr. light mil. electronics dept. Gen. Electric Co., Utica, N.Y., 1958-64, research engr. laminated products dept., Coshocton, O., 1964-66, systems specialist radiation effects spacecraft dept., Phila., 1966-67, mgr. design rev. reentry systems, 1967-69, mgr. parts, materials, and processes engring. space systems orgn., 1969-70; staff scientist Nat. Materials Adv. Bd., Nat. Acad. Scis., Washington, 1970—. Guest instr. Pa. State U., 1956. Recipient Golden Key Man award Gen. Electric Co., 1961. Fellow Am. Soc. Testing and Materials (hon.); mem. Am. Chem. Soc., Am. Nuclear Soc., Am. Inst. Chem. Engring., Am. Soc. Metals. Mason. Author: Space Radiation Effects on Materials, 1962; Testing for Prediction of Material Performance in Structures and Components, 1972. Contbr. articles to tech. jours. Patentee vitamin synthesis. Home: 7821 Carrleigh Pkwy Springfield VA 22152 Office: 2101 Constitution Av NW Washington DC 20418

SHANEYFELT, SHIRLEY NADENE FEARN, artist; b. Hastings, Neb.; d. Oris C. and Calla (Wary) Fearn; student Hastings Coll., Corcoran Sch. Art, George Washington U.; pvt. study with Andrea Di Zerega, Laura Douglas, Joseph Pielage, Yolande Mayhall; m. Lyndal L. Shaneyfelt, June 16, 1940; 1 son, Terry Leroy. One-man shows at Lee Galleries, Alexandria, Va., 1961, FBI, Washington, 1965—, Heron House Gallery, Reston, Va., 1966, Galleries, Art League No. Va., 1967, others; exhibited in group-shows at Smithsonian Instn., Washington, 1952, 57, Georgetown U., Washington, 1963, Old Towne Gallery, Alexandria, 1965, Washington Gallery Art, 1965, U. Va., Charlottesville, 1965, Hadassah Invitational Shows, Alexandria, Va., 1967-74, Alexandria br. Pen Women Group Show, Gallery on Mall, 1969, Gilliam Show, Alexandria Art League, 1972, Rehoboth By-the-Sea Cottage Tour and Art Show, 1972, others; represented in permanent collections Gen. Testing Labs., Alexandria, Crestwood Elementary Sch., Springfield, Va., Atlantic Research Corp., Alexandria; also pvt. collections; tchr., dir. Shane Painters, 1962-74. Recipient 1st prize Springfield Contemporary Show, 1956; 4th prize No. Va. Art League, 1959, 2d, 3d prizes, 1959; 1st prize (2), 2d prize Women's Club of Va., 1959; 1st prize Art League Marshall Show, 1961; 1st prize Art League, 1963, 3d prize, 1963; 3d prize Picasso Show, Hecht's Washington, 1963; 1st prize Galleries, Art League, 1967; hon. mention Corcoran Art Sch. Spring Show, George Washington U., 1972; named Artist of Year No. Va. Cotillion, 1973. Mem. Nat. League Am. Pen Women (1st v.p., 1964-65), Art League No. Va. (2d v.p. 1962-63; gallery hanging chmn. 1967), Am. Art League. Clubs: Women's Belle-Haven (art chmn. Alexandria 1963-65). Address: 6125 Vernon Terrace Alexandria VA 22307

SHANK, RUSSELL, librarian; b. Spokane, Sept. 2, 1925; s. Harry and Sadie (Hytowitz) S.; B.S., U. Wash., 1946, B.A. in L.S., 1949; M.B.A., U. Wis., 1952; D.L.S., Columbia, 1966; m. Doris Louise Hempfer, Nov. 9, 1951; children—Susan Marie, Peter Michael, Judith Louise. Reference librarian U. Wash., 1949; asst. engring. librarian U. Wis., 1949-52; chief in-service tng. and personnel Milw. Pub. Library, 1952; engring.-phys. scis. librarian Columbia, 1953-59; asst. univ. librarian U. Cal. at Berkeley, 1959-64; sr. lectr. Columbia Sch. Library Service, 1964-66, asso. prof., 1967; dir. libraries Smithsonian Instn., 1967—; vis. asst. prof. U. Wash., summer 1956; officer of instrn. Columbia Sch. Library Service, 1954-59; lectr. U. Cal. at Berkeley, 1959-64. Dir. sci. library project N.Y. Met. Reference and Research Library Agy., 1966-68. Served with USNR, 1943-46. Recipient Distinguished Alumnus award U. Wash. Sch. Librarianship, 1968. Council on Library Resources fellow, 1973-74. Mem. A.L.A. (chmn. personnel adminstrn. sect. 1965-66, pres. information sci. and automation div. 1968-69, mem. council 1961-65), Assn. Coll. and Research Libraries (pres. 1972-73), Spl. Libraries Assn. (chmn.

engring. div. 1968-69), Am. Soc. Information Sci., A.A.A.S. Author: Regional Access to Scientific and Technical Information, 1966; also articles. Home: 1054 Dalebrook Dr Alexandria VA 22308 Office: Smithsonian Instn Washington DC 20560

SHANKLE, ROBERT JACK, educator, dentist; b. Walker County, Ga., Sept. 17, 1923; s. Robert Davis and Ada (Goodson) S.; student North Ga. Coll., 1941-43, U. Ga., 1943, Washington U., 1944; D.D.S., Emory U., 1948; m. Nancy Lee Bruckman; children—Robert Davis II, Jane Lewis. Instr., Emory U. Sch. Dentistry, 1949-51; asso. prof. U. N.C., 1951-61, prof., 1961-66, prof., dept. chmn., 1966—, also dir. admissions Dental Sch.; cons. Womack Army Hosp., dir. admissions; cons. Ft. Knox, Ky., Ft. Benning, Ga. Served with AUS, 1943-44, capt. USAF, 1955-57. Diplomate Am. Bd. Endodontics (past dir.). Fellow Am. Assn. Endodontists, Am. Coll. Dentists, Internat. Coll. Dentists; mem. Omicron Kappa Upsilon (pres. supreme chpt.), Alpha Epsilon Delta. Republican. Episcopalian. Author (with Brauer and Richardson) The Dental Assistant, 1964; (with others) The Art and Science of Operative Dentistry, 1968. Editor: N.C. Dental Jour. Home: 1306 Mason Farm Rd Chapel Hill NC 27514

SHANKLIN, ROBERT LEE, chemist; b. Terre Haute, Ind., June 16, 1926; s. Vernon A. and Olive Paulette (Mann) S.; B.S., Ind. State U., 1950; m. Patricia Anne Burrell, May 23, 1947; 1 son, Robert Lee Shanklin II. Lab. supr. E.I. duPont de Nemours, Dana, Ind., 1951-57, Wilmington, Del., 1957-58, New Johnsonville, Tenn., 1958-64; chief chemist Mosites Rubber Co., Fort Worth, Tex., 1964—. Served with USNR, 1944-46. Mason. Developer non-burning elastomers used in space exploration. Home: 3716 Orchard St Fort Worth TX 76119 Office: 2720 Tillar St Fort Worth TX 76107

SHANNON, BUFORD STANLEY, JR., computer service co. exec.; b. Paris, Tex., Feb. 11, 1939; s. Buford Stanley and Frances (Jones) S.; B.S. in Math. Engring., So. Meth. U., 1961, M.S. in Statistics (NIH fellow), 1963; m. Nanette Odom, Jan. 25, 1961; children—Clark Lamar, Stacy. Elec. engr. Dallas Power & Light Co., 1958-59; research asst. Socony Mobil Field Research Labs., Duncanville, Tex., also engring. research asst. Southwestern Med. Sch., Dallas, 1960-61; lectr. dept. math. and exptl. statistics So. Meth. U., Dallas, 1963-64; dir. Goddard Computer Sci. Inst. of Wadley Insts. Molecular Medicine, Dallas, 1963-69, controller Wadley Insts., 1967-69; cons. Cons. Assos., Inc., Dallas, 1969; v.p., also gen. mgr. and treas. TELPAR, Inc., Dallas, 1969-70; pres. Alpha Systems, Inc., Dallas, 1970—, treas., 1970-72, chmn. bd., 1972—. Cons. in computing, finance and statistics, 1964-69; asst. prof. Grad. Research Inst. of Baylor U., Dallas, 1963-69. Mem. Assn. for Computing Machinery (pres. Dallas-Fort Worth chpt. 1967-69; referee Communications 1966—), Am. Statis. Assn. (pres. North Tex. chpt. 1964-65). Contbr. articles to tech. jours. Home: 3513 Milton St Dallas TX 75205 Office: 6400 N Central St Dallas TX 75206

SHANNON, DAVID LEROY, lawyer; b. Cin., Apr. 26, 1906; s. William David and Martha Norris (Rowland) S.; A.B., Case Western Res. U., 1928; J.D., Stetson U., 1932; m. Dorothy Welland Conner, Feb. 19, 1971; children by previous marriage—Ruth Alice (Mrs. R.G. Harrison), Sally (dec.). With advt. dept. Procter & Gamble Co., Cin., 1928-29; admitted to Fla. bar, 1932, Ohio bar, 1933; practiced in Cin., 1933-49, New Smyrna Beach, Fla., 1949—; municipal judge New Smyrna Beach, 1955-59, City of Edgewater, 1970-71. Chmn. S.E. Volusia County service unit Salvation Army, 1969—; youth dir. Fla. region Christian Ch. (Disciples of Christ), 1960-68, mem. regional bd., 1968-74; pres., chmn. bd. Christian Ch. (Disciples of Christ) (Internat.), 1971-74, mem. adminstrv. com., 1969-72, mem. gen. bd., 1969-74. Recipient Man of Yr. award Fla. Christian Men's Fellowship, 1968. Mem. Am. Bar Assn., Fla. Bar, Delta Tau Delta, Phi Alpha Delta. Republican. Mason (32 deg., Shriner). Home: 110 Columbus Av New Smyrna Beach FL 32069 Office: 399 Canal St PO Box 846 New Smyrna Beach FL 32069

SHANNON, DONALD SUTHERLIN, educator; b. Tacoma Park, Md., Dec. 28, 1935; s. Raymond Corbett and Elnora Pettit (Sutherlin) S.; B.A., Duke, 1957; M.B.A., U. Chgo., 1964; Ph.D., U. N.C., 1972; m. Virginia Ann Lloyd, June 24, 1961; children—Stacey Eileen, Gail Allison. Mem. auditing staff Price Waterhouse & Co., N.Y.C., 1957-61; sr. accountant Price Waterhouse, Chgo., 1964-65; instr. Duke U., Durham, N.C., 1964-69; asst. prof. bus. adminstrn. U. Ky., Lexington, 1969—. Served with AUS, 1958-59, 61-62. Mem. Am. Accounting Assn., Am. Inst. C.P.A.'s, Ill. Soc. C.P.A.'s, So. Econ. Assns., Am. Finance Assn., Beta Gamma Sigma. Club: University Chicago. Home: 3304 A Wood Valley Court Lexington KY 40502

SHANNON, JACK THOMAS, lumber co. exec.; b. Memphis, Feb. 25, 1924; s. James Egbert and Anna May (Strube) S.; student Vanderbilt U., 1942, Memphis State U., 1946-47; m. Amelia Russell, June 15, 1950; children—Jack Thomas, Carroll, Richard L. With Shannon Bros. Lumber Co., Memphis, 1947—, pres., 1970—; v.p. Shannon Bros. Enterprises, Memphis, 1965—; dir. Union Planters Nat. Bank, Memphis. Pres. Memphis Cotton Carnival Assn., 1967; commr. Auditorium and Conv. Center, Memphis; mem. adv. com. Shelby County Sheriff Dept., 1968—. Bd. dirs. Hutchison Sch. for Girls, Memphis. Served with USAAF, 1942-46. Mem. Beta Theta Pi. Republican. Episcopalian. Clubs: Memphis Country, Memphis Hunt and Polo. Home: 45 S Norwall St Memphis TN 38117 Office: PO Box 619 1684 Florida St Memphis TN 38101

SHANNON, JOHN SANFORD, ry. exec.; b. Tampa, Fla., Feb. 8, 1931; s. George Thomas and Ruth (Garrett) S.; A.B., Roanoke Coll., 1952; J.D., U. Va., 1955; m. Elizabeth Howe, Sept. 22, 1962; children—Scott Howe, Elizabeth Garrett, Sandra Denison. Admitted to Va. bar, 1955; asso. mem. firm Hunton, Williams, Gay, Powell & Gibson, Richmond, Va., 1955-56; with Norfolk & Western Ry. Co., Roanoke, Va., 1956—, solicitor, 1956-60, asst. gen. solicitor, 1960-64, gen. solicitor, 1965-68, gen. counsel, 1968-69, v.p. law, 1969—; dir. Wheeling & Lake Erie Ry. Co., Roanoke, Trailer Train Co., Chgo. First Fed. Savs. and Loan Assn., Roanoke, Nickel Plate Improvement Co., Roanoke. Pres. Legal Aid Soc. Roanoke Valley, 1970—; bd. dirs. Help, Inc., Roanoke; pres. bd. trustees North Cross Sch. Mem. Am., Va., Roanoke bar assns., Roanoke C. of C., Order Coif, Sigma Chi, Omicron Delta Kappa, Phi Delta Phi. Episcopalian (chancellor Diocese S.W. Va.). Clubs: Roanoke Country, Shenandoah (Roanoke); Metropolitan (Washington). Home: 507 Audubon Rd SW Roanoke VA 24014 Office: 8 N Jefferson St Roanoke VA 24042

SHANNON, ROBERT EDWARD, educator; b. Blackwell, Okla., Sept. 6, 1932; s. Edward Vincent and Emma Stella (Buellsfeld) S.; B.S., Okla. State U., 1955, Ph.D., 1965; M.S., U. Ala., 1960; m. Gayle Marion Day, July 9, 1955; children—Kelly Anne, Edward Vincent. Operations research analyst Coleman Co., Inc., Wichita, Kan., 1955-56; systems engr. U.S. Army Ballistics Missile Agy., Huntsville, Ala., 1956-59, G.C. Marshall Space Flight Center, Huntsville, 1959-65; prof. engring. U. Ala., Huntsville, 1965—; v.p. Acad. Assos. Cons. to industry, U.S. Army Missile Command. Chmn. research com. Manpower Area Planning Council. Pres. bd. Cath. Social Services, 1972-73. Served with AUS, 1956-58. Mem. Am. Inst. Indsl. Engrs., Am. Soc. Engring. Edn., Operations Research Soc. Am., Inst. Mgmt. Scis., World Future Soc., Sigma Xi, Alpha Pi Mu, Delta Chi. Roman Catholic. Author: Systems Simulation—The Art and Science, 1975. Contbr. articles to profl. jours. Home: 2221 Briarcliff Rd Huntsville AL 35801

SHANNON, ROBERT MCDONALD, JR., architect, planner; b. Bristol, Va., Oct. 2, 1917; s. Robert McDonald and Helen Izetta (Coyner) S.; B.S., Va. Poly. Inst. and State U., 1939, M.S., 1940; postgrad. Woodrow Wilson Sch. Princeton, 1949-50, Ohio State U., 1954-56; m. Anne MacGowan, June 20, 1953 (div. May 1964); children—Christopher, Alexandra, Nicholas. With U.S. Army C.E., 1940-61, comdg. officer 109th Engring. Bn., Mannheim, Germany; adviser Chinese Chief of Engrs., Taiwan; engr. N.Y. Engr. Dist.; dir. community shelter planning Hays, Seay, Mattern & Mattern, Roanoke, Va., 1961-63; dir. Roanoke Valley Regional Planning Commn., Roanoke, 1964-68; exec. dir. Fifth Planning Dist. Commonwealth of Va., 1969-72; asst. planning and constrn. Va. Commonwealth U., Richmond, 1973—; asst. prof. Ohio State U., 1953-56; instr. U. Md. Far East, 1958, U. Va. Roanoke Center, 1962-65. Mem. Arts Com. City of Roanoke, 1970-73; mem. com. Roanoke Valley Museum, 1970-73; U.S. observer UN Interregional Seminar, Madrid, Spain, 1972. Bd. dirs. Va. Citizens Planning Assn. Decorated Bronze Star. Registered architect, Va. Mem. A.I.A., Am. Inst. Planners, Asia Soc. (Southeast Asia adv. group), Tau Beta Pi. Author met. area planning studies. Home: 9304 Groundhog Dr Richmond VA 23235 Office: Va Commonwealth U Box 805 MCV Sta Richmond VA 32398

SHAO, STEPHEN PINYEE, educator; b. I-hing, Kiangsu, China, Jan. 24, 1924; s. Chu Tang and Shawyuen (Wang) S.; B.S., Nat. Hunan U. China, 1946; M.A., Baylor U., 1949; Ph.D., U. Tex., 1956; m. Betty Lucille Outen, June 18, 1953; children—Stephen Pinyee, Dale Hilton, Lawrence Peter, Alan Terence, Patricia Sue. Came to U.S., 1948, naturalized, 1956. Chief accountant Bd. for Tex. State Hosps. and Spl. Schs., 1952-54; prof., head bus. adminstrn. dept. Bluefield (Va.) Coll., 1954-56; lectr. Univs. Taiwan (Formosa), Hong Kong, summer 1961; sr. statistics and mgmt. cons. U.S. Naval Supply Center, Norfolk, Va., 1962-68; prof. mgmt. and statistics Coll. William and Mary, Norfolk, 1956-62; prof., chmn. dept. quantitative scis. in bus. econs. Old Dominion U., Norfolk, 1962—. Mem. Am. Econ. Assn., Am. Accounting Assn., Am. Statis. Assn., So. Mgmt. Assn., Alpha Kappa Psi. Author: Mathematics of Finance, 1962; Statistics for Business and Economics, 1st edit., 1967, 2d edit., 1972; Mathematics for Management and Finance, 1969. Home: 5161 Lake Shore Rd Virginia Beach VA 23455 Office: Sch Bus Old Dominion U Norfolk VA 23508

SHAPER, CHARLES HARRY, mfg. co. exec.; b. Camden, N.J., Mar. 11, 1899; s. Max and Molly Shapiro; B.S., U. Colo., 1920; LL.B., South Tex. Coll. Law, 1936; m. Saralee Pollock, Aug. 26, 1973; children (by previous marriage)—Steve, Roger, Susan (Mrs. Don G. Rehmeyer). Engr., State of Okla., 1920-22; chief metallurgist Reed Roller Bit Co., Houston, 1922-45; with Metal Window Products Co. adn affiliates, Houston, 1945—, pres., 1945-65, chmn. bd., 1965—. Cons. Am. Soc. for Metals, 1925-73. Home: 2004 Buffalo Terrace Houston TX 77019 Office: Box 125 Houston TX 77001

SHAPIRO, ALFRED BRUCE, lawyer; b. Alexandria, La., Dec. 29, 1942; s. Morris and Mary Fern (Clyde) S.; B.A., La. State U., 1965, J.D., 1968; m. Janice Ruth Lea, Sept. 26, 1967; children—Melissa Lea, David Bruce. Admitted to La. bar, 1968; practice law, Alexandria, 1968-71; law clk. to U.S. Dist. Judge Nauman S. Scott, 1971-73; asst. dist. atty. Rapides Parish, La., 1973—. Mem. City of Alexandria Housing Code Com., 1972; mem. Republican Polit. Action Com. Mem. Am., La., Alexandria bar assns., Alexandria Jaycees (v.p. 1971), Alexandria-Pineville C. of C., Phi Alpha Delta. Jewish religion. Mason. Home: 542 Hummingbird Lane Alexandria LA 71301 Office: PO Box 1365 Alexandria LA 71301

SHAPIRO, CAROL SADIE, plastic surgeon; b. Pitts., Sept. 24, 1939; d. Leo I. and Charlotte H. (Heller) Shapiro; B.S., U. Pitts., 1961; M.D., Woman's Med. Coll. Pa., 1965; m. Donald E. Morgan, May 1974. Intern, Phila. Gen. Hosp., 1965-66; resident gen. surgery Georgetown U. Hosp., Washington, 1966-69, resident plastic surgery, 1969-71, post tng. fellow, 1971-72; practice medicine specializing in plastic surgery Dumfries (Va.) Med. Center, 1972—; mem. staff Potomac Hosp., Woodbridge, Va., Prince William Hosp., Manassas, Va., Commonwealth Hosp., Fairfax, Va.; clin. instr. Georgetown U. Sch. Medicine, 1972—. Vol. team physician Garfield High Sch. Football Team, 1971—. Home: 6120 Shiplett Blvd Burke VA 22015 Office: Dumfries Med Center Dumfries VA 22026

SHAPIRO, LEONARD, former air force officer, bus. exec., govt. ofcl.; b. Rochester, N.Y., Feb. 1, 1917; s. Sam and Rose (Tomkin) S.; B.A., U. Ill., 1939; M.A., Georgetown U., 1948, Ph.D., 1949; m. Judith Torruella, Aug. 16, 1947; 1 son, John L. Commd. 2d lt., advanced through grades to col. USAF, 1951, chief operations Missile Test Center, 1959-61, Congo, 1961-62, tech. tng., Amarillo, Tex., 1962-65, ret.; dir. Internat. Bus. Devel., Northrop Corp., Beverly Hills, Cal., 1965-69; asst. adminstr. Econ. Devel. Adminstrn., Govt. P.R., 1970—, Mem. Cal. Citizens Committee, Nat. Council on Crime and Delinquency. Active Boy Scouts. Bd. govs. Georgetown U. Decorated Legion of Merit D.F.C., Air medal with 13 oak leaf clusters. Fellow Am. Inst. Aeros. and Astronautics. Roman Catholic. Club: Wings (N.Y.C.). Author Soviet Treaty Series, 2 vols., 1949, 52. Home: 860 Ashford Av Apt 9 A Santuree PR 00907 Office: Econ Devel Adminstrn GPO Box 2350 San Juan PR 00936

SHAPIRO, MYRON (MIKE) FREDERICK, communications co. exec.; b. Mpls., Dec. 16, 1918; s. Leo and Miriam (Levin) S.; student Duluth Jr. Coll., 1937-38, U. Minn., 1939; m. Conway Helen King, Oct. 24, 1942; 1 dau., Lynne Carole (Mrs. Duke Covert). Mgr. KTXL-Radio, San Angelo, Tex., KECK-Radio, Odessa, Tex., 1945-52; sales rep. WFAA-TV, Dallas, 1952-53; comml. mgr. KDUB, Lubbock, Tex., 1953-54; account exec. Avery Knodel, Chgo., 1954-55; v.p., mng. dir. Griffin Telecasting Properties, Tulsa and Little Rock, 1956-58; mgr. WFAA-TV, 1958-60, gen. mgr., 1960—; exec. v.p. Belo Broadcasting Corp. (owners WFAA), Dallas, 1970—. Chmn. Dallas March of Dimes, 1970-71; mem. devel. bd. Jacksonville Lon Morris Coll., Jacksonville, Tex., 1971—, mem. adv. bd. Communications Sch., U. Tex. at Austin, 1969—. Bd. dirs. Family Guidance Center, 1967-69, Am. Cancer Soc., 1965—. Served with A.C., AUS, 1941-45. Recipient Outstanding Broadcaster award Assn. Broadcast Execs. Tex., 1962. Mem. Nat. Assn. Broadcasters (chmn. bd. dirs. TV 1965-66), ABC-TV Affiliates Assn. (chmn. bd. govs. 1961-63), Assn. Broadcast Execs. Tex. (pres. 1959-60), Dallas Ad Club (bd. dirs. 1968-69), Dallas Ad League (bd. dirs. 1968-69), Better Bus. Bur. (bd. dirs. 1965—), Salesmanship Club. Initiated weekly TV show pub. service Let Me Speak To The Manager, 1961—. Home: 6911 Waggoner Pl Dallas TX 75230 Office: WFAA AM-FM-TV Communications Center Dallas TX 75202

SHAPIRO, RAYMOND ELIHU, govt. ofcl.; b. N.Y.C., Oct. 20, 1927; s. Isaiah W. and Julia (Goldstein) S.; B.S., Coll. City N.Y., 1948; Ph.D., Ohio State U., 1952; m. Dorothy Ann Norman, June 28, 1964; children—Richard Irving, Sharon Beth. With U.S. Dept. Agr., Beltsville, Md., 1953-65; with office scis. Bur. Foods FDA, Washington, 1965—. Served with AUS, 1946-47. Guggenheim fellow, 1961-62. Fellow A.A.A.S.; mem. Am. Chem. Soc., Geochem. Soc. Jewish religion (pres. synagogue). Mason. Home: 2205 Greenery Lane Silver Spring MD 20906 Office: 200 C St SW Washington DC 20204

SHARE, LEONARD, physiologist; b. Detroit, Oct. 14, 1927; s. Jacob and Mildred (Tobachnick) S.; A.B., Bklyn. Coll., 1947; A.M., Oberlin Coll., 1948; Ph.D., Yale, 1951; m. Carol R. Robey, Aug. 28, 1949; children—Michael E., Donald S., Frederick C. USPHS postdoctoral fellow Western Res. U., 1951-52, instr. physiology, 1952-54, sr. instr., 1954-57, asst. prof., 1957-63, asso. prof., 1963-68; prof. physiology Case Western Res. U., 1968-69; prof., chmn. dept. physiology and biophysics U. Tenn., 1969—; researcher Inst. Biol. Chemistry of U. Copenhagen (Denmark), 1962-63; mem. gen. medicine Bstudy sect. NIH, 1965-69. Mem. Am. Physiol. Soc., Endocrine Soc., Memphis Heart Assn., A.A.A.S., Internat. Soc. Neuroendocrinology, Sigma Xi. Contbr. articles to profl. jours. Home: 340 Shady Woods Cove Memphis TN 38117

SHARMA, DULI CHANDRA, civil engr.; b. Sherpur, India, June 8, 1942; s. Murari Lal and Rumali (Devi) S.; B.Sc. cum laude, Aligarh Muslim U., India, 1963; M.S., U. Miami (Fla.), 1969; m. Nirmala Gaur, May 15, 1965; children—Amit, Anjali. Lectr. civil and structural engring. Aligarh U., 1963-65, Jaipur U., 1965-67; grad. asst. U. Miami, 1967-69; structural designer M. Noble & Assos., Miami, 1969-70, Connell Assos., Miami, 1970-72; structural project engr. Ferendino, Grafton, Spillis, Candela, Architects, Engrs., Planners, Coral Gables, Fla., 1972-73; structural engr. Inter-Am. Center Authority, Miami Lakes, Fla., 1973—. Sec.-treas. India Assn. Miami, 1967-68, pres., 1971-72. Registered profl. engr., Fla. Mem. Fla. Engring. Soc. (sr.), Nat. Soc. Profl. Engrs., Am. Soc. C.E., Am. Concrete Inst. Home: 10070 SW 4th St Miami FL 33144 Office: 14440 NW 60th Av Miami Lakes FL 33014

SHARMAN, GEORGE ALBERT, dentist; b. Houston, July 13, 1917; s. George Robert and Cora Jane (Duke) S.; student U. Houston, 1935; D.D.S., Tex. Dental Coll., 1940; postgrad. Am. Sch. Applied Hypnotherapy, Hypnoanesthesia, 1952; m. Margie Eloise Worsham, June 22, 1940; 1 son, Robert Wayne. Practice dentistry, Houston, 1940—. Served to capt. USAAF, 1942-46. Fellow Royal Soc. Health; mem. Am. Endodontic Soc., Am. Soc. Clin. Research Dental Materials, Houston Dist., Tex., Am. dental assns., Hon. Order Good Fellow, Psi Omega. Home and Office: 2110 Airline Dr Houston TX 77009

SHARP, JOHN THOMAS, physician, educator; b. Dalhart, Tex., Nov. 16, 1924; s. John Robert and Laura Ellen (James) S.; M.D., Columbia U., 1947; m. Marjorie Sue Glinn, June 3, 1949; children—John R., Thomas G., Jeffrey D. Intern, Presbyn. Hosp., N.Y.C., 1947-48, resident, 1948-49; resident VA Hosp., White River Junction, Vt., also Mary Hitchcock Hosp., Hanover, N.H., 1949-51; fellow arthritis unit Mass. Gen. Hosp., Boston, 1953-57, asst. physician, 1957-60; research asso. Harvard Med. Sch., Boston, 1957-60; asso. physician Henry Ford Hosp., Detroit, 1960-62; asso. prof. medicine, chief section rheumatic disease Baylor Coll. Medicine, Houston, 1962-65, prof., 1965—. Cons., Methodist Hosp., Houston, 1963—. Bd. dirs. Tex. Gulf Coast chpt. Arthritis Found., 1963—, chmn. med. and sci. com., 1964-66, chmn. med. adminstrv. com., 1970-72. Served with USNR, 1951-53. Arthritis Found. fellow, 1954-56. Mem. A.C.P., Am. Rheumatism Assn., Am. Assn. Immunologists, Am. Soc. Microbiology, Tex. Rheumatism Assn. (pres. 1958). Editorial bd. Arthritis and Rheumatism, 1968—; editor The Role of Mycoplasmas and L Forms of Bacteria in Disease, 1970. Home: 5314 Mandell St Houston TX 77005

SHARP, PAUL FREDERICK, univ. pres.; b. Kirksville, Mo., Jan 19, 1918; s. Frederick J. and L. Blanche (Phares) S.; A.B., Phillips U., 1939; Ph.D., U. Minn., 1947; LL.D. (hon.), Tex. Christian U., 1961; L.H.D. Buena Vista Coll., 1967; Litt. D., Limestone Coll., 1971; m. Rosella Ann Anderson, June 19, 1939; children—William, Kathryn, Paul Trevor. Instr. U. Minn., 1942, 46-47, vis. lectr., 1948; asso. prof. Am. history, chmn. Am. Instns. program U. Wis., 1954-57, vis. lectr., 1953; vis. lectr. San Francisco State Coll., 1950, U. Ore. 1955; Fulbright lectr. Am. Instns., univs. Melborne and Sydney, Australia, 1952; pres. Hiram Coll., 1957-64; chancellor U. N.C., Chapel Hill, 1964-66; pres. Drake U., Des Moines 1966-71, U. Okla., 1971—. Served from ensign to lt. (s.g.), USNR, 1943-46; naval liaison officer Royal Australian Navy, 1944-45. Research grants Minn. Hist. Soc., 1947, 48, Social Sci. Research Council, 1949, 51; Ia. State U. Alumni Fund award, 1952; Fulbright award to Australia, 1952; Ford Faculty fellow, 1954; recipient award of merit Am. Assn. State and Local History, 1955; Silver Spur award Western Writers Am., 1955; Guggenheim fellow, 1957. Mem. Phi Beta Kappa, Phi Kappa Phi, Pi Gamma Mu, Phi Alpha Theta. Mem. Disciples of Christ Church. Author of Agrarian Revolt in Western Canada, 1948; Old Orchard Farm; Story of an Iowa Boyhood, 1952; Whoop-Up Country; Canadian American West, 1955. Editor: Documents of Freedom, 1957. Cons. author: Heritage of Midwest, 1958; regional editor Montana mag., editorial cons. Americana Press, 1955—. Contbr. articles profl. jours. Home: 1200 S Pickard St Norman OK 73069

SHARP, RUTH COLLINS (MRS. CHARLES S. SHARP), civic worker; b. Dallas; d. Carr P. and Ruth (Woodall) Collins; B.A., So. Meth. U., 1948; m. Charles S. Sharp, June 21, 1947; children—Sally, Stanton, Susan. Pres. Jr. League, 1961-62, ofcl. hostess Internat. Conf. in Dallas, 1961; pres. Vis. Nurse Assn., 1956-58; pres. Dallas Day Nursery Assn., 1964-66. Sec. bd. dirs. YMCA, 1961-62; bd. dirs. KERA Ednl. TV, Grand Jury Assn., Salvation Army, Dallas; trustee So. Meth. U., Hockoday Sch. Recipient Zonta award as Dallas Woman of Year, 1965, Golden Plate award Am. Acad. Achievement for Community Service, 1965; Woman of Achievement award So. Meth. U., 1966; Arete award for community service, 1969. Methodist. Club: Dallas Woman's (pres. 1967-69). Home: 5227 Meaders Lane Dallas TX 75229

SHARPE, JOHN ALLEN, JR., newspaper editor; b. Lumberton, N.C., Oct. 20, 1912; s. John Allen and Daisy (Courtney) S.; A.B., Duke, 1932; m. Helen Allen Seawell, Jan. 1, 1950; children—John Allen III, Clifford Seawell, Hal Courtney. Newspaper reporter Robesonian, Lumberton, 1932-39, asso. editor, 1940-43, 46-48, editor, 1948—; pres. Robeson Broadcasting Co. Served with USAAF, 1943-46. Mem. N.C. Press Assn. (v.p. 1967-68). Methodist. Home: 1015 Riverside Blvd Lumberton NC 28358 Office: 121 W 5th St Lumberton NC 28358

SHARPE, MITCHELL RAYMOND, historian, author; b. Knoxville, Tenn., Dec. 22, 1924; s. Mitchell Raymond and Katie Grace (Hill) S.; B.S., Auburn U., 1949, M.A., 1954; postgrad. Emory U., 1955; m. Virginia Ruth Lowry, Dec. 21, 1952; children—Rebecca Ann, Rachel Ruth, David Mitchell. Instr. English, Auburn U., 1952-54, U. Ala. at Huntsville, 1957-65; tech. writer U.S. Army Missile Command, Huntsville, 1955-60; supervisory tech. writer Marshall Space Flight Center, Huntsville, 1960-71, sr. historian, 1971—. Cons. history of rocketry Nat. Air and Space Mus., Smithsonian Instn., 1965—; historian Ala. Space and Rocket Center, Huntsville, 1970—. Served with AUS, 1943-46, 50-52. Recipient Robert H. Goddard essay award in history of rocketry Nat. Space Club, 1968. Mem. Am. Inst. Astronautics and Aeros. (tech. com. history of astronautics 1972-73), Nat. Assn. Sci. Writers, Co. Mil.

Historians, Soc. History of Tech., Soc. Tech. Communications, Brit. Interplanetary Soc. Author: Basic Astronautics, An Introduction to Space Science, Engineering, and Medicine, 1962; Applied Astronautics, An Introduction to Space Flight, 1963; Living in Space, The Astronaut and His Environment, 1969; Yuri Gagarin, First Man into Space, 1969; Satellites and Probes, The Development of Unmanned Space Flight, 1970; Dividends from Space, 1971. Asso. editor Space Jour., 1957-59. Home: 7302 Chadwell Rd Huntsville AL 35802 Office: Marshall Space Flight Center Huntsville AL 35812

SHARPE, THOMAS GILBERT, JR., lawyer; b. San Antonio, Dec. 26, 1935; s. T. Gilbert and Dorothy (Stovall) S.; B.A., U. Tex., 1960, LL.B., 1963; m. Shirley Ritter, Aug. 27, 1960; children—John Carlyle, Thomas Steele, James Gilbert. Admitted to Tex. bar, 1963, Colo. bar, 1972, U.S. Supreme Ct. bar; practiced in Brownsville, 1963—; partner firm Hardy & Sharpe, 1963—. Served with 17th inf. regiment, AUS, 1955-57, Korea. Named Outstanding Young Man Brownsville, 1969. Mem. Am. Trial Lawyers Assn. (nat. safety committeeman), Am., Cameron County (pres. 1971-72) bar assns., State Bar Tex. (adv. com. standards on specialization criminal law 1972-74, named Gen. Practitioner Yr. 1972), Nat. Assn. Def. Lawyers in Criminal Cases, Cal. Trial Lawyers Assn., Law-Sci. Acad. Am. (gold medal award 1969; chancellor 1972), Tex. Criminal Def. Lawyers Assn. (dir. 1971—, chmn. amicus curiae com. 1971—), U. Tex. Sch. Law Alumni Assn. (dir. 1971—), Phi Alpha Delta. Clubs: Valley Inn and Country (pres. 1969), Kiwanis (pres. 1969). Home: 2020 Palm Blvd Brownsville TX 78520 Office: 1010 E Washington St Brownsville TX 78520

SHARPE, WILLIAM GRAY, III, ret. ins. agy. exec., lawyer; b. Elm City, N.C., Aug. 4, 1905; s. William Gray and Fannie (Peacock) S.; A.B., Duke, 1926; postgrad. grad. Pell Law Sch., 1933; m. Naomi Cannaday, May 21, 1930; children—Frances Louvenia (Mrs. Charles Franklin Ritch II), William Gray IV. Teller, Toisnot Banking Co., Elm City, 1927-31; admitted to N.C. bar, 1933; asst. cashier Br. Banking & Trust Co., Elm City, 1931-33, cashier, 1933-54; owner Sharpe Ins. Agy., Elm City, 1954-70; pres. Elm City Devel. Corp., 1963-67, v.p., 1967—. Active various community drives. Mem. Bd. Edn. Elm City, 1948-66. Mem. Lambda Chi Alpha. Methodist (lay leader 1965-71, chmn. ofcl. bd. 1966-67). Rotarian. Elk. Home: PO Box 465 Elm City NC 27822 Office: 121 1/2 E Main St Elm City NC 27822

SHARPLEY, JOHN MILES, lab. exec.; b. Norfolk, Va., Jan. 28, 1918; s. John Edward and Annie Carter (Miles) S.; B.A., Hampden-Sydney Coll., 1941; M.S., U. Richmond, 1949; Ph.D., U. London (Eng.) 1951; m. Virginia Leah Tarpin, July 16, 1941. Chief microbiologist Froehling and Robertson Inc., Richmond, Va., 1945-47; dir. microbiol. research, Buckman Labs., Inc., Memphis, 1950-60; pres. Sharpley Labs. Inc., Fredericksburg, Va., 1960—; prof. dept. biology, Va. Commonwealth U., 1965—. Vis. lectr. Am. Inst. for Biol. Scis. Served to lt. col., USAF, 1941-45. Decorated Purple Heart medal. Fellow Am. Inst. Chemists, A.A.A.S.; mem. Soc. Indsl. Microbiology (dir. 1949-52), Am. Chem. Soc., Soc. Am. Bacteriologists, Soc. for Gen. Microbiology. Author: Applied Petroleum Microbiology, 1960, Elementary Hydrocarbon Microbiology, 1964. Contbr. articles to profl. publs. Home: Belle Plains Belle Plains Rd Fredericksburg VA 22401 Office: Box 846 Fredericksburg VA 22401

SHAUCK, MAXWELL EUSTACE, JR., educator; b. Sandusky, O., Oct. 7, 1935; s. Maxwell Eustace and Gertrude Kennedy (Fisher) S.; B.A., Miami U., 1960, M.A., 1962; Ph.D. (NSF fellow 1964-66), Tulane U., 1966; m. Pamela Jean Todd, Sept. 12, 1969; children—Kimberly Wynn, Kristin Alane. Research instr. Yale, 1966-68; asst. prof. Duke, 1968-70; asso. prof. math. N.C. Central U., 1970—, also postdoctoral fellow N.C. State U., 1972—. Pres. Carolina Sport Aviation, Inc.; chief flight instr. Air East. Served with USNR, 1957-59. NIH postdoctoral fellow, 1972—. Mem. Am. Math. Assn., Soc. Indsl. and Applied Math., Am. Math. Soc., Sigma Xi. Contbr. articles to profl. jours. Home: 729 Tinkerbell Rd Chapel Hill NC 27514 Office: Biomathematics Program University of North Carolina Raleigh NC 27514

SHAUGHNESSY, WINSLOW MORSE, mus. dir.; b. Springfield, Ill., Oct. 27, 1935; s. Howard John and Grace (Heck) S.; B.S. in Botany, U. Wis. at Madison, 1957; postgrad. zoology So. Ill. U., 1957-58; m. Judith Smith, June 15, 1957; children—Anne, Geoffrey, Susan. Curator natural sci. Pa. State Mus., Harrisburg, 1961-67; mus. adminstr. Acad. Natural Scis. Phila., 1967-71; dir. Children's Mus., Nashville, 1971—. Fellow Del. Valley Ornithol. Club; mem. Am. Ornithologists' Union, Assn. Interpretive Naturalists. Rotarian. Home: 6413 Currywood Dr Nashville TN 37205 Office: PO Box 7067 Nashville TN 37210

SHAW, CHARLES SAXON, owner real estate and ins. co.; b. Greensboro, Ala., May 11, 1939; s. Walter Melvin and Olive Zoe (Mathers) S.; B.S., U. So. Miss., 1961; m. Shirley Jean Copeland, Nov. 17, 1961; children—Tamela Jean, Sharon Kae, Patricia Dee. Owner, Shaw Real Estate and Ins., Mobile, Ala., 1961—. Bd. dirs. Am.'s Jr. Miss Pageant, 1969-70, Ala. Gov.'s Beach Home, 1963-64. Recipient outstanding president award Ala. Jaycees, 1970. Mem. Mut. Agts. Assn. U.S., Jaycees (city pres. 1969-70, nat. dir. 1970-73, v.p. met. affairs U.S., 1972-73), Delta Sigma Pi. Mason (Shriner). Home: 2016 Archer Lane Mobile AL 36605 Office: 1540 S Beltline Hwy Mobile AL 36609

SHAW, CLINTON ROBERT, economist, govt. ofcl.; b. Springfield, Mass., Oct. 2, 1932; s. Arthur Merrill and Enid (Eves) S.; A.B., U. Mass., 1959; J.D., George Washington U., 1964; m. George Fisher Collins, Mar. 30, 1956; 1 son, Clinton Robert. Economist, U.S. Tariff Commn. Washington, 1959—. Served from 2d lt. to capt. USAF, 1952-56. Mem. Am. Econ. Assn., Delta Theta Phi. Author tech. reports for U.S. Tariff Commn. Home: 3106 N Taylor St Arlington VA 22207 Office: US Tariff Commn Washington DC 20436

SHAW, EMIL GILBERT, environmental scientist; b. San Antonio, June 22, 1922; s. Arthur Dee and Dorothy Cameron (Johnson) S.; B.S., S.W. Tex. State U., 1947, M.A., 1948; Ph.D., Tex. A. and M. U., 1967; m. Dora Lee Whitley, June 27, 1970; children by previous marriage—Alexis (Mrs. William E. West, Jr.), Emil G., Robert B.; stepchildren—Deena L., Leah M. With U.S. Air Force Sch. Aerospace Medicine, Brooks AFB, Tex., 1958—, chief chem. support sect., 1958-66, dep. chief environmental systems br., also chief tech. and adminstrv. support office, 1966-68, dep. chief environmental scis. div., 1968-72, dir. environmental scis., also chief environmental scis. div., 1972—. Vis. prof. Tex. A. and M. U., College Station, 1968; adj. prof. Va. Poly. Inst., Blacksburg, 1970. Served with USNR, 1941-44, AUS, 50-58. Recipient Spl. Act of Service award Brooks AFB, 1964. Mem. Am. Chem. Soc., Aerospace Med. Soc. Mason. Home: 10606 West Av San Antonio TX 78213 Office: USAFSAM Environmental Sciences Div Brooks AFB TX 78235

SHAW, GEORGE VINCENT, JR., data processing co. exec.; b. Rochester, N.Y., Sept. 6, 1928; s. George Vincent and Katherine Louise (McGreal) S.; B.A., Yale, 1950; m. Eva Darlene Blue, Nov. 30, 1957; children—Cynthia, Sally, George Vincent III, Jennifer. Asst. controller Allied Stores Corp., Dey Bros. & Co., 1951-56; controller, v.p. Maverick Clarke, San Antonio, 1956-62; accountant Haskings & Sells, Houston, 1962-63; partner Holmes & Raquet, San Antonio, 1963-68; v.p. Holmes & Shaw, Inc., San Antonio, 1968—; dir. S. States Oil & Gas Co. C.P.A., Tex. Mem. Am. Inst. C.P.A.'s. Roman Catholic (finance chmn. 1968, 71). Clubs: San Antonio, Northern Hills Country (San Antonio). Home: 9003 Valley View Lane San Antonio TX 78217 Office: Century Bldg West San Antonio TX 78216

SHAW, HENRY OVERSTREET, transp. exec.; b. Adel, Ga., Oct. 21, 1893; s. Archibald Hiram and Elizabeth (Overstreet) S.; intensive course U.S. Naval Acad., 1918; m. Vivian Izona Riggs, June 19, 1920 (dec. May 1967); 1 dau., Sylvia Byron (Mrs. David Nicholas Blount); m. 2d, Mary H. Gardner, Apr. 28, 1971. With Ga. Lumber & Supply Co. and Shaws, Inc., Miami, Fla., 1914-29, v.p., treas., 1923-29; with Shaw Bros. Oil Co. and predecessor cos., Miami, Fla., 1916—, chmn. bd. dirs., exec. officer, 1950-61; land developer, 1916—; partner Shaw Bros. Docks and Shaw Bros. Shipping Co., 1943—; pres. Shaw Bros. Shipping Co., 1955—, Shaw Marine Co., Shaw Gold Coast Co.; owner Shaw Fgn. Trade Warehouse; dir. Fla. Nat. Bank & Trust Co. of Miami, Fla. First Nat. Bank of Opa Locka. Chmn. Dade County chpt., A.R.C. war fund drive, 1942, dir. county chpt., 1942-43, vice chmn., 1943; dir. Dade County Community Chest, 1950-51. Pres. South Atlantic and Fla. Ports Conf., 1945-47; chmn. Miami Rate and Traffic Bd., 1927-33, Port and Harbor Bd., 1937-38, 1939; mem. Am. and Fla. petroleum industries coms., 1931—; mem. Gov. spl. com. on freight rates (Fla.), 1940-45. Mem. Citizens bd. U. Miami, 1946—, pres., 1950. Served as ensign Supply Corps, USNRF, 1918-19; mem. Civilian aide com. of comdg. gen. AAF, 1942. Mem. Miami C. of C. (dir. 1944-49, pres. 1944-46), Greater Miami Traffic Assn., Internat. Platform Assn. Mason (K.T., Shriner), Elk, Rotarian (pres. Miami club 1934-35). Home: 881 Ocean Dr Key Biscayne FL 33149 Office: 501 NE 1st Av Miami FL 33132

SHAW, JO EDWARD, JR., lawyer; b. Houston, Apr. 26, 1934; s. Jo Edward and Will Rivers (Smith) S.; B.A., Rice U., 1955; LL.B., U. Tex., 1958; m. Betty J. Harden, July 3, 1960; children—Jana, Jason, Justin. Admitted to Tex. bar, 1958; U.S. Supreme Ct. bar; practiced in Houston, 1959—; asso. firm Dyche, Wheat, Thornton, 1959-64; mem. firm Dyche, Wheat, Thornton & Wright, 1964-71, Wheat, Thornton & Shaw, 1971—; municipal judge City of Southside Place, 1964—. Dir. Statewide Title Co., Farmers & Mchts. State Bank, Moulton, Tex., Starnes Group, Inc., Tex. Land Title Assn., Northwest Park Corp. Mem. city council City of Bunker Hill Village, Tex., 1970—. Served to capt. AUS, 1958. Mem. Am., Tex., Houston bar assns., Am. Judges Assn., Am. Judicature Soc., Sigma Alpha Epsilon (pres. 1957-58). Presbyn. (chmn. bd. diaconate 1972—). Club: Houston Racquet. Home: 11614 Starwood St Houston TX 77024 Office: 3610 One Shell Plaza Houston TX 77002

SHAW, MARGERY WAYNE SCHLAMP, physician, lawyer, educator; b. Evansville, Ind., Feb. 15, 1923; d. Arthur George and Louise (Meyer) Schlamp; student Hanover Coll., 1940-41; A.B. magna cum laude, U. Ala., 1945; M.A., Columbia, 1946; postgrad. Cornell U., 1947-48; M.D., U. Mich., 1957; J.D., U. Houston, 1973; 1 dau., Barbara Rae (Mrs. Frederic L. Ferri). Intern St. Joseph Mercy Hosp., Ann Arbor, Mich., 1957-58; practice medicine specializing in human genetics, Ann Arbor, 1958-67, Houston, 1967—; instr. dept. human genetics Med. Sch. U. Mich., 1958-61, asst. prof., 1961-66, asso. prof., 1966-67; asso. prof. dept. biology Grad. Sch. Biomedical Scis. U. Tex., Houston, 1967-69, prof., 1969—; dir. Med. Genetics Center, Houston, 1971—; mem. genetics study sect. NIH, Bethesda, Md., 1966-70, mem. genetics tng. com. 1970-73, chromosome studies astronauts NASA, 1970-71; mem. adv. bd. Nat. Genetics Found., 1972—, research adv. bd. Planned Parenthood, Houston, 1972—. First aid instr. A.R.C., 1962-67; unit chmn. United Fund, 1966. Recipient Billings Silver medal A.M.A., 1966; Achievement award Am. Assn. U. Women, 1970-71. Mem. Am. Soc. Human Genetics (past sec., dir.), Genetics Soc. Am. (sec. 1971-73), Tissue Culture Assn. (trustee 1970-73), Environmental Mutagen Soc. (dir. 1972-74), Am. Soc. Cell Biology, Phi Beta Kappa, Alpha Omega Alpha. Asso. editor: Am. Jour. Human Genetics, 1962-68; editorial bd. In Vitro. Cons. editor: Cytogenetics, 1962—. Contbr. articles to profl. jours. Home: 3614 Montrose Blvd Houston TX 77006 Office: MD Anderson Hosp and Tumor Inst Houston TX 77025

SHAW, PHILIP EUGENE, organic chemist; b. St. Petersburg, Fla., July 21, 1934; s. Paul David and Frances (Beacham) S.; B.S. in Chemistry, Duke, 1956; Ph.D. (Eli Lilly fellow in chemistry), Rice U., 1960; m. Marilyn June Robertson, June 27, 1959; children—Maurlyn, Cheryl, Jonathan. Pharm. research Sterling-Winthrop Research Inst., Rensselaer, N.Y., 1960-65; organic chemist Citrus and Subtropical Products Lab., U.S. Dept. of Agr., Winter Haven, Fla., 1965—. Mem. Am. Chem. Soc. (chmn. Lakeland subsect. 1973), Inst. Food Technologists, Fla. State Hort. Soc. Democrat. Methodist. Kiwanian (dir. 1972). Contbr. articles to sci. jours. Patentee in field. Home: 2116 John Arthur Way Lakeland FL 33803 Office: Box 1909 Winter Haven FL 33880

SHAW, PHILIP SIDDEL, cons.; b. Montpelier, Vt., Jan. 17, 1915; s. William and Bertha (Clark) S.; A.B., Duke, 1937; M.A., U. Fla., 1944; postgrad. Fla. State U., 1959-60; m. Lois Cleveland, Mar. 26, 1936; children—Philip S., William A. Asst. auditor to auditor Fla. Auditing Dept., Tallahassee, 1942-54; comptroller Bd. County Commrs., Pinellas County (Fla.), 1955-60; asst. div. dir. finance Fla. Dept. Edn., Tallahassee, 1964-65, comptroller, 1965-73; cons., 1974—. Sci. tchr., prin. Fla. pub. schs., 1938-42; cons. handbook devel. sect. U.S. Office Edn., 1964—, mem. com. revision of forms, grant and loan mgmt. br., 1965-66; mem. Nat. Com. on Financial Accounting for Pub. Schs., 1965—; cons. Ednl. Information Systems, P.R., 1967; mem. tech. adv. com. Ala. Dept. Edn., 1970—. Mem. Assn. Ednl. Data Systems (dir., treas. 1964—), Southeastern Edn. Lab. (chmn. data systems group 1966-67). Co-author: Principles of Public School Accounting. Address: 1221 Brandt Dr Tallahassee FL 32303

SHAW, ROBERT, music condr.; b. Red Bluff, Cal., Apr. 30, 1916; s. Shirley Richard and Nelle Mae (Lawson) S.; A.B., Pomona Coll., 1938, Mus.D. (hon.), 1953; Mus.D. (hon.), Coll. Wooster, 1951, St. Lawrence U., 1955, Mich. State U., 1960, Cleve. Inst. Music, 1966, Western Res. U., 1966, Emory U., 1967, Fla. State U., 1968; D.F.A. (hon.), U. Alaska, 1963; L.H.D., Kenyon Coll., 1963; m. Maxine Farley, Oct. 15, 1939; children—Johanna, Peter Thain, John Thaddeus; m. 2d, Caroline Sauls Hintz, Dec. 19, 1973. Dir. Fred Waring Glee Clubs, 1938-45; choral dir. Aquacades, 1942-43, Carmen Jones, 1943, Seven Lively Arts, 1944, My Darlin Aida, 1953; guest condr. CBS Symphony series, 1944-45, ABC Symphony series, 1945, NBC Symphony, 1946, N.Y.C. Symphony, 1946, Boston Symphony Orch., 1958, N.Y. Philharmonic, 1970, Nat. Symphony Orch., 1959, Chgo. Symphony Orch., 1960, Houston Symphony, 1970, Dallas Symphony, 1969, Minn. Orch., 1972, Richmond (Va.) Symphony, 1971; dir. choral music Berkshire Music Center, 1946-49; dir. choral activities Juillard School Music, 1946-49; condr. San Diego Summer Symphony, 1953-58; asso. condr. Cleve. Orch., 1956-67; music dir., condr. Atlanta Symphony Orch., 1967—; artistic dir. Alaska Festival of Music, 1956—; dir. Meadow Brook Sch. Music, 1965-67, Blossom Festival Sch., Cleve. Orch.-Kent (O.) State U., 1968—, Brevard (N.C.) Music Center, 1972-73. Founder, dir. Robert Shaw Chorale, which has made ann. tours of U.S., 1948—, Middle East and Europe, 1956, USSR, 1962, S.Am., 1964. Recipient Nat. Assn. Am. Composers and Condrs. award for outstanding Am. born condr., 1943; Guggenheim fellow, 1944, founder-dir. The Collegiate Chorale, 1941. Mem. Ga. Art Commn., 1967—. Address: 3707 Randall Mill Rd Atlanta GA 30327

SHAW, ROBERT JENNINGS, chmn. Ga. Republican Com.; b. Bronwood, Ga., Aug. 21, 1929; s. Robert Edward and Vesta (Jennings) S.; student Ga. Inst. Tech., 1947, U. Ga. at Atlanta, 1948-50; m. Mary Elaine Smith, Dec. 25, 1950; children—Maria Elena, Melanie Dawn, Susan June, Bobbie Elizabeth Ann. Gen. agt., Pan-Am. Life Ins. Co., 1961—. Pres., Bolton Civic Assn. 1966—. Vice chmn. finance com. Fulton County (Ga.) Rep. com., 1963, chmn. speakers' bur., 1964, ho. dist. chmn. also campaign mgr. for candidate for Ga. state representative, 1965, first vice chmn. also chmn. candidate com., 1966, chmn., 1968—, chmn. exec. com., 1970—, chmn., Rep. Central Com., 1970—; vice chmn. So. region Rep. Nat. Com., 1973—; mem. exec. com. Fifth Congl. Dist. Rep. Com., 1965—; mem. Ga. State Rep. Centennial Com., 1966-68; first vice chmn. Fulton County Rep. Party, 1970—; first vice chmn. Ga. Rep. Com., 1970-71, chmn., 1971—; first vice chmn., Ga. Rep. Exec. Com., 1970—. Bd. dirs. Atlanta Hosp. Served as staff sgt. USAF, 1950-51; PTO. C.L.U. Mem. Atlanta Assn. Life Underwriters, Gen. Agts. and Mgrs. Assn. of Atlanta, South Cobb Jaycees (hon. life), Phi Sigma Epsilon (hon.) Baptist (music dir.). Home: 295 Glen Lake Dr NW Atlanta GA 30327 Office: 1819 Peachtree St NE Atlanta GA 30309

SHAW, THOMAS NEVILLE FAWCETT, sch. adminstr.; b. N.Y.C., June 19, 1925; s. William Fawcett and Margaret (Nicholson) S.; A.B. cum laude Princeton, 1949; M.A., Columbia, 1956; m. Peggy Wolfe, Sept. 2, 1950; children—Anne Gibson, Peter Wolfe. Ordained priest Protestant Episcopal Ch., 1966; tchr. English and history, dir. studies Wooster Sch., Danbury, Conn., 1949-61, dir. Wooster Summer Sch. Reading Skills, 1957-61; dir. Camp Pequot, Ivoryton, Conn., 1951-56; headmaster Trinity Episcopal Sch., New Orleans, 1961—. Trustee St. Martin's Episcopal Sch., New Orleans. Served with AUS, 1943-46. Mem. Nat. Assn. Episcopal Schs. (pres. 1971-73), La. Episcopal Sch. Assn. (pres. 1969-71), Ind. Schs. Assn. of Southwest (mem. standards and research com. 1966-70, chmn. research com. 1972-74). Author: A Manual for Reading, 1955. Home: 1305 Jackson Av New Orleans LA 70130 Office: 2111 Chestnut St New Orleans LA 70130

SHAW, WILLIAM FREDERICK, statistician; b. Bklyn., Feb. 24, 1920; s. Charles Peter and Josephine Veronica (Seusing) S.; B.B.A., U. Miami, 1949; M.A., George Washington U., 1953; m. Josephine Cannington Kerbey, Jan. 18, 1947; children—William Frederick, Teresa Anne. With Research and Statistics div. FHA, Washington, 1950—, chief statistician, 1969—. Served with F.A., AUS, 1943-45. Decorated Bronze Star medal for heroism. Mem. Am. Statis. Assn., Am. Econ. Assn., Alpha Kappa Psi. Home: 6527 Byrnes Dr McLean VA 22101 Office: 7th and D Sts SW Washington DC 20411

SHAW, WILLIAM HARLAN, educator; b. Tulia, Tex., Apr. 3, 1922; s. Willie Sample and Delia (Harlan) S.; B.A., Hardin-Simmons U., 1943, M.A., 1949; Ph.D., La. State U., 1955; m. Majorie Lee McQuade, Nov. 1, 1945; children—Delia Belle, Morgan Roe. Grad. asst. La. State U., Baton Rouge, 1948-49, 53-54; instr. Hardin-Simmons, Abilene, Tex., 1949-50, asst. prof., 1955-56, Ill. State U., Normal, 1950-53; asst. prof. Washington U., St. Louis, 1956-61; asst. prof. Fla. State U., Tallahassee, 1961-67, asso. prof., 1967-68; asso. prof., coordinator grad. studies dept. drama U. New Orleans, 1968-72, prof., 1972—. Costume dir. Asolo Theater Festival, State Theater of Fla., 1962-68. Served with USNR, 1943-46. Presbyn. (deacon). Home: 7450 Fieldston Rd New Orleans LA 70126

SHAW, WILLIAM WESLEY, educator; b. Phila., Oct. 19, 1910; s. William Henry and Mary (Burt) S.; B.A., Dickinson Coll., 1932; M.A., Princeton, 1934, Ph.D., 1935; m. Mary Elizabeth Cole, June 8, 1938; children—Judith C. (Mrs. Steven A. Davidow), William Wesley, Regina E. (Mrs. Gerard P. van As). Tech. asst. N.J. State Civil Service Dept., Trenton, N.J., 1936-38; dir. personnel San Diego County, Cal., 1938-41; asso. dir. Municipal Service Bur., N.Y. State Civil Service Commn., Albany, N.Y., 1941-42; dir. personnel City New Orleans, 1942-70; prof. polit. sci. Tulane U., New Orleans, 1947—, dir. Urban Studies Center, 1971—. Bd. dirs. United Fund Greater New Orleans, 1967-73. Mem. Pub. Personnel Assn. (pres. 1957, 58), Am. Polit. Sci. Assn., Am. Soc. Pub. Adminstrs. Home: 1721 Robert St New Orleans LA 70115

SHAWCROFT, BRIAN, architect; b. Nottingham, Eng., Feb. 24, 1929; s. Herbert Thomas and Annie (Tatman) S.; grad. Southwest Essex Tech. Coll. and Sch. of Art, 1953; M.Arch., Mass. Inst. Tech., 1959-60; m. Anne Marie Rogers, Sept. 13, 1968. Came to U.S., 1959, naturalized, 1965. Architect, Slater, Uren & Pike, Architects, London, Eng., 1954-56, Page & Steele, Architects, Toronto, Ont., Can., 1956-59; partner MacMillan, MacMillan, Shawcroft & Thames, Raleigh, N.C., 1968-70; partner Environmental Planning Assos., Raleigh, 1971—. Asso. prof. architecture Sch. Design N.C. State U., Raleigh, 1960-68; Cons. architect Holloway-Reeves Architects, Raleigh, 1964—. Mem. State Capitol Planning Commn., Raleigh, 1963-65, Heritage Sq. Planning Commn., Raleigh, 1963-65. Served with Ednl. Corps, Royal Army, 1947-49. Mem. A.I.A. (N.C. chpt. award of merit 1962, 68, House and Home House for Better Living award of merit 1962), Royal Inst. Brit. Architects (asso.). Home: 210 Ashe Av Raleigh NC 27605 Office: 333 Fayetteville St Raleigh NC 27601

SHAWHAN, JOHN FRANKLIN, engring. exec.; b. Cin., Feb. 4, 1912; s. Frank and Emma Rose (Meyer) S.; E.E., U. Cin., 1935; m. Etha Heller, June 1, 1937; 1 dau., Nancy Elizabeth. Test engr. Cin. Gas & Elec. Co., 1935-37; elec. design engr. Shepard Elevator Co., 1937-45, chief engr., 1945-58; chief engr. elevator div. Dover Corp., Memphis, 1958-66, engring. adminstrv. officer, 1966-72, v.p. engring. elevator div., 1973—. Chmn., Memphis Bd. Elevator Rules, 1967—. Mem. Cin. Engring. Soc. (life), Am. Nat. Standards Inst., Eta Kappa Nu, Tau Beta Pi. Presbyn. (elder). Home: 1301 Hayne Rd Memphis TN 38117 Office: PO Box 2177 Memphis TN 38101

SHAY, VIOLET AMELIA BROWN (MRS. JOHN HENRY SHAY, JR.), artist, poet, writer; b. New Orleans; d. Thomas Beggs and Ethel (Schultz) Brown; grad. bus. coll., New Orleans, 1929; Famous Writers Sch.; m. John Henry Shay, Jr., June 15, 1940. Free lance writer, 1940—; poetry published in anthologies including Avalon, Am. Sonnets and Lyrics, New Voices in American Poetry, 1972, others; prose pub. in mags. including Coronet, Canadian Home Jour., Seventeen, Pathfinder, The Pen Woman, Town Jour.; juvenile stories in publs. including Stories for Children, Council Fires, Trailblazer; editor little mags., 1945-50; ceramics exhibited Pirate's Alley Art Show, New Orleans, 1950-51. Recipient awards for writing Nat. League Am. Pen Women, La. Press Women; hon. mention ceramics Pirate's Alley Art Show, 1950; award Deep South Writers Conf., 1968. Founding fellow Intercontinental Poetry Soc.; mem. Avalon World Arts Acad. (La.) (pres. 1952-54), Nat. Hist. Soc. (founding asso.), Composers, Authors and Artists Assn. Am., Nat. Poetry Day Com. (state chmn. 1949-56), Nat. League Am. Pen Women (br. pres. 1951-53), Avalon World Arts Acad., United

Amateur Press Assn. Am. (past chief lit. dir.), Wendell Willkie Found. Contbg. author: Louisiana Vignettes, 1967; Louisiana Leaders, 1970. Address: 1231 Congress St New Orleans LA 70117

SHEA, MARTIN COYLE, JR., physician; b. Memphis, Dec. 24, 1929; s. Martin Coyle and Ethel Marie (Fredette) S.; B.S., U. Tenn., 1952, M.D., 1952; m. Trina Kay McKeithen, Dec. 29, 1972; children—Marc, Melinda, Madeline, Alison, Rachel, Jeff. Intern, U.S. Naval Hosp., Oakland, Cal., 1953; resident gen. surgery U.S. Naval Hosp., Bethesda, Md., 1955-57, resident otolaryngology, 1957-59; head dept. otolaryngology U.S. Naval Hosp., Memphis, 1959-62; otologist Memphis Otologic Clinic, 1962-67, Shea Otologic Group, Memphis, 1967—, also pres.; asst. prof. otolaryngology U. Tenn.; cons. U.S. Naval, Vets. hosps.; mem. asso. staff Bapt. Meml. Hosp. Served to lt. comdr. M.C., USNR, 1952-62. Diplomate Am. Bd. Otolaryngology. Mem. Memphis and Shelby County Med. Soc., A.M.A., Am. Acad. Ophthalmology and Otolaryngology, Am. Council Otolaryngology, So., Tenn., Pan Am. med. assns., Tenn. Acad. Otolaryngology, Pan. Am. Soc. Otolaryngology, Memphis Soc. Otolaryngology, Flying Physicians Assn., Alpha Omega Alpha. Research on mastoid obliteration with bone. Home: 5925 Poplar Pike Extension Memphis TN 38138 Office: 1215 Poplar Av Memphis TN 38104

SHEA, MICHAEL, elec. engr.; b. Bonham, Tex., Aug. 1, 1940; s. James Elbert and Hazel (Barron) S.; B.S. in Elec. Engring., U. Houston, 1963, B.S. in Indsl. Engring., 1971; m. Margaret Helen Cullen, Mar. 24, 1967; children—David Lawrence, Christine Elizabeth, Patrick Michael. With Houston Lighting & Power Co., 1963—, engr., 1965-71, sr. engr., 1971-73, supr. maintenance/tech. div. energy control and dispatching dept., 1973—. Registered profl. engr., Tex. Mem. I.E.E.E., Gulf Meadows Civic Club. Home: 7726 Folkestone St Houston TX 77034 Office: PO Box 1700 Houston TX 77001

SHEAKS, BARCLAY, artist; b. East Chicago, Ind., Oct. 22, 1928; s. Earl L. and Jeanie (Rice) S.; B.F.A., Va. Commonwealth U., 1949; m. Edna Mae Daniel; 1 son, Owen James. Art tchr., 1949—; head art dept. Va. Wesleyan Coll., Norfolk, 1970—; artist-in-residence Humanities Center, Richmond, Va., 1971—; art cons. for Hunt Mfg. Co., Inc. Phila., 1968—; lectr. Va. Mus. Exhibited in one-man shows at Va. Mus., 1969, Columbia (S.C.) Mus., 1971, Mobile (Ala.) Mus., 1968; exhibited in group shows Nat. Acad., Corcoran Gallery, Norfolk, Va. mus., Butler Inst. Am. Art, others; represented in permanent collections Va. Mus., Columbia Mus., Butler Inst. Am. Art, Youngstown, O. Mem. Va. Mus., Norfolk Mus., Peninsula Arts Assn., Tidewater Artists, La. Watercolor Assn. Author: Painting in Acrylics From Start to Finish, 1972. Home: 51 Hopkins St Newport News VA 23601

SHEAR, SIDNEY KINGSBURY, operations analyst; b. Akron, O., Apr. 16, 1912; s. Verne Warren and Grace Addison (Kingsbury) S.; A.B., Western Res. U., 1934, M.A., 1936; Ph.D. in Physics, Brown U., 1939; m. Charlotte Virginia Krick, June 13, 1943; children—Warren Krick, Eugene Kingsbury. Physicist U.S. Dept. of Navy, 1941-45; operations analyst Operations Evaluation Group of Center for Naval Analyses, Arlington, Va., 1945-54, dir. operations research group, 1954-57, field rep., London, Eng., 1958—, Mediterranean area, 1964, Washington, 1959-60, 62-63; dir. naval warfare analysis group, Arlington, 1960-62, sr. sci. analyst Operations Evaluation Group, 1965—. Bd. dirs. Arlington Met. Chorus, Kindler Found. Mem. Operations Research Soc. Am. Democrat. Mem. United Ch. of Christ (mem. bd. social action). Author research papers. Home: 6035 28th St North Arlington VA 22207 Office: 1401 Wilson Blvd Arlington VA 22209

SHEARER, JOHN CLYDE, educator; b. Phila., June 24, 1928; s. John Dwight and Edna Mildred (Moser) S.; B.S., Cornell U., 1952; Fulbright fellow U. Manchester, Eng., 1952-53; A.M., Princeton, 1958, Ph.D., 1960; m. Mary Ann Shafer, Apr. 30, 1955; children—John Peter, Rachel Alicia. Adminstrv. asst. indsl. relations Union Carbide Metals Co., Marietta, O., 1952-56; research asst. indsl. relations Princeton, 1957-60; asst. prof. econs. Carnegie Inst. Tech., 1960-65; asso. prof. econs. Pa. State U., 1965-67; prof. econs., dir. Manpower Research and Tng. Center of Okla. State U., 1967—; labor arbitrator. Prof., economist Latin Am. Inst. Econ. and Social Planning, UN Econ. Commn. for Latin Am., Santiago, Chile, 1962-63; cons. Orgn. Am. States, UN, Ford Found., Inter-Am. Devel. Bank, Council Internat. Progress in Mgmt., A.M.A., Okla. Municipal League, others. Served with USMC, 1946-48. Owen D. Young fellow, 1956-57, 57-58; Ford Found. fellow, 1958-59. Mem. Nat. Acad. Arbitrators, Am. Econ. Assn., Indsl. Relations Research Assn., Soc. Internat. Devel., Okla. Civil Liberties Union, Southwestern Regional Manpower Adv. Com., Fed. Mediation and Conciliation Service, Am. Arbitration Assn., Phi Kappa Phi. Author: High-Level Manpower in Overseas Subsidiaries, 1960. Contbr. articles profl. jours., chpts. in books. Home: 2020 Crescent Dr Stillwater OK 74074

SHEARIN, FORREST GREENE, assn. ofcl.; b. nr. Weldon, N.C., Mar. 13, 1903; s. John Wesley and Eugenia (Kilpatrick) S.; student pub. schs., Weldon; m. Virgie Elizabeth Grizzard, Dec. 23, 1923; children—Beatrice Eugenia, Forrest Greene. Mem. N.C. Jr. Order United Am. Mechanics, 1924—, sec., gen. mgr. state council ins. dept., 1940—, state mgr. ins. dept., nat. council, 1949—, controller, bd. trustees N.C. Jr, O.U.A. M. Children's Home, nat. council bd. trustees Children's Home, mem. ritual com. nat. council, 1955-59, chmn. Good of the Order com. nat, council, 1957; nat. vice councilor Jr. O.U.A.M., 1961-63, nat. councilor, 1963-65, mem. nat. council bd. control com. on investments and program, 1967—, mem. exec. bd. nat. council bd. of officers, nat. council treas., 1972—; owner, sec. treas. Colonial Frozen Foods, Inc.; owner Forrest G. Shearin, finance bus., gen. real estate bus.; owner, operator Forrest G. Shearin, Ins. Agy.; pres. Investment Enterprises, Inc., 1961—, also dir., sec., treas. Scotland Neck Devel. Corp.; dir. Br. Bank & Trust Co. Mem. Halifax Devel. Commn., 1965—, Region L Council of Govts., 1965-69. Sec.-treas. Scotland Neck Bus. Bur., 1959—; mem. City Council, Scotland Neck, 1946—, finance officer, 1949—; chmn. Local Democrats Pct.; mem. County Dem. Exec. Com., N.C. Dem. Exec. Com. Bd. trustees, finance com. Chowan Coll., Murfreesboro, 1947-50; trustee Bapt. Orphanages N.C., 1951-55; chmn. bd. trustees Our Community Hosp., Scotland Neck, 1955-58, chmn., acting adminstr., 1961-64; served as mem. Health Com. Lower Halifax County; mem. Bicentennial Com. Halifax County, 1958. Named Mr. Jr. Order N.C., 1969. Mem. North Roanoke Bapt. Assn. (treas. 1958-63, chmn. constn. and by-laws com. 1956; gen. bd. state conv. 1957-60; chmn. social service com.; exec. com.); mem. exec. and budget com. State Bapt. Conv. N.C.; mem. corp. bd. Bapt. Home for Aging. Democrat. Baptist (deacon, trustee). Home: W 17th St Scotland Neck NC 27874 Office: N Main St Scotland Neck NC 27874

SHEARIN, HENRY LLOYD, financial analyst; b. Danville, Ky., Aug. 1, 1942; s. J.T. and Georgia Winefred (Tuttle) S.; student Centre Coll. Ky., 1961-62; B.S., Eastern Ky. U., 1965; m. Brenda Carroll Crews, Oct. 21, 1961. With Yeager, Ford & Warren, C.P.A.'s, Louisville, 1965-71, mgr., 1970-71; financial analyst Extendicare, Inc., Louisville, 1971—. Served with AUS, 1970-73. C.P.A., Ky. Mem. Ky. Soc. C.P.A.'s, Am. Inst. C.P.A.'s, Louisville Jaycees. Home: 3808 Old Brownsboro Hills Rd Louisville KY 40222 Office: Extendicare Inc One Riverfront Plaza Louisville KY 40202

SHEEHAN, JAMES HARLEY, lawyer, accountant; b. Macon, Ga., May 4, 1931; s. James B. and Frances (Harley) S.; B.S. with honors, U. Fla., 1961; J.D. with high honors, Fla. State U., 1971; m. Caroline Martha Smith, Nov. 2, 1952; children—James Gregory, Kelly Elizabeth. Agt., Internal Revenue Service, Jacksonville, Fla., 1961-65; tax mgr. Milligan & Burke, C.P.A.'s, Jacksonville, 1965-68; lectr. fed. income taxation Fla. State U., Tallahassee, 1968-71; partner Arthur Young & Co., Jacksonville, 1971—; admitted to Fla. bar. Mem. exec. com. N.E. Fla. Estate Planning Council, 1968-69; active Community Chest, United Fund. Served with USNR, 1949-53. C.P.A., Fla. Mem. Fla. (Jacksonville chpt. award for excellence 1967, state taxation com.) Am. insts. C.P.A.'s, Fla. Bar, Am. Bar Assn., Delta Theta Phi. Beta Alpha Psi, Alpha Kappa Psi. Methodist. Contbr. articles to profl. jours. Home: 8342 Calento St Jacksonville FL 32211

SHEEHAN, ROBERT JAMES, assn. exec.; b. Pitts., May 13, 1937; s. Regis James and Helen (O'Leary) S.; B.S. in Econs., U. Pitts., 1966, M.A. in Econs., 1970; m. Marie Elizabeth Yoskovich, Apr. 24, 1965; children—Stephanie Ann, Robert James III. Engaged as a research analyst with ACTION-Housing, Inc., Pitts., 1960-62; adminstrv. asst. Dept. City Planning, Pitts., 1962; project rep., Urban Redevel. Authority Pitts., 1963-65, devel. coordinator, 1965-67, director rehab., after 1968; now dir. econs. Nat. Assn. Homebuilders, Washington. Mem. Jr. C. of C. (dir. 1963-64), Soc. for Advancement Mgmt. (treas. 1964-65), Am. Econ. Assn., Regional Sci. Assn., Bldg. Ofcls. Conf. Am., Pi Kappa Alpha. Roman Catholic. K.C. (financial sec. 1962-65). Home: 1606 Wrightson Dr McLean VA 22101 Office: Nat Assn Homebuilders 15th and M Sts NW Washington DC 20005

SHEEHAN, WILLIAM HAROLD, lawyer; b. Childress, Tex., Mar. 6, 1928; s. Gerald and Mazzie (Lewis) S.; LL.B., Baylor U., 1951; m. Mary Louise Mayers, May 30, 1948; children—Mary Margaret, Kathleen J., John P., Jack Hale. Admitted to Tex. bar, 1950; pvt. practice, Friona, Tex., 1950-65; partner Dubuque & Meredith, Dumas, Tex., 1966—; county atty. Parmes Co. (Tex.), 1955-57; dist. atty. 154th Jud. Dist., 1957-61. Chmn. March of Dimes, Friona, 1954-55, Community Chest, Friona, 1960-61; pres. Dumas Concert Assn., 1966—; pres. Dumas YMCA, 1969-70. Served with AUS, 1946-47, 52-54. Mem. Dumas C. of C. (pres. 1968-69), Am., Dumas, 69th Dist, bar assns., State Bar Tex. (council mem., chmn. gen. practice sect.). Baptist (deacon). Lion. Home: 601 Bennett Dr Dumas TX 79029 Office: 105 W 7th St Dumas TX 79029

SHEEHAN, WILLIAM JOHN, librarian; b. Syracuse, N.Y., Jan. 1, 1937; s. William Jeremiah and Margaret Mary (Horrigan) S.; B.A., U. Toronto, 1960; S.T.B., U. St. Michael's Coll., 1965; M.S. in L.S., Case Western Res. U., 1968. Joined Congregation of Priests of St. Basil, 1955, ordained priest Roman Catholic Ch., 1966; tchr. Aquinas Inst., Rochester, N.Y., 1960-62; tchr. Catholic Central High Sch., Detroit, 1962-63; asst. librarian St. Basil's Sem., Toronto, Ont., Can., 1963-67; asst. librarian U. St. Thomas, Houston, 1968-69, dir. libraries, 1969—. Mem. A.L.A., Catholic Library Assn. Address: 3812 Montrose Blvd Houston TX 77006

SHEEHY, MARIE ANN PAVELKA (MRS. VINCENT THOMAS SHEEHY), govt. ofcl.; b. Kyjov, Czechoslovakia, Apr. 1, 1920; d. Joseph Louis and Marie (Navratil) Pavelka; came to U.S., 1924, naturalized, 1930;; student Bryant and Stratton Bus. Coll., Chgo., 1938; m. Vincent Thomas Sheehy, May 13, 1941; 1 dau., Marie W. (Mrs. Thomas M. Lisi). Sec., Ingersoll-Rand Machinery Co., Chgo., 1939-40; sec. Internat. Boundary Commn. U.S. and Can., Dept. State, Washington, 1940—, adminstrv. asst., 1956-63, adminstrv. officer 1963—. Asst. financial drives Trinity Coll. Alumni, Washington, 1968. Roman Catholic. Home: 2205 Beechwood Rd Lewisdale-Adelphi MD 20783 Office: GAO Bldg 441 G St NW Washington DC 20548

SHEELEY, EUGENE CHARLES, educator, audiologist; b. Tiffin, O., Jan. 4, 1933; s. Carl Frank and Mable Serena (Reedy) S.; B.A., Heidelberg Coll., 1954; M.A., Case-Western Res. U., 1955; Ph.D., U. Pitts., 1964. Dir., Hearing Test and Child Study Center, N.M. Sch. for the Deaf, 1964-67; prof. speech U. Ala., 1967—; cons. Partlow State Sch. and Hosp., Tuscaloosa, Ala., Ala. State Crippled Children's Services. Mem. Am. Speech and Hearing Assn., Am. Assn. Mental Deficiency, Conv. Am. Instrs. Deaf, Acoustical Soc. Am. Contbr. articles profl. jours. Research in psychoacoustics. Home: PO Box 26 Ralph AL 35480 Office: PO Box 1965 University AL 35486

SHEETS, NAN, artist; b. Albany, Ill.; d. George Duffield and Orvilla (Booth) Quick; Ph.G., Valparaiso U., 1905; postgrad. Utah U., 1908-09, Broadmoor Art. Acad., 1921-24; m. Fred C. Sheets, June 28, 1909. Art column Daily Oklahoman Sun Edn., Oklahoma City, 1934-62; dir. Oklahoma Art Center, Oklahoma City, 1935-65, ret., 1965, trustee; exhibited one-man shows Okla. Art Center, 1950, Ft. Worth Arts Center, 1929, Mus. Art, Okla. U., 1930; Philbrook Art Center, Tulsa, 1949, 1952, Witte Meml. Mus., San Antonio, 1929, Mus. Fine Arts, Houston, 1929; exhibited group shows State Fair of Okla., 1927, Tulsa U., 1932, Philbrook Art Center, 1952, Okla. Art Center, 1967. Named to Okla. Hall of Fame, 1953; named Woman of Year in Radio and TV, Okla. Sooner chpt. Am. Women in Radio and TV, 1959; named Outstanding Citizen Greater Oklahoma City, 1962. Fellow Royal Soc. Arts (Eng.); mem. Okla. Art League (hon.), U. Okla. Alumni Assn. (hon.), Ill. Acad. Fine Arts (hon. life), Beta Sigma Phi (hon.), Delta Kappa Gamma (hon.), Kappa Pi (hon.). Club: Altrusa (hon). Address: 401 NW 18th St Oklahoma City OK 73103

SHEFELMAN, THOMAS WHITEHEAD, architect; b. Seattle, Oct. 3, 1927; s. Harold Samuel and Lilly Madolene (Whitehead) S.; B.Arch., U. Tex., 1950; M.Arch., Harvard, 1957; m. Janice Vera Jordan, Sept. 18, 1954; children—Karl, Daniel. Designer archtl. firms, Austin, Tex., 1951-57; travel to Far East, 1954-55; asso. Fehr & Granger, Austin, 1957-59; individual practice architecture, Austin, 1959-69; partner Taniguchi, Shefelman, Vackar & Minter, Austin, 1970—; asso. prof. architecture and planning U. Tex., 1964-72. Dir. Community Devel. Corp. of Austin, 1969-70, Austin Natural Sci. Center, 1972—. Served with USNR, 1945-46. Recipient community service award Human Opportunities Corp., Hogg Found. grantee, design honor award A.I.A., 1970. Mem. A.I.A., Beta Theta Pi, Tau Delta Sigma. Episcopalian. Club: Austin Yacht. Author: Architectural Studies, 1968. Home: 2717 Woolridge Dr Austin TX 78703 Office: 105 E 3d St Austin TX 78701

SHEFFER, L. MILES, architect; b. Athens, Ga., Feb. 15, 1925; s. Lafayette Miles and Marguerite (Beattie) S.; student U. Ga., 1942-43, 45-46; B.S., B. Arch., Ga. Inst. Tech., 1950; m. Marie Lewallen, July 20, 1946; children—Melisande, Miles Lewallen, Deirdre. Designer J.N. Pease Co., Columbus, Ga., 1950-51; acting dir. sch. planning div. Ga. State Dept. Edn., 1951-53; chief architect Ga. State Sch. Bldg. Authority and Univ. System Bldg. Authority, 1953-55; individual archtl. practice, Atlanta, 1955—; dir. Motel Properties, Inc. Vice pres. United Cerebral Palsy of Atlanta, 1971-73, now dir. Served with USAAF, 1943-44. Mem. A.I.A., Constrn. Specifications Inst., Council Ednl. Facilities Planners, Pi Kappa Alpha. Presbyn. (deacon, elder). Lion. Home: 81 Peachtree Circle Atlanta GA 30309 Office: 1315 W Peachtree St Atlanta GA 30309

SHEFFEY, JOHN PRESTON, govt. ofcl.; b. Marion, Va., Apr. 21, 1919; s. John Preston and Virginia (Harrington) S.; student Marion Coll., 1935-37; B.S., U.S. Mil. Acad., 1942; M.A., George Washington U., 1962; m. Shirley Vera Jennings, Dec. 19, 1948; children—Katherine Jean, Shirley Theresa. Commd. 2d lt. U.S. Army, 1942, advanced through grades to col., 1962; instr. U.S. Mil. Acad., 1945-48; gen. staff officer and armor unit comdr., 1954-58; adviser to Army of South Vietnam, 1959-60; gen. staff officer Dept. Army, 1961-65; ret., 1965; exec. sec. Atlantic-Pacific Interoceanic Canal Study Commn., Washington, 1965-66, exec. dir., 1967-70; spl. adviser Dept. of State, 1971—. Bd. dirs. Colombian Prep. Sch. Found. Decorated Bronze Star medal, Legion of Merit; recipient Civilian awards for outstanding achievement Combined Fund Drive, 1966, 67, 68. Mem. Assn. Grads. U.S. Mil. Acad. (past trustee), Ret. Officers Assn. Republican. Presbyn. Home: 1313 Kingston Av Alexandria VA 22302 Office: Dept of State Washington DC 20520

SHEFFIELD, CHARLES WILLIAM, corp. exec.; b. Ridley Park, Pa., Feb. 21, 1934; s. Walker and Marion (Hicks) S.; B.C.E., U. Fla., 1957; M.S. in San. Engring., U. Cin., 1966; m. Barbara Jean Greis, Feb. 8, 1958; children—Michelle, Jonathen, Kerry, Tamey. Design engr. Michaels Engring. Co., Orlando, Fla., 1959-60; dir. san. engring. dept. Orange County Health Dept., Orlando, Fla., 1960-65; pollution control officer Orange County Pollution Control Dept., Orlando, 1966-74; pres. BioEngring. Services, Inc., 1974—. Chmn., Gov's. Lake Apopka Tech. Com., 1966-69; mem. Gov's. Aquatic Research and Devel. Com., 1966-70. Served to lt. (j.g.) USPHS, 1957-59. Recipient Govt. Conservation award 1969, Outstanding Tech. Engr. award, 1974; named Engr. of Year, 1972. Registered profl. engr., Fla. Mem. Nat. Soc. Profl. Engrs., Am. Soc. C.E., Fla. Engring. Soc. (past chmn. engrs. in govt. sect., mem. exec. com.), Fla. Pollution Control Assn. (indsl. waste com. 1972—), Conservation 70 (tech. com. 1969), C. of C. (conservation-environmental com. 1966—). Contbr. articles to profl. jours. Home: 3509 Edland St Orlando FL 32806 Office: 95 W Jersey St Orlando FL 32806

SHEFFIELD, VERNON GERALD, accountant; b. Houston, Oct. 7, 1913; s. Norris and Mary Benjamin (Rowe) S.; B.B.A., S. Tex. Coll., 1937; m. Marjorie Carlock, July 24, 1965; children—Walter, Robert, Carol. Accountant Tex. Co., Houston, 1930-37; sr. accountant Ernst & Ernst, Houston, 1937-47, mgr. tax dept., 1949-51; accountant, supr. Touche, Niven, Bailey & Smart, Detroit and St. Louis, 1947-48; partner Aubrey Farris Co., Houston, 1948-49, Alwin Adam & Co., Houston, 1951-53; pvt. accounting practice, Houston, 1953-54; partner Sheffield, Garrett & Carter, Houston, 1954-67; partner Sheffield, Pridgen & Iverson, Houston, 1967-72, merged with Alexander Grant & Co., 1972, partner, 1972—; treas., dir. Preston Exterminating Co., Inc., Arcas Co. Sec.-treas., dir. LaPorte Utility Dist., 1971-72. Mem. devel. council Southwestern U., 1973—. Mem. Am. Inst. C.P.A.'s, Tex. Soc. C.P.A.'s, Nat. Assn. Accountants (pres. Houston chpt. 1955-56, nat. dir. 1965-67), Bus. and Estate Planning Council. Methodist (adminstrv. bd.). Clubs: Pine Forest Country of Houston (pres. 1953-54), Downtown Houston Exchange (v.p. 1962), Houston, University, Warwick, Pelican (Galveston). Home: 8925 Memorial Dr Houston TX 77024 Office: 1200 Milam St Houston TX 77002

SHEFTEL, HARRY BERNARD, govt. ofcl.; b. Clinton, Mass., July 9, 1906; s. Morris and Molly (Siff) S.; A.B., Clark U., 1927; M.A., Am. U., 1944; m. Alice Naistat, Sept. 21, 1935; children—Janice S. (Mrs. Ira L. Plotkin), Rosalyn L. (Mrs. Alan I. Stiefel). Chief analysis sect. Bur. Labor Statistics, Washington, 1935-41; asst. chief constrn. research div. WPB, 1941-45; dir. econ. research Fed. Works Adminstrn., 1945-50; bus. economist Def. Prodn. Adminstrn., 1950-52; program analyst Dept. Def., 1952-55; asso. clearance officer, Office of Mgmt. and Budget, Exec. Office of Pres., Washington, 1956-74; cons. Gen. Accounting Office, Office Mgmt. and Budget, 1974—. Pres. Coolidge High Sch. Home and Sch. Assn. Mem. Am. Econ. Assn., Am. Statis. Assn., Tau Kappa Alpha. Toastmaster. Club: Nat. Press. Home: 5813 3d Pl NW Washington DC 20011 Office: New Exec Office Bldg Washington DC 20503

SHEILD, FRANCIS WARREN, dentist; b. Newport News, Va., Aug. 15, 1935; s. George Henry and Katherine Warren (Houston) S.; A.B., Va. Mil. Inst., 1957; D.D.S., Med. Coll. Va., 1961; m. Margaret Phelps Dixon Posey, Aug. 20, 1960; children—Katherine Elizabeth, George Cabell. Dentist, Hampton, Va., 1963—. Co-owner Rhododendron Nursery, Newport News, 1970—. Mem. adv. bd. Am. Cancer Soc., 1963-66, Thomas Nelson Community Coll., Hampton, 1965—, also budgetary and finance chmn. Served with AUS, 1957-63. Mem. exec. bd. Hampton Rds Cotillion, 1966—; charter mem. Hampton Rds. Assembly, 1952—. Mem. Am., Va., Peninsula dental assns., Fedn. Dentaire Internat., Am. Rhododendron Soc., Hampton Horticulture Soc., So. Appalachian Bot. Club. Episcopalian. Clubs: Hampton Roads German, Lafayette Gun, Hampton Yacht, Chesapeake Bay Yacht Racing Assn., Cruising of Va. Author: A Star To Guide You, 1968. Contbr. column to Yachting mag. Patentee, mfr. navigational computer. Home: 118 Woodland Dr Newport News VA 23606 Office: 1610 Aberdeen Rd Hampton VA 23366

SHELBURNE, C. DANIEL, banker; b. Green Bay, Va., Mar. 31, 1915; s. Thomas Pettus and Mabel (Daniel) S.; B.S., Hampden-Sydney Coll., 1936; M.B.A., U. Pa., 1939-40; postgrad. Stonier Grad. Sch. Banking, Rutgers U., 1946-49; m. Edith McDanel, Dec. 27, 1941; children—John Daniel, Edward McDanel, Thomas Maynard. Bank examiner Fed. Res. Bank, Richmond, Va., 1945-48, sr. bank examiner, 1949-50; with Wachovia Bank & Trust Co., N.A., Winston-Salem, N.C. and Raleigh, N.C., 1950—, v.p. in charge loan adminstrn. dept., 1955-69, sr. v.p. in charge loan adminstrn. dept., 1969—. Dir. Bus. Devel. Corp. N.C. Instr., Grad. Sch. Consumer Banking, U. Va., 1961—, trustee, 1972—. Active United Fund; past pres. adv. bd. Wake County Salvation Army, Boy Scouts Am.; past pres. Mental Health Bd. Wake County, Raleigh. Bd. dirs. W.W. Holding Tech. Inst. Found., 1971—, v.p., 1973—; bd. dirs. N.C. Episcopal Ch. Found., 1973—. Served with Supply Corps, USNR, 1941-45; lt. comdr., ret. Recipient Silver Beaver award Boy Scouts Am., 1969. Mem. C. of C., Robert Morris Assos. (past pres. Carolinas-Va. chpt.), Sigma Chi. Episcopalian. Clubs: Carolina Country, Executives (Raleigh). Home: 2551 Wake Dr Raleigh NC 27608 Office: PO Box 27886 Raleigh NC 27611

SHELBY, BILLY LEE, engring. exec.; b. Memphis, Feb. 2, 1936; s. John Earven and Mary Erlyne (Gregory) S.; student Memphis State U., 1958—; m. LaVada Joy Maples, Oct. 16, 1963; children—John Marc, Terry Lynn, RaMona Gay, Eric Malcolm. Mgr. elec. engring. ITT Am. Elec. Co., Southaven, Miss., 1962—. Served with USNR, 1954-56. Mem. Illuminating Engring. Soc., I.E.E.E., Am. Nat. Standards Inst. Mem. Ch. of God (councilman). Home: 1588 Hutson Av Memphis TN 38116 Office: PO Box 100 Southaven MS 38671

SHELBY, CHARLES EDWIN, geneticist; b. Salem, Ky., July 19, 1925; s. Richard Romeo and Amy (Gibbs) S.; B.S., U. Ky., 1948, M.S., 1949; Ph.D., Ia. State U., 1952; m. Dorothy Ellen Scott, Sept. 11, 1955 (dec. Feb. 4, 1972); children—Mary Christine, Dorothy Ellen, Susan

Marie, Richard Romeo; m. 2d, Janet Doreen Schonert, June 2, 1973. Research geneticist U.S. Range Livestock Expt. Sta., Miles City, Mont., 1952-55; research geneticist Beef Cattle Breeding research Agrl. Research Service U.S. Dept. Agr., Denver, 1955-59; investigations leader, dir. regional Swine Breeding Lab. U.S. Dept. Agr. Agrl. Research Service, Ames, Ia., 1959-70, mem. grad. faculty Ia. State U., 1966-70, asso. prof., 1965-70; liaison officer U.S. Dept. Agr. Ky. State Coll., 1970—. Served with USNR, 1944-46. Mem. Am. Genetic Assn., Am. Meat Sci. Assn., Am. Soc. Animal Sci., Genetic Soc. Am., Biometric Soc., Am. Inst. Biol. Sci., A.A.A.S., Am. Assn. U. Profs., Central Ky. Geneal. Soc. (pres.), Sigma Xi, Alpha Gamma Rho. Mem. Christian Ch. Contbr. articles to sci. jours. Home: 431 Tatato Trail Frankfort KY 40601 Office: Ky State U Frankfort KY 40601

SHELBY, MCDALTON, hwy. research engr.; b. Austin, Tex., July 5, 1910; s. Lemeul Evart and Mabel (Wright) S.; B.S. in Elec. Engring., U. Tex., 1931; m. Frances Jeanette Campbell, Apr. 8, 1934; children—Donald M., Robert N., Lilas Janice (Mrs. Sam E. Kinch, Jr.), Judith Ann (Mrs. J. Q. Edwards, Jr.). With Tex. Hwy. Dept., Austin, 1931-65, successively asst. engr., 1931-41, resident engr., Brownwood, Tex., 1941-47, structural found. design engr., Bridge div., Austin, 1947-54, research engr., 1954-65; hwy. research engr. Tex. Transp. Inst., Tex. A. and M. U., College Station, 1965—. Fellow Am. Soc. C.E. (pres. Austin br. 1963); mem. Nat. Soc. Profl. Engrs. (pres. Travis chpt. 1957), Am. Soc. Testing and Materials, Nat. Acad. Sci. (mem. dept. design Hwy. Research Bd., and chmn. gen. design div.), Internat. Platform Assn., Sigma Xi. Methodist. Rotarian. Home: 2103 Vinewood Bryan TX 77801 Office: Hwy Research Bldg Tex Transp Inst Tex A and M Univ College Station TX 77843

SHELDON, ANSON HOISINGTON, polit. worker, bus. exec., farmer; b. Nehawka, Neb., June 5, 1905; s. George Lawson and Rose (Higgins) S.; student pub. schs.; m. Beatrice Everett, Feb. 5, 1939; children—Patricia Ann (Mrs. Harry Strauss), Anson Holsington, Lawson Everett. Various positions to service sta. mgr. Standard Oil Co. of Ky., 1921-22; dealer Internat. Harvester Co., 1924-26, road engr., sales southeastern U.S., 1926-29; sales Allis Chalmers Mfg. Co., Memphis br., 1930-36; distbr. Miss. and Ark., Massey Harris Co., 1938-39; dirt contractor and heavy equipment rentals, 1945-50; mfrs. agt. Baker Plow Co., 1957-67; factory rep. Howard Rotavator Co., 1961-68; Miss. state real estate broker, 1968—; chmn. bd. Machinery, Inc., 1968—; distbr. Grove Mfg. Co., 1962-66; farmer, 1923—. Commr. Washington County Soil Conservation Dist., 1947—. Mem. legislative com. Delta Council Water Resources Com., 1964-65. Mem. Miss. state exec. com. Republican Party, 1944-64, state chmn., 1948-52, vice chmn., 1952-60; del Rep. Nat. Conv., 1956, 60. Mem. Miss. Soil Conservation Commrs. Episcopalian. Elk. Address: Avon MS 38723

SHELDON, BEATRICE EVERETT (MRS. ANSON H. SHELDON), polit. worker; b. Gunn, Miss., May 16, 1915; d. John Broadus and Pency Ann (Wooley) Everett; R.N., Dr. Willis Walley Sch. Nursing, Jackson, Miss., 1937; m. Anson H. Sheldon, Feb. 5, 1939; children—Patricia Ann (Mrs. Harry C. Strauss), Anson H., Lawson. Nurse, Kings Daus. Hosp., Canton, Miss., 1937, Greenville, Miss., 1937, Helena (Ark.) Hosp., 1938-39; sec.-treas. Machinery, Inc., 1966—. Mem. county com. Miss. Republican Party, 1944-60; alternate del. to Rep. State Conv., 1948, 52, 56, 60. Trustee South Washington County Hosp. Mem. Miss. Registered Nurse Assn., Miss. Fedn. Women's Clubs. Episcopalian. Home: Keystone Plantation Avon MS 38723

SHELDON, CHARLES STUART, II, govt. ofcl.; b. Shanghai, China, May 18, 1917 (parents Am. citizens); s. Sidney Roby and Eunice (Fife) S.; B.A. magna cum laude, U. Wash., 1936, M.A., 1938; A.M., Harvard, 1939, Ph.D., 1942; m. Margaret Jean Reed, Mar. 21, 1942; children—Margaret (Mrs. David L. Mallino), Pamela (Mrs. Robert K. Morris), Nancy Jean. Asst. prof. transp. econs. U. Wash., 1940-55; chief Pacific sect. cargo requirements War Shipping Adminstrn., 1942-43; chief fgn. and domestic commerce, research and programs Econ. and Sci. Sect., Gen. Hdqrs., Supreme Comdr. Allied Powers, Tokyo, Japan, 1948-49; sr. specialist transp. Legislative Reference Service, Library Congress, 1955-58; tech. dir. House Com. on Sci. and Astronautics, 1959-61; sr. staff Space Council, White House, Washington, 1961-66; chief sci. policy research div. Library of Congress, Washington, 1966—. Cons. Sabena Belgian World Airlines, 1953-55; commentator on Soviet space program NBC and CBS TV, 1965—. Mem. planning commn., Puget Sound, Wash., 1940-42, chmn. road commn., 1942-43; mem. Municipal League, Seattle, 1946-50. Served to capt. USNR, 1943-46, 50-52. Recipient Commendation U.S. Congress House Com. on Sci. and Astronautics, 1961. Fellow Am. Astronautical Soc., British Interplanetary Soc., Am. Inst. Aeronautics and Astronautics (distinguished traveling lectr. 1968-74); mem. Am. Econ. Assn., Pan Xenia (internat. sec. 1937-42), Internat. Acad. Astronautics (corr.), Phi Beta Kappa. Presbyn. Author: Soviet Economic Growth, 1957; Review of the Soviet Space Program, 1967; The Soviet Space Program, 1971. Home: 3507 N Piedmont St Arlington VA 22207 Office: Congl Research Service Library Congress Washington DC 20540

SHELDON, ROGER ALPHA, printing and pub. co. exec.; b. Baton Rouge, May 12, 1922; s. William Hannaman and Arta (Sims) S.; B.A., La. State U., 1942, postgrad., 1946; m. Suzanne R. Eaton, Jan. 30, 1972; children by previous marriage—Mark, Elizabeth (Mrs. Alan Danneman), Bonnie (Mrs. Craig Eaton), Paul, David, Patricia. Dep. information officer Houston regional office WAA, 1946-47; account exec. George Kirksey & Assos., Houston, 1947-49; pub. relations counsel Tex. div., Am. Cancer Soc., Houston, 1949-51; editor-writer Merkle Press, Inc., Washington, 1951-61, v.p., editorial dir., 1962-71, v.p. spl. projects, 1971—; information officer Pres.'s Commn. on Status of Women, Washington, 1962. Troop committeeman Nat. Capitol Area council Boy Scouts Am., 1968—; community relations chmn. Allied Civic Group, Montgomery County, Md., 1955-56. Democratic precinct chmn., Montgomery County, 1968-70. Served with USAAF, World War II. Decorated Air medal; recipient Service certificate Boy Scouts Am., 1960. Mem. Washington Newspaper Guild (mem. bd. 1959-60), Internat. Platform Assn. Unitarian. Club: Nat. Press. Editor: The Carpenter, United Brotherhood Carpenters and Joiners Am. Editorial cons. Popular Archeology. Home: 3828 Calvert St NW Washington DC 20007 Office: 810 Rhode Island Av NE Washington DC 20018

SHELP, RONALD KENT, trade assn. ofcl.; b. Cartersville, Ga., Sept. 29, 1941; s. Clarence Harrison and Willie Marion (Puckett) Mulkey; A.B. cum laude, U. Ga., 1964; M.A. (Crown-Zellerbach fellow 1964-65, Francis Bolton fellow 1965-66), Johns Hopkins Sch. Advanced Internat. Studies, 1966; m. Gail Joan Deschner, Mar. 11, 1972. Sr. asso. C. of C. of U.S.A., Washington, 1966—, exec. sec. Assn. Am. Chambers Commerce in Latin Am., 1969—; exec. sec. Internat. Ins. Adv. Council, trade assn. U.S. ins. cos. operating overseas, Washington, 1966—. Exec. v.p., also partner Art Enterprises Internat. U.S. expert del. Bus. Adv. Council OAS, Caracas, Venezuela, 1970. Mem. Pres.'s Peru Earthquake Vol. Assistance Group. Co-chmn. Young Execs. for Humphrey-Muskie, Greater Washington area, 1968. Served with AUS, 1966-72. Mem. Blue Key, Phi Beta Kappa, Phi Kappa Phi, Phi Eta Sigma, Pi Sigma Alpha, Omicron Delta Kappa. Democrat. Club: International (Washington). Contbr. articles to internat. jours. Home: 560 N St SW Washington DC 20024 Office: 1615 H St NW Washington DC 20006

SHELTON, JAMES MAURICE, educator; b. Collinwood, Tenn., July 27, 1924; s. Arch M. and Beulah Ethel (Pigg) S.; B.S., U. Tenn., 1948; M.S., Tex. A. and M. U., 1953, Ph.D., 1957; m. Lucy Vise, Aug. 28, 1950; children—Larry H., Michael V., Donald M., Stephen Andrew. Instr., U. Tenn., 1948-50; instr. Tex. A. and M. U., College Station, 1950-53, prof. animal sci., 1957—; asso. prof. Am. U. Beirut (Lebanon), 1954-56. Served with USNR, 1943-46. Mem. Am. Soc. Animal Sci., Am. Genetic Assn., Soc. for Study Reprodn., Research Soc. Am. (pres. Central Tex. br. 1969-70), Sigma Xi. Republican. Lion. Home: 2939 Cumberland St San Angelo TX 76901 Office: RFD 1 Box 950 San Angelo TX 76901

SHELTON, JOHN BANNER, broadcasting exec.; b. Mayodan, N.C., July 5, 1916; s. Walter Roscoe and Minetti (Fulton) S.; A.A., Mars Hill Coll., 1939; m. Mary Helen Carter, Nov. 15, 1941. Order clk. Gam Dandy, Inc., Madison, N.C., 1939-40, asst. supt., 1940-48; founder pres., dir. Mayo Broadcasting Corp., Madison, 1948—. Chmn., Republican Party 5th Dist. N.C., 1958—. Trustee Morehead Meml. Hosp. Mem. Rockingham County Fine Arts Festival Assn. (membership chmn. 1958-60, pres. 1960-62), Mars Hill Bus. Club Alumni Assn. (pres. 1939-40, 63-64), A.I.M. (fellow pres.'s council). Baptist. Clubs: Rotary; Deep Springs Country (Madison, N.C.). Home: Rural Route 1 Stoneville NC 27048 Office: PO Box 311 Madison NC 27025

SHELTON, LEWIS SAMUEL, mus. adminstr.; b. Jacksonville, Fla., Nov. 19, 1933; s. Lewis Samuel and Mattie (Wansley) S.; B.S., U. Ga., 1955, M.A., 1963, Ed.D. (NSF fellow 1964-65), 1965; m. Patricia Clarke Rae, Aug. 20, 1955; children—Barbara, Catherine, Jeffrey. Prof. dept. biology DeKalb Coll. and Oglethorpe U., Atlanta, 1964-66; dir. Fernbank Sci. Center, Atlanta, 1966—. First v.p. Druid Hills Civic Assn., 1969—. Bd. dirs. Druid Hills Civitan Club. Mem. Nat. Sci. Tchrs. Assn., Am. Mgmt. Assn. Home: 1036 Oxford Rd NE Atlanta GA 30306 Office: 156 Heaton Park Dr NE Atlanta GA 30307

SHELTON, ROBERT DUANE, educator; b. Dublin, Tex., Sept. 14, 1938; s. Duane McAfee and Bertie Ella (Honea) S.; B.S. in Elec. Engring., Tex. Tech. U., 1960; S.M. (Kaiser Aluminum fellow 1960-61, NSF fellow 1961-62), Mass. Inst. Tech., 1962; Ph.D., U. Houston, 1967; m. Ruth Klein, Nov. 28, 1963; 1 son, Duane Edward. Engr. Tex. Instruments, Inc., Dallas, 1962-63; aerospace technologist NASA Johnson Space Center, Houston, 1963-64; asst. prof. U. Houston, 1964-68; asso. prof. Tex. Tech. U., Lubbock, 1968-70; asso. prof. elec. engring. and computer sci. U. Louisville, 1970—. Cons. to Univac Inc., Houston Research Inst., Gulf Aerospace Corp. NASA and NSF grantee in communications and computer research, 1967-73. Mem. I.E.E.E., Instn. Elec. Engrs. (London), Assn. Computing Machinery, Am. Soc. Engring. Edn. Home: 1006 Old Cannons Lane Louisville KY 40207 Office: Dept Electrical Engineering U Louisville Louisville KY 40208

SHENK, CHARLOTTE PATTON FORGEY (MRS. DONALD H. SHENK), genealogist; b. nr. Columbia, Tenn., Aug. 30, 1901; d. William Shorter and Lena (Jones) Forgey; B.S. in English and History, Middle Tenn. State U., 1935; B.S. in L.S., Emory U., 1938; m. Robert Bruce Chesnut, Mar. 1, 1940 (dec. Sept. 1944); m. 2d, Donald H. Shenk, Dec. 29, 1960; stepchildren—William E., Howard F. Tchr. pub. schs., Tenn., Ga., 1922-36; sch. librarian, Chamblee, Ga., 1938-44, Nashville, 1944-46; tchr., tech. librarian Office Tech. Services, Washington, 1946; with C.E., Manhattan Dist., Oak Ridge, Tenn., 1946-47, AEC, Oak Ridge, 1947-56; chief Army Ballistic Missile Agy., Tech. Library, Huntsville, Ala., 1956-63; research librarian, tech. librarian Marshall Space Flight Center Library Service, Huntsville, 1963-65; cons. geneologist, record searcher, 1965—. Founding mem., bd. dirs. Am. Indian Heritage Assn., 1968-72; mem. research team Ala. Sesquicentennial Celebration, 1969. Recipient Distinguished Alumni award Middle Tenn. State U., 1966. Mem. A.L.A., Spl. Libraries Assn., Southeastern Library Assn., Spl. Libraries and Information Bureaux (London), Am. Inst. Aeros. and Astronautics, Am. Documentation Inst., Assn. U.S. Army, Huntsville Lit. Soc., Living Descents Blood Royal, Friends of Winchester Cathedral. Presbyn. Club: Culture (Huntsville, sec. 1968-72). Author: (with husband) The First Presbyterian Church, Huntsville, Alabama, Sesquicentennial, 1818-1968, 1968. Home: 2208 Lytle St Huntsville AL 35801

SHENK, DONALD HUGH, govt. ofcl.; b. nr. Kokomo, Ind., Apr. 9, 1901; s. William Ellsworth and Elizabeth Margaret (Trees) S.; B.S., Pudue U., 1924, M.S., 1940; m. Ruth Aletha Swartz, Aug. 30, 1929 (dec. Oct. 1957); children—William Earle, Howard Fred; m. 2d, Charlotte Forgey, Dec. 29, 1960. With Westinghouse Airbrake, Co., Wilmerding, Pa., 1924-26; mem. faculty Purdue U., Lafayette, Ind., 1926-29, Clemson (S.C.) Coll., 1929-43; mem. faculty U. Ala., Tuscaloosa, 1943-49; also head dept.; with Redstone Arsenal, Huntsville, Ala., 1949-68. Registered profl. engr., Ala. Mem. North Ala. Genealogic Soc. (v.p. 1965, dir. 1965-68), Am. Indian Heritage Assn. (v.p. 1967-69), Pi Tau Sigma. Mason. Patentee in field. Address: 2208 Lytle St S E Huntsville AL 35801

SHENTON, ALTON O'NEIL, clergyman; b. Cambridge, Md., Mar. 6, 1935; s. Anthony William and Aline (Brown) S.; B.A., Western Ky. U., 1964; B.D., Emory U., 1967, M.Div., 1972; m. Nina Pauline Felts, Apr. 4, 1961; children—Paula Michelle, Gregory O'Neil. Ordained to ministry Meth. Ch., 1965; pastor, Bowling Green, Ky., 1960-64, Douglasville, Ga., 1964-67, Sonora, Ky., 1967-69, Kenwood United Meth. Ch., Louisville, 1969—. Mem. Louisville Conf. Bd. Social Concerns, 1968-72. Served with USN, 1955-59. Named Louisville Minister of Week, 1972. Mem. S.A.R. Optimist (Pres.'s Golden Circle award 1968). Clubs: A.M. Stickles History (Western Ky. Univ., Bowling Green); NATO Sportsman's (Naples, Italy). Home: 6815 Homestead Dr Louisville KY 40214 Office: 7032 Southside Dr Louisville KY 40214

SHENTON, LEONARD ROY, statistician, educator; b. Staffordshire, Eng., Feb. 4, 1909; s. John William and Sarah (Adams) S.; student Manchester U., 1927-32; B.S., Edinburgh U., 1932, Ph.D., 1940, D.Sc., 1959; m. Margaret Elaine Jackson, Aug. 23, 1935. Mathematician, lectr., reader Manchester U., 1948-60; prof. Va. Poly. Inst., 1961-62; research statistician Nat. Lab., Oak Ridge, 1963; prof. Computer Center, U. Ga., Athens, 1965—; statis. cons., 1963—. Served with RAF, 1939-45. Mem. Am., Manchester statis. socs., Edinburgh Math. Soc., Math. Assn. Asso. editor Jour. Am. Statis. Assn., 1973—. Contbr. articles profl. jours. Home: 210 Pine Valley Dr Athens GA 30601

SHEPARD, ALAN BARTLETT, JR., astronaut; b. Derry, N.H., Nov. 18, 1923; s. Alan Bartlett and Renza (Emerson) S.; grad. Pinkerton Acad., Derry, N.H., 1940; student Admiral Farragut Acad., 1940; B.S., U.S. Naval Acad., 1944; grad. Naval War Coll., 1958; m. Louise Brewer, Mar. 3, 1945; children—Juliana, Laura. Commd. ensign U.S. Navy, 1944, advanced through grades to rear adm., 1971; designated naval aviator, 1947; assigned destroyer U.S.S. Cogswell, Pacific, World War II, Fighter Squadron 42, 1947-49, aircraft carriers in Mediterranean, 1947-49; with U.S. Navy Test Pilot Sch., 1950-53, 55-57; took part in high altitude tests, experiments in test and devel. in-flight refueling system, carrier suitability trials of F2H3 Banshee, also trials angled carrier deck; operations officer Fight Squadron 193, Moffett Field, Cal., and in carrier U.S.S. Oriskany, Western Pacific, 1953-55; test pilot for F3H Demon, 1956, F8U Crusader, 1956, F4D Skyray, 1955, F11F Tigercat, 1956; project test pilot F5D Skylancer, 1956; instr. Naval Test Pilot Sch., 1957; aircraft readiness officer staff Comdr.-in-Chief Atlantic Fleet, 1958-59; joined Project Mercury man in space program, NASA, 1959; first American in space May 5, 1961; chief of astronaut office, 1965—, comdr. Apollo 14 Lunar Landing Mission, until 1971; del. to UN 1971. Decorated D.S.M, D.F.C.; recipient NASA Distinguished Service Medal; recipient Langley medal Smithsonian Instn., 1964. Fellow Soc. Exptl. Test Pilots; mem. Order Daedalians, Soc. Colonial Wars. Lion, Kiwanian, Rotarian. Address: Manned Spacecraft Center NASA Houston TX 77058

SHEPARD, CHARLES C., physician; b. Ord. Neb., Dec. 18, 1914; B.S., Northwestern U., 1936, M.S., 1938, M.B., 1940, M.D., 1941. Commd. med. officer USPHS, 1941; with NIH, 1942-48, 49-50, Biochem Inst., Uppsala, Sweden, 1948-49, Rocky Mountain Lab., 1950-53; chief leprosy and rickettsial disease sect. virology br. Center for Disease Control, Atlanta, 1954—. Vis. prof. U. Ala., 1956-60; mem. Rickettsial Disease Commn., Armed Forces Epidemiol. Bd., 1959—; chmn. leprosy panel Japan-U.S. Coop. Med. Sci. Program, 1965—. Recipient Kimble Methodology award and Gorgas medal, 1963; World Leprosy Day award, 1970. Mem. A.A.A.S., Am. Soc. Microbiology, Soc. Exptl. Biology, Am. Assn. Immunology. Research in infectious diseases, especially rickettsiae and leprosy. Office: Center for Disease Control Atlanta GA 30333

SHEPARD, HENRY BURGARD, constrn. exec.; b. New Orleans, May 9, 1916; s. Theodore Howell and Helen (Burgard) S.; B.S. in Civil Engring., Tulane U., 1937; m. Janet Johnstone, June 10, 1938; children—Helen W. (Mrs. Norman D. Stockwell), Cheryl A., Leslie L., Henry. Vice pres. R. P. Farnsworth & Co., New Orleans, 1937-57; pres. H.B. Shepard & Co., 1957-65; exec. v.p. George Farnsworth Constrn. Corp., New Orleans, 1965-67, dir., 1965-67; pres. Shepco, Inc., New Orleans, 1968—; mgr. heavy constrn. div. T. L. James & Co., Inc., Kenner, La., 1969—. Presbyn. (elder). Home: 5018 Bancroft Dr New Orleans LA 70122 Office: PO Box 51986 New Orleans LA 70151

SHEPARD, KATHARINE, art mus. curator; b. Bristol, Conn.; d. Charles Norman and Marguerite (Dunbar) Shepard; B.A., Bryn Mawr Coll., 1928, M.A., 1929, Ph.D., 1936; student Am. Sch. Classical Studies, Athens, Greece, 1930-31 Pvt. tutoring, research, N.Y.C., 1936-41; mus. aide Nat. Gallery Art, Washington, 1941-43, asst. registrar, 1943-55, asst. curator graphic arts, 1955—; lectr. grad. sch. dept. art Catholic U. Am., 1960-69. Mem. Am. Assn. Museums, Archaeol. Inst. Am. (sec. Washington chpt.), Print Council Am. Episcopalian. Home: 1260 21st St NW Washington DC 20036 Office: Nat Gallery of Art Washington DC 20565

SHEPARDSON, DAVID LEONARD, banker; b. Birmingham, Ala., Dec. 16, 1938; s. Vene Phillip and Ione (VonDroskie) S.; B.A., Randolph-Macon Coll., 1961; m. Melinda Luck, Jan. 6, 1962; children—Linda Montague, David Leonard. With Bank Va.-Tidewater, Norfolk, 1961—, v.p., 1968-70, sr. v.p., 1970-74, exec. v.p., 1974—. Mem. Am. Cancer Soc., 1968-69, Big Bros. Richmond, 1968-70; campaign chmn. March Dimes, 1970-71; pres. Richmond Community Service Center, 1971—. Mem. Richmond City Council, 1969-70; mem. Richmond Human Relations Commn., 1969—. Bd. dirs. Multiple Sclerosis, 1968-70, Region 19 Community Coll., Richmond, 1969-70, Atlantic Rural Exposition, 1971—; trustee Markets Diversified, Richmond, 1968—. Recipient Mem. Richmond Jr. C. of C. (Distinguished Service award 1970), Central Richmond Assn., Phi Kappa Sigma. Methodist. Rotarian. Home: 29 Maxwell Rd Richmond VA 23226 Office: 800 E Main St Richmond VA 23219

SHEPHERD, CHARLES WESLEY, hosp. adminstr.; b. nr. Theadville, Miss., Apr. 25, 1934; s. Hamilton W. and Lois (Rolison) S.; student Gradwohl Sch. Lab. Technique, 1953; A.A., Meridian Jr. Coll., 1957; student U. So. Miss., 1957-58; LL.B., Jackson Sch. Law, 1961; certificate, U. Ala. in Birmingham, 1972; m. Lora Gossard, July 16, 1955; children—Charles Wesley, Susanne, Sherri. Admitted to Miss. bar, 1961; lab. asst. St. Luke's Hosp., St. Louis, 1952-53; med. technologist Watkins Meml. Hosp., Quitman, Miss., 1953-55, hosp. adminstr., 1955-58, 1967—; med. technologist St. Dominics Hosp., Jackson, Miss., 1959-61; gen. ins. agt., Meridian and Quitman, Miss., 1961-67. Chmn., Clarke County Home Health Adv. Com., 1969-70; pres. Clarke County Wildlife Conservation League, 1955-56; sec., treas., dir. Miss. Wildlife Fedn., 1961-63; chmn. Clarke County Heart Assn., 1957-58; active Clarke County Red Cross, Clarke County March of Dimes; sec., treas., dir. Clarke County Planning Commn., 1966-69. Recipient Miss. Wildlife/Sears-Roebuck Found. State Game and Fish Conservation award, 1963; Outstanding Alumni award U. So. Miss., 1966-67; Distinguished Achievement award Am. Med. Technologists, 1956. Mem. Am., Miss. (chmn. council emergency service 1969-70) hosp. assns., East Miss. (pres. 1965-66), Miss. assns. ins. agts., Quitman Jr. C. of C., Nat. Wildlife Fedn. Methodist (commn. chmn. 1962—, lay speaker 1962—). Lion (Outstanding Pres. award Quitman 1965, pres. 1964-65), Mason (master 1965—). Club: Quitman Country. Home: PO Box 93 Quitman MS 39355 Office: 120 E Water St Quitman MS 39355

SHEPHERD, MARK, JR., electronics co. exec.; b. Dallas, Jan. 18, 1923; s. Mark and Louisa Florence (Daniell) S.; B.S. in Elec. Engring., So. Meth. U., 1942; M.S. in Elec. Engring., U. Ill., at Urbana, 1947; m. Mary Alice Murchland, Dec. 21, 1945; children—Debra Aline (Mrs. Rowland K. Robinson), MaryKay, Marc Blaine. With Gen. Electric Co., 1942-43, Farnsworth TV and Radio Corp., 1947-48; with Tex. Instruments Inc., Dallas, 1948—, v.p., gen. mgr. semicondr.-components div., 1955-61, exec. v.p. co., 1961-67, pres., 1967—, chief exec. officer, 1969—, also dir.; dir. Republic Nat. Bank Dallas. Mem. industry adv. council Dept. Def.; mem. exec. com. Adv. Council on Japan-U.S. Econ. Relations; chmn. Found. for Sci. and Engring. So. Meth. U.; mem. Pres.'s Export Council. Trustee, So. Meth. U., Com. for Econ. Devel. Served to lt. (j.g.) USNR, 1943-46. Registered profl. engr., Tex. Fellow I.E.E.E.; mem. Am. Mgmt. Assn. (dir. 1967-70), Soc. Exploration Geophysicists, Newcomen Soc., Council on Fgn. Relations, Internat. C. of C. (trustee U.S. Council), Nat. Acad. Engring., Sigma Xi, Eta Kappa Nu (dir. 1969-71). Home: 5006 Middlegate Rd Dallas TX 75229 Office: 13500 N Central Expressway PO Box 5474 Dallas TX 75222

SHEPHERD, RICHARD BUTLER HOOKE, civil engr.; b. Pond, Miss., Feb. 10, 1905; s. Arthur Merson and Louise Maria (Hider) S.; student Cornell U., 1922-23, Miss. State U., 1924, U. Mo., 1925-27, U. Tenn., 1945. Insp. C.E., Vicksburg, Miss., 1928-31, Memphis, 1931-32, civil engr., Memphis, 1932-47; geod. engr. 29th Engring. Ba. Base Topo, Manila, P.I., 1948-54; cartographer U.S. Army Map Service, Far East, Tokyo, Japan, 1954-60; ret. 1960; vol. ednl. therapy VA Hosp., Memhis, 1961-63, 69—; registered rep. White & Co., Memphis, 1964-69. Extension instr. U. Tenn., 1942-46, U. Ark., 1944. Bd. dirs. Travellers Aid. Fellow Am. Soc. C.E. (life), Am. Congress on Surveying and Mapping (life); mem. Memphis Engrs. Club (life).

A.I.M., Soc. Am. Mil. Engrs., Cornell Soc. Engrs., Pi Tau Sigma. Episcopalian. Clubs: Memphis University; Tokyo Lawn Tennis, Memphis Civitan. Home: 1380 Lamar Av Apt 707 Memphis TN 38104

SHEPHERD, ROBERT ASHLAND, lawyer; b. Huntsville, Tex., July 7, 1894; s. James L. and Julia (Josey) S.; grad. Sam Houston State U., 1914; student U. Tex. at Austin, 1916-17; m. Opal Powell, July 8, 1922; children—Robert Ashland, William Leftwich. Admitted to Tex. bar, 1921; with James L. Shepherd, Cisco, Tex., 1921; with Vinson, Elkins, Searls, Connally & Smith, Houston, 1921-70, partner, 1929—, mng. partner, 1951-59. Vice pres., dir. Duval Corp., 1947-70; chmn. bd., dir. Heights State Bank, Houston. Trustee Tex. Med. Center, Meth. Hosp., Houston, Tex. Meth. Found., Lon Morris Coll., Jacksonville, Tex. Served as 2d lt., F.A. and aviation, U.S. Army, World War I. Mem. Am., Tex., Houston bar assns., S.A.R., Sons Republic Tex. Democrat. Methodist (trustee). Mason (Shriner, K.T.). Home: 2136 Inwood Dr Houston TX 77019 Office: First City Nat Bank Bldg Houston TX 77002

SHEPHERD, ROBERT ASHLAND, JR., lawyer; b. Mexia, Tex., Nov. 6, 1923; s. Robert Ashland and Opal (Powell) S.; LL.B., U. Tex., 1948; m. Estelle Streetman Lindsey, July 28, 1945; children—Marion Lindsey, Robert A. III, David Powell. Admitted to Tex. bar, 1948, since practiced in Houston; mem. firm Vinson, Elkins, Searls, Connally & Smith, 1948—, partner, 1959-67; pres. Austral Oil Co., Houston, 1967-69. Trustee Meth. Hosp., South Tex. Jr. Coll. Served with AUS, 1943-45; ETO. Decorated Purple Heart. Mem. Am. Judicature Soc., Am., Houston bar assns., State Bar of Tex., Phi Delta Phi, Kappa Sigma. Presbyn. Clubs: River Oaks Country, Houston Country, Ramada; Links (N.Y.C.). Home: 3414 Overbrook Lane Houston TX 77027 Office: Cullen Center Bank Bldg Houston TX 77002

SHEPHERD, ROBERT LENWARD, TV exec.; b. Atlanta, Aug. 21, 1933; s. Earl Lenward and Linda (Grubbs) S.; A.B., U. Ala., 1959; m. Beverly Joyce Crowell, Oct. 1, 1960; children—Nancy Lynn, Scott Lenward and Susan Leigh (twins). Dir., announcer U. Ala. Broadcasting Services, Tuscaloosa, 1958; producer, dir. WEDU-TV, Tampa, Fla., 1959; prodn. mgr. St. Petersburg, Fla., 1959-63; program prodn. mgr. WDCN-TV, Nashville, Tenn., 1963-65; gen. mgr., 1965—; exec. v.p. Nashville Pub. TV Council, Inc., 1971—. Dir. summer lab workshops in ednl. TV, Belmont Coll., Nashville, 1966-67; coordinator Vanderbilt U. M.A. in Teaching Seminars, Nashville, 1966—. Bd. dirs. Middle Tenn. Radio and TV Council, 1965-67; bd. dirs., pub. edn. dir. Pinellas County Unit, Am. Cancer Soc., St. Petersburg, Fla., 1962-63; bd. dirs. So. Ednl. Communications Assn., 1973—; bd. mgrs. Pub. Broadcasting Service, 1972—. Served with CIC, AUS, 1955-57; PTO. Mem. Internat. Platform Assn., Nat. Assn. Ednl. Broadcasters, Pi Kappa Phi (pres. 1958, treas. 1957). Recipient George Washington Honor Medal awards Freedoms Found., Valley Forge, 1964, 66. Home: 713 Georgetown Dr Nashville TN 37205 Office: Box 12555 15th and Compton Avs Nashville TN 37212

SHEPPARD, ALBERT PARKER, JR., univ. dean; b. Griffin, Ga., June 6, 1936; s. Albert Parker and Cornelia S. (Cooper) S.; B.S. summa cum laude, Oglethorpe Coll., 1958; M.S. (Woodrow Wilson fellow), Emory U., 1959; Ph.D., Duke, 1965; m. Judith Prosser, Sept. 9, 1957; children—Albert Parker III, Frank Philip. Sr. engr. Orlando (Fla.) research div. Martin Marietta Co., 1960-63; physicist U.S. Army Research Office, Durham, N.C., 1963-65; prin. research engr., also head spl. techniques br. electronics div. Ga. Inst. Tech., Atlanta, 1965-71, chief chem. scis. and materials div., 1971-72, asso. dean engring., also prof. elec. engring., 1972—; faculty DeKalb Coll., Clarkston, Ga., 1967-71. Partner Microwave Cons., Atlanta, 1969—. Mem. I.E.E.E. (sr.), Am. Soc. Engring. Edn., Engring. Research Council, Internat. Microwave Power Inst., Sigma Xi, Sigma Pi Sigma. Contbr. articles to sci. jours. Home: 2665 Hawthorne Dr NE Atlanta GA 30345 Office: Georgia Institute of Technology 225 North Av Atlanta GA 30332

SHEPPARD, JAMES DANIEL, banker; b. Houston, Feb. 29, 1928; s. George B. and Priscilla (Spaulding) S.; grad. Hill Sch., 1946; A.B., Princeton, 1950; grad. Stonier Grad. Sch. Banking, 1967; m. Frances Boggs, Mar. 14, 1962. With S.C. Nat. Bank, Greenville, 1954—, mgr. comml. credit dept., 1961—, v.p., 1967—. Served with USNR, 1950-53. Mem. Robert Morris Assos. Home: 209 W Mountain View Av Greenville SC 29609 Office: PO Drawer 969 Greenville SC 29602

SHEPPERD, JOHN BEN, lawyer; b. Gladewater, Tex., Oct. 19, 1915; s. Alfred Fulton and Berthal (Phillips) S.; LL.B., U. Tex., 1941; LL.D., North Tex. State Coll., 1951, Chapman Christian Coll., Los Angeles, 1953, Southwestern U., 1955; m. Mamie Strieber, Oct. 6, 1938; children—Alfred Lewis, John Ben, Marianne and Suzanne (twins). Admitted to Tex. bar, 1941, mem. Kenley, Sharp, Shepperd and Ritter, Longview, Tex., 1941—; Tex. sec. state, 1950-52; atty. gen. of Tex., 1952-56; gen. counsel Rodman-Noel oil interests, Odessa, after 1957; now with El Paso Products Co., Odessa, Tex. Mem. Bd. Edn. Tex., 1949-50; sec. Tex. Economy Commn., 1950-51; pres. Sabine River Watershed Assn., 1949-52; mem. Tex. Indsl. Commn., Tex. Civil War Centennial Commn.; v.p. Tex. Tourist Council, 1961. Pres. Tex. Jr. C. of C., 1941, U.S. Jr. C. of C., 1947; nat. council rep. East Tex. area Boy Scouts Am., 1948-51; pres. Tex. Hist. Survey Com., 1963—. Mem. Nat. Assn. Attys. Gen. (pres. 1956). Democrat. Mem. Christian Ch. Author: The President's Guide to Club and Organization Management and Meetings. Home: 3107 Windsor Dr Odessa TX 79760 Office: PO Box 3908 Odessa TX 79760

SHERFEY, JAMES DANIEL, electric utility exec.; b. Glasgow, Ky., Apr. 14, 1934; s. Ray Mitchell and Sally Vern (Matthews) S.; B.S., U. Ky., 1956; m. Nancy Sue Lickert, May 25, 1957; children—Karen, Susan. Dir. power sales and pub. relations Farmers Rural Electric Coop. Corp., Glasgow, 1957-61, gen. mgr. Glasgow Electric Plant Bd., 1961-67; gen. mgr. Bristol Tenn. Electric System, Bristol, Tenn., 1967—. Served with AUS, 1957. Named Outstanding Young Man of Year, Barren County (Ky.) Jaycees, 1964, Boss of Year, Nat. Secs. Assn., 1971. Mem. Am. Pub. Power Assn. (dir. 1970—), Aircraft Owners and Pilots Assn., Washington C. of C. Baptist (deacon 1969—). Clubs: Rotary (pres. 1970-72), Country of Bristol. Home: 525 Vance Dr Bristol TN 37620 Office: 37 4th St Bristol TN 37620

SHERIDAN, PAUL FRANCIS, lawyer; b. Bklyn., Mar. 22, 1937; s. Edward Joseph and Eileen (Jackson) S.; B.A., Columbia, 1958; J.D., Georgetown Law Center, 1963; m. Jeanette Mager, Aug. 16, 1969; children—Paul Francis, Michelle Maureen. Admitted to Va. bar, 1963, D.C. bar, Fed. bars, 1964; clk. U.S. Dist. Ct., 1963-64; pvt. practice law specializing in civil litigation, 1964—; partner law firm Siciliano, Ellis, Sheridan & Dyer, Arlington, Va., 1964—; instr. Georgetown Law Center, 1965-67. Served to capt. USMCR, 1958-60. Mem. Arlington County Bar Assn. (pres. 1973-74), Va. State Bar (mem. 10th dist. com. 1970-73). Home: 2399 N Kenmore St Arlington VA 22207 Office: 1911 Fort Myer Dr Arlington VA 22209

SHERIDAN, ROBERT HOWARD, JR., investment banker; b. Mpls., July 17, 1933; s. Robert Howard and Nora L. (McIntyre) S.; B.A., Rice U., 1954; postgrad. U. Tex., 1954-55; grad. Investment Bankers Assn. course Wharton Sch. Finance U. Pa., 1968; m. Mary Ellen Woodruff, Jan. 27, 1962 (div. Nov. 1971); children—Robert Howard III, Phillip Douglas. Vice pres. investments Tex. Nat. Bank, Houston, 1955-64; sr. v.p., dir. Moroney, Beissner & Co., Inc., Houston, 1964-74; sr. v.p., dir. Rotan Mosle Mortgage Co., 1974—; v.p. Rotan Mosle Inc., 1974—; sr. v.p., dir. Moroney, Beissner Mortgage Co.; dir. Enrivo Service, Inc., Rice Grads. Enterprises, Inc. Mem. Houston Soc. Financial Analysts, Nat. Assn. Securities Dealers, Securities Industry Assn., Phi Delta Theta. Clubs: River Oaks Country, Plaza (Houston). Home: 2828 Bammel Lane Houston TX 77006 Office: 2200 Bank of Southwest Bldg Houston TX 77002

SHERIDAN, ROGER WILLIAMS, civil engr.; b. Dallas, Jan. 26, 1921; s. Lawrence V. and Grace E. (Emmel) S.; student Purdue U., 1940-42, U.S. Mil. Acad., 1942, U. Utah, 1946-50; B.S. in Civil Engring., Westminster Coll., 1955; m. Shirley Parsons, June 12, 1944; children—Kathleen, Richard Parsons, Margaret Grace (Mrs. Duane Woody), Susan Fisher, Sherrie Ann (Mrs. Charles Vaughn), Charles Lawrence. Field engr. L.V. Sheridan, Los Alamos, 1948-52; pres., dir. Met. Engrs., Inc., 1952-56; gen. supt. Utah Constrn. Co. (Peru), project mgr. Kaiser Engrs., Volta River Project (Ghana), 1959-61; v.p. constrn. Homesmith, Inc., 1963-64; dir. engring. Khuzestan Water & Power, 1964-67; mgr. constrn. S.-E. Asia, Philco-Ford, 1967-68; asst. v.p., project mgr. Boise-Cascade Corp., 1968-70; v.p. Realtec, Inc., 1970-72; exec. v.p. Metro Surveying & Engring. Co., 1972-73; v.p. gen. mgr. Eastern Pa. Marine Properties, Inc.; exec. v.p. Drums, Inc.; v.p. Lake of Four Seasons, Inc., Acqua Constrn. Co., 1973—. Cons. civil engring. Served to capt. C.E., AUS, World War II; ETO. Decorated Purple Heart, Bronze Star medal. Registered profl. engr., Ga., Ala., N.C., S.C., Fla., Pa., Utah, N.J., Tex., Ariz., Colo., Wyo., Nev., Okla., Cal. Fellow Am. Soc. C.E., Beavers. Episcopalian. Elk. Home: Route 4 Deerfield Covington GA 30209 Office: PO Box 656 Hazleton PA 18201

SHERIN, ROBERT MORRIS, computer co. exec.; b. Boston, Apr. 17, 1939; s. Marcus Leon and Sarah (Burwen) S.; student Johns Hopkins, 1958-60, Emerson Coll., 1960-62; m. Gerda Buchholz, Oct. 21, 1965, children—David Daniel, Susan Jenifer. Copywriter, announcer radio sta. WNBP, Newburyport, Mass., 1960-62; planneranalyst Eastern Airline, Inc., Miami, Fla., 1965-68; pres. Nova Computing Services, Inc., Miami, 1968—. Cons. data conversion for numerous cos. Served with AUS, 1962-65. Mem. Assn. for Systems Mgmt. (publicity chmn. 1972-73), Data Processing Mgmt. Assn. (newsletter editor 1971-72). Contbr. articles on data processing to profl. publs. Home: 15805 SW 101 Av Miami FL 33157 Office: 16201 SW 95 Av Miami FL 33157

SHERMAN, GERALD HOWARD, lawyer; b. N.Y.C., Aug. 29, 1932; s. Abraham and Jean (Rose) S.; B.B.A., Coll. City N.Y., 1953; LL.B., Harvard, 1958; m. Lola Barbara Kay, Mar. 19, 1961; children—Jonathan, Ann. Admitted to N.Y. bar, 1959; D.C. bar, 1960; practiced in Washington, 1958—; mem. firm Cooper & Silverstein, 1958-61, partner Silverstein & Mullens, 1961—; adj. prof. Georgetown U. Law Center, 1974—, also mem. adv. bd. tax mgmt., 1960—. Mem. Am. Bar Assn., Bar Assn. D.C. Home: 11112 Whisperwood Lane Rockville MD 20852 Office: 1776 K St NW Washington DC 20006

SHERMAN, GORDON RAE, univ. computer center dir.; b. Menomenee, Mich., Feb. 24, 1928; s. Gordon Everett and Myrtle Harriet (Evanson) S.; B.S. in Statistics, Ia. State Coll., 1953; M.S. in Statistics, Stanford, 1954; Ph.D. in Math., Purdue U., 1960; m. Lois E. Miller, July 3, 1951; children—Karen, Thor. Instr. Purdue U., Lafayette, Ind., 1956-60; dir. computing center, also head computer sci. dept. U. Tenn., Knoxville, 1960—; program dir. NSF, Washington, 1971-72. Served with USAF, 1946-49, 50-51. Mem. Assn. Computing Machinery (S.E. regional rep., also council mem. 1971—; chmn. spl. interest group univ. computing centers 1971—), Data Processing Mgmt. Assn. (chpt. pres. 1972-73), Am. Statis. Assn., Ass. Ednl. Date Systems, Inst. Math. Statistics, Operations Research Soc. Am., Soc. Indsl. and Applied Math., Inst. Mgmt. Sci., Sigma Xi, Phi Kappa Phi. Club: Holston Hills Country (Knoxville). Contbr. articles on computing, mgmt. sci., operations research, statistics and applied math. to profl. jours. Home: 5408 Smoky Trail Knoxville TN 37919

SHERMAN, HAROLD MORROW, author, lectr.; b. Traverse City, Mich., July 13, 1898; s. Thomas Henry and Alcinda E. (Morrow) S.; student U. Mich., 1918-19; m. Martha Frances Bain, Sept. 26, 1920; children—Mary Alcinda (Mrs. Bernard J. Kobiella), Marcia Anne (Mrs. Wendell R. Smith). Reporter, Marion (Ind.) Chronicle, 1921-24, free lance writer, N.Y.C., 1924-35; author Your Key to Happiness radio program CBS, 1935-36, The Adventures of Mark Twain produced by Warner Brothers, 1942; founder, pres., dir. ESP Research Assos. Found., Little Rock, 1964—; investigator, experimenter, authority on extra-sensory perception; co-developer Blanchard Springs Caverns, Stone County, Ark. Mem. Authors League Am. (life), Dramatists Guild. Lion. Author: Know Your Own Mind, 1953; How to Make ESP Work for You, 1964; How to Solve Mysteries of Your Mind and Soul, 1965; The New TNT—Miraculous Power Within You, 1966; Wonder Healers of the Philippines, 1967; Your Mysterious Powers of ESP, 1969; How to Foresee and Control Your Future, 1970; How to Take Yourself Apart and Put Yourself Together Again, 1971, (with Ambrose and Olga Worrall) Your Power to Heal, 1972; You Live After Death, 1972; (with Sir Hubert Wilkins) Thoughts Through Space; You Can Communicate with the Unseen World, 1974; numerous others. Record albums include: How to Develop ESP, 1964; Advanced Techniques of ESP, 1964; How to Foretell Your Future 1964. Experiments in long distance telepathy with Arctic explorer Sir Hubert Wilkins. Home: Kahoka Route Mountain View AR 72560 Office: ESP Research Assos Union Nat Plaza Bldg Little Rock AR 72201

SHERMAN, JEROME NATHANIEL, psychologist; b. Everett, Mass., Nov. 13, 1936; s. Abraham and Anna (Grunberg) S.; B.A., Harvard, 1958; B.A. in Hebrew Lit., Hebrew Union Coll., 1960, M.A., 1963; M.A. in Sci. and Edn., Boston U., 1964; Ph.D., U. Houston, 1968; m. Ruth Goldberger, Aug. 26, 1962; chileren—Marc Owen, Scott Allen, Rhonda Sue. Ordained rabbi, 1962; rabbi Temple Beth Israel, Houston, 1963-68, Temple Isaiah, Lafayette, Cal., 1968-72; psychologist, Houston, 1972—; lectr. psychology and religious studies Houston Community Coll., 1972—, Rice U., 1973—. Pres. Contra Costa County Mental Health Assn., 1967-68; mem. Jewish Family Service, Oakland, Cal., 1969-72. Mem. sch. bd. Houston Model Sch., 1967-68. Bd. dirs. Houston Jewish Community Council, 1966, Contra Costa County Planned Parenthood Assn., 1970-72, Cal. State Mental Health Assn., 1971-72. Recipient spl. service award Houston Blue Bonnet Bowl, 1967, distinguished citizens award Contra Costa County Mental Health Assn., 1971. Mem. Houston Rabbinical Assn. (past pres.), Am., Tex., Western psychol. assns., Centra Conf. Am. Rabbis, Council Marriage and Family Living, Pacific Assn. Reform Rabbis. Rotarian. Clubs: Harvard (Houston), San Francisco Press. Home: 14811 Cindywood St Houston TX 77024 Office: Meml City Profl Bldg 902 Frostwood St Suite 204 Houston TX 77024

SHERMAN, JOHN HARVEY, JR., engring. physicist; b. Roanoke, Va., Aug. 12, 1918; s. John Harvey and Mary (Stephens) S.; student Oberlin Coll., 1936-37; A.B., U. Tampa, 1940; M.S., Lehigh U., 1947; postgrad. Cornell U., 1940-41, N.C. State Coll., 1950-51; m. Marie Louise Weill, Mar. 31, 1943; children—Mary Esther (Mrs. John Taube), Ida Leah Cole. Optician Spencer Lens Co., Buffalo, 1941-42; asst. prof. elec. engring. N.C. State Coll., 1947-50; quartz crystal engr. Gen. Electric Co., Lynchburg, Va., 1951—, tech. leader quartz crystal design, 1957—. Mem. Electronic Industries Assn. Working Group P5.4, 1960—, chmn., 1970—. Founder Lynchburg Fine Arts Symphony Orch., 1965. Bd. dirs. Lynchburg Community Concert Assn., 1968—, pres., 1970—. Mem. I.E.E.E., Assn. Lynchburg Gen. Electric Engrs., Sigma Xi, Eta Kappa Nu. Unitarian. Home: 2022 Woodcrest Dr Lynchburg VA 24503 Office: Mountain View Rd Lynchburg VA 24502

SHERMAN, JOSEPH DALE, univ. computer center dir.; b. Boston, Ga., May 31, 1936; s. Claude Payton and Nina Mae (Smith) S.; A.A., Ga. Southwestern Coll., 1956; B.S., Valdosta State Coll., 1961; M.Ed., U. Ga., 1969; m. Jan Strobel, Nov. 10, 1958; children—Mark Christopher, Jeffery, Girard. Announcer radio sta. WMTM, Moultrie, Ga., 1956-59; accountant Jaco Pants, Inc., Tifton, Ga., 1961-62; inventory accountant Abraham Baldwin Coll., Tifton, 1962-66, instr., 1966-68, dir. computer center, 1968-73; head dept. software services Computer Center, U. Ga., Athens, 1973—. Cons. in computer installations, 1969—. Recipient Carlton Award of Excellence Greater Baldwin Assn., 1973, Distinguished Service award Bus. Div. Abraham Baldwin Coll., 1973. Presbyn. (deacon 1965—). Kiwanian (treas. Tiftarea 1968-73). Home: 1607 Tyson St Tifton GA 31794 Office: University of Georgia Computer Center Athens GA 30602

SHERMAN, ROGER JOE, univ. ofcl.; b. Roswell, N.M., Nov. 21, 1934; s. Roger Bennett and Bessie Lorena (Atkinson) S.; B.S. in Journalism, So. Meth. U., 1957, M.A. in English, 1969; m. Judith Ann Renard, Apr. 17, 1957; children—Mark Alan, Kathleen Ann. Reporter, Dallas Times Herald, 1957-64; news bur. dir. So. Meth. U., Dallas, 1964-65, information services dir., 1965—. Pub. relations cons. Presbyn. Village, Dallas Bapt. Assn., Dallas N.E. Meth. Dist.; makeup and editorial cons. All-Ch. Press, Inc., 1960-64. Recipient Journalism award State Bar Tex., 1962. Mem. Am. Coll. Pub. Relations Assn. (Nat. Case Study award 1973), Press Club of Dallas (Dallas News Story award 1963), Pi Kappa Alpha. Presbyn. (ruling elder 1967—). Interim editor The Tex. Meth. newspaper, 1959. Home: 9860 Elmcrest Dr Dallas TX 75238 Office: Information Services Dept Southern Methodist University Dallas TX 75275

SHERMAN, RUSSELL EDSEL, lawyer; b. Abington, Pa., Sept. 9, 1936; s. Russell Edward and Mildred Tomlinson (Hughes) S.; B.A., Duke U., 1958; J.D., George Washington U., 1963; m. Janice Medley, Mar. 21. 1959; children—Scott Michael, Christoper William, Shaun Andrew. With Defense Intelligence Agy., U.S. Govt., 1960-63; topographic draftsman Arlington County, Pa., 1963; admitted to Va. bar, 1963, D.C. bar, 1963, U.S. Supreme Ct., 1965; asso. McGinnis, Berg, Shadyac & Nolan, Arlington, Va., 1963-68; partner Shadyac, Berg, Nolan & Sherman, 1968—. Vice-pres. Olde Creek P.T.A., 1972, pres., 1973; chmn. Duke U. Alumni Admissions Commn. for Arlington County, 1968-73. Commnv. YMCA Youth Football, 1973. Served with USMCR, 1958-60. Mem. Am. Judicature Soc., Va. Trial Lawyers Assn., Arlington County Bar Assn. (mem. exec. com. 1972), Phi Delta Theta, Delta Theta Phi. Republican. Episcopalian. Home: 4415 Glenn Rose St Fairfax VA 22030 Office: 2014 N 16th St Arlington VA 22216

SHERMAN, WAYNE HERSHEL, computer co. exec.; b. Oklahoma City, Feb. 4, 1934; s. Hershel and Leoon Pearl (Button) S.; B.S. in Mech. Engring, 1957; M.B.A., Oklahoma City U., 1971; m. Patricia Louise Richardson, July 15, 1961 (div. Mar. 1973); children—Paul Wayne, Sherri Lynn. Data sales mgr. S.W. Bell Telephone Co., Oklahoma City, 1964-68; mgr. terminal product planning Gen. Electric Co.-Honeywell, Oklahoma City, 1968-71; sr. systems analyst Honeywell Information Systems, Inc., Washington, 1971-73; sr. mem. tech. staff Computer Scis. Corp., Washington, 1973—. Mem. Del City (Okla.) Park Commn., 1967-69. Served to lt. AUS, 1957-59, 61-62. Registered profl. engr., Okla. Home: 7901 Harwood Pl Springfield VA 22152 Office: 6565 Arlington Blvd Falls Church VA 22042

SHERMAN, WILBUR BROWN, oil co. exec.; b. Turner, Kan., Nov. 4, 1911; s. S. Franklin and Inez (Byers) S.; A.B., U. Cal. Los Angeles, 1939; m. Virginia LaRue Tucker, Nov. 28, 1936; children—Dorothy Virginia, Richard Allyn, Elizabeth Ann. Geophys. computer Am. Petroleum Corp., Los Angeles, 1940-41; field geologist Superior Oil Co., 1941-42; v.p., dir. engring. and geol. cons. De Goyer & McNaughton, Dallas, 1948-58; pres. Panoil Co., 1958-70, chmn. bd., 1971; dir. Premier Consol. Oil fields, Ltd., London, Eng., 1959-72. Petroleum cons., 1971—. Served from 1st lt. to lt. col., USAF, 1942-47. Registered profl. engr., Tex. Mem. Am. Inst. Mining and Metallurgy, A.A.A.S., Am. Assn. Petroleum Geologists, Am. Geophys. Union, Am. Meterol. Soc., Dallas Geol. Soc. Republican. Methodist. Clubs: Dallas Country, Preston Trail Golf, Petroleum; Athletic (N.Y.). Contbr. profl. mags. Home: 3716 Caruth Blvd Dallas TX 75225 Office: Preston State Bank Bldg Dallas TX 75225

SHERMAN, WILLIAM EURASTI, lawyer; b. Tampa, Fla., Apr. 28, 1927; s. William Eurasti and Maryetta (Abbott) S.; B.A., U. Fla., 1950, J.D., 1953; m. Frances Jeannette Rogers, Feb. 1, 1950 (div. 1973); children—William Eurasti III, Valerie Ann. Admitted to Fla. bar, 1953; spl. asst. to Atty. Gen. Fla., Tallahassee, 1953; asso. Francis P. Whitehair, DeLand, Fla., 1954-57; practiced in DeLand, 1958—; mem. firm Hall, Sweeney & Godbee, 1958-59, Hull, Landis, Graham & French, 1961-66, Landis, Graham, French, Husfeld and Sherman, 1966-69, Landis, Graham, French, Husfeld, Sherman & Ford, PA., 1969—. Mem. Volusia County Charter Study Commn., 1969-71. Bd. dirs. Internat. Music Festivals, Inc., 1969-71, Montreat (N.C.)-Anderson Coll., 1961-71, Mountain Retreat Assn., 1961-71. Served with Signal Corps, AUS, World War II. Mem. Fla. Bar (gov. 1970—, chmn. legislative com. 1973, exec. com. real property probate and trust sect., mem. Uniform Probate Code Study Commn.), Am., Volusia County (pres. 1969-70) bar assns., DeLand C. of C. (v.p. 1970-71), Phi Delta Phi, Pi Kappa Alpha, Alpha Delta Sigma. Democrat. Presbyn. (elder). Rotarian. Clubs: Lake Beresford Yacht (commodore 1966), Deland Golf and Country; Halifax. Home: 549 N Hayden St PO Box 329 DeLand FL 32720 Office: 110 W Indiana Av DeLand FL 32720 also 412 N Wild Olive Daytona FL 32018

SHERRILL, JAMES FENTON, mfg. co. exec.; b. Columbus, Miss., Dec. 19, 1924; s. Leon T. and Bertha E. (Geer) S.; student engring. U. Ala., 1946-54; LL.B., LaSalle Extension U., 1966; m. Hazel Joyce Kilgore, July 30, 1949; children—James Fenton, William Lynn, Julia LuAnn. Prodn. and material control mgr. Butler Mfg. Co., Birmingham, Ala., 1951-62; prodn. specialist Chrysler Corp., Huntsville, Ala., 1962-69; div. plant mgr. Thomas Industries, Inc., Johnson City, Tenn., 1969-70; v.p. mfg. Mor-Flo Industries, Inc., Johnson City and Cleve., 1970—; also dir.; gen. mgr. Tenn. Tank Co., Johnson City. Served with USNR, 1943-46, 50-51. Mem. Am. Prodn. and Inventory Control Soc., Civitan Internat. (program dir. 1960-62), Exchange Club (dir. 1968-69). Baptist. Club: Johnsity City Country.

Home: 1900 Sinking Creek Rd Johnson City TN 37601 Office: PO Box 788 Johnson City TN 37601

SHERRILL, LARRYMORE, civil engr.; b. Jacksonville, Fla., Oct. 16, 1942; s. Oliver Lee and Margaret (Logan) S.; B.S. in Civil Engring., Tenn. Tech. U., 1965; m. Sandra Kay Johnson, Mar. 19, 1965; 1 dau., Lisa Michelle. Engring. trainee Am. Bridge div. U.S. Steel, Pitts., 1965-66; job engr. Dravo Corp., Pitts., 1966-71; chief engr. Lenoir Industries, Inc., modular mfg., Lenoir City, Tenn., 1971—. Registered profl. engr., Ala., Ark., Fla., Ga., Ind., Ky., La., Miss., N.C., Ohio, Pa., S.C., Tenn., Va., W.Va. Mem. Am. Soc. C.E. (asso.). Design and analysis modules for motel constrn., 1971. Home: 832 Sanders Rd Knoxville TN 37919 Office: PO Box 190 Lenoir City TN 37771

SHERRILL, LEROY, physician; b. Big Spring, Tenn., Oct. 9, 1929; s. Jesse Henry and Ethel Pearl (Blankenship) S.; B.S., U. Tenn., 1949, M.D., 1952; m. Margaret Cameron Marshall, Aug. 23, 1958; children—David, Nancy. Intern Jefferson Davis Hosp., Houston, 1953; resident VA Hosp., Houston, 1956-57; practice medicine specializing in gen. practice, Rossville, Ga., 1958-67, Chattanooga, 1967—; mem. staff Tri-County Hosp., Ft. Oglethorpe, Ga. Served with USAF, 1954-56. Mem. Walker-Catoosa-Dade County (Ga.) Med. Soc. Home: 520 S Crest Rd Chattanooga TN 37404 Office: 4802 14th Av Chattanooga TN 37407

SHERRILL, ROBERT GLENN, journalist; b. Frogtown, Ga., Dec. 24, 1925; s. Henry Clifton and Susan Olive (McGinley) S.; B.A., Pepperdine Coll., 1949; M.A., U. Tex., 1956; M.A., U. Minn., 1960; m. Mary Elizabeth Bergeson, May 5, 1950. Reporter Ariz. Times, Phoenix, 1948-49, Standard Times, San Angelo, Tex., 1951, Am.-Statesman, Austin, Tex., 1954-55, Nashville Tennessean, 1957-58; instr. English, U. Tex. at Austin, 1955-56, Tex. A. and M., Bryan, 1956-57, U. Mo., Columbia, 1958-59; asso. editor Tex. Observer, Austin, 1960-63; polit. writer Miami Herald, 1964-65; Washington editor, The Nation, 1965—. Contbr. polit. articles to Sunday N.Y. Times, Playboy, Pageant, other mags. Served with U.S. Mcht. Marine, 1942-46. So. Rockefeller fellow, 1957; Duke fellow in communications, 1973-74; recipient ann. award Soc. Mag. Writers, 1967, Edit. Ann. award Playboy, 1970; nominee Nat. Book award, 1974; recipient N.Y. Newspaper Guild Page One award, 1974. Author: The Accidental President, 1967; Gothic Politics in the Deep South, 1968; The Drugstore Liberal, 1968; Military Justice Is to Justice as Military Music Is to Music, 1970; Why They Call It Politics, 1972; The Saturday Night Special, 1973. Address: 617 North Carolina Av SE Washington DC 20003

SHERRILL, ROBERT GRADY, JR., hosp. med. dir.; b. Decatur, Ala., Aug. 26, 1924; s. Robert Grady and Ethel (Corsbie) S.; B.S., Fla. So. Coll., 1949; M.A., Vanderbilt U., 1950; M.D., U. Tenn., 1955; m. Lanette Crumpton, Mar. 30, 1973. Intern City of Memphis Hosp., 1955-56; med. dir. Hillsborough County Hosp., Tampa, Fla., 1956-72; practice medicine, Tampa, 1960-72; med. dir. Mercy Hosp., Birmingham, Ala., 1972—; pres. Jefferson Clinic, 1972-74. Asst. prof. Ga. State Tchrs. Coll., 1950-51; mem. med. adv. bd. to Hosp. and Welfare Bd. Hillsborough County, 1961-65; mem. Community Coordinating Council and Mental Health Com., Tampa, 1963-70; mem. Fla. Com. Alcoholism, 1971-72; mem. Mental Health Bd., Jefferson County, Ala. Dist. dir. Boy Scouts Am., 1968-69. Bd. dirs. Curtis Hixon Rehab. Center, 1965-70, Suicide Prevention Com., Tampa, 1970-72, Jefferson County Alcoholic Com., Tri-County Regional Health Planning Council. Served as surg. technician AUS, 1943-46; ETO. Recipient Alcoholic Rehab. citation State of Fla., 1966, certificate of commendation Interprofl. Family Council, 1961. Mem. A.M.A., Ala., So. med. assns., Jefferson County Med. Soc., Am. Acad. Gen. Practice, Ala. Acad. Family Practice, Am., Jefferson County heart assns., Nat. Rehab. Assn., Am. Assn. Study Headache (dir., treas.), Fla. Thoracic Soc. (dir. 1967-70), Am. Cancer Soc. (profl. edn. com.), Internat. Platform Assn., Mental Health Assn. (dir., also profl. adv. bd. 1968-72), Sigma Xi. Rotarian. Home: 725-D Raleigh Villa Birmingham AL 32209 Office: Mercy Hospital 1515 6th Av S Birmingham AL 35233

SHERROD, KY, sch. adminstr.; b. Swenson, Tex., Sept. 3, 1929; s. Lester Algie and Claudie Belle (Hall) S.; B.S., W. Tex. State U., 1951, M.E., 1952; m. Frances Bussard, Aug. 23, 1952; children—Randall, Brent, Mark. Coach, tchr. Channing (Tex.) High Sch., 1952-53, prin., 1953-56; supt. schs. Channing Ind. Sch. Dist., 1956—. Mem. Am. Assn. Sch. Adminstrs., Tex., Panhandle sch. leaders assns., Tex. State, Dallam-Hartley (past pres.) tchrs. assns. Mason, Lion (past pres.). Home: PO Box A Channing TX 79018

SHERROD, ROBERT LEE, writer; b. Thomas County, Ga., Feb. 8, 1909; s. Joseph Arnold and Victoria Ellen (Evers) S.; A.B., U. Ga., 1929; m. Elizabeth Hudson, Oct. 8, 1936 (dec. Dec. 1958); children—John Hudson, Robert Lee; m. 2d, Margaret Carson Ruff, May 5, 1961 (div. 1972); m. 3d, Mary Gay Labrot Leonhardt, Aug. 26, 1972. Reporter Atlanta Constitution, Palm Beach (Fla.) Daily News, others, 1929-35; with Time and Life mags. as Washington corr., asso. editor, war and Far East corr., 1935-52; Far East corr. Sat. Eve. Post, 1952-55, mng. editor, 1955-62, editor, 1962, and editor-at-large, 1963-64; v.p., editorial coordinator Curtis Pub. Co., 1965-66; writing on fgn. affairs and history, 1966—; contract writer Life mag., N.Y.C., 1966-68. Mem. Pres.'s Com. to Employ Handicapped; mem. USMC History Adv. Com., 1973—. Trustee Corrs. Fund. Commended by U.S. Navy Dept., Battle of Attu, May 1943, Battle of Tarawa, Nov. 1943; recipient Headliners Club award, for war reporting, 1944; Benjamin Franklin award U. Ill., 1954; Overseas Press Club certificate, 1955. Mem. Mil. Order of Carabao. Episcopalian. Clubs: Federal City, National Press (Washington); Overseas Press, Century (N.Y.C.). Author: Tarawa, the Story of a Battle, 1944, new edit., 1973; On to Westward, 1945; History of Marine Corps Aviation in World War II, 1952; also of text for Life's Picture History of World War II, 1950 and Kobunsha's Picture History of the Pacific War (in Japanese), 1952. Home: 4000 Massachusetts Av NW Washington DC 20016

SHERWOOD, EDWARD READ, II, civil engr.; b. New Orleans, July 7, 1937; s. Edward Read and Katherine Mary (Ernst) S.; B.S., Tulane U., 1960; m. Nancie Cecelia Summerville, Sept. 6, 1958; children—Edward Read, Christopher, William, Katherine, Nancie, Julianne. Field engr. Williams-McWilliams, New Orleans, 1960-61; operations mgr. Lane & Co., Inc., New Orleans, 1962-67; chief estimator H.B. Fowler & Co., Inc., Harvey, La., 1967-72; exec. v.p. LeGardeur Internat. Inc., Belle Chasse, La., 1972—. Served to 2nd lt., AUS, 1961-62. Recipient Certificate of Achievement, Transp. Research Command, 1961-62. Mem. Am. Soc. C.E., La. Engring. Soc., Am. Welding Soc., Am. Concrete Inst., Am. Soc. Testing Materials, Kappa Alpha. Democrat. Roman Catholic. Clubs: Pickwick, Windsor (New Orleans). Home: 1622 Pine St New Orleans LA 70118 Office: PO Box 269 4011 Woodland Hwy Belle Chasse LA 70037

SHERWOOD, ELMER WILLIAM, ins. and real estate exec.; b. Linton, Ind., Feb. 22, 1896; s. Elmer Tip and Hattie (Price) S.; A.B., Ind. U., 1921; m. Lucille Smith, Sept. 27, 1924; children—Jean, Robert Elmer. Tchr. English Linton High Sch., 1922-23; pres. Sherwood Sales Co., Linton, 1932-34; pub. relations rep. Sherwood-Templeton Coal Co. and Central Ind. Coal Co., 1935-37; editor Nat. Legionaire, Publ. Am. Legion, 1937-42; dir. Nat. Americanism Commn. Am. Legion, 1945-46; pres. Ind. Mut. Fire Ins. Co.; treas. Sherwood Assos. pub. relations counsellors, also Sebring Devel. Corp.; exec. Am. Travelers Life Ins. Co.; dir. Midwest Devel. Co., Bloomfield State Bank. Active Boy Scouts Am.; treas. A.R.C. Clk. Green County, Ind., 1927-35; former mem. Ind. Ho. of Reps.; del. Republican nat. conv., 1936; organizer Democrats for Ike, 1952; nat. chmn. Vets. for Eisenhower, 1952. Served with U.S. Army, World Wars I and II; brig. gen. Res. ret.; adj. gen. Ind., 1944-45. Mem. Res. Officers Assn., Mil. Order Loyal Legion, U.S. Mil. Order World Wars, Am. Legion (mem. nat. child welfare com. 1922-26, del. to nat. conv. 1923, 24, 26, 45, del.-at-large 1921-50; chmn. nat. legislative com., chief coordinator Congress and Senate com., Rep. Nat. Com.), 40 and 8, V.F.W., Ind. Soc. Chgo., Sons Ind., N.Y. City, Nat. Ski Assn., Rainbow Div. Soc. Ind. (pres. 1922—), Sigma Delta Chi, Beta Theta Pi. Mason, Rotarian. Clubs: Army and Navy (Washington); Armed Forces (Ft. Harrison, Ind.); Writers, Aeons and Sphinx (Ind. U.); Sno Birds (Lake Placid, N.Y.); Columbia (Indpls.); Sebring Shores Country (Sebring, Fla.). Author: Rainbow-Hoosier, 1918; Diary of a Rainbow Veteran, 1928; The Shibboleth, 1942; American Citizenship, 1943; Analysis of Communism, 1946. Home: Rural Route 1 Box 167 Sebring FL 33870 Office: Sebring Shore Club Bldg Sebring FL 33870

SHETLER, STANWYN GERALD, botanist; b. Johnstown, Pa., Oct. 11, 1933; s. Sanford Grant and Florence (Young) S.; student Eastern Mennonite Coll., 1951-53; B.S. with distinction, Cornell U., 1955, M.S., 1958; postgrad. U. Mich., 1958-62; m. Elaine Marie Retberg, Feb. 2, 1963. Staff, asst. curator Smithsonian Instn., Washington, 1962-63, asso. curator Phanerogams, 1963—, sci. adminstr. botany, 1969—. Mem. A.A.A.S., Am. Inst. Biol. Scis. (sec. flora N.Am. program 1966-71, dir. 1972—, governing bd. 1973—), Arctic Inst. N.Am., Biol. Soc. Washington (council 1969-70), Bot. Soc. Am., Internat. Soc. Plant Taxonomy, Am. Soc. Plant Taxonomists, Audubon Naturalist Soc. Washington (program chmn. natural history forum 1968-70; dir. 1971-74), also other profl. socs. Author: The Komarov Botanical Institute: 250 Years Of Russian Research, 1967; also papers. Home: 142 Meadowland Lane E Sterling VA 22170 Office: Dept Botany Smithsonian Instn Washington DC 20560

SHIELD, CHARLES FRANKLIN, JR., computer corp. exec.; b. Ontario, Cal., Apr. 2, 1919; s. Charles Franklin and Esther Amelia (Liller) S.; B.S., U. Cal. at Los Angeles, 1950; m. Annabelle Wingo, Dec. 12, 1944; children—Charles Franklin III, Linda Kay, Anita Louise (Mrs. Douglas Lee), James Floyd, Terra Lea. With IBM Corp., 1950—, tech. asst., Owego, N.Y., 1960-62, staff engr., 1962-63, staff engr., Huntsville, Ala., 1963-65, project engr., 1965-69, staff engr., 1969-72, staff program evaluation analyst, 1972—. Tchr. summer course Samford U., USAF, IBM Corp. Active Boy Scout Am. Served to lt. col USAAF, 1941-46. Decorated D.F.C., Air medal with 7 oak leaf clusters. Mem. I.E.E.E. (sr.), Air Force Assn. (state sect.-treas. 1966), Res. Officers Assn. (nat. membership dir.). Comml. pilot. Home: 5611 Woodridge St Huntsville AL 35802 Office: 150 Sparkman Dr Huntsville AL 35805

SHIELDS, CHARLES CLAY, accountant; b. Frankford, Ky., June 10, 1921; s. Charles Austin and Mary Clay (Perkins) S.; B.S. in Commerce, U. Ky., 1949; m. Betty Morgan Wilson, Mar. 18, 1948; children—Gregory C., Sherrie C. Jr. accountant W.W. Thorp., Co., 1949-51; spl. agt. Internal Revenue Service, 1951-53; partner Shields, Tuttle & Batsel and predecessor firms, C.P.A.'s, Lexington, Ky., 1953-71; partner Potter, Hisle, Sugg & Nolan, C.P.A.'s, Lexington, 1971—. Treas. Ky. Bd. Accountancy, 1971-72, pres., 1972-73; mem. Lexington Estate Planning Council, 1966—. Served with USAAF, 1942-46. C.P.A., Ky. Mem. Ky. Soc. C.P.A.'s (v.p. 1966-67, pres. 1967-68), Am. Inst. C.P.A.'s (council 1967-68), So. States Conf. C.P.A.'s (exec. com. 1960-69), Central Ky. Assn. C.P.A.'s, Ky. Hist. Soc. Democrat. Mem. Christian Ch. (deacon 1966—). Mason (K.T., Shriner). Clubs: Lexington Country, Lafayette. Home: 1626 Meadowthorpe Av Lexington KY 40505 Office: 2228 Young Dr Lexington KY 40505

SHIELDS, CHARLES L., advt. agy. exec.; b. Lombard, Ill., Apr. 3, 1926; s. Charles Emerson and Janet Lucile (Kepner) S.; student U. Ga., 1946-47; m. Mildred Reynolds, Dec. 22, 1951; children—Patricia Ann, Charles Jonathan, Richard Scott. Script writer Pearltone Studio Prodns., Des Moines, 1945; copywriter, announcer radio sta. WMJM, Cordele, Ga., 1946; copywriter radio sta. KCBC, Des Moines, 1947, radio sta. KRNT, Des Moines, 1948-50; writer Gen. Pictures Prodns., Des Moines, 1947-48; free lance radio copy Lessing Advt. Co., Des Moines, 1950; radio, TV copy specialist Bozell & Jacobs, Inc., Omaha, 1952, Burke Dowling Adams, Inc., Atlanta, N.Y.C., 1952-53; radio, TV copy dir. Kirland, White & Schell, Atlanta, 1953-55; copy dir. Liller, Neal, Battle & Lindsey, Atlanta, 1955-59; pres. Chuck Shields Advt., Inc., Atlanta, 1960-69, Clearwater, Fla., 1969—, Shields Properties, 1972—. Co-chmn. advt. Atlanta United Appeal, 1963. Advt. cons. Ga. Congressman Charles L. Weltner, 1962, 64, 66; advt. dir. Fulton County Democratic exec. com., Atlanta, 1964. Bd. dirs. Pinellas County United Way, 1972, creative dir., 1971-72. Mem. Clearwater Advt. Fedn. (1st v.p. 1972). Home: 1203 Bay Dr Belleair Beach FL 33535 Office: Colonial Park 2601 Jewel Rd Belleair Bluffs FL 33540

SHIELDS, CHARLIE DEWITT, savs. and loan exec.; b. Center, Miss., Mar. 26, 1909; s. Charlie Walter and Mary Natie (Price) S.; grad. So. Bus. Coll., Vicksburg, Miss., 1929; law degree, Am. Law Sch., Chgo., 1930; m. Beatrice Williams, Sept. 2, 1934; children—Camille (Mrs. Lenman Key), Sharlynn (Mrs. A.P. Baltzell). Admitted to Miss. bar, 1930, since practiced in Meridian; ins. agt. So. Guaranty Ins. Co., Meridian; founder, pres. First Savs. & Loan Assn., Meridian 1952-69; pres. Bankers Trust Savs. & Loan Assn. (merger First Savs. & Loan Assn. 1969), Jackson, Miss., 1969—; dir. So. Guaranty Ins. Co., Montgomery, Ala., Nat. Gen. Ins. Co., others. City councilman, Meridian, 1956-60; chmn. Meridian Selective Service Draft Bd., 1952-72; chmn., sec. Lauderdale County Democratic exec. com., 1938—. Bd. dirs. Meridian area Salvation Army; trustee Clarke Coll., Newton, Miss., also pvt. founds. Served with U.S. Army, 1927-28. Mem. Miss. State Bar, Lauderdale County Bar Assn., Miss. Savs. and Loan Inst. Mason, Lion (pres. 1969-70). Home: 2715 28th St Meridian MS 39301 Office: 2105 6th St Meridian MS 39301 also Bankers Trust Savings and Loan Association Box 918 Jackson MS 39205

SHIELDS, DAVID WILLIAM, JR., lawyer; b. Rensselaer, Ind., Jan. 12, 1899; s. David William and Emma (Gay) S.; student Sch. Law, Vanderbilt U.; m. Arlie Cox, May 8, 1930; children—David William III (dec.), John Alfred, James Edward, Sam Jarrett. Tchr. county schs., 1922-25; county supt. schs., 1927-32; admitted to Tenn. bar; pvt. practice law, Manchester, 1932-62, 65—; county judge, Coffee County, 1951-65. Dir. Coffee County Fair Assn., 1933-53; mem. Coffee County Bd. Edn., 1939-40; chmn. County Hwy. Com., 1947-51; chmn. Coffee County Hosp. Commn., 1954-62, Citizens Welfare Council. Mem. Tenn. Ho. of Reps., 1941-43. Mem. Am. Bar Assn., Bar Assn. Tenn., Am. Legion, World War I Vets. Mason, Odd Fellow, K.P. Home: Route 4 Manchester TN 37355 Office: Peoples Bank Bldg Manchester TN 37355

SHIELDS, FLETCHER DOUGLAS, educator; b. Nashville, Oct. 27, 1926; s. Ben Cockrill and Sarah Alice (Srygely) S.; B.S., Tenn. Poly. U., 1947, M.S., Vanderbilt U., 1948, Ph.D., 1956; m. Cora Beal Hardison, Oct. 2, 1948; children—Alice McKay (Mrs. Lambert Murray), Fletcher Douglas, Anne, Ben. Physicist, Union Carbide Co., Oak Ridge, 1948-49; faculty Middle Tenn. State U., Murfreesboro, 1949-59; prof. physics U. Miss., Oxford, 1959—. Sec. bd. dirs. Univ. Christian Student Center, 1962—. Served with USAAF, 1945. Mem. Sigma Xi. Mem. Ch. of Christ (elder 1965—). Club: Oxford Rotary (pres. 1971). Home: Box 246 Route 6 Oxford MS 38655 Office: Physics Dept University of Mississippi Oxford MS 38677

SHIELDS, HARVEY GERALD, ednl. adminstr.; b. Yorktown, Va., Nov. 27, 1937; s. Harvey and Eliza Lorraine (Amory) S.; B.A. cum laude, Washington and Lee U., 1960; M.A., Tulane U., 1962; M.Ed., Harvard, 1969. Asst. headmaster Asheville (N.C.) Sch., 1963-69; head counselor Brandon Hall Sch., Atlanta, 1969-70; dean Litchfield (Conn.) Prep. Sch., 1970-71; dir. Ednl. Adv. Service, Atlanta, 1971-72; dir. admissions Sewanee Acad. of U. of South, Sewanee, Tenn., 1972—. Mem. Secondary Sch. Admission Test Bd., 1964-69. Chmn. United Fund, Litchfield, 1971. Mem. Am. Assn. U. Profs., Lambda Chi Alpha. Republican. Episcopalian. Clubs: Harvard (N.Y.C.). Home: Rebel's Rest Sewanee TN 37375 Office: Sewanee Academy Sewanee TN 37375

SHIELDS, JOHN EDGAR, editor; b. Camden, N.J., May 8, 1924; s. Emmett Paxton and Marion Amy (Kilheffer) S.; B.A., U. Md., 1950; m. Louisa Conaway Room, Mar. 24, 1951; children—David Sanford, Richard Paxton, Diane Karen. Producer, dir. CBS, Washington, 1946-49; sec. to Ambassador William C. Bullitt, 1950; with CIA, 1950-52; exec. Asia Found., various Far Eastern countries, 1952-55; fgn. corr., author, editor various media, 1952-60; with Nat. Geog. Soc., 1960-62; asso. editor Congl. Digest, Washington, 1962-68, editor, 1968—; dir. mining, pub. corps. Served with USNR, 1942-45. Mem. S.A.R., Mensa, Phi Kappa Phi, Alpha Phi Omega, Sigma Alpha Epsilon. Methodist. Clubs: Nat. Press. Author books on local history, genealogy, including A History of the Shields Family, 1968; East Tennessee Migrations: Factors and Families, 1969; The Scotch-Irish in Augusta County, Virginia, 1971; Narratives of Westward Movement, 1973. Home: 19128 Roman Way Gaithersburg MD 20760 Office: 3231 P St NW Washington DC 20007

SHIELDS, LESTER HOWARD, physician; b. Isabella, Tenn., Sept. 4, 1908; s. Robert Martin Van Buren and Ellen Rose (Carver) S.; B.S., U. Tenn. at Knoxville, 1928; M.D., U. Tenn. at Memphis, 1930; m. Esther Workman, June 5, 1931; children—Lester Howard, Patricia Anne (Mrs. Andre Nowacki). Intern Bapt. Hosp., Memphis, 1930-31; gen. practice medicine, Athens, Tenn., 1938-74; mem. staff Epperson Hosp., Athens Community Hosp.; owner, operator Shields Hosp. and Med.-Surg. Clinic. McMinn County med. examiner. Dir. Spurling Fire Alarm & Indicator Co. Served to capt., AUS, 1942-45. Decorated Bronze Star. Mem. A.M.A., Tenn., McMinn County, Mid South, So. Med. socs. Baptist. Club: Chestuee Golf and Country (Etowah, Tenn.). Home: Airport Rd Athens TN 37303 Office: P O Box 508 Athens TN 37303

SHIELS, JAMES HENRY, JR., advt. and indsl. art. co. exec.; b. Dallas, Feb. 19, 1930; s. James Henry and Mary (Robbins) S.; B.A., So. Methodist U., 1957; m. Gay Nell Steelmen, June 28, 1957; 1 son, James Henry, III. Staff artist, sales rep., 1956-58; owner, art dir. Henry Shiels Indsl. and Advt. Art Studio, Dallas, 1958—. Vice pres., vice chmn. bd. Mary Shiels Hosp., 1966—. Served to 1st lt. USAF, 1952-56, capt. USAF Res., 1960-65. Mem. Nat. Soc. Art Dirs., Dallas-Ft. Worth Art Dirs. Club, Dallas-Ft. Worth Soc. Visual Communications (dir.). Presbyn. Home: 2905 Purdue Dallas TX 75225 Office: Dallas Athletic Club Bldg Dallas TX 75201

SHIH, CHIA SHUN, educator; b. Kiangsi, China, July 14, 1938; s. I Ming and Chih-Yung (Chang) S.; came to U.S., 1963, naturalized, 1973. B.S., Taiwan Cheng Kung U., 1960; M.S., U. Tex. at Austin, 1966, Ph.D., 1967; m. Hester F. Chiao, Aug. 6, 1966; children—R. Liren, Rainee L. Engr., Taiwan Water Supply Commn., Taipei, 1961-63; supr. research dept. Roy F. Weston, Inc., West Chester, Pa., 1967-70; asso. prof. indsl. engring. dept. Tex. A. and M. U., College Station, 1970-73; prof., also dir. environmental studies div. U. Tex. at San Antonio, 1973—. Partner, Devel. through Applied Sci. Co., San Antonio, 1972—; partner Marco Polo Assos., Corpus Christi, 1971—. Served as engring. officer Chinese Army, 1960-61. Registered profl. engr., Tex. Mem. Am. Inst. Indsl. Engrs., Water Pollution Control Fedn., Am. Water Resources Assn., Am. Water Works Assn., Tex. Assn. Profl. Engrs., Sigma Xi, Phi Kappa Phi, Alpha Pi Mu, Chi Epsilon. Contbr. chpts. to books on environmental pollution. Research in environmental quality and water resources systems analysis. Home: 7010 Evening Sun Dr San Antonio TX 78238 Office: 4242 Piedras Dr E San Antonio TX 78228

SHINDLER, THOMAS OSBORNE, orthopedic surgeon; b. Hempstead, Tex., Dec. 11, 1919; s. J.T. and Louise (Osborne) S.; B.A., U. Tex., 1941, M.D., 1943; m. Betty Randal, Dec. 29, 1950; children—Byron, John. Intern, Hosp. P.E. Ch., Phila., 1943-44; research fellow U. Tex. Med. Br., Galveston, 1947-48, resident, 1948-50; resident Arabia Temple Crippled Childrens Hosp., Houston, 1950-51; pvt. practice medicine specializing in orthopedic surgery, Houston, 1951—; clin. asso. prof. orthopedic surgery U. Tex. Med. Sch., Houston; sr. attending Hermann Hosp.; lectr. U. Tex. Postgrad. Sch. Medicine; instr. Baylor U. Coll. Medicine; orthopedic surgeon Houston Oiler Profl. Football Team, 1960-70. Adviser Liberty Mut. Ins. Co. Served to capt. AUS, 1944-46. Decorated Bronze Star medal; recipient Gold medal for research Am. Acad. Orthopedic Surgeons, 1949. Mem. Am. Acad. Orthopedic Surgery, A.C.S., A.M.A., Assn. Bone and Joint Surgery, Clin. Orthopedic Soc., Houston Surg. Soc. (past v.p.), Houston Orthopedic Soc. (past pres.), Internat. Soc. Orthopedic Surgery and Traumatology, Singleton Surg. Soc. (past pres.), Profl. Football Physicians Soc. (past pres.), Phi Beta Pi. Episcopalian. Clubs: River Oaks Country, Petroleum. Contbr. articles to profl. jours. Home: 3609 Meadow Lake Lane Houston TX 77027 Office: Hermann Profl Bldg Houston TX 77025

SHINGLETON, ROYCE GORDON, educator, writer; b. Stantonsburg, N.C., Oct. 25, 1935; s. Wiley Thomas and Lossie Ellen (Vick) S.; B.S., East Carolina U., 1958; M.A., Appalachian State U., 1964; Ph.D., Fla. State U., 1971; m. Ruth Bennett, June 10, 1962; children—Royce Gordon, Justin Thomas. History tchr. Dinwiddie (Va.) High Sch., 1960-61; social studies tchr. Greene Central High Sch., Snow Hill, N.C., 1961-63; dean of men Lees-McRae Coll., Banner Elk, N.C., 1964-65; instr. history Ga. State U., Atlanta, 1968-73; freelance writer, 1973—. Vis. prof. Oglethorpe U., summers 1973, 74. Served with AUS, 1958-60. Mem. Am., So. hist. assns., Pi Gamma Mu, Phi Alpha Theta, Theta Chi. Democrat. Editor: America in the Making, 1969. Contbr. articles to hist. jours. Home: D27-6851 Roswell Rd Atlanta GA 30328

SHINTON, MORGAN EVAN, JR., sch. adminstr.; b. Lansford, Pa., Jan. 15, 1931; s. Morgan Evan and Elizabeth (McMichael) S.; B.S., East Stroudsburg Coll., 1958; M.Ed., Fla. Atlantic U., 1967, Edn. Specialist, 1973; m. Maxine J. Wilson, Aug. 1, 1959; children—Michelle, David, Sharon. Tchr. Halifax (Pa.) Area Joint

Schs., 1958-59; mem. faculty The Mills Sch., Ft. Lauderdale, Fla, 1963—, adminstr., 1966—, trustee, 1968—. Served with USMCR, 1948-52. Episcopalian. Mason. Club: Broward Football Officials (treas. 1969—) (Ft. Lauderdale). Home: 3420 NW 35th St Fort Lauderdale FL 33309 Office: 1512 E Broward Blvd Fort Lauderdale FL 33301

SHIPMAN, DAVID LEON, mgmt. scientist; b. Dallas, Tex., Apr. 18, 1931; s. Hubert Lyle and Bessie Margaret (King) S.; student Arlington State Coll., 1948-50; B.S., U. Tex., 1958; postgrad. U. Ala., 1963-70; Ph.D. (NASA scholar), Okla. State U., 1972; m. Sandra Rosa Vogt, Aug. 29, 1953; children—Cynthia Gale, Connie Lynn, David Anthony. Project engr. Tex. Hwy. Dept., Waco, 1958-61; design engr. Bur. Pub. Rds., Gatlinburg, Tenn., 1961-62; planning engr. Dept. of Army, Ft. Campbell, Ky., 1962; aerospace engr., mgmt. scientist NASA, Huntsville, Ala., 1962—. Asso. prof. Ala. A. and M. Bus. Sch., 1972—. Bd. dirs. Huntsville Community Chorus, 1969—; v.p. Internat. Little League, Huntsville, 1973—. Served with USNR, 1950-55. Mem. Am. Inst. Indsl. Engrs., (dir. programs 1973). Mem. Ch. Christ (deacon 1967—). Contbr. to profl. publs. in field. Home: 516 Cleermont Dr SE Huntsville AL 35801 Office: GC Marshall Space Flight Center A & PS-CP-A Huntsville AL 35812

SHIPMAN, HAROLD LEO, JR., accountant; b. Abilene, Tex., Mar. 17, 1940; s. Harold Leo and Katherine Mercedes (Gavin) S.; student Rice U., 1957-58, Pan Am. Coll., 1959; B.B.A., U. Tex. at Austin, 1962; M.B.A. (teaching fellow), N. Tex. State U., 1964; m. Diane Roberts, June 1, 1962; children—Harold, Christopher. With Arthur Young & Co., Dallas and Houston, 1964-73, tax mgr., Dallas, 1969-71, Houston, 1971-73; controller Joe A. McDermott Inc., Houston, 1973—. Mem. Am. Inst. C.P.A.'s, Tex. Soc. C.P.A.'s, Am. Civil Liberties Union. Democrat. Unitarian. Home: 2932 Lafayette St Houston TX 77005 Office: 1803 Allen Pkwy Houston TX 77019

SHIPMAN, HAROLD R., civil engr.; b. Rock Rapids, Ia., Feb. 20, 1911; s. Elvin Laforester and Leora (Macdonald) S.; B.S., U. Minn., 1937, M.S., 1948; m. Lois M. Brown, Aug. 22, 1938; children—Bruce Macdonald, Richard Pierce. Asst. engr. Minn. Dept. Health, 1937-40, dist. engr., Mankato, 1942-44, dir. div. hotels, resorts and restaurants, 1946-50; asst. engr. FSA, Minn., 1940-42; san. engr. adviser UN Civil Assistance Command, Korea, 1950-51; san. engr. adviser to Turkish Govt., WHO, 1951-54, san. engr. adviser to Govt. of Egypt, 1954-58; chief engr. Pan Am. Health Orgn., 1958-62; chief water supply div. World Bank, Washington, 1962-72, water supply and waste adviser, 1972—. Chmn. UN's Interagy. Subcom. on Water Resources, 1971. Trustee Environmental Engring. Intersoc. Bd. Served from capt. to lt. col., San. Corps, AUS, 1944-46. Recipient Govtl. citation Egypt, 1958. Registered profl. engr., Minn. Diplomate Am. Acad. Environmental Engrs. Fellow Am. Soc. C.E., Am. Pub. Health Assn.; mem. Nat. Soc. Profl. Engrs., Am. Water Works Assn., Interam. Assn. San. Engrs., Internat. Water Supply Assn., Am. Photogrammetry Soc. Contbr. articles to profl. jours. Home: 7108 Edgevale St Chevy Chase MD 20015 Office: 1818 H St Washington DC 20433

SHIPP, BERT NICOLO, television news coordinator; b. Artesia, N.M., Nov. 26, 1929; s. Bert N. and Anna Mae (Bruce) S.; student Abilene Christian Coll., 1952-55, So. Meth. U., 1955-56; m. Shirley Ann Upham, Aug. 29, 1953; children—Bruce Edward, Brett Ramsey, Stefanie Ann. Reporter, Abilene (Tex.) Reporter, 1955, Dallas Times Herald, 1956-57; editor Garland (Tex.) Times Reporter, 1958; newsman WBAP-TV, Ft. Worth, Tex., 1959-60; asst. news dir. WFAA-TV, Dallas, 1961-65, news dir., 1965-74, news coordinator, 1974—. Adviser to pub. relations bd. North Tex. Tb and Respiratory Assn.; committeeman Cub Scouts Circle 10 council Boy Scouts Am., 1968—. Mem. Radio-TV News Dirs. Assn., Sigma Delta Chi. Mem. Ch. of Christ (trustee). Club: Press Dallas (pres.). Home: 4902 Abbott Av Dallas TX 75205 Office: Communications Center Dallas TX 75202

SHIPPEY, ORRLINE ELLIS (MRS. WOODROW W. SHIPPEY), librarian; b. Italy, Tex.; d. Forest Pierce and Mary Ella (Orr) Ellis; B.A., Trinity U., 1936; B.L.S., Tex. Woman's U., 1938; postgrad. George Peabody Coll., summer 1941; m. Woodrow W. Shippey, Oct. 21, 1945. Librarian pub. schs., Jefferson, Tex., 1936-39, White Oak Pub. Schs., Longview, Tex., 1939-58; cataloger Engring. Library, Tex. A. and M. Coll., College Station, summer 1942; dir. Nicholson Meml. Pub. Library, Longview, 1958—. Mem. Am. Assn. U. Women, A.L.A., Tex. Library Assn. (chmn sch. div. 1944-45, chmn. children's div. 1950-51, dist. chmn. 1968). Methodist. Contbr. articles profl. jours. Home: PO Box 1311 Longview TX 75603 Office: 400 S Green St Longview TX 75601

SHIRCLIFF, ROBERT THOMAS, bus. cons. co. exec.; b. Vincennes, Ind., May 20, 1928; s. Thomas Maxwell and Martha (Somes) S.; B.S., Ind. U., 1950; m. Carol Reed, May 9, 1953; children—Laura Howell, Elizabeth Somes. Vice pres., gen. mgr. Pepsi-Cola Bottling Co., Bloomington, Ind., 1950-55, v.p., treas., Charleston, W. Va., 1955-63; pres. Pepsi-Cola Allied Bottlers, Inc., Jacksonville, Fla., 1963-73; pres. Robert T. Shircliff & Assos., 1973—; dir. General Cinema Corp., Boston, 1968-73, Atlantic Nat. Bank, Jefferds & Moore, Inc., Shoney's Big Boy Enterprises, Inc. Chmn. bd. Duval County chpt. A.R.C., 1972, YMCA, United Fund; pres. Speech and Hearing Clinic, Jacksonville, 1972-73. Mem. Nat. Pepsi-Cola Bottlers Assn. (dir., pres. 1971), Jacksonville C. of C. (v.p.), Sigma Alpha Epsilon. Rotarian (dir., pres. 1969-70). Clubs: River, Timuquana Country, University (Jacksonville). Home: 4918 Prince Edward Rd Jacksonville FL 32210 Office: 2529 Gulf Life Tower Jacksonville FL 32207

SHIRES, GEORGE THOMAS, educator, surgeon; b. Waco, Tex., Nov. 22, 1925; s. George Thomas and Donna Mae (Smith) S.; student U. Tex. at Austin, 1944; M.D. (life ins. med. research fellow 1946-47), U. Tex. Southwestern Med. Sch., Dallas, 1948; m. Robbie Jo Martin, Nov. 27, 1948; children—Donna Jacquelyn (Mrs. James G. Blain), George Thomas III, Jo Ellen. Intern, Mass. Meml. Hosp., Boston, 1948-49; research investigator U.S. Naval Med. Research Inst., Bethesda, Md., 1949-50; surg. resident Parkland Meml. Hosp., Dallas, 1950-53, surgeon-in-chief surg. services, 1960—; asso. surgeon U.S. Naval Hosp. Ship Haven, 1953-55; clin. instr. surgery U. Tex. Southwestern Med. Sch. at Dallas, 1955-57, asst. prof., 1957-60, asso. prof., also acting chmn. dept. surgery, 1960-61, prof. surgery, also chmn. dept., 1961—; mem. staff Presbyn. Hosp. Dallas; cons. surgeon St. Paul Hosp., Meth. Hosp., Baylor U. Med. Center, Children's Med. Center, Dallas VA Hosp., Gaston Episcopal Hosp.; instr. cons. med. staff Tarrant County Hosp. Dist., 1969—. Chmn. Am. Bd. Surgery, 1972-74, mem. exam. com., 1968-72, chmn. com., 1971-72, rep. Am. Bd. Med. Specialties, 1971-77; cons. to surgeon gen. Nat. Inst. Gen. Med. Scis., 1965—; cons. to surgeon gen. U.S. Army, 1965—; mem. com. on trauma Nat. Acad. Scis.-NRC, 1964-71; mem. research program evaluation com. VA Career Devel. program, 1972—; mem. gen. med. research program NIH. Served as lt. (j.g.), M.C., USNR, 1949-50, as lt., 1953-55. Diplomate Am. Bd. Surgery. Mem. Dallas County Med. Soc., Dallas Heart Assn., Dallas Soc. Gen. Surgeons (pres.-elect 1972-74), Dallas So. Clin. Soc. (vice chmn. council for continuation med. studies 1969-70, mem. numerous coms.), Pan-Am. (council on surgery 1971—), Am., Tex. (mem. com. med. careers) med. assns., Internat., Tex. surg. socs., Am. Assn. for Surgery of Trauma, A.C.S. (bd. regents 1971-74, also mem. numerous coms.), Am. (sec. 1969-74), Pan-Pacific, So., Western surg. assns., Digestive Disease Found. (founder), Halsted Soc., Internat. Soc. Burn Injuries, Soc. Clin. Surgery, Soc. for Surgery Alimentary Tract, Soc. Surg. Chairmen (sec. 1968-70, pres. 1972-74, rep. to Council Acad. Socs. 1972—), Soc. Univ. Surgeons (chmn. publs. com., also mem. exec. council 1969-71), Surg. Biology Club (sec. 1968-70), Allen O. Whipple Surg. Soc., Alpha Omega Alpha, Alpha Pi Alpha, Phi Beta Pi. Baptist. Editor: Care of the Trauma Patient, 1966; (with others) 1971 Year Book of Surgery; asso. editor Principles of Surgery, vols. 1 and 2, 1969; mem. editorial bd. Am. Jour. Surgery, 1968—, Year Book Med. Pubs., 1970—, Annals of Surgery, 1972—; cons. to editorial bd. Jour. Trauma, 1968—. Contbr. articles to med. jours., chpts. to books. Home: 7107 Blairview St Dallas TX 75230 Office: 5323 Harry Hines Blvd Dallas TX 75235

SHIRK, GEORGE HENRY, lawyer; b. Oklahoma City, May 1, 1913; s. John H. and Carrie (Hinderer) S.; A.B., U. Okla., 1935, LL.B., 1936. Admitted to Okla. bar, 1936, since practiced in Oklahoma City; spl. justice Supreme Ct. Okla., 1963; mayor Oklahoma City, 1964-67. Pres., Oklahoma City Safety Council, 1959-63; mem. Okla. Civil War Centennial Commn., 1961-65. Bd. dirs., exec. com. United Fund Oklahoma City, 1961—; trustee Nat. Trust Hist. Preservation. Served to Col. Gen. Staff Corps, AUS, 1944-45. Decorated Bronze Star medal, Legion of Merit (U.S.); Legion of Honor (France). Mem. Okla. Hist. Soc. (pres. 1959—), Phi Delta Theta, Phi Delta Phi. Lutheran. Mason (Jester). Author: Oklahoma Place Names, 1965. Home: 5201 Vernon Rd Oklahoma City OK 73111 Office: Colcord Bldg Oklahoma City OK 73102

SHIRK, MILDRED ROCKWELL (MRS. FRANK CHARLES SHIRK), librarian; b. Inverness, Md., Apr. 2, 1918; d. Charles Berman and Mildred (Bennett) Rockwell; B.S., Mary Washington Coll. of U. Va., 1939; B.L.S., Drexel Inst. Tech., 1940; m. Frank Charles Shirk, Apr. 30, 1942; children—David Frederick, Linda (Mrs. Wood). Library asst. Morristown (N.J.) Pub. Library, 1940-42; head librarian Caldwell (N.J.) Pub. Library, 1942-44; librarian pub. elementary sch., Blacksburg, Va., 1950-59; reference librarian Va. Poly. Inst. Library, Blacksburg, 1959-61; regional dir. Montgomery-Radford Regional Library, Radford, Va., 1961-70; library dir. Radford Pub. Library, 1970-72; librarian Montgomery County Hosp., 1972—; library dir. New River Valley Community Coll., Radford, 1967-69. Mem. Blacksburg Jr. Woman's Club, 1945-53, pres., 1953; co-founder, v.p. Blacksburg Intermediate Woman's Club, 1952-55; mem. Town and Country Garden Club, Blacksburg, 1950—, sec., 1954-55; chmn. cancer crusade Blacksburg, 1953; bd. dirs. Mary Washington Coll. Alumni Assn. Mem. Va., Southeastern library assns., Zeta Tau Alpha. Home: 111 Country Club Dr Blacksburg VA 24060 Office: Montgomery County Hosp Blacksburg VA 24060

SHIRLEY, PRESTON, lawyer; b. Fort Worth, Nov. 14, 1912; s. James Preston and Nevra (Boykin) S.; student Tex. Christian U., 1928-30; LL.B., U. Tex., 1933; m. Elizabeth Hodgson, Nov. 13, 1936; children—Susan (Mrs. John Eckel), Carolyn (Mrs. Bryan Wimberly), Sarah. Admitted to Tex. bar. 1933; partner firm Boykin, Ray & Shirley, Fort Worth, 1933-36; asso. prof. law U. Tex., Austin, 1936-40; partner firms Kelley & Looney, Edinburg, Tex., 1940-41, Holloway, Hudson & Shirley, Fort Worth, 1945-47, Mills, Shirley, McMicken & Eckel, Galveston, Tex., 1947—. Dir. First Hutchings-Sealy Nat. Bank, Galveston, mem. exec. com., 1967—; dir. Am. Indemnity Financial Corp., Galveston. Mem. U. Tex. Devel. Bd., Austin, chmn., 1965-66, 66-67; mem. devel. bd. U. Tex. Med. Br., Galveston, 1967—; pres. First Bapt. Found., Galveston. Chmn. Galveston Charter Rev. Commn., 1968, 72, mem., 1970; mem. Planning Commn. City of Galveston, 1961-69; mem. Tex. Constl. Revision Commn., 1973—. Bd. dirs. Sealy & Smith Found. for John-Sealy Hosp., Galveston; bd. dirs. U. Tex. Found., Pres., 1970-72; trustee U. Tex. Law Sch. Found. Served from 2d lt. to lt. col. AUS, 1942-45; CBI. Fellow Am. Coll. Trial Lawyers, Am. Coll. Probate Counsel, Am., Tex. bar founds.; mem. Tex. Assn. Def. Counsel (pres. 1963-64), Galveston County (pres. 1954-55), Am. bar assns., State Bar Tex. (com. adminstrn. justice 1952-72), Internat. Assn. Ins. Counsel, Assn. Ins. Attys., Order of Coif, Phi Delta Phi, Phi Kappa Psi. Club: Galveston Artillery. Author: Texas Pattern Jury Charges, vols. 1 and 2, 1969. Home: 4602 Sherman Blvd Galveston TX 77550 Office: First Hutchings-Sealy National Bank Bldg Galveston TX 77550

SHIVE, ROBERT ALLEN, JR., ednl. adminstr.; b. Dallas, Oct. 27, 1942; s. Robert Allen and Kathryn Evelyn (Saunderson) S.; B.A., So. Methodist U., 1964, M.S., 1966; Ph.D., Ia. State U., 1969; m. Lynda Jean Fowler, June 20, 1964; children—Robert Allen III, Hampton Fowler, Allyson Elizabeth. Teaching asst. So. Meth. U., 1964-66; teaching asst. Ia. State U., 1966-67, instr., 1967-69; asst. prof. Millsaps Coll., Jackson, Miss., 1969-74, asso. prof., 1974—, dir. computing center, 1973—. Cons. Honeywell Research Center, Mpls., 1973, Honeywell Information Systems, Mpls., 1974. Recipient fellowship NSF, 1965. Mem. Am. Math. Soc., Math. Assn. Am. (state vice-chmn. 1972), Phi Gamma Delta. Methodist (adminstrv. bd. 1972—). Contbr. to profl. publs. in field. Home: 5246 Suffolk Circle Jackson MS 39211

SHIVLER, JAMES FLETCHER, JR., civil engr.; b. Clearwater, Fla., Feb. 17, 1918; s. James Fletcher and Estelle (Adams) S.; B.S. in Civil Engring., U. Fla., 1938, M.S. in Engring., 1940; m. Katherine Lucille Howlett, Feb. 2, 1946; children—James Fletcher III, Susan (Mrs. William J. Schilling). Mem. engring. faculty U. Fla., 1940-41; with Reynolds, Smith & Hills, Architects-Engrs.-Planners, Inc. (formerly Reynolds, Smith & Hills, architects and engrs.), Jacksonville, Fla., 1941—, partner, 1950—, pres., 1970—; partner Lewis-Eaton Partnership, Archi- tects-Engrs. & Planners, Jackson, Miss., 1969—; dir. Environmental Sci. & Engring., Inc., Gainesville, Fla. Mem. Fla. Bd. Engr. Examiners, 1964-70, v.p., 1964-65, pres., 1965-70. Served as lt. j.g., Civil Engr. Corps, USNR, 1943-46; PTO. Recipient Outstanding Service award Fla. Engring. Soc., 1971, Distinguished Alumnus award U. Fla., 1972, citation for service to constrn. industry Engring. News Record, 1973. Registered profl. engr., Fla., Ga., N.C. Fellow Am. Soc. C.E. (pres. Fla. sect. 1952), Fla. Engring. Soc. (pres. 1960-61); mem. Nat. Soc. Profl. Engrs. (pres. 1972-73), Am. Inst. Cons. Engrs., Fla. State (dir.-at-large 1971—), Jacksonville Area chambers commerce, Tau Beta Pi. Presbyn. Clubs: Jacksonville Exchange, University, River, Deerwood, Baymeadows Golf, Florida Yacht, Florida Aero, Jacksonville Power Squadron. Home: 8191 Hollyridge Rd Jacksonville FL 32216 Office: PO Box 4850 Jacksonville FL 32201

SHNEIDEROV, ANATOL JAMES, cosmophysicist; b. Ekaterinburg, Russia, July 29, 1894; s. James G. and Alexandra (Petukhov) S.; C.E., Petrograd Mil. Engring. Sch., 1917, Mag. Mil. Eng., 1918; B.Elec. Engring., George Washington U., 1944; M.A., Tchrs. Coll., Columbia, 1948; postgrad. Johns Hopkins U., 1945-46, Cath. U. Am., 1944-45, 55-58; m. Siren O. Martirosiantz, Sept. 30, 1930 (dec. Dec. 1958); 1 dau., Svetozara Anatol'evna (Mrs. Maxim D. Persidsky). Came to U.S., 1941, naturalized 1950. Owner, Izida Assns., Harbin-Shanghai, China, 1924-41; mng. dir. Shneider Process Co., Ltd., Hong-Kong, Shanghai, Washington, 1941-45; chmn., pres. Polycultural Instn. Am., Washington, 1945—, prof. Russian lang. and culture, 1950—; geophysicist U.S. Geol. Survey, 1958-62; fellow European Center for Research on Gravitation, Rome, Italy, 1961, del. to U.S., 1962, prof., 1964; engr.-geophysicist arctic bibliography Arctic Inst. N. Am., Washington, 1962—. World lectr., 1964-65. Mem. Am. Geophys. Union, Am. Phys. Soc., Philos. Soc. Washington, Fedn. Am. Scientists, A.A.A.S., Am. Def. Preparedness Assn., Arctic Inst. N.Am., Am. Inst. Aeros. and Astronautics, Washington Acad. Scis. Author: The Dreams I Dreamt & the Life I Lived, 1927; The Little Blue Book of Shanghai, 1932; editor: Dynamics and Mobilism of an Expanding Earth. Author radional field theory; pioneer in earth's expansion theory; author of expulsion planetery theory. Home: 1673 Columbia Rd NW Washington DC 20009 Office: care Arctic Inst N Am 406 E Capital St Washington DC 20003

SHOCKLEY, GILBERT RALPH, aluminum products co. exec.; b. Rosebud, Mo., Sept. 20, 1919; s. Ernest and Verena Flora (Baur) S.; B.S. in Chem. Engring., U. Mo. at Rolla, 1942, Chem. Engr. (hon.), 1960, Dr.Engring. (hon.), 1970; postgrad. U. Cal. at Los Angeles, 1943-44, Washington U., St. Louis, 1946-47, Ga. Sch. Tech., 1947-48; m. Louise McNaron, Dec. 29, 1943; children—Ann Lacy (Mrs. Charles C. McBride), Gilbert Ralph. Mgr. filter div. Eimco Corp., Salt Lake City, 1951-53; dir. chem. process dept. Gen. Research Orgn., Olin Mathieson Chem. Corp., New Haven, 1953-57, v.p. research and devel. Metals Div., N.Y.C., 1957-58, v.p. metals Internat. Div., N.Y.C., 1958-61; Reynolds Metals Co., gen. dir. product devel. div., Richmond, Va., 1961—, exec. v.p. Reynolds Research Corp., Richmond, 1966—; dir. High Voltage Power Corp., Westboro, Mass. Served as lt. j.g. USNR, 1943-46. Mem. Am. Soc. for Metals, Am. Inst. Chem. Engrs., Am. Chem. Soc., Engrs. Club Richmond (dir. 1971—), Va., N.Y. acads. scis., Soc. Automotive Engrs., Am. Mgmt. Assn. (research planning council 1970—), Assn. U.S. Army, Air Force Assn., U.S. C. of C. (mem. patent system adv. panel 1968-71), Indsl. Research Inst. (chmn. pension com. 1973—), Tau Beta Pi, Alpha Chi Sigma. Clubs: University (N.Y.C.); Country of Virginia (Richmond); Cercle Interalliée, Union Interalliée (Paris, France). Patentee in field. Home: 207 Nottingham Rd Richmond VA 23221 Office: Reynolds Research Corporation 5th and Cary Sts Richmond VA 23261

SHOCKLEY, THOMAS DEWEY, JR., educator; b. Haynesville, La., Nov. 2, 1923; s. Thomas Dewey and Inez (Hudson) S.; B.S., La. State U., 1950, M.S., 1952; Ph.D., Ga. Inst. Tech., 1963; m. Willie Belle Austin, Feb. 13, 1947; children—Dainne, Cecilia (Mrs. Thomas P. Walters). Instr. La. State U., 1952-53; aerophysics engr. Gen. Dynamics, 1953-56; research engr., asst. prof. Ga. Inst. Tech., 1962-63; asso. prof. U. Ala., 1963-64; prof. U. Okla., 1964-67; prof., chmn. dept. chem. engring. Memphis State U., 1967—; systems cons. Served with AUS, 1942-46, 50. Mem. I.E.E.E. (chmn. Memphis sect.), Am. Soc. Engring. Edn., Sigma Xi, Phi Kappa Phi (pres. Memphis State chpt.). Contbr. articles profl. jours. Home: 1526 Poplar Estates Pkwy Germantown TN 38138 Office: Memphis State University Memphis TN 38152

SHOEMAKER, DONALD HOWARD, educator; b. LaPorte, Ind., Sept. 19, 1926; s. Harry Cecil and Wanda (Rosenbaum) S.; student Rose Poly. Inst., 1944-45; B.S., Ind. U., 1950, M.S., 1953, Ed.D., 1964; m. Evelyn Helen Gembala, June 18, 1949; children—Gregory, Pamela. Sci. tchr., prin. Ind. pub. schs., 1950-57; lectr., program supr. Ind. U., Bloomington, 1957-62; dir. regional bur. teaching materials U. Va., Charlottsville, 1962— asst. prof. to prof. edn., 1962-70, prof. edn., 1970—; cons. audio-visual communications pub. schs. Va. Served with USAAF, 1945-46. Mem. N.E.A., Assn. Ednl. Communications and Tech. (bd. dirs. 1969-71, Outstanding Media Educator of Yr. award Va. chpt. 1970-71), Va. Edn. Assn. (pres. dept. teaching materials 1963-64), Nat. Assn. Ednl. Broadcasters, Phi Delta Kappa (faculty advisor 1967-71; Distinguished Service award 1972). Home: 2511 Smithfield Rd Charlottesville VA 22901

SHOEMAKER, JAMES MARSHALL, JR., lawyer; b. LaJolla, Cal., Aug. 25, 1932; s. James Marshall and Frances (Little) S.; B.A., U. Va., 1955, J.D., 1965; m. Mary Hunter Sloan, Jan. 3, 1959; children—James Marshall III, Edward Sloan, Jonathan Evans. Fgn. service office U.S. Dept. State, Bur. Cultural Affairs, Washington, 1958-60, vice consul Am. Embassy, Tokyo, Japan, 1960-62; admitted to S.C. bar, 1965; mem. firm Wyche, Burgess, Freeman & Parham, Greenville, 1965—. Dir. Engineered Custom Plastics Corp., Palmetto Spinning Corp. Pres., Family and Children Service, Greenville County, S.C., 1968-69; mem. Little Theatre Council, 1967-71; chmn. United Fund div., 1969-70. Mem. Greenville City Council, 1971-73. Served with USMCR, 1955-58. Mem. Am., S.C., Greenville County bar assns., Greenville C. of C. (dir. 1970-71). Republican. Episcopalian. Kiwanian (dir. 1970-73). Clubs: Greenville County Country; Poinsett. Home: 109 Pine Forest Dr Greenville SC 29605 Office: 44 E Camperdown Way Greenville SC 29603

SHOEMAKER, LEONARD WILEY, cons. engr.; b. Long Beach, Cal., Nov. 11, 1937; s. Leonard Miller and Josephine (Berry) S.; B.S., Tex. A. and M. Coll., 1961; m. Bobby Jean Foster, June 1, 1958; 1 dau., Sharon Dawn. Civil engr. U.S. Forest Service, Lufkin, Tex., 1961-64, supervisory civil engr., Cleve., 1964-66; asso., v.p. Dannenbaum Engring. Corp., Houston, 1966-69; prin. R.G. Miller Engrs., Houston, 1969-70; pres. Leonard W. Shoemaker & Assos., Inc., Houston, 1970—. Mem. Nat., Tex. (pres. Sam Houston chpt. 1970-71, Outstanding Young Engr. 1969) socs. profl. engrs., Am. Soc. C.E., Harris County Heritage Soc. Presbyn. (elder, deacon). Club: Optimist (v.p. 1969-70). Home: 127 Plantation St Houston TX 77024 Office: 9235 Katy Freeway Houston TX 77024

SHOEMAKER, RALPH JOSEPH, library cons., author; b. East Lansdowne, Pa., July 13, 1906; s. Frank W. and Harriet (Mathews) S.; m. Elsie M. DeGraff, Dec. 9, 1951. Asst. librarian Phila. Pub. Ledger, 1920-34; asso. librarian Phila. Evening Ledger, 1934-42; chief librarian Courier-Jour. and Louisville Times, 1947-62; now library cons. and author. Vice chmn. of Phila. Library Council, 1933-34. Served from pvt. to capt., AUS, 1942-46. Named Ky. col., 1963. Mem. Ky. Library Assn. (pres. 1955-56), Spl. Libraries Assn. (chmn. newspaper div. 1935-36), Louisville Library Club (pres. 1950-51). Author: Memorial Tribute to Joseph F. Kwapil, 1934; The Presidents Words, vols. 1-7, 1954-61; Subject Classifications for Clipping and Picture Files, 1958; Newspaper Library Filing Systems, 1962; East Lansdowne: Early Facts and Fond Recollections, 1969; In the Classics series, part I, 1970, part II, 1973. Contbr. articles and book revs. to mags., newspapers. Address: 5136 28th Av N St Petersburg FL 33710

SHOEMAKER, WILLIAM MILLARD, r.r. exec.; b. Lake Cormorant, Miss., July 6, 1909; s. William Millard and Floy (Buford) S.; B.S.C., U. Miss., 1931-35; m. Alice Denman, Feb. 18, 1939; children—William Millard, Susan, Richard. Various positions I.C. R.R., 1936-51; gen. traffic mgr. Meridian & Bigbee R.R., Meridian, Miss., 1952-56, exec. v.p., gen. mgr., 1956—, dir., mem. exec. com., 1957—; dir. Citizens Nat. Bank. Mem. adv. bd. Choctaw Area council Boy Scouts Am., 1957—, v.p., 1960—; mem. exec. com. Research and Devel. Council, 1972. Trustee Instns. Higher Learning Miss.; bd. dirs. Miss. Econ. Council. Named Boss of Year, Meridian chpt. Nat. Assn. Secs., 1962; Ky. col.; hon. lt. col. Ala. Mem. Am. Short Line Assn. (legislative com. 1962-67, dir. 1972), Birmingham Traffic and Transp.

Club, Meridian C. of C. (dir.), Pi Kappa Alpha. Baptist. Rotarian. Clubs: Downtown, Northwood Country (Meridian); Club (Birmingham). Home: 3131 29th Av Meridian MS 39301 Office: 119 22d Av S Meridian MS 39301

SHOFFNER, ARTHUR RAY, real estate exec.; b. Hodgenville, Ky., May 14, 1895; s. William Henry and Sarah Janie (Morris) S.; m. Nellie Tate, Apr. 25, 1917 (dec. 1957); children—Roy Morris, Nellie (Mrs. William French), Irene (Mrs. Courtwright), Mary J.; m. 2d, Frances T. Newman; children—Thomas R., Jean F. Real estate broker, also auctioneer, Crestview, Fla., 1945—; founder, pres. A.R. Shoffner & Co., Frankfort, Ky. and Crestview, 1922—; founder, pres. Lincoln Lumber & Mfg. Co., Hodgenville and Crestview, 1936—; founder, pres. Farmers Union Oil & Royalty Co., Hodgenville and Crestview, 1930—; founder, pres. Morris Realty Co., Inc., Henderson, Ky.; founder, pres., also chmn. bd. Opportunities, Inc., Crestview, 1943—; founder, pres. Nat. Real Estate & Bus. Jour., Huntsville, Ala., 1950—; founder, pres. Shoffner Printing & Pub. Co., Inc., Crestview, 1954—. Address: Route 1 Box 280 Crestview FL 32536

SHOFFNER, CLARENCE LORENZO, dentist; b. Greensboro, N.C., Dec. 13, 1921; s. Ira Benjamin and Lelia Bernice (Harriston) S.; B.S., A. and T. U., Greensboro, 1942; D.D.S., Howard U., 1951; postgrad. U. Pa., 1946-47; m. Carrie Tena Carter, Nov. 13, 1943; children—Selia Lorene, Annah Yvonne. With div. oral hygiene N.C. Dept. Health, Raliegh, 1951-52; practice gen. dentistry, Weldon, N.C., 1952—. Pres., Hillcrest Realty Subdiv., Roanoke Rapids, N.C. Mem. N.C. Human Relations Commn., 1970—, Halifax County Selective Service Bd., 1969—. Bd. dirs. Weldon Bus. Bur., Rheasville Vol. Fire Dept.; trustee Halifax Tech. Inst. Served with USAAF, 1942-45. Recipient Howard U. Coll. Dentistry Alumni award, 1974. Mem. Acad. Gen. Dentistry, Am. Dental Assn., N.C., Old North State dental socs., Eastern Carolina Med., Dental and Pharm. Soc., Rocky Mount Acad. Medicine, Roanoke Rapids C. of C., Nat. Negro Golf Assn., Nat. Guardsman Inc., Basilius Omega Psi Phi. Democrat. Roman Catholic. Mason. Club: Meadowbrook Country (life). Home: PO Box 266 Weldon NC 27890 Office: 100 Elm St Weldon NC 27890

SHOFNER, GEORGE EDWIN, JR., govt. ofcl., structural engr.; b. Memphis, Aug. 7, 1930; s. George Edwin and Aimee (Myers) S.; B.S. in Civil Engring., U. Tenn., 1952; m. Mildred Marie Gibson, Sept. 12, 1952; 1 dau., Mildred Gibson. Structural engr. Ford Motor Co., Nashville, 1959-60; chief structural-civil br. facilities office Marshall Space Flight Center, NASA, Huntsville, Ala., 1960—. Cons. engr. fallout shelter analysis, 1967—. Scoutmaster, Tenn. Valley council Boy Scouts Am., 1953-58, commr., 1967—. Served to lt. SAC, USAF, 1953-55. Registered profl. engr., Ala., Tenn. Mem. Am. Soc. C.E., Ala. Soc. Profl. Engrs. (Engr. of Year 1967-68, 72 Huntsville chpt., Outstanding Service award 1968, chpt. pres. 1971-72; nat. dir. 1972-74). Home: 914 Fagan Springs Dr Huntsville AL 35801 Office: Marshall Space Flight Center AL 35812

SHOFNER, ORMAN EUGENE, radiobiologist; b. Houson, Nov. 1, 1938; s. Amos Eugene and Mary (Witcher) S.; B.S., Mid-Western U., 1964; postgrad. S.W. Found. Research and Edn., 1954-56, U. St. Thomas, Mo. Sch. Medicine, 1958, Phillips U., 1964-65; M.S., Ohio State U.; M.L.S., U. Okla.; m. Shirley Ann Ricks, June 1, 1968. Chief technologist Des Moines Gen. Hosp., 1960-61; dir. dept. radiology Sam Houston Meml. Hosp., 1963-65; computer scientist McDonnell Aircraft MACTEX, Houston, 1965-68; radiobiologist, computer scis. Computer Concepts, Inc., Houston, 1968—; former angiographic radiobiologist, Detroit cons. Am. Para-Med. Accrediting Commn., instr. coordinator, radiol. clin. asso. Grandview Hosp., Dayton, O. Decorated Order Golden Ray; recipient Internat. Radiography award, 1960, Order of Blue Cathode European Assn. Radiology Technologists. Diplomate Am. Bd. Bio-Analysts. Fellow Internat. Coll. Med. Tech. (v.p.); mem. Am. Radiography Technologists (trustee, v.p.), Nat. Coll. Radiography Technologists (pres.), A.A.A.S., Am. Med. Writers Assn., Am. Heart Assn. Radiol. Council, Ohio Soc. Med. Technologists, Internat. Soc. Radiographers and Radiologic Technologists (lectr.), Am. Inst. Documentation, Brit. Inst. Radiology, Assn. Am. Med. Personnel (pres. bd. trustees), Soc. Nuclear Medicine, Soc. Radiographers, Mensa, Am. Soc. Med. Technologists, Mich. Soc. Radiologic Technology, Aerospace Med. Assn., Am. Assn. Allied Health Personnel (pres. bd. trustees), Internat. Platform Assn., U.S. Jr. C. of C., Gamma Delta, Sigma Zeta, Beta Beta Beta, Alpha Psi Omega. Author: The Art and Science of Angiography, 1973; Angiography for the Radiologic Technologist, 1974. Editor Jour. Am. Radiography Technologists, 1964—, jour. Assn. Allied Med. Personnel; contbg. editor Internat. Clin. Pathology News, 1965—. Contbr. articles to profl. jours. Home: 9875 Audelia St Apt 1098 Dallas TX 75238

SHOFSTAHL, ROBERT MAXWELL, savs. and loan exec.; b. New Orleans, Feb. 8, 1942; s. Maxwell Fredrick and Ellen Anna (Falkenstein) S.; B.A. cum laude, Tulane U., 1964, postgrad, in law, 1966; m. Lois Alice Berrigan, June 6, 1964; children—Tyson Brahm, Elisia Ellette. Traffic supr. South Central Bell Telephone Co., New Orleans, 1964-67, traffic mgr., Baton Rouge, 1967-69, traffic mgr., Shreveport, La., 1969-71; asst. to pres. Pelican Homestead & Savs. Assn., New Orleans, 1971, v.p., 1971-73, sec., also exec. v.p., 1973—, dir., 1973—. Mem. Inter-Industry Flood Ins. Com., 1973—. Mem. League Savs. and Loan-Homestead Assns. Greater New Orleans (pres. 1973-74), Home Builders Assns. Greater New Orleans (asso.), Internat. House (asso.), New Orleans C. of C., Phi Beta Kappa, Phi Eta Sigma, Eta Sigma Phi. Home: 3613 Ridgeway Dr Metairie LA 70002 Office: Pelican Homestead & Savings Assn 344 Carondelet St New Orleans LA 70112

SHOLAR, MAURICE ALLEN, qualifying agt.; b. Bainbridge, Ga., Aug. 4, 1930; s. Elisha Everett and Gretchen Gertrude (McCullough) S.; B.S., U. Miami, 1963, M.S., 1965; m. Betty Joann Batten, July 19, 1951; children—Duane Allen, Robin Lynn. Design engr., v.p. Ray L. Hart & Asso., Coral Gables, Fla., 1964-72; qualifying agt., gen. mgr. C.-Jann Devel. Corp., also J.A. Clark Plastering Co., Inc., Miami, Fla., 1972—; chmn. bd. Surfside Challenge, Inc. Served with USCG, 1950-53. Recipient N.S. Found. award, 1964; named young engr. of year State of Fla., 1966. Engring. Contractors of Dade County scholar, 1962, 63. Mem. Nat. Soc. Profl. Engrs., Fla. Engring. Soc., Iron Arrow, Omicron Delta Kappa, Tau Beta Pi, Phi Kappa Phi, Tau Beta Epsilon, Pi Mu Epsilon. Research on ammonia-nitrogen relations during anarobic digestion, 1965. Home: 8505 SW 58th St Miami FL 33143 Office: 5300 NW 72d Av Miami FL 33166

SHOLES, DILLARD MCCARY, JR., physician; b. Richmond, Va., Aug. 29, 1915; s. Dillard McCary and Elizabeth Reeves (Bragg) S.; A.B., Duke, 1938; postgrad. U. N.C., 1940, Va. Poly. Inst., 1942-45; M.D., Med. Coll. Va., 1949; m. Mattie Lou Edwards, Dec. 23, 1939; children—Dillard McCary III, Susan (Mrs. Kenneth Kelly), Thomas Earle, Christopher Warren, Keith Edward, William McNeil, Phillip Charles. Intern Med. Coll. Va. Hosps., practiced medicine, Fredericksburg, Va., 1950; research fellow in obstetrics and gynecology Jefferson Med. Sch. Hosp., Phila., 1952-53; resident obstetrics-gynecology Meth. Epis. Hosp., Phila., 1952-55; resident U. Tenn. Meml. Hosp., Knoxville, 1957-60; practice medicine specializing in obstetrics and gynecology, Elizabethton, 1950-69, Johnson City, Tenn., 1969—; attending staffs Carter County Meml. Hosp., Elizabethton, Johnson City Hosp. Mem. Elizabethton City Council, 1962-67. Trustee Blue Cross-Blue Shield Tenn. Served with USPHS, 1956. Diplomate Am. Bd. Obstetrics and Gynecology. Mem. Tenn. Med. Soc., A.M.A., Knoxville Surg. Soc., Am. Coll. Obstetricians and Gynecologists, A.C.S., Endocrine Soc., Am. Soc. Cytology, Sigma Xi. Research in gynecologic oncology. Home: 1100 Hillrise St Johnson City TN 37601 Office: Professional Bldg Johnson City TN 37601

SHOOK, CLIFTON AUGUSTUS, JR., mech. engr.; b. Portsmouth, Va., Apr. 17, 1919; s. Clifton Augustus and Florence Rosemond (Wilson) S.; B.S., Va. Poly. Inst. and State U., 1950; m. Frances Caroline Chesson, Oct. 15, 1940; children—Caroline Stuart, John Clifton, Gary Ross. Enlisted USN, 1944, advanced through grades to comdr., 1967, tchr. math. Norfolk Naval Air Sta., Norfolk, Va., 1950-51; safety engr. Norfolk Naval Air Sta. and Norfolk Naval Shipyard, 1951-55; supr., engr. Naval Air Sta., Norfolk, Va., 1955-60; chief mech. br., utilities sect. USAF Hdqrs. Tactical Air Command, Langley AFB, Va., 1960—. Active Boy Scouts Am.; spl. asst. Girl Scouts Am., active local charitable orgns. Registered profl. engr., Vt. Mem. Nat., Va., Tidewater socs. profl. engrs., Ret. Officers Assn., Phi Kappa Phi, Alpha Zeta. Methodist (mem. adminstrv. bd. 1965—). Club: Good Sam (Chesapeake, Va.). Home: 228 Mann Dr Chesapeake VA 23320 Office: HQ TAC DEMU Langley AFB VA 23665

SHOOLBRED, AUGUSTUS WAITE, JR., civil engr.; b. Columbia, S.C., Dec. 29, 1926; s. Augustus Waite and Margaret (Fowler) S.; B.S., Clemson U., 1949; m. Mary Britton Shoolbred; children—William Augustus, Margaret Louise, Mary Ann, Mary Chestnut, Frances Elizabeth, Richard Fowler. Insp., S.C. Hwy. Dept., 1949-50; design engr. LBC & W-Harwood Beebe Co., Spartanburg, S.C., 1950-60, chief engr., sec., dir., 1960-63, v.p., 1963-72, exec. v.p., 1972—; exec. v.p., dir. Spartan Assos., Inc.; v.p., dir. Lyles, Bissett, Carlisle & Wolff. Served with C.E., AUS, 1945-47. Recipient certificate of meritorious service S.C. Soc. Profl. Engrs., 1966, 69, 73. Mem. Nat., S.C. (v.p., past dir., past chpt. pres.) socs. profl. engrs., Am. Water Works Assn. Episcopalian. Club: Ramsgate Country. Home: 125 Fernbrook Circle Spartanburg SC 29302 Office: PO Box 2646 2000 E Main St Spartanburg SC 29302

SHORE, JOSEPH NATHAN, govt. ofcl.; b. N.Y.C., Sept. 7, 1925; s. Morris and Eva (Fuchs) S.; B.A., N.Y. U., 1945; M.A., Ohio State U., 1948; m. Rita M. Feldstein, Feb. 8, 1947; children—Carol Lee, (Mrs. Stephen Berman), Laurence. Social worker N.Y. State Tng. Sch. Delinquent Boys, Warwick, 1946-50; social worker youth parole D.C. Bd. Pub. Welfare, Washington, 1950-52; case analyst Dept. Army Office Provost Marshal Gen. Corrections Div., Washington, 1952-57; supervising analyst U.S. Bd. Parole, Dept. Justice, Washington, 1957-61, parole exec., 1961-69; mem. D.C. Bd. Parole, Washington, 1969—. Supr. grad. students Cath. U. Sch. Social Work, Washington, 1950-52; professorial lectr. Am. U. Coll. Pub. Affairs, Center Adminstrn. Justice, Washington, 1970—. Treas. Banockburn Community Club and Civic Assn., 1963-64. Recipient Civilian Meritorious Service award Dept. Army, 1953-54. Mem. Assn. Paroling Authorities (sec. 1972-73). Am. Correctional Assn., Nat. Council Crime and Delinquency, Middle Atlantic States Corrections Assn., Alpha Phi Omega. Jewish religion. Home: 6206 E Halbert Rd Bethesda MD 20034 Office: Suite 503 614 H St NW Washington DC 20001

SHORKEY, ALBERT FREDERICK, chem. plant mgr.; b. Bethlehem, Pa., July 7, 1914; s. Edward Louis and Helen Elizabeth (Lennox) S.; B.S., Kenyon Coll., 1935; M.S., Ohio State U., 1937; m. Sidney A. Horstmann, June 20, 1938 (dec.); children—Charles E., Allen L.; m. 2d, Maurine Grayson, Dec. 3, 1944; children—Robert G., Margaret R. Engr., Dow Chem. Co., Midland, Mich., 1937-66, mgr. tech. services Tex. div., 1961-66; plant mgr. Dow Badische Co., Anderson, S.C., 1966—. Vice pres. Blue Ridge council Boy Scouts Am.; mem. adv. bd. Salvation Army; pres. Anderson County United Fund. Trustee, v.p. Anderson Meml. Hosp. Registered profl. engr., Tex., S.C. Mem. Am. Inst. Chem. Engrs., Am. Soc. M.E., Anderson C. of C. (past pres.). Episcopalian (jr. warden). Club: Anderson Country. Home: 508 Timber Lane Anderson SC 29621 Office: Box 3025 Anderson SC 29621

SHORT, ELMER EUGENE, feed ingredients co. exec.; b. nr. Fountain Run, Ky., Mar. 2, 1931; s. Gibb Barton and May (Patterson) S.; student Western Ky. U., 1954-56; m. Lou Schrodt, July 23, 1956; children—Stephen, David, Linda, Michael, Gerald. Feed ingredient merchandiser Pillsbury Co., Memphis, 1956-65; pres., dir. So. Feed Ingredients Co., Memphis, 1965—. Grad. asst. Dale Carnegie courses, 1973—. Served with USAF, 1950-54. Mem. Memphis Feed and Grain Club (sec. 1959-60, dir. 1960-61). Club: Colonial Country. Home: 5954 Haymarket St Memphis TN 38138 Office: Box 17526 Memphis TN 38117

SHORT, HERMAN B., police ofcl.; b. Gauley Mills, W.Va., May 22, 1918; s. Enos Herman and Freda Mae (Black) S.; grad. Am. Detective Sch. and Am. Finger Print System N.Y., 1939; m. Nettie Lucille Kesterson, Aug. 3, 1949; 1 son, Robert Enos. Mem. Houston Police Dept., 1945—, insp., 1963-64, chief police, 1964—; engaged as real estate broker, Houston, 1966—. Bd. dirs. Houston Farm and Ranch Club, 1965-67, Houston Livestock Show and Rodeo, 1965-67. Served with USCGR, 1942-45. Mem. Houston Police Officers Assn., Tex. Police Assn., Internat. Assn. Chiefs Police, Tex. Municipal Police Officers Assn. Baptist. Home: 9106 Almeda Genoa Rd Houston TX 77034 Office: 61 Reisner St Houston TX 77002

SHORT, JAMES DAVID, mfg. co. pres.; b. Abington, Pa., Mar. 1, 1942; s. William Howard and Rita Mary (Kauffman) S.; B.S., So. Meth. U., 1964, M.S. in Engring., 1967; m. Suzanne Potter, Nov. 23, 1963; children—Kristina Kay, Suzanne Pauline, Joanna Nicol. Student engr. Collins Radio Co., Dallas, 1960-64; engr. Microwave Physica Corp., Garland, Tex., 1964-66; staff engr. Collins Radio Co., Dallas, 1966-67; pres., dir. Electro/Data, Inc., Garland, 1967-73; v.p., dir. Care Electronics, Inc. Huntsville, 1971-73; pres., dir. Am. Time Co., Garland, Tex., 1973—. Mem. I.E.E.E., Assn. Old Crows, Phi Gamma Delta. Republican. Home: 11915 Brookmeadow Dr Dallas TX 75218 Office: 3401 W Kingsley Rd Garland TX 75041

SHORT, JAMES NEWTON, petroleum co. exec.; b. Dayton, O., Nov. 14, 1922; s. Joseph B. and Myrtle M. (Emrick) S.; B. Chem. Engring., U. Cin., 1945, M.S., 1947, D.Sc., 1949; m. Jean Schott, June 23, 1945; children—William T., Charles E., John R., Ronald P. With pharm. research Warren Teed Lab., Columbus, O., 1949-51; with Phillips Petroleum Co., Bartlesville, Okla., 1951—, mgr. chem. processes branch, 1969-72, mgr. polyolefins branch, 1972—. Mem. Am. Chem. Soc., Soc. Plastics Engrs. (sect. treas. 1973). Patentee in field. Contbr. articles to profl. publs. Home: 2360 Windsor Way Bartlesville OK 74003 Office: Phillips Petroleum Co Bartlesville OK 74003

SHORT, ROBERT BROWN, educator; b. Changsha, China, Feb. 28, 1920; s. Samuel McClelland and Rachael Elizabeth (Brown) S. (parents U.S. citizens); B.A., Maryville Coll., 1941; M.S., U. Va., 1945; Ph.D., U. Mich., 1950; m. Lavinia Louise Mullinnix, June 10, 1947; children—Sally Brown, Rebecca Ann, Robert Timothy. Instr. Sewanee Mil. Acad., 1941-43; tchr. Va. Episcopal Sch., 1943-44; asst. prof. biology Fla. State U., 1950-53, asso. prof., 1953-57, prof., 1957—; cons. NIH. NIH spl. research fellow, 1970-71; NSF grantee, 1957-73, NIH research grantee, 1952—. Mem. Am. Soc. Parasitologists (council 1967-71), Am. Soc. Tropical Medicine and Hygiene, Am. Micros. Soc. (exec. com. 1972-74), Assn. Southeastern Biologists (exec. com. 1958-61, 65-68, pres. 1968-69), Phi Beta Kappa, Phi Kappa Phi. Contbr. articles profl. jours. Home: 2407 Miranda St Tallahassee FL 32304

SHORT, WILLIAM ARTHUR, educator; b. West Chester, Pa., Feb. 18, 1925; s. Clarence Albert and Irma Mary (Manley) S.; B.S., Furman U., 1950; M.S., U. S.C., 1952; M.S., U. Ala., 1957, Ph.D., 1961; m. Jessie Mays Cox, June 6, 1950; children—John W., Steven N. Research chemist So. Research Inst., Birmingham, Ala., 1952-61; mem. faculty Athens (Ala.) Coll., 1961—, prof. chemistry, 1961—, chmn. div. natural scis. and math., 1961—. Trustee Gorgas Scholarship Found., Inc. Served with USNR, 1940-43. Fellow Am. Inst. Chemists; mem. Am. Chem. Soc., Sigma Xi, Chi Beta Phi (bd. dirs. 1968—, treas. 1969—). Methodist. Contbr. articles on organic chemistry and biochemistry to sci. jours. Home: Route 10 Box 23 Athens AL 35611 Office: Athens College Athens AL 35611

SHORT, WILLIAM EDWARD, cons. elec. engr.; b. Manistee, Mich., Mar. 6, 1909; s. Leonard and Sara Lulu (Bedford) S.; B.S. in Elec. Engring., Mich. State U., 1933; m. Laura Jane Welsh, Nov. 7, 1937. Draftsman, Black, Sivalls & Bryson, Oklahoma City, 1934-37, Tulsa Boiler Co., Tulsa, 1937-39; jr. engr. Jones Laughlin Steel Co., Tulsa, 1939-40; cons. engr. Tulsa, 1946—. Served with AUS, 1940-46; PTO. Club: Sertoma. Home: 3337 S Wheeling Av Tulsa OK 74105 Office: Mayo Bldg Tulsa OK 74103

SHORT, WILLIAM GILBERT, educator, author; b. Des Moines, N.M., June 26, 1928; s. William Thomas and Geneva (House) S.; B.A., U. Tex., 1951; M.Ed., Trinity U., 1952; Lic., U. Madrid (Spain), Ph.D., 1968; diploma Colgate U., 1965; postgrad. U. Heidelberg, Germany, 1955, U. N.Y. at Albany, 1971-72; Dr. Polit. Sci. (hon.), El Salvador-Academia de Bejar, 1972; m. Maria Pilar Molina Martin, Nov. 29, 1956; m. 2d, Rosa Maria Ceruera Valencia, Nov. 29, 1969. Expediter, interpreter U.S. Mission to Spain, 1956-58; with U.S. Civil Service, 1958-63, edn. officer U.S. Forces in Eng., 1958-59, edn. officer, San Antonio, 1959-63; lang. tchr. San Antonio Coll., 1960-64; dir. Inter-Am. Inst., Freeport, N.Y., 1964-72; coordinator modern fgn. lang. edn., supr. Spanish edn. State U. N.Y., Albany, 1969—. Fgn. lang. specialist Central High Sch. Dist. 3, Merrick, L.I.; dir. 1st Yucatan Inter-Am. Studies Program for U.S. High Sch. Students; asso. dir. Instituto Inter-Americano de Yucatan. Mem. med. adv. bd. Care-Medico, San Antonio, 1964-69. Served with AUS, 1946-47, USAF, 1951-54. Recipient John F. Kennedy award, 1962; Alliance for Progress award, 1962; Presdl. citation, 1962; Vice presdl. citation, 1962; Bolsa de Estudios, Inst. de Cultura Hispanica, 1963, others; decorated La Orden de Bejar. Mem. N.Y. Fedn. Lang. Tchrs., Am. Assn. Tchrs. Spanish and Portuguese, Internat. Platform Assn. Author: La Politica educativa de los Estados Unidos entre los indios Navajo, 1968; El Hombre Folsom, 1970; El Pueblo Navajo, 1969; Junior Year in Spain, 1971; Experimento Inter-cultural, 1973, others. Contbr. articles to jours., also monographs. Home: 722 Weizmann Blvd San Antonio TX 78213 Office: 1400 Washington Av Albany NY 12203

SHORTER, EDWARD SWIFT, artist, museum dir. emeritus; b. Columbus, Ga., July 2, 1902; s. Dr. James Hargraves and Elizabeth (Swift) S.; A.B., Mercer U., 1924; student Corcoran Sch. Art, 1924-28, Boston Museum Sch., 1925, Fontainebleau (France), with Andre Lhote (Paris), Wayman Adams, Hugh Breckenridge; LL.D., Mercer U., 1971; m. Mildred Watts, Oct. 3, 1953. Mem. staff Corcoran Sch. Art, 1930; exec. dir., also instr. art Columbus Mus. Arts and Crafts, 1952-70; now cons. in the arts Columbus Mus. and Hist. Columbus Found.; past lectr. U. Ga. Extension; represented in museums in cities throughout U.S., including: Atlanta, Montgomery, Macon, Columbus, Savannah (all Ga.), N.Y.C., Washington, New Orleans, Waco (Tex.), Ft. Hays (Kan.). Trustee Boys' Club, Shorter Coll., Symphony Orch., Coweta Meml. Assn., Columbus, Ga., Ga. Mus. Art (Athens), Atlanta Art Assn.; Ga. Hist. and Fine Arts Commn.; bd. dirs. Atlanta Art Inst., Columbus Symphony, Brookstone Sch. Corcoran Art scholar, Paris, 1931, Algenon Sydney Sullivan award, Mercer U.; recipient Gari Melchers medal Artists Fellowship Inc. Mem. Shorter Coll. Hall of Fame. Mem. Assn. Ga. Artists (pres.), S.E. Art Mus. Dirs. Assn. (dir.), Assn. Am. Mus. Dirs., Am. Fedn. Arts, Ga. Hist. Soc., Artists Equity Assn., Am. Artists Profl. League, Nat. Art Club, 3 Arts League (mem. bd.), Nat. Audubon Soc., Sigma Alpha Epsilon. Baptist. Clubs: Green Island Country, Bid Eddy, Candun; Salamagundi (N.Y.C.). Home: Folly Hill River Rd Columbus GA 31904 Office: 1251 Wynnton Rd Columbus GA 31906

SHORTT, HUBERT LAFAYETTE, electronic engr.; b. Damascus, Va., Jan. 18, 1910; s. Americus deLafayette and Ada Josephine (Salmon) S.; B.S. in Elec. Engring., U. Cin., 1930; m. Rosemary Gerard Viggiano, Feb. 22, 1958; children—Barbara Joan, Richard Alexander. Engr., Crosley Radio Corp., Cin., 1930-31, RCA, Camden, N.J., 1931-33; chief engr. Lafayette Radio Corp., N.Y.C., 1933-36; pres., chief engr. Transformer Corp. Am., N.Y.C., 1936-38, Wire Broadcasting Corp. Am. (now Muzak), N.Y.C., 1938-42; v.p. charge mil. electronic prodn. Airadio, Inc., Stamford, Conn., 1942-46; founder, pres. Polytron Corp., White Plains, N.Y., 1946-51; pres. Technograph, Inc., patent licensing all Eisler U.S. printed circuits patents, Winston-Salem, N.C., 1951—. Cons. in field. Fellow Radio Club Am.; mem. I.E.E.E. (sr.), Licensing Execs. Soc. Home: 3018 Cambridge Rd Winston-Salem NC 27104 Office: 920 Northwest Blvd Winston-Salem NC 27103

SHOSTAK, ARNOLD, operations analyst; b. Syracuse, N.Y., Oct. 13, 1913; s. Jacob Meyer and Julia (Goldberg) S.; B.S., Coll. City N.Y., 1935, E.E., 1936; M.S. in Physics, U. Md., 1950; Ph.D., Cath. U. Am., 1955; m. Bertha Gortenburg, Feb. 14, 1942; children—G. Seth, Robert E., David A. Radio engr. FCC, 1937-44; physicist Office Naval Research, 1946-55; dir. electronics program Office of Naval Research, Arlington, Va., 1955-73; sr. physicist Lulejian & Assos., Falls Church, Va., 1973—. Research prof. U. Cal., 1957; vis. prof. elec. engring. Stanford, 1972. Served to capt. USNR, 1944-73. Mem. Sigma Xi. Author: Preparing for Radio Operator Examinations, 1948. Contbr. articles to sci. jours. Patentee in field. Home: 3017 S Buchanan St Arlington VA 22206 Office: Skyline Towers Falls Church VA 22041

SHOSTECK, ROBERT, mus. curator; b. Newark, Apr. 25, 1910; s. Saul and Bessie (Rubin) S.; A.B., George Washington U., 1937, M.A., 1953; m. Dora Rabinovitz, May 9, 1936 (dec. May 1969); children—Herschel, Sara Williams; m. 2d, Ruth Dub, Dec. 1970. Dir. research B'nai B'rith Vocation Service, 1945-59; asst. chief placement Nat. Roster Sci. and Specialized Personnel, 1940-45; curator B'nai B'rith Exhibit Hall, Washington, 1959—. Mem. Am. Jewish Hist. Soc., Am. Assn. Museums, Am. Assn. State and Local History, Jewish Hist. Soc. Greater Washington (pres. 1960-62), Audubon Soc., Am. Hort. Soc. Author: Careers in Retail Business Ownership, 1946; Small Town Jewry Tell Their Story, 1953; College Finder, 1959; College Guide for Jewish Youth, 1959; Potomac Trail Book, 1968;

Weekender's Guide, 1969; Dr. John de Sequeyra—The Portugese—Jewish Physician of Colonial Williamsburg, 1971; Words for Flowers and Plants, 1974. Home: 5100 Alta Vista Rd Bethesda MD 20014 Office: 1640 Rhode Island Av NW Washington DC 20035

SHOULTZ, JAMES CLARK, govt. ofcl.; b. Nacogdoches, Tex., May 9, 1919; s. James Clark and Lorena (Wright) S.; B.A., Tex. A. and M. U., 1940; m. Alice Catherine Hucke, Dec. 10, 1943; children—James Clark III, Catherine Alice. Commd. 2d lt. U.S. Army, 1942, advanced through grades to col., 1965; dep. provost marshal U.S. Army Europe, 1965-67; dep. to Army Provost Marshal Gen., Washington, 1968-70; comdr. U.S. Army Spl. Tng. Brigade, Ft. Riley, Kan., 1970-72; ret., 1972; dir. corrections Orange County, Orlando, Fla., 1972—; prof. corrections Rollins Coll., Winter Park, Fla., 1973—. Cons., Sch. Pub. Adminstrn., U. Ga., 1973—. Bd. dirs. Thee Door, Orange County Health Assn., Orange County Law Enforcement Council. Decorated Legion of Merit (3); recipient distinguished service award Fla. Council Crime and Delinquency, 1973, officer of year award Orlando Exchange Club, 1973. Mem. Am. Correctional Assn., Lambda Alpha Epsilon. Democrat. Methodist. Mason (Shriner). Clubs: Rolling Hills Country. Home: PO Box 965 Longwood FL 32750 Office: 1 N Court Av Orlando FL 32801

SHOWALTER, DONALD EUGENE, lawyer; b. Broadway, Va., Feb. 23, 1941; s. Carl Grove and Louise Eleanor (Mensch) S.; A.B., Eastern Mennonite Coll., 1962; LL.B., U. Va., 1965; m. Marlene Frances Collins, Aug. 8, 1964; children—Carl Grove II, Anne Louise, Philip Edward. Admitted to Va. bar, 1965; asso. firm Wharton, Aldhizer & Weaver, Harrisonburg, Va., 1965-70, partner, 1970—; dir. Mennonite Broadcasts, Inc., Broadway Drug Store, Inc., Massanutten Broadcasting, Inc.; tchr. Eastern Mennonite Coll. Town atty. Town of Broadway. Bd. dirs. Community Park Corp. Mem. Am., Va., Rockingham-Harrisonburg (pres. 1972-73) bar assns., Delta Theta Phi. Home: Broadway Av Broadway VA 22815 Office: Virginia National Bank Bldg Harrisonburg VA 22801

SHOWS, CLARENCE OLIVER, dentist; b. nr. Brantley, Ala., Oct. 17, 1920; s. John Oliver and Cora (Nichols) S.; student Wis. State Coll., 1946-47; D.D.S., Northwestern U., 1951; m. Rachel LaRene Price, July 24, 1943; children—Toni Cherie (Mrs. August F. Dennig), Kristin Clare, Bradley Scott, Gregory Norman, Jeffery Ryan. Individual practice dentistry, Valparaiso, Fla., 1951-53, Pensacola, 1953—. Mem. Pensacola Art Assn.; past pres. Escambia County Unit Am. Cancer Soc., now bd. dirs. Fla. unit; mem. Eagle Scout Bd. Rev., Escambia County. Served with USCG, 1939-46. Fellow Am. Acad. Gen. Dentistry (pres. Fla. unit), Royal Soc. Health; mem. Internat. Orthodontic Assn., Gulf Breeze C. of C. (past pres.), Fla. Soc. Dentistry for Children (past pres.), Acad. Gen. Dentistry, Am. Assn. Dentists, Am. Dental Assn., Am. Soc. Preventive Dentistry, Fedn. Dental Internat., Am. Inst. Oral Biology, Am. Assn. Clin. Hypnosis, Northwestern U. Alumni Assn., Navy League, Psi Omega. Democrat. Presbyn. Mason (Shriner), Elks. Clubs: Pensacola, Exchange. Home: 516 Navy Cove Blvd Gulf Breeze FL 32561 Office: 3090 Navy Blvd Pensacola FL 32505

SHRADER, EDWARD FRANKLYN, educator; b. Martinsburg, W.Va., Dec. 24, 1917; s. Edward Franklin and Mary (Blake) S.; B.A., Randolph Macon Coll., 1940; S.T.B., Westminster Sem., 1943; M.A., George Washington U., 1962, D.Ed., 1966; A.P.C., Hunter Coll. Coll. City N.Y., 1963; m. Elaine Loretta Shinners, Aug. 23, 1958; children—Heather Ann, Thurston Drew, Mimi Victoria. Ordained to ministry Meth. Ch., 1943; minister Camp Hill Ch., Harpers Ferry, W.Va., 1946-50, St. Mathews Episcopal Ch., Wheeling, W.Va., 1955-56; sales rep. Interwoven Stocking Co., New Brunswick, N.J., 1951-56; tchr. Storer Coll., Harpers Ferry, Brooklyn Park, Annapolis, Md., Golden Ring Sch., Baltimore County, Md., Loudoun County, Va., 1956-59; counselor High Point Sr. High Sch., Beltsville, Md., 1959-67; prof. counselor edn. Coll. Edn., Fla. Atlantic U., Boca Raton, 1967—, acting head of guidance, 1973. Committeeman Boy Scouts Am., Martinsburg, W.Va., 1943-46, Harpers Ferry, 1946-50; county com. mem. March Dimes, Loudoun County, Va.; zone chmn. Harpers Ferry P.T.A., 1946-47, 56-62; program chmn. bridge dedication ceremonies, Harpers Ferry, 1949. Served with USNR, 1944-46, 50-51. Mem. Nat. Honor Soc., N.E.A., Acad. Tchrs. Occupations, Am. Personnel and Guidance Assn., Md., Prince George's County tchrs. assns., Am. Assn. U. Profs., Omicron Delta Kappa, Tau Kappa Alpha, Phi Delta Theta, Phi Delta Kappa. Author: Readings in Counseling: Process, Practice and Projections, 1970; New Dimensions in Thinking: Counseling—The Different, The Disadvantaged, and Marginal Student, 1974. Home: 2210 NE 48th Ct Lighthouse Point FL 33064 Office: Fla Atlantic U Boca Raton FL 33432

SHREVE, ETHEL M. MCGUIRE (MRS. E. CARL SHREVE), civic worker; b. Piedmont, W.Va.; d. Thomas and Mary (Murphy) McGuire; grad. Potomac State Coll.; m. E. Carl Shreve, Oct. 21, 1940. Financial sec. Potomac State Coll., Keyser, W.Va., 1920-40. Vol. worker A.R.C., Balt., 1948-56, U. Md. Hosp., Balt., 1949-53, Mercy Hosp., Balt., 1954-56, Christ Child Soc., Balt., 1946-56; aux. worker St. Marys Hosp., Knoxville, Tenn., 1956—, treas., 1957, v.p., 1960; aux. treas., social worker U. Tenn. Hosp., Knoxville, 1961-62; vol. social worker Eastern State Psychiat. Hosp., Knoxville, 1969; founder, chmn. layette program Ladies of Charity, Knoxville, 1964—. Mem. Womens Aux. Tenn. Soc. Profl. Engrs. (pres. 1960), U. Tenn. Faculty Womens Club (treas. 1960-61), Our Lady of Fatima Soc. (sec. 1959-60). Roman Catholic. Home: 4 Brookview Lane Knoxville TN 37919

SHREVES, MELVIN LANKFORD, JR., coll. exec.; b. Nassawadox, Va., May 30, 1942; s. Melvin Lankford and Virginia (Odam) S.; B.A., Elon Coll., 1966; m. Peggy Hill, May 27, 1966; children—Michael David, Christopher Melvin. Dir. pub. relations Hargrave Mil. Acad., Chatham, Va., 1966; instr. English-journalism Dan River High Sch., Ringgold, Va., 1966-69; mgr. bus., advt. Star-Tribune, Chatham, 1969-70; dir. news bur. Elon Coll., 1970—. Cub master Chatham Cub Scouts, 1969-70; pres. Hargrave Alumni Assn., 1969-71. Named Outstanding Sertoman, 1967. Mem. Kappa Sigma. Presbyn. Rotarian (sec. 1973—). Home: Box 801 Gibsonville NC 27249 Office: Box 2208 Elon College NC 27244

SHRIVER, EDGAR LOUIS, psychologist, scientist; b. Canton, O., Apr. 1, 1927; s. Elmer George and Clara (Kellogg) S.; B.A., Washington and Jefferson Coll., 1950; M.A., U. Rochester, 1951; Ph.D., U. Pitts., 1953; m. Beatrice Melrowin, 1951 (div. 1961); 1 son, John Adam; m. 2d, Sara Baker Eden, Aug. 15, 1961; children—Katherine Louise, Craig Edgar, Paul Kellogg. Research psychologist Am. Inst. for Research, Pitts., 1951-52; sr. staff scientist Human Resources Research Office, Washington, 1953-68; v.p., dir. Matrix Corp., Alexandria, Va.; pres. Tech. Tng. Corp., Washington, 1961-73; pres. Alexandria Community Sch., 1972-73; pres., chmn. bd. Kinton Inc., 1973—; cons. Westinghouse Corp., Am. Tel & Tel. Served with USNR, 1945-46. Fellow Am. Psychol. Assn.; mem. A.A.A.S., Eastern, D.C. psychol. assns., Phi Kappa Sigma. Presbyn. Home: 100 Prince St Alexandria VA 22314 Office: 100 Prince St Alexandria VA 22314

SHRIVER, THOMAS A., judge; b. Wartrace, Tenn., Feb. 4, 1895; s. Thomas A. and Elizabeth (Holt) S.; student U. of Va., 1915-16; grad. Govt. Sch. Marine Engring., 1917-18; LL.B., Cumberland U., 1920; J.D., Cumberland Law Sch. of Sanford U., 1969; m. Attie G. Humphreys, Aug. 6, 1926; children—Thomas H., Richard V., Don Albert. Tchr., prin. high sch., Bedford County, Tenn., 3 yrs.; practice law, 1920-40, partner Shriver and Shriver; apptd. Chancery Ct., Tenn., 1940, elected 1942-50, 50-55; judge Tenn. Ct. Appeals, 1955—, presiding judge, 1962—. Pres. Nashville Fgn. Relations Com. Mem. S.A.R. (pres. chpt.; pres. Tenn.). English Speaking Union (pres. chpt.), Tenn. Hist. Soc. Democrat. Methodist. Clubs: Exchange, Freolac, Shakespeare. Author articles; Published Opinions. Home: 1709 Bonner Av Nashville TN 37215 Office: Supreme Ct Bldg Nashville TN 37219

SHRODER, MORRIS, govt. ofcl.; b. Buffalo, June 3, 1918; s. Max and Fannie (Mildwoff) S.; B.S., Cornell U., 1939; LL.B., Georgetown U., 1955; m. Florence L. Davis, Mar. 28, 1953; children—Mark Davis, Susan Joy, and David Lewis. Tng. officer VA, Buffalo, 1946-50; analytical statistician VA, Washington, 1950-54; chief resources analysis br., directorate of plans, supplies and operations Office of Surgeon Gen., Dept. Army, 1954-63; statistician Pub. Housing Adminstrn., 1963-65, dep. asst. commr. for program planning, 1965-68; dir. program devel. div. Housing Assistance Adminstrn., Dept. Housing and Urban Devel., 1968-70, dir. publicly financed housing div., 1970—; dir. Navy Fed. Credit Union, 1959, asst. treas., 1960, treas., 1961-63, chmn. supervisory com., 1957-59. Served from pvt. to sgt. AUS, 1942-46. Mem. Am., Fed. bar assns. Home: 407 Deerfield Av Silver Spring MD Office: 451 7th St SW Washington DC 20410

SHRONCE, LESTER NORMAN, county ofcl.; b. Granite Falls, N.C., Feb. 7, 1938; s. Lester Judston and Edna Mae (Setzer) S.; A.B. in Bus. Adminstrn., Lenoir Rhyne Coll., 1963; m. Betty Jeanne Stoutt, Aug. 27, 1963; children—Lecia, Jeffrey, Neil. Corporate accountant Cushion Oil Co., Inc., North Wilkesboro, N.C., 1963-64; accountant Caldwell County (N.C.), 1965-66, data processing mgr., 1966-70, county mgr., 1970—. Div. chmn. March of Dimes, 1968; active United Fund. Sec. Republican Exec. Com., Caldwell County, 1971-73; candidate for N.C. State Auditor, 1972. Served with USAF, 1957-61. Mem. Aircraft Owners and Pilots Assn., N.C. Assn. of County Accountants, Catawba Valley Data Processing Mgmt. Assn. Lion (pres. club 1971-72). Home: Route 4 Box 43 Granite Falls NC 28630 Office: PO Box 757 Lenoir NC 28645

SHROPSHIRE, WILLIAM TUCKER, coll. adminstr.; b. Douglasville, Ga., Nov. 22, 1923; s. Jim Henry and Eddie (Dobbs) S.; A.B., Morehouse Coll., 1947; M.B.A., St. Edwards U., 1972; student U. Neb., 1953, U. Tex., 1963, 1970-71; m. Verona Baxter, Aug. 23, 1949; children—Willa, Rodney, Eric. Budget asst., chief accountant Savannah State Coll., 1947-54; comptroller Albany State Coll., 1954-61; bus. mgr. Huston-Tillotson Coll., 1961—; cons. So. Assn. Colls. and Schs., Moton Found. Mgmt. Improvement Program. Bd. dirs. Austin Human Opportunities Corp. Served with USNR, 1943-46. Ford Found. Advanced Study grantee, 1970—. Mem. Nat. Assn. Coll. and U. Bus. Officers, Nat. Accountants Assn. (dir. Austin chpt. 1971-72), Nat. Assn. Ednl. Buyers, Phi Beta Lambda, Kappa Alpha Psi. Mem. African Methodist Episcopal Ch. Lion. Home: 5509 Tipton Dr Austin TX 78702 Office: Huston-Tillotson Coll Austin TX 78702

SHRULL, ROSWALD ERNEST, lawyer; b. Delta, O., Dec. 27, 1929; s. Leslie Francis and Violet Beatrice (Zimmerman) S.; B.A. in Econs., Ohio Wesleyan U., 1952; LL.B., U. Tex. at Austin, 1959; m. Charlene Jo Fruth, July 9, 1960; children—Stephen Ernest, Stephanie Elissa. Admitted to Tex. bar, 1959; asso. firms Wilson & Hight, Dallas, 1959-60, R.E. Green, Fort Worth, 1960-61, Crumley & Green, Fort Worth, 1961, Frank E. Crumley, Fort Worth, 1961-62, Crumley & Hooper, Fort Worth, 1962-64; partner Crumley, Murphy & Shrull, Inc. and predecessor firms, Fort Worth, 1964—, pres., 1961—. Served with USAF, 1947-48, 52-54, 62; col. Res. Mem. State Bar Tex., Am. Bar Assn., Tex. Assn. Def. Counsel, Air Power Council, Fort Worth C. of C. (mil. affairs com.), Res. Officers Assn. U.S. (exec. sec., nat. councilman 1973—, pres. Tex. 1972-73), Chi Phi. Republican. Presbyn. (ruling elder 1963—, clk. of session 1969—; moderator Presbytery of the Trinity 1972-73, mem. adminstrv. commn. Presbytery of the Covenant 1973—). Home: 3500 Park Hollow St Fort Worth TX 76109 Office: Crumley Murphy & Shrull Inc WT Waggoner Bldg Fort Worth TX 76102

SHRUM, ROBERT MARSHALL, architect; b. Jeanette, Pa., Sept. 29, 1921; s. Lawrence Emmett and Mary Margaret (Gongaware) S.; student Seton Hill Coll., 1946-47; B.Arch., Carnegie Inst. Tech., 1952; m. Shirley Ann Larimer, Sept. 10, 1948; children—Deborah Ann, Beverly Louise, Karen Lynn, Robin Denise. Architect, Sorber & Hoone, Greensburg, Pa., 1952-55, Bennett Assos., Morgantown, W.Va., 1955-57, Edwin T. Reeder Assos., Miami, Fla., 1957-58, S. L. Shephard & Assos., Miami, 1958-60, Rader & Assos., Miami, 1960-61; pvt. practice architecture, North Miami, Fla., 1961—. Mem. North Miami Archtl. Rev. Bd., 1970—. Bd. dirs. North Dade YMCA, 1967-70. Served with AUS, 1941-46; PTO. Decorated Purple Heart. Certified Nat. Council Archtl. Registration Bds. Mem. A.I.A. (Fla. Assn.), Am. Defenders Bataan and Corregidor (Fla. chpt.). Lutheran. Home: 401 NE 103d St North Miami FL 33161 Office: 13205 NE 16th Av North Miami FL 33161

SHTOFMAN, NORMAN MAURICE, merchant; b. Dallas, Sept. 19, 1928; s. Joseph and Ethel (Levine) S.; B.B.A., U. Tex., 1948; m. Charlotte Pauline Grenader, June 28, 1948; children—Susan Jean (Mrs. Marvin Krasner), Alexander, Michael Allen. Pres., Shtofman Shoe Co., Tyler, Tex., 1955—; sec.-treas. San Shu, Inc.; owner Norman Shtofman Stores; gen. mgr. Joseph Shtofman Co.; dir. Peoples Nat. Bank. Campaign chmn., v.p. United Fund, 1969, pres., 1970; vice chmn. East Tex. Area council Boy Scouts Am., 1971; mem. Bi-Racial Com., 1971-72; chmn. maintenance fund Tyler Art Mus., 1971; community adviser Jr. League, 1972. Chmn. Sanders for Senate, Smith County, 1972. Pres., bd. dirs. East Tex. Symphony; pres. YMCA, Tyler Federated Jewish Welfare Fund, Tyler chpt. Am. Jewish Com.; bd. dirs. Dallas council Girl Scouts Am., Tyler Civic Theatre, CODAC; bd. dirs., v.p. Camp Fire Girls; sec. East Tex. Hosp. Found.; mem. adv. bd. Salvation Army; community adviser Jr. League; chmn. adv. bd. Mother Francis Hosp.; bd. govs. Med. Center Hosp.; bd. dirs. Stewart Blood Bank, Smith County Area Health Council. Mem. C. of C. (dir., chmn. bldg. com.), 210 Assos. (life). Jewish religion (pres., dir. temple, pres. Mens Club). Lion (pres.). Home: 621 Green Lane Tyler TX 75701 Office: 1905 W Bow St Tyler TX 75701

SHTULMAN SIDNEY, statistician; b. N.Y.C., Aug. 13, 1920; s. Isadore and Minnie (Singer) S.; B.B.A., Coll. City N.Y., 1940; postgrad. Columbia U., 1950, Am. U., 1956-58, George Washington U., 1958-60; m. Helene Rosenzweig, Jan. 19, 1947; children—Mary (Mrs. Robert Gerdes), Kathy, Michael. Head operations research br. U.S. Naval Weapons Lab., Dahlgren, Va., 1942-59; dir. advanced warfare research div. Office Naval Research, Washington, 1959-66; dir. div. survey planning and analysis Office Edn., Washington, 1966—. Served with AUS, 1945-47. Mem. Am. Statis. Assn., Inst. Math. Statistics, Operations Research Soc. Home: 6415 Rivington Rd Springfield VA 22152 Office: 400 Maryland Av Washington DC 20202

SHU, PAUL PHILLIP, cons. civil engr.; b. Tuscaloosa, Ala., Dec. 12, 1942; s. Paul Clifford and Rebecca (Wedgworth) S.; B.S. in Civil Engring., Va. Mil. Inst., 1965; m. Elizabeth Anne Hall, June 19, 1965; children—Jeffrey Phillip, Stacy Anne. Lubrication engr. Humble Oil & Refining Co., New Orleans, 1965-66, Knoxville, Tenn., 1966-68; constrn. engr. Johnson & Galyon, Inc., Knoxville, 1968-71; civil cons. engr., Wise, Va., 1971—. Mem. exec. com. Wise-Lee County chpt. Nat. Humanities Series, 1972-73. Registered profl. engr., Tenn., Va. Mem. Va. Soc. Profl. Engrs. (sec.-treas. Mountain Empire chpt. 1973-74), Am. Soc. C.E., Cons. Engrs. Council. Baptist (chmn. bd. deacons 1972—). Club: Wise Kiwanis. Designer sewage treatment plants, Va.; also project mgr. recreation and devel. projects. Home: PO Box 57 Crestview Dr Wise VA 24293 Office: PO Box 1307 Wise VA 24293

SHUBAT, KENNETH DON, radio sta. exec.; b. San Francisco, Jan. 1, 1928; s. Frank and Bertha Irene (Evans) S.; student San Francisco State Coll., 1947-49; m. Alice Pauline Spradley, June 12, 1947; children—Glenda (Mrs. Ted Molman), Deborah, Kim, Melodie, Melissa. Sr. accountant U. Cal., 1949-50; profl. skater, 1950-57; treas. Nutri Bio Co., 1957-60; with radio sta. CKLG, Vancouver, B.C., 1960-62; salesman radio sta. KOMA, Oklahoma City, 1962-73, sales mgr., 1964—. Mem. Oklahoma City C. of C., Sales and Marketing Execs. Club, Oklahoma City Ad Club. Lion. Club: Pyramid Tip (Oklahoma City). Home: 5933 NW 81st St Oklahoma City OK 73138 Office: PO Box 1520 Oklahoma City OK 73101

SHUEY, HENRY MILLER, phys. chemist; b. Louisville, Aug. 13, 1920; s. Arthur Ferguson and Mary Willis (Miller) S.; B.S., Centenary Coll., 1941; M.S., U. Wis., 1944, Ph.D. in Phys. Chemistry, 1949; m. Eudare Belle Schocke, Sept. 1, 1946; children—Henry Miller, Paul Charles, Lora Elizabeth. Research asso. Explosive Research Lab., U.S. Bur. Mines, Pitts., 1944-45; phys. chemist Rohm & Haas Co., Phila., 1947-49, head ballistics sect., Huntsville, Ala., 1949-64, dir. tech. liaison, Huntsville, 1964—, cons. to Army and Navy on solid propulsion, 1947—. Pres. Huntsville Symphony Orch. Assn., 1972-73. Recipient 41 for Freedom award Navy Dept., 1967; certificate of appreciation for patritotic civilian service U.S. Army, 1970, Outstanding Civilian Service medal, 1971. Mem. Am. Inst. Aeros. and Astronautics (research award 1964), Am. Ordnance Assn., Am. Chem. Soc., Sigma Xi. Rotarian. Patentee propellants. Home: 3115 Panorama Dr Huntsville AL 35801 Office: 1312 Meridian St Huntsville AL 35801

SHUFFLEBARGER, DAVID TAYLOR, pub. relations adminstr., educator; b. Hampton, Va., Feb. 26, 1944; s. Charles Cosby and Emily (Taylor) S.; B.A. (Baker scholar, McElwee scholar) in Polit. Sci., Washington and Lee U., 1969; m. Patricia Grace Delk, June 8, 1968; children—Christopher Scott, Timothy Todd. Sports writer Daily Press, Newport News, Va., 1961-65; copy editor Virginian Pilot, Norfolk, 1965-67; dir. athletic publicity Va. Mil. Inst., Lexington, 1968; sch. tchr. Fairfield Sch., Lexington, 1969, also pastor; dir. pub. relations Va. Employment Commn., Richmond, 1969-70; asst. prof., dir. univ. relations Old Dominion U., Norfolk, 1970—, also asst. to pres. for pub. affairs. Dir. Communications Virginians for Constn., Richmond, 1970; campaign mgr. for candidate in Dem. primary for U.S. Senate, Richmond, 1970. Bd. dirs. Tidewater council Boy Scouts Am. Div. fellow, Duke, 1969, Univ. fellow, Yale, 1969. Mem. Pub. Relations Soc. Am., Am. Acad. Polit. Sci., Edn. Writers Assn., Am. Coll. Pub. Relations Assn., Am. Assn. U. Profs., Am. Soc. Pub. Adminstrn., Am. Alumni Council. Home: 1115 Manchester Av Norfolk VA 23508 Office: PO Box 6173 Norfolk VA 23508

SHUFFLEBARGER, FRANK ALBERT, accountant; b. Happy, Ky., July 18, 1921; s. Henry A. and Goldia Mae (Parsons) S.; student Alice Lloyd Jr. Coll., 1939-41, U. Minn., 1942-43, Cornell U., 1943-44; B.S. in Bus. Adminstrn., Berea Coll., 1948; postgrad. U. Ky., 1948-49; m. Janet J. Justice, Feb. 27, 1965. Tchr., McDowell (Ky.) High Sch., 1950-51; accountant Gen. Motors Corp., Hamilton, O., 1951-53; sales engr. U.S. Radiator Co., Louisville, 1953-56; sr. accountant Heffner & Cecil, C.P.A.'s, Louisville, 1956-58; controller Ky. Telephone Co., London, 1958-63; pvt. practice accounting, Glasgow, Ky., 1963—; dir. Charles W. Knight & Sons, Louisville. Investment adviser to bus. firms; adviser to Fountain Run (Ky.) and Marrowbone (Ky.) water dists., 1970—. Pres. McDowell P.T.A., 1950. Served with USNR, 1942-46. Decorated Navy Commendation medal. C.P.A., Ky. Mem. Ky. Soc. C.P.A.'s, Am. Inst. C.P.A.'s, V.F.W. Democrat. Baptist. Mem. Hon. Soc. Ky. Mountain Men. Home: PO Box 203 Glasgow KY 42141 Office: 204 E Washington St Glasgow KY 42141

SHUFORD, FORREST HERMAN, II, state ofcl.; b. Gastonia, N.C., Nov. 3, 1923; s. Forrest H. and May (Renfrow) S.; student Wake Forest Coll., 1941-43; LL.B., Duke-Wake Forest Law Sch., 1946; m. Grace McD. Ray, Sept. 7, 1946; children—Forrest Herman III, May Janice. Admitted to N.C. bar; staff atty. N.C. Atty. Gen.'s Office, Raleigh, 1946-49; atty., adviser, solicitor's office U.S. Dept. Labor, Washington, 1949-53; dep. commr. N.C. Indsl. Commn., 1953-62, commr., 1962—. Mem. N.C. State Bar, N.C. Bar Assn. Presbyn. Rotarian. Home: 1212 Bancroft Dr Raleigh NC 27609 Office: NC Indsl Commn Raleigh NC 27601

SHUFORD, GORDON ERIC, JR., elec. engr.; b. Hickory, N.C., Feb. 17, 1943; s. Gordon Eric and Vera Barber (Shuford) S.; B.S. in Elec. Engring. with honors, N.C. State U., 1965; postgrad. Rensselaer Poly. Inst., 1965-66; m. Julia Kay Eckard, Mar. 25, 1967; children—Kimberly Karol, Kristina Kay. Sr. engr. distbn. power system design Carolina Power & Light Co., Raleigh, N.C., 1968—. Served as lt., Security Agy., AUS, 1966-68. Named Distinguished Mil. Grad. N.C. State U., 1965. Registered profl. engr., N.C., S.C. Mem. I.E.E.E., Nat. Rifle Assn., Am. Legion, Raleigh Engrs. Club, Eta Kappa Nu, Tau Beta Pi. Home: 3501 Crofton Ct Raleigh NC 27604 Office: 336 Fayetteville St Raleigh NC 27602

SHUFORD, PAUL MASON, banker; b. Richmond, Va., July 2, 1922; s. Jesse Franklin and Lois (Wright) S.; B.S., Washington and Lee U., 1943, J.D., 1948; m. Mary Campbell Gant, June 7, 1947; children—David Gant, Mark Campbell. Admitted to Va. bar, 1948; partner firm Wicker, Baker & Shuford, Richmond, 1948-60, Wallerstein, Goode, Dobbins & Shuford, Richmond, 1960-72; sr. v.p., sr. trust officer Central Nat. Bank of Richmond, 1973; corporate v.p., gen. counsel Central Nat. Corp., Richmond, 1974—; instr. Washington and Lee U., 1948; instr. Richmond Coll. Law, 1950-54. Vice-chmn. Richmond Area Community Council, 1956-59; chmn. Vol. Service Bur., 1954-56; dir., counsel Nat. Tobacco Festival, 1949—. Served with USAAF, 1943-45. Decorated D.F.C., Air medal with two oak leaf clusters, Purple Heart. Mem. Washington and Lee Alumni Inc. (nat. pres. 1960-61), Am., Va., Richmond (pres. 1972) bar assns., Am. Judicature Soc., Phi Beta Kappa, Order Coif, Phi Delta Phi, Phi Kappa Sigma. Democrat. Mem. Christian Ch. (moderator 1970-72, trustee 1966—, elder 1964—). Clubs: Commonwealth, Hermitage Country. Author weekly editorial column "Letter on the Law" Richmond News, 1958-60. Home: 8 Glenbrooke Circle W Richmond VA 23229 Office: 219 E Broad St Richmond VA 23219

SHULA, DON FRANCIS, profl. football coach; b. Grand River, O., Jan. 4, 1930; s. Dan and Mary (Miller) S.; B.S., John Carroll U., Cleve., 1951; M.A., Western Res. U., 1953; m. Dorothy Bartish, July 19, 1958; children—David, Donna, Sharon, Anne, Michael. Profl. football player, Cleve. Browns, 1951-52, Balt. Colts, 1953-56, Washington Redskins, 1957; asst. coach U. Va., 1958, U. Ky., 1959, Detroit Lions, 1960-62; head coach Balt. Colts, 1963-70; head coach, v.p., part owner Miami Dolphins (winner Super Bowl 1972, 73), 1970—. Served with Ohio N.G., 1952. Recipient Coach of Yr. award, 1964, 67, 68, 70, 71, 72, 73. Roman Catholic. Address: Miami Dolphins-Biscayne Coll 16400-D NW 32d Av Miami FL 33054

SHULMAN, ARNOLD, lawyer; b. Phila., Apr. 12, 1914; s. Edward Nathaniel and Anna (Leshner) S.; student Emory U., 1931; J.D., U. Ga., 1936; m. Mary Frances Johnson, Nov. 26, 1943; children—Diane (Mrs. Elliot Lifshey), Warren Scott, Amy Lynn (Mrs. Stephen Moorman). Admitted to Ga. bar, 1937; mem. firm Shulman & Shulman, Atlanta. Tchr. Atlanta Law Sch., 1964—. Chmn. DeKalb County (Ga.) Sch. Study Commn., 1962-64, DeKalb County Sch. Salary Commn., 1960-62; mem. Fulton County-Atlanta Ct. Study Commn., 1961-62. Served to capt. AUS, 1941-46. Mem. Am., Atlanta bar assns., Ga. State Bar. Club: Lawyers (Atlanta). Author: (with Wiley H. Davis) Georgia Practice and Procedure, 1948, 3d edit., 1968. Contbr. articles to legal jours. Home: 1420 Stephens Dr NE Atlanta GA 30329 Office: 2216 Peachtree Center Bldg Atlanta GA 30303

SHULTS, OTTO A., accountant; b. Wayland, N.Y., Feb. 6, 1898; s. Conrad D. and Elizabeth (Pirrung) S.; student Rochester Bus. Inst., 1916, Pace Inst. Accountancy, 1917-19; C.P.A., U. State N.Y., 1929; m. Alma Jessie Roseberry, May 11, 1920 (dec. June 1969); m. 2d, Mabel A. Perdue Eaton, Dec. 8, 1971. With Wilson, Shults & Co. and predecessors, C.P.A.'s, 1919-60, exec. dir., 1925-60; partner Peat, Marwick, Mitchell & Co., C.P.A.'s, 1961-64, merger 1961, cons., 1964—; dir. Central Trust Co. of Rochester (N.Y.), Genesee Brewing Co., Inc. chmn. bd. emeritus, trustees Nazareth Coll.; trustee emeritus St. John Fisher Coll. Mem. Rochester Mus. Assn. (life), Rochester Meml. Art Gallery, Am. Inst. C.P.A.'s, Am. Ordnance Assn. (life), N.Y. State Soc. C.P.A.'s, Nat. Assn Accountants, Rochester C. of C. (life), Acad. Polit. Sci. N.Y. (life mem.). K. C. (4 1/2), Order Alhambra (life), Elk (life). Clubs: Automobile (dir.), City, Locust (hon.), Oak Hill Country, Rochester, Genesee Valley, Country (Rochester, N.Y.); Westchester Country (Rye, N.Y.); N.Y. Athletic (N.Y.C.); Union League (Chgo.); Coral Ridge Yacht, Coral Ridge Country (Ft. Lauderdale). Home: 2601 NE 37th Dr Fort Lauderdale FL 33308 Summer 1400 East Av Rochester NY 14610

SHULTS, WILBUR DOTRY, II, chemist; b. Atlanta, Nov. 24, 1929; s. Wilbur Dotry and Eva Katherine (Jones) S.; B.S., Emory U., 1950, M.S., 1951; Ph.D. (Union Carbide-AEC fellow), Ind. U., 1966; m. Suereta Jean Fagan, Dec. 26, 1950; children—Susan Dee, Sheri Kay, Stephan Alan. Jr. chemist Oak Ridge Nat. Lab., 1951-53, chemist, 1955-62, asst. group leader, 1966-67, group leader, 1967-72, asst. div. dir. analytical chemistry, 1972—; lectr. in field. Vice chmn. Environmental Quality Adv. Bd., Oak Ridge, 1971—; vice chmn. Oak Ridge Civic Ballet Assn., 1972—. Served with AUS, 1955-57. Mem. Am. Chem. Soc. (pres. East Tenn. sect. analytical group 1970-71, councillor 1972-73). Club: Oak Ridge Country. Editor: Determination of Air Quality, 1972. Contbr. articles to tech. jours., chpts. to books. Home: 1011 W Outer Dr Oak Ridge TN 37830 Office: Oak Ridge National Laboratory PO Box X Oak Ridge TN 37803

SHULTZ, GEORGE PRATT, former govt. ofcl.; b. N.Y.C., Dec. 13, 1920; s. Birl E. and Margaret Lennox (Pratt) S.; B.A., Princeton, 1942; Ph.D. in Indsl. Econs. (fellow Social Sci. Research Council 1947-48), Mass. Inst. Tech., 1949; m. Helena M. O'Brien, Feb. 16, 1946; children—Margaret Ann, Alexander George. Mem. faculty Mass. Inst. Tech., 1946-57, asso. prof. indsl. relations, 1955-57; prof. indsl. relations Grad. Sch. Bus., U. Chgo., 1957-69, dean sch., 1962-69; sec. of labor, 1969-70; dir. Office of Mgmt. and Budget, Washington, 1970-72; sec. treasury, 1972-74. Dir. Borg-Warner Corp., Stein, Roe & Farnham Stock Fund, Inc., Gen. Am. Transp. Corp., Stein, Roe & Farnham Balanced Fund, Inc. Chmn. task force to rev. U.S. Employment Service programs; sr. staff economist Pres.'s Council Econ. Advisers, 1955-56; cons. Office Sec., Dept. Labor, 1959-60, mem. steering com. study collective bargaining in basic steel industry, 1960; staff dir. nat. labor policy study Com. Econ. Devel., 1961; cons. Pres.'s Adv. Com. Labor-Mgmt. Policy, 1961-62; mem. Gov. Ill. Com. Unemployment, 1961-69; co-chmn. Automation Fund Com., 1962-69; mem. various arbitration panels, 1960—. Bd. dirs. Nat. Opinion Research Center, Chgo., 1962-69. Served to capt. USMCR, 1942-45. Mem. Am. Econ. Assn., Indsl. Relations Assn., Nat. Acad. Arbitrators. Author: (with T. A. Whisler) Management Organization and the Computer, 1960; (with Arnold R. Weber) Strategies for the Displaced Worker, 1966; also articles, chpts. in books, reports. Home: 273 S Fort Scott Dr Arlington VA 22202 Office: Exec Office of the President Washington DC 20503

SHUMAN, HAROLD DEAN, lawyer; b. El Dorado, Kan., June 9, 1929; s. Leroy and Avis Crela (Hix) S.; student El Dorado Jr. Coll., 1947-49; A.B., Washburn U., Topeka, 1954, J.D., 1954; m. Joyce Ann Sparks, July 6, 1956; children—Rebecca, Dee Anne, Harold Dean. Admitted to Kan. bar, 1954, Tex. bar, 1955; tax examiner State of Kan., Topeka, 1952-54; gen. legal counsel Central Am. Life Ins. Co., Lubbock, Tex., 1957; asst. dist. atty. Lubbock County, 1957-58; practiced law, Lubbock, 1958—. Bus. law instr. Tex. Tech U., 1959-71. Bd. dirs. S.W. Lighthouse for Blind, treas., 1967, pres., 1968, 71-72; bd. dirs. Lubbock Symphony, 1966. Served to 1st lt. USAF, 1954-56. Mem. Lubbock County Bar Assn., State Bar Tex., Lubbock C. of C., Phi Alpha Delta. Republican. Mem. Ch. of Christ. Kiwanian (pres. 1963), Rotarian (dir. 1971-72). Club: Lubbock. Home: 3316 55th St Lubbock TX 79413 Office: 1601 Broadway Lubbock TX 79401

SHUMATE, CHARLES ROLANE, clergyman; b. Meridian, Miss., July 6, 1946; s. James Rolane and Evelyn (White) S.; student Meridian Jr. Coll., 1964, B.A., Anderson Coll., 1968; postgrad. Louisville Presbyn. Sem., 1968-69, Lexington Theol. Sem., 1970-72; m. Laretta Airgood, Mar. 18, 1967; 1 dau., Chausette Dawn. Ordained to ministry Ch. God, 1970; protestant minister Bryce Canyon (Utah) Nat. Park, 1967; asso. pastor First Ch. God, Louisville, 1968-70; Eastland Pkwy. Ch. God, 1970-72; pastor First Ch. God, Kingsport, Tenn., 1972—. State youth dir. Ky. Youth Ch. of God, 1969-71; Tenn. sec. Ch. God, 1972—; chmn. youth com. Kingsport Preaching Mission, 1972, Greater Kingsport Area Crusade, 1973—. Mem. adv. bd. Sr. Citizens Kingsport, 1973-74; participant Nat. Drug Abuse Tng. Seminar, Washington, 1974. Recipient sr. award Anderson Coll., 1968; Lexington Theol. Sem., 1971-72. Mem. Kingsport Ministerial Assn. (pres. 1972). Clubs: Civitan (chaplin Kingsport 1973-74), Amici (Anderson Coll.). Home: 2740 Polk St Kingsport TN 37664 Office: 2316 Memorial Blvd Kingsport TN 37664

SHURBET, DESKIN HUNT, JR., educator; b. Lockney, Tex., Aug. 27, 1925; s. Deskin Hunt and Ethel (Ewing) S.; B.A., U. Tex. at Austin, 1950, M.A., 1951; m. Larke Ann Harrington, Dec. 27, 1958; children—Pamela Lynn, Patricia, Kari Larke. Seismologist in charge Columbia Seismograph Sta., St. George's Bermuda, 1951-56; mem. faculty Tex. Tech U., Lubbock, 1956—, prof. geophysics, 1956—, dir. seismol. obs., 1956—. Served with USNR, 1942-44. Fellow A.A.A.S., Tex. Acad. Scis.; mem. Seismol. Soc. Am., Am. Geophys. Union, Soc. Exploration Geophysicists, N.Y. Acad. Scis. Home: 5002 46th St Lubbock TX 79414 Office: Seismological Observatory Tex Tech Univ Lubbock TX 79409

SHURE, JACQUES C., bus. exec.; b. Paris, France, Aug. 27, 1940; s. Harold J. and Florence M. (Myers) S.; came to U.S., 1948, naturalized, 1953; B.S., Dartmouth, 1963; M.B.A., Syracuse U., 1965; m. Mitzi Ann Miron, Oct. 1, 1967; children—Deborah Jane, Amy Rebecca. Vice pres. Dowman-Jenches Oil Operators, Houston, 1967-69; LA-CO, Inc., Little Rock, 1969-70; pres., dir. Beaver Creek Industries, Inc., Atlanta, 1970—; dir., chief operating officer Gen. Plywood Corp., Atlanta, 1971—; dir. Atla. Nat. Investment Corp., Interstate Credit Corp. Home: 1716 Barkston Ct Atlanta GA 30341 Office: 3355 Lenox Rd NE Atlanta GA 30326

SHUSTER, CARL NATHANIEL, educator; b. Frenchtown, N.J., Feb. 16, 1890; s. Nathaniel Rittenhouse and Catharine (Draucker) S.; diploma Normal Sch., 1913; B.S., Tchrs. Coll. Columbia, 1915, A.M., 1918; Ph.D., Columbia, 1940; m. Edith Gilman, June 5, 1918; children—Carl, Nathaniel, John Gilman, Jean Wessner. Instr. Bowling Green U., summer 1920, 21, Pa. State U., summer 1925; instr. Columbia, 1926-52, prof., head dept. math. N.J. State Coll., Trenton, 1929-56; head dept. math. Pennington Sch., 1956-57; tchr. Sch. Indsl. Arts, Trenton, 1956-57; vis. prof. Yeshiva U., 1953-57; head math. dept. U. Tampa (Fla). 1957-60; prof. emeritus Trenton State Coll.; head math. dept., dir. Adirondack So. Sch., St. Petersburg, Fla.; vis. prof. Coll. Advanced Sci., N.H. summer 1962, U. Fla., summer 1963; also sr. sci. editor. Served with USNRF, 1917-18. Recipient alumni citation Trenton State Coll., 1961; Columbia Press Assn. Gold Key. Fellow A.A.A.S., Fla. Council Sci.; mem. Fla. Acad. Sci., Assn. Math. Tchrs. N.J. (council 1926, permanent mem. 1955—, pres. 1952), Nat. Council Tchrs. Math. (dir. 1946-48, pres. 1948-49), Am. Math. Soc., Math. Assn. Am., Phi Delta Kappa. Mason, Lion. Club: Torch (chmn. exec. com.). Author: How to Use the Sextant, 1934; How to Use the Hypsometer and Clinometer, 1934; Field Work in Mathematics, 1936; Real Life Mathematics, Grades 3-8, 1938; Problems in Teaching the Slide Rule, 1940; Plane Geometry, 1955; The Scribner Arithmetics, Grade 7-8, 1955; Functional Mathematics, Grades 7-12, 1956. Editorial bd. Mathematics Mag., 1946-60. Contbr. numerous articles to jours. and mags. Home: 2035 26th Av N St Petersburg FL 33713

SIAPNO, WILLIAM DAVID, geologist; b. Norfolk, Va., Aug. 29, 1926; s. Generoso H. and Alice Lithia (Russell) S.; B.S. in Geology, Va. Poly. Inst., 1951; M.S. in Geology, U. Colo., 1953; postgrad. U. So. Cal., part time 1962-65; m. Elsie Ruth Martin, Feb. 8, 1963; stepchildren—Herbert Lee Martin, Myron W. Martin, Kathryn S. Martin. Geologist, pilot, adminstr. U.S. AEC, Rocky Mountain and far west, 1953-59; cons., Denver, 1960-61; space scientist N.Am. Aviation, Downey, Cal., 1962-66, chief geologist, 1966-68; Ocean Systems Operations; chief scientist Deepsea Ventures, Inc., Gloucester Point, Va., 1968—. Mem. adv. bd. Cape Fear Tech. Inst., Wilmington, N.C. Served with USAAF, 1945-46. Registered profl. engr., Colo., Va.; registered profl. geologist, Cal. Mem. Geol. Soc. Am., Am. Inst. Mining Engr. Home: Star Route Box 133 Gloucester Point VA 23062 Office: Deepsea Ventures Inc Gloucester Point VA 23062

SIBLEY, JAMES ASHLEY, JR., educator; b. Shreveport, La., Oct. 21, 1916; s. James Ashley and Lucian Katherine (Hammond) S.; B.A., Centenary Coll., 1940, postgrad., 1941-53; M.Ed., La. State U., 1963; m. Anna May Switzer, Feb. 1, 1963. Asst. mgr. Sibley's Hardware and Variety Stores, 1935-41; farmer, Shreveport, 1941-45; tchr. sci., phys. edn. supr. Lab. Sch., Centenary Coll., Shreveport, 1941-42; tchr. pub. schs., Shreveport, 1942-44, Baton Rouge, 1958-71; dir. VITAL Career Information Center, Dept. Edn., Baton Rouge, 1971—; coordinator cultural resources Unit Project for humanities East Baton Rouge Parish Sch. Bd.; personnel technician, examiner La. Civil Service Dept., Baton Rouge, 1944-48; employment counselor, test technician La. Employment Service, Shreveport, 1948-57; ednl. cons. Gulf S. Research Inst.; coordinator La. Arts and Sci. Center Planning Project, East Baton Rouge Parish Schs. Mem. econ. council East Baton Rouge Parish Sch. Bd., 1963-64; exec. asst. region 7, La. Jr. Acad. Scis., 1963-64; adviser Nat. Conf. on Employment Am. Indian. Past mem. bd. dirs. Found. for Hist. La. Co-founder, sponsor Jr. Archeol. Soc., Inc., Meml. Mus. and Library Fund. Recipient Merit award for outstanding service to pub. La. chpt. Internat. Assn. Personnel in Employment Security, 1952. Mem. Assn. Childhood Edn. Internat. (cons. elementary sci. and social studies sect. 1963-64), Nat. Social Studies Council (pres. East Baton Rouge Parish chpt. 1964-65), Assn. Supervision and Curriculum Devel., Am. Personnel and Guidance Assn., La. Personnel and Guidance Assn. (exec. com., bd. 1972-73), Nat. Vocational Guidance Assn., (del.), La. Guidance Assn., Nat. Sci. Tchrs. Assn., Archeol. Inst. Am., Soc. for Am. Archeology, La. Acad. Scis., La. Tchrs. Assn., La. Sch. Counselors Assn., Nat. Congress Parents and Tchrs., La., La. Sci. tchrs. assns., Am. Assn. Museums, La. Vocational Guidance Assn. (pres. 1971-73), Nat. Assn. for Humanities Edn., Am. Anthrop. Assn., East Baton Rouge Classroom Tchrs. Assn., La., No. La. (charter, past pres.) hist. assns., Ark., Okla., La. (past dir.), Tex. archeol. socs., Phi Delta Kappa, Psi Chi (charter mem. L.S.U. chpt.). Episcopalian (past treas. and vestryman). Author: Louisiana's Ancients of Man, 1967; The Junior Archeological Society, 1967; Geology of Baton Rouge and Surrounding S.E. La. Area, 1972, others. Editor: Cultural Heritage of East Baton Rouge Parish, 1969; Handbook of Vital Career Information Center; The Development and Use of Behavioral Objectives, 1970. Contbr. articles to profl. publs. Home: 2007 Cloverdale Av Baton Rouge LA 70808 Office: PO Box 44064 Baton Rouge LA 70804

SIBLEY, MARILYN MCADAMS (MRS. J. DALE SIBLEY), educator; b. Bedias, Tex., Sept. 30, 1923; d. Horace A. and Nevada Ann (Stuart) McAdams; B.A., Sam Houston State U., 1942; M.A., U. Houston, 1961; Ph.D., Rice U., 1965; m. J. Dale Sibley, June 24, 1944; children—David, Stuart, Mark. Instr., U. Houston, 1961-62; editorial asst. Jour. So. History, Rice U., Houston, 1964-65; asso. prof., now prof. history Houston Bapt. Coll., 1966—, chmn. dept., 1971—; vis. prof. U. Tex. at Austin, 1973; pres., dir. H.A. McAdams Ranch, Inc., Huntsville, 1966—. G.W. Brackenridge fellow Brackenridge Found., San Antonio, 1969, 70. Mem. Am. Assn. U. Profs., Orgn. Am. Historians, So. Tex. (editorial adviser 1969—) hist. assns. Author: Travelers in Texas, 1761-1860 (S.G. Roberts award Sons Republic Tex.), 1967; The Port of Houston: A History, 1968; George W. Brackenridge: Maverick Philanthropist, 1973. Contbr. articles to profl. jours. Home: 702 Bison St Houston TX 77024

SIBLEY, WILLIAM ARTHUR, physicist; b. Fort Worth, Nov. 22, 1932; s. William Franklin and Sada (Rasor) S.; B.S., U. Okla., 1956, M.S., 1958, Ph.D., 1960; m. Joyce Elaine Gregory, Dec. 21, 1957; children—William Timothy, Lauren Shawn, Stephen Marshall. Research physicist Inst. Metal-physics, Tech. U. Aachen (Germany), 1960-61, solid state div. Oak Ridge (Tenn.) Nat. Lab., 1961-70; prof., chmn. dept. physics Okla. State U., Stillwater, 1970—. Served to lt. AUS, 1951-53. Fellow Am. Phys. Soc.; mem. Sigma Xi. Baptist. Home: 3119 W 27th Stillwater OK 74074

SICILIANO, NESTOR REINALDO, architect; b. Buenos Aires, Argentina, Feb. 2, 1928; s. Arturo and Clotilde (Corte) S.; B.A., Nat. Sch. Tech. Edn., 1947; M.Arch., U. Buenos Aires, 1956; sutdent Ga. State U., 1973; m. Manuela Ashfield, June 6, 1963; children—Jarl R., Claudia B. Asst. architect Atlanta Bd. Edn., 1964-66; archtl. coordinator, 1966-73, coordinator planning and arch., 1973—. Pan Am. planning cons., 1967—; cons. architect T.E. Stivers Orgn., Inc., 1968—; cons. sch. planning UNESCO. Mem. A.I.A. (mem. internat. com. 1970; visitor chmn. 1971-72). Address: PO Box 38042 Capitol Hill Station Atlanta GA 30334

SICK, WILLIAM NORMAN, JR., electronics co. exec.; b. Houston, Apr. 20, 1935; s. William Norman and Gladys Phylena (Armstrong) S.; B.A., Rice U., 1957; B.S. in Elec. Engring., 1958; m. Stephanie Anne Williams, Sept. 14, 1963; children—Jill Melanie, David Louis. With Tex. Instruments, Inc., 1958—, applications and sales engr., Dallas, Washington, Phila., 1948-61, marketing mgr. silicon transistors, Dallas, 1961-64, gen. mgr. power products, 1964-68, mgr. strategic planning, 1968-70, mgr. microwave and custom programs, 1970-71, asst. v.p. corporate devel., 1974—; pres. Tex. Instruments, Asia Ltd., Tokyo, Japan, 1971-74. Guest lectr. Sophia U., Tokyo, 1973. Recipient Francis award Rice U., 1956. Mem. I.E.E.E., Am. C. of C. of Japan, Sigma Xi, Tau Beta Pi, Sigma Tau (award 1955). Episcopalian. Club: American (Tokyo). Contbr. articles to profl. jours. Home: 6923 Briar Cove Dr Dallas TX 75240 Office: Tex Instruments Inc Box 5474 Dallas TX 75222

SIDBURY, JAMES BUREN, JR., pediatrician, educator; b. Wilmington, N.C., Jan. 13, 1922; s. James Buren and Willie Wellington (Daniel) S.; B.S., Yale, 1943; M.D., Columbia, 1947; m. Alice Lucas Rayle, Aug. 31, 1953; children—Anne, Mary, Patricia, James, Robert. House officer Roosevelt Hosp., N.Y.C., 1947-49; intern Johns Hopkins Hosp., 1949-50; resident Western Res. U. Hosp., 1950-51; sr. asst. surgeon USPHS, 1951-53; practice medicine specializing in pediatrics, Wilmington, 1953-54; research fellow, asst. prof. pediatrics Johns Hopkins Hosp., 1954-61; asso. prof. pediatrics Duke Med. Center, Durham, N.C., 1961-65, prof. pediatrics, 1965—, dir. clin. research unit, 1961—; cons. Watts Hosp., Durham. Mem. study sect. Nat. Inst. Child Health and Human Devel., 1972—. Bd. dirs. N.C. Diabetes Assn. Served with USNR, 1943-45. Diplomate Am. Bd. Pediatrics. Mem. Am. Acad. Pediatrics, Soc. for Pediatric Research, Am. Pediatric Soc., Am. Soc. for Pediatric Endocrinology, Lawson Wilkins Pediatric Endocrine Soc. (founder 1972), Am. Chem. Soc., Sigma Xi. Home: 4044 Nottaway Rd Durham NC 27707 Office: Box 3215 Duke Med Center Durham NC 27710

SIDDIQUE, IRTAZA HUSAIN, educator; b. Budaun, India, July 4, 1929; s. Tasadduq H. and Ajaib (Bano) S.; G.B.V.C., Bihar Vet. Coll., 1950; M.S., U. Minn., 1961, Ph.D., 1963; m. Siddiqa Syed, July 4, 1954; children—Najeeb, Asim. Veterinarian Govt. of India, 1950-59; asst. prof. Sch. Vet. Medicine, Tuskegee Inst., Ala., 1964-65, asso. prof., 1965-71, prof. microbiology, 1971—. Dir. research grants on listeriosis NIH, 1965, NSF, 1974—. Mem. Am. Soc. Microbiology, Am. Vet. Med. Assn., Conf. Research Workers Animal Diseases, Assn. Am. Vet. Med. Colls., Phi Zeta. Home: 414 Parker Av Tuskegee Institute AL 36088

SIDES, JACK DAVIS, JR., lawyer; b. Dallas, Sept. 18, 1939; s. Jack Davis and Edith Eugenia (Lowrie) S.; B.B.A., U. Tex., 1962, J.D. with honors, 1963; m. Nancy Pauline Cantwell, July 22, 1967; children—Mary Katharine, Jack Davis III. Admitted to Tex. bar, 1963; mem. firm Jackson, Walker, Winstead, Cantwell & Miller, Dallas, 1963-68, White, McElroy, White & Sides, 1968—. Active crusade Am. Cancer Soc., 1966-72; judge of moot ct. competition So. Meth. U., 1968-71. Mem. Am., Tex., Dallas (ethics com. 1972-73) bar assns., Dallas Def. Assn. (sec. 1972-73), Tex. Assn. Def. Counsel, Tex. Law Rev. Assn., Phi Gamma Delta, Phi Delta Phi. Club: Brook Hollow Golf. Home: 4217 Shenandoah St Dallas TX 75205 Office: Republic Bank Tower Dallas TX 75201

SIDLINGER, BRUCE CHESTER, mfg. co. exec.; b. Cedar Rapids, Ia., Dec. 10, 1927; s. Paul E. and Ruth (Wilson) S.; student U. Ia., 1948, U. Ill., 1949-51; m. Joanne Leonard, May 16, 1956; 1 son, Bruce Douglas. Pres., Sidlinger Products Co., Inc., Garland, Tex., 1948—; profl. trampolinist, 1951-67; appeared at Radio City Music Hall, 1955, Gary Moore Show, 1957, Paul Winchell Show, 1957. Served with AUS, 1946-48. Mem. Theta Xi. Patentee in field. Home: 2810 Country Club Rd Garland TX 75041 Office: 208-214 International Rd Garland TX 75040

SIDRANSKY, HERSCHEL, educator; b. Pensacola, Fla., Oct. 17, 1925; s. Ely and Touba (Bear) S.; B.S., Tulane U., 1948, M.D., 1953, M.S., 1958; postgrad. U. Chgo., 1948-49; m. Evelyn Lipsitz, Aug. 18, 1952; children—Ellen, David Ira. Rotating intern Charity Hosp., New Orleans, 1953-54; instr. pathology Tulane U. Sch. Medicine, New Orleans, 1954-58; pathologist Nat. Cancer Inst., Bethesda, Md., 1958-61; prof. pathology U. Pitts. Sch. Medicine, Pitts., 1961-72; prof., chmn. pathology U. South Fla. Coll. Medicine, Tampa, 1972—. Vis. scientist Weizmann Inst., Rehovoth, Israel, 1967-68; cons. Divisional Biologics Standards Contracts Com. NIH, 1966-67; mem. pathology B study sect. NIH, 1968-72, mem. nutrition study sect., 1973—. Served with Aus, 1944-46. Recipient Borden Undergrad. Research award in medicine Tulane U., 1953. Life Inst. med. research fellow, 1956-57; USPHS tng. fellow, 1957-58, spl. research fellow, 1967-68; Eleanor Roosevelt Internat. Cancer fellow travel award, 1967-68. Mem. Am. Assn. Pathologists and Bacteriologists, Am. Soc. for Exptl. Pathology, Soc. for Exptl. Biology and Medicine, Am. Assn. Cancer Research, Am. Inst. Nutrition, Internat. Acad. Pathologists, Med. Mycol. Soc. Ams., Reticuloendothelial Soc., A.A.A.S., N.Y. Acad. Scis., Am. Assn. U. Pathologists, Sigma Xi (prize for research 1957). Home: 11710 Lipsey Rd Tampa FL 33618

SIEFEN, HOWARD THEODORE, chem. engr.; b. Bridgeport, Conn., June 29, 1919; s. Theodore Henry and Lillian E. (Woerner) S.; B.S. in Chemistry, U. Mich., 1940, M.S., 1942, Ph.D., 1944; m. Virginia Marie Smith, Feb. 17, 1968. Research chemist E.I. duPont de Nemours & Co., Inc., La Porte, Tex., 1943-49, sr. chemist, 1949-54, tech. specialist, 1954-62, sr. engr., 1962—. Councilman, City of El Lago (Tex.), 1972-74. Bd. dirs. Clear Lake Emergency Med. Corp., 1973-74. Mem. Alpha Chi Sigma (pres. profl. chpt. South Tex. 1956-58, councilor So. dist. 1966-71). Home: 315 Whitecap Dr Seabrook TX 77586 Office: PO Box 347 La Porte TX 77571

SIEGEL, GERALD WILLIAM, newspaper co. exec.; b. Waterloo, Ia., Sept. 21, 1917; s. Samuel and Rebecca (Wartey) S.; A.B. magna cum laude, U. Ia., 1941; LL.B., Yale, 1947; m. Helene L. Jacober, Aug. 22, 1948; children—Robin Elizabeth, Robert Arthur. Exec. asst. to chmn. U.S. Securities and Exchange Commn., 1947-53; chief counsel U.S. Senate Democratic Policy Com., Washington, 1953-58; lectr. Harvard Bus. Sch., 1958-61; v.p., counsel, dir. Washington Post Co., 1961-71; v.p., counsel Washington Post, 1971—. Trustee, Fed. City Council; bd. dirs. Nat. Conf. Christians and Jews; bd. dirs. Childrens Hosp. Mem. Fed. Bar Assn., Yale Law Sch. Assn., Phi Beta Kappa. Democrat. Home: 4921 30th Pl NW Washington DC 20008 Office: 1150 15th St NW Washington DC 20005

SIEGEL, JEROME SEYMOUR, physician; b. Memphis, Oct. 2, 1937; s. Max and Sophie Rebecca (Rosen) S.; student U. Pa., 1955-57, Southwestern Coll. Memphis, 1957-58; M.D., U. Tenn., 1961; m. Gloria Beryl Shubow, Dec. 22, 1957; children—David Alan, Karen Lynn. Rotating intern U. Chgo., 1961-62; gen. med. officer Barksdale AFB, La., 1962-64; resident internal medicine Wilford Hall USAF Hosp., Lackland AFB, Tex., 1964-67; chief internal medicine sect. USAF Hosp., Tackikawn AB, Japan, 1967-70; practice medicine specializing in internal medicine, Memphis, 1970—; active staff Wm. F. Bowld, City Memphis hosps.; jr. staff Meth. Hosp.; cons. staff St. Joseph's Hosp., Memphis. Clin. instr. medicine U. Tenn. Coll. Medicine, 1970—; mem. teaching staff, asso. Bapt. Meml. Hosp., Memphis. Served to lt. col. USAF, 1962-70. Diplomate Am. Bd. Internal Medicine. Fellow Memphis Acad. Internal Medicine; mem. A.C.P., Am. Soc. Internal Medicine, Memphis, Shelby County med. socs., So., Mid South med. assns., Tenn. Med. Soc., Tenn. Soc. Internal Medicine, Nat. Assn. Residents and Interns, A.M.A., Am., Memphis heart assns., Phi Delta Epsilon. Republican. Jewish religion. Contbr. articles to med. jours. Home: 6624 Westminster Rd Memphis TN 38138 Office: 5050 Poplar Memphis TN 38157

SIEGEL, JOSEPH HERMAN, psychologist; b. Tyler, Tex., Dec. 31, 1924; s. Maurice and Annie (Eisenberg) S.; B.S. in Biology, So. Meth. U., 1948, M.A. in Psychology, 1949; Ph.D. in Psychology, U. Okla., 1954; m. Eve Peristein, Aug. 19, 1945; children—Jeffrey, Drew, Brett. Staff psychologist Dallas Child Guidance Clinic, 1949-50; psychologist Tex. Dept. Pub. Welfare, Dallas, 1949-50; asst. psychologist Central State Hosp., Norman, Okla., 1950-52; instr. U. Okla., 1952-53, instnl. counselor, 1953-54; cons. psychologist Family Consultation Service, Tuckahoe, N.Y., 1954-56; clin. psychologist Dallas Soc. Crippled Children, 1956-57; clin. dir. Children's Devel. Center, Dallas, 1956-62; cons. psychologist Angels, Inc., 1963—; chmn. profl. adv. com. Dallas Council Retarded Children; individual practice of clin. psychology, Dallas, 1956—. Lectr. psychology So. Meth. U., 1956, 62. Bd. dirs. Planned Parenthood of Dallas; adviser Trustees Lena Callier Trust Fund. Served with AUS, 1943-46. Certified psychologist Tex. Bd. Examiners of Psychologists. Mem. Am., S.W., Tex., Dallas (pres. 1961-62) psychol. assns., Am. Assn. on Mental Deficiency, Nat. Rehab. Assn., Am. Acad. Psychotherapists, Am. Group Psychotherapy Assn., Rorschach Inst., Dallas Soc. Clin. Psychologists, Am., N.Y. acads. sci. Home: 11330 Hillcrest Rd Dallas TX 75230 Office: 3519 Cedar Springs St Dallas TX 75219

SIEGEL, MALCOLM RICHARD, educator; b. New Haven, Nov. 5, 1932; s. Meyer and Isabel (Leaf) S.; B.S., U. Conn., 1955; M.S., U. Del., 1959; Ph.D., U. Md., 1963; m. Carolyn Joan Friedman, June 17, 1962; children—Erik, Mark. Postdoctoral fellow U. Md., 1963-66; asst. prof. plant pathology U. Ky., 1966-68, asso. prof., 1968-73, prof., 1973—. Served with AUS, 1955-57. USPHS grantee, 1966-73. Mem. Am. Phytopath. Soc., Sigma Xi, Gamma Sigma Delta. Asso. editor Phytopathology, 1973—. Contbr. articles profl. jours. Home: 247 Tahoma Rd Lexington KY 40503

SIEGLER, HOWARD MATTHEW, physician; b. N.Y.C., May 26, 1932; s. Samuel Lewis and Shirley Kendall (Matthews) S.; B.A., Hofstra U., 1951; postgrad. Yale, 1949, St. Andrews U., 1958; M.D., N.Y. Med. Coll., 1965; m. Toinette Andrau, Dec. 1, 1953; children—Samuel Lewis II, Karel Lynn, Jacqueline Andrau, Todd Bradford. Intern, N.Y.U. Med. Center, N.Y.C., 1965-66, New Rochelle (N.Y.) Hosp., 1966-67; asst. to dean U. Tex. Med. Sch., Dallas, 1967-68; sr. fellow dept. phys. medicine Baylor Coll. Medicine, 1968-69; gen. practice medicine, Houston, 1970—; clin. fellow in obstetrics and gynecology St. Lukes Episcopal Hosp., Houston, 1971—; mem. staff St. Joseph, Center Pavilion, Med. Arts, St. Anthony's hosps. (all Houston). Co-chmn. Muscular Dystrophy Soc., 1966-67; active Assn. to Help Retarded Children, Protestant Charities N.Y.; asso. trustee The Kinkaid Sch. Col. aide de camp Gov.'s staff, Tenn., Miss., La., 1971; lt. col. aide de camp Gov.'s staff Ala., 1971. Mem. Am. Fertility Soc., Royal Soc. Health, Am. Geriatrics Soc., A.A.A.S., N.Y. Acad. Sci. (life), Am. Diabetes Assn., Am. Social Health Assn., Am. Soc. Bariatrics, Christian Med. Soc., So. Med. Assn. (life), Am. Med. Soc. Alcoholism, Phi Chi. Episcopalian. Home: 1 Longfellow Lane Houston TX 77005 Office: Hermann Profl Bldg Suite 1020 6410 Fannin St Houston TX 77025

SIERGIEJ, EDWARD STANLEY, aerospace co. exec.; b. Nanticoke, Pa., Jan. 14, 1928; s. John and Stasia (Fiar) S.; B.E.E., U. Colo., 1958; B.S. in Communication Engring., U.S. Naval Post Grad. Sch., 1960; M.A. in Internat. Affairs, George Washington U., 1963; m. Mary Olwen Vaughan, Sept. 16, 1952; children—Nancy Jean, E. David, Wendy Ann. Commd. ensign USN, 1948, advanced through grades to comdr., 1964; planning specialist LTV Electrosystems, Greenville, Tex., 1968-71; requirement coordinator Greenville div. E-Systems, Inc., 1971—. Mem. Citizens Transp. Com., Greenville, 1970-71. Mem. U.S. Naval Inst., Ret. Officer's Assn., Assn. Old Crows, Eta Kappa Nu, Sigma Tau. Club: Oak Creek Country (Greenville). Home: 108 Oak Glen Dr Greenville TX 75401 Office: Box 1056 Greenville TX 75401

SIERK, HERBERT ALLEN, educator; b. St. Louis, May 11, 1932; s. Waldemar and Lucille Louise (Zell) S.; diploma Moody Bible Inst., 1954; B.A., Bryan Coll., 1956; M.S., U. Tenn., 1958; Ph.D. (Sci. Faculty fellow), U. Wis., 1963; m. Elizabeth Carolyn Powers, June 12, 1954; children—Ruth Ann, David Allen, Phillip Anthony. Instr. biology MacMurray Coll., Jacksonville, Ill., 1958-62; asst. prof. biology, 1963-67, asso. prof. biology, 1967-70; prof. biology Union U., Jackson, Tenn., 1970—, chmn. dept. biology, 1970—, chmn. div. natural scis., 1971—, dir. Self-Study, 1973—. Dir. Coll. Sci. Improvement Program Grant, 1968-70. NSF grantee, 1965-67. Mem. Am. Bryological and Lichenological Soc., A.A.A.S., Am. Inst. Biol. Scis., Bot. Soc. Am., Brit. Lichen Soc., Internat. Assn. for Plant Taxonomy, Tenn. Acad. Sci., Sigma Xi (asso.), Phi Kappa Phi. Baptist (deacon 1972—). Kiwanian (dir. Jackson Club 1971-72, chmn. youth services com. 1972-73). Home: 677 N Pkwy Jackson TN 38301

SIFONTES, ORVAL EMILIO, architect; b. Arecibo, P.R., May 22, 1932; s. Jose E. and Josefa (Fontan) S.; student U. P.R., 1951-53; B.Arch., Tulane U., 1957; m. Gladys Louise Smith, 1956; children—Carmen, Roxanne, Vanessa, Maria Dolores, Orval E., Maria del Pilar. Asso. in charge of design, firm Pedro A. Miranda, San Juan, P.R., 1958-62; partner Sarriera Sifontes Assos., San Juan, 1963-66; prin. firm Orval E. Sifontes, Hato Rey, P.R., 1967—. Mem. A.I.A., P.R. Coll. Engrs., Architests and Surveyors, Inter-Am. Planning Soc. Home: 372 Edie Caceria St Hato Rey PR 00918 Office: 531-A Sergio Cuevas St Hato Rey PR 00918

SIGEL, M(OLA) MICHAEL, educator; b. Nieswiez, Poland, June 24, 1920 (came to U.S. 1937; naturalized 1941); s. Zundel and Helen (Lubecka) S.; B.A., U. Tex., 1941; Ph.D., Ohio State U., 1944; m. Mary Elizabeth Wynne, Dec. 22, 1941; children—Suzanne Lee (Mrs. Robert Hood Barth, Jr.), Vicki Adelaide Breina (Mrs. Mitchell Sroka), Rachel Delelaw Sarah, Valerie Harriet Louise, David Edward Burl. Officer in charge bacteriology Army Service Command Lab., 1943-46; asso. virology U. Pa., 1946-50, asst. prof. virology, 1950-53; in charge virus diagnostic lab. Children's Hosp., Phila., 1946-53; chief reference diagnosis and research unit USPHS, Montgomery, Ala., 1953-55; spl. cons. WHO, Europe, 1956; asso. prof. U. Miami, Fla., 1955-58, prof. microbiology, sch. medicine, 1958—. Dir. Virus Labs., Variety Children's Research Found., 1955-60, research dir., chmn. research staff, 1960-70; research asso. Lerner Marine Lab., Bimini, Bahamas, 1963—; mem. editorial staff Translation Project Fedn. Am. Socs. Exptl. Biology, 1963-67; mem. research council U. Miami, 1964-66; hon. prof. U. W.I., 1960—. Served to col. AUS. Diplomate Am. Bd. Microbiology. Fellow A.A.A.S., N.Y. Acad. Scis.; mem. Am. Soc. Microbiology (vice chmn. nat. meeting 1969; pres. So. Fla. br. 1969-70; councillor 1971-72); Soc. Exptl. Biology and Medicine, Soc. Pediatric Research, Am. Assn. Immunologists, Soc. Gen. Microbiology, Reticuloendothelial Soc., Am. Soc. Cell Biology, Am. Assn. Cancer Research, Tissue Culture Assn. (program chmn. 1969-70, councilor-at-large), Phi Beta Kappa, Sigma Xi. Author: (with A.R. Beasley) Viruses, Cells and Hosts, 1962. Editor: Lymphogranuloma Venereum, 1962; Differentiation and Defense Mechanisms in Lower Organisms In Vitro, 1968; asso. editor Cancer Research, 1969-72; editor (with R.A. Good) Tolerance, Autoimmunity and Aging, 1972. Contbr. articles to profl. jours. Home: 7980 SW 58th St Miami FL 33143

SIGUR, FREDERICK JOSEPH, real estate corp. exec.; b. New Orleans, Apr. 8, 1917; s. Sidney Charles and Ida (Prevost) S.; student Loyola U., 1947-48; m. Marguerite Bradbury, June 29, 1941; children—Frederick J., Carolyn Ann, Kenneth M., David J., Daniel P. Condr., N.O. Pub. Service, Inc., New Orleans, 1936-40; custom guard U.S. Govt., New Orleans, 1941-42; tool and die maker Consol. Vultee Aircraft Corp., New Orleans, 1942-45; salesman Dutel Real Estate, New Orleans, 1945-48; broker Frederick J. Sigur Realty Co., Arabi, La., 1948—; pres. Carolyn Homes, Inc., Arabi, 1952-55, Ridgeland Terrace, Inc., Arabi, 1954-66, Carolyn Park, Inc., 1955—, Boulevard Homes, Inc., Arabi, 1955—, Mid-South Land Corp., Arabi, 1962—, Delta Dredging Corp., Chalmette, La., 1962—, Arabi Properties, Inc., 1962—, Carolyn Devel. Corp., New Orleans, 1964—, Fred J. Sigur & Sons, Inc., Chalmette, 1964—; treas. Southeast Properties, Inc., New Orleans, 1962—; v.p. Normand Co., New Orleans, 1959—, Fazzio Excavating Corp., New Orleans, 1966—, Chalmette Marina, Inc., 1969—; v.p. dir. St. Bernard Bank & Trust Co., 1964—; dir. La. So. Rwy. Co. Mem. St. Bernard Port Authority, 1962—; dir. New Orleans Area Health Planning Council, 1969; chmn. St. Bernard Easter Seal Soc., 1969. Bd. dirs. A.R.C., St. Bernard Parish. Recipient Outstanding Citizen award C. of C., 1965, Man of Year award St. Bernard Parish Bus. and Profl. Women's Orgn., 1970. Mem. C. of C. (dir. met. area com. 1967—), St. Bernard Hist. Soc. K.C., Kiwanian. Club: Braithwaite (La.) Golf. Home: 2301 Paris Rd Chalmette LA 70043 Office: 100 Rowley Blvd Arabi LA 70032

SIKES, FRANK, savs. and loan exec.; b. Cobbtown, Ga., Nov. 27, 1930; s. Elie and Zelma B. (Brown) S.; grad. high sch.; m. Bessie Alice Patton, Apr. 12, 1959; 1 son, Jeffrey Frank. With First Fed. Savs. & Loan Assn., Lake Wales, Fla., 1951—, v.p., 1968—; owner S & W Ranch Supply, Lake Wales, 1968—. Pres., Little League Baseball, Lake Wales, 1971-72. Home: 1151 Lakeshore Blvd Lake Wales FL 33853 Office: 40 W Park Av Lake Wales FL 33853

SIKES, L. B. T., supt. schs.; b. Leonard, Tex., Sept. 10, 1915; s. Richard Green and Hattie (Tefteller) S.; B.S., Tex. A. and M. U., 1938; M.S., East Tex. State U., 1945; m. Geraldine Thrasher, Feb. 24, 1939; children—David, Richard, Betsy. Tchr., coach Rosebud Schs., 1938-40; high sch. prin. Ozona (Tex.) Pub. Schs., 1940-48; supt. Crockett County schs., Ozona, 1953—; supt. Wortham Ind. Sch. Dist., 1948-51; supt. Calvert Ind. Sch. Dist., 1951-53. Mem. N.E.A., Am., Tex. assns. sch. adminstrs., Tex. Tchrs. Assn. (pres. Dist. XI). Mason, Lion. Home: 1303 Av C Ozona TX 76943 Office: 797 Av D Ozona TX 76943

SIKES, MELVIN PATTERSON, educator; b. Charleston, Mo., Dec. 24, 1917; s. Dorothy Edward and Kimmie (Patterson) S.; B.A., N.C. Coll., 1938; M.A., U. Chgo., 1948, Ph.D., 1950; m. Zeta Bledsoe, Oct. 17, 1953; children—Cheryl Lynn, Bertha Kimeta. Prof., dean Bishop Coll., 1952-55, Wiley Coll., 1955-60; supr. Gt. Southwest Life, 1955-60; clin. psychologist VA Hosp., 1960-68; asst. regional dir. Dept. Justice, 1968-69; prof. psychology, U. Tex., Austin, 1969—. Pvt. practice psychology, part-time, 1950-69; dir. Houston Co-op. Crime Prevention Program, 1967-68; dir. Program for Treatment of Alcoholism, VA Hosp., Houston, 1960-68. Mem. Austin Human Relations Commn.; chmn. 1st Nat. Congress Black Profls. in Higher Edn. Served to 2d. lt. USAF, 1943-46. Recipient Meritorious Service award VA, 1968. Mem. Am., Tex., Houston, Southwestern psychol. assns., N.Y. Acad. Scis., N.E.A., Nat. Council Alcoholism, Houston Council Human Relations. Home: 8703 Point West Dr Austin TX 78736

SIKES, ROBERT L. F., congressman; b. Isabella, Ga., June 3, 1906; s. Benjamin Franklin and Clara Ophelia (Ford) S.; B.S., U. Ga., 1927; M.S., U. Fla., 1929; LL.D., Stetson U., 1969, U. W. Fla., 1970; L.H.D., St. Leo Coll., 1969; Hon. Doctorate, U. Inca Garcilaso de la Vega (Peru), 1970; m. Inez Tyner; children—Mrs. Bobbye S. Wicke, Robert Keyes. Agrl. and indsl. research, 1928-32; pub. Oklaloosa News-Journal, Crestview, Fla., and other newspapers, 1933-40. Mem. State legislature, 1936-40; chmn. County Dem. Com., 1934; mem. 77th to 92nd Congresses from 1st Fla. Dist. Chmn. Fla. delegation Dem. Nat. Conv., 1956-60, del., 1972. Del. Pan Am. Rds. Conf., Venezuela, 1954, Interparliamentary Conf., Warsaw, 1959; dir., v.p. Nat. Rivers and Harbors Congress, 1959-71; mem. exec. com. Water Resources Congress, 1971; del. to Sixth World Forestry Congress, Madrid, 1966, Seveneth Congress, Buenos Aires, 1972. Bd. visitors USAF Acad., Civil Air Patrol; adv. com. Am. Enterprise Inst. Served to maj. gen. AUS, World War II; ETO. Decorated Legion of Merit; recipient Nat. Affairs Leadership award, 1951, Nat. Leadership award Am. Gun Dealers Assn., 1959, Distinguished Service award Res. Officers Assn. U.S., 1958, 66, Gov.'s Conservation Award, 1960, Guatemalan Order Merit, 1961, Young Dem. Clubs Fla. award, 1961, Am. Legion Distinguished Service award, 1962, Navy Times Good Neighbor award, 1962; Fla. Council of 100 Distinguished Service award, 1962, Humanitarian award Children's Asthma Research Ins., 1963, Outstanding Service award Fla. Nat. Guard, 1963, George Washington Meml. award, 1966, Good Govt. award Pensacola Realty Bd., 1966, Defender of Free Enterprise award Life Underwriters, 1966, Hon. State Farmer award Fla. Assn. Future Farmers Am., 1967, alumni award Alpha Gamma Rho, 1968, Fla. Public Service award U.P.I., 1968, Distinguished Service award Water Resources Congress, 1972, Gen. Louis E. Brereton award Fla. Air Force Assn., 1972, numerous others; hon. faculty chair in govt. Okaloosa-Walton Jr. Coll. named in his honor. Mem. Mil. Order World War, Am. Legion, V.F.W., Nat. Assn. Suprs. (hon.), Fla. Hist. Soc. (dir., v.p.), Res. Officers Assn. (Hall of Fame 1963, minute man hall of fame 1964, man of year 1967), Fleet Res. Assn. (hon. life mem.), Navy League (hon. life mem.), Naval Aviation Mus. Assn. (trustee), Am. Soc. Arms Collectors, Am. Fedn. Govt. Employees, United Fedn. Postal Clks. (hon.), Nat. Rifle Assn. (life), 40 and 8, Nat. Sojourners, Nat. Assn. Master Mechanics and Foreman Assn. (hon.), S.C.V., Blue Key, Phi Kappa Phi, Sigma Delta Chi, Alpha Zeta, Phi Sigma, Alpha Gamma Rho. Methodist. Mason (33 deg., Shriner, K.T., Grotto; grand orator Fla. lodge 1968-69), K.P., Elk, Moose; mem. Order of Ahepa (hon. mem., leadership award 1969). Clubs: Kiwanis (lt. gov. 1940), Lions (hon.), Rotary (hon.), Civitan (hon.), Toastmasters Internat. (award 1971). Home: Crestview FL 32536 Address: Rayburn House Office Bldg Washington DC 20515

SIKORA, EUGENE STANLEY, profl. engr.; b. Duquesne, Pa., July 21, 1924; s. Adam Joseph and Helen (Pietrowska) S.; student Okla. Bapt. U., 1943-44; B.S. in Indsl. Engring., U. Pitts., 1949; C.E., Carnegie Inst. Tech., 1951; m. Corinne Mary Coliane, Sept. 7, 1946; children—Karyn Ann, Leslie Ann. Bridge design engr. Gannett, Fleming, Corddry & Carpenter, Pitts., 1949-50; structural designer Rust Engring. Co., Pitts., 1950-51, chief field engr., 1951-52, asst. project engr.; project engr. Frank E. Murphy & Assos., Bartow, Fla., 1952-55; v.p. Wellman-Lord Engring. Co., Lakeland, Fla., 1955-61; pres. Gulf Design Co., Lakeland, 1961—; v.p. Badger Co. Inc., Cambridge, Mass., 1968—; dir. Southeastern Chem. Corp., Lakeland, 1962—, Nat. Office Bldgs. Corp., Lakeland, 1962—, Largo Vista, Inc., Lakeland, 1962—, Bus. Computers, Inc., Dallas, Continental Chem. Processors, Inc., N.Y.C. Served with USAAF, 1943-45. Mem. Nat. Soc. Profl. Engrs., Am. Inst. Mining, Metall. and Petroleum Engrs., Am. Mgmt. Assn., Am. Inst. Chem. Engrs., Am. Inst. Indsl. Engrs., Fla. Engring. Soc. Democrat. Roman Catholic. Rotarian. Home: 1400 Seville Pl Lakeland FL 33803 Office: US Hwy 98 S and Reynolds Rd Lakeland FL 33801

SILBER, ROBERT LEE, ednl. assn. exec.; b. Mt. Vernon, Ind., July 30, 1928; s. Fred Joseph and Evelyn Carey (Morelock) S.; B.S., Evansville Coll., 1950; M.S., So. Ill. U., 1953; postgrad. Brown U., 1959, Johns Hopkins, 1963-64; m. Wanda Mae Maier, Dec. 26, 1948; children—Deborah June (Mrs. Thomas Insel), Randall R., Gregory K. With metallurgy lab. Servel, Inc., Evansville, Ind., 1951-52; tchr. Shawnee High Sch., Wolf Lake, Ill., 1952-55, Central High Sch., Evansville, 1955-60; adminstr. Am. Chem. Soc., Washington, 1960-73; exec. dir. Nat. Sci. Tchrs. Assn., Washington, 1973—. Cons. U.S. ednl. projects, 1962—; pres. Concern Group, Inc., Washington, 1971—. Pres., P.T.A., Takoma Park, Md., 1962. Recipient Star award Nat. Sci. Tchrs. Assn.; Trail award Jr. C. of C., 1964. Mem. Am. Chem. Soc., Nat. Sci. Tchrs. Assn., A.A.A.S. Methodist. Contbr. articles to various publs. Home: 12106 Jan Lane Silver Spring MD 20904 Office: 1201 16th St NW Washington DC 20036

SILBERMAN, DONALD JARED, pediatric psychiatrist; b. Birmingham, Ala., June 4, 1915; s. Louis and Dora (Gingold) S.; B.S., Samford U., 1934; M.D., U. Md., 1938; m. Anne Copeland, Dec. 6, 1959; children—Claire, Connie. Intern, Ill. Masonic Hosp., Chgo., 1938-39, Hillman Hosp., Birmingham, Ala., 1939-40; resident Hillman Hosp., 1940-41, Univ. Hosp., Birmingham, 1946-47; practice medicine specializing in pediatrics, Birmingham, 1947-64, specializing in gen. and pediatric psychiatry, Birmingham, 1964—; pres. med. staff Childrens Hosp., 1963-64, Hill Crest Hosp., 1970-71. Clin. asso. prof. pediatrics U. Ala., Birmingham, 1955—, clin. asst. prof. psychiatry, 1968—. Served from 1st lt. to maj. AUS, 1941-46. Decorated Bronze Star medal. Nat. Inst. Mental Health fellow in psychiatry, 1964-68. Diplomate Am. Bd. Pediatrics. Fellow Am. Acad. Pediatrics, Am. Psychiat. Assn. (pres. Ala. dist. br. 1973-74, mem. exec. com. 1971—, alternate del. to Assembly dist. brs. 1971—, editor Ala. Dist. br. Newsletter 1971—); mem. Jefferson County Med. Soc. (chmn. athletic com. 1970—), Ala. Acad. Neurology and Psychiatry (trustee), Birmingham Acad. Medicine, Birmingham Area C. of C. (chmn. football com. 1955-62). Clubs: Club, Pinetree Country (Birmingham). Home: 3773 Locksley Dr Birmingham AL 35223 Office: 1717 11th Av Birmingham AL 35205

SILBERT, BURTON, radiologist; b. N.Y.C., July 8, 1933; s. David and Donnice (Rahinsky) S.; B.A., N.Y. U., 1954; M.D., Vanderbilt U., 1958; m. Estelle Kushner, June 19, 1954; children—Diedra, Michael, Michelle, Daniel. Intern, Butterworth Hosp., Grand Rapids, Mich., 1958-59; resident radiology Grace Hosp., Detroit, 1959-62; instr. radiology Vanderbilt Med. Sch., Nashville, 1962-63; practice medicine, specializing in radiology, Nashville, 1962—; radiologist in chief Park View Hosp., Nashville, 1962—; mem. staff West Side Hosp., Miller Hosp., Madison Hosp., Nashville; clin. instr. radiology Vanderbilt Med. Sch., 1963—. Jewish religion (trustee synagogue). Home: 5925 Sedberry Rd Nashville TN 37205 Office: Park View Hosp 230 25th Av N Nashville TN 37203

SILCOX, GORDON BRUCE, banker; b. Takoma Park, Md., May 11, 1938; s. Walter Bruce and Ruth May (Davis) S.; A.B., Princeton, 1960; M.B.A., U. Pa., 1965; m. Judith Andrea Smith, Mar. 7, 1970; 1 dau., Andrea Davis. Asst. trust investment officer Am. Security Bank, Washington, 1965-69; trust investment officer, head investment dept. Union Trust Co. D.C., Washington, 1969—. Instr. mgmt. edn. Washington chpt. Am. Inst. Banking. Served to lt. (j.g.) USN, 1960-63. Mem. Financial Analysts Fedn. Methodist. Clubs: University, Princeton (treas. 1972—) (Washington). Home: 6329 N 19th St Arlington VA 22205 Office: Union Trust Co DC 15th and H Sts NW Washington DC 20005

SILER, EUGENE, lawyer; b. Williamsburg, Ky., June 26, 1900; s. Adam Troy and Minnie (Chandler) S.; A.A., Cumberland Coll., 1920, LL.D., 1972; A.B., U. Ky., 1922; postgrad. Columbia, 1923; m. Lowell Jones, Oct. 17, 1925; children—Carolyn Browning, Annette Hungerford, Dorothy White, Eugene. Admitted to Ky. bar, 1924; practiced in Williamsburg, 1924—; mem. firm Tye, Siler, Gillis & Siler, 1925-39; judge Ct. Appeals Ky., 1945; pvt. practice law, 1948-54; mem. U.S. Congress, 1955-65; v.p. Bank Williamsburg (Ky.), 1940—; dir., sec.-treas. Jellico Grocery Co. Pres., Ky. Bapt. Conv., 1952-53. Served to capt. AUS, 1942-45. Mem. Am. Legion (dist. comdr. 1935). Mason (dist. gov. 1973-74). Rotarian. Contbr. column Corbin Daily Tribune and Whitley Republican. Address: Box 97 Williamsburg KY 40769

SILER, EUGENE EDWARD, JR., lawyer; b. Williamsburg, Ky., Oct. 19, 1936; s. Eugene Edward and Lowell (Jones) S.; B.A. cum laude, Vanderbilt U., 1958; LL.B., U. Va., 1963; LL.M. (E. Barrett Prettyman fellow), Georgetown U., 1964; m. Christy Dyanne Minnich, Oct. 18, 1969; 1 son, Eugene Edward III. Admitted to Ky. bar, 1963, Va. bar, D.C. bar; legal intern, Washington, 1963-64; practice in Williamburg, 1964-65; county atty. Whitley County, Williamsburg, 1965-70; U.S. atty., Lexington, Ky., 1970—. Sec., dir. Whitley Republican, Inc., 1968-70; co-chmn. Rep. campaign 5th Congl. Dist., 1966; pres. 5th Congl. Dist. Lincoln Club, 1969-70. Trustee, Cumberland Coll., Williamsburg, 1965-74. Served with USN, 1958-60, now lt. comdr. Res. Recipient Freedom's Found. medal, 1968. Mem. Ky., Va., Fed. bar assns., Bar Assn. D.C., Naval Reserve Assn., S.A.R., Gideons. Baptist. Optimist. Home: 820 Walnut St Williamsburg KY 40769 Office: Federal Bldg Lexington KY 40501

SILLIMAN, JULIAN WINTHROP, san. engr.; b. Palestine, Tex., Aug. 15, 1909; s. John Calvin and Bertha (Umstead) S.; A.B., Stanford, 1930, engr., 1932; m. Anne Marie Tucker, Sept. 27, 1936; children—Jay Robert, Nancy Fortino. Surveyor, resident engr., designer Cal. Div. Hwys., 1932-40; commd. lt. C.E., U.S. Navy, 1940, advanced through grades to capt., 1953; engr. constrn. of fld. base, 1941-42; with U.S. See Bee program, 1943-47; assigned to Spain, 1954-56; ret., 1960; chief engr. Mills Petticord & Mills., Washington, 1960-64; project engr. George Washington U. Hosp., Washington, 1964-66; chief engr. Airways Engring., Washington, 1966-70; asst., now dir. Dept. San. Sewers, Tampa, Fla., 1970—. Fellow Am. Soc.

C.E.; mem. Water Pollution Control Fedn., Tau Beta Pi. Registered profl. engr. Fla., N.Y., Cal., Va. Home: 2413 S Dundee St Tampa FL 33609 Office: Dept Sanitary Sewers Tampa FL 33602

SILLIMAN, RUSSELL AFTON, architect; b. Warren, O., June 26, 1925; s. Frederick Afton and Lillian Beatrice (Penry) S.; B.A., Denison U., 1949; B.Arch., U. Mich., 1952; m. Judith Ann Leonard, June 22, 1950; children—Margaret Ann, Janet Carol, Kathryn Jean, Jeri Ann. Archtl. draftsman Austin Co., Cleve., 1952-53; architect Osborn Engring. Co., Cleve., 1953-55; asso. architect Outcalt-Guenther Architects, Cleve., 1955-61; architect Austin Co., Cleve., 1961-65, Atlanta, 1965—, v.p., mgr. S.E. dist., 1966—. Trustee Holy Innocents Sch., Atlanta. Served with USNR, 1943-46. Mem. Atlanta C. of C. Episcopalian. Club: Riverside Swim and Tennis (Atlanta). Home: 1115 Winding Creek Trail NW Atlanta GA 30328 Office: 2970 Peachtree Rd NW Atlanta GA 30305

SILVEY, THOMAS JESSE, supt. schs.; b. Roston, Ark., June 21, 1912; s. Jesse B. and Viola S. (Bailey) S.; B.S., U. Ark., 1937, M. Ednl. Adminstrn., 1963; m. Bobbie Nell Martin, June 5, 1938; 1 dau., Fredrica Nell. High sch. tchr., basketball coach, Patmos, Ark., 1933-35; adminstrv. officer Agr. Adj. Adminstrs. Office, Faulkner County, Ark., 1937; asst. county agt. Washington County, supr. U. Ark. Agr. Srs. majoring in agrl. extension, 1938, county agrl. agt., 1939-42; tchr. vets. on farm tng., 1945-51; high sch. prin., 1952-53; supt. Bodcaw Schs., 1953-64; supt. Calico Rock (Ark.) Schs., 1964—; operator farm, 1945-64. Co-organizer, pres. U. Ark. Boys 4-H House, 1936, v.p. Agr. Day Assn. U. Ark., 1937; chmn. Joint State Adv. Council on Sch. Health, 1959-61; dist. commr., mem. exec. com. Boy Scouts Am., 1958-63; mem. Calico Rock City Planning Commn., 1969. Bd. dirs. White River Planning and Devel. Dist. Served with USNR, 1942-45. Recipient State Community Devel. Leadership award, 1968. Mem. N.E.A., Ark. Edn. Assn., Supts. Assn., Am., Ark. sch. adminstrs. assns., Ark. Sch. Bds. Assn., Assn. Sch. Curriculum Devel., Ark. Activities Assn. (exec. com., parliamentarian), Am. Legion (past post comdr.), 40 and 8, S.W. Ark. Schoolmasters Club, S.W. Ark. Poultry Producers Assn. (past pres.), U.S. Poultry and Egg Producers Assn. (past nat. v.p.), Izard County Tchrs. Assn. (past pres.), Calico Rock C. of C. (past pres.). Baptist (deacon). Lion. Home: Karla St Calico Rock AR 72519 Office: College St Calico Rock AR 72519

SILVIOUS, OWEN FRANKLIN, music pub., record mfg., mail order co. exec.; b. Luray, Va., Jan. 15, 1939; s. Omey F. and Effie (Jewell) S.; student pub. schs.; m. Nancy A. Gochenour, Aug. 12, 1961 (div.); children—Owen F. II, Eugene F. Pres., Luray Industries, Inc. (Va.), 1966—, Luray Music Co., 1966—, Frankie Record Co., Luray, 1966—. Songwriter, Broadcast Music, Inc., N.Y.C. and Nashville, 1967—; mng. dir. World Real Estate Investment Fund Ltd., Bahamas, 1971—, Diamonds Investment Fund Ltd., Bahamas, 1971—. Served with AUS, 1956-65. Mem. Nat. Songwriters Guild. Home: Luray VA 22835 Office: PO Box 62 Luray VA 22835

SIMCAK, ANDREW, JR., clergyman; b. Garfield, N.J., Aug. 15, 1930; s. Andrew and Justina (Pollack) S.; student Concordia Collegiate Inst., 1944-50, Valparaiso U., summer 1953; B.D., Concordia Sem., St. Louis, 1955; m. Jacqueline Jennie Cardaro, June 5, 1955; children—Timothy Andrew, Sharon Ann, Deborah Marie, Christine Ruth. Ordained to ministry Lutheran Ch., 1955; pastor Grace Luth. Ch., Sequin, Tex., 1955-58, St. Matthew Luth. Ch., San Antonio, 1958-61, St. John Luth. Ch., Corpus Christi, Tex., 1961-69, St. Michael Luth. Ch., Houston, 1969-73; organizer, pastor St. Timothy Luth. Ch., Houston, 1973—. Pastoral adviser Lone Star dist. Luth. Laymen's League, 1971—; chmn. Tex. dist. Pastor's-Tchrs. Conf., 1971-73, Tex. dist. Commn. on Fraternal Orgns., 1965—; mem. ad hoc com. to study pastoral approach to lodge problem Mo. Synod Luth. Ch., 1969-71. Home: 14710 Enchanted Valley Dr Cypress TX 77429 Office: 18530 W Montgomery Rd Houston TX 77070

SIMMEN, EDWARD ROBERT, educator; b. Galveston, Tex., Nov. 27, 1933; s. Frank Emil and Homoiselle (Tolex) S.; B.A., U. Tex., 1955, M.A., 1959; Ph.D., Tex. Christian U., 1966. Instr. English, Frederick Coll., Portsmouth, Va., 1959-60, Tyler (Tex.) Jr. Coll., 1960-63; asso. prof. English, Pan Am. State U. Tex., Edinburg, 1966—; vis. prof. lit. La. Universidad de las Americas, Puebla, Mexico, 1973-74. Served to lt. USNR, 1955-57. Mem. South Central Modern Lang. Assn., Rio Grande Valley Council Tchrs. English (dir.), Delta Tau Delta. Editor: The Chicano: From Caricature to Self-Portrait, 1971; Pain and Promise: The Chicano Today, 1972; A Chicano Bibliography: The Decade of the Sixties, 1973; Toward Readable Writing, 1974. Contbr. articles to profl. jours. Home: Route 1 Box 179 McAllen TX 78501 Office: Pan Am U Edinburg TX 78539

SIMMONS, CHARLES BAILEY, mus. dir.; b. Bristol, Conn., Oct. 9, 1931; s. Kenneth Harleston and Kathryn Antoinette (Gabb) S.; B.A., Yale, 1953, postgrad., 1953-54; postgrad. U. Del., 1965-66; m. Martha Wardwell Swain, Aug. 29, 1953; children—Kate Gabb, Hannah Swain, Jonathan Swain. Sect. mgr. G. Fox & Co., Hartford, Conn., 1957-58; asst. charge prints and framing Moyer Gallery, West Hartford, Conn., 1958-61; pres. Simmons Gallery, Avon-New Hartford, Conn., 1962-65; curator Hist. Soc. York County, Pa., 1966-69; dir. Henry Morrison Flagler Mus., Palm Beach, Fla., 1970—. Cons. York House Found. (Pa.), 1967-68. Trustee Sci. Mus. and Planetarium, West Palm Beach, Fla., 1970—. Served with AUS, 1954-56. H.F. DuPont Winterthur Mus. fellow, 1965-66. Mem. Nat. Trust Historic Preservation, Am. Assn. Mus., Victorian Soc. Am., S.E. Mus. Conf., Fla. Art Mus. Dirs. Assn., Soc. Archtl. Historians, Smithsonian Instn., Conn. Hist. Soc., Am. Assn. State and Local History. Address: The Henry Morrison Flagler Mus Palm Beach FL 33480

SIMMONS, EUGENE LYNN, educator; b. Post, Tex., Dec. 7, 1942; s. Henry Eugene and Norma Ruth (Trueblood) S.; B.S., Eastern N.M. U., 1964; M.S., Tex. Tech U., 1966, Ph.D., 1968; m. Judith Guyrene Turner, Aug. 28, 1967; 1 dau., Heather Elaine. Research asso. Queen's U., Belfast, No. Ireland, 1967-69; asst. prof. Northwestern State Coll., Alva, Okla., 1969-70; research asso. U. Houston, 1970-71, U. Tex. M.D. Anderson Hosp. and Tumor Inst., 1971-72; vis. scientist NASA Manned Spacecraft Center, 1972-73; vis. lectr. U. Natal, Durban, South Africa, 1973—. Recipient fellowships USAF, 1964, NASA, 1965, British Sci. Research Council, 1967, Sandia Corp., 1970, NIH, 1971, Nat. Research Council, 1972, grants NASA, 1965, Nat. Research Council, 1972, African Explosives, 1973. Mem. Am. Chem. Soc., The Chem. Soc., A.A.A.S., Sigma Xi. Contbr. to profl. publs. in field. Home: 4211 University St Houston TX 77004 Office: Dept Chemistry U Natal Durban South Africa

SIMMONS, FREDERICK MARTIN, architect; b. Paris, Tex., Jan. 21, 1915; s. John Fred and Rosa (Mauney) S.; student N.C. State U., 1934-35, Warren Sch. Aeronautics, 1936, Aero Industries Tech. Inst., 1937, The Citadel, 1940-44; m. Eunice May Sharpe, Dec. 17, 1937; children—Fredrika Carol, Suzanne Sharpe. Draftsman SP2-8, U.S. Naval Base, Charleston, S.C., 1938-46, V.W. Breeze, Architect, Shelby, N.C., 1946-49; architect Fred M. Simmons, Shelby, N.C., 1949-53, 56—, J.N. Pease & Co., Charlotte, 1953-56; pres. Cleveland Aircraft Co., 1970—. Comml. pilot, 1944—; instr. CAA Flight & Ground Sch., 1948—; chief engring. and pub. works Cleve County Dept. Civil Def., 1959—; mem. fine arts com. N.C. Luth. Synod, 1967—; dir. county fire vol. dept., 1961-70. Democratic candidate N.C. Ho. Reps., 1964. Mem. A.I.A., Nat. Geog. Soc., Antique Airplane Assn. Found. Lutheran. Comdr. first Coast Guard Aux. Air Squadron organized Charleston, S.C., 1946; designed first air conditioned sch. in N.C. with fallout protection for 1200 students. Home: Route 5 Box 129 Shelby NC 28150 Office: 924 E Dixon Blvd Shelby NC 28150

SIMMONS, GEORGE BENTON, educator; b. Nashville, Aug. 3, 1931; s. Avery Benton and Alice (Burnley) S.; B.A., U. Louisville, 1953; M.B.A., Ind. U., 1957, D.B.A., 1961; m. Mira Wilkins, June 15, 1968. Asst. prof. marketing adminstrn. U. Tex., 1961; cons. AID, Mexico, 1962; asst. prof. bus. Columbia, 1962-66; dir. Center for Bus. and Econ. Research, also asso. prof. bus. adminstrn. U. Mass., Amherst, 1966-68, prof., chmn. dept. mgmt., 1967-73; dean Sch. Bus. and Organizational Scis. Fla. Internat. U., 1974—. Served to lt. (j.g.) USNR, 1953-56. Mem. Am. Inst. Decision Scis., Acad. of Mgmt., Internat. Center Miami, Beta Gamma Sigma, Kappa Alpha. Author: A Bibliography of International Business, 1964. Address: Sch Bus and Organizational Scis Fla Internat U Tamiami Trail Miami FL 33144

SIMMONS, HOWARD HELMUTH, educator; b. N.Y.C., June 26, 1915; s. Frederick Herbert and Martha Marie (Winkler) Simon; certificate in commerce U. San Francisco, 1941; A.B., George Washington U., 1949; M.B.A., Stanford, 1951; postgrad. Am. U., 1966-69, N.Y.U., 1954-56; m. Ruth Ellen Barnett, Dec. 27, 1941; children—Marla (Mrs. Bruce Betzel), Howard Keith. Commd. 2d lt. U.S. Army, 1937, advanced through grades to col., 1958; comptroller Seventh Army, 1953-54; mem. joint programs office Joint Chiefs Staff, 1959-61; pres. Finance Corps Bd., 1963-64; dir. accounting Comptroller of the Army, 1965-66; chmn. social sci. dept. No. Va. Community Coll., Annandale, 1966, dean student services, 1967-71, prof. bus. mgmt., 1971—. Adj. prof. Southeastern U., 1964-66, chmn. dept. financial adminstrn., 1965-66. Pres. Anglo-Am. Schs., Athens, Greece, 1952-53. Decorated Legion of Merit with oak leaf cluster; recipient Outstanding award Fed. Govt. Accountants Assn., 1965. Mem. Am. Soc. Mil. Comptrollers (v.p. 1965-66), Am. Econ. Assn., Am. Accounting Assn., North Ridge Citizens Assn., Alpha Phi Omega. Democrat. Lutheran. Home: 3202 Old Dominion Blvd Alexandria VA 22305 Office: 8333 Little River Turnpike Annandale VA 22003

SIMMONS, JAMES BENJAMIN, lawyer; b. Whiteville, Tenn., Aug. 11, 1908; s. James Thomas and Mary Elizabeth (Sammons) S.; LL.B., Cumberland U., 1927; J.D., George Washington U., 1938, LL.M., M.P.L., 1939; m. Dorothy Payne, Feb. 26, 1943; children—Mary Sue, Jo Ann, Nancy Marie, Kathie Lorraine. Admitted to D.C. bar, 1939, Va. bar, 1945, Md. bar, 1948; practiced in D.C., 1949—; now partner Ward & Simmons; officer, dir., White Hall Manor, Inc., 1948—. Mem. Am., D.C., Md., Va. bar assns., Am. Judicature Soc., Internat. Platform Assn., Am. Acad. Polit. and Social Sci., Phi Beta Gamma (chief justice of the Washington alumni chpt. 1956-57). Office: 850 Sligo Av Silver Spring MD 20910

SIMMONS, JOHN WALTON, govt. ofcl.; b. Orange, Tex., Jan. 17, 1911; s. Walton Byron and Lucile (Ball) S.; B.S. in Chem. Engring., Tex. A. and M. Coll., 1931; m. Daisy B. Simmons; 1 son, Barre W. Chem. engr. The Tex. Co., 1931-47, on Bahrein Island, Persian Gulf, 1938-41; dir. Orange Indsl. Devel. Commn., exec. v.p. Orange C. of C. 1947-56; exec. v.p., gen. mgr. Sabine River Authority of Tex. (state agy.), Orange, 1956—. Spl. cons. to Gov. Tex. on Water affairs, 1970-71. Dir. Tex. Water Conservation Assn., 1949—, pres., 1962-69; pres., dir. Sabine River Authority of Tex., 1949-56; mem. Gov.'s Water Com., 1953-54, 57; v.p. Nat. Rivers and Harbors Congress, Washington, 1954-68, nat. dir. 1968-71; dir. Water Resources Congress, 1971—; mem. exec. com., 1972—, treas., 1973-74, pres., 1974—; mem. U.S. nat. commn. Internat. Commn. on Irrigation and Drainage. Served from 2d lt. to lt. col., USAAF, 1942-46; PTO, 1945; dep. air chem. officer Hdqrs. AAF, Washington, 1946. Recipient Outstanding Citizen award Greater Orange Area C. of C., 1967, Conservation Service award U.S. Dept. Interior, 1967; TWCA Ann. Conv. Dedication award 1970; Water Conservation Individual award Ft. Worth C. of C., 1970. Mem. Am. Chem. Soc., Tex. Soc. Profl. Engrs., Am. Water Works Assn., Nat. Water Resources Assn. (nat. dir. 1969—, treas. 1972), Municipal Finance Officers Assn. Club: Sportsmen of Texas. Home: 1955 Camelot Dr Apt 7 Orange TX 77630 Office: PO Box 579 Orange TX 77630

SIMMONS, KENNETH ROLAND, constrn. exec.; b. Tulia, Tex., Feb. 14, 1918; s. Clarence and Lelia Ann (Putnam) S.; student Texarkana Jr. Coll., 1936-37, U. Ark., 1937-39; m. Mary Marie Allen, Sept. 20, 1941; children—Kenneth Oran, Eugene Carl. With Robert E. McKee Gen. Constrn., Inc., El Paso, 1939—, gen. supt., 1963—, v.p., 1965—. Mem. Disciples of Christ Ch. Supr. numerous constrn. projects including Grady Gammage Meml. Auditorium, Ariz. State U., Tempe, 1942; Francisco Grande Guest Tower, Casa Grande, Ariz., 1957; L.E.M. Test Facilities, White Sands (N.M.) Missile Range, 1965; U.S.A.F. Acad., nr. Colorado Springs, Colo., 1956-59; William Beaumont Army Hosp., El Paso, 1970; U. Tex. at El Paso Engring. Scis. complex, 1974. Home: 9824 Trinidad St El Paso TX 79925 Office: 1918 Texas Av El Paso TX 79998

SIMMONS, RICHARD GLENN, city mgr.; b. Kissimmee, Fla., Aug. 6, 1928; s. Henry T. and R. L. (Fletcher) S.; B.S., U. Fla., 1950, M.A., 1951; m. Kay Upson, July 2, 1955; children—Sandra, Susan. City mgr., Melbourne, Fla., 1954-55, 67-69, Haines City, Fla., 1956-59, Winter Park, Fla., 1959-67, West Palm Beach, Fla., 1969—; intern, Kissimmee, Fla., 1950, Phoenix, 1952-53. Past pres. Central Fla. Council for Hard of Hearing Children. Bd. dirs. United Fund of Palm Beach County. Mem. task force on solid waste Nat. League Cities U.S. Conf. Mayors, Washington, 1973; adv. com. on solid waste Nat. Commn. on Productivity, Washington, 1973. Served from 1st lt. to capt. USAF, 1955-57. Recipient Distinguished Service award Jr. C. of C., 1964, awards of merit City of Winter Park, 1967, Melbourne, 1969. Mem. Internat., Fla. (past pres., dir.) city mgrs. assns., West Palm Beach C. of C., Fla. Chi Phi Assn. (bd. mem.). Methodist (past chmn. adminstrv. bd.). Kiwanian (past pres., dir.). Home: 356 Potter Rd West Palm Beach FL 33405 Office: City Mgr's Office City Hall West Palm Beach FL 33402

SIMMONS, ROBERT HOMER, tool co. exec.; b. McBride, Miss., Mar. 25, 1916; s. Homer Hirman and Nonnye Armildia (Cobb) S.; Asso. Sci. with honors, Copiah Lincoln Coll., 1936; B.S., La. State U., 1938, postgrad. bus. adminstrn., 1939. With Hunt Tool Co., Houston, 1939—, dir., sec., 1960, sec.-treas., 1961, v.p., sec.-treas., 1972—; sec.-treas. Hunt Engine & Equipment Co., Houston, 1958—, also dir.; sec.-treas. Reagan Tool Co., Morgan City, La., 1963-64, also dir.; v.p., sec.-treas. Internat. Tool Co., Inc., Houston, 1963—, also dir.; v.p. Clegg & Hunt, Inc., Houston, 1965—. Mem. Nat. Assn. Purchasing Agts., Sigma Nu, Kappa Mu Epsilon. Clubs: Cleveland (Miss.) Country; Houston Turn-Verein, Warwick, University (Houston). Home: 1539 Castle Ct Houston TX 77006 Office: PO Box 1436 Houston TX 77001

SIMMONS, SAMUEL WILLIAM, govt. ofcl.; b. Benton County, Miss., June 5, 1907; s. Britt L. and Ida E. (Pegram) S.; B.Sc. with honors, Miss. State U., 1931; A.M., George Washington U., 1934; Ph.D., Ia. State U., 1938; m. Lois Grantham, Aug. 5, 1928; children—Samuel William, Grant P. With U.S. Dept. Agr., Bur. Entomology, 1931-44; with USPHS, 1944-71, dir. Carter Meml. Lab., 1944-47, chief tech. devel. br., 1947-53, chief technology br. communicable disease center 1953-66; chief pesticides program Nat. Communicable Disease Center Atlanta, 1966-68; dir. div. pesticide community studies FDA, 1968-71; dir. div. pesticide community studies U.S. Environmental Protection Agy., 1971-72, ret. Vis. lectr. tropical pub. health Harvard, 1952-67; asso. preventive medicine and community health Emory U., 1957—. USPHS rep. Fed. Com. on Pest Control. Recipient Alumni Achievement award George Washington U., 1946, Alumni Centennial Citation award Ia. State U., 1958, Distinguished Service medal USPHS, 1965, William Crawford Gorgas medal Assn. Mil. Surgeons U.S., 1968, Distinguished Career award U.S. Environmental Protection Agy., 1972. Hon. cons. Army Med. Library, 1940-53. Adv. bd. Inst. Agrl. Medicine, U. Ia. Sch. Medicine, U.S.-Japan Com. on Sci. Cooperation. Diplomate Am. Bd. Microbiology. Fellow Am. Soc. Tropical Medicine and Hygiene (councilor 1953), Chem. Specialties Mfrs. Assns. (interdepartmental com. pest control, subcom. vector control inter-agy. com. water resources, chmn. 1964-66), U.S.-Mexico Border Health Assn., WHO (chmn. com. on pesticides 1951, 56, 57), A.M.A., (com. on insecticides 1950-59, com. on toxicology 1960), Research Soc. Am., Entomol. Soc. Am., Nat. Malaria Soc. (sec.-treas. 1951), Nat. Environmental Health Assn., Agrl. Research Inst., Horological Socs., Am. Mosquito Control Assn., Armed Forces Pest Control Bd., Nat. Research Council, Sigma Xi, Phi Kappa Phi, Gamma Sigma Delta, Los Hidalgos. Contbr. articles profl. jours. Editor and co-author, The Insecticide DDT and Its Significance, vol. II. Contbr. to Human and Veterinary Medicine, 1959. Home: 2050 Blackfox Dr NE Atlanta GA 30345

SIMMONS, STACY EARL, architect; b. Jackson, Miss., July 26, 1938; s. Andrew Henry and Ercell Lucille (Putnam) S.; B.Arch., Auburn U., 1961; m. Sara Jo Shields, Dec. 19, 1957; 1 dau., Rache Michelle. Draftsman, Painter, Weeks & McCarty, Knoxville, Tenn., 1961-63; architect Freeman-White Assos., Charlotte, N.C., 1964-70; architect, interior designer, pres. Omnia Design, Inc., Charlotte, 1970—. Recipient South Atlantic Regiona Design award A.I.A., 1966, South Atlantic Regional Design award, 1970. Mem. A.I.A. (dir. Charlotte sect., mem. nat. com. on design), Am. Inst. Interior Designers, Guild Religious Architecture, Phi Kappa Tau, Phi Mu Alpha. Democrat. Presbyn. Designer, Hamlet (N.C.) Sch. Nursing, 1965, Omnia Design Offices, Charlotte, 1968; Farmville (N.C) United Methodist Ch., 1971, A.C. Monk & Co. Interiors, 1973. Office: PO Box 1843 Charlotte NC 28201 Home: 9331 Providence Rd Matthews NC 28105

SIMMONS, WILLIAM ISAAC, dentist; b. Waco, Tex., Feb. 14, 1924; s. Jared Claude and Blanche (Schwarz) S.; D.D.S., Loyola U., New Orleans, 1946; certificate in orthodontics, U. Pa., 1950; m. Evelyn Kottle, June 11, 1967; children—Jared Claude, Walter Neil, Gina Denise, Nancy Dayan. Tchr., U. Tex. Dental Sch., 1951; individual practice dentistry, specializing in orthodontics, Shreveport, La., 1951—. Served with USAF, 1946-48. Mem. Am. Dental Assn. (v.p. 4th Dist.), Am. Orthodontic Soc., Royal Soc. Health. Jewish religion. Mason. Clubs: Pieremont Oaks Tennis, Petroleum (Shreveport); Barksdale Air Force Officers. Office: 2042 Line Av Shreveport LA 71104 also 3019 Old Minden Rd Bossier City LA 71010

SIMMS, JOHN MEREDITH, lawyer, ry. exec.; b. Raleigh, N.C., Jan. 17, 1923; s. Robert Nirwana and Virginia Adelaide (Egerton) S.; B.S. (Herbert Worth Jackson scholar), U. N.C., 1948, J.D., 1950; m. Lorraine Glenn, July 7, 1944; children—Sarah Haskew, John Meredith. Admitted to N.C. bar, 1950; gen. law practice, Raleigh, 1950-64; div. counsel Norfolk So. Ry. Co. (merged with So. Ry. Systems 1974), Raleigh, 1950-64, gen. counsel, 1965-74, v.p., 1970-74; with legal dept. So. Ry. Systems, Washington, 1974—; spl. counsel Atlantic Coast Line R.R. Co., Raleigh, 1950-64; gen. counsel Norfolk So. Indsl. Devel. Corp., 1965-69, v.p., gen. counsel, 1970-73; gen. counsel Durham and S.C. Railroad, 1965-69, v.p., gen. counsel, 1970-73. Bd. dirs. Hilltop Home for Retarded Children, 1964-74, N.C. Baptist Found., 1970-74; trustee Raleigh Bapt. Assn., 1964-74; trustee Meredith Coll., 1958-61, bd. assos., 1967—. Served to capt. AUS, 1943-46. Mem. Am., N.C., Wake County bar assns., Raleigh C. of C. Baptist (deacon 1952—). Clubs: Raleigh Executives (1st v.p. 1973-74), Raleigh Civitan (internat. judge adv. 1959-60, 64-65). Author: (with others) N.C. Manual of Law and Forms, 1951. Home: 6304 Ft Hunt Rd Alexandria VA 22307 Office: So Ry System 920 15th St PO Box 1808 Washington DC 20013

SIMMS, LEROY ALANSON, editor, publisher; b. Emelle, Ala., Sept. 17, 1905; s. John Thomas and Minnie Epes (Thomas) S.; student U. Ill., 1924-25; m. Flora Virginia Hammill, June 30, 1926 (dec. Oct. 1966); 1 dau., Lucie Grey (Mrs. Charles Clifford Grubbs); m. 2d, Martha H. Richardson, May 17, 1969. Reporter Birmingham (Ala.) News, 1925; reporter, asst. city editor Tampa (Fla.) Morning Tribune, 1925-26; city editor Birmingham Post, 1927-29, mng. editor, 1930-31; copy editor Newspaper Enterprise Assn. Service, Inc., Cleve., 1931-32; day editor Asso. Press, Birmingham, 1933-38, corr., 1939-58; mng. editor Birmingham News, 1959-61; editor Huntsville (Ala.) Times, 1961—, v.p., dir., 1963—, pub., 1964—. Bd. dirs. United Givers Fund; bd. dirs. Huntsville Indsl. Expansion Com., pres. 1970. Mem. Ala. Asso. Press Assn. (sec. 1939-58, pres. 1965-66), Birmingham Press Club (past v.p., past dir.), Ala. Press, Assn. (dir. 1964-65), Am., So. newspaper pubs. assns., Am. Soc. Newspaper Editors, Sigma Delta Chi (pres. Ala. profl. chpt.; chmn. Ala. 1960), Theta Chi. Clubs: Rotary, Huntsville Country, Valley Hills Country. Home: 1 Cruse Alley SE Huntsville AL 35801 Office: Huntsville Times Meml Pkwy Huntsville AL 35807

SIMMS, RUSSELL KEITH, synthetic fiber mfg. co. exec.; b. Beaman, Ia., Feb. 24, 1913; s. Thomas William and Dolly Ellen (Oliver) S.; B.A., State U. Ia., 1935; postgrad. Okla. State U., 1935-36; m. Ida May Wilson, Aug. 16, 1937. Apprentice engr. Phillips Petroleum Co., 1936; dist. engr. natural gas and gasoline dept., Borger, Tex., 1941-45, cons. chem. engr. patent div., Bartlesville, Okla., 1945-50; chief process engr. Phillips Chem. Co., 1950-63, br. mgr. engring. dept., Bartlesville, Okla., 1963-67; dir. corporate engring. Phillips Fibers Corp., Greenville, S.C., 1967—. Registered profl. engr., Okla. Mem. Am. Inst. Chem. Engrs. Mason. Home: 103 Shallowford Rd Greenville SC 29607 Office: Box 66 Greenville SC 29602

SIMON, BERNARD, assn. exec.; b. West New York, N.J., May 7, 1920; s. Max and Mary (Kell) S.; B.S. in Journalism, N.Y. U., 1941; m. Dorothy Ligeti, May 24, 1942; children—Gary Leonard, Linda Fran, David Judah. Reporter Religious News Service, N.Y.C., 1946-47; asso. dir. pub. relations anti-defamation league B'nai B'rith, N.Y.C., 1947-55, dir. pub. relations B'nai B'rith, 1955—; editor The Nat. Jewish Monthly mag., Washington, 1970-71. Served with AUS, 1942-46. Mem. Pub. Relations Soc. Am., Am. Jewish Pub. Relations Soc. Jewish religion. Mem. B'nai B'rith. Club: National Press

(Washington). Home: 2405 Colston Dr Silver Springs MD 20910 Office: 1640 Rhode Island Av NW Washington DC 20036

SIMON, DOROTHEA JONES (MRS. GEORGE MANNING SIMON), Christian Sci. practitioner; b. Rayville, La.; d. Claude Charles and Ada (Ellis) Jones; certificate home econs. St. Mary's Sch., Raleigh, N.C., 1924; m. George Manning Simon, Jan. 2, 1927; 1 son, George Manning. Joined Christian Sci.; Christian Sci. practitioner, Baton Rouge, 1947—. Mem. Com. Arsenal Museum, 1960; mem. Baton Rouge Found. Hist. La., Inc. (life). Chmn. bldg. trustees Christian Sci. Orgn., La. State U., 1961—. Mem., Young Women's Christian Orgn. (life), Colonial Dames of Am. (life), D.A.R., Delta Delta Delta. Club: Woman's. Home: 2995 Reymond Av Baton Rouge LA 70808

SIMON, H(UEY) PAUL, lawyer; b. Lafayette, La., Oct. 19, 1923; s. Jules and Ida (Rogers) S.; B.S., U. Southwestern La., 1943; J.D., Tulane U., 1947; m. Carolyn Perkins, Aug. 6, 1949; 1 son, John Clark. Admitted to La. bar, 1947, since practiced New Orleans; asst. prof. advanced accounting U. Southwestern La., 1944-45; prin. in C.P.A. firm Haskins & Sells, New Orleans, 1945-57; partner law firm Deutsch, Kerrigan & Stiles, New Orleans, 1957—. C.P.A., La., Miss. Mem. Am. Judicature Soc., Internat. (com. on securities issues and trading 1970—), Inter-Am., Am. (mem. com. ct. procedure 1958—), La., New Orleans bar assns., Am. Inst. C.P.A.'s, New Orleans Assn. Notaries, Soc. La. C.P.A.'s, C. of C. (mem. council), Tulane Tax Inst. (program com 1960—), Bur. Govtl. Research, Am. Accounting Assn., Nat. Assn. Accountants, Am. Assn. Atty.-C.P.A.'s, Tulane Alumni Assn., Phi Delta Phi (past pres. New Orleans chpt.), Sigma Pi Alpha. Clubs: Young Men's Business (legislation com.), Lamplighter, Press, Toastmasters, New Orleans Country, Petroleum (New Orleans); International House; Paul Morphy Chess, Pendennis. Author: Changes Effected by the Louisiana Trust Code, 1965; Gifts to Minors And the Parent's Obligation of Support, 1968. Asso. editor La. C.P.A., 1956-60; mem. bd. editors Tulane Law Rev., 1945-46. Home: 6075 Canal Blvd New Orleans LA 70124 Office: One Shell Sq Suite 4700 New Orleans LA 70139

SIMON, KENNETH ALAN, govt. ofcl.; b. Mt. Jewett, Pa., Feb. 28, 1916; s. George Preston and Bertha Irene (Rathburn) S.; B.S., Lock Haven State Coll., 1950; M.Ed., Pa. State Coll., 1953; Ed.D., Pa. State U., 1959 div.; children—Kenneth A., Carol (Mrs. William Norfolk). Prin., Lafayette Twp. Sch. Dist., McKean County, Pa., 1951-55; research and statis. program specialist Pa. Dept. Pub. Instrn., Harrisburg, 1955-59; chief Reference, Estimates and Projections br. Nat. Center for Edn. Statistics, U.S. Office Edn., Washington, 1959—, presently on assignment UNESCO Edn. Devel. Program, Jakarta, Indonesia. Cons., Ministry Edn., Jamaican Govt., 1965; part-time lectr. Am. U., 1964, U. Md., 1965. Served with USMCR, 1943-45; PTO. Recipient Superior Service award Dept. Health, Edn. and Welfare, 1970. Mem. N.E.A. (life). Club: Capitol Yacht (Washington). Contbr. articles to profl. lit. Home: 1301 Delaware Av SW Washington DC 20024 Office: 400 Maryland Av SW Washington DC 20202

SIMON, LORENA COTTS (MRS. SAMUEL C. SIMON), music tchr.; b. Sherman, Tex., Jan. 16, 1897; d. George Godfrey and Willie (Jones) Cotts; student Am. Conservatory, summer 1938; Julliard Music Sch., summer 1939; diploma Sherwood Music Sch., 1941; D. Lit. Leadership, Internat. Acad. Leadership, Philippine Islands, 1967; Mus. D., St. Olav's Acad., Sweden, 1969; L.H.D., Nother Pontifical Acad.; m. Samuel C. Simon, Nov. 6, 1918 (dec.). Tchr. violin, piano, theory and harmony, Port Arthur, Tex., 1919—. Organizer, dir. Schubert's Violin Choir, Port Arthur, 1919-55. Judge Internat. Poetry Peace Award Contest, 1965. Works of poetry in Internat. Poetry Archives, Manchester Central Library, Eng., 1965. Named Poet Laureate of Tex. 1961; Poet Laureate of Magnolia Dist., 1962-64; Poet Laureate of Port Arthur, 1962—; recipient gold plaque Tex. Fedn. Women's Club, 1962, spl. award 1st place in poetry and music Tex. heritage dept., 1963, spl. award in music and fine arts and outstanding service awards, 1965; 1st place in poetry, 1966; Medal of Honor and Diploma of Merit, Centro Studi Scambi Internat., Rome, Italy, 1965, Silver, Gold medals of merit, 1967, diploma of merit, 1966, 67; Hon. Poet Laureate-Musician, United Poets Laureate Internat., 1966, Karte of award, 1968, Hon. Internat. Catholic Poet Laureate, 1968; Contemporary Internat. Poet Hall of Fame, 1968; honored by Tex. Senate and Ho. of Reps., 1967. Mem. Internat. Platform Assn., Nat., Tex. press womens assns., Nat. Council Cath. Women, Nat. Guild Piano Tchrs. (charter mem.; adjudicator), Am. Coll. Musicians (adjudicator), Am. Poetry League, Poets Soc. Tex. (counselor 1967—, critic judge), Am. Poets Fellowship Soc. Corp., U.S., UN Assn.-U.S.A., Alpha Delta Kappa. Clubs: Writers' (pres. 1963-64), Symphony. Author: The Golden Key, 1958; From My Heart (1st place award Ann. Poetry Writers Contest of Tex. Press Women's Assn. 1961), 1959; Children's Story Hour (1st place award Nat. Fedn. Press Women's Ann. Writers' Contest 1962), 1960; In Music Land, 1965; That Blessed Night, 1966. Songs pub. include Live Expectantly, 1962, In Search for Growth, 1963, Freedom's Light, 1963, What Can I Do for Jesus, 1963. Donor funds for constrn. of churches in Africa. Address: 411 Fifth Av Port Arthur TX 77640

SIMON, ROY MICHAEL, architect; b. Delray Beach, Fla., Oct. 24, 1930; s. Alexander A. and Linda (Zaine) S.; B.S., Ga. Inst. Tech., 1952, B.Arch., 1953; m. Mary Elizabeth Wilder, July 29, 1961; children—Roy Michael, Laura Lee, John Christopher. Apprentice Kenneth Jacobson, architect, Delray Beach, Fla., 1949-58, asso., 1958-59; individual practice architecture, Delray Beach, 1959—. Mem. Recreation Adv. Bd., 1957-59; sec. Bd. Adjustments, 1959, 61, 63, chmn., 1960, 62, 64, 66; mem. Delray Beach (Fla.) Planning and Zoning Commn. Bd. dirs. Community Chest, 1959-68. Served to capt., USAF, 1954-56. Named one of 5 outstanding young men of year Delray Beach, 1962; Mem. Jr. C. of C. (pres. 1959-60; state dir. 1960-61, 1963-64, Jaycee of Year, 1961, 63, recipient Distinguished Service award 1962, 65); C. of C. (dir. 1959—; pres. 1964-65, 68-69), Ga. Tech. Alumni Assn. (pres. 1961-62), A.I.A. (pres. Spanish River sec. 1971), Fla. Assn. Architects, Fla. Assn. Am. Inst. Architects (mem. exec. com. Palm Beach chpt. 1967—, sec. 1971—; Architect Community Service award 1971), Sigma Phi Epsilon. Episcopalian (vestry 1960-64). Lion (dir. 1957-67; pres. 1965-66). Home: 1110 NW 2d Av Delray Beach FL 33444 Office: 94 NE 5th Av Delray Beach 33444

SIMON, WILLIAM LEONARD, film writer; b. Washington, Dec. 3, 1930; s. Isaac B. and Marjorie (Felstiner) S.; B.E.E., Cornell U., 1954; m. Arynne Lucy Abeles, Sept. 18, 1966; 1 dau., Victoria Marie; 1 stepson, Sheldon M. Bermont. Writer documentary and indsl. films TV programs, 1958-64; pres. William L. Simon Film Scripts, Inc., Washington, 1964—. Cons. films, TV Dem. Central Com., 1966-67; lectr. George Washington U., 1968-70. Pres. Foggy Bottom Citizens Assn., 1963-65, mem. exec. bd., 1965-69; v.p. Shakespeare Summer Festival, 1966-67, trustee, 1965-70. Served to lt. with USNR, 1954-58. Recipient 5 Golden Eagle awards Cine Film Festival, numerous other awards. Mem. Nat. Acad. TV Arts and Scis. (gov. D.C. chpt. 1970-73), Am. Film Inst., Univ. Film Assn., Eta Kappa Nu (chpt. pres. 1953-54), Tau Beta Pi. Writer numerous produced works for motion pictures and TV. Home: 2407 1/2 Eye St NW Washington DC 20037

SIMONS, ALBERT, JR., lawyer; b. Charleston, S.C., Nov. 20, 1918; s. Albert and Harriet Porcher (Stoney) S.; A.B., Princeton, 1940; LL.B., Yale, 1947; m. Caroline Pinckney Mitchell, June 18, 1948; children—Albert III, Julian Mitchell, Cotesworth Pinckney, Caroline Pinckney. Admitted to S.C. bar, 1947; practiced in Charleston, 1948—; asso. Sinkler & Gibbs, 1948; partner Sinkler, Gibbs & Simons, 1949-70; partner Sinkler, Gibbs, Simons & Guerard, 1970—. Dir. Charleston Rubber Co. Mem. City Council of Charleston, 1954-59; Charleston County Bd. Assessment Control, 1965—. Bd. dirs. Charleston Library Soc., S.C. Hist. Soc., Carolina Art Assn., Legal Aid Soc., Family Agy., S.C. Municipal Council. Served from pvt. to maj. F.A., U.S. Army, 1941-46. Decorated Bronze Star medal. Fellow Am. Coll. Probate Counsel; mem. Am., S.C., Charleston County bar assns., St. Cecilia Soc., S.C. Soc., Soc. of Cin., Soc. Colonial Wars, Hibernian Soc., Alpha Tau Omega, Phi Delta Phi. Episcopalian. Mason, Rotarian. Clubs: Carolina Yacht, Charleston. Home: 8 S Battery St Charleston SC 29401 Office: 2 Prioleau St Charleston SC 29402

SIMONS, CHARLES EDWIN, trade assn. exec.; b. Lafayette, Ind., Nov. 2, 1906; s. Charles Adam and Myrtle (Wetherill) S.; student pub. and parochial schs.; m. Mary Ann Yeazell, Oct. 19, 1929; children—Charles Lewis (dec.), Carol Jayne (Mrs. Dan R. Currens), Susan Bland (Mrs. Robert M. Caron), Charles Wetherill. Reporter, writer, editor newspapers in Lima, O., also Springfield, O., Huntington, W.Va., 1925-29; wire editor, capitol corr., polit. writer AP, Columbus, O., Austin, Tex., 1929-36; editor Tex. Parade, Austin, 1936-42; exec. v.p. Tex. Mid-Continent Oil and Gas Assn., Dallas, 1947-71; mem. Tex. Hwy. Commn., 1971—. Sec., Texas Democratic Party, 1942-44; presdl. elector, 1960, 68. Mem. bd. dirs. Gonzales Warm Springs Found. Mem. Tex. Aeros. Assn. (past pres.), Am., Tex. (past pres.) socs. trade execs., Am. Acad. Social and Polit. Sci., Tex. Good Rds. Assn., (dir. pub. relations Austin 1936-42, exec. v.p. 1942-46), Sheriffs' Assn. Tex. (hon. life), Sigma Delta Chi. Clubs: Headliners, Austin; Dallas Country, Dallas Petroleum (all Dallas); Petroleum (Houston); Ft. Worth. Home: 4428 Southern Av Dallas TX 75205 Office: 902 Preston State Bank Bldg 8111 Preston Rd Dallas TX 75225

SIMONS, HOWARD, journalist; b. Albany, N.Y., June 3, 1929; s. Rubin and Mae (Chesler) S.; B.A., Union Coll., 1951, Litt.D. (hon.), 1973; M.S., Columbia, 1952; Nieman fellow Harvard, 1958-59; m. Florence Katz, Nov. 11, 1956; children—Anna, Isabel, Julie, Rebecca. Reporter, editor Sci. Service, Washington, 1954-59; free-lance writer, 1959-61; reporter Washington Post, 1961-66, asst. mng. editor, 1966-69, dep. mng. editor, 1969-71, mng. editor, 1971—. Am. columnist New Scientist, London, Eng., 1963-67. Cons. Nat. Acad. Scis. Office of Information, 1959-61. Served with AUS, 1952-54. Mem. Overseas Writers, Council on Fgn. Relations. Club: Federal City (Washington). Contbr. articles to Harper's, Saturday Review, Saturday Evening Post, others. Home: 906 N Overlook Dr Alexandria VA 22305 Office: 1150 15th St NW Washington DC 20005

SIMONTON, WILLIAM CHRISTOPHER, editor; b. Covington, Tenn., Nov. 10, 1928; s. William C. and Emma (Long) S.; B.A., Centre Coll., 1950; m. Elizabeth Jane Butler, Aug. 18, 1949; children—Gail M., Kevin W. News editor Covington Leader, 1950-57, mng. editor, 1957-65, editor, 1965—. Football ofcl. Tenn. Secondary Sch., 1950—; mem. Covington Bd. Edn., 1957-71, chmn., 1961-69. Bd. dirs. Tenn. Sch. Bds. Assn., 1969-71; bd. dirs. Civington Indsl. Devel. Commn., chmn. 1970—. Mem. Tenn. Press Service (dir.), Am. Newspaper Reps. (dir. 1962-66), Tenn. Press Assn. (pres. 1967-68), Big Ten Ofcls. Assn. (pres. 1966-67), Covington C. of C. (pres. 1965, indsl. chmn. 1965—), Sigma Delta Chi, Sigma Alpha Epsilon. Home: 1 King Circle Covington TN 38019 Office: 2001 Hwy 51 S Covington TN 38019

SIMPSON, BRUCE LISTON, engring. co. exec.; b. Chgo., Nov. 14, 1912; s. Herbert Spencer and Edith (Moeller) S.; student Hobart Coll., 1930-33; B.S.L., Northwestern U., 1934, J.D., 1936; m. Madeleine Edith Holmes, Apr. 17, 1937; children—Judy T. (Mrs. Henry W. Dienst), Pamela L. (Mrs. John C. Anderson), Peter Liston III. Admitted to Ill. bar, 1937; asso. firm Ashcraft & Ashcraft, Chgo., 1933-37; with Nat. Engring. Co., 1937—, pres., dir., 1942-71, chmn. bd., 1972—; pres., dir. Nat. Engring. of Can., 1957—; chmn. Simpson Maschinen AG, Zurich, Switzerland, 1968—. Hon. life mem. Am. Foundrymens Soc. (past pres.). Unitarian. Clubs: Mid-America Union League, Chicago Yacht (Chgo.); Royal Poinciana, Naples Yacht (Naples, Fla.); Geneva Golf, Dunham Woods (Geneva). Home: 2701 N Gulfshore Blvd Naples FL 33940 Office: 20 N Wacker Dr Chicago IL 60606

SIMPSON, CHARLES FLOYD, vet. pathologist; b. East Orange, N.J., Jan. 29, 1919; s. Charles Floyd and Josephine (Reuttner) S.; B.Sc., Rutgers U., 1940; D.V.M., Cornell U., 1944; M.Sc., Ohio State U., 1955; Ph.D., U. Minn., 1961; m. Lucy Virginia Allport, Apr. 22, 1947; children—Vicki Ann, Kim Charles. Practice vet. medicine, Summit, N.J., 1947-48; asso. pathologist U. Fla., Gainesville, 1948-54, pathologist, 1955-58, 61—. Served with Vet. Corps, AUS, 1944-47. Spl. NIH grantee Recipient award Am. Vet. Med. Assn. Research, 1971. Fellow Am. Vet. Med. Assn.; mem. Electron Microscope Soc. Am., Internat. Acad. Pathologists, Soc. Exptl. Biology and Medicine, Sigma Xi (award 1971, pres. Fla. chpt. 1972-73), Gamma Sigma Delta (award 1970, sec. 1970-71), Phi Zeta. Kiwanian (dir., chmn. various coms.). Contbr. articles to sci. non-profl. jours. Home: 2225 NW 6th Pl Gainesville FL 32603

SIMPSON, DONALD STEWART, sign co. exec.; b. Chgo., Aug. 29, 1910; s. Thomas Stanley and Florence May (Stewart) S.; student Oberlin Coll., 1928-29; A.B., Dartmouth, 1932; m. Esther Norma Wentzler, Feb. 24, 1950; children—David, James. With Sears, Roebuck & Co., 1932-56, asst. zone mgr. Mid-Atlantic zone, Phila., 1948-50, mgr. Phila. store, 1950-56; mgr. Big Town Shopping Center, Mesquite, Tex., 1959-62; pres. MCAX Sign Co., Inc., Dallas, 1962—. Served to lt. comdr. USNR, 1942-46. Mem. Tex. Mfrs. Assn., Psi Upsilon. Republican. Presbyn. Rotarian. Home: 3612 Lexington Av Dallas TX 75205 Office: 4122 Commerce St Dallas TX 75226

SIMPSON, FRED BRYAN, govt. ofcl.; b. Birmingham, Ala., Sept. 4, 1935; s. Joseph Woodly and Nellie (Ware) S.; B.S., Howard Coll., 1961; LL.B., Vanderbilt U., 1964; m. Peggy Ann Holloway, Aug. 20, 1961; children—Bryan, Cynthia, Derek. Admitted to Ala. bar, 1964; atty. U.S. Army Redstone Arsenal, Huntsville, Ala., 1964-65; pvt. practice law firm Morring, Giles, Watson & Willisson, Huntsville, 1965-69; dist. atty. 23d Jud. Circuit Ala., Huntsville, 1969—. Alternate del. Democratic Nat. Conv., 1972. Vice-pres. Huntsville Christmas Charities, 1973-74. Served with USAF, 1953-57. Mem. Am., Fed., Madison County, Ala. bar assns., Nat., Ala. (v.p. 1973-74), dist. attys. assns., Am. Judicature Soc., Fraternal Order Police. Baptist. (trustee). Home: 724 Mira Vista Dr SE Huntsville AL 35802 Office: Madison County Courthouse Huntsville AL 35801

SIMPSON, HAROLD BROWN, ret. air force officer, educator; b. Hindsboro, Ill., Apr. 3, 1917; s. Harry Leon and Louise (Brown) S.; B.S., U. Ill., 1940, A.M., 1950, M.S., 1950; Ph.D., Tex. Christian U., 1969; m. Lorraine Hennings, Mar. 1, 1941; children—Jeffrey, Harold Brown, Gregory, Georganna, Deborah. Commd. 2d lt., USAF (formerly USAAF), 1941, advanced through grades to col., 1954; intelligence analyst Directorate of Intelligence Hdqrs., 1950-54; dir. statis. services Hdqrs. USAFE, 1955-58; comptroller 12th Air Force, 1959-63; ret., 1963; chmn. dept. social sci. Hill Jr. Coll., Hillsboro, Tex., 1963—; adj. prof. history Tex. Christian U., 1970—. Decorated Commendation medal with oak leaf cluster. Fellow Co. Mil. Historians, Tex. Hist. Soc.; mem. Air Force Assn., Tex. Hist. Assn., Pi Kappa Phi, Alpha Phi Theta. Author: Brawling Brass North and South, 1960; Gaines' Mill to Appomattox, 1963; Texas In The War, 1861-1865, 1965; Gray Granite For Gray Heroes, 1968; Hood's Texas Brigade In Poetry and Song, 1969; Hood's Texas Brigade: Lee's Grenadier Guard, 1970. Home: 4913 Westhaven Dr Fort Worth TX 76132 Office: PO Box 619 Hillsboro TX 76645

SIMPSON, JOANNE GEROULD (MRS. ROBERT H. SIMPSON), meteorologist, educator; b. Boston, Mar. 23, 1923; d. Russell and Virginia (Vaughan) Gerould; B.S., U. Chgo., 1943, M.S., 1945, Ph.D., 1949; m. W.V.R. Malkus, 1948 (div. 1964); children—David, Steven, Karen; m. 2d, Robert H. Simpson, Jan. 6, 1965. Asst. prof. physics, meteorology Ill. Inst. Tech., Chgo., 1945-51; meteorologist Woods Hole (Mass.) Oceanographic Instn., 1951-61; prof. meteorology U. Cal. at Los Angeles, 1961-65; chief exptl. br. Environmental Sci. Services Adminstrn., Coral Gables, Fla., 1965-70, dir. Exptl. Meteorol. Lab., 1970-74; adj. prof. atmospheric scis. U. Miami, Coral Gables, 1967-74; prof. environmental scis. Center Advanced Studies U. Va., 1974—. Mem. Fla. Gov.'s Environmental Coordination Council, 1971—. Guggenheim fellow, 1954. Recipient Meisinger award, 1962; Dept. Commerce gold medal, 1972, Women in Communications award, 1973. Fellow Am. Meteorol. Soc., Royal Meteorol. Soc. (Britain). Author: (with Herbert Riehl) Cloud Structure and Distributions Over the Tropical Pacific Ocean, 1964. Home: Top Sargeant Charlottesville VA 22904

SIMPSON, LEWIS PEARSON, educator; b. Jacksboro, Tex., July 18, 1916; s. John Pearson and Grace (Sidebottom) S.; B.A., U. Tex., 1938, M.A., 1939, Ph.D., 1948; m. Mary Elizabeth Ellis, July 14, 1941; 1 son, Lewis David. Instr. U. Tex., 1941-42, 44-48; civilian instr. U.S. Navy Flight Sch., 1942-44; asst. prof. La. State U., 1948-53, asso. prof., 1953-60, prof., 1960-64, prof. and co-editor Southern Rev., Baton Rouge, 1964-71, William A. Read prof. English lit., 1971—; Lamar Meml. lectr. So. lit. Mercer U., 1973. John Simon Guggenheim Meml. Found. fellow, 1954-55; La. State U. Found. Distinguished Faculty fellow, 1971-72. Mem. Am. Assn. U. Profs., Modern Lang. Assn., Am. Studies Assn., Soc. for Study So. Lit. (exec. council 1968-70), Orgn. Am. Historians, So. Hist. Assn., South Central Modern Lang. Assn., Thoreau Soc., Emerson Soc. Author: The Federalist Literary Mind, 1962; Profile of Robert Frost, 1971; The Poetry of Community, 1972; The Man of Letters in New England and The South, 1973. Editor: Library of Southern Civilization; adv. editor, Southern Writers Series, Arlington Quar.; co-editor The So. Rev., 1971—. Editorial bd. Am. Lit., George Washington Cable. Contbr. articles in field to profl. jours. Home: 965 Aberdeen Av Baton Rouge LA 70808

SIMPSON, RICHARD LEE, sociologist, educator; b. Washington, Feb. 2, 1929; s. Donald Dake and Lottie (Lee) S.; A.B., U. N.C., 1950, Ph.D., 1956; M.A., Cornell U., 1952; m. Ida Ann Harper, July 10, 1955; children—Robert Donald, Frank Daniel. Instr. sociology Pa. State U., University Park, 1956-57; asst. prof. sociology Northwestern U., Evanston, Ill., 1957-58; asst. prof. sociology U. N.C. at Chapel Hill, 1958-61, asso. prof., 1961-65, prof., 1965—. Cons. editor sociology Charles E. Merrill Pub. Co., Columbus, O., 1967-72. Mem. bd. U. N.C. Press, 1962—. Mem. Am., So. (1st v.p. 1968-69, pres. 1971-72) sociol. assns., Soc. for Study of Social Problems. Author: Attendants in American Mental Hospitals, 1961. Editor Social Forces, 1969-72; co-editor, contbr. Social Organization and Behavior, 1964—, Institutions and Social Exchange, 1971—. Home: 604 Brookview Rd Chapel Hill NC 27514

SIMPSON, ROBERT HOMER, meteorologist; b. Corpus Christi, Tex., Nov. 19, 1912; s. Clyde Robert and Annie Laurie (Rainey) S.; B.S., Southwestern U., 1932; D.Sc., 1963; M.S., Emory U., 1935; Ph.D., U. Chgo., 1962; m. Joanne Gerould, Jan. 6, 1965. Tchr., Tex. Pub. Schs., 1935-40; with U.S. Weather Bur., 1940-73, dep. dir. research div., 1960-62, asso. dir. Weather Bur., Washington, 1963-67, dir. Nat. Hurricane Center, Miami, Fla., 1967-73; research prof. environmental sci. U. Va., Charlottesville, 1973—. Mem. Am. Meteorol. Soc., Sigma Xi. Contbr. articles to profl. jours. Home: PO Box 5508 Charlottesville VA 22903

SIMPSON, VICTORIA MAGALINE, home economist; b. Fernandina Beach, Fla., Sept. 19, 1923; d. Leroy and Catherine D.E. (Wilson) Simpson; B.S., Fla. A. and M. U., 1945; postgrad. summers Mich. State U., 1947, Prairie View A. and M. U., 1950. Tchr. home econs., Marion County, Fla., 1945-47, Fla. A. and M. U., Tallahassee, 1947-49; extension home econs. agt., Columbia County, Fla., 1949-50, Dade County, Miami, Fla., 1950—. Adv. com. Booker T. Washington Community Sch., Miami, 1971—; active Dade County Assn. Retarded Children, Greater Miami, Urban League, Dade County Youth Fair, Dade County 4-H Youth Found., Dade County YMCA, Carver br. Recipient Distinguished Service award Nat. Assn. Extension Home Economists, 1961. Mem. Am. Home Econs. Assn., Nat., Fla. assns. extension home econs. agts., Epsilon Sigma Phi, Alpha Kappa Mu, Delta Sigma Theta. Home: 13840 Monroe St Miami FL 33158 Office: 2690 NW 7th Av Miami FL 33127

SIMS, BENNETT JONES, clergyman; b. Greenfield, Mass., Aug. 9, 1920; s. Lewis Raymond and Sarah Cosette (Jones) S.; A.B., Baker U., 1943; postgrad. Princeton Theol. Sem., 1946-47; B.D., Va. Theol. Sem., 1949, D.D., 1966; postgrad. Cath. U., 1969-71; D.D., U. of South, 1972; m. Beatrice May Wimberly, Sept. 25, 1943; children—Laura (Mrs. John P. Boucher), Grayson, David. Ordained to ministry Protestant Episcopal Ch. as deacon, 1949, priest, 1950; recotr Ch. of Redeemer, Balt., 1951-64; dir. continuing edn. Va. Theol. Sem., 1966-72; bishop, Atlanta, 1972—; priest-in-charge St. Alban's Ch., Tokyo, 1962; spl. lectr. Diocesan Confs., U.S., overseas, 1969. Trustee U. of South. Served with USNR, 1943-46. Named Young Man of Year, Balt. C. of C., 1953, Distinguished Alumnus of Year, Baker U., 1972. Merrill fellow Harvard, 1964-65. Home: 108 17th St NE Atlanta GA 30309 Office: 2744 Peachtree Rd NW Atlanta GA 30305

SIMS, EDITH MARIE, librarian; b. Baton Rouge, Jan. 27, 1928; d. Lyle Wood and Thelma Kathleen (Tillman) Sims; B.S., La. State U., 1949, B.L.S., 1951. Tchr. pub. schs., Haynesville, La., 1949-50; newspaper librarian La. State U. Library, Baton Rouge, 1949-56, geology librarian, 1956-57, govt. documents librarian, 1957-68, asso. librarian, head social sci. div., 1968—, vis. asso. prof. Sch. Library Sci. Sec., Baton Rouge chpt. La. Mental Health Assn., 1962; mem. Baton Rouge Symphony Aux., 1968—. Mem. Am., La. library assns., Spl. Libraries Assn., La. Hist. Assn., Geosci. Information Soc., Phi Alpha Theta. Baptist. Home: 1475 W Chimes St Baton Rouge LA 70802

SIMS, ERNEST THEODORE, JR., scientist, educator; b. Atlanta, Aug. 29, 1932; s. Ernest Theodore and Louise (Miller) S.; B.S.A., U. Ga., 1954; M.Sc., Ohio State U., 1959, Ph.D., 1962; grad. basic research course Oak Ridge Inst. Nuclear Studies, 1965; m. Margaret Elizabeth Richter, Dec. 28, 1963; children—Ernest Theodore III,

John Christopher Richter. Pomologist, Sims Fruit Farms, Conyers, Ga., 1956-57; grad. research asst. Ohio State U., 1957-62; asst. prof. horticulture Clemson (S.C.) U., 1962-67, asso. prof. horticulture, postharvest physiologist, 1967-72, prof., 1972—, mem. grad. faculty, 1968—, faculty senate, 1969-71. Troop committeeman Boy Scouts Am., 1967-69. Served with AUS, 1954-56; maj. Res. Mem. Assn. Southeastern Biologists, Res. Officers Assn. U.S., Am. Soc. Hort. Sci. (S.C. reporter nat. jour. 1966—), Am. Soc. Plant Physiologists, Internat. Soc. Hort. Sci., Sigma Xi, Phi Kappa Phi, Alpha Zeta, Gamma Sigma Delta. Presbyn. Lion. Contbr. articles to profl. jours. Home: 117 Poole Lane Clemson SC 29631

SIMS, EUGENE FELIX, welding co. exec.; b. Crockett, Tex.; Nov. 7, 1924; s. Martin C. and Bethel A. (Parsley) S.; student Oklahoma City U., 1942-43, U. Houston, 1947-48, 50-51; m. Linda Powers, Dec. 2, 1967; children—Sandra (Mrs. Richard Lambert, Jr.), Rosemary Gregg, Eugene Felix. With Crutcher Resources Corp., Houston, 1957—, chief pilot, 1957-67; v.p., gen. mgr. automatic welding div. CRC-Cross Internat., Houston, 1967—, pres. CRC-Automatic Welding div., 1974—, mem. exec. operating com. parent co., 1973—. Served with USAAF, 1943-46. Mem. Am. Welding Soc. Home: 506 Rancho Bauer Houston TX 77024 Office: 10522 Old Katy Rd Houston TX 77043

SIMS, JAMES NATHAN, petroleum co. exec.; b. Orange, Tex., Jan. 16, 1918; s. James Nathan and Nora (Baker) S.; B.S., U. Houston, 1940; m. Nelda Fagan, Oct. 24, 1947; children—Gail, Howard. Petroleum geologist Phillips Petroleum Co., Houston, 1941-56, exploration geologist, 1945-48, sr. exploration geologist, 1948-56; partner Acorn Oil Co., Houston, 1956-64; owner, prin. Acorn Oil and Gas Co., Houston, 1964—. Mem. Houston Geol. Soc., Am. Assn. Petroleum Geologists, Soc. Ind. Profl. Earth Scientists, Houston Assn. Petroleum Landmen. Methodist. Home: 4 Valley Forge St Houston TX 77024 Office: 935 San Jacinto Bldg 911 Walker St Houston TX 77002

SIMS, WILLIAM EDWARD, univ. pres.; b. Chickasha, Okla., Mar. 28, 1921; A.B., Lincoln U., 1949; M.A., Colo. State Coll., 1952, Ed.D., 1963; m. Muriel Crowell, June 27, 1945; 1 dau., Dana Rae. Tchr., Tulsa Pub. Schs., 1948-53; asso. prof. music, chmn. dept. Langston (Okla.) U., 1963-65, dean acad. affairs, 1965-69, pres., 1970—. Bd. dirs. State Fair Okla., Okla. Humanities Task Force, Okla. Heart Assn. Served with USNR, 1942-46. Mem. N.E.A., Higher Edn. Alumni Council, Okla. Edn. Assn., Soc. for Advancement of Mgmt., Kappa Delta Pi, Phi Delta Kappa, Kappa Alpha Psi. Lion. Home: P O Box 907 Langston OK 73050

SINCLAIR, CLARENCE BRUCE, educator; b. Independence, Mo., Jan. 28, 1924; s. Glen William and Mabel Mariliz (Kearns) S.; B.A. in Biology-Chemistry, U. Kansas City, 1949, M.A. in Zoology, 1950; Ph.D. in Botany, U. Mo., 1967; m. Carlotta Alice Ballantyne, Dec. 22, 1947; children—Susan A. (Mrs. Stephan E. Himmell), Scott W., Sherry L. Grad. asst. U. Kansas City, 1949-50; prof. biology Nat. Coll., Kansas City, Mo., 1950-64; prof. botany U. Ark., Little Rock, 1964—, dean div. life scis., 1969—, asst. dean Sch. Health Related Professions Med. Sch., 1972—. Instr., Rockhurst Coll., summer 1958; lectr. plant taxonomy U. Mo., Kansas City, evenings 1963-64. Served with inf. AUS, 1943-46. NSF Edn. grantee, summers 1960, 71; A.H.I. grantee, 1970, 71; O.W.R.R. Dept. Interior grantee, 1969-73; Pvt. Ind. APL grantee, 1968—; U.S.A. Corp. Engring. grantee, summer 1972. Mem. A.A.A.S., Am. Inst. Biol. Scis., Bot. Soc. Am., Internat. Assn. Plant Taxonomy, Mo. Acad. Sci., Ark. Acad. Sci., Rocky Mountain Biol. Lab. Assn., Nat. Woodcarvers Assn., Sigma Xi. Contbr. articles to sci. jours. Home: 6827 Dahlia Dr Little Rock AR 72209

SINCOX, FRANCIS JOHN, JR., physician; b. Saginaw, Mich., May 11, 1932; s. Francis John and Erna (Hefke) S.; B.A., Emory U., 1954, M.D., 1958; m. Frances Barker, June 21, 1958; children—Douglas John, Kathleen Barker. Intern U.S. Naval Hosp., St. Albans, N.Y., 1958-59; practice medicine McGill Clinic, Kings Mountain, N.C., 1963—; mem. staff Kings Mountain Hosp. FAA med. examiner, 1963—. Mem. Kings Mountain Police Res., 1969—. Bd. dirs. A.R.C., 1964-65. Served with USNR, 1959-63. Diplomate Am. Bd. Family Practice. Mem. Am. Acad. Gen. Practice, Cleveland County Med. Soc. (v.p., 1966-67), Kings Mountain C. of C. (dir., 1970—), A.M.A., N.C. Med. Soc. Presbyn. (deacon). Mason (32 deg.), Kiwanian. Home: 404 Edgemont Dr Kings Mountain NC 28086 Office: PO Box 392 Kings Mountain NC 28086

SINGER, MARKUS MORTON, assn. exec.; b. N.Y.C., Dec. 20, 1917; s. Isadore and Nettie (Stromer) S.; B. Comml. Sci., N.Y. U., 1939; postgrad. George Washington U., 1951-55; m. Phyllis Berger, June 26, 1945; children—Fredric, Robert. With Nat. Food Brokers Assn., Washington, 1946—, exec. v.p., 1965-71, pres., 1972—. Asst. sec. Nat. Food Brokers Assn. Found. Inc., 1957—. Served with AUS, 1942-46. Mem. Am. Mgmt. Assn., Am. Marketing Assn., Am. Soc. Assn. Execs., Washington, Am. Socs. assn. execs., Washington Food Group, Old Guard, Young Guard. Home: 3304 Shirley Lane Chevy Chaee MD 20015 Office: 1916 M St NW Washington DC 20036

SINGER, STUART ALAN GORDON, chem. engr.; b. Toronto, Ont., Can., May 19, 1922; s. Joseph George and Hazel Ellen (Marshall) S.; B.A.Sc., U. Toronto, 1943, M.A.Sc., 1945, Ph.D., 1947; m. Rosalie Jacqueline Holling, June 12, 1948; children—Gayle Joanne, Sherry Leigh. Came to U.S., 1947, naturalized, 1956. Devel. engr. Research Enterprizes, Ltd., 1943-44, asst., Toronto, 1944-46, instr. chem. engring., indsl. chemistry, 1947; research engr. rayon dept. E.I. duPont de Nemours & Co., Buffalo, 1947-50, tech. investigator film dept., Wilmington, Del., 1950-52, tech. supt., Columbia, Tenn., 1952-55, Buffalo, 1955-59, dir. Film Research & Devel. Lab., Richmond, Va., 1959-69, research mgr., 1969—. Mem. Am. Inst. Chem. Engrs. Episcopalian (vestryman). Home: 3206 Stratford Rd Richmond VA 23225 Office: PO Box 27222 Richmond VA 26261

SINGH, HARINDER S., computer co. cons.; b. Patiala, India, Dec. 23, 1941; s. Nihal and Lajwanti (Devi) S.; B.A. with honors, Punjab U., 1959; M.S., U. N.C., 1962; Ph.D., St. Louis U., 1965; m. Harriet Mae Varnum, Dec. 31, 1963; children—Sarita, Sushila. Came to U.S., 1960, naturalized, 1968. Research geophysicist Digital Seismic Corp., 1965-69; dir. research and devel., dir. tng. Digital Resources Corp., 1969-70; sr. cons., educator University Computing Co., Dallas, 1970—. Tchr., Tulane U., 1962-63, Tex. Christian U., 1971-73, U. Tex., Arlington, 1974—. Vol. fireman, Pantego, Tex., 1972—. Air Force Office Sci. Research grantee, 1963. Mem. Soc. Exploration Geophysicists, Am. Geophys. Union, World Affairs Council, Jr. C. of C. Home: 3400 Peachtree St Arlington TX 76013 Office: 2910 Av F E Arlington TX 76013

SINGH, RAGHBIR, educator; b. Punjab, India, Nov. 1, 1931; s. Amar and Inder (Kaur) S.; B.Sc., Punjab U., India, 1952, M.Sc., 1955; Ph.D., U. Minn., 1964; m. Jean Marie Gustafson, Dec. 28, 1966; 1 son, John Dwight. Came to U.S., 1959, naturalized, 1972. Research asst. Ministry Agr., India, 1955-59, U. Minn., Mpls., 1959-64; postdoctoral research fellow U. Minn., Mpls., 1964-65; asst. prof. biology Chadron (Neb.) State Coll., 1965-66, asso. prof., 1966-67; prof. biology Benedict Coll., Columbia, S.C., 1967-68, prof. biology, chmn. div. sci. and math., 1968—. John Cowles fellow, 1960-61, NSF grantee, 1966. Mem. A.A.A.S., Neb., S.C. acads. scis., Honor Soc. Agr., Sigma Xi. Mason (Shriner). Home: 210 S Gregg St Columbia SC 29205

SINGLETARY, JOHN N., ins. co. exec.; b. Henderson, Tex., Nov. 9, 1917; s. John N. and Lillian P. (Beam) S.; B.A., U. Okla., 1938, LL.B., 1941; m. Virginia Southwell, Oct. 17, 1942; children—Anita Jo, John N. III. Admitted to Okla. bar, 1941; practiced in Oklahoma City, 1941-42, 45-51; co-founder Globe Life & Accident Ins. Co. Oklahoma City, 1951—, chmn. bd., pres., 1951—; dir. Globe Color Press, 1st Nat. Bank & Trust Co. Oklahoma City, other indsl. firms; pres. Carport, Inc., Hudson Hotel, Globe Realty Devel. Corp.; chmn. bd. Am. Life & Accident Ins. Co., Fort Worth. Served to capt. USAAF, 1942-45. Mem. Oklahoma City C. of C. (dir., 1966-73), Optimists (pres., 1948-49), Alpha Tau Omega. Home: 1704 Bedford Dr Oklahoma City OK 73116 Office: 311 W Sheridan St Oklahoma City OK 73102

SINGLETARY, OTIS ARNOLD, JR., univ. pres.; b. Gulfport, Miss., Oct. 31, 1921; s. Otis Arnold and May Charlotte (Walker) S.; B.A., Millsaps Coll., 1947; M.A., La. State U., 1949, Ph.D., 1954; m. Gloria Walton, June 6, 1944; children—Bonnie, Scot, Kendall Ann. Mem. faculty U. Tex., 1954-61, prof. history, 1960-61, asso. dean arts and scis., 1956-59, asst. to pres., 1960-61; chancellor U. N.C. at Greensboro, 1961-66; v.p. Am. Council on Edn., Washington, 1966-68; dir. Job Corps, Office Econ. Opportunity, Washington, 1964-65; exec. vice chancellor acad. affairs U. Tex. System, 1968-69; pres. U. Ky., Lexington, 1969—. Bd. dirs. Am. Assn. Higher Edn., 1969-72, Ednl. Change Inc., 1968—, Inst. Services to Edn., 1969—, So. Regional Edn. Bd., 1970—, Fed. Reserve Bank Cleve., 1973—. Regional chmn. Woodrow Wilson Nat. Fellowship Found., 1959-61; chmn. N.C. Rhodes Scholarship Com., 1964-66, chmn. Ky. com., 1970-72; bd. visitors Air U. MAFB, 1973—. Served with USNR, 1943-46, 51-54; comdr. Res. Recipient Scarborough Teaching Excellence award U. Tex., 1958, Students Assn. Teaching Excellence award, 1958, 59; Grantee Carnegie Corp., 1961. Mem. Am., So. hist. assns., Am. Mil. Inst. (Moncado Book Fund award 1954), Phi Beta Kappa, Phi Alpha Theta, Pi Kappa Alpha. Democrat. Methodist. Author: Negro Militia and the Reconstruction, 1957; The Mexican War, 1960; American Universities and Colleges, 1968. Office: U Ky Lexington KY 40506

SINGLETON, EUSTACE BYRON, lawyer; b. Lufkin, Tex., Oct. 3, 1909; s. James Madison and Carolyn Elizabeth (Haygood) S.; A.B., U. Tex., 1933, J.D., 1933; m. Elsie Adeline Bell, May 16, 1936; children—Eustace Byron II, Savannah Adeline. Admitted to Tex. bar, 1933, U.S. Supreme Ct. bar, 1941, U.S. Ct. Claims bar, 1952, U.S. Ct. Customs and Patent Appeals bar, 1956, also others; mem. firm Underwood, Strickland & Singleton, Amarillo, Tex., 1933-38, Monning & Singleton, Amarillo, 1939-49, Singleton & Trulove, Amarillo, 1950-60; practiced in Amarillo, 1961—; atty. corp. counsel City of Amarillo, 1941-48; part-time referee in bankruptcy U.S. conciliation commn., 1933-40; mgmt. exec., gen. counsel Beef Industries, Inc., BC & M Drilling Co. of Mesa, Continental Dynamics Ltd., Las Vegas, Ark. Valley Feed Yards, Inc., Southwestern Grain-Soweco, Inc., Food & Fiber Research & Devel., Inc., TransEra Research Dallas, Inc. Pres. Venture-Assos. Mgmt. Corp. Exec. committeeman Young Dems. of Tex., 1935-46; finance committeeman Amarillo Dem. Com., 1936-40. Chmn. Amarillo chpt. A.R.C.; dep. dir. War Savs. Staff, Austin, Tex., 1939-43; nat. committeeman War Finance Com., Dallas, 1943-46. Bd. dirs. Edna Gladney Home, Draughon's Bus. Coll., Lubbock and Amarillo; bd. govs. Arthritis and Rheumatism Found. Mem. Am., Fed., Amarillo bar assns., State Bar Tex., Am. Judicature Soc. Home: 2405 Lipscomb St Amarillo TX 79109 Office: 1408 Am Nat Bank Bldg Box 12055 Amarillo TX 79101

SINGLETON, GEORGE TERRELL, physician; b. Wichita Falls, Tex., Dec. 16, 1927; s. George Terrell and Lillian (Fain) S.; B.A., Midwestern U., 1949, B.S., 1949; M.D., Baylor U., 1954; m. Jacqueline Green, July 12, 1952; children—Marsha, Thomas, Robert. Intern, Henry Ford Hosp., Detroit, 1954-55, resident, 1955-58; practice medicine specializing in otolaryngology, 1958—; chief div. otolaryngology U. Fla., 1961—; chief of staff Shands Teaching Hosp., 1971—. Served with AUS, 1958-60. Recipient Triological Soc. H.P. Mosher Meml. award, 1967. Mem. Alachua County Med. Soc. (pres. 1970-72), Am. Acad. Opthalmology and Otolaryngology (Research award 1960), Am. Bd. Otolaryngology, Am. Otol. Soc., Am. Laryngol., Rhinol. and Otol. Soc., Soc. U. Otolaryngologists, Soc. Acad. Chmn. Otolaryngology, Sigma Xi. Home: 1421 NW 47th Terrace Gainesville FL 32601 Office: Box 725 U Fla Gainesville FL 32601

SINGLETON, HELEN MARIE MCKINNEY (MRS. ARTHUR GLEN SINGLETON), county ofcl.; b. Ballinger, Tex., Dec. 8, 1914; d. Curtis B. and Annie Frances (Harmon) McKinney; grad. Draughon's Bus. Coll., 1934; m. Arthur Glen Singleton, June 22, 1936; 1 son, Curtis Fred. With First Nat. Bank, Edinburg, Tex., 1935; 1st asst. county auditor Hidalgo County, Edinburg, 1942; treas. Hidalgo County, Edinburg, 1947—. Hostess to Conf. County Treas's State Tex., 1964. Active mem. Edinburg Hosp. Aux. Recipient Gold Medallion of Mexico, 1963; named Outstanding County Treas. of Tex., 1971-72. Mem. County Treas.'s Assn. Tex. (pres. 1964; dir. 1964), Nat. Assn. County Treas. and Finance Officers (sec., treas. 1966, pres. 1972-73). Presbyn. (chmn. bus. and profl. women's circle 1969). Club: Zonta (pres. 1963). Home: PO Box 564 810 S 8th St Edinburg TX 78539 Office: Court House Edinburg TX 78539

SINGLETON, RUDOLPH GRANTLEY, JR., lawyer; b. Lexington, Ky., May 24, 1930; s. Rudolph Grantley and Eula (Peterson) S.; student Mars Hill Coll., 1948-50; A.B., Wake Forest U., 1952, J.D., 1954; m. Jennette Johnston, Sept. 20, 1958; children—Sarah Scott, Rudolph Grantley III. Admitted to N.C. State bar, 1954; pvt. practice law, Fayetteville, 1954-56; asst. solicitor Cumberland County Superior Ct., 1955-56; partner Nance, Collier, Singleton, Kirkman & Herndon, Fayetteville, 1958—; city atty. Fayetteville, N.C., 1972—. Chmn. So. dist. Boy Scouts Am., 1963-64; pres. Cumberland County Heart Assn., 1966-67. Chmn. pub. relations com. City Fayetteville, 1968-69. Pres. Cumberland County Young Dem. Club, 1958-59; precinct chmn. Dem. party, 1966-68; mem. county Dem. Exec. Com., 1966-68. Served with AUS, 1956-57. Mem. N.C., Am. bar assns., Am. Arbitration Assn. (panel, 1971—), Fayetteville C. of C. (dir. 1967—, pres. 1970), Sigma Phi Epsilon, Phi Alpha Delta. Democrat. Baptist. Clubs: Exchange of N.C. (dist. gov. 1963-64), Exchange of Fayetteville (pres. 1962-63), Highland Country (dir. 1972—). Home: 1 Skye Pl Fayetteville NC 28303 Office: PO Drawer 1210 First Union Nat Bank Bldg Fayetteville NC 28301

SINGLEY, JOHN EDWARD, educator; b. Wildwood, N.J., July 31, 1924; s. John Edward and Dorothy Mae (Pfrommer) S.; B.S., Ga. Inst. Tech., 1950, M.S., 1952; Ph.D., U. Fla., 1966; m. Virginia Hyland Ragsdale, Mar. 17, 1950; children—Gladys (Mrs. Gary Nason), Ann, Margaret, Patricia. Phys. chemist Army Ordnance Rocket Research Center, Huntsville, Ala., 1950-51; dir. tech. service Tenn. Corp., College Park, Ga., 1951-64; instr. Ga. State U., Atlanta, 1953-63, asst. prof., 1963-66, asso. prof., 1966-67; asso. prof. dept. environmental engring. scis. U. Fla., Gainesville, 1967-70, prof., 1970—. Cons., Marineland Studios, 1967—, WHO, 1972—, Pres.'s Council on Environmental Quality, 1973—, Nat. Acad. Sci., 1971-72, Water and Air Research, Inc., 1970—. Bd. dirs. Gainesville Young Life, Alachua County Assn. Retarded Children. Served with USNR, 1943-45. Recipient Ambassador award Am. Water Works Assn., 1971, Water Quality Div. award Am. Water Works Assn., 1973; named Civitan of Year, 1970. Fellow Am. Inst. Chemists; mem. Am. Water Works Assn. (trustee Fla. sect. 1971-74), Am. Chem. Soc. (chmn.-elect Gainesville subsect. 1973-74). Club: Civitan (pres. Gainesville 1972-73). Patentee in field. Home: 1852 NW 10th Av Gainesville FL 32605

SINKO, LOUIS, govt. ofcl.; b. Chgo., Jan. 23, 1928; s. Louis and Ethel (Horvath) S.; B.S., Ill. Inst. Tech., 1949; m. Elaine E. Butler, July 30, 1960 (div. Nov. 1969); children—Louis IV, Gellert. Jr. engr. Riechel & Drews, Inc., Chgo., 1950; engr. C.E. U.S. Army, Chgo., 1952-57, Army Ballistic Missile Agy., 1957-59; sr. engr. Missile and Space Systems Div., United Aircraft Corp., East Hartford, Conn., 1959-60; supr. Marshall Space Flight Center, Ala., 1960—. Served with AUS, 1950-52. Registered profl. engr., Ala., Ill. Mem. Nat. Council State Bds. Engring. Examiners, Nat. Rifle Assn. (life). Home: P O Box 1074 Huntsville AL 35807 Office: Marshall Space Flight Center AL 35812

SINTZ, EDWARD FRANCIS, library adminstr.; b. New Trenton, Ind., Feb. 6, 1924; s. John and Edith (Rudicil) S.; B.A., U. Kan., 1950; M.A. in L.S., U. Denver, 1954; M.S. in Pub. Adminstrn., U. Mo., 1965; m. Donna Norris, Apr. 12, 1952; children—Ann Kriston, Lesley Elisabeth, Julie Melinda. Various positions Kansas City (Mo.) Pub. Library, 1954-64, asst. librarian, 1964-66; asst. librarian St. Louis Pub. Library, 1966-67, asso. librarian, 1967-68; dir. Miami-Dade Pub. Library System, 1968—; instr. library sci. Washington U., St. Louis, 1966-67. Served with USAAF, 1942-45. Mem. Am., Fla. library assns. Editor: Mo. Library Assn. Quar., 1956-58. Home: 5730 SW 56th Terrace Miami FL 33143 Office: 1 Biscayne Blvd Miami FL 33132

SIPES, SAMUEL SEYMOUR, lawyer; b. Canadian, Tex., Sept. 13, 1939; s. Ernest Franklyn and Ruby Hellen (Blackman) S.; B.A., Yale, 1966; J.D., Tex. U., 1969; m. Doris Ann Deere, Aug. 18, 1967; children—Allison Anne, Christopher Hugh. Admitted to Tex. bar, 1969; practiced in mem. firm. Potash & Bernat, Inc., El Paso, 1969—, partner, 1971—. Served with AUS, 1959-62. Mem. Young Lawyers Assn. (pres. 1973—). Kiwanian. Home: 5751 Valley West Dr El Paso TX 79932 Office: SW Bank Bldg El Paso TX 79901

SIPIORA, LEONARD P., museum dir.; b. Lawrence, Mass., Sept. 1, 1934; s. Walter and Agnes (Kolodziej) S.; A.B. cum laude, U. Mich., 1955, M.A., 1956; m. Sandra Joyce Coon; children—Alexandra W., Erika. Faculty State U. Ia., 1956-60, U. Tex. at El Paso, 1961-67. Sec., treas. El Paso Council for Internat. Visitors, 1968-71; pres. El Paso Arts Council, 1969-71. Trustee, El Paso Mus. of Art, Community Concert Assn., El Paso Symphony. Mem. Hist. Soc. El Paso, Nat. Soc. Arts and Letters (1st v.p. El Paso chpt.), Symphony Assn., Tex. Mus. Conf. (dir.), Mountain-Plains Mus. Conf. (membership chmn.), Am. Assn. Museums, Assn. Art Mus. Dirs., Am. Fedn. Arts, Internat. Platform Assn., Kappa Pi. Republican. Lutheran. Home: 1012 E Blanchard El Paso TX 79902 Office: 1211 Montana El Paso TX 79902

SIQUEIROS, DAVID ALFARO, painter; b. Mexico City, Mexico, 1896; student Escuela Nacional de Bellas Artes, also schs. in Spain, France, Italy, 1917-22. Officer, Carranza's Army, 1910-16; mil. attache, Paris, 1917; editor Vida Americana, Spain; sec.-gen. Sindicato de Pentores, also editor house organ El Machte; organizer (with Amado de la Cueva) Alianza de Obreros Pintores, Guadalajara, 1925; founder Federacion Minera de Jalesco; rep. various Mexican workers' orgns. to Russia, 1928, del. workers' meetings in S.A., 1929; polit. exile, 1931; prof. Chouinard Sch. Art, Los Angeles, 1932-33; developed method for use air brushes to apply paint to outdoor murals; del. Congress Mexican Artists to Congress Revolutionary Artists, N.Y.C., 1936; established art sch., N.Y.C., 1936; prin. works include Fresco Chouinard Sch. Art, Plapa Art Center, Los Angeles, Mus. Modern Art, N.Y.C., Museo de Sao Paulo, Museo de Rio De Janeiro; murals in Bellas Artes, Hosp. de la Raza, Centro Medico, Museo de Historia, Castillo de Chapultepec, Escuela Nacional Preparatoria, U. Guadalajara (all Mex.), also in Argentina, Chile, Cuba. Served with Spanish Republican Army, 1937. Contbr. articles on art Mexican, European, South American periodicals. Address: care Revista de Mexico 3 Uruguay Mexico City DF Mexico

SIRCAR, ANIL KUMER, research chemist; b. Calcutta, India, Jan. 1, 1928; s. Aswini Kumer and Provabati (Sen) S.; B.Sc., Dacca U., 1948, M.Sc., 1949; D.Phil., Calcutta U., 1955; m. Smriti Palit, Aug. 7, 1951; children—Tamali, Manash, Tapash. Came to U.S., 1965. Chemist, Sindri Fertilizers & Chems. Ltd., Sindri, India, 1951-52; research officer Indian Assn. for Cultivation Sci., Calcutta, India, 1952-57, 58-59; research fellow U. Minn., Mpls., 1958; sr. sci. officer Indian Rubber Mfrs. Research Assn., Poona, India, 1960; mgr. lab. Nat. Rubber Mfrs. Ltd., Calcutta, 1960-65; research asso. So. Regional Research Lab., New Orleans, 1965-67; research chemist J.M. Huber Corp., Borger, Tex., 1967—. Hon. lectr. in rubber chemistry and examiner in polymer chemistry U. Calcutta, 1962-65. Named Outstanding Toastmaster Dist. 44 Toastmasters Internat., 1973. Fellow Royal Inst. Chemistry, London; mem. Am. Chem. Soc. (sec. Panhandle Plains sect. 1971, program chmn. 1972, pres. 1973; mem. rubber div., polymer chemistry div., organic coatings and plastics div.), N.Am. Thermal Analysis Soc. Club: Toastmasters (edn'l. v.p. Club 218 1972, pres. 1972, area gov. area VI dist. 44 1973—). Contbr. articles to sci. jours. Home: 304 Houston St Borger TX 79007 Office: PO Box 831 Borger TX 79007

SIRICA, JOHN J., U.S. judge, b. 1904; LL.B., Georgetown U., 1926; m. Lucile M. Camalier, Feb. 26, 1952; children—John J., Patricia Ann, Eileen Marie. Former mem. firm Hogan & Hartson, Washington; now judge U.S. Dist Ct. for D.C.; adj. prof. law Georgetown U. Law Center. Mem. Am. Bar Assn., Bar Assn. D.C. (hon.), Phi Alpha Delta. Clubs: Congressional Country, Nat. Lawyers, Lido Civic. Home: 5069 Overlook Rd NW Washington DC 20016 Office: US Ct House Washington DC 20001

SISK, HENRY LYBRAN, educator; b. Los Angeles, June 22, 1914; s. Joseph L. and Henrietta (Berry) S.; A.B., Ariz. State U., 1935; M.A., U. Ariz., 1937; Ph.D., Cornell U., 1939; m. Hazel Swain Halladay, Apr. 6, 1946; 1 son, Duncan L. Cons., Stevenson Jordan & Harrison, Inc., Chgo., 1947-49; dir. indsl. relations Milprint, Inc., Milw., 1949-52; supt. orgn. devel. Continental Can Co., Chgo., 1952-56; asst. to v.p. Dresser Co., Dallas, 1956-59; prof. bus. adminstrn. N. Tex. State U., Denton, 1960—. Labor arbitrator, also cons.; mem. Fed. Mediation Conciliation Service, Nat. Mediation Bd. Served to capt. AUS, 1942-46. Author: Principles of Management: A Systems Approach to The Management Process, 1969; Management and Organization, 1973. Home: 2803 Foxcroft Circle Denton TX 76201

SISK, JOHN KELLY, communications exec.; b. Cookeville, Tenn., Mar. 3, 1913; s. Thurman Kelly and Martha Jane (Sewell) S.; B.S., U. Ala., 1934; m. Isbell Lane, Sept. 30, 1936; children—John Kelly, Isbell Lane (Mrs. Lawton Irick, Jr.). Pres., chief exec. officer Multimedia

Inc., 1968-73, chmn., chief exec. officer, 1973—; chmn., pub. Greenville News-Piedmont Co. (S.C.); pres. Advertiser Co., Montgomery, Ala.; chmn. exec. com. Asheville Citizen-Times Printing Co. (N.C.), Multimedia Broadcasting Co., Greenville; dir. S.C. Nat. Bank, Liberty Life Ins. Co., A.P. Past bd. dirs. YMCA; past chmn. Greenville County Planning and Devel. Bd.; past chmn. Greenville County chpt. A.R.C. Trustee Converse Coll., Duke Endowment; adv. trustee Furman U.; past chmn. bd. trustees Greenville Gen. Hosp. C.P.A. N.Y., S.C. Mem. Downtown Greenville Assn. (dir. 1957), Am., So. (chmn. bd. 1964) newspaper pubs. assns., S.C. Press Assn. (pres. 1962), Greater Greenville C. of C. (pres. 1953), Phi Gamma Delta. Methodist. Clubs: Nat. Press; Poinsett, Greenville Country, Green Valley Country, Cotillion (Greenville); Biltmore (N.C.) Forest Country; Mountain City (Asheville, N.C.); Plantation (Hilton Head, S.C.). Home: 104 Parkins Lake Rd Greenville SC 29607 Office: 305 S Main St Greenville SC 29601

SISKIN, MILTON, dentist; b. Cleveland, Tenn., May 14, 1921; s. Max and Gertrude (Jacobson) S.; B.A., U. Tenn., 1942, D.D.S., 1945; m. LaVerne Lazarov, June 20, 1948; children—Milton, Gregory. Intern Walter G. Zoller Meml. Dental Clinic, Billings Hosp., Chgo., 1946-47, resident, 1947; instr. Coll. Dentistry, U. Tenn., 1947-51, asst. prof., 1951-58, asso. prof., 1958-64, prof., 1964—, chief div. oral medicine and surgery, head dept. oral medicine, 1955-58, lectr., dept. gen. anatomy and embryology Orthodontics; Grad. Sch. cons., VA Hosp., Lamar, 1951-57, VA Hosp., Kennedy br., Memphis, 1953—, John Gaston Hosp., Memphis, 1953—, central office VA, 1965—, Dental Adv. Service, Little People of Am., Harvard Sch. Dental Medicine, Indian Health Service; endodontic cons. Tenn. State Bd. Examiners, 1967—; others; cons. endodontics test constrn. com. Nat. Bd. Dental Examiners, 1972—. Rep. Regional Library Adv. Com. Served as lt. (j.g.) USNR, 1947. Recipient Thomas P. Hinman medallion, 1966; Tenn. Dental Assn. fellow, 1967. Diplomate Am. Bd. Oral Medicine, Am. Bd. Endodontics (com. on constn. and by-laws 1971—). Fellow A.A.A.S., Internat., Am. colls. dentists, Am. Acad. Oral Pathology, Am. Assn. Endodontics (dir. registry periapical lesion, chmn. edn. com. 1969-70, com. constn. and by-laws 1971—); mem. Am. Acad. Oral Roentgenology, Am. Acad. Dental Medicine (edn. com. 1962—, pres. tri-state sect. 1962, 63), Am. Assn. Dental Editors, Inst. Dental Medicine, Am. Inst. Oral Sci. (exec. com.), Am. Soc. Dentistry Children, N.Y. Acad. Scis., So. Endodontics Study Group, Am. Med. Writers' Assn., Am. Soc. Clin. Hypnosis, Am. Dental Assn. (cons. council on dental edn. 1967—, cons. council on hosp. dental service 1968—, council on fed. dental service 1971—, del. 13th and 14th Internat. Dental Congress), Fedn. Dentaire Internationale, Am. Cancer Soc. (local unit dir. 1958-62, 64-68, 70, exec. com. 1971—, elected to Hall Fame Memphis and Shelby County unit 1966, hon. dir. 1963-64, profl. edn. com. Tenn. div. 1971—, dir. 1971—), Zeta Beta Tau, Alpha Omega, Omicron Kappa Upsilon. Club: Executives (Memphis), Century, President's. Editorial staff Jour. Tenn. Dental Assn., 1951-55; guest editor Am. Profl. Pharmacists, 1962; asst. editor Jour. Dental Medicine, 1963—; cons. editor, contbr. Dental Clinics of N.Am.; editorial bd. Am. Assn. Endodontists, 1964; editor Proc. Conf. on Biology Human Dental Pulp, 1970-72. Contbr. articles profl. jours. and books. Home: 5209 Walnut Grove Rd Memphis TN 38117 Office: U Tenn Coll Dentistry 847 Monroe Av Memphis TN 38163

SISSOM, LEIGHTON ESTEN, univ. adminstr.; b. nr. Manchester, Tenn., Aug. 26, 1934; s. W.E. and Bertha Sarah (Davis) S.; B.S., Middle Tenn. State U., 1956; B.S. in M.E., Tenn. Poly. Inst., 1962; M.S. in M.E., Ga. Inst. Tech., 1964, Ph.D., 1965; m. Evelyn Janelle Lee, June 13, 1953; children—Terry Lee, Denny Leighton. Draftsman, Westinghouse Electric Corp., 1953-57; mech. designer Aro, Inc., Arnold Air Force Sta., Tenn., 1957-60; prof., chmn. dept. mech. engring. Tenn. Technol. U., Cookeville, 1965—. Bd. dirs., sec.-treas. Tenn. Technol. Engring. Devel. Found. NASA trainee 1962-65. Mem. Am. Soc. for Engring. Edn. (chmn. mech. engring. div. S.E. sect. 1973-74), Am. Soc. M.E. (chmn. mech. engring. dept. heads com. 1972-74, sec. nat. mech. dept. heads com. 1973-74). Nat. Tenn. socs. profl. engrs., Sigma Xi, Phi Kappa Phi, Tau Beta Pi, Pi Tau Sigma. Mem. Ch. of Christ. Author: (with D.R. Pitts) Elements of Transport Phenomena, 1972. Home: Gainesboro/Shipley Rds Cookeville TN 38501

SISTRUNK, WALTER EVERETT, educator; b. Montbrook, Fla., Apr. 6, 1920; s. Odis Carlos and Ruby Letillie (Howard) S.; A.A., Central Fla. Jr. Coll., 1960; B.A. in Edn. with honors, 1962, M.Ed., 1963; Ed.D., U. Fla., 1966; m. Marian Godwin, Feb. 6, 1943; children—Mary Kathryn, Michael E., David F., Carlos L., Walter Eugene, Brenda Gail. Farmer, mcht., 1945-55; asst. circulation mgr. Fla. Times Union, 1955-58; credit mgr. Marion Hardware Co., Ocala, Fla., 1958-62; head dept. social studies Bradford High Sch., Starke, Fla., 1962-65; dir. continuing edn. Brunswick Coll. (Ga.), 1965-66; asst. prof. elementary and secondary edn., dir. student tchrs. Miss. State U., 1966-68, asso. prof. edn. adminstrn., dir. learning labs., 1968-72, prof. ednl. adminstrn., 1972—. Cons., 1971-73, Choctaw Indian Schs., and many pub. sch. dists. Trustee Wood Jr. Coll., 1967-72. So. Edn. fellow, 1963-66; Fla. Tchr. scholar, 1959-62; named Bradford County Tchr. of Year, Fla. Edn. Assn., 1965. Mem. Am. Assn. Sch. Adminstrs., Miss. Edn. Assn., Miss. Assn. Sch. Adminstrs., Southeast Regional Assn. Tchr. Educators (pres. 1972-73), Assn. Tchr. Educators, Kappa Delta Pi, Phi Kappa Phi, Phi Delta Kappa. Democrat. Methodist. Mason, Rotarian. Author: (with Robert C. Maxson) A Practical Approach to Social Studies, 1972; (with Robert Maxson) A Systems Approach to Educational Administration, 1973; Instructional Planning, 1973; Principles of Secondary Teaching, 1973. Home: 1103 Robin Hood Rd Starkville MS 39759 Office: Drawer LH State College MS 39762

SITES, JOHN EDWARD, educator; b. Dayton, O., June 27, 1938; s. John Wilber and Peggy (Hunter) S.; B.A. in Edn., U. Fla., 1960; J.D., U. Miami, 1966; M.A., Appalachian State U., 1970; m. Joan Marie Paris, Sept. 24, 1965; 1 son, Jack Clinton. Classroom tchr. social studies Dade County (Fla.) Pub. Schs., 1960-63, inst. TV tchr. history, 1963-65, asst. prin. for adminstrn., 1965-66; research asst. Bradley, Johnson, Nelson & Young, Attys., Fla., 1966-67; prof. social scis. Brenau Coll., Gainesville, Ga., 1967-68, dean coll., prof. social scis., 1968—. Cons. Gainesville Model Cities, 1968—, U. Miami Endowment Com., 1969—, Ga. Council on Edn., 1968—, So. Assn. Colls. and Schs., 1972-73, Ga. Dept. Edn., 1973—, numerous others. Mem. Ga. Gov.'s Interagy. Child Care, 1974—; mem. Gainesville-Hall County Bicentennial Commn., 1974—. Recipient Outstanding Educator award Brenau Coll., 1971. Mem. Am., Ga. sociol. assns., So. Sociol. Soc., Ga. Conf. on Social Welfare (dir.), Acad. Deans So. States, Am. Conf. Acad. Deans, Am. Assn. for Higher Edn., Nat. Orgn. Legal Problems Edn., Ga. Adult Edn. Assn., A.A.A.S., Pi Kappa Alpha, Delta Theta Phi, Phi Delta Kappa, Phi Alpha Theta. Kiwanian. Author: (with others) Teacher's Guide to Basic Education, 1961; Teacher's Guide to World Geography, 1964; Teacher's Guide to ITV American History, 1965. Home: 916 Chattahoochee Dr NE Gainesville GA 30501

SITES, JOHN WILBUR, horticulturist, univ. dean.; b. Syracuse, N.Y., July 11, 1912; s. John Milton and Kathryn McKee (Hillery) S.; B.S., Ohio State U., 1935, M.S., 1940, Ph.D., 1950; m. Peggy Hunter, July 11, 1936; children—John Edward, Sharon Eleanor (Mrs. Joseph Pesek III), Kathryn Hunter (Mrs. Robert T. Shewey). Jr. horticulturist Dept. Agr., Zanesville, O., 1935-36, asst. horticulturist, 1936-42; asso. horticulturist U. Fla. Agrl. Expt. Stas., Lake Alfred, 1942-45, horticulturist, 1946-55, Gainesville, 1955-67, asst. dir., 1955-57, head fruit crops dept., 1957-60, asso. dir., 1960-67, dir., dean for research, 1967—. Pres., Winter Haven Pops (Fla.) Orch. Assn., 1954. Recipient Agrl. award for meritorious service Charles H. DuPont Found., 1970. Fellow Am. Soc. Hort. Sci.; mem. Am. Soc. Hort. Sci. (Gourley award for pomol. research 1951), Fla. Hort. Soc. (Krome Meml. Inst. award 1962), Soil and Plant Soc. Fla., Nat. Research Inst., Internat. Platform Assn., Sigma Xi, Alpha Gamma Rho, Gamma Sigma Delta, Pi Alpha Xi. Episcopalian (vestryman 1968—). Kiwanian (pres. Winter Haven 1950). Club: University of Fla. Faculty (pres. 1963-64). Home: 1819 SW 35th Av Gainesville FL 32608

SITWELL, PHRONSIE IRENE MARSH (MRS. HERBERT CECIL FITZROY SITWELL), poet, feature writer, educator; b. nr. Lynchburg, Va., Apr. 1, 1907; d. Peter Addison and Constance (Fisher) Marsh; student Lynchburg Coll., 1924-26; B.S., Mary Washington Coll., Fredericksburg, 1927; M.A., Columbia, 1932; summer study U. Va., 1925, 71, Inst. on World Affairs, Geneva, Switzerland, 1935, N.Y.U., 1940-41, U. Pa., 1957; postgrad. Va. Poly. Inst., 1966-67, U. Va., 1970-71; m. Erik Solling Monberg, Apr. 25, 1943 (div. 1947); 1 son, Edmund Marsh; m. 2d, Herbert Cecil FitzRoy Sitwell, May 14, 1961 (dec. Aug. 1965). Tchr. Salem (Va.) High Sch., 1927-28, E. C. Glass High Sch., Lynchburg, 1928-30, Oyster Bay, N.Y., 1930-34, Washington, 1934-44, 50-62; adminstrv. asst. TVA, 1933; gen. supr. edn. Wythe County Schs., Wytheville, Va., 1945-46; instr. Phillips Coll., Lynchburg, 1946-47; ednl. adviser Sullins Coll., Bristol, Va., 1947-49; social studies chmn. Capitol Page Sch., 1949-50; Ofcl. visitor 3d Internat. Congress on Comparative Law, The Hague, Netherlands, 1937; mem. Columbia Writers' Conf., 1966. Del. Va. Dem. Conv., 1970; mem. Dem. Com. of Bedford County. Recipient fellowship to Nat. Music Camp, Interlochen, Mich., to write scripts for NBC broadcast, 1940, fellowship to N.Y.U., 1941, U. Pa., summer 1957. Mem. Am., Phila. acads. polit. sci., Modern Lang. Assn., Soc. Archtl. Historians, Poetry Soc. Va., Nat. Trust Historic Preservation, Nat. League Am. Pen Women (v.p. charge creative activities D.C. br. 1939-41), Arts Club Washington, U.D.C., Internat. Platform Speakers Assn., Poetry Soc. Bedford (co-founder, pres. 1961-62, 70-71), English Speaking Union, Charlottesville Va., Lynchburg, Bedford hist. socs., Pi Gamma Mu, Episcopalian. Clubs: Specs, Writers of Va., Woman's (pres. Oyster Bay, N.Y. 1932-34). Contbr. poems Maelstrom, VPI, 1966, newspapers, mags., others; also articles. Home: Three Otters Estate RFD 2 Bedford VA 24523 also 1106 Federal St Lynchburg VA 24504

SIVLEY, ROBERT BENTON, psychologist; b. Chattanooga, Feb. 2, 1934; s. Grover Benton and Alma (Boyd) S.; B.A., David Lipscomb Coll., 1955; M.A., George Peabody Coll., 1956, Ph.D., 1960; m. Barbara Outten, Apr. 23, 1960; children—Bobby, John, William. Chief psychologist Central State Hosp., Nashville, 1960-61; psychologist VA Hosp., Murfreesboro, Tenn., 1961-67; exec. dir. Pennyroyal Regional Mental Health Center, Hopkinsville, Ky., 1967—; vis. lectr. U. Ky., Hopkinsville Community Coll.; cons. Western State Hosp., Outwood State Hosp. and Sch. Mem. Human Relations Commn., 1969—. Mem. Am., Southeastern, Ky. psychol. assns. Rotarian. Home: 131 S Sunset Circle Hopkinsville KY 42240 Office: 735 North Dr Hopkinsville KY 42240

SIZER, PHILLIP SPELMAN, oil field service co. exec.; b. Whittier, Cal., Apr. 11, 1926; s. Frank Milton and Helen Louise (Saylor) S.; B.S. in Mech. Engring., So. Meth. U., 1948; m. Evelyn Sue Jones, Aug. 16, 1952; children—Phillip Spelman, Ves W. With Otis Engring. Corp., Dallas, 1948—, project engr., 1958-62, chief devel. engr., 1962-70, v.p. research and devel., 1970-73, v.p. engring. and research, 1973—. Fellow Am. Soc. M.E. (named Engr. of Yr. N. Tex. sect. 1971); mem. Soc. Petroleum Engrs., Kappa Sigma, Kappa Mu Epsilon, Sigma Tau, Tau Beta Pi. Club: Petroleum Engineers (Dallas). Patentee in field. Home: 14127 Tanglewood Dr Dallas TX 75234 Office: PO Box 34380 Dallas TX 75234

SJOBERG, SIGURD ARNOLD, aerospace engr.; b. Mpls., Sept. 2, 1919; s. John and Anna Charlotte (Erickson) S.; B.S. in Aero. Engring., U. Minn., 1942; D.Sc. (hon.), DePauw U., 1972; m. Elizabeth Jane Ludwig, Jan. 8, 1944; children—Eric, Stephen, Robert. Aero. engr. NACA, 1942-59, operations coordinator NASA-Manned Spacecraft Center, Houston, 1959-62, asst. to chief flight operations div. Manned Spacecraft Center, Houston, 1962-63, test dir. Apollo abort test operations White Sands Missile Range, N.M., 1963, dep. dir. flight operations, Houston, 1963-69, dir. flight operations, 1969-72, dep. dir. Johnson Space Center (former Manned Spacecraft Center), 1972—. Recipient NASA Exceptional Service medals (2), 1969; NASA Distinguished Service medal, 1971; Outstanding Achievement award U. Minn., 1973. Home: 203 Pine Shadows Dr Seabrook TX 77586 Office: NASA-Johnson Space Center Houston TX 77058

SKAGGS, HORACE GRANT, dentist; b. Sublett, Ky., Sept. 11, 1912; s. Doctor Randolph and Sallie Mandy (Lemaster) S.; student U. Ky., 1932-33, postgrad., 1935-39; D.M.D., U. Louisville, 1939; m. Mildred Louise Mansfield, Sept. 2, 1933; children—William Randolph, Horace Grant. Pvt. practice dentistry, Paintsville and Lynch, Ky., 1939-41, Ashland, Ky., 1945—; mem. staff Kings Daus. Hosp., Ashland. Mem. YMCA, 1953—. Bd. dirs. Tb Assn. Served with AUS, 1941-45; capt. Res. Fellow Royal Soc. Health; mem. Ky. Dental Assn., Eastern Dist. Dental Soc. (pres. 1956), Am. Dental assn., S.A.R., Internat. Platform Assn., Psi Omega. Baptist. Mason (32 deg.), Rotarian, Toastmaster (past pres.). Home: 2638 Virginia Av Ashland KY 41101 Office: 307-8 2d Nat Bank Bldg Ashland KY 41101

SKEITH, JACK THERON, utility co. exec.; b. Colorado Springs, Colo., Aug. 9, 1921; s. Jess Arthur and Blanch Louise (Ryan) S.; B.S., U. Okla., 1949; m. Bezelia May Harrison, July 9, 1945; children—Barbara (Mrs. John Edwin Guinn III), Richard. With Okla. Natural Gas Co., Tulsa, 1949—, mgr. gas supply and reserves, 1964-73, v.p. gas supply, 1973—. Mem. Natural Gas Men of Okla. (pres. 1970-71), Petroleum Club of Tulsa (pres. 1973-74). Kiwanian (chmn. new club extensions 1972-73). Home: 6735 S 67th St Tulsa OK 74133 Office: PO Box 871 Tulsa OK 74102

SKELTON, DOROTHY GENEVA SIMMONS (MRS. JOHN WILLIAM SKELTON), educator; b. Woodland, Cal.; d. Jack Elijah and Helen Anna (Siebe) Simmons; B.A., U. Cal., 1940, M.A., 1943; m. John William Skelton, July 16, 1941. Sr. research analyst War Dept., Gen. Staff, M.I. Div. G-2, Washington, 1944-45; vol. researcher, monuments, fine arts and archives sect. Restitution Br., Office Mil. Govt. for Hesse, Wiesbaden, Germany, 1947-48; vol. art tchr. German children in Bad Nauheim, Germany, 1947-48; art educator, lectr. Dayton (O.) Art Inst., 1955; art educator Lincoln Sch., Dayton, 1956-60; art edn. instr. U. Va. Sch. Continuing Edn., Charlottesville, 1962—; researcher in genealogy; exhibited in group shows, Cal., Colo., Ohio, Washington and Va. Represented in permanent collections Madison Hall, Charlottesville, Madison Center, Madison, Va. Mem. Nat. League Am. Pen Women, Am. Assn. Museums, Coll. Art Assn. Am., Nat. Soc. Arts and Letters, Inst. for Study of Art in Edn., Dayton Soc. Painters and Sculptors, Va. Mus. Fine Arts, Cal. Alumni Assn., Am. Assn. U. Women, Air Force Officers Wives Club. Republican. Methodist. Clubs: Army Navy Country; Lake of the Woods (Va.) Golf and Country. Address: Lotos Lakes Brightwood VA 22715

SKELTON, HOWARD CLIFTON, marketing exec.; b. Birmingham, Ala., Mar. 6, 1932; s. Howard C. and Sarah Ethel (Holmes) S.; B.S., Auburn U., 1955; m. Winifred Harriet Karger, May 19, 1962; 1 dau., Susan Lynn. Copywriter Rich's, Inc., Atlanta, 1955-59; copywriter Ga. Power Co., Atlanta, 1959-61; dir. advt. and sales promotion Callaway Mills, Inc., LaGrange, Ga., 1961-65; dir. advt. and sales promotion Thomasville Furniture Industries (N.C.), 1965-66; v.p. in charge of fashion and textiles Gaynor & Ducas, N.Y.C., 1966-70; dir. communications Collins & Aikman, N.Y.C., 1970-73; exec. v.p. Marketplace, Inc., Atlanta, 1973-74; dir. marketing and communications Internat. City Corp., Atlanta, 1974—. Served with Signal Corps, AUS, 1956-58. Recipient Danforth Found. award, 1950. Mem. Omicron Delta Kappa, Lambda Chi Alpha, Sigma Delta Chi. Home: 5276 Willow Point Pkwy Mariet.a GA 30062 Office: First Nat Bank Tower Atlanta GA 30303

SKELTON, JESSE DANIEL, petroleum co. exec.; b. Wichita, Kan., Apr. 24, 1923; s. Jesse Albert and Anne (Goodman) S.; B.E.E., Kan. State U., 1948; M.E.E., Okla. State U., 1954; m. Gloria F. Mulcahy, May 21, 1944; children—Janet Sue (Mrs. Reed Wood), Linda Kae (Mrs. Ellis Clark III), Karen Ann (Mrs. Russell Mai). Research engr. Carter Oil Co., Tulsa, 1948; div. mgr. Jersey Prodn. Research, Tulsa, 1958-64; dir., v.p. exploration research Esso Prodn. Research, Houston, 1964-67; asst. div. exploration mgr. Humble Oil & Refining Co., Houston, 1967-69; exploration data processing mgr. Exxon Co., U.S.A., Houston, 1969—. Served to 1st lt. USAAC, 1943-46. Mem. Am. Assn. Petroleum Geologists, Internat. Assn. for Math. Geology, Marine Tech. Soc., Soc. Exploration Geophysicists (v.p. 1973—), Sigma Tau, Eta Kappa Nu, Phi Kappa Phi. Republican. Baptist (deacon 1955-73, tchr. 1960-73). Home: 13902 Pinerock Lane Houston TX 77024 Office: PO Box 2180 Houston TX 77001

SKINNER, EDGAR ROBERT, accountant; b. St. Louis, Jan. 13, 1908; s. Edgar Ritter and Anna Marie (Byrne) S.; B.C.S., St. Louis U., 1930; m. Katherine Marie Byers, Sept. 21, 1935; children—Carroll Ann (Mrs. Joseph A. Savarino), Katherine Marie (Mrs. Wade William Beckman III). C.P.A., Price, Waterhouse & Co., St. Louis, 1930-45; mgr. Slick Airlines, San Antonio, 1945-50, treas. Slick Oil Co., San Antonio, 1945-54; financial and tax mgr. George W. Strake, Houston, 1954-63; self-employed as C.P.A., Houston, 1963—. Lectr. cost accounting St. Louis U., 1942-44. Bd. dirs. Bering Homecenter, Houston, Nat. Found. March of Dimes, Houston. C.P.A., Mo., Tex. Home: 2670 Marilee St Houston TX 77027 Office: 805 Bankers Mortgage Bldg Houston TX 77002

SKINNER, FRANK DOUGLAS, editor; b. Shreveport, La., May 13, 1926; s. Douglas N. and Charlotte (Rohrbough) S.; B.A. in Journalism, U. Okla., 1947; m. Anna Jean Gray, Dec. 12, 1953; children—Douglas Gray, Mary Craig. News editor, Anadarko (Okla.) Daily News, 1948-53; asst. news editor Mich. State U., 1953-56; univ. news editor, 1956-62; pub. information officer Chatham Coll., 1963-66; editor Higher Edn. and Nat. Affairs, Am. Council on Edn., Washington, 1966—. Recipient feature writing, make-up awards Okla. Press Assn., 1949, 1951, Edn. News award Am. Coll. Pub. Relations Assn., 1960. Mem. Edn. Writers Assn. Contbr. to profl. jours. Home: 6319 Utah Av NW Washington DC 20015 Office: 1 Dupont Circle Washington DC 20036

SKINNER, HUBERT C(LAYTON), educator; b. Tulsa, Oct. 3, 1929; s. Orlo C. and Onamae (Hood) S.; B.S. in Geology, U. Okla., 1951, M.S., 1953, Ph.D., 1954; m. Judith Ann Miller, Dec. 27, 1958; children—Susan, Sharon, Kathryn. Museum technician U. Okla., 1951-52, grad. asst., 1952-53, teaching asst., summer 1953, instr. geology, 1953-54, summer 1954; supr. Paleontol. Lab. La. div. Texaco, Inc., 1954-57; asst. prof. Tulane U., 1954-57, asso. prof., 1957-62, prof., 1962—, editor Tulane Studies in Geology and Paleontology, 1962—; vis. prof. U. Okla., summer 1965. Served with USAFR, 1951-58. Fellow Geol. Soc. Am.; mem. Paleontol. Soc., Paleontol. Assn. Great Britain, Am. Assn. Petroleum Geologists, Soc. Econ. Paleontologists and Mineralogists, Sigma Xi, Sigma Gamma Epsilon (nat. pres. 1965-70, nat. historian, 1970—), Phi Sigma. Research, numerous pubs. sci., tech. jours. Home: 3737 Napoleon Av New Orleans LA 70125

SKINNER, ROY GENE, basketball coach; b. Paducah, Ky., Apr. 17, 1930; s. Marion Henry and Ruby (Tapp) S.; diploma Paducah Jr. Coll., 1950; A.B., Presbyn. Coll., 1952; M.A., George Peabody Coll., 1958; m. Betty Jo Ledford, June 3, 1952; children—Kim Henry, Brad Steven, Chris, Joe Brant, Tapp Blaine, Dea. Dir., Found. Boys' Club, Portsmouth, Va., 1953; tchr., coach Cradock High Sch., Portsmouth, 1954-56, Paducah Jr. Coll., 1957; asst. coach Vanderbilt U., Nashville, 1957-61, head basketball coach, 1961—. Lectr., coach under U.S. State Dept. specialist grant, Taipei, Taiwan, 1963. Named Coach of Year, Nashville Banner, 1963, Young Man of Year, Jr. C. of C., 1963, S.E. Conf. Coach of Year, 1965, 1967, 74, Nat. Collegiate Athletic Assn. Dist. III Coach of Year, 1974. Mem. Nat. Collegiate Athletic Assn., Basketball Assn. Republic China (hon.). Mem. Christian Ch. Contbr. articles to sports publs. Office: Vanderbilt U Nashville TN 37203

SKIPPER, HOWARD EARLE, biochemist; b. Avon Park, Fla., Nov. 21, 1915; B.S., U. Fla., 1938, M.S., 1939, Ph.D. in Nutrition and Biochemistry, 1941; m. 1941; two children. Head biochemistry div., So. Research Inst., 1946-48, asst. dir., 1948-63; v.p. also dir. Kettering-Meyer Labs, 1964—; prof. exptl. pathology Med. Center, U. Ala., 1955—. Mem. adv. com. isotopes, AEC, 1953-56; pharmacological and exptl. therapeutical study sect. USPHS, 1954-56; pharmacological-biochem. panel Cancer Chemotherapy Nat. Service Center, 1956-59, drug evaluation panel, 1958-59, also chmn. cancer chemotherapy rev. bd. NIH, 1958-60; nat. adviser Cancer Council, 1958-60, 64—, dissemination, field testing com., U.S. Army Chem. Corps., 1961-63, also bd. sci. cons. Nat. Cancer Inst., 1961-64; sci. adv. com., Sloan-Kettering Inst. Cancer Research. Trustee, C.F. Kettering Found. Served with CWS, AUS, 1941-46. Mem. Chem. Soc., Soc. Biol. Chem., Assn. Cancer Research. Address: 703 Euclid Av Birmingham AL 35213*

SKJONSBY, HAROLD SAMUEL, histologist, educator; b. Sisseton, S.D., July 6, 1937; s. Alfred Bernard and Elna Louise (Carlson) S.; B.S., Concordia Coll., 1959; M.S., U. N.D., 1962, Ph.D., 1964; m. Barbara Jean Stenberg, Aug. 20, 1961; children—Adam, Nathan, Amy. Asst. prof. dept. histology U. Tex Dental br., Houston, 1964-69, asso. prof., 1969—, also head dept. histology. Pres., Willow Creek Little League, 1972-73. Bd. dirs. Fun Football. Nat. Def. fellow, 1959-62. Mem. A.A.A.S., Sigma Xi. Lutheran (pres. 1970-72). Home: 4325 Hummingbird St Houston TX 77035

SKLAR, ALEXANDER, bus. cons.; b. N.Y.C., May 18, 1915; s. David and Bessie (Wolf) S.; student Cooper Union, N.Y.C., 1932-35; m . Hilda Rae Gevarter, Oct. 27, 1940; 1 dau., Carolyn Mae (Mrs. Louis M. Taff). Chief design engr. Aerovox Corp., New Bedford,

Mass., 1933-39; mgr. mfg., engring. Indsl. Condenser Corp., Chgo., 1939-44; owner Capacitron, Inc., 1944-48; v.p. mfg. Jefferson Electric Co., Bellwood, Ill., 1948-65; v.p., gen. mgr. electro-mech. div. Essex Wire Corp., Detroit, 1965-67; v.p. operations Circle F. Industries, 1968; adviser, dir. various corp., 1969—; adj. prof. mgmt. Fla. Atlantic U., Boca Raton, 1970—; lectr. profl. mgmt. U. Cal., Los Angeles, Harvard Grad. Sch. Bus. Adminstrn., U. Ill. Coll. Dentistry. Chmn., Century Club Community Fund, 1961; mng. com. Oak Park Community Lectures, 1963-66. Vice pres., bd. dirs. Nat. Conf. Christians and Jews. Address: 4100 Galt Ocean Dr Fort Lauderdale FL 33308

SKOLNICK, ALFRED, naval officer; b. Bklyn., Aug. 15, 1930; s. Samuel and Florette Gladys (Doktor) S.; B.S., Queens Coll., 1951; M.A., Columbia, 1952; M.S., U.S. Naval Postgrad. Sch., Monterey, Cal., 1960; Ph.D., Poly. Inst. Bklyn., 1965; m. Sara Heloise Hatcher, June 8, 1957; children—David Harold, Susan Alyn. Aerophysicist, chance Vought Aircraft, Dallas, 1952-53; commd. ensign USN, 1953, advanced through grades to capt., 1974; surface to air missile officer Johns Hopkins Applied Physics Lab., 1953-56; missile fire control officer U.S.S. Boston, 1956-57; systems integration officer ships inertial nav. Polaris Project, Washington, 1960-62; spl. asst. for design, deep submergence systems project, Washington, 1965-66; dir. tech. Joint Navy/Commerce SES Project Office, Washington, 1967-72; asst. project mgr. for combat systems Surface Effect Ships Project Office, Bethesda, Md., 1972-74, dir. combat systems integration div. Naval Sea Systems Command, 1974—. Mem. adj. faculty U. Va. Sch. Continuing Edn., Falls Church, 1967—; lectr. No. Va. Community Coll., Alexandria, 1965—; mem. steering com. radio tech. commn. on marine scis. FCC, 1971—. Pres., Northpoint Civic Assn., Dix Hills, L.I., 1963-64. Mem. I.E.E.E., U.S. Naval Inst., Sigma Xi, Phi Epsilon Pi. Unitarian (trustee ch. 1972—). Mason. Home: 5432 N Carlin Springs Rd Arlington VA 22203 Office: PO Box 34401 Bethesda Md 20034

SKOLNICK, MALCOLM HARRIS, med. sch. adminstr.; b. Salt Lake City, Aug. 11, 1935; s. Max Cantor and Charlotte Sylvia (Letman) S.; B.S. in Physics (Ford Found. scholar), U. Utah, 1956; M.S. in Physics, Cornell U., 1959, Ph.D. in Theoretical Physics, 1962; m. Lois Marlene Ray, Sept. 1, 1959; children—Michael, David, Sara, Jonathan. Formerly with ednl. materials devel. Edn. Service Inc., Watertown, Mass.; researcher Inst. Advanced Study, Princeton, N.J.; sci. researcher, tchr. Mass. Inst. Tech.; math. and sci. tchr. tng. Endl. Devel. Center, Newton, Mass.; mem. staff Health Sci. Center State U. N.Y. at Stony Brook; now adminstr., instructional tech. dir. biomed. communications U. Tex. Med. Sch., Houston; chmn. health care systems and tech. study sect. Nat. Center Health Services Research Dept., Dept. Health, Edn. and Welfare, 1974-76; cons. in field. Dir. Pub. Systems Research, Inc. Mem. Three Village Sch. Bd., Setauket, N.Y., 1970-71. Served with USNR, 1961. Cornell U. teaching and research fellow. Mem. Am. Phys. Soc., Am. Assn. Physics Tchrs., A.A.A.S., Assn. Computing Machinery, Biophys. Soc., Assn. Devel. Computer-based Instructional Systems, N.Y. Acad. Sci., Am. Assn. Physicists in Medicine, Sigma Xi. Research biomed. image processing thermodynamics biomonolayers, instructional tech. and electronic data processing. Home: 733 Brogden Rd Houston TX 77024 Office: U Tex Med Center 6400 W Cullen St Houston TX 77025

SKONBERG, CARL MARLING, govt. ofcl.; b. Paxton, Ill., June 21, 1909; s. Carl J. and Hilma Clarinda (Skog) S.; Ph.B., U. Chgo., 1932, M.B.A., 1941; m. Charlotte L. Meyer, Apr. 3, 1937; 1 son, John. Sec., Builders & Mfrs. Casualty Co., Chgo., 1934-38; mem. research staff Marshall Field & Co., Chgo., 1938-42, expense asst., 1948; economist OPA and WPB, Washington, 1942-46; def. prodn. adminstr. SBA, Washington, 1949-54; economist Bur. Econs., FTC, Washington, 1954—. Lectr., Am. U., Washington, 1961-69. Mem. Am. Econ. Assn., Am. Marketing Assn. Home: 6655 Van Winkle Dr Falls Church VA 22044 Office: FTC Washington DC 20580

SKRABANEK, ROBERT LEONARD, sociologist, educator; b. Snook, Tex., Nov. 18, 1918; s. John T. and Frances (Bravenec) S.; B.S., Tex. A. and M. U., 1942, M.S., 1946; Ph.D., La. State U., 1949; m. Kathryn A. Kohler, Dec. 1, 1943; children—John, Marian. Grad. asst. Tex. A. and M. U., 1946-47; research asst. and instr. La. State U., 1947-49; asst. prof. sociology to prof. sociology Tex. A. and M. U., College Station, 1949—, chmn. sociology div., 1963-70, head dept. sociology and anthropology, 1970-72, prof., 1972—; vis. prof. So. Meth. U., 1961, Iliff Sch. Theology, 1964; cons. U.S. AID in Colombia and Ecuador, 1962, Ford Found. in Dominican Republic, 1963. Mem. bd. dirs. Brazos County Counselling Service, 1965—, Tex. Social Welfare Assn., 1967. Served to lt. USNR, 1942-46; PTO. Mem. Am., Southwestern (past pres.) sociol. assns., Population Assn. Am., Southwestern Social Sci. Assn., Tex. Acad. Sci., Rural Sociol. Soc., Phi Kappa Phi, Sigma Xi, Alpha Kappa Delta, Gamma Sigma Delta, Delta Tau Kappa. Contbr. articles in field to profl. jours., also books. Home: 307 Gilchrist Av College Station TX 77840

SKYE, WILLIAM EMILE, lawyer; b. Alexandria, La., Feb. 26, 1921; s. Emile and Ethel (Hemphill) S.; student Tulane U., 1937-38, La. Coll., 1938-39; B.A., U. Wis., 1942; J.D., La. State U., 1950; m. Sue Bennye Gilham, Apr. 9, 1970; 1 dau., Julie Roberta. Admitted to La. bar, 1950; since practiced in Alexandria, 1950—. Mem. Rapides Parish Sch. Bd., 1966-73. Served with USMC, 1942-45. Mem. Am., La., Alexandria (pres. 1965-66) bar assns., Am. Legion, Am. Judicature Soc., Order Coif., V.F.W. Democrat. Mason (Shriner). Home: 2702 Elliott St Alexandria LA 71301 Office: 608 Murray St Alexandria LA 71201

SLACK, DERALD ALLEN, educator, plant pathologist; b. Cedar City, Utah, Dec. 22, 1924; s. Fredrick and Marscella (Perry) S.; B.S., Utah State U., 1949, M.S., 1950; Ph.D., U. Wis., 1952; m. Betty Lue Stevens, Dec. 5, 1944; children—Steven Allen, Bonnie Lue. Asst. prof. U. Ark., Fayetteville, 1952-54, asso. prof., 1954-59, prof., 1959-64, prof., head dept., 1964—. Bd. mem., sec. Ark. State Plant Bd., 1964—. Served with USAF, 1943-45. Recipient Outstanding Instr. award U. Ark., 1956; Distinguished Achievement award for research and teaching U. Ark., 1961. Mem. Am. Phytopath. Soc., Soc. Nematologists (charter; editor Nematology Newsletter 1958-62), Ark. Hort. Soc., Ark. Pesticide Assn., Helminthological Soc. Washington, Ark. Acad. Sci., Sigma Xi (pres. Ark. chpt. 1961-63), Gamma Sigma Delta, Farm House (pres. Ark. Farm House Assn. 1961—). Author: (with others) Plant Pathology Laboratory Manual, 3d edit., 1968. Contbr. articles to sci. jours. Home: 1535 Hefley Fayetteville AR 72701

SLACK, MARY KNOX PULLIAM (MRS. RICHARD JOHN SLACK), librarian; b. San Angelo, Tex., Oct. 1, 1912; d. Mark Bell and Mary Knox (Powell) Pulliam; student So. Meth. U., 1929-30; B.J., U. Mo., 1933; postgrad. Shorter Coll., 1968; M. Librarianship, Emory U., 1970; m. Richard John Slack, Aug. 19, 1935; children—Ann Knox (Mrs. Richard R. Lorelle), Mary Susan (Mrs. Robert Wycliffe Cheatham, Jr.). Corr., Dallas Jour., 1934-35; copywriter Robert E. Martin Co., Atlanta, 1943-44; serials librarian Shorter Coll., Rome, Ga., 1968-70, reference, serials librarian, 1970-72, asst. prof. ednl. media, 1971-72; founder, head bus. library Tri-County Regional Library, Rome, 1972-74; med. librarian N.W. Ga. Regional Hosp., Rome, 1974—. Founder, Floyd Hosp. Sch. Nursing Library, Rome, 1968, cons., 1968—. Vol. A.R.C., 1957-67. Mem. Am. (regional audiovisual rev. com. Booklist 1970-73), Southeastern, Ga. (2d v.p. 1973—), library assns., Am. Assn. Higher Edn., Ga. Assn. Educators, N.E.A., Med. Library Assn., Spl. Libraries Assn., D.A.R., Gamma Alpha Chi, Delta Gamma. Democrat. Episcopalian. Home: 600 Redmond Rd Apt B-2 Rome GA 30161 Office: NW Ga Regional Hosp Rome GA 30161

SLADCZYK, GEORGE, JR., lawyer; b. Port Arthur, Tex., Mar. 28, 1930; s. George and Mary Cleo (Claycomb) S.; B.B.A., U. Tex., 1955, J.D. with honors, 1956; m. Eleanor McIlwain Stevens, June 23, 1951; 1 dau., Amy. Admitted to Tex. bar, 1956; asso. firm Orgain, Bell & Tucker, Beaumont, Tex., 1956-59; pvt. practice law, Port Arthur, 1959-72; mem. firm Sladczyk, Peckham & Walker, Port Arthur, 1972—. Bd. dirs. Simbolo, Inc. Served to 1st lt. USAF, 1951-55. Mem. State Bar Tex., Tex. Assn. Def. Counsel, Maritime Law Assn., Jefferson County Bar Assn. (chmn. grievance com. 1961-69). Club: Port Arthur. Casenote editor Tex. Law Rev., 1955-56. Home: 5930 Gladys Beaumont TX 77706 Office: 3015 Plaza Circle Port Arthur TX 77640

SLADE, ROY, artist, ednl. adminstr.; b. Cardiff, U.K., July 14, 1933; s. David Trevor and Millicent (Stone) S.; N.D.D., Cardiff Coll. Art, 1954; A.T.D., U. Wales, 1954; m. Rona Jones, July 20, 1957. Came to U.S., 1967. Tchr. art and crafts Heolgam High Sch., Wales, 1956-60; lectr. art Clarendon Coll., Nottingham, Eng., 1960-64; sr. lectr. fine art Leeds Coll. Art, Eng., 1964-67; prof. painting Corcoran Sch. Art, Washington, 1967-68, asso. dean, 1969-70, dean, 1970—; acting dir. Corcoran Gallery of Art, Washington, 1972, dir., 1973—; sr. lectr. Leeds Coll. Art, Eng., 1968-69; exhibited one-man shows Howard Roberts Gallery, Cardiff, Wales, 1958, New Art Center, London, Eng., 1960, U. Birmingham, 1964, 69, Herbert Art Gallery and Museum, Coventry, 1964, Va. State Art League, 1967, Museum of Arts and Crafts, Columbus, Ga., 1968, Jefferson Place Gallery, Washington, 1968, 70, 72, 73, Park Sq. Gallery, Leeds, 1969, St. Mary's Coll. (Md.), 1971, Guelph U. (Ont., Can.), 1971; exhibited group shows U.K., N.Y.C., Can.; represented in permanent collections Arts Council Gt. Britain, Contemporary Art Soc., Nuffield Found., Ministry of Works, Eng., Brit. Embassy, Washington, Brit. Overseas Airways Corp., U. Birmingham, Wakefield City Art Gallery, Clarendon Coll., Cadbury Bros. Ltd., Eng., Lord Ogmore, Local Education Authorities; vis. Boston Museum of Fine Arts, 1970. Served with Brit. Army, 1954-56. Recipient award Welsh Soc., Phila., 1974. Fulbright scholar, 1967-68. Club: George Washington University. Address: Corcoran Gallery of Art 17th St and New York Av Washington DC 20006

SLAPPEY, MARY MCGOWAN, journalist; b. Kittrell, N.C., Nov. 22, 1914; d. Walter Gordon and Mary Jouvette (McGowan) Slappey; student Am. U., 1938-39; A.B. in Polit. Sci., George Washington U., 1947; student Corcoran Sch. Art, 1950-57. Tchr. in charge Nat. Bus. Sch., Washington, 1952-59; asst. to editor nat. publs. Nat. Council Catholic Men, Washington, 1959-66; exec. editor Nat. Newman Apostolate, U.S. Cath. Conf., 1966-69; free-lance reporter, writer, Washington, 1969—. Served with WAVES, 1942-46. Mem. Fed. Poets Washington, Internat. Platform Assn., Am. Artists Profl. League, Nat. Writers Club, Columbian Women George Washington U., Pi Gamma Mu. Author: Firelosophy & Inspiration, 1932, Crossroads of Eternity, 1947; editor Cath. Traveler, 1967. Home: 4500 Chesapeake St N W Washington DC 20016 Office: 1250 Connecticut Av NW Washington DC 20036

SLATER, ALTON RAY, elec. engr.; b. Gandy, La., Jan. 15, 1926; s. Sidney Troy and Arizona (Coburn) S.; B.S. in Elec. Engring., U. Houston, 1955; m. Jeannette Robinson, Nov. 17, 1951; children—Alton Ray, Calvin Dale, Ronald Paul, Gerald Mark. Elec. engr. Walter Kidde Engrs., Houston, 1956-58, Sip Engrs., Inc., Houston, 1958-59; elec. project engr. Brown & Root, Inc., Houston, 1950-56, 59—. Served with USAAF, 1944-46. Sr. mem. I.E.E.E.; mem. Instrument Soc. Am., Lazybrook Civic Club, Timbergrove Dads Club. Baptist (tchr., pres. brotherhood, dir. tng.). Home: 1823 Greengrass Ct Houston TX 77008 Office: PO Box 3 Houston TX 77001

SLATER, OLIVER EUGENE, bishop; b. Sibley, La., Sept. 10, 1906; s. Oliver Thornwell and Mattie (Kennon) S.; A.B., So. Meth. U., 1930, B.D., 1932; D.D. (hon.), McMurry Coll., Abilene, Tex., 1951; L.H.D., Southwestern Coll., Winfield, Kan., 1961; LL.D., Baker U., 1962, So. Meth. U., 1964; m. Eva B. Richardson, Nov. 25, 1931; children—Susan (Mrs. H. Kipling Edenborough), Stewart Eugene. Ordained to ministry Methodist Ch., 1932; pastor in Rochelle, Tex., 1932-33, Menard, Tex., 1933-36, Ozona, Tex., 1936-42, San Antonio, 1942-44, Houston, 1944-50, Polk St. Ch., Amarillo, Tex., 1950-60; consecrated bishop, 1960; bishop of Kan. Area Meth. Ch., 1960-64, of San Antonio-N.W. Tex. area, 1964-68; bishop San Antonio area, 1968—. Mem. Interbd. Commn. for Enlistment Ch. Occupations, 1968-72. Mem. jurisdictorial confs., Meth. Ch., 1948, 56, 60, gen. confs., 1956, 60, pres. gen. bd. edn., 1964-72. Mem. Bd. Edn., 1960-72; pres. Council of Bishops, 1972-73. Chmn. Commn. on Archives and History, 1972—. Liaison bishop from United Meth. Council Bishops to Korean Meth. Ch., 1968—. Mem. bd. Global Ministries, 1972—; trustee So. Meth. U., Southwestern U. Home: 4022 Fawnridge Dr San Antonio TX 78229 Office: 535 Bandera PO Box 28509 San Antonio TX 78228

SLATER, TERRENCE LYONS, lawyer; b. Syracuse, N.Y., Dec. 20, 1928; s. Joseph Harold and Marie (Argus) S.; B.A., Georgetown U., 1951, LL.B., 1954; m. Joan Salomone, Oct. 8, 1960; children—Katherine Marie, Maureen Anne. Admitted to D.C. bar, 1954; atty. Fed. Communications Commn., Washington, 1956-66; atty. Internat. Tel. & Tel. Corp., Washington, 1966—. Served with AUS, 1954-56. Mem. Fed., Am. bar assns., Fed. Communications Bar Assn., Eta Sigma Phi. Home: 6320 N 24th St Arlington VA 22207 Office: 1707 L St NW Washington DC 20036

SLATON, GAYNELL RAY, state ofcl.; b. Baton Rouge, July 30, 1939; s. Earl E. and Marjorie (Braithwaite) S.; B.S., Southeastern La. U., 1963; m. Edith E. Appell, Aug. 18, 1962; children—Margaret Ann, James Edward. Mgr., So. States Coop., Richmond, Va., 1965; exec. dir. U.S. Dept. Agr.-Agrl. Stblzn. Conservation Service, Covington, La., 1966—. Active Jr. C. of C., held all local office positions, state chmn., 1969, internat. dir., 1970, state internal v.p., 1971-72, nat. dir., 1971; mem. State Manpower Com., 1972—, La. Alliance, 1971—, St. Tammany Fair Assn., 1966—; mem. State Adv. Bd. for Employment Security, 1972—. Kellogg Found. scholar. Recipient Keyman award La. Jr. C. of C., 1970, 71; named Outstanding State Chmn. La. Jaycees, 1969. Democrat. Presbyn. (elder 1970—). Home: 309 E 5th Av Covington LA 70433

SLATON, PAUL ERNEST, JR., physician; b. Hopkinsville, Ky., Jan. 29, 1932; s. Paul Ernest and Lilly (Cooper) S.; B.A. magna cum laude, Vanderbilt U., 1954, M.D., 1957; m. Martha Helen Keene, Sept. 6, 1955; children—Paul Ernest III, Susan, Keene, Joel. Intern, asst. resident Vanderbilt U. Hosp., Nashville, 1957-59; asst. resident U. Cal., San Francisco, 1959-60, chief resident, 1961-62, fellow in endocrinology, metablism, 1960-64, asst. prof., 1964-69; dir. div. continuing edn., asso. prof. Vanderbilt U., 1969—. Served to maj. USPHS, 1961-63. Fellow A.C.P.; mem. Endocrine Soc., Am. Fedn. Clin. Research, Phi Beta Kappa, Alpha Omega Alpha, Alpha Tau Omega. Contbr. articles to med. jour. Home: 3919 Kimpalong Dr Nashville TN 37205

SLAUGHTER, ELBERT RAY, JR., lumber co exec.; b. Edgewood, Tex., Apr. 15, 1920; s. Elbert Ray and Kathleen (Valentine) S.; B.S., So. Meth. U., 1942; m. Mary Louise Holdsworth, July 7, 1943; children—Mary Kathleen (Mrs. James Adam Nolte), Christopher Ray, John Steven. With inventory control EMSCO Derricks & Equipment Co., Dallas, 1944-46; salesman Anderson-Hanson Co., Dallas, 1946-49; prin. Slaughter Lumber Sales, Dallas 1949—, Slaughter Bros., Inc., Dallas, 1952—; dir., pres. Tex. Pacific Lumber Co., Inc., 1967—; dir. Northwest Bank, Ft. Worth. Bd. dirs. Sunnyside, Inc., Dallas. Mem. N.Am. Wholesale Lumber Assn. (dir. mem. exec. com. 1972—), Alpha Tau Omega. Republican. Christian Scientist. Club: Northwood. Home: 9116 Clearlake St Dallas TX 75225 Office: 8124 Westchester Dallas TX 75225

SLAUGHTER, ELMER CUNNINGHAM, mfg. exec.; b. Houston, Sept. 12, 1920; s. Elmer Carlton and Margaret (Cunningham) S.; student N. Tex. State U., 1936-37; E.E., U. Cin., 1942; m. Jeannette Kearney, June 27, 1942; children—Jean (Mrs. M. Johnson), Susan (Mrs. H. Sachs), Dorothy (Mrs. M. Ashmead), Edward, Mary, John, Richard, Michael, Doris, Rebecca, Nancy, Janet. Established test lab. Lear, Inc., Piqua, O., 1942-45, chief design engr., 1945-46, chief engr., Grand Rapids, Mich., 1946-47; chief engr. Piqua Machine & Mfg. Co., 1948-54; pres. E-M Corp., Fletcher, O., 1947-48, Slaughter Co., Ardmore, Okla., 1954—. Cons., Lear, Inc., Grand Rapids, Mich., 1947-48, Polo Pump Co., Ill., 1947-49, Safa Alarm Co., Orrville, O., 1948-50; chmn. Mayor's Indsl. Adv. Com., 1971-72. Commr., Piqua Boys Baseball Assn., 1958-61; chmn. Ardmore Edn. Council, 1970—; pres. bd. dirs. Ardmore Sheltered Workshop, 1970-72. Mem. I.E.E.E., A.A.A.S., Ardmore C. of C. (pres., dir. 1972—), Tau Beta Pi, Eta Kappa Nu, Sigma Xi. Office: Moore and Hailey Sts Ardmore OK 73401

SLAUGHTER, FREEMAN CLUFF, dentist; b. Estes, Miss., Dec. 30, 1926; s. William Cluff and Vay (Fox) S.; student Wake Forest Coll., 1944;; student Emory U., 1946-47, D.D.S., 1951; m. Genevieve Anne Parks, July 30, 1948; children—Mary Anne, Thomas Freeman, James Hugh. Practice gen. dentistry, Kannapolis, N.C., 1951—. Mem. N.C. Bd. Dental Examiners, 1966—, pres., 1968-69, sec.-treas., 1971—; chief dental staff Cabarrus Meml. Hosp., Concord, N.C., 1965-66; mem. N.C. Adv. Com. for Edn. Dental Aux. Personnel-N.C. State Bd. Edn., 1967-70. Pres. Kannapolis chpt. N.C. Symphony Soc., 1961, trustee, 1962-68; active Boy Scouts Am. Served with USNR, 1944-46; ETO, MTO. Fellow Am. Coll. Dentists; mem. Am. Legion, Kannapolis Jr. C. of C. (v.p. 1952), Toastmasters Internat. (pres. Kannapolis 1963-64), Am. Dental Assn., Am. Assn. Dental Examiners (chmn. nat. dental Liaison com.), So. Conf. Dental Deans and Examiners (v.p. 1969), N.C. Dental Soc., N.C. Dental Soc. Anesthesiology (pres. 1964), Southeastern Acad. Prosthodontics, So. Acad. Oral Surgery, Am. Soc. Dentistry for Children (pres. N.C. unit 1957), Internat. Assn. for Dental Research, Cabarrus County Dental Soc. (pres. 1953-54, 63-64, 69), Omicron Kappa Upsilon, Alpha Epsilon Upsilon. Mason (Shriner). Club: Kannapolis Music (pres. 1962-63), Rotary. Home: 506 Dawn St Kannapolis NC 28081 Office: Professional Bldg Kannapolis NC 28081

SLAUGHTER, HOWARD FLANARY, bldg. materials exec.; b. Dallas, July 5, 1932; s. Lee Roy, Sr. and Emily F. Slaughter; B.B.A., So. Meth. U., 1954; m. Carolyn Bethmann, June 8, 1956; children—Kevin, Greg. Traveling adviser Kappa Alpha Order active chpts., 1954-55; exec. v.p. Slaughter Industries, Inc., Dallas, 1957—. Active So. Meth. U. sustentation drive, United Way, Am. Cancer Soc., Heart Fund, Baylor Hosp. fund drive, YMCA fund drive. Served with USAF, 1955-57. Mem. Tex. Council on Econ. Edn. (dir.), Sales and Marketing Execs. Dallas (pres. 1972-73), So. Forest Products Assn., Lumbermen's Assn. Tex., Tex. Forestry Assn., Kappa Alpha Alumni Assn. (pres. 1960), Pi Sigma Epsilon. Presbyn. Club: Salesmanship, Royal Oaks Country (Dallas). Home: 3306 Bryn Mawr St Dallas TX 75225 Office: 2801 Lombardy Lane Dallas TX 75220

SLAUGHTER, ROBERT LOUIS, ednl. adminstr.; b. Laredo, Tex., Jan. 4, 1942; s. Julian Louis and Pilar Feliz (Macias) S.; B.A., St. Edward's U., 1964; m. Judy Johnson, Dec. 22, 1973. Head coach middle sch. Trinity Valley Sch., Ft. Worth, 1965-70, dir. testing, 1966-67, dir. admissions and testing, 1967—, dir. summer sch., 1968-70, 73, 74, head lower sch., 1968-70, athletic dir., 1970-71, head varsity basketball coach, 1970-71, varsity football coach, 1970-72, middle sch. basketball coach, 1971-72, 73-74, middle sch. football coach, 1972-73, coordinator middle sch. athletic facilities, mem. headmaster's council, 1968—. Sec. Tex. Ind. Schs. Conf., 1969-70. Instr., Confrat. Christian Doctrine, 1964-65. Named Tchr. of Year St. Edwards U., 1964. Republican. Roman Catholic. Clubs: Central Catholic (Fort Worth); Press, International-Latin American, Texas (Austin). Home: 5716 Wales St Fort Worth TX 76133 Office: 6101 McCart St Fort Worth TX 76133

SLAVICK, JOHN PHILIP, broadcasting co. exec.; b. Memphis, May 21, 1929; s. Henry William and Rose Lenore (O'Hara) S.; student U. Notre Dame, 1947-48; B.Mus., N. Tex. State Coll., 1951, M. 1952; Music Edn., m. Zula Ann Regenold, Aug. 20, 1955; children—Deborah Lynn, Ann Elaine, Larry Alan, Helen Marie, David Lee, John William. Band dir. Millington High Sch., Memphis, 1952; floorman Scripps-Howard Broadcasting Co., WMC-TV, Memphis, 1954-55, producer-dir., 1955-62, prodn. mgr., 1962-72, program mgr., 1972—. Served with AUS, 1952-54. Mem. Television Program Conf. (dir. 1974). Roman Catholic (dir. 1973-74). Home: 1546 W Crestwood Memphis TN 38117 Office: 1960 Union Av Memphis TN 38104

SLAVIN, JOSEPH WILLIAM, govt. ofcl.; b. Boston, Feb. 8, 1927; s. Ambrose and Evelyn (Tuttle) S.; B.S., U.S. Mcht. Marine Acad., 1948; m. Arlene Harris, June 4, 1949; children—Elaine, JoAnne, Patricia. Engr., U.S. Lines, N.Y.C., 1949-50; mech. engr. Stone & Webster Engring. Corp., Boston, 1954; engr. Tech. Lab., Dept. Interior, Gloucester, Mass., 1954-59, asst. lab. dir., 1960, lab., 1961-66; acting asst. dir. indsl. research Dept. Interior, Washington, 1966, asst. dir. indsl. research, 1967-69, asst. dir. utilization and engring., 1969, asst. dir. operations, 1970; asso. dir. resource utilization Nat. Marine Fisheries Service, Washington, 1971—. Mem. U.S. nat. com. Internat. Inst. Refrigeration, 1963—; sci. adviser Refrigeration Research Found., 1957—. Pres., Camelot Civic Assn., 1969-71, Camelot P.T.A., 1973. Fellow Am. Soc. Heating, Refrigerating and Air Conditioning Engrs.; mem. Marine Tech. Soc., A.A.A.S., Am. Soc. Heating, Refrigeration and Air Conditioning Engrs. Contbr. articles to profl. jours. Home: 8203 Excaliber Ct Annandale VA 22003 Office: Dept Commerce NOAA Nat Marine Fisheries Service Washington DC 20235

SLAWSON, BOBBY JOE, pub. co. exec.; b. Jacksonville, Tex., Apr. 19, 1939; s. Harvey E. and Eva (Hammonds) S.; student Baylor U., 1958-59; A.A., Lon Morris Coll., 1960; B.B.A., Sam Houston State U., 1962; M.B.A., So. Meth. U., 1971; m. Harriet N. Whigham, Sept. 1, 1961; children—Steven Edward, Susan Eleanor. Mgr. gen.

accounting, budgeting and cost accounting Tex. Instruments, Dallas, 1965-71; controller Taylor Pub. Co., Dallas, 1971—. Served to lt. USAF, 1965-68. C.P.A., Tex. Mem. Am. Inst. C.P.A.'s, Tex. Soc. C.P.A.'s. Home: 1106 Park East Dr Garland TX 75041 Office: PO Box 597 Dallas TX 75221

SLAYTON, DONALD KENT, astronaut; b. Sparta Wis., Mar. 1, 1924; s. Charles Sherman and Victoria Adelia (Larson) S.; B.Aero. Engring., U. Minn., 1949; Sc.D. (hon.), Carthage Coll., 1960; D. of Engring. (hon.), Mich. Technol. Inst.; m. Marjory Lunney, May 15, 1955; 1son Kent Sherman. Served to capt., USAAF, 1942-46; engr. Boeing Aircraft Co., 1949-51; commd. capt. USAF, 1951, advanced to maj., 1959, resigned, 1963; fighter pilot, maintenance officer, Germany, 1952-55; fighter test pilot Edwards AFB, Cal., 1955-59; joined Project Mercury, manned space flight, NASA, 1959, chief astronaut, 1962-63, asst. dir. flight crew operations, 1963-66, dir. flight crew operations, 1966-74, docking module pilot Apollo Test Project, 1974—. Assoc. fellow Soc. Exptl. Test Pilots; fellow Am. Astronautical Soc.; mem. Order of Daedalians, Exptl. Aircraft Assn., Am. Fighter Aces, Nat. Rifle Assn. Home: Box 637 Friendswood TX 77546 Office: Manned Spacecraft Center NASA Houston TX 77002

SLAYTON, WILLIAM LAREW, assn. exec.; b. Topeka, Dec. 2, 1916; s. Clarence Harvey and Mary (Larew) S.; student U. Omaha, 1937-39; A.B., U. Chgo., 1940, M.A., 1942; D.H.L. (hon.), Clarkson Coll. Tech., 1965; m. Mary Prichard, Aug. 30, 1941; children—Mary Elizabeth (Mrs. Ronald McKean), Barbara (Mrs. Peter Shelton). Polit. sec. Alderman Paul H. Douglas, Chgo., 1940-42; planning analyst Milw. Planning Commn., 1944-45, 46-47; municipal reference librarian, Milw., 1947-48; asso. dir. Urban Redevel. Study, Chgo., 1948-50; field rep. div. slum clearance and urban redevel. HHFA, Washington, 1950; dir. redevel. Nat. Assn. Housing and Redevel. Ofcls., Washington, 1950-55; v.p. planning, redevel. Webb & Knapp, Inc., Washington, 1955-60; partner planning I.M. Pei & Partners, N.Y.C., 1956-61; commr. Urban Renewal Adminstrn., Housing and Home Finance Agy., Dept. Housing and Urban Devel., Washington, 1961-66; dir. Urban Policy Center, Urban Am., Inc., Washington, 1966; exec. v.p. Urban Am., Inc., 1966-69, pres., 1969; exec. v.p. A.I.A., Washington, 1969—, exec. v.p. A.I.A. Found., 1970—, pres. A.I.A. Corp., 1970—, chmn. A.I.A. Research Corp., 1973—. Chmn. urban devel. adv. com. Dept. Housing and Urban Devel., 1967-68; mem. U.S. delegation Econ. Commn. for Europe, 1970. Served with USNR, 1945-46. Recipient Gold medal Royal Instn. Chartered Surveyors, Gt. Britain, 1965. Mem. Potomac Inst. (dir.), Am. Inst. Planners, Nat. Assn. Housing and Redevel. Ofcls., A.I.A. (hon.), Washington Drama Soc. (dir.). Home: 3411 Ordway St NW Washington DC 20016 Office: AIA 1785 Massachusetts Av NW Washington DC 20036

SLEADD, FRANKLIN BLAND, pathologist; b. Shelbyville, Ky., Jan. 30, 1930; s. Bernard Bland and Annabell (Gladwell) S.; A.B. in Zoology, U. Louisville, 1951, M.D., 1955; m. Betty Lois Baldwin, Jan. 21, 1956; children—Bernard, James, Kathleen, Wendy, Robert, Clinton. Intern, St. Joseph Hosp., Lexington, Ky., 1955-56; resident in pathology U. Louisville Sch. Medicine and VA Hosp., Louisville, 1965-69; dir. labs. Henry County Gen. Hosp., Paris, Tenn., 1969—. Pres. Franklin B. Sleadd M.D.-Prof. Corp., 1972—. Med. examiner Henry County, Tenn., 1969—. Served to lt. comdr. M.C. USN, 1956-65. Diplomate Am. Bd. Pathology. Fellow Coll. Am. Pathologists, Am. Soc. Clin. Pathologists. mem. A.M.A., Tenn., So. med. assns., Tenn. Soc. Pathologists. Home: 509 Blanton Paris TN 38242 Office: Henry County Gen Hosp Paris TN 38242

SLEDGE, BARNETT JENKINS, JR., real estate exec.; b. Memphis, Nov. 3, 1942; s. Barnett Jenkins and Rachael Pauline (Davis) S.; B.S. in Mech. Engring., U. Tenn., 1965; Engr., McDonnell Douglas Corp., St. Louis, 1965-67; partner Bond-Sledge Bldg. Contractors, Aspen, Colo., 1968; v.p., dir. Pyramid Properties Corp., Dallas, 1969-70; v.p., dir. Pyramid Corp., Dallas, 1970-72; pres. Lakecroft, 1973—. Mem. Kappa Sigma, Pi Tau Sigma. Episcopalian. Office: 1003 NE Loop 410 San Antonio TX 78209

SLEIGHT, ROBERT BENTON, psychologist; b. Hemlock, N.Y., Sept. 16, 1922; s. Edson F. and Marian (Hoppough) S.; B.Ed., State U. N.Y. Tchrs. Coll. at Geneseo, 1946; M.S., Purdue U., 1947, Ph.D., 1949; m. Dorothy M. Barden, May 7, 1944; 1 son, Robert Barry. Research fellow Purdue U., 1946-48; asst. prof., research psychologist Johns Hopkins, 1948-51; research scientist and cons. Naval Research Lab., 1952; pres., chmn. bd. Century Research Corp., 1952—. Mem. Citizens zoning adv. com. D.C., 1955-57; mem. Arlington County Sch. Bd. Curriculum Council. Bd. dirs. Arlington Com. 100, Arlington A.R.C. Served as naval aviator USNR, 1943-45. Fellow Am. Psychol. Assn., A.A.A.S., Human Factors Soc.; mem. Eastern, D.C. psychol. assns., Internat. Assn. Applied Psychology, Sigma Xi. Contbr. articles to textbooks and profl. jours. Home: 3717 N 27th St Arlington VA 22207 Office: 4113 Lee Hwy Arlington VA 22207

SLENKER, NORMAN FREDERICK, lawyer; b. Washington, Pa., Oct. 12, 1929; s. Fred William and Esther Lenore (Lamp) S.; A.B., Ohio Wesleyan U., 1951; J.D., George Washington U., 1955; certificate, Seminar for Lawyers Med. Coll. Va., 1959; m. Berta King Ray, Sept. 20, 1952; children—Susan G., Donald P., Martha B. Ins. investigator-adjuster Kemper Ins. Co., Ins. Co. N.Am., and an ind. firm, Washington, 1951-56; admitted to Va. bar, 1956; since practiced in Arlington; partner firm Russell & Hulvey, 1956-69; trial atty. Jesse, Phillips, Kendrick others, 1960-62; partner firm Duff & Slenker, 1962-72, Slenker, Brandt & Jennings, 1972—. Instr. U. Va. Extension, Arlington, 1956-57; tchr. history and govt. Arlington Pub. Sch. System Night Sch., 1957-59. Mem. Am., Va. Arlington County bar assns., Am. Judicature Soc., Delta Theta Phi, Beta Theta Pi. Home: 3861 N Ridgeview Rd Arlington VA 22207 Office: 1012 N Utah St Arlington VA 22201

SLESINGER, MORRIS LEONARD, chem. co. exec.; b. Bishopville, S.C., Jan. 15, 1919; s. Otto and Bessie (Jolson) S.; B.S., N.C. State Coll., 1940; m. Ann Moscovitz, Nov. 18, 1949; children—Cathy, Joel, Margaret. Vice pres. Dexter Chem. Corp., Charlotte, N.C., 1965—; dir. United Mills Corp. Served to lt. col. inf. AUS, 1940-46. Mem. Am. Assn. Textile Chemists and Colorists, Sigma Alpha Mu. Mem. B'nai B'rith. Home: 4116 Silver Bell Dr Charlotte NC 28211 Office: PO Box 801 Charlotte NC 28251

SLEVIN, JOSEPH RAYMOND, journalist; b. N.Y.C., Nov. 27, 1918; s. Theodore and Katherine (Bluh) S.; B.A., Yale, 1939, postgrad., 1939-40; postgrad. U. Neb., 1940-41; M.A., U. Ill., 1942; m. Katherine Day, Dec. 8, 1943; children—Ann Day, Michael Scott, Jonathan Day, Peter Day. Staff editor Kiplinger Mag., 1946-47; Washington corr. Jour. Commerce, 1947-55; nat. econs. editor N.Y. Herald Tribune, 1955-66; editor, pub. Washington Bond Report, 1962—; syndicated columnist Newsday, Washington, 1966-71, Phila. Inquirer, Washington, 1971—. Commentator Voice Am., 1960-62, Westinghouse Broadcasting, 1973—. Served to lt. USNR, 1942-45. Mem. Am. Polit. Sci. Assn., Overseas Writers, White House Corr. Assn., Nat. Press Club. Clubs: Federal City, Exchequer, Yale (Washington). Home: 16 E Melrose St Chevy Chase MD 20015 Office: Nat Press Bldg Washington DC 20004

SLIDER, JOHN ROBERT, optometrist; b. Gorman, Tex., Nov. 11, 1941; s. William Hardie and Eula (Clarke) S.; student Austin Coll., 1960-62; B.S., U. Houston, 1965, O.D., 1966; m. Betty Jo Suddith, Aug. 31, 1968. Partner with D.W. Leach, optometric practice, Odessa, Tex., 1968—. Bd. dirs. Odessa Council for the Blind, 1969, Ector County Cancer Assn., YMCA. Served to capt. AUS, 1966-68. Mem. Tex., Am. optometric assns., S.W. Contact Lens Soc., W. Tex. Optometric Soc. (pres. 1969, 70, 73), Jr. C. of C. Presbyn. (elder). Lion. Home: 3003 Eastover St Odessa TX 79762 Office: 415 N Sam Houston St Odessa TX 79761

SLITOR, RICHARD EATON, economist; b. St. Paul, July 1, 1911; s. Ray Francis and Nelle (Eaton) S.; student U. Wis., 1928-30; S.B. magna cum laude, Harvard, 1932, Ph.D., 1940; M.A. (Carnegie Teaching fellow), Colgate U., 1934; m. Louise Bean, Dec. 24, 1937; children—Prudence Van Zandt (Mrs. William Marshall Crozier, Jr.), Deborah Beckwith, Nicholas Wentworth, Christopher Wells Eaton. Instr., tutor econs. Harvard, 1934-41, Radcliffe Coll., 1940-41; asso. prof., chmn. dept. econs. and bus. adminstrn. Mt. Union Coll., 1941-42; economist U.S. Treasury Dept., 1942-72, chief bus. taxation staff, office tax analysis, 1961-63, asst. dir., 1963-72; prof. econs. U. Mass. at Amherst, 1967-68; econ. cons. Rand Corp., NSF, Dept. Housing and Urban Devel., N.C. State Tax Study Commn., others. Adv. Commn. Intergovtl. Relations, Washington, 1973-74. Cons. Nat. Commn. on Urban Problems, Colombian Fiscal Commn., Bogota, 1968. Fed. exec. fellow The Brookings Instn., 1963-64. Mem. Am. Statis. Assn., Am. Econ. Assn., Internat. Inst. Pub. Finance, Royal Econ. Soc., Nat. Tax Assn., Phi Beta Kappa. Episcopalian. Club: Harvard (Washington). Author: Federal Income Tax in Relation to Housing. Contbr. articles and studies on taxation to profl. jours. Home: 9000 Burning Tree Rd Bethesda MD 20034 Office: 726 Jackson Pl NW Washington DC 20575

SLOAN, EARL LEROY, civil engr.; b. Boise City, Okla., Apr. 25, 1909; s. Dudley C. and Neva (Powell) S.; B.S. in Civil Engring., Kan. State Coll., 1929; M.S., Mass. Inst. Tech., 1930; m. Geneva Landrum, Apr. 2, 1933. Engr. constrn. pub. bldgs. Underhill Constrn. Co., Wichita, Kan., 1930-32; engr. rd., bridge constrn. Okla. Hwy. Dept., 1933-35, design engr. bridges, 1935-39; with Phillips Petroleum Co., Bartlesville, Okla., 1939-74, project engr., 1958-74; with Petrochim N.V., Antwerp, Belgium, 1966-70; on loan to Alyeska Pipeline Service Co., Houston, 1970-74. Mem. Nat., Okla. socs. profl. engrs. Baptist (deacon). Club: Hillcrest Country (Bartlesville). Home: 1401 Hampden Rd Bartlesville OK 74003

SLOAN, EUGENE HOLLOWAY, educator; b. Lebanon, Tenn., Sept. 14, 1907; s. Henry Churchill and Effie (Holloway) S.; A.B., Cumberland U., 1927, LL.B., 1928, J.D., Samford U., 1969; M.A., Peabody Coll., 1939; m. Lillian Rachel White, June 12, 1929; children—Gene H., Joseph White, William Henry, Lilli Anne Twining. Editor, Lebanon (Tenn.) Democrat, 1926-28; prin. Gladeville (Tenn.) High Sch., 1928-31; tchr., coach Lebanon (Tenn.) High Sch., 1931-36, prin., 1938-45; city supt. schs., Lebanon, 1937-38; state editor Nashville (Tenn.) Banner, 1945; pub. relations dir. Tenn. Dept. Edn., 1945-46; tchr., dir. pub. relations Middle Tenn. State U., 1946—, prof. bus. law, 1946—. Admitted to Tenn. bar, 1928. Mem. Am. Bus. Law Assn., Pi Omega Pi, Sigma Delta Kappa, Pi Mu Sigma, Alpha Kappa Psi. Mem. Ch. of Christ. Democrat. Mason. Club: Lions. Author: Personages in American History, 1939; With Second Army in Tennessee, 1956; co-author: Business Law, 1962, Modern Journalism, 1963, History at Wilson County, 1965 articles pub. in profl. jours., mags., newspapers. Home: 728 Greenland Dr Murfreesboro TN 37130

SLOAN, JAMES PARK, educator; b. Clinton, S.C., Oct. 2, 1916; s. Eugene Blakely and Janie Pressly (Lindsay) S.; B.A., Erskine Coll., 1937; M.A., Tulane U., 1938; m. Alice Catherine Gaines, June 26, 1941; children—James Park, Edwin Gaines. Tchr. econs., govt., sociology, English, Ga. Mil. Acad., College Park, 1938-39; tchr. history, govt. Clinton (S.C.) High Sch., 1939-41; asst. to chmn. S.C. Def. Council, Clinton, 1941-42; paymaster Joanna Mills Co. (S.C.), 1942, personnel dir., 1946-58, dir. indsl. relations, 1958-64; editor co. monthly mag. The Joanna Way, 1950-64; asst. prof. polit. sci. Coll. of Charleston (S.C.), 1964-67; asst. prof. polit. sci., asst. dir. acad. affairs Spartanburg regional campus U. S.C. 1967-73. Mem. adv. council S.C. Employment Security Commn., 1955—; mem. planning bd. S.C. Accident Prevention Conf., 1954-57; mem. edn. task force Model Cities Program, City of Spartanburg, 1971-72; mem. long-range planning com. City of Spartanburg, 1970—. Vice chmn. Laurens County S.C. Heart Assn., 1953-64; mem. Laurens County Tri-Centennial Com., 1970; vice chmn. Laurens County Am. Cancer Soc., 1956-64, exec. dir. Joanna Community Chest, 1950-64; mem. standing com. on communications Asso. Reformed Presbyn. Synod, 1970-72, mem. standing com. on publications, 1973—; mem. Laurens County Bd. Election Commrs., 1970—. Mem. S.C. Ho. of Reps., 1940-42; mem. Clinton City Council, 1954-60, mayor pro tem, 1958-60; mem. Clinton City Employee Appeal Bd., 1973—, Clinton City Mgr. Adv. Com., 1973—; del. Nat. Dem. Conv., 1956; del. S.C. Dem. Conv., 1942, 46, 48, 52, 54, 56, 60; mem. Laurens County Dem. Exec. Com., 1950-60, chmn., 1948-50; county chmn. S. Carolinians for Ind. Electors, 1956; del. to S.C. Republican Conv., 1968, 70, 72; chmn. Laurens County Rep. Conv., 1972. Trustee Erskine Coll., 1949-53, Joanna Found., 1955-66; bd. dirs. Clinton-Newberry Natural Gas Authority, 1954-60. Served from apprentice seaman to lt. USNR, 1942-46; ETO, PTO. Recipient George Washington Honor medal Freedoms Found., 1963. Mem. South Caroliniana Soc., Am. Assn. Indsl. Editors (dir. 1950, 58-60, pres. 1960-61), So., S.C. polit. sci. assns., Laurens County Hist. Soc. (charter). Mem. Asso. Ref. Presbyn. Ch. (ruling elder, 1947-70, life ruling elder 1971, supt. Sunday sch. 1939-60, now tchr. men's class). Club: Piedmont (Spartanburg, S.C.). Author articles trade jours., religious publs. Home: 103 Maple St Clinton SC 29325 Office: Univ South Carolina Spartanburg SC 29303

SLOAN, JOHN, merchant; b. Nashville, June 28, 1904; s. Paul Lowe and Anne (Joy) S.; grad. Wallace U. Sch., 1921; B.A., Vanderbilt U., 1925; m. Margaret Howe, Feb. 7, 1935; children—John, George A. II, Thomas Howe, Paul Lowe, III. With Cain-Sloan Co., Nashville, 1925—, successively salesman, dept. mgr., v.p., pres., 1937-70, chmn., 1970—; dir. First Am. Nat. Bank, First Amten Corp. Magistrate 15th dist. Williamson County (Tenn.), 1948—. Trustee Vanderbilt U.; pres. bd. trustees Montgomery Bell Acad. Mem. Vanderbilt Alumni Assn. (pres. 1941-45), Kappa Alpha. Rotarian. Clubs: Coffee House, Hillsboro Hounds, Belle Meade Country. Home: Maple Grove Farm Route 1 Brentwood TN 37027 Office: Cain-Sloan Co Nashville TN 37027

SLOAN, MARY KATHLEEN LEWIS (MRS. EUGENE BLAKELY SLOAN), author; b. Winnsboro, S.C.; d. Thomas Walter and Mary Ellen (Street) Lewis; student U. S.C., 1936-38, then postgrad.; A.B., Furman U., 1940; m. Eugene Blakely Sloan, Aug. 4, 1951 (dec. Apr. 1969); children—Mary Lindsay, Laura Lewis. Free-lance photo-journalist, 1942—; editor Oliver Beacon, and pub. relations dept. Oliver Gen. Hosp., Augusta, Ga., 1943-47; editorial staff News and Herald, Winnsboro, 1951; mng. editor S.C. Meth. Adv., Columbia, 1956-63; editor U. S.C. Press, 1965-68, advt., promotion dir., 1967-68; travel writer S.C. Dept. Parks, Recreation and Tourism, 1968-69; pres. Lewis-Sloan Pub. Co. Cons. writing, book and related publishing. Mem. Richland County Tricentennial Commn. Recipient spl. award for periodical lit. S.C. Fedn. Women's Cubs, 1970. Mem. South Caroliniana Soc., Historic Columbia Found., S.C., Fairfield County hist. socs., Nat. Trust for Historic Preservation, Outdoor Photographers League. Presbyn. Co-editor: A Documentary Profile of the Palmetto State, 1971. Compiler: South Carolina: A Journalist and His State, 1974. Contbr. articles to profl. jours. Home: 215 S Harden St Columbia SC 29205

SLOAN, SAMUEL JOSEPH, mech. engr.; b. Waynesville, N.C., Apr. 23, 1914; s. Hugh Johnston and Ginny Linda (Stringfield) S.; student South Ga. State Coll., 1932-33; certificate Emory Jr. Coll., 1943; B.S., U. S.C., 1951; m. Mary Louise Spires, June 20, 1942; children—Sarah (Mrs. Keith Kreutziger), Mary Jo (Mrs. Bill L. Perkins). Area engr. E.I. duPont, Augusta, Ga., 1951-53; mech. engr. U.S. Army C.E., Tripoli, Libya, Vicenza, Italy, 1953-59; constrn. coordinator Campion Paper & Fiber Co., Canton, N.C., 1959-62; chief estimating and specifications br. NASA, Huntsville, Ala., 1962—. Cons., Foy & Lee, architects, Waynesville, N.C., 1959-62. Mem. Tennessee Valley Hist. Soc., 1968-73; hon. mem. Ala. Sheriff Assn., 1967-73. Chmn. programs Young Democrats Haywood County (N.C.), 1959-60. Served to 1st lt. AUS, 1940-47. Decorated Bronze Star, Purple Heart. Registered profl. engr., Ala. Recipient Sustained Superior Performance award NASA, 1964. Mem. Ret. Officers Assn., Disabled Officer Assn., V.F.W., U. S.C. Alumni Assn. (chmn. bldg. com. 1972-73). Democrat. Methodist. Mason. Club: Am. Contract Bridge Assn. (pres. 1965-66, nat. Goodwell com. 1970-73). Home: 1305 Lowell Dr Huntsville AL 35801 Office: NASA George Marshall Space Flight Center Huntsville AL 35812

SLONE, DENNEY WOOD, lawyer; b. Mascotte, Fla., Mar. 6, 1907; s. R.W. and Roalia P. (Carter) S.; student U. Fla., Troy State Tchrs. Coll., Valdosta State Coll., 1950-51; LL.B., Atlanta Law Sch., 1946; m. Voncile Fleming, Nov. 5, 1941; children—William L., Albert E. Tchr. pub. schs., 1925-26; clk. U.S. P.O., 1940-42, admitted to Ga. bar, 1946; gen. practice law, Atlanta, 1946-47, Lakeland, Ga., 1947—; Lanier County atty., 1952-56, 65—; councilman City of Lakeland, Ga., 1965-68; atty. City of Lakeland, 1969—. Served with USCGR, 1942-45. Mem. Am. Bar Assn., Am. Judicature Soc., Ga. Municipal Assn., Ga. Assn. County Commrs., 8th Congl. Dist. Ga. County Officers Assn. (exec. com. 1965), Internat. Platform Assn., Am. Legion, Sigma Delta Kappa. State Bar Ga. Democrat. Baptist. Lion. Home: 443 Pecan St Lakeland GA 31635 Office: 105 N Center St Lakeland GA 31635

SLONECKER, WILLIAM THOMAS, pediatrician; b. Nashville, July 20, 1931; s. Herman Leroy and Stella Mae (Small) S.; A.B., Trevecca Nazarene Coll., 1953; M.D., U. Tenn., 1958; postgrad. George Peabody Coll., 1952-53, Vanderbilt U., 1953-54; m. Betty Elaine Jewell Slonecker, June 18, 1956; children—William Gregory, Susan Lyn, Christopher Thomas. Intern, Bapt. Hosp., Nashville, 1958-59, resident, 1959-61; practice medicine specializing in pediatrics, Nashville, 1961—; partner Drs. Kirby & Slonecker, 1961—; mem. staffs Bapt., St. Thomas, Vanderbilt hosps. Med. dir. Blood Bank Found.; faculty Trevecca Nazarene Coll., part time, 1961—, also pres. devel. council. Mem. Gov.'s Com. on Revision Day Care and Infant Care Standards, 1970-71. Bd. dirs. Nashville Neurol. Inst., Nashville Christian Services. Diplomate Am. Bd. Pediatrics. Mem. Am., Tenn. med. assns., Nashville Acad. Medicine, Nashville Pediatric Soc. Mem. Ch. Nazarene (ch. bd. 1962—). Home: 5875 Fredericksburg Dr Nashville TN Office: 3725 Nolensville Rd Nashville TN 372- 11

SLOUGH, WILLIAM FRED, city ofcl.; b. Kingsport, Tenn., Oct. 15, 1944; s. Fred William and Mary Dixie (Greer) S.; B.S. in Polit. Sci., East Tenn. State U., 1966, M. City Mgmt., 1972; m. Sandra Ollie Phibbs, June 27, 1970. Adminstrv. asst. City of Johnson City (Tenn.), 1971—. Asso. mem. Internat. City Mgmt. Assn. Club: Optimist (dir. 1972-73, v.p. 1973-74) (Brevard, N.C.). Home: 102 Franklin St Brevard NC 28712 Office: 151 W Main St Brevard NC 28712

SMALL, FREDERICK ARTHUR, govt. ofcl.; b. Cumberland, Md., June 8, 1928; s. Frederick Trouton and Mary Devereux (Call) S.; B.A., Goddard Coll., 1952, postgrad. McGill U., 1952; m. Margaret Murphy, Jan. 13, 1951; children—Colleen Tara, Kim Collier, Susan Joy (Mrs. Billie White), Dawn Michelle. Glaciologist, U.S. Army, 1952-55; computer systems specialist Gen. Motors Co., 1955-59; sr. computer systems specialist system Devel. Corp., 1959-62; spl. asst. to pres. Ocean Sci. and Engring., 1962-63; dir. Ocean Center, oceanographer USN, 1964-69; dir. computer information systems Ocean Data Systems, Inc., 1969-71; chief systems and programs Dept. Justice Drug Enforcement Adminstrn., Washington, 1971—. Sci. adviser arctic and mountain environments Juneau Ice Field, Alaska, 1950—. Community commr. E. Detroit council Boy Scouts Am., 1955-59. Club: Explorers (N.Y.C.). Home: 4005 Lee Pl Annandale VA 22003 Office: 1405 Eye St Washington DC 20537

SMALL, KENNETH FREDERICK, broadcasting exec.; b. Camden, N.J., Apr. 5, 1909; s. Harry A.C. and Ethel (Hollingshead) S.; student Cornell U., 1926-28, Pa. Acad. Fine Arts, 1928-30; m. Elizabeth C. Adams, Jan. 14, 1932; children—Elizabeth C. (Mrs. Gordon D. Price), Kenneth H. Exec. v.p. Newman, Lynde & Assos., Inc., Jacksonville and Miami, Fla., 1945-52; asst. gen. mgr. radio sta. WPDQ, Jacksonville, also sec. Jacksonville Broadcasting Corp., 1952-56; mng. dir. radio stas. WRUF, WRUF-FM, U. Fla., 1956—, asst. prof. Coll. Journalism and Communications. Pres. Civic Round Table, Jacksonville, 1949-52. Mem. Fla. Assn. Broadcasters (exec. v.p. 1962—), Jacksonville Advt. Club (past pres.). Democrat. Rotarian (dir.). Clubs: Propeller (Jacksonville); Torch (Gainesville, Fla.). Home: 1936 NE 7th St Gainesville FL 32601

SMALL, MELVIN D., physician, educator; b. Somerville, Mass., May 22, 1925; s. Sidney J. and Ida (Gelbsman) S.; student Boston U., 1942, U. Colo., 1942-43, Ga. Tchrs. Coll., 1943, U. N.H., 1943, State U. Ia., 1943-44, Boston Coll., 1950; A.B., U. Wis., 1950; postgrad. U. Vt., 1950-51, U. Lausanne, 1954-56, Harvard, 1958; M.D., Duke U., 1959; m. Judith Nogee, Dec. 23, 1962; children—Michael Dorian, Michele. Fellowship in gastrointestinal research with F. Ingelfinger, Mass. Meml. Hosp., Boston, 1951-53, with N. Zamchek, Boston City Hosp., 1953-59; research asst. Boston U. Sch. Medicine, 1956-57; intern Georgetown U. Hosp., 1959-60, resident in medicine, 1960-61, chief gastrointestinal research, 1961-64; chief gastroenterology service Georgetown div. D.C. Gen. Hosp., 1964-69; pres. Gastroenterology Assos. Corp.; chmn. continuing edn. com. Alexandria (Va.) Hosp.; instr. Georgetown U., 1961-67, clin. asst. prof. medicine, 1967; bd. dirs. Jefferson Meml. Hosp., 1965-71. Witness, U.S. Senate Small Bus. Subcom. on Drug Pricing; chmn. Internat. Faculty for Postgrad. Med. Edn. Served with AUS, 1943-45. Mem. Am. Physiol. Soc., Am. Inst. Nutrition, A.A.A.S., A.M.A., Am. Coll. Gastroenterology, A.C.P., Am. Gastroent. Assn., Am. Fedn. for Clin. Research, Am. Soc. Internal Medicine. Contbr. articles in field to profl. jours. Home: 2914 N 27th St Arlington VA 22207 Office: 5021 Seminary Rd Alexandria VA 22311

SMALLHORST, DAVID FRANCIS, city ofcl.; b. St. Louis, Oct. 2, 1911; s. David E. and Frances S. (Smith) S.; B.S. in C.E., U. Tex., 1936; m. Blanche Lundquist, Dec. 18, 1937 (dec. Oct. 1965). With Tex. State Dept. Health, 1936-66, dir. water pollution control div., 1948-66, exec. sec. Water Pollution Control Bd., 1961-66; staff engr. water and wastewater dept., City of Austin, Tex., 1966—. Trustee V. M. Ehlers Meml. Fund, Inc. Served to maj., San. Corps, AUS, 1942-46. Registered profl. engr., Tex. Diplomate Am. Acad. Environmental Engrs. Mem. Water Pollution Control Fedn. (life), Am. Soc. C.E., Am. Water Works Assn., Nat. Soc. Profl. Engrs., Tex. Pub. Health Assn. (life), Tex. Water and Sewage Assn. (life), Tau Beta Pi, Chi Epsilon. Home: 4811 Caswell Av Austin TX 78751 Office: PO Box 1088 Austin TX 78767

SMARTT, JOHN MADISON, lawyer; b. Smartt, Tenn., Feb. 24, 1919; s. Robert White and Sarah Alma (Roggli) S.; B.S., U. Tenn., 1942, J.D., 1948; m. Harriet Chapin, June 9, 1943; children—John Madison, Jane (Mrs. Roy D. Stroud), Douglas D., Robert W., III. Admitted to Tenn. bar. 1948; since practiced in McMinnville; dir. alumni affairs U. Tenn., Knoxville, 1948-69; mem. firm Fowler, Rowntree, Fowler & Robertson, Knoxville, 1969—. Served to capt. AUS, 1942-46. Mem. Phi Delta Phi. Democrat. Presbyn. (mem. session 1970-73). Kiwanian. Home: 4603 Holston Hills Rd Knoxville TN 37914

SMATHERS, JAMES BURTON, educator; b. Prairie du Chien, Wis., Aug. 26, 1935; s. James Levi and Irma Marie (Stindt) S.; B.Nuclear Engring., N.C. State Coll., 1957, M.S., 1959; Ph.D., U. Md., 1967; m. Sylvia Lee Rath, Apr. 20, 1957; children—Kristine Kay, Kathryn Ann, James Scott, Ernest Kent. Research engr. Atomics Internat., Canoga Park, Cal., 1959; Walter Reed Army Inst. Research, Washington, 1961-67; prof. nuclear engring. Tex. A. and M. U., College Station, 1967—. Cons. U.S. Army. Served with AUS, 1959-61. Recipient Gen. Dynamics Excellence in Teaching award, 1971. Mem. Am. Nuclear Soc., Health Physics Soc., Am. Assn. Physicists in Medicine, Am. Soc. for Engring. Edn., Sigma Xi, Sigma Pi Sigma, Phi Kappa Phi. Home: 1402 Glade St College Station TX 77840

SMEDBERG, MERLE WILLIAM, cons. engr.; b. Jamestown, N.Y., June 11, 1909; s. John William and Marie (Anderson) S.; B.S. in Elec. Engring., Carnegie Inst. Tech., 1931; m. Elizabeth Maxwell, Mar. 3, 1937; Engring. aide Jamestown Bd. Pub. Utilities, 1931-34, mgr., 1955-71; cons. engr., Gatlinburg, Tenn., 1971—; engring. aide TVA, Knoxville, Tenn., 1934-35; engring. aide to regional constrn. engr. Rural Electrification Administrn., Washington, 1935-43, 46-50; chief elec. engr. Frank Horton & Co., Lamar, Mo., 1950-52; asst. chief power and radio br. AEC, Oak Ridge, 1952-55. Chmn., Allegheny River Regional Water Resources Planning Bd., 1968-71. Served to lt. comdr. USNR, 1943-45. Mem. I.E.E.E. (sr.), Nat. Soc. Profl. Engrs., Am. Pub. Power Assn. (dir. 1961-65), Municipal Electric Utilities Assn. N.Y. State (pres. 1965-66), Jamestown Area C. of C. (dir. 1962-68, v.p. 1968-71). Home: PO Box 465 Gatlinburg TN 37738

SMEETON, CECIL BROOKS, ret. educator; b. Chgo., Apr. 3, 1903; s. Cecil Brooks and Marie (Jensen) S.; B.Sc., Northwestern U., 1926, M.B.A., 1946; m. Florence Rooney, Sept. 23, 1933; children—Thomas, John, Peggy (Mrs. J. William Stanton), Mary Ann. Promotion mgr. Star-Peerless Wall Paper Mills, Chgo., 1931-35; account exec. Evans Assos. Advt. Agy., Chgo., 1935-37; asst. dir. promotion Meredith Pub. Co., Des Moines, 1937-40; instr. marketing Ohio State U., 1940; asst. prof. Ind. U., 1940-46; asso. prof. U. Notre Dame, 1946-50; prof. marketing coll. bus. adminstrn. Marquette U., Milw., 1950-65, dir. market dept., 1952-58, prof. advt. Coll. Journalism, 1965-68; prof. marketing and advt. Lake Superior State Coll., Mich. Tech. U., Sault Ste. Marie, 1968—. Am. Assn. Advt. Agys. fellow, 1954-55; recipient Advt. Fedn. Am. and Printers' Ink silver medal, 1961. Mem. Acad. Advt., Beta Gamma Sigma, Alpha Kappa Psi, Alpha Delta Sigma. Author: Profile of the Modern Sales-Marketing Executive, 1948, rev. edit., 1961; Sales and Marketing Executives International, 1948, rev. edit., 1961; Times Change So Does Distribution, 1949; Outdoor Advertising Association of America, 1949; Rapidly Changing Markets: Their Challenge to Salesman, 1959; (with others) Principles of Marketing, 1961; (with others) Principles of Advertising, 1963; (with others) Creative Imagination, 1970. Address: 4222 2d Rd North Arlington VA 22203

SMELLEY, CAROL BARCLAY LINDSAY (MRS. FRANCIS AARON SMELLEY), govt. ofcl.; b. Atlanta, Oct. 17, 1922; d. John Samuel and Florence Gertrude (Hand) Lindsay; student U. Ala., 1952; m. Francis Aaron Smelley, June 30, 1948; children—Dorothy Ann Echols (Mrs. Richard Raymond), Susan Grace. With Dept. Health, Edn. and Welfare, Social Security Adminstrn., Tuscaloosa, Ala., 1946—, claims rep., 1947-55, field rep., 1955—. Neighborhood chmn. Tombigbee council Girl Scouts U.S.A., 1959-62. Mem. Tuscaloosa County Preservation Soc. (trustee 1969—, recording sec. 1970—), Birmingham Geneal. Soc. Methodist. Clubs: Altrusa (dir. 1968—, 1st v.p. 1970-71, pres. 1971-72), Tuscaloosa (Ala.) Country; Woodland Hills Garden (pres. 1964-65) (Tuscaloosa), Woodland Hills Swim (Tuscaloosa). Home: 171 Woodland Hills Tuscaloosa AL 35409 Office: 1118 Greensboro Av Tuscaloosa AL 35401

SMELLEY, F(RANCIS) AARON, banker; b. Tuscaloosa, Ala., July 4, 1919; s. Francis M. and Fannie (Busby) S.; B.S., U. Ala., 1947; postgrad. Alexander Hamilton Inst., 1965-67, Sch. Banking, U. Wis., 1971; m. Carol Lindsay, June 30, 1948; children—Dorothy Echols (Mrs. Richard Raymond), Susan. With Social Security Bd., Washington, 1941; storekeeper Northington Gen. Hosp., Tuscaloosa, 1943-44; accountant Ala. Binder & Chem. Co., Tuscaloosa, 1947-49, asst. comptroller, 1949-51, asst. treas., 1951-59, comptroller, 1959-60, treas., 1960-66; asst. comptroller City Nat. Bank Tuscaloosa, 1966—. Active various community drives. Chmn. Expo 1972 Black Warrior Council Boy Scouts Am.; treas. Tuscaloosa Heritage Week, 1973. Served with AUS, 1942. Mem. Am. Inst. Banking (treas. Tuscaloosa chpt. 1967), Bank Adminstrn. Inst., Tuscaloosa Preservation Soc., Commerce Exec. Soc., U. Ala. Alumni Assn., Am. Legion. Methodist (treas.). Clubs: Tuscaloosa Country, Kiwanis (dir. 1966), Toastmaster (pres. 1962). Home: 171 Woodland Hills Tuscaloosa AL 35401 Office: PO Box 2509 Tuscaloosa AL 35401

SMELO, LEON SAMUEL, physician; b. Phila., Feb. 22, 1911; s. William and Anna (Steinberg) S.; A.B., U. Pa., 1931, M.D., 1935; m. Mary Ann Carver, Sept. 11, 1940; 1 dau., Martha (Mrs. Richard Wagoner). Intern, Phila. Gen. Hosp., 1936-37, metabolic dept. resident physician, 1938; asst. med. dir. Renziehausen Found., Children's Hosp. Pitts., U. Pa. Med. Sch., 1939-41; practice medicine specializing in internal medicine, Birmingham, Ala., 1942—; chief sect. on metabolism and endocrinology dept. medicine Bapt. Med. Center, 1966—; asso. prof. medicine Med. Coll. Ala., 1971—. Chmn. med. adv. bd. Birmingham Indsl. Health Council; asso. dir. Camp Seale Harris, 1948—; physician Univ. Group Diabetes Program, 1960—. Diplomate Am. Bd. Internal Medicine. Fellow A.C.P., Internat. Coll. Physicians; mem. Am. Fedn. Clin. Research, A.M.A., Am. (mem. council 1958—). Ala. (pres. 1971-72) diabetes assns., So., Ala. med. assns., Birmingham Acad. Medicine, Birmingham Soc. Internists (v.p., dir. 1948-49), Jefferson County Med. Soc., Birmingham Metabolic and Diabetes Assn. (pres., dir. 1948-49). N.Y. Diabetes Assn. Home: 2523 Mt Brook Circle Birmingham AL 35223 Office: 1211 27th Pl S Birmingham AL 35205

SMELTZER, JOHN FROST, educator; b. Shamokin, Pa., Jan. 23, 1909; s. Frost Edwin and Emma (Williamson) S.; B.S., Franklin and Marshall Coll., 1931; B.D., Lancaster Theol. Sem., 1934; postgrad. (grantee), Harvard Div. Sch., 1938-39, U. Pitts., 1939-40; M.A., Middle Tenn. State U., 1967; m. Thelma Kathryn Lytle, Nov. 29, 1934; children—Paul N., John P., James F. Ordained to ministry Evang. and Ref. Ch., 1934; pastor Evang. and Ref. Ch., Pa., Md., 1934-42, Denver, Pa., 1946-51; asst. prof. psychology Cleveland (Tenn.) State Coll., 1967—; psychol. testing and evaluation Headstart, 1969-70. Dist. commnr. Boy Scouts Am., 1969-71. Served as chaplain USAAF, 1941-46, ETO; from lt. col. to col. USAF, 1951-67. Decorated Bronze Star medal. Mem. Hist. Soc. Pa., Tenn. Ednl. Assn., Sigma Pi. Democrat. Mem. United Ch. of Christ. Mason, Lion. Home: 3602 Belmont Circle Cleveland TN 37311 Office: PO Box 1205 Cleveland State Coll Cleveland TN 37311

SMETANA, JOSEPH LAWRENCE, orgn. exec.; b. Temple, Tex., Mar. 8, 1930; s. Joseph Edward and Alice Annie (Gerngross) S.; student Temple Jr. Coll., 1949-50, U. Tex., 1951-52; B.S. in Vocational Agr., Sam Houston State U., 1953; m. Sybel Faye Rankin, Sept. 21, 1972. Insp. Tex. Dept. Agr., 1953-54, bus. mgr. seed div., asst. to chief seed div., 1954-60; safety dir. Tex. Farm Bur., Waco, 1960—. Mem. safety-loss control com. Southwestern Ins. Information Service. Recipient Citizenship award Am. Farm Bur., 1962; Dist. Service award Tex. Safety Assn., 1963; TV film award Nat. Safety Council, 1966. Mem. Falls County Farm Bur., Nat. Inst. for Farm Safety, Am. Soc. for Safety Engring. (asso.), Pub. Relations Soc. Am., Farm-Ranch-Tex. Safety Assn. (v.p. 1968—), Tex. Farm and Ranch Safety Council (pres. 1969-70). Roman Catholic. K.C., Elk. Home: 3920 Rolando Waco TX 76711 Office: Box 489 Waco TX 76703

SMIDDY, JOSEPH CHARLES, food co. exec.; b. Jellico, Tenn., Feb. 16, 1926; s. Sillus David and Emma Elizabeth (West) S.; m. Wilma Jean Marion, Nov. 16, 1946; children—Gloria (Mrs. Robert Clinton Price), Robert Milton, Nancy Carolyn. Co-owner, mgr. S.D. Smiddy & Son Grocery, Jellico, 1946-48; salesman Remfro Wholesale Grocery, Williamsburg, Ky., 1948-52; salesman J. Allen Smith & Co., Knoxville, 1952-53, sr. salesman, 1953-54, ty. mgr., 1954-55, dist. mgr., 1955-60; co-owner Mymatt-Smiddy Brokerage Co., Knoxville, 1960-62; merchandising mgr. J. Allen Smith Co., Knoxville, 1962-66; sales mgr. Gt. Western Foods Co., Knoxville, 1966—. Served with USMCR, 1944-46; PTO. Baptist. Mason (32 deg.), Lion. Home: 4028 Longwood Dr Knoxville TN 37918 Office: 108 Depot St NE Knoxville TN 37917

SMILEY, GARY RAY, educator, dentist; b. Spartanburg, S.C., Sept. 13, 1936; s. Harry and Rose (Hecklin) S.; B.S. in Dentistry, U. N.C., 1958, D.D.S., 1961, M.Sc. in Orthodontics, 1965; m. Sandra Lee Margolis, July 3, 1960; children—Steven Jay, Karen Beth, Suzanne Cheryl. Asst. prof. orthodontics U. N.C. at Chapel Hill, 1965-67, asso. prof., 1967-71, prof., 1971—, asst. dean research, 1971—, dir. orthodontic grad. research, 1967—. Orthodontic cons. N.C. Bd. Health, 1966—. Served to capt. USAF, 1961-63. USPHS grantee, 1967—. Mem. Am. Assn. Orthodontists, So. Soc. Orthodontists, Am. Cleft Palate Assn., Internat. Assn. Dental Research, A.A.A.S., Am. Dental Assn., Teratology Soc., Am. Cleft Palate Assn. (sec. 1971—), Phi Beta Kappa, Omicron Kappa Upsilon, Sigma Xi. Research and publs. on normal and abnormal growth and devel. of craniofacial complex especially formation of secondary palate. Home: 1704 Fountain Ridge Rd Chapel Hill NC 27514

SMILEY, GERALD THOMAS, space products co. exec.; b. Bristol, Que., Can., Sept. 23, 1925; s. Harold Ephriam and Charlotte Elizabeth (Russell) S.; B.E.E., Clarkson Coll. Tech., 1950; m. Sarah Elizabeth Meeker, Sept. 6, 1948; children—David, Linda, Steven, Patrick. Engr. heavy mil. elec. dept. Gen. Electric Co., 1951-55, program mgr., 1955-59, mgr. systems engring. def. systems div., 1959-62, program mgr. Apollo systems dept., Daytona Beach, Fla., 1962-63, mgr. Kennedy operations, Cape Canaveral, Fla., 1963-68, gen. mgr. Apollo and ground systems dept., Daytona Beach, 1968-73, gen. mgr. Earth Stas. dept., 1973—. Chmn. World Affairs Forum, Daytona Beach, 1970; mem. Civic League Halifax Area, 1968—. Bd. dirs., dep. campaign chmn. United Fund Brevard County, 1966-67. Served with USNR, 1943-46. Recipient Pub. Service award NASA, 1969. Mem. Am. Inst. Aeros. and Astronautics (membership chmn. 1967), Air Force Assn., I.E.E.E., Am. Ordance Assn., Nat. Space Club, Eta Kappa Nu. Rotarian. Home: 230 Landmark Circle Ormond Beach FL 32074 Office: PO Box 2500 Daytona Beach FL 32015

SMILEY, ROBERT LEE, entomologist; b. Birmingham, Ala., June 14, 1929; s. James and Cherry (Fuller) S.; B.S., Ala. A. and M. U., 1959; postgrad. Ohio State U., 1962-67; M.S., U. Md., 1973; m. Cleeretta L. Henderson, Sept. 21, 1955; children—Consuela, Robert, Lisa, Joan. Agrl. research technician U.S. Agr. Dept., Washington, 1961-67, research entomologist, 1967—. Scoutmaster, Boy Scouts Am., 1962-63, committeeman, 1963-64. Served with AUS, 1951-53. Alpha Kappa Mu scholar, 1968; named hon. citizen Minn., 1968. Mem. Entomol. Soc. Am., Entomol. Soc. Washington (custodian 1963-68), A.A.A.S., Acarology Assn. Baptist. Contbr. articles to profl. jours. Home: 1444 Primrose Rd NW Washington DC 20012 Office: Agr Research Sta US Agr Dept Beltsville MD 20705

SMIT, CHRISTIAN JACOBUS BESTER, educator; b. Piet Retief, S. Africa, Jan. 10, 1927; s. Cornelis Johannes and Jeanetta Jacoba (Bester) S.; B.Sc., Pretoria U., S. Africa, 1946, H.E.D., 1947; Ph.D., U. Cal. at Berkeley, 1953; m. 2d Wanda Anna Storath, 1968; children—Elizabeth, Jeanne, Christian. Came to U.S., 1963, naturalized, 1969. Research scientist Fruit and Food Tech. Inst., S. Africa, 1953-59; prof., head dept. food sci. U. Stellenbosh (S. Africa), 1960-63; research scientist Sunkist Growers Inc., Corona, Cal., 1963-68; prof. food sci. U. Ga., Athens, 1968—; div. chmn., dept. head, 1973—. Mem. Am. Chem. Soc., Inst. Food Technologists, A.A.A.S., S. African Assn. for Food Sci. and Tech. (hon. life), Sigma Xi, Gamma Sigma Delta. Contbr. articles to sci. jours. Patentee in field. Home: 485 Forest Rd Athens GA 30601

SMITH, ALAN JOHN, real estate investment trust co. exec.; b. Greenwich, Eng., July 21, 1931; s. John James and Minnie Margaret (Allen) S.; B.Sc. in Econs., U. Coll., London, Eng., 1954; m. Mary G. Russell, Aug. 26, 1960; children—Russell A., Katherine M. Came to U.S., 1961, naturalized, 1966. Sr. securities analyst Gt.-West Life Assn. Co., Winnipeg, Man., Can., 1956-60; corporate finance asso. F. Eberstadt & Co., 1961-62, N.Y. Securities Co., 1962; pres. So. Financial Services Inc., Greensboro, N.C., 1962-65; mortgage cons. Coral Gables, Fla., 1965-67; founder, treas. Asso. Mortgage Investors (ASE), Coral Gables, 1967-73; pres. Asso. Mortgage Mgrs., Inc., Coral Gables, 1967—; pres. Constrn. Funding Service, Inc., Coral Gables, 1973—. Served with Brit. Army, 1950-51. Mem. N.Y. Soc. Securities Analysts, Am. Soc. Appraisers (asso.). Clubs: Univeristy, British Luncheon (N.Y.); Coral Reef Yacht (Miami). Home: 443 Barbarossa Av Coral Gables FL 33146 Office: 120 Giralda Av PO Box 1998 Coral Gables FL 33134

SMITH, ALBERT HENRY, JR., metallurgist; b. Anniston, Ala., Mar. 10, 1928; s. Albert Henry and Eunice (Kitchens) S.; student Auburn U., 1948-49; B.S., Jacksonville State U., 1951; m. Sara Anne Geier, Sept. 7, 1950; children—David Albert, Sheila Ann. Chemist, Ala. Pipe Co., Anniston, Ala., 1950-53; research chemist Monsanto Chem. Co., Anniston, Ala., 1953; metallurgist, chief metallurgist, asst. plant mgr. Ala. Pipe Co., Anniston, Ala., 1954-67; tech. and quality control dir. SPARM, Woodward Iron Co., Anniston, Ala., 1967-71; mgr. quality control and metallurgy Woodward Soil Pipe group Woodward Co., Anniston, 1971-73; tech. dir. Charlotte Pipe & Foundry Co. (N.C.), 1973—. Troop committeeman Boy Scouts of Am., 1967—. Served with AUS, 1946-48. Mem. Am. Soc. for Testing and Materials, Am. Standards Assn., Am. Foundrymens Soc. (chpt. chmn. 1968-69), Cast Iron Pipe Research Assn., Cast Iron Soil Pipe Inst. Baptist. Home: 6716 Pleasant Dr Charlotte NC 28211 Office: 1400 NC Nat Bank Bldg Charlotte NC 28202

SMITH, ALEXANDER MARTIN, II, textile research co. exec.; b. Junction City, Ark., Oct. 23, 1918; s. Richard Gwyn and Margaret Ray (Harvison) S.; student Davidson Coll., 1935-36, N.C State U., 1936-39; B.S. in Chem. Engring., Mass. Inst. Tech., 1941, Sc.D., 1943; m. Ida Claire Purcell, Oct. 6, 1945; children—Clare Purcell, Ray Harvison, Martha Marshall. Devel. engr. Esso Standard Oil Co., Baton Rouge, 1943-46; asst. prof. Mass. Inst. Tech., Cambridge, 1946-48; pres. Chemurgy Corp., Elkin, N.C., 1948-59; pres. Technic Engring. Corp., Elkin, 1952—; dir. devel. Chatham Mfg. Co., Elkin, 1959-69; exec. v.p. Carolina Bloomer Co., Elkin, 1967—; pres. Chatham Research and Devel. Corp., Elkin, 1970—; chmn. bd. Yadkin Valley Bank & Trust Co., Elkin, 1968—. Trustee N.C. Symphony Soc. Mem. Am. Chem. Soc., Textile Research Inst., Fiber Soc. Methodist. Kiwanian. Club: Cedarbrook Country (Elkin). Inventor fiberwoven process and machine, 1960-64, Tanera man made leather, 1969-73. Home: 131 Gwyn Av Elkin NC 28621 Office: 125 W Robin Elkin NC 28621

SMITH, ALFRED GLAZE, JR., economist, educator; b. Urbana, Ill., Dec. 28, 1913; s. Alfred Glaze and Lucy Catharine (Prutsman) S.; A.B., Columbia, 1934, A.M., 1939, Ph.D., 1954; m. Katharine Cushing Brown, May 9, 1936; children—Alfred Glaze III, LeRoy Fairchild. With personal div. S.H. Kress & Co., 1936-38; instr. econs. U. S.C., 1938-42, asst. prof., 1942-47, asso. prof., 1947-54, prof., 1954—, head dept. econs., 1958-70; discussant First Ann. Conf. Econ. Devel. South, 1960; Fulbright prof., Bologna, Italy, 1963-64. Owner, operator farm, Lexington County, S.C. Served as officer USNR, 1943-46; comdr. Res. Mem. Am., So. econ. assns., Econ. History Assn. Club: Torch (pres.). Author: Economic Readjustment of an Old Cotton State: South Carolina, 1820-1860, 1958. Home: 1816 Enoree Av Columbia SC 29205

SMITH, ALLIE MAITLAND, research scientist; b. Lumberton, N.C., June 9, 1934; s. Allie McCoy and Emma Hattie (Wright) S.; B.S. with honors in Mech. Engring., N.C. State U., 1956, M.S., 1961, Ph.D., 1966; m. Sarah Louise Whitlock, June 16, 1957; children—Sara Leianne, Hollis Duval, Meredith Lorren. Asso. engr. Martin Co., Balt., 1956-57; mem. tech. staff Bell Telephone Labs., Burlington, N.C., 1957-62; research project engr. Research Triangle Inst., Durham, 1962-66; research supr. Arnold Research Orgn., Inc., Arnold Air Force Sta., Tenn., 1966—. Instr. N.C. State U., 1958-60, asst. prof. (extension), Raleigh, 1961-62; asso. prof. U. Tenn., Tullahoma, part-time 1966-73, Knoxville, 1974—. Asso. fellow Am. Inst. Aeros. and Astronautics (thermophysics tech. com. 1973—); mem. Sigma Xi, Phi Kappa Phi, Tau Beta Pi, Pi Tau Sigma. Democrat. Baptist. Author: Fundamentals of Silicon Integrated Device Technology, Vol. 1: Oxidation, Diffusion and Epitaxy, 1967. Contbr. articles to profl. jours. Reviewer for Am. Inst. Aeros. and Astronautics Jour. and Internat. Jour. Heat and Mass Transfer; proposal reviewer NSF. Home: 1714 Country Club Dr Tullahoma TN 37388 Office: ARO Inc Arnold Air Force Station TN 37389

SMITH, ALVA EUGENE, lawyer; b. Dallas, Feb. 1, 1940; s. William Alva and Willie Ruth (Taylor) S.; B.B.A. (Acad. scholar 1961-62), So. Meth. U., 1962, LL.B., 1965. Admitted to Tex. bar, 1965; mem. tax staff Arthur Young & Co., Dallas, 1969-70; tax mgr. Centex Corp., Dallas, 1970-73; mgr. taxes and ins. Baker-Crow Co., Dallas, 1973; partner Tudor, Smith & Co., C.P.A.'s, Dallas, 1973—. Bd. dirs. Angles, Inc., 1963-64; adv. com. Thelma Boston Found. for Handicapped Children, 1973—. Served with AUS, 1966-69. C.P.A., Tex. Mem. Am. Inst. C.P.A.'s, Tex. Soc. C.P.A.'s, Am., Tex. State bar assns. Home: 8426 Van Pelt Dr Dallas TX 75228 Office: 810 LTV Tower Dallas TX 75201

SMITH, AMELIA HALL, musician; b. Oklahoma City; d. Charles Jordan and Marie Helen (Ferris) Hall; grad. Drew Sem. for Young Women, Carmel, N.Y., 1930; summer student Woman's Coll., Greensboro, N.C., Julliard Sch. Music, N.Y.C.; certificate Am. Guild of Organists, 1954; student operatic seminar Manhattan Sch. Music, 1970; m. Willard Cardwell, Nov. 18, 1936 (div. Nov. 1954); children—Marie Lorraine (Mrs. James Albert Harrill, Jr.), Christine Amelia (Mrs. Ray D. Dodge); m. 2d, Harry Logan Smith, Jr., Aug. 19, 1956. Profl. accompanist, 1925—; soprano soloist, 1934—, appeared with Piedmont Festival Orch., 1943-49, Jacksonville (Fla.) Symphony Orch., 1957, others; appeared as Marie, Bartered Bride, 1941; founder, leading soprano Music Theatre Repertory Group, 1947-52; founder, dir. Opera Workshop, Jacksonville U. Coll. Music, 1956-61; founder, music dir., mng. dir. Opera Repertory Group (TV and touring opera co.), 1961—, also pres.; music columnist N.C. and Fla. newspapers; pianist Jacksonville Symphony Orch., 1963-67; music faculty Edward Waters Coll., Jacksonville, 1967-68; organist, choirmaster 1st Meth. Ch., 1954-59, Grace Chapel Parish, 1959-67, Presbyn. Ch. Southside Estates, 1968-72, San Jose Episcopal Ch., 1972—. Active Arts Festival of Jacksonville Council Arts, 1958—, music chmn., 1958-59; dean. Am. Guild Organists, Jacksonville, 1958-61, chmn. Southeastern regional conv., 1963; mem. Am. Bicentennial Commn. of Jacksonville, 1973—. Mem. Music Tchr. Assn. Jacksonville, Am. Guild of Organists, Jacksonville Council Arts, Nat. Assn. Tchrs. Singing, Nat. Assn. Am. Composers and Condrs., Jacksonville Opera Guild (founder), Central Opera Service, Am. Guild Mus. Artists, Musicians Assn. Jacksonville. Episcopalian (mem. music commn. Diocese of Fla. 1966-67). Club: Altrusa (pres. 1967-68, com. 1963-64) (Jacksonville). Music columnist The Trend, Jacksonville, 1969—; corr. Mus. Am. Home: 4227 Peachtree Circle E Jacksonville FL 32207 Office: 7423 San Jose Blvd Jacksonville FL 32217

SMITH, ANDERSON BENSKIN, JR., lawyer; b. Richmond, Va., Aug. 25, 1922; s. Anderson Benskin and Otelia Nimmo (Branch) S.; student Duke, 1943-44; B.Sc., U. N.C., 1946; postgrad. U. Va. Law Sch., 1947-48; B.C.L., Coll. William and Mary, 1949; m. Edwina Young Myers, July 1, 1960; children—Gwendolyn Coleman, Susan Branch, Anderson Benskin, III, Helen Young. Admitted to Va. bar, 1948; partner firm Carneal, Smith & Athey, Toano, Va. and Williamsburg, Va., 1948-60, Williamsburg, 1960—. Dir. First Fed. Savs. & Loan Assn. Richmond, 1971—. Mem. James City County Bd. Suprs., 1951-54; mem. James City County Sch. Bd., 1960-61; U.S. commr., 1954-60; U.S. magistrate, parttime, 1972—. Bd. dirs. Jamestown Acad., 1962-71. Served with USNR, 1943-46. Mem. Am., Va. bar assns., Va. State Bar, Delta Theta Phi. Mason. Club: Ruritan

Nat. (pres. Williamsburg 1949, dist. gov. 1951, nat. bd. dirs. 1953-57). Home: 608 College Terrace Williamsburg VA 23185 Office: PO Box 440 124 N Henry St Williamsburg VA 23185

SMITH, ANGIE FRANK, JR., lawyer; b. Detroit, Tex., Nov. 3, 1915; s. A. Frank and Bess Patience (Crutchfield) S.; B.A., Rice U., 1937; LL.B., U.Tex., 1940; m. Mary Hannah, June 15, 1939; children—Tweed, Karen, A. Frank III, Alison, Leslie Ann. Partner Vinson, Elkins, Searls, Connally & Smith and predecessor; dir. Cullen Center Bank & Trust. Quintana Petroleum Corp., Austral Oil Co., Crutcher Resources Corp. Adv. bd. Internat. Oil and Gas Edn. Center. Trustee, mem. exec. com. Meth. Hosp., Houston, Southwestern U., Georgetown, Tex.; trustee Cullen Found.; bd. dirs. Houston Symphony Soc. Served with USNR, 1942-45. Fellow Am. Bar Found.; mem. Sons Republic Tex., Knight San Jacinto, Am., Tex., Houston bar assns., Order of Coif, Phi Delta Phi, Phi Delta Theta. Methodist. Clubs: River Oaks Country; Broadmoor Golf, Garden of Gods (Colorado Springs). Home: 3420 Piping Rock Lane Houston TX 77027 Office: First City Nat Bank Bldg Houston TX 77002

SMITH, AUBURN PINKNEY, coll. athletic dir., educator; b. Louann, Ark., Dec. 13, 1913; s. Andrew Pinkney and Anna (Neeley) S.; B.A., Hendrix Coll., 1938; M.S., George Peabody U., 1953; postgrad. U. Ark., 1964-65 Tchr., coach Morrilton High Sch., 1938-41, Camden High Sch., 1941-42, 1946-47; instr., coach So. State Coll., Magnolia, Ark., 1947-54, head coach, athletic dir., asst. prof., 1954-69, athletic dir., asso. prof. phys. edn., 1969—, dir. financial aids, 1972—. Pres. Ark. Athletic Dirs. Intercollegiate Conf., 1972. Served with USAAF, 1942-46. Decorated Bronze Star medal. Mem. Nat., Ark., Southwest assns. student financial aid adminstrs., Magnolia C. of C., Am. Legion, V.F.W., Ark. Edn. Assn., N.E.A., A.A.H.P.E.R., Ark. Coaches Assn., Nat. Assn. Intercollegiate Coaches Assn., Nat. Assn. Intercollegiate Athletics (chmn. exec. com. 1967-73, award of merit 1974). Methodist (chmn. ofcl. bd. 1961-62). Kiwanian, Rotarian. Home: 1305 Lacari St Magnolia AR 71753

SMITH, AUGUST WILLIAM, educator; b. Austin, Tex., Oct. 10, 1940; B.B.A., U. Tex., 1963, M.B.A., 1965, Ph.D. in Bus. Adminstrn., 1971; married; 2 sons. Mfg. engr. Tex. Instruments Inc., Houston, 1965, cons., 1967-68; cons.-researcher Mgmt. Research Internat., Austin, Tex. and N.Y.C., 1967; asst. prof. mgmt. Tex. A. and M. U., College Station, 1969—. Staff selective service sect., adj. gen. Tex., 1967—. Served with AUS, 1965-67; Vietnam. NASA resident fellow, 1969. Mem. Acad. Mgmt. (also Southwest div.), Am. Inst. Indsl. Engrs. (sr.), Southwestern Social Sci. Assn., Soc. Information Mgmt., Assn. Systems Mgmt., Am. Inst. Decision Scis., Am. Soc. Advancement Sci., Soc. Advancement Mgmt., Nat. Defense Transp. Assn., Armed Forces Communication and Electronics Assn., N.G. Assn. Tex. (life), Ex-Students Assn. U. Tex. (life), Old Crows Soc., Beta Gamma Sigma, Sigma Iota Epsilon. Contbr. articles to profl. publs. Home: 2301 Devonshire St Bryan TX 77801 Office: Dept Mgmt Tex A and M U College Station TX 77843

SMITH, B. J., educator, art gallery ofcl.; b. Beaver, Okla., Aug. 22, 1931; s. Oliver Lindell and Mattie Sue (Harper) S.; B.F.A., Okla. State U., 1955; M.F.A., U. Okla., 1959. Asst. to dir. Okla. Art Center, Oklahoma City, 1961-65; asst. prof. art Okla. State U., Stillwater, 1965—, dir. Gardiner Art Gallery, 1965—. Exhibited one-man shows Town and Gown Theater, Stillwater, 1967, Summit Gallery, Oklahoma City, 1972, U. Okla. Mus. Art, Norman, 1973; two-man shows CAF Gallery, Oklahoma City, 1968, Gardiner Art Gallery, Okla. State U., Stillwater, 1971; exhibited in group shows Philbrook Art Center, Tulsa, 1958, 64, 65, 67, 68, 73, Okla. Art Center, Oklahoma City, 1962-64, 68, 70, Springfield (Mo.) Art Mus., 1966, 70, 71, CAF Gallery, 1966, others. Served with AUS, 1955-57. Recipient Purchase award 9th Midwest Biennial Joslyn Art Mus., Omaha, 1966; Okla. Biennial 1967 Okla. Art Center, 1967, painting award 38th Okla. Artists Ann., Philbrook Art Center, Tulsa, 1968. Home: 2132 W Sunset Dr Stillwater OK 74074

SMITH, B. FRANK, JR., marketing engr., analyst, cons.; b. Sturgis, Miss., Aug. 26, 1916; s. B. Frank and Florence (Kornegay) S.; B.A., B.S., U. Tenn., 1949, postgrad., 1949-50; m. Emily Edith Berryhill, Nov. 28, 1946. U.S. dep. collector Internal Revenue Service, Memphis, 1944-45; territory sales W. A. Shaeffer Pen Co., Ga., S.C., 1950-52; profl. pharm. service rep. Stuart Pharms., Tenn., Ga., N.C., Ky., 1952-66, Treasure Island, Fla., 1966-72; terr. mgr. Stuart Pharm. div. ICI America Inc., 1972—. Unit leader Shrine Crippled Children, 1964-65; adviser, dir., contbr. Easter Seal Soc., 1962-63; asst. chmn. com. Elk Crippled Children Rehab., 1968—; adviser, dir., mem. Scottish Rite Masons Underprivileged Children's Soc. Served with AUS, 1940-44. Mem. Pharm. Reps. Assn. (dir.), Tampa Bay Pharm. Reps. Assn., Am. Security Council, Found. Econ. Edn., Am. Legion, Disabled Am. Vet. Republican. Lutheran. Mason (32 deg., Shriner), Elk. Clubs: Seminole Country, Bath. Home: 10215 3d St E Treasure Island FL 33706

SMITH, BARNETT FRISSELL, biologist, educator; b. Montgomery, Ala., Jan. 17, 1909; s. Thomas J. and Alice (Johnson) S.; B.S., Morehouse Coll., 1932; M.S., Atlanta U., 1934; Ph.D., U. Wis., 1944; m. Grace Burley Boggs, Aug. 22, 1962; children—Barnett Frissell, Olivia Boggs. Tchr. biology, gen. sci. city schs., Atlanta, 1935-36; asso. prof. biology Ala. State Coll., 1937-45; prof. biology Spelman Coll., Atlanta, 1945—. Ford Found. fellow, 1954-55; La. State U. fellow, Central Am., summer 1966. Contbr. articles to sci. jours. Home: 1198 Fountain Dr SW Atlanta GA 30314

SMITH, BENJAMIN DENNIS, research chemist; b. Norfolk, Va., July 16, 1938; s. Prentis P. and Edwyne (Parker) S.; B.S. in Chemistry, Coll. William and Mary, 1960; Ph.D. in Chemistry, Ga. Inst. Tech., 1966. Research chemist Naval Weapons Lab., Dahlgren, Va., 1960—. Recipient Outstanding Young Man of Year award, 1971-72; Naval Weapons Lab. Outstanding Performance award, 1972. Home: Potomac Gardens Apts 93A PO Box 1026 Dahlgren VA 22448 Office: Naval Weapons Lab Code FCC Dahlgren VA 22448

SMITH, BENJAMIN FRANKLIN, council ofcl.; b. Holcomb, Miss., Dec. 22, 1917; s. Ben F. and Allene (DeShazo) S.; B.S., Delta State Tchrs. Coll., 1939; grad. student George Peabody U.; m. Mary Alyce Bounds, Aug. 31, 1941; children—James Winfred, Lelia Elaine. Instr. biol. sci., Arcola (Miss.) Sch., 1939-41, Jackson City Sch., 1941-42; tng. officer V.A., 1946-47; asst. mgr. Delta Council, 1947-49, secretary, mgr., 1949-57, exec. v.p., 1957—. Mgmt. rep. Labor Mgmt. Manpower Com. Region IV, 1957-64; mem. Nat. Cotton Adv. Com. Served as capt. AUS, 1942-46. Recipient Man of Year award Progressive Farmer, 1962; Spl. Service award U. S. Weather Bur., 1964; Outstanding Alumni award Delta State Coll., 1964; Golden Anniversary Fed. Land Bank award, 1967; Silver Beaver Boy Scouts Am. Mem. Miss., Nat., So. assns. C. of C. execs., Delta State Alumni Assn. Methodist. Club: Lions. Author articles in tech. jours. Contbr. Delta Looks Forward, 1949; Flood Control in the Mississippi Valley, 1952. Editor: Delta Council News. Home: Leland MS 38756 Office: Stoneville MS 38776

SMITH, BENJAMIN SHAW, JR., petroleum co. exec.; b. Mexia, Tex., Jan. 23, 1917; s. Benjamin Shaw and Natalie (Machon) S.; student Rice U., 1934-35, Met. Bus. Sch., 1935-36; m. C. Ruth McDonald, Dec. 30, 1942; children—Benjamin Shaw III, C. Rebecca. Dir. indsl. relations Lion Oil Co., El Dorado, Ark., 1937-55; dir. personnel research Monsanto Co., St. Louis, 1955-58; gen. mgr. adminstrv. services Murphy Oil Corp., El Dorado, 1958-69, v.p., 1969—; dir. Nat. Bank Commerce, El Dorado. Chmn. El Dorado Airport Commn., 1962—; gen. chmn. United Campaign, 1967. Bd. dirs. Greater El Dorado Com. Mem. Am. Petroleum Inst., Am. Mgmt. Assn., El Dorado C. of C. Methodist. Rotarian. Home: 101 Fairway Lane El Dorado AR 71730 Office: Murphy Bldg El Dorado AR 71730

SMITH, BUDD ELMON, coll. pres.; b. Benson, N.C., Feb. 9, 1910; s. James L. and Hettie (Lee) S.; A.B., U. N.C., 1931, M.A., 1934, Ph.D., 1942; postgrad. Duke U., 1950-51; LL.D., Wake Forest Coll., 1961; m. Ethel Lillie Knott, Dec. 27, 1943; children—James Fielding, William Budd. Prof. biology Coker Coll., 1935-35, 39-46; plant breeder Coker's Pedigreed Seed Co., Hartsville, S.C., 1935-39; prof. biology Wake Forest Coll., 1946-51; supt. schs., Ocford, N.C., 1951-53; pres. Wingate Coll., 1953—. Dir. Wingate State Bank. Mem. Nat. Accrediting Commn. Higher Edn.; chmn. Christmas Seals; chmn. N.C. Transfer Studies. Trustee Union Meml. Hosp.; mem. indsl. commn. Union County, 1954-57; pres. Union County Indsl. Devel. Commn., 1960-61. Served from petty officer 2d class to lt. USNR, 1942-45. Named Man of Year, Union County, 1961. Mem. A.A.A.S., Am. Assn. Sch. Adminstrs., Bot. Soc. Am., Am. (dir.), So. (pres.), N.C. (pres., organizer) assns. jr. colls., N.C. Assn. Ind. Colls. and Univs. (exec. com.), So. Assn. Schs. and Colls. (chmn. standards com.), Nat. Council Ind. Two-Yr. Colls. (exec. com.), N.C. Acad. Sci., Southeastern Assn. Biologists, Union-Monroe C. of C. (pres. 1972), Phi Beta Kappa, Sigma Xi, Beta Beta Beta, Omicron Delta Kappa, Alpha Sigma Phi, Alpha Epsilon Delta. Democrat. Baptist (deacon, lay leader). Clubs: Lions, Rotary. Home: Northwood Wingate NC 28174

SMITH, CALVIN MILES, dentist; b. Atlanta, Dec. 11, 1924; s. Harvey Miles and Stella Idaray (Bryant) S.; B.S., Morehouse Coll., 1948; D.D.S., Howard U., 1953; m. Margaret Odessa Nixon, Sept. 22, 1949; children—Calvin Miles, Stephen La Coste, Lynn Lavada, Kim Clarice. Tchr. gen. scis. Ballard High Sch., 1948-49; practice dentistry, Atlanta, 1953—; dental cons. Atlanta Residential Man-Power Tng. Center, 1969—. Panel chmn. Atlanta Community Chest, 1966-67; pres. N.A.A.C.P., Atlanta, 1963, 64, treas., 1962, 65-66, life mem., 1970—; mem. Atlanta Com. Cooperative Action, 1961—, Mayor's Com. for Hotel and Restaurant Desegregation, 1961; mem. exec. com. Atlanta Model Cities Program, 1967—, Atlanta Youth Council, 1968—. Vice pres. Fulton County Democratic Club, 1963-71. Chmn. bd. Atlanta Home for Convalescing and Aged, 1953—. Served with USMCR, 1944-46; PTO. Named Atlanta Citizen of Year, 1964; recipient Achievment award Guardsmen, 1964. Mem. Am., Ga. (pres. 1964, 65), N. Ga. (pres., 1963-64) No. Dist. dental assns., Omega Psi Phi. Baptist. Mason (32 deg., Shriner). Club: Graduate Bridge. Contbr. articles to newspapers, periodicals. Home: 469 Haldane Dr SW Atlanta GA 30311 Office: 2380 Sewell Rd SW Atlanta GA 30311

SMITH, CAMERON EARL, electronics exec.; b. Columbia, S.C., Mar. 16, 1942; s. George Earle and Lily Summers (White) S.; B.S., U. S.C., 1965; M.S., U. Ala., 1967, postgrad., 1967-68; m. Shirley Lorene Creamer, Jan. 30, 1965; children—Teresa L., Denise C. With Fed. Systems div. Internat. Bus. Machines, aerospace, Huntsville, Ala., 1965-67; cons. engr. F.A. Smith, Charleston, S.C., 1967; aerospace electronics engr. Sperry Rand, Huntsville, Ala., 1967-68; indsl. electronics engr. Milliken Electronics, Greenville, S.C., 1968-71; with Steel Heddle Mfg. Co., indsl. electronics, Greenville, S.C., 1971—electronics mgr. 1973—. Registered profl. engr., S.C., N.C., Ala. Mem. I.E.E.E., Eta Kappa Nu. Contbr. to profl. publs. in field. Patentee in field. Home: 205 Highbourne Dr Greenville SC 29607 Office: Box 1867 Greenville SC 29602

SMITH, CARLOS CLIFFORD, lawyer; b. Chattanooga, Nov. 6, 1939; s. Clarence Roy and Catherine Ellen (Henegar) S.; B.S., U. Chattanooga, 1961; J.D., U. Cin., 1964; m. Ann Christine Windhorn, Feb. 27, 1965; children—Mark, Catherine Ann. Admitted to Tenn. bar, 1964; asso. firm Strang, Fletcher, Carriger, Walker & Hodge, Chattanooga, 1964-68, partner, 1968—, mng. partner, 1971—. Counsel, Tenn. Credit Union League, 1971—; spl. counsel to Atty. Gen. Tenn., 1971—, to Tenn. Dept. Transp., 1971—. Gen. counsel Met. Govt. Charter Commn., 1969-70; chmn. probate com. Tenn. Law Revision Commn., 1971—; pres. Blood Assurance, Inc., 1971—; treas. Team Eval. Center, 1971—. Bd. dirs. Chattanooga Speech and Hearing Center, Auditorium Bd. City of Chattanooga. Mem. Chattanooga (pres.-elect 1974—, bd. govs. 1969-71), Tenn. (tax sect.), Am. (real estate, probate and trust sect.) bar assns., Tenn. Def. Lawyers Assn., Chattanooga Jaycees (v.p. 1967-69, state dir. 1960-70), Chattanooga C. of C. (air pollution task force 1966-68, vice chmn. govt. affairs com.). Lutheran. Home: 1117 Applewood Circle Signal Mountain TN 37377 Office: Maclellan Bldg Chattanooga TN 37402

SMITH, CAROL CROSSWELL, lawyer; b. Buffalo, Dec. 21, 1928; d. Albert L.L. and Helen (McDowell) McCormick; student Radcliffe Coll., LL.B. cum laude, U. Buffalo, 1947; postgrad. Columbia, 1960, Harvard, 1961; m. William J. Crosswell (dec. 1947); m. 2d, Gilbert Wheatland Smith, Feb. 2, 1952 (div. Feb. 1969); children—Carol, Linda. Admitted to N.Y. bar, 1948, Washington bar, 1953, Fla. bar, 1967; mem. legal staff UN, 1947-51; mem. U.S. Govt. Psychol. Strategy Bd., 1951-53; U.S. del. Inter Am. Council Jurists, Santiago, Chile, 1960; practiced in N.Y.C., 1950—, Palm Beach, Fla., 1967—; mem. firm Weidon and Crosswell, 1950-66. Mem. Fla. Marine Commn., 1968—. Bd. dirs. Jr. League, Millard Fillmore Hosp., Buffalo, Save the Children Fedn., Gebbie Found.; bd. govs. Nova U. Law Center. Mem. Soc. Women Geographers, Fellows of Harvard. Clubs: Indian Harbor Yacht (Greenwich, Conn.); Buffalo Country; N.Y. Skating; Palm Beach Yacht, Sail Fish (Palm Beach, Fla.); Royal Canadian Yacht (Toronto, Ont.); Trident Yacht (Ont.). Author: Protection of International Personnel, 1956; Financing Foreign Investment, 1962; International Business Techniques, 1962. Home: 1204 N Ocean Blvd Palm Beach FL 33480 also Cherrycroft Burt NY Office: 60 E 42d St New York City NY 10017 also 629 Peruvian Av Palm Beach FL 33480

SMITH, C(HARLES) CARNEY, trade assn. exec.; b. Kalamazoo, Nov. 17, 1912; s. Henry and Helen (Carney) S.; student Kalamazoo Coll., 1929-31; A.B., Western Mich. U., 1933; M.A., U. Mich., 1938; postgrad. Northwestern U., 1940; LL.D., Alma Coll., 1972; m. Mildred Krohne, June 18, 1934; children—Patricia Marie (Mrs. M. Kent Barker), Clark Krohne. With Kalamazoo City Welfare Dept., 1933-35; head dept. speech and forensics No. High Sch., Flint, Mich., 1935-38; chmn. dept. speech Alma (Mich.) Coll., 1938-42; regional dir. Eastern area A.R.C., Washington, 1942-46; dir. mgmt. tng. program Mut. Benefit Life Ins. Co., Newark, 1946-48, gen. agt., Washington, 1948-63; exec. v.p. Nat. Assn. Life Underwriters, Washington, 1963—. Chmn., Gen. Agts. and Mgrs. Conf., 1962-63. Bd. dirs. D.C. chpt. A.R.C.; trustee Detroit Inst. Tech., Life Underwriters Tng. Council. Recipient John Newton Russell Meml. award for outstanding contbn. to life ins. industry, 1970; Distinguished Alumnus award Western Mich. U., 1972. Mem. U.S., D.C. chambers commerce, Tau Kappa Alpha. Republican. Conglist. Lion. Clubs: Capitol Hill, University (Washington); University (N.Y.C.); Congressional (Potomac, Md.). Contbr. articles to profl. jours. Home: 809 Vassar Rd Alexandria VA 22314 Office: 1922 F St NW Washington DC 20006

SMITH, CHARLES EDWARD, physician; b. Omaha, Nov. 16, 1917; s. Maurice I. and Rebecca (Ratner) S.; student U. Md., 1934-37; A.B., George Washington U., 1939, M.D., 1941; postgrad. Columbia, 1950-51; m. Phyllis Stein Lange, June 12, 1941; children—Timothea Ann (Mrs. Jurgen-Harald Zimmermann), Jonathan Charles. Intern, USPHS Hosp., Balt., 1941-42; staff psychiatrist VA Hosp., Northport, N.Y., 1945-49; chief med. officer, psychiatrist Fed. Correction Inst., Ashland, Ky., 1949-50; resident USPHS Hosp., S.I., N.Y., 1950-51; chief Psychiat. Service Med. Center for Fed. Prisoners, Springfield, Mo., 1951-55; asst. med. dir. Fed. Bur. Prisons, Washington, 1956-62, med. dir., 1962-66; chief of service West Side div. St. Elizabeth Hosp., Washington, 1966-67; asso. prof. psychiatry U. N.C. Sch. Medicine, Chapel Hill, 1967-73, prof., 1973—; sr. psychiat. cons. N.C. Dept. Corrections, 1967—. Mem. profl. council Nat. Council on Crime and Delinquency, 1965—, mem. adult corrections panel, adv. council N.C. Council, 1968—. Served as capt. M.C., AUS, 1943-46. Fellow Am. Psychiat. Assn., A.A.A.S.; mem. A.M.A. Democrat. Conglist. Mason (Shriner), Kiwanian. Contbr. numerous articles to profl. jours. Home: S Lakeshore Dr and Rolling Rd Chapel Hill NC 27514 Office: Dept Psychiatry U NC Sch Medicine Chapel Hill NC 27514

SMITH, CHARLES FOSTER, accountant; b. nr. Scranton, S.C., Nov. 14, 1919; s. Wade H. and Kizzie (Marlowe) S.; B.S., U. S.C., 1940; m. Sarah Virginia Fore, Nov. 15, 1947; children—Sarah Dianne, Rebecca Elaine, Caroline Virginia. Practice pub. accounting, Myrtle Beach, also Conway, S.C., 1947—; dir. Peoples Nat. Bank, Conway, 1959-69; mem. action bd. C & S Bank, Myrtle Beach, 1969—. Mem. S.C. Bd. Accountancy, 1969—, chmn., 1971—. Treas., bd. dirs. Coastal Ednl. Found. Served with AUS, 1944-46; PTO. C.P.A., S.C. Mem. S.C. Assn. C.P.A.'s (pres. 1959-60), Am. Inst. C.P.A.s, Phi Beta Kappa, Omicron Delta Kappa. Methodist (chmn. adminstrv. bd. 1956-57). Home: 3400 N Kings Hwy Myrtle Beach SC 29577 Office: 401 12th Av N Myrtle Beach SC 29577

SMITH, CHARLES G., JR., editor; b. Shreveport, La., Feb. 27, 1925; s. Charles G. and Annie (Browning) S.; B.A., Miss. Coll., 1949, M.A., 1952; postgrad. U. So. Miss., 1953, La. State U.; m. Sara C. Smith, Nov. 27, 1957. Instr. Journalism Central High Sch., Jackson, Miss., 1952-62; staff writer, contbg. mem. Clarion-Ledger, Jackson, Miss., 1957-65, city editor, 1965-73, news editor, 1973—. Served with AUS, 1943-46. Mem. Miss. Journalism Assn. (past pres.), Sigma Delta Chi (chpt. past pres.), C. of C. Episcopalian. Miss. Wing staff mem. Civil Air Patrol, 1957—. Office: 311 E Pearl St PO Box 40 Jackson MS 39205

SMITH, CHARLES H., JR., pub. co. exec. Pres., publisher Roy N. Lotspeich Pub. Co Inc., Knoxville, Tenn. Office: 210 W Church Av Knoxville TN 37901*

SMITH, CHARLES LEAVELL, JR., city engr.; b. Pensacola, Fla., Mar. 4, 1914; s. Charles Leavell and Marie (McGill) S.; B.S. in Elec. Engring., Ga. Inst. Tech., 1935; m. Sara Lewis, Sept. 7, 1940; children—Sara Lewis (Mrs. Michael J. Grode), Charlotte Jon. Asst. sales engr. Westinghouse Elec. Corp., 1935-38; engr. Wright & Logez, Cedartown, Ga., 1938-41, Smith-Bittenbring, Inc., Cedartown, 1945-50; supt. light, water and sewage dept. City of Griffin (Ga.), 1950—. Served to comdr. USNR, 1941-45. Mem. I.E.E.E., Tau Beta Pi, Sigma Alpha Epsilon, Phi Kappa Phi, Phi Eta Sigma, Omicron Delta Kappa. Democrat. Episcopalian. Elk. Club: Exchange (pres. Griffin 1957, dist. gov. 1958-59). Contbr. article to profl. publ. Home: 652 Brook Circle Griffin GA 30223 Office: Light and Water Dept Griffin GA 30223

SMITH, CHARLES ULLMAN, educator; b. Birmingham, Ala., Oct. 16, 1923; s. William Pernell and Ella Marzetta (Johnson) S.; B.S., Tuskegee Inst., 1944; M.A., Fisk U., 1946; Ph.D., Wash. State U., 1950; postgrad. U. Conn., 1958; m. Marolyn Camille Warner, Aug. 21, 1951 (div.); 1 dau., Shauna Yvonne. Faculty Fla. A. and M. U., Tallahassee, 1950—, prof., chmn. sociology dept., 1951—; adj. prof. sociology Fla. State U., 1964—. Pres., Tallahassee Council Human Relations, 1960-62; mem. Gov.'s Interagy. Law Enforcement Planning Council, 1967-71, Fla. Commn. on Human Relations, 1969-73; Fla. del. White House Conf. on Children, 1970, White House Conf. on Aging, 1971. Vice chmn., mem. exec. com. Leon County Democratic Party, 1966—. Trustee Fla. Council on Aging. Grantee, coordinator sever coll. study on student unrest Russell Sage Found., 1967—. Recipient Silver medallion Mental Health Assn. Fla., 1968, Gold medallion, 1971, Meritorious Achievement award Fla. A. & M. U., 1973, DuBois award Assn. Social and Behavioral Scientists, 1973. Mem. Am., So. (v.p. 1967-68, pres. elect 1974) sociol. socs., Am. Assn. U. Profs., N.E.A., Fla. Edn. Assn., Fla. (bd. dirs.), Leon County (bd. dirs.) assns. mental health, Am. Acad. Polit. Social Sci., Alpha Phi Alpha. Presbyn. Editor: Diamond Anniversary Essays, 1962. Adv. editor Social Forces, 1971-72; asso. editor Jour. Health and Social Behavior, 1973—. Editorial bd. Agewise, 1969-71, Jour. Health and Social Behavior, Jour. Social and Behavioral Scis., 1973—. Contbr. articles to books and profl. jours. Home: 3039 Cloudland Dr Tallahassee FL 32303

SMITH, CHLOETHIEL WOODARD, architect; b. Peoria, Ill., Feb., 2, 1910; d. Olliver Ernest and Coy Blanche (Johnson) W.; B.Arch. with honors, U. Ore., 1932; M.Arch., Washington U., 1933; m. Bromley Keables Smith, Apr. 5, 1940; children—Bromley Keables, Susanne Woodard. Various drafting positions, Portland, Ore., Seattle, 1929-32, drafting and design, N.Y.C., 1933-36; chief research and planning FHA, Washington, 1936-39; asso., pvt. practice architecture, Washington, 1939-40; city planning exhibit, drafting, Montreal, Can., 1940-41; prof. architecture U. San Andres, cons. Servicio Cooperativo de Salud Publica, La Paz, Bolivia, 1942-45; prin. Chloethiel Woodard Smith & Assos., Washington, 1945—; prin. works include Am. Embassy Chancery and Residence, Asuncion, Paraguay, Chestnut Lodge, Rockville, Md., Capitol Park apt. and town houses, Washington, bookstore Harcourt, Brace & World, Inc., N.Y.C., master plan for Washington Channel Waterfront, E St. Expressway, Washington, numerous pvt. residences, also urban renewal plans. Jury mem. house awards A.I.A., Nat. Assn. Home Builders; design review panel Boston Redevel. Agy.; participated exhibits City for Living, Montreal, Can., 1940, German Bldg. Expn., Hanover, 1951; mem. architects adv. com. Nat. Capital Downtown Com. Inc.; mem. President's Adv. Council on Pennsylvania Av., 1963. Trustee Fred L. Lavanburg Found. Recipient Award of Merit, A.I.A., 1960; 1st honor award, award of merit FHA, 1963; John Simon Guggenheim Meml. Found. fellow, 1944. Fellow A.I.A. (chmn. 1965 Pan-Am. Congress com.); mem. Am. Inst. Planners Com. of 100 on Fed. City, Washington Bldg. Congress, Washington Planning and Housing Assn., Columbia Hist. Soc., Met. Washington Bd. Trade, Am. Fedn. Arts, Soc. Archtl. Historians, Alpha Omicron Pi. Home: 2328 Massachusetts Av NW Washington DC 20008 also Monterey Blue Ridge Summit PA Office: 1056 Thomas Jefferson St NW Washington DC 20007

SMITH, CLAUDE KENNETH, educator; b. Gray Hawk, Ky., Feb. 10, 1932; s. Robert S. and Martha Jane (Farmer) S.; B.S., Eastern Ky. U., 1954; M.R.E., So. Bapt. Theol. Sem., 1958; M.B.A., U. Ky., 1966; m. Wanda M. Cox, June 17, 1956; children—Sherilyn Rhea, Claude Kenneth. Mem. faculty McKee (Ky.) High Sch., 1954-55; chmn. bus. dept. Bluefield (Va.) Coll., 1957-61; staff accountant Haskins and Sells, Indpls., 1961-62; sr. accountant George S. Olive & Co., CPA's, Indpls., 1962-64; chmn. dept. accounting Eastern Ky. U., Richmond, 1964—, mem. faculty senate, 1969-72, chmn. faculty senate, 1969-70. Bd. dirs., sec.-treas. Home Care Centers, Inc., Richmond. Recipient YMCA-YWCA award for citizenship, 1954. Mem. Ky. Soc. C.P.A.'s (chmn. career opportunities com. 1970-71), Am. Inst. C.P.A.'s (membership com. 1968-71), Am. Accounting Assn., Central Ky. Assn. C.P.A.'s. Baptist (deacon 1960—; chmn. deacons 1963-64). Home: 109 Meadowlark Dr Richmond KY 40475

SMITH, CLIFFORD WELDON, banker; b. Greensboro, Ga., Apr. 3, 1918; s. Clifford Alexander and Olive (Cawthon) S.; grad. high sch.; m. Marjorie Taylor, Apr. 6, 1941; children—Clifford Weldon, Laurence D., Cecily (Mrs. John R. Callaway). With Bank Greensboro (Ga.), 1937—, v.p., 1965-66, exec. v.p., 1966-72, pres., 1972—. Pres. Greensboro Indsl. Corp., 1948-71; dir. Greensboro Investment Corp. Mayor, Greensboro, 1968—. Served with AUS, 1943-46; ETO. Methodist. Mason, Lion. Home: Appalachee Av Greensboro GA 30642 Office: Greensboro Bank Greensboro GA 30642

SMITH, DALLAS GLEN, JR., educator; b. Jackson County, Tenn., June 25, 1940; s. D.G. and Margaret E. (Ramsey) S.; B.S., Tenn. Poly. Inst., 1963; M.S., Tenn. Tech. U., 1967; Ph.D., Va. Poly. Inst., 1969; m. Sarah Jo Agee, Feb. 3, 1961; children—Rory Mitchell, Jill Margot. Bridge design engr. bridge div. Tenn. Dept. Hwys., Nashville, 1963-65; asst. prof. dept. engring. mechanics Va. Poly. Inst., Blacksburg, 1969-70; asst. prof. dept. engring. sci. Tenn. Technol. U., Cookeville, 1970—. Cons. in fracture mechanics Army Missile Command, Redstone Arsenal, Ala., summers 1971, 72. Nat. Def. Edn. Act fellow, 1967-69. Registered profl. engr., Va., Mem. Soc. Exptl. Stress Analysis (papers com.), Am. Soc. Engring. Edn., Order Engr., Sigma Xi. Contbr. articles to tech. mags. Home: Route 8 Cookeville TN 38501

SMITH, DAVID FLOYD, JR., city ofcl.; b. Mexia, Tex., Mar. 4, 1926; s. David Floyd and Georgia Hazel (Scott) S.; B.B.A., Baylor U., 1949; m. Betty Jane Bradford, Aug. 29, 1948; children—David B., William S. Purchasing agt. City Waco (Tex.), 1960, asst. dir. pub. works, 1962-65, dir. finance, 1965-68, asst. city mgr., 1968-70, city mgr., 1970—. Bd. dirs. United Fund, Hillcrest Bapt. Meml. Hosp., 1965. Served with USMCR, 1944-52. Recipient Service awards local Little League orgn. Mem. City Mgmt. Assn. (state and nat. chpts.). Democrat. Baptist. Mason, Rotarian (citizenship award 1970), Lion. Home: 5631 Lake Jackson Dr Waco TX 76710 Office: PO Box 1370 Waco TX 76701

SMITH, DAVID NEELY, pub. co. exec.; b. Canton, O., Oct. 2, 1937; s. William Everett and Goldie Iva (Neely) S.; B.S. in Bus. Adminstrn., Miami U., Oxford, O., 1959; m. Judith Ann Leone, Sept. 16, 1963. Ency. salesman P.F. Collier Inc., Cleve., 1959-65; sales mgr. Grolier Inc., Jacksonville, Fla., 1965-68; exec. v.p. finance Communication and Studies, Atlanta, 1968-70; pres. Internat. Horizons Inc., Atlanta, 1970—. Mem. Delta Sigma Pi, Phi Kappa Tau. Republican. Presbyn. Home: 238 15th St NE Atlanta GA 30309 Office: 2525 1st Nat Bank Tower Atlanta GA 30303

SMITH, DAVID V., educator, forester; b. Lumpkin, Ga., July 12, 1921; s. David V. and Nelle (Siddall) S.; B.S.F., U. Ga., 1946; M.F., Duke U., 1950, postgrad. 1950-52; Ph.D., Coll. Forestry at Syracuse, 1968; m. Mary Frances Evans, June 8, 1947; children—Susan C., Mary Katherine. Jr. forest technician S.C. Commn Forestry, Walterboro, S.C., 1947, sr. forest technician, 1948, asst. forester, 1949; grad teaching asst. Duke U., 1950-51, instr., 1952, vis. asst. prof. summer 1953; asst. prof. forestry Va. Poly. Inst., Blacksburg, 1952-57, asso. prof., 1957-70; prof. forest engring. Stephen F. Austin State U., Nacogdoches, 1970—. Forest cons. cities Pulaski and Martinsville, Va.; Norfolk and Western Rys., Roanoke, Va., Barnes Lumber Co., Charlottesville, Va., Appalichian Power Co., Roanoke, Lester Brothers Lumber Co., Martinsville, Freeport Sulphur Co., N.Y.C., Allied Chem. Co., Morristown, N.J., Temple Industries, Diboll, Tex. Served to 1st lt. with AC, AUS, 1942-45; ETO. Mem. Am. Soc. Photogrammetry, Am. Congress on Surveying and Mapping, Photogrammetric Soc. (London), Soc. Photo-optical Instrumentation Engrs., Soc. Am. Foresters (chmn. chpt. 1958), Sigma Xi, Alpha Gamma Rho, Phi Sigma Xi. Methodist. Home: 2101 Creek View Bend Nacogdoches TX 75961

SMITH, DEWITT CLINTON, JR., optometrist; b. Statesboro, Ga., Nov. 4, 1924; s. DeWitt C. and Ruth (Dunaway) S.; student Augusta Coll., 1942, U. Ky., 1943, U. Ga., 1944; D. Optometry, Sou Coll., 1948, postgrad., 1963-64; postgrad. U. Rome, Italy, 1967; m. Elizabeth Ansley, June 6, 1954; children—Melanie Ruth, DeWitt C. Practice optometry, Augusta, Ga., 1948—. Sec. Richmond Homes & Investment, 1962—. Cons. in visual care Columbia County schs., Ga. Bd. dirs. Ways and Means for the Blind, Augusta. Served with AUS, 1943-44. Fellow Am. Acad. Optometry; mem. Nat. Soc. for Prevention of Blindness, Am., Ga. (pres. 10th dist. 1964-65, trustee 1965-66), optometric assns., Better Vision Inst., D.A.V., Am. Legion, Beta Sigma Kappa, Sigma Chi, Omega Epsilon Phi. Elk, Mason (Shriner). Club: Civitan. Home: 2223 Kings Way Augusta GA 30904 Office: Smith Bldg 2479 Wrightsboro Rd Augusta GA 30904

SMITH, DOCK GARNER, JR., lawyer; b. Clayton, N.C., May 20, 1935; s. Dock Garner and Helen (Rains) S.; B.S., E. Carolina U., 1957; J.D., U. N.C., 1960; m. Peggy Faye Smith, 1957; children—Dock Garner III, Douglas G., Sandra Kay, Daniel G. Admitted to N.C. bar, 1960; individual practice in Robbins, N.C., 1961—. Pres. Robbins Improvement Co., Inc. Pres. Robbins Mchts. Assn., 1963-64. Pres. Moore County Young Democrats, 1964-66. Sec., dir. Northmoore Student Loan Found., Inc.; mem. Gov.'s N.C. Task Force on Adjudication; mem. Moore County Planning Bd., 1973. Mem. N.C., Moore County bar assns., Jr. C. of C. (pres. 1963-64). Methodist. Elk, Lion. Clubs: Montgomery County Country; Golden Sands Golf and Country, Pinehurst Golf and Country. Home: 310 Frye St Robbins NC 27325 Office: 118 E Salisbury St Robbins NC 27325

SMITH, DUDLEY, trade assn. exec., sugar cons., author; b. Campbellsville, Ky., Dec. 6, 1904; s. Herbert G. and Addie (Feather) S.; B.S., U. Ky., 1931; postgrad. U.S. Dept. Agr. Grad. Sch., 1931-35; m. Verta Enid Templeton, June 9, 1935; children—Mary Lou (Mrs. John William Harrell Brown), Dudley Templeton, Elizabeth Verta (Mrs. Phillip A. Jones). Specialist tobacco marketing U. Ky., 1929-31, Fed. Farm Bd., 1931-32; with U.S. Dept. Agr., 1933-36; with Washington Office Assn. Sugar Producers P.R., 1936-72, v.p., 1941-72; tobacco and livestock farmer, Mitchellville, Md., 1941-68; cons. sugar and tobacco U.S. and fgn. countries, 1940—. Chmn., Md. Tobacco Authority, 1960-66; mem. Gov.'s Commns. on Utilization Water Resources, Feasibility of State Dept. Agr.; mem. Task Group on Sugar, Pres.'s Bi-Partisan Commn. on Increased Indsl. Use Agrl. Products; chmn. Sugar Research and Marketing Adv. Com., 1951-58; chmn. Chairmen All Agrl. Research Service Adv. Coms., 1954; bd. dirs. Md. Tobacco Co-op., 1956-67; lay com. Prince George (Md.) Jr. Coll., 1962-69; exec. bd. Tobacco Growers Information Com., 1962-67. Recipient award for outstanding service to agr. Prince George's C. of C., 1962. Mem. Internat., P.R., Queensland sugar technologists assns., Md. Agrl. Soc., Md. Farm Bur. (past county pres., dir. Md.), Sugar Club, Alpha Gamma Rho, Alpha Zeta. Democrat. Methodist. Mason. Club: University. Editor, Sugary Azucar Yearbook, 1971—. Contbr. articles on sugar and tobacco to trade publs. Home: 3001 Veazey Terrace NW Washington DC 20008 Office: 3003 Van Ness St NW Washington DC 20008

SMITH, DWIGHT HAZELTON, physician; b. Saluda, S.C., Dec. 13, 1921; s. George William and Naomi (Burnett) S.; B.S., Furman U., 1943; M.D., Med. U. S.C., 1946; m. Miriam King, Sept. 27, 1942; children—Preston, Brende, Judith, Dwight Hazelton, King. Intern, Med. Coll. Va. Hosp., 1946-47; practice medicine specializing in family practice, Williamston, S.C., 1950—; owner Williamston Hosp., 1950—; med. examiner FBI, 1948; FAA, 1960; team physician Palmetto High Sch., Williamston 1950—. Chmn. bd. dirs. Saluda Velley Fed. Savs. & Loan Assn., Williamston, 1964—; dir. So. Bank & Trust Co., Greenville, S.C. Pres., Anderson County Property Owners Assn. 1971; mem. Anderson County (S.C.) Bd. Edn., 1966-70. Served to lt (j.g.) USNR, 1943-46, 57-59. Diplomate Am. Assn. Family Practice. Fellow Am. Acad. Family Physicians (charter); mem. Am., So. med. assns., Am. Acad. Gen. Practice, Greenville County Med. Soc. Methodist (chmn. ofcl. bd. 1965-66). Home: 219 Hamilton St Williamston SC 29697 Office: PO Box 246 Williamston SC 29697

SMITH, EARL WESLEY, lawyer; b. nr. Memphis, Tex., Nov. 6, 1919; s. James William and Sallie Elizabeth (Baskin) S.; student Schreiner Inst., Kerrvelle, Tex., 1938-40; A.A. U. Tex., 1947; m. Mozelle Owens, Aug. 31. 1941; children—Robert Earl, Janice (Mrs. John Moss), Martha. Admitted to Tex. bar, 1947; practiced in San Angelo, Tex., 1947—; mem. firm E.E. Murphy, 1947-48; atty. San Angelo, 1949-50, dist. atty., 1951-53; with firm Smith & Foy, 1953-55, Runge, Hardeman, Steib, Smith & Foy, 1955-60, Hardeman & Foy, 1960-65, Hardeman, Smith & Kever, 1965-72; 51st dist. judge, San Angelo, 1973—. Mem. Law Enforcement Study Commn., 1957, Bar Com. to Revise Code of Criminal Procedure, 1957-71, Penal Code Revision Com., 1970—; mem. juvenile delinquency com. Family Law Counsel, 1970-73. County chmn. Democratic party, 1961; state dist. committeeman, 1968-72. Trustee Abilene Christian Coll. Mem. Fellows Tex. Bar Found., Home: 129 S Irving St San Angelo TX 76901 Office: Ct House San Angelo TX 76901

SMITH, EDDIE GLENN, JR., dentist, med. found. exec.; b. Palatka, Fla., Nov. 13, 1926; s. Eddie Glenn and Mamie (Jenkins) S.; B.S., Howard U., 1952, D.D.S., 1959; m. Callie Glasby, June 20, 1954; children—Katressia M., Katherine J. Intern, Crownsville (Md.) State Hosp., 1959-60; gen. practice dentistry, Washington; 1960—; dental dir. Community Group Health Found., Washington, 1968-70, dir. health services, 1970, project dir., 1971—. Asst. prof. dept. community dentistry Howard U. Coll. Dentistry, 1969—; pres. Nat. Dental Assn., 1972—; cons. Am. Dental Assn., Nat. Urban Coalition, Washington; cons. to sec. Dept. Health, Edn. and Welfare, 1968-72. Tech. adviser Washington Model Cities Program, 1969-70; parliamentarian Citizens for Better Health Care, 1971; 1st vice-chmn. bd. mgmt. YMCA, Washington, 1971. Bd. dirs. Health and Welfare Council, D.C., 1972; bd. regents Nat. Library Medicine, 1972—. Adv. bd. dirs. Nat. Med. Assn. Found. Served with USAAF, 1945-47. Recipient Meritorious award Howard U. Coll. Dentistry, 1969; Zone v.p. award Nat. Dental Assn., 1967, Dentist of Year award, 1969; Pub. Service award Washington Urban League, 1971. Mem. N.A.A.C.P., Fedn. Civic Assns., Robert T. Freeman Dental Soc. (award 1970, pres. 1968-71, editor Newsletter 1965-67), D.C. Dental Soc. (chmn. speaker's bur. 1968-69), Howard U. Dental Alumni Assn. (nat. pres. 1967-69), Omega Psi Phi. Baptist (trustee). Home: 7815 Orchid St NW Washington DC 20012 Office: Community Group Health Found 3308 14th St NW Washington DC 20010

SMITH, EDMUND CHRISTIAN, mfg. co. exec.; b. Clarksville, Tenn., Mar. 16, 1910; s. Frederick Norman and Corinne (Northington) S.; B.A., Vanderbilt, 1931, LL.B., 1934; m. Nelle McMahan, June 7, 1938; children—Barbara (Mrs. Doyle J. Smith, Jr.), Edmund Christian. Admitted to Tenn. bar, 1934; with Conwood Corp. (formerly Am. Snuff Co.), Memphis, 1934-74, v.p., 1956-64, sec., 1964-74, also dir., ret., 1974. Recording sec. So. Baptist Brotherhood Com., 1936-48, exec. com., 1936-48; vol. worker Shelby United Fund, 1964—, sect. chmn., 1972, 73; bd. dirs. Memphis and Shelby County Tb Health Assn., 1952-70, pres., 1966-67; bd. dirs. Memphis Met. YMCA, 1958-64. Mem. Memphis and Shelby County Bar Assn., Am. Soc. Corp. Secs., Delta Tau Delta, Phi Delta Phi. Baptist. Rotarian. Club: Memphis Country. Home: 4262 Tuckahoe Rd Memphis TN 38117

SMITH, ELIZABETH WIESS (MRS. LLOYD H. SMITH), civic worker; b. Beaumont, Tex., Jan. 29, 1916; d. Harry Carothers and Olga (Keith) Wiess; student Miss Porter's Sch., Miss Helen Stout's Schs.; m. Lloyd Hilton Smith, on May 25, 1940; children—Sandra K. (Mrs. Robert A. Mosbacher), Sharon L. (Mrs. David William Keller), Sydney C. Trustee Ballet Found., 1950-70, Southampton Hosp., 1958-70, Houston Mus. Fine Arts, 1951—, Houston Ballet Found., 1957—, Vis. Nurse Assn., 1947-52, Michael E. DeBakey Med. Found., 1970—, art assos. St. Thomas U., 1963—; bd. dirs. Inst. for Antiquities and Christianity of Claremont grad. sch., 1970—. Mem. Am. Fedn. Art, Southampton Hist. Soc. Clubs: Houston Garden, Assembly, Bayou, Ramada Allegro (Houston); River (N.Y.C.); Southampton Garden; Curzon House (London, Eng.). Home: 2 Longfellow Lane Houston TX 77005

SMITH, ETHEL LILLIE KNOTT (MRS. BUDD ELMON SMITH), librarian; b. nr. Oxford, N.C., July 21, 1915; d. Fielding and Lillie (Overton) Knott; student Queens Coll., 1933-34; A.B., Meredith Coll., 1937; B.L.S., U. N.C., 1942; M.A., Appalachian State Tchrs. Coll., 1955; postgrad. U. Chgo.; m. Budd Elmon Smith, Dec. 28, 1943; children—James Fielding, William Budd. Tchr., Guilford (N.C.) Coll. High Sch., 1937-38, Roanoke Rapids (N.C.) High Sch., 1938-42; librarian Gastonia (N.C.) High Sch., 1942-43, U.S. Army, Camp Butler, N.C., 1943-44, Cornell Library Assn. Library, 1944-45; instr. Wake Forest Coll., 1946-51; librarian Oxford City Schs., 1952-53; instr. Wingate (N.C.) Coll., 1953-55, librarian, 1955—. Exec. sec. N.C. Nat. Library Week, 1963. Sec., Wingate P.T.A., 1957-58, Woman's Missionary Union, 1958-60, Union County Planning Bd., 1964—; mem. com. Self-Study Baptist Colls. N.C., 1964-65. Mem. Am. Assn. U. Women (pres. N.C. 1970-72), Am., Southeastern, N.C. (past chmn. jr. coll. sect., chmn. coll. and univ. sect.) library assns., Nat. Council Tchrs. English, Modern Lang. Assn., Delta Kappa Gamma. Democrat. Baptist. Clubs: Woman's Garden. Asso. editor: The Junior College Library Collection. Contbr. articles to profl. jours. Address: Route 2 Box 121A Benson NC 27504

SMITH, FRANCIS PALMER, architect; b. Cin., Mar. 27, 1886; s. Henry Howard and Eva Belle (Kendall) S.; B.S. in Architecture, U. Pa., 1907; m. Ella Sorin, June 15, 1910 (dec. 1930); children—Margaret Ella (Mrs. Henry Rauh Kingdon), Francis Palmer, Jr. (dec.), Robert, Henry Howard. Draughtsman, Cin. and Columbus, O., 1907-08; travel and study in Europe, 1909; prof. architecture Ga. Sch. of Tech., Atlanta, 1909-22; mem. firm Pringle & Smith, architects; designer 1st Nat. Bank, Wm. Smith, Atlanta, 1922-34; pvt. practice, 1934—; now partner firm Francis P. Smith & Henry H. Oliver; works include Doctors Bldg., Rhodes Haverty Bldg., Whitehead Bldg., Cox Carlton Hotel, Atlanta, Lynch Bldg., Jacksonville, Venetian Hotel, Miami, (Pringle & Smith), Druid Hills Presbyterian Ch., annex to Trust Co. of Ga. Bldg., Cathedral of St. Philip (Ayers & Godwin Assos.), Atlanta Comml. Bank & Trust Co., Ocala, Fla., Decatur br. First Nat. Bank, Atlanta, Ga., also numerous churches, residences, comml. works in the South and S.E. Recipient Brooke Silver medal U. of Pa., Walter Cope Meml. Prize. Served from capt. to maj. C.E., AUS, 1942-46; asst. to dist. engr., Atlanta, exec. and engring. officer with Post Engr., Troop Supply officer, Post. Engr., and Custodial officer, Camp Tyson, Tenn. Fellow A.I.A. (past pres. Ga. chpt.), Stained Glass Assn. of Am. (asso. mem.), Sigma Xi, Phi Kappa Phi. Episcopalian. Translator and publisher of Voillet-le-Duc's Mediaeval Stained Glass. Home: 1135 Lullwater Rd Atlanta GA 30307 Office: Whitehead Bldg Atlanta GA 30303

SMITH, FRANK PRINCE, lawyer, banker; b. Albion, Okla., Jan. 19, 1931; s. Thomas H.P. and Hazel (Looper) S.; B.S., Okla. State U., 1958; LL.B., Okla. U., 1958; m. Audrey L. McQuigg, June 4, 1959; 1 dau., Janet. Admitted to Okla. bar, 1958; practiced in Ponca City, Okla., 1958-59; trust examiner Fed. Res. Bank of Kansas City (Mo.), Kansas City Life Ins. Co., 1963-65; v.p., trust officer N.M. Bank & Trust Co., Hobbs, 1965-67; v.p., trust officer Arlington (Tex.) Bank & Trust Co., 1967-72; v.p., trust officer Calcasieu-Marine Nat. Bank, Lake Charles, La., 1973—. Past mem. adv. bd., treas. Salvation Army, Hobbs, former mem. adv. bd., Arlington, Tex. Served with USAF, 1951-54. Mem. Okla., Am. bar assns., Delta Theta Phi. Republican. Methodist (past steward). Home: 1539 John Lake Charles LA 70601

SMITH, FREDERICK ALLEN, elec. engr.; b. Tavares, Fla., Jan. 1, 1929; s. George Earle and Pearl Emily (Ayers) S.; grad. Capitol Radio Engring. Inst., 1950; student Lake Coll. of Commerce, 1953; m. Alma Charlotte Etheredge, Jan. 24, 1951; children—Deborah Anne, Frederick Allen, Ronald Earle. Staff engr. Radio Sta. WRNO, Orangeburg, S.C., 1950; field engr. Philco Corp., Phila., 1951-54; electronics engr. U.S. Navy, Charleston, S.C., 1954-57, supr. radar engring. br., 1957-61, supr. radar and communications engring. br., 1961-64, head aero. engring. div., 1964-65; owner, dir. Allen Wired Music Co., Charleston, 1954-59; cons. Frederick A. Smith, cons. engr., 1961—; owner Burgla-Matic Alarm Co., 1970—, Ashley Marina Co., 1970—. Expert engr. FCC, 1966—; mem. adv. bd. S.C. Tech. Edn. Center. Trustee James Island Pvt. Sch. Found., Charleston, S.C. Served with USNR, 1946-48. Registered profl. engr. S.C. Mem. I.E.E.E. (sect. treas. 1963-64, pres. 1964-65), Nat. Soc. Profl. Engrs., Constrn. Specification Inst., U.S. Power Squadron. Mason (32 deg.), Elk. Club: Exchange (pres. 1960, v.p. 1959). Home: 863 Robert E Lee Blvd Charleston SC 29412 Office: Ashley House Charleston SC 29401

SMITH, FREDERICK WILLIAMS, physician; b. Mooresville, Ala., Sept. 6, 1922; s. James Samuel and Mabel Allene (Williams) S.; A.B., Vanderbilt U., 1942, M.D., 1944; m. Frances Anne Bottoms, Oct. 26, 1966; children—Sharyn (Mrs. Thomas McCartrie Nolen), Linda Allene, Erich Wolfe, Benjamin Conrad. Intern, Duke Hosp., Durham, N.C., 1944-45; resident surgery Med. Coll. Ala., Birmingham, 1947-50, instr. surgery, 1950-52; practice medicine specializing in surgery, Huntsville, Ala., 1952—; mem. staff Huntsville Hosp., chief surgery, 1961-63, v.p. staff, 1963-65, pres. staff, 1965-67; mem. staff Crestwood Hosp., chief surgery, 1965-68; staff Fifth Av., Med. Center hosps. Served to capt. AUS, 1945-47. Diplomate Am. Bd. Surgery. Fellow A.C.S. (chpt. pres. 1972), Southeastern Surg. Congress; mem. Am., So. med. assns., Madison County Med. Soc. (pres. 1959—). Rotarian. Home: 1110 Apalachee St Huntsville AL 35801 Office: 116 Sivley Rd Huntsville AL 35801

SMITH, GARY LOCKE, optometrist; b. Fargo, N.D., Feb. 13, 1944; s. Robert Francis and Mary Carolyn (Hector) S.; B.A., U. N.D., 1966; D.Optometry, So. Coll. Optometry, 1969; m. Marjorie Kay Odegard, July 3, 1966; 1 dau., Mary Locke. Partner with Dr. Jack Runningur, optometrists, Rome, Ga., 1969—. Mem. Ga. Com. on Children and Youth, 1970—. Bd. dirs. N.W. Ga. Speech and Hearing Clinic, vice chmn., 1972—. Mem. Ga. Optometric Assn. (dist. pres. 1972—), Rome Jr. C. of C., Phi Delta Upsilon. Home: 13 Ridgewood Rd Rome GA 30161 Office: 206 E 3d St Rome GA 30161

SMITH, GEORGE PATRICK, II, lawyer; b. Wabash, Ind., Sept. 1, 1939; s. George Patrick and Marie Louise (Barrett) S.; B.S. (Wade Meml. scholar), Ind. U., 1961, J.D. with honors, 1964; certificate Academie De Droit International, De La Haye, Palais De La Paix, The Netherlands, summer 1965. Krannert teaching fellow law Ind. U., Bloomington, 1964-65; admitted to Ind. bar, 1965, D.C. bar, 1966, U.S. Supreme Ct. bar, 1968; gen. ltd. practice law, 1965—; spl. counsel Environmental Protection Agy., Washington, 1971-73; dep. dir. Adminstrv. Conf. U.S., 1974—; Instr. law U. Mich. at Ann Arbor, 1965-66; legal adviser fgn. claims settlement commn. Dept. State, Washington, 1966; asst. prof., asst. dean Law Sch. State U. N.Y. at Buffalo, 1967-69; vis. prof. law George Washington U. Law Center, summer 1968; asso. prof. law U. Ark., Fayetteville, 1969-71; adj. prof. Georgetown Law Center, Washington, 1971—, Catholic U. Law Sch., 1973—; cons. Ark. Planning Commn., 1970-71. Ombudsman, U. Ark., 1969-70; spl. counsel environmental control legislation Gov. Ark., 1970-71; mem. Ark. Waterway Study Commn., 1970-71; chmn. Commn. on Environmental Control, State Arts and Sci. Com. Ark., 1970-71; life mem. Ind. U. Found., 1962—; mem. NRC-Nat. Acad. Scis.; active Smith Meml. Law Collection, Wabash County Library (Ind.), 1963—, Smith Bicentennial Collection Am. Lit., Hampden-Sydney Coll., 1974—. Mem. Am. (chmn. Young Lawyers sect. environmental quality 1971—), Ind. bar assns., Fed. Bar Council, Soc. Legal History, Am. Soc. Internat. Law, Nat. Lawyers Club, Am. Judicature Soc., Environmental Def. Fund, Selden Soc., World Wildlife Fund, Nat. Cathedral Soc., Ind. Soc. Washington, Sigma Alpha Epsilon, Phi Alpha Delta, Alpha Kappa Psi, Order of Omega. Episcopalian. Club: Cosmos (Washington). Contbr. articles to profl. jours. Home: 1400 S Joyce St Apt C 1607 Arlington VA 22202 Office: Adminstrv Conf US 2120 L St NW Suite 500 Washington DC 20037

SMITH, GEORGE SEVERN, lawyer; b. Van Wert, O., Jan. 31, 1901; s. Harvey C. and Nella (Severn) S.; LL.B., Nat. U., 1928; m. Thelma Gertrude Horst, Jan. 12, 1935; 1 son, George Severn. Admitted to D.C. bar, 1931; chief license div. Fed. Radio Commn., 1929-32; asso. with Paul M. Segal, 1932-41; partner Segal, Smith & Hennessey, attys., Washington, 1942-57, Smith, Hennessey & McDonald, Washington, 1958-62; legal adviser to commr. FCC, 1962-66, chief broadcast bur., 1966-70; cons. Marmet Profl. Corp., Washington, 1971-74. Del. Fed. Communications Bar Assn. to house of dels. Am. Bar Assn., 1958-59. Served with Med. Dept., U.S. Army, 1918-19. Mem. Am. Bar Assn., Fed. Communications Bar Assn. (Washington pres. 1957), Bar Assn. D.C. Republican. Methodist. Home: Chesapeake Ranch Club Box 154 Lusby MD 20657

SMITH, GILBERT BRISTOL, aviation equipment co. exec.; b. Mapleton, Ia., June 28, 1912; s. Gilbert Max and Bessie Marie (O'Connell) S.; grad. Philips Acad., 1931; B.S., Northwestern U.,

1935; m. Annie Warren Mason, Jan. 30, 1937; children—Janet (Mrs. William N. Walker), Elizabeth (Mrs. Ralph Lawson III). With CAA, 1939-45, liaison officer for central and S.Am., 1945; dir. indsl. aid div. Trans-Marine Airlines, Inc., N.Y.C., 1945-46; operations mgr. Roosevelt Field, Inc., 1946-47; salesman Investors Syndicate, Heampstead, N.Y., 1947-48; with Frank Ambrose Aviation Co., Inc., Flushing, N.Y., 1948-53, sales mgr., 1950-51, v.p., 1952-53; pres., Internat. Assos., Inc., Miami, 1953—. Asso., Glen A. Gilbert & Assos., 1957—. Group chmn. United Fund, 1960-70. Pres., Republican Club Coral Gables, 1965-68. Served with USNR, 1935-39. Recipient Gen. Billy Mitchel award Aviation Writer, 1972. Mem. Hist. Assn. So. Fla. (dir. 1966-70, chmn. aviation com. 1968-70), Greater Miami Aviation Assn. (dir. 1962-73), Quiet Birdman, Aerospace Council (mem. internat. affairs council 1964-68), Miami Dade County C. of C. (chmn. aviation action com. 1973), OX-5 (dir. Fla. wing). Home: 3581 E Glencoe St Coconut Grove FL 33133 Office: PO Box 453 Miami FL 33148

SMITH, GORDON LAIDLAW, JR., mfg. oil and gas prodn. co. exec.; b. Chattanooga, Jan. 29, 1926; s. Gordon Laidlaw and Sara (Simmons) S.; grad. McCallie Sch., 1944; B.C.E., Duke, 1948; m. Frances Lowrance Street, Aug. 22, 1951; children—Gordon Laidlaw III, Preston Lowrance, Sara Frances. With Wheland Co. (merged into Gordon Street, Inc. 1961), Chattanooga, 1948-61, trainee, 1948-50, supt. prodn. planning and material control, 1950-53, asst. sales mgr., 1953-56, sales mgr., 1956-58, sec., 1958-61, dir., 1959-61; sec., dir. Gordon Street, Inc. (merged into N.Am. Royalties, Inc. 1969), Chattanooga, 1961-69, sec.-treas., 1964-69; sec.-treas. N.Am. Royalties, Inc., Chattanooga, 1969-72, v.p., finance, treas., 1972—, also dir.; dir. First Fed. Savs. & Loan Assn. Chattanooga, Chattanooga Gas Co. Chmn. Chattanooga-Hamilton County chpt. A.R.C., 1962-64, mem. exec. com., 1958—; mem. Met. Bd. YMCA, 1966-67, mem. campaign cabinet New YMCA Fund, 1966—. Mem. Duke U. Alumni Admissions Adv. Com. Bd. dirs. Boys' Club Chattanooga. Served with USNR, 1944-46. Mem. Am. Petroleum Inst., C. of C. U.S., Greater Chattanooga Area C. of C. (v.p. 1972—), Chattanooga Mfgr. Assn. (pres. 1966-67), Chattanooga Automobile Club (pres. 1973—), Phi Delta Theta, Omicron Delta Kappa. Presbyn. (deacon 1954—, trustee 1964—). Kiwanian (pres. Chattanooga 1963). Clubs: Chattanooga Golf and Country, Mountain City (Chattanooga). Home: 1609 Edgewood Circle Chattanooga TN 37405 Office: 200 E 8th St Chattanooga TN 37402

SMITH, HANK TODD, advt. co. exec.; b. Port Arthur, Tex., Jan. 24, 1939; s. John Harold and Jessie (Homeyer) S.; B.B.A., Lamar U., 1960; postgrad. So. Meth. U., 1962-64, U. Tex., 1968; m. Jane Jordan, Nov. 24, 1967. Mgmt. trainee Sears Roebuck & Co., Port Arthur, Dallas, 1960-62; reporter U.P.I., Dallas, 1963-65; field rep., asst. dir. pub. relations Republican party Tex., Dallas, Tyler and Austin, 1965-68; owner adv. agy. Writers' Ink, Austin, 1969-71; creative dir. Neal Spelce Assos., Austin, 1971-72; creative dir. Media Communications Inc., Austin, 1972—. Recipient Gold Addy, Austin Advt. Club, 1971, 72, 73; Gold Addy, 10th Dist. Am. Advt. Fedn., 1973. Mem. Austin Advt. Club (dir., pres. 1973-74), 10th Dist. Am. Advt. Fedn. (dir.), Dallas-Ft. Worth Soc. Visual Communications, Am. Inst. Graphic Arts, Pub. Relations Soc. Am., Sigma Phi Epsilon. Episcopalian. Club: Town Lake Breakfast (pres. 1967-68), Headliners. Home: 1604 Forest Trail Austin TX 78703 Office: Mut Savs Bldg Austin TX 78701

SMITH, HARMON LEE, JR., educator, theologian; b. Ellisville, Miss., Aug. 23, 1930; s. Harmon Lee and Mary M. (O'Donnell) S.; A.B., Millsaps Coll., 1952; B.D., Duke, 1955, Ph.D. (Gurney Harris Kearns Found. fellow, Lilly Found. fellow Cooper Found. fellow), 1962; m. Bettye Joan Watkins, Aug. 21, 1951; children—Pamela, Amy, Harmon. Asst. to dean Duke U. Div. Sch., Durham, N.C., 1959-65, asst. prof. Christian ethics, 1962-68, asso. prof., moral theology, 1968-73, prof., 1973—. Pres., Durham Human Relations Council, 1966-67. Bd. dirs. N.C. Council on Human Relations, 1968—. Postgrad. fellow Soc. Religion in Higher Edn., 1973. Fellow Am. Assn. Theol. Schs.; mem. Am. Acad. Religion, Am. Soc. Christian Ethics. Author: Personal Decision Making, 1964; The Christian and His Decisions, 1969; Ethics and the New Medicine, 1970. Asso. editor: Science, Medicine and Man, 1973. Contbr. articles to profl. publs. Home: 3510 Randolph Rd Durham NC 27705

SMITH, HAROLD GLENN, physicist; b. Lafayette, La., July 3, 1927; s. William Newton, Sr., and Beulah (Fuller) S.; B.S., U. Southwestern La., 1949; M.S., Tulane U., 1951; Ph.D., Ia. State U., 1957; m. Marion Francis Batty, Feb. 18, 1950, children—Lorie Janet, Brian Alan, Lynette Elaine. Jr. research asso. Ames Lab., AEC, 1951-54; physicist Oak Ridge Nat. Lab., 1957—. Treas. Oak Ridge Civic Ballet Assn., 1968-70. Bd. dirs. Tenn. Citizens Wilderness Planning, 1970, v.p., 1973. Served with USNR, 1944-46. Fellow Am. Phys. Soc.; mem. Am. Crystallog. Assn., A.A.A.S., Research Soc. Am. Editor: Transactions Am. Crystallog. Assn., 1967. Contbr. articles profl. jours. Developer Polaroid film holder for neutron and x-ray diffraction photographs. Home: 103 Walton Lane Oak Ridge TN 37830 Office: Oak Ridge Nat Lab PO Box X Oak Ridge TN 37830

SMITH, HAROLD OGDEN, JR., food merchandisers assn. exec.; b. Indpls., Dec. 27, 1901; s. Harold Ogden and Elizabeth Miles (Carroll) S.; student Va. Poly. Inst., 1925, Washington and Lee U., 1927; m. Dorothy Dial, July 2, 1935; children—Harold Ogden III, Dorothy (Mrs. George William Troxler), Lisa (Mrs. John Henry Trainor II), Judith (Mrs. Thomas F. Haney). Mgr. Washington office Nat. Confectioners' Assn., 1945-47; exec. v.p. U.S. Wholesale Grocers Assn., Inc., 1947-69; exec. dir. Food Merchandisers Am., Inc., Washington, 1969—; pres., Mite-T-Mart Food Stores Corp., 1971—; chmn. Master Gourmets Inst., 1971—. Vice-chmn. mil. sub-com., prodn. exec. com. WPB, 1943-45. Mem. Am. Soc. Assn. Execs., S.A.R., Sons Revolution, Alpha Tau Omega. Presbyn. (deacon 1962-72). Club: Kenwood Golf and Country (Bethesda, Md.). Home: 5315 Oakland Rd Kenwood Chevy Chase MD 20015 Office: Suite 1026 1511 K St NW Washington DC 20005

SMITH, HARRY LEROY, JR., broadcasting co. exec.; b. Topeka, Mar. 22, 1924; s. Harry L. and Mary Jane (Tribble) S.; B.A., Wichita State U., 1950; m. Virginia Dotts, Jan. 30, 1943; children—Virginia Marie, Janet Lee. Sales, Procter & Gamble, 1953-61; with Pioneer Broadcasting Co., Austin, 1961—, v.p., 1969—; gen. mgr. KNOW, Austin, 1969—. Mem. Traffic Safety Commn., 1971-73. Served to lt. col. USAF, 1950-53. Mem. Nat., Tex. assns. broadcasters, Sales and Marketing Execs. Democrat. Episcopalian. Mason (Shriner), Rotarian. Club: Country (Austin). Home: 2114 Fordham Lane Austin TX 78723 Office: 1907 N Lamar St Austin TX 78767

SMITH, HENRY JEFFERSON, horticulturist; b. Bradenton, Fla., Mar. 28, 1922; s. Oscar and Bessie (Thomason) S.; B.S., M.S.A., U. Fla., 1949; m. Sara Louise Bays, May 16, 1953; children—Jeff, Sally Elizabeth. Instr., asst. greenhouse mgr. Miss. State U., Starkville, 1949, landscape specialist, 1950-66; landscape editor So. Living Mag., Birmingham, Ala., 1966-70; landscape horticulturist N.C. State U., Raleigh, 1970—. Cons. landscape of pvt. homes, pub. bldgs., Ala., Miss., Fla., Tex., N.C., 1950—; lectr. on ecology, environment, horticulture. Served with AUS, 1953-56. Mem. Am. Soc. for Hort. Sci., Garden Writers Assn. Am., Am. Hort. Soc., Nat. Council Instrs. in Landscape Architecture (asso.), Internat. Platform Assn., Epsilon Sigma Phi, Sigma Delta Chi. Baptist (deacon). Club: Civitan. Home: 2901 Augusta Ct Raleigh NC 27607

SMITH, HENRY JOSEPH, astronomer; b. Boston, Jan. 10, 1928; s. Robert Paul and Bertha (Fonseca) S.; B.S., Harvard 1950, M.A., 1951, Ph.D., 1955; m. Elske von Panhys, Sept. 10, 1950; children—Geoffrey, Kenneth. Supt. Harvard U. Boyden Sta., S. Africa, 1952-54; astronomer-in-charge Harvard Coll. Obs. Field Sta., Sunspot, N.M., 1955-59; physicist Sacramento Peak Obs., Sunspot, 1959-62; supervisory physicist Central Radio Propagation Labs., Nat. Bur. Standards, Boulder, Colo., 1962-63; chief solar physics, physics and astronomy programs Office Space Sci. and Applications, NASA Hdqrs., Washington, 1963-66, dep. dir. physics and astronomy programs, 1966-68, dep. asso. adminstr. space sci., 1968—. Served with USAF, 1946-47. Mem. Am. Geophys. Union, Am. Astronom. Soc., Internat. Astron. Union. Office: 400 Maryland Av SW Washington DC 20546

SMITH, HERMAN ELMO, JR., mech. engr.; b. Spiro, Okla., Nov. 26, 1918; s. Herman Elmo and Lula Marie (Scargall) S.; B.S., Okla. State U., 1939; m. Lois Maurine King, May 2, 1943; 1 son, Brian Lee. With Hudgins, Thompson, Ball & Assos., Inc., archtl., engring., planning, Oklahoma City, 1948—, v.p., 1964-69, sec.-treas., 1964—, dir., 1964—, sr. v.p., 1969—; pres. Northwest Engrs., Inc., Enid, Okla., 1968—; v.p., sec.-treas. Car Rentals, Inc. and Profl. Equipment Co., Oklahoma City, 1966—; v.p., asst. sec.-treas. Hudgins, Thompson, Ball of Ark., Inc., Little Rock, 1973—. Mem. Okla. Bd. Registration for Profl. Engrs. and Land Surveyors, 1972—. Bd. visitors Sch. Civil Engring., Okla. State U., 1972—. Served to maj. USAAF, 1942-46, USAF, 1951-53. Registered profl. engr., Okla., Ark., Kan., La., N.M., Tex., Ga., Miss., D.C., Md., Ia., Mo., Pa., Tenn., Neb., Ill., Ind., Va., Ariz., Nev., Ohio., Colo. Fellow Am. Soc. C.E.; mem. Nat. Council Engring. Examiners, Am., Cons. Engrs. Council, Nat. Soc. Profl. Engrs., Am. Water Works Assn., Am. Rd. Builders Assn., Am. Pub. Works Assn., Cons. Engrs. Council Okla., Pi Tau Sigma, Sigma Tau. Mason (32 deg. Shriner, Jester). Club: Quail Creek Golf and Country, Petroleum, Sportsman's Country (Oklahoma City). Contbr. to profl. publs. in field. Home: 2612 Warwick Dr Oklahoma City OK 73116 Office: PO Box 1845 Oklahoma City OK 73101

SMITH, HERMAN JARED, constrn. co. exec.; b. Campbell, Tex., Mar. 23, 1930; s. Herman Hubert and Maude Genevieve (Jared) S.; student East Tex. U., 1947-49; m. Patsy Ruth McDonough, July 14, 1950; children—Vicki Lynn, Karla Gay. Pres., Herman J. Smith, Inc., Fort Worth, 1963—; chmn. bd. S.W. Bank, Fort Worth, Mansfield (Tex.) State Bank. Bd. chmn., Tarrant County Conv. Center, Fort Worth, 1967-74. Mayor, City of Hurst, Tex., 1965-66. Trustee Howard Payne Coll., Brownwood, Tex., 1962-74. Served with USNR, 1950-52. Mem. Nat. Assn. Home Builders Assn. Gen. Contractors (dir. Tex. 1967-74) Tex. Assn. Builders (pres. 1974). Home: Box 123 Hurst TX 76053 Office: 13427 Box Fort Worth TX 76118

SMITH, HERSCHEL LEROY, JR., physicist; b. Oklahoma City, Apr. 18, 1921; s. Herschel LeRoy and Wilhelmina (Erickson) S.; A.A., Oklahoma City Jr. Coll., 1940; B.S. in Engring. Physics, Okla. U., 1943; postgrad. U. Md., intermittently 1946-52; m. Ina Modena Fowler, Jan. 23, 1943; children—Herschel Larry, Alan Wayne, James David. Instr. lab. physcis U. Okla., 1942-43; physicist armor materials U.S. Naval Research Lab., Washington, 1943-46, physicist fracture mechanics area, 1946—, head fracture study sect., 1958—. Pres., chmn. bd. Potomac Heights Mut. Home Owners Assn., Inc., 1953-54. Served as ensign USNR, 1945; now lt. comdr. Res. Recipient Am. Soc. Testing Materials award, 1960. Mem. Am. Phys. Soc., Am. Inst. Aeros. and Astronautics, Research Soc. Am., Am. Soc. Testing and Materials, Sigma Pi Sigma. Baptist (chmn. deacons 1960-67). Club: Toastmasters (pres. 1964-65). Contbr. articles to tech. publs. Patentee micro-tensile machine. Home: 3804 Hemlock Pl SE Temple Hills Park MD 20031 Office: 4555 Overlook Av SW Washington DC 20375

SMITH, HERSHEL FRANCIS, investment banker; b. Birmingham, Ala., Mar. 31, 1933; s. Hershel Francis and Alta Odessa (Arnold) S.; student Ga. State Coll. Bus. Adminstrn., 1955-56; 1 dau., Sarah Frances. Registered rep. Johnson, Lane Space Corp., Atlanta, 1951-62; v.p. Pierce, Wulbern, Murphey Corp., Jacksonville, Fla., 1962-70; v.p. First Equity Corp. Fla., Jacksonville, 1970-74; pres. The Smith House, Inc., Jacksonville, 1974—. Mem. Jacksonville Financial Analysts Soc. Mason. Clubs: Atlanta Athletic; Ponte Vedra (Fla.); University (Jacksonville). Home: 1560 Lancaster Terrace Jacksonville FL 32204 Office: Gulf Life Tower Jacksonville FL 32207

SMITH, HOWARD EDWARD, educator; b. San Francisco, Aug. 1, 1925; s. Charles Augustus and Gertrude Bernadette (Higgins) S.; B.S., U. Cal. at Berkeley, 1951; M.S., Stanford, 1954, Ph.D., 1957; m. Louise Meier, Nov. 18, 1960; children—David Charles, Marie-Louise, Erika Bernadette. Asst. research chemist Cal. Research Corp., Richmond, Cal., 1951-52; research asso. Stanford, 1956; USPHS postdoctoral fellow Wayne State U., Detroit, 1956-57, Swiss Fed. Inst. Tech., Zurich, 1957-59; asst. prof. chemistry Vanderbilt U., Nashville, 1959-63, asso. prof., 1963-71, prof., 1971—. Mem. A.A.A.S., Am. Assn. U. Profs., Am. Chem. Soc. (chmn. Nashville sect. 1971), Chem. Soc. (London), Tenn. Acad. Sci., Sigma Xi, Phi Lambda Upsilon, Theta Xi. Contbr. articles to sci. jours. Home: 2012 Sweetbriar Av Nashville TN 37212

SMITH, HOWARD KINGSBURY, news commentator; b. Ferriday, La., May 12, 1914; B.A., Tulane U., 1936, LL.D., 1955; L.H.D., Alfred U., 1959, Thiel Coll., 1961, U. Md., 1970; LL.D., Roosevelt U., 1961, Centenary Coll., 1971, U. Md., 1973, Ripon Coll., 1974; D.Litt., St. Norbert's Coll., 1958; H.H.D., Pikeville Coll., 1973; L.H.D., St. Michael's Coll., 1973; m. Benedicte Traberg, Mar. 1942; children—Jack, Catherine. Studied Nazism, Berlin, 1936; reviewer fgn. dispatches New Orleans Item-Tribune; Rhodes scholar Merton Coll., Oxford, Eng., 1937, revisited Germany, Russia, Holland and Austria; fgn. corr. in London, United Press, 1939; Berlin corr. CBS, Switzerland, 1941, war corr. 9th Army, 1944, covered Nuremberg trials, 1946, chief European corr., European dir., London, Eng., 1946-57, corr. Washington bur., 1957-61, chief corr., gen. mgr., 1961-62; news analyst ABC, Washington, 1962—. Recipient Overseas Press award for best radio reporting from abroad, 1951-54; DuPont award, 1955, 63; Sigma Delta Chi award for radio journalism, 1957, George Polk Meml. award documentary The Population Explosion, 1960, co-recipient George Peabody award, 1960; Sylvania award, 1959; Emmy award TV Acad. Arts and Scis., 1960; Radio-TV Daily award as commentator of yr., 1960; Am. Jewish Congress award, 1962; Overseas Press award, best radio interpretation fgn. affairs, 1961, best TV interpretation, 1963; Radio-TV News Dirs. Assn. Paul White Meml. award, 1962. Author: Last Train from Berlin, 1942; The State of Europe, 1949; Washington, D.C., 1967. Office: 1124 Connecticut Av Washington DC 20036

SMITH, ISAAC DAVID, JR., soil cons.; b. Petersburg, W.Va., Sept. 29, 1930; s. Isaac D. and Elizabeth (Groce) S.; student Strayor Bryant and Stratton Bus. Coll., Balt., 1950-51; B.S. in C.E., The Citadel, 1960; m. W. Ann Clark, Feb. 27, 1954; children—Elizabeth Ann, Isaac David III, Michael Wayne. Estimator, Hardman Constrn. Co., Mount Pleasant, S.C., 1960-62; with Soil Cons., Inc., Charleston, S.C., 1962—, dir. labs., 1967-73, v.p. labs., 1973—. Served with USNR, 1951-55. Registered profl. engr., S.C. Mem. Am. Soc. C.E. (state v.p. elect), Charleston Civil Engrs. Club, Am. Soc. Testing Materials, Constrn. Specifications Inst. (dir., past pres.), S.C. Soc. Engrs. Club: Nat. Railway Historical Society. Home: 133 Sampa Rd Mount Pleasant SC 29464 Office: PO Drawer 698 Charleston SC 29402

SMITH, IVAN HERBERT, lawyer; b. Downs, Kan., Jan. 9, 1921; s. Zeb Herbert and Carrie Lorena (Williams) S.; B.A., Hastings Coll., 1947; postgrad. U. Mich. Law Sch., 1947-48; J.D., U. Ark., 1950; m. Wanda Dale Leatherman, June 4, 1943 (div. June 1968); children—Diana Dale, Debra Dawn; m. 2d, Middie True (Poteete) Moore, Jan. 30, 1970. Admitted to Ark. bar, 1950; practiced in Little Rock, 1950, 51; departmental atty. Ark. Dept. Pub. Welfare, Little Rock, 1952-63, state information officer under reciprocal support act, 1953—, program coordinator, dir. legal services, 1962—. Vice pres. Ark. Conf. on Social Welfare, 1956, treas., 1958-64; area cons. Ark. Plan for Mental Health, 1963—; emergency welfare coordinator State of Ark., 1962—; chmn. exec. com. Nat. Reciprocal Support Conf., 1957, mem. exec. com., 1957—; dist. committeeman Boy Scouts Am., 1957-59; Ark. dep. compact adminstr. Interstate Compact on Juveniles. Served to lt. col. AUS, 1942-46; now col. Res. Decorated Bronze Star. Mem. Ark., Pulaski County bar assns., Am. Jurisprudence Assn., Am. Legion (vice comdr.), Am. Pub. Welfare Assn., Res. Officers Assn. Democrat. Methodist (ofcl. bd.). Mason (Shriner); mem. Order Eastern Star. Author: Manual of Procedure on Reciprocal Support Act, 1961; Manual on Statute Draft, 1950. Home: 500 S Summit Apt 13 Little Rock AR 72202 Office: Employment Security-Welfare Bldg Little Rock AR 72201

SMITH, IVAN JUAN, realtor; b. Corbin, Ky., Apr., 9, 1930; s. Alvy and Ruby (Candy) S.; A.A., U. Fla., 1954; m. Gene Frances Wynne, Sept. 28, 1951; children—Stephanie Kay, Kelly Sue (Mrs. William Gill), Cary Lynn. Asso. mem. M.N. Weir & Sons, Inc. realty, Pompano Beach, Fla., 1954-59, v.p., 1959-64; pres., 1965-69; pres., chmn. bd. Ivan J. Smith & Co., Inc. Realtors, Pompano Beach, 1969—; dir. 1st Nat. Bank, Pompano Beach, Beach 1st Nat. Bank. Mem. South Fla. council Boy Scouts Am., 1970-73. Served with USCGR, 1951-54. Named Outstanding Young Man, Jr. C. of C. Pompano Beach, 1963; Pompano Beach Realtor of Year, 1967. Mem. Nat. Inst. Farm and Land Brokers, Nat. Assn. Realtors, Pomano Beach-Deerfield Beach Bd. Realtors (pres. 1967), Greater Pompano Beach C. of C. (pres. 1972). Clubs: Hundred of Broward County; Century of Univ. Fla.; Coral Springs (Fla.) Country; Lake Toxaway (N.C.) Country; Lighthouse Point (Fla.) Yacht; Tower (Ft. Lauderdale, Fla.). Home: 2495 SE 6th St Pompano Beach FL 33062 Office: 3350 E Atlantic Blvd Pompano Beach FL 33062

SMITH, JACK CARROLL, C. of C. exec.; b. Meridian, Miss., Mar. 22, 1923; s. Elmo and Dora (Connor) S.; B.B.A., U. Ga., 1948; m. Melissa Moultrie Smith, July 30, 1948; children—Carroll, Jack Carroll, Claire. Staff supr. personnel Newport News Shipbuilding & Dry Dock Co., 1948-60; exec. v.p. Roanoke Valley C. of C., Roanoke, Va., 1960—. Chmn. Indsl. Devel. Authority, City of Roanoke; sec. Greater Roanoke Valley Devel. Found.; mem. City of Roanoke Airport Adv. Commn.; sec.-treas. Miss Virginia Pageant, Inc., 1964—, also exec. dir.; indsl. prodn. commr. Emergency Indsl. Prodn. Resource Agy. Mem. World Trade Conf. Com., Gov.'s Travel Adv. Com., Bicentennial Commn.; mem. indsl. devel. com., chmn. travel devel. com. Va. State Chamber. Bd. dirs., v.p. Nat. Assn. Miss America State Pageants; bd. dirs. Va. Thanksgiving Festival, Roanoke Symphony Soc. Served with AUS, 1943-45. Mem. Newcomen Soc. Club: Roanoke Valley Booster (past pres.). Home: 201 Parkcrest Rd SW Roanoke VA 24014 Office: PO Box 20 Roanoke VA 24001

SMITH, JACK CURTIS, biostatistician; b. Breckenridge, Tex., Mar. 25, 1941; s. Mark Curtis and Gertrude Elizabeth (Smith) S.; B.A., Howard Payne Coll., 1963; M.S., Tulane U., 1965; m. Doris Jane Russell, May 26, 1963; 1 son, Mark Curtis. Survey dir., statistician La. State Health Dept., New Orleans, 1965-66; served to sr. asst. Epidemic Intelligence Service, USPHS, 1966-68; chief statis. services activity Family Planning Evaluation Br. Center for Disease Control, Atlanta, 1968—. Faculty, Emory U. Sch. Medicine, 1970-71, U. N.C. Sch. Pub. Health, 1969, 71-72; cons. WHO, Geneva, Switzerland, 1972; tech. adviser AID, Taichung, Taiwan, 1971; mem. tech. cons. panel Nat. Center for Health Statistics, Dept. Health, Edn. and Welfare, 1971-73. NIH fellow, 1963-65. Recipient Dept. Health, Edn. and Welfare Superior Work Performance award, 1971. Mem. Am. Assn. Planned Parenthood Physicians, Am. Pub. Health Assn., Population Assn. Am., Population Reference Bur., So. Regional Demographic Group. Club: Decatur-DeKalb Men's Garden. Contbr. articles to nat. jours., also monographs. Home: 3952 Woburn Dr Tucker GA 30084 Office: Family Planning Evaluation Br Center for Disease Control Atlanta GA 30333

SMITH, JACK DARLING, machinery co. exec., publisher; b. Madison, Fla., Jan. 25, 1920; s. Amos Charles and Ida Mae (Gissendaner) S.; student South Ga. Coll., 1948-50; A.B., Valdosta State Coll., 1952, B.S., 1952; B.D., Emory U., 1955, M.Div., 1972; LL.B., Blackstone Sch. Law, 1970, J.D., 1971; m. Jane Frances Kappel, Dec. 13, 1970; children by previous marriage—Lyndell Darling, Joan Renice (Mrs. Kenneth Cole), Walton Earle. Vice pres., gen. mgr. Nat. Pub. Relations, Inc., Thomasville, Ga., 1946-48; ordained to ministry Meth. Ch., 1952; pastor, Ludowici, Ga., 1948-52, Stockbridge, Ga., 1952-55, Wadley (Ga.) 1st Ch., 1955-60, Sylvania, Ga., 1960-64, Dublin, Ga., 1964-68; v.p. pub. relations Fulghum Industries, Inc., Wadley, 1968—, also dir.; pres. Dixie Publs. & Arts Co., Inc. County chmn. Gov. Carter's campaign, 1970. Trustee Ga. Magnolia Manor, Americus, 1965—; trustee Epworth-by-the-Sea. Served with USAAF, 1940-45. Mem. Ga. gov.'s staff, 1966-68, 68-70, 71; named Adm. Ga. Navy, 1971—. Mem. C. of C. (pres.). Democrat. Mason, Rotarian. Pub., Dixie Logger, Lumberman Mag., 1969—, Woodchuck, 1973—. Home: Box 703 Wadley GA 30477 Office: Box 487 Wadley GA 30477

SMITH, JACK GILLESPIE, engr.; b. Kansas City, Mo., Aug. 17, 1917; s. Harvey H. and Della (Gillespie) S.; student Ga. Inst. Tech., 1935-40, U. Minn., 1943-44; m. Myra Louise Johnson, Nov. 27, 1941; children—Mary Louise (Mrs. James J. Johnson), Jack Gillespie, Davie Clarissa (Mrs. James E. Milsted). Elec. engr. TVA, Knoxville, 1940-58, Army Ballistic Missile Agy., Huntsville, Ala., 1958-60; supr. aero. engr. NASA, MSFC, Huntsville, 1960—, now attached to Plant Engring. and Materiel Mgmt. Office. Ordained as deacon Presbyn. Ch. U.S., mem. North Ala. Presbytery, mem. council Camp Maranatha. Served with AUS, 1942-46. Registered profl. engr., Tenn. Mem. Nat. Soc. Profl. Engrs., Internat. Platform Assn. Home: 1310 Kennamer Dr Huntsville AL 35801 Office: MSFC EM 34 Bldg 4200 Huntsville AL 35812

SMITH, JAMES BURT, JR., hosp. found. adminstr.; b. Galveston, Tex., July 13, 1937; s. James Burt and Mamie (Teutsch) S.; student Tarleton State Coll., 1954-56; B.B.A., N. Tex. State Coll., 1958; m. Nancy Fay Strickland, June 21, 1958; 1 dau., Jenny Beatrice. Plant mgr. Tex. Milling Co., Clifton, 1961-66; hosp. adminstr. Goodall-Witcher Hosp. Found., Clifton, 1966—. Mem. Clifton City Council, 1963—; mayor, Clifton, 1973-75; pres. Heart of Tex. Council

Govts., Waco. C.P.A., Tex. Mem. Tex. Soc. C.P.A.'s, Tex. Hosp. Assn. Mason, Lion. Home: 415 Northern Av R Clifton TX 76634 Office: 503 W 5th St Clifton TX 76634

SMITH, JAMES HADLEY, data control co. exec.; b. Mount Airy, N.C., Aug. 17, 1928; s. James Raymond and Annie Jamie (Hadley) S.; grad. Woodberry Forest Sch., 1946; A.B., Duke, 1950; m. Emily Elizabeth Blum, Feb. 24, 1951; children—Emily Elizabeth, Helen Blum. Office mgr. Nat. Furniture Co., Mount Airy, 1952-60; pres. Skyline Motors, Inc., Mount Airy, 1960—; dir. Electronics Data Controls Corp., Winston-Salem, N.C., 1963-70, chmn. bd., 1970—. Chmn., Mount Airy United Fund, 1958-59. Served with AUS, 1950-52. Methodist. Mason, Elk. Club: Mount Airy Country. Home: 216 Howard St Mount Airy NC 27030 Office: PO Box 430 Mount Airy NC 27030

SMITH, JAMES LONNIE, lawyer; b. Hattiesburg, Miss., Sept. 26, 1936; s. Lonnie and Velma (Waldrop) S.; B.A., U. Miss., 1958, LL.B., 1960. Admitted to Miss. bar, 1960; asso. Bobby J. Garraway, Lumberton, Miss., 1960-61; gen practice Poplarville, Miss., 1962; with Magnolia Title Co., Picayune, Miss., 1963-65; partner firm Williams & Smith, Picayune, Miss., 1965—. Mem. Miss. Ho. of Reps., 1968—. Bd. dirs. Poplarville (Miss.) Pub. Library. Mem. C. of C., Phi Delta Phi. Baptist. Mason. Rotarian. Home: 205 N Hickory St Popularville MS 39470 Office: 109 N Main St Picayune MS 39466

SMITH, JAMES OTIS, landscape architect; b. Longview, Tex., Dec. 12, 1936; s. Ralph Alexander and Ruby Mae (Snearly) S.; B.S., Tex. A. and M., 1963; m. Linda Margaret Watkins, Aug. 30, 1958; children—Cheryl Lyn, James Pruett. Head design Naud Burnett Asso., Dallas, 1963-67; principal James O. Smith Asso., Richardson, Tex., 1967-70; head dept. landscape architecture and planning B.H.A. Architects & Engrs., N.Y.C. and Dallas, 1970—; site design coordinator Dallas/Ft. Worth Airport, 1970-72, project engr., 1972—, asst. office mgr. for constrn., 1973—. Mem. Am. Soc. Landscape Architects (asso.), Tex. Soc. Landscape Architects (pres. 1967-71). Home: 1 Shadywood Pl Richardson TX 75080 Office: 1949 N Stemmons St Dallas TX 75207

SMITH, JEAN CHANDLER, librarian; b. Phila., Apr. 13, 1918; d. Chandler White and Philena P. (Cheetham) Smith; A.B., Bryn Mawr Coll., 1939; M.S., Yale, 1953. Circulation librarian, reference librarian D.C. Pub. Library, Washington, 1939-43; translator U.S. Office Censorship, Panama Canal Zone, 1943-44; librarian Kaneohe (T.H.) Naval Air Sta., 1944-46; reference asst., asst. reference librarian, research asst. Yale U. Library, New Haven, 1947-58; reference librarian biol. scis., acting chief acquisitions sect. NIH, Library, Bethesda, 1959-63; chief reference services dept. library Dept. Interior, Washington, 1963-65; asst. dir. libraries Smithsonian Instn., Washington, 1965-68, spl. asst. to dir. libraries for biol. sci. programs, 1968-72, asst. dir. libraries for bur. services, 1972—. Guest investigator Osborn Meml. Lab., Yale, 1953-57. Mem. Am. Soc. Information Sci., Spl. Libraries Assn. (treas. D.C. chpt. 1966-69, 2d v.p. D.C. chpt. 1969—, nat. sec., treas. natural resources div. 1969—), Conn. Acad. Arts and Scis., Am. Soc. Limnology and Oceanography, Bibliog. Soc. Am. Home: 3601 Connecticut Av NW Washington DC 20008 Office: Smithsonian Instn Washington DC 20560

SMITH, JEROME ARNOLD, pub. relations exec.; b. Glendive, Mont., Sept. 6, 1929; s. Charles Thomas and Esther Margaret (Bauer) S.; B.A. in Psychology and Philosophy, U. Mont., 1956; m. Lorilee Ruth Stark, Oct. 5, 1957; 1 dau., Stacey Lorraine. Pres., Finefrock, Goebel Smith, Inc., Lafayette, Cal., 1964-68; reporter KGO, San Francisco, 1968-70; news dir. sta. KXYZ, Houston, 1970—. Guest lectr. U. Houston, 1970-73. Mem. code com. Harris County Med. Soc., Houston, 1971—; mem. adv. com. Houston Bay area Boy Scouts Am., 1971—. Served with USAF, 1948-51. Recipient Silver Gavel award Am. Bar Assn., 1972, Abe Lincoln award So. Baptist Radio-TV Commn., 1972. Mem. Houston News Dirs. Assn. (pres. 1971—), Radio-TV News Dirs. Assn., U.P.I. Broadcastors of Tex., Sigma Delta Chi (pres. Tex. Gulf Coast chpt. 1972—). Home: 12633 Memorial St Houston TX 77024 Office: 1602 Fannin Bank Bldg Houston TX 77025

SMITH, JERRY MILLARD, savs. and loan exec.; b. Oklahoma City, Aug. 20, 1931; s. M. W. and Lucille (Tipton) S.; B.S., Kan. U., 1954, M.Pub. Adminstrn., 1960; m. Erma Lee Lutz, Jan. 26, 1951; children—Stephanie, Sara. Asst. city mgr., city planner, Lawrence, Kan., 1958-60; city mgr., Parsons, Kan., 1960-62, Pittsburg, Kan., 1963-68, Norman, Okla., 1968-72; exec. v.p. Western Home Service Corp., Norman, 1972-73; sr. exec. v.p. Sooner Fed. Savs. and Loan, Tulsa, 1973—. Instr. Sch. Engring. U. Kan., 1955-58. Served with USMCR, 1953-54. Mem. Internat. City Mgrs. Assn., Scarab, Pi Sigma Alpha. Rotarian. Home: 441 Thorton St Norman OK 73069 Office: 404 S Boston Av Tulsa OK 74103

SMITH, JIM, radio-TV exec.; b. Oklahoma City, Oct. 11, 1933; s. Leonard James and Faye Rachel (Anderson) S.; student Okla. A. and M. U., 1951-52, George Williams U., 1952-53, Whittier Coll., 1953-54; B.A., Cal. Theol. Sem., 1955; m. Karel Lane Carter, Jan. 17, 1957; children—Phillip Wayne, James Frank, Scott Oden. With various radio and TV stas., 1961-64; mgr. KIEU, KWOW radio, Los Angeles, 1964-69; host syndicated TV show, Dallas, Ft. Worth, 1967-68; TV personality, Tulsa, 1965-68; part owner radio sta. KVIN, 1969-72; dir. news and spl. events sta. KUHI-TV, Joplin, Mo., 1973—. Pres. Family Plan, Tulsa, 1971—. Active Democratic party, Okla., 1965-73, campaign coordinator U.S. Congressman Ed Edmondson, 1970; spl. radio cons., 1970-72. Bd. dirs. P.I.P.E. Inc., Indian self-help orgn. Recipient Man of Year award So. Cal. Am. Radio Broadcasting Co., 1964. Mem. Northwest Okla. Broadcasting (dir. 1970-72), TV News Dirs. Unitarian. Lion (pres. 1963). Address: PO Box 527 Ozark AR 72949

SMITH, JOEL PERRY, physician; b. Richland, Ga., Aug. 15, 1912; s. Joel Olin and Mary (Perry) S.; O.D., So. Coll. Optometry, 1937; O.D., Emory U., 1942; B.S., LaGrange Coll., 1944; M.D., U. Ga. 1947; m. June Goforth, June 5, 1933; children—Joel Perry II, Michael Gordon, Ellen Janet, Lynda Jean. Owner, LaGrange Optical & Jewelry Co. (Ga.), 1934-44; intern Norfolk (Va.) Gen. Hosp., 1947-48; resident surgery Crawford W. Long Hosp., Atlanta, 1948-49; pvt. practice medicine specializing in ophthalmology and otolaryngology Atlanta, 1949—; staff mem. Ga. Bapt., Grady, Crawford W. Long, Henrietta Egleston hosps., Atlanta; clin. instr. otolaryngology Emory U. Med. Sch., 1956—; founder, med. dir. Drs. Meml. Hosp., Atlanta, 1969—. Dir. Electronic Equipment Co. Atlanta. Sec., dir. Ga. Found. Otolarnygology; mem. Deafness Research Found., N.Y.C. Served as capt. AUS, 1953-55. Fellow Soc. Mil. Ophthalmology; mem. A.M.A., So., Ga. med. assns., Alpha Kappa Kappa. Democrat. Methodist. Mason (32 deg., Shriner), Lion. Club: Atlanta Athletic. Contbr. article to profl. jours. Home: 1618 Lady Marion Lane NE Atlanta GA 30309 Office: 573 W Peachtree St NW Atlanta GA 30308

SMITH, JOHN GETTYS, pub. relations exec.; b. York, S.C., Nov. 24, 1932; s. Clyde B. and Ora (Gettys) S.; A.B., U. S.C., 1956; m. Nelle Elliott McCants, June 25, 1955; children—John Gettys, Spencer McCants, Ora Elliott. Tchr., York High Sch., 1956-57; with York County Health Dept., 1957-59; York bur. chief Rock Hill (S.C.) Evening Herald, 1959-61; salesman Smith Furniture, York, 1961-63; dir. pub. relations Sea Pines Plantation Co., 1963-64, v.p. pub. relations, community devel. Sea Pines Co., Hilton Head Island, S.C., 1964-74, also dir.; v.p. Sea Pines Investment Co., 1969-74; pres. John Gettys Smith Assos., Pub. Relations Cons., 1974—; pres. Harbour Ventrues, Inc., Caliboque Properties Inc. Coordinator, Internat. Inst. Advancement Creative Arts, 1967-70; founder York Mus. Assn. 1956, York County Meml. Mus., 1958; dir. ann. tour York homes; mem. York County Hist. Commn., 1960-63; chmn. Western York County Crippled Children's Soc., 1959-63; adv. mem. S.C. Confederate Centennial Commn., 1961-65; exec. com. Savannah Symphony Sec., 1969—; mem. Beaufort County Bd. Edn., 1967-69; pres. Carolina Low Country Hist. Found.; v.p. Sea Pines Acad., Sea Pines Ednl. Found.; chmn. Gov.'s Conf. on Travel and Tourism, 1971-72, CBS Tournament Tennis Champions, 1971, CBS Tennis Classic, 1972-73, P.G.A. Sea Pines Heritage Golf Classic, 1969-74, NBC-Family Circle Tennis, 1973; pres. S.C. Travel Council, 1973-74. Served with AUS, 1954-56. Recipient award Am. Travel Orgns., 1967, 1st pl. award Discover Am. travel orgn., 1973. Mem. Historic Beaufort Found. (fund raising com. 1971-72), York County (charter) hist. socs., Artists' Guild York, Chester, Lancaster Counties S.C. (exec. com.), S.C. (adv. com. for tourist promotion 1959-61), Hilton Head Island (v.p. 1964-66, pres. 1967), Beaufort County (tourist promotion com. 1966) chambers commerce, Hugenot Soc., Hilton Head Island Homebuilders' Assn. (sec.-treas. 1965-66), Sigma Nu, Kappa Pi. Episcopalian (vestryman). Clubs: Chatham, Oglethorpe (Savannah, Ga.); Plantation (Hilton Head Island); Pinacle (Augusta). Author: A Family of York, 1967. Contbr. articles to mags., newspapers. Home: Sea Pines Plantation 48 Beach Lagoon Hilton Head Island SC 29928 Office: Sea Pines Co Hilton Head Island SC 29928

SMITH, JOHN JOSEPH, lawyer; b. Pitts., Nov. 14, 1911; s. John Joseph and Alta Ethel (McGrady) S.; A.B., Birmingham So. Coll., 1931; A.M., U. Va., 1932; J.D., U. Ala., 1937; m. Ruth Lee Snavely, July 11, 1942; children—John Joseph, Robert William. Instr., U. Ala., 1934-37; admitted to Ala. bar, 1937, bar Supreme Ct. U.S.; asso. Murphy, Hanna & Woodall, 1937; asst. prof. U. Va., 1937-39; atty. Office Solicitor Labor, U.S. Dept. Labor, 1939-42; enforcement atty. rent div. OPA, 1942-43; legal counsel aircraft div. Bechtel-McCone Corp., Birmingham, 1943-46; pvt. practice law, Birmingham, 1946—. Mem. gov.'s staff, 1963-71. Active Community Chest, YMCA, Better Bus. Bur.; committeeman Boy Scouts Am.; founder, commr. Homewood Joy Open Baseball League, 1958-72, chmn. bd., 1972—; chmn. Homewood Citizens Action Com. Against Annexation. Recipient Nat. Pop Warner award for service to youth, 1961. Mem. Am., Ala., Birmingham bar assns., Farrah Order Jurisprudence (founder, nat. pres. 1969-71, historian 1973—), Am. Econ. Assn., U. Va., U. Ala. alumni assns., Homewood C. of C., Pi Gamma Mu, Tau Kappa Alpha, Delta Sigma Phi. Methodist (founder, dist. dir. young adult fellowship classes). Mason (Shriner). Club: The Club. Author: Selected Principles of the Law of Contracts, Sales and Negotiable Instruments, 1938. Home: 1506 Primrose Pl Birmingham AL 35209 Office: First Nat Bldg Birmingham AL 35203

SMITH, JOHN MALCOLM (MAC), lawyer; b. Marion, Ark., July 20, 1911; s. Dolph and Annabele (Nance) S.; student U. Ark., 1929-32, LL.B., 1934; m. Gladys Wright, Apr. 18, 1942. Admitted to Ark. bar, 1934; pvt. practice, Marion, 1934-41, West Memphis, Ark., 1942; partner Rieves & Smith, Marion, 1946-49, West Memphis, 1949-62, individual practice, 1963—; dir., gen. counsel 1st Nat. Bank, West Memphis; dir., sr. v.p., gen. counsel Cooper Communities, Inc. (formerly Cherokee Village Devel Co., Inc.), Belle Vista, Ark.; dir. Union Planters Corp., Memphis. Spl. justice Supreme Ct. Ark., 1955; spl. legal counsel agr. com. U.S. Ho. of Reps., 1961; mem. Ark. Ho. of Reps., 1939-42. Bd. dirs. West Memphis Boys Club, Meth. Found. Ark.; trustee Crittenden Meml. Hosp., West Memphis. Served from capt. to lt. col. AUS, 1942-46. Mem. Am., Ark. bar assns., Law-Sci. Acad. Am., Urban Land Inst., Am. Land Devel. Assn. (dir. 1973—), Am. Judicature Soc., Am. Legion, V.F.W., Judge Advs. Assn., West Memphis C. of C. (v.p., dir. 1974), Blue Key, Sigma Alpha Epsilon. Methodist (trustee, sec.). Clubs: Meadowbrook Country (West Memphis); Summit (Memphis); National Lawyers (Washington). Home: 415 Cooper St West Memphis AR 72301 Office: PO Box 830 West Memphis AR 72301

SMITH, JOHN MARLIN, ednl. adminstr.; b. Gainesville, Ga., Jan. 23, 1939; s. Alvin and Willa (Smith) S.; B.S., North Ga. Coll., 1963; Ednl. Adminstrn., U. Ga., 1967, Specialist Ednl. Adminstr. Degree, 1967; m. Evelyn Hurley, Mar. 16, 1958; children—Johnie Belinda, Rickey Marlin. Tchr. pub. schs. Gainesville, Ga., 1958-63; prin. pub. schs. Dahlonega, Ga., 1963-69, supt., 1969—. Chmn. steering com. 9th Dist. Ednl. Services Center, Cleveland, Ga., 1970—. Mem. Lumpkin County Edn. Assn. (pres. 1967-68), 9th Congl. Dist. Supt.'s Orgn. (pres.), N.E.A., Ga. Assn. Educators, Ga. Assn. Sch. Supts., Dahlonega-Lumpkin County C. of C. (past dir.), Kappa Delta Pi. Democrat. Baptist. Club: Lins (Dahlonega). Home: Rte 2 Dahionega GA 30533 Office: PO Box 277 Dahlonega GA 30533

SMITH, JOHN RANDALL, interior designer; b. Jacksonville, Fla., Oct. 27, 1941; s. John Albert and Fanney Elizabeth (West) S.; student Fla. State U., 1960-62, Edison Jr. Coll., evenings 1967; B.F.A., Ringling Sch. Art, 1967; m. Jane Leonard, Mar. 29, 1964; children—Randall Bryan, John Clayton, Lesley Anne and Lorie Jane (twins). Designer, Holland Salley Interior Designs, Inc., Naples, Fla., 1966-72; interior designer Killearn Properties Inc., Tallahassee, 1972—, asst. v.p., 1973—, also dir. design and single family housing; pres. J. Randy Smith., A.I.D.-Interior-Designs, Tallahassee, 1974—. Mem. publs. bd. Collier Democrat, Naples, 1971—; co-chmn. Com. to Elect Askew-Adams, 1971; vice chmn. Gov. Askew Adv. Com. Collier County, 1970. Mem. Am. Inst. Interior Designers, Jr. C. of C., Tallahassee Home Builders Assn., Gulf Coast Investment Club Naples, Alpha Tau Omega. Democrat. Baptist. Club: Killearn Golf and Country (Tallahassee). Home: 1801 Myrick Rd Tallahassee FL 32303

SMITH, JOSEPH CHARLES, real estate devel. co. exec.; b. Palestine, Tex., Nov. 26, 1940; s. Sidney H. and Mary Ellen (Smith) S.; B.B.A., U. Tex., 1963; M.S. (Grad. Teaching fellow), Tex. Coll. Arts and Industry, 1966; m. Nancy Clare Williams, Dec. 30, 1967; children—Jennifer, Michael, C.P.A., Price Waterhouse & Co., Houston, 1966-69, Main Lafrentz & Co., Houston, 1969-72; exec. v.p. Scott Mann & Co., Houston, 1972—, also dir.; v.p. Nat. Leisure Corp., Houston, 1972—, also dir.; dir. Mann Properties, Inc., N.W. Park Corp. Served with USCGR, 1963-64. Mem. Am. Inst. C.P.A.'s, Tex. Soc. C.P.A.'s, Sigma Chi. Methodist. Clubs: Exchange, Houston (Houston). Home: 647 Electra St Houston TX 77024 Office: 711 Houston Club Bldg Houston TX 77002

SMITH, KEN MCFARLANE, lawyer; b. Kokomo, Ind., Feb. 12, 1927; s. James McFarlane and Pearl (Johnston) S.; B.S., Ind. U., 1948, LL.B., 1950, J.D., 1967; m. Mildred Alice Howell, Aug. 16, 1953; children—Timothy McFarlane, James Michael. Admitted to Ind. bar, 1950, Va. bar, 1954; practiced in Arlington, Va., 1954—; asst. pub. defender State Ind., 1950; law clk. U.S. Civil Service, 1953; pvt. practice, 1954—; asst. commonwealth atty. Arlington County, 1955-59, substitute judge, 1961-66, 67—, asst. commr. accounts, 1960—; tchr. bus. law U. Va. Extension, 1957; mem. Va. Adv. Legislative Council Study on Consol. Local Govts., 1959; mem. Nat. Traffic Ct. Conf. for Judges Northwestern U., 1963; mem. Va. Adv. Legislative Council Study Group on Commrs. of Fiduciaries and Accounts, 1963—. Sec.-treas., Universal Bldg. Co., Inc., 1960-72; chmn. bd. Bank Arlington, 1969-73. Chmn., Ct. of Honor Arlington council Boy Scouts Am., 1955-59, area explorer chmn., 1971-72; chmn. March of Dimes, 1959; vice chmn. YMCA, 1959-61; chmn. Heart Assn., 1962. Pres., Arlington (Va.) Young Democrats, 1958-29, chmn. 10th dist., 1959-60; exec. v.p. Va. Young Democrats, 1960-61, dist. v.p., 1962-63, counsel, 1964-65. Pres. Inter-Service Club Council Arlington, 1965; bd. dirs. Alcoholics Rehab., Inc., 1965—; chmn. adv. bd. Salvation Army, 1963-67; mem. adv. bd. Mental Hygiene Center, 1963-66, Council Ind. Colls. Va., 1971—; adv. com. Arlington Sch. Bd., 1972—; asso. bd. U. Richmond, 1973, trustee, 1974—. Served with Signal Corps, AUS, 1950-52. Recipient Distinguished Service award Jr. C. of C., 1962; named Kiwanis Man of Year, 1964, 71; named Man of Yr., Inter Service Club Arlington, 1971. Mem. Am., Va., Arlington bar assns., Arlington Outdoor Edn. Assn. (dir. 1972—), Phi Kappa Psi, Phi Delta Phi. Baptist (Clarendon moderator 1971—, bd. deacons 1972—). Home: 4056 N 27th Rd Arlington VA 22207 Office: 2007 N 15th St Arlington VA 22216

SMITH, KILLOUGH KING, JR., lawyer; b. Sherman, Tex., Feb. 16, 1920; s. Killough King and Leta (Barker) S.; LL.B., U. Tex., 1947; m. Mary Marshall Mitchell, May 12, 1946; children—Kathleen (Mrs. James T. Stafford), Melinda, Kent, Frances. Admitted to Tex. bar, 1948; asso., partner Thompson, Walker, Smith & Shannon, 1948-60; partner Hudson, Keltner, Smith & Cunningham, Ft. Worth, 1961—. Served as capt. AUS, 1942-46. Mem. Phi Gamma Delta. Clubs: Rotary, Century II, Colonial Country (Ft. Worth). Home: 3821 Overton Park E Fort Worth TX 76109 Office: Continental Life Bldg Fort Worth TX 76102

SMITH, LARRY JAMES, elec. engr.; b. Waverly, Tenn., Nov. 19, 1944; s. Walter James and Delilah Elease (McClure) S.; B.S. cum laude, U. Tenn., 1969; m. Joy Delaine Spencer, Aug. 28, 1966; children—Jennifer Dawn, John Wayne. Elec. engr. TVA, Chattanooga, 1969-70, New Johnsonville, Tenn., 1970-71, Cumberland City, Tenn., 1971-73, Chattanooga, 1973—. Served with AUS, 1962-65. Mem. I.E.E.E., Tau Beta Pi, Eta Kappa Nu. Home: 101 Lucas St Waverly TN 37185 Office: TVA Office of Power 805 Edney Bldg Chattanooga TN 37402

SMITH, LAWRENCE EVERETT, educator; b. Rossburg, O., Aug. 20, 1920; s. Emerson E. and Ida (Hittle) S.; B.A., U. Louisville, 1943; postgrad. Cornell U., 1946; M.A., U. Mich., 1952; Ed.D. (grad. fellow 1954-56), U. Fla., 1956; m. Timothy C. Riggs, Nov. 11, 1944; children—Kay Frances (Mrs. Keith W. Leonard), Wayne Errol. Prin. Marlow (Ga.) High Sch., 1945-54; asst. dir. Bur. Ednl. Research, U. Ala., University, 1956-59; asso. prof. Glasboro (N.J.) State Coll., 1959-61, 62-65; vis. asso. prof. U. Fla., 1961-62; prof. Inst. Ednl. Research, Fla. Atlantic U., Boca Raton, 1965—, dir., 1965-71. Exec. sec. 1st dist. Ga. High Sch. Assn., 1952-54; cons. Ala. Legislative Commn., 1958-59; research dir. Curriculum Devel. Council So. N.J., 1963-65; mem. adv. council Southeastern Ednl. Lab., Atlanta, 1966—. Served with USMCR, 1943-45. Mem. Am., Fla. ednl. research assns., Am. Assn. Sch. Adminstrs., Am. Assn. U. Profs., N.E.A., Fla. Edn. Assn., Franklin Inst. Sci. and Mechanic Arts, Phi Delta Kappa, Kappa Delta Pi, Phi Kappa Phi. Mem. Ch. of Nazarene. Producer instructional TV series on ednl. supervision Fla. Atlantic U., 1966—. Home: 899 SW 9th Terrace Boca Raton FL 33432

SMITH, LAWRENCE NORFLEET, banker; b. Roanoke, Va., June 1, 1937; s. Norfleet A. and Margaretta (Brady) S.; B.S., Hampden-Sydney Coll., 1959; postgrad. U. Richmond, 1960, Stonier Grad. Sch. Banking, Rutgers U., 1968; m. Sally Birdsong, Apr. 15, 1961; children—Lawrence N., Harvard B., Susan N. Salesman, F.W. Craigie & Co., Richmond, 1959-61; investment banker, mgr. municipal bond dept. Mason & Co., Inc. (now Legg-Mason), Newport News, Va., 1961-64; with United Va. Bank/Seaboard Nat., Suffolk, Va., 1964-70, v.p., 1968-70, exec. v.p., Norfolk, Va., 1971—, sec. bd. dirs., 1967—; dir. Empire Machinery & Supply, Norfolk, Buck Equipment Inc., Twenty, Inc. Mem. Suffolk/Nansemond Cons. Study Commn., 1970—; mem. Suffolk Zoning Bd. Appeals, 1969—; co-chmn. Suffolk-Nansemond Devel. Commn. Group chmn. United Fund Norfolk; devel. com. Eastern Va. Med. Coll. Bd. dirs. Suffolk Recreational and Charitable Assn., Norfolk YMCA. Mem. Va. Bankers Assn. (dir. Group I), C. of C., Tri-County, Regional Emergency (exec. mgr.) clearing house assns. Episcopalian (asst. treas.). Rotarian. Clubs: Suffolk Sports, German, Suffolk Golf Assn., Suffolk Tennis (Suffolk), Cedar Point Country (Crittenden, Va.); Harbor; Princess Anne Country. Home: 826 Riverview Dr Suffolk VA 23434 Office: Box 3127 Norfolk VA 23514

SMITH, LAWTON HARCOURT, mammalian physiologist; b. Poughkeepsie, N.Y., Nov. 15, 1924; s. Frank Irving and Dorothy (Harcourt) S.; B.S., U. Conn., 1950; M.A., Syracuse U., 1952, Ph.D., 1954; m. Jeanette Anderson Parke, Oct. 6, 1946; 1 son, Lawton Bradley. Research asso. biology Oak Ridge Nat. Lab., 1955-56, staff biologist, 1957-70, research group leader, 1970—. Lectr. physiology U. Tenn. Grad. Sch. Biomed. Scis. NSF fellow, 1960-61. Mem. Am. Physiol. Soc., Radiation Research Soc., Soc. Exptl. Biology and Medicine. Home: 124 Dartmouth Circle Oak Ridge TN 37830 Office: Biology div Oak Ridge Nat Lab Oak Ridge TN 37830

SMITH, LEMUEL AUGUSTUS, JR., justice; b. Holly Springs, Miss., Aug. 30, 1904; s. Lemuel Augustus and Louise (Robertson) S.; LL.B., U. Miss., 1926; m. Chesley Thorne, Dec. 2, 1931; children—Caffey (Mrs. E.E. (Litkenhous), Lemuel Augustus. Admitted to Miss. bar, 1926, practiced in Holly Springs, 1926-65; dir. First State Bank Holly Springs. County pros. atty., 1935-50; atty. Marshall County Bd. Suprs., 1948-65; asso. justice Supreme Ct. of Miss., 1965—. Spl. chancellor 3d Chancery Ct. Dist. Miss., 1958-59. Pres. bd. trustees Holly Springs Municipal Separate Sch. Dist., 1946-57. Mem. Miss. Ho. of Reps., 1929, 32, 33, 36. Served as lt. comdr. USNR, 1942-45. Mem. Am., Miss. (past complaint commr.), Marshall County (pres. 1957) bar assns., Kappa Alpha. Episcopalian (former vestryman). Home: 631 Chulahoma Av Holly Springs MS 38635 Office: Dept Justice Bldg Jackson MS 39205

SMITH, LEROY FLEMING, JR., physician; b. Savannah, Ga., Oct. 7, 1935; s. Leroy Fleming and Helen (Tuten) S.; A.B., King Coll., 1956; M.D., Med. Coll. Ga., 1960; m. Elizabeth Hilsman, July 18, 1959; children—Leslie, Powell, Edward. Intern, Harrisburg (Pa.) Hosp., 1960-61; resident Cleve. Clinic Found., 1963-67; practice medicine specializing in hematology, med. oncology, Alexandria, Va., 1967—; asst. clin. prof. medicine Georgetown U. Med. Sch., 1970—. Pres. bd. trustees Alexandria Community Health Center, 1970—. Served with USAF, 1961-63. Diplomate Am. Bd. Internal Medicine. Mem. A.C.P. Home: 1105 Vassar Rd Alexandria VA 22314 Office: 4801 Kenmore Av Alexandria VA 22304

SMITH, LEROY VICTOR, football coach; b. Lexington, Ky., Aug 4, 1938; s. Henry Clay and Mary (Byrd) S.; B.S., Jackson (Miss.) State Coll. 1958; M.S., U. Ky., 1963 ; m. Mary Levi, Mar. 14, 1958;

children—Darryl Victor, Angela Maria, Danee LaVon. Surp., Lexington (Ky.) Recreation Dept., summers 1956-63; with Miss. Valley State Coll., 1958-59; head football coach Randolph High Sch., Pass Christian, Miss., 1959-63; with Meigs High Sch., Nashville, 1963-64; head football coach Tuskegee Inst., 1964-70, Ky. State U., 1970—. Cons. community edn. program, Tuskegee, 1966. Mem. Am. Football Coaches Assn., Kappa Alpha Psi. Alpha Kappa Mu. Democrat. Episcopalian. Author articles. Home: 410 College Park Dr Frankfort KY 40601

SMITH, LESLIE MITCHELL, automotive co. exec.; b. Woodlake, Cal., Mar. 18, 1922; s. Victor Ellis and Mildred Marguerite (Mitchell) S.; grad. high sch.; m. Hilda Norvell, June 12, 1954; children—Emily (Mrs. Jerry B. Jackson), Joseph Scott. With Nat. Bank Commerce, Memphis, 1960-61; programmer Plough, Inc., Memphis, 1961-65; systems analyst Gen. Electric Computer Div., Memphis, 1965-66; mgr. data processing dept. Third Nat. Bank, Nashville, 1966-68; mgr. data center Scovill-Schrader Automotive Products Div., Nashville, 1968—. Adv. com. Nashville State Tech. Inst.-Continuing Edn. Div. Served with USN, 1941-60. Decorated D.F.C., Air medals (5). Mem. Soc. Computer Programmers (founder, 1st pres. 1964-65), Automotive Electronic Data Processing Council, Assn. Systems Mgmt., Am. Prodn. and Inventory Control Soc. (chpt. pres. 1971-72, v.p. region IV 1973—), Fleet Res. Assn. Home: 909 Neartop Dr Nashville TN 37205 Office: 2000 Richard Jones Rd Nashville TN 37215

SMITH, LEVIE DAVID, JR., realtor; b. Lakeland, Fla., Oct. 19, 1924; s. Levie David and Grace (Ross) S.; student U. Miami, 1943-44; B.S., Fla. So. Coll., 1947; m. Annie Laurie Hogan, Aug. 29, 1948; children—Nancy Carol, Levie David III, Judith Ann. Appraiser, Smith & Smith, Realtors, Lakeland, Fla., 1948-50, 52-73; now pres. Levie D. Smith & Assos., Inc., Lakeland. Mem. exec. bd. Gulf Ridge council Boy Scouts Am. Served as ensign USNR, 1943-46, as lt., 1950-52. Mem. Nat. Assn. Realtors (dir. 1974-76), Fla. Assessment Adminstr. (rev. comm. 1974) Am. Inst. Real Estate Appraisers (v.p. Fla. chpt. 1961, pres. 1962), Soc. Real Estate Appraisers (pres. West Coast chpt. 1957), Am. Right-of-Way Assn., Lakeland Bd. Realtors (pres. 1958), Fla. Assn. Realtors (v.p. 10th dist. 1968, pres. 1970), Lakeland C. of C. (dir. 1974). Democrat. Presbyn. (elder). Rotarian. Home: 515 Laurel Lane Lakeland FL 33803 Office: 223 S Florida Av Lakeland FL 33802

SMITH, LLOYD THOMAS, JR., lawyer; b. Petersburg, Va., Sept. 18, 1932; s. Lloyd Thomas and Ella Hilah (Hinton) S.; B.A., U. Va., 1955, LL.B., 1960; m. Willie Ashlin Wyatt, S.; B.A., U. Va., 1955, LL.B., 1960; m. Willie Ashlin Wyatt, Aug. 6, 1960; children—Garrett, Ashlin Wyatt, Hilah White. Admitted to Va. bar, 1960; asso. McGuire Wood & Battle, Charlottesville, Va., 1961-67, Tremblay & Smith, Charlottesville, 1968—. Dir., mem. exec. com. Va. Broadcasting Corp. Trustee Jefferson-Madison Regional Library; bd. dirs. Charlottesville-Albermarle Soc. for Prevention Cruelty to Animals. Served with USMCR, 1951-52. Mem. Am., Va., Albermarle-Charlottesville bar assns., Va. State Bar, Clubs: Farmington Country, Greencroft (Charlottesville). Home: 620 Park St Charlottesville VA 22901 Office: 105 E High St Charlottesville VA 22902

SMITH, MALCOLM CRAWFORD, JR., govt. ofcl.; b. Kingsville, Tex., Jan. 2, 1936; s. Malcolm Crawford and Bessie Valerie (Walker) S.; D.V.M., Tex. A. and M. U., 1959; M.S., Purdue U., 1965; m. Mary Arline Jones, May 27, 1961; children—Gavin Paul, Natasha Meadows. Chief NASA Food and Nutrition Br., Johnson Space Center, Houston, 1969—; sec.-treas. Spar Chems., Inc., Houston, 1971—. Bd. dirs., vice-chmn. Internat. Vet. Med. Found. Served to maj. USAF, 1959-69. Decorated Legion of Merit. Recipient Col. Rohland Isker award Research & Devel. Assos., Inc., 1972; NASA Outstanding Achievement award, 1972. Fellow Am. Inst. Chemists; mem. Am. Vet. Med. Assn., Am. Chem. Soc., Aerospace Med. Assn., Poultry Sci. Assn., Inst. Food Technologists, Assn. Mil. Surgeons. Home: 3410 Miramar St LaPorte TX 77571 Office: NASA Johnson Space Center Houston TX 77058

SMITH, MALCOLM DUNKIN, farmer; b. Montgomery, Ala., Nov. 2, 1939; s. Albert Fay and Evelyn (Dunkin) S.; student Auburn U., 1957-59, Belhaven Coll., 1960-61; m. Jane Drinkard, Aug. 6, 1966. With McQueen Smith Farms, Prattville, Ala., 1965—, farm mgr., 2d v.p., 1970—. Supr. Autanga County com. Agr. Stblzn. Conservation Service, 1972—. Mem. city council, Prattville, Ala., 1971—. Bd. dirs. Montgomery Area Mental Health Bd. Served with U.S.N.G., 1962-70. Mem. Autauga County Hog Producers Assn. (pres. 1969-71), Ala. Cattleman's Assn., Presbyn. (chmn. bd. deacons 1968-69). Home: 1257 Huie St Prattville AL 36067 Office: Route 6 Box 277 Prattville AL 36067

SMITH, MARIAN ADAMS (MRS. JULIUS CLARENCE SMITH III), civic worker; b. Winston-Salem, N.C., June 6, 1928; d. Roger Lee and Blanche Evelyn (Brann) Adams; B.F.A., U. N.C., 1951; m. Julius Clarence Smith III, June 21, 1951; children—Stephen Manly, Thomas Julius, Marian Keith. Art supr. Raleigh (N.C.) Pub. Schs., 1951; art tchr. Greensboro (N.C.) Pub. Schs., 1952-55. Pres., Southeastern Theatre Conf., 1970-71, chmn. children's theatre div., 1964-66, chmn. endowment fund, 1969—, now adminstrv. dir.; pres. N.C. Theatre conf., 1970-71; regional dir. Am. Coll. Theatre Festival, 1971-73; v.p. Pixie Theatre for Young People, Greensboro, 1962—; chmn. adv. com. of theatre U. N.C. at Greensboro, 1962—; chmn. children's theatre Jr. League of Greensboro, 1962-63, chmn. TV, 1964-65; v.p. Jr. League sustainers, 1970-71. Bd. govs. Nat. Childrens's Theatre Conf., 1967-69. Mem. Am. Theatre Assn. (dir. 1972), Children's Theatre Assn. (chmn. bicentennial festival com.), Greensboro Women's Investment Club (pres. 1965-66). Club: Greensboro Study (pres. 1964-65). Home: 310 Irving Pl Greensboro NC 27408 Office: 1209 W Market St U NC at Greensboro NC 27412

SMITH, MORRIS RUDOLPH, ednl. adminstr.; b. Lockhart, Tex., May 11, 1905; s. Joseph Edgar and Julia (Osteen) S.; B.S., S.W. Tex. U., 1932; M.Ed., U. Tex., 1939; m. Carleta Elizabeth Tunnell, Sept. 1, 1931; children—Jack Morris, Elizabeth Ann, Richard K. Tchr., coach Lytle, Tex., pub. schs., 1931-35; prin. Macdona (Tex.) Sch., Tex., 1935-37, Pharr, Tex., 1937-43; area supr. Tex. Bd. Vocational Edn., Austin, 1946-47; county coordinator, Pharr, 1948-52; elementary prin. Clover Sch., San Juan, Tex., 1952-55; supt. Hidalgo County schs., Edinburg, Tex., 1955—. Pres. Valley Retarded Sch. Bd., 1955-56. Served to capt. USAAF, 1943-46. Mem. N.E.A. (dist. membership chmn.), Nat. Assn. Sch. Adminstrs. Mason, Kiwanian. Home: 217 E Jones St Pharr TX 78577 Office: Courthouse Bldg Edinburg TX 78539

SMITH, NEALE ERICSON, mfg. co. exec.; b. Douglas, Ariz., Nov. 6, 1932; s. Roy Ellsworth and Beatrice (Neale) S.; B.S., Cal. Inst. Tech., 1954; M.S. in Elec. Engring., Ariz. State U., 1966, M.S. in Physics, 1967; m. Ana Elva Cornejo Gardner, Nov. 21, 1969; children—Neale Ricardo, Eric David, Odin Alonso. Radar devel. engr. Goodyear Aerospace, Litchfield Park, Ariz., 1963-66; physicist, information theory Lawrence Radiation Lab., Livermore, Cal., 1968; with Macromex, S.A., Aqua Prieta, Sonora, Mex., 1968—, tech. dir., 1968—. Served with USMCR, 1954-56. Mem. I.E.E.E. Home: 905 Calle Ira Agua Prieta Sonora Mexico Office: Av Panamericana Calle 2 Agua Prieta Sonora Mexico

SMITH, ORMA RINEHART, judge; b. Booneville, Miss., Sept. 25, 1904; s. Jefferson Davis and Lena (Rinehart) S.; LL.B., U. Miss., 1927; m. Margaret Elizabeth Fernandez, June 17, 1930; 1 son, Orma Rinehart. Admitted to Miss. bar, 1927; practice in Corinth, 1928-68; mem. firm Smith & Smith, 1959-68; U.S. dist. judge No. Dist., 1968—. Fellow Miss. Bar Found.; mem. Am., Alcorn County bar assns., Miss. State Bar (past pres.), U. Miss. Alumni Assn. (pres. 1961-62), Alpha Tau Omega. Baptist. Mason (33 deg., Shriner, K.T.), Rotarian. Home: 812 Gloster St Corinth MS 38834

SMITH, OSCAR DALLAS, JR., circuit ct. judge; b. Columbus, Ga., July 21, 1920; s. Oscar D. and Marie (Bertling) S.; student Ga. Southwestern Coll., 1938-40, U. Va., 1946-47; m. Jane Latane Bryan, Jan. 10, 1948; 1 son, Oscar Dallas III. Admitted to Ga. bar, 1947, practiced in Columbus, 1947-62; judge City Ct. Columbus, 1962-69; 3d judge Superior Ct. of Chattahoochee Circuit (Ga.), 1970—. Served with USAF, 1941-45. Decorated D.F.C., Air medal with 2 oak leaf clusters. Mem. Am. Bar Assn., Am. Judicature Soc., State Bar of Ga., Mil. Order of World Wars, Assn. of the U.S. Army. Presbyn. (elder). Clubs: Columbus Lawyers, Columbus Executive. Office: Govt Center Columbus GA 31901

SMITH, OSCAR FRANCIS, IV, dredging co. exec.; b. Norfolk, Va., Apr. 12, 1942; s. Oscar Francis III and Marjorie (Goodwin) S.; student Va. Poly. Inst., 1960-63; B.S. in Finance, Old Dominion U., 1971; m. Sharon Smith, May 13, 1967; children—Oscar Francis V., Susan Lee. Clk. Norfolk Dredging Co., 1960, asst. supt., Cape Charles, Va., 1961, asst. supt., Charleston, S.C., 1963, supt., Miami, Fla., 1964, supt., Merritt Island, Fla., 1965, supt., Norfolk, 1966-68, personnel mgr., safety dir., 1968-73, dir. loss control, 1973—, also dir. Mem. Y's Mens Club YMCA, Norfolk, 1964-68; mem. Norfolk Safety Council, 1971-73; mem. exec. com. constrn. sect. Nat. Safety Council, 1972—, editor newsletter, 1973—. Mem. Am. Soc. Safety Engrs. (sec. Greater Tidewater chpt. 1972-73, pres. 1974—), Nat. Safety Mgmt. Soc., Soc. Am. Mil. Engrs., Omicron Delta Epsilon. Episcopalian (vestryman 1973—). Club: Engineers Hampton Roads (Norfolk). Home: 6136 Powhatan Av Norfolk VA 23508 Office: PO Box 539 Norfolk VA 23501

SMITH, PATRICK CHESLEY, state govt. ofcl.; b. Easley, S.C., Mar. 25, 1914; s. Roy R. and Fay (Sellers) S.; B.S. in Commerce, U. S.C., 1936; m. Nell Bewley Keith, June 15, 1940; children—William Chesley, James Keith, Luta Catherine (Mrs. William L. Watson, III). With S.C. State Govt., Columbia, 1936—, supr. schoolbook commn., 1936-43, dir. finance Dept. Edn., 1943-51, asst. dir. Edn. Finance Commn., 1951-60, asst. state auditor, 1960-66, state auditor, 1966—. Presbyn. Rotarian. Home: 2609 Stratford Rd Columbia SC 29204 Office: Wade Hampton Bldg Columbia SC 29211

SMITH, PAUL EDMUND, JR., educator; b. Northampton, Mass., Feb. 6, 1927; s. Paul Edmund and Mary Jane (Murphy) S.; B.A., U. Mass., 1948; postgrad. Harvard, 1948-49; M.A., Boston U., 1957; B.D., Columbia Theol. Sem., 1957, M.Div., 1971; postgrad. U. N.C., 1967-68. Instr. Latin and French, Chester (Vt.) High Sch., 1949-53, Loris (S.C.) High Sch., 1953-54; lectr. U. Ga., Albany, 1957-59; instr. Latin Rocky Mount (Va.) High Sch., 1959-61; asst. prof. religion Ferrum (Va.) Coll., 1961-68; vis. lectr. history John Tyler Community Coll., Chester, Va., 1968-69; asst. prof. philosophy and religion Richard Bland Coll., Petersburg, Va., 1968-71, asst. prof., chmn. dept., 1971—. Mem. Am. Hist. Assn. Democrat. Presbyn. Home: Lakewood Estates 3774 Westwood Dr Petersburg VA 23803

SMITH, PETER FRANCIS, govt. ofcl.; b. New Brunswick, N.J., June 29, 1942; s. George Francis and Theresa (Krysl) S.; B.S., Rutgers U., 1964, M.S., 1966; Ph.D., Pa. State U., 1970; m. Patricia Bayly, July 23, 1966; children—Justin, Courtney. Agrl. economist U.S. Dept. Agr., Washington, 1969-71; sr. staff mem. Office of Fed. Activities, U.S. Environmental Protection Agy., Washington, 1971—. Mem. Am. Econ. Assn., Am. Marketing Assn., Am. Council on Consumers Interests, Alpha Zeta, Omicron Delta Epsilon. Home: 518 Tennessee Av Alexandria VA 22305 Office: 401 M St SW Washington DC 20460

SMITH, PETER GARTHWAITE, natural gas co. exec., lawyer; b. South Orange, N.J., July 22, 1923; s. Karl Garthwaite and Fannie A. (Jones) S.; A.B., Princeton, 1948; LL.B., Yale, 1951; m. Anne Allerton Ward, Dec. 23, 1950; children—Allerton G., Thomas G., Amy G., Abigail G. Admitted to N.Y. bar, 1951; practiced in N.Y.C., 1951-54; atty. So. Natural Gas Co., Co., Birmingham, Ala., 1955-58, asst. sec., atty., 1958-62, sec., atty., 1962-65, sec., gen. counsel, 1966-67, v.p., sec., gen. counsel, 1967-71, exec. v.p., 1971—, dir., 1969—; exec. v.p., dir. So. Natural Resources, Inc., 1973—; v.p., sec., dir. Mesopotamian Petroleum Corp., 1964-68; dir. Offshore Co., So. Natural Resources, Inc., So. Ocean Exploration Co. So. Prodn. & Refining Co.; mem. mgmt. com. Boise So. Co., Sea Robin Pipeline Co. Vice pres., bd. dirs. Birmingham Jr. Programs, 1959-61; pres. bd. trustees Ala. Found. for Hearing and Speech, 1967-69; trustee Birmingham council Camp Fire Girls. Served with USAAF, 1943-46. Mem. Am. Bar Assn., Independent Natural Gas Assn., Phi Delta Phi. Episcopalian. Clubs: Relay House, Princeton of N.Y., Mountain Brook. Home: 3710 Montrose Rd Mountain Brook AL 35213 Office: First Nat So Natural Bldg Birmingham AL 35202

SMITH, RANKIN MCEACHERN, ins. co. exec., football exec.; b. Atlanta, Oct. 29, 1925; ed. Emory U., U. Fla., U. Ga. With Life Ins. Co. Ga., 1943—, tng. asst.. 1950, dist. mgr., 1951, asst. v.p., 1954, corporate sec., 1954, v.p., 1957, exec. v.p., 1963, sr. v.p., 1968-70, pres., chief exec. officer, 1970—; owner, chmn. bd. Atlanta Falcons football team; dir. Greyhound, Inc., Trust Co. Ga. Assos. Mem. exec. bd. Atlanta council Boy Scouts Am.; exec. com. Central Atlanta Progress, Inc.; Ga. chmn. Nat. Soc. Prevention Blindness, 1973-74; div. chmn. United Way campaign, 1973-74. Trustee U. Ga. Found., Reinhardt Coll., Lovett Sch. bd. dirs. Ga. Heart Assn. Mem. Atlanta C. of C. (dir.), Atlanta Assn. Life Underwriters, Chi Phi. Methodist. Mason (Shriner), Rotarian. Clubs: Piedmont Driving Capital City (bd.). Home: 77E Andrews Dr NW Apt 327 Atlanta GA 30305 Office: Life Ga Tower Atlanta GA 30308

SMITH, RAYMOND ALFRED, furniture mfg. co. exec.; b. Mount Airy, N.C., July 4, 1924; s. James Raymond and Annie James (Hadley) S.; grad. Woodberry Forest Sch., 1942; B.A. in Bus. Adminstrn., Duke, 1945; m. Love Banner Diffee, June 10, 1950; children—James Raymond II, Michael David. Dir., sec.-treas. Nat. Furniture Co., Inc., Mount Airy, N.C., 1953-72, v.p., 1972—; dir. Northwestern Bank, Mount Airy. Mem. Mount Airy urban Redevel. Commn., 1959-63; treas. Mount Airy-Surry Count Airport Authority, 1963—; chmn. adv. bd. Surry Community Coll. Nursing Sch., 1969-70; pres. No. Surry Hosp. Found., 1969. Bd. dirs. Mount Airy Youth Found., Reeves YMCA. Named Young Man of Year, Jr. C. of C., 1955. Mem. So. Furniture Mfrs. Assn. (dir. 1961—). Methodist (steward 1955—, bldg. fund chmn. 1960—). Rotarian. Club: Mount Airy Country (dir. 1948-65). Home: 1309 Crescent Dr Mount Airy NC 27030 Office: 215 Factory St Mount Airy NC 27030

SMITH, ROBERT DEAN, banker; b. Arkansas City, Kan., Aug. 20, 1935; s. Willy S. and Grace Lee (Dawson) S.; B.S., Tex. Tech U., 1958; m. Elizabeth Wilson, Feb. 14, 1959; 1 son, Christopher Dean. Asst. cashier Citizens Nat. Bank, Lubbock, Tex., 1957-62; v.p. Bank of Tex., Houston, 1962-71; exec. v.p. Fidelity Bank & Trust Co., Houston, 1971-73, pres., 1973—, also dir. Bd. dirs. Tex. Children Hosp., 1970—, Pin Oaks Charity Horse Show, 1970—, Woodland North Water Dist., 1970— (all Houston). Mem. Kappa. Sigma. Democrat. Roman Catholic. Club: Valley Lodge. Home: 7727 Osage St Houston TX 77036 Office: 1602 Milam St Houston TX 77002

SMITH, ROBERT EARL, mfg. co. exec.; b. Duncan, Okla., Oct. 9, 1927; s. Floyd E. and Cassie Gladys (Cleveland) S.; B.B.A., U. Okla., 1951; m. Shirley Yvonne Land, July 20, 1947; children—Robert Land, Phillip Scott, Carter Blake. Auditor Arthur Andersen & Co., Houston, 1951-54; pres. Ancon Oil & Gas Inc., Houston, 1954-65; ind. oil producer, 1965-67; v.p. Butte Gas & Oil Co., Houston, 1967-70; pres. Dixel Industries, Inc., Houston, 1970—; dir. Memorial Bank, Houston. Served with USMC, 1946. Mem. Beta Gamma Sigma. Methodist. Clubs: Coronado, University (Houston). Home: 12414 Cobblestone St Houston TX 77024 Office: 4545 Post Oak Pl Houston TX 77027

SMITH, ROBERT JACKSON BATES, JR., govt. ofcl.; b. Augusta, Ga., Nov. 9, 1941; s. Robert Jackson Bates and Mary (Willis) S.; B.B.S., U. Ga., 1963, LL.B., 1965; m. Kittie Potter Graham, Aug. 11, 1962; children—Robert Jackson Bates III, Samuel T.G., Mary Willis. Admitted to Ga. bar, 1965; partner firm Yow, Lee & Smith, Augusta, 1966-67; partner Allgood & Childs, Augusta, 1968-69; U.S. atty. So. Dist. Ga., 1969—. Part time instr. law Augusta Coll., 1966-69. Legal counsel, mem. exec. com. Richmond County (Ga.), 1967-69. Bd. dirs. Augusta Easter Seal Soc., 1965-69, 1st v.p. 1967-68. Named Outstanding Young Man of Richmond County, Jr. C. of C., 1969-70. Mem. Am., Augusta, Fed. bar assns., Augusta Trial Lawyers Assn., Phi Alpha Delta. Home: 1138 Glenn Av Augusta GA 30904 Office: PO Box 1703 Augusta GA 30903

SMITH, ROBERT SULLINS, physician; b. Del Rio, Tenn., May 28, 1929; s. Robert Taylor and Ollie Lillie (Moore) S.; B.S., Randolph-Macon Coll., 1951; M.D., Med.Coll. Va., 1956; m. Nancy Virginia Kibler, Aug. 26, 1950; children—Carol, Michelle, Robert Sullins, Janet. Intern, Mercy Hosp., Springfield, O., 1956-57; gen. practice medicine Dinwiddie, Va., 1958-69; Va. med. examiner, med. examiner FAA, Dinwiddie, 1958-69, State Va., Dinwiddie County, Dinwiddie, 1958—; mem. staff Petersburg (Va.) Hosp., Mem. Va. Com. Study Abortion, 1969-70, Physician Shortage, 1970-71. Vice pres. Dinwiddie Citizens Orgn. for Better Edn. and Other Improvements, 1963-64. Bd. dirs. Ruritan Civic and Recreation Assn., John Tyler Community Coll., Chester, Va. Served to capt. M.C., USAF, 1957-58. Named Most Outstanding Sr. Citizen Dinwiddie County, 4 Ruritan clubs Dinwiddie County, 1964. Diplomate Am. Bd. Family Practice. Mem. Randolph Macon Alumni Assn., A.M.A., 4th Dist. med. socs., Med. Soc. Va., Va. (sec. 1970-73, v.p. 1973), Tri City Area (pres. 1968-73), Am., acads. family physicians, Va. (dir. 1968-70, v.p. 1973-74, pres. elect 1974-75) Am. Med. Polit. Action Com., Med. Coll. Va. Alumni Assn., Am. Coll. Emergency Physicians, Va. Council Health and Med. Care, Omicron Delta Kappa, Chi Beta Phi, Beta Beta Beta, Alpha Sigma Chi, Lamba Chi Alpha, Theta Kappa Psi. Methodist. Mason. Club: Walter Hines Page. Address: Route 1 Box 16 Dinwiddie VA 23841

SMITH, ROGER CROWELL, psychologist; b. Pitts., May 28, 1937; s. Arthur Crowell and Mabel (Fields) S.; A.B., U. Ky., 1960, M.S., 1963, Ph.D., 1967; m. Alice Ann Champion, July 14, 1962. Research asst. dept. psychology U. Ky., Lexington, 1960-64, intern clin. psychology, 1964-65, teaching asst., 1965-66; instr. U. Tex., El Paso, 1967-68; chief clin. psychology, learning processes research psychology lab. Civil Aero. Inst., FAA, Oklahoma City, 1968—. Cons. Family Service, El Paso, 1967-70, Child Treatment Center, El Paso, 1967-68, adolescent clinic Children's Meml. Hosp., Oklahoma City, 1970—, com. psychiat. evaluation pilots Flying Physicians Assn., 1969—; adj. asso. prof. med. psychology U. Okla. Sch. Medicine, Oklahoma City, 1968—, adj. asso. prof. child psychology, 1970—, adj. asso. prof. psychology, Norman, 1972—. Served with AUS, 1966-68. Recipient Certificate Achievement; USPHS fellow, 1960-64. Mem. Am., Midwestern, Southwestern, Western, Rocky Mountain, Okla. (editor Newsletter 1972-73) psychol. assns., A.A.A.S., Aerospace Med. Assn., Psychonomic Soc., Assn. Aviation Psychologists, N.Y. Acad. Scis., U. Ky. Alumni Assn. (dir.), Am. Assn. State Psychology Bds. (pres. 1974-75), Okla. State Bd. Examiners Psychologists (chmn. 1972-73), Sigma Xi. Contbr. articles to profl. jours. Home: 2724 Ann Arbor Oklahoma City OK 73127 Office: AAC-118 CAMI-FAA PO Box 25082 Oklahoma City OK 73125

SMITH, RUSSELL CALVIN, city ofcl.; b. Haines City, Fla., Feb. 26, 1925; s. George Rosse and Grace (Kelly) S.; B.S. in C.E., U. Fla., 1950; M.S. in Mgmt., Rollins Coll., 1971; m. Frances E. McGehee, Sept. 4, 1949; children—Stephen Kelly, Holly Elizabeth. Constrn. engr. Bur. Reclamation, Grand Coulee, Wash., 1950-51; asst. city engr. City Daytona Beach, Fla., 1953-55, city engr., 1955-63, dir. pub. works, 1963-68, dir. pub. services, 1968-71, city mgr., 1971—. Served to 1st lt. USAF, 1942-46, 1951-52. Decorated D.F.C., Air medal with two oak leaf clusters. Registered profl. engr., Fla. Mem. Am. Pub. Works Assn. (chpt. pres. 1970), U. Fla. Alumni (pres. 1969), Internat. City Mgmt. Assn., Jr. C. of C. (first v.p. 1960), Fla. Engring. Soc. Presbyn. (elder). Rotarian. Club: Daytona Beach Quarterback. Home: 536 S Seneca Blvd Daytona Beach FL 32014 Office: 209 Orange Av Daytona Beach FL 32014

SMITH, SAM MAYER, childrens home adminstr.; b. Saluda, S.C., Oct. 24, 1907; s. Robert Louis and Happie (Berry) S.; A.B., Furman U., 1930, H.H.D., 1958; postgrad. N.Y. Sch. Social Work, 1932; m. Ann Wilkerson, Apr. 2, 1936; children—June (Mrs. Henry Summerall, Jr.), Jeanie (Mrs. C. G. Mitchell), Mary Linca (Mrs. James M. Holt, Jr.). Field rep. Connie Maxwell Children's Home, Greenwood, S.C., 1930-36, asso. supt., 1937-46, supt., treas., 1946—. Chmn., Juvenile and Family Ct., Greenwood, 1956-62; mem. adv. bd. Child Welfare League Am., N.Y.C., 1962-67. Named Man of Year, Greenwood Rotary, 1968, Greenville Lions, 1969. Mem. Child Care Assn. So. Bapts. (pres.), Southeastern Child Care Assn. (pres.), S.C. Bapt. Conv. (pres.), S.C. Conf. Social Work (pres.), Nat. Assn. Social Workers. Rotarian (pres. Greenwood club, dist. gov.). Home: 605 North St Greenwood SC 29646 Office: Connie Maxwell Childrens Home Greenwood SC 29646

SMITH, SAMUEL ELBERT, JR., dentist; b. Fordoche, La., Oct. 14, 1922; s. Samuel Elbert and Andrea (Vedross) S.; student La. State U., 1939-40, La. Poly. U., 1941, Southwestern La. Inst., 1941-43, U. Chgo., 1943-44; D.D.S., Emory U., 1948; postgrad. U. So. Cal., 1952, U. Ind., 1966; m. Mary Martin Brown, May 3, 1941; children—Lauree Faith, Samuel Kemper; m. 2d, Eva Mae Jackson, July 22, 1972. Practice gen. dentistry, Shreveport, La., 1948-51, 54—; mem. staff Confederate Meml. Med. Center, Pines Sanitarium, Highland, Willis-Knighten Meml. hosps. Dir. dental asst. tng. program La. Dept. Edn., temporary chmn. 4th Dist., State La., 1958; instr. pilot sch. Vocational Sch., Shreveport, 1948—. Speaker Americanism forum

P.T.A., 1955—; mem. John Birch Soc., 1967-69. Bd. dirs. YMCA, Shreveport. Served with inf. AUS, 1942-44, Dental Corps, USNR, 1951-53; PTO. Mem. Am., La. dental assns., 4th Dist. Dental Soc., Internat. Acad. Orthodontics, Am. Legion, Gideons Internat., Delta Sigma Delta. Democrat. Baptist. Clubs: East Ridge Country, Shreveport Parks and Recreation. Home: 3825 Pines Rd Shreveport LA 71108 Office: 3834 Southern Av Shreveport LA 71106

SMITH, SIDNEY M., securities co. exec.; b. Anniston, Ala., Dec. 25, 1904; s. Columbus and Sallie (March) S.; B.S., in M.E., Ga. Sch. Tech., 1927; m. Adele Metzler, June 6, 1939; children—Wendy (Mrs. Charles Sheron), Cathie. Vice pres. Clement A. Evans & Co., Inc. investment bankers, Atlanta, 1933-60; v.p., Robinson-Humphrey Co., Inc., Atlanta, 1960—; also dir.; asso. mem. N.Y. Stock Exchange, 1952—; pres., dir. Traffic Equipment Co., Atlanta, 1941—, Interstate Bond Co., Chgo., 1968—. Trustee Levi Nat. Meml. Hosp., Hot Springs, Ark. Mem. Commerce Club. Mem. B'nai B'rith. Club: Standard Town and Country. Home: 3680 Tuxedo Rd NW Atlanta GA 30305 Office: 2 Peachtree St NE Atlanta GA 30303

SMITH, SOL, cons. petroleum engr.; b. Balt., Aug. 27, 1913; s. Hyman and Betty (Katz) S.; B.S., U. Tex., 1935, M.S., 1937; m. Dorothy Rose Cohen, Dec. 30, 1945; children—Larry, Darrell, Randy. Dist. engr. R.R. Commn. of Tex., Pampa, and Wichita Falls, Tex., 1937-42, asst. chief engr. Austin, 1946-48; engr. chem. warfare U.S. War Dept., Huntsville, Ala., 1942-45; dist. engr. Mobil Oil Corp., Edna, Tex., 1945-46; cons. petroleum and natural gas engr., Austin, 1948—. Tchr. natural gas course U. Okla., Norman, 1949. Mem. Am. Inst. Mining and Metall. Engrs., Soc. Petroleum Engrs; Am. Gas Assn., Am. Petroleum Inst. Mason (Shriner). Contbr. to profl. publs. in field. Home: 3221 Cherry Lane Austin TX 78703 Office: 815 Brown Bldg Austin TX 78701

SMITH, SPURGEON EUGENE, research exec.; b. San Marcos, Tex., July 17, 1925; s. Charles Spurgeon and Grace Rebekah (Berry) S.; B.S., S.W. Tex. State U., 1946; m. Linnea Bergquist, Aug. 27, 1948 (div. Feb. 1972); children—Thomas Spurgeon, Marian Elizabeth. Systems specialist Def. Research Lab. of U. Tex., 1951-56; v.p. research Textran, Inc., Austin, Tex., 1956-61; research dir., v.p. advanced research scis. and systems group Tracor, Inc., Austin, 1961—. Dir. KMFA-FM. Served to lt. (j.g.) USNR, 1943-46. Mem. Am. Math. Soc., Acoustical Soc. Am., Assn. Old Crows. Episcopalian. Research on radar and countermeasures; patentee in field. Home: 1305 Bradwood Rd Austin TX 78722 Office: 6500 Tracor Lane Austin TX 78721

SMITH, STANFORD, assn. exec.; b. Macon, Ga., Apr. 6, 1919; s. William Stanford and Willie (Leggett) S.; A.B. in Journalism, U. Ga., 1941; m. Martha L. Cooper, Oct. 4, 1942; children—Marion C., Mary Elizabeth, Lucinda L. Reporter Chronicle, Augusta, Ga., 1945-47; sec., mgr. Ga. Press Assn., Atlanta, 1947-53; asst. to gen. mgr. Am. Newspaper Publishers Assn., N.Y.C., 1953-60, gen. mgr., 1960-72, pres., gen. mgr., 1972—. Vice pres. Am. Newspaper Pubs. Assn. Found. Served to capt. AUS, 1941-45; PTO; brig. gen. Res. Decorated Bronze Star, Legion of Merit. Mem. Internat. Fedn. Newspaper Publishers, Sigma Delta Chi. Episcopalian. Clubs: Overseas Press, (N.Y.C.); Nat. Press, Metropolitan (Washington). Home: 11744 Indian Ridge Rd Reston VA 22091 Office: Am Newspaper Publishers Assn 11600 Sunrise Valley Dr Reston VA 22070

SMITH, STANLEY WOOD, elec. products co. exec., elec. engr.; b. Jacksonville, Fla., Oct. 21, 1926; s. Stanley and Ethel Winifred (Wood) S.; B.E.E., U. Fla., 1950; postgrad. U. Pitts., 1950-51, Ga. Inst. Tech., 1957-58; m. Eugenia Beatrice Bridges, Dec. 30, 1950; children—Thomas Eugene, Brian Gregory. Purchasing engr. Westinghouse Electric Corp., Balt., 1950-53; sales engr., dist. mgr. Reliance Electric Co., Atlanta, 1953-63; sr. engr. Bendix Corp., Cape Kennedy, Fla., 1963-67; regional mgr. GTE Sylvania, Inc., Atlanta, 1967-73; area mgr. Leeds & Northrup Co., Atlanta, 1973—. Active Boy Scouts Am. Served with USNR, 1944-46; PTO. Registered profl. engr., Fla., Ga. Mem. Nat. Soc. Profl. Engrs., Instrument Soc. Am., Sigma Tau, Kappa Sigma, Phi Eta Sigma. Republican. Episcopalian. Home: 3280 Henderson Creek Rd Atlanta GA 30341 Office: 2150 Parklake Dr NE Atlanta GA 30345

SMITH, THOMAS HARPER, educator; b. Ashland, Wis., Jan. 19, 1934; s. Harper H. and Inga (Olsen) S.; A.A., San Antonio Coll., 1953; B.S., S.W. Tex. State U., 1955, M.A., 1958; postgrad. U. Tex. at Austin, 1956—; m. Carlie Theresa Sutton, Sept. 3, 1955; children—Dana Kay, Kirk Allen, Suzanne. Tchr., coach high sch., Poteet, Tex., 1955-56; mem. faculty San Antonio Coll., 1956—, instr., asst. basketball coach, 1956-58, head basketball coach, 1958-70, asso. prof. health phys. edn., 1965—. Mem. Tex. Assn. Health, Phys. Edn. and Recreation, Tex. Jr. Coll. Tchrs. Assn., S.W. Basketball Ofcls. Assn. (pres. 1973—), S.W. Football Ofcls. Assn. Lutheran. Mason (32 degree, Shriner). Home: 10907 Mt Ida San Antonio TX 78213

SMITH, THOMAS WYATT, hosp. adminstr.; b. Campbellsville, Ky., May 9, 1937; s. Samuel Garnett and Mary Lee (Rice) S.; A.A., Campbellsville Jr. Coll., 1955; B.S. in Commerce, U. Louisville, 1966; certificate in Health Adminstrn., Ohio State U., 1973; m. Malinda Susan Parker, Dec. 15, 1956; children—Gregory Thomas, Bradley Wyatt, Brentley Parker. Salesman, Louisville Gas and Electric Co., 1955-63, advt. and pub. relations mgr., 1963-69; dir. pub. relations and devel. Jewish Hosp., Louisville, 1969-73, asst. dir., 1973—. Pres. Buechel Little League, 1973; active Boy Scouts Am., United Way, various other civic activities. Served with AUS, 1959. Mem. Am. Marketing Assn. (pres. Louisville chpt. 1966), Louisville Advt. Club (dir. 1970-73, v.p. 1972-73), Nat. Assn. Hosp. Devel., Am. Soc. Hosp. Pub. Relations Dirs., Ky. Hosp. Assn. Baptist (deacon 1962—; dir. Sunday sch. 1972—). Home: 2915 Sheldon Rd Louisville KY 40218 Office: 217 E Chestnut St Louisville KY 40202

SMITH, TIMOTHY LEE, accountant; b. Jacksonville, Tex., Feb. 5, 1943; s. Oscar Lee and Christene (Grimes) S.; A.A., Lon Morris Coll., 1963; B.B.A., Stephen F. Austin State U., 1965; m. Ruth Eilene Ball, July 3, 1964; children—Timmy L., Troy L., Tiffany L. With Sheffield, Garrett & Carter, CPA's, Houston, 1965; staff accountant Triangle Refineries, Inc., Houston, 1965-66; accounting supr. Squyres, Johnson, Squyres & Co., CPA's, Tyler, Tex., 1966-72; self-employed C.P.A., Jacksonville, Tex., 1972—. Sec. Lon Morris Coll. Boosters Club, 1972-73. Mem. Am. Inst. C.P.A.'s, Tex. Soc. C.P.A.'s East Tex. Estate Council, Stephen F. Austin Alumni Assn. Kiwanian. Home: Lenora St Jacksonville TX 75766 Office: Jacksonville Bldg and Loan Bldg PO Box 1897 Jacksonville TX 75766

SMITH, TOM E., oil co. exec.; b. Burlington, Tex., Dec. 18, 1908; s. Vinny L. and Carrie A. (Barnes) S.; B.S., So. Meth. U., 1929; M.D., Baylor U., 1933; m. Marianna McKamy, June 2, 1937; children—McKamy, Tom, Marianna (Mrs. Jerry Powell), Sally (Mrs. Dan Wolfe). Intern Baylor U. Hosp., Dallas, 1933-34; resident St. Mark's Hosp., London, Eng., 1934-35; practice medicine specializing in proctology, Dallas, 1935-64, Tyler, Tex., 1965-69; mem. staff various hosps.; ret. from medicine, 1969; sr. v.p. Harding Oil Co., Dallas, 1962—, dir. corporate planning, 1971—. Asso. prof. proctology Baylor U., 1935-42. Dir. Middle Sabine River Authority, 1971—. Bd. dirs. Tex. Chest Found., Tyler State Coll. Ednl. Found. Served to lt. col. AUS, 1942-46. Fellow A.C.S., Am. Proctologic Soc.; mem. Tyler C. of C. (v.p. bd. dirs. 1968-71), Alpha Omega Alpha, Lambda Chi Alpha, Phi Chi. Rotarian (dist. gov. 1959-60); Mason (Shriner, K.T., Jester). Clubs: Willowbrook Country, Petroleum (Tyler); Northwood Country, Chaparral (Dallas). Home: Hide-A-Way Lake Route 1 Box 881-A Lindale TX 75771 Office: Carillon Tower West 13601 Preston Rd Dallas TX 75240

SMITH, TROY A., civil engr.; b. Sylvatus, Va., July 4, 1922; s. Wade Hampton and Augusta Mabel (Lindsey) S.; B.C.E., U. Va., 1948; M.S. in Engring., U. Mich., 1952, Ph.D. in Engring. Mechanics, 1970. Structural engr. C.E., U.S. Army, 1948-59; chief structural engr. Brown Engring Co., Inc., Huntsville, Ala., 1959-60; structural research engr., then aerospace engr. U.S. Army Missile Command, Redstone Arsenal, Ala., 1960—. Served with USNR, 1942-46. Registered profl. engr., Va., Ala. Mem. Soc. Am. Mil. Engrs., Sigma Xi (asso.). Elk. Contbr. tech. articles to profl. jours. Home: 2406 Bonita Dr SW Huntsville AL 35801 Office: Directorate of Research Devel Engring and Missile Systems Lab US Army Missile Command Redstone Arsenal AL 35809

SMITH, WALTER GOLD, mech. engr.; b. Palmyra, Va., July 19, 1919; s. Wilmer Irwin and Luster (Gold) S.; B.S., Duke, 1941; m. Kathryn Felton, July 20, 1943; 1 son, Walter Gregory. Design engr. Westinghouse Electric Co., Balt., 1946-47; v.p. foundry Walter James Corp., Durham, N.C., 1947-49; engr. Arrow Plumbing & Heating Co., Durham, 1949-53; mem. faculty Duke, 1953-54; cons. engr., Durham, N.C., 1954—. Served to lt. comdr. USNR, 1941-45. Registered profl. engr., N.C., Va., S.C., Fla. Mem. Nat., N.C. socs. profl. engrs., N.C. Soc. Engrs., Durham Engrs. Club. Clubs: Durham City (past dir.), Durham Wildlife, Sertoma. Home: 507 Brookwood Dr Durham NC 27707 Office: NC Bank Bldg PO Box 2165 Durham NC 27702

SMITH, WALTON RAMSEY, forest products cons.; b. Charlotte, N.C., Aug. 21, 1910; s. Frank Brandon and Cora May (McNinch) S.; student Davidson Coll., 1928-29; B.S. in Forestry, N.C. State U., 1934; m. Annie Dee Leatherman, July 3, 1936; children—Deanne (Mrs. James Winiarski), Patricia (Mrs. John H. Adams), Dorothy (Mrs. John Sullivan), Sylvia (Mrs. Patterson Calhoun), Walton Ramsay. With adminstrn. U.S. Forest Service, Franklin, N.C., and Jackson, Miss.; 1936-39, research, New Orleans, Madison, Wis. and Asheville, N.C., 1939-50; pres. Walton Lumber Co., Mebane, N.C., 1950-52; engaged in research U.S. Forest Service, Asheville, 1952-68, ret., 1968; forest products cons. to wood industries, 1969—. Adj. prof. Sch. Forest Resources N.C. State U., Raleigh, 1965—. Pres. N.C. Forestry Found., 1965-73. Recipient Superior Service award U.S. Dept. Agr., 1969; Distinguished Alumnus award N.C. State U. Sch. Forestry Research, 1970; Gottschalk award Forest Products Research Soc., 1967; Borden award for research Borden Co. and Forest Products Research Soc., 1969. Mem. Forest Products Research Soc. (nat. bd. mem. 1958-62), Soc. Am. Foresters. Contbr. articles to profl. jours. Home: Route 4 Box 570 Franklin NC 28734

SMITH, WALTON WRIGHT, realtor; b. Selma, N.C., Feb. 5, 1909; s. William Exum and Addie Beatrice (Wellons) S.; student Duke, 1927-30; m. Geraldine Mavis Bezant, Aug. 2, 1945; children—Pamela (Mrs. David Exum James), Janet (Mrs. Stephen Porter Darnell), Walton Wright. Clk., J.C. Penney Co., Wilson, N.C., 1930-32; partner Smith-Anderson Service Sta., Wilson, 1933-35; investigator Retail Credit Co., Wilson, Burlington, Winston-Salem and Greenville, N.C., 1935-40; operative builder, Wilson, 1940-42; builder, realtor, developer, Wilson, 1945—. Pres., Wilson Bd. Realtors, 1971; v.p. Multiple Listing Service, 1973. Served to capt. USAAF, 1942-45. Mem. Eastern N.C. Home Builders Assn. (pres. 1967). Club: Wilson Country. Home: 1208 Brookside Dr Wilson NC 27893 Office: 729 Ward Blvd NW Wilson NC 27893

SMITH, WARREN HUNTINGTON, architect; b. Spokane Wash., Jan. 23, 1925; s. Earl Robert and Esther (Hines) S.; student Wash. State U., Pullman, 1942-43; B.Arch., U. Ore., 1949; M.Arch., Mass. Inst. Tech., 1950; m. Margaret Isabel Griffiths, June 17, 1949; children—Christopher Earl, Theodore Jesse. Architect, Bindon & Wright, architects, Seattle, 1950-55; project architect Arabian-Am. Oil Co., The Hague, Netherlands, 1955-57; chief architect Bechtel Assos., N.Y.C., 1957-60; mgr. bldg. product devel. U.S. Plywood Corp., N.Y.C., 1960-62; cons. architect Wellman-Lord Engring., Inc., Lakeland, Fla., 1962-64; prin. Warren H. Smith & Assos., Lakeland, 1964; now sr. partner Smith & Swilley, Architects, Lakeland, also Delray Beach. Chmn., City Lakeland Bd. Standards and Appeals; mem. pub. adv. panel on archtl. services Gen. Services Adminstrn.; mem. Polk County Citizen's Adv. Com. for Econ. Devel. Assistance. Bd. dirs., pres. Lakeland YMCA. Served with USAAF, 1943-45; ETO. Decorated Purple Heart; recipient Award for Excellence in Indsl. Design, Factory Mag., 1961. Mem. A.I.A. (corporate mem., pres. Polk County sect.), Nat. Soc. Interior Designers, Delta Upsilon. Episcopalian. Kiwanian. Clubs: Fla. Sailing Assn. (St. Petersburg); Lakeland Yacht. Prin. works include: Fla. Technol. U., Orlando, Delray Beach Club Apts., Sci. and Tech. Bldg. U. South Fla., Tampa. Home: 2725 Oakland Dr Lakeland FL 33803 Office: 2401 Florida Av Lakeland FL 33803

SMITH, WARREN THOMAS, clergyman, educator; b. Knoxville, Tenn., Oct. 20, 1923; s. Warren T. and Lola May (Jones) S.; student Maryville Coll., 1942-43; B.A., Ohio Wesleyan U., 1945; B.D., Emory U., 1948; Ph.D., Boston U., 1953; D.D., Lincoln Meml. U., 1958; m. Barbara Ann Sullards, Dec. 27, 1949; 1 son, James Warren. Ordained deacon Methodist Ch., 1947, elder, 1949; asso. minister Peachtree Rd. Meth. Ch., Atlanta, 1950-53; minister Sharp Meml. Meth. Ch., dir. religious life, head dept. religion Young Harris Coll., 1953-57; minister Trinity Meth. Ch., Atlanta, 1957-60; mem. staff Bd. Edn., Meth. Ch., 1960-64; minister Young Harris Meml. Ch., Athens, Ga., 1964-66, N. Decatur Meth. Ch., 1966-68; sr. minister First United Meth. Ch., College Park, Ga., 1968-74; asst. prof. ch. history Interdenominational Theol. Center, Atlanta, 1974—. Recipient grant Nat. Endowment for Humanities for in depth biography Thomas Coke, 1969. Mem. Am. Soc. Ch. History, Wesley Hist. Soc. (Eng.), Am. Hist. Assn., Omicron Delta Kappa, Delta Tau Delta. Mason. Author: Thomas Coke, Foreign Minister of Methodism, 1959; Heralds of Christ, 1963; At Christmas, 1969. Contbr. articles profl. jours. Home: 3460 Hemphill St College Park GA 30337 Office: 671 Beckwith St SW Atlanta GA 30314

SMITH, WAYNE OSMER, dentist; b. Elyria, O., Nov. 15, 1926; s. Charles Gerald and Marjorie Elizabeth (Osmer) S.; student Princeton, 1946, Ohio U., 1947; B.S., Western Res. U., 1955, D.D.S., 1959; m. Yvonne Peairs, Sept. 5, 1952; children—Courtney, Bradford, Whitney, Kent. Endodontist, Jacksonville, Fla., 1959-61, West Palm Beach, Fla., 1961—. Pres., owner Ohio Battery Warehouse, Cleve., 1970—, Cumberland Batteries Inc. (Md.), 1968—; dir. endodentic sect. research group Palm Beach Jr. Coll., 1965—. Served as test pilot USNR, 1952-54. Diplomate Assn. Am. Endodentists (dir.). Mem. Am., Fla. dental socs., Psi Omega. Rotarian. Republican. Patentee fixed removal safety cover for outdoor swimming pool. Home: 222 Monterey Rd Palm Beach FL 33480 Office: Citizens Bldg West Palm Beach FL 33401

SMITH, WENDELL EUGENE, hardware wholesale co. exec.; b. Albuquerque, Nov. 4, 1909; s. Frank Joseph and Ollie (McDonald) S.; student W. Tex. State Coll., 1935; m. Esther Doris Evans, Sept. 29, 1928; 1 son, Wendell Eugene. With Morrow-Thomas Hardware Co., Amarillo, Tex., 1928-50, exec. v.p., 1942-50, gen. mgr., 1945-50; pres., chmn. bd. Okla. Hardware Co., Oklahoma City, 1951-73, also dir.; chmn. bd. Nash Hardware Co., Fort Worth, 1962—, also dir.; vice chmn., dir. B.H. & L. Industries, Inc.; exec. v.p., gen. mgr. Peden Industries, Inc., Houston, also dir. Mem. Oklahoma City Bond Adv. Com., Oklahoma City Symphony. Recipient Outstanding Achievement in Hardware Wholesaling award Canadian Wholesale Hardware Assn., 1959. Mem. Nat., So., Tex. wholesale hardware assns., Nat. Tax Equality Assn. (dir.), Oklahoma City C. of C., Frontiers of Sci. Republican. Mason (Shriner), Rotarian. Clubs: Petroleum, Sirloin, Touchdown. Home: 2200 Willowick Dr Houston TX 77027 Office: 700 N San Jacinto Houston TX 77001

SMITH, WENDELL ROWE, elec. engr.; b. Brownfield, Tex., Feb. 14, 1919; s. Fred Clarence and Mattie (Rowe) S.; student So. Meth. U., 1936-37; B.S., Tex. Tech. Coll., 1942; m. Montez Marie Hudson, May 29, 1968; children (by previous marriage)—Patricia Ann (Mrs. Richard L. Renko), Barbara Lea (Mrs. John E. Melde III), Wendell Kaye (Mrs. Jimmie Vaughan), Nancy Virginia (Mrs. Kim McGregor); stepchildren—Randall L. Howard, Jeri Sue Howard. Engr., Curtis Wright Corp., Louisville, 1943; tchr. Tex. Technol. Coll., Lubbock, 1944; computer Petty Geophys. Co., San Antonio, 1944; engr. Southwestern Pub. Service Co., Plainview, Tex., 1946-48, sr. design engr. Plains div., 1948-70, So. div., 1970—. Mem. Civil Def. Com., Plainview, 1964-73, chmn., 1969—. Served with USNR, 1944-45; PTO. Registered profl. engr., Tex. Mem. I.E.E.E. (chpt. chmn. 1963-64), Hi Plains Geol. Soc. (pres. 1971-73). Methodist. Mason (dist. dep. 1963); mem. Order Eastern Star. Home: 1200 Travis St Plainview TX 79072 Office: 304 W 6th St Plainview TX 79072

SMITH, WILLARD JOAL, wood processing co. exec.; b. Zanesville, O., Sept. 16, 1887; s. Joal Kirk and Laura (Hibbs) S.; student Ohio State U., 1966-67; m. Mayme Kinsall, Sept. 17, 1917 (dec.). Chmn. bd. W.J. Smith Wood Preserving Co., Denison, Tex., 1929—; chmn. bd. Citizens Nat. Bank, 1945—, Citizens Investment Co., Denison, 1951—; v.p. Fed. Bldg. & Loan Co., Denison, 1950—. Chmn. Denison Zoning Bd., 1962—. Bd. dirs. Cedar Lawn Cemetary, Denison. Mem. Denison C. of C. (past pres.). Mason. Clubs: Rod and Gun (past pres.) (Denison); Tanglewood Country. Home: 1401 Woodard St Denison TX 75020 Office: Box 703 1700 Morton St Denison TX 75020

SMITH, WILLARD NEWELL, parasitologist; b. Wellington, Kan., Jan. 27, 1926; s. Jesse Clyde and Mabel Ethel (Connelly) S.; B.S., U. Md., 1950, M.S., 1953, Ph.D., 1966. Asst. parasitologist Ga. Agrl. Expt. Sta., Griffin, 1954-57; parasitologist U.S. Dept. Agr. Regional Parasite Lab., Auburn, Ala., 1957-60; parasitologist-in-charge Dept. Agr. Parasite Div., Tifton, Ga., 1960-62; asst. mem. U. Tex. Dental Sci. Inst., Houston, 1966—. Served with USNR, 1944-46. USPHS Spl. fellow, 1967-70. Mem. Internat. Assn. Dental Research, Helminthol. Soc. Washington, Am. Soc. Parasitologists, S.W. Theater Guild (pres. 1972), Sigma Xi. Home: 5206 Sanford Rd Houston TX 77035 Office: 1018 Blddgett St Houston TX 77004

SMITH, WILLIAM ARTHUR, supt. schs.; b. Converse, S.C., June 26, 1908; s. Charles W. and Annie (Jones) S.; B.A., Furman U., 1929; Ed.M., Duke, 1940; postgrad. Tchrs. Coll. Columbia, 1953; m. Ollie Sanders, Nov. 28, 1934; 1 son, Arthur O. Tchr. Hartsville High Sch., 1934-45, prin., 1945-50; supt. Bennettsville City Schs., 1950-55, Conway Area Schs., 1955-61, Florence County Sch. Dist. 3, Lake City, S.C., 1961—. Dir. S.C. Edn. Investors Corp., Columbia, S.C. Mem. S.C. Edn. Assn. (pres. 1963-64), S.C. Sch. Supts. Assn. (pres. 1958-59), Am. Assn. Sch. Adminstrs. Baptist (deacon, chmn. bd. 1965-66). Rotarian (dir.) Home: 205 Palmetto St Lake City SC 29560

SMITH, WILLIAM BREVARD, banker; b. Woodbury, Tenn., June 10, 1918; s. George Stanton and Linda (Brevard) S.; certificate Am. Inst. Banking; grad. Sch. Banking La. State U., 1959; m. Dorothy Dell, Oct. 12, 1940 (dec. 1969); children—William Michael, Steve Alexander. With various trucking firms including McBroom Truck Co., Tenn. Motor Lines, Nashville, Tenn. Carolina Transp., Nashville, 1937-50; with Bank Commerce, Woodbury, 1950—, cashier, v.p., 1955-66, pres., 1967—; also dir. Chmn. Heart Fund, 19——, March of Dimes. Trustee bd. devel. Middle Tenn. State U., Murfreesboro, 1970—. Mem. Ch. of Christ. Lion. Home: 416 Murfreesboro Rd Woodbury TN 37190 Office: 200 Public Sq Woodbury TN 37190

SMITH, WILLIAM FRANCIS, educator; b. McDonogh, Md., June 21, 1905; s. William Ballard and Emmette (Brooks) S.; A.B., Washington and Lee U., 1926; M.A., Tulane U., 1930; postgrad. Universidad Central de Madrid, 1929, U. N.C., summer 1932; Ph.D., U. Tex., 1940; m. Ruth Alice Sheilds, Aug. 18, 1931; children—Margaret Lyle (Mrs. James William Keating). Instr., Tulane U., New Orleans, 1926-43, asst. prof., 1943-46, asso. prof., 1946-65, prof., 1965-71, prof. emeritus, 1971—; acting head Spanish dept. Coll. Arts and Scis., 1943-46, 50-51, 59-60, acting chmn. dept. Spanish in Grad. Sch., 1959-60. Ford Found. fellow, 1951-52. Mem. Modern Lang. Assn., Am. Assn. Tchrs. Spanish and Portuguese (past com. chmn.), S.C. Modern Lang. Assn. (past pres., mem. exec. com.), Phi Sigma Iota (past nat. treas.), Delta Sigma Pi, Pi Kappa Phi. Presbyn. (elder). Contbr. articles to profl. jours. Home: 1119 Jefferson Av New Orleans LA 70115 Office: Tulane U New Orleans LA 70118

SMITH, WILLIAM HOWARD, physician; b. Woodward, Okla., Jan. 15, 1925; s. Charles Bernard and Catherine (Campbell) S.; B.S., Northwestern State Coll., 1944; M.D., U. Okla., 1947; m. Joy Stafford, Nov. 21, 1946 (div. 1960); children—Su Su, Kelly, Joel; m. 2d, Joy Mock, June 13, 1971; 1 adopted dau., Karla Kay, 1 son, Tyre Smith. Intern Kansas City Gen. Hosp., 1947-48; practice medicine, Lindsay, Okla., 1948-51, 53-62, practice medicine, surgery, Pasadena, Tex., 1962— mem. staff Pasadena Bayshore, Pasadena Gen., Bapt. Meml. hosps., Houston; med. dir. Southmore Hosp. Mem. Lindsay Pub. Sch. Bd., 1953-54. Served as capt. M.C., AUS, 1951-53. Diplomate Am. Bd. Family Practice. Fellow Am. Acad. Family Practice; mem. Am., Tex., Indsl. med. assns., Harris County Med. Soc., Assn. Mil. Surgeons, Assn. Ry. Surgeons, Houston Acad. Medicine. Home: 2312 Lillian St Pasadena TX 77502 Office: 901 E Curtis St Pasadena TX 77502

SMITH, WILLIAM MASSIE, lawyer; b. Richmond, Va., Apr. 17, 1920; s. James Gordon and Ella Williams (Buek) S.; B.A., U. Va., 1948, J.D., 1948; m. Elizabeth Catherine Haden, Dec. 27, 1941); children—Elizabeth (Mrs. Leo S. Sullivan), William Massie, Sallie Cameron (Mrs. James W. Foster), David Gordon. Admitted to Va. bar, 1948; practiced in Charlottesville; partner firm Smith & Danielson, 1948-51, Paxon, Marshall & Smith, 1951-73; prin. firm Paxon, Smith, Boyd, Gilliam & Gouldman, Inc., Charlottesville, 1973—; mem. bd., exec. com. Citizens Bank & Trust Co., Charlottesville, Citizens Commonwealth Corp.; mem. bd. Blue Ridge Finance Corp. Pres. United Community Funds and Councils Va., 1963-64. Bd. dirs., mem. exec. com. Martha Jefferson Hosp. and Sanatorium. Served with USMCR, 1942-46. Mem. Am. Judicature Soc., Am. Legion, Navy League, Am., Va. (v.p. 1958) bar assns., Va. State Bar, Alumni Assn. U. Va. (pres. 1971-72). U. Va. Law Sch.

Alumni Assn. (sec. 1948-68), Raven Soc., Beta Theta Pi, Phi Delta Phi, Omicron Delta Kappa. Episcopalian. Elk. Clubs: Farmington Country, Greencroft, Red-Land (Charlottesville); Commonwealth (Richmond, Va.). Home: 1834 Westview Rd Charlottesville VA 22903 Office: 500 Citizens Commonwealth Center Charlottesville VA 22902

SMITH, WILLIAM OGDEN, physicist; b. Ithaca, N.Y., Aug. 19, 1898; s. John Hays and Johanna (Leidner) S.; B.S., U. Pitts. 1921, postgrad., 1921-25; postgrad. U. Cal. at Berkeley, 1925-26, Cal. Inst. Tech., 1926-27, 32-33; m. Ruby Virginia Dempster (dec. Jan. 1953); 1 son, William Moore. Instr. U. Pitts., 1921-25; fellow Mellon Inst. Indsl. Research, Pitts., 1927-29; physicist Gulf Research & Devel. Co., Pitts., 1929-32; physicist U.S. Dept. Agr., Washington, 1934-42; mem. staff radiation lab. Mass. Inst. Tech., 1942-46; physicist U.S. Geol. Survey, Washington, 1946-69; individual practice, 1969—. Project chief Lake Mead sedimentation survey, 1947-50, Chgo. bedrock survey, 1950-51, Passamaquoddy bedrock survey, 1951-52, Chesapeake Bay studies, 1952-53; adviser geol. studies Channel Tunnel Study. Fellow Geol. Soc. Am.; mem. N.Y. Acad. Sci., Am. Geophys. Union, Philos. Soc. Washington, Geol. Soc. Washington. Presbyn. Contbr. articles in physics, soils, geophysics, hydrology to profl. publs. Home: 8508 Springvale Rd Silver Spring MD 20910

SMITH, WILLIAM PERNELL, educator; b. Birmingham, Ala., Oct. 2, 1919; s. William Pernell and E. Marzetta (Johnson) S.; B.S., Tuskegee Inst., 1939; M.Ed., Rutgers U., 1947, Ed.D., 1959; m. Dorothy Horton, Jan. 16, 1944; children—Barbara J., William Pernell III, Eric B. Instr. Tuskegee (Ala.) Inst., 1947-51, asso. prof. edn., 1960-69; clk. VA, Constrn. Cos., Newark, N.J., 1951-52; asst. prof. Ala. State Coll., Montgomery, 1952-55, asso prof. edn., 1956-60; prof. edn., chmn. div. tchr. edn. and psychology Ala. State U., Montgomery, 1969-71, area coordinator guidance and psychology, 1971—. Vis. lectr. Rutgers U., 1957-58; regional rep. Stanford Research Inst., 1968—. Cons. in guidance and psychology Office of Econ. Opportunity and other fed. projects, 1964—. Vice pres. Com. for Greater Tuskegee, 1969-70, pres. 1970-71. Served with AUS, 1942-46. Mem. Ala. Edn. Assn., Am. Personnel and Guidance Assn., Nat. Vocational Guidance Assn., Student Personnel Assn. for Tchrs in Edn., Assn. for Measurement and Evaluation in Guidance, N.E.A. (life), Phi Delta Kappa, Kappa Delta Pi. Address: 2502 Howard Rd Tuskegee Institute AL 36088 Office: Div Tchr Edn and Psychology Ala State U Montgomery AL 36104

SMITH, WILLIAM PERRY, JR., engring. and contracting co. exec.; b. Dublin, Va., Feb. 25, 1928; s. William Perry and Maxine Elizabeth (Farmer) S.; B.S. in Mech. Engring., Va. Polytech. Inst., 1951; m. Betty Joyce Cooper, Dec. 10, 1966; children—William Perry III, Stacey Finette; 1 step-dau., Cindy Kaye Watkins. Field engr. TVA, New Johnsonville, 1951; service engr., contract engr. Combustion Engring., Inc., Windsor, Conn., 1951-61; pres., owner Perry Smith Co., Inc., Chattanooga, 1962—; pres. Tenn. Steel Tank Co., Chattanooga, 1970—. Mem. Indsl. Com. 100, 1969-73. Served with USAF, 1946-47. Mem. Am. Soc. M.E., Nat. Soc. Profl. Engrs., Chattanooga C. of C. Republican. Mason, Elk. Club: Chattanooga Engineers. Home: 7121 Saratoga Lane Chattanooga TN 37421 Office: 1910 Polymer Dr PO Box 8177 Chattanooga TN 37411

SMITH, WILLIAM SPENCER, JR., tobacco co. exec.; b. Blackstone, Va., Dec. 23, 1918; s. William Spencer and Nancy (Williamson) S.; student Rutgers U. Grad. Sch. Sales Mgmt., 1965-66; m. Dorothy Clements, Jan. 30, 1942; children—Katherine Lavassuer, Nancy Clements, William Spencer III. With R.J. Reynolds Tobacco Co., 1939-42, 46—, asst. div. mgr., 1952-53, sales staff, Winston-Salem, N.C., 1953-58, asst. sales mgr., 1958-59, sales mgr., 1959-61, v.p., 1961-66, exec. v.p., 1966-70, pres., chief exec. officer, 1970-72, chmn., chief exec. officer, 1972—, also dir.; dir. Hanes Corp., Reynolds Industries, Carolina & Northwestern Ry. Co., Wachovia Bank & Trust Co. Trustee Old Salem; bd. dirs. Winston-Salem chpt. A.R.C. Served with AUS, 1942-46. Named Tobacco Man of Year So. Tobacco and Candy Assn., 1966; named to Nat. Assn. Tobacco Distbrs. Hall of Fame, 1972. Mem. Am. Soc. Corporate Execs., Honorable Order Ky. Cols. Democrat. Methodist. Rotarian. Clubs: Old Town, Bermuda Run Golf and Country (Winston-Salem); Lone Palm Golf (Lakeland, Fla). Home: 349 N Pine Valley Rd Winston-Salem NC 27104 Office: Corner 4th and Main Sts Winston-Salem NC 27102

SMITH, WILLIAM STANFORD, assn. exec.; b. Macon, Ga., Apr. 6, 1919; s. W. Stanford and Willie (Leggett) S.; A.B., U. Ga., 1941; m. Martha L. Cooper, Oct. 4, 1942; children—Marion C. (Mrs. Jeff R. Hills), Mary Elizabeth (Mrs. Peter P. Wallace), Lucinda L. (Mrs. Stephen Warnick). Reporter, Augusta (Ga.) Chronicle, 1945-47; sec.-mgr. Ga. Press Assn., Atlanta, 1947-53; asst. to gen. mgr. Am. Newspaper Pubs. Assn., N.Y.C., 1953-60, gen. mgr., 1960-71, pres., gen. mgr., Reston, Va., 1971—. Vice pres. Am. Newspaper Pubs. Assn. Found. Served to capt. AUS, 1941-45; PTO. Decorated Legion of Merit, Bronze Star; officer's cross Order of Merit of Fed. Republic of Germany, 1971. Mem. Internat. Fedn. Newspaper Pubs. (mem. council), Internat. Press Telecommunications Council (1st chmn.). Clubs: Nat. Press, Metropolitan (Washington); Overseas Press (N.Y.C.). Home: 11744 Indian Ridge Rd Reston VA 22091 Office: Sunrise Valley Dr Reston VA 22091

SMITH, WILLIE TESREAU, JR., lawyer; b. Sumter, S.C., Jan. 17, 1920; s. Willie T. and Mary (Moore) S. ; student Benedict Coll., 1937-40; A.B., Johnson C. Smith U., 1947; LL.B., S.C. State Coll., 1954; m. Anna Marie Clark, June 9, 1955; 1 son, Willie T. III. Admitted to S.C. bar, 1954; began gen. practice, Greenville, 1954; now exec. dir. Legal Services Agy. Greenville County, Inc. Mem. adv. bd. Greenville Tech. Edn. Center Adult Edn. Program and Para-legal program, S.C. Regional Med. Program; mem. Greenville County Redevel. Authority. Bd. dirs. Nat. Alliance Bus. Men, Greenville Family and Childrens Service, Southeastern Biophys. and Anthrop. Found. Served with AUS, 1942-45, USAF, 1949-52. Mem. Am., Nat., S.C., Greenville County bar assns., Southeastern Lawyers Assn., Am. Legion, Greater Greenville C. of C. (dir.), N.A.A.C.P., Omega Psi Phi. Presbyn. Mason (Shriner). Home: 601 Jacob Rd Greenville SC 29605 Office: 135 S Main St Greenville SC 29601

SMITHER, CHARLES GABRIEL, ins. exec., state senator; b. New Orleans, Nov. 28, 1914; s. James William and Louise (Person) S.; B.A., Tulane U., 1936; m. Charlotte Mary Hardie, Oct. 17, 1939; children—Charles Hardie, Louise Person (Mrs. Denis H. McDonald), Charlotte Sanders. Spl. agt. Union Central Life Ins. Co., New Orleans, 1936-40, mgr., 1967-71, spl. agt., 1971—; partner James W. Smither & Sons, gen. agts., New Orleans, 1940-67; v.p., dir. Ferd, Marks-Smither & Co., Ltd., ins. agts. and brokers, New Orleans, 1969—; chmn. bd. Kalvar Corp., New Orleans, 1959-64, 67—; dir. Asso. Cold Storage, Inc., So. Microfilm Corp., Metro-Kalvar, Inc., Date Processing Center, Inc.; mem. La. Senate, 1968—. Campaign chmn. Community Chest, 1952-53. Chmn. New Orleans Pub. Library Bd., 1946-61; mem. Sewerage and Water Bd., 1949-51; mem. La. Ho. of Reps., 1962-68. Bd. dirs. Internat. House, 1948-51; bd. adminstrs. Tulane U. Ednl. Fund, 1967—; pres. bd. Metairie Park Country Day Sch., 1955-57, Crippled Children's Hosp., 1959-60. Served to maj. AUS, 1942-45; ETO. Decorated Silver Star, Bronze Star, Purple Heart; Croix de Guerre (France). C.L.U. Mem. Nat. Assn. Life Underwriters, Am. Soc. Chartered Life Underwriters. Republican. Episcopalian (trustee Diocese of La. 1960-70). Clubs: Boston; New Orleans Country, Stratford (New Orleans). Home: 440 Audubon St New Orleans LA 70118 Office: 1600 Canal St New Orleans LA 70112

SMITHERS, RAYMOND JOHN, broadcaster; b. Melrose Park, Ill., Sept. 20, 1942; s. James Joseph and Maudie (Peed) S.; student pub. schs. With radio sta. WOPA, Oak Park, Ill., 1958, WBKB-TV, Chgo., 1958-59, WKFM, Chgo., 1960-61, WFMQ, Chgo., 1961-63, WNWC, Arlington Heights, Ill., 1963-65, WFMF, Chgo., 1965-67, WEXI, Arlington Heights, 1967-69, WIND, Chgo., 1970-71; program mgr. WYEN Radio, Des Plaines, Ill., 1971-73; pres. Love Central Pet Centers, Inc. Recipient Clio award for comml. prodn., Am. TV and Radio Commercials Festival, 1969, med. journalism award, A.M.A., 1969, news award, A.P., 1970. Mem. A.F.T.R.A., Nat. Thespian Soc. (life). Author, producer radio documentaries: Both Feet on the Ground, 1970; Emerald of Dirt, 1970; The Moon or Bust, 1971; From Bobby Sox to Sugar Cubes, 1969; Chicagoland Sings, 1971. Composer, performer: I'll Remember, 1968. Home: 1916 N 56th Av Hollywood FL 33020

SMITHWICK, ROBERT WALTER, JR., fibers mfg. exec.; b. Louisburg, N.C., May 13, 1923; s. Robert Walter and Dorothy Lee (Johnson) S.; grad. Fishburne Mil. Sch., Waynesboro, Va., 1940; B. Chem. Engring., N.C. State Coll., 1946; m. Kathryn Owen Evans, July 15, 1944; children—Kay (Mrs. R.B. Craft), Bob, Ann. Prodn. supr. Tenn. Eastman Co., Kingsport, 1946—. Served to capt. AUS, 1943-45, 50-52; ETO, Korea. Registered profl. engr., Tenn. Episcopalian. Kiwanian. Home: Crown Colony I-13 Kingsport TN 39660 Office: Eastman Rd Kingsport TN 39660

SMOKE, WILLIAM GLADDEN, JR., cotton oil co. exec.; b. St. Matthews, S.C., Aug. 28, 1938; s. William Gladden and Aurelia (Antley) S.; B.S., Clemson U., 1960; m. Sheila M. Hampton, Aug. 22, 1970; 1 dau., Elizabeth Hampton. Project engr. indsl. gas and cryogenics sect. Army Research and Devel. Lab., Ft. Belvoir, Va., 1960-62, fuel cell sect. electric power br., 1962-65; asst. gen. mgr. Victor Cotton Oil Co., Gaffney, S.C., 1965-67, partner, gen. mgr., 1967—; pres. Humphries Gin Corp., 1967-71; owner Smoke Chem. Co., 1965—, W.G. Smoke Oil Co.; partner Cooksey Oil Co.; mgr. State Commodity Warehouse, 1965—. Dist. adv. bd. Small Bus. Adminstrn. Explorer scout adviser Boy Scouts Am., 1967-69; capt. profl. div. Cherokee County Community Chest, 1969. Mem. S.C. Republican Exec. Com.; Rep. nominee S.C. Senate, 1972; dist. chmn. Westmoreland for Gov., 1974. Bd. dirs. Cherokee County Boys Club, 1970-72; bd. visitors S.C. Meth. Homes, 1971—. Served to 2d lt. AUS, 1960-61. Mem. Gaffney Jr. C. of C. (1st v.p. 1969, Distinguished Service award 1970, Young Man of Yr. award 1970), Am. Inst. Chem. Engrs., Western S.C. Chem. Engrs. Club, Gaffrey (dir. 1971-73), Cherokee County (dir. 1972-74, treas. 1973, 74) chambers commerce, Cherokee Historic Preservation Soc. Methodist (ofcl. bd. 1968—, lay leader). Kiwanian (pres. Gaffney 1970-71). Home: 312 E Frederick St Gaffney SC 29340 Office: 314 E Frederick St Gaffney SC 29340

SMOLKIN, STEPHEN WILLIAM, univ. ofcl.; b. San Antonio, Aug. 30, 1941; s. Harry A. and Carolyn (Ghetzler) S.; B.B.A., U. Tex., 1964; m. Sandra von Werssowetz, Jan. 27, 1964; 1 dau., Sheryl Wynne. Computer systems analyst W.R. Smolkin & Assos., Inc., New Orleans, 1964-65, data processing dir., 1966-67, v.p., 1968-69; admistrv. systems mgr. Tulane U., faculty Univ. Coll., New Orleans, 1970—. Bd. advisers Mobile Home Communities, Inc., Denver, 1968-69. Mem. Am. Mgmt. Assn., Assn. for Systems Mgmt., Sigma Alpha Mu. Home: 302 Bella Dr Metairie LA 70005 Office: Computer Lab Tulane U New Orleans LA 70118

SMOOT, GEORGE FITZGERALD, JR., research hydrologist; b. Wetumpka, Ala., Jan. 16, 1922; s. George Fitzgerald and Ethel (Fuller) S.; student Tulane U., 1939-42; B.S., Auburn U., 1950; m. Talicia Diane Crawford, July 14, 1943; children—George Fitzgerald III, Sharon Diane, Jack Edward Bowie. Engr. technician U.S. Geol. Survey, Ala. dist., 1948-50, hydraulic engr., Ala. dist., 1950-52, Alaska dist., 1952-56, Ohio dist., 1956-62, research hydrologist, Washington, 1962-68, coordinator research on instumentation, Washington, 1968—. Expert adviser representing UN and U.S. AID Program to developing nations on problems relating to hydrology. Served with USNR, 1942-45. Mem. Am. Soc. C.E., Am. Geophys. Union, Internat. Assn. Hydrological Scis. (hydrometry com. 1968—), Internat, Orgn. for Standardization (chmn. work group on instruments for measurement flow in open channels 1966—). Developed moving-bost method measuring flow in large rivers, 1968. Home: 3010 Ashburton Av Herndon VA 22070 Office: U S Geol Survey Nat Center Reston VA 22092

SMOOT, JOE ASHLEY, osteo. physician; b. Laverne, Okla., Apr. 10, 1916; s. Edward M. and Mary Etta (Browning) S.; A.B., Phillips U., 1936; D.O., Kansas City Coll. Osteopathy and Surgery, 1941; m. Kathryn Mae McArron, Dec. 24, 1940; children—Susan Kay (Mrs. Daniel G. Staudt), Paula Jeanne (Mrs. James W. Ogg), Sammye Jo (Mrs. David E. Sullivan), Ashley Anne (Mrs. William M. Hurlbutt). Intern, Lakeside Hosp., Kansas City, Mo., 1941-42, resident, 1942-43; gen. practice osteo. medicine, surgery, Tulsa, 1943—; chief of staff Okla. Osteo. Hosp., Tulsa, 1962, 63. State chmn. Osteo. Medicare and Med. Rev. Bd., 1968—; pres. SGH Bldg. Corp., Tulsa, 1962—; dir. Nat. Equity Life Ins. Co., 1967-72. Admissions com., adj. prof. surgery Okla. Coll. Osteo. Medicine and Surgery, 1974—. Bd. dirs., mem. exec. com. Okla. Christian Home, Edmond, 1954-62. Mem. Am., Okla. (pres. 1967-68, legislative com. 1970—) osteo. assns., Tulsa Dist. Osteo. Soc. (pres. 1951), Am. Osteo. Acad. Orthopedics (asso). Mem. Christian Ch. (elder). Optimist (dir. 1945—). Club: Tulsa (pres. 1951-52). Home: 2838 S Florence Av Tulsa OK 74114 Office: 1936 S Harvard Av Tulsa OK 74112

SMOOT, LUCILLE D. HEIN (MRS. CHARLES EFFINGER SMOOT), govt. ofcl.; b. West Pittston, Pa., July 25, 1920; d. John Jonas and Elizabeth Boam (Coffee) Hein; student Am. U., 1940-45, Cornell U., 1969; m. Gerald Arthur Butler, Oct. 7, 1942 (div. July 1946); 1 son, Gerald Allan; m. 2d, Charles Effinger Smoot, Sept. 9, 1961. With Personnel Div., Internal Revenue Service, Washington, 1942—, successively asst. clerk, sr. clerk, personnel technician, personnel officer, 1942-59, employee relations specialist, 1959-66, labor mgmt. and employee relations specialist, 1967-70, program leader for employee relations, 1970-72, chief conduct and appeals sect. 1972-74, spl. adviser labor relations, 1974—. Vice pres. Young Peoples League, 1946-48; chmn. Information Bur., Community Chest, 1948-50. Mem. Soc. Personnel Adminstrn., Nat. Trust Historic Preservation. Republican. Presbyn. Club: Government Girl. Home: 2006 Columbia Rd Washington DC 20009 Office: Treasury Dept Washington DC 20224

SMOTHERMAN, HAROLD MONROE, banker; b. Coffeyville. Kan., Apr. 21, 1928; s. Claude Stanford and Cecile Marie (Barnett) S.; B.S., Okla. U., 1950; postgrad. Southwestern Grad. Sch. Banking, 1967; m. Juanita Janette Moeller, Nov. 22, 1950; children—Ann Lynn, John Stanford. Sr. petroleum engr. Cities Service Oil Co., Bartlesville, Okla., 1950-58; petroleum engr., Merc. Nat. Bank, Dallas, 1958-64; v.p., Citizens First Nat. Bank, Tyler, Tex., 1964—. Pres., YMCA, Tyler, 1969, E. Tex. Symphony Assn., 1968. Registered profl. enger., Okla., Tex. Mem. Ind. Petroleum Assn. Am. (v.p. 1973). Am. Inst. Mining, Metall. and Petroleum Engrs., Am. Assn. Petroleum Geologists, Robert Morris Assos., Mid Continent Oil and Gas Assn., E. Tex. Estate Council, Tyler Petroleum Club (pres. 1973), Petroleum Engrs. Club Dallas (pres. 1964). Methodist. Mason, Rotarian. Club: Willowbrook Country (Tyler). Home: 624 Windsor Pl Tyler TX 75701 Office: Box 2020 Tyler TX 75701

SMOTHERS, JAMES LLEWELLYN, educator; b. Jackson, Tenn., Aug. 30, 1930; s. James Frazier and Ruby LaVerne (Williams) S.; B.S., Lambuth Coll., 1952; M.S., U. Tenn., 1953, Ph.D, 1961; m. Elizabeth Anne Colley, Aug. 29, 1964. Nat. Heart Found. fellow in marine biology Inst. Marine Sci. of U. Miami, 1961-62; asst. prof. biology U. Louisville, 1962-66, asso. prof., 1966-71, prof., 1971—. Served with M.S.C., AUS, 1955-57. Mem. Am. Soc. Zoologists, Assn. Southeastern Bilogists, Internat. Oceanographic Found., Sigma Xi. Home: 3501 Illinois Av Louisville KY 40213 Office: University of Louisville Louisville KY 40208

SMOUSE, THOMAS HADLEY, research scientist; b. Cumberland, Md., July 10, 1936; s. Thomas Stanton and Bernetta May (Hadley) S.; B.S., Pa. State U., 1958; M.S., Rutgers U., 1964, Ph.D., 1965; m. Elizabeth Madore, June 21, 1959; children—Thomas Madore, Deirdre Anne, Robert Hadley. Analytical chemist Nat. Biscuit Co., Fairlawn, N.J., 1958-61; research fellow Rutgers U., New Brunswick, N.J., 1961-65; sr. research chemist Campbell Inst. for Food Research, Camden, N.J., 1965-67; research scientist Anderson Clayton Foods, Richardson, Tex., 1967—. Lectr. Internat. Soc. for Fat Research, 1972, Food Tech. Conf., 1973. Pres. Plano Fine Arts League, 1971-72; pres. Plano Friends of Library, 1970-71. Trustee Plano Pub. Library, 1971—, chmn., 1972—. Recipient Honor Student award Am. Oil Chemists, 1964. Mem. Am. Oil Chemists Soc., Am. Chem. Soc., Inst. Food Technologist, Agr. and Food Div., Sigma Xi, Delta Theta Sigma. Mason. Home: 1505 Westlake Dr Plano TX 75074 Office: 3333 N Central Expressway Richardson TX 75080

SMYLIE, THOMAS MELVILLE, mfg. co. exec.; b. Brookhaven, Miss., Oct. 31, 1916; s. Thomas Melville and Dora (Hubbard) S.; B.S., Miss. State U., 1939; postgrad. La. State U., 1947, Harvard, 1956; m. Patricia Clare O'Brien, Apr. 19, 1941; children—D'Arcy Clare, John Hubbard. With Ethyl Corp., Baton Rouge, N.Y.C., 1940—, corporate v.p., 1966—; pres., chief exec. officer William L. Bonnell Co., Inc., 1965-66, dir. 1966—, chmn., chief exec. officer Capitol Products Corp., 1969—; chief exec. officer, dir. Ethyl Mining Co.; dir. Bromet Co., Magnolia, Ark. Mem. Lead Industries Assn. (v.p., dir.), Am. Petroleum Inst., Am. Inst. Chem. Engrs. (past sect. chmn.), Blue Key, Kappa Alpha, Tau Beta Pi. Clubs: Baton Rouge Country; Canadian, Metropolitan (N.Y.C.). Home: 5937 Goodwood Av Baton Rouge LA 70806 Office: Ethyl Tower 451 Florida Baton Rouge LA 70801

SMYLIE, VERNON GUY, JR., pub. relations cons., author; b. Houston, Aug. 10, 1920; s. Vernon Guy and Alice (Marshall) S.; A.B. in Govt. and Journalism, Tex. Christian U., 1941; grad. Pub. Relations Inst., 1959; m. Arlene Frances Simon, Nov. 14, 1949; children—Eric, Alisa Ann, Regina. Reporter, Houston Press, 1942, investigative writer, 1948-50; investigative writer Albuquerque Tribune, 1945-46, El Paso (Tex.) Herald-Post, 1946-48; capitol corr. Scripps-Howard Newspapers, Austin, Tex., 1950, Santa Fe, 1951; Tex. dir. pub. relations Aluminum Co. Am., Port Lavaca, Tex., 1951-53; pub. relations cons., Corpus Christi, Tex. 1953—. Pres., Montclair P.T.A., 1958-59, Corpus Christi Fine Arts Colony, 1961, Nueces County Hist. Soc., 1967-69; chmn. Nueces County chpt. March of Dimes, 1959; mem. Tex. State Hist. Commn., 1973—. Served with USAAF, 1942-45. Recipient A.P. Community Service citation, 1947. Episcopalian. Club: Corpus Christi Knife and Fork (pres. 1970-71). Author: Padre Island Report, 1960; Thirteenth Grade, 1961; Taming of the Texas Coast, 1963; The Secrets of Padre Island, 1964; The Moon Belongs to Houston, 1966; Edward C. Lasater, Texas Trail Blazer, 1968; A Noose for Chipita, 1970; Texas in Fact, 1972. Home: 425 University Dr Corpus Christi TX 78412 Office: Six Hundred Bldg Corpus Christi TX 78403

SMYTHE, JULES WALKER, dentist; b. Gale City, Va., Sept. 2, 1924; s. Clarence Alexander and Effa M. (Johnson) S.; B.S., Emory and Henry Coll., 1947; D.D.S. magna cum laude, U. Tenn., 1951; m. Andrea Cory Adams, July 30, 1971; children—Jules Walker, Preston. Practice dentistry Smythe Dental Clinic, Bristol, Tenn., 1951—. Joint owner Holston Plaza Real Estate Devel. Mem. Sullivan County Bd. Health. Served with AUS, 1943-46. Recipient 1st Place award dental exhibits Tenn. Dental Meeting, 1962. Mem. Am. Acad. Oral Medicine, Pierre Fauchard Acad., 1st Dental Dist. Tenn. (pres.), Omicron Kappa Upsilon. Contbr. articles to profl. jours. Home: 700 Vance St Bristol TN 37620 Office: 800 Hill St Bristol TN 37620

SNAPP, HARRY FRANKLIN, educator, historian; b. Bryan, Tex., Oct. 15, 1930; s. H.F. and Ethel (Manning) S.; B.A., Baylor U., 1952, M.A., 1953; Ph.D., Tulane U., 1963; m. Elizabeth Mitchell, June 1, 1956. Instr., U. Coll. Tulane U., 1960-62; asst. prof. history Wofford Coll., 1963-64; asst. prof. history North Tex. State U., Denton, 1964-69, asso. prof., 1969—. Mem. Friends Winchester Cathedral, Am. Com. for Irish Studies. Recipient North Tex. State U. Faculty Research award, 1966, 67. Mem. Am. Assn. U. Profs. (pres. North Tex. chpt. 1968-69, pres. Southwestern regional conf. 1971-72), So. Conf. on Brit. Studies (sec.-treas.), Am., So. hist. assns., Hist. Assn. (London), Northamptonshire Record Soc., Butler Soc. (Ireland), Econ. History Soc., Ch. Hist. Soc., Tex. Assn. Coll. Tchrs., Tulane U. Alumni Assn., Alpha Chi. Episcopalian. Editor: Brit. Studies Mercury, 1970—, Tex. Academe, 1973—. Contbr. to profl. jours. Home: PO Box 1427 Denton TX 76201

SNAVELY, GUY EVERETT, coll. chancellor; b. Antietam, Md., Oct. 26, 1881; s. Charles Granville and Emma (Rohrer) S.; A.B., Johns Hopkins, 1901, Ph.D., 1908; Alliance Francaise, Paris, summer 1905; LL.D., Emory U., 1925, Stetson U., 1936, Washington Coll., 1937, Allegheny Coll., 1938, MacMurray Coll., 1942, Marietta Coll., 1945, U. Pitts., 1946, Alfred U., 1948, U. Chattanooga, 1949, Mt. Mary Coll., Valparaiso U., Tex. Christian U., 1950, U. Detroit, Ripon Coll., 1952, Barry Coll., 1957, Lafayette Coll., 1959; Ed.D., Whitman Coll., 1945; D.C.L., Birmingham-So. Coll., 1938; L.H.D., Boston U., 1937, Albion Coll., 1946, Cornell Coll., 1953; Litt.D., Fla. So. Coll., 1930, Cumberland U., 1932; m. Ada Rittenhouse, Sept. 27, 1905 (dec. 1948); children—Guy Everett, Brant Rittenhouse, Charles Albert; m. 2d, Louise Hutcheson, 1950 (dec. 1963); m. 3d, Madelyn T. Hale, July 17, 1964. Instr., Md. Nautical Acad., Easton, 1901-02; vice prin. Milton Acad., Balt., 1902-05; mem. faculty Allegheny Coll., 1906-19, prof. Romance langs., lit., 1910-19, registrar, 1908-19, on leave of absence as dir. so. div. A.R.C., Atlanta, 1917-19; asst. to gen. mgr. A.R.C., Washington, 1919; dean Converse Coll., Spartanburg, S.C., 1919-21; pres. Birmingham (Ala.) So. Coll., 1921-38, 55-57, chancellor, 1957—; interim pres. Lafayette Coll., 1957-58, Athens Coll., 1966. Hon scholar in edn. Tchrs. Coll. Columbia, vis. prof. Romance langs. N.Y. U., 1914-15. Exec. dir. Assn. Am. Colls., 1937-54; mem. Jefferson County Civil Service Bd.; mem. Birmingham Housing Commn.; chmn. State NRA Bd. for Ala.; v.p. Nat. Service Fund; chmn. Nat. Com. Colls. and Civilian Def.; lt. col. Ala. N.G. on staff of gov., 1923-26. Pres. Birmingham S.S. Assn., 1922-24; vice chmn. Internat. Sunday Sch. Exec. Com. Trustee Miles Coll., Hood Coll., Am. U. Mem. Modern Lang. Assn. Am., Nat. Adv. Com. on Edn., Ala. Coll. Assn. (pres. 1926-27), So. Assn. Colls. and Secondary Schs. (sec., treas. 1926-37), Assn. Am. Colls. (pres., 1929-30), Am. Council on Edn. (exec. com. 6 years, vice chmn. 1937-38), Assn. Urban Univs. (pres. 1936-37); chmn. scholarship dept. Presser Found.; trustee, exec. com Nat. Conf. Christians and Jews; v.p. Citizens Nat. Com.; chmn. Ala. YMCA State Com., 1931-33, Joint Meth. Hymnal Com.; del. So. Meth. Gen. Conf., 1934, 38. Decorated Officer d'Academie, 1941; Officer French Legion of Honor, 1947. Methodist. Corr. mem. Royal Spanish Am. Acad., Cadiz, Spain; mem. Alliance francaise of U.S. and Canada (pres.), Phi Beta Kappa, Phi Beta Kappa Alumni N.Y. (pres.), Phi Beta Kappa Alumni D.C., Nat. Phi Beta Kappa Com. Assns. (chmn.), Kappa Phi Kappa (nat. pres. 1927-31), Phi Gamma Delta, Omicron Delta Kappa (nat. pres. 1935-37), Phi Sigma Iota, Pi Tau Chi (nat. pres.). Club: Cosmos (Washington). Author: Choose and Use Your College, History of Southern College Assn.; The Church and The Four Year College; A Search for Excellence: Memoirs of a College Administrator. Editor: Alarcon's El Capitan Veneno, 1917; Valdez, Jose (with R. C. Ward), 1919. Contbr. articles to philos. and ednl. jours. Address: Birmingham-So Coll Birmingham AL 35204

SNAVELY, GUY EVERETT, JR., orgn. exec.; b. Baldwin, Md., June 30, 1906; s. Guy E. and Ada (Rittenhouse) S.; A.B., Birmingham-So. Coll., 1927; L.H.D., Athens Coll., 1950; m. Helen McNeill, June 3, 1930; children—Sherry Louise, Dan McNeill. Bus. mgr. Ala. Inst. for Deaf and Blind, 1933-38; exec. sec., trustee Pickett & Hatcher Ednl. Fund, Inc., Columbus, Ga., 1938-62, exec. v.p., 1962—. Mem. adv. com. Higher Edn. Act 1965, U.S. Office Edn., 1965-69, mem. adv. com. Nat. Vocational Student Loan Ins. Act 1965, 1965-69; mem. membership com., coll. scholarship service Coll. Entrance Exam. Bd., 1966-68. Treas., Ga.-Ala. council Boy Scouts Am., 1955-63, treas. Chattahoochie council, 1964—; chmn. Columbus Citadel, Salvation Army, 1974—; dir. Family Service Bur., 1939-41, 54-58; counselor Miss Ga. Scholarship Fund, 1947-53; dir. Nat. Conf. Christians and Jews, 1950-53; dir. Columbus Appeals Rev. Bd., 1951-53; chmn. Ga. com. Am. Assn. for UN, 1952-56; pres. Columbus Community Chest, 1948-50; pres. Muscogee Mental Health Assn., 1953, v.p., 1958, 62-65. Bd. dirs. Jr. Achievement, Columbus Sch. Speech; trustee Ga. Found. Ind. Colls. Served as maj. F.A., AUS, 1942-46; ETO, 1944-45. Decorated Bronze Star. Mem. Columbus C. of C. (chmn. edn. com. 1948-49), Mil. Order World Wars (chpt. adj. 1961-62, comdr. 1965-66), Assn. U.S. Army (dir. chpt. 1968-71), Brimingham-So. Coll. Alumni Assn. (past pres.), So. Assn. Student Financial Aid Adminstrs. (sec.-treas. 1963-70), Omicron Delta Kappa, Alpha Tau Omega. Presbyn. (vice chmn. com. on homes and ednl. instns. Synod Ga. 1962-66, mem. com. on campus Christian life 1965-66, elder). Kiwanian (sec. Ga. dist. 1950). Club: Big Eddy. Home: 2619 Habersham Av Columbus GA 31906 Office: 1800 Buena Vista Rd Columbus GA 31906

SNEAD, HAROLD FLEMING, state justice; b. Richmond, Va., June 16, 1903; s. Edloe Gathright and Ada (Riddell) S.; B.A., U. Richmond, 1925, LL.B., 1929, LL.D., 1958; m. Elizabeth Somerville Call, Apr. 2, 1937; 1 dau., Elizabeth Call (Mrs. David C. Dorset). Admitted to Va. bar, 1929; practiced in Richmond, 1929-48; trial justice Henrico County, 1935-48; judge Circuit Ct. Henrico County, Circuit Ct. Richmond, 1948-57; asso. justice Va. Supreme Ct. Appeals, 1957—, now chief justice. Dir. Franklin Fed. Savs. & Loan Assn., Richmond. Bd. dirs. Christian Children's Fund, Richmond; trustee U. Richmond. Mem. Phi Beta Kappa, Omicron Delta Kappa, Kappa Sigma, Delta Theta Phi. Democrat. Baptist. Home: 9301 River Rd Richmond VA 23229 Office: Supreme Ct Bldg Richmond VA 23219

SNEAD, ROBERT R., constrn. co. exec.; b. Daytona Beach, Fla., Oct. 19, 1927; s. Walter S. and Lillie G. (Mabbette) S.; B.S. in Architecture, Rensselaer Poly. Inst., 1950; m. Peggy Liggett, June 14, 1969; children—David, Donna, Terry, Patrick, Kenneth. Sr. partner Snead & Wiggert Mapping Service, Daytona Beach, 1950-51; constrn. engr. E.I. DuPont de Nemours & Co., Jackson, S.C., also Circleville, O., 1952-54; v.p., gen. mgr. Richardson Constrn. Co., Ft. Lauderdale, Fla., 1954-61; v.p. Ackerman Bldg and Devel. Co., Ft. Lauderdale, 1962; pres., chmn. bd., chief exec. officer Snead Constrn. Corp., Ft. Lauderdale, 1963—. Mem. Asso. Gen. Contractors (dir. South Fla. chpt., also mem. Tampa chpt.), Broward, Miami, Tampa, Daytona Beach, Mut. builders exchanges, Sommellier Guild, Broward Com. of 100. Elk. Clubs: Coral Ridge Country, Inverrary Racquet and Country, Le Club International, Exchange (chpt. pres., state pres.) (Ft. FLauderdale). Home: PO Box 23691 Fort Lauderdale FL 33307 Office: 1164 E Oakland Park Blvd PO Box 23580 Fort Lauderdale FL 33307

SNEAD, WALTER HAROLD, city ofcl.; b. Covington, Va., Apr. 15, 1933; s. Walter Andrew and Mary Elizabeth (Craft) S.; A.A., Mars Hill Coll., 1958; C.E., Va. Poly. Inst., 1960; div. Nov. 1970; children—Yvonne Marie, Tracy Karen. City engr. City Galax, Va., 1961-69, city mgr., 1969—. Pres., Community Action Agy., 1972, 73; adminstr. Park Commn., 1968—; chmn. Welfare Bd., 1973; tech. adv. bd. Wytheville Community Coll., 1969-70. Served with AUS, 1953-56. Mem. Internat. City Mgmt. Assn., Va. Municipal League (legislative bd. 1971-72), Va. C. of C. Baptist. Lion, Elk. Home: 124 Armory Rd Galax VA 24333 Office: 123 N Main St Galax VA 24333

SNEED, HENRY LEE, JR., sch. adminstr.; b. Troy, Ala., Apr. 11, 1914; s. Henry Lee and Delia (Osborne) S.; B.A., Erskine Coll., 1936; M.A., U. S.C., 1943; postgrad. Duke, 1938-39, U. Chgo., 1962, Columbia, 1964, Kent State U., 1969; m. Addie Meador, Dec. 21, 1937; children—Henry Lee, William Daniel. Teaching prin., coach, Clover, S.C., 1938-42; supt. Piedmont (S.C.) Pub. Schs., 1942-44, 46-49; prin. Chester (S.C.) High Sch., 1949-51; supt. Chester Area Schs., 1951-60, Bennettsville (S.C.) Schs., 1960-61, Florence (S.C.) Sch. Dist. 1961-73; cons. sch. house planning Smith & Fuller, A.I.A., Florence, 1973—. Mem. S.C. Adv. Com. Title III, 1969—, S.C. Vocational Adv. Commn., 1971—; mem. numerous evaluation coms., 1948—. Bd. dirs. S.C. Children's Bur., 1956-60, chmn., 1960; bd. dirs. YMCA, Pee Dee Edn. Supplemental Center. Served with USNR, 1944-46. Mem. S.C. Assn. Sch. Adminstrs. (past pres.), Am., S.C. assns. sch. supts., N.E.A., S.C. Edn. Assn., Erskine Coll. Alumni Assn. (pres. 1973-75), Florence C. of C. (dir., Leadership, Service award 1971), S.C. High Sch. League (past pres.). Presbyn. (elder). Rotarian. Home: 1101 Melrose Av Florence SC 29501 Office: 204 W Pine St Florence SC 29501

SNEED, RONALD ERNEST, engr.; b. Oxford, N.C., Nov. 23, 1936; s. Henry Ernest and Jewel (Hughes) S.; B.S., N.C. State U., 1959, Ph.D., 1971; m. Shelba Jean Walters, June 8, 1958; children—Kathy Geneva, Jennie Leigh. Sales trainee John Deere Co., Monroe, Ga., 1959-60; extension agrl. engr. N.C. State U., Raleigh, 1960-69, 70—; grad. fellow U.S. Army C.E., Wilmington, N.C., 1969-70; cons. in field. Served with AUS, 1960. Mem. Am. Soc. Agrl. Engrs., N.C. Irrigation Soc., Soil Sci. Soc. N.C., Res. Officers Assn., Sprinkler Irrigation Assn., Sigma Xi, Alpha Zeta, Epsilon Sigma Phi. Baptist (deacon 1971—). Home: 3405 Malibu Dr Raleigh NC 27607 Office: PO Box 5906 NC State U Raleigh NC 27607

SNELL, DAVID, writer; b. Minden, La., Mar. 28, 1921; s. John Barnard and Ada Jack (Carver) S.; student La. State U., 1939-43; children by previous marriage—Barry, Jan Whitfield; m. 2d, Dixie Baye Oliver, Sept. 1, 1956; children—Steven Mark, Sandra Robin. Reporter, Minden Herald & Webster Rev., 1936-37, Atlanta Constn., 1943-44; rewrite man U.P., N.Y.C. bur., 1946-47; reporter N.Y. Sun, 1947-50; radio and TV commentator WOR-Mut., 1950-52; reporter, feature writer N.Y. World Telegram & Sun, 1950-55; mem. staff Life mag., 1955-69, corr. Europe, Africa and Middle East, Paris, France, 1957-61, London, Eng., 1961-62, asso. editor, 1962-63, sr. editor, 1963-69, author column Dateline America; writer under contract to Life mag., 1969-71, Time-Life Books, 1972—; pres. Internat. Writers, Ltd., 1971—; dir. Internat. Spl. projects consultants, Inc. Served with AUS, 1945-46. Recipient George Polk Meml. award, 1952, Sportsmanship Brotherhood award, 1954, Citizenship award Am. Legion, 1938, Sci. award Bausch & Lomb, Inc., 1938; cited by Inst. Edn. by Radio-TV, Ohio State U., 1951. Mem. A.A.A.S., Sigma Nu. Methodist. Club: Press (Houston). Artist in oil, also cartoonist pub. nat. mags. Contbr. articles to Saturday Rev./World, Smithsonian, Signature, other nat. mags. Office: 440 Pinehaven Houston TX 77024 also care Harold Matson Co Inc 22 E 40th St New York City NY 10016

SNELL, JAMES DANIEL, JR., physician; b. Memphis, Sept. 6, 1933; s. James Daniel and Goldena (Hardy) S.; B.S., Centenary Coll. La., 1954; M.D., Vanderbilt U., 1958; m. Catherine Cheatham, June 7, 1958; children—Elizabeth, Margaret. Intern, Vanderbilt Hosp., Nashville, 1958-59, resident, 1960-63; practice medicine specializing in pulmonary medicine, Nashville, 1963—; asst. prof. medicine Vanderbilt U., 1966-70, asso. prof. medicine, 1970—, chief pulmonary medicine, 1966—. Recipient Pulmonary Acad. award, 1971—. Mem. A.C.P. Episcopalian. Home: 1151 Crater Hill Dr Nashville TN 37215

SNELL, JOHN NEWTON, JR., dist. judge; b. Latexo, Tex., July 30, 1912; s. John N. and Linnie (Garrett) S.; LL.B., Houston Sch. Law, 1934; m. Jean James, June 1, 1935; children—James Allen, John Newton III. Admitted to Tex. bar, 1935, since practiced law in Houston; asst. dist. atty., 1942-45; judge County Ct. at Law No. 2, 1948-54; judge 152d Dist. Ct., Harris County, Tex., 1954—. Mem. State Bar Tex., Houston Bar Assn. Democrat. Baptist. Mason (32 deg., Shriner). Home: 4611 Dunsmere St Houston TX 77018 Office: Civil Cts Bldg Houston TX 77002

SNELLGROVE, JAMES COLUMBUS, elec. engr.; b. Newberry, S.C., Oct. 12, 1920; s. John William and Charlcy Levina (Rhoden) S.; student Spartanburg Jr. Coll., 1939-41; B.S. in Elec. Engring., U. S.C., 1951; m. Rosa Lee Emanuel, Dec. 31, 1950; children—Janice, James Columbus, Susan, Brian. With Army Ballistic Missile Agy., U.S. Govt., Huntsville, Ala., 1956-60, elec. engr. Marshall Space Flight Center, 1960—. Active Little League. Served with USNR, 1942-45, 50-51; PTO. Baptist. Mason. Home: 8009 Strong Dr Huntsville AL 35802 Office: Marshall Space Flight Center Huntsville AL 35812

SNELLING, RICHARD KELLY, telecommunications co. exec.; b. St. Petersburg, Fla., Nov. 12, 1931; s. William Henry and Estelle Eula (Hall) S.; B.S. in Indsl. Engring., U. Fla., 1955; postgrad. Clemson U., 1963-64; m. Barbara Ann Mulligan; children—Deborah Jane, Richard Kelly, Laura Ann. With So. Bell Tel. & Tel. Co., Atlanta, 1956—, student engr., jr. engr., West Palm Beach, 1956-59, jr. engr., engr., Orlando, Fla., 1959-64, supervising engr., dist. engr., Cocoa, Fla., 1964-69; plant extension engr., Jacksonville, Fla., 1969-71, div. engr., Ft. Lauderdale, Fla., 1971-72, engring. dir., Atlanta, 1972—. Mem. industry liason com. U. Fla. Registered profl. engr., Fla. Mem. I.E.E.E. (sr.; sect. chmn. Cape Canaveral 1968-69), Fla.-Ga., Nat. socs. profl. engring. U. Fla. Alumni Assn. (v.p. Cocoa chpt. 1968). Clubs: San Jose Country; Boca Raton. Home: 2624 Leslie Dr NE Atlanta GA 30345 Office: 535 Hurt Bldg Atlanta GA 30303

SNELLINGS, FRANK WINN, JR., newspaper co. exec.; b. Richmond, Va., Feb. 14, 1937; s. Frank Winn and Lucille (Barr) S.; student U. Richmond, 1955-57, U. Coll., evenings 1957-65; m. Dinah Moore, Aug. 17, 1963; children—Kim, Valda, Leigh, Adele, Charles Moore. Asst. v.p. Wheat First Securities, Richmond, 1960-71, Computer Co., Richmond, 1971-73; project dir. Media Gen., Richmond, 1973—. Mem. Data Processing Mgmt. Assn. Lion. Home: 12212 Owls Hollow Chester VA 23831 Office: 301 E Grace St Richmond VA 23219

SNELSON, ROBERT MICHAEL, architect; b. Kansas City, Mo., July 24, 1935; s. Grover M. and Robbie R. (Baskin) S.; student Okla. A. and M. Coll., 1953-55; B.Arch., Okla. State U., 1963; m. Carol Dee Bockelman, July 2, 1955; children—Robert Michael, Mark. Job capt. Atchison, Kloverstrom, Saul & Atchison, Denver, 1963-66; project architect Slater, Saul & Spenst, Denver, 1965-67, Faxon, Gruys & Sayler, Los Angeles, 1967-71; prin. Dan F. Stowers, Architect, Little Rock, 1971—. Cub master, Los Angeles, 1967-71. Served with USAF, 1955-59. Mem. A.I.A., Ark. Archeol. Soc., Ark. Gem and Mineral Soc. Presbyn. Club: Grande Maumelle Sailing (Little Rock). Home: 43 Walnut Valley Dr Little Rock AR 72205 Office: 1516 W 3d St Little Rock AR 72203

SNELSON, SIGMUND, geologist; b. Santa Paula, Cal., June 22, 1932; s. Clifton Earl and Eugenie (Riegler) S.; B.S., U. Redlands, 1953; M.S., U. Wash., 1955, Ph.D., 1957; postgrad. U. Graz, Austria, 1957-58; m. Ann Elizabeth Hull, Dec. 17, 1960; children—Kermit, Karin. Geologist, Shell Oil Co., Seattle, 1959-64, Ventura, Cal., 1964-67, staff geologist, Midland, Tex., 1970-72, Houston, 1972—; sr. geologist Shell Devel. Co., Ventura, 1967-70. Fulbright fellow, Austria, Mem. Geol. Soc. Am., Am. Assn. Petroleum Geologists (A.I. Levorsen Meml. award 1972); Geologischen Vereinigung. Clubs: Houston Athletic, Memorial Drive Country (Houston). Office: PO Box 2099 Houston TX 77001

SNETHEN, ROLLIN KENNETH, ret. city ofcl., cons. engr.; b. Pontiac, Ill., Oct. 19, 1908; B.S. in Ry. Elec. Engring., U. Ill., 1930; postgrad. Command and Staff Coll. Army, 1956-62; m. Lucille Hortense Myer, Oct. 1, 1929; children—James Alan, Marilyn Suzanne (Mrs. Ralph Earnest Clark), Barbara Dolores (Mrs. Robert David Leonard), Carol Louise (Mrs. Richard Willis Reed). Jr. engr. Ill. Hwy. Dept., Ottawa, 1936-40; engr. Hasie & Green, Engrs., Lubbock, Tex., 1947; city engr., mgr. City Plainview, Tex., 1948-56; mgr. City Colorado City, Tex., 1956-60, City of Corsicana, Tex., 1960-69; mgr. City Sapulpa, Okla., 1969-73, cons. engr., 1973—. Mem. Okla. Planning Congress; mem. exec. com. Central Okla. Crime Commn.; mem. Tulsa Met. Long-range Water and Sewer Planning Com., Tulsa Met. Manpower Commn. Bd. dirs. Okla. Municipal League, United Fund, Central Okla. Devel. Dist. Served to lt. col. AUS, 1940-47. Registered profl. engr., Tex., Okla., Colo. Mem. Internat., Tex., North Tex. (pres. 1964), Okla. (dir. 1971-73) city mgrs. assns., U.S. Mil. Engrs. Soc., Tex. Water Conservation Assn., Corsicana (dir., chmn. water resources 1967), Sapulpa (dir.) chambers commerce, Nat., Okla. socs. profl. engrs. Baptist. Research on chilled car wheels. Home: 2018 Bellaire Circle East Corsicana TX 75110

SNIDER, CHARLES VAN, pediatrician; b. Knoxville, Tenn., Mar. 15, 1937; s. Charles Frederick and Frances Elizabeth (Vineyard) S.; B.S., U. Tenn., 1958; M.D., U. Ark., 1962; m. Vicki Ann Park, June 23, 1962; children—Jay, Sherri, John. Intern, Baptist Meml. Hosp., Memphis, 1962-63; resident, 1963; City Memphis Hosps., U. Tenn., 1967-68; practice medicine specializing in pediatrics, Memphis, 1968—; mem. staff Bapt. Meml., Meth., City Memphis, LeBonheur Childrens hosps.; faculty dept. pediatrics U. Tenn., 1969—, staff pediatrician, 1970—. Served with USPHS, 1963-65. Diplomate Am. Bd. Pediatrics. Mem. A.M.A., Am. Acad. Pediatrics, Shelby County Pediatric Soc. Baptist (dir.). Home: 920 Tranquil Lane Memphis TN 38116 Office: 1129 Hale Rd Memphis TN 38116

SNIDER, ROBERT LARRY, electronics co. exec.; b. Muskogee, Okla., Aug. 10, 1932; s. George Robert and Kathryn (Smiser) S.; student Phillips U., 1950-51, Tex. A. and M. Coll., 1952; B.S. in Indsl. Engring., U. Houston, 1955, postgrad., 1956; postgrad. Pomona Coll., 1960; m. Gerlene Rose Tipton, Nov. 26, 1953; children—Melody Kathryn, Rebecca Lee. Instr., Coll. Engring., U. Houston, 1955-56; sr. indsl. Sheffield Steel Corp., Houston, 1955-59, Kaiser Steel Co., Fontana, Cal., 1959-60; cons. Arthur Young & Co., Los Angeles, 1960-61; mgmt. analyst Iranian Oil Exploration & Producing Co., Masjidi-Suliman, Iran, 1961-62, cons., 1962-64, asso., 1964-65; v.p. operating methods div. Booz, Allen & Hamilton, Inc., Dallas, 1965-67, v.p., mng. officer internat. prodn. and inventory control div., 1967-69; prin., gen. cons. practice Peat Marwick Mitchell, Houston, 1969-71; exec. v.p., dir. Sterling Electronics Co., Houston, 1971-72, pres., chief operating officer, dir., 1972—. Served with C.E. AUS, 1956. Recipient Outstanding Mil. Engr. award Soc. Mil. Engrs., 1955. Sr. mem. Am. Inst. Indsl. Engrs.; mem. Am. Mgmt. Assn. (mem. pres.'s assn.), Phi Theta Kappa, Phi Kappa Phi. Home: 530 Ramble Wood Rd Houston TX 77024 Office: 4211 Southwest Freeway Sterling Electronics Bldg Houston TX 77001

SNIDER, TED LOWELL, radio sta. exec.; b. Rockwood, Tex., Dec. 16, 1928; s. Andy Jasper and Julia (Hull) S.; B.A., Baylor U., 1949, M.A., 1950; certificate U. Cal. at Los Angeles, NBC-TV Inst., 1950; m. Jane Julian, Dec. 6, 1950; children—Cathron Julaine, Ted Lowell. Mgr. KOAT-TV, Albuquerque, 1953-55, KXOC, Chico, Cal., 1955-57; program dir. WTCN-TV, Mpls., 1957-59; mgr. KBST, Big Spring, Tex., 1959-61, KPAY, Chico, 1961-66; pres. gen. mgr. KARN/KKYK/ARN, Little Rock, 1966—; owner KFIN, Jonesboro, Ark.; owner, pres. Snider Corp., Bus. Music of Ark., Inc., Pub. Bench Ads, Inc. Mem. City Council, Chico, 1965-66. Pres. adv. bd. Salvation Army, Chico, 1964; pres.-elect Butte County (Cal.) chpt. Am. Cancer Soc., 1964; pres., bd. dirs. Chico YMCA, 1962; v.p. bd. dirs. Little Rock YMCA, 1971—. Served with USMCR, 1951-52. Recipient Community Service award Chico Rotary Club, 1963; named Broadcaster of Distinction, Baylor U., 1969. Mem. Ark. Broadcasters Assn. (pres. 1974). Baptist (mem. exec. bd. So. Bapt. gen. conv. Cal. 1962-64). Rotarian. Home: 571 Valley Club Circle Little Rock AR 72207 Office: 1001 Spring St Little Rock AR 72203

SNIDER, WADE THOMAS, land surveyor; b. Denton, N.C., July 11, 1940; s. Arthur Roosevelt and Nettie Josephine (Davis) S.; student Wingate Coll., 1958-60; m. Nancy Hendren, Aug. 3, 1963; children—Warren Thomas, Melody Rose, Amiee Annette. Supr. surveying dept. Moore Gardner & Assos., Asheboro, N.C., 1962-67; partner individual land surveying practice, Lexington, N.C., 1968-70; prin. Wade T. Snider Surveying Services, Lexington, 1970—. Served with AUS, 1964. Mem. N.C. Soc. Surveyors. Baptist (deacon 1964-71; chmn. 1967-70). Home: 134 Eastside Dr Lexington NC 27292 Office: 308 W Center St Lexington NC 27292

SNIDER, WALTER DARRELL, lawyer; b. Beaumont, Tex., June 2, 1942; s. Darrell Langston and Leatha (Yankie) S.; B.A., Baylor U., 1964, LL.B., 1966; m. Lois Ann Debney, Dec. 18, 1965; 1 son, Wade Darrell. Admitted to Tex. bar; asso. firm Evans J. Karpenko, Hurst, Tex., 1969-71, Karpenko, Handy, Hill & Morgan, Hurst, 1971-72; pvt. practice law, Hurst, 1972—. Municipal ct. judge City Colleyville, Tex., 1973—. Served with AUS, 1967-69. Decorated Bronze Star medal. Mem. Am., N.E. Tarrant County (pres. 1973—), Tarrant County-Ft. Worth bar assns., State Bar Tex., Tex. Trial Lawyers Assn. Club: Mid-Cities Optimist (Hurst). Home: 1729 Brown Trail Hurst TX 76053 Office: 813 Trailwood Dr Hurst TX 76053

SNODGRASS, JAMES LEE, ednl. adminstr.; b. Osaka, Va., Sept. 9, 1936; s. John Henry and Bessie Ellen (McCann) S.; A.B., Lincoln Meml. U., 1958; M.A., U. Tenn., 1961; m. Donna Faye Marsee, Aug. 8, 1958; children—Bill, Brent. With Webb Sch. of Knoxville (Tenn.), 1959—, headmaster. Active Am. Field Service. Slemp Found. grantee, 1954-58. Mem. Assn. Coll. Admissions Counselors. Home: 109 Sanwood Rd Knoxville TN 37919 Office: Webb Sch Knoxville Route 21 Knoxville TN 37919

SNOOK, JOHN LLOYD, bus. exec.; b. Troy, O., Nov. 25, 1896; s. Clarence Guy and Anna B. (Counts) S.; Ph.B., Kenyon Coll., 1919; m. Alice V. Winger, June 21, 1923 (dec. Dec. 1967); children—John Lloyd, Elizabeth Anne, Julia Winger, Alice Winger; m. 2d, Mary C. Gayler, Jan. 29, 1972. Sec., treas., plant mgr. Kitchen Aid Mfg. Co., Springfield, O., 1919-24; prof. indsl. research Antioch Coll., Yellow Springs, O., 1924-30; pres., gen. mgr. J. L. Snook Co. (formerly Antioch Shoe Project, Inc.), 1930-60. Cons., SCORE, 1966—, project adminstr. Lakeland Ret. Sr. Vol. program, 1974—. Chmn., Scioto County chpt. A.R.C., 1946-59, Greater Lakeland (Fla.) chpt., 1965-69; mem. nat. nominating com., 1948-49, Eastern area adv. council, 1950-52, vice chmn. mems. and funds Ohio, 1953-55, mem. nat. bd. govs., 1957-61, mem. Fla. conf. com., 1965-68; dir. YMCA, 1957-62, pres. Clay Twp. br., 1960-62, dir. Lakeland Family YMCA, 1968—; chmn. Scioto County Community Chest, 1950; dir. Scioto County Crippled Children's Soc., 1948-60, pres., 1950-56; Ohio Soc. Crippled Children, 1949-55, pres. 1951-52; dir. Nat. Soc. Crippled Children, 1951-52; pres. Scioto County Council Social Agys., 1953-55; chmn. Com. for Ministry to Def. Community in Scioto Valley, 1952-56; mem. Portsmouth Town Hall Forum Com., 1942-60, chmn., 1955-59; exec. com. Ohio Citizens Council for Health and Welfare, 1954-59; dir. United Cerebral Palsy of Polk County, Fla., 1962—, v.p., 1964—; bd. dirs. United Fund of Greater Lakeland, 1964—, exec. com., 1970—; chmn. adv. bd. Salvation Army, 1969-71; 1971—. Past sr. warden Episcopal Ch., mme. bishop and chpt. Diocese of So. Ohio, 1956-59, del. ho. of deps., 1955, chmn. dept. stewardship and every mem. canvas Diocese South Fla., 1964-70; pres. Portsmouth Assn. Chs., 1949-50; adminstrv. com. Ohio Council Chs., 1954-61, trustee Found., 1961-62; mem. Lakeland Com. on Creative and Performing Arts, 1972—, Fla. Ancillary Manpower Planning Bd., 1972—. Mem. Portsmouth City Charter Revision Com., 1951-52. Served as ensign AC, USN, 1918-19; lt. comdr. USNR, 1944-46. Recipient citation for outstanding performance Navy Dept., 1945. Mem. Nat. Mgmt. Assn. (charter), Delta Kappa Epsilon. Episcopalian (vestryman, jr. warden 1966—, exec. bd. Diocese South Fla. 1966-69). Mason, Rotarian (past pres., past dist. gov.). Home: 1342 Edgewater Beach Dr Lakeland FL 33801

SNOOK, JOHN MCCLURE, telephone co. exec.; b. Toledo, May 31, 1917; s. Ward H. and Grace (McClure) S.; student Ohio State U., 1936-43; m. Marjorie Louise Younce, Jan. 15, 1974. Instr. history, fine arts and scis. Ohio State U., Columbus; exec. v.p. Gulf Telephone Co., Foley, Ala., 1955-70, pres., 1970—. Chmn., Baldwin (Ala.) Sesquicentennial, 1969; mem. hon. staff Gov. Ala., 1967—; active civil def., community projects; asst. civil def. dir. Baldwin County, 1974.

Hon. a.d.c. lt. col. Ala.; hon. Ala. state trooper; recipient Citizen of Year award Gulf Shores, 1956-57. Mem. Nat. Rifle Assn. (life), Am. Ordnance Assn., South Baldwin C. of C., Delaware County, Baldwin County (pres.) hist. assns., Friends of Library Assn. (pres. 1973-74), Ohio State Alumni Assn., Ala. Ind. Telephone Assn., Telephone Pioneers, Ind. Pioneers. Kiwanian, Lion. Office: Box 670 Foley AL 36535

SNOW, CORBIN LEE, JR., lawyer; b. Marshall, Tex., July 12, 1934; s. Corbin Lee and Lela Mae (Bassett) S.; B.B.A., U. Tex., 1956, LL.B., 1961; m. Ellen Genevieve Munson, Mar. 11, 1962; children—Ellen, Corbin Lee III, Sarah, Stephanie. Landman Union Oil Cal., 1961-63; admitted to Tex. bar, 1962; practiced in Austin, Tex., 1963-67, San Antonio, 1967—; asst. atty. gen. Tex., 1963-69; corp. ct. judge, Alamo Heights, Tex., 1971-72; city atty., City of Alamo Heights, 1973. Bd. dirs. Texans for Ednl. Excellence. Served with USAF, 1957-58. Mem. Tex., San Antonio bar assns., Phi Delta Theta. Presbyn. (deacon 1971-74). Mason. Home: 217 College Blvd San Antonio TX 78209 Office: 8000 Broadway San Antonio TX 78209

SNOW, JOEL ALAN, physicist; b. Brockton, Mass., Apr. 1, 1937; s. George Herbert and Mary Wilson (Sproul) S.; B.S., U. N.C., 1958; M.A., Washington U., St. Louis, 1963, Ph.D., 1967; m. Laetitia Mary Harrer, June 27, 1959; children—Jonathan, Nicholas. Instr. physics and electronics U.S. Naval Power Sch., Conn., 1958-61; instr. physics Washington U., summer 1962; asst. program dir. theoretical physics NSF, Washington, summer 1966, asso. program dir. theoretical physics, 1967-68, head Office Interdisciplinary Research, 1969-70, dep. asst. dir. for sci. and tech., 1971—; research asso. physics U. Ill., 1967-68. Served to lt. USNR, 1958-61. Recipient NSF Meritorious Service award, 1972, William A. Jump Found. meritorious award, 1973. Fellow A.A.A.S.; mem. Am. Phys. Soc., Am. Assn. Physics Tchrs., Philos. Soc. Washington, Com. for Environmental Information (sci. div.), World Future Soc., Phi Beta Kappa, Sigma Xi. Home: 6619 Byrnes Dr McLean VA 22101 Office: Nat Sci Found 1800 G St NW Washington DC 20550

SNOW, JOHN THOMAS, indsl. research organic chemist; b. St. Petersburg, Fla., Dec. 29, 1943; s. Sydney Thomas and Cynthia (Reeves) S.; B.S. in Chemistry, Earlham Coll., 1965; M.S. in Chemistry, Middlebury Coll., 1967; Ph.D., U. Cal. at Davis, 1970; m. Carol Anne Johnston, June 11, 1966. Chemist U.S. Naval Weapons Center, China Lake, Cal., 1967; postdoctoral research asso. chemistry dept. U. Cal., Davis, 1970-71; chief chemist research U.S. Sugar Corp., Clewiston, Fla., 1971—. Mem. Am. Chem. Soc., Am. Soc. Sugarcane Technologists, Internat. Soc. Sugarcane Technologists, Sigma Xi. Home: 505 S Deane Duff Clewiston FL 33440 Office: PO Box 1207 Clewiston FL 33440

SNOW, THOMAS WAYNE, JR., state ofcl.; b. Old Hickory, Tenn., Jan. 10, 1936; s. Thomas Wayne and Johnnie Pearl-(Huffine) S.; A.B., U. Ga., 1958, LL.B., 1960. Admitted to Ga. bar, 1959; practice in Rossville, 1960—; city atty. Ft. Oglethorpe, Ga., 1964—, Chickamauga, Ga.; atty. Chickamauga Sch. Bd.; mem. Ga. Ho. of Reps., 1962—, chmn. ho. judiciary com., 1969—. Ga. del. Nat. Legislative Leadership Conf., Washington, 1966, Atlanta, 1969. Mem. 7th Dist. Legislative Assn. (past pres.), Rossville Jr. C. of C. (past pres.), Rossville Boosters, Hon. Future Farmers Am., Am. Judicature Soc., Ga. Bar Assn., Lookout Mountain Jud. Bar Assn., U. Ga. Alumni Assn. (pres. Walker County chpt.). Democrat. Methodist (lay leader, Sunday sch. tchr.). Elk. Club: Exchange (Rossville). Home: Route 2 Chickamauga GA 30707 Office: 308 Spring Rossville GA 30741

SNOWDEN, JACK BENTLEY, dentist; b. Paris, Tex., Mar. 24, 1928; s. Leonard Alley and Minnibel (Bentley) S.; B.A., Tex. Tech. Coll., 1949; D.D.S., Baylor U., 1957; m. Elizabeth Jean Seward, Apr. 8, 1955; children—John Seward, Mary Anne, Allen Bentley. Practice dentistry, Arlington, Tex., 1957—; asso. clin. prof. periodontics Baylor Coll. Dentistry, 1957—. Bd. dirs. YMCA, 1965-67. Served with M.C., AUS, 1950-52. Fellow Am., Internat. colls. dentists, Acad. Gen. Dentistry; mem. Am., Tex. dental assns., Southwestern Soc. Dental Medicine (pres. 1968-69), Fort Worth Dist. Dental Soc. (sec.-treas. 1971-72; pres. 1973-74), Fort Worth (pres. 1971), Tex. (v.p. 1972-74, pres. 1974-75) acads. gen. dentistry, Arlington Dental Study Club (pres. 1969-70), C. of C. (dir. 1965-66), Omicron Kappa Upsilon. Presbyn. (ruling elder 1961—; gen. supt. Sunday Schs. 1965-68). Mason (Shriner). Clubs: Sportsman, Civitan (pres. 1963-64) (Arlington). Home: 4101 Curry Rd Arlington TX 76016 Office: 801 E Border St Suite A Arlington TX 76010

SNUGGS, HERSCHELL FRANCIS, county mgr.; b. Badin, N.C., June 18, 1919; s. Walter Artis and Lettie (Russell) S.; B.A. in Pub. Adminstrn., U. N.C., 1950; m. Christine Tyson Hellen, June 21, 1947; children—Frances Christine, Charles Russell. City mgr. Highland Park, Ill., 1951-54, Penn Twp., Pa., 1954-55, Lake Worth, Fla., 1955-57, Thomasville, Ga., 1957-63, Colonial Heights, Va., 1963-66, Mooresville, N.C., 1966-70; county mgr. Stanly County, Albemarle, N.C., 1970—. Bd. dirs. Entertainment Found., Youth Center, 1958—, treas., 1960-61; bd. dirs. Salvation Army. Served with inf. AUS, 1941-45, PTO. Mem. Internat., Ga. (pres.) city mgrs. assns., Am. Soc. Pub. Adminstrn., C. of C. (dir. 1958—), Ga. Municipal Assn. (dir. 1958—), P.T.A. (v.p. 1967), Band Boosters (pres. 1968). Baptist. Kiwanian (pres. 1963, 66). Home: Box 128 Crestview Dr Albemarle NC 28001 Office: County Courthouse Albemarle NC 28001

SNYDER, DICK PHILIP, accountant; b. Covington, Okla., Aug. 11, 1936; s. William Bryan and Edith (Kirk) S.; B.S., Okla. State U., 1958, M.S., 1960. Staff accountant Haskins & Sells, Tulsa, 1960-61, 62-63; asst. treas. U.S. Liquidgas, Inc., Tulsa, 1963-66; sr. accountant Peat, Marwick, Mitchell & Co., Tulsa, 1966-72; asst. controller Williams Energy Co., Tulsa, 1972—. Vice pres. Stillwater Delta Tau Delta Housing Corp. Served with USAF, 1961-62. C.P.A., Okla. Mem. Am. Inst. C.P.A.'s, Okla. Soc. C.P.A.'s, Beta Alpha Psi, Delta Tau Delta, Alpha Kappa Psi, Alpha Kappa Psi Alumni. Mem. Christian Ch. Home: 1623 S Utica Av Tulsa OK 74104 Office: Nat Bank of Tulsa Bldg Tulsa OK 74103

SNYDER, EDWINA HUNTER, educator; b. Coushatta, La., Apr. 4, 1932; d. Edison Everett and Cora Lee (Jones) Hunter; B.A., La. Coll., 1952; M.R.E., Southwestern Bapt. Theol. Sem., 1955; M.A., Northwestern U., 1958, Ph.D. (Univ. scholar), 1965; m. James Robert Snyder, June 2, 1960; 1 dau., Wendy Jo. Youth dir. Parkview Bapt. Ch., Shreveport, La., 1952-53; youth dir. Univ. Bapt. Ch., Fort Worth, 1954-55; ednl. dir. First Bapt. Ch., Galax, Va., 1955-57; speech instr. Bapt. Missionary Tng. Sch., Chgo., 1957-58; faculty speech dept. Georgetown (Ky.) Coll., 1958—, prof., 1971—, chmn. dept., 1964-67, 72—. Creator Wordmasters, choral group. Trustee Visitation Montessori Sch. Georgetown, chmn. faculty and acad. coms., 1970-71, v.p. bd. trustees, 1971-72, pres. bd. trustees, 1972-73. Georgetown Coll. research and writing grantee, 1969. Mem. Am. Assn. U. Profs., Am., So. speech communication assns., Ky. Assn. Communication Arts (pres. 1971-72), Pi Kappa Delta, Alpha Chi, Alpha Lambda Delta. Democrat. Baptist (deacon 1969-72). Contbr. papers to profl. convs. Organizer Wordmasters, speech performing ensemble touring U.S., abroad, 1958—. Home: 1113 Choctaw St Georgetown KY 40324

SNYDER, FALLON, printing exec.; b. Dallas, July 28, 1925; s. Bryan and Margurite (Shumate) S.; student Tex. A. and M. U., 1942, Ga. Inst. Tech., 1943; B.B.A., So. Meth. U., 1948; m. Shirlee Doris Stovall, July 17, 1947; children—Anna Victoria, Nancy Margaret, Cartier Fallon, Stuart Webster. With Johnston Printing Co., Dallas, 1947—, v.p., sales mgr., 1956-66, pres., 1966—. Served with USMCR, 1943-46. Decorated Purple Heart; named Most Valuable Mem., Dallas Advt. League, 1957. Mem. Printing Industries Tex., Advt. Club Dallas (pres. 1964), Kappa Sigma. Episcopalian. Home: 10949 Candlelight St Dallas TX 75229 Office: 2700 N Haskell St Dallas TX 75206

SNYDER, GEORGE FREDERICK (JERRY), JR., horse breeder; b. Indpls., Jan. 9, 1941; s. George Frederick and Charlotte Jane (Casady) S.; student U. Colo., 1959-60, Ind. U., 1960-61. IBM Computer Programming, 1965, stud mgr. course U. Ky., 1970; m. Martha Louise Adkins, Apr. 2, 1966; children—Scott Frederick, Stacy Louise, Suzanne Robyn. Self-employed bill collection agy., Indpls., 1961-62; research and marketing Am. Fletcher Bank, Indpls., 1962-66; sales S.E. Ind. Josten's, Owatonna, Minn., 1966-68; mgr., trainer, driver Holly Lane Farm, Lexington, Ky., 1969—. Served with AUS, 1963-64. Mem. Ky. Standardbred Assn. (sec.-treas. 1972-73), Ky. Harness Horseman's Assn. (dir.), Gentlemen's Driving Club (dir.). Republican. Mem. Christian Ch. Address: Rural Route 4 Versailles KY 40383

SNYDER, JOHN LEMOYNE, govt. ofcl.; b. Lansing, Mich., June 23, 1930; s. LeMoyne and Louise (Drew) S.; B.S., Mich. State Coll., 1951; A.M., Dartmouth, 1953; Ph.D., Northwestern, 1957. Instr. geology U. Tex., Austin, 1957, asst. prof., 1957-62; dir. edn. Am. Geol. Inst., Washington, 1962-69; program mgr. div. higher edn. in sci. NSF, Washington, 1969—. Faculty, Grad. Sch. U.S. Dept. Agr., 1972—. Fellow Geol. Soc. Am., A.A.A.S.; mem. Nat. Assn. Geology Tchrs., Geol. Soc. Washington, Sigma Xi, Phi Kappa Phi, Sigma Gamma Epsilon, Psi Upsilon. Author: (with others) Geology-Science and Profession, 1965. Home: 3914 S 12th Arlington VA 22204 Office: NSF Washington DC 20550

SNYDER, JOSEPH FREMONT, dentist; b. Deland, Fla., Dec. 5, 1931; s. Joseph Fremont and Mildred Humphrey (Barnes) S.; A.A., U. Fla., 1957; D.D.S., Med. Coll. Va., 1961; m. Alynn Cordell, Dec. 17, 1955; children—Joseph Fremont III, Suzanne Alynn. Practice dentistry, Daytona Beach, Fla., 1961—. Commr. South Penisula Zoning Comm., 1968—. Trustee Museum of Arts and Scis., pres., 1966—. Served with AUS, 1949-53. Mem. Am., Fla. dental assns., Am. Soc. Preventive Dentistry, Acad. Gen. Dentistry, Fla. Acad. Dental Practice Adminstrn. Presbyn (elder 1968—). Home: 2424 S Peninsula Av Daytona Beach FL 32018 Office: 159 Broadway Daytona Beach FL 32018

SNYDER, LENARD DAVID, engring. exec.; b. Bristow, Okla., Dec. 27, 1920; s. Earl P. and Julia E. (Ladd) S.; B.S., Okla. State U., 1943; m. Beatrice Mae Strom, Jan. 17, 1943; children—Donna B., David R. Design engr. George E. Failing Supply Co., Enid, Okla., 1946-51; mech. engr. Continental Oil Co., Ponca City, 1952-53; chief engr. Drilling Accessory & Mfg. Co., Dallas, 1953-55; chief engr., product mgr. oil field drill div. Joy Mfg. Co., 1955-58; with Dodge Mfg. Corp. div. Reliance Electric Co., Dallas, 1958—, dist. mgr., 1965-71, area mgr., 1971—. Served to capt. AUS, 1943-46, 51-52. Registered profl. engr., Okla., Tex. Mem. Am. Soc. M.E. Patentee drilling equipment. Home: 8944 Lockhaven Dr Dallas TX 75238

SNYDER, MARION GENE, congressman; b. Louisville, Jan. 26, 1928; s. M. G. and Lois (Berg) S.; J.D., U. Louisville, 1950, LL.B. cum laude, Jefferson Sch. Law, Louisville, 1950; m. Patricia Creighton Robertson, Apr. 10, 1973; 1 son, Mark; 3 stepchildren. Admitted to Ky. bar, 1950, D.C. bar, 1970; real estate broker, 1948—; practiced in Louisville, 1950—; engaged in residential constrn. bus., 1958-67, in farming, 1957-67; city atty. Jeffersontown, 1953-57; magistrate 1st dist. Jefferson County, 1957-61; mem. 88th Congress, 3d Dist. Ky.; mem. 90th-93d Congresses from 4th Dist. Ky. Vice pres. Ky. Magistrates and Commnrs., 1958. Pres., Jeffersontown Civic Center, 1953-54, legal adviser Jeffersontown Community Council, 1951-52. Pres. Lincoln Republican Club Ky., 1960-61, 1st Magisterial Dist. Rep. Club, 1955-57; mem. South End Rep. Club. Mem. Ky., D.C. bar assns., Louisville C. of C., Ky. Farm Bur., Louisville Bd. Realtors, Nat. Inst. Real Estate Brokers, Flying Realtors Assn. Optimist (pres. Jeffersontown 1957-58). Home: 8405 Old Brownsboro Rd Brownsboro Farms Louisville KY 40222 Office: 140 Chenoweth Lane Louisville KY 40207 also Cannon Bldg Washington DC

SNYDER, RICHARD WESLEY, computer co. exec.; b. Kansas City, Mo., Apr. 12, 1938; s. Leonard Lewis and Agnes E. (Grittinger) S.; B.S., Ind. U., 1960; M.B.A., U. Detroit, 1964; m. Roberta Marie Lloyd, Nov. 28, 1958; children—Richard, Robert, Stacey. Financial analyst, marketing coordinator Ford Motor Co., Dearborn, Mich., 1960-66; internat. sales mgr. Frigiking, Inc., Dallas, 1966-74, dir. sales, 1968-69, v.p. marketing, 1969-72, pres., 1972-74; pres. Gen. Computer Systems, Inc., Dallas, 1974—. Mem. Dallas Sales and Marketing Assn. Home: 10039 Pensive Dr Dallas TX 75229 Office: Gen Computer Systems Inc PO Box 6251 Dallas TX 75222

SNYDER, ROBERT MURRAY, oceanographic engr.; b. Penn Yan, N.Y., Feb. 19, 1932; s. Theodore Adelbert and Stella (Stow) S.; B.S. in Physics, Rensselaer Poly. Inst., 1959; m. Beatrice Stelle Miller, May 5, 1969; children—Kenneth Edward Baxter, David Robertson Baxter. Research asst. Woods Hole (Mass.) Oceanographic Instn., 1959-60, 63-63; mohole staff engr. Nat. Acad. Sci., Washington, Houston, Los Angeles, 1960-61; project engr. Ocean Sci. & Engring., Washington, 1963-69; dir. technol. research Oceanography Mariculture Industries, Riviera Beach, Fla., 1969-70; pres. Snyder Oceanography Services, 1970—, Offshore Mooring Services, Inc.; chmn. bd. S.O.S. Foods Internat., Inc.; v.p., dir. Eotech, Inc. Served with USCG, 1951-54. Registered profl. engr., Fla. Mem. Marine Tech. Soc. (chpt. vice chmn. 1967-68), Nat. Security Indsl. Assn., Sigma Xi. Co-author: Handbook of Ocean and Underwater Engineering, 1969. Contbr. articles to profl. jours. Home: 169 Beacon Lane Jupiter FL 33458 Office: 169 Beacon Lane Jupiter FL 33458

SNYDER, THEODORE ALLEN, JR., lawyer; b. Greenville, S.C., Dec. 17, 1932; s. Theodore Allen and Rebecca Wilson (Clark) S.; B.A., U. Chgo., 1952; LL.B. with distinction, Duke, 1955; m. Ann Sherwood Timberlake, Jan. 31, 1970; 1 son, Theodore Allen III. Admitted to S.C. bar, 1955; practiced in Greenville, 1959—; mem. firm Wofford & Snyder, Greenville, 1962—. Mem. citizens adv. com. Greenville Urban Renewal Commn., 1972—. Trustee, Trustees for Conservation; bd. dirs. Legal Service Agy of Greenville County. Served with Judge Adv. Gen's Corps, AUS, 1955-58. Mem. Sierra Club (region v.p. 1970-74, chmn. nat. land use com. 1972-74, dir. 1974—). Home: 2 Whitsett St Greenville SC 29601 Office: PO Box 232 Greenville SC 29602

SNYDER, THOMAS DANIEL, electronics engr.; b. Phila., Aug. 30, 1925; s. Thomas Daniel and Edith May (Lees) S.; Asso. in Applied Sci. in Radio and TV Tech., Milw. Sch. Engring., 1951; m. Mary Ann Wilson, Aug. 28, 1954; children—Thomas Daniel, Ellen Mary, John W. Foreman Prime Mfg. Co., Milw., 1951; with engring. dept. No. Light Co., Milw., 1951-52; communications clk. fgn. service U.S. Dept. State, 1952-55; electronics engr. U.S. Dept. Def., Warrenton, Va., 1955—. Cons. accoustics and magnetics govt. agys., 1964—; lectr. metric conversion; participant Solid States Application Conf., Fla. Atlanta U., 1971; participant profl. seminars Mass. Inst. Tech., 1962, 64, 66, Columbia, 1963, Pa. State U., 1967, U. Wis., 1969. Pres., P.T.A., Fairfax, Va., 1971, county rep., 1972. Served with USNR, 1943-46; PTO. Recipient Meritorious award for outstanding design in electronics equipment, U.S. Govt., 1969. Mem. A.A.A.S., I.E.E.E., Optical Soc. Am., Metric Assn., Am. Nat. Metric Council, Am. Legion, Cath. War Vets. (adj. 1964-67). Roman Catholic. Contbr. articles to profl. jours. Patentee in field. Home: 4246 Worcester Dr Fairfax VA 22030 Office: Warrenton Tng Center Warrenton VA 22186

SNYDERMAN, RALPH, clin. immunologist; b. Bklyn., Mar. 13, 1940; s. Morris and Ida (Candeub) S.; B.S., Washington Coll., 1961; M.D. magna cum laude, State U. N.Y. Downstate Med. Center, 1965; m. Judith Ann Krebs, Nov. 19, 1967; 1 son, Theodore Benjamin. Intern, Duke Med. Center, Durham, N.C. 1965-66, resident, 1966-69, asst. prof. medicine and immunology, 1972—; sr. investigator NIH, Bethesda, Md., 1969-72; chief div. rheumatology Durham VA Hosp., 1972—. Adv. bd. NIH. Served to lt. comdr. USPHS, 1967-69. Howard Hughes Med. investigator, 1972—. Mem. Am. Assn. Immunologists, Am. Fedn. Clin. Research, Am. Rheumatology Assn., Sigma Xi, Alpha Omega Alpha. Office: Dept Medicine Duke U Med Center Durham NC 27710

SOBRINO, JOSEPHINE, educator; b. San Antonio, Aug. 1, 1915; d. Fausto and Maria (Gutierrez de la Vega) Sobrino; A.B., Incarnate World Coll., 1936; diploma (U.S. State Dept. grantee), U. Mexico, 1945; M.A., U. Tex., 1946; Ed.D., U. Houston, 1960; postgrad. U. Valladolid, 1953, (Instituto Spanish cultural grantee) U. Madrid, 1954. Chmn. dept. modern langs. Tex. Southmost Coll., Brownsville, 1942-59; chmn. dept. Spanish, U. Houston, 1959-72; dir. profl. edn., prof. Spanish U. Houston at Clear Lake City, 1973—. Cons., Spanish for Modern Lang. Assn., 1963-65, Tex. Edn. Agy., 1960-63; del. conv. Internat. Fedn. U. Woman, Paris, 1956. Bd. dirs. Brownsville Library Assn., 1954-59, Charro Days, Inc., Brownsville, 1949-59, Mercy Hosp. Nursing Sch., Brownsville, 1955-59, Inst. Hispanic Culture. Nat. Conf. Christians and Jews grantee, 1954. Recipient Magnificate Medal award Mundelein Coll., Chgo., 1962; Spanish Consulate Gen. award, 1962; Matrix award Theta Sigma Phi, 1965; Faculty Research grantee U. Houston, 1968; Tex. Fgn. Lang. Assn. award, 1974. Mem. Internat. Fedn. Cath. Alumnae (state sec. 1940), Am. Assn. U. Women (Brownsville pres. 1954-56, state conv. chmn. 1958), Tex. Fgn. Lang. Assn. (pres. 1954-56, 66-68), Houston Council Tchrs. Fgn. Langs. (pres. 1962-63), Alliance Francaise (mem. bd. Houston 1964—). Author: Influence of Continuing Cultural Patterns Reflected by Pertinent Folklore of Selected Indian Tribes on the Education in Mexico, 1960; The Bilingual Child, 1961; (with others) Espanol: La Teoria y la Practica, 1971, Repaso de Espanol: Lo esencial, 1972. Contbr. articles to profl. jours. Home: 1022 Willowdale St Seabrook TX 77586

SOCOLOW, SANFORD, broadcasting exec.; b. N.Y.C., Nov. 11, 1928; s. Adolph and Sarah (Mindich) S.; B.A., Coll. City N.Y., 1950; m. Anne Grace Krulewitch, May 26, 1960; children—Jonathan Levin, Helen Elisabeth, Michael Joseph. With N.Y. Times, 1949-51; fgn. corr. in Far East, Internat. News Service, 1953-56; with CBS News, 1956—, covered all polit. convs., 1956—, covered manned space flight program, 1961—, producer CBS Evening News with Walter Cronkite, 1963-71, v.p., dep. dir., exec. editor CBS News, 1972-74, v.p., dir. news, Washington, 1974—. Served to 1st lt. AUS, 1951-53; Korea. Mem. Sigma Delta Chi. Clubs: National Press, International (Washington). Home: 3026 Newark St NW Washington DC 20008 Office: CBS News 2020 M St NW Washington DC 20036

SODERBERGH, PETER ANDREW, univ. dean, educator; b. Bklyn., Nov. 14, 1928; s. Sven Eric and Mary Margaret (Mc Gowan) S.; B.A., Amherst Coll., 1950; M.A. in Teaching, Harvard, 1959; Ph.D., U. Tex., 1966; m. Mary Ann Bernard, May 12, 1953; children—Susan, Mary, Peter, Katherine, Steven Charles. Tchr. pub. schs., Andover, Mass., 1959-60, prin. Andover Jr. High Sch., 1960-61; instr. English, Phillips Andover Acad., summers, 1959-61; lectr. in edn. Emory U., Atlanta, 1961-63; asst. prof. edn. U. Tex., Austin, 1966-67; prof. edn. U. Pitts., 1967-73; asso. dean Sch. Edn., U. Va., Charlottesville, 1973—. Served with USMCR, 1950-58; Korea. Decorated Purple Heart. Markoe scholar, 1958-59. Mem. Soc. for Cinema Studies, Soc. for Study of So. Lit., Phi Delta Kappa, Kappa Delta Pi, Phi Kappa Phi, Alpha Delta Phi. Democrat. Roman Catholic. Contbr. articles to profl. jours. Home: 712 Highland Av Charlottesville VA 22903 Office: 405 Emmet St Charlottesville VA 22903

SODOLSKI, JOHN, assn. exec.; b. Menasha, Wis., Apr. 11, 1931; s. Leo Vincent and Laone (Pinkowsky) S.; B.S. in Polit. Sci., U. Wis., 1953; m. Carol Jeannette Eppard. With Stanford Paper Sales Corp., Washington, 1957-59, Atlantic Research Corp., Alexandria, Va., 1959-62; dir. indsl. electronics div. Electronic Industries Assn., Washington, 1962-69, v.p. communications indsl. electronics div., 1969—. Served to 1st lt. USMCR, 1953-55. Mem. Washington Opera Soc., Sigma Chi. Club: National Press (Washington). Home: 1310 Swan Harbour Rd Washington DC 20022 Office: 2001 I St NW Washington DC 20006

SOENNEKER, HENRY JOSEPH, clergyman; b. Melrose, Minn., May 27, 1907; s. Henry and Mary (Wessel) S.; B.A., Josephinum Coll. and Sem., Worthington O., 1930; J.C.L., Cath. U. Am., 1950. Ordained priest Roman Catholic Ch., 1934; asst. parish of St. Anthony, St. Cloud, Minn., 1934-40, also tchr. Cathedral High Sch., St. Cloud, and chaplain VA Hosp.; chaplain Sisters of St. Francis, Little Falls, Minn., 1940-48; spiritual dir. St. John's Major Sem., Collegeville, Minn., 1950-61; bishop Diocese of Owensboro (Ky.), 1961—. Home: 1535 Frederica St Owensboro KY 42301 Office: PO Box 773 Owensboro KY 42301

SOFIA, SABATINO, educator; b. Episcopia, Italy, May 14, 1939; s. Ulisse and Carmela (Costanzo) S.; B.S., Yale, 1963, M.S., 1965, Ph.D., 1966; came to U.S., 1961; m. Tara L. Sibilia, Aug. 18, 1963; children-Tamara Lynn, Ulysses John. Nat. Acad. Scis.-NRC postdoctoral research asso. Goddard Inst. for Space Studies, N.Y.C., 1966-67; asso. prof. astrophysics U. South Fla., Tampa, 1967-70, prof., 1970—. Cons., Observatorio Cagigal and Concit, Caracas, Venezuela, 1970—. NSF grantee, 1967-69, 69-72; Jila fellow, 1973-74. Mem. Am. Astron. Soc., Internat. Astron. Union, Sigma Xi. Contbr. profl. jours. Home: 401 Lakewood Av Tampa FL 33612 Office: Dept Astronomy Univ South Florida Tampa FL 33620

SOGIN, HAROLD HYMAN, educator; b. Chgo., Dec. 14, 1920; s. Samuel and Sadie (Cohen) S.; B.S. in Mech. Engring., Ill. Inst. Tech., 1943, M.S., 1950, Ph.D., 1952; m. Ruth Reinberg, Dec. 26, 1946; children—Sarah (Mrs. Edward Allen Berman), Cecilia, David, Daniel. Asst. prof. Ill. Inst. Tech., Chgo., 1953-55; asst., then asso. prof. Brown U., Providence, R.I., 1955-60; prof. dept. mech. engring. Tulane U., New Orleans, 1960—. Cons. AVCO, Wilmington, Mass., 1957-60, Boeing Co., 1964-67. Served with USNR, 1944-46. NSF grantee, 1962-64, 69-71, 72—. Mem. Am. Soc. M.E., Am. Soc. Engring. Edn., Sigma Xi. Democrat. Jewish religion. Club: Echec Carre (New Orleans). Contbr. profl. jours.

SOHL, NORMAN FREDERICK, paleontologist; b. Oak Park, Ill., July 14, 1924; s. Fred John and Florence Martha (Wray) S.; B.S., U. Ill., 1949; M.S., 1951, Ph.D., 1954; m. Dorothy Martha Jansen, June 5, 1947; 1 son, Norman Frederick. Research asst. Ill. Geol. Survey, 1949-50; instr. Bryn Mawr (Pa.) Coll., 1952-53; instr. geology U. Ill., 1953-54; geologist U.S. Geol. Survey, Washington, 1954-68, chief paleontologist, 1968—. Adj. prof. George Washington U., Washington, 1963; vis. prof. geology U. Kan., Lawrence, 1966, U. Miami, 1972. Bd. overseers Harvard, pres., trustee Inst. Malacology. Served with AUS, 1943-45. Decorated Bronze Star medal, Purple Heart. Mem. Soc. Econ. Mineralogists and Paleontologists, Paleontol. Soc. Am., Paleontol. Soc. Washington (pres. 1966), Internat. Paleontol. Union (treas. 1968), Soc. Study Evolution, Geol. Soc. Jamaica, Soc. Systematic Zoology, Smithsonian Institution (hon. research asso. 1967—). Contbr. to profl. publs. in field. Home: 7105 Vermillon Place Annandale VA 22003 Office: Room E 501 U S Mus Natural History Washington DC 20242

SOHLER, KATHERINE BEATRICE BERRIDGE, pub. health educator; b. Cambridge, Mass., May 31, 1919; d. William Arthur and Ruth (Reid) Berridge; B.A., Radcliffe Coll., 1941; M.A., Yale, 1943, Ph.D., 1950, M.P.H., 1961, Dr. P.H., 1966; m. Theodore Paul Sohler, May 31, 1941 (div. June 1953); children—Edith, Theodore Berridge. Research asst. Yale, 1942-47, Sterling fellow, 1947-48, research asst. 1956-60, post-doctoral fellow, 1960-61, 63-66, research asso. dept. epidemiology and pub. health, 1966-67; study dir. Community Health Information Center, Mendocino State Hosp., Talmage, Cal., 1967-69; asst. prof. biostatistics and epidemiology Sch. Health, U. Okla., Oklahoma City, 1969-71, asso. prof., 1971—; dir. field office Dutchess County Evaluation Studies, Hudson River State Hosp., Poughkeepsie, N.Y., 1961-63; research asso. Columbia, 1961-63. Fellow Am. Pub. Health Assn.; mem. Am. Statis. Assn., A.A.A.S., Am. Assn. U. Profs., Am. Acad. Polit. and Social Sci., Soc. Epidemiologic Research, Phi Beta Kappa. Unitarian. Clubs: Sierra. Home: 324 NW 86th St Oklahoma City OK 73114 Office: BSE Dept PO Box 26901 Oklahoma City OK 73190

SOILEAU, JOHN MILLARD, govt. soil scientist; b. Washington, La., July 10, 1934; s. Valmont and Melba Ann (Doucet) S.; B.S. in Agronomy, U. Southwestern La., 1956; M.S. in Soils, Ia. State U., 1958; Ph.D. in Soils, N.C. State U., 1962; m. Joanne King Piper, Feb. 8, 1964; children—John Mark, Jeffery Millard, Christopher James, Trevor Valmont. Research asso. dept. agronomy Ia. State U., Ames, 1956-58; grad. asst. N.C. State U., Raleigh, 1958-62; research soil scientist TVA, Muscle Shoals, Ala., 1962—. Mem. Am. Soc. Agronomy, Soil Sci. Soc. Am., Soil Conservation Soc. Am., Blue Key, Phi Kappa Phi, Gamma Sigma Delta. Contbr. articles to profl. jours. Home: 262 McGough Blvd Florence AL 35630 Office: F137 NFDC Tennessee Valley Authority Muscle Shoals AL 35660

SOJKA, NICKOLAS JOSEPH, educator; b. Page, Neb., June 15, 1934; s. Walter and Anna (Boguz) S.; B.S., Kan. State U., 1958, D.V.M., 1958; M.S., U. Va., 1969; m. Eleanor June Cox, Apr. 23, 1960; children—Nickolas Joseph, Thomas John. Gen. vet. practice, Storm Lake, Ia., 1960; plant supt. agrl. marketing service U.S. Dept. Agr., Phila., 1961-62; asso. in vet. medicine Duke, 1962-65; asso. prof. surgery Sch. Medicine U. Va., Charlottesville, 1966—. Com. chmn. Cub Scouts Stonewall Jackson council Boy Scouts Am., 1970-72. Served to maj. AUS, 1958-60. Mem. Va. Acad. Sci. (sec. med. sect. 1970-71), Am. Assn. Lab. Animal Sci. (program chmn. 1967, 69), Am., Va., N.C., Blue Ridge vet. med. assns., Am. Soc. Animal Sci., Va. Acad. Sci., A.A.A.S., Alpha Zeta, Gamma Sigma Delta. Home: 305 Eastbrook Dr Charlottesville VA 22901 Office: Sch Medicine U Va Charlottesville VA 22901

SOKOLOFF, BORIS THEODORE, med. scientist, author; b. St. Petersburg (now Leningrad), Russia, Nov. 12, 1889; s. Theodore and Maria (Verchovtzev) S.; Ph.D. U. St. Petersburg, 1913; M.D., 2d Med. Sch., Petrograd, Russia, 1917; Sc.D., U. Charles, 1916; m. Alice Hunt, June 3, 1912; children—Boris Theodore, Kiril. Came to U.S., 1929, naturalized, 1933. Head exptl. medicine Nat. Inst. Sci., 1918-20; fellow U. Brussels (Belgium), 1923-24, Pasteur Inst., Paris, France, 1925-26, U. Prague (Czechoslavakia), 1927; with Rockefeller Inst. Med. Research, N.Y.C., 1929-30; with Cancer Inst., Columbia, 1930-31, research fellow physiology and chemistry Columbia, 1935-42; research fellow dept. pathology Med. Sch. Washington U., St. Louis, 1931-35; dir. So. Bio-Research Inst., Fla. So. Coll., Lakeland, 1947—. Served to capt. M.C., Russian Army, 1917-18. Decorated St. Vladimir Order. Mem. Royal Soc. Medicine, Royal Soc. Arts and Letters, Am. Assn. Cancer Research, Am. Chem. Soc., N.Y. Acad. Scis., Am. Soc. Biol. Editors, A.A.A.S. Author: The Achievement of Happiness, 1936; Napoleon, Medical Biography, 1937; The Story of Penicillin, 1945; Science and the Purpose of Life, 1950; August Comte, Biography, 1961; Careinoid and Serotonin, 1968; The Permissive Society, 1972. Mng. editor Jour. Growth, 1963—. Home: 825 Vistabula St Lakeland FL 33801 Office: So Bio-Research Inst Fla So Coll Lakeland FL 33802

SOKOLSKI, ALAN, govt. ofcl.; b. N.Y.C., Jan. 5, 1931; s. Irving and Pearl (Herzig) S.; B.M.E., Cornell U., 1953; M.B.A., Columbia, 1959, Ph.D. (Eastman Kodak Bus. fellow, Carnegie Travel fellow), 1962; m. Carol Stitt, July 27, 1956; children—Lynn, Lauren. Project engr., contract adminstr. Foster Wheeler Corp., N.Y.C., 1957-59; economist, bd. govs. Fed. Res. System, 1962-63; asst. program economist, acting program officer for capital devel. U.S. AID, Lagos, Nigeria, 1963-65; sr. economist, dep. dir. Office Econ. Research and Analysis, Dept. State, 1965-70; econ. research officer CIA, Washington, 1970—; lectr. Fgn. Service Inst., 1965-68; professorial lectr. Cath. U. Am., 1967-69. Served as 1st lt. USAF, 1954-56. Fellow African Studies Assn.; mem. Am. Econ. Assn., Sierra Club. Author: The Establishment of Manufacturing in Nigeria, 1965. Home: 915 Hyde Rd Silver Spring MD 20902 Office: CIA Washington DC 20505

SOLES, EDITH MARIE EDMONDSON HOBBS (MRS. JAMES HENRY SOLES), educator; b. Hanceville, Ala., Mar. 11, 1918; d. James Robert and Margaret Zuella (Howell) Edmondson; B.S., U. Ala., 1940, Ph.D., 1969, M.A., N.Y. U., 1960; m. Lindsey Maurice Hobbs, Aug. 4, 1940 (dec.); children—Lindsey Maurice, Janet Anna (Mrs. David Alan Norton), Ruth Bright; m. 2d, James Henry Soles, Apr. 24, 1970. Lectr., Reading Inst. N.Y. U., N.Y.C., summer 1959; reading cons. pub. schs., Highland Park, N.J., 1959-61; lectr. Pa. State U., Erie, summer 1961; reading cons. pub. schs., Bennettsville, S.C., 1961-63; asst. prof. elementary edn. St. Andrew's Presbyn. Coll., Laurinburg, N.C., 1963-64; reading clinician Macomb County Sch. Dist., Mt. Clemens, Mich., 1965-66; supr. instrn. Madison County Schs., Huntsville, Ala., 1966-67; tchr. psychology DeKalb Coll., Clarkston, Ga., 1969—. Home: 1502 Sagewood Circle Stone Mountain GA 30083 Office: DeKalb College Clarkston GA 30021

SOLI, ORLAN ALTON, airline exec.; b. River Falls, Wis., Jan. 6, 1918; s. Henry Curtis and Nina (Ramburg) S.; B.S., Wis. State U., 1940; M.S., Cal. Inst. Tech., 1946, Profl. Engring. Degree, 1947; m. Eleanor Dorothy Schuelke, Mar. 1, 1942; 1 son, Todd Orlan. Commd. ensign USN, 1940, advanced through grades to capt., 1960, ret., 1965; gen. mgr. Naval Air Rework Facility Navy Dept., 1950-65; asst. v.p. materials mgmt. Am. Airlines, Tulsa, 1965-71, v.p. maintenance and engring., 1972—. Bd. dirs. Okla. Maritime Adv. Bd., Goodwill Industries, Decorated Air medal; recipient Gold Knight award Nat. Mgmt. Assn., 1972. Mem. A.I.M., Nat. Mgmt. Assn., U.S. Navy League (dir. 1970-73), Nat. Soc. Profl. Engrs., Sigma Xi. Lutheran. Mason. Club: Indian Springs Country (Tulsa). Home: 5206 S Harvard Av Tulsa OK 74135 Office: 3800 N Mingo Rd Tulsa OK 74151

SOLKA, JACK, urban planner, architect; b. Mexico City, Mexico, May 20, 1935; s. Isaac and Rose (Neumann) S.; B. Arch., Tex. A. and M. U., 1958; M.S., Columbia, 1962; m. Davie Lou Ettelman, Feb. 28, 1960; children—Michael Benjamin, Steven Morris, Gary Leonard. Came to U.S., 1945, naturalized, 1952. Instr. architecture Columbia 1963; with Morris Ketchum & Assos., N.Y.C., 1964, Hans & Bennett Assos., Corpus Christi, Tex., 1964-66; partner Martin & Solka, Corpus Christi, Tex., 1967-68, Bennett, Martin & Solka, Corpus Christi, 1967-68, Bennett, Martin, & Solka, 1969—. Housing cons., 1969—. Co-ordinator Tex. Gov.'s Conf. on Community and Urban Affairs, 1969; exec. dir. Community Devel. Corp., Corpus Christi, 1967-69; chmn. Municipal Arts Commn., 1968-69; leader Boy Scouts Am., 1967-69. Bd. dirs. Tex. A. and M. Hillel Found. Served with AUS, 1958-59. Mem. A.I.A. (pres. chpt. 1971), Tex. Soc. Architects (dir. 1972—), Nat. Assn. Nonprofit Housing Orgns. (dir. 1969). Rotarian. Home: 501 Bermuda St Corpus Christi TX 78411 Office: 4707 Everhart Rd Corpus Christi TX 78411

SOLLENBERGER, CHARLES THOMAS, dairyman; b. Fayetteville, Pa., May 30, 1918; s. Charles William and Evelyn Hannah (Ausherman) S.; student Washington and Lee U., 1936-38; m. Elizabeth Louise Dalke, Mar. 17, 1939; children—Jean Ehlman, Conee Walser, Margaret George, Thomas, Richard. Owner, Woodstock Poultry Co. (Va.), 1939-65, Shenwood Farms, Woodstock 1960—, Shenwood Office Bldg., 1967—; pres. Pennmarva Dairymen's Fedn. Coop., 1974—. Mem. Va. Agrl. Stblzn. Bd., 1958-61. Mem. Woodstock Town Council, 1946-52, vice mayor; chmn. Shenandoah County Republican Party, 1966-69; mem. Shenandoah County Bd. Suprs., 1968-70, chmn., 1968-70. Treas., Shenandoah County Meml. Hosp., 1955—. Trustee, v.p. Massanutten Acad.; bd. dirs. Shenandoah Valley Music Festival, Inc. Recipient Man of Year award Woodstock C. of C., 1972, Outstanding Achievement award Lord Fairfax County Soil and Water Conservation Dist., 1973, citation A.R.C., 1973. Mem. Va. Dairymen's Assn. (pres. 1973-75), Md. and Va. Milk Producers Assn. (1st v.p. 1973—). Mem. United Ch. of Christ (past deacon, elder, trustee). Rotarian (past pres. Woodstock). Home: Shenwood Farms Box 427 Woodstock VA 22664 Office: 505 N Main St Woodstock VA 22664

SOLLIDAY, ALBERT LAFAYETTE, petroleum co. exec.; b. Watertown, Wis., Dec. 3, 1898; s. Albert Fay and Emma (Habbeggar) S.; B.S. in Petroleum Geology, U. Okla., 1923; m. Octavene Neely, Apr. 16, 1936; children—Anne (Mrs. Robert White), Albert, Fay Neely. With Dixie Oil Co., Tulsa, 1923-31; with Stanolind Oil & Gas Co., Wichita Falls, Tex., and Tulsa, 1931-58, v.p. operations, 1944-48, exec. v.p., 1948-58; pres. Pan Am. Petroleum Corp. (name changed to Amoco Prodn. Co.), then v.p. exploration dept. Amoco, Tulsa, 1958-63; dir. Knight Industry, Tulsa, Antelope Oil Co., Denver; sr. dir. Utica Nat. Bank & Trust Co., Tulsa; dir., sec., treas. Indonesia Nat. Consortium Activity, Djakarta. Bd. dirs. Salvation Army, Tulsa. Served with U.S. Marine Corps, 1918. Mason (Shriner, Jester). Home: 2856 E 34th St Tulsa OK 74105 Office: 616 Amoco Bldg N Tulsa OK 74103

SOLOMON, ERNEST, gas co. exec.; b. Winnipeg, Man., Can., Mar. 25, 1911; s. Samuel and Mollie (Katz) S.; B.S., U. Man., 1930, M.S., 1932; Ph.D., McGill U., 1934; postgrad. U. Manchester, 1934-35, Stanford, 1935-36; m. Rachael Minerva Schecter, Sept. 6, 1934; children—Marcia (Mrs. James F. Simon), Judith Anne. Came to U.S., 1936, naturalized, 1942. Research chemist M. W. Kellogg Co., 1936-60; asso. dir. research, 1960-65, asst. to exec. v.p., 1965-72; mgr. econs. dept. Coastal States Gas Corp., Houston, 1972—; sr. v.p., Coastal States Energy, Houston, 1973—. 1851 Exhibition scholar, 1934. Fellow Am. Inst. Chemists; mem. Am. Chem. Soc., Engrs., Research Soc. Am. Patentee in field. Home: 10015 Doliver Dr Houston TX 77042 Office: 5 Greenway Plaza E Houston TX 77027

SOLOMON, FREDERIC, lawyer, banker; b. Ft. Valley, Ga., Aug. 1, 1911; s. Aaron Moses and Mayme (Wice) S.; B.S. summa cum laude, U. Ga., 1933, J.D. with honors, 1933; certificate banking Rutgers U., 1941; m. Anita Ostrin, July 4, 1954; children—Andrew Mark, Laurie Ann. Admitted to Ga. bar, 1933, U.S. Supreme Ct. bar, 1938, D.C. bar, 1949; practice law, Atlanta, 1933-34; with legal div. bd. govs. Fed. Res. System, Washington, 1934-42, 45-59, dir. div. supervision and regulation, 1959—; asst. gen. counsel to bd. govs. Fed. Res. System and Fed. Open Market Com., 1948-59. Adviser, Bur. Budget, 1947; lectr. U. Wis., Madison, 1960—. Served from 1st lt. to maj. USMCR, 1942-45; col. Res. (ret.). Recipient Ross Essay award Am. Bar Assn., 1948, Honor medal Freedoms Found., 1950. Mem. Am., Fed. bar assns., U. Ga. Alumni Assn. (v.p. 1963), Am. Econ. Assn., Sphinx, Gridiron, Blue Key, Phi Beta Kappa, Phi Kappa Phi. Jewish religion (bd. mgrs. congregation). Club: Woodmont Country. Contbg. Author; Bankers' Handbook, 1966; contbr. articles in field. Home: 7517 Holiday Terrace Bethesda MD 20034 Office: Fed Res Bldg 20th St and Constitution Av Washington DC 20551

SOLOMON, MARTIN B., JR., univ. adminstr.; b. Chgo., Aug. 8, 1933; s. Martin B. and Beatrice A. (Neufeld) S.; B.S., U. Ky., 1955, M.B.A., 1960, Ph.D., 1967. Asst. dir. U. Ky. Computing Center, Lexington, 1960-67, dir., 1967—, asso. prof. bus. adminstrn., 1967—, chmn. dept. computer sci., 1967-68, chmn. coordinating com. Systems Planning Project, 1968-69, chmn. adv. computing com., 1968-70. Mem. Higher Edn. Information Mgmt. Systems, So. Regional Edn. Bd., 1968—; vis. scientist Assn. Computing Machinery and NSF, 1969; editorial adviser Jour. Econ. Studies, Glasgow. Served with USAF, 1955-57. Mem. Am. Econ. Assn., Assn. Computing Machinery, Am. Mgmt. Assn., Am. Statis. Assn., Inst. Mgmt. Sci., Beta Gamma Sigma. Author: Investment Decisions in Small Business, 1963; (with N. G. Lovan) Annotated Bibliography of Films in Automation, Data Processing and Computer Science, 1967; (with M.A. Kennedy) Ten Statement Fortran, 1970, Eight Statement PL/C. Contbr. chpts. to Management: Cases and Concepts, 1969, Essentials of Management, 1965. Contbr. articles to profl. jours. Office: U Ky Computing Center Lexington KY 40506

SOLOMON, SOLOMON SIDNEY, endocrinologist; b. N.Y.C., Dec. 2, 1936; s. Nathan and Irene (Oransky) S.; A.B. (scholar), Harvard, 1958; M.D. (Whipple scholar), U. Rochester, 1962; m. Linda Marcia Shaw, June 17, 1962; children—Joan Geller, Rebecca Karen. Intern, Tufts New Eng. Med. Center Hosp., Boston, 1962-63; resident Boston City Hosp., 1963-65; USPHS fellow, U. Wash. Med. Sch., Seattle, 1965-67; research and edn. asso. VA Hosp., Memphis, 1969-71, chief endocrinology and metabolism, 1971—. Spl. teaching fellow Tufts U. Med. Sch., 1964-65; asst. prof. medicine U. Tenn. Med. Units, Memphis, 1969-73, asso. prof., 1973—. Served to capt. USAF, 1967-69. Recipient VA Hosp. research career devel. award, 1969-71, and grants from NIH. Diplomate Nat. Bd. Med. Examiners. Mem. Am. Fedn. Clin. Research, Am. Diabetes Assn., Endocrine Soc., So. Soc. Clin. Investigation, Central Soc. Clin. Research, Sigma Xi. Contbr. profl. jours. Home: 5196 Longmeadow Dr Memphis TN 38134 Office: 1030 Jefferson Av Memphis TN 38104

SOLSTAD, ARNOLD KALMAR, educator; b. Viking, Alta., Can., Nov. 1, 1917; s. Eilert and Marie (Aamodt) S.; came to U.S., 1933, naturalized, 1941; B.S., Wis. State U. at River Falls, 1941; Ph.D., U. Minn., 1964; m. Mildred Rien, Oct. 15, 1940; children—Edward, Mary Heine, John, Ronald. Tchr. trainer ICA, Panama, 1954-57; mgr. Pierce Co. Breeders Coop., Plum City, Wis., vocational agr. tchr., Ark., Wis., 1948-57; asst. prof. U. Minn. at St. Paul, 1957-66; asso. prof. agr. Chico (Cal.) State Coll., 1966-68; prof. Tex. A. and I. U., Kingsville, 1968—, coordinator bilingual degree program, 1970—. Cons., Escuela Agricola Panamericana, Honduras, summer 1964. Sec., SW Alliance for Latin Am., 1973. Mem. Tex. Tchrs. for Mechanized Agr. (pres. 1972), Am. Soc. Agrl. Engrs., A.A.A.S., Alpha Tau Alpha, Phi Delta Kappa, Gamma Sigma Delta, Sigma Delta Pi. Home: 715 W Nettie St Kingsville TX 78363

SOLZBACHER, WILLIAM ALOYSIUS, linguist, govt. ofcl.; b. Honnef, Germany, Feb. 1, 1907; s. Carl and Josepha (Schmitz) S.; student U. Bonn, 1926-28; Ph.D., U. Cologne, 1931; m. Regina Reiff, July 27, 1931; children—Josephine (Mrs. Patrick Evetts Kennon), Irene (Sister Irene Marie), Regina (Mrs. Richard O. Rouse), Eve (Mrs. Richard D. Cuthbert). Came to U.S., 1941, naturalized, 1947. Interpreter, organizer internat. confs., 1925-39; founder, editor La Juna Batalanto (internat. youth mag. in Esperanto), 1926-34; faculty Am. Peoples Coll. in Europe, Oetz, Tyrol, 1932-37; lecture tours, Europe, 1925-40, U.S., 1933; exiled by Nazis, as free lance writer, journalist, lectr. in Luxembourg and Belgium, 1933-40; escaped from Nazi occupied Belgium and France, 1940; asso. editor Cath. Intercontinental Press, N.Y.C., 1942-50, treas., 1947-48, v.p., 1948-49; asst. prof. history and polit. sci. Coll. Mt. St. Vincent, 1950-51; fgn. lang. editor, chief program schedule sect. Voice of Am., Dept. of State, 1951-53; ednl. dir. study tours ASSIST, 1953-54; chief monitoring staff Voice of Am., 1954-67, policy application officer, 1967—, dir. worldwide Esperanto broadcasts, 1960-61. Led internat. delegation presenting Esperanto petition to UN, 1950; attended World Esperanto congresses, 1953-73; del. 3d conf. U.S. Nat. Commn. UNESCO, 1952, World Congresses Sociology, Liege, Belgium, 1953, Amsterdam, 1956, Stresa, 1959, Washington 1962, Varna, Bulgaria, 1970. Fellow Am. Sociol. Assn.; mem. Esperanto Assn. N.Am. (past pres.) Internat. Commn. Esperanto and Sociology (chmn.), Esperanto Acad., Am. Assn. for Advancement Slavic Studies, Speakers Research Com. for UN, Polynesian Soc., A.A.A.S., Modern Lang. Assn., Soc. for Sci. Study Religion, Linguistic Soc. Am., Am. Hist. Assn., Am. Acad. Polit. and Social Sci. Author: Walther Rathenau als Sozialphilosoph, 1932; Devant Hitler et Mussolini, 1933; Pie XI contre les Idoles, 1939; Rome en de Afgoden van Onzen Tijd, 1940; (with George Alan Connor, Doris T. Connor) Esperanto: The World Interlanguage, 1948, 55, 66; Say It In Esperanto, 1954. Contbr. to encys. Home: 6030 Broad St Washington DC 20016 Office: 330 Independence Av Washington DC 20547

SOMBERG, SEYMOUR IRA, coll. dean; b. Bklyn., May 15, 1917; s. Sidney Jack and Rose (Zuckerman) S.; B.S.F., Ia. State Coll., 1941; M.S., Duke U., 1946, Ph.D. (fellow 1960-62), 1962; m. Nedra Harriet Goldstein, May 6, 1947; children—Debra Lynn (Mrs. Alan Journet), Benjamin Lawrence, Sandra Jeanne, Steven Jay. Internat. cons. forester, 1941-60; asso. prof. forestry So. Ill. U., Carbondale, 1962-64; forestry officer, adviser to Peruvian Govt., FAO/UN Devel. Program, Lima, Peru, 1964-67; asso. prof. forest econs. and biometrics Auburn (Ala.) U., 1967-70; asst. dean, dir. research Sch. Forestry, Stephen F. Austin State U., Nacogdoches, Tex., 1970—. Reviewer research proposals Environmental Protection Agy., 1972—, forestry com. East Tex. C. of C., 1971—; cons. Govt. Venezuela, 1967—. Served with USAAF, World War II. Loeb Found. Research grantee, 1960-62, Forestry Service Research grantee, 1965-72, FAO/UN travel grantee, 1968—. Mem. Soc. Am. Foresters (nat. chmn. licensing com. 1971—), Am. (exec. council, 1971—), So. econs. assns., Am. Statis. Assn., Am. Soc. Appraisers, Am. Assn. U. Profs., Assn. Cons. Foresters (pres. 1960-62), Sigma Xi, Xi Sigma Pi. Elk, Lion. Club: Civitan (past pres.), Author over 70 books. Contbr. profl. jours. Editor, The Consultant, 1948-60. Home: 4124 Raguet St Nacogdoches TX 75961

SOMMER, LEONARD SAMUEL, physician; b. Springfield, Mass., July 3, 1924; s. Nathan and Jennie (Turbiner) S.; B.S., Yale, 1944; M.D., Columbia U., 1947; m. Anita Friedman, Dec. 21, 1963; children—Babette, Anne. Intern, Peter Bent Brigham Hosp., Boston, 1947-48, resident, 1948-49; research fellow Columbia-Presbyn. Med. Center, Cornell, N.Y. Hosp., 1949-50, 53-56, Harvard Med. Sch., 1954-56, London Hammersmith Hosp., 1952-53; practice medicine, specializing in cardiovascular diseases, Miami, Fla., 1956—; dir. cardiovascular lab. Jackson Meml. Hosp.; asso. prof. Dept. Medicine, U. Miami, 1962—. Pres., Heart Assn. Greater Miami, 1972-73; bd. dirs. Fla. Heart Assn., 1969—; mem. analysis com. S. Fla. Health Planning Council, 1971-72. Served with USPHS, 1950-52. Fellow A.C.P., Am. Coll. Cardiology; mem. Sigma Xi, Alpha Omega Alpha. Home: 2451 Brickell Av Miami FL 33129 Office: Box 875 Biscayne Annex Miami FL 33152

SOMSEN, ROGER ALAN, paper co. exec.; b. River Falls, Wis., May 4, 1931; s. John Henry and Doris Leola (Wahl) S.; student Wis. State U., 1949-51; B.S., U. Wis., 1953; M.S., Inst. Paper Chemistry, 1955, Ph.D., 1958; m. Marilyn Dallman, June 25, 1956; 1 son, Jon. Supr. process engring. research, research and devel. Olinkraft, Inc., West Monroe, La., 1962-68, tech. services mgr. pulp and paper div., 1968-72, tech. dir., 1972—. Mem. Am. Chem. Soc., T.A.P.P.I. (chmn. S.W. sect. 1965-67), Ouachita Power Squadron (comdr. 1973-74), Phi Lambda Epsilon, Alpha Chi Sigma, Alpha Phi Omega. Lutheran (vice chmn. ch. council 1964-72). Home: 3906 Forsythe Av Monroe LA 71201 Office: PO Box 488 West Monroe LA 71291

SONES, CHARLES GAYLON, petroleum co. exec.; b. Marshall, Tex., Feb. 5, 1922; s. Henry Jackson and Roxie (Williams) S.; B.S., Tex. A. and M. U., 1946; m. Lillian Pilat, Sept. 4, 1948; children—Charles R., Kenneth W., Robert A. With Texaco, Inc., Houston, 1947; with Ada Oil Co., Houston, 1948—, v.p., 1962—, dir., 1970—; dir. Houston Oilers, 1970—, Riffe Petroleum Co., Tulsa, 1971—, Ada Securities Corp., Houston, 1969—; v.p. Adams Petroleum Center, Houston, 1970—. Served to 1st lt. C.E., AUS, 1943-46, to capt. USAF, 1950-52. Decorated Bronze Star medal. Methodist (trustee 1960-74). Club: Golfcrest Country (Pearland, Tex.). Home: 3012 Country Club Dr Pearland TX 77581 Office: PO Box 844 Houston TX 77001

SONFIELD, RICHARD HUBER, accountant; b. Houston, July 16, 1934; s. Robert Leon and Dorothy (Huber) S.; student U. Houston, 1955-61; m. Carlene Rae Sump, July 16, 1962; children—J. Mark, Patricia Lynn, Dorothy Rae, Sandra Lane. Accountant, Peat, Marwick, Mitchell & Co., Houston, 1960-61; with Richard H. Sonfield, Inc., Houston, 1961—, pres., chmn. bd., 1973—; sec., Mortgage Capital Corp., Houston, 1972—; v.p. T.N.K. Corp., Humble, Tex., 1967—. Served with USMCR, 1952-55. C.P.A., Tex. Mem. S.A.R., Tex. Soc. C.P.A.'s, Am. Inst. C.P.A.'s, Delta Sigma Phi.

Home: 815 St Andrews Rd Humble TX 77338 Office: 1200 Milam Suite 446 Houston TX 77002

SONGSTER, GERARD FRANCIS, elec. engr.; b. Darby, Pa., Aug. 29, 1927; s. John J. and Florence (Schaeff) S.; B.S., Drexel Inst. Tech., 1951; M.S., U. Pa., 1956, Ph.D., 1962; m. Elizabeth R. Uhl, Apr. 11, 1953; children—Sheila, Claudia. Elec. engr. Philco Corp., Phila., 1951-52; staff engr. Moore Sch. Elec. Engring., U. Pa., 1952-56; asso. prof. elec. engring. Drexel Inst. Tech., 1956-63, acting dir. biomed. engring., 1963; sr. scientist Melpar, Inc., Falls Church, Va., 1963-64; elec. engr. U.S. Naval Research Lab., Washington, 1964-65; NIH spl. fellow Mass. Inst. Tech., Cambridge, 1965-67; biomed. engr. NASA Electronic Research Center, Cambridge, 1967-70; prof., chmn. dept. elec. engring. Old Dominion U. Sch. Engring., Norfolk, 1970—. Dir. Life Sci. Engring. Corp., Waltham, Mass. Served with USNR, 1945-46. Mem. I.E.E.E., A.A.A.S., Sigma Xi. Am. Home: Sch Engring Old Dominion U Norfolk VA 23508

SONI, MARIANO, lawyer; b. Mexico City, Mex., Dec. 28, 1936; s. Mariano and Carmen (Cassani) S.; B. Humanities, Centro Universitario Mexico, 1953; LL.B., Universidad Autonoma de Mexico, 1958; m. María de la luz Fernandez, Aug. 25, 1959; children—Mariano, Luz del Carmen, Alejandra. Admitted to Mexican bar, 1959; asso. Baker, Botts & Miranda, Mexico City, 1956-63; partner Woodson, Pattishall, Garner & Perez Vargas, Mexico City, 1963-65, Woodson, Pattishall, McAuliffe & Perez Vargas, Mexico City, 1966-68, Pattishall, McAuliffe, Perez Vargas & Soni, Mexico City, 1969, Perez Vargas & Soni, Mexico City, 1970—; alternate pres. bd. H.K. Porter Co. de Mexico, S.A.; sec. bd. Seven-Up Mexicana, S.A. Prof. tax law Universidad Ibero Americana, Mexico City, 1963-66. Mem. Ilustre y Nacional Colegio de Abogados de Mexico (pro-treas. 1966-69), Interam. Bar Assn., Asociacion Interamericana de la Propiedad Industrial (founder mem., treas. pro tem 1964), Asociacion Mexicana de la Propiedad Industrial (pres. 1966-67), Asociacion Mexicana para la Protection de la Propiedad Industrial (founder), Internat. Assn. Indsl. Property (exec. com. 1972—). Club: Cuicacalli A.C. University. Home: 120 Alberto J Pani Circuito Economistas Cdad Satelite Edo Mexico Mexico Office: 120 Paseo de la Reforma Mexico 6 DF Mexico

SONNENFELD, RICHARD JOHN, chemist; b. Britton, Okla., Apr. 29, 1919; s. Ernst and Mame (Myer) S.; B.S., U. Pitts., 1941; M.S., U. Okla., 1955, Ph.D., 1956; m. Birddean Virginia Martin, Mar. 14, 1942; children—Linda (Mrs. James R. Coates), R. Bruce, Carol (Mrs. Joe D. Phelps), Barry E. Chemist, Gen. Chem. Co., East St. Louis, Ill., 1941; foreman TNT prodn. Hercules Powder Co., Weldon Spring, Mo., 1941-43; with Philipps Petroleum Co., Bartlesville, Okla. and Borger, Tex., 1946—, sr. rubber research chemist, Bartlesville, 1956-63, sct. mgr., 1963—. Bd. dirs. Cherokee Area council Boy Scouts Am., 1969—. Served with AUS, 1943-46. Eastman Kodak fellow, 1955-56. Mem. Am. Chem. Soc., A.A.A.S., Alpha Chi Sigma, Sigma Xi, Phi Lambda Upsilon, Sigma Pi Sigma, Kappa Sigma. Presbyn. Patentee in synthetic rubbers. Home: 842 SE Concord Dr Bartlesville OK 74003 Office: Phillips Petroleum Co Bartlesville OK 74003

SONNER, HENRY THOMAS, metal fabricating co. owner; b. Island, Ky., Oct. 27, 1934; s. Joseph Howell and Eura Elizabeth (Nall) S.; student East Chicago Roosevelt Trade Sch., 1957-61; m. Shirley Jean Stringer, Aug. 30, 1957; children—Venea, Sabrina, Karen. Owner, pres. A & S Fabricating Co., Livermore, Ky., 1969—. Served with USMCR, 1954-57. Mason. Home: Box 126 Livermore KY 42352 Office: A & S Fabricating Co Hwy 431 N Livermore KY 42352

SONNER, JOHN LOUIS, II, physician; b. Knoxville, Tenn., June 23, 1937; s. John Boyd and Evelyn Ruth (Burkhart) S.; B.A., U. Tenn., 1962; M.D., U. Tenn., 1962; m. Jewel Dean Clark, July 22, 1964; children—John Boyd, II, Robert Louis, Andrew Clark. Intern U. Tenn. Meml. Research Center and Hosp., Knoxville, 1962-63; gen. practice medicine, Buena Vista, Ga., 1964-65, Sevierville, Tenn., 1965—; chief staff Sevier County Hosp., Sevierville, 1971-73. Bd. govs. Peninsula Center, Louisville, Tenn., 1973—. Served to capt. M.C., AUS, 1963-65. Diplomate Am. Bd. Family Practice. Mem. Sevier County Med. Soc. (pres. 1969, sec., treas. 1970), Tenn. Med. Assn., A.M.A., Am. Coll. Emergency Physicians. Home: Route 4 Sevierville TN 37862 Office: Burchfiel Med Bldg Sevierville TN 37862

SONNINO, MARIO ANTHONY, govt. ofcl.; b. Rome, Italy, May 1, 1915; s. Umberto and Letitia (Amati) S.; grad. Royal Tech. Inst., 1934; C.Sc.D., U. Rome, 1938; M.A., George Washington U., 1946; Ph.D., Am. U., 1949, M.B.A., 1955; postgrad. N.Y. U., 1940-42, Am. U., 1955-65; m. Frances Cosimano, June 3, 1945; children—Daniel Frank, Anthony Stephen. Came to U.S., 1940, naturalized, 1942. Treas., Motor Corp. Aircraft Co., 1939-40; pub. accountant, 1940-42; v.p., treas. S.W. Airlines, 1953; air transport examiner CAB, Washington, 1943-53, chief econ. research, 1954-60, supervisory economist and chief comml. rates, 1960-69, spl. asst. for research and planning, 1970-71; rate adviser Postal Rate Commn., Washington, 1971—. Professorial lectr. bus. econs. and mgmt. Am. U., 1949—, mem. dissertation com., 1950—, admissions com., 1960-66; lectr. Prince Georges Coll., 1960—, mem. coll. senate exec. com. 1965-68. Mem. Suitland Citizens Council, 1955-60; active Prince Georges County chpt. A.R.C., 1955—. Recipient Distinguished Service award CAB, 1968, Superior Performance awards, 1948, 51, 54, 64. Mem. Am. Econ. Assn., Nat. Planning Assn., Am. Soc. Traffic and Transp., Am. Transp. Assn., Soc. Advancement of Mgmt., NRC, Alpha Kappa Psi, Delta Nu Alpha. Home: 2023 Jameson St Washington DC 20031 Office: 2000 L St NW Washington DC 20268

SOPHER, CHARLES DUANE, educator; b. Dahinda, Ill., Aug. 15, 1939; s. Amos O. and Trella Irene (Sunbburg) S.; B.S., Western Ill. U., 1961; M.S., U. Ill., 1963; Ph.D., N.C. State U., 1969; m. Sharron Lee Washabaugh, Dec. 29, 1957; children—Kellie Dawn, Matthew Todd. Instr. soil sci. N.C. State U. at Raleigh, 1965-69, asst. prof., 1969—. Mem. Planning and Zoning Bd., Cary, N.C., 1972—. Mem. Soil Sci. Soc. N.C. (pres. elect 1973-74), Am. Soc. Agronomy, Sigma Xi, Gamma Sigma Delta. Contbr. articles to profl. jours. Home: 1100 Reedy Creek Rd Cary NC 27511 Office: Dept Soil Science North Carolina State Univ Raligh NC 27607

SOPKIN, RONALD BARTON, apparel mfg. co. exec.; b. Chgo., Feb. 17, 1922; s. Alvin A. and Sadie (Hall) S.; student Nichols Coll., 1940-41; m. Doris Lenore Wald, Apr. 6, 1946; children—Nancy (Mrs. James R. Pettit), Gail (Mrs. Donald Kemp), Bonnie. With Wentworth Mfg. Co., Lake City, S.C., 1945—, pres., 1964—; dir. Peoples Bank S.C., Florence, Sparkle Mill, Olanta, S.C., 1969-70. Commr., Florence City/County Airport, 1970-73. Bd. dirs. Florence Little Theater, 1962—, chmn. bd. trustees, 1967—. Served with USAAF, 1942-45. Home: 510 Ridgewood Dr Florence SC 29501 Office: Blanding St Lake City SC 29560

SORELLE, ANDREW CURRIE, JR., engr.; b. Rosenberg, Tex., May 18, 1920; s. Andrew Currie and Nita Ray (SoRelle) SoR.; B.S., Tex. A. and M. U., 1942; m. Maxine Chambers, Mar. 22, 1943; children—Virginia Lee, Andrew Currie III. Ind. oil operator and producer, 1945-57; investments, 1957—. Bd. dirs. Star of Hope Mission, Houston, Com. of Fourteen. Served from 2d lt. to maj. USAAF, 1942-45. Decorated Silver Star, D.F.C., Air medal with 17 oak leaf clusters. Mem. Am. Inst. Mining, Metall. and Petroleum Engrs., Full Gospel Bus. Men's Fellowship Internat. (dir.), Clubs: Petroleum, Lakeside Country, Houston. Home: 10220 Memorial Dr Houston TX 77024 Office: 300 Jackson Hill Houston TX 77007

SORENSEN, ANTON MARINUS, JR., educator; b. Granger, Tex., Feb. 5, 1925; s. Anton Marinus and Odie Bertha (Cobb) S.; B.S., Tex. A and M U., 1949; M.S., Cornell U., 1951, Ph.D., 1953; m. Tommie Mae Moorman, June 3, 1944; children—Susan (Mrs. Thomas Dee Davenport), Walter Frank. Grad. asst. Cornell U., 1949-53; asst. prof. dairy sci. dept. Miss. State U., 1953-55; asst. prof. animal sci. dept. Tex. A and M U., 1955-57, asso. prof., 1957-65, prof., 1965—. Cons. Wortham Research Found., 1960-65, Eli Lilly Co., 1966—; cons. internat. programs AID, Dominican Republic, 1966. Mgr., coach Little League, 1963-64, umpire-in-chief, 1966; chmn. bd. equalization A and M Consol. Sch. Dist., 1970. Served with AUS, 1943-46; ETO. Recipient Faculty Distinguished Achievement award Tex. A and M Former Students Assn., 1968, Distinguished Tchr. award Am. Soc. Animal Sci., 1969, Distinguished Service to Agr. award Gamma Sigma Delta, 1972; named Piper Prof., Minnie Stevens Piper Found., 1970, Hon. Prof., Coll. Agr., Tex. A and M U., 1971, Outstanding Prof., Tex. A and M U., 1971. Mem. Am. Soc. Animal Sci. (chmn. teaching award com. 1971), Am. Dairy Sci. Assn., Soc. Study Fertility, Am. Assn. Lab. Animal Sci., A.A.A.S., Soc. Study Reproduction, Tex. Acad. Sci. Baptist (deacon 1958—). Author: (with W. T. Berry and L. D. Wythe, Jr.) Basic Animal Science Laboratory Manual, 1956, revised edits., 1958, 62, 68; Repro Lab, A Laboratory Manual for Animal Reproduction, 1971, rev. edit., 1973. Home: Route 5 Box 618 Bryan TX 77801

SORRELL, STERLING NORMAN, lawyer; b. Laredo, Tex., May 2, 1938; s. Norman W. and Elizabeth (Nye) S.; student Rice U., 1955-56; B.A., U. Tex., 1959, LL.B., 1964; m. Martha Frances Barrett, Apr. 16, 1966; children—Virginia, Andrew. Admitted to Tex. bar, 1964; mem. legal staff Gulf Oil Corp., Midland, Tex., 1965; staff atty. Latin Am. Gulf Oil Co., Coral Gables, Fla., 1966-67; practiced in Houston, 1967-74; partner Dillingham, Schleider & Masquelette, 1973-74; mem. legal staff Occidental Petroleum, Inc., Bakersfield, Cal., 1974—; dir. Nyco, Inc. Served to lt. USNR, 1959-67. Mem. Am., Houston (mem. internat. and comparative law com. 1972) bar assns., Am., Houston rose socs., Delta Upsilon, Delta Theta Phi. Democrat. Episcopalian (treas. vestry 1968-70). Home: 4423 Woodlake Dr Bakersfield CA 93309 Office: 5000 Stockdale Hwy Bakersfield CA 93309

SORRELLS, BOBBY GENE, pub. co. exec.; b. Hartford, Ala., Oct. 18, 1937; s. F. L. and Ruby (White) S.; B.A., Auburn U., 1961; postgrad. Columbia U., 1965; m. Theresa Dancy, Mar. 22, 1956; children—Robert, Jeffrey, Sandra. Cost Accountant St. Marys Kraft Corp. (Ga.), 1961-62; asst. comptroller Ledger-Enquirer Co., Columbus, 1962-66; comptroller R.W. Page Corp., Columbus, 1966—. Bd. dirs. Boys Club. Served with USNR, 1956-58. Mem. Inst. Newspaper Controllers (membership com. 1971—). Republican. Baptist (supt. young people 1971-72, Sunday sch. dir.). Lion (dir.). Club: Country (Columbus). Home: 2504 Brookwood Circle Phenix City AL 36867 Office: 17 W 12th St Columbus GA 31901

SORRELLS, JOHN HARVEY, newspaper editor; b. Oklahoma City, Jan 14, 1923; s. John Harvey and Ruth (Arnett) S.; B.S. in Bus. Adminstrn., Washington and Lee U., 1948; m. Mary Morris Blakely, Jan. 4, 1944; children—John Harvey III, Mary Morris, Nancy Gordon. Research dir. Knoxville (Tenn.) News-Sentinel, 1948-50, gen. advt. salesman, 1950-55; gen. advt. salesman Memphis Pub. Co., 1955-58; spl. sects. editor Comml. Appeal, Memphis, 1958-60, gen. assignment reporter, 1960-61, night city editor, also asst. city editor, 1961-63, promotions editor, 1963—. Mem. pub. affairs com. Memphis chpt. A.R.C., 1964—; sec.-treas. Am. Legion-Comml. Appeal Christmas Basket Fund, 1963—. Bd. dirs. Boys Town. Served with AUS, 1942-46; ETO; col. Res. Decorated Bronze Star medal with V, Purple Heart with oak leaf cluster, Combat Infantry badge, Meritorious Service medal. Mem. C. of C., Mil. Order World Wars, Am. Legion, Internat. Newspaper Promotion Assn., Sigma Delta Chi, Phi Kappa Psi. Presbyn. (elder). Home: 4209 Waymar Dr Memphis TN 38117 Office: 495 Union St Memphis TN 38101

SORRELS, WILLIAM WRIGHT, newspaper editor; b. Cordova, Tenn., July 28, 1924; s. Chelsea Howard and Mary (Wright) S.; student Miss. State U., 1946-47; B.J., U. Mo., 1949; M.A., Memphis State U., 1969; m. Carolyn Ramsey, June 28, 1954; children—Deborah, John Clarke, Reporter, editor West Point (Miss.) Daily Times Leader, 1949-53; reporter Honolulu Star-Bull., 1953-54; reporter, asst. city editor Comml. Appeal, Memphis, 1954-61, asst. mng. editor, 1962-68, mng. editor, 1968—; mng. editor Evening Ind., St. Petersburg, Fla., 1961-62. Owner, Indian Mound Farm, Starkville, Miss.; instr. journalism Memphis State U. Bd. dirs. Mile-O-Dimes. Served with USNR, 1943-46. Mem. Sigma Delta Chi (pres. Mid-South chpt. 1965-66), Kappa Alpha Tau. Presbyn. Kiwanian. Club: Summit. Author: Memphis' Greatest Debate, 1970. Home: 1453 Finley St Memphis TN 38116 Office: 495 Union St Memphis TN 38101

SORRIER, ISABEL LANE, librarian; b. Statesboro, Ga., Aug. 13, 1917; d. Brooks Blitch and Caroline Viola (Moore) Sorrier; B.S., Ga. So. Coll., 1938; postgrad. U. Ga., 1940; B.S., George Peabody Coll., 1942. Intern, Warder Pub. Library, Springfield, O., 1942; librarian Homerville (Ga.) High Sch., 1939-41; head librarian Waycross (Ga.) Pub. Library, 1942; librarian Newnan (Ga.) High Sch., 1943; dir. Statesboro (Ga.) Regional Library, 1944—. Mem. library adv. com. bldg. constrn. Ga. Dept. Edn., mem. book selection com. Sec. chpt. A.R.C., 1945-48. Mem. A.L.A., S.E., Ga. (exec. bd. 1960, chmn. sect. 1960-62) library assns., Ga. Edn. Assn., Bus. and Profl. Women's Club (treas. 1950-52). Presbyn. Home: 112 Park Av Statesboro GA 30485 Office: 124 S Main St Statesboro GA 30458

SOSEBEE, JAMES WILSON, instnl. adminstr.; b. Atlanta, Feb. 24, 1919; s. Arbelia and Mary Augusta (Bell) S.; A.B., Tex. Christian U., 1944; B.D., Luth. So. Sem., 1954; m. Mildred Crook, Nov. 22, 1942; children—Marcia (Mrs. Houston A. Butler), Richard James. Ordained to ministry Christian Ch., 1938; minister First Christian Ch., Columbia, S.C., 1950-55, First Christian Ch., Atlanta, 1955-66, Central Christian Ch., Waco, Tex., 1966-67, Brookhaven Christian Ch., Atlanta, 1967-70; exec. dir. Atlanta Union Mission, 1970—; pres. Arch Corp., Atlanta, 1973—. Chmn. bd. Nat. Benevolent Assn. Christian Chs. Am., 1973-75. Trustee Christian Coll. Ga., Athens, 1958-66, chmn. trustees, 1960-64; chmn. bd. trustees Campbell-Stone Apts., sr. citizens home, Atlanta, 1962-66. Served with AUS, 1945-50; now col. Res. Mem. Mil. Order World Wars. Club: Atlantic Athletic. Home: 1502 Epping Forest Dr NE Atlanta GA 30319 Office: 624 Healey Bldg Atlanta GA 30303

SOTERIADES, MICHAEL COSMAS, educator; b. Istanbul, Turkey, Mar. 25, 1923; s. Cosmas and Evouli (Tsaoussoglou) S.; student Athens (Greece) Coll., 1933-41; Diploma Engr., Nat. Tech. U. Athens, 1948, Dr. Engring., 1952; Sc.D., Mass. Inst. Tech., 1954; m. Rose Marie Rentroia, Aug. 5, 1962. Asso. engr. A. Woolf Assos., Boston, 1954-55; Greek Govt. in charge of Aseismic Design and Specifications for rebuilding City of Volos, Greece, 1955-56; chief engr. Universal Engring. Corp., Boston, 1956-58; v.p. engring. Doxiadis Assos., Inc., Washington, 1958-61, dir., treas., 1959-61; prof. Cath. U. Am., 1961—; cons. Nat. Acad. Scis., Dept. Commerce, Dept. Navy, 1961—. Served to 2d lt. Greek Army, 1948-52. Fellow Am. Soc. C.E.; mem. Tech. Chamber of Greece, Sigma Xi, Tau Beta Pi. Author: Aseismic Construction—Design, Erection, 1956. Home: 3380 Stephenson Pl NW Washington DC 20015 Office: Cath U Washington DC 20017

SOTTILE, JAMES III, mining co. pres.; b. Miami, Fla., Aug. 3, 1940; s. James and Ethel (Hooks) S.; B.S. cum laude, U. Fla., 1962; m. Judith Horne, Dec. 5, 1959; children—James IV, Michael, Scott, Thomas, Jennifer. Vice pres. Goldfield Corp., Melbourne, Fla., 1970-71, pres., dir., 1971—; dir. Treasure Salvors, Key West, Fla. Vice pres., dir. Canaveral Indian River Groves, Inc., Micco, Fla., 1964-70, Brevard-Indian River Groves, Inc., Micco, 1964-69, Indian River Shores Groves, Inc., 1964; pres., dir. Indian Mound Corp., Micco, 1963-69, Original 51 Corp., Micco, 1966-69; v.p. Lake Byrd Citrus Packings Co., Micco, 1963-71, pres., 1971—, also dir.; v.p. Indian River Orange Groves, Inc., Micco, 1963-69, pres., 1969—, also dir.; pres., dir. Citrus Growers Fla., Inc., Micco, 1970—; v.p., dir. No. Goldfield Investments Inc., Ltd., Melbourne, Fla., 1971—, Mamba Engring Co., Inc., Titusville, Fla., 1972—; pres. dir. Black Range Mining Corp., Albuquerque, 1972—, San Pedro Mining Corp., Albuquerque, 1972—, Goldfield Consol. Mines Co., Albuquerque, 1972—; v.p., dir. Valencia Center, Inc., Coral Gables, Fla., 1964—. Supr., sec. San Sebastian Draignage Dist., Melbourne, 1965—. Mem. Fla. C. of C. (dir. 1972). Democrat. Roman Catholic. Clubs: Eau Gallie Yacht, Port Malabar Country (Melbourne). Home: 846 Malibu Lane Indialantic FL 32903 Office: 65 E NASA Blvd Melbourne FL 32901

SOULE, GEORGE, coll. pres.; b. New Orleans, Nov. 24, 1896; s. Albert Lee and Anna Sophronia (Cooper) S.; student Isadore Newman Sch., Georgia Mil. Acad., Soule Coll., La. State U.; m. Mary Brooks Ragland, Feb. 21, 1922; children—George, Evan R., Mary Brooks. Clk. and asst. instr. Soule Coll., 1919, successively tchr., asst. treas., treas. (1926), sec. and mgr. in charge adminstrn., 1929—, partner firm A. L., E. E. and George Soule, owners of Soule Coll., Inc., 1936-48, pres., 1948—; past v.p. Am. Empire Ins. Co.; dir. Union Savs. & Loan Assn.; dir., past v.p. Bur. Govtl. Research New Orleans. Past pres. New Orleans chpt. Nat. Officers Mgmt. Assn.; past bd. dirs. Magnolia Sch. for Exceptional Children, pres., 1945, 46; chmn. campaign execs. com., United Community and War Chest, 1945; past pres. New Orleans Community Chest; chmn. New Orleans Ednl. Found; past vice chmn. City Planning and Zoning Commn. New Orleans; organizer, exec. officer New Orleans regiment U.S. Coast Guard Vol. Port Security Force, World War II. Campaign vice chmn. United Fund, 1952. La. elector at large on George Wallace Presdl. ticket, 1968. Served to 2d lt. F.A., U.S. Army, 1917-18. Recipient Americanism award Am. Legion, 1960. Mem. New Orleans C. of C., Young Men's Bus. Club. Discussions Unltd. (hon. life), Soc. War 1812 (historian La.). Episcopalian (sr. warden; pres. St. Thomas). Clubs: Gyro of New Orleans (past pres., past dist. gov.), New Orleans Executive of La. (pres. 2 terms, hon. life), Juanita, Boston, Pendennis (past pres.) (New Orleans). Home: 4825 Carondelet St New Orleans LA 70115 Office: 1410 Jackson Av New Orleans LA 70130 also PO Box 53306 New Orleans LA 70153

SOULEN, ROBERT LEWIS, educator; b. Chgo., Jan. 19, 1932; s. Harold Lewis and Martha Elizabeth (Nevins) S.; A.B., Baker U., 1954; Ph.D., Kan. State U., 1960; m. Lola Lee Hendrickson, Oct. 9, 1954; children—Karin E., Stephen L., Julia K. Sr. research chemist Jefferson Chem. Co., Austin, Tex., 1960-64; Lillian Nelson Pratt prof. chemistry Southwestern U., Georgetown, Tex., 1964—. Dir. classical music program radio sta. KGTN, Georgetown, Tex., 1972—; cons. Diamond Shamrock Corp., 1971—. Mem. Georgetown Housing Authority, 1968-71, chmn., 1970-71. Chmn. bd. Williamson Land Devel. Corp., 1972—. Served with AUS, 1954-56. NSF grantee, 1965, Robert A. Welch grantee, 1966-72; Dow fellow, 1958-60; recipient Phi Lambda Upsilon scholarship award, 1958, Bausch Lomb award, 1950. Mem. Am. Chem. Soc. (chmn. elect Central Tex. sect. 1973), A.A.A.S., Am. Assn. U. Profs., Tex. Acad. Sci., Sigma Xi, Phi Lambda Upsilon. Methodist. Lion (rep. Tokyo Conv. 1969). Patentee in field. Home: 1501 Olive St Georgetown TX 78626 Office: Dept Chemistry Southwestern Univ Georgetown TX 78626

SOULES, LUTHER HUGH, JR., food brokerage co. pres.; b. nr. San Antonio, Aug. 11, 1915; s. Luther Hugh and Frances Blanche (Harper) S.; student Draughon's Comml. Coll., 1932-34; m. Bessie Merle Myers, June 12, 1937; children—Luther Hugh III, Barbara (Mrs. James B. Young), Joe Carlton. Bookkeeper, Bruner Brothers & Runnels, Mineola, Tex., 1933-37; office mgr. Van Winkle Motor Co., Dallas, 1937-43; SW regional mgr. Canada Dry Ginger Ale, Inc., Dallas, 1943-58; v.p. Great Western Foods Co., Fort Worth, 1958-62; pres., owner Luke Soules Inc. food broker, San Antonio, Tex., 1962—. Mem. San Antonio Sales and Marketing Execs. (v.p. 1967-69; dir. 1967-73), Soc. Mayflower Decs., Sons Republic Tex., S.A.R. Rotarian. Presbyn. Home: 511 Larkwood St San Antonio TX 78209 Office: 98 Brees Blvd San Antonio TX 78209

SOUTHARD, SAMUEL, mental health inst. exec.; b. Lincolnton, N.C., Feb. 10, 1925; s. Samuel and Stella (Miller) S.; A.B., George Washington U., 1948; B.D., So. Bapt. Theol. Sem., 1951, Th.D., 1954; m. Frances Allen, May 6, 1950; children—Pamela, Melanie. Ordained to ministry Bapt. Ch., 1950; pastor, Ft. Mitchell Bapt. Ch., 1954; prof. Inst. Religion, Tex. Med. Center, 1955-58; prof. pastoral care So. Bapt. Theol. Sem., 1958-66; dir. research Presbyn. Ch. U.S., 1966-69; dir. profl. services Ga. Mental Health Inst., Atlanta, 1969-72, dep. supt. manpower and tng. 1973—. Dir. Lilly Endowment Conf. on Motiviation for Ministry, 1958; chmn. standards and constitution So. Bapt. Assn. on Clin. Pastoral Edn., 1957; dir., lectr. E. Asia Conf. on Marriage and Family Counseling, Bangkok, 1968; mem. Assn. Theol. Schs. Com. on Clin. Pastoral Edn., 1960-66; mem. editorial com. Research on Religious Devel., 1966-69. Served with AUS, 1943-46. Author: Family and Mental Illness, 1957; Counseling for Church Vocations, 1957; Pastoral Evangelism, 1962; Religion and Nursing, 1959; Pastoral Authority in Personal Relationships, 1969; Christians and Mental Health, 1972; Family Counseling in East Asia, 1969; Every Child Has Two Fathers, 1971; People Need People, 1972; Anger in Love, 1973; Like the One You Love, 1974; Your Guide to Group Experience, 1974. Home: 2588 Grand Prix Ct NE Atlanta GA 30345 Office: 1256 Briarcliff Rd NE Atlanta GA 30306

SOUTHER, ROY HOBART, water pollution research cons.; b. nr. Elkin, N.C., July 25, 1897; s. William A. and Fannie (Norman) S.; B.S. in Chem. Engring. and Chemistry, U. N.C., 1920, postgrad., 1941-42, 44, 56. With Cone Mills Corp., Greensboro, N.C., 1920-59, research dir., 1944-59; sci. and engring. research cons. in water conservation, Greensboro, 1960—. Mem. adv. bd. Inst. Textile Tech., Charlottesville, Va., 1948-51, Textile Research Inst., Princeton, N.J., 1957-60; chmn. chem. processing industries task group Nat. Tech. Task Com. on Indsl. Waste, USPHS, 1960—. A founder, sec.-treas. Greensboro Evening Coll., 1947-53; mem. adv. bd. Greensboro div. Guilford Coll., 1947-70, bd. visitors, 1970—; recipient Coll.

Adminstrn. award, 1960; mem. N.C. adv. com. on sci., engring. and specialized personnel SSS, 1957-71. Precinct chmn. Democratic party Guilford County, N.C., 1940-52. Mem. Am. Assn. Textile Chemists and Colorists (chmn. nat. com. on stream sanitation tech. 1962-64), Water Pollution Control Fedn. (Indsl. Waste medal 1959), Am. Chem. Soc., Am. Soc. Quality Control, N.C. Acad. Sci., Greensboro C. of C., U. N.C. Alumni Assn. (pres. Greensboro chpt. 1949-50), Textile Quality Control Assn. (founding mem.), Civitan Internat., Toastmasters (N.C. Community Service award 1971), Phi Beta Kappa, Alpha Chi Sigma. Presbyn. Mason. Club: Greensboro Writers. Contbr. articles on research in water conservation, pollution abatement, statis. quality control and textile processing to profl. jours., chpts. to books. Developer indsl. waste-water control system used by world-wide industries, municipalities. Home: 3116 Summit Av Greensboro NC 27405 Office: 3116 Summit Av Greensboro NC 27405

SOUTHERN, DONN ALAN, lawyer; b. Knoxville, Tenn., Feb. 4, 1934; s. Martin Holmes and Mary (Bowling) S.; B.A., U. Tenn., 1955; J.D., 1957; m. Faye MacGregor, June 21, 1962; children—Pamela Gaye, Todd Fuller. Admitted to Tenn. bar, 1957; mem. firm Quick, Buchignani & Greener, Memphis, 1958-63; partner Buchignani, Greener & Southern, 1963-65, Bruce & Southern, 1965-72, Bruce, Southern, Perkins & Johnson, 1972—. Tchr. real estate courses Practicing Law Inst., N.Y.C., 1972. Chmn. Memphis Air Pollution Control Hearing Bd., 1969-72; chmn. Memphis and Shelby County Air Pollution Control Hearing Bd., 1972—. Served with AUS, 1957-58; now maj. Res. Mem. Am., Tenn., Memphis-Shelby County (dir. 1970-73, mem. exec. com. 1973), Memphis bar assns., Order of the Coif, Kappa Sigma, Phi Delta Phi. Presbyn. (ruling elder 1972—). Club: Chickasaw Country. Home: 218 Colonial Rd Memphis TN 38117 Office: 3201 100th St N Main Bldg Memphis TN 38103

SOUTHERN, THOMAS MARTIN, chemist; b. Beaumont, Tex., June 19, 1942; s. Haskell Larry and Earline (Shaw) S.; B.S., Lamar U., 1960-64; M.S., Tex. Tech. U., 1966; Ph.D., U. Houston, 1969; m. Barbara Marie Lewis, June 4, 1966; children—Michelle Lea, John Wesley. Chemist, Tex. Eastman Co., Longview, 1969—. Partner, East Tex. Graphics, Longview, 1970-73. Mem. Am. Chem. Soc. Home: 2207 Paul St Longview TX 75601 Office: PO Box 7444 Longview TX 78601

SOUTHEY, DAVID LUDGATE, architect; b. Bridgeport, Conn., Aug. 17, 1911; s. Ernest Guy and Lena Frances (Dean) S.; B.Arch., U. Pa., 1936; m. Ann Kathleen Robertson, June 20, 1945. Partner E.G. Southey, Bridgeport, 1936-41; prin. David L. Southey, Bridgeport, 1947-52; architect, bur. medicine and surgery Dept. Navy, Washington, 1951—. Served to lt. comdr. USNR, 1943-46. Recipient Meritorious Civilian Service award Navy Dept., 1965, Superior Civilian Service award, 1968, Outstanding Performance awards, 1964, 65, 66, 67, 70. Mem. A.I.A., Conn. Soc. Architects, Archtl. Assn. London, Am. Hosp. Assn., Ret. Officers Assn., Res. Officers Assn. U.S., Alpha Tau Omega. Club: Brooklawn Country (Fairfield, Conn.). Home: 2801 Quebec St NW Washington DC 20008 Office: Bur Medicine and Surgery Navy Dept 23d and E Sts NW Washington DC 20390

SOVDE, ROGER LINTON, newspaper exec.; b. Archie Henry and Esther (Zelke) S.; student Minn. Sch. Bus., 1954; m. Joy Dorothy Eberspacher, Apr. 30, 1955; children—David Arthur, Jon Hugh, Steven Craig, Susan Carol. Vice pres. Richardson-Sovde Co., Inc., Mpls., 1954-62; salesman Twin City Lino, Inc., Mpls., 1962; asst. to pub. Mankato Free Press (Minn.), 1962-67; gen. mgr. Evening Herald, Rock Hill, S.C., 1967—, asst. pub., 1970—; sec. Herald Pub. Co., Rock Hill; dir. Pat-Print, Inc. Mem. adv. com. Mankato Bd. Edn., 1965; mem. All Am. Cities Com., Rock Hill, 1967. Editor city newspaper Republican Party, Bloomington, Minn., 1961, city vice chmn., 1962. Chmn. Rock Hill Better Bus. Bur. Com, 1969. Bd. dirs. York County unit Am. Cancer Soc., 1972—; mem. adv. com. Community Pre-release Center, Rock Hill, 1972—; trustee Friendship Jr. Coll., 1974. Served with USNR, 1951-54. Mem. Rock Hill C. of C. (chmn. retail task force com. 1970). Home: 2386 Ferncliff Rock Hill SC 29730 Office: 132 W Main St Rock Hill SC 29730

SOWA, EVA INGERSOLL LONG (MRS. WALTER D. SOWA), social worker; b. Birmingham, Ala., Sept. 4, 1910; d. John Hamner and Fannie (Ingersoll) Long; B.A., U. Pitts., 1930, M.A., 1933; M.S. in Social Service Adminstrn., 1941; m. Walter D. Sowa, Apr. 4, 1942; children—Peter William, Thomas Michael. Tchr., Bentleyville (Pa.) High Sch., 1930-32; social worker Allegheny County (Pa.) Emergency Relief Bd., Pitts., 1934-36, Mothers' Assistance, Old Age Pension, Blind Pension, Pitts., 1936-38, Travelers Aid Soc., Pitts., 1938-40; probation officer Allegheny County Juvenile Ct. Pitts., 1940-43; case worker Childrens Aid Soc., Birmingham, 1960-67; supr. Travelers Aid Soc., Birmingham, 1967—. Active P.T.A. Mem. Nat. Assn. Social Workers, Acad. Certified Social Workers, Sigma Kappa Phi, Pi Lambda Theta. Club: Social Workers. Home: 2121 16th Av S Birmingham AL 35205 Office: 3600 8th Av S Birmingham AL 35222

SOWA, WALTER D., educator, lawyer; b. McKeesport, Pa., Jan. 17, 1907; s. Peter and Anna (Jankowska) S.; A.B., U. Pitts., 1928, Litt.M., 1940; J.D., Duquesne U., 1933; m. Eva Ingersoll Long, Apr. 4, 1942; children—Peter William, Thomas Michael. Tchr. elementary sch., Alliquippa, Pa., 1928-30, high sch., Pa., 1930-42; probation officer Juvenile Ct., Allegheny County, Pa., 1940-41; joined U.S. Army, 1942, advanced through grades to lt. col., 1962; acad. coordinator Baylor U., 1943-44, Tex. A. and M. Coll., 1944-46; judge adv. Korea Base Command, 1946-48; at Pa. State Coll., 1948-50; asst. judge adv. X Corps, Korea, 1950-51; sec. gen. staff X Corps, 1951-52; chief contracting div. Hdqrs. 3d Army, 1952-56; legal assistance adviser, 1956-60; trial observer-lawyer, 1960-62, ret., 1962; prof. criminal law Cumberland Law Sch. Howard Coll., Birmingham, Ala., 1963—; prof. criminal law and evidence Samford U., Birmingham, 1963—. Decorated Bronze Star. Mem. Am., Ga., Ala. bar assns., Pa. Edn. Assn. Methodist. Mason. Home: 2121 16th Av S Birmingham AL 35205

SOWDER, WILSON THOMAS, state health ofcl.; b. Callaway, Va., 1910; M.D., U. Va., 1932; M.P.H., Johns Hopkins, 1939. Intern U. Ia. Hosps., 1932-33; asst. resident physician St. Luke Hosp., San Francisco, 1933-34; practice medicine specializing in preventive medicine and pub. health; mem. staff USPHS Hosps., 1934-38; state health officer Fla. Div. Health (formerly Fla. Bd. Health), Jacksonville, 1945-61, 63-69, dir. div. health Dept. Health and Rehab. Services, 1969—; chief office aging USPHS, 1961-62. Diplomate Am. Bd. Preventive Medicine and Rehab. Fellow Am. Pub. Health Assn.; mem. A.M.A. Office: PO Box 210 Jacksonville FL 32201

SOWELL, KATYE MARIE OLIVER (MRS. JESSE CLARENCE SOWELL), educator; b. Winston-Salem, N.C., Apr. 6, 1934; d. William Manton and Katye (Price) Oliver, Sr.; B.A., Flora Macdonald Coll., 1956; M.S., U. S.C., 1958; postgrad. U. So. Miss., 1961-62; Ph.D., Fla. State U., 1965; m. Jesse Clarence Sowell, Sept. 7, 1957 (dec. Feb. 1961); 1 son, David Clarence. Instr. Flora Macdonald Coll., Red Springs, N.C., 1958; asst. prof. Elon (N.C.) Coll., 1958-60; instr. U. So. Miss., Hattiesburg, 1960-63, Fla. State U., Tallahassee, 1965; faculty East Carolina U., Greenville, N.C., 1965—, asst. prof. math., 1965-67, asso. prof. math., 1967-72, prof., 1972— supr. student teaching math., 1966—, dir. NSF Inst. for Secondary Tchrs. Math., 1968-69, NSF Inst. for Jr. High Sch. Tchrs. Math., 1970-71, 72-73. Lectr., cons. Mem. Math. Adv. Council N.C. Dept. Pub. Instrn., 1970—. Mem. Math. Assn. Am., Am. Math. Soc., Nat. Council Tchrs. Math., N.C. Council Tchrs. Math. (pres. Eastern region 1971-73), Am. Assn. U. Profs., N.C. Assn. Educators, Pi Mu Epsilon. Democrat. Presbyn. Home: 103 Garrett St Greenville NC 27834

SOWELL, W. R., (BILL), aviation co. exec.; b. Chipley, Fla., Nov. 8, 1920; s. Claude Tee and Eunice (Richardson) S.; student Centenary Coll., 1940-42; grad. Norton Bus. Coll., Shreveport, La., 1942; m. Nadine Martin, Sept. 1942 (div. Feb. 1971); children—J. Donald, Dorris Diane (Mrs. Diane Sowell Ansley), Deborah K., Sheri Denise. Owner, pres. Panama Airways, Inc., Panama City, Fla., 1946-53; pilot instr., flying supr. So. Airways, Bainbridge, Ga., 1950-53; founder, owner, pres., pilot, instr. Sowell Aviation Co., Inc., Panama City, 1954—; chmn. bd. Sowell Aircraft Service, Inc., Panama City, 1964—; founder, pres., owner Pensacola Aviation Inc., Pensacola, Fla., 1964-72; pres., co-owner Sowell Rent-A-Car, Inc., Panama City. Airplane and instrument pilot examiner FAA, 1946—; mem. Panama City Airport Bd., 1959-61, chmn., 1959-61; mem. Fla. Gov.'s Aviation Com., 1972—. Served with AC, AUS, 1940-45. Mem. Nat. Aviation Trades Assn., Airplane Owners and Pilots Assn., Quiet Birdmen, Fla. Aviation Trades Assn. (pres. 1970-72, dir.), Bay County C. of C. (dir. 1956-66, chmn. aviation com. 1962-63). Baptist. Rotarian, Mason (Shriner), Elk. Club: St. Andrew Bay Yacht. Home: 213 Wilson Av Panama City FL 32401 Office: Panama City Bay County Municpal Airport Panama City FL 32401

SOWELL, WENDELL LORAINE, educator; b. Pemberton, W.Va., Aug. 17, 1917; s. Larkin Andrew and Sallie Lee (Brewer) S.; B.S., Auburn U., 1947, M.S., 1955; LL.B., Jones Law Sch., 1960; Ph.D. in Preventive Medicine, U. Okla., 1967; m. Alva Loree Webb, July 7, 1936; children—Bashaba (Mrs. Joseph Thomas Gibbons), Wendell Loraine, Darrell B. Toxicologist Ala. Dept. Toxicology and Criminal Investigation, Auburn, 1947-60; dir., establisher Crime Lab., Ft. Worth, 1960-65; asst. supt., dir. crime lab. Bur. Criminal Identification and Investigation, State Ohio, London, 1968; asso. prof. biol. scis. Livingston (Ala.) U., 1968-71; asso. prof. Sch. Law Enforcement, Jacksonville, State U., 1971—. Pres. Sowell Realty, Inc., Birmingham and Jacksonville, Ala., 1972—; tchr. real estate Gadsden (Ala.) State Jr. Coll., 1973; dir. N.E. Ala. Police Acad., Jacksonville, Ala., 1972. Served with U.S. Army, 1942-44. NIH trainee environmental health, U. Okla., 1965-67. Mem. Am. Chem. Soc., Soc. Applied Spectroscopy, Forensic Sci. Soc., Internat. Assn. Forensic Toxicologists, Am. Acad. Forensic Scis., Ala. Peace Officers Assn., Gamma Sigma Delta, Sigma Delta Kappa. Baptist. Author; (with Robert A. Wilson) Institute on Homicide Investigation Techniques, 1961. Home: 328 5th Av Jacksonville AL 36265 Office: School Law Enforcement Jacksonville State Univ Jacksonville AL 36265

SOWER, FRANK WILLIAM, retail trade co. exec., city ofcl.; b. Frankfort, Ky., Dec. 10, 1910; s. John Rodman and Rose Elma (Edwards) S.; B.S., Northwestern U., 1933; m. Minnie Lynn Evans, Aug. 22, 1937; children—Frank William, Lynn (Mrs. Michael E. Bufkin), John. Owner Sower Hardware, Frankfort, 1937-59, Sower Office Equipment, Frankfort, 1940—; mayor of Frankfort, 1968-72; dir. Farmers Bank & Capital Trust Co. of Frankfort. Mem. Capital Planning and Zoning Commn., 1950-59. Mem. adv. bd. Kings Daus. Hosp. Served to lt. USNR, 1944-46. Mem. Ky. Retail Hardward Assn. (pres. 1957), Capital City Softball Assn. (pres. 1952), Ky. Hist. Soc. (pres. 1966-68), S.A.R., Ky. Civil War Round Table, Am. Legion, V.F.W., C. of C. (pres. 1947), Sigma Nu. Democrat. Roman Catholic (mission committeeman 1961-62). Rotarian (pres. 1958). Home: 112 Wilkinson St Frankfort KY 40601 Office: 217 St Clair St Frankfort KY 40601

SOWERS, WADE ANDREW, dentist; b. nr. Lexington, N.C., Apr. 29, 1899; s. Luther Columbus and Fannie Florence (Long) S.; B.A., Wake Forest Coll., 1921; M.A., Lincoln Meml. U., 1923; D.D.S., Med. Coll. Va., 1924; m. Lena Maye Beck, Aug. 26, 1924; 1 son, Wade Philip. Asst. prin., then prin. Liberty-Piedmont Inst., 1921-24; prin. Arcadia High sch., 1925, Mineral Springs High Sch., Forsyth County, N.C., 1925-27; practice dentistry, Lexington, 1921—. Pres., organizer, trustee Daniel Boone Meml. Park, 1957. Mem. Pierre Fauchard Acad., Acad. Internat. Medicine and Dentistry, N.C., Davidson County dental socs., Am. Dental Assn., Davidson County Hist. Soc., Second Dist. Dental Soc. (pres. 1952). Mason. Home: Route 5 Lexington NC 27292 Office: Courthouse Sq Lexington NC 27292

SPACH, JOHN THOM, editor; b. Winston-Salem, N.C., Mar. 5, 1928; s. William Mathias and Evelyn Alexander (Thom) S.; student U.S. Mil. Acad., 1947-49; A.B., Duke, 1955. Rep. field advt. Proctor & Gamble, Santa Monica, Cal., 1955-57; supr. Cal. Test Bur., Hollywood, 1957-59; asso. editor Furniture South, High Point, N.C., 1959-61; sales rep. Aldrman Studios, High Point, N.C., 1961-67, Newsfoto Pub. Co., San Angelo, Tex., 1968-71; mng. editor Sports Digest N.C., Winston-Salem, 1972—. Served with CIC, AUS, 1951-53. Recipient Founders award N.C. Heart Assn., 1964. Mem. United Comml. Travelers, Travelers Protective Assn., N.C. Writers Assn., Wachovia Hist. Assn. Clubs: Twin City, Forsyth Country (Winston-Salem). Author: Time Out From Texas, 1969. Office: PO Box 2996 Winston-Salem NC 27102

SPADARO, JAMES JOSEPH, food scientist, govt. ofcl.; b. Albany, N.Y., Apr. 26, 1915; s. Samuel and Mary (Pagano) S.; B.S., N.Y. State Coll. Forestry, 1940; m. Catherine Virginia Corte, June 10, 1948; children—Mary (Mrs. Charles H. Miller), James, Nancy, Cathy, Jean. Tech. asst. Am. Writing Paper Corp., Holyoke, Mass., 1940-42; research leader So. Regional Research Center, U.S. Dept. Agr., New Orleans, 1942—. Recipient awards U.S. Dept. Agr., 1956, 58, 63. Mem. Inst. Food Tech. (chmn. 1971), Am. Oil Chemists Soc., Research Soc., Am., Am. Peanut and Edn. Asso., Am. Assn. Cereal Chemists, Fed. Bus. Assn., Toastmasters Internat. (Toastmaster of Year award 1960, pres. local 1966-67). Author numerous articles on chemistry of foods, comml. food processes. Patentee in field. Home: 1455 Gardena Dr New Orleans LA 70122 Office: 1100 Robert E Lee Blvd New Orleans LA 70179

SPAIN, ELMER LEE, clay co. exec.; b. Tulsa, Aug. 12, 1922; s. Leslie L. and Cleola May (Lindsay) S.; M.E., Okla. State U., 1948; B.S., Tulsa U., 1950; m. Wanda J. Brooks, Apr. 12, 1947; children—Leslie, Denzil, Kathryn. Sales mgr. Sapulpa Brick & Tile Co. (Okla.), 1950-56; editor Brick and Clay Record mag., Chgo., 1956-59; sales mgr. Chambers Bros. Co. mfg., Phila., 1960-66; mgr. Bell Clay Co., Gleason, Tenn., 1967—. Vice pres., dir. Bell Research, Inc., Chester, W.Va., 1967—. Served with Air Corp, AUS, 1942-46. Mem. Am. Ceramic Soc., Pi Tau Sigma. Mason. Home: 16 Hillcrest Dr Paris TN 38242 Office: Box 151 Gleason TN 38229

SPALDING, BILLUPS PHINIZY, educator; b. Atlanta, Sept. 29, 1930; s. Hughes and Bolling (Phinizy) S.; A.B., U. Ga., 1953, M.A., 1957; Ph.D., U. N.C., 1963; m. Margaret Anne Roscoe, Aug. 18, 1969; children—Billups Phinizy, David Bushrod. Asst. prof. history Coll. Charleston (S.C.), 1963-66; asso. prof. U. Ga., Athens, 1966—. Chmn., Ferdinand Phinizy Lectureship Com. Bd. sponsors Atlanta Symphony Orch.; trustee Athens-Clarke Heritage Found.; bd. dirs. U. Ga. Found. Served with USNR, 1953-55. Mem. S.C., Ga. (curator 1968—), Athens (pres. 1970) hist. socs., Ga. Conservancy, Nat. Trust, Am. Assn. U. Profs., Gridiron Secret Soc., Nine O'Clocks, So. Hist. Assn., Kappa Alpha. Democrat. Clubs: Le Petite Francais (London); Piedmont Driving (Atlanta); Athens. Editor: Ga. Hist. Quar. Home: 573 Hill St Athens GA 30601

SPALDING, HENRY A., mining engr.; b. Ky., Mar. 20, 1899; s. J.D. and Alice (Estes) S.; studied under personal tutors; m. Gertrude Petrey, Feb. 8, 1923; children—Jack P. (dec.), Richard D. Gen., widely diversified engring. practice; inventor metall. processes; pres. H.A. Spalding, Inc.; mgr., part owner Old Va. Land Co. Recipient Outstanding Citizen award Hazard (Ky.) civic clubs, 1958. Registered profl. engr. Mem. Am. Soc. C.E., Am. Inst. Mining Metall. and Petroleum Engrs. (Legion of honor), Ky., Soc. Profl. Engrs. (pres. 1949-50, hon.), Ky. Acad. Sci., Appalachian Geol. Soc., Ky. Hist. Soc., Nat. Rifle Assn. (exec. com., dir.). Club: Filson. Co-author: Engineers Vest Pocket Book. Contbr. articles to profl. jours. Home: Broadway Hazard KY 41701 Office: Baker Bldg Hazard Ky also 1928 Connecticut Av NW Washington DC 20009

SPALDING, HENRY CANNON, JR., investment banking firm exec.; b. Richmond, Va., July 5, 1938; s. Henry Cannon and Sue Metcalf (Sharp) S.; B.A., Hampden-Sydney Coll., 1960; postgrad. U. Pa., 1970-72; m. Kaye Culver Brinkley, Aug. 5, 1961; children—Mary Parke, Henry Cannon III, Maria Blair. Asst. trust officer United Va. Bank State-Planters, 1960-66; gen. partner Scott & Stringfellow, Richmond, Va., 1968—; dir. Investors Savs. & Loan Assn. Mem. Am. Philatelic Soc., Am., N.Y. stock exchanges. Richmond Soc. Financial Analysts, Hampden-Sydney Alumni Assn. (pres. 1971-72). Episcopalian. Clubs: Commonwealth, Country (Richmond). Home: 204 Hillwood Av Richmond VA 23226 Office: PO Box 1575 Richmond VA 23213

SPALDING, HUGH C., supt. schs.; b. Raywick, Ky., Aug. 13, 1912; s. Thomas Elder and Elizabeth (Mattingly) S.; A.B., Western Ky. State Coll., 1935; M.A., U. Ky., 1949; m. Bernadette Hill, June 12, 1942; children—Sarah, Elizabeth, Catherine, Rose, Hugh. Tchr. schs., Marion County, Lebanon, Ky., 1931-36, supr., 1936-38; supt. Marion County Schs., Lebanon, 1938—. Served with AUS, 1942-46. Mem. Nat., Ky. edn. assns., Am. Legion. Roman Catholic. K.C. Home: 335 Spalding Av Lebanon KY 40033 Office: 344 Spalding Av Lebanon KY 40033

SPALDING, JOHN FRANKLIN, physicist; b. Aug. 4, 1926; s. John F. and Anne (Harvey) S.; B.S., Mich. State U., 1951; student U. Chgo., 1946-49; postgrad. U. Cal., 1953-55; m. Jean Jackson, May 29, 1952; children—Katherine, Nancy, Nicholas, Kenneth. Jr. optician Lick Obs., Mt. Hamilton, Cal., 1951-53; engr. Gen. Electric Co., gen. engring. lab., Schenectady, 1955-64; physicist Perkin-Elmer Co., Wilton, Conn., 1964-67; optical physicist Range Measurements Lab., Eastern Test Range USAF, Patrick AFB, Fla., 1968-72, chmn. com. optical drawing standards, 1971; mgr. GEOSC, Inc., 1973—. Instr. Mohawk Valley Tech. Inst., evenings and adult edn., 1956-57; G.E. Co., adult edn. courses, 1959-64. Served with inf. AUS, 1944-46. Recipient Outstanding Performance award USAF, 1971. Fellow A.A.A.S.; mem. Soc. Photog. Instrumentation Engrs., Am. Astron. Soc., Sigma Pi Sigma, Alpha Delta Phi. Presbyn. (deacon 1970, elder 1973). Pioneer in application image orthicons to astronomy, 1962. Home: PO Box 303 Melbourne Beach FL 32951

SPALDING, LESTER HELM, lawyer; b. Lebanon, Ky., June 16, 1920; s. Bennie Grant and Hazel (Helm) S.; A.B., Western Ky. State Coll., 1941; J.D., U. Louisville, 1948; m. Nell Terry, Sept. 12, 1942; children—Larry Helm, Susan Terry, Steven Lynn. Tchr., Phillipsburg (Ky.) Graded Sch., 1941-42; admitted to Ky. bar, 1948; practiced in Lebanon, 1948-51, 53—; atty. Marion County Bd. Edn., 1957—; city atty., Lebanon, 1956-58; commonwealth's atty. 11th jud. dist., Marion, Washington, Green, Taylor counties, 1958—; pres. Masonic Temple Co., 1957—; dir. Marion Nat. Bank. Mem. Lincoln Trail Crime Commn., 1969—. Bd. dirs. Marion County Pub. Library. Served to 1st lt. USAAF, 1942-46; from capt. to maj., 1951-53; now maj. USAF Res. Mem. Ky. (pres. 1972—), Marion County, Lebanon bar assns., Am. Legion (comdr. 1954-55), V.F.W. (dept. staff judge adv. 1955-58), Ky. Hist. Soc., Phi Alpha Delta, Omicron Delta Kappa. Methodist (steward, mem. finance com.; dist. lay speaker). Kiwanian (v.p. 1956). Home: Park Heights Lebanon KY 40033 Office: 7 Court Sq Lebanon KY 40033

SPALDING, RICHARD LEROY, hosp. adminstr.; b. LaGrange, Mo., Apr. 18, 1936; s. Edward William and Thelma (Keith) S.; student Culver-Stockton Coll., 1955-56, Hardin-Simmons U., 1964, Columbia 1965; m. Beulah Kaye Barrigar, June 3, 1956; children—Kathleen J., Richard L., John E. Announcer, account exec. radio sta. WCAZ, Carthage, Ill., 1954-58; exec. v.p. Circle-S, Inc., Eastland, Tex., 1959-61; adminstr. Eastland (Tex.) Meml. Hosp., 1961-62; adminstrv. asst. Hendrick Meml. Hosp., Abilene, Tex., 1962-66; exec. dir. Meml. Hosp., Denison, Tex., 1966-73; sr. v.p. Hendrick Med. Complex, Abilene, 1973—; instr. Grayson Coll. Pres., North Grayson unit Am. Cancer Soc., 1968-69, Denison Concert Assn., 1969-70; chmn. community relations Profile for Ednl. Progress Denison Pub. Schs., 1968-69; chmn. Texoma Area Health Services Planning Council, 1969-73; mem. Gov.'s Conf. Health Care Costs. Bd. dirs. Abilene Philharmonic Assn., Abilene Community Theatre. Recipient Winner-Speak Up Jr. C. of C. award, 1963. Mem. Tex. Hosp. Assn. (chmn. council pub. edn. 1969—, chmn. Blacklands div. 1969-70), Am. Coll. Hosp. Adminstrs. Baptist. Mason. Home: 1850 Elmwood Dr Abilene TX 79605 Office: PO Box 88 Abilene TX 79604

SPALDING, ROSS DEAN, elec. engr.; b. Puyallup, Wash., Mar. 27, 1927; s. Ralph Carter and Viola Ester (Yeager) S.; student Coll. Puget Sound, 1946-48; B.S., Wash. State U., 1951; m. Caroline Josephine Potter, Mar. 10, 1951; children—Patrice (Mrs. J.B. Davis), Celeste, Janice, Phillip. Test engr. Gen. Electric Co., Schenectady, 1951-52, systems application engr., 1952-59, product-bus. planner, Waynesboro, Va., 1959-61, numerical control instr., 1961—. Dir. Sweet Adeline Chorus, Waynesboro, 1963-71. Served with USNR, 1945-46. Registered profl. engr., N.Y., Va. Mem. I.E.E.E. (sr.), Soc. for Preservation and Encouragement of Barber Shop Quartet Singing in Am. (chorus dir. 1971-72). Club: Shenandoah Sport Parachute (Waynesboro). Home: PO Box 155 Stuarts Draft VA 24477 Office: General Electric Co ICPD Waynesboro VA 22980

SPALTEN, ROBERT GEORGE, dentist; b. San Antonio, Apr. 2, 1929; s. Edward Henry and Hilda Ann (Mueller) S.; student St. Mary's U., 1946-49, U. Tex., 1949-50; D.D.S., St. Louis U., 1954; m. Jacqueline Barbara Jacobson, Nov. 29, 1954; children—Robert George, Steven Joseph, Jill Marie, John Edwin. Individual dental practice, San Antonio, 1956—, also lectr. Bd. dirs. Ursline Acad., 1966-71. Served with USAF, 1954-56. Mem. Internat. Coll. Dentists, Am., Tex. dental assns., San Antonio Dist. Dental Soc. (dir. 1966-68), Southwestern Dental Assembly, Austin and San Antonio Dental Study Club. K.C., Kiwanian (dir. 1966-68). Contbr. articles to profl. jours. Home: 111 Wyndale St San Antonio TX 78209 Office: Milam Bldg San Antonio TX 78205

SPANGENBERG, THEODORE SANDERS, state ofcl.; b. Miami, Fla., Sept. 22, 1924; s. Carl Henry and Lily May (Pettyjohn) S.; B.C.E., U. Fla., 1951; m. Marion Averett Hawthrone, June 5, 1950; children—Mary Sandra, Theodore S., Mayrene Caryl, Marion Diane, Erin Lee. Engring. insp., engring. trainee, maintenance engr., asst. engr. Fla Rd. Dept., Chipley, 1951-61; dist. maintenance engr. Fla. Dept. Transp., 1962—. Dist. commr. Boy Scouts Am., 1965-67, asst. dist. commr., 1968-73, dist. chmn., 1973—. Served with AUS, 1944-46. Decorated Purple Heart. Registered profl. engr., surveyor, Fla. Fellow Fla. Engring. Soc.; mem. Nat. Soc. Profl. Engrs., Am. Civil Engring. Soc., Fla. Soc. Profl. Land Surveyors. Baptist (deacon). Home: PO Box 446 Chipley FL 32428 Office: PO Box 607 Chipley FL 32428

SPANGLER, CHARLES DAVID, project engr.; b. Chgo., Feb. 20, 1912; s. Charles H. and Addie E. (Evinger) S.; B.S. in Civil Engring, Ill. Inst. Tech., 1934; M.S. in Bacteriology, U. Ill., 1936; Ph.D. in Pub. Health, Yale, 1940; m. Hilda B. Hudgins, Nov. 12, 1937; children—Charles Thomas, Carol Patricia (Mrs. Joseph White), David Paul, John Jefferson. Research bacteriologist Proctor & Gamble Co., Chgo., 1935-36; engr. Ill. State Health Dept., Springfield, 1936-39, USPHS, various locations, 1941-69; with Pan Am. Health Orgn., Washington, 1965-68; engr. World Bank, Washington, 1969—. Served with AUS, 1942-52. Mem. Am. Acad. Environmental Engrs., Commd. Officers Assn. of USPHS. Home: 10212 Brookmoor Dr Silver Spring MD 20901 Office: 1818 H St NW Washington DC 20433

SPANGLER, GEORGE WESLEY, physicist, educator; b. Roanoke, Va., Oct. 20, 1928; s. Charles and Lola Bell (Amos) S.; B.A. in Physics, U. Chattanooga, 1957; certificate (U.S. A.E.C. fellow), U. Washington, 1959; Ph.D. (USPHS fellow), U. Cal. at Los Angeles, 1965; m. Lorrayne Bernice Brakhage, July 30, 1952; children—Karen Kae (Mrs. Ronald Herbert Blair), Nathan Joe, Kala Noelle, Chem. engr. Wallace and Tiernan Co., Inc., Newark, 1952-54; photographer Boyd & Ogden Agy., Chattanooga, 1954-57; research engr. Atomics Internat., Canoga Park, Cal., 1959-62; research dir. R.S. Landauer Jr. & Co., Matteson, Ill., 1962-63, research specialist, 1963-67; asso. prof. physics U. Tenn., Chattanooga, 1967—. Cons. in radiology and nuclear medicine Erlanger Hosp., Chattanooga, 1967—; lectr. U. Cal., Los Angeles, 1963-67, U.S. Dept. Def., Los Angeles, 1964-65, various civic and profl. orgns., 1952—. Mem. TV Panel programs for Adult Edn. Council, 1968-70. Bd. dirs. Project Vision, Chattanooga, 1972—. Served with USNR, 1948-52. Decorated Korean medal with two clusters. NSF grantee, 1969. Mem. Am. Phys. Soc., Am. Nuclear Soc., Health Physics Soc., Tenn. Acad. Sci., Sigma Xi, Sigma Pi Sigma, Pi Mu Epsilon. Home: 115 North Bragg Av Lookout Mountain TN 37350 Office: Univ of Tenn Chattanooga TN 37401

SPANN, RONALD DEVOYE, dentist; b. Little Rock, Oct. 25, 1942; s. Clyde DeVoye and Lera Lorece (James) S.; student State Coll. of Ark., 1960-63; D.D.S., U. Tenn., 1966; m. Nancy Smith, June 16, 1964; children—Shannon Paige, Ashli Tara. Dentist Memphis Pub. Health Dept., 1966; pvt. practice dentistry, Arkadelphia, Ark., 1968—; cons. Riverwood Nursing Home, 1968—. Served as capt. USAF, 1966-68. Mem. Ark. Football Ofcls. Assn., Am., Ark. Dental assns., C. of C., Ark. Alumni Assn., Sigma Tau Gamma (dir. 1970-71). Baptist. Rotatian, Kiwanian. Club: Arkadelphia Country (pres. 1971-72, dir.). Home: 104 Forrest Park Dr Arkadelphia AR 71923 Office: 3004 W Pine Rd Arkadelphia AR 71923

SPARKMAN, JOHN, U.S. senator; b. Morgan County, Ala., Dec. 20, 1899; s. Whitten J. and Julia Mitchell (Kent) S.; A.B., U. Ala., 1921, LL.B., 1923, A.M., 1924, LL.D., 1958; LL.D., Auburn U., Spring Hill Coll., Seoul Nat. U. (Korea); m. Ivo Hall, June 2, 1923; 1 dau., Julia (Mrs. Tazewell Shepard, Jr.). Admitted to Ala. bar, 1925; YMCA sec. U. Ala., 1923-25; instr. Huntsville Coll., 1925-28; practicing atty., Huntsville, Ala., 1925-37; U.S. commr., 1930-31; mem. 75th to 79th Congresses (1937-47), 8th Ala. Dist.; elected to U.S. Senate, Nov. 1946 to fill unexpired term late Senator John H. Bankhead, reelected for full terms, 1954, 60, 66, 72. U.S. del. UN, 1950-51, Japanese Peace Treaty Conf., 1951, signed for U.S.A. Democratic nominee v.p. U.S., 1952. Trustee Athens Coll., Am. U. Served S.A.T.C., 1918; col. U.S. Res. Corps. Mem. Am. Legion (past comdr.), Huntsville C. of C. (pres. 1935-36), Phi Beta Kappa, Pi Kappa Alpha, Phi Alpha Delta. Democrat. Methodist (dist. lay leader). Woodman, Kiwanian (ex-dist. gov.), Mason; mem. Eastern Star. Home: Huntsville AL 35801 also 4928 Indian Lane NW Washington DC 20016

SPARKMAN, ROBERT SATTERFIELD, surgeon, educator; b. Brownwood, Tex., Feb. 18, 1912; s. Ellis Hugh and Ola (Stanley) S.; B.A., also M.D., Baylor U., 1935; m. Willie Ford Bassett, Feb. 21, 1942. Intern, Cin. Gen. Hosp., 1935-36, resident in surgery, 1938-40; intern Good Samaritan Hosp., Lexington, Ky., 1936-37; resident in pathology Baylor Hosp., Dallas, 1937-38; practice medicine, specializing in surgery, Dallas, 1946—; chief dept. gen. surgery Baylor U. Med. Center, Dallas, 1969—; mem. staff Parkland Meml. Hosp., Dallas; clin. prof. surgery U. Tex. Southwestern Med. Sch., Dallas, 1963—; chief civilian surg. cons. 5th U.S. Army Area, 1950—, also cons. to surgeon gen. U.S. Army, 1950—. Mem. med. adv. council Dallas County Hosp. Dist., 1969—. Chmn. exec. com. Friends of Med. Library of U. Tex. Southwestern Med. Sch., 1964—. Bd. dirs. Friends of Dallas Pub. Library, Assos. of So. Meth. U. Libraries; trustee Dallas and Mae Smith Found., v.p., 1971—. Served from 1st lt. to col., M.C., AUS, 1940-46; PTO. Decorated Bronze Star. Diplomate Am. Bd. Surgery. Fellow A.C.S. (bd. govs. 1962-70); mem. Am., So. (v.p. 1959), Okla. (hon.) surg. assns., Tex. Surg. Soc. (pres. 1965), Dallas Gen. Surgeons Soc. (pres. 1961), Internat. Soc. Surgery, Dallas So. Clin. Soc., Dallas County Med. Soc., Tex. State Med. Assn., A.M.A., Soc. Med. Cons. to Armed Forces, James D. Rives Surg. Soc., John Shaw Billings History of Medicine Soc. (hon.), Soc. for Surgery Alimentary Tract, Société Internationale de Chirurgie, Alpha Omega Alpha. Club: Chaparral (Dallas). Editor, also prin. author: The Texas Surgical Society, The First Fifty Years, 1965; editor Minutes of the American Surgical Association 1880-1968, 1972. Contbr. numerous articles to sci. jours. Home: 5351 Wenonah St Dallas TX 75209 Office: 1004 N Washington St Dallas TX 75204

SPARKMAN, WENDELL BURL, san. engr.; b. Coleman, Tex., Mar. 21, 1913; s. William Burl and Beulah (Parker) S.; B.S. in Civil Engring., Tex. Technol. U., 1939; M.C.E., U. Okla., 1956; m. Lela Ruth Woolf, July 22, 1944; children—Mary Beth (Mrs. Donald Kennedy), John Wendell, Roy Burl. Office asst. Tex. Hwy. Dept., Sanderson, 1939; jr. hydraulic engr. U.S. Dept. Housing and Urban Devel., Houston, 1939-42, asst. hydraulic engr., 1942-48, asso. hydraulic engr., 1948-56, civil engr., 1956-58, san. engr., 1958-62, civil engr., 1962-67, san. engr., 1967—. Mem. Long Range Water Supply Com. Oklahoma City, 1953-54. Baptist (deacon 1959-64, 70—). Modern Woodman of Am. Home: 15419 W Hampton Circle Houston TX 77071 Office: 2 Greenway Plaza E Houston TX 77046

SPARKS, BRYAN, chemist; b. Shreveport, La., Sept. 25, 1937; s. Casper Bryan and Merrie Margret (Stowell) S.; B.S. cum laude, Centenary Coll., 1959; Ph.D. (NSF fellow), U. Ark., 1965; m. Bessie Ruth Risinger, Dec. 23, 1959; children—John Douglas, Stephanie Lyn. Chemist, N.Am. Rockwell, Tulsa, 1964-65, Borg-Warner Corp., Washington, W.Va., 1965-68, Ethyl Corp., Baton Rouge, 1968—. Monsanto fellow, 1960-61. Mem. Am. Chem. Soc., Sigma Xi. Patentee copolymers, peroxides, polymerizations, stabilization and applications of polyvinyl bromide. Home: 860 Sinclair St Baton Rouge LA 70815 Office: Ethyl Corp Box 341 Baton Rouge LA 70821

SPARKS, CECIL RAY, physicist; b. Lochwood, W.Va., Nov. 16, 1930; s. Cecil Ralph and Vida Marie (Summers) S.; B.S. in Mech. Engring., U. Tex., 1953; M.S. in Mech. Engring., U. Pitts., 1956. postgrad., 1956-57; m. Judith Carol Eckstein, Aug. 10, 1956; children—Claudia Ruth, Nancy Leigh, Paul Daniel. Research engr. Westinghouse Electric Corp., Pitts., 1953-57; sr. research engr. dept. applied physics S.W. Research Inst., San Antonio, 1957-66, sect. mgr., 1966-69, asst. dir., 1969—. Mem. Soc. Automotive Engrs. (mem. small engine noise com. 1968-70, mem. operator noise exposure subcom. 1970-73), Acoustical Soc. Am., Am. Inst. Physics, Tau Beta Pi, Pi Tau Sigma. Methodist (chmn. evangelism 1972-74). Author: (with others) Noise Abatement at Gas Pipeline Installations. Patentee in field. Home: 10906 Janet Lee Dr San Antonio TX 78230 Office: PO Drawer 28510 8500 Culebra Rd San Antonio TX 78284

SPARKS, CHARLES PAUL, indsl. psychologist; b. nr. Louisa, Ky., Oct. 9, 1915; s. Charles Clarence and Fannie (France) S.; B.S., Ohio State U., 1936, M.A., 1938; postgrad. Tulane U., 1949-51; m. Jean Case, Nov. 19, 1941; children—Paul E., Steven D. Psychologist pub. schs., Mansfield, O., 1937-40; dir. psychol. services Indpls. Pub. Schs., 1940-42; unit head personnel research Adj. Gen. Office, U.S. Army, 1946-48; project dir. Richardson, Bellows, Henry & Co., 1948-50, regional dir., 1951-54, v.p., 1955-62, pres., 1963; personnel research coordinator Exxon Co. U.S.A., Houston, 1964—; adj. prof. U. Houston, 1970—. Served to capt., AUS, 1942-46. Fellow Am. Psychol. Assn. Author: (with D.H. Fryer, E.R. Henry) Outline of General Psychology, 1951. Home: 7715 Dashwood Dr Houston TX 77036 Office: 800 Bell St Houston TX 77001

SPARKS, CHRISTIAN BENJAMIN, coll. adminstr.; b. Beaumont, Tex., Nov. 4, 1922; s. James Chester and Inez Sarah (Derwin) S.; B.S., U. Houston, 1948; M.Edn., 1949; D.Edn., U. N.M., 1973; m. Viola May Joines, June 26, 1942 (div. Aug. 1956); children—Steven Christy, Vicki Lynn (Mrs. Holbert F. Hawkins); m. 2d, Elizabeth Davison Cleland, Dec. 28, 1956. Tchr., athletic coach South Park Ind. Sch. Dist., Beaumont, Tex., 1946-49, Galena Park (Tex.) Sch. Dist., 1949-52, Houston Ind. Sch. Dist., 1953-56; asst. to supt., coach Peekskill (N.Y.) Mil. Acad., 1958-64; dir., coach Chris Sparks' Swim Club, Penn Hills, Pa., 1965-66; instr. phys. edn. Amarillo (Tex.) Coll., 1966-67, chmn. phys. edn., dir. athletics, 1968—. Mem. Potter-Randall County Group Work and Recreation Council, 1968-70; vice chmn. La. Jr. Olympics, 1952; pres. Amarillo Potter County Heart Assn., 1970-71. Mem. Potter-Randall County Regional Planning Commn., 1969-70, City Recreation Commn., Galena Park, Tex., 1950-52. State bd. dirs. Am. Heart Assn., 1970—. Served with USAAF, 1942-45. Mem. Tex. Assn. Health, Phys. Edn. and Recreation (state bd. dirs. 1970—, chmn. nominating com. 1973), Tex. Jr. Coll. Tchrs. Assn. (chmn. phys. ed. 1969-70), Am. Coll. Sports Medicine, Internat. Platform Assn., Tex. Tchrs. Assn. Rotarian. Author: (with Phil Moriarty) Springboard Diving, 1959. Syndicated column, Sparks on Swimming, 1966. Home: 2400 Polk St Apt B Amarillo TX 79109 Office: 2201 S Washington St Amarillo TX 79178

SPARKS, MEREDITH PLEASANT, chemist, patent atty.; b. Palestine, Ill., Dec. 9, 1905; d. John L. and Laura (Bicknell) Pleasant; A.B. with distinction, Ind. U., 1927, A.M., 1928; Ph.D., U. Ill., 1936; J.D. Rutgers U., 1958; m. William J. Sparks, Dec. 31, 1930; children—Ruth (Mrs. James W. Foster), Katherine (Mrs. Richard L. Albrecht), Charles, John. Tchr. chemistry Rochester (Ind.) High Sch., 1928-29; chemist Du Pont Co., Niagara Falls, N.Y., 1929-34; research on cosmetics Northam Warren Co., N.Y.C., 1939; chem. patents Am. Cyanamid Co., Bound Brook, N.J., 1941-46. Admitted to Fla. bar, 1958, U.S. Supreme Ct. bar, also other fed. cts. Mem. Assn. Ind. U. Chemists (pres. 1950-51), Internat., Am. bar assns., Am., N.J. patent law assns., Internat. Patent and Trademark Assn., Am. Chem. Soc., Nat. Assn. Women Lawyers, Am. Assn. U. Women, Phi Beta Kappa, Sigma Xi, Iota Sigma Pi. Contbr. articles to profl. jours. Patentee in field. Home: 5129 Granda Blvd Coral Gables FL 33146 Office: Alfred I Du Pont Bldg 169 E Flagler St Miami FL 33131

SPARKS, SHERMAN PAUL, osteo. physician, surgeon; b. Toledo, Ill., Jan. 23, 1909; s. Ernest Melvin and Nancy Jane (Keller) S.; B.S., U. Ill., 1932, M.S., 1938; D.O., Kirksville Coll. Ostepathy and Surgery, 1945; m Joyce Marie Patterson, Jan. 23, 1965; children—by previous marriage—James Earl, Randal Paul, Robert Dale, Paul David. Intern Sparks Hosp., Dallas, 1945; practice osteo. medicine specializing in surgery, Rockwall, Tex., 1946—. Tchr. High Sch. Mt. Olive, Ill., 1932-42. Civil Def. coordinator, Rockwall County, 1950—; pres. P.T.A., Rockwall, 1958-59, Band Boosters, 1960-61, Rockwall Centennial Celebration, 1954; Republican chmn. Rockwall County, 1964—. Mem. Am., Tex. (v.p. 1954), Rockwall (pres. 1955-56), Dist. 5 osteo. assns., Am. Coll. Gen. Practitioners. Mason (Shriner). Inventor photo-electric turbidimeter for quick quantitative counting bacteria. Home: 406 W Rusk St Rockwall TX 75087 Office: 106 N 2d St Rockwall TX 75087

SPARKS, THOMAS EVERETT, lawyer; b. Crossett, Ark., Aug. 15, 1911; s. Albert Theodore and Clara (Morton) S.; A.B., Hendrix Coll., 1932; LL.B., Washington and Lee U., 1935; m. Julia Benton, June 29, 1940; children—Thomas Everett, Julianna Dickey, Helen Benton. Admitted to Ark. bar, 1935, since practiced in Fordyce; mem. Ark. Ho. of Reps., 1967—. Pres., Benton Realty Co., Inc., Benton Hardware Co., Inc., Benton Casket Mfg. Co., Inc., Benton Furniture Co., Inc.,; owner Morton Abstract Co. Pres., Dallas County Indsl. Devel. Corp. Served to lt. USNR, 1943-46. Fellow Am. Bar Found.; mem. Am., Ark. (ho. dels.) bar assns., Ark. Trial Lawyers Assn., Fordyce C. of C. (past pres.). Democrat. Methodist. Rotarian. Home: RFD 2 Fordyce AR 71742 Office: PO Box 784 Fordyce AR 71742

SPARLING, JOSEPH JAMES, educator; b. Umatilla, Fla., Dec. 19, 1935; s. Joseph Paul and Elizabeth (Hamrick) S.; B.S., Fla. State U., 1957, M.S., 1958; Ph.D., U. Mich., 1968; m. Marilyn Claire Bull, June 22, 1963; children—Kimberly, Christina. Tchr., Fla., Cal., Mich., 1958-63; curriculum cons. community schs., Grand Blanc, Mich., 1963-64, prin., 1964-65; asso. dir. Frank Porter Graham Child Devel. Center, U. N.C., Chapel Hill, 1967—, asst. prof. edn., 1969—. Mem. Am. Ednl. Research Assn., Assn. Supervision Curriculum Devel., A.A.A.S. Author: (with J.J. Gallagher) Research Directions for the 70's in Child Development, 1971. Contbr. articles to profl. jours. Home: Bayberry Dr Chapel Hill NC 27514

SPAUGH, HERBERT, bishop, newspaper columnist; b. Winston-Salem, N.C.; s. Rufus A. and Louise (Hege) S.; A.B., LL.D., Moravian Coll.; B.D. Moravian Theol. Sem.; M.A., D.D., Davidson Coll.; m. Ida Brown Efird; children—Earle, Herbert, Mrs. Robert Farmer, Jr. Furniture mfr., Winston-Salem; ordained to ministry Moravian Ch., pastor Little Ch. on Lane, Charlotte, N.C., 1924-66; columnist Charlotte News, 1933—. Bishop, past mem. various exec. bds. Moravian Ch. Am.; bd. govs., past v.p. Moravian Ch. Am. South, mem. finance bd. Past chmn. Consol. Sch. Bd. Charlotte and Mecklenburg County; chaplain Charlotte Police Dept.; past pres. Charlotte-Mecklenburg Ministerial Assn., Mecklenburg A.R.C.; organizer Charlotte Pub. Sch. Music System; mem. N.C. Sch. Bd. Assn., N.C. Council Chs., Charlotte Alcohol Edn. Com., Groves Conf. Marriage and Home, Charlotte Mental Hygiene Soc., Charlotte Family Life Council. Moravian Ch. Archives Bd. Trustee Moravian Coll., Bethlehem (Pa.), Salem (N.C.) Coll. Served with mil., World War I. Recipient Silver Beaver award Boy Scouts Am.; Rotary citizenship award. Mem. Am. Legion (hon. life chaplain), Order of St. Luke the Physician. Clubs: Executives, City (Charlotte); Civitan (citizenship award, past chaplain Carolina dist., past chaplain internat.). Author: The Pathway to Contentment; Everyday Counsel for Everyday Living; The Pathway to a Happy Marriage; The Boy, the Man, the Bishop; Psalms for Everyday Living. Contbr. articles to numerous mags. Address: 130 N Canterbury Rd Charlotte NC 28211

SPAULDING, AARON LOWERY, business exec.; b. Durham, N.C., Mar. 16, 1943; s. Asa Timothy and Elna (Bridgeforth) S.; student N.C. Central U., 1960-64, U. Pa., 1966-68, Naval Officers Candidate Sch., 1969, Naval Supply Corps Sch., 1969-70; m. Patricia Gwendolyn Alford, Sept. 30, 1972. Financial and systems analyst RCA, N.Y. and N.J., 1964-66, budget analyst, N.Y., summer 1967; co-founder, treas., dir. Re-Con Services, Inc., Phila., 1968-69; instr. progress mgmt. and econ. devel., 1968-69; commd. ensign USN, 1969; with Naval Command Systems Support Activity, Washington, 1970-72; comptroller John F. Kennedy Center for Performing Arts, 1972-74; exec. dir. Boyden Bd. Dir. Services, 1974—. Cons. to Manpower and Edn. Task Force, Phila. Urban Coalition, 1969, Human Resources Center U. Pa., 1969. Mem. Wharton MBA Assn. (pres. 1968). Home: 441 N St SW Washington DC 20024 Office: Boyden Bd Dir Services 1730 K St NW Washington DC 20006

SPAULDING, ASA TIMOTHY, JR., exec. mgmt. cons.; b. Durham, N.C., Sept. 21, 1934; s. Asa Timothy and Elna (Bridgeforth) S.; A.B., Morehouse Coll., 1956; M.B.A., N.C. Central U., 1965; grad. exec. program, U. N.C., 1973; m. Shirley B. Atwell, Sept. 6, 1958; children—Pamela Frances, Asa Timothy III. With controller's dept. N.Y. Life Ins. Co., N.Y.C., 1956-57; sr. systems analyst U.S. Trust Co., N.Y.C., 1959-60; methods rep. Electronic Data Processing div. RCA, N.Y.C., 1960-61; asst. planning dir., later asst. v.p. systems and policy services N.C. Mut. Life Ins. Co., Durham, 1961-69; pres., chief exec. officer Information Services Corp., Durham, 1968—; chief exec. officer Asa Spaulding and Assos. Mem. Durham Council on Human Relations, N.C. Task Force on Planned Variations; pres. Emorywoods Community Assn., 1971. Chmn. bd. dirs. Found. for Econ. and Environmental Devel., 1968—. Served with AUS, 1957-59. Recipient Distinguished Service award Durham Jr. C. of C., 1964. Mem. Assn. for Systems Mgmt. (dir. 1965-67, Nat. Distinguished Service award 1971), Data Processing Mgmt. Assn., Durham C. of C. (chmn. manpower devel. com. 1970), Durham Bus. and Profl. Chain, Omega Psi Phi. Republican. Baptist. Mason. Clubs: Durham Striders Track, Durham Sports. Contbr. articles on systems and data processing to profl. publs. Home: 1110 Jerome Rd Durham NC 27707 Office: 5529 Chapel Hill Blvd PO Box 1010 Durham NC 27702

SPAULDING, GEORGE EDWARD, advt. and pub. relations exec.; b. St. Louis, Sept. 1, 1913; s. George S. and Alice (Botefuhr) S.; student N.Y. U., 1942; m. Mary Louise Hager, Mar. 3, 1944 (dec. June 1973); children—John Edward, William Bryant. Sr. copywriter Johns-Manville Corp., N.Y.C., 1940-53; sales promotion mgr. McLean Trucking Co., 1953-67, dir. advt. and pub. relations, 1967—. Served to 1st lt. AUS, 1942-46. Mem. Sales and Marketing Council, Am. Trucking Assn., N.C. Motor Carriers Assn. (chmn. communications adv. council 1971-72), Winston-Salem Traffic Club. Presbyn. (mem. bd. ushers 1970—, deacon 1974). Lion. Editor: The McLean Stockholder, 1956—. Home: 2340 Apt E Bay Meadows Apts Winston-Salem NC 27103 Office: PO Box 213 Winston Salem NC 27102

SPEAKES, LARRY MELVIN, journalist; b. Cleveland, Miss., Sept. 13, 1939; s. Harry Earl and Ethlyn Frances (Fincher) S.; student U. Miss., 1957-61; m. Laura Christine Crawford, Nov. 3, 1968; children—Sondra LaNell, Barry Scott, Jeremy Stephen. News editor Oxford (Miss.) Eagle, 1961-62; news editor Bolivar Comml., Cleveland, 1962-63, mng. editor, 1964-66; dep. dir. Bolivar County Civil Def., Cleveland, 1963-64; gen. mgr. Progress Publishers, Leland, Miss., 1966-68, editor Leland Progress, Hollandale Herald, Bolivar County Democrat, Sunflower County News; mem. staff U.S. Senate, Press Sec. Sen. J. O. Eastland, Washington, 1968-74; staff asst. to Pres., White House, 1974—. Active Girl Scouts Am., Boy Scouts Am. Recipient Gen. Excellence award Miss. Press Assn., 1968; named Reporter of Year The Mississippian, U. Miss., 1958; Lambda Sigma award, 1960. Mem. Kappa Sigma, Lambda Sigma, Omicron Delta Kappa, Sigma Delta Chi. Methodist. Home: 1000 6th St SW Washington DC 20024 Office: Old Exec Office Bldg Pennsylvania Av NW Washington DC 20050

SPEAR, ADOLPH FLATAUER, financial exec.; b. Apalachicola, Fla., Apr. 29, 1917; s. Emory M. and Tessie (Flatauer) S.; A.B., Oglethorpe U., 1939; postgrad. Harvard, 1943; m. Edith Jane Knight, Mar. 5, 1949; children—Barbara, LLoyd, Robert, James, Kenneth. Auditor, Ernst & Ernst, C.P.A.'s, Atlanta, 1939-43, 1945-46; with Am. Standard, N.Y.C., 1947-52; sec., treas., dir. Gen. Plywood Corp., Louisville, 1953-62, Consider H. Willett, Inc., Louisville, 1963; pres., dir. Adolph F. Spear & Co., Inc., Louisville, Ft. Lauderdale, 1964—; mgr. finances Indsl. Services Am., Inc., Louisville, 1969-70; chmn. Casa Madero, Inc., 1971—; dir. Internat. Resources Corp., Internat. Acquisitions, Inc., Corporate Enterprises, Inc., Certified Realty, Inc. Chmn., United Cerebral Palsy Fund drive, 1959. Served from ensign to lt. USNR, 1943-45; PTO. C.P.A., Ga., Ky. Mem. Order Confederate Cols. Ky. (gen. 1956—), Order Ky. Cols., Am. Inst. C.P.A.'s, Tax Execs. Inst. (v.p. 1960-61), So. Inst. Mgmt. (founding mem.), Financial Execs. Inst. Kiwanian (chmn. underprivileged childrens com. 1961-62). Clubs: Admirals (Louisville); Le Club Internat. (Ft. Lauderdale). Home: 3021 NE 42d Fort Lauderdale FL 33308 Office: 1040 Bayview Dr Fort Lauderdale FL 33304

SPEARMAN, JAMES TYRON, coll. adminstr.; b. Tifton, Ga., Sept. 23, 1945; s. James Monroe and Polly (Drake) S.; Asso. degree, Abraham Baldwin Agrl. Coll., 1965; B.S., U. Ga., 1967, M.S., 1969; m. Sandra Nichols, June 27, 1971. House dir., U. Ga., Athens, 1966-68; dir. pub. relations Abraham Baldwin Agrl. Coll., Tifton, Ga., 1968—, tchr. poultry sci., 1969—. Active Boy Scouts Am. Mem. Baldwin Alumni Assn. and Found. (exec. sec. 1969-73), Tifton C. of C., Ga. Soc. Assn. Execs., Southeastern Poultry and Egg Assn., Gridiron Secret Soc., Phi Kappa Phi, Alpha Xeta. Clubs: Exchange (state dir. 1973), Toastmasters (pres. 1971), X. Home: 517 E 18th St Tifton GA 31794 Office: Box 262 Abraham Baldwin College Tifton GA 31794

SPEARS, GEORGE HARRISON, JR., textile co. exec.; b. Bruceville, Tex., June 20, 1915; s. George Harrison and Martha Eunice (Walraven) S.; A.A., Schreiner Inst., 1935; B.B.A., U. Tex.; m. Jane Thompson, Jan. 23, 1948; children—Craig, Rebecca, Mark, David. Accountant United Fruit Co., Guatemala, 1938-39; chief accountant Campbell, Taggart, Dallas, 1940-53; self-employed as C.P.A., Dallas, 1954-70; treas., Facho, Inc., Dallas, 1970—, also dir.;

dir. Freestone County Mfg., Inc., Betsy Ross Flag Girls, Inc. Served to lt. USNR, 1942-46. C.P.A., Tex. Mem. Soc. C.P.A.'s. Methodist (trustee 1950-52). Home: 1239 Danville St Richardson TX 75080 Office: 2315 Alamo St Dallas TX 75201

SPEARS, GRAYSON ELDRIDGE, carpet mill exec.; b. Spearsville, La., Dec. 20, 1928; s. Grayson Lee and Lillian (Rockett) S.; student Northwestern State Coll., 1948, Centenary Coll., 1949, So. Meth. U., 1963—; m. Geraldine Carter; children—Linda, Duane, Don, David, Mark, Dawn. With Hemenway Furniture Co., Shreveport, La., 1948-53, Frank Lyon Co., 1953-56, Jay's Furniture Co., Dangerfield, Tex., 1956-57; v.p., gen. mgr. Colonial South Life Ins. Co., Ruston, La., 1957-63; v.p., gen. mgr. Cherokee Carpet Mills, Inc., Lewisville, Ark., 1965-70; co-organizer Marlin Mills, Inc. (Tex.), 1970—, v.p. mfg., 1970-71; organizer Spears Carpet Mills, Inc., 1971, Spears Carpet Mills, Hugo, Okla., 1973. Served with AUS, 1946-47. Mem. Ch. of Christ. Rotarian. Home: 404 E 17th St Hope AR 71801 Office: Hwy 29 N N Indsl Park Hope AR 71801

SPEARS, J. DANIEL, architect, educator; b. Dallas, Oct. 3, 1937; s. Leonard Daniel and Melba Fay (Proctor) S.; B.Arch., U. Tex. at Austin, 1960; M.S. in Arch. (Acad. grantee 1962-63), Columbia, 1963; postgrad. Technische Hochschule, Vienna, Austria, 1961. Mem. design and prodn. staff Bowman, Swainson & Heister, Harlingen, Tex., 1961, Harrell & Hamilton, Dallas, 1960, 64-65; supr. design and prodn. Enslie O. Oglesby architect, Dallas, 1963, 64, summer 1966; asso. prof. architecture U. Tex. at Arlington, 1965—, asst. chmn. dept. 1969-72. Mem. Soc. Archtl. Historians, Tex. Soc. Archtl. Historians, A.I.A., Tex. Soc. Architects. Address: PO Box 2932 Dallas TX 75221

SPEARS, JACK, assn. exec.; b. Fort Smith, Ark., Dec. 23, 1919; s. Clifford Grady and Josephine (Ferguson) S.; B.S. cum laude, U. Ark., 1941; m. Helen Jeanne Jackson, May 14, 1942; children—Jack, Richard Thomas. Exec. dir., Tulsa County Med. Soc., 1942. Mem. bd. Tulsa County Pub. Health Nursing Service, 1959-67. Bd. dirs. Am. Cancer Soc., Tulsa County, 1945-55, Tulsa Lakes Area Health and TB Assn., 1952-68. Recipient Distinguished Service award Salvation Army Tulsa, 1973. Mem. Am. Assn. Med. Soc. Execs. (trustee 1967-69), Beta Gamma Sigma, Alpha Kappa Psi. Author: Hollywood-The Golden Era, 1971. Contbr. numerous articles on history of motion pictures, films and book reviews to Films in Review, 1955—. Home: 6208 S Utica St Tulsa OK 74136 Office: Tulsa County Med Soc 104 Utica Sq Medical Center Tulsa OK 74114

SPEARS, JAMES WILLIAM, lawyer, educator; b. Jasper, Ark., July 21, 1934; student Ark. Poly. Coll., 1952-54; B.S. in Indsl. Engring., U. Ark., 1958, J.D., 1964; L.I.M., U. Tex., 1972. With Guy A. Moore's Ozark Abstract Co., Jasper, 1958-60; admitted to Ark. bar, 1964; partner Walker, Villinies & Spears, Harrison, Ark., 1965; asst. prof. law, U. Ark., Fayetteville div., 1965, Little Rock div., 1966-69, asso. prof., 1969-73, prof. law, 1973—. Mem. research staff 7th Ark. Constl. Conv. Mem. Ark. Bar Assn., Nat. Rifle Assn., Pi Kappa Alpha, Phi Alpha Delta. Democrat. Jewish religion. Mason, Elk. Home: 800 N Van Buren St Little Rock AR 72205 Office: 300 Broadway Little Rock AR 72201

SPEARS, JOHN HERMAN, lawyer; b. Imboden, Ark., Oct. 10, 1901; s. Ben and Kate (Odom) S.; student U. Ark., 1927-28, Memphis State Coll., 1928-29; m. Willie Sue Robertson, Jan. 4, 1930. Admitted to Ark. bar, 1935, since practiced in West Memphis; dep. pros. atty. Crittenden County, Ark., 1940-44; city atty., West Memphis, 1945-52. Dir., atty. West Memphis Fed. Savs. & Loan Assn., Bank of West Memphis. Mayor, Turrell, Ark., 1938-39. Chmn., Local Draft Bd., 1946-71. Trustee So. Bapt. Coll., Walnut Ridge, Ark., Bapt. Meml. Hosp., Memphis. Mem. Crittenden County Bar Assn. (past pres.). Baptist (trustee, Sunday sch. tchr.). Club: West Memphis Country. Home: 217 Roosevelt St West Memphis AR 72301 Office: 500 E Broadway West Memphis AR 72301

SPEARS, WILLIAM EUGENE, JR., clergyman, author; b. Union, S.C., June 7, 1927; s. William Eugene and Edna (Moore) S.; A.B., U. S.C., 1948; B.D., So. Baptist Theol. Sem., 1951, M.Div., 1973; Ph.D., U. Edinburgh (Scotland), 1953; m. Lillian Wilson Adams, Sept. 9, 1952; children—Sally Adams, William Eugene III. Ordained to ministry Bapt. Ch., 1949; pastor First Chs., Mooresville, N.C., 1953-58, North Augusta, S.C., 1958-64, Emerywood Ch., High Point, N.C., 1964-69, First Bapt. Ch., Chattanooga, 1969-72, Bapt. Ch. Beaufort (S.C.), 1972—. Preacher, S.C. Bapt. Pastor's conf., 1961, Tenn. Bapt. Evangelistic Conf., Nashville, 1971. Served with USNR, World War II. Named High Pointer of Week, High Point Enterprise, 1969; recipient keys to city High Point Mayor, 1969, certificate Chattanooga Mayor, 1972. Mem. Aiken Bapt. Assn. (moderator), Omicron Delta Kappa, Sigma Chi, Kappa Sigma Kappa. Author: Seventy Feet Nearer the Stars, 1964; also Sunday Sch. lessons Bapt. Courier S.C., 1973—. Contbr. articles to profl. jours. Address: Charles St and King St PO Box 869 Beaufort SC 29902

SPEED, EDWIN MAURICE, coll. dean; b. Enterprise, Miss., Aug. 17, 1918; s. Benjamin Thomas and Lela Alma (Davis) S.; B.A., Birmingham So. Coll., 1950; student Trinity U., 1946-47; D.M.D., U. Ala., 1954, M.S., 1965; postgrad. Cumberland Law Sch., 1965-66; m. Adele Marie House, Aug. 16, 1941; children—Edwin Michael, Ann Marie. Pvt. practice dentistry, Birmingham, Ala., 1954-61; mem. faculty Sch. Dentistry U. Ala., Birmingham, 1965—, asso. prof., 1968—, asst. dean, 1966—. Pres., South Hill Corp., real estate devel., Birmingham, 1970—. Active United Appeal. Mem. Park and Recreation Bd., 1960-72; mem. City Council Bestavia Hills, Ala., 1960-72, pres., 1960-64. Bd. dirs. Vestavia Library, 1960-72. Served with USAAF, 1941-45, USAF, 1961-62; col. Res. (ret.). Decorated Air medal with 5 oak leaf clusters and 1 silver cluster. Mem. Ala. Dental Assn. (trustee 1967-69), Am. Assn. Dental Schs. (pres. 1973-74), Am. Dental Assn., Am. Acad. Periodontology, Kappa Alpha, Delta Sigma Delta, Omicron Kappa Upsilon. Roman Catholic. Contbr. profl. jours. Home: 1325 Willoughby Rd Birmingham AL 35216 Office: 1919 7th Av S School Dentistry Univ Ala Birmingham AL 35294

SPEED, GROVER CLEVELAND, glass mfg. co. exec.; b. Collins, Miss., Mar. 23, 1918; s. Grover Cleveland and Emma (Welch) S.; B.S., Miss. State U., 1940; m. Christine M. Pickering, Apr. 12, 1941; children—Doris (Mrs. Mohamad-Salem Mobarak), Dorothy (Mrs. Michel L. Meek), Mary (Mrs. Thomas Weissinger). With Gen. Elec. Co., Jackson, Miss., 1940—, supr. engring., 1945-64, mgr. Jackson Glass Plant, 1964—. Registered profl. engr., Miss. Mem. I.E.E.E. Methodist (steward). Rotarian. Home: 234 Shady Circle Jackson MS 39204 Office: PO Box 8457 Bettlefield St Jackson MS 39204

SPEED, JOHN SACKETT, ins. exec.; b. Dubuque, Ia., Aug. 29, 1927; s. Lloyd Jeter and Marion (Whitbread) S.; A.B., Princeton, 1950; M.B.A., Harvard, 1955; m. Anne Carter Stewart, Apr. 28, 1951; children—Virginia, Lloyd, Anne Carter. With Commonwealth Life Ins. Co., Louisville, 1955—, exec. v.p., 1968-72; exec. v.p. Capital Holding Corp., 1973—; dir. 1st Nat. Bank Louisville, 1st Ky. Trust Co. Bd. dirs., pres. Inst. Physical Medicine and Rehab., Louisville, 1971-73. Served with USNR, 1945-46. Home: 2531 Ransdell Av Louisville KY 40204 Office: PO Box 1085 Louisville KY 40201

SPEEL, HENRY CHARLES, chemist; b. Phila., Nov. 21, 1908; s. John Field and Clara (McClatchey) S.; A.B., Harvard, 1930, spl. student, 1931-33; m. Mary Ella Urquhart, Sept. 1, 1934; 1 dau., Gwen (Mrs. Gerald P. Kaplan). Chem. engr. Atlas Powder Co., 1934-45; new comml. products research Gen. Mills, Inc., 1945-46; tech. rep. Alrose Chem. Co., 1947-48, Gen. Aniline & Film Corp., 1948-50; dir. devel. Wyandotte Chem. Corp., 1951-52; cons. Speel & Asso., 1952—, pres., 1952-60; v.p. Schwarz, Speel & Assos., 1959-60; marketing research adviser Universal Oil Products Co., Des Plaines, Ill., 1960-63; became staff specialist chems. products and process evaluation staff, Office Adminstr., Agrl. Research Service, U.S. Dept. Agr., Washington, 1963, now indsl. analyst program devel. staff. Fellow Am. Inst. Chemists (life); mem. Am. Chem. Soc., Am. Oil Chemists Soc. (nat. chmn. joint com. with Am. Soc. Testing and Materials on analysis soaps and detergents 1961-68), Am. Soc. Testing and Materials (councillor Middle Atlantic dist.), Comml. Chem. Devel. Assn., Midwest Chem. Marketing Assn. (founder, chmn. group 1963-64), Soc. Cosmetic Chemists, Chem. Market Research Assn., Am. Assn. Textile Chemists and Colorists (sec. Western New Eng. sect. 1959-60). Presbyn. (treas. New Eng. synod council Presbyn. Men 1955-58). Clubs: Chesapeake; Harvard Varsity; Chemists (N.Y.C.). Editor: 2 edits. Textile Chems. and Auxs., 1952, 57, Japanese edit., 1962. Contbr. to tech. publs. Patentee in field. Home: 821 S Lee St Alexandria VA 22314 Office: ARS OA PDS US Dept Agr Washington DC 20250

SPEER, FRIDTJOF ALFRED, govt. engring. mgr.; b. Berlin, Germany, Aug. 23, 1923; s. Alfred Fedor and Gerda Juliane (Radmann) S.; Dipl. Ing., Tech. U. Berlin, 1950, Dr. Ing., 1953; m. Margret Hillemann, Mar. 22, 1951; children—Sabine, Susanne, Beate. Came to U.S., 1955, naturalized, 1960. Asst. prof. Tech. U. Berlin, 1950-55; br. chief Army Ballistic Missile Agy., Huntsville, Ala., 1955-60; project mgr. NASA, Marshall Space Flight Center, Huntsville, 1960—. Recipient Exceptional Service medals NASA, 1969. Asso. fellow Am. Inst. Aeros. and Astronautics. Home: 4303 Panorama Dr SE Huntsville AL 35801 Office: NASA Marshall Space Flight Center Huntsville AL 35812

SPEIDEL, JOHN JOSEPH, physician, govt. ofcl.; b. Iowa City, Sept. 17, 1937; s. Thomas Dennis and Edna (Warweg) S.; A.B. cum laude, Harvard, 1959, M.D., 1963, M.P.H., 1965; m. Brook Seawell, July 11, 1967; 1 dau., Sabrina Brett. Intern St. Luke's Hosp., N.Y.C., 1963-64; resident N.Y.C. Dept. Health, 1965-67, dep. dir. maternal and infant care project, 1966-67; chief research div. Office of Population, Bur. Population and Humanitarian Assistance, AID, Dept. State, Washington, 1970—. Lectr. population and family planning Georgetown U., U. Cal., George Washington U. Served to maj. AUS, 1967-69. Recipient meritorious unit citation Office of Population, 1969-71, Arthur S. Flemming award Washington Downtown Jr. C. of C., 1972. Diplomate Nat. Bd. Med. Examiners, Am. Bd. Preventive Medicine. Mem. Am. Pub. Health Assn., Population Assn. Am., Assn. Planned Parenthood Physicians, Soc. Study Reproduction, Internat. Union Sci. Study Population, Soc. Study Fertility, Am. Fertility Soc. Contbr. to profl. publs. in field. Editor: (with others) Female Sterilization, 1971; Hysteroscopic Sterilization, 1974. Home: 2531 Eye St NW Washington DC 20037 Office: PHA/POP/R AID Dept State Washington DC 20523

SPEIGHT, FRANK YOUNG, assn. exec.; b. Thomasville, Ga., June 8, 1914; s. Frank Young and Julia Aleen (Ernest) S.; B.S. in Chem. Engring., Auburn U., 1938; m. Jeanne Lambert, Jan. 27, 1945; 1 son, David Eugene. Tech. aide Nat. Acad. Scis., 1946-54; sci. coordinator Am. Soc. Testing Materials, Phila., 1954-64; dir. information program Engrs. Joint Council, N.Y.C., 1964-70; mgr. safety and health Am. Welding Soc., Miami, Fla., 1970—. Chmn. com. on thesaurus rules Am. Nat. Standards Inst., 1969. Fellow Am. Inst. Chemists, A.A.A.S. Contbr. articles profl. jours. Home: 725 Catalonia Av Coral Gables FL 33134 Office: 2501 NW 7th St Miami FL 33125

SPELCE, WILLIAM BENNETT, advt. co.; b. Clarksville, Ark., Sept. 4, 1937; s. Neal Leslie and Fannie Lou (Bennett) S.; B.B.A., U. Tex. at Austin, 1963, postgrad. Sch. Law, 1960-63. Supervising auditor State Tex., Austin, 1963-68; asst. to v.p. for bus. affairs Tex. Tech. U., Lubbock, 1963-68; system auditor U. Tex. System, Austin, 1969-73; v.p., controller Neal Spelce Assos. advt. and pub. relations, Austin, 1973—. C.P.A., Tex. Mem. Am. Inst. C.P.A.'s. Home: 101 Blue Ridge Trail Austin TX 78746 Office: PO Box 1905 Austin TX 78767

SPELL, DANIEL MELVIN, JR., aerospace co. engring. exec.; b. Brunswick, Ga., Nov. 13, 1931; s. Daniel Melvin and Grace (Reed) S.; B.Indsl. Engring., Ga. Inst. Tech., 1959; postgrad. U. South Fla., 1968—; m. Anne Marie Petri, Aug. 22, 1953; children—Dawn Marie, Daniel Melvin III, Regina Anne, Richard Scott. Indsl. engr. Westinghouse Electric Corp., Fairmont, W.Va., 1959-62; with Honeywell, Inc., St. Petersburg, Fla., 1962—, chief indsl. engr., 1967-72, prodn. mgr., 1972—. Cons. mgmt., engring. Committeeman, Boy Scouts Am., Dunedin, Fla., 1969—; mgr., v.p. Little League, Dunedin, 1963-67. Served with USAF, 1950-54. Registered profl. engr., Fla. Mem. Nat. Soc. Profl. Engrs., Fla. Engring. Soc., Am. Inst. Indsl. Engrs. Democrat. Baptist. Toastmaster. Home: 66 Lexington Dr Dunedin FL 33528 Office: 13350 US Hwy 19 St Petersburg FL 33733

SPELL, WILLIAM MARCUS, TV exec.; b. Wrightville, Ga., Oct. 24, 1942; s. Artis Moore and Wunelle (Curry) S.; B.B.A., Ga. State U., 1969, M.B.A., 1971; m. Julia Raye Clark, Nov. 13, 1966; children—Edison Clark, Curry Louise. Asst. editor Wrightsville (Ga.) Headlight, 1958-61; machine operator Life Ins. Co. Ga., Atlanta, 1961-62; test technician Ga. Hwy. Dept., Atlanta, 1962-63; adminstrv. asst. Citizens & So. Nat. Bank, Atlanta, 1963-66; customer accounts auditor So. Ry. Co., Atlanta, 1966-67; salesman 3M Co., Atlanta, 1967-68; merchandising mgr. WAGA-TV, Atlanta, 1969-71, account exec., 1971—. Active Forward Atlanta Campaign, United Appeal; chmn. DeKalb council Boy Scouts Am. Served with USAF, 1967-68. Mem. Food Mfrs. Sales Execs. Club, Izaak Walton League, Atlanta Broadcast Execs. Club, Kappa Psi, Pi Sigma Epsilon. Baptist. Home: 773 Willivee Dr Decatur GA 30033 Office: PO Box 4207 Atlanta GA 30302

SPELLER, BILLY WAYNE, elec. engr.; b. Dozier, Ala., Oct. 12, 1943; s. Billy James and Annie (Butler) S.; B.S. in Elec. Engring., Auburn U., 1964, M.S. (USPHS fellow), 1966; M.B.A., U. Tenn., 1974; m. Nancy Melrose Cooper, Jan. 19, 1963; children—Timothy Wayne, Amanda Kristi. Mem. devel. engring. staff nuclear div. Union Carbide Corp., Oak Ridge, 1966—, adminstrv. asst. to supt. lab. devel. dept., 1968-70, group supr. instrumentation devel. sect., 1970—. Mem. I.E.E.E., Sigma Xi, Eta Kappa Nu, Phi Kappa Phi. Sigma Pi. Home: 112 Colgate Rd Oak Ridge TN 37830 Office: PO Box Y Oak Ridge TN 37830

SPELLMEYER, LEONARD HARLEY, utility co. exec.; b. Stuttgart, Ark., July 20, 1916; s. Leo Carl-John and Margaret Ann (Niewold) S.; grad. Internat. Corr. Schs., 1954; m. Mildred Edna Price, Sept. 19, 1964; 1 dau.—Judith Lynn (Mrs. Gregory Boyd). Draftsman, No. Ill. Gas Co., 1947-51, dist. asst., 1951-55, supt. transp., 1955-62, indsl. gas engr., 1962-65, architect rep., 1965-66; sales mgr. Brevard div. City Gas Co. Fla., 1966-67, gen. sales mgr. all divs., 1967-70, asst. v.p. operations, 1970, v.p. operations, Hialeah, 1970—. Active Dade County Civil Def. Served with AUS, 1944-46; PTO. Mem. Nat. Assn. Corrosion Engrs., Gas Inst. Great Miami, Hialeah-Miami Springs C. of C. Mason, Kiwanian. Home: 15300 SW 78th Pl Miami FL 33157 Office: 955 E 25th St Hialeah FL 33013

SPELMAN, JON WHITE, theatre dir.; b. Kansas City, Mo., July 10, 1942; s. Norman L. and Elizabeth S. (Schneider) S.; B.A. with honors, Williams Coll., 1964; M.A., Purdue U., 1966. Actor, dir. Merry-Go-Round Theatre, Sturbridge, Mass., 1963-66, Williamstown (Mass.) Theatre, 1964; tri-founder, dir. Montserrat Festival Theatre, Montserrat, B.W.I., 1965; asst. prof. theatre U. Tenn., Chattanooga, 1966-68; dir. edn., staff dir. Asolo State Theatre Co., Sarasota, Fla., 1968-73; artistic dir. Fla. Studio Theatre Co., Sarasoto, 1973—. Cons. to State Fla. Theatre Edn. in Schs., 1968—; vis. profl. dir. Nat. Playwrighting Conf., 1970; rep. Am. Profl. Theatre, 4th World Conf. Internat. Assn. Theatre for Children and Young People, 1972; program leader nat. convs. Am. Theatre Assn., 1971-72. Grantee theatrical prodns. and related activities. Mem. Fla. Theatre Conf., Fla. League Arts, Tenn. Arts Commn., Southeastern Theatre Conf., Univ. Resident Theatre Assn., Am. Nat. Theatre and Acad. Contbr. to profl. publs. in field. Office: 4619 Bay Shore Rd Sarasota Fl 33580

SPENCE, DALE WILLIAM, educator; b. Beaumont, Tex., Apr. 8, 1934; s. William and Dovie Alice (Byrd) S.; B.S., Rice U., 1956; M.S., N. Tex. State U., 1959; Ed.D., La. State U., 1966; m. Alice Marie Henslee, Aug. 5, 1955; children—D'Anne, Susan Lee, Dale William. Instr. N. Tex. State U., Denton, 1958-59, Hardins-Simmons U., Abilene, Tex., 1959-62; mem. faculty Rice U., Houston, 1963—, asso. prof. health, phys. edn. and anatomy, 1969-72, prof., 1973—; dir. exercise rehab. and research St. Joseph Hosp., Houston, 1973—. Vis. asso. prof. Baylor Coll. Medicine, Houston, 1970—. Served with USMCR, 1956-58. Muscular Dystrophy Assns. Am. and NIH postdoctoral fellow, Baylor Coll. Medicine, 1968-69; NASA/Am. Soc. Engring. Edn. research fellow, 1969-70. Fellow Am. Coll. Sports Medicine; mem. A.A.A.S., Am. Assn. U. Profs., Marine Corps Res. Officers Assn. Author: Get Fit and Stay That Way, 1965; Essentials of Kinesiology, 1974; (with others) A Study Guide for Human Dissection, 1972. Editorial bd. Jour. Health, Phys. Edn. and Recreation, 1965-68. Home: 2912 Georgetown St Houston TX 77005 Office: Dept Health Phys Edn Rice Univ Houston TX 77005

SPENCE, FLOYD DAVIDSON, congressman; b. Columbia, S.C., Apr. 9, 1928; s. James Wilson and Addie (Lucas) S.; A.B., U.S.C., 1952, J.D., 1956; grad. nat. security seminar Indsl. Coll. Armed Forces; m. Lula Hancock Drake, Dec. 22, 1952; children—David, Zack, Benjamin, Caldwell. Admitted to S.C. bar, 1956; partner firm Callison and Spence, West Columbia, 1956—; mem. S.C. Ho. Reps., 1956-62; mem. S.C. Senate, 1966-70, minority leader, 1966-70, chmn. joint com. investigate communist activities, 1969; mem. 92d-93d Congresses from S.C.; mem. Armed Services Com. Past chmn. Ridge dist. Central S.C. council Boy Scouts Am., 1965-66, exec. bd., 1963—; chmn. Lexington County Mental Health Assn., 1959; mem. exec. com. Columbia Bd. dirs. Mid-Carolina Mental Health Assn., 1970. Served with USNR, 1952-54. Mem. Am. Legion, (mem. counter-subversive activities com. 1966, 67), V.F.W., Res. Officers Assn., Navy League, Columbia Carillon (dir. 1966-70), West Columbia-Cayce, Lexington, S.C. chambers commerce. Lutheran. Contbr. articles on communism to profl. jours.; lectr. in field. Home: Box 815 Lexington SC 29072 Office: Box 11378 Columbia SC 29211

SPENCE, JAMES ROBERT, banker; b. Lillington, N.C., Sept. 25, 1927; s. George Broughton and Lillie (Patterson) S.; LL.B., U. N.C., 1953;; m. Marilyn S. Younce, Jan. 10, 1953; children—Helyn S., James Robert, Louise Y. Admitted to N.C. bar, 1953; v.p. High Point (N.C.) Bank & Trust Co., 1967-71; pres. Southeast Nat. Bank of Orlando (Fla.), 1971—; vis. lectr. banking High Point Coll., 1969-70. Chmn. High Point (N.C.) Democratic Party, 1968-69. Served with USNR, 1945-47. Mem. N.C. State Bar. Kiwanian. Author: The Making of a Governor, 1968. Home: 1394 Stewart St Winter Park FL 32789 Office: PO Box 80 Orlando FL 32801

SPENCE, JOHN MORGAN, JR., utility co. exec.; b. LaFayette, Ala., Jan. 2, 1923; s. John Morgan and Edna E. (McCarley) S.; B.S., Auburn U., 1949; m. Norma Lee Chadwick, Aug. 4, 1945; 1 dau., Deborah Ellen. Extension farm agt. Ala. Extension Service, Florence, 1949; asst. mgr. Lauderdale County Coop., Florence, 1949-52; dist. and div. rural service engr. Ala. Power Co., Tuscaloosa, 1952-63; sr. agrl. engr., Birmingham, 1963-67, supr. sales tng., 1968—. Served with AUS, 1943-45. Recipient hon. state farmer degree Future Farmers Am., 1959, hon. mem. Ala. 4-H Clubs, 1963. Registered profl. engr., Ala. Mem. Nat. Mgmt. Assn. (recipient Leadership award 1969), Am. Soc. Tng. and Devel., Indsl. Audio Visual Assn., Am. Soc. Agrl. Engrs., Gamma Sigma Delta. Presbyn. Home: 4521 Linwood Dr Birmingham AL 35222 Office: 600 N 18th St Birmingham AL 35291

SPENCER, DONALD FORD, electronics engr.; b. Bellevue, Ky., Apr. 16, 1924; s. Merle Wilson and Mildred (Ford) S.; B.S., U. Cin., 1951; m. Phyllis Esther Parry, Dec. 30, 1950; children—Barton Parry, Sherra Ford, Wendra. Electronic engr. USN Bur. Ships and Naval Research Lab., Washington, 1951-56; head air-to-surface missile guidance unit USN Bur. Aeros., 1956-59; chief avionics and guidance div. Office Communications and Electronics, Office Dir. Def. Research and Engring., 1959-70; electronics indsl. specialist Office Asst. Sec. Def., 1970—; pres. Va. Execs. Investments. Served with USNR, 1943-46. Registered profl. engr., D.C. Asso. fellow Am. Inst. Aeros. and Astronautics; mem. I.E.E.E. (sr.), Inst. of Nav., Cal. State Soc., Soc. Va. (v.p.). Presbyn. Mason. Clubs: Mt. Vernon Yacht Annapolis Yacht. Home: 6621 Wakefield Dr Alexandria VA 22307 Office: The Pentagon Washington DC 20301

SPENCER, EMORY MAURICE, lawyer, oil operator; b. Redwater, Tex., Mar. 13, 1905; s. Cuthbert and Thursey (McBeth) S.; A.B., Rice Inst., 1926; postgrad. U. Tex. Law Sch., 1931-33; m. Mildred Farrow, Sept. 17, 1943; children—Sandra Carol, James Darrell (adopted), Mary, Alicia. Geophysicist, Sun Oil Co., S.W. U.S., 1927-34; admitted to Tex. bar, 1936, since practiced in Rockport; city atty., 1943-45; county judge Aransas County, 1948-49; county atty., 1939-43, 45-48; oil operator, 1948—; dir. Portland State Bank (Tex.). Chmn., Ark. County Democratic Exec. Com., 1955-58. Mem. State Bar Tex., Tex. Bar Found., Delta Tau Delta. Episcopalian. Home: Majorca Rockport TX 78382 Office: PO Drawer 1207 Rockport TX 78382

SPENCER, FERN E. SMITH (MRS. LUCIAN W. SPENCER), civic worker; b. Wheeler, Tex., May 13, 1920; d. Bonner and Laura (Lamberth) Smith; student Amarillo Jr. Coll.; m. Lucian Witten Spencer, May 20, 1949; children—Patricia Ann (Mrs. W.C. McElhannon), Laura Beth (Mrs. Robert D. Hill, Jr.), Lucian W. Bd. dirs. Moore County Concert Assn., Girl Scout council, Dallas Civic Ballet; vol. worker Presbyn. Hosp., mem. San Antonio Little Theatre, Dallas Symphony Orch. League. Named Woman of Year, Beta Sigma Phi, 1962. Mem. Christian Ch. (deaconess.). Clubs: Woodlawn Garden; Dumas Garden, 1932 Study; Tanglewood Hills Country. Home: 1119 Western Blvd Arlington TX 76013

SPENCER, JERRY DEAN, landscape architect; b. Dimmitt, Tex., Apr. 24, 1938; s. Truman C. and W. Pauline (Andrew) Armor; B.S. in Landscape Architecture, La. State U., 1962; M. Landscape Architecture, Harvard, 1964; m. Nora Sue Wise, May 27, 1963; children—Jennifer Ashley, Christopher Andrew. Landscape architect firm Sasaki, Dawson, De May Assos. Inc., Watertown, Mass., 1964-68, Boston Redevel. Authority, 1968-69; sr. planner Chatham County-Savannah (Ga.) Met. Planning Commn., 1969-73; new community planner Sea Pines Co., Hilton Head, S.C., 1973-74; prin. Savannah Design Group Inc., 1974—. Mem. Hist. Savannah Found., 1971-74. Recipient merit of excellence award landscape architecture, 1962. Mem. Am. Soc. Landscape Architects. Home: 215 E Gwinnett St Savannah GA 31401 Office: 12 East Bay St Savannah GA 31401

SPENCER, MARY MILLER, civic worker, club woman; b. Comanche, Tex., May 25, 1924; d. Aaron Gaynor and Alma (Grissom) Miller; B.S., North Tex. State U., 1943; 1 dau., Mara Lynn. Cafeteria dir. Mercedes (Tex.) Pub. Schs., 1943-46; home economist coordinator All-Orange Dessert Contest, Fla. Citrus Commn., Lakeland, 1959-62, 64; children's services worker Fla. Div. Family Services, Lakeland, 1969-70, social worker, 1970—. Tchr. purchasing sch. lunch dept. Fla. Dept. Edn., 1960. Clothing judge Polk County (Fla.) Youth Fair, 1951-68, Polk County Federated Women's Clubs, 1964-66; pres. Dixieland Elementary Sch. P.T.A., 1955-57, Polk County Council P.T.A.'s, 1958-60; dist. 7. Fla. Congress Parents and Tchrs., 1961-63; chmn. pub. edn. com. Polk County unit Am. Cancer Soc., 1959-60, bd. dirs., 1962—; charter mem., bd. dirs. Lakeland YMCA; sec. Greater Lakeland Community Nursing Council, 1965-69; trustee, vice chmn. Polk County Eye Clinic, 1962-64, pres., 1964—; bd. dirs. Polk County Scholarship and Loan Fund, Inc.; mem. exec. com. West Polk County (Fla.) Community Welfare Council, 1960-62, 65-68; mem. budget and audit com. Greater Lakeland United Fund, 1960-62; mem. adv. bd. Polk County Juvenile and Domestic Relations Ct., 1960-69,; mem. exec. com. Sun Coast Health Council, 1968—, vol., disaster res. social worker A.R.C., 1970—; mem. Fla. Health and Welfare Council, 1970—, Polk County Mental Health Assn., 1970—. Sec. bd. dirs. Fla. West Coast Ednl. Television, 1960—. Mem. Fla. Congress Parents and Tchrs. (hon. life, pub. relations chmn. 1962-66.), Fla. Pub. Health Assn., Alumni Assn. North Tex. State U. Democrat. Methodist. Mem. Order Eastern Star. Home: 535 W Beacon Rd Lakeland FL 33803 Office: PO Box 2161 Lakeland FL 33803

SPENCER, RONALD SMITH, JR., assn. exec.; b. Pensacola, Fla., Dec. 23, 1929; s. Ronald Smith and Louise (Zuber) S.; B.A., Stetson U., 1951; m. Barbara Jean Robbins, Mar. 30, 1952; children—Susan Page, Ronald Smith III. Sec.-treas. Dixie Lime & Stone Co., Ocala, Fla., 1958-64; chmn. Fla. Indsl. Commn., Tallahassee, 1964; exec. dir. Fla. Forestry Assn., Tallahassee, 1965-69; exec. v.p. Fla. State C. of C., Jacksonville, 1969—. Mem. Fla. Citizens Adv. Commn. Banking, Fla. Adv. Commn. Tourism, Fla. Savs. and Loan Study Commn., Fla. Council Internat. Devel., 1972. Served with USAF, 1951-55. Recipient Stetson U. Distinguished Alumni award, 1971; award for best article Fla. Realtor mag., 1973. Mem. Fla. (dir.), Am. socs. assn. execs., Council State Chambers Commerce, Fla. C. of C. Execs., Pi Kappa Phi. Democrat. Baptist. Clubs: River (Jacksonville); Capital City Country, Tiger Bay (Tallahassee). Home: 3057 Carlow Circle Tallahassee FL 32303 Office: PO Box 5497 Tallahassee FL 32301

SPENCER, SHERWOOD, lawyer; b. Ashland, Ky., Jan. 23, 1913; s. Holmes A. and Mary (Baker) S.; B.B.A., U. Fla., 1933, J.D., 1936; m. Jean Rowe, Dec. 15, 1939; children—William Sherwood, Carol Ann. Admitted to Fla. bar, 1936, U.S. Supreme Ct. bar, 1963; practice law, Hollywood, Fla., 1939—; city atty. Hollywood, 1949-53. Dir. gen. counsel Hollywood Fed. Savs. & Loan Assn.; chmn. bd., gen. counsel Southeast Bank Hollywood Hills, Southeast Bank of Miramar. Mem. grievance com. 15th Jud. Circuit, 1950-55; mem. com. of 100. Mem. Broward County (pres. 1949), Fla. (bd. govs. 1953-63, dir. real property sect. 1971—), Am. (standing com. unauthorized practice of law) bar assns., Fla. Title Assn. (chmn. title examiners' div. 1950-51). Rotarian. Clubs: Emerald Hills Country, Yacht (vice commodore 1948), Lauderdale Yacht. Home: 1600 Rodman St Hollywood FL 33021 Office: Hollywood Fed Bldg Hollywood FL 33022

SPENCER, THOMAS MORRIS, coll. pres.; b. Nolan County, Tex., Nov. 30, 1916; s. Thomas Monroe and Dell (Whitley) S.; B.S., Sam Houston State Tchrs. Coll., 1935, M.A., 1939; Ed.D., U. Houston, 1947; m. Rachel Bradham, Nov. 26, 1936; children—Betty Dell (Mrs. W. M. Von-Maszewski), Thomas Morris, Anna Lou (Mrs. Robert Bragg), Vera Sue (dec.), Willie Jo (Mrs. Gerald Mace). High sch. prin., Holland, Tex., 1935-37; supt. Thrall (Tex.) Ind. Sch. Dist., 1937-41, Llano (Tex.) Ind. Sch. Dist., 1941-42; dep. supt. pub. instrn. State of Tex., 1942-43; supt. Cypress Fairbanks Ind. Sch. Dist., Cypress, Tex., 1943-47; pres. Blinn Coll., Brenham, Tex., 1947-57, South Plains Coll., Levelland, Tex., 1957-61; pres. San Jacinto Coll., Pasadena, Tex., 1961—. Mem. Tex. Adv. Bd. for Nurses Tng., 1951-57; mem. adv. com. to Tex. Commn. on Higher Edn., 1965—; mem. liaison com. Tex. Coordinating Commn. Higher Edn., 1965—; mem. steering com. Tex. Conf. on Edn.; mem. Tex. Council on Aerospace Edn. Chpt. chmn. Washington County A.R.C., 1950—; dist. chmn. Boy Scouts Am., 1956—; dir. United Fund drives. Bd. dirs. House Speaker's Com. of 100. Dist. Salvation Army. Mem. Am. Assn. Jr. Colls. (commn. govt. affairs), Tex. Pub. Jr. Coll. Assn. (pres. 1949—, chmn. legislative com.), Assn. Tex. Colls. and Univs. (dir.), Pasadena C. of C. (past pres.), Woodmen of World, Kappa Delta Pi, Pi Kappa Delta. Mem. Christian Ch. (past chmn. ofcl. bd.). Lion, Rotarian, Mason (Shriner). Home: 706 Cherokee Dr Pasadena TX 77502 Office: 8060 Spencer Hwy Pasadena TX 77505

SPENCER, WARREN FRANK, educator; b. Swan Quarter, N.C., Jan. 27, 1923; s. Carroll Baxter and Lucille Gertrude (Mann) S.; student George Washington U., 1942, U. Fla., 1942-43; B.S.S. cum laude, Georgetown U., 1947; M.A., U. Pa., 1949, Ph.D., 1955; m. Elizabeth Jolanda Toth, Sept. 6, 1947; children—Lucille Mann, Carroll Baxter. Instr. history Salem Coll., Winston-Salem, N.C., 1950-53, asst. prof., 1953-56; asst. prof. Old Dominion U., Norfolk, Va., 1956-57, asso. prof., 1957-61, prof., 1961-67, chmn. div. social studies and dept. history, 1961-67; prof. history U. Ga., Athens, 1967—. Served with AUS, 1943-45. Vis. scholar, Duke, 1952; Am. Philos. Soc. fellow, 1958, 70; recipient 1st Ann. Faculty award Old Dominion U., 1961-62, Best History Book Published in 1970 award Phi Alpha Theta, 1971. Mem. Am. Hist. Assn., So. Hist. Assn. (chmn. European History sect. program com. 1970), Soc. French Hist. Studies, Phi Alpha Theta. Democrat. Episcopalian. Co-founder, pres. Norfolk Hist. Soc., 1966-67. Author: (with Lynn M. Case) The United States and France: Civil War Diplomacy, 1970. Contbr. to profl. jours. Home: 290 Fortson Dr Athens GA 30601 Office: Dept History Univ Georgia Athens GA 30601

SPENCER, WILLA BELLE, educator; b. Chickasha, Okla, July 22, 1913; d. Jefferson Lee and Jessie (Condron) Carter; B.S., Okla. Coll. for Women, 1935; M.S., Okla. State U., 1939; m. Lee Bowen Spencer, Aug. 19, 1939; children—Lee Bowen, Mary Ann, Sarah Margaret. Tchr. Konawa (Okla.) High Sch., 1935-36; instr., asst. prof., asso. prof., dir. women's phys. edn. Okla. Bapt. U., 1936-63; asst. prof. phys. edn. State Coll. Ark., 1963—. Dir. Community Swimming Program, Shawnee, Okla., 1953-63. Bd. dirs. Pottawatomie County chpt. A.R.C., 1950-63, Campfire Girls, U.S.A., Shawnee, 1958-63. Mem. Am. Assn. U. Women (past pres. Shawnee br.), Okla. Soc. Mayflower Descs. (state elder), Am., Ark., Okla. (state chmn. coll. sect. 1961-62) assns. health, phys. edn. and recreation, Delta Kappa Gamma (pres. 1974—). Home: 2002 Prince St Conway AR 72032

SPERBER, PERRY ARTHUR, physician; b. Providence, Oct. 11, 1907; s. Hugo and Hattie (Mann) S.; B.A., Brown U., 1928; M.D., N.Y. U., 1932; m. Muriel Hope Reed, Sept. 28, 1939; children—Gayle Patricia (Mrs. Thomas Eugene Freeman), Perry Reed. Intern N.Y.C. Hosp., 1932-33, resident, 1933-34; resident Correction Hosp., N.Y.C., 1934-35; practice medicine specializing in dermatology, allergy, Providence, 1937-50, Daytona Beach, Fla., 1951—; former mem. staff R.I., Jane Brown hosps., Providence, mem. staff Halifax Dist., Ormond Beach Meml. hosps., Daytona Beach. Curator, Daytona Beach Sea Zoo, 1951-61. Chmn. patrons com. Am. Heart Assn., Daytona Beach, 1967. Fellow Am. Assn. Clin. Immunology and Allergy (pres. Southeastern region 1971-72), A.A.A.S., Am. Med. Writers Assn., Am. Geriatrics Soc., Am. Acad. Allergists; mem. A.M.A., Fla., So. med. assn., Am. Acad. Dermatology, Assn. Mil. Dermatologists, Assn. Cosmetic Plastic Surgeons, Soc. Contemporary Medicine and Surgery. Baptist (deacon). Kiwanian (past pres., lt. gov. 5th div. Fla. 1973-74). Author: Treatment of the Aging Skin and Dermal Defects, 1965; Sex and the Dinosaur, 1970; Drugs, Demons, Doctors and Disease, 1973. Contbr. articles to profl. jours. Address: 816 Wells Dr South Daytona FL 32019

SPERELAKIS, NICK, educator; b. Joliet, Ill., Mar. 3, 1930; s. James and Arestea (Kayadakis) S.; B.S., U. ill., 1951, M.S., 1955, Ph.D., 1957; m. Dolores Martinis, Jan. 28, 1960; children—Nicholas, Mark Demetri, Christine Marie, Sophia Ann, Thomas Andreas and Anthony James (twins). Instr. physiology Western Res. U., Cleve., 1957-59; asst. prof. physiology, 1959-66, asso. prof., 1966; prof. physiology U. Va. Med. Sch., Charlottesville, 1966—. Served with Project Hope in Peru, 1962. Served with USMC, 1951-53. Mem. Am. Physiol. Soc., Biophys. Soc., Am. Soc. Zoologists, Am. Assn. U. Profs., A.A.A.S., I.E.E.E., Soc. Neuroscis., Soc. Gen. Physiologists, Cardiac Muscle Soc., Sigma Xi, Phi Kappa Phi. Mem. Greek Orthodox Ch. Asso. editor Sci. Jour. Contbr. articles in field to profl. jours. Home: 1615 Cedar Hill Rd Charlottesville VA 22901

SPERLING, FREDERICK, educator; b. N.Y.C., Jan. 16, 1913; s. Ben and Ann (Sinkin) S.; S.M., U. Chgo., 1941, Ph.D., 1952; m. Hazel Cooper, May 1, 1972; children—Barry L., Norman. Instr. pharmacology Med. and Dental Sch. Georgetown U., Washington, 1945-48; pharmacologist NIH, Bethesda, Md., 1948-56, U.S. Dept. Agr., Beltsville, Md., 1956; dir. Sperling Lab. div. Foster D. Snell, Inc., Balt., 1956-62; asso. prof. pharmacology Howard U. Med. Sch., Washington, 1962-70, prof., 1970—. Vis. lectr. Howard U., 1956-62; resident vis. scientist FDA, 1968-69; cons. toxicology Nat. Library Medicine, 1967-69; vis. scientist Armed Forces Inst. Pathology, 1972—. Served with AUS, 1942-45. Fellow Am. Inst. Chemists, A.A.A.S., Washington Acad. Sci.; mem. N.Y. Acad. Sci., Soc. Toxicology (chmn. edn. com. 1969-70), Soc. Exptl. Biology and Medicine (nat. com. mem. 1970—), Am. Soc. Pharmacology and Exptl. Therapeutics. Contbr. profl. jours. Home: 1131 University Blvd W Silver Spring MD 20902 Office: College Medicine Howard Univ Washington DC 20001

SPERLING, HARRY GEORGE, educator; b. N.Y.C., Aug. 26, 1924; s. Edward and Beatrice Kellar (Baer) S.; A.B., U. Pa., 1944; M.S., New Sch. Social Research, 1946; Ph.D., Columbia, 1953; m. Doris Newman, June 16, 1950; children—Linda, Diane. Sect. head psychophysics and colorimetry, vision br. USN Med. Research Lab., New London, Conn., 1949-59; mgr. manned systems research Honeywell Co., Mpls., 1959-67; prof., dir. sensory scis. center U. Tex., Houston, 1967—. Adj. prof. physiol. optics Baylor Med. Coll., 1967—; adj. prof. math. scis. Rice U., 1973—. Bd. dirs. Inst. Ophthalmology, Tex. Med. Center, Inc. Fellow Optical Soc. Am.; mem. Internat. Research Group Colour Vision Deficiencies (dir. 1973—). Contbr. to profl. publs. Office: Texas Medical Center 6420 Lamar Fleming Blvd Houston TX 77025

SPERO, MORTON BERTRAM, lawyer; b. N.Y.C., Dec. 6, 1920; s. Adolph Otto and Julia (Strasburger) S.; B.A., U. Va., 1942, LL.B., 1946; m. Louise Thacker, May 1, 1943; children—Donald Steven, Carol (Mrs. Steven A. Roen). Admitted to Va. bar, 1946, U.S. Supreme Ct. bar, 1961; mem. legal staff NLRB, 1946-48; partner Nat-Sales Co., Petersburg, Va., 1948-61; practice, Petersburg, 1961-71; partner firm Spero & Levinson, Petersburg, 1971—. Chmn. campaign United Fund Petersburg, 1960, pres., 1964-65; chmn. Dist. IV Va. Council on Social Welfare, 1969; mem. profl. adv. staff Southside Mental Health Assn., 1963; co-chmn. Nat. Conf. Christians and Jews, Petersburg, 1951-55; mem. council USO, Peterburg, 1965—; organizer cub scout pack 152 Robert E. Lee council Boy Scouts Am. Chmn. Howell for Gov., Petersburg, 1973. Served with USNR, 1942-45. Recipient Service to Law Enforcement citation Petersburg Police Dept., 1965; named Outstanding mem. B'nai B'rith Petersburg, 1966. Mem. Va. State Bar (chmn. criminal law sect 1972-73), Va. Trial Lawyers Assn. (v.p. 1972—), Petersburg Bar Assn. (sec.-treas. 1964-66), Am. Judicature Soc., Tau Epsilon Phi, Jewish religion (pres. congreation 1973—). Elk (exalted ruler 1969), Rotarian; mem. B'nai B'rith (state v.p. 1954). Home: 33 Ivy Lane Petersburg VA 23803 Office: Union Trust Bldg Suite 203 Petersburg VA 23808

SPERONIS, STEPHEN LOUIS, educator; b. Lowell, Mass., Dec. 1, 1920; s. Louis Stephen and Katherine (Theodorou) S.; B.A., Boston U., 1947, M.A., 1948; Ph.D., U. Mich., 1956; m. Constance Anne Hatges, June 25, 1950. Teaching fellow U. Mich., 1950-54; prof. U. Tampa, Fla., 1956—, dean evening div., 1959-61, v.p. for devel., 1961-68, spl. asst. to pres., 1969-73, prof. contemporary Am. history, Russian, Middle East, Far East, polit. sci. Resident news analyst WFLA-TV and radio sta., Tampa, 1958; mem. Young Ams. Freedom Staff Radio Free Europe, 1958. Middle East editor, mem. Am. Security Council. Am. Served with AUS, 1942-45. Mem. Mchts. Assn. Tampa (dir.), Sales and Marketing Execs. of Tampa, Phi Alpha Theta, Phi Kappa Phi, V.F.W., Am. Legion, Res. Officers Assn., Lambda Chi Alpha. Mason (32 deg.), Rotarian. Home: 5012 San Miguel St Tampa FL 33609

SPERRY, JOSEPH AUSTIN, II, assn. adminstr.; b. Woodbury, N.J., Jan. 14, 1899; s. Washington Elliot Langley and Sarah (Ridgely) S.; student Washington Coll. Accounting, 1919-21; m. Myrtle Onice Palmer, Sept. 4, 1920; children—Helen (Mrs. R.R. Zimmerman), Myrtle, Joseph Austin III, Dorothy (Mrs. R.V. Legere). With Bur. Internal Revenue, 1919-22; accountant, West Palm Beach, Fla., 1922-36, Fla. Auditing Dept., 1936-39, Bradenton and Tampa, Fla., 1939-41; asst. sec. Superior Fertilizer Co., Tampa, 1941-45; accountant, Sulphur Springs, Fla., 1946—, Dade City Fla., 1951—; mgr. sec. North Tampa C. of C., 1965—. C.P.A., Fla. Home: 6106 Branch Av Tampa FL 33604 Office: PO Box 8247 Tampa FL 33604

SPICKERMAN, WILLIAM REED, educator; b. Council Bluffs, Ia., Dec. 28, 1925; s. Rudolph and Rosina Marie (Smith) S.; B.A., Omaha U., 1949, M.A., 1953; M.S., Xavier U., 1957; Ph.D., U. Ky., 1965; m. Mazuri Sylvene Osteen, June 18, 1957. Tchr. Neola (Ia.) Pub. Schs., 1949-50; engr., 1951-52; tchr., Council Bluffs, Ia., 1952-56; tech. engr. Gen. Elec. Co., Cin., 1956-57; tchr., Cin., 1957-58; engr. Avco Corp., Cin., 1958-60; specialist engr. Goodyear Aircraft, Akron, O., 1960-61; sr. scientist Spindletop Research, Lexington, Ky., 1965-67; asso. prof. math. E. Carolina U., 1967-70, prof., 1970—. Served with AUS, 1944-46. Mem. Am. Math. Assn., Math. Assn. Am., Soc. Indsl. and Applied Math., Operations Research Soc. (asso.), Am. Assn. Univ. Profs., N.E.A. Moose. Author: (with T.J. Dignani) Basic Geometry, 1969. Home: 1302 E 14th St Greenville NC 27834

SPICOLA, GUY WILLIAM, lawyer, state legislator; b. Tampa, Fla., Feb. 27, 1938; s. Joseph G. and Alma (Norona) S.; B.A., U. Fla., 1960, LL.B., 1962; m. Bonnie Sharon Wallace, Aug. 19, 1961; children—Brandon Sean, Betsy Sue; m. 2d, Georgie Ann Blevins, Sept. 1, 1973. Admitted to Fla. bar, 1962; atty. finance and taxation coms. Fla. Ho. of Reps., 1963, mem., 1967—, majority whip, 1969—, chmn. environmental protection com.; atty. City of Temple Terrace (Fla.), 1963-66. Pres., bd. dirs. Young Democrats Hillsborough County, 1965-66; alternate del. Dem. Nat. Conv., 1968. Mem. Am., Tampa-Hillsborough County bar assns., Fla. Bar, Am., Bay Area (pres.) trial lawyers assns., Acad. Fla. Trial Lawyers, Am. Judicature Soc., Tampa, Tampa Jr chambers commerce, Phi Delta Phi, Alpha Tau Omega. Roman Catholic. Clubs: Palma Ceia Golf and Country, Merrymakers. Address: 725 E Kennedy Tampa FL 33602

SPIELVOGEL, BERNARD FRANKLIN, chemist; b. Ellwood City, Apr. 23, 1937; S. Rudolph and Johanna Walberger (Frank) S.; B.S. in Chemistry and Physics, Geneva Coll., 1959; Ph.D. (Univ. Scholar fellow), U. Mich., 1963; m. Donna Katherine Scandlin, Aug. 10, 1963; children—Karl, Jan, Jeffrey. Inst. chemistry U. N.C. at Chapel Hill, 1963-64, asst. prof., 1964-67; program dir. Army Research Office, Durham, N.C., 1967—. Adj. asso. prof. chemistry Duke, 1972—. Petroleum Research Fund grantee, 1964; Army Research Office grantee, 1972. Mem. Am., London chem. socs., Elisha Mitchell Sci. Soc., Am. Assn. U. Profs., Sigma Xi. Contbr. research articles on chemistry to sci. publs. Home: 100 Ashe Place Chapel Hill NC 27514 Office: Box CM Duke St Durham NC 27706

SPIERS, JAMES MONROE, plant physiologist; b. Wiggins, Miss., July 31, 1940; s. Irvin P. and Vivian (O'Neal) S.; Asso. Sci., Peekinston Jr. Coll., 1961; B.S., Miss. State U., 1963, M.S., 1966; Ph.D., Tex. A. and M. U., 1969; children—Gina E., Wendi K. Research plant physiologist U.S. Research Lab., Poplarville, Miss., 1969—, location and research leader, 1972—. Mem. Am., Internat. socs. hort. sci., Am. Soc. Agronomy. Home: Route 1 Box 20 Wiggins MS 39577 Office: Box 287 Poplarville MS 39470

SPIEWAK, IRVING, nuclear engr.; b. Bklyn., Jan. 5, 1928; s. Meyer and Ethel (Teichteil) S.; B. Chem. E., Cooper Union, 1947; M.S., Mass. Inst. Tech., 1948; m. Mary Bryan, July 19, 1953; children—Alan Richard, Jonathan Andrew, Leah. With Oak Ridge Nat. Lab., 1949—, dep. dir. nuclear desalination program, 1965—. Pres. Oak Ridge Playhouse, 1957; concertmaster Oak Ridge Symphony, 1953; mem. Anderson County (Tenn.) Sch. Bd., 1967—. Mem. Am. Inst. Chem. Engrs., Am. Nuclear Soc. Jewish religion (pres. congregation, 1965-68). Mem. B'nai B'rith. Home: 712 S Main St Clinton TN 37716 Office: Oak Ridge Nat Lab PO Box Y Oak Ridge TN 37830

SPIGAI, DANIEL JOHN, cons. engr.; b. Bronx, N.Y., Mar. 4, 1933; s. James and Victoria (Abbate) S.; B.S., Manhattan Coll., 1954; m. Jacqueline Elizabeth Parisi, Jan. 18, 1958; children—Lisa, Victoria, David, Daniela. Engr. trainee N.Y. Central R.R., Weekaukee, N.J., 1954; with Howard, Needles, Tammen & Bergendoff, N.Y. and N.J., 1957-70, project mgr., to 1970; asso. Howard, Needles, Tammen & Bergendoff, Fairfield, N.J. and Alexandria, Va., 1971-73, partner, 1974—. Mem. planning bd. Borough of Oakland (N.J.), 1967. Served with AUS, 1955-57. Registered profl. engr., N.Y., N.J., Pa., Conn., Del., Va., Ga., Me., Vt., Fla., Mass., N.H. Mem. Am. Soc. C.E., Nat., N.Y. State socs. profl. engrs., Airport Operators Council Internat., Am. Assn. Airport Execs. Home: 1304 Chancel Pl Alexandria VA 22314 Office: 130 N Royal St PO Box 186 Alexandria VA 22313

SPILDE, LULU MARY CASLEY (MRS. OTIS SPILDE), educator; b. Flandreau, S.D.; d. Hugh and Elizabeth (Lane) Casley; B.S., S.D. State U., 1914; M.A., U. S.D., 1925; Ed.D., N.Y. U. 1942; m. Otis Spilde, June 8, 1921. Prin pub. schs., Bryant, S.D., 1914-21, Vienna, S.D., 1921-23; dean women, dir. tchr. tng. U. S.D. at Springfield, 1925-39, Fordham U., N.Y.C., 1944-46; prof. edn., dir. tchr. tng. St. John's U., Jamaica, N.Y., 1946-65; prof. edn. Niagara U., Niagara Falls, 1966-68, Ft. Lauderdale (Fla.) U., 1968—. Lectr., dir. testing and guidance, dir. extension centers; cons. state dept., Pierre, S.D.; active sch. surveys Nassau County, N.Y., 1961-62, Pres. So. dist. P.T.A., S.D., 1937-39, Am. Legion Aux., Vienna, S.D., 1923-25; supreme nat. dir. edn. Cath. Daus. Am., 1940-65. Mem. Am. Assn. U. Women, Am. Assn. U. Profs., N.E.A., Nat. Cath. Edn. Assn. Author: Audio-Visual Aids in Education, 1958, Observation and Student Teaching, 1961, Techniques of Oral Book Reviews, 1963. Contbr. articles to profl. mags. Home: 1201 SE 2d St Fort Lauderdale FL 33301

SPILHAUS, ATHELSTAN, meterologist and oceanographer; b. Cape Town, Union of S. Africa, Nov. 25, 1911; s. Karl Antonio and Nellie (Muir) S.; B.Sc., U. Cape Town, 1931, D.Sc., 1948; S.M., Mass. Inst. Tech., 1933; D.Sc., Coe Coll., 1961, Hahnemann Med. Coll., 1968, U. R.I., 1968, Phila. Coll. of Pharmacy and Sci., 1969, Hamilton Coll., 1970, Southeastern Mass. U., 1970, Durham (Eng.) U., 1970, U. S.C., 1971, Southwestern at Memphis, 1972; LL.D., Nova U., 1970; m. Gail Griffin, 1964; children by previous marriage—Athelstan F., Mary Muir, Eleanor, Margaret Ann, Karl Henry. Came to U.S., 1931, naturalized, 1946. Research asst. Mass. Inst. Tech., 1934-35; asst. dir. tech. services Union of S. Africa Def. Forces, Pretoria, 1935-36: research asst. Woods Hole Oceanographic Instn., Woods Hole, Mass., and Cambridge, Mass., 1936-37, investigator in phys. oceanography, 1938, phys. oceanographer, 1940—; asst. prof. meterology N.Y. U., 1937, asso. prof., 1937-42, prof., 1942, dir. research, 1946; meteorol. adviser to Union S. Africa Govt., 1947; dean Inst. Tech. U. Minn., 1949-66, prof. physics, 1966-67; pres. Franklin Inst., Phila., 1967-69; Woodrow Wilson fellow Internat. Center for Scholars Smithsonian Instn., Washington, 1972—. Science Service, Inc.; trustee Aerospace Corp., Los Angeles; U.S. commr. Seattle World's Fair, 1961-62; chmn. nat. fisheries center and aquarium adv. bd. U.S. Dept. Interior. Mem. adv. coms. for armed forces; mem. nat. com. Internat. Geophys. year; mem. com. on oceanography, com. on polar research Nat. Acad. Scis.; mem. exec. bd. UNESCO, 1955-58. Trustee Woods Hole Oceanographic Instn., St. Paul Inst.; mem. Nat. Sci. Bd., 1966-72. Served from capt. to lt. col. USAAF, 1943-46. Decorated Legion of Merit, Exception Civilian Service award Dept. Army. Fellow Royal Meterol. Soc., Am. Inst. Aeros. and Astronautics; mem. Am. Soc. Limnology and Oceanography, Am. Soc. Engring. Edn., Minn. Soc. Profl. of Engrs., Am. Meteorol. Soc., Royal Soc. So. Africa, A.A.A.S. (pres. 1970, chmn. bd. 1971), Am. Philos. Soc., Am. Geophys. Union, Tau Beta Pi, Sigma Xi, Iota Alpha. Episcopalian. Clubs: Racquet (Phila.); Cosmos (Washington). Inventor of Rathythermograph., 1938. Contbr. Jour. of Marine Research. Jour. of Meterology; author: Workbook of Meteorology: Weathercraft: Meteorological Instruments; Satellite of the Sun, Our

New Age, Turn to the Sea, The Ocean Laboratory. Home: 2815 28th St NW Washington DC 20008 Office: NOAA Room 629 425 13th St Washington DC 20004

SPILLANE, LEO JEROME, asphalt co. pres.; b. New Richland, Minn., Aug. 23, 1916; s. John Jerome and Anastasia Florence (Gossman) S.; B.S., St. Thomas Coll., 1937; M.S., U. Minn., 1940, Ph.D., 1942; m. Kathryn Frances Grady, June 16, 1945; children—Stacia, Margaret (Mrs. Henry Steinhoff), Leo Jerome, Kathleen, Janet, John, James. Group leader research Allied Chem. Corp., Morristown, N.J., 1942-49; chief chemist Reaction Motors, Inc., Rockaway, N.J., 1949-51; asst. dir. research Lion Oil Co., El Dorado, Ark., 1951-55; mgr. research Monsanto Co., El Dorado, and St. Louis, 1955-69; pres. Gulf States Asphalt Co., Houston, 1969—; also dir. Mem. Am. Chem. Soc. (chmn. local sects. 1955, 66), Am. Inst. Chem. Engrs., Am. Petroleum Inst., Am. Mgmt. Assn., Petroleum Club Houston, Sigma Xi, Phi Lambda Upsilon. Chmn. troop com. DeSoto and St. Louis councils Boy Scouts Am., 1953-66, asst. scoutmaster Houston council, 1971-72. Patentee in field. Home: 13134 Kimberley Lane Houston TX 77024 Office: 1212 Main Bldg Houston TX 77002

SPILLMAN, JOHN HARRY, dentist; b. Jackson, Miss., Jan 15, 1923; s. Louis Cromwell and Lula (Melvin) S.; student Millsaps Coll., 1941-42; D.D.S., Emory U., 1950; m. Nancy Elizabeth Fairley, Mar. 2, 1957; children—John Harry, Catherine Fairley, Thomas Archie. Individual practice dentistry, Winston-Salem, N.C., 1950—. Mem. Winston-Salem Bd. Health, 1968—; mem. adv. com. Winston-Salem Animal Shelter, 1970—; commnr. Community Devel. Program, 1971—, Bd. dirs. N.C. Dental Found. Served to lt. col. USAF, World War II. Fellow Internat. Coll. Dentists; mem. N.C. Assn. Professions (dir.), Am. Coll. Dentists, N.C. (sec.-treas. 1972-74, exec. com. 1972-74), Forsyth County (pres. 1958, pres. 2d dist. 1968) dental socs. Episcopalian (vestryman). Rotarian. Clubs: Twin City, Old Town. Home: 2860 Holyoke Pl Winston-Salem NC 27106 Office: 140 Lockland Av Winston-Salem NC 27103

SPILMAN, LOUIS, editor; b. Crawfordsville, Ind., Jan. 7, 1899; s. Theodore Bruce and Susan Dale (Boughner) S.; student Wabash Coll.; m. Emily Jane Moon, Sept. 15, 1920; children—Susan (Mrs. V.F. Reynolds), Mary Emily (Mrs. E.O. Davisson), William, Louis, Robert, Martha (Mrs. Paul R. Clark). City editor Marion (Ind.) Chronicle, 1920-24; editor-mgr. Lyman Publ. Corp. div. Fed. Bus. Publ., N.Y.C., 1924-29; pres., editor, pub. News-Virginian, Waynesboro, Va., 1929-64, chmn. bd., 1964—; daily columnist, 1934—; sec., dir. Waynesboro Hotel Corp., 1937-41; corr. U.S. Atomic Bomb Tests, Bikini, 1946; chmn. bd. Glasgow (Ky.) Daily Times, 1957—; Mem. Meth. Com. Overseas Relief, 1952-64, mem. pub. relations and Meth. Information com., 1964-68; chmn. Gov.'s Study Commn. on Vocational Rehab., 1967-69; mem. U.S. Dept. Commerce Trade Mission to Germany, 1962. Chmn., Augusta County Flood Control Commn., 1972-73. Bd. dirs. Germanna Found. Served as sgt. U.S. inf., 1916-17, 2d lt. USAAC, 1917-18. Mem. Va. Press Assn. (pres. 1933-35), Va. UN Assn. (dir.), So. Newspaper Pub. Assn., Va. Farm Bur., Am. Legion, Phi Gamma Delta, Sigma Delta Chi. Democrat. Mason (Shriner), Rotarian. Author: So This Is South America, 1962. Home: 700 Locust Av PO Box 747 Waynesboro VA 22980 Office: 544 W Main St PO Drawer 1027 Waynesboro VA 22980

SPILMAN, WILLIAM BRUCE, newspaper exec.; b. N.Y.C., July 28, 1927; s. Louis and Emily (Moon) S.; A.B., Wabash Coll., 1950; m. Patricia Elaine Black, Feb. 3, 1951; children—Rebecca Elaine, Elizabeth Jane, Barbara Ellen, William Black. With Waynesboro Pub. Co. (Va.), 1937—, rural editor, 1952, sports editor, 1953-54, mech. supt., 1955-58, bus. mgr., 1958-63, pres. corp., 1963—. Chmn. fund drive A.R.C., Waynesboro, E. Augusta County, 1953; presdl. appointee Ann. Assay Commn., Phila., 1967; treas. Waynesboro YMCA, 1971—; mem. adv. com. Blue Ridge Community Coll.; chmn. Old Dominion Advt. Conf., 1961. Served with USMCR, 1944-46, to 2d lt., 1950-51. Mem. Va. Press Assn. (pres. 1968-69), Waynesboro C. of C., Waynesboro Retail Mchts. Assn. (pres. 1971-72), Am., Va. (life) numis. assns., Marine Corps Res. Officers Assn., Token and Medal Soc. (nat. pres. 1966-68), Marine Corps League (central Va. detachment), Sigma Delta Chi, Phi Gamma Delta, Pi Delta Epsilon. Democrat. Methodist. Mason (Shriner), Rotarian. Club: U.S. Auto (life mem.). Home: 1837 Cherokee Rd Waynesboro VA 22980 Office: 544 W Main St Waynesboro VA 22980

SPINELLA, NICHOLAS ANTHONY, lawyer; b. Richmond, Va., Feb. 22, 1924; s. Anthony and Florence (Rovigo) S.; J.D., U. Richmond Law Sch., 1949; m. Zelda M. Passeri, Sept. 11, 1948; children—Debra Anne, Joan Marie. Admitted to Va. bar, 1949; sr. partner Spinella, Spinella & Owings, Richmond, 1949—. Bd. dirs., atty. St. Mary's Hosp., Richmond, 1968—; atty. Cath. Diocese Richmond, 1963—. Bd. dirs. Nurses Profl. Registry, Richmond, 1962—; bd. dirs., treas. Seton House Home for Un-Wed Mothers, Richmond, 1958—. Mem. Am., Va., Richmond bar assns., Va. Trial Lawyers Assn. K.C. Club: Serra Internat. (dist. gov. 1973). Home: 8955 Wishart Rd Richmond VA 23229 Office: 5421 Patterson Av Richmond VA 23226

SPINK, WILLIAM THOMAS, educator; b. Bay City, Mich., Oct. 3, 1910; s. Henry and Inez (Richardson) S.; B.S., U. Miami, Coral Gables, Fla., 1953; M.S., U. N.C., 1955, Ph.D., 1958; m. Nellie Mary Barron, Oct. 3, 1932. Mem. faculty dept. entomology La. State U., Baton Rouge, 1958—, asso. prof., 1962-68, prof., 1968—. Served to maj. USAAF, 1942-46. Decorated Medal Commendation. Mem. Entomol. Soc. Am., Am. Biol. Assn., La. Entomol. Soc., La. Pest Control Assn., Sigma Xi, Gamma Sigma Delta. Home: 336 Baird Dr Baton Rouge LA 70808 Office; Life Scis Bldg La State Univ Baton Rouge LA 70803

SPINKS, JOHN DAVIDSON, JR., pub. relations firm exec.; b. Winston-Salem, N.C., July 16, 1924; s. John D. and Sarah (Boals) S.; student N.C. State Coll., 1942, 46-47, U. N.C., 1947-49; m. Edith L. Forbes, Aug. 26, 1950; children—Claire P., Rebecca H. City editor Daily Reflector, Greenville, N.C., 1950-51; asst. state editor News and Observer, Raleigh, N.C., 1951-53; spl. writer Twin City Sentinel, Winston-Salem, 1953-56; supr. employee communications McLean Trucking Co., Winston-Salem, 1956-64; mgr. pub. relations services firm Long, Haymes & Carr, Winston-Salem, 1964-72; pres., owner John Spinks Pub. Relations, Winston-Salem, 1972—. Sec. YMCA, Winston-Salem, 1963; chmn. pub. relations com. United Fund, Winston-Salem, 1972. Served with AAC, 1942-46. Mem. Am. Assn. Indsl. Editors (pres. 1963-64), Pub. Relations Soc. Am., Pub. Relations Roundtable Winston-Salem (past pres.). Presbyn. (edler). Home: 4072 Beaver Brook Rd Clemmons NC 27012 Office: 708 1st Center Bldg Winston-Salem NC 27104

SPINKS, PAUL CALHOUN, ins. co. exec.; b. Campbell, Tex., Feb. 1, 1934; s. Brittian Calhoun and Bertha (Fitzgerald) S.; B.B.A., East Tex. U., 1957; m. Molly-Jane Sinkule, Mar. 12, 1959; children—Paula Michele, Michael Calhoun, Donna Gayle. With Fidelity Union Life Ins. Co., Dallas, 1959—, asst. v.p., 1971-72, v.p. investment operations, 1972—; pres., dir. Continental Properties Inc., Dallas, 1973—; v.p., treas. May Tex, Inc., Dallas, 1970—; treas. Mayflower Trust, 1971—. Bd. dirs. Neighborhood Housing Services Dallas. Served with AUS, 1954-55. C.P.A., Tex. Mem. Nat. Assn. Accountants (dir. profl. devel. Dallas), Tex. Soc. C.P.A.'s, Am. Inst. C.P.A.'s. Home: 311 Meadowcrest St Richardson TX 75080 Office: 411 N Akard St Dallas TX 75201

SPINN, ROGER WILLIAM, lawyer; b. Brenham, Tex., Apr. 25, 1939; s. Richard Charles and Helena (Schieffer) S.; student Southwestern U., Georgetown, Tex., 1957-58, Blinn Jr. Coll., 1958-59; B.S., Sam Houston State U., 1961; LL.B., U. Tex. at Austin, 1964; m. Margie Ann Hinze, June 13, 1959; children—Matthew William, Mark Wesley, June. Admitted to Tex. bar, 1964; partner firm Spinn, Ehlert, Spinn, Weisler & Weisler, Brenham, 1964—; atty. City of Brenham, 1968—. Chmn. Washington County Democratic Com., 1968-72. Recipient Distinguished Service award Brenham Jr. C. of C., 1967. Mem. Tex., Am. bar assns., Tex. Trial Lawyers Assn. Kiwanian. Home: 900 Geney St Brenham TX 77833 Office: PO Box 1118 Brenham TX 77833

SPINNER, ERNEST, chemist; b. Bklyn., Apr. 20, 1944; s. Irving and Geraldine (Chernick) S.; B.S. cum laude, L.I. Univ., 1965; Ph.D., U. Pa., 1970; m. Linda Barychewsky, Oct. 5, 1969; 1 dau., Clotho Alexis. Research asso. Internat. Paper Co., Mobile, Ala., 1970—. Recipient honor award in chemistry, L.I. Univ., 1965; NSF trainee, 1965-68, Allied Chem. fellow, 1969. Mem. Am. Chem. Soc. (treas. sect. 1972-74), Sigma Xi. Home: Route 3 Box 1105 Theodore AL 36582 Office: PO Box 2328 Mobile AL 36601

SPIRTES, MORRIS ALBERT, physician; b. N.Y.C., July 11, 1911; s. Samuel and Ida (Albert) S.; B.S., Coll. City N.Y., 1931; M.D., U. Zurich, 1936; m. Cecile Vaughan, Jan. 15, 1945; children—Judy (Mrs. Ronald Hale), Richard, David, Peter. Intern, Lincoln Hosp., Bronx, N.Y., 1936-37; resident internal medicine Montefiore Hosp., Bronx, 1937-39; postdoctoral studies biochemistry, 1946-49; research asso. Biochem. Cancer Inst., Phila., 1949-53; asso. prof. pharmacology Hahnemann Med. Coll., 1953-65; prof. pharmacology U. Pitts., also asso. chief staff for research VA, 1965-71; prof. pharmacology Tulane U., also research physician, chief neuropharmacology VA, 1971—; lectr. Anzac Postgrad. Med. Soc., 1970. Served with M.C., AUS, World War II; PTO. Fellow Am. Cancer Soc. for Research. Home: 2116 Octavia St New Orleans LA 70115 Office: 1430 Tulane Av New Orleans LA 70112

SPITZER, CARY REDFORD, instrumentation engr.; b. New Hope, Va., July 31, 1937; s. Clyde Burke and Marion Jeanette (Redford) S.; B.S., Va. Poly. Inst., 1958; M.S. in Adminstrn., George Washington U., 1970; m. Carrie Laura Ruth Logan, June 18, 1960; 1 son, Stiegel Logan. Instrumentation engr. NASA, Hampton, Va., 1962-69, molecular analysis expts. mgr. Project Viking, 1969-70, phys. and magnetic properties investigations mgr., 1970—. Served with USAF, 1959-62. Mem. I.E.E.E. (sr.), sect. chmn. 1968-69), Aerospace and Electronic Systems Soc. (v.p. tech. operations, 1969-72, pres. 1973), Pi Delta Epsilon, Rho Tau Sigma. Methodist (lay leader 1966-67, chmn. adminstrv. bd. 1972—). Patentee in field. Home: Route 1 Box 227B Williamsburg VA 23185 Office: Langley Sta MS 159 Hampton VA 23665

SPITZER, CHARLES EDGAR, JR., metals co. exec.; b. Lynchburg, Va., May 11, 1924; s. Charles Edgar and Ora (Monroe) S.; B.S. in Archtl. Engring., Va. Poly. Inst., 1949; m. Jean Lucille Hess, July 20, 1946; children—Charles E., J. Garry, B. Scott, Cynthia Jean. Engr., draftsman Va. Metal Products, Orange, Va. 1949-50; with So. Iron Works, Inc., Springfield, Va., 1950—, exec. v.p., 1963-64, pres., 1964—; dir. UVB First & Citizens Nat. Bank, Alexandria, Va., 1972—. Bd. dirs. Alexandria Hosp. Corp., 1966-69. Served to 1st lt. C.E., AUS, 1943-46; PTO. Mem. Va.-Carolinas Structural Steel Fabricators Assn. (pres. 1969), Tau Beta Pi, Tau Sigma Delta. Methodist. Club: Belle Haven (Alexandria, Va.). Home: 1606 Mason Hill Dr Alexandria VA 22307 Office: 6600 Electronic Dr Springfield VA 22150

SPITZNAGEL, JOHN KEITH, educator; b. Peoria, Ill., Apr. 11, 1923; s. Elmer Florian and Anna (Kolb) S.; B.A., Columbia, 1943, M.D., 1946; m. Anne Moulton Sirch, Feb. 2, 1947; children—John, Jean, Margaret, Elizabeth, Paul. Intern Johns Hopkins Hosp., Balt., 1946-47; resident Barnes Hosp., St. Louis, 1949-51; vis. investigator Rockefeller Inst., N.Y.C., 1951-52; mem. faculty Sch. Medicine, U. N.C. at Chapel Hill, 1957—, prof. microbiology and infectious diseases, 1957—; mem. staff N.C. Meml. Hosp., Chapel Hill, Watts Hosp., Durham, N.C. Ad hoc adviser NIH, 1971—, cons., 1974—. Served with M.C., U.S. Army, 1947-57. USPHS postdoctoral fellow, 1968; grantee USPHS, AEC. Diplomate Nat. Bd. Med. Examiners, Am. Bd. Internal Medicine. Fellow A.C.P.; mem. Am. Assn. Immunologists, Infectious Disease Soc., A.A.A.S., A.M.A., Am. Assn. U. Profs., So. Soc. Clin. Research, Sigma Xi. Editor: Infection and Immunity, 1970—, Jour. Immunology, 1973—. Discoverer of chem. nature of bacteria-killing substances in white blood cells. Home: Iris Lane Chapel Hill NC 27514 Office: 140 McNider Hall Chapel Hill NC 27514

SPIVAK, LAWRENCE E(DMUND), TV-radio producer; b. N.Y.C.; s. William B. and Sonya (Bershad) S.; A.B., Harvard; LL.D., Wilberforce U.; D.Litt., Suffolk U.; L.H.D., Tampa U.; m. Charlotte Beir Ring; children—Judith (Mrs. Wm. Lee Frost) (dec.), Jonathan. Bus. mgr. Antiques Mag., 1921-30; asst. to the pub. Hunting and Fishing, Nat. Sportsman mags., 1930-33; bus. mgr. Am. Mercury, 1934-39, pub. 1939-44, editor, pub., 1944-50; founder, pub. Ellery Queen's Mystery Mag., The Mag. of Fantasy and Science Fiction, Mercury Mystery Books, Bestseller Mysteries, Jonathan Press Books, until 1954. Producer-founder TV program Meet the Press, radio, 1945—, TV, 1947—. Recipient two Peabody awards, Emmy award for outstanding achievement in coverage of spl. events. Home: Sheraton Park Hotel Washington DC 20008 Office: 2660 Woodley Rd NW Washington DC 20008

SPIVEY, CARL BASCOM, supt. schs.; b. Pensacola, Fla., Apr. 13, 1927; s. Bascom C. and Anna Nancy (Crews) S.; A.B., Asbury Coll., 1951; M.A., U. Ky., 1955; specialist in phys. sci. teaching Washington U., St. Louis, 1960; certificate in adminstrn., U. Ky., 1970; m. Jo Ann Naylor, May 30, 1951; children—Denise Dale, Shelley Jay, Aletha Gay. With Fayette County Pub. Schs., Lexington, Ky., 1955—, tchr. physics, 1955-61, dir. pupil transp. dept., 1961-69, asso. supt., 1969—. NSF fellow Murray State U., 1958-59, Washington U., 1959-60. Mem. Am. Assn. Sch. Adminstrs. (nat. adv. com. 1969—), Am. Assn. Physics Tchrs., Ky. Assn. sch. Adminstrs., Phi Delta Kappa. Home: 3136 Trinity Rd Lexington KY 40503 Office: 400 Lafayette Pkwy Lexington KY 40503

SPIVEY, JAMES SHERWOOD, exporter; b. Lufkin, Tex., Mar. 2, 1915; s. Madden Calender and Lillie (Hennington) S.; B.S., Tex. A. and M. U., 1937; m. Marilyn Patterson, Nov. 4, 1939; children—Susan, Peter. Mgr., Terrell (Tex.) C. of C., 1939-42; pres., chief exec. officer James S. Spivey, Inc., Washington, 1946—; dir. Haranel Internat. Pty., Ltd., Melbourne, Australia. Pres., Spivey Internat., Inc., Washington, 1950—. Served to lt. col. AUS, 1942-46. Decorated Silver Star, Purple Heart, Bronze Star medal with oak leaf cluster (U.S.); Croix de Guerre (France). Mem. Ind. Telephone Pioneer Assn., Washington Bd. Trade, 90th Div. Assn. Presbyn. (elder). Rotarian (pres. Washington). Clubs: Congressional Country (Washington). Home: 10828 Alloway Dr Potomac MD 20854 Office: 3817 Livingston St NW Washington DC 20015

SPIVEY, JOHN B., lawyer; b. Adrian, Ga., Jan. 29, 1897; s. Levi and Katharine (Drew) S.; student pub. schs., Adrian, Ga.; m. Florrie Dean Ricks, Apr. 12, 1918; children—Julia Christine (Mrs. Walter Hodges Rountree), Ruby Kathryn (Mrs. Ernest Alexander Grindler). Admitted to Ga. bar, 1915; practiced in Swainsboro, 1919—; mem. firm Spivey and Carlton, 1919—; judge Superior Ct., Middle Judicial Circuit, 1966. Pres., 1st Fed. Savings & Loan Assn., Swainsboro, 1965—. Spivey State Bank, Swainsboro, 1965—; chmn. bd. Swainsboro Gas Co., 1950—. City councilman, Swainsboro, 1925, mayor pro-tem, 1925-30; mem. Ga. Ho. of Reps., 1930-36; pres. Ga. State Senate, 1937-41. Served with inf. U.S. Army, 1918. Mem. Am., Ga., Middle Jud. bar assns. Methodist (trustee). Rotarian. Home: 326 W Main St Swainsboro GA 30401 Office: 102 N Main St Swainsboro GA 30401

SPIVEY, SHERMAN REX, real estate broker; b. Texhoma, Okla., Aug. 26, 1921; s. Joseph Randolph and Alice (James) S.; student univ. student, 1939-41; m. Adeline Martha Hintlian, May 4, 1958; children—Joseph, Margaret, Christopher, Michael, Edward, Martha. With Geophys. Service Inc., India, Saudi Arabia, U.S., 1946-59, party chief, 1954-59; owner, broker Rivercliff Realty Co., Rogers, Ark., 1959—; owner, mgr. Rivercliff Farms, War Eagle, Ark., 1963—; dir. Carroll Electric Co-op Corp. Treas., Benton County Com. Republican party, 1966-67. Bd. dirs. Benton County Farm Bur., 1964-68. Served with USAAF, 1942-46. Mem. Rogers C. of C. (dir.), Soc. Exploration Geophysicists, Rogers Bd. Realtors (pres. 1972, Realtor of Year 1972). Roman Catholic. Elk, Rotarian. Home: 1 Rivercliff Rd Rogers AR 72756 Office: PO Box 825 Rogers AR 72756

SPOERL, EDWARD SCHNURR, govt. ofcl.; b. Knowles, Wis., Apr. 3, 1918; s. Edward Jacob and Myrtle Ida (Schnurr) S.; B.S., U. Wis., 1940; postgrad. Cornell U., 1943-44; Ph.D., U. Wis., 1947; m. Barbara M. Gray, Oct. 19, 1946; children—Patricia M., Robert E. Asst. prof. botany dept. U. Ariz., Tucson, 1947-48; chief biochemistry section Mound Lab., Miamisburg, O., 1948-54; chief cell research branch Army Med. Research Lab., Fort Knox, Ky., 1954-62; dir. biophysics div. Army Med. Research Lab., 1962-72; chief biol. branch Army Foreign Sci. and Tech. Center, Charlottesville, Va., 1973—. Lectr., Univ. Coll., U. Louisville, 1958-63. Mem. A.A.A.S., Biophysi. Soc., Am. Soc. Microbiology, Am. Chem. Soc., Am. Soc. Cell Biology, Radiation Research Soc., Am. Soc. Plant Physiology, Bot. Soc. Am., Sigma Xi. Contbr. numerous articles to profl. publs. Home: 1834 Yorktown Dr Charlottesville VA 22901 Office: Army Foreign Sci and Tech Center 220 7th St NE Charlottesville VA 22901

SPOONER, ARTHUR ELMON, educator; b. Lucedale, Miss., Dec. 12, 1920; s. William Webster and Mamie (Driskell) S.; B.S., Miss. State U., 1951, M.S., 1952; Ph.D., Purdue U., 1955; m. Mamie Lou Pierce, Sept. 19, 1942; children—Mary Alice (Mrs. Douglas Charles Loberg), Arthur Elmon Jr. Mem. faculty dept. agronomy U. Ark., Fayetteville, 1955—, asso. prof., 1959-64, prof., 1964—. Chmn. bd. dirs. Ark. Enterprises for Blind, 1968-69. Served with USAAF, 1943-46. Decorated Purple Heart, Air Medal with 2 oak leaf clusters; recipient certificate merit Am. Forage and Grassland Council, 1969. Mem. Am. Soc. Agronomy (pres. So. br.), Am. Forage and Grassland Council, Acacia. Lion, Mason, Elk. Contbr. profl. jours. Home: 2272 Briarwood Lane Fayetteville AR 72701 Office: Dept Agronomy Univ Ark Fayetteville AR 72701

SPOONER, RONALD LEE, research co. exec.; b. Detroit, Oct. 8, 1939; s. Clarence D. and Eleanor (White) S.; M.S. in Engring. (I.F.C. fellow 1962, Gannett fellow 1963), U. Mich., 1963, M.S. in Math., 1965, Ph.D. in Engring., 1967; m. Linda Ethel Ellis, June 15, 1962; children—Lisa, Susan. Research engr. Cooley Electronic Lab, Ann Arbor, Mich., 1964-68; asso. dir. Bolt Beraner & Newman Co., Washington, 1968-72; v.p., treas. Planning Systems Inc., Washington, 1972—. Adj. prof. dept. elec. engring. Catholic U. Am., Washington, 1968—. Treas. Annandale (Va.) Coop. Nursery Sch., 1972; mem. For Love of Children, Washington, 1968—. U. Fla. grantee, 1964. Mem. I.E.E.E., Acoustical Soc. Am., Washington Acad. Scis., U.S. Naval Inst., Sigma Xi, Eta Kappa Nu, Tau Beta Pi, Phi Kappa Phi, Alpha Tau Omega. Club: Fairfax Tennis (Va.) Contbr. to profl. jours. Home: 3804 King Arthur St Annandale VA 22003 Office: 7900 W Park Dr McLean VA 22101

SPORRE, ROBERT ALFRED, educator, performing arts adminstr.; b. Mpls., June 25, 1922; s. Alfred and Catherine (Holzemer) S.; student Grinnell Coll., 1940-42; B.A., U. Ia., 1949; M.F.A., Tex. Christian U., 1957; Ph.D., Ohio State U., 1963. Dancer Anna Sokolow's Co., N.Y.C., 1950-51; dir. Ethan Allan Players, Brandon, Vt., summers, 1952, 53; instr. drama U. Tex., Austin, 1957-60, also asst. to Dean Coll. Fine Arts; prof. speech and drama U. Wis.-Platteville, 1963-70, mem. faculty senate, 1963-66; guest lectr. drama Central Washington State Coll., 1970-72; prof. drama Eastern Ky. U., Richmond, 1972—. Owner, mgr. drama workshops, Bremerton, Wash., Pasco, Wash., Grand Junction, Colo. Mem. gov.'s com. on Arts in Wis., 1966. Served with inf. AUS, 1942-46. Research grantee U. Wis., 1967. Mem. Am. Theatre Assn. (chmn. stage movement, dance project 1964-69), Speech Communication Assn. Conglist. (bd. deacons 1966-69). Principle prodns. include Twelfth Night, 1965, Richard II, 1967, Macbeth, 1969, The House of Bernarda Alba, 1968, Lysistrata, 1972, Midsummer Night's Dream, 1973, Home: Route 7 Village Sq Townhouse #10 Richmond KY 40475 Office: Dept of Drama and Speech Eastern Ky Univ Richmond KY 40475

SPOTO, ANGELO PETER, JR., physician; b. Tampa, Fla., Mar. 25, 1933; s. Angelo Peter and Zillah Marie (Renfroe) S.; student U. Fla., 1950-53, Fla. So. Coll., 1953; B.S., Duke, 1956, M.D., 1957; m. Carolyn Jeanette Barbee, Aug. 30, 1958; children—Keith Peter, Elizabeth Anne, Jacqueline Marie. Intern Duke Hosp., 1957-58, med.-allergy fellow, 1958-59; resident internal medicine USAF Hosp., Lackland AFB, Tex., 1960-62, allergy resident Walter Reed Army Med. Center, Washington, 1962-63; physician Watson Clinic, Lakeland, Fla., 1966—, partner, 1968—; clin. asso. prof. medicine U. South Fla., Tampa; mem. staff Lakeland Gen. Hosp. Served to maj. USAF, 1959-66. Recipient Triangle award YMCA, 1971. Fellow Am. Acad. Allergy (chmn. host com. 1973-74), Am. Assn. Certified Allergists (bd. govs. 1970—, co-chmn. certification com. 1972—); mem. Polk County, Fla., So. med. Assns., A.M.A., Fla. (pres.-elect 1973-74), Southeastern allergy assns., Fla., Am. socs. internal medicine. Presbyn. (elder). Research in sickle cell anemia, antihistamine drugs, respiratory failure drug therapy. Contbr. articles to profl. jours. Home: 2515 Hollingsworth Hill Lakeland FL 33803 Office: Watson Clinic 1600 Lakeland Hills Blvd Lakeland FL 33802

SPRABERY, ARCHIE PATRICK, physician; b. Tupelo, Miss., Dec. 18, 1942; s. Archie Trevelin and Anne Rae (Burch) S.; student U. Miss., 1960-63, M.D., 1967; m. Carol Ann Forister, May 29, 1967; 1 son, Scott Ellis. Intern Miss. Bapt. Hosp., Jackson, 1967-68; pvt. practice medicine, specializing in family practice, Fulton, Miss., 1968—; chief staff Itawamba County Hosp., Fulton. Mem. Itawamba

County Jr. C. of C., A.M.A., Miss. Med. Assn., Alpha Epsilon Delta. Republican. Baptist. Address: PO Box 280 Fulton MS 38843

SPRADLEY, JULIAN ROY, food broker, relator; b. Hawkinsville, Ga., Aug. 2, 1907; s. Mack Duron and Lula (Smith) S.; student Dale Carnegie Schs., 1941-42; m. Sybil Ruth Soar, July 5, 1937; children—Margaret Lavinia (Mrs. Anthony F. Mielczarski, Jr.), Julian Roy. With Hoskins & Green, Inc., food brokers, Miami, Fla., 1935-37; chmn. bd., sec. Spradley, Riley & Slaughter, Inc., Miami, 1937—; realtor Keyes Co., Miami. Mem. Miami Civic Music Assn., 1954—. Mem. exec. com. Miami Bapt. Assn. Served with U.S. Army, 1928-31. Recipient Exceptionally Meritorious Service awards Miami Food Brokers Assn., 1968, Nat. Food Brokers Assn., 1961-62. Mem. Nat. (regional dir.), Miami (pres.) food brokers assns. Bapt. (deacon). Mason. Home: 1416 Murray Av Tifton GA 31794

SPRADLIN, SIDNEY FRED, accountant; b. Clayton, N.M., Jan. 3, 1928; s. Fred B. and Anne (Lambert) S.; B.S., U. Denver, 1952; m. Mary E. Kingsley, Dec. 8, 1951; children—Tomas, Steven, Letha, James. With Arthur Young & Co., accountants and auditors, Tulsa, 1952-70, Dallas, 1970—. Served with AUS, 1947-48. Mem. Am. Inst. C.P.A.'s, Nat. Assn. Accountants, Beta Gamma Sigma. Home: Route 2 Box 111B Plano TX 75074 Office: 2800 Republic Tower Dallas TX 75201

SPRAGENS, THOMAS EUGENE, banker; b. Ellisburg, Ky., July 12, 1897; s. William Arthur and Frances (Reynierson) S.; B.S., Georgetown Coll., 1917; m. Edna Grace Clark, Feb. 26, 1924; children—William Clark, Thomas Eugene, Ruth (Mrs. Russel Fred Gilbert). Tchr., Richmond (Ky.) High Sch., 1923-24; bookkeeper Farmers Nat. Bank, Lebanon, Ky., 1924-30, teller, 1930-36, asst. cashier, 1936-42, cashier 1942-59, pres. 1959-65, chmn. bd. 1965—. Sponsor, fund raiser Boy Scouts Am., 1966-69. Trustee W. C. McChord Estate, 1957-68. Mem. Am. Bankers Assn. (v.p. 1948-51), Ky. Bankers Assn. (pres. group six 1958), Alpha Lambda (pres. 1916-17), Pi Kappa Alpha. Baptist. Home: 236 S Proctor Knott Av Lebanon KY 40033 Office: 136 W Main St Lebanon KY 40033

SPRAGUE, DAVID CARTER, dept. store exec.; b. Lawton, Okla., July 28, 1929; s. Robert S. and Zelpha (Carter) S.; B.A., Abilene Christian Coll., 1950; postgrad. Tex. Christian U., 1952-53; m. Wilma Jean Neal, July 23, 1950; children—Angela, Robert. Partner, mgr. Sprague's Furniture Mart, Lawton, 1955-60; v.p. Trade Mart Dept. Stores, Oklahoma City, 1961-65, pres., 1970—, also dir.; exec. v.p. IHC, Inc., Oklahoma City, 1966-70, dir., 1967-70. Dir. Nat. Playtime Villages, Inc., Oklahoma City, chmn., dir. First Bank Atoka, Okla. Bd. dirs. Okla. State Mental Health Assn., 1964-65. Served to 1st lt. AUS, 1953-55. Home: 1820 Drury Lane Oklahoma City OK 73116 Office: 1830 NW 4th Dr Oklahoma City OK 73106

SPRAGUE, JAMES TRUMAN, civil engr.; b. Des Moines, Aug. 31, 1906; s. James A. and Maud (Davis) S.; B.S., Ia. State U., 1930; m. Mildred L. Bishop, June 11, 1929; 1 dau., Dixiana (Mrs. William F. Hanks). Engr., materials insp. Mo. Hwy. Dept., 1930-33; jr. engr. Kan. Hwy. Dept., 1936-41; constrn. engr. Def. Constrn., 1941-43; city engr. City Miami (Okla.), 1946—. Instr. san. engring. Sch. Mil. Govt., Princeton, N.J., 1945-46. Served with USNR, 1943-46. Recipient Hatfield award Water and Pollution Control Fedn., 1962. Registered profl. engr., Ia., Okla. Home: 40 F NW Miami OK 74354 Office: 129 5th Av NW Miami OK 74354

SPRAGUE, ROBERT SUMMERS, mcht.; b. Cache, Okla., June 28, 1904; s. Roger Alger and Luella (Wycoff) S.; student LaSalle Extension U., 1926; m. Zelpha Chestine Carter, Sept. 1, 1923; children—Mary (Mrs. John McNayr), David, Robert Paul, Martha (Mrs. Edwin Mitchell). Accountant, Payne-McGee Grocery Co., 1922-24; owner, operator Sprague's Food Mart, 1924-50, Sprague's Furniture Mart, 1950-60; co-owner Trade Mart Dept. Store, Inc., 1960-70; sec. Eastern Indsl. Sites, Inc., 1960—, Indsl. Sites, Inc., 1965—; v.p., chmn. bd. Geronimo Property, Inc., 1964—; pres. Westgate Devel. Co., Inc. 1961-70 (all Lawton, Okla.); co-owner Ark. Seawey Indsl. Complex, Ozark. Mem. adv. bd. Abilene Christian Coll., 1954-72, lectr., 1962; lectr. Pepperdine Coll., Los Angeles, 1963-64. Bd. dirs. Columbia Christian Coll., Portland, Ore. Mem. Lawton C. of C. (past v.p.), Lawton Grocery Assn. (past pres.), Lawton Retail Mchts. Assn. (past pres.), Internat. Platform Assn. Mem. Ch. of Christ (past elder). Democrat. Author: Grass Money, 1970; Ghosts of Palo Duro Canyon, 1972. Contbr. articles to ch. publs. Home: 1 N 35th St Lawton OK 73501 Office: 425 S 11th St Lawton OK 73501

SPRAGUE, WILLIAM GEORGE, oral pathologist; b. Cleve., Apr. 15, 1923; s. George William and Ella Virginia (Stubbs) S.; student Ohio U., 1941-43; B.S., Western Res. U., 1945, D.D.S., 1947; m. Harriet Ida Rice, June 19, 1948; children—Barbara (Mrs. David Allen Miller), Patricia Alice, Nancy Lyn. Intern Cleve. State Hosp., 1947-48; resident Western Res. U. Inst. Pathology, 1948-52; commd. 1st lt. USAF, 1952, advanced through grades to col., 1964; staff oral pathologist USAF Sch. Aviation Medicine, 1952-54; asso. oral pathologist, dental and oral pathology div. Armed Forces Inst. Pathology, Washington, 1954-57, 65-69; chief oral pathology USAF Hosp., Lackland AFB, 1957-65; chief oral pathology div., dir. dental services Ramey AFB, P.R., 1969-72, command dental surgeon Hdqrs. AFSC-SGD, Washington, 1972—. Instr. operative dentistry Western Res. U., 1947-48, instr. pathology, 1948-52; asso. clin. prof. pathology U. Tex., 1957-65, Med. Coll. Va., 1965-69; nat. mil. cons. USAF, 1969—. Pres., Bd. Edn., Ramey AFB Sch. Systems, 1971-72. Decorated USAF Commendation medal, Meritorious Service medal. Fellow A.A.A.S., Am. Acad. Oral Pathology, Am. Coll. Dentists; mem. Am. Dental Assn., Am. Soc. Clin. Pathologists, Am. Acad. Oral Pathologists (past pres.), Omicron Kappa Upsilon. Mason. Contbr. chpt. to Oral Pathology, 1964. Contbr. articles to profl. jours. Home: 1112-1 Columbus Circle Andrews AFB MD 20335 Office: Hdqrs AFSC-SGD Washington DC 20334

SPRAGUE, WILLIAM WALLACE, JR., food co. exec.; b. Savannah, Ga., Nov. 11, 1926; s. William Wallace and Mary (Crowther) S.; B.S., Yale, 1950; m. Elizabeth Louise Carr, Oct. 3, 1953; children—Lauren and Courtney (twins), William Wallace III, Elizabeth. With Savannah Sugar Refining Corp. (name changed to Savannah Foods & Industries, Inc., 1970), 1952—, sales mgr. indsl. products, 1959, asst. sec., 1959-60, sec., 1961-62, v.p., 1962-72, pres., chief exec. officer, 1972—, also dir.; pres., chief exec. officer Everglades Sugar Refinery, Clewiston, Fla.; chmn. bd., chief exec. officer Jim Dandy Co., Birmingham, Ala., Adeline Sugar Factory Co., Ltd., Jeaneretta, La.; dir. Citizens & So. Nat. Bank, Atlanta, Atlantic Towing Co., Savannah. Asso. chmn. div. United Community Appeal, 1970-72. Bd. dirs. Savannah Port Authority. Served with USNR, 1945-46. Mem. Savannah Area C. of C., Carolina Plantation Soc. Clubs: Oglethorpe, Century, Cotillion (Savannah). Home: 24 E 50th St Savannah GA 31405 Office: PO Box 339 Savannah GA 31402

SPRAKER, HAROLD STEPHEN, educator; b. Cedar Bluff, Va., May 13, 1929; s. Stephen Marco and Cynthia (Cook) S.; B.S., Roanoke Coll., 1950; M.Ed., U. Va., 1955, D.Advanced Grad. Study, 1959, D.Ed., 1960; postgrad. Peabody Coll., 1956; m. Betty Jean Conley, Oct. 2, 1954; children—John S., Mark Conley. Tchr. math. Falls Church (Va.) High Sch., 1950-51, Richlands (Va.) High Sch., 1953-57; asst. prin. Richlands High Sch., 1955-57; apprentice coordinator Tazewell and Buchanan Counties, Va., 1953-57; research asso. U. Va., Charlottesville, 1958-60, instr. extension, 1959-60; asst. prof., asso. prof. math. Middle Tenn. State U., Murfreesboro, 1960-65, prof., 1965—, chmn. dept. math., 1967—, dir. NSF Inst., 1966-67, NSF Math. Inst. Mem. vis. scientist program Tenn., 1964—. Served with AUS, 1951-53. Mem. Math. Assn. Am., Am. Math. Soc., Nat. Council Tchrs. Math., Tenn. Math. Tchrs. Assn., N.E.A., Tenn. Edn. Assn., Pi Mu Epsilon. Lutheran (council). Home: Route 6 Murfreesboro TN 37130

SPRAY, PAUL ELLSWORTH, surgeon; b. Wilkinsburg, Pa., Apr. 9, 1921; s. Lester Ellsworth and Gertrude (Hull) S.; B.S., U. Pitts., 1942; M.D., George Washington U., 1944; M.S. in Orthopedic Surgery, U. Minn., 1950; m. Louise Conover, Nov. 18, 1943; children—David Conover, Thomas Laton, Mary Lynn. Intern, Stapleton U.S. Marine Hosp., S.I., N.Y., 1944-45; resident Mayo Found., Rochester, Minn., 1945-46, 48-50; pvt. practice medicine specializing in orthopedic surgery, Oak Ridge, 1950—; staff Oak Ridge Hosp., cons. med. div. Oak Ridge Asso. Univs., Cumberland Clinic, Chamberlain Meml. Hosp., LaFollette (Tenn.) Community Hosp.; courtesy staff E. Tenn. Bapt., U. Tenn., Park West hosps. Mem. bd. orthopedics overseas div. Medico-Care, 1961—, sec. bd., 1971—, chmn. Nigeria Orthopedic Project, 1965-70; cons. Daniel Arthur Rehab. Center, Oak Ridge, 1971—; mem. area adv. group Knoxville Area Regional Med. Program, 1970—; mem. Anderson County Health Council, 1968—; mem. medico adv. bd. CARE, 1969—; A.M.A. vol. physician, Viet Nam, 1967, 72. Bd. dirs. Council So. Mountains, 1961-68, sec., 1965-66; bd. dirs. Medico, 1971—. Served as capt. AUS, 1946-48. Recipient Service to Mankind award Sertoma, 1968. Diplomate Am. Bd. Orthopedic Surgeons. Fellow A.C.S., Internat. Coll. Surgery; mem. A.M.A., Roane-Anderson County Med. Soc. (past pres.), Tenn. Orthopedic Soc., Knoxville Surg. Soc., Knoxville Orthopedic Club, Orthopedic Letters Club, Am. Acad. Orthopedic Surgeons, Am. Fracture Assn., Am., So. med. assns., Société Internationale Chirurgie Orth y Traumatologie, UN Assn. (past pres. Tenn.). Mem. Soc. of Friends. Lion (Humanitarian Service award dist. 12N 1968). Home: 507 Delaware Av Oak Ridge TN 37830 Office: 145 E Vance Rd Oak Ridge TN 37830

SPRINGER, JACK G., assn. exec.; b. Norman, Okla., Sept. 11, 1926; s. Charles S. and Mary A. (Goff) S.; B.S., U. Okla., 1950; m. Doris M. Lebow, Apr. 14, 1945; children—Carol (Mrs. F.B. Power), Sheryl, Jane, Cynthia. With Pauls Valley (Okla.) C. of C., 1950-51, Seminole (Okla.) C. of C., 1951-53; Bryan-College Station (Tex.) C. of C., 1953-61, Galveston (Tex.) C. of C., 1961-63, West Regional Tex. C. of C., 1963-71; exec. v.p. Okla. State C. of C., Oklahoma City, 1971—. Served with AUS, 1944-46. Mem. Assn. Am. C. of C. Execs., Okla. C. of C. Execs. (dir.), Council State Chambers Commerce (v.p.), U.S. C. of C. (pub. affairs com.). Home: 6224 NW 85th St Oklahoma City OK 73132 Office: 101 Am Gen Bldg 621 N Robinson St Oklahoma City OK 73102

SPRINGER, JIMMY NORVEL, radio sta. exec.; b. Dallas, Nov. 8, 1938; s. James Buford and Ernestine (Richardson) S.; B.F.A., U. Tex. at Austin, 1961; m. Virginia Kay Jordan, Apr. 17, 1959 (div. Jan. 1972); children—Kimberlee Dawn, Phyllis Jeaninne; m. 2d, Diana Faye Ashton, Sept. 8, 1972. Newsman sta. KRIS-TV, Corpus Christi, Tex., 1964; with radio sta. KRYS, Corpus Christi, 1964—, sales mgr., 1967-70, gen. mgr., 1970—. Music dir., bd. dirs. Corpus Christi Harmonaire Barbershop Chrous, 1968. Dir., v.p. Lakewood Village Council Co-owners; mem. Corpus Christi Leadership Council. Bd. dirs. Corpus Christi Tourist Bur., 1972; pres. bd. trustees Corpus Christi Osteo. Hosp. Mem. Corpus Christi (pres. 1971), Am. (del.) advt. fedns., Coastal Bend Media Council (pres.), Soc. Preservation and Encouragement Barbershop Quartet Singing in Am. (v.p. 1968-69), Aircraft Owners and Pilots Assn. Clubs: Sunset Lake Recreation Center (Portland, Tex.), Tips, Sales and Marketing Executives, Bon Vivants (Corpus Christi), National Aero Club: Home: 1917 Hidden Way Corpus Christi TX 78412 Office: PO Box 9698 Corpus Christi TX 78408

SPRINGFIELD, MELVIN EUGENE, realtor; b. Greenville, S.C., May 24, 1938; s. Homer Lamar and Elise Ramsey (Funderburk) S.; student Clemson U., 1959; m. June Caudell, May 6, 1956; children—Sherry Le June, Debbie Elaine, Melvin Eugene. Service mgr. Shealy Elec. Wholesalers, Greenville, 1959-66; salesman, So. Electric Service, Greenville, 1966-69; salesman, Holder Electric Supply Greenville, 1969-71, Colonial Real Estate, Greenville, 1971-73; self-employed as realtor, Greenville, 1973—. Chmn. Cleveland Park Zoo Commn., 1970-73; exec. dir. Holdiay Festival Parade, 1971, Greenville Soap Box Derby, 1965. Named Key Man, Greenville Jr. C. of C., 1966, 72, Jaycee of Year, 1964, 65. Mem. Greater Greenville C. of C., (dir. 1970-71), S.C. (v.p. 1970-71; internat. senator 1970), Greenville (pres. 1969-70) jr. chambers commerce. Baptist. Home: 20 Woodvale Av Greenville SC 29605 Office: Box 2401 Greenville SC 29602

SPROUL, HARVEY LEONARD, judge; b. Williamsburg, Ky., Oct. 8, 1933; s. Harvey LaFayette and Ruth (Renfro) S.; B.S., U. Tenn., 1955, J.D., 1957; student Judge Adv. Gen.'s Sch., 1958; m. Sylvia Ann Moulton, May 31, 1958; children—Daniel, Susan, Jane Anne, Lyda B. Admitted to Tenn. bar, 1957; claims adjustor U.S. F & G Ins. Co., Knoxville, Tenn., 1957; partner law firm Dannel, Fowler & Sproul, Lenoir City, Tenn., 1961-63, Daniel & Sproul, 1963-65, Sproul & Russell, 1968-70, Sproul & Bailey, 1973—; pvt. practice law, 1965-66; judge Loudon County, Tenn., 1966-74. Chmn., E. Tenn. Devel. Dist., 1966-68; mem. State Adv. Com. for Local Planning, 1971-74; chmn. Tellico Area Planning Council, 1967-74. Served with AUS, 1958-60. Named Tenn.'s Outstanding Young Man, 1966; Lenoir City Distinguished Service award, 1962. Mem. Tenn. County Judges Assn. (v.p. 1972-74), Loudon County Bar Assn. (pres. 1966-67), Lenoir City C. of C. (dir.), Phi Delta Phi, Kappa Sigma, Delta Sigma Phi. Democrat. Methodist. Rotarian. Home: Route 5 Lenoir City TN 37771 Office: 109 W Broadway Lenoir City TN 37771

SPROULL, ROBERT CHRISTLEY, dentist, researcher, ret. officer; b. New Cumberland, W.Va., Nov. 5, 1920; s. Bert Christley and Emma (Allen) S.; D.D.S., U. Pitts., 1950; postgrad. U. So. Cal., 1956-57; m. Mary M. Moran, June 3, 1949; children—Robert M., Elizabeth A., William A., Brian E. Enlisted man U.S. Army, 1942-46; commd. officer U.S. Army, 1950, advanced through grades to col., 1967; chief fixed prosthodontic service William Beaumont Gen. Hosp., El Paso, Tex., 1966-72, chief hosp. dental clinic, 1970-72. Asst. to Dr. Berndmark Heukemes, archaeologist, Heidelberg, Germany, 1961-65. Decorated Bronze Star medal, Legion of Merit. Diplomate Am. Bd. Prosthodontics. Fellow Am. Coll. Dentists, Am. Coll. Prosthodontists (inter-soc. color council); mem. Am. Acad. History Dentistry (v.p. 1973-74), Am. Dental Assn., Colour Group (Gt. Britain). Club: Prospectors (pres. 1972) (El Paso). Contbr. articles to profl. jours. Research on color matching in dentistry, laser and holography. Home: 2405 Gairloch St El Paso TX 79925 Office: Box 640 El Paso TX 79920

SPROUSE, ERNEST GILBERT, social worker; b. nr. Staunton, Va., June 9, 1935; s. Ernest and Virginia (Buchanan) S.; B.A., King Coll., 1961; postgrad. Va. Commonwealth U., 1966; m. Linda Carol McGlamary, Feb. 1, 1965; children—Robin Michelle, Tamara Lin. Child welfare worker Bristol (Va.) Dept. Pub. Welfare, 1961-65, sr. social worker, 1966, supt., 1966—. Supr. undergrad. students East Tenn. State U., Johnson City, 1967-71; dir., treas. Bristol Speech and Hearing Center, Bristol, 1968-71. Served with AUS, 1956-58. Mem. Tenn.-Va. Council Social Agys. (treas. 1969-71), Child Devel. Center (mem. adv. com. 1967—, chmn. 1969-71), Va. Council Social Welfare (bd. dirs. 1969—). Baptist (bd. dirs. 1971—). Club: Optimist (pres. 1970-71, Optimist of Yr. 1970, bd. dirs. Bristol). Home: 1627 Pineview St Bristol VA 24201 Office: 36 Moore St Bristol VA 24201

SPRUELL, GEORGE MUTHA, ednl. adminstr.; b. Americus, Ga., Feb. 9, 1942; s. Lucius Mutha and Laura Eugenia (Walker) S.; A.B., Clemson U., 1965; m. Elizabeth Stokes Wallenburg, Jan. 29, 1966; 1 dau., Hope Lewton. Dean students Brandon Hall Sch., 1966-68; asst. headmaster Aiken (S.C.) Prep. Sch., 1968—. Home: 248 Florence St Aiken SC 29801 Office: PO Box 317 Aiken SC 29801

SPRUIELL, JOSEPH EARL, educator; b. Knoxville, Tenn., Oct. 13, 1935; s. Joseph Samuel and Margaret (Claiborne) S.; B.S., U. Tenn., 1958, M.S., 1960, Ph.D., 1963; m. Rhonda Pauline Ownby, June 20, 1958; children—Teresa, Janet. Mem. faculty dept. chem., metall. engring. U. Tenn. at Knoxville, 1960—, asso. prof., 1967-71, prof., 1971—. Cons., Oak Ridge Nat. Lab., 1960—. Mem. Am. Soc. Metals (chmn. 1969-70), Am. Crystallographie Soc., Sigma Xi, Phi Kappa Phi, Tau Beta Pi. Home: 9705 Tunbridge St Concord TN 37720 Office: Dept Chem. and Metall Engring. Univ Tenn Knoxville TN 37916

SPURLOCK, DWIGHT ROSS, elec. engr.; b. Temple, Okla., July 21, 1932; s. Henry Franklin and Edrie Marue (Ross) S.; B.S. in E.E., U. Okla., 1959; m. Karen Joyce Mawkins, Feb. 14, 1961; children—Russell D., Rebecca Dee. Engr., Community Pub. Service Co., Texas City, Tex., 1959-62, substation and transmission engr., 1962-69, div. elec. supt., 1969—. Served with USNR, 1951-54. Registered profl. engr., Tex. Mem. I.E.E.E., Tex. Soc. Profl. Engrs. (dir. Galveston County chpt.), Texas City C. of C. (ir. 1973). Elk, Kiwanian. Home: 1708 16th Av N Texas City TX 77590 Office: PO Box 2190 Texas City TX 77590

SPURLOCK, JACK MARION, engring. research cons.; b. Tampa, Fla., Aug. 16, 1930; s. Joseph Marion and Gertrude (Saffold) S.; B.Chem. Engr., U. Fla., 1952; M.S., Ga. Inst. Tech., 1958, Ph.D., 1961; m. Phyllis Lowene Ridgway, June 30, 1952; children—Barbara Lynn, Scott Edward, Paul Andrew, Teresa Anne. Quality control engr. Auto-Lite Battery Co., East Point, Ga., 1954-55; research asso., asst. prof. Ga. Inst. Tech., Atlanta, 1955-62; mgr. aeroscis. research dept. Martin Co., Orlando, Fla., 1962-64; dir. engring. research dept. Atlantic Research Corp., Alexandria, Va., 1964-69; exec. v.p. Health and Safety Research Inst., Springfield, Va., 1969-72, pres., 1972—; engring cons. Theodore Jonas and Assos., Washington, 1971—. Mem., chmn. SAE Com. on Spacecraft Environmental Control and Life Support Systems, 1965—. Served to lt. USAF, 1952-54. Fellow Am. Inst. Chemists, Royal Soc. Health, Aerospace Med. Assn.; asso. fellow Am. Inst. Aero. and Astronautics; mem. Am. Inst. Chem. Engrs., Aerospace Med. Assn., Am. Chem. Soc., A.A.A.S. Presbyn. (elder). Author: (with Thomas W. Jackson) Research and Development Management, 1966. Home: 6144 Roxbury Av Springfield VA 22152 Office: Suite 201 2009 N 14th St Arlington VA 22201

SPURR, STEPHEN HOPKINS, univ. pres.; b. Washington, Feb. 14, 1918; s. Josiah Edward and Sophia Clara (Burchard) S.; B.S. with highest honors, U. Fla., 1938, D.Sc. (hon.), 1971; M.F. cum laude, Yale, 1940, Ph.D. (Oberleander Trust fellow), 1950; m. Patricia Chapman Orton, Aug. 18, 1945; children—Daniel Orton, Jean Burchard. Instr., asst. prof., acting dir. Harvard Forest, Harvard, 1940-50; asso. prof. U. Minn., 1950-52; prof. U. Mich. at Ann Arbor, 1952-71, asst. to v.p. acad. affairs, dean Sch. Natural Resources, 1962-65; dean Horace H. Rackham Sch. Grad. Studies, 1964-71, v.p., 1969-71; prof. botany and pub. affairs, pres. U. Tex. at Austin, 1971—. Chmn., Grad. Rec. Exam. Bd., Council Grad. Schs., 1969-71; mem. Commn. on Non Traditional Study, 1971; mem. Nat. Bd. Grad. Edn. Mem. Pres.'s Adv. Panel Timber and the Environment, 1971-73. Trustee Carnegie Found. for Advancement of Teaching, Inst. Internat. Edn. Sci. faculty fellow NSF, 1957-58; Fulbright research scholar, New Zealand and Australia, 1960; vis. scholar Center for Advanced Studies Behavioral Scis., 1966-67. Fellow Soc. Am. Foresters (mem. council, founding chmn. div. forest mgmt.); mem. New Zealand Inst. Foresters (hon.), Ecol. Soc. Am., Conf. Biol. Editors (exec. com.), Lake States Forest Tree Improvement Com. (chmn.), Orgn. for Tropical Studies (pres. 1967-68), Mich. Acad. Sci., Arts and Letters (pres. 1968-69), Nature Conservancy (gov. 1972—), Am. Forestry Assn. (dir. 1971—). Unitarian. Author: Aerial Photographs in Forestry, 1948; Forest Inventory, 1952; Photogrammetry and Photo-Interpretation, 1960; Forest Ecology, 1962; Academic Degree Structures, 1970. Founding editor Forest Sci., 1955-60. Inventor photogrammetric devices. Home: 2101 Meadowbrook Dr Austin TX 78703

SPURRIER, MARGARET NORVELL (MRS. KEITH MCCAULEY SPURRIER), Republican nat. committeewoman; b. Nashville, Apr. 7, 1919; d. Richard and Margaret (Parker) Norvell; ed. Wellesley Coll., Vanderbilt U.; m. Keith McCauley Spurrier, June 26, 1940; children—Lucia Parker (Mrs. William Lee Drier), Irene LeJau (Mrs. John Alan Pendergrast). Co-chmn. Shelby County (Tenn.) Republican party, 1962-66; mem. Tenn. Rep. Exec. Com., 1966-70, Rep. nat. committeewoman, 1968—. Mem. Tenn. Commn. Status of Women. Bd. dirs. Shelby United Neighbors, Tenn. Bot. Gardens and Fine Arts Center. Mem. Nat. Fedn. Rep. Women, Memphis Symphony League, Memphis Jr. League, Nat. Congress Parents and Tchrs., Kappa Alpha Theta, Chi Delta Phi. Episcopalian. Address: 89 Goodwyn St Memphis TN 38111

SQUIBB, SAMUEL DEXTER, educator; b. Limestone, Tenn., June 20, 1931; s. Ben B. and Pearl (Harris) S.; B.S. in Chemistry, East Tenn. State U., 1952; Ph.D., U. Fla., 1956; m. Jo Ann Kyker, Dec. 15, 1951; children—Sandra Lavanne, Kevin Dexter. Asso. prof. chemistry Western Carolina U., Cullowkee, N.C., 1956-60; asst. prof., coordinator dept. chemistry Eckerd Coll., St. Petersburg, Fla., 1960-63, asso. prof., coordinator, 1963-64; prof., chmn. dept. chemistry U. N.C. at Asheville, 1964—. Fellow Am. Inst. Chemists (profl. accredited); mem. Am. Chem. Soc., Am. Assn. U. Profs., Nat. Sci. Tchrs. Assn., Phi Beta Kappa, Alpha Chi Sigma, Gamma Sigma Epsilon. Presbyn. (deacon 1968-71). Author: Experimental Modern Chemistry, 1969; Experimental Modern Chemistry II, 1971; Experimental Modern Organic Chemistry, 1970; Chemistry I, 1972; Chemistry II, 1974. Home: 8 Honey Dr Asheville NC 28805

SQUIRE, PETER WEAVER, physician; b. Fairmont, W.Va., Mar. 25, 1926; s. Edward Allen and Sara Lewis (Waters) S.; B.S., Hampden Sydney Coll., 1948; M.D., Med. Coll. Va., 1952; m. Nancy Hall Barker, Apr. 12, 1953; children—Harry Edward, William Byron, Peter Weaver, Robert Hall. Intern Stuart Circle Hosp., Richmond,

Va., 1952-54; pvt. practice medicine, specializing in family practice, Emporia, Va., 1954—; mem. staff Roanoke Rapids (N.C.) Hosp.; chief of staff Greensville Meml. Hosp., Emporia, 1972-73. Dir. Citizens Nat. Bank, Emporia. Mem. Old Dominion Area council Boy Scouts Am., 1956-68. Served to lt. (j.g.) USNR, 1943-46. Diplomate Am. Bd. Family Practice. Fellow Am. Acad. Family Physicians; mem. Med. Soc. Va., A.M.A., Am., Va. acads. gen. practice, Theta Chi, Omicron Delta Kappa, Phi Chi. Presbyn. (deacon 1964—). Rotarian. Home: 428 Laurel St Emporia VA 23847 Office: 219 Weaver Av Emporia VA 23847

SQUIRES, WARREN GLENN, elec. engr.; b. Sioux City, Ia., Sept. 11, 1913; s. Glenn Samuel and Beulah Warren (Greene) S.; student U. Colo., 1932-35; B.S. in E.E., U. Tex., 1938; m. Alice Carolyn Butts, June 15, 1946. Substa. operator Dallas Power & Light Co., 1938-42; engr. Brown & Root Constrn. Co., McAlester, Okla., 1942-44; research engr. N. Am. Aviation Co., Dallas, 1944-45; mgr. S.W. Engrs., San Antonio, 1949; div. engr. Tex. Power & Light Co., Sherman, 1950—. Named Engr. of the Year, N.E. Tex. chpt. Tex. Soc. Profl. Engrs., 1972. Registered profl. engr., Tex. Mem. I.E.E.E., Nat., Tex. socs. profl. engrs., Sigma Pi Sigma (alumnus mem.). Mem. Christian Ch. (chmn. bd. 1961-62, 65-66, elder 1961-74). Home: 519 N Holly Av Sherman TX 75090 Office: PO Box 640 Sherman TX 75090

SRERE, PAUL ARNOLD, biochemist, educator; b. Davenport, Ia., Sept. 1, 1925; s. Jacob and Margaret (Weinstein) S.; B.S. in Chemistry, U. Cal. at Los Angeles, 1947; Ph.D. in Comparative Biochemistry, U. Cal. at Berkeley, 1951; m. Marjorie Laslo, Sept. 1, 1953; children—Margot, Elizabeth Ann, Mark, Hilary. Biochemist, Mass. Gen. Hosp., Boston, 1951-53; asst. prof. biochemistry U. Mich., Ann Arbor, 1956-61, asso. prof., 1961-63; research biochemist Lawrence Radiation Lab., U. Cal., Livermore, 1963-66; prof. biochemistry U. Tex. Health Sci. Center, Dallas, 1966—; chief pre-clin. sci. unit VA Hosp., Dallas, 1966. Mem. admissions com. U. Tex. Health Sci. Center, Dallas, 1969—; coordinator faculty seminar, U. Tex., Dallas, 1971-72; VA liaison rep. to NIH biochemistry study sect., 1971—. Mem. Town Lake Project Com., 1971—. Served with USNR, 1944-46. Jane Coffin Childs Fund Med. Research fellow, 1953-54; USPHS fellow, 1954-56; VA research grantee, 1972-73. Mem. Am. Heart Assn. (research com. 1971—), Internat. Union of Biochemists (commn. biochem. nomenclature 1971—), Fed. Am. Soc. for Exptl. Biology, Am. Soc. for Cell Biology, Am. Assn. U. Profs., Am. Chem. Soc. Editorial bd. Jour. Biol. Chemistry, 1973—, Biochem. Medicine, 1969—. Contbr. articles on biochemistry to sci. jours. Home: 3600 Lindenwood St Dallas TX 72505 Office: 4500 S Lancaster Rd Dallas TX 75216

STAAB, WILLIAM CARL, banker; b. Springfield, Ill., Feb. 12, 1927; s. Carl Herman and Helen Katherine (Metzger) S.; A.B., Springfield Jr. Coll., 1948; B.S. in Commerce, St. Louis U., 1949, J.D., 1954; m. Nancy Mae Wright, July 28, 1956; children—William Carl., Jennifer, Patrick. Accountant, Union Electric Co., St. Louis, 1949-55; admitted to Mo. bar, 1954, Ill. bar, 1955; mem. firm Sullivan, Staab & Joyce, St. Louis, 1955-56; with Merc. Trust Co., St. Louis, 1956-61; with Ouachita Nat. Bank, Monroe, La., 1961—, trust officer, 1961—, v.p., 1961—. Active A.R.C., Boy Scouts Am., United Givers Fund, Monroe Area Guidance Center, Alexandria Diocese Cath. Charities Bd. Chmn. adv. bd. St. Joseph's Home for Aged; mem. adv. bd. St. Frederick High Sch. Served with USNR, 1945-46. Mem. Ill. Bar Assn., Mo. Bar. Roman Catholic (pres. adv. council). K.C. Clubs: Lotus, Bayou Desiard Country (Monroe). Home: 3800 Loop Rd Monroe LA 71201 Office: PO Box 1412 Monroe LA 71201

STACEY, TRUMAN, editor; b. Port Arthur, Tex., Dec. 8, 1916; s. James H. and Billie (Davis) S.; Ph.B., U. Detroit, 1946, M.A., 1951; postgrad. Cath. U. Am., 1951, George Washington U., 1951; m. Dorothy Mary Piboin, May 25, 1963; step-children—Patricia, Cheryl. Reporter, Beaumont (Tex.) Enterprise, 1937-42, Okla. City Daily Oklahoman, 1943-44, Detroit Free Press, 1944-45, Washington Times-Herald, 1950-51; pub. relations dir. U. Detroit, 1945-49; sports editor, Lake Charles (La.) Am. Press., 1951-60, editor, 1961—. Organizer, co-chmn. Lake Charles chpt. Nat. Conf. Christians and Jews, bd. dirs., 1973—; mem. Nat. Com. Cath. Scouting; lay chmn. Com. Cath. Scouting Diocese of Lafayette; pres. S.W. La. chpt. Council Devel. French in La. Mem. La. Bicentennial Commn., 1973—; mem. Commn. on Communications, Diocese of Lafayette, 1973—. Bd. dirs. La. Council for Music and Performing Arts. Served to sgt. AUS, 1942-43. Recipient Civic Service award Greater Lake Charles C. of C., 1971; Distinguished Service award K.C., 1972; Distinguished Service cross Serra, 1973; Southwest La. Patriot of Yr. award, 1973; decorated knight Order St. Gregory, knight comdr. Order of Fleur de Lis. Mem. Am. Soc. Newspaper editors, Nat. Conf. Editorial Writers, Asso. Press Mng. Editors Assn. Democrat. Roman Catholic. K.C. Club: Serra Internat. (pres. local chpt. 1971-72, gov.-elect dist. 13 1973-74). Home: 814 W McNeese St Lake Charles LA 70601 Office: 327 Broad St Lake Charles LA 70601

STACK, RONALD JOSEPH, county ofcl.; b. Phila., July 22, 1934; s. John Joseph and Madalyn (Russell) S.; student Assos. Investment and Financial Inst., 1958; Inst. Criminal Justice S. Fla., 1973; m. Edith L. Houser, June 20, 1964; children—Stephen, Karen, Kristi, Michael. Mgr., Assos. Financial Services, Miami, Fla., 1955-67; exec. v.p. Island Finance Co., Key West, 1967-70; city mgr., dir. pub. safety City Key West, 1970-73; chief adminstrv. officer Monroe County Sheriffs Dept., Key West, 1973—. Chmn., Monroe County Sheriffs Civil Service Bd., 1968-70. Sec., Monroe County March of Dimes, 1970; adv. bd. Salvation Army, 1972—. Mem. Fla., Internat. city and county mgrs. assns., Nat. Sheriffs Assn., Fraternal Order Police, Am. Legion. Mason (32 degree). Home: 3732 Cindy Av Key West FL 33040 Office: 500 Whitehead St Key West FL 33040

STADLER, JOHN BUCHAN, realtor, mortgage banker; b. Cleve., Oct. 25, 1907; s. John Louis and Angeline (Hauserman) S.; B.S. in Bus. Adminstrn., U. Fla., 1930; m. Lucille P. Rose, Aug. 11, 1938; children—Angeline (Mrs. William Fox Eckbert, Jr.), Linda Marleen (Mrs. Howard Richard Bates), John William. Asst. sec., dir. First Fed. Savs. & Loan Assn., Miami, Fla., 1933—; pres. Stadler Assos., Inc.; realtor John B. Stadler, Coral Gables, Fla., 1943—. Mem. Fla. Blue Key, Kappa Sigma, Alpha Kappa Psi. Home: 3272 Riviera Dr Coral Gables FL 33134 Office: 375 Miracle Mile Coral Gables FL 33134

STAFFORD, DONALD BENNETT, educator; b. Forsyth County, N.C., Oct. 30, 1938; s. Samuel Bennett and Lillie Pearl (Teague) S.; B.S.C.E., N.C. State U., 1961, M.S. (Engring Found. fellow), 1963, Ph.D., 1968; m. Marilyn Ann Kimball, June 9, 1962; 1 son, Shannon Dale. Instr. civil engring. N.C. State U., Raleigh, 1963-68; asst. prof. Clemson (S.C.) U., 1968-71, asso. prof. civil engring., 1971—. Cons. part-time Miller, Warden-Western Cons. Engrs., Raleigh and Lincoln, Neb., 1964-66, S.C. Appalachian Regional Planning and Devel. Commn., Greenville, S.C., 1969—. Recipient NSF sponsored Geometronics Inst., Purdue U., 1966; NASA Summer Faculty fellow Manned Spacecraft Center, Houston, summer 1970. Mem. Am. Soc. C.E., Hwy. Research Bd., Am. Soc. Photogrammetry, Am. Soc. Engring. Edn., Inst. Traffic Engrs., Sigma Xi, Chi Epsilon, Tau Beta Pi, Phi Kappa Phi. Home: S Woodbury Rd Bayshore Box 279 Route 2 Seneca SC 29678 Office: Dept Civil Engring Clemson U Clemson SC 29631

STAFFORD, GEORGE TIMOTHY, JR., trailer mfg. co. exec.; b. Birmingham, Ala., Sept. 30, 1907; s. George Timothy and Margaret (Berry) S.; B.S. in Mech. Engring., Auburn U., 1929; m. Agnes Evelyn Coffin, Mar. 31, 1934; children—Evelyn (Mrs. Burns Johns), George Timothy III, Harry Coffin. Mgr. heating dept. Birmingham Gas Co., 1930-42; engr. WpB, 1943, Continental Gin, 1944; v.p. Fontaine Truck Equipment, 1945; pres. Birmingham Mfg. Co. Inc., 1946—, Birmingham Totemall Inc., 1962—. Treas., mem. bd. trustees Southeastern Bible Coll., Birmingham, 1960—. Patentee in field. Mem. Tau Beta Pi. Home: 3632 Montevallo Rd Birmingham AL 35213 Office: PO Box 289 Springville AL 35146

STAFFORD, HARRY WILKINSON, lawyer; b. Jacksonville, Tex., Apr. 20, 1939; s. M. V. and Helen Louise (Wilkinson) S.; B.B.A., U. Tex. at Austin, 1961, LL.B., 1963; m. Elizabeth Kelton, Aug. 26, 1961; children—Todd Kelton, Elizabeth. Admitted to Tex. bar, 1963; mem. firm Wheat, Wheat & Stafford, Tyler County, Woodville, Tex., 1963—. Sec., Tyler County Indsl. Corp., 1967—. Mem. exec. council Trinity Neches council Boy Scouts Am., 1966-72, dist. chmn., 1969. Mem. State Bar Tex., Tyler County Bar Assn. (pres. 1972-73). Rotarian. Home: PO Box 12 Woodville TX 75979 Office: PO Box 156 Woodville TX 75979

STAFFORD, ROY ELMER, geneticist; b. Republic, Kan., Dec. 28, 1930; s. Clarence E. and Clara G. (McClure) S.; B.S., Kan. State U., 1953; M.S. in Plant Genetics, U. Minn., 1962, Ph.D., 1964; m. Marlene Ann Reed, June 14, 1959; children—Rebecca Ann, John David, Matthew Reed, Stephen Earl, Philip Roy. Research asst. U. Minn., 1959-65; plant breeder Am. Crystal Sugar Co., Rocky Ford, Colo., 1965-68; research geneticist U.S. Dept. Agr., Lubbock, Tex., 1968-72, research leader, Vernon, Tex., 1972—. Mem. Am. Soc. Agronomy, Crop Sci. Soc. Am., Am. Soc. Sugar Beet Technologists, Sigma Xi, Phi Kappa Phi, Alpha Zeta, Gamma Sigma Delta. Contbr. articles to profl. jours. Home: 3901 Bismarck St Vernon TX 76384 Office: Tex A and M U PO Box 1658 Vernon TX 76384

STAFFORD, THOMAS PATTEN, astronaut; b. Weatherford, Okla., Sept. 17, 1930; B.S., U.S. Naval Acad., 1952; student USAF Exptl. Flight Test Sch., 1958-59; m. Faye Laverne Shoemaker; children—Dionne, Karin. Commd. 2d lt. USAF, 1952, advanced through grades to brig. gen.; chief performance br. Aerospace Research Pilot Sch., Edwards AFB, Cal., with Manned Spacecraft Center NASA, Houston, 1962—, now chief U.S. astronauts; pilot Gemini VI, command pilot Gemini IX, comdr. Apollo X; dept. dir. flight crew operations. Co-author: Pilot's Handbook for Performance Flight Testing, Aerodynamics Handbook for Performance Flight Testing. Address: Manned Spacecraft Center NASA (CA) Houston TX 77058

STAFFORD, WILLIAM BANE, elec. engr., govt. ofcl.; b. Mallory, W.Va., May 2, 1930; s. Fred Hardiman and Gwendolyn Edith (Shumate) S.; student W.Va. U., 1947-48, U.S. Naval Acad., 1951-54; B.E.E., Ga. Inst. Tech., 1955; m. Shirley Jeannine Husson, Mar. 19, 1953; 1 dau., Jeannine Marie. Engr., Fla. Power & Light Co., Miami, 1955-57, Sarasota, Fla., 1957-59; asst. to plant elec. engr. U.S. Indsl. Chem. Co., Deer Park, Tex., 1959-60, chief quality assurance br., 1960-63; valuation engr. Hdqrs. U.S. Army Corps Engrs., Washington, 1963-64; elec. utilities contract cons. Directorate Civil Engring., U.S. Air Force, Washington, 1964—, also elec. engr. Pres. U.S.I. Fed. Credit Union, 1961-63. Served with AUS, 1948-50, 50-51. Mem. I.E.E.E. Toastmaster, Optimist (treas. 1958-60). Home: 11162 Oak Leaf Dr Silver Spring MD 20901 Office: Headquarters United States Air Force Engineering Div Washington DC 20332

STAGG, BRIAN LEE, historian, hist. assn. adminstr.; b. St. Louis, May 19, 1948; s. Thaddeus Severin and Dorothy Kathleen (Geiger) S.; B.A., U. of South, 1973. Exec. dir. Rugby Restoration Assn., Rugby, Tenn., 1966—; librarian Thomas Hughes Pub. Library, Rugby, 1970—. Mem. Morgan County Parks and Recreation Commn., 1973—. Recipient Moore Meml. award for best article of the year Tenn. Hist. Quar. 1968. Mem. Nat. Trust Historic Preservation (publs. com), Am. Assn. State and Local History, Sigma Upsilon. Episcopalian (lay reader 1970—, organist 1971—). Author: History of Deer Lodge, Tenn., 1964; The Distant Eden, 1973. Editor: An Anthology of Rugby Verse, 1974. Home: Roslyn Rugby TN 37733 Office: PO Box 8 Rugby TN 37733

STAGG, FREDERICK RAYMOND, steel co. exec.; b. Irondequoit, N.Y., Feb. 14, 1918; s. Philip Walter and Edith (Burkin) S.; Secretarial Diploma, Rochester Sch. of Commerce, 1938; Structural Engring. degree, Internat. Correspondence Schs., 1947; m. Phyllis Marie Chandley, May 12, 1946; children—Susan (Mrs. Robert Boyd Pamplin), Frederick Raymond. Small sales, drafting dept. Asheville Steel Co. (N.C.), 1945-53, head draftsman, 1953-59, engr. sales mgr. 1959-63, v.p. prodn., 1964—, also dir. Bd. dirs. Y.M.C.A., 1964. Served with M.C., AUS, 1941-45. Mem. Engrs. Soc. (pres. 1963), Welding Soc. (pres. 1969). Conglist. (deacon 1950—, chmn. 1969). Kiwanian (pres. 1963). Home: 69 Edwin Pl Asheville NC 28801 Office: Box 691 Meadow Rd Asheville NC 28802

STAGGERS, RUCKER LEWIS, physician; b. Birmingham, Ala., Aug. 30, 1930; s. William Llewellyn and Frances (Howe) S.; B.S., Auburn U., 1953; M.D., Med. Coll. Ala., 1957; m. Nettie Simpson Mayo, June 6, 1951; children—Sara Howe, William Rucker, Caroline Mayo, Robert Jackson. Intern Univ. Hosp., Birmingham, 1957-58; resident Carraway Meth. Hosp., Birmingham, 1958-59; gen. practice medicine, Benton, Ala., 1959-63, Eutaw, Ala., 1963—; mem. courtesy staff New Vaughan Meml. Hosp., Selma, Ala.; mem. staff Greene County Hosp., Eutaw. Pres. Warrior Pvt. Sch. Found., 1967-70, bd. dirs., 1967—; bd. dirs. Ala. Soc. Crippled Children, 1959-69, county chmn., 1959—. Served with AUS, 1948-49. Mem. Alpha Omega Alpha, Pi Kappa Alpha, Nu Sigma Nu, Alpha Epsilon Delta. Presbyn. (ruling elder 1960—). Lion (pres. 1968-69). Home: 508 Wilson St Eutaw AL 35462 Office: 202 Pickens St Eutaw AL 35462

STAHL, BEN, artist, writer; b. Chgo., Sept. 7, 1910; s. Ben F. and Grace (Meyer) S.; student pub. schs.; m. Ella M. Lehocky, Dec. 19, 1940; children—Ben F., Gail, Regina, David. Illustrator Sat. Eve. Post, other nat. mags., 1933—; mem. founding faculty Famous Artists Schools (now Famous Schs. Internat.), Westport, Conn., 1949—; mem. Fla. Art Commn.; bd. advisers Am. Art. Found.; v.p. Sarasota Mus. of the Cross (creator all paintings and drawings exhibited); exhibitor Nat. Acad. Design, Art Inst. Chgo., Audubon Museum, others; one-man shows Soc. Ill., N.Y.C., 1945, Stevens Gross Galleries, Chgo., 1950, Scarab Club, Detroit, 1951, Sarasota Art Assn., 1950, Cellar Gallery, Chgo., 1971, U. Brigeport, 1971, Parker Playhouse, Ft. Lauderdale, 1971, Top Flight Gallery, Sarasota, 1971, Darro Gallery, Wilmette, Ill., 1971, others; painted and exhibited the 14 stas. of the cross for Cath. Bible and Catholic Press, Chgo., 1955; illustrated 2 volumes Bible, also ltd. edit. of Gone With the Wind, 1960. Recipient numerous nat. awards, including Saltus gold medal Nat. Acad. Design, 1949, Sequoyah Book Award (for Blackbeard's Ghost), Okla. Library Assn., 1969. Mem. Soc. Illustrators, Artists and Writers, Westport Artists (co-founder, 1st pres.), Sarasota Art Assn. (v.p. 1953), Internat. Platform Assn. Club: Players (N.Y.C.). Author, illustrator: Blackbeard's Ghost, 1965 (Walt Disney film, released 1968); The Secret of Red Skull, 1971. Home: Tenerias 29 San Miguel de Allende Mexico

STAHL, CHARLES FREDRIC, architect; b. Rockford, Ill., Oct. 20, 1931; s. Charles Jacob and Ruth (Stephens) S.; student North Tex. State U., 1948-50; B.Arch., U. Tex., 1955; m. Joyce Lorayne Davis, Aug. 28, 1954; children—Charles Gregory, Lisa Kathryn. Draftsman Neggli & Riley, architects, Austin, Tex., 1957-60; with Barrow & Stahl, architects, Austin, 1960—, partner, 1960—. Dir. N.W. Savs. Assn., Austin. Mem. teaching staff Tex. Assn. Realtors, 1973-74. Pres. N.W. Highlands Assn., 1968-69; chief West Austin Nation Y-Indian Guides, 1970; campaign chmn. Travis County unit Am. Cancer Soc., 1971. Bd. dirs. Austin YMCA. Served with AUS, 1955-57. Mem. Am. Inst. Architects (pres. Austin chpt. 1972), Tex. Soc. Architects (dir. Austin chpt. 1973, v.p. 1974), Phi Kappa Sigma (pres. Austin alumni 1969). Home: 1906 Mountainview Rd Austin TX 78703 Office: 3637 Far West Blvd Austin TX 78731

STAHL, RAY EMERSON, coll. adminstrn. exec.; b. Latrobe, Pa., Mar. 24, 1917; s. Curtis E. and Josephine (King) S.; A.B., Bethany Coll., 1938; B.D., Butler U., 1943; Ed.M., U. Pitts. 1946; postgrad. St. Vincent Coll., 1939. Pitts. Sch. Accountancy, 1939-40, U. Ky., 1955; M.A., Ohio State U., 1969; m. Faith Worrell, Aug. 25, 1941; children—Ellen Josephine (Mrs. Lawrence Carpenter), Ray Emerson. Ordained to ministry Disciples of Christ Ch., 1941; minister Brentwood Christian Ch., Pitts., 1943-46, First Christian Ch., Erwin, Tenn., 1946-50; exec. sec. in charge bus. adminstrn., pub. relations Milligan Coll., Tenn., 1950-68; dir. pub. relations E. Tenn. State U., Johnson City, 1968—. Bd. dirs. Reece Mus., Johnson City Symphony Orch. Mem. Council for Advancement Small Colls. (chmn. pub. relations 1957-61), Johnson City C. of C. (dir.), Kappa Alpha, Theta Phi, Kappa Tau Alpha. Republican. Mem. Christian Ch. Kiwanian. Club: Johnson City Country. Author: How to Finance the Local Church, 1953. Contbr. articles to profl. jours. Home: 108 Park Ct Johnson City TN 37601

STAHLMAN, JAMES GEDDES, publisher; b. Nashville, Feb. 28, 1893; s. Edward Claiborne and Mary (Geddes) S.; grad. Webb Sch., Bell Buckle, Tenn., 1912; A.B., Vanderbilt U., 1916; postgrad. U. Chgo., 1916; LL.D., Atlanta Law Sch., 1939; m. Mildred Thornton, Jan. 20, 1917; children—Ann Geddes (Mrs. George R. Hill), Mildred Stahlman; m. 2d, Effye Chumley, Jan. 10, 1939 (dec.); m. 3d, Gladys P. Breckenridge, June 1, 1953. Pres., pub. Nashville Banner, 1930—; chmn. bd. Newspaper Printing Corp., 1937—. Mem. nat. council Boy Scouts Am. Trustee Vanderbilt U., Cordell Hull Found., MacArthur Meml. Found., Hermitage, Home Andrew Jackson. Served as pvt. U.S. Army, World War I; capt. USNR, World War II. Recipient Am. award Americas Found., 1956, Freedoms Found. Washington medal, 1961, 65, 4th Estate award Am. Legion, 1970. Mem. Inter-Am. Press Assn. (pres. 1955-56), Am. (pres. 1937-39), So. (pres. 1932-33, chmn. bd. 1933-34) newspaper pubs. assns., Am. Soc. Newspaper Editors, Phi Beta Kappa, Sigma Chi, Sigma Delta Chi, Omicron Delta Kappa, Sigma Upsilon. Presbyn. Mason (33 deg., K.T., Shriner, past potentate). Clubs: Belle Meade Country, Hillsboro Hounds, Cumberland; Army-Navy, Army Navy Country, Nat. Press (Washington); Metropolitan, University, Dutch Treat (N.Y.C.); Circumnavigators. Home: 815 Tyne Blvd Nashville TN 37220

STALCUP, JOE ALAN, lawyer; b. Hooker, Okla., Feb. 13, 1931; s. Herbert I. and Ruby (Gantt) S.; B.B.A. cum laude, So. Methodist U., 1951, J.D. magna cum laude, 1959; m. Nancy Jo Vaughn, Sept. 3, 1950; children—Melinda (Mrs. James L. Lundy Jr.), Sondra Jo, Cheri Ann. Tchr. Dallas Ind. Sch. Dist., 1951-57; admitted to Tex. bar, 1959; asso. mem. firm Locke, Purnell, Boren, Laney & Nealy, Dallas, 1959-66; asso. atty., partner firm Geary, Brice & Lewis, Dallas, 1966-67; founder, sr. partner firm Stalcup, Johnson, Meyers & Miller and predecessor firm, Dallas, 1968—. Pres. Dallas County Young Democrats, 1952-54. Bd. dirs., mem. exec. com. N. Tex. Christian Communications Commn., 1972—; bd. dirs., v.p. Greater Dallas Council Chs., 1972—. Mem. Am., Tex., Dallas bar assns., Am. Judicature Soc., Phi Alpha Delta. Mem. Christian Ch. (elder). Home: 6950 Tokalon St Dallas TX 75214 Office: 2700 2001 Bryan Tower Dallas TX 75201

STALEY, KENNETH EUGENE, automobile mfg. co. exec.; b. Western, Neb., Nov. 26, 1904; s. Ernest Grant and Ruby (Steven) S.; student U. Neb., 1922-24, Armed Forces Indsl. Coll., 1947-48; m. Nell Dowd, Oct. 23, 1928. With Gen. Motors Corp., various locations, 1929-66, gen. sales mgr., Detroit, 1959-62, v.p. distbn., marketing, 1962-66, ret., 1966, mem. Gen. Motors Speakers Bur., 1966—; dir. First Fed. Savs. & Loan, Lake Worth, Fla. Sec. treas., mem. bd. govs. Nat. Hwy. User Conf., Washington, 1962-66, living endowment gold key Nova U., Ft. Lauderdale, 1973—. Bd. dirs. Auto Industry Hwy. Safety Com., 1962-66; trustee Fla. Atlantic U. Found., Boca Raton, (Fla.) Community Hosp.; gov. U. Miami (Fla.); mem. bd. regents Gen. Motors Inst., 1962-66, Marymount Coll., Boca Raton, 1967—. Served to col. AUS, 1941-45; ETO. Decorated Bronze Star. Mem. Soc. Univ. Founders. Automotive Orgn. Team, Lambda Chi Alpha. Republican. Roman Catholic. Clubs: Royal Palm Yacht and Country, 150 (Boca Raton); D.A.C. (Detroit). Home: 1200 S Ocean Blvd Boca Raton FL 33432 Office: Gen Motors Bldg W Grand Blvd Detroit MI 48202

STALEY, THOMAS F., educator, univ. dean; b. Pitts., Aug. 13, 1935; B.A., B.S., Regis Coll., 1957; M.A., U. Tulsa, 1958; Ph.D. (fellow), U. Pitts., 1962; m. 1960; 4 children. Asst. prof. English, Rollins Coll., 1961-62; vis. prof. U. Pitts., summers 1962, 67; Fulbright resident prof., Trieste, Italy, 1966-67; asso. prof. English, U. Tulsa, 1968-70, pres., 1970—, dean Grad. Sch., 1969—. Co-chmn. Internat. James Joyce Symposium, Dublin, 1967, chmn., 1969; Danforth asso. Am. Council Learned Socs. grantee, 1969. Mem. South Central Modern Lang. Assn. (chmn. comparative lit. sect. 1965-66). Author: Approaches to Ulysses, 1970; also chpts. in books. Editor: James Joyce Today, 1966; Dubliners: A Critical Handbook, 1969; co-editor U. Tulsa Monograph Series; mem. bd. editors 20th Century Lit. Research on James Joyce, comparative lit., modern European and Brit. fiction. Office: Office of Dean Graduate School University of Tulsa Tulsa OK 74104

STALLARD, HARLEY TRIGG, supt. schs.; b. Wise, Va., May 12, 1917; s. Jerry Trigg and Flora Belle (Taylor) S.; student Miligan Coll., 1934-35, 36-37; B.S., Radford Coll., 1947; M.S., Va. Poly. Inst., 1951; m. Bunnie Frances Robinette, May 8, 1941; children—Harley, Robert, Anita (Mrs. Gary Dorton), Michael, Larry, Nancy, Addie. Elementary head tchr. Wise County Sch. Bd. (Va.), 1937-43, 45-49, tchr. high sch., 1949-51, bd. clk., 1951-53, prin. elementary schs., 1953-54, prin. high schs., 1954-61, elementary supr., 1961-63, dir. instrn., 1963-71, div. supt., 1971—. Mem. Wise County com. Democratic party, 1954. Served with AUS, 1943-45. Mem. Va. (pres. Dist. 0 1951, dir. 1951), Wise County (sec. 1947-51) edn. assns., S.W. Suprs. (pres. 1966-67). Baptist (tchr. men's bible class 1954—, Sunday sch. supt. 1960-62, chmn. bd. deacons 1967-70). Moose, Lion (charter pres. 1953-54) (dep. dist. gov. 1958-59, 62-63). Home: Box 418 Big Stone Gap VA 24219 Office: PO Box 1217 Wise VA 24293

STALLINGS, FRANK HALL, educator; b. Smith's Grove, Ky., Feb. 8, 1909; s. William Marion and Lina Thomas (Hall) S.; student Ky. Wesleyan Coll., 1926-27, U. Ky., 1927-28; A.B., U. Louisville, 1931, M.A., 1937; Ed.D., U. Ky., 1959; m. Evalyn Mae Strange, Jan. 30, 1932; children—William Marion II, Linda Lee (Mrs. Gregory P. Grantham). Tchr. pub. schs., Clark County, Ky., 1928-29, Louisville, 1942-58; lectr. U. Louisville, 1951-58, mem. faculty, 1958—, prof. edn., head dept., 1961-68, chmn. unit for adminstrn. and supervision, 1968—. Cons. 2d annual conf. schs. in transition U.S. Comm. Civil Rights, 1960; ofcl. del. White House Conf. Children and Youth, 1960; adv. mem. Ky. Council Pub. Higher Edn., 1966—. Mem. Mallon Com. Met. Govt. Louisville and Jefferson County, 1956-58; chmn. Peoples Com. for Annexation, 1948-51. Mem. Ky. Dept. Elementary Sch. Prins. (pres. 1956), Ky. Assn. Colls., Elementary and Secondary Schs. (pres. 1965—), N.E.A., Kappa Delta Pi, Phi Delta Kappa. Democrat. Baptist. Author: Let's Take a Field Trip, 1955; A Study of the Effects of Integration on Scholastic Achievement in the Louisville Public Schools, 1958: Development of Alternative Models for the Preparation of Elementary School Guidance Personnel (with others), 1967. Home: 3717 Norbourne Blvd Louisville KY 40207

STALLINGS, JAMES CAMERON, educator, chemist; b. Denton, Tex., Jan. 16, 1919; s. Arthur Bunyan and Mona (Coker) S.; B.S., North Tex. State U., 1942, M.S., 1943; Ph.D. (Gen. Aniline fellow 1948-49), U. Tex., 1950; m. Otelia Olga Limmer, Dec. 18, 1949; children—Stephanie Ann, Deborah. Chemist Wilson Labs., Denton, Tex., 1942-43; prof. chemistry dept. Sam Houston State U., Huntsville, Tex., 1949-57, prof., dir. chemistry dept., 1959—; sr. research chemist Celanese Chem. Co., Corpus Christi, Tex., 1957-59. Served to comdr. USNR, 1943-46; PTO. Fellow Am. Inst. Chemists; mem. Am. Chem. Soc., Phi Lambda Upsilon. Lutheran. Home: 1912 18th St Huntsville TX 77340

STALLINGS, JAMES HENRY, govt. ofcl.; b. Bryan, Tex., Sept. 20, 1892; s. William Daniel and Emma Elizabeth (Josey) S.; B.S., Tex. A. and M. U., 1914; M.S. (Research fellow), Ia. State U., 1917, Ph.D., 1926; m. Pearl Louise Drummond, Aug. 1, 1923; children—George Drummond, James Henry. Asst. prof. Ia. State U., 1919-20; head soils dept. Tex. A. and M. U., 1920-26; agronomist Penny-Gynn Inst., 1926-28, Nat. Fertilizer Assn., 1929-33; regional dir. Soil Conservation Service, U.S. Dept. Agr., 1934-37, organizer, dir. flood control program, Washington, 1937-42; dir. fertilizer program War Food Adminstrn., Washington, 1942-44; prin. research specialist Soil Conservation Service, 1945-59; soil sci. editor Biol. Abstracts, 1952—, Webster's Internat. Dictionary. Mem. N.Y. Acad. Scis., Soil Sci. Soc. Am., Agronomy Assn., Internat. Platform Assn., Sigma Xi. Author: Soil Conservation, 1957; Soil Use and Improvement, 1957. Contbr. articles to profl. jours. Address: 5146 Nebraska Av NW Washington DC 20008

STALLINGS, JOHN HARRISON, govt. ofcl.; b. Oklahoma City, July 1, 1940; s. Harry Coburn and Ruby (Berry) S.; B.Engring. Sci. in Chem. Engring., Brigham Young U., 1963; m. Claudia Lynnette Harvey, Dec. 23, 1963; children—Sherri Lynnette, Patricia Louise, John Berry, Traci June, Claudia Dawn. Environmental protection engr. Air Pollution Control Bur. State Ill., Springfield, 1965-71, also acting chief episode and standards sect., 1970-71; head engring. sect. Air Pollution Control div. Okla. Dept. Health, Oklahoma City, 1971—. Dir. Thomas N. Berry & Co., Stillwater, Okla. Registered profl. engr., Okla., Ill. Mem. Am. Inst. Chem. Engrs. (asso. mem.), Nat., Ill., Okla. socs. profl. engrs., Huguenot Soc. Mem. Ch. Jesus Christ Latter-day Saints (ward clk.).

STALLINGS, NELL ALLEN, educator; b. Louisburg, N.C., July 15, 1915; d. George B. Haywood and Christiana (Lacy) Stallings; B.S., U.N.C., 1936, M.A., 1942. Tchr. sr. high sch., High Point, N.C., 1936-42; Lenoir Rhyne Coll., Hickory, N.C., 1942-43; faculty E. Carolina U., Greenville, N.C., 1943—, prof. phys. edn., 1963—. Staff mem. Nat. Aquatic Sch., 1958-72. Water safety chmn. Pitt County chpt. A.R.C., 1962—. Recipient Honor award N.C. Assn. for Health, Phys. Edn. and Recreation, 1968. Fellow A.A.H.P.E.R.; mem. N.E.A., Am. Assn. U. Women (pres. 1953-54), Nat., So. assns. phys. edn. for coll. women, N.C. Edn. Assn., N.C. Assn. Health, Phys. Edn. and Recreation (pres. 1954-55). Home: 2411 Umstead Av Greenville NC 27834

STALLINGS, REX PATRICK, state ofcl.; b. Dallas, Tex., Jan. 11, 1934; s. Rufus H. and Francis Marie (Eubanks) S.; B.B.A., U. Tex., 1956; m. Doris Rudell Bletsch, June 3, 1956; children—Ray Patrick, Rex Patrick, Russell Patrick. Account rep. IBM Corp., Amarillo, Tex., 1961-65, Dallas, 1965-66; area mgr. Xerox Corp., Dallas, 1966-67; sr. cons. Peat, Marwick, Mitchell, C.P.A. firm, Dallas, 1969; dir. Office of Information Services, Office of Gov. Tex., Austin, 1969—. Served to lt. (j.g.) USN, 1956-59. Recipient Noteworthy Contbn. award Am. Soc. C.E., 1971. Mem. Tex. State Agy. Bus. Adminstrs. Assn., Nat. Assn. for State Information Systems (mem. exec. com. 1971—, fed. state local liaison com. chmn. 1971-73). Home: 4104 North Hills Dr Austin TX 78731 Office: PO Box 13224 Austin TX 78711

STALNAKER, LEO, JR., educator; b. Tampa, Fla., Oct. 18, 1923; s. Leo and Judson (Vest) S.; student U. Tampa, 1941-42, Coll. William and Mary, 1943-44; B.A., U. S. Fla., 1962, also M.A.; m. June Esther Kuebler, Oct. 5, 1946; children—Lance K., Jeffrey Clay. Staff writer, Tampa Times, 1946-49, city editor, 1950-55, asso. state editor Tampa Tribune, 1955-57, night city editor, 1957-65, city editor, 1965-66, asst. mng. editor, 1966-70; asst. prof. mass communications U. S. Fla., 1970—. Served with AUS, 1943-46. Decorated Purple Heart, 3 battle stars; ETO, combat medal. Mem. Sigma Delta Chi. Lutheran. Home: 1907 Heather Av Tampa FL 33612

STAMBAUGH, JOHN FRANKLIN YEAGER, accountant; b. Archbold, O., July 30, 1914; s. Harry Francis and Elizabeth Cecil (Yeager) S.; B.S., U. Okla., 1936; m. Elizabeth Lorene Busey, Jan. 4, 1941; children—Jananne (Mrs. Peter Silcher), John Franklin Yeager. Mng. partner Frazer & Torbet, Tulsa, 1946-67, Touche Ross & Co., Tulsa, 1967—; instr. U. Tulsa Downtown Coll., 1947-54. Mem. budget com. Community Chest, 1950-52. Chmn. bd. dirs. U. Okla. Alumni Devel. Fund, 1967-70; bd. visitors U. Okla., 1968-72. Served to lt. USNR, 1942-46. Mem. U. Okla. Hall of Fame; charter mem. and exec. com. U. Okla. Bd. Fellows; recipient Outstanding Service award U. Okla. Alumni Devel. Fund, 1965, 70. C.P.A., Okla., Wis., Ia., Tex., N.Y., Md., Va., La., N.C. Mem. Tulsa C. of C., Okla., Tex., N.Y., Md., Va., La., N.C., Tulsa (pres. 1950-51) socs. C.P.A.'s. Mason (Shriner). Clubs: Tulsa, Meadowbrook Country, Cedar Ridge Country (Tulsa); Garden of the Gods (Colorado Springs). Contbr. articles to profl. jours. Home: 2206 E 38th St Tulsa OK 74105 Office: Nat Bank of Tulsa Bldg Tulsa OK 74103

STAMPER, JOE ALLEN, lawyer; b. Okemah, Okla., Jan. 30, 1914; s. Horace Allen and Ann (Stephens) S.; B.A., U. Okla., 1933, LL.B., 1935; m. Johnnie Lee Bell, June 4, 1936; 1 dau., Jane Allen (Mrs. Ernest F. Godlove). Admitted to Okla. bar, 1935; practiced in Antlers, Okla., 1935-36, 46—; atty. Pushmataha County, 1936-39; mem. Okla. indsl. commn., 1939-40; spl. justice Okla. Supreme Ct., 1948. Pres., Antlers Sch. Bd., 1956-67, Pushmataha Found., 1957—; mem. Okla. Bicentennial Commn. Mgr., Okla. Democratic party, 1946; chmn. dist., 1946-50; alternate del. Dem. Nat. Conv., 1951. Served from 2d lt. to col. AUS, 1935-46, ETO. Decorated Bronze Star. Mem. Am., Okla. (bd. govs.) bar assns., S.A.R., Pi Kappa Alpha. Baptist (deacon). Mason (32 deg., Shriner), Lion. Club: Whitehall (Oklahoma City). Home: 1000 NE 2d St Antlers OK 74523 Office: PO Box 100 Antlers OK 74523

STAMPS, HERMAN FRANKLIN, dentist; b. Washington, Jan. 20, 1924; s. Herman Franklin and Alice Beatrice (Bowman) S.; B.S., Howard U., 1945, D.D.S., 1948; M.Sc., U. Mich., 1953; m. Pauline Duvall, Oct. 2, 1948; children—Eric, Alisa. Gen. practice dentistry, Washington, 1948—. Mem. faculty Howard U., Washington, 1948—, dir. clinics, 1967-70, prof. Coll. Dentistry, 1969—; coordinator facilities, systems and planning, 1970—; cons. Montgomery County Jr. Colls., 1966, Washington Bd. Edn., 1963-65, Manpower Bd. Labor Dept., 1964-67. Chmn. supervisory com. Armstrong Neighborhood Fed. Credit Union, 1964-66; Bd. dirs. Washington Urban League, 1958—, chmn. membership drive, 1960-61, bd. dirs. COIN, 1962-65. Served with AUS, 1942-44. Diplomate Am. Bd. Endodontics. Mem. Robert T. Freeman Dental Soc. (pres. 1959-61), Nat., Am. dental assns., D.C. Dental Soc., Am. Dental Assn., Am. Soc. History Dentistry (charter), Am. Assn. Endodontics, Omicron Kappa Upsilon. Author: Modern Prescription Writing, 1954. Home: 7541 16th St NW Washington DC 20012 Office: 2328 Georgia Av NW Washington DC 20001

STANALAND, WILLIAM WHIT, JR., accountant; b. Benson Junction, Fla., Mar. 15, 1930; s. William Whit and Goldie (Merritt) S.; B.S. in Bus. Adminstrn., U. Fla., 1957, postgrad., 1959; postgrad. Rollins Coll., 1964; m. Norma Lee Ober, June 24, 1961; children—Sherry D., William Whit III, Terence B., Dana Lee; m. 2d, Sandra L. Swann, Dec. 1, 1971. Jr. accountant Pepsi Cola Bottling Co., 1957-58; accountant Wells, Laney, Earlich & Baer, 1958-59, A.J. Mixner, C.P.A., 1961-63; controller Halco Products, Inc., 1959-61; C.P.A., Orlando, Fla., 1963—. Served with USMC, 1948-52. C.P.A., Fla., Ga. Mem. Am., Fla. insts. C.P.A.'s. Kiwanian, Toastmaster. Home: Route 1 Box 178F Lake Dr Sanford FL 32771 Office: 5400 Diplomat Circle Orlando FL 32810

STANBERY, CECIL HENLEY, dentist; b. nr. Chattanooga, Apr. 12, 1929; s. William Cecil and Etta Moyers (Henley) S.; B.A., U. Tenn., 1952, M.S., 1954, D.D.S., 1958; m. Johnnie Annette Richardson, June 15, 1957; children—William Cecil II, John Samuel. Faculty, U. Chattanooga, 1953-54; practice dentistry, Cleveland, Tenn., 1958—. Instr. geography Cleveland State Community Coll., 1968. Dental missionary, Bolivia, 1969. Chmn. 3d dist. Tenn. Republican party, 1972—; Bradley County campaign mgr. for Richard Nixon, 1968. Mem. Am., Tenn. dental assns., Third Dist. Dental Soc., Pierre Fauchard, S.A.R., Sigma Nu, Delta Sigma Delta. Rotarian, Elk. Home: North Lee Hwy Cleveland TN 37311 Office: 423 Central Av NW Cleveland TN 37311

STANCZYK, MARTIN HENRY, govt. ofcl., metallurgist; b. Jersey City, Jan. 26, 1930; s. Martin John and Mary Josephine (Sajkowski) S.; B.S., U. Ariz., 1957, M.S., 1958; m. Mary Lu Sauer, Nov. 28, 1957; children—Cynthia, Rebecca, Jeanette, Brooks. Metallurgist, U.S. Bur. of Mines, Tucson, 1957-60, research metallurgist, Tuscaloosa, Ala., 1960-68, supervisory metallurgist, College Park, Md., 1968-73, chief of research, Tuscaloosa, 1973—. Coach, (Kettering) Md. Boys and Girls Club; football coach boys Club Tuscaloosa. Served with USAAF, 1949-53. U.S. Bur. of Mines fellow, 1957. Mem. Am. Inst. Mining Engrs. (sec. treas. 1968-70, award 1973), Sigma Xi, Phi Lambda Upsilon. Elk. Contbr. articles to profl. publs. Home: 82 Arcadia Dr Tuscaloosa AL 35401 Office: PO Box L University AL 35486

STANDER, ROBERT ANGUS, chem. co. exec.; b. Balt., July 7, 1928; s. Henricus Johannes and Florence Mary (Creelman) S.; student Cornell U., 1946-47; A.B. in Physics, Colby Coll., 1950; m. Maurine Masal Maust, June 4, 1951; children—Mary (Mrs. John G. Landry), Linda, Robert Angus, Timothy. Trainee physicist Texaco, Inc., 1950-51; with Chem. Service, Inc., 1955-62, br. mgr., Baton Rouge, 1956-58, gen. mgr., Lafayette, La., 1958-62; founder, Chem. Applicators of Lafayette, Inc., 1963, chmn. bd., pres., gen. mgr., 1963—; dir. Burlastan. Served with USAF, 1952-55; Korea. Mem. Nat. Assn. Corrosion Engrs. (chpt. pres. 1960-61), Nat. Assn. Power Engrs. (custodian 1970—), Natural Gas Processors Assn., Am. Petroleum Inst., Nat. Pilots Assn., Aircraft Owners and Pilots Assn., Air Force Assn., Am. Legion. Republican. Presbyn. Rotarian. Inventor chem. and mechanic procedures. Home: 313 Thibodeaux Dr Lafayette LA 70501 Office: PO Box 52803 Lafayette LA 70501

STANFIELD, CECIL EMMETTE, architect; b. Vinita, Okla., Sept. 30, 1918; s. Cecil Abram and Rachel (Hammett) S.; B.Arch., Okla. State U., 1942; postgrad. Am. Acad., Rome, Italy, 1944-45; m. Ramona Sue Shaw, Aug. 30, 1966; children—Tracy Lynn, Judith Ann, Terri Lynn, Ramona Yvette. Designer, Parr & Aderhold, Oklahoma City, 1942-43; chief designer, draftsman Leon B. Senter, Tulsa, 1946-47; chief draftsman-chief designer Arthur B. Atkinson, Tulsa, 1947-48; pvt. practice architecture, Tulsa, Corpus Christi and Brownsville, Tex., Norman, Okla., 1948—; mng. dir. Belize Cotton Industries, British Honduras, 1963—. Served to capt. USAAF, 1943-46. Decorated Bronze Star medal. Mem. A.I.A., Am. Orchid Soc., Kappa Alpha. Mason. Kiwanian, Rotarian. Author: Sun, Land and Water, 1965. Numerous archtl. works include: Oral Roberts U. Campus Plan and 4 bldgs.; Abundant Life bldg.; Okla. U. Fine Arts Bldg. Home: 2831 S Florence St Tulsa OK 74112 Office: 720 Buffalo St Corpus Christi TX 78403 also 1940 E Elizabeth St Brownsville TX 78520 also Coronado Inn Norman OK 73069 also 1424 S Utica St Tulsa OK 74104

STANFORD, BOB EDWARD (ROBERT EDWARD STAMETS), advt. exec.; b. Braddock, Pa., July 29, 1918; s. Russell Curl and Cecilia (Hager) Stamets; student So. Meth. U., 1936-38; m. Jeanne Burney, 1949 (div. 1966); children—Katherine, Russell, Mollie. With Gen. Motors Corp., 1940-42, Columbia Pictures, 1942-45, A.H. Belo Corp., 1945-49, KBTV, Dallas, 1949-52; ind. TV-radio producer, 1952-54; advt. dir Southland Corp., Dallas, 1954—, pres. subsidiary Stanford Agy., 1972—. Recipient Am. TV Comml. Festival awards for best S.W. market and best local retail, 1962, Hollywood Advt. Club awards for internat. broadcast, 1965, 70, 71, Clio awards for local low-budget, retail and retail dealers, 1972. Home: 5860 Dexter Dr Dallas TX 75230 Office: 2828 N Haskell St Suite 300 Dallas TX 75204

STANFORD, CHARLES WHITSON, JR., mus. exec.; b. Durham, N.C., Sept. 13, 1924; s. Charles Whitson and Mary (McIver) S.; A.B., U. N.C., 1947; postgrad. Columbia, 1948-49, Princeton, 1949-53. Curatorial asst. Colonial Williamsburg, Inc., 1955-56; curator edn. N.C. Mus. Art, Raleigh, 1958-70, dir., 1970—. Mem. Gov.'s Bldg. Commn. Head, State Agy., 1970—; dir., v.p. Redfields, Inc., Chapel Hill; lectr. art history on TV, radio. Vice chmn. Exec. Mansion Fine Arts Commn. Bd. dirs. Mary Duke Biddle Gallery for Blind, N.C. Mus. Art, Raleigh, N.C. Symphony Soc. (exec. com.), N.C. Art Soc. (exec. com.), Historic Hillsborough Commn.; dir. adv. bd. N.C. Ednl. TV, div. humanities N.C. Dept. Pub. Instrn.; bd. dirs. Reynolds House, Winston-Salem. Recipient N.C. award (Gold medal) in fine arts, 1969. Mem. N.C. Mus. Council (past dir.), Coll. Arts Assn., N.C. Art Soc., Assn. Art Mus. Dirs. Clubs: Princeton (N.Y.); Nassau (Princeton, N.J.). Democrat. Author: Masterpieces in the North Carolina Museum of Art, 1966, 2d edit., 1972; Selections from British and American Painting, 1967. Contbr. articles to profl. periodicals. Home: Redfields Route 1 Box 79 Chapel Hill NC 27514 Office: Dirs Office NC Mus Art Raleigh NC 27601

STANFORD, DONALD ELWIN, educator; b. Amherst, Mass., Feb. 7, 1913; s. Ernest Elwood and Alice Lyndon (Carrol) S.; A.B., Stanford, 1933, Ph.D., 1953; M.A., Harvard, 1935; m. Maryanna Peterson, Aug. 14, 1953. Instr. English, Colo. State Coll., 1935-37, Dartmouth, 1937-41, U. Neb., 1941-42; instr. La. State U., Baton Rouge, 1948-49, asst. prof., 1953-55, asso. prof., 1955-62, prof. English, 1962—, editor Humanities Series, La. State U. Press, 1962-67, editor So. Rev., 1963—. Guggenheim fellow, 1958-59. Mem. Modern Lang. Assn., Melville Soc., P.E.N. Author: The New England Earth (poems), 1941; The Traveler (poems), 1955; Edward Taylor, 1965. Editor: The Poems of Edward Taylor, 1960. Home: 776 Delgado Dr Baton Rouge LA 70808

STANFORD, HARRY WRIGHT, ednl. adminstr.; b. San Antonio, Sept. 3, 1923; s. Edward Rosemond and Elizabeth Gooch (Wright) S.; B.S., North Tex. State U., 1942; M.S., Cal. Inst. Tech., 1944; postgrad. U. Tex., Austin, 1946-47, 66; m. Katheryne Lucille Belser, Aug. 15, 1948; children—Rebecca (Mrs. Gene B. Christy), Janice (Mrs. Robert K. Hickman), Teresa (Mrs. John J. Davis, Jr.), Nancy Jo. Tchr., prin. Elkhart (Tex.) Pub. Schs., 1942-43; asst. state auditor, Austin, 1947-49; chief accountant, auditor N.Tex. State U., Denton, 1949-55; asst. supt., bus. mgr. Midland (Tex.) Pub. Schs., 1955-69, San Antonio Pub. Schs., 1969—. Chmn. supervisory com. Tchr. Credit Union, 1950-61; chmn. shelter com., disaster plans A.R.C., 1963-66; govt. agys. chmn. United Fund, 1964-65; sec. finance com. Midland Citizens Adv. Com. for Pub. Schs., 1965; mem. adv. com. Tex. Bd. Edn., Edn. Mgmt. Information System, 1968—. Served with USAAF, 1943-46; PTO. C.P.A., Tex. Mem. Tex. Assn. Sch. Bus. Ofcls. (pres. Bexar County 1973—), Assn. Sch. Bus. Ofcls. of U.S. and Can., Tex. Soc. C.P.A.'s, Tex. Tchrs. Assn. (life). Methodist. Mason, Lion. Author: Financial Accounting Manual, 1971. Office: 141 Lavaca St San Antonio TX 78210

STANGER, ALLEN BORDEN, clergyman, educator; b. Blacksburg, Va., Sept. 15, 1909; s. Robert Preston and Ida (Bingham) S.; A.B., Lynchburg (Va.) Coll., 1933; B.D., Yale, 1936; M.A., Hartford Sem., 1936; D.D., Christian Theol. Sem., 1961; m. Nellie DeJarnette Gray, June 13, 1937. Ordained to ministry Christian Ch., 1929; pastor West End Christian Ch., Danville, Va., 1934, 35, 36-42; dir. religious edn. for Christian Chs., Chesapeake area, Va., Md., D.C., 1942-47; tchr. Lynchburg Coll., 1947-50, asso. prof. religion, 1950-73, tchr. speech, 1970-74, chaplain, 1971-74, dir. ministerial tng., 1966-74; now supply minister, ch. cons. Active YMCA, 1947—. Mem. Blue Key, Tau Kappa Alpha, Alpha Phi Omega. Author: Prayer and Poems, 1962; This and That, 1965. Home: 349 College St Lynchburg VA 24501

STANGER, RUSSELL, orch. condr.; b. Boston; grad. New Eng. Conservatory Music; student Tanglewood. Condr. Cecelia Soc. Boston, 1953; organizer Boston Little Orch., 1958; asst. condr. N.Y. Philharmonic, 1960; Mpls. Symphony Orch. (name now Minn. Orch.), 1964-66; music dir. Norfolk (Va.) Symphony Orch., 1966—. Guest condr. leading Am. and European orchs., including Phila. Orch., N.Y. Philharmonic, CBC Symphony, Buffalo Philharmonic, Oslo Philharmonic, Bergen (Norway) Philharmonic, Royal Philharmonic, London Philharmonic, Orchestre Symphonique des Reims, Societe des Concerts du Conservatoire (Paris). Composer: Buffoons (A Merry Overture), 1963; Childhood Images, 1968; Rock Opus (for Symphony Orch. and Optional Rock Group), 1970. Office: PO Box 26 Norfolk VA 23501

STANLEY, CARL MEADOWS, lumber co. exec.; b. Spencer, Tenn., May 27, 1935; s. John Kendrick and Mary R. (Bennett) S.; B.S., Tenn. Tech. U., 1955; m. Reita Chandler, Sept. 17, 1954; children—Shannon Stanley, Mary Ann. Staff auditor Ernst & Ernst, McMinnville, Tenn., 1960-63; pres. Burroughs-Ross-Colville Co., McMinnville, 1963—; dir. Whitson Land Co., McMinnville, 1st Nat. Bank, McMinnville. Pres. United Givers Fund, 1967-69. Govs. campaign mgr. Dem. Party, 1964. Served with AUS, 1957-59. Named Outstanding Young Man of Year, Jaycees, 1968. Mem. Jr. C. of C. (pres. 1962). Mem. Ch. of Christ. Rotarian. Home: 318 Post Rd McMinnville TN 37110 Office: 301 Depot St McMinnville TN 37110

STANLEY, CURTIS E., educator; b. Valdosta, Ga., Mar. 26, 1917; s. Odis and Emma (Byron) S.; A.B., Johnson C. Smith U., 1939; M.A., Fisk U., 1949; postgrad. U. Pitts., 1951-54, N.Y. U., 1959, 65; LL.D., Daniel Payne Coll., 1972; m. Louise Murray, Feb. 3, 1943. Dist. mgr. Afro Am. Life Ins. Co., 1946-47; prin. Darwin High Sch., Cookeville, Tenn., 1948-52, Washington High Sch., Blakely, Ga., 1952-60; freshman dean Ala. State U., Montgomery, 1960-63, asso. prof. edn., 1953—. Dir. Am. Cancer Soc., 1954-56, Ala. State U. Credit Union, 1961-69. Served to 1st lt. AUS, 1942-46; PTO. Mem. Ga. Tchrs. and Ednl. Assn., Am. Assn. U. Profs., N.E.A., Assn. for Supervision and Curriculum Devel., Ala. Edn. Assn., Omega Psi Phi. Mem. A.M.E. Ch. (steward 1960—). Elk, Mason (32 deg., Shriner). Home: 2952 Vandy Dr Montgomery AL 36110

STANLEY, DAVID TAYLOR, researcher; b. East Orange, N.J., Aug. 18, 1916; s. Edward Otis and Mary (Taylor) S.; A.B., Princeton, 1937; M.A., Am. U., 1961; m. Helen H. Swan, Apr. 19, 1941; children—David H., Margaret (Mrs. K. Peter Henrickson), Mary Elizabeth (Mrs. Lee F. Feinberg). Personnel officer FCA, 1938-42, VA, 1946-48, Dept. Def., 1948-53; mgmt. analyst AEC, 1953-56, Pub. Health Service, 1956-58; dir. mgmt. policy Dept. Health Edn. and Welfare, 1958-61; sr. fellow Brookings Instn., Washington, 1961—. Served with USAAF, 1942-45. Named Layman of Year, Greater Washington Assn. Unitarian Universalist Chs., 1968. Mem. Am. Polit. Sci. Assn., Am. Soc. Pub. Adminstrn., Soc. Personnel Adminstrn., Pub. Personnel Assn. Unitarian (chmn. commn. appraisal 1961). Author: Professional Personnel for the City New York, 1963; The Higher Civil Service, 1964; Changing Administrations, 1965; Men Who Govern, 1967; Bankruptcy: Problem, Process, Reform, 1971; Managing Local Government Under Union Pressure, 1972. Home: 1720 Brookside Lane Vienna VA 22180 Office: 1775 Massachusetts Av NW Washington DC 20036

STANLEY, DONALD SANFORD, elec. engr.; b. Portland, Me., Feb. 6, 1932; s. Herbert Arthur and Marion Louise (Manks) S.; B.E.E., U. Fla., 1960; m. Joanne Holmwood Case, Sept. 21, 1963; children—Edmund W., Robert H., Melinda L., Jennifer L. Field service engr. Honeywell, Mpls., 1960-62, sr. systems engr., St. Petersburg, Fla., 1962-67, 72—; co-founder, v.p., dir. Aero Comm. Systems, Inc., St. Petersburg, Fla., 1967-74; with Honeywell Inc., St. Petersburg, 1974—. Bd. dirs. Seminole Jr. Warhawk Athletic Assn. Served with USAF, 1951-54. Presbyterian (elder 1974—, pres. bd. trustees 1974—). Home: 13575 101st Terrace N Seminole FL 33542 Office: Honeywell Inc 13350 US Hwy 19 St Petersburg FL 33733

STANLEY, DOROTHY EVELYN, educator, artist, author, lectr.; b. Nuremberg, Germany, Sept. 18, 1909; d. William H. Sellings and Lucie (Danziger) Peiser; came to U.S., 1937, naturalized, 1943; B.A., Maidenhead Coll., London, 1928; M.A., Hunter Coll., 1951; postgrad.

Columbia, 1946-47, U. Heidelberg, U. Munich, U. Paris, 1930-34; m. Jan. 31, 1932; children—Brigitte Strauss (Mrs. Saunders), Frank Strauss. Head proofroom George Grady Press, N.Y.C., 1939-42; asst. head monitoring sect. Overseas Radio div. U.S. State Dept., N.Y.C., 1942-45; tchr. French, English, Lycee Francais, N.Y.C., 1945-46; tchr. French, Latin, Acad. Sacred Heart, N.Y.C., 1946-49; tchr. French, German, Acad. Lang., N.Y.C., 1949-52; translator, interpreter 1st Nat. City Bank N.Y., 1952-59; asst. prof. fgn. langs. and lit. Old Dominion U., Norfolk, Va., 1960—. Exhibitor art galleries N.Y.C., 1954-59, Va., 1960—; lectr. creative living, 1959—; translator local orgns., bus., 1940. Recipient Grand Nat. Finalist award Am. Artists Profl. League, 1956, 57. Mem. Am. Assn. U. Women, Alliance Francaise, Am. Fedn. Astrologers, Va. Astrol. Assn., Am. Assn. Ret. Persons, Tidewater Sr. Citizens Center. Lutheran. Author: Die Kunterbunte Spielkiste, 1929, Das Lustige Kinderbuch, 1931, They Call It Courage, 1968. Home: 330 W Brambleton Av Norfolk VA 23510

STANLEY, DUFFY BROCK, architect; b. Midland, Tex., Feb. 14, 1923; s. Benjamin M. and Mary (White) S.; student Tex. A. and M. U., 1941-43, B.Arch., 1948; m. Irene Marie Muller, July 31, 1948; children—Sheila, Lars, Brock, Sonya, Sharon. Draftsman-designer J.J. Black, Architect, Midland, 1948-51; job capt. Carroll & Daeuble, Architects, El Paso, Tex., 1951-57; prin. Duffy B. Stanley, Architects, El Paso, 1957—. Mem. El Paso Zoning Bd. Adjustment, 1959-69, chmn., 1970; mem. Open Space Com. El Paso, 1970-71; vice chmn. Citizens Environmental Council, 1971-72. Served to capt. AUS, 1943-46. Decorated Bronze Star, Silver Star. Presbyn. Mason. Author: Open Space in the El Paso Region, 1970. Home: 3120 Wheeling St El Paso TX 79930 Office: Bassett Tower El Paso TX 79901

STANLEY, HAROLD DALLAS, III, ednl. adminstr.; b. Kinston, N.C., Dec. 29, 1929; s. Harold Dallas and Lila Maude (Meacham) S.; B.A., N.C. Wesleyan U., 1965; M.Div., Duke, 1969; m. Jean Stout Watlington, Jan. 27, 1951; children—David Meacham, Judith Elizabeth. Gen. mgr. radio sta., Wilmington and Clinton, N.C., 1954-58; clothier, Clinton, 1958-60; ordained to ministry Meth. Ch., 1961, served as minister, 1960-69; pres. Carolina Mil. Acad., Maxton, N.C., 1969-72; headmaster James F. Byrnes Acad., Florence, S.C., 1972—. Pres., Assn. for Mentally Retarded, 1968-69. Served with AUS, 1951-53. Mem. S.C. Ofcls. Ind. Sch. Assn. Democrat. Mason (32 deg., Shriner), Rotarian (past pres.). Home: 30 York St Florence SC 29501 Office: James F Byrnes Academy Route 1 Florence SC 29501

STANLEY, JOSEPH ANDREW, JR., san. engr.; b. Ft. Worth, Sept. 30, 1915; s. Joseph Andrew and Florence (Lewis) S.; student Sul Ross Coll., 1933-35; grad. Tex. Tech. U., 1939; postgrad. Vanderbilt U., 1940; m. Mildred Dutton Knox, July 28, 1940; children—Carole Ann, Joseph A. III. Jr. engr. Tex. Hwy. Dept., Pecos, Odessa, 1937-40; jr. engr., dist. san. engr. Tex. Dept. Health, Lubbock, 1940-46; san. engr. City of Lubbock, 1946-47; owner-mgr. Hygeia Bottled Water Co., Lubbock, 1947—; owner Hygeia Sprinkler & Equipment Co., Lubbock, 1949—. Chmn., City County Bd. Health, Lubbock, 1951-54; mem., chmn. Municipal Utilities Bd., 1959-65; chmn. City-County Health Bd., Lubbock, 1966-68; chmn. Citizens Adv. Com., 1966-69. Del., Tex. State Democratic Conv., 1954; mem., sec. bd. mgrs. Lubbock County Hosp. Dist., 1968—. Bd. dirs., sec.-treas. bd. Lubbock Boys Clubs, 1968—; pres. bd. dirs. YMCA, 1957. Served with USPHS, 1954-56. Named One of 5 Outstanding Young Men, Tex. Jr. C. of C., 1946; Engr. of Year, 1970. Mem. Nat., Tex. socs. profl. engrs., Am. (pres. 1966, sec.-treas. 1967), Tex. (pres. 1963, 65) bottled water assns., Tex. Turf Irrigation Assn. (pres. 1967), Am. Water Works Assn., Sales and Marketing Execs. Internat., Phi Kappa Psi. Baptist. Rotarian, Mason. Clubs: Lubbock, Lubbock Country. Patentee water purification equipment. Home: 28 Country Pl Lubbock TX 79407 Office: 405 Av U Lubbock TX 79401

STANLEY, LILA GAIL, polit. scientist; b. Marietta, Ga., Mar. 23, 1941; d. James Miller and Louise (Land) Stanley; A.B., Randolph-Macon Woman's Coll., 1963; M.A., Emory U., 1964; postgrad. Am. U., 1967-68. Instr. polit. sci. W. Ga. Coll., Carrollton, 1964-66; tchr. Am. history dept. Foxcroft Sch., Middleburg, Va., 1966-67; staff asst., caseworker Congressman John J. Flynt, Jr., Washington, 1967-74; staff asst., caseworker Senator Robert C. Byrd, Washington, 1974—. Mem. Am., So. polit. sci. assns., D.A.R., Phi Sigma Alpha, Zeta Tau Alpha. Democrat. Methodist. Home: 2450 Virginia Av NW Washington DC 20037 also 297 Freyer Dr Marietta GA 30060 Office: Russell Senate Office Bldg Washington DC 20510

STANLEY, ROBERT ALTON, educator; b. Steiner, Tex., May 3, 1917; s. Lawrence B. and Margie K. (Adcock) S.; B.S., N. Tex. State U., 1946; M.A., Sul Ross State Coll., 1949; m. Anna Marie Seljos, Dec. 23, 1938; children—Lee Burnett, Randall Leighton, Warren Llewellyn. Tchr. pub. schs. Tex., 1937-42; prin. high sch. Granfills Gap, Tex., 1946-51, Brewer High Sch., Fort Worth, 1951-58; supt. Granbury Ind. Sch. (Tex.), 1958-71; tchr. Cleburn (Tex.) Ind. Sch. Dist., 1971-73; supt. Blum (Tex.) Ind. Sch. Dist., 1973—. Served with C.E., AUS, 1942-46; PTO. Mem. Tex. Tchrs. Assn., Tex. Assn. Sch. Adminstrs., N.E.A., Am. Iris Soc., Am. Assn. Sch. Adminstrs. Home: 1210 Hemphill Cleburne TX 76031 Office: Blum Ind Sch Dist Box 548 Blum TX 76627

STANLEY, WILLIAM DANIEL, educator; b. Bladenboro, N.C., June 13, 1937; s. John D. and Sallie (Dowless) S.; B.S., U. S.C., 1960; M.S., N.C. State U., 1962, Ph.D., 1963; m. Mary Louise Nichols, Aug. 26, 1962; 1 dau., Karen Louise. Devel. engr. Elecro-Mech. Research, Inc., Sarasota, Fla., 1963; asst. prof. Clemson (S.C.) U., 1964-66; asso. prof. elec. engring. Old Dominion U., Norfolk, Va., 1966-72, prof., 1972—, dir. grad. program elec. engring., 1969-70, chmn. dept. engring. tech., 1970—. Cons. NASA, Hampton, 1967-69. Mem. Am. Soc. Engring. Edn., I.E.E.E. (subsect. program chmn. 1966), Phi Beta Kappa, Sigma Xi, Phi Kappa Phi, Tau Beta Pi, Eta Kappa Nu, Pi Mu Epsilon. Author: Transform Circuit Analysis for Engineering and Technology, 1968. Home: 1315 Milton St Norfolk VA 23505

STANONIS, FRANCIS LEE, geologist; b. Louisville, July 9, 1931; s. Frank and Lelia (Lehman) S.; B.S., U. Ky., 1951, M.S., 1956; Ph.D., Pa. State U., 1958; m. Gia Denton Nicholson, July 7, 1956; children—Frank L., Virginia N. Owner, Frank L. Stanonis Oil Co., Henderson, Ky., 1964—; pres. Enviro-Sci. Corp., Evansville, Ind., 1970—. Prof. geology and geography Ind. State U., Evansville, 1969—; chmn. div. sci. and math., 1973—. Served with inf. AUS, 1951-53. Mem. Am. Inst. Profl. Geologists, Am. Inst. Mining and Metal. Engrs., Geol. Soc. Am., Geol. Soc. Ky., Geol. Soc. Ill., A.A.A.S., Alpha Chi Sigma. Home: 142 N Arlington St Henderson KY 42420

STANTON, CURTIS HENDERSON, utility exec., elec. engr.; b. Key West, Fla., June 3, 1918; s. Curtis Harvey and Sarah Belle (Knowles) St.; B.S. in Mech. Engring., U. Fla., 1940; m. Claire Ann Tillman, Apr. 4, 1942; children—Claire (Mrs. Robert T. Sutton), Gail (Mrs. Watson W. Dyer), Sarah Kathryn. Test engr. Gen. Electric Co., Schenectady, 1940-41, turbine engr., 1941-45, sales tng. dir., 1945-47; exec. v.p., gen. mgr. Orlando (Fla.) Utilities Commn., 1947—. Pres. Central Fla. Fair, 1960-62, Fla. Industries Expn., 1970-71. Bd. dirs. United Appeal, 1956. Mem. Am. Water Works Assn. (chmn. nat. dir. Fla. sect. 1969-71), Fla. Municipal Utilities Assn. (pres. 1959-60, chmn. Fla. electric power coordinating group 1974), I.E.E.E., Orlando C. of C. (pres. 1964-65), Am. Soc. M.E. Clubs: Orlando Country, University, Citrus, Executives. Home: 740 Alba Dr Orlando FL 32804 Office: 500 S Orange Av Orlando FL 32801

STANTON, GEORGE EDWIN, biologist, educator; b. Danville, Pa., Mar. 28, 1944; s. Robert L. and Helen A. (Fairchild) S.; B.S., Bucknell U., 1966; Ph.D., U. Me., 1969; m. Susan Jeanne Merritt, Dec. 28, 1965; children—Deborah Jeanne, Kay Suzanne. Dir. nature and conservation Orange Mountain council Boy Scouts Am., 1960-65; grad. research asst. U. Me., Orono, 1966-69; asst. prof. biology Columbus (Ga.) Coll., 1969-72, asso. prof., 1972—; adj. asso. prof. biology Ga. State U., 1972—. Faculty adviser NSF supported student originated study in aquatic ecology, 1972. Mem. Ga. Environmental Adv. Commn., 1972—, Columbus-Phenix City Transp. Study-Citizens Adv. Bd., 1972—. Bd. dirs. Chattahoochee Valley Humane Soc.; trustee, pres. Columbus chpt. Ga. Conservancy, Inc., 1970-72. Recipient Sertoma Cleaner Environment award, 1971; named Columbus Coll. Distinguished Profl., 1973. Mem. A.A.A.S., Am. Inst. Biol. Scis., Entomol. Soc. Am., Ecol. Soc. Am., Am. Soc. Limnology and Oceanobraphy, Assn. S.E. Biologists, Ga. Acad. Sci., Ga. Entomol. Soc., Am. Assn. U. Profs. (pres.), Nat., Columbus (pres.) Audubon socs., Phi Sigma, Omicron Delta Kappa. Presbyn. (deacon). Contbr. articles profl. jours. Home: 4123 Steam Mill Rd Columbus GA 31907

STANTON, ROBERT LOWELL, physician; b. Des Moines, Feb. 18, 1924; s. Judson Horatio and Ozella (Hull) S.; B.S., U. Miami, 1948; M.D., Temple U., 1953; m. Betty Mae Tyrell Phillips, Sept. 15, 1945; children—Michael Phillips, Peter Wares, Scott Hull. Intern Temple U. Hosp., Phila., 1953-54; resident Dade County Hosp., Miami, Fla., 1954-55, resident internal medicine, VA Hosp., Miami, 1955-56; practice medicine, specializing in family practice, Miami, 1957—; mem. attending med. staff Am. Hosp., Larkin Gen. Hosp., Baptist Hosp., all Miami. Served with USNR, 1942-45. Decorated Silver Star. Mem. A.M.A., Dade County, Fla. med. assns., So. Med. Group (co-founder), Am. Acad. Family Practice, Beta Beta Beta, Alpha Epsilon Delta, Phi Chi. Unitarian (pres. congregation). Club: Kings Bay Yacht (Miami). Home: 9430 SW 53d St Miami FL 33165 Office: 9090 SW 87th Ct Miami FL 33156

STAPH, HORACE EUGENE, research lubrication engr.; b. Petrolia, Tex., Jan 8, 1921; s. Eugene William and Alice (Dammer) S.; B.S., Rice Inst., 1943; M.S., U. Tex., 1951; Ph.D., U. Minn., 1959; m. Rachel Evelyn Ruth, June 29, 1950; children—Catherine, Dana, Eric. Design draftsman Douglas Aircraft Co., Long Beach, Cal., 1943-45; instr. U. Tex., Austin, 1946-51, asst. prof., 1951-60; lectr. U. Minn., Mpls., 1953-55; sr. research engr. S.W. Research Inst., San Antonio, 1960—. Cubmaster, Boy Scouts of Am., 1966-69. Served with AUS, 1945-46. Mem. Am. Soc. M.E., Am. Soc. Lubrication Engrs., Sigma Xi, Tau Beta Pi, Pi Tau Sigma. Lutheran. Home: 6526 Redbird Lane San Antonio TX 78228 Office: 8500 Culebra Rd San Antonio TX 78228

STAPLES, ROBERT ROGERS, indsl. mgmt. engr.; b. Middle Granville, N.Y., Feb. 11, 1905; s. Parker Jonathan and Flora Antoinette (Rogers) S.; B.S. in Civil Engring., U. R.I., 1931; M.Mgmt. Engring., Rensselaer Poly. Inst., 1955; m. Marjorie Lois Hughes, July 17, 1937 (dec. 1964); children—Park Jonathan II, Maveret (Mrs. David Albert Daigle); m. 2d, Beatrice Edith Welton, Feb. 10, 1968. Various engring. positions, 1931-41; vocational adviser VA, 1946-51; civil engr. Naval Supply Depot, 1954; sr. civil service indsl. engr. U.S. Navy, 1955-65; cons. indsl. mgmt. engr., Arlington, Va., 1965—. Cons. on engineered performance standards to naval dists. Served to lt. col. AUS, 1941-46; lt. col. Res. ret. Mem. Am. Inst. Indsl. Engrs. (chpt. pres. 1966-67, dir. 1965, 68-69), Nat. Soc. Profl. Engrs., Soc. Am. Mil. Engrs., Am. Legion. Methodist. Mason (Shriner, K.T.). Clubs: Army Navy Country (Arlington). Author navy engineered performance standards, Engrs. Manual. Address: 2443 S Culpeper St Arlington VA 22206

STAPLES, WILLIAM RUSSELL, oral-maxillo-facial surgeon; b. Rumford, Me., Nov. 28, 1922; s. Russell James and Mildred Bernice (Westcott) S.; D.M.D., Tufts U., 1946; postgrad. Naval Dental Sch., 1950-52, Georgetown U., 1951-52, Temple U., 1955-56; m. Alice Elizabeth Maynard, July 27, 1946; children—Jane Elizabeth (Mrs. George Thomas Gantt), David William. Enlisted U.S. Navy, 1942, commd. ensign, 1943, advanced through grades to capt., 1962, ret. 1966; faculty Emory U., 1966-67; practice oral-maxillo facial surgery, Jacksonville, Fla., 1967—. Exec. dir. Delta Dental Plan Fla., Fla. Dental Services, Inc. Fellow Royal Soc. Health; mem. Am., Fla. dental assns., Southeastern Soc. of Oral Surgeons, Am. Dental Soc. of Anesthesiology, Internat., Am., Fla. socs. oral surgeons, Jacksonville Acad. Oral and Maxillo-Facial Surgeons (pres.). Mason. Club: Hidden Hills Country (Jacksonville). Contbr. articles to profl. jours. Home: 4005 Cove St Johns Rd Jacksonville FL 32211 Office: 3434 Atlantic Blvd Jacksonville FL 32207

STAPP, WILLIE LEE BROOME (MRS. CARL HERBERT STAPP), accountant; b. Snyder, Okla., Mar. 4, 1913; d. William Benjamin and Kate (Ross) Broome; grad. Draughon's Bus. U., 1935; student Okla. State U. Extension Div., 1936-37; m. Carl Herbert Stapp, Nov. 23, 1938; children—Bruce Michael, Patricia Kay (Mrs. Bert Walker, Jr.), Roger Leon. Sec., Rev. H. C. Ownbey, Bible Bapt. Ch., Oklahoma City, 1935-36; with Okla. Edn. Assn., Norman, 1935-36; office sec. Okla. Congress of Parents and Tchrs., Norman, 1936-44, asso. exec. sec., 1957-59, exec. sec., 1959-69; asst. editor, bus. mgr. Okla. Parent-Tchr., Norman, 1936-44, mng. editor, 1963-69; real estate saleslady Carl H. Stapp Co., Oklahoma City, 1948-56; accountant athletic dept. U. Okla., 1969—. Mem. Okla. Congress Parents and Tchrs. (life), Okla. Edn. Assn. (asso.). Baptist. Mem. Order Eastern Star. Home: 200 W Symmes St Norman OK 73069 Office: 180 W Brooks St Norman OK 73069

STARBUCK, SHIRLEY, artist; b. Bklyn.; d. Sidney Hilton and Maria Ponce de Leon (French) Starbuck; student Art Students League, 1945-46; m. Baxter Ragsdale Still, Jr., May 27, 1949 (div. Apr. 1954); 1 dau., Susan. Art dir. Ted. Bates & Co., N.Y.C., 1944-49, Doherty, Clifford, Steers & Shenfield, N.Y.C., 1954-59, Norman, Craig & Kummel, N.Y.C., 1959-62; free lance designer, illustrator. Red Cross vol., sketching patients in mil. hosps. Mem. D.C. League Republican Women. Mem. D.A.R., Soc. Mayflower Descs. in State N.Y. Club: Tavern Cay Sailing. Address: 2022 Columbia Rd NW Washington DC 20009

STARK, CARL ELLROY, physician; b. Poughkeepsie, N.Y., Sept. 28, 1921; s. Howard Cyrus and Hilda Mary (Roe) S.; B.S., U. Va., 1948, M.D., 1952; m. Katharine Grason Reynolds, June 14, 1947; children—Katharine Blair, Hilda Roe. Chemist Naval Research Lab., Washington, 1942; biochem. pollution cons. Am. Viscose, Front Royal, Va., 1948; intern Reading (Pa.) Hosp., 1952, resident, 1952-53; gen. practice medicine, Wytheville, Va., 1953—; mem. staff Chatwood Meml. Hosp., Wytheville Hosp., Pulaski (Va.) Hosp. Bd. dirs. Chitwood Meml. Hosp. Corp., pres., 1968; bd. dirs. Mt. Rogers Devel. Corp., Marion, Va., 1967-68; med. examiner State of Va., 1964—. Chmn. Wythe-Bland Water and Sewer Authority, 1967—; chmn. Mt. Rogers Regional Planning Commn., 1968-71; 2d. v.p. Great Lakes to Fla. Hwy. Assn., 1968-71; pres. Va. Municipal League, 1972-73; mem. Gov.'s Adv. Com. Emergency Med. Service, Commonwealth Va., 1968-71, mem. govs. adv. com. state and local affairs, 1970-71; mayor Town of Wytheville, 1962—. Bd. dirs. Upward-Bound Va. Poly. Inst., Mountain Community Action Program. Served with AUS, 1943-46. Decorated Corix De Guerre (Belgium). Mem. State Soc. S.A.R. (pres. 1971-72), Southwestern Va. Med. Soc. (pres. 1967-68), Va. State Med. Soc. (dir.), Wythe Baseball Assn. (exec. mem. 1968-71), Med. Soc. Va. (pres. 1972-73), Va. Farm Bur., V.F.W., Iron Boot Soc., Soiree Soc., Phi Chi, Sigma Alpha Epsilon. Episcopalian (lay reader, vestryman 1952, exec. com. 1968-71). Mason, Lion; mem. Order Eastern Star (worthy patron 1966, 70). Home: 805 W Fulton St Wytheville VA 24382 Office: Main St Wytheville VA 24382

STARK, JOHN REGAN, govt. ofcl.; b. S.I., N.Y., Jan. 18, 1918; s. Raymond Sylvester and Mary Catherine (Regan) S.; B.A., Cornell U., 1938; M.A., N.Y. U., 1941; J.D., George Washington U., 1952; m. Edna Fay Kolberk, Dec. 28, 1940; children—Suzanne (Mrs. Richard Krause), Brian. Economist, U.S. Bur. Budget, Washington, 1946-56; admitted to Va. bar and D.C. bar; asst. dir. price div. Bur. Labor Statistics, Washington, 1956-57; individual practice law, Washington and McLean, Va., 1958-61; clk., economist Joint Econ. Com. U.S. Congress, Washington, 1961-64; gen. counsel Banking and Currency Com., U.S. Ho. of Reps., Washington, 1964-65; exec. dir. Joint Econ. Com., U.S. Congress, Washington, 1967—; prof. law George Washington U., Washington, 1965—. Served to lt. (j.g.) USCGR, 1942-46. Mem. Am., Fed. bar assns., Am. Soc. Pub. Adminstrn. Democrat. Unitarian. Author: (with Phillip B. Yeager) Your Inalienable Rights, 1959. Co-author syndicated column Law in the News, 1954-60. Contbr. articles to mags. and profl. jours. Home: 4815 Grantham Av Chevy Chase MD 20015 Office: New Senate Office Bldg Washington DC 20510

STARKS, FRANKLIN FERGUSON, JR., bldg. operations co. exec.; b. Louisville, Feb. 17, 1924; s. Franklin Ferguson and Mary Gunn (Powell) S.; grad. Woodberry Forest Sch., 1942; B.S., Yale, 1948; m. Noell Marvin, Dec. 8, 1951; children—Seashols Noell, Franklin Ferguson III, Henry Powell. With Starks Bldg. Co., Louisville, 1948—, sec., 1949-53, v.p., 1953-57, pres., 1957—. Dir. First Nat. Bank of Louisville, 1st Ky. Trust Co., Louisville Investment Co. Bd. dirs., YMCA, 1966-71, Boy Scouts Am., 1962-69; pres. dirs. Child Guidance Clinic, 1950-71. Served with 11th Airborne div. Signal Corps, AUS, 1943-46; PTO. Mem. So. Conf. Bldg. Owners and Mgrs. (pres. 1957-58), Louisville Assn. Bldg. Owners and Mgrs., Louisville C. of C. (dir. 1971—), Louisville Central Area (dir. 1957-74). Rotarian. Clubs: Louisville Country, Pendennis (Louisville). Home: 512 Club Lane Louisville KY 40207 Office: 823 Starks Bldg Louisville KY 40202

STARKS, RALPH JAMES, research engr.; b. Gentry, Ark., July 2, 1923; s. David and Viola Ethyl (Boaz) S.; A.A., Joplin Jr. Coll., 1950; B.S. in Physics, Kan. State Coll., 1952, M.S. in Math., 1953, postgrad. in Solid State Physics, 1961-63; m. Mary Louisa McDaniel, Sept. 5, 1947; 1 son, Ralph James. Research engr. exploratory research sect. Joplin research dept. Eagle-Picher Industries, 1952-56, sr. research engr. Miami Research Labs. (Okla.), 1956-70, dir. research, 1970—. Served with USAAC, 1942-45; ETO Decorated Air medal with two oak leaf clusters. Mem. Am. Soc. for Testing and Materials, Am. Soc. for Quality Control, Am. Nuclear Soc., V.F.W. Mem. Christian Ch. (elder 1970—). Mason (32 deg., Shriner). Contbr. articles to profl. jours. Home: 2602 Illinois St Joplin MO 64801 Office: 200 9th Av NE Miami OK 74354 Mailing Address: PO Box 1090 Miami OK 74354

STARR, DAVID WRIGHT, educator; b. Anna, Tex., Dec. 8, 1912; s. Walter Benjamin and Edna Earle (Wright) S.; B.A., So. Meth. U., 1933; M.A., U. Ill., 1937, Ph.D., 1940; m. Elsie Ritchey, Nov. 23, 1961; children—(by previous marriage) David Wright, Sally (Mrs. Glenn Howard Tucker). Tchr., principal Sadler (Tex.) High Sch., 1933-34; tchr. Denison (Tex.) High Sch., 1934-37; asst. in math. U. Ill., Champaign-Urbana, 1938-40, fellow, 1937-38; instr. math. and aviation So. Meth. U., Dallas, 1940-43, coordinator aviation, 1941—, asst. prof. math., 1943-46, assoc. prof., 1946-48, prof., 1948—, chmn. dept. math., 1963—; coordinator CAA War Tng. Program, 1941-44. Fellow Tex. Acad. Scis.; mem. Am. Math. Soc., Math. Assn. Am. (chmn. Tex. sect. 1951-52), Nat. Council Tchrs. Math., Blue Key, Phi Beta Kappa, Kappa Mu Epsilon, Pi Mu Epsilon, Sigma Alpha Epsilon. Methodist. Mason, Lion. Contbr. articles to profl. jours. Home: 3503 Normandy St Dallas TX 75205

STARR, HOWARD ALLEN, educator; b. Waco, Tex., Apr. 7, 1938; s. Clarence J. and Ouida (Bowman) S.; B.A., U. Dallas, 1960; M.A., So. Meth. U., 1963; Ph.D., E. Tex. State U., 1969; m. Julie King Ellis, Aug. 1970; 1 son, Brandon Blair. Tchr. biology Richardson (Tex.) High Sch., 1960-65, counselor, 1962-65; became admissions counselor Austin Coll., 1965, now asso. prof. psychology, chmn. dept. psychology and sociology, asst. dean for ednl. advising, 1972—, coordinator individual devel. program, 1972, coordinator mentor tng., 1972. Mem. Am., Tex. (pub. relations com.) personnel and guidance assns., Nat. Assn. Biology Tchrs., A.A.A.S., Tex. Tchrs. Assn., Am. (asso.), S. Western, Tex. (asso.) psychol. assns., Phi Delta Kappa, Kappa Delta Pi. Mem. Disciples of Christ Ch. Home: 1802 Skyline Dr Sherman TX 75090 Office: Austin Coll Dept Psychology Box 1595 Sherman TX 75090

STARR, STEVE DAWSON, photographer; b. Albuquerque, Sept. 6, 1944; s. Richard Vernon and Carol (Harley) S.; student Antioch Coll., 1962-63, Bethel Coll., 1963-64; B.A., San Jose State Coll., 1967; m. Marilynne Sue Anderson, Aug. 6, 1965; 1 son, Stephen Richard. Photographer San Jose (Cal.) Mercury-News, 1966-67; now photographer, picture editor A.P., Albany, N.Y., Los Angeles, N.Y.C., Miami, Fla. Recipient Pulitzer prize spot news photography, 1970, Nat. Headliners award, 1970, George Polk Meml. award, 1970, Pictures of the Year hon. mention, 1970. Mem. Nat. Press Photographers Assn., Sigma Delta Chi. Home: 256 Carlisle Dr Miami Springs FL 33166 Office: 2125 Biscayne Bldg Miami FL 33137

STARS, WILLIAM KENNETH, educator, mus. adminstr.; b. DePauw, Ind., Mar. 13, 1921; s. Robert Emmett and Edna Mary (Crider) S.; B.A. in Philosophy, Duke, 1948; M.A. in Art History, U. N.C., 1950; postgrad. in art edn. N.Y. U., 1953-67; m. Martha Jane Vickers, Oct. 2, 1945. Tchr. art Durham (N.C.) High Sch., 1950-66; instr. studio art Duke, Durham, 1953-67, asst. prof. art, 1967—, also conservator Duke Mus. Art., 1967—, dir., 1973—, dir. Duke's Arts and Crafts Workshop, 1967—. Pres. Durham Art Guild, 1954-55, 60-61. Bd. dirs. Allied Arts, Durham, 1960-62. Served with AC, USNR, 1942-45. Mem. Nat. Art. Edn. Assn., Coll., Southeastern Coll. art assns., Internat. Inst. for Conservation, Am. Assn. U. Profs., Kappa Delta Pi. Contbr. articles to profl. jours. Patentee weaving loom and accessories. Home: 1916 Glendale Av Durham NC 27701

STASAVICH, BECKY ANN, ednl. adminstr.; b. Hickory, N.C., June 5, 1940; d. Clarence and Helen (Warlick) Stasavich; A.B. in English and History, Catawba Coll., 1961; M.A. in Eng. E. Carolina U., 1967. Tchr. English various high schs., Albemarle, N.C., 1961-66, Greenville, 1966-67; asso. dean students, instr. psychology Pfeiffer

Coll., Misenheimer, N.C., 1967-72; asso. dean students Lenoir Rhyne Coll., Hickory, N.C., 1972—. Mem. program com., student personnel com. Piedmont Univ. Center, Winston-Salem, N.C. Bd. dirs. Heart Assn. Catawba County, N.C., 1973—, sec., 1974-75. Mem. Nat., N.C. (program com. chmn. 1970-71, mem. nominating com., v.p. 1972-74) assns. women deans, adminstrs. and counselors, Am. Personnel and Guidance Assn., Am. Coll. Personnel Assn., So. Coll. Personnel Assn., Alpha Delta Kappa (v.p. Xi chpt.). Democrat. Presbyn. Clubs: Pfeiffer Woman's (pres. 1969-71); Altrusa (dir., 2d v.p. 1974—) (Hickory Hills). Home: 7 Sharlton Manor 410 10th Avenue Dr NE Hickory NC 28601

STATEN, GEORGE COWDEN, JR., architect; b. El Paso, Tex., July 2, 1931; s. George Cowden and Ruth (Cummings) S.; student U. Tex. at El Paso, 1949; B.A. (Jesse Jones scholar), Rice U., 1953, B.Arch. (L.S. Mewhinney scholar), 1954; m. Shirley Gore, Oct. 11, 1958; children—Gregory Gore, James Burleson. Designer, Percy W. McGhee, Architect, El Paso, 1947-53; draftsman Dunaway and Jones Architects, Houston, 1953-54; designer, draftsman Carroll, Daeuble & Assos., Architects, El Paso, 1957-58; prin. George Staten, Jr., Architect, 1959-62; partner Middleton and Staten, Architects, 1962-68; partner Kuykendall, McCombs, Middleton & Staten, Architects, El Paso, 1969-70; pres. George Staten & Assos. Inc., Architects and Planners, 1970-74; pres. Staten/Pierce-Lacey, Inc., Architects and Planners, 1974—. Mem. Zoning Bd. Adjustment, El Paso, 1959-70; co-chmn. Citizens Adv. Council, El Paso, 1955-56; chmn. Citizens Adv. Impact Study Com., El Paso, 1973-74. Bd. dirs. El Paso County Assn. for Blind, 1960-74, pres., 1974; bd. dirs. Am. Cancer Soc., El Paso, 1969-72. Served with USN, 1954-57; PTO. Recipient Walsh 2d prize Rice U., 1953, A.I.A. runner up award Henry Adams Fund, 1954. Mem. Navy League El Paso, Naval Res. Assn., El Paso C. of C., A.I.A. (chpt. pres. 1969), Constrn. Specifications Inst. (chpt. pres. 1963-64), Tex. Soc. Architects (dir. 1972-74), Sigma Alpha Epsilon. Kiwanian (dir. 1965). Home: 237 Viking Dr El Paso TX 79912 Office: Suite 225 Koger Bldg 444 Executive Center Blvd El Paso TX 79902

STATON, JON TOM, sch. adminstr.; b. Hollis, Okla., Jan. 7, 1933; s. William Francis and Sarah (Clark) S.; B.S., Okla. Bapt. U., 1956; Ed.M., U. Okla., 1959, Ed.D., 1962; m. Carolyn Brown, Sept. 28, 1954; children—Kelsey, Kevin, Sarah. Tchr. Caney High Sch., Caney, Kan., 1956-57, Roswell (N.M.) High Sch., 1957-60; Kellogg fellow U. Okla., 1960-61, dir. gen services, 1961-62; supt. schs., Mountain Grove, Mo., 1963-67, Muskogee, Okla., 1967—; vis. prof. sch. adminstrn, Drury Grad. Sch. Edn., 1965—. Bd. dirs. Okla. chpt. Soc. Crippled Children. Served with AUS, 1954-56. Mem. Am. Assn. Sch. Adminstrs. (life), Okla. Bapt. U. Alumni Athletic Assn. (pres.), N.E.A., Assn. Student Teaching, Am. Childhood Edn., Phi Delta Kappa. Rotarian. Home: 4301 W Broadway Muskogee OK 74401

STATON, WILLIAM WAYNE, state senator; b. Olive Branch, N.C., Oct. 11, 1916; s. Oscar M. and Addie Mae (Young) S.; B.S., Wake Forest Coll., 1938, J.D., 1941; grad. student U. N.C., 1946; m. Ellen Douglas Boone, June 28, 1947; children—William Wayne, Allyn Moore. Admitted to N.C. bar, 1941; practice in Sanford, 1946—; mem. firm Pittman, Staton & Betts, 1946—; county atty. Lee County, 1956-60; city atty., Sanford, 1963-66; now atty. Central Carolina Tech. Inst.; mem. N.C. senate, 1969—. Pres. Young Democratic Clubs N.C., 1952; asst. campaign mgr. Frank P. Graham for U.S. Senate, 1952; personal campaign mgr. Gov. Terry Sanford in elections, 1960; del. Nat. Dem. Conv.,Com., 1960-64; mem. Dem. Nat. Com. from N.C., 1962-66; mem. Ho. of Reps, N.C., 1966-68. Mem. N.C. Commn. Improved Cts., 1958, N.C. Vets. Commn., 1957-60; mem. N.C. Commn. for Rules of Civil Procedure, 1967-68; pres. Lee County United Fund; mem. N.C. Jud. Council, 1969—, N.C. Capitol Planning Commn., 1971—. Mem. exec. bd. Occoneechee council Boy Scouts Am., 1956—; trustee Wake Forest Coll., 1955—. Served to capt. F.A., AUS, 1942-46, ETO; col. N.C. N.G. Decorated Purple Heart, Bronze Star medal. Mem. Am., N.C., Lee County bar assns., Am. Legion (past judge advocate N.C.), Sanford C. of C. (past pres.), Omicron Delta Kappa. Baptist (past bd. deacons). Club: Sanford Executive (past pres.). Home: 636 Palmer Dr Sanford NC 27330 Office: 205 Courtland Dr Sanford NC 27330

STAUB, BROTHER ROBERT JOSEPH, educator; b. Chgo., Jan. 29, 1922; s. Joseph Anthony and Helen (Kordick) S.; B.S. in Biology cum laude, St Mary's Coll., Minn., 1943; M.A. in Botany and Zoology, U. Minn., 1949, Ph.D. in Ecology (MacMillan fellow, So. Fellowship Fund fellow), 1966. Joined Fratres Scholarum Christianarum (Bros. Christian Schs.); tchr. pvt. high schs., Mo., 1943-46, Minn., 1946-49, 53-59, Ill., 1949-50; instr. biology and math., asst. dean men Christian Bros. Jr. Coll., Memphis, 1950-53; prof., chmn. dept. biology Christian Bros. Coll., Memphis, 1959—. Founding mem. bd. dirs. Environmental Action Council Memphis, 1969—, pres., 1973-74; mem. founding com. Memphis Project Vol. Recycle, 1973—; mem. adv. bd. Ave Maria Home for Aged, Memphis, 1965—, water pollution research Environmental Protection Agy., 1967-72. Bd. Citizens To Preserve Overton Park, 1972—. Fellow Tenn. Acad. Sci.; mem. Ecol. Soc. Am., Nat. Assn. Biology Tchrs., Bot. Soc. Am., Am. Bryological and Lichenological Soc., Am. Forestry Assn., Am. Inst. Biol. Scis. Democrat. Roman Catholic. K.C. (4 deg.). Address: 650 East Pkwy South Memphis TN 38104

STAUBER, LESLIE EDWIN, mfg. exec.; b. Rural Hall, N.C., Mar. 28, 1903; s. William Edwin and Lillian (Felts) S.; A.B., U. N.C., 1925; m. Jessie Louise Brown, May 10, 1930; children—Leslie Edwin, Barbara June (Mrs. Fred Mexwell Fultz). Owner, Rural Telephone Co., 1927-28; partner Rural Hall Veneer Co., 1928-53, owner, 1954—, mfr. wood veneers, 1928—, plywood, 1936—. Organizing mem., sec.-treas. Rural Hall San. Dist., 1938-50; charter mem. Rural Hall Fire Dept., 1938-50; justice of peace, 1932-34. Charter rep. from Moravian Ch. on com. Rural Hall Meml. Park. Club: Civic (pres. 1947). Home: Corner Broad and Wall Sts Rural Hall NC 27045 Office: 1st St Rural Hall NC 27045

STAVISKY, SAMUEL ELLIOT, pub. relations cons.; b. Chelsea, Mass., Dec. 6, 1914; s. Jacob Zedel and Jennie (Cohen) S.; B.S. in Journalism, Boston U., 1936; m. Bernice Ruth Seigle, Dec. 31, 1946; children—Robin, Judith. Reporter, editor, columnist Boston Am., Rochester (N.Y.) Jour., Washington Herald, Washington Post, 1933-54; pres. Samuel E. Stavisky & Asso., Inc., pub. relations, Washington, 1954—. Cons. Cuban Sugar Industry, U.S. Cuban Sugar Council, Banco Nacional de Cuba, 1954-60, Internat. Coffee Agreement, 1961-63, U.S. Cane Sugar Refiners Assn., Pan Am. Coffee Bur., 1963—, Colombian Center, N.Y.C., 1965-66; cons. govt. agys. and industry Mexico, Brazil, Colombia, Portugal, U.K., Sweden; exec. dir. World Coffee Information Center, Washington, 1965—. Trustee Experiment in Internat. Living. Served USMCR, 1942-45; PTO. Mem. Pub. Relations Soc. Am. Clubs: International, National Press, Broadcasters (Washington). Contbr. numerous articles to popular mags. Home: 7021 Oak Forest Lane Bethesda MD 20034 Office: 1100 17th St NW Washington DC 20036

STAYMAN, HAROLD WILLIAM, JR., civic orgn. exec.; b. Tamaqua, Pa., Mar. 27, 1933; s. Harold William and Elinor Mae (Wagner) S.; student U. Md., 1952-54, 56; m. Veronica Van Allen, Nov. 23, 1967; children—Veronica, Valerie Elizabeth. Nat. Yellow Page rep. So. Bell Telephone Co., Miami, Fla., 1957-65; from dir. pub. relations to exec. dir. Republican State Exec. Com., Fort Lauderdale, Fla., 1966-67; exec. dir. Fla. Turnpike Authority, Ft. Lauderdale, 1967-69, Fla. Council of 100, Tampa, 1970—; sec. dep. profl. and occupational regulation State of Fla., Tallahassee, 1969-70. Mem., dist. coordinator Fla. Gov.'s Com. for Employment of Handicapped, 1970—; founder, dir., vice chmn. Ams. for Constl. Action, 1965-68; mem. Bicentennial Commn. Fla., 1972—, mem. exec. com., 1973—. Nat. committeeman Fla. Fedn. Young Republicans, 1965-66; 1st v.p. Dade County Young Rep. Club, 1965-66; founder, editor-in-chief Fla. Rep. Challenger (newspaper), 1966-67. Bd. dirs., treas. Fla.-Colombia Alliance; bd. dirs. Tampa Easter Seal Soc., 1973—. Served with AUS, 1953-57. Named One of Outstanding Young Men in Am., U.S. Jr. C. of C., 1969, Fla. Young Rep. of Year, Dade County Young Rep. Club, 1965. Mem. Fla. Pub. Relations Assn., Fla. Indsl. Devel. Council, Fla. Agrl. Bus. Inst., Fla. Soc. Assn. Execs., Confrerie de la Chaine des Rotisseurs (vice senechal 1973—). Clubs: Killearn Country (Tallahassee); Executive (Orlando, Fla.); River (Jacksonville, Fla.); Tampa Yacht and Country. Home: 5116 Homer Av Tampa FL 33609 Office: 1211 N Westshore Blvd Suite 105 Tampa FL 33607

STEARMAN, LEWIS ARTHUR, newspaper exec.; b. Alexandria, Va., Feb. 8, 1924; s. Joseph and Esther (Rose) S.; student pub. schs.; m. Mildred Ruth Myers, Oct. 8, 1950; children—David Warren, Douglas Alan, Joseph Michael. Mem. exec. staff Alexandria Gazette, 1940—, gen. mgr., 1952—, bus. editor, 1955, v.p., treas., 1966—, also dir.; dir. Park & Shop, Inc., Alexandria. Corp. mem. Alexandria Hosp. Corp., 1965—; mem. Friendship Fire Co. (life), 1953—. Bd. dirs. Am. Cancer Soc., Alexandria Boys Club (v.p.), Alexandria A.R.C., Mental Hygiene Adv. Bd., Alexandria Civic Orch., Salvation Army (pres. 1961-63). Pres., Alexandria Community Mental Health Center, 1968-69, Sr. Citizens Employment Service Alexandria, 1970-71; divisional v.p. Alexandria Bd. Trade, 1968-69. Recipient Outstanding Merit award in promoting better community relations Maurice D. Rosenberg Lodge B'nai B'rith, 1953; Outstanding Merit award Salvation Army Alexandria, 1959; Pub. Service award U.S. P.O., 1967; Community Service award Boys Clubs Am., 1971, Torch award, 1972, others; named Man of Year, Salvation Army, 1965, 67. Mem. Retail Mchts. Assn. (sec.-treas., 1960-61), Alexandria (v.p. 1966-67), Fairfax County chambers commerce, Inst. Newspaper Controllers and Finance Officers (tech. adv. bd.), So. Newspaper Assn., Va. Press Assn., Nat. Press Club, Nat. Editorial Assn. Mem. B'nai B'rith (Outstanding Community Service award 1968, trustee lodge). Club: Optimist (Alexandria). Home: 6421 Bluebill Lane Alexandria VA 22307 Office: 717 North St Asaph St Alexandria VA 22313

STEBBINS, ARTHUR PETER, psychiatrist; b. Charlotte, Vt., July 17, 1912; s. Warren J. and Lillian (Desany) S.; B.S., U. Vt., 1935, M.D., 1939; m. Louise Nancy Chadbourne, May 24, 1942; children—Sharon Elizabeth, Arthur Peter, Marguerite Ann. Rotating intern Eastern Me. Hosp., Bangor, 1939-40; asst. physician Bangor State Hosp., 1940-41, sr. physician, 1941-44; sr. staff physician VA Psychiat. Hosp., Coatesville, Pa., 1941; practice medicine specializing in psychiatry, Bangor, 1944-56, also mem. staff Eastern Me. Gen., St. Joseph's hosps.; owner, operator Russell Psychiat. Hosp., Brewer Me., 1950-56; pvt. practice Portland, Me., 1956-63, also staff psychiatry Mercy Hosp.; clin. dir. Baldpate, Inc., psychiat. practice, Georgetown, Mass., 1963-64; Westwood (Mass.) Lodge, Inc., psychiat. hosp., 1964-65; clin. dir. Bournewood (Mass.) Hosp., 1965-66, med. dir., 1966-73; pvt. practice, Brookline, Mass., 1965-73; sr. physician psychiatry VA Hosp., Salem, Va., 1973-74; chief mental hygiene clinic VA Hosp., Huntington, W.Va., 1974—. Fellow Am. Geriatrics Assn., Acad. Psychosomatic Medicine, Mass. Med. Soc.; mem. Am. Psychiat. Assn., A.M.A., New Eng. Soc. Psychiatry, Norfolk County Dist. Med. Soc., N.Y. Acad. Scis. Home: 121 Valley View Dr Huntington WV 25704 Office: VA Hosp Huntington WV 25701

STEED, TOM, congressman; b. nr. Rising Star, Tex., Mar. 2, 1904; m. Hazel Bennett, Feb. 26, 1923; 2 sons (Roger, officer USMCR dec. China, May 1947). Connected with Okla. daily newspapers, 20 yrs.; mng. editor Shawnee News & Star, 4 yrs. Mem. 81st to 93d Congresses, 4th Okla. Dist. Served from pvt. to 2d lt. A.A.A., AUS, 1942-44, with OWI, 1944-45; CBI. Home: 1904 N Pennsylvania Shawnee OK 74801 Office: Rayburn House Office Bldg Washington DC 20515

STEEL, CHARLES EUGENE, chem. co. exec.; b. Anson, Tex., July 8, 1934; s. Herman T. and Gladys (Propst) S.; B.S., Tex. Tech. U., 1957; m. Anne Akers, Aug. 25, 1954; children—Gary Lee, Frances Anne, Julie Marie. Chemist, Celanese Chem. Co., Pampa, Tex., 1957-60, supr. personnel 1960-62, labor relations rep. Celanese Fibers Co., Cumberland, Md., 1962-63, labor relations supr., Pearisburg, Va., 1963-65, indsl. relations mgr., 1965-69, dir. adminstrn. Celanese Chem. Co. Tech. Center, Corpus Christi, Tex., 1969-72; plant mgr. Celanese Chem. Co., Pampa, 1970—. Dir. Security Fed. Savs. & Loan Assn. Mem. Ind. Sch. Bd., Pampa, Tex., 1967-68; exec. bd., v.p. Coastal Bend United Fund, 1970-71; pres. Adobe Walls council Boy Scouts Am., 1974. Bd. dirs. Pampa Indsl. Found., 1972-74, Salvation Army, 1972-74, Pampa Youth Center, 1972-74, Pampa United Fund, 1973-74. Recipient Adult Order of the Arrow award, Boy Scouts Am., 1971. Mem. Pampa C. of C. (v.p. 1973-74). Methodist (chmn. council on ministries 1970-71).

STEELE, BENNIE WESLEY, state ofcl.; b. Edna, Kan., Aug. 10, 1918; s. Jessie Lee and Mattie May (Poteet) S.; B.A., Oklahoma City U., 1954, postgrad., 1965; m. Ethelynn Belle Bales, Aug. 29, 1936; children—Patricia (Mrs. Boyce Dwain Montgomery), Pamela (Mrs. James Maurice Crawford). With Star Mfg. Co., 1936-37; self employed truck driver, 1937-40; welder, welding foreman Robinson Steel Co., 1940-43; mgr., co-owner Steele Brothers Machine Shop, Oklahoma City, 1946-51; jr. draftsman, sr. draftsman, design squad boss Okla. Hwy. Dept., Oklahoma City, 1951-56, mgr. data services, 1956-72, head spl. services div., 1972—; mem. indsl. art faculty Oklahoma City U., 1956-57. Ordained minister Ch. of Christ, 1959, elder, 1972. Mem. Gov. Bellman's Com. on Centralization, 1964. Served with USAAF, 1943-45; ETO. Mem. Am. Assn. State Hwy. Ofcls. Club: Toastmasters International (past pres., named Outstanding Toastmaster 1964, Best Speaker Area 2 1965) (Oklahoma City). Home: 4906 N Asbury St Bethany OK 73008 Office: Jim Thorpe Bldg Oklahoma City OK 73105

STEELE, BERNADINE BROWN (MRS. JOHN L. STEELE), educator; b. nr. Central City, Ky., Mar. 1, 1912; d. Charles and Bernice (Millard) Brown; B.S., Western State U., 1949, M.A., 1957; postgard Peabody Coll., 1959, U. Hawaii, 1961; m. John L. Steele, Sept. 26, 1931. Tchr. elementary sch., Muhlenberg County, Ky., 1937-43; supr. Lanham Act Nursery Schs., Fayetteville, N.C., 1943-45; elementary tchr. Central City Ind. Schs., 1946-62, counselor, supr., 1962—. Mem. Mid-western Regional Mental Health-Mental Retardation Bd., 1967—; life mem. P.T.A. Mem. N.E.A. (life, mem. adv. council 1966-67), Ky. edn. Assn. (life, pres. 1966-67), Bus. and Profl. Womens Club, Central City C. of C., Delta Kappa Gamma (state chmn. 1967-68). Home: 312 W 2d St Central City KY 42330 Office: W Main St Central City KY 42330

STEELE, CLARENCE ATKINSON, hwy. engr.; b. Brailey, O., Apr. 19, 1906; s. James R. Laird and DeEtta (Atkinson) S.; B.S. in Civil Engring., Purdue U., 1929; M.Philosophy, U. Wis., 1933; m. Elizabeth Marie Garrison, May 25, 1935; children—James J., Richard G., Thomas A., William J. With Wabash R.R., 1925-26, 27-28, 29, 31; surveyor Ind. Hwy. Commn., 1930; with U.S. Bur. Pub. Rds., 1933-70, dep. chief, econs. and requirements div. Office Research and Devel., Washington, 1962-70; spl. asst. to chief transp. econs. dir. and to dir. program and policy planning Fed. Hwy. Adminstrn., Washington, 1971—. Mem. dept. econs., finance and adminstrn. Hwy. Research Bd., 1957-70, mem. adv. com. conf. on transp. and community values, 1968—. Mem. adv. council No. Va. Center, U. Va., 1949-59, chmn., 1954-59; mem. Overlee Community Assn. Methodist. Mason. Contbr. articles to profl. publs. Home: 5901 18th St N Arlington VA 22205 also RFD St David's Church VA 22652 Office: Fed Hwy Adminstrn Washington DC 20591

STEELE, EARL LARSEN, educator; b. Denver, Sept. 24, 1923; s. Earl Harold and Jennie Louise (Larsen) S.; B.S. cum laude, U. Utah, 1945; Ph.D., Cornell U., 1952; m. Martha Hennessey, June 27, 1953; children—Karl Thomas, Earl Robert, Karen Lynn, Kevin Douglas, Lisa Louise, Colleen Carol. Research scientist, electronics lab. Gen. Electric Co., Syracuse, N.Y., 1952-56; dept. chief semiconductor div. Motorola Inc., Phoenix, 1956-58; mgr. devel. lab. Hughes Aircraft Co., Newport Beach, Cal., 1958-63; group scientist Autonetics div. N. Am. Rockwell, Anaheim, Cal., 1963-69; prof., chmn. dept. elec. engring. U. Key., Lexington, 1969—. Affiliate prof. U. Cal. at Irvine, 1956-68; associated faculty mem. So. Cal. Coll., Costa Mesa, 1962-63; affiliate asso. prof. Ariz. State U., 1957-58. Fellow I.E.E.E.; mem. Am. Phys. Soc., Am. Soc. Engring. Edn., Engring. Council for Profl. Devel., Sigma Xi, Tau Beta Pi, Eta Kappa Nu. Mem. Church Jesus Christ Latter-day Saints. Kiwanian. Author: Optical Lasers in Electroncis, 1968. Home: 313 Blueberry Rd Lexington KY 40503 Office: 452 Anderson Hall Dept Electrical Engineering Univ Kentucky Lexington KY 40506

STEELE, (HENRY) MAX(WELL), author, educator; b. Greenville, S.C., Mar. 30, 1922; s. John M. and Minnie (Russell) S.; student Furman U., 1939-41, Vanderbilt U., 1943; B.A., U. N.C., 1946; postgrad. Academie Julienne, Paris, France, 1951-52, Sorbonne, U. Paris, 1952-55; m. Diana Whittinghill, Dec. 31, 1960; children—Oliver Whittinghill, Keven Russell. Lectr. creative writing U. N.C., Chapel Hill, 1956-58, writer-in-residence, 1966—, lectr., 1967-68, asso. prof., 1968-72, prof., 1972—, dir. creative writing program, 1968—; lectr. creative writing U. Cal. Extension, 1963-64; mem. staff Writer's Community, Squaw Valley, 1970—. Served with USAAF, 1942-46. Recipient O'Henry Prize Story award Doubleday Pub. Co., 1955, 69; named distinguished alumnus Furman U., 1971. Nat. Endowment for Arts grantee, 1967. Author: Debby, 1960 (reissued as The Goblins Must Go Barefoot, 1966) (Harper prize novel 1960, Harper's Eugene F. Saxton Meml. Trust award, Mayflower Cup for best book by a North Carolinian); Where She Brushed Her Hair, and Other Short Stories, 1968; (juvenile) The Cat and the Coffee Drinkers, 1969. Adv. editor Paris Rev., 1952—. Contbr. short stories to Atlantic, Harper's, New Yorker, Colliers, Cosmopolitan, Esquire, Mademoiselle, Quar. Rev. Lit., also other lit. jours. Home: Mason Farm Rd Chapel Hill NC 27514 Office: Dept of English University of NC Chapel Hill NC 27514

STEELE, JACK, journalist; b. North Manchester, Ind., Sept. 15, 1914; s. Roscoe and Dessie (Wonderly) S.; A.B., Middlebury (Vt.) Coll., 1936; M.S. in Journalism, Columbia, 1937; m. Barbara Louise Lyons, Sept. 30, 1939; children—Jeffrey L., Peter C. Reporter, N.Y. Herald Tribune, 1937-53; chief polit. writer Scripps-Howard Newspaper Alliance, 1953-67, mng. editor, 1967-74, editor, 1974—. Recipient Raymond Clapper award, 1949, Sigma Delta Chi award, 1949. Heywood Broun award, 1951, Ernie Pyle award, 1963. Clubs: Nat. Press, Gridiron (Washington). Presbyn. Home: 5824 Osceola Rd Washington DC 20016 Office: 777 14th St NW Washington DC 20005

STEELE, JAMES COLUMBUS, JR., machinery mfg. co. exec.; b. Statesville, N.C., July 10, 1913; s. Henry Oscar and Annie (Parker) S.; grad. U. N.C., 1935; m. Grace Shelton Carpenter, May 4, 1940; children—James Columbus III, Henry Forest, John Shelton, Thomas Parker. With J.C. Steele & Sons, Inc., Statesville, 1935—, now chmn. bd.; dir. Pine Hall Brick & Pipe Co., Inc., Winston-Salem, N.C.; dir. Pub. Service Co. of N.C., Gastonia, Northwestern Bank, Statesville. Past chmn., Statesville Planning and Zoning Bd.; chmn. Statesville Redevelopment Commn., 1966—. Bd. dirs. N.C. Engring. Found. Served to lt. USNR, World War II; PTO. Fellow Am. Ceramic Soc.; mem. Kappa Sigma. Presbyn. (elder). Rotarian (past pres.). Clubs: Statesville Country; Blowing Rock (N.C.) Country (past pres.). Home: 429 Summit Av Statesville NC 28677 Office: 710 S Mulberry St Statesville NC 28677

STEELE, JOHNNIE HUGH, ins. exec.; b. Covington, Ga., Nov. 3, 1925; s. Johnnie James and Ada (Kitchens) S.; student Emory at Oxford Coll., 1946-47; m. Dorothy Virginia Lassiter, Aug. 10, 1947; children—Johnnie Hugh, Margaret Susan. Teller, Bank of Covington (Ga.), 1947-58; owner Steele Ins. Agy., Covington, 1958-66; partner Steele-Prescott Ins. Agy., Covington, 1966—; chmn. bd. First Nat. Bank of Newton County, Covington, 1963—. Tax receiver Newton County (Ga.), 1960-64. Mem. bd. visitors Emory U., Atlanta, 1969—; trustee Piedmont Acad., Monticello, Ga., 1971—. Served with AUS, 1945-46. Named Agt. of Year, Ga. Mutual Ins. Assn., 1969. Mem. Ga. Assn. Mutual Ins. Agts. (dir.), Am. Legion, Newton County C. of C. (pres. 1969). Baptist (deacon). Mason, Rotarian (pres. 1967-68), Elk. Home: 3135 Ellen Ct Covington GA 30209 Office: 1132 Floyd St NE Covington GA 30209

STEELE, JOSEPH RODGERS, coast guard officer; b. Birmingham, Ala., Jan. 20, 1920; s. George Curtis and Anne (Rodgers) S.; student Birmingham-So. Coll., 1936-39; B.A., U. Ala., 1940; B.S. in Engring., U.S. Coast Guard Acad., 1943; postgrad. U. Ill., 1949-50; M.S. in Aero. Engring., U.S. Air Force Inst. Tech., 1952;; m. Jeanne Marie Drake Smith, Apr. 15, 1967; 1 son, Joseph Rodgers. Commd. ensign, U.S. Coast Guard, 1943, advanced through grades to rear adm., 1971; chief engring. div. 17th Coast Guard Dist., Juneau, Alaska, 1967-69; chief operations div. 2d Coast Guard Dist., St. Louis, 1970-71; chief, office of personnel U.S. Coast Guard Hdqrs., Washington, 1971—. Mem. Soc. Am. Mil. Engrs., U.S. Naval Inst., Pi Kappa Alpha. Presbyn. Clubs: Army-Navy (Washington); Army-Navy Country (Arlington, Va.). Home: 6357 Crosswoods Dr Falls Church VA 22044 Office: Coast Guard Hdqrs 400 7th St SW Washington DC 20590

STEELE, MARION ARCHIBALD, cons. engr.; b. Nashville, Sept. 9, 1938; s. Marion A. and Mary (Daniel) S.; student Vanderbilt U., 1957-58; Ga. Inst. Tech., 1958; B.S.C.E. Va. Mil. Inst., 1961; postgrad. W. Va. U., 1964-65; m. Brenda Elizabeth Gantt, Nov. 9, 1963; children—Mary Margaret, Marion Archibold Jackson. Office engr. Ingersoll-Rand Co., Richmond, Va., N.Y.C., 1960-1961-62; engr. mgr. Morgantown (W. Va.) San. Bd., 1965-66; design engr. Wiley & Wilson, cons. engrs.-architects-planners, Lynchburg, Va., 1966-71, project mgr., 1966-67, mgr. Manassa, Va., 1967-69, asst. dir. constrn. adminstrn., Lynchburg office, 1969-70, head civil engring. dept., Lynchburg, 1970-71; mgr. offices Stottler Stagg and Assos.,

Brevard Engring. Co., Winter Haven and St. Petersburg, Fla., 1971-72; sales engr. Taulman Co., Charlotte, N.C., 1972—. Mem. Va. Adv. Legislative Council, 1968-70. Served to capt. AUS, 1962-64. Recipient Army Commendation Medal, V-Corps Certificate Achievement. Registered profl. engr., W. Va., Va., N.C. Mem. Nat., Va. (sec., treas. Lynchburg 1967-68, dir. 1969) socs. profl. engrs., Fla., Va. (v.p. 1971), W.Va. Water pollution control assns. Home: 10709 Forest Dr Matthews NC 28105 Office: 201 S Tryon St Box 2447 Charlotte NC 28201

STEELE, RICHARD KENNETH, photog. equipment cons.; b. Geneva, N.Y., May 26, 1940; s. Lewis Crawford and Florence (Guest) S.; B.S. in Optical Engring., U. Rochester, 1963; m. Georgia Ann Yaw, May 4, 1963; children—Richard, Elizabeth, Robert. Engr. aeronutronics div. Philco-Ford, Newport Beach, Cal., 1963-64; optical design engr. Perkin-Elmer, Costa Mesa, Cal., 1964-65; chief optical engr. applied optics and mechanics div. Electro-Optical Systems, Arcadia, Cal., 1965-66; founder pres. Optek Inc., Costa Mesa, 1967—, Optek div. mgr. SEACO Computer-Display, Inc., Garland, Tex., 1971—; founder R.K. Steele, Consultants, 1972—; founder, pres. Optical Assos., Dallas, 1973—; dir. SEACO Computer-Display Inc. Cons., Bausch & Lomb, Rochester, N.Y., 1968—, Poly-Optics, Santa Ana, Cal., 1967—, Tex. Instruments, Dallas, 1972—, Tracor Inc., Austin, 1973—. Mem. Optical Soc. Am., Soc. Photo. Scientists and Engrs., Soc. of Photo-Optical Instrumentation Engrs. Home: 7117 Briar Cove Dr Dallas TX 75240

STEELMAN, ALAN WATSON, congressman; b. Little Rock, Mar. 15, 1942; s. Ples C. and Flossie (Watson) S.; B.A., Baylor U., 1964; M.L.A., So. Methodist U., 1971; fellow John F. Kennedy Inst. Politics, Harvard, 1972; m. Carolyn Findley, Aug. 29, 1962; children—Robin, Kimble, Alan Watson and Allison (twins). Exec. dir. Republican Party Dallas County, 1966-69; exec. dir. Sam Wyly Found., Dallas, 1969; exec. dir. Pres.'s Adv. Council on Minority Bus. Enterprise, Washington, 1969-72; mem. 93d Congress from 5th Tex. dist. Mem. Spl. White House Speakers Task Force on Phases I and II, Adminstrn.'s Econ. Program, 1969-72. Mem. Speakers Bur. Dallas United Fund, 1966; chmn. donors div. Dallas Symphony, 1967. Bd. dirs. Dallas Civic Opera, UCC Venture Corp., Dallas, Inst. for Early Childhood Edn., Dallas, Dallas Big Brothers; bd. councilors Bus. Sch., Fed. City Coll., Washington; trustee, dir. KERA-TV, 1969-72. Named Congressman of Month, May 1973. Mem. L.Q.C. Lamar Soc. (dir.), Pi Sigma Alpha. Home: 3507 Springland Lane NW Washington DC 20008 Office: 437 Cannon House Office Bldg Washington DC 20515

STEEN, ROBERT FREDERICK, elec. engr.; b. Atlanta, Aug. 19, 1942; s. Frederick Henry and Marion Steele (Rodger) S.; B.S., U. Rochester, 1964; M.E.E., N.C. State U., 1967, Ph.D., 1972; m. Ruth Elisabeth Decker, Aug. 10, 1965; children—Douglas Richard, Mark Frederick. Market and engring. planning IBM, Kingston, N.Y., 1964-65, design engr., 1965-68, advanced tech., 1968-70, adv. engr., Research Triangle Park, N.C., 1970—, also tchr. co. sponsored edn. program. NSF grantee, 1963. Mem. I.E.E.E. Patentee in field. Home: 2021 Mallard Lane Raleigh NC 27609 Office: IBM Research Triangle Park NC 27709

STEERE, BRUCE MIDDLETON, truck line exec.; b. Evanston, Ill., Dec. 29, 1918; s. Kenneth David and Grace (Duffield) S.; B.A., Yale, 1942; indsl. adminstrn., Harvard Bus. Sch., 1943; m. Anne MacCuen Bullivant, July 5, 1968; children—Lucy Duffield, Grace McLaurin, Mrs. Douglas E. Kliever, Richard M. H. Harper III, Patricia B. Harper, Stuart L. Harper. Indsl. engr. Chance Vought Aircraft, Bridgeport, Conn., 1943-45; pres. Steere Tank Lines, Dallas, 1945—. Pres., dir. So. Ins. Co., Dallas, 1952—; dir. Republic Financial Services, Inc., Allied Finance Co., Indsl. Life Ins. Co., (all Dallas). Mem. Tex. Tank Truck Carriers Assn. (past pres.), Tex. Motor Transp. Assn. (past pres.), Beta Theta Pi. Democrat. Mem. Christian Ch. Clubs: Brook Hollow Golf (Dallas); Koon Kreek (Athens, Tex.) N.Y. Yacht, Cruising of Am. (N.Y.C.); Stone Horse Yacht (Harwich Port, Mass.); Athletic (Dallas). Home: 4412 N Versailles St Dallas TX 75205 Office: 2808 Fairmount St Dallas TX 75201

STEFANIK, THEODORE MARTIN, elec. engr.; b. Johnstown, Pa., Oct. 16, 1932; s. Martin Anthony and Catherine (Strazik) S.; B.S. in Elec. Engring., U. Pitts., 1959; M.S. in Elec. Engring., Drexel U., 1964; M.S. in Mgmt., Rollins Coll., 1971; m. Jeannie Agnes Milavec, Feb. 2, 1957; children—Susan, Theodore J., Christina, John, Ramona. With Martin Marietta Corp., various locations, 1959—, chief engr., Ocala, Fla., 1969-72, sr. staff engr., Orlando, Fla., 1972—. Instr., Harford Jr. Coll., Belair, Md., 1965-67; notary pub. Served with USN, 1951-55. Registered profl. engr., Fla. Mem. I.E.E.E. (chmn. profl. activities com.), Nat. Soc. Profl. Engrs., Fla. Engring. Soc., Fla. Acad. Sci. Inventor in field. Home: 743 London Rd Winter Park FL 32789 Office: MP 476 Orlando FL 32805

STEFFEN, STEVE, interior designer; b. Chgo., Mar. 8, 1918; s. Louis Joseph and Emilia Josephine (von Dvorak) S.; student Northwestern U., 1936-37, U. Turin (Italy), 1946-47, Parsons Sch. of Design, 1948-50, N.Y. U., 1948-50. Interior designer Marshall Field & Co., Chgo., 1950-54, Richard Plumer Co., Miami, 1954-64, Beresford Interiors, 1964-67; partner, designer Steve Steffen Assos., 1968—; instr. interior design Miami Dade Jr. Coll., 1969. Served with USCG, 1941-43. Mem. Am. Inst. Interior Designers (pres. Fla. dist. chpt. 1960). Address: 5901 SW 50th St Miami FL 33155

STEFFENS, ROGER CHARLES, landscape architect; city planner; b. Milw., May 18, 1934; s. Raymond Charles and Helen Anna (Jahn) S.; student St. Petersburg Jr. Coll., 1958-59; B.Landscape Architecture cum laude, U. Fla., 1962; M. City and Regional Planning, U. N.C., 1964; m. Huguette Ann Bourgery, Sept. 27, 1957; children—Marc Charles, Ashley Noelle. Prin. Planner City of Huntsville (Ala.), 1964-67; city planner asso. Ewald Assos., Memphis, 1967-68; div. mgr. Reynolds, Smith & Hills, Jacksonville, Fla., 1968-72; v.p. Reynolds, Smith Hills, 1972—; partner PLD LTD., Jacksonville, 1972—; trustee BNC Investors, Jacksonville. Mem. Huntsville Beautification Bd., 1965-67; spl. adviser Huntsville Bd. Adjustment, 1965-67. Bd. govs. Deerwood Homeowners Assn., Jacksonville, Fla., 1971-72. Served with USAF, 1954-58. Named Hon. Citizen of Huntsville, 1967; recipient state and nat. awards for excellence in community planning and land devel. Mem. Am. Inst. Planners, Am. Soc. Landscape Architects, Am. Soc. Landscape Architecture (mem. nat. com. on edn. and policy planning 1973-74), Am. Soc. Planning Ofcls., Urban Land Inst., Fla. Planning and Zoning Assn., World Future Soc., Porsche Club Am., Gargoyle, Phi Kappa Phi. Home: 7640 Windward Way W Jacksonville FL 32216 Office: PO Box 4850 Jacksonville FL 32201

STEGALL, DAVID LAWRENCE, dentist; b. Ft. Worth, Aug. 6, 1942; s. Eugene Thomas and Marion (Goodman) S.; student Tex. Christian U., 1960-61, Tex. Wesleyan of Ft. Worth, 1961-63; D.D.S., Baylor U., 1967; m. Sandra Camille Powers, May 26, 1967; children—Britton Lawrence, Kathryn Camille, Emily Elizabeth. Practice dentistry, Ft. Worth, 1967-68, Dallas, 1968—; instr. gnathology. Active, Dallas Civil Opera Co. and Guild, Dallas Mus. of Fine Arts, Dallas Theater Center. Recipient Horace Beachum award for denture prosthesis Baylor U. Coll. Dentistry, 1967. Mem. Am., Tex. dental assns., Dallas County Dental Soc., Peter K. Thomas Gnathological Study Group (pres. 1968—), Dr. Charles Stuart's Gnathological Soc. (pres. 1967—). Episcopalian. Home: 5322 Montrose Dr Dallas TX 75209 Office: 8226 Douglas St Dallas TX 75225

STEGALL, WHITNEY, lawyer; b. Rockvale, Tenn., Feb. 17, 1916; s. Benjamin Duggan and Nannie (Love) S.; B.S., Middle Tenn. State U., 1937; LL.B., Vanderbilt U., 1950; m. Orene Cowan, Dec. 29, 1956; children—Whitney, Amy. Admitted to Tenn. bar, 1949; practiced in Murfreesboro, 1949-74; partner firm Stegall, Daniel, Burton, Bolin & LaRoche; chancellor 8th jud. dist. State of Tenn., 1974—. Dir. Nat. Bank Murfreesboro, Nat. Health Corp. Chmn. Heart of Tenn. dist. Mid-Cumberland council Boy Scouts Am., 1971-72. Mem. Tenn. Senate, 1965-66. Bd. dirs. Rutherford Hosp., Inc., Met. Airport Authority; trustee Middle Tenn. State U. Loan, Scholarship and Devel. Fund. Served to maj. AUS, 1942-47. Mem. Murfreesboro C. of C. (past pres.), Middle Tenn. State U. Alumni Assn. (past pres.), Murfreesboro (past pres.), Cannon County (past pres.) bar assns. Democrat. Kiwanian (past pres., lt. gov.). Home: 132 Park Circle Murfreesboro TN 37130 Office: 401 W Main St Murfreesboro TN 37130

STEHLIN, JOHN SEBASTIAN, JR., physician; b. Brownsville, Tenn., June 16, 1923; s. John Sebastian and Princess (King) S.; M.D., Marquette U., 1947; m. Mary E. Cleary, Sept. 1950 (div. Sept. 1962); children—Mary Cleary, Criss William, Gary Parker; m. 2d, Jean Waggoner, Apr. 7, 1973. Intern Milw. Hosp., 1947-48, resident, 1949-52; resident Bapt. Hosp., Memphis, 1948-49; fellow surgery Lahey Clinic, Boston, 1952-53, 56; mem. staff U. Tex. M.D. Anderson Hosp. and Tumor Inst., Houston, 1955-67, sr. fellow, 1955-56, asso. prof. surgery, 1963-67, asso. surgeon, 1961-67; clin. asso. prof. surgery Baylor Coll. Medicine, Houston, 1967—, also sci. dir. St. Joseph Labs. for Cancer Research, 1970—. Mem. surg. staff St. Joseph Hosp., Houston; hon. prof. Faculty Medicine U. Republic Uruguay. Diplomate Am. Bd. Surgery. Fellow A.C.S.; mem. Am. Assn. Cancer Research, A.A.A.S., A.M.A., Cancer Assn. Argentina (hon.), Cancer Soc. Chile (hon.), Harris County Med. Soc., Houston Surg. Soc., Internat Platform Assn., James Ewing Soc., N.Y. Acad. Scis., Pan Am. Med. Soc., Salem Surg. Soc. (hon.), Soc. Dermatology Uruguay (hon.), Southwestern Surg. Congress, So. Med. Assn., Surg. Soc. Chile (hon.), Tex. Med. Assn., Tex. Surg. Soc., Western Surg. Assn., Royal Soc. Medicine. Home: 3705 Inverness St Houston TX 77019 Office: 777 St Joseph Profl Bldg Houston TX 77002

STEHLING, ALVIN JAMES, educator; b. Fredericksburg, Tex., May 12, 1931; s. Alvin Adam and Emmie (Blum) S.; B.B.A., St. Mary's U. San Antonio, 1954, M.A. in Econs., 1973; m. Jeanette Frances Weidenfellow, Sept. 27, 1958; children—Stephen, Sharon, Sandra, Tod. Analyst machine accounting dept. City Pub. Service Bd., San Antonio, 1956-63, supt. machine accounting, 1963-66; instr. data processing dept. San Antonio Coll., 1966-68, chmn. data processing dept., 1968—. Dir. Stehling Bros., Fredericksburg. Scoutmaster, Boy Scouts Am., 1960-61; pres. Better Service Club, San Antonio, 1959-60. Served to 1st lt., arty., AUS, 1954-56. Mem. Data Processing Mgmt. Assn. (past pres.), Omicron Delta Epsilon. Toastmaster. Home: 15607 Oak Grove St San Antonio TX 78228

STEIN, BERNARD REUBIN, program analyst; b. Boston, Aug. 5, 1927; s. Harry and Miriam (Orent) S.; B.S., Northeastern U., 1949; M.S., U. Tenn., 1950; postgrad. Catholic U. Am., 1952-54; Dr. Rer. Nat., U. Göttingen (Germany), 1957; m. Eleonora Elena Scarpa, May 22, 1957; children—Costanza, David, Raffael. Post-doctoral fellow U. Ottawa, 1957-58; phys. chemist U.S. Army Research Office, 1958-60; chief chemistry br. U.S. Army Research and Devel. Group, 1960-63; phys. chemist U.S. Army Research Office, 1964-65; program analyst NSF, Washington, 1965—. Served with AUS, 1945-47. Mem. Am. Chem. Soc., A.A.A.S., Sigma Xi. Home: 6727 Rosewood St Annandale VA 22003 Office: 1800 G St NW Washington DC 20550

STEIN, CHARLES HOWARD, recreation co. exec.; b. N.Y.C., Dec. 13, 1927; s. Gilbert and Fritzie (Lieberman) S.; student U. Miami, 1945-46, N.Y. U., 1946-47; m. Rusty Senft, Nov. 27, 1953; children—Bradley, Clifford, Candice. Pres., prin. shareholder Orange State Processing Corp., 1951-56; gen. mgr. citrus div. Kraft Foods Co., Lakeland, Fla., 1956-65; pres. Kitchens of Sara Lee, dir., v.p. Consol. Food Corp., Deerfield, Ill., 1965-67; pres., chmn. bd. Hardwicke Cos., Inc., N.Y.C., 1968—. Mem. Fla. Council of 100, 1965—. Mem. Young Presidents Orgn. Home: 5345 Pinetree Dr Miami Beach FL 33140 Office: 42d Floor 9 W 57th St New York City NY 10022

STEIN, GILBERT TAYLOR, constrn. co. exec.; b. Chattanooga, Feb. 20, 1928; s. John Gilbert and Evelyn Douglass (Taylor) S.; B.S., U. Tenn., 1950; m. Virginia June Harris, Oct. 4, 1952; children—Virginia Evelyn, Frank Douglas, John Taylor. Partner, Porzelius & Stein, cons. engrs., Chattanooga, 1955-71; partner Stein Constrn. Co., 1950—; v.p. Chattanooga Indsl. Devel. Corp., 1960—. Founder, mem. Scenic Cities Beautiful Commn., Chattanooga, 1962—. Bd. dirs. Hamilton County Sch. Bd., 1967—, Mental Health Assn., Chattanooga Psychiat. Clinic. Served to lt. (j.g.) USNR, 1954-56. Registered profl. engr., Tenn. Mem. Asso. Gen. Contractors Am., Nat. Soc. Profl. Engrs., Am. Soc. C.E., Chattanooga C. of C. (exec. com., dir.), Phi Kappa Phi, Chi Epsilon, Tau Beta Pi, Kappa Sigma. Republican. Episcopalian (supt. Sunday sch.). Clubs: Mountain City, Civitan, Chattanooga Yacht; Lookout Mountain Fairyland. Home: 281 Stephenson Av Lookout Mountain TN 37350 Office: 3611 Amnicola Hwy Chattanooga TN 37406

STEIN, MARTIN MATTHEW, economist; b. Bad Gastein, Austria, Feb. 21, 1946; s. Leon and Bess (Kicis) S.; brought to U.S., 1949, naturalized, 1955; B.S. with high honors, U. Md., 1967, postgrad. in econs., 1968-72. Computer programmer U. Md., College Park, 1965; economist U.S. Dept. of Commerce, Washington, 1966; economist U.S. Dept. of Transp., Washington, 1967-73; mgr. socio-econ. studies Md. Dept. Transp., Balt., 1973—. Investment counselor; coordinator U.S. C. of C. Coll.-Bus. Symposium, 1967. Del. to Md. Fedn. Young Republicans, 1968, Rep. Leadership Tng. Inst., 1970, 71, 72. Named one of Outstanding Young Men Am. U.S. Jaycees, 1972. Mem. Soc. Govt. Economists (founder 1970, pres. 1972, chmn. bd. 1973, recipient award 1973), Nat. Council Assns. for Policy Scis. (v.p. 1972), Nat. Economists Club, Omicron Delta Epsilon, Delta Sigma Pi (scholarship award 1967, pres. Washington Alumni Assn. 1971-73, dist. dir. 1973). Republican. Jewish religion. Research on social and econ. impact of transp. Home: 1250 4th St SW Washington DC 20024 Office: PO Box 8755 Balt-Washington Internat Airport MD 21240

STEINBACH, KARL HEINRICH, physicist; b. Bonn, Germany, Feb. 19, 1928; s. Franz and Mathilde (Braunshausen) S.; M.S. in Physics, U. Munich (Germany), 1953; Ph.D. in Engring., Tech. U. Hannover (Germany), 1971; m. Dobrila Bojanovic, Dec. 28, 1955; children—Bernhard Zdravko, Carlo Franz, Boris John. Came to U.S., 1959, naturalized, 1965. Physicist, Pintsch Electro Co., Konstanz, Germany, 1953-57; chief electronics lab. Telefunken Co., Munich, also Konstanz, 1957-59; chief microwave, electronics unit U.S. Army Research and Devel. Lab., Ft. Belvior, Va., 1959-65, chief research design br., barrier, intrusion detection div., 1965-67, chief research div., intrusion detection and sensor lab. U.S. Army Mobility Equipment Research and Devel. Center, 1967-71, chief mine detection div., 1971—. Recipient award for outstanding achievement Army Sci. Conf., West Point, 1962; research and devel. award Dept. Army, 1969, research and study fellow, 1971. Mem. I.E.E.E., Research Soc. Am. Patentee in field. Home: 9115 Coronado Terrace Fairfax VA 22030 Office: US Army MERDC Fort Belvoir VA 22060

STEINBERG, JOSEPH, statistician, govt. ofcl.; b. N.Y.C., Mar. 22, 1920; s. Solomon and Sophie (Sauer) S.; B.S., Coll. City N.Y., 1939; postgrad. U.S. Dept. Agr. Grad Sch., 1940-41; Am. U., 1940-42, Catholic U., 1947; m. Ruth Cohen, Oct. 30, 1949; children—Steven L., Seth M. With Census Bur., U.S. Dept. Commerce, 1940-42, 44-63, chief statis. methods div., 1959-63; statistician Social Security Bd., 1942-44; chief math. statistician Social Security Adminstrn., U.S. Dept. Health Edn. and Welfare, Washington, 1963-72; asst. commr. survey design Bur. Labor Statistics, Dept. Labor, Washington, 1972—. Lectr., Grad. Sch. U.S. Dept. Agr., Washington, 1942—; mem. assembly behavioral and social scis. NRC-Nat. Acad. Scis., 1971—, mem. com. on fed. agy. evaluation research, 1971—. Recipient Meritorious Service award U.S. Dept. Commerce, 1955, Distinguished Service award Dept. Health, Edn. and Welfare, 1968. Fellow Am. Statis. Assn., A.A.A.S.; mem. Internat. Assn. Survey Statisticians, Inter-Am. Statis. Inst., Population Assn. Am., Inst. Math. Statistics, Phi Beta Kappa. Contbr. articles to profl. jours. Home: 1011 Roswell Dr Silver Spring MD 20901 Office: Bur Labor Statistics 2116 441 G St NW Washington DC 20212

STEINBERG, LARRY JAY, accountant; b. Columbia, Mo., Dec. 3, 1942; s. Simon Carl and Margaret Carolyn (Strunck) S.; B.S. cum laude, A.B., U. Mo., 1964; m. Rita Susan Hymson, Aug. 23, 1964; children—Scott Hymson, Laura Frances. With Ernst & Ernst, Louisville, 1964-71, supr., 1969-71; mgr. Touche Ross & Co., Louisville, 1971—. Treas., Louisville Hebrew Sch., 1966-68, Chance's Nursery and Kindergarten, Inc., 1973-74. Treas., City of Bancroft, 1973, trustee, 1974—; precinct capt. Republican party, 1973—. C.P.A., Ky. Mem. Ky. Soc. C.P.A.'s, Am. Inst. C.P.A.'s, Louisville Jr. C. of C. (treas. 1968-69). Jewish religion. Home: 7500 Adler Way Louisville KY 40222 Office: 510 W Broadway Louisville KY 40202

STEINDL, FRANK GEORGE, educator; b. Chgo., Aug. 26, 1935; s. Frank and Anna (Bumeder) S.; B.A., DePaul U., 1957; A.M., U. Ill., 1958; Ph.D., U. Ia., 1963; m. Joyce Becker, Aug. 26, 1961; children—David F., Andrew M., Peter E., Matthew T. Instr. econs. St. Benedict's Coll., Atchison, Kan., 1958-59; mem. faculty Okla. State U., Stillwater, 1962—, asso. prof. econs., 1965-70, prof., 1970—. Vis. economist Fed. Res. Bank Cleve., 1966-67. Mem. Am. Assn. U. Profs., Am., Midwest (v.p. 1973-74), Southwestern (pres. 1974-75), So. econ. assns., Econometric Soc., Southwestern Social Sci. Assn., Beta Gamma Sigma, Omicron Delta Epsilon. Contbr. articles to profl. jours. Home: 902 Osage Dr Stillwater OK 74074

STEINER, BECKWITH, JR., optometrist; b. Palacios, Tex., Dec. 2, 1937; s. Beckwith and Bessie (Linville) S.; B.S., U. Houston, 1965, certificate optometry, 1966, O.D., 1967; m. Macella Mae Lowe, Sept. 5, 1958; children—Beckwith Wayne, Paul Isaac, Deborah Shannan, Sherri Alacia. Optometrist, Bay City, Tex., 1967—. Lectr. U. Houston, 1968-69. Precinct chmn. Democratic party, 1972—, mem. Matagorda County Exec. Com., 1972—. Served with USAF, 1958-62. Recipient award Freedoms Found. for Outstanding article, 1972. Fellow Am. Acad. Optometry; mem. Am., Tex. optometric assns., Bay City Jr. C. of C. (pres. 1970), U.S. Jr. C. of C. (nat. dir. 1971-72), Phi Theta Upsilon. Baptist. Rotarian. Home: 4314 Doris St Bay City TX 77414 Office: 1015 Av G Bay City TX 77414

STEINER, LEO KEITH, JR., former banker; b. Birmingham, Ala., Mar. 3, 1903; s. Leo Keith and Dian (Holzer) S.; grad. Culver (Ind.) Mil. Acad., 1920; B.S. in Econs., Wharton Sch. U. Pa., 1924; m. Sylvia Forman, Oct. 15, 1924 (div.); children—Leo Keith III, Dorothy Forman (Mrs. Jacob W. Schott). Exec. v.p. Steiner Bros. Bank, 1940-62; pres. Guardian Realty Co., Birmingham, 1942-62; dir. Old Republic Life Ins. Co., Chgo. Served as maj. USAAF, 1942-44. Clubs: Xanadu Yacht and Tennis (Freeport, Grand Bahama Island); Jockey (Miami, Fla.). Home: Jockey Club Apt 1805 11111 Biscayne Blvd North Miami FL 33161

STEINFELD, SAMUEL SIMONS, state justice; b. Louisville, Feb. 16, 1906; s. Emile and Florence (Simons) S.; LL.B., U. Louisville, 1928; m. Flora Loebenberg, July 24, 1929; children—Helene S. (Mrs. Howard B. Grossman), James F. Admitted to Ky. bar, 1928; asso. Gifford & Steinfeld, 1928-33; partner Steinfeld & Steinfeld, Louisville, after 1933; former judge Ky. Ct. Appeals, Frankfort; now chief justice Ky. Supreme Ct. Vice pres., dir. Llewellyn St. Matthews Laundry; pres., dir. Lorenza Realty Co.; sec., dir. Coin Laundromat, Inc., Modern Loan Co., Financial Investment Corp., Mid-Land Warehouse Co.; dir. Sympson Bros. Coal Co. Civic sec. Jewish Community Center Louisville, 1956, v.p., 1957, trustee, 1951—. Pres. Louisville Young Men's Republican Club, 1939; alternate del. Rep. Nat. Conv., 1940, 56; mem. Jefferson County Rep. Exec. Com. Mem. Ky., Louisville (legal chmn. jud. and rules com. 1950-57) bar assns., Comml. Law League Am. Jewish religion. Clubs: L (U. Louisville); Adath Israel Men's (past pres.), Lincoln. Home: 1856 Princeton Dr Louisville KY 40205 Office: Supreme Ct Bldg Frankfort KY 40601

STEINICHEN, JOHN, architect; b. Stone Mountain, Ga., Apr. 29, 1907; s. John and Ada (Wallace) S.; apprentice in sculpture under Herman Steinichen, 1922-26; student Ga. Inst. Tech., 1945; m. Laura Octavia Johnson, Aug. 5, 1929; children—John III, Joyce Kay (Mrs. Glenn E. Wiltsey). Designer, sculptor, 1926-31; freelance artist, sculptor, musician, 1931-41; with Firestone Aircraft Plant, Atlanta, 1942-45; architect with various archtl. firms, Atlanta, 1945-50; asso. architect Finch, Alexander, Barnes, Rothschild & Paschal and predecesser firms, Atlanta, 1950-73. Sculptures and paintings exhibited in group shows, Atlanta, Washington, N.Y.C., others, 1931—; represented in pvt. collections. Mem. Am. Fedn. Musicians, A.I.A., Soc. Mil. Engrs., Allied Artists Am. (asso.), Rockdale C. of C. Presbyn. Rotarian (dir. local club). Home: PO Box 59 3131 Dennard Rd Conyers GA 30207

STEINLE, LEON FRANCIS, lawyer; b. Jourdanton, Tex., Mar. 22, 1918; s. Alfred Ney and Cedalia Frances (Wurzbach) S.; student St. Mary's U., 1935-37; LL.B., U. Tex., 1940; m. Virginia Franklin, June 5, 1937; children—Angela (Mrs. T.L. Hairston III), Leon Franklin. Admitted to Tex. bar, 1940; with Martin Abstract Co., Jourdanton, 1940-41, land dept. Humble Oil & Refining Co., Corpus Christi, Tex., 1941-43; practice law, Jourdanton, 1946—; dir. Jourdanton State Bank; pres., chmn. bd. Atascosa Savs. Assn., Jourdanton. Pres., Jourdanton Vol. Fire Dept., 1948-50; pres. Atascosa Hosp. Assn., 1968—. Served from ensign to lt. USNR, 1943-46; ETO. Mem. Jourdanton C. of C. (pres. 1958-59), Atascosa County Bar Assn. (pres. 1960—). Roman Catholic (pres. parish council 1969—). K.C. Home: 814 Zanderson Av Jourdanton TX 78026 Office: 101 Main St Jourdanton TX 78026

STEINMAN, LOUIS CLAUDE, broadcasting exec.; b. Grand Rapids, Mich., Apr. 22, 1922; s. Claude Vernon and Susie (Noble) S.; grad. pub. high sch.; m. Jane LaNelle Davis, Dec. 2, 1960. Mgr. photo finishing Va. Dare Photo Co., Fort Lauderdale, Fla., 1955-60, Photo Print Inc., Fort Lauderdale, 1960-63; mgr. camera dept. Gold-Silver

Co., Nashville, 1963-65; film dir. WDCN-TV, Nashville, Tenn., 1966—; prodn. engr. Spotland Prodns., Nashville, 1969—. Served with USNR, 1940-41. Mem. Soc. Preservation Encouragement Barbershop Quartet Singing Am. (past pres.), Soc. Motion Picture and TV Engrs. Home: PO Box 37 Whites Creek TN 37189 Office: 15th and Compton Pl Nashville TN 37212

STEINSCHULTE, THILO, architect; b. Berlin, Germany, July 4, 1926; s. Josef and Nora (Cleff) S.; B.A. (scholar), Tech. U. Munich (Germany), 1950; M.A. (scholar), 1953; postgrad. (exchange scholar urban planning), U. Wash., 1950-51; m. Izora Elisabeth Rikard, Nov. 24, 1954; 1 dau., Nora E. Came to U.S., 1953. Architect Bain & Overturf, Seattle, 1953-54; partner Barron, Heinberg & Brocato, architects and engrs., Alexandria, La., 1954—. Various exhbns. paintings arts shows La., 1968—. Pres. Rapides Symphony Orch., Alexandria, 1971; v.p. Central La. Art Assn., 1971. Trustee Wesley Found. La. State U., Alexandria, 1971; bd. dirs. Central La. Community Theatre, Alexandria, 1969-70, Rapides Arts Council, 1973-74. Served with German Armed Forces, 1943-45. Mem. A.I.A. (pres. Central La. chpt. 1968), La. Architects Assn. (v.p. 1970-71), Am. Inst. Archeology. Methodist (trustee, chmn. bd. trustees 1969-70). Rotarian (pres. 1973-74). Clubs: Alexandria Investment, Alexandria Aquatic. Home: 3107 Pershing St Alexandria LA 71301 Office: 1015 Wisteria St Alexandria LA 71301

STEISS, ALAN WALTER, educator; b. Woodbury, N.J., Feb. 15, 1937; s. Walter and Martha (Schroeder) S.; B.A. in Sociology, B.A. in Psychology, Bucknell U., 1959; M.A. in Urban and Regional Planning, U. Wis., 1966, Ph.D., 1969; m. Patricia Foster McClintock, June 13, 1959; children—Carol Jean, Darren Christopher, Todd Alan. Asst. planner N.J. Planning Bur., Trenton, 1960-61, sr. planner, 1961-62; prin. planner N.J. Div. State and Regional Planning, Trenton, 1962-63, supervising planner, 1963-64; chief statewide planning State of N.J., Trenton, 1964-65; state planning adviser State of Wis., Madison, 1965-67; mem. faculty dept. urban planning Va. Poly. Inst. and State U., Blacksburg, 1967—, asso. prof., 1969-72, prof., 1972—, also asso. dean, chmn. div. environmental and urban systems, 1969—. Partner, Planning Scis. Orgn. Inc., Atlanta, 1967—; cons. to several states on field regional planning. Mem. Assn. Collegiate Schs. Planning (exec. com.), Am. Assn. U. Profs., Am. Soc. Pub. Adminstrn., Urban Am., Nat. Urban Coalition, Psi Chi, Tau Sigma Delta, Lambda Alpha. Author: (with others) Planning Administration, 1966; A Framework for Planning in State Government, 1968; (with A.J. Catanese) Systemtic Planning: Theory and Application, 1970; Public Budgeting and Management, 1972; Urban Systems Dynamics: Models for Analysis and Planning, 1974. Contbr. articles to profl. jours. Home: 1397 Locust Av Blacksburg VA 24060

STEM, MARTHA SNOWDON, editor, author; b. Oil City, Pa., July 2, 1908; d. Wayne Compton and Nettie (Snowdon) Stem; grad. Va. Jr. Coll. Sch. Journalism, 1927; A.B., Pa. Coll. for Women, 1929. Columnist dir. spl. edits. schs., coll. and chs. Pitts. Press, 1932-41, St. Petersburg (Fla.) Times, 1941-42; free lance writer pub. relations, 1942-51; exec. sec. Dept. Pub. Information, Am. Optometric Assn., Pitts., 1951-53; dir. profl. relations Optometric Extension Program Found., Duncan, Okla., 1953—, co-organizer, cons., editor Optometric Extension Program Asst.'s Course, 1958—. Tchr. introductory psychology pvt. high sch., St. Petersburg, Fla., 1945-49. Corr. Acad. Therapy Publs., San Rafael, Cal., 1966—. Bd. dirs. Volunteers for Vision, 1968—. Mem. Chatham Coll. Alumnae Assn., Omega. Presbyn. Author: Optometric Extension Program Course series Professional and Patient Relations, 21 vols. Editor: Optometric Extension Program NEWS. Contbr. articles to various optometric publs. Home: 445 29th Av North St Petersburg FL 33704 Office: Box 911 Duncan OK 73533

STENBERG, ROBERT THEODORE, physician; b. Austin, Tex., Feb. 23, 1923; s. Theodore Thorson and Elizabeth (Noble) S.; B.A. with honors, U. Tex., 1943, M.D., 1946; m. Johnnie Mae Gable, Nov. 19, 1953; 1 son, Gary Morris. Intern Kansas City (Mo.) Gen. Hosp., 1946-47; resident psychiatry U. Mich., 1949-50; staff psychiatrist Ft. Custer (Mich.) VA Hosp., 1950; asst. chief psychiatry and neurology service VA Hosp., Ft. Benjamin Harrison, Ind., 1950-51; staff psychiatrist Richmond (Ind.) State Hosp., 1951; supt. Spencer (W.Va.) State Hosp., 1951-52; psychiatrist VA Regional Office Mental Hygiene Clinic, Huntington, W.Va., 1952; staff psychiatrist, dir. Harris County unit Austin State Hosp., 1953-60, 62—, resident, 1960-62. Cons. psychiatry, neurology Brown Schs. for Exceptional Children, 1962-67. Served to capt. M.C., USAF, 1947-49. Fellow Am. Psychiat. Assn.; mem. Tex. Neuropsychiat. Assn., Austin Psychiat. Soc., Am., Tex. med. assns., Travis County Med. Soc., Acad. for Religion and Mental Health, Am. Group Therapy Assn., N.Y. Acad. Sci., A.A.A.S., Phi Beta Kappa, Alpha Epsilon Delta, Alpha Kappa Kappa. Home: 1512 Wayford Dr Austin TX 78758 Office: Box 96 4110 Guadalupe St Austin TX 78751

STENGER, WILLIAM WALTER, art dealer; b. Atlanta, May 2, 1925; s. Carl Robert and Eleanor Clair (O'Beirne) S.; B.A., U. Ga., 1948. Antique dealer and appraiser porcelain, china, crystal and art works, Atlanta, 1950—; estate evaluation, documentation of decorative arts. Served with USAAF, 1942-45. Mem. Atlanta Arts Alliance, Met. Mus. Art, Am. Soc. Appraisers. Club: Optimist Internat. Home: 2282 Peachtree St NW Atlanta GA 30309 Office: 2205 Peachtree Rd NE Atlanta GA 30309

STENNIS, JOHN CORNELIUS, U.S. senator; b. Kemper County, Miss., Aug. 3, 1901; s. Hampton H. and Cornelia (Adams) S.; B.S., Miss. State Coll., 1923; LL.B., U. Va., 1928; Ph.D. (hon.), Millsaps Coll., U. Wyo.; LL.D., Miss. Coll., Belhaven Coll., 1972; m. Coy Hines, Dec. 24, 1929; children—John Hampton, Margaret Jane. Pvt. practice law, DeKalb, Miss.; mem. Miss. Ho. of Reps., 1928-32; dist. pros. atty., 1931-35; apptd. circuit judge, 1937, elected to same office, 1938, 42, 46; mem. U.S. Senate, 1947—, chmn. Senate Armed Services, mem. Ethics Com., mem. Appropriations, Space coms. Mem. Am. Bar Assn., Miss. Bar Assn., Phi Beta Kappa, Alpha Chi Rho, Phi Alpha Delta. Presbyn. Mason, Lion. Home: DeKalb MS 39328 Office: US Senate Washington DC 20510

STEPHAN, CHARLES ROBERT, ret. naval officer, educator; b. Bklyn., Sept. 30, 1911; s. Charles Albert and Ella (Wallendorf) S.; B.S. in Engring., U.S. Naval Acad., 1934; m. Eleanor Grace Stronck, Feb. 14, 1937; children—Yvonne (Mrs. U.T. Brown), Joan Diane (Mrs. E. Cathcart), Charles Royal, Robert Warren. Commd. ensign USN, 1934, advanced through grades to capt., 1953; air def. officer in U.S.S. Raleigh, Pearl Harbor, 1941; comdg. officer U.S.S. Woodworth, South Pacific, 1943-44; asso. prof. naval sci. Rensselaer Poly. Inst., 1945-46; exec. officer in U.S.S. Iowa, 1951-52; comdr. Destroyer Squadron 8, 6th Fleet, 1959-60; ASW research and devel. dir. Staff Chief Naval Operations, Washington, 1960-63; prof., chmn. ocean engring. dept. Fla. Atlantic U., 1964—. Trustee Fla. Ocean Scis. Inst. Decorated Navy Cross, Bronze Star medals (2). Mem. Marine Technol. Soc. (charter), U.S. Naval Inst., I.E.E.E. (sr.), Am. Soc. Engring. Edn., Am. Assn. U. Profs., Navy League, Fla. Acad. Sci., Soc. Naval Architects and Marine Engrs. Kiwanian (past pres. Sunrise, Boca Raton). Home: 1010 NW 6th Terrace Boca Raton FL 33432

STEPHAN, DAVID GEORGE, govt. ofcl.; b. Columbus, O., Feb. 8, 1930; s. Paul Raymond and Bess (Long) S.; B.Ch.E., Ohio State U., 1952, M.Sc., 1952, Ph.D., 1955; m. Dorothy Spetnagel, June 10, 1951; children—Douglas, Donn, Dean. Technologist AEC Feed Materials Prodn. Center, Fernald, O., 1955; chief air pollution control research USPHS, Cin., 1956-60, dep. chief Advanced Waste Treatment Research Program, 1961-64, dep. chief br. basic and applied scis., 1965-66; dir. research Fed. Water Pollution Control Adminstrn., Dept. Interior, Arlington, Va., 1966-68, asst. commr. research and devel. Fed. Water Quality Adminstrn., 1968-71; dir. research program mgmt. Environmental Protection Agy., Washington, 1971—. Served with USPHS, 1955-64. Mem. Am. Inst. Chem. Engrs., Am. Chem. Soc., Water Pollution Control Fedn., Am. Pub. Works Assn., A.A.A.S., Internat. Assn. for Water Pollution Research, Fed. Water Quality Assn., Ohio State U. Assn., Sigma Xi, Phi Lambda Upsilon, Tau Beta Pi, Texnikoi. Mem. Ch. of Christ (deacon). Home: 9127 Christopher St Fairfax VA 22030 Office: US Environmental Protection Agy Washington DC 20460

STEPHENS, ARIAL AVANT, librarian; b. Charlotte, N.C., July 23, 1932; s. Leroy Chapman and Ibbie Annie (Lowe) S.; A.A., Charlotte Coll., 1952; B.A. in History, U. N.C., 1960, M.S. in Library Sci., 1968; m. Laurie Anne Brockmann, Mar. 26, 1960; children—Laurie Reid, Duncan Gray. Library asst. Mecklenburg County Sch. Library Dept., Charlotte, 1947-52; library asst. Pub. Library Charlotte and Mecklenburg County, Charlotte, 1960-61, asst. dir., 1962-71, dir. libraries, 1971—. Served with USN, 1952-56. N.C. State Library scholar, 1961-62. Mem. Am., Southeastern (chmn. pub. library sect. 1972-74), N.C., Metrolina (pres. 1965-67), Mecklenburg (pres. 1965-66) library assns., Community Execs. Congress (pres. 1971-72). Rotarian. Clubs: Torch (Charlotte, N.C.). Home: 810 Sunnyside Av Charlotte NC 28204 Office: 310 N Tryon St Charlotte NC 28202

STEPHENS, BOBBY GENE, chemist; b. Glendale, S.C., Mar. 8, 1935; s. Dewey and Bertha (Mott) S.; B.S., Wofford Coll., 1957; M.S., Clemson U., 1961, Ph.D., 1964; m. Sandra Elizabeth White, June 27, 1957; children—Barbara, Edward, Robert, Adam. Textile chemist Reeves Bros., Inc., Fairforest, S.C., 1957-58; asst. prof. chemistry Wofford Coll., 1963-67, asso. prof., 1967-72, dean Coll., 1972—; research chemist Dept. Health, Edn. and Welfare, Cin., 1964. Chmn. Spartanburg (S.C.) Environmental Pollution Tech. Adv. Bd., 1968—; v.p. Spartanburg County Pollution Control Authority, 1971—. Served to 1st lt. AUS, 1958-60. Mem. Am. Chem. Soc., S.C. Acad. Sci. (Jefferson award 1969), Am. Soc. Testing and Materials (mem. com. sampling and analysis atmospheres). Methodist. Home: 129 Bellwood Lane Spartanburg SC 29302

STEPHENS, CHARLES ANTHON, physician; b. Camden, Tex., Oct. 13, 1925; s. Buford Dured and Carrie (Collins) Stephens; B.A., U. Tex., 1950, M.D., 1954; m. Nancy Raisch, June 25, 1954; children—Deborah, Claudia, Charles Anthon II, Barbara, Jerry. Intern Univ. Hosp., Little Rock, 1954-55; resident U. Tex. Med. Br., Galveston, 1955-58; practice medicine specializing in obstetrics-gynecology, Odessa, Tex., 1958—; mem. staff Med. Center Hosp., chief of staff 1962. Bd. dirs. Odessa Community Chest and United Fund, 1959-60, Ector County Assn. Retarded Children, Midland-Odessa Mental Health-Mental Retardation Bd. Served with USNR, 1943-46. Diplomate Am. Bd. Obstetrics and Gynecology. Fellow Am. Coll. Obstetrics-Gynecology; mem. Am., Tex. med. assns., Andrews, Ector County med. socs., Willard R. Cooke Obstetrics-Gynecology Soc., Pi Kappa Alpha, Phi Chi. Home: 3204 Blossom Lane Odessa TX 79760 Office: 808 Tower Dr Odessa TX 79760

STEPHENS, EDGAR JACOB, JR., lawyer, state legislator; b. New Albany, Miss., May 26, 1916; s. Edgar Jacob and Annabel (Wiseman) S.; student Erskine Coll., 1934-35; B.A., U. Miss., 1938, J.D., 1940. Admitted to Miss. bar, 1940; practiced in New Albany, 1941—; real estate broker, 1962—; pros. atty. Union County, New Albany, 1945-51; mem. Miss. Ho. of Reps., 1952—. Mem. Miss. Commn. Budget and Accounting, Miss. Medicaid Commn. Trustee, Pub. Employees' Retirement System. Served with USNR, 1942-45. Mem. Miss. State Bar, Am. Legion, Phi Delta Phi, Sigma Chi. Democrat. Presbyn. Home: Glenwood New Albany MS 38652 Office: PO Box 330 New Albany MS 38652

STEPHENS, ELVIS CLAY, educator; b. Childress, Tex., Jan. 9, 1934; s. Leslie and Dell (Farrow) S.; B.B.A., North Tex. State U., 1958, M.B.A., 1959; D.B.A., Ind. U., 1966; m. Loleta Joyce Perkins, Feb. 4, 1956; children—Daryl Lynn, Jennifer Sue. With field advt. dept. Procter & Gamble Co., Cin., 1951-53; instr. Austin Coll., 1959-61; asst. prof. North Tex. State U. Sch. Bus., Denton, 1963-69, asso. prof., 1969-71, prof., 1971—, chmn. dept., 1969—. Served to 1st lt. AUS, 1953-56. Mem. Indsl. Relations Research Assn. (chpt. sec.-treas. 1966-68), Am. Soc. for Personnel Adminstrn. (chpt. pres. 1969), Dallas Personnel Assn., Am. Soc. for Tng. and Devel. (pres. chpt. 1972), Beta Gamma Sigma. Methodist. Home: 2321 Kayewood Dr Denton TX 76201

STEPHENS, FRANCIS LEE, food store corp. exec.; b. Nacogdoches, Tex., Mar. 5, 1938; s. Edward C. and Edith (Gray) S.; student Stephen F. Austin State Coll., 1955-56, Syracuse U., 1956-57, San Antonio Coll., 1959-60; B.A. in Econs., U. Tex., 1962; m. Pollyanna Allison, Sept. 21, 1958; children—Susan Camille, Elizabeth Dawn. With Town & Country Food Stores, Inc., 1960—, v.p., 1964—, partner, 1965—, also dir. Dir. 1st Nat. Bank. Pres. county chpt. Am. Cancer Soc., 1969-71, state bd. dirs., 1971-72; co-chmn. with wife 1st Ann. Fiesta del Concho, 1973, 2d Ann. Fiesta, 1974. Mem. city commn., San Angelo, 1972-74. Bd. dirs. Tex. Jr. C. of C. Hosp. Found., 1968-69, Fort Concho Mus., San Angelo, Tex., 1968-71; trustee MH-MR Center Greater West Tex., 1970-71; trustee Tex. Law Enforcement and Youth Devel. Found., 1970-71, pres., 1972. Served with USAF, 1956-60. Recipient awards including Sparkplug of Year award Tex. Jr. C. of C., 1967; named One of Five Outstanding Young Texans, Tex. Jaycees, 1971. Mem. U.S. (nat. dir. 1968-69), Tex. (v.p. 1968-69), San Angelo (pres. 1967-68) jr. chambers commerce, Tex. Retail Grocers Assn. (dir. 1971-73), San Angelo C. of C. (v.p. 1971, dir. 1969-71), West Tex. C. of C. (dist. v.p. 1970-74), Angelo State U. Ram Club (pres. 1971-72). Presbyn. (bd. deacons, tchr. Sunday Sch.). Home: 2738 Briargrove St San Angelo TX 76901 Office: 2021 Austin St San Angelo TX 76901

STEPHENS, JAMES CLAYTON, lawyer, judge; b. nr. Dublin, Ga., July 19, 1941; s. James Clayton and Nita (Luke) S.; A.B., Mercer U., 1963; LL.B., Walter F. George Sch. Law, 1965; m. Helena Lee Reeves, July 24, 1969; 1 son, William Pinckney. Admitted to Ga. bar, 1965; gen. practice law, Soperton, Ga., 1965—; judge Ct. Ordinary, Treutlen County, Ga., 1967—; solicitor-pro-tem, State Ct. Treutlen, 1969—; city atty., Soperton, 1969—. Chmn. Treutlen County A.R.C., 1966—. Mem. bd. dirs. Heart Ga. Planning and Devel. Commn., 1967-69. Served with AUS, 1965. Recipient Outstanding Citizen award Heart of Ga. Planning and Devel. Commn., 1968. Mem. Am. Judicature Soc., Lambda Chi Alpha, Phi Delta Phi. Lion (sec., treas. 1966—). Clubs: Treutlen Boosters (v.p. 1968), Treutlen County Sportsmen's (pres. 1969). Home: 114 New St Soperton GA 30457 Office: Treutlen County Courthouse Soperton GA 30457

STEPHENS, JOHN AMOS, physician; b. Monticello, Ga., June 10, 1914; s. Amos Mack and Lucille (Shell) S.; grad. Ga. Mil. Acad., 1930; student Emory U., 1930-34; A.B., U. Tenn., 1936; M.D., George Washington U., 1942; m. Eva Curtis Williamson, June 5, 1943; 1 dau., Dorothy Arnett (Mrs. Raymond L. Barnes). Intern Grady Hosp., Atlanta, 1942-43; practice medicine, Laurel, Md., 1946-50, Waycross, Ga., 1950-52; resident internal medicine Riverside Hosp., Jacksonville, Fla., 1952-54; practice specializing in internal medicine, Jacksonville, 1954-69; emergency room Bapt. Meml. Hosp., 1969-70; med. dir. Gulf Life Ins. Co., Jacksonville, 1970—; med. officer U.S. P.O., Jacksonville, 1970—. Courtesy staff Bapt. Meml., Methodist, St. Vincent's, St. Luke's hosps., Duval Med. Center. Trustee Bapt. Home for Children. Served to capt. USAAF, M.C., AUS, 1943-46. Mem. A.C.P. (life), Am. Soc. Internal Medicine, Assn. Life Ins. Med. Dirs. Am., Fla. Med. Assn., A.M.A., Duval County Med. Soc. (chmn. com. medicine and religion, 1965-66), Sigma Nu, Phi Chi. Baptist (deacon). Clubs: South Jacksonville Civitan, San Jose Country; Pontevedra, University. Home: 4382 San Jose Lane Jacksonville FL 32207 Office: Gulf Life Tower Jacksonville FL 32207

STEPHENS, JOHN CARNES, hydraulic engr.; b. Attalla, Ala., Sept. 22, 1910; s. John J. and Margaret Editha (Carnes) S.; B.S., Ala. U., 1931; postgrad. Stanford, 1931-32; m. Phelia Frances Walker, Sept. 10, 1936; children—John Carnes, Mary Louise, Margaret Editha. Agrl. engr. Soil Conservation Service, U.S. Dept. Agr., Dadeville, Ala., 1933-39, asst. project engr. Everglades Project, Ft. Lauderdale, Fla., 1939-42, project engr., 1942-46, research project supr., 1949-54, research project engr. Agrl. Research Service, 1954-61, research investigations leader, watershed engr. So. br. Soil and Water Conservation, Ft. Lauderdale, 1961-62; research investigations leader, dir. S.E. Watershed Research Center, Athens, Ga., 1962-70; chief N.W. br. Soil and Water Conservation, Agrl. Research Service, Boise, Ida., 1970-72, research area dir. Mississippi Valley area So. region Agrl. Research Service, Stoneville, Miss., 1972—; water control engr. Dade County (Fla.), 1946-49. Collaborator Central-So. Fla. Flood Control Dist., 1949—. Registered profl. engr., Fla. Mem. Am. Geophys. Union, Am. Soc. Agrl. Engrs., Am. Soc. C.E. (exec. com. irrigation and drainage div. 1964-72, mem. mgmt. group D water resources 1972—), Am. Water Resources Assn., Soil Conservation Soc. Am., Scabbard and Blade, Sigma Phi Epsilon. Presbyn. Rotarian. Contbr. articles to profl. jours. Home: 114 Plantation Dr Leland MS 38756 Office: Room 104 US Delta State Agrl Research Center Stoneville MS 38776

STEPHENS, JOHN KIRKER, educator; b. Chgo., July 10, 1941; s. Rothwell and Margaret (Clark) S.; B.A. with high honors, Swarthmore Coll., 1962; M.A., U. Ill., 1963, Ph.D., 1967; postdoctoral research fellow, Yale, 1971-72; m. Dorothy Claire Faust, June 9, 1961; children—Fern Margaret, Owen Kirker Clifford. Mathematician, U.S. Naval Missile Center, Pt. Mugu, Cal., summers 1965, 66; asst. prof. econs. U. Okla., Norman, 1967-71, asso. prof., 1971—. Cons. economist Bur. for Bus. and Econ. Research, 1968-71. Cons. Okla. Gov.'s Adv. Com. on Taxation, 1968-70. Fellow NSF Cooperative. Nat. Merit scholar. Mem. Am., Western econ. assns., Royal Econ. Soc., Econometric Soc., Math. Assn. of Am., Am. Assn. U. Profs., Phi Beta Kappa, Sigma Xi (asso.), Omicron Delta Epsilon, Pi Mu Epsilon, Beta Gamma Sigma, Tau Alpha Omicron. Republican. Episcopalian. Contbr. articles to profl. jours. Home: 1206 Classen Blvd Norman OK 73069

STEPHENS, LEVIE BURDESHAW, state ofcl.; b. Skippersville, Ala., Dec. 5, 1905; s. James Arthur and Martha (Burdeshaw) S.; B.S., U. Ala., 1926; LL.B., Jones Law Sch., 1949; m. Lottie Jackson, June 1, 1930; children—Martha (Mrs. William Stancik), Janella (Mrs. Thomas Esslinger). Admitted to Ala. bar, 1950; tchr., coach high schs. Ala., 1926-34; social case worker, A.R.C. and Jefferson County Dept. Pub. Welfare, 1934-37; probation officer Juvenile and Domestic Relations Ct., Birmingham 1937-39; probation and parole officer Ala. Bd. Pardons & Paroles, Montgomery, 1939-40, supr. probation and parole officers, 1940-43, exec. dir., 1944—; dir. Ga. Bd. Pardons and Paroles, 1943-44. Mem. profl. council Nat. Council Crime and Delinquency, mem. adv. council on parole. Mem. Ala. Probation and Parole Assn. (pres. 1952), So. States Probation and Parole Conf. (pres. 1949), Parole and Probation Compact Adminstrs. Assn. (adminstr. 1949—), Nat. Probation and Parole Assn., Assn. Paroling Authorities (exec. com.), Am. Correctional Assn. (dir. 1962—). Kiwanian. Home: 3049 Cloverdale Rd Montgomery AL 36106 Office: 654 State Adminstrn Bldg Montgomery AL 36104

STEPHENS, MCDONALD LEE, automobile dealership exec.; b. Richmond, Va., Apr. 15, 1926; s. Ennolls A. and Ann (Lee) S.; student Washington and Lee U., 1942-43; B.B.A., Tulane U., 1946; m. Mary Elizabeth Holmes, July 11, 1947; children—Ann Lee (Mrs. N.C. Curtis III), Elizabeth, Martha, Mary. Part-owner Tides Inn Hotel, Irvington, Va., 1947—, Stephens Buick (named changed to Stephens Chevrolet 1959), New Orleans, 1947—; owner Tchoupitoulas Plantation Restaurant, New Orleans, 1968—; pres. Stephens Mercedes-Benz Imports, New Orleans, 1971—. Mem. Internat. House, New Orleans. Past pres. Louis S. McGehee Sch. Bd., New Orleans. Mem. alumni bd. dirs. Tulane U., New Orleans. Served with USNR, 1942-46. Mem. Nat., La., New Orleans automobile dealers assns., New Orleans Restaurant Assn., New Orleans C. of C., YMCA. Episcopalian (vestryman). Club: New Orleans Country. Home: 2858 Chestnut St New Orleans LA 70115 Office: 840 Carondelet St New Orleans LA 70130

STEPHENS, ROBERT GRIER, JR., U.S. congressman; b. Atlanta, Aug. 14, 1913; s. Robert Grier and Martha Lucy (Evans) S.; A.B., U. Ga., 1935, M.A., 1937, LL.B. cum laude, 1941; exchange student U. Hamburg (Germany), 1935-36; m. Grace Winston, July 20, 1938; children—Grace Winston (Mrs. D.R. Bianchi), Robert Grier III, Mary Winston, Lawton Evans. Mem. staff dept. history and polit. sci. U. Ga., 1938-41, 46; admitted to Ga. bar, 1941; practice in Athens, 1946-60; city atty., Athens, 1947-50; mem. Ga. Senate, 1951-53, Ga. Ho. of Reps., 1953-59; mem. 87th-93d congresses from 10th Dist. Ga. Gen. counsel Ga. Press Assn., 1959-61. Mem. Ga. Democratic Exec. Com. Bd. dirs. Athens YMCA. Served with AUS, 1941-46; legal staff Nuremberg Trial, 1945; lt. col. Res. Mem. Am. Legion, V.F.W., Athens C. of C. (dir.), Phi Beta Kappa, Phi Kappa Phi, Omicron Delta Kappa, Kappa Alpha. Presbyn. (elder). Kiwanian (lt. gov.). Home: 435 Woodward Way Athens GA 30601 Office: House Office Bldg Washington DC 20515

STEPHENS, ROBERT JOEL, diversified industry co. exec.; b. Nocona, Tex., Feb. 20, 1925; s. Joel Morgan and Susan (Simpson) S.; B.S., Okla. A. and M. Coll., 1949; M.S., Okla. State U., 1958; m. Lorene Shirley Robertson, Dec. 22, 1949; children—Robert Joel, David Arthur, Karen Sue. County agt. extension div. Okla. State U., Stillwater, 1954-57; property appraiser Okla. Hwy. Dept. and Fed. Bur. Roads, Oklahoma City, 1957-58; founder, pres. Robert J. Stephens Co., Anadarko, Okla., 1951—; chmn. bd. pres. 27 corps., including Preferred Mut. Inc., Oklahoma City, 1969—, So. Pub. Co., Apache, Okla., 1972—, Soil Conservation Contractors, Nocona, Tex., 1971—. Mem. Okla. Bd. Nursing Homes, 1963—; adviser transp. to Gov. Okla., 1970—. Bd. dirs. J.M. Stephens Scholarship Trust. Served with USNR, 1944-46; PTO. Mem. Anadarko C. of C. (past pres.), Okla. State Nursing Home Assn. (v.p.). Mason (Shriner). Home: 412

Country Club Dr Anadarko OK 73005 Office: 201 W Kansas St Anadarko OK 73005

STEPHENS, ROBERT KENNETH, accountant; b. Newbern, Tenn., Nov. 23, 1914; s. Thomas David and Mary Louise (Denton) S.; B.S. in Commerce, U. Tenn., 1937; postgrad. accounting LaSalle Extension U., 1939-42; m. Lillian Magdalene Leigh, July 2, 1938 (dec. Mar. 1973); children—Linda Louise (Mrs. Steven Hodges Brasfield), Mary Catherine (Mrs. Donald Estes). Tchr., Miller-Hawykins Bus. Coll., Memphis, 1937-38; dean, tchr. Tupelo (Miss.) Bus. Coll., 1938-39; auditor U.S. Dept. Agr., Little Rock, 1940-42, Jackson, Miss., 1942-46; individual practice pub. accounting, Jackson, 1946—; sec.-treas. Underwood Glass Co., New Orleans, 1956—. C.P.A., Miss., Tenn. Mem. Am. Inst. C.P.A.'s, Miss. Soc. C.P.A.'s, Miss. Econ. Council, Jackson C. of C. Baptist (clk.). Club: Jackson Country. Home: 3939 Hawthorn Dr Jackson MS 39206 Office: 2715 N State St Jackson MS 39216

STEPHENS, ROBERT OREN, educator; b. Corpus Christi, Tex., Oct. 2, 1928; s. Joseph Key and Mary Emma (Robertson) S.; student Del Mar Coll., 1945-47; B.A., Tex. Coll. Arts and Industries, 1949; M.A., U. Tex., 1951, Ph.D., 1958; m. Carey Virginia Jones, Sept. 8, 1956; children—Nancy Leigh, Melissa Ann, Robert Allan. Tchr. English, Shiner (Tex.) High Sch., 1949-50; spl. instr. English, U. Tex., 1957-58, 58-61; asst. prof. English, U. N.C. at Greensboro, 1961-66, asso. prof., 1966-68, prof., 1968—. Served to lt. USNR, 1951-55. Mem. Am. Studies Assn., Am. Assn. U. Profs., Modern Lang. Assn., South Atlantic Modern Lang. Assn. Presbyn. (elder 1965). Author: Hemingway's Nonfiction: The Public Voice, 1968; Ernest Hemingway: The Critical Reception, 1974. Contbr. articles to profl. jours. Home: 1706 Sylvan Rd Greensboro NC 27403

STEPHENS, STEVE, pub. relations, advt. co. exec.; b. Newport, Ark., Apr. 22, 1930; s. Owen and Allie Mae (Rozzell) S.; student U. Little Rock, 1948; B.S. in Bus. Adminstrn., U. Ark., 1951; postgrad. U. Miss., 1954-55; L.H.D., Southwestern Coll., Oklahoma City; m. Ellen Beede, Apr. 21, 1957; children—Stanton, Steele. With CBS-TV, Little Rock, 1957-65; spl. asst. to U.S. Senator John L. McClellan, Washington, 1965-68; corporate v.p. pub. relations and advt. Nat. Investors Life Ins. Co., Little Rock, 1968-69; pres., chmn bd. Stephens Internat., Ltd., Little Rock, 1969—; chmn. bd., chief exec. officer Stephens & Goodwin Investments, Inc., Stephens Investments, Inc., Stephens Internat. Travel Inc.; dir. Bolivian Internat. Devel., Sociedad Anomina. State adviser Nat. Found., 1960-64; mem. exec. com. Radio Free Europe, 1961-62; state chmn. Arthritis Found., 1969; state adviser Youth Leadership Council, 1961-65; chmn. Little Rock City Beautiful Commn., 1961-62; mem. Pulaski County Health and Welfare Council, 1961-62; del. Inter-Am. Partners Alliance for Progress Conf., Lima, Peru, Partners of Ams. Hemispheric Conf., San Jose, Costa Rica, 1968; chmn. publicity United Fund campaign, 1968, bd. dirs., 1969-71; publicity chmn., dist. vice chmn. Pioneer dist. Boy Scouts Am., 1969-70; state chmn. March Dimes, 1973-74; state chmn. Internat. Youth for Understanding; bd. adv. trustees Direct Relief Found.; bd. dirs. Internat. Services for Blind, Inc.; bd. visitors Army-Navy Acad. Named Bolivian Consul Gen. for Ark., Bolivian Pres., 1969. Served with USMC, 1951-54. Recipient Service to Humanity award Little Rock Jaycees. Mem. Internat. Assn. Polit. Consultants, Little Rock C. of C., Brit. Inst. Pub. Relations (overseas asso.), Sales and Marketing Execs. Pub. Relations Soc. Am. Mason (Shriner, 32 deg.). Clubs: Little Rock, Racquet, Capitol, Pleasant Valley Country; Bahama Sound Beach. Home: 2823 Painted Valley Dr Little Rock AR 72207 Office: Tower Bldg Little Rock AR 72201

STEPHENS, WILLIAM DAVID, chemist; b. Paris, Tenn., Nov. 11, 1932; s. Claude Elmer and Lillian (Cole) S.; B.S., Western Ky. State U., 1954; Ph.D., Vanderbilt U., 1959; m. Marilyn Jean Miller, Sept. 11, 1954; children—William Daniel, Steve-Anna, Jennifer Lynn. Chief organic chem. sect. Thiokol Chem. Co., Redstone Arsenal, Huntsville, Ala., 1959-63, supr. synthetic chemistry and propellant research group, 1966—; head basic materials research lab. Goodyear Tire & Rubber Co., Akron, O., 1963-66. Asso. prof. chemistry U. Ala., Huntsville, 1966—. Mem. Am. Chem. Soc. (sect. dir.). Home: 8912 Willow Hills Dr Huntsville AL 35802 Office: Thiokol Chem Corp Redstone Arsenal Huntsville AL 35807

STEPHENS, WILLIAM THEODORE, lawyer; b. Balt., Mar. 31, 1922; s. William A. and Mildred (Griffin) S.; student Balt. City Coll., 1939-41, U. Md., 1946-47; A.B., J.D., George Washington U., 1950, postgrad., 1951; m. Arlene Alice Lesti, June 2, 1958; children—William Theodore, Renee Adena. Admitted to Md. bar, 1950; also D.C., Va. bars; mem. firm J.L. Green, Washington, 1950-51, J.M. Cooper, Washington, 1952-54; own law firm William T. Stephens, Washington, 1955—. Dir. Exotech, Inc., Gaithersburg, Md., Financial Services Holding Corp., Wichita, Kan., KHI Corp., Fairfax, Va., Hamilton Bank & Trust Co., Bailey's Cross Roads, Va., Inter Financial Corp. Del. Mem. adv. bd., exec. com. Nat. Com. on Uniform Traffic Laws and Ordinances. Trustee Ophthalmic Research Found., Washington, Fairfax-Brewster Sch., Falls Church, Va., Am. Bikeways Found., Washington. Served to 1st lt. AUS, 1941-46. Mem. Am. Bar Assn. (sec. taxation 1959—, sec. corps., banking and bus. law 1960—). XVI Corps Assn. (pres. 1967), Kappa Alpha order (Ct. of Honor), Delta Theta Phi. Clubs: Commonwealth (Cal.), University, Capitol Hill (Washington); Fairfax Racquet (dir.); Racquet International, Jockey (Miami, Fla.). Home: 6636 Tansey Dr Falls Church VA 22042 #also 881 Ocean Dr Key Biscayne FL 33149 Office: 1000 Vermont Av Washington DC 20005

STEPHENSON, ALEXANDER BASIL, banker; b. Jacksonville, Fla., Oct. 9, 1925; s. John Edmond and Marie (Lohse) S.; student The Citadel, 1943; B.S. in Banking and Finance, U. Fla., 1949; m. Barbara Wickham, June 18, 1948; children—Robert, James, William. Loan officer Atlantic Nat. Bank, Jacksonville, 1950-52; 1st v.p., dir. Springfield Atlantic Bank, Jacksonville, 1952—. Served with USNR, World War II; PTO. Clubs: Jacksonville Marine Assn., St. John's River Yacht, North Florida Cruising. Home: 5525 Lakewood Circle E Jacksonville FL 32207 Office: W Bay Sta Jacksonville FL 32206

STEPHENSON, ALLEN DECOSTA, JR., assn. exec.; b. Raleigh, N.C., May 6, 1927; s. Allen D. and Georgia (Smith) S.; student N.C. State Coll., 1946-47; B.B.A., Wake Forest Coll., 1950; m. Betty Jean Herrington, Oct. 8, 1960; children—Lisa Marie, Sandra Jean. Asst. mgr. Rocky Mount (N.C.) C. of C., 1954-55; mgr. Carrollton (Ga.) C. of C., 1955-59; dir. indsl. relations Assn. Industries Ga., Atlanta, 1959-61; exec. dir. Athens (Ga.) Area C. of C., 1961—. Sec.-treas., dir. N.E. Ga. Area Planning and Devel. Assn., 1962—; exec. dir. Athens-Clarke County Indsl. Devel. Authority. Served with USNR, 1945-46. Mem. Am., So., Ga. (pres. 1967) chamber commerce execs. assns., Ga. Indsl. Developers Assn. (pres. 1972). Baptist. Rotarian. Home: 201 Woodward Way Athens GA 30601 Office: PO Box 948 Athens GA 30601

STEPHENSON, CHARLES MILLARD, govt. ofcl.; b. Kite, Ga., Oct. 23, 1910; s. Jubilee S. and Annie (Hatcher) S.; B.B.A. cum laude, Emory U., 1930; M.A., U. Ky., 1932, postgrad., 1932-34; m. Laura Norwood Roberson, May 1, 1936; children—Ann Marie (Mrs. Bruce Lynn Welch), Peter Martin, Hilary, Laura Paine, Elizabeth. Research accountant Ky. Tax Reduction Assn., Louisville, 1933; state supr. municipal and county finance study Civil Works Adminstrn., Ky., 1933-34; adminstrv. asst. Bur. Bus. Research, U. Ky., Lexington, 1934; economist TVA, Knoxville, Tenn., 1934-68, chief govt. research staff, div. nav. devel. and regional studies, 1968—. Mem. Nat. Tax Assn.-Tax Inst. Am. (mem. intergovt. fiscal relations com.), Am. Soc. for Pub. Adminstrn., Delta Sigma Pi, Beta Gamma Sigma. Democrat. Unitarian-Universalist. Author: Industrial Sites: A Community Problem, 1961. Editorial adv. bd. Nat. Tax. Jour. Home: 1803 Westchester Dr Knoxville TN 37918 Office: Arnstein Bldg Knoxville TN 37902

STEPHENSON, DAVID CARTER, clergyman; b. Morganton, N.C., July 3, 1938; s. Oscar Lee and Edith Mae (Woodward) S.; B.Th., Gulf Coast Bible Coll., Houston, 1962; m. Georgetta Sansil Harrington, Nov. 6, 1959; children—Ronnie Earl, Andy Lee. Ordained to ministry Ch. of God, 1963; pastor, Conroe, Tex., 1960-62, First Ch. of God, Darlington, S.C., 1964—. Evangelist, music dir., conf. leader across Am.; vice chmn. So. Ministers Conv., 1973-74; host daily radio program WDAR, Darlington, 1972—; singer with Gospel Four Singers. Mem. adv. com. Darlington County Sch. Bd. Recipient Alumnus of Year award Gulf Coast Bible Coll., 1973. Kiwanian. Home: 509 Shearin St Darlington SC 29532 Office: N Main St Darlington SC 29532

STEPHENSON, FRED DOUGLAS, psychiat. social worker; b. Pontiac, Mich., Sept. 21, 1939; s. Leonard Earl and Myrland (Coleman) S.; A.B., U. Mich., 1961; postgrad. U. Cal., 1962; A.M., U. Chgo., 1965; diploma, Gestalt Inst. Cleve., 1972; m. Kay S. Donald, June 3, 1962; children—Shawn, Anne. Pub. health program asso. Tb and Health Assn., Santa Ana, Cal., 1961-63; psychiat. social worker Chgo. State Hosp., 1964, Tinley Park (Ill.) State Hosp., 1965-67; chief psychiat. social worker Community Mental Health Services, Gainesville, Fla., 1967-69; individual practice in individual marriage and family psychotherapy, Gainesville, 1969—; instr. psychiatry U. Fla. at Gainesville, 1969—; field faculty mem. Goddard Coll., Plainfield, Vt., 1972—. Mem. Nat. Assn. Social Workers, Nat. Alliance Family Life (clin.), Am. Assn. Marriage and Family Counselors (clin.), Acad. Certified Social Workers. Editor Gestalt Therapy Primer, Readings in Gestalt Therapy. Home: Route 5 Box 464 Gainesville FL 32601

STEPHENSON, JIMMYE MITCHELL, educator; b. Oklahoma City, June 18, 1928; d. Harold Gentry and Vera (Mitchell) Stephenson; B.A., John Brown U., 1950; B.S.N., Tulane U., 1953; diploma Mather Sch. Nursing, 1953; M.N., Emory U., 1960; Specialist in Coll. Teaching degree Murray State U., 1971. Staff nurse So. Bapt. Hosp., New Orleans, 1953; asst. instr. Northwestern St. Coll. La., Natchitoches, 1954-59, asst. prof., 1959-61; chmn. dept. nursing N.E. Miss. Jr. Coll., Booneville, 1962-63; asst. prof. nursing Berea (Ky.) Coll., 1963-69, student acad. adviser student nurse recruitment programs, 1963-69, adviser Berea Coll. Assn. Student Nurses, 1964-69; asso. prof. dept. nursing Murray (Ky.) State U., 1969-73; dean Sch. Nursing and Allied Health Scis. Florence (Ala.) State U., 1973—. Mem. Am., Ky., Ala. nurses assns., Ala., Nat., Ky. leagues for nursing. Democrat. Baptist. Home: Box 634 Florence State U Florence AL 35630

STEPHENSON, MALVINA, syndicated columnist, radio reporter; b. Paris, Tex.; d. Robert E. and Allie (King) Stephenson; A.B. in Govt. History, Southeast State Coll.; M.S. in Journalism, U. Okla. Feature writer, reporter Tulsa World; columnist; with Stephenson News Bur., 1963—; radio reporter ABC, Washington; editorial and research asst. to Senator R.S. Kerr, 1951-63; syndicated columnist Washington Offbeat, Knight Newspapers Wire Service, 1969—; with Chgo. Tribune Syndicate, Washington, 1970—; commentator all-news radio sta. WTOP, Washington, 1972—. Mem. Delta Delta Delta. Clubs: Washington Press, Am. Newspaper. Co-editor: Land, Wood and Water (Sen. Robert S. Kerr), 1960. Home: 330 A St SE Washington DC 20003

STEPHENSON, PHIL, finance co. exec.; b. Gaffney, S.C., Oct. 24, 1912; s. George L. and Osie (Simmons) S.; student Mars Hill Jr. Coll., 1932-33, U. S.C., 1933-37; m. Edna Louise Mottern, Aug. 12, 1937 (div. 1964); children—Phil, Robert, Kathy. Vice pres. Dixie Glove Mfg. Co., Gaffney, 1937-39; Ford dealer, Gaffney, 1939—; organized Stephenson Finance Co., Inc., 1947, now operating 100 brs. in South; organizer Superior Automobile Ins. Co., Florence, S.C., 1952, Superior Life Ins. Co., 1954; organizer, chmn. bd. Westchester Nat. Bank of Dede County, Miami, Fla., 1964, Peoples Bank of S.C., Florence, 1965; organizer, dir. Midway Nat. Bank, Miami, Fla.; dir. NCNB Corp., Charlotte, N.C. Bd. dirs. S.C. Found. Ind. Colls., Inc., So. States Indsl. Council, Nothville, Tenn.; trustee Limestone Coll., Gaffney; mem. devel. adv. council U. S.C. Mem. Am. Indsl. Bankers Assn. (dir. at large). Episcopalian. Clubs: City (Charlotte), Poinsetta (Greenville, S.C.); Racquet, Palm Bay, Jockey (Miami, Fla.); Florence Country. Home: 950 Park Av Florence SC 29501 Office: 518 S Irby St Florence SC 29501

STEPHENSON, RICHARD MURRELL, clergyman; b. nr. Ivor, Va., Dec. 1, 1921; s. Edgar Vick and Eleanor (Daughtrey) S.; B.A., Hampden-Sydney Coll., 1943; Th.M., So. Bapt. Theol. Sem., 1946; D.D., U. Richmond, Va., 1966; m. Noralee Mellor, Feb. 1, 1949; children—Vivian, Lee, Richard. Ordained to ministry Bapt. Ch., 1944; pastor First Bapt. Ch., Ft. Myers, Fla., 1946-50; pastor Columbia Bapt. Ch., Falls Church, Va., 1950-67; exec. sec. Bapt. Gen. Assn. Va., Richmond, 1968—; dir. So. Bapt. Found., Nashville. Trustee So. Bapt. Theol. Sem., Louisville, Hon. chaplain Army, 1965. Mem. Omicron Delta Kappa, Eta Sigma Phi. Kiwanian. Home: 8951 Bellefonte Rd Richmond VA 23229 Office: PO Box 8568 Richmond VA 23226

STEPHENSON, ROBERT EDWARD, librarian; b. Katonah, N.Y., June 22, 1923; s. John and Etta Lillian (Adams) S.; A.B., Hamilton Coll., 1948; M.S. in L.S., Columbia, 1950; m. Mary White Thompson, June 17, 1961; children—Thomas Robert, Barbara Ann. With Va. Poly. Inst. and State U. (formerly Va. Poly. Inst.), Blacksburg, 1949—, documents librarian, acting asso. librarian tech. services, 1961-62, asso. librarian tech. services, 1962-71, architecture librarian, 1972—, mem. faculty senate, senate cabinet, 1973—. Vice pres. Blacksburg Regional Art Assn., 1970-71, pres., 1971-72; mem. Blacksburg Council on Human Relations, 1959-63; mem. Blacksburg Ministerial Assn., 1955—. Served with USAAF, 1943-46. Mem. A.L.A., Va. (2d v.p. 1966-67), Southeastern library assns., Potomac Tech. Processing Librarians (exec. com. 1964-65), Am. Assn. U. Profs. (membership com. chpt. 1965-66). Christian Scientist. Clubs: Va. Polytechnic Institute University, Blacksburg Country (Blacksburg). Home: 1206 Highland Circle SE Blacksburg VA 24060

STEPHENSON, ROBERT JUBILEE, civil engr.; b. Vidalia, Ga., Apr. 8, 1932; s. Jubilee Smith and Annie (Hatcher) S.; B.C.E., Ga. Inst. Tech., 1954; postgrad. soil mechanics Harvard, 1963; m. Patricia Ann Kent, June 9, 1954; children—Daniel Kent, Barbara Eleanor. Coop. student-worker Ga. Hwy. Dept., 1950-52; jr. engr. C.E., Atlanta, 1954-57, staff soil mechanics br. South Atlantic div. lab., Marietta, Ga., 1957-68, br. chief, 1968-71, dir. South Atlantic Div. Lab. C.E., Marietta, 1971—; cons. in field. Served with AUS, 1955-57. Registered profl. engr., Ga. Mem., Nat., Ga. socs. profl. engrs., Am. Soc. C.E., Am. Soc. Testing and Materials, Contbr. article to profl. jour. Home: 399 Seminole Dr NE Marietta GA 30060 Office: PO Box 51 Marietta GA 30060

STEPHENSON, ROYCE LEE, realtor; b. Jasper, Tex., Aug. 19, 1930; s. William Jennings and Euleen (Orton) S.; student Lamar U., 1957; m. Fay Hardy, Oct. 29, 1949; children—Reagan, Kit, Chris, Kirk. Asst. mgr. Oxford Bldg. Mfg. Co., Beaumont, Tex., 1950-59; mgr. Chambers County Lumber Co., Winnie, Tex., 1959-66, Jasper Investment Corp. (Tex.), 1966-72; owner Royce Stephenson Co. realty and bldg., Jasper, 1972—. Charter v.p. Winnie Med. Center, 1965. Mem. state com. Tex. Realtor mag., 1972—. Mem. Nat. Assn. Real Estate Bds., Tex. Assn. Realtors, Deep E. Tex. Bd. Realtors (pres. 1970-71). Lion (pres. 1962-63). Home: Route 2 Box 330 Jasper TX 75951 Office: US 190 S Jasper TX 75751

STEPHENSON, WILLIAM HAYWOOD, state ofcl.; b. Johnson County, Willow Springs, N.C., Nov. 26, 1927; s. William P. and Lois (Partin) S.; student Hoyles Bus. Sch., 1947-48; m. Della F. Coates, Mar. 10, 1949; children—William Timothy, John Phillip. With U.S. Mcht. Marines, 1945-46; with N.C. Indsl. Commn., Raleigh, 1948—, exec. sec., 1960-70, dep. commr., 1970, commr., 1970—. Chmn. Wake County (N.C.) Bd. Elections, 1964-70. Mem. N.C. Shorthand Reporters Assn. (organizer, sec. 1957), So. Assn. Workmen's Compensation Adminstrs., Internat. Assn. Indsl. Accident Bds. and Commns., Woodmen of World. Democrat. Methodist (chmn. pastor-parish relations com. 1974—). Elk. Club: Colonial (Garner; pres. 1967-68). Home: 1207 Poplar Av Garner NC 27529 Office: Eastgate Office Center Raleigh NC 27611

STEPP, EVERETT HOLMES, power plant design engr.; b. Hatfield, Ky., Oct. 4, 1916; s. Mose G. and Cosbie (Alley) S.; B.E.E., U. Ky., 1941; student Harvard U., 1943; m. Mary Margaret Royce, June 20, 1942; children—Mary (Mrs. George Dewey Schou), John Everett, Joseph Thomas. Tchr., Bent Branch Sch., Hatfield, Ky., 1937-39; jr. engr. TVA, Knoxville, 1941-42; engr. draftsman Frasier Brace Engrng. Co. Inc., Holston Ordnance Works, Kingsport, Tenn., 1942-43; W. C. Olsen Engrng., Raleigh, N.C., 1947; asst. chief electrician, engr. charge AC power div. Island Creek Coal Co., Holden, W. Va., 1948-52; area engr. Atomic Energy Program, Aiken, S.C., 1952-54; engr. draftsman Reynolds Smith & Hills, Engrs., Architects, Planners, Jacksonville, Fla., 1954-57, design engr., 1957-64, sr. design engr., 1964—; pres. 8th St. Coin Laundry, Jacksonville, 1959-63; Sterling Enterprises Inc., Jacksonville, 1959-63. Served with AUS, 1943-46. Registered profl. engr., W.Va. Home: 2660 Forest Blvd Jacksonville FL 32216 Office: PO Box 4850 Jacksonville FL 32201

STEPP, JAMES MARVIN, educator; b. Old Fort, N.C., July 26, 1913; s. John Marvin and Florence (Pendergrass) S.; B.A., Berea Coll., 1937; M.A., U. Va., 1938, Ph.D., 1940; m. Vivian Olivia Pittman, June 21, 1942; children—James Marvin, John E., Kenneth S., Benjamin T. Mem. faculty Clemson (S.C.) U., 1940—, Alumni prof. agrl. econs., 1966—. Econs. cons. Nat. Security Resources Bd., 1952, S.C. State Devel. Bd., 1962, Marine Resources Com. of Coastal Plains Regional Com., 1968, S.C. Water Resources Com., 1967—. Mem. Am., So. (v.p. 1954-55) econ. assns., Am., So. agrl. econ. assns., So. Regional Sci. Assn. (pres. 1974-75). A.A.A.S., S.C. Acad. Sci. Methodist. Club: Torch. Co-author Economics of Environmental Quality, 1972. Editor (with James C. Hite) Coastal Zone Resource Management, 1971. Contbr. to publs. in field. Home: 252 Riggs Dr Clemson SC 29631

STERLING, W. DAWSON, life ins. exec.; b. Waco, Tex., Dec. 29, 1922; s. Marion and Ruth (Esser) S.; student Baylor U., 1939-40; B.B.A. with highest honors, U. Tex., 1947; LL.B., So. Meth. U., 1953; student exec. program Columbia, 1958; m. Lynn; children—Clare, Evelyn. With Southwestern Life Ins. Co., Dallas, 1947-69, v.p., sec., 1958-62, pres., 1962-69; pres. Am. Gen. Life Ins. Co., Houston, Am. Gen. Life Ins. Co. of Del., Houston, 1972—; dir. Patriot Life Ins. Co. N.Y.; v.p., dir. Am. Gen. Ins. Co., Houston, 1969—; dir. No. Ins. Co. N.Y., Variable Annuity Life Ins. Co., Assurance Co. Am. Admitted to Tex. bar, 1953. Mem. exec. com. Am. Life Conv., 1966-69; dir. Internat. Ins. Seminars, Tex. Life Conv., 1962-64. Mem. Dallas Citizens Council, 1962-69; gen. chmn. Dallas United Fund campaign, 1967; pres., dir. Dallas Assembly, 1962-63. Served to 1st lt., pilot USAAF, World War II. Fellow Life Office Mgmt. Assn. (pres. 1967-68); mem. Dallas C. of C. (v.p., dir. 1962-65), State Bar Tex., Order Woolsack, Beta Gamma Sigma, Rotarian. Address: PO Box 1931 Houston TX 77001

STERLING, WALTER GAGE, mfg. co. exec.; b. Anahuac, Tex., May 20, 1901; s. Ross Shaw and Maude (Gage) S.; LL.B., U. Tex., 1925; m. Ruth Dermody, Jan. 30, 1941. With Royalty Properties, Houston, 1927—, v.p., 1946—; pres. Sterling Oil & Refinery 1935-50, Richmond Mfg. Co., 1951—; with Richmond Sales, 1952—; dir. Citizens Nat. Bank & Trust Co., Baytown; trustee Mortgage & Trust Investors. Trustee Hermann Hosp. Estate, 1950—, pres. bd. trustees, 1965—; bd. dirs. Tex. Med. Center. Served to capt. USAAF, 1941-44. Mem. S.A.R. (pres. gen. 1968-69), Delta Kappa Epsilon. Clubs: Lakeside Country (past pres.), Petroleum (past pres.) (Houston). Home: 5701 Jackson St Houston TX 77004 Office: PO Box 2891 Houston TX 77001

STERN, ALFRED, philosopher, educator; b. Baden bei Wien, Austria, July 19, 1899; s. Julius and Rose (Kohn) S.; Bachelor, Piaristengymnasium, Vienna, 1919; Ph.D. with honors, U. Vienna, 1923; m. Gloria Maria Pagan y Ferrer, Nov. 15, 1946. Came to U.S. 1944, naturalized, 1949. Lectr., Sorbonne, Paris, 1934-39; prof. philosophy Inst. High Studies of Belgium, Brussels, 1935-40, Cal. Inst. Tech., Pasadena, 1947-68, U. P.R., Mayaguez, 1968—. Adv. Folia Humanistica, Barcelona, Spain, Atenea, Mayaguez. Served to lt., Austrian Army, 1917-18; French Army, 1940. Decorated knight Legion of Honor (France); officer Order of Leopold II (Belgium); officer of Academic Palms (France). Mem. Am. Philos. Assn. (pres. Pacific div. 1964-65), Alliance Francaise (v.p. Los Angeles, 1962-68). Author: Philosophical Foundations of Truth, Reality and Value, 1932; Philosophy of Values, 1936; Philosophy of Politics, 1943; Philosophy of Laughter and Tears, 1949; Philosophy of History and the Problem of Values, 1962; Sartre—His Philosophy and Existential Psychoanalysis, 1967; The Search for Meaning, 1971. Home: 270 Luna St San Juan PR 00901 Office: U PR Mayaguez PR 00708

STERN, HAROLD P., art museum dir.; B.A., U. Mich., 1943, M.A., 1948, Ph.D., 1959. Mem. curatorial staff Freer Gallery Art, Smithsonian Instn., Washington, 1951, asst. dir., 1962-71, dir., 1971—. Hon. lectr. Japanese art U. Mich. Author: Masterpieces of Korean Art, 1957; Hokusai: Paintings and Drawings in the Freer Gallery of Art, 1960; Master Prints of Japan Ukiyo-e Hanga, 1969; Freer Gallery of Art: Japan, 1971; Rimpa: Masterworks of the Japanese Decorative School, 1971; The Magnificent Three: Lacquer, Netsuke and Tsuba, 1972; Ukiyo-e Painting, Freer Gallery Art, 1973. Research on Chinese art, Japanese painting, ceramics and decorative arts. Office: Freer Gallery Art Washington DC 20560

STERNBERG, DANIEL ARLE, musician, condr., coll. dean; b. Lwow, Poland, Mar. 29, 1913; s. Philipp and Eva (Makowska) S.; baccalaureate, Realgymnasium, Vienna, 1931; student U. Vienna,

1931-35; diploma of condr. Vienna State Acad. Music, 1935; composition study with Karl Weigl, 1931-35; conducting with Fritz Stiedry, 1935-36; m. Felicitas Gobineau, July 29, 1936. Came to U.S., 1939, naturalized, 1946. Lectr. Vienna Volkshochschule, 1933-34; condr. Vienna Vets. Orch., 1934-35; asst. condr. Leningrad Philharmonic and Grand Opera, 1935-36; guest condr. Leningrad and Moscow radio orchs., 1936, Dallas Symphony Orch., 1952, 65; music dir. Tiflis State Symphony Orch., Russia, 1936-37; head piano dept. Hockaday Inst. Music, Dallas, 1940-42; dean sch. music Baylor U., Waco, Tex., 1942—; mus. dir., condr. Waco Symphony Orch., 1963—; concert accompanist; lectr. mus. subjects. Awarded Abrams Meml. award for orchestral composition by Dallas Symphony Orch., 1948. Mem. Am. Assn. U. Profs., Music Tchrs. Nat. Assn. (pres. Southwestern div.), Sinfonia, Phi Mu Alpha, Omicron Delta Kappa. Contbr. articles to mags. Home: 3108 Robin Rd Waco TX 76708

STERNBERG, HANS JOACHIM, dept. store exec.; b. Aurich, Germany, July 4, 1935; s. Erich and Lea (Knurr) S.; A.B. magna cum laude, Princeton, 1957; m. Donna Gail Weintraub, Feb. 19, 1967; children—Erich, Julie Ellen, Deborah Ann, Mark Samuel. Came to U.S., 1937, naturalized, 1943. With Goudchaux's, Inc., Baton Rouge, 1960—, exec. v.p., sec.-treas., 1963—; partner Insa Sternberg & Bros., Baton Rouge, 1960—; pres. 1550 Realty Co.; v.p. Erich Sternberg Realty Co., Inc.; dir. WLCS Radio Sta. Mem. adv. council marketing dept. La. State U., 1971—; pres. Baton Rouge Jewish Welfare Fedn., 1971-72; mem. young leadership cabinet United Jewish Appeal, 1970—. Bd. dirs. La. Heart Assn., 1970-71, La. Capital Area Health Planning Council, 1970-71, Anglo-Am. Art Museum, 1973—; bd. dirs. Baton Rouge Art Gallery, 1967—, pres., 1972. Served to lt. (j.g.) USNR, 1957-59. Jewish religion (treas. temple 1971-72, sec. Men's club 1969). Clubs: City, Bocage Racquet, Toastmasters, Round Table (Baton Rouge). Home: 2375 Kleinert Av Baton Rouge LA 70806 Office: PO Drawer 3478 Baton Rouge LA 70821

STERNBERG, MARY JO PATRICIA, gift store owner; b. Montgomery, Ala., Mar. 17, 1928; d. Edward Martin and Mary Frances (Discher) Sternberg; student Gulf Park Coll., 1944-46, Nazareth Coll., 1946-48; B.F.A., Newcomb Coll. Tulane U., 1950. With Hardy Dabbs, Inc., interior decorators, Gulfport, Miss., 1950-52; salesman Young Ages, 1952; salesman, gift buyer Northrops, 1952-55; owner, operator Purple Lantern, Gulfport, 1955—, br., Biloxi, Miss. Mem. PACT com. Urban Renewal, Gulfport, 1971—; exec. com. Gulfport Mchts. Com., 1970—; exec. com. Very Important Visitors Assn., 1972—. Named Queen Ixolib, Gulf Coast Carnival Assn., 1955. Mem. Gift and Decorative Assn. (nat. winner 1st pl. 1969, nat. v.p. 1974—), Am. Booksellers Assn., Miss. Retail Mchts. Assn., Nat. Fedn. Ind. Bus., Gulf Coast Arts Festival, Miss. Art Assn., Gulfport C. of C. (v.p. 1970—), Better Bus. Bur., Gulfport Little Theatre (pres. 1956-67, bldg. bd. 1971—). Roman Catholic (parish council 1970—). Home: 1640 E Beach Gulfport MS 39501 Office: 1217 25th Av Gulfport MS 39501 also 130 Magnolia Mall Biloxi MS

STERNER, JOHN, med. instrument mfr.; b. London, Eng., Oct. 26, 1912; s. Lawrence E. and Bleema (Levy) S.; came to U.S., 1915; B.S., Mass. Inst. Tech., 1933, D.Sc., 1950; m. Delphine T. Leary, Feb. 4, 1956; stepchildren—Patricia E. Leary, Pamela A. Leary. Vice pres., dir. Baird Atomic, Inc., Cambridge, Mass., 1939-54; dir. flight test operations Space Tech. Labs., TRW, Inc., Patrick Air Force Base, Fla., 1955-59; exec. v.p., dir. Cordis Corp., Miami, Fla., 1960—. Served to lt. col. ordnance, AUS, 1942-45. Mem. Am. Phys. Soc., Optical Soc. Am., Am. Mgmt. Assn. Home: 8930 SW 52d Av Miami FL 33156 Office: 125 NE 40th St Miami FL 33137

STERNER, MICHAEL EDMUND, govt. ofcl.; b. N.Y.C., Dec. 26, 1928; s. Harold Walther and Leonie (Knoedler) S.; A.B., Harvard, 1951; m. Courtenay Read, Mar. 30, 1957; children—Lucian, Marcelin. Govt. relations rep. Arabian-Am. Oil Co., Dhahran, Saudi Arabia, joined Fgn. Ser., 1956; vice consul, Aden, 1957-58; polit. officer, Cairo, 1960-64; desk officer Near Eastern Affairs, Dept. State, 1964-71, country dir. United Arab Republic Affairs, 1971—. Served with AUS, 1954-56. Home: 2712 36th St Washington DC 20007 Office: NEA/UAR State Dept Washington DC 20520

STERNGOLD, HENRY, constrn. co. exec.; b. Detroit, Sept. 20, 1923; s. Harry and Minnie (Schultz) S.; B.S. in Civil Engring., U. Mich., 1943; m. Levona Levy, Apr. 4, 1948; children—Nancy, Arthur, James, Paul. Gen. contractor Sam Bldg. Co., Detroit; pres. Fla. Scholz Homes, Inc., Boca Raton, 1958-61; prin. Henry Sterngold, Cons., West Palm Beach, Fla., 1961-65; v.p., chief engr. Snead Constrn. Corp., Fort Lauderdale, 1965—. Served to lt. (j.g.) C.E., USNR, 1943-46; PTO. Decorated Bronze Star. Registered profl. engr., Mich., Fla., Ga., Cal. Mem. Am. Soc. C.E., Nat. Soc. Profl. Engrs., Constrn. Specifications Inst., Assn. Gen. Contractors. Club: Inverarry Racquet (Fort Lauderdale). Home: 1031 Tennessee Av Fort Lauderdale FL 33312 Office: 1164 E Oakland Park Blvd Fort Lauderdale FL 33307

STEVENS, A(DOLPH) EDWARD, assn. exec.; b. Glasgow, Scotland, May 19, 1899; s. Joseph John and Anna Josephine (Brewer) S.; came to U.S., 1909, naturalized, 1925; student DeLaSalle Inst., 1913-16; LL.B., DePaul U., 1922; m. Tynie Blazer, Mar. 3, 1935. Admitted to Ill. bar, 1922; practiced in Chgo., 1922-28; owner Eagle Music & Radio, Chgo., 1929-39, Eagle Radio & TV, Miami, Fla., 1939-70. Sec., treas. Central Brevard Christian Businessmen's Com., 1972—. Mem. TV and Electronic Service Assn. Miami (recipient Merit award 1957, treas. 1950-59, pres. 1959-61), Profl. TV Assn. Inc. (hon.), Nat. Alliance TV and Electronic Service Assns. (gov. South Atlantic, dir., gov. Fla. 1963-64; v.p. Eastern div. 1962-63), Fla. Electronic Service Assn. (charter and hon. life mem., pres. 1963-65, 74-75, 1st ann. award plaque 1965, exec. dir. 1971—), South Fla. Indsl. Editors Assn. (treas. 1963-66), Better Bus. Bur. South Fla. (dir. 1965-68), Brevard Electronic Service Assn. (hon. life). Editor: TESA Miami News, 1960-64, FESA News, 1964-65, Fla. Electronic Technician, 1969-70. Address: 1250 Leslie Dr Merritt Island FL 32952

STEVENS, ALBERT DONALD, banker; b. Jackson, Miss., Dec. 6, 1919; s. Albert and Margaret (Finn) S.; student U. Ky., 1936-40; LL.D., U. Louisville, 1951; m. Amanda Jane Hines, May 13, 1944; children—Margaret Jane (Mrs. Philip Herndon), Albert Donald. With Loan Guaranty, U.S. VA., Louisville, 1945-48; with So. Trust Co., Louisville, 1949-50; v.p. Louisville Trust Co. (Ky.)., 1952—. Served with USAF, 1943-45, 50-52. Decorated Air medal with 2 oak leaf clusters. Mem. Ky., Louisville bar assns., Nat. Assn. Real Estate Bds. (sect. v.p.), Nat., La. bd. realtors. Club: River Road Country (Louisville). Home: 606 Club Lane Louisville KY 40207 Office: 1 Riverfront Plaza Louisville KY 40202

STEVENS, DAVID BRUCE, orthopaedic surgeon; b. Louisville, July 11, 1929; s. Albert Clyde and Sue A. (Schan) S.; A.B., DePauw U., 1951; M.D., Northwestern U., 1955; m. Sarah Ann Symon, Sept. 1, 1952; children—Scott D., Patricia Sue. Intern U. Mich., 1955-56, asst. resident in surgery, 1956-57; resident orthopaedics U. Mich., 1957-60; practice medicine specializing in orthopaedic surgery, Lexington, Ky., 1960— mem. staffs Good Samaritan, St. Joseph's, Central Baptist, Shriner's, Cardinal Hill hosps.; asst. clin. prof. surgery U. Ky. Sch. Medicine, Lexington, 1962—; dir. Wallace's Bookstores, Inc., Lexington, 1965—. Cons., Bur. Hearings and Appeals, Social Security Adminstrn., 1967—; surgeon, pres. Ky. Commn. Handicapped Children, 1961—. Mem. Ky. Central Com. Republican party, 1965-67. Bd. dirs. Opportunity Workshop of Lexington. Mem. A.M.A. (del. 1971—), Ky. Med. Assn. (trustee), Orthopaedic Soc. (pres. 1965), Fayette County Med. Soc. (pres. 1968), Phi Beta Kappa, Alpha Omega Alpha, Sigma Nu. Rotatian. Club: Idle Hour Country (Lexington). Home: 346 Jesselin Dr Lexington KY 40503 Office: 201 Nicholasville Rd Lexington KY 40503

STEVENS, DON LORENZO, JR., naval architect; b. New Rochelle, N.Y., May 1, 1928; s. Don Lorenzo and Emily (Crandon) S.; B.C.E., U. Va., 1951; M. Engring., U. Cal. at Berkeley, 1960; m. Barbara Louise Thayer, June 16, 1951; children—Richard Alan, David Owen, Douglas Moore, Kathryn Diane. Naval architect preliminary design br. Bur. Ships, U.S. Navy, Washington, 1951-60, head structural and hydrofoil sect., 1960-66, project dir. ship concept design div. Naval Ship Engring. Center, 1966-70, dir. planning and coordination Undersea Long-Range Missile (Trident) Submarine Design Project Office, Hyattsville, Md., 1970-73, dep. ship design mgr. Aux. Ships, Naval Ship Engring. Center, 1973—. Troop leader Boy Scouts Am., 1966-73. Bd. dirs. Claremont Citizens Assn., 1957-59. Registered profl. engr., Va. Mem. Soc. Naval Architects and Marine Engrs., Am. Soc. Naval Engrs. (officer flagship sect. council 1969—, nat. council 1973—), Royal Instn. Naval Architects, Assn. Sr. Engrs. (exec. bd. 1961-62, 68-70), Instituto Panamericano Engenharia Naval, Trigon, Delta Upsilon. Episcopalian. Home: 1212 S Forest Dr Arlington VA 22204 Office: Naval Ship Engring Center Hyattsville MD 20782

STEVENS, ELBERT MERVIN, finance and ins. exec.; b. Harper, Tex., Apr. 14, 1902; s. Joseph Martin and Eva (Delavan) S.; student pub. schs., San Antonio; m. Thelma Riley, Oct. 31, 1928. Pres., chmn. bd. Gt. Western Loan & Trust Co., San Antonio, 1947—. Gt. Western Life Ins. Co., 1947—, Gt. Western Mut. Ins. Co., 1947—, Gt. Western Underwriters, 1956—, Gt. Western Leasing Co., 1960—, Gt. Western Finance Co., 1958—. Trustee S.W. Research Inst. San Antonio; bd. govs. Tex. Rural Communities, Dallas; bd. dirs. Keystone Sch., San Antonio Boys Clubs, Livestock Expn. Mem. Tex. Finance Conf. (past pres.), Am. Automobile Assn. (past nat. v.p.), C. of C. (past dir.), Tex. Farm Bur., Exotic Wildlife Assn. (pres.), Am. Indsl. Bankers Assn. (dir.), San Antonio Council Pres., Jr. C. of C. (past pres.), St. Hubertus Soc. Lion, Mason (K.T., Shriner). Clubs: Breakfast (past pres.), Alamo Motor (past pres.), Lions, San Antonio Gun. Office: 1000 N Alamo St San Antonio TX 78215

STEVENS, H. MORRIS, state ofcl.; b. Omaha, Tex., Oct. 19, 1913; s. Harvey Bun and Nona (Boyet) S.; student Burleson Coll., 1930, Tyler Jr. Coll., 1931, Tex. U., 1931-32, Tex. Western U., 1934; m. Gwendolyn Schieffer, Dec. 27, 1941; children—Nancy Jeanette (Mrs. Thomas Hrin, Jr.), Mildred Nona (Mrs. Richard K. Rogers), Harvey Morris, Michael Richard. With Tex. Treasury Dept., Austin, 1936—, chief clk., 1946—. Mem. Tex. Pub. Employees Assn. (dir., 1st v.p. 1946-51), Nat. Assn. Unclaimed Property Adminstrs. (treas.). Home: 3901 Brookview Rd Austin TX 78722 Office: State Finance Bldg Austin TX 78711

STEVENS, JAMES TRAXEL, ednl. assn. editor; b. Shreveport, La., Mar. 28, 1917; s. Samuel Clement and Nevah (Hill) S.; B.A. in Music, La. Coll., Pineville, 1942; postgrad. U. Tex., 1946-49; m. Evelyn Maxine Fowler, Mar. 6, 1942; children—Linda (Mrs. Harry Menn, Jr.), Barry Clemens. Newsreporter, writer Sta. KVET, Austin, 1947-49; capitol corr. Long News Service, Austin, 1949-54; dir. journalsim Univ. Interscholastic League, U. Tex., Austin, 1954-56; dir., mng. editor div. publs. Tex. Tchrs. Assn., Austin, 1956—. Served with AUS, 1942-46. Recipient award of distinction Nat. Sch. Pub. Relations Assn., 1970. Mem. Soc. Austin Indsl. Editors (pres. 1958), Internat. Council Indsl. Editors (Mid-Continent 1st award 1958, 62), Internat. Assn. Bus. Communicators, Edn. Press Assn. Am. (regional dir., 1971-73), State Edn. Editors (sec. 1969), Sigma Delta Chi. Democrat. Methodist. Home: 4202 Gnarl Dr Austin TX 78731 Office: 316 W 12th St Austin TX 78701

STEVENS, ROGER TEMPLETON, research engr.; b. Syracuse, N.Y., Jan. 11, 1927; s. Raymond Alfred and Mabel (Templeton) S.; B.A., Union Coll., Schenectady, 1949; M.A., Boston U., 1959; LL.B., Blackstone Sch. Law, 1966; m. Mildred Lorraine Hasbrouck, June 12, 1948; children—Margaret Ann, David Keith. Sr. engr. Spencer-Kennedy Labs., Boston, 1955-56, Avco Mfg. Co., Boston, 1956-57, Electronics Systems, Inc., Boston, 1957-60; staff asst. to chief engr. and supr. video and display sect. Sanders Assos., Nashua, N.H., 1960-65; mem. tech. staff advising USAF on Command & Control Systems, Mitre Corp., Bedford, Mass., 1965-67; sr. research engr. Dikewood Corp., Albuquerque, 1967-70; mem. tech. staff, group leader Mitre Corp., McLean, Va., 1970—. Mem. I.E.E.E. (sr. mem., sec. 1963-64, vice chmn. N.H. sect. 1964-65). Mason. Contbr. articles to profl. jours. Home: 1701 Fox Run Ct Vienna VA 22180 Office: Mitre Corp Westgate Research Park McLean VA 22101

STEVENS, ROY ARTHUR, county mgr.; b. Benson, N.C., Aug. 30, 1924; s. Arthur Festus and Lalon (Strickland) S.; grad. Worth Bus. Coll., Fayetteville, N.C., 1942, Southeastern Inst. for Orgn., 1958, Bus. Mgmt. Inst., Jacksonville, N.C., 1959; m. Nora Alma Wood, June 21, 1947; children—Roy Arthur, Gloria Delilah. Clk., A.E. Rankin Co., Inc., Fayetteville, 1942-43, bookkeeper, 1946-49; chief clk., office mgr. Becker County Sand & Gravel Co., Cheraw, S.C., 1949-55; owner, operator Stevens Bookkeeping Service, 1955; asst. mgr. C. of C., Fayetteville, 1956; mgr. Jacksonville C. of C., 1957-64; dir. Resources Devel. Commn. for Brunswick County, Southport, 1965-69; mgr. Onslow County, 1969-71; dir. Carteret County Econ. Devel. Council, Morehead City, N.C., 1971—. Mem. exec. bd., past pres. Ocean Hwy. Assn.; past pres., bd. dirs. Travel Council N.C.; former dir. N.C. Indsl. Developers Assn. Served with USAAF, 1943-46. Named Tarheel of Week, 1964. Baptist. Home: West Car Meadows Morehead City NC 28557 Office: 913 Shepard St Morehead City NC 28557

STEVENS, WILLIAM DALE, computer exec.; b. Topeka, Nov. 8, 1929; s. Floyd Wayne and Flossie (Northup) S.; B.S. in Chem. Engring., Kan. State U., 1952; m. Mary Charlotte Anderson, Sept. 18, 1954; children—John Stewart, Charles David. Chemist, Sunray Oil Co., Duncan, Okla., 1954-56; process engr. DX Sunray Oil Co., Duncan, 1956-58, computer econs. engr., Tulsa, 1958-61; process econs. engr. Skelly Oil Co., Tulsa, 1961-62, supr. process econ. engring., 1962-67, tech. asst. to computer dept. mgr., 1967-73, mgr. sci. applications, 1973—. Project mgr. SHARE, 1967-69, div. mgr., 1969-71; project mgr. GUIDE, 1967-71. Served with AUS, 1952-54. Registered profl. engr., Okla. Mem. Inst. Mgmt. Scis. (pres. southwestern chpt. 1967-68), Am. Inst. Chem. Engrs., Mensa (Tulsa test adminstr.), INTERTEL (asst. internat. gen. sec. 1970-73, chmn. membership com. 1971—, pres. chpt. 1969-70, internat. gen. sec. 1974—), Assn. for Computing Machinery, Tulsa Computing Soc. Republican. Episcopalian (lay reader; sch. supt.). Home: 218 S 102d East Av Tulsa OK 74128 Office: 15th St at Boulder Av Tulsa OK 74102

STEVENSON, ALMIRA ABBOT (MRS. H.E. STEVENSON), adminstrv. law judge; b. Fayetteville, W.Va., July 8, 1916; d. Alois Bahlmann and Nona (Reynolds) Abbot; B.A., Randolph-Macon Women's Coll., 1937; student Student's Internat. Union, Geneva, Switzerland, 1937; J.D., U. Chgo., 1948; m. Henry Edwin Stevenson, Oct. 15, 1949; children—Henry Edminster, Abbot. Admitted to W.Va., D.C. bars, 1948; research analyst Office Def. Transp., Washington, 1942, Office Civilian Def., Washington, 1941; atty. office solicitor U.S. Dept. Labor, Washington, 1949-50; atty. adviser to NLRB, Washington, 1951-72, trial examiner, 1972, adminstrv. law judge, 1972—; equal employment opportunity appeals examiner Civil Service Commn., 1970—. Served from 2d lt. to maj. USMC Res., 1943-54. Home: 5512 30th St NW Washington DC 20015

STEVENSON, CHESTER JOHN, elec. utility co. exec.; b. Scranton, Pa., Jan. 17, 1924; s. John George and Sophia (Zychal) Sobonski; student Wharton Sch. Bus., U. Pa., 1947-49, marketing Internat. Corr. Schs., 1956; certificate elec. engring., U. Ky., 1957; m. Helen Ruth Schweitzer, Nov. 3, 1951; children—Cathy, Wayne, Paul, Nancy. Field mgr. Fuller Brush Co., Lexington, Ky., 1954-55; comml. service adviser Ky. Utilities Co., Lexington, 1955-59, local mgr., Georgetown, Ky., 1959-60, Flemingsburg, Ky., 1960-66, div. mgr. customer services, Lexington, 1966—. Mem. beautification com. Ky. Dept. Natural Resources, 1964-71. Assembly rep. Lexington United Community Fund, 1966-69. Bd. dirs. Jr. Achievement Blue Grass area, 1973—. Served with AUS, 1943-45; ETO. Decorated Purple Heart, Soldier's Medal; recipient Five Star awards, Sons Am. Legion, 1940; named Man of Year, Jr. C. of C. Scott County (Ky.), 1959, Man of Year, Fleming County (Ky.), 1963. Mem. Ky. (co-chmn. community devel. 1966—), Fleming County (pres. 1963), Fayette County chambers commerce. Republican. Lutheran (supt. Sunday sch. 1967-69, deacon 1969—). Mason, Lion (zone chmn. 1964-65, pres. 1972-73). Home: 1029 Whitehall Pl Lexington KY 40507 Office: 120 S Limestone St Lexington Ky 40502

STEVENSON, CLARENCE NEAL, lawyer; b. Pettus, Tex., Oct. 9, 1934; s. R.A. and Mary (Ballard) S.; B.A., U. Tex., 1959, J.D., 1960; m. Sandra J. Sitterle, June 6, 1964; children—Neal Wayne, Morgan Lee. Admitted to Tex. bar, 1960; asso. mem. firm Fly, Moeller & Stevenson and predecessor firms, Victoria, Tex., 1960-64, partner, 1964—. Dir. Swain-Kovar Ford Co., Victoria, S. Tex. Savs. Assn., Victoria; instr. real estate law Victoria Coll., 1973—. Chmn. Victoria Child Welfare Unit, 1970; pres. Youth Home Victoria, 1973—. Del., Tex., Nat. Democratic convs., 1972. Bd. dirs. S. Tex. Race Assn. Served with AUS, 1954-56. Mem. State Bar Tex., Victoria Bar Assn. (Pres. 1966), Delta Chi, Phi Alpha Delta, Friar Soc. Episcopalian. Home: Route 1 Box 69-S Victoria TX 77901 Office: 1908 N Laurent St Victoria TX 77901

STEVENSON, DWIGHT ESHELMAN, clergyman, educator; b. Cuba, Ill., Mar. 6, 1906; s. Luther and Mabel (Eshelman) S.; B.A., Bethany (W.Va.) Coll., 1929, D.D., 1947; B.D., Yale, 1933; m. DeLoris Ray, Apr. 28, 1928; children—Virginia (Mrs. Marcus Bryant), Dwight Ward. Ordained to ministry Christian Ch. (Disciples of Christ), 1929; minister Bethany Meml. Ch., 1933-44; instr. Bethany Coll., 1933-44, prof., head dept. philosophy and religion, 1944-47; prof. homiletics Lexington (Ky.) Theol. Sem., 1947-74, interim pres., 1964, 74, dean, 1969-74, dean emeritus, 1974—; coordinator team A, Theol. Edn. Assn. Mid-Am., 1974- Vis. prof. Union Theol. Sem. Philippines, Manila, 1953-54, World Campus Afloat, 1965-66, Clarement (Cal.) Sch. Theology, 1968. Mem. Assn. Profl. Edn. Ministry. Author 20 books including: In the Biblical Preacher's Workshop, 1967; A Way in the Wilderness, 1968. Home: 592 Bellcastle Rd Lexington KY 40505 Office: 631 S Limestone St Lexington KY 40508

STEVENSON, EARL, JR., cons. engr.; b. Rayston, Ga., May 8, 1921; s. Earl and Compton Helen (Randall) S.; diploma Emmanuel Coll., 1948; student U. Ga., 1950; B.S., Ga. Inst. Tech., 1953; m. Sue Roberts, Apr. 25, 1956; children—Catherine Helen, David Earl. Engr., Merritt & Welker Engrs., Marietta, Ga., 1954-57, Keck Engring. Assos., Atlanta, 1957-59, Gen. Services Adminstrn., Atlanta, 1959-60; v.p., dir. Miller Stevenson & Steinichen, Inc., cons. engrs. and planners, Atlanta, 1960—; sec., dir. Windy Hill Devel. Corp., Atlanta; treas., dir. Lakeshore Land Co., Inc., Atlanta. Served with USAAF, 1944-45. Registered profl. engr., Ga., Ala., Miss., S.C. Mem. Ga. Soc. Profl. Engrs., Ga. Water Pollution Control Assn. Home: 140 Orchard Rd Smyrna GA 30080 Office: 75 8th St NE Atlanta GA 30309

STEVENSON, ELBERT KENNETH, JR. chem. co. exec.; b. Butler, Mo., Oct. 10, 1931; s. Elbert Kenneth and Sarah Elizabeth (Williams) S.; B.S. in Petroleum Engring., U. Kan., 1954, M.S., 1956; m. Doris Darlene Mitchell, Feb. 7, 1951; children—Periann, Mitchell Scott, Nancy, Kenna. Petroleum engr. Texaco, Inc., Tulsa, Okla., 1956-65; pres. En-Geo Corp., Tulsa, 1965-67; v.p. Stonehenge Oil Co., Tulsa, 1967-70; sr. project leader Dow Chem. Co., Houston, 1970—. Recipient E.A. Stephenson award for Outstanding senior student U. Kan., 1954. Registered profl. engr., Okla. Mem. Soc. Petroleum Engrs., Sigma Nu, Sigma Tau. Methodist (dir. 1963-69). Home: 9226 Stroud St Houston TX 77036 Office: 3636 Richmond Av Houston TX 77027

STEVENSON, FRANK GEORGE, JR., securities dealer; b. Americus, Ga., Apr. 21, 1932; s. Frank George and Dorothy (Baugh) S.; B.B.A., U. Ga., 1954; m. Joan Wilson Askew, Sept. 7, 1957; children—Mary Kathryn, Karen, John Askew. With Wood, Struthers & Winthrop, Inc., Atlanta, 1963—, now v.p. sales; exec. v.p., treas., dir. Hawick Fund, Inc., Atlanta, 1968—; dir. Castleberry's Food Co., Augusta, Ga. Precinct chmn. Fulton County Republican Com., 1971-72. Served with USAF, 1954-56. Mem. Nat. Assn. Security Dealers. Clubs: Peachtree Golf, Peachtree Racket, Piedmont Driving, Commerce (Atlanta). Home: 3872 Randall Ridge Rd NW Atlanta GA 30327 Office: 2 Peachtree St Atlanta GA 30303

STEVENSON, FRANK MOODY, real estate exec.; b. Birmingham, Ala., Aug. 11, 1920; s. Horace Adlai and Maude (Moody) S.; A.B., Birmingham So. Coll., 1941; m. Evelyn McClain Lewis, July 31, 1943; children—Frank Moody, Edward Lewis. Sec., dir. Westside Lumber Co., Huntsville, Ala., 1961-62; sr. real estate appraiser FHA, Birmingham, 1949-59; partner Thomas & Stevenson Constrn. Co., Huntsville, 1959—; real estate appraiser Frank M. Stevenson, Huntsville, 1959—; pres. Frank & Stevenson Realty Co., Inc., Huntsville, 1966—; v.p., dir. Huntsville Asso., Inc., 1966—; sec.-treas., dir. Stak Devel. Co., Inc., 1962-66, Stakbilt Homes, Inc., 1963-66. Mem. Huntsville Indsl. Expansion Com., 1967—. Mem. Nat. Soc. Real Estate Appraisers, Am. Soc. Real Estate Appraisers, Birmingham-So. Coll. Alumni Assn. (dir. 1970-73), Nat. Assn. Real Estate Bds., Huntsville, C. of C., Kappa Alpha. Presbyn. Home: 2903 Drexel Dr SE Huntsville AL 35801 Office: 915-C Franklin St SE Huntsville AL 35801

STEVENSON, HANCIE, city ofcl., data processor; b. Anna, Tex., Oct. 16, 1915; s. Guy and Nora (Cromer) S.; diploma Draughts Bus. Coll., 1938; student Tex. Tech., 1954-56; m. Margie E. Shorter, Dec. 13, 1939; children—Bobby Guy, Neva Gayle. Mgr. utility services, billing City of Lubbock, Tex., 1950-56, data processing co-ordinator,

1957—. Cons. systems work in municipal utility billing; mem. Computer Informations Systems Adv. Com. Served with USNR, 1944-46; PTO, ETO. Mem. Data Processing Mgmt. Assn. (chpt. pres. 1962—, internat. dir. 1963—, div. vice chmn. 1967—). Home: 3004 37th St Lubbock TX 79413 Office: PO Box 2000 Lubbock TX 79457 also 3004 37th St Lubbock TX 79413

STEVENSON, HENRY EDWIN, editor; b. Moorhead, Minn., May 25, 1916; s. Henry Ebeneezer and Nina Lillian (Edminster) S.; B.S., Moorhead State Coll., 1939; postgrad. U. Chgo., 1946-49; m. Almira Abbot, Oct. 15, 1949; children—Henry Edminster, Abbot. Reporter, Moorhead Daily News, 1936-38; reporter Fargo (N.D.) Forum, 1938-39; tchr. pub. schs., Burtrum, Minn., 1940-42; tchr. Sidwell Friends Sch., Washington, 1949-51; edn. specialist Navy Tng. Publs. Center, Washington, 1951-54; supervisory editor Naval Photog. Interpretation Center, Washington, 1954-62; asst. for res. officer tng. Bur. Naval Weapons, Washington, 1962-63; program mgr. various tng. manuals Bur. Naval Personnel, Washington, 1963-72; mem. staff Nat. Center Housing Mgmt., Washington, 1972—. Served from 2d lt. to 1st lt., USMCR, 1942-45, from 1st lt. to lt. col. Res., 1945-67. Mem. Marine Corps Res. Officers Assn., Gamma Theta Upsilon, Beta Theta Pi. Author: (with others) The Marine Corps Reserve-A History, 1966. Editor: The Reserve Weaponeer, 1962-63; Naval Tng. Bull., 1963-72). Home: 5512 30th St NW Washington DC 20015 Office: Nat Center Housing Mgmt 1133 15th St NW Washington DC 20005

STEVENSON, JAMES PRESTON FANT, clergyman; b. Hartselle, Ala., Oct. 5, 1919; s. James Preston and Claribel (Fant) S.; grad. Fort Smith Jr. Coll., 1939; A.B. (Kneeland Theol. award), Coll. of Ozarks, 1941, D.D., 1950; B.D., Columbia Theol. Sem., 1944, M.Div., 1971; m. Kathryn McGee, Jan. 3, 1942; children—Victoria Fant (Mrs. Phillip Land II), Sarah Kay. Ordained to ministry Presbyn. Ch., 1944; pastor First Presbyn. Ch., Uniontown, Ala., 1944-46, Canal St. Presbyn. Ch., New Orleans, 1946-50, First Presbyn. Ch., Clarksdale, Miss., 1952-68, Central Presbyn. Ch., Bristol, Va., 1968-73; family relations counselor, Bristol, Va., 1972-73; pastor Tirzah Presbyn. Ch., Waxhaw, N.C., 1973—. Vice pres. New Orleans Ministerial Assn., 1949; pres. Coahoma County Ministerial Assn., Clarksdale, 1958; mem. edn. study com. Presbyn. Ch. in U.S., chmn. standing com. woman's work, 1958, chmn. permanent com. of minister and his work in gen. assembly, 1964—; chmn. com. on minister and work Presbyn. Ch. State of Miss.; chaplain Miss. Ho. of Reps., 1959; chaplain of day Ho. of Reps., Washington, 1969; Va. State chaplain. Camp chaplain Boy Scouts Am.; chaplain City of Coahoma County, City of Bristol, Va., Appalachian Crime Clinic; clergy rep. Coahoma County Parents League; youth counselor Youth Court, Coahoma County; dir. religious affairs Va. Civil Def. Col. staff Gov. Johnson of Miss., Gov. Ellington of Tenn. Bd. dirs. Columbia Theol. Sem., Decatur, Ga. A.R.C., Highlands; bd. dirs., mem. exec. com. Va. Highlands Community Coll., Bristol Meml. Hosp.; chmn. bd. dirs. Coahoma County Nursing Sch. Served as capt., chaplain, USAF, 1950-52, Korea. Recipient Alumnus of Year award Coll. of Ozarks, 1949. Mem. Nat. Council Family Relations. Mason (chaplain New Orleans shrine 1948—). Mem. Coahoma County, Bristol chambers commerce, S.A.R., Alumni of Columbia Theol. Sem. (v.p. 1955-57). Co-author: The Manual for Ordination and Installation of Ministers, 1963. Home: RFD 4 Box 84 Waxhaw NC 28173

STEVENSON, JOHN MOTE, paper co. exec.; b. Cin., May 17, 1930; s. Frank E. and Neva (Mote) S.; A.B., Harvard, 1952, M.B.A., 1954; m. Roxanna Louise Harrington, June 25, 1954; children—Frank, John, Amy, Sarah, David. With Champion Internat. Corp. and subsidiary cos., 1954—, v.p., Southwestern div. mgr. DairyPak, Paper Converting div., Fort Worth, 1966—; dir. Continental Nat. Bank Fort Worth. Pres., Retarded Children Services Assn. Tarrant County, 1966-67; mem. Mayor's Com. for Streams and Valleys. Bd. dirs. Fort Worth Park and Recreation Dept., 1969-73; trustee Fort Worth Country Day Sch., 1971—; bd. dirs., past pres. Child Study Center, Ft. Worth; mem. exec. council Longhorn council Boy Scouts Am.; v.p. United Fund of Tarrant County; bd. dirs. Ft. Worth Symphony Orch. Assn.; asso. trustee W.I. Cook Children's Hosp. Mem. Sales and Marketing Execs. Fort Worth (v.p. 1969—, dir.), Fort Worth C. of C. (dir.). Republican. Presbyn. (elder). Clubs: Hasty Pudding Harvard, Harvard Business School (Dallas-Fort Worth), Fort Worth; Chaparral, Rivercrest Golf, Ridglea Golf, Webhannet Golf. Home: 1207 Hillcrest St Fort Worth TX 76107 Office: 1901 Windsor Pl Fort Worth TX 76110

STEVENSON, JOHN WILLIAM, educator; b. Rhome, Tex., Mar. 8, 1924; s. Forrest Taulbee and Euna (Wright) S.; B.S. in Commerce, Tex. Christian U., 1952, M.B.A., 1961; LL.B. (scholar), So. Methodist U., 1955; Ph.D., U. Tex., 1968; m. Nell Eugenia McCall, May 11, 1956; children—John W., Susan Donnell. Accountant, Alford, Meroney & Co., Dallas, 1952-55, Leatherwood & Ward, Fort Worth, 1955-59; asso. prof. dept. accounting Tex. Christian U., Ft. Worth, 1959-68; prof. Stephen F. Austin State U., Nacogdoches, Tex., 1968—, chmn. dept. accounting, 1968—. Pres. Stevenson & White, Nacogdoches, 1973—; cons. Exxon Corp., 1971. Vice pres. Friends of Library, Nacogdoches, 1973—. Served with USNR, 1943-46. C.P.A., Tex. Mem. State Bar Tex., Tex. Soc. C.P.A.'s, Nat. Assn. Accountants, Phi Kappa Phi, Beta Alpha Psi, Beta Gamma Sigma, Phi Alpha Delta. Presbyn. (elder). Kiwanian. Home: 1720 York Dr Nacogdoches TX 75961

STEVENSON, LARRY CLAYTON, auditor; b. Watertown, S.D., Nov. 7, 1942; s. Olaf Sigard and Ella (Nesheim) S.; B.S. in Bus. Adminstrn. with honors, U. S.D., 1965; Staff auditor firm Haskins & Sells, Houston, 1965-69, Tenneco, Inc., Houston, 1969—. C.P.A., Tex. Mem. Am. Inst. C.P.A.'s, Tex. Soc. C.P.A.'s, Beta Gamma Sigma. Home: 1505 Woodhead Houston TX 77019 Office: PO Box 2511 Houston TX 77001

STEVENSON, WILLIAM DAMON, JR., elec. engr., educator; b. Pitts., July 21, 1912; s. William Damon and Margaret (Watson) S.; B.S. in Engring., Princeton, 1934; B.S. in Elec. Engring., Carnegie-Mellon U., 1939; M.S., U. Mich., 1942; m. Anne Mary Kilcourse, Dec. 17, 1951; children—John Scott, Margaret Haven. Instr. Clemson (S.C.) U., 1939-42, asst. prof., 1942-43; asst. prof. Princeton (N.J.) U., 1943-46; asso. prof. dept. elec. engring. N.C. State U. at Raleigh, 1946-51, prof., 1951—, asso. head dept., 1967—. Dir. Troxler Elec. Labs., Raleigh. Cons. editor elec. power engring. McGraw-Hill Ency. Sci. & Tech., 1963—. Recipient Ordnance Devel. award U.S. Navy, 1946. Fellow I.E.E.E.; mem. Am. Soc. Engring. Edn., Phi Beta Kappa, Sigma Xi, Tau Beta Pi, Eta Kappa Nu, Phi Kappa Phi. Author: Elements of Power System Analysis, 1955. Home: 2706 White Oak Rd Raleigh NC 27609

STEVES, SAM BELL, constrn. co. exec.; b. San Antonio, Tex., Feb. 15, 1911; s. Albert and Annie (Bell) S.; A.B., Washington and Lee U., 1932; m. Joan Cahill, May 6, 1933 (dec. Jan. 1972); children—Joanne (Mrs. F.F. Devine Jr.), Annie (Mrs. Virgil Rosser III), Martha (Mrs. Edwin Jones Peet), Elizabeth (Mrs. Clyde Frederick Shannon Jr.), Julie; m. 2d, Louise Laux Anderson, July 21, 1973. Mgr. Ed Steves & Sons Lumber Co., San Antonio, 1939-54; pres. Steves Industries Inc., San Antonio, 1954-58; pres. Tampo Mfg. Co., Inc., San Antonio, 1958-73, now chmn. db. Mem. adv. bd. Incarnate Word Coll., San Antonio. Mayor San Antonio, 1951-52. Bd. dirs. Joan and Sam Bell Steves Found. Decorated Knight St. Gregory Great. Mem. San Antonio C. of C., San Antonio Mfrs. Assn. Rotarian, Kiwanian. Clubs; Texas Cavaliers, San Antonio German, Order Alamo, Merry Knights, Pilon, San Antonio County. Home: 532 Terrell Rd San Antonio TX 78209 Office: 1146 W Laurel St San Antonio TX 78285

STEWARD, CARL WARREN, citrus processing co. exec.; b. Cardington, O., Mar. 4, 1922; s. Harry Burton and Mary Elizabeth (Daily) S.; B.B.A., Ohio State U., 1943; postgrad. U. Cal. at Berkeley, 1946, Princeton, 1964, Rollins Coll., 1971—; m. Ethel Grace Billingham, Oct. 23, 1946 (dec. Mar. 15, 1974); children—Dorothy Lee, Carl Warren, William Charles. Mgr. accounting Farm Bur. Coop., Columbus, 1946-56; controller Mt. Vernon Bridge Co. (O.), 1956-60, Pa. Farm Bur., Harrisburg, 1960-65; controller B.C. Cook & Sons Enterprises, Inc., Haines City, Fla., 1965—, asst. gen. mgr., 1971—; sec., treas. Growers Processing Service, Inc., Highland City, Fla., 1968—. Mem. Haines City Planning Commn. Served with AUS, 1943-46. Decorated Bronze Star medal, Bronze Arrowhead. Mem. Nat. Assn. of Accountants (dir. 1961—, pres. Mid-Fla. chpt. 1971-72), C. of C., Delta Sigma Pi. Mem. Christian Ch. (chmn. bd. 1953-55). Home: 1017 E Ledwith St Haines City FL 33844 Office: 413 N 12th St Haines City FL 33844

STEWART, ALBERT, JR., physician; b. Fayetteville, N.C., Sept. 23, 1920; s. Albert and Winnie Davis (Bruton) S.; student U. S.C., 1936-37; A.B., U. N.C., 1941; M.D., Washington U., 1944; m. Mary Inglesby DuBose, Oct. 5, 1951; children—Albert III, David DuBose, Paul Finley, Charles Inglesby, James Bruton. Intern Barnes Hosp., St. Louis, 1944-45; fellow medicine Washington U., St. Louis, 1946-47; ships surgeon Grace Line, N.Y.C., 1947; resident physician Meml. Hosp., Charlotte, N.C., 1948; fellow gastroenterology Lehey Clinic, Boston, 1949; practice medicine specializing in internal medicine, Fayetteville, 1950—; attending physician Highsmith, Cape Fear Valley hosps.; cons. VA Hosp.; clin. asso. prof. medicine U. N.C. Sch. Medicine, 1968—. Served with M.C., USNR, 1945-46, 52-54. Diplomate Am. Bd. Internal Medicine. Fellow A.C.P.; mem. A.M.A., N.C., Cumberland County med. socs., Am., N.C. socs. internal medicine. Episcopalian. Kiwanian. Home: 1507 Morganton Rd Fayetteville NC 28305 Office: 114 Broadfoot Av Fayetteville NC 28305

STEWART, BOBBY ALTON, soil scientist; b. Erick, Okla., Sept. 26, 1932; s. William David and Anna Maude (Howard) S.; B.S., Okla. State U., 1953, M.S., 1957; Ph.D., Colo. State U., 1961; m. Jane Ann Nelson, Aug. 5, 1956; children—Steven Mark, Gregory Neal, Judith Ann. Soil scientist Dept. Agr. and Okla. Expt. Sta., Stillwater, 1953-57, soil scientist, Ft. Collins, Colo., 1957-68, research leader Southwestern Gt. Plains Research Center, Bushland, Tex., 1968—; tchr. soils course Colo. State U., 1962; tchr. grad. course soils Tex. A. and M. U., 1973. Mem. Soil Sci. Soc. Am. (asso. editor Procs. 1967-73, div. chmn. 1972), Soil Conservation Soc. Am. (div. chmn. 1973). Contbr. articles profl. jours. Home: 6712 Jameson St Amarillo TX 79106 Office: US Dept Agr Research Center Bushland TX 79012

STEWART, BURTON GLOYDEN, JR., banker; b. Clayton, N.C., Mar. 14, 1933; s. Burton Gloyden and Evelyn I. (Stallings) S.; B.A., Duke, 1955; grad. student Sch. Banking of South, La. State U., 1968-70; m. Patricia Taylor, June 16, 1956; children—Burton III, Herbert Taylor. Trainee, Allstate Ins. Co., Charlotte, 1957, agt., 1957, sales trainer, 1958-59, dist. sales mgr., Columbia, S.C., 1959-60, Greensboro, N.C., 1960-64, field sales mgr., Jackson, Miss., 1964, Charlotte, N.C., 1964, regional sales mgr., 1964-66; v.p. Branch Banking & Trust Co., Wilson, N.C., 1966-72, mgr. marketing dept., 1967-71, mgr. bus. devel. div., 1971-72, sr. v.p., 1972-73, exec. v.p. corporate planning and marketing div., 1973—; dir. Branch Corp., 1974—. Treas., Wilson Arts Council, 1969-71; active United Fund, N.C. Heart Assn. Served as lt. USNR, 1955-57. Mem. N.C. Bankers Assn. (mem. marketing com. 1970), Bank Marketing Assn. Methodist (adminstrv. bd. 1968-71). Home: 1134 Knollwood Dr Wilson NC 27893 Office: 223 W Nash St Wilson NC 27893

STEWART, CHESTER ORVILLE, govt. ofcl.; b. Madisonville, Tex., Apr. 12, 1938; s. Wade Welton and Kathleen (Scott) S.; B.B.A., U. Tex., 1960; postgrad. Coll. Law, Houston U., 1964-67; m. Mary Janice Fisher, Oct. 28, 1961; children—Lisa Lynnette, Wade Fisher. With IRS, various locations, 1960—, estate, gift tax examiner, Houston, 1964-70, appellate conferee, New Orleans, 1972—. C.P.A., Tex., La. Mem. Am. Inst. C.P.A.'s, Tex., La. Socs. C.P.A.'s. Baptist. Home: 6141 Bellaire Dr New Orleans LA 70124 Office: Rm 444 600 South St New Orleans LA 70130

STEWART, CORNELIUS JAMES II, mfg. co. exec.; b. Houston, June 27, 1925; s. Ross and Catherine (Rial) S.; student Spartan Sch. Aeros., 1943, U. Tex., Austin, 1946; certificate in Econ. Moblzn., Indsl. Coll. Armed Forces, 1952; m. Gretchen Elizabeth Braun, Nov. 27, 1947; children—Cornelius James III, Richard Ross, David Rial, Gretchen Elizabeth, Catherine Maria. Purchasing agt. Stewart & Stevenson Services, Inc., Houston, 1947-56, v.p., sec., 1956-73, pres., 1973—; purchasing agt. C. Jim Stewart & Stevenson, Inc., 1947-56, pres., 1956—; pres. Bayou Bldg. Corp., 1948—; chmn. bd. Machinery Acceptance Corp.; v.p., sec.-treas. Internat. Switchboard Corp.; dir. Mangone Shipbldg. Corp., So. State Bank, Reagan Commerce Bank. Chmn., Houston Planning Commn., 1955—. Bd. dirs. Holly Hall. Served with USAAF, 1944-45. Mem. Purchasing Agts. Assn. Houston (pres. 1959-60), nat. dir. 1961-62), Houston C. of C., Kappa Sigma. Presbyn. Rotarian. Clubs: Houston (chmn. finance com. 1972, pres. 1973), Houston Country, Ramada. Home: 5957 Shady River St Houston TX 77027 Office: 1719 Preston St PO Box 1637 Houston TX 77001

STEWART, DAVID KEITH, educator; b. Olathe, Kan., May 22, 1921; s. Bernard and Louverna Adele (Brown) S.; B.A., Central Mo. State Coll., Warrensburg, 1948; M.A., Tchrs. Coll., Columbia, 1950; postgrad. U. Ia., 1952-58, Cornell U., Ithaca, N.Y., summer 1968; Ed.D., N.Y. U., 1970; m. Nina Farmer, Aug. 15, 1942; children—Judith (Mrs. Charles L. Brader, Jr.), Diane Kathryn, Jeanne Elizabeth. Teaching prin. Plainville (Kan.) Elementary Sch., 1948-49; tchr. Greenwich (Conn.) pub. schs., 1949-50; prin. sch., Muncie, Kan., 1950-52; dir. elementary edn. Iowa City Pub. Schs., 1952-58; instr. State U. Ia., summers 1955-57; dir. elementary edn. Kenosha (Wis.) pub. schs., 1958-64; prin. Murray Av. Sch., Mamaroneck, N.Y., 1964-68; asst. supt. personnel Mamaroneck Pub. Schs., 1968-70; supt. McCracken County Pub. Schs., Paducah, Ky., 1970-73; prof. edn. psychology U. So. Miss., Hattiesburg, 1973—. Vis. prof. Carthage Coll., Kenosha, summers 1963-64; editor, host Chalk Dust, ednl. radio series, weekly, Iowa City, 1955-57. Served with USAAF, 1942-45; PTO. Contbr. articles to profl. jours. Home: 3422 W Adeline Hattiesburg MS 39401 Office: PO Box 293 So Sta U So Miss Hattiesburg MS 39401

STEWART, EASTON, civil engr.; b. Wybark, Okla., Sept. 11, 1922; s. Voistes Lee and Zella (Fears) S.; B.S. in Civil Engring., U. Okla., 1953; m. Maralynn E. Robertson, Dec. 29, 1949; children—Stephen, Charles, Barbara, Cheryl. Owner, Easton Stewart & Assos., Cons. Engrs., Baton Rouge, 1969—. Served with USNR, 1942-45; PTO. Registered profl. engr., Okla., Miss., La., Tenn. Mem. Cons. Engrs. Council, Am. Soc. C.E., Nat., La. socs. profl. engrs., Am. Pub. Works Assn., Inst. Transp., Inst. Municipal Engrs. Specialist in maj. hwy. design. Home: 11433 Archery Dr Baton Rouge LA 70815 Office: 6717 Goya Av Baton Rouge LA 70806

STEWART, FLYNN WHEELER, accountant; b. Bowie, Tex., Jan. 26, 1915; s. Cap Smith and Annie Bell (Wheeler) S.; student Draughons Bus. Coll., 1936; m. Dewey Adaline Hatchett, Jan. 27, 1940; children—Roland, Flynn Wheeler II, James, Nancy, Elizabeth (Mrs. Robbie C. Edmondson). Accountant, Northwestern Supply Co., Burkburnett, Tex., 1936-37; comptroller White Stores, Inc., Clinton, Okla., 1937-44; internal auditor Consol. Vultee Aircraft, San Diego, 1944-45; comptroller White Stores, Inc., Wichita Falls, Tex., 1945-46; partner Stewart, Rariden & Miller, Wichita Falls, 1946—; dir. 1st Nat. Bank, Bowie, Tex. C.P.A., Tex. Mem. Am. Inst. C.P.A.'s, Tex. Soc. C.P.A.'s, Am. (past pres.), Tex. (past pres.) angus assns. Club: Exchange. Home: 3505 Harrison St Wichita Falls TX 76308 Office: 1220 Oiland Gas Bldg Wichita Falls TX 76301

STEWART, G KINSEY, psychologist; b. Des Moines, Sept. 9, 1925; s. Lloyd George and Gladys (Kinsey) S.; student Millsaps Coll., 1943-44, Franklin and Marshall Coll., 1944; B.A., Drake U., 1948; M.S., Tulane U., 1956, Ph.D., 1960;; m. Marguerite Stanley, July 7, 1945; children—Kathryn Lynn (Mrs. Mark Blasingame), Karen Lee, Maureen Kay. Psychologist, La. Dept. Hosps., Shreveport, 1950-53; field rep., asst. dir. La. Assn. for Mental Health, New Orleans, 1953-56; guidance officer Tulane U., New Orleans, 1956-60; asst. prof. La. State U., New Orleans, 1960-62; sr. psychologist Kennedy Child Study Center, Santa Monica, Cal., 1962-68; clin. psychologist, Gulfport, Miss., 1968-70; dir. Gulf Coast Mental Health Center, 1970—. Bd. dirs. Juvenile Delinquency Commn. Santa Monica, Harrison County Assn. for Mental Health, Nat. Council Community Mental Health Centers, 1972-74, Harrison County Drug Council. Served with USMCR, 1943-46. Mem. Am., La. (sec. 1961-62), Cal., Miss. psychol. assns., Am. Assn. U. Profs., Am. Assn. on Mental Deficiency, Mental Health Assn. Staff Council, Sigma Xi. Home: Route 1 Box 328 Saucier MS 39574 Office: 1326 Broad Av Gulfport MS 39501

STEWART, GUSTAVUS HOFFMEYER, power and light co. exec.; b. Florence, S.C., Oct. 23, 1913; s. Alexander Toland and Agnes Margaret (Hoffmeyer) S.; B.S., Clemson U., 1935; M.S., Va. Poly. Inst., 1938; m. Juanita Gladys Mitchell, Sept. 2, 1944; children—Patricia Diane (Mrs. Leaman Gerarde Norris), William Alexander, Julian Gustavus. Leader agr. engring. extension work Clemson U., 1936-56; mgr. S.C. area devel. Carolina Power & Light Co., Florence, 1956-72, dir. pub. affairs for S.C., 1972—; treas. Greater Carolinas Corp., 1971; pres. Gem Cove Inc., 1966—, Stewart Enterprises, 1963—; sec., dir. Greater Carolinas Life Ins. Co., 1972—; dir. Enterprise Devel. Co., Bristol, Tenn., 1972—. Mem. Gov.'s Mgmt. and Rev. Commn., 1971; tchr. Florence Darlington Tech., 1963-66. Chmn., Florence County Resources Devel. Commn., 1963—; vice-chmn. Gov's Beautification and Community Improvement Bd., 1973-74; chmn. congl. dist. Student Tchr. Achievement Recognition Program, 1966-71; mem. S.C. Traffic Council, 1967—; mem. U.S. Sec. of Commerce Regional Export Expansion Council, 1969—; bd. visitors Coker Coll. Served from 2d lt. to col., AUS, World War II. Decorated Bronze Star; recipient Plaque for meritorious service 4-H, 1970, Community Leader of Am. award, 1969-71, Distinguished Service award, 1972; Distinguished Service award S.C. Assn. Future Farmers, 1972; Community Devel. award S.C. Jaycees, 1969-70. Registered profl. engr., S.C. Mem. Am. Soc. Agrl. Engrs. (chmn. S.E. sect. 1956), Res. Officers Assn. (pres. 1963), S.C. State C. of C. (dir. 1963-64), Southeastern Community Devel. Assn. (pres. 1969-70), V.F.W., Am. Legion, Alpha Zeta, Sigma Epsilon. Methodist. Elk, Rotarian. Clubs: Kilowatt, Country (Florence); Palmetto (Columbia, S.C.). Home: 809 W Palmetto St Florence SC 29501 Office: Florence Mall Florence SC 29501

STEWART, HENRY ALLEN, SR., lawyer; b. Aragon, Ga., Sept. 19, 1910; s. F. M. and Willie Mae (Turner) S.; B.S., U. Ga., 1933, J.D. and M.A., 1934; m. Rebecca Henslee, Jan. 31, 1937 (dec.); 1 son, Henry Allen. Admitted to Ga. bar, 1934; instr. history U. Ga., 1933-34; dep. commr. revenue, Ga., 1934-37; practice law, Cedartown, Ga., 1934—; vice chmn., dir. Comml. Nat. Bank, Cedartown Loan & Finance Co., Colonial 5, 10 and 25 cent Stores, Inc., Cedartown; v.p., dir. Ga. Solite Corp., Richmond, Va.; dir. Guaranty Title Ins. Co., Atlanta. Vice chmn. Ga. State Bd. Edn.; vice chmn. State Democratic Exec. Com. Mem. Polk County (pres.), Tallapoosa Circuit (pres.), Tallapoosa, Ga., Am. bar assns., C. of C., Sigma Delta Kappa, Alpha Kappa Psi. Elks. Mason (Shriner). Clubs: Cherokee County, Legion, Exchange (state pres.), Gridiron. Home: 728 N College St Cedartown GA 30125 Office: Stewart Building Cedartown GA 30125

STEWART, JAMES RAYMOND, JR., judge; b. Chgo., Feb. 15, 1933; s. James Raymond and Virginia (Supple) S.; B.S., U. Ill., 1954; LL.B., U. Miami, 1960; m. Jane M. Poole, June 23, 1954; children—Lynn C., John R., Nancy J. Admitted to Fla. bar, 1960, since practiced in Miami; asso. firm Dixon, Dejarnette, Bradford, Williams, McKay and Kimbrell, 1960; practiced West Palm Beach, Fla.; asso. firm Wood and Cobb, 1961-63, mem. firm Wood, Cobb, Robinson, Falcon and Letts, 1963-67; asst. atty., Palm Beach County, Fla., 1965-67; county judge Palm Beach County, 1967-69; circuit judge State of Fla., 1969—, chief judge, 1973—. Pres. Assn. Religious Orgns., 1968-69, bd. dirs., 1968-72. Bd. dirs. Family Service Agy. Palm Beach County, 1963, Mental Health Assn., 1968-69, YMCA, 1969-71. Served to 1st lt. USMC, 1954-57. Methodist. Home: 6599 Katherine Rd West Palm Beach FL 33406 Office: Courthouse West Palm Beach FL 33401

STEWART, JOE LOWERY, govt. ofcl.; b. Towns, Ga., Jan. 7, 1918; s. John Quincey and Mary Gustava (Clements) S.; student Capitol Radio Engring. Inst., 1937-39, U.S. Coast Guard Res. Acad., 1944; m. Louise Matilda Kielbasa, Feb. 14, 1947; children—John Davis, Walter Mason, Bette Jo. Chief engr. Sta. WMOG, Brunswick, Ga., Sta. WFTL, Ft. Lauderdale, Fla., 1937-42; sr. engr. electronic engring. Sta. USCG, Washington, 1946-52, chief frequency mgmt., 1952—. Rep., interdept. radio adv. com. Treasury Dept., 1952-67, Dept. Transp., 1967—; mem. nat. com. Internat. Radio Consultative Com., 1970—. Served to ensign USCGR, 1942-46; ETO. Recipient Gold medal for exceptional service Treasury Dept., 1963, Gallatin award, 1967. Mem. I.E.E.E. (sr.), Nat. Rifle Assn. (life). Home: 9322 E Parkhill Dr Bethesda MD 20014 Office: 400 7th St SW Washington DC 20590

STEWART, JOHN CRAIG, educator, author; b. Selma, Ala., Jan. 20, 1915; s. Horace H. and Mary (Craig) S; B.A., U. Ala., 1948, M.A., 1950; m. Lila Harper, Oct. 15, 1960; 1 son, Bruce Craig. Instr. U. Ala., Tuscaloosa, 1950-55, asst. prof. English and creative writing, 1955-60; asst. prof. English and creative writing U. Ala. Extension Center Mobile, 1960-64; asst. prof. U. So. Ala., Mobile, 1964-66, asso prof. English and creative writing, 1967-71, prof., dir. creative writing program, 1971—, acting chmn. dept. English, 1964-66. Cons. faculty Air U., Maxwell Field, Ala., 1951; dir. publs. div. Army Ballistic Missle Agy., Huntsville, Ala., summer 1960. Served to maj. USAAF, 1941-45. Mem. Am. Assn. U. Profs., South Atlantic Modern Lang. Assn., Phi Delta Theta. Author: Through the First Gate, 1950; Muscogee Twilight, 1965; Know Alabama, 1957; Prose and Poetry for Enjoyment, 1955. Contbr. short stories in popular mags., as Atlantic

Monthly, Am. Mercury, Saturday Evening Post, True, Comment, New Writers, many others. Home: Route 2 Box 328-C Theodore AL 36582 Office: U So Ala Gaillard Dr Mobile AL 36608

STEWART, JOHN ELLIOTT, investment counsel; b. Chgo., Dec. 1, 1912; s. Robert Wright and Maude (Elliott) S.; ed. Yale, 1935; m. Mary Terry Schlamp, May 9, 1936; children—James Jeremiah, Sara Royall, John Elliott. Salesman Colonial Beacon Oil Co., N.Y.C., 1935-36; pres. Stewart, Warren & Co., N.Y.C., 1937-40; comml. aviation pilot, flight instr. A & H Flying Service, Asheville, N.C., 1940-42; asst. supt. stas. operations and flight dispatch mgr. Pan Am. Airways, Inc., Atlantic div., N.Y.C., 1947-50; asso. Neergard, Miller & Co., N.Y.C., 1950-57, Coffin & Burr, Inc., N.Y.C., 1957-61, Laird, Bissell & Meeds, 1961-62; formed own investment counseling firm, Madison, 1962; dir. North Madison Representative Orgn., 1966-68, pres., 1967-68. Sec. Federated Assns., Greenwich, 1952-54; dir. Am. Coalition, Washington, 1957-60; chmn. U.S. Day Com. Greenwich, 1954; v.p. Madison Land Conservation Trust, 1966-67, pres., 1968-70, dir., chmn. land acquistion com., 1968-71, justice of peace, 1964-71; mem. Conn. Power Facility Evaluation Com., 1971; mem. Conn. Am. Revolution Bicentennial Council, 1971—; vice chmn. Bicentennial Commn. Palm Beach, 1974—. Mem. Republican Town Com. Madison, 1964-71; dir. Palm Beach Rep. Club, 1972-74, pres., 1972-74. Served as lt. comdr., naval aviator USNR, 1942-46. Mem. Greenwich C. of C. (past v.p., dir. 1956-60, chmn. legislative com., edn. com.), S.A.R. (bd. mgrs., sr. v.p. Conn. soc. 1962-64, pres. Conn. Soc. 1964-66, nat. trustee for Conn., 1965-67, v.p. Palm Beach chpt. 1972), C.A.R. (mem. bd. Conn. soc.; sr. pres. Lt. William Stewart Soc.). Republican. Clubs: Metropolitan (gov. 1958-62) (N.Y.C.); Racquet (Chgo.); Madison Rotary (dir. v.p. 1966-67, pres. 1968-69) (Madison); Biltmore (N.C.) Forest Country; Everglades, Beach (Palm Beach, Fla.); Marbella (Spain). Home: La Casa Pequena 730 North County Rd Palm Beach FL 33480

STEWART, JOHN WESLEY, supermarket exec.; b. Trent, Tex., Mar. 3, 1918; s. George Thomas and Zadie E. (Estep) S.; student pub. schs.; m. Bennie Fee Stone, Jan. 14, 1940; children—Johnnie Ray, Jimmie V., Ronald Wesley. Owner grocery story, Quemado, Tex., 1938-39, Borden & Ray Grocery, Asherton, Tex., 1939-48; owner Stewart's I.G.A. Store, Cotulla, Tex., 1941-42; rancher, Asherton, 1939-48; owner Stewart's I.G.A. Foodliner, Uvalde, Tex., 1948-66, Stewarts United Supermarket, Uvalde, after 1967, now owner, pres. J.W. Stewart & Co. Inc.; partner radio sta. KPSO, Falfurrias, Tex., 1955-65, radio sta. KSOX, Raymondville, Tex., 1959-65; rancher, Uvalde County, 1965—, Catarina, Tex., 1969—; dir. Uvalde Nat. Bank. Baptist (deacon). Mason, Lion (past pres.). Home: PO Box 1633 Uvalde TX 78801 Office: 600 E Main St Uvalde TX 78801

STEWART, JOSEPH GORDON, dentist; b. Anniston, Ala., Mar. 8, 1929; s. James Douglas and Mamie Louise (McClellan) S.; B.S., Birmingham So. Coll., 1952; D.M.D., U. Ala., 1954; m. Roxie Catherine Grace, Aug. 24, 1952; children—Labella, Roxanna, Joanna, Joseph Gordon. Practice pediatric dentistry, Montgomery, Ala., 1956—. Cons. Montgomery Children's Center, 1957—. Pres., Montgomery Community Action Com., 1967, Central Ala. Timberland Inc., 1970-71. Mem. Ala. Dental Polit. Action com., chmn. bd., 1973. Bd. dirs. Tukabatchee Area council Boy Scouts Am., pres. 1968-70; bd. dirs. Montgomery Children's Center, Ala. Dental Found., Ala. Heart Assn.; bd. dirs. United Appeal Ala., v.p., 1974-75. Served to capt. Dental Corps, AUS, 1954-56. Named one of four outstanding young men of Ala., Ala. Jr. C. of C., 1964, Most Distinguished Alumnus, U. Ala. Sch. Dentistry, 1968; recipient Silver Beaver award Boy Scouts Am., 1964, Distinguished Service award Montgomery Jr. C. of C., 1964. Fellow Am. Coll. Dentists; mem. Am. (del. 1964-70), Ala. (trustee 1962-72, pres. 1970-71) dental assns., Ala. Dental Alumni Assn. (pres. 1961), Montgomery County Dental Soc. (pres. 1959), Am. Soc. Dentistry for Children (pres. 1962, pres. dist. 1974-75), Alpha Tau Omega, Psi Omega. Methodist (steward 1964-68). Home: 2052 Myrtlewood Dr Montgomery AL 36111 Office: 330 S Ripley St Montgomery AL 36104

STEWART, LAWRENCE GORDON, mining engr.; b. Coxtox, Ky., Nov. 18, 1927; s. James Lee and Ollie Geneva (Tolliver) S.; B.S. in Mining Engring., U. Ky. 1954; m. Lola Bailey, Dec. 7, 1951; children—Lawrence Gordon, Patricia Lee. Mining engr., foreman U.S. Steel Corp., Lynch, Ky., 1954-62; chief engr. Princess Coals Inc., Mallory, W.Va., 1962-63; Omar Mining Co. (W.Va.), 1963-71; chief engr. Eastovar Mining Co., Brookside, Ky., 1971—. Scoutmaster, mem. troop com. Boy Scouts Am. Served with AUS, 1945-47; ETO. Mem. Ky. Mining Inst., Ky. C. of C. Address: Brookside KY 40811

STEWART, LINDA JOAN WILLIAMS, educator; b. Monterey Park, Cal., Oct. 17, 1938; d. Ralph F. and Maude (Spicer) Williams; B.A. in Edn., Northwestern State Coll., 1962, M.Ed., 1964; Ed.D., Okla. State U., 1970; m. Douglas Stewart, Dec. 22, 1962 (div. 1973). Tchr. English, speech Medicine Lodge (Kan.) High Sch., 1963; tchr., counselor Harper (Kan.) High Sch., 1964-66; instr. speech Northwestern State Coll., Alva, Okla., 1968, acting chmn. speech dept., 1969-71, prof. speech, 1971—, also dir. drama prodns. Sponsor, Castle Players; mem. Nesatunga Arts and Humanities Council. Mem. Bus. and Profl. Guidance Assn., Alvah C. of C., Am. Ednl. Theatre Assn., Speech Assn. Am., N.E.A., Am. Assn. U. Women, Alpha Psi Omega (sponsor). Republican. Conglist. Mem. Order Eastern Star. Home: 1202 2d St Alva OK 73717

STEWART, LLOYD MAY, newspaper editor; b. Port Arthur, Tex., Jan. 15, 1924; d. Lloyd Martin and May (Cowart) Stewart; B.J., U. Tex., 1945. Reporter, Wichita Falls (Tex.) Record News, 1945, Marshall (Tex.) News Messenger, 1946-47; editor Cleburne (Tex.) Times-Rev., 1947-49; with Ft. Worth Star-Telegram, 1949—, soc. editor, 1950—, art editor, 1959-63, woman's editor, fashion editor, 1963—. Recipient 1st place award, women's news Tex. A.P. Mng. Editors Assn., 1966. Mem. Am. Assn. U. Women, Tex. Congress Parents and Tchrs., Fashion Group, Inc., Women in Communications (chpt. pres. 1962-64, nat. bd. 1964—, nat. pres. 1968-71). Episcopalian. Clubs: Zonta, Woman's, Woman's Shakespeare (Ft. Worth). Home: 710 N Main St Cleburne TX 76031 Office: 400 W 7th St Fort Worth TX 76101

STEWART, LOUIS ALVIN, govt. ofcl.; b. Flatonia, Tex., Feb. 28, 1928; s. George A. and Albina Elizabeth (Weidel) S.; B.S., Tex. A. and M. U., 1953; M.A. in Corrections, Sam Houston State U., 1971; m. Della Polly Laqua, June 2, 1951; children—Debra Gayle, Louis Alvin. Asst. probation officer Travis County Juvenile Ct., Austin, 1953-54; sr. group adviser Travis County Juvenile Home, 1954-57; supt. Gardner House, Travis County Juvenile Ct., Austin, 1957—. Vice pres. St. Ignatius Parent Tchrs. Guild, 1964-65, pres., 1965-66; v.p. Holy Cross High Sch. P.T.A., 1969-70, pres., 1970-71. Served with USAAF, 1946-47. Mem. Am., Tex. Corrections Assns., Tex. Inst. on Children and Youth (chmn. 1964), Tex. Probation and Parole Assn. (chmn. 1961, 63). Address: 2515 S Congress Av Austin TX 78704

STEWART, MARCUS CROWDER, utilities exec.; b. Whiteville, Tenn., Dec. 14, 1907; s. Marcus Jefferson and Mattie Sue (Crowder) S.; B.S., U. Tenn., 1929, postgrad., 1953, 61; m. Mattie Reeves Patton, June 18, 1936; 1 son, Marcus Crowder. Local mgr. Tenn. Electric Power Co., 1929-39; property recorder TVA, 1939-40; mgr. Sand Mountain Electric Coop., Ft. Payne, Ala., 1940-71, mgr. emeritus, 1971-73, mgmt. cons., 1973—; engring. cons. Sand Mountain Water Authority; co-organizer Farmers Telephone Coop. and Water Systems. Bd. dirs. Choccolocco council Boy Scouts Am., United Givers Fund DeKalb County. Served to 1st lt. Officers Rec. Corp., 1929-46. Registered profl. engr., Ala. Mem. Am. Inst. Mgmt. (asso), North Ala. Pub. Power Distbrs. (chmn. pub. relations com., Outstanding Mgr. grantee 1972), North Ala. Indsl. Devel. Assn. (pres., dir.), Tenn. Valley Pub. Power Assn. (pres., dir.), Ala. Rural Electric Assn. Coops., Nat. Rural Elec. Coops. Assn. (com. chmn.), Ft. Payne (dir. 1951-54), Rainsville (dir. 1965-68) chambers commerce. Democrat. Methodist (mem. adminstrv. bd., also chmn.). Mason; mem. Order Eastern Star (past worthy patron). Home: 206 Forrest Av S Fort Payne AL 35967 Office: PO Box 581 Fort Payne AL 35967

STEWART, POTTER, asso. justice U.S. Supreme Ct.; b. Jackson, Mich., Jan. 23, 1915; s. James Garfield and Harriet Loomis (Potter) S.; student Hotchkiss Sch.; B.A. cum laude, Yale, 1937, LL.B. cum laude, 1941, LL.D., 1959; fellow Cambridge U., Eng., 1937-38; m. Mary Ann Bertles, Apr. 25, 1943; children—Harriet Potter (Mrs. Richard Virkstis), Potter, David Bertles. Admitted to Ohio bar, 1941, N.Y. bar, 1942; asso. firm Debevoise, Stevenson, Plimpton & Page, N.Y.C., 1941-42, 45-47; asso. Dinsmore, Shohl, Sawyer & Dinsmore, Cin., 1947-50, mem. firm, 1951-54; U.S. judge Ct. Appeals, 6th Circuit, 1954-58; asso. justice U.S. Supreme Ct., 1958—. Mem. com. White House Conf. on Edn., 1954-55. Mem. Cin. City Council, 1950-53, vice mayor, 1952-53. Served as lt. USNR, 1942-45. Mem. Am., Ohio, Cin. bar assns., Am. Law Inst., Yale Law Sch. Assn. (exec. com.), Order of Coif, Phi Beta Kappa, Delta Kappa Epsilon, Phi Delta Phi. Episcopalian. Clubs: Camargo, Commonwealth, Commercial, University (Cin.); Chevy Chase (Washington); Century (N.Y.C.); Bohemian (San Francisco). Home: 5136 Palisade Lane Washington DC 20016 Office: Supreme Ct Bldg Washington DC 20543

STEWART, ROBERT H., III, banker; b. Dallas, Dec. 3, 1925; s. Robert H. Stewart; B.B.A. in Banking, So. Meth. U., 1949; m. Cynthia Giesecke, 1949; children—Cynthia Caroline, Alice Partee. With Empire State Bank, Dallas, 1949-50; with First Nat. Bank, Dallas, 1951—, v.p., 1953-59, sr. v.p., pres., now chmn., chief exec.; dir. Dallas Hotel Co., Allied Finance Co., Republic Ins. Co., Southwestern Life Ins. Co., Gifford-Hill & Co., Inc., Dallas, Braniff Airways, Inc., Pepsi-Cola Co. Bd. dirs. Dallas Citizens Council. Served to 1st lt. inf. AUS, 1944-46, also Korea. Clubs: Brook Hollow Golf (dir.), Terpsichorean (dir.), Idlewild (dir.) (Dallas). Home: 4626 N Lindhurst St Dallas TX 75229 Office: First Nat Bank Box 6031 Dallas TX 75222

STEWART, ROBERT PERCY, JR., ins. co. exec.; b. Natchez, Miss., Nov. 12, 1922; s. Robert Percy and Virginia Lowry (Hodge) S.; B.F.A., U. Ga., 1943; student So. Meth. U., 1953-56, South Tex. Coll. Law, 1956-57, U. Houston Law Sch., 1956-57; m. Betty Lou George, Aug. 12, 1950; children—Katherine Louise, Virginia Anne, Robert Percy, Owen Thomas. Asst. sales mgr. S.W. div. Kraft Foods Co., Garland, Tex., 1947-53; partner George & Stewart, attys., Dallas, 1953—; pres. S.W. Title Ins. Co., Dallas, 1963—, also dir.; dir. North Dallas Bank and Trust Co., AAA Dallas Auto Club. Served with inf., AUS, 1942-46. Decorated Bronze Star with 2 oak leaf clusters. Mem. Am. Bar Assn., Title Underwriters of Tex. (pres., 1965), Tex. Land Title Assn. (v.p. 1966, dir. 1971), Delta Theta Phi, Phi Delta Theta. Presbyn. Clubs: Chaparral, City, Top-of-the Cliff (Dallas). Home: 4348 Shenandoah Av Dallas TX 75205 Office: 701 Elm St Dallas TX 75202

STEWART, ROBERT WILLIAM, III, constrn. co. exec.; b. Plainview, Tex., June 14, 1940; s. Robert William and Marian (McDowell) S.; student Schreiner Inst. (Kerrville, Tex.), 1958, Spartin Sch. Aeros., 1959, Yingling Sch. Aeros., 1960, Lubbock Christian Coll., 1963; B.B.A. in Accounting, Tex. Tech. U., 1966; m. Margaret Fay Chapman, Dec. 2, 1960; children—Robert William IV, Paul William. Auditor firm Ernst & Ernst, Lubbock, Tex., and Ft. Worth, 1966-68; dir. finance Mitchell Industries, Inc., Mineral Wells, Tex., 1968-70; owner Moon & Hall, Inc., Mineral Wells, 1969-70; asso. Zack Burkett Co., Graham, Tex., 1971—. Sponser Cub Scouts Am., Mineral Wells, 1971-72; adviser Jr. Achievement, Ft. Worth, 1968-69. C.P.A., Tex. Mem. Tex. Soc. C.P.A.'s, Nat. Skeet Shooting Assn. Presbyn. Club: Brazos River Gun and Archery (Mineral Wells). Home: 2001 NW 4th Av Mineral Wells TX 76067 Office: PO Box 209 Graham TX 76046

STEWART, WALTER BINGHAM, educator; b. Evanston, Ill., Aug. 15, 1913; s. Walter Morgan and Elizabeth (Bingham) S.; student U. Ill., 1932-33, Northwestern U., 1939-40, U. Wis., 1961-63, Upper Ia. U., 1962-63; A.B., U. N.C., 1938; B.S., Radford Coll., 1964; postgrad. U. Fla., 1966-68; m. Janie Veda Sinclair, July 3, 1939; children—Sinclair, Donald. Account exec. Erwin, Wasey, Chgo., 1939-40; advt. mgr. The Parker Pen Co., Janesville, Wis., 1940-44; sales and advt. mgr. Louis Melind Co., Chgo., 1945-47; advt. mgr. Reynolds Pen Co., Chgo., 1947-50; advt. mgr. H.W. Gossard Co., Chgo., 1950-61; mgr. Travelmats-Press Pub. Co., Prairie du Chien, Wis., 1961-63; chmn. journalism dept. Radford Coll., 1965-73; freelance newspaperman; advt. cons. to Western Auto Stores, Travel Bur. Fla.; radio broadcaster. Mem. Pi Delta Epsilon, Kappa Delta Pi, Phi Delta Kappa, Phi Gamma Delta. Rotarian. Author: Do You Pass the Model Test, 1957; Do You Dress Like a Model, 1958; Do You Have a Model Figure, 1959; Adventures in Travel, 1962; The Complete Book of Modeling, 1974. Home: 101 Dogwood Lane Radford VA 24141

STIBBS, JOHN HENRY, univ. dean; b. Chgo., Feb. 10, 1909; s. Henry Howard and Bertha (Hemingway) S.; Ph.D., U. Mich., 1942; m. Phyllis Miner, May 25, 1941; children—Virginia Helen, Henry Howard II, John Henry. Teaching fellow U. Mich., 1937-42; instr. U.S. Naval Acad., 1946; with Tulane U., 1946—, successively asst. prof. English, asst. dean Coll. Arts and Scis., 1946-49, prof. and dean of students, 1949—. Mem. exec. com. Assn. Naval R.O.T.C. Colls., 1967-70; acad. council Coll. Student Personnel Inst., 1966-70. Dir. Louise McGehee Sch. 1953-66. Served with USNR, 1942-46, now comdr. Mem. Nat. Assn. Student Personnel Adminstrs. (pres. 1954-55), Am. Personnel and Guidance Assn., Am. Coll. Health Assn., Am. Assn. U. Profs., Orleans Audubon Soc. (pres. 1951-69), Modern, South Central lang. assns., Renaissance Soc., S.R., Soc. War 1812, Delta Kappa Epsilon, Phi Kappa Phi, Omicron Delta Kappa. Clubs: Internat. House, Boston, South Louisiana Gun (dir.), Southern Yacht, New Orleans Lawn Tennis (New Orleans). Author short stories. Contbr. articles to profl. jours. Home: 6901 Willow St New Orleans LA 70118

STICKLEY, ELMER EUGENE, educator; b. Brackenridge, Pa., Jan. 23, 1915; s. Eugene Franklin and Mary Ann (Crawford) S.; B.S., Carnegie Inst. Tech., 1937; M.S., U. Pitts., 1940, Ph.D., 1942; m. Olivia Horner, Dec. 27, 1939; 1 son, Spencer Eugene; m. 2d, Marilyn Anderson Edwards, Jan. 27, 1973. Instr., Pa. Coll. for Women (now Chatham Coll.), part-time, 1938-42; fellow Mellon Inst., Pitts., 1942-43; research physicist Pitts. Plate Glass Co., 1943-51; med. physicist Brookhaven Nat. Lab., 1951-61; attending physicist Presbyn. Hosp., N.Y,C., 1961-66, radiation safety officer, 1961-66, tchr. physics of radiology, diagnostic X-ray physics, nuclear medicine physics, 1961-66; asso. prof. radiology Coll. Physicians and Surgeons, Columbia U., 1961-66; prof. radiation, physics Med. Coll. Va., Richmond, 1966—. Cons. in radiol. physics. Fellow Am. Coll. Radiology; mem. Am. Assn. Physicists in Medicine, Soc. Nuclear Medicine, Health Physics Soc., Am. Inst. Physics, Va. Acad. Sci., Radiol. Soc. N.Am., Radiation Research Soc., Am. Radium Soc., Am. Roentgen Ray Soc., Sigma Xi. Home: 2750 Stratford Rd Richmond VA 23225 Office: 1200 E Broad St Richmond VA 23298

STIEG, ROBERT WILSON, ednl. adminstr., b. Clintonville, Wis., Mar. 12, 1943; s. Robert Wilson and Jane Ellen (Gibson) S.; student Faculte Catholique de Lyon, 1964-65; B.S. in Fgn. Service, Georgetown U., 1966; m. Louise Fannie Blatt, Feb. 3, 1968. Novice Communaute de Taize, 1963-66; research asso. R.R.Bowker Assos., Washington, 1966-67; asst. headmaster Grafton Sch., Berryville, Va., 1968-71, headmaster, 1970—. Mem. Nat. Assn. of Pvt. Schs. for Exceptional Children (dir. 1973—, rec. sec. 1973—), Va. Assn. of Ind. Spl. Edn. Facilities (dir. 1973—, treas. 1973—, v.p., chmn. standards and membership com. 1974—), Northwestern Mental Health Assn. (dir. 1973—), Orton Soc., Assn. for Children with Learning Disabilities, Council for Exceptional Children, Nat. Soc. for Performance and Instruction. Home: Route 2 Box 781 Front Royal VA 22630 Office: Box 469 Berryville VA 22611

STIEGLER, THEODORE DONALD, mech. engr.; b. Balt., May 28, 1934; s. August and Helene (Giese) S.; B.S. in Mech. Engring., Duke, 1956; postgrad. U. Va., 1962-63; m. Beth Collins Sutton, July 6, 1957; children—Linda Catherine, Sally Collins. With E.I. duPont de Nemours & Co., Richmond, Va., 1958—, staff engr., 1973—. Served as lt. (j.g.) USNR, 1956-58. Registered profl. engr., Va. Mem. Nat. Rifle Assn., Delta Tau Delta. Mem. United Ch. of Christ. Co-inventor film winding apparatus, other film accessories. Home: 1329 Pulliam St Richmond VA 23235 Office: PO Box 27222 Richmond VA 23261

STIFF, ASHBY GORDON, JR., educator; b. Balt., Oct. 18, 1930; s. Ashby Gordon and Mary Ellen (Waring) S.; A.B., Johns Hopkins, 1951; M.S., Fla. State U., 1957. Mgmt. trainee Sheraton Corp. Am., Balt., 1956; mgmt. trainee Hotel Corp. Am., Washington, 1957; asst. mgr. Many Glacier Hotel, Glacier Park Co., Glacier, Mont., summer 1958, gen. mgr., 1959-60; gen. mgr. Canyon Village Yellowstone Park Co., Yellowstone Park, Wyo., summers 1961, 64, gen. mgr. Lake Hotel, summer 1962; dir. food, housing Nat. Def. Edn. Act French Insts., Tallahassee, 1963; instr. Sch. Bus., Hotel Adminstrn. Fla. State U., Tallahassee, 1957-61, asst. prof., 1961-68, asso. prof., 1968—, dir. European study program, 1970—. Served with USAF, 1951-55. Named Ky. col. Mem. S.A.R. (past chpt. sec.-treas.), Soc. War 1812 in Md., Order First Families Va., Council Hotel, Restaurant and Instl. Edn. (mem. research com. 1968—, head research project new concepts comml. food edn. 1968, charter mem.), Soc. Hosts, League Hospitality Execs., Soc. Scullions (past pres.), Am. Assn. U. Profs., Navy League, Alpha Kappa Psi, Alpha Psi Omega, Lambda Chi Alpha. Elk. Club: Johns Hopkins (Balt). Publs. editor League Hospitality Execs., 1964—. Contbr. articles to profl. jours. Home: 1481 Marion Av Tallahassee FL 32303

STIFF, JOHN STERLING, city mgr.; b. McKinney, Tex., Feb. 14, 1921; s. James Harrison and Elva (Boone) S.; student Tex. A. and M. Coll., 1938-41; B.E., Yale, 1947; m. Harriet Raschig, May 21, 1946; children—Mark, Justin. Office engr. City of Big Spring, Tex., 1938-39, 41-42; city engr., Abilene, Tex., 1947-51, city mgr., Irving, Tex., 1953-57; gen. mgr. Hardee-Pipkin Constrn. Co., Irving, 1957-58; city mgr., Garland, Tex., 1958-63, Amarillo, Tex., 1963—. Mem. Tex. Gov.'s Com. on Intergovtl. Relations, 1970. Served with USNR, 1942-46, 51-52. Registered profl. engr., Tex. Mem. Internat. (v.p. 1968), Tex. (past pres.) city mgrs. assns., Internat. City Mgmt. Assn. (pres. 1970-71), Amarillo, Dallas (central hwy. com.) chambers commerce, Garland Home Builders Assn. Methodist (steward). Rotarian (past dir. Garland). Clubs: Amarillo A. and M., Amarillo Yale. Home: 7100 Dreyfuss Amarillo TX 79106 Office: PO Box 1971 Amarillo TX 79105

STIGERS, ROBERT WINSTON, dentist; b. Shelbyville, Ky., July 7, 1925; s. Willie Edgar and Mary Francis (Young) S.; student Centre Coll., 1946-49; D.M.D., U. Louisville, 1959; m. Anne McWilliams, Sept. 16, 1951; children—Stephen, David, Lee Anne. Practice of dentistry, 1959-60; staff dentist VA Hosp., Lexington, Ky., 1960—, chief dental service, 1968—; part-time faculty Coll. Dentistry, U. Ky., 1968—. Pres., P.T.A., 1968-69. Served with USAAF, 1943-45. Mem. Christian Ch. Lion, Optimist. Club: Spindletop Hall (Lexington). Home: 1620 Kensington Way Lexington KY 40504 Office: VA Hosp Lexington KY 40507

STIGLER, WILLIAM ARTHUR, museum dir.; b. Ruleville, Miss., July 15, 1910; s. William Arthur and Frances (Word) S.; LL.B., U. Miss., 1936; m. Jeanette Louise Amidon, July 1, 1938. Admitted to Miss. Bar, 1936; practiced in Tunica, 1936-39, spl. agt., supr. FBI, 1939-51; asst. dep. adminstr. Maritime Adminstrn., Washington, 1952-60; dir. Bur. Fgn. Regulation, Fed. Maritime Commn., Washington, 1960-65; exec. dir. Miss. Nursing Home Assn., Jackson, 1968-71; supt. Jefferson Davis Shrine and Museum, Biloxi, Miss., 1971—. Address: Box 200 W Beach Blvd Biloxi MS 39531 Office: 200 W Beach Blvd Biloxi MS 39531

STILES, RAEBURN BRACKETT, state ofcl.; b. Middlebury, Vt., Mar. 14, 1915; s. John E. and Caroline (Brackett) S.; A.B., Middlebury Coll., 1938; M.A., Peabody Coll., 1949; B.S., Vanderbilt U., 1958; m. Carolyn Louise Flascher, Dec. 19, 1941; 1 dau., Susan B. (Mrs. Richard B. Sibley). Tchr. math., coach Green (N.Y.) Central High Sch., 1938-41; tchr., recreation dir. Southfield Sch., Shreveport, La., 1941-42; asso. prof. applied math. Vanderbilt U., 1946-64; engr., dir. computer services div. Tenn. Dept. Hwys., Nashville, 1964-72; dir. regional computing State of Tenn., Nashville, 1972—; meteorologist U.S. Air N.G. Served with Air Corps, 1942-46; ETO: with USAF, 1951-53; to lt. col. Tenn. Air N.G., 1960-71. Registered profl. engr., Tenn. Mem. Am. Math. Assn., Am. Soc. Engring. Edn., Assn. Systems Mgmt., Nat. Soc. Profl. Engrs. Presbyn. (deacon, elder). Home: 3911 Trimble Rd Nashville TN 37215 Office: Andrew Jackson Bldg Nashville TN 37219

STILES, WARREN OAKLEY, cons. engr.; b. Alma, Mich., July 18, 1928; s. Charles Edward and Helen Lucile (Hayner) S.; student Eastern Mich. U., 1957; B.S.E. in Mech. Engring., Mich., 1960; m. Constance Ann Patrick, Sept. 11, 1952; 1 son, Jonathan. Engr., Cutler-Hammer, Milw., 1960-65, Koppers Co., Pitts., 1966; indsl. systems cons., Ypsilanti, Mich., 1966-68; with Aqua-Chem., Inc., Wrightsville Beach, N.C., 1968-71; cons. engr., Wrightsville Beach, 1971—. Pres., Aqua-Labs. of Wrightsville Beach, Inc., 1970—; v.p., dir. Arcon Devel. Corp., Wilmington, N.C., 1971-73). Served with AUS, 1950-54. Mem. Nat. Assn. Professions, Profl. Engrs. N.C., Am. Soc. M.E., Am. Water Works Assn., Water Pollution Control Fedn., Assn. Iron and Steel Engrs., Pi Tau Sigma. Democrat. Club: Wilmington Engineers. Designer elec. motive system for stage wagon drives at New Met. Opera House, Lincoln Center for Performing Arts, N.Y. Home: 7000 Wrightsville Av Wrightsville Sound NC 28480 Office: PO Box 437 Wrightsville Beach NC 23480

STILES, WILLIAM BARNARD, elec. engr., educator; b. Custer City, Okla., Oct. 25, 1909; s. Leslie Earl and Amy Lee (Barnard) S.; B.S. in Elec. Engring., Ia. State U., 1932, M.S. in Elec. Engring., 1937, Ph.D., 1945; m. Myrna M. Cadwell, Mar. 19, 1932; children—Anne M. (Mrs. George Behler), Mary E. (Mrs. Harry Rook). Instr. engring. mechanics Ia. State U., Ames., 1934-37, asst. prof. 1937-46, asso. prof., 1946-49; prof. engring. mechanics U. Ark., Fayetteville, 1949-53, also asso. dir. engring. exptl. sta., 1949-53; prof. engring. mechanics U. Ala., University, 1953-61, 69—, also head mechanics dept., 1953-61, prof., dir. Grad. Inst. Tech., U. Ark., Little Rock, 1961-69. Cons. Wright-Patterson AFB, Dayton, O., summer, 1954, Boeing Airplane Co., Seattle, summer, 1955. Registered profl. engr., Ark. Fellow Am. Soc. M.E. (pres. Ark. sect. 1967-68); mem. Am. Soc. Engring. Edn. (v.p. S.E. sect. 1972-73), Nat., Ark. (pres. 1965-66) socs. profl. engrs., Soc. Exptl. Stress Analysis, Sigma Xi, Phi Kappa Phi, Pi Mu Epsilon, Tau Beta Pi. Rotarian. Clubs: Exchange (Tuscaloosa); Little Rock Engineers (pres. 1968-69). Author: (with A. Higdon) Engineering Mechanics, 1949; (with others) Mechanics of Materials, 1960. Home: 1215 Northwood Lake Northport AL 35476 Office: Box 2908 University AL 35486

STILL, CHARLES NEAL, physician; b. Richmond, Va., Apr. 15, 1929; s. Charles Wright and Ruth (Kemp) S.; B.S., Clemson U., 1949; M.S., Purdue U., 1951; M.D., Med. U. S.C., 1959; m. Dorothy Lee Varn, Dec. 27, 1958; children—Charles Herbert, Carl Nelson. Sara Alice. Lab. chemistry Clemson (S.C.) U., 1948-49; teaching fellow biochemistry Purdue U., Lafayette, Ind., 1949-51; instr. chemistry Clemson U., 1951-52, U.S. Mil. Acad., West Point, N.Y., 1953-55; intern U. Chgo. Clinics, 1959-60; resident Johns Hopkins Hosp. and Balt. City Hosp., 1960-63; postgrad. fellow Johns Hopkins, 1960-63; USPHS research fellow Harvard Med. Sch. and McLean Hosp. Research Lab., Belmont, Mass., 1963-65; chief neurology service William S. Hall Psychiat. Inst., Columbia, S.C., 1965—; vis. asst. clin. prof. neurology Med. U. S.C., 1967-72, asso. clin. prof. neurology, 1973—; cons. S.C. Bapt. Hosp., Columbia, 1966—. Chmn. grants rev. com. S.C. Dept. Mental Health, 1973—. Served to 1st lt. Q.M.C., AUS, 1952-55. Diplomate Am. Bd. Psychiatry and Neurology, Pan Am. Med. Assn. (neurology council). Fellow Am. Geriatrics Soc.; mem. Am. Acad. Neurology, Gerontological Soc., A.M.A., Internat., Am. socs. for neurochemistry, S.C., So. med. assns., Johns Hopkins Med. and Surg. Assn., Sigma Xi. Baptist. Home: 2 Culpepper Circle Columbia SC 29209 Office: WS Hall Psychiat Inst Drawer 119 Columbia SC 29202

STILL, WILLIAM JAMES SANGSTER, pathologist, educator; b. Aberdeen, Scotland, Sept, 16, 1923; s. William and Jean (Sangster) S.; M.B. Ch.B., U. Aberdeen, 1951, M.D., 1960; m. Mary E.A. Duguid, Mar. 27, 1951; children—Mary J.E., William John Peter. Lectr. pathology U. London, 1956-60, sr. lectr., 1962-65; asst. prof. pathology Washington U., St. Louis, 1960-62; prof. pathology Med. Coll. Va., Richmond, 1965—. Served to lt. Royal Navy, 1941-46. Fellow Council on Arteriosclerosis, Am. Heart Assn.; mem. Coll. Pathologists Gt. Britain. Home: 4207 Kensington Av Richmond VA 23221

STILL, WILLIAM LEONARD, aerospace co. exec.; b. LaPanza, Cal., Sept. 16, 1919; s. Mently Frederick and Annabella (Ross) S.; B.S. in Aero. Engring., Air Force Inst. Tech., 1949, M.S. in Elec. Engring., 1954; m. Mary Cathryne Wilson, Aug. 17, 1945; children—William T., Robert J., Patricia A. Commd. 2d. lt. AC, U.S. Army, 1942, advanced through ranks to lt. col. USAF, 1962; research and devel. through the earth communications and ground communications and control minutemen missile, 1958-62; asst. to v.p. Deco Electronics div. Westinghouse, Leesburg, Va., 1962-67; chmn. bd., pres. Aerospace Indsl. Assos., Inc., Purcellville, Va., 1967— . Decorated Bronze Star. Mem. Am. Inst. Aeros. and Astronautics, Am. Ordnance Assn., Air Force Assn., Ret. Officers Assn. Patentee in field. Cons. editor Control Engring., 1962-67. Contbr. articles in field to profl. jours. Home: RFD 2 Box 73 Purcellville VA 22132 Office: PO Box 875 Purcellville VA 22132

STILLWELL, WALTER BROOKS, JR., dentist; b. Savannah, Ga., Dec. 27, 1919; s. Walter Brooks and Jane Caroline (Shuptrine) S.; student U. Md., 1938-39; D.D.S., Balt. Coll. Dental Surgery, 1943; m. Selpha Theresa Everson, Sept. 17, 1945; children—Walter Brooks, Caroline Marie, Serena Everson. Individual practice dentistry, Balt., 1946-49, Savannah, 1949—, specializing in pedodontia, 1955—; mng. partner Shuptrine Co., drug mfg. co., Savannah, 1961—; pres. Pedodontic Asso. of Savannah, 1970—. Mem. Ga. Dental Examiners Bd. Active United Community Appeal, Boy Scouts Am., YMCA, Cancer Soc.; mem. Savannah Symphony Soc., Little Theatre of Savannah. Served to capt., Dental Corp, AUS, 1943-46. Fellow Am. Acad. Pedodontics, Am., Ga. dental assns., Internat. Coll. Dentists, Southeastern Soc. Pedodontics, Ga. Soc. Pediatric Dentistry, Savannah Dental Soc. (pres. 1955-56), Southeastern Dist. Dental Soc. (pres. 1964), Ga. Soc. Dentistry for Children (pres. 1969), Soc. Colonial Wars in Ga. Baptist (deacon 1952—). Clubs: Civitan, Savannah Yacht, Chatham, Cotillion. Home: 1 Marsh Dr Savannah GA 31404 Office: 211 E 31st St Savannah GA 31401

STILTZ, HARRY LANGLEY, housing cons. co. exec.; b. Hereford, Md., Aug. 7, 1920; s. Emory Holton and Mamie (Langley) S.; student U. Chattanooga, 1948-49; B.S. in Elec. Engring., U. Tenn., 1951; m. Mary Alleen, June 9, 1965; 1 dau., Lea Ann. Project engr. E.I. du Pont de Nemours & Co., Inc., Chattanooga, asst. prof. U. Chattanooga, 1951-53; field test engr. TVA, Chattanooga, 1953-56; project engr. Lockheed Ga. Co., Marietta, 1956-58, group engr., 1959-62; group engr. Martin Co., Orlando, Fla., 1958-59; pres., chmn. bd. dirs. Aerosci. Electronics, Inc., Atlanta, 1962-66; founded Aerospace Telementry Sch., Atlanta, 1962, dir., 1962-68; pres. Stiltz Sales & Engring. Co., Atlanta, 1966-68; research engr. Ga. Inst. Tech., 1968-69; sr. partner Manufactured Housing Cons., Atlanta, 1969—; v.p., gen. mgr. W.P. Atkinson Industries, Inc., Shawnee, Okla., 1969-71; v.p., gen. mgr. TBR Homes, Inc., Pelham, Ga., 1972-73; div. mgr. C.O. Smith Industries, Inc., Moultrie, Ga., 1973—. Bd. dirs. Orchid Bowl Assn., Chattanooga, 1947-48; neighborhood commr. Boy Scouts Am., Marietta, 1960-62. Served with USAAF, 1942-45. Recipient Gen. Electric Zero Defects award Aerosci. Electronics, Inc., 1966. Registered profl. engr., Tenn., Ga., Okla. Mem. I.E.E.E., Instrument Soc. Am., V.F.W., Eta Kappa Nu, Tau Beta Pi. Methodist. Author, editor: Aerospace Telemetry, vol. I, 1962, vol. II, 1966. Home: 500 Hillcrest Moultrie GA 31768 Office: Peachtree Housing Moultrie GA 31768

STIMSON, DEPARX, cons. engr.; b. Florence, S.C., Dec. 13, 1908; s. Samuel Carl and Mary DeParx (Parks) S.; B.S., N.C. State U., 1930; B.S. in Mech. Engring., Auburn U., 1931; B.S. in Elec. Engring., Wofford U., 1932, M.S., 1933; m. Ethel Susan Williams, Oct. 3, 1939 (dec. May 1956); children—Samuel Edward, Richard Barrett; m. 2d, Emily Gail Sparks, Oct. 20, 1968; 1 dau., Maggi V. Tchr. S.C. Sch. for Deaf and Blind, Cedar Spring, 1931; instr. Wofford U., 1932; supervising prin. Francisco Dist. Pub. Schs., 1934-35; research engr., dir. tech. sales Bahnson Co., Winston-Salem, N.C., 1935-52; owner, chief engr. DeParx Stimson Engrs., cons. engrs., 1952—. Founder Cross and Crescent award Wake Forest U. Registered profl. engr. Mem. Am. Soc. Heating, Air-Conditioning and Refrigeration Engrs. (past pres.), Nat. Soc. Profl. Engrs., Winston-Salem Engrs. Club (past v.p.), N.C. Soc. Engrs., Profl. Engrs. N.C. (charter), Asso. Professions N.C., Lambda Chi Alpha. Baptist. Research on heat pump and refrigeration cycles, auto-incremental electrostatic precipitators; originator application of large incremental-centrifugal refrigeration for industry. Home: 121 Idlewilde Dr Winston-Salem NC 27106

STIMSON, RICHARD ALDEN, pub. relations exec.; b. Hamden, Conn., Jan. 18, 1923; s. Frank Giles and Susie Alden (Brown) S.; B.A., Yale, 1943; postgrad. Am. U., Biarritz, France, 1945, Yale, 1947-50; m. Joan Daffodil Crabb, Apr. 19, 1947; 1 son, Richard Edgar Frank. Research asso., State of Conn., Hartford, 1946-50; exec. dir. state council for Pa. Fair Employment Practices Commn., Harrisburg, 1950-51; dir. pub. information Fedn. Protestant Welfare Agys., N.Y.C., 1951-52; asst. dir. pub. relations Am. Inst. C.P.A.'s, N.Y.C., 1952-56; asst. exec. dir. Am. Textbook Pubs. Inst., N.Y.C., 1956-59; pres. Stimson Asso., Pub. Relations, N.Y.C., 1959-64; exec. asst. communications Price Waterhouse & Co., N.Y.C., 1960-64; pub. relations dir. Wool Bur., Inc., N.Y.C., 1964-69; account mgr. Kofoed Pub. Relations Assos., Hollywood, Fla., 1969-70; pres. Stimson Assos., Inc., Fort Lauderdale, Fla., 1970—. Treas., Information Council on fabric flammability, 1967-68, vice chmn., 1968-69. Cons. ednl. relations Jones, Brakeley & Rockwell, Inc., N.Y.C., 1961-64; advisor U.S. Army Information Sch., Ft. Slocum N.Y., 1962. Treas., Council for Edn., Valley Stream, L.I., N.Y., 1954; v.p., trustee dist. 13 Bd. Edn., Valley Stream, 1955-58. Served with AUS, 1943-46; ETO; maj. U.S. Army Res. ret. Mem. Pub. Relations Soc. Am. (charter mem. counselors sect. mem. grievance bd. 1963-66); Nat. Investor Relations Inst., Fla. Pub. Relations Assn. (state dir. 1971—). Unitarian. Club: Yale of Fort Lauderdale (Fla.). Contbg. editor Pub. Relations Quar., 1963-72. Home: 4701 Hawthorne Circle Hollywood FL 33021 Office: 4485 Stirling Rd Fort Lauderdale FL 33314

STINCHCOMB, HAROLD RUSSELL, city ofcl.; b. Columbia Station, O., Dec. 28, 1925; s. Harry Clayton and Elsie Elletta (French) S.; student Fla. State Fire Coll., 1965-66, ann. seminars, 1955-71, Internat. Assn. of Fire Chief's Ann. Adminstrv. Seminar, 1966-70; m. Marjorie Martine Drake, Jan. 5, 1960; children—Marjorie, Susan, William. Soloist Orpheus Chorus, Cleve., 1945-51; second class fireman, City of Sarasota, Fla., 1954-55, 1st class fireman and dept. electrician, 1955-56, lt., 1956-58, battalion capt. 1958-66, fire chief, 1966—; cons. Exec. Dir. Internat. Fire Adminstrv. Inst., State U. N.Y., 1969—; chief coordinator fire rescue Sarasota County (Fla.), 1971—, coordinator emergency med. grants, 1973—, asst. civil emergency coordinator civil def., 1972—. Area safety dir. Boy Scouts Am., 1969-70; camp com. YMCA, 1966-68. Bd. dirs. Sarasota chpt. A.R.C., 1974—. Recipient Civic Service award Fraternal Order of Eagles, 1969. Mem. Fla. State Fire Chiefs' Assn. (pres. 1972—), Internat. Assn. of Fire Chiefs, S.E. Fire Chiefs' Assn. (v.p. 1970-74). Methodist (adminstrv. bd. 1969-73). Home: 3136 Browning St Sarasota FL 33580 Office: 1445 4th St Sarasota FL 33577

STINGILY, JAMES RAY, physician; b. Vicksburg, Miss., Nov. 6, 1928; s. Ernest Ray and Dixie Field (Collins) S.; B.B.A., U. Miss., 1953; postgrad. Miss. Coll., 1954-55; M.D., U. Miss., 1959; m. Margaret Jane Vance, June 2, 1956; children—Rebecca Susanne, Sharon Diane, James Ray. Intern, Miss. Baptist Hosp., 1959-60; practice medicine, partner, asso. Family Med. Clinic, Hazlehurst, Miss., 1960—; chief staff Hardy Wilson Meml. Hosp., 1965—. Sec., treas. ASC Realty Co. Inc., 1966—. Served with USN, 1946-49. Hon. col. on staff gov. Miss., 1972—. Mem. C. of C. (pres. 1967), Miss., County, Am. med. assns., Phi Chi. Baptist (chmn. deacons bd. 1970-72). Office: Family Med Clinic Hazlehurst MS 39083

STIRSMAN, WILLIAM ANDREW, state ofcl.; b. Greenville, Ky., Nov. 19, 1923; s. Hubert Altha and Lola Gladys (Adkins) S.; student Nashville Bus. Coll., 1946-47; m. Dorothy N. Settle, Nov. 3, 1944; children—William E., Jennifer (Mrs. Samuel Dean Sears). Lab. technician Gt. Lakes Steel Corp., Ecorse, Mich., 1942-43; claims examiner Ky. Dept. Econ. Security, Madisonville, 1947-48; with Ky. Dept. Hwys., 1948—, now sr. resident engr. Chmn., Muhlenberg Water Dist., 1967—. Served with USNR, 1943-46. Registered profl. engr. Ky. col. Mem. Assn. Ky. Hwy. Engrs. Baptist (deacon, chmn. brotherhood, treas., song dir.). Mason (Shriner). Home: Rural Route 1 Box 375 Central City KY 42330 Office: PO Box 130 Madisonville KY 42431

STIRZAKER, NORBERT ARTHUR, educator; b. Lorain, O., July 20, 1928; s. Herbert Aidan and Sara (Smith) S.; B. Mus. Edn., Murray State U., 1950; M.M., Ind. U., 1951; M.Ed., U. Miss., 1957, Ed.D., 1958; m. Mildred Elizabeth Parsons, July 28, 1951; children—Kim Elizabeth, Thomas Duncan, Ellen Ann, Amy Grace. Band dir., supr. music Holland (Mo.) Pub. Schs., 1951-52, band dir., county supr. music Brownsville (Tenn.) Pub. Schs., 1954-56; head dept. social scis., prof. edn. Rio Grande (O.) Coll., 1958-59; asst. supr. course programs U. Mich. Extension Service, Ann Arbor, 1959-61; dir. div. extended services, asst. prof. edn. Ind. State U., Terre Haute, 1961-67; chief adminstrv. officer Ind. State U. at Evansville, 1965-67, dir. U. S.C. at Spartanburg, 1967-73, asso. prof. ednl. adminstrn., 1973—. Mem. Spartanburg City Long Range Planning Com., 1969—. Bd. dirs. Spartanburg chpt. United Fund, 1969-72, Charles LeaCenter, Spartanburg; chmn. bd. dirs. Speech and Hearing Clinic, Spartanburg, 1969-71. Served with AUS, 1952-54. W.K. Kellogg research fellow, 1956-58. Mem. C. of C. Greater Spartanburg (dir. 1972—), Sigma Pi Mu, Kappa Delta Pi, Phi Mu Alpha, Phi Delta Kappa. Rotarian. Contbr. to profl. jours. Home: 527 Royal Oak Dr Spartanburg SC 29302 Office: Univ SC Spartanburg SC 29303

STOBAUGH, ROY L., supt. schs.; b. Choctaw, Ark., July 15, 1917; s. Mark L. and Lillian (Huie) S.; student Ark. Tech. U., 1937-40; B.S., State Coll. Ark., 1945; M.Ed., Memphis State U., 1955; m. Wilma West, May 9, 1941; children—Suzanne (Mrs. Berkley Baker), Sara Jane (Mrs. Danny Flowers). Coach, Wilson (Ark.) High Sch., 1941-52; gen. mgr. Crain & Co., chain store, 1952-54; supt. schs., Turrell, Ark., 1954-59, Hughes, Ark., 1959—. Bd. dirs. Athletic Dist. 3, pres. 1947-49. Mem. Nat., Ark. (dir. 1955-58) edn. assns., Northeast Ark. Baseball Assn. (pres. 1960-61), P.T.A. (life), Am. Assn. Sch. Adminstrs. Methodist (bd. stewards 1945—; trustee 1970—). Home: Box 368 Hughes AR 72348

STOBS, JAMES ROBERT, constrn. co. exec., artist; b. Logan, Ia., Nov. 30, 1913; s. Matthew and Bonnie (Twiford) S.; B.F.A., U. Fla., 1937; m. Ruby Lee Wentworth, Mar. 5, 1939; children—James Robert II, Barbara Lee (Mrs. Fredrick Merrill Macy), Gayle Anne, Partner-founder Stobs Bros. Constrn. Co., Miami, Fla., 1937—; sec.-treas. Forming Services, Inc., Miami, 1965—; developer-promoter acreage ltd. partnerships; exhibited in group art shows Tri-County Fair, Tampa, Fla., Soc. Four Arts, Palm Beach, Fla.; others; mem. Miami Art League Jury, 1972, Ann. Dade County Poincianna Art Exhbn., Jury, 1972, 73. Mem. Miami Shores (Fla.) Planning Bd., 1950-53, Dade County Grand Jury Assn. Recipient Blue Ribbon, Tri-County Fair, Tampa, 1936, Cash prize Soc. Four Arts Exhbn., Palm Beach, 1937, others. Mem. Asso. Gen. Contractors (Safety award 1968-72, treas. nat. conv. 1952), Internat. Platform Assn., Delta Sigma Phi. Republican. Presbyn. (deacon 1961-63). Kiwanian. Club: Miami Shores Country. Home: 429 NE 101st St Miami Shores FL 33138 Office: 7010 NE 4th Ct Miami FL 33138

STOCKARD, RALPH REAVIS, educator; b. Graham, N.C., July 23, 1939; s. Lee R. and Nellie Graham (Reavis) S.; B.S. in Elec. Engring., N.C. State U., 1962, postgrad. in Advanced Math., 1965-67; m. Hilda Gray Cantrell, Feb. 29, 1964; children—Susan, Ralph. Engr., Brown Engring. Co., Huntsville, Ala., 1962-64; engr. Research Triangle Inst., Durham, N.C., 1964-67; instr. Tech. Inst. Alamance, Burlington, N.C., 1967—. Mem. Graham City Council, 1971—. Registered profl. engr., N.C. Mem. Graham Jr. C. of C. (Distinguished Service award 1972). Home: 307 E Harden St Graham NC 27253 Office: 411 Camp Rd Burlington NC 27215

STOCKER, EDWARD EUGENE, banker; b. Media, Pa., Dec. 17, 1917; s. George Patrick and Anna Katharine (Mengel) S.; B.S., U. Ark., 1938; J.D., Georgetown U., 1941; m. Margaret Elizabeth Jacoway, Oct. 1, 1948; children—Edward Eugene, Bronson Jacoway, Margaret Cooper. Admitted to D.C. bar, 1942, Ark. bar, 1947, Tex. bar, 1964; practice law, N.Y.C., 1946-47, Little Rock, 1947-50, 52-54; asst. trust officer First Nat. Bank, Dallas, 1954-56; exec. v.p., sr. trust officer Continental Nat. Bank, Fort Worth, Tex., 1956—. Mem. faculty Southwestern Grad. Sch. Banking, So. Meth. U., Dallas, 1959-60, 71. Mem. Tarrant County Community Council, 1971—. Trustee, Tarrant County Charitable Found. Trust, pres. 1968; bd. dirs. Child Study Center, pres. 1970; bd. dirs. Easter Seal Soc., Multiple Sclerosis chpt.; bd. dirs. Tarrant County Heart Assn., chmn. 1963; bd. dirs. Retarded Childrens' Services; bd. dirs. Bell Hosp. Trust, chmn. 1970—; trustee W.I. Cook Meml. Hosp., 1971—. Panther Boys Club. Served to lt. comdr. USNR, 1942-46. Mem. Am., Tex., Fort Worth, Tarrant County bar assns., Sigma Nu, Alpha Kappa Psi, Delta Theta Phi, Pi Gamma Mu. Roman Catholic. Democrat. Rotarian. Clubs: River Crest Country, Fort Worth. Author: (with Paul C. Cook and Arch B. Gilbert) Manual for Preparation of Wills and Administration of Trusts in Texas, 1967. Home: 3517 Dorothy Lane S Fort Worth TX 76107 Office: Box 910 Fort Worth TX 76101

STOCKHAM, RICHARD JAMES, mfg. co. exec.; b. Birmingham, Ala., Apr. 20, 1904; s. William Henry and Kate (Clark) S.; student U. Ill., 1922-25, various other univs., 1925-42; m. Charlotte Louise Rushton, Nov. 27, 1927 (dec. Aug. 1965); children—Richard James, William Henry II, Charlotte (Mrs. Cecil G. Murdock, Jr.); m. 2d, Thelma C. Stockham, Feb. 17, 1968. With Stockham Valves & Fittings, Birmingham, 1925—, sec., 1927-45, v.p., 1945-53, pres., 1953—, also dir. Gen. chmn. United Appeal, Birmingham, 1963. Mem. adv. bd. Cumberland Law Sch.; trustee Samford U., William H. and Kate F. Stockham Found. Served from maj. to lt. col. AUS, 1942-45. Decorated Legion of Merit. Mem. So. Indsl. Relations Conf. Bd. (dir.), Ala. Hist. Assn. (mem. exec. com.), Asso. Industries Ala. (dir.). Baptist. Home: 2862 Stratford Rd Birmingham AL 35213 Office: 4000 10th Av N Brimingham AL 35202

STOCKTON, JOHN ROBERT, educator; b. Leon, Ia., Oct. 19, 1903; s. John Collins and Emma Isabel (McCready) S.; A.B., Maryville Coll., 1925, LL.D., 1956; M.A., U. Ia., 1927, Ph.D., 1932; D.Litt., Tex. Christian U., 1971; m. Anna Beulah Vaughn, Dec. 24, 1928; children—Joanne Beatrice (dec.), John Robert, Eileen Doris (Mrs. Drew Hearn). Tchr., Clay County High Sch., Celina, Tenn., 1925-26; instr. Coe Coll., 1927-29; asst. prof. Drake U., 1929-32; statistician, Meredith Pub. Co., Des Moines, 1932-35; asst. prof. bus. statistics U. Tex., Austin, 1935-37, asso. prof., 1937-39, prof., 1939—, statistician Bur. Bus. Research, 1946-49, dir., 1949-69. Mem. Tex. Commn. on State and Local Tax Policy, 1959-69; mem. adv. group to commr. internal revenue, 1966-67. Served to maj., AUS, 1942-46. Fellow Am. Statis. Assn.; mem. Am. Econ. Assn., Asso. Burs. Bus. and Econ. Research (pres. 1957-58), Western Council Travel Research (pres. 1960). Club: Town and Gown (Austin). Author: Introduction to Business and Economic Statistics, 1968; (with others) Economics of Natural Gas in Texas, 1952, Water for the Future, 1959. Home: 1010 Gaston Av Austin TX 78703

STOCKTON, RODNEY MAURICE, cosmetic co. exec.; b. St. Louis, Feb. 3, 1913; s. Rodney M. and Martha Julia (Harkins) S.; student Asbury Coll., 1930-33; m. Joan Denise Barnes, Feb. 15, 1963; 1 dau., Denise Twinkle. Indsl. sales engr. Sylvania Indsl. Corp., Chgo., 1937-41; chem. sales engr. L. Sonneborn & Sons, Chgo., 1941-47; pres., founder, chmn. bd. Aloe Creme Labs., Inc., Ft. Lauderdale, Fla., 1953—. Mem. council of 100 Ft. Lauderdale U.; mem. U.S. Pres.'s Com. on Employment Handicapped, Fla. Gov.'s Com. for Handicapped; life mem. Fla. Sheriffs Boys Ranch. Recipient Gold Key to City Miami Beach, Achievement award Rep. J. Herbert Burke. Ky col. Mem. A.I.M. (fellow pres.'s council), Sales and Marketing Execs. Assn., Ft. Lauderdale Mail Users' Council, Cosmetics, Toiletries and Fragrance Assn., Aerospace Med. Assn., Fla., Ft. Lauderdale chambers commerce, Fla. Police Athletic Fedn., Inc. Home: 4120 NE 25th Av Fort Lauderdale FL 33308 Office: PO Box 5847 Fort Lauderdale FL 33310

STOCKWELL, BENJAMIN EUGENE, lawyer; b. Oklahoma City, Aug. 28, 1931; s. Benjamin Paul and Anna (Cunningham) S.; B.A., U. Okla., 1952, LL.B., 1956; m. Marjorie Ethel Ribble, Apr. 4, 1952; children—Margaret Lynn, David Alan. Admitted to Okla. bar, 1956; practiced in Oklahoma City, 1956-60, Norman, Okla., 1961—; mem. firm Benedum and Stockwell, 1961-62; now mem. firm, Stockwell and Pence; asst. prof. law, legal adviser to pres.'s office U. Okla., 1960-61. Chmn. Okla. State Bd. Examiners Ofcl. Shorthand Reporters. Chmn. Celveland County Bd. Health, 1963-64. Bd. dirs. Cleveland County Cancer Soc. Served to 1st lt. AUS, 1952-54. Mem. Okla. State (mem. exec. council 1965—; chmn. spl. com. on implementation of jud. reform amendments 1967; v.p. 1969), Cleveland County (past pres.) bar assns., Okla. Inst. for Justice, Scabbard and Blade, Pi Kappa Alpha, Pi Gamma Mu. Episcopalian. Mason; mem. Order DeMolay. Home: 2247 60th Av SE Norman OK 73069 Office: 119 E Main St Norman OK 73069

STOEPLER, GEORGE RICHARD, supt. schs.; b. Eden, Tex., July 26, 1913; s. Albert Richard and Gladys Ethel (Bingham) S.; B.S., S.W. Tex. State U., 1940, M.A., 1950; m. Syble Alvenia Belk, Sept. 24, 1936; children—Anna Idell (Mrs. Benjamin M. DeSopo), Annette (Mrs. Donald Lloyd Spalinger). Tchr. social studies Laredo (Tex.) Pub. Schs., 1941-42; prin. clk. War Dept.-Ordnance, 1942-45; supt. schs., Millersview, Tex., 1945-50, Blackwell, Tex., 1952-59; mgr. Farm and Ranch Enterprises, 1960-66; prin. Melvin Pub. Schs., Eden, Tex., 1966-70, dir. in-service, 1967-71, supt. schs., 1971—. Cons. phys. edn. Blackwell Schs. Community dir. Girl Scouts Am., Blackwell, 1951-59, Boy Scouts Am., Blackwell, 1951-59. Recipient Distinguished Service award Tex. Pub. Schs., 1955. Mem. Edwards Plateau Hist. Assn. (pres. 1969-73), Tex. Old Forts and Missions Restoration Soc., Tex. State Assn., Tex. Assn. Sch. Adminstrs., Tex. State Hist. Soc. Author: Blue Norther, 1944. Address: Broadway and Maddox Eden TX 76837

STOESS, RAY HAMPTON, hotel exec.; b. PeeWee Valley, Ky., June 10, 1931; s. Carl Raymond and Margaret (Smith) S.; student U. Ky., 1949; U. Louisville, nights 1955-61; m. Donna Newcomb, June 22, 1951; children—Pamela, Janet, Sandra, Teri, Bucky. With Sealtest, Louisville, 1954-68, sales mgr. home service routemen, 1964-66, mgr. food store sales, 1966-68; asst. v.p. prodn. Hubbuch in Ky., Louisville, 1968-69; gen. mgr. Ramada Inn, Louisville, 1969-71, mgr. pub. relations and group sales, Fort Myers, Fla., 1971-72; dir.

sales Ramada Inn, Louisville, 1972—. Chmn. Bluegrass Indsl. Park, Louisville, 1973-74. Chmn., City-County All-Star Football Game (Crippled Childrens Bowl), 1965; founder Ky. Hall of Fame, Ky. State fairgrounds, 1965; orginator, pres. Mini Bd. Assn. Atherton High Sch., Louisville, 1973-74; active Russell Area council Poverty Program. Served with USMCR, 1950-54; Korea. Named retail salesman of year Sealtest, 1958, salesman of year, 1960-62, recipient Pres.'s Cup award, 1961; named outstanding young man in commerce and industry by bus. leaders Louisville, 1966; recipient Flying Dutchman award Met. Parks & Recreation, 1969, Louisville Gen. Hosp. award for staring Pro-Celebrity Golf Tournament, 1971. Mem. Louisville (dir., 1965-66), Jefferstown (pres., 1973-74, chmn. gaslight festival 1974) chambers commerce, Am. Legion, V.F.W. Methodist. Home: 2367 Valley Vista Rd Louisville KY 40205 Office: 9700 Bluegrass Pky Louisville KY 40299

STOESSEL, CAROLE JEAN (MRS. ALEXANDER W. ZVONAR), physician, pianist; b. Salisbury, N.C., July 14, 1936; d. Frank William and India Beatrice (Aldredge) Stoessel; student piano with Raymond Lewenthal, 1954-55; B.A. magna cum laude, Catawba Coll., 1959; M.D. (Nancy Lybrook Lasater Reynolds scholar), Bowman Gray Sch. Medicine, Wake Forest U., 1963; m. Alexander W. Zvonar, Nov. 2, 1963. Concert pianist recitals, concerts, 1950-59, 71—; various tv and radio appearances, 1950-55; intern pathology Columbia Presbyn. Med. Center, N.Y.C., 1963-64, resident fellow dept. microbiology, 1964-65; physician A.R.C. Bloodmobile unit, Rowan County, N.C., 1972—. Dealer antique dolls, 1967—. Mem. Children Am. Revolution, Historic Salisbury Found., Inc. (charter). Democrat. Lutheran. Address: 329 S Fulton St Salisbury NC 28144

STOKELD, FREDERICK WILLIAM, internat. bus. cons.; b. Middlesbrough, Eng., June 15, 1933; s. Frederick William and Beryl (Metcalf) S.; B.Sc., London Sch. Econs., 1955; M.B.A., Ind. U., 1959; m. Laura Renfro, Aug. 4, 1962; children—Frederick William, Amanda Clare. Came to U.S., 1958, naturalized, 1973. Instr. internat. econs. Portland (Ore.) State Coll., 1961-62; mgr. world trade and transp. dept. Portland C. of C., 1962-68; sr. asso. internat. group U.S. C. of C., Washington, 1968—. Served with RAF, 1955-58. Mem. Regional Export Expansion Council. Home: 5537 N 10th St Arlington VA 22205 Office: 1615 H St NW Washington DC 20006

STOKER, RAYMON CHARLES, JR., lawyer; b. Odessa, Tex., Feb. 19, 1939; s. Raymon Charles and Claudene (Goodall) S.; B.B.A., Baylor U., 1962, J.D., 1964; m. Carole Jo Fannin, Aug. 24, 1964; children—Carole Camille, Raymon Charles III. Admitted to Tex. bar, 1964; practiced in Odessa, 1965—; atty. for chief justice Tex. Supreme Ct., Austin, 1964-65; asso. firm Shafer, Gilliland, Davis, Bunton and McCollum, 1965-70; mem. firm Shafer, Gilliland, Davis, Bunton, McCollum and Stoker, 1970—. Dir. Gen. Diversified Investments, Inc., Odessa, 1971—, sec., 1972—. Com. chmn. Sunset Trail council Boy Scouts Am., 1969. Named Boss of the Year Odessa Legal Secs. Assn., 1970. Mem. Ector County Bar Assn. (dir. 1967), State Jr. Bar Tex. (dir. 1968-69), State Bar Tex., Tex. Assn. Defense Counsel. Presbyn. (deacon 1966-69), Kiwanian (dir. 1969-70). Club: Permian Gun (pres. 1971—). Home: 1435 Sweetbriar St Odessa TX 79761 Office: 201 First National Bank Bldg Odessa TX 79761

STOKER, RUPERT RANDOLPH, hardware mfg. co. exec.; b. Zephyr, Tex., Apr. 10, 1907; s. Edgar E. and Ellie Brown (Couch) S.; student So. Meth. U., 1942; m. Thelma Jo Cavitt, Sept. 1, 1935; children—Carolyn (Mrs. John T. Shinn), Lindley Randolph. Partner, Cavitt Store, Red Oak, Tex., 1935-42; co-mgr. quality control staff N.Am. Aviation, Dallas, 1942-47; pres. Trego Industries, Inc., Red Oak, 1947—; owner Stoker & Pritchett Developers, Red Oak, 1966—. Active Ellis County Democratic Party. Mem. Ellis County Hist. Soc., Tex. Builders Hardware Club, Nat. Builders Hardware Assn., Builders Hardware Mfrs. Assn. Mem. Christian Ch. (chmn. bd. stewardship 1966—, worship com. 1965—). Lion. Clubs: Waxahachie Country; Riverlake Country. Home: 610 W Marvin St Waxahachie TX 65165 Office: Box 85 Red Oak TX 75154

STOKES, AUBREY DOYLE, lawyer; b. Waco, Tex., Mar. 28, 1921; s. Dink K. and Ollie Marie (Lloyd) S.; student Baylor U., 1940-41, J.D., 1950; student Tex. Wesleyan Coll., 1946-48; m. Wave Estelle Rhodes, Sept. 6, 1944; children—Ted Randolph, Steven Doyle. Admitted to Tex. bar, 1950, U.S. Dist. Ct., 1951, U.S. Ct. Appeals bar, 1972; practice law, San Angelo, Tex., 1950—; asst. dist. atty. 119th and 51st Jud. Dists. Tex., 1951-52, dist. atty., 1953-57; individual practice, San Angelo, 1957-58; mem. firm Webb & Stokes San Angelo, 1958—; owner, propr. El Rancho Contento, quarter horse farm, nr. San Angelo, 1960—. Instr. bus. law San Angelo Jr. Coll., 1951, 53. Active San Angelo council Boy Scouts Am. Served with USNR, 1941-45, 52-53. Mem. Am., Tom Green County (v.p. 1966-67, pres. 1971-72, chmn. ethics com. 1972) bar assns., Am., Cal., Okla., Tex. (dir. 1970-73) trial lawyers assns., Tex. Conf. Bar Pres.'s, West Central Tex. Law Enforcement Assn. (dir., pres. 1955), San Angelo Jr. C. of C. (dir. 1950-51), V.F.W. (dist. judge advocate 1958), Tex. Horse Council (dir. 1972—), Quarter Horse Assn. West Tex. (v.p. 1970, pres. 1971, high point award 1967), Tex. Quarter Horse Racing Assn. (sec. 1971-72, dir. 1971—), Quarter Horse Breeders Assn., Quarter Horse Racing Owners Am., Am. Legion, Delta Theta Pi. Democrat. Baptist. Mason (32 degree, Shriner). Clubs: Hoolihan, Inc. (San Angelo); San Angelo Riding. Home: 3231 Woodland Circle San Angelo TX 76901 Office: PO Box 1271 San Angelo TX 76901

STOKES, CARL NICHOLAS, lawyer; b. Memphis, Jan. 26, 1907; s. John William and Edith Isabell (Burgess) S.; student Draughton's Bus. Coll., 1929-30; LL.B., U. Memphis, 1933; m. Laverne Judson, Aug. 21, 1930; 1 dau., Vicki Laverne (Mrs. Dennis Neff Koehn). Admitted to Tenn. bar, 1934; mem. firm Norvell & Monteverde, Memphis, 1934-38; with legal dept. Tenn. Unemployment Compensation Div., 1937-38; clk. City Ct. Memphis, 1938-42, Criminal Cts. Shelby County, 1946-50; judge City Ct. Memphis, 1950-52; mem. firm Shea & Pierotti, Memphis, 1952-62; v.p., gen. counsel Allen & O'Hara, Inc., Memphis, 1962-72; now mem. firm McDonald, Kuhn, Smith, Gandy, Miller & Tait, Memphis. Dir. First Fed. Savs. and Loan Assn. Adv. bd. Salvation Army, chmn., 1973-74; trustee Shrine Sch. for Handicapped Children. Served to capt., inf. AUS, 1942-46. Recipient award of merit Tenn. Bar Assn., 1958. Mem. Am., Tenn., Memphis and Shelby County bar assns., Am. Legion, Mil. Order World Wars, Navy League, Memphis Area C. of C. (chmn. welcome com. 1972-73). Mem. Christian Ch. Mason (33 deg., K.T., Shriner), Kiwanian (pres. 1971-72). Home: 2237 Massey Rd Memphis TN 38138 Office: Law Offices McDonald Kuhn Smith Gandy Miller & Tait 150 E Court St Memphis TN 38103

STOKES, COLIN, tobacco mfg. co. exec.; b. Winston-Salem, N.C., Apr. 4, 1914; s. Henry Straughan and Eloise (Brown) S.; grad. McCallie Sch., 1931; B.S., U. N.C., 1935; m. Mary Louise Siewers, Jan. 1, 1943; children—Louise Siewers (Mrs. Philip G. Kinken), Henry Straughan II, Daniel Shober. With R. J. Reynolds Tobacco Co., 1935—, asst. to supt. mfg., 1947-53, asst. supt. mfg., 1953-56, supt. mfg., 1956-59, dir., 1957—, v.p., 1959-61, exec. v.p., 1961-70, chmn. bd., 1970-72; pres. R.J. Reynolds Industries, 1972-73, chmn., chief exec. officer, 1973—, also dir.; dir. Winston-Salem Savs. & Loan Assn., Integon Corp., N.C. Nat. Bank, NCNB Corp. Bd. dirs. YMCA, 1946-52; campaign chmn. United Fund Forsyth County, 1957, dir., 1957-59; trustee N. C. Bapt. Hosps., 1958-61, 63-66, 68-71, chmn. trustees, 1960, 61, 69, 70, chmn. finance com., 1959; trustee Wake Forest U., 1971—, Salem Coll. and Acad., 1966-74; dir. William and Kate B. Reynolds Meml. Park, 1958-64, Child Guidance Clinic, 1959-61. Served from pvt. to capt., inf. AUS, 1942-46. Mem. Winston-Salem C. of C. (dir. 1952-55, 68-71), Zeta Psi. Baptist (deacon, finance com.). Kiwanian (pres. 1963, dir.). Home: 2701 Reynolds Dr Winston-Salem NC 27104 Office: RJ Reynolds Industries Inc Winston-Salem NC 27102

STOKES, DAVID KERSHAW, JR., physician; b. Camden, S.C., Feb. 3, 1927; s. David Kershaw and Mary Belle (Smith) S.; B.S., Clemson U., 1948; M.S., U. Ga., 1952; Ph.D., Tex. A. and M. U., 1955; M.D., Med. U. S.C., 1957; m. Louise Wingo, June 9, 1950; children—Donna, David, Tina. Intern Spartanburg (S.C.) Gen. Hosp., 1958, dir. family practice residency, 1972—; practice medicine specializing in family practice, Inman, S.C., 1959—. Chmn. bd. trustees, Dist. 1 Schs., Spartanburg County, S.C., 1966—. Served with AUS, 1945-47. Diplomate Am. Bd. Family Practice. Mem. Am., S.C. med. assns., Spartanburg County Med. Soc. (pres. 1972), Am. Assn. Physicians and Surgeons, Am. Heart Assn., So. Med. Assn. Home: 8 Canaday St Inman SC 29349 Office: 43 N Main St Inman SC 29349

STOKES, JACK AVERY, physician; b. Lincoln County, Miss., Feb. 10, 1931; s. Ernest Gayle and Ida Mae (Grant) S.; student Miss. Coll., 1950; B.S., U. Miss., 1957, M.D., 1960; m. Sammie J. Wiseman, May 29, 1955; children—Mickey Eugene, Janet Michal. Intern, U. Miss. Med. Center, Jackson, 1960-61; pvt. practice family medicine, Pontotoc, Miss., 1961—; mem. staff Pontotoc Community Hosp., North Miss. Hosp., Tupelo. Chmn. Pontotoc County Home Health Care Program, 1970—; tchr. cardiopulmonary resuscitation, 1970—. Bd. dirs. Pontotoc County Appalachian Devel. Served with USN, 1950-54. Fellow Am. Acad. Family Physicians; mem. A.M.A., Am. Geriatrics Soc., Am., Miss. heart assns., Nat., Miss. (pres. 1971-73) flying physicians assns., Aircraft Owners and Pilots Assn., Aviation Med. Examiner Council on Med. Services, Miss. Med. Assn. (v.p. 1967-68), N.E. Miss. Med. Soc. (pres. 1968-69, sec.-treas. 1971-74), Miss. Acad. Family Practice (dir. 1972-74), Pontotoc County Devel. Assn., Nu Sigma Nu. Baptist. Lion. Clubs: Flying, Pontotoc Country. Home: 1019 N Brooks St Pontotoc MS 38863 Office: 207 Holmes Rd Pontotoc MS 38863

STOKES, JAMES PORTER, clergyman; b. Greer, S.C., Mar. 14, 1926; s. Albert Broadus and Nannie Cora (Bright) S.; B.A., Furman U., 1946; B.D., So. Bapt. Theol. Sem., 1949; m. Marjorie Ussery, May 12, 1949; children—James Porter II, Mark Singleton, David Thomas, Marjorie Nanelle. Ordained to ministry Bapt. Ch., 1948; pastor Bethune (S.C.) Field of Chs., 1949-51, First Bapt. Ch., Blacksburg, 1951-56, Seneca (S.C.) Bapt. Ch., 1956—. Bd. dirs., tchr. Beaverdam Bapt. Sem. Extension Center, 1964—; chmn. com. on coms. S.C. Bapt. Conv., 1970, mem. gen. bd., 1956, chmn. stewardship com., 1973; mem. S.C. Bapt. spl. student study com. Furman U., 1967—. Trustee S.C. Bapt. Hosps., So. Bapt. Theol. Sem., Louisville; chmn. adminstrn. com. Easley (S.C.) Bapt. Hosp. Mem. Beaverdam Bapt. Assn. (moderator). Lion. Home: 114 E South 2d St Seneca SC 29678 Office: 201 S Fairplay St Seneca SC 29678

STOKES, JOHN MYERS, lawyer; b. Lufkin, Tex., Sept. 4, 1939; s. Caroll Myers and Evelyn (Brister) S.; A.B., Tex. Tech. Coll., 1961; J.D., George Washington U., 1964; m. Nancy Joan Baldwin, July 1, 1961; 1 son, John Myers. Law clk. Chief Judge Wilson Cowen, U.S. Ct. of Claims, Washington, 1964-66; admitted to D.C. bar, 1965, Tex. bar, 1969; practiced in Washington, 1966-68; legislative research dir. Republican Party of Tex., Austin, 1968, exec. dir., spl. counsel, 1968-70; officer grants mgmt. and budget control Office Child Devel., Dept. Health, Edn. and Welfare, Dallas, 1970, regional atty., 1970—. Vice chmn. Tex. Young Republican Fedn., 1961-62; pres., organizer Tex. Tech. Young Republican Club, 1960-61. Mem. Am., Fed., D.C. bar assns., State Bar Tex., George Washington Law Sch. Alumni Assn., Phi Delta Phi, Delta Tau Delta. Contbr. articles in field to profl. jours. Home: 2812 Crest Ridge Dallas TX 75228 Office: 1114 Commerce St Dallas TX 75702

STOKES, MACK (MARION) BOYD, bishop; b. Wonsan, Korea, Dec. 21, 1911; s. Marion Boyd and Florence Pauline (Davis) S.; came to U.S., 1928; student Seoul Fgn. High Sch., Korea; A.B., Asbury Coll., 1932; B.D., Duke, 1935; postgrad. Boston U. Sch. Theology, 1935-37, Harvard, 1936-37; Ph.D., Boston U., 1940; LL.D., Lambuth Coll., Jackson, Tenn., 1963; m. Ada Rose Yow, June 19, 1942; children—Marion Boyd III, Archie Yow and Elsie Pauline. Resident fellow systematic theology Boston U., 1936-38, Bowne fellow in philosophy, 1938-39; ordained to ministry Meth. Ch. as deacon, 1938, elder, 1940; vis. prof. philosophy and religion Ill. Wesleyan U., 1940-41; prof. Christian doctrine Candler Sch. Theology, Emory U., 1941-56, asso. dean, Parker prof. systematic theology, 1956-72, chmn. exec. com. div. of religion grad. sch., 1956-72, acting dean Candler Sch., 1968-69; created bishop United Meth. Ch., 1972, now bishop, Jackson, Miss.; mem. faculty Inst. Theol. Studies, Oxford U., 1958, Del., Meth. Ecumenical conf., 1947, 52, 61, 71, Holston, Gen. confs., S.E. Jurisdictional Conf., 1956, 60, 64, 68, 72; chmn. com. ministry Gen. Conf. Meth. Ch., 1960; nat. com. Nature Unity We Seek, 1956—; mem. gen. com. ecumenical affairs theol. study com. United Meth. Ch., 1968-72, com. on Cath.-Meth. relations, 1969—. Mem. Am. Philos. Assn., Am. Acad. Religion, Am. Assn. U. Profs., Metaphys. Soc. Am., Theta Phi (nat. sec.), Pi Gamma Mu. Author: Major Methodist Beliefs, 1956; The Evangelism of Jesus, 1960; The Epic of Revelation, 1961; Our Methodist Heritage, 1963; Crencas Fundamentals Dos Methodistas, 1964; Study Guide on the Teachings of Jesus, 1970; The Bible and Modern Doubt, 1970; Major United Methodist Beliefs, 1971. Address: PO Box 931 Jackson MS 39205

STOKES, OSCAR BARKER, city mgr.; b. Durham, N.C., Aug. 28, 1928; s. Oscar Montague and Arline Bernice Feezor (Spencer) S.; ed. Ashmore Bus. Coll., U. N.C.; m. Lois Ann Marley, Oct. 26, 1956; children—Sharon Kay, Anne Carol. Mem. City of Lexington (N.C.) Police Dept., 1952-57, adminstrv. asst., tax collector, 1957-61; city mgr., dir. pub. housing Town of Valdese, N.C., 1961-67; city mgr. City of Roanoke Rapids (N.C.), 1967-72, City of Sanford (N.C.), 1972—. water safety dir. Lexington A.R.C., 1950-52; dir. Roanoke Rapids Council Govtl. Law and Order, 1970-72; mem. bd. selectors Burke County Community Coll., 1965-67. Chmn. bd. Valdese Community Center. Served with USNR, 1944-46, PTO; AUS, 1949-52. Democrat. Methodist. Moose, Elk, Rotarian (dir., past pres.). Home: 615 Brinn Dr Sanford NC 27330 Office: PO Box 338 Sanford NC 27330

STOLAR, ROBERT, physician; b. Lithuania; s. Elias and Lana (Tobias) S.; brought to U.S., 1911, naturalized, 1916; A.B., George Washington U., 1931; M.D., Georgetown U., 1935; m. Frances Moore, Aug. 23, 1945. Intern, Gallinger Municipal Hosp., Washington, 1935-36; fellow Georgetown U., 1936-38; clin. asst. vis. dermatologist and syphilologist Bellevue Hosp., N.Y.C., 1938-40; practice medicine, specializing in dermatology, Washington, 1940-41, 46—; clin. prof. medicine (dermatology) Georgetown U. Med. Sch., 1947—; clin. prof. dermatology Howard U. Sch. Medicine, 1968—. Served with AUS, 1941-46; col. Res. (ret.). Mem. Balt.-Washington Dermatol. Soc. (pres. 1953-54), Internat. Soc. Tropical Dermatology (treas.-gen. 1964-70). Mason. Clubs: George Washington University, Cosmos (Washington). Office: Washington Medical Science Bldg 916 19th St NW Washington DC 20006

STOLEE, MICHAEL JOSEPH, educator; b. Mpls., Aug. 22, 1930; s. Gullik R. and Adeline (Thomason) S.; B.A., St. Olaf Coll., 1952; M.A., U. Minn., 1959, Ph.D., 1963; m. Marilyn K. Sandbo, June 6, 1952; children—Margaret Kay, Paul Andrew, Anne Marie. Tchr., Adams (Minn.) High Sch., 1952-54; prin. Welcome (Minn.) High Sch., 1954-56; supt. schs., Russell, Minn., 1956-59, Clarkfield, Minn., 1959-61; instr. U. Minn., 1961-63; asst. prof. edn. U. Miami, Coral Gables, Fla., 1963-65, prof. edn., 1966—, coordinator grad. studies Sch. Edn., 1968-70, asso. dean, 1969—; asst. prof. edn. U. Mass., 1965-66. Dir. Fla. Sch. Desegregation Cons. Center, 1966-69. Mem. N.E.A., Am. Assn. Sch. Adminstrs., Nat. Soc. for Study Edn., Nat. Assn. Secondary Sch. Prins. Phi Delta Kappa. Home: 6618 San Vicente Av Coral Gables FL 33146

STOLLEY, CHARLES ARTHUR, cons. engr.; b. Chgo., Feb. 4, 1923; s. Louis D. and Marion (Twigg) S.; student Central YMCA Coll., 1940-42; B.S., U. Ill., 1949; m. Ruth Elizabeth Krueger, Nov. 3, 1951; children—Kent Charles, Scott Louis. Mech. engr. Babcock & Wilcox Co., Chgo., 1949, Gerlitz Constrn. Co., Itasca, Ill., 1949-51, Racnar Benson, Inc., Chgo., 1951-55; project engr. Summer Sollitt Co., Chgo., 1955-65; asso. partner Engrs. Collaborative, Chgo., 1965-68; mech. engr. Alexander & Assos., Ft. Lauderdale, Fla., 1968-69; mech. engr., pres. Stolley & Assos., Ft. Lauderdale, 1969—. Served with AUS, 1943-46. Registered profl. engr. Fla., Ill., Ind., Mich., Ohio, Pa., Wis. Mem. Am. Soc. Heating, Refrigeration and Air Conditioning Engrs. U.S. Power Squadron, Pi Tau Sigma. Office: 2404 W Davie Blvd Fort Lauderdale FL 33312

STOLT, ROBERT HOWARD, physicist; b. Oakland, Cal., Oct. 21, 1944; m. Stanley Sherwood and Irma Fern (Howard) S.; B.S., U. Wyo., 1966; Ph.D. (Nat. Def. Edn. Act fellow), 1970; m. Donna Lee Royal, Sept. 5, 1964; 1 son, Robert Howard. Research asso. U. Colo., Boulder, 1970-71; research scientist Continental Oil Co., Ponca City, Okla., 1971—. Mem. Phi Beta Kappa, Phi Kappa Phi, Sigma Pi Sigma. Republican. Mem. Ch. of Jesus Christ of Latter-day Saints. Contbr. articles on physics to profl. pubis. Home: 2116 Canary Dr Ponca City OK 74601 Office: Continental Oil Company Ponca City OK 74601

STONE, BEN HARRY, lawyer, state ofcl.; b. Gulfport, Miss., Jan. 18, 1935; s. William Harry and Tressie (Lancaster) S.; B.B.A., Tulane U., 1957; LL.B., J.D., U. Miss., 1961; m. Nancy Jane Reed, Nov. 14, 1958; children—Nancy Jane, Virginia Louise, Kathleen Lancaster. With devel. dept. Tulane U., 1958-59; admittted to Miss. bar, 1961; practiced in Jackson, 1961-63; mem. firm Eaton, Cottrell, Galloway & Lang, Gulfport, 1963—; mem. Miss. Senate, 1968—. Teaching fellow U. Miss. Sch. Law. Fed. coordinator for City of Gulfport, Miss. Council Devel. Marine Resources 1969-72. Chmn. Harrison County chpt. Am. Cancer Soc., 1965; bd. dirs. Salvation Army, Gulfport, 1965. Cath. Charities, Inc., 1968—. Bd. mem. Westminster Acad., Gulfport. Served with USAF, 1957-58. Mem. Am., Harrison County (pres. 1967) bar assns., Miss. State Bar, Miss. Jr. Bar Assn. (dir.), Miss. Econ. Council, Miss. Soc. Prevention Blindness, Miss. Research and Devel. Council (mem. exec. com. 1968—), Council State Govts. (exec. com. 1973—), Gulfport Area C. of C. (dir.), Jr. C. of C. (dir. 1969—), Sigma Alpha Epsilon, Phi Delta Phi. Presbyn. Home: 1320 E Beach Blvd Gulfport MS 39501 Office: 2300 14th St Gulfport MS 39501

STONE, CECIL JEROME, JR., plywood mfg. co. exec.; b. Bristol, Tenn., Apr. 24, 1926; s. Cecil Jerome and Edna May (Shumaker) S.; student U. Tex., 1945, King Coll., 1946, Internat. Corr. Schs., 1957-61; m. Dorothy Louise Carmody, July 25, 1946; children—Kathryn (Mrs. Randall Lee Wyatt), Dorothy (Mrs. Michael Dockery), Nancy. Carrier helper U.S. Post Office, 1944; laborer, Old Dominion Plywood Corp., Bristol, Va., 1947-49, foreman, 1949-54, treas., 1954—, pres., 1960—; dir. Bristol br. Va. Nat. Bank. Bd. dirs. Vol. Blind Industries, Inc., Morristown, Tenn. Served with AUS, 1944-46; ETO. Decorated Bronze Star, Purple Heart. Mem. Bristol C. of C. (dir. 1973-75). Lion. Clubs: Country (Bristol, Tenn.); High Meadows Golf and Country (Roaring Gap, N.C.). Home: 161 Kingsbridge Bristol TN 37620 Office: PO Box 674 Bristol VA 24201

STONE, EDWIN CHESTER, lawyer; b. Bassett, Va., Feb. 28, 1939; s. Wilbert Morris and Laura (Nolen) S.; B.A., Bridgewater Coll., 1961; LL.B., U. Va., 1964; m. Eleanor Jean Muntzing, Dec. 26, 1960; children—Margaret, Lorri, Edwin Chester. Admitted to Va. bar, 1964; since practiced in Radford; mem. firm Dalton, Poff & Turk, 1964-66: partner, Dalton, Poff, Turk & Stone, 1966-72. Dalton, Stone & Clay, Radford, Va., 1972—. Dir. First & Merchants Bank of Radford. Chmn. Radford (Va.) Planning Commn., 1969-71. Chmn. Radford City Republican Com., 1965. Bd. Dirs. United Fund, Radford, Va., 1966-71; bd. dirs., mem. exec. com. St. Albans Psychist. Hosp.; bd. dirs. Radford Coll. Found. Mem. Va., Radford, Montgomery, Floyd (v.p. 1971) bar assns., Bridgewater Coll. Alumni Assn. (pres. 1966). Kiwanian. Home: 27 Fieldale Dr Radford VA 24141 Office: Box 1089 Radord VA 24141

STONE, HAZEL LUCY ROTH (MRS. NORREL L. STONE), purchasing exec.; b. Des Moines; d. William and Verne (Fessler) Roth; student U. Ia., 1937-39, Drake U., 1939-41, U. Kansas City Sch. Law, 1941-43; m. Norrel L. Stone, Jan. 8, 1954. Buyer regional office Montgomery Ward, 1941-43; citrus grower, Haines City, Fla., 1943-48; buyer Maas Bros., St. Petersburg, Fla., 1950—. Instr. marketing Jr. Coll., St. Petersburg, evenings 1950-58; prof. econs., English and reading comprehension, Am. Inst. Banking, St. Petersburg, evenings 1956—. Active various community fund drives; state adviser distributive edn., 1945-65, 69—. Charter mem. Republican Congl. Club. Named Outstanding Bus. and Profl. Woman of Year, 1956. Mem. Am. Inst. Banking (Service award Holiday Isle chpt. 1972), Fla. League Arts, Mus. Fine Arts, Smithsonian Assos., Internat. Platform Assn., Kappa Alpha Theta. Club: Bath. Contbg. author to textbooks. Home: 1330 North Shore Dr NE St Petersburg FL 33701 also Box 331 Highland Park FL 32401

STONE, HUBERT DEAN, journalist; b. Maryville, Tenn., Sept. 23, 1924; s. Archie Hubert and Annie (Cupp) S.; student Maryville Coll., 1942-43; B.A., U. Okla., 1949; m. Agnes Shirley, Sept. 12, 1953 (dec. Mar. 1973); 1 son, Neal Anson. Sunday editor Maryville-Alcoa Daily Times, 1949; mng. editor Maryville-Alcoa Times, 1949—; v.p. Maryville-Alcoa Newspapers, Inc., 1960—; pres. Stonecraft, 1954—. Mem. mayor's adv. com. City of Maryville. Bd. dirs. United Fund of Blount County, 1961-63, vice chmn. campaign, 1971—; bd. dirs. Nat. Hillbilly Homecoming Assn., Alkiwan Crafts, Inc., Tee Bee Cee Corp., Inc., Maryville Utilities Bd.; trustee Smoky Mountain Passion Play Assn. Served from pvt. to staff sgt. AUS, 1943-45. Decorated Bronze Star; named Outstanding Sr. Man of Blount County, 1970. Mem. Profl. Photographers of Am., Tenn. Profl. Photographers Assn., Great Smoky Mountains Conservation Assn., Ft. Loudoun Assn., Tenn. Jaycees (editor 1954-55, life mem., sec.-treas. 1955-56), Jr. Chamber Internat. (senator) Maryville-Alcoa Jaycees (life mem., pres. 1953-54), Blount County (v.p. 1971), Townsend (dir. 1969-71) chambers commerce, Tenn. Asso. Press News Execs. Assn. (v.p.), Asso. Press Mng. Editors Assn., Am. Legion, V.F.W., Chilhowee

Bapt. Assn. (chmn. history com.) U. Okla. Alumni Assn. (life mem., pres. E. Tenn. chpt. 1954-55), Sigma Delta Chi (life). Baptist (trustee, deacon, chmn. finance com.). Mason, Kiwanian (pres. 1969-70). Club: Green Meadow Country. Author articles in field. Home: 1510 Scenic Dr Maryville TN 37801 Office: 307 E Harper Av Maryville TN 37801

STONE, ISAAC G., govt. ofcl.; b. Boston, Aug. 30, 1902; s. Jacob and Esther (Linsky) S.; B.S. summa cum laude, Tufts Coll., 1925; LL.B., Washington Coll. Law, 1928, M.P.L., 1929; J.D., Am. U., 1968; m. Lily Mickelson, May 20, 1935; 1 dau., Harriet Marsha. Admitted to D.C. bar, 1928; asst. patent examiner U.S. Patent Office, 1925-46, prin. examiner pharm. div., 1946-51, supervisory examiner, 1951-58, dir. patent research and exam. chem. group, 1958-62, acting examiner-in-chief, 1962-67, examiner-in-chief, 1967—. Mem. Patent Office Soc. Home: 7928 Orchid St NW Washington DC 20012 Office: US Patent Office Washington DC 20231

STONE, JEREMY JUDAH, assn. exec.; b. N.Y.C., Nov. 23, 1935; s. I.F. and Esther M. (Roisman) S.; student Mass. Inst. Tech., 1953-54; B.A. with high honors, Swarthmore Coll., 1957; Ph.D. (NSF fellow), Stanford, 1960; m. Betty Jane Yannet, June 16, 1957. Research mathematician Stanford Research Inst., Menlo Park, Cal., 1960-62; mem. profl. staff Hudson Inst., Croton-on Hudson, N.Y., 1962-64; research asso. Harvard Center Internat. Affairs, Cambridge, Mass., 1964-66; asst. prof. math. Pomona Coll., Claremont, Cal., 1966-68; Social Sci. Research Council fellow Stanford, 1968-69, Council on Fgn. Relations and Internat. Affairs fellow, 1969-70; dir. Fedn. Am. Scientists, Washington, 1970—. Mem. Council Fgn. Relations, Phi Beta Kappa, Sigma Xi. Author: Containing the Arms Race: Some Specific Proposals, 1967; Strategic Persuasion, 1968. Home: 5615 Warwick Pl Chevy Chase MD 20015 Office: 307 Massachusetts Av NE Washington DC 20002

STONE, JOHN FLOYD, educator; b. York, Neb., Oct. 13, 1928; s. Harry F. and Anna (Klima) S.; student Neb. Wesleyan U., 1948-50; B.S., U. Neb., 1952; M.S., Ia. State U., 1955, Ph.D., 1957; m. Carol O. Youngson, Aug. 2, 1953; children—Mary, Margaret, David, Jana. Research asso. Ia. State U., Ames, 1955-57; asst. prof. Okla. State U., Stillwater, 1957-60, asso. prof., 1960-69, prof., dept. agronomy, 1969—. Commr., City of Stillwater, 1974—. Served with USN, 1946-48. Mem. Am. Soc. Agronomy, Soil Sci. Soc. Am. (asso. editor 1968—), Am. Geophys. Union, Internat. Soil Sci. Soc., Sigma Xi. Office: Dept Agronomy Okla State U Stillwater OK 74074

STONE, (MARY) KATHARINE GANN (MRS. ERNEST STONE), educator; b. Sylacauga, Ala.; d. William C. and Mary (Twilley) Gann; B.S., Jacksonville State U., 1933; M.A., U. Ala., 1944, postgrad., 1960, 62; m. Ernest Stone, Aug. 18, 1934; 1 son, William Ernest. Prin., tchr., DeKalb County Schs., 1934-44; tchr. Jacksonville (Ala.) State U., 1944-46, dir. elementary lab. sch., 1948—. Condr. workshops for tchrs. Jefferson, Calhoun, Marshall, Butler, Cherokee counties; tchr. inst. numerous counties, cities; mem. Title III Adv. Council, State of Ala., 1968—; mem. Gov.'s Com. on Adult Edn., 1968—. Recipient Alumnus of Year award Jacksonville State U., 1961-62. Mem. Ala. Edn. Assn. (dist. pres. 1944-46), Edn. Profl. Standards Commn. (tchr. 1944-50), Am. Assn. U. Women (pres. 1950-52), N.E.A., Dept. Elementary Sch. Prins. (pres. dist. V 1971-72), Assn. Childhood Edn., Nat. Assn. Parliamentarians, Ala. Assn. Parliamentarians (historian 1963-65, sec. 1971-73, v.p. 1973—), Nat. Council Tchrs. Math., Am. Assn. Sch. Adminstrs. Ala. Fedn. Women's Clubs (exec. bd. 1945—), Delta Kappa Gamma (pres. chpt. 1940-44), Kappa Delta Pi, Alpha Xi Delta. Club: Progressive Study (pres. 1951-52). Home: President's Mansion Jacksonville State U 730 N Pelham Rd Jacksonville AL 36265

STONE, OLEN JERRY, ins. agy. exec.; b. Huntsville, Ark., July 22, 1916; s. Alison C. and Pearl (Ledbetter) S.; student Northeastern State Tchrs. Coll., 1933; grad. Chillicothe Bus. Coll., 1934-35, David Rankin Jr. Sch., 1938-39; student Mo. U., 1942; m. Alice E. Summerfield, Sept. 21, 1935; children—Carole Jean, David J. Sales engr, Mid-Valley Supply Co., St. Louis, 1935-58; ins. agt., real estate broker Fansher & Stone, Inc., 1959—, pres., 1967—; real estate broker, ins. agt. Fansher & Stone Real Estate Co., Okmulgee, Okla., 1959—, pres., 1967—; dir. Okmulgee Land Title Co., Citizens Nat. Bank, Okmulgee, Nat. Found. Life Ins. Co., Oklahoma City. Sec., treas. Okmulgee Realtors Bd., 1966-67, v.p., 1968-69, pres., 1970, 71; pres. Flordell Hills Improvement Assn., St. Louis, 1941. Bd. dirs. Salvation Army, Okmulgee, v.p. 1968-69, pres., 1970-71. Mem. Retail Mchts. Assn. (dir. 1962-68, pres. 1964). Baptist (deacon 1945-58, 1963-66, supt. Sunday sch. 1946-58, 63-64, 67-69). Lion (pres. 1964-66). Home: 1911 E 10th St Okmulgee OK 74447 Office: 215 E 8th St Okmulgee OK 74447

STONE, ROBERT WILLIAM, pharm. co. exec.; b. Glasgow, Ky., Oct. 4, 1943; s. Robert and Alice Pauline (Bowles) S.; student Western Ky. U., 1960-62; B.S., U. Ky., 1965; m. Joyce Kaye Matthews, Aug. 15, 1964; children—Joseph Harlan, Robert Matthew, Wade Redford. Pharm. intern Begley Drugs, Somerset, Ky., 1965-66; pharmacist Taylors Prescription Service, Inc., Glasgow, 1966-70; organizer Glasgow Prescription Center, Inc., 1970, pres., 1970—, chmn. bd., 1970—. Mem. Citizens Adv. Com. City of Glasgow, 1968-70. Named Outstanding Jaycee of Jr., Glasgow Jr. C. of C., 1967, 68. Mem. Am., Ky., 4th Dist (treas. 1967-68) pharm. assns., Glasgow Jr. C. of C. (pres. 1968-69, dir 1969-70). Methodist (dir. 1967-70). Kiwanian (treas. 1967-68). Home: 555 Lexington Dr Glasgow KY 42141 Office: Glasgow Prescription Center Inc W Public Square Glasgow KY 42141

STONE, ROY MAXWELL, record co. and publishing co. exec.; b. Live Oak, Fla., Jan. 9, 1916; s. William E. and Lola (Miller) S.; student U. Fla., 1938-39, South Tex. Law Sch., 1954-55; m. Lulu Pryor Cloud, Dec. 8, 1940; children—Maxwell Pryor, William Robert, Mary Alice. Religious songwriter J. H. Henson Music Co., Atlanta, 1950; with Baxter Music Co., Dallas, 1950-52, Stamps Quartet Music Co., Dallas, 1952-54, Country Music Band, 1934-39; owner R & M Record Shops, Inc., 1956—, Stoneway Record Co., Houston, 1964—, Roy M. Stone Pub. Co., 1964—, Stoneway Pub. Co., 1970—; pres. Wide World Records, 1969—. Mem. Country Music Assn. Baptist. Mason. Author, Composer: Our Hymns and Gospel Songs. Composer many songs including I Know That God is Real, Out of Order. Home: 10414 Shady Lane Houston TX 77016 Office: 2817 Laura Koppe Houston TX 77016

STONECIPHER, ELMER THOMAS, socio-econ. devel. cons.; b. LaCrosse, Ind., Feb. 6, 1920; s. Samuel Oliver and Mary Etta (McKim) S.; student Ind. U., 1938-40; B.A., Tulane U., 1949; M.A., George Washington U., 1964; postgrad. Naval War Coll., 1964; m. Rebecca Louise Lehner, Sept. 23, 1943; children—Susan Kögel, Charles, Sarah, Rebecca, Henry, Daniel. Commd. ensign USN, 1941, advanced through grades to capt., 1960, ret., 1965; dir. tech. tng. Dept. of Def. nuclear program, N.M., 1951-54, 57-60, dir. NATO Sch., Europe, 1960-63, mem. Joint Staff and Exec. Office Sec. Navy, 1964-65; civilian service Exec. Office of Pres., 1965-67; v.p. Avco Corp., socio-econ. devel., Washington, 1968-73; v.p. Inst. of Rockies, 1973—. Guest lectr. NATO Def. Coll., 1960-63. Active in youth oriented orgns. Decorated commendation medal. Recipient Freedom Found. medal, 1964. Mem. Am. Mgmt. Assn., Am. Soc. Tng. and Devel., Pa. German Soc., St. Andrew's Soc., S.A.R. (state dir. 1958-59), Fedn. German Am. Men's Clubs (dir. 1962-63). Methodist. Clubs: George Washington University, Army and Navy, Internat. (Washington). Home: 3118 Wynford Dr Fairfax VA 22030 Office: 1901 N Moore St Arlington VA 22209

STONEY, WILLIAM SHANNON, JR., physician; b. Gainesville, Fla., Apr. 21, 1928; s. William Shannon and Martha (Hunt) S.; B.A., U. South, 1950; M.D., Vanderbilt U., 1954; m. Marian Elizabeth Tilley, June 3, 1953; children—Elizabeth Shannon, Martha Carol, William S., Marian T. Intern, Vanderbilt U. Hosp., Nashville, 1954-55, resident, 1955-56, 58-62; sr. registrar cardiac surgery Gen. Infirmary, Leeds, Eng., 1962-63; practice medicine, specializing in cardiac surgery, Nashville, 1963—; mem. staff St. Thomas, Vanderbilt U., Parkview hosps., asst. clin. prof. dept. surgery Med. Sch., Vanderbilt U., Nashville, 1963-72, asso. clin. prof., 1972—. Bd. dirs. Middle Tenn. Heart Assn., Cardiovascular Fund St. Thomas Hosp., Nashville. Served to lt. M.C., USNR, 1956-58. Rudolph Light surg. fellow, 1962-63. Diplomate Am. Bd. Surgery, Am. Bd. Thoracic Surgery. Fellow Am. Coll. Cardiology; mem. Soc. Thoracic Surgeons, So. Surg. Assn., So. Thoracic Surg. Assn. Home: 3822 Brighton Rd Nashville TN 37205 Office: 2108 West End St Nashville TN 37201

STOPHEL, GLENN CARLTON, lawyer; b. Bristol, Tenn., Jan. 22, 1937; s. Oscar William and Cora Lee (Frye) S.; B.S., Bob Jones U., 1957; J.D., U. Tenn., 1961; m. Jacqueline Hudgins, Mar. 24, 1958; children—Rhonda, Kimberly, Leslie. Admitted to Tenn. bar, 1962; atty. Stophel, Caldwell & Heggie, 1962-65; partner Stophel, Caldwell & Heggie, Chattanooga, 1965—; chmn. bd. trustees Legal Aid Soc. Chattanooga, 1971-73. Sec. Fellowship of Christian Athletes, 1972-73; pres. Community Action Agy., 1971; v.p., dir. Reach Out, Inc. Sec. bd. trustees Bethel Bible Sch., 1972-73; chmn. Brainerd Bapt. Sch. Bd., 1971—. Served with AUS, 1957-59. Named young man of year for Chattanooga, Jaycees, 1972, outstanding young man for Tenn., 1972. Mem. Estate Planning Council Chattanooga, Am., Tenn., Chattanooga bar assns., Order of Coif. Clubs: Mountain City, Kiwanis (Chattanooga). Home: 1 Lynncrest Dr Chattanooga TN 37411 Office: MacLellan Bldg W Chattanooga TN 37402

STORCK, AMBROSE HOWELL, surgeon; b. New Orleans, July 8, 1903; s. Jacob Ambrose and Minnie Edna (Howell) S.; B.S., Tulane U., 1923, M.D., 1925, M.S., 1934. Intern Charity Hosp. of La., New Orleans, 1925-27, house surgeon, 1927-31, vis. surgeon, 1932-40, sr. vis. surgeon, 1940—; practice medicine specializing in surgery, New Orleans, 1931—; instr. clin. surgery, Tulane U., 1931-39, asst. prof. clin. surgery, 1939-47, prof. clin. surgery, 1947-64, prof. surgery, 1964-72, prof. surgery emeritus, 1973—; hon. staff surgeon Touro Infirmary, 1969—; cons. surgeon So. Bapt. Hosp., 1970—. Cons. gen. surgery for VA, Tex. and La., 1946-54; surg. cons. 4th Army Station Hosp., New Orleans; mem. local unit La. Cultural Resources Commn.; mem. Charity Hosp. Tumor Registry Bd. Commd. maj., U.S. Army Med. Res., 1940, advanced through grades to Col., 1948; asst. cons. in surgery Office of The Surgeon Gen., March 14, 1942, later cons. in gen. surgery, E.T.O., and chief surg. service De Witt Gen. Hosp. Recipient Distinguished Service award American Cancer Soc., also research grants. Diplomate Am. Bd. Surgery. Fellow A.C.S. (gov. 1959-62); mem. Am., So. surg. assns., Surgeons Club, So. Surgeons Club, Soc. Univ. Surgeons, Soc. for Vascular Surgery, Soc. Med. Cons. to Armed Forces, A.M.A., Internat. Soc. Surgery, La. Surg. Assn. (pres. 1954), Southeastern Surg. Congress, Soc. Surgery Alimentary Tract (founder mem.), Am. Assn. Cancer Research, So. Med. Assn., La. State Med. Soc. (chmn. cancer commn.), A.A.A.S., New Orleans Acad. Scis., Assn. for Surgery of Trauma, La. Soc. S.A.R., Ednl. Council Orleans Parish Unit Am. Cancer Soc. (hon. dir. for New Orleans and La.), New Orleans Surg. Soc. (pres. 1958), Royal Soc. Medicine (Eng.), Nat. Trust Historic Preservation, Assn., Internat. House, La. Landmarks Soc. (dir.), Phi Delta Theta, Nu Sigma Nu. Democrat. Presbyn. Clubs: Boston, Louisana, Lake Shore, Pickwick. Author (book) Military Surgical Manual—Abdominal and Genito-Urinary Injuries; contbg. author, history U.S. Army Med. Dept. during World War II; Cancer of the Digestive Tract; also author med. articles in Annals of Surgery, Archives of Surgery, Gynecology and Obstetrics, New Orleans Med. and Surg. Jour. Co-editor Tulane Medicine. Editorial bd. Am. Surgeon. Home: 1458 Nashville Av New Orleans LA 70115 Office: 1430 Tulane Av New Orleans LA 70112

STORER, JOHN JAMES, physician; b. Iowa, La., July 17, 1919; s. James Lawrence and Juanita Rae (McKinley) S.; B.S., U. So. La., 1940; M.D., La. State U., 1944; m. Cleta M. Tanquis, Apr. 11, 1945; children—Cleta Ann, John, Claire Rae, George, Ilene, Clarence, William, Kathleen. Teaching fellow Tex. A. and M. U., 1940; intern Mercy Hosp., New Orleans, 1944; gen. practice medicine, Kinder, La., 1946-71; chief staff Allen Parish Hosp., 1969-71; med. dir. Charity Hosp., Lake Charles, La., 1971—. Served with USNR, 1945-46. Fellow Am. Acad. Family Physicians, Am. Geriatrics Soc., Royal Soc. Health; mem. A.M.A., Am. Quarter Horse Assn., Am. Legion, Woodmen of World, Allen Parish Farm Bur., La. State, Allen Parish med. socs., Phi Chi. Home: Kinder LA 70648 Office: Charity Hosp 1000 Walters St Lake Charles LA 70601

STORER, MORRIS BREWSTER, educator; b. Pitts., Nov. 14, 1904; s. Norman Wilson and Mary Elizabeth Wyman (Perry) S.; B.S., Dartmouth, 1926; M.A., U. Chgo., 1929; M.A., Harvard, 1932, Ph.D., 1937; m. Gretchen Geuder Schneider, Aug. 18, 1935; children—John Winthrop, Christopher Martin, Thomas Perry. Instr. philosophy U. Pitts., 1927-28, Lafayette Coll., 1929-30, Dartmouth Coll., 1932-35; social scientist U.S. Dept. Agr., 1936-46; dean instrn. Mt. Vernon Jr. Coll., 1946-47; prof. humanities U. Fla., Gainesville, 1947-73, emeritus, 1973—. Pres., Santa Fe Telephone Co., 1950-52. Served to capt. AUS, 1943-44. Mem. Am. Assn. U. Profs., Am. Fedn. Tchrs. (sec. local chpt. 1970-71), Am., Fla. philos. assns., Grange, Delta Upsilon. Unitarian (chmn. 1965-66). Club: Melrose (Fla.) Civic (pres. 1949-50). Home: Swan Lake PO Box 148 Melrose FL 32666

STOREY, BEN CHARLES, physician; b. Washington, Ind., Aug. 3, 1933; s. Thomas G. and Mary (Russo) S.; student Wabash Coll., 1954; grad. Med. Sch. Ind., U., 1958; m. Mary Emma Farr, Sept. 2, 1955; children—Mark, Matthew, Todd, Troy, Monique. Intern Tampa (Fla.) Gen. Hosp., 1958-59; practice gen. medicine, Titusville, Fla., 1959—; mem. staff Jess Parrish Meml. Hosp., 1959—. Dir. Lantern Hills Devel. Corp., Fisher Constrn. Co., Superior Cabinet & Supply Co., Titusville Med. Facilities, Inc. Mem. Brevard Ednl. Com., 1971-72. Bd. dirs. Brevard Heart Loan Fund; bd. dirs., physician Pop Warner Hurricane League, Inc., Titusville. Recipient Distinguished Service award Titusville Jr. C. of C., 1969. Mem. Am., Fla., Canaveral (pres. 1968-70) heart assns., Fla. (chmn. pharmacy com. 1968-71), Brevard County (pres. 1968) med. assns., Phi Gamma Delta, Nu Sigma Nu. Moose. Home: Burkholm Rd Route 1 Box 386 Titusville FL 32780 Office: 500 N Washington Av Titusville FL 32780

STOREY, BILL HENRY, chemist; b. Cameron, Tex., Oct. 30, 1938; s. Bill Bean and Frances Sedonia (Sefcik) S.; B.S., S.W. Tex. State Coll., 1962; m. Elizabeth Louise Carleton, July 14, 1959; children—Bruce Wayne, Susan Lynn, Lori Ann. Chemist, Southwestern Portland Cement Co., Odessa, Tex., 1962-65, chief chemist, El Paso, Tex., 1965-70; chief chemist Southwestern Cement Co., Odessa, 1970—. Mem. Am. Soc. Testing Materials, Am. Petroleum Inst., Am. Concrete Inst., Baptist. Eagle. Home: 3731 Boulder St Odessa TX 79762 Office: PO Box 1547 Odessa TX 79760

STOREY, CLYDE HERBERT, glass co. exec.; b. Lynch, Ky., Sept. 28, 1934; s. Watson and Mildred Pearl (McIntire) S.; student Ga. Inst. Tech., 1952-53, U.S. Naval Acad., 1954-55; B.S. in Mining Engring., U. Ky., 1958; m. Betty Jo Groh, May 27, 1958; children—Rebecca Lillian, Lora Dawn, Rachel Ramona. Dir. indsl. engring. Princess Coals, Inc., 1959-61; with Corning Glass Works, Harrodsburg, Ky., 1961—, successively jr. glass technologist, foreman melting tank maintenance, shift melting foreman, sr. glass technologist, supr. optical properties, supr. glass tech., 1967—. Part-time land surveyer, 1963-66. Served with USNR, 1954-55. Registered profl. engr., Ky. Research in photochromic glass. Home: 774 Cane Run St Harrodsburg KY 40330 Office: 680 E Office St Harrodsburg KY 40330

STOREY, WILLIAM MARION, bar assn. exec.; b. Savannah, Ga., Aug. 16, 1924; s. William Marion and Rubye (McDonald) S.; student Cornell Midshipmans Sch., 1943-44; A.B., U. N.C., 1947, J.D., 1950; m. Lucille Ann Tucker, Apr. 19, 1952; children—James McDonald, Ann Tucker. Admitted to N.C. bar, 1950, practiced in Raleigh until 1955, gen. counsel N.C. Bd. Pharmacy, 1950-55; exec. sec.-treas. N.C. Bar Assn. and N.C. Bar Found., Raleigh, 1955-69, exec. v.p., treas., 1969—. Mem. N.C. adv. com. Practicing Law Inst., 1967—; mem. N.C. Penal System Study Commn., 1969—. Mem. U. N.C. adv. TV com., 1959—. Active Wake County Civil Def. Authority. Bd. dirs. N.C. Bar Found. Served to lt. USNR, 1942-46; lt. comdr. Res. Recipient Judge John Parker Meml. award for unusually outstanding and conspicuous service to cause of jurisprudence N.C. Bar Assn., 1971. Mem. Am., Wake County, N.C. (gov. 1955—) bar assns., Internat. Assn. Continuing Legal Edn. Adminstrs. (exec. com. 1970—), Am. Judicature Soc., Nat. Assn. Bar Execs., Am., N.C. State bars. Methodist (steward 1958—). Clubs: Raleigh Kiwanis (dir., sec. 1957-60, 63-65), Raleigh City, Carolina Country, Esquires. Home: 701 Yarmouth Rd Raleigh NC 27607 Office: North Carolina Bar Center 1025 Wade Av Raleigh NC 27605

STORMS, JOHN WEBB, accountant; b. Washington, July 13, 1944; s. Louis Wilson, Jr., and Marie Elizabeth (Webb) S.; B.B.A., U. Tex., 1966; M.B.A., Coll. City N.Y., 1968; m. Charlene Raye Butler, Aug. 6, 1965; children—Shannon Leigh, Collyne Ann. Staff tax accountant Arthur Young & Co., Houston, 1968-69; controller Taylor & Assos., Inc., Houston, 1969-71; tax mgr. W.M. Mischer Co., Houston, 1971; asst. to pres. Hycel, Inc., Houston, 1971-72; pvt. accounting practice, Houston, 1972—; v.p., dir. Thompson Irrigation, Inc.; treas., dir. G.O.T., Inc.; tchr. tax course U. Houston, 1972. Arthur Andersen merit scholar, 1965. Mem. Am. Inst. C.P.A.'s, Tex. Soc. C.P.A.'s, Phi Delta Theta, Beta Gamma Sigma, Beta Alpha Psi. Home: 12638 Taylorcrest St Houston TX 77024 Office: 3229 D'Amico St Houston TX 77019

STORRS, THOMAS IRWIN, banker; b. Nashville, Aug. 25, 1918; s. Robert Williamson and Addie Sue (Payne) S.; B.A., U. Va., 1940; M.A., Harvard, 1950, Ph.D., 1955; m. Kitty Stewart Bird, July 19, 1948; children—Thomas, Margaret. With Fed. Res. Bank, Richmond, Va., 1934-60, v.p. charge research, 1957-59, v.p. charge Charlotte br., 1959-60; exec. v.p. N.C. Nat. Bank, Greensboro, 1960-67, vice chmn. bd. dirs., 1967-69, pres., 1969-73, chmn. exec. com., 1974—; pres. NCNB Corp., 1968-73, chmn. bd., 1974—; dir. Texfi Industries, Inc., Greensboro, Black and Decker Mfg. Co. Mem. Fed. Adv. Council, pres., 1974. Trustee, U. N.C. at Charlotte. Served to lt. comdr. USNR, 1941-45, 51-52, comdr. Res. ret. Mem. N.C. Citizens Assn. (pres. 1971-72), Assn. Res. City Bankers, Raven Soc. Episcopalian. Clubs: Greensboro Country, Greensboro City; Charlotte Country, Country of N.C., Charlotte City. Home: 330 Eastover Rd Charlotte NC 28207 Office: NCNB Corp NCNB Plaza PO Box 120 Charlotte NC 28201

STOTHART, JAMES LONNIE, dentist; b. Greensboro, Ala., July 20, 1929; s. James Lonnie and Alice Creswell (Seed) S.; B.S., U. Ala., 1951, D.M.D., 1955; m. Gloria Burks McKeon, Sept. 11, 1954; children—Richard Burks, Alice Amanda. Gen. practice dentistry, Selma, Ala., 1957—; mem. staff New Vaughan Meml. Hosp., Selma Med. Center. Bd. dirs., sec. bd. Sturdivant Mus. Assn. Served from 1st lt. to capt. USAF, 1955-57. Mem. Am., Ala., Dallas County dental assns., U. Ala. Alumni Assn. (pres. Dallas County 1967), Psi Omega, Sigma Alpha Epsilon. Republican. Episcopalian. Club: Selma Country. Home: 2011 Church St Selma AL 36701 Office: PO Box 455 Selma AL 36701

STOUDEMIRE, STERLING A(UBREY), ret. educator; b. Concord, N.C., Sept. 4, 1902; s. Palmer and Frances (Cranford) S.; A.B., U. N.C., 1923, M.A., 1924, Ph.D., 1930; m. Irene Slate, 1925 (dec. 1940); 1 dau., Marian S. (Mrs. James A. Hawlans); m. 2d, Mary Arthur Billups, 1946; 1 son, Sterling Cranford. Instr. Spanish U. N.C., 1924-30, asst. prof. Spanish, 1930-35; asso. prof. Spanish, 1935-41, prof. Spanish, 1941-72, head dept. Romance langs., 1949-64. Served as lt. comdr. USNR, 1942-45. Mem. Modern Lang. Assn., S. Atlantic Modern Lang. Assn. (pres. 1962), Am. Assn. Tchrs. Spanish and Portguguese, Am. Name Soc., Phi Gamma Delta. Episcopalian. Author articles and book revs. on Spanish Romanticism; author and editor Spanish texts and anthologies. Translator: Oviedo's Natural History of the West Indies, 1959; Cuentos de Espana y de America, 1942; Christian Doctrine (Pedro de Cordoba), 1970. Home: 712 Gimghoul Rd Chapel Hill NC 27514

STOUT, JOE FRANCIS, boot co. exec.; b. Granville, Tenn., Sept. 5, 1933; s. Clifford D. and Sally B. (Huff) S.; student pub. schs., Putnam County, Tenn.; m. Anita Sue Dye, Sept. 22, 1956; children—Jerry Morgan, Amy Renee. Machine operator Continental Aviation & Engring. Co., Detroit, 1951-56; exptl. hand former Mercury Metalcraft Co., Detroit, 1956-58; with Ga. Boot Co., Baxter, Tenn., 1958-64, now gen. mgr. Ga. div., Blairsville, Ga. Mem. com. Heart Fund, 1963. Bd. dirs. Am. Cancer Soc. Lt. col. on staff gov. Ga., 1968—. Mem. Ga. Sheriffs Assn. Mason; mem. Order Eastern Star. Clubs: North Ga. Sportsman, Quarterback (Blairsville). Home: Deep South Farm Rd Blairsville GA 30512 Office: Gainesville Hwy Blairsville GA 30512

STOUT, RICHARD ALAN, mus. adminstr., artist; b. Lenoir City, Tenn., Mar. 4, 1941; s. Reese Huston and Viola (Green) S.; B.S. with honors in Sci. and English, Carson-Newman Coll., Jefferson City, Tenn., 1963; m. Linda Ellen Canipe, Mar. 29, 1964; 1 son, Richard Shane. Tchr. biology South Point Sr. High Sch., Belmont, N.C., 1963-65; asst. dir. Schiele Mus. Natural History and Planetarium, Gastonia, N.C., 1965—. Tchr. field ecology workshops, Gastonia, 1971—; designer earth-space scis. program for pub. schs., Gaston County, N.C., 1967; one-man shows Carson-Newman Coll., 1962, Gaston County Regional Library, 1972; exhibited in group shows as Hallmark artist, 1957, Starving Artists Festival, Gastonia, 1971-73, Realism in N.C., Charlotte, 1974. Mem. Heart Assn. Com., 1969-72, Bicentennial Com., 1973. Mem. N.C. Mus. Council, N.E.A., Am. Assn. Museums, Nat. Wildlife Fedn., Conservation Council N.C., N.C. Watercolor Soc., Gaston County Conservation Soc. (adv. com. 1970-73). Democrat. Baptist. Home: Route 1 Ashebrook Park Dallas NC 28034 Office: 1500 E Garrison St PO Box 953 Gastonia NC 28052

STOVALL, GUY FRANKLIN, JR., investment exec.; b. El Campo, Tex., Jan. 13, 1934; s. Guy Franklin and Edith I. (Perterka) S.; B.B.A., U. Houston, 1956; m. Kay Kuhn, Feb. 7, 1956; children—Guy Franklin III, Becky, Linda, David, Eric. Trader in oil, land, cattle, rice investments; dir., chmn. bd. 1st Nat. Bank, El Campo, Tex.; pres. bd. Carancahua Bay Properties, Inc. Trustee Gulf Coast Med. Found., former pres. and chmn. bd., now pres. bd., chmn. exec. com.; trustee numerous trusts. Recipient Elk of year award, 1969-70. Mem. Petroleum Club. Methodist (trustee 1965-71). Elk (trustee). Club: Houston. Home: El Campo TX 77437 Office: 202 E Jackson St El Campo TX 77437

STOVALL, JAMES WATTS, clergyman; b. Mobile, Ala., Apr. 27, 1912; s. Albert Bee and Rosa Lee (McDowell) S.; student pub. schs.; m. Janet Elizabeth Myers, June 19, 1935 (dec. Aug. 1967); 1 dau., Mary Elizabeth. Blacksmith's helper Mobile County, Ala., 1930-38; asst. warehouseman Mobile County, 1938-43, warehouseman, 1943; minister Belforest Christian Ch., 1953-54, Robertsdale Christian Ch., 1955-65, 67—, Azalea Christian Ch., 1966-67. Lifetime blood donor A.R.C., 1957—. Recipient Town and Country Minister of Yr. award Ala. Christian Chs., 1963. Mason. Home: 300 Stocking Mobile AL 36604

STOVALL, REGINALD MORRIS, mayor; b. Tupelo, Okla., Aug. 1, 1916; s. William Dudley and Grace (Allen) S.; ed. Tex. Christian U., 1936; m. Amelia Zich, Sept. 9, 1939; children—Linda (Mrs. Robert Paul Guminski), Marsha, Peggy, Nancy (Mrs. S.R. Sanders). Pres., Panther City Office Supply Co., 1944—; mayor, Fort Worth, 1969—. Mem. Fort Worth City Council, 1963-68. Episcopalian. Mason (Shriner). Home: 2428 Medford Ct E Fort Worth TX 76109 Office: 3001 W 7th St Fort Worth TX 76107

STOVALL, THELMA L., state ofcl.; b. Munfordville, Ky., Apr. 1, 1919; d. Samuel Dewey and Addie Mae Hawkins; student LaSalle Extension U., U. Ky., Eastern State Coll.; m. Lonnie Raymond Stovall, Sept. 30, 1936. Mem. Ky. Ho. of Reps., sec. of state State of Ky., 1956-60, 64-68; treas. State of Ky., 1960-64, 68-72, sec. of state, 1972—. Active State Labor Movement; sec. Tobacco Workers Internat. Union; liaison officer Louisville Community Chest and labor unions; state chmn. Muscular Dsytrophy, 1957-70; v.p. Muscular Dystrophy Assn. Am., 1970-72, chmn. legislative com., 1972—; mem. Pres.'s Commn. on Status of Women, 1964-68. Nat. committeewoman Young Democratic Clubs Ky., 1952-56, pres., 1956-58. Bd. dirs. edn. dept. Ky. Fedn. Labor. Mem. Bus. and Profl. Women's Club. Democrat. Baptist. Moose; mem. Order Eastern Star. Club: Altrusa. Home: 104 Valley Rd Louisville KY 40204 Office: State Capitol Frankfort KY 40601

STOVER, CARL FREDERICK, found. exec.; b. Pasadena, Cal., Sept. 29, 1930; s. Carl Joseph and Margarete (Muller) S.; B.A. magna cum laude, Stanford, 1951, M.A., 1954; m. Catherine Swanson, Sept. 3, 1954 (div. Jan. 1973); children—Matthew Joseph, Mary Margaret, Claire Ellen; m. 2d, Jacqueline Kast, Sept. 7, 1973. Instr. polit. sci. Stanford, 1953-55; fiscal mgmt. officer Office Sec. Dept. Agr., 1955-57; asso. dir. conf. program pub. affairs Brookings Instn., 1957-59, sr. staff mem. govtl. studies, 1960; fellow Center for Study Democratic Instns., Santa Barbara, Cal., 1960-62; asst. to chmn. bd. editors Ency. Brit., 1960-62; sr. polit. scientist Stanford Research Inst., 1962-64, dir. pub. affairs fellowship program Stanford, 1962-64; pres. Nat. Inst. Pub. Affairs, Washington, 1964-70; pres. Nat. Com. U.S.-China Relations, 1971-72; pres., dir. Federalism Seventy-Six, Inc., 1972—; pvt. profl. cons., 1970—. Cons. to govt., 1953—. Treas., Nat. Com. U.S.-China Relations, 1966-71, dir., 1966—; treas., dir. Coordinating Council Lit. Mags., 1966-68. Trustee Inst. Nations, 1962—, Nat. Inst. Pub. Affairs, 1967-71. Fellow A.A.A.S.; mem. Am. Soc. Pub. Adminstrn., Am. Polit. Sci. Assn., Am. Soc. for Cybernetics, Fedn. Am. Scientists, Soc. Internat. Devel., Nat. Acad. Pub. Adminstrn. (hon.), Phi Beta Kappa Assos., Phi Beta Kappa. Democrat. Presbyn. Author: The Government of Science, 1962; The Technological Order, 1963. Founding editor Jour. Law and Edn., 1971-73. Home: 1280 21st St NW Washington DC 20036

STOVER, CHARLES OSCAR, educator, band dir.; b. Coffeyville, Kan., Apr. 15, 1913; s. Charles Robert and Addie (Wood) S.; B.S., Kan. State Tchrs. Coll., 1940, M.S., 1946; postgrad. Mich. State U., 1949-53; m. Catherine Elizabeth Cooper, Aug. 23, 1936. Dir. vocal music, Roosevelt Jr. High Sch., Coffeyville, Kan., 1935-42; band dir. Kan. State Tchrs. Coll., Pittsburg, 1942-47; supr. music, dir. jr. coll. bd. dir. Coffeyville Pub. Schs., 1947-52; asst. dir. bands Mich. State U., 1953-60; asso. prof. Northwestern State Coll., Alva, Okla., 1960—, chmn. music dept., 1960—, band dir., 1960—. Band clinician Slingerland Drum Co. Mem. Bd. Advisers, Niles, Ill., 1957-67; bd. advisors J.F. Kennedy Center for Performing Arts, 1970—. Served with AUS, 1943-46. Named Outstanding Tchr., Coffeyville Pub Schs., 1952, All Am. Bandmaster's Band, Chgo., 1956; named Tchr. of Year Northwestern State Coll., 1968-69. Mem. N.E.A., Okla. Edn. Assn., Music Educators Nat Conf., Okla. Music Educators Assn., Okla. Bandmaster's Assn., Coll. Bandmaster's Nat. Assn., Kappa Kappa Psi, Phi Beta Mu (state pres. 1971—), Phi Mu Alpha. Republican. Presbyn. (elder, choir dir.). Rotarian (pres. 1967—). Home: 716 Apache Dr Alva OK 73717

STOVER, HERMAN DINSMORE, distillers assn. exec.; b. Portland, Me., Nov. 14, 1918; s. Herman Dinsmore and Leona Frye (Johnson) S.; student Northwestern Bus. Coll., Portland, 1938; certificate pub. adminstr. U. Me., 1967; m. Faith Janice Clark, Sept. 15, 1940; children—Carole (Mrs. Stanley Roger Tupper, Jr.), Susan Elaine. Purchasing agt. New Eng. Shipbldg. Corp., 1941-43, 45-46, Baker Refrigeration Corp., 1947-53; adminstr. Me. State Liquor Commn., 1953-68; v.p. adminstrn. Distilled Spirits Council U.S., Inc., Washington, 1972—. Mem. Me. Gov's. Standardization Com., 1962-68; mem. Sch. Bldg. Com., Augusta, Me., 1967-68. Trustee Ft. Western, Augusta, Me., 1967-68. Served with USAAF, 1943-45. Mem. Am. Soc. Assn. Execs., Mason (Shriner). Club: Nat. Press (Washington). Home: 8525 Milford Ct Springfield VA 22152 Office: 538 Pennsylvania Bldg Washington DC 20004

STOVER, LLOYD VERNON, educator; b. Belfast, Me., May 30, 1922; s. Walter Raymond and Neva Evelyn (Armstrong) S.; B.S., U. N.H., 1948; LL.B., U. Miami, 1951, J.D., 1964; m. Betty Jean Curry, May 21, 1955; children—Kim, Nan, Jil. Mgr. guided missile range operations Pan Am. Airlines, 1954-57; mgr. allied communications Europe Internat. Tel.; Tel., 1957-60; mgr. Titan site activation Martin Co., 1960-62; mgr. marine systems and technologies Gen. Electric Co., 1962-67; v.p. Oceans Gen., 1967-70, now dir., sr. research scientist U. Miami Inst. Atmospheric and Ocean Sci., 1967-70; pres. Ocean Marine Products, 1967-70; mgr. environmental systems Sanders & Thomas, Inc., 1970; prof. urban and environmental studies Fla. Internat. U., Miami, 1970—. Cons. Nat. Marine Sci. Commn., 1968-70, Ho. of Reps. Mcht. Marine and Fisheries Com., 1967-70, Senate Commerce Com., 1967-70; mem. Aspen Inst. Humanistic Studies, 1971; mem. Dade County Environmental Action Com., 1970-71; adviser Inter-Am. Inst. Ecology, 1970-71, Miami-Dade Jr. Coll., 1967-71. Served with USN 1940-46. Decorated Air Medal. Mem. Marine Tech. Soc. (chmn. Fla. chpt. 1967-70), Am. Trucking Assns. (asst. gen. council 1951-54), A.A.A.S., Fla., D.C. bars. Home: 9621 SW 62d Ct Miami FL 33156

STOVER, VERGIL G., transp. research exec.; b. Lake Park, Minn., June 7, 1933; s. Vergil D. and Edna (Larsen) S.; B.S., Ohio U., 1958; M.S., Purdue U., 1960, Ph.D., 1963; m. Mary Sue Punkar, Dec. 30, 1955; children—Kenneth, Terrance, Curt. Project engr. Ohio Dept. Hwys., Cleve., 1957-58; prin. investigator Joint Hwy. Research Project, instr. civil engring. Purdue U., Lafayette, Ind., 1958-63; asst. prof. U. S.C., Columbia, 1963-66; program mgr. transp. planning Tex. Transp. Inst., Tex. A. and M. U., College Station, Tex., 1966—, asst. prof., 1966-67, asso. prof., 1967-71, prof., 1971—. Project engr. Wilbur Smith & Assos., Columbia, S.C., 1963-65. Served with inf. AUS, 1951-53. Mem. Inst. Traffic Engrs., Am. Marketing Assn., Hwy. Research Bd., Am. Soc. Planning Ofcls., Sigma Xi. Home: 1017 Holt St College Station TX 77840 Office: Tex Transp Inst Tex A and M U College Station TX 77843

STOVER, WILLIAM REITZEL, educator, condominium cons.; b. Waynesboro, Pa., June 8, 1906; s. Harry Edgar and Antoinette (Reitzel) S.; B.S., Temple U., 1938, Ed.M., 1940; Litt. D., Wagner Coll., 1953; m. Anna Mary Miller, June 5, 1928. Prin. Amon Heights and Jr. High Sch., Pennsauken, N.J., 1928-47, supt., 1947-55; supt. Central Regional High Sch. Dist., Bayville, N.J, 1955-58, Mainland Regional High Sch. Dist., Linwood, 1958-64. Ofcl. local congregation Luth. Ch., 1931—, ofcl. N.J. Synod, 1953-64; mem. personnel commn. Fla. Synod; instr. Christian edn., 1950—, del. Luth. Ch. Convs., 1952-64; mem. Luth. Laymen's Movement. Troop com. chmn. Boy Scouts Am., 1936-42, mem. bd. review 1941-42; pres. Condominium Assn. and area council, 1970-72; active various civic or charity drives. Bd. dirs. Wagner Coll., Mt. Airy Sem., Phila., Community Mobile Meals. Mem. N.E.A. (life), P.T.A. (life), N.J. Edn. Assn. (pres. 1951-53), Nat., N.J. assns. sch. adminstrs., Assn. Ret. Persons (local pres. 1966-68), Phi Delta Kappa. Lutheran. Mason (Shriner). Author: What You Should Know Before Buying a Condominium, 1972. Home: 3272 Southfield Lane Sarasota FL 33580

STOWE, JAMES JUNIOR, advt. agy. exec.; b. Drumright, Okla., Mar. 5, 1921; s. James R. and Myrtle Louise (Pruitt) S.; student U. Md., 1955-60, Hills U., 1961-63; m. Mozel Aleen Staton, Nov. 30, 1940; children—James, Patricia, Pamela. Commd. officer U.S. Army, 1940, advanced through grades to maj., 1960; self-employed Sundries Store, 1960-61; accountant, auditor Ackerman Assos., Oklahoma City, 1963-65, sec.-treas., 1965—; dir. Ackerman Inc. Adviser, Call-A-Teen Summer Youth Employment Program, 1970—, Jr. Achievement Program, 1971—. Decorated Purple Heart with cluster, Silver Star, Bronze Star with cluster. Mem. Am. Accountants Assn. Mason. Home: 5912 Tiffany Circle Oklahoma City OK 73132 Office: 5708 Mosteller Dr Oklahoma City OK 73112

STOWE, JOHN JOEL, JR., clergyman; b. Clarksville, Tenn., June 11, 1908; s. John Joel and Myra Anderson (McFarrin) S.; Ph.B., Emory U., 1929; M.A., Peabody Coll., 1930; postgrad. Duke Div. Sch., 1935-36, Vanderbilt U., 1938-40; D.D., Oklahoma City U., 1963; m. Evalyn Walker, Sept. 3, 1932; children—John Joel III, Myra Evalyn (Mrs. Husni Khallfa), Betse, Kay (Mrs. W. Don Moore), Louise (Mrs. R.D. Johns). Ordained to ministry Meth. Ch., 1935; pastoral services N.C., Ark., Tex., Okla., 1933—; Woodward Dist., 1972—; dist. supt. United Meth. Ch., 1974—, pres. ministerial alliances, 1945-65, mem. or officer conf. bds. edn., missions and others. Founder chaplaincy Okla. Hwy. Patrol, 1950-52; chaplain Okla. Senate, 1956-71. Active A.R.C.; mem. exec. bd. various Boy Scout councils, recipient Silver Beaver award, 1958. Bd. dirs. Woodward Meml. Hosp., Sr. Citizens, Okla.; bd. dirs., officer Wesley Found., Cameron Coll. Southeastern Coll., U. Tulsa; Mem. Sigma Chi (pres. alumni assn. 1956-58). Mason (K.T., 32 deg., royal grand chaplain 1957-58), Rotarian, Lion, Kiwanian. Contbr. articles to profl. publs. Address: 3344 Cheyenne Dr Woodward OK 73801

STOWE, WILLIAM MCFERRIN, clergyman; b. Franklin, Tenn., Jan. 28, 1913; s. John Joel and Myra Anderson (McFerrin) S.; A.B., Hendrix Coll., Conway, Ark., 1932, D.D., 1956; B.D., Duke, 1935, D.D., 1967; Ph.D., Boston U., 1938; D.D., Oklahoma City U., 1955; L.H.D., Southwestern Coll.; LL.D., So. Meth. U.; LL.D., Baker U., 1966; m. Twila Farrell, July 28, 1943; children—William McFerrin, Twila Gayle, Martha Elizabeth. Ordained to ministry Meth. Ch., 1937; pastor Meth. Ch., Alta Loma, Tex., 1938-40, Garden Villas Meth. Ch., Houston, 1940-44; mem. staff Bd. Edn., Meth. Ch.; dir. youth work Tex. Cont. Meth. Ch., 1940-44; dir. spl. tng. enterprises, 1944-49, sec. personnel service, 1946-49; sec. vocational counsel Meth. Ch., 1946-48; pastor First Meth. Ch., Stillwater, Okla., 1949-51, St. Luke's Meth. Ch., Oklahoma City, 1951-64; bishop The Meth. Ch., Kansas Area, 1961-72, Dallas, 1972—. Vis. prof. The Iliff Sch. Theol., Denver, summer 1945-47, Scarritt Coll., Nashville, 1944-46; spl. lectr. Boston U. Sch. Theology, 1945, Perkins Sch. Theology, So. Meth. U., 1944-46, Westminster Theol. Sem., 1946-47, Grad. Sch. Religion, U. So. Cal., 1946, Gammon Sch. Theology, 1944-45; dean Okla. Meth. Pastors' Sch. Mem. exec. com. Okla. Council Chs.; pres. Okla. City Council Chs., 1955-56; pres. Okla. Conf. bd. edn. The Meth. Ch.; mem. exec. com. jurisdictional bd. edn., mem. co-ordinating council, del. to world conf., 1956, 61, 66, 71, jurisdictional conf., 1956, 60, 64, del. gen. conf., 1956, 60, 64; mem. world council; del. World Meth. Theol. Inst., Oxford, Eng., 1958, 62; exec. com. Okla. Meth. Conf. Council; pres. Okla. Conf. Meth. Commn. Christian Higher Edn., 1956-60. Trustee So. Meth. U., Southwestern U., Huston-Tillotson Coll., Lydia Patterson Inst., Perkins Sch. Theology, Kan. Wesleyan, St. Paul Sch. Theology. Recipient Distinguished Alumnus award Boston U. Sch. Theology. Mem. Sigma Chi. Mason. Club: The Mokus (Boston). Author: Characteristics of Jesus, 1962; Power of Paul, 1963; It All Began With God. Contbr. articles to religious jours. Home: 4123 Echo Glen Dallas TX 75234 Office: PO Box 8124 3300 Mockingbird Lane Dallas TX 75205

STRACENER, NEALON, savs. and loan exec.; b. Kipling, La., June 29, 1916; s. James Monroe and Mary Evelyn (Higginbotham) S.; B.A. in Journalsim, La. State U., 1942, J.D., 1948; m. Mary Helen Langlois, June 2, 1943; children—Douglas Nealon, Carol Elizabeth. Admitted to La. bar, 1947; U.S. Supreme Ct.; practiced in Baton Rouge, 1947—; founder, pres. Guaranty Fed. Savs. & Loan Assn., 1957—. Chmn. 6th Dist. Republican Exec. Com., East Baton Rouge Parish Exec. Com.; gen. counsel Rep. State Central Com.; editor La. Republican, 1952-62; del. Rep. Nat. Convs., 1956, 60. Pres. Alpha Xi Delta House Corp. Mem. Am., La. State, East Baton Rouge Parish bar assns., Am. Judicature Soc., Theta Xi, Sigma Delta Chi. Baptist (deacon). Mason (Shriner). Home: 9461 Woodbine Dr Baton Rouge LA 70815 Office: 3155 Weller Av Baton Rouge LA 70805

STRADER, HUNTER GORDON, JR., physician; b. Burlington, N.C., May 3, 1932; s. Hunter Gordon and Alline Elizabeth (Hay) S.; B.S., Davidson Coll., 1954; M.D., Duke, 1958; m. Helen Haynes, Dec. 18, 1955; children—Hunter Gregg, Richard Haynes, Pamela Lynn. Intern, Moses Cone Meml. Hosp., Greensboro, N.C., 1959-60; resident internal medicine Tulane Med. Service, New Orleans, 1960-61; gen. practice medicine, Lexington, N.C., 1962—; mem. staff Lexington (N.C.) Meml. Hosp., 1962, mem. exec. com., 1963-65. Med. cons. Pitts. Plate Glass, Lexington, 1969—, Henry Link Corp., Lexington, 1971—. Dir. Davidson County Little League. Served to capt. USAF, 1960-62. Recipient A.M.A. Physicians Recognition award, 1973. Diplomate Am. Bd. Family Practice. Fellow Am. Acad. Family Practice; mem. A.M.A., So. Med. Assn., N.C. State (v.p.), Davidson County med. socs., Phi Beta Kappa, Omicron Delta Kappa. Methodist. Kiwanian. Home: 208 Overbrook Dr Lexington NC 27292 Office: 2 Cherry St Lexington NC 27292

STRAHLE, ROLF GULLMAR, educator, architect; b. Gothenburg, Sweden, May 21, 1919; s. Gunnar W. and Gerda C. (Hedlund) S.; M.Arch., Swedish State Coll. Tech., 1944; postgrad. U. Gothenburg, 1948-49; m. Ivy Soriano de Strahle, Nov. 21, 1956; children—Bjorn Gullmar, Jeanne-Marie Karin. Came to U.S., 1947. Expert, adviser UN Tech. Assistance, Nigeria, Dahomey, 1961, Ethopia, Kenya, 1964-66, Peru, 1969-73; chief architect Inst. Urban Housing, San Salvador, El Salvador, C.A., 1950-57; prof. Sch. Architecture, U. El Salvador, 1950-57; cons. architect, design and planning dept. suburbs City Gothenburg, 1957-58; asso. prof. Sch. Architecture, Syracuse U., N.Y., 1958-59; prof. Sch. Architecture Tulane U., New Orleans, 1959-69; now prof. Sch. Architecture U. Southwestern La., Lafayette. Served with Royal Engrs. (Sweden), 1940-44. Mem. Swedish Inst. Architects, A.I.A., Am. Assn. U. Profs. Address: U SW La PO Box 3868 Lafayette LA 70501

STRAIN, DAVID LEROY, bank exec.; b. Washington, Feb. 23, 1921; s. David Leroy and Ethel Lois (Ross) S.; LL.B., U.N.C., 1952; postgrad. Stonier Grad. Sch. Banking, 1958; m. Marian Frances Lance, May 7, 1955; children—Karen J., Susan M. Vice-pres. Nat. Bank Commerce (name now Va. Nat. Bank), Norfolk, Va., 1952-60; sr. v.p. Br. Bank & Trust Co., Wilson, N.C., 1960-62; pres. Charles F. Cates & Sons, Inc., 1962-64; exec. v.p. First Nat. Bank, Norfolk, Va., 1965-70, Peoples Nat. Bank, Greenville, S.C., 1970-72; pres., dir. So. Bank & Trust Co., Greenville, 1973—; dir. So. Bancorp., Inc., Greenville, Charles F. Cates & Sons, Inc., Faison, N.C., Asso. Distbrs., Charleston, S.C. Bd. dirs. Goodwill Industries Upper S.C., Greenville. Served with USAAF, 1941-46. Mem. Newcomen Soc., Phi Delta Phi, Alpha Tau Omega. Presbyn. Clubs: Greenville Country, Poinsett. Home: 9 Stonybrook Dr Greenville SC 29607 Office: PO Box 1329 Greenville SC 29602

STRAIN, PAULA MARY, librarian; b. Brooke County, W. Va.; d. Paul Russell and Margaret (Evans) Strain; A.B, Bethany Coll., 1937; B.S., Carnegie Inst. Tech., 1938; postgrad. U. Pitts., 1940-41. Asst. librarian Westminster Coll., 1939-40; asst. librarian Carnegie-Ill. Steel Corp., Pitts., 1940-42; librarian, 1942-44; librarian U.S. Naval Photog. Interpretation Center, Washington, 1946-48, liaison and selection officer Library of Congress, 1948-57; sr. research analyst Library of Congress, 1957-60; tech. librarian Electronics Systems Center, IBM, Owego, N.Y., 1960-68; head librarian Booz Allen Applied Research, Inc., Bethesda, Md., 1968-70; mgr. library services MITRE Corp., McLean, Va., 1970—. Served with USNR, 1944-46. Bd. mgrs. Finger Lakes Trail Conf., 1962-68, editor, 1962-67, pres., 1967-68. Mem. Am. Assn. U. Women, Women's Nat. Book Assn., Appalachian Trail Conf., Spl. Libraries Assn. (editor geography and map div. 1962-65, chmn. 1968-69, pres. Upstate N.Y. chpt. 1967-68). Clubs: Potomac Appalachian Trail (pres. 1970-72) Washington; Adirondack Mountain. Author articles various periodicals and jours. Home: 8315 N Brook Bethesda MD 20014 Office: 1820 Dolley Madison Blvd McLean VA 22101

STRAIN, RICHARD EDGAR, physician, educator; b. Perry, Ia., Feb. 22, 1909; s. Robert S. and Katherine (McIntyre) S.; B.A., Maryville Coll., 1931; M.D., Vanderbilt U., 1935; m. Anne Price, Nov. 6, 1938; children—Mary Katherine (Mrs. A.L. King), Robert Sterling, and Richard Edgar Strain. Intern Stanford U. Hosp., San Francisco, 1935-36; asst. resident in surgery Stanford (Cal.) U. Hosps., 1936-37, fellow, asst. resident in neurosurgery Harvard Service, Boston City Hosp., 1946-48, Lahey Clinic, Boston, 1948-49; resident neurosurgery Harvard Service, Boston City Hosp., 1949; practice medicine, specializing in neurosurgery, Coral Gables, Fla., 1949—; med. missionary, Huchow, China, 1937-38, Miraj, India, 1939-42; asst. vis. surgeon Vanderbilt U. Med. Sch., Nashville, 1942-46; mem. Coll. Physicians and Surgeons, Man., Can., 1939; asst. prof. neurosurgery U. Miami, Coral Gables, 1952—, asso. prof., 1958; sr. neurosurgeon Jackson Meml. Hosp., Coral Gables, 1955; mem. staffs Doctors, Varsity Childrens hosps., Coral Gables, 1949, Baptist Hosp., Miami, Fla., 1960, South Miami Hosp., 1960; dir. neuro-physiol. research Eastern State Psychiat. Hosp., Knoxville, Tenn., 1968—; lectr. health edn. U. Tenn., Knoxville, 1968, asst. prof., 1969—. Bd. dirs. East Tenn. Council on Alcohol and Drug Abuse. Served with Chinese Nat. Army, 1938. Diplomate Am. Bd. Neurol. Surgery. Fellow A.C.S.; mem. Harvey Cushing Soc., Congress Neurol. Surgeons, So. Neurosurg. Soc., Southeastern Surg. Soc., Fla. Med. Soc (del. 1958-60), Coral Gables C. of C. (dir. 1959-62). Methodist. Rotarian (pres. 1959-60, dir., pres. Coral Gables 1960-61), Civitan (sec.-treas. Maryville). Contbr. numerous articles med. jours. Author: (with Mayshark, Kirk and Hornsby) Personal Health from the Ecological Perspective, 1972. Home: 1829 Westwood Dr E Maryville TN 37801

STRAKA, EDWARD ANTON, JR., dentist; b. Cicero, Ill., Nov. 3, 1930; s. Edward Anton and Alice Caroline (Nikola) S.; B. Gen. Edn., Morton Jr. Coll., 1950; postgrad. U. Ill., 1950-51; D.D.S., Northwestern U., 1955; m. Carleen Ann Ettinger, Aug. 8, 1953; children—Ann, Sally. Practice dentistry, Sarasota, Fla., 1957-68; pres. Edward A. Straka, D.D.S., Profl. Corp., 1968—. Dir. Marshall Motors Inc., M. M. Land Corp. Pres. Sertoma Speech and Hearing Clinic, 1966-72; mem. Local Govt. Study Commn., Sarasota Charter Commn., 1970-77; pres. Cardinal Mooney High Sch. Club, P.T.A., 1971-72; mem. adv. com. Sarasota County Sch. Bd., 1968-69; v.p. Commence, 1968; mem. finance com. L. D. Pankey Dental Found., 1968—; mem. Sarasota County Charter Rev. Bd., 1972—; vice chmn. Cardinal Mooney High Sch., 1973—. Bd. dirs. Sarasota Guidance Clinic, Health and Welfare Council. Served to capt., Dental Corps, AUS, 1955-57. Mem. Soc. Oral Physiology and Occlusion, Acad. Electro-Surgery and Dentistry, West Coast Dental Soc. (program chmn. 1970-71), South Gate (dir. 1963-64), Forest Lakes (dir. 1966-69) community assns., Family Motor Coach Assn. (dir. Fla. chpt. 1970-71). Club: Sertoma (pres. 1963-64) (Sarasota). Home: 2920 Pony Lane Sarasota FL 33580 Office: 1851 Arlington St Sarasota FL 33579

STRANAHAN, ROBERT PAUL, JR., lawyer; b. Louisville, Oct. 29, 1929; s. Robert Paul and Anna May (Payne) S.; A.B., Princeton, 1951; LL.B., Harvard, 1954; m. Louise Perry, May 12, 1956; children—Susan Diai, Robert Paul III, Carol Payne. Admitted to D.C. bar, 1954, Md. bar, 1964; practiced in Washington, 1957—; asso. firm Wilmer & Broun, 1957-62; partner, Wilmer, Cutler & Pickering, 1963—; professorial lectr. Nat. Law Center George Washington U., 1969-72. Served to 1st lt., USMCR, 1954-57. Mem. Am., Fed. bar assns., Bar Assn. D.C. Clubs: Princeton, Metropolitan, Gridiron (Washington); Chevy Chase (Md.). Home: 5316 Cardinal Ct Washington DC 20016 Office: 1666 K St NW Washington DC 20006

STRANGE, BUFORD BENNETT, broadcasting co. exec.; b. Mansfield, La., July 18, 1936; s. Buford Zack and Josie (Griffith) S.; B.A., La. Coll., 1958; M.A., U. So. Miss., 1959; postgrad. U. Minn., 1960-61; m. Mayme Vera Stone, May 30, 1959; children—Jo-Ruth, Vera-Zee, Clinton Buford. Reporter Mansfield Enterprise, 1956-57, Interstate Progress, Logansport, La., 1956-57, Shreveport (La.)

Times, 1955-57, 66—; news dir. WDAM-TV, Hattiesburg and Laurel, Miss., 1961-66; asst. prof. dept. communications, dir. radio-TV U. So. Miss., Hattiesburg, 1958-66; pres. Heart Dixie Broadcasting Corp., gen. mgr. KDXI radio, Mansfield, 1967—; pres. Mansfield Cablevision. Recipient several civic awards, including La.'s Sound Citizen award La. Jr. C. of C., 1966, La. Sch. Bell award La. Tchrs. Assn., 1969. Mem. Mansfield (hon. life), La. (regional v.p. 1970-71), U.S. (dir. 1970-71) Jaycees, Pi Kappa Delta, Alpha Psi Omega, Sigma Delta Chi. Baptist (supt.). Lion. Author: (with W.E. Simonson) Techniques of Debate, 1960. Contbr. articles to profl. jours. Home: 114 Gibbs St Mansfield LA 71052 Office: Drawer 740 Mansfield LA 71052

STRANSKY, JOHN JANOS, forester; b. Budapest, Hungary, Sept. 2, 1923; s. Janos and Ellionor (Milne) S.; student Poly. Inst., Hungary, 1941-45; B.F., Ludwig Maximilian U., Munich, Germany, 1947; M.F. (Bliss scholar, Fisher fellow), Harvard, 1954; m. Eva Gorgey, June 6, 1947; children—John H., Nicholas B. Came to U.S., 1950, naturalized, 1955. Research asst. Bussey Inst., Harvard, 1954-57; forester div. forest econs. research So. Forest Expt. Sta., U.S. Forest Service, 1957-58, research forester Wildlife Habitat and Silviculture Lab., 1958—, lectr. forest game mgmt. Stephan F. Austin State U. Sch. Forestry, Nacogdoches, Tex., 1967—. Mem. Soc. Am. Foresters (group chmn.), Wildlife Soc., Ecol. Soc. Am. (chpt. sec.), Am. Assn. U. Profs., Nat. Rifle Assn., Tex. Forestry Assn. Contbr. articles to profl. jours. Home: 1533 Redbud St Nacogdoches TX 75961

STRASBURGER, LEROY, wholesale trade exec.; b. Columbia, S.C., Mar. 10, 1922; s. Lafayette and Augusta (Bruggeman) S.; student U. S.C., 1939-40, Mass. Inst. Tech., 1941; B.S., Columbia U., 1947; m. Edith Donaldson, Apr. 17, 1948; children—Carol, Richard, Frank. Marketing trainee Gen. Electric Co., 1947-48; asst. to marketing v.p., dist. sales mgr. Hotpoint Co., Chgo. and Cin., 1948-50; So. regional mgr. NESCO, Atlanta, 1950-52; partner, gen. mgr. L. Strasburger & Sons, wholesale trade, Columbia, S.C., 1952—; Pres. L. Strasburger's Inc., 1958—; chmn. distbr. panel Admiral Corp., 1970-71; adv. bd. Am. Bank and Trust Co. Pres., Columbia Music Festival, 1959-60; pres. Columbia Philharmonic Orch., 1967-68. Served with USMCR, 1942-46. Mem. Columbia C. of C. (dir. 1963-65, v.p. 1964-65). Presbyn. (chmn. bd. deascons 1963-64). Rotarian. Clubs: Palmetto, Spring Valley, Litchfield Columbia Executive (pres. 1966-67). Home: 1621 Adger Rd Columbia SC 29204 Office: 711 Bluff Rd Columbia SC 29201

STRATTON, HENRY DAVIS, lawyer; b. Pikeville, Ky., Aug 9, 1925; s. Pem Burton and Minnie M. (Davis) S.; student Asbury Coll., 1943, Pikeville Coll., 1946-47; LL.B., U. Louisville, 1950; m. Lois Jean Shipley, June 14, 1947; children—David Carey and Daniel Pemberton (twins), Teresa Louise. Admitted to Ky. bar, 1950; practice, Pikeville, Ky., 1950—; pres., dir. Citizens Bank of Pikeville; v.p., dir. East Ky. Broadcasting Co.; dir. Campbell County Broadcasting Co., Lawrence County Broadcasting Co., Greater Ky. Broadcasting Co. Mem. Ky. Crime Commn., 1968—. Bd. dirs. Meth. Hosp. Ky., also gen. counsel; regent Eastern Ky. U., 1970—; trustee Pikeville Coll. Served with AUS, 1943-46. Mem. U.S. (dir.), Ky. (v.p.) jr. chambers commerce, Am., Ky. (mem. house dels. 1964-65, gov. 1966—, v.p. 1974—) bar assns., Ky. Hist. Soc., Phi Alpha Delta, Omicron Delta Kappa. Methodist. Mason. Club: Filson; Greenmeadows. Home: 110 Cedar Dr Pikeville KY 41501 Office: 2d St Pikeville KY 41501

STRATTON, JAMES CURTIS, ret. educator; b. Pueblo, Colo., Sept. 12, 1908; s. James P. and Georgia (Curtis) S.; B.A. cum laude, U. Colo., 1931; M.S. in Journalism, Northwestern U., 1940. Instr. English, journalism, publications adviser Pueblo Central High Sch., 1931-39; instr., asst. prof. English, journalism U. Wyo., Laramie, 1940-46; asst. to asso. prof. journalism Okla. State U., Stillwater, 1946-74, asso. prof. emeritus, 1974—, also dir. music ednl. radio sta. KOSU-FM; desk, exec. editor Laramie (Wyo.) Daily Bulletin (arrangement U. Wyo.), 1942-45; fine arts writer, editor Stillwater Daily News-Press, 1946—; broadcaster spl. recorded shows Radio KSPI, Stillwater, 1950-74; music editor, program annotator Oklahoma City Symphony Orchestra, 1962—. Mem. Sigma Delta Chi, Pi Gamma Mu, Alpha Tau Omega, Kappa Tau Alpha, Omicron Delta Kappa. Lion. Home: 605B Bennett Stillwater OK 74074

STRAUSS, ALMA CAROLINE BROWDER (MRS. HARVEY STRAUSS), theatrical producer; b. Lincoln, Neb.; d. David and Ellen Elizabeth (Murphy) Browder; B.F.A. cum laude, Wesleyan Coll., 1958; postgrad. U. Ga., 1959-60; m. Harvey Strauss, Aug. 31, 1960; children—Benjamin Browder, Jon Harvey, Susan Beth, Guy Simon. Commentator WMAZ Radio, Arcadia, Fla., 1958; actress indsl. movie Ga. Center for Continuing Edn., Athens, 1959; tchr. Palmetto High Sch., Bradenton, Fla., 1958-59; studio traffic co-ordinator, slide librarian, asst. children's program WDBO-TV, Orlando, Fla., 1959-60; tchr. adult workshop in drama Tobay Players, Plainview (N.Y.) High Sch., 1963; dir. Waltz of Toreadors Tobay Players, Plainview, 1964, Oh Men, Oh Women, 1964; dir., tchr. Surfside Sch. Theatre, Surfside Players, Cocoa Beach, Fla., 1967-68, tchr. Surfside Mems. Continuing Workshop, 1968-69; dir. two original mus. galas Cocoa (Fla.) Jr. Women's Club, 1968-69; dir., tchr. drama puppetry program North Palm Beach Recreation Center, 1969-74; co-dir., co-producer original script children's play cultural enrichment program Palm Beach County Schs. Coastal Players, Jupiter, Fla., 1971; dir. Barefoot in Park, Coastal Players, Jupiter, 1970. Mem. com. cultural devel. No. Palm Beach Community Devel. Action Plan, 1971; founding mem. Music, Art, Drama, Dance North County, 1971. Sec. North County Democratic Club, Palm Beach County, 1971-72. Bd. govs. Surfside Playhouse, Cocoa Beach, 1966-67. Mem. Am. Theatre Assn., Children's Theatre Assn., Am. Community Theatre Assn., Parent Tchr. Orgn., League Women Voters, Alpha Psi Omega. Unitarian. Home and office: 6641 Emerald Lake Dr Miramar FL 33023

STRAUSS, CLIFFORD MARCUS, bank dir.; b. Memphis, Tenn., May 17, 1904; s. Fred and Carrie (Schuster) S.; grad. high sch.; m. Roselyn Lieber, Aug. 5, 1926; children—Jean (Mrs. Saul A. Mintz), Peggy S. (Mrs. James R. Greenbaum). Chmn. bd. Strauss Liquor Corp., Monroe, La., 1926-69; pres. Strauss Liquor Corp., Shreveport, La., 1946-69; pres. Gulf Inland Corp., Houston, 1931-69; chmn. bd. F. Strauss & Son, Inc., Tallulah, La., 1959-69, Strauss Distbrs., Little Rock, 1937-69, F. Strauss & Son, Inc., New Orleans, 1939-69; dir. Peoples Homestead & Savings Assn., Ouachita Nat. Bank. Pres. Wine and Spirits Found. La., 1952-53; developer, operator Eastgate, Northgate shopping centers, Monroe, 1964—. Pres. Ouachita Parish chpt. A.R.C., 1944-45; United Givers Fund, 1958-59; mem. Ration Bd., 1943-44; pres. Pub. Affairs Research 1967-68. Bd. dirs., chmn. bd. Carolyn Rose Strauss Rehab. Center, Monroe; bd. dirs. Council for Better La. Mem. Wine and Spirits Wholesalers Am. (chmn. bd. 1945-46), C. of C. (pres. 1950-51). Jewish religion (pres. 1960-61). Mason (32 deg., Shriner). Clubs: Lotus, Bayou Desiard Country. Home: 3706 Deborah Dr Monroe LA 71201 Office: PO Box 6058 Commerce Av Monroe LA 71201

STRAUSS, JOSEPH RICHARD, wholesale co. exec.; b. San Antonio, Nov. 24, 1899; s. David J. and Ida (Oppenheimer) S.; B.Sci. and Engring., U. Pa., 1921; m. Emilie Fies Straus, Nov. 1, 1922; children—David J., Joe R. With Straus-Frank Co., San Antonio, 1921—, pres., 1932-62, chmn. bd., 1962—; dir. Bank San Antonio. Bd. dirs. San Antonio Zoo, 1953—, San Antonio Livestock Exposition, 1953—. Served with USNR, 1918-19. Mem. San Antonio C. of C. (past dir.). Jewish religion. Mason (Shriner). Club: San Antonio Country, Argyle (San Antonio). Home: 700 Grandview Pl San Antonio TX 78209 Office: PO Box 600 San Antonio TX 78292

STRAUSS, RICHARD CHARLES, real estate exec.; b. Dallas, Aug. 3, 1943; s. Robert S. and Helen (Jacobs) S.; student Parsons Coll., 1963-66; m. Daniele Bagon (div.); 1 dau., Tania. Asso., Henry S. Miller, 1967-68; partner Crawford-Strauss Properties, Dallas, 1968-73; propr. Strauss Investments, 1973—; dir. Main St. Nat. Bank, Dallas, Dallas-Ft. Worth Airport Bank. Mem. law enforcement com. Dallas Greater Community Relations Bd., 1971—; steering com. Dallas Forum. Chmn. Texans for Ben Barnes, Dallas Com., 1970. Served with Tex. Air N.G., 1965. Mem. Apt. Owners and Mgrs. Assn., Dallas Apt. Assn. (dir.), Home and Apt. Builders (state dir.), Nat. Apt. Assn., Asso. Gen. Contractors, Dallas C. of C. (chmn.'s council). Address: 4432 Walnut Hill Lane Dallas TX 75220

STRAWBRIDGE, CECIL HOWARD, lawyer; b. Vernon, Ala., Feb. 24, 1906; s. S.R. and Tezzie (Holliday) S.; LL.B., U. Ala., 1931; postgrad. U. Nev., 1970; m. Sarah Autense Rector, May 11, 1941; children—Ronnie, Shirley (Mrs. Phillip Latimore). Admitted to Ala. bar, 1931; practiced in Vernon; circuit judge, Vernon, 1952; county atty., Pickens, Fayette, Lamar counties. Bd. dirs., chmn. bd. dirs. Lamar County Hosp. Served with USAAF, 1942-45. Mem. Dist. Attys. Assn. (v.p. 1949), Circuit Judges Assn. (state pres. 1969-70), Delta Kappa, Sigma Phi Epsilon. Methodist. Mason (Shriner), Odd Fellow, Kiwanian. Home: Star RFD Vernon AL 35592 Office: Circuit Judge's Office Courthouse Vernon AL 35592

STREAM, LAWRENCE, physician; b. Kansas City, Kan., Mar. 13, 1923; s. Lawrence Peter and Ruth Edith (Wiberg) S.; student U. Kan., 1941-43, Tex. A. and M. U., 1943-44, Baylor U., 1944; M.D., U. Okla., 1949; m. Millicent Anita Marrs, June 11, 1949; 1 son, Lawrence Wyatt. Intern St. Anthony Hosp., Oklahoma City, 1949-50; resident anesthesiology Univ. Hosp., Oklahoma City, 1952-54, mem. teaching staff, 1954-58; practice medicine specializing in anesthesiology, Oklahoma City, 1958—; mem. staff Mercy Hosp., Oklahoma City, Drs. Gen. Hosp., Oklahoma City, Univ. Hosp., Oklahoma City. Served with AUS, 1943-46, 51-52. Decorated Bronze Star medal. Diplomate Am. Bd. Anesthesiology. Mem. A.M.A., Am., Okla. (sec.-treas. 1956-58) socs. anesthesiologists, Okla. State, Okla. County med. socs., Phi Chi, Sigma Phi Epsilon. Conglist. Home: 2316 NW 118th St Oklahoma City OK 73120 Office: 1411 Classen St Oklahoma City OK 73106

STREEB, GORDON LEE, fgn. service officer; b. Windsor, Colo., Dec. 24, 1935; s. Gerhard Ottmar and Amelia (Martin) S.; B.S., U. Colo., 1959, B.S. in Bus., 1959; postgrad. U. Minn., 1968-72; m. Alice Junette Thomas, Aug. 11, 1962; children—Kurt, Kent, Kerry-Lynn. Design engr., Dow Chem. Co., Rocky Flats, Colo., 1961-62; fgn. service officer Dept. State, Washington, 1962-69, service assignments U.S. Mission, Berlin, Germany, 1963-65, Am. Consulate Gen., Guadalajara, Mexico, 1965-67, consul. U. Minn., 1968-69; tchr. econs. Normandale State Jr. Coll., Bloomington, Minn., 1969-72; fgn. service officer Dept. State assigned as internat. economist Office Trade Agreements, 1972—. Mem. Am. Econ. Assn. Served with USAF, 1961. Lutheran. Home: 14721 Algretus Dr Centreville VA 22020 Office: State Dept Washington DC 20520

STREET, ROBERT DECATUR, ednl. adminstr.; b. Hickory, N.C., May 3, 1934; s. Monroe Garland and Amie Elizabeth (Britain) S.; B.B.A., Wake Forest Coll., 1960; M.Ed., U. N.C., 1967, postgrad. (Research fellow), 1967—; m. Ann Marie Tillotson, June 12, 1960; children—Stephen Bradley, Sheila Kaye. Dept. mgr. Maas Bros. Dept. Store, St. Petersburg, Fla., 1961-62; tchr., Greensboro, Winston-Salem, Mocksville, N.C., 1963-68; dir. bus. affairs Richmond Tech. Inst., Hamlet, N.C., 1969—. Served with USNR, 1952-56: ETO. Mem. N.E.A., Am. Vocational Assn., N.C. Assn. Community Coll. Bus. Ofcls., N.C. Assn. Educators. Mason. Club: Civitan (treas. 1970-71) (Rockingham, N.C.). Home: 208 E Temple Av Rockingham NC 28379 Office: PO Box 1189 Hamlet NC 28345

STREET, WILLIAM PAUL, ednl. adminstr.; b. Bloomfield, Mo., Sept. 22, 1907; s. William Terry and Minnie Florence (Chasteen) S.; B.E., No. Ill. State Tchrs. Coll., 1932; M.A., Northwestern U., 1936, Ph.D., 1947; m. Lina Esther Luhtala, Dec. 23, 1933; 1 son, David Paul. Tchr., Vine Hill Rural Sch., Cuba, Mo., 1925-26, Proviso Twp. High Sch., Maywood, Ill., 1933-38; tchr.-dir. regional services No. Ill. U., DeKalb, 1938-55; dir. centennial observance N.E.A., 1955-57; dir. Bur. Sch. Service, U. Ky., Lexington, 1957-74, editor Bull., 1957-74; tchr. Georgetown (Ky.) Coll., 1974—. Dir. evaluation Office Econ. Opportunity, Knox County, Ky., 1965-68; dir. numerous sch. dist. surveys in Ky., 1957-74, studies in W.Va., Tenn., S.C.; dir. 3 year evaluation U. Ky. Coop. Extension Appalachian Community Impact Project, 1969-72. Chmn. Community Action, Fayette County, Ky., 1970-72. Trustee, Chgo. chpt. Nat. Hemophilia Found., 1954-57. Mem. Nat., Ky. edn. assns., Ky. Council Edn. (sec.-treas. 1958—), Sch. Facilities Council, Am. Ednl. Research Assn., Phi Delta Kappa, Kappa Delta Pi. Methodist. Kiwanian. Editor: Edn. Today, 1951-54, alumni jour. quar. No. Ill. U., 1938-55. Home: 709 Waco Ct Lexington KY 40503 Office: Georgetown Coll Georgetown KY

STREIT, MAE HELEN GLASCOCK (MRS. JOHN SAM STREIT), editor; b. Hamilton, Ala., June 27, 1914; d. James Oscar and Lula (Owen) Glascock; grad. pub. schs.; m. John Sam Streit, Aug. 27, 1939 (dec. June 1953); 1 son, Samuel Allen. With Franklin County Times, Russellville, Ala., 1961—, soc. editor, 1962-63, city editor, 1963-65, editor, 1965—; corr. Birmingham (Ala.) Post-Herald newspaper, 1962—. Bd. dirs. Franklin County chpt. A.R.C. Recipient 1st pl. news writing award Ala. Press Assn., 1973. Mem. Sigma Delta Chi. Mem. Ch. of Christ. Clubs: Cultura Garden (pres. 1956-57). Home: 408 High St Russellville AL 35653 Office: 142 US 43 Bypass Hwy Russellville AL 35652

STRELAU, CONRAD ANDREW, computer co. exec.; b. Houston, Aug. 15, 1931; s. August Ernest and Florence Elizabeth (Wasson) S.; B.S., Tex. A. and M. U., 1953; m. Carol Catherine Walker, Aug. 3, 1951; children—Gary Dale, Shari Carol, Teri Suzanne, Cathy Marie. Customer engr. IBM Corp., Houston, 1953-58, field mgr., Houston, 1959-61, mgr. customer engring., Beaumont, Tex., 1962, San Antonio, 1963, mgr. personnel planning, White Plains, N.Y., 1964, asst. to pres. field engring. div., 1965-66, area mgr., San Francisco, 1967-68; v.p. field engring. Recognition Equipment, Inc., Dallas, 1969-70, sr. v.p. field operations, 1971, sr. v.p. operations, 1971-73, group v.p., 1973—. Presbyn. (deacon 1969). Home: 7206 Desco Dr Dallas TX 75225 Office: PO Box 22307 Dallas TX 75222

STRELLA, GEORGE GALEN, san. engr.; b. Salina, Kan., July 21, 1929; s. James and Laura Virginia (Turner) S.; B.A., U. So. Cal., 1951; B.C.E., U. Kan., 1959, M.C.E., 1962; m. Jeanne Frances Nettleton, June 20, 1954; 1 son, Steven. Film dir. KETC, St. Louis, 1954-56; Design engr. Servis, Van Doren & Hazard, cons. engrs., Topeka, 1956-60, Greeley & Hanson, engrs., Chgo., 1962-65; dist. engr. Kan. Dept. Pub. Health, Topeka, 1960-62; dir. water pollution control City of Kansas City (Kan.), 1965-68; chief civil engr. W.R. Holway & Assos., Inc., Tulsa, 1968-74; v.p. Mansur-Daubert-Williams, Inc., Tulsa, 1974—. Served to lt. (j.g.) USNR, 1951-54. Registered profl. engr., Ill., Okla. Mem. Am. Soc. C.E., Water Pollution Control Assn. Okla., Am. Water Works Assn., Tulsa C. of C. Mason, Kiwanian. Home: 2150 S 80th E Av Tulsa OK 74129 Office: 1648 S Boston Av Tulsa OK 74119

STRENCH, DONALD DAVIS, r.r. exec.; b. Ketchikan, Alaska, Mar. 14, 1921; s. William Gotfried and Mary (Minthorne) S.; student U. Hawaii, 1939-41; B.S., W.Va. U., 1944; student advanced mgmt. Northwestern U., 1961; grad. Advanced Mgmt. Program, Harvard, 1962; m. Mary Bibb Lamar, Jan. 14, 1956; children—Donald Davis, William Godfry, Bibb Lamar. With So. Ry. System, Atlanta, 1946-65, gen. mgr., 1962-65; exec. v.p. Atlanta's West Point, Western of Ala., Ga. R.R., Atlanta, 1965-66, pres., 1966-68; gen. mgr. Louisville & Nashville R.R., Louisville, 1968-69, v.p. operations, 1969-73, exec. v.p., 1973—; dir. Louisville Trust Bank, Terminal R.R. St. Louis, Ky. and Ind. Terminal Co. Served as 1st lt. C.E., AUS, 1944-46. Republican. Episcopalian. Clubs: Hunting Creek Country (Louisville); Pendennis (Louisville). Home: 2910 Glen Hill Circle Louisville KY 40222 Office: 908 W Broadway Louisville KY 40202

STRICKLAND, ALICE DENINGTON (MRS. CLARENCE A. STRICKLAND), savs. and loan exec.; b. nr. Clinton, Ky., May 21, 1919; d. William Edward and Lovie Marie (Dean) Denington; student Manatee Jr. Coll., 1966-68; grad. Am. Savs. and Loan Inst., 1974; m. Clarence A. Strickland, Aug. 2, 1936; children—John Edward, William T. Bookkeeper, ins. clk. DeSoto County Hosp., Arcadia, Fla., 1948-52, asst. bookkeeper, 1952-56; teller First Fed. Savs. & Loan Manatee County, Bradenton, Fla., 1957-59, asst. head teller, 1959-60, asst. controller, 1960-61; treas., controller Manatee Fed. Savs. & Loan, Bradenton, 1961-72, v.p., treas., 1972—. Tchr. ednl. classes Am. Savs. & Loan Inst., Bradenton, 1968-71, bd. govs., 1966, sec., 1967. Named Boss of Year, Credit Women Bradenton, 1964. Mem. Nat. Soc. Controllers (mem. com. branching 1973-74). Beta Sigma Phi (pres. 1968, service chmn. 1969). Baptist (supt. Young Peoples Dept. 1959-61). Club: Zonta (sec. Bradenton 1969). Home: 4903 26th Av W Bradenton FL 33505 Office: PO Box 4166 Cortez Plaza Bradenton FL 33507

STRICKLAND, ALLEN MCGILL (MRS. GEORGE M. STRICKLAND), artist; b. Washington; d. I. J. Nota and Frances M. (Maloy) McGill; student pvt. schs.; m. George Marion Strickland, Nov. 11, 1947. Salon in Paris Artistes Francais; one-man show at Daytona Beach (Fla.) Art League, Cinema Theatre Gallery, Daytona Beach; 2-man show Daytona Beach Art League, 1972; represented in pvt. collections in U.S. and France. Recipient numerous prizes Daytona Beach Art League. Mem. Nat. League Am. Pen Women (pres. Daytona Beach br.), Fla. Fedn. Art, Daytona Beach Art League, St. Augustine Art Assn., Garden Club Am. (pres. Halifax County). Home: 487 John Anderson Hwy Ormond Beach FL 32074

STRICKLAND, MAURICE ALEXANDER, physician; b. Moultrie, Ga., Sept. 25, 1910; s. Matthew Lee and Mary (Nesbitt) S.; B.S., U. Ga., 1935; M.A., N.Y.U., 1936; Ph.D., 1939; M.D., Emory U., 1948; m. Irma Surovy, Mar. 5, 1938 (dec. Mar. 1970); children—Daniel Matthew, Maurice Henry, John Arthur. Grad. asst. econs. dept. N.Y.U., N.Y.C., 1937-39; instr. Coll. Engring., U. N.C. at Raleigh, 1939-40; asso. prof. Ga. Inst. Tech., Atlanta, 1940-43; intern U.S. Marine Hosp., Stapleton, N.Y., 1948-49; resident surgery Atlanta VA Hosp., 1949-50; asst. resident surgery Nassau Hosp., N.Y.C., 1951-52; sr. resident surgery Jefferson Hosp., Detroit, 1952-53; sr. resident surgery Buffalo VA Hosp., 1954-55; staff surgeon Bay Pines (Fla.) VA Hosp., 1955-56; staff surgeon Columbia (S.C.) VA Hosp., 1956-57; practice medicine specializing in surgery, Atlanta, 1957-60; resident and matriculate in cancer and dermatology N.Y.U., Pastgrad. Hosp. and Bellevue Hosp., N.Y.C., 1960-62; practice medicine specializing in dermatology and cancer surgery, Bakersfield, Cal., 1963-64, Houston, 1965—; staff mem. dermatology skin cancer surgery sect. Meml. Hosp. Houston, Meml. Hosp. System, Bellaire Gen. Hosp., Sharptown Gen. Hosp., attending physician Houston Social Hygiene Clinic; staff mem. Ben Taub Gen. Hosp., Houston; instr. dermatology Baylor U. Med. Sch. Surgeon and commd. officer USPHS, Hosp., Tuba City, Ariz., 1953. Fellow A.C.S., Am. Geriatric Soc., Societas Internat. Dermat. Tropicae, Internat. Acad. Cosmetic Surgeons; mem. Royal Coll. Physicians, Am., So., Tex. med. assns., Harris County Med. Soc., Harris County Acad. Medicine, Acad. of Dermatology (asso.), Houston Dermatol. Soc., Pub. Health League, Bellaire C. of C., Beta Gamma Sigma, Delta Mu Delta. Rotarian. Home: 6801 Bellaire Blvd Houston TX 77036 Office: 6441 High Star Houston TX 77036

STRICKLAND, RENNARD JAMES, educator; b. St. Louis, Sept. 26, 1940; s. Ruel James and Adell Gwendolyn (Tucker) S.; B.A., Northeastern Coll., 1962; J.D., U. Va., 1965, S.J.D., 1970; M.A., U. Ark., 1966. Asst. prof. U. Ark., Fayetteville, 1965-69; asst. prof. U. West Fla., Pensacola, 1970-71; asso. prof. St. Mary's U., San Antonio, 1971-72, Sylvan Lang distinguished vis. prof. law, summer, 1973; asso. prof. U. Tulsa, 1972—, acting dean Sch. Law, 1974—. Cons. Duke Found Indian Oral History Project, U. Fla., 1970-72; juror Am. Indian Art Ann., Philbrook Art Center; Heritage Juror Five Civilized Tribes Indian Art Annual. Fellow Am. Bar Found., Am. Council Learned Soc., Selden Soc.; mem. Indian Heritage Assn. (founder 1967, dir. 1967—), Communication Assn. Am., Am. Soc. Legal History, Delta Sigma Rho, Tau Kappa Alpha, Rho Theta Sigma, Phi Kappa Delta, Phi Delta Phi. Author books including: Sam Houston with the Cherokees, 1967, Hell on the Border, 1972, Adventures of a Cherokee Boy, 1972, Choctaw Spirit Tales, 1972, How to Get into Law School, 1973, The Cherokee People, 1973, Fire and the Spirits: Cherokee Law from Clan to Court, 1974, American Indian Spirit Tales, 1974. Home: 1722 S Carson St #2110 Tulsa OK 74104

STRICKLAND, ROBERT LOUIS, business exec., author; b. Florence, S.C., Mar. 3, 1931; s. Franz M. and Hazel (Eaddy) S.; A.B., U. N.C., 1952; M.B.A. with distinction, Harvard, 1957; m. Elizabeth Ann Miller, Feb. 2, 1952; children—Cynthia Anne, Robert Edson. Advt. mgr. Lowe's Cos., Inc., North Wilkesboro, N.C., 1957-58, operations mgr., 1958-60, marketing mgr., 1960-61, dir. marketing, 1961-69, v.p. marketing, 1969-70, sr. v.p., 1970—, office pres., 1970—, mem. exec. com., dir., 1961—; founder Sterling Advt., Ltd., 1966. Vice pres., mem. adminstrv. com. Lowe's Profit-Sharing Trust, 1961—, chmn. operations com., 1972—. Panelist Nat. Investor Relations Inst. Ann. Conf., 1972, Grt. Ideas in Consumer Relations Brand Names Found. Ann. Conf., 1972. Mem. N.C. Ho. of Reps., 1962-64; mem. Republican exec. com. N.C., 1963-73. Trustee, sec. bd., mem. personnel Com. Wilkes Community Coll.; v.p. bd. dirs. Nat. Home Improvement Council. Served with USNR, 1952-55; lt. Res., 1955-62. Named Wilkes County (N.C.) Young Man of Yr., Wilkes Jr. C. of C., 1962; recipient Bronze Oscar of industry award Financial World, 1969, 70, 71, 72, 73, Silver Oscar of Industry award, 1970, 72, 73, Gold Oscar, 1972; recipient certificate of Distinction, Brand Names Found., 1970, Distinguished Mcht. award, 1972. Mem. Newcomen Soc., Scabbard and Blade, Phi Beta Kappa, Pi Kappa Alpha. Clubs: Twin City (Winston-Salem, N.C.); Roaring (N.C.) Gap. Author: Lowe's Cybernetwork, 1969; Lowe's a Living Legend, 1970;

Ten Years of Growth, 1971; The Growth Continues, 1972, 73. Contbr. articles to profl. jours. Home: 226 N Stratford Rd Winston-Salem NC 27104 Office: Box 111 North Wilkesboro NC 28656

STRICKLAND, THOMAS JOSEPH, artist; b. Keyport, N.J., Dec. 27, 1932; s. Charles and Clementine (Grasso) S.; student Newark Sch. Fine and Indsl. Arts, 1951-53, Am. Art Sch., 1956-59, Nat. Acad. Fine Arts, N.Y.C., 1957-59. One man show Hollywood (Fla.) Art Mus., 1972; exhibited in group shows at Studio Gallery, N.Y.C., 1959, 60, Le Monde, Palm Springs, Cal., 1960, 61, Binderton House, Phila., 1962, Internat. Art Exchange, N.Y.C., 1962, Art Fair Galleries, Holmdel, N.J., 1963, Libyan Gallery, N.Y.C., 1963, 64, Galerie 19, Roslyn, N.Y., 1963, Old Queens Gallery, New Brunswick, N.J., 1964, Elion Art Found., Princeton, N.J., 1965, Galerie des Deux Mondes, N.Y.C., 1967, Gabriel's Gallery, Hillsdale, N.J., 1968, 1st Ann. Met. Young Artists Show, Nat. Arts Club, 1958, Am. Artists Profl. League, Nat. Arts Club, 1958, 61, Parke-Bernet Galleries, N.Y.C., 1959, 61-64, Hashomer Hatzair, N.Y.C., 1961-64, Jewish Labor Com. Art Sale, N.Y.C., 1963-65, Butler Inst. Am. Art, Fine Arts Festival, Youngstown, O., 1963, Orchestral Workshop of Westchester, White Plains, N.Y., 1964-65, Art Fair 65, Garden City, N.Y., 1965, Art 66 Sisterhood of Temple Beth El, Closter, N.J., 1966, Harmons of Guilford (Conn.), 1969, Gramercy Art Gallery, N.Y.C., 1966, Salon Rouge du Casino, Dieppe, 1967, Expn. Intercontinentale, Monaco, 1966-68, New York Galerie, Nice, 1971, 7e Grand Prix internat. de peinture de la Cote d'Azur, Cannes, 1971, Grove House, Coconut Grove, 1971-72, Art Show Temple Beth Am, Miami, 1972, Beaux Arts of Lowe Art Mus., Miami, 1972; represented in numerous pvt. collections including St. Vincent Coll., Latrobe, Pa. Recipient Julius Hallgarten prize Nat. Acad. Fine Arts, 1956, Dr. Ralph Weiler prize Nat. Acad. Fine Arts, 1957, Bertrum R. Hulmes Meml. Medal award Am. Vets. Soc. Artists, N.Y.C., 1965, First prize Hollywood Arts and Crafts Guild Ann. Mems. Art Exhbn., 1972, First prize Seven Lively Arts Festival Circle Art Show, Hollywood, 1972. Mem. Grove House, Hollywood Arts and Crafts Guild. Club: Miami Palette. Address: 2598 Taluga Dr Miami FL 33133

STRICKLAND, WILLIAM EDWARD, equipment corp. exec.; b. Fayetteville, N.C., July 31, 1929; s. Edward Lee and Catherine (Johnson) S.; A.A., U. N.C., 1955; m. Harriet Gallup, Dec. 18, 1953; children—Harriet Allison, Susanne Lee, William Edward. With Sealtest Foods div. Kraftco Corp., 1954-72, dist. gen. mgr., Wilson, N.C., 1968-72; v.p. sales and marketing sect. Simpson Equipment Corp., 1973—; sec.-treas. Elpercare Inc., Kisco Corp. Bd. dirs. United Fund Wilson County (N.C.); bd. dirs., mem. exec. com. N.C. Dairy Found., 1968—. Served to 1st lt. AUS, 1950-53. Decorated Bronze Star medal. Mem. So. Assn. Dairy Food Mfrs. (dir. N.C. chpt.), N.C. Dairy Products Assn., Sales and Marketing Execs. (pres. 1968-69), Fabulous Fishermen (pres. 1960-61). Rotarian (pres. 1969-70). Elk. Club: Wilson Country (dir.). Home: 1010 Ensworth Rd Wilson NC 27893 Office: US Hwy 301 S Wilson NC 27893

STRIEF, HARRY JOSEPH, JR., real estate exec.; b. Sioux City, Ia., Mar. 8, 1916; s. Harry Joseph and Mable Edna (Rabdau) S.; B.A. in Journalism, So. Meth. U., 1938; postgrad. Northwestern U., 1938-39; m. Doreen Elisa Mawson, Oct. 30, 1943; 1 son, Paul Arthur. Corr., U.P., Rio de Janeiro, Brazil, Buenos Aires, Argentina, 1939-41; with M.I., Office of Mil. Attache, Am. embassy, Buenos Aires and Washington, 1941-44; partner Sitco Lumber Co., Dallas, 1946-67; owner The Strief Co., Dallas, 1954—; partner Strief Enterprises, Dallas, 1954—; pres. Wichita Investment Co., Dallas, 1954—; vice pres. Boston Realty Co., Dallas, 1954-68. Pres., Greenway Parks Home Owners Assn., 1956-57. Served with AUS, 1944-46. Mem. Nat. Assn. Real Estate Bds., Inst. Real Estate Mgmt., (pres. Dallas-Ft. Worth chpt. 1963-64), Internat. Council Shopping Centers, Nat. Inst. Real Estate Brokers, Tex. Real Estate Assn., Sertoma Internat. (pres. Dallas 1951-52; life), Internat. Trade Assn. Dallas (charter mem., pres. 1954), Dallas Real Estate Bd. (dir. 1958-59), Dallas C. of C. (dir. 1960-62). Clubs: Athletic, Country, Dallas, Chaparral, Petit, Trader Vics (Dallas). Home: 5515 Montrose Dallas TX 75209 Office: Republic Bank Tower Dallas TX 75201

STRINGER, ELLIS ARNOLD, librarian; b. Florien, La., Feb. 6, 1914; s. Silas Deane and Sarah Vilona (Arnold) S.; B.A., La. Coll., 1936; B.L.S., La. State U., 1941; B.D., New Orleans Bapt. Theol. Sem., 1950; m. Mary Lois Irby, Aug. 29, 1948; children—Mary McKeithen, Letitia Rose. Ordained to ministry Bapt. Ch., 1948; pastor Bapt. Chs., Sandy Hook, Miss., 1948-50, Holden, La., 1950-52, Deerford, La., 1952-57, Sicily Island, La., 1957-59, Jonesville, La., 1960—; adminstrv. librarian Catahoula Parish Libraries, 1959—; tchr. Madisonville Jr. High Sch., St. Tammany Parish, La., 1938-40; prin. Tunica Jr. High Sch., West Feleciana Parish, 1941-42. Served with AUS, 1942-46. Mem. La. Library Assn., Pi Gamma Mu. Democrat. Mason. Home: 1302 N Park St Jonesville LA 71343 Office: PO Box 218 Harrisonburg LA 71340

STRINGER, ROBERT LYNN, banker; b. Killeen, Tex., Dec. 11, 1923; s. James Benjamin and Myrtle Lucille (Arnold) S.; B.B.A., Baylor U., 1949; grad. Rutgers U. Grad. Sch. Banking, 1955; m. Ora Belle Sharp, June 6, 1947; 1 son, Robert Lynn. Asst. cashier to v.p. Nat. City Bank, Waco, Tex., 1946-57; v.p. Tex. Nat. Bank, Houston, 1957-58; pres. Waxahacie Bank & Trust Co. (Tex.), 1958-60, Fed. Nat. Bank, Shawnee Okla., 1960-65, Ark. Valley Bank, 1965-70, 1st Nat. Bank of Mena (Ark.), 1971—; v.p. FABCO. Dir. West Ark. council Boy Scouts Am., 1965-70. Served with AUS, 1943-46. Mem. Mena C. of C. (dir. 1973). Baptist. Mason (Shriner), Lion. Home: 205 Reine St Mena AR 71953 Office: 807 S DeQueen St Mena AR 71953

STRINGFELLOW, SAM PRICE, JR., newspaperman; b. Jefferson, Tex., Mar. 30, 1914; s. Sam Price and Mary Lea (Freeman) S.; A.A., E. Tex. Bapt. Coll., 1934; B.A., Baylor U., 1936; postgrad. N. Tex. State Tchrs. Coll., 1936, Syracue U., 1936; m. Judy Burbage Weidman, June 2, 1954; step-children—Julie (Mrs. J. Stewart Gent), Jon Howard Weidman. Reporter The Herald, Syracuse, N.Y., 1937; reporter Daily News, Galveston, Tex., 1937-39, state editor, 1939-41; courthouse reporter Times Herald, Dallas, 1941; reporter News Messenger, Marshall, 1945-50, city editor, 1950-51, co-mng. editor, 1951-55; news dir. radio station KMHT, 1955-64; corr. The Times, Shreveport, La., 1954-64, asst. city editor, 1964-68, city editor, 1968-70, night city editor, 1970—; A.P. corr., Dallas, 1945-64, New Orleans, 1968—. Adv. council Caddo Parish 4-H Clubs. Served with AUS, 1941-45. Decorated Bronze Star medal. Mem. Am. Legion, Sigma Delta Chi. Methodist. Kiwanian (pres.). Clubs: Shreveport Press; Capitol Correspondents (Baton Rouge). Home: 3943 Balcom St Shreveport LA 71109 Office: Shreveport Times PO Box 222 Shreveport LA 71130

STRINGFIELD, HEZZ, JR., corp. and financial co. exec.; b. Heiskell, Tenn., Oct. 4, 1921; s. Hezz and Cecil Willie (Williams) S.; grad. bus. adminstrn. Draughon Coll., 1939; student finance and bus. U. Tenn.; m. Helen Louise Hinton, Mar. 20, 1939; children—Carolyn Mae Jolce (Mrs. James M. Corum), Don Wayne, Gail Louise (Mrs. John D. Gamble), Debra June (Mrs. Patrick T. Cassidy). Finance and bus. adminstrn. exec. Clinton Engring. Works, E.I. duPont de Nemours & Co., 1943-44, Manhattan Dist. metall. project, U. Chgo., 1944-45, Monsanto Chem. Co., 1945-48, nuclear div. Union Carbide Corp., 1948—; ind. bldg. contractor, real estate developer, 1946-56; cons. gen. bus., real estate financing, 1946—; mgmt. cons. mission to Middle East, Gen. Treaty Orgn., 1965; dir. Film Badge Fabricators, Inc. Bd. dirs. Found. Mgmt. Edn., Advanced Mgmt. Corp., Council Internat. Progress in mgmt., 1964-67, Found. Internat. Progress in Mgmt., 1964-67; mem. Adv. Council Univs. and Colls. Comdr. USCG Aux., 1962-63. Registered pub. accountant, Tenn. Fellow Soc. Advancement Mgmt. (Profl. Mgr. citation 1963; v.p. 1958-62; exec. v.p. 1962-63; pres. 1963-64; chmn. bd. 1964-65); mem. Am. Mgmt. Assn., Am. Inst. Accountants, Soc. for Advancement Mgmt. (top mgmt. adv. council 1972—). Methodist. Contbr. articles to profl. jours. Home: 5000 Trent Lane Knoxville TN 37922 Office: PO Box K Oak Ridge TN 37830

STRITE, JACOB JAY MILLER, clergyman; b. Greencastle, Pa., Dec. 19, 1904; s. John Calvin and Daisy Belle (Miller) S.; A.B., Lynchburg Coll., 1930; student Christian Theol. Sem., Indpls., 1933-37; B.D., Lexington Theol. Sem., 1958, Th.M., 1959; m. Anna Irene Eckert Foltz, Aug. 9, 1929 (dec. 1953); children—Georgia Annabelle (Mrs. Carl Ray Flock), Martha Eckert (Mrs. Tony Lee Trexler); m. 2d, Clara Belle Fleishman, Oct. 23, 1954. Ordained to ministry Disciples of Christ Ch., 1933; minister North Eastwood Christian Ch., Indpls., 1933-35, Daleville (Ind.) Christian Ch., 1935-44, Corydon (Ind.) Christian Ch., 1945-50, Melrose Christian Ch., Roanoke, Va., 1950-57, Mt. Carmel Christian Ch., Winchester, Ky., 1957-60, Christian Coll. Ga., Athens, Ga., 1960-61 (also counselor, tchr.), Friendship Christian Ch., Athens, 1962-64, minister at large, 1964-69; asso. Bethany Christian Ch., Roanoke, Va., 1969—. Mem. Disciples of Christ Hist. Soc. Home: 1678 Springbrook Rd NW Roanoke VA 24017 Office: 3115 Fleming Av NW Roanoke VA 24012

STROBEL, JOSEPH JULIUS, chem. engr., govt. ofcl.; b. Washington, Mar. 12, 1914; s. Luther W. and Martha A. (Nichols) S.; B.S. in Chem. Engring,, Va. Poly. Inst., 1935; m. Evelyn G. Fraley, Aug. 9, 1947; children—Russell A., Gene L. Chem. engr. Dow Chem. Co., Midland, Mich., 1936-42; chem. engr. C.W.S., Washington, 1946; chemist, chem. engr., sr. project engr. Naval Ordnance Lab., White Oak, Md., 1947-52; chem. engr. Office Saline Water, U.S. Dept. Interior, Washington, 1952—, chief div. Processes devel., 1959-65, chief program analysis and coordinating staff, 1965-67, chief desalting feasibility and econs. studies staff, 1967-72, asso. dir., 1972—. Served to maj. AUS, 1942-46; ETO. Registered profl. engr., D.C. Mem. Am. Chem. Soc., Am. Inst. Chem. Engrs., Soc. Plastics Engrs., Soc. Am. Magicians. Research on cellulose ethers, plastics applications, fresh water from salt water. Address: 2106 Wakefield St Alexandria VA 22307

STROMAN, JOSH HAMPTON, librarian; b. Ardmore, Okla., Oct. 11, 1938; s. Ewing Melvin and Velma Katharine (Foster) S.; B.A., Okla. State U., 1960; M.L.S., U. Okla., 1964. Jr. documents librarian Okla. State U., Stillwater, 1964-67, sr. documents librarian, 1967-72, head documents librarian, 1972-74; asst. librarian in charge tech. services U. Tulsa, 1974—. Participant, Inst. on Govt. Publs., U.S. Office Edn., Emory U., 1969. Mem. A.L.A., Okla. Library Assn. (editor quar. jour. 1967-69, treas. 1974-75). Office: U Tulsa McFarlin Library 600 S College St Tulsa OK 74104

STRONG, ANNIE D. SINGFIELD (MRS. LEONARD V. STRONG), social worker; b. Augusta, Ga.; d. Archie E. and Della (Ayers) Singfield; B.A. cum laude, Paine Coll., 1930; grad. Atlanta U. Sch. Social Work, 1940; m. Leonard V. Strong, Aug. 19, 1948. Tchr., Duplin County Tng. Sch., Faison, N.C., 1930-38; child welfare worker Five Points House, N.Y.C., 1940-42, Anson County Dept. Pub. Welfare, Wadesboro, N.C., 1942-46; social worker VA Hosp., Nat. Assn. Social Workers, Am. Acad. Certified Social Workers, Ala. Conf. Social Work. Home: PO Box 314 Tuskegee Institute AL 36088 Office: VA Hosp Tuskegee AL 36083

STRONG, FRANK RANSOM, educator; b. Lawrence, Kan., Apr. 4, 1908; s. Frank and Mary Evelyn (Ransom) S.; B.A., Yale, 1929, J.D., 1934; m. Gertrude Elizabeth Way, Aug. 31, 1929; children—John William, Mary Elizabeth (Mrs. Lawrence J. Brennan). Instr. econs. U. Del., 1929-31; instr., asst. prof. law U. Ia., 1934-37; asst. prof., asso. prof., prof. law Ohio State U., 1937-65, dean, 1952-65, dean, prof. emeritus, 1965—; prof. law U. N.C., Chapel Hill, 1965—, Cary C. Boshamer Distinguished Univ. prof., 1970—, vis. asso. prof. law Duke, 1940-41; J. DuPratt White prof. law Cornell U., 1963; faculty, orientation program in Am. law Princeton, 1966-67, seminar chmn., 1967; dir. law teaching clinics Assn. Am. Law Schs., 1968—. Mem. faculty Salzburg Seminar Am. Studies, 1959; summer vis. prof. law Duke, U. Mich., U. N.C., Northwestern U., U. Tex., Tex. Tech U., Willamette U.; vis. prof. Sixty-Five Club, Hastings Coll. Law, 1974. Chmn. bd. trustees Ohio Legal Center Found., 1961-65. Recipient Distinguished Service award Ohio State U., 1956, fellows award Ohio Bar Assn. Found., 1964. Mem. Assn. Am. Law Schs. (pres. 1960), Order of Coif (nat. sec.-treas. 1970—), Phi Beta Kappa. Independent. Home: 211 Markham Dr Chapel Hill NC 27514

STRONG, JACK PERRY, physician, educator; b. Birmingham, Ala., Apr. 27, 1928; s. Larkin B. and Mary Louise (Perry) S.; B.S., U. Ala., 1948; M.D., La. State U., 1951; m. Patricia Powers, Jan. 26, 1951; children—Mary Louise, Margaret Patricia, Martha Jane, Maury Elizabeth. Rotating intern Jefferson Hillman Hosp., Birmingham, Ala., 1951-52; asst. dept. pathology La. State U. Sch. Medicine, New Orleans, 1952-53, instr., 1955-57, asst. prof., 1957-60, asso. prof., 1960-64, prof. pathology, 1964—, chmn. dept. pathology, 1966—. Cons. Pathology Southwest Found. Research and Edn., 1954-55; sabbatical with Social Medicine Research unit Med. Research Council, London, Eng., 1962-63; assisting vis. pathologist Charity Hosp. La., New Orleans, 1952-53, 55-58, vis. pathologist, 1958-66, sr. vis. pathologist, pathologist-in-chief La. State U. div., 1966—; with pathology A study sect. USPHS, 1965-69, chmn., 1967-69. Mem. epidemiology and biometry adv. com. NIH, 1971—; mem. sci. adv. bd. cons. Armed Forces Inst. Pathology, 1971—. Vice pres. Jefferson Com. Better Schs., Metairie, La., 1964. Served to capt. USAF, 1953-55. Recipient Research Career Devel, award USPHS, 1962-64. Sr. research fellow USPHS, 1957-62. Diplomate Am. Bd. Pathology. Mem. Coll. Am. Pathologists, Am. Assn. Pathologists and Bacteriologists, Am. Soc. Exptl. Pathology, Internat. Acad. Pathology (mem. council 1968-71), Am. Soc. Clin. Pathologists, Am. Assn. Chmn. Med. Schs. Depts. Pathology (v.p. 1969, pres. 1970), Internat. Soc. Cardiology (mem. sect. epidemiology and prevention), La. (research com. 1960—, dir. 1967), Am. (fellow councils arteriosclerosis and epidemiology, mem. pathology research com. 1969—) heart assns., Phi Beta Kappa, Alpha Omega Alpha, Phi Kappa Phi, Sigma Chi. Methodist. Contbr. articles publs. Home: 4117 Cleveland Pl Metairie LA 70003 Office: 1542 Tulane Av New Orleans LA 70112

STRONG, MARLIN JEROME, physician, educator; b. Saginaw, Mich., Aug. 17, 1929; s. Marlin Bertram and Helen May (Tefft) S.; A.B., Calvin Coll., 1951; M.D., Boston U., 1956. Intern, U. Mich., 1956-57; resident anesthesiology Hosp. U. Pa., 1957-60; asst. anesthesiology U. Pa., 1960-63; instr. anesthesiology Baylor U. Coll. Medicine, Houston, 1963-64, asst. prof., 1964-68, asso. prof., 1968—; mem. staffs St. Luke's, Tex. Childrens, Meth., Ben Taub, Jefferson Davis hosps. (all Houston). Served to capt. M.C., AUS, 1960-62. Diplomate Am. Bd. Anesthesiology. Fellow Am. Soc. Pediatrics, Am. Soc. Anesthesiologists. Home: 3614 Montrose St Houston TX 77006 Office: Baylor Coll Medicine Houston TX 77025

STROTHER, DORA DOUGHERTY (MRS. LESTER J. STROTHER), aviation psychologist, pilot; b. St. Paul, Nov. 27, 1921; d. John Maynard and Esther Lucile (Wardle) Dougherty; A.A., Cottey Coll., Nevada, Mo., 1941; Ph.B., Northwestern U., 1949; M.S., U. Ill., 1953; Ph.D., N.Y. U., 1955; m. Lester J. Strother. Flight instr., ferry pilot airports in N.Y. and Ill., 1944-49; flight instr. Inst. Aviation, U. Ill., 1949-50, research pilot, research asso. Aviation Psychology Lab., 1950-54, 56-57; human engring. specialist Martin Co., Balt., 1957-58; human factors engr. Bell Helicopter Co., Ft. Worth, 1958-62, chief human factors group, 1962—; holder feminine world record altitude in rotorcraft, 1961-66, feminine world record point-to-point distance in rotorcraft, 1961-66; v.p., asst. treas. Tex. Met. Publs., Inc. Adv. council Tex. Aero. Comm., 1963-64; mem. gen. aviation safety com. Nat. Safety Council; judge Internat. Sci. Fair, Dallas, 1966; chmn. women's adv. com. on aviation FAA. Panel mem. Coll. Town Hall Programs, 1962. Chmn. bd. trustees Amelia Earhart Meml. Scholarship Fund of Ninety-Nines. Served as pilot WASP, USAAC, 1943-44; lt. col. USAF Res. Recipient Achievement award N.Y. U., 1955, Amelia Earhart award Am. Women's Assn., 1957, Alumni award Cottey Coll., 1957, Recognition certificate Ft. Worth C. of C., 1961, Lady Hay Drummond-Hay trophy Women's Internat. Assn. Aeros., 1961, Aviation Woman of Year award Women's Nat. Aviation Assn., 1961; Achievement award, Am. Assn. U. Women, 1966, 67; merit award Northwestern U. Alumni Assn. Fellow Human Factors Soc. Am. (editorial bd. jour.), asso. fellow Am. Inst. Aeros. and Astronautics (tech. judge student papers 1961, mem. tech. com. on life scis. and systems 1970—); mem. Am., Southwestern, Tex., Tarrant County (pres.) psychol. assns., Assn. Aviation Psychologists (pres.), Am. Helicopter Soc., Assn. U.S. Army, Soc. Engring. Psychologists, Soaring Soc. Am., Tex. Soaring Assn., 99s (chmn. Ft. Worth), P.E.O., Whirly-Girls. Episcopalian. Mem. Order Eastern Star. Editor: Tex. Metro mag. Contbr. numerous articles, papers in field. Home: 3616 Landy Lane Fort Worth TX 76118 Office: Bell Helicopter Co Fort Worth TX 76101

STROTHER, HAZEL B., accountant; b. Akron, O., June 29, 1929; d. Lawrence McCauley and Josei (Friend) Beall; student W.Va. Wesleyan Coll., 1947-49; A.A., George Washington U., 1951, A.B.; m. Samuel L. Strother, Oct. 23, 1953 (div. Feb. 1971). Sec., jr. accountant C. B. Stovall & Co., Washington, 1951-52; sec., ins. underwriter Washington Ins. Agy., Inc., 1952-57; accountant U.S. AEC, 1957-62; accountant, asst. chief, accounting and analysis br. Hdqrs. Marine Corps, Washington, 1962-66; staff accountant Hdqrs. NASA, Washington, 1966-68; staff accountant Hdqrs. Dept. Health, Edn. and Welfare, Washington, 1968—. Mem. Am. Accounting Assn., Fed. Govt. Accountants Assn. (nat. chmn. pub. relations com. 1972, 73), Internat. Platform Assn., George Washington U. Alumni Assn., W.Va. U. Alumni Assn., W.Va. State Soc., Alpha Beta Gamma. Democrat. Clubs: Braxton County (W.Va.) Young Democrats, George Washington University (charter mem.). Home: 1600 S Eads St Arlington VA 22202 Office: 300 Independence Av SW Washington DC 20201

STROTHER, JACK WILHOIT, JR., banker; b. Louisa, Ky., Sept. 24, 1943; s. Jack Wilhoit and Edith Evelyn (Sparks) S.; B.A., Centre Coll. Ky., 1965; postgrad. La. State U., 1973; m. Celia Otero Coll, May 12, 1968; 1 son, Mark David. Asst. cashier Comml. Bank, Grayson, Ky., 1969-70, v.p., 1970—, also dir. Treas., Cancer Soc., 1972—. Served with USNR, 1966-69; Vietnam. Mem. Am. Inst. Banking (pres. 1972-73), Bank Adminstrn. Inst. (v.p. 1973—), Ky. Bankers Assn. (edn. com. 1973—), Grayson Jaycees (pres. 1973—, dir. 1970—). Home: 219 Johnson Av Grayson KY 41143 Office: 106 E Main St Grayson KY 41143

STROTHER, LESTER JAMES, publisher; b. Elizabeth, La., Mar. 9, 1924; s. Theodore H. and Ella (Laird) S.; B.J., U. Mo., 1950; m. Dora Jean Dougherty, Nov. 23, 1966; children—David Lester, Grant Douglas. Night editor El Dorado (Ark.) Daily News, 1950-51; news editor Lake Charles (La.) Am. Press, 1951-52; staff corr. U.P.I., Dallas, 1952-57; free lance writer, Dallas and Forth Worth, 1957-64; asst. city editor Ft. Worth Star Telegram, 1959-63; asso. dir. pub. relations, asso. editor Ft. Worth Mag., 1963-65; pres., chmn. bd., chief exec. officer Tex. Met. Publs. Inc., 1965—, pub. Tex. Metro Mag., Arlington, Tex., 1965—; lectr. in field. Mem. Postal Commn., Arlington, 1968—; mem. communication adv. bd. U. Dallas, 1969—. Del. Tarrant County (Tex.) Democratic conv., 1968, 72. Served with USNR, 1943-46; comdt. Dallas/Fort Worth Metroplex Sta., Tex. Navy, 1970—. Mem. Ft. Worth (mem. Trinity River devel. com. 1971—), Dallas, Haltom Richland Area (dir. 1968—), Grand Prairie, Arlington chambers commerce, Indsl. Editors Assn. (v.p. 1965-66), Dallas Sales and Marketing Exec., Mag. Pubs. Assn., Dallas Advt. League, Sigma Delta Chi, Sigma Phi Epsilon, Kappa Alpha Mu. Episcopalian (del. diocesan conv. 1971). Clubs: Fort Worth Advertising, Fort Worth Knife and Fork, Fort Worth Press; Dallas Press. Home: 3616 Landy Lane Fort Worth TX 76118 Office: PO Drawer 5566 Arlington TX 76011

STROUD, DAVID, JR., wholesale co. exec.; b. Kennett, Mo., July 2, 1913; s. David and Mary Maude (Striffler) S.; student S.E. Mo. State Coll., 1931-34; m. Mildred Ward Harrison, Jan. 14, 1939; 1 dau., Susan Elizabeth. Asst. purchasing agt. Mo. Utilities Co., Cape Girardeau, Mo., 1934-37; purchasing agt. Ark. Utilities Co., Helena, 1937-42; gen. mgr. A. S. Kelly Co., West Helena, Ark., 1946-47; comptroller, Lewis Supply Co., Inc., Helena, Ark., 1947-52; sec.-treas. Helena Wholesale, Inc. (Ark.), 1952-73, financial v.p., 1968-73, also dir.; chief accountant Eagle River Chem. Corp., West Helena, 1973—. Chmn. West Helena Mayor's Adv. Council, 1966-68; West Helena Planning Commr., 1962—; ex-officio mem. Phillips County Planning Commn., 1964—, Area Planning Commn., 1966—; vice-chmn. West Helena Water Commn., 1964-71, chmn., 1971—, West Helena Sewer Commn., 1964-71, chmn., 1971—; v.p. West Helena Promotional Assn., 1971, vice chmn. Phillips County Port Authority 1971—. Bd. dirs., v.p. Mid-South Sight Service Inst., Memphis, 1962-70. Served to lt. (j.g.) USNR, 1942-46. Decorated Bronze Star medal; recipient Key to City West Helena, 1971, award Mid-South Sight Service Inst., 1971. Mem. Ark. Wholesale Grocers Assn. (com. chmn. 1962—). Republican. Methodist. Lion. Club: Ark. Razorback Booster. Home: 216 Richmond Hill West Helena AR 72390 Office: 201 York St Helena AR 72342

STROUD, DONALD DEAN, artist, educator; b. Clarsville, Tex., July 18, 1928; s. Albert Graydon and Virgie Bell (Bean) S.; student U. Houston, 1949; B.A. in Art, Tex. Technol. U., 1956, M. Ed., 1959; postgrad. U. Tex., 1969—; m. Loris Lamonte Leddy, Apr. 7, 1950; children—Patrice (Mrs. Lynn Searsy), Jeffrey Graydon, Robert Warren. Comml. artist Coca-Cola, Lubbock and Paris, Tex., 1947-49; free-lance artist, tchr., Lubbock, 1950-59; free-lance artist, Levelland, Tex., 1959—; faculty South Plains Coll., Levelland, 1959—, coll. one-man shows, 1965—, also others. Work includes relief sculpture numerous bldgs. Levelland; executed mosaic murals Cook Meml. Hosp., 1971, South Plains Hosp., 1972, College Av Floral, 1973; also represented in pvt. collections. Served with C.E., AUS, 1951-53. Recipient $1500.00 excellence in teaching award First Nat. Bank

Levelland, 1967. Baptist (deacon). Home: 1621 Grant St Levelland TX 79336

STROUD, HOWARD BURNETT, SR., ednl. adminstr.; b. Athens, Ga., Mar. 31, 1930; s. George Edward and Emma Mae (Flanigan) S.; B.S., Morehouse Coll., 1956; M.A., Atlanta U., 1968; m. Victoria Lee Baker, Oct. 10, 1960; 1 son, Howard Burnett. Classroom tchr. Union Inst., 1956, Burney Harris High Sch., 1956-65; guidance counselor, asst. prin., tchr. Lyons Jr. High Sch., Athens, 1965-67, prin., 1967—; sec. Frontline Corp., Fledgling Black Corp. Adult instr. Civil Def., 1960; pres. Harris br. YMCA, 1956—; mem. Athens-Clarke Charter Commn., 1968-69; lay v.p. Athens-Clarke County Cancer Soc., 1971—. Bd. dirs. Athens (Ga.) Regional Library, Athens Clarke County United Way Inc.; bd. dirs., regional chmn. Ga. div. Am. Cancer Soc. Served with AUS, 1951-53. Recipient Plaque for leadership YMCA, 1959. Certificate of Appreciation Am. Cancer Soc., 1970, 73, Certificate of Appreciation V.F.W. 1961, 62. Mem. Nat. Assn. Secondary Sch. Prins., N.E.A., Ga. Clarke County edn. assns., Ga. Assn. Middle Sch. Prins. (dir. Central region), Phi Delta Kappa, Kappa Alpha Psi (polemarche 1973-74). Baptist (deacon, mem. finance com., trustee). Elk, Mason. Club: Athens Breakfast Optimist (v.p. 1971-73, pres. 1973—). Home: 175 Jones Dr Athens GA 30601 Office: 2190 Winterville Rd Athens GA 30601

STROUD, JAMES ERNEST, devel. co. exec., mayor; b. Weatherford, Okla., May 8, 1912; s. Jess W. W. and Samantha (Allbright) S.; student Southwestern State Coll., Weatherford, 1931; m. Nell Hume Stroud, Dec. 1, 1912; children—Richard, James Ernest, II, Timothy Hume, Sherelle S. (Mrs. Charles F. Culp), Gaynor (Mrs. L. Dean Tucker). Owner, N.M. Welding Supply Co., 1932-41; owner, pres. Tex-Air Gas Co., 1947-55, J. Ernest Stroud & Co., Amarillo, Tex., 1941—; pres. Stroud Devel. Co., Amarillo, 1960—; pres., owner Trades Fair Center. Mayor, Amarillo, 1967—. Del. to Republican Nat. Conv., 1964, elector, 1968. Mem. Amarillo C. of C. Club: Amarillo Country. Home: 1520 Bryan St Amarillo TX 79102 Office: 215 Buchanan St Amarillo TX 79105 also 503 Bank SW Bldg Amarillo TX 79109

STROUD, JAMES WILLIAM, state legislator; b. Denison, Tex., June 4, 1914; s. Lynn and Rose (Hickman) S.; m. Sara Frances White, Aug. 20, 1938 (div. Aug. 1954); children—James William, Robert Lynn, George Winton; m. Mary Ellon Birdwell, Oct. 7, 1960; children—Douglas Alan, Paul Jeffrey. Dep. to regional accountant Home Owner Loan Corp., Dallas, 1935-42; pres. Liberty Packing Co., 1940-50; regional ration banking officer, region mgr. dist. center OPA, 1942-47; regional dir. U.S. Census Bur., Dallas, 1948-64; mem. Tex. Ho. of Reps., 1964—, chmn. state electron code com., 1968-70. Mem. regional coordinating com. Tex. Vocational Rehab.; mem. Dallas Council on Alcoholism. Mem. Phi Sigma. Home: 5507 McCommas St Dallas TX 75206 Office: Ho of Reps State Capitol Austin TX 75201

STROUD, ROBERT EDWARD, lawyer; b. Chester, S.C., July 24, 1934; s. Coy Franklin and Leila (Caldwell) S.; A.B., Washington and Lee U., 1956, LL.B., 1959; m. Katherine E. Clark, Apr. 8, 1961; children—Robert Gordon, Margaret Lathan. Admitted to Va. bar, 1959; asso. McGuire, Woods & Battle, Charlottesville, 1959-64, partner 1964—. Lectr. Grad. Sch. Bus. Adminstrn., U. Va., legal edn. insts., others. Pres. Charlottesville Housing Found., 1968—. Trustee Presbyn. Found., 1972-73; mem. gen. exec. bd. Presbyn. Ch. U.S., 1972-73. Served to 2d lt. with AUS, 1957. Mem. Am., Va. bar assns., Tax Inst. Am., Am. Judicature Soc., Am. Acad. Polit. and Social Sci., Phi Eta Sigma, Omicron Delta Kappa, Phi Delta Phi. Presbyn. Home: 104 Woodstock Dr Charlottesville VA 22901 Office: PO Box 1191 Charlottesville VA 22902

STROUSS, GENE BARTON, indsl. relations exec.; b. Drummond, Wis., Nov. 17, 1934; s. Glen O. and Vanessa M. (Piety) S.; B.A., David Lipscomb Coll., 1964; m. Rosemary Harris, June 27, 1959; children—Lisa Kimberly, Barton Alan. Ordained to ministry Ch. of Christ, 1955; minister chs., Clarington, O., 1955-56, St. Mary's, W.Va., 1956-58, Crawfordsville, Ind., 1958-59, Brookston, Ind., 1959-62, Elk Grove Village, Ill., 1965-68; tchr. history Roycemore Sch., Evanston, Ill., 1964-66; employment mgr. Methode Electronics, Inc., Chgo., 1966-69; indsl. relations asst. Midwest div. Vulcan Materials Co., Chgo., 1968-69, mgr. adminstrn. metallics div., Clark, N.J., 1969-72, rep. indsl. relations dept., Brimingham, Ala., 1972—. Co. rep. N.J. Self Insurers Assn., 1969-72. Cub Scout den leader Watchung Area council Boy Scouts Am., 1972. Mem. Mid-State Personnel Assn., Westfield Area C. of C. (dir. 1970-72, vice chmn. polit. action com. 1972). Mem. Ch. of Christ (deacon 1965-66). Home: 3458 Heather Lane Birmingham AL 35216 Office: One Office Park Circle Birmingham AL 35223

STROZIER, AUGUSTUS BUENAVISTA, III, dentist; b. Houston, Mar. 9, 1918; s. Augustus Buena Vista and Era (Weaver) S.; student U.S. Mil. Acad., 1936-37; U. Houston, 1937-39; D.D.S., Tex. Dental Coll., 1943; m. Helen Geers Willis, Mar. 30, 1943. Pvt. practice gen. dentistry, Houston, 1946—; pres., dir. Automotive Finance Corp., Houston, 1956—; pres., dir. Lone Star Trust Co., Houston, 1956-58; chmn. bd. dirs., 1958-59. Pres. Houston Property Owners Assn., 1948-49. Organizer, Democratic Party, S.E. Houston, 1948. Served to capt. D.C., AUS, 1943-46. Mem. Am. Dental Assn., Am. Acad. Gen. Dentistry., Tex., Houston dental socs., U. Houston Alumni Assn., U. Tex. Alumni Assn., Am. Legion, Zi Psi Phi. Club: Houston Morphy Chess (pres. 1950). Home: 2534 Yorktown St Houston TX 77027 Office: 7338 McHenry St Houston TX 77017

STRUBA, DAVID, elec. engr., govt. ofcl.; b. Johnstown, Pa., Oct. 14, 1942; s. John Joseph and Marie (Paska) S.; B.S.E.E., 1965; postgrad., George Washington U., 1965—. Electronics engr. FCC, Washington, 1964—, frequency spectrum mgr., 1964—. Mem. I.E.E.E. Home: No 1003 2030 N Adams Arlington VA 22201 Office: No 710 1919 M St NW Washington DC 20554

STRUBY, BERT, newspaper exec.; b. Macon, Ga., Jan. 19, 1917; s. Chester Albert and Julia (Riley) S.; A.B. magna cum laude, Mercer U., 1938; m. Jane Whitfield Spearman, May 24, 1947; children—Cynthia Jane, Neil Albert. Reporter, Macon Telegraph, 1938-40, state editor, 1940-41, asst. to publisher Macon Telegraph and Macon News, 1947-48, exec. editor Macon Telegraph, 1948-54, editor, 1954-58, gen. mgr. both papers, 1957—, exec. v.p. Macon Telegraph Pub. Co., 1958—, also dir. Chmn., Ga. Asso. Press, 1963-64; chmn. bd. So. Edn. Reporting Service, 1962-64. Chmn. Ga. citizens com. Nat. Council on Crime and Delinquency, 1961-65, mem. nat. bd. trustees, 1962-64; bd. Macon Housing Authority, 1952—, chmn. bd. commrs., 1961-64; mem. Ga. Bd. for Children and Youth, 1963—; mem. Gov.'s Youth Study Com., 1962; pres. Macon Big Bros. Assn., 1962, named Big Brother of Year, 1962, bd. dirs., 1959-65; mem. adv. bd. Bibb County Juvenile Ct., 1949-59; mem. steering com. Macon Council on World Affairs, 1954-62. Served to lt. comdr. USNR, 1941-46. Recipient Certificate of Merit, Freedoms Found., 1950; citation Anti-Defamation League of B'nai B'rith, 1951; Mil. Service Cross, U.D.C., 1954; Silver Beaver award Boy Scouts Am., 1967. Mem. So. Newspaper Publs. Assn. (pres. 1966-67), Macon C. of C. (chmn. Downtown Council 1970-71, v.p. 1971-72, pres. 1974), Mercer U Alumni Assn. (pres. 1956-57, mem. exec. com. 1960-65), Nat. Alliance Businessman (chmn. Macon Metro area 1971-72), Am. Legion. Baptist (deacon). Elk, Rotarian. Club: Idle Hour Country (Macon). Home: 1855 Waverland Dr Macon GA 31201 Office: 120 Broadway Macon GA 31201

STRUELENS, MICHEL MAURICE JOSEPH GEORGES, fgn. affairs cons.; b. Brussels, Belgium, Mar. 10, 1928 (came to U.S. 1960, naturalized 1966); B.A., Coll. St. Pierre, Brussels, 1944; M.A., Antwerp (Belgium) U., 1949; Ph.D., Am. U., Washington, 1968; m. Godelieve De Wilde, Aug. 2, 1949; children—Alain, Patricia, Brigitte, Bernard, Jean Paul. Insp. econ. affairs Congo Govt., Leopoldville, 1950-54, chief insp. econ. affairs, 1954-55, dep. commr. transp., 1955-57; dir. Information and Pub. Relations Office for Congo, Brussels, 1957-58, Congo Tourism Pavillion, Internat. World's Fair, Brussels, 1958-59; dir. gen. Belgian Congo and Ruanda Urundi Tourist Office, Congo, 1959; chmn. African Commn. Internat. Union Ofcl. Travel Orgns., Geneva, Switzerland, 1959-60; ofcl. Katanga rep. in U.S., N.Y.C., 1960-63; dir. gen. Internat. Inst. for for African Affairs in Can., 1963-64; spl. asst. to prime minister Democratic Republic Congo, fgn. affairs minister, adviser to Congo UN delegation, adviser Congo embassy, Washington, N.Y.C., 1964-65; dir. Eurafrica, Consultants on Fgn. Affairs, Washington, 1966—. Prof. polit. sci., French, Am. U., 1968—, dir. Center Research and Documentation on European Community, 1971; adminstr. Congo Touring Clubs, Brussels, Leopoldville, 1959—; adminstr. French parish, exec. v.p. Eglise Saint Louis Corp., French-Speaking Union Inc., Washington. Recipient Internat. Union Ofcl. Travel Orgns. Poster award, Brussels, 1958; Etoile de Service en Argent, King of Belgium, 1956, chevalier de l'Ordre Royal du Lion, 1957. Mem. Phi Sigma Alpha. Rotarian. Club: Bukavu Royal Sports (founder Congo 1950; pres. 1951-54; hon. pres. 1957). Author: (with Inforcongo) Congo Belge et Ruanda-Urundi, 1958; (monograph) Le Canada a l'Heure de l'Afrique, 1964. Home and office: 1374 Woodside Dr McLean VA 22101

STRULL, NORMAN JAMES, oral surgeon; b. Louisville, July 2, 1937; s. Charles H. and Sarah B. (Baron) S.; D.M.D., U. Louisville, 1962; m. Nancy Dock, June 25, 1961; children—Gregory Evan, Dana Michelle, Vicki Lynn. Oral surgery intern U. Ala., Birmingham, 1962-63; resident in oral surgery U. Louisville Hosps., 1963-65; pvt. practice oral surgery, Louisville, 1965—; instr. U. Louisville Sch. Dentistry, 1965—. Mem. Am. (del. 1971—), Southeastern, Ky. (sec.-treas 1971—) socs. oral surgeons, Am., Ky. dental assns., Ky. Med. Assn., Jefferson County Med. Soc. Home: 6210 Innes Trace Louisville KY 40207 Office: 4122 Shelbyville Rd Louisville KY 40207

STUART, BROOKS SWYGERT, county ofcl.; b. Coronaca, S.C., May 13, 1904; s. Robert Lee and Alice (Rice) S.; A.B., Wofford Coll., 1926; m. Lois Elizabeth Pettit, Oct. 14, 1933; s. Brooks Swygert, Alice Elizabeth. Bookkeeper, Nat. Loan & Exchange Bank, 1926-30, Central Union Bank, Greenwood, S.C., 1930-33; with County Bank, Greenwood, S.C., 1933-42, 46-69, sr. v.p., 1965-69, now dir.; treas. Greenwood County, 1969—; dir. Mut. Savs. & Loan Assn., Greenwood. Mem. Fed. Housing Authority, Greenwood, 1968—; chmn. Civil Def. Greenwood County, 1969—; commr. pub. works, Greenwood, 1963-65; mem. Commn. of Cokesbury Hist. and Recreational Commn.; chmn. bldg. com. Brewer Hosp., 1955. Mem. County Bd. Edn., 1947-48; mem. City Council, 1948-58. Bd. dirs., treas. A.R.C., 1955—; bd. dirs. YMCA, Community Chest; trustee, treas. Greenwood Meth. Home. Served with AUS, 1942-46. Mem. Am. Legion, Newcomen Soc. U.S., S.A.R. (pres. Cambridge chpt. 1966-68, state v.p. 1967-69), Greenwood C. of C. (dir. 1956-61, pres. 1962), Sigma Alpha Epsilon. Methodist (past com. world service and finance S.C. Conf., chmn. bd. stewards 1956, 67). Kiwanian (pres. Greenwood 1960). Club: Greenwood Country (pres. 1951). Home: 407 Jennings Av Greenwood SC 29646 Office: County Courthouse Monument St Greenwood SC 29646

STUART, EDWARD, JR., forest engr.; b. Boston, June 15, 1917; s. Edward and Helen (Fox) S.; B.S. in Forestry, U. Me., 1937; F.E. (hon.), Biltmore Forest Sch., Weisbaden, Germany, 1946; children—Edward, Diane and Bruce. Forester, Me. and Can., 1937, with U.S. Forest Service, in Mass., Colo., S.D., Wyo., 1938-42; cons. and practicing forester, Va., N.C., S.C., Md. W.Va., 1946-56; pres. chmn. bd. dirs. Eastern Forestry, Inc., Hampton, Va., 1956—; consulting and practicing forestry and real estate appraiser. Served from lt. to capt. AUS, 1942-46; mil govt. Forestry Office, Great Hesse, Germany, 1945-46. Decorated Commendation Medal Croix Militaire (Belgium). Mem. Nat. Assn. Cons. Foresters (pres. 1948-50; exec. council 1950-60, exec. sec. 1960—, editor The Consultant), Nat. Council Forestry Assn. Execs., Am. Soc. Appraisers, Am. Forestry Assn. (forest progress adv. council 1950-51), Soc. Am. Foresters (chmn. Rappahannock sect. 1960), Mil. Govt. Assn., Va. Forestry Council (sec.), Practicing Forestors Inst. (dir.), Gloucester, Mathews, Middlesex Realty Bd. (dir.), Nat. Assn. Real Estate Bds., Va. Real Estate Assn., S.A.R., Nat. Forest Products Assn. (mem. forestry adv. com.), Nat. Def. Exec. Res., Am. Legion. Author numerous tech. articles on forestry and appraising. Home: Stuart Landing Wake VA 23176 Office: Box 6 Wake VA 23176

STUART, HAL MARTIN, physician; b. Elkin, N.C., June 5, 1931; s. Luther Martin and Hallie Mae (Gilliam) S.; B.S. cum laude, Wake Forest Coll., 1953; M.D., Bowman Gray Sch. Medicine, 1956; m. Bonnie Jane Hall, Dec. 20, 1955; children—Amanda, Robinette. Intern, N.C. Bapt. Hosp., Winston-Salem, 1956-57; resident obstetrics-gynecology City Meml. Hosp., Winston-Salem, 1959-60; gen. practice medicine, Elkin, N.C., 1960—; mem. staff Hugh Chatham Meml. Hosp., Elkin; med. examiner, Surry County, 1971—. Dir. Yadkin Valley Bank & Trust Co., Elkin, N.C. Mem. N.C. Gov's Com. to Bd. Air and Water Resources, 1970. Bd. dirs. Surry County Tb Assn. Served with USNR, 1957-59. Recipient Shepardson award Bowman Gray Sch. Medicine, 1956. Diplomate Am. Bd. Family Practice. Mem. A.M.A., Am. Acad. Gen. Practice, So. Med. Assn., N.C. State, Surry-Yadkin (v.p. 1970-71) med. scos., Alpha Omega Alpha. Methodist. Mason. Home: 306 Ivy Circle Elkin NC 28621 Office: 180-C Parkwood Dr Elkin NC 28621

STUART, JESSE HILTON, author; b. W-Hollow, near Riverton, Ky., Aug. 8, 1907; s. Mitchell and Martha (Hilton) S.; A.B., Lincoln Meml. U., Harrogate, Tenn., 1929, hon. D.H.L., 1950; student Vanderbilt U., 1931-32, Peabody Coll.; D.Litt., U. Ky., 1944; D.Litt., Marietta (O.) Coll., 1952; LL.D. Baylor U.; D.Litt. (hon.), Morris Harvey Coll., 1959; Marshall U., 1962, No. Mich. U., 1964, Eastern Ky. State Coll., 1964; Dr. Pedagogy (hon.), Murray State U., 1968; m. Naomi Deane Norris, Oct. 14, 1939; 1 dau., Jessica Jane (Mrs. Julian Juergensmeyer). Tchr. sch., lectr. colls. and univs., 1940—, supt. city schs. Greenup, Ky., 1941-43; vis. lectr., prof. Am. U. Cairo, 1960-61; taught in Grad. Coll. Edn., U. Nev., summer 1958; writer in residence Eastern Ky. U. 1965-66; author short stories, poetry, articles. Specialist U.S. Dept. State, USIS, 1962-63. Am. representative Asian Writers' Conf., 1962. Mem. group to revise Ky. State Constn. chmn. health, welfare and edn. com. Bd. dirs. Ky. Heart Assn., state chmn., 1964. Served as apprentice seaman USN, March 1944, commd. lt. (j.g.), Aug. 1944, stationed in Washington, D.C. Awarded Guggenheim fellowship for European travel, 1937; Jeanette Sewal Davis Poetry Prize, 1934; $5000 prize, Acad. of Arts and Scis., 1941; $5000 prize Acad. Am. Poets, 1961. Mem. Poetry Soc. Am. Republican. Methodist. Author: Man With a Bull-Tongue Plow (poems), published 1934; Head O'W-Hollow (stories) 1936; Beyond Dark Hills (autobiography), 1938; Trees of Heaven (novel), 1940; Mem of the Mountains (stories), 1941; Taps for Private Tussie (Thomas Jefferson Southern Award, $500; Book-of-the-Month, Dec. 1943); Mongrel Mettle (autobiography of a dog), 1944; Album of Destiny (poems), 1944; Foretaste of Glory (novel), 1946; Tales From the Plum Grove Hills (Stories), 1946; The Thread That Runs So True, 1949 (N.E.A. selection as best book of 1949); Hie to the Hunters, 1950; Clearing in the Sky, 1950; Kentucky Is My Land (poems), 1952; The Good Spirit of Laurel Ridge, 1953; The Beatinest Boy, 1953; A Penny's Worth of Character; 1954; Red Mule (juvenile), 1954; The Year of My Rebirth, 1956; Plowshare in Heaven (collection of short stories), 1958; The Rightful Owner, 1960; God's Oddling, 1960; Andy Finds A Way, 1961; Hold April, 1962; A Jesse Stuart Reader, 1963; Save Every Lamb, 1964; Daughter of the Legend (novel), 1965; My Land Has A Voice, 1966; Ride with Huey the Engineer (junior book), 1966; Mr. Galhon's Novel, 1967; Come Gentle Spring, (story collection), 1969; To Teach to Love, 1969. Author of short stories in anthologies: Best Short Stories, O. Henry Meml. Collection., Co-editor: Outlooks Through Literature (textbook). Contbr. to Harpers, Atlantic Monthly, Esquire, Ladies' Home Journal. Poetry, etc. Home: Greenup KY 41144

STUART, VIRGIL SAMUEL, city ofcl.; b. Atlanta, Dec. 29, 1907; s. James R. and LeNora (Holt) S.; student North Ga. Coll., 1925-27; m. Lillian Justice, July 4, 1931; children—Phyllis Ann, Virgil Samuel. Mcht., St. Augustine, Fla., 1928-33; police officer, St. Augustine, 1933, chief of police, City of St. Augustine, 1958—. Bd. dirs. St. Johns Assn. Mem. Fla. Peace Officers Assn. (sec., treas. 1945—, spl. legislative rep.), Internat. Assn. Chiefs Police, St. Augustine and St. Johns County C. of C. (dir.). Democrat. Methodist, Mason (Shriner, K.T.). Club: Shrine (pres. 1947) (St. Augustine). Home: 10 Hibiscus St Saint Augustine FL 32084 Office: PO Box 75 Saint Augustine FL 32084

STUART, WILLIAM HARRIS, JR., San. engr., govt. ofcl.; b. Nashville, July 7, 1940; s. William H. and Maxie Helen (Allen) S.; B.S. in Civil Engring., Tenn. State U., 1962; M.S. in Water Resources and Environmental Engring., Vanderbilt U., 1970; m. Charlene McClain, Aug. 30, 1966; 1 son, William H. Civil engr. U.S. Bur. Reclamation, Denver, 1962-65, U.S. Soil Conservation Service, Nashville, 1965-68; san. engr. U.S. Environmental Protection Agy., Atlanta, 1970—. Mem. High Mus. of Art, Butler St. YMCA. Registered profl. engr., Tenn., Ga. Mem. Am. Soc. C.E., Tenn. State U. Alumni Assn. Home: 2934 Piney Wood Dr East Point GA 30344 Office: 1421 Peachtree St Atlanta GA 30309

STUBBEMAN, DAVID GRAVES, lawyer; b. Midland, Tex., Aug. 28, 1938; s. Frank Diedrich and Violet (Graves) S.; B.A., So. Methodist U., 1960; LL.B., U. Tex., 1963, J.D., 1963; m. Sue Edmunda Swenson, Aug. 19, 1961; children—William Frank, Susan Kay. Admitted to Tex. bar; practice law, Abilene, Tex., 1966—; asso. atty., Wagstaff, Harrell, Alvis, Erwin & Stubbeman, 1966-69, partner, 1970—. Chmn. Citizens for Better Govt., Abilene, 1972—. Bd. dirs. West Tex. Rehab. Center, Abilene. Served to lt. comdr. Judge Adv. Gen. Corps, USNR, 1963-66. Mem. Abilene Jr. C. of C. (past treas.), Abilene Jr. Bar Assn. (pres.), Tex. Jr. Bar. Assn. (state dir. 1970-71), Abilene (sec. treas. 1970), Am. bar assns., State Bar Tex., Tex. Assn. Def. Counsel, Tex. Utility Lawyers Assn. Presbyn. (deacon). Rotarian. Home: 1241 Leggett Dr Abilene TX 79605 Office: 605 Citizens Nat Bank Bldg Abilene TX 79601

STUBBLEFIELD, DAVID EDWARD, holding co. exec.; b. Fayetteville, Ark., May 26, 1937; s. William Hugh and Evelyn (Robertson) S.; B.S. in Bus. Adminstrn., U. Ark., 1958; m. Suzanne Scudder, Dec. 27, 1958; children—David, Tracy. With Ark. Best Freight System, Inc., Ft. Smith, 1959-67, dir. research and planning, 1965-67; v.p. Data Tronics Corp. subsidiary Ark. Best Corp., 1967-70, pres., 1970-73, treas. parent co., 1974—. Mem. exec. bd., v.p. Western Area council Boy Scouts Am.; mem. Ft. Smith Sch. Bd., 1970—. Bd. dirs. Sebastian County chpt. A.R.C. Served to capt. AUS, 1958-66. Baptist (deacon). Home: 3501 S 35th St Fort Smith AR 72901 Office: 310 Towson Av Fort Smith AR 72901

STUBBLEFIELD, FRANK ALBERT, congressman; b. Murray, Ky., Apr. 5, 1907; s. Vernon C. and Virginia (Wilson) S.; student U. Ariz., 1927; B.S. in Commerce, U. Ky., 1932; m. Odessa Boaz, Feb. 4, 1934; children—Jennye Sue, Frankie Ann, Mary B. Retail druggist, Murray, Ky., 1935-58; mem. 86th-92d Congresses, 1st Dist. Ky. Mem. city council, Murray, Ky., 1939-43; mem. Ky. R.R. Commn., 1951-58. Served as lt. (j.g.) USNR, World War II. Mem. Murray C. of C. (dir.), Alpha Tau Omega. Democrat. Methodist. Elk, Rotarian. Home: 716 Poplar St Murray KY 42071 also 4619 Albemarle St Washington DC 20016 Office: House Office Bldg Washington DC 20525

STUBBS, HAL SESSION, physician; b. Douglas, Ga., Apr. 26, 1930; s. Clyde McDonald and Allie (Fales) S.; student S. Ga. Coll., 1947-49; B.S., Tulane U., 1951, M.D., 1955; m. Barbara A. Brown, June 22, 1956; children—Philip, Missy, Mark, Molly. Intern, Ohio State U. Hosps., 1955-56; resident urology Med. Coll. Ga., 1958-62; practice medicine, specializing in urology, Bristol, Tenn.; chief staff Bristol Meml. Hosp., 1974—. Served with AUS, 1956-58. Diplomate Am. Bd. Urology; mem. A.M.A., Am. Urology Assn., Tenn. Med. Assn., Southwestern Va., Sullivan County med. socs., Alpha Omega Alpha. Home: 1728 Holston Dr Bristol TN 37620 Office: 28 Midway St Bristol TN 37620

STUBBS, ROBERT SHERWOOD II, educator, govt. ofcl.; b. St. Louis, Nov. 11, 1922; s. Sherwood Obear and Marie Clifton (deVaux) S.; student Johns Hopkins, 1939-41; A.B., U. Ala., 1942; J.D., George Washington U., 1952; m. Laura Ann Cobb, June 26, 1943; children—Robert Sherwood III, Anna Lucille. Commd. 2d lt. U.S. Marine Corps, 1943, advanced through grades to lt. col., 1959; ret., 1962; admitted to Ala. bar, 1952, D.C. bar, 1952, Hawaii bar, 1957, Ga. bar, 1968; instr. East Carolina Coll., 1959-62; asst. prof. law Emory U., Atlanta, 1963, asso. prof., 1964, prof., 1965-73; exec. asst. atty. gen. Ga., 1973—; spl. cons. Ga. State Bar Spl. Com. on Assistance to Indigent Criminal Defendants, 1964-67, Am. Bar Assn. standing com. on Legal Aid and Indigent Defendants, 1965-66; spl. cons. criminal justice com. State Bar Ga., 1967-68, mem., 1968-69; counsellor So. Regional Edn. Bd., 1967; mem. legal com. Ga. Com. on Crime and Delinquency, 1963-69, chmn. legal com., 1967-68; mem. Ga. Juvenile Ct. Law Study Com., 1967-71; cons. profl. adv. panel Ga. Council Crime and Delinquency, 1969-73; asso. counsel Met. Atlanta Commn. Crime and Delinquency, 1972; cons. Ga. Dept. Family and Children Services, 1969, Ga. Dept. Edn., 1971-72, Ga. Dept. Human Resources, 1972; research cons. Gov.'s Commn. Jud. Processes, 1972-73. vice chmn. Criminal Justice Supervisory Bd., Atlanta Region Met. Planning Commn., 1971-72. Mem. Am., Ga. (mem. com. law schs. and practicing attys. 1971-73), Decatur-DeKalb bar assns., Am. Trial Lawyers Assn., Am. Judicature Soc., Am. Assn. U. Profs., Nat. Council on Family Relations, Scribes, Tudor and Stuart Soc., Order of Coif, Kappa Alpha, Phi Delta Epsilon, Omicron Delta Kappa, Phi Delta Phi. Club: Atlanta Lawyers. Author: Marriage and Divorce in Georgia, 1964; Under the Gun, 1966; Georgia Law of Children, 1969; Criminal Practice and Procedure in Georgia in 1863, 1971; (with Lucy Henritze) Social Worker in Deprivation

Proceedings, 1973; Georgia Appellate Court Jurisdiction, 1973. Contbr. articles to profl. jours. Home: 2630 Woodwardia Rd NE Atlanta GA 30345

STUCKEY, BYRON WELDON, computer co. exec.; b. Fort Worth, July 18, 1932; s. Herbert Floyd and Mollie Lee (Still) S.; B.B.A., U. Tex., 1964; J.D., So. Meth. U., 1968; m. Delores Ann Estes, June 6, 1951; children—Dave Weldon, Keith Alan. Sec. to corporate treas. Richardson Oils, Inc., Fort Worth, 1956-61; accountant, controller Campbell, Henderson & Co., Dallas, 1961-65; sec.-controller Moran Bros., Inc., Shaft Drillers, Inc., Wichita Falls, Tex., 1965-67; pres. Nat. Data Communications, Inc., Dallas, 1967—. Served with USCG, 1952-56. Mem. Am. Judicature Soc., Am., Tex., Dallas bar assns., Dallas Forum, Delta Theta Phi. Baptist. Home: 3720 Pallos Verdas Dr Dallas TX 75229 Office: 2997 LBJ Freeway Dallas TX 75234

STUCKEY, JASPER L., geologist; b. Princeton, N.C., July 24, 1891; s. John Haywood and Betty Eliza (Bunn) S.; A.B., U. N.C., 1918, Am., 1920; student Grenoble U., 1919; Ph.D., Cornell U., 1924; D.Sc., N.C. State U., 1965; m. Anabel Stephenson, June 23, 1920 (dec.); m. 2nd, Gladys Brinkley, July 24, 1936; 1 son, William Jasper. Tchr. pub. sch., Johnston County, 1910-11; supt. Limestone Plant, N.C. Dept. Agr., Bridgeport, Tenn., 1917-18; asst. geologist, N.C. Geol. Survey, 1920, 21, 24 and summers 1922-23; instr. geology, U. N.C., 1921, Cornell U., 1922-24; state geologist, N.C. Dept. Conservation and Devel., 1925-26, acting dir., 1925; prof. geology, N.C. State Coll., 1926-55; mem. adminstrv. council Greater U. N.C., 1937-41; sr. geologist U.S. Army Engrs., 1930; became state geologist N.C. Dept. Conservation, 1940, head div. mineral resources, 1955, now retired; emergency co-ordinator of mines for N.C., 1941-43. Dir. N.C. State Coll. Minerals Research Lab., 1946-54, Served as cpl. Co. E., 323d Inf., A.E.F., 1918-19. Recipient Gov.'s Distinguished Citizens award, 1964. Fellow A.A.A.S., Mineral. Soc. Am., Geol. Soc. Am. (chmn. Southeastern sect. 1964-65), Am. Geog. Soc.; mem. N.C. Acad. Sci. (pres. 1940), Am. Ceramic Soc., Am. Inst. Mining, Metall. and Petroleum Engrs., Assn. Am. State Geologists (pres. 1958-59), Soc. Econ. Geologists, N.C. Soc. Engrs., Carolina Geol. Soc. (pres. 1947), Keramos (hon.), Sigma Gamma Epsilon, Phi Kappa Phi, Sigma Xi, Sigma Chi. Clubs: Engineers, Civitan, Torch (Raleigh, N.C.). Contbr. to bulls. and tech. jours. Home: 1911 Sunset Dr Raleigh NC 27608

STUCKEY, KENNETH FAIRCHILD, ednl. adminstr.; b. Columbia, S.C., Nov. 11, 1930; s. William Louis and Mable (Jackson) S.; B.A., U. N.C., 1953; postgrad. Boston U., 1961; M.Ed., U. S.C., 1971; postgrad. Middle Tenn. State U., 1971, U. S.C., 1972—; m. Josephine Elizabeth Watts, Jan. 3, 1960. French and English instr. Charlotte (N.C.) Country Day Sch., 1954-56; head lower sch. Aiken Prep. Sch., 1957-68; grad. asst. U. S.C., 1968-70; prin., headmaster Webb Sch., Bell Buckle, Tenn., 1970-73; founding headmaster Univ. Heights Acad., Hopkinsville, Ky., 1973—. Founder, co-dir. Aiken (S.C.) Reading Clinic, 1961-68; resident dir. Camp Agawan-Kezar, Lovell, Me., 1962-63. Pres. honor council Aiken County dist. Boy Scouts Am., 1968. Mem. Phi Delta Kappa. Episcopalian. Rotarian. Address: Box 812 Hopkinsville KY 42240

STUCKEY, WALTER JACKSON, JR., physician; b. Fairfield, Ala., Mar. 6, 1927; s. Walter Jackson and Lena (Brackin) S.; B.S., U. Ala., 1947; M.D., Tulane U., 1951; m. Mildred Creel Roberts, Nov. 27, 1952; children—Walter Jackson III, John Hamlin, James Allan. Intern, Charity Hosp. La., New Orleans, 1951-52; resident in gen. practice Lafayette (La.) Charity Hosp., 1952; resident in internal medicine Tulane med. service Charity Hosp. La., VA Hosp. New Orleans, 1955-57; fellow, instr. dept. medicine Tulane U. Sch. Medicine, 1958-60, asst. prof., 1960-62, asso. prof., 1962-68, prof., 1968—, chief sect. hematology, 1963—, sr. vis. physician, 1968—; practice medicine specializing in hematology, New Orleans; cons. VA, USPHS, Meth., Mercy hosps., Hotel Dieu, New Orleans, Huey P. Long Charity Hosp., Pineville, La., VA Hosp., Alexandria, La., Lallie Kemp Charity Hosp., Independence, La., East Jefferson Hosp., Touro Infirmary. Served with USNR, 1952-54. Bd. dirs. New Orleans chpt. Leukemia Soc., Inc., Cancer Assn. Greater New Orleans. Fellow A.C.P.; mem. A.A.A.S., Am. Assn. Cancer Edn., A.M.A., Am. Soc. Internal Medicine, La., Orleans Parish med. socs., New Orleans Acad. Internal Medicine, N.Y. Acad. Scis., La. Heart Assn. (undergrad. and postgrad. research coms. 1966—), Am. Soc. Hematology, Am. Soc. Clin. Oncology, So. Med. Assn. Methodist. Home: 7325 Cameo St New Orleans LA 70124 Office: 1430 Tulane Av New Orleans LA 70112

STUCKEY, WILLIAMSON SYLVESTER, JR., congressman; b. Eastman, Ga., May 25, 1935; s. Williamson S. and Ethel (Mullis) S.; B.B.A., U. Ga., 1956, LL.B., 1959; m. Ethelyn McMillan, July 16, 1963; children—Williamson Sylvester III, Stuart Anne, Scott M., Stephanie, Jay-Gould. Former exec. v.p. Stuckey's Stores, Inc.; former pres. Stuckey Pecan Co., Stuckey Timberlands, Inc.; adviser to Stuckey div. Pet Milk Co.; mem. 90th-93d congresses from 8th Ga. Dist., mem. House Interstate and fgn. commerce com., finance and commerce subcom., D.C. com. Vice chmn. Central Ga. council Boy Scouts Am.; mem. Alumni Council. Bd. govs. Woodward Acad. Named Ga. Jaycee Man Yr., 1969. Mem. Nat. Young Presidents Orgn., Eastman Jr. C. of C. (past pres.), Gridiron, Sigma Alpha Epsilon, Phi Delta Phi. Democrat. Episcopalian. Mason, Elk, Rotarian. Home: College St Eastman GA 31023 Office: PO Box 310 Eastman GA 31023

STUDDARD, DON EDWARD, lawyer; b. Brownwood, Tex., Oct. 5, 1932; s. John Rue and Fannie Lou (Bird) S.; B.B.A., U. Tex., 1953, LL.B., 1958; m. Susan Newcombe, Aug. 10, 1957; children—Linda, Randall, Wesley. Admitted to Tex. bar, 1957; practiced in El Paso, Tex., 1958—; mem. firm Potash, Cameron, Bernat & Studdard, 1958-69, Studdard, Melby and Schwartz, 1969—. Trustee McMurray Coll.; bd. dirs. El Paso Christian Home for Girls. Served with AUS, 1953-55. Mem. Am., Tex., El Paso bar assns. Methodist (pres. bd. trustees 1968). Home: 604 Satelite St El Paso TX 79912 Office: 924 Southwestern Nat Bank Bldg El Paso TX 79901

STUDER, DALE FREDERICK, coal co. exec.; b. nr. New Philadelphia, O., Oct. 2, 1921; s. John W. and Louise (Finzer) S.; grad. high sch.; grad. Dale Carnagie course, 1973; m. Kathryn L. Anreas, Aug. 25, 1946; children—Paula Gay, Deborah Elaine. Prin. owner Walden's Ridge Coal Co., 1953—; pres., prin. owner, Tri-State Coal Sales, Chattanooga, 1957—; prin. owner Pioneer Coal Co., Chattanooga, 1974—. Republican Central committeeman, Sugarcreek, O., 1947-49. Served with USAAF, 1942-46; ETO. Mem. Inst. Mining Engrs. Republican. Methodist (dir. 1955-58). Home: 952 Runyan Dr Chattanooga TN 37405 Office: Box 69 Chattanooga TN 37401

STULL, RAYMOND EUGENE, govt. ofcl.; b. Tuscarawas, O., Aug. 15, 1922; s. John Gabriel and Grace (Frantz) S.; B.S. in Edn., Ohio State U., 1947; m. Margaret Kathleen Meese, Dec. 14, 1941; children—David, Karen, Mark, Kris, Kim, Jon. Tchr. high sch., Bowerston, O., 1947-49; reporter Daily Reporter, Dover, 1949-50, sports editor, 1950-52; sports editor Daily Jeffersonian, Cambridge, 1952-54; state-regional editor Internat. News Service, Columbus, 1954-58; pub. relations dir. Republican State Hdqrs., Columbus, 1961-65; asst. pub. relations dir. Rep. Nat. Com., 1965-69; dir. pub. information Small Bus. Adminstrn., Washington, 1969-71, dir. pub. affairs, 1971—. Free-lance writer, 1964—. Served with AUS, World War II. Republican. Mem. Moravian Ch. Home: 1632 Macon St McLean VA 22101 Office: 1441 L St NW Washington DC 20006

STULLKEN, DONALD EDWARD, aerospace operations exec.; b. Sullivan, Ill., Apr. 11, 1920; s. Edward H. and Mary (Shumacher) S.; B.A., DePauw U., 1941; M.S., Purdue U., 1942, Ph.D., 1950; D.Sc., DePauw U., 1967; m. Elizabeth Russell, Mar. 7, 1942; children—Russell E., William G., W. Kurt. Asst. prof. Purdue U., Lafayette, Ind., 1953-54; aviation physiologist Chief Naval Air Tng. Staff, U.S. Navy, Pensacola, Fla., 1954-62; chief flight operations and recovery NASA, Johnson Space Center, Houston, 1962—. Mem. Seabrook (Tex.) Vol. Fire Dept., 1962-70, pres., 1965; chmn. Clear Creek Swim League, 1966-67. Bd. dirs. Gulf Coast Sci. Found. Served with USNR, 1943-46, 50-53. Mem. A.A.A.S., U.S. Naval Inst., Sigma Xi. Methodist. Home: 839 Timbercove Dr Seabrook TX 77586 Office: NASA Johnson Space Center Houston TX 77058

STUNTZ, HOMER CLYDE, physician; b. Lahore, Punjab, India, Feb. 25, 1923 (parents Am. citizens); s. Clyde Bronson and Florence Ada (Watters) S.; came to U.S., 1941; student Wesleyan U., 1941-43, Mich. State Coll., 1944, U. Tex., 1946-48; M.D., Southwestern Med. Sch., 1952; m. Billie Jean Williams, June 7, 1952; children—Beverly Ann, Jean Allison, Philip Williams. Intern, Baylor U. Hosp., Dallas, 1953; resident in surgery McKinney VA Hosp., 1954; gen. practice medicine, Orange, Tex., 1954—; chief staff Orange Meml. Hosp., 1959. Bd. dirs. Orange County Cancer Soc., Commn. on Alcoholism. Served to 2d lt. USAAF, 1943-46. Mem. A.M.A., So., Tex. med. assns., Orange County Med. Soc. (pres. 1958), C. of C., Conservative Union, Econ. found. Home: 2223 24th St Orange TX 77630 Office: 1214 16th St Orange TX 77630

STURDEVANT, JOHN URQUHART, public relations exec.; b. N.Y.C., Nov. 2, 1913; s. John Thomson and Mary Pauline (Bannon) S.; B.A. Columbia, 1934. Asso. editor Am. Weekly, N.Y.C., 1935-60, mng. editor, 1960-63; editor Pictorial Living Mag., N.Y.C., 1963-66; pub. relations cons., account exec. Carl Byoir & Assos., N.Y.C., 1966-69; pub. relations cons. Sturdevant Assos., Palm Beach, Fla., 1969—. Mem. Pub. Relations Soc. Am. Clubs: Silurians, Dutch Treat, Overseas Press (N.Y.C.). Address: 596 N County Rd Palm Beach FL 33480

STURDIVANT, LAURA DRAKE SATTERFIELD (MRS. EDWIN COLEMAN STURDIVANT), hist. and med. writer; b. Port Gibson, Miss., Aug. 31, 1913; d. Milling Marion and Laura (Drake) Satterfield; B.A. magna cum laude, Millsaps Coll., 1934; m. William Harrell, Oct. 12, 1933 (dec. 1969); m. 2d, Edwin Coleman Sturdivant, Nov. 17, 1973. Research and editorial asst. Miss. Dept. Archives and History, Jackson, 1941-47, 50, research asst., 1961-63, asst. dir. information and edn. div., 1973—. med. sec. VA Hosp., Little Rock, 1950-52; publs. writer med. scis. army med. service Army Med. Service Sch., Brooke Army Med. Center, San Antonio, 1952-58; publs. writer med. scis. bur. state services Communicable Disease Center, USPHS, Atlanta, 1959-60. Mem. Miss. history adv. Com. Miss. Authority Ednl. TV, 1973—. Recipient Gautier Hist. Article award South Miss. Festival of Arts, 1967, Old Spanish Fort Poetry award, 1968, 69. Mem. Soc. Am. Archivists, Am., So. hist. assns., Miss. Folklore Soc. (pres. 1971-72), Internat. Platform Assn., Am. Med. Writers Assn., Nat. League Am. Pen Women (pres. Magnolia br. 1971-74), Med. Library Assn., Miss. Hist. Soc., Miss. Geneal. Soc., Colonial Dames Am. (chpt. v.p.), A.A.A.S., Millsaps Coll. Alumni Assn. (dir. 1971-74). D.A.R., Kappa Delta. United Methodist (mem. archives and history commn). Club: Jackson Yacht. Author: (with J.H. Hendrix, Jr.) A. History of the American Association of Plastic Surgeons, 1971. Asst. editor Jour. Miss. History, 1963—; cons. editor Enchantment of Am. series; asst. editor, contbr. to A History of Mississippi, 2 vols., 1972; indexer, author preface reprint Recollections of Mississippi and Mississippians (Reuben Davis), 1972. Contbr. to hist. publs. Home: 820 Arlington St Jackson MS 39202 Office: Miss Dept Archives and History PO Box 571 Jackson MS 39205

STURGEON, BENJAMIN LEE, lawyer; b. Pampa, Tex., Mar. 20, 1937; s. Aaron Anderson and Marie Elizabeth (Bastin) S.; B.S., Tex. Christian U., 1959; J.D., So. Methodist U., 1962; m. Sandra Hartman, Aug. 30, 1958; children—Benjamin Britt, John H., Lee Scott. Admitted to Tex. bar, 1962, practiced in Pampa, 1966—; mem. firm Sturgeon and Sturgeon, 1966-72, Smith, Waters, Sturgeon and Holt, 1972-74, Stokes Carnahan & Fields, Amarillo, 1974—. Pres., dir. Panhandle Plains Devel. Corp., Pampa, 1969—; sec., treas. Pampa Furniture Co., 1972—. Chmn. Gray County Republican Com., 1969-71. trustee, pres. Pampa Ind. Sch. Dist., 1971-74. Served with USNR, 1962-66; lt. comdr. Res. Mem. Am., Tex. trial lawyers assns., Tex. Criminal Def. Lawyers Assn., Tex., Porter County bar assns. Home: 5505 Brinkman Amarillo TX 79106 Office: 1002 Amarillo Nat Bank Bldg Amarillo TX 79106

STURM, DOROTHY, artist, educator; b. Memphis, Aug. 2, 1911; d. Frank Falls and Charlie Owen (Weddle) Sturm; student Art Students League, N.Y.C., 1930-33; student in biol. scis. and med. illustration Columbia, 1931-32. Illustrator in pathology Columbia Coll. Phys. and Surg., N.Y.C., 1932-34; TVA malarial research for Rockefeller Found. at U. Tenn. Med. Sch., Memphis, 1940-41, malarial research for War Emergency Council, 1942-43; instr. drawing and painting Memphis Acad. Arts, 1937-39, 42, asso. prof., 1966-70, prof. metal arts, 1970—; exclusive contract Betty Parsons Gallery, N.Y.C., 1952-70; hematology study Abbott Labs., 1968—. Saunders Pubs. grantee for blood morphology study, 1954-55. Author: (with Diggs and Bell) Morphology of Human Blood, 1956. Home: 3525 Oakley St Memphis TN 38111 Office: Memphis Academy of Arts Overton Park Memphis TN 38112

STURTEVANT, WILLIAM CURTIS, anthropologist; b. Morristown, N.J., July 26, 1926; s. Alfred Henry and Phoebe (Reed) S.; B.A., U. Cal., Berkeley, 1949; Ph.D., Yale, 1955; m. Theda Maw, July 26, 1952; children—Kinthi D.M., Reed P.M., Alfred B.M. Instr. dept. anthropology, asst. curator anthropology Peabody Mus., Yale, 1954-56; ethnologist, gen. anthropologist Bur. Am. Ethnology, Smithsonian Instn., Washington, 1956-65, gen. anthropologist, curator Nat. Mus. Natural History, 1965—, mem. Center for Study of Man, 1968—. Fulbright lectr. U. Oxford, 1967-68. Served with USNR, 1945-46. Home: 7009 Florida St Chevy Chase MD 20015 Office: Smithsonian Instn Washington DC 20560

STYNE, ALEXANDER FREDERICK, cons. indsl. designer; b. Karisruhe, Germany, Nov. 15, 1913; s. Nathan and Recha (Straus) S.; student Munich (Germany) and Bern (Switzerland) univs., 1932-33; B.Arch., Brussels, Belgium, 1938; m. Mercedes Tarrida-Bertran; children (by previous marriage)—Joanna. Philip. Came to U.S., 1940, naturalized 1944. Mgr. display studio, instr. Reiman Sch., London, Eng., 1939; asst. to Joseph Aronson, designer and author, N.Y.C., 1940; pres. Styne & Ballard, Inc., N.Y.C., 1947-59; instr. N.Y. Sch. Interior Design, 1947-59; indsl. design cons. specializing in lighting and color problems, Miami, Fla., 1959—; instr. Miami Dade Jr. Coll., 1964-68; vis. lectr., critic, U. Miami, 1964—, co-chmn. advanced lighting course, 1971—, adj. prof. elec. engring., 1972—; vis. prof. Sch. Architecture and Art, Auburn (Ala.) U., 1970, U. N.C. at Greensboro, 1971. Pres. Jr. Mus., Hempstead, N.Y., 1957-58. Served with C.E., AUS, 1942-43. Recipient 1st prize lighting competition Southeastern region, 1970. Mem. Am. Inst. Interior Designers (bd. govs. N.Y. chpt. 1956-59, v.p., 1958-59), Municipal Art Soc. N.Y. (com. interior design 1950-53), Indsl. Designers Soc. Am., Inter-Soc. Color Council (del., chmn. problem sub-com. on human response to color), Illuminating Engring. Soc. (nat. allied arts com. 1964—, nat. com. on color 1972—, nat. residence lighting com. 1973—, nat. council judges internat. awards program 1973—), Internat. Commn. on Illumination (fundamentals of visual signalling com). Patentee in field. Contbr. articles profl. jours. Research and devel. work in marine lighting, 1970—. Office: 15206 NE 8th Av Miami FL 33162

SUBAT, JOHN EDWARD, govt. ofcl.; b. Elmhurst, Ill., Dec. 16, 1941; s. John Edward and Mary (Mierzwa) S.; B.S. in Agrl. Econs., U. Ill., 1964; postgrad. Purdue U., 1964-70; m. Nancy Alice Norris, Nov. 27, 1970; 1 son, Ashley. Grad. instr. dept. agrl. econs. Purdue U., Lafayette, Ind., 1966-70; agrl. economist Econ. Research Service, U.S. Dept. Agr., Washington, 1970-71, program analyst Office Planning and Evaluation, Office of Sec., 1971—. Home: 5414 Phelps Luck Dr Columbia MD 21045 Office: Office Planning and Evaluation US Dept Agr 14th and Independence Sts SW Washington DC 20250

SUBERMAN, JACK, educator; b. N.Y.C., June 18, 1920; s. Alex and Frieda (Caskill) S.; B.A., U. Fla., 1946, M.A., 1947; Ph.D., U. N.C., 1954; m. Marcella Kaufman, Jan. 30, 1942; 1 son, Rick Ian. Instr., U. N.C., 1949-50, 52-53; editorial chief Extension Course Inst., USAF, Montgomery, Ala., 1950-52; prof. English, N.C. State U., Raleigh, 1953-67, dir. summer sessions, 1959-67, dir. continuing edn. div., 1965-67; dean Coll. Humanities, Fla. Atlantic U., Boca Raton, Fla., 1967—. Served to capt. USAAF, 1942-45. Decorated Air medal with oak leaf cluster. Mem. Nat. Assn. Coll. and Univ. Summer Sessions (regional v.p. 1964-66), S. Atlantic Modern Lang. Assn., Assn. for Higher Edn., N.E.A. Author: Basic Composition, 1956, 2d edit., 1968; A Language Reader for Writers, 1966. Home: 700 NE 5th Av Boca Raton FL 33432

SUBLETT, CARL CECIL, educator; b. nr. Paintsville, Ky., Feb. 4, 1919; s. Tandy Taylor and Beulah (Fitzpatrick) S.; student Western Ky. State Coll., 1938-40, Univ. Study Center, Florence, Italy, 1945, U. Tenn., 1955-56; m. Helen Crawford Davis, Aug. 20, 1942; children—Carol Taylor (Mrs. Bert Edwin Witham), Eric Davis. Editorial artist Bristol (Va.) Newspaper Corp., 1949-52; asst. mgr. Bristol (Va.) Art Engravers, 1951-53; art dir. Charles S. Kane Co., Knoxville, Tenn., 1954-65; prof. art U. Tenn., 1966—. Exhibited Southeastern Ann., Atlanta, 1954-58, 60, Mid-South Exhbn., Memphis, 1956-58, Va. Intermont Coll., 1949-60, Provincetown Art Festival, 1958, Nashville Festival, 1958-60, Miss. Art Assn., 1958-59, Painters of New South, Birmingham, 1959, Butler Inst. Am. Art., 1959, Smithsonian Instn., 1960, Watercolor U.S.A., 1964-72, Am. Watercolor Soc., N.Y.C., 1972, 73, Tenn. Watercolor Soc., 1972-74, others; work rep. in permanent collections E. Tenn. Coll., Knoxville Art Center, Stephens Coll., Columbia, Mo., Tenn. Botanical Gardens and Fine Arts Center, Hunter Gallery, Chattanooga, others. Served with AUS, 1943-45. Mem. Tenn. Coll. Art Assn., Mus. Modern Art, Birmingham Art Assn., Arts and Craft Soc., Dulin Gallery of Art, Knoxville Water Color Soc., Huntsville Art League. Methodist. Contbr. editorial art Kingsport Times. Home: 2104 Lake Av Knoxville TN 37916

SUBLETT, CHARLES WILLIAM, publishing co. exec.; b. Danville, Va., Jan. 1, 1906; s. Charles William and Martha Ethel (Smith) S.; J.D., U. Va., 1927; m. Marian Lucille Pace, Jan. 8, 1950; children—Charles William, Martha Susan. Admitted to Fla. bar, 1928, Va. bar, 1931; mem. editorial staff Michie Law Pub. Co., Charlottesville, Va., 1927-28, 31-35, editor-in-chief, 1935-44, v.p., 1939—; practiced in West Palm Beach, Fla., 1928-31; pres. dir. Michie City Publs. Co., Charlottesville, 1943—. Mem. Gov's. Democratic Steering Com., 1961. Mem. Am., Va., Charlottesville, Albemarle bar assns., Jefferson Lit. Soc., Phi Alpha Delta. Democrat. Methodist. Mason. Clubs: Farmington Country, Falcon (Charlottesville). Home: 106 Minor Rd Charlottesville VA 22903 Office: 914 Emmet St Charlottesville VA 22902

SUELL, ROBERT MAY, wholesale dry goods co. exec.; b. Nicholasville, Ky., July 7, 1917; s. Albert and Sarah Frances (English) S.; student pub. schs.; m. Nona Christine Brumfield, June 15, 1957. Mgr., Park Theatre, 1941-43, 46-47; asst. credit mgr. Ades-Lexington Dry Goods, Co., Inc., Lexington, Ky., 1947-57, credit mgr., 1957—. Chmn., Jessamine County (Ky.) Republican Party, 1972—, campaign chmn., 1972-73. Served with AUS, 1943-46. Mem. Nat., Ky., Jessamine County (2d v.p., dir. 1973—) hist. socs. Mem. Christian Ch. Mason (32 degree, Shriner), Odd Fellow, Home: 121 Bell Ct Nicholasville KY 40356 Office: 249 E Main St Lexington KY 40507

SUGERMAN, HARRY GERSHON, wholesale co. exec.; b. Chgo., Aug. 15, 1902; s. Louis and Rose (Sharfman) S.; student Chgo. Bus. Coll., 1919-20; m. Sylvia Fisher, Aug. 22, 1929 (dec. Aug. 1972); children—Charles Fisher, Judy (Mrs. Sidney Stahl). With Louis Sugerman & Son, Inc., Chgo., 1920-42; mgr. Dixie Supply Co., San Antonio, 1942-45; owner Harry Sugerman, Inc., wholesale military insignia, accessories and supplies, 1945—, chmn. bd., 1945—; chmn. bd. Vision Electronics, Inc., 1951—, Cadet Mfg. Corp., 1955—. Mem. San Antonio chpt. U.S.O., 1963—; mem. San Antonio chpt. Jewish Social Service Fedn., 1958—; co-chmn. bldg. com. Golden Manor Home for Aged, 1957—. Home: 700 E Hildebrand St Olmos Towers Apts 405 San Antonio TX 78212 Office: 3419 E Commerce St San Antonio TX 78219

SUGG, HAROLD GRAY, newspaper editor; b. Greenville, N.C., Apr. 14, 1916; s. B. B. and Lillian (Gray) S.; B.S., Davidson Coll., 1937; M.A., Old Dominion U., 1971; m. Mary Jane Nesbitt, Feb. 12, 1944 (dec.); children—Harold Gray, William N., Elizabeth E. City editor Stanly News and Press, Albemarle, N.C., 1938; polit. reporter, asso. editor The Virginian-Pilot, Norfolk, Va., 1939-57, asst. pub., 1957-65; sr. v.p., dir. Landmark Communications, Inc., Norfolk, 1965-71; editor editorial page Roanoke (Va.) Times, 1971—. Pres. Friends of Norfolk Pub. Library, 1955-61; bd. dirs. Norfolk Pub. Library, 1955-61; bd. dirs. Norfolk Pub. Library, 1962—. Served to capt. AUS, 1942-46. Mem. Phi Gamma Delta. Clubs: Norfolk (Va.) Yacht and Country; Shenandoah, Roanoke Rotary. Home: 1810 Greenwood Rd Roanoke VA 24015 Office: PO Box 2491 Roanoke VA 24010

SUGG, ROBERT WHITTINGTON, dentist; b. Durham, N.C., July 15, 1926; s. Avery Gordon and Cammie Elizabeth (Whittington) S.; A.B., Duke, 1949; D.D.S., U. N.C., 1955; m. Dorothy Maria Dezern, June 10, 1950; children—Deborah Anne, Patricia Louise, Robert W. Gen. practice dentistry, Durham, 1955—. Mem. N.C. State Bd. Dental Examiners, 1971—. Bd. dirs. Gov. Morehead Sch. Served with USNR, 1944-46. Mem. Am. Dental Assn., N.C. Dental Soc., Am. Assn. Dental Examiners, Am. Soc. Dentistry Children, Omicron Kappa Upsilon, Beta Theta Pi, Psi Omega. Home: 510 Brookwood Dr Durham NC 27707 Office: 209 S Gregson St Durham NC 27701

SUGGS, MARION JACK, clergyman, educator; b. Electra, Tex., June 5, 1924; s. Claude Frank and Lottie Maye (Gibson) S.; B.A., U. Tex., 1946; B.D., Tex. Christian U., 1949; Ph.D., Duke, 1954; m. Ruth Lee Barge, Nov. 13, 1943; children—Adena (Mrs. Jerry Beck), James Robert, David Nathan. Ordained to ministry Christian Ch. (Disciples of Christ), 1948; minister churches in Austin, Tex., 1943-46, Gladewater, Tex., 1948-50, Wendell, N.C., 1950-52; mem. faculty Tex. Christian U., Ft. Worth, 1952—, prof. N.T., 1956—. Chmn. Am. Textual Criticisn Seminar, 1965, Gospel Seminar, 1969-72; mem. exec. com. Internat. Greek N.T. Project, 1963-74. Recipient Distinguished Alumnus award Tex. Christian U., 1973. Am. Council Learned Socs. fellow, 1963-64. Mem. Am. Acad. Religion (pres. S.W. sect. 1960), Am. Assn. Theol. Schs. (fellow 1963-64), Soc. Bibl. Lit. (pres. S.W. sect. 1968), Studiorum Novi Testamentum Societas, Phi Beta Kappa, Alpha Gamma Delta, Pi Gamma Mu, Theta Phi. Author: The Gospel Story, 1960; Wisdom, Christology and Law in Matthew's Gospel, 1970. Co-editor: Studies in the History and Text of the New Testament, 1967; mem. editorial bd. Jour. Bibl. Lit., 1970—. Contbr. numerous articles to profl. jours. Home: 5605 Winifred Dr Fort Worth TX 76133

SUH, MOON WON, statistician; b. Seoul, Korea, Sept. 30, 1936; s. Hee Suk and Woo Soon (Lee) S.; B.S., Seoul Nat. U., 1961; M.S., N.C. State U., 1964, Ph.D., 1969; m. Chisook Kim, Sept. 14, 1963; children—John D., Carolyn E. Came to U.S., 1962, naturalized, 1970. Research fellow Nat. Knitwear Mfrs. Assn., Sch. Textiles, N.C. State U., 1963-67, Themis research fellow U.S. Dept. Def., 1968-69; research analyst Burlington Industries, Inc., Greensboro, N.C., 1969—. Mem. Am. Statis. Assn., Inst. Math. Statistics, Biometric Soc., Sigma Xi. Home: 1907 Forest Valley Rd Greensboro NC 27410 Office: 3330 W Friendly Av Greensboro NC 27420

SUITERS, LARRY THOMAS, lawyer; b. Washington, Sept. 18, 1940; s. Franklin Thomas and Kathryn (Otwell) S.; A.B. with honors, Coll. William and Mary, 1962; LL.B., U. Va., 1965; m. Diane Stuart Lovewell, July 6, 1972; 1 son, Tyler Paige. Admitted to Va. bar, 1965; mem. firm Kinney, Smith, Barham, Arlington, Va., 1965-74; sr. partner Barham, Radigan & Switers, Arlington, 1974—. Mem. Arlington County Planning Commn., 1969—. Republican nominee for Va. Senate, 1971; mem. Arlington County Rep. Com., 1967-73, vice chmn., 1971—. Bd. dirs. Arlington Com. of 100, 1973-74. Served with AUS, 1967. Mem. Arlington County (treas., exec. com., pres.-elect 1974-75), Va., Am. bar assns., Va. State Bar (10th dist. grievance and ethics com. 1973—), Va. Trial Lawyers Assn., Arlington Jr. C. of Co. (Outstanding Young Man 1971). Club: Civitan. Home: 4745 Little Falls Rd Arlington VA 22207 Office: 2009 N 14th St PO Box 966 Arlington VA 22216

SUKI, WADI NAGIB, physician; b. Khartoum, Sudan, Oct. 26, 1934; s. Nagib Khalil and Fahima Hamdi (Hariz) S.; B.S., Am. U. Beirut, 1955, M.D. with distinction, 1959; m. Lailah Janet Stephan, May 6, 1967; children—Leila, Ramzy, Lenora, Wade. Came to U.S., 1959, naturalized, 1964. Fellow in exptl. medicine U. Tex. Southwestern Med. Sch., Dallas, 1959-61; resident in internal medicine Parkland Meml. Hosp., Dallas, 1961-63; fellow in nephrology U. Tex. Southwestern Med. Sch., 1963-65, instr., 1965-66, asst. prof. internal medicine, 1966-68; asso. prof. medicine Baylor Coll. Medicine, Houston, 1968-71, prof., 1971—, chief renal sect., 1968—; practice medicine, specializing in internal medicine and kidney diseases, Dallas, 1965-68, Houston, 1968—; chief renal sect. Meth. Hosp., Houston; attending physician Ben Taub Gen. Hosp., Houston; cons. medicine VA Hosp., Houston. Chmn. med. adv. bd. Kidney Found. Houston and Greater Gulf Coast, 1969-71; chmn. nat. med. adv. council Nat. Kidney Found., 1971-73, mem. sci. adv. bd., 1972—; mem. exec. com. council on kidney in cardiovascular disease Am. Heart Assn., 1971—; cons. in nephrology Wilford Hall USAF Med. Center, Lackland AFB, Tex. Recipient Research and Training Grants, NIH, USPHS, 1968—. Fellow A.C.P.; mem. Internat., Am. socs. nephrology, A.A.A.S., Am. Fedn. Clin. Research, Am. Physiol. Soc., Am., So. (sec.-treas.) socs. clin. investigation, European Dialysis and Transplantation Assn. (asso.), Alpha Omega Alpha. Mem. editorial bd. The Kidney, 1970—. Contbr. articles to profl. jours. Home: 4926 Glenmeadow St Houston TX 77035 Office: 6516 Bertner St Houston TX 77025

SULLENBERGER, ARA BROOCKS COX (MRS. HAL J. SULLENBERGER), educator; b. Amarillo, Tex., Jan. 3, 1933; d. Carl Clarence and Ara Frances (Broocks) Cox; student Randolph-Macon Woman's Coll., 1951-52, So. Meth. U., 1952-53, Arlington State Coll., 1953, Amarillo Coll., 1953-54; B.A., Tex. Technol. U., 1955, M.A., 1958; postgrad. Tex. Christian U., 1963-64, North Tex. State U., 1969—; m. Hal Joseph Sullenberger, Nov. 2, 1952; children—Hal Joseph, Ara Broocks. Tchr. math. Lubbock (Tex.) High Sch., 1955-56; instr. math. Tex. Technol. Coll., 1956-63; chmn. dept. math. Ft. Worth County Day Sch., 1964-67; instr. Tarrant County Jr. Coll., Ft. Worth, 1967-70, asst. prof. math., 1970—; cons. math. Project Change, 1967-68; speaker numerous math. councils. Sec. Alcoholics United, 1970-71. Recipient award for teaching excellence Gen. Dynamics of Ft. Worth, 1966. Mem. Math. Assn. Am., Nat. Council Tchrs. Math., Tex. Jr. Coll. Tchrs. Assn., Am. Assn. U. Profs., Jr. League, Pi Beta Phi. Episcopalian. Club: Ft. Worth Architects Wives. Home: 600 Eastwood Av Fort Worth TX 76107 Office: 5300 Campus Dr Fort Worth TX 76119

SULLENBERGER, HAL JOSEPH, architect; b. Stephenville, Tex., Mar. 26, 1933; s. Hal McCallom and Madeline (Funkhouser) S.; student Arlington State Coll., 1952-53, Amarillo Coll., 1953-54; B.Arch., Tex. Technol. U., 1962; m. Ara Broocks Cox, Nov. 2, 1952; children—Hal Joseph Jr., Ara Broocks. Archtl. draftsman firm Wilson, Patterson, Sowden, Dunlap, & Epperly, Fort Worth, 1962-63; draftsman firm Preston M. Geren, Fort Worth, 1963-67, job. capt., 1968-71; field supr. firm Albert S. Komatsu, Fort Worth, 1967; job capt. firm Lawrence D. White, Fort Worth, 1967-68, 71-72; asso. architect firm Robert L. Wright, Fort Worth, 1972-73; project architect firm Thomas E. Stanley, Dallas, 1973, chief prodn. architect, 1973—. Served with USNR, 1950-64. Mem. A.I.A. (corporate mem.; chmn. edn. com.), Constrn. Specifications Inst. (dir. 1973-75). Episcopalian. Designer Arlington (Tex.) Community Center, 1971. Home: 600 Eastwood Dr Fort Worth TX 76107 Office: PO Box 1554 Dallas TX 75219

SULLINS, JOHN KENNETH, environmental engring. firm exec.; b. Ogden Center, Mich., Nov. 27, 1923; s. David Wilkerson and Eletra (Sallows) S.; student East Tenn. State Coll., 1940-42; B. Sc. in Chem. Engring., U. Tenn., 1948; m. Betty Sue Starr, June 6, 1947; children—Glenn Kenneth, Douglas Alan, Carma Starr. With The Mead Corp., various locations, 1949-73; pres. Aquatair Appalachian Corp., Kingsport, Tenn., 1968-73; pres. Sullins Ecology Engring., Inc., Kingsport, Tenn., 1973—. Registered profl. engr., Tenn. Mem. Nat., Tenn. socs. profl. engrs., Am. Inst. Chem. Engrs., Water Pollution Control Fedn., Air Pollution Control Assn., T.A.P.P.I., Am. Legion. Elk, Moose. Clubs: Ridgefields Country, Metropolitan Dinner (Kingsport). Patentee in field. Home: 2005 E Sevier Av Kingsport TN 37664 Office: 1451 E Center St Kingsport TN 37664

SULLINS, ROBERT, real estate broker; b. Terrell, Tex., Nov. 25, 1933; s. Robert Timothy and Rossie (Crawford) S.; B.S., Tex. A. and M. U., 1955; m. Sue Parnell, June 18, 1954; children—Robert David, Dan Crawford, Michael Ross, Patrick Hogan, Susan Maureen. Design engr. Gen. Dynamics Co., Ft. Worth, 1957-62; real estate salesman Morris & Pruitt, Inc., Arlington, Tex., 1963-64; pres. Sullins Co., real estate, Arlington, 1965—. Tarrant County chmn. Milford for U.S. Congress, 1972; mem. Arlington Bd. Equalization, 1972. Served with AUS, 1955-57. Recipient Distinguished Community Service award City of Arlington, 1973. Mem. Nat., Tex. (dir. 1972-74) assns. realtors, Nat. Assn. Homebuilders, Tex. Assn. Builders, Ft. Worth Builders Assn. (dir. 1971-73), Arlington Bd. Realtors (dir. 1970-73, pres. 1971, Realtor of Year award 1972). Home: 1511 Tatum St Arlington TX 76012 Office: 812 E Park Row Arlington TX 76010

SULLIVAN, A(NNA) MANNEVILLETTE, metallurgist, govt. ofcl.; b. Washington, Aug. 18, 1913; d. Francis Paul and Vilette (Anderson) Sullivan; student Wellesley Coll., 1931-33; A.B., George Washington U., 1935; postgrad. Cath. U., 1935-36, M.S., U. Md., 1955. Asst. metallurgist Carnegie Inst. Washington, 1942-45; metallurgist Nat. Bur. Standards, Washington, 1945-46, U.S. Naval Research Lab., Washington, 1947—. Mem. Research Soc. Am., Am. Soc. Metals, Am. Soc. Testing Materials, Alpha Delta Pi. Iota Sigma Pi. Club: Altrusa Internat. Research in fracture of metals with spl. reference to fracture mechanics. Home: 4000 Massachusetts Av NW Washington DC 20016 Office: Naval Research Lab Washington DC 20375

SULLIVAN, CHARLES ANDREW, corp. exec.; b. Washington, Nov. 3, 1920; s. Michael Francis and Gertrude Lavinia (Miller) S.; student George Washington U., 1938-42, Cambridge U., 1943-44; m. Katharine Reynolds McCarthy, Apr. 3, 1943. Comml. specialist Treasury Dept., 1940-43; economist RFC, War Assets Adminstrn., 1946-48; internat. economist Munitions Bd., 1948-51; staff Office Sec. Def. for Internat. Security Affairs, 1951-57, chief Far East div., 1951-52, chief Western hemisphere Far East and South Asian affairs, 1952-53, dir. Office Fgn. Politico-Mil. Policy, 1953-55, dir. Office Internat. Affairs, 1955-57; asst. dir. ODM, 1957-59; dep. spl. asst. to sec. of state for disarmament and atomic energy, 1959-60; spl. asst. to under sec. of state, 1960-61; asst. to sec. of treasury, 1961-66; pres., chmn. bd. dirs. Hispano Corp. Am., 1967-71; pres. Charles A. Sullivan Assos., 1970—; dir. Chemalloy Minerals, Ltd., Templet Industries; mem. internat. adv. bd. Am. Security & Trust Co. Chmn. indsl. moblzn. com. NATO, 1950-51; def. adviser to delegations ANZUS, NATO and SEATO councils, 1952-57, fgn. minister's confs. in Berlin, 1954, Geneva, 1954, 55, 59, Summit Conf., Geneva, 1955, Tripartite Heads of Govts. Conf., Bermuda, 1957; mem. Presdl. Base Rights Survey Group, 1956-57. Served with AUS, 1943-45. Home: 1539 29th St NW Washington DC 20007 Office: Barr Bldg 910 17th St NW Washington DC 20006

SULLIVAN, DANIEL DAVID, lawyer; b. Bellville, Tex., Feb. 6, 1930; s. Pitman Z. and Dolores (Stroud) S.; student George Washington U., 1950-54; LL.B., U. Tex., 1956; m. Barbara Ann Anderson, Nov. 27, 1957; children—Julia Elizabeth, Jane Melissa. Admitted to Tex. bar, 1956; partner Sullivan & Sullivan, Odessa, Tex., 1956-57; individual practice, Andrews, Tex., 1958—; dist. atty. 109th Judicial Dist. Tex., 1960-65. Dir., v.p. Antex Oil & Gas Co., Inc., Andrews, 1973—. Adminstrv. asst. Senator Ralph Yarborough, 1963; at-large Democratic candidate U.S. Ho. of Reps., 1964. Pres. bd. dirs. Community Gen. Hosp., Andrews; trustee Andrews Ind. Sch. Dist. 1967-69. Mem. State Bar Tex., Andrews Bar Assn. (v.p.) Tex. Trial Lawyers Assn., Phi Alpha Delta, Sigma Phi Epsilon. Democrat. Kiwanian. Home: 1119 Golf Course Rd Andrews TX 79714 Office: 119 NW Av A Andrews TX 79714

SULLIVAN, GEORGE DENNIS, lawyer; b. Elmira, N.Y., Mar. 6, 1938; s. John Leo and Louise (O'Neil) S.; B.S. in History and Polit. Sci., Coll. Holy Cross, 1959; postgrad. Law Sch., Notre Dame U., 1959-62; LL.B., So. Meth. U., 1963; m. Beverly Jane Knapp, Aug. 25, 1962; children—Patricia Ellen, Mark Edward, Molly O'Neil. Admitted to Tex. bar, 1963; asso. firm Goldberg, Alexander & Sullivan and predecessor firms, Dallas, 1963-67, partner, 1967-74; partner firm Zimmerman, Minick & Sullivan, 1974—. Mem. Dallas, Tex., Am. bar assns., Jr. Bar Tex. (mem. environmental com.), Comml. Law League Am., Phi Delta Phi. Roman Catholic. K.C. (4 degree). Home: 6431 Westlake St Dallas TX 75214 Office: 4230 LBJ Freeway Dallas TX 75234

SULLIVAN, HELEN ESTELLE (STELLA SULLIVAN), artist; b. Houston, Oct. 11, 1924; d. Maurice Joseph and Anne (King) Sullivan; B.A., Rice U., 1945; student Mus. Sch. Art, 1949-50, Sch. Detroit Soc. Arts and Crafts, 1950-51; M.F.A., Cranbook Acad. Art, 1954. One-man shows in Columbus, O., Houston; exhibited in group shows in Houston; instr. Mus. Fine Arts Sch., Houston, 1961-70, U. Houston, 1962-66, Spring Br. Sch. Adult Edn., 1962-66; asst. prof. art Sam Houston State U., Huntsville, Tex., 1970-71; owner Stella Sullivan Sch. Art and Gallery, Houston, 1971—; instr. Post Oak YMCA, Houston, 1973—; vis. asst. prof. art U. Del., 1963; faculty Brazasport Art League, Freeport, Tex., 1961; Outdoor Painting Workshop, Sante Fe, summer 1970, Landscape Painting Workshop, Telluride, Colo., Summer 1971; co-founder, sec., treas. pres. Handmakers, Inc., Houston, 1957-60; asso. in formation of Galley 75, Conroe, Tex.; designer print room Rice U., 1966; executed murals and prints Flagship Hotel, Galveston, Tex.; executed prints Menger Hotel, San Antonio, Hotel Intercontinental, Manila, P.I., Fredonia Hotel, Nacogdoches, Tex. Recipient Shlumberger award Houston Artists 26th Ann., 1951, Fabric award Tex. Crafts 7th Ann., 1955. Roman Catholic. Club: Houston Yacht, (Houston). Home: 5353 Institute Lane Houston TX 77005 Office: 2409 Times Blvd Houston TX 77005

SULLIVAN, JIMMIE DONALD, ednl. adminstr.; b. Seminole, Okla., Sept. 13, 1933; s. Emmitt H. and Cordelia V. (Ingold) S.; B.S., Central State U., Edmond, Okla., 1955; M.S., Okla. State U., 1958, postgrad., 1963; postgrad. U. Ia., 1961; m. Janet Sue Berry, Aug. 1, 1959; children—Terri Lynn, Michael Jay. Asst. information dir. Central State U., Edmond, 1957-58; news dir. Eastern Okla. State Coll., Wilburton, 1958—. Served with AUS, 1955-57. Mem. Okla. Coll. Pub. Relations Assn. (pres. 1968-69). Democrat. Baptist. Mason (Shriner), Lion (dist. gov. 1970-71, state chmn. 1971-72). Home: 128 Jensen St Wilburton OK 74578

SULLIVAN, JOHN HANSELL, JR., banker; b. Atlanta, June 25, 1942; s. John Hansell and Genivieve (Muirhead) S.; A.B., Duke, 1964; M.B.A., U. N.C., 1967; m. Dorothy L. Smith, June 4, 1965; children—John O'Shea, David Tyson. Investment analyst Prudential Ins. Co., Jacksonville, Fla., 1967-68; dir. investment research 1st Nat. Bank Atlanta, 1968—. Chartered financial analyst. Mem. Atlanta Soc. Financial Analysts. Home: 946 Dean Dr Atlanta GA 30318 Office: PO Box 4148 Atlanta GA 30302

SULLIVAN, L. M., sch. adminstr.; b. Crescent, Okla., June 11, 1924; s. Roy Hampton and Lillis Martha (Prosser) S.; B.A., Northwestern State Coll., Alva, Okla., 1950; M.Ed., Phillips U., 1952; Ed.D., Okla. State U., 1968; m. Peggy Louise Rowley, Mar. 5, 1945; children—Michael, Steven. Adminstr. schs. in Okla., 1949—, sch. adminstr. Harrah pub. schs., 1968—. Mem. City-County Bd. Health, Oklahoma County, 1969—. Served with USAAF, 1942-45. Decorated D.F.C., Air medal with five clusters. Mem. Nat. Acad. Sch. Execs., Am. Assn. Sch. Adminstrs. (tour Soviet Union 1971), Panhandle Edn. Assn. (pres. 1960-61). Democrat. Methodist (lay leader). Lion, Rotarian. Home: 119 Gold St Harrah OK 73045

SULLIVAN, RICHARD LYLES COBLE, lawyer; b. Chester, S.C., Aug. 25, 1940; s. John Lee and Sarah (Glenn) S.; A.B. in History, U. S.C., 1964, J.D., 1968; m. Marion Stewart Boyd, May 22, 1963; children—Richard Lyles, Marion Stewart. Admitted to S.C. bar, 1968; asso. mem. firm Glenn Porter & Sullivan and predecessor firm, Columbia, S.C., 1968-70, partner, 1970—. Mem. Tex. State Bd. Rev., 1974-78. Vice pres. S.C. Young Democrats Club, 1967-69; mem. S.C. Ho. Reps., 1971-72; alternate del. Nat. Dem. Conv., 1964, 68; chmn. Richland County Dem. party, 1974—. Bd. dirs. Creative Factory, Columbia; trustee Columbia Mus. Art. Mem. S. Caroliniana Soc., Alston Wilkes Soc., Columbia Sertoma Club, Phi Delta Phi. Dem. Episcopalian. Club: Forest Lake Country (Columbia). Home: 432 Springlake St Columbia SC 29206 Office: PO Box 11588 Columbia SC 29211

SULLIVAN, WILLIAM CLINTON, judge; b. Birmingham, Ala., Sept. 3, 1926; s. Archie H. and Louise (Montgomery) S.; LL.B., U. Ala., 1949; m. Helen Lob, Sept. 28, 1951. Admitted to Ala. bar, 1949; gen practice, Talladega, Ala., 1949-58; mayor, Lincoln, Ala., 1952-58; circuit judge Talladega County, 1958—. Mem. Ala. Pattern Jury Instructions Com. Served with USNR, 1944-46. Mem. Am., Talladega County (past pres.) bar assns., Ala. State Bar, Nat. Conf. State Trial Judges, Internat. Platform Assn., Chi Phi. Democrat. Methodist. Club: Talladega Country. Home: PO Box 235 Lincoln AL 35096 Office: Ct House Talladega AL 35160

SULLIVAN, WILLIAM LITSEY, lawyer, state senator; b. Harrodsburg, Ky., Nov. 1, 1921; s. Charles Blount and Anne (Litsey) S.; B.A., Centre Coll. of Ky., 1949; LL.B., U. Ky., 1948; m. Elizabeth Dorsey, Apr. 21, 1951; children—William Litsey, John Charles. Admitted to Ky. bar, 1948; with firm Dorsey and Sullivan, Henderson, Ky., 1956-74; commr. aeros. State of Ky. 1958-60; mem. Ky. Senate, 1954-57, 66—, majority leader, 1956, pres. pro tem, 1968—. Served with USAAC, 1942-45; ETO. Named Outstanding Young Man of Ky., U.S. Jr. C. of C., 1956. Rotarian (pres. 1962). Home: 517 N Main St Henderson KY 42420 Office: 140 N Main St Henderson KY 42420

SULLIVAN, WILLIAM NICHOLAS, JR., govt. ofcl.; b. Lawrence, Mass., June 23, 1908; s. William Nicholas and Catherine (Lynch) S.; B.S.C., U. Mass., 1930, M.S.C., 1937. Jr. entomologist Entomology Research Div., Agrl. Research Service, Dept. of Agr., Beltsville, Md., 1931-37, entomologist, 1937-42, research entomologist, 1947—; cons. WHO. Served to maj. AUS, 1942-47. Recipient John Scott award City of Phila., 1945, Chem. Specialists Mfrs. Assn. Achievement award, 1954, Eric Rotheim award Fedn. European Aerosol Assn., 1970, Distinguished Service award U.S. Dept. Agr., 1973. Mem. A.A.A.S., Am. Inst. Biol. Scis., Entomol. Soc. Am., Washington Entomol. Soc., Insecticdal Soc. Washington, Sigma Xi. Co-Inventor insecticidal aerosol bomb, World War II. Home: 3601 Wisconsin Av NW Washington DC 20016 Office: Room 110 Bldg 307 ARC Beltsville MD 20705

SULLIVAN, WILLIAM ROYCE, physician; b. Bells, Tenn., Mar. 9, 1918; s. William Bryant and Lucy (Speight) S.; student Cumberland U., 1937-40; M.D., U. Tenn., 1949. Intern, Ga. Baptist Hosp., Atlanta, 1949-50; resident Lloyd Nolan Hosp., Fairfield, Ala., 1955; gen. practice medicine, Bells, 1952-67, Cauldwell, Tex., 1967-70; anesthesiologist Haywood County Meml. Hosp., 1956-67; staff physician, asso. med. dir., anesthesiologist Western State Psychiat. Hosp., Western State Hosp., Bolivar, Tenn., 1970—. Past pres. Crocker County Cancer Soc. mem. Am., Tex., Tenn. med. assns., Nacogdoches Med. Soc., Consol. Med. Assembly of West Tenn. Mason. Rotarian. Address: Western State Hosp Bolivar TN 38074

SULLIVAN, WILLIAM STANLEY, lawyer; b. Birmingham, Ala., Sept. 17, 1931; s. Andrew J. and Era Kathryn (Stanley) S.; student Va. Poly. Inst., 1947; B.A., U. Richmond, 1951, LL.B., 1954; m. Jacquelyn Scott Bryant, Aug. 17, 1954; children—William Stanley, Elizabeth Scott. Admitted to Va. bar, 1954; practiced in Richmond, Va., 1958—; partner, William, Sullivan & Cabell, 1958-61, Sadler, Parker & Sullivan, 1962-63, Parker, Parker & Sullivan, 1963-71, Sullivan & Kane, 1971—; pres. Rox Industries, 1968-69. Mem. staff A.R.C. Nat. Aquatics Sch., 1968—. Bd. dirs. Saints and Sinners, 1961-64, pres., 1965. Served with USNR, 1954-58. Mem. Assn. Trial Lawyers Am., Am., Va., Richmond bar assns., Press Club Va., MacNeil Law Soc., Phi Gamma Delta, Delta Thgta Phi. Methodist. Home: 4012 Hermitage Rd Richmond VA 23227 Office: 1508 Willow Lawn Dr Richmond VA 23230

SULZBY, JAMES FREDERICK, JR., realtor; b. Birmingham, Ala., Dec. 24, 1905; s. James Frederick and Annie (Dobbins) S.; student Howard Coll., Birmingham, 1925-26, A.B., Birmingham-So. Coll., 1928; grad. Am. Inst. Banking, 1934; Litt.D., Athens Coll., 1953; m. Martha Belle Hilton. Nov. 9, 1935; children—James Frederick III, Martha Hilton (Mrs. Robert J.B. Clark). Mem. staff trust dept. First Nat. Bank of Birmingham, 1929-43; pres. Sulzby Realty Co., 1943—; dir. Fidelity Savs. & Loan Assn.; pres. Norwood Gardens, Inc., 1948-49, sec.-treas. 1950, v.p., 1951. Trustee Birmingham Civic Symphony Assn.; mem. Jefferson County Personnel Bd. bd. dirs. Birmingham Sunday Sch. Assn.; chmn. Planning Com., 1948-61; dir. Ala. Bapt. publ., 1945—; historian 75th anniversary celebration for Birmingham, 1946, also treas. deacon, mem. exec. com. Southside Baptist Ch.; pres. Ala. Baptist Young Peoples Union, 1932-33; chmn. Jefferson County Nat. Found. Infantile Paralysis, 1951-52. Bd. govs. Civic Theatre of Birmingham, 1946-48. Recipient Distinguished Service award Ala. Hist. Commn., 1972. Mem. Newcomen Soc. N.Am. (Ala. com.), Ala. Hist. Assn. (pres. 1947-49), Ala. Baptist (pres. 1947-49), Birmingham (sec. 1945-50, trustee) hist. socs., Avondale Civic Assn. (pres. 1946), Am. Planning and Civic Assn., Nat. Assn. Real Estate Bds. (dir. 1952-56), Birmingham Real Estate Bd. (pres. 1953), Ala. Assn. Realtors (pres. 1952), Ala. Writers Conclave (pres. 1950), Birmingham Area Ednl. Television Assn. (treas., dir.), Ala. Acad. Sci. (pres. 1965-66), Birmingham C. of C. (chmn. edn. com. 1949-51), Birmingham So. Coll. Alumni Assn. (pres. 1960). Phi Beta Kappa, Delta Sigma Phi, Omicron Delta Kappa. Clubs: Mountain Brook Country; University (Tuscaloosa); The Club, Downtown. Author: Birmingham As It Was in Jackson County, 1944; Birmingham Sketches, 1945; Annals of the Southside Baptist Church. 1947; Historic Alabama Hotels and Resorts, 1960; Authur W. Smith: A Birmingham Pioneer, 1855-1944, 1961. Democrat. Baptist. Home: 3121 Carlisle Rd Birmingham AL 35213 Office: Massey Bldg Birmingham AL 35203

SULZER, ALEXANDER JACKSON, immunoparasitologist; b. Emmett, Ark., Feb. 13, 1922; s. Eugene A. and Edna J. (Weaver) S.; student Ia. Poly. Inst., 1940-41; B.A., Hardin-Simmons U., 1949; postgrad. Vanderbilt U., 1950-51; M.S., Emory U., 1960, Ph.D., 1962; m. Fay Catherine Ross, Oct. 3, 1942; children—Danny Lynn, Harry Eugene. Instr. biology Hardin-Simmons U., Abilene, Tex., 1949-50; AEC fellow Vanderbilt U., Nashville 1950-51; parasitologist U.S. Communicable Disease Center, Atlanta, 1951-59; NIH fellow Emory U., Atlanta, 1959-62; microbiologist U.S. Nat. Communicable Disease

Center, Atlanta, 1962—. Prof. honorario Universidad Peruana Cayetano Heredia, Lima. Served with AUS, 1942-43. Fellow Royal Soc. Tropical Medicine and Hygiene; mem. Research Soc. Am., Am. Soc. Tropical Medicine and Hygiene, Am. Soc. Parasitologists. Home: 3711 Canadian Way Tucker GA 30084 Office: 1600 Clifton Rd Atlanta GA 30333

SUMMAR, DWAYNE, utility holding co. exec.; b. Murfreesboro, Tenn., Mar. 4, 1939; s. B.H. and Mae (Groom) S.; B.S. in Journalism, U. Tenn. at Knoxville, 1961. Reporter writer Nashville Tennessean, 1961-62, Knoxville News-Sentinal, 1962-69; advt. copywriter Ga. Power Co., Atlanta, 1964-66, advt. asst., 1966-67, supr. spl. services sect., 1967-68; mgr. pub. relations So. Services Co., Atlanta, 1968-72, v.p., mgr. pub. relations and advt., 1972—. Mem. Edison Electric Inst. (mem. pub. relations com.), Pub. Relations Soc. Am. (certified mem.), Sigma Delta Chi. Home: 525 Spring Valley Rd NW Atlanta GA 30318 Office: PO Box 720071 Atlanta GA 30346

SUMMER, ALBIOUN F., lawyer, state ofcl.; b. Pelahatchie, Miss., Nov. 2, 1921; s. Sydney Lamar and Iva Lee (Hardy) S.; diploma Hinds Jr. Coll., 1942; student U. Miss. Law Sch., 1946-47; LL.B., Jackson Sch. Law, 1950; m. Mary Lois Campbell, June 1945; 1 son, Carl Bennison. Admitted to Miss. bar, 1950; atty. Town of Pelahatchie, 1950-51; mem. Miss. Bd. Vet. Affairs, 1957; exec. asst., legal adviser to gov. State of Miss., Jackson, 1958, chief asst., legal adviser, 1968-69; chancery judge 5th Dist. of Miss., 1958-61; atty. gen. State of Miss., 1969—. Mem. Beta Theta Pi, Phi Delta Theta. Office: State Capitol Jackson MS 39201

SUMMERFELT, ROBERT CLAR, educator; b. Chgo., Aug. 2, 1935; s. Clarence Glen and Ernestina Clara (Henschel) S.; B.S. cum laude U. Wis., 1957; M.S., So. Ill. U., 1959, Ph.D., 1964; postgrad. Duke, 1962; m. Deanne E. Walsh, June 25, 1960; children—Scott, Steven, Sloan. Grad. research and teaching asst. So. Ill. U., Carbondale, 1957-62, lectr. zoology, 1962-64; asst. prof. zoology Kan. State U., 1964-66; asso. prof. zoology Okla. State U., Stillwater, 1966-70, prof., 1970—. Leader coop. fishery unit div. fishery research Bur. Sport Fisheries and Wildlife, US Dept. Interior, 1966-73; cons. Peace Corps, Ministry Agr., Guatemala, 1967-72. Active Little League Baseball. Named Conservationist of Year, Rotary Club, 1973. Mem. Am. Fisheries Soc. (pres. state chpt. 1970-71. chmn. divisional com. 1971, 1st place citation So. div. 1971), Wildlife Disease Assn., Ecol. Soc. Am., Midwest Benthological Soc., Izaak Walton League, Wilderness Soc., Kan., Ill. acads. sci., Sigma Xi, Phi Kappa Phi. Lion. Club: Sierra. Contbr. articles to profl. jours. Home: 1721 Sunset Dr Stillwater OK 74074

SUMMERLIN, GLENN WOOD, JR., advt. exec.; b. Dallas, Ga., Apr. 1, 1934; s. Glenn Wood and Flora (Barrett) S.; student Ga. Inst. Tech., 1951-52; B.B.A., Ga. State U., 1956, M.B.A., 1967; m. Rebecca Anne Valley, Oct. 16, 1971; 1 son, Wade Hampton; children by previous marriage—Glenn Wood III, Edward Lee. Prodn. mgr. Fred Worrill Advt., Atlanta, 1956-65; v.p. sales Grizzard Advt., Inc., Atlanta, 1965—. Trustee Ga. State U. Found. Named Outstanding Young Man in DeKalb County N. DeKalb Jr. C. of C., 1967; recipient C.S. Bolen award So. Council Indsl. Editors, 1967; Humane award Atlanta Humane Soc., 1971. Mem. Internat. Council Bus. Communicators, Asso. Mail Advt. Agys., Ga. Assn. Bus. Communicators (pres. 1966-67), Mail Advt. Service Assn. (pres. N. Ga. chpt. 1959-60), Sales and Marketing Execs. (dir. Atlanta 1969-71), Am. Marketing Assn. (dir. Atlanta chpt. 1969—, pres. 1973-74), Ga. Bus. and Industry Assn. (gov.), Atlanta Humane Soc. (dir. 1970—, treas. 1973-74), Ga. State U. Alumni Assn. (pres. 1971-72). Ga. State U. Grad. Bus. Club (v.p. 1969-70), Omicron Delta Kappa, Sigma Phi Epsilon. Home: 1133 Ragley Hall Rd NE Atlanta GA 30319 Office: 1144 Mailing Av SE Atlanta GA 30315

SUMMERS, ANNIE RUTH (MRS. WALTER JEROME SUMMERS), realtor; b. Bradley Junction, Fla., Feb. 25, 1915; d. Lonnie Edward and Alice Elmina (Allen) Harvey; student Fla. State Coll. for Women, 1930-31; m. Walter Jerome Summers, Nov. 9, 1933 (dec.); 1 dau., Mary Alice (Mrs. Harry L. Pender). Sales mgr. Arboretum Lychee Orchards, Laurel, Fla., 1946-66; real estate broker, mgr. branch office H.N. Wimmers, Venice, Fla., 1956-65; pres., mgr. Summers Nursery & Landscaping, Inc., Laurel, Fla., 1960-65; mgr. Basswood, Inc., Okeechobee, Fla., 1965-68; owner, broker and realtor Summers Realty, Nokomis, Fla., 1968—. Mem. Venice C. of C. (dir. 1965—), Venice Bd. Realtors (v.p. 1972-73, pres. 1973). Inventor spl. propogation container for growing plants. Home: 205 E Palm Av Nokomis FL 33555 Office: 229 N Tamiami Trail Nokomis FL 33555

SUMMERS, JAMES WILLIAM, judge; b. Rusk, Tex., July 8, 1914; s. James Lee and Constance (Rook) S.; B.B.A., J.D., U. Tex., 1937; m. Inez Thompson Steed, Nov. 22, 1969; children—Julia Ann (Mrs. Charles E. Tucker), Raymond C. Steed. Admitted to U.S. Supreme Ct. bar, Tex. bar, 1937, practiced in Rusk, 1937-56; city atty., 1937-41; county atty. Cherokee County, 1941-42, 47-48, county judge, 1949-56; judge 2d Jud. Dist. Tex., Rusk, 1957—. Dir. First State Bank, Southwestern Title & Guaranty Co.; partner Summers Bros., land, cattle, timber. Dir. Civil Def., Cherokee County, 1949-56; mem. Cherokee County Heritage Assn.; mem. adv. council Criminal Justice Program, Stephen F. Austin U., vice chmn. Rusk Housing Corp.; chmn. Nacogdoches-Cherokee Counties Probation Bd. Bd. dirs. East Tex. area council Boy Scouts Am., Rusk Indsl. Found., Rusk United Way. Served as lt. USNR, 1942-46. Fellow Tex. Bar Found.; mem. Am. Judicature Soc., Am., East Tex., Cherokee County bar assns., State Bar Tex., Nat. Conf. State Trial Judges, County Judges and Commrs. Assn. Tex., Nat. Assn. County Ofcls., Am., Tex., East Tex. Aberdeen-Angus assns., U. Tex. Ex-Students Assn. (exec. council Austin, past pres. Cherokee County alumni club), Rusk C. of C. (chmn. govt. affairs com.), Tex. Farm Bur. Fedn., Cherokee County Hist. Soc. (dir.), Am. Legion, Beta Gamma Sigma, Phi Delta Phi, Phi Eta Sigma, Phi Delta Theta (v.p. East Tex. alumni). Methodist (chmn. ofcl. bd.), Mason (Shriner), Kiwanian (past pres.). Home: 200 W 5th St Rusk TX 75785 Office: Courthouse Rusk TX 75785

SUMMERS, JOSEPH FRANK, petroleum co. exec.; b. Newnan, Ga., June 26, 1914; s. John Dawson and Anne (Blalock) S.; B.A. in Math., U. Houston, 1942; profl. certificate meteorology, U. Cal. at Los Angeles, 1943, U. Chgo., 1943; postgrad., U. P.R., 1943-44; M.A. in Math., U. Tex. at Austin, 1947; postgrad. (fellow math.) Rice U., 1947-49; m. Evie Margaret Mott, July 8, 1939; children—John Randolph, Thomas Franklin, James Mott. With Texaco Inc., Houston, 1933-42, 49—, mgr. data processing, 1957-67, asst. gen. mgr. computer services dept., 1967—; instr. math. AAC, Ellington Field, Tex., 1941-42, U. Tex. at Austin, 1946-47. Pres. Houston Esperanto Assn., 1934-39. Served to capt. AAc, 1942-46. Mem. Assn. Computing Machinery (pres. 1956-58), Nat. Assn. Accountants (past dir.), Am. Petroleum Inst. (mem. data processing and computing com. 1955-59). Author: Mathematics for Bombadiers and Navigators, 1944. Home: 5517 Tilbury Dr Houston TX 77027 Office: PO Box 52332 Houston TX 77052

SUMMERS, JOSEPH KEITH, educator; b. Wilkes-Barre, Pa., Dec. 6, 1920; s. Samuel and Rose (Deutsch) S.; B.S., N.Y.U., 1951, M.B.A., 1960; m. Harriet Jacobs, Sept. 1, 1946; children—Laureen, Sheldon. Marketing dir. Am. Fluoride Corp., N.Y.C., 1955-56; prof. mgmt. U. P.R., San Juan, 1957—; adminstr. Clinica Antillas, Inc. P.R., 1958-62; adminstr. Presbyn. Hosp., Inc., 1962-69; dir., cons. Intermar Marketing Group, Inc., N.Y.C.; cons. IBEC Realty, Inc. Vice pres., dir. Las Colinas Devel. Corp.; asst. treas., dir. Internat. Life Ins. Co. P.R. Mem. Food Distbn. Com. for Gov. P.R., 1958-60; adviser, cons. Coop. Movement P.R., 1958-62. Bd. advisers Robinson Sch. Served with USAAF, 1942-45. Columnist, San Juan Star; feature writer San Juan Review. Contbr. articles to profl. jours. Home: 1223 Rafael Arcelay Rio Piedras PR 00924 Office: Box 249 San Juan PR 00902

SUMMERS, THOMAS EUGENE, entomologist; b. Seneia, Ga., June 7, 1919; s. Elijah Gary and Tinie (Cheek) S.; B.S.A., U. Ga., 1941; M.S., Ia. State Coll., 1947, Ph.D., 1950; m. Edith Hernandez, June 30, 1961; children—Thomas Morgan, Gary Robert, Ruth Anne, Elizabeth Christine. Plant pathologist Dept. Agr., State College, Miss. Belle Glade, Fla., 1950-65, entomologist sugarcane insects investigations Agrl. Research Sta., Canal Point, Fla., 1965—. Mem. grad. faculty U. Fla., 1966. Served with USAAF, 1941-46. Decorated Purple Heart, Air medal, D.F.C. Mem. Entomol. Soc. Am., A.A.A.S., Internat. Orgn. for Biol. Control, Fla. Entomol. Soc., V.F.W. Elk, Rotarian. Research on small grains diseases, diseases of stem and leaf fiber crops. Home: Lakeshore Dr Canal Point FL 33438 Office: Sugarcane Field Station Canal Point FL 33438

SUMMERS, VICTOR LAWRENCE, ednl. adminstr.; b. St. Joseph, Mo., Apr. 29, 1928; s. Victor Lawrence and Viola Mae (Cline) S.; A.B., Rockhurst Coll., 1953; M.A., Am. U., 1966. Instr., Woodward Sch., Washington, 1956-57, U.S. Mil. Acad. Prep. Sch., Ft. Belvoir, Va., 1957-58; headmaster, Ascension Acad., Alexandria, Va., 1958—. Served with USN, 1946-49. Mem. Va. Assn. Secondary Sch. Prins., Va. Assn. Ind. Elementary Schs. (v.p. 1971-72), Va. Assn. Ind. Schs. (pres. 1972-73), No. Va. Fine Arts Assn. (pres. 1966), Pi Sigma Alpha. Roman Catholic. Office: 4401 W Braddock Rd Alexandria VA 22304

SUMMERSELL, CHARLES GRAYSON, educator; b. Mobile, Ala., Feb. 25, 1908; s. Charles Fishweek and Sallie Rebecca (Grayson) S.; A.B., U. Ala., 1929, A.M., 1930; Ph.D., Vanderbilt, 1940; m. Frances Sharpley, Nov. 10, 1934. Instr. history U. Ala., University, 1935-40, asst. prof., 1940-46, asso. prof., 1946-47, prof., 1947—, head dept. history, 1954-71. Radio commentator, Tuscaloosa and Selma, Ala., 1941-43. Commd. lt. (j.g.), USNR, 1942; active duty, 1943; served with U.S. Navy in PTO; lt. comdr.; comdr. Res., 1954; officer charge Naval Tng. School, Norfolk, Va., 1951-53; mem. steering com. organizing Tuscaloosa unit Organized Res. of Navy, 1947. Recipient Letter of Commendation USNR, 1945. Mem. So., Mississippi Valley, Ala. (pres. 1955-56) hist. assns., U.S. Naval Inst., Naval Hist. Found., S.A.R., (pres. Ala. 1957-58), Am. Assn. State and Local History (council 1965-71), Am. Hist. Assn., Hakluyt Soc., Phi Beta Kappa (pres. Ala. chpt. 1953-54), Phi Alpha Theta. Democrat. Club: University. Author: Historical Foundations of Mobile, 1949; Mobile History of a Seaport Town, 1949; Alabama History for Schools, 1957, rev., 1965, 70; (with Howard W. Odum and G.H. Yeuell) Alabama Past and Future, 1941, rev. edit. (with G.H. Yeuell and W.R. Higgs), 1950; (with Frances C. Roberts) Exploring Alabama, 1957, rev., 1961; (with Frances S. Summersell) Alabama History Filmstrips, 1961; (with F.S. Summersell and Rembert W. Patrick) Florida History Filmstrips, 1963; (with others) Texas History Filmstrips, 1965; The Cruise of the C.S.S. Sumter, 1965; Ohio History Filmstrips, 1967; (with others) California History Filmstrips, 1968, Illinois History Filmstrips, 1970; (with others) Atlas of Alabama, 1973. Editor: The Journal of George Townley Fullam: Boarding Officer of the Confederate Sea Raider Alabama, 1973. Mem. editorial adv. bd., Am. Neptune, 1946—; mem. editorial bd. Ala. Rev., 1964—. Contbr. articles and revs. to encys. and profl. jours. Home: 1411 Caplewood Dr Tuscaloosa AL 35401 Office: PO Box 1936 University AL 35486

SUMMERSELL, FRANCES SHARPLEY (MRS. CHARLES GRAYSON SUMMERSELL), club woman; b. Birmingham, Ala.; d. Arthur Croft and Thomas O. (Stone) Sharpley; student Ala. Coll., Montevallo, Peabody Coll., Nashville; m. Charles Grayson Summersell, Nov. 10, 1934. Partner, artist, writer Asso. Educators, 1959—. Mem. D.A.R., Magna Charta Dames, U. Women's Club (pres. 1957-58), U.D.C. (state historian 1956-58, pres. Robert Emmet Rodes chpt. Tuscaloosa 1953-55), Daus. Am. Colonists (organizing regent Tuscaloosa 1956-63), English Speaking Union, Marquis Biog. Library Soc. (adv. mem.). Mem. Ft. Morgan Hist. Commn., 1959-63. Mem. Tuscaloosa County Preservation Soc. (trustee 1965—), West Ala. Art Assn., Nat. Trust. Clubs: Universtiy (Tuscaloosa); Birmingham Metropolitan Dinner. Co-author: Alabama History Filmstrips, 1961; Viewing Alabama History Flimstrips, 1961; Florida History Filmstrips, 1963; Texas History Filmstrips, 1965-66; Ohio History Filmstrips, (Merit award Am. Assn. State and Local History 1968), 1967; California History Filmstrips, 1968; Illinois History Filmstrips, 1970. Home: 1411 Caplewood Tuscaloosa AL 35401

SUMMERSON, GEORGE WILLIAM, hotel exec.; b. Richmond, Va., Nov. 18, 1903; s. George Ralph and Eula Mead (Ford) S.; B.S., Washington and Lee U., 1927; m. Champe Grant, Dec. 24, 1932; children—Champe (Mrs. Don Hyatt), Sue (Mrs. Irvin Wells III), George William. Gen. auditor Robert E. Lee Hotel, Winston-Salem, N.C., 1929-35; mgr. Washington Duke Hotel, Durham, N.C., 1935-39; gen. mgr. Hotel Gen. Shelby, Hotel Bristol (Va.), 1939-56; pres., gen. mgr. Martha Washington Inn, Abingdon, Va., 1956—. Pres. Bristol Community Chest, 1950-51, Washington County United Fund, 1964-65; mem. state adv. com. Salvation Army, 1972—, vice chmn. div. adv. bd., 1973-74. Mayor, mem. City Council, Bristol, 1951-57; vice mayor, mem. Town Council, Abingdon, Va., 1968-70, 71-72, mayor, 1972—. Bd. visitors Sullins Coll., Bristol, Va.; bd. dirs., exec. com. Mt. Rogers Planning Commn., 1969-72, chmn., 1973-74. Recipient Bristol's Outstanding Citizen award V.F.W., 1953; City of Bristol Pub. Service Recognition award, 1954-56; Bristol Centennial Celebration award, 1956; Distinguished Service award Hotel-Motel Greeters, 1969, Va. Hotel-Motel Assn., 1971. Mem. Am. Hotel and Motel Assn. (trustee ednl. inst. 1958—, pres. inst. 1967-69), Am. (dir. 1949), Va. (pres. 1948), So. (pres. 1952) hotel assns., Hotel Greeters (chpt. pres. 1932), Bristol C. of C. (pres. 1952), Va. Travel Council (pres. 1950-51, outstanding service citation 1952), Abingdon C. of C. (pres. 1959-60), Va. State C. of C. (certificate appreciation 1961, v.p. 1969-71). Methodist (chmn. adminstrv. bd. 1966-69, lay leader 1970-72). Mason (Shriner), Kiwanian. Club: Glenrochie Country (pres. 1961) (Abingdon). Home: 150 W Main St Abingdon VA 24210 Office: Martha Washington Inn 150 W Main St Abingdon VA 24210

SUMMITT, ROBERT LAYMAN, physician, educator; b. Knoxville, Dec. 23, 1932; s. Robert Luther and Mary (Layman) S.; student Davidson Coll., 1950-51; M.D., U. Tenn., 1955, M.S. in Pediatrics, 1962; USPHS postdoctoral fellow U. Wis., 1963; m. Joyce Ann Sharp, Dec. 23, 1955; children—Robert Layman, Susan Kelly, John Blair. Intern Meml. Research Center and Hosp., U. Tenn., Knoxville, 1956; resident Coll. Medicine, U. Tenn., City Memphis hosps., 1959-60, chief resident, 1960-61; practice medicine, specializing in pediatrics and med. genetics, Memphis, 1964; mem. faculty dept. pediactrics, anatomy and child devel. U. Tenn. Center Health Scis., Memphis, 1964—, asso. prof., 1968-71, prof., 1971—, also chief genetics sect., dept. genetics Child Devel. Center, both 1964—, dir. Nat. Found. Birth Defects Center, 1970—; mem. staff City Memphis, Le Bonheur Children's, St. Joseph hosps., all Memphis; cons. several other hosps. Served with USNR, 1957-59; capt. Res. USPHS grantee, 1964-67, 71—, March Dimes Nat. Found. grantee, 1968—. Diplomate Am. Bd. Pediatrics. Fellow Am. Acad. Pediatrics; mem. Memphis and Shelby County Pediatric Soc. (pres. 1970), A.M.A., Tenn., Memphis and Shelby County med. assns., Tenn. Pediatric Soc., So. Soc. Pediatric Research, Am. Soc. Human Genetics, N.Y. Acad. Scis., A.A.A.S., Soc. Pediatric Research, Sigma Xi. Contbr. articles to profl. jours. Home: 3102 Glenfinnan Rd Memphis TN 38128 Office: 848 Adams Av Memphis TN 38103

SUMNER, BILLY TAYLOR, cons. civil engring. and planning co. exec.; b. Chgo., July 13, 1923; s. Lawton Taylor and Adele (Shelton) S.; B.E. magna cum laude, Vanderbilt U., 1946; m. Mary Sue Williams, Nov. 23, 1951; children—Kimberly Suell, Shelton Williams. Resident engr. Polk, Powell & Hendon, Nashville, 1946-51; Southeastern engring. rep., mgr. Nashville plant Universal Concrete Pipe Co., Columbus, O., 1951-53; cons. Dixie Poultry Processors, Franklin, Tenn., 1953-54; resident mgr. Nashville office Geo. P. Rice, New Orleans, 1954-55; prin. firm Barge, Waggoner, Sumner & Cannon, cons. civil engrs. and planners, Nashville, Knoxville, Morristown, Tenn., 1955—. Pres. Tenn. Bot. Gardens and Fine Arts Center, 1967-69; chmn. architect-engr. div. United Givers Fund, 1972; mem. steering com. Middle Tenn. Young Life Campaign, 1973-74. Trustee, v.p. Children's Museum, Nashville. Served with AUS, 1943-46. Mem. Am. Soc. C.E., Am. Water Works Assn., Water Pollution Control Fedn., Am. Pub. Works Assn., Soc. Am. Mil. Engrs. Am. Inst. Cons. Engrs. (councilor 1972-73, v.p. 1973), Am. Cons. Engrs. Council (v.p. 1973—), Nat. Soc. Profl. Engrs. (vice chmn. 1967-69, chmn. 1969-70), Tau Beta Pi, Sigma Nu. Presbyn. Rotarian. Clubs: Belle Meade Country, Nashville City, Cumberland (Nashville). Home: 801 Robertson Academy Rd Nashville TN 37220 Office: 404 James Robertson Pkwy Nashville TN 37219

SUMNER, GEORGE CLAIBRONE, elec. engr.; b. Potosi, Tex., Oct. 6, 1921; s. Charles Lynn and Emmie (Harris) S.; B.S., Tex. A. and M. U., 1942; M.S., Mass. Inst. Tech., 1949, M.B.A., Tex. Christian U., 1973; m. Sue White, Jan. 6, 1963; children—Nancy, Stephanie. Mem. staff Mass. Inst. Tech., 1947-50; mgr. elec. and support systems Gen. Dynamics Corp., Ft. Worth, 1950—. Served to capt., Signal Corps, AUS, 1942-46. Registered profl. engr., Tex. Mem. I.E.E.E. (chmn. Ft. Worth sect. 1956-58), Sigma Xi, Beta Gamma Sigma. Home: 4000 Harlanwood Dr Fort Worth TX 76109 Office: Box 748 Fort Worth TX 76101

SUMRELL, GENE, research chemist; b. Apache, Ariz., Oct. 7, 1919; s. Joe B. and Dixie (Hughes) S.; B.A., Eastern N.M. U., Ph.D., U. Cal. at Berkeley, 1951. Asst. prof. chemistry Eastern N.M. U., 1951-53; sr. research chemist J. T. Baker Chem. Co., Phillipsburg, N.J., 1953-58; sr. organic chemist S.W. Research Inst., San Antonio, 1958-59; project leader Food Machinery & Chem. Corp., Balt., 1959-61; research sect. leader El Paso Natural Gas Products Co. (Tex.), 1961-64; project leader So. utilization research and devel. div. U.S. Dept. Agr., New Orleans, 1964-67, investigations head, 1967—. Served from pvt. to staff sgt., AUS, 1942-46. Mem. Am. Chem. Soc., A.A.A.S., N.Y. Acad. Scis., Am. Inst. Chemists, Am. Oil Chemists Soc., Am. Assn. Textile Chemists and Colorists, Research Soc. Am., Am. Assn. U. Profs., Sigma Xi, Phi Kappa Phi. Home: PO Box 24037 New Orleans LA 70184 Office: 1100 Robert E Lee Blvd New Orleans LA 70179

SUMTER, FREDERICK NEAL, JR., savs. and loan exec.; b. Albany, Ga., May 21, 1938; s. Frederick Neal and Georgian Mae (Eckerman) S.; B.B.A., U. Ga., 1960; m. Mary Frances Palmer, July 9, 1961; children—Frederick Neal III, Anna Kathryn. Mgmt. trainee First Fed. Savs. & Loan Assn., Albany, 1961-65, asst. v.p., 1965-68, v.p., treas., 1968-73, sr. v.p., treas., 1973—. Mem. Dougherty County Bd. Registrars, 1971. Bd. dirs. United Fund, Albany, 1973, A.R.C., 1970. Mem. Soc. Real Estate Appraisers (pres. 1972), Ga. Assn. Savs. and Loan Personnel (pres. 1969). Home: 1814 Green Valley Dr Albany GA 31705 Office: 401 Pine Av Albany GA 31702

SUMWALT, ROBERT LLEWELLYN, JR., constrn. co. exec.; b. Columbia, S.C., Dec. 29, 1927; s. Robert Llewellyn and Caroline M. (Causey) S.; B.S. in Civil Engring., U. S.C., 1949; M.S. in Civil Engring., Mass. Inst. Tech., 1950; m. Mary Joyce Mills, Mar. 8, 1952; children—Elizabeth Ladson, Robert Llewellyn III. Area engr. E. I. duPont de Nemours & Co., Camden, S.C., 1950-52; constrn. engr. Columbia City Sch. System, 1952-58; pres. Gen. Bldg. Div., dir. McCrory-Sumwalt Constrn. Co., Columbia, 1958—. Pres. Richland County unit Am. Cancer Soc., 1956, Carolina Carillon Ball, 1963; sect. chmn. United Community Services, 1957; div. chmn. constrn. div. United Way, 1973. Bd. dirs. Am. Cancer Soc., S.C. chpt., 1957, Richland County unit A.R.C., 1955-56. Named Young Man of the Year, Columbia Jr. C. of C., 1958. Registered profl. engr., S.C. Mem. Asso. Gen. Contractors Am., Am. Inst. Constructers, Columbia Contractors Assn. (pres. 1969), S.C. Soc. Engrs., S.C. Soc. Profl. Engrs., Sigma Alpha Epsilon, Phi Beta Kappa, Omicron Delta Kappa, Tau Beta Pi. Presbyn. (chmn. bd. deacons 1968). Kiwanian (pres. 1962). Clubs: Forest Lake Country, Palmetto, Cotillion, Centurion (Columbia). Home: 1420 Belmont Dr Columbia SC 29205 Office: 2801 Devine St Columbia SC 29205

SUNKEL, GEORGE FOREMAN, retail trade exec.; b. Paris, Ill., June 18, 1904; s. John William and Beatrice (Foreman) S.; student Austin Coll., 1922-23; m. Margaret Sue Smith, June 17, 1926; children—Marian (Mrs. Joseph L. Frank), Margaret (Mrs. Maxey Kyle Russell, Jr.). Partner, McCulloch Grocery Co., Clarksville, Tex., 1923-40; owner Piggly Wiggly Stores, Clarksville, 1940—; pres. Piggly Wiggly Operators Warehouse, Shreveport, La., 1965; chmn. bd. Piggly Wiggly Red River Co., Inc., Clarksville, 1957—; dir. Piggly Wiggly Operators Warehouse, Shop Rite Foods, Inc., Dallas. Alderman, Clarksville, 1935-40. Bd. dirs. Red River County Indsl. Found.; trustee Synod of Tex. Presbyn. Found. Mem. Nat. Piggly Wiggly Operators Assn. (pres. 1952), Clarksville C. of C. (pres. 1955). Presbyn. (ruling elder 1940). Mason (Shriner). Home: 1500 W Main St Clarksville TX 75426 Office: 800 W Main St Clarksville TX 75426

SUNS, WAYNE EDWARD, banker; b. Huntsville, Ala., Oct. 24, 1941; s. James Henry and Mollie (Lewis) S.; student U. Ala., 1963-64, U. Wis. at Madison, 1973-75; m. Jerri Ann Martin, May 14, 1966; children—Stephanie Michelle, Jennifer Anne, Wayne Edward Jr. With First Nat. Bank, Huntsville, 1963—, asst. v.p., 1968-71, v.p. data processing, 1971—. Instr. data processing North Ala. Coll. Commerce, Huntsville, 1971—; cons. data processing field. Chmn. Gov.'s Com. Employment Handicapped, Huntsville area, 1973—; mem. Pres.'s Com. Employment Handicapped, 1973—; sec., dir. budgets Community Umbrella Program Adolescent Behavior and Drug Abuse Prevention, 1972—. Served with AUS, 1960-63. Mem. Huntsville Jr. C. of C., Nat. Rehab. Assn., Mensa. Mason. Home: 100 Wingate Av Huntsville AL 35801 Office: PO Box 680 Huntsville AL 35804

SURACI, CHARLES XAVIER, JR., govt. ofcl.; b. Washington, Feb. 10, 1934; s. Charles Xavier and June (Hunter) S.; student Pa. Mil. Coll., 1952-53; grad. Nat. Acad. Broadcasting, 1959; Columbia Union Coll., 1961-62, student Catholic U., 1969; m. Florence Patricia

DeMino, May 23, 1970. With Harry Diamond Lab, U.S. Army, Washington 1963—, material publs. asst., 1963-68, adminstrv. asst., head dispatcher for operations transp. officer, 1968—; served to lt. col. Civil Air Patrol, 1957-74, col., 1974—, now wing comdr. Nat. Capitol Wing. Mem. youth com. YMCA, Silver Spring, Md., 1962-69, mem. bd. mgmt., 1967—. Served with USAF, 1953-57. Recipient certificate of commendation from Pres. Nixon, 1970, Exceptional Service award Congressman Lester Wolff, 1972; named Air Man of Month USAF, 1956. Roman Catholic. Club: Andrews AFB Officers (Washington). Home: 3906 Halsey St Kensington MD Office: Conn Av and Van Ness St Washington DC 20438

SURRATT, JERRY LEE, coll. dean; b. Winston-Salem, N.C., Oct. 18, 1936; s. Robert Lee and Cleo Shirley (Phelps) S.; A.A., Wingate Coll., 1957, B.A., Wake Forest Coll., 1959; B.D., Southeastern Baptist Theol. Sem., 1962; Ph.D., Emory U., 1968; m. Alice Andrea Allen, June 16, 1963; children—Andrea Leigh, Emily Elizabeth. Instr. and acting chaplain, Salem Coll., Winston-Salem, 1965-67; prof. Wingate Coll. (N.C.), 1967—, acad. dean, 1968—. Chmn. joint com. on coll. transfer N.C. Bd. Higher Edn., 1970; v.p. N.C. Assn. Jr. Colls., 1971, pres., 1973; mem. exec. com. N.C. Assn. Colls. and Univs., 1973; sec. Charlotte Area Ednl. Consortium, 1973. Mem. Am. Acad. Religion, Am. Soc. Ch. History, Moravian Hist. Soc., N.C. Hist. and Lit. Soc., Wachovia Hist. Soc., Assn. Acad. Deans N.C., Conf. Acad. Deans So. States. Mason. Home: PO Box 487 Wingate NC 28174

SURVANT, WILLIAM GREGORY, educator; b. Owensboro, Ky., Aug. 26, 1907; s. Ellis and Lina Elizabeth (Gregory) S.; B.S., U. Ky., 1931, M.S., 1945; Ph.D., Ohio State U., 1951; m. Rubye Jean Bellamy, Nov. 27, 1936. Tchr. vocational agr. Whitesville High Sch., Daviess County, Ky., 1931-38; soil conservationist Soil Conservation Service, Morganfield, Ky., 1939-42; prof. agronomy U. Ky., Lexington, 1942—, acting asso. dean instrn. Coll. Agr., 1966-68, acting chmn. dept. forestry, 1969-70. Mem. Am. Soc. Agronomy, Soil Sci. Soc. Am., Soil Conservation Soc. Am. Home: 120 Tahoma Rd Lexington KY 40503

SUSMAN, MORTON LEE, lawyer; b. Detroit, Aug. 6, 1934; s. Harry and Alma (Koslow) S.; B.B.A., So. Methodist U., 1956, LL.B., 1958; m. Nina Meyers, May 1, 1958; 1 son, Mark Lee. Admitted to Tex. bar, 1958, Fed. bar, 1961; law clk. Wynne & Wynne, Dallas, 1958; asst. U.S. atty., Houston, 1961-65, 1st asst. U.S. atty., 1965-66, U.S. atty., 1966-69. Past mem. bd. dirs. Am. Jewish Com. Houston, S.W. Regional council Am. Jewish Com. Houston Council Human Relations, Planned Parenthood Houston, S.W. Region Planned Parenthood; bd. dirs. Ct. Vol. Services, Houston, 1969—. Mem. Tex. Bill of Rights Found., 1967-69. Served to lt. with USNR, 1958-61. Recipient Younger Fed. Lawyer award Fed. Bar Assn., Washington, 1968. Mem. Am., Fed., Houston bar assns., State Bar Tex., Barristers, Sigma Alpha Mu (pres. 1954), Phi Eta Sigma, Phi Alpha Delta, Delta Sigma Pi. Jewish religion (trustee congregation 1968-72). Rotarian. Club: Houston. Case note editor Southwestern Law Jour., 1957-58. Home: 11003 Landon Lane Houston TX 77024 Office: 2290 Two Shell Plaza Houston TX 77002

SUSSMAN, MARION BEATRICE BAUM (MRS. IRVING SUSSMAN), counseling psychologist, ednl. cons.; b. Paterson, N.J.; d. Samuel and Adele (Gerstein) Baum; student U. Ala., 1940-42; B.Ed. cum laude, U. Miami, 1953, M.Ed., 1956, Ph.D., 1973; postgrad. U. N.C., 1969; m. Irving Sussman, Nov. 21, 1943; children—Nicki (Mrs. Steve Charles Horowitz), Roberta Joy. Sci. tchr. Kinloch Park Jr. High Sch., Miami, Fla., 1953-56, counselor, guidance chmn., test chmn., 1956-63, asst. prin. for guidance, 1969-73; counselor, test chmn. S.W. Miami High Sch., 1963-68; grad. asst. U. Miami, Coral Gables, Fla., 1968-69; mem. staff Piedmont summer program Wake Forest U., Winston-Salem, N.C., 1972-74; asso. dir. Piedmont winter program Biscayne Coll., Miami, 1974; pvt. practice as counselor, 1973—; sch. services conc. N.C. Advancement Sch., Winston-Salem, 1974—. Cons. on peer-group counseling. Active various community drives. Mem. N.E.A., Am., Fla., South Fla., Dade County (pres. 1967-68) personnel and guidance assns., Fla. Edn. Assn., Am. Psychology Assn., Assn. for Humanistic Psychology, Common Cause. Mem. B'nai B'rith Women. Home: 8951 SW 60th Terrace Miami FL 33143 also 317 Hanover Arms Ct Winston-Salem NC 27104

SUTHERLAND, EARL WILBUR, JR., physician, educator; b. Burlingame, Kan., Nov. 19, 1915; B.S., Washburn Coll., 1937; M.D., Washington U., St. Louis, 1942; div.; 3 children. Intern Barnes Hosp., St. Louis, 1942; asst. in pharmacology Washington U. Sch. Medicine, 1940-42, instr., 1945-46, biochemist, 1946-50, asst. prof., 1950-52, asso. prof., 1952-53; with OSRD, 1943-45; prof. pharmacology, dir. dept. Case Wastern Res. U. Sch. Medicine, Cleve., 1953-63; prof. physiology Vanderbilt U. Sch. Medicine, Nashville, 1963—. Mem. panel on metabolism sect. biochemistry com. on growth NRC, 1953-54; pharmacologist, exptl. therapeutist USPHS, 1954-58; mem. pharmacological tng. com. NIH, 1958-62, 63-65, mem. arthritis and metabolic disease program com., 1966—. Recipient Nobel prize in medicine and physiology for research in hormones, 1971. Mem. Nat. Acad. Sci., A.A.A.S., Soc. Biol. Chemists, Am. Chem. Soc., Soc. Pharmacology. Research on enzymatic and hormonal aspects of carbodhydrate metabolism, mechanism of action of hormones and drugs, intermediary carbohydrate metabolism, cyclic nucleotides. Office: Dept Physiology Vanderbilt University School of Medicine Nashville TN 37203*

SUTHERLAND, FRANK, editor; b. nr. Smyrna, Tenn., May 31, 1945; s. Ernest Franklin and Fontelle (Moore) S.; B.A. in Philosophy, Vanderbilt U., 1970; m. Ann Katherine Sparkes, Dec. 28, 1967 (div.). Campus corr. Nashville Tennessean, 1963, gen. assignment reporter, 1964, youth page editor, 1965-66, reporter, 1966-69, edn. editor, 1969—. Mem. Sigma Delta Chi (pres.). Home: 3436 Love Circle Nashville TN 37212 Office: 1100 Broadway Nashville TN 37202

SUTHERLAND, JOHN ALFRED, petroleum co. exec.; b. Kansas City, Mo., Feb. 16, 1924; s. Jesse Dick and Grace (Slaughter) S.; student Kansas City Jr. Coll., 1941-43; B.S., U. Mo., 1948; m. Norma Elenore Doerner, June 25, 1949; children—Ellen Laura, Karen Lee. Jr. mech. engr. Stanolind Oil & Gas Co., Okla., Wyo., 1948-51; sr. engr. Sunray Oil Corp., La., Okla., 1951-55; v.p. Union Tex. Petroleum div. Allied Chem. Corp., Houston, 1955—; v.p., dir. Uno-Tex Petroleum Corp. Served with USNR, 1943-46. Registered profl. engr., Okla., La. Mem. Am. Petroleum Inst. (mem. gen. com. div. refining 1968-73), Nat. Gas Processors Assn. (v.p. 1970-73, dir.), Tau Beta Pi. Patentee in field. Home: 415 Coachman Lane Houston TX 77024 Office: 3000 Richmond Av Houston TX 77001

SUTHERLAND, JOHN PATRICK, journalist; b. Kansas City, Mo., June 12, 1920; s. Joseph Frederick and Hazel Marie (Hogan) S.; A.B., U. Mo., 1947, B.Jour., 1948; m. Virginia Claire Shockley, Oct. 19, 1942. Reporter, Spirit Lake (Ia.) Beacon, 1937; asst. editor Barrick Pub. Co., 1948-50; mem. Washington staff Wall Street Jour., 1951-52; White House corr. U.S. News and World Report, Washington, 1953—. Chmn. bd. trustees Merriman Smith Meml. Fund, Washington, until 1972. Served to lt. F.A. AUS, World War II; PTO. Mem. White House Corrs. Assn. (pres. 1971-72), Mil. Order Carabao. Roman Catholic. Club: Nat. Press (Washington). Author: Men of Waterloo, 1966. Office: US News and World Report 2300 N St NW Washington DC 20037

SUTHERLAND, RAYMOND CARTER, educator; b. Horse Cave, Ky., Nov. 5, 1917; s. Raymond Carter and Ruth (Veluzat) S.; student Transylvania Coll., 1935-36; A.B., U. Ky., 1939, M.A., 1950, Ph.D., 1953; grad. Gen. Theol. Sem., 1942. Ordained to ministry Episcopal Ch., 1942; curate St. Luke's Ch., Anchorage, Ky., 1942-44; prof. U. Tenn., 1953-57, Ga. State U., Atlanta, 1957—; research grant U. Oxford, 1959. Served as chaplain, capt. AUS, 1944-47, PTO, ETO. Recipient research grant from Georgia State Coll. for work on medieval manuscripts. Mem. Am. Archaeol. Assn., Heraldry Soc. Eng., Medieval Acad. Am., Modern Lang. Assn., Oriental Ceramic Soc. (London), Heraldry Soc. (London). Am. Author: Medieval English Conceptions of Hell as Derived from Biblical, Patristic, and Native Germanic Sources, 1953; The Religious Background of Swift's A Tale of A Tub, 1958; Mechanics of Versification, 1963, 2d edit., 1964; The Celibate Beowulf, the Gospels and the Liturgy (Ga. State Coll. Monograph series), 1964. Contbr. articles profl. jours. Home: 50 Polo Dr NE Atlanta GA 30309

SUTHERLAND, THOMAS ALLEN, librarian; b. Owensboro, Ky., Oct. 24, 1940; s. Adron Cohen and Ruth Moina (Christian) Sutherland; B.A., Ky. Wesleyan Coll., 1964; M.L.S., U. Ky., 1965; m. Gayle Moss, Aug. 28, 1965; children—Ginna Ruth, Todd Allen. Library asst. Ky. Wesleyan Coll., 1963-64; regional dir. Ky. Dept. Libraries, Frankfort, 1965-68; dir. Paducah (Ky.) Pub. Library, 1968—. Instr., Sch. Library Sci., U. Ky., 1970—; mem. Ky. State Adv. Council on Libraries, 1971-73, chmn., 1974. Served with AUS, 1958-59, 61-62. Recipient trustees award Ky. Library Assn., 1970. Mem. Am., Ky. (exec. sec. 1971—; trustees award 1970), Southeastern library assns., Phi Delta Theta. Methodist. Rotarian. Book reviewer Library Jour., 1970—. Contbr. articles to profl. pubs. Home: 285 Sycamore Dr Paducah KY 42001 Office: 555 Washington St Paducah KY 42001

SUTOW, WATARU WALTER, physician; b. Guadalupe, Cal., Aug. 31, 1912; s. Yasaku and Yoski (Sato) S.; A.B., Stanford U., 1939; M.D., U. Utah, 1945; m. Mary Hideo Korenaga, Sept. 7, 1937; children—Ollie Ellen (Mrs. Philip C. Williams), Chiyono Jean (Mrs. Philip M. Van Dam), Edmund Keith. Intern, resident pediatrics Salt Lake County Gen. Hosp., 1945-47; pediatrician Atomic Bomb Casualty Commn., Japan, 1948-50, 52-54; asso. pediatrician, asso. prof. pediatrics U. Tex. M.D. Anderson Hosp. and Tumor Inst., Houston, 1954-69, pediatrician, prof. pediatrics, 1969—; research collaborator Brookhaven Nat. Lab.; clin. asso. prof. pediatrics Baylor U. Served with M.C., AUS, 1951-53. Recipient research career award in pediatric oncology, USPHS, 1963—. Mem. Am. Assn. Cancer Research, Am. Soc. Clin. Oncology, Am. Fedn. Clin. Research, A.M.A., Am. Acad. Pediatrics. Editor: Clinical Pediatric Oncology. Research on cancer chemotherapy. Home: 4371 N MacGregor Way Houston TX 77004 Office: MD Anderson Hosptal Houston TX 77025

SUTTERLIN, FRANK WILLIAM, surgeon; b. Frankfort, Ky., Feb. 2, 1914; s. Frank Joseph and Rebecca Roseanna (Salyers) S.; B.S. cum laude, U. Fla., 1935; M.D., Johns Hopkins, 1939; m. Jeanelle Carter, Apr. 29, 1939; children—Frank William, Jon Christopher. Intern, Union Meml. Hosp., Balt., 1939-40; resident obstetrics and gynecology and surgery Hosp. for Women Md., 1940-43; practice medicine, specializing in gen. surgery, Bristol, Tenn. and Va., 1947—; chief surg. sect. Bristol (Tenn.) Meml. Hosp., 1959-60. Pres., Bristol (Tenn.) Tb Assn., 1951-53. Served to maj., M.C., AUS, World War II. Decorated Bronze Star. Fellow A.C.S.; mem. So., Tenn. med. assns., Sullivan-Johnson County Med. Soc. Kiwanian. Home: 217 Maple Tree Dr Bristol TN 37620 Office: 4-N Doctors Bldg Bristol TN 37620

SUTTLE, STEPHEN HUNGATE, lawyer; b. Uvalde, Tex., Mar. 17, 1940; s. Dorwin Wallace and Elizabeth (Barrett) S.; B.A. cum laude, Washington and Lee U., 1962; J.D. U. Tex., 1965; m. Rosemary Davison, Aug. 3, 1963; children—Michael Barrett, David Paull, John Stewart. Admitted to Tex. bar, 1965; briefing atty. Judge Leo Brewster, U.S. Dist. Ct. No. dist. Tex., Fort Worth, 1965-67; asso. mem. firm McMahon, Smart, Wilson, Camp, Lee & Surovik, Abilene, 1967-70, partner, 1970—. Dir. Zavala County Bank, Crystal City, 1964-65. Sec. bd. dirs. Boys Clubs Abilene, 1970—; active Abilene chpt. United Fund, 1970—. Chmn. Taylor County Dolph Briscoe for Gov. campaign, 1972, 74, Citizens for Better Govt., 1974—. Bd. dirs. Abilene Fine Arts Mus., 1971-72, Community Action Program, 1972. Mem. Jr. Bar Tex. (chmn. bd.; sec., treas.), Abilene (sec., treas. 1968-69), Tex., Am. bar assns., Abilene C. of C., Delta Tau Delta. Democrat. Episcopalian. Club: Westwood Raquet (Abilene). Home: 1405 Woodland Trail Abilene TX 79605 Office: PO Box 1440 Abilene TX 79604

SUTTLES, WILLIAM MAURRELLE, clergyman, educator; b. Ben Hill, Ga., July 25, 1920; s. Wiley Maurrelle and Eddie Lou (Campbell) S.; B.C.S., Ga. State U., 1942; M.R.E., Emory U., 1953, M.Th., 1947; M. Div., Yale, 1946; Ed.D., Auburn U., 1958; D.D., Mercer U., 1972; m. Julia Lanette Lovern, Jan. 28, 1950. Ordained to ministry Baptist Ch., 1938; pastor Haralson (Ga.) Bapt. Ch., 1950—, Luthersville Bapt. Ch., 1951-62; faculty Ga. State U., Atlanta, 1942—, prof. speech, 1957—, exec. v.p., provost, 1970—, also prof. ednl. adminstrn. and higher edn., Dir. First Ga. Bank, Atlanta Fed. Savings and Loan Assn. Mem. Ga. Sci. and Tech. Commn., 1964-72, Citizens Bond Study Commn., 1965—; past chmn. men's council Atlanta League Women Voters, 1963; past chmn. Walter H. and Marjorie M. Rich Scholarship Fund; mem. Christian Council Met. Atlanta. Mem. Com. 100 for Better Edn. in Atlanta; chmn. Joint Citizens Adv. com. to study Atlanta and Fulton County govts.; mem. southwestern regional manpower adv. com. U.S. Dept. Labor, 1972—. Trustee Ga. State U. Athletic Assn., Ga. State U. Found., George M. Sparks Scholarship Fund, John and Mary Franklin Found., Tift Coll., Hillside Cottages; past bd. trustees Marion Howard Sch.; past bd. dirs. Fulton County chpt. Am. Cancer Soc., Fulton-DeKalb chpt. March of Dimes. Served with USNR, 1944-46. Named Rural Minister of Year, State of Ga., 1959; Alumnus of Year, Ga. State U., 1964; Clergyman of Yr., Ga. region Nat. Conf. Christians and Jews, 1971; Faculty Mem. of Yr., Delta Zeta, 1964-65. Mem. Ga. State U. Alumni Assn. (trustee, pres.), Ga. Press Assn. (hon.), N.E.A., Ga. Assn. Educators, Atlanta C. of C., Sigma Nu, Alpha Kappa Psi, Kappa Phi Kappa, Phi Delta Kappa, Kappa Delta Pi, Phi Eta Sigma, Sigma Pi Alpha, Phi Kappa Phi, Beta Gamma Sigma, Omicron Delta Kappa, Sigma Tau Delta. Mason (Shriner), Kiwanian (pres. 1966). Club: Commerce (Atlanta). Home: 2734 Piney Wood Dr East Point GA 30344

SUTTON, FREDERICK ISLER, JR., realtor; b. Greensboro, N.C., Sept. 13, 1916; s. Fred I. and Annie (Fry) S.; grad. Culver (Ind.) Mil. Acad., 1934; A.B., U. N.C., 1939, postgrad. Law Sch,, 1939-41; grad. Realtor's Inst., 1956, postgrad. Grad. Sch., 1957; m. Helen Sykes Morrison, Mar. 18, 1941; children—Fred I. III, Frank Morrison. Propr., Fred I. Sutton, Jr., realtor, Kinston, N.C., 1946—; dir. Hotel Kinston; dean Realtors Inst., U. N.C., 1966, 67. Chmn. Kinston Parking Authority; v.p., dir. Ednl. Found., 1966; sec. Indsl. Devel. Com.; chmn. Kinston Water Resources Commn.; pres. United Fund, 1969-71. Trustee Florence Crittenton Services, 1971, bd. dirs., 1972-74. Served from ensign to lt. comdr., USNR, 1941-46. Mem. N.C. (v.p. 1957), Kinston (pres., Realtor of Year 1963) bds. realtors, N.C. Assn. Real Estate Bds. (dir.), Nat. (rep. N.C. Realtors State Assns. com. 1969, 70), N.C. (v.p. 1959, 61-63, chmn. edn. com. 1964, regional v.p. 1966) assns. realtors, Realtor's Inst. (trustee 1961-63, v.p. 1966), S.R., Kinston C. of C. (v.p. 1967, 69). Presbyn. (deacon). Mason (32 deg., Shriner), Kiwanian (pres. 1964). Home: 1101 N Queen St Kinston NC 28501 Office: Sutton Bldg Kinston NC 28501

SUTTON, IRVING CLARENCE, JR., furniture mfg. co. exec.; b. Oklahoma City, Dec. 29, 1910; s. Irving Clarence and Cornelia (White) S.; student Capitol City Bus. Coll., Little Rock; Ruby Gordon Hefley, June 1929 (div. Apr. 1953); children—Cornelia (Mrs. Bill Bates), Bobby L.; m. 2d, Audie M. Henson, Mar. 8, 1958. Asst. postmaster, Lurton, Ark., 1927-52; propr. Lurton Gen. Store, 1941-52; gen. mgr. I.C. Sutton Handle Factory (name changed to Sutton Products, Inc., 1958), Harrison, Ark., 1952—, pres., 1958—; trustee Sutton Estate Trust. Mem. Boone County Republican Com., 1960—. Mason, Lion. Home: 1214 Berry St Harrison AR 72601 Office: 1200 N Spring St PO Box 191 Harrison AR 72601

SUTTON, ORUS RICHARD, ednl. adminstr.; b. Granville, Tenn., June 12, 1916; s. Thomas Benjamin and Ethel Maye (Brown) S.; B.S., Tenn. Tech. U., 1938; M.A., Northwestern U., 1942; Ed.D., U. Tenn., 1967; m. Frances DeLyle Weller, Aug. 24, 1949; children—Thomas Weller, Elizabeth Ann. Tchr., asst. dean of men, bookkeeper, Baxter Sem., Baxter, Tenn., 1938-39; instr. Bus. Jackson County High Sch., Gainesboro, Tenn., 1939-40, Morristown (Tenn.) High Sch., 1940-42; head. dept. Bus. Middle Ga. Coll., Cochran, 1942-44; supr. student tchrs. Murray (Ky.) State Coll., 1944-45; head dept. bus. adminstrn. East Tenn. State U., Johnson City, 1945-56; head dept. bus. edn. and bus. adminstrn. Appalachian State U., Boone, N.C., 1956-70, head dept. bus. edn., coordinator grad. programs, 1970—. Recipient Outstanding Tchrs. award Appalachian State U., 1971. Mem. Nat., Nat. Bus., So. Bus., Am. Vocational edn. assns., Internat. Soc. Bus. Edn., N.C. Assn. Educators, Delta Pi Epsilon, Phi Delta Kappa, Pi Omega Pi. Mason. Home: 205 Pine St Boone NC 28607 Office: College of Business Appalachian State Univ Boone NC 28607

SUTTON, PHILIP GARLAND, JR., marketing cons.; b. New Albany, Ind., May 8, 1936; s. Philip Garland and Ona (Tucker) S.; student Western Mich. U., 1954-56; B.S., Purdue U., 1958; postgrad. Northeastern U., 1962-63, Union Coll., 1964-65; m. Marsha Anne McCauley, June 10, 1961; children—Philip Garland III, David Maurice, Elizabeth Tucker. Tech. rep. Am. Cyanamid Co., Boston, 1958-63; market devel. specialist Gen. Electric Co., Waterford, N.Y., 1963-66, mgr. southwestern dist., Dallas, 1966-69, mgr. plastic additive project, Waterford, 1969-71, mgr. fluids sect., 1971-72; pres. Sutton Assos., marketing cons., Houston, 1972—. Served with USCGR, 1959-60. mem. Soc. Plastics Industries, Soc. Aerospace Materials and Process Engrs. Delta Chi. Unitarian. Lion. Home: 10711 Creektree Dr Houston TX 77070 Office: 9800 NW Freeway Houston TX 77018

SUTTON, ROBERT HAROLD, juvenile probation, group care cons.; b. Mathews, Va., May 16, 1942; s. Freeman Walter and Virginia Hurst (Callio) S.; student Ferrum Jr. Coll., 1964-65; B.S., Va. Commonwealth U., 1971; m. Lois Jane Mitchell, Aug. 21, 1965; 1 son, Scott Dale. Supr. Study Home for Boys, Va. Dept. Welfare and Instns., Richmond, 1965-66, asst. supt., 1966-69, supt. Pinecrest Center, 1969-73, cons. probation, detention Tidewater Region, Norfolk, 1973—. Served with USAF, 1960-63. Mem. Va. Juvenile Officers Assn., Norfolk Jr. C. of C. Home: 1078 Level Green Blvd Virginia Beach VA 23462 Office: Div. Youth Service 9 Koger Exec Center Suite 222 Norfolk VA 23502

SUTTON, WILLIAM WALLACE, biologist, educator; b. Monticello, Miss., Dec. 15, 1930; s. Talmon Lawrence and Bessie (Lewis) S.; B.A., Dillard U., 1953; M.S., Howard U., 1959, Ph.D., 1965; postgrad. U. Ore., summer 1960, U. Rochester, summer 1961; m. Leatrice Hubbard, Aug. 28, 1954; children—William Wallace, Jr., Averell Hubbard, Sheryl Lynn, Alan David, Allison Maria, Gavin Jerome. Med. technician D.C. Gen. Hosp., Washington, 1955-59; instr. biology Dillard U., New Orleans, 1959-65, asst. prof., 1965-66, asso. prof., 1966-69, prof. biology, acting chmn. div. natural scis., 1969-70, chmn. div. natural scis., 1970—. Mem. troop com. Boy Scouts Am. Past pres. Pan Hellenic Council New Orleans; mem. Library Improvement Com. La. Trustee WYES-TV, La. Health Plan; bd. dirs. Urban League Greater New Orleans, New Orleans chpt. Nat. Conf. Christians and Jews, New Orleans Community Relations Council; mem. com. undergrad. research La. Heart Assn. Nat. Def. Edn. Act fellow, 1962-63; asso. Danforth Found. Mem. N.Y., La. acads. sci., Nat. Inst. Sci., (pres. 1973—), A.A.A.S., Am. Inst. Biol. Sci., Soc. Protozoologists, Sigma Xi, Beta Beta Beta, Omega Psi Phi, Beta Kappa Chi. Home: 1837 Pratt Dr New Orleans LA 70122 Office: 2601 Gentilly Blvd New Orleans LA 70122

SVANAS, GEORGE WILLIAM, lawyer; b. El Reno, Okla., Nov. 10, 1925; s. George Andrew and Martha M. (Judenschwager) S.; student El Reno Jr. Coll., 1943, J.D., U. Okla., 1950; m. Gloria Tanner, Dec. 23, 1949; children—Gregory W., Galen T. Admitted to Tex. bar, 1951, since practiced in Odessa; with Phillips Petroleum Co., Odessa, 1950-53; asso. firm Stowe and Harman, 1953-59; mem. firm Stowe, Harman, Svanas, Farnsworth and McCrea, 1959-65, Stowe and Svanas, 1965-66, Svanas and Svanas, 1966—. Dir., officer Tank Service & Constrn. Co., Inc., Odessa, 1958—, Anderson Base Co., Inc., Odessa, 1961—, San Angelo (Tex.) Raceway Park, Inc., 1973—. Served with USAAF, 1943-46; ETO, MTO. Mem. State Bar Tex., Am., Tex., Okla., Ector County (sec. 1956, dir. 1963-67, 71-72) bar assns., Delta Theta Phi. Eagle (v.p. 1952-53), pres. 1953-54), Lion (v.p. 1964-65, dir. 1967-69). Club: Am. Bus. (sec. 1954-55). Home: 2100 Bonham St Odessa TX 79760 Office: 418 W 4th St Odessa TX 79760

SVARLIEN, EARLE OSCAR, educator; b. Overhalla, Norway, Mar. 25, 1906 (came to U.S. 1926, naturalized 1934); s. Johan and Charlotte (Kolberg) S.; student Western Wash. Coll., 1933-36; B.A., U. Wash., 1937, M.A., 1939; Ph.D., U.N.C., 1942; m. Mattie Stinson, June 7, 1942; 1 son, John Earle. Social sci. analyst Library of Congress, Washington, 1942-46; asso. prof. polit. sci. U. Fla., 1946-55, prof., 1955—; cons. pub. internat. law Govtl. Affairs Inst., Washington, 1969—. Decorated Knight's Cross 1st class Royal Order St. Olav (Norway), 1966. Mem. Am. Assn. U. Profs., UN Assn. (pres. chpt. 1966), Am. Soc. Internat. Law (exec. council 1962-65), World Peace through Law Center, Consular Law Soc. Author: Introduction to Law of Nations, 1955; Eastern Greenland Case in Historical Perspective, 1964. Contbr. articles to profl. jours. Home: 1635 NW 5th Av Gainesville FL 32601

SWAFFORD, WILLIAM BRYSON, educator; b. Monterey, Tenn., Aug. 23, 1912; s. William Carlin and Pearl (Kidwell) S.; B.S., U. Tenn., 1948; M.S., U. Miss., 1955; M.A., Memphis State U., 1958; LL.B., So. U., 1962; m. Violet Jeannette Lain, Nov. 28, 1943; children—Barbara Lain (Mrs. Jon Stanton), William Bryson, Patricia Ann (Mrs. Mark Grill). Instr., U. Tenn. Coll. Pharmacy, Memphis, 1945-55, asst. prof., 1955-61, asso. prof., head dept. pharm. adminstrn., 1961-63, prof., chmn. dept. pharmaceutics, 1963-71, asst. dean, 1971—. Cons. VA hosps., Memhis, Nashville; mem. research team Marion Labs. Indsl.

Pharm. Research; sec.-treas. dist. 3 Nat. Assn. Bds. Pharmacy-Am. Assn. Colls. Pharmacy. Served to maj. AUS, 1941-46; ETO; col. Res. ret. Decorated Silver Star medal, Bronze Star medal, Purple Heart; French Fouragerre; named hon. citizen Knoxville, 1973. Dilomate Am. Bd. Pharm. Dilomates. Fellow Am. Coll. Apothecaries; mem. Am., Tenn. (Pharmacist of Year 1973), Memphis, Shelby County pharm. assns., Mil. Order World Wars, Res. Officers Assn., Am. Assn. Colls. Pharmacy (chmn. conf. tchrs.), Delta Chi Delta, Phi Delta Kappa, Kappa Psi, Rho Chi. Author: Pharmacy and the Law, A Manual For Practicing Pharmacists, 1969; A Correspondence Course in Pharmaceutical Law, 1969; A Correspondence Course Non-Prescription Drugs, 1971; co-author other corr. courses. Home: 1840 Poplar Estates Pkwy Germantown TN 38038 Office: 874 Union Av Memphis TN 38103

SWAIM, GUY WINFIELD, architect; b. Little Rock, Sept. 2, 1906; s. Guy Winfield and Annie Lillian (Cook) S.; B.Arch., Auburn (Ala.) U., 1932; m. Mildred Elizabeth Cox, Sept. 1, 1934; children—Sylvia (Mrs. Michael McWilliams), Cecilia (Mrs. Oliver Crary). Founder, Swaim, Allen, Wellborn & Assos., architect-engrs., Little Rock, 1933—. Mem. Pulaski County Planning Bd., 1955-61, North Little Rock Planning Commn., 1956-60. Bd. dirs. Pulaski County chpt. A.R.C. Served as 2d lt., F.A., U.S. Army, 1931-38. Mem. A.I.A. (past pres. Ark. chpt.), North Little Rock C. of C. (dir., past pres.), Sigma Nu. Elk, Lion. Address: 215 Louisiana St Little Rock AR 72201

SWAIM, JOHNNY RAY, basketball coach; b. Jean, Tex., Sept. 9, 1929; s. Erin Ray and Dollie (Allen) S.; B.S. in Phys. Edn., Tex. Christian U., 1953, M.Ed., 1956; m. Joan Hewatt, Nov. 7, 1953; children—Michael Ray, Susan Elizabeth. Head basketball coach La Vega High Sch., Waco, Tex., 1955-56; asst. basketball coach Tex. Christian U., Ft. Worth, 1956-67, head basketball coach, 1967—. Bd. dirs. Panther Boys' Club, Fort Worth. Served to 1st lt. USMCR, 1953-55. Named championship coach for team championship Southwestern Conf. Nat. Collegiate Athletic Assn., 1967-68, 70-71; named Southwestern Conf. Coach of Year, 1971, Nat. Collegiate Athletic Assn. Dist. VI Coach of Year, 1971. Mem. Tex. High Sch. Coaches Assn., Tex. Christian U. Ex-Lettermen's Assn. Mem. Christian Ch. Home: 3721 Fenton St Fort Worth TX 76133

SWAIN, ALICE MARIE MCNEELY, reading specialist; b. Oklahoma City, Feb. 3, 1924; d. William Henry and Lucy Bruce (McCuiston) McNeely; B.S., Langston U., 1946; M.E., U. Okla, 1952; m. Robert Alphonso Swain, Aug. 24, 1946; children—Robert Alphonso II, Lecia Danee. Tchr. schs., Oklahoma City, 1950—; pres. Together Enterprises, Oklahoma City, 1971—; asst. prof. edn., coordinator reading Langston (Okla.) U. Recipient S.W. Regional Sigma of Year award, 1962, U. Okla. math. grantee, 1963, Livingtext book grantee, 1964; named one of 10 outstanding nat. Sigma women, 1965. Mem. Urban League Guild, N.A.A.C.P., YWCA, Okla. Edn. Assn., N.E.A., Nat. Pan-Hellenic Council (sec. 1970-72, v.p. 1972—, nat. pres. 1974-75), Sigma Gamma Rho (past chmn. bd. dirs., Hall of Fame). Mem. Christian Ch. Club: Tes Trams Social (Oklahoma City). Editor: Alice's Short Stories, 1972. Contbr. column The Black Dispatch, 1974. Home: 3016 Norcrest Dr Oklahoma City OK 73111 Office: 3016 Norcrest Dr Oklahoma City OK 73111

SWAIN, DWIGHT VREELAND, educator; b. Rochester, Mich., Nov. 17, 1915; s. J. Edgar and Florence (Vreeland) S.; A.A., Jackson Jr. Coll., 1935; B.A., U. Mich., 1937; M.A., U. Okla., 1954; m. Joye Raechel Boulton, Feb. 12, 1969; 1 son, Thomas McCray. Newspaper and mag. editor, Mich., Pa., Cal., 1937-41; scriptwriter motion picture unit U. Okla., Norman, 1949-65, prof. journalism, 1952—; v.p. BHS Prodns., Inc., 1961-71. Book critic Sunday Oklahoman, 1950-60; cons., mem. nat. adv. bd. Palmer Writers Sch., Mpls., 1966—; judge film and novels Nat. Cowboy Hall of Fame and Western Heritage Center, Oklahoma City, 1960—. Served with AUS, 1942-46. Mem. Sci. Fiction Writers Am., Univ. Film Prodns. Assn., Am. Med. Writers Assn., Am. Assn. U. Profs. Author: Tricks and Techniques of the Selling Writer, 1965. Producer, writer film Stark Fear, 1963. Contbr. articles to profl. jours. Home: 1304 McKinley Av Norman OK 73069

SWAIN, JAMES MAURICE, physician; b. San Jose, Costa Rica, June 19, 1924 (parents Am. citizens); s. James Obed and Nancy (Cox) S.; M.D., U. Tenn., 1947; m. Barbara Halsted, July 15, 1955; children—Thomas Lester, Michael Lee. Intern St. Joseph Hosp., Memphis, 1948-49; research asst. anatomy U. Tenn., 1948, instr. anatomy, 1950; fellow radiology Cleve. Clinic, 1950, 53-54; pvt. practice, Lake Charles, La., 1954—; clin. instr. radiology La. State U., 1961; chief of radiology Lake Charles Meml. Hosp.; vis. radiologist La. State U. Sch. Medicine. Served from pvt. to pfc, AUS, 1943-46; to capt. USAF, 1951-52. Diplomate Am. Bd. Radiology. Mem. Am. Coll. Radiology, Radiol. Soc. La., A.M.A., La. Med. Soc., So. Med. Assn., A.A.A.S., La.-Tex. Gulf Coast Radiol. Soc., Am. Musicological Assn., Am. Mus. Instrument Soc., Flying Physicians Assn., Nuclear Med. So. Home: 3929 Bayouwood Dr Lake Charles LA 70601 Office: 2900 2d Av Lake Charles LA 70601

SWAIN, JAMES O(BED), educator; b. Greenfield, Ind., Dec. 31, 1896; s. Ashbell Willard and Laetitia (Lambert) S.; A.B., Ind. U., 1921, A.M., 1923; Ph.D., U. Ill., 1932; student U. Madrid, summer 1933, U. Chile, 1951-52; m. Nancy Jane Cox, June 19, 1923; children—James Maurice, Juan Robert. Mem. faculty Mich. State Coll., 1931-37, asst. prof. modern langs., 1935-37; prof. chmn. dept. Romance langs. U. Tenn. 1937-58; guest dir. summer langs. sch. Western Colo. Coll., 1937; guest lectr. Am. lit. U. Chile, summer session, 1952; guest lectr. U. Madrid, summer 1958, Maracaibo, Venezuela, 1959; exec. sec. Mountain Interstate Fgn. Lang. Conf., 1963-64; vis. prof. U. Ky., 1964—, Maryville Coll., 1966, Roanoke Coll., 1967, Lee Coll., 1969-70. Served with C.E., U.S. Army, 1918-19. Mem. Modern Lang. Assn. Am. (sectional officer various times), Central, So. States, South Atlantic (pres. 1948-49) modern lang. assns., Am. Assn. Tchrs. Spanish (exec. com. 1949-52), Am. Assn. Tchrs. French, Am. Assn. Tchrs. Italian, Institute de Literature Iberoamericana, Sigma Delta Pi (nat. exec. sec. 1947-63). Methodist (deacon). Author: Rumbo a Mexico, 1942; Ruedo Antillano, 1946; Vicente Blasco Ibanez, Realistic Techniques, 1959; Juan Marin-Chilean, the Man and his Writings, 1971. Co-editor: Les Chemins de la Mer. Asso. editor Hispania, 1936-42; asst. bus. mgr. Modern Lang. Jour., 1938-51. Travel Europe, Latin Am., South Am. Contbr. to Compton's Pictured Ency., Latin Am. and Spanish Lit. Home: 414 Forest Park Blvd Carlton Towers Knoxville TN 37919

SWAIN, ROBERT OLIVER, assn. exec.; b. Clinton, Conn., Jan. 11, 1910; s. Oliver Black and Everetta (Dowd) S.; B.A., Denison U., 1933; certificate in research, Harvard, 1938; m. Beth Bower, Aug. 7, 1933; children—Anne (Mrs. Thomas W. McNeill), Robert Oliver, Peter J. Engr., Tex. Dept. Hwys., Austin, 1933-42; sr. hwy. engr. Bur. Pub. Rds., Washington, 1946-47; transp. adviser State Dept., Washington, 1947-48; pres. Internat. Road Fedn., Washington, 1948—. Patron Sch. Engring., Am. U. Beirut (Lebanon), 1962—; mem. bd. consultants Eno Found. Hwy. Traffic Control, 1963—; adviser Nat. Hwy. Inst., 1971—; mem. steering com. hwy engring. developing countries U. Surrey (Eng.), 1972—. Bd. dirs. Asian Inst. Tech. Found., N.Y.C., 1971—. Served with C.E., AUS, 1942-46; ETO. Decorated Bronze Star; chevalier Legion of Honor (France); Grand Cross of Merit (Spain), Order of Merit (Peru), Order of Hwy. Merit (Cuba), Order of Occident (Austria), Order of Manuel Amador Guerrero (Panama); recipient Man of Year award Mexican Hwy. Assn., 1964; Gold medal award Assn. of Hwys. (Spain), 1971; Distinguished Alumnus award Denison U., 1957. Mem. Inst. Traffic Engrs., Am. Soc. Mil. Engrs., Automotive Orgn. Team, Kappa Sigma, Omicron Delta Kappa. Clubs: Army and Navy, Washington Golf and Country (Washington). Contbr. articles to profl. jours. Home: 1001 Wilson Blvd Arlington VA 22209 Office: 1023 Washington Bldg Washington DC 20005

SWAIN, SAMUEL CURTIS, ins. agt., retail trade exec.; b. Sherman, Tex., Aug. 17, 1918; s. Samuel Curtis and Frances Marie (Hogan) S.; student So. Meth. U., 1938-39, Dallas Sch. Bus. Adminstrn., 1936-40; m. Jean Sanders, July 7, 1945; 1 dau., Jean Martha (Mrs. Ray Barrett Baldwin III). With Proctor & Gamble Co., Dallas, Houston and Lufkin, Tex., 1936-42; prin. Curtis Swain Ins., Lufkin, 1947—; with Perry Bros., retail trade, 1947—, chmn. bd., 1965—; dir. First Bank & Trust Co., Tex. Foundries, Inc. Chmn., Angelina County Airport Bd., 1963—. Served with USAAF, 1942-45 (prisoner of war Germany 1943-45). Decorated Air Medal, Purple Heart. Roman Catholic. Home: 712 Jefferson St Lufkin TX 75901 Office: 318 Perry Bldg Lufkin TX 75901

SWALIN, BENJAMIN FRANKLIN, orchestral dir.; b. Mpls., Mar. 30, 1901; s. Benjamin N. and Augusta (Johnson) S.; B.S., Columbia, 1928, M.A., 1930; Ph.D., U. Vienna, 1932; diplomas, Inst. Mus. Art, N.Y.C., 1926, 28; fellow for study in Europe, Inst. Internat. Edn., 1930-32; diploma Hochschule für Musik, Vienna, 1932; m. Martha Maxine McMahon, Jan. 1, 1935. Violinist, Mpls. Symphony Orch., 1919-21; prof. violin and theory DePauw U., Greencastle, Ind., 1933-35; asso. prof. music U. N.C., 1935-49; dir. N.C. Symphony Orch., 1939—. Recipient N.C. Gold Medallion award, 1967; Morrison award for performing arts N.C., 1968. Mem. Am. Musicol. Soc., MacDowell Colony, Nat. Fedn. Music Clubs, Delta Chi, Phi Mu Alpha Sinfonia. Clubs: Columbia University; Torch (Durham, N.C.). Author: The Violin Concerto: a Study in German Romanticism, 1941. Contbr. articles to music assn. jours. and books; composer of several orchestral works, and compositions for violin and piano, chamber music and voice. Guest dir. in Guadalajara and Mexico City, Mexico. Home: Chapel Hill NC 27514

SWALIN, MAXINE MCMAHON (MRS. BENJAMIN F. SWALIN), musician; b. Waukee, Ia., May 7, 1903; d. George Thomas and Mary E. (Wilson) McMahon; student Stephens Coll., 1922, Drake U., 1923; diploma in piano and theory Inst. Mus. Art Juilliard Sch. Music, 1928; B.A., U. Ia., 1932; M.A., Radcliffe Coll. 1936; m. Benjamin F. Swalin, Jan. 1, 1935. Dir. theory dept. Hartford Sch. Music, Conn., 1928-30; high sch. tchr., Oxford and Chapel Hill, N.C., 1936-38; adminstrv. asst. N.C. Symphony Soc., Chapel Hill, 1939—; musician (piano, celesta, harpsichord), commentator children's concerts N.C. Symphony Orch., 1942—. Recipient Distinguished Citizen award Gov. N.C., 1964. Mem. Am. Assn. U. Women, Radcliffe Alumnae Assn. Home: Maxaben Jones Ferry Rd Chapel Hill NC 27514 Office: 3031/2 N Columbia St Chapel Hill NC 27514

SWAN, JACK TURNER, physician; b. Greenville, S.C., Mar. 20, 1931; s. Robert Patterson Wren and Grace (Turner) S.; B.A., Vanderbilt U., 1952; M.D., 1956, postgrad., 1956-57, 58-59; postgrad. U. Cal. at San Francisco, 1957-58; M.P.H., Johns Hopkins U., 1960; m. Lou Thomas Klein, Sept. 13, 1958; children—Thomas P., Molly H., Sally W., Reed L., Kate T. Intern, Vanderbilt U., Nashville, 1956-57, resident 1958-59; resident U. Cal. at San Francisco, 1957-58; practice medicine, specializing in pediatrics, Nashville, 1964-72; mem. staff Nashville Meml. Hosp., Vanderbilt Univ. Hosp.; clin. instr. dept. pediatrics Med. Sch., Vanderbilt U., 1964—. Cons. Head Start program Office Econ. Opportunity, 1966—, Walter Reed Hosp., 1966—. Served with USPHS, 1960-63. USPHS fellow, 1959-60. Mem. Tenn. Med. Assn., Sigma Nu. Episcopalian. Club: Old Hickory (Tenn.) Golf and Country. Author (with L.B. Altstatt) Tumescence-Invisibility Theory, 1969. Home: 1104 Riverside St Old Hickory TN 37138 Office: 612 W Due West St Madison TN 37115

SWAN, MARCUS EDISON, JR., savs. and loan exec.; b. Lufkin, Tex., Aug. 9, 1941; s. Marcus Edison and Mary (Cochran) S.; B.B.A., North Tex. State U., 1964; m. Fredna Null, Aug. 20, 1966; 1 son, Gregory Kevin. Analytical revision reporter Dun & Bradstreet, Inc., Dallas, 1965-67; with Home Savs. and Loan Assn., Lufkin, 1967—, exec. v.p., 1970—, dir., 1973—; dir. Royal Underwriters, Inc., Home Savs. Investment Co. Mem. Lufkin Planning and Zoning Bd., 1972-74. Mem. Lufkin Jr. C. of C. Mem. Christian Ch. (mem. ch. bd. 1973-74). Home: 6 Trailwood Ct Lufkin TX 75901 Office: PO Box 448 Lufkin TX 75901

SWANSON, CHARLES HALLBERG, petroleum co., exec.; b. Luck, Wis., June 11, 1924; s. Charles and Annie (Hallberg) S.; B.C.S., Okla. Sch. Accountancy, 1948; m. Mertyce Christenson, Sept. 26, 1942; 1 dau., Toni (Mrs. George H. Meason III). Sales mgr. Anchor Petroleum Co., Tulsa, 1947-59; sr. v.p. Wanda Petroleum Co., Houston, 1959-71; owner, pres. Swanee Petroleum Co., Houston, 1971—. Served with AUS, 1943-46. Decorated Bronze Star. Mem. Nat. Liquified Petroleum Gas Assn. (dir., exec. com. 1968—). Mason. Home: 6314 Riverview St Houston TX 77027 Office: Swanee Petroleum Co 2200 Southwest Hwy Suite 40D Houston TX 77006

SWANSON, DAVID H(ENRY), economist; b. Anoka, Minn., Nov. 1, 1930; s. Henry Otto and Louise Isabell (Holiday) S.; B.A., St. Cloud State Coll., 1953; M.A., U. Minn., 1955; m. Suzanne Nash, Jan. 19, 1952; children—Matthew David, Christopher James. Economist area devel. dept. No. States Power Co., Mpls., 1955-56, staff asst., v.p. sales, 1956-57, economist indsl. devel. dept., 1957-63; dir. area devel. dept. Ia. So. Utilities Co., Centerville, 1963-67, dir. econ. devel. and research, 1967-70; dir. New Orleans Econ. Devel. Council, 1970-72; mgr. Kaiser Aetna Texas, New Orleans, 1972-73; dir. corp. research United Services Auto Assn., 1973—. Vice chmn. planning commn. Roseville, Minn., 1961; mem. Ia. Airport Planning Council; mem. adv. council office Comprehensive Health Planning; mem. adv. com. Center for Indsl. Research and Service, Advanced Mgmt. Research, Inc., 1967-70; mem. exec. council So. Ia. council Boy Scouts Am. County finance chmn. Republican Party, 1966-67. Bd. dirs. So. Indsl. Devel. Council, 1972-73, La. Indsl. Devel. Execs., Urban League New Orleans; bd. mgrs. Eastern New Orleans YMCA; mem. exec. com. La. State U. at New Orleans. Served with USAF, 1951-52. Mem. N.A.M., Am. Econ. Assn., Regional Sci. Assn., Am. Indsl. Devel. Council, Edison Electric Inst. (chmn. area devel. com.), Nat. Assn. Bus. Economists, Soc. for Ins. Research, Air Force Assn. Republican. Espiscopalian. Club: Toastmasters (past pres.). Address: United Services Auto Assn San Antonio TX 78288

SWANSON, DEAN CHARLES, telephone co. exec.; b. Mpls., Apr. 26, 1932; s. Dean Leroy and Laurene Grace (Johnson) S.; B.S., U.S. Naval Acad., 1957; m. Helen Kay Stewart, June 9, 1957; children—Sabrina, Dean, Christopher. Exec. v.p., dir. Standard Telephone Co., Cornelia, Ga., 1963—; dir. Teledata Corp., Cornelia Bank; sec.-treas. Multi-View TV, Inc. Chmn. Habersham County Indsl. Authority, 1970—; mem. Cornelia Planning Commn., 1965—; regional adviser Goals for Ga., 1971—; dist. chmn. Stay and See Ga., 1974. Served to capt. USAF, 1957-63. Mem. U.S. Ind. Telephone Assn. (small bus. com. 1968—), Ga. Telephone Assn. (pres. 1969-70), Ga. Mountain Assn. (pres. 1969-71), Cornelia C. of C. (pres. 1967), Ga. C. of C. (dir. indsl. devel. council 1968—). Methodist. Rotarian. Club: Kingwood Country (Clayton, Ga.). Home: Box 43 Cornelia GA 30531 Office: Box 400 Cornelia GA 30531

SWANSON, ELLIS LESTER, architect; b. San Antonio, Feb. 12, 1927; s. William Lester and Minnie Maud (Smith) S.; student U. Houston, 1946-48; B. Arch., U. Tex., 1952; m. Betty Jean Armstrong, July 19, 1953; children—Eric Lyle, Elisa Lynn. Draftsman, Ned. A. Cole, Austin, Tex., 1952, Robert L. Vogler, Corpus Christi, Tex., 1952-53, Walter C. Bowman, Harlingen, Tex., 1954-57; partner Bowman Swanson Hiester, Harlingen, 1953-66, Swanson Heister Wilson Boland, architects and engrs., 1966—; dir. BSH Service Corp., Harlingen. Pres., United Fund, Harlingen, 1969; Served with USNR, 1945-46, 50, 53-54. Mem. A.I.A. (chpt. pres. 1961). Episcopalian (sr. warden 1970). Clubs: Toastmasters (pres. 1960) (Harlingen). Lion (dist. gov. 1967). Prin. archtl. works include Mercedes High Sch., 1966, Harlingen Air Terminal, 1967, Harlingen Tourist Center, 1969, Harlingen C. of C. Office, 1969, LaJoya High Sch., 1971. Home: 1627 Sam Houston Dr Harlingen TX 78550 Office: 1220 W Harrison St Harlingen TX 78550

SWANSON, WALLACE MARTIN, lawyer; b. Fergus Falls, Minn., Aug. 22, 1941; s. Marvin Walter and Mary Louise (Lindsey) S.; B.A. with honors, U. Minn., 1962; LL.B. with honors, So. Meth. U., 1965; m. Janet Middleton, Jan. 21, 1964; 1 dau., Kristen Lindsey. Admitted to Tex. bar, 1965, since practiced in Dallas, 1965—; partner Hewett, Johnson, Swanson & Barbee, attys., Dallas, 1970—. Mem. Am., Dallas bar assns., State Bar Tex. (mem. securities subcom. corp., banking and bus. law com. 1972—), Barristers, Phi Alpha Delta, Phi Beta Kappa, Order of Woolsack. Articles editor Southwestern Law Jour., 1964-65. Home: 4611 Irvin Simmons Dr Dallas TX 75229 Office: Two Eleven N Ervay Bldg Ninth Floor Dallas TX 75201

SWARTHOUT, GERARD, JR., constrn. co. exec., civil engr.; b. Ft. Clayton, C.Z., May 14, 1922; s. Gerard and Marguerite Simmons (Downman) S.; B.C.E., Ga. Inst. Tech., 1947; m. Evelyn L. Presler, Nov. 10, 1945; children—Edith S. Norton, Gerard III. Engr. Ga. Hwy. Dept., 1947-54; engr. B.P. Lamb Co., Statesboro, Ga., 1954-65; engr., adminstr. Scott Bridge Co., Opelika, Ala., 1965—, exec. v.p., 1969—. Served to sgt., AUS, 1942-46. Registered profl. engr., Ga., Ala. Mem. Ala. Road Builders Assn. (dir. 1967-71, treas. 1971, sec. 1972, v.p. 1973). Episcopalian (vestryman, layreader 1950—). Elk. Home: 407 N 4th St Opelika AL 36801 Office: PO Box 2038 Opelika AL 36801

SWARTZ, HARRY, physician; b. Detroit, June 21, 1911; s. Isaac and Anne (Srere) S.; A.B., U. Mich., 1930, M.D., 1933; postgrad. N.Y. U., 1936-38; m. Eve Sutton, Oct. 3, 1942; 1 son, Mark Sutton. Intern, Michael Reese Hosp., Chgo., 1933-35; resident allergy N.Y. U. Med. Colls. and Clinics, 1936-38; asst. attending physician Inst. of Allergy, Roosevelt Hosp., N.Y.C., 1946-74; chief allergy clinic, asso. attending physician, adj. prof. medicine N.Y. Polyclinic Med. Sch. and Hosp., N.Y.C., 1957-74; med. dir. Soluble Products Corp., Bklyn., 1965-74; pres. Health Field Validation Corp., N.Y.C., 1965—; sci. dir. Ediciones P-L-M-S-A, 1974—. Med. editor Med. Opinion and Rev., 1965-74; editor-in-chief Investigacion Medica Internacional, 1974—. Served from 1st lt. to maj. M.C., AUS, 1942-46. Diplomate Am. Bd. Clin. Immunology and Allergy. Fellow Am. Acad. Allergy, Am. Coll. Allergists, Am. Assn. Clin. Immunology and Allergy, Am. Geriatric Soc., Internat. Acad. Applied Nutrition; mem. N.Y. Allergy Soc., Internat. Allergologic Soc., N.Y. Acad. Sci., A.A.A.S., A.M.A., N.Y. State, N.Y. County med. socs., Phi Beta Kappa, Alpha Omega Alpha, Phi Kappa Phi. Author: Allergy: What It Is and What To Do About It, 1949, rev. 1966; Your Hay Fever, 1951, rev., 1962; The Allergic Child, 1954; Laymans Medical Dictionary, 1956; The Allergy Guide Book, 1962, rev., 1966; Your Body (juvenile), 1962. Patentee safety and med. devices. Home: APDO 752 Cuernavaca MOR Mexico Office: 155 E 55th St New York City NY 10022 also Medellin 184-1 Mexico City 7 Mexico

SWARTZ, WILLIAM PERRY, JR., diversified indsl. co. exec.; b. Seven Mile Ford, Va., Sept. 21, 1911; s. William Perry and Elva Blanche (Worrell) S.; E.E., Va. Poly. Inst., 1933; m. Suelle McKellar, Mar. 29, 1935; children—William Perry III, Elva Ann (Mrs. James H. Simmons), Charles Eugene, Suelle Marie (Mrs. Jack Hall). Chmn. bd. William P. Swartz, Jr. & Co., Inc., Roanoke, Va., 1936-72; chmn. bd. Swartz Enterprises, diversified industries, Roanoke, 1966—; chmn. bd. Gen. Automation Corp., Gen. Service Industries Corp., Peak Industries Inc., United Va. Bank, 1963-66. Chmn. Roanoke Stadium Adv. Com., 1960-68; mem. Roanoke Bd. Health, 1955-69. Chmn. bd. trustees Ferrum (Va.) Coll., 1960-62. Mem. Gideons, Pocket Testament League, YMCA, Ashram Movement, Faith at Work, Lay Witness Missions, Internat. Prayer Fellowship. Methodist. Author: The Key to the Kingdom, 1968; God is in Business, 1971. Home: 1341 Sewell Lane SW Roanoke VA 24015 Office: PO Box 22 420 W Church Av Roanoke VA 24001

SWAYZE, THOMAS RANDOLPH, realtor; b. New Orleans, Sept. 16, 1924; s. Nelson Ryan and Golda (Glass) S.; student Tulane U., 1941-43, 46-47; m. Martha Anne Taylor, Feb. 4, 1950; children—Thomas Randolph, N. Taylor, Robert L. Floor broker New Orleans Cotton Exchange, 1947-59; v.p. Hardie Meric Realtors, New Orleans, 1959; v.p. sales Gertrude Gardener Inc., New Orleans, 1960-62; owner firm Richards & Swayze Inc., New Orleans, 1962-70; v.p. Latter & Blum, Inc. Realtors, 1971—. Served to 2d lt. USMCR, World War II, to capt. Korean Conflict. Decorated Air medal with gold star. Mem. New Orleans, Jefferson Parish real estate bds., Nat. Inst. Real Estate Brokers (pres. chpt.), Am. Inst. Real Estate Appraisers (residential mem.), Kappa Alpha. Club: Southern Yacht. Home: 1321 Nashville Av New Orleans LA 70115 Office: 7835 Maple St New Orleans LA 70118

SWEARINGEN, HAROLD LYNDON, petroleum co. exec.; b. Independence, Kan., Sept. 17, 1937; s. Lynn and Dorothy Grace (Swalley) S.; A.A., Independence Jr. Coll., 1957; B.S. in Elec. Engring., Kan. State U., 1960; m. Charlene Faye Meyer, Oct. 17, 1959; children—Renee, Lisa, Shari, Kurtis. Microwave technician Sinclair Pipe Line Co., Independence, 1960-61, sr. engr. communications dept., 1962-63, sr. engr. telecommunications dept., 1963-67; adminstr. operations telecommunications Sinclair Oil Co., N.Y.C., 1967-69; sr. telecommunications system design engr., 1967-69, Trans Alaska Pipeline, Houston, 1969-71; project mgr. telecommunications Atlantic Richfield Co., Tulsa, 1972—. Mem. I.E.E.E. Lutheran. Home: 6911 E 62d Pl Tulsa OK 74133 Office: 909 South Boston St Tulsa OK 74102

SWECKER, CHARLES EMMETT, physician; b. Salem, Va., Feb. 20, 1925; s. James Allen and Alice Gladys (Given) S.; student Va. Poly. Inst., 1942-43; B.S., Roanoke Coll., 1949; M.D., Med. Coll. Va., 1954; m. Betty Jane Alexander, June 14, 1952; children—Charles Emmett, Suzanne, Melanie, Stephanie. Student physician Juvenile Detention Home, Richmond, Va., Va. State Penitentiary, 1951-54; intern DePaul Hosp., Norfolk, Va., 1954-55; practice medicine, specializing in family practice, Wise, Va., 1954-62, Roanoke, Va.,

1962—, owner, operator Poages Mill Med. Clinic, Roanoke, 1968-72; mem. staffs Roanoke Meml. Hosp., Community Hosp. of Roanoke Valley, Shenendoah Hosp., Roanoke, Lewis-Gale Hosp., Roanoke; med. examiner Wise County and City of Norton, 1962; med. cons. Armed Forces Exam. and Entrance Sta., Roanoke, 1963-68; compensation physician U.S. Govt. Employes, 1969—, Eaton, Yale & Towne, Inc., 1967—, McLean Trucking Co., Inc., 1970—; exam. physician Roanoke County and City sch. bds., 1967—; med. dir. Roanoke Meth. Home, 1964—, Estate Life Ins. Co. of Am., 1970—; med. examiner City of Roanoke, 1967—; guest lectr. Ga. Police Acad., 1973; cons. Regional Medicare Office, 1971-72; pres., chmn. bd. Med. Services, Inc., 1967—. Mem. town council, Wise, Va., 1961. Bd. dirs. P.T.A. Served with Air Corps, USNR, 1943-46. Decorated D.F.C., Air Medal with five Stars. Mem. Am., Va. Acads. gen. practice, Med. Soc. Va., Roanoke Acad. Medicine. Methodist (youth counselor 1957-71). Home: 1117 Oakwood Dr SW Roanoke VA 24015 Office: 2026 Brambleton Av SW Roanoke VA 24015

SWECKER, DONALD BRYAN, advt. and sales exec.; b. Huttonsville, W. Va., Mar. 19, 1920; s. Holt Samuel and Lucy (Kittle) S.; grad. Potomac State Coll. of W. Va. U., 1940; postgrad. Davis Elkins Coll., 1941; student 149th Life Ins. Agy. Mgmt. Sch., 1947; m. Charlotta Irene Deets, Oct. 4, 1943; children—Mark, Edith, Benjamin, Emily, Kim, Lisa, Jeffrey, Andrew. With Peoples Life Ins. Co., Washington, 1946-72, agt., 1946-50, asst. dist. mgr., 1950-55, field tng. supr., 1955-57, sales promotion mgr., 1957-66, asst. v.p. advt., 1966-70, 2d v.p. advt., 1970-72, editor co. mag. PLICO, 1958-72; 2d v.p. pub. relations Capital Holding Corp., Louisville, 1972—. Moderator, instr. Communications Workshop, Coll. William and Mary, Williamsburg, Va., 1967. Pres. P.T.A., Elkins, W. Va., 1947. Served with AUS, 1941-45; PTO. Recipient Award of Merit, United Givers Fund, 1959. Mem. Life Ins. Advertisers Assn. (chmn. Eastern Round Table 1966; ednl. com. 1967; chmn. membership com. 1969; nat. sec., nat. exec. com. 1970-72), Financial Pub. Relations Council of Greater Washington, D.C. Life Underwriters, Assn., (program chmn. Mid-Atlantic Sales Congress 1966), Internat., Mid-Atlantic councils indsl. editors, Am. Wildlife Fedn., V.F.W., Phi Sigma Nu. Episcopalian (supt., vestryman 1962-66, 68-72, lay reader). Contbr. articles to profl. jours., poetry, non-fiction to Rotarian Mag., Poetic Voice Am., West Va. Review, newspapers, others. Home: 305 Marengo Dr Middletown KY 40243 Office: 674 S 4th St Louisville KY 40202

SWEENEY, JAMES BARTHOLOMEW, govt. ofcl.; b. Phila., July 7, 1910; s. Anthony Joseph and Bertha (Collins) S.; B.S. in Econ., U. Villanova, 1952; m. Helen Ver, Dec. 2, 1944; 1 son, Frank James. Free lance author-photographer; commd. lt. col. USAAF, 1942, advanced through grades to lt. col., ret., 1965; pub. relations officer U.S. Forces in Japan; dir. pub. affairs U.S. Naval Oceanographic Office, 1965-72; dir. pub. information Def. Mapping Agy., 1972—. Decorated Bronze Star, others. Mem. Internat. Assn. Boating Writers, Armed Forces Writers League, Internat. Oceanographic Found., Nat. Press Club. Author: Pictoral History of Oceanographic Submersibles, 1970; Pictoral History of Sea Monsters and Other Dangerous Marine Life, 1972; Vessels for Underwater Exploration, 1973. Contbr. profl. jours. Home: 7205 Burtenwood Dr Alexandria VA 22307 Office: Defense Mapping Agency Bldg 56 Naval Observatory Washington DC

SWEENEY, JOSEPH FRANCIS, sch. adminstr.; b. Bklyn., Sept. 17, 1927; s. Joseph Francis and Ann (McDonough) S.; A.B., Spring Hill Coll., 1950; A.B. Woodstock Coll., 1951. Ordained in priest Roman Catholic Ch., 1957; tchr. St. Joseph's Prep., Phila., 1951-54; dir. admissions, Georgetown U. Undergrad. Sch., 1959-68; pres. Gonzaga Coll. High Sch., Washington, 1968—. Workshop dir. Internat. Inst. Edn., Washington, 1963; mem. Counselling Com. Entrance Exam. Bd., 1962-65; chmn. Opportunity Project for Edn., 1967-70. Chmn. Sursum Corda Corp., 1968—. Trustee Georgetown U. Address: 19 Eye St NW Washington DC 20001

SWEET, ROBERT THOMAS, banker; b. Hartford, Conn., June 18, 1938; s. Howard Francis and Catherine Elizabeth (Chesanek) S.; B.A., Trinity Coll., 1960; LL.B., U. Balt., 1966; M.A., Cath. U., 1973; m. Bonita Neumeister, June 29, 1963. Asst. dir. research, asst. v.p. Dean Witter, Investment Bankers, N.Y.C., 1969-71; v.p., trust investment officer Riggs Nat. Bank of Washington, 1971—. Mem. Community Planning Bd., N.Y.C., 1970. Served with AUS, 1962. Mem. Washington Soc. Investment Analysts (dir. 1972-73), N.Y. Soc. Security Analysts, Nat. Economists Club. Club: Hyannis (Mass.) Yacht. Home: 4934 Western Av Chevy Chase MD 20016 Office: 800 17th St NW Washington DC 20006

SWEETEN, JOHN MARBROOKS, JR., extension agrl. engr.; b. Rocksprings, Tex., Jan. 11, 1944; s. John Marbrooks and Johnnie Rachel (Johnson) S.; student Austin Coll., 1961-62, U. Tex. at Austin, 1963; B.S., Tex. Tech. U., 1965; M.S., Okla. State U., 1967, Ph.D., 1969; m. Mary Claire Kinney, Mar. 25, 1967; children—Jessica Lynn, Patrick Kinney. Grad. research asst. Okla. State U., 1965-68, Nat. Sci. Found. grad. fellow, 1968-69; san. engr. USPHS, Cin., 1969, U.S. Environmental Protection Agy., Cin., 1970-71; extension agrl. engr. Tex. A. and M. U., 1971—; engring. and edn. cons. livestock waste mgmt. and feedlot pollution control; cattle feeder and rancher. Served to lt. comdr., USPHS, 1969-71. Plains Cotton Ginners scholar, 1964. Registered profl. engr. Mem. Am. Soc. Agrl. Engrs. (paper award 1970), Nat., Tex. socs. profl. engrs., Sigma Xi, Phi Kappa Phi, Alpha Zeta. Presbyn. Contbr. articles profl. jours. Home: 1804 Leona St College Station TX 77840

SWEIGERT, MILTON EDWARD, architect; b. Atlanta, Mar. 2, 1934; s. Ray Leslie and Edna (Powers) S.; B.S., Ga. Inst. Tech., 1956, B. Arch., 1959; m. Helen LaRue Horne, June 16, 1956; children—Vicki LaRue, Valerie Lea. Designer, L. Miles Sheffer, Architect, Atlanta, 1960; job capt. Cunningham & Forehand, Architects, Inc., Atlanta, 1961-65; project architect Lockwood Greene Engrs., Inc., Spartanburg, S.C., 1965-67, archtl. dept. head, Atlanta, 1967-68; v.p., chief architect Zachary W. Henderson & Assos., Atlanta, 1968-70; chief architect Sheetz & Bradfield, Architects, Inc., 1970-73; corporate architect Financial Bldg. Consultants, Inc., Atlanta, 1973-74; individual practice architecture, 1974—. Supporting mem. Arthritis Found., 1969—; sponsor Campus Crusade for Christ Internat., 1970—, Christian Children's Fund, 1965—. Served with USNR, 1956-58. Registered architect, Ga., Ala., Fla., S.C. Mem. A.I.A., Constrn. Specifications Inst., Ga. Archtl. and Engring. Soc. (1st v.p. 1975), Ga. Assn. Architects, Ga. Conservancy, Ga. Tech. Nat. Alumni Assn., Nat. Campers and Hikers Assn., Tau Sigma Delta, Delta Tau Delta. Republican. Mem. Christian and Missionary Alliance. Club: Dunwoody N Driving (dir., v.p. 1973). Home: 4518 Kingsgate Dr NE Atlanta GA 30341 Office: 11 Dunwoody Park NE Suite 1Z1 Atlanta GA 30341

SWENSSON, EARL SIMCOX, architect, master planner; b. Nashville, July 28, 1930; s. Earl Ebenezer and Viola La Zelle (Simcox) S.; B.S. in Bldg. Design with honors, Va. Poly. Inst., 1952, M.S. in Arch., 1953; M.S. in Arch., U. Ill., 1955; m. Suzanne Dickenson, June 6, 1953; children—Krista, Lin, Kurt. Designer Perkins & Will Architects, Chgo., 1956-60; jr. partner Donald E. Stoll, Architect, Nashville, 1960-61; pres. Earl Swensson Architects, Nashville, 1961-73, chmn., 1973—; adj. prof. grad. studies div. Va. Poly. Inst. Coll. Arch. at Blacksburg, 1971-72; pres. Better Environments, Inc., Nashville, 1969—; chmn. bd. Investment Property Services, Inc., Nashville, Coordinating Services, Inc., Nashville. Lectr. grad. studies dept. civil engring. Vanderbilt U., 1974. Mem. adv. bd. Salvation Army, Nashville, 1963-70; mem. Martha O'Brien Community Center, 1968-72, vice chmn., 1971-72. Mem. com. Met. Zoning Ordinance, 1967-69. Recipient design awards profl. orgns. Mem. A.I.A. (pres. middle Tenn. chpt. 1971-72), Tenn. Soc. Architects (dir. 1967-71), Nashville C. of C. (gov.), Phi Kappa Phi, Tau Sigma Delta, Phi Delta Epsilon. Presbyn. (elder). Prin. works include Tenn. Bapt. Conv. Hdqrs., Brentwood, 1969; campus master plan Union U., Jackson, Tenn., 1970, Nashville campus U. Tenn., 1971, Roosevelt Community, Springfield, Ill., 1973. Home: 6530 Curreywood St Nashville TN 37205 Office: 2303 21st Av S Nashville TN 37212

SWETMAN, GLENN ROBERT, educator, poet; b. Biloxi, Miss., May 20, 1936; s. Glenn Lyle and June (Read) S.; B.S., U. So. Miss., 1957, M.A., 1959; Ph.D., Tulane U., 1966; m. Margarita Ortiz, Feb. 8, 1964; children—Margarita June, Glenn Lyle Maximilian, Glenda Louise. Teaching fellow U. So. Miss., 1957-58, asst. prof., 1964-66; instr. Ark. State U., 1958-59, McNeese U., 1959-61; instr., teaching fellow Univ. Coll. Tulane U., 1961-64, spl. asst. dept. elec. engring., 1961; asso. prof. La. Inst. Tech., 1966-67; prof., head dept. langs. Nicholls State Coll., Thibodaux, La., 1967-69, head dept. English, 1969-71, prof., 1971—. Partner, Breeland Pl., Biloxi, Miss., 1960—; stringer corr. Shreveport (La.) Times, 1966—; cons. tech. writing Union Carbide Corp. Subdiv. coordinator Republican party, Hattiesburg, Miss., 1964. Served with AUS, 1957. Recipient Poetry awards KQUE Haiku contest, 1964, Coll. Arts contest, Los Angeles, 1966, Black Ship Festival, Yoqosuka, Japan, 1967; Green World Brief Forms award Green World Poetry Editors, 1965. Mem. Modern Lang. Assn., S. Central Modern Lang. Assn., Coll. Writers Soc. La. (pres. 1971-72), I.E.E.E., Am. Assn. Engring. Edn., La. Poetry Soc. (pres. 1971—), Internat. Boswellian Inst., Nat. Fedn. State Poetry Socs. (2d v.p., nat. membership chmn. 1972—), Phi Eta Sigma, Omicron Delta Kappa. Book reviewer Jackson (Miss.) State Times, 1961. Poems pub. in various publs. including Poet, Prairie Schooner, Trace, Ball State U. Forum, Film Quar.; (books of poems) Tunel de Amor, 1973; Deka # 1, 1973. Home: 638 Fairway Dr Thibodaux LA 70301

SWICK, LEO EMMETT, JR., geologist; b. Lima, O., July 2, 1917; s. Leo E. and Mildred May (Kennedy) S.; B.A., Ohio State U., 1939; M.S., 1941; m. Margaret Kathryn Nunemaker, Sept. 28, 1938; children—Sue (Mrs. Robert Henry), Nancy (Mrs. W. James Carmichael), Kathryn (Mrs. Wayne Locke), David Edward. Geol. engr. Mickel Plate R.R., Cleve., 1941-43; indsl. engr. B. & O. R.R., Balt., 1943-44; geologist Magnolia Petroleum Co., Mt. Vernon, Ill., 1944-46, Gainesville, Tex., 1946-48; prin. L.E. Swick, geologist, oil operator, Gainesville, Tex., 1948—. Cons. in petroleum geology, 1948—. Mem. Gainesville City Council, 1951-52; chmn. bd. edn., Gainesville, 1954-59. Mem. Am. Assn. Petroleum Geologists (life), Am. Inst. Profl. Geologists, Gainesville C. of C. (pres. 1954), Petroleum Club Ft. Worth. Home: 820 S Dixon St Gainesville TX 76240 Office: Box 734 411 E California St Gainesville TX 76240

SWIFT, GILBERT, elec. engr.; b. Bklyn., Apr. 10, 1912; s. William Edgar and Eve Gertrude (Gilbert) S.; B.S. in Elec. Engring., U. Pa., 1933, E.E., 1949; m. Virginia Dare Harner, Oct. 31. 1943; children—Jill (Mrs. Michael A. Donnelly). Engr., RCA Mfg. Co., Camden, N.J., 1935-40; sr. project supr. Well Surveys, Inc., 1940-60; asst. tech. dir. Dresser Research, 1960-62; mgr. spl. projects Lane Wells div. Dresser Industries, Inc., 1962-67; research instrumentation engr. Tex. Transp. Inst., Tex. A. and M. U., College Station, 1967—. Served with Signal Corps, AUS, 1941-46. Mem. I.E.E.E., Soc. Exploration Geophysicists, Sigma Tau, Eta Kappa Nu. Patentee in field. Home: Route 3 Box 26A Bryan TX 77801 Office: Tex Transp Inst College Station TX 77843

SWIFT, ROY ERWIN, educator; b. Elgin, Ill., Nov. 4, 1911; s. Louis Swift and Theresa (Fallenbichle) S.; B.S., Mo. Sch. Mines, 1934; M.S., U. Wash., 1940; M.S., U. Utah, 1940; D.Eng., Yale, 1949; m. Beryl Elizabeth Madison, Apr. 25, 1942. Engr. mineral industries, 1934-39; instr. mech. engring. La. State U., 1939-41; asso. prof. chemistry U. Alaska, 1941-43; asso. prof. metall. engring. Purdue U., 1945-46; research asso. Battelle Meml. Inst., Columbus, O., 1947-49; asst. prof. mining and metallurgy U. Nev., 1949-51; asso. prof. mining and metall. engring. U. Ky., 1951-56, prof. metall. engring., 1956—; cons. in field. Mem. Am. Soc. Engring. Edn., Am. Soc. Metals, Am. Inst. Mining, Metall. and Petroleum Engrs., Ky. Soc. Profl. Engrs., Am. Inst. Chem. Engrs. (nuclear div.), Sigma Xi, Tau Beta Pi, Sigma Gamma Delta, Alpha Sigma Mu, Chi Alpha Sigma. Toastmaster (adminstrv. v.p., pres. 1967-68). Club: Lexington Exchange (v.p. 1968—). Home: 321 Melbourne Way Lexington KY 40502

SWIGERT, JOHN LEONARD, JR., former astronaut, govt. ofcl.; b. Denver, Aug. 30, 1931; s. John Leonard and Virginia (Seep) S.; B.S. in Mech. Engring., U. Colo., 1953; M.S. in Aero. Space Sci., Rensselaer Poly. Inst., 1965; postgrad. U. Cal. at Los Angeles, 1965-66; M.B.A., U. Hartford, 1967; D.Sc. (hon.), Am. Internat. Coll., 1970, Western Mich U., 1970; LL.D., Western State U., 1970. Served to capt. USAF, 1953-56; engring. test pilot Pratt & Whitney Aircraft, East Hartford, Conn., 1957-64, Space and Information Systems div. N.Am. Aviation, Downey, Cal., 1965-66; astronaut NASA-Johnson Space Center, Houston, 1966-73; exec. dir. Com. Sci. and Astronautics, U.S. Ho. of Reps., Washington, 1973—. Mem. Mass Air N.G., 1957-60, Conn. Air N.G., 1960-65. Recipient Presdl. medal for Freedom, 1970, U. Colo. Distinguished Alumnus award, 1970; City N.Y. gold medal, 1970; City Houston medal for Valor, 1970; City Chgo. gold medal, 1970. Asso. fellow Soc. Exptl. Tests Pilots, Am. Inst. Aeros. and Astronautics (Octave Chanute award 1966, Haley Astronautics award 1971), Am. Astronautical Soc. (Flight Achievement award 1971), Pi Tau Sigma, Sigma Tau, Phi Gamma Delta. Roman Catholic. Office: Suite 2321 Rayburn House Office Bldg Washington DC 20515

SWIHART, JOHN DONALD, JR., elec. engr.; b. Hobart, Okla., Aug. 3, 1936; s. John D. and Mary (Madden) S.; B.S. in Elec. Engring., U. Okla., 1959; postgrad. U. Fla., 1967, Tarrant County Jr. Coll., 1969, N. Tex. State U., 1970—; m. Mary Ann Nixon, Jan. 30, 1958; children—Susan LaRue, Timothy George, David Gerard, Mary Kathryn. Electronic engr. FAA, Oklahoma City, 1959-66, elec. engr. aircraft systems, Fort Worth, 1967—; electronic engr. Naval Tng. Device Center, Orlando, Fla., 1967. Asst. cubmaster, Webelos den leader, scoutmaster Boy Scouts Am., 1967—; class rep. U. Okla. Alumni Devel. Fund. campaign, 1968. Served to lt. AUS, 1959. Registered profl. engr., Okla., Tex. Mem. I.E.E.E., Nat. Soc. Profl. Engrs., Toastmasters Internat., Tau Beta Pi, Eta Kappa Nu, Sigma Tau. Democrat. Roman Catholic. K.C. Home: 7313 Janetta Dr Fort Worth TX 76118 Office: FAA PO Box 1689 Fort Worth TX 76101

SWINFORD, MAC, judge; b. Cynthiana, Ky., Dec. 23, 1899; s. McCalla C. and Allie (McKee) S.; LL.B., U. Va., 1925, postgrad., 1924-25; LL.D., Chase Coll. Sch. Law, 1965; m. Benton Peterson, Nov. 17, 1927; children—Mary Jouett (Mrs. McKay Reed, Jr.), John McKee, Sarah Hanson (Mrs. Hall Kinney), Alice Jane (Mrs. Bruce Kolbe), Ann Gregg (Mrs. Delmer Dunn). Admitted to Ky. bar, 1922; practiced at Cynthiana, 1922-35; U.S. dist. atty. Eastern Dist. Ky., 1933-37; judge U.S. Dist. Ct. for Eastern and Western Dists. Ky., 1937—. Mem. Ky. Ho. of Reps., 1926-28. Mem. Am., Ky., Fed., Harrison County bar assns., Sigma Nu. Democrat. Presbyn. Author: Kentucky Lawyer. Home: 440 E Pike St Cynthiana KY 41031 Office: Fed Bldg Box 1489 Lexington KY 40501

SWING, ANN T. (MRS. WILLIAM E. WILLIAMSON), physician; b. Millpoint, W.Va., June 9, 1910; d. Leonard G. and Mary (Matuzeck) Swing; A.B., U. W.Va., 1931, B.S., 1932; M.D., Med. Coll. Va., 1934, postgrad. (Immunology fellow), 1941-42; m. William E. Williamson, July 22, 1950. Intern, Med. Coll. Va., 1935-36; intern Willard Parker Hosp., N.Y.C., 1936-37, resident 1937-38; resident physician N.Y. Tng. Sch. for Girls, 1939-40, Farmville (Va.) State Tchrs. Coll., 1940-41; attending physician Bur. Maternal and Child Welfare, D.C. Pub. Health Dept., 1943-50; med. officer. Preventive Medicine div., Dept. Army Surgeon Gen., 1950-51; cons. pediatrician U.S. Army, Am. Hosp., France, 1952-54; med. officer U.S. Army Dispensary, Ft. Meyer, Va., 1955-67, chief pediatrics, 1967—. Mem. A.M.A., Am. Med. Women's Assn., Med. Women's Internat. Assn., Women's Med. Soc. D.C., Med. Soc. D.C., Bus. and Profl. Womens Club. Home: 1870 Wyoming Av NW Washington DC 20009 Office: Andrew Rader US Army Clinic Fort Myer VA 22211

SWINSKY, GREGOR WILLIAM, statistician; b. Milw., Oct. 16, 1938; s. Milton Oscar and Catherine (Hickey) S.; B.S. in Elec. Engring. (Western Electric Co. Scholar, Univ. Scholar), Marquette U., 1960, M.S., 1962; Ph.D. in Math. (NIH fellow), Catholic U. Am., 1970; m. Patricia I. Steinberg, Apr. 20, 1963; children—Andrew, Elizabeth, Matthew. Statistician, Melpar, Inc., Falls Church, Va., 1967-70, Def. Communications Agy., Arlington, Va., 1970—. Adj. asst. prof. Va. Poly. Inst., Reston, 1971-72. Served to 1st lt. AUS, 1962-64. Mem. Am. Statis. Assn., Inst. Math. Statistics, Wis. State Soc. (pres. 1971—), Pi Mu Epsilon, Tau Beta Pi, Eta Kappa Nu. Home: 10806 Colton St Fairfax VA 22030 Office: Def Communications Engring Center Def Communications Agy 1860 Wiehle Av Reston VA 22090

SWOPE, MARY MARGARET RICHARDS (MRS. KING SWOPE), club woman; b. Morganfield, Ky.; d. Lewis R. and Margaret Blue (Cromwell) Richards; student Centre Coll., 1912-15, Pa. Coll. for Women, 1915-18; m. King Swope, Mar. 22, 1918 (dec. Apr. 1961); children—William Richards, King. Sec., Nat. Soc. Daus. Barons of Runnymede; nat. councillor Daus. Founders and Patriots Am., 1958-62; Ky. pres. Daus. Colonial Wars. 1959-62; pres. chpt. IX Colonial Dames Am., 1952-58. Mem. Nat. Soc. Arts and Letters (Ky. chpt.), Colonial Daus. 17th Century (nat. councillor 1967-70, pres.), Ky. Hist. Soc., Lexington Jr. League, Daus. Am. Colonists, D.A.R., Order of Crown (4th nat. v.p.), Ams. of Royal Descent, Magna Charta Dames, First Families Va., Ky. Burgess. Republican. Presbyn. Clubs: Lexington (Ky.) Country; Filson; Idle Hour Country. Home: 247 S Hanover Av Lexington KY 40502

SWORDS, HENRY LOGAN, physician; b. Terrell, Tex., May 12, 1918; s. John Henry and Mattie Ethel (Logan) S.; B.S., East Tex. State U., 1939; M.S., 1947; M.D., Southwestern Med. Sch., 1947; m. Ruth C. Riley, June 20, 1940; children—Henry Logan II, Sylvia Lorraine. Tchr., Ft. Worth (Tex.) Pub. Schs., 1939-41, prin., 1941-44; intern John Peter Smith Hosp., Ft. Worth, 1947-48; gen. practice medicine, Ft. Worth, 1948—; mem. staff St. Joseph's, Harris Meml., All Saints hosps., Ft. Worth; chief div. gen. practice St. Joseph Hosp., 1970-71. Served as cadet USAAF, 1942. Mem. Am., Tex. med. assns., Am., Tex. acads. gen. practice, Am. Geriatric Soc., Tarrant County Med. Soc. (v.p. 1967), Phi Beta Pi. Methodist (chmn. bd. 1957-58, pres. bd. trustees 1959-60). Rotarian (pres. N. Ft. Worth 1969-70). Home: 5808 Blue Ridge Dr Fort Worth TX 76112 Office: 301 W Central St Fort Worth TX 76106

SYLVESTER, BARBARA BOLEN (MRS. JOSEPH G. SYLVESTER), nat. Democratic committeewoman, civic worker; b. Florence, S.C., Mar. 8, 1929; d. Hugh Bernard and Ola Mae (Williamson) Thornton; student Mars Hill Coll., 1946, Western Carolina U., summers; m. Joseph Gerg Sylvester, June 30, 1954; children—Pamela Mae, Elsa April. Sec., S.C. State Bd. Juvenile Corrections, 1969-71, chmn., 1971—; chmn. S.C. Dept. Youth Services, 1971—. S.C. Democratic exec. committeewoman, 1968—; chmn., Florence County White House Conf. on Children and Youth, 1970; chmn. 1st Step Kindergarten-Red Brick Sch., 1972—. Bd. dirs. S.C. Assn. Retarded Children, 1968-70; pres. Florence County Assn. for Retarded Children, 1969. Home: 510 Camellia Circle Florence SC 29501

SZABO, BERNARD, apparel mfg. exec.; b. Male Hutovo, Czechoslovakia, Aug. 7, 1923; s. Menhard and Helen (Roth) S.; m. Shirley Dorothy Fine, June 5, 1949; children—Lynette (Mrs. Michael R. Green), Valerie. Came to U.S., 1948, naturalized, 1954. Mgr., Jolly KidsTogs, Belding, Mich., 1954-58, Gerson & Gerson, Lawrenceville, Va., 1958-60; owner, pres. Emporia Garment Co., Inc. (Va.), 1960—, Roxobel Garment Co. (N.C.), 1971—, Franklin Garment Co. (Va.), 1973—. Served with AUS, 1948. Mason. Address: 405 Laurel St Emporia VA 23847

SZERYNG, HENRYK, violinist; b. Poland, 1921; pupil Carl Flesch, Berlin, Germany, Gabriel Bouillon, Paris Conservatoire, also Nadia Boulanger. Pub. appearances, Warsaw, Bucharest, Vienna and Paris, 1933-39; Polish Army giving concerts 1940-45; world tours, 1952—; prof. a.h. Nat. Music Conservatory and Music Faculty, Mexico City. Decorated officer Order of Arts and Letters (France); comdr. Order of Lion (Finland); knight comdr. Order of Polonia Restituta (Poland); recipient Grand Prix du Disque, 1955, 57, 59, 60, 61, 67; Medal of City of Paris; others. Home: Arenida JM Marroqui 28 Mexico City Mexico Office: care Hurok 730 Fifth Av New York City NY 10019

TABB, HORACE ENGLISH, savings and loan exec.; b. Elizabethtown, Ky., Jan. 3, 1915; s. Edwin J. and Hattie (English) T; A.B., Duke, 1936; LL.B., U. Mich., 1939; m. Helen E. Nall, Nov. 15, 1941; children—Katherine T. (Mrs. James R. Lanz), Linda Sue. Admitted to Ky. bar, 1939, since practiced in Elizabethtown; with OPA, 1941-45; pres., atty., dir. 1st Fed. Savs. & Loan Assn., Elizabethtown, 1956—; pres. Ky. Bldg., Savs. & Loan League, 1966—. Co-owner Radio Stas. WIEL and WLBN, 1952—, Mid-Ky. Poster Co., Elizabethtown, 1959—. Bd. dirs. Southeastern Conf. U.S. Savs. and Loan League, 1966—, U.S. Savs. and Loan League, 1967—. Mem. Am. Judicature Soc., Ky., Hardin County bar assns., Ky. C. of C. (dir. 1970—), Sigma Nu. Clubs: Lions (past pres.), Rotary, Pendennis, Filson. Home: 1120 Oak St Elizabethtown KY 42701 Office: 202 W Dixie Av Elizabethtown KY 42701

TABB, JAMES HUGH, banker; b. Houston, Miss., Jan. 16, 1908; s. James Pounds and Katherine Blanche (Sanderson) T.; B.A., U. Miss., 1929; postgrad. Harvard, 1930-31; m. Eva Eudora Collins, Dec. 27, 1936; children—James Collins, Nancy (Mrs. Jack Ray Dendy). Establisher, J.H. Tabb & Co., Houston, Miss., 1936, pres., 1936—; pres. Houston State Bank 1939-73; dir. Grenada Bank, Natchez Trace Electric Power Assn., Houston. Alderman, City of Houston, 1940-60. Trustee Miss. Meth. Found., Miss. Forestry Assn. Found. Recipient Silver Beaver award Boy Scouts Am., 1969. Mem. Ry. Tie Assn. (Man of Year award 1971, pres. 1955-56), Miss. Econ. Council, Miss. Mfrs. Assn., Pi Kappa Phi. Methodist (chmn. adminstrv. bd.). Mason. Club: Exchange (Houston). Home: 792 N Pontotoc St Houston MS 38851 Office: 105 W Washington St Houston MS 38851

TABB, JOHN DUANE, govt. ofcl.; b. Hayden, Colo., Aug. 24, 1936; s. Glenn Lee and Pauline (Purcell) T.; B.S. in Agrl. Engring., Colo. State U., 1959; m. Patricia Ann Turner, Nov. 24, 1963; children—Brenda Jean, Jeffrey Lynn. Dist. engr. Bur. Land Mgmt., Denver and Glenwood Springs, Colo., 1962-66, design and constrn. engr., Santa Fe, 1966-70, civil engr., Washington, 1970—. Served with AUS, 1960-62. Recipient Bausch & Lomb award, 1954, Superior Performance award Bur. Land Mgmt., 1967, 71, 72. Mem. Am. Soc. Agrl. Engrs., Farm House. Home: 14608 Baugher Dr Centreville VA 22020 Office: Interior Bldg Bur Land Mgmt Washington DC 20240

TABLER, KENNETH AMBROSE, statistician; b. Martinsburg, W.Va., July 18, 1926; s. Henry John and Pauline Winifred (Ambrose) T.; student Potomac State Coll., 1944-46; B.S., W.Va. U., 1948, M.S., 1949; Ph.D., U. Ill., 1954; m. Patricia Jean Webster, Sept. 9, 1950; children—David Lee, Bonnie Jean, Roberta May, Mark Alan. Dairy husbandman, U.S. Dept. Agr., Urbana, Ill., 1949-56, analytical statistician, Beltsville, Md., 1956-67; math. statistician U.S. Office Edn., Washington, 1967—. Treas. Galway P.T.A., Beltsville, 1969-71. Mason, Toastmasters (area gov. 1965-66). Home: 2700 E Randolph Rd Silver Spring MD 20904 Office: 400 Maryland Av SW Washington DC 20202

TABOR, BRITTON DUNCAN, bank dir.; b. Checotah, Okla., Aug. 29, 1914; s. Britton Hamilton and Bessie (Duncan) T.; B.A., U. of South, 1936; postgrad. Harvard U., summer 1936, Northwestern U., 1936-37, U. Va., 1940-41, U. N.M., 1948-49. Sr. credit man C.I.T. Corp., Chgo. also Dallas, 1937-39; tchg. fellowship U. Va., 1940-41; reporter, feature writer Muskogee (Okla.) Phoenix and Times-Democrat, 1942; mem. news and editorial staff Kingsport (Tenn) Times and News, 1946; news and editorial staff Knoxville (Tenn.) News Sentinel, 1946-47; press sec., legislative asst. to Congressman Ed Edmondson, Washington, 1955-60; free-lance writer, 1960—; dir. Peoples Nat. Bank, Checotah, Okla., 1961—. Fund drive chmn. North McIntosh County chmn. A.R.C., 1952; mem. Nat. Rivers and Harbors Congress, 1956-66. Served with AUS, 1942-45. Mem. S.A.R. (pres. Muskogee chpt. 1965), Am. Legion, Okla. Hist. Soc., Am. Mus. Natural History (asso.), Phi Beta Kappa, Omicron Delta Kappa, Pi Gamma Mu, Delta Tau Delta. Democrat. Episcopalian. Club: Nat. Press. Home: 631 W Lafayette Av Checotah OK 74426 Office: 631 W Lafayette Av Checotah OK 74426

TABOR, MICHAEL MILLS, lawyer; b. Waco, Tex., Sept. 5, 1943; s. Marion Mills and Dora Faye (Looney) T.; B.B.A., So. Meth. U., 1966, J.D., 1969; m. Mary Maud Coleman, Jan. 3, 1970; 1 son, David Benson. Admitted to Tex. bar, 1969; roughneck Tucker Drilling Co., San Angelo, Tex., 1962; roustabout Pool Well Servicing Co., San Angelo, 1963; salesman Kenray Ford Sales, Inc., Dallas, 1964-65; atty. James, Ingram & Glenn, Attys., Dallas, 1968-70; asso. firm Blanchette, Shelton & James, Attys., Dallas, 1970—. Active various civic drives. Recipient U.S. Law Week award Bur. Nat. Affairs, Inc., 1969; Am. Jurisprudence Fed. Cts. award, 1969. Mem. Am. Dallas (chmn. subcom. 1973) bar assns., Dallas Jr. Bar (chmn. com. 1971; v.p. 1973), Tex. Jr. Bar (dir. 1973), Phi Alpha Delta (treas. 1968), Phi Delta Theta. Methodist (mem. adminstrv. bd. 1971-73; mem. com. 1972-73). Home: 7072 Arboreal St Dallas TX 75231 Office: 40th Floor First Nat Bank Bldg Dallas TX 75202

TACHMINDJI, ALEXANDER JOHN, naval architect, marine engr.; b. Athens, Greece, Feb. 16, 1928 (came to U.S. 1950; naturalized 1958); s. John and Athena (Andreades) T.; B.Sc., Kings Coll. Durham (Eng.) U., 1949, B.Sc. (hons.); 1950; M.S., Mass. Inst. Tech., 1951; postgrad. U. Md., 1951-54; m. Diane Primeau, Dec. 4, 1965. Head research and propeller br. D.W. Taylor Model Basin, U.S. Navy Dept., Washington, 1951-59; with Inst. for Def. Analyses, Arlington, Va., 1959—, asst. dir. sci. and tech. div., 1963-67, dep. dir., 1967-69, dir. systems evaluation dir., 1969-72, dir. Tactical Tech. Office, Def. Advanced Research Projects Agy., 1972-73, dep. dir. DEF Advanced Research Projects Agy., 1973—; U.S. mem. Internat. Cavitation Com., 1955-59, also U.S. chmn. Am. Cavitation Com. Recipient U.S. Navy Meritorious Civilian award, 1955. Fellow Am. Inst. Aeros. and Astronautics, Royal Instn. Naval Architects; mem. Soc. Naval Architects and Marine Engrs. (chmn. panel hydroelasticity 1967-73, mem. hydrodynamics com. 1967—), N.E. Inst. Engrs., A.A.A.S., N.Y. Acad. Sci., Sigma Xi. Club: Cosmos (Washington). Patentee ventilated propeller. Home: 4915 Sedgwick St Washington DC 20016 Office: Advanced Research Projects Agy Def Dept Pentagon Washington DC

TACHMINDJI, DIANE ELIZABETH PRIMEAU (MRS. ALEXANDER J. TACHMINDJI), civic worker, assn. exec.; b. Davenport, Ia., Dec. 3, 1936; d. Carl Donald and Fern (Elofson) Primeau; B.A., Marygrove Coll., 1962; m. Alexander J. Tachmindji, Dec. 4, 1965, U.S. congl. sec., 1957-59; legislative liaison Gen. Motors Corp., Washington, 1962-63; exec. sec. Inst. for Def. Analyses, Washington, 1963-64; asst. to dir. community relations service U.S. Conf. Mayors, Washington, 1964-65. Vol. canteen worker A.R.C., 1962-63; vol. Albert Deutsch Center, 1967-69, dir. vols., 1967-69, bd. dirs., sec., 1968-69, v.p., 1969-72; chmn. membership and vol. recruitment com. D.C. Mental Health Assn., 1968-69, mem. publicity com., 1969, mem. legislation and pub. policy com., 1970-71, bd. dirs., 1970-72, del. to health and welfare council, 1970-72, vice chmn. Mental Health Ball, 1971; rec. sec. Womens Com. Nat. Ballet, 1967-68, corr. sec., 1968-69, vice chmn., 1969-71, womens com. Nat. Symphony, 1967-68; bd. dirs. Washington Area Council on Alcoholism and Drug Abuse, 1972-73, mem. Finance Com., 1972-73. Mem. Nat. Ballet Soc. Home: 4915 Sedgwick St Washington DC 20016

TACKET, HALL SANFORD, physician; b. Dyer, Tenn., Apr. 12, 1921; s. John Otis and Lucile (Sanford) T.; student U. Miss., 1939-40; B.S., U. Tenn., 1943, M.D., 1944; m. Jeanne Snedecor, June 21, 1947; children—Lynn, Carol, Hall Sanford. Intern Phila. Gen. Hosp., 1944-45, 47; resident John Gaston Hosp., Memphis, 1947-50; practice medicine specializing in internal medicine, Memphis, 1950—; clin. prof. medicine U. Tenn., 1964—; mem. staff Bapt. Meml. Hosp., City Memphis Hosp. Trustee Memphis Theol. Sem. Served to capt. AUS, 1945-47. Fellow A.C.P. (gov. Tenn. 1967-73), Am. Coll. Cardiology. Presbyn. (elder 1972—). Club: Delta Sailing. Contbr. articles to med. periodicals. Home: 4338 Chickasaw Cove Memphis TN 38117 Office: 910 Madison St Memphis TN 38103

TADLOCK, FRANCES AYERS (MRS. WILLIAM RAY TADLOCK), educator; b. Pickens County, S.C., May 2, 1926; d. Frank Jackson and Lucy Elizabeth (Blackerby) Ayers; B.S., Winthrop Coll., 1946; grad., 1947, 49, 52-53; grad. Furman U., 1965-67, U. S.C., 1967, La Verne Coll., 1971, 73, Clemson U., 1973, 74; m. William Ray Tadlock, Apr. 27, 1946; children—William Ray, Connie Lorraine. Tchr. home econs. Greenville County (S.C.) Sch. Dist., 1946-57, tchr. 1965-74. Mem. Childhood Edn. Assn. (state v.p. 1970-72), Delta Kappa Gamma. Baptist. Home: 20 Westbrook Lane Greenville SC 29605 Office: Sch Dist Greenville County Greenville SC

TAEUBER, CONRAD, govt. ofcl.; b. Hosmer, S.D., June 15, 1906; s. Richard E. and Emmy (Mussgang) T.; A.B., U. Minn., 1927, M.A., 1929, Ph.D., 1931; postgrad. U. Heidelberg (Germany), 1929-30, U. Wis., 1929-30; m. Irene Barnes, July 26, 1929; children—Richard Conrad, Karl Ernst. Asst. prof. Mt. Holyoke Coll., 1929-33; asso. econ. analyst Fed. Emergency Relief Adminstrn., 1934-35; various positions to head agrl. economist Bur. Agrl. Economies, U.S. Dept. Agr., 1935-46; chief of statistics br. FAO of UN, 1946-51; asst. dir. charge demographic fields Bur. of Census, Washington, 1951-68, asso. dir., 1968-73; dir. Center Population Research Georgetown U., Washington, 1973—. Recipient Outstanding Achievement award U. Minn., 1951, Exceptional Service award Dept. Commerce, 1963. Fellow Am. Statis. Assn.; mem. A.A.A.S. (past v.p.), Am. Sociol. Assn. (past sec.), Population Assn. Am. (past pres.), Inter-Am. Statis. Inst. (pres.), Internat. Statis. Inst. Club: Cosmos (Washington). Author: (with C.E. Lively) Rural Migration in the United States, 1939; (with Irene B. Taeuber) The Changing Population of the United States, 1958; The People of the United States in the 20th Century, 1960. Contbr. articles profl. jours. Home: 4222 Sheridan St Hyattsville MD 20782 Office: Center Population Research Georgetown U Washington DC 20007

TAFT, KINGSLEY ARTER, JR., forester; b. Cleve., Nov. 17, 1930; s. Kingsley Arter and Louise (Dakin) T.; A.B., Amherst Coll., 1953; B.S., U. Mich., 1957; M.S., N.C. State U., 1962, Ph.D., 1966; m. Eva Eileen Burkett, Mar. 4, 1955; children—Charisse Ann, Lynette Louise, Tiffany Norena. Forester, Nebo Oil Co., Minden, La., 1957-59; grad. asst. N.C. State U., Raleigh, 1959-63; forester geneticist TVA, Norris, 1963—. Served as pvt. 1st class AUS, 1953-55. Mem. Soc. Am. Foresters, A.A.A.S. Home: 55 Dogwood Rd Norris TN 37828 Office: Ridgeway Rd Norris TN 37828

TAFT, PAUL F., fiber glass co. exec.; b. Nashville, Oct. 10, 1933; s. James Maurice and Alois (Herndon) T.; B.S., Middle Tenn. State U., 1957; M.S., Vanderbilt U., 1958; m. Joyce Power, Jan. 31, 1958; children—Sheryl Dianne, James Warren. Research chemist Girdler Catalyst Co., Louisville, 1958-59, U.S. Tobacco Co., Nashville, 1959-65; tech. dir. Ferro Fiber Glass Co., Nashville, 1965—, adminstrv. asst. to pres. Winner Corp., 1972-73; pres. All Glass Inc., Goodlettsville, Tenn., 1973—. Served with USMCR, 1951-54. Mem. Am. Chem. Soc., Soc. Plastic Engrs., Am. Assn. Quality Control. Home: 1310 McChesney Av Nashville TN 37216 Office: Fiber Glass Rd Nashville TN 37211

TAHIR, ABE MAHMOUD, JR., art dealer; b. Greenwood, Miss., Feb. 18, 1931; s. Mahmoud and Mary (Ollie) T.; B.B.A., U. Miss., 1953; M.B.A., George Washington U., 1960. Supply mgmt. specialist U.S. Gen. Services Adminstrn., Washington, 1958-64; supply adviser Turkish govt. AID, Ankara, Turkey, 1964-66; owner, dir. Tahir Gallery, New Orleans, 1966—. Served with USAF, 1954-56. Mem. Delta Sigma Pi, Omicron Delta Kappa. Roman Catholic. Home: 1401 St Andrew St New Orleans LA 70130 Office: 823 Chartres St New Orleans LA 70116

TAHIR, ASH HUSSAIN, physician; b. Bahawal Pur, West Pakistan, Sept. 16, 1940; s. Zia Mohammad and Mumtaz (Begum) Khan; B.Sc., Govt. Coll., Lahore, West Pakistan, 1959; M.B.B.S., King Edward Med. Coll., Lahore, West Pakistan, 1964; m. Dixie Ann Webb, Apr. 17, 1970; children—Lisa Shawn, Michael Ash. Came to U.S., 1964, naturalized, 1974. Intern, Youngstown (O.) Hosp., 1964-65; resident surgery Lewis Gale Hosp., Roanoke, Va., 1965-66, St. Francis Hosp., Wichita, Kan., 1966-67; resident anesthesiology Charity Hosp., New Orleans, 1967-70, clin. instr. anesthesiologist, 1970—; clin. asst. prof. dept. surgery Tulane U. Sch. Medicine, New Orleans, 1972—; cons. anesthesiologist Lallie Kemp Charity Hosp., Independence, La., 1970—. Recipient physicians recognition award A.M.A., 1969, 74, numerous grants for research in anesthesiology. Fellow Royal Coll. Physicians (Can.), mem. Am., La. socs. anesthesiologists, Internat. Anesthesia Research Soc., Royal Soc. Health (Eng.) (hon.). Club: Roving and Mountaineering (sec. 1963-64). Contbr. articles to profl. pubs. Home: 7061 Mayo Rd New Orleans LA 70126 Office: 1532 Tulane St New Orleans LA 70140

TAIT, COLUMBUS DOWNING, JR., psychoanalyst, educator; b. Valdosta, Ga., Sept. 3, 1923; s. Columbus Downing and Mary L. (Jacobs) T.; B.A., U. Va., 1943, M.D., 1947; m. Nancy Kirk Reep, Aug. 25, 1956; children—Carl Downing, Jennifer Bradshaw. Intern, Bellevue Hosp., N.Y.C., 1947-48; resident in psychiatry Compton (Cal.) Sanitarium, 1948-49, Rockland (N.Y.) State Hosp., 1950; AEC postdoctoral research fellow in med. scis. Duke, 1949, Yale, 1950; psychoanalytic student Columbia, N.Y.C., 1950, 53-57; practice medicine specializing in psychiatry and psychoanalysis, N.Y.C., 1953-64; instr. Psychoanalytic Clinic, Columbia, 1957-64; asso. prof. psychiatry Emory U. Sch. Medicine, Atlanta, 1964-67; prof. 1967—; dir. research Ga. Mental Health Inst., 1965-71; part-time practice psychoanalysis; Atlanta, cons. local juvenile cts. Research and cons. psychiatrist Washington Youth Council, 1954-61, Mblzn. for Youth, N.Y.C., 1962-64. Served to lt., M.C., USNR, 1951-53. Diplomate Am. Bd. Psychiatry and Neurology. Fellow Am. Psychiat. Assn. (com. on history of psychiatry 1969—); mem. Am., Internat. psychoanalytic assns., A.M.A., A.A.A.S., Ga., Atlanta med. socs., Phi Beta Kappa, Alpha Omega Alpha. Author: (with Hodges) Delinquents, Their Families, and the Community, 1962. Contbr. articles to profl. jours. Home: 820 Douglas Rd NE Atlanta GA 30342 Office: Dept Psychiatry Emory U Atlanta GA 30322

TAKES, DONALD EUGENE, elec. engr.; b. Rockwell City, Ia., Feb. 11, 1924; s. Nicholas Eugene and Etta (Grove) T.; B.S. in Elec. Engring., Ia. State U., 1948; m. Dolores Barrett, Aug. 31, 1946; children—Thomas, Terri, Julie, Steven. Jr. engr. Curtiss-Wright Corp., Columbus, O., 1948-49; project aerosystems engr. Gen. Dynamics, Ft. Worth, 1949-62; mgr. elec. engring. Harris Intertype Corp., Ft. Worth, 1962—. Served with USAAF, 1942-45. Decorated Air medal with five oak leaf clusters. Registered profl. engr., Tex. Mem. Eta Kappa Nu, Tau Beta Pi, Alpha Tau Omega. Home: 6805 Gammer Dr Fort Worth TX 76116 Office: Box 15247 Fort Worth TX 76119

TALBOT, DAVID ARLINGTON ROBERTS, educator; b. Guyana, Jan. 25, 1917; s. David Patterson and Maude (Roberts) T.; B.A., Morris Brown Coll., 1939; M.A., Columbia, 1951; Ed.D. (So. Edn. fellow), U. Ark., 1966; D.D., Jackson Theol. Sem., 1960; m. Phyllis Snow Willis, June 19, 1945; children—David Arlington, James Patterson, Eric Maurice. Instr. Morris Brown Coll., 1939-40; social worker N.Y.C. Dept. Welfare, 1946-51; chmn. div. lang., lit., arts, prof. English, Shorter Coll., 1952-57, dir. guidance, 1954-57; asso. dir. guidance U. Ark., Pine Bluff, 1957-60, dean students, 1960-68; prof. student personnel and guidance East Tex. State U., 1968—; cons. U. Ark., 1970; dir. Multi-Cultural Tchr. Tng. Inst., summer 1969; ordained to ministry A.M.E. Ch. Mem. Commn. IV Ark. Council Chs., 1962-68; mem. exec. com. Jean's Addition Civic and Polit. Organ., Pine Bluff, 1965-68; mem. Mayor's Commn. on Community Affairs, Pine Bluff, 1967-68. Trustee Tex. Assn. Developing Colls. Served with AUS, 1942-45. Decorated Bronze Star medal. Mem. Am. Coll. Personnel Assn., Nat. Assn. Personnel Workers (nat. treas. 1966-70), Omega Psi Phi, Phi Delta Kappa. Democrat. Mason, Lion. Home: 3011 Tanglewood St Commerce TX 75428 Office: East Tex State U Counseling Center Commerce TX 75428

TALBOT, DOUGLAS WILLIAM, engring. and developing co. exec.; b. Beacon, N.Y., Feb. 20, 1935; s. Douglas Francis and Margret (O'Keefe) T.; B.C.E., Va. Mil. Inst., 1957; m. Dolores Ribera, Nov. 23, 1957; children—Elizabeth, Marianne, Cynthia, Douglas. Cons. engr. Gen. Electric Co., Schenectady, 1957-59; design engr., asst. to chief engr. City of Richmond, Va., 1959-63; city engr., City of Independence, Mo., 1963-66; dir. pub. works City of Hopewell, Va., 1966-68; pres. Talbot & Assos., Engrs., Planners, Surveyors, Virginia Beach, Va., 1968—. Commnr. Hampton Rds. Sanitation Commn., 1970-72; mem. Com. 100, 1972-74. Served with AUS, 1968-69. Named Young Engr. Mo., 1968. Registered profl. engr., Va., Mo., N.Y. Mem. Am. Soc. C.E. (chmn. urban planning and devel. div. 1968-70), Va. Soc. Profl. Engrs. (pres. Hopewell-Petersburg chpt. 1966-68), Am. Pub. Works Assn. (chmn. tech. specifications and standards com. 1964-65, hwy. and urban planning com. 1965-66), Home Bldrs. Assn. (dir. 1971-74), Virginia Beach Assn. Home: 1816 N Alanton Dr Virginia Beach VA 23454 Office: PO Box 2224 100 Landmark Sq Virginia Beach VA 23452

TALBOT, LEE MERRIAM, ecologist; b. New Bedford, Mass., Aug. 2, 1930; s. Murrell Williams and Zenaida (Merriam) T.; student Deep Springs Coll., 1948-49; A.B., U. Cal. at Berkeley, 1953, M.A., 1963, Ph.D., 1963; m. Martha Walcott Hayne, May 16, 1959; 1 son, Lawrence Hayne. Staff ecologist Internat. Union for Conservation, Europe, Asia, Africa, 1954-56, dir. S.E. Asia Project, 1964-65; ecologist, dir. East African Ecol. Research Project, U.S. Nat. Acad. Scis., N.Y. Zool. Soc., Govts. of Kenya, Tanzania, 1959-63; wildlife adviser UN Spl. Fund, Africa, 1963-64; resident ecologist and Smithsonian field rep. for internat. affairs in ecology and conservation Smithsonian Instn., Washington, 1966-70; sr. scientist Council Environmental Quality, Exec. Office of Pres., Washington , 1970—. Cons. U.S. Nat. Acad. Scis., UNESCO, UN Spl. Fund, Peace Corps, AID, Internat. Union for Conservation, Life Mag., fgn. govts.; dep. convener Internat. Biol. Program Conservation Sect. Trustee Population Reference Bur., Am. Com. for Internat. Wildlife Protection; mem. exec. bd. Internat. Union for Conservation. Served with USMCR, 1953-54. Recipient Outstanding Publ. award Wildlife Soc., 1963. Fellow A.A.A.S., N.Y. Zool. Soc.; mem. Wildlife Soc. (com. chmn.), Am. Soc. Mammalogists, Assn. for Tropical Biology (com. chmn.), Pacific Sci. Assn. (conservation chmn.) Soc. Range Mgmt. (dir.), Assn. Am. Geographers, Ecol. Soc. Am., Am. Com. for Internat. Wildlife Protection (chmn.), Zool. Soc. Korea, Fauna Soc. London, East African Wildlife Soc., Order Golden Bear, Phi Kappa Sigma. Clubs: Explorers (N.Y.C.); Cosmos (Washington); Boone and Crockett, Sports Car of America. Author: books, monographs; (television documentary film) Man, Beast and the Land, 1968 (Cine Golden Eagle award 1969). Contbr. articles to profl. jours. Home: 6656 Chilton Ct McLean VA 22101 Office: Council Environmental Quality Exec Office President 722 Jackson Pl Washington DC 20006

TALBOT, MARTHA WALCOTT HAYNE (MRS. LEE MERRIAM TALBOT), conservationist, biologist; b. San Francisco; d. Francis Bourn and Anna (Walcott) Hayne; B.A., Vassar Coll., 1954; m. Lee Merriam Talbot, May 16, 1959; 1 son, Lawrence Hayne. Co-founder, co-dir. student conservation program U.S. Nat. Parks Assn., Washington, 1955-59; asst. dir. East African Ecol. Research Project, U.S. Nat. Acad. Scis., N.Y. Zool. Soc., Govts. of Kenya and Tanzania, East Africa, 1959-64; asst. dir. S.E. Asia Project, Internat. Union for Conservation, various Asian countries, 1964-65; research asso. Office of Ecology, Smithsonian Instn., Washington, 1966-70, cons., 1971. Cons. Club Tours, N.Y.C., 1969—; mem. organizational staff internat. scientific and tech. confs. in Africa, Asia, U.S.; leader tour to East Africa, 1969-70. Mem. Fairfax County (Va.) Park Authority, 1972—, sec.-treas., 1974. Bd. dirs. Student Conservation Assn., Inc., also mem. exec. com. Co-recipient Outstanding Publs. award Wildlife Soc., 1963, Cine Golden Eagle award, 1969. Mem. Soc. Women Geographers (exec. council 1972—), La Leche League, Nat. Parks Assn., Vassar Alumni Assn. Clubs: Sierra (San Francisco); Cosmos (Washington). Author: (with others) An Introduction to the Landscape of East Africa, 1961; The Wildebeest in Western Masailand, 1963; Renewable Natural Resources in the Philippines, 1964; Meat Production Potential of Wild Animals in Africa, 1965; Conservation of the Hong Kong Countryside, 1966. Co-editor: Conservation in Tropical South East Asia, 1968. Contbr. articles to profl. jours. Home: 6656 Chilton Ct McLean VA 22101

TALBOT, MORGAN KRAEMER, lawyer; b. Jonesboro, La., July 29, 1928; s. Shelby Morgan and Vyvyen (Kraemer) T.; A.A., Lamar U., 1947; B.B.A., U. Tex., 1950, J.D., 1957; m. Jane C. Mitchell, Feb. 21, 1959; children—Mark Mitchell, Morgan Keith (dec.). Admitted to Tex. bar, 1957; partner firm Ewers, Toothaker, Ewers, Abbott, Talbot, Hamilton & Jarvis, McAllen, Tex., 1957—. Instr. bus. law Pan Am. U., Edinburg, Tex., part-time 1971—. Pres., founding dir. McAllen Trade Zone, 1965-73; pres. McAllen United Fund, 1966, McAllen Heart Fund, 1967—, McAllen Opera Soc., 1966. State del. Tex. Democratic party, 1972. Dir. McAllen Pub. Housing Authority, Roselawn Cemetery Assn., McAllen. Mem. Am., Hidalgo County (pres. 1964-65) bar assns., State Bar Tex. (chmn. com. 1973-74), McAllen C. of C. (dir.). Episcopalian (lay reader 1972—, vestryman 1973—). Rotarian. Club: McAllen Country. Home: 1500 Kerria St McAllen TX 78501 Office: Box 3670 McAllen TX 78501

TALBOTT, FRANK, III, textile co. exec., lawyer; b. Danville, Va., Mar. 26, 1929; s. Frank and Margaret (Jordan) T.; B.A., U. Va., 1951, LL.B., 1953; m. Mary Beverley Chewning, July 11, 1952; children—Beverley, Frank IV. Admitted to Va. bar, 1952; gen. practice law, Danville, 1956-66; with Dan River Mills, Inc., 1966—, v.p., gen. counsel, 1968—; dir. First Nat. Bank Danville. Vice chmn. Danville Sch. Bd., 1964-70. Sec. Danville Democratic Com., 1962-63. Trustee U. Va. Student Aid Found., 1963-68; bd. dirs. United Fund Danville, 1959-63; bd. mgrs. U. Va. Alumni Assn., 1971-73. Served with AUS, 1953-56. Decorated Commendation medal. Mem. Am., Va. (v.p. 1965-66, exec. com. 1967-70), Danville (pres. 1965-66) bar assns., Am. Judicature Soc., Newcomen Soc., Delta Psi, Phi Alpha Delta. Methodist. Clubs: Golf, German (Danville). Home: 420 Maple Lane Danville VA 24541 Office: 2291 Memorial Dr Danville VA 24541

TALKINGTON, PERRY CLEMENT, physician; b. Waco, Tex., 1909; M.D., Baylor U., 1934. Intern, Hamot Hosp., Erie, Pa., 1934-35; resident in neurology and psychiatry Taunton (Mass.) State Hosp., 1935-37; resident in organic neurology Phila. Orthopedic Hosp. and Infirmary Nervous Diseases, 1937-38; chief psychiatrist Timberlawn Sanitarium, Dallas, 1949-68, cons. in psychiatry, 1968—; chief neurology and psychiat. service Baylor Hosp., Dallas, 1955-69; civilian cons. U.S. Surgeon Gen., 1946-73; asst. clin. prof. neurology and psychiatry Baylor U., 1938-40, instr. clin. neurology and psychiatry, 1940-43; clin. asst. prof. neuropsychiatry Southwestern U., 1945-50, clin. asso. prof. neuropsychiatry, 1950-69, clin. prof. psychiatry, 1969—. Served as lt. col. M.C., AUS, 1941-45. Diplomate Am. Bd. Psychiatry and Neurology. Mem. A.M.A., Central Neuropsychiat. Assn. (pres. 1971-72), Am. Psychiat. Assn. (pres. 1972-73), So. Med. Assn., So. Psychiat. Assn., Am. Coll. Psychiatrists. Office: 4645 Samuell Blvd Dallas TX 75228

TALLANT, HAROLD DONALD, clergyman; b. Chattanooga, Oct. 29, 1916; s. Rev. Joseph Bernard and Laura Jane (Green) T.; A.B., Carson-Newman Coll., 1938; Th.M., So. Bapt. Theol. Sem., 1941; D.D., Georgetown Coll., 1957; m. Rhoda Ellen Haun, May 14, 1939; children—Marilynn Sue (Mrs. Tallant Friel), Harold Donald. Music dir. Beechmont Bapt. Ch., Louisville, 1938; ordained to ministry, Bapt. Ch., 1939; asst. pastor Ninth and O Bapt. Ch. Louisville, 1938-41; asso. pastor First Bapt. Ch., Frankfort, Ky., 1941-42; pastor First Bapt. Ch., London, Ky., 1942-47, Madisonville, Ky., 1947-63, First Bapt. Ch., Daytona Beach, Fla., 1963-67; evangelist, cons. So. Bapt. Ch., 1967-68; pastor Farmdale Bapt. Ch., Louisville, 1968-70; evangelist Highview Bapt. Ch., Louisville, 1970—. Pres. tng. Ky. Bapt. Conv., 1947, 48, 49, vice chmn., bd. missions, 1953-54, 56-58, chmn. music com., 1952-54, hosp. commn., 1949-51, mem. exec. com., 1953-54, 57-58, 58-59, 59-60, chmn. exec. bd., 1959, 60, chmn. appropriations com., 1959, adminstrv. com., 1962, chmn. wage scale adminstr., 1961, 62; mem. Ky. Baptist Exec. Bd., 1972—, chmn. evangelism com., 1972-73; pres. Madisonville Ministerial Assn. 1960-63; trustee Fgn. Mission bd. So. Bapt. Conv., 1963; faculty Ridgecrest Bapt. Assembly of So. Bapt. Conv., 1947—, time and place com., 1954, trustee Sunday Sch. bd., 1954-62, teller, 1959, program, 1961, com. on coms. 1962—; moderator Little Bethel Baptist Assn., 1949-51, asst. moderator Gen. Assn. Ky. Bapts., 1956-57; exec. bd. Fla. Bapt. Conv., 1966—; moderator Halifax Bapt. Assn., 1965-66; dir. World Missions Conf., Long Run Bapt. Assn., 1969-71, mem. evangelism com., 1971-72. Mem. Social Service Adminstrn., Commonwealth of Ky., 1956-59; trustee Ky. Temperance League, 1955-63, Hopkins County chpt. A.R.C., 1959-65. Hopkins County Com. Retarded Children, 1960; instl. rep. Boy Scouts Am., 1949—. Trustee Georgetown Coll., 1948-64. Kiwanian (dir. Madisonville 1963; Distinguished Service award 1963, Legion of Honor award, Daytona Beach, Fla. 1968, dir. Louisville 1970, 74). Home: 6204 Richiewayne Dr Louisville KY 40219 Office: 7711 Fegenbush Lane Louisville KY 40228

TALLEY, JAMES STATON, banker; b. Clarksburg, W.Va., Oct. 23, 1922; s. Nathan Maurice and Blanche Elizabeth (Staton) T.; student Benjamin Franklin U., 1940-41; B.A., George Washington U., 1949; m. Marilyn Jean Hunter, June 8, 1949; children—Anne-Elizabeth, Patricia, Michael, Jennifer. Various supervisory positions Gen. Motors Acceptance Corp., 1949-63, asst. sec., credit mgr., Washington, 1963-64; asst. v.p. First Va. Bankshares, indirect credit, Arlington, Va., 1964-69, v.p., 1969-71; v.p. First Va. Finance Plan, 1968-71, First Va. Bank, br. adminstrn., 1971—. Mem. Va. Bankers Installment Credit Com., 1968-69; moderator panels, credit confs., 1968-69; designer, instituted operations First Va. Finance Plan, 1967-69, developer loan adminstrn. program direct field, 1971. Served with USCGR, 1942-46. Mem. Kappa Sigma. Methodist (teller 1971-74). Home: 8929 Stark Rd Annandale VA 22003 Office: 1st Va Plaza 6400 Arlington Blvd Falls Church VA 22046

TALLEY, JERRY LEALAND, bank exec.; b. Kerens, Tex., Sept. 1, 1928; s. Milton E. and Gertrude Marie (Newsom) T.; A.A., Arlington State Coll., 1948; grad. Southwestern Grad. Sch. Banking, So. Meth. U., 1960; m. Rita Evelyn Pierce, July 17, 1950; children—Jan Ell, Jerri Kay. Radio announcer KGAF, Gainesville, Tex., 1948-50, program dir., 1952-54; farm dir. KFDX-TV, Wichita Falls, Tex., 1954-56; sales mgr. Gainesville Retail Establishment, 1956-58; asst. v.p. Grayson County State Bank, Sherman, Tex., 1958, v.p., dir., 1959, exec. v.p., 1960, pres., trust officer, 1964—; pres., chmn. Texoma Savs. Assn., Sherman, Tex., 1962-64, also dir.; dir. Day Mfg. Co., Medco, Inc., Constn. Village, Pylon Farms, DMC, Inc., Zona Leasing Corp.; dir., pres. Central S.W. Corp.; dir. v.p. Recovery Co.; pres. Gainesville Devel. Corp.; dir., treas. Grayson Computer Service. Mem. adv. com. S.W. Employees Incentive Plan, 1971—. Active Am. Cancer Soc., Sherman United Fund, Boy Scouts Am., Camp Fire Girls, Salvation Army, Texoma Expn. and Livestock Show; mem. devel. bd. Austin Coll., 1962-66; mem. Area and State Soil Conservation Selection Panel, 1962. Bd. dirs. Sherman Council on Drug Edn.; trustee Austin Coll., Sherman. Served with USAF, 1950-52. Named Outstanding Young Man of Sherman, Jr. C. of C., 1959; nominated Outstanding Young Texan, Jr. C. of C., 1961. Mem. Sherman C. of C. Am. Legion. Presbyn. (elder). Mason (32 degree, Shriner), Rotarian. Home: 1610 Lakewood St Sherman TX 75090 Office: 400 N Crockett St Sherman TX 75090

TALLEY, NEVA BENNETT (MRS. J.H. MORRIS), lawyer; b. Judsonia, Ark., Aug. 12, 1909; d. John W. and Erma (Rhew) Bennett; B.A. magna cum laude, Ouachita Coll., 1930; M.Ed., U. Tex., 1938, postgrad., 1939-41; m. Cecil C. Talley, Jan. 1, 1946 (dec. Oct. 1948); m. 2d, Joseph H. Morris, Mar. 22, 1952. Tchr. high sch., prin. White County, Ark., 1930-42; student asst. U. Tex., summers, 1937-41; ordnance insp. war service appointment U.S. Army Service Forces, 1942-45; law office apprentice, pvt. tutorship, North Little Rock, Ark., 1945-47; admitted to Ark. bar, 1947, pvt. practice in Little Rock. Chmn. Ark. Council of Children and Youth, 1952-54; pres. Nat. Women Lawyers Found., 1958-60; Recipient ann. award, Nat. Assn. Women Lawyers, 1962; Distinguished Service award Ark. Bar Assn., 1970. Fellow Am. Acad. of Matrimonial Lawyers (bd. govs. 1969—), Ark. Bar Found.; mem. Nat. (life, council del. 1952—, pres. 1956-57, exec. council family law sect. 1958—), Little Rock (pres. 1950-51) assns. women lawyers, North Little Rock Bus. and Profl. Women's Club (pres. 1951-52), Am. Assn. U. Women (v.p. Little Rock br. 1955), Am. (council family law sect. 1958—, chmn. family law sect. 1969-70, mem. ho. dels. 1957-58, 70—, state membership chmn.), Ark. (chmn. family law reform com. 1960-61, del. 1972-75), Pulaski County bar assns., Am. Judicature Soc., Nat. Conf. Lawyers and Social Workers (mem. nat. exec. bd. 1962-67, 70—), Phi Alpha Delta (hon.), Delta Kappa Gamma. Author: Family Law Practice and Procedure Handbook, 1973; Appellate Civil Practice and Procedure Handbook, 1975. Home: 101 N State St Little Rock AR 72201 Office: 722 W Markham St Little Rock AR 72201

TALLEY, WILLIAM GILES, JR., container mfg. co. exec.; b. Adel, Ga., Sept. 25, 1939; s. William Giles and Mary (McGlamry) T.; B.S. in Bus. Adminstrn., U. S.C., 1961; m. Jacqueline Vickery, Apr. 14, 1962; children—William Giles III, John Lindsey, Bronwyn Ashley. Mgmt. trainee Talley Veneer & Crate Co., Inc., Adel, 1961-62, plant mgr., salesman, Waynesboro, Ga., 1965-67; Talley's Box Co., Leesburg, Fla., 1962-65, plant mgr. 1967-69; partner, gen. mgr. Growers Container Cooperative, Inc., Leesburg, 1969—; dir. First Nat. Bank Leesburg. Bd. dirs. Leesburg Hosp. Assn. Served with USAAF, 1961. Mem. Leesburg C. of C. (dir.), Sigma Alpha Epsilon. Democrat. Methodist. Elk, Kiwanian. Home: Lake Griffin Leesburg FL 32748 Office: PO Box 817 Leesburg FL 32748

TALMADGE, HERMAN E(UGENE), U.S. senator; b. McRae, Ga., Aug. 9, 1913; s. Eugene and Mattie Thurmond (Peterson) T.; grad. Druid Hills Sch., Atlanta, 1931; LL.B., U. Ga., 1936; student Midshipman's Sch., Northwestern U., 1942; m. Leila Elizabeth Shingler, Dec. 24, 1941; children—Herman Eugene, Robert Shingler. Admitted to Ga. bar, 1936, practiced with father, Atlanta, 1936-41, 45-48; gov. Ga., 1948-55; gen. practice law, Atlanta, 1955-57; U.S. senator, 1957—. Served with USN, 1941-45; commd. ensign and advanced through grades to lt. comdr.; participated in invasion of Guadalcanal aboard U.S.S. Tryon; served as flag sec. to comdt. of Naval Forces at New Zealand, June 1943-Apr. 1944; exec. officer U.S.S. Dauphin, participated in engagements with Japanese Fleet and in Battle of Okinawa; entered Tokyo Bay, V-J Day. Mem. Navy League, Am. Legion, V.F.W., S.C.V., S.A.R., Am., Ga., Atlanta bar assns., Farm Bur., Sigma Nu, Sigma Delta Kappa, Sphinx. Democrat. Baptist. Mason (Shriner), Elk. Club: Touchdown (Athens, Ga.). Author: You and Segregation. Home: Lovejoy GA 30250 also 2801 New Mexico Av NW Washington DC 20007 Office: 275 W Peachtree St NE Atlanta GA 30303

TALTON, ALMANDA R. (MRS. FURMAN CARLTON ANDERSON), educator; b. Sterlington, La., Dec. 12, 1930; d. Henry Joseph and Katie (Moses) Talton; B.S., Grambling Coll., 1954; M.A., Columbia, 1958, profl. diploma, 1964; m. Furman Carlton Anderson, Aug. 23, 1966. Tchr., Grambling (La.) Coll. Nursery Sch., 1954-56, dir., tchr., 1956-63, tchr. Coll., 1964-66, coordinator head start staff tng. programs, 1966; head tchr., supervising tchr. Queens Coll. Early Childhood Edn. Center, Flushing, N.Y., 1963-64; regional tng. officer State of La.-Office Econ. Opportunity, Grambling, 1966-67; part-time tchr. Grambling Coll., part-time supr. kindergarten programs Lincoln Parish, cons. S. Central Regional Edn. Lab., Little Rock, 1967—. Cons. S.W. region Office Child Devel. Mem. La. Edn. Assn., Assn. for Childhood Edn. Internat., So. Assn. for Children Under Six, Nat. Assn. for Edn. Young Children, Am. Assn. U. Profs., Am. Home Econs. Assn., Day Care and Child Devel. Council Am., Alpha Kappa Alpha. Address: Box 314 Grambling LA 71245

TALTON, GORDON TYLER, dentist; b. Apopka, Fla., Dec. 25, 1915; s. William Goode and Julliett (Pollard) T.; B.S., Wake Forest Coll., 1940; D.D.S., Med. Coll. Va., 1943; m. Mildred Lyell James, Sept. 18, 1945; children—Catharine, Grace, Gordon, David, Bettye. Pvt. practice dentistry, Orlando, Fla., 1947—. Bd. dirs. Bapt. Terrace. Served with USNR, World War II. Mem. Am., Fla. dental assns., Central Dist. (pres. 1968-69), Orange County dental socs. Baptist. Lion. Home: 77 Interlaken Rd Orlando FL 32801 Office: 1017 E Robinson Av Orlando FL 32802

TAMAYO, RUFINO, painter; b. Oaxaca, Mexico, Aug. 26, 1899; s. Manuel Arellances and Florentina Tamayo; ed. Sch. Fine Arts, Mexico City; m. Olga Flores Rivas, Jan. 24, 1934. Head dept. ethnographic drawing Nat. Mus. Archaeology, 1921-26; tchr. drawing, painting Mexico City pub. schs., 1926; head dept. plastic arts Mexican Secretariat Edn., 1932; art instr. Dalton Sch., N.Y.C., 1938—, Bklyn. Mus. Art Sch., 1946; painter, one man shows Weyhe Gallery, N.Y.C., 1926, Art Center, N.Y.C., 1927, Nat. Theatre, Mexico City, 1929, John Levy Galleries, N.Y.C., 1931, Carolina Amor Gallery, Mexico City, 1935, Valentine Gallery, N.Y.C., 1939-47, Arts Club Chgo., 1945, Pierre Matisse Gallery, N.Y.C., 1948, Knoedler Gallery, N.Y.C., 1951—, Mus. Fine Arts, Houston, 1956, Palais des Beaux Arts, Brussels, 1950, Galeriedes Beaux Arts, Paris, 1950, and many others U.S., Europe, S.Am. and Mexico; rep. permanent collections Mus. Modern Art, N.Y.C., Phillips Meml. Gallery, Washington, Art Inst. Chgo., N.Y. Pub. Library, Musee Nat. d'Art Moderne, Paris, and others in Europe, Mexico, U.S. Recipient 3d prize Carnegie Internat., Pitts., 1952, 2d prize, 1955; recipient 1st prize. San Paulo (Brazil) Biennal, 1954. Decorated chevalier de la Legion d'Honneur (France). Hon. mem. Am. Acad. Arts and Letters. Home: Malintzin 20 Coyoacan Mexico

TAMBLYN, LEWIS RALPH, assn. exec.; b. St. Neot, Cornwall, Eng., June 16, 1923; s. Horace John and Henrietta Grace (Hancock) T.; came to U.S., 1924, naturalized 1946; student Muskegon Jr. Coll., 1946-48, Alma Coll., 1948; B.A., U. Mich., 1949, M.A., 1951, Ed.D., 1961; m. Audrey Florence Cornell, Dec. 22, 1946; children—Jane, Annette, Mary. Tchr., prin. Huron Valley Schs., Milford, Mich., 1953-55, prin., 1955-62; asst. dir. rural service N.E.A., Washington, 1962-68, coordinator rural service, 1968-72, organizational specialist, 1972—. Vis. prof. Ohio U., 1962; cons. Office Commr. U.S. Office Edn., 1967-70, Bur. Research, 1968; mem. adv. com. Ednl. Resources Information Center/Clearinghouse on Rural Edn. and Small Schs., 1968. Served with RCAF, 1942-45. Mem. Am. Country Life Assn. (dir.), Council Nat. Orgns. Children and Youth (dir.), N.E.A., Am. Assn. Sch. Adminstrs., Phi Delta Kappa. Methodist. Mason. Author: Rural Education in the U.S., 1971; Research Abstracts in Rural Education, 1969; Inequality: A Portrait of Rural America, 73; (with others) Rural Schools As A Mechanism for Rural Development, 1974. Home: 13122 Foxhall St Silver Spring MD 20906 Office: 1201 16th St NW Washington DC 20036

TAMM, EDWARD A(LLEN), U.S. circuit judge; b. St. Paul, Apr. 21, 1906; s. Edward Allen and Lucille Catherine (Buckley) T.; student Mt. St. Charles Coll., Helena, Mont., 1923-25, U. Mont., 1926-28; LL.B., Georgetown U., 1930, LL.D., 1965; J.S.D. (hon.), Suffolk U., 1971; m. Grace Monica Sullivan, Jan. 30, 1934; children—Edward Allen, Grace Escudero. Admitted to Minn. bar, U.S. Supreme Ct. bar; ofcl. FBI, 1930-48; judge, U.S. Dist. Ct. for D.C., 1948-65, U.S. Ct. Appeals for D.C. Circuit, 1965—, chief judge Temporary Emergency Ct. Appeals of U.S. Trustee, St. Joseph Coll.; bd. dirs. Police Boys Club, Washington. Served as lt. comdr., USNR. Decorated comdr. Legion of Merit (Ecuador); Order of Balboa (Panama). Mem. Met. Bd. Trade, USCG Aux., Am., Fed. bar assns., Bar Assn. D.C., Am. Judicature Soc., Friendly Sons St. Patrick, Sons Union Vets., John Carroll Soc., La Confrerie des Chevaliers du Tastevin, Confrerie de la Chaine des Rotisseurs, Newcomen Soc., Am. Law Inst., Sigma Nu. Roman Catholic. Clubs: Columbia Country, Ocean City Light Tackle, Nat. Lawyers, Lawyers, Seaview Country. Home: 3353 Runnymeade Pl NW Washington DC 20015 Office: US Ct Appeals DC Circuit Washington DC 20001

TANENBAUM, HERBERT LOUIS, physician; b. Washington, Oct. 20, 1927; s. Samuel and Tessie (Silberman) T.; B.S. cum laude, Georgetown Coll., 1948, M.D. magna cum laude, 1952; m. Elaine Rhoda Bresler, July 27, 1958; children—Bruce, Michael, Robert, Steven, Mark. Intern, Boston City Hosp., 1952-53; resident Georgetown U. Hosp., 1953-54, Charity Hosp., New Orleans, 1954-55; clin. asso., investigator Nat. Heart Inst., Bethesda, Md., 1955-57; practice medicine, specializing in cardiology, Washington, 1958—; mem. staff Washington Hosp. Center; asst. clin. prof. medicine Georgetown Med. Sch., 1958—. Cons. Nat. Heart Inst., Bethesda, Md. Served with USPHS, 1955-57. Fellow A.C.P.; mem. Am. Coll. Cardiology, Am. Coll. Chest Physicians, Am. Heart Assn., Am. Fedn. for Clin. Research. Home: 9812 Belhaven Rd Bethesda MD 20034 Office: 4400 Connecticut Av Washington DC 20008

TANIGUCHI, ALAN YAMATO, architect; b. Stockton, Cal., Sept. 13, 1922; s. Isamu and Sadayo (Miyagi) T.; B.Arch., U. Cal. at Berkeley, 1949; student Detroit Inst. Tech., 1944-45; m. Leslie Honnami, Apr. 29, 1949; children—Evan Key, Keith. Designer-draftsman firm Hillmer & Callister, Architects, San Francisco, 1949-50, Anshen & Allen, Architects, San Francisco, 1950-51; pvt. practice architecture Alan Y. Taniguchi, Assos., Harlingen, Tex., 1951-60, Austin, Tex., 1961-69; partner firm Taniguchi & Croft, Harlingen, 1960-61; prin., pres. TSVM, Inc., Architects, Austin, 1969—, asst. prof. arch. U. Tex. Sch. Architecture, Austin, 1961-63, asso. prof., 1963-65, prof., 1965-72, dean, 1967-72; prof., dir. Rice U. Sch. Architecture, 1972—. Mem. Tex. Com. for Humanities, 1973—, City of Austin Planning Commn., 1968-72, Austin Zoning Bd., 1970-72; mem. architecture adv. panel Tex. Commn. Arts and Humanities, 1973—. Bd. dirs. Houston Urban Bunch. Fellow A.I.A. (dir. Houston chpt., Austin chpt. awards 1969-71), Tex. Soc. Architects (Honor awards 1960-62), Tau Sigma Delta, Phi Kappa Phi. Home: 3508 Stanford St Houston TX 77006 Office: 105 E 3d St Austin TX 78701 also Rice U Houston TX 77001

TANKERSLEY, JAMES INGRAM, food processing co. exec.; b. Knoxville, Tenn., Apr. 30, 1942; s. James O. and Ella (Ingram) T.; B.S. in Mech. Engring., U. Tenn., 1964; m. Edna Mae Weaver, July 25, 1960; children—Darla Ann, Kelle Leigh, James Wood. Pres. Winter Garden Inc., Bells, Tenn., 1972—; v.p., dir. United Foods, Inc., Memphis, 1972—. Dir. Agrl. Services Assn., Inc., Bells. Registered profl. engr., Tenn. Mem. Am. Soc. M.E., Phi Kappa Phi, Phi Eta Sigma, Tau Beta Pi. Methodist. Home: PO Box 299 Bells TN 38006 Office: PO Box 119 Bells TN 38006

TANKSLEY, JEPTHA CHARLES, judge; b. nr. Lula, Ga., Dec. 18, 1920; s. Adger Lee and Esther (Eller) T.; student North Ga. Coll., 1938-40; B.S., U.S. Mil. Acad., 1943; LL.B., Emory U., 1949; B.B.A., U. Ga., 1952; m. Frances McKay Rowan, May 13, 1948; children—Jeptha Reid, Charles Branch, Thomas Rowan. Admitted to Ga. bar, 1949, practice, Atlanta, 1949-52; asst. solicitor gen., Ga., 1952-56; judge Fulton Superior Ct., 1957—. Served from 2d lt. to capt., inf., AUS, 1947, ETO. Decorated Purple Heart, Silver Star. Mem. Am. Bar assn., State Bar Ga. (treas. 1964-70), Alpha Tau Omega, Phi Alpha Delta. Presbyn. Lion. Club: Lawyers. Home: 3440 Paces Forest Rd NW Atlanta GA 30327 Office: Court House Atlanta GA 30303

TANNENWALD, THEODORE, JR., judge; b. Valatie, N.Y., July 28, 1916; s. Theodore and Myra (Barnet) T.; A.B. summa cum laude, Brown U., 1936; LL.B. magna cum laude, Harvard, 1939; m. Selma Peterfreund, Aug. 3, 1940; children—Peter, Robert. Admitted to N.Y. bar, 1939, D.C., 1946; staff atty. Weil, Gotshal & Manges, N.Y.C., 1939-42, partner, 1947-65; judge U.S. Tax Ct., Washington, 1965—; lectr. George Washington U. Sch. Law, 1968—; prin. legal cons. Lend Lease Adminstrn., 1942; acting asst. chief, fgn. funds control div. Dept. State, 1942-43; spl. cons. Sec. War, 1943-45. Cons., Sec. Def., 1947-49; counsel to spl. asst. to Pres., 1950-51; asst. dir., chief of staff to dir. for mut. security Exec. Office Pres. 1951-53; spl. counsel to the Moreland Commn., 1955-58; N.Y. mem. Tri-State Tax Commn., 1958-59; mem. President's Task Force on Fgn. Aid and spl. asst. to sec. of state, 1961. Chmn. bd. govs. Hebrew Union Coll.-Jewish Inst. Religion; chmn. nat. adv. panel Am. Jewish Com.; trustee U. State N.Y., 1958-59. Mem. Am., Fed., D.C. bar assns., Council Fgn. Relations, Assn. Bar City N.Y., Phi Beta Kappa, Sigma Xi, Delta Sigma Rho. Home: 2916 Albemarle St NW Washington DC 20008 Office: US Tax Court Washington DC 20044

TANNER, EMERSON BECK, savs. & loan assn. exec.; b. Union City, Tenn., June 17, 1921; s. Tyree Walker and Dorothy (Beck) T.; B.B.A., U. Tenn., 1943; m. Edith Adelle Summers, Sept. 11, 1943; children—John Sumners, Robert Tyree, Rodger Beck. Pres., Union City Ins. Agy. Inc., 1946-51, First Fed. Savs. & Loan Assn., Union City, 1951—; chmn. bd. dirs. Tennesco; sec. Dyersburg Coca Cola Bottling Co.; pres. Tech. Corp. Served to capt. AUS, 1943-46. Decorated Bronze Star medal. Mem. Tenn. Savs. and Loan League (pres. 1973), Am. Legion, V.F.W., Union City C. of C. (pres. 1960-61). Mason (Shriner), Moose, Eagle, Rotarian. Club: Poplar Meadows Country. Home: Pleasant Valley Rd Union City TN 38261 Office: 215 S 1st St Union City TN 38261

TANNER, JOHN MAYO, radiologist, educator; b. Ashland, Ky., Oct. 5, 1926; s. Lawrence Marion and Martha Elizabeth (Watson) T.; B.A. cum laude, Vanderbilt U., 1949; M.D., Vanderbilt U., 1952; m. Helen Killebrew Rooney, June 7, 1951; children—Helen Elizabeth, Donna Katherine, Sally Lawrence, Martha Watson, Mary Ellen. Intern Harper Hosp., Detroit, 1952-53, resident radiology, 1953-56; practice medicine specializing in radiology, Ashland, Ky., 1956-58; radiologist Radiology Assos., Nashville, 1958—; mem. staff Nashville Bapt. Hosp.; clin. instr. radiology Vanderbilt Med. Sch., 1963—. Bd. dirs. Home, Inc., Nashville, 1972—. Served with USNR, 1945-46. Diplomate Am. Bd. Radiology. Mem. Radiol. Soc. N.Am., A.M.A., Tenn., So. med. assns., Nashville Acad. Medicine, Tenn. Radiol. Soc., Phi Beta Kappa, Sigma Chi, Phi Chi. Presbyn. (deacon 1962-65; elder 1966-71). Club: Belle Meade Country (Nashville). Home: 300 Walnut Dr Nashville TN 37205 Office: 321 Mid-State Med Center Nashville TN 37203

TANNER, JOHN PAUL, electronics co. exec.; b. Cleve., Sept. 22, 1927; s. William and Lucille (McKenney) T.; B.B.A., U. Miami, 1951, B.S., 1954; M.B.A., Rollins Coll., 1965; m. Mary Magdalen Johnson, Nov. 6, 1948; children—Timothy, Thomas, Christina, John, Roy, William, Joseph, Julia, Daniel, David, Mary Ellen. Engr., Chemstrand Corp., Pensacola, Fla., then sr. engr. Bendix Corp., South Bend, Ind., 1951-58; supr. prodn. engring. Radiation Inc., Melbourne, Fla., 1958-64; chief plans and programs LTV Aerospace Corp., Kennedy Space Center, Fla., 1964-67; dir. indsl. and prodn. engring. Electronic Communications Inc., St. Petersburg, Fla., 1967—; pres. John P. Tanner & Assos., Cons. engrs., Orlando, Fla., 1969—. Lectr. engring. tech. St. Petersburg Jr. Coll., 1968-70, Valencia Community Coll., 1973—. Served to lt. USNR, 1951-53; Korea. Registered profl. engr., Fla., Ga. Mem. Am. Inst. Indsl. Engrs. (sr.). Democrat. Roman Catholic. Home: 1410 Pinar Dr Orlando FL 32807 Office: 1501 72d St N St Petersburg FL 33733

TANNER, NATHAN HERBERT, JR., holding co. exec.; b. Radford, Va., May 30, 1922; s. Nathan Herbert and Bessie (Bond) T.; student Internat. Corr. Schs., 1940-41; m. Mary Grace Jones, Nov. 25, 1949; children—Stephen, David, Tommy. With Norfolk & Western Ry., Roanoke, Va., 1940-56; with Roanoke Photo Finishing Co., Inc., 1956-65, sales mgr., mgr., v.p., 1961-65; v.p., gen. mgr. photo subsidiaries div. Swartz Enterprises, Roanoke, 1965—, also dir. subsidiaries. Mem. Parents' Council Va. Mil. Inst., Lexington, 1970—; mem. devel. council Ferrum (Va.) Coll., 1966-68. Bd. dirs. Va. Jr. Miss pageant. Served with USAAF, 1942-45; ETO. Mem. Roanoke Valley C. of C., Master Photo Dealers and Finishers Assn., Graphic Arts Assn. Va., Printing Industries Va. Assn., Nat. Assn. Broadcasters. Methodist (lay speaker). Club: United Commercial Travelers (Roanoke). Home: 3460 Grandin Rd Extension Roanoke VA 24018 Office: PO Box 22 Roanoke VA 24001

TANNER, PAUL FRANCIS, clergyman; b. Peoria, Ill., Jan. 15, 1905; s. Frank John and Laura (McGowan) T.; A.B., St. Francis (Wis.) Sem., 1930, A.M., 1931, S.T.B., 1931; student Marquette U., 1923-25, 33-36, Kenrick Sem., St. Louis, 1925-27. Ordained priest Roman Catholic Ch., 1931; sec. Cath. Action, also dir. Confrat. Christian Doctrine, and dir. Cath. Youth activities Archdiocese Milw.; asst. dir. youth dept. 1940-42, dir., 1942-45, asst. gen. sec. N.C.W.C., 1945-58, gen. sec., 1958-68; bishop, St. Augustine, Fla., 1968—. Apptd. Papal Chamberlain, 1948; domestic prelate, 1954; consecrated Titular Bishop Lamasba, 1965. Author: (with Dr. Edward Fitzpatrick) Methods of Teaching Religion in Elementary Schools, 1939. Editor Catholic Action, 1943-53. Home: 5051 Atlanta Blvd Jacksonville FL 32200 Office: Gulf Life Tower Jacksonville FL 32201

TANNER, RALPH M., coll. pres.; b. Jefferson County, Ala., Dec. 10, 1926; A.B., Birmingham-So. Coll., 1954, M.A. in History, 1957; Ph.D. in History, U. Ala., 1967; postgrad. Cumberland Sch. Law, Samford U., 1968-70; m. Judith Berry; 3 children. Head tchr. Jefferson County Pub. Schs., 1950-53; tchr. Warrior High Sch., 1953-56; prof. history and govt. Walker Jr. Coll., Jasper, Ala., 1956-60, dean coll., 1956-60; vis. asst. prof. history and polit. sci. Birmingham-So. Coll., 1960, asst. prof., 1960-67, asso. prof., 1967-72, dir. admissions, 1961-64, registrar, 1961-62, chmn. dept. history, 1970, dean coll., 1970-71, exec. v.p., chief exec. officer, 1971-72, pres., 1972—. Head edn. div. Jefferson County Heart Appeal; mem. Ala. region exec. com. Nat. Conf. Christians and Jews. Bd. dirs. Birmingham Civic Ballet; mem. adv. com. Ala. Hist. Commn.; mem. commn. archives and history N. Ala. Conf. United Meth. Ch., chmn. commn., 1969-72; bd. dirs. Ala. Partners of Americas; v.p. Birmingham Symphony Assn.; mem. Citizens Adv. Commmn. Jefferson County Personnel Bd. Mem. So. Hist. Assn., So. Polit. Sci. Assn., Ala. Hist. Assn. (mem. exec. com. 1969—, chmn. program com. 1966-67, 70-71), Am. Assn. U. Profs., Ala. Assn. Collegiate Registrars and Admission Officers (pres., 1959-62), Ala. Assn. Coll. Adminstrs., Jefferson County Classroom Tchrs. Assn. (pres. 1952-54), So. Assn. Colls. and Schs. Evaluating Coms., Birmingham C. of C. (mem. com. on higher edn. 1972), Kappa Phi Kappa, Phi Alpha Theta, Pi Sigma Alpha, Omicron Delta Kappa. Contbr. numerous articles, book revs. to profl. jours. Address: Birmingham-Southern Coll Birmingham AL 35204

TANNER, TERRELL BENSON, physician; b. nr. Clermont, Ga., July 25, 1932; s. Fred Homer and Alice (Haynes) T.; student Emory Jr. Coll., 1949-51; B.A., Emory U., 1959; M.D., U.S. Naval Sch. Aerospace Medicine, 1960; m. Jane Davidson, 1954 (dec. 1967); children—William Davidson, Sarah Rogers, Robert Benson, John Cash; m. 2d, Martha Cash, Apr. 11, 1969. Intern. U.S. Naval Hosp., Pensacola, Fla., 1959-60; resident U.S. Naval Sch. Aerospace Medicine, 1960-61; pvt. practice medicine, specializing in family medicine, Hartwell, Ga., 1964-69, Gatlinburg, Tenn., 1969—; mem. staff Anderson (S.C.) Meml. Hosp., 64-69; pres. Hart County Hosp. Staff, 1967-69; mem. Sevier County Hosp. med. staff. Sec. Hart County (Ga.) Republican Party, 1967-68; speaker E. Tenn. Heart Assn., 1973-74. Bd. dirs. Gatlinburg Community Chest. Served with USN, 1958-64. Fellow Am. Acad. Family Physicians; mem. Royal Soc. Health (London), Ga. Acad. Gen. Practice (dir. 1964-67), Omicron Delta Kappa, Phi Chi. Republican. Methodist (teacher youth Sunday sch., vice-chmn. adminstrv. bd. 1972-73, chmn. council on ministries 1971-72). Kiwanian. Home: 279 Airport Rd Gatlinburg TN 37738 Office: 277 Airport Rd Gatlinburg TN 37738

TANNER, WILLIAM BROWN, JR., radio program dir., operations mgr.; b. Vicksburg, Miss., Dec. 6, 1944; s. William Brown and Laura Nelson (Sharkey) T.; student Millsaps Coll., 1963-65, Hinds Jr. Coll., 1964. Announcer, WQBC Radio, Vicksburg, 1959-62; radio time salesman WJQS, Jackson, Miss., 1963; announcer, copywriter WSLI, Jackson, 1963-66; announcer, music dir. WNSL, Laurel, Miss., 1966-68; program dir. WKOR, Starkville, Miss., 1968; sta. mgr. KNOE-FM, Monroe, La., 1969-70; program dir. WJDX, Inc., Jackson, 1970—, operations mgr. 1970—, host Bill Tanner Show, 1970-74; program dir. Y-100, WHYI, Miami, Fla., 1974—, also host Bill Tanner Show. Home: 4200 Sheridan St Apt 208 Hollywood FL 33020 Office: 2741 N 29th Av Suite 300 Hollywood FL 33020

TANZER, LESTER, mag. editor; b. N.Y.C., Aug. 3, 1929; s. Charles and Clara (Ente) T.; A.B., Columbia, 1951, M.S., 1952; postgrad. George Washington U., 1965—; m. Marlene June Luckton, June 29, 1949; children—Stephen, Jeffrey, Andrew, David. Reporter, Wall St. Jour., Washington, 1952-59; asso. editor Changing Times mag., Washington, 1959-64; asso. exec. editor U.S. News and World Report, Washington, 1964—. Mem. Nat. Press Club, Am. Polit. Sci. Assn., Columbia Coll. Alumni Assn. Met. Washington (pres. 1962-64). Club: Nat. Press (Washington). Author: (with Stefan Ilok) The Brotherhood of Silence, 1962; Stretching Your Auto Dollar, 1964; Ten Champions, 1965. Editor: The Kennedy Circle, 1961. Home: 4859 N 30th St Arlington VA 22207 Office: 2300 N St Washington DC 20037

TANZLER, HANS G., JR., mayor; b. Charlotte, N.C., Mar. 11, 1927; s. Hans G. and Dorrette (Walker) T.; B.A., U. Fla., 1949, LL.B., 1951; m. La Mercedes Woodard, Jan. 26, 1973; 1 son from previous marriage, Hans G. III. Admitted to Fla. bar; with firm Tanzler and Maddox; then 1st county solicitor; gen. counsel Fla. State Bd. Health, 1961-63; judge criminal ct., 1963-67; mayor Jacksonville, Fla., 1967—. Served on Governor's Adv. Com. on Decent Lit.; past pres. Fla. League Cities; bd. govs. U.S. Conf. Mayors. Active Big Bros. Served with USNR, 1945-46. Mem. Jacksonville C. of C., Am., Fla., Jacksonville bar assns., Kappa Alpha. Mason (32 deg., Shriner), Moose. Presbyterian. Home: 7901 Bay Meadows Circle East #319 Jacksonville FL 32216 Office: 1401 City Hall Jacksonville FL 32202

TAPP, JAY COWAN, mfg. co. pres.; b. Oklahoma City, June 17, 1935; s. Felix Cowan and Virginia (Filson) T.; B.A., Rice Inst., 1957; B.S. in M.E., 1958; M.B.A., Harvard, 1960; m. Jacquelyn Louise Bartell, Nov. 23, 1957; children—Felix C., Filson B., Jay Bertell. Asst. to pres. Helmerich & Pay, Inc., Tulsa, 1960-63; treas. F.H. Maloney Co., Houston, 1963-65; financial v.p. Kirby Industries, Houston, 1966-68; pres. Kirby Bldg. Systems, Kirby Real Estate Investment Corp., Houston, 1968—; dir. Caribbean Finance Co., San Juan, P.R.; exec., dir. Nat. Bank, Houston. Bd. dirs. Rice Design Alliance, Children's Mental Health Center, Houston; chmn. bd. Palmer Drug Abuse Program, 1973—. Episcopalian. Home: 1647 S Boulevard Houston TX 77006 Office: PO Box 36429 Houston TX 77036

TARANTOLA, CHARLSIE LOVELL (MRS. MICHAEL NICHOLAS TARANTOLA), educator; b. Weatherford, Tex., Aug. 16, 1920; d. James Thomas and Pauline (Harris) Bradshaw; student George Washington U., U. Va., Am. U. Washington, North Tex. State Tchrs. Coll.; B.S., Smith Hughes, 1945; postgrad. Trenton State Tchrs. Coll., 1954-57; M.S. in Edn., Va. Poly. Inst. and State U., 1974; m. Michael Nicholas Tarantola, June 3, 1944; children—Michael Roy, John Terry. Tchr., Muenster (Tex.) Pub. Schs., 1941-43, Breckenridge (Tex.) Pub. Schs., 1945, Faruell (Tex.) Pub. Sch., 1947, Sasebo (Japan) Am. Sch., 1948-49; adult ednl. instr. TI— Div., Gelenhausen, Germany, 1954; elementary tchr. Gelenhausen Am. Sch., 1952-54, Pemberton (N.J.) Twp., 1954-57, Fort Myer (Va.) Elementary Sch., 1957-65; sci. tchr. Oakridge Elementary Sch., Arlington, Va., 1965-71; secondary sci. tchr. Thomas Jefferson Jr. High Sch., 1971—. Mem. V.I.S.T.A., Nat. Va., Arlington edn. assns., Nat. Sci. Tchrs. Assn., Delta Kappa Gamma. Roman Catholic. Home: 515 N Longfellow St Arlington VA 22203

TARAVELLA, JOSEPH PHILIP, community devel. co. exec.; b. N.Y.C., Jan. 19, 1919; s. James and Margaret (Capuccio) T.; B.S., Fordham U., 1940; M.S., Columbia, 1940-41; m. Florence E. Wright, May 27, 1944; children—Joseph Philip, Mark James. Sales mgr. R.H. Macy Co., N.Y.C., 1940-41; exec. v.p., gen. mgr. Coral Ridge Properties, Inc. subsidiary Westinghouse Electric Corp., Ft. Lauderdale, Fla., 1945-66, pres., chmn. bd., 1960—, also dir., also gen. mgr. Community Devel. div., Coral Springs, Fla.; pres., chmn. Half Moon Bay Properties, San Francisco; dir. Fla. Power & Light., Financial Life Ins. Co., Southeast Bank of Galt Ocean Mile, Southeast Bank of Broward, Bank of Coral Springs, Half Moon Bay, Cal., Curacao Properties, N.V.; dir., mem. exec. com. Bank of Coral Springs. Mem. Fla. Environmental Land Mgmt. Bd.; trustee, mem. new communities council Urban Land Inst.; mem. Fla. Environmental Standards Com. Mem. exec. bd. S.E. Council Boy Scouts Am. Served to lt. USCGR, 1941-45. Mem. Urban Land Inst., Fla. C. of C. (dir.), Fla. Council 100 (chmn.), Fla. Land Sales Bd. Democrat. Roman Catholic. Clubs: Coral Springs (Fla.) Golf and Tennis; Coral Ridge Yacht (Ft. Lauderdale); Broken Woods Country. Home: 2641 Yacht Club Blvd Fort Lauderdale FL 33304 Office: 9500 W Sample Rd Coral Springs FL 33065

TARBET, DONALD GENTRY, educator; b. Shelbyville, Mo., May 15, 1917; s. J. Omer and Lucile (Gentry) T.; student Culver Stockton Coll., 1934-37; B.S., U. Mo., 1938, M.Ed., 1946, Ed.D., 1952; student Wash. U., summers 1947, 48; m. Justeen Bales, Nov. 20, 1941. Teacher Ellington (Mo.) High Sch., 1938-40; teacher, prin. Pattonville (Mo.) High Sch., 1940-42, 46-48; prin. Warrensburg (Mo.) High Sch., 1948-51; prof. edn. U. N.C., 1952—, dir. summer session, 1969—. Served with AUS, 1942-45. Mem. Am. Assn. U. Profs., Nat. Assn. Secondary Sch. Prins., Horace Mann League Am., N.E.A., N.C. Assn. Educators, Phi Delta Kappa, Phi Mu Alpha. Democrat. Baptist (deacon 1972-74). Author: Television and Our Schools, 1961; Teacher In-Service Education by Television, 1958. Contbr. articles to nat. ednl. publs. Home: 904 Christopher Rd Chapel Hill NC 27514

TARBETT, JAMES ALLAN, JR., computer engr.; b. Takoma Park, Md., June 15, 1941; s. James Allan and Margaret (Dyer) T.; B.E.E., Lamar U., 1966, M.E.F., 1970; m. Frances Mary McBride, Feb. 22, 1964; children—Patrice Charlene, Shannon Cathleen. Asso. engr. elec. and instrument design Mobil Beaumont Refinery, 1966-69, engr. elec. and instrument design, 1969-70, engr. process computer control, 1970-73, sr. engr. process computer control, 1973—. Pilot Civil Air Patrol, 1969; team mgr. S. Little League, 1973. Registered profl. engr., Tex. Mem. I.E.E.E. (pres. Beaumont sect. 1972-73, v.p. 1971-72, sec.-treas. 1970-71), Gulf Coast Engring. and Sci. Soc. Inc. (dir. 1972-73, v.p. 1970-71, sec. 1969-70), Aircraft Owners and Pilots Assn., Nat. Rifle Assn. Roman Catholic. Clubs: Magnolia Investor (pres. 1973—). Home: 6230 Daisy Dr Beaumont TX 77706 Office: Mobil Oil Corp PO Box 3311 Beaumont TX 77704

TARBOX, FREDERICK CHARLES, JR., computer co. exec.; b. Columbus, O., May 11, 1942; s. Frederick Chalmers and Grace (Guth) T.; B.S. in Mech. Engring., Case Inst. Tech., 1964; postgrad. Ohio State U., 1964-65, N.C. State U., 1967; m. Christina Kay, Nov. 28, 1964. Owner, Upper Arlington Lawn Service Co. (O.), 1951-60; mech. engr. Columbus & So. Ohio Electric Co., 1960-65; plant engr. Carolina Power & Light Co., Goldsboro, N.C., 1965-67; pres. Hydra Computer Corp., Raleigh, N.C., 1967—. Fallout shelter analyst Office Civil Def., Columbus, O., 1965—. Sponsor indsl. coop. tng. Enloe High Sch., Raleigh, 1969—. Mem. Am. Soc. M.E., Alpha Phi Epsilon. Republican. Mem. United Ch. of Christ. Home: 300 Cedar Crest Dr Raleigh NC 27609 Office: PO Box 17883 Raleigh NC 27609

TARBOX, GURDON LUCIUS, JR., museum dir.; b. Plainfield, N.J., Dec. 25, 1927; s. Gurdon Lucius and Lillie (Hodgson) T.; B.S., Mich. State U., 1952; M.S., Purdue U., 1954; m. Milver Ann Johnson, Sept. 25, 1952; children—Janet Ellen, Joyce Elaine, Paul Edward, Lucia Ann. Asst. dir. Brookgreen Gardens, Murrells Inlet, S.C., 1954-59, trustee, 1959—, dir., 1963—. Chmn. Georgetown County Mental Health Commn., 1964-66. Trustee Kaminski House. Served with AUS, 1946-48. Mem. Soc. Am. Foresters, Am. Assn. Bot. Gardens and Arboreta (dir. 1971—), Georgetown County Hist. Soc. (pres. 1970—). Episcopalian. Home: Brookgreen Gardens Murrells Inlet SC 29576 Office: Brookgreen Gardens Murrells Inlet SC 29576

TARIN, EDWARD I., realtor; b. Texas City, Tex., Nov. 11, 1932; s. Joseph Edward and Lottie (Zander) T.; student Tex. A. and M. U., 1950; children—David, Daryl. Owner E.I. Tarin & Co., Texas City, also Alta Loma, Tex., 1965—; instr., lectr. appraisal methods and techniques Coll. Mainland, 1967. Served with USNR, 1951. Mem. Texas City-La Marque Bd. Realtors, Nat., Tex. assns. realtors, Am. Inst. Real Estate Appraisers. Mason. Home: 631 7th Av N Texas City TX 77590 Office: PO Box 2277 Texas City TX 77590

TARKENTON, DONALD LEE, city ofcl.; b. Norfolk, Va., Feb. 7, 1948; s. James Theodore and Elsie Mae (Lilley) T.; B.A. in Polit. Sci. and Social Sci., Elon Coll., 1970; M.P.A., W.Va. U., 1971; m. Margaret Anne Johnson, Sept. 16, 1972; 1 child, Stephanie Renee. Adminstrv. asst., Graham, N.C., 1969-70; town mgr. Town Siler City, N.C., 1971—. Recipient George C. Franklin Meml. award U. N.C. Inst. Govt., Chapel Hill, 1973. Mem. Siler City Jr. C. of C. (pres. 1973-74), Internat. City Mgmt. Assn., Am. Soc. Pub. Adminstrn., Am. Pub. Works Assn., Internat. Personnel Mgmt. Assn., Nat. League Cities. Baptist. Mason, Moose. Home: PO Box 682 Siler City NC 27344 Office: PO Box 769 Siler City NC 27344

TARPLEY, JOHN WILLIAM, elec. engr.; b. Bonham, Tex., Nov. 8, 1919; s. William Everett and Cora (Bivans) T.; B.S., U. Tex., 1942; m. Alice Dora Morgan, Sept. 11, 1941 (div.); children—Bill, Joy Alice (Mrs. Carl H. Moneyhon). Asst. div. engr. Tex. Power & Light Co., McKinney, 1945-48; design engr., Austin, Tex., 1948-50; distbn. engr. Lubbock, Tex., 1950-52; elec. engr. for phys. plant U. Tex., 1952-58; cons. engr., Austin, 1958—. Chmn. troop com. Boy Scouts Am., 1954-65. Served to lt. USNR, 1942-45. Mem. I.E.E.E. (sr.), Tex. Soc. Profl. Engrs. (sec.-treas. sect. 1968-70). Lion (sec. 1955-56), Kiwanian (dir. 1968-70). Club: Ramshorn (sec. 1958-59). Address: 1512 1/2 S Congress Austin TX 78704

TARPLEY, THOMAS JOSEPH, real estate co. exec.; b. Rome, Ga., Mar. 24, 1939; s. Joseph Chaney and Rachel (Wall) T.; student Ga. Inst. Tech., 1957-58; Ga. Banking Sch., 1964; Ga. Inst. Real Estate, 1964, 1966; m. June Faye Cantrell, Mar. 21, 1959; children—Thomas Joseph, Susan Annette, Christopher Lee. Loan officer Nat. City Bank, Rome, 1961-64; with advt. dept. J.L. Todd Auction Co., Rome, 1964, real estate salesman, 1965, asso. broker, asst. treas., 1966-67, exec. v.p., 1967—; partner P & T Builders; asst. sec., dir. Gilmer Estates, Inc.; treas. W-W Investments, Inc. Mem. Gov.'s staff Youth for Christ Module Support Com., 1973; pres. Maple St. Community Center, 1973-74, v.p., 1971-72, sec., 1968-71; chmn. bd. dirs. Rome YMCA; adv. dir. Northwest Ga. council Boy Scouts Am., 1973—; adv. dir. Star House; pres. North Heights Elem. PTA, 1973. Bd. dirs. Floyd County unit Am. Cancer Soc. Named Realtor Yr., Rome Bd. Realtors, 1971; Outstanding Young Layman award Rome Jaycees, 1971, Distinguished Service award, 1972. Mem. Rome Bd. Realtors (pres. 1970-71), Ga. Assn. Realtors (dir. 1970-72), Nat. Assn. Realtors, Nat. Assn. Real Estate Appraisers, Ga. Tech. Alumni Assn., Peach Bowl Assn. Methodist (chmn. bd. trustees 1974—, chmn. adminstrv. bd. 1974—, mem. council on ministries 1969—, counselor elementary fellowship 1974—, mem. bldg. com. 1969—, jr. high sch. Sunday sch. tchr. 1964-72, chmn. finance com. 1969-72). Lion. Club: Coosa Country. Home: 107 Wells Dr Rome GA 30161 Office: 531 Broad St Rome GA 30161

TARRANT, JOHN EDWARD, lawyer; b. Dyersburg, Tenn., Nov. 25, 1898; s. John Morgan and Penelope A. (Fumbanks) T.; B.S., U. Va., 1921; LL.B., Harvard, 1923; m. Mary Park Kaye, May 26, 1928; children—Mary Kaye (Mrs. Edwin Durham II), Eleanor (Mrs. Phillip B. Newman III), Penelope (Mrs. Clay L. Morton). Admitted to Ky. bar, 1923; asso. Simpson, Thacher & Bartlett, N.Y.C., 1922, Bruce, Bullitt & Gordon, Louisville, 1923-26; partner Bruce & Bullitt, 1926-40, Ogden Tarrant, Galphin & Street, 1940-48, Bullitt, Dawson & Tarrant, 1948-70, Tarrant, Combs, Blackwell & Bullitt, 1970—; gen. counsel Fed. Land Bank, Fed. Intermediate Credit Bank, Louisville, 1930; spl. judge Ct. Appeals, Ky., 1948; chmn. bd. Louisville Investment Co., 1958—; dir. Churchill Downs Inc., Louisville Transit Co.; dir. Citizens Fidelity Bank & Trust Co., 1957-69, adviser, 1969-71. Trustee U. Louisville, 1966-70, Norton Children's Hosps., YWCA, 1939-63; bd. dirs. Louisville Central Area Assn., 1966—. Served O.T.C., Camp Fortress Monroe, Va., 1918. Fellow Am. Bar Found.; mem. N.C. Soc. Cincinnati, Ky. Soc. Colonial Wars, S.A.R., Am., Ky., Louisville bar assns., Am. Law Inst., Am. Judicature Soc., Phi Beta Kappa, Kappa Sigma. Republican. Episcopalian. Clubs: Pendennis, River Valley, Wynn Stay, Filson, Country (Louisville); Jefferson; Frankfort (Ky.) Country; Broad Street (N.Y.C.); Metropolitan (Washington); Union (N.Y.C.). Home: Beech Grove 3740 Upper River Rd Louisville KY 40207 Office: Kentucky Home Life Bldg Louisville KY 40202

TARVER, JACK MCLANE, lawyer; b. Waco, Tex., Nov. 8, 1940; s. Jackson McLane and Frances Ella (Wheelis) T.; B.A., U. Tex., 1963; LL.B., U. Tex. Sch. Law, 1966; m. Georgia Lee Monroe, Aug. 27, 1966; children—John David, Robert Madison. Admitted to Tex. bar, 1966; asso. Daniel, Brown & Tarver, Temple, Tex., 1966-70, partner, 1970—. Fellow Tex. Bar Found., 1973—. Mem. Am. Bar Assn., State Bar Tex., Bell-Lampasas-Mills Counties Bar Assn. (pres. 1972-73), Am. Judicature Soc., Tex. Assn. Def. Counsel (dir. 1973—). Home: 3413 Buffalo St Temple TX 76501 Office: Temple Nat Bank Bldg Temple TX 76501

TARVER, JAMES DONALD, educator; b. Canyon, Tex., Dec. 23, 1921; s. Clyde James and Cloma Aliene (Foster) T.; student Weatherford Jr. Coll., 1939-40; B.S., Tex. A. and M. U., 1947; Ph.D., U. Wis., 1951; m. Mildred Louise Cotten, Sept. 17, 1943. Asst. prof. U. Ark. at Fayetteville, 1950-51; mem. faculty Okla. State U., Stillwater, 1951-66, asso. prof., 1953-57, prof., 1957-66; prof. sociology and agrl. econs. U. Ga., Athens, 1966—, dir. Demographic Research and Tng. Center, 1966-72; vis. prof. Utah State U., summers 1964, 65. Vice chmn. southeastern regional manpower adv. com. U.S. Dept. Labor, 1972-74, agr. rep., 1972-74. Served with AUS, 1942-45. A.M.A. research fellow, summer 1965. Mem. Am. Sociol. Assn., Population Assn. Am., Nat. Research Council, Nat. Acad. Scis., Rural Sociol. Soc., So. Regional Demographic Group. Home: Route 1 Box 56C Bishop GA 30621 Office: Dept Sociology Univ Georgia Athens GA 30602

TARWATER, JAN DALTON, educator; b. Ft. Worth, Sept. 30, 1937; s. Roy L. and Margie (Dalton) T.; B.S., Tex. Tech. U., 1959; M.A., U. N.M., 1961, Ph.D., 1965; m. Nancy Pat Houston, Aug. 15, 1958; children—Jay D., Paul H., Patrick M. Asst. prof. math. Western Mich. U., Kalamazoo, 1965-67, North Tex. State U., Denton, 1967-68; asso. prof. math. Tex. Tech U., Lubbock, 1968—, asso. chmn. dept., 1972-73, chmn., 1973—. Dir. History Am. Math. Project Tex. Colls. and Univs. Bicentennial Program, 1972—. Mem. Am. Math. Soc., Sigma Xi, Phi Kappa Phi, Kappa Mu Epsilon, Phi Sigma Tau. Contbr. articles to profl. jours. Home: 3823 53d St Lubbock TX 79413

TATE, ALBERT, JR., state supreme ct. justice; b. Opelousas, La., Sept. 23, 1920; s. Albert and Adelaide (Therry) T.; student La. State U., 1938-39, certificate, 1948; B.A., George Washington U., 1941; LL.B., Yale, 1947; m. Claire Jeanmard, Apr. 23, 1949; children—Albert III, Emma Adelaide, George J., Michael F., Charles E. Admitted to La. bar, 1948, practiced in Ville Platte, 1948-54; judge Ct. of Appeal, 1st Circuit of La., Baton Rouge, 1954-60; presiding judge Ct. Appeal, 3d Circuit, Lake Charles, 1960-70; asso. justice La. Supreme Ct., 1958, 70—; prof. law La. State U., 1967-68. Mem. Jud. Council of State of La., 1960-70; mem. com. and council La. State Law Inst., 1954-59; faculty Inst. Jud. Adminstrn. N.Y.U., 1965—, Appellate Judges Seminar, U. Ala., 1966, 70, U. Nev., 1967; chmn. La. Judiciary Commn., 1969—; mem. adv. council Nat. Center for State Cts. Chmn. La. Commn. on Aging, 1956-59; pres. La. Cotton Festival, 1955-57; mem. Evangeline Area council Boy Scouts Am., 1948—, dist. chmn., 1949-50. Served with AUS, 1942-45. Recipient Am. Trial Lawyers judiciary award, 1971. Mem. Am. (chmn. exec. com. appellate judges conf. 1966—), La. bar assns., Am. Judicature Soc. (dir. 1969—), La. Conf. Ct. of Appeal Judges (pres. 1967-70), Am. Legion, V.F.W., Order of Coif (hon.), Blue Key (hon.). Delta Kappa Epsilon. K.C., Woodmen of World, Rotarian. Author: Louisiana Civil Procedures, 1968; Treatises for Judges, 1971. Contbr. articles to profl. jours. Home: Box 409 Ville Platte LA 70586 also 2414 Octavia St New Orleans LA 70115 Office: Supreme Court La 301 Loyola Av New Orleans LA 70112

TATE, ALLEN (JOHN ORLEY), critic, poet; b. Clark County, Ky., Nov. 19, 1899; s. John Orley and Nellie (Varnell) T.; B.A., magna cum laude, Vanderbilt U., 1922; Litt.D., U. Louisville, 1948, Colgate U., 1956; U. Ky., 1960; M.A., Oxford, 1958; Litt.D., Carleton Coll., 1963, U. of South, 1970; m. Caroline Gordon, novelist, Nov. 3, 1924; (div.); dau., Nancy Meriwether (Mrs. Percy Woods, Jr.); m. 2d, Isabella Gardner, Aug. 27, 1959 (div.); m. 3d, Helen Heinz, July 30, 1966. Free lance writer, 1924—; Guggenheim Found. fellow 1928-30; lectr. English lit. Southwestern U., Memphis, 1934-36; prof. English, Woman's Coll., U. N.C., 1938-39; resident fellow in writing, creative arts program Princeton, 1939-42; incumbent chair of poetry Library of Congress, 1943-44; editor The Sewanee Review, 1944-46; editor poetry and belles lettres Henry Holt & Co., 1946-48; lectr. English, N.Y. U., 1947-51; prof. English U. Minn., 1951-66, Regents' prof. English, 1966-68; vis. prof. humanities U. Chgo 1949; Fulbright prof. U. Oxford, 1958-59; vis. prof. Vanderbilt U., 1967; sr. fellow Ind. Sch. Letters Recipient Midland Author's prize (Chgo.), 1933; Bollingen prize in Poetry, 1956; Brandeis U. Medal award for poetry, 1961; Medaglio D'Oro, Dante Soc. (Florence), 1962; $5,000 award Acad. Am. Poets, 1963. Mem. Am. Acad. Arts and Letters, Nat. Inst. Arts and Letters (pres. 1968—), Am. Acad. Arts and Scis., Soc. Am. Historians, So. Hist. Assn., Phi Beta Kappa, Sigma Upsilon, Phi Delta Theta So. editor Hound and Horn, 1932-34, Democrat. Clubs: Princeton, Century Assn. (N.Y.C.); Authors (London). Author or co-author books since 1928; latest publs.: On the Limits of Poetry, 1948; The Hovering Fly, 1949; (with Caroline Gordon) The House of Fiction, 1950; The Forlorn Demon, 1953; The Man of Letters in the Modern World, 1955; Collected Essays, 1960; Poems, 1960; Essays of Four Decades, 1969; The Swimmers and Other Selected Poems, 1971; also articles and verse in various publs. Editor: Man and His Work (T.S. Eliot), 1966. Adv. editor Kenyon Rev., 1938-42. Regular mem. CBS radio program, Invitation to Learning, 1940-41. Address: Running Knob Hollow Rd Sewanee TN 37375

TATE, HAROLD SIMMONS, JR., lawyer; b. Taylors, S.C., Sept. 19, 1930; s. Harold Simmons and Cleone (Clayton) T.; A.B. cum laude Harvard, 1951, J.D., 1956; postgrad. Clemson U., 1953; m. Elizabeth Anne Coker, Dec. 22, 1952; children—Mary Elizabeth Anne, Martha Coker, Virginia Clayton. Admitted to S.C. bar, 1956; partner firm Boyd, Knowlton, Tate & Finlay, Columbia, S.C., 1962—. Chmn. Richland County Mental Health Center, 1965-66; co-chmn. Columbia Hearing and Speech Center, 1962-64; mem. admission and scholarship com. Harvard, 1961—; chmn. subcom. on legislation of legislation and finance study commn. Gov.'s Adv. Group on Mental Health Planning, 1963-65; chmn. Columbia Bd. Supervisory of Registration, 1961-70; pres. Columbia Philharmonic Orch., 1966-67; pres. Town Theatre, 1967-70. Trustee Richland County Pub. Library, Historic Columbia Found. Served to capt. AUS, 1951-53. Mem. Harvard Law Sch. Assn. S.C. (sec.-treas. 1958-70). Episcopalian. Clubs: Tarantella, Forest Lake Country, Columbia Drama (pres. 1963-64), Palmetto (sec. 1963-70, pres. 1973—). Contbr. articles, book revs. to profl. jours. Home: 15 Gibbes Ct Columbia SC 29201 Office: 1250 SCN Center Columbia SC 29201

TATE, JAMES OLIVER, psychologist, educator; b. Dallas, Apr. 29, 1929; s. Otho Stanley and Gertrude (Stevens) T.; student Abilene Christian Coll., 1949-51; B.B.A., So. Meth. U., 1952-53; Ed.D., North Tex. State U., 1961; m. Janet Elaine Gerleman, Nov. 29, 1957; children—James, Gregory, Carter, Blair. Supr. Bell Telephone Co., Dallas, 1956-58; asso. prof. psychology East Central State Coll., Ada, Okla., 1961-68; cons. Oklahoma City Neuropsychiat. Clinic, 1967-73, psychologist, 1973—; clin. and counseling psychologist VA Hosp., Denver, 1968-69; mem. staff U. Okla., Norman, 1969-73, coordinator of evaluation, dir. adult guidance, evaluation and testing dept.; psychologist Oklahoma City Neuropsychiat. Clinic, 1973—; practice cons. psychologist, 1964—. Bd. dirs. Pontotoc County Mental Health Bd., 1962-65. Served with AUS, 1953-55. Named Tchr. of Year, East Central State Coll., 1962. Mem. Am. Psychol. Assn., Psi Chi, Sigma Tau Gamma. Home: 2517 Wildwood St Norman OK 73069 Office: 1111 N Lee Ave Oklahoma City OK 73103

TATE, WILLIS MCDONALD, coll. chancellor; b. Denver, May 18, 1911; s. Robert Spence and Grace (Brown) T.; A.B., So. Meth. U., 1932, A.M., 1935; postgrad. U. Chgo., 1945, U. Tex., 1946-55; LL.D., Tex. Wesleyan Coll., 1951, Centenary Coll., 1954, U. Denver, 1957; L.H.D., Oklahoma City U., 1954; Sc.D., U. Tulsa, 1959; Ped.D., Albright Coll., 1974; m. Joel Estes, Dec. 24, 1932; children—Willis McDonald, Joel Ann (Withers). Tchr. elementary sch. and prin. jr. high sch., Alamo Heights, San Antonio, 1932-43; exec. asst. to pastor First Methodist Ch., Houston, 1943-45; with So. Meth. U., 1945—, successively asst. dean students, dean, v.p., 1945-54, pres., 1954-71, chancellor, 1971—. Pres. Tex. Council Chs., 1960; pres. Nat. Assn. Schs. and Colls. of Meth. Ch., 1960; pres. Univ. Senate of Meth. Church, 1960; mem., past pres. Dallas Council World Affairs, Dallas Citizens Council; bd. dirs. Am. Council Edn.; bd. cons. Nat. War Coll. Recipient Meiklejohn award Am. Assn. U. Profs., 1965. Fellow Am. Sociol. Soc.; mem. Tex. Assn. Colls. (past pres.), Council Protestant Colls. and Univs. (past chmn. 1966), So. U. Conf. (pres. 1963), Philos. Soc. Tex. (pres. 1971), Assn. Am. Colls. and Univs. (past chmn. bd.). Clubs: Petroleum, Cosmos. Author: (with A. Q. Sartain and W. W. Finlay) Human Behavior in Industry, 1954. Home: 3600 Marquette St Dallas TX 75225

TATLOCK, LLOYD EUGENE, clergyman; b. Jeffersonville, Ind., Aug. 21, 1925; s. Raymond Logan and Ora Ethel (Shanks) T.; A.B. in Religion, Butler U., 1949; M.R.E., Coll. of Bible, Lexington, Ky., 1952; postgrad. U. Ky., 1953; m. Janice Kiser, Sept. 3, 1949; children—Wayne L., Charles D., William. Ordained to ministry First Christian Ch., 1951; missionary for missions bd. Christian Ch., 1953—; served in Paraguay, 1953-56, Jacksonville, Fla., 1957-59, Argentina, 1959-70; tchr. Colegio Ward, Buenos Aires, 1959-65; now field rep. Mexico div. Overseas Ministries Disciples of Christ. Served with USNR, 1943-46. Mem. Kappa Kappa Psi. Author articles in field. Home: 2414 Clemson Av Orlando FL 32808 Office: care Christian Ch 202 S Downey Av Indianapolis IN 46219

TATUM, CLARENCE ALBERT, JR., utility exec.; b. Dallas, June 25, 1907; s. Clarence Albert and Annie Elizabeth (Wright) T.; B.A. in Physics, So. Meth. U., 1928; m. Caroline King, Dec. 16, 1936; children—Clarence Albert III, Henry King. Mem. staff comml. dept. Dallas Power & Light Co., 1928-39, comml. mgr., 1939-50, v.p., asst. to pres., 1950-53, pres., dir., gen. mgr., 1953-67; pres., chief exec. officer, dir. Tex. Utilities Co., 1967-72, chmn. bd., 1972—; dir. Tex. Power & Light Co. Hon. trustee Com. Econ. Devel. Mem. exec. bd. and nat. council Circle Ten council Boy Scouts Am.; v.p. Callier Hearing and Speech Center; adv. mem. Dallas Citizen Council. Bd. dirs. State Fair of Tex., Dallas Theatre Center, Dallas Summer Musicals, Dallas Symphony Orch., Excellence in Edn. Found. Chmn. bd. trustees So. Meth. U.; trustee So. Meth. U. Found. for Sci. and Engring., Salk Inst., Southwestern Med. Found., Tex. Research Found., Dallas Mus. Fine Arts. Mem. The Conf. Bd., Sigma Alpha Epsilon, Beta Gamma Sigma (hon.). Methodist. Clubs: City, Chaparral, Northwood, Salesmanship, Dallas Country, Petroleum (Dallas). Home: 10 Willow Wood Dallas TX 75205 Office: 1506 Commerce St Dallas TX 75201

TATUM, DONALD EDWARDS, ins. exec.; b. Clover, S.C., Jan. 1, 1924; s. William Otis and Elizabeth (Mayo) T.; student La. State U., 1940-42; C.L.U., Am. Coll. Life Underwriters, 1955, C.L.U. M., 1958; m. Sally J. Marsteller, Mar. 13, 1964; children—William Otis IV, Timothy B., Elizabeth E., Donald Edwards. With Conn. Gen. Life, Hartford, Conn., 1946-62, mgr., Pitts., 1956-62; v.p. Nat. Union Ins. Cos., 1962-67; pres., dir. South Coast Life Ins. Co., Houston, Gt. Nat. Life Ins. Co., Grenat Corp., 1968-70; sr. v.p. U.S. Life Corp., N.Y.C., 1967-70; pres. dir. Peninsular Life Ins. Co., George Washington Life Ins. Co., 1970-74; pres., dir. Lincoln Am. Life Ins. Co., 1974—; chmn. Peninsular Securities, Inc.; dir. Peninsular Fire Ins. Co., Am. Annuity Life Ins. Co., Am. Automobile Dealers Assn., Jacksonville Nat. Bank. Active United Fund. Served to lt. USNR, 1943-46. C.L.U. Mem. Jacksonville Area C. of C. (v.p., gov.), Assn. Life Underwriters (chpt. dir. 1960-62), N.Am. Newcomen Soc., Life Ins. Trust Council, Pa. Ins. Fedn. (dir.). Presbyn. Clubs: San Jose Country, River, Ponte Vedra; Tenn. Contbr. to publs. Home: 2749 Forest Circle Jacksonville FL 32217 Office: 60 N Main St Memphis TN 38101

TATUM, FRANCIS LLOYD, lawyer; b. Jackson, Tenn., Aug. 7, 1925; s. James Royal and Olive Irene (Leggett) T.; student Union U., 1943-45; J.D., Cumberland U., 1947; m. Mary Inadene Rogers, Mar. 15, 1949; children—Aaron, Janice, Lloyd R., Timothy, Suzanne. Admitted to Tenn. bar, 1947; spl. agt. FBI, Washington, New Haven, Phila., 1950-53; pvt. practice law, Henderson, Tenn., 1953—. Bd. dirs. numerous local corps.; atty. Chester County, 1958-69. Mem. Tenn. Jud. Standards Commn. Served with USAAF, 1943-45. Mem. Am., Tenn. bar assns., Am. Trial Lawyers. Home: O'Neal Lane Henderson TN 38340 Office: 130 Main St Henderson TN 38340

TATUM, JOSEPH FRANKLIN, gas co. exec.; b. Hattiesburg, Miss., Apr. 6, 1925; s. Will Sion and Bernice (Sarphie) T.; B.Engring., Vanderbilt U., 1945; m. Lady Barker, Apr. 6, 1946; children—Dawn (Mrs. W. Christie Hauck), Joseph Franklin, Deborah. Pres. C.E. Equipment Co., Inc., Hattiesburg, 1952—; pres. Trade Mart Devel. Co., Inc., Hattiesburg, 1972—; pres. So. Garden Estates Mobile Home Parks, Hattiesburg, 1969—; sec.-treas. Willmut Gas & Oil Co., Hattiesburg, 1955—. Mem. engring. adv. council Miss. State U., 1973-76; engring. council Vanderbilt U., Nashville, 1972-75. Pres. United Givers Fund, 1955-56, bd. dirs. 1972-75; trustee YWCA, Hattiesburg, 1964—. Registered profl. engr., Miss. Mem. Hattiesburg Area C. of C. (pres. 1963-64), Miss. Econ. Council (pres. elect 1974-75), Hattiesburg Area Hist. Soc. (pres. 1970-71), dir. 1974—, Methodist (steward). Kiwanian (dist. gov. 1969-70). Home: 2600 Mimosa Lane Hattiesburg MS 39401 Office: 315 S Main St PO Box 1649 Hattiesburg MS 39401

TATUM, RICHARD DURHAM, electronic engr.; b. Kermit, Tex., Jan. 17, 1947; s. Dyess C. and Maxine (Durham) T.; B.S. (Cabot Corp. scholar 1964-68), La. State U., 1969; postgrad. Va. Poly. Inst., 1971—. Electronic engr. Naval Weapons Lab., Dahlgren, Va., 1969—. Mem. Eta Kappa Nu. Club: Fredericksburg Camera. Home: PO Box 713 Dahlgren VA 22448 Office: Naval Weapons Lab Dahlgren VA 22448

TAUB, THEODORE CALVIN, lawyer; b. Springfield, Mass., Jan. 1, 1935; Samuel and Sara Lee (Daum) T.; B.A., Duke, 1956; J.D., U. Fla. 1960; m. Roberta Ginsburg, Aug. 23, 1959; children—Andrew Louis, Tracy Leigh, Adam Samuel. Admitted to Fla. bar, 1960; practiced Tampa, Fla., 1961—; partner Gibbons, Tucker, McEwen, Smith, Cofer & Taub, Tampa, 1969—. Asst. city atty., Tampa, 1963-67; city. atty., Oldsmar, 1968-69, Temple Terrace, Fla., 1973—. Mem. Hillsborough County Charter Commn., 1966-67; vice chmn. Tampa Bd. Housing Rev., 1972—. Mem. exec. bd. Gulf Ridge council Boy Scouts Am., 1973—. Served with USNR, 1961. Recipient Seldon Waldo Meml. award Fla. Jr. C. of C., 1965-66, Clayton Frost Meml. award U.S. Jr. C. of C., 1969-70. Mem. Tampa and Hillsborough County Bar Assn. (sect. pres. 1964-65), Fla. Bar, Am. Bar Assn., Am. Judicature Soc., Tampa Jr. C. of C. (pres. 1965-66), Fla. Jr. C. of C. (nat. dir. 1966-67, legal counsel 1968-69, pres. 1969-70), U.S. Jr. C. of C. (legal counsel 1970-71), Tau Epsilon Phi (pres. 1956). Mason (Shriner). Clubs: University, Tower, Palma Ceia Golf and Country (Tampa). Home: 4937 Lyford Cay Rd Tampa FL 33609 Office: 606 Madison St Tampa FL 33601

TAVEL, ROBERT FREDERICK, real estate broker; b. Johnston City, Ill., June 7, 1943; s. James Robert and Vivian Lee (Brown) T.; student Alvin Jr. Coll., 1961-63; m. Lillie Faye Moffett; children—Phillip Jeffery, Sherry Michelle. With Brockman's Dept. Store, Lake Jackson, Tex., 1964, asst. mgr., Alvin, Tex., 1965, mgr., West Columbia, Tex., 1966-71, Deer Park, Tex., 1971-73; gen. mgr. Deer Park Realty, owner Tavel Ins. Agy., 1973—. Charter chmn. West Columbia Library Bd., 1968-71; chmn. West Columbia Beautification Assn., 1970; div. chmn. Brazoria County United Fund Communities, 1971; chmn. Sch. Dist. Drug Edn. Bd., 1970-71; mem. dist. com. Bay Area council Boy Scouts Am., 1969-70. Named West Columbia's Outstanding Young Man, Jr. C. of C., 1970, Deer Park Jr. C. of C., 1974; recipient First Outstanding Service award West Columbia City Council, 1971, citation Tex. Gov. Preston for service to Tex. Indsl. Commn., 1970. Mem. Tex. (pres. 1968), West Columbia, Deer Park (pres. 1974) chambers commerce. Baptist (Sunday Sch. supt. 1966-71). Mason, Rotarian (pres. 1970—). Home: 3456 Hickory St Deer Park TX 77536 Office: 1014 San Augustine St Deer Park TX 77536

TAVERNER, DONALD VARDY, TV exec.; b. Ashland, Me., Mar. 7, 1919; s. Harold Godwin and Isabel (Young) T.; B.A., U. Me., 1943; LL.D., Allegheny Coll., 1970; m. Ruth Olive Rowell, Jan. 24, 1943; children—Margaret Elizabeth (dec.), Theodore Gilbert, Frederic Walter. No. New England rep. Nat. Found. for Infantile Paralysis, Portland, Me., 1946-49, asst. nat. dir. fund raising, N.Y.C., 1950-51; exec. dir. Gen. Alumni Assn., U. Me., Orono, 1951-59; dir. devel. U. Me., 1959-62; pres. Met. Pitts. Ednl. TV WQED-TV and WQEX-TV, 1962-70, Nat. Cable TV Assn., Washington, 1970-72; pres. sta. WETA-TV/FM, Washington 1972—. Asso. Media Center, Grad. Library Sch., U. Pitts., 1963—. Mem. pres.'s council Mt. Mercy Coll.; dir. Pitts. Council on Pub. Edn.; mem. Pitts. Council on Econ. Edn.; trustee Eastern Ednl. Network, 1962—, pres., 1964-67, chmn. bd., 1967—; chmn. bd. Allegheny County chpt. Nat. Found., 1965-67; chmn. adv. council Vt. Coll., 1969-72. Trustee Robert Morris Coll., Pitts. Served to 1st lt. AUS, 1943-46. Decorated Bronze Star, Purple Heart; named Man of Yr. in Communications, Pitts., 1969. Mem. Nat. Assn. Ednl. Broadcasters (dir. 1964-67), Sigma Alpha Epsilon. Sigma Delta Chi. Rotarian. Clubs: University, Spectators (Orono, Me.). Home: 8512 Canterbury Dr Annandale VA 22003 Office: 3620 27th St S Arlington VA 22206

TAXON, JORDAN IRVING, clergyman; b. Columbus, O., May 12, 1917; s. Morris Nathan and Edyth Irene (Schottenstein) T.; B.A., B.S. in Edn., Ohio State U., 1938; M.A., Northwestern U., 1940; LL.B., So. Law U., 1942; M.H.L., Jewish Inst. Religion, 1947; m. Gloria Grace Seidel, July 3, 1949; children—Janet Deborah, Morse Nathan, Naomi Sue. Rabbi, 1947; rabbi Temple Beth El, Cranford, N.J., 1946-52, Tri City Jewish Center, Rock Island, Ill., 1954-64, Synagogue Emanu-El, Charleston, S.C., 1964—. Chaplain, Graystone State Hosp., Morris Plains, N.J., 1950-52, Lyons (N.J.) VA Hosp., 1951-52, Clinton (Ia.) VA Hosp., 1954-64, V.A. Hosp., Charleston, 1964—. Vice chmn. Rock Island Park Bd., 1960-64; v.p. Southeast region Rabbinical Assembly, Miami, Fla., 1971—. Mem. bd. Blackhawk Coll., Moline, Ill., 1962-64. Served with AUS, 1952-54. Tanenbaum scholar Hebrew U., 1947-48. Mem. Assn. Jewish Chaplains, Greater Carolina Assn. Rabbis, N.Y., Chgo. bds. rabbis, Rabbinical Assembly, Mil. Chaplains Assns., Assn. Mental Health Chaplains. Mason; mem. B'nai B'rith. Club: Exchange (Charleston). Contbr. articles to various publs. Home: 42 6th Av Charleston SC 29403 Office: 78 Gordon St Charleston SC 29403

TAYLOR, ALONZO CLASON, cons. engr.; b. McKinney, Tex., Oct. 4, 1903; s. Alonzo Green and Sue (Border) T.; B.S., Tex. A. and M. U., 1924; m. Virginia Wood, May 29, 1932; 1 son, Lonn Wood. Insp. Miss. River Commn., Vicksburg, Miss., 1924-25; jr. engr. to asst. engr. U.S. Bur. Pub. Rds., Washington and Ft. Worth, 1925-29; insp. Tex. Hwy. Dept, Sherman, 1929-30; asst. engr. to hwy. engr. U.S. Bur. Pub. Rds., 1930-46, programming and planning engr., Manila, Philippines, 1946-49, supervising hwy. engr., Washington, 1949-51, div. engr., Manila, 1951-55, chief Office Fgn. Projects, Washington, 1955-56, regional engr., regional fed. hwy. adminstr., Ft. Worth, 1956-70; cons. engr. to Fed. Hwy. Adminstrn., Ft. Worth, 1971-73, ret. Recipient Adminstrs. award Fed. Hwy. Adminstrn., 1969, Pub. Works Man of Year award Kiwanis Internat. and Am. Pub. Works Assn., 1964; Award of Merit, Philippine Contractors Assn., 1955; decorated officer Legion of Honor (Philippines). Registered profl. engr., Pa., Tex. Life mem. Am. Soc. C.E.; fellow Inst. Traffic Engrs., Nat. Soc. Profl. Engrs., Philippine Better Rds. Assn. (hon. life), Tau Beta Pi, Chi Epsilon. Club: Army and Navy (Manila). Home: 3961 Weyburn Dr Fort Worth TX 76109

TAYLOR, ARCHER SAVOYE, cable television cons. engr.; b. Longmont, Colo., Feb. 14, 1916; s. Archibald and Martha (Savoye) T.; B.S., Antioch Coll., 1938; m. M. LaVerne Wise, June 17, 1944; children—David S., Lawrence K., Kenneth M., Margaret S. Physicist, engr. Nat. Bur. Standards, Washington, 1938-43; engr. Paul F. Godley Co., Cons. Engrs., Montclair, N.J., 1944-48; engr. Archer S. Taylor, Cons. Engr., Missoula, Mont., 1948-65; v.p. engring. firm Malarkey, Taylor & Assos. Inc., Consultants, Washington, 1965—; part-time mem. faculty U. Mont., 1951-63; owner, operator Northwest Video Inc., Kalispell, Mont., 1953-68. Mem., engring. cons. Mont. Gov.'s Com. on Ednl. TV, 1960-63. Sr. mem. I.E.E.E.; mem. Nat. Cable TV Assn. (dir. 1961-67, vice-chmn. 1964), Soc. Motion Picture and TV Engrs. Home: 1522 Forest Villa Lane McLean VA 22101 Office: 1225 Connecticut Av NW Washington DC 20036

TAYLOR, BARBARA JO ANNE HARRIS (MRS. RICHARD POWELL TAYLOR), civic and polit. worker; b. Providence, Sept. 9, 1936; d. Ross Cameron and Anita (Coia) Harris; student Tex. Christian U., 1952, Salve Regina Coll., 1952-53, Our Lady of the Lake Coll. and Convent, 1953-54, St. Mary's U., summer 1954, Incarnate Word Coll., 1954-55; B.S., Georgetown U., 1963; m. Richard Powell Taylor, Dec. 19, 1959; 1 son, Douglas Howard. Adminstrv. asst. profl. devel. and welfare N.E.A., Washington, 1956-59; asst. to dir. Georgetown U., Washington, 1956-59; exec. asst. All Am. Conf. to Combat Communism, Washington, 1960. Mem. exec. bd. Salvation Army Aux., D.C., 1967—, chmn. membership com., 1969-70, co-chmn., 1970—, chmn. fund-raising com., 1968-69, co-chmn., 1971-72, 73-74, mem. exec. com. of exec. bd., 1970—, treas., mem. finance com., 1970-71, v.p., 1971-72, historian, 1972—, editor Our Watchword Newsletter, 1968-69; mem. exec. bd. Welcome to Washington Internat., 1969—, bd. advisers, 1969—, dir. workshop, 1969—; exec. bd. Am. Opera Sch. Soc., Washington, 1970—, Episcopal Ch. Home for Aged Women's Aux., 1970—, Episcopal Center for Emotionally Disturbed Children Women's Aux., 1970—; exec. bd. St. David's Episcopal Ch. Aux., 1970-72, 73-74, v.p., 1970-72, 73-74, chmn. program com., 1970-72, 73-74; bd. dirs., treas. Spanish-Portuguese Study Group, 1970-72. Mem. exec. bd. League Republican Women D.C., 1964-67, treas., 1964-67; mem. nat. council Womens Nat. Rep. Club, N.Y.C., 1969—, chmn. Washington-Md.-Va. legislative com., 1970—, co-chmn. ann. conf., 1971, 74; mem. Nat. Fedn. Rep. Women, 1964—; mem. governing bd. Capital Speakers Club, 1973—, chmn. by laws com., 1973—. Mem. Internat. Platform Assn., Spanish-Portuguese Study Group, Nat. Lawyers Wives, Lawyers Wives D.C., D.A.R. (chpt. nat. def. rep. 1972—, chpt. exec. bd. 1974—, vice regent 1974—). Clubs: International, Capitol Hill, Washington (mem. internat. com. 1971—); Congressional Country (Potomac, Md.). Home: 6007 Corewood Lane Sumner Washington DC 20016

TAYLOR, BILL EDWARD, dentist; b. Clinton, Okla., May 20, 1935; s. Raymond W. and Elsie L. (Behnke) T.; student U. Okla., 1953-57; D.D.S., U. Md., 1961; m. Eleanor Louise Stewart, Aug. 26, 1956; children—Louis Edward, Cynthia Elaine. Individual practice gen. dentistry, Enid, Okla., 1963—. Chmn., Enid Semi-pro Baseball, 1969-70; chmn. econ. devel. program Mayor's Goals Program, 1971-72. Trustee Okla. Dental Found. Served with USAF, 1961-63. Recipient Mosby award for Scholarship, Gold medal Thesis award, 1961. Mem. Am. Acad. Gold Foil Operators, Am., Okla., Garfield County dental assns. Methodist. Kiwanian (pres. 1972). Club: Oakwood Country. Patentee Futures, 1971. Home: 1217 Indian Dr Enid OK 73701 Office: 617 S Quincy St Enid OK 73701

TAYLOR, BOB BYRON, cartoonist; b. Stockton, Cal., July 21, 1932; s. Orla J. and Bertha (Friesen) T.; A.A., Grant Tech. Jr. Coll.; B.A., Sacramento State Coll.; m. JoAnne B. Femling, Jan. 31, 1955; children—Kevin Scott, Cameron Matthew. Sports cartoonist Sacramento Union, 1950-54; editorial cartoonist Dallas Times Herald, 1958—. Served with USAF, 1954-58. Recipient several awards for boosting service morale Dept. Def., award Nat. Conf. Christians and Jews, 1964, Southwest Journalism Forum; Best Cartoon award Dallas Press Club, 1968, 72; Grenville Clarke award, 1968. Home: 13843 Waterfall Pl Dallas TX 75240 Office: Herald Square Dallas TX 75221

TAYLOR, BOYD EUGENE, writer, newspaper exec.; b. Atlanta, July 31, 1901; s. Eugene Helm and Minnie (Jarrell) T.; B.S., Emory U., 1923; M.S., Sorbonne, 1926; Certificate, Louvre Mus. (France), 1926, Prado Mus., Spain; M.A., U. Madrid, 1925; m. Cora Mina Moses, Feb. 22, 1922 (dec. 1927). Sci. writer Hearst Newspapers, 1919-40; tchr. Fulton High Sch., Atlanta, 1922-27; asst. night chief Atlanta bur. A.P., 1920; city editor Atlanta Constn., 1941-44; gen. mgr. Ind. Press, Atlanta, 1944—; pres. Southland, Inc., Stone Mountain Food Products, Inc., Community Newspapers, Inc. Pres. Separate Schs., Inc., Pvt. Sch. Found., Nat. Laymens Com. to Crush Communism in Chs.; co-founder Hartsfield Internat. Airport, 1925. Bd. dirs. Ga. Taxpayers Relief Assn., Genetics Research Library; chmn. Historic House Mus. Corp. Served to 2d lt., Signal Corps, U.S. Army, World War I; to maj. USAAF, World War II. Recipient plaque Fulton County Tchrs. Assn., 1963. Life fellow Royal Soc. (London); mem. Am. Soc. Human Genetics, Genetics Soc. Am., Am. Genetic Assn., Population Assn. Am., Ga. Acad. Sci., Am. Inst. Biol. Scis., A.A.A.S., Brit. Assn. for Advancement Sci., Anglican Soc., Soc. For Study Evolution, Internat. Assn. for Advancement Eugenics and Ethnology, Am. Soc. Health Assn., Council For Basic Edn., Planned Parenthood Fedn. Am., Am. Acad. Polit. and Social Sci., Soc. for Preservation English Lang. and Lit. (founder), Nat. Wildlife Fedn., Nat. Rifle Assn. (life), Nat. Trust for Historic Preservation. Anglican Orthodox (co-founder, trustee). Club: Atlanta Billiard (pres.). Home: 327 St Paul Av SE Atlanta GA 30312 Office: PO Box 1 Atlanta GA 30301

TAYLOR, CARROLL AUBREY, city mgr.; b. Snyder, Tex., Mar. 19, 1922; s. Sterling A. and Elizabeth (Payne) T.; student Tex. Tech. Coll., 1942, 46; m. Zanalee Jones, Oct. 23, 1943; children—Zee Lyn, Carol, Zana. Resident engr. H. N. Roberts & Assos., cons. engrs., 1947; city engr., Lamesa, Tex., 1948-49, city mgr., 1949—. Treas. Lamesa dist. Girl Scouts Am., chmn. property bd. trustees. Chmn. bd. health South Plains Health Unit, 1954-60; mem. gov.'s Hwy. Safety Commn., 1958-61. Served from 2d lt. to capt. USMC, 1942-46. Mem. Internat., Tex. (regional dir. 1961, pres. 1965-66) city mgrs. assns., C. of C. Presbyn. (elder, clk. of sessions). Lion (dir. 1955, pres. 1962-63). Home: 812 N 15th St Lamesa TX 79331 Office: City Hall Lamesa TX 79331

TAYLOR, CARSON ELROY, physician; b. St. Louis, July 31, 1924; s. Byron Hawthorne and Faye Pauline (Carson) T.; student Vanderbilt U., 1941-42, Duke, 1943-45; M.D., U. Tenn., 1949; m. Bernice Marguerite Russell, June 18, 1947; 1 son, Carson Elroy. Intern, USN Hosp., Pensacola, Fla., 1949-50, resident obstetrics and gynecology, 1950-51; gen. practice medicine, Lawrenceburg, Tenn., 1952—; mem. staff Lawrence County Hosp., 1952—, chief of staff, 1967, 72; co. physician Murray O. Mfg. Co., Lawrenceburg, 1956—, Union Carbide Corp., Lawrenceburg, 1957—. Pres., Crockett Bowl, Inc. Chmn. bd. trustees Crockett Gen. Hosp., Lawrenceburg, 1973-74. Served with USCG and USNR, World War II, USNR, 1949-51; now lt. col. U.S. Army Res. Mem. Am. Acad. Family Practice, Tenn. Acad. Gen. Practice (pres. 1968), Am., Tenn., Middle Tenn. (pres.) med. assns., Lawrence County Med. Soc. (pres.). Presbyn. (elder, past deacon). Lion (past dir.). Home: 248 Parkes Av Lawrenceburg TN 38464 Office: PO Box 430 Lawrenceburg TN 38464

TAYLOR, CECIL G(RADY), univ. ofcl.; b. Williamston, N.C., May 20, 1909; s. Henry Dawson and Laura Elizabeth (Peele) T.; A.B., U. N.C., 1929, A.M., 1930, Ph.D., 1935; student U. Paris (Am. Field Service fellow 1935-36), 1935-36; m. Ellen Eakin Albright, May 26, 1937; children—Vickie Albright, Ellen Albright, John Howell. Instr. romance langs. U. N.C., 1931-35; mem. faculty La. State U., 1936—, prof. romance langs., 1949—, dean Coll. Arts and Scis., 1949-65, chancellor, Baton Rouge campus, 1965—. Served as lt. (j.g.) and lt. USNR, 1943-46. Decorated Palmes Academiques (France). Mem. Modern Lang. Assn., South Atlantic, South Central modern lang. assns., Phi Beta Kappa, Omicron Delta Kappa, Phi Kappa Phi. Home: 2105 Kleinert Av Baton Rouge LA 70806

TAYLOR, CHARLES HART, state ofcl., real estate co. exec.; b. Brevard, N.C., Jan. 23, 1941; s. Robert G. and Loee (English) T.; B.A., Wake Forest U., 1963, J.D., 1966; m. Elizabeth Bryan Owen, Nov. 21, 1970. Mng. dir., gen. counsel Transylvania Tree Farms, Brevard, 1966—; Southeastern Real Estate and Discount Co., Brevard, 1966—, mem. N.C. Ho. of Reps., 1967-73, house minority leader, 1968-73; mem. N.C. senate, 1973—, minority leader, 1973—. Dir. N.C. Consumers Council, 1971. Dir., Nat. Republican Legislators Conf., 1969—; mem. N.C. Rep. Central Com., 1968-71, exec. com., 1967-71. Bd. visitors Western Carolina U., Wake Forest U.; trustee Brevard Music Center, 1967—; mem. N.C. Bapt. Found., 1966—; bd. dirs. 4-H Devel. Fund, 1971. Recipient citation for Outstanding Service 4-H Club, 1969, Alumni award State 4-H Club, 1967, Outstanding Student award Phi Alpha Delta, 1966. Mem. Brevard C. of C. (dir.), 4-H Club State Honor Club, Phi Alpha Delta (mem. internat. bd.). Author: Timber Mortgage Loans, 1966, also articles. Home: Burrell Mountain Rd Brevard NC 28712 Office: PO Box 66 Brevard NC 28712

TAYLOR, CLARENCE EVERETT, librarian; b. Pratt, Mo., Oct. 30, 1914; s. General Franklin and Nora Susan (Lewis) T.; B.S. in Edn., Ohio State U., 1937; B.S. in L.S., Western Res. U., 1940, M.S. in L.S., 1956; m. Kathryn Elizabeth Mallett, Sept. 2, 1940; children—Karen Sue (Mrs. John F. Maxwell, Jr.), Ellen Elizabeth (Mrs. Joel F. Greenwell). Tchr., Green Rural High Sch., Laings, O., 1937-39; library asst. D.C. Pub. Library, 1940-41; cataloger Social Security Adminstrn., Washington, 1941, 45-46, Armed Forces Staff Coll. Library, Norfolk, Va., 1947, VA, Washington, 1948; gifts and exchange librarian Ohio State U., 1949; asso. librarian USAF Inst. Tech., Wright-Patterson AFB, O., 1950-53, librarian, 1954-55; asst. prof., asst. librarian Abilene (Tex.) Christian Coll., 1956-62, asso. prof., asst. librarian, 1963—. Served to 2d lt., Signal Corps, USAAF, 1942-45. Mem. Am., Tex. library assns., Beta Phi Mu. Home: 1001 Washington Blvd Abilene TX 79601

TAYLOR, CLIFTON BRADLEY, dentist; b. Lebanon, Ky., Feb. 11, 1912; s. Robert Elmer and Grace Evelyn (Murphy) T.; student Mars Hill Coll., 1931-33; B.S., Wake Forest U., 1935; D.M.D., U. Louisville, 1940; m. Vera Elizabeth Chesolm, Aug. 3, 1939; children—Barbara (Mrs. George Bond Jr.), Grace (Mrs. Jim Tillotson), Martha, Virginia. Practice of dentistry, Hendersonville, N.C., 1940—; mem. staff Margaret Pardee Hosp. Commr. Town Laurel Park, 1950—. Vol. Hill Fire Dept. Bd. dirs. Henderson County YMCA, Henderson County Teen-Age Canteen. Served with dental corps., AUS, 1953-55. Mem. Am., N.C. dental assns., So., Henderson County, First Dist. dental socs., Internat. Acad. Dentistry, Am. Legion. Lion. Clubs: Cotillion, (Hendersonville). Hendersonville Country. Home: 128 Silver Pine Dr Hendersonville NC 28739 Office: 560 Fleming St Hendersonville NC 28739

TAYLOR, DALLAS JEFFREY, architect; b. Abington, Pa., Dec. 24, 1944; s. William C. and Helen S. (Schmidt) T.; B.S. in Engring., John Brown U., 1966; B.A. with honors in Architecture, B.Arch. with honors, U. Ark., 1969; m. Veta Ruth Sneed, Dec. 21, 1965; 1 son, Dallas Christopher. Housing coordinator Woodward, Cape & Assos./Envirodynamics, Inc., Dallas, 1969-72; project mgr. urban housing Southwestern Dynamics, Inc., Dallas, 1972—. Housing cons. Delta Pacific Corp., Dallas, 1970-71, Structex Corp., Dallas, 1971-72; Amron Corp., Dallas, 1972-73. Waid Found. fellow A.I.A., 1969; research grantee Am. Iron and Steel Inst., 1968-69. Recipient Nat. Council Archtl. Registration Bd. certificate, 1973. Mem. A.I.A. (sch. medal U. Ark. 1969), Tex. Soc. Architects. Home: 1324 Sylvan Plano TX 75074 Office: 3635 Noble St Dallas TX 75204

TAYLOR, DONALD RANSONE, curator; b. Hampton, Va., July 8, 1930; s. William Rosser and Marion (Ransone) T.; student Washington and Lee U., 1947-48; A.B., Coll. William and Mary, 1951, M.Ed., 1957; m. Johanna Ernestine Williams, June 16, 1951; children—David Littleton, Stephen Dudley. Instr. world history Hampton (Va.) High Sch., 1952-62; curator Syms-Eaton Museum, Hampton, 1960-62; curator of edn. Tryon Palace, New Bern, N.C., 1962—. Coordinator 350th Anniversary Celebration, Hampton, 1959-60. Mem. N.E.A., Soc. Archtl. Historians, Nat. Trust for Historic Preservation, Hampton, New Bern hist. socs., Phi Delta Kappa. Presbyn. (deacon 1966-69, elder 1969-72, 73-75). Author: History of Hampton, Va., 1960; Out of the Past . . . The Future, 1972. Home: 3536 Canterbury Rd New Bern NC 28560 Office: 613 Pollock St New Bern NC 28560

TAYLOR, DYER JUSTICE, judge; b. Columbia, S.C., Sept. 25, 1922; s. Dyer John and Marymagdalene (Laws) T.; student Johns Hopkins, 1942, U. N.C., 1948; J.D., George Washington U., 1951; m. H. Patricia Owens, June 11, 1949; children—Kathleen Johanna, Janet Maria. Asso. firm Ballard & Beasley, Washington, 1951-55; with Justice Dept., Washington, 1955-57; asst. U.S. atty., D.C., 1957-58; jr. partner firm John Laskey, Washington, 1958-60; asst. solicitor Interior Dept., Washington, 1960-61; hearing examiner ICC, 1961-63; trial examiner FPC, 1963-70; asso. judge Superior Ct. of D.C., 1970—. Chmn. Municipal affairs Beverly Hills Citizens Assn., 1958. Served with USNR, 1943-45. Mem. Fed. Trial Examiners Conf., Nat. Conf. State Trial Judges, Am., Fed., D.C. bar assns. Home: 1946 Creek Crossing Rd Vienna VA 22190 Office: 613 G St NW Washington DC 20001

TAYLOR, EDDIE THOMAS, banker; b. Lubbock, Tex., Dec. 2, 1929; s. Jess H. and Lois (Eubank) McWherter; B.S., Tex. Technol. U., 1955; m. Martha Ann Chrisholm, Aug. 31, 1959; children—Carrie Sue, Stacy Ann. County supr. loan dept. Farmers Home Adminstrn., Plains, Tex., 1959-65; v.p. loan dept. Yoakum County State Bank, Denver City, Tex., 1965—. Served with AUS, 1951-53. Baptist. Mason (32 deg.), Lion. Home: 1315 N Av F Denver City TX 79323 Office: 221 Av B Denver City TX 79323

TAYLOR, ELIZABETH DALE DABBS (MRS. JAMES L. TAYLOR), pharmacist, educator, farmer; b. Shannon, Miss., 1914; d. Rome Grafton and Jessie (Prude) Dabbs; student Blue Mountain (Miss.) Coll., 1933, postgrad., 1959, 65; student Millsaps Coll., 1936; B.S. in Pharmacy, U. Miss., 1937, B.A., 1938, M.S. in Pharm. Chemistry, 1955, postgrad., 1962, 66, 67, 70—, Triple A Teaching Certificate, 1972; postgrad. Miss. State U., 1943, 60, 64-67, 70-71; m. James Leroy Taylor, Jan. 21, 1941; children—Elizabeth Dale, Jessie Roma. Pharmacist drugstores rural Miss., 1937-56; tchr. Shannon Consol. Sch., 1947-59; tchr. Tupelo (Miss.) pub. schs., 1959—, chmn. sci. dept., 1960; chmn. sci. dept. Milam Jr. High Sch., Tupelo, 1961-64, adviser Jr. Engring. Tech. Soc., 1962—; tchr. sci. N.E. Miss. TV Council Tupelo, 1964-71, cons. ednl. programs TV sta. WTWV, drug abuse, 1966, safety, 1967; sci. cons. Blue Mountain Coll., 1959, symposium George Marshall Space Flight Center, Huntsville, Ala., 1965; cons. Miss. Instructional Curriculum Lab., Jackson, 1968-69; sci. curriculum adv. tchr. Lee County Farm Bur., Tupelo, 1957-66. Leader Tupelo troops Girl Scouts Am., 1957-62, 55-63; instr. nursing, family health Shannon A.R.C., 1951; mem. Shannon Home Demonstration Club, Shannon, 1950-61, P.T.A., Tupelo, 1959—, Lee United Neighbors, 1963—. Miss. rep. to NASA. Named Miss Shannon, 1932, Outstanding Jr. Engring. Tech. Adviser, Miss. State U. engring. extension service, 1963; recipient Miss. Merit Community Program award edn. Miss. Econ. Council, Tupelo, 1963, Pacemaker award Parade Mag., N.E.A., Tupelo, 1965. Mem. Miss. Acad. Sci., Tupelo Ednl. Assn., U. Miss. Alumni Assn., Miss. Sci. Tchrs. Assn., Miss. Pharm. Assn., Nat. Sci. Tchrs. Assn., Internat. Platform Assn., D.A.R. Baptist. Club: Shannon (Miss.) Women's (v.p. 1963, 68; pres. 1969). Contbr. articles to profl. jours. Home: Box 133 Verona MS 38879 Office: Tupelo High Sch Varsity Dr Tupelo MS 38801

TAYLOR, ELLA LOUISE RICHARDS (MRS. HOWARTH E. TAYLOR), bus. exec.; b. Cumberland, Md., Apr. 2, 1925; d. William Carl and Emma (Wolfe) Richards; B.S., Wheaton Coll., 1947; Ph.D., U. Ill., 1952; m. Howarth E. Taylor, Sept. 27, 1952; children—David, Martha, Rebecca, Mary, Stephen, Ruth. Teaching asst. Wheaton (Ill.) Coll., 1944-47; chemist Celanese Corp. Am., Cumberland, 1947-48; teaching asst. U. Ill., 1948-52; tchr. Hickory Ridge (Ark.) High Sch., 1952-53; sec.-treas. Hickory Ridge Farm Supply Inc., 1962—, Hickory Ridge Rice Farms, Inc., 1961—, Taylor Seed Farms, Inc., 1958—, Taylor Seed Processing Plant, Inc., 1958—, Big T Oil Co., 1974—. Mem. Hickory Ridge P.T.A., 1959—, pres., 1962-64; leader 4-H CLUBS, Hickory Ridge, 1968—; mem. Cross County Miss Fluffy Rice Com., 1970—; mem. Cross County High Sch. Band Boosters, 1967—, v.p., 1972-74; mem. Cross County Health Com. Bd., 1972—. Recipient Ark. Farm Family of Year award, 1969. Mem. Sigma Xi, Sigma Pi Sigma, Sigma Delta Epsilon, Iota Sigma Pi. Baptist. Address: Hickory Ridge AR 72347

TAYLOR, ERNEST AUSTIN, JR., textile co. exec.; b. Balt., Jan. 18, 1918; s. Ernest Austin and Alma (Robinson) T.; B.E.E., Ga. Inst. Tech., 1948; m. Rachel Charleen Morgan, Feb. 14, 1944; children—Rachel (Mrs. Harold Clay), Charles Ernest. Elec. engr. Phillips Petroleum Co., Bartlesville, Okla., 1948-51, Electrical Equipment Co., Augusta, Ga., 1951-52; elec. design engr. Patchen & Zimmerman, Augusta, 1952-56; engr. Monsanto Textiles Co., Decatur, Ala., 1956-61, sr. engr., 1961-66, devel. asso., 1966-72, sr. research specialist, 1972—. Bd. dirs. Internat. Bible Coll., Florence, Ala. Served with USNR, 1943-45. Registered Profl. Engr., Ala. Mem. I.E.E.E., Fluid Power Soc. Mem. Ch. Christ (elder 1967-71, ednl. dir. 1971—). Patentee in field. Home: 2202 Cleveland Av SW Decatur AL 35601 Office: Monsanto Textiles Co PO Box 2204 Decatur AL 35601

TAYLOR, ETHEL MAE HENDERSON (MRS. JOHN BENJAMIN TAYLOR), educator, broadcaster; b. nr. Laurens, S.C.; d. James William and Ella (Dendy) Henderson; B.A., Benedict Coll., 1946; summer study U. S.C., 1966; m. John Benjamin Taylor, Feb. 10, 1946; children—John B., Gwendolyn Bernice (Mrs. Robert Hall), James Howard, Ludwald Clifton, Audriene Denise, Deborah Elizabeth, Melonie Joyce, Cheryl Kaye, Missy Carol. Sec., Hampton Printing Co., Columbia, S.C., 1949-52; tchr. Richland County Sch., Eastover, S.C., 1953-60, Columbia (S.C.) city schs., 1961—; part-time radio announcer radio sta. WOIC, Columbia, 1954—. Pub. relations dir. Fairwold Jr. High Sch., 1967—. Mem. Columbia Urban League, Nat., Richland Co. ednl. assns., Nat., S.C. councils tchrs. English, S.C. Tchr. Assn., Nat. Assn. TV and Radio Announcers, Internat. Platform Assn., Am. Bus. Womens Assn. Baptist (organist). Home: 2221 Mance St Columbia SC 29203 Office: 830 Laurel St Columbia SC 29201

TAYLOR, EVERETTE LESTER, JR., physician; b. Scottsville, N.C., Jan. 23, 1925; s. Everette Lester and Malissa Cox (Hill) T.; student U. N.C., 1942, U. Ala., 1943, Washington and Jefferson Coll., 1943-44, Yale, 1944; A.B., Washington and Lee U., 1949; M.D., Duke, 1955; m. Carol Snow Anderson, Oct. 25, 1953; children—Mark Anderson, Mary Carol. Rotating intern Greenville (S.C.) Gen. Hosp., 1955; resident gen. practice Bluefield (W.Va.) sanitarium, 1956; gen. practice medicine, Sparta, N.C., 1957—; mem. staff Alleghany County Meml. Hosp. Cons., New River Mental Health Clinic, Boone, N.C., 1966—, Alleghany County Health Dept., Sparta, 1966—; med. examiner Alleghany County, 1970—; coroner Alleghany County, 1962-66, 70—. Served with C.E., AUS, 1943-46; CBI. Mem. A.M.A., Am. Acad. Family Practice, So. Med. Assn., N.C., Ashe-Alleghany (pres. 1971) med. socs., Phi Kappa Psi, Chi Phi, Alpha Epsilon Delta. Democrat. Presbyn. (deacon). Mason, Lion. Home: 305 Taylor St Sparta NC 28675 Office: Cleveland Meml Hosp Shelby NC 28150

TAYLOR, FLONNIA CHAMBERS (MRS. RHEA A. TAYLOR), social worker; b. Williamsburg, Ky.; d. James Henry and Lassafaye (Hicks) Chambers; A.B. cum laude, Carson-Newman Coll., 1926; M.A., Ohio State U., 1933; M.A., U. Chgo., 1952; m. Rhea A. Taylor, June 26, 1930. Tchr. English and dramatics Bethel Coll., 1931-32, U. Ky., 1945, English, Georgetown Coll., 1955-56; social work cons. Ky. Child Welfare Div., Frankfort, 1937-42; area rep. A.R.C., Alexandria, Va., 1942-46; psychiat. social worker VA, Lexington, Ky., 1946-51; spl. supervisory and adminstrv. work A.R.C., Washington chpt., Family Service, Lansing, Mich., 1952-55; social worker Shriners Hosp., Lexington, Ky., 1955-57; exec. dir. United Cerebral Palsy of Bluegrass Agy., 1958—. Mem. Gov.'s Adv. Com. Child Welfare of Ky., 1960—, v.p., 1970; chmn. Gov.'s Adv. Com. Day Care, Ky., 1963—; mem. Nat. Adv. Com. on Social Service to Nat. United Cerebral Palsy Assn., 1959—; profl. cons. coms. on children and family Ky. White House Conf. Bd. dirs. Community Chest, Family Service, County Child Welfare, Florence Crittenden Home (pres.). Mem. Am. Assn. U. Women (pres. 1960-62), Ky. Welfare Assn. (pres. 1959-60), Central Ky. Philharmonic Orch. (sec. 1961-62, dir. 1961—), League Women Voters, Am. Assn. Social Workers, Nat. Assn. Social Workers, Acad. Certified Social Workers, State Mental Health Orgn., P.E.O. Clubs: Zonta, University of Kentucky Woman's. Home: Tayraf Hill Route 2 Harrodsburg Rd Lexington KY 40504 Office: 465 Springhill Dr Lexington KY 40503

TAYLOR, FRANK B(RAVITY), editor, writer; b. Clarington, O., Mar. 3, 1905; s. Frank Bravity and Leila (Urpman) T.; student U. Wyo., 1924-25; m. Katherine Maurine Grabill, Apr. 23, 1933; 1 dau., Virginia Kay (Mrs. Kenneth J. Sherk). Writer miscellaneous fiction, articles on business, engring., industry scis., 1928—; dist. editor, feature writer Gulf Pub. Co., Tulsa office, 1936-42; editor, editorial mgr. Ind. Petroleum Assn. Am., monthly, Tulsa, 1945-60, research analyst, Washington, 1960-64, research analyst, Tulsa, 1964-70; exec. v.p. Nat. Stripper Well Assn., Tulsa, 1970—. Recipient honor for editorial excellence Internat. Council Indsl. Editors, 1947, Distinguished Service award Okla. Petroleum Council, 1969. Mem. Tulsa Geol. Soc., Engrs. Soc. Tulsa (pres. 1942-43). Clubs: Young Men's (hon. life mem., pres. 1941-42), Petroleum (founder) (Tulsa). Home: 5902 S 68th East Av Tulsa OK 74145

TAYLOR, FRANK HART, mech. engr.; b. San Antonio, Feb. 1, 1930; s. William H. D. and Alice (Hart) T.; student U. Md., 1947-49; B.Ch.E., Ga. Inst. Tech., 1958; m. Kay Lynette Riley, Jan. 26, 1957; children—Donna Marie, Lisa Lynn, Frank Mark. Wireline helper Otis Engring. Corp., Liberty, Tex., 1958-59, draftsman, Dallas, 1959-60, jr. design engr., 1960-61, design engr., 1961-67, project engr., 1967-72, sr. design engr., 1972—. Served with USAF, 1952-57. Registered profl. engr., Tex. Mem. Tex. Soc. Profl. Engrs., Am. Soc. M.E., Assn. Wellhead Mfrs. (mem. control equipment com.). Republican. Presbyn. (deacon). Author: (with others) Wireline Operations and Procedures, 1964. Patentee oil well tools. Home: 2024 Reagan St Carrollton TX 75006 Office: PO Box 34380 Dallas TX 75234

TAYLOR, GERALD HERMAN, hosp. adminstr.; b. Asheville, N.C., Jan. 8, 1937; s. Herman Melvin and Grace (Crook) T.; student U. Chattanooga, 1964; B.S., Mars Hill Coll., 1967; M.S., Samford U., 1968; m. Sandra Dianne Cole, May 28, 1967; children—Michael David, Kathy Jean, Gary Bruce. Tchr. mgmt. Vocational Tech. Sch., Asheville, 1966-67; dir. admitting U. Ala. Hosps. and Clinics, Birmingham, 1968; adminstr. Hancock Meml. Hosp., Sparta, Ga., 1968-69, Meml. Hosp., Adel, Ga., 1969-72, Gilman Hosp., St. Marys, Ga., 1972—. Cons. N.E. Fla. Broadcasting, Inc. Served with USMCR, 1955-59. Elk, Lion. Home: 102 W Conyers St St Marys GA 31558 Office: PO Box 805 Dillworth St St Marys GA 31558

TAYLOR, GERRY MAILAND, librarian; b. Eustis, Me., July 7, 1913; s. Everett Bowen and Amy Maria (Wilber) T.; student Farmington State Tchrs. Coll., 1930-32; B.A. cum laude, Baylor U., 1951, M.A. with honors, 1952; M.L.S., U. Tex., 1955; m. Myra Fairhead, Aug. 6, 1948. Grad. library asst. Baylor U., 1951-52; documents asst. U. Tex. Library, 1952-53; revisor Grad. Sch. Library Sci., U. Tex., 1953-54, sr. library clk. Law Sch. Library, 1954-55; asst. librarian Tex. Agrl. and Indsl. Coll., 1955-56; asso. librarian Sam Houston State U., 1956-66; head librarian Ark. State U., State University, 1966—. Library bldg. cons., City of Huntsville, Tex., 1965-66. Served with AUS, 1940-45; PTO. Mem. Am., N.E. Ark., Ark. (chmn. intellectual freedom com. 1967-68) library assns., Phi Delta Kappa, Psi Chi, Beta Phi Mu, Alpha Chi, Ark. Council on Library Edn., Ark. Sch. Masters Assn. Baptist. Mason (32 deg., Shriner). Contbr. articles to nat. profl. library jours. Home: Box 1017 State University AR 72467

TAYLOR, HENRY SPLAWN, author, educator; b. Lincoln, Va., June 21, 1942; s. Thomas Edward and Mary Marshall (Splawn) T.; B.A., U. Va., 1965; M.A., Hollins Coll., 1966; m. Frances Ferguson Carney, June 29, 1968; 1 son, Thomas Edward. Instr. Roanoke Coll., Salem, Va., 1966-68; asst. prof. U. Utah, Salt Lake City, 1968-71, dir. Writers' Conf., 1969-72; asso. prof. lit. Am. U., Washington, 1971—. Recipient Poetry prize Acad. Am. Poets, 1962, 64, Utah State Inst. Fine Arts, 1969, 71. Author: (poetry) The Horse Show at Midnight, 1966; (poetry) Breakings, 1971; (textbook) Points of Departure, 1974. Founder, poetry editor Roanoke Rev., 1967-68; contbg. editor Hollins Critic, 1970—; asso. editor Masterplots Ann., 1971—. Home: 6931 Hector Rd McLean VA 22101 Office: Dept Literature Am U Massachusetts and Nebraska Ave NW Washington DC 20016

TAYLOR, HERMAN, JR., agrl. co. exec.; b. Natchitoches, La., Oct. 31, 1932; s. Herman and Sadie (Cook) T.; student Northwestern St. U. La., 1951; B.S., La. State U., 1954; m. Evelyne Campbell, June 26, 1954; children—Herman, Mary Evelyne, Elizabeth Lynn. Pres., Taylor & Co., 1954—; C-T-C Land Corp., 1955—, H-T Stock Farms, Inc., 1954—, Cook-Taylor Land Corp.; v.p. Delta South Oil Co., Inc., 1970—, Hickory Ridge Devel. Co., 1968—, Hickory Ridge Shopping Centers, 1971—, People's Realty Co., 1969—, Broadmoor Shopping Cen. 1959-68; v.p., dir. People's Bank & Trust Co. Nat. trustee, mem. exec. com. Ducks Unlimited, 1969—, now pres.; pres. Natchitoches Farm Bur., Natchitoches Wildlife Assn.; chmn. Natchitoches Cancer Soc., Agrl. Stblzn. and Conservation Service, Natchitoches, 1965—; vice chmn. La. Beef Promotion Commn., 1968, Natchitoches Water Bd. Dist. 1, 1961-72; v.p. Red River Valley Improvement Assn., 1961—; mem. La. Sovereignty Commn., 1960-64, La. com. Farmers Home Adminstrn., 1971—, Red River Nav. Commn., 1966—, Culver Ednl. Found., 1969—, La. State U. Found., 1964—, Northwestern State U. La. Found., 1969—, livestock adv. bd. La. State U., 1967—. Bd. dirs. Fed. Land Bank, Natchitoches County Fair, Ducks Unlimited (Can.). Recipient Gov. James H. Davis award outstanding future farmer, 1947-48; Gov. Earl K. Long award for livestock prodn., 1949, for outstanding farmer, 1950; State Farmer degree award Future Farmers Am., 1949, 1st prize La. pub. speaking contest La. Future Farmers, 1949, 50. Mem. La. Cotton Producers Assn., Nat. Cotton Council, Am. Brahman Breeders Assn., La. (past v.p.), Am. (finance com. 1962-63) cattlemen's assns., La. Farmer Elected Com. Assn. (v.p.), La. Brahmans Assns., La. Bankers Assn., Sigma Alpha Epsilon, Delta Zeta. Democrat. Methodist. Mason (32 degree, Shriner), Elk, Rotarian. Democrat. Methodist. Clubs: Culver (Ind.) Fathers Assn., Natchitoches Country. Home: Hickory Hill Natchitoches LA 71457 Office: PO Box 947 Natchitoches LA 71457

TAYLOR, HOWARD GREENWOOD, JR., motel co. exec.; b. Frederick, Md., Jan. 4, 1913; s. Howard Greenwood and Flora (Rippeon) T.; D.D.S., U. Md., 1934; m. Lorraine Virginia Watkins, Feb. 22, 1941; 1 dau., Tamara Olivia (Mrs. Richard Newman). Practice gen. dentistry, Frederick, 1934-42, Damascus, Md., 1946-69; pres. Ridge Ct., Inc., Largo, Fla., 1969—. Served to lt. comdr., Dental Corps, USNR, 1942-45. Mem. Am., Md. (past v.p.), Frederick (past pres.) dental assns., Gorgas Odontological Soc., Psi Omega, Omicron Kappa Upsilon. Lion. Home: 158 Ridge Rd NW Largo FL 33540 Office: Ridge Rd and 2d Av NW Largo FL 33540

TAYLOR, HOYT PATRICK, JR., state ofcl.; b. Wadesboro, N.C., Apr. 1, 1924; s. Hoyt Patrick and Inez (Wooten) T.; B.S., U. N.C., 1945, LL.B., 1948; m. Elizabeth Lockhart, Mar. 17, 1951; children—Elizabeth Ann, Hoyt Patrick III, Adam Lockhart. Admitted to N.C. bar; mem. N.C. Ho. of Reps., 1955-66, speaker, 1965-66; lt. gov. of N.C., 1969—. Served to 1st lt. USMCR, 1945-46, 51-52. Mem. Phi Gamma Delta, Delta Sigma Pi, Phi Delta Phi. Democrat. Methodist. Office: State Capitol Raleigh NC 27601

TAYLOR, IRVING HENRY, oil co. exec.; b. Detroit, Aug. 18, 1922; s. Irving Henry and Lavinia (Startzman) T.; student Swarthmore Coll., 1940-41; B.A., George Washington U., 1949; M.A., Columbia, 1951; m. Katherine Louise Needham, Feb. 6, 1943; 1 dau., Leslie Ann. Financial analyst Standard Oil Co. (N.J.), N.Y.C., 1952-55, mgr. Western Hemisphere and internat. finance div., 1966; financial adviser Internat. Petroleum Co., Ltd., Bogota, Colombia, 1956-57, treas., Lima, Peru, 1957-59, treas., Coral Gables, Fla., 1966—, also dir.; asst. treas. Esso Internat., Inc., N.Y.C., 1959-63, mgr. fgn. sales, 1963-64, asst. gen. sales mgr., 1964-66; treas. Esso Inter-Am., Inc., 1966—. Bd. dirs. Dade County Jr. Achievement. Served with USAAF, 1942-46. Mem. Am. Econ. Assn., Artus, Coral Gables C. of C., Phi Beta Kappa, Pi Gamma Mu, Phi Sigma Kappa. Club: Riviera Country (Coral Gables). Home: 12751 Old Cutler Rd Coral Gables FL 33156 Office: 396 Alhambra Circle Coral Gables FL 33134

TAYLOR, JAMES BRYANT, civil engr.; b. Lenoir, N.C., Oct. 27, 1943; s. Charles Bruce and Mabel Irene (Laney) T.; student N.C. State U., 1962-67; m. Mary Ann Heffner, June 6, 1965; 1 son, Andrew Bryant. Sr. designer atomic power div. Newport News Shipbuilding & Dry Dock Co. (Va.), 1967-69; mgr. pre-engineered homes div. Taylor Lumber Co., Lenoir, 1969-71; job supt. Lenoir Constrn. Co., 1971-73; gen. mgr., treas. Taylor Constrn. Co., 1973—. Tchr. constrn. apprentice program Caldwell Community Coll., Lenoir, evenings 1971—. Presbyn. Home: 104 Amhurst Park Lenoir NC 28645 Office: 2075 Morganton Blvd SW Lenoir NC 28645

TAYLOR, JAMES LYNN, educator; b. Rogers, Tex., June 16, 1945; s. Ervin Daniel and Gwendolyn Yvonne (James) T.; A.A., Temple Jr. Coll., 1965; B.S. in Edn., U. Tex., 1967, M.A., 1969; m. Nancy Rae Koehn, Mar. 21, 1970. Grad. asst. U. Tex., Austin, 1967-68; tchr. Burnet (Tex.) pub. schs., 1968-69; instr. biology Temple (Tex.) Jr.

Coll., 1969—. Faculty adviser Sci. Club and Nat. Intercollegiate Rodeo Assn., Temple Jr. Coll., 1972—; cons. Am. Desk Mfg. Co., Temple, 1969-70. Mem. S.W. Basketball Ofcls. Assn., Tex. Acad. Sci., A.A.A.S., Bot. Soc. Am., Am. Inst. Biol. Sci., Tex. Jr. Coll. Tchrs. Assn., Temple Jr. Coll. Ex-Students Assn. (sec. 1971, v.p. 1972, pres. 1973), Phi Theta Kappa, Kappa Delta Pi, Phi Kappa Phi. Baptist. Home: 2606 N 15th St Temple TX 76501 Office: 2600 S 1st St Temple TX 76501

TAYLOR, JAMES RODNEY, univ. adminstr.; b. Pensacola, Fla., Nov. 3, 1940; s. Herbert Jackson and Ruth (Stuart) T.; A.B., Samford U., 1962; B.D., Southeastern Bapt. Theol. Sem., 1965, Th.M., 1966; m. Catherine Patricia West, Dec. 26, 1960; children—Leigh Ann, Brian Rodney, Julie Patricia. Ordained to ministry So. Bapt. Ch., 1961; manuscript editor Bapt. Sunday Sch. Bd., Nashville, 1966-68; staff asst., field sec. Tenn. Med. Assn., Nashville, 1968-69; asso. dir. devel. Vanderbilt U., 1968-69; dir. devel. Va. Intermont Coll., Bristol, 1969-70; dir. devel. U. W. Fla., Pensacola, 1970—. Exec. sec. U. W. Fla. Found., 1970—. News sec. for congl. candidate, 1969—. Mem. Pensacola C. of C., Fellowship Christian Athletes, Fla. High Sch. Activities Assn., Soc. Bibl. Lit., Am. Schs. Oriental Research. Republican. Editor: Young People's Life and Work Curriculum Materials, 1966-68. Contbr. to religious, hist. essays to various jours. Home: 5430 Primrose Dr Pensacola FL 32504

TAYLOR, JOHN ALLEN, geologist, engr.; b. Oklahoma City, Apr. 22, 1926; s. Ralph Staddan and Mary Ellen (Swift) T.; B.S., U. Okla., 1945, M.S., 1949; advt. bus. mgmt. Yale; m. Jo Ann Eaton, June 18, 1945; children—Jerry Alan, Douglas Lee, Kay Susan, Jacqueline Ann. Geologist, Shell Oil Co., LaJunta, Colo., 1946-47; instr. geology U. Okla., 1948-49; geologist Magnolia Petroleum Co., San Antonio, 1949-52, Houston, 1952, asst. exploitation geologist, Dallas, 1953-54, dist. geologist, Lake Charles, La., 1954-57, Mt. Vernon, Ill., 1957-59; dist. expln. supt. Mobil Oil Co., Oklahoma City, 1959-65; cons. geologist, petroleum engr., 1965—. Chmn. elect research com. Interstate Oil Compact Commn.; mem. task force for preparation efficiency study oil industry U.S. Sec. of Interior, 1964-65. Vice chmn. U. Okla. Sch. Geology Found. Served to lt. (j.g.) USNR, 1943-46; PTO. Named Hon. Col., Gov. of Okla., 1962, Gov. of Ind., 1964. Mem. Mid Continent Oil and Gas Assn., Am. Assn. Petroleum Geologists (v.p. 1971-72), Am. Inst. Profl. Geologists (sec. pres. 1965-66, nat. exec. com. 1967), Soc. Petroleum Engrs., Soc. Expln. Geophysicists, U. Okla. Alumni Assn. (nat. pres. 1963-64, chmn. Oklahoma City alumni devel. fund 1965-66, dir. fund 1967), Geol. Soc. Am., S. La. (pres. 1956), Oklahoma City, Ardmore, Tulsa geol. socs., Oklahoma City C. of C. (dir. 1964-65, vice chmn. oil and gas com.), Oklahoma City Petroleum Club (dir. 1963-66, pres. 1966), Ind. Petroleum Assn. Am. (dir. 1972), Okla. Ind. Petroleum Assn. (v.p. 1969-71), Sigma Xi, Sigma Gamma Epsilon. Episcopalian. Club: Oklahoma City Golf and Country. Contbr. articles to profl. jours. Home: 1607 Norwood Pl Oklahoma City OK 73120 Office: Liberty Tower Oklahoma City OK 73102

TAYLOR, JOHN GRANVILLE, architect; b. Russellville, Ky., Feb. 16, 1937; s. John Henry and Willie (Cassady) T.; student Western Ky. Coll., 1955-57, U. Ky., 1957-59; B.Arch., La. State U., 1965; m. Teresa Cummings, June 24, 1967; children-John Michael, Heather Kathleen. Designer firm Gassner, Nathan, Browne, Architects, Memphis, 1965-66; project architect Mel O'Brien, Architect, Memphis, 1966-70; pres. Taylor & Crump, Architects, Inc., Memphis, 1970—. Mem. A.I.A. (dir. Memphis br.), Tenn. Soc. Architects (dir., chmn. pub. relations 1974), Memphis C. of C., Sigma Alpha Epsilon. Democrat. Baptist. Clubs: Tennessee, Woodmen of World. Home: 760 Roland St Memphis TN 38104 Office: Falls Bldg Memphis TN 38103

TAYLOR, JOHN HUME, JR., lawyer; b. Norfolk, Va., Dec. 20, 1931; s. John Hume and Cecilia Ahston (Taylor) T.; grad. Woodberry Forest Sch., 1950; LL.B., U. Va., 1960; m. Martha McRee Pender, Feb. 23, 1963; children—Martha McRee, Richard Calvert, John Hume III. Admitted to Va. bar, 1960, U.S. Dist. Ct. bar, 1960, U.S. Ct. Appeals bar, 1961; asso. mem. firm Rixey & Rixey, Norfolk, 1960-63; partner Cocke & Taylor, Norfolk, 1963-72; individual practice, Norfolk, 1972—. Pres., Norfolk Forum, 1971-73. Sec., Electoral Bd. City Norfolk, 1971—; mem. Planning Commn. City Norfolk, 1967—; mem. 2d Dist. Dem. Com., 1964-68, State Dem. Central Com., 1964-68. Chmn. lay bd. DePaul Hosp., 1973—. Served with USNR, 1955-57. Mem. Norfolk-Portsmouth, Va., Am. bar assns. Clubs: Harbor, Norfolk Yacht and Country. Home: 1309 Westover Av Norfolk VA 23507 Office: 1805 Va Nat Bank Bldg Norfolk VA 23510

TAYLOR, JOHN MAXWELL, govt. ofcl.; b. West Point, N.Y., May 3, 1930; s. Maxwell Davenport and Lydia (Happer) T.; B.A., Williams Coll., 1952; M.A., George Washington U., 1954; m. Priscilla Mary Sheppard, July 6, 1957; children—Alice Spaulding, Katharine Maxwell, James Sheppard. With CIA, Seoul, Korea, Bangkok, Thailand, 1952-64; with Dept. State, including Singapore and Rangoon, Burma, 1964-70; project devel. officer Export-Import Bank, Washington, 1970—. Mem. Manuscript Soc. (chpt. pres. 1965-66), Theta Delta Chi, Delta Sigma Rho. Mem. United Ch. Christ. Author: Korea's Syngman Rhee, 1960; From The White House Inkwell, 1968; Garfield of Ohio, 1970. Home: 1939 Lorraine Av McLean VA 22101 Office: 811 Vermont Av NW Washington DC 20571

TAYLOR, JOSEPH TALIAFERRO, III, physician; b. Charleston, S.C., July 24, 1937; s. Joseph Taliaferro and Eloise (Lanier) T.; B.S., Coll. Charleston, 1959; M.D., Med. U. S.C., 1961; m. Susan Dwight Walker, July 11, 1959; children—Ellen Walker, Susan Sloan, Joseph Taliaferro. Intern, Med. U. S.C. Teaching Hosps., 1961-62; gen. practice medicine, Ridgeville, S.C., 1962-63, Summerville, S.C., 1963—; chief staff Dorchester County Hosp., 1969-72. Trustee, Summerville Acad., pres., 1968—. Served as capt. M.C., AUS, 1966-68. Decorated Bronze Star medal. Diplomate Am. Bd. Family Practice. Fellow Am. Acad. Family Physicians; mem. Am., S.C. med. assns., Am. Acad. Family Practice, Dorchester County Med. Soc. (pres. 1969-71), Alpha Omega Alpha. Episcopalian (vestryman 1971-74). Lion. Home: 108 Old Country Club Rd Summerville SC 29483 Office: 435 N Cedar St Summerville SC 29483

TAYLOR, JOSHUA CHARLES, educator, museum dir., art historian; b. Hillsboro, Ore., Aug. 22, 1917; s. James Edmond and Anna L.M. (Scott) T.; student Mus. Art Sch., Portland, Ore., 1935-39; B.A., Reed Coll., 1939, M.A., 1946; M.F.A., Princeton, 1949, Ph.D., 1956. Designer for theatre, 1936-41, for San Francisco Opera Ballet, 1936-37; tchr. theatre Reed Coll., 1939-41; tchr. history art Princeton, 1948-49; mem. faculty U. Chgo., 1949—, chmn. 1st yr. program humanities in coll., 1954-58, William Rainey Harper prof. humanities, also prof. history art. 1963—; dir. Nat. Collection Fine Arts, Smithsonian Instn., Washington, 1970—; lectr., U.S., on TV, 1953—; lectr. Inst. Interuniversitario, Argentina, 1962; spl. research 19th and 20th century painting and artistic theory Italy and U.S. Former mem. adv. com. 20th century art Art Inst. Chgo.; mem. faculty adv. com. Ency. Brit.; mem. adv. bd. Lillie P. Bliss Internat. Study Center Mus. Modern Art. Served to maj., inf., AUS, 1941-46; ETO. Mem. Coll. Art Assn. Am. (dir.), Assn. Art Museum Dirs., Am. Assn. Museums, Royal Soc. Arts, Internat. Inst. Conservation Historic and Artistic Works, Phi Beta Kappa. Author: William Page, the American Titian, 1957; Learning to Look, 1957; Futurism, 1961; Graphic Works of Umberto Boccioni, 1961; Vedere prima di credere, 1970; also articles, revs. Home: 1250 31st St NW Washington DC 20007

TAYLOR, LEON MCCORD, ednl. adminstr.; b. Knoxville, Tenn., Dec. 15, 1916; s. William Henry and Era Irene (Kennedy) T.; B.A. cum laude, Trinity U., 1955; m. Annie Juanita Thompson, Feb. 1, 1941; children—James Allan, Thomas Stuart, Douglas Lee, Carolyn Sue, Joseph Michael, William Andrew. Bookkeeper, Consumer Ice & Coal Co., Port Arthur, Tex., 1935-37; announcer, continuity dir. sta. KFDM, Beaumont, Tex., 1937-41; dir. promotion KRNT Radio and Radio Theater, Des Moines, 1945-47; dir. pub. relations Trinity U., San Antonio, 1947—, v.p. univ. relations, 1969—, asso. prof. journalism, 1967—. Served with USAAF, 1941-45; Col. Res. ret. Recipient Best Motion Picture Film award for higher ednl. instns. Am. Coll. Pub. Relations Assn., 1961; decorated AF Commendation medal with 2 oak leaf clusters. Mem. Pub. Relations Soc. Am. (chpt. pres. 1952), San Antonio C. of C., Sigma Delta Chi. Baptist. Home: 447 E Rosewood St San Antonio TX 78212

TAYLOR, LILLIAN ROSS MCCULLOCH (MRS. DAVID WYATT AIKEN TAYLOR), librarian; b. Elizabethtown, N.C., Mar. 29, 1928; d. Edgar F. and Jessie Lee (Sugg) McCulloch; A.B., Queens Coll., 1949; M.A., Presbyn. Sch. Christian Edn., Richmond, Va., 1951; M.A., Peabody Library Sch. of George Peabody Coll., 1963; Ednl. Specialist degree, 1970; m. David Wyatt Aiken Taylor, Aug. 25, 1951; children—Frances Bland, David W.A. Tchr. pub. schs., Richmond, Va., 1951-52, Harlingen, N.J., 1952-53; librarian Peabody Demonstration Sch. George Peabody Coll., Nashville, 1963-70, pres. faculty orgn., 1967-70; librarian Montgomery Bell Acad., Nashville, 1970—; instr. L.S. Belmont Coll., Nashville, 1973. Recipient Algernon Sydney Sullivan award, 1949. Mem. Am., Southeastern (pres. elect sch. libraries div.), Tenn. (edn. com.) library assns., Nashville Library Club (v.p. 1970—), Women's Nat. Book Assn. Beta Phi Mu. Home: 2669 Rangewood Ct NE Atlanta GA 30345

TAYLOR, LLOYD CHAMBERLAIN, educator; b. Richmond, Va., Dec. 31, 1923; s. Lloyd Chamberlain and Marcia (Estes) T.; A.B., Lehigh U., 1949, A.M., 1951, Ph.D., 1956. Faculty, Tex. A. and M. U., College Station, 1956—, prof. history, 1968—. Served with M.I., AUS, 1943-46. Mem. Am. Hist. Assn., Am. Studies Assn., Southwestern Social Sci. Assn., Phi Kappa Phi. Contbr. articles to profl. jours. Home: 401 Cross St College Station TX 77840

TAYLOR, LOUIS HERMAN, educator; b. nr. Glasgow, Ky., Nov. 22, 1914; s. Philip Hershel and Lena Wallace (Tinsley) T.; A.B., Georgetown (Ky.) Coll., 1946; B.D., So. Bapt. Theol. Sem., 1951, Th.D., 1955; m. Lula Bicknell, Nov. 25, 1937; 1 dau., Linda Sue. Truck driver Hayes Grocery Co., Glasgow, 1931-36; salesman, Albany, Ky., 1936-40; salesman Waggener Grocery Co., Burkesville, Ky., 1940-43; prin. Woodford County (Ky.) Elementary Sch., 1946-48; ordained to ministry Bapt. Ch., 1943; pastor Bradfordsville (Ky.) Bapt. Ch., 1949-53, New Hope Bapt. Ch., 1953-55; prof. religion and philosophy Va. Intermont Coll., Bristol, Va., 1955—, acad. dean, 1963, 67. Fellow archeology So. Bapt. Theol. Sem., 1954-55; vis. prof. philosophy King Coll., Bristol, Tenn., summer 1956. Mem. Soc. Bibl. Lit. and Exegesis. Mason, Rotarian, Lion. Club: Civitan (Bristol). Author: The New Creation, 1958. Home: 127 Brookdale Circle Bristol VA 24201

TAYLOR, LUCILLE FARMER, accountant; b. Richmond, Va.; d. Charles Elam and Agnes Susan (Fry) Farmer; certificate accounting, bus. administrn. Va. Mechanics Inst., 1942; m. Allen Lynwood Taylor, Nov. 3, 1928. Accountant, agt. U.S. Internal Revenue Service, Richmond, 1944-54, group supr. audit div., 1955-71, br. chief stblzn. div., 1971-72; bus. mgr. Va. Meth. Sch. Christian Mission, 1972—. Treas. Wilson Inn, Richmond, 1974—. Mem. Am. Soc. Women Accountants (chpt. pres. 1954-56), Nat. Assn. Accountants (chpt. dir. 1963-65, sec. 1966-67, v.p. 1967-70; pres. 1970-71, sec. Va. council 1972—), Nat. Fedn. Fed. Employees (dir. 1947-49; v.p. 1950-51), Va. Soc. C.P.A.'s. Am. Women's Soc. C.P.A.'s Wesleyan Service Guild (pres. 1962-64; Richmond dist. chmn. 1968-70; Va. conf. sec. 1970-71, vice chmn. 1971—). Methodist (sec. bd. trustees 1959—; chmn. commn. finance and stewardship 1963-64; chmn. com. wills, legacies 1962-64). Club: Zonta (pres. 1963-64). Home: 5524 Westower Dr Richmond VA 23225 Office: 5524 Westower Dr Richmond VA 23225

TAYLOR, MARVIN ELLIOTT, hosp. adminstr.; b. Greenville, S.C., Oct. 13, 1920; s. Robert Lafayette and Theodosia (McCall) T.; grad. George Washington U., 1950; m. Roberta Lou Owen, Nov. 26, 1954; children—Davis Hamilton, Jonathan Elliott, Gregory Franklin. Reporter, Greenville News, 1939-43; writer Dept. State, Washington, information officer U.S. embassy, Pusan, Korea, 1952-54; spl. asst. in edn. and cultural affairs officer U.S. embassy, Bonn, Germany, 1954-59; with USIA, Dept. State, Washington, 1959-62; consul U.S. embassy, Nairobi, Kenya, 1962-63; dir. pub. relations Greenville Hosp. System, 1963—. Chmn. pub. information Greenville County (S.C.) Found., 1968-72; mem. exec. com. S.C. Health and Sci. Fair, 1965—. Served with AUS, 1943-46; PTO. Mem. S.C. (pub. relations cons.), Am. (adv. com. pub. relations) hosp. assns., C. of C., Am. Soc. for Hosp. Pub. Relations, Advt. Club Greenville. Republican. Lutheran. Kiwanian. Home: 53 Woodvale Av Greenville SC 29605 Office: 100 Mallard St Greenville SC 29601

TAYLOR, MARVIN FRED, architect; b. Sesser, Ill., July 5, 1936; s. Clarence Oral and Geneverett Lea (Dorrough) T.; student U. Cin., 1954-56, Lee Coll., 1958; m. Loretta Sue Sanders, Aug. 15, 1959; children—Mark Fred, Marlene Faye. Asso., Haglund & Venable Architects, Memphis, 1966-67; jr. partner Doggett/Taylor Assos., 1967-68; design asso. George A. Thomason & Assos., 1968; individual practice architecture, planning, Memphis, 1968—. Mem. archtl. adv. com. Memphis-Shelby County, 1970—. Registered architect, 16 states, Nat. Council Archtl. Registration Bds. Mem. Memphis Jr. C. of C. (dir.), A.I.A., Tenn. Soc. Architects, Am. Soc. Registered Architects. Mem Ch. of God (mem. nat. archtl. bd. 1960-68, profl. advisor 1968—). Author: Plans for Churches, 1969, 71. Prin. works include women's Residence Hall Lee Coll., Cleveland, Tenn., U.S. Post Office and Vehicle Facility, Texarkana, Tex., Post Offices, Olive Branch, Miss., Starkville, Miss., Nursing Home, Forrest City, Ark., U.S. Post Office, Enterprise, Ala., Oak Forest Ch. of God, Memphis, Home for Children, Sevierville, Tenn., Keller Oil Co. office bldg., Effingham, Ill., Ch. of God, Buford, Ga. Home: 2228 Kingsrow Parkway Cordova TN 38018 Office: First Am Bank Bldg Memphis TN 38103

TAYLOR, MARY ANNE SMITH (MRS. RALPH EMERSON TAYLOR), civic worker; b. Port Gibson, Miss., Jan. 9, 1917; d. William Myles and Agnes (Pawlick) Smith; A.A., Copiah-Lincoln Jr. Coll., Miss., 1935; postgrad. Mich. State U., 1945; m. Ralph Emerson Taylor, July 15, 1934; 1 dau., Anne Lavin (Mrs. Christopher John Cannon). With Red Cross Motor Service, 1952-57; pres. Shoreacres Womens Club, 1958; v.p., program chmn. La Porte Bayshore Garden Club, 1959-60, pres., 1960-61, librarian, 1962-63, artistic com. chmn. and Flower Show chmn., 1963-64, publicity chmn., 1964-65; mem. Planning Commn., Shoreacres, 1960-64; chmn. Bd. Inspection, Shoreacres, 1962-64; councilman City of Shoreacres, Tex., 1964-68; mem. Gulf Coast Regional Planning Conf., 1966-68; mem. pub. relations com. Houston-Harris County Transp. Study, 1966—; geol. field asst., Western Australia, 1970-71, 73. Recipient Five Year Service award Red Cross Motor Service, 1957. Mem. Houston Geol. Aux. (past com. chmn.), Womens Aux. Am. Inst. Mining and Metal. Engrs., Am. Civil Liberties Union, Tex. Conservation Council, Bay Area League Women Voters, Shoreline Art League. Democrat. Episcopalian. Clubs: Petroleum, Houston Yacht (past chmn. childrens sailing com.). Compiler, editor: Index to Geological Serials, 1965. Home: PO Drawer A LaPorte TX 77571

TAYLOR, MARY ANN HAMPTON (MRS. GERALD THOMAS TAYLOR), physician; b. Forest City, N.C., June 19, 1935; d. James Miles and Lavonia (Butler) Hampton; B.S. cum laude, Wake Forest Coll., 1956; M.D., 1960; m. Gerald Thomas Taylor, Dec. 20, 1962; children—Lisa Ann, Gregory Thomas, Mary Lynne. Intern Med. Coll. Va., Richmond, 1960-61; staff physician Wake Forest U. Student Health Service, Winston-Salem, N.C., 1961—, asst. dir., 1964—; staff physician N.C. Sch. Arts, 1973. Bd. dirs. ARC. Mem. N.C., Forsyth med. socs. Methodist. Home: Green Meadows Route 8 Winston-Salem NC 27106 Office: Box 7386 Reynolds Sta Winston-Salem NC 27109

TAYLOR, MARY CURTIS SMITH (MRS. JOHN GORDON TAYLOR), musician; b. Shepherdsville, Ky., Jan. 9, 1937; d. Curtis Waldo and Hazel Dell (Trunnell) Smith; student U. Louisville, 1955; B.S. in Music, Murray State Coll., 1958, M.Ed., 1960; m. John Gordon Taylor, Aug. 16, 1958; children—John Gordon, Tiffany May, Whitney Adams. Soloist Louisville Orch., 1954, mem., 1963—; music educator, Benton, Ky., 1958-60, Jefferson County, 1960-64; concertmaster Louisville Civic Orch., 1963—; pvt. violin instrn.; mem. profl. strolling violinists; instr. music appreciation Alice Lloyd Coll., Pippa Passes, Ky. summer 1967; violinist Ky. Opera Assn., 1967—; 1st violinist Nashville Symphony, 1969-72, prin. 2d violin, 1972—. Mem. Colonial Dames XVIII Century, Sigma Alpha Iota. Club: Murray (Ky.) Woman's. Home: Route 7 Box 13 Murray KY 42071

TAYLOR, PAUL PEAK, dentist, educator; b. Childress, Tex., May 11, 1921; s. Noah Peak and Lois (Vinson) T.; student W. Tex. State Coll., 1940; D.D.S., Baylor U., 1944, M.S., U. Mich., 1951; m. LaVerne Countryman, Aug. 11, 1945; children—Peri Ann, Scott Vinson. Pvt. practice pedodontics, Dallas, 1952-69; prof., chmn. grad. pedodontics, Baylor U. Coll. Dentistry, 1960-69, prof., chmn. pedodontic dept., 1969—; dir. dentistry Childrens Med. Center, Dallas, 1960—. Served to capt. AUS, 1951-53. Recipient Mott Found. fellowship. Diplomate Am. Bd. Pedodontists. Fellow Am. Coll. Dentists; mem. Am. Soc. Dentistry for Children (pres. Tex. unit 1946-47), S.W. Soc. Pedodontists, Am. Dallas County dental assns., Am. Acad. Pedodontics, Am. Assn. Sheriff Posses and Riding Clubs (regional v.p. 1969-70), Dallas Execs. Assn. (pres. 1970—). Mason (Shriner). Episcopalian. Contbr. articles to dental jours. Home: 2615 Briarcove Plano TX 75074 Office: 1935 Amelia St Dallas TX 75235

TAYLOR, RAYMOND MASON, lawyer, librarian; b. Washington, N.C., Jan. 1, 1933; s. Thaddeus Raymond and Mary Ada (Mason) T.; A.B. in Polit. Sci., U. N.C. at Chapel Hill, 1955, J.D., 1960; m. Evelyn Rachel High, Apr. 3, 1965; 1 dau., Elizabeth Lee. Staff reporter Washington Daily News., summers 1952, 54; adminstrv. asst. Civil Def. Orgn., Winston-Salem and Forsyth County, N.C., 1955; adminstrv. intern City Winston-Salem, summer 1958; admitted to N.C. bar, 1960; U.S. Supreme Ct. bar, 1970; research asst. to justice Supreme Ct. N.C., 1960-61; asso. firm Gardner, Connor & Lee, Wilson, N.C., 1961-64; adj. instr., then adj. prof. bus. law Atlantic Christian Coll., Wilson, 1962-64; marshal, librarian Supreme Ct. N.C., 1964—; spl. lectr., econs. N.C. State U., 1967—; dir. N.C. Law Research Facilities Study, 1970; chmn. State and Ct. Law Libraries U.S. and Can., 1973—. Mem. library services com. Am. Bar Found., 1969-73. Sec. Southeastern Area council Am. Jr. Red Cross, 1949-50, study visitor to Europe, 1950; chmn. cultural affairs com. Wilson (N.C.) Jr. C. of C., 1963-64; N.C. rep. civil def. unit Nat. Def. Exec. Res., 1967-70. Democratic precinct chmn. Beaufort County, N.C., 1954-57; parliamentarian Wilson County Dem. Exec. Com., 1962-64; mem. Beaufort County Dem. Exec. Com., 1954-57, N.C. 2d Solicitorial Dist. Dem. Exec. Com., 1962-64. Served with AUS, 1955-57. Recipient awards editorial, news and feature writing U. N.C. Press Club, 1955, award hist. feature writing N.C. Soc. County and Local Historians, 1955, named Tar Heel of the Week, 1971. Mem. Am. (mem. spl. com. law book pub. practices 1970—), N.C., Wake County bar assns., N.C. State Bar (chmn. spl. com. law book publs. and rev. bd. 1971), Am. Assn. Law Libraries (certified law librarian, 1968—; co-chmn. com. relations with pubs. and dealers 1970-72), Order Golden Fleece (pres. 1958-59), Pi Sigma Alpha, Phi Delta Phi. Presbyn. Author: History of the North Carolina Supreme Court Library, 1969; also articles. Asst. editor Tar Heel Barrister, 1958-59; mem. student bd. editors N.C. Law Rev., 1960. Home: 3073 Granville Dr Raleigh NC 27609 Office: 500 Justice Bldg PO Box 1841 Raleigh NC 27602

TAYLOR, RICHARD DOUGLAS, lawyer; b. Nashville, May 31, 1931; s. Carl Douglas and Kathryn Cornelia (Hagerty) T.; student U. Notre Dame, 1949-50; B.A., Vanderbilt U., 1953; J.D., Vanderbilt U., 1955; m. Cynthea Braly, Aug. 29, 1953; children—Richard Douglas, Geoffrey Alan, Steven Scott, Mary Kathryn. Admitted to Tenn. bar, 1955; mem. firm Glasgow, Adams & Taylor, Attys., Nashville, 1958—, partner, 1969—. Partner, Moss Rose Devel. Co., 1972—, Sunnyside Devel. Co., Nashville, 1972-73; legal counsel Cath. Diocese Nashville, 1973—. Mem. Met. County Council, Nashville and Davidson County, 1962-71; mem. Met. Traffic Commn., Pub. Records Commn., Nashville, 1962-66; pres. St. Bernard Sch. for Handicapped, Nashville, 1971—. Bd. dirs. Dede Wallace Center, Nashville. Served to lt. USNR, 1955-58. Mem. Internat. Assn. Ins. Counsel, Am., Tenn., Nashville (sec. 1963-64) bar assns., Fedn. Ins. Counsel. K.C. Clubs: Cedar Creek Yacht (Mt. Juliet, Tenn.); City (Nashville). Home: 6720 Rodney Ct Nashville TN 37205 Office: 300 James Robertson Pkwy Nashville TN 37201

TAYLOR, RICHARD LARRY, elec. engr.; b. Jackson, Miss., Jan. 11, 1940; s. William Davis and Lillian Maude (Lomax) T.; B.S., Miss. State U., 1961; postgrad. Rollins Coll., 1966-67, Fla. Atlantic U., 1972—; m. Dianne Elaine Ladner, July 7, 1962; children—Judith Marilyn, Amanda Ellen, Therese Lynn. With Fla. Power & Light Co., Miami, 1964—, human resources specialist, 1973, asst. system operator, 1973, mgr. system protection system, 1973—. Served as ensign USNR, 1961-63. Registered profl. engr., Fla. Mem. I.E.E.E., Fla. Engring. Soc. Home: 4719 SW 34th Terrace Fort Lauderdale FL 33312 Office: Box 3311 Miami FL 33101

TAYLOR, RICHARD POWELL, lawyer; b. Phila., Sept. 13, 1928; s. Earl Howard and Helen (Martin) T.; student Cornell U., 1946-48; B.A., U. Va., 1950, J.D., 1952; m. Barbara Jo Anne Harris, Dec. 19, 1959; 1 son, Douglas Howard Martin. Admitted to Va. bar, 1952, D.C. bar, 1956; law clk. Judge Armistead M. Dobie, U.S. Ct. Appeals 4th Circuit, 1952-53, practiced in Washington, 1956—; asso. firm Steptoe and Johnson, 1956-61; partner, 1962—; sec., corp. counsel Slick Corp., 1963-69, asst. sec., 1969-72, dir., 1965-68; sec., corp. counsel Slick Indsl. Co., 1963-72; sec., dir. Slick Indsl. Co. Can. Ltd., 1966-72;

gen. counsel Intercontinental Forwarders, Inc., 1969—, sec., 1969-72, dir., 1972—. Served to lt. (j.g.) Air Intelligence, USNR, 1953-56. Mem. Am. (vice chmn. aviation com. pub. utility sect. 1974—), Fed., Fed. Power, D.C., Va. bar assns., Am. Judicature Assn., Internat. Platform Assn., Order of Coif, Raven Soc., Chi Phi, Delta Theta Phi. Republican. Episcopalian (vestryman). Clubs: International, Capitol Hill, Congressional Country. Home: 6007 Corewood Lane Sumner Washington DC 20016 Office: 1250 Connecticut Av NW Washington DC 20036

TAYLOR, ROBERT ELLIOTT, psychologist; b. Barre, Vt., May 6, 1931; s. Harold Elliott and Hazel (Locke) T.; B.A., U. Tenn., 1956, M.A., 1957, Ph.D., 1961; m. A. Catharine Parisi, Dec. 28, 1950; children—Jennifer Lyn, Johnathan Elliott. Prof., Radford (Va.) Coll., 1960-62; asst. prof. U. Ga., Athens, 1962-67; psychologist Avalon Psychiat. Clinic, Athens, 1966-68; individual practice clin. psychology, Macon, Ga., 1968—; adj. prof. Mercer U., Macon, 1968-71; cons. Macon Hosp., 1969—. Served with USMCR, 1952-54. Diplomate Am. Bd. Profl. Psychology. Mem. C. of C., Ga. Human Relations Council, Am. Acad. Psychotherapists, Am., So., Ga. (pres. 1973-74) psychol. assns., Am. Civil Liberties Union. Contbr. to profl. jours. Home: 4518 Beechwood Dr S Macon GA 31204 Office: Live Oaks 2437 Vineville Av Macon GA 31204

TAYLOR, ROBERT KILE, telephone co. exec.; b. Austin, Tex., Dec. 24, 1937; s. Kermit Robert and Grace (Kile) T.; B.A., Tex. Christian U., 1964; m. Carol Ann Sullivan, May 26, 1962; children—Christy, Richard, Randall, Ryan and Connie (twins). Writer sports dept. Ft. Worth Star-Telegram, 1959-60, copywriter promotion dept., 1962-63, police reporter, 1963-65, fed. reporter, 1965; pub. relations asst. Alcoa, Point Comfort, Tex., 1966-68, pub. relations asst., Rockdale, Tex., 1968-69, pub. relations mgr. Cleve. Works, 1969-70; pub. relations dir. Gulf-States-United Telephone Co., Tyler, Tex., 1970—. Served with AUS, 1960-63. Mem. Tex. Pub. Relations Assn., Pub. Relations Soc. Am., Sigma Delta Chi. Methodist (chmn. bd. 1967-68, Sunday sch. supt. 1968-69). Lion (sec.-treas. Port Lavaca 1967-68, 1st v.p. Rockdale, 1968-69, pres. 1969, zone chmn. 1971-72, dep. dist. gov. 1972-73, pres. Tyler Evening Lions 1972-73). Author: Fort Worth, 1800 to Now, 1963. Home: 1331 Powers Dr Tyler TX 75701 Office: 120 S College St Tyler TX 75701

TAYLOR, ROBERT L., judge; b. Embreeville, Tenn., Dec. 20, 1899; s. Alfred Alexander and Florence Jane (Anderson) T.; Ph.B., Milligan Coll., 1921; student Vanderbilt Law Sch., 1922-23; LL.B., Yale, 1924; m. Florence Fairfax McCain, May 27, 1933; children—Ann, Robert. Admitted to Tenn. bar, 1923; practiced law, Johnson City, 1924-49; U.S. judge Eastern Dist. of Tenn., 1949—. Mem. Tenn. State, Am., Fed. bar assns., Am. Judicature Soc., Corby Ct., Sigma Alpha Epsilon, Phi Delta Phi. Mem. Christian Ch. Home: 3567 Talahi Dr Knoxville TN 37919 Office: Federal Bldg Knoxville TN 37902

TAYLOR, ROBERT TIECHE, entomologist; b. San Diego, June 29, 1932; s. Clifford Harris and Hazel Marie (Gobar) T.; B.S., Okla. State U., 1954, M.S., 1957, Ph.D., 1960; m. Ellen Clare McAulay, Apr. 11, 1964; children—Suzanne Clare, Kathryn Marie. Engaged in vector control Tulsa City-County Health Dept., summers 1956, 57, 60; engaged in malaria project Pan Am., Health Orgn., Bogota, Colombia, 1960-61; with U.S. Navy Pub. Works, Washington, 1961-63; with malaria project AID, State Dept., Port-au-Prince, Haiti, 1963-65; research entomologist USPHS, Savannah, Ga., 1965-73, Atlanta, Ga., 1973—. Served with Med. Service Corps, AUS, 1954-56. Mem. Entomol. Soc. Am., Am. Mosquito Control Assn., Am. Soc. Tropical Medicine and Hygiene, Royal Soc. Tropical Medicine and Hygiene. Contbr. articles to profl. jours. Home: 3268 Woodrow Way Atlanta GA 30319 Office: Center for Disease Control Atlanta GA 30333

TAYLOR, RONALD WAITMAN, govt. ofcl.; b. Ashland, Ky., Apr. 11, 1922; s. Henry Martin and Bessie (Warman) T.; B.S. in Petroleum Engring., U. Tex., 1947; m. Jessie Elsie Meyers, June 1, 1947; children—Randolph W., Joanna. Petroleum engr. Gulf Oil Corp., Crane, Tex., 1947-49; gas engr. Warren Petroleum Co., Tulsa, 1949-50; petroleum engr. Sinclair Oil & Gas Co., Enid, Okla., 1951-68; petroleum engr. U.S. Geol. Survey, New Orleans, 1968-71, head gas processing group, 1971-73; valuation engr. Internal Revenue Service, Houston, 1973—. Served with USAAF, 1944-46; CBI. Registered profl. engr., Tex., Okla. Mem. Nat. Soc. Petroleum Engrs. Methodist (past steward, lay leader, supt. Ch. sch.). Mason. Home: 6620 Westchester St Houston TX 77005 Office: 2102 New Federal Bldg 515 Rusk St Houston TX 77002

TAYLOR, ROY ARTHUR, congressman; b. Vader, Wash., Jan. 31, 1910; s. Arthur A. and Lola (Morgan) T.; A.B., Maryville (Tenn.) Coll., 1931; law license Asheville (N.C.) U., 1936; m. Evelyn Reeves, May 8, 1932; children—Alan F., Toni R. (Mrs. John F. Robinson). Admitted to N.C. bar, 1936, practiced in Asheville and Black Mountain, 1936-60; mem. N.C. Legislature from Buncombe County, 1947-49, 51-53; atty. Buncombe County, 1949-60; mem. 86th-87th Congresses 12th Dist. N.C., mem. 88th-93d Congresses 11th dist. N.C.; mem. House Fgn. Affairs Com.; chmn. nat. parks and recreation subcom. House Com. Interior and Insular Affairs. Served to lt. (s.g.) USNR, 1943-46. Baptist (deacon). Lion (dist. gov. 1951-52). Home: 110 Connally St Black Mountain NC 28711 Office: House Office Bldg Washington DC 20515

TAYLOR, RUTH E. PETERSON (MRS. CLOYD VERON TAYLOR), home economist; b. Olivia, Tex., Feb. 23, 1923; d. Charley Emil and Ellen (Cavallin) Peterson; B.S., N. Tex. State U., 1944; M.S. U. Md., 1967; m. Cloyd Veron Taylor, Aug. 22, 1945; children—Mary Elizabeth, Cloydia Opal, Cloyd Veron. Tchr. home econs. high sch., Arlington County, Va., 1962-64; mgmt. tng. Marriott Hot Shoppes, Washington, 1965-66; program asst. Dairy Council Met. Washington, 1967-73; nutrition cons. Northern Va., 1973—. Leader, Girl Scouts, Frankfurt, Germany, 1957-59, Arlington County, Va., 1959-60. Mem. Am. Home Econs. Assn., D.C. Dietetic Assn. (chmn. pub. relations 1969-70), Home Economists in Bus., Am. Pub. Health Assn., Electrical Women's Round Table, Internat. Platform Assn., Altrusa, Phi Delta Gamma. Home: 2631 N Kenmore St Arlington VA 22207 Office: 1511 K St NW Washington DC 20005

TAYLOR, WILLIAM REED, JR., textile co. exec.; b. Cleve., Jan. 29, 1918; s. William Reed and Katherine M. (Kelley) T.; B.S., Mass. Inst. Tech., 1940; m. Elizabeth M. Bricker, Dec. 28, 1940 (dec. Aug. 1969); 3 children; m. 2d, Mary Cecilia Leary, Dec. 21, 1969; 4 adopted children. Student engr. Chrysler Corp., Highland Park, Mich., 1940-41; project engr. Perfection Stove Co., Cleve., 1946-48; with Universal Wire Spring Co., Bedford, O., 1948-61, quality control mgr., 1950-53, supt., 1953-57, mgr. main plant, 1957-61; pres., chief engr. Geometric Spring Co., Cleve., 1961-66; prodn. control and personnel mgr. Jackson Products Co., Tampa, Fla., 1966-67, pres., 1968-71; pres. Gallagher Textile Mills, Inc., Tarpon Springs, Fla., 1971—. Served with AUS, 1941-46. Presbyn. Club: Carrollwood Country (Tampa). Patentee spring mfg. machinery. Home: 10702 Carroll Lake Dr Tampa FL 33618 Office: 425 E Spruce St Tarpon Springs FL 33589

TAYLOR, WILLIAM REGINALD, JR., cattle feeder; b. Elkins, W.Va., Aug. 17, 1930; s. William Reginald and Molissia Lorene (Moore) T.; student Tex. Tech. U., Lubbock, 1949; m. Molly Margaret Wegenhoft, Aug. 4, 1950; children—Molissia Kay, Terry Lyn, William Reginald III. Cattle order buyer, speculator, feeder, Houston, 1950-61; cattle feeder, co-owner Sealy Feed Yard (Tex.), 1961-70, cattle feeder, 1970—; dir. Citizens State Bank, Sealy. Democrat. Methodist. Home: 103 Briar Circle Sealy TX 77474 Office: Box 668 Sealy TX 77474

TAYLOR, WINSTON HOWARTH, ch. ofcl.; b. Brunswick, Neb., Oct. 24, 1921; s. Milo Elmer and Jessie May (Howarth) T.; student Willamette U., 1938-43; B.B.A., Tulane U., 1947; M.A. in Journalism, U. Md., 1973; m. Betty Frances Terroy, Sept. 9, 1946; children—Alan W., Hope C., Brian D., Meredith E., Graham A. Reporter, news editor Ore. Statesman, Salem, 1939-43, 47-53; dir. pub. relations and promotion San Francisco Area, Methodist Ch., 1953-60; dir. Washington Office, United Meth. Communications, 1960—; lectr. pub. relations Am. U., 1966-67, instr. journalism U. Md., 1971-72. Served with AUS, 1943-46; ETO. Mem. Religious Pub. Relations Council (past nat. pres.). Home: 1014 Woodside Pkwy Silver Spring MD 20910 Office: 100 Maryland Av NE Washington DC 20002

TAZEWELL, CALVERT WALKE, ret. air force officer, author, historian; b. Wilmington, Del., Apr. 13, 1917; s. Calvert W. and Sophie (Goode) Tazewell; student Air Corps Tech. Sch., 1940, Air Tactical Sch., 1948, Sophia U., Tokyo, 1951, Air Command and Staff Sch., USAF Air. U., 1952, Ind. U., 1956; m. Beverly Mae LaCour, Jan. 14, 1943 (div. Apr. 1959); children—Lyn Diane, Patricia Marie, Beverly Ann; m. 2d, Belle Gordon, July 7, 1959 (div.); 1 son, William Bradford. Pvt., Va. N.G., 1934-35; radio technician, San Antonio, 1936-37; pvt., USAC, 1937, m/sgt. weather observer and forecaster, 1941; commd. 2d lt., U.S. A.A.F. (by direct appointment while overseas), 1942, advanced through grades to lt. col.; Airways and Air Communications Service; comml., multi-engine pilot; as communications specialist on U.S.A.F. meteorol. flight, flew over North Pole, 1947; during World War II developed and supervised for USAAF pioneer worldwide weather communications system, which principles and techniques have been accepted by World Meteorol. Orgn. and Internat. Civil Aviation Orgn.; apptd. officer Regular Army, 1947; transferred to Air Force, 1948; comdr. 1951st AAGS Squadron, Nagoya, Japan, 1950-51; dep. dir. plans and requirements Hdqrs. 1808th AACS Wing, Tokyo, Japan, 1951-52; comdr. 1300th Student Squadron, Great Falls, Mont., 1953-54; 818th AC & W Squadron, Randolph, Tex., 1955-56, Kangnung Air Base, Korea, 1957, Takaoyama Air. Sta., Japan, 1958; dir. communications-electronics 314th Air div. Oson, Korea, 1956-57. Duluth Air Def. Sector, 1958-59; ret., 1959; civil def. coordinator Dade County, Fla., 1961; organizer chmn. Met. Dade County Pub. Library Adv. Bd., 1963-64; instn N.Y. U., 1962-63, Old Dominion U., 1964-65. Trustee Assn. for Preservation Va. Antiquities, 1967-69. Decorated Bronze Star medal. Mem. Norfolk (1st pres., founder), Va. hist. socs., Common Cause, Am. Civil Liberties Union, UN Assn., Am. Radio Relay League, Natural Food Associates, Nat. Health Fedn., Voicespondence Club, Worldwide Tapetalk, Global Tape Rec. Exchange Amateur radio sta. operator, 1935—. Address: 520 Oak Grove Rd Norfolk VA 23505

TEAGUE, EDWARD LINDELL, JR., athletic dir.; b. Washington, Dec. 14, 1921; s. Edward L. and Virginia (Simmers) T.; student N.C. State U., 1940-43; A.B., U. N.C., 1946, M.A., 1947; postgrad. U. Md., 1953-54; m. Rita Mae Smith, Apr. 7, 1945; children—Peggy Diane, Joanne Rita. Asst. football coach Guilford Coll., 1947-49, head coach, dir. athletics, 1949-50; backfield coach U. Md., 1952-56, U. N.C., 1956; head football coach The Citadel, Charleston, S.C., 1957-65, dir. athletics, 1966—, asso. prof. phys. edn., 1957—. Served to 1st lt. USMCR, 1943-46; PTO; to maj., 1950-51; Korea. Named S.C. Coach of Year, 1960, So. Conf. Coach of Year, 1961. Mem. Am. Assn. Health, Phys. Edn. and Recreation, Am. Football Coaches Assn., Coll. Athletic Bus. Mgrs. Assn., Nat. Assn. Coll. Dirs. Athletics, Phi Delta Kappa. Kiwanian (past pres., dir. Charleston). Author: (with Wm. C. Brown) Handbook of Football Scouting and Film Analysis, 1953; The Unbalanced Line Open End T, 1964. Home: 8D The Citadel Charleston SC 29409

TEAGUE, GARY JEAN, city ofcl.; b. Ft. Worth, Tex., Aug. 8, 1943; s. Harvey Jean and Margaret (Brooks) T.; B.C.E., Arlington State Coll., 1966; postgrad. Tex. Christian U., 1967-68; m. Ruth Ann Courtade, July 3, 1964; children—Stephanie, Brett. Jr. engr. stress analysis Gen. Dynamics Corp., Ft. Worth, 1966-67; with City of Ft. Worth, 1967—, chief design engr., 1972—. Chmn. Tarrant County Com. for Standardization of Roadway Standards, 1973-74. Mem. Am. Pub. Works Assn., Am. Soc. C.E., Tex. Pub. Works Assn. Baptist (clk. 1970-74, Sunday sch. teacher 1964-74). Home: 5000 White Oak Lane Fort Worth TX Office: 1000 Throckmorton St Fort Worth TX 76102

TEAGUE, HYMAN FARIS, pub. co. exec.; b. San Angelo, Tex., Jan. 14, 1916; s. John Henry and Minnie (Gauldin) T.; B.A., McMurry Coll., 1935, postgrad., 1940; postgrad. Hardin-Simmons U., 1935-36; m. Sophia Golda Harvey, Dec. 26, 1944; children—Carl Robin, Alan Cole. Tchr. pub. schs. Tex., 1935-43; with The Steck Co. (name changed to Steck-Vaughn Co., 1965), Austin, Tex., 1946—, v.p., 1965, pres., 1965—, also dir. Served with USNR, 1943-46. Mem. Assn. Am. Pubs., Nat. Council Tchrs. English. Democrat. Baptist. Rotarian. Home: 4906 Rollingwood Dr Austin TX 78746 Office: 807 Brazos St Austin TX 78701

TEAGUE, JAMES UDELL, drilling co. exec.; b. Caldwell, Tex., Oct. 23, 1909; s. Oliver Ransom and Mary Frances (Rollins) T.; B.A., Rice U., 1930; m. Margot Elizabeth Terry, Dec. 26, 1935; children—James Oliver, Margot Terry. Div. petroleum engr. Humble Oil & Refining Co., Houston, 1930-40; supt. Hogg Oil Co., Houston, 1940-48; chief exec. officer, prin. owner Columbia Drilling Co., Houston, 1948—. Life trustee, vice chmn. bd. govs. Rice U. Served to lt. comdr. USNR, 1942-45. Registered profl. engr., Tex. Mem. Am. Petroleum Inst. (mem. gen. com. div. prodn., 1955—), Am. Assn. Petroleum Geologists, Am. Inst. Mining and Metall. Engrs., Tex. Ind. Producers and Royalty Owners Assn. (exec. com. 1955—), Am. Assn. Oilwell Drilling Contractors (nat. pres. 1958, permanent dir.), Mid-Continent Oil and Gas Assn. Episcopalian. Kiwanian. Clubs: Houston, Houston Petroleum (pres. 1966), Lakeside Country (Houston). Patentee in oilfield tech. Home: 3203 S Braeswood St Houston TX 77025 Office: Columbia Drilling 3700 Buffalo Speedway Houston TX 77006

TEAGUE, OLIN EARL, congressman; b. Apr. 6, 1910; s. James Martin and Ida (Sturgeon) T.; student A. and M. Coll. of Tex., 1928-32; m. Freddie Dunman, Dec. 30, 1932; children—James M., John O., Jill Virginia. Sta. supt. U.S. P.O., College Station, Tex., 1932-40; elected, 1946, to fill unexpired term of Luther A. Johnson, as mem. 79th Congress from 6th Tex. Dist., mem. 80th to 93d congresses from 6th Tex. Dist., mem. house com. vet. affairs, chmn. house com. astronautics and space scis., mem. com. on standards of ofcl. conduct. Served to col. 314th Inf., 79th Div., AUS, World War II. Decorated Silver Star with 2 clusters, Bronze Star with 1 cluster, Purple Heart with 2 clusters, Combat Infantryman's Badge, Army Commendation Ribbon (U.S.); Croix de Guerre with palm (France). Democrat. Baptist. Lion. Home: 6015 Massachusetts Av Woodacres MD 20901 Office: House Office Bldg Washington DC 20525

TEAGUE, SARAH ANN CRUMBLEY (MRS. DONALD WAYNE TEAGUE), journalist; b. Holly Pond, Ala., Aug. 17, 1938; d. James Burr and Alma (Reid) Crumbley; B.A., Howard Coll., 1959; m. Donald Wayne Teague, Feb. 20, 1960. Asst. in pub. relations Howard Coll., Birmingham, Ala., 1959-64; fashion editor Birmingham Post-Herald, 1964-72, women's editor, 1972—. Co-chmn. state publicity Birmingham Festival Arts, 1963-64; nat. sec. Howard Coll. Alumni Assn., 1963-64; mem. U. Alumni Assn. Scholarship Com., 1964-67; mem. Birmingham's Fall Fashion Time Com., 1964—. Mem. Chi Omega, Sigma Delta Chi. Baptist. Home: 1429 S 28th St Birmingham AL 35205 Office: 2200 4th Av N Birmingham AL 35202

TEAGUE, THOMAS SWANN, educator; b. High Point, N.C. Dec. 9, 1937; s. Thomas Carrick and Ethel (Swaim) T.; A.A., Mars Hill Coll., 1958; B.Mus., Fla. State U., 1961, M.Mus., 1962, Mus.D., 1969; m. Rebecca Holder, June 24, 1960 (div.); children—Julia Leigh, Thomas David. Asst. prof. music Carson-Newman Coll., Jefferson City, Tenn., 1962-69, asso. prof., 1969—, dir. opera, 1965—. Recitalist, opera and oratorio performer. Recipient Malcolm Miller award for Outstanding Student Projects Knoxville Jour., 1965. Mem. Nat. Assn. Tchrs. of Singing; Phi Kappa Lambda, Phi Mu Alpha. Democrat. Baptist. Author: Diction Manual for Singers, 1966. Home: Route 1 Jefferson City TN 37760

TEAGUE, WILLIAM CHANDLER, music dir.; b. Gainesville, Tex., July 8, 1922; s. John Abner and Martha Leo (Chandler) T.; student Gainesville Jr. Coll., 1938-39, So. Meth. U., 1939-41; Mus. B., Curtis Inst. Music, 1948; m. Lucille Ridinger, Sept. 5, 1943; children—Lynda Gayle, William Chandler. Mem. faculty Episcopal Acad., Overbrook, Pa., 1945-48; dir. music St. Mark's Episcopal Ch., also prof. music Centenary Coll., Shreveport, 1948—; concert artist, 1955—, tours throughout Europe, Eng., 1966, 69, 72, 74. Mem. concerto contest com. Shreveport Symphony Soc.; mem. Commn. Ch. Music, Diocese of La., 1949, Liturgical Commn.; adviser Camp Hardtner Choir Camp, 1950; adv. com. 4th Province Conf. Ch. Music, 1951—; mem. Shreveport Cultural Affairs Com. Bd. dirs. Shreveport Community Concerts; asso. trustee Evergreen Conf. Center. Served with USAAF, 1942-45. Named Shreveport Outstanding Musician of Year, 1969; recipient Cultural award Shreveport Jour., 1969, Shreveport Music Tchrs. Assn., 1970. Mem. Am. Guild Organists (dean North La. chpt., S.W. regional chmn. 1969—, nat. council 1970—), Hymn Soc. Am., Am. Assn. U. Profs., La. Music Tchrs. Assn., Music Tchrs. Nat. Assn., Am. Cathedral Organists and Choirmasters Assn., Phi Mu Alpha. Episcopalian. Home: 547 Broadmoor Blvd Shreveport LA 71105

TEARE, GEORGE WILLIAM, JR., computerized typesetting firm exec.; b. Cleve., Oct. 15, 1930; s. George William and Catharyn (Hall) T.; A.B., Dartmouth, 1953; M.B.A., U. Pa., 1957; m. Nancy Underwood Sawin, June 26, 1954; children—Catharyn Hall, Susan Elizabeth. Salesman, IBM Corp., Phila., 1957-62; data processing sales mgr. Fisher-Stevens Inc., Clifton, N.J., 1964-68; pres. Bru-El Graphic, Inc., Springfield, Va., 1968—; dir. William Byrd Press, Richmond, Va., Time Share Corp., Hanover, N.H. Bd. dirs. Del. County chpt. Am. Cancer Soc., 1960-62. Served to 1st lt. USMCR, 1953-55. Mem. Nat. Composition Assn. (pres.), Printing Industries Washington (treas.), Master Printers Washington (sec.-treas.). Home: 913 Rail Ct McLean VA 22101 Office: 5265 Port Royal Rd Springfield VA 22151

TEARLE, RICHARD VINCENT, traffic safety engr.; b. N.Y.C., June 25, 1942; s. Vincent Richard and Lillian (Gartner) T.; B.A., Hofstra U., 1966; M.B.A., Fla. State U., 1970; student U. Md., 1972-73; m. Marguerite Parker Messick, Feb. 24, 1968; children—Richard Vincent, David. Tech. and engring. analyst Am. Automobile Assn., Falls Church, Va., sec. 1970—, subcom. on signs, 1971—, nat. adv. com. to U.S. Dept. Transp. on uniform traffic control devices, 1971—. Mem. North Springfield Civic Assn., 1971—. Served with AUS, 1966-68. Mem. Internat. Municipal Parking Congress, Nat. Safety Council, Inst. Traffic Engrs., Hwy. Users Fedn. (hwy. safety adv. panel). Home: 5516 Kathleen Pl Springfield VA 22151 Office: 8111 Gatehouse Rd Falls Church VA 22042

TEARS, CLAUDE FREDERICK, JR., engring exec.; b. Cambridge, Mass., May 13, 1919; s. C. F. and Gwendolyn (Jones) T.; B. Chem., Cornell U., 1940; postgrad. Syracuse U., 1941, Columbia, 1942-44; m. Ruth E. McCulley, May 25, 1945 (div.); children—Claude Frederick III, Lisa Michele. Control chemist Semet-Solvay Co., 1941-42; process engr. Celanese Corp. Am., 1942-44, Kellex Corp., 1944-45; project engr. Bahrein Petroleum Co., 1945-47; chief engr. Process Engrs., Inc., 1947-51; v.p. process and project engring. Tears Engrs., Dallas, 1951-59, exec. v.p., 1959-64, pres., 1964-66, dir., 1951—, chief engr. Chem. Producers Corp., Dallas, 1966-69, v.p. engring., 1970-72. Tex. chess champion, 1950, 56; mem. U.S. chess team for World Corr. chess Olympiades III and IV, 1958-66; N.Am. champion Flying Scot Class Yacht, 1971. Mem. Am. Inst. Chem. Engrs. (sr.), Am. Petroleum Inst. Home: 8626 Inwood Rd Dallas TX 75209

TEASLEY, EDGAR WILLIAM, assn. exec.; b. Toccoa, Ga., Oct. 7, 1912; s. Edgar Carl and Pearle (Brown) T.; A.B. in Econs., George Washington U., 1936; m. Margaret Pitney, Sept. 15, 1939; children—Stewart P., Russell W. Exec. trainee W.R. Grace & Co., N.Y.C., 1936-41; gen. mgr., owner radio sta. WTNT, Augusta, Ga., 1947-49; self-employed land developer, home builder, realtor, Greenville, S.C., 1950-63; exec. v.p. Home Builders Assn., Greenville, 1963—. Trustee Home Builders Ins. Trust, Home Builders Self Insurers Fund, Home Builders Pension Fund.; bd. dirs. Greenville Housing Found. Served with USNR, 1941-46. Recipient 8 awards as exec. v.p. Home Builders Assn. Greenville. Mem. Am. Soc. Assn. Execs., Nat. Assn. Home Builders (life dir., econ. adviser), Home Builders S.C. (dir.). Presbyn. (ruling elder). Editor, pub. Home Building Newsletter, 1962—. Home: 8 Sunset Dr Greenville SC 29605 Office: 702 E McBee Av Greenville SC 29601

TEDDER, CHARLES COOPER, city ofcl., real estate exec.; b. Sardis Community, S.C., Aug. 27, 1929; s. Nolan Heywood and Lena Bell (Locklair) T.; B.A., Presbyn. Coll., 1952; m. Joy Streett, June 12, 1954; children—Dawn, Matthew, Amy. Partner, Tedder-Jones Ins. Agy., Florence, S.C., 1961-73; founder, owner C. Cooper Tedder Co., Florence, 1973—; mayor Florence, 1971—. Pres., Christian Bus. Men's Club, Florence, 1963, United Fund, Florence, 1965, Big Bros. Assn., 1966-69, YMCA, 1970-71; v.p. Boys Club, Florence, 1970—; chmn. Cancer Crusade, 1962-63; mem. Brookland Plantation Home for Boys, Orangeburg, 1964—. Bd. dirs. Glad Tidings, Inc., Charlotte, N.C. Served with USMCR, 1953-54. Named Florence Young Man of Year, Jr. C. of C., 1962. Mem. S.C. Municipal Assn. (v.p. 1973), C. of C. (pres. 1967-68). Presbyn. Lion. Home: 1337 Clarendon Av Florence SC 29501 Office: PO Box 4900 Second Loop Rd Florence SC 29501

TEDDER, KENNETH ALLEN JOE, mfg. co. exec.; b. Rockwood, Tenn., Oct. 30, 1922; s. Thomas Charles and Ruth Dexter (LaRue) T.; student U. Tenn., 1940; U. Cal. at Berkeley, 1943-44; m. Elizabeth Louise Nickle, Oct. 24, 1942; children—Jodie (Mrs. Robert Millard Stamey), Claudia (Mrs. Barry Steven Owens). Salesman, Herbert & Nickle Furniture Co., Knoxville, Tenn., 1945-49; owner, mgr. Henshaw Furniture Hosp., Knoxville, 1949-55; salesman Covert

Textiles, High Point, N.C., 1955-59; salesman Fulton Cotton Mills, Atlanta, 1959-68, sales mgr., 1968-72; mdse mgr. Bibb Co., Macon Ga., 1972-73, v.p. marketing Fabrics div., 1973—. Served with AUS, 1943-45. Decorated Purple Heart. Mem. Christian Ch. Mason. Home: 230 Stone Mill Trail Atlanta GA 30328 Office: Bibb Co Atlanta GA 30328

TEDDLIE, STELLA MAYE HARWELL (MRS. HORACE TEDDLIE), educator; b. Cedar Hill, Tex.; d. Josiah Clayton and Myrtle Mae (Trees) Harwell; B.A., U. Wyo., 1945; postgrad. So. Meth. U., 1953-56, 63—; Ph.D. (hon.), Colo. Christian Coll.; m. Horace Teddlie, Apr. 1, 1926; children—Albert Harwell, Merritt Bonar. Binding librarian Dallas Pub. Library, 1934-42; tchr. pub. schs., Okla., Colo., Wyo., Tex., 1944-53, Dallas, 1953-56, 60—. Mgr. Preston Center Travel Office, Dallas, 1956-57, Dallas Travel Service, 1957-60. Chmn. City Blood Bank for Tchr. of Dallas. Chmn. bd. dirs. Thorp Spring Christian Coll. Mem. N.E.A. (textbook com. for Dallas schs.), Tex. Tchrs. Assn., Dallas Classroom Tchrs. Assn. (chmn. 1970-72), Phi Kappa Phi, Psi Chi, Alpha Delta Kappa (charter Kappa chpt. 1956; internat. transp. chmn. 1957—; organizer Mexico City chpt. 1963, state historian Tex.). Democrat. Mem. Ch. of Christ. Clubs: Dallas Export-Import, Zonta (program chmn. Dallas 1958-59). Author: (handbook) Practical Handicraft, 1942. Home: 2718 Overcrest St Dallas TX 75211

TEELE, ARTHUR EARLE, educator; b. Vaughan, N.C., Nov. 11, 1910; s. George Washington and Cora (Williams) T.; A.B., N.C. Coll., 1934; A.M., Cornell U., 1941, Ph.D., 1953; m. Florazelle Swayze, Dec. 11, 1937; children—Synthia Florabeale, Arthur Earle. Instr., chmn. dept. social studies Warren County Tng. Sch., Wise, N.C., 1934-39; ednl. therapist. VA Hosp., Roanoke, Va., 1946-50; prof. edn., history, head dept. edn. St. Augustine's Coll., 1953-54; prof., chmn. dept. edn. Prairie View (Tex.) A. and M. Coll., 1954-57; prof., head dept. secondary edn. Fla. A. and M. U., Tallahassee, 1957-70, dir. prins., suprs. workshop 1964-66, prof., dean of grad. studies, 1970—; dir. Hardee County Curriculum Workshop, 1960; dir. Hampton Jr. Coll. Workshop, 1962; mem. research council Coop. Coll. Projects (Land Grant TVA), 1963-64. Mem. United Fund steering com. Fla. A. and M. U., 1961-67. Bd. dirs. Leon County United Fund, 1962-69, N.E. Fla. Summer Camp, Jacksonville, 1966-69; pres. Coll. Terrace Community, 1963-68. Served with USAAF, 1943-45. Recipient Grant-in-Aid for Research, Cornell U., 1952; named Distinguished Alumnus, N.C. Coll., 1960. Mem. N.E.A., Assn. Supervision and Curriculum Devel., Fla. Edn. Assn., Nat. Assn. Secondary Sch. Prins., Tallahassee Club Frontiers Internat. (pres. 1972), Kappa Alpha Psi (dir.), Phi Delta Kappa, Kappa Delta Pi, Sigma Pi Phi. Contbr. to numerous publs. in field. Home: 620 Howard Av Tallahassee FL 32304

TEELE, RAY PALMER, profl. engr.; b. Washington, July 12, 1903; s. Ray P. and Mary (Hazard) T.; B.S. in Elec. Engring., U. Mich., 1927; M.S. in Physics, George Washington U., 1929; m. Marion Beth Johnson, Apr. 12, 1927; 1 dau., Audrey (Mrs. Ronald A. Ryder). With Nat. Bur. Standards, Washington, 1923-65, physicist-in-charge research on photometry, 1965; cons. profl. engr., Washington, 1966-74; cons. Am. Assn. Motor Vehicle Adminstrs. Fellow Illuminating Engring. Soc., Optical Soc. Am., Washington Acad. Scis.; mem. Illuminating Engring. Soc. Gt. Britain, Soc. Automotive Engrs., Inst. Traffic Engrs. (affiliate). Died Feb. 17, 1974. Address: 3713 Jenifer St NW Washington DC 20015

TEER, NELLO LEGUY, JR., constrn. co. exec.; b. Durham, N.C., Mar. 8, 1914; s. Nello Leguy and Gertrude (Adcock) T.; student U. N.C., 1932-35; LL.D., N.C. State U., 1968; m. Dorothy Foster, Nov. 10, 1934; children—Sondra (Mrs. Reece A. Robertson), Nello Leguy III, Dorothy (Mrs. Stephan H. Snider), Michael Page. Pres. Nello L. Teer Co., Durham, 1952—, Nello L. Teer Internat., Inc., Durham, 1952—, Central Engring. and Contracting Corp., Durham, 1952—. Pres. Occoneechee council Boy Scouts Am., 1964; pres. Friends of Watts Hosp., 1965-68. Founder, bd. dirs. Better Hwys. Information Found.; pres. N.C. Engring. Found., 1963-65. Recipient Civilian Meritorious Service award U.S. Bur. Yards and Docks USN, World War II, Silver Beaver award Boy Scouts Am., 1963, Silver Antelope award, 1969. Mem. Asso. Gen. Contractors Am. (nat. pres. 1973), Am. Road Builders Assn. (pres. 1959-60; award greatest contbn. 1962), Internat. Road Fedn. (dir., mem. exec. com., world council), Carolina Road Builders Assn., Durham C. of C. (civic award 1972). Episcopalian (sr. warden). Home: 3200 Rugby Rd Durham NC 27707 Office: PO Box 1131 Durham NC 27702

TEETER, BENJAMIN LUKE, govt. ofcl.; b. Johnstown, Pa., Apr. 6, 1916; s. Luke and Isabel Hope (Aiken) T.; student Johns Hopkins, 1943, Indsl. Coll. Armed Forces, 1972-73; m. Hazel Leona Higley, Oct. 24, 1941; children—Roger M., Barbara (Mrs. Richard Kennamer). Loader shipping dept. Bethlehem Steel Co., Johnstown, 1936-37; with U.S. Army Missile Command, Redstone Arsenal, Ala., 1940—, transp. specialist, 1960—. Historian, rec. sec. Rocket City Astronom. Soc., Huntsville, Ala., 1961-72. Served with Ordnance Corps, AUS, 1934-40. Mem. Am. Ordnance Assn. (life), von Braun Astronom. Soc. (exec. sec. 1965—), Nat. Model R.R. Assn., Nat. Wildlife Fedn., Nat. Rifle Assn. Mason. Clubs: Blue and Gray Gun, Radio Amateur (Huntsville). Home: 3103 Caldwell Rd NW Huntsville AL 35805 Office: US Army Missile Command Redstone Arsenal AL 35809

TEETER, THOMAS ALLEN, librarian; b. Dumas, Ark., Oct. 4, 1943; s. Charles Ruskin and Neva Katherine (Taylor) T.; B.S., U. Ark., 1965; M.L.S., U. Miss., 1967, Ed.D., 1971; m. Carolyn Flossie Umsted, July 30, 1967. Social studies tchr. Little Rock Pub. Sch. Dist., Little Rock Central High Sch., 1965-66, head librarian, 1966-70; grad. asst. in secondary edn. U. Miss., 1971; asso. dir. libraries, asst. prof. U. Ark., Little Rock, 1972—. Mem. N.E.A., Assn. for Ednl. Communication and Tech., Am., Ark. library assns., Ark. Edn. Assn., Phi Delta Kappa. Home: 25 Bradford Dr Little Rock AR 72207 Office: U Ark 33d and University Sts Little Rock AR 72204

TEETS, FRANK DAVID, agrl. co. exec.; b. Minot, N.D., Mar. 23, 1936; s. Miles Francis and Esther (Olsen) T.; B.S., Stetson U., 1961; m. Carolyn Sue Crawford, Aug. 2, 1958; children—Frank David, James Crawford, Kelly Sue, Rebecca Leeann. Staff accountant W.O. Daley & Co., Orlando, Fla., 1961-64; sec., gen. mgr., dir. South Bay Growers, Inc. (Fla.), 1964—; dir. Thomas Bros., Inc., Fla. Lettuce, Inc., Sobay Crispheart, Inc., Paul Eskew & Assos., Inc. Pres., Belle Glade Beautification Com., 1967. Bd. dirs. Glades Day Sch., Pahokee, Fla. Served with USCGR, 1953-57. Mem. Fla. Celery Exchange (dir.), Fla. Council Farmer Coops. (v.p. 1968), Council Farmer Coops. (treas. 1968), Pi Kappa Alpha. Republican. Elk. Home: 709 NE 3d St N Belle Glade FL 33430 Office: PO Box 56 South Bay FL 33493

TEIPEL, JOHN ALBERT, civil engr.; b. Dallas, Nov. 8, 1923; s. Albert Henry and Mary Frances (Bland) T.; student Tex. A. and M. U., 1941-42; B.S. in Civil Engring., So. Meth. U., 1947; postgrad. Command and Gen. Staff Coll., 1959, Urban Exec. program, Mass. Inst. Tech., 1971; m. Ellen Louise Townsend, June 21, 1943; children—John Randolph, Ellen Lorraine (Mrs. Richard P. Evans), Philip Andrew. Civil engr. Tex. Hwy. Dept. and City of Dallas, 1947-52; civil engr. Hyden Engring. Co., Dallas, 1953-61; lt. col., bn. comdr. 49th Armored Div., Tex. N.G., 1961-62; dep., then asst. dir. pub. works, dir. Dept. Streets and Sanitation Services, Dallas, 1963—. Comdg. officer Dallas Police Res., 1953-59. Bd. dirs. City Employees Credit Union, Dallas. Served with AUS, 1942-45; ETO. Registered profl. engr., Tex. Fellow Am. Soc. C.E. (pres. Dallas br., state dir.); mem. Tex. Pub. Works Assn. (pres. 1972). Mason (master). Club: Bass. Contbr. articles to profl. jours. Home: 5835 Sunnywood Dallas TX 75228 Office: 2721 Municipal Dallas TX 75215

TEJWANI, ASAN, utility co. engr.; b. Bhiria, Nawabshah, India, Aug. 7, 1938; s. Gianchand and Jhami T.; B.Tech. with honors Indian Inst. Tech., Kharagpur, 1961, M.Tech., 1962; M.S., U. Ill., 1966; m. Indu H. Rawtani, June 11, 1968; 1 dau., Sujata. Came to U.S., 1964, naturalized, 1973. Civil engr. Gannon Dunkerley & Co. Ltd., New Delhi, India, 1962-64; civil engr., design interstate bridges, retaining walls, computer applications Harland Barthalomew & Assos., Memphis, 1966-71; structural engr. Memphis Light, Gas & Water Div., Memphis, 1971—. Registered profl. engr., Tenn. Mem. Internat. Group of Memphis, Am. Soc. C.E. Home: 3149 Estes St Memphis TN 38118 Office: 220 S Main St Memphis TN 38101

TELEKI, PAUL GEZA, geol. oceanographer; b. Budapest, Hungary, Apr. 30, 1937; s. Geza and Yolanda (Daranyi) T.; B.S., U. Fla., 1961, M.S., 1966; Ph.D., La. State U., 1970; m. Laurilla Elizabeth Howie, Dec. 17, 1960; children—Alexia, Ilona. Asst. in research dept. coastal engring. U. Fla., 1961-65; geologist Coastal Engring. Research Center, Washington, 1970—. Mem. Am. Geophys. Union, Internat. Assn. Hydraulic Research, Internat. Assn. Sedimentologists, Internat. Assn. Math. Geology, Soc. Econ. Paleontology and Mineralogists, Internat. Water Resource Assn., Am. Soc. Photogrammetry (chmn. geol. oceanography com. 1973—, chmn. symposium on remote sensing in oceanography 1973). Office: Div Engring Devel Coastal Engring Research Center Kingman Bldg Ft Belvoir VA 22060

TELESCA, FRANCIS EUGENE, architect; b. Scranton, Pa., Oct. 22, 1921; s. Joseph J. and Bernetta (Bocchiccio) T.; B.Arch. summa cum laude, Catholic U. Am., 1953; m. Dianne Willis, July 31, 1968; children—Celeste (Mrs. Robert Stokes), Anthony, Cheryl, Glenn, Francis Eugene II, Tina Lee. Employed by various archtl./engring. firms, Washington, also Miami, 1951-59; pvt. practice architecture, Miami, 1959-63; v.p., dir. architecture Greenleaf/Telesca, engrs. and architects, Miami, 1964—; dir. Greenleaf Enterprises, Inc., Bonefish Towers, Inc. Mem. Nat. Com. on Architecture for Commerce and Industry, 1965-66. Mem. Fla. Planning and Zoning Assn., 1963-72; mem. South Fla. Hosp. Council, 1963-70; mem. Inst. Urban Affairs, U. Miami, 1965-66; mem. citizens adv. com. South Fla. Bldg. Code Survey, 1965-66; mem. archtl. adv. com. Miami-Dade Jr. Coll., 1967-69. Bd. dirs. South Fla. Interprofl. Council, 1966-68; bd. dirs., pres. Coconut Grove Assn., 1961-63, Grove House, 1962-63. Served with AUS, 1940-45, 50-51; ETO. Decorated Bronze Star medal; recipient spl. citation Am. Assn. Sch. Adminstrs., 1969, Grand Nat. award Nat. Community Fallout Shelter Competition, 1964. Mem. A.I.A. (pres. Fla. chpt. 1965, dir. 1966-68, award of merit 1968), Soc. Coll. and U. Planning, Coconut Grove C. of C. (dir. 1960-65), Phi Eta Sigma. Roman Catholic. Home: 7299 SW 79th St Miami FL 33143 Office: 1451 Brickell Av Miami FL 33131

TELFAIR, JOHN SPIER, JR., cons. engr.; b. Jacksonville, Fla., Apr. 27, 1916; s. John Spier and Ann (Willard) T.; student Marion Inst., 1936, U.S. Mil. Acad., 1937-39; B.C.E., U. Fla., 1942; m. Lesley Lucille Bremer, Aug. 27, 1956; children—Judith Johnson (Mrs. B. J. Adkins), Peter Johnson, Janice Johnson, Ann. Engr. Corps of Engrs., U.S. Army, Jacksonville, Fla., 1942-43, 1945-47; asst. prof. civil engring. U. Fla., 1943-44; engr. U.S. Maritime Service, 1944-45; research hydraulic engr. State of Fla., Jacksonville, 1948-49; san. engr. Fla. Bd. Health, Vero Beach, 1949-51, Smith & Gilespie, Jacksonville, 1951-53, J.S. Telfair, 1953-54; chief engr. Central and S. Fla. Flood Control Dist., West Palm Beach, 1954-56; sr. engr. Maurice H. Connell & Assos., Inc., cons. engrs., Miami, 1956-60, mem. firm, dir., 1960—; partner Connell, Pierce, Garland & Friedman, architects-engr., Miami, 1963-72; chief engr. Inter-Am. Center Authority State of Fla., 1972—. Cons. in hydrology and environmental engring. Harland Bartholomew & Assos., Memphis, St. Louis, Atlanta; mem. Fla. Bd. Engr. Examiners, 1960-68, pres., 1964. Registered profl. engr., Fla., Ga., Cal., N.Y., Md., Ariz., Ala. Diplomate Am. Acad. Environmental Engrs. Fellow Am. Soc. C.E., Fla. Engring. Soc.; mem. Am. Water Works Assn., Sigma Tau, Tau Beta Pi. Episcopalian. Rotarian. Address: 4924 Alhambra Circle Coral Gables FL 33146

TELFORD, JOSEPH CHARLES, furniture co. exec.; b. Alma, Ill., Aug. 4, 1920; s. Emory Charles and Edna Marie (See) T.; student Curtiss-Wright Aircraft Sch., 1941, New Eng. Aircraft Sch., 1943, Embry-Riddle Sch. Aviation, 1945, Pitts. U., 1944; B.S. in Edn., So. Ill. U., 1947, postgrad., 1947-48; m. Virginia McLaurin, May 25, 1946 (dec. 1972); children—Penelope Ann, Joseph Charles III; m. 2d, Brookie Taylor, Nov. 21, 1973; 1 son, James Edward. Designer, store planner Hotchkiss Store Fixtures, San Antonio, 1947-52; pres. Telford Store Fixtures, Inc., San Antonio, 1952—, San Antonio Store Equipment Sales, Inc., 1956—. Comdr. Shrine Hosp. Unit for Crippled or Burned Children, San Antonio, 1962-67. Served to 1st lt. USAF, 1942-46. Recipient Distinguished Service award for pharmacy Tex. Pharm. Assn., 1960. Mem. U.S., San Antonio chambers commerce, San Antonio Exec. Assn., Nat. Assn. Mfrs. Mason (Shriner), K.T. Home: 2206 Briarwood St San Antonio TX 78209 Office: PO Box 1131 San Antonio TX 78294

TEMERLIN, JULIUS LIENER, advt. agy. exec.; b. Ardmore, Okla., Mar. 27, 1928; s. Pincus and Julia (Kahn) T.; B.A. in Journalism, U. Okla., 1950; m. Karla Sue Samuelsohn, July 23, 1950; children—Dana Michelle, Lisa Babette. Editor Sponsor Mag., N.Y.C., 1950-51; copywriter Glenn Advt., Dallas, 1952-54, TV dir., 1954-56, v.p., creative dir., 1957-70, chief operating officer, 1970-74; pres., chief exec. officer Glenn, Bozell & Jacobs, Inc., Dallas, 1974—. Active Dallas Mus. Fine Arts, Am. Cancer Soc., Nat. Assn. for Retarded Children; mem. Nat. Council of Christians and Jews. Served to 1st lt. AUS, 1951-52. Decorated Bronze Star medal. Mem. Am. Assn. Advt. Agys. (chm. southwest council 1969-70), Advt. League Dallas. Club: Dallas, Columbian Country. Home: 9301 Sunnybrook St Dallas TX 75220 Office: 1750 Regal Row Dallas TX 75247

TEMPLE, ARTHUR, JR., lumber co. exec.; b. Texarkana, Tex., Apr. 8, 1920; s. Arthur and Katherine (Sage) T.; student U. Tex., 1938; m. Mary MacQuiston, Apr. 20, 1939 (div.); children—Charlotte Ann Spencer, Arthur III; m. 2d, Charlotte Dean, Sept. 4, 1963. Bookkeeper, Temple Lumber Co., Lufkin, Tex., 1938-41, mgr., 1941-48; mgr. So. Pine Lumber Co. (name changed to Temple Industries, Inc.), Diboll, Tex., 1948, v.p., gen. mgr., 1949, pres., dir., 1951-72, chmn. bd., chief exec. officer, 1972—; chmn. bd. Sabine Investment Corp. Tex., Scotch Investment Co., Temple Assos., Inc., Topaz Oil Co., all Diboll, Tex. Gypsum Co., Inc., Dallas; pres., dir. Woodward, Inc., Austin, Angelina Free Press, Home Owners Trust, Diboll Housing Found., Inc., all Diboll; exec. v.p., dir. Tex. South-Eastern R.R. Co., Temple-White Co., Inc., Diboll; mem. exec. com., dir. Wheelabrator-Frye, Inc., N.Y.C.; dir. Time, Inc., N.Y.C., Chattanooga Container Corp., Temple Mfg. Co., Dallas, Lumbermen's Investment Corp., Austin; adv. dir. Diboll State Bank, First Bank & Trust, Lufkin, Pineland State Bank (Tex.), Love Woods Products Co., Diboll. Dir. Angelina County Water Control and Improvement Dist. No. 2, Diboll; v.p. Sportsmen's Clubs Tex., Austin; mem. adv. com. Multiple Use of Nat. Forests, Washington; mem. Lufkin City Council; dist. chmn. Boy Scouts Am.; mem. Area Council; chmn. Angelina County Community Chest Fund, Lufkin. Trustees Temple Found.; mem. bd. A.R.C., Lufkin, Salvation Army, Lufkin, Angelina County Tb Assn., Lufkin, Angelina County Heart Assn., Lufkin; trustee Meml. Hosp., Lufkin. Recipient Medal of Merit, V.F.W.; Forest Farmer Ann. award Forest Farmers Assn., 1965. Mem. Delta Kappa Epsilon. Episcopalian (mem. vestry). Rotarian, Lion. Clubs: Confrerie des Chevaliers du Tastevin; Headliners University; Pineland Service. Office: Temple Industries Inc Diboll TX 75941

TEMPLE, GRAY, clergyman; b. Lewiston, Me., Mar. 13, 1914; s. Charles Hosea and Eleanor (Gray) T.; A.B., Brown U., 1935; B.D., Va. Theol. Sem., 1938, D.D., 1961; m. Maria Drane, Jan. 29, 1940; children—Gray, Robert Brent, Charles Adams. Ordained priest P.E. Ch., 1939; rector, Rocky Mt., N.C., 1942-53, Charlotte, N.C., 1953-56, Columbia, S.C., 1956-61; bishop of S.C., 1961—. Successively mem. standing com., exec. council and bd. exam. chaplains P.E. Diocese N.C., 1942-56; successively mem. standing com., exec. com. and bd. exam. chaplains P.E. Diocese S.C., 1956-61; del. Gen. Conv. P.E. Ch., 1949-52, 55, 58; mem. nat. exec. council P.E. Ch. U.S.A., 1970—. Vice pres. East Carolina council Boy Scouts Am., 1950-53. Chmn. trustees Porter Acad.; trustee Voorhees Coll., St. Mary's Sch., Raleigh, York Orphanage, Ch. Home Ladies; trustee, mem. exec. council Kanuga Conf. Center. Home: 1000 S Main St Summerville SC 29483 Office: PO Drawer 2127 Charleston SC 29403

TEMPLE, JAMES PITTS, physician; b. Sylacauga, Ala., June 28, 1927; s. William Frank and Mary Hannah (Pitts) T.; student Howard Coll., 1945, 47; B.S. in Pharmacy, Auburn U., 1950; postgrad. Huntingdon Coll., 1955; M.D., U. Ala., 1959; m. Alice Fay Shepherd, June 22, 1947; children—Linda Fay, James Pitts. Intern, Carroway Meth. Hosp., Birmingham, Ala., 1959-60; practice medicine, Alexander City, Ala., 1960—; chief staff Russell Hosp., Alexander City. Pres., Marble City Nursing Home, Sylacauga, 1966—, Temple Med. Clinic, Alexander City, 1968—. Served with USAAF, 1945-47. Fellow Am. Acad. Gen. Physicians; mem. Tallapoosa County Med. Soc. (pres. 1970-71), A.M.A., Beta Beta Beta, Rho Chi. Home: 916 Pineview Dr Alexander City AL 35010 Office: PO Box 268 Alexander City AL 35010

TEMPLE, KEITH ROE, cartoonist; b. Glasgow, Scotland, Feb. 11, 1899 (came to U.S. 1919, naturalized 1925); s. Edward and Lily (Roe) T.; J.D., Loyola U., New Orleans, 1927; m. Anice Phillips, Feb. 13, 1935. Reporter-artist The Times-Picayune, New Orleans, 1919-22, editorial cartoonist, 1923-67; artist New Orleans Item, 1922. Admitted to La. bar, 1927. Served with 2d Austrailian Bn., 1916-18. Decorated Victory medals (Gt. Britain, Australia). Mem. La. Bar Assn. Home: 1906 Napoleon Av New Orleans LA 70115

TEMPLE, LARRY EUGENE, lawyer; b. Plainview, Tex., Dec. 26, 1935; s. Herman and Grace (Ivey) T.; B.B.A., U. Tex., 1957, LL.B., 1959; m. Louann Atkins, Feb. 23, 1963; children—Laura Allison, John Lawrence. Admitted to Tex. bar, 1959; exec. asst. to Tex. Gov. John B. Connally, 1963-67; spl. counsel to Pres. U.S., 1967-69; pvt. practice law, Austin, Tex., 1969—. Chmn. bd. dirs. Chevy Chase Nat. Bank, Austin, 1972—. Mem. Tex. Constl. Revision Commn., 1967; mem. Nat. Democratic Policy Com., 1969-72; chmn. Tex. Dems. for Nixon, 1972. Chmn. adv. council to U. Tex. Sch. Social Work, Austin, 1972-73. Mem. Order of Coif, Phi Alpha Delta. Home: 2606 Escondido Cove Austin TX 78703 Office: PO Box 261 Austin TX 78767

TEMPLE, WINNIE LAVENIA, dietitian; b. Killeen, Tex.; d. John Thomas and Fannie (Dockray) Temple; B.S. in Nutrition, Tex. Technol. Coll., 1940; pvt. tutoring, Sinaloa, Mexico, 1931. Asst. dietitian Lubbock Gen. Hosp., 1933-40, chief dietitian, 1941-43; dietetic intern Grassland Hosp., 1941; dietitian Coll. Food Service, Tex. Technol. Coll., 1946; dir. dietetics Scott and White Hosp. and Clinic, Temple, Tex., 1946-70; head nutrition therapy and edn. VA Hosp., Waco, 1970—. Served to lt. M.C. AUS, 1943-46. Mem. Am., Tex. (state pres. 1965-66, state del. 1967-69, state exec. bd. 1955—), Central Tex. dietetic assns., State Nutrition Council, St. Mary Altar Soc., Am. Assn. U. Women, Cath. Daus. Am. Roman Catholic. Home: 2501 West Av Z Temple TX 76501 Office: VA Hosp Waco TX 76703

TEMPLETON, ARTHUR WILLIAM, aviation service co. exec.; b. Ashburn, Ga., Jan. 10, 1925; s. Ralph N. and Maggie (Story) T.; grad. tech. high sch.; m. Madie Pauline Wrenn, May 29, 1948; children—Betty Sue, Joanne, William Nolan, Charles David. Vice pres. Hangar One, Inc., Atlanta Airport, 1947—, also dir. Served with AUS, 1942-46. Lutheran. Rotarian. Club: Lakeshore Country. Home: 3314 S Bay St Jonesboro GA 30236 Office: PO Box 20718 AMF Atlanta GA 30320

TEMPLETON, CHARLES CLARK, chemist; b. Houston, Oct. 4, 1921; s. David H. and Miriam (Clark) T.; B.S. in Chemistry, La. Poly. Inst., 1942 M.S., U. Wis., 1947, Ph.D., 1948; m. Ann Hathaway Lewis, Dec. 23, 1944; children—Charles Clark, Robert Dudley, John Foster, Thomas Wofford. Instr. chemistry U. Mich., 1948-50; with exploration and prodn. research div. Shell Devel. Co., Houston, 1950—, research asso. in chemistry, 1963—. Mem.-at-large, dist. commr. Sam Houston Area council Boy Scouts Am., 1956—. Served to lt. USNR, 1942-46. Recipient Turner prize Electrochem. Soc., 1951. Mem. Am. Chem. Soc., Soc. Petroleum Engrs., Sigma Xi, Phi Lambda Upsilon, Phi Kappa Phi, Alpha Chi Sigma. Democrat. Presbyn. (elder). Mason. Contbr. articles to profl. lit. Home: 6119 Reamer St Houston TX 77036 Office: PO Box 481 Houston TX 77001

TENER, GEORGE EVANS, land developer; b. Edgeworth, Pa., May 5, 1917; s. Alexander Campbell and Marion (Clement) T.; B.A., Yale, 1940; student Fgn. Service Inst., 1951-52; m. Patricia Ann Buehner, Apr. 13, 1946 (div. Jan. 1962); children—Roberta Harrison (Mrs. James G. Kekam), Jenifer Evans; m. 2d, Anne Powell Potts Faber, Oct. 11, 1966. With State Dept. 1949-54, vice consul Am. Consulate Gen., Naples, Italy, 1949-51, 2d sec., sec. of embassy, Manila, P.I., 1952-54; security analyst J. & W. Seligman & Co., N.Y.C., 1956-63; dir. Aircraft Engine Parts, Inc.; now pres. Middleburg Lake, Inc. (Va.) Served from vol. to 1st lt. Am. Field Service, World War II. Mem. Orange County Hunt Assn. Democrat. Episcopalian. Clubs: University (N.Y.C.); Metropolitan (Washington); Potomac Valley Yale (past pres.). Home: Ardarra Middleburg VA 22117

TENNANT, BILLY GLENN, health ofcl.; b. Atmore, Ala., Aug. 15, 1918; s. Andrew and Mollie (Collins) T.; student pub. health U. Fla., 1947-48; m. Evelyn Givhan, June 2, 1938; children—Glenn Allen, Cynthia Ann, Susan Patricia. Finance officer WPA, Pensacola, Fla., 1941-42; dir. environmental health Escambia County Health Dept., Fla., 1946—. Adviser, Escambia County Plumbing and Gas Control Bds., 1953—. Mem. Escambia County Community Council, 1957-60; pres. State Fla. Sanitarians Registration Bd., 1960, sec., 1961—. Served with USNR, 1942-45. Recipient Good Govt. award Jr. C. of C., 1953; Outstanding Sanitarian award U.S., 1955, State Fla.,

1958-59. Mem. Fla. Assn. Sanitarians (pres. 1954-55), County Environmental Health Dirs. (chmn. 1963), Fla. Pub. Health Assn. (pres. 1971), Nat. Assn. Sanitarians. Mason (Shriner). Home: 4 Teakwood Dr Pensacola FL 32506 Office: 2251 N Palafox St Pensacola FL 32502

TENNANT, DAISY MAE ELMORE, poet; b. Senatobia, Miss., Aug. 27, 1910; d. John Charlie and Nora (Wimberly) Elmore; student U. Tex., 1930, Odessa (Tex.) Evening Coll., various periods, Rutherford Bus. Coll., 1967; m. Tracy W. Tennant, Feb. 17, 1934 (div. 1945); children—Nancy Jo (Mrs. James E. Stiles), Sharon Annora (Mrs Mitchell R. Gause). Part time sec. to chmn. bd., chief exec. officer, office mgr. Ormand Industries, Inc., Odessa, Tex., 1955-64, Dallas, 1964—; office mgr. Main Lafrentz & Co. Poetry workshop leader Odessa Evening Coll. 1957-59; poetry chm. Odessa Coll. Writer's Roundup, 1957-63; Spl. adv. com. services Women's dept. Tex. Bank and Trust Co., Dallas, 1966—; judge various poetry contests. Recipient numerous poetry awards, including Hadra Meml. award, 1965, Chapbook award, 1963, Globe Peace award, 1966, Lyric award, 1966, Grand Prix award Nat. Fedn. State Poetry Socs., 1966, Old South award, 1967, Hurley Meml. award, 1967, and many others. Mem. Poetry Soc. Am., Nat. Fedn. State Poetry Socs., Acad. Am. Poets (affiliate), Poetry Soc. Tex. (rec. sec. 1968—, chmn. Tex. Poet's Meml. Collection Baylor Coll., 1966—, program chmn. 1967—; treas. 1969), Writer's Workshop (pres. Odessa 1961-62), Shakespeare Club (v.p. Odessa Coll. 1962), Avalon World Arts Acad., Vachel Lindsay Assn., Compatriots Dallas. Author books of verse: Shifting Sands, 1954, Miss Fitts and Miss Cellany, 1960; contbr. poems to anthologies, including Anthology of American Poetry, 1959; Avalon Anthologies, 1962; National Federation Anthology, 1968; also to newspapers, mags., radio, television. Home: 7131 Casa Loma St Dallas TX 72514 Office: Bryan Tower Dallas TX 75201

TENNANT, HARRY LARENZE, editor; b. Seymour, Ia., Aug. 17, 1909; s. Frank E. and Myrtle (Tennant) Rouse; B.A., State U. Ia., 1933; postgrad. U. Cal. at Berkeley, 1936; m. Margaret Alice Free, Feb. 14, 1942. Reporter, S.W. Newspress, Los Angeles, 1934; pub. relations Shuberts Theatrical Co., Los Angeles, San Francisco, 1935-38; writer U.P.I, Omaha, Lincoln, Neb., Phila., 1940; city editor Ames (Ia.) Daily Tribune, 1941; corr. Chgo.-N.Y. Jours. of Commerce, Washington, 1945-50; editor Watson Publs., Washington, 1952—; U.S. editorial dir. Interavia Pubs., Geneva, 1955-69; editor Cahners Publs., Washington, 1965—; editor Biomed. News, Washington, 1971—. Served with AUS, 1942-45. Recipient Explorer I 10th Anniversary medal, 1969. Mem. Nat. Space Club, White House, State Dept. corrs. assns., Aviation and Space Writers Assn., Nat. Space Writers Assn., Aero Club. Club: Nat. Press. Contbr. articles to profl. jours. Home: 3705 Mill Creek Rd Haymarket VA 22069 Office: Nat Press Bldg Washington DC 20004

TEPPER, BERNARD, physician; b. Cordele, Ga., Nov. 15, 1923; s. William and Anna (Aronowitz) T.; B.S., Emory U., 1945, M.D., 1947; m. Marjorie Oxman, June 20, 1948; children—Eric F., Patricia Ann. Intern Beth Israel Hosp., Newark, 1947-48; resident in medicine Sinai Hosp., Balt., 1948-50, chief resident, 1950-51; practice medicine specializing in internal medicine, Chattanooga, 1953—; chief of medicine Meml. Hosp., Chattanooga, 1965-69, vice chief of staff, 1970-71, chief of staff, 1972-73. Chmn. Social Welfare com. Jewish Welfare Fedn., 1958-62, v.p., 1962-64; mem. alumni council Emory U., 1969—. Bd. dirs. Meml. Hosp., Chattanooga. Served with USNR, 1943-44, AUS, 1951-53. Mem. Chattanooga-Hamilton County Med. Soc. (mem. house dels. 1973), A.C.P., Am. Soc. Internal Medicine, N.Y. Acad. Sci., A.M.A., So., Tenn. med. assns., Chattanooga Soc. Internal Medicine (pres.). Home: 869 Belvoir Crest Dr Chattanooga TN 37412 Office: 511 McCallie St Chattanooga TN 37402

TEPPER, MORRIS, govt. ofcl.; b. Jerusalem, Palestine, Mar. 1, 1916 (came to U.S. 1922; naturalized 1926); s. Benjamin and Anna (Goldman) T.; B.A., Bklyn. Coll., 1936, M.A., 1938; Ph.D., Johns Hopkins, 1952; m. Sandra Levin; children—Andrew S., Bradford M. Research meteorologist U.S. Weather Bur., Washington, 1946-51. chief severe local storms research unit, 1951-59; dep. dir. Earth Observation programs, dir. meteorology NASA, Washington, 1959—; tchr. fluid mechanics, mem. phys. sci. com. U.S. Dept. Agr. Grad. Sch., 1952-59. Served with USAAF, 1943-46. Recipient Meissinger award Am. Meteorol. Soc., 1950, Distinguished Alumni award of honor Bklyn. Coll., 1961, NASA Exceptional Service medal, 1966, Spatiales Gold medal Centre National D'Etudes, 1972. Mem. Am. Meteorol. Soc., Am. Inst. Aeros. and Astronautics, Washington Acad. Scis. Home: 107 Bluff Terrace Silver Spring MD 20902 Office: 400 Maryland Av SW Washington DC 20546

TERMES, MIGUEL SALVADOR, banker; b. Havana, Cuba, Apr. 14, 1905; s. Salvador and Mercedes (Gonzalez) T.; B.B.A., Havana Bus. Sch., Cuba, 1922; extension courses and seminars on banking and finance U.S. univs.; m. Hortensia Cabrera, May 9, 1942; 1 dau., Silvia C. Pro-mgr. 1st Nat. City Bank of N.Y., Havana, 1919-49; chief supr. comml. banks Banco Nacional de Cuba, Havana, 1950-52; controller Banco Nunez, Havana, 1952-58, adminstrv. gen. mgr. Trust Co. of Cuba, Havana, 1958-60; v.p. Banco de Ponce (P.R.), comml. bank, 1961—. Mem. P.R. Bankers Assn. (pres. operation com. 1969, 71, 72), P.R. Clearing House Assn. (v.p. 1972-73). Roman Catholic. Club: Deportivo de Ponce (P.R.). Home: 12 2d St San Jorge Ponce PR 00731 Office: Banco de Ponce Plaza Degetau Ponce PR 00731

TERRELL, CHARLES OLIVER, physician; b. Quincy, Ill., Oct. 9, 1935; s. Hoydt Brooks and Ina Marie (Hamner) T.; B.S. in Medicine, U. Ill., 1956, M.D., 1960; m. Frances Ann Pfeiffer, Dec. 27, 1958; children—Charles Oliver, Gregory Allen, Susan Marie. Intern, Tampa (Fla.) Gen. Hosp., 1960-61; resident anesthesiology U. Tex., Galveston, 1963-65; anesthesiologist anesthesia dept. Med. Center Clinic, Pensacola, Fla., 1965; practice medicine specializing in anesthesiology, Pensacola, 1965—; chief anesthesia dept. Sacred Heart Hosp., Pensacola, 1969—. Served with USAF, 1961-63. Diplomate Am. Bd. Anesthesiology. Fellow Am. Coll. Anesthesiologists; mem. A.M.A., Fla., Escambia County med. socs., Am., Fla. socs. anesthesiologists, Internat. Anesthesia Research Soc. Methodist (ofcl. bd.). Home: 1221 Durnford St Pensacola FL 32503 Office: 1750 N Palafox St Pensacola FL 32501

TERRELL, DUNNING R., coll. adminstr.; b. Bowling Green, Fla., Sept. 17, 1923; s. John Wesley and Rosa (DeLoach) T.; student U. Miami, 1943-44; B.S., La. Poly. Inst., 1949; M.S., La. State U., 1952; m. Nita Lyvon Turley, Aug. 19, 1945; children—Dunning Michael, Judith Lynn. Athletic dir., coach Gibsland (La.) High Sch., 1949; athletic dir., coach Calhoun (La.) High Sch., 1949-55; athletic dir., coach Hardee High Sch., Wauchula, Fla., 1955-66; athletic dir., coach South Fla. Jr. Coll., Avon Park, 1966—. Served with USNR, 1943-46. Mem. Fla. Assn. Pub. Jr. Colls., A.A.H.P.E.R. Baptist (Sunday sch. tchr. 1947—, tng. union worker 1955—, deacon 1958—, mem. choir 1958—, mem. finance com. 1972—). Home: PO Box 743 Wauchula FL 33873 Office: South Fla Jr Coll Avon Park FL 33825

TERRELL, EDGAR ALLEN, JR., machinery mfg. co. exec.; b. Charlotte, N.C., July 19, 1920; s. Edgar Allen and Jane (Johnson) T.; B.S., The Citadel, 1941; m. Emmie Louise Jennings, Nov. 5, 1949; children—Robert Edgar, William Jennings, Jon Allen. Personnel mgr. Terrell Machine Co., Charlotte, 1941-52, plant mgr., 1952-66, exec. v.p., 1967-72, pres., 1972—, also dir.; dir. Charlotte br. N.C. Nat. Bank. Chmn. bd. trustees Central Piedmont Community Coll. Found. Served to maj. AUS, 1941-45. Decorated Bronze Star medal. Mem. Charlotte Engrs. Club, Am. Ordnance Assn. Republican. Episcopalian. Clubs: Charlotte Country, Charlotte City. Home: 2820 Rothwood Dr Charlotte NC 28211 Office: PO Box 928 8801 S Pineville Rd Charlotte NC 28201

TERRIS, BRUCE JEROME, lawyer; b. Detroit, Aug. 3, 1933; s. Charles Zachary and Ruth (Singer) T.; A.B. summa cum laude, Harvard, 1954, LL.B. magna cum laude, 1957; postgrad. Georgetown U., 1957-60; m. Shirley Duval, Aug. 1958; children—Elizabeth, Jessica, Robert. Admitted to D.C. bar; asst. to solicitor gen., Washington, 1958-65; asst. dir. Nat. Crime Commn., 1965-67; asst. to Vice Pres. U.S., 1967-68; cons. crime, poverty, legal service to poor, Washington, 1967; vis. prof. law Cath. U. Am., Washington, 1967-68; exec. dir. Anacostia Assistance Corp., 1968-69; cons. crime, poverty, law, housing, urban problems, 1969; sr. atty. Center for Law and Social Policy, 1969-70; now head pub. interest law firm. Chmn., Nat. Conf. on Law and Poverty, 1965; mem. campaign staff Robert Kennedy, 1968; chmn. Washington Dem. central com., 1968-72. Mem. Phi Beta Kappa. Contbr. articles to profl. jours. Home: 1855 Shepherd St NW Washington DC 20011

TERRY, GEORGE ALVIN, bank exec.; b. Oneida, Tenn., Dec. 19, 1926; s. William Claude and Paralee Long (Cowan) T.; student Auburn U., 1943, Ala. U., 1944; B.A., U. Tenn., 1950; m. Sarah Ellen Winn, June 9, 1950; children—Stephanie Rhea, Saralee Winn, Sereessa Louise, Rachel Cowan. Vice pres. Terry Motor Co., 1950-60, v.p., 1950—; part owner, mgr. Ben Franklin Store, Sparta, Tenn., 1960-73; v.p. First Trust and Savs. Bank, Oneida, 1963—. Mem. Nat. Com. for Support Pub. Schs., 1961-70; dir. fed. and state surplus property for State of Tenn., 1972—; active P.T.A., Hillbrook Camp, Knoxville, Tenn. Mem. Tenn. Ho. of Reps., 1957-59, Tenn. Senate, 1961-65. Bd. dirs. Mid-South Youth Camp, Henderson, Tenn. Served to 2d lt. AUS, 1943-46. Mem. Conservation League, Am. Legion, Nat. Trust for Historic Preservation, Smithsonian Assos., Lambda Chi Alpha. Republican. Mem. Ch. of Christ. Kiwanian. Home: Box 337 304 Highland Heights Dr Goodlettsville TN 37072

TERRY, JEAN RAYMOND, chem. co. exec.; b. Jerseyville, Ill., Feb. 27, 1924; s. Jesse Raymond and Rena Barbara (Parsell) T.; B.S., Fla. So. Coll., 1950; postgrad. Harvard Bus. Sch., 1970-71; m. Lois Harris, Nov. 22, 1950; children—Alison Parsell, Vance Stallings. Safety dir. W.R. Grace & Co., Bartow, Fla., 1950-59, asst. gen. mgrs., 1961-70, gen. mgr., 1970—; mgr. Terry Ladder Works, Bartow, 1959-61. Bd. dirs. Polk County Property Owners League, 1971-73. Served with USMCR, 1942-46. Registered profl. engr., Fla. Mem. Bartow C. of C. (v.p., 1972-73). Presbyn. Home: 1880 Hermosa St Bartow FL 33830 Office: Hwy #60 Bartow FL 33830

TERRY, JOHN JOSEPH, transp. leasing co. exec.; b. Chgo., July 29, 1937; s. Michael Parnell and Honore (Ryan) T.; B.S.C., Loyola U., Chgo., 1959; postgrad. U. Chgo., 1964, U. S.Fla., Terese Rose Mulkern, Dec. 31, 1960; children—Michael, Gregory, Deirdre. C.P.A., Touche Ross & Co., Chgo., 1959-65; v.p. finance Nat. City Lines, Inc., Denver, 1965-71; v.p. finance transp. div. Pepsico, Inc., Tulsa, 1971—, dir. several subsidiaries. Mem. U.S. Army N.G., 1960. C.P.A., Ill. Mem. Am. Inst. C.P.A.'s, Am. Trucking Assn. Home: 4718 S Lewis Ct Tulsa OK 74105 Office: 525 S Main St Tulsa OK 74151

TERRY, JOHN VERLIN, educator; b. Hagerstown, Ill., Oct. 8, 1920; s. William Bergen and Clester (Hopkins) T.; B.A., John Brown U., 1949; M.B.A., U. Ark., 1966; L.H.D., Linda Vista Bapt. Coll. and Sem. (San Diego), 1967; m. Fern Nadine Stradley, Feb. 14, 1942; children—John Mark, Joan Elizabeth, Luanne, Clay Thomas. Ordained to ministry Bapt. Ch., 1946; pastor chs. Tex., Ark., 1948-58; asst. to pres. Peterson Industries, Decatur, Ark., 1958-62; head bus. dept. John Brown U., Siloam Springs, Ark., 1966-70, head div. devel., 1971—. Guest lectr. U. Ark., 1966—; prin. firm John V. Terry & Assos., Siloam Springs, 1969—. Mem. exec. com., bd. dirs. Ark. Council Econ. Edn., 1968—; commr. Edn. Commn. U.S., 1969—; chmn. adv. council Small Bus. Adminstrn., Ark., 1970—. Served with AUS, 1942-44; PTO. Mem. Am., So., econ. assns., Southwestern Social Sci. Assn., Ark Coll. Tchrs. Econs., Bus. (pres. 1969), Modern Woodmen Am., Beta Gamma Sigma. Contbr. articles to profl. jours. Home: 1242 W Jefferson St PO Box 28 Siloam Springs AR 72761

TERRY, OLIN BRYAN, advt. agy. exec.; b. Mineral Wells, Tex., Dec. 15, 1929; s. Olin Asbury and Nancy (Bryan) T.; B.A., So. Methodist U., 1950; m. Dorothy Kale, Mar. 2, 1956; 1 son, Steven Wayne. Asst. program dir. sta. KIXL, Dallas, 1949-53; dir. sta. WFAA-TV, Dallas, 1954-56; prodn. mgr. sta. KFJZ-TV, Ft. Worth, 1957-60; operations mgr. sta. WJBK-TV, Detroit, 1960-61; radio/TV dir. Bloom Advt., Dallas, 1961-64; v.p. radio/TV Glenn Advt., Dallas, 1965-73, sr. v.p., 1973—. Office: 4700 Republic Bank Tower Dallas TX 75201

TERRY, REGINALD NATHANIEL, ednl. adminstr.; b. Norfolk, Va., Jan. 17, 1946; s. Moses and Hattie (Mack) T.; B.S., Norfolk State Coll., 1964-69; M.A., N.C. Central U., 1970-72; m. Joyce Juline Tankard, July 20, 1968; 1 son, Onuwa Djyata. Student asst. atty. U.S. Post Office, Norfolk, 1967, clk. U.S. PO., 1967-68; student tchr. John F. Kennedy High Sch., Suffolk, Va., 1968; tchr. W.E. Waters Jr. High Sch., Portsmouth, Va., 1969; counselor Norfolk City Sch., 1969; dir. athletics, dean men, coach, instr. phys. edn. and psychology Durham (N.C.) Coll., 1969-71, dean student affairs, 1971—. Pres. Groove Phi Groove Social Fellowship, Inc., Norfolk State Coll., 1967-68; South Atlantic regional dir. Nat. Little Coll. Athletic Assn., 1969-70, nat. bd. dirs., 1970-71, nat. pres., 1971-72. Mem. A.A.H.P.E.R., N.E.A., N.A.A.C.P., Am. Assn. for Higher Edn., Nat. Assn. Collegiate Dir. Athletics, Nat. Jr. Coll. Athletic Assn., Nat. Assn. Baseball Coaches Assn., Nat. Assn. Basketball Coaches U.S., Nat. Assn. Student Personnel Adminstrs., Kappa Alpha Psi. Home: 921 Windcrest Rd Durham NC 27707 Office: 3128 Fayetteville St Durham NC 27707

TERRY, WARREN BERGEN, bottling co. exec.; b. Patoka, Ill., Aug. 11, 1918; s. William Bergen and Clester (Hopkins) T.; student U. Tex., 1939-44; m. Frances LaVerne Schnasse, Feb. 14, 1938; children—Warren Bergen, Sumner Patrick, William Michael, Timothy Edward. With Am. Bottling Co., Corpus Christi, Tex., 1936-49; co-owner, mgr., v.p. Coca-Cola Bottling Co., San Jose, Cal., 1949-53, also dir.; co-owner, v.p., gen. mgr. Quaker State Bottling Co., Pitts., 1953-59; advt. bus., Boston, 1959-61; co-owner, pres., gen. mgr. Ft. Wayne Coca-Cola Bottling Co. (Ind.), 1961-68; pres., owner Blue Grass Coca-Cola Bottling Co., Inc., Lexington, Ky., 1963—, Mount Sterling, Richmond and Somerset, Ky., 1965—, Champaign Coca-Cola Bottling Co., Inc. (Ill.), 1973—; pres. Coca-Cola Bottling Co., Peoria, Inc. (Ill.), 1973—, Sprite-Flite Jets, Inc., Lincoln, Neb., 1973—; dir. First Security Nat. Bank, Lexington. Bd. dirs. Lexington unit Nat. Multiple Sclerosis Soc., 1967—; mem. adv. com. Lexington Jr. League Horse Show, 1972—. Bd. curators Transylvania U., 1969—. Fellow U. Ky., 1968—. Mem. Lexington C. of C. (dir. 1969—, mem. devel. com. 1970—), Newcomen Soc. Clubs: Le Club International (Ft. Lauderdale, Fla.); Country (Lexington). Home: Russell Cave Pike PO Box 11761 Lexington KY 40511 Office: 541 W Short St Lexington KY 40501

TERRY, WARREN BERGEN, JR., soft drink co. exec.; b. Corpus Christi, Tex., Feb. 26, 1939; s. Warren Bergen and Loma (Schulze) T.; B.A., U. Tex., 1962; postgrad. Harvard Bus. Sch., 1969, U. Ky., 1970; m. Dianne Smyth, June 7, 1962; children—Samuel Eric, Shawn Marie, Jenny Christine. Rep. Ft. Wayne Coca-Cola (Ind.), 1962-65; br. plant mgr. Blue Grass Coca-Cola, Danville, Ky., 1965, v.p., gen. mgr., Lexington, Ky., 1969—, also dir. Bd. dirs. Cardinal Hill Hosp., Lexington, Jr. Achievement of Blue Grass. Methodist. Home: 839 Glendover Rd Lexington KY 40502 Office: PO Box 1149 Lexington KY 40501

TESTERMAN, JACK DUANE, univ. adminstr.; b. Marietta, Okla., Dec. 13, 1933; s. Jesse D. and Lillie (Holt) T.; A.A., Murray Jr. Coll., 1953; B.A., Okla. State U., 1955, M.S., 1957; Ph.D., U. Tex., Austin, 1972; m. Lou Donaghe, Feb. 12, 1953; children—Kenny Ray, Sherri Gail, Jay Darrell; m. 2d, Edwyna Pace, Aug. 30, 1968. Research statistician Jersey Prodn. Research, Tulsa, 1957-62; statistician Phillips Petroleum, Bartlesville, Okla., 1962-63; prof. math., statistics U. Southwestern La., Lafayette, 1963—, registrar, 1965—; dir. institutional research, 1970-73, v.p. for university relations, 1973—. Mem. Am. Statis. Assn., Internat. Platform Assn., Math. Assn., La. Acad. Scis., Assn. Computing Machinery, Data Processing Mgmt. Assn., Sigma Xi, Pi Mu Epsilon, Phi Theta Kappa, Phi Delta Kappa, Omicron Delta Epsilon. Address: Box 940 Lafayette LA 70501

TETI, JOHN JOSHUA, mech. engr.; b. Winchester, Ky., June 24, 1914; s. Marco Antonio and Nannie (Bush) T.; B.S. in Mech. Engring., W.Va. U., 1940; m. Wilma Marie McDermott, June 7, 1941; children—John J. Jr., Michael J., Patrick A. Plant designer Island Creek Coal Co., Holden, W.Va., 1940-52; mgr. contract engring. coal plants div. Kanawha Mfg. Co., Charleston, W.Va., 1952-69; engring. dir. underground mine equipment design div. Kersey Mfg. Co., Bluefield, Va., 1969—. Served to maj. C.E., AUS, 1942-46; ETO. Mem. Am. Inst. Mining Engrs. Rotarian. Patentee in field. Home: Route 3 Box 134A Bluefield VA 24605 Office: PO Box 151 Bluefield VA 24605

TEUNISSON, JOHN HENRY, civil engr.; b. Monticello, Miss., Feb. 12, 1911; s. John Henry and Rilla (Reed) T.; B.S., Miss. State U., 1933; m. Beth Murphy, Nov. 29, 1946; 1 dau., Elizabeth (Beth) Ann. Project engr. Miss. State Hwy. Dept., Jackson, 1933-41, 45-49; city engr. City of Greenville, Miss., 1949—. Pres. S. Delta Econ. Devel. Dist., 1967—. Served to maj., C.E., AUS, 1941-45. Decorated Bronze Star medal with oak leaf cluster. Mem. Miss. Soc. Profl. Engrs. (past pres.), Am. Soc. C.E. (dir. mid south sect. 1953-54), Am. Pub. Works Assn. (Miss. rep. 1958-68), Alpha Tau Omega, Scabbord and Blade. Presbyn. (elder). Home: 1285 Kirk Circle Greenville MS 38701 Office: 340 Main St Greenville MS 38701

THAGARD, THOMAS WERTH, judge; b. Greenville, Ala., Apr. 10, 1902; s. James Lee and Minnie (Roach) T.; B.S., Auburn U., 1924; LL.B., Cumberland U., 1929; m. Beverly Preuit, July 5, 1934; children—Thomas Werth, Josephine Thagard. Admitted to Tenn. bar, 1929, Ala. bar, 1929; practiced in Greenville, 1929-52; judge Circuit Ct., 1952-69, presiding judge Ala. Ct. Civil Appeals, Montgomery, 1969-72; judge State of Ala., 1972—. Chmn. Legislative Council Ala., 1951. County solicitor, Butler County, Ala., 1931-46; mem. Ala. Ho. of Reps., 1946-50; mem. Ala. Senate, 1950-52. Bd. dirs. L.V. Stabler Meml. Hosp.; mem. Walter O. Parmer Scholarship Bd. Mem. Ala. Assn. Circuit Judges (pres.). Democrat. Methodist. Rotarian. Home: 411 Balaclava Dr Greenville AL 36037 Office: Box 462 Greenville AL 36037

THARP, HENRY ELLIOTT, theatre tech. dir., designer; b. Winfield, Kan., Apr. 23, 1932; s. Kenneth and Margaret (Murray) T.; B.A., B.S. in Edn., Emporia (Kan.) State Coll., 1958; M.A., U. Ill., 1959, postgrad., 1962-64. Asst. tech. dir. Hofstra U., Hempstead, N.Y., 1958-59; asst. costumer theatre dept. U. Ill. at Urbana, 1962-64; tech. dir. theatre U. Louisville, 1960-62, 64-66, Louisville Children's Theatre, 1966—. Bd. dirs. Louisville Youth Performing Arts Center, 1972—. Served with USAF, 1952-56. Mem. U.S. Inst. for Theatre Tech., Am. Theatre Assn., Children's Theatre Conf., Louisville Theatrical Assn., Nat. Trust for Historic Preservation, Theatre Hist. Soc., Am. Soc. for Theatre Research. Home: 1809 Eastern Pkwy Louisville KY 40204

THARPE, WILLIAM LEE, paper co. exec.; b. Chipigy, Fla., Aug. 11, 1919; s. Charles and Luvonia (Creamer) T; B.S., Western Ky. State U., 1948; m. Frances Arnold, Apr. 11, 1944; children—William Blalne, Arnold Craig. Gen. mgr. St. Joe Paper Co., Jacksonville, Fla., 1949-65; cons. St. Regis Paper Co., Atlanta, 1965; pres. Birmingham Packaging Corp. (Ala.), 1965—; Jackson Packaging Corp. (Miss.), 1965—. Served with USAAF, 1941-45. Mem. N.A.M., Ala. Assn. Industries, C. of C. Lion. Clubs: Chase Lake Country, The Club. Home: 325 Shenandoah Dr Birmingham AL 35226 Office: 1701 31st Pl SW Birmingham AL 35201

THAXTON, CARLTON JAMES, librarian; b. Tucson, May 23, 1935; s. Carl Newton and Daisy (Conard) T.; A.B., U. Ga., 1957; M.S., Fla. State U., 1958; m. Donna Jean Bradley, Aug. 25, 1957; children—James Bradley, Carl Stanton. Dir. Coastal Plain Regional Library, Tifton, Ga., 1958-60, 61-68, Kingsport (Tenn.) Pub. Library, 1960-61; dir. div. pub. library services Ga. State Dept. Edn., Atlanta, 1968—; instr. library sci. U. Ga. Sch. Edn. at off campus centers in Albany and Tifton, 1960—. Mem. Am., Ga., Southeastern library assns. Democrat. Methodist. Home: 3207 Oxbridge Way Lithonia GA 30058 Office: 156 Trinity Av SW Atlanta GA 30303

THAXTON, JAMES RALPH, ret. coll. pres.; b. Griffin, Ga., Mar. 23, 1901; s. James Reece and Frances Louise (Jones) T.; A.B., U. Ga., 1921, A.M., 1924; diploma, U. Grenoble, France, 1922; Ph.D., U. Ind., 1937; m. Helen Clarkson, Dec. 30, 1922; children—James Edwin, William Herlot. High sch. teacher, Griffin, 1921; instr. Romance langs. U. Ga., 1922, adjunct prof., 1923, asso. prof., 1926, prof., 1939, dean Co-ordinate Coll. (women's jr. coll., U. Ga.), 1941-43, prof. history, 1942-48; dir. admissions 1943-48; registrar, U. Ga., 1945-48; acting pres. Ga. State Woman's Coll., 1948-49, pres. Valdosta State Coll., 1949-66, pres. emeritus, 1966—; ednl. cons., 1966—. Dir. March of Dimes campaign 8th Congl. dist., 1950, co-dir., 1951. Mem., pres. Valdosta Bd. Edn.; dir. Ga. Sch. Bd. Assn. Mem. So. Hist. Assn., Am. Assn. Tchrs. Spanish, Am. Assn. Collegiate Registrars, Com. on Uniform Curriculum, Ga. Coll. Assn., Chmn. of Com. on Evaluation of Vet. Edn. So. U. Conf., Am. Assn. Teachers of Fren South Atlantic Modern Lang. Assn., Assn. Ga. Colls. (pres. 1953, v.p. 1954), Ga. Edn. Assn. (pres. coll. div. 1955), Pi Kappa Phi, Phi Beta Kappa, Phi Kappa Phi, Kappa Delta Pi, Alpha Chi, Phi Eta Sigma. Mem. Disciples of Christ Ch. Democrat. K.P., Kiwanian (lt. gov. Ga. dist.). Address: 305 E Jane St Valdosta GA 31601

THAYER, LLOYD YATES, supt. schs.; b. Troy, N.C., June 28, 1911; s. Whitmund Lafayette and Theodocia Ernest (Leach) T.; A.A., Wingate Jr. Coll., 1929; A.B., Wake Forest Coll., 1931, M.A., 1939; Ed.D., U. N.C., 1957; m. Georgia Griffin, Aug. 12, 1942. Tchr., Union County (N.C.) Pub. Schs., 1931-35, prin., 1935-37; prin. Wake

County (N.C.) Pub. Schs., 1937-39; prin. High Point (N.C.) Pub. Schs., 1939-59, dir. instrn, 1959-60, asst. supt. schs., 1960-68, asso. supt. schs., 1968—. Mem. N.C. Textbook Commn., 1957-61. Bd. dirs. Family Service Bur., Tb Assn.; trustee Wingate Coll., 1968—, chmn. scholarship com., 1968—. Recipient Distinguished Service award High Point Jr. C. of C., 1946, Kiwanis Internat., 1964, Certificate of Appreciation Nat. Assn. Secondary Sch. Prins., 1956. Mem. Am. Assn. Sch. Adminstrs., N.C. Edn. Assn. (pres. div. prins. 1955-56, state pres. 1961-62), Horace Mann League (N.C. pres. 1962-63), Phi Delta Kappa. Kiwanian (pres. High Point 1974). Home: 1601 Country Club Dr High Point NC 27260 Office: 900 English Rd High Point NC 27260

THEDE, MARION DRAUGHON (MRS. JOHN FREDERICK THEDE), writer, violinist, violist; b. Davis, Okla., Nov. 11, 1903; d. James and Lena (Erdwurm) Draughon; B.Mus., U. Okla., 1922; postgrad. Chgo. Mus. Coll., 1929, Murray Sch. Agr., 1923-24, Okla. City U., 1938-39; pvt. study violion with Leon Sametini, 1929, Max Fischel, 1929; m. John Frederick Thede, Mar. 12, 1960; children—Johnston Murray, Jr., James H. Buchanan. Violinist, violist Oklahoma City Symphony Orch., 1937-67, Oklahoma City Lyric Theatre, 1961-66, Tulsa Philharmonic, 1967-70; various radio, TV appearances; rec. artist; producer folk festivals. Music historian folk and ethnic music U.S., 1929—. Chmn. Okla. State folk music Okla. Fedn. Music Clubs, 1964—; organizer Okla. Folk Council, 1965; nat. chmn. Folk Music and Folk Archives for Nat. Fedn. Music Clubs, 1968-71, mem. nat. com., 1971—. Recipient Merit awards Nat. Fedn. Music Clubs, 1965—, Okla. Fedn. Music Clubs, 1968. Mem. Soc. Ethonomusicology, Internat. Musicol. Soc., Nat. Folk Festival Assn., Okla. Fiddlers' Assn. (organizer 1971), Am. Fedn. Musicians, Acad. Am. Educators, Mu Phi Epsilon, Alpha Gamma Delta. Democrat. Author: The Fiddle Book, 1967. Contbr. articles to mus. publs., Western mags. Address: 1824 NW 23d St Oklahoma City OK 73106

THEIS, PAUL ANTHONY, pub. relations exec.; b. Fort Wayne, Ind., Feb. 14, 1923; s. Albert Peter and Josephine Mary (Kinn) T.; B.A., Notre Dame U., 1948; B.S., Georgetown U., 1949; m. Nancy Wilbur, Aug. 21, 1971. Reporter, Fairchild Publs., 1951-53; Washington corr. Newsweek Mag., 1953-54; exec. asst. U.S. congressman, 1955-57; pub. relations dir. Nat. Republican Congl. Com., Washington, 1957—. Served with USAAF, 1943-45; ETO. Decorated Air medal with two clusters. Mem. Pub. Relations Soc. Am., Nat. Press Club, Congl. Flying Club. Club: Capitol Hill (bd. govs.) (Washington). Author: (with William L. Steponkus) All About Politics. Editor: (with Edmund L. Henshaw, Jr.) Who's Who in American Politics. Inventor: (with Donald M. Zahn) Hat in The Ring Game. Home: 38 Ivy St SE Washington DC 20003 Office: 300 New Jersey Av SE Washington DC 20003

THIEDEMAN, DOUGLAS JOHN, dentist; b. Lansing, Mich., Oct. 17, 1940; s. John Herman and Marjorie Irene (Finkhouse) T.; student Western Res. U., 1958-60; D.D.S., U. Mich., 1964; m. Bette Ann Johnson, June 15, 1963; children—Michelle Lynn, Patrick David. Pvt. practice dentistry, Boynton Beach, Fla., 1966-69; staff dentist VA Hosp., Salisbury, N.C., 1969—. Served to capt. AUS, 1964-66. Mem. Am. Dental Assn., Rowan County Dental Soc., Sigma Chi, Psi Omega. Republican. Episcopalian (lay reader 1968-69). Office: VA Hosp 1601 Brenner Av Salisbury NC 28144

THIELE, MILDRED DORCAS BRADFORD (MRS. WALTER H. THIELE), nurse; b. Walnut, Miss.; d. Blythe Thompson and Ellen (Davis) Bradford; diploma in nursing Bapt. Hosp., Memphis, 1938; student U. Mich., 1940; B.S., U. Wash., 1950; m. Walter H. Thiele, Apr. 15, 1968. Pub. health nurse, Miss., 1938-40; head nurse to chief nurse VA hosps., Jackson, Miss., Grand Island, Neb., N.Y.C., Chgo. Mpls., Lake City, Fla., Gainesville, Fla., 1945-69. Served to capt. U.S. Army Nurse Corps, Korean War. Recipient commendation Dir. VA Hosp., Grand Island, 1953. Mem. Am., Fla (chmn. membership com., 1968, dir.) nurses assns., Bus. and Profl. Womens Club Lake City (past pres.), Alpha Tau Delta. Republican. Episcopalian. Club: Ponte Vedra (Fla.) Address: 5347 Noble Circle S Jacksonville FL 32211

THIELE, WALTER HENRY, ret. hosp. adminstr., govt. ofcl.; b. Frankfort, Germany, Oct. 13, 1905 (came to U.S. 1906, naturalized 1916); s. Ludwig A. and Henrietta Maria (Braam) T.; student U. Mich., 1926-28; Ohio State U., 1928-29; U. Basie, 1929-30; M.D., U. Heidelberg, 1932; m. Anne P. Pfeffer, Sept. 17, 1934 (dec. June, 1965); 1 son, Richard Frederick; m. 2d, Mildred D. Bradford, 1968. Intern St. John's Hosp., Nyack (N.Y.) Hosp., 1933-34; resident St. Elizabeths Hosp., Washington, 1934-35; internist Lake City, Ia., also chief medicine Fayetteville (N.C.) VA Hosp., 1934-52; dir. Atlanta VA Hosp., 1952-60, Lake City VA Hosp., 1960-66, Clarksburg (W.Va.) VA Hosp., 1966-67. Served to col., M.C., AUS, 1942-47. Mem. Am. Hosp. Assn., A.M.A., Phi Gamma Delta. Episcopalian. Mason (K.T., Shriner), Rotarian. Home: 5347 Noble Circle S Jacksonville FL 32211

THIELMAN, DOROTHY LOUISE, library adminstr.; b. Paris, Tex., Sept. 12, 1919; d. Albert Birtes and Olga (Rutherford) Webb; A.A., Paris Jr. Coll., 1938; B.A., Tex. Woman's U., 1940; M.A., George Peabody Coll., 1947; m. Charles Eugene Thielman, June 1, 1947; 1 son, Albert Lee. Librarian Paris (Tex.) Jr. Coll., 1941, also dir. learning resources center, 1969—. Mem. Am., Tex. library assns., Tex. Jr. Coll. Tchrs. Assn., Tex. Assn. Ednl. Tech., Assn. Ednl. Communications and Tech., Beta Sigma Phi. Presbyn. Home: 275 28th St SE Paris TX 75460 Office: Paris Jr Coll Paris TX 75460

THIES, AUSTIN COLE, utility co. exec.; b. Charlotte, N.C., July 18, 1921; s. Oscar Julius and Blanche (Austin) T.; B.S. in Mech. Engring., Ga. Inst. Tech., 1943; m. Marilyn Joy Walker, June 26, 1945; children—Austin Cole, Robert Melvin, Marilyn Loone. With Duke Power Co., Charlotte, 1946—, mgr. steam prodn., 1963-65, asst. v.p., 1965-67, v.p. prodn. and operation, 1967-71, sr. v.p. prodn. and transmission, 1971—, also dir. Chmn. prodn. com., chmn. engring. and operating div. Southeastern Electric Exchange; chmn. tech. adv. com. Carolinas Va. Nuclear Power Assos. Served with USNR, 1943-46. Decorated Purple Heart. Mem. Edison Electric Inst., Charlotte C. of C., Am. Soc. M.E. (past chmn. Piedmont Carolina sect.), N.C. Soc. Engrs. (pres. 1973), Charlotte Engrs. Club, Pollution Control Assn., Am. Nuclear Soc., Nat. Rifle Assn. (life), Kappa Sigma. Presbyn. (elder). Rotarian (dir., pres. North Charlotte). Clubs: Cowans Ford Country, Charlotte Executives, Charlotte Ga. Institute Technology (past pres.), Charlotte Rifle and Pistol (past pres.), Charlotte City. Home: 2429 Red Fox Trail Charlotte NC 28211 Office: 422 S Church St Charlotte NC 28201

THIGPEN, GEORGE EDWARD, ednl. adminstr.; b. Huhtsville, Tex., May 16, 1916; s. John R. and Margaret P. (Burnett) T.; B.S., Sam Houston State Coll., 1939; M.E., U. Houston, 1951; m. Joyce Hines, June 18, 1942; children—George Michael, David Hines. Tchr. Grand Saline (Tex.) Ind. Sch. Dist., 1939-41; math. tchr. Tomball Ind. Sch. Dist., 1946-47; prin. high sch., Pearland, 1947-51; prin. El Campo (Tex.) Ind. Sch. Dist., 1951-53; supt., 1953—. Mem. legislative council U. Tex. Interscholastic League. Served with USNR, 1941-45. Mem. C. of C. (dir.), Am., Tex. assns. sch. adminstrs., Am. Legion, V.F.W. Mason. Lion. Home: 816 Av 1 El Campo TX 77437 Office: 700 W Norris El Campo TX 77437

THIGPEN, SILAS FORREST, JR., merchant, city ofcl.; b. Bay Springs, Miss., Jan. 2, 1907; s. Samuel F. and Julia C. (Arledge) T.; student La. State U., 1928; m. Tattie Mae Smith, Oct. 21, 1932; 1 dau., Tommiann (Mrs. Ronald V. Henagan). Mcht., farm supply, 1929—; mayor, Bay Springs, Miss., 1940-73. Mem. Miss. Geol. Survey Bd., 1956; v.p. exec. com. Miss. Municipal Assn., 1963-65, pres., 1965—. Bd. trustees sch. system, 1935-57. Recipient Gov.'s award, 1963; plaque for work as chmn. Geol. Survey Bd., 1970-71. Mem. Retail Mchts. Assn., Miss C. of C. (chmn. com. marine resources, chmn. com. study govtl. purchasing procedures), Nat. League Cities (com. govt. and administrn.), Miss. Seedmens Assn. Baptist. Mason, Rotarian. Address: Bay Springs MS 39422

THOBURN, ROBERT, dentist; b. Phila., Dec 23, 1909; s. Robert and Barbara (Tunstall) T.; student U. Fla., 1929-30; D.D.S., Atlanta-So Dental Coll. (name changed to Emory U. Dental Sch.), 1934; m. Marguerite Emma Steele, June 2, 1936; children—Robert and Thomas Edward (twins), Barbara Kaye (Mrs. Richard M. Davies), Donald William. Individual practice dentistry, Daytona Beach, Fla., 1934—; mem. dental staff Halifax Dist. Hosp. Fla. del. Am. Dental Assn., 1952-71; mem. Fla. Bd. Dentistry, 1958-69, also chmn., 1961, 66. Dir. South Peninsula Taxpayers Assn., 1953-55; commr. South Peninsula Zoning Bd., 1953-55; mem. South Peninsula Appeal Bd., 1957-58; area chmn. merit program fund drive Emory U., 1967-69. Recipient Distinguished Alumni award Emory U. Dental Sch., 1971. Fellow Am. Coll. Dentists (chmn. Fla. sect. 1959-60), Fla. Dental Assn. (hon.; historian 1946-60, pres. 1954-55); mem. Am. Dental Assn. (council on dental edn. 1966-72), Central Dist. Dental Soc. (legislative com.), Fla. Bd. Dentistry (certificate merit 1969), Volasia County Dental Soc. (life, past pres.), Am. Acad. History Dentistry (pres. 1958-59), Acad. 100 Sch. Dentistry of Fla., Am. Assn. Dental Examiners, Delta Sigma Delta, Lambda Chi Alpha. Presbyn. (deacon, elder). Mason. Author (with Helen S. Haines) 75 Years of Dentistry-History of the Florida State Dental Society, 1960. Home: 1908 S Peninsula Dr Daytona Beach FL 32018 Office: 227 Orange Av Daytona Beach FL 32014

THOM, JOHN LEROY, ednl. adminstr.; b. Walker, La., Aug. 24, 1920; s. Wesley and Eleze Bradford (Wire) T.; B.A., La. State U., 1940; M.A., Roosevelt U., 1966; m. Erin Elaine Hyde, Dec. 11, 1943; children—John Leroy, Jr., Juliet, Jennifer, Robert. Classified advt. mgr. Houma (La.) Daily Courier, 1940-41; midshipman U.S. Navy, 1941, advanced through grades to comdr., 1955, ret., 1966; dir. information services Pensacola (Fla.) Jr. Coll., 1966—, exec. dir. Alumni Assn., 1966—. Recipient Pensacola Jr. Coll. Alumni Assn. Service award, 1969. Mem. Fla. Pub. Relations Assn. (chpt. pres. 1968-69). Republican. Methodist. Club: Exchange (v.p. 1968-69) (Pensacola). Home: 4405 Scenic Hwy Pensacola FL 32504

THOMAN, CHARLES LEA, engring. co. exec., civil engr.; b. Birmingham, Ala., Aug. 27, 1929; s. Lewis Turner and Irma Lea (Hardaway) T.; B.C.E., Auburn U., 1957; m. Katherine Ross, Aug. 1, 1967; children—Barbara C., John Gano Winter, Katherine Alice. Cons. engr. J.B. Converse & Co., Mobile, Ala., 1957-58, Fromherz Engrs., New Orleans, 1964-65; v.p. Nat. Equities Land Developer, New Orleans, 1965-66; engr. Dunn Constrn. Co., Birmingham, Ala., 1966-68; pres. Thoman Engrs., Inc., Birmingham, 1968—. Chmn. Oak Mountain Devel. Co., 1972—. Bd. dirs. Horizon Med. Care, Inc., v.p., 1970—. Served to lt. USNR, 1950-55. Decorated Air medal. Registered profl. engr., La., Miss., Cal. Mem. Am. Soc. C.E., Nat. Soc. Profl. Engrs., La. Engring. Soc. Planned 5,000 acre Lake Forrest Devel., New Orleans, 1965. Home: 3545 Victoria Rd Birmingham AL 35223 Office: PO Box 729 Alabaster AL 35007

THOMAN, JOHN RICHARD, cons. engr.; b. Columbus, O., Aug. 11, 1920; s. Albert and Clara (Krug) T.; B.S., Case Inst. Tech., 1942; m. Alice Duvall, Feb. 10, 1945; children—Barbara E. (Mrs. T. H. Howell), John R., Patricia A., Daniel P. Commd. officer USPHS, 1944-67, chief san. engr. U.S. Operations Mission to Ethiopia, 1951-57, mem. Imperial Ethiopian Med. adv. bd. of Health, Div. of Water Supply & Pollution Control, Washington 1949-51, 57-59, regional program dir., Atlanta, 1959-64, dir. Southeast Water Lab., Athens, 1963-69; regional dir. Southeast region Fed. Water Quality Adminstrn., 1966-70; acting regional adminstr. Environmental Protection Agy., 1970-71; mgr. Engring.-Sci., Inc., Atlanta, 1971-73; project devel. cons. Black, Crow & Eidsness, Inc., Atlanta, 1973—. Lectr. civil engring. U. Fla., 1963-67; research asso. U. Ga., 1966-68. Diplomate Am. Acad. San. Engrs. Fellow Am. Soc. Civil Engrs.; mem. Am. Water Works Assn., Water Pollution Control Fedn., Am. Pub. Works Assn., A.A.A.S., Tau Beta Pi, Theta Tau, Sigma Alpha Epsilon. Registered profl. engr., D.C., Ga., Miss. Home: 1176 Hampton Hall Dr Atlanta GA 30319 Office: 1261 Spring St Atlanta GA 30309

THOMAS, ALAN TOY, chem. engr.; b. Louisville, May 15, 1921; s. M(oses) A(lan) and Ruth (Lacefield) T.; B. Chem. Engring., U. Louisville, 1943, M. Chem. Engring., 1947, Ph.D., 1964; m. Joycelyn Jane Markert, Mar. 18, 1945; children—Thomas Douglas, Tucker Craig. With Brown-Forman Distillers Corp., 1943—, apprentice supr., tech. supr., research engr. and statistician, research asso., project and devel. engr., asst. to the v.p. dir. prodn., 1943-64, asst. dir. prodn., 1964-73, asst. v.p., dir. prodn., 1973—. Lectr. math. U. Louisville, 1957-59, lectr. bus. mgmt., 1964—. Registered profl. engr., Ind. Fellow A.A.A.S.; mem. Am. Chem. Soc., Am. Mgmt. Assn., Am. Math. Soc., Operations Research Soc. Am., Distillers Feed Research Council, Inst. Mgmt. Sci., Am. Soc. Quality Control, Inst. Math. Statistics, N.Y. Acad. Sci., Phi Lambda Upsilon, Sigma Xi. Presbyn. Contbr. articles to profl. jours. Home: 708 Arbor Dr N Anchorage KY 40223 Office: PO Box 1080 Louisville KY 40201

THOMAS, MRS. CLARENCE A., investment bus. exec.; b. Cleburne, Tex., July 17, 1914; d. Martin Coppage II and Florence (Campbell) Sanders; student U. Tex. 1931-33, Tex. Woman's U., 1933-34, U. Tex. at Arlington 1948-49; m. E. O. Nichols, June 2, 1935 (div. Aug. 1947); 1 dau., Judy Nichols (Mrs. Gerald J. Roberts, Jr.); m. 2d, Clarence A. Thomas, Oct. 29, 1950. Tchr., therapeutic dietitian, also interior decorator Plainview (Tex.) Sanitarium, 1941-47; owner, dir. Food Services, Carters Cafeteria, Ft. Worth, 1950-60; asso. exec. investments Carter Investments, Fort Worth, 1950—; owner, operator ranch. Active A.R.C., Jr. League, Art Assn. Mem. Internat. Platform Assn., Kappa Alpha Theta. Mem. Ch. of Christ. Clubs: Kappa Alpha Theta Mothers, North Texas Riding. Home: 3601 Wooten Dr Fort Worth TX 76133 Office: 109 1/2 Main St Fort Worth TX 76102

THOMAS, COLIN GORDON, JR., educator, Iowa City, July 25, 1918; s. Colin G. and Eloise (Brainerd) T.; B.S., U. Chgo., 1940, M.D., 1943; m. Shirley Forbes, Sept. 14, 1946; children—Karen, Barbara, James G., John F. Intern, U. Ia. Hosp., 1943-44, resident in surgery, 1944-45, 47-50, asso. in surgery, 1950-51, asst. prof., 1951-52; asst. prof. surgery U. N.C., Chapel Hill, 1952-55, asso. prof., 1955-61, prof., 1961—, chmn. dept. surgery, 1966—; chief of surgery N.C. Meml. Hosp. Served with M.C. AUS, 1945-47. Diplomate Am. Bd. Surgery. Mem. A.M.A., A.C.S., Am. Thyroid Assn., Am. Assn. Cancer Research, Durham-Orange County Med. Soc., Soc. U. Surgeons, So. Soc. Clin. Research, Am. Surg. Assn., So. Surg. Soc., N.Y. Acad. Scis., Am. Assn. U. Profs., Halsted Soc., Soc. Exptl. Biology and Medicine, Soc. Internat. de chirurgie, Allen Whipple Surg. Soc., Womack Surg. Soc., Soc. Surg. Chairmen, Nat. Bd. Med. Examiners (Surgery), Soc. for Surgery Alimentary Tract, Alpha Omega Alpha. Editoral bd. Rev. Surgery. Contbr. numerous articles to med. jours. Home: Morgan Creek Rd Chapel Hill NC 27514 Office: NC Meml Hospital Chapel Hill NC 27514

THOMAS, DIANE, journalist. Motion picture-theatrical editor Atlanta Constitution, 1966-69; editorial asso. Atlanta Mag., 1970—. Home: 838 Virgil St NE Atlanta GA 30307 Office: 1104 Commerce Bldg Atlanta GA 30302

THOMAS, DONALD WAYNE, govt. ofcl.; b. Bradenton, Fla., Aug. 19, 1935; s. Jesse and Lydia Emma (Merkens) T.; B.Indsl. Engring., U. Fla., 1958; M.S., George Washington U., 1968. Staff indsl. engr. Robins AFB, Ga., 1959-60, 62-64, U.S. Naval Ordnance Plant, Macon, Ga., 1960-61, Brookley AFB, Ala., 1961-62, Hdqrs. USAF, Washington, 1964-67; staff indsl. engr., staff Office Sec. Navy, Office Civilian Manpower Mgmt., Washington, 1967-69, adminstrv. officer, 1969-72, spl. asst. for manpower utilization, 1972—. Recipient Superior Achievement award Dept. Navy, 1969. Registered profl. engr., Vt. Mem. Am. Inst. Indsl. Engrs. (sr.), Nat. Soc. Profl. Engrs., Am. Soc. for Pub. Adminstrn. Club: University (Washington). Home: 4101 Cathedral Av NW Washington DC 20016 Office: Civilian Manpower Mgmt Dept Navy Washington DC 20390

THOMAS, EDDIE FRANKLIN, aerospace exec.; b. Charlotte, N.C., Jan. 15, 1929; s. Eddie Franklin and Mary (Prince) T.; B.S. in Elec. Engring., N.C. State U., 1953; M.S., So. Methodist U., 1966; M.S., U. Dallas; m. Barbara Ann Henderson, Sept. 12, 1950; children—Deborah Ann, Victor Michael. Electronic engr. Bell Aerospace, Buffalo, N.Y., 1953, engring. tech. rep., 1954; design engr. Convair Aerospace div. Gen. Dynamics, Ft. Worth, Tex., 1957-59, sr. design engr., 1959-61, sr. aerosystems engr., 1961-63, project aerosystems engr., 1963, reliability design splst., 1963-64, reliability-maintainability and safety, 1964-68, chief reliability, maintainability and safety, 1968-70, chief quality engring., 1970-71, chief product assurance, 1971-73, mgr. product assurance, 1973—; instr. Tarrant County Jr. Coll., 1973—. Served with USAF, 1946-49. Registered profl. engr., Tex. Mem. Nat. Security Indsl. Assn. (ann. reliability and maintainability symposium mgmt. com.), Am. Soc. Quality Control, Am. Soc. Metals (engring. reliability com.), I.E.E.E., Nat. Mgmt. Assn. Contbr. articles to sci. jours. Home: 4629 Owendale Dr Fort Worth TX 76116 Office: Gen Dynamics PO Box 748 Fort Worth TX 76101

THOMAS, EMORY FLOYD, utility exec.; b. Savannah, Tenn., Feb. 28, 1916; s. John Streaty and Katherine T. (Morris) T.; student Southeastern La. U., 1936; B.S. in Mech. Engring., Miss. State U., 1939; m. Mildred Woodson Key, Sept. 5, 1944; children—Patricia, Emory Floyd, Jr., Katherine, Frederick. Jr. engr. Hales Bar Plants TVA, Guild, Tenn., 1939-43, mech. engr., Nashville Steam Plant, 1943-48, asst. supt., Wilson Steam Plant, Wilson Dam, Ala., 1948-49, Watts Bar Steam Plant, Spring City, Tenn., 1949-50, asst. supt., Johnsonville Steam Plant, New Johnsonville, Tenn., 1950-52, supt., 1952-60, asst. dir. div. Power Prodn., Chattanooga, 1960-62, dir. power prodn., Chattanooga, 1962—. Mem. USA-USSR Tech. Exchange Group, 1973. Mem. Am. Soc. M.E., Am. Nuclear Soc., Kappa Alpha, Pi Tau Sigma. Methodist (chmn. bd. 1968-71). Mason. Club: Exchange (Chattanooga). Home: 3589 Kings Rd Chattanooga TN 37416 Office: Room 716 Edney Bldg Chattanooga TN 37401

THOMAS, ERNEST SAWAYA, II, mfg. exec.; b. Jackson, Miss., Aug. 8, 1937; s. Ernest Sawaya and Esmer (Joseph) T.; B.S., U. Notre Dame, 1959; m. Margo Saba, July 28, 1962; children—Deborah Lynn, Sharon Marie, Ernest David, John Joseph. Sec. treas. Norman Shirtmakers, Inc., Jackson, 1960—. Served with AUS, 1959-60. Elk, Rotarian (dir.) Home: 4024 Eastwood Dr Jackson MS 39211 Office: I-55 South Byram Exit Jackson MS 39212

THOMAS, FAY MATHEW, bank ofcl.; b. Creston, Ia., July 9, 1890; s. Lincoln and Fannie Elizabeth (Brenanstal) T.; m. Willa Mae Adams, July 19, 1919; children—Clinton L., Jean-Faye. Mgr. Richmond (Va.) Cafeterias, Inc., 1920-22; gen. mgr. United Hotels Corp. Cafeterias, Toronto and Montreal, Can., 1922-25; mgr. Cavalier Hotel, Virginia Beach, Va., 1925-27; gen. mgr. Hotel Roanoke (Va.), 1927-29, Hotel Patrick Henry, 1929-32, Exchange Buffet Corp., N.Y.C., 1932-35; v.p., gen. mgr. Hotel Carter, Cleve., 1935-39; asst. to pres. Hotel New Yorker, N.Y.C., 1939-41; v.p., gen. mgr. Hotel Roosevelt, New Orleans, 1941-42, Hotel Book—Cadillac Detroit, 1942-52; v.p. for bus. devel. Broward Nat. Bank Ft. Lauderdale, Fla., 1955-72; dir. Key Biscayne Hotel and Villas, Miami, Jacksonville Coach Co., Jacksonville, Fla. Col. Civil Air Patrol, 1941-50, Mich. wing comdr., Midwest regional comdr., then mem. nat. exec. com.; dir. funding bd. Internat. Swimming Hall of Fame. Served with U.S. Army, World War I. Mem. Am. Legion, D.A.V., Mil. Order World Wars, Detroit Bd. Commerce, So., Ohio, Ft. Lauderdale (hon. life). Detroit hotel assns., Mich. Aeros. and Space Assn. (hon. life). Mason. Clubs: Detroit Athletic; Aero of Michigan (hon. life); Wings (N.Y.C.); Army and Navy (Washington); Ft. Lauderdale (Fla.) Lauderdale Yacht (dir.); Lago Mar Country. Home: 1750 E Las Olas Blvd Fort Lauderdale FL 33301

THOMAS, GEORGE, clergyman; b. Mavromati Messinias, Greece, Mar. 3, 1911; s. Thomas and Vangelia (Mistriotis) Thomopoulos; B.A., Holy Cross Theol. Sem., 1931. Ordained priest, Greek Orthodox Ch., 1942, named Archimandrite, 1953; instr., organizer Greek edn., Grand Island, Neb., 1934-37; asst. prin. Greek-Am. Koraes Sch., Chgo., 1938-41; priest St. John's Ch., Omaha, Grand Island and Lincoln, Neb., 1942-44, Sts. Constantine and Helen Ch., Milw., 1944-67, St. Nicholas, Tarpon Springs, Fla., 1967-68, Holy Trinity Ch., Tulsa, 1968—; spl. insp. Greek edn., Wis., 1952-54; adviser youth activities 2d dist. Chgo. area, 1962-64; co-chmn. Eccles. divorce hearings and ct. 2d dist., 1963-66. Mem. steering com. Greater Milw. Area on Religion and Race, 1963-67; chaplain VA, Wood, Wis., 1952-67; religious cons. psychology dept. Eastern Orthodox patients, Milw. County, 1950-67. Recipient hon. citizen award, Tarpon Springs, 1968. Mem. Greek Am. Progressive Assn., U.S. Mil. Chaplains Assn. Home: 611 W 15th St Tulsa OK 74119 Office: PO Box 2821 Tulsa OK 74101

THOMAS, GEORGE HERBERT, radio broadcasting co. exec.; b. Zwolle, La., Aug. 10, 1904; s. Henry Herbert and Evie George (Woods) T.; student N.W. State Coll., Natchitoches, La., 1926-27; m. Katherine Florence Porter, Dec. 7, 1933; 1 dau., Joan Katherine (Mrs. Charles W. Brakefield). Hotel mgr., Shreveport, La., Ft. Smith, Ark., Lafayette, La., 1929-44; owner, dir., radio sta. KVOL, Lafayette, 1935-64; owner, pres. radio sta. KANE, New Iberia, La., 1946—; pres. New Iberia Broadcasting Co.; dir. Evangeline Broadcasting Co. (Lafayette), 1935-64; charter mem. bd. dirs. Guaranty Bank & Trust Co. (Lafayette). Active A.R.C., chmn. Lafayette Parish chpt., 1958-60; mem. adv. bd. Salvation Army, Lafayette, 1948-60. Mem. Lafayette Recreation Commn., 1940-56, 57-62, chmn., 1948-56; bd. dirs. S.W. La. Rehab. Center, 1960-62; bd. dirs. Lafayette area Safety Council. Recipient Bronze Plaque award Lafayette City Ofcls., 1959; named King of S.W. La. Mardi Gras, Lafayette, 1960. Hon. life mem. Nat. Recreation Assn.; mem. Nat. La. (pres. 1952-53) assns.

broadcasters, Radio Broadcast Pioneers, Am., La. (pres. 1957-58, dir.), So., Western senior golf assns. C. of C., La. Hotel Assn. (pres. 1941-42). Methodist. Shriner. Club: Oakbourne Country (pres. 1969) (Lafayette). Home: 1228 Myrtle Pl Lafayette LA 70501 Office: 450 E Main New Iberia LA 70560

THOMAS, HARRY AMOS, banker; b. Lincoln, Neb., Apr. 27, 1929; s. Harry N. and Marie (Kinneberg) T.; B.A., Amherst Coll., 1951; M.B.A., Am. U., 1959; m. Margaret Roberts, May 14, 1955; children—Betsy C., Jeffrey N. Insp. Retail Credit Co., Washington, 1954-56; financial analyst SEC, Washington, 1956-58; asst. treas. Equitable Life Ins. Co., Washington, 1958-64; asst. v.p. Michelman & Hanf, N.Y.C., 1964-65; with investment officer United Va. Bank, Richmond, 1965-72; asst. v.p. Capitoline Investment Services, Richmond, 1973—. Served with AUS, 1952-54. Presbyn. (elder, deacon). Home: 708 West Drive Circle Richmond VA 23229 Office: 900 E Main St Richmond VA 23214

THOMAS, HARRY EMILE, theatre chain exec.; b. Monroe, La., May 22, 1920; s. Haleem and Hazel (Heider) T.; student La. State U., 1938-41; m. Yvonne Solomon, Jan. 26, 1947; children—H. Kinnon, H. Steve. With Gulf States Theatres, McComb, Miss., 1946-69, New Orleans, 1969—, asst. gen. mgr., 1950-69, sr. v.p., 1969—; dir. Bank McComb. Served with USAAF, 1943-46. Mem. Miss. (past sec.-treas., past pres., past chmn. bd.), La. (dir., treas.) theatre owners assns. Clubs: Exchange (Yazoo City and McComb), Variety Internat. (New Orleans). Home: 6737 Catina St New Orleans LA 70124 Office: 510 O'Keefe St New Orleans LA 70150

THOMAS, HENRY ASHTON, physician, assn. exec.; b. New Orleans, July 9, 1903; s. Joseph Andrew and May Stuart (Birss); B.S., Tulane U., 1925, M.D., 1929; m. Inez Buckingham, Apr. 10, 1933; children—Margaret Dewey, Edward Dewey, James, Linda (Mrs. Frank Bordelov), Harold. Resident eye, ear, nose and throat medicine Charity Hosp., New Orleans, 1929-33; practice medicine, New Orleans, 1933-65; sec.-treas. La. State Med. Soc., New Orleans, 1965—; mem. faculty La. State U., 1933-74, now asso. clin. prof. emeritus. Trustee Philip H. Jones Estate, La. Regional Med. Program; regent Uniformed Services Univ. Health Scis. Recipient citation U.S. govt. Diplomate Am. Bd. Otolaryngology. Mem. A.M.A., So. Med. Assn., La. State, Orleans Parish med. socs., Am. Acad. Facial Plastic and Reconstructive Surgery, Am. Acad. Ophthalmology and Otolaryngology. Home: 5968 Canal Blvd New Orleans LA 70124 Office: 1700 Josephine St New Orleans LA 70113

THOMAS, JAMES DAVID, educator; b. Holliday, Tex., July 20, 1910; s. William Albert and Angie Belle (Wisdom) T.; A.B., Abilene Christian Coll., 1943; M.A., So. Methodist U., 1944; Ph.D., U. Chgo., 1957; m. Mary Katherine Payne, Feb. 22, 1931; children—Deborah (dec.), Hannah (Mrs. Dwayne Kissick), John Paul. Asst. city mgr. Lubbock, Tex., 1939-42; minister Northwest Ch. Christ, Chgo., 1945-49; prof. Bible, Abilene (Tex.) Christian Coll., 1949—, head dept., 1970—, lectureship dir., 1952-70; pub., owner, mgr., editor Bibl. Research Press, Abilene, 1958—; staff writer Gospel Adv., 20th Century Christian. Mem. adv. council Am. Bible Soc. Mem. Am. Acad. Religion, S.W. Philos. Soc., Am. Sci. Affiliation, Evangelical Theol. Soc., Soc. Bibl. Lit. (sect. pres. 1967-68). Mem. College Church of Christ (elder 1969—). Kiwanian (dir. 1967-68, program dir. 1968). Mem. editorial bd. Restoration Quar. Home: 774 NE 15th St Abilene TX 79601

THOMAS, JAMES EDWARD, lawyer; b. Maryville, Tenn., Nov. 19, 1918; s. H. Charles and Mary Alice (Mills) T.; B.A., Maryville Coll., 1941; LL.B. cum laude, Harvard, 1948; m. Jean White, Aug. 15, 1941; 1 son, James Edward. Admitted to Ga. bar, 1950; practiced in Atlanta, 1948—; asso firm Alston, Miller & Gaines, 1948-53, partner, 1954—. Dir. Citizens and So. Bank of Sandy Springs (Ga.). Served to capt. AUS, World War II; maj. Res. ret. Decorated Bronze Star medal. Mem. Am., Ga., Atlanta bar assns. Republican. Episcopalian. Clubs: Atlanta Lawyers, Commerce, Cherokee Town Country. Home: 5 Westchester Sq So 238 15th St NE Atlanta GA 30309 Office: Citzens and So Nat Bank Bldg Atlanta GA 30303

THOMAS, JERRY, pres. Fla. senate; b. West Palm Beach, Fla., Apr. 30, 1929; s. Larry A. and Irene (Lee) T.; A.A., Palm Beach Jr. Coll., 1949; B.S., Fla. State U., 1951, postgrad., 1952; M.E., Fla. Atlantic U., 1968; m. Jeannie Hair, Nov. 21, 1951; children—Robbie, Larry, Kenny, Jerry, Cindy. Chmn. bd. dirs., pres. Gen. Financial Systems, Inc., Riviera Beach, Fla., 1963—; mem. Fla. Ho. of Reps., 1960-64; mem. Fla. Senate, 1964—, pres., 1970—. Chmn., pres. United Capital Corp., First Nat. Bank & Trust Co. of Lake Worth, Capital Leasing Corp.; chmn. bd. First Marine Bank & Trust Co. of Riviera Beach, First Nat. Bank & Trust Co. of Jupiter/Tequesta, First Comml. Bank of Live Oak, Marine Nat. Bank of Jacksonville, Congress Nat. Bank of Palm Springs, First Community Bank of Boca Raton, Peoples Bank of Gainesville, Tri-City Bank of Palm Beach Gardens; former adminstr. dir. Fla. Securities Commn.; Palm Beach chmn. U.S. Savs. Bond Div., 1961—. Bd. dirs. Children's Home Soc. of Fla., South Fla. Fair and Exposition. Served with USMCR, 1952-54, also USNR. Mem. Greater West Palm Beach, No. Palm Beach County chambers commerce, Am. Legion. Presbyn. (elder 1963-66). Home: Route 1 Box 19960 Jupiter FL 33458 Office: First Marine Bank & Trust Co Box 9787 Riviera Beach FL 33404

THOMAS, JERRY PAUL, educator; b. Birmingham, Sept. 22, 1943; s. John Leon and Lola (Logan) T.; B.S., U. Montevallo, 1965; M.S., U. Ala., 1969, Ed.S. in Biology, 1971, Ph.D. in Biology, 1973; m. Susan Elizabeth Newbold, Jan. 25, 1969; children—Collin Newbold, Scott Logan. Mem. faculty, research staff U. Ala., Tuscaloosa, 1967-73, research asst., 1968, 71, supr. gen. biology labs., 1972-73; asst. prof. dept. biology Palm Beach Atlantic Coll., West Palm Beach, Fla., 1973—. Recipient research award Assn. Southeastern Biologists, 1971; Sigma Xi grantee, 1972, recipient research award, 1973. Mem. Am. Bot. Soc., Assn. Southeastern Biologists, Am. Soc. Plant Physiologists, Sigma Xi. Baptist. Home: El Pomar Trace West Palm Beach FL 33406 Office: 1101 S Olive Av West Palm Beach FL 33401

THOMAS, JOE, educator; b. Panama, Okla., Aug. 20, 1931; s. Earl David and Anna (Hollycross) T.; B.A., Northeastern State Coll., 1952; M.Ed., U. Okla., 1962; m. Patricia Lee Tobey, Aug. 9, 1952; children—David, Christina, Margaret, Charles. Coach Spiro (Okla.) High Sch., 1952-55; coach Shawnee (Okla.) High Sch., 1955-56; coach Stigler (Okla.) High Sch., 1956-62; athletic dir., chmn. liberal arts div. Eastern Okla. State Coll., 1962—; football, basketball ofcl., high sch. and coll. games, 1952—. Pres. Latimer County Recreation Assn., 1972—. Mem. Okla. Ofcls. Assn. (dir. 1970-74), Wilburton (Okla.) C. of C., Nat. Intramural Assn., Higher Edn. Alumni Assn., N.G. Assn. of U.S., 45th Infantry Div. Assn. Baptist (deacon 1959). Mason (32 deg.). Author: Eastern Oklahoma State College Orientation Handbook, 1972. Home: Box 1126 Eastern Oklahoma State Coll Wilburton OK 74578 Office: Box 1126 Eastern Oklahoma State Coll Wilburton OK 74578

THOMAS, JOHN CAMPBELL, lawyer; b. Detroit, Feb. 28, 1928; s. William John and Belle Bernetta (Thompson) T.; B.B.A., U. Mich., 1950, J.D., 1953; m. Margaret Yvonne Stults, Sept. 1, 1951; children—John Campbell, Jeffrey F., Laurel A., Lynda D., Lisa B. Admitted to Mich. bar, 1954, Fla. bar, 1968, mem. legal staff Chrysler Corp., Detroit, 1953-60; trust officer Detroit Bank & Trust Co., 1960-66; v.p., sr. trust officer 1st Bank & Trust Co., Boca Raton, Fla., 1966-71; practiced in Boca Raton, 1971—. Chmn. bd., pres. J. Thomas Boca Raton, Inc. Lectr. Fla. Atlantic U., Boca Raton, 1968—. Served with AUS, World War II. Mem. Am., Fla., Mich., Supreme Ct. bar assns., Boca Raton C. of C., Chi Phi. Presbyn. Clubs: Boca Raton; University of Mich. (Ann Arbor). Home: 1149 A1A Opal Towers Hillsboro Beach FL 33062 Office: Amdur Bldg 40 SE 1st Av Boca Raton FL 33432

THOMAS, JOHN HANSFORD, JR., physician; b. Greenville, Va., June 19, 1909; s. John Hansford and Ella Blanche (Burnett) T.; student Washington and Lee U., 1927-30; M.D., U. Va., 1934; m. Mary Johnston Lasley, June 19, 1941; children—Gail (Mrs. Richard Charles Zug), Sarah (Mrs. DuPont Guerry IV), Mary Lasley, John Hansford III, Thomas Randall. Intern, Balt. City Hosps., 1934-35; practice medicine specializing in family medicine, Greenville, 1936—; mem. staff Kings Daus. Hosp., Staunton, Va. Mem. adv. bd. Va. Nat. Bank. Mem. U. Va. Devel. Fund Com., 1966—. Chmn. local com. Democratic party, 1971. Mem. Am., World, So., Va. med. assns., Augusta County Med. Soc. (pres. 1944), Sigma Alpha Epsilon, Phi Beta Pi. Presbyn. (trustee). Clubs: Staunton Cotillion; Windmill Point (Va.) Yacht; Irvington, Cheasapeake (Irvington, Va.); Circus Saints and Sinners (Staunton). Address: Meddock Greenville VA 24440

THOMAS, JOHN PELHAM, educator; b. Ashby, Ala., Apr. 18, 1922; s. John Pelham and Rebecca Jane (Hudson) T.; B.S., Auburn U., 1946; M.A.T., U. Va., 1961; Ph.D., U. S.C., 1965; m. Beulah Marie Hawks, Sept. 23, 1945; children—Sarah Jane, Susan Marie, Nancy Lynn, Mary Elizabeth, Martha Louise, James Paul. With Agrl. Extension Service, Auburn U., 1946-52; farmer, Opp, Ala., 1953-59; tchr. Covington County (Ala.) Schs., 1955-59, Tuscaloosa City Schs., 1959-60; mem. faculty U. N.C., Charlotte, 1964-67; prof., head math. dept. Western Carolina U., Cullowhee, N.C., 1967—. Served with USMCR, 1943-45. Baptist. Home: Route 67 Box 35B Cullowhee NC 28723

THOMAS, JOHN RUSSELL, bank exec.; b. Alexander City, Ala., Aug. 1, 1937; s. Russell and Crawford (Anthony) T.; B.S. in Textile Engring., Ga. Inst. Tech., 1960; postgrad. U. Ala., 1961; m. Francis Tate Jordan, Dec. 8, 1962; children—Russell L., John Jordan. Textile engr. Russell Mills, Inc., Alexander City, 1964-70, v.p., 1970-73; vice chmn. First Nat. Bank, Alexander City, 1973—; dir. 1st Nat. Bank, Alexander City, Cotton States Life, Tuscaloosa, Ala., Russell Lands, Inc., Alexander City. Chmn. Bd. Edn. Alexander City, 1970—. Bd. dirs. Central Ala. Rehab. Center, Montgomery. Served to 1st lt. AUS, 1962-64. Baptist. (deacon). Clubs: The Club (Birmingham); Willow Point Golf and Country (Alexander City). Home: 107 N Central Av Alexander City AL 35010 Office: PO Drawer 272 Alexander City AL 35010

THOMAS, JOHN THEKKEMANNIL, librarian; b. Chetheckal, India, Mar. 31, 1933; s. Mathew Thekkemannil and Annamma (Thekkemannil Chacko) John.; B.A., U. Travancore, 1955; nat. diploma in commerce All India Council for Tech. Edn., 1959; LL.B., U. Bombay, 1967; M.L.S., U. Western Ont. Came to U.S., 1970. Accountant, cost investigator Govt. India Civil Service, Bombay, 1956-67; jr. accountant Marcus & Co., chartered accountants, London, Ont., Can., 1958; library asst. U. Western Ont., Can., 1969; asst. catalog librarian N.C. Agrl. and Tech. State U., Greensboro, 1970, head reference dept., 1971—. Mem. Am., Canadian, South Eastern Regional, N.C. library assns., India Cultural and Ednl. Assn. (hon. sec. 1971-73), Am. Assn. Law Libraries, Chartered Inst. Secs. and Adminstrs. (Eng.). Clubs: Guilford Library (Greensboro). Contbr. articles to profl. publs. Editor: Library Booklist, Library Newsletter, N.C. Agrl. and Tech. State U., 1971—. Home: 211 N Cedar St Greensboro NC 27401

THOMAS, JULIAN BALDWIN, pub. utilities cons.; b. San Marcos, Tex., July 19, 1891; s. John Adelphus and Nellie Rebecca (Julian) T.; B.S., Tex. A. and M. Coll., 1911, M.E., 1931; m. Beatrix Hemkens, Nov. 20, 1920 (dec.); 1 dau., Nellie Frances. Apprentice, Greenville Foundry & Machine Co., 1907-08; student engr. Houston Cotton Oil Co., 1911-12; supt. Municipal Electric Plant Greenville, Tex., 1912; supt. Tex. Power & Light Co., 1912-17, engr., chief engr., 1919-30; v.p. Tex. Electric Service Co., Ft. Worth, 1930-38, dir., 1933-63, exec. v.p., 1938-40, pres., gen. mgr., 1941-61, chmn. bd., 1961-63; engring. cons., 1963—; v.p., dir. Tex. Utilities Co., Ft. Worth, 1945-61; dir. Old Ocean Fuel Co., pres., 1959-61. Cons. AID, Taiwan, Korea, Philippines, 1963-66. Mem. Tex. Bd. Registration Profl. Engrs., 1941-51, chmn., 1949. Chmn., Tex. Gov.'s Com. on Water Conservation, 52-57, Tex. Research League, 1958. Bd. dirs. YMCA; bd. dirs. Tex. Atomic Energy Research Found., 1957-62, pres., 1958-59; trustee Mary Couts Burnett Trust, 1948—, chmn., 1965—. Served to capt. USAAF, 1917-19. Fellow I.E.E.E., Am. Soc. M.E.; mem. Tex. A. and M. Ex-Students Assn. (past pres. Tex.), W.Tex. C. of C. (past dir.), Edison Electric Inst. (past dir.), Tau Beta Pi. Episcopalian. Clubs: Fort Worth, Steeplechase, River Crest Country, Colonial Country, Exchange (Ft. Worth). Home: 2222 Huntington Lane Fort Worth TX 76110 Office: First Nat Bank Bldg Fort Worth TX 76102

THOMAS, KENNETH WILBUR, wholesale trade exec.; b. Cainesville, Mo., June 12, 1922; s. William Perry and Amy C. (Reeder) T.; B.S. in Mech. Engring., Ia. State Coll., 1950—; m. Barbara Jean Dial, Feb. 16, 1947; children—Dwight, Sidney, Christina. Field engr. Square D Co., Rockford, Ill., 1950-58, dist. mgr., Moline, Ill., 1958-62, Tulsa, 1962-71; pres. Asso. Engring. & Supply Co., Tulsa, 1971—; dir. Three Forks Elec. Co., Muskogee, Okla. Pres. Handicapped Opportunity Workshop, Tulsa, 1969-70, chmn. bd., 1970-71. Served with USAAF, 1943-46. Decorated Air medal with three clusters, D.F.C. Registered profl. engr., Okla. Republican. Mem. Christian Ch. (deacon 1964-70). Club: Sertoma (pres. Tulsa Southside 1967-68). Home: 3725 S 93d E Av Tulsa OK 74145 Office: 208 S Norfolk St Tulsa OK 74101

THOMAS, LEE BALDWIN, mfg. exec.; b. Alma, Neb., Sept. 17, 1900; s. Rees and Fannie (Baldwin) T.; B.B.A., U. Wash., 1923; m. Margaret Thomas, 1924; children—Lee Baldwin, Margaret Ellen (Mrs. Wallace Dunbar), Susan Jane (Mrs. A. Scott Hamilton). Advt. mgr. Ernst Hardware Co., Seattle, 1923-24, sales mgr., 1926-29; buyer R. H. Macy Co., N.Y.C., 1924-25; dir. home goods merchandising Butler Bros., Chgo., 1929-41; pres. Ekco Products Co., Chgo., 1941-47, Am. Elevator & Machine Co., Louisville, 1947-48; chmn. bd. Vermont Am. Corp. and subsidiaries, Am. Saw & Tool Co., Louisville, Vt. Tap & Die Co., Lydonville, Vt., Multi Metals, Inc., Louisville, DeLuxe Saw & Tool Co., Louisville and High Point, N.C.; chmn. exec. com. Thomas Industries, Inc. and subsidiaries; owner Honey Locust Valley Farms, Cloverport, Ky., Thomas Shaker Farms, South Union, Ky. Bd. dirs. Honey Locust Found., Louisville. Mem. N.A.M. Clubs: Skokie County (Glencoe, Ill.); Owl Creek Country (Anchorage, Ky.); Harmony Landing Country (Prospect, Ky.); Pendennis (Louisville); Union League, Mid-day (Chgo.); Lake Region Country (Winter Heaven, Fla.); Mountain Lake (Lake Wales, Fla.). Home: Evergreen Rd Anchorage KY 40223 Office: 207 E Broadway Louisville KY 40202

THOMAS, NOAH OSCAR, JR., real estate co. exec.; b. Center, Tex., Dec. 10, 1907; s. Noah Oscar and Mary (Beckham) T.; A.B., Baylor U., 1930. Vice pres. Travis-Edwards, Inc., Shreveport, 1956—. Pres., Shreveport Civic Opera Assn., 1958-; mem. Shreveport Met. Planning Commn., 1955-56, Downtown Devel. Commn., 1966-69. Bd. dirs. Schumpert Meml. Hosp., Shreveport. Served with USNR, 1942-46. Recipient Outstanding Citizenship award City Council Shreveport, 1955. Mem. Shreveport C. of C., Order Cincinnati, S.A.R. Clubs: Shreveport; Tulsa. Home: 3806 Highland Av Shreveport LA 71106 Office: Beck Bldg Shreveport LA 71101

THOMAS, PAT FRANKLIN, Democratic state chmn.; b. Quincy, Fla., Nov. 21, 1933; s. Pat and Verna (Peacock) T.; grad. U. Fla.; m. Mary Ann Jolley; children—Anne Jolley, John Pat. Service rep. Fla. Farm Bur., 1960-62; owner Gen. Ins. Agy., 1962—; Democratic state committeeman, Gadsden County, Fla., 1966—; chmn. Dem. Exec. Com., Fla., 1966—, organizing chmn. delegation Dem. Conv., Chgo., 1968. Mem. Fla. Ho. of Reps., 1972—. Served with AUS, Korean War. Named one of five Outstanding Man of Fla., Fla. Jr. C. of C., 1968. Mem. Fla., Gadsden County assns. ins. agts., Quincy Jr. C. of C. (one of Five Outstanding Young Men 1967), Quincy C. of C. (mgr.), Am. Legion, Am. Cancer Soc., Blue Key, Alpha Gamma Rho. Presbyn. Mason (32 deg., Shriner), Rotarian. Club: Sawano Country (Quincy). Home: Hwy 90 Quincy FL 32351 Office: PO Box 629 Quincy FL 32351

THOMAS, REYNOLD, JR., elec. engr.; b. Burlington, N.J., May 17, 1930; s. Reynold and Alice (Scott) T.; B.S., U.S. Mil. Acad., 1952; M.S. in Elec. Engring., Purdue U., 1960; m. Nancy Lou Bushnell, June 3, 1952; children—Leslie C., Linda W., Melissa A., Reynold III. Commd. 2d lt. U.S. Army, 1952, advanced through grades to maj.; ret., 1966; digital switching systems engr. Def. Communications Agy., Washington, 1963-66, ADP systems engr., 1966-70, design engr., chief devel. div. office MEECN system engring., 1970—; cons. NEO Corp., 1964-67. Pres. Fairfax County (Va.) Fedn. Citizens Assns., 1971-72; program commnr. Soccer Vienna Youth Inc., 1970-73; mem. Fairfax County Fair Housing Bd., 1969-73, vice chmn. 1970, 74; mem. Zoning Ordinance Study Commn., Fairfax County, 1970-73. Mem. I.E.E.E. (sr.), Alpha Phi Omega. Episcopalian (lay reader 1970—). Home: 2546 Villanova Ct Vienna VA 22180 Office: Defense Communications Agy Washington DC 20305

THOMAS, ROY WELDON, elec. contractor; b. nr. Mt. Airy, N.C., Jan. 10, 1929; s. John Samuel and Annie (Mathis) T.; grad. high sch.; m. Mary Magdalene Blackard, Dec. 23, 1950; 1 dau., Mary Lynn. With Floyd S. Pike Elec. Contractor, Inc., Mt. Airy, 1947—, v.p., 1963—, also dir.; dir. Mt. Airy Hosiery Mill, Mt. Airy Aviation. Served with AUS, 1946-47. Mason. Club: Mount Airy Country. Home: 513 Ridgeway Mount Airy NC 27030 Office: 418 Smith St Mount Airy NC 27030

THOMAS, RUBLE ANDERSON, utility co. exec.; b. Birmingham, Ala., July 14, 1921; s. James A. and Grace (Smith) T.; B.S. in Mech. Engring., Ga. Inst. Tech., 1947, B.S. in E.E., 1948, M.S. in E.E., 1949; student Oak Ridge Sch. Reactor Tech., 1953-54; m. Mary Jo Bass, Feb. 16, 1941; children—James, Janice (Mrs. Peter M. Graffeo). Electric design engr. Commonwealth & So. Corp., Birmingham, 1948; with So. Services Inc., Birmingham, Ala., 1949—, mgr. nuclear power, 1959-65, asst. to pres., 1965-66, v.p., 1966—. Mem. So. Interstate Nuclear Bd., 1966-73; dir. Power Reactor Devel. Co., Detroit, 1968-73; trustee High Temperature Reactor Devel. Assos., 1967-73. Served to 1st lt. AUS, 1943-44, USAAF, 1944-46. Registered profl. engr., Ala., Fla., Ga., Mich., Miss. Mem. Am. Nuclear Soc., Am. Soc. M.E., Edison Electric Inst., Electric Power Research Inst., I.E.E.E. Kiwanian. Club: Downtown. Home: 713 Mountain Dr Birmingham AL 35206 Office: PO Box 2625 Birmingham AL 35202

THOMAS, WARREN MILNER, mech. engr.; b. La Jolla, Cal., Sept. 2, 1920; s. Warren Wilkinson and Laura (Milner) T.; B.S., U. Kan., 1942; m. Amy Lee Hill, Apr. 8, 1944; children—David Warren, Gregory Lee, Nancy Ruth. With Phillips Petroleum Co., Bartlesville, Okla., 1942—, mgr. mech. design br., engring. dept., 1956—. Dir. 66 Fed. Credit Union, 1956-65; pres. P.T.A., Bartlesville, 1964-65. Precinct chmn. Republican Party, 1950-57. Registered profl. engr., Okla. Mem. Am. Soc. M.E., Am. Nat. Standards Inst. (com., group chmn. 1965—), Nat., Okla. (chpt. v.p. 1960) socs. profl. engrs., Am. Petroleum Inst. (sec. piping subcom. 1965—), Tau Beta Pi, Sigma Tau, Pi Tau Sigma, Delta Tau Delta. Methodist (ofcl. bd. 1965-69). Lion. Club: Hillcrest Country (Bartlesville). Home: 1455 Valley Rd Bartlesville OK 74003 Office: Phillips Petroleum Co Bartlesville OK 74003

THOMAS, WAYNE ELVIN, lawyer; b. Silverton, Tex., Feb. 16, 1928; s. Zerrell and Bertha (Edwards) T.; B.A., West Tex. State U., 1947; LL.B., U. Tex., 1951; m. Mary Hodges, Sept. 26, 1947; children—David Wayne, Shyla, Trent Hodges. Admitted to Tex. bar, 1951; partner firm Thomas and Burdett, Hereford, Tex., 1951—. Dist. committeeman Boy Scouts of Am., 1954-56; chmn. United Fund, 1963-64; chmn. Indsl. Devel. Com., 1967-68. Pres., Deaf Smith County Hosp., 1957, dir., 1954-67; pres. West Tex. Ex-Students, Inc., 1966, dir., 1963-67; mem., chmn. coordinating bd. Tex. Coll. and Univ. Systems, 1969—. Served to 1st lt. USAF, 1951-52. Fellow Am. Coll. Probate Counsel, Tex. Bar Found.; mem. Tex. State Bar, Am. Bar Assn., Am. Judicature Soc., Deaf Smith County C. of C. (pres. 1965), Order of Coif, Delta Theta Phi (pres. 1950-51). Baptist. Contbr. articles in field to profl. jours. Home: 206 Sunset Dr Hereford TX 79045 Office: 116 S 25 Mile Av Hereford TX 79045

THOMAS, WILLIAM FRED, telephone co. exec.; b. Thomston, Ala., Oct. 31, 1913; s. Earl Gaines and Stella (Holt) T.; B.S., Auburn U., 1936; m. Dorothy Perkins, Oct. 17, 1942; children—Dorothy E., Frances Susan. Elec. engr. So. Bell Telephone Co., Columbus, Ga., 1937-47; pres. Elmore Coosa Telephone Co., Eclectic, Ala., 1947—. Cons. engr. Engring. Assos., 1972—. Served with AUS, 1942-46. Decorated Bronze Star medal. Republican. Methodist. Address: Eclectic AL 36024

THOMAS, WILLIAM GRIFFITH, lawyer; b. Washington, Nov. 1, 1939; s. Henry Phineas and Margaret (Carr) T.; student Williams Coll., 1957-59, Richmond Coll., 1959-60; J.D., U. Richmond, 1963; m. Suzanne Campbell Foster, June 7, 1960; children—William Griffith III, Alexander Young, Margaret Campbell. Admitted to Va. bar, 1963; partner firm Thomas, Haddock & Sewell, Alexandria, Va., 1973—. Dir. Dominnion Nat. Bank No. Va.; dir., gen. counsel Washington-Lee Savs. & Loan Assn., 1963—. Sec. Va. Democratic Party, 1968-70, chmn., 1970-72. Recipient Distinguished Service award Alexandria Jr. C. of C., 1969. Mem. Alexandria, Va., Am. bar assns., Pi Sigma Alpha. Episcopalian (vestryman). Clubs: University (Washington); Commonwealth (Richmond). Editor: Univ. Richmond Law Notes, 1963. Home: 318 N Quaker Lane Alexandria VA 22304 Office: 607 Prince St Alexandria VA 22313

THOMAS, WILLIAM MARION, dentist; b. Troy, Ala., Oct. 19, 1928; s. Norman Marion and Jewel (Tadlock) T.; B.S., U. Ala., 1950, D.M.D., 1954; m. Hilda Smith, Mar. 14, 1964; children—Norma Wilynn, William Marion, Kimberly Jewel, James Norman. Practice of dentistry, Troy, Ala., 1954—; mem. staff Edge Meml. Hosp. Mem.

Selective Service Bd., 1969—. Served with Dental Corps, USNR, 1954-56. Mem. Am., Ala. dental assns., Third Dist. Dental Soc., Acad. Gen. Dentistry, C. of C., Am. Legion, Psi Omega, Alpha Epsilon Delta. Democrat. Baptist (deacon). Moose, Lion (pres. 1969). Home: 200 Monroe Dr Troy AL 36081 Office: 541 Elm St Troy AL 36081

THOMAS, WILLIAM NEIL, JR., lawyer; b. Chattanooga, Tenn., Dec. 14, 1918; s. William Neil and Mary (Allison) T.; B.A., U. Chattanooga, 1940; LL.B., Harvard, 1943; m. Elizabeth Jean Marus, Aug. 22, 1941; children—William Neil III, Gail (Mrs. John Trent Pollock). Admitted to Tenn. bar, 1948, since practiced in Chattanooga; asso. mem. firm Charles A. Noone, 1947-49; asso. mem. firm Thomas, Leitner, Mann, Warner & Owens and predecessor firms, 1949-52, partner, 1952—; spl. judge Tenn. Ct. Appeals, 1962; atty. Town Lookout Mountain, Tenn., 1949—. Chmn. bd. Boston Banch, Inc., Chattanooga. Trustee Lookout Mountain Meml. Community Center. Served to capt. AUS, 1942-45; ETO. Decorated Bronze Star. Fellow Am. Coll. Probate Council; mem. Chattanooga (sec. treas. 1953-54), Tenn., Am. bar assns. Republican. Episcopalian. Clubs: Mountain City (Chattanooga); Fairyland (Lookout Mountain). Home: 100 Whiteside St Lookout Mountain TN 37350 Office: 330 Pioneer Bldg Chattanooga TN 37402

THOMASON, BERENICE MILLER, microbiologist; b. Birmingham, Ala., Mar. 10, 1924; d. Henry Herbert and Lillian (Martin) Miller; student Huntingdon Coll., 1941-43; B.S., Ga. State Coll., 1960; m. Earl Luther Thomason, Dec. 4, 1944 (div. June 1948); 1 son, Thomas Stephen. Med. technologist War Dept., Sta. Hosp., Ft. Benning, Ga., 1943-45; pub. health technologist Muscogee County Health Dept., Columbus, Ga., 1948-51; bacteriologist Communicable Disease Center, Atlanta, 1951-53, 3d Army Med. Lab., Ft. McPherson, Ga., 1953-54; microbiologist Communicable Disease Center, Atlanta, 1954-61, research microbiologist, 1961—. Mem. DeKalb Humane Soc., 1967—. Mem. Am. Soc. for Microbiology, Research Soc. Am., Ga. Conservancy, Nat. Wildlife Assn. Research on devel. immunofluorescent techniques for rapid detection of pathogenic bacteria. Contbr. articles in field to profl. jours. Home: 4202 Hambrick Way Stone Mountain GA 30083 Office: Center for Disease Control Atlanta GA 30333

THOMASON, JOHN JOSEPH, lawyer; b. St. Louis, July 28, 1929; s. Joseph Jefferson and Clara (Galyean) T.; student Southwestern Coll., 1947-49; LL.B., U. Tenn., 1952; student U. Va. Coll. Law, 1953; m. Sally Palmer, June 24, 1956; children—Jeffery, Palmer, Susan. Admitted to Tenn. bar, 1952; asst. pub. defender Shelby County, Tenn., 1955-57; asso. firm Nelson, Norvell & Floyd (firm name later changed to Nelson, Norvell, Wilson & Thomason), Memphis, 1955-57, partner, 1957-67; partner firm Thomason, Crawford & Hendrix, Memphis, 1967—; chmn. Tenn. Appellate Ct. Nominating Commn., 1971—. Pres. Memphis Arts Council, 1971-73; pres. Central Garden Area Assn., 1967-68; pres. Memphis Citizen Assn., 1967-68; chmn. Tenn. Lawyers for U.S. Sen. Howard Baker, 1966; chmn. Tenn. Lawyers for Gov. Winfield Dunn, 1970; Shelby County Campaign mgr. for Pres. Richard Nixon, 1972. Bd. dirs. Boys Club of Memphis; bd. dirs. Tenn. Arts Commn.; bd. dirs. Memphis Boys Club Assn.; bd. dirs. Memphis Arts Council. Served to capt. AUS, 1952-55. Mem. Am. (ho. dels. 1965, council gen. practice session 1969—), Memphis (dir. 1971-73), Shelby County, Tenn. (chmn. young lawyers sect. 1964, gen. practice sect. 1970) bar assns., Sigma Alpha Epsilon, Omicron Delta Kappa. Republican. Presbyn. (chmn. bd. deacons). Club: Memphis U. Home: 1584 Carr Av Memphis TN 38104 Office: 100 N Main St Memphis TN 38103

THOMASON, JOHN MELVIN, physician; b. Olanta, S.C., Nov. 18, 1935; s. Eddie Houston and Kate Goodwin (Ordiorne) T.; B.S., Clemson U., 1958; M.D., Med. U. S.C., 1965; m. Martha Elizabeth Bruce, June 20, 1958; children—Katherine Kim, Karen Bruce, Kristie Elizabeth. Landscape constrn. Jack Clark Co., Charlotte, N.C., 1958-59; tchr. Charleston (S.C.) Pub. Schs., also football coach, 1960-61; intern Meml. Hosp., Savannah, Ga., 1965-66; family practice medicine, also med. dir. Bruce Hosp., Florence, S.C., 1966—; mem. med. staff Florence Gen. Hosp., McLeod's Meml. Hosp. Mem. Florence City Park Commn. Served with AUS, 1959-60; mem. Res. Mem. S.C. Med. Assn., Florence County Med. Soc., Alpha Kappa Kappa. Lion. Home: 1170 S Edisto St Florence SC 29501 Office: 514 S Dargan St Florence SC 29501

THOMASSET, WILLIAM KAPPES, army officer; b. Los Angeles, Nov. 17, 1922; s. Charles Artheme and Mary (Kappes) T.; B.S. in Mil. Sci., U.S. Mil. Acad., 1946; M.S. in Civil Engring., U. Cal. at Berkeley, 1953; m. Katherine Miriam Rowson, June 5, 1946; children—Katherine (Mrs. Michael Kasper), William R., Julia M. Commd. 2d lt. C.E., U.S. Army, 1946, advanced through grades to col., 1968; dep. dist. engr. N.Y. Engr. Dist., N.Y.C., 1964-66; engr. adviser 3d Turkish Army, Erzurum, Turkey, 1966-67; project officer, br. chief, div. chief Inst. Combined Arms and Support, Fort Leavenworth, Kan., 1967-70; dir. facilities engring. Fort Sill, Okla., 1970-72, Fort Hood, Tex., 1972—. Decorated Army Commendation medal with oak leaf cluster, Bronze Star medal, Meritorious Service medal, Legion Merit. Registered profl. engr., Okla. Home: 6776 24th St Fort Hood TX 76544 Office: Dir Facilities Engring Fort Hood TX 76544

THOMASSON, JAMES NELSON, physician; b. Rock Hill, S.C., Feb. 12, 1918; s. Walter DeBrue and Nancy Elizabeth (Long) T.; B.S., Furman U., 1939; M.D., Vanderbilt U., 1943; m. Mildred Raymond, Nov. 26, 1942; children—James Nelson, Nancy Anne (Mrs. Arthur J. Laib III), Raymond Young. Intern, asst. resident, resident U. Va., Charlottesville, 1943-47; practice medicine, specializing in internal medicine, Nashville, 1947—; mem. staff St. Thomas Hosp., Bapt. Hosp., Park View Hosp., West Side Hosp. (Nashville); asst. prof. clin. medicine Vanderbilt U. Med. Sch., 1973—; cons. VA Hosp., Nashville, 1950-60. Diplomate Am. Bd. Internal Medicine. Mem. Nashville Soc. Internal Medicine, Nashville Acad. Medicine (pres. 1964), Tenn. Med. Assn., A.M.A., A.C.P. Elk. Clubs: University, Cumberland Yacht. Home: 6526 Currywood Dr Nashville TN 37205 Office: 1918 Hayes St Nashville TN 37203

THOMPSON, BRENT DRUIEN, banker; b. Donansburg, Ky., Oct. 4, 1930; s. Veachil Ira and Lucille Mae (Higgason) Thompson; B.S., U. Ky., 1950, M.S., 1958; m. Dorothy Mae Spencer, June 5, 1952; children—Risé Carol, John Mark. Tchr. vocational agr. Ky. Pub. Schs., 1950-57; with Trigg County Farmers Bank, Cadiz, 1957—, v.p., 1969-71, pres., 1972—, also dir.; dir. Trigg County Ins. Agy., Inc., Cadiz. Sec., Trigg County Planning and Devel. Assn., 1963-73, Pennyroyal Regional Mental Health-Mental Retardation Bd., 1968-71; adv. dir. Cumberland Valley council Girl Scouts U.S.A., 1973-74; mem. Ky. Gov.'s Council on Pub. Higher Edn., 1966. Bd. dirs. Ky. Bapt. Found., Audubon council Boy Scouts Am. Served to 1st lt. USAF, 1954-56; now lt. col. Res. Recipient Hon. Ky. Farmer degree Ky. Assn. Future Farmers Am., 1966. Mem. N.E.A. (life), Am., Ky. (regional pres. 1970-71) bankers assns., Cadiz-Trigg County C. of C. (charter mem., chmn. indsl. devel. com. 1963-76), U. Ky. Alumni Assn. (dir. 1970-73), So. Ky. Pkwy. Assn., Nat. Block and Bridle Club, Alpha Gamma Rho. Batpist (deacon 1957—). Rotarian (charter mem., pres. 1969-70). Club: Civitan (sec. Cadiz 1959-62). Office: 38 Main St Cadiz KY 42211

THOMPSON, BUFORD DALE, horticulturist; b. Lake Wales, Fla., Oct. 22, 1922; s. Sheldon Stringer and Bonnie (Durrance) T.; B.S. in Agr. with honors, U. Fla., 1948, M.S., 1949, Ph.D., 1954; m. Margaret Virginia Cody, Aug. 20, 1944; children—Margaret D., James G., Michael L. Asst. horticulturist Agrl. Expt. Stas., Inst. Food and Agrl. Scis., U. Fla., Gainesville, 1948-60, asso. prof., asso. horticulturist, 1960-66, prof., horticulturist, 1966—. Served to capt. AUS, 1943-46; ETO; Col. Res. Mem. Am. Soc. Hort. Sci. (Vaughan award 1962), Am. Soc. Plant Physiologists, Fla. Hort. Soc., Caribbean Region Hort. Soc. Club: University Florida Alumni (pres.). Home: 725 NW 40th Terrace Gainesville FL 32601

THOMPSON, CARSON R., leather co. exec.; b. Wilson, Okla., Feb. 10, 1939; s. Silas and Della (Wood) T.; B.S. in Social Sci., Tex. Wesleyan Coll., 1962; m. Charlotte Ann Arwine, Dec. 26, 1959; children—Shelley, Susan. With Tandy Leather Co., Fort Worth, 1957-74, warehouse mgr., 1964-70, mdse. mgr., leather buyer, 1970-74; pres. Tex-Tan Welhausen Co., Yoakum, Tex., 1974—. Baptist. Home: Yoakum TX 77995 Office: Tex-Tan Welhausen Co Yoakum TX 77995

THOMPSON, CHARLES BENJAMIN, JR., civil engr.; b. Auburn, Neb., Oct. 22, 1917; s. Charles Benjamin and Thelma Tolinda (Call) T.; B.S. in Civil Engring., U. N.M., 1940; M.S., State U. Ia., 1948; m. Kathryn Lois Hanlan, Aug. 3, 1938; children—Charles Hugh, Carolyn Louise, Marilyn Kay. Clk. Woods Bros. Constrn. Co., Omaha, 1935-38; insp., dept. roads and irrigation State Neb., Lincoln, 1940; jr. insp. ordinance material, War Dept., St. Louis Ordnance Dist., 1941, jr., asso., sr., chief insp. ordnance material, St. Louis Ordnance Plant, 1941-43; civil engr. Horner & Shifrin, cons. engrs., St. Louis, 1943; ordnance engr., indsl. specialist, indsl. engr., tech. editor War Dept. Office, Chief of Ordnance, Washington, 1943-46; asst. prof. civil engring. U. N.M., Albuquerque, 1948-51; sr. engr. N.M. Interstate Stream Commn., Santa Fe, 1951-53; chief, tech. div. N.M. State Engr. Office, 1953-58; civil engr.-planner, Litchfield Whiting Bowne Assos., Bangkok, Thailand, 1958-59; hydraulic engr. U.S. Study Commn.-Texas, Houston, 1959-61; water resources engr. U.S. State Dept., AID, Washington, 1961—. Registered profl. engr. Alaska, Ariz., Colo., D.C., N.M., Md., Okla., Tex., La., Miss., Mass. Fellow Am. Soc. C.E.; mem. Internat. Commn. Irrigation and Drainage, Internat. Assn. for Hydraulic Research, Permanent Internat. Assn. Navigation Congresses, Am. Ordnance Assn., Nat. Soc. Profl. Engrs., Internat. Commn. on Large Dams, Internat. Water Supply Assn., Am. Legion, Sigma Tau, Chi Epsilon. Methodist. Author numerous manuals, reports and tech. papers. Address: 5705 Indian Ct Alexandria VA 22303 Office: US Dept State AID SER ENGR (SA) Washington DC 20523

THOMPSON, CLARK WALLACE, JR., investment exec.; b. Galveston, Tex., Aug. 28, 1919; s. Clark Wallace and Libbie (Moody) T.; B.B.A., U. Tex., 1947; m. Rosalie Anne Meador, Aug. 30, 1941; 1 dau., Anne Meador (Mrs. F. J. Whitley, Jr.). With Arthur Anderson & Co., Houston, 1947-56, partner, 1956-61; personal investment mgmt., Houston, 1961—; now also dir. Southwestern Savs. Assn., Houston. Mem. accounting adv. com. U. Tex., Austin, 1958—. Mem. adv. com. Salvation Army; bd. dirs. Community Welfare Planning Assn. Houston, Assn. Community TV; trustee Northwood Inst., Midland, Mich.; steering com. Texas Futures, Austin. Served to capt. AUS, 1943-46. Mem. Am. Inst. C.P.A.'s, Fat Stock Show Assn., Beta Theta Pi, Beta Alpha Psi. Democrat. Episcopalian. Clubs: Houston Country, Houston; Port Bay (Rockport, Tex.); Broadmoor Golf, Garden of The Gods, Country of Colorado (all Colorado Springs). Home: 2700 S Post Oak Rd Houston TX 77027 Office: Transco Tower Houston TX 77027

THOMPSON, CLYDE CLINTON, dentist; b. Thompson, Ark., Mar. 30, 1898; s. Edwin Staton and Lucy Ardelia (Hall) T.; D.D.S., Vanderbilt U., 1919; m. Oza Brace Leeper, Nov. 20, 1920; children—Betty Anne (Mrs. George Clark Read), Margaret Ellen (Mrs. J.T. Sharp), Clyde Clinton. Dentist, DeQueen, Ark., 1919—, partner with son, 1949—. Dir. 1st Nat. Bank DeQueen. Leader, Caddo Area council Boy Scouts Am., 1923-68, mem. council, 1926-68; mem.-at-large nat. council, 1962, 63; mem. Sch. Bd. DeQueen, 1931-40, pres., 1935-40. Chmn., Sevier County Republican Central Com., 1932-45; mem. Rep. State Com., 1945-63. Recipient Silver Beaver award Boy Scouts Am., 1948. Fellow Am. Coll. Dentists (vice-chmn. for Ark.); mem. Ark. (life mem., pres. 1936), S.W. Dist. (sec. 1921-30), Am. (life) dental assns., Am. (champion 1931), Ark. (champion 1933) dental golf assns., Phi Kappa Sigma, Psi Omega. Republican. Baptist (deacon). Mason (32 degree, K.T.), Rotarian (pres. DeQueen Club 1936). Club: DeQueen Country. Home: 619 Vandervoort Av DeQueen AR 71832 Office: 111 N 4th St DeQueen AR 71832

THOMPSON, CORTEZ LEMONTE, radio exec.; b. Sumter, S.C., Apr. 15, 1946; s. Everett Joseph and Geneva Wilber (Davis) T.; B.A., Fisk U., 1967; m. Jean Iris Nelson, July 6, 1967. Sales rep. Frank's Distbg., Washington, 1968-69; dir. programming, pub. affairs WOL Radio, Washington, 1969—. Chmn. radio promotional com. United Negro Coll. Fund, Washington, 1973—. Recipient outstanding service award Washington Urban League, 1973. Mem. Omega Psi Phi. Home: 490 M St SW Washington DC 20024 Office: 1680 Wisconsin Av NW Washington DC 20007

THOMPSON, DAN FOX, elec. products mfg. co. exec.; b. Savannah, Ga., Mar. 15, 1920; s. Levy John and Mary Alice (Fairchild) T.; student U. Ill., 1951; B.S., Air Force Inst. Tech., 1954; m. Jane Thomas, Feb. 22, 1964; children—Dan Fox, John Phillip, Merri Lynn, Gay Elizabeth, Jan. Served to col. USAAF, then USAF, 1939-64; organized, trained and equipped the first Air Force unit to teach advanced instrument flying techniques, 1943-44; planned and implemented the first multiple count down procedure for Missile launches Cape Canaveral, 1957-62; mem. original team to recover five million dollars in Spanish Galleon treasure, 1964; devel. engr. IBM, Cape Canaveral, Fla., 1964-68; v.p., dir. Real Eight Co., Inc., elec. products, Melbourne, Fla., 1968-73. Adv. oceanography curriculum Brevard Community Coll., 1969-70. Decorated Legion of Merit. Mem. Cape Canaveral chpt. Tech. Socs., Missile Range and Space Pioneers, Inc. (pres. 1970-71), Ret. Officers Assn. Clubs: Eau Gallie Yacht (gov., sec.) (Indian Harbour Beach, Fla.), PAFB Officers Patrick AFB, Fla.). Home: 117 Cat Cay Lane Indian Harbour Beach FL 32935

THOMPSON, DAVID LEE, banker; b. Lebanon, Mo., July 11, 1943; s. D.A. and Signey Bill (Carothers) T.; B.B.A., Tex. Christian U., 1967; m. Lana Kay Harris, July 29, 1967; children—David Allen, Suzanne Lee. Asst. comptroller Ft. Worth Nat. Bank, 1969-71; v.p., controller Capital Nat. Bank, Austin, Tex., 1971-73, sr. v.p., controller, 1973—. Mem. Austin chpt. C.P.A.'s, Nat. Assn. Accountants, Am. Inst. C.P.A.'s, Tex. Soc. C.P.A.'s. Toastmaster. Home: 8611 Willowick St Austin TX 78759 Office: PO Box 550 Austin TX 78701

THOMPSON, DONNELL MILBURN, candy mfg. co. exec.; b. Ft. Worth, Jan. 27, 1930; s. Hugh Donnell and Mary Katherine (Shook) T.; grad. Tarrant County Jr. Coll., 1973; m. Patsy Genelle Thomas, Jan. 3, 1948; children—Pat, Mike, Marlyss, Malaree, Catha. With Pangburn Co., Inc., Ft. Worth, 1949—, mgr. materials supply, 1952-56, purchasing mgr., 1956-71, materials mgr., 1972-73, prodn. services mgr., 1973—. Committeeman, Ft. Worth Young Life Campaign, 1964—. Served with USNR, 1947-50. Mem. Nat. Assn. Purchasing Mgmt., Ft. Worth Purchasing Mgmt. Assn. (past pres., past nat. dir.). Baptist. Home: 2656 S Kingsbury Av Fort Worth TX 76118 Office: PO Box 65 Fort Worth TX 76101

THOMPSON, DOUGLAS HERSCHEL, JR., state ofcl.; b. Alexandria, Va., Aug. 8, 1942; s. Douglas Herschel and Ruth (Burdette) T.; B.S. in Bus. Adminstrn., U. Fla., 1965; m. Sara Parks. Legislative auditor State of Fla., Gainesville, 1966-72; exec. dir. Fla. State Bd. of Accountancy, Gainesville, 1968, 72. Div. chmn. United Way; mem. Alachua County Charter Commn.; chmn. Heart Fund, 1972; pres. Alachua County Heart Assn.; regional dir. Nat. Assn. State Bds. Accountancy; mem. local govt. study commn. C.P.A., Fla. Mem. Am. Inst. C.P.A.'S, Fla. Inst. C.P.A.'s., Gainesville Jr. C. of C. (dir., named Outstanding Young Man 1973), U. Fla. Alumni Assn. (pres.). Rotarian. Methodist. Home: 1817 NW 23d St Gainesville FL 32605 Office: 3131 NW 13th St Gainesville FL 32602

THOMPSON, EDWARD K(RAMER), editor and pub.; b. Mpls., Sept. 17, 1907; s. Edward T. and Bertha E. (Kramer) T.; A.B., U. N.D., 1927, H.H.D., 1958; m. Marguerite M. Maxam, May 14, 1927 (div.); children—Edward T., Colin R.; m. 2d, Lee Eitingon, Apr. 1, 1963. Editor Foster Co. Independent, Carrington, N.D., 1927; city editor Fargo (N.D.) Morning Forum, 1927; picture editor, asst. news editor Milw. Jour., 1927-37; asso. editor Life, 1937-42, asst. mng. editor, 1945-49, mng. editor 1949-61, editor, 1961-68; spl. asst. to Sec. State, 1968; editor, pub. Smithsonian (Instn.) mag., Washington, 1969—. Served to lt. col. USAAF, 1942-45, Decorated Legion of Merit; Order Brit. Empire; named to N.D. Hall Fame, 1968, Editor of Year, Nat. Press Photographers Assn., 1969; recipient Smithsonian's Joseph Henry medal, 1973. Mem. Phi Beta Kappa, Sigma Delta Chi. Home: 1601 28th St NW Washington DC 20007 Office: Smithsonian Institution Washington DC 20560

THOMPSON, FRANK HODGE, transp. co. exec.; b. Stephens, Ark., Aug. 9, 1921; s. Robert Herbert and Irene (Hodge) T.; student Ouachita Bapt. U., 1940-43; m. Lurline Turbeville, Feb. 23, 1944; children—Celia (Mrs. Artie Gregory), Carolyn, Frank Hodge. Agt., terminal mgr. Wheeling Pipe Line, Inc., Helena, Ark., 1952-58; pres., Frank Thompson Transport, Inc., El Dorado, Ark., 1958—. Chmn., Union County FHA Com., 1966-69, Union County Devel. Council, 1964—. Chmn. bd. dirs. Union County Soil and Water Conservation Dist., 1973—; bd. dirs. Meth. Found. Ark. Served to capt., cav. AUS, 1943-46; PTO. Mem. Recipient Soil Conservation award Goodyear Co., 1965; named Union County Farm Family of Year, Ark. Power & Light Co. and El Dorado C. of C., 1967. Mem. Ark. Bus and Truck Assn., C. of C. U.S., Rotary Internat. Democrat. Methodist (mem. bd. laity 1970-72). Home: Route 5 Box 240 El Dorado AR 71730 Office: Paxton Rd PO Box 29 El Dorado AR 71730

THOMPSON, FRANK MAY, airline co. exec.; b. Indpls., Sept. 26, 1923; s. Frank D. and June (May) T.; B.A., U. Va., 1950; M.B.A., Harvard, 1952; m. Betsy Craig Smith, Sept. 6, 1952; children—Craig, Kerry, Amy, Jay. City reporter Dun & Bradstreet, Inc., N.Y.C., 1950; with Gen. Electric Co., 1952-56; mgmt. cons. McKinsey & Co., Inc., N.Y.C., 1956-61; dir. personnel and indsl. relations Bulova Watch Co., Inc., N.Y.C., 1961-64; v.p. Am. Express Co., N.Y.C., 1964-68; v.p. personnel relations Eastern Airlines, 1968—; dir. Lawrence Tufts Co., Briarcliff, N.Y. Instr. extension div. Sch. Indsl. and Labor Relations, Cornell U., 1959-62. Served with USMCR, 1942-46. Mem. Am. Mgmt. Assn., Indsl. Mgmt. Club. Clubs: Harvard Business School of N.Y.; Harvard of Westchester (N.Y.). Home: 4510 Santa Maria Coral Gables FL 33146 Office: Eastern Airlines Internat Airport Miami FL 33148

THOMPSON, GARRIS ARCHIBALD, JR., engring. constrn. exec.; b. Olanta, S.C., Apr. 26, 1924; s. Garris Archibald and Myrtle (Humphrey) T.; B. Mech. Engring., Clemson U., 1949; m. Emily Florence Whitmire, Dec. 21, 1947; children—Elizabeth Ann (Mrs. Michael D. Layman), Katherine Rebecca, Judith Lee, Emily Jane. Maintenance engr. Duke Power Co., Great Falls, S.C., 1949-50; asst. field project mgr. E.I. duPont de Nemours, Inc., Wilmington, Del., 1950-67; v.p. operations Applied Engring. Co., Orangeburg, S.C., 1967—. Served with C.E., U.S. Army, 1942-46. Mem. Southeastern Gas Assn., Nat., S.C. socs. profl. engrs., Am. Legion. Methodist. Club: Country of Orangeburg (S.C.). Contbr. tech. articles to trade publs. Home: 2575 Jackson Blvd Orangeburg SC 29115 Office: 1525 Charleston Rd Orangeburg SC 29115

THOMPSON, GEORGE ALFRED, JR., ret. county govt. ofcl.; b. Providence, Feb. 21, 1909; s. George Alfred and May Josephine (Heath) T.; B.S., R.I. State Coll., 1932, M.S., 1934; m. Elisabeth Sorensen Willard, Apr. 24, 1939; 1 dau., Joann Elisabeth. 1932-38, With R.I. Dept. Agr., U.S. Dept. Agr., 1938-42, USPHS, 1942-53; dir. Jefferson County Mosquito Control Dist., Nederland, Tex., 1953-74. Med. entomologist. Served with USPHS, 1942-53. Mem. Am. Registry Certified Entomologists, Sci. Research Soc. Am. Contbr. articles to profl. jours. Home: 2313 Av B Nederland TX 77627

THOMPSON, GERALD ELLISON, supt. schs.; b. Hubbard, Tex., Nov. 4, 1909; s. Oscar Scott and Mary (Kitura) T.; A.B., Trinity U., 1932; M. Ed., Tex. U., 1942; m. Louise Baird, June 29, 1935; children—Barry Baird, Gerald Dan. Coach, tchr., Pecos, Tex., 1932-34; prin. Kermit (Tex.) High Sch., 1934-48; supt. schs., Kermit, 1948—. Served from ensign to lt. comdr. USNR, 1942-45. Mem. C. of C. (pres.), Tex. Tchrs. Assn. (past pres.), Am., Tex. (past pres.) assns. sch. adminstrs., N.E.A., Am. Legion. Methodist. Mason, Lion (dist. gov.). Home: 848 Jeffee St Kermit TX 79745 Office: 701 S Poplar St Kermit TX 79745

THOMPSON, GUY PATRICK, electronic engr.; b. Guston, Ky., Mar. 17, 1921; s. Joseph Albert and Eva (Ritchie) T.; B.S., U. Ky., 1949; m. Helen Dean Cummings, Aug. 25, 1944; children—Guy P., Susan Gail, Alan Ray, Theresa Joan. Design engr. General Electric Co., Schenectady, 1951-53; process engr., Owensboro, Ky., 1953-58; process engr. Am. Printing House for the Blind, Louisville, 1958; electronic engr. Army Missile Command, Huntsville, Ala., 1958—. Active Boy Scouts Am. Served with USNR, 1942-45. Registered profl. engr., Ala. Mem. Nat. Geographic Soc., Assn. U.S. Army, Scabbard and Blade. Democrat. Roman Catholic. Home: 10005 Lily Flagg Circle Huntsville AL 35803 Office: AMCPM-MDER Redstone Arsenal AL 35803

THOMPSON, HAROLD FONG, architect; b. Memphis, Sept. 1, 1943; s. Joe Luther and Althera (Jones) T.; B.Arch., Howard U., 1967; m. Judy Armieta Brown, Dec. 24, 1966; children—Alan Craig, Kimberly Jean. Fallout shelter analyst, project architect firm Lyles, Bissett, Carlisle & Wolff, Washington, 1964-68; project architect firm Walk Jones & Francis Mah, Memphis, 1968-69, job capt., 1969-72; partner firm Clair Jones & Harold Thompson, Memphis, 1972—.

Mem. Vollintine-Evergreen Community Assn.; v.p. Memphis Community Design Center, 1972—. Mem. Nat. A.I.A., Tenn. Soc. Architects, Constrn. Specifications Inst., Nat. Trust Hist. Preservation, Alpha Phi Alpha. Home: 883 Kensington Pl Memphis TN 38107 Office: 1420 Union Av Memphis TN 38104

THOMPSON, HERMAN ORA, pharmacist, educator; b. Earl Park, Ind., Jan. 21, 1911; s. Ora and Dora T. (Linzbach) T.; B.S., U. N.C., 1937; M.S., Purdue U., 1940, Ph.D., 1944; m. Wilora (Billie) Pike, Mar. 18, 1939; children—Beverly Carol (Mrs. Rudy Watkins Barker), Herman Ora. Practicing pharmacist, N.C., 1937-38; med. service rep. Eli Lilly Co., Durham, N.C., 1938-39; grad. teaching asst. Purdue U., Lafayette, Ind., 1940-43; asst. prof. pharmacy U. Ga., Athens, 1944-45; asso. prof. pharmacy, hosp. pharmacist U. Ill., Chgo., 1945-46; asso. prof. pharmacy U. N.C., Chapel Hill, 1946-51, prof., 1951—. Mem. Am., N.C. pharm. assns., Acad. Pharm. Scis., E. Mitchell Sci. Soc., N.Y. Acad. Sci., Am. Assn. Colls. Pharmacy, Sigma Xi, Rho Chi. Home: 900 Xtopher Rd Chapel Hill NC 27514

THOMPSON, HOWARD ELLIOT, coll. pres.; b. Dobbs Ferry, N.Y., Mar. 4, 1914; s. Harry E. and Anna (French) T.; student Pa. State U., 1934-35; B.S., Springfield (Mass.) Coll., 1938; M.A., Ohio State U., 1940; Ph.D., U. N.C., 1952; m. Helen L. West, Feb. 13, 1939; children—Toni L., C. Scott, Prof., head dept. athletics Cedarville (O.) Coll., 1939-41; dir. health and phys. edn. Bethlehem Central Schs., Albany, N.Y., 1941-43; dir. athletics and phys. edn. Plattsburgh (N.Y.) Schs., 1946-50; prof., head div. health and phys. edn. Mo. State Tchrs. Coll., Kirksville, 1952-53, dir. athletics, 1952-53; prin. Wilkes Central High Sch., North Wilkesboro, N.C., 1953-62; supt. schs. Chapel Hill, N.C., 1962-65; pres. Wilkes Community Coll., Wilkesboro, N.C., 1965—; prof. Grad. Sch. Western Caroline U., summers 1955, 62, Appalachian State U., summer 1956, N.C. Central U., summer 1963, U. N.C., spring 1963. Chmn. Plattsburgh City Youth Commn.; edn. com. Appalachian Regional Commn. adv. council Community Coll.; bd. visitors Western Carolina U. Served from ensign to lt. comdr. USNR, 1943-46. Decorated Philippine Liberation Medal. Mem. No. N.Y. Coaches Assn. (chmn. 1946-50), N.W. Carolina Prins. Assn. (pres.), N.C. Assn. Educators, Am. Assn. Sch. Adminstrs., N.C. Assn. Community Coll. Presidents (chmn.), So. Assn. Secondary Schs. and Colls. (central reviewing com.), C. of C. (dir.), V.F.W. (past post comdr.), Am. Legion, Phi Delta Kappa. Methodist. Home: Country Club Rd Wilkesboro NC 28697

THOMPSON, JACK ELDERS, mfg. co. exec.; b. Glennville, Ga., Dec. 31, 1923; s. Henry Lucious and Lucille (Kicklighter) T.; student Atlanta Retail Credit Assn., 1952, Ga. Assn. Credit Mgmt., Inc., 1953, Nat. Office Credit Analysis, 1956; m. Jewell Deanne Hutto, Dec. 31, 1948; children—Jeffery Elders, Michael Lee. Stock clk. Hubbard Pants Co., Bremen, Ga., 1942, shipping clk., 1942, corr. coordinator, 1947-55, asst. credit mgr., 1955-59, asst. sec., 1959-66, sec., credit mgr., 1966—; salesman Higgins Slacks, Lineville, Ala., 1946; sec. Ga. Converters, Inc., Bremen, 1959—. Served with AUS, 1943-46; ETO. Mem. V.F.W., Am. Legion. Lion. Home: 200 Coats Dr Bremen GA 30110 Office: 119 Hamilton Av Bremen GA 30110

THOMPSON, JACK WINSTON, mech. engr.; b. Dallas, Aug. 12, 1925; s. Willis Elmer and Opal (Loftis) T; student Tex. A. and M. U., 1943-44; B.S., So. Meth. U., 1949; m. Bettye Jeanne Decatur, Feb. 16, 1947; children—Sharon Layne, Jon Randall, Susan Gay, Jay Rodger. Draftsman C. Wallace Plumbing Co., Dallas, 1947-49; sales engr. Tex. Distbrs., Inc., Dallas, 1949-51; gen. mgr., chief engr. Fagan Air Conditioning Co., Little Rock, 1951-59; v.p., mgr., chief engr. Natkin & Co., Lincoln, Neb., 1959-64; exec. v.p. George Linskie Co., Inc. (merged with Sam P. Wallace Co., Inc. 1971), Dallas, 1964—, now v.p., mgr. Dallas div. Co-founder dir. North Tex. Contractors Assn. 1968-72; chmn. mech. code com. city of Dallas, 1968-71; past pres., v.p., mem. Constrn. Employees Council N. Tex., 1968-70; mem. Dallas Plumbing/Mech. Code Adv. and Appeals Bd., 1971—. Democratic precinct chmn. Dallas County, 1968—; mem. Dallas County Dem. Exec. Com., 1968-74; dir. Dem. Com. Responsible Govt., Dallas, 1969-74. Served to 1st lt. AUS, 1944-47. Registered profl. engr., Tex., Ark., Neb., Ia. Fellow Am. Soc. Heating, Refrigerating and Air Conditioning Engrs. (dir.; regional chmn., past chmn. bd., pres., sec. Ark. chpt., past treas., Distinguished Service award 1971, sec. Neb. chpt.); mem. Mech. Contractors Assn. Dallas (dir. 1972—, v.p. 1967, pres. 1968), Am. (dir.), Tex. (dir.) mech. contractors assns., Am. Soc. M.E. (charter mem., past vice chmn. Ark. sub.-sect.), Nat., Tex. socs. profl. engrs., Former Students Assn. and Aggie Club Tex. A. and M. U., Alumni Assn. So. Meth. U. Dallas C. of C. Baptist. Mason (32 deg., K.T., Shriner, Jester), Rotarian. Clubs: Las Colinas Country (Irving, Tex.); Engineers (Dallas) Address: 5035 Royal Lane Dallas TX 75229

THOMPSON, JAMES ERVIN, JR., banker; b. Betsy Layne, Ky., June 22, 1924; s. James E. and Mary (Ratliff) T.; A.B., Union Coll., 1950, B.S., 1952; student Ky. Sch. Banking, 1960; m. Hazel Marie Yeager, Dec. 24, 1950; children—David Mark, Michelle Marie. Tchr.-coach Pike County Bd. Edn., Pikeville, Ky., 1950-53; teller Citizens Bank of Pikeville, Ky., 1953-56; with Union Nat. Bank, Barbourville, Ky., 1956—, exec. v.p., 1971—. Bd. dirs. Knox Pub. Bldg. Corp., Barbourville Pub. Bldg. Corp., Knoxco. Bd. dirs. Knox County Gen. Hosp. Served with U.S. Army, 1942-46. Mem. Knox County C. of C. (dir. 1970-73), Southeastern Ky. Banking Adminstrn. (dir. 1970-71), Ky. Bankers Assn. (group v.p. 1972-73, pres. 1973-74). Democrat. Baptist (deacon). Mason (Shriner), Kiwanian. Home: 245 Sampson Lane Barbourville KY 40906 Office: PO Box 320 Barbourville KY 40906

THOMPSON, JAMES GRANT, physician; b. Carthage, Miss., 1902; M.D., U. Tenn., 1931. Intern U.S. Marine Hosp., New Orleans, 1931-32; postgrad. course skin and cancer unit N.Y. Postgrad. Med. Sch., 1935-36; resident in dermatology N.Y.C. Hosp., Welfare Island, 1939-40; mem. staff Miss. Bapt. Hosp., Doctors Hosp., St. Dominics Hosp., Hinds Gen. Hosp., Univ. Hosp., all Jackson; cons., mem. attending staff VA Hosp., Jackson; clin. prof. medicine and chief dermatology sect. dermatology U. Miss. Diplomate Am. Bd. Dermatology. Mem. A.M.A., So. Med. Assn., S.E. Dermatol. Soc., Am. Acad. Dermatology, Pan Am Med. Assn., Internat. Soc. Tropical Dermatology, Soc. Investigative Dermatology, Internat. Congress Dermatology, S.W. Dermatol. Congress. Office: 710 E Fortification St Jackson MS 39201

THOMPSON, JAMES HOWARD, librarian; b. Memphis, Aug. 20, 1934; s. Curtis Barnabas and Clara (Terry) T.; B.A., Southwestern U., 1955; M.A. (fellow, Ford Found. fellow), U. N.C., 1957, Ph.D., 1961; M.S. (fellow), U. Ill., 1963; m. Margareta Ortenblad, Nov. 24, 1961; children—Ralph, Anna, Howard. Cataloger, bibliographer Duke, 1963-65; asst. prof. history U. Southwestern La., Lafayette, 1965-66, U. Colo., Boulder, 1966-68; dir. house undergrad. library, lectr. dept. history U. N.C., Chapel Hill, 1968-70, dir. libraries, asso. prof. dept. history, Greensboro, 1970—. U. Colo. grantee, Eng., 1967. Mem. Am., Southeastern, N.C. library assns., Am. Hist. Assn., Phi Beta Kappa, Beta Phi Mu. Home: 3006 New Hanover Dr Greensboro NC 27408 Office: Jackson Library U NC Greensboro NC 27412

THOMPSON, LEE BENNETT, lawyer; b. Miami, Indian Terr., Mar. 2, 1902; s. P.C. and Margerie Constance (Jackson) T.; B.A., U. Okla., 1925, LL.B., 1927; m. Elaine Bizzell, Nov. 27, 1928; children—Lee Bennett, Jr., Ralph Gordon, Carolyn Elaine. Admitted to Okla. bar, 1927, since practiced in Oklahoma City; mem. firm Cantrell, Douglass, Thompson & Wilson; spl. justice Okla. Supreme Ct., 1967-68; sec., gen. counsel Mustang Fuel Corp. and other corps. Past sec. Masonic Charity Found. Okla.; chmn. Okla. County chpt. A.R.C., 2 terms; chmn. resolutions com. Nat. A.R.C. Conv., 1953. Served from capt. to col., AUS, 1940-46; PTO. Decorated Legion of Merit; recipient Distinguished Service citation U. Okla., 1971. Fellow Am. Bar Found., Am. Coll. Trial Lawyers; mem. Oklahoma City C. of C. (past dir.), Oklahoma City Jr. C. of C. (past pres.), U.S. Jr. C. of C. (past dir. and v.p.), Oklahoma City Symphony Orch. (past dir.), Oklahoma City. Community Fund (past dir.), Okla. County (past pres.), Am. (ho. of dels.), Okla. (pres. 1972) bar assns., U. Okla. Alumni Assn. (past mem. exec. com.), U. Okla. Meml. Student Union (pres.), Okla. City Zool. Soc. (past dir.), Am. Judicature Soc., Mil. Order World Wars, Mil. Order Carabao, Am. Legion, Beta Theta Pi (past v.p., trustee), Phi Beta Kappa. Democrat. Mem. Christian Ch. (past elder). Mason (Shriner, Jester, 33 deg.), Rotarian (past pres.). Clubs: Seventy Five, Men's Dinner (past mem. exec. com.), Beacon, Oklahoma City Golf and Country. Home: 539 NW 38th St Oklahoma City OK 73118 Office: First Nat Bldg Oklahoma City OK 73102

THOMPSON, LEROY, JR., army res. officer, radio engr.; b. Tulsa, July 7, 1913; s. LeRoy and Mary (McMurrain) T.; B.S. in Elec. Engring., Ala. Poly Inst., 1936; m. Ola Dell Tedder, Dec. 31, 1941; 1 son, Bartow McMurrain. Commd. 2d lt., U.S. Army Res., 1935, advanced through grades to col., 1963; signal officer CCC, 1936-40; radio engr. Officer Hdqrs. 4th C A., 1941, signal officer OSS, Burma, 1945, signal officer Hdqrs. OSS, China, 1945, radio engr., tech. liaison officer, Central Intelligence Group, CIA, 1945-50; chief radio br. Hdgrs. FEC, Tokyo, 1950-53, chief radio engring br. Signal C Plant Engring. Agy., 1953-55; radio cons. to asst. dir. def. research and engring. communications, 1960-62; pvt. research and devel. on communication and related problems, 1963—; owner Thompson Research & Exptl. Devel. Lab. Licensed profl. radio engr., Ga. Mem. I.E.E.E. (sr.), Vet. Wireless Operators Assn., Am. Radio Relay League, Nat. Rifle Assn., Res. Officers Assn., Am. Motorcycle Assn., Nat. Wildlife Fedn. Baptist. Home: 6450 Overlook Dr Alexandria VA 22312

THOMPSON, LEROY EARL, educator; b. Lithium, Mo., May 22, 1934; s. Henry Hubert and Hazel (Feltz) T.; B.S. in Civil Engring., Mo. Sch. Mines and Metallurgy, 1956; M.S., U. Mo. at Rolla, 1965; Ph.D., Rice U., 1971; m. Freida Joanne Medley, Feb. 8, 1958; children—Julie Kay, Karen Lynne, Michael Lee. Structural engr. McDonnell Aircraft Co., St. Louis, 1956-60; instr. dept. civil engring. U. Mo. at Rolla, 1960-71, asst. prof., 1971-73; founding faculty, asso. prof. Fla. Internat. U. Sch. Tech., 1973—. Cons. structural engring. field. Mem. sch. bd. St. Patrick's Sch., Rolla, Mo., 1972; pres. St. Patrick's Home and Sch. Assn., 1972. Served to capt. C.E., AUS, 1956-65. NSF trainee, 1966-68, summer faculty fellow, 1962, 64; Am. Inst. Steel Constrn. fellow, 1968-69; recipient Outstanding Tchr. Year award U. Mo. at Rolla, 1970, 71, 72, 73, U. Mo. Rolla Alumni Assn., 1971; Outstanding Alumnus award Mo. Gamma chpt. Sigma Phi Epsilon, 1972. Mem. Am. Soc. Civil Engrs. (jr. dir. 1971-72), Soc. Exptl. Stress Analysis, Internat. Assn. Housing Sci. (internat. treas. 1972-73), Sigma Xi, Chi Epsilon, Sigma Phi Epsilon, Blue Key. Home: 5860 SW 89th Pl Miami FL 33143

THOMPSON, LIBBIE MOODY (MRS. CLARK W. THOMPSON), civic worker; b. Galveston, Tex., Nov. 22, 1897; d. William Lewis and Libbie Rice (Shearn) Moody; student Holton-Arms, Washington, 1915; m. Clark W. Thompson, Nov. 16, 1918; children—Clark W., Libbie (Mrs. James I. Stansell) (dec.). Former dir. YWCA, Galveston chpt. A.R.C.; founding mem. chancellor's council U. Tex.; nat. bd. Med. Coll. Pa., also mem. pres.'s assos.; mem. fine arts commn. U.S. Dept. of State; adv. council fine arts, mem. chancellor's com. U. Tex.; bd. dirs. Meridian House Internat. Mem. Colonial Dames, Daus. Republic of Tex., Am. Legion Aux., Am. Newspaper Women's Club, League Women Voters (past dir.), Huguenot Soc., U.D.C., Soc. Sponsors USN (life), Magna Charta Dames, Plantagenet Soc., Opera Soc. of Washington, Smithsonian Assos. (life), Salvation Army Aux. Washington (life), Friends Kennedy Center (a founder), Order Washington, Friends Rosenberg Library, UN Assn. U.S.A., Jr. League (hon. life), Order of Washington, Descs. of Most Noble Order of Garter. Clubs: Women's Nat. Democratic, Sulgrave, 1925 F Street, George Town (Washington); Galveston Artillery. Home: 1616 Driftwood Lane Galveston TX 77550 also 3301 Massachusetts Av NW Washington DC 20008

THOMPSON, LUTHER JOE, clergyman; b. Watertown, Tenn., Nov. 9, 1918; s. Eli Wilson and Lucille Smith (Neal) T.; A.B. summa cum laude, Carson-Newman Coll., 1941; Th.M., So. Bapt. Theol. Sem., 1945; Ph.D., U. Edinburgh, 1951; m. Mary Evelyn Wingo, Aug. 23, 1945; children—Joseph Mark, Luther Kent. Ordained to ministry Bapt. Ch., 1938; student pastor, 1938-45; pastor 1st Bapt. Ch., Springfield, Tenn., 1945-50, McAlester, Okla., 1950-54, Calvary Bapt., Jackson, Miss., 1954-60, 1st Bapt. Ch., Chattanooga, 1960-68, 1st Bapt. Ch., Richmond, Va., 1968—. Vis. preacher Ridgecrest and Glorieta Bapt. assemblies; Gheens lectr. preaching So. Bapt. Theol. Sem., Louisville; guest preacher USAF, Spiritual Life Confs., 1965. Mem. Gov.'s Adv. Com. in Pub. Welfare, Chattanooga, 1964-68, Mayor's Com. for Community Improvement, 1963-68. Bd. dirs., exec. com., adv. bd. Richmond Bapt. Assn. Recipient George Washington Honor medal for outstanding sermons, 1960, 64. Author: Monday Morning Religion, 1961; Through Discipline to Joy, 1966. Home: 8905 Highfield Rd Richmond VA 23229 Office: Monument and Boulevard Richmond VA 23220

THOMPSON, MARGUERITE MYRTLE GRAMLING (MRS. RALPH B. THOMPSON), librarian; b. Orangeburg, S.C., Apr. 23, 1912; d. Thomas Laurie and Rosa Lee (Stroman) Gramling; B.A. in English cum laude, U. S.C., 1932, postgrad., 1937; B.A. in Library Sci., Emory U., 1943; m. Ralph B. Thompson, Sept. 17, 1949 (dec. Oct. 1960). Tchr. English pub. high schs., S.C., 1932-43; librarian Rockingham (N.C.) High Sch., 1943-45, Randolph County (N.C.) Library, Asheboro, 1945-48, Colleton County (S.C.) Library, Walterboro, 1948-61; chief librarian Florence (S.C.) County Library, 1961—. Sec. com. community facilities, services and instns. Florence County Resources Devel. Com., 1964-67; vice chmn. Florence County council on Aging, 1968-70, corr. sec., 1971, exec. bd., 1968—. Mem. A.L.A. (council 1965-72), Southeastern, S.C. (pres. 1960, chmn. assn. handbook revision com. 1967-69, sect. co-chmn. com. standards for S.C. pub. libraries 1966—, fed. relations coordinator 1972-73) library assns., Delta Kappa Gamma (state scholarship chmn. 1967-73, internat. scholarship com. 1970-74; 2d v.p. 1971-73, 1st v.p. 1973-75), Florence County Hist. Soc., Greater Florence C. of C. (div. vice chmn. 1968; women's div. chmn. 1969-70), Southeastern Regional Conf. Women in Chambers Commerce (dir. 1970-71), Florence Lit. Club (pres. 1970-72, v.p. 1972-74). Methodist (chmn. ch. library com. 1965-71, chmn. com. ch. history, 1968-69). Club: Florence Literary (sec. 1964-66). Home: 1012 Woodstone Dr Florence SC 29501 Office: 319 S Irby St Florence SC 29501

THOMPSON, MARION CURTIS, orgn. exec.; b. Lexington, Okla., Nov. 22, 1930; s. Tommie Curtis and Kate (Harshberger) T.; B.S., Central State U., 1957; m. Vera Jean Cox, Mar. 29, 1956; children—Todd, Teri. Program dir. South Oklahoma City YMCA, 1957-61, phys. dir. Central YMCA, 1961-65, exec. dir. North Side YMCA, Oklahoma City, 1965—; instr. Am. Mgmt. Assn. Served with USCGR, 1951-54. Mem. Assn. Profl. Dirs. YMCA. Baptist (dir. high sch. dept. 1970-73, tchr. 1962-69). Kiwanian (pres. 1969-70). Club: J Mac Booster. Home: 1428 NW 106th St Oklahoma City OK 73114 Office: 10000 N Pennsylvania Av Oklahoma City OK 73120

THOMPSON, MARVIN CULLUM, ins. co. exec.; b. Dallas, May 11, 1924; s. Robert William and Llora (Cullum) T.; student So. Methodist U., 1941-43; B.S. in Econs., U. Pa., 1944; m. Elizabeth Burgher, Mar. 12, 1949; children—Barbara, Lynda, Marvin Cullum, Beth, Robert Cedric. With Home Ins. Co., N.Y.C., 1944, Standard Accident Co., Detroit, 1945; partner Kirkpatrick-Thompson Co., Dallas, 1946-57; mem. faculty Dallas Coll., So. Methodist U., 1954-58; sec. United Fidelity Life Ins. Co., Dallas, 1957, v.p., 1958-60, exec. v.p., 1960, pres., 1961—; dir., mem. exec. coms. Citizens Nat. Bank, Dallas, Byerly Foods, Inc., Dallas, S.W. Title Ins. Co., Dallas. Bd. dirs. Met. YMCA, 1968-74, chmn. finance com., 1970-74; bd. dirs. Citizens' Traffic Commn.; chmn. bd. trustees Trinity Christian Acad., Dallas. Mem. Dallas Council on World Affairs, Central Bus. Dist. Assn., Young Presidents Orgn., Cotton Bowl Council, Newcomen Soc., So. Methodist U. Alumni Assn. (exec. com.). Presbyn. Clubs: City (dir., chmn. membership com.), Idlewild, Dallas Country (Dallas). Office: 1025 Elm St Dallas TX 75202 Home: 3612 Beverly Dr Dallas TX 75205

THOMPSON, MARY ANN (MRS. THOMAS R. BLANKS, JR.), lawyer; b. Nashville, Nov. 3, 1934; d. William Terry and Gladys (Mitchell) Thompson; student U. Chattanooga, 1954-58; LL.B., Cumberland U., 1960, J.D., 1969; m. Thomas R. Blanks, Jr., June 29, 1974. Office mgr. Lookout Beverages, Inc., Chattanooga, 1961-63; admitted to Tenn. bar, 1961; asso. counsel Provident Life & Accident Ins. Co., Chattanooga, 1963—; dir. Provident Employees Credit Union. Bd. dirs., Big Sisters, Big Bros., Inc., Orange Grove Day Care Center; active Nat. Retarded Children's Assn., Tenn. Retarded Children's Assn., Chattanooga Retarded Children's Assn. Mem. Am., Tenn., Chattanooga-Hamilton County Bar Assn., Zonta Internat., Alpha Lambda Delta, Pi Gamma Mu, Iota Tau Tau (dean Zeta chpt. 1959-60). Republican. Episcopalian. Home: 909 S Crest Rd Chattanooga TN 37404 Office: Provident Life & Accident Ins Co Fountain Square Chattanooga TN 37402

THOMPSON, MILTON STRONG, orthopaedic surgeon; b. Newbury, Mass., Oct. 26, 1901; s. Milton Strong and Abigail Adams (Johnson) T.; A.B., Harvard, 1924, M.D., 1931; m. Elizabeth Paige, Jan. 20, 1940; 1 dau., Phoebe (Mrs. Phoebe Neesham); (stepchildren) Mary (Mrs. James Donald), Caroline Howe (Mrs. George Erwin). Intern Boston City Hosp., Boston, 1931-33, Mass. Gen. Hosp. and Children's Hosp., Boston, 1933-35; grad. asst. Harvard Med. Sch., Mass. Gen. Hosp., 1936-40; chief orthopaedic service Me. Gen. Hosp., 1940-46; commd. maj. M.C., U.S. Army, 1941, lt. col. 1944, col., 1949; chief orthopaedic service Brooke Gen. Hosp., Ft. Sam Houston, 1946-53; cons. USAREUR, 1953-56, Walter Reed Army Hosp., Washington, 1956-58; ret., 1958; prof. orthopaedic surgery Baylor U. Grad. Sch., 1949-53; vis. prof. forensic orthopaedics Sch. Law, U. Tex., 1959-62, clin. prof. orthopaedics, 1967—. Spl. lectr. Georgetown U., 1956-58; cons. AID, Formosa, 1962. Pres., Easter Seal Soc., San Antonio, 1968. Bd. dirs. Rogerson House, Boston, 1934-65. Diplomate Nat. Bd. Med. Examiners, Am. Bd. Orthopedic Surgery. Fellow A.C.S. Royal Soc. Medicine (London), Am. Acad. Orthopedic Surgeons, I.C.S., Am. Assn. Surgery Trauma, Am. Orthopedic Assn., Internat. Soc. Orthopedics and Traumatology. Clubs: Argyle, Oak Hills Country (San Antonio); Army and Navy (Washington); Harvard (N.Y.C.). Contbr. articles to med. jours. Home: 441 Burr Rd San Antonio TX 78209 Office: Nix Profl Bldg San Antonio TX 78205

THOMPSON, NED ATLAS, elec. contractor; b. Pine Bluff, Ark., Aug. 20, 1909; s. Truman and Annie May (Franks) T.; B.S., U. West, 1956; student Marquette U.; m. Hazelle Jolly, Mar. 25, 1938; children—Sandra (Mrs. Ray Lee), Glenda (Mrs. Robert Gomez). Tchr. indsl. electronics Texarkana Coll., 1942; elec. supt. Lone Star Ordnance Plant, 1942-46; owner Thompson Electric Co. contracting, mfg., Texarkana, Tex., 1946—. Mem. I.E.E.E. (sr.), Elec. Apparatus Service Assn. (pres. 1970-71). Mem. 1st Ch. of Nazarene. Rotarian. Author: Electrical Testing in Shop and Field, 1971; Electricians Formulas and Tables, 1973. Contbr. profl. jours. Home: 2021 W 14th St Texarkana TX 75501 Office: 1307 W 7th St Texarkana TX 75501

THOMPSON, PAUL ANDREW, physician; b. Jackson, Tenn., Apr. 13, 1936; s. R. Clyde and Ruth (Holt) T.; B.S., U. Tenn. at Knoxville, 1958, M.D., 1960; m. Mary Lou Bonham, Dec. 22, 1957; children—Alix, Audrey, Andrew. Intern, John Gaston Hosp., Memphis, 1960-61; resident Bapt. Meml. Hosp., Memphis, 1961-64; practice medicine specializing in internal medicine The Med. Group, Memphis, 1964, 67—; mem. staff Bapt. Meml. Hosp. Asst. prof. U. Tenn. Coll. Medicine, 1967—. Bd. dirs. Dixie Homes Goodwill Boys Club, 1968—. Served to capt., M.C., USAF, 1964-67. Mem. A.C.P., Am., Tenn. socs. internal medicine, Sigma Alpha Epsilon, Phi Chi. Republican. Methodist. Home: 35 Belleair Dr Memphis TN 38104 Office: 1734 Madison Av Memphis TN 38104

THOMPSON, RALPH GORDON, lawyer; b. Oklahoma City, Dec. 15, 1934; s. Lee Bennett and Elaine (Bizzell) T.; B.B.A., U. Okla., 1956, J.D., 1961; m. Barbara Irene Hencke, Sept. 5, 1964; children—Lisa, Elaine, Maria. Admitted to Okla. bar, 1961; spl. agt. Office of Spl. Investigations, 1957-60; gen. practice with Cantrell, Douglass, Thompson & Wilson, Oklahoma City, 1961—; mem. Okla. Ho. of Reps., 1966-70, asst. minority floor leader, 1969-70; spl. justice supreme ct. Okla., 1970-71. Mem. Okla. Crime Commn., 1968-70, gov.'s council on narcotics and drug abuse, 1968-70. Republican nominee for lt. gov. Okla., 1970; Okla. co-chmn. Friends of Richard Nixon, 1971-73. Trustee Okla. Bar Found., 1966-70; pres., Okla. Young Lawyers Conf., 1965; Chmn. bd. dirs. A.R.C., 1970-72, vice chmn., 1968-70, chmn. Midwestern area adv. council, 1973-74. Served as lt. USAF, 1957-60; maj. Res. Named Oklahoma City's Outstanding Young Man, 1967; one of three Outstanding Oklahomans, 1968. Mem. Am., Okla. (chmn. gen. practice sect. 1974—, chmn. internat. law com. 1973—), Oklahoma County bar assns., Beta Theta Pi, Phi Alpha Delta. Episcopalian. Home: 1109 Huntington Oklahoma City OK 73116 Office: First Nat Bldg Oklahoma City OK 73102

THOMPSON, RICHARD FORD, accountant; b. Dallas, Nov. 20, 1938; s. Atlas Haynes and Maurine (Ford) T.; student (scholar 1956-57) Schreiner Inst., 1952-57; B.B.A., U. Tex., 1968; m. Noel Lutes, Nov. 20, 1965; children—Mary Noel, Laurel. Vice pres. Ice Sports, Inc., Dallas, 1963-66; staff accountant Alford Meroney & Co., C.P.A.'s, Dallas, 1968-69; accountant Arnold N. Ablon & Co., C.P.A.'s, Dallas, 1969—. Owner RICHCO, Dallas, 1962—. Served with AUS, 1958-60. C.P.A., Tex. Mem. Tex. Soc. C.P.A.'s, Am. Inst. C.P.A.'s. Episcopalian. Mason (32 deg., Shriner, K.T.). Club: 500

(Dallas). Home: 6167 Danbury Lane Dallas TX 75214 Office: 1620 Republic Nat Bank Bldg Dallas TX 75201

THOMPSON, ROBERT BROCK, hemotalogist, oncologist, educator; b. Sarnia, Ont., Can., June 24, 1929; s. Howard Bell and Margaret (McDonald) T.; M.D., U. Western Ont., 1953; Masters in Human Biology, U. Paris, 1971; D.Sc. (hon.), London Inst., 1973; pupil immunology Dr. G. Mathe, Paris, France, 1970-71; m. June Margaret Cutt, Apr. 20, 1957; children—Robert Brock, Arthur Cameron, Bruce Warren Charles, Phyllis Margaret. Intern Victoria Hosp., London, Can., 1953-54; resident Victoria Hosp., 1954-58, Mt. Auburn Hosp., Cambridge, Mass., 1958-59, Eugene Talmaldege, Augusta, Ga., 1959-61; practice medicine, specializing in clin. pathology, oncology, hematology, Jackson, Miss., 1963-72; mem. staff U. Miss. Hosp.; asst. dir. clin. labs. U. Miss., 1963-71; instr., Med. Coll of Ga., 1962-63; asst. prof. clin. lab. scis. U. Miss. Med. Center, Jackson, 1963-68, dir. med. oncology clinic, asso. prof., 1968-72; dir. immunohematology Scott White Clinic, Temple, Tex., 1972—, also mem. dept. internal medicine. Scoutmaster, Boy Scouts of Am., 1965-71. Served with RCAF, 1954-58. Mem. Order of Arrow. Home: PO Drawer 1285 Temple TX 76501 Office: Scott White Clinic Temple TX 76501

THOMPSON, ROBERT EUGENE, physician; b. Jackson, Miss., Dec. 10, 1930; s. Robert Lamar and Gladys Aletrice (Cooper) T.; B.S., Tulane U., 1952, M.D., 1955; m. Mary Susan Auguste Sherwood, June 5, 1954; children—Jeffrey Robert, Nanette Kathleen, Virginia Ann. Intern, Charity Hosp. of La., 1955-56; gen. practice medicine, 1956—; with Toccoa (Ga.) Clinic Med. Assos,., 1958—, sr. partner, 1959—, chmn. exec. com., 1970. Pres., Ampo, Inc.; dir. Franklin Discount Co. Chmn., United Fund, 1963, Salvation Army Adv. Bd., 1964; v.p. Little League Council, 1970. Trustee Toccoa Housing Authority; trustee, chmn. Library Bd. Served to capt. USAF, 1956-58, Named Jaycee Outstanding Young Man of Year, 1964. Diplomate Am. Bd. Family Practice. Mem. A.M.A., Am. Acad. Family Practice. Presbyn. (deacon, elder). Lion. Home: 175 Pine Valley Dr Toccoa GA 30577 Office: 800 E Doyle St Toccoa GA 30577

THOMPSON, SAMUEL ASBURY, chem. co. exec.; b. Davidson, N.C., June 25, 1918; s. Samuel Asbury and Mary Lavina (Proctor) T.; B.S. in Chemistry, Davidson Coll., 1939; m. Margaret Elizabeth Brothers, June 29, 1946; children—Susan Keith, Robert Brothers. Operations supr. Dupont-Kankakee (Ill.) Ordnance Works, 1942-43; research chemist Am. Bemberg Co., Elizabethton, Tenn., 1946-52; with Union Carbide Corp., Oak Ridge, 1952—, supr. chem. engrs. nuclear div., 1971—; profl. potter, Oak Ridge, 1965—. Trustee Oak Ridge Community Art Center, 1965, Arts Council, Oak Ridge, 1969-72. Served with USNR, 1943-46; PTO. Registered profl. engr., Tenn. Mem. Nat. Soc. Profl. Engrs., So. Highland Handicraft Guild, Piedmont Craftsmen, Inc., Foothills Craft Guild (co-founder, pres. 1969—), Plum Nelly Clothesline Art Show, Tenn. Archeol. Soc. Club: Country (Oak Ridge). Home: 993 W Outer Dr Oak Ridge TN 37830 Office: Union Carbide Corp Nuclear Div PO Box P Oak Ridge TN 37830

THOMPSON, SOPHUS, univ. dean; b. nr. Hatton, N.D., Mar. 13, 1902; s. Christopher and Ida (Anderson) T.; B.S., N.D. State U., 1925; postgrad. U. Minn., Ia. State U.; m. Dagny H. Aasgaard, Dec. 29, 1926; children—Sophus Aasgaard, Erik Grinde. Jr. engr. Ill. Dept. of Hwys., 1924-26; instr. civil engring. U. Ark., 1926-28; asst. prof. civil engring. So. Meth. U., Dallas, 1928-32, asso. prof., 1932-34, prof., chmn. civil engring. dept., 1934-64, dean of engring., 1964-67; pres. Thompson, Abney & Schoeller, Cons. Engrs., 1967-69; staff specialist Forrest & Cotton Inc., Cons. Engrs., Dallas, 1969—. Cons. engr., Dallas, 1940—. Fellow Am. Soc. C.E. (Tex. pres. 1964-65), Am. Assn. Engring. Edn., Nat. Soc. for Profl. Engrs.; mem. Am. Concrete Inst., Technical Club Dallas. Contbr. articles in field to profl. jours. Home: 2936 Dyer St Dallas TX 75205

THOMPSON, WARREN E., sci. adminstr.; b. Joliet, Ill., June 15, 1930; s. David E. and Edna M. (Templeton) T.; student Joliet Jr. Coll., 1947-49; B.S., U. Wis., 1951; M.A., Harvard, 1953, Ph.D., 1956; m. Ellen E. Coon, June 9, 1962; children—Barbara E., Douglas J. Fulbright scholar U. Leiden, Netherlands, 1955-57; postdoctoral fellow, instr., asst. prof. chemistry U. Cal. at Berkeley, 1957-59; asst. prof. chemistry Case Inst. Tech., Cleve., 1959-65; sci. adminstr. Office Internat. Programs, NSF Washington, 1965—. Mem. Am. Chem. Soc., A.A.A.S., Sigma Xi, Phi Lambda Upsilon. Contbr. articles in field to profl. jours. Home: 4509 Amherst Lane Bethesda MD 20014 Office: 1800 G St NW Washington DC 20550

THOMPSON, WILLIAM ALBERT, JR., cons. engr.; b. Bluefield, W.Va., June 9, 1930; s. William Albert and Mary Elizabeth (Draper) T.; B.S. in Civil Engring., Va. Mil. Inst., 1952; m. Betty Presley Atkins, Aug. 1, 1952; children—William Albert III, James Carroll, Robert Ryland. Pres., Thompson & Litton, Inc., cons. engrs., architects and planners, Wise, Va., 1956—. Dir. 1st Nat. Exchange Bank, St. Paul, Va. Trustee Johnston Meml. Hosp., Abingdon, Va. Served as officer USAF, 1952-55. Registered profl. engr., Va., N.C., N.J., Ky., W.Va., Tenn. Fellow Am. Soc. C.E.; mem. Va. Soc. Profl. Engrs. (Outstanding Service award 1970), cons. engrs. counsils Va. (pres. 1969-70), U.S. (dir. 1970-71), Am. Arbitration Assn. (panelist). Presbyn. (elder). Mason. Home: 128 Orchard Dr Wise VA 24293 Office: PO Box 1307 Wise VA 24293

THOMPSON, WILLIAM BERT, ednl. adminstr.; b. Columbus, Miss., Nov. 5, 1920; s. Samuel David and Lucy (Daves) T.; B.S., U. Miss., 1947, M.A., 1950, Ed.D., 1968; m. Mary Etta Powell, June 5, 1949; children—William J., Lelon David, Mary Anne. Tchr. history, coach S.D. Lee High Sch., Columbus, 1947; prin. Amory Elementary Sch., 1948-49, Aberdeen Jr.-Sr. High Sch., 1950-55, Greenville High Sch., 1956-60; asst. supt. Greenville (Miss.) Pub. Schs., 1960-64, supt., 1965—. Mem. Miss. Accrediting Com., 1955-61; mem. Pres. Nixon's Commn. on Sch. Finance, 1970-72. Served with AUS, 1942-45. Mem. N.E.A., Assn. for Supervision and Curriculum Devel., Miss., Greenville edn. assns., Miss. Assn. Sch. Adminstrs. (pres. 1971-72), Miss. Assn. Sch. Supts., Miss. Prins. Assn. (pres. 1956-57), Pi Delta Kappa. Home: 263 Bermuda Dr Greenville MS 38701 Office: Box 749 Greenville MS 38701

THOMPSON, WILLIAM JOEL, county agt.; b. Cragford, Ala., Apr. 5, 1914; s. William Abb and Zula (Alford) T.; student So. Union Jr. Coll., 1935-36; B.S., Auburn U., 1939, M.S., 1952, postgrad., 1957-62; m. Arminda Howell, Dec. 20, 1941. Vocational agr. tchr. Blount County Bd. Edn., Oneonta, Ala., 1939-46, Jefferson County Bd. Edn., Birmingham, Ala., 1946-54; asst. county agt. Auburn U., Jefferson, Walker, Shelby Counties, 1954-71; county extension chmn., Cleburne County, Heflin, Ala., 1971—. Recipient Distinguished Service award Nat. County Agts. Assn., 1972. Mem. Phi Delta Kappa, Epsilon Sigma Phi. Kiwanian. Clubs: Buxahatchee Country (Calera, Ala.); Civitan (pres. Warrior, Ala. 1951-52). Home: PO Box 158 Heflin AL 36264

THOMPSON, WILLIAM LESTER, electronic mfg. exec.; b. Midland, Tex., Dec. 18, 1932; s. William Lester and Mamie (Jordan) T.; B.S. in Electronic Engring., Tex. Tech. Coll., 1957; postgrad. So. Meth. U., 1957-59; m. Barbara Dillen, July 5, 1953; 1 son, Marc Bradford. Communciations engr. City of Lubbock, Tex., 1955-57; electronic engr. Tex. Instruments Inc., Dallas, 1957-59, tech. marketing engr., 1959-61, marketing mgr. Germanium Products div., 1961-65, gen. mgr. bus. calculator dept., 1973—; exec. v.p. Thermalloy Inc., Dallas, 1965-69, now dir.; pres. Bradford Industries, Dallas, 1969-70, also dir; v.p. operations LTV Edn. Systems Inc., Dallas, 1970-73. Served with USN, 1951-55. Registered profl. engr., Tex. Mem. A.A.A.S., I.E.E.E., Tau Beta Pi, Eta Kappa Nu, Kappa Kappa Psi. Developer thermafilm dielectric film; inventor thermacote thermal joint compound. Home: 819 Lockwood Dr Richardson TX 75080 Office: 13500 N Central Expressway Dallas TX 75222

THOMS, HAROLD HERMAN, broadcasting exec.; b. Indpls., July 9, 1899; s. George Rudolph and Matilda (Goth) T.; B.S., Purdue U., 1921; m. Meredith Selene Jelks, Dec. 18, 1925; children—Matilann Selene (Mrs. Nathaniel C. W. Gennett, Jr.). Pres. Arlington-Fairfax Broadcasting Co., Arlington, Va., 1948—; pres. The Thoms Broadcasting Cos., Greensboro, N.C., 1956—; pres. Thoms Cablevision, Asheville, N.C., 1967—; pres. sta. WANC-TV, Asheville, N.C., 1953—; pres. Thoms Services Corp., Thoms Radio-TV Enterprises, CATV Inc., Thomsland, Inc., CATV Engring. Services, Inc.; mem. exec. com. Radio Advtg. Bur.; past pres. N.C. CATV Assn. Bd. dirs., pres. Asheville Orthopedic Hosp. and Rehab. Center. Served with USNR, 1918. Recipient N.C. Rehab. Assn. pub. service award, 1971, Sertoma Club Service to Mankind award, 1971. Mem. So. CATV Assn., Nat. Cable TV Assn., N.C. Assn. Broadcasters. Clubs: Am. Business (pres. 1935-36), Asheville Country, Biltmore Forest Country. Address: 75 Scenic Hwy Asheville NC 28804

THOMSON, JAMES MCILHANY, lawyer; b. New Orleans, Aug. 9, 1924; s. Paul J. and Gretchen (Bigelow) T.; B.A., Va. Mil. Inst., 1947; LL.B., U. Va., 1950; m. Sarah Jennings, Nov. 15, 1952; children—Sally J., Teresa L. Law clk. Judge Bennett C. Clark, 1950-51; admitted to Va. bar, 1951, since practiced in Alexandria; mem. profl. staff U.S. Senate Jud. Com., 1951-52; partner firm Clarke, Richard Moncure & Whitehead, 1953-63, Thomson, Gannon, Thomas & Cacheris, 1965-67; mem. Va. Ho. of Dels., 1955—, majority leader, 1968—; founder, chmn. City Bank & Trust Co. Alexandria, 1964-71; dir. Dominion Nat. Bank, 1972—, Dominion Bankshares Corp., 1969—; founder, sec., dir. Fidelity Savs. & Loan Assn. (now Washington & Lee Savs. & Loan Assn.), Alexandria, 1961-64, 72—. Mem. adv. bd. George Mason Coll. Served with USMCR, World War II. Recipient Distinguished Service award Jr. C. of C., 1955. Mem. Am. Va., Alexandria bar assns., Am. Legion, Alexandria C. of C., S.A.R., S.C.V., Forty and Eight, Civitan, Beta Theta Pi. Eagle, Odd Fellow. Home: 801 N Pitt St Apt 1101 Alexandria VA 22314 Office: 201 N Washington St Alexandria VA 22314

THOMSON, WILLIAM ALEXANDER, JR., dentist; b. Hattiesburg, Miss., June 22, 1928; s. William Alexander and Monroe Joseph (Tate) T.; student Va. Poly. Inst., 1946-48; B.Engring., Vanderbilt U., 1951; postgrad. U. So. Miss., 1961-62; D.D.S., U. Tenn., 1965; certificate orthodontics U. Pa., 1967. Mech. engr. Chance Vought Aircraft Corp., Dallas, 1951-52, Freeport Sulphur Co., Port Sulphur, La., 1952-53, 56-61; dentist Fla. State Bd. Health, Sarasota, 1965-66; pvt. practice dentistry specializing in orthodontics, Hattiesburg, Miss., 1968—. Served to lt. (j.g.) C.E., USNR, 1953-56. Mem. Am., Miss. dental assns., Am. Assn. Orthodontists, So. Soc. Orthodontists, Richard Doggett Dean and Marguerite Taylor Dean Hon. Odontological Soc., Delta Sigma Delta. Kiwanian (chmn. achievement com. 1971-72). Address: 405 S 37th Av Hattiesburg MS 39401

THORINGTON, JOHN TAYLOR, marketing exec.; b. Birmingham, Ala., Sept. 26, 1930; s. Fletcher and Ruth (Glass) T.; A.B., Birmingham So. Coll., 1952; m. Martha Jean Schaier, Sept. 17, 1955; children—John, Laura. With Ala. Gas Corp., Birmingham, 1948-52; with U.S. Pipe and Foundry Co., Birmingham, 1956-67; with Jim Walter Corp., Tampa, Fla., 1969—, dir. marketing research and econ. planning, marketing research dept., 1969—. Active youth baseball group, 1969-74. Served to lt. (j.g.) USNR, 1952-56. Recipient Most Valuable Mem. award Birmingham chpt. Am. Marketing Assn., 1968. Mem. Am. Marketing Assn. Home: 5019 Dickens Av Tampa FL 33609 Office: 1500 N Dale Mabry St Tampa FL 33607

THORNBURG, RICHARD HART, elec. engr.; b. Canton, O., Apr. 23, 1940; s. Glenn Thompson and Margaret (Hart) T.; B.S. in Elec. Engring., Ohio U., 1963; m. Barbara Ann Houpt, Aug. 5, 1972. Test supr. launch operations Apollo and Skylab, 1967-73, mgr. shuttle work control and information mgmt. systems planning Shuttle Program Office, Kennedy Space Center, Fla., 1974—. Served to capt. Ordnance Corps, AUS, 1963-66. Mem. Soc. Preservation and Encouragement Barber Shop Quartet Singing Am. Home: 2351 Snead Ct Titusville FL 32780 Office: SP-OPN NASA Kennedy Space Center FL 32899

THORNE, JOHN THOMAS, indsl. instrument control system designer; b. Port Arthur, Tex., Apr. 17, 1926; s. Ernest Eugene and Mary (Wooldridge) T.; student Tex. Coll. Mines, 1944-45; LeTourneau Tech., 1949-50; Lamar Coll., 1952-53; Lee Coll., 1964-65; U. Houston, 1967-68; m. Patricia McBride, Feb. 12, 1949; children—John Thomas, Ernest E., Alida Diane, Jerry Allen. Instrument technician Texas City Refining Inc. (Tex.), 1953-63; instrument and electronics instr. Lee Coll., 1963-66; instrument supr., technician (part-time) Tech. Maintenance, Inc., Pasadena, Tex., 1963-67; ind. cons., Houston area, 1967-68; ind. cons. Diamond-Shamrock, Tenneco, U.S. Indsl. Chems., Olin Corp., 1967-68; instrument tech. dept. head San Jacinto Coll., 1966-68; regional systems sales mgr. Robertshaw Controls Co., Houston, also Anaheim, Cal., 1968-70; ind. cons. Olin Corp., Pasadena Ind. Sch. Dist., 1970-72; mgr. tng. sales Tex-A-Mation Engring., La Porte, Tex., 1971-72; ind. cons. Forney Engring., Dallas also J.E. Sierenne Co., Houston, 1972; instrument designer Stubbs, Overbeck & Assos., Houston, assigned to Celanese Chm. Co., Bishop, Tex., 1972; instrument designer, job boss S.I.P., Inc., Houston, assigned to Shell Chem. Co., Houston, 1972-74; instrument engr., system designer Tellepsen Petro-Chem. Constrn. Co., Houston, 1974—. Mem. Tex. Senate Com. for Tech. and Vocational Edn., 1971—; Tex. rep. for instrumentation U.S. Dept. Health Edn. and Welfare Conf., Los Alamos, 1967. Served with AUS, 1946, 50-53; with USAAF, 1946-49. Mem. Instrument Soc. Am. (edn. dir. Houston sect. 1972—), Am. Soc. Engring. Technicians, Internat. Platform Assn. Mason. Home: 2118 Flynn Dr Pasadena TX 77502 Office: PO Box 2536 Houston TX 77001

THORNE, PHILIP TRUMAN, clergyman; b. Youngstown, O., Jan. 26, 1917; s. Charles Morris and Hazel (Partridge) T.; A.B., Western Res. U., 1945; diploma McCormick Theol. Sem., 1947; m. Pauline Hollar, Dec. 26, 1942; 1 son, Charles Paul (dec.). Dir boy's work Hiram Social Settlement House, Cleve., 1943-45; ordained to ministry Presbyn. Ch., 1947; minister, Lorain, O., 1947-59, 1st Presbyn. Ch., Hubbard, O., 1959-72; minister Rio Vista United Presbyn. Ch., St. Petersburg, Fla., 1972—. Christian edn. examiner Presbytery of Cleve., 1947-59; chmn. nat. mission com. Presbytery of Mahoning, 1966-67; organizer Deacons Work Program, Lorain, 1952-59, Hubbard, 1963; commr. Gen. Assembly Presbyn. Ch., 1969. Bd. dirs. Presbyn. Towers, St. Petersburg, 1972—. Club: Hubbard 400 Investment (past pres.). Home: 7700 11th St N St Petersburg FL 33702

THORNTON, CHARLES DEWANE, govt. ofcl.; b. Brownsville, Pa., Mar. 3, 1915; s. De Wane and Sadie (McCune) T.; B.S., U. Pitts., 1939; postgrad. U. Rochester, 1940-41, U. Tenn., 1946; D.Sc., Ind. Inst. Tech., 1957; m. Dakota Wheeler, Oct. 14, 1935; children—D. Darlene (Mrs. David F. Sutter), Charles De Wane, Constance D. (Mrs. Edward J. Frautschi), Janice (Mrs. Richard T. Olsen), Holly V. Tech. asst. Source and Fissionable Materials accountability to chief, Office Operations Analysis and Planning, U.S. AEC, 1948-56; tech. asst. to v.p. Internat. Tel. & Tel., 1965-67, v.p. indsl. labs., 1958-60, N. Am. tech. dir., 1960-63; exec. v.p., dir. Clevepak Corp., 1967-70; chmn. Thornton Industries, Inc., Kingston, Tenn., 1966—, cons. tech. mgmt. group, 1970; dir. div. nuclear materials safeguards AEC, Washington, 1970-72, spl. asst. for energy policy Office Planning and Analysis, 1972—. Dir. Venture Systems, Inc., Whitehall, Pa.; trustee Stamford Investment Fund. Cons. U.S. AEC, 1956—, mem. adv. com. on nuclear safeguards, 1966—; mem. Communications Panel; mem. 1966 White Ho. Conf. on Internat. Cooperation. Fellow A.A.A.S., Am. Inst. Chemists; mem. Am. Chem. Soc., Am. Nuclear Soc., Inst. Nuclear Materials Mgmt., Operations Research Soc. Am., Wilderness Soc., Pa. Soc. Home: 404 Chesapeake Dr Great Falls VA 22066 Office: US AEC Washington DC 20545

THORNTON, J. EDWARD, lawyer; b. Starkville, Miss., Nov. 25, 1907; s. Marmaduke Kimbrough and Annie (Knox) T.; A.B., Miss. Coll., 1928; LL.B., Harvard, 1933; m. Mary Belle Quinn. Admitted to Ala. bar, 1934, Mass. bar, 1936; asst. circuit solicitor, Jefferson County, 1936-39; asst. gen. counsel Ala. Dept. Revenue, 1939-42; mem. firm Vickers, Leigh & Thornton, Mobile, Ala., 1945-56, Thornton & McGowin, Mobile, 1956—; mem. Spl. Supreme Ct. Ala., 1967-68. Mem. adv. com. on proposed new appellate rules Supreme Ct. of Ala., 1972-74; mem. Mobile area adv. council Comprehensive Health Planning, 1970. Mem. Ala. Democratic Com., 1950-54. Served to lt. comdr. USNR, 1942-45. Fellow Am. Bar Found.; mem. Am. (ho. dels., state del. for Ala. 1958-59), Ala. (pres. 1963-64, chmn. com. jurisprudence and law reform 1951-63, chmn. sect. practice and proc. 1969-72), Mobile (pres. 1955, editor bull. 1966—) bar assns., Am. Law Inst., Jud. Conf. for 5th Circuit U.S., Selden Soc., Mobile Arts Council (1st pres. 1956), English-Speaking Union (pres. Mobile 1960-61), Mobile Opera Guild (pres. 1963-65), Mobile Chamber Music Soc. (pres. 1972-74), Mobile C. of C., Scribes. Baptist. Clubs: Athelstan, Internat. Trade. Contbr. articles to profl. publs. Address: PO Box 23 Mobile AL 36601

THORNTON, JOHN CARMAN, architect; b. Sturgis, Mich., Nov. 27, 1888; s. James Braithwait and Julia (Carman) T.; B.Arch., U. Mich., 1913; m. Barbara Mae Irvine, Apr. 8, 1916; children—James Irvine, Kenneth George. Draftsman, John Graham, 1914-15; archtl. engr. Detroit Edison, 1916-38, architect, 1938-53; self-employed as architect, Royal Oak, Mich., 1953-65; cons. on masonry and plaster problems and fire safety, Royal Oak, 1953-65, St. Petersburg, Fla., 1965—. Mem. Mich. Bldg. Safety Council, 1951-55; trustee Royal Oak Safety Council, 1958-64; mem. adv. com. to Mich. State Fire Marshal, 1958-62; chmn. home safety conf. Washington, 1956. Recipient Alex Dow award for research Detroit Edison Co., 1952. Mem. A.I.A. (Gold medal Detroit chpt. 1962, chmn. com. human safety 1954-61), Suncoast Gem and Mineral Soc., Nat. Safety Council (dir. 1957), Nat. Fire Protection Assn. (safety to life com. 1959-65), Am. Standards Assn. (chmn. study com. 1950-53), Alpha Rho Chi, Tau Sigma Delta. Republican. Baptist (chmn. bd. trustees 1926-27). Mason. Club: High Twelve (Royal Oak, St. Petersburg). Home: 6909 9th St S St Petersburg FL 33705

THORNTON, JOSEPH HARDIN, navy officer; b. Atlanta, Oct. 28, 1920; s. Joseph H. and Mabel Jane (Dixon) T.; B.S., Webb Inst. Naval Arch., 1943; M.Naval Engring., Mass. Inst. Tech., 1947-50; postgrad. U.S. Naval War Coll., 1959-60; m. Gertrude Lacey, Dec. 4, 1943; children—Elaine (Mrs. G. Thomas Todd), John, Janet (Mrs. Stephen Rust), Barbara. Commd. ensign USN, 1943, advanced through grades to capt., 1963; prodn. mgr. Mare Island Naval Shipyard, 1969-71; supr. shipbldg., conversion and repair Draw T Mayport Naval Sta., Jacksonville, Fla., 1971—. Vice pres., dir. Navy Mayport Fed. Credit Union, 1971-73. Decorated Bronze Star medal. Mem. Soc. Naval Architects and Marine Engrs. Kiwanian. Home: 39 Fairway Lane Jacksonville Beach FL 32250 Office: Draw T Mayport Naval Sta Jacksonville FL 32228

THORNTON, O. FRANK, state ofcl.; b. Mullins, S.C., July 26, 1905; s. O.F. and Lucendia (Cooper) T.; LL.B., U. S.C., 1928; m. Rosa Waring, Aug. 19, 1933; children—Rosa (Mrs. J.M. Cherry, Jr.), Frances C. (Mrs. Roy H. Shelton, Jr.). Admitted to S.C. bar, 1928, practiced in Clover, 1930-50; editor Clover Herald, 1931-50; sec., bus. mgr. Salisbury-Spencer Baseball Club, Piedmont League, 1927-29; city atty. Clover, 1940-50; mem. S.C. Ho. of Reps., 1935-36, reading clk. of Ho., 1936-50; sec. of state S.C., Columbia, 1950—. Chmn. S.C. fund drive Crippled Children's Soc., 1960-61. Mem. S.C. Election Bd., 1940-50; mem. County Democratic Exec. Com., 1940-50. Bd. dirs. United Fund Richland-Lexington Counties, Travelers Aid Soc. Mem. Nat. Assn. Secs. of State (pres. 1959-60). Methodist. Elk, Mason, Lion (dir. 1961-62, 66-67). Home: 712 Arbutus Dr Columbia SC 29205 Office: Wade Hampton Office Bldg Columbia SC 29202

THORNTON, OTIS BROOKS, educator; b. Union Point, Ga., Nov. 12, 1918; s. Percy Heard and Marianna (Brooks) T.; diploma U.S. Air Force Inst. Tech., 1956; M.B.A., U. Chgo., 1961; m. Angela Mae Watts, Sept. 15, 1945; children—Marianna Ruth (Mrs. David H. Rotroff III), Lawrence Brooks, John Vance. Commd. 2d lt. U.S. Air Force, 1941, advanced through grades to col., 1966; ret., 1968; programming and planning dir. U. Ga., 1968-70, asst. prof. engring., chmn. career edn. div., 1971—; owner Beach Builders, Mexico Beach, Fla., 1970-71; cons. engr. Decorated Air medal with six oak leaf clusters. Registered profl. engr., Tenn. Mem. Nat. Soc. Profl. Engrs., Air Force Assn. Home: PO Box 297 Tullahoma TN 37388 Office: Motlow State Community Coll Tullahoma TN 37388

THORNTON, PERCY, JR., judge; b. Clinton, N.C., Apr. 4, 1921; s. Percy Haywood and Mamie (Darden) T.; student Campbell Coll., 1938-39; A.A., George Washington U., 1949, J.D., 1952; m. Estelle Byrd, Mar. 29, 1945; children—William Byrd, Pamela Lee, Marsha Darden. With CIA, 1946-56; admitted to Va. Bar, 1953; partner firm Owens & Thornton, Manassas, Va., 1956-68; judge 16th Judicial Circuit Va., Manassas, 1968—; acting commonwealth atty. Prince William County, Va., 1958. Dir. Piedmont Fed. Savs. and Loan Assn., 1972—. Atty. Prince William Hosp., 1960—, various other civic orgns., 1962—; mem. No. Va. Community Coll. Bd., 1970. Bd. dirs. sta. WNVT, 1972—; trustee Va. Baptist Homes. Served with USNR, 1942-45. Decorated Purple Heart. Mem. Am., Va. (8th dist. com. 1964-67), various local bar assns., Phi Alpha Delta. Democrat. Baptist (lay preacher). Kiwanian. Designer, builder contemporary homes. Home: PO Box 416 Briarmont Estates Manassas VA 22110 Office: 9302 Peabody St Manassas VA 22110

THORNTON, SUE BONNER, librarian; b. nr. Fairfield, Tex.; d. John Carder and Mary (Bonner) Thornton; A.B., U. Okla., 1920, A.B. in L.S., 1938, Mus.B. in Piano, 1921; M.A., Columbia, 1932; postgrad. U. Hawaii, summer 1936. Music supr. Okla. pub. schs., 1921-25; head music dept. Northeastern State Coll., Tahlequah, Okla., 1925-32, librarian, 1932—. Freestone county chmn. hist. markers and landmarks Tex. Hist. Survey Com. Mem. N.E.A., A.L.A., Daus. Am. Colonists, Colonial Dames 17th Century (rec. sec. Okla. state chpt.), Nat. Soc. Magna Charta Dames, Tahlequah C. of C., United Ch. Women Tahlequah (chmn. 1960), D.A.R. (chmn. good citizens com. for state 1958-60), Huguenots of S.C., U.S. Daus. War 1812, Daus. Colonial Wars, Ams. Royal Descent, Colonial Order of Crown, Platagenet Soc., Tex. Federated Women's Clubs (chmn. edn. dept.) Order of Washington, Soc. Descs. Order of Garter, P.E.O., Okla., Tex. geneal. socs., Tex. Hist. Found., Tex., Southwestern Cattle raisers assns., Alpha Gamma Delta. Democrat. Presbyn. (pres. local women's dept. 1965—). Clubs: Dallas Garden, History (Fairfield), Pan American Round Table, Freestone County Country; Harvey Woman's (Palestine, Tex.). Home: Fairfield TX 75840

THORNTON, WILLIAM E., astronaut; b. Faison, N.C., Apr. 29, 1929; ed. U. N.C.; m. Elizabeth Jennifer Fowler; two sons. Dir. electronics div. Del Mar Engring. Labs., Los Angeles, 1956-62; instr. U. N.C. Med. Sch., 1963-64; intern Wilford Hall, USAF Hosp., Lackland AFB, San Antonio, 1964-65; with aerospace med. div. Brooks AFB, San Antonio, 1965-67; scientist-astronaut NASA, 1967—. Address: Lyndon B Johnson Space Center 2101 NASA Rd Houston TX 77058*

THORPE, JACOB OLIVER, dentist; b. Charlotte, N.C., Oct. 2, 1924; s. Jacob Hoots and Sara Elizabeth (Simpson) T.; A.A., Belmont Abbey Coll., 1948; D.D.S., Georgetown U., 1953; m. Dorothy Marie Heinz, Nov. 20, 1943; children—John Oliver, William Dennis, Mary Elizabeth. Dental health officer Mecklenburg County Health Dept., Charlotte, 1953-54; pvt. practice dentistry Randolph Med. Center, Charlotte, 1955—; mem. dental staff Charlotte Meml. Hosp., 1954—, instr. clin. dentistry, 1954—, chief staff dental div., 1964-66; mem. dental staff Mercy Hosp., Charlotte, 1954—. Mem. dental adv. com. Central Piedmont Community Coll., Charlotte, 1964—; research cons. Pelton & Crane Dental Mfg. Co., Charlotte, 1968—. Pres., Mecklenburg County unit Am. Cancer Soc., 1970-71; active YMCA, United Appeal. Served to maj. Dental Corps, USAAF, 1943-45; PTO. Recipient Mary Louise Reilly Service award Am. Cancer Soc., 1972. Mem. Am. Dental Assn., Am., N.C. socs. dentistry for children, Dental Found. N.C., N.C. Soc. Dental Anesthesiology (pres. 1967), Am. Inst. Oral Scis., So. Acad. Periodontology, N.C., Charlotte (pres. 1969) dental socs., N.C. Cath. Laymans Assn., N.C. Assn. Professions, N.C. Pub. Health Assn., Charlotte C. of C., Charlotte Execs. Club, Georgetown U., Belmont Abbey Coll. alumni assns., Delta Sigma Delta, Phi Theta Kappa, Omicron Kappa Upsilon. Republican. Roman Catholic. Mason. Club: Catawba County Country (Newton, N.C.) Home: Route 2 Box 502 Denver NC 28037 Office: 1928 Randolph Rd Charlotte NC 28207

THORPE, MARION DENNIS, univ. pres.; b. Durham, N.C., Sept. 25, 1932; B.A. in Psychology magna cum laude, N.C. Coll. at Durham (now N.C. Central U.), 1957, M.A. in Psychology, 1958; Ph.D. in Adminstrv. Ednl. Services, Mich. State U., 1961; postgrad. U.S. Mcht. Marine Acad., 1965, U.S. Dept. Def. Staff Coll., 1965; m. Lula Glenn; children—Pamela Monique, Marion Dennis. Grad. asst. Mich. State U., 1959-60, asst. instr. ednl. psychology, 1959-61; asst. prof., then asso. prof. psychology N.C. Coll., 1961-65; asst. dir., then dir. Neighborhood Youth Corps, Office Field Operations, Dept. of Labor, Washington, 1965-66, nat. leader Job Devel. Task Force, Washington, 1966; asst. dir. N.C. Bd. Higher Edn., 1966-67; v.p. Central State U., Wilberforce, O., 1967-68; pres. Elizabeth City (N.C.) State U., 1968—. Mem. Nat. Lab. for Higher Edn.; mem. Citizens Adv. Com. Edn. Professions Devel. Act, adv. com. to N.C. Gen. Assembly, 1970; mem. Pres. Nixon's N.C. Com. Pub. Edn.; chmn. edn. com. Mayor's Growth Center Devel. Com., Elizabeth City, 1971; commr. Edn. Commn. States; mem. Appalachian Regional Student Internship program. Mem. Durham Com. Negro Affairs, 1961, Durham Community Planning Council, 1962, Action for Durham Devel. Com., 1962, Mayor's Com. Jobs for Vets., Elizabeth City. Bd. dirs. Manpower Devel. and Tng. Project, Wilberforce, 1967, Martin Luther King Scholarship Com. Woodrow Wilson Found., United Fund., So. Regional Edn. Bd. Mem. N.C. Assn. Colls. and Univs. (mem. com. govtl. relations; mem. exec. com.), Assn. Eastern N.C. Colls. (past mem. exec. com.), Am., N.C. psychol. assns., Am. Personnel and Guidance Assn., So. (commr.), Am. Assns. state colls and univs., Alpha Kappa Mu, Psi Chi, Omega Psi Phi. Home: 1201 Parkview St Elizabeth City NC 27909

THRAILKILL, BENJAMIN EDWARD, JR., dentist; b. Chester, S.C., May 25, 1923; s. Benjamin Edward and Mary (Hall) T.; B.S., Clemson Coll., 1947; D.D.S., Med. Coll. Va., 1954; m. Peggy Braddy, Nov. 26, 1955; children—Benjamin Edward III, William Robert. Pvt. practice dentistry, Hemingway, S.C., 1954—. Mem. regional adv. com. Health Services and Mental Health Adminstrn., Dept. Health, Edn. and Welfare, 1971—. Mem. troop com. Pee Dee Area council Boy Scouts Am., 1956-63. Vice-chmn. Williamsburg County Republican party, 1965-70, chmn., 1970—. Served with inf. AUS, 1943-46. Decorated Purple Heart, Bronze Star medal (2). Mem. Am., S.C. dental assns., V.F.W., Am. Legion, Delta Sigma Delta. Methodist. Club: Civitan (pres. 1958). Address: Box 518 Hemingway SC 29554

THRAILKILL, GEORGE MARVIN, elec. engr.; b. Union, Miss., Aug. 9, 1924; s. Clifford and Ewa Juanita (Mathia) T.; B.S. in Elec. Engring., Miss. State U., 1957; M.S., George Washington U., 1968; m. Betty Jo McElvoy, June 2, 1950; children—Donald Bruce, Joni Lynn, Vicki Carol, David. Apprentice engr. Allen & Hashall, Cons. Engrs., Memphis, 1948-51; instr. elec. engring. Miss. State U., Starkville, 1957-61; pub. works elec. engr. USN Civil Service Pub. Works Dept., Naval Air Sta., Meridian, Miss., 1961—. Registered fallout shelter analyst Def. Civil Preparedness Agy., 1964—. Bd. dirs. Meridian Small Bus. Assn., 1971-72; chmn. bd. dirs. East Miss. Sportsman's Assn., Meridian, 1972-73; mem. Inter-Alumni Council, State Colls. and Univs., 1966—. Served with USAF, 1942-47, 51-53, 61-62, 67-68. Registered profl. engr., Miss. Mem. Nat., Miss. (pres. 1962-64) socs. profl. engrs., I.E.E.E., Meridian Swimming Assn. (pres. 1971—). Home: 3524 34th St Meridian MS 39301 Office: Pub Works Dept Engring Div Naval Air Sta Meridian MS 39301

THRAILKILL, WARREN MARCUS, accountant; b. Waycross, Ga., Oct. 11, 1920; s. Vesper Houston and Clara Beatrice (Gaylor) T.; B.S. in Accounting, U. Ala., 1947; diploma Command and Gen. Staff Coll., 1971; m. Mary Louise Pogue, Mar. 21, 1947; children—Katherine Louise (Mrs. Charles Duncan), Margaret Allan, Warren Marcus. With Price, Waterhouse & Co., C.P.A.'s, N.Y.C., 1947-48, Arnold, Keller & Smith, C.P.A.'s, Birmingham, Ala., 1948-53, George C. Baird & Co., C.P.A.'s, Augusta, Ga., 1953-56; with So. Elec. Steel Co., Birmingham, 1956-58; prof. St. Bernard Coll., Cullman, Ala., 1958-62; v.p.-treas. King Pharr Canning Operations, Inc., Cullman, 1962-70; self-employed C.P.A., Cullman, 1970—. Tchr., Cullman Coll., 1968—. Bd. dirs. Tennessee Valley council Boy Scouts Am., Girl Scouts N. Ala.; trustee Cullman Hosp., 1968—, vice chmn., 1970—. Served to lt. col. AUS, 1942-45. Mem. Am. Inst. C.P.A.'s, Ala., Ga. socs. C.P.A.'s, Cullman County C. of C., Am. Legion, Assn. U.S. Army, Res. Officers Assn., Sigma Phi Epsilon, Beta Alpha Psi. Methodist (past chmn. bd. stewards). Rotarian. Home: 606 1st SE Cullman AL 35055 Office: PO Box 1054 Cullman AL 35055

THRASHER, EMMA REID (MRS. HAROLD MORGAN THRASHER), city extension agt.; b. East Orange, N.J., Nov. 8, 1921; d. William Albert and Hope (Forman) Reid; B.S. in Child Devel. and Home Econs., Pa. State U., 1940-44; student Coll. William and Mary, 1955, 58, U. Va., 1957, Va. Poly. Inst., 1962; m. Harold Morgan Thrasher, June 22, 1944; children—Henry Taylor, William Seay, Lee-Hope. Tchr. Friend's Community Sch., West Chester, Pa., 1944-45; tchr. Chesapeake (Va.) Pub. Sch., 1951-53, 55-61; extension agt. Extension div. Va. Poly. Inst. and State U. Coop. Extension Service, 1961—, supr. 4-H youth program, 1970—; saleswoman, unit mgr. Tupperware Home Parties, Inc., 1953-56; treas. Seay Hope Taylor Corp., Chesapeake, Va., 1970-72; adv. bd. J.C. Penney, Inc. Pres. Gt. Bridge Band Parents Assn., 1968; patron Norfolk Civic Ballet, 1968-72; mem. Chrysler Museum, Norfolk, Va. Museum, Richmond. Bd. dirs. S.E. dist. 4-H Edn. Center, Chesapeake. Mem. Nat. (Distinguished Service award 1973), Va. (mem. policy com. 1971, 4-H com. 1971) assns. extension home economists, Nat., Va. (dir. 1964-69, dist. chmn. 1962-65) home econs. assns., Nat., Va. (pres. elect 1974) assns. extension 4-H agts., Pa. State U. Alumni Assn. (life mem., area chmn. 1969-70), Am. Bible Soc., Chesapeake C. of C., Epsilon Sigma Phi (unit citation 1973). Home: 710 Sign Pine Rd Chesapeake VA 23322 Office: Agent Dept 300 Cedar Rd Chesapeake VA 23320

THUNBERG, PENELOPE HARTLAND, research adminstr.; b. Stoneham, Mass.; B.A. in Econs., Brown U., 1940, LL.D., 1966; M.A., Ph.D., Radcliffe Coll.; m. Howard E. Thunberg. Mem. faculty Wells Coll., Mt. Holyoke Coll., Brown U.; internat. economist, staff President's Council Econ. Advisers, 1951-53, rep. interagency internat. econ. programs, 1963-64; econ. research analyst Soviet Bloc internat. econ. activities CIA, 1954-65, dep. chief internat. div., 1962-65; commr. U.S. Tariff Commn., 1965-70; mem. Bd. Nat. Estimates, CIA, 1970-74; dir. econ. research Center for Strategic and Internat. Studies, Georgetown U., 1974—. Recipient Fed. Woman's award Civil Service. Office: 1800 K St NW Washington DC 20505

THURMAN, LLOY DUANE, educator; b. Oconto, Neb., Sept. 3, 1933; s. Jesse Lloy and Mabel Ione (Parrish) T.; B.S., U. Neb., 1959, M.S. (Arthur W. Sampson fellow 1960-61), 1961; Ph.D. in Botany, U. Cal. at Berkeley, 1966; m. Barbara Joan Patterson, May 19, 1957; children—Sonya Renee, Daniel Keith, Linda Michelle. Asst. prof. biology So. Cal. Coll., Costa Mesa, 1965-67; asst. prof. biology Oral Roberts U., Tulsa, 1967-69, asso. prof. biology, 1969-72, prof. biology, 1972—, chmn. dept. natural scis., 1969-73. Cons. U. Tulsa, Corps of Engrs. Bd. govs. Okla. Coalition for Clean Air, 1973, mech. tech. com., 1973. Served with USAF, 1953-57. Mem. A.A.A.S., Am. Inst. Biol. Scis., Am. Soc. Plant Taxonomists, Bot. Soc. Am., Cal. Bot. Soc., Ecol. Soc. Am., Okla. Assn. for Undergrad. Edn. in Biology (pres. 1972—), Soc. for Study Evolution, Sigma Xi. Republican. Methodist. Home: 2520 E 57th St Tulsa OK 74105

THURMON, HARRY LYNN, electronics co. exec.; b. Kilgore, Tex., Mar. 2, 1941; s. Merida Eldridge and Mary (Jones) T.; student Kilgore Jr. Coll., 1959-60; B.E.E., So. Methodist U., 1964, postgrad., 1966-70; m. Barbara Sue Moore, June 1, 1962; children—Russell, Philip, Jeffrey. Internal auditor Westinghouse Elec. Corp., Pitts., 1964-65; sr. internal auditor LTV Electrosystems div. LTV Corp., Dallas, 1966-67, sr. internal auditor LTV Corp., 1967-68; adminstrv. asst. to treas. E-Systems Inc., Dallas, 1968-70, dir. financial operations, asst. treas., 1970-71, treas., 1971—, v.p., 1973—; v.p., treas. Eagle Transport, 1971—, ESY Export Co., (both Dallas), 1972—; v.p. finance Continental Electronics Systems Inc., Dallas, 1970—. Mem. Financial Exec. Inst., Phi Theta Kappa. Club: Royal Oaks Country.

THURMOND, STROM, U.S. senator; b. Edgefield, S.C., Dec. 5, 1902; s. John William and Eleanor Gertrude (Strom) T; B.S., Clemson Coll., 1923, LL.D., 1961; LL.D., Bob Jones U., 1948, Presbyn. Coll., 1960, Lander Coll., 1973; Dr. Mil. Sci., The Citadel, 1961; D.Humanities, Trinity Coll., 1965; Litt.D., Cal. Grad. Sch. Theology, 1970; m. Jean Crouch, Nov. 7, 1947 (dec. Jan. 1960); m. 2d, Nancy Moore, Dec. 22, 1968; children—Nancy Moore, Juliana Gertrude, J. Strom. Tchr. in S.C. schs., 1923-29; supt. edn., 1929-33; admitted to S.C. bar, 1930; city atty., county atty.; state senator, 1933-38; circuit judge, 1938-46; gov. S.C., 1947-51; mem. Thurmond, Lybrand & Simons, 1951-55; U. S. senator, 1954—. Del. Democratic Nat. Conv., 1932, 36, 48, chmn. S.C. delegation and nat. committeeman, 52, 56, 60; chmn. S.C. delegation Republican Nat. Conv., 1968, del., 1972; States' Rights Dem. candidate for Pres., 1948. Served with U.S. Army, 1st Army, ETO and PTO; attached to 82d Airborne Div. for invasion of Europe, 1942-45; ret. maj. gen. U.S. Army Res. Decorated 18 medals and awards, including Legion of Merit with oak leaf cluster, Bronze Star medal with V., Purple Heart, Presdl. Distinguished Unit Citation, 5 battle stars (U.S.), Croix de Guerre (France), Order of Crown (Belgium). Recipient Patriots award Congl. Medal of Honor Soc., 1974. Past trustee Winthrop Coll. (S.C. Coll for Women). Mem. Am. Bar Assn., Res. Officers Assn. (past nat. pres.; Minuteman of Year award 1971), Am. Legion (nat. def. com.), Mil. Govt. Assn. (past nat. pres.), numerous other vets., civic and fraternal orgns. Baptist. Republican. Author: The Faith We Have Not Kept, 1968. Office: Senate Office Bldg Washington DC 20510 Home: Aiken SC 29801

THURSTEN, RUBEN LOUIS, ret. sch. counselor; b. Waynesville, Mo., May 11, 1908; s. Charles William Louis and Myrtle May (Luter) T.; B.S., Murray (Ky.) State Coll., 1930, M.A., 1958; Ed.D., George Peabody Coll., 1962; m. Barbara Kaiser McClurg, Jan. 13, 1967; children—Louis, Rose, Charles Michael. Pub. safety officer TVA, 1941-42; sch. supt., Grandrivers, Ky., 1938-41, 43-44; tchr. U.S. Air Force, Ramney, P.R., 1959-60; men's counselor L'Ans Creuse High Sch., Mt. Clemens, Mich., 1960-72, ret. Pres. C.I.O. Union, Calvert City, Ky., 1953-54. Mem. Am. Personnel and Guidance Assn., Nat. Vocational Guidance Assn., Mich. Edn. Assn., Mich. Psychol. Assn., Mich. Personnel and Guidance Assn., Am. Civil Liberties Union, Kappa Delta Pi, Phi Delta Kappa. Mason, Rotarian. Club: Hi Twelve (Mt. Clemens). Home: Box 281 Olive Hill KY 41164

THURSTON, EARLE LAURENCE, educator; b. N.Y.C., Jan. 17, 1943; s. Earle Harold and Doris (Watkinson) T.; B.S., State U. N.Y., 1964; M.S., Ia. State U., 1967, Ph.D., 1969; postgrad. U. Tex., 1970; m. Jacquelynn Joan Newman, Jan. 31, 1962; children—Brian, Kevin, Patti. Asso., U. Tex., Austin, 1969-70; mem. faculty Tex. A. & M. U., College Station, 1970—, asst. prof., dir. Electron Microscopy Center, 1970—. Sigma Xi grantee, 1967, NSF postdoctoral grantee, 1969-70. Mem. Am. Soc. Cell Biology, Bot. Soc. Am., Electron Microscopy Soc. Am., Tex. Soc. Electron Microscopy (exec. council 1973—), Sigma Xi, Phi Kappa Phi. Contbr. articles to profl jours. Home: 1507 Barak Lane Bryan TX 77801 Office: Tex A & M U College Station TX 77843

THUSS, LOUISE BENEDICT (MRS. WILLIAM GETZ THUSS), civic worker; b. Nashville, Feb. 8, 1899; d. Chauncey B. and Sara (Byrns) Benedict; student Ward-Belmont Coll., 1916; Vanderbilt U., 1920; m. William Getz Thuss, Sept. 25, 1923; children—William Getz, Chauncey Benedict, Robert Wilkey. Organizer, 1st pres. Vis. Nursing Assn., Birmingham, Ala., 1937, bd. dirs., 1937-43, 49-55; bd. mgrs. Mercy Home, 1930—, pres., 1953-55, treas., 1964-68; mem. Jefferson County Coordinating Council, 1950—, pres. children's com. 1929-30; mem. spl. com. on juvenile delinquency Jefferson County Assn. for Mental Health, 1960—, mem. planning com., 1963-64; mem. edn. com. Jefferson County unit Am. Cancer Soc.; past v.p. Radio-TV Council; mem. Home Garden Club; active A.R.C., 1942—; charter mem. U. Hosp. Aux., Cauldron Lit. Club; pres. Jefferson County Med. Soc. Woman's Aux., 1952-53, bd. dirs., 1956-62, hon-mem., 1965—, Community Service award, 1967; pres. Ala. Med. Assn. Woman's Aux., 1955-56, bd. dirs., 1956-62 hon. mem., 1967—; mem. nat. bd. dirs. A.M.A. Woman's Aux., 1954-57, 1st v.p. nat. membership chmn., 1960-61, nat. pres., 1962-63, bd. dirs., 1963-64, nat. chmn. 1972 Golden Anniversary; 1st v.p. So. Med. Assn. Woman's Aux., 1963-64, pres., 1965-66; charter mem., v.p. U.S. sect. Internat. Coll. Surgeons Woman's Aux., 1958-60, 61-63, pres., 1963-64, bd. dirs., chmn. Southeastern region, 1958-60; charter mem., 2d v.p. Southeastern Surg. Congress Woman's Aux., 1960-61, Ala. councilor, 1955-62, chmn. luncheons Women's Com. of 100 for Birmingham, corr. sec., 1967-68, bd. dirs., 1968—, 1st v.p., 1970, pres., 1972-74; steering com. Comprehensive mental Health Planning Com. 1964-65; mem. Salvation Army, v.p. women's aux., 1967-68; bd. dirs. Birmingham Festival of Art. Recipient certificates of appreciation numerous orgns., 1962-70; named Birmingham Woman of Year, 1972. Mem. Birmingham Art Mus. Birmingham Art Assn. (corr. sec. for bd. 1966-68), Birmingham Music Club, Arlington Hist. Assn. (v.p. 1968-71; pres. 1972-74), Ala. Opera Assn., Family Counseling Assn. Jefferson County, Am. Assn. U. Women, Birmingham Jr. League (sustaining), Internat. Platform Assn., Ala. Consumers Assn., English Speaking Union, Kenmore Hist. Soc., Nat. Hist. Assn., Nat. Trust for Hist. Preservation, Am. Heritage Soc., Birmingham Bot. Soc., Common Cause, Ala. Pro-Am., Kappa Alpha Theta. Methodist. Home: 2837 Southwood Rd Birmingham AL 35223

THUSS, WILLIAM GETZ, JR., physician; b. Birmingham, Ala., Nov. 18, 1924; s. William and Louise (Benedict) T.; M.D., U. Md., 1948; Sc.D. (fellow) U. Cin., 1956; m. Gene Bradley Connell, Jan. 22, 1949; children—Pamela Connell, William G. III, Gene Bradley. Intern, New Haven and Grace-New Haven Community Hosps., Yale, 1948-49; resident in pathology Baylor U., VA Hosp., 1949-50; asso. clin. prof. pub. health and epidemiology, chief, occupational med. sect. Med. Coll., Ala., 1956—. Aviation med. examiner FAA, 1961—; pvt. practice specializing in occupational medicine, Birmingham, 1956—. Served to lt. (j.g.) M.C., USNR, 1951. Mem. Indsl. Med. Assn., Indsl. Hygiene Assn., Assn. Tchrs. Preventive Medicine, Acad. Occupational Medicine, Am. Pub. Health Assn., Am. Coll. Preventive Medicine, Birmingham Acad. Medicine, N.Y. Acad. Sci., Royal Soc. Health. Address: Thuss Clinic 2124 4th Av S Birmingham AL 35233

THWEATT, GEORGE BOOKER, constrn. co. exec.; b. Little Rock, Sept. 22, 1926; s. Charles B. and Mable (Smith) T.; B.S., U. Ark., 1949; m. Elizabeth Walker, Aug. 12, 1948; children—Kay, Steve. With Ben M. Hogan Co., Inc., Little Rock, 1949—, sec.-treas., 1964—; dir. Ark. Travelers Baseball, Little Rock; pres. R.T., Inc., Little Rock, 1968—; sec.-treas. C.R.T., Inc., 1968—. Served with USNR, 1944-46. Mem. Kappa Sigma. Mason (Shriner). Home: 507 Valley Club Circle Little Rock AR 72203 Office: 1100 Fairpoint St Little Rock AR 72202

THWING, RAILTON CLARE, constrn. co. exec.; b. San Antonio, May 14, 1921; s. James Marvin and Lillie (Childress) T.; B.S., Tex. A. and M. U., 1943; m. Lillian Alma Needles, Feb. 19, 1949; children—James Roland, Dale David, William Hollis. With Loyd W. Richardson Constrn. Corp., Aransas Pass, Tex., 1946—, mng. partner, 1958-60, pres., 1960—; dir. Portland Savs. & Loan Assn. (Tex.). Vice pres. Gulf Coast council Boy Scouts Am., 1966-68, council pres., 1969-71. Mem. City Council Aransas Pass, 1963—. Served to capt. AUS, 1943-45; ETO. Mem. C. of C. (pres. 1962). Methodist. Moose. Clubs: Knife and Fork, Propeller (Corpus-Christi); 20-30 (Aransas Pass). Home: 1059 S McCampbell St Aransas Pass TX 78336 Office: 1054 S Rife St Aransas Pass TX 78336

TICE, DOUGLAS OSCAR, JR., lawyer; b. Lexington, N.C., May 2, 1933; s. Douglas Oscar and Lila (Wright) T.; B.S., U. N.C., 1955, LL.B., 1957; m. Janet N. Capps, Feb. 28, 1959; children—Douglas Oscar III, Janet E. Exec. sec. N.C. Jud. Council, Raleigh, 1958-59; admitted to N.C. bar, 1957; practiced in Raleigh, 1959-61; atty. Office Regional Counsel, U.S. Internal Revenue Service, Richmond, Va., 1961-70; v.p. counsel Carlton Industries, Inc., Richmond, 1970—. Served with AUS, 1957-58. Mem. Am., N.C., bar assns., N.C., Va. state bars, Civil War Round Table Richmond (pres. 1968), S.C.V., Va. Hist. Soc., N.C. Lit. and Hist. Soc., Confederate Meml. Lit. Soc. Presbyn. Club: Sertoma (pres. 1968-69). Home: 7901 Three Chopt Rd Richmond VA 23229 Office: 5001 W Broad St Richmond VA 23230

TIDBALL, CHARLES STANLEY, physiologist, computer scientist, educator; b. Geneva, Switzerland, Apr. 15, 1928 (parents Am. citizens); s. Charles Taylor and Adele (Desmaison) T.; diploma Choate Sch., 1946; student Worcester Poly. Inst., 1946-47; B.A. in Chemistry, Wesleyan U., 1950; M.S. in Pharmacology, U. Rochester, 1952; Ph.D. in Physiology, U. Wis., 1955; M.D., U. Chgo., 1958; m. Mary Elizabeth Peters, Oct. 25, 1952. Asst. in physiology U. Wis., Madison, 1953-55, U. Chgo., 1955-58; rotating intern Madison Gen. Hosp., 1958-59; physician Mendota (Wis.) State Hosp., 1959; with George Washington U., Washington, 1959—, asst. research prof. physiology, 1959-63, asso. prof., acting chmn. dept. physiology, 1963-64, prof., 1964-65, chmn. physiology dept., 1964-71, Henry D. Fry prof. physiology, 1965—, research prof. medicine, 1972—, dir. computer assisted edn. (Med. Center), 1973—; mem. faculty Am. Youth Found. Confs., 1967—. Cons. Washington VA Hosp., 1966-69, VA Center, Martinsburg, W.Va., 1960-62, Smith Kline and French Labs., Phila., 1964-66, NASA, Washington, 1964-65, FDA. Washington, 1966-68. Bd. dirs. Half Way House for Women, Washington, 1965-67; bd. dirs., mem. finance com. YMCA of Met. Washington, 1972—, exec. com., 1973—; bd. dirs. Camp Letts (YMCA), Washington, 1968—, chmn., 1972—; pres. Regional Assembly YMCA, 1974—. USPHS spl. fellow in gastroenterology, 1960-61; recipient USPHS research career devel. award, 1961-63, Brandenburg Intern award Madison Gen. Hosp., 1959; (with Dr. Marie M. Cassidy) Sci. Achievement award Washington Acad. Scis., 1967. Fellow Washington Acad. Scis.; mem. A.A.A.S., Biophys. Soc., Am. Physiol. Soc. (rep. to pub. information com. Fedn. Am. Socs. Exptl. Biology 1965-70, rep. to publs. com. 1973—, sec., treas., gastrointestinal sect. 1965-68, chmn. 1968-69), Am. Gastroenterological Assn., Digital Equipment Computer Users Soc., Assn. for Devel. of Computer Based Instructional Systems, Cathedral Choral Soc., Canoe Cruisers Assn. Episcopalian. Contbr. articles to profl. jours. Mem. editorial bd. American Jour. Physiology, Jour. Applied Physiology, 1967-69, Jour. Computer-Based Instrn., 1974—. Home: 4100 Cathedral Av NW Washington DC 20016

TIDMORE, WILLIAM EWING, air pollution control engr.; b. Collinsville, Ala., Apr. 17, 1900; s. William John and Allie (Albright) T.; B.S., Ga. Sch. Tech., 1930; postgrad. U. Heidelberg; m. Mildred Victoria Jordan, Oct. 25, 1935; children—Anne, William Ewing. Student engr. Ala. Power Co., Anniston, 1925-30, supt. installation and service Automatic Coal Burning Corp., Atlanta, 1931-40; dir. Smoke Abatement Bur. City of Atlanta, 1940-52, air pollution control engr., 1952—. Mem. adv. bd. State Fire Commr., 1949-63, asst. dist., neighborhood commr. Boy Scouts Am., 1955-65. Served to lt. col. AUS, 1940-45. Registered profl. engr., Ga. Mem. Ga. Architect and Engring. Soc., Air Pollution Control Assn. (dir. 1950-53), Ga. Tech. Alumni Assn., C. of C. (mem. life quality steering com.), Res. Officers Assn., Ret. Officers Assn. Methodist (adminstrv. bd.). Author: (with Silver Burdette) People Use the Earth, 1967. Home: 1097 Amsterdam Av NE Atlanta GA 30306 Office: City Hall Atlanta GA 30303

TIDWELL, BILLIE DEE, banker; b. Denton, Tex., Aug. 24, 1927; s. George D. and Willie E. (Miller) T.; student Draughon's Bus. Coll., 1946-47, LaSalle U., 1950-52, Banking Sch., So. Methodist U., 1961; m. Ava Ruth Smith, Apr. 22, 1950; children—Karen Sue, Lana Kay. Bookkeeper, Frederick Implement Co. (Okla.), 1946-51; cashier 1st Nat. Bank, Frederick, 1954—, also dir. Treas. Frederick Sch. Dist., 1963—. Served with AUS, 1952-54. Mem. Bank Adminstrv. Inst., Frederick C. of C. (pres. 1967), Frederick Future Farmers Am. Mem. Ch. of Christ. Rotarian. Home: 404 Circle Dr Frederick OK 73542 Office: 200 W Grand St Frederick OK 73542

TIDWELL, DONAVON DUNCAN, clergyman, educator; b. Iredell, Tex., Feb. 16, 1906; s. Charles L. and Fannie Stell (Harris) T.; B.A., Howard Payne Coll., 1931; Th.M., Southwestern Bapt. Theol. Sem., 1936, Th.D., 1940; m. Thelma Turner, Apr. 30, 1930; children—David, Truett. Student pastor Spurlin, Center Valley, Pleasant Valley, Duffau, Clairette, Spring Creek, Thurber, Valley Grove, Oak Dale, Cresson, 1926-38; ordained to ministry Baptist Ch., 1925; pastor 1st Bapt. Ch., De Leon, Tex., 1938-41, Walnut St. Bapt. Ch., Carbondale, Ill., 1941-44; instr. ch. history Bapt. Foundation, So. Ill. Normal U., Carbondale, 1941-44; prof. Bible and Greek Hannibal-La Grange Coll., Hannibal, Mo., 1944-46; prof. Bible and Greek Howard Payne Coll., Brownwood, Tex., 1946-63, chmn. div. religion, 1957-62, research prof. religion, 1962-63; chmn. div. Christianity, Houston Bapt. Coll., 1963-71. Mem. Am. Acad. Religion (pres. S.W. sect. 1954), Tex. Bapt. Bible Tchrs. (pres. 1953), So. Bapt. Hist. Soc. (v.p., 1942-44). Mason (33 deg., K.T.). Author: A History of the Baptists in Erath County, Tex., 1937; Freemasonry in Brownwood, 1966; A History of the Baptists of Iredell (Texas), 1968; A History of Gray Lodge 329 A.F. & A.M., Houston, Texas, 1870-1970. Editor The Tex. Free-Mason, 1970—. Home: 3702 Castle St Waco TX 76710

TIDWELL, HAZEL ELIZA HAWPE (MRS. MARION LEONARD TIDWELL), anesthetist; b. Anadarko, Okla.; d. Charlie Bartlett and Addie Allen (Kesterson) Hawpe; student Southwestern Jr. Coll., Keene, Tex., 1923; grad. Boulder (Colo.) Sanitarium and Hosp., 1924, Western Res. U. Hosp. Sch. Anesthesia, 1927; m. Marion Leonard Tidwell, Feb. 5, 1946. Supt., Brown Hosp., Mexia, Tex., 1924-35; adminstr., anesthetist Christoffer, Edgar & Willford Hosp., Mexia, 1937-62; anesthetist Gen. Mexia Hosp., also Mexia State Sch. Hosp., 1963—. Anesthetist, A.R.C., 1963—. Recipient Woman of Year award Mexia Bus. and Profl. Women's Club, 1963. Mem. Am., Tex. State nurses assns. Seventh Day Adventist. Mem. Order Eastern Star. Home: 817 Holly Lane Mexia TX 76667

TIDWELL, JAMES CHARLES, mfg. co. exec.; b. Louisville, Sept. 9, 1928; s. Charles Raymond and Lucile (Sanders) T.; B.S., Tri-State Coll., 1950; m. Dorothy Isabel Lorenz, Apr. 24, 1954; children—David Edward, Nancy Sue. With CTS Corp., various locations, 1950—, v.p. sales and engring., Paducah, Ky., 1969-71, v.p., gen. mgr., 1971—. Vice pres. Paducah McCracken County Community Chest, 1967—; v.p. St. Mary High Sch. P.T.A., 1970-71, pres., 1971-72; mem. Paducah Labor-Mgmt. Com., 1971—, Mayors Com. for Paducah Progress, 1971—; mem. health studies adv. com. Paducah-Tilghman Area Vocational Sch., 1971-72. Served with AUS, 1951-53. Named Duke of Paducah, Ky. col. Mem. Am. Loudspeaker Mfrs. Assn. (pres., dir. 1971-72). Democrat. Roman Catholic. Lion. Club: Rolling Hills Country. Home: 128 Vine St Paducah KY 42001 Office: 1565 N 8th St Paducah KY 42001

TIDWELL, JAMES HAROLD, supt. schs.; b. Brilliant, Ala., Oct. 21, 1928; s. James Monroe and Reatha (Cochran) T.; B.S., Livingston State U., 1952; M.S., U. Ark., 1961; m. Willie Evelyn Adams, Jan. 8, 1951; children—James Thomas, Mitchell Edwin, Steven Leslie. Coach, tchr., Laurel, Miss., 1951-53, Dermott, Ark., 1953-55; coach, tchr., Star City, Ark., 1955-59, supt. schs., 1959-67; adminstrv. asst., Pine Bluff, Ark., 1967-68; supt. schs., Dumas, Ark., 1968—. Served with USNR, 1946-48. Mem. S.E. Ark. Schoolmasters Club (pres. 1960-61), S.E. Ark. Athletic Assn. (pres. 1961-62), Ark. Edn. Assn. (coordinating chmn. S.E. Ark. 1959-60), N.E.A., Am. Assn. Sch. Adminstrs. Clubs: Lions (pres. 1973-74) (Dumas); Optimist (lt. gov. 1965-66) (Star City, Ark.). Home: 114 N College St Dumas AR 71639 Office: 315 S Adams St Dumas AR 71639

TIDWELL, JOHN EDWARD, JR., civil engr.; b. Nashville, Oct. 2, 1940; s. John Edward and Anabel (Easley) T.; B.E., Vanderbilt U., 1962; M.S., U. Tenn., 1969; m. Janet Elizabeth Malone, Sept. 15, 1962; children—Janet Blaire, Anne Elizabeth. With Fed. Hwy. Adminstrn., 1962—, hwy. engr. trainee, 1962-65, area engr., Nashville, 1965-70, planning and research engr., Jackson, Miss., 1970-74, dist. engr., 1974—. Registered profl. engr., Tenn., Miss. Mem. Am. Soc. C.E., Inst. Traffic Engrs. Home: 1131 Primrose St Jackson MS 39212 Office: 666 North St Jackson MS 39201

TIDWELL, OSCAR CROMWELL, dentist; b. Nashville, June 15, 1914; s. Oscar Cromwell and Corene (Mebane) T.; B.A., Vanderbilt U., 1936; D.D.S., U. Tenn., 1940; m. Mary Louise Lea, May 1, 1948; children—Percie Corene, Mary Louise Lea, Oscar Cromwell. Gen. practice dentistry, Nashville, 1946—; mem. staff Jr. League Home for Crippled Children, Nashville. Dental rep. United Givers Fund, 1951-53, Nat. Adv. Council to Selective Service System, Tenn., 1972—; chmn. dental sect. Heart Fund drive, 1955; dental mem. council Community Agy., 1961. Bd. dirs. St. Augustines Chapel, Vanderbilt U. Served to maj. AUS, 1941-45. Fellow Royal Soc. Health; mem. Am. (del. 1967—, mem. council 1965-67), Tenn. (v.p. 1960-61, sec. 1967-72, pres. 1974, ann. fellowship award 1972) dental assns., Nashville Dental Soc. (pres. 1955-56), Pierre Fauchard Acad., Am. Coll. Dentists, Soc. Mil. Surgeons, A.A.A.S., Federation Dentaire Internat., Nashville Songwriters Assn., C. of C., Alpha Tau Omega, Psi Omega. Episcopalian. Kiwanian. Club: Belle Meade. Contbr. articles to profl. jours., hist. quar. Home: 905 Westview Av Nashville TN 37205 Office: Midstate Med Center Nashville TN 37203

TIDWELL, REX LYON, JR., elec. engr.; b. Houston, Mar. 11, 1936; s. Rex L. and Ruth (Caruthers) T.; B.A., Rice U., 1958, B.S. in Elec. Engring., 1959; m. Elizabeth Cannan, May 26, 1962; children—Mark A., Ross L. Engr., Commonwealth Services, Inc., Houston, 1960-61; engr. Tenn. Gas Pipeline Co., Houston, 1961-72; sr. engr. energy planning and conversion Tenn. Gas Transmission Co., Houston, 1972—. Registered profl. engr., 19 states. Mem. Nat. Soc. Profl. Engrs. Home: 5635 Delmonte St Houston TX 77027 Office: Box 2511 Houston TX 77001

TIDWELL, ROBERT EARL, ednl. adminstr.; b. Blount Springs, Ala., July 21, 1883; s. Robert and Nannie (Graves) T.; B.S., U. Ala., 1905; A.M., Columbia, 1925, supts. diploma, Tchrs. Coll., 1925; LL.D., Birmingham-So. Coll., Ala., 1923, U. Ala., 1927; m. Bessie Sargent, July 6, 1906 (dec. Apr. 1928); m. 2d, Bessye Veach, Feb. 3, 1930. Prin. Ensley High Sch., Birmingham, Ala., 1906-12; supt. Tenn. Coal, Iron & R.R. Co. Schs., Birmingham, 1912-18; dir. tchr. tng. State Dept. Edn., Montgomery, Ala., 1918-27; asst. state supt. edn., Ala., 1920-27, state supt. edn., 1927-29; dean extension div. and prof. edn. U. Ala., 1930-54, emeritus; asst. to pres. Stillman Coll., 1954, acting dean, 1957-60, prof. edn., chmn. div. social sci., coordinator of self-study, 1964; lectr. edn. Summer Tng. Sch., Halifax, N.S., 1928. Mem ednl. survey groups Columbia, mem. dept. supervision and curriculum devel.; chmn. U. Ala. War Tng. Com., World War II; mem. U.S. Armed Forces Inst. Com. on Tng.; cons. on teaching by TV Ala. Dept. Edn. U. Ala. Extension Center Bldg. named for him, 1954. Mem. Ala. Ednl. Assn., N.E.A. (exec. com. dept. rural edn.), Nat. U. Extension Assn. (pres. 1947-48), Nat. Soc. Study Edn., Am. Assn. Adult Edn., Am. Assn. Sch. Adminstrs., Phi Beta Kappa. Phi Delta Kappa, Kappa Delta Pi, Kappa Phi Kappa, Kappa Sigma. Democrat. Baptist. Mason, Rotarian (del. to Phila. 1954, Japan 1961). Clubs: University, University. Author ann. reports State Bd. Education of Ala., 1927-30, Ala. Unified Equalization Ednl. Program 1927, Teacher Training in Alabama, 1927; Planning Improvement in Rural Living through the Schools, 1941; Adult Education in a Free Society, 1955; also articles in mags. Travelled India, Egypt, Israel, Jordan, others. Home: 1602 Alaca Pl Tuscaloosa AL 35401

TIEDEMANN, ALBERT WILLIAM, JR., chemist; b. Balt., Nov. 7, 1924; s. Albert William and Catherine (Madigan) T.; B.S., Loyola Coll., Balt., 1947; M.S., N.Y.U., 1949; Ph.D., Georgetown U., 1958; m. Mary Therese Sellmayer, Apr. 6, 1953; children—Marie Therese, Donna Elise, Albert William III, David Lawrence. Teaching fellow N.Y.U., 1947-50; instr. chemistry Mt. St. Agnes Coll., 1950-55; chief chemist Emerson Drug div. Warner Lambert Pharm. Co., Balt., 1955-60; analytical supr. Hercules Powder Co., Allegany Ballistics Lab., Cumberland, Md., 1960-68; tech. service supt. Hercules Inc., Radford, Va., 1968-72; dir. Div. Consol. Labs., Commonwealth of Va., Richmond, 1972—. Served to lt. (j.g.) USNR, 1943-46; capt. Res., 1946—. Fellow Am. Inst. Chemists; mem. Am. Mgmt. Assn., Am. Chem. Soc., Am. Soc. Quality Control, U.S. Naval Inst., Naval Res. Assn. (dist. pres. 1954-57; nat. v.p. 1962-63, 65-69; Nat. Meritorious Service award 1971). Home: 10511 Cherokee Rd Richmond VA 23235 Office: Div Consolidated Labs 1 N 14th St Richmond VA 23219

TIEDEMANN, JOHN GEORGE, psychologist; b. Washington, Dec. 12, 1927; s. Berthold Diedrich and Eula (Gootee) T.; student U. Del., 1945-46, 48-50; A.A., George Washington U., 1951; B.A., 1953, M.S., 1954; Ph.D., Am. U., 1961; m. Sheila Mary Sloan, Apr. 27, 1957; children—Patricia Ann, John Scott. Research asst. Human Resources Research Orgn., Washington, 1952-53; intern Mansfield State Hosp., 1954-55; sch. psychologist pub. sch. system, Washington, 1955-61; supervising psychologist Army Behavioral Sci. Research Lab., Washington, 1961-68; personnel research mgr. employee and labor relations group U.S. Postal Service, Washington, 1968—. Lectr. D.C. Tchrs. Coll., Washington, 1958-59; teaching asst. Am. U., Washington, 1957-61. Pres., mem. bd. Tempo ABC-Ft. McNair Fed. Credit Union, 1963-69. Served with USNR, 1946-48. Mem. Am., D.C. (treas. 1963-67), psychol. assns., Kappa Alpha, Psi Chi. Contbr. articles to profl. jours. Home: 2938 McKinley St NW Washington DC 20015 Office: US Postal Service 475 L'Enfant Plaza West SW Washington DC 20260

TIEDT, L.O., univ. adminstr.; b. Warrenton, Tex., Feb. 17, 1932; s. Otto Fritz and Leola (Kiel) T.; B.S., Tex. A. and M. U., 1952; m. Dolores Krupa, Aug. 17, 1952; children—Mark, Barry, Sharon. Broadcaster farm news KTRH Radio, Houston, 1954-62; mgr. agr. Houston C. of C., 1962-63; exec. v.p. mgmt. Rice Council for Marketing Devel., Houston, 1963—. Served with AUS, 1952-54. Home: 9846 Briarwild St Houston TX 77055 Office: 3917 Richmond St Houston TX 77029

TIEDTKE, JOHN MEYER, ret. coll. adminstr.; b. Toledo, Sept. 15, 1907; s. Ernest and Mamie (Meyer) T.; A.B., Dartmouth Coll., 1930; M.C.S., Dartmouth Tuck Sch. Bus. Adminstrn., 1931; m. Sylvia Southard, Oct. 30, 1948; children—Philip Ernest, Marie Christine. Treas., bus. mgr. Rollins Coll., Winter Park, Fla., 1948-51, v.p., 1951, financial v.p., 1969-70, trustee, 1970—. Owner, Shawnee Farms, Clewiston, Fla., 1937—; dir. Orlando Fed. Savings & Loan, Orlando, Fla., 1960—, Sugar Cane Growers Coop. Fla., Belle Glade, 1960—, Fla. Fruit and Vegetable Assn., Gainesville, 1940—; chmn. sugar com. Fla. Farm Bur., Gainesville, 1940—. Supr. Diston Island (Fla.) Drainage Dist., 1950—. Bd. dirs. Fla. Symphony Orchestra, 1950—; bd. trustees Coll. Wooster (O.), 1940—; pres. Bach Festival Soc. Winter Park, 1952—. Recipient Rollins Coll. Medal of Honor, 1949, C.H.I.E.F. award Ind. Colls. and Univs., 1972, First Govs. award for Arts, 1973. Home: Isle of Sicily Winter Park FL 32789 Office: Rollins College Winter Park FL 32789

TILFORD, JAMES DEAN, JR., aviation exec.; b. Boston, Jan. 15, 1921; s. James Dean and Helen Morewood (Ferguson) T.; student Princeton, 1939-41; m. Emily Jane Meyer, June 22, 1946; children—James Dean III, Diana Leigh, Richard Ferguson. With Nat. Airlines, 1941, 46-60, sta. agt., Norfolk, Va., 1946-47, Tampa, Fla., 1947-48, sta. mgr., Marianna, Fla., 1948-50, West Palm Beach, Fla., 1950-54, sales mgr., Palm Beach, Fla., 1954-60; partner Palm Beach Aviation, Lantana, Fla., 1958-61, partner 1960-61; partner Aviation Sales & Service, Inc., Palm Beach, 1961-62; pres., owner Tilford Flying Service, West Palm Beach, 1962—. Commr., Palm Beach Shores, Fla., 1958-59, head Palm Beach Community Chest Dr. 1961; bd. dirs. Palm Beach Civic Assn., 1961—, Internat. Flying Fellowship of Rotarians. Nat. Air Transp. Confs., 1968—, chmn. bd., 1970-71; adv. bd. Flight Freedoms Found., 1973—. Served to maj. USAF, Mem. Nat (dir. 1965-67), Fla. (pres. 1964-65) aviation trades assns., C. of C. (dir. 1957-66), Internat. Flying Farmers, Aircraft Owners and Pilots Assn., Airline Passengers Assn. (nat. adv. council 1971—), Nat. Pilots Assn., Sportsman Pilots Assn., Nat. Bus. Aircraft Assn., Nat. Air Taxi Conf. Rotarian. Clubs: Islander (pres. 1959), Everglades, Sailfish of Fla. (Palm Beach, Fla.); Home: 266 Southland Rd Palm Beach FL 33480 Office: PO Box 1658 Palm Beach Internat Airport West Palm Beach FL 33402

TILLERY, MARGIE FREEMAN (MRS. LEE ROY TILLERY, JR.), banker; b. West Point, Ga., Aug. 9, 1921; d. Arthur Roy and Sadie (Clem) Freeman; grad. LaGrange (Ga.) Bus. Coll., 1939; student U. Ga., 1946-47; m. Lee Roy Tillery, Jr., July 19, 1947; 1 son Roy Lewis. Sec., Callaway Mills, LaGrange, Ga., 1939-47; legal sec. Cantey & Huff, Attys., West Point, 1947-48; bookkeeper First Nat. Bank, West Point, 1949-50; mgr. bus. office Valley Med. Group, Langdale, Ala., 1950-55; asst. cashier Valley Nat. Bank, Lanett, 1956-63; cashier Citizens Nat. Bank, Shawmut, Ala., 1963—. Early treatment edn. chmn. West Point area Am. Cancer Soc. Sec., bd. dirs. United Fund, Inc., West Point. bd. dirs. Troup County unit Am. Cancer Soc., Goodwill Industries, Inc., West Point, United Fund, Inc., West Point. Named Key Banker, Chambers County, Ga. Mem. Nat. (membership chmn. Central Ala., v.p. So. region 1972-73), Ala. assns. bank women, Ala. Bankers Assn. (ins. com. 1971—), Am. Inst. Banking, Beta Sigma Phi. Mem. Christian Ch. Clubs: West Point Junior Woman's (charter mem.), Contemporary. Home: 400 E 4th St West Point GA 31833 Office: Citizens Nat Bank of Shawmut PO Box 708 Shawmut AL 36876

TILLEY, RICE M., lawyer; b. Huntsville, Tex., Aug. 28, 1899; s. J.R. and Lillie Tilley; tchrs. certificate Sam Houston State Tchrs. Coll., 1919; LL.B., U. Tex., 1922; m. Lucille Kelly, Dec. 29, 1932; children—Rice M., Nancy S. Admitted to Tex. bar, 1921; practiced law in Corsicana, Tex., 1922-27; asst. atty. gen. Tex., 1927-29, 1st asst. atty. gen., 1929-30; legal adviser State Senate, 1931; practice law, Ft. Worth, 1931—. Chmn. Am. Cancer Soc.; active Infantile Paralysis Found., Red Cross, others; chmn., pres. dir. various civic and charitable instns. Chmn., del. Democratic State Conv., 1944; chmn. Dem. Nat. Conv., 1944. Served with U.S. Army, 1918. Recipient Presdl. award Outstanding Service, Selective Service Bd., 1956. Home: 3565 Bellaire Dr N Fort Worth TX 76109 Office: Ft Worth Nat Bank Bldg Fort Worth TX 76102

TILLEY, RICE MATTHEWS, JR., lawyer; b. Ft. Worth, June 21, 1936; s. Rice M. and Lucille (Kelly) T.; grad. Phillips Andover Acad., 1954; B.A., Washington and Lee U., 1958; LL.B., So. Meth. U., 1961; LL.M., N.Y. U., 1962; m. Clara Susan Begby, June 11, 1960; children—Marisa Lynn, Angela Ainsworth, Lisa Scott. Admitted to Tex. bar, 1961; shareholder Law, Snakard, Brown & Gambill, Ft. Worth, 1964—. Bd. dirs. Civic Music Assn. Ft. Worth, 1965-69, v.p., campaign chmn., 1966, 67; bd. dirs. Lena Pope Home, 1966—, pres., 1970-71; bd. dirs. Casa Manana Mus., Inc., 1969—; bd. dirs. Future Ft. Worth, 1969—; bd. dirs. Easter Seal Soc. Crippled Children and Adults Tarrant County, Tarrant County Assn. Mental Health, Van Cliburn Found., Arts Council, Ft. Worth Opera Assn.; bd. dirs. Ft. Worth and Tarrant County unit Am. Cancer Soc., exec. v.p., 1969. Served to 1st lt. arty. AUS, 1962-64. Recipient Matthews, Fisher, Budd and Sands award for excellence in writing in field of taxation So. Meth. U. Law Sch., 1961. Mem. Am. Judicature Soc., Am., Ft. Worth-Tarrant County bar assns., State Bar Tex., Ft. Worth Jr. Bar, Tarrant County All-Sports Assn. (dir. sec. 1966), Ft. Worth Bus. and Estate Council (v.p. 1967; pres. 1969-70), Beta Theta Pi, Phi Alpha Delta. Mem. Disciples of Christ Ch. Home: 44 Valley Ridge Rd Fort Worth TX 76107 Office: Fort Worth Nat Bank Bldg Fort Worth TX 76102

TILLMAN, LEONARD, elec. engr.; b. Mobile, Ala., Nov. 19, 1931; s. Charles Manuel and Rosa Viola (Easley) T.; B.E.E., Auburn U., 1960; M.S. in E.E., U. Ark., 1964; postgrad. U. Cal. at Los Angeles, 1966, U. Ala., 1966-67; m. Sarah Cook, Sept. 1, 1959; children—Leonard Charles, Paul Daniel. Field service engr. Am. Bosch Arma, Garden City, N.Y., 1960-63; with Sperry Rand Corp., Huntsville, Ala., 1964-72; sr. staff engr. Martin Marietta Corp., Orlando, Fla., 1972-74; instrument design engr. Ciba-Geigy Corp., McIntosh, Ala., 1974—. Coach football YMCA, 1966-73, coach baseball, 1971-72. Chmn. scholarship fund Auburn U., Orlando, 1972-74. Served with USAF, 1951-55. Registered profl. engr., Ala. Mem. Am. Inst. Aeros. and Astronautics. Clubs: Alumni, Auburn Alumni (Orlando). Home: 1205 W Carre Dr Mobile AL 36618

TILLMAN, MASSIE MONROE, lawyer; b. Corpus Christi, Tex., Aug. 15, 1937; s. Clarence and Artie Lee (Stewart) T.; B.B.A., Baylor U., 1959; LL.B., Baylor U. Sch. Law, 1961; m. Jerra Sue Comer, July 27, 1957; children—Jeffrey Monroe, Holly. Admitted to Tex. bar, 1961, since practiced in Ft. Worth; partner Herrick & Tillman, 1961-66, Brown, Herman, Scott, Dean & Miles, 1970—. Mem. Fort Worth-Tarrant County Bar Assn. (dir. 1970-72, chmn. med.-legal liaison com. 1968—), Tex. Assn. Def. Counsel, Fort-Worth-Tarrant County Trial Lawyers Assn., Am., Tex. bar assns., State Bar of Tex. (chmn. pilot project Right of Trial by Jury 1969—). Democrat. Presbyn. Author: Tillman's Trial Guide, 1970. Home: 4612 Briarhaven Rd Fort Worth TX 76109 Office: 203 Fort Worth Club Bldg Fort Worth TX 76102

TILLMAN, SETH PHILLIP, govt. ofcl.; b. Springfield, Mass., Aug. 26, 1930; s. Samuel and Rose (Austin) T.; A.B., Syracuse U., 1951, M.A., 1952; M.A., Fletcher Sch. Law and Diplomacy, 1956, Ph.D., 1959. Instr. polit. sci. Mass. Inst. Tech., Cambridge, 1956-58, asst. prof., 1958-60; cons. Senate Com. on Fgn. Relations, U.S. Senate, Washington, 1961—; lectr. European diplomacy Johns Hopkins U. Sch. Advanced Internat. Studies, Washington, 1964—. Served with AUS, 1952-54. Mem. Council on Fgn. Relations. Home: 1527 44th St NW Washington DC 20007 Office: Com on Fgn Relations US Senate Washington DC 20510

TILTON, KENNETH LEE, banker; b. Baytown, Tex., Dec. 26, 1940; s. Raymond Lee and Geraldine (Childers) T.; grad. Lamar State Coll. Tech., 1963; m. Gayle Wallace, June 5, 1964; children—Kyle David, Kathy Leigh, Kerry Lynne. Sr. accountant Price Waterhouse & Co., Houston, 1963-67; v.p., controller, cashier 1st Nat. Bank Baytown (Tex.), 1967-70; v.p., mgr. accounting Tex. Commerce Bank, Houston, 1970—. C.P.A., Tex. Mem. Tex. Soc. C.P.A.'s, Am. Inst. C.P.A.'s. Home: 2407 Mockingbird Lane Baytown TX 77520 Office: 712 Main St Houston TX 77002

TILTON, WEBSTER, JR., gen. contractor; b. St. Louis, Sept. 11, 1922; s. Webster and Eleanor (Dozier) T.; student St. Marks Prep. Sch., 1936-40, Pawling Prep. Sch., 1940-42; master brewers degree, U.S. Brewers Acad., 1949; m. Grace Drew Wilson, Feb. 14, 1948 (div. Oct. 1959); 1 son, Webster III; m. 2d, Nancy McBlair Payne, Jan. 5, 1963. Asst. brewing technologist F&M Schaffer Brewing Co., Bklyn., 1948-52; factory sales rep. Cole Steel Equipment Co., N.Y.C., 1957-68; dist. sales mgr. Scantlin Electronics, Inc., Washington, 1968-70; sales rep. Comml. Washer's Dryer Sales Co., Washington, 1970-73; gen. contractor, Washington, 1973—. Served from cadet to chief mate, USNR, 1942-45. Episcopalian. Home: 3719 Fulton St NW Washington DC 20007

TIMBERLAKE, LORA DELL (MRS. MARLIN C. TIMBERLAKE), librarian; b. Mansfield, La., June 26, 1934; d. Thomas Lewis and Georgie Lee (Gilliam) White; B.A. magna cum laude, So. U., 1954; M.L.S., La. State U., 1969; m. Marlin C. Timberlake, June 27, 1954; children—Marlin C., Oberon Denise. Tchr., librarian Washington Parish High Sch., Franklinton, La., 1954-55; tchr. Phoenix (La.) High Sch., 1956-62, Herdon (La.) High Sch., 1962-63; librarian Walnut Hill High Sch., Shreveport, La., 1963—. Vol. leader 4-H Club, 1970—, mem. home econs. adv. council, 1971—. Chmn. Modisette Award Sub-Com., 1970-71. Recipient Modisette award La. Library Assn., 1969; named Educator of Year, Caddo Edn. Assn. and Shreveport Times, 1969. Mem. Caddo Librarians Orgn. (sec. 1965-67), Caddo Edn. Assn. (bldg. rep. 1970—), Nat., La. edn. assns., Am. Internat. Charolais Assn., Kappa Delta Pi, Beta Phi Mu. Democrat. Baptist (dir. youth activities 1968—). Home: Route 6 Box 659 Dawson Rd Shreveport LA 71109 Office: Route 2 Box 85 Woolworth Rd Shreveport LA 71109

TIMBERLAKE, MARY ESTELLE, librarian; b. Durham, N.C., Dec. 2, 1910; d. Joe Elmore and Estelle (Flintom) Timberlake; student Winthrop Coll., 1929-30; A.B., U. S.C., 1932; M.A., George Peabody Coll. Tchrs., 1943. File clk. Fed. Land Bank, Columbia, S.C., 1933-42;

librarian Lander Coll., Greenwood, S.C., 1943-45; reader's services librarian Vassar Coll., Poughkeepsie, N.Y., 1950-54; librarian Newberry (S.C.) Coll., 1954-57; reference librarian U. S.C., Columbia, 1957-59, asst. reference librarian, 1945-50, 60-71, documents librarian Univ. Library, 1971—. Mem. Am., Southeastern, S.C. library assns., Am. Assn. U. Women, D.A.R. Republican. Methodist. Club: Adirondack Mountain (Poughkeepsie). Home: 1041 Marion St Columbia SC 29201 Office: Univ Library U South Carolina Columbia SC 29208

TIMBERLAKE, WAYT BELL, JR., lawyer; b. Staunton, Va., Nov. 23, 1908; s. Wayt Bell and Frances Stuart (Yates) T.; B.A., Va. Mil. Inst., 1929; LL.B., U. Va., 1932; m. Susan Lewis Marshall, Apr. 28, 1934; children—Frances (Mrs. Clyde L. Meares), Susan (Mrs. Colin S. Thomas), Wayt Bell III. Admitted to Va. bar, 1931; mem. firms Timberlake & Smith, Staunton, 1948-62; sr. partner Timberlake, Smith, Thomas & Moses, Staunton, 1962—. Dir. First Va. Bank Augusta, Staunton, First Va. Bankshares Corp., Arlington. City councilman City Staunton, 1950-54, vice mayor, 1952-54. Served with USNR, 1943-45. Fellow Am. Coll. Trial Lawyers; mem. Am., Va. (v.p. 1948-49), Staunton-Augusta County bar assns. Home: 1525 Dogwood Rd Staunton VA 24401 Office: Box 2566 Staunton VA 24401

TIMMERMAN, JOHN HODGES, dentist; b. Hartsville, S.C., Mar. 12, 1940; s. Washington Price and Margaret Griffin (Jordan) T.; student Clemson U., 1958-61; D.D.S., Med. Coll. Va., 1965; m. Jewel Garland Hoffmeyer, July 28, 1962; children—Marian Jordan, John Hodges, Elizabeth Garland, Margaret Marian. Pvt. practice dentistry, Chesterfield, S.C., 1965-66, Columbia, S.C., 1968—. Dir., sec. bd. dirs. Carolina Enterprises Columbia, Inc. Active Boy Scouts Am. Served to capt. Dental Corps, AUS, 1966-68. Mem. Am. Soc. Dentistry for Children (exec. com. S.C. chpt. 1971-75, pres. 1974-75), Am., S.C. dental assns., Greater Columbia, Central Dist. (sec.-treas.) dental socs., Internat. Assn. Orthodontics, S.C. Acad. Gen. Dentistry, Clemson U., Med. Coll. Va. alumni assns. Baptist (deacon 1969-72, 73—). Clubs: Country of Lexington (Lexington, S.C.); Greater Columbia Clemson (dir. 1971—, pres. 1973-74). Home: 727 Westover Rd Columbia SC 29210 Office: 1513 Morninghill Dr Columbia SC 29210

TIMMONS, HARRY MOTTE, newspaper exec.; b. Charlotte, N.C., July 22, 1936; s. Paul and Erlene (Hightower) T.; B.S., N.C. State Coll., 1959; m. Ruth Ann Cliff, Jan. 20, 1956; children—Harry Motte, Gary Arthur, Shari Lee. With data reduction div. Hercules Power Co., Bacchus, Utah, 1959-61; supr. customer support NCR Co., Atlanta, 1961-64; mgr. computer dept. Sentinel Star Co., Orlando, Fla., 1964-66, asst. gen. mgr., 1966-68, gen. mgr., 1968—. Exec. v.p. United Appeal Orange County, 1968-74; v.p. Central Fla. Devel. Com., 1970-72. Pres. bd. trustees Holiday Hosp., 1972—. Mem. Orlando Area C. of C. (dir. 1970-71), Boone Boosters Athletic Assn. (pres. 1973—). Clubs: Executives, Citrus, University, Rio Pinar Country (Orlando). Elk. Home: 1800 Lorena Lane Orlando FL 32806 Office: PO Box 2833 Orlando FL 32802

TIMMONS, HERALD AUSTIN, museum ofcl.; b. Ohatchee, Ala., Nov. 21, 1912; s. Coke Williams and Wallace Flora (Bryant) T.; student Lawrence Sch. Art, 1931, U. Ala., 1958, 65, 70; m. Sadie Mae Fox, July 15, 1939; children—Barbara, Mary (Mrs. James Ricky Bobo), Frances (Mrs. Alvin Parris), Harold, Eugene. With maintenance dept. Anniston Bd. Edn., 1932-40; with Anniston Police Dept., 1940-52; with Anniston Detective Dept., 1951-66; curator Regar Museum, Anniston, 1966—. Mem. Anniston Rescue Squad, Fraternal Order Police, 1950—. Bd. dirs. Glen Addie Recreation Center, Anniston, 1952-61. Mem. Ala. Archaeologia Soc., Choccolocca Archaeol. Soc. (dir. 1969-73). Club: Saks Art (dir. 1968-73). Home: 4114 Sprague Anniston AL 36201 Office: 1411 Gurnee St Anniston AL 36201

TIMMONS, PAT FRANCIS, lawyer; b. Texarkana, Ark., Nov. 26, 1917; s. Pat F. and Janet (Spidel) T.; B.A., Baylor U., 1939; J.D., South Tex. Coll., 1947; m. Clara Virginia Penick, Aug. 25, 1940; children—Claire Janet, Patrick F., Terence P. Pub. accountant P. F. Timmons, Houston, 1940-45; staff counsel Superior Oil Co., Houston, 1945-49; tax counsel Transcontinental Gas Pipeline Corp., Houston, 1950-57; admitted to Tex. bar, 1947; practice in Houston, 1957—. Dist. com. mem. Boy Scouts Am., 1965-66. C.P.A., Tex. Mem. Tex. Soc. C.P.A.'s, Am. Inst. C.P.A.'s, State Bar Tex., Am. Bar Assn. Home: 7706 Woodway St Houston TX 77042 Office: 1350 One Allen Center Houston TX 77002

TIMMS, DONALD EDWIN, bank exec.; b. Lake City, Ark., Sept. 6, 1927; s. Dudley Earnest and Edna Mae (Hooper) T.; student Sch. of Banking of South, La. State U., 1956-58, Nat. Comml. Lending Sch., U. Okla., 1969; m. LaWanda Eloise Thomas, Dec. 27, 1947; 1 dau., Rhonda Suzanne. Teller Farmers State Bank, Lake City, 1950-53, asst. v.p., 1953-56, v.p., 1956-59; v.p. Citizens Bank Jonesboro, Ark., 1959-69, sr. v.p., 1969—. City Councilman City Lake City, 1954-58; treas., 1958-72; sec. bd. Lake City pub. schs., Lake City, 1965—; Central committeeman County Democratic Central Com., Craighead County, Ark., 1969—. Served with AUS, 1946-47. Baptist (deacon 1964—). Mason (Shriner), Lion (sec. 1970-73; sec., treas. 1973—). Home: Buffalo St Lake City AR 72437 Office: Box 1090 Jonesboro AR 72401

TIMMS, JAMES DONNIE, mil. acad. adminstr.; b. Greenville, S.C., Feb. 7, 1910; s. James Harrison and Carrie (Morgan) T.; A.B., Furman U., 1941; M.S., Barry Coll., 1961; m. Mildred Della Johnson, Sept. 16, 1936; children—Bobbie (dec.), Darlene (Mrs. Rogers T. Hornsby), Cheryl (Mrs. Thomas Meyer). Tchr. Cedar Grove High Sch., Belton, S.C., 1934-39; prin. Chappells (S.C.) High Sch., 1940-41; prin. Elliott (S.C.) High Sch., 1942-43; dean, prin. Miami (Fla.) Mil. Acad., 1943—. Mem. Nat. Assn. Secondary Sch. Prins., Am. Assn. Ret. Persons, Advs. Internat. Trade Comity. Mem. Ch. of God (Sunday sch. tchr. 1935—). Home: 196 E 13th St Hialeah FL 33010 Office: 10601 Biscayne Blvd Miami FL 33138

TIMS, GEORGE BARTON, JR., univ. adminstr.; b. Purcell, Okla., June 23, 1918; s. George Barton and Kate Rebecca (Lewis) T.; B.S., Okla. State U., 1947, M.S., 1949; m. Virgie Adelyn Short, Dec. 29, 1941; children—Rebecca Laura (Mrs. Barrie C. Collins), Georgann (Mrs. Raymond Hudler). Asst. prof. indsl. engring. Okla. State U., Stillwater, 1946-51; prof., head dept. indsl. engring. Lamar U., Beaumont, Tex., 1951-66, asso. dean engring., dir. coop. edn., 1966-73, dir. vets. affairs, 1973—. Research collaborator Okla. Agrl. and Indsl. Devel. Service, 1950-51; chief-of-party Western Mich. U. AID Nigerian project, Ibadan, 1962-64, U. Houston India project, Madras, 1965, Patna, 1966. Councilman, Veterans Village, Stillwater, Okla., 1948. Served from pvt. to maj. C.E., AUS, 1941-46. Registered profl. engr., Tex. Mem. Am. Inst. Indsl. Engrs., Am. Soc. Engring. Edn., Blue Key, Sigma Xi, Alpha Pi Mu, Tau Beta Pi, Sigma Tau. Mason, Rotarian. Home: 5570 Sul Ross Lane Beaumont TX 77706

TINDELL, BILLY EUGENE, architect; b. Springfield, Mo., Jan. 21, 1925; s. Benjamine F. and Effie M. (McClure) T.; B.Arch., U. Okla., 1959; m. Zola Ernestine Biggs, Jan. 8, 1950; children—Lee Ann, Billy Stephen. Sr. research architect Southwest Research Inst., San Antonio, 1965-67; chief architect Hudgins Thompson Ball, Tulsa, 1967-69, Cooper Communities, Inc., Bentonville, Ark., 1969-71; architect B.E. Tindell, Rogers, Ark., 1971-73; sr. architect Bechtel Power Corp., Houston, 1974—. Served with AUS, 1943-46. Decorated Purple Heart. Mem. A.I.A., U. Okla. Alumni Assn. (life). Address: 2111 Teague St Houston TX 77055

TINGLEY, GLENN VINCENT, clergyman; b. Fields Corner, O., July 31, 1901; s. Nelson Eugene and Edith G. (Gage) T.; student Los Angeles Sem., 1915-20, Los Angeles Pacific Coll., 1919-20; A.B., Mt. Vernon U., 1942, Th.B., 1942; D.D., Christ Sem., 1944; m. Elva Eunice Allen, Sept. 10, 1921; children—Ruth Eunice (Mrs. Bruce Teer), Pauline Elsie (Mrs. John Thomas Sawyer), Alice Mae (Mrs. William Schafer), Marjorie (Mrs. Herman Cano), Peggy Glenn Iris (Mrs. Richard Barker), Glenn Vincent. Ordained to ministry, Christian and Missionary Alliance, 1926; pastor Birmingham Gospel Tabernacle, 1929-56; pres. Birmingham Bible Inst., 1930-50; pastor Alliance Ch., Rochester, N.Y., 1956-60; pres. Radio Revival, Inc., 1929—; pastor Fort Payne; Ala., 1969—; pres. Courier Broadcasting Service, Inc., 1944-51, Fair Haven Conf. Grounds, Birmingham, Ala., 1952-60. Evangelist interdenominational crusades various countries, 1959—; conf. speaker for The Evang. Alliance Mission, Aruba and Curacao, 1961; speaker Slovak Bapt. Union of Europe, 19 countries, 1954, Oriental Missionary Soc. in Greece, 1954; evangelist Christian and Missionary Alliance, Lebanon, Syria, Jordan in Ivory Coast. French West Africa, 1954, nat. evangelist, 1963-64; crusades in Peru, Colombia, Japan, Hong Kong, Philippines, Singapore, Malaysia, Israel. Pres. DeKalb County Mental Health Assn., 1967-68, 71-72. Trustee Toccoa Falls Bible Coll. Mem. Christian and Missionary Alliance, Nat. Religious Broadcaster (dir. 1941-61), Rochester Ministers Fellowship (pres. 1957-58), Rochester Fedn. Chs. (dir. 1957-58), Fort Payne Ministerial Assn., Pastors' Assn. Ft. Payne (pres. 1972). Home: PO Box 656 309 NW 21st St Fort Payne AL 35967 Office: PO Box 1928 Birmingham AL 35201

TINKLE, LON (JULIEN LON TINKLE), educator, editor; b. Dallas, Mar. 20, 1906; s. James Ward and Mary (Gardenhire) T.; A.B., So. Meth. U., 1927, A.M., 1932; Diplome de phonetique, Sorbonne, U. Paris, 1933; grad. student Columbia, 1936, 37; LL.D., St. Mary's U., 1963; m. Maria Ofelia Garza, Dec. 27, 1939; children—Jon Richard, James Alan, Anthony Robert. Instr., asst. prof., then prof. French and comparative lit. So. Meth., U., 1932—; guest prof. Columbia, summer 1947; asst. lit. editor Dallas News, 1942-47, lit. editor, 1947—. Vice pres. Margo Jones Theatre in the Round, Dallas, 1945-57; mem. bd. Dallas Mus. Fine Arts, Dallas Civic Music Assn., Dallas Friends of Library. Decorated Palmes Academiques (France); recipient Faculty Achievement award So. Meth. U,, 1959; prize Tex. Inst. Letters, 1959; Book award Sons Republic of Tex., 1959. Mem. Philos. Soc. Tex., Tex. Inst. Letters (pres. 1949-52), C. of C. Democrat. Mem. Christian Ch. Author: (with C. F. Zeek) Les Deux Idoles; 13 Days to Glory; The Alamo, 1958; The Story of Oklahoma, 1962; The Valiant Few, 1964; The Key to Dallas, 1965; Mr. De, 1970. Co-editor: The Cowboy Reader, 1959. Home: 3615 Amherst St Dallas TX 75225

TINKLE, MAYBELLE, educator; b. Henrietta, Tex., Dec. 20, 1909; d. George and Carrie Mae (Heindel) Tinkle; B.S., Tex. Wesleyan Coll., 1931; M.Ed., U. Tex., 1932; postgrad. U. Colo., 1937, U. Wis., 1938; D.Ed., U. Mich., 1955. Co-owner, M.B. Tinkle Dept. Store, Ft. Worth, 1932-38; asst. prof. phys. edn. Tex. Wesleyan Coll., Ft. Worth, 1937-46; asso. prof. phys. edn. Tex. Christian U., Ft. Worth, 1946—. Summer camp counsellor Camp El Tesoro, Granbury, Tex., 1942, Camp Waldemar, Hunt, Tex., 1943-49. Mem. Am. Assn. U. Women (pres. 1959-61), N.E.A., Tex. State Tchrs. Assn., Am., Tex. assns. health, phys. edn. and recreation, Nat., So. assns. phys. edn. coll. women, Ft. Worth Womens Phys. Edn. Assn., English Speaking Union, Delta Psi Kappa, Alpha Chi, Pi Lambda Theta, Delta Kappa Gamma. Methodist. Club: Womans Altrusa (pres. 1973-74) (Fort Worth). Home: 4900 Staples Av Fort Worth TX 76133

TINNELL, LEONARD EDWARD, accountant; b. Stamps, Ark., Oct. 4, 1916; s. Oscar H. and Gertrude (Tisdale) T.; grad. Internat. Accountants' Soc., Inc., Chgo., 1944; m. Jewell Orleans Wright, Mar. 16, 1935; children—Myrna Evelyn (dec.), James Edward, Sharon Diaine. Comptometer operator to gen. auditor Lion Oil Co., El Dorado, Ark., 1934-49; sec.-treas. Wheeling Pipe Line, Inc., 1949-51, Newell-White Motors, 1949-51; asst. to v.p. Lion Oil Co., El Dorado, 1951-55; asst. to v.p. to dir. supply and transp. Monsanto Chem. Co. - Lion Oil Co., 1955-60, personnel mgr., accounting dept. Monsanto Chem. Co., St. Louis, 1960-67; gen. mgr. Bear Brand Roofing, Inc., Bearden, Ark., 1967—; dir. Citizen's Bank, Bearden. accounting cons. El Dorado, 1940—. Sec. El Dorado Water & Sewer Commn., 1951-60. Pres. Jr. C. of C., El Dorado, 1944-46. Mem. Am. Inst. C.P.A'S., La. Tank Truck Carriers, Inc., Ark. Purchasing Agts. Assn. (v.p.), Ark. C. of C., Asphalt Roofing Mfrs. Assn., Nat. Assn. Purchasing Agts. (vice chmn. dist. 7, pub. relations, 1958-60). Mem. Ch. of Jesus Christ of Latter-day Saints (pres. Ark. dist. 1952-60; patriarch state 1969—). Home: PO Box 358 Bearden AR 71720 Office: Bear Brand Roofing Inc Bearden AR 71720

TINNEY, EDWARD EARL, historian; b. Norwood, W.Va., Jan. 2, 1928; s. Steve and Elizabeth (Wheeler) T.; B.A., W.Va. Inst. Tech., 1953; m. Lore Stoll, Oct. 4, 1948; children—Helena (Mrs. Steve Dozier), Edward Earl. Tchr., Clay (W.Va.) High Sch., 1953-54, Shenandoah (Va.) High Sch., 1954-55, DeMotte (Ind.) High Sch., 1956-57; prin. Brandy Station (Va.) Elementary Sch., 1957-59, Lignum (Va.) Elementary Sch., 1959-60; recreation leader, Augusta, Ga., 1960-61; historian Horseshoe Bend Nat. Mil. Park, Dadoville, Ala., 1961-63; historian Nat. Park Service, Cumberland Gap, 1963-66; historian Shiloh (Tenn.) Nat. Mil. Park, 1966-69; historian Chickamauga-Chattanooga Nat. Mil. Park, Fort Oglethorpe, Ga., 1969—. Pres. John Ross House Assn., home of Cherokee Indian Chief in the 1830's. Served with AUS, 1946-48, 1950-51. Mem. Chattanooga Hist. Soc. Methodist. Home: 1738 S Clayton Av Chattanooga TN 37412 Office: Chickamauga Chattanooga Nat Mil Park Fort Oglethorpe GA 30741

TINNIN, HELEN LOU, community health scientist; b. Austin, Tex., Feb. 1, 1933; d. Hugh and Mattie May (Carter) Tinnin; A.B., U. Cal. at Berkeley, 1952, M.P.H., 1961; Ph.D., Ohio State U., 1964. Pharm. mfrs. rep. Pfizer Lab. of N.Y., Youngstown, O., 1952-54, Ayerst Labs of N.Y., Birmingham, Ala., 1954-59; instr. personal and community health Ohio State U., 1961-63; health edn. cons., project dir. Tri-Agy. Health Edn. Council, Canton, O., 1963-64; asst. prof. preventive medicine and pub. health, cons. scientist Univ. Hosp. and Clinics, U. Ala. Med. Center, 1964-66; asso. prof. health edn. and asst. to dean program planning U. Tex. Grad. Sch. Biomed. Scis., Tex. Med. Center, Houston, 1966-67; prof. community health and med. practice U. Mo. Med. Sch., Columbia, 1967-70; exec. dir. Forsyth Health Planning Council, also prof. community medicine Bowman Gray Sch. Medicine, Wake Forest U., Winston-Salem, N.C., 1971—. Cons. Westinghouse Learning on Population Dynamics, Program Methodology U. Mo. Regional Med. Program, Health Service Research sect. U. Mo. Med. Sch. Adviser youth groups Episcopal Ch. Mem. Assn. Am. Med. Colls., Am. Assn. U. Profs., N.C. Pub. Health Assn., Soc. Pub. Health Educators, Am. Sch. Health Assn., Council on Med. Television, Assn. Tchrs. Preventive Medicine, Am. Pub. Health Assn., Assn. Sch. Allied Health, Am. Assn. U. Women, League Women Voters. Home: 2934-B St Mark's Rd Winston-Salem NC 27103 Office: Bowman Gray School of Medicine Allied Health Bldg 1990 Beach St Winston-Salem NC 27103

TINSLEY, NORMA ELISE ROBINSON (MRS. JAMES MADISON TINSLEY), mfg., wholesale co. exec.; b. Shreveport, La., July 18, 1909; d. James Malcolm and Effie (Estes) Robinson; A.B. magna cum laude, Centenary Coll., 1930; postgrad. U. Colo., 1931; m. James Madison Tinsley, Apr. 26, 1943; 1 son, James Robinson. Asso. prof. English, psychology Dodd Coll., Shreveport, 1930-41; mng. partner Robinson-Tinsley Co., Shreveport, 1936—. Sec., Little Theater Guild, 1936-37; mem. com. Preservation Fort Hudson Battlefield, 1959-61; mem. Soc. Preservation Fort Del., 1959-61. Named hon. Ky. Col., hon. Ky. Adm. Mem. U.S., Shreveport chambers commerce, L'Alliance Francaise, La., N. La. hist. assns. (mem. bd. 1959-61, sec. 1959), Internat. Platform Assn., Am. Assn. U. Women (hospitality chmn. Shreveport br. 1969—), Ky. Hist. Soc., Centenary Coll. Alumni Assn. (chpt. bd. dirs. 1965-67). Chi Omega (Shreveport chpt. pres. 1935-37), Alpha Chi, Pi Gamma Mu. Baptist. Home: 1039 Sheridan Av Shreveport LA 71104 Office: 2101 Seymour St Shreveport LA 71104

TIPPENS, STEPHEN COOPER, publishing co. exec.; b. Nashville, Jan. 26, 1937; s. Arthur Cliffe and Mary Lou (Cooper) T.; B.A., Vanderbilt U., 1959; postgrad. U. Tenn., 1962-63; m. Patricia Jean DeSart, Sept. 2, 1962; children—Michael Sean, Christopher Stephen, Jennifer Louise. Exec. trainee Third Nat. Bank, Nashville, 1962-63; life ins. underwriter Penn Mut. Ins. Co., Nashville, 1963; pub. relations asst. United Meth. Pub. House, Nashville, 1963-65, pub. relations mgr., 1965-68, dir. pub. relations, 1968—. Vice chmn. bd. Wesley Found., Nashville, 1968-70, treas., 1973—; v.p. Tenn. Conf. Young Adult Assembly, United Meth. Ch., 1969-70. Served with AUS, 1959-62. Mem. Religious Pub. Relations Council (chpt. pres. 1966-67, nat. bd. govs. 1967-73), Pub. Relations Soc. Am. Home: 3905 Valley Rd Nashville TN 37205 Office: 201 8th Av S Nashville TN 37202

TIPTON, STUART GUY, trade assn. exec.; b. Knightstown, Ind., Dec. 26, 1910; s. Guy Stuart and Bessie (Walters) T.; A.B., Wabash Coll., 1932; J.D., Northwestern U., 1935; m. Lorraine Arnold, May 15, 1937; children—Susan, Judith, Ann, Patience. Admitted to Ind. bar, 1935, D.C. bar, 1940; atty. legislative sect. Office of Gen. Counsel, Treasury Dept., Washington, 1936-38; atty. CAA, Washington, 1938-40, asst. gen. counsel, 1940-44; gen. counsel Air Transport Assn., Washington, 1944-55, pres., 1955-72, chmn. bd., 1972—. Trustee Holton-Arms Sch., Bethesda, Md. Clubs: Internat., Nat. Aviation, Metropolitan, Capitol Hill (Washington); Wings (N.Y.C.); Congressional Country, Burning Tree (Bethesda). Home: 11761 Glen Rd Potomac MD 20854 Office: 1709 New York Av NW Washington DC 20006

TISDALE, THOMAS SUMTER, JR., lawyer; b. Florence, S.C., May 10, 1939; s. Thomas Sumter and Rebecca Wright (Roberts) T.; B.A., U. South, 1961; LL.B., U. S.C., 1964, J.D., 1967; m. Courtenay Cordes McDowell, Feb. 6, 1965; children—Thomas Sumter III, Frederick Reese. Admitted to S.C. bar, 1964, also U.S. Supreme Ct. bar; asso. firm Young, Clement & Rivers, 1964-68, partner, 1968—; asst. solicitor 9th Jud. Circuit S.C., 1970; judge Charleston (S.C.) Municipal Ct., 1970-72. Chmn., Charleston Democratic Party, 1971—. Bd. dirs. A.R.C., 1971—, Am. Cancer Soc., 1971—; trustee U. South, 1970—. Mem. Am., S.C. (v.p. 1973—), Charleston County (exec. committeeman 1970—) bar assns., Charleston Lawyers Club (pres. 1971), Soc. Colonial Wars, Omicron Delta Kappa, Blue Key. Episcopalian (mem. vestry 1969—, warden 1973—). Home: 109 Broad St Charleston SC 29401 Office: 28 Broad St Charleston SC 29401

TITUS, FRANK LLOYD, clergyman; b. Deposit, N.Y., Aug. 15, 1906; s. Lloyd Clarke and Sadie (Couse) T.; A.B., Syracuse U., 1930; student Delancey Div. Sch., Buffalo, 1932, Coll. of Preachers, Washington, 1937; grad. Command and Gen. Staff Coll., Ft. Leavenworth, 1952; grad. advanced course Chaplain Sch., Ft. Slocum, N.Y., 1957; m. Frieda Burlingame, Nov. 24, 1926; children—Donald Frederick, Marilyn (Mrs. Ernest Seaton, Jr.). Ordained to ministry Episcopal Ch., 1933; curate Trinity Ch., Watertown N.Y., 1932-35; rector Emmanuel Ch., Little Falls, N.Y., 1935-40; overseas sec. Nat. Council Episcopal Ch., 1946-50; rector Holy Cross Ch., Miami, Fla., 1952-65, Calvary Ch., Indian Rocks Beach, Fla., 1965—. Dean Miami Episcopal Deanery, 1957-65; hon. canon St. Luke's Cathedral, Orlando, 1967-68; hon. canon St. Peter's Cathedral, St. Petersburg, 1969; mem. standing com. Diocese of So. Fla., 1960-61, S.W. Fla., 1972-73, mem. diocesan council, 1970-71, mem. com. of the statee of ch., 1961-64; del. Episcopal Gen. Conv., 1970-73. Bd. dirs. Florence Crittenton Home Dade County, 1962-65; trustee Windham House, N.Y., 1948-50; dir. promotion Diocese of So. Fla., 1953-56, trustee, 1966-70; mem. citizens adv. com. Miami, 1963-65. Bd. dirs. chmn. Allupatah YMCA, bd. mgrs., 1963-64; bd. dirs. Greater Miami YMCA, 1954-65. Mem. Aux. Fla. Hwy. Patrol, 1960-65. Served as chaplain, lt. col. AUS, 1940-46, PTO; lt. col. Res. (ret.). Mem. Greater Miami Ministerial Assn. (treas. 1961-62, pres. 1962-63), Miami Clericus, Am. Legion, 40 and 8, Acad. Religion and Mental Health, Navy League (chaplain Miami chpt. 1964-65), Mil. Order World Wars (chaplain), Res. Officers Assn., Holiday Isles C. of C. (dir. 1970-71), Ret. Officer's Assn. Democrat. Mason (32 deg., Shriner), Elk, Rotarian. Author: Cross on My Collar, 1955; Oil From the Beard of Aaron, 1961; Descendants of Selah Titus, 1971. Contbr. numerous articles to mags. Home: 107 25th St Belleair Beach FL 33535 Office: 1615 1st St Indian Rocks Beach FL 33535

TITUS, GEORGE FRANCIS, accountant; b. Clarendon, Pa., Jan. 2, 1898; s. Smith Luther and Mary Frances (McBride) T.; B.S., U. Okla., 1927, M.S., Columbia, 1928; postgrad. Harvard Grad. Sch. Arts and Sci., 1932, Yale, 1933; m. Edna Mae Brown. Accountant various accounting firms, N.Y.C., 1928-32; chief field auditor, Dept. Agr., 1934-35; financial analyst, Dept. Internal Revenue, 1935-40; chief auditor Dept. Navy, Phila., 1941-45, mem. Navy Contract Renegotiation Bd., 1945-46, chief accountant Pearl Harbor Naval Shipyard Hawaii, 1947-49, dep. controller Mil. Sea Transport Service N.Y., 1949-50; financial analyst ECA, 1950-53; deptl. internal auditor, Treasury Dept., Washington, 1953-63; former prof. econ. history Southeastern U., now ret. Mem. Am. Inst. C.P.A.'s, Yale Engring. and Sci. Assn., Acacia, Chi Beta. Home: 4501 Arlington Blvd Arlington VA 22203

TITUS, ROBERT LEE, educator; b. Blackwell, Okla., Dec. 11, 1927; s. Banner Shawhan and Eva May (Flood) Titus; A.B., William Jewell Coll., 1951; M.S., Ind. U., 1955, Ed.D., 1964; m. Geraldine Ruth Park, May 25, 1952; children—Robert William, Diane Louise. Tchr. Kinsley (Kan.) pub. schs., 1951-54; asso., asst. prodn. supr., Audio-Visual Center, Ind. U., Bloomington, 1956-57; faculty ednl. media and tech. dept. East Tex. State U., Commerce, 1957—, prof., 1968—. Cons. on media equipment, facilities and utilization; condr. workshops. Served with AUS, 1946-47. Mem. N.E.A., Assn. for Edn. Communication and Tech., Tex. Assn. for Edn. Tech. (pres. 1966-67, dir. 1967-73, mem. exec. com. 1971-73), Area Ten Assn. for Edn. Tech. (pres. 1971-72), Tex. Assn. Coll. Tchrs., Tex. Soc. Coll. Tchrs.

of Edn., Phi Delta Kappa (pres. 1973-74). Baptist (deacon). Kiwanian (pres. 1966, dir. 1964-68). Home: 2305 Bois d'Arc Commerce TX 75428

TOAN, CHARLES SCOTT, food co. exec.; b. Rochester, N.Y., Dec. 11, 1919; s. Lewis A. and Jessie C. (Scott) T.; B.S. in Agr., Cornell U., 1942; m. Eleanore V. Reed, June 12, 1943; children—Brenda, Douglas, Elizabeth, Sylvia. Plant mgr. Coop GLF, Inc., Macedon, N.Y., 1947-48, Waterloo, N.Y., 1948-49; plant mgr. Nat. Fruit Product Co., Winchester, Va., 1949-59, v.p. prodn., 1967—; exec. sec. Frederick Co. Fruit Growers, Inc., Winchester, 1960-66. Pres., dir. Nat. Council Agrl. Employers, Washington, 1967-68. Pres. Shenandoah Apple Blossom Festival, Winchester, 1962-64, mem. exec. com., 1960—. Bd. dirs. Winchester Meml. Hosp., 1963—. Served with USNR, 1942-46. Mason, Rotarian. Home: 629 Tennyson Av Winchester VA 22601 Office: 550 Fairmont Av Winchester VA 22601

TOBER, GLENN, oceanographer; b. Springfield, Ill., June 2, 1943; s. Henry and Mollie (Broida) T.; B.S. in Elec. Engring., U. Fla., 1966, M.S. in Elec. Engring., 1971, postgrad., 1972—; m. Pamela Ziccardi, July 1, 1968; 1 son, Ryan Michael. Research asst. oceanography dept., coastal and oceanographic engring. U. Fla., Gainesville, 1970—. Served to lt. (j.g.) U.S. Coast and Geodetic Survey, Environmental Sci. Services Adminstrn., Dept. Commerce, 1966-69. Mem. I.E.E.E., Eta Kappa Nu. Home: 319 SW 12th St Gainesville FL 32601 Office: Dept Coastal and Oceanographic Engring Univ Fla Gainesville FL 32601

TOBIASSEN, THOMAS JOHAN, state legislator, mech. engr.; b. Omaha, Nov. 21, 1931; s. Thoralph Johan and Goldie (Marie) T.; B.S., Ohio State U., 1959; postgrad. U. Fla., 1967-68; m. Audrey I. Neumann, Nov. 27, 1959; children—Thomas Johan, Todd Johan. Sr. engr. Monsanto Co.; mem. Fla. Ho. of Reps., 1968—. Served with C.E., AUS, 1953-55. Mem. C. of C., Sigma Chi. Republican. Lutheran. Kiwanian. Patentee in field. Address: 8010 Woodbine Dr Pensacola FL 32503

TOBOLOWSKY, JACK LEHMAN, textile co. exec.; b. Dallas, Jan. 16, 1917; s. Reuben and Etta Gertrude (Tobolowsky) T.; B.B.A., U. Tex., 1937; m. Josephine Pergament, Feb. 7, 1943; children—Dona (Mrs. Robert Stiffel), Ira, George, Myra. Sr. engr. Western Electric Co., N.Y., 1944-49; gen. mgr. Tex Style Mfg. Co., Midlothian, 1949-59; pres. Midlo Textile Co., Midlothian and Dallas, 1959-63; pres. Wolf Textile Co., Dallas, 1963—; also engaged in ranching. Served with AUS, 1942-44. Mem. Phi Sigma Delta. Home: 5909 Waggoner Dr Dallas TX 75230 Office: 2214 Pacific Av Dallas TX 75201

TOBUREN, LAWRENCE RICHTER, transp. co. exec.; b. Cleburne, Kan., July 11, 1915; s. Edward Franklin and Anna Fredericks (Richter) T.; student U. Denver, 1937-41; m. Ella Joyner Brame, Dec. 16, 1942; children—Lawrence Richter, William Brame, Luanne Brame, Gwendolyn Brame. Dispatch clk., dispatcher Continental Airlines, Denver, 1943-48; dispatcher Pacific Intermountain Express, Denver, 1948-52, dir. dispatch, Oakland, Cal., 1952-57, Western region operations mgr., 1957-58; with Pilot Freight Carriers, Inc., Charlotte, N.C. and Winston-Salem, N.C., 1958—, dir. operations, 1963-67, v.p. operations, 1967-71, exec. v.p., 1972—. Served with USAAF, 1942-43. Mem. Equipment Interchange Assn. (dir.). Republican. Methodist. Home: Route 1 Wedge Dr Pfafftown NC 27040 Office: N Cherry Extension and Polo Winston-Salem NC 27102

TODD, EDWARD PAYSON, govt. ofcl.; b. Newburyport, Mass., Jan. 26, 1920; s. Glendon Forrest and Stella May (Cashman) T.; B.S., in Physics, Mass. Inst. Tech., 1942; Ph.D., U. Colo., 1954; m. Barbara Adams Wright, June 17, 1950; children—Glendon Gardner, Nathaniel Adams, Charles Payson. Research physicist United Shoe Machinery Corp., Beverly, Mass., 1946-49; supr. applied research Pitney Bowes, Inc., Stamford, Conn., 1954-57; tech. dir. Upper Air Lab., U. Colo., Boulder, 1957-63; asso. program dir. for atmospheric scis. NSF, Washington, 1960-61, program dir. for aeronomy, atmospheric scis. sect., also NSF-Nat. Center Atmospheric Research liaison, Washington, 1963-65, acting head atmospheric scis. sect. Math. and Phys. Scis. div., 1963-64, spl. asst. to asso. dir. for research, 1965-66, dep. asso. dir. for research, 1966-70, dep. asst. dir. for research, 1970—, chmn. interdeptl. com. for atmospheric scis., 1972—. Mem. Falls Church (Va.) Sch. Bd., 1968—. Served to capt. Signal Corps, AUS, 1942-46. Recipient Distinguished Service award NSF, 1971. Mem. Am. Geophys. Union (council mem. 1970-72), Am. Meteorol. Soc. Home: 312 Van Buren St Falls Church VA 22046 Office: NSF 1800 G St NW Washington DC 20550

TODD, FRANK LESESNE, brick mfg. exec.; b. Hendersonville, N.C., Jan. 18, 1922; s. John Haywood and LeNorah (Bennett) T.; B.S., Wake Forest U., 1943, LL.B., 1948, J.D., 1970; m. Betty Anne Drysdale, Oct. 23, 1948; children—Frank Lesesne, Barbara Anne, John Bruce, Elizabeth Drysdale. Admitted to N.C. bar, 1948; practiced in Hendersonville, N.C., 1948-55; pres. Fletcher Brick Co., Hendersonville, 1955-64; pres. Moland-Drysdale Corp., Hendersonville, 1964—; dir. Northwestern Bank, Hendersonville and North Wilkesboro, N.C. Chmn. Hendersonville Planning and Zoning Bd., 1965-69; commr. Hendersonville, 1969—; mayor pro tem, Hendersonville, 1969—. Trustee, Montreat Anderson Coll., Flat Rock Playhouse; bd. visitors Western Carolina U. Served to lt. USNR, 1943-46. Mem. N.C. Bar Assn., N.C. Brick and Tile Assn. (dir. 1964—), Structural Clay Products Inst. (dir. 1966-69), Phi Alpha Delta, Lambda Chi Alpha. Presbyn. Elk, Kiwanian. Clubs: Etowah (N.C.) Golf (pres., also owner); Hendersonville Country. Address: PO Box 2150 Hendersonville NC 28739

TODD, JERRY FOCH, mech. engr.; b. Ft. Worth, Sept. 23, 1924; s. Arthur Totter and Mae (Kearney) T.; B.S. in Mech. Engring., Stanford, 1949; m. Leta Kate Maclin, Mar. 19, 1946; children—Reginald, Tera (Mrs. Don Albert), Teresa (Mrs. Dale Hogue), Robert, Elizabeth. Sales engr. Continental Supply Co., Dallas, 1949-50; engr. trainee Magnolia Petroleum Co., Dallas, 1950-51, plant engr., 1951-52, project constrn. engr., 1952-54, project engr., 1954-58, maintenance engr., 1958-60; project engr. Sid Richardson Carbon & Gasoline Co., Ft. Worth, 1960-68; chief engr. Trend Constrn. Corp., Oklahoma City, 1968-69, v.p., 1969—; pres. Process Packages, Inc., Oklahoma City, 1973—. Chmn. summer art show Hurst Art Assn., 1964-65. Registered profl. engr., Okla., Tex. Mem. Natural Gas Processors Assn., Stanford Alumni Assn. Presbyn. (deacon 1955-57, elder 1958-59, 63-65). Club: O.S. U. Posse. Home: 2317 NW 112th Terrace Oklahoma City OK 73120 Office: Box 14503 Oklahoma City OK 73114

TODD, LUTHER BEDFORD, paint co. exec.; b. Dallas, June 1, 1937; s. Benjamin Henry and Catherine Amanda (Dodson) T.; B.B.A., So. Meth. U., 1961; postgrad. bus. adminstrn. U. Tex., 1964-65; m. Beverly Ann Hopkins, Sept. 8, 1962; children—Stephen Wayne, Patricia Anne. Traveling auditor U.S. Gen. Accounting Office, Dallas, 1961-64; jr. accountant Wade, Barton & Marsh, C.P.A.s, Austin, Tex., 1964-65; accountant Touche Ross & Co., C.P.A.s, Houston, 1965-69, audit supr., 1969-72; internal auditor Napko Corp., paint mfg. and sales, Houston, 1972—. Mem. supervisory com. Napko Fed. Credit Union, 1973-74. Adviser, Jr. Achievement, Houston, 1966-69, treas. Advisers' Assn., 1969; sec. Sharpstown Country Club Estates (E.) Homeowners' Assn., 1971-72. Served with USNR, 1957-59. C.P.A., Tex. Mem. Am. Inst. C.P.A.s, Tex. Soc. C.P.A.s (chmn. Houston chpt. com. invocations 1972-73), Nat. Assn. Accountants (asst. sec. Houston chpt. 1968-69), Hosp. Financial Mgmt. Assn. Methodist (counselor youth fellowship 1966-68, mem. ch. adminstrv. bd. 1972—). Home: 7710 Sands Point Houston TX 77036 Office: 5300 Sunrise St Houston TX 77021

TODD, MERYL LYNN, cons. engr.; b. Edgewood, Ia., May 12, 1909; s. Charles Samuel and Marie (Martin) T.; B.S., Ia. State U., 1931; m. Margaret Gilchrist Moore, Oct. 27, 1931; children—Winifred Lee (Mrs. William H. Findley), Stephen Randolph. Engr., Trane Co., La Crosse, Wis., 1931-36; cons. engr., Waterloo, Ia., 1936-40; partner firm Todd, Hedeen & Assos., Waterloo, 1940-68; chief mech. engr., architect Engr. Group, Bomber Base, Sioux City, Ia., also Naval Air Sta., Ottumwa, Ia., 1942-44; pres. Todd-Hedeen Internat. Inc., Waterloo, Ia., also Miami, Fla., 1954—; dir. Compania Cubana Primadera S.A., N.Y.C., Primadera Internat., N.Y.C., also Miami. Mem. Nat. Soc. Profl. Engrs., Am. Soc. Mech. Engrs., Am. Soc. Heating, Ventilating, Refrigeration and Air Conditioning Engrs., Am. Soc. Agrl. Engrs., Fla. Engring. Soc., Delta Tau Delta. Republican. Methodist. Home and office: 12050 Moss Ranch Rd Miami FL 33156

TODD, STANLEY EARL, dentist; b. Detroit, Feb. 10, 1923; s. Earl B. and Oca (Logsdon) T.; student U. Eastern Ky., 1940-41; D.M.D., U. Louisville, 1949; m. Esta Newman, June 21, 1946; children—Stanley Earl, Rebecca Newman. Pvt. practice dentistry, Richmond, Ky., 1949—. Pres. Ken Rich, Inc.; dir. Bank of Richmond. City commr. Richmond, 1969-71. Bd. dirs. Ky. River Foothill Council. Served with USAAF, 1943-45. Mem. Pierre Fauchard Acad., Am., Ky. dental assns., Beta Delta, Psi Omega. Republican. Mem. Christian Ch. (chmn. bd. 1969-70). Club: Exchange (Richmond). Home: 304 Barnes Mill Rd Richmond KY 40475 Office: 527 W Main St Richmond KY 40475

TODD, THOMAS CARMEL, ednl. adminstr.; b. Dotham, Ala., Jan. 9, 1929; s. Alda Thomas and Ada Estelle (Tharp) T.; B.S., Troy State U., 1955; M.S., Fla. State U., 1957; m. Barbara Sheen, May 15, 1973; children—Kimberly, Thomas Edward, Teri Jan. Prin., Telogia (Fla.) Sch., 1955-57, Ponce de Leon Elementary Sch., Clearwater, Fla., 1957-63; supt. schs. Bay County, Panama City, Fla., 1966-72; exec. asst. to the commr. of edn., Tallahassee, 1972—. Mem. Bay County Council on Aging, 1970-71. Served with AUS, 1951-53. Decorated Air medal. Recipient Good Govt. award Panama City Jr. C. of C., 1969. Mem. Fla. Assn. County Sch. Supts. (pres. 1971-72), Audubon Soc., Sierra Club, Lynn Haven C. of C. (pres. 1968-69), Kappa Delta Pi, Phi Delta Kappa. Democrat. Baptist. Mason, Elk, Lion. Home: Box 2073 Tallahassee FL 32304 Office: Dept Edn Tallahassee FL 32304

TOERNER, PAUL EMILE, constrn. co. exec.; b. Creole, La., Oct. 1, 1926; s. Earl Eugene and Eucharist Katherine (Theriot) T.; grad. high sch.; m. Edna E. Hale, Feb. 15, 1947; children—Paula (Mrs. Richard Metts), Richard, William, Katherine (Mrs. Rodney Browne), Marie. Splicer, So. Bell, Lake Charles, La., 1949-55; supt. Lindsey Constrn., 1955-58; splicer U.S. Govt., Ft. Polk, La., 1959-61; splicer, supt. Burnup & Sim Inc., West Palm Beach, Fla., 1961-70, v.p., 1970-71; owner, pres. Call Burnup & Sims of P.R., Burnup & Sims of St. Croix and St. Thomas, 1971—; pres. Burnup & Sims, Continental Honduras, 1971—. Served with paratroopers AUS, 1945-49. Mem. Tampa C. of C. Democrat. Methodist. Mason, Moose. Home: 10465 Acme St West Palm Beach FL 33406 Office: 2011 Okeeschobee Blvd West Palm Beach FL 33401

TOGIE, DAVID, advt. firm exec.; b. Plant City, Fla., Sept. 23, 1934; s. David and Othell (McQuinn) T.; B.A., U. Md., 1970; M.A., Am. U., 1971; m. Carolyn Virginia Turner, May 9, 1959; children—Jeffrey Adam, Marc Darren. Producer, dir. WTVT-TV, Tampa, Fla., 1957-66; prodn. mgr. WVTV-TV, Milw., 1966-67; tv producer, dir. Def. Dept., Washington, 1967-71; prodn. mgr. WTOG-TV, St. Petersburg, Fla., 1971; owner, pres. David Togie Advt., Tampa, 1971—; pres. Togie-Hill Property Investments, 1971—. Mem. Tampa C. of C. Served with USMCR, 1953-56. Mem. Tampa C. of C. Democrat. Home: 4231 Beachway Dr Tampa FL 33609 Office: 105 S Gomez St Tampa FL 33609

TOLAR, JOHN NEEDHAM, lawyer; b. Ocala, Fla., Apr. 14, 1912; s. John N. and Adeline Virginia (Eminisor) T.; student U. Fla., 1930-31; LL.B., Columbus U., 1937, LL.M., 1938; J.D., Catholic U. Am., 1967; m. Marye N. Walker, July 2, 1941. Admitted to D.C. bar, 1937, Fla. bar, 1940, U.S. Supreme Ct. bar, 1957; clk. Fed. Home Loan Bank, 1933-38; sec. to personnel com. HOLC, 1938-39; with Pub. Works Adminstrn., 1939-40; spl. agt. Dept. of Agr., 1940-46; instl. property specialist War Assets Adminstrn., 1946-48; practice, Ft. Lauderdale, Fla., 1948—. Pres. trustees Presbytery of South, Synod of Fla., 1956-69; mem. permanent jud. commn., United Presbyn. Ch., U.S.A., 1962-67. Served as officer USAAF, 1942-45. Mem. Am. Bar Assn., Fla. Bar. Home: 2124 Middle River Dr Fort Lauderdale FL 33305 Office: Bayview Bldg Fort Lauderdale FL 33304

TOLBERT, VIRGINIA STANSEL (MRS. EARL PEEBLES TOLBERT), physician; b. Ruleville, Miss., Aug. 10, 1918; d. Horace Sylvan and Dovie Pearl (High) Stansel; B.A. cum laude, Miss. State Coll. for Women, 1937; med. certificate, U. Miss., 1948; M.D., U. Tenn., 1950; m. Earl Peebles Tolbert, June 7, 1953; 1 son, Henry Lawrence. Intern U. Ala. Hosp., Birmingham, 1950-51; gen. practice medicine, Ruleville, Miss., 1951—; mem. staff North Sunflower County Hosp., Ruleville; cons. physician Sunflower County Health Dept. Alderman, mem. town bd., Ruleville, 1970-73, mayor, 1973—. Pres. Sunflower County Heart Assn., 1960—. Mem. Am., Miss. med. assns., Miss. Municipal Assn. (exec. com. 1973—), Delta Med. Soc., Alpha Omega Alpha. Methodist. Home: 220 E Oscar St Ruleville MS 38771 Office: 601 N Oak St Ruleville MS 38771

TOLER, JAMES EDWARD, elevator co. exec.; b. Greensboro, N.C., Nov. 20, 1931; s. Morell Bryant and Edie Alma (Gillespie) T.; student in bus. adminstrn. U. N.C., 1950-52; m. Nina Marie Ritcey, May 5, 1956; children—Robin R., James Edward. With So. Elevator Co., Greensboro, 1956—, sales mgr., 1960—, exec. v.p., 1966—. Vice pres. Greensboro Community Center, 1968—. Vice chmn. City of Greensboro Wildlife Resources Commn., 1968—. Bd. dirs. Jr. Achievement of Greensboro, sec. exec. com., 1971—; bd. dirs. Young Life in Greater Greensboro. Served with USCGR, 1952-55. Mem. U.S. Power Squadron (sec. Winston-Salem squadron 1969-70), U.S. Boating Assn., Internat. Yachting Fellowship Rotarians, Piedmont Sales Execs. Club, Sigma Chi (pres. Greensboro alumni assn. 1960-61). Methodist. Mason (Shriner). Clubs: Summit Rotary (pres. 1970-72), Sedgefield Country (Greensboro); Washington (N.C.) Yacht and Country; Montgomery Country (Troy, N.C.). Home: 5516 Mecklenburg Rd Greensboro NC 27407 Office: Southern Elevator Co PO Drawer 20206 Greensboro NC 27420

TOLES, JAMES LAFAYETTE, JR., educator; b. Monrovia, Liberia, May 9, 1933; s. James LaFayette and Angeline Patricia (Toles) T.; came to U.S., 1954, naturalized, 1968; B.S., Clark Coll., 1958; M.B.A., N. Tex. State U., 1962; Ph.D., U. N.D., 1970; m. Barbara R. Gallashaw, Dec. 24, 1958; children—Patricia Ann, Cynthia Annette, James Lafayette III, Celia A. Asst. prof. Miles Coll., Birmingham, Ala., 1958-59; asst. prof. Wiley Coll., Marshall, Tex., 1960-62; prof. accounting, chmn. div. bus. and econs. Fort Valley (Ga.) State Coll., 1962—. Cons. in acad. adminstrn. United Bd. for Coll. Devel.; mem. com. on real estate law and policy devel. Ga. Bd. Regents. Mem. regional exec. com. Boy Scouts Am., 1973—. Recipient Outstanding Service award Ga. Bus. and Office Edn. Assn., 1973; Liberian Govt. scholar, 1954-58; Ford Found. fellow, 1964; Republic Steel fellow, 1964; So. Fellowship Fund grantee, 1969-70; NSF summer fellow; others. Mem. Am. Accounting Assn., Am. Mgmt. Assn., Nat. Bus. Tchr. Edn. Assn., Am. Vocational Edn. Assn., Operations Research Soc. Am., Am. Ednl. Research Assn., Am. Assn. Collegiate Schs. Bus., Phi Omega Pi, Delta Pi Epsilon, Phi Beta Lambda, Phi Delta Kappa, Alpha Phi Alpha. Episcopalian (mem. vestry bd.). Mason. Contbr. to profl. publs. Home: 1327 Jones St Fort Valley GA 31030

TOLLEY, AUBREY GRANVILLE, psychiatrist, state ofcl.; b. Lynchburg, Va., Nov. 15, 1924; s. Aubrey Thomas and Nonnie Isabell (Pinion) T.; student Duke, 1942-43; M.D., U. Va., 1952; m. Jeannette Leigh Poindexter, Mar. 21, 1947; children—Barbara Leigh, Stuart Granville, Leslie Carroll, Anna Catherine. Intern, St. Elizabeth's Hosp., Washington, 1952-53; resident psychiatry U. Va. Med. Sch., Charlotteville, 1953-56; instr. dept. psychiatry U. N.C. 1956-61, asst. prof., 1961-66; dir. residency edn. John Umstead Hosp., Butner, 1966-67; dir. profl. tng. and edn. N.C. Dept. Mental Health, Raleigh, 1967-72, asst. commr., 1972-73; dir. Dorothea Dix Hosp., Raleigh, 1973—, dir. psychotherapy, 1961-67; cons. psychiatry VA Hosp., Fayetteville, 1956—. Served with USNR, 1943-46. Diplomate in psychiatry Am. Bd. Psychiatry and Neurology. Mem. A.M.A., Am. Psychiat. Assn., N.C., Durham-Orange County med. socs., N.C. Neuropsychiat. Assn. Home: 1504 Halifax Rd Chapel Hill NC 27514 Office: Dorothea Dix Hosp Raleigh NC 27602

TOLMAS, HYMAN CYRIL, pediatrician; b. New Orleans, Feb. 1, 1922; s. Charles and Cecile (Bressler) T.; B.S., Tulane U., 1943; M.D., Tulane Med. Sch., 1945; m. Constance D. Cohen, July 9, 1950; children—Jean Ann, Alan Leon. Intern, Charity Hosp. La., New Orleans, 1945-46, resident pediatrics, 1946, 48-50; practice medicine, specializing in pediatrics, New Orleans, 1950—; mem. med. adv. com. New Orleans Speech & Hearing Center, 1964—; chief, coordinator pediatrics Hosel Dieu Hosp., New Orleans, 1960-65; sr. vis. pediatrician Touro Infirmary, New Orleans, 1950—; mem. staff Mercy, East Jefferson Gen., Lakeside Hosps., New Orleans; pres. med. staff Mercy Hosp., 1972; asso. clin. prof. pediatrics Tulane Med. Sch., 1965—. Bd. dirs. A.R.C., 1953-54. Served to lt. (j.g.) USNR, 1946-48. Recipient Med. award City New Orleans, 1963, Orleans Parish Med. Soc., 1967. Fellow Am. Acad. Pediatrics; mem. New Orleans Pediatric Soc. (pres. 1963-65), La. Pediatric Soc. (sec. 1968-70), Orleans Parish Med. Soc., A.M.A., La. Med. Soc., New Orleans Grad. Med. Assembly. Club: Bacchus Carnival (New Orleans). Contbr. articles to nat. jours. Home: 466 Crystal St New Orleans LA 70124 Office: 2017 Metairie Rd Metairie LA 70005

TOM, JAMES ROBERT, outdoor furniture mfg. co. exec.; b. Odessa, Tex., Apr. 21, 1939; s. George Ellison and Mattie (Inez) T.; student Tex. A. and M. U., 1957; B.B.A., Tex. Technol. U., 1961; m. Frances Kay Mackey, Sept. 16, 1961; children—Susan Kay, James Robert Jr., Emily Christian. Asst. trust officer Midland Nat. Bank (Tex.), 1966-67, v.p., trust officer, 1969-72; sr. accountant Main LaFrentz & Co., Midland, 1967-68; pres. Gibson Mfg. Co., Midland, 1972—, also dir. parent co. Magnatex Corp. Bd. dirs. Midland chpt. Am. Heart Assn., 1966, Arthritis Found, 1971-72, A.R.C., 1970—, Boys Club Midland, 1971-72, Midland County Livestock Assn., 1966-72; trustee Trinity Sch. Midland. Served with AUS, 1963-65. C.P.A., Tex. Mem. Am. Inst. C.P.A.'s, Tex. Soc. C.P.A.'s, Delta Sigma Pi. Democrat. Roman Catholic. Home: 2407 Neely St Midland TX 79701 Office: PO Box 6242 Midland TX 79701

TOMLINSON, JOE GRAHAM, architect; b. Dallas, June 20, 1938; s. L.G. and Lois (Graham) T.; student Sch. Arts Dallas Mus. Fine Arts, 1951-52, (scholar) 1954-56; N.Tex. State U., 1957-58; B.Arch., Tex. Inst. Tech., 1963; m. Judith Ann Marting, Aug. 16, 1969; children—Julie, Janet, Steve, Christina, Gary. Archtl. design cons. Collins Radio Corp., Richardson, Tex., 1967-68; self-employed archtl. designer, Dallas, 1968-72; pres. Concept Arts, Inc., Dallas, 1972—. Design cons. Tippetts-Abbett-McCarthy-Stratton for Dallas/Ft. Worth Regional Airport, 1968-70, airport proposal City Hobbs, N.M., 1970-71, Varo Corp., Garland, Tex., 1968-70. Recipient Dallas Mus. Fine Arts Book award, 1955. Home: 3970 Cedar Brush Dallas TX 75229 Office: 3003 LBJ Fwy Dallas TX 75234

TOMLINSON, LAMBUTH, pub. co. exec.; b. Ft. Worth, July 22, 1923; s. Douglas and Mary (Capers) T.; B.S. in Commerce, Tex. Christian U., 1943; m. Mary Jean Vance, Aug. 28, 1943 (div. 1968); children—John Douglas, Jean Elizabeth; m. 2d, Sally McClanahan Redwine, Sept. 30, 1968; stepchildren—Julia Ann Redwine, Jimmy Redwine. With All-Ch. Press, Ft. Worth, 1939—, dir., 1959—, pres., 1960—. Newspaper tech. cons. Jackson (Miss.) State-Times, 1954-55; pres., S.W. Sch. Printing, Sam Houston State Coll., 1959-61. Pres. Joint Bd. Christian Chs. Tarrant County, 1960-62; mem. Zoning Bd. Adjustment, City of Ft. Worth; 1st mayor Edgecliff, Tex., 1951-52. Trustee St. Joseph's Hosp., Tarrant County Mental Health-Mental Retardation Center; bd. dirs. Fort Worth Downtown Assn., 1962-63. Served with USAAF, 1942-45. Decorated Air medal. Mem. Christian Ch. (elder). Clubs: Ft. Worth; Colonial. Home: 4912 Stacey Fort Worth TX 76132 Office: 1200 W Berry St Fort Worth TX 76110

TOMMIE, WILLIAM THOMAS, civil engr.; b. Duncanville, Ala., Dec. 31, 1922; s. James Thomas and Emma (Arnold) T.; B.S. in C.E., U. Ala., 1951; m. Colleen Reynolds, June 17, 1950; children—Carol T., William Thomas. Design engr. TVA, Knoxville, 1951, Am. Bridge, Birmingham, Ala., 1951-59; chief engr. Temerson Steel Warehouse, Tuscaloosa, Ala., 1959-72; dir. sales, engring. Cain Steel & Supply, Tuscaloosa, 1972—. Bd. dirs. West End Christian Sch., Tuscaloosa, 1970-71. Served with AUS, 1946-47; Korea. Mem. Sub-Contractors Assn., Chi Epsilon. Baptist (deacon). Lion (dir. Tuscaloosa 1970-71, 73-74). Home: 22 Woodridge Tuscaloosa AL 35401 Office: PO Box 1369 Tuscaloosa AL 35401

TONAHILL, JOE HALBERT, lawyer, banker; b. Hughes Springs, Tex., Nov. 4, 1913; s. Joseph Emmett and Annie (Crump) T.; student U. Tex., 1938; LL.B., Washington Coll., 1941; m. Violett Smith, Mar. 31, 1941; children—Mildred, Rebecca, Susan, Smithy, Joey, Anne. Admitted to Tex. bar, 1941; practiced in Jasper, Tex., 1946—; mem. firm Fisher & Tonahill, 1946-56. Chmn. bd. 1st Nat. Bank, Jasper, Tex., 1960—; lectr. U. Tex., 1952-63. City atty., Jasper, Tex., 1947—. Served with USNR, 1942-45. Mem. Am. Trial Lawyers Assn. (bd. govs. 1955-56), Nat. Assn. Defense Lawyers in Criminal Cases, State Bar Tex. (dir. 1958-61, sect. chmn. 1961-62), Internat. Acad. Trial Lawyers, Tex. Assn. Plaintiffs Attys. (pres. 1951-52), Am., 1st Judicial Dist. (pres. 1951) bar assns., Internat. Soc. Barristers (dir. 1965), Am. Judicature Soc., Am. Legion, Delta Kappa Epsilon, Sigma Nu Phi.

Episcopalian. Mason (Shriner). Clubs: Lions. Contbr. numerous articles in field to profl. jours. and books. Home: Kirbyville Hwy Jasper TX 75951 Office: Tonahill Bldg Jasper TX 75951

TONIETTE, SALLYE JEAN, physician; b. Sulphur, La.; d. Eugene Augusta and Sallye (Tanner) Toniette; student John McNeese Jr. Coll., 1946-47; B.S., La. State U., 1949; tchrs. certificate La. State U., 1950, M.D., 1955. Intern, Crawford W. Long Meml. Hosp., Emory U., Atlanta, 1955-56, resident obstetrics and gynecology, jr., sr., chief residencies, 1956-59; practice obstetrics and gynecology, Sulphur, 1959—; bd. dirs. Holly Hill Nursing Home; mem. med. staff W. Calcasieu Cameron, 1959—. Bd. dirs. Calcasieu Parish Cancer Soc. 1963-67. Named Woman of Distinction, Calcasieu Parish Police Jurors-Bus. and Prof. Women's Club of West Calcasieu, 1969. Fellow Am. Coll. Obstetrics and Gynecology; mem. Am., So. med. assns., La., Calcasieu Parish med. socs., La. Wildlife Fedn., Am. Quarter Horse Assn., Assn. Am. Physicians and Surgeons, Alpha Chi Omega, Beta Tau Mu, Iota Sigma Pi, Phi Theta Kappa. Democrat. Methodist. Contbr. articles to profl. jours. Home: 301 W Verdine St Sulphur LA 70663 Office: 521 Cypress St Sulphur LA 70663

TOOHIG, MICHAEL FRANCIS, elec. products co. exec.; b. Lawrence, Mass., Dec. 9, 1924; s. Timothy Michael and Catherine (Walsh) T.; B.S. cum laude, Boston Coll., 1949, M.S., 1950; postgrad. Ind. U., 1964; m. Barbara Jean Bissonnette, June 30, 1956; children—Delsina M., Timothy J., Terrence M., Michele T., Aimee L. Supr. def. research div. Firestone Tire & Rubber Co., Akron, O., 1950-53; v.p., gen. mgr. ITT Tube and Sensor Labs., Fort Wayne, Ind., 1953-72; v.p., dir. engring. Electron Tube div. ITT, Roanoke, Va., 1972—. Chmn. radiation def. Ft. Wayne Civil Def., 1957-60. Served with AUS, 1943-46. Decorated Bronze Star. Mem. I.E.E.E., Assn. U.S. Army. Roman Catholic. Patentee in field. Home: 5207 N Spring Dr Roanoke VA 24019 Office: 7635 Plantation Rd Roanoke VA 24019

TOPPING, MARVIN WOODROW, ednl. cons.; b. Poquoson, Va., July 17, 1911; s. Joseph and Amelia (Bunting) T.; B.A., Randolph-Macon Coll., 1932; S.T.B., Boston U., 1936, postgrad., 1937-39; m. Louise E. Marshall, Dec. 3, 1938; children—John Marvin, Jean Carol. Dir. admissions, pub. relations Union Coll., Barbourville, Ky., 1943-47; dir. pub. relations Med. Coll. Va., 1947-50; exec. dir. Am. Coll. Pub. Relations Assn., Washington, 1950-56; vice chancellor Neb. U., 1956-57; asst. dir. devel. George Washington U., 1957-62; founder, pres. Coll. & Univ. Personnel Cons., Washington, 1962—. Contbr. articles to profl. publs. Pioneer 1st ann. Survey Philanthropy to Higher Edn. Home: 9909 E Bexhill Dr Kensington MD 20795 Office: 1629 K St NW Washington DC 20006

TORO, HAROLD, lawyer; b. Ponce, P.R., June 7, 1938; s. Harold J. and Irma (Toro) T.; B.A. cum laude, U. P.R., 1960, LL.B. magna cum laude, 1963; m. Mary Ann Tulla, Nov. 22, 1968; children—Marianne, Harold Jose, Ivan. Admitted to P.R. bar, 1963; asso. mem. firm Goldman & Santiago, San Juan, P.R., 1963-64, Cohen & Lespier, Hato Rey, P.R., 1964-72; partner firm Lespier & Toro, Hato Rey, 1972—. Mem. P.R. Bd. Law Examiners, 1970-74. Mem. P.R. C. of C. (chmn. labor relations sect. 1971-72), Phi Sigma Alpha. Editor: Law Rev. U. P.R., 1962-63. Home: K-2 San Patricio Av Urb Los Caobos Guanabo PR Office: PO Box 1441 Hato Rey PR 00919

TORRE, MOTTRAM PETER, social psychiatrist; b. New Orleans, Feb. 6, 1919; s. Peter and Juanita (Mottram) T.; B.S., Tulane U., 1940, M.D., 1943; M.P.H., Columbia U., 1949; m. Elizabeth Lassiter, Apr. 13, 1957. Intern, Phila. Gen. Hosp., 1947; resident Pa. Hosp., 1944, Payne Whitney Hosp., 1947; vis. Fulbright prof. U. Paris Sch. Medicine, 1949-50; psychiat. cons. on selection and tng. of overseas personnel Dept. Def. USPHS, Washington, 1953-54; asso. in psychiatry Columbia U. Coll. Phys. and Surg., 1955-59; psychiat. cons. to med. service UN, N.Y.C., 1955-62; chief psychiat. out-patient dept. St. Luke's Hosp., N.Y.C., 1955-56, asst. attending psychiatrist, 1955-61; spl. cons. World Fedn. for Mental Health, London, Eng., 1956-58, asst. dir., 1958-61, project dir., 1958-63; lectr. Coll. City N.Y., 1959-61, prof., 1961-63, acting chmn., 1961-62; vis. lectr. Tulane U., 1963-64, lectr., 1964, asso. clin. prof. Sch. Pub. Health, 1971—; psychiat. cons. La. Bd. Health, 1964-66; chief mental health program Jefferson Parish Health Unit, New Orleans, 1964-66; asso. dir. Touro Community Mental Health Center, New Orleans, 1966-67; dir. tng. and research DePaul Community Mental Health Center, 1967-69, chief community psychiatry, 1969—. Vice pres. Research Inst. for the Study of Man, 1959-63; pres. Human Potential Research Inst. Served to lt. (j.g.) USNR, 1945-46. Nat. Inst. Mental Health fellow, 1958. Diplomate Am. Bd. Psychiatry and Neurology. Mem. Am. Psychiat. Assn. (chmn. pub. health com. 1967-69), Group for Advancement Psychiatry (chmn. internat. relations com. 1961-67), Delta Tau Delta. Home: 806 Esplande Av New Orleans LA 70116

TORRES, PETER, JR., lawyer; b. San Antonio, Dec. 2, 1933; s. Peter and Lola (Whitten) T.; B.A. cum laude, St. Mary's U., 1957, LL.B., 1963; m. Yolanda Parga, June 3, 1958; children—Denise Yvonne, Peter Alan, Tina Cheryl, Paul Andre. Tchr. history and civics Edgewood High Sch., San Antonio, 1957-60; admitted to Tex. bar, 1963, since practiced in San Antonio. Mem. San Antonio city council, 1967-71. Served with USMCR, 1951-54. Mem. Tex., San Antonio bar assns., Tex., San Antonio (dir. 1968—) trial lawyers assns., Tex. (dir. 1965), San Antonio (dir. 1964-65) civil liberties unions, Am., Tex. (dir. 1973—) criminal def. lawyers assns. Methodist. Home: 414 North Dr San Antonio TX 78215 Office: 1014 San Pedro Av San Antonio TX 78212

TORRES SEPULVEDA, ANIBAL, agrl. research center adminstr.; b. Adjuntas, P.R., Jan. 15, 1930; s. Cristobal and Jovita (Sepulveda de Torres) Torres Delgado; B.S., La. State U., 1958, M.S., 1963; m. Eva Elena Arce, Dec. 27, 1963; children—Evelyn Yolanda, Anibal Luis. Mem. staff Agrl. Expt. Sta. U. P.R., 1958—, adminstr. in charge Fortuna Research Substa., 1968—. Served with inf. AUS, 1950-52. Mem. Am. Soc. Agrl. Scis., Coll. Agronomists (pres. Utuado chpt. 1959-60), Am. Soc. Hort. Scis., Gamma Sigma Delta, Alpha Zeta. Lion (pres. Adjuntas chpt. 1963-64). Contbr. articles to sci. jours. Home: 6 A-26 Ponce PR 00731 Office: RFD 1 Buzon 101 Juana Diaz PR 00665

TORRES-AGUIAR, MANUEL AUGUSTO, psychiatrist; b. Fajardo, P.R., May 29, 1920; s. Francisco and Aurora (Torres) A.; B.S.A., U. P.R., 1941, M.S.S., 1944; M.D., Creighton U., 1950; m. Irma Isabel Diaz, Nov. 13, 1944; children—Irmarilis I., Manuel A., Roberto H., Maritza A. Pub. health office, Lares, P.R., 1951-52; psychiat. resident Neb. Psychiat. Inst., U. Neb., 1952-55; staff psychiatrist Norfolk (Neb.) State Hosp., 1955-56; co-dir. social psychiatry project, Social Sci. Research Center, U. P.R., 1956-59, asst. prof. clin. psychiatry, Sch. Medicine, 1956-60, prof. hosp. adminstrn., asso. prof. psychiatry, dir. Univ. Hosp., asst. dean Med. Sch. U. P.R., 1960-62; dep. sec. health Commonwealth of P.R., 1957-60, sec., 1967-69, regional dir. Health and Welfare, 1960-62. Asst. supt., med. dir. Rio Piedras Psychiat. Hosp., 1962-65; cons. comprehensive mental health planning, 1965-67. Diplomate Am. Bd. Psychiatry and Neurology. Mem. P.R. Med. Assn., Am. Psychiat. Assn., P.R. Pub. Health Assn. Democrat. Roman Catholic. Club: Exchange (pres. 1962). Home: Violeta 164 Urb San Fco Rio Piedras PR 00927 Office: Darlington Bldg Rio Piedras PR 00925

TORRES LAO, JUAN EDUARDO, civil engr.; b. Ponce, P.R., Sept. 21, 1928; s. Juan Torres and Francisca (Lao) T.; B.S. in C.E., Coll. Agr. and Mech. Arts, Mayaguez, P.R., 1958; m. Dulcinea Marrero, Apr. 21, 1951; children—Juan E., Frances Ileana, Frankly A. Owner, J.E. Torres Lao & Assos., Ponce, 1959—. Pres., Coliseo Shopping Center, JET Realty, Inc., Ponce, 1973—. Served with AUS, 1951-53. Decorated Purple Heart. Mem. Am. Soc. C.E., Am. Concete Inst., Nat. Soc. Profl. Engrs., Phi Epsilon Chi. Home: 110 A Buena Vista Development Ponce PR 00731 Office: Coliseo Shopping Center Ponce PR 00731

TORRES-OLIVER, JUAN FREMIOT, clergyman; b. San German, P.R., Oct. 28, 1925; s. Luis N. and Amalia (Oliver) Torres; student St. John's Sem., 1944-50; M.A. in Musicology, Cath. U. Am., 1952; LL.B., U. P.R., 1959; LL.M., St. John's U., 1964. Instr., Cath. U. P.R., Ponce, 1952-56; vice chancellor Diocesan Curia, 1961-64; prof., asso. dean Sch. Law, Cath. U. P.R., 1961-64; apptd. bishop Ponce, 1964; installed and consecrated bishop Ponce, 1964—. Decorated Cross of Order Juan Pablo Duarte, Dominican Republic. Mem. Academia de Artes y Ciencias, Phi Alpha Delta. Club: Ponce Yacht. Home: 19 Obispado Av Ponce PR 00731 Office: PO Box 1430 Ponce PR 00731

TOSTENGARD, STANFORD ORVIND, pipeline co. exec.; b. Dovray, Minn., Sept. 1, 1922; s. Gilbert and Ruth Olive (Hager) T.; B.A. cum laude, St. Olaf Coll., 1947; M.B.A. with distinction, Harvard, 1949; m. Ardyce Aws, Sept. 3, 1950; children—Stephen, Anne. With Gulf Oil Corp., Pitts., 1949-50, Houston, 1951-59, area foreman, New Orleans dist., 1959-61, dist. mgr., 1961-64; v.p., dir., mgr. operations Gulf Refining Co., Houston, 1964-71, v.p., dir., mgr. joint interest pipe lines, 1971—; dir. Four Corners Pipe Line Co., Laurel Pipe Line Co., West Tex. Gulf Pipe Line Co., Cherokee Pipe Line Co., Toronto Pipe Line Co., Okan Pipeline Co., Platte Pipeline Co. Chmn. bd. regents Tex. Luth. Coll., Seguin. Dir. Luth. Brotherhood Frat. Ins. Soc. Served with AUS, 1943-46. Mem. Am. Petroleum Inst., Mid-Continent Oil and Gas Assn., Houston C. of C. Lutheran. Clubs: Houston, Riverbend Country (Houston). Home: 5006 Lymbar St Houston TX 77035 Office: Gulf Bldg PO Box 2100 Houston TX 77002

TOUPS, HERMAN THOMAS, real estate investor grocer; b. Luling, La., Dec. 18, 1921; s. Wilson T. and Laura (Mongrue) T.; grad. high sch.; m. Florence Ryan, May 2, 1942; children—Florence Patricia, Herman Thomas, Evelyn Frances. Operator, Am. Oil Co., Texas City, Tex., 1938-47; owner Toups Ice Service, Texas City, 1947—; pres. Polar Ice & Food Co., LaMarque, Tex., 1955—, Toups Realty, Texas City, 1961—; Served with USAF, 1942-46, Mem. Tex., Galveston County (pres. 1964-65, v.p. 1967—) retail grocers assns., C. of C. (dir. 1963-64). Roman Catholic. Rotarian. Home: 1805 11th St N Texas City TX 77590 Office: 1002 Main St La Marque TX 77568

TOURTELLOTTE, MILLS CHARLTON, mech. elec. engr.; b. Great Falls, Mont., Dec. 16, 1922; s. Nathaniel Mills and Frances (Charlton) T.; B.S., Ill. Inst. Tech., 1947, M.S., 1952; m. Dorothy Gray, Sept. 26, 1947; children—Jane Frances, Kathryn Louise, Thomas Nathan. Co-op. engr. student Acme Steel Co., Riverdale, Ill., 1940-43; engr. Automatic Electric Co., Chgo., 1947-49, Inland Steel Co., East Chicago, Ind., 1952-56; engr. Gulf States Tube Corp., Rosenberg, Tex., 1956—; pres. Fabricators, Inc., 1967. Vice chmn., then chmn. Fort Bend County Program Bldg. Com., 1967-70. Mem. Tex. Republican Com., Fort Bend County, 1962—. Sec., South Lyon (Mich.) Citzen's Adv. Com., 1960; mem. Gary (Ind.) Symphony Orch., 1941-43; leader 4-H Electric Club, 1964-69; pres. Ft. Bend County 4-H Adult Leaders Assn., 1965-68. Vice chmn. bd. dirs., chmn. music com. Federated Ch., Harvey, Ill. Served with USNR, 1944-46. Recipient award for tech. article Welded Steel Tube Inst., 1964; Friend of 4-H award, Ft. Bend County, 1968. Registered profl. engr., Ill., Mich., Tex. Mem. Am. Soc. M.E., Assn. Iron and Steel Engrs., V.F.W. (post adj. 1964-68, quartermaster 1968-70), Tex. (chmn. edn. com. 1968-69), Nat. socs. profl. engrs., Am. Soc. for Engring. Edn. (chmn. relations with industry com. Houston chpt. 1968-69). Methodist. Patentee in field. Home: 1114 Inwood Dr Richmond TX 77469 Office: PO Box 952 Rosenberg TX 77471

TOUSSIENG, POVL WINNING, child psychiatrist; b. Nysted, Denmark, Sept. 5, 1918 (came to U.S. 1949, naturalized 1963); s. Povl W. and Ingeborg (Hansen) T.; M.D., U. Copenhagen, 1945. Intern, Denmark 1945-46, Frederiksborg County Central Hosp., Kansas City, Mo., 1949-50; gen. practice medicine, Denmark, 1946-49; fellow Menninger Sch. Psychiatry, Topeka, 1950-53, John Harper Seeley fellow in child psychiatry Menninger Found., Topeka, 1953-55, mem. staff, 1955-65; cons. Kan. Boys Indsl. Sch., Topeka, 1957-61; asso. prof. child psychiatry and pediatrics U. Okla. Med. Center, Oklahoma City, 1965-69, prof., 1969—; clin. dir. Youth Counseling and Child Devel. Center, Oklahoma City, 1966—, dir. child psychiatry, 1974—; pres. bd. Paseo Center Inc., 1970—. Bd. dirs. Psychiat. Outpatient Centers Am., Troubled Children's Found. Served with Royal Danish Navy, 1943, 45-46. Fellow Am. Psychiat. Assn., Am. Orthopsychiat. Assn. (bd. 1968-71); mem. Soc. for Research in Child Devel., Midcontinent Psychiat. Assn., Med. and Correctional Assn. Contbr. articles to profl. jours., textbooks. Home: 4030 N Lincoln St Oklahoma City OK 73105

TOWER, JOHN GOODWIN, U.S. senator; b. Houston, Sept. 29, 1925; s. Joe Z and Beryl (Goodwin) T.; A.B. in Polit. Sci., Southwestern U. Tex., 1948, also LL.D.; M.A. in Polit. Sci., So. Meth. U., 1953; student London Sch. Econs. and Polit. Sci. U. London, 1952-53; LL.D., Howard Payne Coll., Alfred U.; m. Joza Lou Bullington, Mar. 21, 1952; children—Penelope, Marian, Jeanne. Announcer radio sta. KFDM, Beaumont, Tex., 1948, KTAE, Taylor, Tex., 1948-49; ins. agt., Dallas, 1950-51; asst. prof. polit. sci. Midwestern U., Wichita Falls, Tex., 1951-60; U.S. senator from Tex., 1961—, mem. banking, housing and urban affairs, armed services, joint def. prodn. coms., chmn. senate Republican Policy Com., 1973—. Del., Republican nat. convs., 1956, 60, 64, 68, 72, mem. platform com., 1960, 64, 68, 72, chmn. tax delegation, 1972, chmn. senatorial campaign com., 1969-70. Trustee So. Meth. U., Southwestern U. Enlisted man USNR, World War II, PTO. Mem. Am. Polit. Sci. Assn., S.W. Social Sci. Assn., Tex. Hist. Soc., Am. Legion, U.S. Naval Inst., Am. Assn. U. Profs., Kappa Sigma. Methodist. Kiwanian, Mason (32 deg., Shriner). Home: Wichita Falls TX 76302 Office: Old Senate Office Bldg Washington DC 20510

TOWLER, MARTIN LEE, physician; b. Hockley, Tex., Sept. 18, 1910; s. Ernest William and Ellen (Shoquist) T.; M.D., U. Tex. Sch. Medicine, 1935; m. Hetta G. Jockusch, Sept. 28, 1940; children—Hetta E., Martin H., Julie G., Sally J., William L. Intern, resident John Sealy Hosp., Galveston, Tex.; resident Colo. Gen. Hosp., Denver; practice medicine, specializing in neurology and psychiatry, Galveston, 1946—; prof. dept. neurology and psychiatry U. Tex. Med. br., Galveston, 1946—, dir. dept. EEG, 1947—. Served with AUS, 1942-46. Home: 5115 Av T Galveston TX 77550 Office: 200 University Blvd Galveston TX 77550

TOWLER, WILLIAM RUSSELL, elec. systems designer; b. Chatham, Va., Aug. 17, 1921; s. Joab Washington and Nannie (Pickrel) T.; B. Elec. Engring., U. Va., 1951, M. Elec. Engring., 1967; postgrad. U. Cal. at Los Angeles, 1952-54; m. Virginia Anne Wood, Feb. 16, 1949 (div. Apr., 1961); children—Antonia Russell, Sam Channing, Barbara Hayes. Elec. engr. Convair div. Gen. Dynamics Corp., San Diego and Pomona, Cal., 1951-57; project. engr. Sperry Piedmont Co., Charlottesville, Va., 1957-63; research scientist Research Labs. for Engring. Scis., U. Va., Charlottesville, 1963—. Mem. elec. adv. group Danville (Va.) Community Coll. 1968—. Served with USAAF, 1942-46. Mem. I.E.E.E., A.A.A.S. Patentee in field. Office: RLES Thornton Hall Univ Va Charlottesville VA 22903

TOWLES, DONALD BLACKBURN, newspaper exec.; b. Lawrenceburg, Ky., Sept. 10, 1927; s. Joseph Sterling and Marjorie (Blackburn) T.; A.B., U. Ky., 1948; m. Geraldine Gooch, Dec. 20, 1947; children—Sally Blackburn, Rebecca Neale. Asst. dir. Ky. div. publicity and editor In Kentucky mag., Frankfort, 1948-55; asst. dir. pub. service and promotion dept. Courier-Jour. and Louisville Times, Louisville, 1956-66, dir. pub. service and promotion, 1966-71, dir. circulation, 1971—. Served with AUS, 1952-54. Mem. Internat. Newspaper Promotion Assn. (pres. so. region 1969-70, dir. 1968-71), Ky. Press Assn. (dir.). Mem. Christian Ch. (elder). Home: 3536 Norbourne Blvd Louisville KY 40207 Office: 525 W Broadway Louisville KY 40202

TOWNES, MILTON HALSEY, food products co. exec.; b. Huntsville, Ala., Apr. 15, 1912; s. Charles Lee and Jeanne (Halsey) T.; B.A., U. Ala., 1933; m. Virginia Grasse, Sept. 5, 1938; children—Beverly (Mrs. Floyd S. Sherman), Virginia Kelly. Agy. sec. Liberty Nat. Life Ins. Co., Birmingham, Ala., 1936-46; with Golden Flake, Inc., Birmingham, 1946—, sales mgr., 1946-69, v.p., 1949-64, sec., 1955-69, exec. v.p., 1964-69, pres., 1970—. Dir. Johnson Rast & Hays, Birmingham, Steel City Bolt and Screw, Birmingham. Served to lt. col. AUS, 1941-45. Mem. Ala. Acad. Sci., Ala. Hist. Assn., S.A.R., Kappa Alpha. Clubs: Exchange, The Club, Vestavia Country (Birmingham). Episcopalian. Home: 2712 Mt Royal Circle Birmingham AL 35216 Office: Golden Flake Inc 110 S 6th St Birmingham AL 35201

TOWNLEY, FINOS JOHN, brokerage co. exec.; b. Birmingham, Ala., Aug. 26, 1902; s. Stephen Mountville and Mellar Elizabeth (Johnson) T.; student Birmingham Med. Coll., 1922; student marketing Miss. So. U., 1943; m. Nellie Estelle Jones, Sept. 25, 1924; children—Finos Jack, Thomas Richard. Salesman Swift & Co., Nashville, 1924, br. mgr., 1927-29, dist. mgr., 1930-36, asst. gen. sales mgr., 1937-46, v.p. sales, 1946-47, dir., 1960—; asst. to pres. Murray Biscuit Co., Augusta, Ga., 1967-70; pres. Nova Sales, Inc., Lakeland, Fla., 1967—, also dir. Dir. Nat. Sales Execs., Chgo. Mayor Lone Palm, Fla., 1968—. Bd. dirs. Am. Meat Inst., Chgo. Mem. Nat. Assn. Food Research (dir. 1955—; pres. 1953-53). Republican. Baptist. Mason. Clubs: Lone Palm Golf (Lakeland, Fla.); Hidden Hills Golf (Jacksonville, Fla.); Lincolnshire Country (Crete, Ill.) (v.p. 1958-59, 60-61). Home: 540 Lone Palm Dr Lakeland FL 33801 Office: 919 Swindell Av Lakeland FL 33802

TOWNSEND, BILLY LYN, historian; b. Brunswick, Ga., May 6, 1943; s. J.R. and Ruth (Lindsey) T.; B.S., Berry Coll., 1966; m. Marvalee Lord, Dec. 19, 1965; 1 son, Curtis Glen. Tchr. social studies, Floyd County, Ga., 1966-69; staff historian Ga. Hist. Commn., Atlanta, 1970-73; chief hist. interpretation parks and hist. sites div. Ga. Dept. Natural Resources, Atlanta, 1973—; cons. Planned Big Shanty Museum Exhibits, Kennesaw, Ga. Recipient Ga. State Teacher's Scholarship, 1962-66. Compiler, editor: Georgia Historial Markers, 1972. Home: 4300 Senoa Dr Kennesaw GA 30144 Office: 707 Washington St Atlanta GA 30334

TOWNSEND, FRANK MARION, physician; b. Stamford, Tex., Oct. 29, 1914; s. Frank M. and Beatrice (House) T.; student San Antonio Coll., 1931-32, U. Tex., 1932-34; M.D., Tulane, U., 1938; m. Gerda Eberlein, 1940 (div. 1944); 1 son, Frank M.; m. 2d, Ann Graf, Aug. 25, 1951; 1 son, Robert N. Intern, Polyclinic Hosp., N.Y.C., 1939-40; commd. 1st lt. M.C., U.S. Army, 1940, advanced through grades to lt. col., 1946; resident instr. pathology Washington U., 1945-47; trans. to USAF, 1949, advanced through grades to col., 1956; instr. pathology Coll. Medicine U. Neb., 1947-48; asso. pathologist Scott & White Clinic, Temple, Tex., 1948-49; asso. prof. pathology Med. br. U. Tex., Galveston, 1949-59; dir. labs. USAF Hosp., Lackland AFB, 1950-54; cons. pathology, chief cons. group Office Surgeon Gen. Hdqrs. SAF, Washington, 1954-55, cons., 1955-63; dep. dir. Armed Forces Inst. Pathology, Washington, 1955-59, dir. 1959-63, now cons. vice comdr. aerospace med. div. Air Force Systems Command, 1963-65; ret., 1965; practice medicine specializing in pathology, San Antonio, 1965—; dir. labs. San Antonio State Chest Hosp., 1965-72; clin. prof. pathology U. Tex. Med. Sch., San Antonio, 1969-72, prof., chmn. dept. pathology, 1972—; cons. Nat. Aeros. and Space Adminstrn., 1967—. Mem. adv. bd. cancer WHO, 1958—; mem. adv. council Civil War Centennial Commn., 1960-65. Bd. dirs. Alamo Area Sci. Fair, 1967—. Decorated D.S.M., Legion of Merit; recipient Founders medal Assn. Mil. Surgeons, 1961. Diplomate Am. Bd. Pathology. Fellow A.C.P., Coll. Am. Pathologists (regional commr. lab. inspection and accreditation 1971—), Am. Soc. Clin. Pathologists, Aerospace Med. Assn. (H.G. Moseley award 1962); mem. A.M.A. Internat. Acad. Aviation and Space Medicine, Internat. Acad. Pathology, Am. Assn. Pathologist and Bacteriologists, Am. Soc. Exptl. Pathologists, Tex. Med. Assn., Bexar County Med. Soc., Tex. Soc. Pathologists. Club: Torch. Contbr. articles to med. jours. Home: 10406 Mt Marcy Dr San Antonio TX 78213 Office: Dept Pathology U Texas Health Science Center 7703 Floyd Curl Dr San Antonio TX 78229

TOWNSEND, GEORGE ROWE, realtor; b. Bennettsville, S.C., Dec. 23, 1922; s. Arthur Douglas and Jayne (Rowe) Townsend; grad. U. Pa. Sch. X-ray Technicians, 1941. X-ray technician, Florence, S.C. 1941-43, Army hosps., Camp Croft and Ft. Jackson, S.C., 1943-45; chief x-ray technician, Florence, 1945-52; sec. Dept. Army, Salzburg, Austria and Frankfurt, Germany, 1952-53; sec. Nat. Security Council, Washington, 1954-56, J.P. Stevens Co., Wallace, S.C., 1956; chief x-ray technician Marlboro County Gen. Hosp., Bennettsville, S.C., 1956-58; sec. Redstone Arsenal, Huntsville, Ala., 1958-59, Litchfield Beach, Inc., Litchfield Beach, Pawley's Island, S.C., 1959-63; owner Townsend Real Estate Co., Pawley's Island, 1963-74; pres., owner Indigo House, Ltd., 1963-74; sec., office mgr. DeBordieu Corp., Georgetown, S.C., 1970—. Sec., Litchfield Beaches Homeowners Assn., 1966-69; sec.-treas. Midway Vol. Fire Dept., 1961-74. Mem. Georgetown County Bd. Realtors (sec.-treas. 1967-69), Nat. Assn. Real Estate Bds., Myrtle Beach and Grand Strand C. of C. Episcopalian. (pres. Ch. Women 1957-58, vestry 1969, mem. Altar Guild 1963—). Home: DeBordieu Colony Club Georgetown SC 29440

TOWNSEND, HAROLD LEE, lawyer; b. Fayetteville, N.C., July 13, 1922; s. Harold Lee and Helen M. (Monroe) T.; B.A., Wake Forest Coll., 1943; LL.B., U. Va., 1948; m. Iris Bear, Sept. 4, 1965; children—Harold Lee III, Linda Ann, Ann Smith, Bruce Lewis. Admitted to Va. bar, 1948; atty. at law, Emporia, Va., 1948—. Mayor Emporia, 1952-56; commonwealth atty. Greensville County, Va.,

1956-64. Named Boy Scout Man of Year, 1969. Mem. Am., Va. (bd. dirs. 1968-70), Richmond trial lawyers assns., Va. State Bar, N.Y. Trial Lawyers Assn., Emporia C. of C. (dir. 1949—), Am. Judicature Soc. Home: 802 Brunswick Av Emporia VA 23847 Office: 300 S Main St Emporia VA 23847 also Route 106 Prince George VA 23875

TOWNSEND, JAMES ROWLAND, banker; b. Dallas, June 13, 1921; s. James Pinckney and Amelia Jessamine (Ward) T.; B.S., North Tex. State U., 1942; LL.B., U. Tex., 1948; postgrad. So. Methodist U., 1957; m. Jane Rhea Gustafson, Aug. 21, 1953; children—Craig Pinckney, Rebecca Rhea, Thomas Neal. Admitted to Tex. bar, 1948; mem. firm Sanders, Lefkowitz & Green, Dallas, 1948-53; mem. law dept. Stanolind Oil & Gas Co., Ft. Worth, 1953-56; atty. TXL Oil Corp., Dallas, 1956-62; v.p., trust officer Merc. Nat. Bank Dallas, 1962—. Worker fund drives United Way, Am. Cancer Soc. and others; pres. P.T.A. Hotchkiss Sch., Dallas, 1966; chmn. troop Com. Circle Ten council Boy Scouts Am., 1967-69. Active precinct affairs Dallas Democratic Com., 1952-56, 68. Bd. dirs. YMCA East Dallas, 1964-68. Served with USAAF, 1942-46. Mem. State Bar Tex., Dallas Bar Assn. (v.p., 1953), Southwestern Legal Found., Dallas Assn. Petroleum Landmen (v.p. 1960), Dallas Estate Planning Council. Mem. United Ch. Christ. (deacon). Mason. Home: 6108 Joyce Way Dallas TX 75225 Office: PO Box 5415 Dallas TX 75222

TOWNSEND, LEWIS FRANKLIN, JR., periodontist; b. Jacksonville, Fla., Nov. 17, 1922; s. Lewis Franklin and Leslie (Beers) T.; D.D.S., Emory U., 1946; student Tufts Sch. Dental Medicine, 1955-56; m. Mary Carr, Apr. 6, 1947; children—Sherrill Ann, Lewis Franklin III. Resident Wilford Hall Med. Center, Lackland AFB, 1958-59; pvt. practice medicine, Jacksonville, Fla., 1946-47; commd. 1st lt., U.S. Air Force, 1948, advanced through grades to col., 1967; ret., 1969; pvt. practice dentistry, specializing in periodontology, Atlanta, 1969—; asso. prof. periodontics Emory U. Sch. Dentistry, 1969—; asst. prof. U. Pa. Dental Sch., 1965-66; clin. prof. periodontics U. Tex., 1966-70; staff officer Atlanta Hosp., 1970—; cons. periodontics VA Hosp., Atlanta; cons., staff periodontist Ga. Retardation Center, Atlanta. Diplomate Am. Acad. Periodontics. Fellow Am. Coll. Dentists; mem. Am., Ga. dental assns., Am. Acad. Periodontics, So. Acad. Periodontics, Ga. Soc. Periodontics. Mason. Home: 1419 Montevallo Circle Decatur GA 30033 Office: 3648 Chamblee-Tucker Rd Atlanta GA 30341

TOWNSEND, MILTON HOUCK, ednl. adminstr.; b. Salem, N.J., Dec. 26, 1923; s. Edward and Carrie May (Brandriff) T.; B.A., Union Coll., 1948; M.A., U. Ky., 1951; m. Betty Kate Miles, June 14, 1952. Dir. pub. relations Union Coll., Barbourville, Ky., 1952—, v.p. for coll. relations and devel., 1965—, part-time instr. history, 1960-63, exec. sec. Alumni Assn., 1951-61. Trustee Wesley Found., Western State Coll., Bowling Green, Ky. Served with USNR, 1942-46. Mem. Am. Coll. Pub. Relations Assn. (past chmn. Ky.), Am. Legion, Ky. Hist. Soc. Republican. Methodist (mem. Ky. Conf. Bd. Edn., sec. Bd. Laity). Clubs: Kiwanis (past pres.), Barbourville Garden. Home: 126 College Park Dr Barbourville KY 40906

TOWNSEND, PAUL SCOTT, petroleum co. exec.; b. Jewett, O., Jan. 20, 1923; s. Leon Fredrick and Wilma Alberta (Shambaugh) T.; student Canton Bus. Coll., 1941-42, Washington and Jefferson Coll., 1943-44; B.S.C., Ohio U., 1948; postgrad. U. Ky., 1959, Syracuse U., 1960; m. Janet Evonne Johnson, Aug. 6, 1949; 1 dau., Darla Lavonne. With Ashland Oil, Inc. (Ky.), 1948—, asst. tax mgr., 1960-65; tax mgr., 1965-70, dir. taxes, 1970—. Instr., U. Ky. at Ashland, part time, 1960-61. Mem. Boyd County Cancer Assn., 1966—. Served with 84th div. AUS, 1943-46. Recipient medals; Ky. Col. Mem. Ky. Oil and Gas Assn. (Merit award 1969, chmn. tax com. 1965—), Ky. Petroleum Council (Appreciation award 1969, chmn. tax com. 1965—), Ky., Ashland chambers commerce, Am. Inst. Real Estate Appraisers (dir. 1969-72, v.p. 1973—), Am. Petroleum Inst. (adv. com. excise taxation 1966—), W.Va. Petroleum Assn. (chmn. tax com. 1965-70, Outstanding Service award 1969), Nat. Assn. Real Estate Bds. Methodist. Contbr. articles to profl. jours. Home: 2925 Forgey St Ashland KY 41101 Office: 1401 Winchester Av Ashland KY 41101

TOWNSEND, RAYMOND ROADES, editor; b. Richmond, Ind., Nov. 7, 1912; s. Edward E. and Rosa May (Roades) T.; B.S., Coll. William and Mary, 1949; m. Ada Lee Kerr, Dec. 19, 1937; 1 dau., Laura Lee. With L & N R.R., Knoxville and Maryville, Tenn., 1941-44; with Colonial Williamsburg Found., Williamsburg, Va., 1946-73, researcher, 1960-73; now chief curator indsl. tech. Nat. Heritage Corp., West Chester, Pa. Editor, Chronicle Early Am. Industries Assn., Williamsburg, 1956—. Cons. tech. Nat. Heritage Ltd., Toronto, Ont., Can., 1973. Served with USNR, 1944-46. Mem. Early Am. Industries Assn., Mid-West Tool Collector's Assn., Antique Crafts and Tools in Vt., Antique Tools and Trades in Conn., Tools and Trades of Mass., Wayne County (Ind.) Hist. Soc., Old Naquaga Hist. Soc. Home: Waters Storehouse Williamsburg VA 23185 Office: Nat Heritage Corp West Chester PA

TOWNSEND, ROBERT GLENN, JR., physician; b. Grayson, Ky., Aug. 30, 1929; s. Robert Glenn and Lois Juanita (Jackson) T.; student U. Ky., 1949-50; B.S., Wake Forest U., 1957; M.D., U. Louisville, 1961; m. Mina Jean Hensley, Aug. 2, 1958; children—Susan Elizabeth, Robert Glenn III, Neil Hensley. Intern, Indpls. Gen. Hosp., 1961-62; partner J. Q. Stovall Meml. Hosp., Grayson, 1962-64; practice gen. medicine, Raeford, N.C., 1964—; family practice medicine, Raeford, 1964-73; pvt. practice, 1973—, mem. staffs Cape Fear Valley Hosp., Fayetteville, Moore Meml. Hosp., Pinehurst. Bd. dirs. Southeastern Econ. Devel. Commn., 1967—, vice chmn., 1970—; bd. dirs. N.C. Cancer Inst., Lumberton, N.C. Served with USAF, 1951-56. Diplomate Am. Bd. Family Practice (charter). Mem. N.C., Hoke County (pres. 1966-68) med. socs., Am., N.C. Acads. family practice, Raeford-Hoke C. of C. (pres. 1966-67), Alpha Omega Alpha, Sigma Phi Epsilon. Methodist (steward 1966—). Home: 313 W Elwood Av Raeford NC 28376 Office: 116 Campus Av Raeford NC 28376

TOWNSEND, THATCHER LOVEJOY, JR., banker; b. Greensboro, N.C., Apr. 11, 1932; s. Thatcher Lovejoy and Eileen (Martin) T.; B.S., U. N.C., 1954; M.B.A., Northwestern U., 1957; m. Marian Faison, Sept. 15, 1956; children—Thatcher Lovejoy III, Allyn. With Wachovia Bank & Trust Co., Winston-Salem, N.C., 1957—, v.p. internat. dept., 1962—; pres. Wachovia Internat. Investment Corp., 1966—; dir. Fomento de Inversiones, S.A., Mexico City, Mexico, Decca Resources Ltd., Sunningdale Oils, Ltd. (all Calgary, Alta., Can.). Served with AUS, 1954-56. Mem. N.C. World Trade Assn. (dir. 1970—). Methodist. Club: Old Town Country (Winston-Salem). Home: 701 Wellington Rd Winston-Salem NC 27106 Office: PO Box 3099 Winston-Salem NC 27102

TOWNSEND, THOMAS JAMES, JR., civil engr.; b. Lake Butler, Fla., Nov. 14, 1917; s. Thomas James and Christine (Lawson) T.; student U. Fla., 1935-42; m. Ellen Catherine Green, Apr. 17, 1947; children—Catherine (Mrs. Gary Allen Jamar), William Thomas. Chief survey party firm Fay, Spofford & Thorndike, Anchorage, 1946-47, asst. dept. engr., chief surveys, 1947-48; with Okla. Dept. Hwys., various locations, 1949—, jr. resident engr., Wewoka, 1956-61, resident engr., Ada, 1961—. Mem. troop com. Boy Scouts Am., 1961—. Served with C.E., USNR, 1942-45; PTO. Registered profl. engr., Okla. Mem. Nat. Soc. Profl. Engrs., Am. Soc. C.E., Okla. Soc. Land Surveyors, Nat. Rifleman's Assn., Nat. Geog. Soc., Nat. Hist. Soc., Smithsonian Instn. Assos. Democrat. Methodist. Mason. Home: 1018 S Highschool St Ada OK 74820

TOWNSEND, WILLIAM HOWARD, lawyer; b. Columbia, S.C., June 17, 1929; s. Fred DuPre and Dollie (Walker) T.; B.A., Washington and Lee U., 1950; LL.B., U. S.C., 1952; m. Patricia Elaine Raley, May 31, 1951; 1 dau., Elaine Walker. Admitted to S.C. bar, 1951; mem. firm Townsend & Townsend, Columbia, 1955-71, McKay, Sherrill, Walker, Townsend & Wilkins, Columbia, 1971—. Vice chmn. East Richland County Pub. Service Dist., 1973—. Served to 1st lt. AUS, 1952-55. Mem. Sigma Nu, Phi Delta Phi. Episcopalian (sr. warden 1968-69). Clubs: Summit, Caprician (Columbia). Home: 1212 Greenhill Rd Columbia SC 29206 Office: PO Drawer 447 Columbia SC 29202

TOWRY, GENE GEORGE, electronics co. exec.; b. Tulsa, Dec. 5, 1928; s. Athel George and Mollie Agnes (Veit) T.; B.B.A., North Tex. State U., 1949; B.S. in E.E. with honors, So. Meth. U., 1958; m. Shirley Marie Collings, July 26, 1949; children—Debra Jean, Robert Bruce. Profl. golfer, Tex., 1949-51; with Tex. Instruments, Inc., Austin, 1954—, co-op. student, 1954-58, engr., 1958-61, project engr., 1962-65, program mgr., 1965-69, product marketing mgr., 1969-71, purchasing, material control mgr., 1971—; dir. Texins Credit Union, Dallas. Served with USNR, 1952-54. Named Sportsman of Month, Dallas C. of C., 1957. Mem. Purchasing Mgrs. Assn. Episcopalian (mem. vestry 1968-69). Clubs: Great Hills Country (dir. 1973—), Balcones Country (Austin). Patentee in field. Home: 4016 Edgerock St Austin TX 78731 Office: Tex Instruments PO Box 2909 Austin TX 78767

TOZER, WILLIAM THOMAS, ins. co. exec.; b. Petersburg, Ill., Jan. 19, 1934; s. Clarence W. and Winona (Armstrong) T.; B.S., U. Ill., 1956; m. Joan Marie Heberlein, July 31, 1955; children—Barbara, Theodore, Marilyn. Acturial asst. State Farm Life Ins. Co., Bloomington, Ill., 1956-60; actuary Am. Republic Ins. Co., Des Moines, 1960-63, v.p., actuary, 1963-69, sr. v.p., actuary, 1969-70, mem. adv. bd. to bd. dirs., 1966-70; v.p., actuary Am. Republic Assurance Co., Des Moines, 1967-70; dir., 1967-70; v.p., actuary United Ins. Co. of Am. Chgo., 1970-72; v.p., chief actuary Ky. Central Life Ins. Co., 1972—. Frequent speaker on computers at profl. meetings, seminars. Mem. actuarial adv. bd. Drake U., 1967-70; chmn. computer adv. com. Ia. Ins. Dept. 1967-68. Mem. Polk County Tax Payers Computer Com., 1965. C.L.U. Fellow Soc. Actuaries, Life Office Mgmt. Inst.; mem. Chgo. Actuaries Club, Am. Acad. Actuaries, Internat. Actuarial Assn., Phi Kappa Phi, Phi Eta Sigma, Beta Gamma Sigma. Presbyn. (elder, deacon, trustee). Contbr. articles in field to profl. jours. Home: 647 Tateswood Dr Lexington KY 40502 Office: 200 E Main St Lexington KY 40507

TRACY, ROBERT EMMET, bishop; b. New Orleans, Sept. 14, 1909; s. Robert Emmet and Margaret Agnes (Cahill) T.; D.D., Notre Dame Sem., New Orleans, 1932, LL.D., 1959. Ordained priest Roman Cath. Ch., 1932; asst. pastor St. Leo the Great Ch., New Orleans, 1932-46; chaplain Newman Club, Tulane U.-Newcomb Coll., 1941-46; dir. Confrat. Christian Doctrine, Archdiocese New Orleans, 1937-46; chaplain La. State U. Newman Club, 1946-59; nat. chaplain Nat. Newman Clubs, 1954-56; pastor St. Mary Madgalen Ch., Abbeville, La., 1959-60; dean Abbeville Deanery, 1959-60; pastor Our Lady of Fatima Parish, Lafayette, La., 1960-61; dean Fatima Deanery, 1960-61; consultor Diocese of Lafayette, 1959-61; apptd. Titular Bishop of Sergentza and Aux. Bishop of Lafayette, 1959; apptd. 1st bishop of Baton Rouge, 1961. Mem. Phi Kappa Theta. Home: Our Lady of the Lake Hosp Baton Rouge LA 70802 Office: PO Box 2028 Baton Rouge LA 78821

TRACY, WARREN FRANCIS, librarian; b. Richmond, Ind., Nov. 26, 1914; s. Timothy Leo and Eleanor (Moore) T.; B.A., Earlham Coll., Richmond, 1938; B.S. in L.S., Western Res. U., 1940; M.A., U. Chgo., 1953, Ph.D., 1958; m. Georgia Garber, May 24, 1941; 1 son, Warren Francis. Dir. Henry County (Ind.) Library Demonstration, 1940-41; asst. librarian Knox Coll., 1946-47, Northwestern State Coll. La., Natchitoches, 1947-51; librarian Coe Coll., 1954-62; librarian, chmn. dept. library sci. U. So. Miss., Hattiesburg, 1962—. Chmn. coll. sect. Ia. Library Assn., 1958, chmn. com. grad. library sch., 1962. Pres. Parent's Assn.-Youth Symphony Orch., Hattiesburg, 1962—. Served to 1st lt. AUS, 1941-46. Mem. Am., Miss. (pres. 1974) library assns., Phi Delta Kappa, Phi Kappa Phi (charter). Presbyn. Author articles in field. Home: Lake Serene Route 4 Hattiesburg MS 39401

TRACZ, RICHARD FRANCIS, educator; b. Kansas City, Mo., Jan. 14, 1944; s. Boley John and Frances (Yoda) T.; A.B., Rockhurst Coll., 1965; M.A., U. Kan., 1967. Asst. instr. English, U. Kan., 1965-67; instr. English, Tarrant County Jr. Coll., 1967-69; instr. English So. Methodist U., 1969—. Recipient U. Kan. Teaching fellowship, 1965-67. Mem. Conf. Coll. Tchrs. of English, Vergilian Soc., South Central Modern Lang. Assn., Nat. Council Tchrs. of English, Conf. Coll. Composition and Communication, Tex. Joint English Com. Roman Catholic. Author: The Responsible Man, 1970; Tempo: A Thematic Approach to Sentence/Paragraph Writing, 1971; The Age of Anxiety, 1972; —30—A Journalistic Approach to Freshman Composition, 1973; Contact: A Textbook in Applied Communications, 1974. Home: 7407 Wellcrest Dr Dallas TX 75230 Office: 213 Dallas Hall So Methodist U Dallas TX 75275

TRAGER, EARL ADAM, geologist; b. South Bend, Ind., June 17, 1893; s. Christian Nicholas and Mary (Raffensperger) T.; student Mich. Agrl. Coll., 1913-14, U. Neb., 1914-15, S.B., U. Chgo., 1917; m. Martelle Wickliffe, Mar. 12, 1932; children—Earl Adam, Mary Frances (Mrs. Robert Burns Moore). Chief sub-surface geologist Empire Gas & Fuel Co., Bartlesville, Okla., 1917-20; chief subsurface geologist Marland Oil Co., Ponca City, Okla., 1920-21, chief geologist, Mexico, 1921-25, chief geologist research dept., 1925-26; chief geologist Earl Oliver & Co., Ponca City, 1926-28, Skelly Oil Co., Tulsa, 1928-30; cons. geologist, Tulsa, 1930-32; chief naturalist div., chief geologist Nat. Park Service, Washington, 1932-40; v.p. Bell & Howell, Chgo., 1940-42; chief liasion officer WPB, U.S. Bur. Mines, 1942-46; pres. Color Craft, Washington, 1946-48; chief geologist Sinclair Petroleum Co., Panama, Africa, Can., 1948-50; sr. geologist Fed. Power Commn., Washington, 1950-55; chief geologist H. Zinder & Assos., Houston, 1955-57; pres. Earl Trager & Assos., Inc., 1957-60; research, technologist inhalation therapy and visual edn. S.W. Med. Sch., Parkland and Woodlawn Hosps., 1960-68, Cardio Pulmonary Inst., Inc. of Meth. Hosp., Dallas, 1960—. Mem. Dallas Council on World Affairs, 1959—. Recipient 1st prize for best med. film Am. Coll. Chest Physicians, 1967. Mem. Am. Assn. Petroleum Geologists, Sigma Nu. Republican. Presbyn. Mason (Shriner), Kiwanian. Contbr. articles to profl. jours. Presently engaged in reassembling study of coal and oil shales to supplement oil reserves. Home: 4526 Glenleigh Dr Dallas TX 75220 Office: Meth Hosp Box 5999 Dallas TX 75222

TRAHAN, HAROLD GEORGE, physician; b. Maurice, La., Sept. 17, 1923; s. Ernest Gustave and Laura (Trahan) T.; B.S., U. Southwestern La., 1942; M.D., La. State U., 1945; m. Bertha Lee Broussard, Dec. 19, 1943; children—Donna (Mrs. Richard Putnam), Harold George, Catherine (Mrs. Weston P. Miller), Henry, Lolette, Thomas. Intern, New Orleans Charity Hosp., 1945-46; gen. practice medicine, Maurice, 1949—; staff Abbeville (La.) Gen. Hosp. Mayor, Village of Maurice, 1950-62. Served to capt. AUS, 1946-48. Mem. A.M.A., La., Vermilion Parish med. socs., La. Acad. Gen. Practice. Address: PO Box 156 Maurice LA 70555

TRAHAN, MICHAEL A., banker; b. Port Arthur, Tex., Dec. 5, 1945; s. Howard A. and B. Elizabeth (Brady) T.; B.B.A., Lamar U., 1968, M.B.A. (teaching fellow), 1970; m. Janice Eloise Townsend, Dec. 16, 1967; 1 dau., Tiffany Nicole. Auditor Arthur Andersen & Co., Houston, 1968-72; controller Gibraltar Savs. Assn., Houston, 1972; v.p., controller Republic Tex. Savs. Assn., Port Arthur, 1972—. C.P.A. Recipient Financial Mgmt. Inst. scholarship award, 1967. Mem. C. of C., Jr. C. of C. (1st v.p. 1973, dir. 1972), Am. Inst. C.P.A.'s, Estate Planning Council, Gulf Coast Controllers Soc., Nat. Controllers Soc., Blue Key, Phi Kappa Phi. Mem. Christian Ch. (deacon). Lion. Home: 14123 Britoak St Houston TX 77024 Office: 2650 Two Shell Plaza Houston TX 77002

TRAINA, PAUL JOSEPH, govt. ofcl.; b. N.Y.C., Mar. 8, 1934; s. Peter and Mary (Panepinto) T.; B.C.E., Manhattan Coll., 1955; M.S., U. Mich., 1960; m. Mary Ann Delehanty, Oct. 8, 1955; children—Peter, Kenneth, Jeanmarie, Julie Ann, Marie. Chief water resource studies region IV, USPHS, Atlanta, 1960-63; chief southeast comprehensive water pollution control, southeast region Fed. Water Pollution Control Adminstrn., Atlanta, 1963-67; dir. tech. programs, Athens, Ga., 1967-71; dir. water programs Environmental Protection Agy. Region IV, Atlanta, 1971-73, dir. enforcement, 1973—. Officer, lt. comdr. USPHS, 1955-67. Mem. Am. Soc. C.E., Water Pollution Control Fedn., N.Y. Acad. Sci. Home: 2366 Wood Creek Ct Tucker GA 30084 Office: 1421 Peachtree St Atlanta GA 30309

TRAINA, ROBERT ANGELO, educator; b. Chgo., Aug. 27, 1921; s. Angelo and Argia (Giovannoni) T.; A.A., Spring Arbor Jr. Coll., 1941; A.B., Seattle Pacific Coll., 1943; S.T.B., The Bibl. Sem. (N.Y.), 1945, S.T.M., 1946; Ph.D., Drew U., 1966; m. Jane Odell, May 31, 1943; children—Robert E., Janis, Lorne Hunt, Judith. Ordained to ministry United Methodist Ch., 1963; prof. Bible, The Bibl. Sem. in N.Y., 1945-66; prof. English Bible, Asbury Theol. Sem., Wilmore, Ky., 1966—, vice-pres., dean, 1967—. Am. Assn. Theol. Schs. fellowship grantee, 1961-62. Mem. Nat. Assn. Profs. of Hebrew, Am. Acad. Religion, Soc. Bibl. Lit., Alpha Kappa Sigma. Author: Methodical Bible Study, 1952; Methodical Bible Teaching, 1953. Home: 505 Bellevue Av Wilmore KY 40390 Office: Asbury Theol Sem Wilmore KY 40390

TRAINOR, GEORGE EDWARD, automobile co. exec.; b. Providence, Aug. 23, 1928; s. George Edward and Helena Regina (Gill) T.; student Md. U., 1948-49, Harvard and Boston U. Summer Sch., 1951, Georgetown U. Dental Sch., 1951-52; B.A. in Journalism and Pub. Relations, George Washington U., 1953; m. Agnes J. Epple, Aug. 22, 1953; children—Sharon Irene, Brenda Jane. With Armed Forces Security Agy., 1952; reporter Washington Post, 1952-53; bur. asst. and feature writer NEA Service, Inc., Scripps-Howard Newspapers Feature Service, 1953-54; reporter news dept. Ford Motor Co., 1954-55, pub. relations field rep., Cleve., 1955-58, sr. pub. relations field rep., N.Y.C., 1958-59, mgr. pub. relations, Washington, 1959-62, European pub. and govtl. affairs mgr., Brussels, Belgium, 1962-65, asst. pub. relations mgr. Ford div., 1965-67, regional pub. relations mgr., Washington, 1967—. Asso. professorial lectr. journalism George Washington U., 1967—; cons. internat. and nat. pub. affairs, parking industry, alcoholic beverage industry. Bd. dirs. Colonials, George Washington U. Served with USMCR, 1945-48. Recipient Extraordinary and Distinguished Service award Colonials, George Washington U., 1962; Alumni Service award George Washington U., 1971. Mem. Pub. Relations Soc. Am. (accreditation bd. 1970-71), Sigma Nu. Clubs: University, George Washington U., National Press (Washington). Home: 2731 N Randolph St Arlington VA 22207 Office: 815 Connecticut Av NW Washington DC 20006

TRALINS, S(ANDOR) ROBERT, author; b. Balt., Apr. 28, 1926; s. Emanuel and Rose (Miller) T.; student Eastern Coll., 1950-51, John Hopkins, 1949; m. Sonya Lee Mandel, Sept. 2, 1945; children—Myles Jay, Alan Harvey. Freelance writer mag. fiction and jour. essays, studies, articles, 1945-54. Served with USMCR, 1943-45. Mem. Sci. Fiction Writers Am. Author numerous books including: Pleasure Was My Business, 1961; Dynamic Selling, 1962; Squaresville Jag, 1965; Beyond Human Understanding, 1966; The Cosmozoids, 1966; Clairvoyant Strangers, 1968; Cairo Madam, 1969; Black Brute, Runaway Slave and Slave's Revenge, 1969; ESP Forewarnings, 1969; Song of Africa, 1969; Panther John, 1970; Clairvoyant Women, 1970; The Mind Code, 1972; Supernatural Warnings, 1972; Black Pirate, 1973; Android Armageddon, 1974. Address: 440 E Dilido Dr Miami Beach FL 33139

TRAMMEL, CHARLES BUFORD, JR., savs. and loan exec.; b. Washington, N.C., Nov. 13, 1927; s. Charles B. and Annie (Hurst) T.; A.A., Mars Hill Coll., 1946; B.B.A., Wake Forest Coll., 1951; student N.C. State Coll., 1949, Ind. U., 1962; m. Sarah Hamrick, Oct. 12, 1952 (dec. Nov. 1962); children—Lucy Dawn, Sarah Beth, John Charles; m. 2d, Kate Harris, Sept. 12, 1964; 1 dau., Anna Alexander. Adjuster, Wachovia Bank & Trust Co., Salisbury, N.C., 1951; examiner Fed. Home Loan Bank, Greensboro, N.C., 1951-54; v.p., chief exec. officer, dir. Elkin-Jonesville Bldg. & Loan Assn., Elkin, N.C., 1954-70; pres., dir. First Fed. Savs. & Loan Assn., Hendersonville, N.C., 1970-74; exec. v.p. Community Fed. Savs. & Loan Assn., Staunton, Va., 1974—. Co-chmn. United Fund, Elkin, N.C., 1962; exec. bd. Daniel Boone council Boy Scouts Am. Bd. dirs. Henderson County United Fund, Hendersonville C. of C., Salvation Army. Trustee Mars Hill Coll. Served with USNR, 1946-48. Mem. N.C. Assn. Realtors, Baptist. Kiwanian (dir. 1963-66), Rotarian (dir. Henderson County). Home: 423 Windemere Dr Staunton VA 24401 Office: PO Box 1238 Staunton VA 24401

TRAMMELL, PHILLIP WAYNE, radio sta. exec.; b. Stonefort, Ill., Sept. 25, 1933; s. Thomas Webb (dec.) and Alene Beatrice (Gay) T.; B.S. in Communications, So. Ill. U., 1957; m. Barbara Jean Chambers, Sept. 8, 1956; children—Teri, Julie. With Storz Broadcasting Co., hdqrs. Omaha, 1961—, gen. mgr. KOMA, Oklahoma City, 1964, WDGY, Mpls., 1964-69, WQAM, Miami, Fla., 1969—. Served with AUS, 1953-55. Decorated Presidential Unit Citation. Mem. Greater Miami Radio Broadcasters Assn. (sec. 1971, v.p. 1972). Methodist (mem. adminstrv. bd. 1971-74). Kiwanian (dir., pres. 1974—). Home: 12921 SW 71st Av Miami FL 33156 Office: 767 41st St Miami Beach FL 33140

TRAMONTE, DOMINICK SAM, JR., apparel co. exec.; b. Galveston, Tex., Nov. 16, 1932; s. Dominick Sam and Ida (Jenkins) T.; LL.B., U. Tex., 1958; B.S. in Commerce cum laude, St. Edward's U., 1954; m. Rosalee Fewell, Aug. 25, 1956; children—Dominick Sam III, Mary Catherine, Christopher Joseph, Sharon Marie. Admitted to Tex. bar, 1958; pres. Tramonte, Apffel, Urbani & Tramonte, Attys. at Law, Galveston, 1958—; pres. Tray-Dart, Inc., Galveston, 1959—, Indcom, Inc., Galveston, 1962—; pres., chmn. bd. Dickson-Jenkins Mfg. Co., Ft. Worth, 1969—. Chmn., Galveston Traffic Adv. Com., 1963, 65, 67, 69, 71, 73; pres. UNICO Nat., 1960-64. Bd. dirs. Del

Barto-Tramonte Found. Named Outstanding Young Man of Am., Montgomery (Ala.) C. of C., 1966. Fellow Am. Mgmt. Inst.; Mem. Am. Apparel Mfrs. Assn., Western Apparel and Equipments and Mfrs. Assn. (award 1972, v.p. 1971, pres. 1972), Ft. Worth C. of C., Galveston C. of C. (1st v.p., dir.). K.C. (4 deg.), Lion. Home: 2623 Christopher St Galveston TX 77550 Office: 2127 Broadway Galveston TX 77550 also 202-08 St Louise Av Ft Worth TX 76101

TRANSUE, DONALD WALTER, oral surgeon; b. Tamaqua, Pa., Aug. 10, 1930; s. Walter and Dorothy (Roth) T.; B.S., East Stroudsburg State Coll., 1952; D.D.S., U. Pa., 1960, postgrad. 1960-61; postgrad. resident in oral surgery Bryn Mawr Hosp., 1961-62, Pa. Hosp., Phila., 1962-64; m. Michele Bonneau Goyette, May 22, 1965; children—Stephanie, Jacqueline, Donald Walter II, Kevin. Oral surgeon, Miami, 1964—, Coral Gables, Fla., 1968—. Pres., Progress Club of Miami, 1971-72. Served with USCG, 1952-56. Recipient hon. med. certificate Lima, Peru, 1970. Diplomate Am. Bd. Oral Surgeons. Mem. Am., Fla. (pres. 1972-73) socs. oral surgeons, Am., Fla., Fla. East Coast, South Dade, Miami (pres. 1974-75) dental socs., Greater Miami Dental Study Group (pres. 1973-74). Kiwanian (chmn. physically handicapped youth com. 1969-70). Home: 7740 SW 70th St Miami FL 33143 Office: 147 Alhambra Circle Coral Gables FL 33134 also Huntington Med Bldg 168 S E 1st St Miami FL 33131

TRANTHAM, GRACE ELEANOR MACDOUGAL (MRS. WALTER E. TRANTHAM, JR.), writer; b. Washington; d. John and Grace Kimball (Douglass) MacDougal; student Dunbarton Coll., 1933-35, Columbia (Tenn.) Inst., 1935-37; m. Walter Earl Trantham, Jr., Oct. 30, 1943; children—Walter Earl III, Duffey Douglass. Publicist, Navy Dept., 1943-45; columnist, reporter Camp Pendleton (Cal.) Scout, Oceanside (Cal.) Blade Tribune, 1947-51; staff columnist Oceanside Blade Tribune, 1952-54; free-lance writer, including ednl. monographs for use in secondary and coll. edn., 1954—. Area co-chmn. March of Dimes campaign, 1966-70, Am. Cancer Soc., 1962-69; co-chmn. Montclair Prep. Sch. Assn., 1968-69. Recipient Merit award Cal. Press Women's Assn., 1955. Republican. Mem. Anglican Ch. (co-chmn. Altar Guild 1961-70). Home: 2605 Faber Ct Falls Church VA 22046

TRANTHAM, WALTER EARL, JR., transp. equipment mfg. exec.; b. Cuero, Tex., July 4, 1920; s. Walter Earl and Mabel (Duffey) T.; student Rice Inst., 1937-39; B.A.E., Tex. A. and M. U., 1942; student Am. U., 1943-44; m. Eleanor MacDougall, Oct. 30, 1943; children—Walter Earl III, Duffey Douglass. Dir. Operations Microwave Tube div. Hughes Aircraft Co., Los Angeles, 1959-61; v.p., dir. marketing Radcom group Litton Industries, Silver Spring, Md., 1961-63; dir. southeast operations U.S. Def. group Internat. Tel. & Tel. Corp., Washington, 1963-66; pres., chief exec. officer Tasker Industries, Van Nuys, Cal., 1966-68; v.p., dir. advanced programs Canoga Electronics Corp., 1968-70; mgr. transp. control systems Comml. Electronics div. Sylvania Electric Products, Inc., subsidiary Gen. Telephone & Electronics, Inc., Waltham, Mass., 1970-71; mgr. transp. control systems GTE Information Systems, Bedford, Mass., 1971-72; dir. govt. operations Servo Corp. Am., Hicksville, N.Y., 1972—. Bd. regents Casa Loma Coll., 1966-71. Served to lt. col. USMC, 1942-55; now col. Res. Fellow A.I.M.; mem. I.E.E.E., Am. Inst. Aero. and Astronautics, Am. Mgmt. Assn., Electronic Industries Assn. (dir. 1966-70, chmn. Mass. transp. bd. 1968-72), Armed Forces Communications Electronics Assn. (v.p., nat. treas. 1959-62, v.p. 1967-70), Nat. Security Indsl. Assn. (mem. mgmt. adv. bd. 1966-68), Assn. Am. Railroads, Marine Corps Res. Officers Assn. (v.p. 1971—). Home: 2605 Faber Ct Falls Church VA 22046 Office: 111 New South Rd Hicksville NY 11802

TRAPOZZANO, VINCENT RUDOLPH, dentist; b. Jersey City, Aug. 15, 1903; s. Vincent and Maria (Juliana) T.; student Valparaiso U., 1923-25, Northwestern U., 1925-27; D.D.S. (fellow in prosthodontics), Med. Coll. Va. Sch. Dentistry, 1931; m. Ruby Fisher Hutchins, Oct. 12, 1960; 1 dau., Barbara (Mrs. James Gerald Simmons). Practice dentistry, Jersey City, 1935-38, N.Y.C., 1939-44, Portsmouth, Va., 1944-45, Phila., 1946-48, New Port Richey, Fla., 1948-54, St. Petersburg, Fla., 1954—. Instr. Med. Coll. Va. Sch. Dentistry, 1931-33; head prosthodontics dept. N.Y. U., 1933-44, U. Pa., 1945-48; dir. postgrad. courses U. Pa., 1945-48; cons. prosthodontia dept. med. and surgery VA Central office, Washington, Fed. Bldg., St. Petersburg, Fla., Bay Pines (Fla.) Med. Center. Diplomate Am. Bd. Prosthodontics. Fellow Royal Soc. Health London (Eng., hon.), Greater N.Y. Acad. Prosthodontics, A.A.A.S., Am. Coll. Prosthodontists, Am. Coll. Dentists; mem. Am. Dental Assn., Fla. Dental Soc., Acad. Denture Prosthetics, Fla. Prosthetics Soc., Fla. Cleft Palate Assn., Xi Psi Phi, Omicron Kappa Upsilon. Mason (Shriner), Elk. Clubs: St. Petersburg Yacht, Wyoming Antelop (St. Petersburg). Author: (with M.G. Swenson) Complete Dentures, 1940. Editor: Review of Dentistry for State Board Examinations, 1960. Contbr. articles to profl. jours. Home: 1909 Brightwaters Blvd St Petersburg FL 33704 Office: 3900 Central Av St Petersburg FL 33711

TRAPP, WILLIAM FRANCIS, elec. engr.; b. Washington, Jan. 16, 1936; s. Francis William and Frances (Quinn) T.; B.E.E., Va. Poly. Inst., 1960; m. Margaret Ann Mason, Dec. 28, 1968; 1 dau., Molly Ann. Engr. Distbn. and Subtransmission sect. Potomac Power Co., Washington, 1962—. Pres. Pepco Fed. Credit Union, 1970-72. Served with AUS, 1960-62. Registered profl. engr., D.C. Mem. I.E.E.E. Home: 1648 Birch Rd McLean VA 22101 Office: 1900 Pennsylvania Av Washington DC 20006

TRASK, JOHN MAURICE, JR., banker; b. Wilmington, N.C., Oct. 12, 1935; s. John Maurice and Flora Murphy (Graham) T.; A.B., Davidson Coll., 1958; M.B.A., Harvard, 1964; m. Caroline Whitehead Clark, Apr. 15, 1961; children—John Maurice III, Caroline Clark, Samuel Clark, Patrick Graham. Asst. dir. alumni pub. relations dept. Davidson (N.C.) Coll., 1959-60; mgr. Kane Island Farms, Beaufort, S.C., 1960-62; pres. Beaufort Broadcasting Co., 1964—, First Carolina Bank, Beaufort, 1971—; dir. W.S. Clark & Sons, Inc., Tarboro, N.C. Vice pres. Beaufort County Open Land Trust, 1971—; chmn. Lowcountry Regional Planning Commn., 1970-71, mem., 1970-73; mem. City Planning Commn. Beaufort, 1967-69; chmn. fine arts com. Beaufort Mus., 1969—. Alternate del. Democratic Nat. Conv., 1968; Trustee Francis Marion Coll., Florence, S.C., Coll. Charleston (S.C.), 1970—, Davidson Coll., 1970—. Served to 1st lt. AUS, 1958-59. Mem. Davidson Coll. Alumni Assn. (pres. 1969-70). Home: PO Box 1063 Beaufort SC 29902 Office: PO Box 230 Beaufort SC 29902

TRAUGHBER, CHARLES EDWARD, traffic exec.; b. Irvin, Ky., June 19, 1923; s. Barney Edward and Ann K. (Lamb) T.; student Ind. U., 1957-60; m. Clara M. Clunie, June 10, 1945; children—Stephen Lee (dec.), Michael Edward, Pamela Ann. Dispatcher, Pa. R.R., Louisville and Indpls., 1940-46, chief clk., 1946-52; rate compiler Central and So. Motor Freight Tarriff Bur., Louisville, 1952-59, exec. asst., 1959-62, gen. mgr., 1962-65; asst. gen. traffic mgr. Tube Turns Div., Chemetrom Corp., Louisville, 1965-69, gen. traffic mgr., 1969—. Dist. chmn., mem. exec. bd., v.p. George Rogers Clark Council, Boy Scouts Am., New Albany, Ind., 1952-65. Served with USNR, 1941-42. Mem. Louisville Transp. Club, Ky. World Commerce Council. Presbyn. (elder). Mason. Home: 1650 Coes Lane New Albany IN 47150 Office: 28th and Broadway PO Box 987 Louisville KY 40201

TRAUTSCHOLD, JEROME FRANCIS, furniture co. exec.; b. Waco, Tex., Mar. 11, 1909; s. Charles Martin and Marie Antoinette (Muhl) T.; grad. parochial schs.; m. Wilma Ann Adam, Oct. 23, 1930; children—Jeannette (Mrs. William E. Brown), Jerome Francis, Marilyn (Mrs. John B. Tolle). With C.M. Trautschold Co., Inc., Waco, Tex., 1926—, sec. bd. dirs., 1934—, v.p., 1966—. Bd. dirs. Lighthouse for Blind; bd. dirs. Providence Hosp. Adv. Bd., Waco, 1970—, 2d v.p., 1971—; trustee Holy Cross Cemetary Found. Decorated knight Equestrian Order Holy Sepulchre. Roman Catholic. Clubs: Serra, Ridgewood Country. Home: 2515 Arroyo Rd Waco TX 76710 Office: 1500 Franklin Av Waco TX 76703

TRAVER, GEORGE WHITE, exec., inventor; b. Chgo., July 8, 1893; s. Frederick Clarence and Grace C. (White) T.; Ph.B., U. Chgo.; m. Elsie Jane Erickson, June 27, 1917. Chmn. Traver Investments (real estate, security and patent holding co.). Trustee U. Chgo. Cancer Research Fund, Music Assos. of Aspen (Colo.), St. Mary's Hosp. (Palm Beach, Fla.); hon. adviser Evanston Hosp. Rehab. Center. Served as ensign USN, World War I. Mem. Chgo. Mus. Natural History, Art Inst. Chgo. (life), Phi Kappa Psi. Mason. Clubs: Church (hon. dir.), Tavern, Chicago Athletic Association, Post and Paddock; Everglades and Bath and Tennis (Palm Beach, Fla.); Aspen Alps; Garden of Gods (Colorado Springs, Colo.). Inventor electronically treating polyethylene so it can be permanently printed. Address: 9 Golf View Rd Palm Beach FL 33480 also Traver Ranch Glenwood Springs CO 81601

TRAVIS, BILL, coll. adminstr.; b. Selma, Ala., Sept. 8, 1931; s. Charlie Monroe and Lorene (Gunter) T.; A.A., East Miss. Jr. Coll., 1952; B.S., Troy State U., 1954, M.S., 1969; postgrad. U. Ala., 1965-66, Ga. State U., 1972-73; m. Joyce Norsworthy, June 12, 1955; children—Keith, Clint, Christopher. Coach, Midland City (Ala.) High Sch., 1956-57, Elba (Ala.) High Sch., 1957-59, Leesburg (Fla.) High Sch., 1959-61, Middle Ga. Coll., Cochran, Ga., 1961-65, DeKalb Coll., Clarkston, Ga., 1965-73; dean students Faulkner State Jr. Coll., Bay Minette, Ala., 1973—. Bd. dirs. Nat. Jr. Collegiate Athletic Assn., Region XVII. Served with USAF, 1954-56. Named Jr. Coll. Coach Year Ga., 1968, 71. Mem. Kappa Delta Pi. Home: Old Daphne Rd Bay Minette AL 36507 Office: Faulkner State Coll Bay Minette AL 36507

TRAVIS, JAMES CAMERON, banker; b. Krum, Tex., Feb. 12, 1931; s. Perry V. and Merle (Simpson) T.; B.S., North Tex. State U., 1952; M.B.A., So. Methodist U., 1961; grad. Sch. Bank Adminstrn. U. Wis., 1965; m. Jo Walker, Nov. 23, 1956; children—Sue Ann, James Cameron. Bookkeeper First State Bank, Frankston, Tex., summers 1948-51; tng. specialist Convair, Ft. Worth, 1952; tchr. Seagoville (Tex.) Schs., 1952-53; asst. examiner Dept. Banking, Austin, Tex., 1956-63; asst. controller Ft. Worth Nat. Bank, 1963-64; cons. Peat, Marwick, Mitchell & Co., 1965-67; sr. v.p., controller Nat. Bank of Tulsa, 1967—; treas. NBT Corp., Tulsa; dir. Mentor Corp.; adv. dir. Mercantile Bank & Trust; adv. dir. City Bank & Trust, Tulsa; adv. dir. Sand Springs (Okla.) State Bank. Served with AUS, 1954-56. Mem. Financial Execs. Inst., Am. Inst. C.P.A.'s, Okla., Tex. State socs. C.P.A.'s, Tulsa C. of C. Mason, Kiwanian. Club: Tulsa, Meadowbrook (pres. 1972-73), University of Tulsa. Home: 6713 E 66th St S Tulsa OK 74133 Office: PO Box 2300 Tulsa OK 74192

TRAVIS, JAMES KEN, govt. ofcl.; b. Dresden, Tenn., Nov. 2, 1936; s. James R. and Virginia L. (Kennedy) T.; degree bus. adminstrn. Lansing Bus. U., 1957-60; postgrad. Mary Hardin-Baylor Coll., part-time, 1961-65, U. Md., Heidelberg, Germany, part-time 1966-68; B.B.A. (Am. Nat. Red Cross scholar 1968-69), Sam Houston State Coll., 1969; m. Barbara Ann Henderson, Nov. 7, 1967; children—Susan, Kendra Ann. Asst. field dir. Am. Nat. Red Cross, Washington, 1963-69; with U.S. Treasury Dept., Dyersburg, Tenn., 1969—, agt., 1969—. Partner Travis Farm, Dresden, Tenn., 1969—. Served with AUS, 1960-62. Mem. Nat. Auctioneers Assn. (life), U.S. Trotting Assn., Phi Theta Pi. Contbr. numerous articles to trade mags. Home: Route 3 Newbern TN 38059 Office: PO Box 748 Dyersburg TN 38024

TRAVIS, JOHN LIVINGSTON, architect; b. Newport News, Va., Sept. 1, 1937; s. Robert Falligant and Frances Jane (Johnson) T.; B.A. in Architecture, U. Tex., 1967; m. Roxana Marie Oughton, Dec. 17, 1960; 1 dau., Ashleigh Singleton. Chief designer, project architect Phelps & Simmons & Assos., 1967-69, Hesson & May & Assos., 1969-72; prin. John L. Travis & Assos., San Antonio, 1972—. Mem. A.I.A., Tex. Soc. Architects. Kiwanian. Home: 418 Evans Av San Antonio TX 78209 Office: GPM Bldg South Tower San Antonio TX 78216

TRAVIS, NEVENNA TSANOFF (MRS. DON C. TRAVIS), realtor; b. Houston, Apr. 16, 1916; d. Radoslay Andrea and Corrinne (Stephenson) Tsanoff; B.A. with distinction, Rice Inst., 1936; M.A., U. Wis., 1938; m. Don C. Travis, June 13, 1940; children—Neven Don Tsanoff, Andrew David Tsanoff. Asso., Bob Bright, Austin, Tex., 1955-57, Ann Miller Crockett, Austin, 1957-66; owner N. T. Travis Real Estate, Austin, 1966—. Vice pres., asst. sec. Travis Ecology Inc., 1973—, also dir. Pres. P.T.A. Am. Dependents Sch., Berlin, Germany, 1952-53. Charter bd. dirs. Tex. System Natural Labs., Inc., sec. bd. 1967-69, treas., 1969—, acting system coordinator, 1973—. Recipient Salesman of Yr. 1962 award Austin Real Estate Bd., 1963. Mem. Austin Real Estate Bd. (pres. women's council 1962), Nat. Assn. Realtors (women's council), Soc. Certified Master Brokers and Certified Master Salesmen (mem. bd. dirs. 1961-64; sec.-treas. 1964; pres. 1965), Tex. Assn. Realtors (chmn. edn. promotion commn. 1963, historian 1964-69), University Ladies, Pan-Am. Round Table, Phi Beta Kappa. Address: 900 Bluebonnet Lane Austin TX 78704

TRAWICK, HENRY PHILIPS, JR., lawyer; b. Balt., July 20, 1926; s. Henry Philips and Margaret (Porterfield) T.; student N.C. State Coll., 1946-48; LL.B., U. Fla., 1950; m. Louise Jones, Dec. 20, 1949. Admitted to Fla. bar, 1950, practiced in Lakeland, 1951-56, Sarasota, 1956—; mem. firm Millican & Trawick 1966—. Vice chmn. Fla. Law Revision, 1967-69, chmn. 1969-72; atty. Sarasota County Sch. Bd., 1961-65; chmn. Fla. Uniform Probate Code Study Commn., 1973-74. Served with USAAF, 1944-45. Mem. Am., Sarasota County bar assns., Fla. Bar. Author: Florida Practice and Procedure, 1973. Home: 2300 Sunnyside Lane Sarasota FL 33579 Office: 2051 Main St Sarasota FL 33577

TRAWICK, JACK DURWARD, wholesale distbg. co. exec.; b. Brownwood, Tex., Dec. 17, 1932; s. Evans Ramah and Josephine (Harwell) T.; B.S., U.S. Mil. Acad., 1955; M.S., U. Tex., 1961, Carnegie Inst. Tech., 1964; m. Virginia Hallum, June 18, 1955; children—Jack David, Virginia Adele, Roy Hallum. Cons. engr. Frank T. Drought, engrs., San Antonio, 1958-59; comptroller, dir. operations San Antonio Fair, Inc., HemisFair 68, 1965-68; v.p., gen. operations mgr. Straus Frank Co., San Antonio, 1968—. Packmaster, Alamo Area council Boy Scouts Am., 1965-68; chmn. adminstrn. com. Straus-Frank Co. Profit-Sharing and Pension Trust, 1971—. Bd. dirs. Alamo council Camp Fire Girls. Served to 1st lt. AUS, 1955-58. Recipient Lillian Gilbreth Mgmt. award U. Tex., 1961. Mem. Tex. Mfrs. Assn. (chmn. nat. affairs com. 1972-73, indsl. relations com. 1973, chmn. S.W. Tex. chpt. 1974), San Antonio C. of C. (chmn. urban improvements com. 1967, budget and finance com. 1973, chmn. finance com. 1973), Sigma Iota Epsilon. Methodist. Kiwanian. Home: 707 Firefly Dr San Antonio TX 78216 Office: 1964 S Alamo St San Antonio TX 78292

TRAYLOR, ORBA FOREST, lawyer, economist, educator; b. Providence, Ky., June 16, 1910; s. Eddie Ewing and Dillie (Stuart) T.; B.A., Western Ky. U., 1930; M.A., U. Ky., 1932, Ph.D., 1948; J.D., Northwestern U., 1936; m. Josephine Zananiri, Nov. 17, 1945; children—Joseph Marion, Robert Forest, John Christopher. Head dept. econs. Ashland Coll., 1935-36; legal asst. trust dept. 1st Nat. Bank, Chgo., 1936-37; asso. prof. econs. and sociology Western Ky. U., 1938-40; research asst. Bur. Bus. Research, U. Ky., 1939; research dir. Ky. Legislative Council, 1939-41; admitted to Ky. bar, 1941; dir. research and statistics Ky. Dept. Welfare, 1941; asso. econ. analyst div. tax research U.S. Treasury Dept.,1942; acting chief accounting UNRRA, Balkan Mission, 1944-45; asst. prof. econs. and bus. U. Denver, 1946-47, U. Mo., 1947-50; tax specialist, asst. econ. commr. ECA, Greece, 1950-53; coordinator exec. devel. programs Ordnance Corps, Dept. Army, 1954; pub. finance expert UN, also lectr. financial adminstrn. Inst. Pub. Adminstrn., UAR, 1954-56; exec. asst. to Ky. lt. gov., dir. Ky. Legislative Research Commn., Frankfort, 1956-58; commr. finance State of Ky., Frankfort, 1958-59; dir. finance Office High Commr. Ryukyu Islands, 1960-64, dir. econ. affairs, 1964-65; prof. econs. and pub. adminstrn. U. Ala., Huntsville, 1965—, chmn. dept. bus. and pub. adminstrn., 1966-68, chmn. econs., 1968-70. Cons. operations research Johns Hopkins, 1957-61; fiscal cons. various orgns.; financial cons. Tenn. Valley Authority, 1972-74; vis. lectr. econs. various univs. and colls.; lectr. U. Md. Far East Div., 1960-65; sr. adviser Bank of Ryukyus, 1960-65; Joint Fgn. Investment Bd., 1964-65; chmn. bd. Ryukyuan Devel. Loan Corp., 1960-65, Joint Petroleum Bd., 1960-65; counsellor Oak Ridge Asso. Univs., 1966-67. Mem. Ala. Edn. Study Commn. Financial Task Force, 1968-69. Served with AUS, 1942-46; lt. col. Res. (ret.). Mem. Am., So. econ. assns. Am. Soc. for Pub. Adminstrn. (council 1973-76), Am., Ky. bar assns., Nat. Tax Assn.-Tax Inst. Am. (dir. 1971-74), Res. Officers Assn., Beta Gamma Sigma, Delta Sigma Pi. Rotarian. Editorial Bd.: Pub. Adminstrn. Rev., 1972-74. Contbr. articles to profl. publs. Address: U Ala PO Box 1247 Huntsville AL 35807

TRAYNHAM, WADE LANIER, dentist; b. Hampton, Va., Sept. 5, 1906; s. William Henry and Lilly (Tuck) T.; student Randolph-Macon Coll., 1925-28; D.D.S., Med. Coll. Va., 1932; m. Irene Sigler, June 5, 1935; children—Mary (Mrs. Robert F. Brosnan), Wade L., Benjamin L. Practice gen. dentistry, Phoebus, 1932-68, Hampton, 1932-40, 68—. Med. adviser Selective Service System, 1948-68; mem. Elizabeth City County Electoral Bd., 1938-59, Hampton Sch. Bd., 1959-62, vice chmn., 1962-64; vice chmn. Eastern dist. Boy Scouts Am., 1944, chmn. Peninsula dist., 1945. Trustee Zeta Lodge Inst., Ashland, Va. Served to 1st lt. Dental Corps, AUS, 1941. Recipient Civic Community Service award, 1969, Dixie Hosp. award, 1972. Mem. Am., Peninsula (past pres.), Va. dental socs., Am. Boxwood Soc., Kappa Alpha, Psi Omega. Methodist (trustee, chmn. adminstrv. bd.). Rotarian, Elk. Developer several dwarf boxwood cultivars. Home: 103 S Bowood St Hampton VA 23369 Office: 90 S Boxwood St Hampton VA 23369

TREADWAY, CHARLES RICHARD, govt. ofcl.; b. Louisville, Oct. 16, 1939; s. Charles F. and Ruby (Peeples) T.; B.A. (Gen. Motors scholar), Vanderbilt U., 1960, M.D., 1964; m. Jane Heifrin, Feb. 10, 1962; children—Catherine, Charles. Intern, Vanderbilt U. Hosp., Nashville, 1964-65; resident psychiatry U. N.C., Chapel Hill, 1965-68, Washington Sch. Psychiatry, 1968-70; practice medicine specializing in psychiatry, Nashville, 1971—; dir. Vanderbilt U. Mental Health Clinic, Nashville, 1970-71; Psychiat. cons. IBM Corp., Washington, 1969; clin. instr. psychiatry Johns Hopkins Sch. Medicine, 1969-70; spl. asst. to dir. Nat. Inst. Mental Health, Md., 1970; commr. Dept. Mental Health State Tenn., Nashville, 1971—. Recipient Anclotte Manor Found. Psychiat. Research award, 1967. Mem. Am., Tenn. med. assns., Am., So. psychiat. assns., Nashville Mental Health Assn., Nashville Acad. Medicine, Davidson County Assn. Retarded Children, Sigma Alpha Epsilon, Phi Chi. Rotarian. Contbr. articles to profl. jours. Home: 385-1821 Bowling Av Nashville TN 37215 Office: Cordell Hull Bldg Nashville TN 37219

TREEN, DAVID CONNER, lawyer; b. Baton Rouge, July 16, 1928; s. Joseph Paul and Elizabeth (Speir) T.; B.A., Tulane U., 1948, LL.B., 1950; m. Dolores Yvonne Brisbi, May 26, 1951; children—Jennifer Anne, David C. and Cynthia (twins). Admitted to La. bar, 1950; with firm Deutsch, Kerrigan & Stiles, New Orleans, 1950-51; v.p. Simplex Mfg. Corp., New Orleans, 1952-57; mem. firm Beard, Blue, Schmitt & Treen, New Orleans, 1957—; mem. 93d congress, 1972—. Republican candidate for Congress from 2d Congl. dist. La., 1962, 64, 68, candidate gov., 1972; del. Nat. Rep. Conv., 1964, 68, chmn. La. delegation, 1968, 72, mem. Rep. State Central Com., 1962—; chmn. Jefferson Parish exec. com., 1962-67; chmn. met. polit. action council La. Rep. party, 1966—; Rep. nat. committeeman, 1972—. Served as 1st lt. USAF, 1951-52. Mem. La. Bar Assn., Order of Coif, Phi Delta Phi, Kappa Sigma. Methodist. Clubs: Metairie (La.) Country. Home: 430 Dorrington Dr Metairie LA 70005 Office: 1408 Longworth House Office Bldg Washington DC 20515

TREGO, LAWRENCE ORLIN, clothing co. exec.; b. Woodward, Okla., July 25, 1921; s. George Laverne and Leatress Lovilla (Wright) T.; student U. Okla., 1939-40; m. Mary Ellen Oates, Jan. 13, 1940; children—Orlin Denney, Terry Dean. With Trego's, Inc., retail men's wear, Woodward, Okla., 1940—, pres., 1948—; v.p. Trego's Westwear, Inc., Woodward, 1948—; owner Trego's, Enid, Okla., 1954—, Trego's Emporium, Cripple Creek, Colo., 1970—; co-owner Woodward Disposal Co., 1970—; pres. Okla. N.W., Inc., 1963. Vice pres. Gt. Salt Plains council Boy Scouts Am., 1971. Democratic precinct chmn., Woodward, 1971. Served to lt. AUS, 1944-45. Mem. Okla. Retail Mchts. Assn. (v.p. 1968—), Okla. (exec. bd. 1974), Woodward (pres. 1958-59) chambers commerce. Mem. Christian Ch. Mason, Elk; mem. Order Eastern Star (past patron). Home: 1805 18th St Woodward OK 73801 Office: 817 Main St Woodward OK 73801

TREICHLER, RAY, agrl. chemist; b. Rock Island, Ill., Sept. 10, 1907; s. Wallace and Pearl (Cushman) T.; B.S., Pa. State U., 1929, M.S., 1929; Ph.D., U. Ill., 1939; m. Kathryn Amelia Blakeley, June 13, 1942. Asst. state chemist Tex. Agrl. Expt. Sta., Tex. A. and M. Coll., College Station, 1929-40; chief Chem. and Biochem. Research Labs., Fish and Wildlife Service, U.S. Dept. Interior, Laurel, Md., 1941-44; chief biol. activities research and devel. div. Office Q.M. Gen., U.S. Army, 1945-53; chief toxic agts. br. Chem. Corps Research and Devel. Comd., Army Chem. Center, Md., 1953-56; asst. to dir. Med. Research Directorate, Chem. Warfare Labs., 1956-58; research adminstr. Services and Support Group, Provisional USAF, 1958-68; mem. staff tech. application H.D. Hudson Mfg. Co., 1968—; vis. scientist U. Ill., Urbana, 1940-41. Fellow N.Y. Acad. Sci., Am. Soc. Microbiology; mem. Am. Soc. for Testing and Materials, Am. Chem. Soc., Am. Inst. Chemists, Entomol. Soc. Am., Mosquito Control Assn., Am. Soc. Agrl. Engrs., Sigma Xi, Gamma Sigma Delta. Mason. Research in food tech., prevention deterioration, chemistry and formulations pesticides, pesticide dissemination systems. Contbr.

articles on vitamins, basal energy and endogenous nitrogen metabolism, nutrition, composition fishery products, toxic compounds, prevention material deterioration. Home: 4740 Connecticut Av NW Washington DC 20008 Office: HD Hudson Mfg Co 1625 I St NW Washington DC 20006

TREISTER, KENNETH, architect, artist; b. N.Y.C., Mar. 5, 1930; s. Arthur and Anita (Weinberg) T.; student U. Miami (Fla.), 1948-49; B.Arch., U. Fla., 1953; m. Helyne Bressler, Jan. 31, 1954; children—Charles, Alan, Eliot. One man shows include Mirell Gallery, Miami, Fla., 1964, 66, 67; exhibited in group shows at Greenwich Gallery, N.Y.C., Columbus (Ga.) Mus. Fine Arts, Lowe Art Gallery, Coral Gables, Fla., Houston Contemporary Art Mus., Atlanta High Mus.; represented in permanent collections at Norton Gallery, Palm Beach, Fla., Miami (Fla.) Mus. Modern Art; Fla. Supreme Ct. Bldg. individual practice architecture, Miami, 1957—. Lectr., dept. architecture U. Miami, 1965-66. Chmn. Citizens Adv. Com., Miami, Fla., 1965-67. Bd. dirs. Am. Jewish Com., Dade County Conf. on Urban Affairs, Friends of U. Miami Library. Served with USNR, 1953-57. Recipient 1st prize Nat. Ceramic Exhibit, Lowe Art Gallery, 1953, award elementary sch. design Nat. Assn. Sch. Adminstrs., 1966; Nat. Merit award for chapel Temple Israel Greater Miami, Guild Religious Architecture, 1968; Gold medal for design low-rise elderly housing S.E. Regional Conf. Housing and Urban Devel., 1968. Mem. A.I.A., Guild Religious Architecture, Richard J. Nautra Inst., Blue Dome Soc., Fla. Sculpture Soc., So. Assn. Sculptors, Zeta Beta Tau. Contbr. articles in field to profl. jours. Home: 3660 Battersea Rd Coconut Grove Miami FL 33133 Office: Office In The Grove 2699 S Bayshore Dr Miami FL 33133

TRENT, EVA MAE MANES (MRS. HORACE MAYNARD TRENT), mathematician; b. Bloomfield, Ind., Mar. 11, 1909; d. Charles Edgar and Eliza (Abrams) Manes; A.B., Ind. U., 1930, postgrad., 1931; postgrad. Miss. State U., 1936-37; m. Horace Maynard Trent, July 29, 1933; children—Marilyn (Mrs. Jerome Roger Grunkemeyer), Sandra (Mrs. Charles J. Rothwell). Counselor, Westminster Found., Bloomington, Ind., 1930-31; rate procedures analyst Pub. Service Co. Ind., Indpls., 1931-33; instr. math. Ind. U., Bloomington, 1934; instr. edn. Miss. State U., State College, 1937; mathematician U.S. Naval Research Lab., Washington, 1956—. Mem. Philos. Soc. Washington, Sci. Research Soc. Am., Acoustical Soc. Am., Internat. Oceanographic Found., Washington Acad. Sci., Zeta Tau Alpha, Gamma Zeta (hon. installation initiate). Contbr. articles in field to profl. jours. Research in atmospheric electricity and its relation to meteorology; U.S. Naval research reports. Home: 413 Tennessee Av Alexandria VA 22305 Office: US Naval Research Lab Washington DC 20375

TREVILLIAN, WILMER THOMAS, banker; b. Richmond, Va., Oct. 31, 1911; s. William Thomas and Martha Wilmer (Roper) T.; B.S., Randolph Macon Coll., 1933; m. Catherine Clifton Newberry, Aug. 23, 1947; children—Elizabeth Jo, Thomas Bird. Clk. fiscal agy. dept. Fed. Res. Bank, Richmond, 1933-40; asst. cashier 1st Nat. Farmers Bank, Wytheville, Va., 1940-63, v.p., 1963—. Pres., A.R.C., 1958-59. Bd. dirs. United Fund, 1963-73. Served with AUS, 1943-46. Decorated Bronze Star; recipient Cross of Mil. Service award U.D.C., 1972. Mem. Lambda Chi Alpha, Chi Beta Phi. Methodist. Lion, Mason (Shriner, K.T., state grand master 1972). Club: Wytheville Golf, Iron Boots Society. Home: 625 W Washington St Wytheville VA 24382 Office: PO Box 514 Wytheville VA 24382

TREVINO, ELIZABETH BORTON DE, author; b. Bakersfield, Cal., Sept. 2, 1904; d. Fred Ellsworth and Carrie (Christensen) Borton; B.A., Stanford, 1925; m. Luis Trevino Gomez, Aug. 10, 1935; children—Luis Federico, Enrique Ricardo. Lectr., 1942—; corr. Religions News Service, 1940—; staff writer Caminos del Aire, 1960—, also free-lance writer, journalist; hon. lectr. Am. Inst. Fgn. Trade, 1960. Recipient medal Kansas City (Mo.) Women's Commn., 1961; named hon. Texan, 1963. Mem. Author's Guild Am., Am. Hispanic Soc., Phi Beta Kappa, Theta Sigma Phi. Author: (juveniles) Our Little Ethiopian Cousin, 1935, Our Little Aztec Cousin, 1934; About Bellamy, 1940; A Carpet of Flowers, 1955; Nacar, the White Deer, 1963; I, Juan de Pareja (Newbery medal 1966) 1965; Casilda of the Rising Moon, 1966; Turi's Poppa, 1968; Here is Mexico, 1970; Beyond the Gates of Hercules, 1971; (adult books) Memoirs: My Heart Lies South, 1953; Where the Heart is, 1962; (novels) Even as you Love, 1957; The Greek of Toledo, 1959; Fourth Gift, 1966; House on Bitterness Street, 1970; The Music Within, 1973. Home: Av Pres Lopez Matos 308 Cuernavaca Mexico Office: Apartado 827 Cuernavaca Morelos Mexico

TREVINO, LEE BUCK, profl. golfer; b. Dallas, Dec. 1, 1939; s. Joe and Juanita (Barrett) T.; ed. pub. schs.; m. Claudia Ann Fenley, Aug. 24, 1964; children—Richard Lee, Lesley Ann, Tony Lee, Troy Liana. Head profl. Hardy's Driving Range, Dallas, 1961-65; asst. profl. Horizon Hills Country Club, El Paso, Tex., 1966-67; chmn. bd. Lee Trevino Enterprises, Inc.; touring profl., 1967—; tournament winner Tex. Open 1965, 66, N.M. Open, 1966. U.S. Open, 1968, 71, Hawaiian Open, 1968, Tucson Open, 1969, 70, Nat. Airlines Open, 1970, World Cup, 1969, 71, Brit. Open, 1971, 72, Canadian Open, 1971, Danny Thomas Memphis Classic, 1971, Sahara Internat., 1971, Tallahassee Open, 1971, Greater St. Louis Classic, 1972, Greater Hartford Open, 1972, Jackie Gleason Classic, 1973, Doral Eastern Open, 1973, Mexican Open, 1973, Chrysler Classic, Australia, 1973, Greater New Orleans Open, 1974; 6th ofcl. money winner, 1968, 1st money winner, 1970; 1st golfer to have scored four sub-par rounds in U.S. Open Competition, 1968; co-holder of all time low scoring record U.S. Open Competition. Hon. chmn. Christmas Seal campaign, 1969, 70, 71, Nat. Sports Ambassador, 1971; hon. chmn. Trans Pecos Tb and Respiratory Disease Assn.; grand marshal Sun Carnival Parade, 1969-70, 71-72; mem. Pres.'s Conf. on Phys. Fitness and Sports; mem. sports com. Nat. Multiple Sclerosis Soc. Served with USMC, 1956-60. Named Tex. Profl. Athlete of Year, 1970, Profl. Golf Assn. Player of Year, 1971, Golf mag. Player of Year, 1971, Sportsman of Year Sports Illus. mag., 1971, Internat. Sports Personality of Year Brit. Broadcasting Assn., 1971, A.P. Male Athlete of Year, 1971; recipient Ann. Hickok Belt award, 1971, Gold Tee award, 1971, Vardon Trophy, 1970, 71, 72. Star TV golf program. Home: 10020 Eastridge Dr El Paso TX 79925 Office: PO Box 12727 El Paso TX 79912

TRIMBLE, JOHN CLIFTON, educator; b. Carters Creek, Tenn., Dec. 8, 1928; s. John Elijah and Mittie G. (Rountree) T.; B.A., David Lipscomb Coll., 1950; M.A., Northwestern U., 1952, Ph.D., 1966; m. Louise Harris, June 10, 1949; 1 son, John Harris. Instr. Purdue U., Lafayette, Ind., 1956-59; asst. prof. Middle Tenn. State Coll., Murfreesboro, 1959-62, Miss. State Coll. for Women, Columbus, 1962-67; asst. prof. dept. speech communication U. South Ala., Mobile, 1967-69, asso. prof., 1969—. Mem. Speech Communication Assn., So. Speech Communication Assn. (mem. exec. council 1970, mem. com. of twelve 1973-74), Ala. Speech and Theatre Assn. (1st v.p. 1970-73). Co-editor Ala. Speech and Theatre Assn. Newsletter, 1967-73. Home: 5521 Vanderbilt Dr N Mobile AL 36608

TRIMBLE, JOHN FREDERIC, accountant; b. Charlottesville, Va., Jan. 18, 1936; s. Frederic Baughman and Elizabeth Evans (Ramsey) T.; B.B.A., U. Tex., 1958; m. Dorothy Frances Guerra, Nov. 20, 1965; children—Nancy Elizabeth, Martha Lea, Linda Cristina. With Price Waterhouse & Co., Houston, 1959-70, mgr., 1965-70; with Main Lafrentz & Co., Houston, 1970—, partner, 1971-73, mng. partner, 1973—. Mem. accounting adv. council U. Tex., Austin, chmn., 1971-72; pres. Mental Health Assn. Houston and Harris County, 1973—; treas. Children's Mental Health Services, Houston, 1973—. Served to 2d. lt. Transp. Corps, AUS, 1958-59. C.P.A., Tex. Mem. Am. Inst. C.P.A.'s, Tex. Soc. C.P.A.'s, U. Tex. Ex-Students Assn., U. Tex. Assn., Phi Delta Theta (pres. 1968). Methodist. Clubs: Breakfast, Alumni, Champions Golf (Houston). Home: 13415 Sea Island Houston TX 77069 Office: 2190 Two Shell Plaza Houston TX 77002

TRIMBLE, LEE SHACKLEFORD, JR., librarian; b. Griffin, Ga., Mar. 14, 1923; s. Lee Shackleford and Effie May (Hutcheson) T.; student U. Fla., 1941-43, Duke, 1943-44; A.B. Journalism, B.A., U. Ga., 1949; M.L.S., Emory U., 1952; m. Mary McKinley Cobb, Dec. 22, 1947; children—Lee Shackleford III, Katherine M., Carlisle C., May H. Head librarian Willow Br. Library, Jacksonville, Fla., 1952-53, Southside Br. Library, 1953-55; dir. Beaufort-Hyde-Martin Regional Library, Washington, N.C., 1955-59; dir. Dalton Regional Library (Ga.), 1959—. Pres., P.T.A., 1961-62, v.p. county-wide, 1962-65; active Boy Scouts Am., 1953-55; mem. Citizen's Adv. Com., Dalton, 1972-73. Served with USMCR, 1943-46. Mem. Ga. (treas. 1962-65), Southeastern library assns., Sigma Chi. Democrat. Presbyn. Home: 206 W Hawthorne St Dalton GA 30720 Office: 101 S Selvidge St Dalton GA 30720

TRINKLE, JAMES LEWIS, real estate broker; b. Roanoke, Va., Apr. 2, 1929; s. Elbert Lee and Helen (Sexton) T.; B.A., Hampden-Sydney Coll., 1950; LL.B., U. Va., 1953; m. Betty Francis, Dec. 27, 1950; children—James Lewis, William Francis, David Ball. Admitted to Va. bar, 1952; asso. law firm Woodrum, Staples & Gregory, Roanoke, 1953-56; sales rep. C.W. Francis & Son, Inc., Roanoke, 1956-61, v.p., 1961-66, pres., 1966—; dir. The Colonial-Am. Nat. Bank of Roanoke; dir. Peoples Fed. Savs. & Loan Assn. of Roanoke. Pres. Central YMCA, Roanoke, 1971-73, Roanoke Fine Arts Center, 1968-70, United Fund of Roanoke Valley, 1963, Downtown Roanoke, Inc., 1962; mem. project com. Roanoke Civic Center, 1964-71; mem. Roanoke City Charter Study Commn., 1961; pres. Young Democratic Clubs of Va., 1959; chmn. Roanoke City Democratic Com., 1962. Bd. dirs. Roanoke Symphony Soc., Roanoke chpt. Am. Cancer Soc., Roanoke Hist. Soc.; trustee Hampden-Sydney Coll. Recipient Distinguished Service award Roanoke Jr. C. of C., 1961. Mem. Roanoke Valley, Va., Nat. real estate bds., Am., Va., Roanoke bar assns., Gen. Alumni Assn. U. Va. (pres.), Omicron Delta Kappa, Pi Kappa Alpha, Phi Alpha Delta. Presbyn. Clubs: Roanoke Country, Shenandoah, Hunting Hills Country, Farmington Country. Home: 5270 Flintlock Rd SW Hunting Hills Roanoke VA 24014 Office: 120 W Kirk Av Roanoke VA 24011

TRIPLITT, RUPERT ANTON, food co. exec.; b. Cisco, Tex., Jan. 23, 1918; s. John William and Ethel Mabel (Limroth) T.; B.B.A., Tex. Tech. U., 1941; grad. Advanced Mgmt. Program Harvard, 1958; m. Katharine Andrews, Oct. 30, 1948; children—Rupert Anton, Mabel Claire, Tom Andrews, Katharine Pearce. Salesman, asst. dist. sales mgr. Tom's, Lubbock, Tex., 1939-41; food broker Sanborn-Holmes, N.Y.C., 1946-47; mem. sales staff Toms Food Ltd., Columbus, Ga., 1947-50, sales mgr., 1951-53, v.p. sales, 1958—; also dir.; pres. Columbus Tom's Sales, 1970—; dir. 1st Fed. Savs. & Loan Assn., 4th Nat. Bank, Columbus, Chattahoochee Valley Fair. Mem. Columbus Met. Airport Commn., 1966-73; pres. Jr. Achievement, 1958-59. Trustee Walter Alan Richards Found., Columbus. Served to lt. comdr. USNR, 1942-46; ETO, CBI. Mem. Peanut Butter Mfrs. and Nut Salters Assn. (past pres.). Baptist (deacon). Rotarian. Clubs: Columbus Country, Green Island. Home: 2730 Averett Dr Columbus GA 31906 Office: 900 8th St Columbus GA 31902

TRIPP, DAVE CHARLIE, ednl. cons.; b. Colfax, Ia., Nov. 7, 1910; s. Charlie S. and Cora Myrtle (Byers) T.; B.A. No. Ia. U., 1931; M.S., Drake U., 1949; postgrad. U. Ia., 1951-52, Ill. State Normal U., 1962; m. Violet LaVerne Alberts, Oct. 8, 1938; 1 dau., Barbara Ann (Mrs. Allan Harrison). Tchr., Delta (Ia.) Pub. Schs., 1931-34, Monroe Jr. High Sch., Mason City, Ia., 1939-44, Fort Dodge (Ia.) Jr. Coll., 1946-47, Pillsbury Acad., Owatonna, Minn., 1947-48; prin. high schs., Rienbeck, Ia., 1948-51, Clarion, Ia., 1951-53, Atlantic, Ia., 1953-56; ednl. cons. Sci. Research Assos., Inc., Chgo., 1953, 56—. Tchr. vocational and ednl. guidance Stetson U., 1966-67. Served to lt. USNR, 1944-46. Mem. Internat. Reading Assn., Am. Ednl. Research Assn., Internat. Platform Assn., Nat. Council on Measurement in Edn., Phi Delta Kappa, Phi Beta Alpha. Mason; mem. Order Eastern Star, Elk. Address: 200 Bedford Trail Apt 200 Kings Point Sun City Center FL 33570

TRIPP, JOHN ALOYSIUS, architect; b. St. Louis, Oct. 8, 1925; s. George Washington and Ella Frances (Broeker) T.; student U. Miami, 1945-48; m. Sally Frances Hand, Jan. 27, 1946; children—Tim Kenneth, Jane (Mrs. Thomas A. Gribbin III). Partner, Tripp & Skrip, architects and planners, A.I.A., Miami, Fla., 1953—. Mem. City of Miami Housing Appeals Bd., 1962-64; mem. City Council West Miami, 1952-58, pres., 1952. Served to lt. USAAF, 1943-45. Mem. A.I.A. Club: Coral Reef Yacht (commodore 1972-73). Home: 1600 S Bayshore Lane Miami FL 33133 Office: 2973 Coral Way Miami FL 33133

TRISCO, ROBERT FREDERICK, educator, clergyman; b. Chgo., Nov. 11, 1929; s. Richard E. and Harriet Rose (Hardt) T.; B.A., St. Mary of the Lake Sem., 1951; S.T.L., Pontifical Gregorian U., Rome, Italy, 1955, D.Ecclesiastical History, 1962; Ordained priest Roman Catholic Ch., 1954; mem. faculty Cath. U. Am., Washington, 1959—, asso. prof. ch. history, 1965—, vice-rector acad. affairs, 1966-68; exec. sec. Am. Cath. Hist. Assn., 1961—. Mem. subcom. for consultation with Baptists, Bishops' Com. Ecumenical and Interreligious Affairs, 1966—, Presbys., 1972—; mem. subcom. history Bishops' Com. Priestly Life and Ministry. Mem. Am. Hist. Assn., Am. Soc. Ch. History. Author: The Holy See and the Nascent Church in the Middle Western United States, 1826-1850, 1962. Editor: The Catholic Historical Review, 1963—. Contbr. to profl. publs. in field. Address: The Catholic University Am Washington DC 20017

TRISDALE, RAYMON, librarian; b. Gainesboro, Tenn., Sept. 11, 1916; s. George F. and Emma (Pharris) T.; student Tulsa U., 1947-49; B.A., U. Okla., 1951; m. Elizabeth Dow, 1951. Librarian, Wakeeney (Kan.) High Sch., 1951-56, Hays (Kan.) High Sch., 1956-58; regional demonstration librarian Mo. State Library, Jefferson City, 1958-59; asst. librarian Keokuk (Ia.) Pub. Library, 1959-60; head librarian Ft. Madison (Ia.) Pub. Library, 1960-61; chief open lit. area Tech. Library, White Sands Missile Range, N.M., 1961-71; chief Logistics Library, Ft. Lee, Va., 1971—. Pres. Miss. Valley Film Co-op, Quincy, Ill., 1961. Served with 90th Inf. Div., AUS, 1942-46. Decorated Purple Heart. Mem. N.E.A., A.L.A., Am. Legion, V.F.W. Democrat. Mem. Ch. of Christ. Mason, Lion. Home: 15017 Horseshoe Bend Dr Chester VA 23831 Office: Logistics Library Fort Lee VA 23801

TRIZNA, FRANK BENEDICT, dentist; b. Newark, Jan. 23, 1932; s. Frank Michael and Gertrude (Mileski) T.; M.Sc. in Dentistry, Fairleigh Dickinson U., 1964; D.D.S., U. Pa., 1962; m. Dona Buckner, Dec. 27, 1969; children—Frank Martin, Dane Forrest (dec.), Dana Cherese. Practice dentistry specializing in orthodontics, Pompano Beach, Fla., 1964—. Served with USNR, 1952-56. Mem. Am., Fla. dental assns., Atlantic Coast, Broward County dental socs., Am. Assn. Orthodontists, Fla. Orthodontic Soc., So. Soc. Orthodontists, Greater Miami Acad. Orthodontists, Am. Soc. Dentistry for Children, Stomatological Soc., U. Pa. Cryer Soc., Pompano Beach C. of C., Pompano Beach Power Squadron, Eta Sigma Sigma, Omicron Kappa Upsilon. Democrat. Roman Catholic. Lion. Club: Lauderdale Athletic; Ft. Lauderdale Tennis; Pompano Beach Optimist. Home: 1238 SE 13th Av Deerfield Beach FL 33441 Office: 2323 NE 26th Av Pompano Beach FL 33062

TROCHE, ALFONSO, petroleum co. exec.; b. San Juan, P.R., Oct. 18, 1937; s. Ildefonso and Dora (Rivera) T.; B.S., N.Y. U., 1959; postgrad. (Community Service Soc. fellow), Columbia, 1959-60; m. Myrtha Ortiz, Feb. 7, 1959; children—Marta Doris, Peggy Ann, Denisse Yvette. Asst. press sec. Office of Mayor City N.Y., 1966-68; pub. relations asst., pub. relations mgr. Esso Standard Oil Co., San Juan, 1968-70, sales supr., 1970—, retail sales mgr., 1971-72, retail sales adviser, 1972—. Pub. relations cons. Sec. Edn., San Juan, 1968. Served as capt. AUS, 1960-66. Recipient bronze medal for outstanding achievement with Spanish community N.Y.C., City N.Y., 1968. Mem. Pub. Relations Soc. Am., Am. Mgmt. Assn., C. of C. P.R. Lion. Club: Overseas Press (asso. mem. San Juan). Home: 14215 SW 73d St Miami FL 33143 Office: 396 Alhambra Circle Coral Gables FL 33134

TROESTER, CARL AUGUSTUS, JR., assn. exec.; b. Kirksville, Mo., May 27, 1916; s. Carl Augustus and Katherine (Magnus) T.; B.S. in Edn., N.E. Mo. State Tchrs. Coll., Kirksville, 1937; M.A., U. Mo., 1938; Ed.D., Columbia, 1942; postgrad. U. Pa., 1945; m. Thelma Schwab, Sept. 3, 1940; children—Carl Augustus III, Thelma Ann, Jeffrey. Instr. phys. edn. N.E. Mo. State Tchrs. Coll., 1937, U. Mo., 1937-39; asst. health and phys. edn. Columbia Tchrs. Coll., 1939-40; dir. health and phys. edn., dean of men, dir. summer session Willimantic (Conn.) State Tchrs. Coll., 1940-46; dual prof. edn. and phys. edn. Syracuse U., 1946-48; exec. sec. A.A.H.P.E.R., Washington, 1948—. Vis. instr. Columbia, summer 1944; vis. instr. health and phys. edn. grad. extension courses health edn. U. Conn., 1945-46; cons. Conn. Dept. Edn., 1945; mem. Citizen's Adv. Com., also Exec. Com. Pres. Eisenhower's Council Youth Fitness, 1956; sec.-gen. internat. council health, phys. edn. and recreation World Confedn. Orgns. Teaching Profession, 1958—. Mem. Conn. Assn. Health, Phys. Edn. and Recreation (hon. life), Coll. Phys. Edn. Assn., Soc. States Dirs. Health, Phys. Edn. and Recreation, Am. Sch. Health Assn., Am. Pub. ealth Assn., Phi Delta Kappa, Kappa Delta Phi. Author: Everyday Games for Children, 1948; (with John H. Shaw) Individual Sports for Men, 1949. Home: 10917 Mariner Dr Silesia MD 20822 Office: 1201 16th St NW Washington DC 20036

TROPP, HARRY ERNEST, ednl. adminstr.; b. St. Louis, Dec. 27, 1912; s. Solomon and Millie (Levin) T.; B.S., St. Louis U., 1935; M.S., Vanderbilt U., 1936; student U. Ill., 1937, Yale, 1959-60; m. Muriel Sidonia Liebmann, Nov. 7, 1943; 1 son, Robert Alan. Prof. physics Buena Vista Coll., 1936-38, dean men, 1938; with Hillsborough County Pub. Schs., Tampa, Fla., 1949—, supr. sci. curriculum, 1958—. Served to lt. col. AUS, 1941-46. Mem. A.A.A.S., Am. Inst. Physics, Nat. Sci. Suprs. Assn., Nat. Sci. Tchrs. Assn. Rotarian (dir. 1968-70). Author (with George R. Tracy and Alfred E. Friedl) Modern Physical Science, 4th edit., 1974. Home: 1906 Brookline St Tampa FL 33609 Office: 1407 E Columbus Dr Tampa FL 33602

TROST, CHARLES ARTHUR, lawyer; b. Montgomery, Ala., Jan. 6, 1938; s. Henry Arthur and Marguerite (Miller) T.; B.A., Vanderbilt U., 1960; J.D., U. Ala., 1963; LL.M. in Taxation, N.Y. U., 1974; m. Annie Howell Orr, June 9, 1962; children—Caroline Thomas, Henry Arthur, Edith Bruder. Admitted to Tenn. bar, 1964; law clk. to chief judge U.S. Dist. Ct., Middle Tenn., Nashville, 1963-64; asso. firm Queener & Courtney, Columbia, Tenn., 1964-66; partner Courtney Trost & Fleming, Columbia, 1966-73. Mem. Lands Condemnation Commn., U.S. Dist. Ct. for Middle Tenn., 1969-73; chmn. Tenn. Law Revision Commn., 1970—. Chmn. Maury County Library Bd., 1966-68; trustee Maury County Hosp., 1971-73. Served with AUS, 1957-59. Named Outstanding Young Man, Tenn. Jaycees, 1972. Mem. Am., Tenn., Maury County bar assns., Phi Delta Phi, Alpha Tau Omega. Episcopalian. Home: 1001 Rolling Fields Columbia TN 38401 Office: 216 W 7th St Columbia TN 38401

TROTTER, DONALD WAYNE, editor; b. York, Ala., Feb. 19, 1939; s. Israel Leonidas and Hazel (Jackson) T.; A.A., Hinds Jr. Coll., 1959; B.A., U. So. Miss., 1961; m. Gloria Lynn Gillenwater, Dec. 26, 1964; 1 son Gregory Scott. Reporter Jackson (Miss.) Daily News, 1962; editorial writer, asso. editor, mng. editor Bristol (Va.) Herald Courier, 1962-66; instr. journalism U. So. Miss., 1964-65; adminstrv. asst. to Rep. William C. Wampler, 9th Dist. VA., 1967; mng. editor Bristol Herald Courier, 1967-69; urban affairs editor Comml. Appeal, Memphis, 1969-70, urban affairs editor, 1970—. Part time instr. Memphis State U. Bd. dirs. Campus Conservative Inc. Served with AUS, 1960. Recipient Freedom Found. Editorial Writing award, 1963. Mem. Memphis Press Club (chmn.), Memphis Gridiron Show, Inc. (exec. chmn.), Omicron Delta Kappa, C. of C. Republican. Baptist. Club: Memphis Press (officer). Home: 2118 University Circle Memphis TN 38112 Office: Memphis Pub Co Memphis TN 38101

TROTTER, JOHN WALLACE, savs. and loan exec.; b. New Iberia, La., June 14, 1917; s. John Alden and Florence Elizabeth (Cherry) T.; B.S., U. Southwestern La., 1939; m. Mary Alice Williams, Apr. 26, 1941. Clk., Duhe-Bourgeois Sugar Co., Jeanerette, La., 1939; cost accountant Jefferson Island Salt Mining Co., Inc., 1939-46; with Iberia Savs. & Loan Assn., New Iberia, 1946—, now exec. v.p., mgr., dir.; dir. Security Mortgage Ins. Co., Baton Rouge, Fed. Home Loan Bank of Little Rock. Chmn., Iberia Parish chpt. A.R.C.; regional v.p. La. Travel Promotion Assn.; mem. Iberia Parish Planning Com.; mem. spl. com. to study finance City of New Iberia; mem. Iberia Indsl. Devel. Com. Trustee Pub. Affairs Research Council La., Wesley Found. U. Southwestern La. Mem. La. Savs. and Loan League (past pres.). Methodist (chmn. bd. trustees, sec.-treas. conf. bd. of laity United Meth. Ch. La.). Rotarian. Club: Iberia Golf and Country. Home: 108 Trotter St New Iberia LA 70560 Office: 301 E St Peter St New Iberia LA 70560

TROTTER, ROBERT WILLIAM, physician; b. Chattanooga, Oct. 14, 1927; s. Lester Samuel and Gertrude (Cox) T.; B.S., U. Chattanooga, 1952; M.D., U. Tenn., 1954; m. Sadie Sue Eldredge, June 18, 1951; children—Patricia Sue, Jane Ida, Robert William, Nancy Carol. Intern, Crawford W. Long Meml. Hosp., Atlanta, 1954-55; resident Univ. Hosp. and Hillman Clinic Med. Coll. Ala., Birmingham, 1955-59; practice medicine, specializing in surgery, Athens, Tenn., 1959—; mem. staff Athens Community Hosp. Mem. McMinn County Bd. of Edn., 1963-71. Bd. dirs. Epperson Hosp., 1961-73, Athens Community Hosp., 1973—. Diplomate Am. Bd. Surgery. Fellow A.C.S.; mem. A.M.A., Tenn. Med. Assn., McMinn County Med. Soc., Southeastern Surg. Congress, Knoxville Surg. Soc. Home: 1208 Woodacres Dr Athens TN 37303 Office: Box 625 Medical Center Athens TN 37303

TROTTER, WILLIAM EDMUNDSON, II, restaurateur; b. Crowley, La., Aug. 27, 1936; s. James M. and Wahneta (Chigley) T.; student Loyola U., New Orleans, 1954-55, Tulane U., 1955-56, La. State U., 1956-57 children—Melissa, Wahneta, William, Deidre; m. Greta Joyce Rabalais, Apr. 17, 1971. Pres., William Trotter & Son, Rice Brokerage, Crowley, 1957-63; v.p. Self Service Restaurants, Inc., New Orleans, 1963-69, chmn. bd., 1969—; pres. Evangeline Downs, Inc., Lafayette, La., 1970—; dir. First Nat. Bank Commerce, New Orleans, First Nat. Bank Lafayette. Mem. New Orleans Tourist and Conv. Commn., 1971—, Delgado-Albania Plantation Commn., 1970—. Roman Catholic. Home: 1 Cromwell Pl New Orleans LA 70118 Office: 4820 Bradley Dr New Orleans LA 70121

TROTTER, WILLIAM PERRY, lawyer; b. Manchester, Ga., Nov. 2, 1919; s. McKie Massenburg and Tudor (Perry) T.; B.A., Vanderbilt U., 1941; LL.B., U. Ga., 1947; m. Julia Thomason, Aug. 5, 1950; children—Jefferson W., William P. Admitted to Ga. bar, 1947, since practiced in La Grange; sr. partner firm Trotter & Zachry; atty. Assn. County Commnrs. Ga., 1962—. Mem. Ga. Senate from 37th Dist., 1951-52, 57-58, Ho. of Reps. from Troup County, 1959; dir. Ga. Dept. Pub. Safety, 1959-61; mem. Dem. Nat. Com. for Ga., 1961-71. Chmn. Ga. Police Acad. Bd., 1961-71. Served to maj. USAAF, World War II. Decorated Air medal. Mem. Am., Ga. bar assns. Home: 323 Lane Circle La Grange GA 30240 Office: 102 Main St La Grange GA 30240

TROUP, ROBERT DALE, ednl. adminstr.; b. Dayton, O., Oct. 28, 1926; s. George Miller and Marcella (Stomps) T.; B.S., Miami U., 1951; postgrad. Stetson U., 1960-62; m. Geraldine Ann Graber, Aug. 20, 1949; children—Jon G., Robert G. Service officer Stark County, O., 1950-55; asst. to pres. Sinclair Coll., Dayton, 1955-57; dir. pub. relations Daytona Beach (Fla.) Community Coll., 1959—. Pub. relations cons. Kellogg Found. Finance chmn. United Fund, Daytona, 1961. Bd. dirs. Halifax Area Citizens Scholarship Found. Served with USAAF, 1944-45. Mem. Nat. Pub. Relations Council, Am. Assn. Community Colls., Fla. Assn. Community Colls. (chmn. pub. relations com. 1966), Beta Phi Gamma. Kiwanian. Home: 1115 Live Oak St Daytona FL 32014 Office: PO Box 1111 Daytona FL 32015

TROUT, RAY CARL, elec. products mfg. co. exec.; b. Kansas, Okla., Oct. 8, 1925; s. Randal Carl and Laura Emma (Beam) T.; student Tulsa U., 1948-49, U. Cal., 1949-50; m. Christine Cervantes, Aug. 5, 1948; children—Robert Ray, Maria Chantel. Engring. dept. Philco Corp., Phila., 1950-54, tele-communications adviser, Saigon, Vietnam, 1954-58; group engr. Philco Western Devel. Lab., Palo Alto, Cal., 1958-63; engring. mgr. Philco Ford Co., Houston, 1963—. Vice-pres., Clear Lake City Community Assn., Houston, 1971-73. Served with USNR, 1943-48. Mem. I.E.E.E. Home: 1330 Bell Grove Seabrook TX 77586 Office: PO Box 58487 Houston TX 77058

TROUT, RONALD PAUL, banker; b. Cape Girardeau, Mo., Sept. 29, 1939; s. Joe Paul and Verda Alma (Jenkins) T.; student S.E. Mo. State Coll., 1957-59; B.S., U. Mo., 1961, M.S., 1963; m. Carole Ann Maes, Nov. 27, 1965; children—Christopher Paul, Anthony Paul. With Peat Marwick, Mitchell & Co., C.P.A.'s, St. Louis, 1965-66; with Edward D. Jones & Co., stock brokers, 1966-70; trust investment mgr. Nat. Bank of Tulsa, 1970—. Bd. dirs. Undercroft Montessori Sch. Mem. Okla. Soc. Financial Analysts (pres. 1972-73), Okla. Bankers Assn. Home: 5327 E 36th St Tulsa OK 74135 Office: 320 S Boston St Tulsa OK 74102

TROUTMAN, EDWIN GLENN, physician; b. Olathe, Kan., July 31, 1927; s. Edwin Glenn and Maude Roxanne (Seaton) T.; student U. Ariz., 1944-45, 46-47; M.D., U. So. Cal., 1952; m. Mary Olena Flesher, Sept. 4, 1949; children—Clinton Edwin, David Glenn. Intern, resident Barlow Sanatorium, Los Angeles, 1951-54; resident 1st Med. Div. Bellevue Hosp., N.Y.C., 1955, 56; teaching resident fellow Nat. Tb. Assn., Am. Trudeau Soc., 1955, 56; practice medicine, specializing in internal medicine, Ft. Worth, 1961—; mem. staff numerous Ft. Worth hosps.; instr. medicine U. So. Cal., 1954; instr. medicine U. Tex. Med. Br., 1957-59, asst. prof. medicine, 1959-61, asst. to dean of medicine 1957-59, med. dir. outpatient dept., asst. dir. for planning, 1959-60; clin. asst. prof. medicine U. Tex. Southwestern Med. Sch., 1961—; dir. med. edn. and research Harris Hosp., Ft. Worth Found., Ft. Worth, 1961-65; pres. Tex. Allergy Labs., Inc., Med. Computers, Inc., Doctors Operational Computer Service, Inc. Bd. dirs. Ft. Worth-Tarrant County Heart Assn. Served with USNR, 1945-46. Mem. Am., Tex. diabetes assns., Am., Tex. State, Tarrant County med. assns., Am. Thor. Soc. Republican. Author various articles pub. in profl. jours. Home: 2026 Ward Parkway Fort Worth TX 76110 Office: 712 7th Av Fort Worth TX 76104

TROUTMAN, MARCUS LLOYD, dentist; b. Iredell County, N.C., Aug. 7, 1882; s. Jacob Calwell and Margaret Louise (Troutman) T.; D.D.S., Atlanta So. Dental Coll., 1917; m. Sudie Steele, May 24, 1911; children—Thelma Marjorie (Mrs. James Augustis Peeler), Julis Beatrice (Mrs. Odis Bennett Summers), Sudie Christine (Mrs. H. Wylie M. Yarborough). With Internal Revenue Dept., Statesville, N.C., 1908-14; practice dentistry, Kannapolis, N.C., 1917—; mem. dental staff Cabarrus Hosp., 1954—. Active P.T.A., YMCA. Mem. Am., Cabarrus dental socs. Rotarian, Mason (Shriner); mem. Order Eastern Star. Republican. Lutheran. Home: 317 S Main St Kannapolis NC 28081 Office: PO Box 162 104 West A St Kannapolis NC 28081

TROUTMAN, MARY OLENA FLESHER (MRS. EDWIN GLENN TROUTMAN), physician; b. Rochester, Minn.; d. Clinton G. and Mary (Dyer) Flesher; A.A., Pasadena Jr. Coll., 1945; B.A., U. So. Cal., 1947, M.D., 1954; m. Edwin Glenn Troutman, Sept. 4, 1949; children—Clinton Edwin, David Glenn. Intern Los Angeles County Harbor Gen. Hosp., Torrance, Cal., 1953-54; resident Manhattan VA Hosp., N.Y.C., 1955-56, U. Tex. Med. Br., Galveston, 1957-58; dir. employees health services James Ewing Hosp., N.Y.C., 1956-57; practice medicine specializing in allergy, Ft. Worth, 1967—. Vice pres. Tex. Allergy Labs., Inc., Ft. Worth, 1967—, Med. Computers, Inc. Ft. Worth, 1969—. Home: 2026 Ward Pkwy Fort Worth TX 76110 Office: 712 7th Av Fort Worth TX 76104

TROWBRIDGE, CYRUS PFEIFFER, judge; b. Ottawa, Ill., Aug. 24, 1928; s. Cyrus Pomeroy and Doris (Merner) T.; B.A., Denison U., 1950; J.D., U. Va., 1953; m. Patricia Winford, Apr. 7, 1974; children by previous marriage—Teri Anne, Leslie Ellen. Admitted to Va. bar, 1952, Fla. bar, 1956; practiced in Stuart, Fla., 1956-60; circuit judge 19th Circuit of Fla., Stuart, 1960—. Exec. officer group 15 Civil Air Patrol. Served to 1st lt. Judge Advocate Gen. Corps. AUS, 1953-56. Mem. Martin County Bar Assn. (pres. 1960), Martin County C. of C. (dir.), USCG Aux., Scribes. Conglist. Mason. Clubs: Rotary, Stuart Sailfish (trustee). Contbr. to legal and flying publs. Home: 920 E 6th St PO Box 445 Stuart FL 33494 Office: Martin County Court House Stuart FL 33494

TROWER, MICHAEL HENRY, architecture and engring. co. exec.; b. Palo Pinto, Tex., Oct. 12, 1937; s. Wilford R. and Mary Catherine (Pierce) T.; B.Arch., Okla. State U., 1961, B.Archtl. Engring., 1961; certificate program for mgmt. devel. Harvard, 1970; m. Betty Anne Davis, Aug. 17, 1957; children—Jeff, Jana, Jennifer, Joan. Job capt. Caudill Rowlett Scott, Houston, 1961-63, project mgr., 1963-66, dept. mgr., 1966-67, project officer mgr., 1967-70, operations mgr., 1970-71, gen. mgr., 1972—, exec. v.p., 1971—, also dir. Mem. A.I.A. Club: Harvard (Houston). Home: 2172 Swift St Houston TX 77025 Office: 1111 W Loop S Houston TX 77025

TROXELL, GEORGE HENRY, oil drilling and exploration co. exec.; b. Swarthmore, Pa., Aug. 21, 1921; s. George Henry and Charlotte Louise (Robertshaw) T.; B.S., U.S. Mil. Acad., 1945; M.S., U. Ill., 1950; m. Nancy Armitage, June 6, 1945; children—George Henry III, Jeffrey Richard, Robert Todd. Vice-pres., gen. mgr. An-Son Drilling Co., Oklahoma City, 1954-58; pres. Hershey Drilling Co., New Orleans, 1959-64; sr. v.p. design and engring. Ocean Drilling & Exploration Co., 1965—. Served to capt. AUS, 1945-54. Home: 3735 Pin Oak St New Orleans LA 70114 Office: 1600 Canal St New Orleans LA 70160

TRUCKS, HOWARD FRANKLIN, aerospace engr.; b. Wilsonville, Ala., Mar. 7, 1938; s. Herbert Howard and Janie Gertrude (Ingram) T.; B.S., U. Ala., 1962, postgrad., 1963-67; m. Judy Alise Boze, July 25, 1974; children from previous marriage—Denise Michelle, Tina Marie. Aerospace engr., spacecraft thermal design NASA, Huntsville, Ala., 1962—. Recipient certificate participation 1st Saturn V launch, 1967, award of achievement for Apollo Lunar landing NASA, 1969. Mem. Ala. Profl. Engring. Soc., Pi Tau Sigma, Tau Beta Pi. Baptist. Contbr. articles to profl. publs. Home: Route 6 Fayetteville TN 37334 Office: MSFC EP44 Huntsville AL 35800

TRUE, CLARENCE HARVEY, civil engr.; b. Boston, Jan. 20, 1893; s. Judson B. and Deborah (Cliff) T.; student Franklin Union, 1910-14, Tufts Coll., 1915; m. Laura E. Robertson, Aug. 13, 1917; children—Mildred, Robert, William, Stanley, Bruce. With Panama Canal Co., 1915-17, Am. Ship Bldg. Corp., 1918-21, Am. Bridge Co., 1922-25; civil engr. Panama Canal Co., U.S. Govt., Balboa, C.Z., 1930-55; structural engr. Ingalls Iron Works, Birmingham, Ala., 1956-58; Rader engr., Miami, Fla., 1959-62; with Weed Johnson, Architect, Miami, 1962-66; with pub. works dept. Coral Gables, Fla., 1965—. Instr. nav. C.Z. Jr. Coll. Extension Div., 1944-46, instr. engring., 1947. Fellow Am. Soc. C.E. Author: Navigation and Astronomic Data, 1948. Home: 1417 Ortega Av Coral Gables FL 33134 Office: Pub Works City Hall Coral Gables FL 33134

TRUE, JAMES ENOS, ret. museum curator; b. Salem, Va., Nov. 25, 1903; s. James J. and Emma (Goodwin) T.; student Roanoke Coll., 1922; Art Students League (N.Y.C.), 1925-26; studied under DuMond, Bridgman, Neilson and Romanovski; m. Beulah Rivers Nalls, Apr. 14, 1927; children—James Enos, Robert Milton, Daniel Marshall, Frances Anne (Mrs. Jack Richard Thomas, Jr.). Exhibited one-man shows Roanoke Fine Arts Center, 1967, Tolliver House, Big Stone Gap., Va., 1974, others; exhibited group shows, Art Club of Middlesboro, Ky., 1965, Highlands Arts Festival, Abingdon, Va., 1966, 70, Bristol Border Guild Exhibit, 1973, Ky.-Va. Fair, 1973; dir. Fed. Art Gallery, Big Stone Gap, 1938-41; designer Dioramas, executed portraits Campbell Bascom Slemp Hist. Collection, 1939-74; curator Southwest Va. Museum, Big Stone Gap, 1946-74; ret., 1974; pvt. art classes. Mem. Roanoke Fine Arts Center, Bristol Art Guild, Southwest Va. Hist. Soc. Democrat. Methodist. Home: 440 Love St Erwin TN 37650

TRUE, ROY JOE, lawyer; b. Shreveport, La., Feb. 20, 1938; s. Collins B. and Lula Mae (Cady) T.; student Centenary Coll., 1957; B.S., (scholar), Tex. Christian U., 1961; LL.B. (scholar), So. Meth. U., 1963, postgrad., 1968-69; m. Patsy Jean Hudsmith, Aug. 29, 1959; children—Andrea Alane, Alyssa Anne, Ashley Alisbeth. Admitted to Tex. bar, 1963; practiced in Dallas, 1963—; pres. Invesco Internat. Corp., 1969-70. Bus. adviser, counselor Mickey Mantle, 1969—. Served with AUS, 1956. Mem. Am., Dallas bar assns., Phi Alpha Delta. Editorial bd. Southwestern Law Jour., 1962-63. Home: 7027 Desco Dr Dallas TX 75225 Office: LTV Tower Dallas TX 75201

TRUITT, MARCUS M., educator; b. Enid, Okla., Oct. 10, 1921; s. Marcus W. and Bertha (McCafferty) T.; B.S., Okla. State U., 1946; M.S., Harvard, 1947, C.E., Stanford, 1951; Ph.D., Johns Hopkins, 1968; m. Mary Lois Ferguson, Nov. 21, 1942; children—Elizabeth, Marcus. Civil engr. United Fruit Co., Central Am., 1947-49; asst. prof. civil engring., U. Ala., Tuscaloosa, 1949-50; asst. prof. civil engring. Tex. A. and I. U., Kingsville, 1951-54, asso. prof., 1954-59, prof., 1959—, chmn. dept. civil engring., 1965—. Cons. civil engr., South Tex., 1952-65. Chmn. bldg. code council, Kingsville, 1953-60; city and county civil def. engr., 1955-65. Served with USAAF, 1942-45. NST grantee, 1965-66. Mem. Am. Soc. C.E. Home: 504 Ailsie Av Kingsville TX 78363 Office: Box 2223 Tex A and I Univ Kingsville TX 78363

TRULUCK, JAMES PAUL, JR., dentist; b. Florence, S.C., Feb. 6, 1933; s. James P. and Catherine (Nesmith) T.; D.D.M., U. La., 1958; m. Kay Bowen, July 26, 1958; children—James P. III, David Bowen, Catherine Ann. Pvt. practice dentistry, Lake City, S.C., 1960—; dir. Palmette Bank & Trust Co.; owner Lake Country Vineyards and Winery; mem. staffs Lower Florence County Hosps. Chmn., Greater Lake City Recreation Commn., 1965—. Del., Republican Conv., 1968. Trustee Florence Mus. Served with USAF, 1958-60. Mem. Am., Pee Dee dental assns., Am. Soc. Dentistry for Children, Am. Soc. Clin. Hypnosis, Delta Sigma Delta, Blue Key. Lion. Home: 114 E Main St Lake City SC 29560 Office: 125 Epps St Lake City SC 29560

TRULUCK, REMBERT SCARBOROUGH, printing exec.; b. Sumter, S.C., Sept. 5, 1910; s. W.Z. and Susan (Boyce) T.; student Internat. Corr. Schs.; m. Mary Frances Scruggs, Sept. 3, 1932; children—Rembert, Georgia J. (Mrs. James M. Cook). Supt., Williams Printing Co., Spartanburg, S.C., 1928-34; supr. pressroom John H. Harland Co., Atlanta, 1934-35; supt. Keys Printing Co., Greenville, S.C., 1944-45, Jacobs Press, Clinton, S.C., 1941-47; owner, operator Truluck Printing Co., Clinton, 1947—. Pres., Greater Clinton Community Chest, 1961—; finance chmn. Laurens Assn. Bapt. Assembly, 1955, v.p. brotherhood, 1956-57; organizer Cub Scout pack Boy Scouts Am., Clinton, 1942, cubmaster, 1942-43. Named Citizen of Year, City of Clinton, 1958. Mem. Am., Carolinas printing industries, Clinton C. of C. (pres. 1948-49). Baptist (chmn. bd. trustees). Lion (pres. Clinton 1959-60, dist. gov. 1958-59; mem. bd. internat. counsellors 1959—). Author: Papa and Me, 1965. Home: 104 Woodrow Dr Clinton SC 29325

TRUMBO, CHARLES BASS, lawyer; b. Fayetteville, Ark., Feb. 23, 1935; s. Donald and Juanita (Bass) T.; B.S. in Bus. Adminstrn., U. Ark., 1957, LL.B., 1959; m. Carolyn Kay Wells, Aug. 20, 1955; children—Jay Hamilton, Carolyn Bass. Admitted to Ark. bar, 1959, since practiced in Fayetteville; city atty., Fayetteville, 1961-65; dep. pros. atty. Washington County, 1963-66. Lectr. bus. law U. Ark. Sch. Bus. Adminstrn., 1959—. Pres. Boy Land of Ark., 1969-71. Mem. Washington County Democratic Central Com. 1968—. Chmn. bd. dirs. Fayetteville Creative Sch., 1970-71; bd. dirs. Washington County Sch. for Retarded Children. Served as 2d lt. AUS, 1957. Recipient Distinguished Service award Fayetteville Jr. C. of C., 1969; names One of 10 Outstanding Young Men in Ark., 1969. Mem. Ark., Washington County (pres. 1965-66) bar assns., Fayetteville C. of C. Episcopalian. Home: 925 Kings Dr Fayetteville AR 72701 Office: Suite 202 First Nat Bank Bldg Fayetteville AR 72701

TRUNDLE, BENTON MCMAHAN, JR., farmer; b. Boyd's Creek, Tenn., Dec. 24, 1934; s. Benton McMahan and Kathleen Elizabeth (Hammer) T.; B.S., U. Tenn., 1957, postgrad., 1971; postgrad. Va. Poly. Inst., 1964; m. Margaret Andrew Ogle, July 16, 1961. Asst. county agt. Va. Agrl. Extension Service, Blacksburg, 1959-64; farmer, Sevierville, Tenn., 1965—; indsl. arts tchr. Sevier County Bd. Edn., Sevier County High Sch., 1971—. Dir. Sevier Farmers Coop. Bd., 1968—. Mem. Sevier County Livestock Assn. (dir. 1968—), Sevier County Farm Bur. (dir. 1968-70), Alpha Gamma Rho, Alpha Zeta, Kappa Kappa Psi. Presbyn. (deacon 1965—). Lion. Club: Boyd's Creek Community. Address: Route 10 Sevierville TN 37862

TRUNDLE, WINFIELD SCOTT, newspaper exec.; b. Maryville, Tenn., Mar. 24, 1939; s. Winfield Scott and Alice (Smith) T.; B.A., Vanderbilt U., 1961, J.D., 1967; m. Diana Shanklin, Feb. 21, 1962; children—Stephen, Allison. Admitted to Tenn. bar, 1967; spl. agt. White House detail U.S. Secret Service, Washington, 1963-66; partner law firm Hunter, Smith, Davis, Norris, Waddey & Treadway, Kingsport, Tenn., 1967-72; v.p., pub., gen. counsel Kingsport Times-News, 1972—. Asso. prof. communications law East Tenn. State U., Exec. com. Appalachian Regional Commn. Healing Arts. Bd. dirs. Palmer Meml. Center, Kingsport Community Chest, Kingsport Boys' Club; Netherland Inn Assn., Jr. Achievement Kingsport. Mem. Am., So. newspaper publs. assns., Tenn., Am. press assns., Bur. Nat. Affairs, Personnel Policy Forum, Am., Tenn. bar assns. Methodist. Lodges: Elks, Moose. Clubs: Kingsport Rotary, Ridgefields Country (Kingsport). Home: Route 9 Hidden Valley Rd Kingsport TN 37663 Office: 701 Lynn Garden Dr Kingsport TN 37662

TRUSCOTT, BASIL LIONEL, physician; b. Chambers, Neb., Aug. 4, 1916; s. Basil Reginald and Annie (Fryer) T.; B.A., Drew U., 1939; M.S., Syracuse U., 1940; M.S., Yale, 1942, Ph.D., 1943, M.D., 1950; m. Elizabeth Jane Worrill, June 19, 1948; children—Elizabeth, Thomas. Instr. anatomy Georgetown Med. Sch., 1943-45, Yale Sch. Medicine, 1947-48; intern Duke Hosp., Durham, N.C., 1950-51; asst. prof. anatomy U. N.C. Sch. Medicine, 1951-54; resident Walter Reed Army Hosp., Washington, 1955-57; practice medicine specializing in neurology, 1959—; asso. prof. neurology Albany Med. Center, 1960-63, prof. neurology, 1963-68; prof. neurology Bowman Gray Sch. Medicine, 1968—, asst. dean for student admissions, 1973—; mem. staff N.C. Bapt. Hosp., Winston-Salem; neurologist VA Hosp., Salisbury, N.C., 1968—. Cons. U.S. Army in Europe, 1958-60. Served with AUS, 1954-60. Fellow Am. Acad. Neurology, A.C.P., Nat. Stroke Council. Methodist. Club: Forsyth Country (Winston-Salem). Contbr. numerous articles to sci., med. jours. Home: 460 Briarlea Rd Winston-Salem NC 27104 Office: Bowman Gray Sch Medicine Winston-Salem NC 27103

TRYON, GARY EUGENE, transp. co. exec., elec. engr.; b. Tallulah, La., Sept. 2, 1943; s. Harold Lyle and Irwina Frances (Loebig) T.; B.S. in Elec. Engring., La. Poly. Inst., 1967; m. Barbara Jean McIntosh, Jan. 28, 1967; children—Brian Anthony, Harold Ivery, Tanya Annette. Elec. engr. Tex. Eastern Transp. Corp., Shreveport, La., 1967-72, tech. safety supr., 1973—. Registered profl. engr., La. Mem. I.E.E.E., Am. Soc. Safety Engrs., U.S. C. of C. K.C. Home: 8871 Hedges Dr Shreveport LA 71108 Office: PO Box 1612 Shreveport LA 71130

TRYON, LAWRENCE EDWIN, lawyer; b. Channahon, Ill., Nov. 25, 1899; s. Allison and Mary (Alexander) T.; student Salt City Bus. Coll., Hutchinson, Kan., 1919, LaSalle Extension U., 1920-28, Northwestern U., 1931; m. Mary A. Bradshaw, Apr. 12, 1925; children—Myrna Jewell (Mrs. Monte L. Thomas), Allison Charles, Mary Kathryn (Mrs. Delbert Carter); m. 2d, Eugenia Shaw, June 11, 1963. Admitted to Okla. bar, 1929; county judge Texas County, Okla., 1931-36, county atty., 1937-38; practice law, Guymon, Okla., 1938—; dir. City Nat. Bank & Trust Co., Guymon. Pres. Guymon Meml. Hosp., 1949-72. Republican candidate Supreme Ct. Okla., 1960; del. Rep. Nat. Conv., 1960, mem. Com. Order of Bus. Served with U.S. Army, World War I. Mem. Am., Okla. bar assns. Methodist (pres. trustees, del. gen. conf. 1936). Mason (32 deg., K.T., Shriner), Lion (dist. gov. 1947-48). Home: 6044 Sunset Dr Guymon OK 73942 Office: Profl Bldg Guymon OK 73942

TSCHOEPE, ELBERT HENRY, civil engr.; b. San Antonio, July 5, 1932; s. Alphonse Joseph and Clara (Fey) T.; B.S., Tex. A. and I. U., 1960; m. Rita Joan Phillips, Aug. 29, 1955; 1 son, Kirby Joseph. Engr., Tex. Hwy. Dept., Corpus Christi, 1961-66; civil engr. U.S. Air Force, Shreveport, La., 1966-69; project engr. Dallas County, Dallas, 1969—. Served with USAF, 1950-54. Registered profl. engr., Tex., Tenn. Mem. Am. Soc. C.E., Nat., Tex. socs. profl. engrs., Am., Tex. pub. works assns. Home: 908 Vinecrest Lane Richardson TX 75080 Office: 613 Records Bldg Dallas TX 75202

TSCHOEPE, EUGENE JULIUS, accountant; b. Eagle Pass, Tex., Sept. 3, 1930; s. Eugene Benjamin and Eleanor Meta (Vordenbaum) T.; student Tex. Lutheran Coll., 1947-49; B.B.A. with honors, U. Tex. at Austin, 1950; m. Joyce Laverne Mueller, Sept. 22, 1951; children—Michael David, Eugene Gregory, Cynthia Gaye. Accountant, George, Thrift & Cockrell, C.P.A.'s, San Antonio, 1950-64; accountant Ernst & Ernst, San Antonio, 1964-65, Austin, 1965—. Vice pres. USO Council of Austin, 1971; v.p. Austin Symphony Orch. Soc., 1970; treas. Goodwill Industries of Austin, 1973. Mem. Am. Inst. C.P.A.'s, Tex. Soc. C.P.A.'s (chpt. pres. 1963-64). Roman Catholic. Home: 7712 Shadyrock St Austin TX 78731 Office: 900 City National Bank Bldg Austin TX 78701

TSCHOEPE, THOMAS, bishop; b. Pilot Point, Tex., Dec. 17, 1915; s. Louis and Catherine (Sloan) T.; student St. Thomas Sch. Pilot Point, 1930, Pontifical Coll. Josephinum, Worthington, O., 1943. Ordained priest Roman Catholic Ch., 1943; asst. pastor in Ft. Worth, 1943-46, Sherman, Tex., 1946-48, Dallas, 1948-53; adminstr. St. Patrick Ch., Dallas, 1953-56; pastor St. Augustine Ch., Dallas, 1956-62, Sacred Heart Cathedral, Dallas, 1962-65; bishop of San Angelo, Tex., 1966-69, Dallas, 1969—. Home: 3915 Lemmon Av Box 19507 Dallas TX 75219

TUBB, LESLIE, dentist; b. Aberdeen, Miss., Dec. 10, 1921; s. Napoleon and Agnes (Davidson) T.; B.S., U. Miss., 1948; D.D.S., Baylor U., 1951; m. Louise Maxcy, Oct. 26, 1943. Practice dentistry, Oxford, Miss., 1953—. Mem. adv. bd. 1st Nat. Bank, Oxford. Served with USAF, 1942-53; Korea, ETO. Mem. Am., Miss., N.E. Miss. dental assns., Omicron Kappa Upsilon, Delta Sigma Delta. Republican. Baptist (deacon 1958-60). Mason. Home: Campground Rd Oxford MS 38655 Office: 713 S Lamar Blvd Oxford MS 38655

TUBBS, HARRY AUGUSTUS, physician; b. Richmond, Va., Sept. 3, 1914; s. William Johnston and Ruth Churchill (Rennie) T.; student U. Tenn., 1930-33, 34-35; M.D., Med. Coll. Va., 1939; m. Joan Ellis, June 11, 1939 (dec. Sept. 1970); children—Charles Gordon, Elisabeth (Mrs. Frank Schmalstieg). Intern, Scott and White Hosp., Temple, Tex., 1939-40; practice medicine specializing in family practice, Fredericksburg, Tex., 1946-52, Post, Tex., 1952—; mem. staff Garza Meml. Hosp., Post; courtesy staff W. Tex. Hosp., Lubbock; med. dir., lab. dir. Med. Center & Lab., Post, 1956—. Pres., Med. Center Found., 1964—; city health officer Post, 1965—; med. cons. Post Ind.

Schs., 1970—. Served with AUS, 1940-46; PTO. Mem. Tex. Acad. Family Physicians (v.p. 1967, chmn. med. sch. liaison com. 1972-73), A.M.A., So., Tex. med. assns., Lubbock-Crosby-Garza Med. Soc., Am. Acad. Gen. Practice (award 1969), Am., Tex. diabetes assns. Contbr. articles to profl. jours. Home: 415 N Av M Post TX 79356 Office: 111 N Av I Post TX 79356

TUBBS, KENNETH PERRY, assn. exec.; b. Toronto, Kan., June 8, 1913; s. Claude Ernest and Martha Lavonia (Johnston) T.; student Wichita Bus. Coll., 1933; m. Mary Elizabeth Edwards, Sept. 20, 1936 (dec.); children—Michael, Martin, Dennis, Sheryl (Mrs. Robert Oliver), Terrence. Clk., Dolese Bros., 1935-36, Wichita, CRI & P R.R., Wichita, 1936-42; asst. traffic mgr. Boeing Airplane, Wichita, 1942-45; asst. traffic mgr. Wichita C. of C., 1945-47; asst. commr. Fort Smith (Ark.) Traffic Bur., 1947-52; mgr. traffic dept. Amarillo (Tex.) C. of C., 1952-56; mgr. transp. dept. Dallas C. of C., 1956—. Instr. transp. Fort Smith Jr. Coll., 1948-51, Amarillo Jr. Coll., 1953-55; chmn. adv. com., Tex. Transp. Inst., Tex. A. and M. U., 1972—. Mem. Assn. ICC Practitioners, Am. Soc. Traffic and Transp. (founding), Transp. Club Dallas (v.p. 1973), Traffic Clubs Internat., Nat. Indsl. Traffic League (pres. 1969-70), S.W. Indsl. Traffic League (sec. 1957—). Rotarian. Home: 10633 Lakemere St Dallas TX 75238 Office: 1507 Pacific St Dallas TX 75201

TUCK, GRAYSON EDWIN, natural gas transmission exec.; b. Richmond, Va., May 11, 1927; s. Bernard Okly and Erma (Wiltshire) T.; B.S., U. Richmond (Va.), 1950; m. Rosalie Scroggs, June 6, 1947; children—Janice Lorrain, Kenneth Edwin, Carol Lynn. Payroll clk., cost clk. Gen. Baking Co., Richmond, 1948-51; jr. accountant Commonwealth Natural Gas Corp., Richmond, 1951-55, sr. accountant, 1956-57, accounting supr., 1957-58, asst. treas., 1959-62, asst. sec., asst. treas., 1963-64, treas., asst. sec., 1965—; sec.-treas. Air Pollution Control Products Inc., Richmond, 1970-73; asst. treas., asst. sec. Commonwealth Gas Distbn. Corp., Richmond, 1969—. Troop sec. Boy Scouts of Am., 1965-69. Served with USNR, 1945-46. Mem. Nat. Assn. Accountants (past asso. dir.), Systems and Procedures Assn. Am. (past treas.). Presbyn. (deacon). Home: 2923 Oakland Av Richmond VA 23228 Office: 200 S 3d St Richmond VA 23219

TUCKER, ALLAN, univ. adminstr.; b. Calgary, Alta., Can., Sept. 29, 1921; s. Frank and Nellie (Chester) T.; B.A., U. Toronto (Ont., Can.), 1943, M.A., 1946; Ph.D., U. Mich., 1952; post-doctoral U. London (Eng.), summer 1955; D.Sc. (hon.), Fla. Inst. Tech., 1971; m. Rebecca Cope Kimber; children—Edwin K., David G. Came to U.S., 1946, naturalized, 1952. Mem. faculty dept. biology Mich. State U., East Lansing, 1946-64, prof., 1962-64, asst. dean advanced grad. studies, asst. to v.p. research, 1959-64; vice chancellor for acad. affairs State U. System Fla., Tallahassee, 1964—, also chmn. council acad. vice presidents, 1964—. Chmn. edn. com. Fla.-Colombia Alliance, 1969—, sec.-treas., 1974—; mem. commn. accreditation service experiences Am. Council Edn., 1969-74, mem. commn. ednl. credit, 1974—; mem. steering com. Navy Campus for Achievement, 1972-74; sci. adviser to U. Ryukyus, Okinawa, 1953-55, cons. to univ. pres., 1957-59. Mem. exec. com. Gov.'s Commn. for Quality Edn. Fla., 1967; mem. panel to select NATO postdoctoral sci. fellows Nat. Acad. Scis., 1969-71; mem. grad. edn. cost com. Council Grad. Schs. U.S., 1969-71, cons. to council, 1969—. Recipient Leadership certificate Adult Edn. Assn. U.S.A., 1971. Mem. Am. Assn. Higher Edn., Nat. Univ. Extension Assn. (mem. nat. com. on govt. relations 1971—), Adult Edn. Assn. U.S.A. (mem. nat. com. on external degrees 1971), Sigma Xi. Author: Pigment Extraction as a Method of Quantitative Analysis of Phytoplankton, 1949; The Relation of Phytoplankton Periodicity to the Nature of the Physico-Chemical Environment, 1957; Attrition of Graduate Students at the Ph.D. Level, 1964; Decentralized Graduate Administration with Centralized Accountability, 1965; also articles. Home: 2301 Delgado Dr Tallahassee FL 32304

TUCKER, BOYCE LYNN, architect; b. Houston, Jan. 12, 1939; s. G. Boyce and Steryl (George) T.; B.Arch., U. Houston, 1963; m. Penelope Flos Meier, June 9, 1961; children—Katherine Ann, Tammy Lynn. Partner firm Musemeche Tucker Davis, Architects, Houston, 1970; prin. Lynn Tucker A.I.A. & Assos., Houston, 1971—. Trustee Jessie A. Tucker Family Trust; bd. dirs. Christ's Mission, Inc. Mem. A.I.A., Nat. Trust for Historic Preservation. Home: 11526 Echo Wood Houston TX 77024 Office: 4615 Post Oak Pl Houston TX 77027

TUCKER, CHARLES CLEMENT, artist; b. Greenville, S.C., Sept. 13, 1913; s. Charles Earl and Myrtle (Clement) T.; student N.Y. Art Student League, 1933-38; m. Virginia Eugenia Smith, Feb. 24, 1954. One man shows at Miami Beach Art Center, Asheville (N.C.) Mus., Hickory (N.C.) Mus., Statesville (N.C.) Mus., Civic Art Gallery, Greenville, S.C., Little Art Gallery, Asheville; exhibited in group shows at Met. Mus. (N.Y.C.), many others throughout U.S.; represented in permanent collections at Capitol Bldg. (Washington), St. Vincent Coll., Wingate Coll., Hickory Mus., Crossnore Coll., U. N.C., Mint Mus. of Art, Charlotte, N.C., Mass. Inst. Tech., numerous others. Served with AUS, 1942-45. Recipient 1st award, N.C. Nat. Exhibit, 1958, 59; Directors award, Council Am. Artist Socs. Nat. Exhbn., N.Y., 1966, Charlotte-Mecklenburg Artist of Year award, 1968, Popular Prize, I.P.A., 1970. Mem. Allied Artists Am., Art Student League N.Y. (life), Am. Artist Profl. League, Western N.C. Conservative Artists, Guild Charlotte Artists (past v.p.), Atelier Conservative Artists (past pres.), Nat. Arts Club (N.Y.C.), Atelier Club (N.Y.C.), Internat. Platform Assn., Hudson Valley Art Assn. Home: 3621 Arborway Dr Charlotte NC 28211

TUCKER, DAISY SNELLGROVE (MRS. WILLIAM C. TUCKER), librarian; b. Pinckard, Ala., Dec. 11, 1912; d. LaFayette and Jessie (Bryant) Snellgrove; grad. Columbus (Ga.) City Hosp. Sch. Nursing, 1934; student U. Ga., 1952; m. William Clifford Tucker, Jan. 12, 1935 (dec. Apr. 1961); children—William Clifford, Frances (Mrs. Eugene Dobson, Jr.). Librarian Ledger-Enquirer Newspapers, Columbus, Ga., 1952—; book review editor Columbus Enquirer, 1954—; head research dept. Ledger-Enquirer, 1952—. Mem. Gov.'s Adv. Com. Mental Instns., 1959-62; bd. dirs. Muscogee Mental Health Assn., 1957—, Ga. Assn. Mental Health (sec.). Recipient Cup of Hope award Ga. Assn. Mental Health, 1958. Mem. C. of C. Baptist. Club: Country (Columbus). Home: 1915 Wildwood Av Columbus GA 31906 Office: Ledger-Enquirer Newspapers Columbus GA 31902

TUCKER, DANIEL LEE, radio announcer; b. Orange, Cal., Feb. 6, 1947; s. Fred Ellis and Lois Ruth (Herrin) T.; self-educated; m. Freddie Merle Coward, Dec. 21, 1970. Staff announcer, religious broadcaster KHCB-FM radio, Houston, 1962—; ind. ins. agent, 1971—. Bd. dirs. Youth for Christ, 1967-73. Home: 1522 Alderbrook Sugarland TX 77478 Office: 126 Almeda Genoa Rd Houston TX 77045

TUCKER, JACK NORRIS, state senator, lawyer; b. Charleston, Miss., May 15, 1921; s. Harry Randolph and Lucy (Rolph) T.; grad. Holmes Jr. Coll., 1942; B.A., U. Miss., 1948, LL.B., 1950, J.D., 1968; m. Pattye Sue Williams, Sept. 12, 1948. Admitted to Miss. bar, 1950; pvt. practice law Tunica, 1950—; mem. Miss. Senate, 1960—. Commr. election Tunica County, Miss., 1952-56, chmn. bd., 1952-56; dir. Miss. Heart Assn., 1952-56, 60-64; chmn. Tunica Heart Fund, 1952—; lay-del. Miss. to Am. Heart Assn., 1960-61; chmn. Tunica County Heart Council, 1961—; Boy Scout commr. Tunica County. Served from ensign to lt. (j.g.), USNR, 1942-46; USNR (ret.). Mem. Am., Tunica, Coahoma County bar assns., Miss. State Bar Am. Legion, V.F.W., Delta Kappa Epsilon, Phi Delta Phi. Democrat. Methodist. Rotarian. Home: PO Box 826 Tunica MS 38676

TUCKER, JAMES RICHARD, electronics co. exec.; b. McKinney, Tex., Jan. 7, 1941; s. Dean Bailey and Alliene (Scott) T.; B.S., Stanford, 1963; m. Ann Shelton, Nov. 24, 1972. Tech. asst. Stanford, 1959-63, research asst., 1963; electronics engr. Continental Electronics div. Ling-Temco-Vought, Inc., Dallas, 1963-66; pres. Tucker Electronics Co., Garland, Tex., 1967—; dir. Inmark, Inc., Kensington, Md. Mem. I.E.E.E., Instrument Soc. Am., Am. Radio Relay League, Aerobics Activity Center, Garland C. of C. Kiwanian (dir. 1969-72, editor newsletter 1969-73). Club: Canyon Creek Country (Richardson, Tex.). Home: 2440 Fairway Circle Richardson TX 75080 Office: 1717 S Jupiter Rd Garland TX 75045

TUCKER, KENNETH WAYNE, contracting co. exec.; b. nr. Pell City, Ala., July 2, 1927; s. Thomas Keaton and Sarah (Campbell) T.; grad. high sch.; m. Anna Lou Meehan, Nov. 1948 (dec. Dec. 1960); 1 dau., Teresa Jean; m. 2d, Betty Ann Colvin, Nov. 22, 1964; children—Toni Celeste, Terri Ann, Tracy Leigh. Supr. Southeastern Contracting Co., Birmingham, Ala., 1950-57; partner T. & H. Constrn. Co., Huntsville, Ala., 1957-59, Tucker Bros. Contracting Co., Birmingham, 1959-70, Pell City, 1970—; pres. Tucker Equipment Co., Birmingham, 1965-70, Pell City, 1970—; v.p. Tucker Enterprises, Birmingham, 1967-70, Pell City, 1970—. Served with USMCR, 1945-48. Mem. Am. Gas Assn., Am. Water Assn., Pell City C. of C. (pres. 1968, dir. 1969). Methodist. Mason (Shriner), Lion, Rotarian. Clubs: Pell City Country (v.p. 1961-75); The Club (Birmingham). Home: Golf Course Rd Pell City AL 35125 Office: PO Box 648 Pell City AL 35125

TUCKER, LAWRENCE JOE, savs. and loan exec.; b. Port Arthur, Tex., Jan. 19, 1923; s. Eliot Payson and Gladys Duke (Avera) T.; student The Citadel, 1941-43; B.B.A., U. Tex., 1948; grad. Southwestern Grad. Sch. Banking, So. Meth. U., 1966; m. Billy Faye Johnstone, Sept. 6, 1948; children—William J., Stuart A., Elizabeth L. Partner, Reid & Tucker Ins. Agy., Corpus Christi, Tex., 1953-57; v.p., regional mgr. First Continental Mortgage Co., Houston, 1957-64; v.p. bus. devel. Corpus Christi Bank & Trust Co., 1964-68; pres., dir. Corpus Christi Savs. & Loan Assn., 1968—. Campaign com. United Fund, Corpus Christi, 1964-65; vice-chmn. Bay Drilling Com., 1973. Bd. dirs. Corpus Christi Area Tourist Bur. Served to 1st lt. USAAF, 1943-45, 50-52. Decorated D.F.C., D.S.C., Air medal with 4 oak leaf clusters. Mem. Sales and Marketing Execs. Assn. (pres. 1968-69), Corpus Christi C. of C. (dir.), Phi Gamma Delta. Episcopalian. Club: Corpus Christi Country. Home: 1 Lakeshore Dr Corpus Christi TX 78413 Office: PO Box 6468 Corpus Christi TX 78411

TUCKER, MARCUS RAY, architect; b. Wichita Falls, Tex., Mar. 26, 1940; s. Farrell Euden and Myrtle Alice (Tabor) T.; B.Arch., Tex. Technol. U., 1964; m. Trena Dee Tucker, May 29, 1960; children—Chance Laden, Kristan Kali. With Richard Colley, Architect, Corpus Christi, 1964-66; asso. Brock & Mabrey Architects, 1966-69; v.p. Neuhaus & Taylor, Architects, Houston, 1969—; dir. interiors Joint Venture III Architects, 1970-73. Mem. Corpus Christi Municipal Arts Commn., 1968-69. Mem. A.I.A. (chmn. Houston chpt. interior architecture awards 1973), Tex. Soc. Architects (co-chmn. design awards 1968). Prin. archtl. work includes interior design Hyatt Regency Hotel, Houston, 1973. Home: 1918 Canterbury St Houston TX 77025 Office: 5051 Westheimer St Houston TX 77027

TUCKER, OLIVER TRUMAN, architect; b. Wichita Falls, Tex., Feb. 3, 1925; s. Sam Houston and Callie Mae (Webb) T.; B.S., U. Tex., 1953; m. Jewell A. Rogers, Aug. 21, 1948; children—John E., James Drew, Mark Oliver. Owner, mgr. Oliver T. Tucker architect and engr., Irving, Tex., 1957—. Mem. Citizens Traffic Commn., 1964—. Served with engrs. USAAF, 1943-45. Registered profl. engr., Tex. Mem. C. of C., Tex., Dallas socs. architects, A.I.A., Soc. Profl. Engrs. Architect jr. high schs. Travis, 1965, Lamar, 1970 (both Irving). Home: 1604 Canyon Oaks Irving TX 75061 Office: 3100 W Airport Freeway Irving TX 75061

TUCKER, WEIR MITCHELL, neurologist, psychiatrist; b. Richmond, Va., Dec. 14, 1914; s. Beverly R. and Elsie (Boyd) T.; M.D., U. Va., 1942; m. Linden Crawford, Oct. 2, 1943; children—Linden Crawford, Pamela Cresson. Resident neurology and psychiatry N.Y. Psychiat. Inst. and Hosp., N.Y.C., 1943-44, Jefferson Hosp., Phila., 1946-49; Inst. Pa. Hosp., Phila., 1949; pres. Tucker Hosp.; prof. clin. neurology Med. Coll. Va., 1963—. Local med. dir. Multiple Sclerosis Assn., 1965—, Muscular Dystrophy Assn., 1950. Bd. dirs. Richmond Area Mental Health Assn., 1965—, pres., 1950—. Served as maj. M.C., AUS, 1943-46. Diplomate Am. Bd. Psychiatry and Neurology. Fellow Am. Acad. Neurology; mem. So. (trustee 1965—, pres. 1973), Southeastern (pres. 1963) psychiat. assns., Va. Neurol. Assn., Assn. Research in Nervous and Mental Diseases, Va. Neuropsychiat. Assn. (pres. 1958), Soc. Cincinnati (Va. pres. 1974). Home: 6208 Tapoun Pl Richmond VA 23226 Office: 212 W Franklin St Richmond VA 23220

TUCKER, WILLIAM EARL, oil and gas drilling, producing co. exec.; b. Montgomery, Ala., Sept. 3, 1932; s. Roland Edwin and Eleanor Elmore (Talbot) T.; B.S., U. Ala., 1965, M.S., 1971; m. Cynthia Ann Clouston, Feb. 18, 1956; children—Cynthia Diane, Thomas Scott, Edwin Ross, William Douglas. Field engr. Halliburton Co., Lafayette, La., 1955-59; petroleum engr. Ala. Oil and Gas Bd., 1959-67; chief research Ala. Oil and Gas Bd., Geol. Survey Ala., 1967-71; pres., chief engr. Warrior Drilling & Engring. Co., Inc., Tuscaloosa, Ala., 1971—; sec.-treas. Moundville Chem. Co., Inc. (Ala.), 1967—. Mem. Interstate Oil Compact Commn. Registered profl. engr., Ala. Mem. Ind. Petroleum Assn. Am. (dir.), Mid Continental Oil and Gas Assn., Am. Inst. Mining Engrs. Lion. Home: 10 Griffin Circle Moundville AL 35474 Office: 526 First Fed Bldg Tuscaloosa AL 35401

TUCKER, WOODSON COLEMAN, ednl. adminstr.; b. Halsey, Ky., Sept. 17, 1908; s. Woodson C. and Annie (Spencer) T.; student U. Ky., 1924-25; B.S., U. Fla., 1929, M.S., 1930, Ph.D., 1953; m. Lillian Stewart, Oct. 8, 1932 (dec. July 1968); children—Woodson Coleman III, Judith Diane (Mrs. William D. Arnett); m. 2d, Lovena Edmonds Wheeless, May 25, 1973. Chemist, Superior Earth Co., Ocala, Fla., 1931-36; asst. gen. mgr. United Prodn. Co., Laurel, Miss., 1936-38; chemist Edgar Plastic Kaolin Co. (Fla.), 1940-41; instr. U. Fla., Gainesville, 1946-53, asst. prof., 1953-58; asso. prof. La. State U., New Orleans, 1958-66, prof., 1966-69, prof. chemistry, asst. dean acad. affairs, 1969-73, asst. vice chancellor for acad. affairs, 1973—. Served from 1st lt. to maj. AUS, 1938-39, 41-46; PTO. Mem. Am. Chem. Soc., Sigma Xi, Gamma Sigma Epsilon, Delta Chi. Methodist (chmn. ofcl. bd. 1963-65, treas. 1969—). Author: (with C.R. McLellan) Lab. Manual Gen. Chemistry, 1961, 66; (with L.M. Trefonas) Integrated Laboratory Series, 1967. Home: 7701 Mayo Rd New Orleans LA 70126 Office: Lake Front New Orleans LA 70122

TUGGLE, RICHARD WILFRED, tobacco co. exec.; b. Blackstone, Va., Feb. 23, 1917; s. Douglas Longstreet and Sue Edward (Armstrong) T.; B.A., Coll. William and Mary, 1938; m. Charlotte Scott Booker, July 19, 1941; children—Pattie A., Richard Wilfred, Edward A. With Universal Leaf Tobacco Co., Inc., Richmond, Va., 1946—, asst. traffic mgr., 1947-50, asst. treas., 1950-59, asst. v.p., 1959-67, v.p., 1967—; dir. Inta-Roto, Inc., Richmond. Bd. dirs. South Richmond-Chesterfield County YMCA, Ch. of Good Shepherd Sch. Served to capt. USAAF, 1942-46. Mem. Leaf Tobacco Exporters Assn. (exec. com. 1969-71), Phi Beta Kappa, Omicron Delta Kappa, Kappa Alpha. Episcopalian. Club: Willow Oaks Country (Richmond). Home: 5111 New Kent Rd Richmond VA 23225 Office: PO Box 25099 Richmond VA 23260

TUGMAN, DANA FRED, agrl. research sta. supt.; b. Boone, N.C., Mar. 31, 1927; s. Stuart Grady and Margaret (Davis) T.; B.S., N.C. State U., 1949; m. Mary Gordon Austin, Nov. 26, 1953; children—Dana, Neal. Asst. county farm agt., Ashe County, N.C., 1949, county farm agt., 1950-52; supt. Upper Mountain Research Sta., Laurel Springs, N.C., 1952—; dir. Skyline Tel. Membership Corp.; dir. Eastern Lamb Produces Co-op. Bd. dirs. N.C. Agrl. Found. Served with USNR, 1945-46. Mem. N.C. Soc. Farm Mgrs. and Rural Appraisers (dir.). Methodist (lay leader 1973—, ch. sch. tchr. 1960—, mem. adminstrv. bd. 1955—, chmn. 1964-68). Rotarian (pres. 1963-64). Address: Upper Mountain Research Sta Laurel Springs NC 28644

TULLIS, EDWARD LEWIS, bishop; b. Cin., Mar. 9, 1917; s. Ashar Spence and Priscilla (Daugherty) T.; A.B., Ky. Wesleyan Coll., 1939; B.D., Louisville Presbyn. Theol. Sem., 1947; D.D., Union Coll., Barbourville, Ky., 1954; m. Mary Jane Talley, Sept. 25, 1937; children—Frank Loyd, Jane Allen (Mrs. William Nelson Offutt IV). Ordained to ministry Methodist Ch., 1941; service chs., Frenchburg, Ky., 1937-39, Lawrenceburg, Ky., 1939-44; asso. pastor 4th Av. Meth. Ch., Louisville, 1944-47, Irvine, Ky., 1947-49; asso. sec. ch. extension sect. Bd. Missions, Meth. Ch., Louisville, 1949-52; pastor First Meth. Ch., Frankfort, Ky., 1952-61, First Meth. Ch., Ashland, Ky., 1961-72; resident bishop United Meth. Ch., Columbia, S.C., 1972—; instr. Bible Ky. Wesleyan Coll., 1947-48; instr. Louisville Presbyn. Theol. Sem., 1949-52. Mem. Meth. Gen. Conf., 1956, 60, 64, 66, 68, 70, 72, Southeastern Jurisdictional Conf., 1952, 56, 60, 64, 68, 72; bd. mgrs. Bd. Missions, 1962-72; mem. bd. discipleship, 1972—. Chaplain, Ky. Gen. Assembly, 1952-61; chmn. Frankfort Com. Human Rights, 1956-61; chmn. Mayor's Adv. Com. Human Relations, Ashland, 1968-72. Pres. bd. dirs. Magee Christian Edn. Found.; trustee Emory U., Alaska Meth. U., Ky. Wesleyan Coll. Recipient Outstanding Citizen award Frankfort V.F.W., 1961, Mayor's award for outstanding service, Ashland, 1971. Kiwanian. Contbr. articles to religious jours. Home: 741 Albion Rd Columbia SC 29205 Office: 1420 Lady St Columbia SC 29201

TULLOSS, JAMES GARRETT, elec. engr.; b. Birmingham, Ala., Nov. 23, 1942; s. Clarence Cotham and Mary Nettie (Jones) T.; B.S., U. Ala., 1966, M.S., 1970; M.B.A., Samford U., 1973; m. Elizabeth Ann Burnett, Apr. 15, 1967; 1 dau., Lisa Ann. Engr., Hayes Internat. Corp., aerospace contractor, Birmingham, Ala., 1966-69; elec. engr. systems devel. So. Services, Inc., utility co., 1969—. Instr., Jefferson St. Jr. Coll., part time, 1966-67. Mem. I.E.E.E., So. Services Leadership Devel. Assn. Republican. Methodist (vice-chmn. adminstrv. bd. 1973-74). Home: 2508 Forestdale Bend Rd Birmingham AL 35214 Office: PO Box 2625 Birmingham AL 35202

TULLY, CHRISTOPHER CARL, JR., dentist; b. Charleston, W.Va., May 30, 1939; s. Christopher Carl and Virginia Bell (Tully) T.; B.S. in Chemistry, Morris Harvey Coll., 1962; M.S. in Biochemistry, W.Va. U., 1965, D.D.S., 1969; m. Judith Ann Fox, Aug. 29, 1959; children—Christopher Carl III, Karen Lynn, Deborah Ann. Practice dentistry, Morgantown, W.Va., 1969; North Augusta, S.C., 1969—. Chmn., North Augusta area Nat. Childrens' Dental Health Week, 1972; dental coordinator United Fund, 1970-71; mem. North Augusta Area Hosp. Planning Com., 1971, Alcohol and Drug Referral Com., 1971-73; chmn. North Augusta Am. Cancer Soc., 1970—, Aiken County Dental Disaster Assn.; chmn. judges com. Miss North Augusta-Miss S.C., 1970; coach Optimist Basketball League, 1969—, Football League, 1970—, Baseball League, 1969-72. Mem. Am., S.C. dental assns., Am. Soc. Dentistry for Children, Am. Endodontic Soc., Am. Soc. Preventive Dentistry, Augusta Dental Soc., W.Va. Dental Alumni Assn., Jr. C. of C., Sigma Nu, Delta Sigma Delta. Republican. Methodist. Lion. Club: North Augusta Booster. Home: 1907 Brynes Rd North Augusta SC 29841 Office: 501 A East Martintown Rd North Augusta SC 29841

TULLY, WOFFORD ROSCOE, accountant; b. Houston, Nov. 29, 1919; s. George Pink and Lucille Annie (Wofford) T.; student Baylor U., 1938, 40; B.B.A., U. Houston, 1947; m. Bette Marie Eddy, Apr. 19, 1963; children—Sharon (Mrs. Kenneth Carr), Sandra (Mrs. Robert E. Morrow). Accountant, Stewart, Burgess & Morris, attys., Houston, 1951-58; sr. accountant T.B. Trotter, C.P.A.'s, Houston, 1958-65; controller Memorial City Shopping City, Houston, 1965-67, Joseph Johnson Enterprises, Houston, 1967-69; practice accounting, Houston, 1969—. Served with USAAF, 1941-45. Decorated D.F.C., Air medal with 4 oak leaf clusters. Mem. Tex. Soc. C.P.A.'s, Am. Inst. C.P.A.'s. Mason. Home: Moscow TX 75960 Office: Citizens State Bank Bldg Corrigan TX 75939

TUMA, GERALD, educator; b. Oklahoma City, July 19, 1914; s. Domonick and Marie (Zimmerman) T.; B.S. in Elec. Engring., U. Okla., 1939; M.E.E., 1941; postgrad. Ia. State U., 1953; m. Eunice Margaerite Furr, Aug. 27, 1938; children—Betty Sharon (Mrs. James W. Swank), Shirley (Mrs. Bruce McFarland). Mem. faculty U. Okla., Norman, 1941—, prof., 1956-66, David Ross Boyd prof., 1966—, dir. Sch. Elec. Engring., 1958-63, acting dir., 1966-67. Served to maj., Signal Corps, AUS, 1942-46. Mem. I.E.E.E. (sr.), Am. Soc. Engring. Edn., Am. Assn. U. Prof., Sigma Xi, Tau Beta Pi, Sigma Tau, Eta Kappa Nu, Pi Mu Epsilon. Home: 1509 Ann Arbor Dr Norman OK 73069

TUMA, JERRY ANDREW, computer center exec.; b. Caldwell, Tex., Apr. 3, 1935; s. Jerry Alvin and Vera (Newcomb) T.; B.S. with highest honors, U. Tex., Arlington, 1963; m. Melba Louise Gradick, Mar. 3, 1965. With Fed. Res. Bank, Dallas, 1952-53, 56-57; with Wyatt Co., Dallas, 1962—, mgr. Wyatt Computer Center, 1965—, dir., 1971-72. Served with AUS, 1953-56. Mem. Data Processing Mgrs. Assn. Republican. Baptist. Home: 7403 Masonville Dr Annandale VA 22003 Office: 1000 16th St NW Washington DC 20036

TUMBLESON, ARTHUR LOUIS, city ofcl.; b. Cin., Oct. 9, 1934; s. Albert Newton and Clara (Watkins) T.; student U. Cin., 1959, U. South Fla., 1965; m. Shirley Richardson, Oct. 4, 1953 (div.); children—Michael Louis, Steven Arthur. Supr. sewer and water engring. City of Cin., 1953-62; agt. Western & So. Life Ins. Co., Cin., 1963-64; dir. bldg. zoning and engring. City of Temple Terrace Fla., 1964—; cons. engr. Active Tampa Little League. Served with AUS, 1952-53. Mason. Club: Temple Terrace Country. Home: 8728 Larkhall Pl Tampa FL 33604 Office: PO Box 16476 Temple Terrace FL 33617

TUNNELL, GRADDY, lawyer; b. Quitaque, Tex., May 1, 1928; s. Ernest B. and Maizine (Graddy) T.; B.A., Baylor U., 1948, LL.B., 1950; m. Gloria Jean Blackburn, Nov. 25, 1950; children—Richard Lynn, Jeffrey Dee, Lindsey Graddy. Admitted to Tex. bar, 1950, since practiced in Plainview; mem. firm LaFont, Tunnell, Formby, LaFont & Hamilton, 1950—; dir. Hale County Savs. Assn., Fed. Land Bank Assn. (both Plainview). Sec.-treas., trustee High Plains Research Found., 1958—. Trustee Wayland Bapt. Coll., Plainview. Served with USAFR, 1953-55. Mem. Hale County Bar Assn. (pres. 1965-67). Baptist (deacon). Mason, Kiwanian. Home: 2800 W 16th St Plainview TX 79072 Office: Skaggs Bldg Plainview TX 79072

TUNSTALL, GEORGE LUCILLE HAWKINS, educator; b. Thurber, Tex., Jan. 17, 1922; d. Harry and Ruth (Martin) Hawkins; B.S., U. Colo., 1943; M.S., Wayne State U., 1959, Ph.D., 1963; m. William Neal Brown, Jan. 19, 1944 (div. Mar. 1946); m. 2d, Edward Haney Tunstall, June 19, 1947 (div. Apr. 1962); children—Ruth Neal, Leslie Diane. Med. tech. U. Colo. Med. Sch., Denver, 1943-45, Presbyn. Hosp. Colo., Denver, 1946-47, Evang. Deaconess Hosp., Detroit, 1950-52, Sinai Hosp. Detroit, 1952-55, Brent Gen. Hosp., Detroit, 1955-58; research teaching asst. biology dept. Wayne State U., 1958-62; asst. prof. Delta Coll., University Center, Mich., 1963-65; asso. prof. Saginaw Valley Coll., University Center, 1965-67; chmn. biology dept. Bishop Coll., Dallas, 1967-71; asso. dir. United Bd. for Coll. Devel., Atlanta, 1971-72; dir. allied health curriculum devel. program Claric Coll., Atlanta, 1972—, adj. prof. dept. biology, 1972—. Edn. cons. Saginaw (Mich.) C. of C., 1966-67, Nat., State, Regional confs., N.A.A.C.P., 1965-67. Active Girl Scouts Am., 1952-62; edn. chmn. Mich. Conf. N.A.A.C.P. brs., 1964-67, pres. Bay City br. 1965-67); exec. sec. Human Relations Commn. Bay City, 1965-67; trustee Mich. Tb. Respiratory Disease Assn., 1965-67; mem. personnel com. YWCA, 1966-67, mem. nominating com. exec. bd., 1967; exec. com. Bay City chpt. Ship Hope, 1966-67. Mem. Bay City Bus. Profl. Women's Club, Am. Soc. Microbiology, Am. Soc. Clin. Pathologists, Mich. Acad. Sci. Arts Letters, A.A.A.S., Am. Inst. Biol. Sci., Am. Soc. for Cell Biology, N.Y. Acad. Scis., Am. Assn. U. Women, Am. Assn. U. Profs., Am. Acad. Polit. Social Sci., Sigma Xi, Alpha Kappa Alpha. Methodist. Contbr. articles profl. jours. Home: 2909 Campbellton Rd SW Atlanta GA 30311

TUNSTILL, GARLAND ALBERT, cons. in finance and govt. relations; b. Eastland County, Tex., Nov. 16, 1901; s. William Austin and Eula (Compton) T.; LL.B., Cumberland U., Lebanon, Tenn., 1923; m. Clover Dell Hill, Feb. 23, 1937 (dec. July 1972). Admitted to Tex. bar, 1924; practice law, Ft. Worth, 1924-26; ind. oil operator, Houston, 1926-40; bus. economist and entrepreneur, 1941-47; financial and govt. relations cons., 1948—. Precinct chmn. Republican party, 1954—. Mem. com. on social. conditions in South, Tulane U. Bd. dirs., cons. Movimiento Pro Federacion Americana. Mem. Tex. Bar Assn. Christian Scientist. Author: (essay) Can the Monroe Doctrine Bring Peace and Prosperity to the Americans? (in library of James Monroe Meml. Found., Fredericksburg, Va.). Home: 2017 Esperanza Houston TX 77023 Office: PO Box 12846 Houston TX 77017

TUPPER, CHARLES FREDERICK, JR., lawyer, state legislator; b. El Paso, Tex., Oct. 1, 1942; s. Charles Frederick and Patsene (Suggs) T.; B.A., U. Tex., El Paso, 1964; J.D., U. Tex., Austin, 1969; m. Cecilia Jo Neely, May 30, 1970; 1 son, Charles Blaine. Admitted to Tex. bar, 1969; since practiced in El Paso; asso. Blackham & Tupper, 1969-70; partner Studdard, Melby, Schwartz & Tupper, 1970—; mem. Tex. Ho. of Reps., 1971—. Guest lectr. Robert Taft Inst. Govt. El Paso dist. chmn. YMCA Youth and Govt., 1971—. Bd. dirs. U. Tex. El Paso Ex-Students, El Paso Mental Health Assn., El Paso Epilepsy Assn.; bd. mgrs. Tex. Youth and Govt. Recipient Student Bar Assn. award U. Tex. Law Sch., 1969; Outstanding Ex-Student award Austin High Sch., 1970; Tex. Intercollegiate Students Assn. Ten Outstanding Legislators award, 1973. Mem. El Paso Young Lawyers Assn., El Paso Bar Assn., Alpha Chi, Phi Alpha Theta, Delta Theta Phi, Sigma Alpha Epsilon. Democrat. Presbyn. Home: 7205 Tierra Alta El Paso TX 79912 Office: 924 Southwest Nat Bank Bldg El Paso TX 79901

TURBERVILLE, FRANK BURTON, JR., elec. engr.; b. Danville, Va., Sept. 17, 1919; s. Frank Burton and Hallie Williams (Connally) T.; student Edwards Mil. Inst., Salemburg, N.C., 1935-39, N.C. State Coll., 1946-48, various courses U.S. Dept. Agr. Grad. Sch., 1959—; m. Wilma Irene Bryant, Feb. 9, 1946; children—Frank Burton III, Charles Gray. Elec. apprentice elec. div. Panama Canal, 1940-44; plant engr. Lexington (N.C.) Telephone Co., 1954; field engr., office engr. Rural Electrification Adminstrn., U.S. Dept. Agr., Washington, 1955—. Served with USNR, 1941-45, 51-53. Mem. Am. Inst. E.E., I.E.E.E., U.S. Naval Inst. Baptist (active various coms.). Mason. Home: 6003 Brandon Av Springfield VA 22150 Office: REA US Dept Agr 14th and Independence Av Washington DC 20250

TURK, JAMES CLINTON, judge; b. Ronaoke, Va., May 3, 1923; s. James Alexander and Geneva (Richardson) T.; A.B., Roanoke Coll., 1949; LL.B., Washington and Lee U., 1952; m. Barbara Duncan, Aug. 21, 1954; children—Ramona Leah, James Clinton, Robert Malcolm Duncan, Mary Elizabeth, David Michael. Admitted to Va. bar, 1952; mem. firm Poff & Turk, Radford, Va., 1952-72; mem. Va. Senate, 1959-72, minority leader; U.S. dist. judge Western Dist. Va., Roanoke, 1972—. Trustee Radford Community Hosp., 1959—. Served with AUS, 1943-46. Mem. Order of Coif, Phi Beta Kappa, Omicron Delta Kappa. Baptist (deacon). Home: 1002 Walker Dr Redford VA 24141 Office: Fed Bldg Roanoke VA

TURK, MALCOLM K., coll. athletic ofcl.; b. Cairo, Ill., May 20, 1942; s. Malcolm and Nelle (White) T.; A.A., Copiah-Lincoln Jr. Coll., 1962; B.S., Livingston U., 1964, M.Ed., 1968; m. Katrina Cade, July 31, 1965. Coach, Cobb County Sch. System, Marietta, Ga., 1965-67; head basketball coach, also athletic dir. Copiah-Lincoln Jr. Coll., Wesson, Miss., 1968—. Mem. Miss., Copiah-Lincoln edn. assns., Am., Miss. assns. health and phys. edn., Wesson Jaycees (pres. 1969). Lion. Club: Co-Lin Golf (Wesson). Home: Box 185 Wesson MS 39191

TURNBULL, JOHN A., lawyer; b. Johnstown, Pa., Apr. 20, 1943; s. Frank Johnson and Ellen Elizabeth (McFeeters) T.; J.D., U. Tenn., 1966; m. Delores Jo Frasier, Sept. 6, 1964; children—Amy Victoria, Karen Belew, John Matthew. Bible salesman Southwestern Co., Nashville, 1962-64; ins. adjuster Tenn. Co., Cookeville, 1966-67; admitted to Tenn. bar, 1967; asso. Roberts & Roberts, attys., Livingston, 1967-69; partner Roberts & Turnbull, attys., 1969—. Alderman, City of Livingston, 1968-70; mem. exec. bd. Upper Cumberland Devel. Dist., 1969—. Mem. Overton County C. of C. (pres. 1973-74). Mem. Christian Ch. (elder 1971—). Home: Route 1 Livingston TN 38570 Office: PO Box 8 Livingston TN 38570

TURNER, CARROLL GLENN, communications exec.; b. El Campo. Tex., June 17, 1909; s. Earl Kirby and Ethel (Van Cleve) T.; E.E., Finlay Engr., 1933; m. Mary M. Turner; children—Robert W. and Carolyn (Mrs. Malford Hierholzer) (twins). Illumination and elec. engr. Kansas City Power & Light Co., 1931-46; regional mgr. Gen. Electric Co., Kansas City, Mo., 1946-52; v.p., gen. mgr. Communications Engring. Co., Houston, 1952-63; pres. Radio Dispatch, Inc. (Tex.), 1963-68, dir.; pres. Mobile Radio, Inc. Served with AUS, 1942-46; lt. col. Res. Decorated Bronze Star medal. Registered profl. engr. Mem. I.E.E.E. (sr.), Houston Engring. and Sci. Soc. Mason (Shriner). Inventor electronic device for controlling linear voltage, apparatus for determining speed of moving object. Home: 1412 Azalea Dr Rosenberg TX 77471 Office: 1717 1st St Rosenberg TX 77471

TURNER, CHARLES SOLOMON, electronics co. exec.; b. Gainesville, Tex., June 9, 1929; s. John Auther and Ruth Anna (Schmidt) T.; B.S. in Elec. Engring., Okla. State U., 1956; postgrad. evening schs. So. Meth. U., 1969, El Centro Coll., 1969; m. Sally Ann Wagoner, Oct. 7, 1962; children—Polly, Robin, Tracy. Engr. computer dept. Gen. Electric Co., Phoenix, 1956-63, project leader, 1960-63; mgr. research and advanced design Recognition Equipment, Inc., Dallas, 1963-67, dir. electronic devel. engring., 1967-69; pres., dir., also chief exec. officer Control Tech., Inc., Garland, Tex., 1969—. Active precinct work Republican party. Served with USN, 1948-52. Mem. Phi Eta Sigma, Sigma Tau. Mem. Unity Ch. Dallas. Patentee amplifiers. Home: 9328 Chiswell St Dallas TX 75238 Office: 620 Easy St Garland TX 75042

TURNER, DEAN WALTON, lawyer; b. Arp, Tex., May 14, 1915; s. Leonard Walton and Rosamond (Dean) T.; student Rice U., 1933-35; J.D., Baylor U., 1938; m. Margaret Robbins, Sept. 28, 1940; 1 son, Raymond W. Admitted to Tex. bar, 1938; gen. civil and criminal law practice, Troup, Tex., 1938-44; partner with T.A. Bath, Henderson, 1946—. City atty. Troup, 1939, 44; asst. county atty. Rusk County, 1946; city atty. Overton, Tex., 1951-60. Chmn., Democratic party Rusk County, 1954-64; mem. State Dem. Exec. Com., 1958-60. Pres., Neches River Conservation Dist., 1961-62; mem. Gov.'s Subcom. to Revise Tex. Election Laws, 1964, State Com. Exam. and Approval of Electronic Voting Machines, 1967, Gov.'s Water Planning Com., 1967; legal adviser Rusk County Draft Bd., 1948—. Trustee Henderson Meml. Hosp. Mem. Am., Rusk County (pres. 1951) bar assns., State Bar Tex., Tex. Assn. Def. Counsel, Def. Research Inst., Rusk County C. of C. (v.p. 1950). Presbyn. (elder 1948—, trustee). Mason, Kiwanian. Home: 1106 E Main St Henderson TX 75652 Office: 107 N Jackson St Henderson TX 75652

TURNER, ELBERT DAYMOND, JR., educator; b. Gainesville, Fla., Nov. 15, 1915; s. Elbert D. and Lena (Baird) T.; B.A. with honors, Davidson Coll., 1937; M.A., U. N.C., 1939, Ph.D., 1949; m. Irma Aboy, Aug. 2, 1945; children—Carmen Irma (Mrs. Joseph Lipe), Ana Maria, Victoria, Elbert D. III, Rosa. Teaching fellow U. N.C., 1937-38, part-time instr. 1938-39; instr. Ga. Tchrs. Coll., 1939-41; instr. Spanish, U. N.C., 1946-49; asst. prof. U. Del., 1949-58, dir. lang. lab., 1955-66, asso. prof. modern langs., 1958-61, prof. modern languages, 1961-66; prof., chmn. dept. fgn. langs. U. N.C., Charlotte, 1966-71, dir. grad. studies, 1970—; vis. prof. NDEA Inst., Utah State U., 1963-64, Utah State U., Oaxaca, Mexico, summer 1966; cons. pub. schs. Del., 1951-52, 56, Delaware Dept. Pub. Instrn., 1959-66, Memphis State U., 1967-70, Profl. Child Care Centers, Inc., 1969-73. Chmn. test devel. Nat. Spanish Exams., 1965-74. Served from 1st lt. to lt. col. AUS, 1941-46; col. Res. Fellow Southeastern Inst. Medieval and Renaissance Studies, 1968. Mem. Am. Assn. Tchrs. Spanish and Portuguese, Assn. for Latin-Am. Studies, Am. Council on Teaching Fgn. Langs., Charlotte Area Ednl. Consortium (sec. 1971-72), S. Atlantic Modern Lang. Assn., Instituto de Literatura Iberoamericana, Phi Beta Kappa, Delta Sigma Pi, Eta Sigma Phi, Sigma Phi Epsilon. Republican. Presbyn. (deacon). Club: Charlotte Swimming. Author: Gonzalo Fernandez de Ovideo y Valdes: An Annotated Bibliography, 1967. Contbr. to various profl. publs. Mem. adv. bd. N.C. Fgn. Lang. Tchr., 1970—. Home: 233 Fenton Pl Charlotte NC 28207

TURNER, ELIZABETH ADAMS NOBLE (MRS. JACK RICE TURNER), ednl. adminstr.; b. Yonkers, N.Y., May 18, 1931; d. James Kendrick and Orrel (Baldwin) Noble; B.A., Vassar Coll., 1953; M.A., Tex. A. and I. U., 1964; m. Jack Rice Turner, July 11, 1953; children—Jay Kendrick, Randall Ray. Ednl. cons. Noble & Noble Pub. Co., N.Y.C., 1956-67; psychometrist Corpus Christi (Tex.) Guidance Center, 1967-70; psychologist Corpus Christi State Sch., 1970-72, dir. programs, 1972, dir. vol. service, 1972—. Real estate salesman Forrest Allen Co., Corpus Christi, 1967-70; coordinator vols. Summer Head Start Program, Corpus Christi, 1967. Mem. allocations com. United Fund, Corpus Christi, 1970. Bd. dirs. YWCA, Corpus Christi Hearing and Speech, Coastal Bend Mental Health Assn., Suicide Prevention Inc., Tb Assn. (all Corpus Christi), Corpus Christi Mus., Art Mus. S. Tex., Corpus Christi. Recipient Love award YWCA, 1970. Mem. Tex. Psychol. Assn. (pres., mem. exec. bd.), Psychol. Assos. (pres.), Am. Psychotherapy Assn., Am. Assn. Mental Deficiency, Leadership Corpus Christi, Jr. League Corpus Christi, Tex. Bookman's Assn., Tex. Assn. Realtors, Kappa Kappa Gamma. Clubs: Corpus Christi Country, Corpus Christi Yacht, Junior Cotillion, Press. Home: 6049 Broadmoor St Corpus Christi TX 78413 Office: 902 Airport Rd Corpus Christi TX 78408

TURNER, GISELA KRAUSE, physician; b. Dortmund, Germany; d. Arthur and Elisabeth (Eckardt) Krause; student U. Muenster (Germany), 1941-42, Strassbourg U. (France), 1942-44; M.D., Heidelberg U. (Germany), 1947; m. Samuel R. Turner, July 10, 1970; children (by previous marriage)—Stephen Arthur, Ralph Eckardt. Intern Hillcrest Med. Center, Tulsa, 1963-64; resident Vanderbilt U. Hosp., Nashville, 1964-67; practice medicine, specializing in anesthesiology, Nashville, 1967—; mem. staff Vanderbilt U. Hosp.; instr. anesthesiology Vanderbilt U., 1967-69, asst. prof., 1969-70. Mem. Am. Soc. Anesthesiologists, Anesthesia and Analgesia Research Soc. Home: 4326 E 103d St S Tulsa OK 74136

TURNER, HENRY BROWN, govt. ofcl.; b. N.Y.C., Sept. 3, 1936; s. Henry Brown III and Gertrude (Adams) T.; B.A., Duke, 1958; M.B.A., Harvard, 1962; m. Sarah Jean Thomas, June 7, 1958; children—Laura, Steven, Nancy. Asst. to pres. Trailor-Murdock Constrn. Co., then controller, Financial Corp. Ariz., Phoenix, 1962-64; asst. to v.p., sec.-treas. Star-Kist Foods, Inc., Los Angeles, 1964-67; mgr. corporate, 1st v.p. finance Mitchum, Jones & Templeton, Inc., Los Angeles, 1967-73, also dir.; asst. sec. commerce, Washington, 1973—; guest lectr. U. Cal. at Los Angeles, Long Beach State U. Co. coordinator Jr. Achievement. Bd. dirs. United Fund. Served to lt. USNR, 1958-60. Republican. Clubs: Harvard Business School of So. Cal., Chadwick School Booster. Home: 1110 Saville Lane McLean VA 22101 Office: Asst Sec Adminstrn Dept Commerce Washington DC 20230

TURNER, HENRY LATHROP, III, financial cons.; b. Cin., July 30, 1931; s. Henry Lathrop Jr. and Nancy (Bosart) T.; grad. Culver Mil. Acad., 1950; B.S., U. Ky., 1954; m. Clara Hoskins, Sept. 24, 1954; children—Catherine (Mrs. Daniel Jonathan Foster), Jacqueline Rae (Mrs. William S. Hamilton), Lucy Elizabeth, Henry Lathrop IV. Ins. agt. Phoenix Mut. Life Ins. Co., Lexington, Ky., 1957-60, Orlando, Fla., 1962-68; pres. Physicians' Adminstrv. Services, Winter Park, Fla., 1968—. Investment cons., 1966—; exec. dir. Nat. Assns. Profl. Corps., Washington, 1969—. Served to 1st lt. USAF, 1955-57. C.L.U. Recipient Certificate Estate Planning and Pensions C.L.U. Am. Coll., 1968. Mem. Assn. Advanced Life Underwriters, Am. Soc. C.L.U.'s (v.p. Central Fla. chpt.), Estate Planning Council, Am. Inst. for Econ. Research. Republican. Mem. Christian and Missionary Alliance Ch. Clubs: Bay Hill, University (Orlando); Ocean Reef (Key Largo, Fla.); Tampa Polo. Pioneer in devel. profl. corps. Home: 810 Juanita Rael Winter Park FL 32789 Office: 807 Morse Blvd Winter Park FL 32789

TURNER, HEYWOOD AXTELL, JR., utility co. exec.; b. Richmond, Va., Mar. 6, 1926; s. Heywood Axtell and Anne Margaret (Pugh) T.; student Duke U., 1944, U. Louisville, 1944-46; B.E.E., U. Fla., 1949; m. Mary Louise Van Dyke, Jan. 26, 1952; children—Sheila, Lee Anne, Heywood III. With Tampa Electric Co. (Fla.), 1947—, adminstrv. asst., 1965-67, gen. mgr. Tampa div., 1967-73, dir. divs., 1973-74, v.p. divs., 1974—. Served with USNR, 1944-46, AUS, 1951-53. Mem. I.E.E.E., Alpha Tau Omega. Presbyn. (ruling elder 1967—). Rotarian (pres. 1973-74). Club: Carrollwood Village Golf and Tennis. Home: 11108 Carrollwood Dr Tampa FL 33618 Office: PO Box 111 Tampa FL 33601

TURNER, JAMES ALEXANDER, JR., lawyer, accountant, educator; b. Kingstree, S.C., Dec. 15, 1937; s. James Alexander and Alice (Ballentine) T.; B.S., U. N.C., 1961; J.D., U. S.C., 1966; m. Betty Morris, June 29, 1963; children—James Alexander III, William Townsend. Accountant, S.D. Leidesdorf & Co., Greenville, S.C., 1961-63; pvt. practice James A. Turner, Jr., C.P.A., Columbia, S.C., 1963-66, 68-71; admitted to S.C. bar, 1966; tax atty. S.D. Leidesdorf & Co., Greenville, 1966-68; asst. prof. indsl. mgmt. Clemson (S.C.) U., 1968-73, asso. prof., 1973—; dir. Turner Lumber Co., LeMoyen, La. Del. Young Rep. Nat. Conv., 1965. C.P.A., S.C. Mem. S.C. Assn. C.P.A.'s (exec. com. 1971, program coordination com. of continuing edn. div.), Am. Inst. C.P.A.'s, S.C. Assn. Accounting Instrs. (pres. 1973-74), Am., Nat. assns. accountants, S.C. Bar Assn., Am. Accounting Assn., S.A.R. (chpt. pres. 1969-71), S.C. Beta Alumni Corp. Sigma Phi Epsilon (pres. 1970—). Presbyn. Clubs: Green Valley Country (Greenville). Home: Route 2 Box 273A Seneca SC 29678 Office: PO Box 303 Clemson SC 29631

TURNER, JAMES EDWIN, farmer; b. Chuckatuck, Va., Nov. 5, 1909; s. William Robert and Ivey Ruth (Johnson) T.; student pub. schs.; m. Mamie Elizabeth Gilliam, Oct. 10, 1931; children—James Edwin, Richard L. Farmer, Carrollton, Va., 1931-65; partner Turner & Turner, Carrollton, 1965-70; pres. Turner Farms, Inc., Carrollton, 1970—; dir. Bank Smithfield (Va.). Treas., Carrollton Vol. Fire Dept., 1965-71; county fire warden, 1945—; mem. Pub. Welfare Dept., 1956—; mem. electoral bd., 1970-71. Named Outstanding Man of Year, Carrollton Ruritan Club, 1970. Mem. Agrl. Stblzn. and Conservation Com. (recipient award certificates), Farm Bur., So. States Tidewater Petroleum, So. States Co-op., Isle of Wight Farmers Co-op. Methodist (trustee). Club: Carrollton Ruritan. Home: RFD 1 Box 219 Carrollton VA 23314 Office: PO Box 56 Carrollton VA 23314

TURNER, JOE DOWERY, ret. mining engr.; b. Adger, Ala., May 29, 1902; s. Henry and Alie (Turner) T.; B.S. in Mining Engring., B.S. in Mining Geology, U. Ala., 1926; postgrad. U. Denver, 1952-54; m. Fannie Mildred Thompson, July 2, 1938. Mining engr. Sloss-Sheffield Co., Bessemer, Ala., 1927-28, Woodward Iron Co., 1928-37, U.S. Geol. Survey, Denver, 1937-44; dist. mining supr. McAlester, Okla., 1944-52, regional mining supr. Denver, 1952-54, chief br. mining operations, Washington, 1954-72. Mem. Joseph A. Holmes Safety Awards Com. Registered profl. engr., Ala., D.C. Mem. Am. Inst. Mining, Metall. and Petroleum Engrs., Fed. Profl. Assn., Nat. Soc. Profl. Engrs., Am. Inst. Profl. Geologists, Soc. Am. Mil. Engrs., Ala. Soc. Profl. Land Surveyors, Am. Congress Surveying and Mapping, Gamma Sigma Epsilon. Mason (K.T., Shriner). Home: 836 Linbard Lane Birmingham AL 35226

TURNER, JOE STEWART, elec. engr.; b. Sherman, Tex., 1909; s. Ethelbert and Annie Lee (Stewart) T.; student Chgo. Radio and T.V. Inst., 1932; B.A. with honors, U. Tex., 1934; m. Vivian Dybwad, Jan. 7, 1932; children—Jo Ann (Mrs. Lawrence Albert Westhaver), Robert Roger. Elec. engr. Cooney Mining Co., Glenwood, N.M., 1934-35, Internat. Milling Co., Greenville, Tex., engr., sect. supr. CAA, Ft. Worth, Tex. and Washington, 1937-47, supt. Pacific area communications, Honolulu, 1948-52; chief radar div. FAA, Washington, 1953-59; project dir. systems div. dir. Collins Radio Co., Dallas, 1960-65; supr. cost control and new tech. reporting Bendix Launch Support, Kennedy Space Center, Fla., 1966—. Coach, Annandale (Va.) Swim Team, 1956. Bd. dirs. Annandale Recreation Center, 1956. Served with AUS, 1943-44. Sr. mem. I.E.E.E. (chmn. Pacific sect. 1951); mem. Bendix Mgmt. Club. Rotarian. Author: DOD/Commerce Joint Use of Radar Agreement, 1958; Airport Surface Detection Equipment, 1959; Performance Standards for Communications Systems, 1960. Home: 2825-614 Washington St Titusville FL 32780 Office: Bendix Launch Support Div PO Box 21086 Kennedy Space Center FL 32815

TURNER, KENNETH AUSTIN, judge; b. Memphis, Mar. 9, 1928; s. William Robert and Pearl (Gwin) T.; student U. Tenn., 1947-49; LL.B., Memphis State U., 1959; m. Mary Sue Ballard, Feb. 6, 1948; 1 dau., Carole Joyce. Wih Memphis Police Dept., 1950-63, detective capt.; juvenile ct. judge, Memphis, 1964—. Served with USMCR, 1946-47, 50-51. Mem. Tenn. Council Juvenile Ct. Judges (pres. 1967-68), Phi Alpha Delta Mason (32 deg.). Home: 1972 Kirby Pkwy Memphis TN 38138 Office: 616 Adams Av Memphis TN 38105

TURNER, LOYD LEONARD, business exec.; b. Claude, Tex., Nov. 5, 1917; s. James Richard and Maude (Brown) T.; B.A., Baylor U., 1939, M.A., 1940; postgrad. U. Pa., 1940-42; m. Lee Madeleine Barr, Apr. 13, 1944; children—Terry Lee, Loyd Lee. Instr., U. Pa., 1940-42; pub. relations counselor Consol. Vultee Aircraft Corp., San Diego, 1946-48, dir. pub. relations, Ft. Worth, 1948-53; asst. to pres. Ft. Worth div. Gen. Dynamics Corp., 1953-71, dir. pub. affairs Convair Aerospace div., Ft. Worth, 1971-72; exec. asst. to chmn. bd. and pres. Tandy Corp., Ft. Worth, 1972—. Pres., Ft. Worth Pub. Library Bd., 1958-63; v.p. Ft. Worth Bd. Edn., 1962-65, pres., 1965-71; mem. exec. com. Tex. Assn. Sch. Bds., 1966-71, v.p., 1970-71; mem. steering com., council big city bds. Nat. Sch. Bds. Assn., 1967-69, mem. Gov's Com. on Pub. Sch. Edn., 1966-69; pres. Tex. Council Maj. Sch. Dists., 1968-69. Bd. dirs. Tarrant County chpt. A.R.C., 1956-59, Tex. Com. Pub. Edn., 1961-69. Bd. dirs. Pub. Communication Found. North Tex., 1970—. Served with USAAF, 1942-46. Named Library Trustee of Year, Tex. Library Assn., 1961, Pres. of Best Bd. of Large Sch. Systems in U.S., N.E.A., 1968; recipient citation Air Force Assn., 1962; Leadership award West Tex. C. of C., 1966, 69. Mem. Pub. Relations Soc. Am., Air Force Assn., Nat. Mgmt. Assn., Advt. Club Ft. Worth, Friends Ft. Worth Library (v.p. 1971—), Ft. Worth C. of C. (dir. 1974—), Arts Council Greater Ft. Worth, Baylor U. Council for Instnl. Devel., Baylor U. Ex-Students Assn. (dir. 1958-61), Sigma Delta Chi (pres. Ft. Worth 1961-62). Baptist. Lion (pres. Ft. Worth 1958-59), Rotarian (pres. Fort Worth 1974-75). Clubs: Knife and Fork (dir. 1963-66, pres. 1965-66), Colonial Country, Century II, Press of Fort Worth. Author: The ABC of Clear Writing, 1954. Home: 3717 Echo Trail Fort Worth TX 76109 Office: 2727 W 7th St Fort Worth TX 76107

TURNER, MYRA BROOKS (MRS. RONALD JOSEPH TURNER), composer; b. Knoxville, Tenn., Jan. 13, 1936; d. Paul David and Lillie Mary (Ray) Brooks; student Juilliard Sch. Music, 1947-51; Mus. B., So. Meth. U., 1955, Mus. M., 1956; m. Ronald Joseph Turner, June 11, 1960; children—Stacy Lynn, Cheryl Leigh,

Teresa Jeanne. Mus. specialist Dallas schs., 1956-60; mus. dir. choral music, Knoxville, 1960-64; composer-in-residence Birmingham (Ala.) Children's Theatre, 1967-69; composer, lectr., performing artist, Atlanta, 1969—. Dir. St. Martin in the Fields Church St. Cecilia Choir, 1973—. Recipient award Seattle Nat. Playwriting Contest, 1968; Nat. Merit award Phi Mu Epsilon, 1972. Mem. Nat., Ga. (dist. festival chmn. 1970—; state festival chmn. 1972) federated mus. clubs, Nat., Ga., Atlanta (v.p. 1972) music tchrs. assns., Mu Phi Epsilon (pres. Atlanta alumnae 1972-74), Pi Kappa Lambda, Alpha Delta Pi. Composer: (three act plays) Cinderella, 1966, Pinocchio, 1965, The Green Dragon, 1965, Mid-Summer Nights Dream, 1965, Flibbertygibbet, 1972, Javoho Junction, 1959; (piano solos) Praise The Lord, Christ Jesus, 1966, Man Speaks Through Music, 1965, The Jazz Man Suite, 1968, Fantasy in A Minor, 1968. Club: Atlanta Woman's. Address: 2433 MacLaren Circle Atlanta GA 30340

TURNER, REX ALLWIN, coll. pres., clergyman; b. Corner, Ala., Feb. 13, 1913; s. Elijah Jesse and Mary Ellen Odessa (Fikes) T.; student U. Ala., 1929-30, Jacksonville State U., 1933-34; A.B., Samford U., 1936; M.S., Auburn U., 1946, Ed.D., 1955; LL.B., Jones Law Sch., 1952; m. Opal Shipp, Dec. 24, 1931; children—June Jacqulin (Mrs. Jesse C. Long), Mary Ellen (Mrs. Phillip D. Hargis), Rex Allwin. Ordained to ministry Ch. of Christ, 1932; prin. Mount High elementary schs., Blount County, Alabama, 1935-36, also instr. city system ofschs., Tarrant, Ala.; minister, Montgomery, Ala., 1936-42; co-founder Ala. Christian Coll., Montgomery 1942, co-pres., 1942-48, pres., 1948—; former minister Panama St. Ch. of Christ, Montgomery. Mem. Am. Assn. Sch. Adminstrs., Am. Assn. U. Profs., Assn. Higher Edn., Am. Assn. Curriculum Devel., Nat. Assn. Secondary Principals, Kappa Delta Pi, Phi Delta Kappa, Sigma Delta Kappa, Staff writer for Gospel Advocate. Author: Milestones in the Restoration Movement, 1955; Principles of School Law and Applications to Alabama's Public School System, 1955; Fundamentals of the Faith, 1973. Home: 10 Watson Circle Montgomery AL 36109 Office: Atlanta Hwy Montgomery AL 36109

TURNER, THOMAS RICHARD, physician; b. Arp, Tex., May 19, 1917; s. Leonard W. and Rosamond (Dean) T.; B.A., Baylor U., 1938, M.D., 1941; M.S., U. Minn., 1945; m. Donnie Martha Goodner, Aug. 29, 1941; children—Nancy Ethel (Mrs. James Clay Lang), Ann Rosemond (Mrs. Robert Wood Jordan), Richard Leonard. Intern, Baylor U. Hosp., Dallas, 1941-42; fellow Mayo Clinic, Rochester, Minn., 1942-45, asso. Springer Clinic, Tulsa, 1945-47, partner, 1947-60; pvt. practice medicine specializing in neurology and psychiatry, Tulsa, 1960—; mem. staff St. John's, Hillcrest, St. Francis hosps. (all Tulsa). Diplomate Am. Bd. Psychiatry and Neurology. Fellow Am. Psychiat. Assn., Am. Acad. Neurology; mem. A.M.A., Am. Med. Electroencephalographic Assn., Central Neurol. Psychiat. Assn., So. Med. Assn. (life), Pan Am. Med. Assn. (diplomate sect. on neurology), Beta Beta Beta, Alpha Chi, Alpha Epsilon Delta. Clubs: Oaks Country, Summit. Home: 1831 E 31st Pl Tulsa OK 74105 Office: 3102 S Harvard Av Tulsa OK 74135

TURNEY, ALFRED WALTER, educator; b. Scott, Miss., Aug. 6, 1916; s. Alfred Walter and Hazel (Brown) T.; Ph.D., U. N.M., 1969; m. Sarah Chidester, Aug. 6, 1926; 1 dau., Mia. Entered U.S. Army, 1938, commd. 2d lt., 1942, advanced through grades to col., 1963, ret., 1963; prof. history Southwestern State Coll., Weatherford, Okla., 1968—. Recipient numerous decorations and awards for mil. service from U.S., South Korea, Germany and others. Author: Disaster at Moscow, 1970, 2d edit., 1971. Home: 1529 Pine Weatherford OK 73096

TUTEN, WILLIAM HOUSTON, ednl. adminstr.; b. DeLand, Fla., June 5, 1928; s. David Bell and Ruth (Houston) T.; B.S., Stetson U., 1950, postgrad., 1952-54; M.P.H., U. Fla., 1962; m. Joanne Waits, Dec. 24, 1932; children—Thomas, Sandra, William Houston, Jonathan. Basketball coach DeLand (Fla.) High Sch., 1952-56; supt. recreation City of Palatka, Fla., 1956-58; mem. faculty St. Johns River Jr. Coll., Palatka, 1958—, coach basketball, 1958-67, dir. health, phys. edn. and athletics, 1958—. Bd. dirs. region VIII, Nat. Jr. Coll. Athletic Assn.; commr. Fla. Jr. Coll. Conf., 1971. Served with USNR, 1950-51. Recipient basketball coach of the year award Mid-Fla. Coll. Conf., 1964, Fla. Jr. Coll. Conf., 1966. Mem. Sigma Phi Epsilon. Methodist. Home: 3225 Blair Dr Palatka FL 32077 Office: 5000 St Johns Av Palatka FL 32077

TUTHILL, BURNET C(ORWIN), musician; b. N.Y., 1888; A.B., M.A., Columbia; Mus.M., Coll. Music, Cin.; Mus.D. (hon.), Chgo. Mus. Coll., Southwestern Coll.; m. Helen Hersey, 1917; m. 2d, Ruth Wood, 1930; 2 daus. Condr., Columbia U. Orch., 1909-13; asst. condr. N.Y. Oratorio Soc., 1914-16; condr. People's Choral Union, N.Y.C., 1913-16, Plandome Singers, 1918-22, U. Cin. Glee Clubs, 1922-30, Southwestern Singers, 1935-59, Memphis Symphony Orch., 1938-46; chief fine arts sect. Shrivenham Am. (Army) U., Eng., 1945; gen. mgr. Cin. Conservatory, 1922-30; dir. music Southwestern Coll., Memphis, 1935-59; rep. Waddell & Reed, Inc., 1959—; composer Concertos for clarinet, string bass, tenor sax, trombone, and orch.; Fantasy Sonata for clarinet and piano, Big River for women's chorus and orch.; sonatas for violin, viola, trumpet, alto and tenor sax, flute, oboe with piano, ensemble music for winds, string quartet, clarinet quintet, others. Founder, Soc. Publ. Am. Music, 1919, treas., 1919-49. Co-founder Nat. Assn. Schs. Music, 1924, sec., 1924-59. Contbr. articles to musical publs. Home: 295 Buena Vista Pl Memphis TN 38312

TUTTLE, FREDERICK BURTON, educator, govt. ofcl.; b. New Haven, July 12, 1908; s. Burton L. and Alta M. (Carter) T.; B.A., Yale, 1930, Ph.D., 1942; postgrad. U. So. Cal., George Peabody Coll., U. Mich.; m. Mary Emily Armstrong, Sept. 3, 1936; children—Frederick Burton, James, Allen, Margaret Emily. Tchr. and prin. New Haven Pub. Schs., 1930-46; adviser edn. CAA, Washington, 1946-49; supt. schs., Westerly, R.I., 1949-52; dir. summer session, dir. placement, prof. edn. State U. Coll., Plattsburgh, N.Y., 1952-58, asso. dean, dir. grad. studies, 1958-63; dep. dir. ednl. programs NASA, 1963-70, dir. ednl. programs, 1970—; vis. prof. U. R.I., George Washington U., R.I. Coll. Edn. Ednl. cons. Nat. Aeronautic and Space Adminstrn.; adviser edn. N.Y. State Bur. Aviation. Served as lst lt. USMC, World War II. Recipient certificate of service Nat. Celebration, Fiftieth Anniversary of Powered Flight; citations N.Y. State Assn. Elementary School Prins. for service to edn. in N.Y.; Plattsburgh Rotary Club for service to community; Plattsburgh Alumni Assn. for service to Coll. Mem. Am. Assn. Sch. Adminstrs., Nat. Sci. Tchrs. Assn., S.A.R., Order Founders and Patriots, N.E.A., Nat. Council Social Studies. Episcopalian. Mason, Lion. Editor: Aviation Education Reports, 1949, 50; aviation edn. number. Nat. Elementary Prin., New Haven Tchrs. Jour., Sci. Edn. in Space Age. Contbr. periodicals. Home: 9229 Forest Haven Dr Alexandria VA 22309

TUTTLE, RICHARD CAROL, engr.; b. Springfield, Mo., Dec. 24, 1906; s. Ulysses Grant and Bessie (Patterson) T.; student in Geology, Tulsa U., 1938-44; m. Lettie Evelyn Nicholson, Mar. 29, 1926; children—Lelia (Mrs. Tom Brown), Richard R., Willard N. With Sinclair Oil Co., Tulsa, 1927-43, successively draftsman, in pipeline, engring., refining, geol., and liaison geol.-geophys. depts.; chief geophysicist, head exploration Sunray Oil Co., Tulsa, 1943-45; pvt. cons. practice, Tulsa, Ada, Okla., 1945-58; head drafting and design and math. Tulsa Tech. Coll., 1960-62, evening class tchr., 1962-70, head drafting and design, 1970—; design engr. Douglas Aircraft, 1962-70. Author profl. papers articles profl. jours. Home: 1915 S Yorktown St Tulsa OK 74104

TWILLIE, CECIL BENODD, wholesale, retail trade exec.; b. Caldwell, Ark., Apr. 20, 1938; s. Allen B. and Hula (Gilliam) T.; B.A., Philander Smith Coll., 1961; M.S., Ark. State U., 1969; m. Ozaree Lowe, July 9, 1961; children—Twyla, Cynthia, Rosalyn. Tchr., Cotton Plant (Ark.) Schs., 1961-62; tchr., coach Forrest City (Ark.) Sch. System, 1962—; gen. distbr. Bestline Products, Inc., Forrest City, 1970—. Vice pres. adv. bd. St. Andrew Day Care Center, Forrest City, 1973-74; commr. Forrest City Little League Baseball, 1972-73. Mem. Forrest City Edn. Assn. (pres. elect, head screening com. local candidates 1970—), Omega Psi Phi. Club: Ambassadors (pres. 1973-74). Address: 618 W Sharpe St Forrest City AR 72335

TWISDALE, HAROLD WINFRED, dentist; b. Roanoke Rapids, N.C., Apr. 28, 1933; s. James Robert and Elma (Smith) T.; B.S., U. N.C., 1955, D.D.S., 1958; m. Barbara Ann Edmonds, Aug. 2, 1958; children—Harold Winfred, Leigh Ann. Individual practice dentistry, Charlotte, N.C., 1961—; mem. dental staff Meml. Hosp., 1961—, head dept. dental prosthetics, 1964-66; lectr., vis. clinician various workshops and confs. Pres. Charlotte Telecasters, Inc., 1965—, Va. Telecasters, Inc., 1966, Augusta Telecasters, Inc., 1966-69, Durham-Raleigh Telecasters, Inc., 1966-70, Memphis Telecasters, Inc., 1966—; partner Twisdale & Steel Assos., 1965-70; proprietor Twisdale Enterprises, 1965—; gen. mgr., pres. WCTU-TV, Charlotte, 1967-69; pres. TV Presentations, Inc., 1967-69; gen. mgr., operator WATU-TV, Augusta, Ga., 1968-69. Mem. N.C. Dental Found., 1958—; transp. chmn. Miss N.C. Pageant, 1965. Trustee Boys Home, Lake Waccomaw, N.C., 1966. Served to capt. USAF, 1958-60. Recipient certificate of Merit Charlotte Jr. C. of C., 1962, 63, Spoke award, 1962, Sparkplug award, 1963, 64, 65, 66. Mem. Am., Southeastern (founder, pres.) analgesia socs., Am., N.C. (mem. fed. dental service com. 1970-72, ednl. com. 1973—), Charlotte (chmn. dental soc. radiation study com. 1970-72), Second Dist. dental socs., N.C. Dental Soc. Anesthesiology, Charlotte Analgesia Study Club, U. N.C. Dental Alumni Assn., Delta Sigma Delta, Lambda Chi Alpha. Democrat. Methodist. Home: 4212 Burning Tree Lane Mathews NC 28105 Office: PO Box 12685 4421 Central Av Charlotte NC 28205

TWYMAN, JOSEPH PASCHAL, univ. pres.; b. Prairie Hill, Mo., Nov. 21, 1933; s. William L. and Hazel (Dry) T.; B.A., U. Mo. at Kansas City, 1955, M.A., 1959, Ph.D., 1962; m. Patricia Joanne Harper, July 26, 1953; children—Mark Kevin, Patricia Lynn. Asst. prof., then asso. prof. Okla. State U., 1960-66, asso. dir. Research Found., 1965-66; dir. research U. Mo. at St. Louis, 1966-67; v.p. U. Tulsa, 1967-68, pres., 1968—; cons. in field, 1960—. Mem. adv. panel Southwestern Coop. Ednl. Lab., 1967-68; adv. bd. Tulsa Opera, 1968—, St. John's Hosp., Tulsa, 1969—. Bd. dirs. Okla Council Econ. Edn., 1968—, Tulsa Community Chest, 1968—, Tulsa Civic Ballet, 1968—, Arts Council Tulsa, 1970—, Thomas Gilcrease Museum Assn., 1970—; trustee Undercroft Montessori Sch., Tulsa, 1967-72, Children's Med. Center, Tulsa, 1968-73; Hillcrest Med. Center, Tulsa, 1969—; mem. exec. com. Frontiers of Sci. Found. Okla., 1968—; bd. dirs. Tulsa Mental Health Assn., 1967—, Mid-Continent Research and Devel. Council, 1967-68. Ford Found. grantee, 1963-66, U.S. Office Edn. grantee, 1958-60, 61-62, 62-63, 64-65, 64-66. Mem. A.A.A.S., Am. Acad. Polit. and Social Sci., Phi Delta Kappa, Omicron Delta Kappa. Presbyn. Rotarian. Clubs: Tulsa, Southern Hills, University and Summit (Tulsa). Author: (with others) The Concept of Role Conflict, 1964; also articles. Home: 1775 E 31st St Tulsa OK 74105

TYER, ARNOLD JEROME, engring. co. exec.; b. McCrory, Ark., Sept. 23, 1923; s. John William and Mary (Love) T.; student Hendrix Coll., 1946-47, Little Rock U., 1948-49; B.S. in Civil Engring., U. Ark., 1951; m. Johnnie Mae Sandago, June 8, 1947; children—David, Lee Ann, John, Paul. Party chief T.J. Fricke Engr., Stuttgart, Ark., 1951-52, constrn. engr. Marion L. Crist & Assos., Inc., Little Rock, 1952-56, roject engr., 1956-58, mem. firm, 1958-68, pres., 1968—. Served with F.A., AUS, 1943-46; ETO. Mem. Am. Water Works Assn., Am. Soc. C.E., Nat., Ark. Socs. profl. engrs., Cons. Engrs. Council Ark. (pres. 1966-67, nat. bd. dirs. 1968-69), Ark. Pollution Control Fedn., Ark., Little Rock chambers commerce. Methodist. Home: 1500 Mountain Dr Little Rock AR 72207 Office: 5100 W 12th St Little Rock AR 72204

TYER, GARL LOGAN, SR., transp. co. exec.; b. Ralls, Tex., Jan. 13, 1934; s. Charles E. and Juanita (Travis) T.; B.B.A., Tex. Tech. Coll., 1955; m. Marion L. Cook, June 19, 1953; children—Garl Logan, Kimberly. Sr. accountant Cassel & Co., C.P.A.'s, Lubbock, Tex., 1958-61; asst. to pres. Luther Transfer & Storage Co., 1961-68, sec.-treas., 1961-68; controller, asst. sec. Zuider Zee Oyster, Bar, Inc., Fort Worth, 1968-70; corporate staff Tyler Corp., holding co., Dallas, 1970-72; v.p., controller, asst. sec. C & H Transp. Co., Inc., Dallas, 1973—. Accounting systems cons. for various firms. C.P.A., Tex. Mem. Nat. Assn. Accountants, Am. Inst. C.P.A.'s, Tex. Soc. C.P.A.'s. Kiwanian (pres. 1965). Home: 6173 Whitman St Fort Worth TX 76133 Office: 2010 W Commerce St Dallas TX 75222

TYLER, EVELYN SILLS, educator; b. Greensboro, N.C., Oct. 16, 1919; d. John Hartsell and Martha (Perry) Sills; B.S., East Carolina Coll., 1956; postgrad., U. N.C., 1960, 68; m. Luther Edward Tyler, Aug. 27, 1940; children—Martha (Mrs. Ronald Webster Leonard), Judith (Mrs. Larry Eugene Dancy). Tchr. pub. elementary schs. Lexington, N.C., 1956-61, Greensboro, N.C., 1961—. Mem. evaluation team students in basic programs Nat. Council for Accreditation Tchr. Edn., 1971—; coordinator Polit. Action Com. for Edn., Greensboro, 1971-72; mem. N.C. Bd. Edn., chmn. policies com.; N.C. rep. Edn. Commn. States, 1974—. Bd. dirs. Learning Inst. N.C., chmn. program com. Recipient Ben L. Smith Tchr. of Year award Greensboro Jr. C. of C., 1972. Mem. N.E.A. (life; del. to constl. conv. 1971-72), N.C. Edn. Assn. (pres. state div. classroom tchrs. 1969-71), Assn. Childhood Edn., Alpha Kappa Delta, Kappa Delta Pi. Presbyn. Democrat. Home: 407 Mimosa Dr Greensboro NC 27403 Office: 300 Raleigh St Greensboro NC 27401

TYLER, JOHNNIE MAE WEEKS, ret. educator, civic worker; b. Ozark, Ala., July 28, 1913; d. John Calvin and Lena Lee (Boyett) Weeks; B.S. in Edn., Troy State Coll., 1946; postgrad. Auburn U., 1955-57; diploma in Christian tng. Baptist Sunday Sch. Bd., Nashville, 1961; m. Saxon DeWitt Dykes, Sr., Sept. 23, 1933 (div. Oct. 1963); children—Saxon DeWitt, Catherine Malissa (Mrs. J. D. Nolin Jr.); m. 2d, William Deval Barefoot, Nov. 25, 1964 (dec. Oct. 1968); m. 3d, E. J. Tyler, June 12, 1969. Tchr. elementary schs. Barbour county, Dale county, Ozark, Ala., 1940-69, 6th group Emma P. Flowers Elementary Sch., Ozark Ala., 1955-69, ret., 1969. Grey lady Dale county chpt. A.R.C., Ozark, 1942-44, 1st aid instr., 1942-69; instr. Civil Def., Ozark, 1963-69; civil Def. coordinator for Ariton, Ala. Notary Pub., Justice Peace, Barbour county, 1963-64. Founding fellow So. Soc. Geneologists; mem. Tex. Geneal. Soc., Fedn. Womens' Clubs (chmn. Dale County 1949-51), Beta Sigma Phi. Baptist (librarian ch. 1963). Clubs: Clio Study (pres. 1956-57), Progressive Study (Clio) (pres. 1959-60); Maud Martin Study (Ozark). Contbr. papers to tech. lit., book reviews Ch. Paper Monthly Publ., Clio, 1963. Home: Route 2 Box 186 Ariton AL 36311

TYNES, VICTOR HORACE, dentist; b. Ivandale, Va., Aug. 20, 1915; s. Joseph Walter and Lucy Jane (Rich) T.; B.S., N.C. A. and T. State U., 1940; D.D.S., Howard U., 1950; m. Blossom Hodge Myers, Feb. 11, 1973; children by previous marriage—Victor Horace, Myron Kevan. Practice dentistry, Greensboro, N.C., 1952-53; pub. health dentist Dental Health Div., State Bd. Health, Raleigh, N.C., 1953-56, Guilford County Health Dept., Greensboro, 1956—. Instr. English, dir. publicity N.C. A. and T. State U., 1940-43, lectr., 1956—. Active YMCA. Served with AUS, 1943-45; ETO; to capt. Dental Corps, AUS, 1950-52. Mem. Am., N.C. (chmn. dental sect. 1972-73) pub. health assns., Nat. Dental Assn., Old North State Dental Soc. (pub. dir. 1953-59), Greensboro Med. Soc., N.A.A.C.P., Alpha Kappa Mu. Baptist (trustee). Home: 2308 Dulaire Rd Greensboro NC 27407 Office: PO Box 4264 Greensboro NC 27406

TYRE, EARL LORAN, state hwy. engr.; b. Alma, Ga., Feb. 23, 1924; s. Marion Cleveland and Sarah Ann (Hyers) T.; student U. Ga., 1950-52, Internat. Corr. Schs., 1954-62, Armstrong Coll., 1960; m. Elizabeth Norton, Feb. 4, 1950; children—Norton, Laurie. Rodman Ga. State Hwy. Dept., 1949-50, chinman, 1950, engring. aide, 1950-51, sr. engring. aide, 1951, hwy. project engr., 1951-54, resident hwy. engr., 1954-55; engr. Coffee Constrn. Co., Eastman, Ga., 1955-56; resident hwy. engr. Ga. State Hwy. Dept., 1956-59, road designer, 1959-62, asst. field div. engr., 1962-68, field div. engr., 1968-71, state hwy. maintenance engr., 1971—. Served with AUS, 1944-46. Registered profl. engr., Ga. Mem. Ga. Hwy. Dept. Engrs. Assn. (pres. 1969-70), Am. Legion, V.F.W., Am. Pub. Works Assn. Home: 2000 Surrey Trail Conyers GA 30207 Office: Dept Transp 2 Capitol Sq Atlanta GA 30334

TYRE, WILLIAM HOWARD, constrn. co. exec.; b. Frostproof, Fla., Mar. 11, 1936; s. R. H. and Margaret Tyre; B.A., Fla., State U., 1964; m. Jill Lee Sovilla, Apr. 21, 1962; children—Ashley Howard and Wesley Lee (twins). Salesman, Liberty Nat. Life Ins. Co., Stuart, Fla., 1961-63; asst. city mgr. West Palm Beach Fla., 1964-66, city mgr., 1966-69; v.p. Perini Land & Devel. Co., West Palm Beach, 1969—. Vice pres. Boys Club Am., 1970—; co-chmn. Heart Fund, 1970—; coach Babe Ruth Baseball, 1966, 67; mem. adv. bd. West Palm Beach Municipal Auditorium, 1970-72. Bd. dirs. United Fund, 1966-70, Gulf Stream Goodwill Industries, 1972, Nelle Smith Residence for Girls, 1972, A.R.C. Served with AUS, 1954-57. Mem. Fla. State U. Alumni Assn. (past dir.), Builders Assn. So. Fla. (dir.), Sigma Phi Epsilon. Republican. Methodist. Kiwanian. Home: 701 Cocoplum Circle Unit 8 Fort Lauderdale FL Office: 2070 NW 141st St Opa Locka FL 33054

TYRRELL, GORDON WOODYARD, auto supply co. exec.; b. Mobile, Ala., June 8, 1932; s. Willis W. and Rebecca (Woodyard) T.; B.S. in Bus., Fla. State U., 1954; m. Anibel Kelsey, Sept. 5, 1953; children—Kay, Janet, Kenneth, Steven. With J.C. Penney Co., Tampa, Fla., 1954; pres. Tyrrell's Auto Supply, Inc., Pensacola, Fla., 1958—. Mem. Fla. Ho. of Reps., 1968-72. Chmn. Northwest YMCA. Bd. dirs. Jr. Achievement, Pensacola Symphony Orch. Served with USAF, 1954-57. Mem. Automotive Service Industry Assn. (dist. dir. Young Execs. Forum), Pensacola C. of C., Nat. Rifle Assn. (life), Navy League. Res. Officers Assn., Alpha Kappa Psi. Rotarian (past pres.). Home: 3331 Summit Dr Apt 42 Pensacola FL 32503 Office: PO Box 5608 Pensacola FL 32505

TYRRELL, TIMOTHY JAY, mathematician; b. Greenwich, Conn., June 24, 1947; s. Wallace Bradley and Ethel Remember (Kennedy) T.; B.A., U. South Fla., 1969; m. Patricia Ann Donohoe, June 6, 1969. Applications programmer Oak Ridge Nat. Lab., 1969-70, mem. research staff, environmental program, energy group, 1971—. Mem. Am. Statis. Assn., Am. Econ. Assn., Assn. Computing Machinery. Home: Route 5 Box 273D Gallaher Ferry Dr Lenoir City TN 37771 Office: Oak Ridge Nat Lab PO Box X Oak Ridge TN 37830

TYSON, CHARLES BOOTH, city ofcl.; b. Sparks, Ga., Oct. 5, 1932; s. Sankey Booth and Ila (Moore) T.; B.B.A., Valdosta State Coll., 1959; m. Pauline C. Lovett, Apr. 10, 1955; children—Charles Todd, Lee Ann. Clk. Valdosta (Ga.) Police Dept., 1957-59; tax appraiser, accountant City of Valdosta, Ga., 1959-61, asst. city mgr., 1961-64; city mgr., Kissimmee, Fla., 1964-72; city mgr., Moultrie, Ga., 1972—. Served with AUS, 1952-56. Mem. Colquit County C. of C. (dir. 1972—), Internat. City Mgmt. Assn. (policy com. 1973). Baptist. Mason, Rotarian. Home: 127 Poplar Terrace Moultrie GA 31768 Office: PO Box 380 Moultrie GA 31768

TYSON, JOHN CAIUS, III, judge; b. Montgomery, Ala., Oct. 7, 1926; s. John Caius and Virginia Bragg (Smith) T.; student Gulf Coast Mil. Acad., Gulfport, Miss., 1942-43, The Baylor Sch., Chattanooga, 1943-44; B.S., also LL.B., U. Ala.; m. M. Mae Martin Bryant; children—Mary Harmon, Marc J. Admitted to Ala. bar, 1951, since practiced in Montgomery; asso. Jones, Murray & Stewart, 1951; individual practice, 1952-56; asso. C. H. Wampold, Jr. in gen. practice law, 1956-60; asst. atty. gen. State of Ala., 1959-71; asso. judge Ala. Ct. Criminal Appeals, 1972—; developer Beaumont Estates; dir. Smith & Tyson, Inc. Lectr. continuing legal edn. program U. Ala. Active A.R.C., United Appeal. Served with USCG, 1944-46. mem. Res., 1947-52. Mem. Am., Ala., Montgomery County (exec. com. 1963) bar assns., Am. Judicature Soc., S.A.R. (past pres. Montgomery County chpt., 1st v.p. Ala.), Soc. Pioneers Montgomery (past pres., dir.), Am. Legion, C. of C. Democrat. Episcopalian (vestryman 1957-61, 69-72). Mason (K.T., Shriner). Kiwanian. Clubs: Montgomery Country, Beauvoir (Montgomery). Contbr. to Ala. Lawyer. Home: 3114 Jasmine Rd Montgomery AL 36111 Office: Ala Court Criminal Appeals 316 Judicial Bldg Montgomery AL 36101

UFEN, CHARLES HENRY, economist; b. Norderney, Germany, Dec. 27, 1921; s. George Juergens and Adeline (Speth) U.; came to U.S., 1928, naturalized, 1931; A.B., U. N.C., 1950, M.A., 1963, postgrad., 1963-68, 70-71; m. Diane Gere Deppen; children—Marya, Geer, Sarah. Bank examiner Fed. Deposit Ins. Corp., 1952-60; instr., lectr. dept. econs. N.C. State U., Raleigh, 1961-64, asst. prof., 1964-70, economist Center for Urban Affairs and Community Services, 1971—, lectr. dept. econs., 1971—. Research cons. Fed. Res. Bank Richmond, 1963, Econ. Devel. Adminstrn., 1968-69. Served with AUS, 1942-46. Decorated Bronze Star medal. Mem. Am., So. econ. assns., Am., So. finance assns., Phi Eta Sigma, Delta Phi Alpha. Home: 4208 Rowan St Raleigh NC 27609

UHL, HENRY STEPHEN MAGRAW, physician, educator; b. Wilkes-Barre, Pa., July 23, 1921; s. John Hamilton and Rebecca (Magraw) U.; A.B., Princeton, 1943; M.D., Harvard, 1947; M.A. (hon.), Brown U., 1967; m. Louise Powell Butler, Nov. 30, 1946; 1 dau., Meredith Louise. Asst. in pathology and anatomy Johns Hopkins Med. Sch., 1947-49; intern, resident pathology Johns Hopkins Hosp., 1947-49; intern medicine Henry Ford Hosp., 1949-50; resident, fellow, research asso. Wayne State U., 1950-53; dir. med. edn. Worcester (Mass.) City Hosp., 1953-58; med. dir., cons. Postgrad. Med. Inst., Boston, 1955-60, dir., 1967—; dir. med. edn. and research Springfield (Mass.) Hosp., 1958-60; asst. dir. regional hosp. program, asso. prof. postgrad. medicine Albany Med. Coll., 1960-66; prof. med. sci., asso. dir. inst. of life scis., dir. continuing med. edn.

Brown U., Providence, after 1966; cons. R.I. Center Gen. Hosp. State coordinator Tri-State Regional Med. Program, after 1968; now dir. Area Health Edn. Center, Asheville, N.C.; prof. medicine U. N.C.; cons. on med. edn. and med. care to numerous hosps. Bd. dirs. R.I. Council of Community Services; trustee St. Joseph's, Lady of Fatima hosps., Providence. Diplomate Am. Bd. Internal Medicine. Fellow A.C.P.; mem. Am. Fedn. Clin. Research, Assn. for Hosp. Med. Edn. (pres. 1958-60), Assn. Am. Med. Colls. Clubs: Downtown City, Biltmore Forest Country (Asheville); Princeton (N.Y.C.). Editorial bd. Hosp. Practice, 1967—. Home: 12 Northwood Rd Asheville NC 28804 Office: 509 Biltmore Av Asheville NC 28801

UHR, ROBERT JONES, gas co. exec.; b. San Antonio, Sept. 15, 1910; s. Robert Frederick and Alvina Augusta (Tampke) U.; B.S. in Elec. Engring., Tex. A. and M. U., 1933; m. Margaret T. Richter, Sept. 15, 1936; children—Barry Wayne, Bonnie (Mrs. Richard E. Denson). Jr. engr. San Antonio Pub. Service Co., 1933-41; div. engr. Entex Inc., New Braunfels, Tex., 1945-55, dist. mgr., 1955—; dir. Guaranty State Bank, New Braunfels. Bd. dirs. New Braunfels Indsl. Found. Served with USAAF, 1941-46. Recipient Friend of 4-H award, 1971. Mem. S. Tex. (dir. 1967-70), Comal County (dir. 1960-63, 69-71), chambers commerce. Mem. United Ch. of Christ (mem. council 1966-72). Home: PO Box 723 New Braunfels TX 78130 Office: PO Box 471 New Braunfels TX 78130

UITERWYK, JAN CHRISTIAAN, shipping exec.; b. Amsterdam, Netherlands, May 16, 1915; s. Daniel and Dina Cornelia (Verhagen) U.; B.A., U. Amsterdam, 1938; m. Maria Alberts, Oct. 4, 1939; children—Robert Hendrik, Jan Daniel, Hendrik. Came to U.S., 1949, naturalized, 1955. Clk., Wels Van Hasselt, Amsterdam, 1935-36; sec. to pres. Klisser & Citroen, Amsterdam, 1936-37; v.p. Alberts & Morel, Amsterdam, 1937-40, exec. v.p., 1940-49, pres., N.Y.C., 1949-52; dept. mgr. W.R. Grace & Co., N.Y.C., 1952-54; br. mgr. Maurice Pincoffs Co., Tampa, Fla., 1954-56; pres. Jan C. Uiterwyk Co., Inc., Tampa, 1956—; pres., chmn. bd. dirs. Jan C. Uiterwyk Co., New Orleans, 1963—, N.Y.C., 1965—, Houston, 1966—, Chgo., 1967—; pres., dir. Uiterwyk Shipping, Ltd., Nassau, Bahamas, 1964—, Uiterwyk Cold Storage Co., Tampa; dir. Pan Am. Bank, Tampa. Hon. consul of Belgium. Past pres. Girls Club, Tampa. Mem. C. of C. Presbyn. Clubs: Palma Ceia Golf and Country, Krewe of Venus, University (Tampa); Plimsoll (New Orleans). Home: 10000 Lindelaan Tampa FL 33618 Office: 715 E Bird St Tampa FL 33604

UJHELY, VALENTINE ANTHONY, physician; b. Budapest, Hungary, July 9, 1886; s. Balint and Emilia (Blaw) U.; Med. diploma, Royal Hungarian U., 1920; m. Olga-Marit Hildeborg Ness, May 16, 1943. Came to U.S., 1923, naturalized, 1930. Resident Met. Sanatorium, Budapest, 1920-23; physician in charge psychotherapy city and state hosps., Phila., Milw., and Providence, 1923-30; physician in charge psychotherapy VA Hosps., N.Y.C., Bath, N.Y., Brecksville, O., and Cleve., 1941-46; neuropsychiatrist Municipal Hosp., Washington, 1946-47; chief neuropsychiatrist Walter Reed Army Hosp., Washington, 1947-48; med. rating specialist, sec. bd. neuropsychiat. cons. Vet.'s Benefit Office VA, Washington, 1948-65; practice medicine specializing in psychiatry, psychoanalysis and neurology, Washington, 1964—; neuropsychiat. dir. Hildeborg House Research Project, Washington, 1950-63; med. dir. Bionomic Research League and Library, 1964—. Served as 1st asst. med. officer Hungarian Army, 1918-19. Recipient pin 30 years service U.S. Govt., 1959, award sustained superior performance VA, 1960. Diplomate Am. Bd. Psychiatry and Neurology. Mem. Acad. Mental Health and Religion (charter), Am. Acad. Neurology, Am. Psychiat. Assn., A.M.A., So. Med. Assn., Cleveland Park Citizens Assn. Contbr. articles to profl. jours. Research visuo-acoustical instrumentation hypoanalysis. Address: 3307 Macomb St NW Washington DC 20008

ULBRICHT, HERBERT HENRY, JR., architect; b. San Marcos, Tex., Jan. 4, 1923; s. Herbert Henry and Stella (Starke) U.; B.Arch., U. Tex., 1949; m. Martha Nunn, Dec. 18, 1947; children—Kirk S., Herbert Henry III. With Nunn, Nunn & Ulbricht, architects, Houston, 1955-61; pvt. archtl. practice as Herbert Ulbricht, Jr., architect, Houston, 1961—. Mem. Bellaire Planning Commn., 1966-68. Served as capt. USAF, 1941-44. Decorated Air medal, D.F.C. (U.S.); Belguique Forte-Guerre. Mem. A.I.A. (chpt. sec. 1956), Tex. Soc. Architects, Houston Power Squadron (comdr. 1968). Kiwanian (pres. 1967). Prin. archtl. works include: Meml. Bank Bldg., Anson Jones Elementary Sch., Lee High Sch. Home: 5239 Loch Lomond St Houston TX 77035 Office: 2727 Kirby Dr Houston TX 77006

ULM, RUBY FLOREE (MRS. ANDERSON C. ULM), librarian; b. Lee, Fla., July 4, 1920; d. William Irwin and Kathleen Tidwell (Lockhart) McCullough; B.S., Fla. State U., 1950, M.S. in L.S., 1957; m. Anderson C. Ulm, July 26, 1940; children—Sandra Wynell, Irwin Anderson. Tchr. Madison County Elementary Schs., Madison, Fla., 1937-54; librarian Madison High Sch., 1954-66; part-time librarian N. Fla. Jr. Coll., Madison, 1959-66, periodicals librarian, 1966—. Mem. vis. com. So. Assn. Colls. and Schs., 1960, 69, 70. Bd. dirs. Fla. Tb. and Respiratory Disease Assn. Mem. Am., Fla. library assns., Nat., Fla., Madison County (pres. 1953-54) edn. assns., Fla. Assn. Sch. Librarians (pres. 1967-68), Fla. Audio Visual Assn., Delta Kappa Gamma, Beta Phi Mu. Club: Madison Woman's (pres. 1970-72). Home: Route 1 Box 129 Lee FL 32059 Office: N Fla Jr Coll Library Madison FL 32340

UMPIERRE-SUAREZ, ENRIQUE, lawyer; b. San Juan, P.R., Oct. 12, 1941; s. Francisco and Felicia (Suarez) U.; B.C.E., Coll. Agr. and Mech. Arts, 1964; LL.B., U. P.R., 1970; m. Aglae Suarez, Mar. 20, 1965; children—Aglae, Enrique II, Denise Marie, Liza Margarita. Project engr. P.R. Water Resources Authority, 1965-68; pres. El Morro Equipment Rental, 1967—; cons. engr. V.M. Garcia Assos., 1969—; admitted to P.R. bar, 1970; counsellor, atty. at law Enrique Umpierre-Suarez, San Juan, 1970—; dir. Golden Mile Restaurants. Precinct pres. Popular Democratic party P.R., 1968—, senatorial dist. rep. to central council, 1968—. Mem. Am. Soc. C.E. (sec.-treas. San Juan chpt. 1968), Inst. Architects, Engrs. and Surveyors P.R. (sec. bd. dirs. 1970-71). Home: 603 El ferrol Apts Hato Rey PR 00918 Office: PO Box 5003 San Juan PR 00936

UNDERHILL, GARY MADISON, credit agy. exec.; b. Richmond, Va., Jan. 20, 1910; s. Ira Dixon and Roselynne E. (Terrell) U.; student U. Richmond, 1929-30; B.S., U. Va., 1932; m. Sarah Jane Reed, Dec. 28, 1936; children—Sarah Reed, Gary M., Thurlow R. Stenographer, clk. So. & C. & O. Rys., Richmond, 1926-28; sec. to pres. Bank of Va., Richmond, 1928-29, asst. to pres., 1932-36, asst. v.p., 1937-44, sec. to Ernest Woodruff, Atlanta, 1936-37; exec. dir. Consumer Bankers Assn., 1945-48; exec. v.p. Charter Bank, Phila., 1948-49; v.p. Girard Trust Bank, Phila., 1949-52; pres., dir. First Nat. Bank of Raleigh (N.C.), 1952-59; sr. v.p. N.C. Nat. Bank, Charlotte, 1959-66; pres. Bus. Devel. Corp. N.C., Raleigh, 1966—. Served as lt. USNR, 1944-45. Mem. Kappa Sigma, Alpha Kappa Psi, Phi Beta Kappa. Episcopalian. Club: Carolina Country. Home: 3111 Eton Rd Raleigh NC 27608 Office: 401 Oberlin Rd Raleigh NC 27605

UNDERHILL, WILLIAM AMORY, lawyer; b. Basinger, Fla., Feb. 21, 1910; s. Wilford Perry and Martha Mabel (Alderman) U.; LL.B., John B. Stetson U., 1936; LL.D., 1969. Admitted to Fla. bar, 1936, D.C. bar, 1952, U.S. Supreme Ct. bar, 1946; practicing lawyer, Deland, Fla., 1936-42, pros. atty., 1940-42; with Dept. Justice, Washington, 1946-52, spl. atty. alien property sect., claims div., 1946-47, spl. atty. vets. affairs sect., 1947, spl. atty., spl. asst. to atty. gen., Office Dept. Atty. Gen., 1947-48, 1st asst. to asst. atty. gen. in charge anti-trust div., 1948-50, acting asst. atty. gen., 1950-51, 1st asst. to dep. atty. gen., 1951, acting dep. atty. gen., 1951, asst. atty. gen. charge lands div., 1951-52; now practicing in Washington, and DeLand, Fla. Asso. dir. Young Democrats Am., 1946. Bd. overseers, Stetson U. Law Sch., St. Petersburg, Fla.; bd. dirs. Law Center Found., St. Petersburg, Inc., pres., 1971—; trustee St. Leo (Fla.) Coll., Bert Fish Testamentary Trust. Served to lt. comdr. USNR, 1942-45. Recipient George Washington Honor medal award Freedoms Found., Valley Forge, 1970, Ben C. Willard award Stetson Lawyers Assn., 1970, C.H.I.E.F. award Ind. Colls. and Univs. Fla., 1974, Distinguished Alumni award Stetson U., 1974; William Amory Underhill Scholarships created Stetson U., 1974. Mem. Deland (pres. 1938), Fla. State (v.p. 1939) jr. chambers of commerce, D.C. Bar, Am., Fed., Volusia County bar assns., Fla. Bar, Fla. Council 100, Stetson U. Alumni Assn. (pres. 1971), Underhill Soc. Am., Mil. Order World Wars, Am. Legion, Phi Alpha Delta, Pi Kappa Phi, Theta Alpha Phi. Elk, Mason (K.T.). Home: 145 N Garfield Av DeLand FL 32720 Office: PO Box 66 DeLand FL 32720 also 1625 K St NW Washington DC 20006

UNDERWOOD, ARTHUR LOUIS, JR., educator; b. Rochester, N.Y., May 18, 1924; s. Arthur Louis and Grace (Porter) U.; B.S., U. Rochester, 1944, Ph.D., 1951; m. Elizabeth Knapp Emery, June 30, 1948; children—Paul, Robert, Susan. Research asso. U. Rochester Atomic Energy Project, 1946-51; research asso. chemistry Mass. Inst. Tech., Cambridge, 1951-52; asst. prof. chemistry Emory U., Atlanta, 1952-58, asso. prof., 1958-62, prof., 1962—; research asso. in chemistry Cornell U., Ithaca, N.Y., 1959-60. Served with USNR, 1944-46. Fellow A.A.A.S.; mem. Am. Chem. Soc., Am. Assn. U. Profs., Phi Beta Kappa, Sigma Xi. Author: (with R.A. Day, Jr.) Quantitative Analysis, 3d edit., 1974. Contbr. articles to research jours. Home: 1354 Springdale Rd NE Atlanta GA 30306

UNDERWOOD, DAVID MILTON, security co. exec.; b. Houston, Mar. 5, 1937; s. Milton Ramon and Catherine (Fondren) U.; grad. Phillips Acad., Andover, Mass., 1954; B.A., Yale, 1958; postgrad. Inst. Investment Banking, Wharton Sch. Finance, U. Pa., 1969; m. Lynda Knapp, Nov. 21, 1964; children—David Milton, Catherine F., Duncan Knapp. With Morgan Stanley & Co., N.Y.C., 1962; with Underwood, Neuhaus & Co., investment bankers, Houston, 1962—, v.p., 1966-74, sr. v.p., 1974—, dir., 1968—; pres. Feliciana Corp., Houston, 1966—, Pano Tech Exploration Co., Houston, 1972—; dir. Fannin Bank. Adv. com. U. Houston, Coll. Bus. Adminstrn., 1966—. Trustee, Fondren Found., Meth. Hosp., Kinkaid Sch. Served to capt. AUS, 1958-60, 61-62. Decorated Army Commendation medal. Mem. Zeta Psi. Republican. Episcopalian Clubs: Houston Country, River Oaks Country, Bayou, Ramada, Houston, Allegro, Sarabande, University (Houston); Yale (N.Y.C.). Home: 3645 Willowick Rd Houston TX 77019 Office: 724 Travis St Houston TX 77002

UNDERWOOD, GREGORY LEE, lawyer; b. Ryan, Okla., Jan. 6, 1939; s. Frank A. and June (Brown) U.; B.A. with honors, U. Tex., 1961, J.D., 1964; m. Norma Jeane Hillyer, Jan. 28, 1961; children—Kenneth Sean, Michael Kevin, Patrick Tyler. Admitted to Tex. bar, 1964; asso. firm Stark & Davey, Gainesville, 1964-68; partner firm Carroll & Underwood and predecessor firm, Gainesville, 1968—; dir. Internat. Polymer Corp., Underwood Mfg. Co., others. Judge City of Gainesville, 1971—; pres. Sam Houston Edn. Found., 1966-67. Recipient Sam Houston award, 1964. Mem. Am., Tex., Cooke County (pres. 1969-71) bar assns. Methodist (chmn. evangelism 1972—). Home: 1804 E California St Gainesville TX 76240 Office: 114 N Dixon St Gainesville TX 76240

UNDERWOOD, JAMES WILBUR, realtor; b. Sebastopol, Miss., May 5, 1921; s. R. Marvin and Della (Shealy) U.; student Draughn's Bus. Coll., 1938-39, U. Mich., 1946, U. Tenn., 1947, U. Ill., 1958, U. Va., 1966; m. Martha Varnado, May 16, 1943; children—Thomas Madison. Pres., J.W. Underwood & Co., Jackson, Miss., 1948—; chmn. bd. Underwood Ins. Agy., Inc., Homestead Savings & Loan Assn., Jackson, Miss.; dir. Deposit Guaranty Nat. Bank, Jackson, Miss. Pres. United Givers Fund, Jackson, 1960; pres. Andrew Jackson council Boy Scouts Am., 1962. Vice-pres. bd. trustees Jackson (Miss.) Pub. Schs., 1967-72. Bd. dirs. Goodwill Industries; trustee, chmn. exec. com. Miss. Bapt. Hosp. Served with USNR, 1942-45. Mem. Nat. Assn. Home Builders (life, dir. 1946—), Miss. Real Estate Assn., Jackson Real Estate Bd., Jackson Home Builders Assn. (pres. 1949-50), Jackson C. of C. (pres. 1960). Kiwanian. Club: Jackson Country (v.p. 1963—). Home: 6049 Woodlea Rd Jackson MS 39206 Office: PO Box 54 Jackson MS 39205

UNGERMAN, IRVINE E., lawyer; b. Leavenworth, Kan., May 12, 1908; s. William and Rachel (Ettleman) U.; LL.B., Washburn U., 1930; m. Hanna Friedberg, Apr. 13, 1929; children—Maynard I., Rowena Mae (Mrs. David Galeaston). Admitted to Okla. bar, 1930; since practiced in Tulsa; mem. firm Ungerman, Grabel, Ungerman and Leiter, 1930—. Gen. counsel, sec., dir. Boulder Bank & Trust Co. Pres. Tulsa Hebrew Sch., 1949-51; pres. Okla. Bd. Corrections, 1971—. Bd. govs. Washburn U. Law Sch. Fellow Am. Coll. Trial Lawyers, Comml. Law League Found.; mem. Internat., Am., Okla., Tulsa County bar assns., Am. Judicature Soc., Nat. Assn. Def-Counsel, Am., Okla. (v.p. 1973-74) trial lawyers assns., Comml. Law League Am. Club: Meadowbrook Country (sec. 1952-65), University, Summit. Jewish religion (pres. congregation). Home: 2230 E 39th St Tulsa OK 74105 Office: Wright Bldg Tulsa OK 74103

UNTERKOEFLER, ERNEST, bishop; b. Phila., Aug. 17, 1917; s. Ernest L. and Anna Rose (Chambers) U; A.B., Cath. U. Am., 1940, S.T.L., 1944, J.C.D,, 1950. Ordained priest Roman Cath. Ch., 1944; asst. pastor Richmond, Va., 1944-47, 50-60, Arlington, Va., 1947-50, sec. Richmond Diocesan Tribunal, 1954-60; moderator Council Cath. Women, 1956-61; chancellor Richmond Diocese, 1960-62, vicar gen., 1962-64, papal chamberlain, 1961; aux. bishop Richmond, titular bishop Latopolis, 1962-64; bishop of Charleston (S.C.), 1965—. Sec., U.S. Cath. Bishops Meeting, 1963; asst. sec. adminstrv. bd. Nat. Cath. Welfare Conf. (now U.S. Cath. Conf.), 1963-66, sec., mem. com. on budget and finance, adminstrv. bd., 1966-69; sec. Nat. Conf. Cath. Bishops, 1966-69, mem. com. for dept. internat. affairs, 1971—, ad hoc com. on women in church and society, 1971—, chmn. region IV, 1972—; mem. Nat. Conf. Cath. Bishops' Commn. for Ecumenical and Interreligious Affairs, 1965-69, cons., 1969—, chmn. sub-commn. for dialogue with Presbyn. and Reform Roman Catholic-Anglican Joint Sub-Commn. on Theology of Marriage, 1967—; mem. Com. on Social Devel. and World Peace, 1971—; chmn. Bishops' Com. on Permanent Diaconate, 1968-71; dir. Center for Applied Research in the Apostolate, 1969—, pres., 1972—; co-chmn. Charleston Religious Com. for Bicentennial. Mem. alumni bd. govs. Cath. U. Am. Recipient Pax Christi award St. John's U., 1970. Home: 114 Broad St Charleston SC 29401 Office: 119 Broad St Charleston SC 29401

UPDEGRAFF, NORMAN CONWELL, refractory co. exec.; b. New Haven, July 6, 1917; s. Robert Rawls and Florence (Engstrom) U.; A.B., Harvard Coll., 1940; m. Patricia Ropke, Jan. 14, 1943; children—Elisabeth (Mrs. Clyde H. Foshee, Jr.), Robert Franklin, David Karl. Chem. engr. Gen. Foods Corp., Hoboken, N.J., 1940-42; chem. engr. E.I. duPont de Nemours & Co., Louisville, 1942-46; asst. tech. dir. Girdler Corp., Louisville, 1946-59; pres. Louisville Fire Brick Works, 1960—. Mem. Am. Ceramic Soc. (chmn. Louisville sect. 1973). Presbyn. Clubs: Louisville Boat, Arts of Louisville. Home: 2564 Cherosen Rd Louisville KY 40205 Office: PO Box 21155 Louisville KY 40221

UPSHAW, JEFFERSON DAVIS, JR., physician; b. Louise, Miss., July 19, 1929; s. Jefferson Davis and Christine (Ferguson) U.; B.S., U. Ala., 1950; M.D., Johns Hopkins U., 1954; m. Grace Hall, July 3, 1953; children—Grace Christine, Jefferson Davis III, Henry Walker. Intern medicine Johns Hopkins Hosp., Balt., 1954-55, asst. resident medicine, 1955-56, 57-59, fellow in medicine, 1959-60, chief resident pvt. med. service, 1960-61; clin. asst. prof. medicine, then asso. prof. U. Tenn. Coll. Medicine, Bapt. Meml. Hosp., Memphis, 1964—, also dir. intern tng. Served to capt. USAF, 1956-58. Fellow A.C.P.; mem. Memphis Acad. Internal Medicine (v.p.), Johns Hopkins Med. and Surg. Assn., Am., Tenn., Memphis, Shelby County med. assns., Am. Soc. Internal Medicine, Phi Beta Kappa, Sigma Xi, Omicron Delta Kappa, Sigma Pi Sigma, Alpha Epsilon Delta, Alpha Omega Alpha, Methodist. Clubs: University, Chickasaw Country (Memphis). Home: 6225 Green Meadows St Memphis TN 38138 Office: 969 Madison Av Memphis TN 38104

UPTON, JOSEPH FURMAN, telephone co. engr.; b. Greenville, S.C., July 19, 1945; s. Julian Foy and Mary (Ashmore) U.; B.E.E., The Citadel, 1966; m. Carolyn Ann Guillotte, Oct. 15, 1966; children—Joel Franklin, Timothy Oneil. Mgmt. asst. So. Bell. Tel. & Tel. Co., Columbia, S.C., 1966-70, engr., 1970-73, supervising engr., 1973—. Served with AUS, 1966-69. Decorated Bronze Star medal. Mem. I.E.E.E. (chmn. membership and transfers com. 1972-73).

URBAN, CURTIS JOHN, accountant; b. Giddings, Tex., Jan. 11, 1940; s. Oscar Wilhelm and Esther (Bigon) U.; student Tex. Luth. Coll., 1958-60; B.B.A., U. Tex., 1962; m. Bernice Evelyn Mitschke, June 9, 1962; children—Trae Anthony, Timothy Aaron. Accounting supr. Cameron Iron Works, Houston, 1963-69; chief accountant Hertz Equipment Rental, Houston, 1969-71; treas. Invader Corp., Giddings, 1971-73; pvt. practice as C.P.A., Giddings, 1973—. Bd. dirs. Lee County Recreation. Served with AUS, 1962-63. C.P.A., Tex. Lutheran (treas. 1966-71.). Lion (v.p. 1972-74). Club: Cummings Creek Country. Home: 550 S Williams St Giddings TX 78942 Office: Hwy 290 E PO Box 204 Giddings TX 78942

URBINA, PEDRO YVO JOSE, corp. cons., lawyer; b. Trujilo, Venezuela, Apr. 2, 1898; s. Pedro Y.J. and Josefa (Delgado) U.; LL.B., Nat. U., 1921, postgrad., 1922-23; LL.M., 1922, Master Patent Law, 1922; J.D., George Washington U., 1968; m. Emily Frances Grigg, May 19, 1923; children—Pepita L. (Mrs. Kenneth M. Kauffman), Pedro Yvo Jose (dec.). Came to U.S., 1919, naturalized, 1922. Admitted to D.C. bar, 1922, Mass. bar, 1928; clk. U.S. Govt. Interior Dept. Bur. Indian Affairs, Washington, 1919-22, law clk., 1922-27; atty. Law Dept. United Fruit Co., Boston, 1927-64, cons. atty., 1965—. Served with USCG Temp. Res., 1942-44. Decorated Medal of Liberty. Mem. Am. Bar Assn. Clubs: National Lawyers (Washington); New Orleans Athletic; University (Boston). Home: The Thames Apt 205 2825 St Charles Av New Orleans LA 70115

URQUHART, SAMUEL LESTER, savs. and loan exec.; b. Norfolk, Va., Feb. 7, 1915; s. Samuel Lawrence and Eva Marion (Lester) U.; B.S., Wilberforce U., 1939; m. Edith Naomi Bedgood, Apr. 3, 1942; 1 dau., Sharon Lynelle. Pvt. practice pub. accounting, Newport News, Va., 1940—; v.p., mgr. Community Savs. & Loan Assn., 1957—. Mem. Newport News-Hampton Bd. Realtors. Chmn. area div., orgn. and extension com. Boy Scouts Am., 1957-59. Served with AUS, 1943-46. Mem. Peninsula C. of C., Nat. Soc. Pub. Accountants, Nat. Bus. League, Nat. Assn. Real Estate Brokers, V.F.W. (past post comdr.), Omega Psi Phi. Baptist. Mason (Shriner). Clubs: 533 (Richmond, Va.), Dochiki Social and Civic. Home: 1347 26th St Newport News VA 23607 Office: 1512 27th St Newport News VA 23607

URRY, DAN WESLEY, biochemist; b. Salt Lake City, Sept. 14, 1935; s. Herbert William and Emma Irene (Swaner) U.; B.A., Ph.D., U. Utah, 1964; m. Janet Ruth Mills, July 3, 1958 (div. July 1970); children—Weston Daniel, Douglas Whitmore, David William. Post doctoral fellow U. Utah, 1964, corp. fellow Harvard, 1964-65; vis. investigator Chem., Biodynamics Lab., U. Cal. at Berkeley, 1965-66; asso. mem. Inst. Biomed. Research, Chgo., 1965-69, mem. 1969-70; prefessorial lectr. U. Chgo., 1967-70; prof. biochemistry U. Ala. Med. Center, Birmingham, 1970—, dir. div. molecular biophysics 1970-72, dir. lab. molecular biophysics, 1972—. Mem. Am. Chem. Soc. (Gt. Lakes area div. chmn. biochemistry, 1969), Am. Soc. Biol. Chemists, A.A.A.S., Sigma Xi, Phi Beta Kappa, Phi Kappa Phi, Phi Eta Sigma. Editor: Spectroscopic Approaches to Biomolecular Conformation. Editorial bd. Research/Devel. mag., 1969—, Biochimica Et Biophysica Acta, 1972—. Research on biomolecular conformation and its relationship to biol. function, e.g., biol. calcification and atherosclerosis, ion transport, structure of biomembranes, antibiotics. Home: 2423 Vestavia Dr Birmingham AL 35216 Office: U Ala University Sta Birmingham AL 35294

USDANE, WILLIAM MILLER, govt. ofcl.; b. Seattle, July 29, 1914; s. Louis and Jennie (Miller) U.; B.A., U. Wash., 1936, M.A., 1940; Ph.D., N.Y. U., 1955; m. Bernice Stusser, Dec. 5, 1943; children—Lynn (Mrs. David Millard), Mark. Vocational adviser VA, Seattle, 1946-50; dir. vocational rehab. Inst. for Crippled and Disabled, N.Y.C., 1950-56; prof. rehab. counseling, San Francisco State Coll., 1956-63; div. chief research and demonstration, Dept. Heatlh, Edn. and Welfare Social and Rehab. Service, Washington, 1963-69; dir. office of research Dept. of Labor, Washington, 1969-70; asst. commr. rehab. services adminstrn. Dept. Health, Edn. and Welfare, Washington, 1970—. Pres. Woodly House, Washington, 1968-69; mem. research bd. Easter Seal Found., Nat. Soc. for Crippled Children and Adults, 1963—. Served with AUS, 1942-45. Fulbright sr. research fellow London Sch. Econs., U. London, 1962-63. Mem. Am. Psychol. Assn. (pres. div.). Contbr. articles to profl. jours. Home: 931 6th St SW Washington DC 20024 Office: Dept of HEW 330 C St SW Washington DC 20201

USDIN, GENE LEONARD, physician, psychiatrist; b. N.Y.C., Jan. 31, 1922; s. I. L. and Eva (Miller) U.; student U. N.C., 1939-40, U. Fla., 1940-41; B.S., Tulane U., 1943, M.D., 1946; m. Cecile Weil, Nov. 8, 1947; children—Cecile Catherine, Linda Ann, Steven William, Thomas Michael. Intern Touro Infirmary, New Orleans, 1946-47; jr. asst., asst. resident psychiatry Cin. Gen. Hosp., 1949-51; fellow psychiatry, Tulane Sch. Medicine, 1951-52; pvt. practice psychiatry, New Orleans, 1952—; asst. prof. clin. psychiatry Tulane Sch. Medicine, 1959-62, asso. prof. clin. psychiatry, 1962-67; asso. prof. clin. psychiatry La. State U. Sch. Medicine, 1967-71, prof. clin. psychiatry, 1971—; prof. psychiatry Notre Dame Sem., 1969—; chief div. neurology and psychiatry Touro Infirmary, New Orleans, 1962-66, dir. psychiat. services, 1966-71; sr. vis. psychiatrist at DePaul & Charity Hosps.; past chmn. psychiat. cons. com. Am. Bar Found. Asst. examiner Am. Bd. Psychiatry and Neurology, 1956—. Trustee United Fund Greater New Orleans, 1966-70. Served to lt.

(j.g.) USNR, 1947-49. Diplomate Am. Bd. Neurology and Psychiatry, Am. Bd. Legal Medicine. Fellow Am. Psychiat. Assn. (chmn. com. psychiatry and law 1964-68, com. on ethics 1970—), Am. Coll. Psychiatrists (bd. regents 1967-70), So. (v.p. 1965-66, pres. 1973-74), La. (past pres.) psychiat. assns., Acad. Psychosomatic Medicine (exec. council), Am. Psychosomatic Soc., New Orleans Soc. Psychiatry and Neurology (past pres.), Group Advancement Psychiatry (chmn. com. psychiatry and law 1963-67, trustee, 1970—), mem. Am., So. (bd. regents 1969-72, chmn. 1971-72) med. assns., Am. Acad. Forensic Scis., La. (chmn. com. mental health), Orleans Parish med. socs., Nat. Assn. Mental Health (profl. adv. council). Rotarian. Author articles in field, Editor-in-chief Psychiatry Digest, 1964-71; bd. editors Mental Hygiene, 1969—, Clin. Medicine, 1965-71, Med. Digest, 1965-71; editor books: Psychoneurosis & Schizophrenia, 1966; Practical Lectures in Psychiatry for the Medical Practitioner, 1966; Adolescence: Care and Counseling, 1967; Perspectives on Violence, 1972; The Psychiatric Forum, 1972; Sleep Research and Clinical Practice, 1973; Psychiatry: Education and Image, 1973. Editor (with Peter A. Martin and A.W. Sipe); A Physician in the General Practice of Psychiatry, 1970. Home: 3 Newcomb Blvd New Orleans LA 70118 Office: 1522 Aline St New Orleans LA 70115

USRY, HERBERT MILTON, hosp. adminstr.; b. Dallas, May 20, 1917; s. Lee Milton and Maude Mae (Goss) U.; B.A. in Social Sci., Howard Payne Coll., Brownwood, Tex., 1945; B.S. in Hosp. Adminstrn., Okla. Bapt. U., 1961; m. Irene Rothell, May 11, 1940; 1 son, William. Commd. 1st lt. U.S. Army, 1945, advanced through grades to maj., 1955; chaplain, 1945-57; ret., 1957; credit and collections mgr. Grand Valley Hosp., Pryor, Okla., 1957-58, adminstrv. asst., 1958-59, asst. adminstr., 1959-62, adminstr., 1962—. N.E. rep. Bapt. Found. Okla. Mem. Am. Coll. Hosp. Adminstrs., Acad. Med. Adminstrs., Protestant Hosp. Assn. Mason, Rotarian. Home: Route 2 Box 23 Adair OK 74330 Office: 1111 E Center St Pryor OK 74361

USRY, LUTHER WALLACE, realtor; b. Gadsden, Ala., Sept. 2, 1913; s. Henry H. and Eliza (Bryant) U.; A.B., Samford U., 1937; m. Lillian Ruth Royal, Oct. 5, 1932; 1 dau., Charlotte Jane (Mrs. Max Seldon Bobo). Ordained to ministry Bapt. Ch., 1936; pastor Bellevue Bapt. Ch., Gadsden, 1936-46, James Meml. Bapt. Ch., Gadsden, 1946-54; broker Harris-Usry, Co., Gadsden, 1964—; now owner Usry Realty Co., Gadsden. Mem. Ala. Real Estate Bd. (dir. 1965—, finance com. 1967—), Gadsden Real Estate Bd. (pres. 1966—, dir. 1967—), Etowah Bapt. Assn. (mem. exec. com. 1935-54, clk., treas., 1949-54), Ala. Real Estate Assn. (dir. 1969), C. of C. Mason. Home: 147 Washington Circle Gadsden AL 35901 Office: 1137 Forrest Av Gadsden AL 35901

USSERY, ROBERT MARSHALL, ednl. adminstr.; b. Rockingham, N.C., Jan. 21, 1943; s. Robert Marshall and Lottie (Croom) U.; A.A., Wingate Coll., 1963; B.S., East Carolina U., 1966, M.A., 1971; m. Sylvia Jane Hancock, Aug. 25, 1963; children—Sahara Mon, Lea Mavourneen. Tchr. math. Grainger High Sch., Kinston, N.C., 1966-68; research asst. East Carolina U., 1968-69, research asso., 1969-70, dir. Office Institutional Research, 1970—; mem. adv. council Nat. Center for Higher Edn. Systems. Mem. N.C. Assn. Instnl. Research (exec. sec. 1972-74), Nat. Assn. Instl. Research, Phi Delta Kappa, Pi Mu Epsilon, Alpha Mu Gamma. Home: Route 3 Box 121 Greenville NC 27834 Office: PO Box 2721 Greenville NC 27834

UTLEY, CLIFTON GARRICK, TV corr.; b. Chgo., Nov. 19, 1939; s. Clifton Maxwell and Frayn (Garrick) U.; B.A., Carleton Coll., 1961; postgrad. Free U. Berlin (Germany), 1962-63. TV corr. news dept. NBC, 1963—, aasignments in Brussels, Belgium, 1963-64, Vietnam, 1964-65, Chgo., 1966, N.Y.C., 1966, Berlin, 1966-68, chief bur., Paris, France, 1968-70, Washington, 1970—. Served with AUS, 1961-62. Office: 4001 Nebraska Av NW Washington DC 20016

UTTERBACK, DONALD DESMOND, oil and mining co. exec.; b. Edmore, Mich., Aug. 18, 1904; s. Chelsey Chalmers and Margaret (Henderson) U.; B.S., U. Ill., 1930, M.S., 1932, Ph.D., 1936; m. Naomi Wyninger, July 23, 1936; 1 dau., Beverly June (Mrs. Eldridge). Sr. geologist Tex. Co., New Orleans, 1936-46; dist. geologist Houston Oil Co. Tex., 1946-51; v.p. exploration Freeport Oil Co., New Orleans, 1951-60, geol. cons., 1960—; v.p. exploration and devel. Basic Resources Internat. Ltd., Toronto, Ont., Can., 1969—. Served to maj. AUS, 1942-46. Fellow Geol Soc. Am., Am. Assn. Petroleum Geologists, Soc. Exploration Geophysicists, Soc. Ind. Profl. Earth Scientists, Am. Inst. Profl. Geologists, Petroleum Club New Orleans (past sec.). Home: 2223 Palmer Av New Orleans LA 70118 Office: Pere Marguette Bldg New Orleans LA 70112

UVACEK, EDWARD, JR., agrl. economist; b. Newark, Sept. 12, 1930; s. Edward and Julia (Lukasik) U.; grad. Seton Hall, 1948; B.S., Rutgers U., 1952, M.S., 1956; Ph.D., Tex. A. and M. U., 1967; postgrad. U.S. Dept. Agr. Grad. Sch., 1958; m. Beatrice Greer, Apr. 18, 1959; children—Debra Theresa, Cynthia Ann, Edward Eugene. Agrl. economist, research div. U.S. Dept. Agr., Washington, Los Angeles, 1956-59; commodity analyst Armour & Co., Chgo., 1959-61; specialist livestock marketing, agrl. extension service, Tex. A. and M. U., College Station, 1961-63, asso. prof. and extension livestock marketing specialist, 1967—; dir. Western Research Inst., College Station, 1960—. Econ. livestock cons. AID, Panama, 1962, Korea, 1963; testified as expert witness Nat. Commn. on Food Marketing, 1965, Nat. Adv. Commn. on Food and Fiber, 1966; research dir. Nat. Livestock and Meat Bd. Task Force Com., 1973-74. Award Trustee Livestock Merchandising Inst., 1971. Served to 1st lt. USAF, 1952-54. Mem. Am., Western agrl. econs. assns., Internat. Assn. Agrl. Economists, Am. Marketing Assn. Home: 1001 Pershing Dr College Station TX 77840 Office: Dept Agrl Econs Tex A and M U College Station TX 77840

UXER, JOHN ELMO, ednl. adminstr.; b. Garrison, N.M., Mar. 31, 1924; s. John and Myrtle Alice (Albright) U.; B.S., N.M. State U., 1949, M.A., 1951, Edn. Specialist, 1962, Ed.D., 1967; m. Wyvonia Oleta Stroud, Aug. 19, 1944; children—John Elmo, Dell Anne. Tchr., House, N.M., 1950-51, Carlsbad, N.M., 1953-54, Artesia, N.M., 1954-57; dir. guidance and counseling, Artesia, N.M., 1957-59, dir. instrn., 1959-61; supt., Jal, N.M., 1961-65; asst. prof. N.M. State U., Las Cruces, N.M., 1966-67; exec. dir. Legislative Finance Com., N.M. Legislature, 1967-68; exec. dir. Region XIX Edn. Service Center, El Paso, Tex., 1968—. Cons. N.M. State Dept. Edn., 1965-68; mem. adv. commn. Tex. Edn. Agy., 1968—; mem. Gov's. Land Use Com., N.M., 1962-63. Bd. dirs. Armed Forces YMCA. Served with USNR, 1942-46, AUS, 1951-53. Decorated Purple Heart, Bronze Star medal; recipient Distinguished Alumnus award Coll. Edn., N.M. State U., 1971. Mem. Am. Personnel and Guidance Assn., N.E.A., Am. Sch. Counselors Assn., Am. Assn. Sch. Adminstrs., Assn. Higher Edn., Tex. State Tchrs. Assn., Tex. Assn. Sch. Adminstrs., N.M. State U. Alumni Assn. (pres. 1974), Phi Delta Kappa. Baptist. Kiwanian, Rotarian. Home: 6404 Westwind St El Paso TX 79912 Office: PO Box 10716 El Paso TX 79997

UZZELL, MINTER, educator; b. Baird, Tex., Aug. 6, 1909; s. Minter Womack and Ada Estelle (Cooke) U.; A.A., Wayland Baptist Coll.; A.B., Hardin Simmons U., 1930; Th.M., S.W. Bapt. Theol. Sem., 1933; Th.M., Berkeley Bapt. Div., 1937; M.A., U. Tulsa, 1951, P.D.E., 1952, Ed.D., 1954; m. Pauline Dykes, Nov. 14, 1937; children—Carol Sue (Mrs. Rex Wayne Kay), Carey Lee. Ordained to ministry Bapt. Ch., 1928; pastor Tex., Ida., Washington, Cal., Okla., 1928; tchr. pub. schs., Muskogee, Okla., 1945-47; asso. sec. YMCA, Ga. Inst. Tech., 1947-48; instr. Bacone Coll., 1949-59; prof. English, Northeastern Okla. State U., Tahlequah, 1959—, formerly dean of students. Active A.R.C. Served with AUS, 1941-45, 53; ETO. Mem. Am. Assn. U. Profs., Nat., Okla. edn. assns., Assn. for Higher Edn., Am. Legion, Res. Officers Assn., Cherokee Hist. Soc., Phi Lambda Chi, Phi Delta Kappa, Kappa Delta Pi. Democrat. Baptist. Kiwanian. Home: 269 Redbud Lane Tahlequah OK 74464

VACCA, JOHN JOSEPH, broadcasting exec.; b. Chgo., Apr. 7, 1922; s. John Joseph and Caroline (Bain) V.; student Northwestern U., 1940-42, Internat. Corr. Schs., 1950-54; m. Alice Isabel Ure, May 2, 1944; children—John Joseph, Dawn Susan, Kim Frances. Editor, Midwest Times, Chgo., 1940-41; with prodn. dept. NBC, Radio, 1946-47; news dir. sta. KECK, Odessa, Tex., 1947-49, chief announcer, 1948-49; program mgr. KOSA-Radio, Odessa, 1949-55, sta. mgr. KOSA-TV, 1955-61, gen. mgr., 1962-72; v.p., dir. Trigg Vaughn Stas., Inc., Odessa, 1962-67; sec. Odessa Broadcasting Co., 1950-72; v.p., asst. sec. Doubleday Broadcasting Co., 1967—; gen. mgr. KDTV, Dallas, 1972-73. Bd. dirs. Odessa Community Chest, 1964-72, Better Bus. Bur., 1956-72; campaign maj. A.R.C., 1951-72; publicity adviser Ector County chpt. Nat. Found. for Infantile Paralysis, 1949-72; campaign coordinator Civic Music Assn., 1950-72; sponsor, adviser Permian Playhouse, 1959-72, v.p., dir., 1971-72. City councilman, Odessa, 1962-64. Bd. dirs. Am. Cancer Soc. Served with USAAF, 1942-46. Recipient Zeus award Epsilon Sigma Alpha, 1971. Mem. Tex. AP Broadcasters Assn., Advt. Club Odessa (pres. 1960-61, dir., 1960-63), C. of C. (publicity adviser 1950-72), Holy Name Soc. Roman Catholic K.C. (sec. Odessa 1950-51). Home: 9330 Emberglow Lane Dallas TX 75231

VADAKIN, JAMES CHARLES, educator; b. Lima, O., Mar. 8, 1924; s. James Charles and Grace (Miller) V.; B.A., Denison U., 1946; M.B.A., Harvard, 1947; Ph.D., Cornell U., 1952; m. Mary Ann Willoughby, Sept. 8, 1946; 1 son, Jeffrey J. Mem. faculty U. Miami (Fla.), 1947—, prof. econs., 1957—, chmn. dept., 1961—, coordinator Cuban Econ. Research Project, 1961—; arbitrator labor-mgmt., 1950—; frequent speaker. Mem. panel arbitrators Fed. Mediation and Conciliation Service; mem. Fed. Ser. Impasses Panel. Served with USNR, 1942-46. First hon. mem. Personnel Assn. Miami, 1954. Mem. Nat. Acad. Arbitrators (bd. govs.), Am. Arbitration Assn., Am. So. econ. assns., Phi Kappa Phi, Omicron Delta Kappa, Lambda Chi Alpha. Club: Harvard (Miami). Author: Family Allowances, 1958; Children, Poverty and Family Allowance, 1968; also articles. Home: 1450 Ancona Av Coral Gables FL 33146

VAGT, JOHN PAUL, coll. dean; b. Jackson, Minn., Nov. 28, 1923; s. John and Dora (Wick) V.; B.A., N. Tex. State U., 1949; M.L.S., U. Tex., 1953; m. Mary Evelyn Hooker, July 29, 1951; children—Janice Evelyn (Mrs. George Smith), Kathryn Juliana. Asst. librarian Tarleton State Coll., 1949-51; librarian, Howard County Jr. Coll., 1953-61, Odessa Coll., 1961-64; dir. libraries Midwestern U., 1964-67; dean learning resources Tarrant County Jr. Coll., Fort Worth, 1967—. Served with AUS, 1945-47. Mem. Am. Assn. Edn. and Communications Tech., Am. Assn. Higher Edn., Am., Tex. library assns., Phi Delta Kappa. Contbr. articles to profl. jours. Home: 3313 Jamestown Dr Fort Worth TX 76119 Office: 5301 Campus Dr Fort Worth TX 76119

VAHLE, CORNELIUS WENDELL, JR., research co. exec.; b. Tracy, Minn., July 15, 1932; s. Cornelius Wendell and Gertrude (Gilronan) V.; B.A., St. Johns U., Collegeville, Minn., 1954; M.A., Cath. U. Am., 1957; Ph.D., Georgetown U., 1967; m. Helen Kate Curry, Feb. 8, 1958; children—Maria, Stephen, Tom More, Peter. Historian, Nat. Park Service, 1958-60; examiner U.S. Bur. of Budget, Washington, 1960-66; v.p. Operations & Policy Research, Inc., Washington, 1966—; mng. editor World Affairs, 1969—; editor Perspective, 1972—. Dir. Heldrez Publications, Helen Dwight Reid Ednl. Found. Pres. Queen of Peace Credit Union, 1963-65. Served with AUS, 1954-56. Home: 5536 N 18th St Arlington VA 22205 Office: 4000 Albermarle St NW Washington DC 20016

VAIL, CHARLES CONRADY, JR., indsl. relations exec.; b. N.Y.C., Oct. 19, 1933; s. Charles Conrady and Virginia (Snow) V.; B.A., Roanoke Coll., 1955; M.S., Radford Coll., 1968; m. Mary Paula Pilkenton, Dec. 22, 1960; children—Charles Conrady III, Elizabeth Risen. Indsl. relations trainee Old Dominion Candies, Roanoke, Va., 1957-60; guidance counsellor Roanoke pub. schs., 1960-64; exec. v.p., treas. Roanoke Valley Industries, 1964—, Indsl. Learning Corp. of Va. Co-chmn. Cancer Crusade, Met. Roanoke Valley, 1967, chmn., 1968. Bd. dirs. Am. Cancer Soc., Roanoke Valley, Va. Coll. Placement Assn., Roanoke Symphony Soc.; trustee Va. Council Econ. Edn. Mem. Nat. Indsl. Council, Nat. Assn. Mfrs. (inter-relations com., urban affairs com.), Am. Soc. Personnel Adminstrs., Personnel Assn. Roanoke, Am. Soc. Assn. Execs., Roanoke Valley C. of C. (chmn. edn. com.). Rotarian (dir. Roanoke). Home: 2614 Richelieu Av SW Roanoke VA 24014 Office: Colonial-Am Bldg Roanoke VA 24011

VAIL, EDWIN GEORGE, scientist; b. Toledo, July 25, 1921; s. Jay Coy and Bernice (Hauman) V.; B.Sc., U. Toledo, 1947; M.Sc., Ohio State U., 1948, Ph.D., 1953; m. Mary Janet McFarland, Nov. 27, 1946; children—Edwin Jay, Thomas Clair, Michael Andrew, Valerie Ann, Richard Austin. With aero. systems div. USAF, Wright Patterson AFB, O., 1951-64; chief human engring. Hamilton Standard, Windsor Locks, Conn., 1964-69; research physiologist Navel Coastal Systems Lab., Panama City, Fla., 1970—; pres. Vail Applied Research Co., Inc., 1973—. Active Boy Scouts Am. Served with AUS, 1951-55. Decorated Air medal with three oak leaf clusters. Mem. Aerospace Med. Assn., Undersea Med. Soc., Sigma Xi, Alpha Epsilon Delta. Mem. Ch. of Christ. Mason. Contbr. articles to profl. jours. Home: 4502 Vista Lane Lynn Haven FL 32444 Office: Naval Coastal Systems Lab Panama City FL 32401

VAIL, FREDERICK SCOTT, rec. co. exec., artist mgr., music pub.; b. San Francisco, Mar. 24, 1944; s. Morgan Willard and Doris (Jacobus) V.; student Cal. State Coll., 1962-64; Indsl. Coll. Armed Forces, 1963; m. Brenda Joyce Howard, June 18, 1972. Radio, TV announcer, program dir., Sacramento, 1957-62; owner, pres. Frederick Vail Prodns., Sacramento and Hollywood, 1962-66; producer Teen-Age Fair, Inc., Hollywood, 1966-68, nat. sales mgr., N.Y.C., 1968; mgr. rec. group The Beach Boys, Hollywood, 1969-71; nat. promotion, sales dir. Brother Records, Hollywood, 1971-72; promotion mgr. Capitol Records, Inc., 1972—. Lectr. youth marketing, impact of youth on economy to civic groups, high schs., colls. through U.S. Del. Govs. Conf. Youth, 1959; mem. exec. bd. El Camino High Sch., Sacramento, 1961-62. Recipient Representative DeMolay award Internat. Supreme Council, Order of DeMolay, 1963. Mem. Country Music Assn., Acad. Country and Western Music, Order of DeMolay (dep. master No. Cal. 1963; sr. councilor central Cal. 1963; chmn. State DeMolay week 1963). Home: 3018 Fairfax Dr Charlotte NC 28209 Office: 1750 N Vine St Hollywood CA 90028

VALDEZ-SABATER, FERNANDO ARTURO, physician; b. Azua, Dominican Republic, May 4, 1927; s. Adriano and Ana Consuelo (Sabater) V.; M.D., U. Santo Domingo, 1956; m. America Ana Franco, Mar. 15, 1958; children—Fernando A., Ana Yanilsa, Harold Valdez Franco. Intern, Hosp. Jose Maria Cabral y Baez, Santiago, Dominican Republic, 1955-56, Paterson (N.J.) Gen. Hosp., 1957-58; resident All Souls Hosp., Morristown, N.J., 1959-60; gen. practice medicine, Salinas, P.R., 1969—; dir. Hosp. Municipal, Juana Diaz, P.R., Hosp. Municipal, Salinas, P.R., Unidad Salud Publica, Salinas. Bd. dirs. A.R.C., Salinas, 1965. Mem. Am. Acad. Family Physicians, Asociacion medica Americana y de P.R., Casa del Medico de Ponce. Mason, Lion. Home: Urbanizacion Salimar A-4 1 Salinas PR 00751 Office: Palmer esquina Union Salinas PR 00751

VALDIVIA, JOSE FRANCISCO, JR., food co. exec.; b. Sancti-Spiritus, Las Villas, Cuba, Jan. 4, 1932; s. Jose F. and Elena A. (Jimenez) V.; Litt.B., Colegio De La Salle, Havana, Cuba, 1949; LL.B., U. Havana, 1954; m. Teresa Hernandez, Feb. 4, 1956; children—Teresita, Jose Frank, Maria Elena. Came to U.S., 1961, naturalized, 1967. Admitted to Cuban Nat. bar, 1954; practiced in Sancti-Spiritus, Cuba, 1954-61; adminstr. fgn. affairs Scott-Mattson Farms, Inc., 1961-70, S. P.R. Sugar Co., 1967-70; v.p. corporate affairs Gulf Western Food Products Co., Ft. Pierce, Fla., 1970-72, sr. v.p., 1973—, also dir. subsidiaries, Bahamas, P.R., Costa Rica, Dominican Republic. Mem. Inter-Am. Bar Assn., Am. Soc. Internat. Law. Roman Catholic. Club: Pelican Yacht (Ft. Pierce). Home: 4017 Greenwood Dr Fort Pierce FL 33450 Office: Gulf and Western Plaza Vero Beach FL 32960

VALENTINE, FOY DAN, clergyman; b. Edgewood, Tex., July 3, 1923; s. John Hardy and Josie (Johnson) V.; B.A., Baylor U., 1944; Th. M., Southwestern Baptist Theol. Sem., 1947, Th.D., 1949; D.D., William Jewell Coll., 1966; m. Mary Louise Valentine, May 6, 1947; children—Mary Jean, Carol Elizabeth, Susan Foy. Ordained to ministry Bapt. Ch., 1942; dir. Bapt. student activities colls. of Houston, 1949-50; pastor First Bapt. Ch., Gonzales, Tex., 1950-53; dir. Christian life commn. Bapt. Gen. Conv. Tex., 1953-60; exec. sec.-treas. Christian life commn. So. Bapt. Conv., 1960—, chmn. So. Bapt. inter-agy. council, 1965-67; Willson lectr. applied Christianity Wayland Bapt. Coll., 1963; Christian ethics lectr. Bapt. Theol. Sem., Ruschlikon-Zurich, Switzerland, 1966. Mem. commn. religious liberty and human rights Bapt. World Alliance, 1966—; trustee Ams. United for Separation of Church and State; bd. dirs. Bapt. Joint Com. Pub. Affairs, Interpreter's House, mem. Nashville Met. Human Relations Commn., 1966—. Mem. Am. Soc. Christian Ethics, Com. So. Churchmen. Democrat. Author: Christian Faith in Action 1956; Believe and Behave, 1964; Citizenship for Christians, 1965; The Cross in the Marketplace, 1966; Peace Peace, 1967; Where the Action is: Studies in James, 1969; also articles. Home: 6354 Torrington Rd Nashville TN 37205 Office: 460 James Robertson Pky Nashville TN 37219

VALENTINE, HENRY LEE II, stockbroker; b. Richmond, Va., Sept. 15, 1927; s. Corbin Braxton and Ida (Massie) V.; B.A., U. Va., 1950; m. Margaret Kane West, Nov. 5, 1955; children—Margaret, Henry, Ida, Edward. Pres. Davenport & Co. of Va., Inc., Richmond, 1950—; dir. First Fund of Va., Mut. Assurance Soc.; dir. Hollywood Cemetery. Mem. Richmond City Council, 1970—. Bd. dirs. Crippled Children's Hosp., Richmond, Richmond Eye Hosp., St. Catherine's Sch., Protestant Episcopal Ch. Home. Served with AUS, 1946-47. Episcopalian (vestryman). Clubs: Country of Va., Commonwealth. Home: 207 Lock Lane Richmond VA 23226 Office: PO Box 1377 Richmond VA 23211

VALENTINE, JOHN PHILLIP, hosp. adminstr.; b. Evanston, Ill., Jan. 11, 1923; s. Frank B. and Margaret P. (Barbutt) V.; B.A., San Francisco State Coll., 1957; M.B.A., Syracuse U., 1958; D.Bus. Adminstrn., George Washington U., 1965; m. Gloria Margo Nelson, Aug. 16, 1948; 1 son, James A. Enlisted as pvt. U.S. Army, 1943, advanced through grades to col., 1970; comdr. Litter Bearer Platoon, 1943-44, Ambulance Co., 1944-45, Collecting Co., 1945-46; exec. officer 25th Med. Bn., 1950-51; exec. officer U.S. Army Hosp., Kyoto, Japan, 1951-53; comptroller Office Surgeon, Hdqrs. Presidio San Francisco, 1953-57, Office Surgeon, Hdqrs. 5th Army, Chgo., 1957-60; spl. asst. to comptroller Office Surgeon Gen., Dept. Army, Washington, 1960-65; dir. U.S. Army-Baylor U. Program in Health Care Adminstrn., 1965-68; dir. dept. adminstrn. U.S. Army Med. Field Service Sch., Brooke Army Med. Center, 1965-69; adminstr. Loudoun Meml. Hosp., Leesburg, Va., 1970—. Bd. dirs. A.R.C. Decorated Bronze Star medal with two oak leaf clusters, Army Commendation medal with three oak leaf clusters. Mem. Am. Acad. Med. Adminstr., Am. Coll. Hosp. Adminstr., Am. Pub. Health Assn., Assn. U.S. Army, Assn. U. Programs in Hosp. Adminstrn. (mem. exec. com. 1967-70), Armed Forces Mgmt. Assn., Am. Mgmt. Assn., Am., Tex. hosp. assns., Alamo Hosp. Div. (v.p. 1965-69). Home: Cattail Ordinary Route 1 Box 468 Leesburg VA 22075 Office: 70 W Cornwall St Leesburg VA 22075

VALIUNAS, ANDREW VYTAUTAS, economist; b. Kaunas, Lithuania, Oct. 20, 1927; s. Domas and Maria (Peciulis) V.; B.A., U. Tuebingen, 1950, M.A., 1950, Ph.D., 1958; m. Colette Rejanne Ducrocq, Oct. 24, 1957. Came to U.S., 1951, naturalized, 1954. Co-founder Vesta G.m.b.H., import-export co., Tuebingen, Germany, 1947-51; research specialist, aerospace engr. Library of Congress, 1958-67; internat. economist Office Econ. Research, U.S. Tariff Commn., Washington, 1967—. Served with USAF, 1952-56; maj. U.S. Army Res. Mem. Am. Econ. Assn., Res. Officers Assn. Author: The Finance Policy of Lithuanian Republic, 1918-40, 1950; The Sovietization of Lithuanian Economy, 1940-41, 1958. Contbr. articles to numerous publications. Home: 2032 Belmont Rd NW Washington DC 20009 Office: 8th and E Sts NW Washington DC 20436

VALLADARES O., RENE, architect, constrn. co. exec.; b. Guatemala City, Guatemala, July 17, 1926; s. Rodolfo and Carmen (Ortiz) V.; grad. Nat. Inst. Guatemala; B.Scis. and Letters, U. St. Carlos, 1944; Architecture, U. Autonoma de Mexico, 1946-50; postgrad. Tulane U., 1953-55; m. Imelda R. Bueno, Apr. 7, 1951; children—Rodolfo, Oscar, Lizette, Rene, Imelda. Came to U.S., 1952, naturalized, 1959. Partner, Cummins-Valladares, New Orleans, 1959-60; prin. Rene Valladares O., A.I.A. Assos., New Orleans, 1960-65, Miami, 1965—, Valladares & Assos., gen. contractors, Coral Gables, Fla., 1965—. Archtl. consultants and planners Spanish and Latin Am. affairs A.I.A., Nat. Council Archtl. Registration Bds., 1964—. Hon. consul Guatemala to Jefferson, La., 1960-68; attache to Embassy Guatemala, Mexico City, 1950-51; consulate Guatemala in San Francisco, 1951-52. Served to lt. USAF, 1944-45. Mem. A.I.A., Amateur Fencers League Am. (dir. Fla. Gold Coast div. 1970-71). Mason. Club: Country (Coral Gables). Prin. archtl. works include Alvin Calendar Field Weather Radar Sta., New Orleans, Metropolitan Bank, Metairie, La., Mary Star of the Sea Ch., Diocese Nassau. Home: 290 SW 71st Av Miami FL 33144 Office: PO Box 971 Coral Gables FL 33134

VALLECILLO, JORGE TEOFILO, mech. engr.; b. Santurce, P.R., July 22, 1918; s. Manuel D. and Felicita (Rivera) V.; B.S. in Mech. Engring., U. P.R., 1939; m. Gladys Samalea, Oct. 12, 1940; children—Gladys C., Donald W. (dec.), Mike. Chief design engr. Sucs

De Abarca, San Juan, P.R., 1939-44; chief engr. Okeelanta Sugar Corp., South Bay, Fla., 1944-49; project engr. U.S. Phosphoric Products, Tampa, Fla., 1949-56; project mgr. Wellman Lord Inc., Lakeland, Fla., 1956-72; project mgr. GM Indsl. Enterprises, 1972-73; pres. Carlau, Inc., Brooksville, Fla., 1973—; pres. Gulf Land Engring., Inc., Brooksville, 1973—. Mem. Nat. Soc. Profl. Engrs., Fla. Engring. Soc., Coll. Engrs. P.R., Nat. Rifle Assn., Phi Eta Mu. Clubs: Associated Tampa Executives, Tampa Police Pistol. Home: 2313 Lila Tampa FL 33609 Office: 1714 Howell Av Brooksville FL 33512

VALLIANOS, LIMBERIOS, coastal engr.; b. N.Y.C., July 19, 1936; s. Spyros and Monte (Livanis) V.; B.S., Poly. Inst. Bklyn., 1958, postgrad., 1961-62; diploma Hydraulic Engr. with distinction, Internat. Course in Hydraulic Engring., Delft, Netherlands, 1968; m. Stella Yasmine Voudiotis, June 15, 1958; children—Alexander Spyros, Tanya Maria. Engr., TVA, Knoxville, Tenn., 1958-59, USPHS, Washington, 1959-60, Reno, 1960-62, Nussbaumer Clark & Velzy-Cons., N.Y.C., 1962-63; chief coastal engring. sect. U.S. Army C.E., Wilmington, N.C., 1963—. Cons. coastal engring. Served with USPHS, 1959-62. Recipient Outstanding Performance award U.S. Army C.E., 1966. Registered profl. engr., N.C. Mem. Am. Soc. C.E., Internat. Assn. for Hydraulic Research, Permanent Internat. Assn. Nav. Congress, Chi Epsilon. Club: Wilmington Engineering. Home: 1618 Robert E Lee Dr Wilmington NC 28401 Office: PO Box 1890 Wilmington NC 28401

VALLOTTON, WILLIAM WISE, surgeon educator; b. Valdosta, Ga., Nov. 26, 1927; s. Joseph Edward and Mattie (Rouse) V.; A.B., Duke, 1947; M.D., Med. Coll. Ga., 1952; postgrad. Harvard; 1956; m. Hulda Roberta Jones, Sept. 3, 1950; children—Stephen Ralph, Amie, Mark Hugh, William Wise. Intern, U. Wis., 1952-53; resident ophthalmology Duke U., 1953-55, instr., 1953-55, asso., 1955-56, asso. prof. ophthalmology Med. Coll. S.C., Charleston, 1958-65, prof., 1965—, dir. residency program ophthalmology, 1960-70, chmn. dept. ophthalmology, 1966—. Cons., USN Hosp., Charleston, 1962—, State Hosp. S.C., Columbia, 1963—, U.S. Vets. Hosp., Charleston, 1966—; faculty home study Am. Acad. Ophthalmology and Otolaryngology. Vice pres. Vallorbe, Inc., Valdosta, Ga., 1955—. Served to lt. M.C., USNR, 1956-58. Diplomate Am. Bd. Ophthalmology. Fellow A.C.S.; mem. S.C. Eye and Ear Assn. (pres. 1965), Charleston Duke Alumni Assn. (past pres.), Assn. Research in Ophthalmology (chmn. S.E. sect. 1966-67), Pi Kappa Phi, Alpha Kappa Kappa, Alpha Omega Alpha. Republican. Methodist. Elk. Research in ophthalmology. Home: 15 Broughton Rd Charleston SC 29407

VALLS, RALPH, customhouse broker; b. Laredo, Tex., Mar. 24, 1909; s. Antonio and Rafaela (Mendiola) V.; grad. high sch.; m. Clotilde Withoff, May 24, 1934; 1 son, Richard R. Farmer, San Rafael Farm, 1928-41; insp. Customs Service, 1941-48; farmer, Laredo, 1948-50; customhouse broker, Laredo, 1950—, Galveston, Tex., 1960—, Houston, 1967—, Corpus Christi, Tex., 1960—; pres. Ralph Valls & Son, Inc., Corpus Christi, 1968—; ocean freight forwarder, 1962—; a founding dir. Gulf Internat. Trader (now Houston Bus. Jours.), Houston, 1964—. Lectr. internat. trade Del Mar Coll., Corpus Christi. Mem. Tex. Internat. Trade Assn. (dir. 1965, 66, 68, 71, 72). Republican. Roman Catholic. Rotarian. Club: Propellers. Home: 4601 Jarvis St Corpus Christi TX Office: Katz Bldg Corpus Christi TX 78403

VANAMAN, RICHARD HENRY LEROY, clergyman; b. Harrisburg, Pa., Nov. 29, 1913; s. Lester Eugene and Sarah (Coxeter) V.; A.B., Dickinson Coll., 1946; S.T.B., Wesley Theol. Sem., Washington, 1951, M.Div., 1971; S.T.M., Colo. Bible Coll. and Sem., 1955; m. Jean Betty Haupt, Nov. 30, 1934; children—Patricia (Mrs. J.A. Schultz), Sara (Mrs. C.C. Morris). Ordained to ministry Methodist Ch., 1948; minister Meth. Chs., Dillsburg, Wellsville, Bendersville (all Pa.), Hampton, Salem Center (both N.H.), 1941-51; minister Episcopal Chs., Harrisburg, Pa., Stuttgart, Tollville (both Ark.), Franklin, Portsmouth, (both Va.), South Miami, Lake Placid, Sebring (all Fla.), Holly Springs, Miss., Woodville, Miss., 1951—; former rector St. Paul's Ch., Woodville; vicar St. Elizabeth's Ch., Zephyrhills, Fla., 1970—; book review editor Hampton Union and Rockingham County (N.H.) Gazette, 1946-49; personnel dept. UGI, N.Y. Life Ins. Co., Nat. Radio Inst. Mem. bd. examining chaplains Diocese of Miss.; mem. dept. stewardship Diocese of So. Fla.; mem. com. Christian social relations Diocese of Southwest Fla., 1971—. Active Boy Scouts Am. Mem. Am. Ch. Union, Lake Placid (pres.), Nat. Geog. Soc., Holly Springs (v.p.) ministerial assns., Alpha Chi Rho. Mason, Odd Fellow, Lion, Rotarian; mem. Order Eastern Star. Clubs: Ruritan, Civitan. Home: PO Box 1115 Zephyrhills FL 33599

VAN APPLEDORN, MARY JEANNE, educator, musician; b. Holland, Mich., Oct. 2, 1927; d. John and Elizabeth (Rinck) van Appledorn; Mus.B., Eastman Sch. Music, U. Rochester, 1948, Mus.M., 1950, Ph.D., 1966. Piano debut Carnegie Recital Hall, N.Y.C., 1957; chmn. dept. music lit. and music theory Tex. Tech. U., Lubbock, 1952—, founder, dir. Symposium of Contemporary Music, 1952-72. Named to Hall of Fame of Tex. Composers. Mem. Mu Phi Epsilon, Alpha Chi Omega, Delta Kappa Gamma (Scholar, 1959-60). Presbyn. Author: Keyboard Singing and Dictation Manual, 1968. Composer various piano and organ selections. Home: 1629 16th St Lubbock TX 79401

VAN ARSDALE, DOROTHY LANGFORD THAYER (MRS. STUART FRANK VAN ARSDALE), art gallery and exhbn. service exec.; b. Malden, Mass., Jan. 14, 1917; d. Arthur Langford and Dorothy (Clark) Thayer; B.S., Simmons Coll., 1938; m. Howard Charles Pritham, Aug. 31, 1939 (div. Sept. 1947); children—Howard George, Eleanor (Mrs. Serge Liros); m. 2d, Stuart Frank Van Arsdale, Aug. 25, 1951 (dec. July 1958); 1 son, Stuart Frank. Sec., Filene's, Boston, 1946-48; exec. sec. Macy's, N.Y.C., 1948-51; sec. John Fox, pub. Boston Post, 1952-54, spl. promotions Boston Post, 1954-55; exec. sec. N.E. Industries, Boston, 1957-60, adminstrv. asst., 1960-62, treas., 1960, also dir.; financial mgr. Smithsonian Travelling Exhbn. Service, Washington, 1962-64, chief, 1964-70; pres. Dorothy T. Van Arsdale Assos., traveling exhbn. service and gallery, Clermont, Fla., 1970—. Decorated Knight Order Dannebrog (Denmark). Mem. Am. Assn. Museums, Internat. Council Museums, Simmons Coll. Alumni Assn., Clermont C. of C. Home: 1676 Bowman St Clermont FL 32711 Office: 630 8th St Clermont FL 32711

VAN ARSDALL, ROBERT EDWARD, ins. co. exec.; b. Monroe, Mich., July 24, 1932; s. Kenneth R. and Margaret (Kimes) Van A.; student Elmhurst Coll., 1951; B.S., Ind. U., 1957; M.B.A., DePaul U., 1963; m. Lydia H. Willinski, Aug. 26, 1956; 1 dau., Christina. Asst. treas. Country Life Ins., Chgo., 1959-65; sr. security analyst Investors Diversified Service Mpls., 1965-66, Union Central Life, Cin., 1966-67; v.p. securities Pan Am. Life, New Orleans, 1967—; dir. Gulf S. Venture Capital Co., New Orleans. Served with USAF, 1952-56. Mem. Financial Analysts New Orleans (pres. 1973-74). Methodist. Home: 310 Jewel St New Orleans LA 70124 Office: 2400 Canal St New Orleans LA 70160

VAN ARSDEL, WILLIAM CAMPBELL III, pharmacologist; b. Indpls., June 27, 1920; s. William Campbell and Mabel (Hedde) Van A.; student Ind. U., 1939-40, Butler U., 1941-42; B.A., Ore. State Coll., 1949, M.S., 1951, Ph.D., 1959; M.S., U. Ore., 1954. Lab. technician, product control lab. U.S. Rubber Co., Indpls., 1941-43, shift supr., 1943-45; teaching fellow zoology, research fellow animal sci. Ore. State Coll., 1954-59, asst. in animal physiology, 1959-63; pharmacologist FDA, Washington, 1963—. Bd. dirs. Parklawn Employees Recreation and Welfare Assn., 1973—. Mem. Research Soc. Am., Under Water Soc. Am. (dir. 1962), Ore. Assn. Underwater Instrs., (chmn. 1963), Ore. Council Skin Diving Clubs (pres. 1962), Atlantic Skin Diving Council (v.p. 1967), Health, Edn. and Welfare Employees Assn. (dir. 1965-73, pres. 1968), A.A.A.S., Japan-Am. Soc. Washington, Ore. State Soc. Washington, Nat. Rifle Assn. Am., N.Y. Acad. Scis., Sea Beavers (hon. life), Sigma Xi. Clubs: Washington Athletic, Toastmasters International. Editor HEW AND YOU, 1965-72. Home: 1000 6th St SW Washington DC 20024 Office: 200 C St SW Washington DC 20204

VANCE, NINA ELOISE WHITTINGTON, theatrical exec.; b. Yoakum, Tex.; d. Perry and Minerva (Dewitt) Whittington; B.A., Tex. Christian U.; postgrad. U. So. Cal., Columbia, Am. Acad. Dramatic Art. Dir. Players Guild, Houston, 1944-46; founder, permanent dir., artistic dir. Alley Theatre, Houston, 1947—; guest dir. Arena Stage, Washington, Playhouse-in-the-Park, Phila. Participant Am. Assembly meeting Asian-Am. Assembly, Kuala Lumpur, Fedn. Malaya; adv. com. Nat. Cultural Center; adv. com. on arts U.S. Adv. Commn. Ednl. and Cultural Affairs. Recipient grant English Speaking Union, 1958; Matrix award for contbn. to field of fine arts Theta Sigma Phi; Personal Dir.'s grant for travel and study Ford Found. Home: 1400 Hermann Dr Houston TX 77004 Office: Alley Theatre 615 Texas Av Houston TX 77002

VANCE, ROBERT MERCER, banker; b. Clinton, S.C., July 9, 1916; s. Robert Berly and Mary Ellen (Bailey) V.; B.S., Davidson Coll., 1937; m. Virginia Sexton Gray, Dec. 27, 1949; children—Mary Bailey, Robert Mercer, Russell Gray. Paymaster, Lydia Cotton Mills, Clinton, 1937-41; with M.S. Bailey & Son, Bankers, Clinton, 1946—, pres., 1948—; dir., asst. treas. Clinton Cotton Mills, 1948-58, v.p., 1956-58, pres., treas., 1958-64; dir., asst. treas. Lydia Cotton Mills, Clinton, 1948-58, v.p., 1953-58, pres., treas., 1958-64; pres., treas. Clinton Mills, Inc., 1964—; dir. Clinton Cottons, Inc., N.Y.C., 1948—, v.p., asst. treas., 1953-58, treas., 1958—; dir. Textile Hall Corp., Greenville, S.C. Pres. Community Chest Greater Clinton, 1958; mem. nominating com. United Community Services S.C., 1959; trustee exec. com. Ednl. Resources Found., 1965; mem. State Adv. Commn. on Higher Edn., 1965-67; mem. State Commn. on Higher Edn., 1967—, chmn., 1968-71. Bd. visitors Davidson (N.C.) Coll., 1959-62; trustee, chmn. bd. Presbyn. Coll., Clinton, 1953-67; trustee, sec. bd. Thornwell Orphanage, Clinton, 1959-67; trustee Inst. Textile Tech., Charlottesville, Va., S.C. Found. Ind. Colls. Served with Signal Corps, AUS, 1941; served to lt. comdr. USNR, 1941-46. Named Man of Year, Clinton Lions Club, 1955. Mem. Am. Textile Mfrs. Inst. (dir. 1965-68), Am. (v.p. 1953-55), S.C. (pres. 1963-64) bankers assns., S.C. Textile Mfrs. Assn. (dir. 1965—), S.C. Textile Assn. (pres. 1967-68), Am. Legion, S.C. State (dir. 1959-60), Clinton (dir. 1951-54) chambers commerce, Kappa Alpha. Presbyn. (elder 1958—). Mason (Shriner), Moose, Kiwanian. Clubs: Lakeside Country (Clinton); Poinsett (Greenville, S.C.); Piedmont (Spartanburg, S.C.). Home: 311 S Broad St Clinton SC 29325 Office: 211 N Broad St Clinton SC 29325

VANCE, ROBERT SMITH, democratic state party chmn.; b. Talladega, Ala., May 10, 1931; s. Harrell Taylor and Mae (Smith) V.; B.S., U. Ala., 1950, J.D., 1952; LL.M., George Washington U., 1955; m. Helen Rainey, Oct. 4, 1953; children—Robert Smith, Charles R. Partner firm Callaway & Vance, Birmingham, Ala., 1956—. Lectr., Cumberland Sch. Law, Samford U., 1967-69. Chmn., Ala. Dem. party, 1966—. Pres. Nat. Assn. Dem. State Chairmen, 1973—. Served to 1st lt. AUS, 1952-54. Mem. Am., Ala., Birmingham bar assns., Omicron Delta Kappa, Beta Gamma Sigma, Delta Chi. Episcopalian. Home: 2824 Shook Hill Rd Birmingham AL 35223 Office: 933 Frank Nelson Bldg Birmingham AL 35203

VANCE, ROY NEWTON, JR., lawyer; b. Paducah, Ky., Nov. 14, 1921; s. Roy Newton and Mary (Bryan) V.; LL.B., U. Ky.; m. Enleen Hamilton, Oct. 20, 1949; children—Linda Barton, Teresa Louise, Roy Newton III. Admitted to Ky. bar, 1946; practiced in Paducah, 1946-70; commr. Ct. of Appeals of Ky., Frankfort, 1970—. Vice pres., gen. counsel Paducah Bank & Trust Co. County atty. McCracken County, Ky., 1949-53; commonwealth atty. 2d Jud. Dist. of Ky., 1953-57. Chmn. bd. trustees Paducah Community Coll. Served to 1st lt., Signal Corps, AUS, 1942-46. Home: 1041 Algonquin St Frankfort KY 40601 Office: Capitol Bldg Frankfort KY 40601

VAN CLEAVE, ROBERT FRANKLIN, geophysicist; b. Indpls., Apr. 28, 1911; s. Benjamin F. and Almeda (Cline) Van C.; student DePauw U., 1928-30; A.B., Wabash Coll., 1933; M.S., U. Okla., 1935; m. Doris Thibodeaux, Apr. 10, 1938; children—Nancy Elizabeth, Margaret Anne, Robert Hamilton. Computer, Western Geophys. Co., Tulsa, 1935-37; supr., party chief Nat. Geophys. Co., Dallas, 1937-46; regional geophysicist, dist. geophysicist Atlantic Refining Co., Dallas, 1946-51; partner Interstate Exploration Co., Tulsa, 1951-59; v.p., chief geophysicist Austral Oil Co., Houston, 1960-72, v.p., mgr. exploration, 1972—. Mem. Soc. Exploration Geophysicists, Am. Assn. Petroleum Geologists, Petroleum Club Houston, Sigma Xi. Club: Houston. Home: 12426 Woodthorpe Lane Houston TX 77024 Office: Exxon Bldg Houston TX 77002

VANDENBERGH, JOHN GARRY, biologist; b. Paterson, N.J., May 4, 1935; s. Garry and Johanna (Hofstede) V.; B.A., Montclair State Coll., 1957; M.S., Ohio U., 1959; Ph.D., Pa. State U., 1962; m. Barbara Ann Doll, June 8, 1958; children—David John, Michael Paul. Research biologist NIH, La Parguera, P.R., 1962-65; research scientist N.C. Dept. Mental Health, Raleigh, 1965—. Adj. prof., dept. zoology N.C. State U., 1965—, cons. Nat. Inst. Mental Health, 1969—; mem. adv. com. Nat. Primate Centers, 1970—. USPHS predoctoral fellow, 1961-62. Mem. Animal Behavior Soc. (program officer 1967-70), A.A.A.S., Am. Soc. Mammalogists, Internat. Soc. Primatology, Sigma Xi. Contbr. articles to profl. jours. Office: Box 7599 Raleigh NC 27602

VANDERHOLT, JAMES FREDERICK, clergyman, sch. supt.; b. Beaumont, Tex., Sept. 4, 1932; s. Charles Edward and Helen Elizabeth (Donahue) V.; student St. Mary's Sem., Houston, Catholic U., 1964, U. Notre Dame, 1966, St. Mary's U., 1967; M.Ed., Our Lady of Lake Coll., 1968. Ordained priest Roman Catholic Ch., 1957. Supt. schs. Diocese of Beaumont, 1967—, counsultor, 1970—; pastor St. Mary's Ch., Port Arthur, Tex., 1971—. Chmn. div. edn. Tex. Catholic Conf., 1970—. Pres., Manpower, Edn. and Tng., Inc., 1967-70. Nat. Cath. Edn. Assn. Rotarian. Address: 528 Augusta St Port Arthur TX 77640

VANDER HORST, JOHN, bishop; b. South Orange, N.J., Jan. 10, 1912; s. Elias and Ella Virginia (Cole) Vander H.; ed. Princeton, 1931-35, St. Stephen's House, Oxford, Eng., 1936; grad. Va. Episcopal Sem., 1938, D.D., 1955; D.D., U. of South, 1955; m. Helen Gray Lawrence, Apr. 17, 1940; children—Helen (Mrs. Peter Gaines Keese), John, Ella Cole, Allston II. Ordained to ministry Episcopal Ch., 1938; rector St. John's Ch., Ellicott City, Md., 1938-42, St. Paul's Ch., Macon, Ga., 1942-45, St. Paul's Ch., Chattanooga, 1945-51; suffragan bishop Diocese Tenn., 1955-61, bishop coadjutor, 1961, bishop, 1961—. Recipient Distinguished Service award Princeton, 1960. Home: 6000 Hillsboro Rd Nashville TN 37215 Office: 528 100 Oaks Tower Nashville TN 37204

VAN DERLASKE, DENNIS PETER, elec. engr.; b. Mineola, N.Y., Jan. 15, 1948; s. Peter Joseph and Emily Gertrude (Shenocka) Van D. B.Engring., State U. N.Y. at Stony Brook, 1969; postgrad. George Washington U., 1969—. Electronic engr. U.S. Army Night Vision Lab., Fort Belvoir, Va., 1969—, project engr., 1971—. Recipient Spl. Act award, 1972. Mem. I.E.E.E. Patentee universal viewer for far infrared. Home: 6366 Hillary Ct Alexandria VA 22310 Office: US Army Night Vision Lab Fort Belvoir VA 22060

VANDERPOOL, WYNANT DAVIS, JR., architect; b. Morristown, N.J., Apr. 12, 1914; s. Wynant Davis and Cornelia Grinnell (Willis) V.; A.B., Princeton, 1936, M.F.A., 1940; m. Ann West Wheeler, Jan. 22, 1965; children—Wynant Davis III, Helena, Madeleine. Designer, J.H. and W.C. Ely, architects, Newark, 1940-42; design, adminstrn. Faulkner, Stenhouse, Fryer & Faulkner, architects, Washington, 1965-68; partner Faulkner, Fryer & Vanderpool, architects, Washington, 1968—. Mem. Bd. Archtl. Consultants for Georgetown, Commn. Fine Arts; pres. Historic Georgetown Inc., Washington, 1971—; v.p. Holland Soc., N.Y., 1972—. Trustee Found. Preservation Historic Georgetown. Served to lt. USNR, 1942-45. Mem. A.I.A., Century Assn. Episcopalian (sr. warden 1973). Club: Mid-Ocean (Tuckerstown, Bermuda); Metropolitan (Washington); Coffee House (N.Y.). Home: 1330 30th St NW Washington DC 20007 Office: 2000 L St NW Washington DC 20036

VANDERVEEN, JOHN EDWARD, nutritionist; b. Prospect Park, N.J., May 13, 1934; s. William John and Lena (Rapp) V.; B.S., Rutgers, The State U., 1956; Ph.D., U. N.H., 1961; m. Ernestine Neuhardt, June 3, 1967. Nutritionist, USAF Sch. Aerospace Medicine, Brooks AFB, Tex., 1964—. Served to 1st lt. USAF, 1961-64. Recipient McLester award Assn. Mil. Surgeons, 1967. Mem. Am. Inst. Nutrition, Am. Inst. Clin. Nutrition, Am. Inst. Food Tech., Am. Chem. Soc., Aerospace Med. Assn., Am. Dairy Sci. Assn., Assn. Mil. Surgeons, Sigma Xi. Presbyn. Home: 100 Kings Crown E San Antonio TX 78233 Office: Box 35306 Brooks Air Force Base TX 78235

VAN DER VOORT, AITCHESON BOWMAR, economist; b. Dunkirk, N.Y., Mar. 15, 1926; s. Henry Ferdinand and Emily (Bowmar) Van Der V.; B.A., Princeton, 1949; M.A., Georgetown U., 1955. Mfrs. rep. Voorhis-Tiebout Co., Red Hook, N.Y., 1949-50; economist Nat. Income div. U.S. Dept. Commerce, Washington, 1955-56; economist Machinery and Allied Products Inst., Washington, 1957—. Instr. econs. Smith Coll., Northampton, Mass., 1956-57. Mem. Alexandria Council Human Relations, 1970—; active The Hopkins House Assn., Alexandria, Va. Mem. Arlington County Democratic Com., 1965-67. Served to 1st. lt. USMCR, 1944-46, 50-52. Mem. Am. Econ. Assn., Nat. Assn. Bus. Economists (v.p., program chmn. local chpt.), Am. Statis. Assn., Internat. Platform Assn., Acad. Polit. Sci., Nat. Economists Club. Asso. editor Capital Goods Review, 1970—. Home: 5021 Seminary Rd Alexandria VA 22311 Office: 1200 18th St NW Washington DC 20036

VANDEVEER, JAMES WELLINGTON, holding co. owner; b. Cleve., May 24, 1925; s. Welzie Wellington and Wilda Ruth Vandeveer; B.S., U. Cal. at Los Angeles, 1949; m. Betty Lou Ober, June 22, 1946; children—Vicki, Cindi. With Allied Oil Co., Cleve., 1949-51; with Vanson Prodn. Corp., Dallas, 1952—, pres., 1957—, chief exec. officer, 1959—; owner, chmn., chief exec. officer Vantex Enterprises, Inc., Dallas, 1964—; dir., mem. exec. com. Ashland Oil Inc. (Ky.). Bd. dirs. Dallas Soc. Crippled Children. Served with inf. AUS, 1943-46: ETO, CBI. Decorated Combat Infantryman Badge. Decorated chavalier du Tastevin, Mem. Wine and Spirits Guild Am., L'Ordre des Coteaux de Champagne, Am. Petroleum Inst., Ind. Petroleum Assn. Am., Am. Fighter Pilot's Assn., Confederate Air Force, Petroleum Club Dallas, Mid Continent Gas and Oil Assn., Quiet Birdmen, Beta Theta Pi. Episcopalian. Club: Northwood Country. Home: 10056 Gaywood St Dallas TX 75229 Office: 540 Meadows Bldg Dallas TX 75206

VANDIVER, FRANK E(VERSON), author; b. Austin, Tex., Dec. 9, 1925; s. Harry Shultz and Maude Folmsbee (Everson) V.; privately ed.; M.A. (Postwar Rockefeller fellow in Humanities, 1946-47, Rockefeller fellow in Am. Studies, 1947-48), U. Tex., 1949; M.A., Oxford U., Eng., 1963; Ph.D. Tulane U., 1951; m. Carol Sue Smith, Apr. 19, 1952; children—Nita, Nancy, Frank. Apptd. historian, San Antonio, Army Service Forces Depot, Civil Service, 1944-45, Air U., 1951-52; prof. history La. State U., summers 1954-57; asst. prof. history Washington U., 1952-55; asst. prof. history Rice U., 1955-56, asso. prof., 1956-58, prof., 1958—, chmn. dept. history and polit. sci., 1962-63, 68-69, Harris Masterson, Jr., chair in history, 1965—, acting pres., 1969-70, provost, 1970—; Harmsworth prof. Am. history Oxford U., 1963-64; vis. prof. history U. Ariz., 1961, U.S. Mil. Acad., 1973-74; master Margarett Root Brown Coll., Rice U., 1964-66, chmn. humanities research council Rice U., 1966-68. Harmon lectr. Air Force Acad., 1963; Walter P. Webb lectr. U. Tex., Arlington, 1967. Mem. Nat. Council on Humanities, 1972—. Adv. council Civil War Centennial Commn.; adv. com. office Chief of Mil. History, Dept. Army, 1970—; chmn. adv. com. U.S. Mil. History Collection, Carlisle, Pa., 1973—. Recipient research grants Am. Philos. Soc., 1953, 54, 60; Guggenheim fellow, 1955-56; Carr P. Collins award Tex. Inst. Letters, 1957; Huntington library research grant, 1961; Harry S. Truman award, 1965; Jefferson Davis award Confederate Meml. Lit. Soc., 1971; Fletcher Pratt award N.Y. Civil War Round Table, 1971, Laureate, Lincoln Acad. Ill., 1973. Mem. Philos. Soc. Tex., Am., So. (asso. editor jour. 1959-62) hist. assns., Tex. Inst. Letters (pres. 1961-63), Jefferson Davis Assn. (pres.; chmn. adv. bd. editors of papers), Soc. Am. Historians (councillor), Civil War Round Table (Chgo.), Phi Beta Kappa. Editor: The Civil War Diary of General Josiah Gorgas, 1947; Confederate Blockade Running Through Bermuda, 1861-65, Letters and Cargo Manifests, 1947; Proceedings of First Confederate Congress, 4th Session, 1954; Proceedings of Second Confederate Congress, 1959; A Collection of Louisiana Confederate Letters; new edit. of J. E. Johnston's Narrative of Military Operations; new edit. J. A. Early's Civil War Memoirs; The Idea of the South, 1964; bd. editors Papers of U.S. Grant. Author: Ploughshares Into Swords: Josiah Gorgas and Confederate Ordnance, 1952; Rebel Brass: The Confederate Command System, 1956; Mighty Stonewall, 1957; Fields of Glory (with W. H. Nelson), 1960; Jubal's Raid, 1960; Basic History of the Confedeacy, 1962; Jefferson Davis and the Confederate State, 1964; John J. Pershing, 1967; Their Tattered Flags, 1970; also hist. articles. Home: 6134 Chevy Chase Houston TX 77027

VANDIVIERE, H(ORACE) MAC, physician, educator; b. Dawsonville, Ga., Mar. 26, 1921; s. Lewis A. and Luna P. (Castleberry) V.; A.B., Mercer U., 1941; M.A., U. Mich., 1944; M.D., U. N.C., 1960; m. Margaret Reynolds, June 5, 1941 (dec. Feb. 1967); children—Christopher, Martin Mac; m. 2d, Irene Graham Melvin, Mar. 23, 1968. Instr., U. Mich., 1944-46; asst. prof. Mercer U., 1946-48; dir. spl. services lab. Ga. Dept. Pub. Health, 1948-51; dir. dept. research N.C. Sanatorium System, Chapel Hill, 1951-67; asst. prof. Duke, 1965-68; med. dir. Haitian Am. Tb Inst., Chapel Hill, also

Jeremie, Haiti, 1962—, pres., 1965—; clin. asso. prof. U. N.C. Sch. Pub. Health, 1967—; asso. prof. U. Ky., Lexington, 1967-71, prof., 1971—; dir. Tb. div. Ky. Bur. Health Services Dept. Human Resources, 1971—. Cons. infectious diseases Sante Publique Dept., Republic of Haiti, 1966—. Vice-chmn. Ky. Comprehensive Health Planning Tb Study Com., 1969-70. Decorated, Pres. of Haiti, 1963. Fellow Am. Pub. Health Assn., Am. Geriatrics Assn.; mem. Nat Tb and Respiratory Disease Assn., Am., Ky. (pres. 1970-71) thoracic socs., A.M.A., Ky., N.C. med. assns. Editor: (with others) Bahama International Conference on Burns, 1964. Contbr. articles to profl. jours. Home: 3429 Brookhaven Rd Lexington KY 40502

VANDOREN, LUCIAN HALL, JR., savs. and loan exec.; b. Washington, Sept. 24, 1925; s. Lucian Hall and Katharine Marvin (Shaw) V.; student Georgetown U., 1946-48; LL.B., Washington Coll. Law, 1951; m. Sue Anne Ring, June 18, 1949; children—Susan Hall, Lucian Kirk, Leslie Ann. With Jefferson Fed. Savs. & Loan Assn., Washington, 1942—, asst. sec., 1951-59, sec., 1959-63, v.p., 1963-71, sr. v.p., treas., dir., 1971—, mem. exec. com., 1972—; v.p., treas., dir. Monticello Service Corp., Washington, 1971—. Pres. Chevy Chase Hills Civic Assn., 1968-69. Chmn. bd. regents Good Counsel High Sch., Wheaton, Md., 1973-74. Served with AUS, 1943-46. Mem. Nat. Soc. Controllers and Financial Officers (chpt. pres. 1959-60), Financial Marketing Council Greater Washington (pres. 1970-73, dir. 1966-74), Met. Washington Bd. Trade, Suburban Md. Home Builders Assn., No. Va. Builders Assn., Advt. Club Met. Washington, Washington Bd. Realtors, Sigma Nu Phi. Rotarian. Clubs: Columbia Country (Chevy Chase, Md.); Touchdown (Washington); Farmington Country (Charlottesville, Va.). Home: 8505 Lynwood Pl Chevy Chase MD 20015 Office: 1680 K St NW Washington DC 20006

VAN DUSEN, CLARENCE RAYMOND, educator, author; b. Elkhart, Ind., Nov. 9, 1907; s. Owen and Caroline (Bolster) Van D.; A.B., Ind. U., 1931; M.A., U. Mich., 1932, D.S., 1937; postgrad. U. Chgo., U. Miami, U. Fla.; m. Norma Louise Rankin, Aug. 1, 1940; 1 dau., Susan Lyn. From instr. to asst. prof. Mich. State U., 1937-42; chmn. dept. speech, dir. Speech and Hearing Clinic, U. Miami, 1946-61; dean instrn. Brevard Jr. Coll., 1961-64; pres. Golden Hills Acad., Ocala, Fla., 1964-65, chmn. faculty, Monroe Jr. Coll. 1965-66; dir. speech and hearing clinic Miss. State Coll. for Women, Columbus, 1966-68, coordinator grad. studies in speech, 1968—. Served to maj. AUS, 1942-46. Fellow Am. Speech and Hearing Assn.; mem. Speech Communication Assn., Mich. Speech Correction Assn. (past pres.), Fla. Speech Assn. (past pres.). Democrat. Conglist. Rotarian. Author: Training the Voice for Speech, 1943, rev. 1953; While You Were Away; (with Howard Van Smith) The New Speech-O-Gram Technique for Persuasive Public Speaking, 1962; (with Harvey Cromwell) Oral Approach to Phonetics, 1969; (with Lee Eggert) Don't Muff The Punch Line, 1973. Contbr. articles to profl. jours. Home: 900 5th Av S Columbus MS 39701

VAN DYKE, GENE, geologist, ind. oil operator; b. Normal, Ill., Nov. 5, 1926; s. Harold and Ruby (Gibson) Van D.; student U. Ill., 1946, Okla. State Coll., 1947; B.S. in Geol. Engring., U. Okla., 1950; m. Theresa Connelly, Dec. 8, 1952; children—Karen, Scott, Janice, Katherine. Geologist, Kerr-McGee Oil Co., Oklahoma City, 1950; chief geologist S. D. Johnson, Wichita Falls, Tex., 1950-51; pvt. practice geologist, ind. oil operator, Wichita Falls, 1951-58; partner Van Dyke & Mejlaender, ind. oil, gas producers, Houston, 1960-62; owner Van Dyke Oil Co., 1962—. Mem. Houston Land men's Assn., Am. Assn. Petroleum Landmen, Am. Assn. Petroleum Geologists, Houston, Geol. Soc., C. of C. Clubs: Houston Petroleum, Houston, Houston Racquet, University, Athletic, Houston. Home: 11100 Meadowick St Houston TX 77024 Office: Southwest Tower Bldg Houston TX 77002

VAN FLEET, DAVID DOMINIC, educator; b. Binghamton, N.Y., Nov. 27, 1940; s. Walter Anthony and Katherine Elizabeth (Beckett) Van F.; B.S., U. Tenn., 1962, Ph.D., 1969; m. Ellamaye Webb, Aug. 27, 1966; 1 dau., Marijke Joi. Jr. planner Tenn. State Planning Commn., Knoxville, 1963; instr. U. Tenn., 1963-67; instr. Kingsport (Tenn.) Grad. Study Program, 1967-70; asst. prof. mgmt. U. Akron, (O.), 1970-73; asst. prof. mgmt. Tex. A. and M. U., College Station, 1973—; participant mgmt. devel. Programs. Mem. Acad. Mgmt., Am., So. econ. assns., Am. Assn. U. Profs. (chpt. exec. com. 1971-73), Scarrabbean Sr. Soc., Nat. Speleological Soc., Nat. Geog. Soc., Zero Population Growth, Omicron Delta Epsilon, Omicron Delta Kappa, Lambda Chi Alpha. Contbr. articles to profl. pubs. Home: 1200 Merry Oaks Dr College Station TX 77840

VAN GELDER, DAVID WILLIAM, physician; b. Grand Rapids, Mich., 1913; M.D., Rush Med. Sch., Chgo., 1938. Intern, Milwaukee County (Wis.) Gen. Hosp., 1938-39; jr. resident Children's Mem. Hosp., Chgo., 1941-42, sr. resident, 1942-43; resident contagious diseases Cook County Hosp., Chgo., 1940-41; resident in pediatrics Ill. Soldiers and Sailors Children's Hosp., Normal, 1939-40; fellow adolescent medicine Children's Hosp., Washington, 1967; mem. pediatric staff Charity Hosp., New Orleans, Our Lady of the Lake Hosp., Baton Rouge Gen. Hosp.; prof. pediatrics Tulane U. Served with USNR, 1944-46. Diplomate Am. Bd. Pediatrics. Fellow Am. Acad. Pediatrics (dist. chmn.); mem. A.M.A. Office: 888 Tara Blvd Baton Rouge LA 70806*

VAN HERPE, LEO B(RYANT), surgeon; b. Bklyn., Oct. 19, 1929; s. Leo J. and Thelma (Kirkendall) Van H.; B.S., Am. U., 1951; M.D., George Washington U., 1955; m. Ann Dieffenbach, June 11, 1955; children—Michael, Christopher, Sandra, Leslie, Pamela. Mem. staff orthopedics Henry Ford Hosp., 1958-62; gen. practice orthopedic surgery Washington, 1962—; asso. prof. orthopedic surgery Georgetown U., 1962—; dir. Childrens Orthopedic Programs Georgetown U., 1962—; med. dir. Kiwanis Crippled Children's Clinic, 1969—; cons. in orthopedic surgery U.S. Naval Hosp., Bethesda, Md. Served as lt M.C., USNR, 1955-58. Fellow A.C.S.; mem. Am. Acad. Orthopedic Surgery, Washington Orthopedic Club (sec.-treas. 1967, pres. 1968). Republican. Episcopalian. Office: 2520 L St NW Washington DC 20006

VAN HERSH, WILLIAM, investment exec.; b. Memphis, May 10, 1920; s. William and Temple Whiten (Cox) Van H.; student So. Law U., 1941-42, U. Tenn., 1943; m. Dorothy Martin, Nov. 3, 1944; children—William Hayes, Pamela (Mrs. Ronald L. Hall), Deborah K., Thomas Null. Partner Collins & Freeman, 1944-47; owner Van Hersh Real Estate & Ins. Corp., 1947-61; vice chmn. bd. Mid Continent Corp., 1961-66; pres., chmn. bd. Bill Van Hersh Enterprises, Memphis, 1966—; chmn. bd. Ark. Motel Corp., Am. Fidelity, Inc.; vice chmn. bd. Music Mountain Water Co.; pres., chmn. bd. Oak Forest Meml. Gardens. Dir. Boys Town. Rep. Tenn. Legislature, 1957-61; mem. Democratic Exec. Com., 1957-60; commr. Memphis and Shelby County Auditorium; chmn. County Utilities Commn. Named outstanding young man of Memphis, 1951, outstanding Jaycee of Memphis and Tenn., 1952. Cons. Health, Edn. and Research Found., Nat. Council Sr. Citizens. Mem. Memphis Bd. Realtors, Nat., Tenn. assns. realtors. Democrat. Baptist. Elk, Mason (Shriner). Clubs: Palm Bay, Jockey, Racket (Miami); Tennessee, Summit (Memphis). Home: 475 N Highland St Memphis TN 38122 Office: 96 N 3d St Memphis TN 38103

VAN HOOK, DAVID HESTER, museum curator, artist; b. Danville, Va., Dec. 25, 1923; s. David D. and Margaret (Vernon) Van H.; student U. S.C., 1949-50; m. Diane Daniels, July 7, 1956; children—Sigmund, Karta. Registrar, Columbia (S.C.) Museum Art, 1951-58, asst. to dir., 1958-60, curator, 1960—; executed 11 panel mural at Kaufman Road Sch., Cola, S.C., 1970; represented in permanent collections at Columbia Mus. Art, Columbia, S.C., Jacksonville, (Fla.) Mus. Art, Security Fed. Home Loan Co., Columbia, others; curator Rudolph Lee Gallery, Sch. Architecture, Clemson (S.C.) U., 1966-67; cons. state scholastic art awards exhibit Liberty Life Ins. Co., 1966-68, state chmn. scholastic art awards exhibit, 1969. Juror various arts festivals and exhibits. Served with AUS, 1945-47. Mem. Am. Assn. Museums, Southeastern Mus. Conf., S.C. Fedn. Museums, Guild S.C. artists (pres. 1968-69). Home: 939 Brantley St Columbia SC 29210 Office: 1112 Bull St Columbia SC 29201

VAN HORN, LAWRENCE VINCENT, steel co. exec.; b. Galena, Kan., Aug. 12, 1913; s. Rob Roy and Pearl May (Page) Van H.; B.S. in Bus. Ed., Central State U., Edmond, Okla., 1935; m. Doretha Lucille Howerton, Aug. 25, 1934; children—Brooke A., Grayson P., Reece M. With Capitol Steel & Iron Co., Oklahoma City, 1935—, chmn. bd., pres., 1963—; dir. Stock Yards Bank; adv. dir. Shepherd Mail State Bank. Mem. adv. bd. Mercy Hosp. Asst sec. Asso. Industries Okla. Mem. Am. Inst. Steel Constrn. (dir. 1966-72), C. of C. (dir.). Kiwanian (pres. 1965). Home: 7601 Dorset Dr Oklahoma City OK 73116 Office: 1726 S Agnew St Oklahoma City OK 73108

VAN HOY, JAMES HAROLD, business exec., mgmt. cons.; b. nr. Garden City, Mo., Apr. 6, 1891; s. Waldo Pleasant and Lutie Dell (West) Van H.; student pub. schs.; m. Inez G., Dec. 19, 1968. Salesman to so. div. mgr. Bird & Son, Inc. of E. Walpole, Mass., Sanford, Fla., 1919-58; pres., dir. Smith Lumber Co., Albany, Ga., East Albany Lumber Co., Flint Homes, Inc., Fernandina (Fla.) Lumber & Supply Co., Amelia Investment Co., Fernandina; dir. Chase & Co., Sanford; dir. East Coast Lumber & Supply Co., Ft. Pierce, Fla.; sec.-treas., dir. Peninsula Paint & Plastic Mfrs., Inc., Sanford; 1st v.p. 1st Fed. Savs. & Loan Assn. Sanford. Chmn. bond holders com. City of Sanford. Democrat. Baptist. Club: River (Jacksonville, Fla.). Home: 900 Magnolia Av Sanford FL 32771

VAN LANDINGHAM, LEANDER SHELTON, JR., patent lawyer; b. Memphis, July 15, 1925; s. Leander Shelton and Bertha (Shumaker) Van L.; B.S. in Chemistry, U. N.C., 1948, M.A. in Organic Chemistry, 1949; J.D., Georgetown U., 1955; m. Henrietta Adena Stapf, July 5, 1959; children—Ann Henrietta, Leander Shelton III. Patent adviser Dept. Navy, Washington, 1953-55; admitted to D.C. bar, 1955, since pvt. practice in Washington. Cons. patent, trademark and copyright law, chem. patent matters, 1955—. Served with USNR, 1943-46, 51-53. Mem. Am. Chem. Soc., Sci. Assn., Am., D.C., Fed. bar assns., Am. Patent Law Assn., Am. Judicature Soc., Sigma Xi, Phi Alpha Delta. Methodist. Home: 10726 Stanmore Dr Potomac Falls Potomac MD 20854

VAN LENNEP, FREDERICK LEAS, horse breeder, mfg. co. exec.; b. Phila., July 6, 1911; s. Gustave A. and Florence (Leas) Van L.; student Haverford Sch., 1920-28; grad. Philips Exeter Acad., 1929; A.B., Princeton, 1933; m. Frances Dodge, Jan. 22, 1950; children—Hector M., Fredericka D., John F.; m. 2d, Mary Hazen Sprow, June 12, 1971. Head, Castleton Farm, Lexington, Ky., horse board and breeding farm, 1946—, Castleton Farm of Trenton (Fla.), 1963—; chmn. bd., pres. Castleton Industries, Inc., Pompano Beach, Fla., 1968—; pres. Castleton, Inc., horse breeding farm, 1949—; chmn. bd. Detroit Race Course, 1970—; dir. Boca Raton Nat. Bank (Fla.). Chmn. adv. com. on horse industry Dept. Agr., 1972—. Trustee St. Andrews Sch., Gulf Stream Sch. Served to lt. USNR, 1942-46. Mem. Am. Horse Show Assn. (dir. 1962—), Am. Saddle Horse Assn. (dir.), Am. Horse Council (trustee 1971—), Hambletonian Soc. (dir. 1951—), Fla. Council of 100. Presbyn. Clubs: Royal Palm Yacht and Country (Boca Raton); Merion Cricket (Haverford, Pa.); Bloomfield Hills (Mich.) Country; Everglades (Palm Beach, Fla.); Metropolitan (N.Y.C.); Iroquois Hunt (Lexington). Home: Castleton Farm Route 3 Lexington KY 40505 Office: PO Box 668 Pompano Beach FL 33060

VANLOH, HAROLD CARL, funeral home and ins. exec.; b. Iowa Park, Tex., Dec. 28, 1907; s. Charles Peter and Martha Katherine (Mueller) Vanl.; student Draughons Bus. Coll., 1924-25; m. Gwinn Elizabet Brumley, Nov. 25, 1935; children—Jerry Jack, Charles Kenneth. Vice-pres. Farmers State Bank, Burkburnett, Tex., 1925-40; cashier First Nat. Bank, Burkburnett, 1940-43; pres. Owens-Brumley Funeral Homes and Ins., Wichita Falls, Tex., 1943—; pres. First Savs. & Loan, 1960-65, Astro Drilling & Producing Co.; dir. First Nat. Bank, Burkburnett. Mem. Burkburnett City Council; mem. Burkburnett Parks and Recreation Bd., 1966-67; former mem. City-County Welfare Bd. Mem. Tex. State Assn. Mut. Ins. Cos. (v.p. 1956-57, 60-61, pres. 1966-67), Burkburnett C. of C. (dir. 1943-62, v.p. 1961-62), Clara (Tex.) Ex Students Assn. (pres. 1958). Democrat. Lutheran. Rotarian. Clubs: Wichita (Tex.); Wichita Falls (Tex.) Country; Burkburnett Swim (pres., dir.). Home: 311 E 6th St Burkburnett TX 76354 Office: 914 Scott St Wichita Falls TX 76301

VAN NESS, MARVIN LEONARD, pump mfg. exec.; b. Welsh, La., Dec. 1, 1903; s. Marvin Brown and Alice Elizabeth (Archer) van N.; student Asbury Coll., 1922-24, McKendree Coll., 1925-26, Rice Inst. Tech., 1926-27; m. Mabel Guzman, Apr. 26, 1929; 1 son, Joseph Leonard. Machinist, Tex. Co., Port Arthur, Tex., 1929-30, Welsh (La.) Machine Shops, 1930-50; owner Lo-Lift Pump Co., Inc., Welsh, 1951-66, pres., mgr., 1974—; owner, operator van Ness Bldgs., Welsh, 1950—; owner, mgr. Lady Fair, Welsh. Alderman, Welsh, 1959-62. Bd. dirs. La. Intracoastal Seaway Assn., 1967, Welsh Gen. Hosp., 1957-60. Lion (pres. 1950, dep. dist. gov. 1953). Home: 602 E South Welsh LA 70591 Office: 208 N Railroad Av Welsh LA 70591

VANNIER, MARYHELEN, educator, author; b. Decatur, Ill., June 18, 1915; d. William H. and Maude (Rockwood) Vannier; B.A., James Millikin U., 1938; M.A., Tchrs. Coll., Columbia, 1943; Ed.D., N.Y.U., 1950. Dir. womens phys. edn. Drake U., Des Moines, 1940-42, St. Lawrence U., Canton, N.Y., 1948-50, Wellesley High Sch., 1940-41; dir. women's health and phys. edn. So. Meth. U., Dallas, 1950—. Mem. Internat. Congress Phys. Edn. Tchrs. Girls and Women, Nat. Conf. Research in Therapeutic Recreation, Am. Sch. Health Assn., A.A.H.P.E.R., Am. Assn. U. Profs., Park and Recreation Assn., Nat. Assn. Phys. Edn. Coll. Women. Author: Teaching Physical Education in Elementary Schools, 1968, 5th edit., 1974; Methods and Materials in Recreation Leadership, 1966, 2d edit., 1974; Individual and Team Sports for Girls and Women, 1969, 3d edit., 1974; Physical Activities for College Women, 1968; Physical Activities for the Handicapped, 1974; many others; articles in profl. jours. Home: 7006 Stefani St Dallas TX 75225

VAN NORMAN, DAVID LAWRENCE, clergyman; b. Gouverneur, N.Y., Mar. 28, 1947; s. Pierson Franklin and Alvena Mae (Jarvis) Van N.; B.A., Anderson Coll., 1969; m. Brenda Joyce Cook, Oct. 26, 1973. Ordained to ministry 1st Ch. of God, 1973; asso. pastor 1st Ch. of God, Mt. Sterling, Ky., 1971-72, minister of youth, Columbia, S.C., 1973—. Exec. bd., state youth dir. Ky. Ch. of God, 1971-72, asst. state youth dir. S.C., 1973—; mem. Ky. Bd. Christian Edn., 1971-72. Instl. rep. Bluegrass council Boy Scouts Am., 1972. Home: 2604 DuBard St Columbia SC 29204 Office: 2665 Covenant Rd Columbia SC 29204

VAN NOSTRAND, ROBERT GAIGE, research co. exec.; b. Oneida, N.Y., Nov. 28, 1918; s. George Peyton and Mildred (Gaige) Van N.; B.S., Mo. Sch. Mines, 1942, M.S., 1949; Ph.D., U. N.C., 1953; m. Colette Marie Regnault, June 19, 1962; children—Chantel, Jean Pierre, Thierry, Dominique, Eric, Gregory. Sr. research geophysicist Magnolia Petroleum Co., Dallas, 1952-56; geophys. supr. Mobil Oil Francaise, Paris, France, 1956-57; chief geophysicist Prepa, Paris, 1957-61; gen. mgr. Exploration Geophysique Roger, Paris, 1961-62; with Teledyne Geotech, 1962—, v.p., 1971; dir. Computer Cartography, Washington. Served to maj. AUS, 1942-47. Mem. Soc. Exploration Geophysics, Am. Geophys. Union. A.A.A.S., Seismological Soc. Am., European Assn. Exploration Geophysics. Contbr. articles to profl. pubs. Editor: Society of Exploration Geophysics, 1966-67. Home: 1424 Kingston Av Alexandria VA 22302 Office: Box 334 Alexandria VA 22313

VANNOY, JOELLENE, nutritionist; b. McLean, Tex., Aug. 30, 1910; d. John Brown and Cora (Mills) Vannoy; B.S., Tex. Tech., 1931; M.A., Columbia, 1936, Ed.D., 1963. Tchr. home econs. McLean (Tex.) High Sch., 1931-33, Plainview (Tex.) High Sch., 1934; home demonstration agt. Stanton, Tex., 1935, Roby, Tex., 1937-38, Crowell, Tex., 1939-41; foods, nutrition specialist Ark. Agr. Extension Service, Little Rock, 1942-45; regional home economist Wheat Flour Inst., Chgo., 1946-55; nutritionist Millers Nat. Fedn., Washington, 1958-63; nutritionist, home economist Wheat Assos., U. S.A., Inc., Bulgur Assos. Inc., 1964-69; pub. health nutritionist D.C. Dept. Pub. Health, 1969—. U.S. technician First World Agrl. Fair, New Delhi, India, 1959-60. Mem. Am. Acad. Polit. and Social Scis., Am. Home Econs. Assn., Am. Dietetic Assn., Am. Pub. Health Assn., Am. Sch. Food Service Assn., Am. Women in Radio and Television, Nat. Acad. TV Arts Scis., Internat. Platform Assn., Nat. League Am. Pen Women, Kappa Delta Pi, Pi Lambda Theta. Mem. Christian Ch. Helped develop nutrition edn. programs in mass communications Colombia, S.Am. Egypt, India, Pakistan, The Philippines, Hong Kong, Taiwan, Vietnam, Thailand, 1958—. Home: 1330 Massachusetts Av NW Washington DC 20005 Office: 1221 M St NW Washington DC 20005

VAN OSTENBERG, PAUL ROGER, dentist; b. Grand Rapids, Mich., Aug. 30, 1941; s. Don Henry and Leonora Franciscus (Rylaarsdam) Van O.; A.A., St. Petersburg Jr. Coll., 1961; student U. Fla., 1961-62; B.A., U. So. Fla., 1963; D.D.S., Med. Coll. Va., 1967. Chief dentist Catawba Sanatorium, Va. State Dept. Health, Roanoke, 1967-68; instr. dept. pediatrics U. Va. Sch. Medicine, Charlottesville, 1968-71, asst. prof. dept. pediatrics, dir. dental services Children and Youth Center, clin. staff, 1971-74; asst. prof. dept. dental ecology U. N.C. Sch. Dentistry, 1973—; vis. dentist, prof. staff U. Va. Hosp., 1971-74. Lt. gov. Civitan Internat., 1972-73. Recipient outstanding service award Charlottesville Civitan Club, 1969-70. Mem. Am., N.C. dental assns., Am. Assn. Dental Schs., Am. Assn. Hosp. Dentists. Presbyn. Club: Civitan (treas. 1969-72) (Charlottesville, Va.). Home: Box 1107 Chapel Hill NC 27514 Office: NC Meml Hosp Box 110 Chapel Hill NC 27514

VAN RYSWYK, CARL WAYNE, elec. engr.; b. Otley, Ia., June 4, 1938; s. Pete and Nellie (Brandenhorst) Van R.; B.S., U. Tex., 1963, M.S, 1969; m. Shirley Elaine Walker, Sept. 30, 1957; children—Carla Jo, Jeffrey Wayne, Craig Wesley, Chris Walker. Asst. engr. White Instruments, Inc., Austin, Tex., 1963-66, chief engr., 1966—. Cons., Millard Research Assos., Austin, Internat. and Pan Am. Inst. Social Sci. and Ednl. Research, Austin. Bd. dirs. Austin Assn. Retarded Children, treas., 1970-71, pres., 1971-72; bd. dirs. Pan Am. Inst. Social Sci. and Ednl. Research. Baptist (Sunday sch. dir. 1968-70). Home: 606 Brookhaven Trail Austin TX 78746 Office: PO Box 698 Austin TX 78767

VAN SANT, GEORGE MONTGOMERY, educator; b. State College, Pa., Nov. 20, 1927; s. Edward Raguet and Beatrice Nordica (Snow) Van S.; A.B., St. John's Coll., Annapolis, Md., 1948; M.A., U. Va., 1955, Ph.D., 1958; postgrad. vis. scholar Cambridge (Eng.) U., 1971-72; m. Peggy Ann Hutchinson, Sept. 12, 1953; children—Edward D., Mary M. Ednl. researcher Nat. Council of Protestant Episcopal Ch., N.Y.C., 1948-49; dir. printing St. John's Coll., 1949-50; information officer Va. Hwy. Research Council, 1956-58; asst. prof. to prof. philosophy Mary Washington Coll. of U. Va., 1958—, chmn. dept., 1969—. Pres. Va. Mus. Fine Arts, Fredericksburg, 1961; v.p. Fredericksburg Cotillion, 1962, 69. Mem. Fredericksburg Democratic Com., 1965-71, 73—. Bd. dirs. Fredericksburg Area United Givers Fund, 1969-71, 73—. Served with USMC, 1945-46, 50-53; col. Res. Decorated Bronze Star, Purple Heart; NSF fellow, 1961. Mem. Am., Va. (pres. 1964) philos. assns., U. Va. Raven Soc., Omicron Delta Kappa. Episcopalian. Contbr. articles to profl. jours. Home: 1407 Washington Av Fredericksburg VA 22401

VAN STONE, LORNE FREDERICK, mgmt. cons.; b. Cairo, Ill., Nov. 2, 1906; s. Lorne Disraeli and Adelaide (Mitchell) Van S.; student Tex. A. & M., 1933; U. Houston, 1938; m. Carmen Elizabeth, June 5, 1929; children—Lorne Frederick, Janice (Mrs. L. B. Hedrick). Salesman, J.E. Rogers, Inc., Houston, 1926-33; mgr. bakery supply dept. Rogers Grain Co., 1933-36; v.p., sales mgr. S. Tex. Feed Co., 1936-38; pres., gen. mgr. Uncle Johnny Mills, Inc., 1938-59; exec. v.p., gen. mgr. United Salt Corp., 1960-65; pres. Lorne F. Van Stone Assos., mgmt. cons. and orgn. devel., 1966—; exec. v.p., dir. C.E. Kaiser Co., 1966—; sec.-treas., dir. Standley Inc., 1948— (all Houston); founder, pres. Lorne F. Van Stone Assos. (U.K.) Ltd., London, Eng., 1970—; pres. Matrex Corp., 1969—; treas. V Inc., 1971; dir. Stillwagon Enterprises, 1969—. Chmn. salt com. for agr. Salt Inst. U.S. and Can., 1964-65; chmn. S.W. Area Conf. Indsl. Relations, 1965. Active various local fund raising campaigns; past mem. adv. coms. U. Houston, U. Kan., Tex. A. & M. U. Bd. dirs. Met. YMCA, Houston, 1964-68, Eye Inst., 1958-68. Mem. Houston C. of C. (past chmn. research com., mem. 1972), Tex. Mfrs. Assn. (dir. 1956-60, chmn. retirement plan and trust fund com. 1963-67, treas. 1961-62), Houston Sales Execs. Club. (life mem., past pres.), Salt Producers Assn. (chmn. agrl. com.), Better Bus. Bur. (life mem., past pres. Houston), Am. (past dir.), Midwest (past dir.), Tex. (pres. 1948, 54) feed mfrs. assns., Execs. Assn. Houston (past pres.), S.W. Sales and Marketing Execs. Assn. (mem. council). Presbyn. (ruling elder). Clubs: Salesmanship of Houston (life mem., past pres.), Houston Farm and Ranch (pres. 1956-57), Houston Yacht (commodore 1959-60). Home: 2736 Werlein St Houston TX 77005

VAN SWEARINGEN, EARL CORNELIUS, color process co. exec.; b. New Cumberland, W.Va., Apr. 2, 1904; s. Clarence Chapman and Carrie Cornelia (Carmen) Van S.; student Cleve. Sch. Art, 1923-24; grad. Cin. Acad. Art, 1926; postgrad., Grand Central Art Sch., N.Y.C., 1933; m. Phyllis Margueritte Andrews, May 18, 1925; children—Barbara Ellen (Mrs. William H. Loescher), Earl Cornelius, Phyllis Margueritte (Mrs. J. Brooks Vallentine). Art dir. J. Walter Thompson Advt. Agy., N.Y.C., Buenos Aires, Argentina, 1928-31; free-lance artist and color cons., N.Y.C., 1931-51; with Batten, Barton, Durstine, Osborn, Inc., advt. agy., N.Y.C., 1953-57; creative dir. A. Asch Co., outdoor advt. agy., N.Y.C., 1958-68; pres. Color

Monitor Corp., N.Y.C., 1968-71; pres. Van Swearingen Corp. Fla., 1971—. Instr. art and painting Grand Central Art Sch., N.Y.C., 1938-40. Recipient Scoutmaster's key Siwanoy Council Boy Scouts Am., Crosley Television Poster award, 1955, Four Roses Poster award, 1962, citation for inventing new printing technique (Van Swearingen Reprodn. Process) Printing Industries of Met. N.Y., 1966. Mem. Soc. Illustrators. Clubs: Orienta Beach and Yacht (Mamaroneck, N.Y., commodore 1967-69, ret. commodore emeritus); Cape Coral Yacht and Racquet (Cape Coral, Fla.). Author: Pictorial Perspectives, 1939; How To Decorate Your Own Home, 1953; inventor E.C. Van Swearingen Reprodn. Process for printing or painting, universal color casting system, 1954, patentee Eng., Can., U.S. Address: 5714 Driftwood Pkwy Cape Coral FL 33904

VAN TUYL, MALCOLM LOUIS, JR., radio broadcasting exec.; b. New Orleans, Aug. 16, 1950; s. Malcolm Louis and Bertha Louise (Enloe) Van T.; student Career Acad. Broadcast, Atlanta, 1968-69, Elkins Sch. Electronics, 1968; m. Camilla Kay Ashcraft, July 30, 1970. Announcer, KLPL Radio, Lake Providence, La., 1969, WWUN Radio, Jackson, Miss., 1969-70, WTIX Radio, New Orleans, 1970—. Home: 3500 Division No 361 Metairie LA 70002 Office: 332 Carondelet St New Orleans LA 70130

VAN VACTOR, DAVID, composer, flutist; b. Plymouth, Ind., May 8, 1906; s. David Ellsworth and Matilda (Fenstermacher) Van V.; Mus. B., Northwestern U., 1928, Mus.M., 1935; student l'Ecole Normale, Paris, summer, 1931; m. Mary Virginia Landreth, May 28, 1931; children—Adriaen, David Landreth. Flutist, Chgo. Symphony Orch., 1931; instr. theory of music Northwestern U., 1935-47; composer, 1928—; asst. condr. Kansas City Philharmonic, 1943-47, also head composition dept. Conservatory of Music, 1945-47; founder condr. Allied Arts Orch. of Kansas City, 1945-47; condr. Knoxville Symphony Orch., 1947-72; prof. dept. fine arts U. of Tenn., 1947—. Guest condr. Nat. Symphony Orch. of Chile, 1945; vis. prof. U. Chile (S.A.); guest condr. Philharmonia Orch. London, 1954; guest condr., flute soloist Palmengarten Orch., Frankfort, Germany, 1961, 62; artist in residence, guest condr. orchs. of Chile, under auspices U.S. Dept. State, 1965. Mem. Am. Wind Quintet League Composers touring Central and S. Am., summer 1941; former mem. conf. bd. Asso. Research Council Com. on Internat. exchange of Persons. Recipient hon. mention for "The Masque of the Red Death" (full orchestra) in Gustavus Swift competition, 1935; 1st award for "Symphony in D" (full orchestra) N.Y. Philharmonic-Symphony competition, 1938; 1st award for "Quintet with Flute, Two Violins, Viola and Cello," Soc. for Publ. of Am. Music, 1941; "Overture to a Comedy No. 2" won 1942 Juilliard Publ. award; Northwestern University Alumni Merit award, 1950. Has composed for full orchestra and chamber orchestra, also chorals and chamber music; works played by Chgo., Rochester, Atlanta, Chattanooga, Pitts., Kansas City, Indpls., San Francisco, Knoxville, Nat. symphony orchs., N.Y. Philharmonic, Cleveland, Phila., St. Louis orchs.; composed under commn. Louisville Orch., Fantasy, Chaconne, Allegro; New Light Composition for Chorus and Orchestra, 1959. Author: Every Child May Hear, 1960. Fulbright Research fellow, Frankfort, Germany, 1957-58. Guggenheim fellow, 1957-58. Mem. Wranglers, Phi Mu Alpha Sinfonia (hon.), Phi Kappa Lambda. Clubs: Arts, Cliff Dwellers (Chgo.) Home: 2824 Kingston Pike Knoxville TN 37910

VAN VLACK, MELVA BULLINGTON (MRS. WILLIAM CLARK VAN VLACK), home economist; b. Vesta Community, Charleston, Ark., Apr. 3, 1909; d. Baxter Lee and Ella Emma (McConnell) Bullington; B.S., U. Ark., 1932, M.S., 1965; postgrad. U. Cal. at Berkeley, 1939, U. Ala., 1948, Jacksonville State U., 1949; m. William Clark Van Vlack, Aug. 9, 1946. Home econs. instr., Prairie Grove, Ark., 1932-33; elementary tchr., Liberty-Tulsa County, Okla., 1933-34; home demonstration agt., Magnolia, Ark., 1934-36, Hope, Ark., 1936-39, Pine Bluff, Ark., 1939-47; jr. high sch. home econs. instr., Atalla, Ala., 1949-57; extension home economist, Ft. Smith, Ark., 1957—. Recipient Distinguished Service award Nat. Assn. Extension Home Economists, 1970. Mem. Am. Home Econs. Assn., Ark. Assn. Extension Home Economists (dist. counselor), Bus. and Profl. Women Pine Bluff and Ft. Smith, Epsilon Sigma Phi, Delta Gamma Sigma. Methodist. Clubs: Sorosis (Magnolia); Soroptimist, Garden (Ft. Smith). Home: 11 Salome St Fort Smith AR 72901 Office: Courthouse Bldg Fort Smith AR 72901

VAN VLEET, DAVID EDWARD, dentist; b. Sharon, Conn., Dec. 16, 1931; s. Henry Lee and Edna Zoe (Cassidy) Van V.; student Agrl. and Tech. Inst., Canton, N.Y., 1949-51, Duke U., 1955-57; D.D.S., U. N.C., 1961; m. Norma June Husted, Nov. 17, 1951; children—Nancy Lynn, David Eric, Lee Morris. Pvt. practice gen. dentistry, Durham, N.C., 1963—; pres., chmn. bd. V & H, Inc., 1970—. Served with USAF, 1951-55, 61-63. Fellow Royal Soc. Health; mem. Delta Sigma Delta. Methodist (steward 1971—). Kiwanian. Home: 2957 Friendship Dr Durham NC 27705 Office: 624 Gary St Durham NC 27703

VARGA, LOUIS PAUL, educator, chemist; b. Portland, Ore., Mar. 25, 1922; s. Joseph and Julia (Demish) V.; B.A., Reed Coll., 1948; M.S., U. Chgo., 1950; Ph.D., Ore. State U., 1960; m. Ruth E. Soehl, June 20, 1948; children—Karis E., Steven H., Deborah J., Leland J. Mem. staff research and devel. Gen. Electric Co., Hanford, Wash., 1950-53; research asso., instr. Reed Coll., 1953-57; coop. fellow U.S. Bur. Mines, Albany, Ore., 1957-60; research asso. Mass. Inst. Tech., 1960-61; asst. prof. Okla. State U., Stillwater, 1961-67, asso. prof. chemistry, 1967—. Asso. Western Univs. faculty research participant Los Alamos Sci. Lab., 1966-67; vis. staff mem., 1968—. Served with AUS, 1940-45. Mem. Am. Chem. Soc., Sigma Xi, Phi Lambda Phi. Research in application of stable isotopes to environmental problems; trace ion analysis; automatic data acquisition and computer methods in analytical chemistry; actinide spetra. Home: 611 Arapahoe Dr Stillwater OK 74074

VARIN, ROSS ARLEN, mech. engr.; b. Birmingham, Ala., Apr. 25, 1934; s. Charles Thomas and Arliene Julia (Callaway) V.; B.S., U. Ala., 1958, postgrad., 1959-62; m. Sara Frances Lokey, Dec. 26, 1955; children—Ross Arlen, Vicki Lynne, Charles Hugh. Design engr. Am. Bridge div. U.S. Steel, Birmingham, 1958-62; design engr. Boeing Co., New Orleans, 1962-63; research engr. Frito-Lay, Inc., Dallas, 1963-64; engring. mgr. Clow Corp., Birmingham, 1964—. Cons. mobile home industry. Mem. C. of C., Assn. Industries Ala., Am. Foundry Soc., Am. Inst. Profl. Engrs. Methodist. Home: 1324 4th Way NW Birmingham AL 35215 Office: 1600 National St Tarrant AL 35217

VARN, WILLIAM LESTER, JR., investment co. exec.; b. Jacksonville, Fla., Dec. 18, 1924; s. William Lester and Myra (Terrell) V.; B.S., Princeton, 1946; postgrad. Renssalaer Poly. Inst., 1943-45; m. Marjorie Hagood Drake, Feb. 5, 1954; children—William Lester III, Eleanor Kenyon. With Varn Investment Co., Jacksonville, 1947—, pres., 1973—; pres. Crescent Financial, Inc., Jacksonville, 1947—; dir. Atlantic Nat. Bank, Fla. Wire & Cable Co., UniCapital Corp., Asbury Realty Co., Jacksonville Fed. Savs. & Loan Assn. Chmn. Greater Jacksonville Open, golf tournament, 1968. Adv. bd. Salvation Army, 1960-74; chmn. bd. trustees Bolles Sch., 1950-74; bd. dirs. St. Luke's Hosp. Assn., Blue Cross of Fla., Riverside Presbyn. Day Sch. Served as lt. (j.g.) USNR, 1944-46. Mem. Jacksonville Area C. of C., Com. of 100, Financial Analysts Soc. Jacksonville, Fellowship Christian Athletes, Ye Mystic Revellers. Presbyn. Clubs: Meninak, River (dir. 1973-74), Timuquana Country (pres. 1969-70), University, Fla. Yacht, Friars (Jacksonville); Ponte Vedra (Fla.). Home: 4075 Timuquana Rd Jacksonville FL 32210 Office: 206 Marine National Bank Bldg 311 W Duval St PO Box 924 Jacksonville FL 32201

VARNEDOE, WILLIAM WHITFIELD, JR., elec. engr.; b. Savannah, Ga., June 11, 1923; s. William Whitfield and Willie (Harmon) V.; B.E.E., Ga. Inst. Tech., 1947; m. Elizabeth Louise Thomas, Nov. 22, 1955; children—Sharon (Mrs. Frank Lindamood, Jr.), William Frank, John Clark, Ker Thomas. Instr. Ga. Inst. Tech., Atlanta, 1947-48; elec. engr. U.S. Navy, Panama City, 1948-52, U.S. Army, Huntsville, Ala., 1952-60, NASA, Huntsville, 1960—. Fire chief, Green Mountain Vol. Fire Dept., 1965—; treas. Madison County Assn. Vol. Fire Depts., 1972—. Served with USAAF, 1943-45. Decorated Air medal with 3 oak leaf clusters. Fellow Nat. Speleological Soc. (bd. govs. 1956, 67). Author: Alabama Caves, 1965, Caves of Madison County Alabama, 1965, Alabama Caves and Caverns, 1973. Home: Route 4 Box 1853 Huntsville AL 35803 Office: EC-11 Marshall Space Flight Center AL 35812

VARNER, JOHN GRIER, historian, educator, author; b. Mt. Pleasant, Tex., Mar. 30, 1905; s. John Grier and Lelia Ada (McConnell) V.; B.A., Austin Coll., 1926; M.A., U. Va., 1932, Ph.D., 1940; m. Jeannette Johnson, Apr. 29, 1939. duPont teaching fellow U. Va., Charlottesville, 1930-38; asst. prof. English, Washington and Lee U., Lexington, Va., 1938-43; dir. Centro Venezolano-Americano, Caracas, 1943-47; asst. cultural attache Am. embassy, Mexico City, Mexico, 1947; prof. English, U. Tex., Austin, 1947-72, emeritus, 1972—. Dept. State lectr., S.Am. and C.Am., 1951-52. Am. Philos. Soc. grantee, U. Tex. Research Council grantee, Spain, 1954. Mem. Real Academia de Ciencias, Bellas Lectras y Nobles Artes (corr., Cordoba, Spain), Tex. Inst. Letters, Latin Am. Studies Assn. Democrat. Presbyn. Author: English Grammar for Venezuelans, 1946; El Inca: The Life and Times of Garcilaso de la Vega, 1968. Editor, translator (with wife): The Florida of the Inca, 1951; Editor: Edgar Allan Poe and The Philadelphia Saturday Courier, 1933. Home: 2510 Jarratt Av Austin TX 78703*

VARNER, KINCH MORGAN, JR., banker; b. Union Springs, Ala., Jan. 7, 1915; s. Kinch Morgan and Estelle Eugenia (McGowen) Varner; student Chillicothe Bus. Coll., 1933-35, La. State U., 1953-56; m. Anne Robison, June 20, 1939; 1 son, Kinch Morgan III. Cashier, dir. First Nat. Bank, Union Springs, Ala., 1936-53; asst. v.p. Birmingham Trust Nat. Bank, 1953-56; v.p. Union Bank &Trust Co., Montgomery, 1956-60; pres., dir. First Nat. Bank, Auburn, 1960—; dir. Birmingham br. Fed. Res. Bank, Nixon Real Estate, University Agy. Pres., Auburn Indsl. Devel. Bd., 1962-70; mayor, Union Springs, Ala., 1952. Bd. dirs. Ala. 4-H Club; state treas. Ala. div. Am. Cancer Soc., 1968-71. Served to 2d lt. AUS, 1944-46. Mem. Auburn C. of C. (pres. 1968), Auburn Downtown Mchts. Assn. (bd. dirs. 1968-71). Lion (dist. gov. 1951-52), Mason. Home: 634 Cary Dr Auburn AL 36830 Office: PO Box 2149 Auburn AL 36830

VASWANI, NARI KALACHAND, govt. engr.; b. Hyderabad, India, Mar. 16, 1920; s. Kalachand H. and Ganga K. (Bhojwani) V.; B.Engring., Bombay U., India, 1943; M.S., Wis. U., 1959; Ph.D., Roorkee U., India, 1964; m. Menghi A. Thadani, June 26, 1948; children—Roma (Mrs. Prem Malkani), Bulbul. Exec. engr. railways, bldg. engr. Indian Railways, 1943-54; prof. Roorkee U., India, 1954-65; mem. Va. Hwy. Research Council, Charlottesville, Va., 1965—. U.S. fellow, 1958-59. Fellow Am. Soc. C.E.; mem. India Road Congress, Am. Soc. Testing Materials, Soc. Soil Mechanics and Found. Engrs., Inst. Engrs., Sigma Xi. Author: Highway Engineering; Railway Engineering; Airport Engineering. Contbr. articles to profl. pubs. Home: 1006 Glendale Rd Charlottesville VA 22901 Office: 3817 University Station Charlottesville VA 22903

VATH, JOSEPH G., clergyman; b. New Orleans, Mar. 12, 1918; ed. Notre Dame Sem. Ordained priest Roman Catholic Ch., 1941; named titular bishop of Novaliciana and aux. bishop of Mobile-Birmingham (Ala.), 1967; now bishop Birmingham. Office: 400 Government St Mobile AL 36606*

VAUGHAN, DAVID ROSS, investment co. exec.; b. Augusta, Ga., June 13, 1931; s. George Marion and Virginia Martha (Moore) V.; student Presbyn. Coll., 1948-52; B.A., Vanderbilt U., 1953; postgrad. Ga. State U., 1956; m. Nancy Finley, Dec. 17, 1952; children—Daniel, Judith, James. With Mut. Benefit Life Ins. Co., 1956-63; 1st v.p., dir. Financial Service Corp. Internat., Atlanta, 1963-72; pres. Balanced Financial Service, Inc., life ins. agy.; v.p. FSC Properties, Inc., 1969-72; pres. Consolidated Resources Corp., 1972—, Real Estate Resources Corp. Chmn. Clairmont Oaks, Inc. Trustee So. Bapt. Annuity Bd. Served to lt. (j.g.) USNR, 1953-55. Mem. Million Dollar Round Table (life), Nat. Assn. Life Underwriters, Assn. Advanced Life Underwriters, Atlanta Estate Planning Council, Pi Kappa Alpha. Republican. Baptist (deacon). Home: 500 Peachtree Battle Dr NW Atlanta GA 30305 Office: Suite 516 100 Colony Sq Atlanta GA 30361

VAUGHAN, JAMES THURMAN, JR., lawyer; b. Hubbard, Tex., Sept. 15, 1927; s. James T. and Johnnie Iola (Orr) V.; B.S., Tex. Christian U., 1950; J.D., So. Meth. U., 1957; m. Henrietta Ann Aikman, Aug. 5, 1950 (div.); 1 dau., Leigh Ann. Exec. dept. Gulf Oil Corp., Ft. Worth, 1950-54; pvt. practice, Dallas, 1957—; gen. counsel Wrather Oil Interests, Eldorado Oil & Gas, Inc., Sovereign Devel. Corp., Sovereign Oil & Gas, Inc., Williams & Wagner Constrn. Co., Inc., Williams & Wagner Investments, inc.; v.p. Republic Leasing Corp. Served with AUS, 1945-47. Mem. Am., Tex., Irving, Dallas bar assns., Tex. Trial Lawyers Assn., Dallas Assn. Petroleum Landmen, State Bar Tex., Ind. Petroleum Assn. Am., Southwestern Legal Found., Delta Theta Phi. Democrat. Baptist. Mason (Shriner). Home: 1008 Hadrian Irving TX 75062 Office: Eldorado Bldg 2929 Cedar Spring Rd Dallas TX 75219

VAUGHAN, KENNETH DOYLE, coll. pres.; b. Highway Highlands, Cal., June 6, 1928; s. Olin B. and Florence (Scott) V.; B.S., W.Tex. State U., 1949, M.Ed., 1953; m. Melba Ruth Grady, July 29, 1949; children—Linda Sue, Stephen Doyle. Tchr., Borger Ind. Sch. Dist., 1949-52; tchr. Clarendon (Tex.) Jr. Coll., 1952-53, pres., 1961—; prin. Clarendon Ind. Sch. Dist., 1952-60; tchr. Amarillo (Tex.) Ind. Sch. Dist., 1960-61. Mem. Tex. Tchrs. Assn., Am. Assn., Sch. Adminstrs., Tex. Jr. Coll. Adminstrs. Assn., Tex. Jr. Coll. Tchrs. Assn. Mason. Home: PO Box 925 Clarendon TX 79226 Office: PO Box 986 Clarendon TX 79226

VAUGHAN, ROGER CONRAD, utility exec.; b. nr. Anniston, Ala., Sept. 17, 1938; s. Boyd and Nora Elane (Green) V.; B.S., Auburn U., 1960; M.S., U. South Ala., 1972; m. Shelby Jean Whatley, Sept. 17, 1959; children—Jefferson Roger, Andrew Boyd. Devel. gr. Union Carbide Corp., Fostoria, O., 1960-61; devel. engr., Lawrenceburg, Tenn., 1963-65; with Ala. Power Co., Anniston and Mobile, Ala., 1965—, indsl. power rep., 1965-73, sr. indsl. power rep., 1973—. Chmn. troup com. Mobile Area council Boy Scouts Am., 1972—; active United Fund, 1972; adviser Jr. Achievement, 1965-66. Bd. dirs. Springhill Little League, 1973—, March of Dimes, Mobile, 1970-73. Served to lt. Signal Corps, AUS, 1961-63. Registered profl. engr., Ala. Mem. Res. Officers Assn., Mobile Area, Ala. chambers commerce, Scabbard and Blade, Pi Tau Sigma. Republican. Episcopalian. Optimist. Clubs: Skyline Country. Home: 3720 Claridge Rd S Mobile AL 36608 Office: PO Box 2247 Mobile AL 36601

VAUGHAN, ROSWELL FAIRBANKS, III, investment banker; b. San Antonio, June 30, 1938; s. Roswell Fairbanks and Helen Stuart (McFarland) V.; B.A., Duke U., 1960; postgrad. N.Y. U., 1961; m. Ann Blake Campbell, Aug. 14, 1965; children—Ann Blake, Helen Stuart. Exec. trainee Irving Trust Co., N.Y.C., 1960-61; with Rauscher Pierce Securities Corp., Houston, 1961-73, v.p., 1969-73; v.p. Reynolds Securities, Inc., 1973—. Bd. dirs. Nat. Cystic Fibrosis Research Found. Mem. Houston Soc. Financial Analysts, Duke U. Alumni (v.p. 1968—). Episcopalian (asso. vestry 1966-67, lay reader 1967—). Clubs: Houston Country, Houston. Home: 5629 Longmont St Houston TX 77027 Office: 600 Jefferson Cullen Center Houston TX 77002

VAUGHAN, STUART (JOHN WALKER VAUGHAN), theatrical dir.; b. Terre Haute, Ind., Aug. 23, 1925; s. John Harwood and Pauletta (Walker) V.; B.A., Ind. State Coll., 1945; M.A., Ind. U., 1946; studied acting with Harold Clurman, 1954-56; m. Gladys Regier, 1948 (div. 1960); m 2d, Helen Quarrier, 1960 (dec. 1963); m. 3d, Anne Thompson, 1965. Profl. acting debut with touring co., 1946; tchr. speech drama Ind. State Tchrs. Coll., 1947-48; dir., actor various stock and repertory cos., N.Y.C., St. Augustine, Fla., Erie, Pa., Nassau, Bahamas, Old Orchard Beach, Me., N.Y. Shakespeare Festival, others, 1948-58; became artistic dir. Phoenix Theatre, N.Y.C., 1958, Seattle Repertory Theatre, 1963; producing dir. Repertory Theatre New Orleans, 1966—; dir. The Lady's Not for Burning, Omnibus, NBC-TV, 1958. Recipient Vernon Rice award, also Village Voice Off-Broadway award for direction N.Y. Shakespeare Co., 1958. Rockefeller artist-in-residence grantee Stanford, 1947; Fulbright grantee for study Brit. repertory theatres, 1949-50; Ford Found. dirs. grantee in Europe, 1961-62. Mem. The Players, Soc. Stage Dirs. and Choreographers, Actors Equity Assn. Co-editor: The Bantam Shakespeare, 1961. Home: 716 St Philip St New Orleans LA 70116 Office: 546 Carondelet St New Orleans LA 70130

VAUGHAN, WALTER WRIGHT, banker; b. Dracut, Mass., Dec. 25, 1932; s. Walter Wright and Margaret Grace (Ryan) V.; student U. Notre Dame, 1950-53, U. Md., 1970; m. Sarah Louise Vance, Jan. 10, 1959; children—Walter Wright III, Daniel Thomas. Asst. treas. Am. Security & Trust Co., Washington, 1956-63, v.p., 1967—; v.p. Mt. Vernon Nat. Bank & Trust Co., Annandale, Va., 1963-67. Faculty, Grad. Sch. Consumer Banking, 1970—; chmn. installment loan adv. com. 5th Fed. Reserve Dist., 1969—. Mem. exec. com. Nat. Found. Consumer Credit; chmn. exec. com. Greater Washington Consumer Counseling and Edn. Service. Vice pres. Annandale Little League, 1972-73. Bd. dirs. Annandale Boys Club. Served with USMCR, 1953-56. Recipient Distinguished Service award Jr. C. of C., 1959; named Young Man of the Year Jaycees, 1959-60. Mem. Consumer Bankers Assn. (dir. 1971—). Home: 4016 Iva Lane Fairfax VA 22030 Office: 7th and Massachusetts Av NW Washington DC 20001

VAUGHN, EARL WRAY, judge, lawyer, former state legislator; b. Reidsville, N.C., June 17, 1928; s. John H. and Lelia (Foster) V.; A.B., U. N.C., 1950, LL.B., 1952; m. Eloise Freeland Maddry, Dec. 20, 1952; children—Mark, John, Stuart, Rose. Admitted to N.C. bar; atty. Draper, N.C., 1953—; solicitor Leaksville Recorder's Ct., 1958-60; mem. N.C. Ho. Reps., 1960-69, speaker, 1967-69; judge N.C. Ct. Appeals, 1969—. Bd. mgrs. Council State Govts., 1963-69. Chmn. Pub. Utilities Com., 1963-65. Bd. trustees Rockingham Coll. Served with inf. AUS, 1946-47. Mem. Phi Delta Phi. Home: 3312 Felton Pl Raleigh NC 27608 Office: 1 W Morgan St Raleigh NC 27602

VAUGHN, EMMA JUAN BELL (MRS. ERASMUS ROSCOE VAUGHN), librarian; b. Cartwright, Ky., Aug. 23, 1908; d. Henry Clay and Nannie (Cooper) Bell; student Transylvania U., 1925-28, Western State U., 1928; B.S., Tenn. Poly. U., 1940; postgrad. Memphis State U., 1950-52, Catheryn Spalding U., 1957-60; Ph.D. (hon.), Hamilton State Coll., 1973; m. Erasmus Roscoe Vaughn, Sept. 25, 1928; children—George Clay, Ann (Mrs. Jere Calvin Robertson), James Erasmus. Prin., Three Forks Sch., Warren County, Ky., 1942-44, Lamont Sch., Robertson County, Tenn., 1944-46; tchr. Alamo (Tenn.) High Sch., 1946-49, pub. schs., Dyer County, Tenn., 1950-54; tchr. English and French, Heath High Sch., Paducah, Ky., 1948-49; librarian Ballard County High Sch., LaCenter, Ky., 1949-50, Hickman High Sch., Clinton, Ky., 1956-57, Fulton County High Sch., Hickman, Ky., 1957-58; tchr. French, biology Byars Hall High Sch., Covington, Tenn., 1954-56; librarian Lowes (Ky.) High Sch., 1958-69. Trustee Stinnett (Ky.) Settlement Sch. Recipient honor award Lowes High Sch. chpt. Future Farmers Am., 1969. Mem. N.E.A., Ky. Edn. Assn., Ky. Hist. Soc., D.A.R. Democrat. Mem. Christian Ch. (pianist 1959-69). Clubs: Woodville (Ky.) Home Makers (charter mem.). Home: 827 W Broadway Mayfield KY 42066

VAUGHN, ERASMUS ROSCOE, educator; b. Monroe, Tenn., May 22, 1900; s. James Francis and Rebecca (Phillips) V.; A.B., Transylvania U., 1926, M.A., 1926; B.D., Vanderbilt U., 1944; postgrad. U. Ky., 1928-29; m. Emma Juan Bell, Sept. 25, 1928; children—George Clay, Ann Stoddard (Mrs. Jere Calvin Robertson), James Erasmus. Head edn. dept. Mt. Berry Coll., 1927-28; supt. Stinnett Settlement Sch., Ky., 1928-34; social sci. and Bible tchr. Livingston Acad., 1936-41; supt. Orlinda (Tenn.) Schs., 1941-46; prin. RoEllen Sch., Dyersburg, Tenn., 1950-56, Western High Sch., Hickman Ky., 1956-58; tchr. history, English, Lowes (Ky.) High Sch., 1958—; pastor Disciples Chs., Livingston, Tenn., Sturgis, Ky., 1934-36. Chmn. Prins. Study Council Tenn., 1950-56; chmn. Crippled Children Camp Program. Recipient Honored Minsters Pin of Disciples, Christian Ch., 1969. Mem. Nat., Ky. edn. assns., Nat. Platform Assos., Pi Kappa Delta, Sigma Upsilon. Lion, Rotarian, Kiwanian. Contbr. articles to profl. jours. Home: 827 W Broadway Mayfield KY 42066

VAUGHN, HUBERT ARNOLD, banker; b. Corbin, Ky., July 30, 1912; s. Jack Lewis and Ollie Mae (Black) V.; student Eastern Ky. U., 1932-35, Ohio State U., 1958; m. Clara Gibson, Feb. 7, 1936; children—Hubert Byron, Judith Ann, Jerry (Mrs. George Litton Kline). With Jellico Grocery Co., Inc., various locations, 1935-68, mgr., Somerset, Ky., 1941-60, mgr. Oneida, Tenn., 1960-68; dir. 1st Trust & Savs. Bank Oneida, Tenn., 1965—, administr. customer service, 1969-72, v.p., trust officer, 1973—. Mem. Oneida Water Works Bd., 1969—. Mem. Scott County C. of C. (dir. 1961-64, treas. 1962-64). Kiwanian. Home: 638 N Main St Oneida TN 37841 Office: 226 S Main St Oneida TN 37841

VAUGHN, ROBERT DONALD, army officer; b. Iola, Kan., Mar. 27, 1925; s. Ralph Herbert and Alice (Dille) V.; B.A., U. Md., 1954; M.B.A., U. Ala., 1960; postgrad. Command and Gen. Staff Coll., 1964, Nat. War Coll., 1970; m. Ruthe Irene De Bow, Aug. 23, 1946; children—Marta Kristine, Robert Donald, John Patrick. Commd. 2d lt. U.S. Army, 1950, advanced through grades to col., 1970; commissary officer SHAPE, 1951-54; co. comdr., 1955-56; adviser MAAG, Iran, 1957-58; staff officer Inventory Control Point,

Germany, 1960-63; chief Civil Schs. Program, 1964-67; bn. comdr. support command comdr. G-4, 1st Cav. Div., Vietnam, 1967-68; monitor M-16 Rifle, 1968; dep. comdr. Atlanta Gen. Depot, 1970-71; comdr. Burtonwood Army Depot, U.K., 1971-73; dir. mgmt. Office Dep. Chief Staff, Logistics Dept. Army, 1973—. Decorated Legion of Merit, Bronze Star medal with oak leaf cluster, Air medal. Mem. Nat. Honor Soc., Beta Gamma Sigma. Democrat. Presbyn. (deacon 1969—). Home: 1516 N Greenbrier St Arlington VA 22205 Office: Pentagon Washington DC

VAUGHN, ROBERT ELI, utility constrn. co. pres.; b. Tampa, Feb. 11, 1930; s. Milton R. and Louise Clairice (Renaud) V.; B.Ch.E., Ga. Inst. Tech., 1951; M.S. in Ch.E., Mass. Inst. Tech., 1952; m. Frances Marie Curry, Feb. 27, 1954; children—Beverly, Robert, Glenn, Frances. Chem. engr., Cabot Corp., Boston, 1951-53, U.S. Phosphoric Products, 1956-58; pres. Mech. & Chem. Equipment Co., Inc., Brandon, Fla., 1958—; v.p., treas. Brandon Chrysler Plymouth, Inc., 1973—; also citrus groves; dir. Barnett Bank Brandon. Chmn., Hillsborough County Cath. Bd. Edn., 1971-72; scoutmaster Boy Scouts Am., 1968—. Bd. govs. S.W. Fla. Water Mgmt. Dist., 1973—. Mem. Am. Inst. Chem. Engrs., Brandon C. of C. Democrat. Roman Catholic. Clubs: Tower, University (Tampa); Brandon Swim and Tennis. Home: 122 Lakewood Dr Brandon FL 33511 Office: PO Drawer 789 Brandon FL 33511

VAWTER, PAUL EDWARD, JR., investment counsel; b. Evanston, Ill., Feb. 7, 1934; s. Paul Edward and Lillian Elizabeth (Ferguson) V.; B.B.A., U. Mich., 1956, M.B.A., 1957; m. Harriet Jane Harper, Aug. 26, 1961; children—Jane Elisabeth, Nancy Jamieson. Investment analyst, Protective Life Ins. Co., Birmingham, Ala., 1957-62; v.p., sr. partner Loomis, Sayles & Co., Washington, 1962—. Instr. econs. and finance part time U. Ala., Birmingham, 1958-61, Samford U., Birmingham, 1959-61. Mem. finance com. Planned Parenthood Assn., 1973—, Episcopal Center for Children, 1973—. Bd. dirs. Glen Echo Fire Dept., 1968-71; trustee Washington Suburban San. Commn., 1973—. Mem. Washington Soc. Investment Analysts (pres. 1973-74), Chartered Financial Analysts, Investment Counsel Assn., Financial Analysts Fedn. Clubs: Metropolitan, George Town Congressional Country (Washington); Racquet (Miami).

VEACH, JOHN BEMIS, JR., lumber co. exec.; b. Pitts., July 21, 1927; s. John Bemis and Jane Craig (Miller) V.; A.B., Yale U., 1949; m. Jean Smith Trainer, June 23, 1951; children—John Bemis III, Margaret Hastings. With Bemis Hardwood Lumber Co., Robbinsbille, N.C., 1952-73, pres., 1965-73; v.p. Whitewater, Inc., 1973—; exec. v.p., dir. Veach May Wilson, Inc., Alcoa, Tenn., 1965—; pres. dir. Veach Wilson Oil Co., Robbinsville, N.C., 1969—. Bd. Trustees Meml. Mission Hosp., Asheville Chamber Music Series. Served with AUS, 1950-52. Mem. N.C. Forestry Assn. (dir. 1970-73), Appalachian Hardwood Mfgs., Inc. (trustee 1970—, pres. 1974—), Appalachian Lumbermen's Club (past pres.), Forest Products Research Soc. (past chmn. sect.). Episcopalian (sec. exec. council diocese Western N.C.). Rotarian. Clubs: Biltmore Forest (N.C.) Country; Mountain City (Asheville, N.C.). Home: 316 Vanderbilt Rd Ashville NC 28803 Office: PO Box 5857 Asheville NC 28803

VEAZEY, JOHN HOBSON, physician; b. Van Alstyne, Tex., June 27, 1901; s. James and Malta Augusta (Blassingame) V.; student Austin Coll., 1918-22; M.D., U. Tex., 1926; m. Elizabeth May Chandler, Mar. 14, 1935; children—Samuel James. Intern Sherman (Tex.) Hosp., 1926-28; pvt. practice medicine, Madill, Okla., 1929-35, Ardmore, Okla., 1935—; one of founders, one of partners Med. Arts Clinic, Ardmore, Okla., 1952—; pvt. practice internal medicine, Ardmore, 1957—; chief staff Meml. Hosp., So. Okla., 1958—, chmn. dept. Internal Medicine, 1973; mem. staff Ardmore (Okla.) Hosp. Co-chmn. profl. div. United Fund, 1969. Mem. Am., Okla. State (council 1944-56) med. assns., Carter-Love-Marshall Med. Soc. (pres. 1955), Ardmore C. of C. (dir., v.p.), Am. Soc. Internal Medicine. Presbyn. (trustee). Mason. Home: 305 D St SW Ardmore OK 73401 Office: 921 14th St NW Ardmore OK 73401

VEGA, JUAN BAUTISTA, tribal chieftain; b. Cozumel Island, Yucatan, Mexico, June 24, 1889; s. Gerarda and Maria (Cen) V.; stepson Ruperto Loria; stepson Florintino Cituk (Mayan chief); reared as a Mayan, Yucatan; translator, sec. to chief; sec. of Saint, supreme Mayan religious authority, 1918—, also custodian Maya holy book; mem. council of chiefs, 1919—, now head chief Mayans, Mexico. Served as gen. Mayan Army, during war between Mexican govt. and Mayans. Address: Chumpon Quintana Roo Mexico

VEGHTE, JACK, ins. agy. exec.; b. Schenectady, May 24, 1935; s. Charles and Ruth (Wurz) V.; B.S., Fla. State U., 1957; m. Nancy Ford, June 8, 1957; children—Melissa, John, Richard, David. Founder, chief exec. officer Veghte Ins. Agy., Clearwater, Fla., 1958—; dir. 1st Fed. Savs. & Loan, Clearwater, 2d Nat. Bank Clearwater. Chmn. March of Dimes, 1965. Kiwanian. Clubs: Carlouel Yacht, East Bay Country, Casado. Home: 1470 Maple Forest Rd Clearwater FL 33516 Office: 601 S Lincoln Av Clearwater FL 33516

VEILLON, EDWARD WARNER, ins. agt., banker; b. Eunice, La., Sept. 11, 1940; s. E. A. and Myrtle (Andrus) V.; student Tulane U., 1958-59; B.S., La. State U., 1962; m. Ann Bordelon, July 10, 1966. Vice pres. E. A. Veillon Agy., Inc., ins., real estate, 1965-69, pres., 1969—; v.p., mgr. Val Realty Corp., 1966-73, pres., 1973—; dir. 1st Fed. Savs. & Loan Assn.; pres. Tri-Parish Bank & Trust Co. Served as 1st lt. U.S. Army, 1962-64. Recipient Jaycee Presdl. citation, 1969; named Outstanding Chmn., 1970, Eunice Outstanding Young Man, 1970. Hon. life mem. 8th U.S. Cav. Mem. Eunice C. of C. (dir., past v.p.), Delta Sigma Phi. Democrat. Roman Catholic. Rotarian. Home: 130 Pinecrest Dr Eunice LA 70535 Office: 220 S 2d St Eunice LA 70535

VELASCO, RALPH ESTEBAN, food co. exec.; b. San Antonio, June 12, 1926; s. Ralph Esteban and Maria (Gonzalez) V.; grad. U.S. Mcht. Marine Acad., 1946; student U. Tex., 1947-50; m. Barbara Juenel Zizelman, Dec. 4, 1953; children—Steven, David. With Amigos Food Co., Inc., San Antonio, 1950—, sales rep., 1950-66, v.p., 1966-67, pres., 1967—. Bd. dirs. N.W. YMCA, San Antonio, 1964-66. Mem. Nat. Canners Assn., Delta Sigma Phi. Club: Turtle Creek County (San Antonio). Home: Route 1 Box 60BB Boerne TX 78006 Office: 4535 W Commerce St San Antonio TX 78237

VELLER, MARGARET PAXTON, physician; b. Beaver Dam, Ky., Dec. 14, 1925; d. Darrell K. and Gladys (Myers) Veller; B.A., Vanderbilt U., 1947, M.D., 1950. Intern, resident Vanderbilt U. Hosp., Nashville, 1950-54; pvt. practice, 1954—. Mem. Am., Miss. (com. maternal and child welfare 1956-73) med. assns., Adams County Med. Soc., Natchez Assn. of Commerce, Miss. Obstet. and Gynecol. Soc., Natchez-Adams County C. of C., Phi Beta Kappa, Alpha Omega Alpha. Baptist. Club: Pilgrimage Garden. Home: 28 S Circle Dr Natchez MS 39120 Office: Natchez Med Clinic 49 Sgt S Prentiss Dr Natchez MS 39120

VELZ, RICHARD ANTHONY, pharm. co. exec.; b. Lagrangeville, N.Y., Aug. 21, 1911; s. Robert and Mary R. (Suwarrow) V.; B.S., Coll. William and Mary, 1936; m. Anya Mishtowt, Aug. 19, 1961. Dir. pub. relations Coll. William and Mary, 1936; corr. A.P., U.P., 1937-39; mem. editorial staff Richmond News Leader, 1936-39; pres., gen. mgr. Colonial Music Corp., Williamsburg, Va., 1939-41; prodn., program dir. Radio Station WRNL, Richmond, Va., 1945-48; adminstr. Va. Mus. Fine Arts, Richmond, 1955-58; dir. pub. relations A.H. Robins Co., Richmond, 1958—, asst. to pres., 1953-70, asst. v.p., 1967-70, v.p., 1970—. Vice-pres., mem. exec. com. Richmond Soc. Prevention Cruelty to Animals, 1968—. Bd. dirs. Richmond Symphony, Nat. Tobacco Festival, Blue Cross of Va. Served to comdr. USNR, 1941-45, 48-53; now capt. Res. ret. Recipient meritorious pub. service citation Sec. Navy, 1963, commendation, 1954, Navy League Scroll of Honor, 1964, Navy Meritorious Service medal, 1972. Mem. Pharm. Mfrs. Assn. (chmn. pub. relations sect. 1970-71), Pub. Relations Soc. Am. (chpt. bd. dirs. 1960-62), Va., Richmond (dir. 1972) chambers commerce, Central Richmond Assn., Va. Mfrs. Assn., Pub. Relations com. YMCA, Am. Ordnance Assn., Ret. Officers Assn., Am., Va. pharm. assns., Naval Acad. Found., Richmond Pub. Relations Assn. (pres. 1960-61), Better Business Bur. (pres. 1962-63), Navy League U.S. (region pres. 1962-67, U.S. Naval Inst., Res. Officers Assn. (chpt. pres. 1965-66), Naval Res. Assn., Greater Richmond C. of C. (exec. com.), Alpha Kappa Psi, Pi Delta Epsilon, Phi Delta Gamma, Tau Kappa Alpha, Phi Kappa Tau. Presbyn. (ruling elder 1966—), (chmn. bd. deacons 1962-65). Clubs: Rotunda (pres. 1969-70) (Richmond); Country of Va.; Press Club of Va. (v.p. 1958-60); Nat. Press, Army-Navy (Washington). Home: 307 N Allen Av Richmond VA 23220 Office: 1407 Cummings Dr Richmond VA 23220

VENABLE, AUSTIN LEWIS, historian; b. Wetumpka, Ala., May 15, 1902; s. William E. and Susan Roberta (Allen) V.; A.B., U. Ala., 1925, A.M., 1929; student U. Chgo., 1930; Ph.D., Vanderbilt U., 1937; m. Nell E. Smith, Dec 21, 1930. Teaching fellow Vanderbilt U., 1935-37; instr. U. Ark., 1937-40, asst. prof., 1940-45; asso. prof. U. Ala., 1954-72, emeritus, 1972—. Mem. Ala. Centennial Commn. Recipient Social Sci. Research grant-in-aid; grant U. Ala. Research Com. Mem. Orgn. Am. Historians, Ala. Hist. Assn., Old South Hist. Soc. (pres. 1964-66), S.A.R. (pres. Ala. 1972-74, nat. trustee 1974—), Am. Hist. Assn., English-Speaking Union (dir. 1963-66), Ala. Acad. Sci., Phi Alpha Theta, Kappa Delta Pi, Pi Kappa Alpha, Kappa Phi Kappa. Club: University. Author monographs, book reviews; editor hist. jours., other publs. Home: Hickory Hill Jasmine Hill Rd Wetumpka AL 36092

VENABLE, CHARLES EDWARD, civil engr., state ofcl.; b. Tyler, Tex., Feb. 8, 1931; s. Robert Shelby and Willie Donna (Lee) V.; student Ark. A. and M. Coll., 1948-50; B.S. in Civil Engring., U. Ark., 1958, M.S. in Civil Engring., 1959; m. Evelylee Harvill, Dec. 6, 1951; 1 son, Robert E. Instr., U. Ark., Fayetteville, 1958-59; civil engr. U.S. Army C.E., Little Rock, 1959; bridge designer Ark. Hwy, Dept., Little Rock, 1959-62, asst. surveys engr., 1962-67, surveys engr. 1967-73, asst. chief engr. planning, 1973—. Vice chmn. Adv. Bd. State Land Surveyor. Chmn., Adv. Bd. Petit Jean Vocational Sch., Morricton, Ark., 1968—. Served with USAF, 1951-55. Registered profl. engr., land surveyor, Ark. Mem. Am. Soc. C.E., Soc. Profl. Engrs., Am. Assn. State Hwy. Ofcls., Tau Beta Pi, Sigma Tau Gamma. Baptist. Home: 9808 Treasure Hill Rd Little Rock AR 72205 Office: New Benton Hwy Little Rock AR 72203

VENABLE, JOHN HEINZ, physician, state ofcl.; b. Atlanta, Dec. 5, 1908; s. Gus Foute and Josephine (Heinz) V.; B.S., Emory U., 1929, M.D., 1933; M.P.H., Tulane U., 1951; m. Louise Ware, Dec. 18, 1934; children—John Heinz, Linda (Mrs. William A. Webb). Faculty, Emory U., 1929-46; commr. health Dalton (Ga.)-Whitfield Health Dept., 1947-50, Griffin (Ga.)-Spalding County Health Dept., 1950-52; dir. tng. Ga. Dept. Pub. Health, Atlanta, 1952-60, dir. dept., 1960-72; asst. dir. Center for Disease Control, 1972—. Mem. Med. Assn. Ga., A.M.A., Ga. Pub. Health Assn., Assn. State and Territorial Health Officers (past pres.), Conf. State and Provincial Health Authorities N.Am. (past pres.), Phi Beta Kappa, Omicron Delta Kappa, Delta Omega. Home: 2418 Howell Mill Rd Atlanta GA 30318 Office: 1600 Clifton Rd NE Atlanta GA 30333

VENABLE, NELL SMITH (MRS. AUSTIN L. VENABLE), ret. educator, clubwoman; b. Butler County, Ala., Nov. 24, 1904; d. William Ward and Elizabeth (Presley) Smith; B.A., U. Ala., 1930; M.A., Vanderbilt U., 1953; m. Austin L. Venable, Dec. 21, 1930. Instr., Coll. of Ozarks, 1943; tchr. Sidney Lanier High Sch., Montgomery, Ala., 1955-72. Mem. Nat., Ala. (v.p. social studies dept. 1958-60), Montgomery (curriculum steering com. 1959-61, chmn. high sch. div. 1959-60) edn. assns., Nat., Ala., Montgomery ret. tchrs. assns., Classroom Tchrs. Assn., Am. Assn. U. Women (exec. bd. 1955-59), Montgomery County Joint Legislative Council (pres. 1955-57), D.A.R. (corr. sec. 1960-64, chaplain 1973—, historian officers club 1974—), Old S. Hist. Soc. (corr. sec. 1961-62, 64-66), English-Speaking Union, Mortar Bd., Phi Beta Kappa. Episcopalian. Home: Hickory Hill Jasmine Hill Rd Wetumpka AL 36092

VENEGAS, EMILIO JOSÉ, constrn. co. exec.; b. Santo Domingo, Dominican Republic, Feb. 4, 1928; s. Emilio V. and Manserrate (del Toro) V.; B.S., Mass. Inst. Tech., 1949; m. Maria del Carmen Vilaro, Dec. 10, 1950; children—Viveca, Emilio, Kim. Engr., design dept. Autoridad Fuentes Fluviales, San Juan, P.R., 1949-50; field engr. Ponce Cement (P.R.), 1950-51; project mgr. Jorge I. Rosso, contractor, Ponce, 1951-55; v.p., chief engr. Ponce Builders, 1955-65; pres. Venegas Constrn. Corp., Ponce, 1965—, Sanson Ready Mix, Ponce, 1964—; dir. Bank of Ponce. Bd. dirs. Colegio Ponceno, Inc. Mem. Am. Concrete Inst., Colegio Ingenieros de P.R., Cursillos de Cristiandad de Ponce (dir.). Clubs: Deportivo de Ponce (dir.), Ponce Yacht. Home: 418 H La Rambla Ponce PR 00731 Office: Edificio Marvesa Ponce PR 00731

VENEZKY, DAVID LESTER, chemist; b. Washington, Sept. 12, 1924; s. Benjamin and Anna (Marks) V.; B.S., George Washington U., 1948; Ph.D. (Eastman Kodak fellow), U. N.C., 1962; m. Evelyn L. Gaver, Sept. 3, 1950; children—Donna Lynn, Mark Edward. Phys. sci. aid, Geol. Survey, Washington, 1948-49; organic chemist Naval Research Lab., Washington, 1949-55; instr. U. N.C., Chapel Hill, 1958-60; asst. prof. Auburn (Ala.) U., 1960-62; research chemist, head inorganic polymer sect. Naval Research Lab., Washington, 1962-69, head reaction mechanisms sect., 1969—. Served with USNR, 1944-46. Mem. Am. Chem. Soc., Sigma Xi, Alpha Chi Sigma. Home: 8707 Bradgate Rd Alexandria VA 22308 Office: Naval Research Lab Washington DC 20375

VENTURA, JACK SAL, economist; b. N.Y.C., Dec. 21, 1943; s. Jose and Mathilde (Algranti) V.; A.B., Columbia Coll., 1964; A.M., U. Pa., 1965; Ph.D. (Univ. fellow), Georgetown U., 1970; m. Stephanie Joan Leavitt, May 29, 1966; children—Daniel Reuben, Jerome Hosea. Economist, sect. of research ICC, Washington, 1965—, chief carrier analysis br., sec. of research Bur. Econs., 1970—. Mem. Am. Econ. Assn., Econometric Soc., Transp. Research Forum, Phi Epsilon Pi. Jewish religion. Home: 1025 Chiswell Lane Silver Spring MD 20901 Office: Interstate Commerce Commn Washington DC 20423

VEREEN, WILLIAM JEROME, uniform mfg. co. exec.; b. Moultrie, Ga., Sept. 7, 1940; s. William Coachman and Mary Elizabeth (Bunn) V.; student Episcopal High Sch.-Va., 1954-57; grad. Culver Mil. Acad., 1959; B.S. in Indsl. Mgmt., Ga. Inst. Tech., 1963; m. Lula Evelyn King, June 9, 1963; children—Elizabeth King, William Coachman. Engr. Riverside Mfg. Co., Moultrie, Ga., 1967-70, v.p., 1970-73, exec. v.p., 1973—, also dir.; v.p., dir. Moultrie Cotton Mills, 1969—; exec. v.p., dir. Riverside Industries, Inc., Moultrie, 1973—; v.p., dir. Riverside Uniform Rentals, Inc., Moultrie, 1971—. Bd. dirs. Moultrie-Colquitt County (Ga.) Devel. Authority, 1973—, Moultrie-Colquitt County United Givers, Moultrie YMCA, Colquitt County Cancer Soc.; trustee Community Welfare Assn., Moultrie, Pineland Sch., Moultrie. Served to capt. USMC, 1963-67. Decorated Bronze Star, Purple Heart. Mem. Am. Apparel Mfrs. Assn., Nat. Assn. Uniform Mfrs., Sigma Alpha Epsilon. Presbyn. (deacon). Elk, Kiwanian. Home: 1817 2d St SE Moultrie GA 31768 Office: PO Box 460 Moultrie GA 31768

VERMILLION, STANLEY EUGENE, physician; b. Goodland, Kan., Feb. 3, 1938; s. Dale D. and Mary (VanVleck) V.; A.B., U. Kan., 1960; M.D., U. Kan., 1964; m. Jane Bird Willey, June 16, 1961; children—Scott, Drew, Wendy. Intern, Mary Imogene Bassett Hosp., Cooperstown, N.Y., 1964-65; resident Mayo Clinic, Rochester, Minn., 1965-68; practice medicine specializing in internal medicine, Johnson City, Tenn., 1970—. Chmn., Renal Adv. Com. State of Tenn., 1972—, regional med. program adviser, 1971—. Served with M.C., AUS, 1968-70. Diplomate Am. Bd. Internal Medicine. Mem. Am. Soc. Nephrology, Internat. Soc. Nephrology, Am., Tenn. med. assns. Home: 107 Ridgemont St Johnson City TN 37601 Office: 106 E Watauga Av Johnson City TN 37601

VERNER, BARTLEY RAY, accountant; b. Commerce, Tex., May 28, 1944; s. John Wesley and Virginia Ruth (Bartley) V.; B.B.A., Tex. Technol. Coll., 1969, M.S., 1970; m. Patricia H. Dorman, June 8, 1963; children—Cynthia Ray, Bartley Ray. Coll. instr. Tex. Technol. U., Lubbock, 1969-70; auditor Touche Ross & Co., Dallas, 1970-73; asst. controller Petrodyne Corp., Longview, Tex., 1973—. Served with USAF, 1962-66. C.P.A., Tex. Mem. Am. Inst. C.P.A.'s, Tex. Soc. C.P.A.'s, Nat. Assn. Accountants. Home: 2404 Balsam St Longview TX 75601 Office: Box 671 Longview TX 75601

VERNEZOBRE, ERNEST FRANCISCO, physician; b. Havana, Cuba, Dec. 4, 1927; s. Francisco and Ysabel (Metz) V.; B.S., Inst. Secondary Edn., Havana, 1945; D. Medicine and Surgery, U. Havana, 1952; m. Diana E. Michael, Dec. 26, 1962; children—Diana Isabel, Rhonda Louise. Came to U.S., 1961, naturalized, 1968. Rotating intern Univ. Hosp., Havana, 1953-54, resident obstetrics and gynecology, 1955-57; cons. gynecology Tb Hosp., Las Villas, Cuba, 1957-59; med. dir. St. Emily Hosp., Havana, 1959-60; nat. dir. Orgn. State Hosps., Cuba, 1957-58; rotating intern Riverside Hosp., Newport News, Va., 1961-62; staff physician Tb Hosp., San Antonio, 1963-64; family practice medicine, Midland, Tex., 1966—; mem. staff Midland, Meml., Parkview hosps., Midland; chief staff Parkview Hosp., 1971, chief medicine, 1972, 73. Prof. U. Havana, summers 1954-55; prof. practical obstetrics 9th Nat. Med. Congress, 1955. Decorated officer Charles J. Finlay Nat. Merit Order (Cuba). Diplomate Am. Bd. Family Practice. Fellow Am. Acad. Angiology, Am. Acad. Family Practice; mem. Am., Pan Am., So., Tex. med. assns., Am., Tex. acads. gen. practice, Am. Acad. Geriatrics, Am. Inst. Hypnosis, Am., Tex. thoracic socs., Am., Tex. diabetes assns., Pan Am. Cancer Soc., Tex. Heart Assn., Midland County Med. Soc. Lion. Club: Downtowners (Midland). Home: 2100 Wadley Apt 132 Midland TX 79701 Office: 1802 W Wall St Midland TX 79701

VERNON, WALTER NEWTON, clergyman, editor; b. Verden, Okla., Mar. 24, 1907; s. Walter Newton and Fannie Hawling (Dodd) V.; student Paris (Tex.) Jr. Coll., 1924-26; A.B., So. Methodist U., 1928, B.D., 1931, A.M., 1934; Litt.D., W.Va. Wesleyan U., 1963; m. Ruth Mason, Dec. 27, 1931; children—Walter Newton III, Kathy (Mrs. Stanley P. Clark). Ordained to ministry Meth. Ch., 1931; pastor Lakewood Ch., Dallas, 1931-38; editor youth publs. Meth. Ch., Nashville, 1938-44; adminstrv. asso. editorial div. Bd. Edn. Meth. Ch., Nashville, 1944-72; rec. sec. TV, Radio, and Film Commn., Nashville, 1948-64; exec. sec. Curriculum Com. Meth. Ch., 1944-72; exec. sec. Meth. Conf. Ch. Edn., 1957-69; spl. news corr. Meth. Ch., 1934—; editor S.C. Jurisdictional Conf. Daily Advocate, 1940-72. Mem. program bd. div. ch. edn. Nat. Council Chs., 1963-72; del. World Council Ch. Edn., Tokyo, Japan, 1958; mem. United Meth. Archives Commn., 1972—. Am. Assn. State and Local History grantee, 1964. Mem. So. Meth. U. Alumni Assn. (past pres. Nashville), Sigma Delta Chi, Tau Kappa Alpha, Author: Methodist Profile, 1959; William Stevenson, Riding Preacher, 1964; Methodism Moves Across North Texas (award merit Am. Assn. State and Local History), 1967; United Methodist Profile, 1968; Resena de la Iglesia Methodita Unido, 1973; Forever Building, the Life and Ministry of Paul E. Martin, 1973. Editor Living With Your Children, 1961; Elmer T. Clark, World Methodist, 1971; The South Central Jurisdiction, 1939-72, 1973. Contbr. articles to hist. and religious publs. Composer numerous hymns. Address: 4013 Dorcas Dr Nashville TN 37215

VERNON, WILLIAM WALLACE, accountant; b. Snyder, Tex., Mar. 1, 1940; s. Alfred E. and Ollie I. (Niedecken) V.; B.B.A., Tex. Technol. U., 1963; m. Emmadell Ewing, Feb. 27, 1960; children—William W., Katherine Frances, Patricia Ann. Staff accountant H.V. Robertson & Co., Amarillo, Tex., 1963-66; partner Lott & Vernon, accountants, Killeen, Tex., 1966—. Dir. ACH, Inc., Killeen, Tex. Treas., Killeen Boys Club, 1971—. Bd. dirs. Tex. Jaycee Hosp. Found., chmn., 1972—. C.P.A., Tex. Mem. Am. Inst. C.P.A.'s, Tex. Soc. C.P.A.'s, Kileen Jr. C. of C. (treas. 1969). Lion. Home: 1202 Crestridge Killeen TX 76541 Office: 109 E Av B Killeen TX 76541

VERROSS, WILLIAM JOHN, paper co. exec.; b. Chgo., Apr. 14, 1921; s. William Mels and Martha (Fraser) V.; B.Chem. Engring., Ohio State U., 1943; m. Marjorie Frances Cottier, Sept. 14, 1946; children—William E., Thomas S., Robert P., Victoria A. Block plant supt. U.S. Gypsum Co., S.I., N.Y., 1946-47; research engr. Westvaco Corp., N.Y.C., 1947-55, prodn. supt., 1955-60, div. prodn. mgr., 1961-66; v.p. gen. mgr. Interstate Paper Corp., Riceboro, Ga., 1966—; pres. Newport Timber Corp., Riceboro, 1967—; dir. Hinesville Bank. Chmn., Covington (Va.) Planning and Zoning Commn., 1954-56; bd. dirs. N.C. State Pulp and Paper Found., 1973—; mem. Covington Sch. Bd., 1957-60, Liberty County (Ga.) Hosp. Authority, 1968-74. Vice chmn. Charleston County Republican party, 1966; chmn. Liberty County Rep. party, 1968. Served with C.E., AUS, 1942-46. Mem. T.A.P.P.I., Paper Industry Mgmt. Assn. (Community Service Award 1969), Liberty County C. of C. (pres. 1967). Home: 512 Martin Rd Hinesville GA 31313 Office: Interstate Paper Corp Riceboro GA 31323

VERTER, HERBERT SIGMUND, educator; b. N.Y.C., Jan. 30, 1936; s. Louis and Bessie (Hochberg) V.; B.S., City Coll. N.Y., 1956; M.A., Harvard, 1957, Ph.D., 1960; postgrad. Imperial Coll. London, 1961; m. Mona Ellen Cowen, July 10, 1960; children—Bradford J., Michael Pippincott, Geoffrey Hantzentrantz Preston, Justine. Teaching asst. Harvard, 1956-60, Imperial Coll. London, 1961; asst. prof. chemistry Central Mich. U., Mount Pleasant, 1961-66; asso. prof. Inter-Am. U. P.R., 1966-67, prof. chemistry, 1967—, chmn. dept. 1967-72, dean grad. studies, 1972—, acting dean acad. affairs, 1973—. Chief scientist ad honorum P.R. Nuclear Center, Mayaguez, 1967—; chmn. med. sch. adv. com., 1966—. Mem. Am. Chem. Soc., Sigma Xi, Phi Beta Kappa. Author: Oxidation of Aldehydes and

Ketones, 1969. Contbr. articles to profl. jours. Home: PO Box 1031 San German PR 00753

VERWOERDT, ADRIAAN, physician, psychiatrist; b. Voorburg, Netherlands, July 5, 1927; s. Christopher and Juliana Margaretha (Busch) V.; M.D., Med. Sch. of Amsterdam, Netherlands, 1952; m. Dorothy Jean Taylor, Oct. 9, 1965; children—Christopher Earl, Mark Adrian. Came to U.S., 1953, naturalized, 1958. Rotating intern Touro Infirmary, New Orleans, 1953-54; resident in psychiatry Duke U. Med. Center, 1954-55, 58-60, fellow in psychiat. research, 1960-61, asst. prof. psychiatry, 1963-67, asso. prof., 1967-71, prof., 1971—, dir. geriatric psychiatry tng. program, 1966—; dir. psychiat. residency tng. John Umstead Hosp., Butner, N.C., 1968—. Served as capt. M.C., AUS, 1955-57. Nat. Inst. Mental Health Career Tchr. Tng. grantee, 1964-66. Diplomate Pan Am. Med. Assn. Fellow Am. Psychiat. Assn.; mem. A.M.A., Gerontol. Soc., Am. Psychosomatic Soc., Am. Geriatrics Soc., Am. Psychoanalytic Assn. Author: Communication with the Fatally Ill, 1966. Contbr. articles to profl. jours. Home: 2747 Sevier St Durham NC 27705 Office: Duke Univ Medical Center Durham NC 27710

VESS, DAVID MARSHALL, educator; b. Birmingham, Ala., Nov. 4, 1925; s. David Walker and Eulalia (Kerby) V.; A.B., Howard Coll., 1948; M.A., Vanderbilt U., 1950; postgrad. (Gen. Edn. Bd. fellow Rockefeller Found.), Harvard, 1950-52; Ph.D., U. Ala., 1965; m. Jean Buchanan, Dec. 30, 1948; 1 son, John Buchanan. Instr., Howard Coll., 1949-50, asst. prof., 1957-65; dir. Americanism, Am. Legion, 1952-57; asso. prof. Samford U., Birmingham, 1965-67, prof. European history, 1967—, dir. Jan. term, 1969, head dept. history and polit. sci., 1970—, chmn. div. social scis., 1970-73. Editorial cons. Am. Assn. Ophthalmology, 1967—; CBS news elections analyst Ala., 1964-66. Bd. mem. Five Points YMCA, 1962-66. Served with USNR, 1943-46; PTO. Mem. Am., So. hist. assns., Ala. Acad. Sci., Societe francaise d'histoire d'outre mer (Paris), Ala. State Council for Social Studies, Kappa Alpha, Omicron Delta Kappa, Pi Gamma Mu, Phi Alpha Theta. Republican. Baptist. Home: 1140 N Shadesview Terrace Birmingham AL 35209

VETTER, HAROLD JOHN, psychologist; b. Buffalo, Mar. 31, 1926; s. Harold J. and Gladys (Bates) V.; B.A. summa cum laude, U. Buffalo, 1949; Ph.D., U. Buffalo, 1955; m. Virginia Rose, Apr. 24, 1964. Instr. psychology U. Buffalo, 1952-54; staff psychologist, psychiat. clinic Erie County Ct., 1954-55; lectr. overseas program U. Md., 1955-63, lectr., 1964-69; asso. prof. criminology Fla. State U., Tallahassee, 1969-71. Cons. editor Internat. Textbook Co., Scranton, Pa. Served with USNR, 1942-46. Mem. Am. Psychol. Assn., Linguistic Soc. Am., Phi Beta Kappa, Psi Chi. Author books, including: Language Behavior in Schizophrenia, 1968; Language Behavior and Communication, 1969; Language Behavior and Psychopathology, 1969; Psychology of Abnormal Behavior, 1972. Asso. editor Jour. Psycholinguistic Research, 1969—. Home: 4370 LaSalle New Orleans LA 70115 Office: Dept Psychology Loyola U New Orleans LA 70118

VETTER, RICHARD CORTRIGHT, oceanography exec.; b. Homer Mich., Apr. 17, 1923; s. Earnest Hunt and Cynthia (Rising) V.; B.A., Albion Coll., 1949; M.S., Scripps Inst. of Oceanography, 1951; m. Betty Ruth McGee, Sept. 4, 1951 (div.); children—David Bruce, Richard Dean, Robert Alan; m. 2d, Sylvia C. Haidari. Instr., U. Cal. Far East Extension Div., 1951; oceanographer Office of Naval Research, Washington, 1951-57; exec. sec. Nat. Acad. Scis. Com. on Oceanography, Washington, 1957-70, exec. sec. Ocean Affairs Bd., 1971—. cons. oceanographic edn., 1965-67. Served with AUS, 1943-45. Mem. Marine Tech. Soc., Nat. Oceanographic Soc. (dir.), Am. Oceanography Assn., A.A.A.S., Am. Geophys. Union, Am. Soc. Limnology and Oceanography, Contbr. articles in field to profl. jours. Office: 2101 Constitution Av NW Washington DC 20418

VEULEMAN, MALCOLM WAYNE, educator; b. Many, La., May 8, 1931; s. Dewey Edward and Violet Kathleen (Parham) V.; B.S. in Accounting, McNeese State Coll., 1959; M.B.A., U. Ark., 1961, Ph.D., 1971; m. Lynda Darylene Leslie, Dec. 20, 1969; 1 son, Michael Wayne. Auditor, Arthur Andersen & Co., Houston, 1960-62; asst. prof. accounting U. Houston, 1962-64, 67-70; instr. U. Ark., Fayetteville, 1964-67; asso. prof. accounting Lamar U., Beaumont, Tex., 1970—. Served with USAF, 1951-55. Earhart fellow, 1966. C.P.A., Tex. Recipient Bd. Regents Merit award Lamar U., 1972-73. Mem. Am. Accounting Assn., Am. Inst. C.P.A.'s, Tex. Soc. C.P.A.'s, Beta Alpha Psi, Beta Gamma Sigma. Republican. Mem. United Pentecostal Ch. Home: 1055 Lilac Lane Beaumont TX 77706

VIBBERT, GEORGE SNEED, JR., banker, city ofcl.; b. Normandy, Tenn., July 11, 1936; s. George Sneed and Susie (Thompson) V.; B.S., Middle Tenn. State U., 1966; postgrad. U. Tenn., 1971-72; m. Elwanda Sawyer, May 30, 1963. With Ryder Truck Lines, Nashville, 1954-66, office mgr., 1957-66; with ARO, Inc., Tullahoma, Tenn., 1966-74, adminstrv. asst., 1971-74; v.p. Am. City Bank, Tullahoma, 1974—. Dir. Arnold Engrng. Devel. Center Fed. Credit Union, 1970-74. Mayor City of Tullahoma, 1972—. Named Outstanding Young Man of Yr., Tullahoma Jaycees, 1971. Mem. Air Force Assn., Soc. Am. Mil. Engrs. Methodist (adminstrv. bd. 1972-73). Kiwanian (pres. 1970-71). Home: 111 S Anderson St Tullahoma TN 37388 Office: City Hall Tullahoma TN 37388

VICHAS, ROBERT PAUL, financial exec.; b. Ft. Lauderdale, Fla., Sept. 26, 1936; s. Peter and Idalene L. (Cooper) V.; B.S., La. State U., 1965; M.A., U. of Ams., Mexico City, 1966; Ph.D., U. Fla., 1967; postgrad. Inst. Hautes Etudes Internationales, 1972; m. Dolores Flores Castellon, June 26, 1965. Financial analyst Dun & Bradstreet, Inc., N.Y.C., 1958-63; asst. prof. econs. and finance East Carolina U., 1967-68; asso. prof. econs. West Ga. Coll., 1968-70; internat. v.p. Exec. Mgmt. Cons., Inc., 1970-71; dir. research Reed & Co., Atlanta, 1973-74. Vis. prof. U. Jose Simeon Canas (San Salvador); cons. to Choice, also Pres. of Nicaragua. Recipient award Dept. of State, 1970. Mem. Am. Econ. Assn., Am. Finance Assn., Assn. Edn. in Internat. Bus., Am. Soc. Psychical Research, Southeastern Conf. Latin Am. Studies, United Comml. Travelers, Beta Gamma Sigma. Author: The Economy of Nicaragua. Editor, contbr.: (with W. Moore) Coeval Economics, 1970; Silver, 1973. Home: PO Box 29 Atlanta GA 30301 Office: Case Postale NR 1211 Geneva 21 Switzerland

VICIEDO, EUSEBIO PERDOMO, biochemist; b. Havana, Cuba, Aug. 14, 1901; s. Mariano and Luisa (Perdomo) V.; B.S., Matanzas Inst., 1918; Ph.Dr., Havana U., 1922; m. Serafina Rodriguez, Mar. 22, 1935; 1 dau., Isis (Mrs. Julio Arrendondo). Came to U.S., 1961, naturalized, 1967. Asst. biochemist Iturrioz Laborat, Havana, Cuba, 1925-30; dir. Plasencia Laborat, Havana, 1932-45, Zimotecnica Corp., Havana, 1945-52; researcher in microbiology Cuban Research Inst., Havana, 1957-61; microbiologist Arroyo Pharm. Corp., 1961-64, Atlas Yeast Corp., P.R., 1964-66, Bacardi Corp., San Juan, P.R., 1966—. Prof. applied microbiology U. Oriente, Cuba, 1953-59. Recipient Gold medal Escuela de Quimica RR.PP. Dominicos Cuba, 1959. Mem. Am. Chem. Soc., Soc. Indsl. Microbiology, Soc. Applied Bacteriology. Home: 585 Independencia St Hato Rey PR 00918 Office: PO Box 3549 San Juan PR 00936

VICK, HAROLD DEAN, cons. traffic engr.; b. Jacksonville, Fla., Dec. 8, 1939; s. Columbus Edwin and Lucretia Webb (Dean) V.; B.S. in C.E., Duke, 1961; M.S. in Transp. Engring., N.C. State U., 1967; m. Judith Patricia Rowe, Oct. 14, 1961; children—Patricia Adair, Michael Dean. Transp. planning engr. Mel Conner & Assos., Tallahassee, 1967-68; v.p., prin. Kimley-Horn Assos., Inc., West Palm Beach, Fla., 1968—. Active YMCA. Served to lt. USNR, 1961-65. Registered profl. engr., Fla., N.C., Ky. Fellow Inst. Traffic Engrs. (sec.-treas. 1973, v.p. 1974, Past Pres.'s award 1969); mem. Am. Soc. C.E. (Engr. of Year 1974), Fla. Engring. Soc., Nat. Soc. Profl. Engrs., Chi Epsilon, Phi Kappa Phi, Delta Tau Delta. Baptist (deacon). Contbr. articles to profl. jours. Home: 10902 Larch Ct Palm Beach Gardens FL 33403 Office: 1252 Old Okeechobee Rd West Palm Beach FL 33401

VICK, ROBERT EDWARD, lawyer; b. Greenville, Ky., Aug. 2, 1918; s. Robert Emory and Ethel (Murphey) V.; student Western Ky. State Coll., 1937-39; LL.B., U. Ky., 1948; m. Geneva Carpenter, June 8, 1946; children—Robert Edward, Ralph Dennis, Frances Annette. With W. G. Duncan Coal Co., Greenville, 1936-37; admitted to Ky. bar, 1948; practiced in Greenville, 1948-51; mem. firm Donan and Vick, 1956—. Served with U.S. Army, 1941-46, 1951-56, 61-62; served to lt. col. Res. ret. Decorated Silver Star, Bronze Star medal. Mem. Greenville Indsl. Devel. Corp. (sec. 1961-62), Am., Ky., 45th Jud. Dist. bar assns., Am. Judicature Soc., U. Ky. Alumni Assn., Am. Legion, V.F.W. (past comdr.), C. of C. (former sec.-treas.). Methodist. Democrat. Kiwanian. Club: Civitan (past pres., sec.-treas.). Home: 148 N Main St Greenville KY 42345 Office: 110 E Court Sq Greenville KY 42345

VICKERS, FRANK NORMAN, physician; b. Hattiesburg, Miss., Mar. 2, 1931; s. Hawkins Ladson and Elizabeth Rose (Gibson) V.; B.A., So. Meth. U., 1952; M.D., Emory U., 1956; m. Elizabeth Ann Dwyer, Dec. 14, 1957; children—Sarah Ellen, Marie, Frank Norman. Intern, New Eng. Center Hosp., Boston, 1956-57; resident internal medicine Tulane U.-Charity Hosp. of La., New Orleans, 1959-61; resident gastroenterology U. Louisville Sch. Medicine, 1961-62, instr. medicine, sect. gastroenterology, 1962-64, asst. prof. medicine, 1964-65; practice medicine, specializing in gastroenterology, Pensacola, Fla., 1965—; mem. staff Baptist Hosp., Univ. Hosps., Pensacola; chief internal medicine Pensacola Ednl. Program, 1969-71. Served as lt. M.C., USNR, 1957-59. Mem. A.C.P., Am. Soc. Gastrointestinal Endoscopy, Am. Coll. Gastroenterology, Am. Fedn. Clin. Research, Fla. Soc. Internal Medicine (pres. 1971-72), Escambia County Med. Soc. (sec. 1971). Home: 281 Beacon Rd Pensacola FL 32503 Office: 14 W Jordan St Pensacola FL 32501

VICKERS, LEE SIDNEY, city ofcl.; b. Avalon, Tex., Jan. 1, 1925; s. Dillard Lee and Nettie Lee (Ellison) V.; student Dartmouth, 1944-46; B.A. in Govt., U. Tex., 1948; m. Dorothy Nell Eaton, Aug. 5, 1946; 1 son, Jerry Lynn. Prin., L.S. Vickers, accountant, Dallas, 1948-50; adminstrv. asst. to dir. pub. works City of Dallas, 1950-55; city mgr. Rosebud, Tex., 1955-56, Gladewater, Tex., 1956-59, Orange, Tex., 1959-60, McKinney, Tex., 1968—. Cons. municipal govt., 1963-68. Mem. adv. council Connally Tech. Inst., Waco, Tex., 1966-68, continuing Edn. Tex. A. and M. U., 1972—. Served with USN, 1942-46; ETO. Mem. E. Tex. (pres. 1957-58), Tex., Internat. (chmn. municipal mgmt. policy com. Tex. 1972, com. on finance 1972-73) city mgrs. assns., Tex. Municipal League (sec. treas. 1968-71), Municipal Finance Officers Assn., McKinney C. of C. (indsl. devel. com. 1968-73). Democrat. Baptist. Lion. Home: 610 Tucker St McKinney TX 75069 Office: 130 S Chestnut St McKinney TX 75069

VICKERS, THOMAS FRANCIS, constrn. co. exec.; b. Houston, June 11, 1943; s. Thomas F. and Betty Jane (Patton) V.; B.A., Southwestern U., 1965; LL.B., U. Tex., 1968; m. Zelda Sue Bitner, Oct. 25, 1964; children—Thomas Francis IV, Stephan Joseph. Exec. v.p. Pecan Valley Properties, San Antonio, 1968-69; pres. Tom Vickers Enterprises, Inc., real estate and constrn., San Antonio, 1969—. Mem. planning session com. San Antonio Capitol Bond Issue, 1970; mem. exec. com. San Antonio Bicentennial Celebration, 1971. Justice of peace, 1971—. Bd. dirs. Alamoa Area council Boy Scouts Am., 1970-72, dist. chmn., 1970—; bd. dirs. Festival San Jacinto Assn., 1971. Mem. Tex. (state v.p. 1971—), San Antonio (dir. 1971—) apt. assns., San Antonio Homebuilders Assn., San Antonio Golf Assn. (dir. 1970—), Phi Delta Theta. Rotarian. Home: 4510 Pecan Grove St San Antonio TX 78223 Office: PO Box 23276 San Antonio TX 78223

VICKERY, KATHERINE, ret. educator; b. Dahlonega, Ga., Mar. 5, 1898; d. Elias Benton and Etta (McMullan) Vickery; A.B., North Ga. Coll., 1918; A.M., George Peabody Coll. for Tchrs., 1919, Ph.D., 1929; D.Sc., Ala. Coll., 1947. Tchr. English and Latin, Millington (Tenn.) High Sch., 1919-22; asst. prof. psychology Ala. Coll., 1922-30, asso. prof., 1930-35, prof. 1935-68, chmn. dept. psychology, 1948-68; vis. prof. U. Ala., summers 1940-41, 51-52, Furman U., 1947. Chmn. edn. sub-com. Ala. Gov.'s Commn. on Status Women. Trustee Shelby Acad.; bd. dirs. Chilton-Shelby County Mental Health Bd. Fellow A.A.A.S. (council 1949-51, 57-64), Ala. Acad. Sci., Am. Psychol. Assn.; mem. So. Soc. Philos. and Psychol., Comparative Edn. Soc., Ala. Assn. for Mental Health (bd. mem.), Am. Assn. U. Women (pres. Ala. div., 1948-50, v.p. S.E. Central region 1963-67), Peabody Alumni Assn. (v.p. 1963-65), Ala. Psychol. Assn. (pres. 1955-56, chmn. bd. certification 1959-61; recipient Distinguished Service award 1962), Southeastern Psychol. Assn., D.A.R. (chpt. regent), Kappa Delta Pi (nat. 1st v.p., 1942-53, pres. 1953-58, exec. counselor, 1958-64; awarded honor Key, laureate). Episcopalian (ch. trustee). Author: A History of Mental Health in Alabama. Author ednl. articles. Home: 311 Nabors St Montevallo AL 35115

VICTOR, JOE MAYER, elec. engr.; b. Houston, Sept. 20, 1939; s. Max M. and Pearl E. (Nason) V.; B.S. in Elec. Engring., U. Tex., 1962, M.S. in Elec. Engring., 1964, Ph.D., 1967; m. Carolyn Harrison, Aug. 23, 1964; children—Kayla, Jeffrey, Melissa, Joshua. Sr. research engr. S.W. Research Inst., San Antonio, 1966—. Councilman, City Council Hill Country Village, 1971-73. Mem. I.E.E.E., Am. Phys. Soc., Research Soc. Am., S.W. Research Recreation Assn. (pres. 1973), Sigma Xi, Tau Beta Pi, Eta Kappa Nu. Jewish religion (trustee congregation). Mem. B'nai B'rith (pres. 1973-74). Home: 112 Cherokee Lane San Antonio TX 78232 Office: 8500 Culebra San Antonio TX 78284

VICTOR, LEONARD BAKER, pathologist, educator; b. Schenectady, N.Y., Aug. 3, 1934; s. Austin and Matilda (Baker) V.; A.B., N.Y.U., 1953; M.D., U. Brussels (Belgium), 1960; T.M.D., Royal Inst. Tropical Medicine, 1960; m. Rona E. Kogan, Dec. 25, 1966; children—Brian Hyde, Sarah Ruth. Rotating intern U. Buffalo, Gen. and Children's hosps., 1960-61; resident in pathology U. Rochester, Strong Hosp., 1961-65; practice medicine specializing in pathology, Rochester, 1965-67, Nashville, 1968-72, Memphis, 1973—; dep. med. examiner, sr. instr. U. Rochester, 1965-67; cons. State Hosp., Rochester, N.Y., 1966-67; asso. prof. pathology Meharry Med. Coll., Hubbard Hosp., Nashville, 1968-72, dir. multitest screening operations, 1968-72; asso. prof. pathology in biomed. engring., Vanderbilt U., Nashville, 1969-72; prof. pathology U. Tenn., 1973—; dep. dir. clin. labs. City of Memphis Hosps., 1973—. Diplomate Am. Bd. Pathology. Fellow Am. Soc. Clin. Pathologists, Coll. Am. Pathologists, Soc. Advanced Med. Systems, Royal Soc. Health; mem. Tenn. Med. Assn., Tenn. Soc. Pathologists, A.M.A., Memphis and Shelby County Med. Socs. Home: 957 Green Oaks Dr Memphis TN 38117 Office: 858 Madison Av Memphis TN 38163

VICTORY, GENE C., oil and gas exec.; b. Leonard, Tex., Nov. 19, 1934; s. Green F. and Avis Dee (Treadway) V.; student So. Meth. U., 1964; m. Pauline Lawrence, May 24, 1957; children—David, Chris. Chief accountant Nortex Oil & Gas Corp., Dallas, 1962-64; treas. Gandy-McAuley Inc., oil and gas producers, 1964-66; v.p. financial Kingwood Oil Co., Oklahoma City, 1966-72; v.p. finance Public leasing Corp., Oklahoma City, 1972-73; v.p., controller Cleary Petroleum Corp., 1974—. Cons. oil and gas accounting. Served with USAF, 1954-57. Mem. U.S., Oklahoma City chambers commerce, Petroleum Accountants Soc. Dallas and Oklahoma City (1st v.p. 1969-70, dir. 1967-70). Baptist (mem. finance com. 1967-69). Home: 4913 NW 62d St Oklahoma City OK 73122

VIDAUD, GUILLERMO ANTONIO, architect; b. Havana, Cuba, Feb. 22, 1929; s. Felix and Flora Fernandes (Vasquez) V.; diploma de arquitecto, U. Havana, 1953; m. Maria Elena de la Vega, Mar. 27, 1955; children—Bill, Freddy, Maria Elena. Came to U.S., 1960. Lectr., N.C. State Coll. Architecture, Raleigh, 1961-62; asst. prof. Tex. A. and M. Sch. Architecture, College Station, 1962-64; asso. prof. Tex. Technol. U., Lubbock, 1964-70; sr. architect City Dallas, 1970—. Partner, Vidadu Troy Architects, Lubbock, 1967-69; mem. adv. com. archtl. div. El Centro Coll., Dallas County Jr. Coll. Dist., 1971—. Sgt., Am. Cancer Soc. campaign, Dallas, 1973. Mem. A.I.A., Tex. Soc. Architects, Colegio de Arquitectos de Cuba en Exilio. Roman Catholic. Home: 11428 Cromwell Ct Dallas TX 75229 Office: 1500 W Mockingbird St Dallas TX 75235

VIEBIG, VAN RICHARD, JR., certified pub. accountant; b. Houston, June 11, 1940; s. Van Richard and Hulda (Alexander) V.; B.A. cum laude, Rice U., 1962 Sr. accountant Voelkel, Simons & Co., C.P.A.'s, Houston, 1962-65; tax and financial adminstr. Jack C. Pollard Enterprises, Houston, 1965-72; sr. partner Viebig & Jones C.P.A., 1973—. Lectr. accounting Rice U., 1969—; Served with USCGR, 1962. Mem. Am. Inst. C.P.A.'s, Tex. Soc. C.P.A.'s Am. Accounting Assn., Tex. Bill of Rights Found., Am. Civil Liberties Assn., Phi Beta Kappa. Episcopalian. Home: 4408 Acacia Bellaire TX 77401 Office: 2419 Fannin St Houston TX 77002

VIERS, JIMMY WAYNE, educator, chemist; b. Grundy, Va., Feb. 26, 1943; s. Milton Elliot and Pauline (Edwards) V.; A.B., Berea Coll., 1965; M.S., Wake Forest U., 1967; Ph.D., Stanford, 1971; m. Virginia Sue McDavid, Aug. 21, 1965; children—Brent Douglas, Dawn Renae. Research asst. U. Utah, Salt Lake City, 1970-71; asst. prof. chemistry Va. Poly. Inst. and State U., Blacksburg, 1971—. Mem. Am. Chem. Soc., Sigma Chi. Home: 519 Alleghany St Blacksburg VA 24061

VIERTEL, JOSEPH MAURICE, real estate exec., author; b. N.Y.C., Aug. 13, 1915; s. Jacob and Daisy (Viertel) Shapiro; A.B. magna cum laude, Harvard, 1936; postgrad. Yale Drama Sch., 1937; m. Janet R. Man, Sept. 13, 1939; children—Thomas Man, John Richard, Alice (Mrs. Dennis Krieger). With Presdl. Realty Corp., White Plains, N.Y., 1940—, mem. exec. com., 1956—, chmn. finance com., dir. corporate planning, 1970—, also dir. Vice-pres. Stamford (Conn.) United Fund, 1955-58, Stamford Anti-Poverty Agy., 1959-63; sec. Stamford Human Rights Commn., 1959-63. Trustee Shapiro-Viertel Found. Clubs: Harvard (N.Y.C., So. Conn.). Author novels: The Last Temptation, 1955, To Love and Corrupt, 1962, Monkey on a String, 1968; play: So Proudly We Hail, 1936; numerous short stories. Home: Box 3081 Christiansted St Croix VI 00820 Office: 180 S Broadway White Plains NY 10605

VIETS, ROBERT COIL, paper co. exec.; b. Vincennes, Ind., Jan. 10, 1916; s. William Andrew and Freda Elizabeth (Freund) V.; student Purdue U., 1935-38; B.S., Ind. U., 1939; postgrad., Tex. A. and M. U., 1942; m. Hanna Christine Offenhausen, Apr. 1, 1972; 1 dau. by previous marriage, Susan (Mrs. Henry Keith Fox). With Packaging Corp. of Am., 1940—, gen. mgr. corrugated shipping container plant, Arlington, Tex., 1965—. Bd. dirs. Jr. Achievement, 1973—. Served to lt. USNR, 1942-45. Mem. Tex. Mfrs. Assn., Fibre Box Assn. (chmn. S. Central Zone 1972-73), Audubon Soc. Presbyn. Mason (32 deg., Shriner), Elk. Home: 2111 Almond St Arlington TX 76011 Office: 1000 Great Southwest Pkway Arlington TX 76011

VILA-BALZAC, MANUEL ANTONIO, constrn. co. exec.; b. Rio Piedras, P.R., June 8, 1926; s. Joaquin Vila-Mayo and Irene Vila Balzac; B.S., U. Ky., 1950; m. Doris C. Schnitzler, Jan. 28, 1950; children—Patricia Ann (Mrs. Richard Mohon), Peggy Jo. Asst. plant engr. Kawneer Co., Lesington, Ky., 1950-51; estimator James E. Smith & Sons, Inc., Louisville, 1951-54, chief estimator, 1967—, v.p., 1967—; estimator George Blanford Co., Louisville, 1955-61. Chmn. Shively Park Commn., 1969, 70-71; mem. Shively Parks Devel. Bd., 1974—. Republican. Roman Catholic (dir. athletic assn. 1970-73). Home: 3446 Janell Rd Shively KY 40216 Office: 7308 Grade Lane Louisville KY 40219

VILLALON, LEONARDO ATANASIO, elec. engr.; b. Havana, Cuba, Nov. 7, 1932; s. Jose Ramon and Elodia (Sorzano) V.; grad. elec. engring. U. Havana, 1955; postgrad. computer sci. Tulane, 1965-66; m. Isabel Marie Urbizu, Oct. 21, 1956; children—Leonardo Atanasio, Alejandro, Gonzalo, Miguel, Isabel. Came to U.S., 1961, naturalized, 1969. Application engr., Internat. Gen. Electric Co., various locations Cuba, U.S., 1955-60; staff engr. Foster Wheeler Corp., engrs. and contractors, N.Y.C., 1961-62; with Waldemar S. Nelson & Co., Inc., New Orleans, 1963—, asst. v.p., 1966—, chief elec. engr., 1970—. Mem. I.E.E.E., Nat. Soc. Profl. Engrs., La. Engrng. Soc. Registered profl. engr., La., Tex. Home: 753 Hermes Pl Gretna LA 70053 Office: 1200 St Charles Av New Orleans LA 70130

VILLANI, CARMEN DOMINICK, cons. data processing; b. Newark, Nov. 26, 1930; s. Raymond Peter and Emily (Ciullo) V.; B.S., Fairleigh Dickinson U., 1952; M.S., N.Y. U., 1961; m. Joan Ellen Mauriello, Nov. 14, 1953; children—Carmen Dominick, Vincent. Asst. project engr. Bendix Aviation Corp., Teterboro, N.J., 1952-58; mgr. data processing Vitro Labs., West Orange, N.J., 1958-63; project engr. ITT data services div., Paramus, N.J., 1963-64; supervising programmer fed. systems div. Univac, Hanover, N.J., 1964-68; sr. systems analyst Standard Oil N.J., Florham Park, N.J., 1968-69; sr. mem. tech. staff Litton Systems Inc., Sunnyvale, Cal., 1969-71; sr. systems analyst Systems Consultants, Inc., Washington, 1971—. Tchr. Fairleigh Dickinson U., Rutherford and Teaneck, N.J., 1961-62, pub. schs. San Jose, Cal., 1969-70, Computer Inst. San Jose, 1969-70. Active Cub Scouts, 1960-61; mgr. P.A.L. baseball team, Parsippany, N.J., 1967-68; committeeman Republican party Morris County, N.J., 1968-69. Served with AUS, 1954-56. Mem. Assn. Computing Machinery, Soc. Indsl. and Applied Math., Am. Mgmt. Assn. Home: 9802 Meadow Dale Ct Vienna VA 22180 Office: 1050 31st St NW Washington DC 20007

VILLARREAL, GILBERT GARZA, radio exec.; b. San Antonio, July 31, 1943; s. Joe Lozano and Carolina (Garza) V.; grad. high sch.; m. Magdalena H. Kosub, July 8, 1967; children—Joseph Kosub, Jason

Kosub. Teen disc jockey KUKA radio, San Antonio, 1959-62; advt. traffic dir., disc jockey KUBO, San Antonio, 1962-64; announcer, copywriter KCCT radio, Corpus Christi, Tex., 1967-68; copywriter KUKA, 1969-72, music dir., 1972—. Dir. Tex. Music Format of Mexican-Am. music, 1972—. Served with AUS, 1964-67. Recipient Pub. Service award for reporting Mayor Corpus Christi, 1967. Home: 430 Thelma St San Antonio TX 78212 Office: 501 Quincy St San Antonio TX 78212

VILLARREAL-GONZALEZ, FIDEL, educator; b. Múzquiz, Coahuila, Mexico, Aug. 5, 1930; s. Fidel and Consuelo (González) Villarreal; B.Sc., Instituto Tecnologico y de Estudios Superiores de Monterrey (Mexico), 1955; M.Sc., U. Cal. at Davis, 1960; m. Teresa Pérez-Maldonado Farías, Sept. 28, 1973. Internat. fellow Southwest Research Inst., San Antonio, 1954-55, mem. staff indsl. research projects, 1955-56; research asst. dept. food sci. and tech. U. Cal., Davis, 1958-60; guest prof. U. Tex. at Austin, 1963-64; coordinator TV chem. courses Monterrey Tech. Inst., 1964-69, prof. chemistry, biochemistry and food chemistry, 1965—, mem. curriculum com. biochem. engring., 1970—. Cons. in field; participant numerous internat. seminars. Mem. Sociedad Química de México (pres. N.E. sect. 1970-72), Inst. Food Technologists, Assn. Tech. Alimentos Mexico, Am. Oil Chemists Soc., Inst. Mexico Quím Aceites y Grasas. Roman Catholic. Author manual: Experimentos en Bioquímica, Resúmenes Química Inorgánica. Contbr. articles to profl. jours. Home: Degollado Sur 802 Monterrey Nuevo Leon Mexico

VILLEMARETTE, TERRY JAMES, social worker; b. New Orleans, May 18, 1939; s. James Joseph and Amy (Firmin) V.; student U. Southwestern La., 1957-61; B.A., La. State U., 1962, M.S.W., 1964; m. Janette Mary Ponthieux, June 8, 1963; 1 son, Keith. Caseworker Forest Glen Mental Health Center, 1964-65; case supr. Hosp. Improvement Project, Pineville, La., 1965-68, asst. coordinator, 1968-70, coordinator, 1970—. Sec. Marksville Econ. Devel. Commn., 1972—. Mem. Nat. Assn. Social Workers (pres. 1970-71), Acad. Certified Social Workers, Rapides Parish Council Social Agys. (pres. 1965-67), La. (adminstrv. v.p. 1969-70, internal v.p. 1970—), Marksville (Key man award 1974; regional v.p. 1968-69), Internat. (senator 1974—) jaycess. K.C. Home: PO Box 474 Marksville LA 71351 Office: PO Box 31 Pineville LA 71360

VILLEPONTEAUX, LORENZ AIMAR, JR., social worker; b. Charleston, S.C., Sept. 1, 1935; s. Lorenz Aimar and Mary (Laurey) V.; A.B., Coll. Charleston, 1958; M.S.W., Tulane U., 1964; Ph.D., U. N.C., 1972; m. Anne Louise Bellinger, Dec. 27, 1957; children—Mary Antonia, Virginia Anne, Laura Marian, Elizabeth Laurey. Probation counselor Charleston Juvenile Ct., 1959-60; dir. probation Rock Hill (S.C.) Juvenile Ct., 1961-62; dir. Horizon House, Charleston, 1964-67; asst. prof. dept. psychiatry Med. U. Hosp., Charleston, 1967—. Chmn. adminstrv. bd. Charleston Area Mental Health Center, 1969-70. Mem. Nat. Assn. Social Workers (pres. coastal Carolina chpt. 1966-68), Acad. Certified Social Workers, Am. Orthopsychiat. Assn., Alumni Assn. Coll. Charleston (pres. 1969-70, mem. exec. com. 1964—). Democrat. Home: 91 Logan St Charleston SC 29401 Office: 80 Barre St Charleston SC 29401

VILLORO, MIGUEL TORANZO, educator; b. Barcelona, Spain, Nov. 21, 1920; s. Miguel Villoro and Maria Luisa Toranzo; Licenciado en Derecho, Escuela Libre de Derecho, Mexico, 1946; Maestro en Filosofia, Universidad Iberoamericana, Mexico, 1946; Doctor en Derecho, Universidad Nacional Autonoma de Mexico, 1973. Joined Soc. of Jesus, 1946, ordained priest, 1958; dir. Law Sch., Universidad Iberoamericana, Mexico, 1960-66, mem. Senate, 1971-74, full prof., 1974—. Vis. prof. Universidad Nacional Autonoma de Mexico, San Luis Potosi, Guadalajara, Querétaro, Zacatecas, Veracruzana, Guanajuato. Mem. Academia Mexicana de Legislacion y Jurisprudence. Author: Metodologia del Trabajo Juridico, 1972; Introduccion al Estudio del Derecho, 1966, 2d edit., 1974; Lecciones de Filosofia del Derecho, 1973. Contbr. articles to profl. jours. Home: 84 Zaragoza Mexico DF 21 Mexico Office: 395 Cerro de las Torres Mexico DF 21 Mexico

VIMONT, RICHARD ELGIN, lawyer; b. Lexington, Ky., Aug. 3, 1936; s. Richard Thompson and Christine (Anderson) V.; B.S., U. Ky., 1958, J.D., 1960; m. Marie Salyer, Sept. 10, 1960; children—Richard Thompson II, Margaret Anderson. Admitted to Ky. bar, 1960; since practiced in Lexington, Ky.; now partner Anggelis and Vimont; vis. prof. bus. law Transylvania Coll., 1963; tennis coach U. Ky., 1963-71. Chmn. bd. Eastern State Hosp., 1970-71. City commr., Lexington, 1972-73; asst. commonwealth atty., 1974—; mem. Regional Crime Council, 1972—, Met. Police and Fire Bds., 1973-74. Mem. Ky. State Tennis Assn. (pres. 1960-62), Patterson Literary Soc., Jr. C. of C., Phi Delta Phi, Sigma Alpha Epsilon. Mem. Christian Ch. (elder). Home: 1412 Lookout Circle Lexington KY 40502 Office: 139 Market St Lexington KY 40507

VINAMATA PASCHKES, CARLOS, lawyer; b. Barcelona, Spain, Sept. 19, 1944; s. Carlos Vinamata Castaner and Martha Paschkes Sibibin; gen. law degree Universidad Nacional Autonoma de Mexico, 1968; m. Carolina Chavez Moran, Jan. 16, 1964; children—Caroline, Claudia Alejandra, Ingrid, Carlos. Admitted to Mexican bar, 1970; mem. firm Basham, Ringe & Correa, Mexico City, 1968-74; partner firm Vinamata, Melesio and Fernandez, 1974—. Dir. internat. studies Confederacion de Profesionistas y Tecnicos Revolucionarios, del Partido Revolucionario Institucional, Mexico City, 1969, 70, 71. Mem. Mexican Assn. Indsl. Property. Home: 6-502 Ixtaccihuatl Mexico City 11 Mexico Office: 123 Liverpool Mexico City 6 Mexico

VINCENT, C. (CHARLES) GEOFFREY, journalist; b. London, Eng., Apr. 14, 1920; s. Charles Bassett and Edith (Vialls) V.; came to U.S., 1928, naturalized, 1942; student U. Buffalo, 1938-39, Washington U., St. Louis, 1947-50; m. Mary Amy Loy, Apr. 12, 1947 (dec. July 1964); children—Wendy Anne, Christopher Loy; m. 2d, Adele Judith Bagnall, Apr. 24, 1965; 1 dau., Mary Jane. Copy boy Buffalo Evening News, 1937, reporter, feature writer, 1939-42; copy editor, feature editor St. Louis Star-Times, 1946, 48-51; copy editor N.Y. Herald Tribune, N.Y.C., 1951-54, asst. night editor, 1954-56; writer News of Week in Review, N.Y. Times, N.Y.C., 1956-61; pub. relations exec. BBDO-Internat., London, 1961-62, Benton & Bowles, London, 1962-63; asso. editor, contbr. N.Y. Times Mag., N.Y.C., 1963-65; Sunday mng. editor Courier-Jour. & Times, Courier-Jour. and Louisville Times Co., Louisville, 1965—. Sec. Louisville Com. on Fgn. Relations. Served with C.I.C., AUS, 1942-46. Mem. English-Speaking Union, Am. Assn. Sunday and Feature Editors (pres. 1970-71). Home: 3900 Fallen Timber Dr Louisville KY 40222 Office: 525 W Broadway Louisville KY 40202

VINCENT, LLOYD DREXELL, coll. adminstr.; b. DeQuincy, La., Jan. 7, 1924; s. Samuel and Lila (Dickerson) V.; student Rice U., 1946-47, 49-50; B.S., U. Tex. (Austin), 1952, M.A., 1953, Ph.D., 1960; m. Johnell Stuart, Aug. 30, 1947; children—Drexell Stuart, Sandra. Asst. prof. U. Southwestern La., 1953-55, asso. prof., 1956-58; instr. Tex. A. and M. U., 1955-56; Danforth Tch. Study grant, NSF Sci. faculty fellowship U. Tex., 1958-59; research scientist Tex. Nuclear Corp., Austin, 1959-60; prof., dir. physics dept. Sam Houston State U., 1960-65, asst. to pres., 1965-67; pres. Angelo State U., San Angelo, Tex., 1967—. Co-owner, mgr. Acme Glass Corp., Baytown, Tex., 1947-49; physics cons. AID, India, summer 1966. Served to 2d lt. USAAF, 1942-45. Fellow Tex. Acad. Sci., mem. Am. Phys. Soc., Am. Assn. State Colls. and Univs. (state rep. 1972-74), Am. Assn. Physics Tchrs. (sect. chmn. 1965-67), Sigma Xi, Sigma Pi Sigma. Democrat. Baptist. Rotarian. Home: 2602 Live Oak St San Angelo TX 76901

VINCENT, ROBERT JERRALD, architect; b. Kilgore, Tex., Jan. 30, 1936; s. Robert E. and Opal B. (Brashear) V.; B.Arch., Tex. A. and M. U., 1959; m. Judith Wilmoth, May 31, 1958; children—Kerry Scott, Robert Layne, Ashley Ann. Architect in tng. George L. Dahl, architects and engrs., Dallas, 1960-62, Prinz & Brooks, Dallas, 1962-63; project architect Pratt, Box & Henderson, architects, planners, Dallas, 1963-65, asso. coordinator, 1967-69, partner 1970-71; staff architect Vincent G. Kling & Assos., Phila., 1965-67; owner Vincent Assn., Architects, Dallas, 1971—. Adj. prof. architecture U. Tex., Arlington, 1972—. Mem. Dallas Park and Recreation Bd. Bd. dirs. Children, Inc., Creative Arts Center, Oak Cliff br. YMCA, Dallas. Served to 2d lt. AUS, 1959-60. Mem. A.I.A., Tex. Soc. Architects, Oak Cliff C. of C. (dir.). Methodist (adminstrv. bd. 1965—). Prin. works: Arlington (Tex.) Childrens Clinic, 1971; Sams House, Arlington, 1973; N.E.T.C. br. Office Bldg., Bedford, Tex., 1973; Portman House, Arlington, 1974. Home: 1934 Kessler Parkway Dallas TX 75208 Office: 3141 Hood St Dallas TX 75219

VINCENT, ROBERT SHELBY, communications co. exec.; b. nr. DeQuincy, La., Dec. 31, 1921; s. George and Clara Louise (Foster) V.; student McNeese Jr. Coll., 1946-47; B.S., La. State U., 1949; m. Velton Nell Long, Apr. 3, 1954; children—Perry Dean, Celia Ann. Installation and service 2-way radio systems, 1950—; propr. La. Radio Communications, Inc., Lake Charles, 1972—. Served with USAAF, 1942-45. Mem. United Pentecostal Ch. Home: 1305 Sunset Dr Lake Charles LA 70601 Office: 629 Hwy 171 PO Box 661 Lake Charles LA 70601

VINEYARD, EDWIN EARLE, coll. pres.; b. Wright City, Okla., Aug. 30, 1926; s. John R. and Bess (Chronister) V.; B.S., Okla. State U., 1949, M.S., 1951, Ed.D., 1955; m. Imogene Mankin, Nov. 6, 1946; children—Louis Ray, Edwin Roy. Jr. high sch. prin., Beggs, Okla., 1949-51; high sch. prin., Mannford, Okla., 1951-52, Davis, Okla., 1952-54; dir. counseling Panhandle State Coll., Goodwell, Okla., 1955-58; dean students, chmn. dept. edn. and psychology Southwestern State Coll., Weatherford, Okla., 1958-61; prof. edn. Okla. State U., Stillwater, 1961-65; pres. No. Okla. Coll., Tonkawa, 1965—. Dir. Service Bank Tonkawa. Mem. Am. Psychol. Assn., Am. Personnel and Guidance Assn. Baptist (deacon 1956-70). Lion, Kiwanian. Author: (with Harold W. Massey) The Profession of Teaching, 1961. Home: 202 S Pine St Tonkawa OK 74653

VINSON, LEWIS CHARLESTON, educator; b. Pineville, La., Sept. 24, 1921; s. Joseph W. and Helen (Elton) V.; A.B., La. Coll., 1939; A.M., La. State U., 1947; postgrad. Tulane U. Prin., Wise Sch., Alexandria, La., 1939-40; teacher Tioga (La.) High Sch., 1940-42; grad. asst. La. State U., Baton Rouge, 1945-47, instr. dept. social sci., 1947-48; asst. prof. psychology Furman U., Greenville, S.C., 1948-49; supr. student tchrs. in social studies, lab. sch., La. Poly. Inst., Ruston, La., 1949-52; asst. prin. Pineville (La.) Elementary Sch.; head dept. social studies John McDonogh Sr. High Sch., New Orleans; coordinator econ. edn. for New Orleans Pub. Sch., now supr. social studies; also TV series Our Econ. Pattern. Bd. dirs. La. Council on Econ. Edn. Served with AUS 1942-45. Mem. Am. Assn. Univ. Profs., Am. Assn. for Supervision and Curriculum, Nat., La. (exec. bd.) councils for social studies, La. Council on Econ. Edn., N.E.A., La. Edn. Assn., Psi Chi, Sigma Delta Pi, Alpha Chi, Phi Delta Kappa, Kappa Delta Pi. Club: Kiwanis. Home: 924 Royal St New Orleans LA 70116 Office: 731 St Charles Av New Orleans LA 70130

VINSON, NELSON, lawyer; b. nr. Birmingham, Ala., July 25, 1923; s. Fred David and Laura (Nelson) V.; student U. Ala., 1941-43, LL.B., 1949; m. Leila Terry Walker, Aug. 11, 1951; children—Hughes Nelson, William Terry. Admitted to Ala. bar, 1949; county dist. atty., Hamilton, Ala., 1949-50; judge Marion County Superior Ct., Hamilton, 1950-59; practice law, Hamilton, 1959—. Mem. Ala. Bd. Bar Commrs., 1968—. Served with AUS, 1943-46. Mem. U. Ala. Alumni Assn. (pres. Marion County chpt. 1954-58), Bar Assn. Ala. (pres. jud. circuit 1958-60), Ala. Bar Assn., Delta Chi. Methodist. Home: Military Rd Hamilton AL 35570 Office: Court Square Hamilton AL 35570

VINSON, RALPH NICHOLAS, cartoonist; b. nr. Trinity, Tex., Oct. 19, 1916; s. Ralph Magee and Leafy (Pruitt) V.; student Tex. A. and M. Coll. and Sam Houston State Coll., 1934-37, Chgo. Acad. Fine Arts, 1938, Tex. Acad., 1953-54; m. Dorothy Leah Ramey, July 27, 1939. Editorial cartoonist Pasadena (Tex.) Daily Citizen, 1960, Fort Worth Star-Telegram, 1963-64, New Orleans States-Item, 1964—. Served with USNR, 1943-45. Mem. Assn. Am. Editorial Cartoonists. Methodist. Mason. Club: New Orleans Press. Home: 324 Arlington Dr Metairie LA 70001 Office: 615 North St New Orleans LA 70130

VINSON, THOMAS GLENN, banker; b. Everton, Ark., Sept. 19, 1923; s. Franklin S. and Chleola J. (Elam) V.; student Draughons Bus. Coll., 1941-42, S.W. Mo. State U., 1942, So. Meth. U., 1960-63; m. Reba Faye Young, Jan. 11, 1946; children—Thomas A., Judy Nanette (Mrs. Allen M. Tucker, Jr.). Cashier, Comml. Bank, Harrison, Ark., 1947-55; pres., dir. First Nat. Bank, Batesville, Ark., 1955—. Bd. dirs. White River Med. Assn. Served with USAAF, 1942-46. Decorated Purple Heart, Air medal with three oak leaf clusters. Mem. Ark. Bankers Assn. (exec. bd. 1960-63), Batesville C. of C. (pres. 1967). Methodist. Mason, Rotarian. Home: 18th St Batesville AR 72501 Office: 250 S Broad St Batesville AR 72501

VIORST, JUDITH (MRS. MILTON VIORST), author; b. Newark; ed. Rutgers U.; m. Milton Viorst; children—Anthony, Nicholas, Alexander. Columnist for Redbook mag. Mem. Phi Beta Kappa. Author: Projects: Space, 1962; 150 Science Experiments Step-By-Step, 1963; The Natural World, 1965; The Changing Earth, 1967; The Village Square, 1967; Sunday Morning, 1968; It's Hard to Be Hip over Thirty and Other Tragedies of Married Life, 1968; Ill Fix Anthony, 1969; (with Milton Viorst) The Washington D.C. Underground Gourmet, 1970; Try It Again, Sam, 1970; People and Other Aggravations, 1971; The Tenth Good Thing About Barney, 1971; Yes, Married, 1972; Alexander and the Terrible, Horrible, No Good, Very Bad Day, 1972; My Mama Says There Aren't Any Zombies, Ghosts, Vampires, Creatures, Demons, Monsters, Fiends, Goblins or Things, 1973; Rosie and Michael, 1974. Address: 3432 Ashley Terrace NW Washington DC 20008

VIORST, MILTON, journalist, author; b. Paterson, N.J., Feb. 18, 1930; s. Louis and Betty (Levine) V.; B.A., Rutgers U., 1951; M.A., Harvard, 1954; M.S., Columbia, 1955; postgrad. U. Lyon; m. Judith Stahl, Jan 30, 1960; children—Anthony Jacob, Nicholas Nathan, Alexander Noah. Washington corr. N.Y. Post, 1961-63; columnist Washington Star Syndicate, 1971—; freelance writer. Chmn. Fund for Investigative Journalism, 1968—. Served to 1st lt. USAF, 1952-54. Author: Liberalism: A Guide to Its Past, Present and Future in American Politics, 1963; Hostile Allies: The Story of Roosevelt and de Gaulle; An Anthology of the Great Documents of Western Civilization; Fall from Grace: The Republican Party and the Puritan Ethic; Hustlers and Heroes: An American Political Panorama. Contbr. to Harper's, Nation, Reporter, New Republic, Science, others. Home: 3432 Ashley Terrace NW Washington DC 20008

VIRANI, SHYAMLAL BECHARBHAI, civil engr.; b. Khad-Khambhalia, India, Apr. 3, 1933; s. Becharbhai Mavji and Otibai Becharbhai (Akabri) V.; diploma in Civil Engring., Birla Engring. Coll., Anand, India, 1957; B.S., U. Mo., 1959, M.S., 1961; m. Kanta Kadva Rola, Mar. 25, 1952; children—Urmila, Anita. Came to U.S., 1958, naturalized, 1971. Resident engr. on sewer project City of Poplar Bluff, Mo., 1961-62; with constrn. and architect depts. M.P. R.R., St. Louis, 1962-65; engr. USAF Titan IIIC and IIIM projects Stearns-Roger Corp., Denver, 1965-67; Apollo program support engr., Skylab program engr. Bendix Launch Support Div., Titusville, Fla., 1967—. Pres., Vista Engring. & Constrn., Inc., Titusville; structural engr. Buccaneer condominium project Boland Devel. Corp., Hover Marine Corp. project. Registered profl. engr., Fla., Colo. Mem. Am. Soc. C.E. Hindu. Home: 2900 Jasmine St Titusville FL 32780 Office: 2111 Garden St Titusville FL 32780

VISSERING, NORMAN HAYDEN, transp. co. exec., ret. army officer; b. Columbus, O., May 16, 1904; s. Harry and Grace Veil (Hayden) V.; B.S., Northwestern U., 1925; m. Nancy Cotter, Aug. 25, 1930; children—Norman, Elizabeth Louise (Mrs. Frederick Lafferty). Citrus grower and shipper, Lake Wales, Fla., 1930-40; exec. v.p. Tampa (Fla.) Union Terminal, 1936-39; commd. maj. U.S. Army, 1940, advanced through grades to maj. gen., 1962; coordinator movement cargo through U.S. embarkation ports; chief land movements sect. G-4 Div., London, Eng., 1944; dep. asst. chief staff ETO, 1945; command line communications, Korea; command New Orleans Port Embarkation; chief plans div. Office Chief Transp.; staff dir. for transp. Office Asst. Sec. Def.; comdr. Army Transp. Center and Army Transp. Sch., Ft. Eustis, Va., 1957-62; ret., 1962; asst. v.p. Seaboard Coast Line R.R., Orlando, Fla., 1962-69; chmn. bd. Fla. Terminals & Trucking Co., Orlando, 1969—. Decorated D.S.M., Bronze Star medal, Legion of Merit; Croix de Guerre (Belgium); Croix de Guerre (France); Order of Brit. Empire; Order of Free Poland; Korean Order of Taiguk. Mem. Nat. Def. Transp. Assn., Central Fla. Traffic Club, Sigma Nu. Mason, Rotarian. Home: 3103 Ardsley Dr Orlando FL 32804 Office: Fla Terminals & Trucking Co PO Box 13607 Orlando FL 32809

VITELLO, JOHN RALPH, pub. relations and fund raising exec.; b. Rochester, N.Y., July 27, 1929; s. Anthony and Josephine (Cornelia) V.; B.B.A., U. Houston, 1954, M.B.A., 1955; m. Alisbel Mills, Aug. 22, 1958. Exec. dir. Tex. div. Am. Cancer Soc., Houston, 1958-63; dir. pub. relations, spl. projects coordinator 17 hosps. Sisters of Charity of Incarnate Word, Houston, 1963—. Cons. pub. relations, fund raising, Houston, 1963—. Mem. pres.'s council U. Houston, 1967—; exec. dir. St. Joseph Hosp. Found., Houston, 1965—; asst. sec., dir. St. Bernardine Hosp. Found., San Bernardino, Cal., 1970—, St. Mary's Long Beach Hosp. Found., 1970—. Served with AUS, 1955-57. Mem. Nat. Assn. Hosp. Devel. Dirs. (pres. 1974-75, named outstanding devel. dir. 1971), Am., Tex. (bd. dirs. 1970) socs. hosp. pub. relations dirs., Pub. Relations Soc. Am., Sigma Chi. Home: 8924 Chatsworth St Houston TX 77024 Office: PO Box 1919 Houston TX 77001

VIVAS, JOSE GUILLERMO, lawyer; b. Ponce, P.R., Apr. 26, 1914; s. Guillermo and Enriqueta (Rosaly) V.; J.D., Georgetown U., 1937; m. Ligia H. Pietri, Aug. 10, 1940; children—Ligia (Mrs. Carlos Martinez-Texidor), Guillermo F., Jose H., Carmen M. Admitted to P.R. bar, 1937, U.S. Supreme Ct. bar, 1945; legal adviser to mayor Ponce, 1938-40; counsel Municipal Housing Authority Ponce, 1938-40, 46-58; sr. partner Vivas, Martinez-Texidor & Limeres, Ponce, 1968—. Faculty, Cath. U. P.R., Ponce, 1968—, prof., 1973—. Bd. dirs. Damas Hosp., Cath. U. P.R. Service Assn. Served to lt. col. AUS, 1940-46. Decorated Legion Merit. Mem. Am. Judicature Soc., Am., P.R. bar assns., Am. Legion (post comdr. 1947). Clubs: Bankers', Ponce Yacht, Deportivo de Ponce. Home: 59 Salud St Ponce PR 00731 Office: Banco de Ponce Bldg Ponce PR 00731

VIZCARRONDO, RAFAEL RENE, lawyer; b. San Juan, P.R., Jan. 24, 1937; s. Rene and Helen (Toro) V.; B.A. cum laude, Harvard, 1959; LL.B., magna cum laude, U. P.R., 1962. Admitted to P.R. bar, 1962; asso. atty. Fiddler, Gonzalesz & Ridriguez, San Juan, P.R., 1962-65, partner, 1965—. Dir. West Indies Indsl. Inst., Ponce, P.R., 1967—. Bd. examiners for Admission to P.R. Bar, 1970—; pres. com. apptd. by gov. to submit amendments to rules of civil procedures, criminal procedure and evidence, 1973—. Served with P.R. Air Nat. Guard, 1958-61. Clubs: AFDA, Bankers, Century (San Juan). Home: Condominio Torre de la Reina Apt 17-C Ponce de Leon #450 Puerta de Tierra San Juan PR 00906 Office: Chase Manhattan Bank Bldg 7th Floor Hato Rey PR 00919 also GPO Box 3507 San Juan PR 00936

VIZZINI, SALVATORE, city ofcl.; b. Pitts., Nov. 29, 1926; s. Samuel Anthony and Lillian Antonette (Wolfe) V.; student pub. schs., Chgo. Law Enforcement Acad., Washington, 1953-54; m. Marginell DeLoach, Mar. 5, 1949; 1 son, Samuel J. Spl. agt. Dept. Air Force, 1951-53, Fed. Bur. Narcotics, Italy, France, Greece, Syria, Turkey, Lebanon, Thailand, Cuba, P.R., U.S., 1953-66; spl. cons. on organized crime U.S. Senate Select Com. To Investigate Organized Crime and Law Enforcement, 1968-69; chief police City of South Miami (Fla.), 1967—. Served with USMC, 1944-50; PTO; CBI. Recipient Spl. Services award U.S. Treasury Dept., 1956, 61, 62, 64, Outstanding Law Enforcement award 20th Dist. Jr. C. of C., 1967, Fla. Gov.'s medal for outstanding law enforcement, 1968. Mem. Internat. Assn. Chiefs Police, Fla. Police Chief's Assn., Dade County Chiefs Police. Home: 6231 SW 58th St South Miami FL 33143 Office: Chief of Police City Hall South Miami FL 33143

VLADIMIR, ANDREW NEAL, advt. exec.; b. New Rochelle, N.Y., Feb. 6, 1932; s. Irwin Alfred and Geraldine (Schulman) V.; grad. Hotchkiss Sch., 1949; student Trinity Coll., Dublin, 1949-50; B.A., Yale, 1954; m. Donna Lynne Perlman, Oct. 9, 1965; children—Allison, Andrea, Jennifer, Thomas Irwin, Alexander. Radio-TV dir. Gotham-Vladimir Advt., N.Y.C., 1954-55, v.p., 1958-60; sales mgr. WAPA-TV, San Juan, P.R., 1955-56; v.p., gen. mgr. Gotham-Vladimir P.R., 1956-58; dir. plans Ruder & Finn, N.Y.C., 1960-61; pres. Vladimir Internat., San Juan, P.R., 1962-65; v.p. Norman Craig & Kummel, N.Y.C., 1965-66; v.p. Kenyon & Eckhardt of Mexico, 1966-67; pres. Vladimir & Evans, Miami, 1967—. Lectr. U. Miami Sch. Bus. Adminstrn. Mem. Am. Assn. Advt. Agys. (govt. relations com.), Assn. Yale Alumni. Clubs: Yale of Miami (sec.), Bankers, Standard, Jockey (Miami); Yale (N.Y.C.). Author: Puerto Rico-The New Life, 1965; Ryder's Family Highway Guide-Handbook of Truck Drivers Secrets, 1969. Home: 11101 SW 72d Av Miami FL 33156 Office: 2801 Ponce de Leon Av Coral Gables FL 33134

VOAS, ROBERT BRUCE, scientist, govt. ofcl.; b. Evanston, Ill., Feb. 21, 1928; s. William Henry and Florence (Williams) V.; Ph.B., U. Chgo., 1946; B.A., U. Cal. at Los Angeles, 1948, M.A., 1951, Ph.D., 1953; m. Carolyn Sylvia Merry, Apr. 11, 1953; children—David William, Jeanette Merry. Research psychologist U.S. Navy Electronics Lab., 1953-54; astronaut tng. officer NASA, 1958-64; dir. Life Sci. Lab., Litton, Inc., 1964-65; dir. field selection, dep. dir. office selection Peace Corps, 1965-68; chief Evaluation Div. OAC, Nat. Hwy. Traffic Safety Adminstrn., Washington, 1968—. Served with USNR, 1954-61. Fellow Am. Psychol. Assn.; mem. Human Factors Soc. Episcopalian (vestryman 1967-69). Home: 1766 Proffit Rd Vienna VA 22180 Office: 6th and D Sts SW Washington DC 22180

VOCELLE, CHARLES, lawyer; b. St. Marys, Ga., Sept. 4, 1923; s. James T. and Mary Della Schmitt) V.; A.A., U. Fla., 1947; J.D., U. Miami, 1950; m. Betty Paige Todd, Feb. 4, 1948; children—Charlene, Douglas. Admitted to Fla. bar, 1950; practiced in Miami, Fla., 1950-60, Lake City, Fla., 1961—; spl. asst. atty. gen. Fla., 1955-60; lectr. U. Miami, 1950-52, Lake City Community Coll., 1962—; pres. Bishop Motels, Inc., 1964—. Mem. Fla. Bd. Bar Examiners, 1970—. Mem. Com. of 100; mem. Lake City Community Coll. Found., 1972—, Fla. tchrs. Adv. Council, 1970-72. Young Democratic nat. committeeman for Fla., 1953; pres. Young Dem. Club of Dade County, 1954. Served with USMCR, 1942-45; PTO. Hon. life mem. Fla. Pest Control Assn.; mem. Lake City, 3rd Jud. Circuit, Am. bar assns., Fla. Bar (chmn. Workmen's Compensation com. 1971—), Lake City-Columbia Country C. of C. (dir. 1965-66), Delta Theta Phi. Kiwanian (pres. 1965). Author of Fla. Pest Control Act of 1959. Home: 825 Evergreen Av Lake City FL 32055 Office: State Exchange Bank Bldg Lake City FL 32055

VOCELLE, JAMES THOMAS, lawyer; b. St. Marys, Ga., Jan. 10, 1897; s. Lucien M. and Jane Elizabeth (Vance) V.; LL.B., Atlanta Law Sch., 1916; m. Mary Della Schmitt, May 12, 1920; children—James Thomas, Mary Delena (Mrs. William D. Shettig), Charles Lucien, Louis B., Angelique (Mrs. Earnest A. Bednar), Marguerite (Mrs. George Siebert, Jr.). Admitted to Ga. bar, 1916, Fla. bar, 1924; pvt. practice, St. Mary's, Ga. 1916-24, Vero Beach, Fla., 1924—; city atty., Vero Beach. Parole commr., 1941-45; state beverage dir., 1945-49; chmn. Indsl. Commn., 1953-61. Served with U.S. Army, 1917-18. Recipient Vercelli medal, 1952. Mem. Am., Fla. bar assns., Am. Legion, Woodmen of World. Democrat. Roman Catholic. K.C. (4 deg.), Rotarian (past pres.). Home: 2635 Carissa Dr Vero Beach FL 32960 Office: 1245 20th St Vero Beach FL 32960

VOELL, RICHARD ALLEN, food co. exec.; b. Chgo., Dec. 29, 1933; s. John H. and Esther A. (Anderson) V.; B.B.A., U. Ill., 1956; M.B.A., U. Hawaii, 1960; m. Virginia Broderick, Dec. 20, 1958; children—David Broderick, Gregory Jon, Jeffrey Scott. Mgmt. trainee Aluminum Co. Am., Chgo., 1956; successively salesman, sales mgr., mgr., v.p., pres., gen. mgr. Meadow Gold Dairies, Hawaii, 1968-71; dist. mgr. Beatrice Foods Co., Hawaii, 1968-71, group mgr., recreational products and mobile homes group, Miami, Fla., 1971-72, v.p. parent co., 1973—; chmn. bd. Island Fed. Savs. & Loan Assn. Active A.R.C., Aloha United Fund; v.p. Big Bros. Hawaii, Inc., 1969-71; dir. Foresight, Inc., Oahu Devel. Conf., 1969-71. Served to 2d lt. AUS, 1956-58. Named one of outstanding young men of Honolulu, Jr. C. of C., 1963, Hawaii, 1968, Am., 1965. Mem. Young Pres.'s Orgn., Hawaii Mfrs. Assn., Soc. Advancement Mgmt., Hawaii Econ. Assn., U. Ill. Alumni Assn., C. of C. of Hawaii (dir. 1962-63). Home: 531 Arvida Pkwy Coral Gables FL 33156 Office: 7100 N Kendall Dr Miami FL 33156

VOGTLE, ALVIN WARD, JR., electric utility exec.; b. Birmingham, Ala., Oct. 21, 1918; s. Alvin Ward and Ollie (Stinger) V.; B.S., Auburn U. 1939; LL.B., U. Ala. 1941; m. Kathryn Drennen, Apr. 20, 1945 (dec.); children—Kathryn D., Anne Moore (Mrs. Bryan Baldwin), Alvin Ward, III; m. 2d, Rachael Giles, 1966; children—Bryant Wade, William Patrick, Rachael Giles, Robert Jackson. Admitted to Ala. bar, 1941; asso. Martin, Vogtle, Balch & Bingham and predecessor firms, Birmingham, 1945-50, mem. firm, 1950-62; exec. v.p., dir. Ala. Power Co., 1962-65; pres. So. Electric Generating Co., 1960-62, dir., 1962—; exec. v.p. The So. Co., 1966-69, pres., dir., 1969—; chmn. bd., dir. So. Services Inc.; dir. Seaboard Coast Line Industries, Inc., Protective Life Ins. Co., Ala., Ga., Gulf, Miss. power cos. Past chmn., mem. exec. com. Edison Electric Inst.; mem. regional adv. com. Fed. Power Commn.; mem. Com. for Constructive Consumerism. Bd. visitors Emory U., Air U.; trustee Com. for Econ. Devel., Tax Found., Mary Baldwin Coll., YMCA of Met. Chgo. Served from 2d lt. to capt. USAAF, 1941-45. Mem. Newcomen Soc. Engr., Newcomen Soc. N.Am., Soc. Colonial Wars, The Conf. Bd., S.A.R., Ala. Hist. Assn., Am. Legion, Sigma Nu. Episcopalian. Clubs: The Club, Mountain Brook Country, Downtown, Birmingham Country (Birmingham); Piedmont Driving, Peachtree Golf, Capital City (Atlanta); Augusta Nat. Golf. Home: Batesville Rd Route 4 Woodstock GA 30188 Office: 64 Perimeter Center E Atlanta GA 30346

VOIGT, ROLAND LAWRENCE, accountant; b. Galveston, Tex., Nov. 1, 1941; s. Herman E. and Jennie Dorothy (Giusti) V.; B.B.A., Lamar U., 1963; m. June Kathleen von Miller, July 13, 1963; children—Wanda Lynn, Martha Elaine. With Haskins & Sells, San Antonio, 1963—, sr. accountant, 1966-70. mgr., 1970—. Beaumont chpt. Tex. Soc. C.P.A.'s scholar, 1962-63. Mem. San Antonio Chpt. C.P.A.'s (chmn. bankers relations com. 1973-74, dir. 1973-76), Nat. Assn. Accountants (treas. 1966-67), Blue Key, Phi Kappa Phi, Delta Sigma Pi. Roman Catholic. Clubs: San Antonio, Alamo Exchange. Editor Tex. C.P.A. mag., 1973-76. Home: 2831 Deer Ledge San Antonio TX 78230

VOLK, LEONARD WILLIAM, II, architect; b. Dallas, Oct. 7, 1928; s. Harold Francis and Florence (Allen) V.; grad. Phillips Acad., Andover, Mass., 1945; B.A., Yale, 1949; M.Arch., Mass. Inst. Tech., 1959; m. Nancy Mae Grove, July 25, 1970. Sales and mgmt. trainee Volk Bros., Dallas, 1950-52; city planner Marvin R. Springer, Dallas, 1959-60; draftsman E.O. Oglesby Jr., Dallas, 1960-62, Harrell & Hamilton, Dallas, 1962-64; with Pratt Box & Henderson, Dallas, 1965-68; prin. Dale Selzer Assos., Architects, Dallas, 1968—; dir. Volk Realty. Draft writer Goals for Dallas, 1966; chmn., organizer Community Design Center of Dallas, 1969—. Vice pres. Inst. for Early Childhood Edn., Dallas, 1973—. Served with USNR, 1948-52, AUS, 1952-55. Mem. A.I.A. (design award 1971), Phi Gamma Delta. Clubs: Brook Hollow, Idlewild, Dallas Fishing and Hunting, Terpsichorean. Architect Denison Med. Clinic, 1970. Home: 3519 Edgewater St Dallas TX 75205 Office: 901 Great American Bldg Dallas TX 75201

VOLKER, ALVIN SEWARD, JR., radio news producer; b. Logan, W.Va., Feb. 26, 1944; s. Alvin Seward and Mary Frances (Chafin) V.; B.J., U. Miami, 1966; m. Sharon Jean Logan, Sept. 1, 1972; 1 son, Eric. Newsman, WIOI radio, Portsmouth, O., 1966-67; news editor WTVR radio TV, Richmond, Va., 1968-69; news producer WLBW-TV, Miami Dade Community Coll. South, Miami, 1969—, sports publicity facilities coordinator, 1970—. Columnist, Record Exchanger mag., 1969—. Mem. Alpha Tau Omega, Sigma Delta Chi. Home: 9404 Sterling Dr Miami FL 33157 Office: 11011 SW 104th St Miami FL 33156

VOLLINTINE, CARY NEAL, accountant; b. St. Paul, July 14, 1942; s. Frank Leach and Juanita (Wright) V.; B.B.A., U. Tex., 1965; M.B.A., U. Wash., 1967; m. Jeanette Sue Johnson, Aug. 14, 1965; children—Heather Diane, Derek Brian. Instr., Highline Coll., Seattle, 1966; sr. auditor Arthur Andersen & Co., Ft. Worth, 1967-70, mgr., 1971—; investment exec. Goodbody & Co., Ft. Worth, 1970-71; pres. Vollintine Land & Cattle Co., 1970—. Active United Fund, Jr. Achievement. Del., Tex. Democratic Conv., 1972. C.P.A., Tex. Mem. Am. Inst. C.P.A.'s, Tex. Soc. C.P.A.'s, U. Wash. Alumni Assn., U. Tex. at Arlington Alumni Assn., Haltom-Richland C. of C. (mem. hwy. com. 1972-73), Phi Sigma Kappa, Phi Sigma Epsilon, Phi Kappa Theta. Mem. Christian Ch. Club: Fort Worth, Fort Worth Farm and Ranch. Home: 504 Oak Hollow Lane Fort Worth TX 76112 Office: 1110 First Nat Bank Fort Worth TX 76102

VOLMAR, PETER JON, architect; b. Northport, L.I., N.Y., Feb. 6, 1938; s. Paul George and Lucille Grace (Bailey) V.; B.Arch., U. Fla., 1962; m. Judith Elliott, Aug. 25, 1958 (div.); children—Jon Robie, Julie Ellen. Designer Harvard & Jolly, 1961-63; asso. architect C. Randolph Wedding & Assos., 1963-71; pvt. practice architecture, St. Petersburg, Fla., 1971—; archtl. cons. St. Petersburg Waterfront Re-devel., 1964; works include 1st Fed. Savs. & Loan Assn. Annex, Sheen residence, John Knox Apartments, Fla. Power Corp. Hdqrs., Treasure Sands Condominium Apts., Chateau Towers. Mem. St. Petersburg Young Reps. Club; chmn. Treasure Island (Fla.) Planning and Zoning Bd. Recipient award A.I.A., 1961, 64, county archtl. awards, 1969, 71. Mem. A.I.A., St. Petersburg Assn. Architects (2d v.p.), Archtl. Prescast Assn., Treasure Island C. of C., Gargoyle. Presbyn. Club: St. Petersburg Yacht. Home: 11750 Capri Circle S Treasure Island FL 33706 Office: 265 108th Av Treasure Island FL 33706

VOLPE, ROBERT WOODARD, rig and equipment mfg. co. exec.; b. Chgo., Dec. 3, 1923; s. Lewis Philip and Inez (McGinity) V.; student Knox Coll., 1941-43; B.S. in E.E., Northwestern U., 1947; m. Jean Ellyn Manley, May 31, 1947; children—Catherine, Barbara, Robert, Patricia. Engr., product planner Gen. Electric Co., Erie, Pa., 1947-67; mgr. product planning Unit Rig & Equipment Co., Tulsa, 1967—, asst. to pres., 1969—. Served with AUS, 1943-45. Recipient Cordiner award Gen. Electric Co., 1965. Mem. I.E.E.E. (mining industry com. 1968—), Soc. Automotive Engrs., Am. Inst. Mining, Metall. and Petroleum Engrs. Home: 3728 S Braden Pl Tulsa OK 74135 Office: PO Box 3107 Tulsa OK 74101

VOLTA, ARMAND JOSEPH, ret. govt. ofcl.; b. N.Y.C., July 30, 1915; s. Carlo and Erminia (Giacchero) V.; B.A., Bklyn. Coll., 1937, M.A., 1941; m. Emma Massoni, Apr. 20, 1947; children—Richard, Carlo, Armand. Instr. math. Bklyn. Coll., 1936-39; jr. marine engr., naval architect U.S. Maritime Commn., Dept of Commerce, Washington, 1942-43, 46-47; mathematician Navy David Taylor Model Basin, Carderock, Md., 1947-50; dir. computation office U.S. Navy, Oceanographic Office, Washington, 1950-73. Served with USNR, 1943-46. Home: 3300 Roslyn Av Washington DC 20028 Office: US Navy Oceanographic Office Washington DC 20390

VON DREHLE, FRANK RAYMOND, furniture, paper and packaging mfg. co. exec.; b. High Point, N.C., May 8, 1928; s. Charles William and Rose Elizabeth (Koester) Von D.; B.S., High Point Coll., 1950; postgrad. Harvard, 1968; m. Patsy Mae Murphy, July 2, 1950; children—Vicki, Raymond, Steve, Terri, Marie, Kim. Sales rep. sch. jewelry Josten's Inc., Owatonna, Minn., 1950-51; sales rep. course paper jobber Spaugh Paper Co., High Point, 1951-53; sales rep. sch. jewelry Josten's, Inc., Owatonna, 1953-57; sales rep. Cellu-Products Co., Patterson, N.C., 1957-61, v.p. sales, 1961-63, v.p. marketing, 1963-71, exec. v.p. marketing, 1971—, also dir.; pres. Widdington, Inc. div. Cellu-Products Cedartown, Ga., 1967-70; exec. v.p., dir. Handico, Inc., N.Y.C., 1973—; exec. v.p. Evergreen Paper Products Inc., Niagara Falls, N.Y., 1972—, Dispotech, Inc., Manchester, Conn., 1972—; pres. von Drehle Enterprises, Inc., Hickory, N.C., 1974—; dir. Hermitage Cabinet Shop, Inc., Cedartown, Ga., Phyl-Pat Inc., Rome, Ga., 1966-67. Mem. Am. Paper Inst. (dir. tissue div. 1973-74), Am. Mgmt. Assn., Nat. Broiler Council (marketing com. 1970—). Elk, Moose, Kiwanian. Home: 425 5th Av Pl NE Hickory NC 28601 Office: Roby-Martin Rd Patterson NC 28661

VON HOFFMAN, NICHOLAS, newspaperman; b. N.Y.C., Oct. 16, 1929; s. Carl and Anna (Bruenn) von H.; grad. Fordham Prep. Sch., 1948; m. Ann Byrne, 1950; children—Alexander, Aristodemos, Constantine. Asso. dir. Indsl. Area Found., Chgo., 1954-63; mem. staff Chgo. Daily News, 1963-66; columnist Washington Post, 1966—. Author: Mississippi Notebook, 1964; Multiversity, 1966; We Are The People Our Parents Warned Us Against, 1968; Left at The Post, 1970; Fireside Watergate, 1973. Office: Washington Post Washington DC 20005

VON OESEN, (ANNA) ELAINE, librarian; b. Wilmington, N.C., Sept. 6, 1913; d. Martin and Adeline (Behrens) von Oesen; A.B., Lenior Rhyne Coll., 1938; B.A. in L.S., U. N.C., 1940, M.A., 1951. Asst. librarian Rockingham County Library, Leaksville, N.C., 1940-42; dir. libraries, Walker County, Lafayette, Ga., 1942-43; chief librarian Camp Davis, N.C., 1943-44; instr., asst. prof. library sci. U. N.C., Chapel Hill, N.C., 1947-52; field librarian N.C. Library Commn., Raleigh, 1952-56; head extension div. State Library, Raleigh, 1956-65, asst. N.C. state librarian, 1965—, also acting N.C. state librarian. Mem. Am., Southeastern (pres. 1968-70) library assns., Am. Assn. State Libraries (sec. 1961-62), N.C. Adult Edn. Assn. (mem. exec. bd. 1958-68), N.C. Library Assn. (chmn. com. on orgn. 1961-66), Beta Phi Mu, Alpha Psi Omega. Democrat. Lutheran (sec. ch. council 1964-67, 69-71). Home: 201 D Boylan Apts Raleigh NC 27603 Office: 109 E Jones St Raleigh NC 27611

VON PLINSKY, ALEXANDER HARRISON, JR., mgmt. cons.; b. Rochester, N.Y., June 10, 1919; s. Alexander Harrison and Carloyne Josephine (Singer) Von P.; grad. high sch.; m. Eleanor Betty Paprocki, May 4, 1943; children—Monica, Alexander Harrison III, Johnathan, Andrew, Mark. Joined U.S. Army, 1940, advanced through grades to 1st lt., 1946; ret., 1960; pres. So. Data Processing Service, Inc., Augusta, Ga., 1960-68; systems analyst Com-Pu-Dat of Augusta; mgmt. cons., systems analyst, Augusta; dir. Cohen-Walker, Inc., J.A. Mullarky Co., Augusta. Instr., U. Ga., Ga. Tech. U., Augusta Coll. Chmn. bd. Aquinas High Sch., Augusta, 1969-70, Immaculate Conception Acad., 1971—. Mem. Am., German philatelic socs., Am. Mgmt. Soc. K.C. Home: 3013 Thomas Lane Extension Augusta GA 30906 Office: Mid South Bldg 370 Bay St Augusta GA 30903

VON STROEBEL, JAMES-MICHAEL, govt. ofcl.; b. Milw., Dec. 14, 1927; s. George Harvey and Margaret Elizabeth (Sullivan) von S.; student Marquette U., 1945-46, 48-49, U. Iberoamericana (Mexico City), 1954; B.S. in Fgn. Service, Georgetown U., 1955, postgrad., 1955-57 Asst. dean U. Iberoamericana, 1955-56; internat. economist Bur. Internat. Commerce, U.S. Dept. Commerce, Washington, Brazilian affairs, 1957-63, Argentine affairs, 1963-66, Central Am., Panamanian and Dominican Republic affairs, 1966-71, Venezuelan affairs, 1971-72, acting dep. dir. Latin Am., 1972, marketing mgr. for Andean and Caribbean countries, 1973; dep. dir. U.S. Trade Center, Mexico City, Mexico, 1973—. Served with AUS, 1950-52. Mem. Soc. Internat. Devel., Am. Polit. Sci. Assn., Am. Acad. Polit. and Social Sci., Acad. Polit. Sci., Internat. Economists Club Washington, Order St. John of Jerusalem, Knights of Malta, Delta Phi Epsilon. Roman Catholic. Home: 820 Salzedo Coral Gables FL 33134 also Am Embassy Mexico City Mexico Office: Latin Am Div O/M Bur Internat Commerce Dept Commerce Washington DC 20230

VON WERSSOWETZ, MURIEL ELIZABETH WILFORD (MRS. ARTHUR J. VON WERSSOWETZ), physician; b. Tzeliutsing, Sze, China, Feb. 1, 1914; d. Edward C. and Claudia (Gaviller) Wilford; M.E.L., Ont. Ladies Coll., Whitby, 1932; M.D., U. Toronto, 1938; m. Arthur J. Von Werssowetz, Oct. 3, 1940 (dec. June 1962); children—Diana (Mrs. William F. Kelsay), Arthur J. Intern, St. Michaels Hosp., Toronto, Ont., 1938-39; resident St. Josephs Hosp., Hamilton, Ont., 1939-40; part-time clinician Chattanooga-Hamilton County (Tenn.) Health Dept., 1941-62, clinician, dir. maternal and child health, 1962—. Mem. Cath. Charities, 1963—; v.p. Newman Club Found., Chattanooga, 1966-67. Mem. A.M.A., Chattanooga-Hamilton County Med. Soc., Am., Tenn. pub. health assns., Cath. Bus. Women's Club (past pres.), Chi Omega Mothers Club (v.p. 1962-63), Lambda Chi Alpha Mother's Club (pres. 1967-68). Club: Altrusa (past pres.). Home: 3412 Alta Vista Dr Chattanooga TN 37411 Office: 921 E 3d St Chattanooga TN 37403

VOS, BERT JOHN, pharmacologist; b. Bloomington, Ind., Sept. 18, 1908; s. Bert John and Rene (Moelker) V.; A.B. cum laude, Ind. U., 1930; Ph.D., U. Chgo., 1934, M.D., 1937; m. Elizabeth Aughey, Oct. 1, 1944; children—Elizabeth Louise, Margaret Anne. Instr., U. Chgo., 1939; with FDA, Dept. Health Edn. and Welfare, Washington, 1939-70, dep. dir. div. pharmacology, 1961-65, dir. div. toxicological evaluation, 1965-68, dep. dir. div. pharmacology and toxicology, 1968-69, dep. dir. div. toxicology, 1969-70; pvt. cons. in pharmacology, 1970—. Recipient Superior Service award Dept. Health, Edn. and Welfare, 1959, Outstanding Service award, 1963. Mem. Am. Soc. Pharmacology and Exptl. Therapeutics, Soc. Exptl. Biology and Medicine, Phi Beta Kappa, Sigma Xi. Home: 6444 Linway Terrace PO Box 569 McLean VA 22101

VOSBECK, WILLIAM FREDERICK, JR., architect; b. Mankato, Minn., May 13, 1924; s. William Frederick and Gladys (Anderson) V.; student Notre Dame U., 1943, Cornell, 1945; B.Arch., U. Minn., 1947; m. Elizabeth Just, Aug. 2, 1947; children—Lee, William Frederick III, Lynn, James Stephen. Partner Vosbeck & Ward, Alexandria, Va., 1957-62, Vosbeck & Vosbeck, 1962-66; mng. partner Vosbeck, Vosbeck, Kendrick, Redinger, archts., engrs., planners, Alexandria, 1966—; dir. United Va./Nat. Bank, Alexandria, United Va. Bankshares, Richmond, Electric Power Co., Richmond. Pres. bd. dirs. Alexandria Hosp., 1966, Sr. Citizens Service, Alexandria, 1969. Served with USMCR, 1942, 50. Recipient Meritorious Service citation Pres.'s Com. on Employment of Handicapped, 1968. Fellow A.I.A. (pres. 1971); mem. Va. C. of C. (bd. dirs. 1970-74, recipient bus. and civic leadership citation 1969), Va. Assn. Professions, Washington Acad. Sci. (Nat. Capitol award for achievement in architecture 1959), Alexandria Jr. C. of C. (Key man award 1960). Architect Tavern Sq. Urban Renewal Project, Alexandria, 1968, Woodrow Wilson Rehab. Center, Staunton, 1965. Home: 7512 Fort Hunt Rd Alexandria VA 22307 Office: 720 N St Asaph St Alexandria VA 22314

VOSS, CHARLES HENRY, JR., elec. engring. educator; b. Kiangyen, China, Sept. 28, 1926 (parents Am. citizens); s. Charles Henry and Mathilde (Easley) V.; B.S. in Elec. Engring., La. State U., 1949, M.S. in Elec. Engring., 1956; Ph.D. in Elec. Engring., N.C. State Coll., 1963; m. Elizabeth Ann Brown, July 24, 1954; children—Elizabeth Ann, Charles Henry III. Asst. chief engr. Sta. WJBO-WBRL-FM, Baton Rouge, 1950-53; div. transmission engr. So. Bell Telephone Co., New Orleans, 1953-54; instr. elec. engring. La. State U., Baton Rouge, 1954-56, asso. prof., 1962-67, prof., 1967—; instr. N.C. State Coll., Raleigh, 1957-61. Served with USNR, 1944-46, Ford Found. fellow, 1961-62; Research Council faculty fellow, 1965. Mem. I.E.E.E., Am. Assn. Med. Instrumentation, Sigma Xi, Phi Eta Sigma, Phi Kappa Phi, Eta Kappa Nu, Tau Beta Pi. Home: 5823 Clematis Dr Baton Rouge LA 70808

VOSS, HERBERT RAYMOND, theater dir. and designer; b. Sheboygan Falls, Wis., Dec. 7, 1932; s. Albert Hugo and Elsa (Bauherr) V.; B.S., Wis. State U., 1955; M.A., U. Minn., 1965; m. Tamara G. Majteles, July 5, 1959; 1 dau., Stephanie Alayne. Designer, tech. dir. Oberlin (O.) Coll. Theater, 1965-67; lighting designer, tech. dir. Am. U. Theater, Washington, 1967—. Mem. Am. Theatre Assn., Children's Theatre Assn., U.S. Inst. Theatre Technicians, Actors Equity Assn. Home: 4501 Everett St Kensington MD 20795 Office: Am U Theatre Massachusetts and Nebraska Avs NW Washington DC 20016

VOYLES, CHARLES NORMAN, ednl. adminstr.; b. Okemah, Okla., Apr. 27, 1928; s. Roy Curtis and Trula Grace (McBrayer) V.; B.S., Okla. State U., 1952, M.S., 1953; m. Mary Claudette Morton, Dec. 27, 1952; children—Tracy Lynn, Trent Morton. Asst. publs. editor Okla. State U., Stillwater, 1953-61, publs. editor, 1961-67, asso. dir. pub. information, extension editor, 1967—. Served with USAF, 1946-49. Recipient Pioneer award Am. Assn. Agrl. Coll. Editors, 1957. Mem. Am. Assn. Agrl. Coll. Editors (dir. 1968-71, pres. 1973-74), Alpha Zeta, Phi Kappa Phi, Kappa Tau Pi. Democrat. Baptist (ch. moderator 1970-71, deacon 1956—). Home: 1101 Brown Av Stillwater OK 74074

WACHTEL, LEO MICHAEL, JR., physician; b. Savannah, Ga., Oct. 5, 1912; s. Leo Michael and Beulah (Weil) W.; A.B., Emory U., 1934; M.D., Jefferson Med. Coll., 1938; m. Helen Ross Dixon, Jan. 7, 1941; children—Leo Michael III, John Dixon. Intern St. Vincent's Hosp., Jacksonville, Fla., 1938-40, now staff mem.; practice family medicine Jacksonville, 1940—; mem. staff St. Lukes, Baptist Meml., Univ. hosps. (all Jacksonville). Dir., Blue Shield Fla., 1956-59, 63-71, treas., 1963-72. Mem. Fla. Bd. Health, 1963-70. Trustee Bolles Sch., Jacksonville, 1956-64. Mem. Duval County Med. Soc. (pres. 1957), A.M.A. (del. 1960-70), Am. (dir. 1972—), Fla. (pres. 1957) acads. family physicians, Fla. Med. Assn. (pres. 1960), Jacksonville Area C. of C. (dir. 1963-65). Presbyn. (elder). Home: 3946 St Johns Av Jacksonville FL 32205 Office: 2708 St Johns Av Jacksonville FL 32205

WACHTEL, SIDNEY BARNETT, investment banking firm exec.; b. N.Y.C., Jan. 3, 1918; s. Isadore and Laura (Spear) W.; B.A., N.Y. U., 1939, M.A., 1941; m. Irma Schocken, Dec. 20, 1947; children—Wendie Lynn, Bonnie Kim. Economist, OPA, Washington, 1942-43, 46-47; statistician U.S. P.O. Dept., Washington, 1947; internat. financial economist Treasury Dept., Washington, 1948-59; economist, account exec. Laidlaw & Co., Washington, 1959-60; mgr. D.C. office, dir. investment adv. dept. A.T. Brod & Co., Washington, 1960-61; pres. Wachtel & Co., Inc., Washington, 1961—, also chmn. bd.; dir. Policyholder Service Corp., Design Specs, Inc., System Sci., Inc., U.S. Time Sharing, Inc. Adviser bus., industry. Served with USAAF, 1943-46. Mem. Washington Soc. Investment Analysts, Nat. Assn. Securities Dealers (chmn. regional dist. com. 1972), D.C. Security Traders Assn. (gov. 1968), Washington Bond Club, Beta Gamma Sigma, Delta Pi Sigma. Unitarian. Home: 7315 Stafford Rd Alexandria VA 22307 Office: 1000 Vermont Av NW Washington DC 20005

WACKENHUT, GEORGE RUSSELL, security services exec.; b. Phila., Sept. 3, 1919; s. William Henry and Frances (Hogan) W.; student U. Pa. Wharton Evening Sch., 1937-38, State Tchrs. Coll., West Chester, Pa., 1938-41; B.S., U. Hawaii, 1942; postgrad. Temple

U., 1946; M.Ed., Johns Hopkins U., 1949; m. Ruth Johann Bell, Apr. 8, 1944; children—Janis Lynn (Mrs. John P. Thorsen), Richard Russell. Dir. phys. edn. profl. program tchrs. tng. Johns Hopkins, 1946-50; civilian cons. recreational sports br. Office Spl. Services, U.S. Army, Washington, 1950-51; spl. agt. FBI, 1951-54; dir. personnel, security and safety Giffin Industries, Inc., Miami, Fla., 1954; pres., chmn. bd. Spl. Agt. Investigators, Inc., Spl. Agts. Security Guards, Inc., Security Services Corp. (all Miami), 1954-58, Wackenhut Corp., Coral Gables, Fla., 1958—, Wackenhut Services, Inc., Coral Gables, 1960—, Wackenhut Protective Systems, 1966—; dir. fgn. subsidiaries. Mem. Fla. Sec. State's Pvt. Investigative, Guard and Patrol Adv. Com., 1963-67, chmn., 1963-64; dir. Fla. Gov.'s War on Crime, 1967-70; mem. law enforcement council Nat. Council on Crime and Delinquency, 1971—. Bd. visitors U.S. Army Mil. Police Sch., 1972-74. Served with AUS, 1941-45. Mem. Soc. Former Spl. Agts. FBI, Inc., Am. Soc. for Indsl. Security, Am. Inst. Mgmt. (presidents council 1964-66). Christian Scientist. Club: Ocean Reef. Home: 20 Casuarina Concourse Gables Estate Coral Gables FL 33143 Office: 3280 Ponce de Leon Blvd Coral Gables FL 33134

WACKENHUT, RUTH JOHANN BELL (MRS. GEORGE RUSSELL WACKENHUT), security services exec.; b. Phila., 1922; m. George Russell Wackenhut, Apr. 8, 1944; children—Janis Lynn (Mrs. John P. Thorsen), Richard Russell. Sec., Spl. Agts. Investigators, Inc., Spl. Agts. Security Guards, Inc., Security Services Corp. (all Miami), 1954-58; sec. Wackenhut Corp., 1958—; dir. Wackenhut Services, Inc., 1960—, Pan Am. Bank Coral Gables, 1973—. Home: 20 Casuarina Concourse Gables Estates Coral Gables FL 33143 Office: 3280 Ponce de Leon Blvd Coral Gables FL 33134

WACKER, ROBERT WILLIAM, elec. engr.; b. Milw., Apr. 3, 1942; s. Ben John and Ruth Ann (Scott) W.; B.S. in E.E., Marquette U., 1964, postgrad., 1965; m. Patricia R. Harrington, Aug. 21, 1965; 1 dau., Lisa Ann. Mem. tech. staff Tex. Instruments, Dallas, 1965-68, project mgr. govt. sponsored work, optoelectronics dept., 1968-72, program mgr. electron device div., 1972—. Mem. I.E.E.E., Homeowners Assn., (v.p. 1972—), Tau Beta Pi, Eta Kappa Nu, Pi Mu Epsilon. Home: 3109 Teakwood Dr Garland TX 75040 Office: PO Box 5012 Dallas TX 75222

WACKS, VIRGIL QUINTON, film producer; b. St. Charles, Va., May 1, 1906; s. William Blanton and Allie Mae (Harber) W.; student Bluefield Coll., 1928-30; photography degree N.Y. Inst. Photography, 1933; m. Jauree Elizabeth McElroy, Nov. 16, 1946; children—Virgil Quinton, Mitchell Rawlin. Owner, Virgil Q. Wacks Agy., producer TV shows, spl. film features for TV and theaters, Pennington Gap, Va., 1960—; owner, operator Lee County Agrl. Fair, Pennington Gap, 1945-63, Lee Block Plant, Inc., 1945-72; v.p. Southwestern Va. R.R. Co., 1972—, Knoxville Sox Baseball Club, 1972—. Nat. chmn., promoter Nat. Press Day Celebration, Cumberland Gap Nat. Hist. Park, 1970—. Mayor, City of St. Charles, Va., 1931-33. Bd. dirs. Lee County Community Action Orgn., Lonesome Pine Devel. Corp., Lee Indsl. Commn. Served with USNR, 1944-45. Recipient Acad. award U.P., 1941; named to Frank D. Lawrence Baseball Hall of Fame, Norfolk, Va., 1950. Mem. Mountain States League Profl. Baseball (pres. 1946-54), Lee County C. of C. (pres. 1970-72, 73-74, exec. dir. 1970-72), Am. Legion (post comdr. 1955). Mason. Club: Civitan (Pennington Gap). Producer films, author articles on snake-handling religious cult in St. Charles, Va. for nat. mags. and newspapers, 1940; producer, promoter Earl Hobson Smith Outdoor Dramas including Trail of Lonesome Pine, Valley Forge, Old Smokey, Davey Crockett, Daniel Boone, others; producer, host weekly TV travel show WKPT-TV, WBLG-TV. Home: Duff St Pennington Gap VA 24277 Office: Main St Pennington Gap VA 24277

WADDELL, EUGENE GARLAND, mus. dir.; b. Sumter, S.C., June 12, 1944; s. Howard Stokes and Edna Earle (Tallman) W.; B.S., Coll. of Charleston, 1967. Dir. Florence (S.C.) Mus., 1969—. Served with AUS, 1967-68. S.C. Arts Commn. grantee, 1969, 70, 71. Mem. S.C. Fedn. Museums (dir. 1971—, v.p. 1973), Am. Assn. Museums, S.C. Archeol. Soc. (dir. 1970), Guild S.C. Artists (dir., 1970-73). Contbr. articles to profl. jours. Home: 600 Spruce St Florence SC 29501 Office: 558 Spruce St Florence SC 29501

WADDELL, WILLIAM LLEWELLYN, pub. relations counsel; b. Macon, Ga., Aug. 29, 1913; s. Oliver Eugene and Charlotte (Brown) W.; A.B., U. Ga., 1935; m. Mary Imogene McCormick, Sept. 7, 1935 (dec. June 1959); children—Esther Lee (Mrs. Declan McCarthy), Mary Anne, Mary Elizabeth; m. 2d, Mary Teresa McGuinness, Jan. 27, 1962. Sports editor Albany (Ga.) Herald, 1935-36; reporter A.P., Tallahassee and Jacksonville, Fla., 1936-37; polit. editor Daytona Beach (Fla.) News Jour., 1937-40; editor, pub. Volusia Mirror, Deland, Fla., 1940-42; city editor Birmingham (Ala.) Post, 1945-49; mem. staff Carl Byoir & Assos., N.Y.C., 1949-57, v.p., account exec., 1957-70, regional office mgr., Atlanta, 1970—. Mem. adv. bd. Grad. Sch. Communications Fairfield U., 1967. Served with USNR, 1942-45. Mem. Pub. Relations Soc. Am. Home: 3464 Wynnton Dr Atlanta GA 30319 Office: 600 W Peachtree St Atlanta GA 30308

WADE, DAVID, govt. ofcl.; b. Jacksonville, Ark., Dec. 18, 1910; s. Thomas Howell and Mable (Corder) W.; B.S., U. Ark., M.D., 1938; m. Hazel Keenzel, Dec. 9, 1934; 1 dau., Sharon (Mrs. Robert A. Shoop). Intern St. Vincent's Infirmary, Little Rock, 1938-39; resident Galveston (Tex.) State Psychopathic Hosp., 1939-42; practice medicine specializing in psychiatry, Austin, Tex., 1945-67; supt. Galveston State Psychopathic Hosp., Austin State Sch., Rusk State Hosp., 1942-44; asst. commr. pub. welfare, 1967-69; dir. comprehensive health planning Gov's. Staff, Austin, 1969-70; commr. Tex. Dept. Mental Health and Mental Retardation, 1970—. Served to maj. M.C., AUS, 1951-52. Fellow Am. Psychiat. Assn. Home: 3215 Exposition Blvd Austin TX 78703 Office: PO Box 12668 Austin TX 78701

WADE, DAVID, automobile sales exec.; b. Homer, La., June 15, 1911; s. Ed and Ola (Crowe) W.; ed. La. Tech. Inst.; m. Marie King, Sept. 28, 1943; 1 dau., Kay (Mrs. MacLeod). Joined USAAF, 1935, advanced through grades to lt. gen. USAF, with USAF Security Service; dep. comdr. 93d Bomb Wing; comdr. 57th Air Div., 303d Bomb Wing, 92d Bomb Wing; chief staff SAC, comdr. 1st Missile Div., 8th Air Force, 2d Air Force, ret., 1967; dir. instns., adj. gen., dir. Dept. Pub. Safety La., 1967-71; adj. gen. State of La., 1971-72; v.p. Internat. Auto Sales, New Orleans, 1972—; guest speaker in field. Decorated D.S.M., D.F.C., Soldier's medal, Legion of Merit, Air medal with oak leaf clusters. Home: 316 Corinne Circle Shreveport LA 71106 Office: 4200 Michoud Blvd New Orleans LA 70129

WADE, GEORGE EMMETT, JR., banker; b. Columbus, Ga., Aug. 19, 1936; s. George E. and Rosa (Smith) W.; B.B.A., U. Ga., 1958; postgrad. Grad. Sch. Banking La. State U., 1972; m. Judith Johnson, Mar. 13, 1971; children—George E. III, Trudy Treanor. Vice pres. marketing First Nat. Bank of Columbus, 1961—; dir. Wade Laundry Inc., So. Lawn & Turf, Inc.; pres. G.E.W., Inc. Bd. dirs. South Columbus Boys Club, Historic Columbus, S.E. Bankcard Assn. Served to lt. USAF, 1958-61. Mem. U. Ga. Alumni Assn., Bank Marketing Assn., Columbus C. of C., Assn. U.S. Army, Ga. Cattlemen's Assn. Rotarian (dist. treas. 1973—). Clubs: Bachelors, Green Island Country. Home: 2310 Fairway Av Columbus GA 31906 Office: PO Box 40 Columbus GA 31906

WADE, LEE FOSHION, ednl. adminstr.; b. Dallas, Aug. 21, 1915; s. Will Gregory and Effie (Neagle) W.; B.S., Southeastern State Coll., 1940; M.S., Okla. State U., 1944; m. Merle Inez Jones, Dec. 23, 1936; children—Wanda (Mrs. Ed. Smith), Billy, Doris (Mrs. Gary Moore). Prin. Bethel Sch., Bayan County, Okla., 1939-43; supt. Cobb Consol. Sch. Dist., Bryan County, 1943-45; coach and tchr. Coalgate (Okla.) and Stringtown State Sch., 1948-56; supt. City View Sch. Dist. 906, Wichita Falls, 1956—. Mem. Govs. Regional Adv. Council on Lifetime Sports. Served with AUS, 1944-45. Mem. Am. Assn. Sch. Adminstrs. Wichita County Tchrs. Assn. (past pres.), Tex. State Tchrs. Assn. Democrat. Baptist. Mason. Home: 2416 Picadilly Wichita Falls TX 76309 Office: 1023 City View Dr Wichita Falls TX 76305

WADE, LENNIS PRESTON, engring. co. exec.; b. Lynchburg, Va., June 30, 1933; s. Lennis Bob and Dolah (Carey) W.; B.C.E., Va. Poly. Inst. and State U., 1955, postgrad., 1955-56; m. Jett Gale Preble, July 1, 1955; children—Gale Preble, Larke Lizzette, Stephanie Preston. Instr. applied mechanics Va. Poly. Inst. and State U., Blacksburg, 1955-56; engr. Wiley & Wilson Engrs., Architects, Planners, Lynchburg, 1958—, partner, 1969-72, v.p., 1973-74, pres., 1974—. Pres. Sandusky Elementary Sch. P.T.A., 1965-66. Served to lt. USAF, 1956-58. Recipient The Societas Cincinnatorum Instituta award, 1955. Mem. Arnold Air Soc., Va. Poly. Inst. and State U. Alumni Assn. (pres. Lynchburg chpt. 1966-67), Va. Soc. Profl. Engrs. (state pres. 1970-71), Nat. Soc. Profl. Engrs., Va. Assn. Professions, Tau Beta Pi, Chi Epsilon, Omicron Delta Kappa, Scabbard & Blade. Presbyn. (deacon 1967-69, elder 1970—). Clubs: Pershing Rifles, Cotillion. Home: 3908 Peakland Pl Lynchburg VA 24503 Office: 2310 Langhorne Rd Lynchburg VA 24501

WADE, MARY CARROLL (MRS. RICHARD R. WADE), govt. ofcl.; b. Rome, Ga., Sept. 1, 1909; d. Seaborn Rosa and Dollie (Hill) Carroll; B.A., Maryville Coll., 1931; postgrad. U. of South, summer 1938; M.A., George Washington U., 1948; Ed.D., Am. U., 1970; m. Richard Rudolph Wade, Apr. 1, 1967. Tchr., Hawkins County, Tenn., 1934-36, Pittman Center, Tenn., 1936-37, Meigs County, Tenn., 1937-38, Chattanooga, 1938-42; clk.-typist War Dept., Washington, 1942-43; library asst. Library of Congress, 1943-44; planner Govt. Printing Office, Washington, 1944-67, planner-in-charge, 1967-72, chief marginally punched continuous forms specifications sect., 1972—. Cons. psychologist Alexandria Vocational Rehab. Dept., 1954-57. Active A.R.C., U.S.O., United Givers Fund; troop leader Girl Scouts U.S.A., Chattanooga. Recipient Distinguished Service award U.S.O., 1946; certificates of merit and hon. award U.S. Govt. Printing Office, 1962, 63, Superior Service award, 1964, 67, 68. Mem. Soc. Personnel Adminstrn., Nat. Vocational Guidance Adminstrn., Am. Personnel and Guidance Assn., Nat. Rehab. Assn., Forms Mgmt. Council U.S. Capitol Hist. Soc., George Washington U., Maryville Coll., Am. U. alumni assns., Pub. Personnel Assn., Franklin Tech. Soc., Washington Club Printing House Craftsmen, Am., Va., D.C. psychol. assns., Columbian Women, Washington Litho. Club, Govt. Printing Office Fed. Women's Program (chmn. 1972-73), Kappa Delta Epsilon, Psi Chi, Phi Delta Gamma (chpt. pres. 1957-58, nat. council rep. 1968-72). Presbyn. Clubs: George Washington University, Americana, Toastmistress (sec. 1972, treas. 1972-73, pres. 1973-74); Fairfax County Business and Professional Women's (v.p. 1974). Home: 614 Bashford Lane Alexandria VA 22314 Office: US Govt Printing Office Washington DC 20401

WADE, WILLIAM IRL, JR., physician; b. Mena, Ark., Sept. 20, 1938; s. William Irl and Wilson (Anderson) W.; student Little Rock Jr. Coll., 1957-59, Little Rock U., 1956-59; M.D. (fellow 1961), U. Ark., 1963; m. Wanda Lee Bates, Jan. 12, 1963; children—Cynthia Carol, Arthur Colin. Intern USPHS and Charity Hosp., New Orleans, 1963-64; resident USPHS Hosp., San Francisco, 1965, asst. chief Out-Patient Clinic, 1965; practice medicine, specializing in general practice, Little Rock, 1966—; mem. staffs St. Vincents Hosp., Baptist Hosp., Meml. Hosp.; family practice preceptorships U. Ark., 1970-72; asso. staff unit family practice U. Ark. Med. Center, 1971-72. Gen. practice state rep. Am. Cancer Soc., 1972; program physician Upward Bound project Philander Smith Coll., 1970-72; vol. physician Office Econ. Opportunity, 1971; pres. U. Ark. Rural Extension Grad. Edn. Program, 1973; chmn. Mead Johnston Award Com., 1973; research mem. Ark Research Found., 1970—. Served to lt. comdr. USPHS, 1963-66. USPHS grantee, 1962. Mem. A.M.A., Am., Ark. (program com. 1969-71, dir. 1973—) acads. gen. practice, Am. Coll. Emergency Room Physicians (charter), Pulaski County Gen. Practicioners Soc. (sec. 1971-72), Little Rock Jr. C. of C., Phi Theta Kappa. Episcopalian. Clubs: Caduceus, Razorback. Editor: Ark. Gen. Practicioners Newsletter, 1970-72. Home: 236 Kingsrow Dr Little Rock AR 72207 Office: 424 N University St Little Rock AR 72205

WAGE, WILLIAM MARTIN, architect; b. Houston, Oct. 27, 1938; s. Paul Edwin and Mary (Rogers) W.; student Memphis State U., 1957-63; m. Dianne Sanders, Aug. 19, 1960; children—Laura Dianne, Julie Elizabeth. Draftsman Sanford & Ellis, Architects, Memphis, 1958-63; sr. draftsman George Awsumb & Sons, Architects, Memphis, 1963-70; architect, head all co. devels. S & W Constrn. Co. of Tenn. Inc., Memphis, 1970-71; pres., chmn. bd. dirs. William M. Wage, Architect, Inc., Memphis, 1971—; chmn. design review com. Star Land Devel. Corp., Memphis, 1971—. Registered architect, Tenn. Mem. A.I.A., Tenn. Soc. Architects. Methodist (treas. Methodist Minute Men of Memphis, 1961, pres. 1962, soloist men's chorus, 1961-67, music dir. 1960-63). Mason. Office: 2600 Poplar Av Memphis TN 38112

WAGENER, LEE EDSON, airport exec.; b. Chgo., June 21, 1920; s. William F. and Charlotte (Williams) W.; B.B.A., Northwestern U., 1941; children—Carol J., David L. With Western Electric Co., 1941-48; dir. airports Broward County, Ft. Lauderdale, Fla., 1948—. Served to lt. comdr. USNR, 1942-46; PTO. Recipient Top Mgmt. award Sales and Marketing Execs. Club, Ft. Lauderdale, 1962. Mem. Southeastern Airport Mgrs. Assn. (pres., 1957), Am. Assn. Airport Execs. (pres., 1968-69), Ft. Lauderdale C. of C., Am. Legion, Quiet Birdmen. Mason. Club: Congressional Flying (Washington). Home: 1668 S Ocean Lane Fort Lauderdale FL 33316 Office: Broward County Dept Airports 290 SW 41st Ct Fort Lauderdale FL 33315

WAGERS, LOIS ELIZABETH HALL (MRS. LYMAN WAGERS), real estate devel. corp. exec.; b. Lexington, Ky., Dec. 14, 1922; d. Forest E. and Elizabeth (Hamilton) Hall; A.B., U. Ky., 1958, M.A., 1960; m. Lyman Wagers, Feb. 21, 1943; children—David L., Lyman Ellsworth, Susan E. Vice pres. Loman Inc., Lexington, 1959-69, pres., 1969—; pres. de Ly Ly Inc., Lexington, 1960-62. Mem. Eisenhowers People-to-People Program, 1958-60. Bd. dirs. Youth Symphony Orch. Lexington, 1969—, pres. bd., 1969. Mem. Lexington Home Builders Assn., Lexington Apt. Council (pres. 1971-72), Philharmonic Guild Lexington, Kappa Delta Pi, Phi Sigma Iota. Republican. Club: Lexington Womans (pres. 1960-61). Home: 1040 Armstrong Mill Rd Lexington KY 40502 Office: 1044 Armstrong Mill Rd Lexington KY 40502

WAGERS, LYMAN ELLSWORTH, orthodontist; b. Bright Shade, Ky., July 27, 1922; s. Floyd and Myrtle (Peters) W.; student U. Ky., 1938-40; D.M.D., U. Louisville, 1943; postgrad. Ohio State U., 1950-52; m. Lois Hall, Feb. 21, 1942; children—David, Lyman Ellsworth, Susan. Gen. practice dentistry, Falmouth, Ky., 1946-47, Lexington, Ky., 1947-52; pvt. practice orthodontics, Lexington, 1952—. Clin. instr. orthodontic dept. U. Ky. Health Center, 1969—. Sec. Ky. Med. Found., 1959; pres. Ohio State U. Orthodontic Alumni Found., 1965. Served to capt., Dental Corps, AUS, 1943-46. Recipient Distinguished Service award Ohio State U. Orthodontic Alumni Found., 1969. Diplomate Am. Bd. Orthodontics. Fellow Am. Coll. Dentists, Internat. Coll. Dentists; mem. Am. Assn. Orthodontists, Am., Ky. (pres. 1959-60) dental assns. Club: Country (Lexington). Home: 1040A Armstrong Mill Rd Lexington KY 40502 Office: 1636 Nicholasville Rd Lexington KY 40503

WAGES, ORLAND JACK, clergyman, librarian; b. Canton, Tex., Aug. 2, 1915; s. Homer DeWitt and Della (Crabtree) W.; student Tex. Tech. Coll., 1936-39; B.S. in L.S., Stephen F. Austin State Coll., 1954; M.S. in L.S., E. Tex. State Coll., 1958, postgrad., 1960-63; m. Alice Ella Humphreys, Aug. 31, 1956. Librarian, instr. speech Jacksonville (Tex.) Coll., 1951-59; asst. librarian, instr. library sci. E. Tex. State Coll., Commerce, 1959-63; librarian, extension instr. library sci. Bridgewater (Va.) Coll., 1963—; extension instr. U. Va., 1967—. Ordained to ministry Baptist Ch., 1951; pastor chs. in Maydelle, Tex., 1953-57, Edom, Tex., 1957-59, Jackson, Tex., 1959-63, Fulks Run, Va., 1963-64, Virginia Av. Bapt. Ch., Harrisonburg, Va., 1967-69. Served to capt. with USAAF, 1940-48. Mem. A.L.A., Southeastern, Va. (editor Va. Librarian 1965-69) library assns., Am. Ednl. Research Assn., Christian Librarians Fellowship (pres. 1967-69), Ministerial Assn., Shenandoah Valley Folklore Soc., Rockingham Hist. Soc., Nat. Geneal. Soc., Phi Delta Kappa. Democrat. Clubs: Civitan (v.p. Jacksonville 1958-59), Rotary (pres. Bridgewater 1966-67). Author: Church Librarian's Handbook, 1961. Home: 210 W Bank St Bridgewater VA 22812 Office: Bridgewater College Bridgewater VA 22812

WAGGONER, JAMES MILAN, clergyman; b. Jacksonville, Fla., Aug. 24, 1933; s. George Jamison and Stella Lorene (Vest) W.; student Temple U., 1951-53; A.B., Elon Coll., 1955; student So. Theol. Sem., 1955-56; B.D., Southeastern Theol. Sem., 1961; m. Margaret Delores Johnson, Sept. 30, 1967; children—Robert, Barbra. Ordained to ministry Meth. Ch., 1958; minister Whitney Cross Meth. Charge, 1957-61, Trinity Ch., 1961-65, Whitley Meml. Ch., 1965-68; chaplain Meth. Home for Children, Raleigh, N.C., 1968—. Chaplain Boy Scouts Am., 1965—. Exec. sec. John A. Wilkinson Meml. Found., 1964-65. Recipient Harvard Book prize, 1948, Citizenship award Am. Legion, 1950, Distinguished Citizen award Belhaven (N.C.) C. of C., 1964, Trailblazer award, Boy Scouts Am., 1967. Mem. Internat. Platform Assn., Group Child Care Assn., Southeastern, N.C. child care assns., Am. Protestant Hosp. Assn., Coll. of Chaplains, Health and Welfare Assn. Composer: Boy Scout Pilgrimage Theme Song, 1968; John A. Wilkinson High School Alma Mater, 1964. Home: 1001 Glenwood Av Raleigh NC 27605

WAGGONER, WILLIAM JOHNSON, lawyer; b. Salisbury, N.C., Oct. 13, 1928; s. James Martin and Julia (Johnson) W.; A.B., U. N.C., 1951, LL.B., 1954; m. Martha Anne Garwood, Aug. 8, 1953; children—William Johnson, Ellen Christine, David Garwood. Admitted to N.C. bar, 1954; asst. U.S. Atty for Western Dist. of N.C., 1957-59; partner Waggoner, Hasty and Kratt, Charlotte. Mem. Republican Speakers Bur., 1959—; gen. counsel Mecklenburg Republican Exec. Com., 1963—; mem. N.C. Bd. Elections, 1973—. Served with AUS, 1946-47. Mem. C. of C., Nat. Assn. Sch. Bd. Attys., Kappa Alpha. Club: Hornet Toastmasters (past pres.). Mem. Am., N.C. Fed. bar assns., N.C. State Bar, Am. Trial Lawyers Assn., Am. Arbitration Assn. (panelist). Lutheran (bd. deacons). Home: 6511 Newhall Rd Charlotte NC 28211 Office: 723 Law Bldg Charlotte NC 28202

WAGGONNER, JOSEPH DAVID, JR., congressman; b. Plain Dealing, La., Sept. 7, 1918; s. Joe David and Elizzibeth (Johnston) W.; B.A., La. Poly. Inst., 1941; m. Mary Ruth Carter, Dec. 14, 1942; children—Carol Jean, David. Mem. 87th-93d Congresses, 4th Dist. La. Mem. Bossier Parish Sch. Bd., 1954-61, pres., 1956-57; mem. La. Bd. Edn., 1960-61. Pres. United Sch. Com. La., 1961, La. Sch. Bds. Assn., 1961. Served to lt. comdr. USNR, World War II, Korea. Mem. Am. Legion, 40 and 8, Kappa Sigma. Democrat. Methodist. Mason (33 deg., Shriner), Elk, Lion. Home: Plain Dealing LA 71064 also 2111 Jefferson Davis Hwy Arlington VA Office: House of Representatives Washington DC 20515

WAGLEY, MARJORIE IRENE CORLEY (MRS. ALTON CADE WAGLEY), educator; b. Florien, La., Nov. 4, 1914; d. Luther Franklin and Nancy (Miller) Corley; B.A., Northwestern U., 1936, U. Houston, 1950; postgrad. S.W. Tex. State Coll., 1946, Brigham Young U., 1958; m. Alton Cade Wagley, Jan. 16, 1937; children—Margie Katherine (Mrs. Gene Barry), Alton Carlin. Tchr. pub. schs., Sabine Parish, La., 1936-42, Beaumont, Tex., 1945-53; dir. spl. edn. S. Parks Sch., Beaumont, 1953—. Dir. Services Unlimited, Beaumont, mem. N.E.A., Tex. Tchrs. Assn., Council Adminstrs. Spl. Edn. (sec. 1967-69), Council for Exceptional Children, Tex. Council for Exceptional Children (pres. 1966; membership chmn. 1967—), Delta Kappa Gamma. Baptist. Club: Soroptimist (charter; corr. sec. pres. chpt. 1972-74) (Beaumont, Tex.). Author: Organizing and Administering Special Education. Home: PO Box 206 Nome TX 77629 Office: 1025 Woodrow St Beaumont TX 77705

WAGNER, AUBREY JOSEPH, engr., govt. ofcl.; b. Hillsboro, Wis., Jan. 12, 1912; s. Joseph M. and Wilhelmina (Filter) W.; B.C.E. magna cum laude, U. Wis., 1933; LL.D. (hon.), Newberry Coll., 1966; D.Pub. Adminstrn., Lenoir Rhyne Coll., 1970; m. Dorothea J. Huber, Sept. 9, 1933; children—Audrey Grace, Joseph Michael, James Richard, Karl Edward. Various positions hwy. engring., surveying, soil erosion control; with TVA, 1934—, beginning as engring. aide, successively jr. hydraulic engr., asst. hydraulic engr., asso. nav. engr., nav. engr., asst. chief river transp. div., acting chief and chief nav. and transp. br., asst. gen. mgr., 1951-54, gen. mgr., 1954-61, became dir., 1961, chmn. bd., 1962—. Mem. Breeder Reactor Corp., 1972—, also vice chmn. Mem. com. domestic water nav. projects and nat. policy Pres.'s Water Resources Policy Commn., 1950; mem. Pres.'s Appalachian Regional Commn., 1963-65, Pres.'s Council Recreation and Natural Beauty, 1965-69; Pres.'s Cost Reduction Council, 1968-69; mem. engring. adv. com. Tenn. Technol. U., 1968—; mem. Tenn. Gov.'s Sci. Adv. Com., 1968-70; mem. nat. adv. council 1974 World Energy Conf., 1971—; mem. adv. com. 1972 UN Conf. Human Environment, 1971—; mem. sr. utility steering com. AEC, 1971—; mem. FPC Exec. Adv. Com. Nat. Power Survey, 1972—; lectr. agr. and natural resources session Salzburg Seminar in Am. Studies, 1968. Mem. nat. council Boy Scouts Am. Recipient Silver Beaver award Boy Scouts Am., 1956, Dougherty award U. Tenn., 1969. Mem. Nat. Acad. Engring., Tenn. Archeol. Soc., Ft. Loudoun Assn., Beta Gamma Sigma, Tau Beta Pi, Chi Epsilon, Phi Kappa Phi, Phi Eta Sigma, Lambda Chi Alpha (Order Achievement 1970), Scabbard and Blade. Lutheran (mem. exec. council Luth. Ch. Am. 1962-70, bd. theol. edn. 1970-72). Home: 201 Whittington Dr Knoxville TN 37919 Office: 403 New Sprankle Bldg Knoxville TN 37902

WAGNER, ELLEN MARIE SEAY (MRS. FREDERIC E. WAGNER), corp. exec.; b. Conway, Ark.; d. Roy R. and Jewel (Belk) Seay; student Ark. State Tchrs. Coll., 1960-62; m. Frederic E. Wagner, Feb. 15, 1963. Asst. dir. Children's Med. Center, Dallas, 1962-64; v.p., dir. Eldorado Oil & Gas, Inc., Dallas, Sovereign Oil & Gas, Inc., Dallas, Williams & Wagner Constrn. Co., Inc., Dallas, Williams and Wagner Investments, Inc., Dallas, Sovereign Devel. Corp., Dallas, Wagner Stables, Dallas, 1965—. Active Dallas Theatre Center. Mem. Braniff Internat. Council, Cal., Tex. thoroughbred breeders assns., USCG Auxiliary, Horsemen's Benevolent Assn. Clubs: Brookhaven Country, 21 Turtle, Cipango, Admirals, Dallas Garden, Listeners Book Review, Dallas Gun, Brook Hollow Golf. Home: 8801 Jourdan Way Dallas TX 75225 Office: 2929 Cedar Springs Rd Dallas TX 75219

WAGNER, FREDERIC EMIL, oil and gas co. exec.; b. Waco, Tex., Aug. 14, 1920; s. Frederic Emil and Ernestine (Clements) W.; student North Tex. Agrl. Coll., 1941-42, So. Methodist U., 1943-45; B.S., U. Tex., 1946; m. Ellen Marie Seay, Mar. 14, 1964; children—Jory Watner, Hilda. Pres. chmn. bd. Williams & Wagner Constrn. Co., Dallas, 1946—. Williams & Wagner Investments, Inc., Dallas, 1946—, Eldorado Oil & Gas, Inc., Dallas, 1956—, Sovereign Oil & Gas, Inc., Dallas, 1965—, Airport Realty Corp., Dallas, 1969—. Chmn. bd. Treasure Island Municipal Dist. Brazoria County, 1968-69; active Dallas Opera Guild. Recipient Distinguished Service award Nat. Exchange Club, 1956. Mem. Council Sci. Socs., Am. Soc. Photogrammetry, Photogrammetry Soc. London, Soc. Petroleum Engrs., Am. Inst. Mining, Metall. and Petroleum Engrs., Petroleum Engrs. Club Dallas, U.S. Power Squadron, USCG Aux., Tex. Thoroughbred Breeders Assn. (pres. 1963-64, 68-69), Horsemen's Benevolent Protective Assn., Nat. Rifle Assn., Nat. Skeet Shooting Assn., Cal. Thoroughbred Breeders Assn. Clubs: Brookhaven Country, Hollow Golf, 21 Turtle, Braniff Internat. Council, Admiral's, Cipango (Dallas); Pala Mesa (Cal.) Golf. Author: Aircraft Lofting Practice, 1943. Home: 8801 Jourdan Way Dallas TX 75225 Office: 2929 Cedar Springs Rd Dallas TX 75219

WAGNER, RALPH PATTERSON, investment co. exec.; b. Beatrice, Neb., Aug. 22, 1893; s. William Henry and Cordelia Harriet (Scherer) W.; B.S. in Civil Engring., B.S. in Elec. Engring., U. Neb., 1917; m. Mary Eleanor Houston, Nov. 20, 1924 (dec.); 1 dau., Eleanor Patterson. With Cities Service Co., N.Y.C., 1920-29, Niagara Mohawk Power Co., Albany, N.Y., 1929-56; pres., dir. Sotexco, Inc., Albany, 1971—; with Wytax Corp., Albany, 1957—, pres., 1965—, dir., 1957—; v.p., dir. Triton Corp., Albany, 1964—; dir. Heartland Devel. Co., Albany, Heartland Leasing Corp., Albany. Bd. dirs. Morton Plant Hosp., Clearwater, Fla., 1963-69; bd. dirs., pres. Albany Med. Center Hosp., 1948—, Huntington's Chorea Found., N.Y.C., 1967—; bd. dirs. Albany Med. Coll., 1949—, v.p., 1949-57. Served with U.S. Army 1917-42. Mem. Sigma Tau. Club: University (Albany). Home: 1408 S Betty Lane Clearwater FL 33516 Office: 66 State St Albany NY 12207

WAGNER, RUSSELL LEE, ins. co. exec.; b. Marengo, Ia., June 17, 1916; s. Charles and Katherine (Schweitzer) W.; B.A., State U. Ia., 1938, M.S., 1940; m. Muriel Darlene Osler, June 21, 1942; children—Vicki Lee (Mrs. Donald A. Rogers), Benjamin Osler. With Nat. Life & Accident Ins. Co., Nashville, 1940—, successively acturial mathematician, asst. actuary, 1945-56, actuary, 1956-58, v.p., 1958-65, sr. v.p., chief actuary ins. standards, 1965-69, exec. v.p., 1969-72, pres., 1972—; pres. NLT Corp.; dir. WSM, Inc.; mem. trust bd. Commerce Union Bank. Bd. dirs. Jr. Achievement Fellow Soc. Actuaries; mem. Southeastern Actuaries. Clubs: Southeastern Actuaries (Atlanta); Bellemeade, Cumberland (Nashville); Internat. (Chgo.). Home: 1066 Lynwood Nashville TN 37215 Office: National Life Center Nashville TN 37250

WAGNER, VERNON LESLIE, JR., film co. exec.; b. New Orleans, July 4, 1936; s. Vernon Leslie and Jean Margaret (Byrne) W.; B.S., Tulane U., 1957; postgrad., 1961-63; M.S., U. Va., 1958; m. Patricia Edith Cole, Apr. 8, 1959; children—Christopher Lee, Gretchen Steele, John Marshall, Stephanie Keller. Chemist, Shell Oil Co., Norco, La., 1956-57; research chemist Freeport Nickel-Sulphur Co., Braithwaite, La., 1959-62; pvt. cons., New Orleans, 1962—, with Kalvar Corp. film mfg. New Orleans 1962—, v.p. research and devel., 1970—; partner Asso. Ideas, Inc., New Orleans, 1963—. Active in civic and polit. activities. Served with USMCR, 1954-62. Recipient Oscar Lee Putnam fellowship Tulane U., 1955-57; award Am. Inst. Chemists, 1957. Mem. T.A.P.P.I., Soc. Photog. Scientists and Engrs., Am. Inst. Aeros. and Astronautics, Sigma Xi, Phi Eta Sigma, Kappa Alpha. Club: Chemists (N.Y.C.). Patentee in field. Home: 1515 DuFossat St New Orleans LA 70115 Office: 909 S Broad St New Orleans LA 70125

WAGNER, WALTER WILLIAM, econ. and marketing research co. exec.; b. Pitts., Dec. 2, 1932; s. Walter William and Martha May (Jamison) W.; B.S., Carnegie-Mellon U., 1953, M.S., 1954; m. Mary Jean Treharne, June 12, 1954; children—Jon Douglas, Sue Allyn, Wendy Lou. Statis. analyst Eastman Kodak Co., 1954-57; sales cons. Met. Life Ins. Co., 1957-60; exec. v.p. Bieley, Wagner & Assos., Inc., 1960-69; pres., Walter W. Wagner & Co., Inc., Miami, 1969—. Mem. Savs. Instns. Marketing Soc. Am. (chmn. market research com. 1973-74). Home: 5221 SW 64th Ct Miami FL 33155 Office: 7600 SW 57th Av Miami FL 33143

WAGONER, EDWARD LOUIS, city ofcl.; b. Sherman, Tex., Mar. 27, 1939; s. Louis M. and Lois Lucille (Arnold) W.; B.A., Austin Coll., 1961; postgrad. Tex. Technol. Coll., 1961-63; m. Danny Ruth LaFollette, Feb. 26, 1962; children—Christopher Dodd, Andrew Shanan, Matthew Darby. Adminstrv. aide City of Lubbock, Tex., 1962-63; asst. city mgr. City of Abilene, Tex., 1963-68; asst. to city mgr. City of Fort Worth, 1968-69; city mgr. City of Greenville, Tex., 1969-72; city mgr. City of Tyler, Tex., 1972—. Mem. com. of future, legislative com. Tex. Municipal League, 1971—; mem. urban study adv. com. Tex. A. and M. U., 1973; chmn. Tex. Municipal Power Pool, 1971. Mem. explorer adv. com. E. Tex. Area council Boy Scouts Am., 1973—; mem. Smith County Area Health Council, 1972-73; active Smith County Assn. Retarded Children. Bd. dirs. Workreation, Tyler; chmn. bd. dirs. Hunt County Opportunity Center, 1971. Clarence Ridley scholar Tex. City Mgmt. Assn., 1962-63. Named Outstanding Com. Chmn., Abilene Jr. C. of C., 1964-65. Mem. Internat., Tex., E. Tex. city mgmt. assns., Tyler C. of C. Presbyn. (elder 1970—). Rotarian. Club: Petroleum (Tyler). Office: 212 N Bonner St Tyler TX 75701

WAID, LUTHER PINKNEY, judge; b. nr. Boaz, Ala., Mar. 2, 1915; s. Luther Pinkney and Roxie (Bynum) W.; student Tenn. Wesleyan Coll., 1933-34; LL.B., U. Ala., 1939; m. Louise Griffith, July 2, 1953. Admitted Ala. bar, 1939, pvt. practice, Guntersville, Ala., 1939-41, Oneonta, 1946-51, 65-67; pros. atty., Blount County, 1949-51; dist. atty. 30th Jud. Circuit, 1951-59, 67-71, circuit judge, 1959-65, 71—. Del., Gen. Conf., Methodist Ch., 1960, Southeastern Jurisdictional Conf., 1960, 64; del. Gen. Assembly, Cumberland Presbyn. Ch., 1974. Served from pvt. to 1st lt. AUS, 1941-46. Mem. Marshall County (pres. 1941), Blount County (sec. 1949-52, pres. 1970-71) bar assns., Am. Legion, C. of C. (dir. 1951-53). Democrat. Presbyn. (elder). Mason. Club: Civitan (pres. Oneonta 1950-51, gov. Ala. dist. N. 1956-57, dist. honor key 1963). Home: 407 4th Av W Oneonta AL 35121 Office: Courthouse Oneonta AL 35121

WAINSHAL, HAROUZI, housing devel. exec.; b. Jerusalem, Israel, Apr. 15, 1932 came to U.S. 1963, naturalized, 1971.; s. Matityah and Zina (Stein) W.; B.S. in Civil Engring., cum laude, Technion, Israel Inst. Tech., 1955; m. Yael Wasser, Sept. 23, 1962; children—Ron, Ruth, Tamar. Project engr. City of Jerusalem, 1956-58; adminstr., tech. dir. Israel Standards Inst., 1958-60; project engr., Iran, 1960-61, Israel, 1961-62; operations mgr. Hampton Devel. Corp., San Juan, P. R., 1963-66; exec. v.p. Devel. Internat. Corp., Coral Gables, Fla., 1966-72, dir., 1969-72; pres. H & W Realty & Devel. Corp., 1972—. Pioneer reinforced concrete modular systems. Home: 11001 SW 75th Ct Miami FL 33156 Office: 1401 Brickell Av Miami FL 33131

WAINWRIGHT, BILL C., savs. and loan assn. exec.; b. Tampa, Fla., Nov. 20, 1913; s. Truby L. and Mabel A. (Britt) W.; B.S. in Bus., U. Fla., 1937; LL.B., Atlanta Law Sch., 1947; postgrad. U. Ind., 1956, Dartmouth, 1963; m. Rebecca Ann Bethel, June 27, 1942; children—Rebecca Ann, Bill C. Pres., Atlanta Fed. Savs. & Loan Assn., 1945—, also dir., mem. exec. com.; dir. United Family Life Ins. Co. Mem. Atlanta Bd. Edn., 1966-69, pres., 1968-69; pres. Atlanta Traffic and Safety Council, 1967, Northside Hosp., 1964-65. Trustee Atlanta Nat. Real Estate Trust. Served as lt. col. AUS, 1941-46. Mem. Am. Savs. and Loan Inst. (nat. pres. 1961), Ga. Savs. and Loan League (pres. 1959), Atlanta C. of C. (dir. 1963-65, chmn. pub. safety and crime abatement task force com.), Lambda Chi Alpha (nat. dir. 1967-71). Presbyn. (ruling elder). Home: 3213 Old Mill Trace SE Marietta GA 30060 Office: 20 Marietta St NW Atlanta GA 30303

WAINWRIGHT, MARY LEE SELLERS (MRS. NEWMAN DAVID WAINWRIGHT, JR.), composer; b. Ruby, S.C., Apr. 24, 1913; d. Samuel Joseph and Martha Ellen Sellers; student Sch. Music, Stetson U., 1947-48; m. Newman David Wainwright, Jr., Nov. 7, 1950; 1 dau., Dolores Ann (Mrs. Clint Kimbrough). Mem. Pres.'s Action Com., Washington, 1958-72; Democratic exec. committeewoman, Broward County, Fla., 1957-62; chmn. edn. Dem. Nat. Exec. Com., Fla., 1957-62. Recipient Spl. awards Fla. Folk Festival, 1957-60; award of merit South Fla. State Hosp., 1966; Superior awards Nat. Fedn. Music Clubs and ASCAP, 1955-72; certificate of appreciation Mayor of Hollywood, Fla., 1962; certificate of appreciation Nat. Police Officers Assn. Am., Police Hall of Fame, 1971. Mem. Am. Soc. Composers, Authors and Pubs., Song Writers Hall of Fame, Internat. Platform Assn., World Home Bible League, Am. Security Council (policy bd.), Hollywood Music Club (pres. 1957-59), Fla. Fedn. Music Clubs (pres. Royal Poincina dist. 1959-61), Nat. Fedn. Music Clubs (mem. nat. com. World of Music 1963-67, pres. Hollywood chpt. past pres.'s assembly 1974—). Author: The Master Key, 1967. Composer: Hollywood, Florida U.S.A., 1955; Education is the Master Key, 1967; Wake Up, Wake Up America, 1959; Our God of All, 1966; The March of Faith, 1965; Rise and Shine, 1964; The Masquerade is Over, 1964; Inspiration is Making all Things New, 1963; Thank You God, 1963; God is Love, 1972 (nat. award 1972); The Meek Shall Inherit The Earth (3 stars, ribbons Parade Am. Music), 1973. Home: 1519 Dewey St Hollywood FL 33020

WAITE, CLAYLAND MOFFATT, transformer co. exec.; b. Ridley Park, Pa., May 4, 1920; s. Oliver Tracy and Laura Virginia (Touchstone) W.; grad. high sch.; student Drexel Evening Sch., 1939-42; m. Mary Edith Hopkins, Apr. 25, 1942; children—Clayland Hopkins, David Ernest. Engring. supr. I-T-E Circuit Breaker Co., Phila., 1944-55, Kuhlman Electric Co., Bay City, Mich., 1955-58, Birmingham, Mich., 1959-68, mgr. materials, Versailles, Ky., 1969—. Dist. magistrate, Woodford County, Ky., 1974—. Mem. I.E.E.E. Methodist (mem. ofcl. bd. 1969-73). Mason, Rotarian. Patentee in field. Home: 121 Ravenwood Rd Versailles KY 40383 Office: 101 Kuhlman Blvd Versailles KY 40383

WAITS, THOMAS POPE, dentist; b. nr. Oxford, Miss., July 13, 1935; s. Tommy Alfred and Thelma (Hawkins) W.; D.D.S., U. Louisville, 1960; B.S., Miss. Coll., 1956; m. Sara Maloy Hodges, May 19, 1968. Pvt. practice dentistry, Gulfport, Miss., 1962-63, Bruce, Miss., 1962—. Mem. Calhoun County Com. Mental Health, 1968—; chmn. Calhoun County Heart Fund, 1967—; guardian Pushmataha Area council Boy Scouts Am., 1968; chmn. Bruce Rotary Club Kidney Found. Col., Gov. John B. Williams staff, 1968-72, Gov. Bill Waller staff, 1972—. Alderman, Bruce, 1973—; mem. Miss. Pub. Welfare Bd., 1974—. Served to capt. USAF, 1960-62. Mem. Am., N.E. Miss. dental assns., Bruce C. of C. Delta Sigma Delta. Baptist. Home: W Johnson St Bruce MS 38915 Office: Calhoun St Bruce MS 38915

WAITZMAN, MORTON BENJAMIN, educator; b. Chgo., Nov. 8, 1923; s. Joseph M. and Anna (Glickman) W.; B.S., U. Miami, 1948; M.S., U. Ill., 1950, Ph.D., 1953; m. Aviva Doris Shedroff, June 9, 1949; children—Sherri, Bradley, Rhonda. Research and teaching asst. dept. physiology U. Ill., 1951-53; instr. dept. pharmacology Western Reserve U., 1954-59, asst. prof., dir. Lab Ophthalmic Research, 1959, asst. prof. dept. pharmacology, 1959-62; asst. prof. dept. physiology Emory U., Atlanta, 1962-67, asso. prof., 1962-68, prof., 1968—, dir. Lab. Ophthalmic Research, 1962—. Chmn. tech. adv. com. Citizens for Clean Air Atlanta, 1970-71; mem. med. adv. com., research adviser Ga. Found. Research in Ophthalmology, Inc., 1964—. Served with AUS, 1943-46. Mem. Assn. Research in Vision and Ophthalmology, Am. Physiol. Soc., Am. Assn. U. Profs. (exec. com. 1964—), Ga. Soc. Prevention Blindness, Sigma Xi, Phi Sigma. Contbr. articles to profl. jours. Home: 1137 Mason Woods Dr NE Atlanta GA 30329

WALDEN, JOHN CLAYTON, educator; b. Clinton, Ill., Sept. 15, 1928; s. Carter Branstetter and Trella Bernice (Bell) W.; A.B., U. Cal. at Los Angeles, 1952; M.A., Cal. State Coll. at Los Angeles, 1957; Ph.D., Claremont Grad. Sch., 1966; m. Shirley Gail Butterfield, Feb. 1, 1952; children—Deanne Carol, Kirk Allen. Tchr. pub. schs., Redlands, Cal., 1952-53; tchr. Monrovia (Cal.) Unified Sch. Dist., 1953-56, jr. high sch. prin., 1956-66; prof. ednl. adminstrn. Auburn (Ala.) U., 1966—, head dept. ednl. adminstrn. and supervision, 1970—. Cons. to sch. dists. in southeast. Pres. Family Service Agy., Monrovia, Cal., 1963. Served with USN, 1946-48. Recipient outstanding young man award Monrovia (Cal.), Jr. C. of C., 1963. Mem. Nat., Ala. edn. assns., Am., Ala. assns. sch. adminstrs., Am. Ednl. Research Assn., Nat. Orgn. Legal Problems of Edn., Am. Assn. University Profs., Nat. Conf. Profs. Ednl. Adminstrn., Phi Delta Kappa, Phi Kappa Tau. Kiwanian. Sect. editor Educational Administration Abstracts, 1969-71. Home: 132 Carter St Auburn AL 36830

WALDO, TOMMY RUTH BLACKMON (MRS. SELDEN FENNELL WALDO), educator; b. Dallas, Jan. 14, 1916; d. Gulie Hargrove and Mary Lee (Craig) Blackmon; B.A., Agnes Scott Coll., 1938; M.A., U. Fla., 1955, Ph.D., 1961; m. Selden Fennell Waldo, Oct. 28, 1941 (dec. Nov. 1950); children—George Selden (dec.), Andrew Blackmon. Grad. asst. U. Fla., Gainesville, 1952-55; instr., 1955-61, asst. prof. English, 1961—, now asso. prof.; pvt. tchr. piano and organ, 1938-55; organist Holy Trinity Episcopal Ch., Gainesville, 1941-42; asso. organist First Bapt. Ch., 1943-58, organist, 1958—. Dir., v.p. League Women Voters, 1947-50. Mem. Modern Lang. Assn., S. Atlantic Modern Lang. Assn., Fla., Gainesville music tchrs. assns., Southeastern Renaissance Conf., Phi Beta Kappa, Delta Kappa Gamma, Sigma Alpha Iota. Democrat. Baptist. Contbr. articles to profl. jours. Home: 719 NE 1st St Gainesville FL 32601

WALDO, WILLIS GERSHAM, cons. engr.; b. Norwood, N.Y., Sept. 8, 1883; s. Gersham Henry and Elizabeth Ellis (Kendrick) W.; student Purdue U., 1901-03; S.B., Mass. Inst. Tech., 1907; postgrad. Vanderbilt U., 1916; m. Irene Aleta Hayward, June 27, 1911 (dec. 1957). Vice pres., chief engr. Tenn. River Improvement Assn., Washington, 1916-30; cons. engr., Washington, 1936-45, West Palm Beach, Fla., 1945—. Technologist, Muscle Shoals Inquiry Commn., Washington, 1928. Served with Ordnance Corps, U.S. Army, 1918. Mem. Am. Soc. C.E. (life), Tenn. (life), Fla. engring. socs., Nat. Soc. Profl. Engrs., Lambda Phi. Republican. Baptist (life deacon). Author: America's Gibraltar, Muscle Shoals, 1916; (with Alexander Kidd) Ramie, a Strategic Material, 1945. Home: 319 Kings Ct West Palm Beach FL 33401

WALDREP, ANDREW JACKSON, clergyman; b. Forsyth, Ga., Aug. 30, 1916; s. Henry Clarence and Wilbur (Walker) W.; student Young Harris Coll., 1933-36; B.Ph., Emory U., 1938, M.Div., 1940; postgrad. U. Wis., 1945-47; m. Hilda Isabelle Wright, Nov. 9, 1941; children—Emory Daniel, Elizabeth Ann, David Jackson, Hilda Isabelle. Ordained to ministry Meth. Ch., 1940; pastor Rabum Gap Coll. and Community Ch., Dillard, Ga., 1940-45, Albany (Wis.) Community Ch., 1945-47; tchr. Young Harris Coll., coordinator Union County Coop. Ministry, 1947-57; dir. Lord's Acre Plan, Asheville, N.C., 1937—; vis. prof. Emory U., Duke, Boston U.; lectr. Yale, U. Ga., U. Wis., Northwestern U., Am. U., U. Tenn., Scarritt Coll., others. Chaplain social conservation service State of Ga. and Western Dist. N.C.; trustee Hinton Rural Life Center. Active United Fund. Named Young Man of Year in field of religion, Rural Minister of Year, State of Ga., 1951; recipient Distinguished Service award N.C. Soil Conservation, 1972. Mem. Rural Sociology Soc. Am., Internat. Speakers Bur., Eta Sigma Phi, Alpha Kappa Delta. Kiwanian. Contbr. articles to ch. publs. Home: Route 1 Box 139 Horse Shoe NC 38742 Office: PO Box 1490 Asheville NC 28802

WALDROP, DENNIS WINFRED, dentist; b. Benton, Tenn., May 6, 1928; s. John Aubrey and Lola (Mitchell) W.; B.S., U. Tenn., 1954, D.D.S., 1955; m. Janie Lee Florance, Dec. 24, 1949; 1 dau., Patricia Ann. Post exchange officer, sales mgr. Army and Air Force Exchange Service, 1946-50; oral surgeon, dental adminstr. Central State Hosp., and dental cons. Petersburg (Va.) Tng. Sch., 1963-64; pvt. practice dentistry, specializing in oral surgery, Colonial Heights, Va., 1965—; dir. Colonial Beach (Va.) Shopping Center; founder, v.p. Historyland Playground, Inc., Colonial Beach, 1963—. Served to lt. col. Dental Corps., AUS, 1955-63. Mem. Am. Dental Assn., Va. Philadelphia County dental socs., Federation Internationale Dentaire, Assn. Mil. Surgeons U.S., Assn. Advancement Gen. Anesthesia in Dentistry, Am. Legion, Omicron Kappa Upsilon, The Deans Soc., Psi Omega, Pi Kappa Alpha. Home: 201 Winston Av Colonial Heights VA 23834 Office: 129 Temple Av Colonial Heights VA 23834

WALDROP, LEWIS ANTHONY, civil engr.; b. Atlanta, Jan. 10, 1941; s. Lewis and Dorothy Lenora Jane (Strickland) W.; B.Civil Engring., Ga. Inst. Tech., 1963, postgrad., 1970-71; m. Eleanor Rebecca Barron, Mar. 3, 1962; children—Eleanor Dee, Liesl Annette. Civil engr. TVA, 1963-64; pres. Lewis Waldrop Contractor, Inc., Marietta, Ga., 1964-67; project engr. Hensley-Schmidt, Inc., cons. engrs., Marietta, 1967-69; v.p. Guillebeau, Britt & Waldrop, Inc., Decatur, Ga., 1969—. Pres. Ga. Baptist Conf. for Deaf, 1971-72. Registered profl. engr., Ga., Ark., Va. Mem. Ga. Soc. Profl. Engrs. (treas. Dekalb chpt. 1971-73), Cons. Engrs. Council, Am. Soc. C.E. (asso.), Ga. Water and Pollution Control Assn., Water Pollution Control Fedn., Chi Epsilon (treas. Ga. Inst. Tech. Chpt. 1962-63). Baptist (trustee). Home: Ross Rd Lithonia GA 30058 Office: 4277-D Memorial Dr Decatur GA 30032

WALES, BILL BARTLETT, oil co. exec.; b. Wink, Tex., Nov. 8, 1927; s. Bartlett Adkinson and Vera (Robinson) W.; B.Arch., Tex. A. and M. U., 1950; m. Elizabeth Fay Waters, Apr. 21, 1951; children—Charissa Lynn, William Bartlett, James Steven. Archtl. draftsman Lynn A. Evans, architect, Corpus Christi, Tex., 1950-51; archtl. planner Engrs. Associated, Corpus Christi, 1951-52; prin. Bill B. Wales, designer, Corpus Christi, 1952; archtl. job chief Kruger & Assos., Santa Fe, 1954-56; chief draftsman Hank Avery architect, Midland, Tex., 1956-58; contract rep. J & C Drilling Co., Corpus Christi, 1959-65, mgr., Refugio, Tex., 1965—, v.p., 1970—; sec. Refugio Enterprises, 1965—. Chmn. Mustang dist. Gulf Coast council Boy Scouts Am., 1966-68, mem., 1968—; mem. lay adv. bd. Refugio Meml. Hosp., 1967—; pres. Refugio Primary Elementary P.T.A., 1967-68, mem., 1968—. Served to 1st lt., inf., AUS, 1952-54: Korea. Mem. A.I.A., Am. Assn. Oilwell Drilling Contractors, V.F.W. Lion (dist. gov., 1968-69). Home: 308 Elm St Refugio TX 78377 Office: 115 Purisima St Refugio TX 78377

WALESKI, ALEXANDER FRANK, sch. adminstr.; b. Chgo., Feb. 8, 1915; s. Alexander Frank and Henrietta Stefanie (Kovalowski) W.; B.A., Randolph-Macon Coll., 1939; M.A., U. N.C., 1949; m. Dorothy Eleanor Wickham, Dec. 26, 1939; 1 son, Arthur Frank. Tchr., coach Southampton County Sch. Bd., Franklin, Va., 1934-41, Henrico County Sch. Bd., Richmond, Va., 1941-43; mem. faculty Augusta Mil. Acad., Ft. Defiance, Va., 1943-45; tchr., coach Martinsville (Va.) City Sch. Bd., 1945-51; prin. Henry County Sch. Bd., Martinsville, Va., 1951—, dir. fed. programs. Mem. N.E.A., Va., Henry County (pres. 1955) edn. assns., Va. High Sch. League (sec., past pres. Blue Ridge Dist., past pres. Piedmont dist. Baptist. Kiwanian (pres. 1957), Lion (charter mem. Martinsville). Home: Box 26A Route 5 Bassett VA 24055 Office: Box 511 Martinsville VA 24112

WALFORD, BESS PATERSON, librarian; b. Richmond, Va.; d. Charles Paterson and Bessie (Williams) Walford; B.A., Westhampton Coll., 1939; B.S. in L.S., Drexel Inst. Tech., 1940. Librarian, Mathews County High Sch. 1940-41; supr. libraries Va. Dept. Mental Hygiene and Hosps., 1941-45; librarian post library 3, Fort Meade, Md., 1945-46, med. and tech. library VA Richmond Regional Office, 1947-49, Fed. Res. Bank of Richmond, Va., 1949-59, Philip Morris U.S.A., Research Library, 1959—. Spl. libraries rep. library adv. com. Va. Council Higher Edn., 1972—. Mem. Va. Library Assn. (chmn. spl. libraries div. 1955-57, pres. 1961-62), Spl. Libraries Assn. (vice chmn. financial div. 1957-58; co-chmn. bus.-finance div. 1958-59, mem. govtl. relations com. 1964-67, chmn. 1968-70; div. liaison officer 1970-72; pres. Va. chpt. 1969-70, mem. consultation com. 1972—. Home: 5014 Sulky Dr Richmond VA 23228 Office: 4201 Commerce Rd Richmond VA 23261

WALHAY, ROBERT DAVIES, assn. exec.; b. Chgo., May 3, 1925; s. Ward and Audrey (Davies) W.; B.A., Mich. State U., 1950; postgrad., London Sch. Econs., 1951; m. Ellen Church, Nov. 22, 1951. Corr., editor Reuters News Agy., London, Eng., 1951-53; editor Am. Daily, London, 1953-54; engaged in pub. relations A.R.C., Washington, 1954—, asst. dir., 1971—. Information officer League Red Cross Socs. Hungarian Refugee Relief, Vienna, Austria, 1956-57, Cuban Refugee Program, 1962-63. Served with AUS, 1943-46; PTO.

Mem. Sigma Delta Chi. Home: 7300 Rollingwood Dr Chevy Chase MD 20015 Office: 17th & D Sts N W Washington DC 20006

WALKER, BURLIAN O'NEAL, coll. adminstr.; b. Magee, Miss., Oct. 31, 1941; s. Cordas Burlian and Arlee (Williamson) W.; student Copiah-Lincoln Jr. Coll., 1960-62; B.S., U. So. Miss., 1964, postgrad., 1965-66, 70-71; postgrad. (Newspaper Fund fellow) U. Miss., 1970. English tchr. Simpson County Schs., 1964-65, 66-67; clk. U.S. Ho. of Reps., 1966; dir. pub. relations, instr. journalism Copiah-Lincoln Jr. Coll., Wesson, Miss., 1967—. Asst. publicity chmn. Miss. Theatre Assn. Conv., 1972; publicity chmn. Am. Cancer Soc., Copiah County chpt., 1972; exec. dir. Miss Co-Lin Pageant, Inc., 1970-73. Alternate del. Miss. Republican party state conv., 1968. Mem. Miss. Assn. Journalism Edn. (pres. 1973-74), Miss., Copiah-Lincoln edn. assns., Miss. Coll. Pub. Relations Assn., Miss. Journalism Assn., Copiah-Lincoln Jr. Coll. (pres. 1970-71), U. So. Miss. alumni assns., Wesson Jr. C. of C., Delta Psi Omega. Contbr. articles to profl. jours. Home: 232 N 2d St Brookhaven MS 39601 Office: Copiah Lincoln Jr Coll Wesson MS 39191

WALKER, SISTER CATHERINE, educator, psychologist; b. Bartlesville, Okla.; d. Ethan Allen and Lula Mae (Kuhn) Walker; B.A., Our Lady of Lake Coll., 1942, B.S. in L.S., 1947; M.A., Cath. U. Am., 1951; Ph.D., Northwestern U., 1955. Jr. high sch. tchr., Alexandria, La., 1941-46; critic tchr. Demonstration Sch., Our Lady of Lake Coll., San Antonio, 1941-46, prin., dean of girls Demonstration Sch., 1946-53, prof. edn. Grad. Sch. Edn., 1955—, dir. student personnel services, 1955-63, dir. counselor edn., 1958—, chmn. grad. edn., 1970-72. Guidance cons. Nat. Cath. Edn. Assn., 1968—; exec. sec. Archdiocesan Guidance Council, 1967—; bd. mgrs. United Colls. San Antonio, 1970-73; cons., speaker, panelist at local, state and nat. profl. meetings. Mem. Nat. Cath. Guidance Conf. (dir. 1962-66), Am., Tex. (conv. coordinator 1968) personnel and guidance assns., Tex. Assn. Counselor Educators and Suprs. (sec.-treas. 1967-69, exec. bd. 1970-72), Tex. Assn. Rehab. Counselors (sec. 1970-72); San Antonio Women Deans and Counselors (pres. 1962-63), South Tex. Personnel and Guidance (pres. 1968-69, exec. bd. 1968-72), Pi Lambda Theta. Mem. editorial bd. The Cath. Counselor, 1958-60, asso. editor, 1960-62, chmn. editorial bd. and staff, 1962-65. Contbr. articles to profl. jours. Address: 411 SW 24th St San Antonio TX 78285

WALKER, CHARLS EDWARD, cons.; b. Graham, Tex., Dec. 24, 1923; s. Pinkney Clay and Sammye (McCombs) W.; B.B.A., U. Tex., 1947, M.B.A., 1948; Ph.D., U. Pa., 1955; m. Harmolyn Hart, June 24, 1949; children—Carolyn, Charls E. Instr. finance U. Tex., Austin, 1947-48, asst. prof., 1950-53, asso. prof., 1954; instr. finance Wharton Sch., U. Pa., Phila., 1948-50; financial economist Fed. Reserve Bank, Phila., 1953; economist, v.p., econ. adv. Fed. Reserve Bank, Dallas, 1954-61; economist Republic Nat. Bank, Dallas, 1955-56; asst. to Sec. of Treasury, 1959-61; exec. v.p. Am. Bankers Assn., N.Y.C., 1961-69; under sec. of Treasury, 1969-72, dep. sec. of Treasury, 1972-73; pres. Charls E. Walker Assos., Inc., Washington, 1973—. Chmn., Pres.'s Council on Minority Bus. Enterprise; vice chmn. Joint Council Econ. Edn. Served to 2d lt. USAAF, 1942-45. Editor: The Bankers Handbook, 1966. Contbr. to econ. jours., newspapers, mags. Home: 1661 Crescent Pl NW Washington DC 20009 Office: 1730 Pennsylvania Av NW Washington DC 20006

WALKER, DALE L., coll. adminstr.; b. Decatur, Ill., Aug. 3, 1935; s. Russell Dale and Eilleen Mary (Guysinger) W.; B.A. in Journalism, U. Tex. at El Paso, 1962; m. Alice McCord, Sept. 30, 1960; children—Dianne, Eric, Christopher, Michael, John. TV newsman KTSM News, El Paso, 1962-66; dir. news and information service U. Tex., El Paso, 1966—. Served with USN, 1955-59. Mem. Nat. Hist. Soc., Am. Soc. World War I Aero Historians, Am. Coll. Pub. Relations Assn. Author: (with Richard O'Connor) The Lost Revolutionary, 1967; The Fiction of Jack London, 1972; C.L. Sonnichsen: Grassroots Historian, 1972; The Alien Worlds of Jack London, 1973; Death Was a Black Horse: The Story of Rough Rider Buckey O'Neill, 1974. also articles. Home: 4569 Skylark Way El Paso TX 79922

WALKER, DANIEL JOSHUA, JR., lawyer; b. Gibson, N.C., Nov. 27, 1915; s. Daniel Joshua and Annie (Hurdle) W.; A.B., U. N.C., 1936, J.D., 1948; m. Sarah Elizabeth Nicholson, June 14, 1941. Claim dept. Barnwell Bros. Trucking Co., Burlington, N.C., 1936-42; admitted to N.C. bar, 1948; clk. Superior Ct., Alamance County, Graham, N.C., 1948-53; partner Long, Ridge, Harris & Walker, Graham, 1953-67; county atty. Alamance County, Graham, 1964—, county mgr., 1971—; sr. mem. firm Walker Harris, Graham, 1967-71. Mem. Human Relations Council, Alamance County, 1963-71, chmn., 1970; mem. N.C. Bd. Water and Air Resources, 1972—. Pres., Alamance County Young Democratic Club, 1950; chmn. Alamance County Dem. Exec. Com., 1956-58; mem. N.C. Dem. Exec. Com., 1958-66. Trustee Tech. Inst. of Alamance, 1964-71; bd. dirs. Alamance County United Fund, Cherokee council Boy Scouts Am., Community YMCA, Burlington; trustee Presbyn. Found., Presbyn. Ch. U.S., 1969-73, mem. Exec. Com., 1971-73; mem. council Orange Presbytery, 1972—. Served with AUS, 1942-46. Decorated Bronze Star medal. Mem. Am. Judicature Soc., Burlington-Alamance C. of C., Am., N.C., Alamance County bar assns., N.C. Assn. County Attys. (v.p. 1971, pres. 1972, named county atty. of yr. 1971), Phi Alpha Delta. Democrat. Presbyn. (elder; trustee ch.). Home: 215 Long Av Graham NC 27253 Office: 124 West Elm Graham NC 27253

WALKER, DAVID, judge; b. Lufkin, Tex., Aug. 7, 1931; s. Howard and Ethel (Cruse) W.; B.B.A., Sam Houston State U., 1952; LL.B., S. Tex. Coll. Law, 1959; m. Virgia Jewell Lindsey, Jan. 10, 1953; children—George, Frank, Dorothy, Larry, Carol. Engaged in real estate bus., Lufkin, 1954-59; admitted to Tex. bar, 1959, practiced in Lufkin, 1959-69; city atty. Lufkin, 1964-69; judge 159th Jud. Dist. for Angelina County (Tex.), 1969—. Pres., Lufkin Bd. Realtors, 1956. Pres. Angelina County Sch. Bd., 1961-66. Trustee Angelina Coll., Lufkin, 1966-69, sec., 1968-69. Mem. Angelina County Bar Assn. (pres. 1969). Kiwanian (pres. Lufkin 1968). Home: Route 10 Box 825 Lufkin TX 75901 Office: Courthouse Sq Lufkin TX 75901

WALKER, DEE BROWN, judge; b. Royse City, Tex., Dec. 3, 1912; s. Dee Alexander and Lela Blanche (Jones) W.; LL.B., So. Meth. U., 1935; m. Ruthe Elizabeth Edwards, Mar. 28, 1942; children—Susan Hays, Stephen Craig; m. 2d, Anna Lee Gandy, Sept. 13, 1952. Admitted to Tex. bar, 1935; atty. Tex. Fire & Casualty Underwriters, 1935-36, Standard Accident Ins. Co., 1936-41, Glens Falls Indemnity Co., 1941-42; gen. practice law, Dallas, 1946-59; atty. Southland Life Ins. Co., 1959-63; judge 162d Jud. Dist. Ct. Dallas County, 1963—. Mem. Dallas County Dem. Com., 1952-63. Trustee Dallas Pub. Library; v.p., dir., trustee Royse City Cemetery Found., Chisholm Cemetery Found., Cottonwood Cemetery Found. Served from pvt. to 1st lt. AUS, 1942-46. Mem. Am., Dallas bar assns., State Bar Tex., Dallas County Criminal Bar Assn., Am. Judicature Soc., Southwestern Legal Found., So. Meth. U. Alumni and Law Sch. Alumni Assn., Res. Officers Assn., Local History and Geneal. Soc. Dallas (pres. dir. 1963-65), S.A.R. (past pres. Dallas), Am. Legion, Mil. Order World Wars, D.A.V., V.F.W., Soc. Colonial Wars, Sons Confederate Vets., Phi Alpha Delta. Mem. Christian Ch. Mason (K.T., 33 deg., Shriner), Lion. Home: 5918 Vanderbilt Dallas TX 75206 Office: 162d Dist Ct House Dallas TX 75202

WALKER, DONALD LEE, chem. co. exec.; b. Bandana, Ky., Aug. 11, 1934; s. Richard and Lottie (Berry) W.; B.S., 1973; m. Eva M. Lofton, Dec. 30, 1955; children—Michael Lee, Linda Gaye. Engr., Air Reduction Chem. Co., Calvert City, Ky., 1960-70, Air Products Chem. Co., Calvert City, 1971—; prin. Walker & Assos., cons. engrs., Paducah, Ky., 1968—. Served with AUS, 1957-59. Registered profl. engr., Ky., Ohio, N.J. Mem. Am. Soc. M.E. Baptist (deacon). Home: Route 1 Bruce Av Paducah KY 42001 Office: PO Box 97 Calvert City KY 42029

WALKER, EMMA MILLS CLEMENT (MRS. SAUNDERS E. WALKER), educator; b. Charlotte, N.C., May 19, 1909; d. George Clinton and Emma (Williams) Clement; A.B., Livingstone Coll., 1930, M.A., Atlanta U., 1941; postgrad. Louisville Municipal Coll.; Ph.D., Ohio State U., 1969; m. Saunders E. Walker, Aug. 28, 1945; 1 dau., Sandra Clementine. Tchr., Dinwiddie (Va.) Normal Sch., 1930-31, Fee High Sch., Maysville, Ky., 1932, Hunt High Sch., Ft. Valley, Ga., 1939-41; faculty Tuskegee Inst., Ala., 1941-67, asst. prof. English, 1943-67, acting chmn. dept. English, 1952-56, 66, 67; prof. coll. edn. achievement project Ft. Valley (Ga.) State Coll., 1967-70, asso. prof. edn., 1970—. Dir. Project Upward Bound, Ft. Valley, 1970-71; sec. Peach County Community Action Program, Ft. Valley, 1970—; sec. Macon County (Ala.) Community Action Program, Tuskegee, 1966-67; chmn. adv. bd., pres. Tuskegee YM-YWCA, 1966-67; mem. Am. Security Council. Mem. Am. Assn. U. Profs., Nat. Council Tchrs. English, So. Atlantic Modern Lang. Assn., Am., Ala. tchrs. assns., Ala. Tchrs. Coll. English, N.A.A.C.P., Links Inc. (area sec. 1968), Phi Lambda Theta, Alpha Kappa Alpha, Lambda Iota Tau. Methodist (chmn. missions Ch. Women United 1965-67). Home: PO Box 1633 FVSC Fort Valley GA 31030

WALKER, ESPER LAFAYETTE, JR., civil engr.; b. Decatur, Tex., Sept. 22, 1930; s. Esper Lafayette and Ruth (Mauldin) W.; B.S., Tex. A. and M. U., 1953; B.H.T., Yale, 1958; m. Sara Lynn Dunlap, Oct. 2, 1955; children—William David, Annette Ruth. Design engr. Tex. Hwy. Dept., Austin, 1956-57; dir. Dept. Traffic Engring., High Point, N.C., 1958-63; v.p. Wilbur Smith & Assoc., Houston, 1963—. Served to 1st lt. C.E., AUS, 1953-56. Registered profl. engr., Tex., S.C. Mem. Nat., Tex. socs. profl. engrs., Inst. Traffic Engrs. (pres. So. sect. 1963). Methodist (adminstrv. bd. 1971—). Home: 14216 Kellywood Lane Houston TX 77024 Office: 1535 West Loop S Suite 200 Houston TX 77027

WALKER, EVELYN, ednl. TV exec., educator; b. Birmingham, Ala.; d. Preston Lucas and Mattie (Williams) Walker; A.B., Huntingdon Coll., 1927, L.H.D., 1974; postgrad. Cornell U., 1927-29; spl. courses U. Ill., 1955; M.A., U. Ala., 1963. Speech instr. Phillips High Sch., Birmingham, Ala., 1930-34; head speech dept. Ramsay High Sch., Birmingham, 1934-52; head instructional TV programming services, Birmingham Pub. Schs., 1969—; staff producer Birmingham Ednl. TV Studios, for Ala. Ednl. TV network, 1954—, acting program dir., 1959; Miss Ann, broadcaster of daily children's program, WSGN Radio, Birmingham, 1946-57. Cons. Gov.'s Ednl. TV Legislative Study Commn., 1953. Mem. Def. Adv. Com. Women in Services, 1959-62, Recall to Duty, 1971; bd. dirs. WAC Found., Freedom Ednl. Found., Festival of Arts; bd. dirs., Women's Com. of 100, sec., 1968-71; internat. competition chmn. Festival of Arts Creative TV, Radio; mem. Birmingham Adv. Com. on Women in Services, co-chmn. TV and radio Gov.'s Adv. Bd. to State Safety Com., 1965—. Nat. del. Asian-American Women Broadcasters Conf., 1966. Recipient alumnae achievement award Huntingdon Coll., 1958, Festival of Arts, Spl. Silver Bowl, Ednl. TV Award, 1962; Educator's Medal Award, Freedoms Found. at Valley Forge, 1963, 68, 69, 70, Nat. Headliner award Women in Communications, 1965, Keys to City Birmingham, 20 year award Ala. ETV Commn.; named Tops in our Town, Birmingham News, 1957, Top TV award Regional A.R.C. Assn., 1964; named State Woman of Achievement, Ala. Bus. and Profl. Clubs, 1964, Birmingham's Woman of Yr., 1965; Ala.'s Woman of Year, Progressive Farmer's Mag., 1967. Mem. Birmingham Tchrs. Club, Nat. Assn. Ednl. Broadcasters, Am. Women in Radio and TV (pres. 1959-60) (area trustee nat. ednl. found. bd.). Am. Assn. U. Women, Nat. League Am. Penwomen, Huntingdon Coll. Alumnae Assn. (internat. pres. 1961-63), Ala. Hist. Assn., Arlington Hist. Soc., Ala. Animal League (dir.), Magna Charta Dames (sec.-treas. 1963-64), D.A.R. (state TV chmn. 1962-64), U.S. Daus. 1812 (state TV chmn. 1963-64), Colonial Dames 17th Century, Daus. Am. Colonists (state TV chmn., 2d v.p. local chpt. 1962—), Ams. Royal Descent, Platagenets Soc., Royal Order Garter, Royal Order Crown, Bot. Soc., Art Mus. Aux., Symphony Women, Women for Patriotic Events, Ala. Dist. Exchange Clubs (hon. life, bronze plaque 1969), Salvation Army Aux., Women in Communications (local pres. 1958), Delta Delta Delta, Delta Kappa Gamma. Methodist. Clubs: Birmingham Country; Press; Altrusa, Downtown (Birmingham); The Club. Home: 744 Euclid Av Birmingham AL 35213 Office: care ETV 2015 N 7th Av Birmingham AL 35203 also Bd Edn Drawer 10007 Birmingham AL 35202

WALKER, FRANCIS CHARLES, psychologist; b. nr. Galesburg, Ill., Feb. 1, 1926; s. Ivan Banks and Hazel Anna (Weiler) W.; B.A., Bradley U., 1949, M.A., 1950; m. Donna Jean Bender, Sept. 1, 1946; children—Gregory C., Taffy Dee (Mrs. Michael W. McCauley). Vocational appraiser Personnel Services Assos., Peoria, Ill., 1949-50; personnel counselor Caterpillar Tractor Co., Peoria, 1950-55; indsl. psychologist Byron Harless and Assos., Tampa, Fla., 1955; indsl. relations cons. Sangamo Electric Co., Springfield, Ill., 1955-60; sec., dir. administrv. service Byron Harless, Schaffer, Reid & Assos, Tampa, 1960-69; v.p. Rutenberg Homes, Inc., Belleair Bluffs, Fla., 1969-70; indsl. psychologist Frank Walker Assos., Tampa, Fla., 1970—. Tchr. eve. div. Bradley U., 1951-53, Springfield Jr. Coll., 1956. Mem. Bd. Edn., Richwoods Township, Peoria, 1951-55; Republican precinct committeeman, 1952-55, 67-68, twp. chmn., 1953-54, dis. chmn., 1967-68. Served with USAAF, 1944-46. Mem. Am., Ill., Southeastern, Fla. (pres. 1972-73), Tampa Bay (pres. 1965-66) psychol. assns., Psi Chi. Presbyn. (clk. of session 1964-67, 71-73). Clubs: University, Exchange (Tampa); Highlands (N.C.) Country. Home: 215 S Hesperides St Tampa FL 33609 Office: 1111 N Westshore St Tampa FL 33607

WALKER, HAROLD WILLIAM, news corr.; b. Darlington, S.C., July 2, 1933; s. Harold Winston and Betty Augusta (Abernathy) W.; B.A., Denison U., 1954; postgrad. Maxwell Sch. Pub. Affairs, Syracuse U., 1960-63; m. children—Stephen, Alison, Sarah. Unemployment ins. examiner N.Y. State Employment Service, N.Y.C., 1958-59; asst. editor N.Y. State Dept. Mental Hygiene, Albany, 1959-61, N.Y. State Edn. Dept., Albany, 1961-63; news reporter WTOP-TV, Washington, 1963-68; news corr. CBS News, Washington, 1968—; adj. prof. journalism Columbia, summer 1969. Served with AUS, 1954-58. Recipient Emmy award Nat. Acad. TV Arts and Scis., 1969. Mem. Blacks in Broadcasting, Am. Fedn. TV and Radio Artists. Home: 3800 Alton Pl NW Washington DC 20016 Office: 2020 M St NW Washington DC 20036

WALKER, HARRY, former baseball mgr.; b. Pasacagoula, Miss., Oct. 22, 1918; s. Ewart and Flossie (Vaughn) W.; student pub. schs.; m. Dorothy Fulmer, Mar. 17, 1941; children—Carole Diane, Mary Sharon, Barbara Anne. Profl. baseball player with St. Louis Cardinals, 1940-43, 46-47, 50-51, 55, Phila. Phillies, 1947-48, Chgo. Cubs, 1949, Cin. Reds, 1949; coach, mgr. St. Louis Cardinal Orgn., 1955; mgr. Pitts. Pirates, 1966-67; hitting instr. Houston Astros, 1967-68, mgr., 1968-72. Served with AUS. Decorated Bronze Star, Purple Heart. Author: How to Bat.*

WALKER, HARRY GREY, judge; b. Ovett, Miss., Sept. 30, 1924; s. Chester A. and Ina (Mangum) W.; LL.B., U. Miss., 1952; m. Carrie Thorne Lang, Apr. 4, 1953; children—Harry Grey, Fred Wallace. Admitted to Miss. bar, 1952; practiced in Gulfport; judge Harrison County Ct., 1964-68; circuit judge 2d dist., 1968-72; asso. justice Miss. Supreme Ct., 1972—. Mem. Miss. Ho. of Reps., 1964. Trustee Cerebral Palsy Assn. Gulf Coast, Good Samaritan Tng. Center. Served with USCG, 1942-44. Mem. Am. Bar Assn., Miss. State Bar, D.A.V., Am. Legion, Paralyzed Vets. Am., Phi Alpha Delta, Kappa Alpha. Democrat. Methodist. Elk. Clubs: Gulfport Yacht, Magnolia Hunting. Home: 2107 Plantation Blvd Jackson MS 39211 Office: Miss Supreme Ct Jackson MS

WALKER, JAMES KENNETH, lawyer; b. Decatur, Tex., Jan. 10, 1936; s. Bluford J. and Elmer Vernice (Clark) W.; LL.B. (J.D.), Baylor U., 1960; m. Mary Frank Garrett, July 9, 1960; children—James Garrett, Steven Wade. Admitted to Tex. bar, 1960; pvt. practice law, Lubbock, Tex., 1960-63; county atty. Cochran County, Tex., 1965-72; pvt. practice law, Morton, Tex., 1972—. Bd. dirs. Morton Indsl. Found. Mem. 19th Bar Dist. Tex. (grievance com. 1972—), Phi Alpha Delta. Methodist. Lion. Home: 507 SE 9th St Morton TX 79346 Office: 109A W Washington St Morton TX 79346

WALKER, JAMES LORENZO, state legislator; b. Marco, Fla., Nov. 1, 1920; s. Forrest Walker and Adnie (Prine) W.; grad. diesel engr. Hemp Hill Diesel Sch.; m. Marguerite Louise Lanier, Jan. 3, 1942; children—Barbara Ann, Carolyn Sue. Mem. Fla. Ho. of Reps., 1956—, speaker pro tem, 1967—; dir. First Nat. Bank & Trust Co. Naples, Citizens Nat. Bank Naples, Vanderbilt Bank, Naples. Mem. Naples-on-the-Gulf Bd. Realtors. Past pres. Collier County TB and Health Assn. Mem. Collier County Bd. Commrs., 1950-56. Served with AC, AUS, 1943-46. Mem. Am. Legion (past post comdr.), mem. Fla., Nat. assns. realtors. Democrat. Mem. Church of God. Lion (past pres. Naples). Home: 720 Banyan Blvd Naples FL 33940

WALKER, JAMES LYNN, JR., state ofcl.; b. Greenville, S.C., May 14, 1924; s. James Lynn, and Ruth (Reaves) W.; student Furman U., 1941-44, 46-48; m. Josephine Breazeale, June 21, 1955; children—Anna Reaves, James Lynn III, and Sallie Mills Walker. With editorial dept. Greenville News, 1941-68, successively reporter, legislative corr., asst. city editor, 1941-55; city editor, 1955-68; asst. dir. pub. relations S.C. Hwy. Dept., 1968-72, dir. pub. relations, 1972—. Served from pvt. to staff sgt. inf. AUS, 1944-46; ETO. Decorated Purple Heart, Bronze Star medal. Mem. Sigma Alpha Epsilon. Home: 1124 Greenridge Lane Columbia SC 29210 Office: SC Hwy Dept PO Box 191 1100 Senate St Columbia SC 29202

WALKER, JAMES WHITTENBURG, oil and gas producer; b. Clayton, N.M., Nov. 10, 1935; s. Basil Eugene and Annie (Whittenburg) W.; B.B.A., U. Tex., 1958; m. Patricia Ann Roberts, Nov. 28, 1959; children—Frances Ann, James Whittenburg, Reid Samuel, Patrick Paul. Reporter, Amarillo (Tex.) Globe News, 1959-62, oil editor, 1962-72, asst. to pres., 1967-72. Pres., Amarillo United Way, 1971, campaign chmn., 1970. Bd. dirs. Amarillo YMCA, pres. 1968; bd. dirs. Children's Rehab. Center, chmn. 1966-67; bd. dirs. Camp Fire Girls of Amarillo, 1969-72, Panhandle Sci. Fair, 1965-72. Mem. Assn. Petroleum Writers (pres. 1971-72), Tex. Daily Newspaper Assn. (dir. 1971-72), Panhandle Producers and Royalty Owners Assn. (exec. com. 1968-71, v.p., 1974—), Amarillo C. of C. (dir. 1968-71), Phi Gamma Delta, Phi Delta Phi. Democrat. Presbyn. (elder 1967-70). Clubs: Amarillo, Amarillo Country, Palo Duro. Home: 6306 Jameson St Amarillo TX 79106 Office: Box 2526 Amarillo TX 79105

WALKER, JOE KEITH, lawyer; b. Springfield, Tenn., May 13, 1931; s. Raymond D. and Genese (Rawls) W.; student Bethel Coll., 1951; B.S., Middle Tenn. State U., 1957; J.D., YMCA Law Sch., 1962; m. Betty Ruth Lipscomb, June 9, 1957; children—Jeff, Pamela Jean. Claim supr. Ins. Co. N.Am., 1957-67; admitted to Tenn. bar, 1962; practiced in Springfield, 1962—; mem. firm Bracy & Walker. Served with USAF, 1951-54. Mem. Tenn. Trial Lawyers Assn., Tenn., Springfield (pres. 1972-73) bar assns., V.F.W. Kiwanian. Home: 103 Tanglewood Lane Springfield TN 37172 Office: 126 S Court St Springfield TN 37172

WALKER, JOHN ALEXANDER, retail co. exec.; b. Phila., June 10, 1922; s. John Anthony and Dorothy (Morrison) W.; student Muhlenburg Coll., 1941-42, U. Pa., 1942-43, Northwestern U., 1944; m. Beryl Audrey Linehard, Apr. 21, 1946; children—Lynn (Mrs. Phil Riker), Dorothy (Mrs. Robert Moynihan), Gail, Debbie, Mary. Dist. mgr. Hotpoint distbg. div. Gen. Electric Co., Chgo., 1946-58; exec. v.p. Lowe's Companies, Inc., North Wilkesboro, N.C., 1958—, also dir.; dir. Lowe's Profit-Sharing Plan and Trust, Lowe's Charitable & Trust Found., Northwestern Security Life Ins. Co., Phoenix, Wilkes Devel. Corp., Alleghany S. A. Mem. plywood adv. council Chgo. Bd. Trade, 1970—; mem. bus. adv. council Appalachian State U., Boone, N.C., 1970-71; Chmn. North Wilkesboro Housing Authority, 1966-71. Chmn. N.C. Republican Finance Com., 1968-71; mem. Republican Nat. Finance Com., 1969-72; Rep. candidate for lt. gov. of N.C., 1972. Served to lt. USNR, 1942-46. Mem. N.C. Home Builders Assn., Nat. Assn. Home Builders, Phi Kappa Sigma. Presbyn. (deacon). Mason (Shriner), Elk. Clubs: Oakwoods Country, Roaring Gap, Blowing Rock Country. Contbr. articles to profl. jours. Home: 104 Coffey St North Wilkesboro NC 28659 Office: Hwy 268 E North Wilkesboro NC 28659

WALKER, JOHN LUTHER, JR., lawyer; b. Roanoke, Va., May 26, 1936; s. John Luther and Katherine Elizabeth (Crawford) W.; B.A. in English (Morehead scholar), U. N.C., 1958; LL.B., U. Va., 1961; m. Mary Louise Bizzell, Aug. 1, 1959; children—John Luther III, Edward Bizzell. Admitted to Va. bar, 1961; asso. firm Woods, Rogers, Muse, Walker & Thornton, Roanoke, 1961-66, partner, 1967—. Bd. dirs. Big Bros. Roanoke, Inc., 1967-69, pres., 1968; bd. dirs. Roanoke Valley Safety Council, 1962-66, pres., 1965; bd. dirs. Blue Ridge council Boy Scouts Am., 1969-71, chmn. Big Lick Dist., 1969-70; bd. dirs. United Fund Roanoke Valley, 1969-73, pres., 1973. Recipient Distinguished Service award Roanoke Jr. C. of C., 1969. Mem. Am., Va. State, Roanoke City (exec. com. 1963-65) bar assns., Va. State Bar, Order of Coif, Raven Soc., Phi Eta Sigma, Omicron Delta Kappa. Presbyn. (deacon 1964-66, chmn. bd. deacons 1966). Club: Shenandoah (Roanoke). Editorial bd. Va. Lawyer, 1968-70. Home: 439 Canterbury Lane SW Roanoke VA 24014 Office: 105 Franklin Rd SW Roanoke VA 24004

WALKER, JOHN T., bishop; b. Barnesville, Ga.,, 1925; A.B., Wayne U., 1951; B.D., Va. Theol. Sem., 1954; m. Rosa Maria Flores; 3 children. Ordained to ministry Episcopal Ch.; rector, St. Mary's Ch., Detroit, 1955-57; tchr. St. Paul's Sch., 1957-66; canon Washington Cathedral, 1966-71; suffragan bishop Diocese of Washington, 1971—; tchr. Bishop Tucker Theol. Coll., Mukono, Uganda, 1964-65. Del. gen. conv. Episcopal Ch., 1970. Trustee, Washington Hosp. Center, Meridan House Found., Potomac Sch., Milton (Mass.) Acad., Va.

Theol. Sch. Home: 3409 Woodley Rd Washington DC Office: Washington Cathedral Mount Saint Albans Washington DC 20016

WALKER, JOSEPH HILLARY, JR., lawyer; b. Birmingham, Ala., Apr. 7, 1919; s. Joseph Hillary and Nora (Arnold) W.; A.B., U. Ala., 1941, LL.B., 1947; m. Ann Tucker, Dec. 31, 1944; children—Joseph Hillary III, Harriet Elizabeth, Mildred Katherine, Bonnie Jo. Admitted to Tenn. bar, 1947; since practiced in Ripley; chmn. bd. Farmers Union Bank, Ripley, Tenn., 1964—; dir. Tucker Agrl. Corp., Ripley. Pres. Tenn. Constnl. Conv., 1959, mem., 1965. Chmn. Lauderdale County Sch. Bd., 1964-67; mem. Tenn. Ho. of Reps., 1949-51, Tenn. Senate, 1951-53. Trustee Lauderdale County Hosp., 1962. Served with USAF, 1941-45. Mem. Sigma Nu. Democrat. Baptist (deacon 1954—, treas. 1960). Rotarian (pres. 1954-55). Home: 1 Lackey Lane Ripley TN 38063 Office: 132 Main St Ripley TN 38063

WALKER, KENNETH ROLAND, ednl. adminstr.; b. Syracuse, Ind., Apr. 12, 1928; s. Carl and Laura Mae (Ford) W.; B.A., Goshen Coll., 1949; M.A., Ind. U., 1950, Ph.D., 1952; M.Ed., U. Ark., 1964; m. Marylou Evelyn Neff, Sept. 10, 1950; children—Elizabeth Ann, Mary Susan. Asso. prof. history and polit. sci. Ark. Poly Coll., Russellville, 1958-64, prof., 1965—, asst. acad. dean, 1958-69, head history dept., 1965-69, chmn. liberal arts div., 1969-70, dean sch. arts and scis., 1970-72, head social scis. and philosophy dept., 1972—. Liaison officer USAF Acad. for Ark., 1964-69, liaison officer coordinator, 1969—. Chmn. Pope County Easter Seal Campaign, 1969—. Served to capt. USAF, 1952-58. Mem. Ark. Dean's Assn. (pres. 1966-67), Ark. Edn. Assn. (pres. dept. higher edn. 1963-64), Ark. Dept. Higher Edn., Orgn. Am. Historians, Southwestern Social Studies Assn., Phi Alpha Theta, Kappa Delta Pi, Phi Delta Kappa. Methodist. Author: Days the Presidents Died, 1966; The History of the Middle West, 1972. Contbr. articles to profl. pubs. Home: Route 2 Box 43 Russellville AR 72801

WALKER, LEE ANNE SEVERY (MRS. SCOTT BARTON WALKER), artist; b. Nashville, July 19; d. P. Lee and Sara M. (Baggott) Severy; B.S. in Art, Middle Tenn. State U., 1968; M.A., Peabody Coll., 1972; m. Scott Barton Walker, June 24, 1967. Tchr. art Nashville Met. Schs., 1969-71, Vol. State Community Coll., 1972, Watkins Inst., 1973—; exhibited one-man shows Peabody Coll., 1971, Centennial Park Art Center, 1972; exhibited group shows MTSO Gallery, 1968, Circle Theater Gallery, 1972, Gallery III, 1973, Studio S Gallery, 1973. Active Project Challenge. Recipient Purchase awards Ann. Tenn. Crafts Fair, 1972, 73, Crafts award Vanderbilt Gallery Arts and Antiques Benefit, 1974. Mem. Tenn. Artists-Craftsmen Assn., Am. Crafts Council, Delta Zeta. Office: Mill Creek Studios 217 Margo Lane Nashville TN 37211

WALKER, LILLIAN WALKER, ins. exec.; b. Meridian, Miss., May 8, 1923; d. Rudolph Blanche and Elizabeth (George) Walker; grad. Meridian Jr. Coll.; m. Edward E. Walker, May 25, 1942; children—Edward T., Betti H. Owner Baton Rouge Agy., 1956—; sec. Southland Concessions, Inc., mem. La. Ho. of Reps., 1964-72, chmn. contingent com., 1964-72; mem. exec. com. Baton Rouge Ins. Exchange Capt. bldg. fund dr. YMCA, Baton Rouge, 1959, 73; bd. dirs., treas. Audubon council Girl Scouts; pres. La. Assn. for Retarded Children, 1960; mem. La Commn. Status Women; So. Central region v.p. Nat. Assn. Retarded Children, 1972-73; mem. La. Baton Rouge assns. retarded children; bd. dirs. Baton Rouge chpt. Nat. Arthritis Found. Del., Nat. Democratic Conv., 1960. Named Louisianian of Year, La. Assn. Broadcasters, 1964, Baton Rouge First Lady of Year Beta Sigma Phi, 1966; Nike award La. Fedn. Bus. and Profl. Women's Clubs; Man of the Quarter award, Am. Assn. Mental Deficiency; Pub. Ofcl. award. La. Assn. Retarded Children. Mem. Nat. Order Women Legislators, Nat. Soc. State Legislators, Am. Legion Aux., La Assn. Ins. Agts., Baton Rouge Bus. and Profl. Women's Club (past pres.), La. State U. Alumni Fedn. (hon.), Zonta (v.p. Baton Rouge), Delta Kappa Gamma. Presbyn. (capt. bldg. fund dr); Home: 655 Cora Dr Baton Rouge LA 70815 Office: 4750 North Blvd Baton Rouge LA 70806

WALKER, LYNN WESLEY, librarian; b. Okeechobee, Fla., Aug. 30, 1928; s. Benjamin Franklin and Neva Gertrude (Williams) W.; B.A., U. Fla., 1950; M.A., Fla. State U., 1953; m. Joyce Roberta Orr, June 9, 1950; children—John Michael, Richard Allen, Jacqueline Lynne. Cataloger U. Tenn. Library, 1950-52; sci. cataloger U. Fla. Libraries, Gainesville, 1952-53, sci. reference librarian, 1953-54, librarian engring. and physics library, 1954-66; dir. libraries Fla. Tech. U., Orlando, 1966—. Tchr. courses in library sci. and engring. graphics U. Fla., 1953-57; cons. microfilm retrieval systems. Mem. Fla. Library Study Commn., 1970—; chmn. State Adv. Council on Libraries, 1971—; v.p. Fla. Assn. Amateur Athletic Union, 1971-74; active YMCA. Mem. Am., (councillor 1971-74), Southeastern, Fla. (pres. 1970-71) library assns., Nat. Microfilm Assn., Beta Phi Mu. Democrat. Episcopalian. Contbr. articles to profl. pubs. Home: 640 Berwick Dr Winter Park FL 32789 Office: PO Box 25000 Orlando FL 32816

WALKER, MARK ANTHONY, judge; b. Covington, Tenn., Sept. 3, 1908; s. Mark Anthony and Ella (Simonton) W.; B.S., U. Tenn., 1931; student U. Tenn. Coll. Law, 1930-31, U. Wis. Sch. Law, 1934; m. Lulie Reynolds Eddins; children—Mark Anthony, Nathalie Eileen, Lawrence Eddins. Admitted to Tenn. bar, 1935; practiced in Covington, 1935-46; circuit judge 16th Jud. Circuit of Tenn., 1946-67; presiding judge Ct. Criminal Appeals, State Tenn., 1967—. Mem. Tenn. Ho. of Reps., 1939-42. Mem. Tenn. Democratic Exec. Com., 1940-43; v.p. Tenn. Young Dem. Club, 1946. Served with USNR, 1942-46; comdr. Res. Mem. Am. Bar Assn., Bar Assn. Tenn., Am. Judicature Soc., Kappa Sigma. Presbyn. Mason (Shriner). Address: 315 S Main St Covington TN 38019

WALKER, ORVILLE CALVIN, educator; b. Roby, Tex., Apr. 20, 1912; s. Ocle C. and Emma (Severfeldt) W.; A.B., Howard Payne Coll., 1933; LL.B., U. Tex., 1936; postgrad. U. Chgo., So. Meth. U.; children—Jack, Jill. Admitted to Tex. bar, 1936; briefing clk. Supreme Ct. Tex., 1936-42; gen. practice San Antonio, 1951-55; prof. law St. Mary's U., San Antonio, 1955—. Mem. rules adv. com. Supreme Ct. Tex. Served with AUS, 1943-46. Mem. Am. Arbitration Assn., Phi Delta Phi, Pi Kappa Delta. Methodist. Contbr. articles to profl. publs. Home: 2302 Blanton Dr San Antonio TX 78216

WALKER, RHEY, II, physician; b. Hillsboro, Tex., May 19, 1924; s. Lawrence Lara and Rose (Grimes) W.; student Hillsboro Coll., 1940-41, Tex. A. and M. Coll., 1941, 43, North Tex. Coll., 1943, Central Mo. Coll., 1943, 44; M.D., Baylor U., 1947; m. Betty Goodwin, June 23, 1947; children—Laneri, Tama. Intern, Ind. U. Med. Center, Indpls., 1947-48; resident internal medicine Meth. Hosp. Southwestern Med. Sch., Dallas, 1948-49, Jefferson Davis Hosp., Houston, 1949-50; practice medicine, specializing in internal medicine, Houston, 1954—; asso. prof. internal medicine, pulmonary diseases Baylor U. Coll. Medicine, Houston, 1963—; asst. prof. internal medicine U. Tex. Med. Sch., Houston; attending physician pulmonary diseases Houston VA Hosp., Houston, 1954—; attending Hermann Hosp., Houston, 1954—; asso. St. Lukes Episcopal Hosp., Houston, 1954—; courtesy and asst. St. Joseph, Meth. hosps. (both Houston); chief medicine 12 Oaks Hosp., 1967, vice chief staff, 1968, chief of staff, 1970-71. Sec.-treas. Houston Diabetes Assn., 1959-60, bd. dirs., 1960—, pres., 1965-66; chmn. Diabetes Detection Drive, 1963; mem. spl. com. aging Community Council Houston, 1958—; mem. exec. com. Meml. Bapt. Hosp. S.W.; mem. Community Council and United Fund Com. Served to lt. (j.g.) USNR, 1943-47; to capt. AUS, 1950-54. Mem. Tex. Med. Assn., Am., Tex. diabetes assns., Am. Heart Assn., Postgrad. Med. Assembly South Tex., Tex. Soc. Aging (charter), Tex. Thoracic Soc., Houston Soc. Internal Medicine, Alumni Assn. Tex., Hind Hagar Soc., Phi Beta Pi, Alpha Phi Alpha. Republican. Clubs: Doctor's (Houston); Internat. Contbr. articles to med. jours. Home: 5319 S Braeswood Houston TX 77035 Office: 3735 Drexel St Houston TX 77027

WALKER, RHONALD DEAN, univ. admisntr.; b. Paducah, Tex., Nov. 16, 1938; s. Doyal Dean and Ada Alyene (Roberts) W.; B.B.A., North Tex. State U., 1962, M.B.A., 1964; J.D., So. Meth. U., 1968; m. Dina Gayle Podnar, Jan. 24, 1965; 1 dau., Ashley Kristin. Mgr., Main, Lafrentz & Co., C.P.A.'s, Dallas, 1962-67; asso. prof. accounting So. Meth. U., Dallas, 1966-73, dir. undergrad. program, 1973—; admitted to Tex. bar, 1968; since practiced in Dallas; partner firm Hampton, Walker & Seward, Dallas, 1968-70. C.P.A., Tex. Mem. Am. Inst. C.P.A.'s, Tex. Soc. C.P.A.'s, Am. Bar Assn., State Bar Tex. Home: 11330 Cotillion Dr Dallas TX 75228

WALKER, ROBERT GERALD, diversified industry exec.; b. Austin, Tex., Feb. 25, 1925; s. Robert Gerald and Bess Woodrin (Patterson) W.; B.B.A., U. Tex., 1959; m. Pauline Burleson, Feb. 11, 1949; children—Keith, Mark, Susan, Wayne, Sally. Mfg. mgr. R.H. Folmar Bldg. Products Co., 1950-55; prodn. control mgr. Waste King Corp., Los Angeles, 1955-56, mfg. services mgr., 1956-59, mfg. mgr. Chgo. plant, 1959-60; mfg. mgr. digital computer div. Litton Industries, Los Angeles, 1960-63, gen. mgr., Lubbock (Tex.) plant, 1963-64, program mgr. econ. devel. div. Beverly Hills, Cal., 1964-65, gen. mgr. Atherton div., Mpls., 1965-67; v.p. Allis-Chalmers Corp., Milw., 1967-72, 67-68, v.p. corporate adminstrn., 1967-68, v.p., gen. mgr. electric controls div., 1968-69, group v.p. 8 utility divs. and 4 consumer product divs., 1970-71; chmn. bd., pres., dir. Kin-Ark Corp., Tulsa, 1972—; dir. Allis-Chalmers Power Systems, Inc., Boyles Galvanizing Corp., Ft. Worth, Camelot Inns of Am. City councilman, mayor, LaMirada, Cal., 1959-60. Served with USAAF, 1943-46, USAF, 1950-51. Home: 3855 S Birmingham Pl Tulsa OK 74105 Office: 2900 E Skelly Dr Tulsa OK 74105

WALKER, ROBERT KIRK, mayor Chattanooga; b. Jasper, Tenn., May 22, 1925; s. Jerry A. and Clemmie (Turner) W.; student U. South, 1943-44; LL.B., U. Va., 1948; m. Miriam Joyce Holt, Aug. 11, 1945; children—Robert Kirk, Marilyn Joy, James Holt. Admitted to Va., Tenn. bar, 1948; practice law, Chattanooga, 1949—; partner firm Strang, Fletcher, Carriger, Walker & Hodge, 1955—; gen. counsel Tenn. Credit Union League, Chattanooga, 1956—; spl. counsel, atty. gen. Tenn. Depts. Ins., Banking and Hwys., 1968-71; sec.-treas., dir. McLaughlin Devel. Co., Chattanooga, 1959—; sec., dir. Southland Fabrics, Inc., Chattanooga, 1959—; sec. Pepsi Cola Bottling Co. Chattanooga; sec. TCUL Service Corp., 1970—; mayor of Chattanooga, 1971—. Exec. bd. Hamilton County Law Enforcement Commn., 1962-67; vice chmn. adv. bd. U. Tenn. Govt.-Industry-Law Center, 1965-66; bd. advisers on criminal justice act U.S. 6th Jud. Circuit, 1965-66; mem. Tenn. Law Revision Commn., 1970-71, Tenn. Law Enforcement Planning Commn., 1971—, Tenn. Manpower Council, 1973—; chmn. Tenn. Local Govt. Study Commn., 1973—; vice chmn. human resources com. Nat. League Cities, 1973—. Exec. bd. Cherokee Area council Boy Scouts Am., 1958—, commr., 1959-60, mem.-at-large nat. council, 1966—, v.p., 1967-69, recipient Silver Beaver, 1966, v.p., 1966-69; exec. bd. Chattanooga Area Heart Assn., 1966—; vice chmn. Bible in Pub. Schs., 1969-71; bd. dirs. Chattanooga Urban Coalition, 1968-71; adv. com. Chattanooga-Hamilton County Health Dept., 1969-71; pres. McCallie Sch. Patrons Assn., 1967-68. Trustee Shepherd Hills Pool Inc.; bd. dirs. Tenn. Municipal League, v.p. 1972—; Allied Arts Council, Chattanooga-Hamilton County Regional Planning Commn., Met. Council for Community Services; bd. dirs. Chattanooga Area Regional Council Govts., pres. 1971-74; bd. dirs., treas. Human Services Inst. for Children and Families, 1974—. Served with USNR, 1943-46; to lt., 1951-52; Korea. Recipient citizenship award Chattanooga Realtors, 1966; George Washington Honor Medals Freedoms Found., 1966, 67, 68, Prin. award, 1969; Service to Mankind award Sertoma Internat., 1969; Outstanding Salesman at Large award Chattanooga Sales and Marketing Execs., 1969; Citizen of Year Chattanooga Edn. Assn., 1970. Fellow Am. Bar Found.; mem. Tenn. (v.p. 1963-64, pres.-elect, 1964-65, pres. 1965-66, bd. govs. 1966-67), Chattanooga (pres. 1962-63, gov. 1959-64) bar assns., Chattanooga C. of C. (bd. dirs. 1969—), Nat. Conf. Bar Presidents, Estate Planning Council Chattanooga (exec. bd. 1960-62), Tenn. Def. Lawyers Assn., U.S. Jud. Conf. Sixth Circuit (life mem.), Order of the Coif, Sigma Nu Phi. Baptist (deacon, dir. Home Mission Bd. So. Bapt. Conv. 1969-74). Optimist (past pres. and past lt. gov. dist. 11, Man of Year, 1956). Club: Mountain City. Home: 3019 Brownwood Dr Chattanooga TN 37404 Office: Municipal Bldg Chattanooga TN 37402

WALKER, RONNIE DERRAL, hosp. adminstr.; b. Sayre, Okla., Nov. 10, 1943; s. Henry Charles and Seaneth Myrtle (Leddy) W.; B.S. in Accounting, Southwestern State Coll. 1966; m. Glenda Carol Moore, Mar. 7, 1970; children—Dana Gayle, Robert Kevin, Ron Henry. Asst. mgr. Spot Restaurant, Weatherford, Okla., 1966; asst. adminstr. Southwestern Meml. Hosp., Weatherford, 1966-68, adminstr. Weatherford Hosp. Authority, 1968—. Mem. Custer County Profl. Adv. Bd., 1970—; mem. Western Okla. Tb and Respiratory Disease Bd., 1971—; mem. Southwestern State Coll. Nursing Program Planning Com., 1969—. Mem. Weatherford Rescue Squad, 1967; dir. Civil Def., 1970—. Named Outstanding Sr. Man, Phi Beta Lambda, 1966. Mem. Am. Coll. Hosp. Adminstrs., U.S., Weatherford chambers commerce, Okla. Hosp. Assn. (dir.), Okla. Pub. Relations Soc. (instl. mem.). Kiwanian (dir. Weatherford). Home: 1214 Lark St Weatherford OK 73096 Office: 215 N Kansas Weatherford OK 73096

WALKER, SCOTT BARTON, III, broadcasting exec.; b. Knoxville, Tenn., July 15, 1944; s. Scott Barton and Virginia (Faulkner) W.; B.A., Middle Tenn. State U., 1968;m. Lee Anne Severy, June 24, 1967. Dir. pub. relations State of Tenn., Nashville, 1968-69; dir. pub. relations Bill Walker & Assos., Nashville, 1970-72; v.p. radio sta. WAMB AM-FM, Nashville, 1972—; dir. Donelson Hermitage Bus. Assn. Office: 1617 Lebanon Rd Nashville TN 37210

WALKER, SIDNEY RAY, lawyer; b. Floydada, Tex., Oct. 4, 1942; s. William Grady and Ruth Estelle (Broyles) W.; student Abilene Christian Coll., 1961-62; B.B.A., Tex. Technol. U., 1965; LL.B., U. Tex., 1968; m. Deborah Joan Wheeler, Dec. 4, 1971. Admitted to Tex. bar, 1968; practiced in partner Wyrick, Rodehaver & Walker, Dallas, 1969—. Vice-pres. S.E. br. Am. Cancer Soc., 1973. Served with AUS, 1968; now lt. Naval Res. Mem. Am., Tex., Dallas Jr. bar assns., Kappa Sigma. Rotarian. Club: Dervish Social (Dallas). Home: 707 Bondstone St Dallas TX 75218 Office: 555 Griffin Sq Dallas TX 75202

WALKER, THURMOND OTTO, physician; b. Winnsboro, S.C., Dec. 9, 1932; s. Tally Otto and Vera (Canady) W.; B.S., U. S.C., 1954; M.D., Med. U. S.C., 1958; children—Thurmond Otto, Leslie. Intern, Columbia Hosp. of Richland County, S.C., 1958-59; staff physician S.C. State Hosp., Columbia, 1959-60; practice medicine, specializing in family practice, Columbia, 1960—; mem. staffs Columbia Hosp., Bapt. Hosp., Lexington County Hosp., Medicenter Hosp., Forest Hills Hosp.; vol. team physician Irmo High Sch., Columbia, 1961-62, 66-68; team physician Stop Polio Oral Vaccine campaign, 1963-64; participating physician Blue Cross-Blue Shield, 1963; dir. Dutch Fork Investment Corp., Columbia. Fellow Am. Geriatrics Soc., Royal Soc. Health; mem. Am. Acad. Family Practice, Am., S.C. med. assns., Columbia Med. Soc., Assn. Family Practitioners of Central S.C., Heart Assn., Phi Rho Sigma. Democrat. Lutheran. Elk, Lion. Club: University of South Carolina Roundhouse. Home: 262 Sandhurst Rd Columbia SC 29210 Office: 1204 Greenville Circle Columbia SC 29210

WALKER, VERNON DELOSS, advt. and pub. relations co. exec.; b. Okean, Ark., Aug. 14, 1931; s. Lonnie G. and Dora G. (Rickey) W.; student So. Baptist Coll., 1952-56; m. Alberta M. Manning, Oct. 31, 1955; children—Curtis Blake, Carla Alane. Announcer, KPOC, Pocahantas, Ark., 1951-52, KRLW, Walnut Ridge, Ark., 1954-55; sales mgr. KNEA, Jonesboro, Ark., 1956-58, gen. mgr., 1960-65; sales mgr. WMC, Memphis, 1958-60; pres. Walker & Asso., Memphis, 1965—; dir. WHAM, Inc. Pres. Sheltered Workshop for Mentally and Physically Handicapped, Jonesboro, 1962-64. Mgr. various polit. campaigns. Bd. dirs. Memphis Heart Assn., 1971-73, Goodwill Industries, Memphis, 1972-73; trustee Pink Palace Mus., Memphis, 1973. Served with AUS, 1952-54. Decorated Bronze Star. Named Man of Year, Jonesboro Jaycees, 1963, West Memphis Jaycees, 1967. Mem. Am. Marketing Assn., Memphis Advt. Fedn. (dir. 1973—), Sales and Marketing Execs. of Memphis. Home: 905 S Roselawn St West Memphis TN 72301 Office: 2605 Nonconnah Blvd Suite 105 Memphis TN 38132

WALKER, WILLIAM MAY, circuit judge; b. Crawfordville, Fla., May 2, 1905; s. Nat R. and Alice (Tully) W.; J.D., Samford U., 1927; m. Pansy Mavis Crosby, Feb. 22, 1937; children—William May, Joseph Stanley. Admitted to Fla. bar, 1927; practiced in Tallahassee, 1927-40; judge Leon County Ct., 1933-40, 2d Jud. Circuit Ct., Tallahassee, 1940—. Mem. examining bd. Fla. Parole Commn., 1960. Mem. Fla. Bar, Am., 2d Jud. Circuit, Tallahassee, Gadsden County (hon.) bar assns., Am. Judicature Soc., Nat. Conf. State Trial Judges, Fla. Circuit Judges Conf. (past pres.), Tallahassee C. of C. (past dir.), Woodmen of World, Phi Alpha Delta. Democrat. Baptist (deacon). Mason (32 deg., Shriner), Lion (past Tallahassee pres., past Fla. dep. dist. gov.). Club: Nat. Seminole. Home: 2117 Jenette St Tallahassee FL 32303 Office: County Courthouse Tallahassee FL 32301

WALKER, WILLIAM RALPH, supt. schs.; b. Ruth, Miss., Feb. 1, 1926; s. Rufus Royd and Leedie Ella (Stewart) W.; B.A., Presbyn. Coll., 1949; M.Ed., U. Tenn., 1953; m. Bertha Rella Prewitt, June 24, 1949; 1 dau. Janella Kaye. Tchr., coach Bradley Central High Sch., 1949-69; supt. schs. Bradley County Schs., Cleveland, Tenn., 1969—. Served with USCGR, 1943-45. Home: 2605 N Henderson St Cleveland TN 37311 Office: PO Box 399 Cleveland TN 37311

WALKINGSTICK, BENJAMIN THACKER, JR., banker; b. Tahlequah, Okla., Oct. 29, 1930; s. Benjamin Taylor and Theone Leah (Grove) W.; B.B.A., U. Okla., 1952; m. Jerry Marshall, June 10, 1952; children—Judith Ann, Jeffrey T., Janet Lee. Gen. ins. agt., Tulsa, Okla., 1954-63; pres. Union Nat. Bank of Chandler, Okla., 1963—; dir. Kin-Ark Corp., Tulsa. Bd. dirs. Lincoln County Indsl. Devel. Authority, Deep Fork Watershed Assn. Served with USAF, 1952-54. Mem. Chandler C. of C. (pres. 1965-66), Lion (pres. 1970-71). Home: 242 Marshall Dr Chandler OK 74834 Office: 1001 Manvel St Chandler OK 74834

WALKINGSTICK, HOWARD CHANDLER, social worker; b. Tahlequah, Okla., Jan. 7, 1915; s. Simon R. and Rebecca (Chandler) W.; B.A., George Washington U., 1946; M.S.W., U. Denver, 1949; postgrad. U. Chgo., 1955. With Bur. Indian Affairs, 1935-70, dir. social work Western Okla., Kan. and Tex., 1952-70; asst. supr. group work cons., coordinator, specialist in a service tng. Bur. Children's Services, Dept. Instns., Social and Rehab. Services, Okla. Social Service System, Oklahoma City, 1970-72, supr. div. pub. assistance, 1972—; asst. prof. U. Okla., 1963. Mem. Okla. Registration Bd. Social Workers, 1965-71; bd. dirs. Okla. Health and Welfare Assn., 1964—; Mental Health Assn., 1961—; Okla. del. to White House Conf. Children and Youth, 1960, 70. Staff tchr. 4th Army Hdqrs., Ft. Sam Houston, Tex. Mem. Okla.'s Com. on Handicapped, 1959—, Com. on Ethnic Minority Groups, Council on Social Work Edn. Served as staff sgt., AUS, 1943-46. Recipient Distinguished Service award Dept. of Interior, 1967. Mem. Am. Soc. Pub. Adminstrn., Nat. Assn. Social Workers, Okla. Health and Welfare Assn. (pres. 1967-68, recipient Distinguished Service award 1967), Tau Kappa Epsilon. Methodist. Mason (32 deg.), Kiwanian. Home: 122 Moore Country Club Dr Holdenville OK 74848 Office: Dept Insts Social and Rehabilitative Services Oklahoma City OK

WALL, ARTHUR EDWARD PATRICK, editor; b. Jamestown, N.Y., Mar. 12, 1925; s. George Herbert and Doris (Olmstead) W.; student pub. schs., Jamestown; m. Marcella Joan Petrine, Nov. 5, 1954; children—John Wright, Marie Ann, David Arthur Edward. Copy editor Worcester (Mass.) Telegram, 1958; Sunday editor Hawaii Island Corr., Honolulu Star-Bull., 1958-59; editor Hilo (Hawaii) Tribune-Herald, 1960-63; Sunday editor Honolulu Advertiser, 1963-65, mng. editor, 1971-72; mng. editor Catholic Rev., Balt., 1965-66, editor, 1966-71; dir. Bur. Information, Archdiocese of Balt., 1965-66; dir., editor-in-chief Nat. Catholic News Service, Washington, 1972—; editor-in-chief Origins and Catholic Trends, 1972—. Chmn., Hawaii Gov.'s Com. on Ednl. TV, 1964-65. Bd. regents Chaminade Coll. of Honolulu, 1959-65, chmn., 1963-65. Named Hilo Young Man of Year, Jaycees, 1960, Father of Year, Honolulu C. of C., 1964. Mem. Internat. Fedn. Catholic Press Agys. (v.p. 1972—), Internat. Catholic Union of Press (council 1972—), Sigma Delta Chi. (past chpt. pres.). Roman Catholic. Club: Nat. Press (Washington). Author: The Big Wave, 1960. Contbr. articles to mags. Home: 10200 Battleridge Pl Gaithersburg MD 20760 Office: 1312 Massachusetts Av NW Washington DC 20005

WALL, BENNETT HARRISON, educator; b. Raleigh, N.C., Dec. 7, 1914; s. Bennett Louis and Evie David (Harrison) W.; A.B., Wake Forest Coll., 1933; M.A., U. N.C., 1941, Ph.D., 1946; m. Neva Olive White, Sept. 7, 1968; children—Maie (Mrs. John E. Clark), Diana (Mrs. John Freckman), Ann Bennett. Instr., N.C. State U., 1942-43; instr. U. N.C., 1943-44; instr. U. Ky., 1944-46, asst. prof., 1946-52, asso. prof., 1952-64; prof. history dept. Tulane U., New Orleans, 1968—, head dept., 1968-73, dir. Tulane Center Bus. History Studies, 1974—. Mem. Am. Hist. Assn., Orgn. Am. Historians, Agrl. History Soc., La. Hist. Assn. (pres. 1974-75), So. Hist. Assn. (sec.-treas. 1953), Omicron Delta Kappa. Co-author: Teagle of Jersey Standard, 1974. Contbr. numerous articles to profl. jours. Home: 6320 S Claiborne New Orleans LA 70125

WALL, BILLY JOE, indsl. engr.; b. Puryear, Tenn., Nov. 26, 1929; s. Alvis Milton and Daisy Lavelle (Gallimore) W.; B.S., U. Tenn., 1956; postgrad. YMCA Law Sch., 1965-66; M.S., U. Tenn., 1973; m. Shirley Redden, July 22, 1961; children—William Jeffrey, Emily Jo.

Project engr. Holley Carburetor Co., Paris, Tenn., 1957-62; indsl. engr. Internat. Tel. & Tel. Corp., Milan, Tenn., 1962-64; mgr. mfg. engring. Scovill Mfg. Co., Dickson, Tenn., 1964—. Tchr., U. Tenn. Extension, 1965-66, Tenn. State Vocational Sch., 1968-69. Served with USAF, 1948-52. Registered profl. engr., Cal., Tenn. Mem. Am. Inst. Indsl. Engrs., Nat. Mgmt. Assn., Dickson County C. of C., U. Tenn. Alumni Assn., Alpha Pi Mu. Baptist. Mason (K.T.). Home: 409 Belwood Dr Dickson TN 37055 Office: Schrader Rd Dickson TN 37055

WALL, FURMAN GRESHAM, JR., investment co. exec.; b. Richmond, Va., Sept. 23, 1944; s. Furman Gresham and Jane Winfield (Pearce) W.; B.B.A., U. Ga., 1966; M.B.A., U. Va., 1968; certificate N.Y. Inst. Finance, 1969; m. Mary Curtis McGregor, June 9, 1965; children—Furman Gresham III, Anne Winfield, Robert Scott. Vice pres. Investment Corp. Va., Norfolk, 1971—; dir. Wedgewood Carpet Co., Richmond, 1971-72. Bd. dirs. Alanton Civic League, 1972-74; trustee, pres. parents group Cape Henry Sch., 1973-74. Mem. Richmond Soc. Financial Analysts, Chi Phi. Republican. Episcopalian. Home: 1405 Cooper Circle Virginia Beach VA 23454 Office: 5 Main Plaza East Norfolk VA 23510

WALL, HENRY BELMA III, traffic engr.; b. Sayre, Okla., Aug. 24, 1943; s. Henry Belma and Anna Mary Louise (Barnard) W.; B.C.E., Ga. Inst. Tech., 1965; certificate Hwy. Traffic Yale Bur. Hwy. Traffic, 1966; m. Marie Ellen Perry, May 29, 1964; children—Laura Lynne, Alex Henry. Regional traffic engr. Tenn. Dept. Hwys., Knoxville, Tenn., 1966-70, asst. state traffic engr., 1970-72; research sect. head Sperry Systems Mgmt., New Orleans, 1972—. Mem. Inst. Traffic Engrs., Chi Epsilon, Sigma Chi. Home: 60 Lisa Av Kenner LA 70062 Office: 1000 Howard Av New Orleans LA 70113

WALL, JAMES EDGAR, JR., wholesale co. dir.; b. Plano, Tex., Dec. 8, 1905; s. James Edgar and Florrie Belle (Bowman) W.; student Emory U., 1923-25; m. Georgia Perry Rudolph, July 20, 1940; children—Erskine Rudolph (Mrs. Frank Anthony James), James Edgar III, John Dixon. With Knight & Wall Co. wholesale hardware, Tampa, Fla., 1946—, pres., 1945-56, chmn. bd., 1956—. Pres., Gulf Ridge council Boy Scouts Am. 1958; chmn. Nat. Found., 1955-61, Mental Health Assn., 1958-62; chmn. H.B. Plant Tampa Municipal Mus., 1953-72, hon. chmn., 1972—. Recipient Pres.'s award beautification com. Greater Tampa C. of C., 1958. Mem. Tampa Hist. Assn. (dir.), Tampa Hist. Soc. (bd.). Methodist. Clubs: Merrymakers (past pres.), Tampa Yacht and Country. Home: 2405 Sunset Dr Tampa FL 33609 Office: 8504 E Adamo Dr Tampa FL 33622

WALL, MARY K(ATE), lawyer; b. Bertram, Tex., Aug. 7, 1912; d. James Francis and Rosalthe (Lawhon) Parker; B.A., U. Tex., 1932, LL.B., 1934; m. Hubert S. Wall, Oct. 18, 1947. Admitted to Tex. bar, 1934; sec. State Tax Bd., 1935-36, Tex. Employment Commn., 1936-37; statistician Tex. Dept. Pub. Safety, 1937-42; briefing atty. Supreme Ct. of Tex., 1942-50; asst. atty gen. Tex., 1950-62; research asso. Tex. Legislative Council, 1962-63; asst. atty. gen. State Tex., 1963-67; dir. elections div. Sec. of State's Office, 1967-70, Legislative Council, 1970—. Mem. Order of Coif, Phi Beta Kappa. Home: 2903 Breeze Terrace Austin TX 78722 Office: care Tex Legislative Council Capitol Station Austin TX 78711

WALL, WENDELL EDGAR, biologist, educator; b. Dover, Fla., Mar. 16, 1938; s. Reid and Cora Lee (Rouse) W.; B.A., U. So. Fla., 1964; M.S., N.C. State U., 1967, Ph.D., 1970; m. Judith Ann Yates, Sept. 5, 1963; children—Julie Lynn, Jason Wendell, Shannon Marie. NIH genetics trainee, 1967; asst. prof. biology Birmingham (Ala.) So. Coll., 1969—. Mem. Bot. Soc. Am., Assn. Southeastern Biologists, A.A.A.S., Am. Inst. Biol. Scis. Home: 1209 Greensboro Rd Birmingham AL 35208

WALL, WILLIAM HENRY, JR., dentist; b. Albany, Ga., Mar. 17, 1937; s. William Henry and Hallie Rebecca (Walker) W.; B.S., U. Ga., 1959; D.D.S., Emory U., 1963, postgrad. 1966-67; m. Barbara Kay Thompson, June 22, 1963; children—William Henry III, Patricia Camille, Stephen Braxton, Kimberly Paige. Intern oral surgery Jackson Meml. Hosp., Miami, Fla., 1965-66; resident oral surgery Duval Med. Center, Jacksonville, Fla., 1967-68; pvt. practice dentistry, specializing in oral surgery, Decatur, Ga., 1968—. Asso. clin. instr. oral surgery Emory U. Sch. Dentistry, 1968—. Served with USAF, 1963-65. Diplomate Am. Bd. Oral Surgery. Mem. Am., Ga., Southeastern socs. oral surgeons, Am. Dental Assn., No. Dist., 5th Dist. dental socs., Chi Phi, Psi Omega. Rotarian. Club: Druid Hills Golf (Decatur). Inventor Wall universal fracture splint used in treating fractured jaws. Home: 3797 Briargreen Ct Atlanta GA 30340 Office: 1275 McConnell Dr Decatur GA 30033

WALLACE, ARCHIBALD, III, lawyer; b. New Orleans, Nov. 6, 1938; s. Archibald and Mildred Loureen (Hardesty) W.; B.A., Furman U., 1960; LL.B., U. Richmond, 1966; m. Eugenia B. Bean, June 16, 1962; children—Archibald IV, John William Hardesty, Mary Caroline. Pub. assistance caseworker Greenville County Dept. Pub. Welfare, Greenville, S.C., 1960-61; caseworker, geriatric placement coordinator City of Richmond (Va.) Dept. Pub. Welfare, 1963; admitted to bar, 1966; partner firm Sands, Anderson, Marks & Clarke, Richmond, 1966—. Tchr., Henrico County, Va., 1969—; owner, founder Old Richmond Co., 1971—, Janma, Inc., 1971. Served with AUS, 1961-63. Mem. McNeill Law Soc., Scabbard and Blade, Kappa Alpha, Phi Delta Phi. Presbyn. (deacon 1968-70, elder 1971—). Kiwanian. Home: 6908 Edmonstone Av Richmond VA 23229 Office: Fidelity Bldg Richmond VA 23219

WALLACE, BENNY RAYMOND, city ofcl.; b. Temple, Tex., May 29, 1945; s. Raymond Ferguson and Bettye Zue (Bourland) W.; B.B.A., N. Tex. State U., 1969; m. Marcia Gail Storm, Aug. 23, 1968; 1 dau., Natalie. City mgr. City of Gatesville, Tex., 1969-71, City of Groves, Tex., 1971—. Mem. Municipal Finance Officers Assn., Internat. Tex. city mgmt. assns. Rotarian. Home: 3122 Woodlawn St Groves TX 77619 Office: PO Box 846 Groves TX 77619

WALLACE, CAMILLE SHIELD (MRS. KARL E. WALLACE), club woman; b. Santa Anna, Tex., Nov. 14, 1897; d. Lee Lafayette and Carrie (Hubert) Shield; grad. Nat. Park Coll., 1918; m. Karl Edward Wallace, Sept. 18, 1918; children—Beryl Camille (Mrs. Jack Golden Wilkinson), Karl Edward, Bruce Elgean, Mary Carolyn (Mrs. Frank Randolph Bass, Jr.), Wayne Earl, Mildred Nichols (Mrs. William Shirley Dameron). Pres., Music Study Club, Santa Anna, 1919-20; mem. bridge clubs, Coleman, Tex., 1926-36, Knife and Fork Club, Eumathian Study Club Burleson, Finesse Bridge Club, Ft. Worth, corr. sec., mem. Woman's Club; corr. sec., mem. Ft. Worth Women's Wednesday Club, Ft. Worth, 1965-67, pres., 1969-70; mem. Ft. Worth Lecture Found., Huguenot Soc. Tex. (state treas.), U.D.C. (v.p. Adm. Raphael Semmes chpt.), D.A.R. (sec., regent Coleman, chaplain, treas., parliamentarian, regent Ft. Worth, chmn. Tex. Student Loan and Scholarship Com., 1958-59, asso. mem. Mt. Vernon chpt., also Our Flag chpt., Washington, chmn. Tex. Soc., 1965—, platform com. 1966-70; vice chmn. organizing new chpts. Tex. 1967—); pres., rec. sec. Women of Ch., 1949-51, corr. sec. Tex. A. and M. Coll. Mother's Club, Ft. Worth, 1938-39; mem. Lily B. Clayton Grammar Sch. Mother's Singer Group, 1937-39; pres. P.T.A., Coleman, 1930-32; organist 1st Christian Ch., Santa Anna, 1913-16; Sunday sch. tchr. 1st Presbyn. Ch., Coleman, 1925-36, pres., rec. sec. Women of Ch., 1925-26; tchr. Sunday sch. classes St. Stephen Presbyn. Ch., Ft. Worth, 1937-59, pres., rec. sec. Women of Ch., 1959-61, corr. sec., 1965—, moderator Bible study; pres. United Ch. Woman Ft. Worth, 1950-53; chmn. scholarship com. Mid-Tex. Presbytery, 1956-57; gray lady Peter Smith Hosp., Ft. Worth, 1957-59. Mem. Tex. Soc. of Huguenot Soc. of the Founders of Manakin in Colony of Va. (rec. sec.), Internat. Platform Assn. Democrat. Home: Route 3 Box 111 Edgecliff Fort Worth TX 76134

WALLACE, CARL LEIGHTON, chem. co. exec.; b. Beverly, Mass., May 15, 1911; s. Russell B. and Effie (Leighton) W.; grad. Bentley Coll., 1930; m. Dorothy Fleser, Nov. 29, 1946; children—Victoria E., Victor C. Prodn. mgr., Norge div. Borg Warner Corp., Muskegon, Mich., 1947-50; mgr. Ford Motor Co., Dearborn and Mt. Clemens, Mich., 1951-61; mgmt. cons. EBS Mgmt. Consultants, N.Y.C., 1962-68; So. sales mgr. Escambia Chem. Corp., Pensacola, Fla., 1968—. Adv. bd. Am. Security Council. Mem. Indsl. Mgmt. Soc., Pensacola Indsl. Mgmt. Assn., Am. Soc. Testing and Materials, Bentley Alumni Assn. (past nat. treas.). Author: Factory, 1948-63. Club: Ford Alumni (a founder). Home: 611 Poinciana Dr Gulf Breeze FL 32561 Office: Pace FL 32502

WALLACE, DON, JR., educator; b. Vienna, Austria, Apr. 23, 1932 (parents Am. citizens); s. Don and Julie (Baer) W.; B.A., Yale, 1953; LL.B., Harvard, 1957; m. Daphne Mary Wickham, May 14, 1963; children—Alexandra Jane, Sarah Anne, Benjamin James. Admitted N.Y. bar, 1957; asso. firm Paul, Weiss, Rifkind, Wharton & Garrison, N.Y.C., 1957-58, 60-62, firm Fleischmann, Jaeckle, Stokes & Hitchcock, N.Y.C., 1959-60; regional legal adviser Middle East dept. AID, State Dept., Washington, 1963-65, dept. asst. gen. counsel, 1965-66; asso. prof. law Georgetown U. Law Center, Washington, 1966-71, prof., 1971—, dir, Inst. Internat., Fgn. Trade Law, 1969—, faculty editor Jour. Law and Policy in Internat. Bus., 1968—; Mem. adv. bd. Jour. Maritime Law and Commerce, 1971—; vis. sr. fellow St. Antony's Coll., Oxford (Eng.) U., 1973—. Mem. hdqrs. campaign staff Adlai Stevenson for Pres., Chgo., 1956; mem. presdl. campaign staff Robert F. Kennedy, 1968; coordinator Anne Arundel County Democratic Nat. Com., 1972; mem. Ward 3 Dem. Com., Washington, 1972—. Sec. bd. dirs. Chesapeake Found., Washington. Fulbright fellow, Turkey, 1967. Mem. Nat. Lawyers Club, Am. Bar Assn. (vice chmn. internat. law sect.), Internat. Law Assn., Am. Soc. Internat. Law. Editor: (with Tugrul Ansay) Introduction to Turkish Law, 1966; International Control of Investment, 1973. Contbr. articles to profl. jours. Home: 2800 35th St NW Washington DC 20007 Office: 600 New Jersey Av NW Washington DC 20001

WALLACE, FRANCES MARIAN (MRS. DEANE D. WALLACE), savs. and loan assn. exec.; b. Lovelock, Nev., Oct. 10, 1917; d. John R. and Estelle (Sullivan) Russell; student Wash. State U., 1935-37; m. Deane D. Wallace, Nov. 29, 1945; children—Michael, Scott, Catherine, Deane Thomas, Susan. Pvt. sec. to pres. Western Gear Works, 1937-44; founder Capital Savs. & Loan Assn., Little Rock, 1962, sec., dir., 1962—. Chmn. Ark. State Savs. and Loan Bd., 1962; gen. mgr., ins. and tax adminstr., trustee profit sharing plan Obstetrics and Gynecology, Profl. Assn. Inc. Vice chmn. program com. of bd. govs. Am. Nat. Red Cross, 1966—; active United Fund, 1966—, co-campaign chmn., 1965. Trustee Ark. Art Center, St. Joseph's Orphanage, North Hills Exceptional Children's Sch., United Community Funds and Councils Am. Named Woman of Year, Ark. Democrat newspaper, Little Rock, 1965; hon. mem. City of San Diego, 1965, City of Oklahoma City, 1966. Home: 6 Edgehill Rd Little Rock AR 72207 Office: 500 S University Little Rock AR 72207

WALLACE, GEORGE CORLEY, gov. Ala.; b. Clio, Ala., Aug. 25, 1919; s. George C. and Mozell (Smith) W.; LL.B., U. Ala., 1942; m. Lurleen Burns, May 23, 1943 (dec. 1968); children—Bobbie Joe, Peggy Sue, George Corley, Janie Lee; m. 2d, Cornelia Ellis Snively, Jan. 4, 1971; stepchildren—Jim, Josh. Admitted to Ala. bar, 1942; asst. atty. gen. Ala., 1946-47; mem. Ala. Legislature from Barbour County, 1947-53; judge 3d Jud. Dist. Ala., 1953-58; pvt. practice, Clayton, Ala., 1958-62; gov. of Ala., 1963-66, 71—. Sponsor Wallace Act for state trade schs., 1947. Candidate Pres. U.S. Am. Ind. party, 1968. Bd. dirs. Ala. Tb Assn. Served with USAAF, 1942-45; PTO. Mem. Am. Legion, V.F.W., D.A.V. Democrat. Methodist (past Sunday sch. tchr. and supt.). Mason (Shriner), Moose, Elk; mem. Order Eastern Star, Modern Woodmen of World. Club: Civitan. Home: 1142 S Perry St Montgomery AL 36104

WALLACE, GEORGE FOSTER, cottonseed mfg. co. exec.; b. Monroe, La., Feb. 9, 1914; s. Charles William and Mable (Foster) W.; student La. State U., 1932-33, La. Poly. Inst., 1933-34, U. Colo., 1934-35; m. Helen Bonnell, June 3, 1935; children—James F., Steven B. Sec.-treas. Union Oil Mill, Inc., West Monroe, La., 1955-67, v.p., gen. mgr., 1967—. Mem. Nat. Cottonseed Products Assn. (pres. 1970-71). Mississippi Valley Oilseed Processors Assn. (pres. 1969-70). Club: Bayou Desiard Country (Monroe). Home: 1606 Island Dr Monroe LA 71201 Office: 520 Trenton St West Monroe LA 71291

WALLACE, GLADYS BALDWIN, librarian; b. Macon, Ga., June 5, 1923; d. Carter Shepherd and Dorothy (Richard) Baldwin; B.S. in Edn., Oglethorpe U., 1961; M.Librarianship, Emory U., 1966; postgrad. U. Ga., 1970-71; m. Hugh Loring Wallace, Jr., Oct. 14, 1941; (div. Sept. 1968); children—Dorothy (Mrs. Robert Nix Archer), Hugh Loring III. Librarian pub. elementary schs., Atlanta, 1956-66; head librarian Northside High Sch., Atlanta, 1966—. Ga. Dept. Edn. grantee, 1950; Nat. Def. Edn. Act grantee, 1963, 65. Mem. A.L.A.; Ga., Southeastern library assns., Atlanta Library Club. Home: 275 Collier Rd NW Apt 15 Atlanta GA 30309 Office: 2875 Northside Dr NW Atlanta GA 30305

WALLACE, JACK EUGENE, pharmacologist; b. Harrisburg, Ill., Jan. 5, 1934; s. Harry H. and Ruby V. (Burroughs) W.; B.S., So. Ill. U., 1955, M.A., 1957; Ph.D., Purdue U., 1961; m. Verla Ann Standerfer, Aug. 14, 1955; children—Michael Eugene, Kimberly Ann. Supervisory pharmacologist USAF, chief forensic toxicology USAF Sch. Aerospace Medicine, Brooks AFB, Tex., 1962-72; pharmacologist, clin. chemist Bexar County Hosp. Dist. and dept. pathology U. Tex. Med. Sch., San Antonio, 1972—, dir. biochem. pathology; dir. research and devel. S.W. Bio-clin. Labs., San Antonio, 1969-72; clin. prof. U. Tex. Med. Sch., San Antonio, 1967-72; asso. prof. Inst. Clin. Toxicology, Houston, 1973—. Cons. Santa Rosa Med. Center, San Antonio, 1968—, Audie Murphy VA Hosp., San Antonio, 1973—, U.S. Army Med. Lab., Ft. Sam Houston, Tex., 1973—. Served with USAF, 1962-64; lt. col. Res. Recipient Sci. Achievement award USAF, 1966. Fellow Am. Inst. Chemists, Am. Acad. Forensic Scis.; mem. Internat. Assn. Forensic Toxicologists, Am. Chem. Soc., Am. Assn. Clin. Chemists, Sigma Xi, Phi Lambda Upsilon. Contbr. numerous articles to profl. jours. Home: 5415 Keystone Dr San Antonio TX 78229 Office: Dept Pathology U Texas Med School San Antonio TX 78229

WALLACE, JAMES ASHFORD, psychiatrist, hosp. adminstr.; b. Memphis, Oct. 14, 1915; s. Walter Richard and Alice Gertrude (Ashford) W.; B.S., U. Va., 1937; M.D., U. Tenn., 1942; postgrad. U. Pa., 1952-53; m. Elizabeth Ann Belote, Nov. 10, 1948; children—James Ashford, Ann Ashford. Intern, Meth. Hosp., Memphis, 1942-43; resident psychiatry U. Ia., 1947-48, 58-59; practice medicine specializing in psychiatry, Memphis, 1946—; med. dir. Wallace Hosp., Memphis, 1949-61; sr. staff psychiatrist Tenn. Psychiat. Hosp., Memphis, 1962-63, supt., 1963—. Asso. prof. psychiatry U. Tenn., Memphis, 1962—. Served to capt. M.C., AUS, 1943-46. Recipient Silver Beaver award Boy Scouts Am., 1955. Diplomate Am. Bd. Psychiatry and Neurology. Fellow Am. Psychiat. Assn.; mem. So. Psychiat. Assn., Tenn. Med. Assn., Memphis Hosp. Assn. (pres. 1955—). Home: 207 E Cherry Circle Memphis TN 38117 Office: 865 Poplar Av Memphis TN 38105

WALLACE, JAMES OLDHAM, ednl. adminstr.; b. San Antonio, Sept. 22, 1917; s. James Vance and Violet Edyth (Oldham) W.; A.A., San Antonio Coll., 1936; B.A., St. Mary's U., 1938, M.A., 1940; B.S. in L.S., Our Lady of the Lake Coll., 1950; m. Lillie Ruth Franklin, July 23, 1948; children—Carolyn (Mrs. S.D. Denning), E. Frances, Thelma. Tchr., Natalia (Tex.) Independent Sch. Dist., 1940-41, Los Angeles Heights, San Antonio, 1941-42; clk. Kelly AFB, 1942-43; certifying officer Randolph AFB, 1943-49; tchr., librarian Lanier High Sch., San Antonio, 1949-50; asst. librarian San Antonio Coll., 1950-51, librarian, 1951-73, dir. learning resources, 1973—. Lectr., Our Lady of the Lake Coll., 1953-55; cons. Office of Edn., Baker & Taylor Co. Trustee, Baptist Meml. Hosp., San Antonio, 1965-67. Named Tex. librarian of year Tex. Library Assn., 1969; boss of year Mission City chpt. Am. Business Women's Assn., 1971. Mem. San Antonio Hist. Assn. (pres. 1970-71), Nat. Soc. Study Edn., Nat. Microfilm Assn., Assn. Ednl. Communications and Tech., Am. Assn. U. Profs., Am. (council 1967-71, constn. and bylaws com. 1970-72), Tex. (chmn. dist. 8, 1970), Southwestern (local arrangements com. 1962), Bexar (pres. 1951-52), library assns., Assn. Coll. and Research Libraries (exec. bd. 1960-63, 67-71, standards com. 1966-73, jr. coll. standards revision com. 1966-72), Am. Assn. Jr. Colls. (joint com. with A.L.A. 1966-70), Council Research and Acad. Libraries (pres. 1966-68, 74—), Collector's Inst., Am. Soc. Eighteenth Century Studies, Tex. Assn. Ednl. Tech., Tex. Jr. Coll. Tchrs. Assn., Librarians in Service to San Antonio. Author: In the Shadow of His Hand, 1961. Home: PO Box 13041 San Antonio TX 78213 Office: 1001 Howard St San Antonio TX 78284

WALLACE, MARVIN JOE, civil engr.; b. Wesson, Miss., Sept. 6, 1926; s. Noah Stephen and Lona Delia (Stewart) W.; B.S. in Civil Engring., U. Ala., 1948; postgrad. Ga. Inst. Tech., 1963-64; m. Sue Harkey, July 3, 1949; children—James Marvin, Katherine Sue. Engr., Phillips Petroleum Co., 1948-69; supr. project control Phillips Fibers Corp., Greenville, S.C., 1969-74, mgr. corporate purchasing, 1974—. Served with AUS, 1944-46. Mem. Am. Soc. C.E., Nat. Assn. Purchasing Mgrs., Theta Tau. Methodist (mem. bd. stewards 1970—). Home: 400 Pimlico Rd Greenville SC 29607 Office: PO Box 66 Greenville SC 29602

WALLACE, MILTON JAY, lawyer; b. Passaic, N.J., Dec. 17, 1935; s. Mark and Regina (Tenny) W.; B.B.A. cum laude, U. Miami, 1956, LL.B., 1959; m. Patricia Radin, July 7, 1963; 1 son, Mark D. Pub. accountant Harry L. Davis, Miami, Fla., 1956-57; office mgr. Lee Constrn. Co., 1957-59; admitted to Fla. bar, 1959; practiced in Miami, 1959—; gen. counsel Fla. Securities Commn., Tallahassee, 1965-68; chmn. bd. Computer Controls Corp., 1968-70; chmn. bd. dirs. Nat. Properties, Inc., 1966—; dir., chmn. exec. com. Biscayne Bank, Miami, 1973—; dir. Consurgico Corp., Brickell Bank, Southeastern Surg. Supply Co., Tallahassee, Aid Auto Stores, Inc., N.Y.C. Judge, City of Miami, 1962-63; asst. atty. gen. State of Fla., 1965-70. Mem. adv. bd. Salvation Army; treas. Miami Philharmonic Soc., 1961-65, v.p., 1966-68, dir., 1961—. Guest lectr. N.Am. Securities Adminstrn., 1966. Served with AUS, 1954-55. Mem. Am., Fla., Dade County bar assns., Fla. Inst. C.P.A.'s C. of C. Clubs: Tiger Bay, Kings Bay Yacht and Country, Jockey, Bankers. Home: 10650 SW 65th Av Miami FL 33156 Office: 2138 Biscayne Blvd Miami FL 33137

WALLACE, RAYMOND BYRD, JR., paper co. exec.; b. Richmond, Va., Mar. 11, 1938; s. Raymond Byrd and Martha (Latane) W.; B.A., Hampden-Sydney Coll., 1960; m. Douglas Louise Laughon, June 5, 1964; children—Douglas Louise, Lee Bristow. With Cauthorne Paper Co., Inc., 1961—, sales rep., 1961-64, asst. v.p., 1964-67, v.p., 1967—. Mem. Richmond., Republican City Exec. Com., 1966-70. Bd. dirs. Richmond Area Inter Club Council, Team of Progress, Richmond Community Mental Health and Retardation Services Bd. Mem. Richmond Printing House Craftsmen. Clubs: Civitan of Richmond (pres. 1970-71, dir. 1966—), Richmond First (membership com. 1970). Home: 4214 Kingcrest Pkwy Richmond VA 23221 Office: PO Box 2059 Richmond VA 23216

WALLACE, ROBERT BARNES, lawyer; b. Paris, Tex., Oct. 11, 1921; s. William Henry and Gertrude Ethyl (Roberts) W.; B.B.A., So. Meth. U., 1943; LL.B., U. Tex., 1948; m. Beverley Bird, July 26, 1947; children—Robert Barnes, Benjamin Bird, John William. Admitted to Tex. bar, 1948; partner Neal, Rachal & Wallace, 1948-50; gen. tax counsel, trial counsel Office of Regional Counsel, U.S. Internal Revenue Service, 1952-57; pvt. practice law specializing fed. income tax matters, Corpus Christi, Tex., 1957—. Chmn. bd. Rineer Hydraulics, Inc. Past pres. Neighborhood Centers; past dist. dir. Little League Baseball. Served with USNR, 1943-46, 50-52. Mem. Am., Tex., Nueces County bar assns., Estate Planning Counsel (past pres.), South Tex. Broadcasting Counsel (exec. com.). Methodist. Club: Corpus Christi Country (past pres.). Home: 203 Jackson St Corpus Christi TX 78411 Office: Guaranty Bank Plaza Corpus Christi TX 78401

WALLACE, RODGER TERRY, physician; b. Cookeville, Tenn., Nov. 5, 1944; s. Oliver Ellis and Marion Ruth (Gernt) W.; B.A., U. South, 1966; M.D., U. Tenn., 1969; m. Barbara Belle Boyer, May 16, 1970. Intern, St. Joseph Hosp., Memphis, 1970—; family practice medicine, Ripley, Tenn., 1971—; chief staff Lauderdale County Hosp., 1972. Mem. Tenn. Med. Soc., Phi Chi, Phi Gamma Delta. Episcopalian. Home: 250 Anthony St Ripley TN 38063 Office: 209 Anthony St Ripley TN 38063

WALLACE, RUSSELL WILLIS, JR., physician; b. Columbia, S.C., Aug. 24, 1934; s. Russell Willis and Mamie (Bell) W.; B.A., Emory U., 1956, M.D., 1960; m. Letitia Crouch, July 6, 1957; children—Victoria, John Mark, Anne-Marie. Intern, Emory U.-Atlanta VA Hosp., 1960-61, med. resident, 1964-65; neurology resident Emory U., 1966-68, clin. instr. medicine, 1968—; pvt. practice medicine specializing in neurology, Decatur, Ga., 1968—; sec. med. staff DeKalb Gen. Hosp., 1972—. Served with USNR, 1961-64. Mem. DeKalb County Med. Soc., Med. Assn. Ga., A.M.A., Am. Acad. Neurology, Am. Bd. Psychiatry and Neurology. Episcopalian. Home: 1276 Balsam Dr Decatur GA 30033 Office: 755 Columbia Dr Decatur GA 30030

WALLACE, SARAH LESLIE, librarian; b. Kansas City Mo., Oct. 28, 1914; d. Leslie Linn and Mary Louise (Shortall) Wallace; A.B. Coll. St. Catherine, 1935, B.S. in L.S., 1936 With Mpls. Pub. Library, 1936-63, pub. relations officer, 1958-63; publs. officer Library of Congress, Washington, 1963—. Instr. Coll. St. Catherine, 1944-60. Recipient St. Joan of Arc award Jr. Catholic League Mpls., 1963, Horace Hart award Edn. Council of Graphic Arts Industry, 1969;

Alexandrine medal, 1972. Mem. A.L.A. (membership chmn. 1962-68), D.C. Library Assn., Franklin Tech. Soc., Am. Inst. Graphic Arts, Fed. Editors Assn., Delta Phi Lambda, Kappa Gamma Pi. Author: So You Want To Be a Librarian, 1963; Definition: Library, 1961. Author, illustrator: Promotion Ideas for Small Public Libraries, 1953; Patrons Are People, 1956. Editor Quarterly Jour. Library of Congress, 1964. Home: 8705 Jones Mill Rd Washington DC 20015 Office: 10 1st St SE Washington DC 20540

WALLACE, WEBB LINDSLEY, financial planner; b. Dallas, Dec. 18, 1940; s. James Edwin and Rose Margaret (Lindsley) W.; B.A., U. of South, 1963; M.B.A., Stanford, 1965; m. Carol Ann Donnohue, June 29, 1963; children—Michael Rhodes, Susan Lindsley. Partner, Bradley Investment Co., Dallas, 1965-70; spl. asst. to pres. Southland Life Ins. Co., Dallas, 1970-71; v.p. Southland Financial Corp., Dallas, 1971—. Mem. Stanford Bus. Sch. Assn., Salesmanship Club Dallas, Phi Beta Kappa, Phi Delta Theta. Presbyn. Home: 3520 Bryn Mawr St Dallas TX 75225 Office: Southland Center Dallas TX 75201

WALLEN, CHARLES MILTON, chem. products co. exec.; b. St. Paul, Sept. 16, 1928; s. Arvid Oscar and Marie Agnes (Groh) W.; B.S., U. Minn., 1951; M.B.A., Northwestern U., 1953; m. Mary Annela Stevens, Aug. 2, 1952; children—Charles, Steven, Gregory, Mary Ellen, Barry, John. Sales mgr. 3M Co., St. Paul, 1953-62; Sales mgr. Com Tech. Corp., Beverly Hills, Cal., 1962-66; sales mgr. West Chem. Products, Los Angeles, 1966-70, mgr. Dallas br., 1970—. Served with USNR, 1945-47. Mem. Tex. Assn. Mfrs. (exec. com.), Dallas C. of C. Roman Catholic. K.C. Home: 5815 Meadowcrest St Dallas TX 75230 Office: 5416 Maple St Dallas TX

WALLER, CHARLIE ERVIN, life ins. exec.; b. Shady Dale, Ga., May 2, 1908; s. Charlie George and Emma Irene (Cook) W.; student Ga. Ala. Bus. Coll., 1927; m. Doris L. Thomas, Sept. 18, 1932; children—Doris Annelle (Mrs. Samuel Spencer Swilling, Jr.), Leland Ervin. Cashier, Inter-Ocean Ins. Co., Jacksonville, Fla., 1927-36; pres. Profl. Ins. Corp., 1937-51; gen. agt. Am. Health Ins. Co., Atlanta, 1952—; pres. First Am. Corp., 1956—, Atlantic and Pacific Life Ins. Co., 1959—. Mason (32 1/2). Home: 2272 Street deVille NE Atlanta GA 30345 Office: 2260 N Druid Hills Rd NE Atlanta GA 30309

WALLER, SAMUEL CARPENTER, lawyer; b. Augusta, Ga., May 3, 1918; s. Harcourt E. and Josephine (Carpenter) W.; A.B., Princeton, 1940; LL.B., Harvard, 1948; m. Anna Bacon Maxwell, Apr. 18, 1952; children—Anna M., Laura G., Amelia C. Admitted to Ga. bar, 194^, since practiced in Augusta; mem. firm Cumming, Nixon & Eve, 1948-51; partner firm Cumming, Nixon, Yow, Waller & Capers, 1951—; city atty. City of Augusta, 1964-69. Dir. Ga. R.R. Bank & Trust Co. Mem. Nat. Conf. of Commrs. on uniform state laws, 1965-72. Pres., Augusta Library, 1956-58; mem., sec. Augusta Coll. Found., 1963—. Mem. Augusta City Council, 1950-56; Mem. Richmond County (Ga.) Democratic Exec. Com., 1962—, chmn., 1962-66. Served to capt. with AUS, 1941-45, now maj. Res. Decorated Bronze Star medal. Mem. State Bar Ga. (bd. govs. 1967—), Am., Augusta (pres. 1971-72) bar Assns., Harvard Law Sch. Assn. Ga. (pres. 1960-61). Episcopalian (sr. warden; registrar Diocese of Ga.). Kiwanian. Clubs: Augusta Country, Pinnacle. Home: 600 Gary St Augusta GA 30904 Office: Ga R R Bank Bldg Augusta GA 30902

WALLER, WILLIAM, gov. Miss; b. Oxford, Miss., Oct. 21, 1926; B.S., Memphis State U., 1948; LL.B. U. Miss., 1950. Admitted to Miss. bar, 1950, U.S. Dist Ct., 1951, U.S. Ct. Mil. Appeals, 1966, U.S. Supreme Ct.; mem. firm Waller & Fox, Jackson, Miss.; dist. atty. 7th Circuit Dist. Miss., 1960-68; gov. Miss., Jackson, 1971—. Mem. Am., Hinds County bar assns., Miss State Bar, Am. Judicature Soc., Am. Trial Lawyers Assn., Nat. Dist. Attys. Assn. Office: Office of the Governor Capitol Bldg Jackson MS 39201

WALLER, WILLIAM, JR., lawyer; b. Nashville, Sept. 18, 1925; s. William and Elizabeth Warner (Estes) W.; B.A., Vanderbilt U., 1947; LL.B., Yale, 1950; m. Margaret Lang Cheves, June 7, 1947 (dec. May 1967); children—Cheves, Courtney; m. 2d, Merrill Lewis McClintock, July 28, 1968. Admitted to Tenn. bar, 1950; since practiced in Nashville; asso. firm Waller Lansden Dortch & Davis, Nashville, 1950-56, partner, 1956—. Lectr. Vanderbilt U. Sch. Mgmt. Trustee Ensworth Sch. Served with USNR, 1944-46, 51-52. Mem. Am. Judicature Soc., Am., Tenn., Nashville, Memphis bar assns., Nashville Com. Fgn. Relations (sec. 1958-70). Clubs: Cumberland, Belle Meade Country, University (Nashville); Le Club (N.Y.C.); Summit (Memphis). Home: 710 Belle Meade Blvd Nashville TN 37205 Office: Am Trust Bldg Nashville TN 37201

WALLERSTEIN, LEIBERT BENET, economist; b. Bklyn., July 5, 1922; s. William Mack and Rachel Leah (Goldberg) W.; B.A., U. N.M., 1950; M.A., U. Minn., 1953; m. Alice Stehle, Mar. 26, 1968. Research asst. U. N.M., 1951; research asst., research fellow U. Minn., 1952-53; asst. employee relations U.S. Dept. Navy, Washington, 1954-55; economist, manpower specialist, editor U.S. Dept. Labor, Washington, 1955-67; economist U.S. Dept. Housing and Urban Devel., Washington, 1967-69, U.S. Dept. Transp., Washington, 1969—. Mem. faculty U. Md., 1966-67, Georgetown U., 1967-69; cons. Comm. on Correctional Manpower, 1967, System Devel. Corp., 1966. Served with AUS, 1946-47. Mem. Am. Econ. Assn., Am. Soc. Govt. Economists. Club: Nat. Economists. Home: 3505 Thornapple St Chevy Chase MD 20015 Office: care Dept Transp 400 7th St SW Washington DC 20541

WALLEY, W. W., physician; b. Richton, Miss., Aug. 2, 1916; s. Joe and Octavia Jane (Smith) W.; B.S., U. Miss., 1946; M.D., U. Pa., 1950; m. Eletha Green, June 7, 1943; children—Eletha Jane (Mrs. Danny Wayne Jenkins), Charlotte Ann, Joseph Claude, W. W., Jr. Intern, U. Ala. Med. Center, 1950-51; pvt. practice of gen. medicine, Waynesboro, Miss., 1951—; mem. staff Wayne Gen. Hosp., chief staff, 1970-71; chmn. bd. Wayne County Funeral Homes, Inc., 1971—. Dist. chmn. Boy Scouts of Am. Alderman, vice mayor City of Waynesboro, 1969—. Served to capt. M.C., AUS, 1941-46, ETO Named Alumnus of Year, Jones County Jr. Coll., 1967. Mem. Miss. State Med. Assn. (past v.p.) C. of C. Mason (Shriner), Rotarian (past pres.). Home: 606 South St Waynesboro MS 39367 Office: 804 Mississippi Dr Waynesboro MS 39367

WALLIN, GENE AMBROSE, physician; b. Stromsburg, Neb., Nov. 5, 1939; s. Eugene Everett and Josephine Louise (Retzlaff) W.; student Am. U., 1957; B.A. in Math., U. Va., 1961; M.D., U. Tenn., 1965; m. Candace Faith Fellows, Nov. 27, 1965; children—Gene Fred, Candace Irene, Kristel Michelle, Stephen Joseph. Intern, Oakland (Cal.) Naval Hosp., 1965-66; regtl. surgeon Camp Le Jeune, N.C., 1966-69; pvt. practice family medicine, Southport, N.C., 1969—; mem. staff J. Arthur Dosher Meml. Hosp., Southport. Sec. Southport Med. Clinic, 1972—. Served as lt. comdr. M.C., USNR, 1966-69. Diplomate Nat. Bd. Med. Examiners. Mem. N.C., Am. acads. family practice, N.C., Brunswick-Pender-New Hanover med. socs., A.M.A. (Physician's Recognition award 1972). Baptist (deacon 1971-73). Home: 409 E Bay St Southport NC 28461 Office: 1004 N Howe St Southport NC 28461

WALLING, ALBERT CLINTON II, clergyman; b. Ft. Lauderdale, Fla., Sept. 24, 1925; s. Jacob Biffle and Nora Maurine (Stone) W.; B.A., Trinity U., 1948; M.Div., Epis. Theol. Sem., 1953; postgrad. Harvard, 1961-63; postgrad. So. Meth. U., 1972; S.T.M., U. of South, Sewanee, Tenn., 1973; m. Carroll Langlois Wicher, Dec. 26, 1964; children—Maurine Carroll, Elizabeth Hancock. Ordained priest Episcopal Ch., 1954; vicar All Saints Ch., Pleasanton, Tex., 1953-54; asst. rector St. Davids Ch., Austin, Tex., 1954-60; vicar Holy Family Ch., prin. St. Saviours Sch., McKinney, Tex., 1960-61; vicar St. Nicholas Ch., Ft. Worth, 1961-64; asso. rector St. Johns Ch., Ft. Worth, 1964-66; rector Ch. of Good Shepherd, Terrell, Tex., 1966-71, Ch. of Ascension, Dallas, 1971-74; asso. rector St. Mark Ch., Houston, 1974—. Mem. ecumenical relations com. Diocese of Dallas, 1969-73; Episcopal chaplain Terrell State Hosp., 1966-71. Marker chmn. Dallas County Hist. Survey Com., 1971-73; pres. Austin Ministerial Alliance, 1957-58, Mental Health Assn. Austin-Travis County, 1958-59, Greater Ft. Worth Gen. Ministers Assn., 1963; bd. dirs. Austin Pre-Sch. Hearing Center, 1957-58; mem. Tex. Hist. Found., 1968—; trustee U. of South; founder, pres. gen., trustee San Jacinto Descendants; diocesan trustee Grace Hall, U. Tex., Austin, 1958-60, Clergy House, Episcopal Diocese Dallas. Hon. Ky. Col. Mem. Sons Republic Tex. (past historian gen., chaplain Dallas chpt., dist. rep. 1971-73), Jamestowne Soc. (life), Huguenot Soc. (Tex. chaplain 1972—), Ch. Hist. Soc., Nat. Soc. Ams. of Royal Descent (life). Democrat. Club: Harvard (Dallas). Contbr. to Internat. Clan Chisholm Soc. Jour., Inverness, Scotland. Home: 2911 University Blvd Houston TX 77005 Office: 3816 Bellaire Blvd Houston TX 77025

WALLING, BERT HEYWARD, JR., physician; b. Union, S.C., July 28, 1921; s. Bert Heyward and Sarah Ethel (Weber) W.; B.S., Coll. of Charleston, 1943; M.D., S.C. Med. Coll., 1945; m. Florence Audrey Hill, Jan. 1, 1943 (dec. 1961); children—Bert Heyward III, Randolph Richard; m. 2d, Sarah Ellen Jones, Nov. 28, 1963. Intern, Columbia (S.C.) Hosp., 1945-46; resident obstetrics and gynecology Columbia Hosp., 1948-50, Charlotte (N.C.) Meml. Hosp., 1950-51; pvt. practice ltd. to obstetrics and gynecology, Walla Walla, Wash., 1951-52, Johnson City, Tenn., 1952, Kingsville (Tex.) Clinic, 1952—; staff Kleberg County Hosp., Kingsville; courtesy staff Meml. Hosp., Corpus Christi, Tex., Brooks County Hosp., Falfurrias, Tex. Served to lt. (j.g.) M.C., USNR, 1946-48. Diplomate Am. Bd. Obstetrics and Gynecology. Fellow Am. Coll. Obstetrics and Gynecology; mem. A.M.A., So., Tex. med. assns., Tex. Assn. Obstetrics and Gynecology, Internat. Fertility Assn., Am. Fertility Soc., Nat. Rifle Assn., Phi Rho Sigma. Episcopalian. Mason. Home: 528 E Shelton Av Kingsville TX 78363 Office: 227 W Kleberg Av Kingsville TX 78363

WALLIS, CARLTON LAMAR, librarian; b. Blue Springs, Miss., Oct. 15, 1915; s. William R. and Tellie (Jones) W.; A.B., Miss. Coll., 1936; A.M., Tulane U., 1946; B.L.S., U. Chgo., 1947; m. Mary Elizabeth Cooper, Feb. 22, 1944; 1 son, Carlton Lamar. Tchr. pub. schs., Miss., 1936-41; instr. Tulane U., 1941-42; librarian Rosenberg Library, Galveston, Tex., 1947-55, Richmond (Va.) Pub. Library, 1955-58; dir. Memphis Pub. Library, 1958—. Bd. dirs. Memphis Project for Aging. Served with AUS, 1942-46. Mem. A.L.A., Tex. (pres. 1952-53), Southeastern (chmn. pub. libraries div. 1960-62, chmn. nominating com. 1962-64), Tenn. (pres. 1969) library assns. Presbyn. (ruling elder). Clubs: Egyptians, Holly Hills Country. Author: Libraries in the Golden Triangle. Home: 365 Kenilworth St Memphis TN 38112 Office: 1850 Peabody Av Memphis TN 38104

WALLIS, ERNEST MARTIN, shoe co. exec.; b. Hamburg, Germany, Aug. 7, 1921; s. Alfred and Janina (Abarbanel) W.; brought to U.S., 1936, naturalized, 1942; student Heinrich Herz Real Gymnasium, Hamburg, 1936; grad. Holderness Sch., Plymouth, N.H., 1937; A.B., Coll. City N.Y., 1941; m. Joan Oettunger, Jan. 13, 1947; children—Jeffrey Allan, David Andrew, Deborah Joy. Mgr., Slty. Importing Co., Inc., Cambridge, Mass., 1946-48; v.p. Embo Casual Footwear Corp., Boston, 1948-63; pres. Marlboro Footwear Co., 1963-65; became regional sales mgr. Eversharp Pen Co., 1965; now pres. Wallis Sales, Inc., Miami. Treas., Parents Blind Children, Inc.; del. Mass. Council for the Blind, Boston; chmn. shoe div. Boston Evening Clinic and Hosp. Served as technician 5th grade, 267th F.A. Bn., AUS, 1942-45, ETO. Decorated Bronze Star, Am. Service medal, European, African, Middle Eastern Service medal with 4 stars, World War II Victory Medal. Mem. Boston Power Squadron (dir. lt. comdr., pub. relations officer), Dale Carnegie Internat. (v.p. Boston chpt.), 210 Assos. (Boston), A.I.M. Clubs: Pleasant Park Yacht; Racquet (Miami), Newton Yacht. Editor: Boston Light. Home: 12840 Hickory Rd Keystone Island 5 North Miami FL 33161 Office: 4730 E 10th Lane Hialeah FL 33013

WALLIS, WILLIAM TURNER, savs. and loan exec.; b. Jacksonville, Fla., Jan. 23, 1926; s. William Turner and Margaret (Phillips) W.; student Washington and Lee U., 1946-50; B.S., Fla. State U., 1951; m. Jean Irene McGinley, Aug. 22, 1952 (dec. Mar. 1974); children—William Turner IV, Laura Day, Michael McGinley, Marshall Bennett. Mgmt. trainee First Fed. Savs. & Loan Assn., West Palm Beach, Fla., 1955-58; pres. First Fed. Savings & Loan Assn. Osceola County, Kissimmee, Fla., 1958—; chmn. bd. Fla. Informgmt. Services, Inc., Orlando, Fla.; pres., dir. Indsl. Devel. Corp. Fla., Orlando. Chmn. East Central Fla. Regional Planning Council, 1962-70; mem. spl. adv. com. Fed. Home Loan Mortgage Corp., 1970-73; mem. community service award com. Walt Disney World, 1972—; mem. Reedy Creek Air and Water Pollution Control Bd., 1971-73; mem. Planning Commn., Kissimmee, 1967-71. Bd. dirs. Osceola Art and Culture Center, Kissimmee, 1960—; bd. dirs., v.p. Central Fla. Devel. Com., 1971-72; bd. dirs. Fla. Tech. U. Found. Served to lt. USNR, 1952-55. Mem. U.S. (dir. 1968-70), Fla. (pres. 1967) savs. and loan leagues, Fla. State (dir. 1970-73), Greater Kissimmee Area (pres. 1973) chambers commerce. Episcopalian (sr. warden 1961-71). Elk. Clubs: University (Orlando, Fla.); Eau Gallie Yacht (Melbourne, Fla.). Home: 1011 Neptune Rd Kissimmee FL 32741 Office: 200 Broadway St Kissimmee FL 32741

WALLS, JOSEPH KYLE, univ. adminstr.; b. Booneville, Ark., Dec. 28, 1946; s. John Hilton and Clara Aline (Warford) Johnson; B.F.A. (Dads Assn. scholar), U. Okla., 1969, M.F.A., 1971; certificate Harvard, 1970; postgrad. Fla. State U., 1971-73. Adminstr., Studio Theatre Program, U. Okla., Norman., 1970-71; adminstrv. intern Nat. Endowment Arts, Washington, 1972; adminstrv. asst. Fla. State U. Sch. Theatre, Tallahassee, 1971—. Del., UNESCO Conf. on Cultural Innovation in Technol. and Post Indsl. Socs., 1973. Recipient Buffalo Mask award for service U. Okla. Drama Sch., 1971. Mem. Internat. Assn. Theatres for Children and Young People, Am. Ednl. Theatre Assn. (vice-chmn. student adv. com. 1970), Am. Theatre Assn. (pres. theatre student assn. 1972). Univ. and Coll. Theatre Assn. (v.p. student interests 1972-73), Young Friends Arts (co-chmn. Fla. chpt. 1972-74, mem. nat. steering com. 1972-74), Fla. League Arts (dir.), Asso. Councils Arts, Am. Film Inst., U.S. Inst. Theatre Tech., Am. Theatre Student League, Southeastern Theatre Conf., Acacia. Home: 610 W Call St Tallahassee FL 32304

WALLS, MARION LEE (MRS. WARREN ANDREW WALLS), finance co. exec. b. Petersburg, Va., Oct. 20, 1922; d. Roland Temple and Fannie Louise (Smith) Lee; grad. high sch.; m. Warren Andrew Walls, Aug. 28, 1943. Cashier, v.p. Bank of Warwick, Newport News, Va., 1941-62; v.p. Asso. Mortgage Cos. Va., Inc., Hampton, 1962—. Mem. Jr. League of Hampton Rds. Home: 16 S Madison Lane Newport News VA 23606 Office: 1120 W Mercury Blvd Hampton VA 23366

WALLS, MARTHA ANN WILLIAMS (MRS. B. CARMAGE WALLS), newspaper exec.; b. Gadsden, Ala., Apr. 21, 1927; d. Aubrey Joseph and Inez (Cooper) Williams; student pub. schs., Gadsden; m. B. Carmage Walls, Jan. 2, 1954; children—Byrd Cooper, Lissa Williams. Sec.-treas., So Newspapers, Inc., Montgomery, Ala., 1954-67, also dir.; pres., dir. Walls Newspapers, Inc., Montgomery, 1967-70; pres. So. Newspapers, Inc., Baytown, Tex., 1970—; sec.-treas. Summer Camps, Inc., Guntersville, Ala., 1954-69, also dir.; v.p., dir. Dixie Newspapers, Inc., Gadsden, Ala., Fort Payne (Ala.) Newspapers, Inc., Scottsboro (Ala.) Newspapers, Inc., McKinney (Tex.) Newspapers, Inc.; v.p. Alvin (Tex.) Sun, Inc., Ft. Payne (Ala.) Newspapers, Inc., Scottsboro (Ala.) Newspapers, Inc.; dir. Bayport Pubs., Inc., Deer Park, Tex., Bayshore Pubs., Inc., LaPorte, Tex., LaMarque (Tex.) Times, Mangum (Okla.) Newspapers, Inc., News-Am., Royse City, Tex., Texco Pub. Co., Inc., Rosenberg, Tex., Tri-County Newspapers, Inc., Katy, Tex. Bd. dirs. Montgomery (Ala.) Acad., 1970-74. Methodist. Home: 18603 Upper Bay Rd Nassau Bay Houston TX 77058 Office: 18100 Upper Bay Rd Houston TX 77058

WALMSLEY, SYLVESTER PIERCE, IV, finance co. exec.; b. Richmond, Va., July 27, 1940; s. Sylvester Pierce and Allie Page (Rhodes) W.; B.S. in Commerce, U. Va., 1963; m. Elizabeth Eyre Ashburner, July 1, 1964; children—Pierce, Page, Christopher. Broker E.F. Hutton & Co., Inc., New Orleans, 1963-67; trust investment officer United Va. Bank, Richmond, 1967-69; pres., investment counsel Thompson, Siegel and Walmsley, Inc., Richmond, 1969—. Served with USCG, 1961. Chartered financial analyst. Mem. Financial Analysts Fedn. Episcopalian. Republican. Club: Country. Home: 5503 Cary St Rd Richmond VA 23226 Office: 801 Mutual Bldg Richmond VA

WALN, RONALD LEE, educator; b. Cedar Rapids, Ia., June 25, 1931; s. George Elbridge and Pauline (Deamer) W.; Mus.B., Oberlin Coll., 1957; M.A., U. Ia., 1959, Ph.D., 1971; m. B. Clara Schlecht, June 16, 1956; children—David George, Robert Earnest. Grad. asst. U. Ia., Iowa City, 1957-59; instr. woodwinds Fla. State U., Tallahassee, 1959-65; asst. prof. woodwinds and music edn. U. Ga., Athens, 1965-72, asso. prof., 1972—, flutist U. Ga. Faculty Woodwind Quintet and Baroque Ensemble, 1966—. Performer with Bklyn., Tallahassee, Jacksonville, Mobile and Augusta symphonys, 1958—. Served with USAF, 1951-55. Mem. Nat. Assn. Coll. Wind and Percussion Instrs. (pres. 1970-72), Ga. Music Tchrs. Assn., Ga. Music Educators Assn., Music Tchrs. Nat. Assn., Music Educators Nat. Conf., Pi Kappa Lambda, Phi Mu Alpha. Methodist (mem. ofcl. bd. 1970—). Home: 499 Brookwood Dr Athens GA 30601

WALNER, ARTHUR H., sci. analyst cons.; b. N.Y.C., Nov. 25, 1928; s. Jack and Anna (Sherman) W.; B.S., Coll. City N.Y., 1951; postgrad. Stevens Inst. Tech., 1951-52, Columbia, 1958, N.Y. U., 1965-66; m. Beverly Block, Apr. 26, 1952; children—Tandi Gwenn, Debra Helene, Phyllis-Jo. Chief quality control Picatinny Arsenal, Dover, N.J., 1951-55; cons. statis. head Applied Sci. Lab., U.S. Naval, Bklyn., 1955-67; dir. operations planning div. Met. Police Dept., Washington, 1967-68; operations analyst Gen. Services Adminstrn., Washington, 1968-71; asst. dir. operational planning Cost of Living Council, 1971-72; sr. program analyst Environmental Protection Agy., 1972—. Cons. in crime analysis and resource planning, 1968—. Mem. Operations Research Soc. Am., Quality Control Soc. Am., Am. Statis. Soc. (div. dir. 1956-67), Internat. Criminology Soc., Internat. Biographers World. Home: 11215 Oak Leaf Dr Silver Spring MD 20901 Office: 401 M St SW Washington DC 20460

WALRAVEN, HAROLD CLAY, JR., dentist; b. Atlanta, May 18, 1928; s. Harold C. and Martha Turner (Jones) W.; B.S., U. Ga., 1950; D.D.S., Emory U., 1954; m. Billie Frances Trunkey, Dec. 27, 1952; children—Terry Frances, Caren Leslie. Med. technician Ga. Bapt. Hosp., Atlanta, 1952; research fellow Emory U., 1952-54, instr., research asso., 1954-69; individual practice gen. dentistry, Atlanta, 1954—. Cons. ceramic engring. Ga. Inst. Tech., 1962—. Mem. Ga. Bd. Dental Examiners, 1969—, pres., 1970—. Dir. Northside Bus. Assn., 1960-65, v.p., treas., 1959-60. Head dental div. United Appeal, 1960, 61, 63, Am. Cancer Soc., 1962, 64, 66, Heart Fund, 1966, 67, 69. Served with AUS, 1945-47. Fellow Am. Coll. Dentists; hon. fellow Ga. Dental Assn.; mem. Interprofl. Council Ga., No. Dist. Dental Soc., Am. Dental Assn., Amateur Athletic Union (officer, committeeman nat. gymnastic championships 1969), Sphinx, Gridiron. Contbr. articles to profl. jours. Patentee coupling agts. Home: 3253 Rilman Dr NW Atlanta GA 30327 Office: 1957 Howell Mill Rd NW Atlanta GA 30318

WALSH, CORNELIUS STEPHEN, corp. exec.; b. N.Y.C., Dec. 27, 1907; s. William Francis and Frances (Murphy) W.; student Eastman-Gaines Sch., 1924-25; m. Edwyna Lois Senter, May 1, 1930; children—Jane Linda, Richard Stephen, Suzanne Patricia. With Dyson Shipping Co., Inc., 1925-27, Interocean Steamship Corp., 1928-30; sec. States Marine Corp., N.Y.C., 1931-38, v.p., 1938-53, pres., 1953-65, dir., 1950-65; pres., dir. States Marine Corp. Del., N.Y.C., 1946-65; chmn. Waterman S.S. Corp., N.Y.C., 1965—, Waterman Industries Corp., 1965—, Hammond Leasing Corp., N.Y.C., 1967—; dir. Oliver Corp.; mem. adv. bd. Mfrs. Hanover Trust Co., N.Y.C. Mem. Met. Mus. Art N.Y.C., Soc. Four Arts Palm Beach (Fla.). Mem. Far East-Am. Council Commerce and Industry (dir.), Soc. Naval Architects and Marine Engrs. (asso.), Japan Soc. (hon. dir.), Am. Bur. Shipping. Clubs: Wall Street, Yacht, Metropolitan Opera, Fifth Avenue (N.Y.C.); Seawanhaka Corinthian Yacht (Oyster Bay, L.I., N.Y.); Pine Valley Golf (Clementon, N.J.); Everglades, Bath and Tennis, Seminole Golf (Palm Beach, Fla.). Home: 220 El Bravo Way Palm Beach FL 33480 Office: Waterman Steamship Corporation 345 Park Av New York City NY 10022

WALSH, GEORGE PAT, food co. exec.; b. Amarillo, Tex., Dec. 17, 1928; s. William D. and Mary (Ellis) W.; student Amarillo Coll., 1949, 56, 65; m. Bobbye Jo Oakley, Aug. 25, 1947; children—Bill Pat, Robbye Jo, Jeffrey Paul. Gen. mgr. Walsh Food Stores No. 3, Amarillo, 1951-56; sales mgr., dealer franchise mgr. Walsh Food Service, Amarillo, 1956-62, gen. mgr., 1962—; v.p. Artic Frozen Foods, Inc., 1962—. Mem. Amarillo Bd. City Devel., 1971; chmn. Council Child Care Agys., 1971; pres. Catholic Family Service, Inc., Amarillo, 1969-70. Mem. Nat. Inst. Locker and Freezer Provisioners (pres., 1968), Amarillo Execs. Assn. (pres., 1971), Frozen Food Council (pres. 1971), Roman Catholic. K.C., Kiwanian. Club: Serra. Home: 1002 Bowie St Amarillo TX 79102

WALSH, GERALD RICHARD, lawyer; b. Scranton, Pa., Sept. 7, 1937; s. Gerald Richard and Mary (Grady) W.; B.S., U. Scranton, 1959; J.D., George Washington U. Law Sch., 1966; m. Ann Eleanor Heffron, May 7, 1966; children—Kieran, Mary Grady, Gerald Richard III. Spl. agt. Office Naval Intelligence, Washington, 1963-65; mem. staff Pres.'s Commn. on Crime in D.C., 1965-66; admitted to Va. bar, 1966; asso. firm L'Hommedieu & O'Grady, Washington, 1966-67; asst. Commonwealth atty., Arlington County, Va., 1967-69; asso. firm McCandlish, Lillard, Church & Best, Fairfax, Va., 1969-70, partner, 1971—; asst. city atty. Fairfax City, 1969—; substitute judge Fairfax County Gen. Dist. Ct., 1973—, Fairfax County Juvenile and Domestic Relations Dist. Ct., 1973—. Served with USNR, 1959-62. Mem. Am., Va. bar assns., Delta Theta Phi. Roman Catholic. Home: 14708 Algretus Dr Centreville VA 22020 Office: 4069 Chain Bridge Rd Fairfax VA 22030

WALSH, GWENDOLYN ELROY, educator; b. Cambridge, Mass., Mar. 19, 1925; d. Chesley and Elizabeth (Furey) Elroy; diploma Bouve Boston Sch. Phys. Edn. and Phys. Therapy, 1946; B.S., Tufts U., 1946; postgrad. San Jose State Coll., 1961, Stanford, 1962; M.Ed., U. Va., 1967; m. Douglas F. Walsh, Sept. 24, 1950 (div. July 1962); children—Kevin Douglas, Robyn Elizabeth. Tchr., Abbot Acad., Andover, Mass., 1946-50, Katherine Delmar Burke Sch., San Francisco, 1951-58, San Carlos (Cal.) High Sch., 1958-62; asst. prof. phys. edn. Mary Baldwin Coll., Staunton, Va., 1962—, co-chmn. dept. phys. edn., 1969—, dance dir., 1962—. Tchr. swimming and canoeing New Eng. summer camps, 1943-49; tchr. Project Opportunity, summer 1969; choreographer Oak Grove Summer Theater, Verona, Va., 1964-67; tchr. fencing Waynesboro YMCA, 1966—; co-dir. Staunton Puppeteers, 1972—. Mem. Am. Assn. U. Profs., Am. Assn. U. Women, Am. Fencers League of Am. (Va. sec.-treas. 1967-68, nat. dir., 1969-70), Am., Va. assns. health, phys. edn. and recreation, So. Assn. Health, Phys. Edn. and Recreation for Coll. Women, Kappa Delta Pi. Club: Blue Ridge Fencers (pres. 1968-70) (Waynesboro, Va.). Episcopalian. Home: 340 E Beverley St Staunton VA 24401

WALSH, JOHN BREFFNI, govt. ofcl.; b. Bklyn., Aug. 20, 1927; s. George Patrick and Margaret Mary (Rigney) W.; B.E.E. summa cum laude, Manhattan Coll., 1948; M.S., Columbia, 1950; postgrad. N.Y.U., 1954-62; m. Marie Louise Leclerc, June 18, 1955; children—George Breffni, John Leclerc, Darina Louise. Asst. in elec. engring. Manhattan Coll., 1947-48; asst. in elec. engring. Columbia, N.Y.C., 1948-49, instr., 1949-51, asst. prof. elec. engring., 1953-58, asst. dir. Electronics Research Labs., 1958-66, lectr. math., 1959-61; asst. chief radar systems br. Rome (N.Y.) Air Devel. Center, 1951-52, chief air def. systems lab., 1952-53, tech. dir. Directorate Intelligence and Reconnaissance, 1953; dep. for research Office Asst. Sec. Air Force, Washington, 1966-71; spl. asst. to President's sci. adviser, sr. mem. NSC staff, Washington, 1971-72; dep. dir. def. research and engring., Washington, 1972—. Cons. to various govt. and indsl. orgns., including Office Dir. Def. for Research and Engring., Army Research Office, Advanced Research Projects Agy., 1953-66. Mem. Cresskill (N.J.) Planning Bd., 1964-66. Served with AUS, 1946-47. Recipient Exceptional Civilian Service award Dept. Air Force, 1969, Meritorious Civilian Service award Dept. Def., 1971, citation of honor as outstanding Air Force civilian employee of year Air Force Assn., 1971. Registered profl. engr., N.Y. State, N.J. Fellow I.E.E.E.; mem. N.Y. Acad. Scis., Sigma Xi, Eta Kappa Nu. Author: (with K. S. Miller) Introductory Electric Circuits, 1960, Elementary and Advanced Trigonometry, 1962; Electromagnetic Theory and Engineering Applications, 1960; also chpts. in books. Contbr. articles to tech. jours., Ency. Americana. Home: 7803 Birnam Wood Dr McLean VA 22101 Office: Pentagon Washington DC 20301

WALSH, MARY D. FLEMING (MRS. F. HOWARD WALSH), club woman; b. Whitewright, Tex., Oct. 29, 1913; d. William and Anna Maud (Lewis) Fleming; B.A., So. Meth. U., 1934; m. F. Howard Walsh, Mar. 13, 1937; children—Richard, Howard, D'Ann (Mrs. William F. Bonnell), Maudi (Mrs. George C. Porter III), William Lloyd. Partner, The Walsh Co. Commr., Tex. Commn. Arts and Humanities, 1968-72. Bd. dirs. Lloyd Shaw Found.; pres. Fleming Found.: v.p. Walsh Found.; bd. dirs. Van Cliburn Internat. Piano Competition, 1964-67; co-founder Am. Field Service, Ft. Worth; bd. dirs. Fort Worth Opera, 1960-73, v.p., 1967-73; bd. dirs. Ft. Worth Ballet Assn., 1973—. Recipient Civic First Lady of Fort Worth award Altrusa Club, 1968; named Patron of Arts in Fort Worth, 1970. Mem. Tex. League Composers (hon. life mem. Ft. Worth guild), Ft. Worth Boys Club, Ft. Worth Children's Hosp., Woman's Club, Jewel Charity Ball, Ft. Worth Pan Hellenic (pres. 1940), Opera Guild, Ft. Worth Art Assn., Ladies Aux. Goodwill Industries, Child Study Center, Tex. Boys Choir Aux., Girl's Service League (hon. life), Round Table, Fine Arts Found. Guild Tex. Christian U., Tarrant County Aux. Edna Gladney Home, William Edrington Scott Theatre Guild, Chi Omega (pres. 1935-36) (financial adviser Rho Epsilon chpt. 1955-69). Baptist. Clubs: Fidelite, Rejebian, Chi Omega Mothers, Kappa Sigma Wives and Mothers, Bankers, Wives, Dinner Dance, Roundelay (founder 1946). Home: 2425 Stadium Dr Fort Worth TX 76109 also 1801 Culebra Av Colorado Springs CO 80907

WALSH, RALPH (PAT) AUGUSTUS, II, broadcasting co. exec.; b. Oklahoma City, Apr. 4, 1932; s. Ralph Augustus and Mary Phyllis (Proffitt) W.; student U. Okla., U. Ark.; m. Bobbie Jean Hill, May 24, 1958; children—Mary, Ralph Augustus, Amy. With KGHI radio, Little Rock, 1957-58, KAJI radio, Little Rock, 1958; successively sales mgr., asst. mgr., mgr., gen. mgr. KAAY radio, Little Rock, now pres. Chmn. bd. Opportunity Group; bd. dirs. Little Rock Unlimited Progress, Little Rock YMCA. Served with AUS, Germany. Mem. Ark. Advt. Fedn. (dir.), Nat. Agrl. Marketing Assn., Ark., Little Rock chambers commerce, Ark. Farm and Ranch Club, Sales and Marketing Execs. Internat., Ark. Broadcasters Assn. Presbyn. (deacon). Clubs: Little Rock, Capital. Home: 208 Hiawatha St Little Rock AR 72205 Office: 1425 W 7th St Little Rock AR 72203

WALSH, WILLIAM EDWARD, JR., lawyer; b. Washington, Pa., Nov. 10, 1909; s. William Edward and Christine (Bochers) W.; student U. Miami, 1927-30, U. Fla., 1930-31, Cumberland U., 1932; m. Natalie Aiken Brooks, Apr. 30, 1951; children—Christine Laury, William Edward III. Admitted to Fla. bar, 1933, since practiced in Miami; pvt. practice, 1933-42; mem. firm Walsh & Walsh, 1946-54, Walsh, Simmonite, Budd & Walsh, 1954-65, Walsh & Walsh, 1965-69, Walsh, Nottebaum & Laks, 1969—. Pres., Key Biscayne Improvement Assn. Served as lt. AUS, 1942-46. Mem. Fla. Bar, Dade County Bar Assn., Mil. Order World Wars. Democrat. Lion (dir. Key Biscayne). Home: 662 Woodcrest Rd Key Biscayne FL 33149 Office: Alfred I du Pont Bldg 169 E Flagler St Miami FL 33131

WALSTAD, PAUL MARION, surgeon; b. Mpls., Mar. 29, 1915; s. Julius Oscar and Hilma (Latt) W.; B.A., U. Minn., 1939, B.S., 1941, M.B., 1943, M.D., 1944; m. Marjorie Jane Vandenberg, Jan. 24, 1945; children—Diana, Marilyn, David, Linda, Paula. Intern Hosp. of Good Samaritan, Los Angeles, 1944; resident in gen. surgery Mary's Help Hosp., San Francisco, 1947-49, U. Pa. Grad. Sch. Medicine, 1949-50; resident in thoracic and cardiovascular surgery Highland-Alameda County Hosp., Oakland, Cal., 1958-59, Children's Hosp., Oakland, 1958-59, U. Ore. Med. Sch., 1959-61; surgeon Travis AFB, Cal., 1950-51; pvt. practice medicine specializing in surgery, Turlock, Cal., 1953-58, 62-64; chief of surgery Stanislaus County Hosp., Modesto, Cal., 1955-56, 63-64; surgeon Daniel Boone Clinic, Harlan, Ky., 1964—; chief of surgery Harlan Appalachian Regional Hosp., 1965—, chief surg. residency tng. program, 1965—, chief staff, 1971-72; cons. in thoracic surgery Hazard, McDowell, Middlesboro, Whitesburg Appalachian Regional Hosps., 1965—; vol. physician, Vietnam, 1969; surgeon Kijabe Med. Center, Kenya, East Africa, 1971. Pres. adv. bd. Harlan County Home Health Service, 1967-70; bd. dirs. County chpt. Am. Cancer Soc., 1962-64. Served with M.C., AUS, 1944-47, 51-53. Diplomate Am. Bd. Surgery, Am. Bd. Thoracic Surgery. Fellow A.C.S. (Ky. cancer liaison fellow), Am. Coll. Chest Physicians (pres. Ky. chpt. 1972), U. Pa. Med. Sch. Grad. Sch. Surg. Soc.; mem. A.M.A., Harlan County Med. Soc. (pres. 1973), Am., Ky. (pres. 1974) thoracic socs., So. Thoracic Surg. Assn., Ky. Med. Assn., Christian Med. Soc., Soc. Thoracic Surgeons. Contbr. articles to profl. jours. Home: Woodland Hills Harlan KY 40831 Office: Daniel Boone Clinic Harlan KY 40831

WALSTON, VIRGIL ALFRED, civil engr.; b. Palestine, Tex., Dec. 20, 1903; s. William Watts and Nora (Featherstone) W.; student Tex. A. and M. U., 1923-26; B.C.E., U. Houston, 1953; m. Dorothy May Darden, July 15, 1928; children—Dorothy Jean (Mrs. Charles W. Alcorn, Jr.), Virgil Alfred, Jr., Sally Darden (Mrs. Sweeney J. Doehring, Jr.). Chainman civil engring. dept. Mo. Pacific R.R., Palestine, Tex., 1926-27, rodman, 1927-29; with Humble Oil & Refining Co., Houston, 1929-68, office sr. supervising engr. Hqrs. Civil Engring. Dept., Houston, 1948-56, regional engr. Southwest Region, 1964-65, sr. tech. adv., Chief Prodn. Engr.'s staff, 1965-68, ret., 1968; now owner Walston Engring. & Realty Co.; engring. cons. Alyeska Pipeline Service Co., Houston, 1969—. Mem. Am. Petroleum Inst., Am. Congress on Surveying and Mapping, Am. Soc. Civil Engrs., Nat., Tex. socs. profl. engrs, Tex. Surveyors Assn., Tex. State Bd. Registration for Public Surveyors (past mem., chmn. bd. 1967-68), Nat., Houston bds. realtors. Baptist. Mason. Home: 3609 Overbrook Lane Houston TX 77027 Office: 3272 Westheimer Rd Houston TX 77006

WALTERS, CALVIN OTIS, JR., diversified co. exec.; b. Savannah, Ga., Jan. 31, 1936; s. Calvin Otis and Mary (Zellner) W.; B.S., Emory U., 1957; m. Jo-Helen Holman, Apr. 11, 1959; children—Helen, Calvin Otis III, Catherine. Chemist, Savannah Foods & Industries, 1957-60, tech. supt., 1960-63, asst. refinery mgr. Everglades br., 1964-66; with Southdown, Inc., Houston, 1966—, pres., chief operating officer Southdown Lands, Inc., 1970—, corp. v.p. for operations, 1971—, chmn. bd., chief exec. officer Santa Clara Vintners, Inc, San Martin Vineyards Co. Instr. Armstrong U., Savannah, 1960-63. Mem. Sugar Industry Technologists (bd. dirs. 1966-70), Am. Sugar Cane League, Am. Soc. Sugar Cane Technology (v.p., dir. sugar information), Wine Inst., Am. Soc. Corporate Planning, Internat. Soc. Sugar Cane Technologists, Sugar Assn., Inc. (v.p., bd. dir. 1970). Methodist. Lion, Rotarian. Contbr. profl. jours. Home: 11910 Broken Bough St Houston TX 77024 Office: 950 Tenneco Bldg Southdown Inc Houston TX 77002

WALTERS, CHARLES RUFUS, textile co. exec.; b. Newton, N.C., Apr. 29, 1907; s. Martin E. and Laura (Scroggs) W.; A.B., Erskine Coll., 1927, LL.D., 1972; LL.B., Fordham U., 1935; J.S.D., N.Y.U., 1938; m. Ruth K. Moore, 1967; children—Anne I. (Mrs. Frederick Richards II), Margaret M. (Mrs. Northrop K. Miyake), Charles R. With Chase Manhattan Bank, N.Y.C., 1929-46; v.p. Abney Mills, Greenwood, S.C., 1947-60; dir. Internat. Div., London, Eng., Burlington Industries, Inc., Greensboro, N.C., 1961-63; pres. Kenneth Mills, Walhalla, S.C., 1964, 67; gen. mgr. Cone Mills Corp., Walhalla, 1967-71; chmn. bd. dirs. Hartness Bottling Works, Spartanburg, S.C., 1964-71, Pepsi Cola Bottling Co., Burlington, N.C., 1968-71, Pepsi-Cola Bottling Co., Durham, N.C., 1969-71, Pepsi Cola Bottling Co., Forest City, N.C., 1970-71; pvt. practice law, Abbeville, S.C., 1971—. Pres. Greenwood Community Chest, 1954-55. Pres. Greenwood YMCA, 1958; trustee, bd. counsellors Erskine Coll., Due West, S.C. Served to lt. col. USAAF, 1942-46. Home: Clemson House Clemson SC 29631 Office: PO Box 926 Abbeville SC 29620

WALTERS, ELEANOR BOYD, mathematician, educator; b. Gunnison, Miss., Mar. 28, 1914; d. Jerry Edward and Loudie (Boyd) Walters; BS. in Edn., Delta State Coll., 1934; M.A., Duke, 1939; Ed.D., Tchrs.; Coll., Columbia, 1956. Tchr. math. Shelby Consol. Sch., Shelby, Miss., 1934-38, Hernando (Miss.) High Sch., 1939-41, Pensacola (Fla.) High Sch., 1941-43; grad. asst. in math. Duke, 1938-39; asso. prof. math. Delta State Coll., Cleveland, Miss., 1943-55, prof., 1955—, acting head dept. math., 1948-55; head dept. 1955—. Mem. adv. com. on secondary math., adv. com. on arithmetic Miss. Dept. Edn., 1960—; math. cons. various Miss. schs., 1961—. Fellow A.A.A.S.; mem. Am. Math. Soc., Math. Assn. Am., Nat. Council Tchrs. Math. (Miss. rep.), Miss. Acad. Scis., Am. Assn. U. Women (v.p. Miss. div. 1959-61, nat. conv. com., 1963, implementation com. 1963-64, br. v.p. 1958-64, sec. S.E. Central region 1963-64, v.p. 1967-71, chmn. nat. conv. com. 1965), Delta Kappa Gamma, Kappa Delta Pi, Pi Gamma Mu. Democrat. Methodist. Home: 1804 Delta State Coll Cleveland MS 38732

WALTERS, FREDERICK J(AMES), mgmt. cons.; b. N.Y.C., Feb. 18, 1906; s. Frederick J. and Laura Patricia (O'Connor) W.; A.B., Princeton, 1927; m. Virginia Cross, Jan. 18, 1934; children—Rosa Lee (Sister Marie Virginia O.P.), Virginia (Mrs. R. M. Stormont), Frederick James (dec.), James Anthony. With Gen. Motors Corp.,1927-45; mem. exec. staff Gen. Electric Co., 1945-46; v.p. Hotpoint, Inc., 1946-52, Packard Motor Car Co., 1952-53; pres. Fred Walters Oldsmobile, Atlanta, 1953-62; v.p. Boyden Assos., Inc., 1962-73; pres. Walters & Co., mgmt. cons., 1973—; dir. Flex-Comm Internat. Guest lectr. Ga. Inst. Tech., U. Ga., Ga. State U. Mem. Small Bus. Adminstrn. Adv. Council for State of Ga. Roman Catholic. Clubs: Capital City, Princeton. Author: Handbook for District Representatives, 1939; A Summary of Veterans' Reemployment Rights, 1944. Home: 4418 Davidson Av NE Atlanta GA 30319 Office: 1102 Lenox Towers Atlanta GA 30326

WALTERS, GEORGE EDWARD, electronics engr.; b. Kewanna, Ind., June 23, 1941; s. Vachael Bailey and Ruth Mildred (Gottschalk) W.; B.A., Ind. Central Coll., 1965; B.S. in E.E., Purdue U., 1965; M.S. in E.E., U. Tex., 1968; m. Carol Nicholson, May 29, 1965; children—Eric Lawrence, Mark Duane. Coop. edn. student LTV Aerospace Corp., Dallas, 1963-65, asst. electronic systems engr., 1965-66, electronic systems engr., 1968-72, electronic systems engr. ground transp. div., 1972—. Grad. teaching asst. U. Tex., Arlington, 1966-68. Pres., chmn. bd. Contact Arlington/Mid Cities. Registered profl. engr., Tex. Mem. I.E.E.E., Com. for Social Responsibility in Engring., Tex. Civil Liberties Union, Tau Beta Pi, Eta Kappa Nu. Democrat. Mem. Christian Ch. Home: 1716 Northbrook Ct Arlington TX 76012 Office: Box 5907 Dallas TX 75222

WALTERS, HOYLE SAGER, wholesale co. exec.; b. Danville, Va., May 9, 1924; s. Archie Hoyle and Mabel Cathryn (Lindsay) W.; B.S., Va. Commonwealth U., 1950; m. Ruby G. Merriman, Nov. 20, 1948; children—Wendra Leigh, Joanne. Salesman, Welmont Electric Corp., 1949-52; advt. mgr. Goldberg Co., Inc., Richmond, Va., 1952-54, territory mgr., 1952-63, sales mgr., 1963-64, v.p. sales, 1964—; v.p. 7200 Corp., 1963—. Served with AUS, 1943-46; ETO. Lutheran (v.p. council 1964-65). Home: 4301 Shirley Rd Richmond VA 23225 Office: 7400 Impala Dr Richmond VA 23228

WALTERS, JAMES NORMAN, graphic arts co. exec.; b. Kansas City, Mo., Feb. 24, 1926; s. Otto Neal and Martha Ellen (Watters) W.; student U. Ark.; m. Rita Marie Ballmann, Aug. 25, 1964. Vice pres. Neal Walters Poster Corp., Bentonville, Ark., 1942-63; pres., 1963—; pres. Gen. Bus. Forms. Inc., 1958—, Offset dir., 1963—; v.p. Graphic Arts Corp., 1963—. Chmn. Bentonville Airport Comm., 1971—, Bentonville Housing Authority, 1966-68; mem. Eureka Springs (Ark.) City Commn., 1961-63; active Boy Scouts Am., 1953-63; Bd. dirs. Econ. Devel. Dist. Benton County, 1967-70, N.W. Ark. dist. Abilities Unltd., 1968—. Served with AUS, 1953-55. Named Man of Year, Eureka Springs C. of C., 1961; recipient award of appreciation Bentonville Jr. C. of C., 1967, Outstanding Civic Leader America award, 1971, 73; award of appreciation Harrison Jr. C. of C., 1970; Mem. Bentonville C. of C. Democrat. Roman Catholic (parish council 1970—, diocesean council 1971—). Mason (Shriner), Elk, Rotarian. Club: Bella Vista Country. Home: 803 NW 8th St Bentonville AR 72712 Office: PO Box 311 Bentonville AR 72712

WALTERS, JAMES VERNON, civil engr., educator; b. Dublin, Ga., May 13, 1933; s. Herbert James and Olive (Chavous) W.; B.C.E. (Gen. Mark Clark scholar), Ga. Inst. Tech., 1955, M.S., 1958; Ph.D., U. Fla., 1963; m. Barbara Ann Daniell, June 18, 1955; children—Daniell Chavous, Eric Carl. Asst. san. engr. USPHS, Atlanta, 1956-59; asst. prof. civil engring. U. Ala., Tuscaloosa, 1959-63, asso. prof., 1963-70, prof., 1970—; Ford Found. engring. resident Internat. Paper Co., Moss Point, Miss., 1966-67; v.p., dir. Tuscaloosa Testing Lab., Inc. Mem. Ala. Adv. Council for Comprehensive Health Planning, 1969-73; mem. Ala. Water Improvement Commn., 1964-65; mem. Ala. Occupational Safety and Health Adv. Bd., 1971-73; mem. Black Warrior River Tech. Adv. Bd., 1965-68; mem. Water and Wastewater Treatment Plant Operators Certification Bd., Ala., 1971-73. Served with USPHS, 1956-59. Mem. Water Pollution Control Fedn. (dir. 1966-69, Arthur Sidney Bedell award 1968), Air Pollution Control Assn., Am. Soc. C.E., Am. Soc. Profl. Engrs., Am. Water Works Assn., Soc. Nematologists, Le Grande Societe de le Sortier, Ala. Acad. Scis., Ala. Water and Pollution Control Assn. (certification bd. mem. 1964-71), Am. Chem. Soc., Sigma Xi, Chi Epsilon, Phi Kappa Phi, Kappa Kappa Psi, Tau Beta Pi. Home: 39 Claymont II Tuscaloosa AL 35401 Office: PO Box AB University AL 35486

WALTERS, JOHN DEWITT, petroleum engr.; b. Bradford, Pa., Oct. 2, 1920; s. John Brandow and Helen (McIntire) W.; B.S., U. Okla., 1947; m. Marjory Jean Anderson, May 8, 1948; children—Marcia Jean (Mrs. Bruce Armstrong), John DeWitt. With Sun Oil Co., Tulsa, 1951—, dist. engr., 1959-63, sr. project engr., 1963-68, sr. engr. adv., 1968-70, region econ. coordinator, 1970—. Served with AUS, 1943-46. Mem. Soc. Petroleum Engrs. Mason. Home: 6765 E 66th Pl S Tulsa OK 74133 Office: Box 2039 Tulsa OK 73102

WALTERS, JOHN SHERWOOD, newspaperman; b. Junction City, Ark., May 15, 1917; s. John Thomas and Cora (McBride) W.; B.A., La. Tech. Inst., 1939; M.A., La. State U., 1941; m. Claire Dailey, June 1, 1941; children—Elizabeth Claire, Mary Dailey (dec.). Editor Ruston (La.) Daily Leader, 1940; reporter Baton Rouge Morning Advocate, 1941; rating examiner Jacksonville Naval Air Sta., 1941-42; reporter Fla. Times-Union, Jacksonville, 1943, 44-53, city editor, 1953-60, exec. editor Times-Union Jacksonville Jour., 1960—; asst. prof. journalism La. Tech. Inst., 1943-44. Chmn. Duval County chpt. A.R.C. Mem. Am. Soc. Newspaper Editors, Fla. Soc. Newspaper Editors (pres. 1971-72), Alpha Lambda Tau, Sigma Delta Chi. Democrat. Methodist. Rotarian (pres. 1971-72). Clubs: Timuquana Country, River, University. Home: 1750 Dogwood Pl Jacksonville FL 32210 Office: Jacksonville Times Union Jour 1 Rvierside Dr Jacksonville FL 32201

WALTERS, LAMAR L., assn. exec. Exec. v.p. La. State C. of C. Address: Capitol House Hotel Suite 201 Baton Rouge LA 70821*

WALTON, CLARENCE, univ. pres.; b. Scranton, Pa., June 22, 1915; s. Leo and Mary (Southard) W.; B.A., U. Scranton, 1937; M.A., Syracuse U., 1938; Ph.D., Cath. U., 1951; m. Elizabeth Kennedy, June 1, 1946; children—Thomas Michael, Mary Elizabeth. Social sci. instr. Duquesne U., 1940, dean sch. bus. adminstrn., 1954-58; asso. dean, prof. Columbia U. Grad. Sch. Bus., 1958-64, dean Sch. Gen. Studies, 1964-68; pres. Cath. U. Am., 1969—; prof., chmn. dept. history and polit. sci. U. Scranton, 1946-53; Penfield fellow Inst. Advanced Internat. Studies, Geneva, Switzerland, 1951-52; vis. prof. U. Buenos Aires, summer 1961, U. Cal. at Berkeley, 1963-64, Ore. State U., summer 1969. Dir. Lincoln Life Ins. of N.Y., 1964-68. Mem. sch. bd., Scranton 1948-52; chmn. Pres.'s panel on non-pub. edn., 1969-72; mem. Nat. Commn. on Sch. Finance, 1969-72. Served as lt. (s.g.) USNR, 1940-46; with Naval Intelligence, communications officer U.S.S. Wisconsin. Mem. Am. Cath. Hist. Assn., Acad. Polit. Sci., A.I.M. Author: Big Government and Big Business, 1968; Corporate Social Responsibilities, 1967; Ethos and The Executive, 1969; Business and Social Progress, 1971; (with Richard Eells) Conceptual Foundations of Business, 1974. Contbr. profl. jours. Home: care Cath U Am Washington DC 20017

WALTON, CONRAD GORDON, SR., architect; b. Houston, June 18, 1928; s. John Edward and Evelyn Lucille (Gordon) W.; B.S. (Walsh scholar), Rice U., 1951; postgrad. U. Houston, 1955; m. Rilda Ellen Akin, Dec. 10, 1954; children—Conrad Gordon, Evelyn Coleman, Roberta Agnes. Asso. mem. firm. Hamilton Brown & Assos., Houston, 1960-61; chief supt. Welton Becket & Assos., Houston, 1961-63; partner Alexander, Walton & Hatteberg, Houston, 1963-68; owner Conrad G. Walton, Houston, 1968—. Co-owner subdiv. Holiday Oaks, Lake Somerville, Tex., 1964—; registered fallout shelter analyst Def. Dept., 1966—. Pres. Woodrow Wilson Elementary P.T.O., Houston, 1969-70; chmn. Troop 345, Roberts Sch., Boy Scouts Am., 1960-71. Republican precinct chmn., 1964-71. Served with AUS, 1952-54; Korea. Mem. A.I.A. (treas. 1968), Tex. Soc. Architects, Constrn. Specifications Inst., Houston C. of C. (civic affairs com.). Methodist. Optimist. Architect U. Houston Arch. Bldg. addition, 1969. Home: 9014 Springview Houston TX 77055 Office: 3203 Mercer St Houston TX 77027

WALTON, EDMUND LEWIS, JR., lawyer; b. Salisbury, Md., Sept. 4, 1936; s. Edmund Lewis and Iris (White) W.; B.A., Coll. William and Mary, 1961, J.D., 1963; student U. Md., 1957-58, Army Language Sch., 1956-57; m. Barbara Post, Sept. 18, 1966; children—Southy Elizabeth, Kristen Post. Admitted to Va. bar, 1963; asso. firm Simmonds, Coleburn, Towner & Carman, Arlington, Va., 1963-68, partner, 1968-72, resident partner Fairfax (Va.) office, 1972—; dir. Aspheronics Inc.; Glare Control of Va. Inc.; Winston Brooks Inc. Pres., dir. Holmes Run Acres Civic Assn., 1965-71, Rocky Run Citizens Assn., 1973—; mem. McLean Citizens Assn., Fairfax County Council on the Arts, Fairfax Fedn. Citizens Assns. Chmn., Fairfax Republican Com., 1970-72; del. Rep. Nat. Conv., 1972; mem. Rep. Va. State Central Com., 1972. Served with AUS, 1956-59. Mem. Am., Va., Fairfax bar assns., Va. State Bar, Va. Trial Lawyers Assn., William and Mary Law Sch. Assn., Pi Kappa Alpha, Phi Alpha Delta. Episcopalian. Clubs: Capitol Hill, Capitol Club of Fairfax. Editor: William and Mary Law Rev., 1962-63. Home: 914 Peacock Station Rd McLean VA 22101 Office: 4021 University Dr Fairfax VA 22030

WALTON, G(EORGE) STOKES, lawyer; b. Helena, Ga., Jan. 3, 1906; s. Merrel Callaway and Lucy (Smith) W.; A.B., Mercer U., 1927, J.D., 1929; m. Dorothy Corinne DuPree, Aug. 27, 1930; children—Dorothy (Mrs. Carroll D. Smith III), Marian A. (Mrs. Douglas M. Duggan). Admitted to Ga. bar, 1929, practiced Macon, 1929-33; atty. legal dept. Fed. Land Bank (Farm Credit Adminstrn.) of Columbia, S.C., 1933-43; gen. practice law, La Grange, Ga.,

1943-54; mem. Allen & Walton, 1945-47; city atty., La Grange, 1949-54; mem. Matthews, Walton, Smith, Shaw & Maddox, Rome, Ga., 1954—. Trustee Shorter Coll., 1954-58; bd. dirs. LaGrange Community Chest, 1950-54. Fellow Am. Coll. Probate Counsel; mem. Am. Judicature Soc., Am., Ga., Rome (pres. 1961) bar assns., C. of C., S.A.R., Delta Theta Phi, Delta Sigma Pi. Democrat. Baptist. Mason. Clubs: Coosa Country, Kiwanis (pres. 1959), Prince. Asst. in compilation Code of Ga. of 1933. Home: 28 Crestwood Dr Rome GA 30161 Office: First Nat Bank Bldg Rome GA 30161

WALTON, MRS. LADY BOGGS, ret. librarian; b. nr. Scottsville, Va., Dec. 5, 1909; d. Walter Francis and Melissa (Frame) Boggs; B.S., Longwood Coll., Farmville, Va., 1935; postgrad. William and Mary, 1939, U. Va., 1953; m. Leslie H. Walton, Aug. 17, 1940. Tchr. Mt. Tabor Sch., Buckingham County, Va., 1927-28, 29-32, Oak Grove Sch., Gilmer County, W.Va., 1928-29, Warren Sch., Albemarle County, Va., 1932-33, Greenwood High Sch., Albemarle County, 1933-35, 51-53, Scottsville High Sch., 1935-47; librarian at Albemarle High Sch., Charlottesville, Va., 1953-63, Greenbrier Sch., Charlottesville, 1963-74. Recipient Rotary Fgn. Travel fellowship for tchrs., 1968. Mem. Am. (mem. recruitment com.), Va. (past chmn. recruitment com., sch. corr. Va. Librarian, 2d v.p., 1st v.p., pres.-elect 1965, pres. 1966) library assns., Nat., Va. edn. assns., Nat. Council English, Math. and Social Studies, Pi Gamma Mu, Kappa Delta Pi, Delta Kappa Gamma (chpt. v.p.). Baptist. Home: RFD 1 Crozet VA 22932

WALTON, MARVIN BEACHER, engring. supr.; b. George West, Tex., Apr. 9, 1929; s. Homer Theophelos and Lura Ethel (White) W.; B.S., U. Tex., Arlington, 1963; m. Mary Louise Smith, Dec. 2, 1956; children—Laurie Ann, Marvin Hiram. Nuclear engr. Gen. Dynamics, Ft. Worth, 1962-65; engring. supr. Lockheed Electronics Co., Houston, 1965—. Coach, All Play Football and Baseball. Served with USAF, 1949-53. Registered profl. engr., Tex. Mem. I.E.E.E., Lockheed Mgmt. Assn., Nat. Mgmt. Assn. Methodist. Research in instrumentation devel. for space research, cosmic ray studies, radiation measurements, lunar surface atmospheric measurement. Home: 16218 Rill Lane Houston TX 77058 Office: 16800 El Camino Real Houston TX 77058

WALTON, PAUL N., lumber and wood products co. exec.; b. Dallas, Aug. 10, 1930; s. Paul N. and Anna (Miller) W.; student A. and M. Bus. Sch., 1947-51, So. Meth. U. Law Sch., 1952-53; m. Beverly C. Piper, Feb. 14, 1952; children—Roseann, Scott. Sales mgr. The Sam A Wing Co. Inc., Dallas, 1952-56; div. mgr. Keller Industries Inc., Miami, Fla., 1956-61; exec. v.p. Wing Industries Inc., 1961-69, pres., 1969—, also dir.; officer, dir. Gen. Forest Products, Inc., Nat. Pacific Inc., Metro Bus. Systems Inc., Metro Bus. Leasing Inc. Home: 14019 Brookcrest Lane Dallas TX 75240 Office: 2929 N Kinsley St Garland TX 75040

WALTON, ROY B., oil and gas co. exec.; b. San Antonio, Tex., May 2, 1943; s. Robert G. and Dorothy L. (Henkes) W.; B.B.A., N. Tex. State U., 1964, M.B.A., 1966; m. Lois Elaine Getz, Dec. 6, 1968; children—Stacy Laureen, Jennifer Leigh, Angela Joy, Christopher Robert. Auditor, Arthur Andersen & Co., 1966-67, tax specialist, 1967-71; asst. to pres. Highland Resources, Inc., Houston, 1971-72, v.p. finance, 1972—; financial dir., sec. Highland North Sea Ltd.; treas. East Camden and Highland R.R. Co. C.P.A., Tex. Mem. Am. Inst. C.P.A.'s, Tex. Soc. C.P.A.'s, Beta Alpha Psi, Kappa Sigma. Home: 7914 Twining Oaks St Spring TX 77373 Office: 800 San Jacinto Bldg Houston TX 77002

WALZ, JERRY ARTHUR, elec. engr.; b. Toledo, Aug. 19, 1936; s. Arthur G. and Margherita (Baum) W.; B.S. in Elec. Engring., U. Toledo, 1961; postgrad. law Loyola U. at New Orleans, 1972-74; m. Linda Jane Mayo, July 12, 1958; children—Mark Louis, Holly Ann. Standards lab. engr., Gen. Dynamics, San Diego, 1961-65; mgr. metrology labs. Gen. Electric, Miss. Test Facility, Bay St. Louis, Miss., 1965-74; chief calibration br. Nat. Oceanographic Instrumentation Center, Nat. Space Tech. Lab., Bay St. Louis, 1974—. Mem. Goals for La. Commn., 1970; pres. Slidell Human Relations Council, 1968, dir., 1970-73; chmn. St. Tammany Democratic Alliance, 1970-74. Bd. dirs. St. Tammany Parish Non-Profit Housing Corp., 1970-71. Col. staff La. Gov. Edwin W. Edwards, 1972-74. Mem. Instrument Soc. Am. (sr.), I.E.E.E., Measurements and Data Soc., L.Q.C. Lamar Soc., Common Cause, Center for Study Democratic Instns., N.A.A.C.P., Am. Civil Liberties Union (v.p. 1972, dir. 1971-74), Phi Delta Phi, Sigma Phi Epsilon. Democrat. Home: 109 Bernay Dr Slidell LA 70458 Office: Nat Space Tech Lab NOIC/NOAA Bay St Louis MS 39520

WALZ, RICHARD JAMES, clergyman, librarian; b. Poplar Bluff, Mo., May 15, 1941; s. Raymond James and Emma Bertha (Husler) W.; A.B., St. Bernard Coll., 1963; postgrad. in philosophy Subiaco Sem., 1963-67; M.L.S., Peabody Coll., 1968. Ordained priest Roman Catholic Ch., 1967; with New Subiaco (Ark.) Abbey, 1967—, head librarian, 1968—, tchr. music and religion, 1968—. Mem. Am., Catholic (chmn. Ark. unit 1973—) library assns. Book reviewer library jour., 1965-71. Address: New Subiaco Abbey Subiaco AR 72865

WAMPLER, MARGUERITE AUSHERMAN LONG (MRS. ROBERT FRANKLIN WAMPLER), educator; b. Harrisonburg, Va.; d. Jacob Owen and Clara (Ausherman) Long; diploma Shenandoah Coll., 1942; B.S. in Edn., Madison Coll., 1958, M.S., 1961; Ed.D., U. Va., 1972; m. Robert Franklin Wampler, Sept. 20, 1942; children—Claranell (Mrs. Phillip Branner), Carolyn L. (Mrs. Gregory Snow). Tchr. elementary sch. 1958-62; tchr. John C. Myers Intermediate Sch., Broadway, Va., 1963-65; prof. edn., supr. middle grade Anthony Seeger Sch. Madison Coll., Harrisonburg, 1966—, now supr. middle grades. Rockingham County chmn. Vol. Services Western State Hosp., 1963-66. Bd. dirs. Harrisonburg-Rockingham Mental Health Assn., 1960—, sec. bd., 1962. Mem. Va. (chpt. chmn. personnel policies 1968), Rockingham County (chmn. pub. relations com. 1964-65) edn. assns., Madison Coll. P.T.A., Delta Kappa Gamma (sec. 1966—), Kappa Gamma. Mem. Ch. Brethren (tchr. jr. class 1966—). Clubs: Pilots Internat., Madison Coll. Woman's, Plains District Woman's (sec.-treas. 1961—, pres. 1963-65). Contbr. article to profl. jour. Home: Route 3 Box 27 Broadway VA 22815 Office: Madison Coll Anthony Seeger Sch Harrisonburg VA 22801

WAMPLER, WILLIAM CREED, congressman; b. Pennington Gap, Va., Apr. 21, 1926; s. John Sevier and Lillian (Wolfe) W.; B.B.A., Va. Poly. Inst., 1948; postgrad. law U. Va., 1948-50; m. Mary Elizabeth Baker, Aug. 29, 1953; children—Barbara Irene, William Creed. Reporter, Bristol Va.-Tennessean, 1950-51; reporter, editorial writer Big Stone Gap (Va.) Post, 1951; reporter, copy editor Bristol Herald Courier, 1951-52; asst. campaign mgr. congl. candidate, 1948; keynote speaker, conv. chmn. 9th Dist. Va., Republican Conv., 1950, nat. vice chmn. congl. campaign com.; mem. 83d, 90th-93d Congresses from 9th Dist. Va.; mem. com. on agr., ranking mem. tobacco subcom., dairy and poultry subcom., oilseeds and rice com. Mem. at large Sequoyah council Boy Scouts Am. Pres. Young Rep. Fedn. Va., 1950; chmn. 9th Va. Rep. Dist., 1965-66. Bd. visitors Emory and Henry Coll., Emory, Va.; bd. dirs. Youth Devel. Found. Served as air cadet USNR, 1943-45. Recipient Freedoms Found. award, 1954; Watchdog of Treasury award Nat. Asso. Businessmen; Appreciation plaque Va. State Letter Carriers Assn., 1968; Outstanding Citizen of Year award Bristol V.F.W. Sesquicentennial award U. Va., 1969; Distinguished Service award Ams. for Constl. Action, 1969. Mem. Am. Legion, Travelers Protective Assn., 40 and 8, Sigma Nu Phi. Moose, Lion. Home: 43 Lee Garden Apts Bristol VA 24201 Office: 323 Cannon Office Bldg Washington DC 20515

WAMPLER, WILLIAM DAVID, food co. exec.; b. Hinton, Va., Apr. 9, 1928; s. Charles Weldon and Zola Estelle (Huffman) W.; student Bridgewater Coll., 1946-48; B.S., Va. Poly. Inst., 1950; m. Bonnie Lou May, Sept. 22, 1951; children—Melinda May, William David, Charles Weldon II, Suzanne. Partner in charge Sunny Slope Hatchery, Harrisonburg, Va., 1950-69, Charles W. Wampler & Sons, Harrisonburg, 1950—; sec., treas. Massanutten Hatchery, Inc., Harrisonburg, 1955-69; partner in charge Farley-Wampler Bros., Harrisonburg, 1964-69; partner Wampler-Bryan Co., Harrisonburg, 1954-69; v.p. head hatchery div. Wampler Foods, Inc., Hinton, 1969—; pres. Rockingham County Sheep and Wool Producers Assn., 1964-67; pres. Staunton Prodn. Credit Assn., Staunton Fed. Land Bank assn. Mem. poultry adv. com. U.S. Sec. Agr., 1961; mem. exec. com. Va. Future Farmers Am., 1949-50; pres. Va. 4-H, 1948-49. Pres. P.T.A., 1962-63. Recipient Distinguished Service award Va. Poultry Fedn., 1962. Mem. Va. Turkey Assn. (pres. 1961-62), Va. Poultry Fedn. (pres. 1965), Nat. Turkey Fedn. (pres. 1966), Va. Angus Assn. (dir. 1965), Va. Charolais Assn. (dir. 1969—), Southeastern Poultry and Egg Assn. (state v.p. 1967), C. of C. (dir. 1966-73), Farm Bur. Assn., Tau Kappa Alpha, Alpha Zeta, Omicron Delta Kappa. Mem. Ch. Brethren (mem. ch. bd. 1967). Democrat. Elk. Club: Block and Bridle (Blacksburg, Va.); Dayton Ruritan (pres. 1955). Home: Route 6 Box 114 Harrisonburg VA 22801 Office: Wampler Foods Inc PO Box 31 Harrisonburg VA 22801

WANG NAI CHI, research co. exec., economist; b. Soochow, China, Mar. 11, 1930; s. Hsueh Yu and Shao Chuan (Chih) W.; came to U.S., 1956; B.A., Nat. Taiwan U., 1954; M.A., Am. U., 1961; Ph.D. (Hopkins Woodrow Wilson fellow, Population Council fellow), U. Md., 1970; m. Amy Fang, Sept. 8, 1962; children—Vivian, Erik. Economist Nat. Planning Assn., Washington, 1963-64; sr. statis. asso. R.L. Banks & Assos., Inc., Washington, 1966—. Mem. Econometric Soc., Am. Statis. Assn., Am. Econ. Assn. Contbr. articles on demography to profl. jours. Home: 11515 Karen Dr Potomac MD 20854 Office: 900 17th NW Washington DC 20006

WANN, LAYMOND DOYLE, petroleum research scientist; b. Magazine, Ark., Apr. 25, 1924; s. Vernon Cecil and Emma (McCrary) W.; B.S. in Physics (Phi Eta Sigma scholar), Okla. State U., 1949, M.S., 1950; m. Betty Lou Brown, Nov. 6, 1948; children—Jacqueline, Lyndall Doyle. With Continental Oil Co., Ponca City, Okla., 1951—, sr. research scientist, 1957-60, research group leader, 1960—. Served with AUS, 1942-46; ETO. Decorated Bronze Star. Mem. Am. Petroleum Inst., I.E.E.E., Aircraft Owners and Pilots Assn., Civil Air Patrol, V.F.W., Phi Kappa Phi, Pi Mu Epsilon, Sigma Phi Sigma. Episcopalian (vestryman). Contbr. articles in fields of elec. and radioactive well-logging, elec. design to profl. jours. Patentee in field. Home: 1501 Monument Rd Ponca City OK 74601 Office: 1000 S Pine St Ponca City OK 74601

WANNAMAKER, WILLIAM WHETSTONE III, chem. engr.; b. Orangeburg, S.C., Nov. 1, 1926; s. William Whetstone and Evelyn (Townsend) W.; grad. The Citadel, 1949; B.Chem. Engring., Cornell U., 1952; postgrad. U. S.C., 1954-55; m. Betty Ray Davis, Sept. 13, 1947; children—Ray (Mrs. Robert Sabalis), Harriet (Mrs. Willis Sheorn III), William Whetstone IV, Preston Davis, Amelia Townsend, Sarah Boyd, Mary DuPre. Tech. engr. E.I. duPont de Nemours & Co., Inc., Camden, S.C., 1952-59; pres. chief chemist Wateree Chem. Co., Lugoff, S.C., 1956—; v.p., asst. gen. mgr. Hynes Chem. Research Corp., Lugoff, 1968-73; sec.-treas Manoa Metals, Inc., Ashepoo, S.C., 1972—. Headmaster, sci. tchr. Thomas Sumter Acad., Dalzell, S.C., 1965-68; lectr. Wade Hampton Acad., Orangeburg, 1969, Joseph Kershaw Acad., 1971-72. Pres., County Republican conv., 1960, 62, 64, 66; chmn. Rep. party Kershaw County, 1961-64, 66; chmn. 5th Congl. Dist., 1961-66; 2d vice chmn. state conv., 1966; alternate del. nat. conv., 1960, 68, 72, del., 1964; state exec. dir. Nixon for Pres., 1968. Bd. dirs. Joseph Kershaw Acad., Camden, chmn., 1971-72. Served with USNR, 1944-46. Registered profl. engr., S.C., Del. Fellow Am. Inst. Chemists; mem. Am. Chem. Soc., V.F.W., Alpha Chi Sigma. Episcopalian. Rotarian. Home: 902 Sunnyhill Dr Camden SC 29020 Office: PO Box 7 Lugoff SC 29078

WANTMAN, JOEL NORMAN, civil engr.; b. Bklyn., June 27, 1941; s. Jack and Edythe (Wecker) W.; B.S., U. Ariz., 1964; M.S., N.Y. U., 1967; m. Ellen Bernice Kolikof, Dec. 29, 1962; children—David Scott, Greg Michael. Designer, Hazen & Sawyer, cons. engrs., N.Y.C., 1965-67; project mgr. Buchart-Horn Cons. Engrs., York, Pa., 1967-68; chief san. engr. Adair & Brady Cons. Engrs., West Palm Beach, Fla., 1968-72; pres. Wantman & Assos., Inc., cons. engrs., West Palm Beach, 1972—. Registered profl. engr., Pa., Fla. Mem. Am. Soc. C.E., Am. Water Works Assn., Nat. Soc. Profl. Engrs., Fla. Engring. Soc., Fla. Inst. Cons. Engrs. Fla. Pollution Control Assn., Bus. Mens' Assn. Palm Beaches (bd. dirs. 1973). Home: 7510 Palm Rd West Palm Beach FL 33406 Office: 2300 Palm Beach Lakes Blvd West Palm Beach FL 33401

WARBURTON, LAWRENCE HENRY, JR., lawyer; b. San Diego, Sept. 6, 1926; s. L. H. and Estellane (Smith) W.; student Coll. Pacific-Stockton, 1945, U. Cal. at Berkeley, 1945-46; B.B.A., U. Tex. at Austin, 1949, LL.B., 1950 ; m. Jeanelle Golden, Sept. 3, 1955; children—Patrick Allison, William Perry, Lane Golden. Admitted to Tex. bar, 1950; individual practice law, Freer, Tex., 1950-54; asst. atty. gen., Tex., 1954-55; asst. dist. atty. 79th Judicial Dist. Tex., 1955-60; partner firm Perkins, Davis, Oden & Warburton, Alice, Tex., 1960—. Mem. exec. bd. Gulf Coast council Boy Scouts Am., 1960—; pres., campaign chmn. United Fund, 1960-62. Served with USNR, 1944-46. Named 1 of 5 Outstanding Young Texans, Tex. Jr. C. of C., 1960; recipient Silver Beaver award Boy Scouts Am., 1968. Mem. State Bar Tex. (mem. grievance com. for dist. 14-A 1968-69, mem. com. on profl. efficiency and econ. research 1968-69, dir. 1969-72, chmn. bar jour. com. 1972—), Coastal Bend Bar Assn. (pres. 1960), Am. Bar Assn., Am. Judicature Soc., Tex. Trial Lawyers Assn., Alice C. of C. (dir., v.p. 1965-66), Alpha Phi Omega (pres. Tex. Alpha chpt. 1949), Sigma Phi Epsilon. Rotarian (pres. 1966). Methodist. Contbr. articles law jours. Home: 1120 Arcadia St Alice TX 78332 Office: Alice Nat Bank Bldg Alice TX 78332

WARD, ALLEN WAYNE, metals industry cons.; b. Decatur, Ala., Aug. 31, 1933; s. Robert Hardy and Grace (Tucker) W.; B.M.E., Clemson U., 1955; M.S., U. Ala., 1968; m. Kay Marie Cowan, Oct. 26, 1957; children—Kelly Wayne, Pamela Kay, Leslie Virginia. Engr., U.S. Pipe and Foundry Co., Birmingham, Ala., 1956-61, head process and product devel. dept., 1962-66, asst. plant mgr., Chattanooga, 1966-69; gen. mgr. Dalton Precision Co., Cushing, Okla., 1971; owner, pres. Ward Assos., Consultants, Stillwater, Okla., 1971—. Mem., co-chmn. Airport Commn. City Stillwater, 1973—; mem. Indsl. Services bd. So. Area council YMCA, Atlanta. Bd. dirs. YMCA, Stillwater. Served as capt. USMCR, 1956-65. Registered profl. engr., Ala., Okla. Mem. Am. Foundrymens' Soc., Am. Soc. Metals, Nat. Soc. Profl. Engrs., So. Area Indsl. Mgmt. Clubs (pres.), Aircraft Owners and Pilots Assn. Presbyn. (elder). Home: 3123 Fox Ledge Lane Stillwater OK 74074 Office: PO Box 249 Stillwater OK 74074

WARD, BENJAMIN PORTER, ret. naval officer, educator; b. LaFayette, Ind., July 2, 1897; s. Harry Van Devanter and Nellie Clara (Armbruster) W. ; B.S., U.S. Naval Acad., 1919; M.S., Columbia U., 1927; m. Mary Ellen Estes, May 6, 1928; 1 son, Benjamin Porter. Commd. ensign USN, 1919, advanced through grades to capt., 1942, ret., 1950; asso. prof. mech. engring. Auburn U., Auburn, Ala., 1950-68, emeritus, 1968—. Decorated Victory Medal, World War I and World War II. Registered profl. engr., N.Y., Washington. Mem. Am. Soc. Naval Engrs., Am. Soc. M.E., Soc. Naval Architects and Marine Engrs., U.S. Naval Acad. Alumni Assn., Pi Tau Sigma. Mason. Clubs: N.Y. Yacht (N.Y.C.); Ponte Vedra (Fla.); Saugahatchee Country (Auburn, Ala.). Home: 815 S College St Auburn AL 36830

WARD, CECIL CLAYTON, ret. govt. chem. engr.; b. Krebs, Okla., Oct. 15, 1910; s. Frank and Mary Anne (McMurdo) W.; B.S. in Chem. Engring., Okla. State U., 1934, M.S., 1947; m. Margye Pryor, Dec. 25, 1935 (dec. Mar. 1972); m. 2d, Leah B. Hayes, Nov. 23, 1973. Chem. engr. Bur. Mines, Bartlesville, Okla., 1935-55, chief br. chemistry and refining, 1955-59, project coordinator, 1959-72, research supr., 1972-74. Pres., Bartlesville Community Concert Assn., 1969-72. Recipient Meritorious Service award Dept. Interior, 1959, Distinguished Service award, 1962. Registered profl. engr., Okla. Mem. Am. Inst. Chem. Engrs., Am. Chem. Soc., A.A.A.S., Am. Soc. Testing and Materials (vice chmn. com. on petroleum 1968—), Nat., Okla. socs. profl. engrs. Club: Hillcrest Country. Contbr. articles to profl. engrs. Home: 2118 Mercury Ct Bartlesville OK 74003

WARD, FORREST LEON, accountant; b. Tulsa, Nov. 26, 1941; s. Joe Davis and Mildred (Carlen) W.; B.S., Okla. State U., 1964; m. Sharon Anne Tharp, Sept. 2, 1962; children—Jerry Darren, Ginger Coleen. Staff auditor Arthur Young & Co., Dallas, 1967-72, audit mgr., 1972—. Instr. Am. Inst. C.P.A.'s. Served with AUS, 1964-67. C.P.A., Tex. Mem. Am. Inst. C.P.A.'s, Tex. Soc. C.P.A.s, Sigma Phi Epsilon, Beta Alpha Psi. Baptist. Toastmasters (adminstrv. v.p. 1972-73, v.p. edn. 1973, pres. 1973-74). Home: 9538 Vinewood Dr Dallas TX 75228 Office: 3800 Republic Nat Bank Tower Dallas TX 75201

WARD, FRED DERYL, lawyer; b. Houston, Aug. 19, 1935; s. Cecil Devane and Mittie Emmaline (Hull) W.; B.A., So. Meth. U., 1957; J.D., U. Tex., 1961; m. Betty Ray Lumpkin, Feb. 17, 1967; 1 son, Fred Deryl. Asst. atty. gen. Tex., Austin, 1961-64; trust officer Merc. Nat. Bank, Dallas, 1964-69; admitted to Tex. bar, 1961; practiced in Austin, 1961-64, Dallas, 1964—; mem. firm Mayo & Ward, Dallas, 1969—. Mem. Am., Dallas bar assns., State Bar Tex. Methodist (mem. bd. 1967-70). Club: Toastmasters (Dallas). Home: 3608 Shenandoah Av Dallas TX 75205 Office: Republic Nat Bank Bldg Dallas TX 75201

WARD, GEORGE TRUMAN, architect; b. Washington, July 24, 1927; s. Truman and Gladys Anna (Nutt) W.; B.S., Va. Poly. Inst., 1951, M.S., 1952; postgrad. George Washington U., 1966; m. Margaret Ann Hall, Sept. 10, 1949; children—Carol Ann, Donna Lynne, George Truman, Robert Stephen. Archtl. draftsman Charles A. Pearson, Radford, Va., 1950; head archtl. sect. Hayes, Seay, Mattern & Mattern, Radford and Roanoke, 1951-52; with Joseph Saunders & Assos., Alexandria, Va., 1952-57, asso. architect, 1955-57; partner Vosbeck-Ward & Assos., Alexandria, 1957-64, Ward & Hall & Assos., Springfield, Va., 1964—; dir. United Va. Bank/Nat. Pres. P.T.A. Burke (Va.) Sch., 1970-71. Bd. mgrs. Fairfax (Va.) County YMCA, 1964—. Served with AUS, 1946-47. Registered profl. architect, Va., Md., D.C., W.Va., Ohio, N.J., Del., Pa., Tenn., Ga., N.C., N.Y., Tex. Mem. A.I.A. (corp.), Guild for Religious Architecture, Va. Assn. Professions, Va. C. of C., Tau Sigma Delta, Omicron Delta Kappa, Phi Kappa Phi, Pi Delta Epsilon. Baptist (deacon). Mason (Shriner, K.T.), Rotarian (charter mem., pres. Springfield 1973-74). Home: 9600 Burke View Av Burke VA 22015 Office: 6320 Augusta Dr Springfield VA 22150

WARD, HAROLD ANSON, III, lawyer; b. Orlando, Fla., Oct. 1, 1933; s. Harold Anson and Elizabeth (Michael) W.; B.A., U. Chgo., 1952, J.D., 1955; m. Mary Elizabeth Lewis, Nov. 8, 1958; children—Catherine Ann, Thomas Harold, Mary Elizabeth. Admitted to Fla. bar, 1955; law clk. to U.S. Supreme Ct. Justice Black, 1955-56; mem. firm Winderweedle, Haines, Ward & Woodman, Winter Park, 1959—. Municipal judge, Winter Park 1969-73. Chmn. bd. Central Fla. Heart Assn.; v.p. Winter Park Youth Center; bd. control Winter Park Meml. Hosp. Found. Treas., trustee Winter Park Meml. Hosp. Assn.; bd. dirs. Edyth Bush Charitable Found. Served to capt. USAF, 1956-59. Recipient Outstanding Young Man of Year award Winter Park Jr. C. of C., 1962. Mem. Am., Fla. (past com. chmn.), Orange County (exec. council) bar assns., Am. Judicature Soc., Winter Park C. of C. (pres.). Conglist. (moderator). Rotarian. Clubs: Winter Park University; Country (Orlando). Home: 2150 Fawsett Rd Winter Park FL 32789 Office: 204 E New England Av Winter Park FL 32789

WARD, JAMES AUDLEY, govt. mathematician; b. Timmonsville, S.C., May 19, 1910; s. Simon Vivian and Grace (Bethea) W.; B.A., Davidson Coll., 1931; M.S., La. State U., 1934; Ph.D., U. Wis., 1939; m. Virginia Kroenke, July 9, 1935; children—James Audley, Frederick R., Wayne D. Asst. prof. math. Davidson Coll., 1937-38; asso. prof. math. Tenn. Poly. Inst., 1939-40; prof. math. Delta State Tchrs. Coll., 1940-42, U. Ga., 1946-49, U. Ky., 1949-55; mathematician Holloman AFB, N.M., 1955-57, chief digital computer br., 1957-59; asst. to v.p. Sperry Rand Corp., 1959-62; computer specialist Office of Dir. Def. Research and Devel., 1962-69; asst. for computer programs Naval Ordnance Systems Command, Washington, 1969—. Served from lt. (j.g.) to lt. comdr. USNR, 1942-46. Mem. Math. Assn. Am. (chmn. La.-Miss. sect. 1942-44, Ky. sect. 1952-53), Am. Math. Soc., Soc. for Indsl. and Applied Math., Assn. for Computing Machinery, I.E.E.E. (sr.), Am. Def. Preparedness Assn., Sigma Xi, Sigma Pi Sigma, Pi Mu Epsilon. Contbr. articles to profl. jours. Home: 5106 Marlyn Dr Washington DC 20016 Office: Naval Ordnance Systems Command Nat Center 2 Washington DC 20360

WARD, JAMES WILLIS, elec. supply co. exec.; b. Amarillo, Tex., Oct. 11, 1930; s. Winford Willis and Grace Alene (Ashcraft) W.; student U.S. Naval Acad., 1950-51; m. Anna La Faun Rankin, Apr. 27, 1952; children—David Garner, Paul Brian. With Nunn Electric Supply Corp., Amarillo, Tex., 1951—, v.p. supply div., 1969—. Pres., Black Lake Water Assn., 1971-74; chmn. Regional Planning Commn. Traffic Land Use Com., 1970-74; mem. state commn. Tex. Mass Transp. Commn., 1972—. Served with USN, 1948-51. Mem. Purchasing Agts. Assn. Tex. Panhandle, Amarillo Exec. Assn., C. of C. (chmn. traffic com. 1969-70). Mason. Clubs: Amarillo; Canyon (Tex.) Country. Home: 6709 Jameson St Amarillo TX 79106 Office: 105 Polk St Amarillo TX 79101

WARD, JAY THOMAS, ins. co. exec.; b. Abilene, Tex., Dec. 27, 1919; s. Joe Thomas and Hilda (Faulke) W.; student Abilene Christian Coll., 1938-40; B.B.A., U. Tex., 1948; m. Jean Marilyn Savage, Sept. 4, 1948; children—Andrea Jean, Angela Ellen. Vice pres. Southland

Life Ins. Co., Dallas, 1948—. Served with AUS, 1940-45. C.P.A., Tex. Fellow Life Office Mgmt. Assn.; mem. Tex. Soc. C.P.A.'s (dir. 1967-70, pres. Dallas chpt. 1972-73). Contbr. articles to profl. jours. Home: 9641 Fieldcrest Dr Dallas TX 75238 Office: Southland Center Dallas TX 75201

WARD, JOHN LEWIS, editor; b. Damascus, Ark., Dec. 17, 1930; s. Roy Wilson and Mamie Lillian (Richardson) W.; student State Coll. Ark., intermittently, 1950-60; B.A., U. Ark., 1968; m. Betty Sue Chandler, Feb. 1, 1957; children—Jennifer Kay, Barry Wilson. Reporter, Log Cabin Democrat, Conway, 1956-58, mng. editor, 1972—; editor, editorial feature page Ark. Democrat, Little Rock, 1958-64; dir. pub. relations Winthrop Rockefeller, Gov. of Ark., 1964-71. Dir. Rockefeller for Gov. campaign, Ark., 1968. Mem. Ark. Inst. Politics (adv. bd.), Sigma Delta Chi. Home: 3 Post Oak Dr Conway AR 72032

WARD, LEW O., oil producer; b. Oklahoma City, July 24, 1930; s. Llewellyn Orcutt and Addie (Reisdorph) W. II; student Okla. Mil. Acad. Jr. Coll., 1948-50; B.S., Okla. U., 1953; m. Myra Beth Gungoll, Oct. 29, 1955; children—Casidy Ann, William Carlton. Dist. engr. Delhi-Taylor Oil Corp., Tulsa, 1955-56; partner Ward-Gungoll Oil Investments, Enid, Okla., 1956—; owner L.O. Ward Oil Operations, Enid, 1963—; v.p. 1420 Lahoma Rd. Inc., Enid, 1967—, also dir.; dir. Community Bank & Trust Co., Pulse Mag. Vice chmn. Indsl. Devel. Commn., Enid, 1968—. Active YMCA. Chmn., Garfield County Republican Com., 1967-69. Bd. dirs. Okla. Polit. Action Com., now chmn. Served as 1st lt. C.E., AUS, 1953-55. Registered profl. engr., Okla. Mem. Am. Inst. Mining and Metall. Engrs., Okla. Ind. Petroleum Assn. (dir.), Ind. Petroleum Assn. Am. (dir.), C. of C. (dir., indsl. devel. com. 1970-72), Am. Bus. Club (pres. 1964), Order Ky. Cols., Alpha Tau Omega. Methodist. Mason (Shriner), Rotarian. Clubs: Metropolitan Dinner (dir. Enid), Falcon, Toastmasters (pres. Enid 1966), Senate. Home: 900 Brookside Dr Enid OK 73701 Office: 1420 Lahoma Rd Enid OK 73701

WARD, (MARY) LUCILE PARRISH (MRS. JACK CHRISTOPHER WARD), club woman; b. Campbellton, Fla.; d. William Albritton and Emma (Hughes) Parrish; B.A., Ala. Coll., 1931; postgrad. Huntingdon Coll., 1937, Wayne U., 1944; m. Jack Christopher Ward, Dec. 2, 1934. Tchr. pub. schs., Abbeville, Ala., 1931-35, Montgomery, 1935-39, Charlotte, N.C., 1945-48. Orientation chmn. Nat. Fedn. Music Clubs, 1963-65, bd. dirs., 1965—, chmn. edn. dept., 1965-69, v.p. in charge southeastern region, 1969-73, also life mem., chmn. membership extension dept. 1973—, exec. bd., 1969—, mem. bicentennial com. 1973—; hon. life mem. Ala. Fedn. Music Clubs; pres. S.C. Fedn. Music Clubs, 1959-63, Guild of Greenville Symphony, 1964-65; bd. dirs. Greenville Symphony Assn., 1957-59, 64-65, 73—; chmn. music and arts com. Greenville County Found., 1965—; mem. S.C. Arts Commn., 1967-68; mem. nat. adv. council Brevard (N.C.) Music Center, 1969—. Named Woman of Year—Music Greenville Piedmont Newspaper, 1960. Mem. Fountain Inn Music Club (life), Delta Omicron (state alumnae chmn. 1965-68, pres. Piedmont alumni chpt. 1967-68, province pres. 1968—), Longview Garden Club (pres. 1953-54), Music Club (Greenville, pres. 1957-59), Greenville Garden Club (pres. 1968-70), Greenville Woman's Club, Garden Club S.C. (life). Methodist. Home: Altamont Rd Paris Mountain Greenville SC 29609

WARD, NELSON DAVID, paper mfg. co. exec.; b. Lubbock, Tex., Aug. 16, 1941; s. Daniel Zigler and Irma (Struve) W.; B.B.A. in Accounting, Tex. Technol. U., 1966; m. Lesa Merril Habbinga, Sept. 5, 1965; children—Joe Dwayne, Shicaire Kay. Sr. auditor firm Peat, Marwick, Mitchell & Co., Dallas, 1967-71; v.p., treas. sec. Ennis Bus. Forms, Inc. (Tex.), 1971—; dir. several cos., including Upco Printing Co., UP Corp., both N.Y.C., Ennis Data Processing Co., So. Bus. Forms Co., Knoxville, Tested Advt. Tech. Co., Burbank, Cal., ABC Bus. Forms, Inc., Miami, and others. Served with USNR, 1959-63. C.P.A., Tex. Mem. Am. Inst. C.P.A.'s, Am. Accounting Assn., Financial Execs. Inst., Am. Mgmt. Assn. Democrat. Methodist. Home: 506 W Denton St Ennis TX 75119 Office: 107 N Sherman St Ennis TX 75119

WARD, RICHARD ARISTA, civil engr.; b. Foss, Okla., Feb. 15, 1920; s. Thomas Hamilton and Dallice (Paris) W.; student East Central Coll., 1946-47; B.S. in Civil Engring., Okla. State U., 1950; m. Ruth Bullock, July 2, 1949; children—Michael Edward, Stephen Richard. With Okla. Hwy. Dept., 1945—, instrumentman, 1949-50, resident engr., 1950-53, asst. div. engr., 1953-64, 65-71, div. engr., 1964, 1965, chief engr., Oklahoma City, 1971—. Mem. Okla. Group Ins. Bd.; trustee Employee Retirement System Okla.; bd. visitors Okla. State U. Served with AUS, 1942-45. Decorated Bronze Star medal with oak leaf cluster. Mem. Am. Soc. C.E., Nat., Okla. socs. profl. engrs. Baptist. Mason. Home: 115 W Dells Av Stillwater OK 74074 Office: Jim Thorpe Bldg Oklahoma City OK 73105

WARD, ROBERT MILLER, lawyer; b. Blacksburg, S.C., Oct. 14, 1916; s. Rembert and Lena Rivers (Miller) W.; grad. U. Cal. at Los Angeles, 1937; m. Carolyn Louise Libby, Apr. 1, 1944; children—Robert Miller, Rembert Brien, Carolyn Libby (Mrs. Gregory Carnohan). Newspaper reporter Rock Hills (S.C.) Herald, Los Angeles Times, 1933-36; sec. to Congressman James P. Richards, S.C. 5th Dist., 1941-45; dir. pub. relations Winthrop Coll., 1945-46; admitted to S.C. bar, 1945, U.S. Supreme Ct. bar, 1949; practiced in Rock Hill, 1945—; mem. firm Roddey & Ward, 1947-53, Ward & Grier, Rock Hill, 1969—. City recorder, Rock Hill, 1962-66; staff asst. Congressman Tom S. Gettys, 1964—. Chmn. York County Library System, 1967. Mem. S.C. Ho. of Reps., 1947-48. Trustee, Rock Hill Sch., 1950-66. Rotarian. Author: Children of King Hagler, 1950; Notary Public in South Carolina, 1969-73. Home: 931 Myrtle Dr Rock Hill SC 29730 Office: 414 W Oakland Av Rock Hill SC 29730

WARD, S(OLOMON) KELLY, dentist; b. Weathersby, Miss., Oct. 21, 1897; s. William Robert and Mary Elizabeth (Stringer) W.; B.A., Miss. Coll., 1923; D.D.S., Emory U., 1928; m. Jimmie Davis Holmes, May 12, 1946. Prin., Hollandale (Miss.) High Sch., 1924-25; practice gen. dentistry, Taylorsville, Miss., 1928—. Miss. dir. Vets.' Farm and Home Bd., 1960-64. Alderman, City of Taylorsville, 1940-48; chmn. Smith County Democratic Com., 1960. Served with USN, 1918-19. Recipient certificates of appreciation, Pres. Roosevelt, 1942-44, Pres. Truman, 1945. Mem. LaSociete des Quarante Hommes et Huit Chevaux, Chef de Gar Locale, Grande de La Porte, Grande Cheminot, Grande Conducteur, LaGrande Medicin, Am. Dental Assn., Am. Legion (gold certificate for service 1973), Miss. Hist. Soc., V.F.W., Miss. Cattlemen's Assn., Delta Sigma Delta. Mason (Shriner, K.T.), Lion; mem. Order Eastern Star. Address: Taylorsville MS 39168

WARD, WILLIAM ARTHUR, coll. adminstr.; b. Oakdale, La., Dec. 17, 1921; s. Albert Winfred and Annie (Williams) W.; B.S., McMurry Coll., 1948; M.S., Okla. State U., 1949; LL.D., Oklahoma City U., 1962; m. Virginia Ella Bell, June 30, 1945; children—Craig, David, Lisa. Dir. pub. relations Schreiner Inst., Kerrville, Tex., 1949-55; asst. to pres. Tex. Wesleyan Coll., Fort Worth, 1955—. Chmn., Tarrant County chpt. ARC, 1971-72. Served to capt. AUS, 1942-46. Methodist. Rotarian. Contbg. editor: Quote Mag., 1970—. Author: Thoughts of a Christian Optimist, 1968; For this One Hour, 1969; Prayer Is, 1969; Fountains of Faith, 1970; Allegiance to America, 1971; Brighten Your Corner, 1973. Home: 2141 Green Hill Circle Fort Worth TX 76112

WARD, WILLIAM FRANKLIN, physician; b. Sumter, S.C., June 16, 1935; s. William Franklin and Mellie Anne (Wells) K.; student Bob Jones U., 1953-55; B.S., U. S.C., 1957; M.D., Med. Coll. S.C., 1961; m. Patricia Lane Fogle, Aug. 27, 1960; children—William Franklin III, Frederick Wells, Darrin Robert. Rotating intern Columbia (S.C.) Hosp., 1961-62; staff physician med.-surg. unit, S.C. State Hosp., Columbia, 1962-63; gen. practice medicine, West Columbia, S.C., 1963—, Springdale, S.C., 1968—; mem. staff vice chief, 1972—; staff Lexington County Hosp., West Columbia Hosp., So. Baptist Hosp., Providence Hosp., Columbia Hosp., (all Richland and Lexington County); sec. Lexington County Hosp., 1971; sch. physician Columbia Bible Coll., 1968—; team physician Airport High Sch., 1968—. Mem. Regional Health Planning Council, 1970—; mem. Drug Abuse Council of Richland-Lexington Counties 1971—; mem. Lexington County Ambulance Commn., 1970—; chmn. Springdale Health Forum, 1971. Bd. dirs. Mid Carolina Council on Alcoholism, 1965-70, Brookland Plantation, Served with M.C., AUS, 1966-68. Mem. A.M.A., So. Med. Assn., Christian, S.C., Columbia med. socs., Am. Acad. Gen. Practice, Am. Heart Assn., Nat. Rehab. Assn., West Columbia C. of C. Baptist (deacon 1965—). Optimist (dist. lt. gov. Cayce-West Columbia 1971—). Home: 1108 Baywater Dr West Columbia SC 29169 Office: 3114 Platt Springs Rd Springdale West Columbia SC 29169

WARD, WINFRED O'NEIL, physician; b. Exmore, Va., Sept. 28, 1933; s. Marvin Omar and Ruth (Kellam) W.; B.S., Coll. of William and Mary, 1954; M.D., Med. Coll. Va., 1958; m. Anne Sexton Martin, June 21, 1958; children—Anne Elizabeth, Susan Terry, Oma. Intern, Mercy Hosp., Springfield, O., 1958-59; practice gen. medicine and psychoanalysis through hypnosis, Franklin, Va., 1961—, hypnoanalysis, 1973—; mem. staff Southampton Meml. Hosp., chief of staff, 1968-70. Mem. Franklin Hwy. Safety Council, 1968, Gov.'s Council on Mental Health, 1965—. Chmn., Franklin Republican City Com., 1965-67, 68-70; vice chmn. 4th Dist. Rep. Com., 1968-70. Bd. dirs. Southampton Meml. Hosp. Served with USNR, 1959-61. Mem. Am. Acad. Gen. Practice, A.M.A., So., Tri-County (pres. 1969-70) med. socs., Med. Soc. Va., Nat. Acad. Med. Hypnosis (charter mem., treas. 1972—), Assn. Advancement Ethical Hypnosis, Richmond Acad. Medicine, Internat. Platform Assn. Home: 2 Twin Lake Lane Richmond VA 23229 Office: 6620 W Broad St Rd Richmond VA 23230

WARDELL, ANTHONY WENTWORTH, govt. ofcl.; b. Bklyn., Jan. 11, 1932; s. Raymond and Constance (Jackson) W.; B.S., Ga. Inst. Tech., 1954; M.S., Chrysler Inst. Engring., Detroit, 1959; m. Emily Ayers, Mar. 21, 1954 (div. May 1974); children—Linda Marie, Mark Douglas. Automotive engr. Chrysler Corp., Detroit, 1957-59; reliability engr. Brown Engring. Co., Inc., Huntsville, Ala., 1959-60; sr. reliability engr. Lockheed Ga. Co., Atlanta, 1960-63; system safety specialist NASA Johnson Space Center, Houston, 1963-69, asst. chief system safety br. 1969—. Served as lt. (j.g.) USN, 1954-57. Recipient Sustained Superior Performance award NASA, 1967, Superior Achievement awards NASA, 1968, 69. Registered profl. engr., Ga. Mem. Tau Beta Pi, Pi Tau Sigma, Phi Eta Sigma, Phi Kappa Phi. Contbr. articles to profl. jours. Home: 18307 Blanchmont Lane Houston TX 77058 Office: Mail Code NS2 NASA Johnson Space Center Houston TX 77058

WARDEN, EDWARD, lawyer, banker; b. Mt. Pleasant, Pa., May 15, 1907; s. Eugene C. and Pleasant (Glessner) W.; B.S., Washington and Jefferson Coll., 1928; LL.B., Duquesne U., 1931; Litt. M., U. Pitts., 1951; m. Emily Bryce, Jan. 30, 1933; children—Mary Bryce, James Bryce, Gerard Bryce. Clk., 1st Nat. Bank, Pitts., 1929-34, asst. trust officer, 1934-37, trust office, 1937-39, v.p., trust officer, 1939-46; v.p. Peoples First Nat. Bank and Trust Co. (merger 1st Nat. Bank and Peoples Pitts. Nat. Bank), 1946-60; v.p. Pitts. Nat. Bank (merger Peoples First Nat. Bank and Trust Co. and Fidelity Trust Co.), 1960-72; practice law, Pinehurst, N.C., 1972; dir. Washington Steel Corp. Mem. Am., Pa., Allegheny County bar assns., Phi Delta Theta, Phi Delta Phi, Pi Delta Epsilon, Phi Alpha Theta. Republican. Episcopalian. Clubs: Pinehurst (N.C.) Country; Duquesne, Fox Chapel Golf (Pitts.); Pike Run Country (Jones Mills, Pa.); Laurel Valley Golf, Rolling Rock (Ligonier, Pa.). Address: 32 Quail Hill Pinehurst NC 28374

WARDER, THOMAS FISHER, obstetrician, gynecologist; b. Carthage, Tenn., Apr. 13, 1915; s. William Henry and Christine Waters (Fisher) W.; B.A., Vanderbilt U., 1936, M.D., 1941; m. Margaret Jeanne Stokes, Sept. 5, 1942; children—Martha Christine (Mrs. Arthur Cory Andreasen), Margaret Jeanne. Intern, Vanderbilt U. Hosp., Nashville, 1941-42, asst. resident, 1942, 46-48, resident, 1948-49, now staff mem., asst. univ. clin. prof. obstetrics-gynecology, 1964—; practice medicine specializing in obstetrics and gynecology, Nashville, 1949—; mem. staff St. Thomas, Bapt., Nashville Gen., Parkview, West Side hosps.; clin. prof. obstetrics-gynecology Meharry Med. Coll., 1967—. Served with M.C., AUS, 1942-46. Diplomate Am. Bd. Obstetrics and Gynecology. Mem. A.M.A., Am. Coll. Obstetrics and Gynecology. Tenn. Med. Assn., Nashville Davidson County Med. Soc., Nashville Obstetrics-Gynecology Soc. (pres. 1966). Presbyn. Home: 214 Hillwood Dr Nashville TN 37205 Office: 104 20th Av N Nashville TN 37203

WARDLEY, JAMES ALAN, accountant; b. Connellsville, Pa., Apr. 16, 1935; s. John Kenneth and Ruth (Weaver) W.; student LaSalle Extension U., 1951-57; B.B.A., U. Tenn., 1956, postgrad., 1968—; m. Molly Laraine Napier, June 8, 1963; children—Linda Gayle, David Kenneth, James Alan II, Marc Scott, Charla Alisha. Jr. accountant, Peat, Marwick, Mitchell & Co., C.P.A.'s, Memphis, 1956-57, sr. accountant, 1957-58; sr. accountant Joe E. Henry & Co. C.P.A.'s, Knoxville, Tenn., 1958-60, partner, 1960-61; partner, dir. John R. Fiser, Inc., Knoxville, 1961-70, controller, 1961-68, v.p., 1968-70; pres. Nova, Inc., Knoxville, 1970—. Bd. dirs. West Side YMCA, Fedn. Chief YMCA Indian Guides, West Central Recreation Commn. C.P.A., Tenn. Mem. Tenn. Soc. C.P.A.'s, Am. Inst. C.P.A.'s, Nat. Assn. Home Builders, Delta Sigma Pi (pres.), Beta Alpha Psi (treas.), Sigma Nu (treas.). Republican. Home: Route 5 9136 Carlton Circle Concord TN 37720 Office: 6910 Kingston Pike Knoxville TN 37919

WARE, CHARLES ARTHUR, ins. exec.; b. Dunnsville, Va., Jan. 20, 1921; s. Catesby and Lila Constance (Maddox) W.; student Lynchburg Coll., 1938-40, William and Mary Coll., 1940-41, U. Ga., 1941-42, Ins. Inst. Am., 1943-44, Columbia U., 1944-45; m. Jeanne Elizabeth Barbour, Oct. 7, 1950; children—Charles Arthur, Keville Barbour, Elizabeth Jeanne. Map clk. Hartford Fire Ins. Co., Atlanta, 1941-42; underwriter Great Am. Ins. Group, N.Y.C., 1943-45, insp., Washington, 1945-46; v.p. South Boston Ins. Agy., Inc. (Va.), 1947-55, pres., 1955—; pres. Randolph Motor Inn, South Boston, 1963—, chmn. bd., 1972; v.p. McDaniel Real Estate Co., Inc., Richmond, 1965-72, Ware Oil Co., Dunnsville, Va., 1959—. Sec.-treas. Martinsville Convalescent Home, Inc., 1965—. Sec. South Boston Electoral Bd., 1960-62, South Boston Planning Commn., 1963—, chmn., 1972—. Mem. Halifax County C. of C. (treas., 1954-58), Va. Hotel and Motel Assn. (bd. dirs. 1966-73), So. Innkeepers Assn. (bd. dirs. 1970-72, v.p. 1971-72), South Boston and Va. Retail Mchts. Assn. (bd. dirs. 1970-73), South Boston Bd. Ins. Underwriters (bd. dirs. 1957, pres. 1960). Club: Brevard Anchor (pres. 1973-74) (Cocoa Beach, Fla.). Presbyn. (deacon). Rotarian. Home: 1412 Hodges St South Boston VA 24592 Office: 325 Main St South Boston VA 24592

WARE, GRAYDON LEROY, educator; b. Springfield, Mass., Oct. 2, 1925; s. George Aaron and Dora Lenora (White) W.; B.S., Adelbert Coll., Case-Western Res. U., 1946, M.S., 1947; postgrad. U. Ill., 1949-50. Instr. Rio Grande (O.) Coll., 1947-49, acting chmn. dept. biology, asst. dean men, 1947-48; instr. Coll. Liberal Arts, Mercer U., Macon, Ga., 1950-52, asst. prof. biology, 1952-59, asso. prof. biology, 1959-74, prof., 1974—. Mem. A.A.A.S., Ga. Acad. Sci., Am. Inst. Biol. Scis., Am. Soc. Mammalogy, Am. Mus. Natural History, Internat. Oceanographic Found., Blue Key, Beta Beta Beta, Sigma Alpha Epsilon (hon. province pres.). Baptist. Author: Laboratory Manual for Comparative Vertebrate Anatomy, 1973; Laboratory Manual of Parasitology, 1973; Laboratory Manual of Microbiology, 1963; Laboratory Manual for Experimental Biology, 1951. Home: 1351 Stadium Dr Apt 201 D Macon GA 31201 Office: Willet Sci Center Mercer U Macon GA 31207

WARE, JAMES WARREN, III, dentist; b. Euharlee, Ga., Feb. 9, 1934; s. James Warren, Jr. and Alma Doris (Nelson) W.; A.B., Shorter Coll., 1956; D.D.S., Emory U., 1960; m. Susie M. Clanton, Aug. 29, 1959; children—Doris Elizabeth, Pamela Anne, John Nelson. Practice dentistry, Carrollton, Ga., 1962-63, Trion, Ga., 1963—; dir. 1st Nat. Bank Chattooga County, Ga. Adviser, Chattooga County Cancer Soc., 1969—. Mem. adv. bd. Shorter Coll., 1971—. Served with USNR, 1960-62. Mem. Am., Ga. dental assns., N.W. Dist. Dental Soc., Xi Psi Phi. Baptist. Rotarian. Home: 1 Greenmeadow Dr Trion GA 30753 Office: Trion Community Hospital Trion GA 30753

WARE, JOHN THOMAS, state senator; b. Chattanooga, Nov. 14, 1931; s. James E. and Marguerite (McQue) W.; student U. Fla., 1949-50; B.S. in Pub. Adminstrn., Fla State U., 1957; J.D., Stetson Coll. Law, 1961; m. Doris Gregory; children—G. Scott, Stacey, Sheryl, Sheila, Steve. Admitted to Fla. bar, since practiced in St. Petersburg; mem. Fla. Ho. of Reps., 1964-66, 68-70; mem. Fla. Senate, 1970—. City atty. St. Petersburg Beach, Fla., 1967. Served with USNR, 1950-54; Korea. Mem. St. Petersburg, Fla., Am. bar assns., Fla. Acad. Trial Lawyers, Lambda Chi Alpha. Home: 211 Sunset Dr N St Petersburg FL 33710 Office: Rutland Central Bank Bldg 55 5th St S St Petersburg FL 33701

WARFIELD, ROBERT EDGAR, JR., banker; b. Atlanta, Oct. 5, 1924; s. Robert Edgar and Mattie Alice (Bragg) W.; student U. Ga. Extension, 1947-50; m. Elaine Grace Bennett, Apr. 18, 1945; children—Robert L., Janice I. Chief clk. Fulton Nat. Bank, Atlanta, 1946-50; asst. v.p. Bank of Zephyrhills (Fla.), 1953-56; pres., chmn. bd. 1st Nat. Bank & Trust Co. Eustis (Fla.), 1963—, Bank of Mt. Dora (Fla.), 1965—; dir. Citizens Nat. Bank Leesburg (Fla.), Burnett Corp., DeLand, Fla., Brown Sugar Corp., Pahokee, Fla., W.M. Igou, Inc., Eustis. Pres., Eustis Little League, 1959, Lake County unit Am. Cancer Soc., 1969—; Lake County chmn. A.R.C., 1963; pres. Lake-Sumter Community Mental Health Center, 1969—; pres. exec. com. Waterman Meml. Hosp. Assn., 1965—; pres. N.E. Lake County Hosp. Dist., 1967—. Served with USNR, 1941-45, 51-52. Mem. Fla. Bankers Assn. (dir. 1971—), Bank Adminstrn. Inst. (pres. 1961), Eustis C. of C. (dir. 1960). Republican. Baptist (tchr. Sunday sch.). Mason (32 deg., Shriner), Elk. Club: Pine Meadows Golf & Country (past pres., dir. 1960—). (Eustis, Fla). Home: 1310 E Crooked Lake Dr Eustis FL 32726 Office: 100 N Bay St Eustis FL 32726

WARFORD, TOMMY GENE, lawyer; b. Gorman, Tex., June 16, 1941; s. Aubrey Whittier and Opal Jo (Fuller) W.; student Ranger Jr. Coll., 1959-61; B.A., U. Tex., 1963, J.D., 1966. Admitted to Tex. bar, 1966; practiced in Eastland, 1969—; atty. Tex. Hwy. Dept., Brownwood, 1967-69; atty. firm Turner, Seaberry & Warford, Eastland, 1969—. Served to 1st lt. AUS, 1966-72. Mem. Am. Bar Assn., State Bar Tex., Phi Alpha Delta. Democrat. Baptist. Lion. Home: 721 Pine St Ranger TX 76470 Office: 408 Exchange Bldg Eastland TX 76448

WARING, JOHN ALFRED, research writer, cons.; b. San Francisco, Dec. 30, 1913; s. John A. and Mary (Wheeler) W.; student pub. schs. Yachting, marine editor Chgo. Tribune, 1934-47; editor Kellogg Messenger, Kellogg Switchboard & Supply Co., Chgo., 1945-49; research cons. Baxter Internat. Econ. Research Bur., Inc., investment counselling, N.Y.C., 1951-52; research asst. marketing research dept. Fuller, Smith & Ross, Inc., advt., N.Y.C., 1953; research writer, cons. Twentieth Century Fund, N.Y.C., 1953-54; research cons. Ford Motor Co., Dearborn, Mich., 1955; chief researcher Internat. Fact Finding Inst., Lawrence Orgn., pub. relations cons., N.Y.C., Washington, 1957-58; lectr. on energy, tech. and history World Power Conf., Montreal, 1958, First Energy Inst., Am. U., Washington, 1960, Nat. Archives, Washington, 1962, Smithsonian Mus. History and Tech., Washington, 1968; guest lectr. social responsibility in sci. U. Md., 1972; lectr. Internat. Conf. on Energy and Humanity, Queen Mary Coll., U. London, 1972; research cons. PARM Project, Nat. Planning Assn., Washington, 1961-62; cons. Sci., Tech. and Fgn. Affairs Seminar, Fgn. Service Inst., U.S. Dept. State, 1965; cons. U.S. energy statistics Smithsonian Instn., U.S. Bur. Census, 1960—; research cons. Program of Policy Studies in Sci. and Tech., George Washington U., 1967-68; del. U.S. commn. UNESCO Conf., San Francisco, 1969; inaugural lectr. Future of Sci. and Soc. in Am. Seminar U.S. Civil Service Commn., Washington, 1970; editorial cons. Nat. Acad. Engring., Washington, 1971; research cons., analyst Seminar Sch., Indsl. Coll. Armed Forces, Ft. Lesley J. McNair, Washington, 1958—. Mem. Soc. History of Tech. (charter), History Sci. Soc., Technocracy Inc., A.A.A.S., Washington Acad. Scis., Phi Beta Kappa Assn. in D.C., Internat. Soc. Gen. Semantics, Am. Humanist Assn., Washington History Sci. Club., Washington Ethical Soc. Contbg. editor: Progressive World Mag., 1962—; technol. trends editor The Futurist Mag., 1968—. Contbr. chpts to books; compiler statis. tabulations. Home: 8502 Flower Av Takoma Park MD 20012 Office: Seminar Sch Indsl Coll Armed Forces Fort Lesley McNair Washington DC 20319

WARING, WILLIAM WINBURN, pediatrician, educator; b. Savannah, Ga., July 20, 1923; s. Antonio Johnston and Sue (Winburn) W.; grad. Hotchkiss Sch., 1942; student Yale, 1942-43; M.D., Harvard, 1947; m. Nell Pape Williams, July 19, 1952; children—William Winburn, Benjamin Joseph Williams, Antonio Johnston, Peter Ayraud, Patrick Houstoun. Intern, Children's Hosp., Boston, 1947-48, Johns Hopkins Hosp., Balt., 1948-49; resident Johns Hopkins Hosp., 1949-52; pvt. practice, Jacksonville, Fla., 1954-56; faculty Tulane U., Sch. Medicine, New Orleans, 1957—, prof. pediatrics, 1965—, lectr. physiology, 1966—; v.p. gen. med. and sci. adv. council Nat. Cystic Fibrosis Research Found., 1970-72; sr. vis. physician Charity Hosp. La., New Orleans; vis. physician New Orleans Crippled Children's Hosp.; dir. New Orleans Cystic Fibrosis Clinic; chief pulmonary diseases sect. pediatrics Tulane U., 1969—. Cons. handicapped children's services La. Dept. Health, 1964—. Served to capt. M.C., AUS, 1952-54. Recipient USPHS Career Devel. award, 1963-67; various research grants. Diplomate Am. Bd.

Pediatrics. Fellow Am. Acad. Pediatrics (chmn. diseases of chest 1970-71), Am. Pediatric Soc., Am. Coll. Chest Physicians; mem. Am. Assn. for Respiratory Therapy (asso. med. cons. editor Respiratory Care 1967—), La. Lung Assn., Cystic Fibrosis Club (pres. 1968, v.p.), Am. Thoracic Soc. (v.p. 1972), So. Soc. Pediatric Research (pres. 1969), New Orleans Pediatric Soc., Orleans Parish Med. Soc. Roman Catholic. Clubs: Boston, So. Yacht, Wyvern (New Orleans). Contbr. articles to profl. jours. Home: 6120 Marquette Pl New Orleans LA 70118 Office: Sch Medicine Tulane U 1430 Tulane Av New Orleans LA 70112

WARMACK, WAYNE PARKER, radio announcer; b. Tampa, Fla., Oct. 12, 1944; s. Wayne Elwood and Marion (Kelly) W.; student Sam Houston State U., 1964-65; grad. U.S. Sch. Music, 1960, Columbia Sch. Broadcasting, 1970; m. Nancy Louise Chilton, Sept. 4, 1965; children—Elissa Rene, Loreli. Announcer, Sta. FLEF-FM, Houston, 1969-70; gen. announcer Sta. KODA-AM-FM, Houston, 1970-72, 73—, Sta. KYND-FM, Pasadena, Tex., 1972-73. Studio orch. violinist Charles Ludwig Sound Rec. Studio, Houston, 1973—. Mem. United Pentecostal Ch. Home: 603 Alvin St Pasadena TX 77506 Office: 4808 San Felipe St Houston TX 77026

WARMAN, MARY KATHERINE OCKERMAN, ednl. adminstr.; b. Burgin, Ky., Sept., 1924; d. Everett Listen and Jenny Katherine (Scifres) Ockerman; student, U. Md., 1959-62; M.A. in Edn., Murray State U., 1962-67, Ed.S. in Sch. Adminstrn., 1972; m. James A. Warman, Apr. 5, 1942 (div. June 1962); children—James A., Everett Michael, Jenny Katherine, Arthur Louis. Substitute tchr. Hopkins County Bd. Edn., Madisonville, Ky., 1962-63; tchr. Outwood Hosp. and Sch., Dawson Springs, Ky., 1963-65, asst. prin., 1965-67, prin., 1967-69, instnl. program dir., 1969-72; unit dir., Oakwood, Somerset, Ky., 1972—. Mem. Am. Assn. Mental Deficiency, Am. Speech Assn., Internat. Platform. Assn., Ky. Personnel and Guidance Assn., Ky. Assn. Tchr. Edn., N.E.A., Bus. Profl. Women's Club, Kappa Delta Pi. Address: 110 Crab Orchard St Somerset KY 42501

WARNDORF, EUGENE ROBERT, plastics mfg. co. exec.; b. Covington, Ky., Jan. 27, 1933; s. Eugene Joseph and Claea (Frey) W.; student Villamadonna Coll., 1956-57, U. Cin., 1958-61; m. Beverly Jean Burkhart, Mar. 2, 1957; 1 dau., Kellie Jean. Pres., Bellevue O.H.M. Inc. (Ky.), 1959—, also chmn. bd.; pres., dir. Thermocor Chem. and Mfg. Co., Erlanger, Ky., 1965-72; pres. Continental Plastics Inc., Covington, Ky., 1972—, also dir.; pres., dir. Acrylo-Craft Mfg. Inc., Sharonville, O.; pres. Cin. Fab-Well Inc., Cin.; v.p., dir. J. G. Roth Inc. Bd. dirs Campbell County Youth Club Inc. Served with USAF, 1952-56. Recipient Distinguished Service awards K.C., 1967, V.F.W., 1968, Outstanding Airmen award of month 1956; named Ky. col. Mem. Soc. Plastics Engrs., Soc. Cosmetic Chemists, V.F.W. (honor degree 1965, comdr. 9th dist. 1968, chmn. Ky. dept. 1969, life), Am. Legion, Cath. War Vets., Newport Shopping Center Mchts. Assn. (v.p., dir. 1969—), Fraternal Order of Police. K.C., Elk. Club: Dayton (Ky.) Golf. Research on water filtration systems, radar height finders, active chem. formulations. Home: 34 Haywood Ct Fort Thomas KY 41075 Office: 930 Martin Pl Cincinnati OH 45202

WARNER, ADDISON WHEELOCK, oil producer; b. Geneva, Ill., June 5, 1899; s. Henry Dimock and Harriette King (Young) W.; student Dartmouth, 1917; B.S., Stanford, 1922; m. Helen Christopher, Dec. 25, 1924; children—Ann Wheelock (Mrs. Kimball), Addison Wheelock. Mgr. investor's aid dept. Chgo. Jour. Commerce, 1922-26; mgr. statis. dept. Stevenson, Perry & Stacy, 1926-27; sales mgr. Robert Stevenson & Co., 1927-28; gen. mgr. Kissell, Kinnicutt & Co., Chgo., 1929-30; sr. partner Addison Warner & Co., 1930-38, pres., 1938-43; now oil producer, also chmn. bd., pres. Imco Dog Food; treas., dir. Aviation Industries. Bd. dirs. Chgo. Area Project, 1934-53; trustee Union League Boys' Club, 1933-53, pres., 1938-40; chmn. finance com., trustee South Side Boys' Club, 1938-53. Served as flying cadet, U.S. Army, 1918-19; apptd. 2d lt., A.S.S. Res. Corps, 1919. Mem. Order Founders and Patriots Am., Chgo. Stanford Alumni Assn. (pres. 1938-47), S.A.R., Mayflower Soc., Chi Psi. Clubs: Adventurers, Union League (Chgo.); Petroleum (Ft. Worth). Address: 4512 Ester Dr Fort Worth TX 76114

WARNER, ALBIN PAUL, educator; b. Chgo., July 11, 1923; s. Roman and Rose (Meger) W.; B.S., U. Ill., 1948, M.S., 1949; Ph.D., U. Mich., 1952; m. Kathleen May Doyle, Feb. 9, 1948; 1 son, Thomas Paul. Instr. physiol. anatomy and phys. edn. U. Ill., Urbana, 1947-49, extension instr., 1951-54; instr. phys. edn. U. Mich., Ann Arbor, 1949-51; dir. health and phys. edn. Champaign (Ill.) Community Schs., 1951-53; prof., dir. DePaul U. Coll. Phys. Edn., Chgo., 1953-62; prof., head dept. health, phys. edn. and recreation Okla. State U., Stillwater, 1962—; prof. grad. sch. Millikin U., 1952. Served with USAAF, 1942-46. Mem. Am., Okla. assns. for health, phys. edn. and recreation, Nat. Coll. Phys. Edn. Assn. for Men, Am. Council Adminstrs. in Health, Phys. Edn. and Recreation, Am. Coll. Sports Medicine. Rotarian (pres. 1966-67), Club: Stillwater Golf and Country. Editorial bd. Physical Educator. Home: 2323 W 9th St Stillwater OK 74074

WARNER, JAN LYNN, lawyer; b. Dunkirk, N.Y., May 9, 1942, s. Warner Tobias and Naomi Arlene (Weisbond) W.; A.B., U. S.C., 1965, J.D., 1968; m. Sheila Kay Wolf, July 24, 1966; 1 son, Monty Seth. Admitted to S.C. bar, 1968; since practiced in Sumter; partner firm Weinberg & Weinberg, Sumter, 1969-71, Weinberg, Weinberg, Bryant, Warner, Sumter, 1971—. Served with USAF, 1960-63. Mem. Am. Judicature Soc., Am., S.C. bar assns., Order Wig and Robe, Sigma Nu, Phi Delta Phi. Home: 782 LeGette St Sumter SC 29150 Office: 111 N Main St Sumter SC 29150

WARNER, JOHN W., lawyer, educator; b. Amarillo, Tex., June 4, 1936; s. Arthur Greeley and Janet (Miller) W.; B.A., Tex. A. and M., 1958; LL.B., U. Tex., 1962; m. Judith Diane Mumma, Dec. 30, 1961; children—Michael, Sandra Kay, Melanie, Patricia. Admitted to Tex. bar, 1962; gen. practice law, Pampa, 1962—; instr. Dale Carnegie Inst., Tex. and Okla., 1964—; municipal ct. judge, 1963-68; atty., county atty., 1969—. Dist. commr. Boy Scouts Am., 1967-70. Incorporator Pampa Youth Council, Inc., 1968—, Southwest Indian Orgn., Inc., 1969. Named Adult Leader of Year, Pampa High Sch. Key Club, 1966, Pampa Outstanding Young Man, 1969. Mem. Am. Trial Lawyers Assn., Am., Gray County bar assns., State Bar Tex., Pampa Jr. C. of C. (pres. 1969-70, state legal counsel 1970-71). Methodist. Club: Democratic (pres. 1963) (Gray County). Home: 2111 Dogwood Pampa TX 79065 Office: 119 E Kingsmill St Pampa TX 79065

WARNICK, J.Q., JR., lawyer; b. Tahoka, Tex., June 1, 1931; s. J.Q. and Alice (Small) W.; B.A., Tex. Tech. U., 1956; J.D., U. Tex., 1959; m. Loretta Ann Stone, Aug. 4, 1962; children—Keri, Holly, Jay. Asst. county atty. Lubbock County (Tex.), 1959-61; admitted to Tex. bar, 1959, since practiced in Lubbock; partner firm Anderson, Edwards & Warnick, Lubbock, 1965—. Mem. electric utilities bd. Lubbock (Tex.) Power and Light, 1969—, chmn., 1972—. Served with USAF, 1951-55. Named Outstanding Young Lawyer in Lubbock, Lubbock Jr. Bar Assn., 1969. Mem. State Bar Tex., Lubbock County Bar Assn. (sec.-treas. 1960), State Jr. Bar Tex. (dir. 1961-63). Episcopalian. Mason. Club: Toastmasters, Hub (Lubbock). Home: 3506 44th St Lubbock TX 79413 Office: PO Box 2487 Lubbock TX 79408

WARNKEN, VERNON LLOYD, govt. ofcl.; b. LaGrange, Tex., July 26, 1933; s. Vernon Henry and Julia Louise (Koenig) W.; student Blinn Jr. Coll., 1950-51; B.B.A., Tex. A. and M. Coll., 1955; m. JoAnn Robertson, Aug. 23, 1953; children—Gary, Deborah, Bryon, Carol, Jeffery. With gen. accounting sect. Tex. Gas Corp., Houston, 1955-60; with U.S. Dept. Justice, Washington, 1960—. C.P.A., Tex. Home: 8108 Carrick Lane Springfield VA 22151 Office: US Dept Justice Bldg Washington DC 20530

WARR, C(LIFFORD) MICHAEL, evangelist, clergyman; b. Ellijay, Ga., Oct. 23, 1918; s. Clifford William and Dorothy O'Della (Kincaid) W.; A.B., Mercer U., 1944; B.D., Southwestern Bapt. Theol. Sem., 1947, M.Ed., 1957; m. Sara Nelle Vaughn, Sept. 3, 1946; 1 son, Daniel Lee. Accountant, Home Owners Loan Corp., Atlanta, 1936-40; ordained to ministry Bapt. Ch., 1941; asso. pastor Met. Bapt. Ch., Washington, 1947-48; pastor Luther Rice Meml. Bapt. Ch., Washington, 1948-53, Coll. Av. Bapt. Ch., Fort Worth, 1953-57, First Bapt. Ch., Rock Hill, S.C., 1957-68; So. Bapt. evangelist, Atlanta, 1968-71; pastor Jackson Hill Bapt. Ch., Atlanta, 1971—. Guest tchr., numerous churchwide and area wide Bible confs. Trustee Southwestern Bapt. Theol. Sem., 1949-54, Midwestern Bapt. Theol. Sem., 1961-69; pres. Pastors Conf., Rock Hill, 1961-62, Fort Worth, 1955-56. Mem. York County Bapt. Assn. (moderator 1963-64), Blue Key. Address: 1403-7 Ponce de Leon Av NE Atlanta GA 30307

WARREN, DONALD LAMAR, mfg. exec.; b. East Tallassee, Ala., Oct. 26, 1933; s. Curtis Lamar and Gracie Mae (Caldwell) W.; student Jacksonville State Coll., 1952-54; B.S. in Textile Mgmt., Ala. Poly. Inst., 1956; postgrad. Auburn U., 1954-56, U. N.C., 1969; m. Mary Ann Powell, June 26, 1954; children—Nena Anne, Janet Alicia. Supr., Deering Milliken, Gainesville, Ga., 1959-66, dept. overseer, 1960-65, yarn mill supt., 1965-66; supt. card/spin Spindale Mills, Inc. (N.C.), 1966-67, plant supt., 1967-72, asst. v.p. mfg., 1972—. Pres., Rutherfordton P.T.A., 1969, New Hope, 1970; gen. chmn. Gardner-Webb Coll. capital gifts campaign, 1970. Chmn. bd. advisers Gardner-Webb Coll. Served with AUS, 1956-58. Mem. Spindale Mills Found., Rutherfordton C. of C. (dir.), N.C. Textile Mfgs. Assn. (vice chmn. research and devel. com. 1971), Inst. Textile Tech. (tech. adv. com. 1967—), Phi Psi. Baptist (deacon, tng. union dir.). Rotarian. Clubs: Bulldog (dir.), Spindale, Rutherford Country. Home: 25 Ivy Dr Rutherfordton NC 28139 Office: PO Box 217 Spindale NC 28160

WARREN, FREDERICK MARSHALL, ret. army officer, judge; b. Newport, Ky., Aug. 23, 1903; s. William Ulysses and Katherine (Lampe) W.; A.B., LL.B., LL.M., LL.D., U. Cin.; m. Peggy Beaton, Feb. 20, 1926; 1 son, Frederick Marshall. Various positions with lumber and millwork cos., 1926-32; police judge, Southgate, Ky., 1932-35; admitted to Ky. bar, 1935; city atty., Southgate, 1935-40, 46-49; city solicitor, Newport, 1950-52; county judge, Campbell County, 1954-58; cons. to under sec. army, 1958; spl. asst. to asst. sec. army for manpower personnel and res. forces, 1959; recalled to active duty as maj. gen. U.S. Army, 1959; chief U.S. Army Res. and ROTC Affairs, 1959-63; circuit judge 17th Jud. Dist. Ky., Newport, 1964—. Field rep. Alcoholic Beverage Control Bd. Ky., 1949; mem. U.S. Army Gen. Staff com. N.G. and army res. policy, 1953-56; mem. res. forces policy bd. Dept. Def., 1958-59. Served to col. AUS, 1941-46. Decorated D.S.M., Silver Star, Bronze Star, Army Commendation medal (U.S.); Croix de Guerre (France, Belgium). Mem. Am., Ky., Campbell County (past pres.) bar assns., Am. Legion, V.F.W., D.A.V., Assn. U.S. Army, Res. Officers Assn. (past nat. v.p.), Mil. Order World Wars. Mason, Elk. Home: 20 Crow Hill Fort Thomas KY 41075 Office: Courthouse Newport KY 40272

WARREN, GEORGE CARLTON, JR., baking co. exec.; b. Metter, Ga., Oct. 8, 1925; s. George Carlton and Hessie (Harper) W.; student Northwestern U. Inst. Mgmt., 1962; children—George Carlton III, Nancy Ann. Salesman, supr. Colonial Baking Co., Augusta, Ga., 1946-51, supr., Gulfport, Miss., 1951-52, sales mgr., Columbus, Ga., 1952-54, Chattanooga, 1954-56, gen. mgr., 1960-61; sales service rep. Campbell Taggart, Inc., Dallas, 1956-60, dir. sales service, 1961-65, v.p. sales and advt., 1965-70, sr. v.p. sales and advt., 1970—. Mem. Dallas Sales and Marketing Execs. Methodist. Mason. Home: 10006 Regal Park Lane Dallas TX 75230 Office: PO Box 2640 Dallas TX 75221

WARREN, JOHN LEAMING, ret. air force officer; b. Holdenville, Okla., Nov. 6, 1906; s. Frank L. and Annie G. (Leaming) W.; student U. Mo., Okla. U., 1923-26; LL.B., Cumberland U., 1928; m. Shelagh D. MacKey, Apr. 30, 1949; 1 dau., Valery Anne. Admitted to Okla. bar, 1928; mem. law firm Warren & Warren, Holdenville, 1928-40. Served with USAF, 1940-63, ret. Decorated Legion of Merit, Republic Korea Mil. Merit Choongmoo medal. Mem. S.A.R., Okla. Bar Assn., Kappa Alpha, Episcopalian. Club: St. Petersburg Yacht. Home: 858 Placido Way St Petersburg FL 33704

WARREN, RAYMOND MCLEOD, JR., engring. co. exec.; b. Rome, Ga., Feb. 16, 1931; s. Raymond McLeod and Nilla Shields (Keith) W.; B.Mech. Engring., Auburn U., 1953; m. Doris Jane Leonard, Dec. 25, 1960; children—Raymond McLeod III, Jane L. Field engr. Babcock & Wilcox Co., 1953-59; v.p. McBurney Stoker & Equipment Co., 1959-67; pres., owner Warren Engring., Inc., Atlanta, 1967—. Served to 1st lt., C.E., AUS, 1953-55. Mem. Kappa Alpha. Baptist (deacon 1965—). Kiwanian. Home: 3140 Arden Rd NW Atlanta GA 30305 Office: 2964 Peachtree Rd NW Atlanta GA 30305

WARREN, RICHARD ERNEST, internat. ednl. television series producer; b. Managua, Nicaragua, Jan. 27, 1942; s. Ernest Reynolds and Marina (Echevirra) W.; B.C.S., Loyola U. South, 1970; m. Betty L. Murray, June 24, 1960; 1 dau., Deborah Marie. Sales office mgr. Avoncraft div. Avondale Shipyards, Inc., 1964-68; bus. mgr. Information Council Ams., New Orleans, 1968-69, exec. dir., 1969-71, internat. dir. gen., 1971—. Cons. Patrolman's Assn. New Orleans, 1969—; producer Spirit 76 internat. TV series, 1973; cons. Metro Pub. Relations, 1973-74, La. Rehab. Assn., 1974. Organizer, Jefferson Parish Am. Revolution Townhall Bicentennial Program, 1973-74; coordinator Freedoms Found-Young Men's Bus. Club Awards Presentation, 1972-73; celebrity chmn. Miss New Orleans Pageant, 1973-74; judge Baton Rouge Pageant, 1973; pres. Avon Guard Security Service, 1972-73. Bd. dirs. Muscular Dystrophy Assn., Goals to Grow Found., Crippled Children's Hosp. Served with USAF, 1960-64. Recipient Citation of Merit, Profl. Bus. Women Am., 1970, Outstanding Bur. Chmn. award Young Men's Bus. Club, 1969; certificate of Appreciation, New Orleans Pub. Sch. System, 1971, citation of Merit, Am. Fedn. Police, 1972, Loyalty Day award V.F.W., 1970, citation of Merit, Execs. Club New Orleans, 1970, certificate of Appreciation, Kiwanis Club, 1969, Award of Merit, Information Council Am., 1968, Plaque of Appreciation, Alton Ochsner Med. Found., 1970, plaque of Merit, Muscular Distrophy Assn. Am. Jerry Lewis Telethon, 1972, Key to City, certificate of Merit, New Orleans, 1973. Mem. Am. Legion, Am. Fedn. Police, Italian Cultural Soc., Radio Free Asia, Information Council Ams., Founder's and Patriot's Am., S.A.R., Adminstrv. Mgmt. Soc., So. Karate Assn., Young Men's Bus. Club Greater New Orleans, New Orleans C. of C. (mem. Americanism com. 1969-72), Loyola U. Alumni Assn., Cross Keys. Mason. New Orleans editor Singles Critique, 1973-74. Contbr. articles to profl. jours. Home: 202 M Central Av New Orleans LA 70121 Office: PO Box 53371 New Orleans LA 70150

WARREN, WILLIAM DAVID, data processor; b. Austin, Tex., Sept. 3, 1931; s. William Frederick and Eleanor Faver (Hill) W.; B.A., U. Tex., 1957. Tabulating equipment operator data processing div. U. Tex., Austin, 1958-61, computer programmer, systems analyst, 1961—. Served with AUS, 1952-53. Mem. Data Processing Mgmt. Assn. (sec. Austin Chpt. 1969-70), Am. Philatelic Soc. (life), U. Tex. Ex-Students Assn. (life). Episcopalian. Club: Stamp (pres. 1951-52) (Austin). Home: 1502 Hardouin Av Austin TX 78703

WARRINER, DAVID DORTCH, lawyer; b. nr. Lawrenceville, Va., Feb. 29, 1929; s. T. Emmett and Maria (Dortch) W.; A.B., U. N.C., 1951; J.D., U. Va., 1957; m. Barbara Ann Jenkins, Jan. 31, 1959; children—Susan Wells, David Thomas Dortch, Julia Cotman. Admitted to Va. bar, 1957; sr. partner, Warriner & Outten, Emporia and Lawrenceville, Va., 1957—; city atty., Emporia, 1969—. Mem. state bd. Va. Assn. Professions, 1968, Va. Assn. Prevention Blindness, 1967—; mem. coll. bd. Southside Va. Community Coll., 1970—, chmn., 1973—; bd. visitors Va. Mil. Inst., 1970—. Co-chmn. State Nixon for Pres. Com., 1968; del. Republican Nat. Convs., 1968, 72; mem. state central com. Rep. party Va., 1963—, mem. exec. com., 1968—, gen. counsel, 1971—; Greensville County Rep. chmn., 1963-71; chmn. 4th Dist. Rep. Com., 1968-71; co-chmn. Va. Com. to Re-Elect Pres., 1972. Served with USNR, 1951-54. Mem. Am., Va. bar assns., Va. State Bar, Va. Trial Lawyers Assn. Lion. Club: Civic (pres. Emporia 1960-61). Home: 100 State St Emporia VA 23847 Office: 314 S Main St Emporia VA 23847

WARRINER, WILLIAM OWEN, JR., tool mfg. co. exec.; b. Houston, July 5, 1929; s. William Owen and Dorothy Sofhia (Hughes) W.; B.S., Tex. A. and M. U., 1951; m. Margaret Lou Scales, July 27, 1973; children—Paul, Susan, Mark. Bookkeeper, S & R Tool & Supply Co., Houston, 1951-54, office mgr., 1954-58, sec.-treas., 1958-72, pres., 1972—. Vice pres. Oak Forest Am., Little League, 1970-72. Mem. Tex. Horse Shoe Pitching Assn. Methodist (mem. adminstrv. bd. 1969-72). Home: 7919 Glenheath St Houston TX 77017 Office: 155 McCarty St Houston TX 77015

WARSHAW, BERTRAM SAUL, cons. civil engr.; b. Bklyn., Mar. 15, 1928; s. Benjamin David and Anna (Wald) W.; B.C.E., Ga. Inst. Tech., 1949; M.S.C.E. U. Miami, 1973; m. Sandra Stein, Sept. 15, 1955; children—Andrew Van, Randy Ladd, Job Lee, Jolie. Area engr. E. I. duPont de Nemours & Co., Savannah River Plant, 1951-53; chief structural insp. Connell & Rader Asso., Miami, 1953-56; structural designer Morton R. Fellman, Cons. Engrs., Miami, 1956-57; structural engr. Jules P. Channing & Asso., Cons. Engr., Miami, 1957-58; staff structural engr. Giller, Payne & Waxman, Miami, 1958-59; pvt. cons. engr. and planner, Miami, 1959—. Active Adult Edn. Program, Dade County, Fla.; asso. structural engr. City Coral Gables, 1963-69; pres. Bertram S. Warshaw & Assos. Inc., cons. engrs., 1969—. Chmn. City Miami Housing Bd. Appeals, 1964-68; chmn. Dade County Bd. Rules and Appeals; v.p. Transp. Terminals Am. Mem. Am. Soc. C.E., Nat. Soc. Profl. Engrs., Fla. Engring. Soc., S.C. Soc. Engrs., Soc. Am. Mil. Engrs., Am. Concrete Inst., N.J. Soc. Profl. Planners, Greater Miami Opera Guild. Club: King's Bay Yacht and Country (Miami, Fla.). Co-patentee in field thin shell concrete constrn. Contbr. articles profl. engring. jours. Home: 4361 Mayfair Dr Miami FL 33133 Office: 1000 NW 57th Av Miami FL 33126

WASCOVICH, GEORGE ELWOOD, clergyman; b. Ankeny, Pa., Jan. 8, 1922; s. George J. and Bertha (Spencer) W.; B.A., Johnson Bible Coll., 1945; B.D., Christian Theol. Sem., 1948, M.Div., 1948; m. Alma Francis Jordan, May 31, 1945; children—Constance (Mrs. David Swinney), Craig, Faith, Kent. Ordained to ministry Christian Ch., 1945; pastor First Christian Ch., Mobile, Ala., 1947-56; sr. minister First Christian Ch., Ft. Wayne, Ind., 1956-66, First Christian Ch., Atlanta, 1966—. Trustee Christian Theol. Sem., Christian Coll. Ga., Campbell-Stone Apts. for Sr. Citizens. Recipient Distinguished Alumni award Christian Theol. Sem., 1969. Mem. Mobile (pres. 1952-53), Fort Wayne (pres. 1962-63) ministerial assns., Druid Hills Chs. Assn. (pres. 1971-72), Theta Phi. Mason (Shriner). Home: 3040 Silva Pine Trail NE Atlanta GA 30345 Office: 999 Briarcliff Rd Atlanta GA 30306

WASHBURN, GENE NEAL, agrl. engr.; b. Santa Rosa, Tex., May 25, 1935; s. Gene Benjamine and Vashti (Blume) W.; B.S., U. Ark., 1958; m. Dana Lee Fitch, Sept. 27, 1958; children—Scott Alan, Guy Austin, Kaka Lyn. Agrl. engr., Soil Conservation Service, Little Rock, 1958-59; hydraulic engr. U.S. Corps Engrs., Little Rock, 1960-68, water resources planner, 1968—. Served with AUS, 1958, 61-62. Registered profl. engr., Ark. Mem. Am. Soc. C.E. (asso.), Nat., Ark. (v.p., 1971-72) socs. profl. engrs. Methodist. Home: Route 1 Box 130AAAA Roland AR 72135 Office: PO Box 867 Little Rock AR 72203

WASHINGTON, JOSEPH REED, JR., educator; b. Iowa City, Oct. 30, 1930; s. Joseph R. and Susie (Duncan) W.; A.B., U. Wis., 1952; B.D., Andover Newton Theol. Sch., 1957; Th.D., Boston U., 1961; D.D., U. Vt., 1969; m. Sophia May Holland, June 28, 1952; children—Bryan Reed, David Eugene. Dean chapel, asst. prof. religion Dillard U., 1961-63; chaplain, asst. prof. religion Dickinson Coll., 1963-66; dean chapel, asso. prof. religion Albion (Mich.) Coll., 1966-69; prof. religion, dean chapel Beloit (Wis.) Coll., 1969-70; prof. religious studies, chmn. Afro-Am. studies U. Va., Charlottesville, 1970—. Served with AUS, 1952-54. Mem. Am. Soc. Christian Ethics, Am. Acad. Religion. Author: Black Religion: The Negro and Christianity in the United States, 1964; The Politics of God, 1967; Black and White Power Subreption, 1969; Marriage in Black and White, 1970; Black Sects and Cults, 1972. Office: Cocke Hall U Va Charlottesville VA 22901

WASHINGTON, WALTER E., mayor; b. Dawson, Ga., Apr. 15, 1915; s. William L. and Willie Mae (Thornton) W.; A.B., Howard U., 1938, LL.B., 1948; postgrad. Am. U., 1939-43; LL.D. (hon.), Fisk U., 1968, Georgetown U., 1968, Catholic U., 1969, Boston U., 1969, George Washington U., 1970, Princeton, 1970; L.H.D., Bishop Coll., Dallas, 1970; m. Bennetta Bullock, Dec. 26, 1941; 1 dau., Bennetta (Mrs. Jules-Rosette). Admitted to D.C. bar, 1948, U.S. Supreme Ct. bar, 1952; ofcl. Nat. Capital Housing Authority, 1941-66, exec. dir., 1961-66; chmn. N.Y.C. Housing Authority, 1966-67; mayor-commr. D.C., 1967—. Mem. adv. bd. U.S. Conf. Mayors; vice chmn. Nat. League Cities; mem. ins. panel Nat. Adv. Commn. Civil Disorders. Vice pres. United Community Funds and Councils Am.; past pres. Washington Home Rule Com., Washington Urban League. Trustee Kennedy Center for Performing Arts; bd. dirs. Washington Council Chs., Nat. Capital Area council Boy Scouts Am., United Planning Orgn., Big Bros. Recipient Career award Nat. Civil Service League, Distinguished Achievement award Howard U.; Nat. Conf. Christian and Jews award; Nat. Bar Assn. award; Washington Archdiocesan award; Community Service award Health and Welfare Council. Mem. Am. Bar Assn., Order of Coif. Clubs: Cosmos, Nat. Lawyers, Federal City (Washington); City (N.Y.C.). Home: 408 T St NW Washington DC 20001 Office: Dist Bldg 14 and E Sts NW Washington DC 20004

WASILEWSKI, VINCENT THOMAS, trade assn. exec.; b. Athens, Ill., Dec. 17, 1922; s. Alex and Anna (Gillespie) W.; A.B. in Polit. Sci., U. Ill., 1948, J.D., 1949; m. Patricia Callery, June 17, 1950; children—Jan, Susan, Catherine, Terese, Thomas, James. Admitted to

Ill. bar, 1950; mem. staff Nat. Assn. Broadcasters, Washington, 1949—, v.p. govt. affairs, 1960-61, exec. v.p., 1961-65, pres., 1965—. Mem. U.S. Nat. Commn. for UNESCO, 1956-60. Served with USAAF, 1942-45. Decorated D.F.C. with oak leaf cluster, Air medal with oak leaf cluster. Mem. Advt. Fedn. Am. (bd. dirs.), Fed. Communications, Am. bar assns., Am. Judicature Soc., Internat. Radio and TV Soc., Order of Coif, Sigma Phi Epsilon, Phi Kappa Phi, Phi Alpha Delta. Roman Catholic. Clubs: Internat. (Washington); Congressional Country (Potomac, Md.). Home: 6608 Bay Tree Lane Falls Church VA 22041 Office: 1771 N St NW Washington DC 20036

WASSERMAN, JACK, lawyer; b. N.Y.C., Feb. 20, 1913; s. Samuel and Sabina (Hoffman) W.; A.B., Coll. City N.Y., 1932; J.D. cum laude, Harvard, 1935; m. Marie Krempa, June 7, 1941; children—Lorraine De Vera, Michael Owen. With Harvard Legal Aid Soc., 1934-35; admitted to N.Y. bar, 1936; practiced law in N.Y.C., 1936-41; atty. Bd. of Immigration Appeals, 1941-42; sr. atty. Alien Enemy Control Unit, 1942-43; mem. Bd. Immigration Appeals, 1943-46; atty. Alien Enemy Litigation Sect., 1946-47; now partner firm Wasserman & Parker. Asst. gen. counsel Citizens Com. on Displaced Persons, 1947-48; past nat. pres. and legislative rep. Assn. Immigration and Nationality Lawyers. Mem. Bars U.S. Supreme Ct., Bd. of Immigration Appeals, ICC, FCC, Am., N.Y. State, Fed., Internat. bar assns., Nat. Lawyers Club, Am. Trial Lawyers Assn., Internat. Law Assn., Phi Beta Kappa. Author: Immigration Law and Practice. Contbr. articles on immigration and citizenship to mags. Home: 4405 Sedgwick St Washington DC 20016 Office: 1707 H St NW Washington DC 20006

WASSILAK, ERWIN JOHN, elec. engr.; b. St. Louis, Dec. 10, 1926; s. John and Clara Caroline (Haas) W.; B.S. in Elec. Engring., Mo. Sch. Mines and Metallurgy, 1950; M.B.A., Oklahoma City U., 1968; m. Lois Jeanne Arkebauer, Aug. 10, 1948; children—Eric Herbert, Kristin Jeanne. Engring. supr. Gen. Elec. Co., Syracuse, N.Y., 1950-70, engring. supr. computer peripheral design, Oklahoma City, 1970—. Served with USNR, 1944-46. Registered profl. engr., N.Y., Okla., Mo. Mem. I.E.E.E. Home: 3737 NW 69th St Oklahoma City OK 73116 Office: PO Box 12313 Oklahoma City OK 73112

WASSON, WOODROW WILSON, sociologist, educator; b. Cottontown, Tenn., June 6, 1915; s. Walter Herman and Zora (Brown) W.; B.A., Vanderbilt U., 1939, M.A., 1940; B.D. (Univ. fellow), U. Chgo., 1943, Ph.D., 1947; M.A., George Peabody Coll., 1967; m. Frances Marie Tallman, June 17, 1944. Prof., Okla. State Coll., Ada, 1947-48, U. Houston, 1948-49; prof., dean Sch. Religion, U. Ga., Athens, 1950-55; research asso., archivist Disciples of Christ Hist. Soc., Nashville, 1959-64; archivist, prof. Vanderbilt U., Peabody Coll., Nashville, 1964-69; prof. sociology, dir. grad. studies in sociology Middle Tenn. State U., Murfreesboro, 1969—. Oxford (Eng.) U. grantee, 1955; mem. Pi Gamma Mu, Beta Phi Mu. Author: James A. Garfield: A Study in the Interrelationship of Religion and Politics, 1952. Editor: Christian-Evangelist Index, 3 vols., 1964. Contbr. articles to profl. jours. Home: 4812 Granny White Pike Nashville TN 37220

WATERS, BETTY HALE (MRS. JULIAN LAFAY WATERS), educator; b. Atlanta, Dec. 21, 1927; d. Robert Lorin and Blondyne (Cooper) Hale; Mus.B., Converse Coll., 1949; M.Elementary Edn. (Optimist scholar 1966), Ga. State U., 1968, Edn. Specialist (Delta Kappa Gamma state fellow 1970, internat. fellow 1972), 1971; Ed.D., U. Ga., 1973; m. Julian Lafay Waters, June 3, 1950; 1 son, John Robert (dec.). Classroom tchr. Dekalb County (Ga.) Schs., 1956-70, in-service lectr., 1965-68, learning disabilities clinician, 1968-70; mem. faculty, coll. supr. Oglethorpe U., Atlanta, 1970-71; coll. supr. U. Ga., Athens, 1971-73; dir.-tchr. learning disabilities program Newton County (Ga.) Pub. Schs., 1973—. Co-chmn. Julian L. Waters Dr. For Retarded Children, Decatur, 1962. Recipient Tchrs. medal Freedoms Found., 1965, Tchr. of Yr. award, Dogwood chpt. Council Exceptional Children, 1970. Mem. Assn. Childhood Edn. (local pres. 1964-66, state pres.), Am. Assn. U. Women, Assn. for Supervision and Curriculum Devel., Assn. Tchr. Educators, Assn. Children with Learning Disabilities, Delta Kappa Gamma, Kappa Delta Epsilon. Home: Route 1 Piedmont Rd Box 492 Hull GA 30646

WATERS, JOHN MAYO, JR., city ofcl.; b. Arapahoe, N.C., Aug. 1, 1920; s. John Mayo and Lela (Bell) W.; student N.C. State U., 1938-39; B.S., U.S. Coast Guard Acad., 1942; postgrad. U. Miami, 1959-61; m. Peggy O'Neal, Jan. 9, 1945; children—Peggy Ann, John Stephen. Commd. ensign U.S. Coast Guard, 1942, advanced through grades to capt., 1964; coast guard officer, 1942-68, chief search and rescue, 1964-66, chief aviation, 1967; chief div. emergency services Nat. Hwy. Safety Bur., 1967-68; ret., 1968; dir. Pub. Safety, Jacksonville, Fla., 1968—; clin. prof. dept. surgery U. Fla. Coll. Medicine, 1973—. Mem. Internat. Assn. Fire Chiefs, Internat. Assn. Police Chiefs, Am. Soc. Safety Engrs., Am. Legion, V.F.W., D.A.V., Navy League, Am. Acad. Orthopedic Surgeons (com. on injuries 1968—), N.E. Fla. Heart Assn. (exec. bd. 1969—, pres. 1972), Nat. Acad. Sci. (emergency med. services com. 1969—), A.C.S. (com. trauma 1969—), Am. Trauma Soc. (exec. bd. 1973—). Rotarian. Author: Rescue at Sea, 1966; Bloody Winter, 1967. Contbr. articles to profl. jours. Home: 4911 Water Oak Lane Jacksonville FL 32210 Office: 107 Market St Jacksonville FL 32202

WATERS, LOUIS ALBERT, banker; b. Beeville, Tex., July 28, 1938; s. William Berry and Lola Mae (Smith) W.; B.A., Rice Inst., 1960; B.S. in M.E., Rice U., 1962; M.B.A., Harvard, 1966; m. Wanda Lyn Phears, June 5, 1962; children—Louis Albert, Laurel Ann, Kristen Leigh. Asso. mem. firm Hornblower, Hemphill, Noyes & Weeks, N.Y.C., 1966-67; v.p. Underwood, Neuhaus & Co., Houston, 1967-69; chmn. Browning-Ferris Industries, Inc., Houston, 1969—, also dir.; chmn. Fannin Bank, Houston, 1970—. Mem. Am. Soc. M.E., Harvard Bus. Sch. Club Houston. Clubs: Houston, Warwick. Office: Fannin Bank Bldg Houston TX 77025

WATERS, RAYMOND PATRICK, advt. exec.; b. Waterbury, Conn., Jan. 27, 1931; s. Harry Joseph and Cathryn Agnes (Williams) W.; B.A. cum laude, Hofstra U., 1960; m. Beatrice Barak, May 27, 1955; children—Tod Joseph, Neal Raymond. Editor, Levittown (N.Y.) Press, 1954-55; advt. asst. Allied Chem. Corp., N.Y.C., 1955-56; v.p., mgr. office, dir. Walther Assos. advt., N.Y.C., 1956-64; Eastern editor Indsl. Marketing Mag., N.Y.C., 1964-66; account exec. Basford Inc. pub. relations, N.Y.C., 1966-68; with M.W. Kellogg Co. div. Pullman, N.Y.C., 1968-70, Houston, 1970—, mgr. pub. relations and publs., 1968—. Tchr. pub. relations pub. schs. Hewlett Woodmere, N.Y., 1961-65; mem. adv. com. Houston Mag., 1970—. Served with USNR, 1950-54. Mem. Assn. Indsl. Advertisers, C. of C., Assn. Petroleum Writers, Pi Delta Epsilon, Alpha Sigma Lambda. Club: Press (Houston). Home: 8834 Winningham Lane Houston TX 77055 Office: M.W. Kellogg Co 1300 Three Greenway Plaza E Houston TX 77046

WATERS, VINCENT S., clergyman. Ordained priest Roman Cath. Ch., 1931; bishop of Raleigh, N.C., 1945—. Address: 600 Bilyeu St Raleigh NC 27606*

WATERS, WALTER KENNETH, JR., educator; b. Kansas City, Mo., Apr. 27, 1927; s. Walter Kenneth and Margaret Elizabeth (Piper) W.; A.B., Park Coll., 1950; M.A. (Field Hotaling fellow), Stanford, 1951, Ph.D., 1964; postgrad. Ind. U., 1956; m. Irene Ruth Holtzinger, Aug. 25, 1956; children—Wendy Kay, Brian David. Instr. English, Doane Coll., 1952-53; instr. speech Dillard U., 1954-57; asst. prof. theatre Portland (Ore.) State Coll., 1958-61; chmn. speech and theatre Monticello Coll., 1962-65; prof. theatre Stephen F. Austin State U., Nacogdoches, Tex., 1965—. Stage dir., set designer New Savoy Opera Co., 1960-62. Served with USNR, 1945-46. Recipient Arts Commn. citation City of Portland, 1960. Mem. Am. Theatre Assn., Speech Assn. Am., Nat. Assn. Schs. Theatre (chmn. ethics com. 1971—, exec. bd. 1973—), Ore. Hist. Soc., Tex. Ednl. Theatre Assn. (pres. 1971-73). Presbyn. (elder 1967-72). Lion. Editor: Tex. Theatre Notes, 1973—. Contbr. articles to profl. jours. Home: 307 Brookshire Dr Nacogdoches TX 75961

WATERS, WILLIAM ALFRED, physician; b. Offerle, Kan., Oct. 27, 1912; s. Earl Evans and Willie Lou (Berry) W.; B.S., Okla. A. and M. Coll., 1933; M.D., U. Okla., 1947; m. Ruth Louise Whitcomb, Jan. 25, 1939. Office salesman, mgr. Oilwell Supply Co., Cushing and Ada., Okla., 1934-36; materials warehouseman Standard Oil Co., Venezuela, 1936-42; intern, Wesley Hosp., Oklahoma City, 1947-48; resident Meth. Hosp., Lubbock, Tex., 1953-54; practice medicine specializing in gen. medicine and surgery, Odessa, Tex., 1948-51, Lubbock, 1953-54, Tulsa, 1954—; mem. staffs Hillcrest Med. Center, Tulsa, Drs. Hosp., Tulsa, St. Francis Hosp., Tulsa. Served with AUS, 1942-46, with M.C., 51-53. Mem. Am., Tulsa County med. assns., Am. Acad. Gen. Practice, Am. Soc. Clin. Hypnosis, Am. Legion, Kappa Alpha. Republican. Mem. Christian Ch. Inventor floss attachment for electric toothbrush, air conditioned headwear. Home: 3648 E 49th St Tulsa OK 74135 Office: 5950 E 31st St Tulsa OK 74135

WATERS, WILLIE ESTEL, horticulturist; b. Smithtown, Ky., Sept. 19, 1931; s. Abraham Lincoln and Mildred Sue (Childers) W.; student Cumberland Coll., 1950-52; B.S., U. Ky., 1954, M.S., 1958; Ph.D., U. Fla., 1960; m. Mary Elizabeth Sumler, May 30, 1952; children—Marie Estel, Alan Lee, Sheila Louise. With Gulf Coast Expt. Sta., Bradenton, Fla., 1960-67; dir. Ridge Ornamental Lab., Apopka, Fla., 1967-70. Agrl. Research and Edn. Center, Bradenton, Fla., 1970—. Served with M.C., AUS, 1954-56. Mem. Am. Soc. Hort. Sci., So. Weed Sci. Soc., Fla. Hort. Soc., Fla. Soil and Crop Sci. Soc., Sigma Xi, Alpha Zeta, Gamma Sigma Delta, Phi Kappa Phi. Baptist. Rotarian. Home: 836 Hillcrest Dr Bradenton FL 33505 Office: 5007 60th St E Bradenton FL 33505

WATKINS, A.J., lawyer; b. Austin, Tex., July 27, 1924; s. Beda D. and Juel (Roper) W.; B.A., U. Tex., 1948; LL.B., Harvard, 1951; m. Jean Voss, May 11, 1946; children—Gregory Lee, Rebecca Lynn. Admitted to Tex. bar, 1951; briefing atty. Supreme Ct. Tex., 1951-52; asso. Baker, Botts, Shepherd & Coates, Houston, 1952-63; partner Baker, Heard, Elledge, & Watkins, Houston, 1963-66, Watkins & Hamilton, Houston, 1966—. Lectr. trial tactics U. Houston Sch. Law, 1967. Mem. Juvenile Adv. Council, Spring Br.-Meml., 1966—. Served with USMCR, 1943-45. Mem. Am., Harris County bar assns., State Bar Tex., Internat. Assn. Ins. Counsel (v.p. casualty ins. com. 1965-66), Tex. Assn. Def. Counsel, Houston C. of C. Methodist. Home: 13002 Indian Creek St Houston TX 77024 Office: Main Bldg Houston TX 77002

WATKINS, ARTY JEWELL, meat packing co. exec.; b. Fairview, Okla., Aug. 3, 1925; s. James S. and Lola Maud (Schriener) W.; student Mo. State U., 1943-44, N.M. State U., 1945-46; m. Jean Schaefer, Oct. 28, 1945; children—Jerry Mack, Marty Jean. Owner, Watkins Packing Co., Dalhart, Tex., 1946-70; mgr. Caviness Packing Co., Inc., Dalhart, 1970—; dir. Nortex Feed Lot. Mem. Bd. Edn. Dalhart Sch. Dist., 1965—. Served with AC, USNR, 1942-45. Home: 1209 Conlen St Dalhart TX 79022 Office: 1900 Chicago St Dalhart TX 79022

WATKINS, CARLTON GUNTER, pediatrician, med. adminstr.; b. Wilmington, N.C., Aug. 25, 1919; s. Edison Lee and Maysie (Gunter) W.; A.B., U. N.C., 1939; M.D., Washington U., St. Louis, 1943; m. Charlotte Jean Metcalf, Mar. 21, 1943; children—Lloyd Dixon Hollingsworth, Carlton Gunter, Mary Melissa, Charlotte Lou. Successively rotating intern, asst. resident, resident pediatrics St. Louis City Hosp., 1943-45; resident pediatrics Duke Hosp., 1945-46; practice medicine specializing in pediatrics Charlotte, N.C., 1946-51, 53-73; chmn. dept. pediatrics Charlotte Meml. Hosp., 1958-61, 63-67; founder, 1963, sr. mem. Charlotte Pediatric Clinic, 1963-73; physician dir. Mecklenburg County Center for Human Devel., Charlotte, 1973—. Mem. Charlotte Mecklenburg Bd. Edn., 1966-74; pres. N.C. Family Life Council, 1966. Served to capt. M.C., AUS, 1951-53. Fellow Am. Acad. Pediatrics; mem. A.M.A., N.C., Mecklenburg County med. socs., N.C., Charlotte (founder, 1st sec. 1950, pres. 1962) pediatric socs., N.C. P.T.A. (life), Alpha Kappa Kappa. Club: Old Catawba (Charlotte). Contbr. articles to med. jours. Home: 6724 Constitution Lane Charlotte NC 28210 Office: 3500 Ellington St Charlotte NC 28211

WATKINS, CHARLOTTE JEAN METCALF, assn. exec.; b. Coffeyville, Kan., Mar. 24, 1921; d. Seward Estel and Amber (Maxson) Metcalf; student Kan. State Coll., 1938-39; R.N., St. Luke's Nursing Sch. (Kansas City, Mo.), 1942; m. Carlton Gunter Watkins, Mar. 21, 1943; children—Lloyd D.H., Carlton G., Jr., Mary Melissa, Charlotte Lou. Pres. N.C. Congress Parents and Tchrs., 1968-70; v.p. region 3 Nat. P.T.A., 1970-72, also nat. commr. Nat. P.T.A., 1972—, mem. exec. com., 1973-75. Mem. adv. council Pres.'s Cabinet Com. on Edn., 1971-73, Gov.'s Task Force on Child Advocacy, 1969-70, on Juvenile Delinquency, 1969-71, on Student Unrest, 1971-72, Gov.'s Com. on State Reorgn., 1970-71; mem. Charlotte Community Relations Commn.; v.p. Charlotte, YWCA, 1972—. Bd. dirs. P.T.A. Mag., Inc., Chgo., Mecklenberg Nat. Conf. Christians and Jews, 1966-72, Mecklenberg Family Life Council, 1962-66. Mem. Charlotte Jaycettes (founder, past pres.), Nat. (life), N.C., Tenn., Fla., Ky. P.T.A.'s, Mecklenberg Med. Aux., Am. Social Health Assn. (mem. N.C. com.), N.C. Zool. Soc. (dir.). Mem. P.E.O. Home and office: 6724 Constitution Lane Charlotte NC 28210

WATKINS, JOHN DAVID, marketing exec.; b. Lakewood, O., Mar. 19, 1946; s. Clayton N. and Kathleen (Karker) W.; A.A., Lake Sumter Jr. Coll., 1967; B.A., U. South Fla., 1969; m. Janice Kay Gehrke, Aug. 9, 1969; children—Sean Thomas, Kenneth Christopher. Dir. marketing and advt. research Canberra TV, Ltd. (Australia), 1969-70; instr. adult edn. Lake County Vocational Sch., Eustis, Fla., 1971; community planner Brevard County (Fla.) Planning Dept., 1971-73; dir. communication and marketing Maj. Design Corp., Orlando, Fla., 1973—. Campaign advt. adviser to mem. Bervard County Democratic Com., 1972—. Mem. Am. Marketing Assn., Pi Sigma Epsilon. Mem. Ch. of Jesus Christ of Latter Day Saints (elder 1971—). Home: 3685 Miriam Dr Titusville FL 32780 Office: 5750 Major Blvd Orlando FL 32805

WATKINS, JOHN EDWARD, III, real estate co. exec.; b. San Antonio, Tex., June 13, 1945; s. John Edward and Jackie Lee (Theis) W.; B.B.A. magna cum laude, St. Mary's U. Tex., 1967. Accountant, Ernst & Ernst, Laredo, Tex., 1967-72; v.p. B.P. Newman Investment Co., Laredo, 1972—. Bd. dirs. Laredo/Webb County Mental Health Adv. Bd., 1970-71. C.P.A., Tex. Mem. Am. Inst. C.P.A.'s, Tex. Soc. C.P.A.'s, Washington Birthday Celebration Assn., Kappa Pi Sigma, Delta Epsilon Sigma. Kiwanian. Home: 2118 Guerrero St Laredo TX 78040 Office: 3517 Arkansas St PO Box 144 Laredo TX 78040

WATKINS, JOHN WILLIAM, county ofcl.; b. Newport News, Va., June 5, 1943; s. William Crane and Elizabeth (Bailey) W.; student Richmond Profl. Inst., 1961-62; m. Gloria Belle Koger, Aug. 13, 1966; children—Eric Paul, Jason Michael, Meaghan Lucia, Todd David. Jr. engr. City of Williamsburg (Va.), 1964-69; asst. county adminstr. County of James City (Va.), 1969-71, 1972—; county adminstr. County of Gloucester (Va.), 1971-72. Sec., Williamsburg Fire Dept., 1965-67; capt. Williamsburg Rescue Squad, 1967-68. Mem. Nat., Va. assns. county adminstrs., Internat. City Mgrs. Assn. Roman Catholic. Lion. Home: 200 John Wythe Pl Williamsburg VA 23185 Office: PO Box JC Williamsburg VA 23185

WATKINS, LOTTIE HEYWOOD, real estate co. exec.; b. Atlanta; d. Eddie and Susie (Wilson) Heywood; student Reid's Bus. Coll., 1943-45; m. J. Elmo Watkins, 1947 (dec. 1951); children—Joyce Rankin (Mrs. Samuel W. Bacote), Judy Yvonne (Mrs. James A. Barnett). Sec., Alexander-Calloway Realty Co., Atlanta, 1945-54; teller-clk. Mut. Fed. Savs. & Loan Assn., Atlanta, 1954-60, now dir.; owner, pres. Lottie Watkins Enterprises, Atlanta, 1960—. Co-chmn. bus. div. Community Chest, 1955-59; YMCA membership campaigns, 1960—, YWCA membership enrollment drive, 1962, centennial fund drive, 1967-68; active Am. Cancer Soc., 1958-59, N.A.A.C.P. membership drive, 1957-59, N.A.A.C.P. freedom fund banquet, 1964, program com. nat. conv., 1962; chmn. cheer fund Atlanta Inquirer, 1961-62; div. leader YMCA centennial fund drive, 1967-68; co-chmn. membership com. Greater Atlanta Council on Human Relations, 1965-66; asst. sec. Atlanta Bus. League, 1960-61; sec. Vis. Nurses Assn.; mem. exec. com. Fulton County Bd. of Registration and Election; mem. Ga. Gov.'s Commn. Voluntarism, 1972. Field dir. Fulton County Citizens Democratic Club, 1960-63; mem. exec. com. 5th Congl. dist. Ga., 1963; vice chmn. Fulton County Dem. party, 1967-68, mem. exec. com., 1967-69. Recipient award for citizenship and progressive bus. leadership College Park Civic League, 1963, C.L. Harper award N.A.A.C.P., 1969; named Woman of Year and Bronze Woman of Year, Iota Phi Lambda, 1962, Woman of Year in bus. Atlanta Negro Bus. and Profl. Womens Club, 1964. Mem. Atlanta Summit Leadership Conf. League Women Voters, Nat. Negro Bus. and Profl. Womens Club (regional sec.)., Women's C. of C. Baptist. Home: 107 Mathewson Pl SW Atlanta GA 30314 Office: 1065 Gordon St SW Atlanta GA 30310

WATKINS, NORRIS WILLIAM, banker; b. Columbia, S.C., Aug. 23, 1930; s. Augustus Samuel and Eva Ann (Taylor) W.; A.B., Lenoir Rhyne Coll., 1956; m. Sybil Cline, Sept. 5, 1953; children—Charlotte Ann, Norris William, Maria Susan, Bradley Steven, Brian Todd. Trainee Wachovia Bank & Trust Co., Winston-Salem, N.C., 1956-60; tech. adv. Lowes Co., Inc., North Wilkesboro, N.C., 1960-61; asst. to pres. Fed. Intermediate Credit Bank, Columbia, 1961-65; sr. v.p. 1st Nat. Bank S.C., Columbia, 1965—. Mem. adv. bd. Midlands Tech. Inst., Columbia. Served with AUS, 1951-53. Club: Spring Valley Country. Home: 7522 Millbrook Rd Columbia SC 29204 Office: Box 111 Columbia SC 29202

WATKINS, WILLIAM LAW, lawyer; b. Anderson, S.C., Dec. 26, 1910; s. Thomas Franklin and Agnes (Law) W.; A.B., Wofford Coll., 1932; LL.B., U. Va., 1933; m. Frances Sitton, Oct. 23, 1937; children—Sarah (Mrs. Allen S. Marshall), Anna (Mrs. Alexander C. Hattaway III), Elizabeth (Mrs. Anderson Mills Kinghorn, Jr.), Jane (Mrs. Roger W. Mudd). Admitted to S.C. bar, 1933; since practiced in Anderson; mem. firm Watkins & Prince, 1936-46, Watkins & Watkins, 1946-54, Watkins, Vandiver & Freeman, 1954-64, Watkins, Vandiver, Kirven & Long, 1964-67, Watkins, Vandiver, Kirven, Long & Gable, 1968—. Dir. Palmetto State Life Ins. Co., Perpetual Bldg. & Loan Assn.; adv. bd. S.C. Nat. Bank. Mem. S.C. Ho. of Reps., 1935-36; mem. S.C. Probation, Parole and Pardon Bd., 1954-69. Trustee Presbyn. Coll., Clinton, S.C., Anderson County Hosp. Assn. Served with AUS, 1942-46. Decorated Bronze Star with oak leaf cluster. Fellow Am. Coll. Trial Lawyers; mem. Am., S.C., Anderson bar assns., Phi Beta Kappa, Sigma Alpha Epsilon. Presbyn. Rotarian. Home: 317 North St Anderson SC 29621 Office: 500 S McDuffie St Anderson SC 29621

WATKINS, WILLIAM MYERS III, mus. dir.; b. Memphis, Aug. 19, 1947; s. William Myers and Lou (Cleveland) W.; student U. Miss., summer 1965; B.S.E. in Art, Delta State Coll., 1969; M.A., N.E. La. U., 1971; m. Catharine Elizabeth Jones, July 10, 1971. Tchr. pub. schs. Greenwood, Miss., 1969; Suwannee High Sch., Live Oak, Fla., 1971-72; exec. dir. Meridian (Miss.) Mus. Art, 1972—. One-man shows Carnegie Pub. Library, Clarksdale, Miss., 1969, Goodwill Industries, Jackson, Miss., 1973, Vicksburg (Miss.) Firehouse Gallery, 1974; exhibited in group shows Downtown Gallery, New Orleans, 1968, John Simmons Gallery, Memphis, 1968, N.Y. U., Buffalo, 1969, Masur Mus. Art, Monroe, La., 1971, Miss. Art Gallery, 1972, 73; represented in permanent collection Miss. Art Assn., Jackson, also pvt. collections; guest artist 6th Pine Grove Festival, East Miss. Jr. Coll., 1972; com. mem. Lively Arts Festival, Meridian, 1972—. Bd. dirs. Miss. Art Colony, Utica, 1973. Mem. Am. Fedn. Arts, Am. Assn. Museums, Kappa Pi. Home: 2310 13th St Meridian MS 39301 Office: Box 5773 Meridian MS 39301

WATKINS, YANCEY LEE, educator; b. Uniontown, Ky., Oct. 12, 1934; s. Jordan Cole and Elizabeth Byron (Yancey) W.; A.B., Western Ky. U., 1956; M.A., George Peabody Coll., 1959; Ed.D., U. Ga., 1970; m. Merle Jean Gray, Mar. 21, 1959; children—Lawrence Jordan, Laura Jean, Lee Ann. Tchr., coach Uniontown High Sch., 1956-58, Henderson (Ky.) County High Sch., 1958-59; head tchr., coach Morganfield (Ky.) Jr. High Sch., 1959-64; asst. prin. Union County High Sch., Morganfield, 1964-66; asso. prof. edn. Murray (Ky.) State U., 1966—. Cons. reading. Served with AUS, 1956, 61-62. Mem. Internat. Reading Assn. (Ky. council pres. 1974-75), Ky. Edn. Assn., N.E.A., Nat. Reading Conf., Res. Officers Assn., Phi Delta Kappa, Kappa Delta Pi. Methodist. Lion (dir.). Murray State U. research and study grantee, 1970—. Home: 803 N 20th St Murray KY 42071

WATLINGTON, JOHN FRANCIS, JR., banker; b. Reidsville, N.C., Mar. 23, 1911; s. John Francis and Frances (Byers) W.; A.B., Washington and Lee U., 1933; m. Margaret Jones, Feb. 22, 1947; children—John Francis III, Anne Wilson. With Wachovia Bank & Trust Co., Winston-Salem, N.C., 1933—, successively transit clk., asst. cashier, asst. v.p., v.p., sr. v.p., 1933-56, pres., 1956—, also chmn. Charlotte office, 1946-56; dir. Colonial Stores, Inc., Piedmont Natural Gas Co., Inc., Piedmont Airlines, Inc., Ga. Pacific Corp., Mass. Mut. Life Ins. Co., Akzona Corp., Carolina Power & Light Co. chmn. Wachovia Corp. Mem. N.C. Bd. Conservation and Devel. Trustee Tax Found., Union Theol. Sem.; chmn. bd. visitors Bowman Gray Sch. Medicine. Mem. Res. City Bankers Assn. (past v.p., dir.), C. of C. (pres. 1953, 58-59, dir. 1957), N.C. Citizens Assn. (dir.). Presbyn. Home: 2020 Virginia Rd Winston-Salem NC 27104 Office: Wachovia Bldg Box 3099 Winston-Salem NC 27102

WATSON, BEN TILLMAN, JR., electronics co. exec.; b. Waycross, N.C., Aug. 26, 1923; s. Ben Tillman and Frances Madlin (Scott) W.; grad. high sch.; m. Thelma Mae Hammitt, May 4, 1946; children—Edanna (Mrs. Douglas Earl Reagor), Ben T. III. Joined USN, 1941, advanced through grades to chief warrant officer, 1962; supr. bidding and proposals CEMC, Dallas, 1962-65; dir. CRF, Dallas, 1965-72; mgr. marketing RF Communications, Inc., Rochester, N.Y., 1971-72; dir. contracts Continental Electronics Mfg. Co., Dallas, 1972—. Mem. I.E.E.E. Methodist. Mason. Club: Duck Creek Golf (Garland, Tex.). Home: 127 Moonlight Dr Plano TX 75074 Office: 4212 S Buckner Blvd Dallas TX 75227

WATSON, BILLY RAY, petroleum exec.; b. Snyder, Tex., Aug. 29, 1928; s. William Miles and Ava Jewel (Sorrells) W.; student Tex. Tech. U., 1948-49; B.B.A., Sul Ross Coll., 1952; m. Delores Earle McCright, July 11, 1952; children—Barry Ray, Brad Allan, Bambi Leigh. With accounting dept. Texas Co., Midland, 1952-55; with Lynes, Inc., packers, Midland, Tex., 1955, Oklahoma City, 1955-56, Duncan, Okla., 1956-61, Healdton, Okla., 1961-62, Midland, 1962; owner Watson Packer Service, Monahans, Tex., 1963; pres. Watson Packer, Inc., 1970—; owner, operator Three-B Oil Co., Monahans, 1965—; partner C & W Mfg., Sweetwater, Tex., 1970—; dir. Boomer's Wire Line Service, Monahans, sec.-treas., 1970—. Bd. dirs. Monahans Indsl. Found. Served with AUS, 1946-48. Mem. Am. Inst. Mining Engrs. (vice chmn. 1969), Ind. Petroleum Assn. Am. Mem. Ch. of Christ (Sunday sch. tchr.). Rotarian (v.p.). Patentee in petroleum field. Home: 1000 S Franklin Monahans TX 79756 Office: Box 756 Monahans TX 79756

WATSON, CHARLES BRYAN, TV sports announcer; b. Hornersville, Mo., July 1, 1927; s. Carl Bryan and Dolly Louise (Wright) W.; ed. pub. schs., Pathfinder Sch. Radio Announcing, Kansas City; m. Julia Sue Chailland, Apr. 27, 1945; 1 son, Craig Bryan. Sports announcer, disc jockey Sta. KBOA, Kennett, Mo., 1950-59; staff announcer Sta. WMPS, Memphis, 1959-68; sports dir. Sta. WHBQ-TV, Memphis, 1968—; guest speaker, master of ceremonies. Served with U.S. Mcht. Marine and AUS, World War II. Mem. V.F.W. Baptist. Club: Kennett Country. Home: 1614 E Barton St West Memphis AR 72301 Office: 485 S Highland St Memphis TN 38111

WATSON, DANIEL MARION, zoo ofcl.; b. Kansas City, Mo., June 3, 1928; s. Holland Otis and Ruby Roberta (Butner) W.; grad. high sch., Kansas City; m. Barbara Jean Richardson, Oct. 25, 1953; children—Diane Marie, Thomas Alan, Kathleen Sue, Kevin Andrew. Journeyman zookeeper, Kansas City Zoo, 1945-58; foreman St. Paul Zoo, 1958-60; dir. Madison (Wis.) Zoo, 1960-62, Essex County (N.J.) Zoo, West Orange, 1962-64, Indpls. Zoo, 1964-66, Abilene (Tex.) Zoo, 1968—. Counselor merit badge Chisholm Trail council Boy Scouts Am., 1969—. Bd. dirs. Abilene Community Theatre, 1971-73. Served with inf., AUS, 1950-52. Fellow Am. Assn. Zool. Parks and Aquariums; mem. Am. Inst. Park Execs. (100 point award, 1960-62), Am. Assn. Zoo Keepers, Am. Soc. Ichthyologists and Herpetologists, Soc. Study Amphibians and Reptiles, Nature Conservancy, Nat. Audubon Soc., Zoo Fauna Assn., Sewellel Soc., Taylor Jones Humane Soc., Herpetologists League, Am. Topical Assn., Abilene Zool. Soc. (exec. dir. 1968—), Nat. Wildlife Fedn., Tex. Ornithol. Soc., Wilderness Soc., Smithsonian Assos. Lion (pres. Abilene). Club: West Texas Camera. Home: 1221 Minter Lane Abilene TX 79603 Office: Box 60 Abilene TX 79604

WATSON, DONALD GEORGE, dentist; b. Birmingham, Ala., Dec. 11, 1933; s. John Edward and Elinor (Robinette) W.; B.S., U. Ala., 1957, D.M.D., 1961, orthodontic certificate, 1966; m. Sandra Sue McCallum, Aug. 28, 1965; children—Donald George, Scott Andrew. Dir. indigent children's orthodontics Med. Center U. Ala., Birmingham, 1966-68; pvt. practice orthodontics, Florence, Ala., 1968—. Instr., clinician Dental Sch. U. Ala., parttime, 1968-73. Served with AUS, 1953-55, to capt. Dental Corps, 1962-64. Mem. Am. Assn. Orthodontists, So. Soc. Orthodontists, Ala. Soc. Orthodontists, Am., Ala. dental assns., Tri-Cities Dental Soc. (pres. 1970-71), Kappa Sigma, Omicron Kappa Upsilon. Methodist. Home: 1832 Ford St Florence AL 35630 Office: 403 N Cedar St Florence AL 35630

WATSON, FLETCHER DRUMMOND, lawyer; b. Tasley, Va., Jan. 11, 1922; s. Major Fosque and Addie (Allen) W.; certificate Bus. Adminstrn., Beacon Bus. Coll., 1941; B.A., U. Va., 1950, J.D., 1952; m. Jane Dyott Holland, Sept. 6, 1947; 1 son, Fletcher Drummond. Admitted to Va. bar, 1952; practiced in Covington, 1952—; partner firm Watson & Carson, 1952-65, Stephenson, Kostel, Watson, Carson & Snyder, 1965—; substitute county judge, Covington, 1953-66. Dir. Covington Nat. Bank, A.A. McAllister & Sons Co., Inc. Mem. Indsl. Devel. Commn. Bd., 1970—. Bd. dirs. Regional Library, United Fund, Covington-Alleghany County, 1952-70. Served with AUS, 1942-46. Mem. Va. (ethics com.), 19th Jud. Circuit (past pres.), bar assns., Delta Theta Phi. Presbyn. (past deacon). Moose, Kiwanian. Clubs: Homestead Golf and Tennis (Hot Springs, Va.), Allegheny Country (Covington). Home: Clearwater Park Covington VA 24426 Office: 251 W Riverside St Covington VA 24426

WATSON, HAROLD FRANCIS, educator; b. Milford, Pa., Apr. 2, 1895; s. John Calvin and Adda (Cole) W.; A.B., N.Y.U., 1918, A.M., 1920; Ph.D., Columbia, 1931; Litt. D., Simpson Coll., 1970; m. Martha Hoyt Tucker, Aug. 23, 1924 (dec. Mar. 2, 1961); children—Robert Francis, Stuart Tucker; m. 2d, Elizabeth White, June 26, 1969. Instr. English, N.Y.U., 1918-19, Hedding Coll., 1919-21; asst. prof. English, U. Me., 1922-24; vis. prof. U. W.Va., summer 1929; prof. English, chmn. div. lang. and lit. Simpson Coll. 1924-55, chmn. div. humanities, 1955-60, chmn. faculty council and dean, 1959, prof. emeritus English. Mem. tech. adv. com. on English Ia. Assn. Coll. Pres., 1928; gen. sec. Ia. Colls. Conf. on English, 1939-41; sec. Ia. Authors Club, 1944-46. Mem. Modern Lang. Assn., Augustan Soc., Heraldry Soc. (Brit.), Phi Beta Kappa, Lambda Chi Alpha, Pi Kappa Delta, Alpha Psi Omega. Mason (32 deg.). Author: The Sailor in English Fiction and Drama, 1550-1800, 1931; Writing for Freshmen (with L.W. Smith), 1930; Adventures in Contemporary Reading (with L. W. Smith), 1932; Coasts of Treasure Island, 1969. Joint editor: Types and Times in English Literature, Book I, 1940. Contbr. articles to profl. jours. Home: 518 E Ash St Fayetteville AR 72701

WATSON, HENRIETTA SUE CARTER (MRS. JACK CROZIER WATSON), lawyer; b. Hayden, Ala., Mar. 5, 1933; d. Henry Zac and Myrtle (Mooneyham) Carter; B.A., La. State U., 1959, J.D., 1959; m. Jack Crozier Watson, Dec. 26, 1958; children—Carter Crozier, Wells Talbot. Admitted to La. bar, 1959; mem. firm Camp & Palmer, Lake Charles, 1959-60, Watson & Watson, Lake Charles, 1960-65; now law clk. Ct. Appeals, 3d Circuit. Dir. Cameron State Bank (La.). Mem. transp. task force Goals for La. Program, 1969-70; mem. bd. commrs. Lake Charles Harbor and Terminal Dist., Lake Charles, 1966—; vice chmn. transp. com. La. Goals Action Program, 1971—. Bd. dirs. Lake Charles Ballet Soc.; trustee Goals for La. Home: 311 Shell Beach Dr Lake Charles LA 70601

WATSON, JACK CROZIER, judge; b. Jonesville, La., Sept. 17, 1928; s. Jesse Crozier and Gladys (Talbot) W.; B.A., U. Southwestern La., 1949; LL.B., La. State U., 1956; m. Sue Carter, Dec. 26, 1958; children—Carter, Wells. Admitted to La. bar, 1956; practiced in Lake Charles, La., 1956-64; mem. firm Watson & Watson, 1960-64; prosecutor City of Lake Charles, 1960; asst. dist. atty. 14th Jud. Dist. La., 1961-64; dist. judge 14th Jud. Dist. La., Lake Charles, 1964-72; judge ad hoc 1st Circuit Ct. Appeal, 1972-73, 3d Circuit Ct. Appeal, 1974—. Faculty, adviser Nat. Coll. State Judiciary, 1970, 73; mem. La. Jud. Council, 1972-74. Served to 1st lt. USAF, 1950-54. Mem. Am., La., S.W. La. bar assns., Nat. Council Juvenile Ct. Judges (pres. La. council 1969-70), Am. Legion, S.W. La. Camellia Soc. (pres. 1973—), Blue Key, Sigma Alpha Epsilon, Phi Delta Phi, Pi Kappa Delta. Club: Lake Charles Yacht (commodore 1970). Home: 311 Shell Beach Dr Lake Charles LA 70601 Office: PO Box 3209 Lake Charles LA 70601

WATSON, JAMES CHESTNUT, physician; b. Trenton, N.J., June 16, 1936; s. Reed and Grace (Chestnut) W.; A.B., Lincoln U., 1958; M.D., Howard U., 1964; M.P.H., U. Tex., 1970; m. Pauline Kathryn Thomas, Apr. 1, 1961; children—Jamie Lyn, Juliette Grace, Paula Elise, Debra Patrice. Intern, Meml. Hosp., South Bend, Ind., 1964-65; practice medicine, specializing in gen. practice and preventive medicine, Houston, 1967-69, 1969—; asst. prof. community medicine Baylor Coll. of Medicine, 1970—; asso. prof. pharmacology Sch. Pharmacy, Tex. So. U., 1972—; mem. active staff Riverside Gen. staff Hosp. Pres., chmn. bd. Freedmen's Pub. Co., Inc., pub. The Informer, Tex. Freemen, 1972—; pres. J. Robb Assos., Inc., health care cons., 1973—; dir. Homestead Bank, Houston. Bd. mgrs. Harris County Hosp. Dist. Served with USAF, 1965-67. Mem. Am., Tex. pub. health assns., Nat. Med. Assn., Houston Med. Forum, Omega Psi, Phi. Democrat. Episcopalian (mem. standing com. Diocese Tex. 1971—). Home: 5339 Trail Lake Dr Houston TX 77045 Office: 8803 Scott St Houston TX 77051

WATSON, JAMES FRANCIS, JR., elec. engr.; b. Newport News, Va., Nov. 13, 1942; s. James Francis and Ethel Lee (Little) W.; B.S. in E.E., Va. Poly. Inst., 1965; M.E.E., Old Dominion U., 1969; m. Merlynn Kay Kunze, May 18, 1965; children—James, Jerry. Elec. engr. Marine Engring. Lab., U.S. Navy, Annapolis, Md., 1965-66; elec. engr., research supr. Newport News Shipbldg. (Va.), 1966—. Mem. I.E.E.E. Home: 3 Holiday Dr Hampton VA 23369 Office: 4107 Washington Av Newport News VA 23607

WATSON, JAMES MILTON, elec. engr.; b. Rio Grande City, Tex., Dec. 24, 1944; s. Robert Lee and Estella (Uribe) W.; B.S. in Elec. Engring., Tex. A. and I. U., 1968; m. Maria Perla Martinez, Aug. 26, 1967; children—Catherine Ann, Robert James. Facilities engr. IBM, Austin, Tex., 1968-71, asso. facilities engr., 1971-72, sr. asso. facilities engr., 1972-73, plant facilities project engr., 1973—. Mem. I.E.E.E., Sigma Tau. Home: 12204 Mustang Chase Austin TX 78759 Office: 11400 FM Rd 1325 Austin TX 78759

WATSON, JOHN BRYDEN, chem. engr.; b. Glasgow, Scotland, Apr. 3, 1938; s. Thomas and Elizabeth (Bryden) W.; grad. chemistry Mungo Acad. Sci. (Scotland), 1957; m. Mary M. Davis, Nov. 19, 1958; children—Teresa, Pauline Frances. Came to U.S., 1966. Sr. technician Can. Wire & Cable Co., Toronto, Ont., 1958-66; chief chemist Electric Parts Corp., Georgetown, Ky., 1966; product devel. engr. Stauffer Chem. Co., Delaware City, Del., 1966-69, sales rep. polymer div., Southfield, Mich., 1969-70; sales mgr. Cardinal Chem. Co., Columbia, S.C. and Dallas, Tex., 1970—. Mem. Soc. Plastics Engrs., Soc. Plastics Industry, Soc. Plastics Wire Assn., Soc. Christian Children's Fund. Roman Catholic. Club: Toastmaster (Dallas). Home: 11430 Glen Cross St Dallas TX 75228 Office: PO Box 28294 Dallas TX 75228

WATSON, JOHN DARGAN, cons. civil engr.; b. Greenwood, S.C., May 23, 1905; s. Harry Legare and Ella (Dargan) W.; A.B., Furman U., 1925; B.C.E., U. N.C., 1928, M.S., 1932; Sc.D., Harvard, 1940; m. Susannah Hawkins Thomas, Jan. 4, 1947; children—Harry Legare, Edgar Thomas, John Dargan. Jr. engr. Ala. Power Co., Phoenix City, 1928-30; instr. civil engring. U. N.C., Chapel Hill, 1930-34, Lehigh U., Bethlehem, Pa., 1934-36; research fellow Harvard Sch. Engring., 1936-39; asst. prof. civil engring. Duke, 1939-42; chief engr. J.A. Jones Constrn. Co., Charlotte, N.C., 1942-45; pres. Watson Engrs., Inc., Greensboro, N.C., 1945-69, LBC&W Assos. of N.C., 1969-72; cons. engr. bldg. industry on structural and foundation problems, Greensboro, 1972—. Mem. N.C. State Bd. Registration for Engrs. and Land Surveyors, 1957-66, 70—. Treas., Guilford Democratic Exec. Com., 1971. Pres., Greensboro Natural Sci. Mus., 1958; pres. Gen. Greene council Boy Scouts Am., Silver Beaver award, 1961-63. Fellow Am. Soc. C.E. (dir.); mem. S.A.R., N.C. Soc. Engr. (pres. 1956), Alpha Tau Omega. Episcopalian. Mason, Rotarian. Club: Greensboro Country. Address: 2300 Princess Ann St Greensboro NC 27408

WATSON, JOHN RAYMOND, structural engr.; b. San Juan P.R., Sept. 7, 1935; s. Edward C. and Stella (Hemsley) W.; B.S.C.E., U. P.R., 1957, B.S., 1958; M.S. in Civil Engring., Mass. Inst. Tech., 1959; m. Brunilda de Jesus Silva, Dec. 28, 1957; 1 son, John Raymond. Instr. gen. and civil engring. U. P.R., Mayaguez, 1957-60; v.p., gen. mgr. Prescon Caribe, Inc., San Juan, 1960-64; asso. Schimmelpfennig, Ruiz & Gonzalez, Rio Piedras, 1964-65; pvt. practice cons. structural engr., Rio Piedras, 1965-69; exec. dir. P.R. Hwy. Authority, 1969-72; pres. Abarca Corps., San Juan, 1973—. Mem. Am. Concrete Inst., Am. Soc. C.E., P.R. Soc. Structural Engrs., P.R. Inst. Engrs., Architects and Surveyors, Met. Opera Guild, Sigma Xi, Tau Beta Pi, Nu Sigma Beta. Mem. New Progressive Party. Episcopalian. Club: Nat. Exchange (nat. dir. 1973—). Home: 1303 Los Patricios Condominium Guaynabo PR 00920 Office: Abarca Box 2352 San Juan PR 00903

WATSON, MURRAY, JR., lawyer, state legislator; b. Mart, Tex., May 14, 1932; s. Murray and Ethel (Bryson) W.; B.B.A., Baylor U., 1952, J.D., 1954; Asso. degree in applied sci. (hon.), Tex. State Tech. Inst., 1970; m. Greta Candace Warren, Aug. 15, 1959; children—Milicent, Marcus Warren. Admitted to Tex. bar, 1955, U.S. Supreme Ct. bar; practice law in Mart, 1955-59, 61-62, Waco, 1959-61, 62—; asso. feed, seed and farming bus. with father, 1949-54, 1963—; prof. bus. law Baylor U., 1959-60; asso. Jones, Boyd, Westbrook & Lovelace, Waco, 1962-67, Watson & Weed, Waco, 1967-71, Watson & Kennedy, 1971—. Vis. instr. McLennan Community Coll., 1967-68; prof. adminstrv. law Baylor Sch. Law, 1969-70. Pres., dir. Central Tex. Indsl. Devel. Council. Bill clk., Tex. Ho. of Reps., 1955; mem. Tex. Ho. of Reps., 1957-62; mem. Tex. Senate, 1963-73; mem. Tex. Legislative Council, 1965. Bd. dirs. Central Tex. Museum, 1962—, pres., 1965-67, v.p., 1967-71; bd. dirs. McLennan Tb Assn., Christmas Seal chmn., 1966. Recipient Distinguished Service award Waco Jr. C. of C., 1963, citation appreciation Tex. Assn. Mental Health, 1963, Distinguished Service award Vocational Agrl. Tchrs. Assn. Tex., 1964, Outstanding Citizenship award Mart C. of C. and Agr., 1964, Outstanding Service to Handicapped award Tex. Rehab. Commn. and President's Council to Employ the handicapped, 1970, many other service awards, gov. for a day, July 12, 1969. Mem. State Bar Tex., Waco-McLennan County, Waco Jr. bar assns., Mart, Waco chambers commerce, Tex. and S.W. Cattle Raisers Assn., McLennan County Farm Bur., Tex. State Firemen and Fire Marshals Assn. (hon. life), Waco Jr. C. of C. (dir. 1958-60, 65-67), Order Artus, Delta Sigma Pi, Phi Alpha Delta. Methodist. Mason (Shriner), K.P., Lion, Kiwanian; mem. Order Eastern Star. Contbr. articles to profl. jours. Home: 308 Texas Av Mart TX 76664 Office: 820 Lake Air Dr Waco TX 76710

WATSON, OPAL JEANNETTE PERRY (MRS. JAMES PARIS WATSON), educator; b. Pickens County, S.C., Oct. 31, 1922; d. Samuel Lee and Sallie Mae (Jewell) Perry; student Anderson Jr. Coll., 1941-43; B.S. in Elementary Edn., Oglethorpe U., 1955; m. James Paris Watson, Nov. 26, 1943; 1 son, James Paris. Elementary tchr. Gwinnett County (Ga.) Schs., 1948-57, Fulton County-Newtown Sch., 1957-63; field worker ch. tng. dept. Ga. Bapt. Conv., Atlanta, 1963—, also presch. cons. Tutor pub. sch. tchrs., 1963—. Dir. day camp Girl Scouts U.S.A., Duluth, Ga., 1957-62; leader Youth Temperance Council, 1968—, ch. tng. dir. Lawrenceville Bapt. Assn., 1956-63, dist. pres. ch. tng. Ga., 1960-65; dist. pres. Woman's Christian Temperance Union, 1964-69, pub. Ga. bull., 1968-72, del. world conv., 1971, state pres., 1968-72; alternate mem. Nat. Temperance and Prohibition Council, 1970; mem. Ga. Safety Council, 1971-72; mem. Gov.'s Conf. on Edn. and Intellectual Enrichment, 1971. Mem. Am. Security Council, Internat. Platform Assn., Ga. Save Sunday Assn. (sec.), Ga. Presch. Assn., W.C.T.U. (pres. Duluth chpt., hon. state pres. 1972—). Baptist (intermediate Sunday sch. supt. 1957-69, peoples dir. 1967-70, mission study chmn. women's group, dir. vacation Bible Sch. 1974). Home: 2923 Pineview St Duluth GA 30136

WATSON, ORES, petroleum co. exec.; b. Haw Creek, Ark., Nov. 16, 1915; s. William and Arizona (Howze) W.; grad. high sch.; m. Doris Bullington, Oct. 20, 1938; children—Jeanie (Mrs. Stuart E. Rosenbaum), Karen. Clk., U.S. P.O., Albuquerque and Wichita Falls, N.M., 1937-54; office mgr. Dual Drilling Co., Wichita Falls, Tex., 1954-64, contracts mgr., 1964-70, v.p. contracts, 1970—. Sec., treas. Priddy Found., 1965—. Mem. N. Tex. Oil and Gas Assn., Internat. Assn. Drilling Contractors. Home: 4400 Cedar Elm Wichita Falls TX 76308 Office: City Nat Bldg Wichita Falls TX 76301

WATSON, SAMUEL ROBERT, JR., utility engr.; b. Henderson, N.C., Nov. 6, 1915; s. Samuel Robert and Roselle (Harris) W.; B.S., N.C. State Coll., 1936, postgrad. physics, 1937-41; m. Lillian Harward, Oct. 19, 1951; children—Samuel Robert III, Bettie, Jane. With Caroline Power & Light Co., Raleigh, N.C., 1936—, dist. engr., 1948-65, div. engr., 1966—. Served with AUS, World War II; ETO. Mem. I.E.E.E., Raleigh Engrs. Club, Civitan (dir.), Theta Tau, Mu Beta Psi. Episcopalian. Clubs: Henderson (N.C.) Country; Carolina Country (Raleigh). Home: 2724 Lakeview Dr Raleigh NC 27609 Office: 115 N Harrington St Raleigh NC 27602

WATSON, THEODORE TALBOT, constrn. co. exec.; b. Cambridge, Mass., Oct. 30, 1912; s. Daniel Harvey and Ella Mary (Talbot) W.; B.S., Boston U., 1936; student U. P.R., 1935; m. Edith Durfee, Aug. 3, 1940; 1 dau., Linda Lee (Mrs. Robert E. McGurk). Dist. sales supr. Scott Paper Co., 1936-42; owner-operator Spring Lake Motor Ct., Rectory, Va., 1946-48; account exec. Research Inst. Am., N.Y.C., 1948-51; pres. T.T. Watson, Inc., Sarasota, Fla., 1952—; dir. Am. Bank Sarasota. Chmn. land use com. Sarasota Brandenton Airport, 1959-72. Chmn. bd. trustees Fla. Constrn. Industries Self Ins. Fund, 1958—; chmn. bd. dirs. County Meml. Pub. Hosp., 1972-73. Pres., United Appeal, chmn.. adv. bd., 1968-71; chmn. A.R.C., 1971-72. Served to lt. USNR, 1942-45; PTO. Mem. Gulf Coast Builders Exchange (bd. mem. 1958-62), Sarasota County C. of C. (pres. 1960-61), Sigma Alpha Epsilon. Clubs: University, Sarabay Country (bd. mem. 1970-72) Field (commodore 1973-74) (Sarasota). Home: PO Box 15466 Sarasota FL 33579 also 1818 Roland St Sarasota FL 33581 Office: 435 S Gulfstream Av Sarasota FL 33577

WATSON, THOMAS PHILIP, state senator; b. Nashville, Ark., Aug. 31, 1933; s. Jordan and Frieda (Pryor) Watson; B.A., Harding Coll., 1959; M.A., U. Mo., 1960; m. Mary Parks, Feb. 20, 1964; children—Rebecca, Phylis. Ordained to ministry Ch. of Christ, 1955; minister chs., Ark., Mo., Okla., 1956—, Edmond (Okla.) Ch. of Christ, 1967-72, Spencer, Okla., 1973—; pres. Red Carpet Real Estate, Edmond, 1972—; mem. Okla. Senate, 1972—. Mem. pres.'s devel. council Harding Coll., Searcy, Ark., 1969—. Bd. dirs. Edmond YMCA, 1969—, chmn., 1969-71; bd. dirs. Edmond Meml. Hosp., 1969-72, chmn., 1971-72. Served with USAF, 1951-55. Republican. Kiwanian. Home: Route 3 Box 284A Edmond OK 73034 Office: 1301 S Broadway Edmond OK 73034 also State Capital Bldg Oklahoma City OK 73105

WATSON, THOMAS SHELBY, broadcasting co. exec.; b. Taylorsville, Ky., July 8, 1939; s. Orville Lee and Bonnie Opal (Snider) W.; student U. Ky., 1958-61; m. Nettie Catherine Hance, Apr. 1, 1961; children—Sharon Elizabeth, Wendy Lynn, Kelly Thomas. Announcer-newsman Sta. WSTL, Eminence, Ky., 1961-62; news editor Sta. WAKY, Louisville, 1961-64, news dir., 1964-67, 69-74; editorialist A.P., Louisville, 1973—; news dir. Sta. WIL, St. Louis, 1967-68. Recipient Robert F. Kennedy Journalism award Nat. Conf. Christians and Jews, 1971. Mem. A.P. Broadcaster's Assn. (newsletter com. 1972-73), Radio Television News Dirs. Assn. (freedom of information com. and newsletter com. 1972-73), A.P. News Dirs. Assn. (pres. Ky. 1971-73), Nat. Headliner's Club, Ky., Mo. hist. socs., Louisville Hist. Preservation League, Louisville Jaycees (dir. 1971). Author: The Silent Riders, 1971. Home: 2505 Colonel Dr Louisville KY 40222 Office: Courier Jour Bldg Louisville KY 40202

WATSON, WILLIAM AUGUSTIN III, textile co. exec.; b. Macon, Ga., Sept. 11, 1927; s. William Augustin, Jr. and Vera (Nottingham) W.; student Auburn U., 1945-46; B.S., U. S.C., 1948; m. Nancy Ellen Claymore, Apr. 8, 1949; children—William Augustin IV, Robert Charles, Virginia Ellen. Salesman, Bibb Mfg. Co., N.Y.C., 1950-60, div. sales mgr., N.Y.C., 1960-62, regional sales mgr., N.Y.C., 1962-64, field sales mgr., Macon, 1964-65, dir. sales and marketing, Macon, 1965-67, v.p. sales and marketing, 1967-71, pres. yarn and rubber industry div., 1970-71; v.p. Shuford Mills, Hickory, N.C., 1971—, dir. Mem. Am. Yarn Spinners Assn. (dir.), N.C. Textile Mfrs. Assn. (dir.), Carpet Yarn Assn. (organizing dir.). Methodist. Home: Route 10 Hickory NC 28601 Office: Shuford Mills Hickory NC 28601

WATTERSON, BRUCE CARTER, dentist; b. Chase City, Va., Oct. 26, 1939; s. George Shual and Ennis James (Carter) W.; B.A., U. Richmond, 1963, postgrad. 1963-64; D.D.S., Med. Coll. of Va., 1968; m. Juanita Rawls, June 17, 1961; children—Scott Hunter, James Carter. Research technician Med. Coll. of Va., 1958-60, med. technologist, 1961-68; practice of dentistry, Norfolk, Va., 1968-70, Virginia Beach, 1970—; with Virginia Beach Health Dept., 1969-72. Mem. Am., Va., Va.-Tidewater dental assns., Virginia Beach Dental Soc., Virginia-Tidewater Dental Study Club, Psi Omega. Home: 4060 Richardson Rd Virginia Beach VA 23455 Office: 760 Independence Blvd Virginia Beach VA 23455

WATTS, ALVA BURL, educator; b. Shreveport, La., Aug. 1, 1918; s. Alva J. and Julia (Thomas) W.; B.S., Southwestern La. Inst., 1939; M.S., La. State U., 1941; Ph.D., Okla. State U., 1950; m. Katherine Wilbanks, Jan. 9, 1942; children—Katherine (Mrs. W.S. Prescott),

Corinne (Mrs. Ed Stone), Alva Burl. Jr. biochemist So. Regional Research Lab., New Orleans, 1941-43; instr. dept. animal industry La. State U., Baton Rouge, 1946-48, asst. prof. dept. poultry industry, 1948-51, asso. prof., 1951-55, prof., head dept. poultry sci., 1955—. Cons. poultry nutrition Agrl. Devel. Bank, Caracas, Venezuela, 1969, 72; cons. animal nutrition AID Contract Program, Managua, Nicaragua, 1972, 73. Served as ensign USNR, 1943-46; now lt. Res. ret. Named Distinguished Alumnus, U. Southwestern La., 1959. Fellow A.A.A.S., Am. Inst. Chemists; mem. Am. Chem. Soc., Am. Inst. Biol. Sci., Am. Inst. Nutrition, Assn. So. Agrl. Workers, Biometrics Soc., Inst. Food Technologists (chmn. Gulf Coast sect. 1967), La Profl. Poultry Workers Soc., La. Tchrs. Assn., Poultry Industries La. (dir. 1960—), Poultry Sci. Assn. (chmn. teaching award com. 1960, dir. 1956, 57), Soc. Animal Sci., Soc. Exptl. Biology and Medicine, Southeastern Poultry and Egg Assn., World's Poultry Sci. Assn. (program com. 1972-74), Am. Legion, Am. Farm Bur., Sigma Xi, Gamma Sigma Delta. Methodist (mem. adminstrv. bd. 1966-68, 72-73). Kiwanian (pres. 1967). Contbr. articles to profl. jours. Home: 1291 Lee Dr Baton Rouge LA 70808

WATTS, HENRY MILLARD, scientist; b. Birmingham, Ala., Oct. 22, 1920; s. Henry Millard and Francis Marie (Weber) W.; Asso. Sci., N.E. Jr. Coll. at Kansas City, Mo., 1939; B.S., U. Mo., 1942; Ph.D., Johns Hopkins, 1952; m. Helena Roselle Long, June 14, 1940; children—Helena (Mrs. John Francis Scott), Patricia (Mrs. James Lawrence Foble). With Bell Telephone Lab., Whippany, N.J., 1942-47; research physicist Johns Hopkins, 1947-52; dir. research, engring. Bendix Radio Div., Towson, Md., 1952-57; chief engr. Martin Co., Orlando, Fla., 1957-60; program mgr. Hughes Aircraft Co., Culver City, Cal., 1961-62; dir. tech. Systems Devel. Corp., Santa Monica, Cal., 1963-64; asst. to v.p. Westinghouse Friendship Airport, Balt., 1965-66; dir. communication systems div. Jerrold Corp., Phila., 1967; dir. biomed. div. Ark Electronics Corp., Willow Grove, Pa., 1967-69; dir. operations Dyad Systems Inc., Columbia, Md., 1969-70; ind. cons. Ellicott City, Md., 1970-71; prin. staff scientist ITT Electro Physics Lab., Columbia, Md., 1972-73; sr. research scientist System Planning Corp., Arlington, Va., 1973—. Recipient U.S. War Manpower Commn. award, 1945. Mem. A.A.A.S., N.Y. Acad. Sci., I.E.E.E., Am. Phys. Soc., Mensa, Sigma Xi, Gamma Alpha, Eta Kappa Nu, Tau Beta Pi. Contbr. articles to profl. jours. Patentee in many fields. Address: 4302 Roberts Av Annandale VA 22003

WATTS, JOHN ROBERT, holding co. exec.; b. Abilene, Tex., Dec. 22, 1926; s. Robert and John Lou (Floyd) W.; B.B.A., U. Tex., 1950; m. Mary Edna Gurley, Sept. 18, 1948; children—John Robert III, Gary Mitchell, Martin O'Dell, Natalie Joan. Indsl. engr. Procter & Gamble Co., Amarillo, Tex., 1950-56; mgr. adminstrn. Tex. Butadiene & Chem. Corp., N.Y.C., 1956-62; pres. Houston Reinforced Plastics Co., 1962-68, Uni-Sun, Inc., Houston, 1969—; pres., dir. Sun-X Mfg., Inc., Sun-X Internat., Inc., Lusterock Internat., Inc., Openings, Inc., Sun-X Plastics, Inc., UniTrade Inc. Served with USNR, 1944-46. Mem. Am. Soc. Indsl. Engrs., Am. Soc. Safety Engrs., Am. Soc. Traffic Engrs., World Trade Assn., C. of C., Ex-Students' Assn. U. Tex., Phi Kappa Psi. Republican. Methodist. Rotarian. Clubs: Longhorn, Presidents (Houston). Home: 11215 Oak Spring St Houston TX 77043 Office: 4125 Richmond Av Houston TX 77027

WATTS, THOMAS ELLINGTON, JR., lawyer; b. Nashville. Oct. 19, 1931; s. Thomas Ellington and Laura Frances (Harris) W., B.A., Vanderbilt U., 1954, LL.B., 1956; m. Mary Louise Miller, May 2, 1959; children—Elizabeth June, Andrew William, Suzanne Laura. Bigelow teaching fellow U. Chgo. Law Sch., 1956-57; admitted to Tenn. bar, 1956, Ill. bar, 1957, U.S. Supreme Ct. bar, 1973; asso. Isham, Lincoln & Beale, Chgo., 1957-59, Van Duzer, Gershon & Jordan, Chgo., 1959-63, Farris, Evans & Evans, Nashville, 1963-68; mem. firm Butler, McHugh, Butler, Tune & Watts, Nashville, 1968-73; pvt. practice, Nashville, 1973—. Bd. dirs. Citizens Advocacy Council for Developmentally Disabled. Served with USAF, 1951-52. Mem. Tenn., Nashville bar assns., Nashville Area C. of C., Phi Beta Kappa. Republican. Mem. Christian Ch. (elder 1972—). Club: Nashville City. Home: 213 Mockingbird Rd Nashville TN 37205 Office: 622 JC Bradford Bldg Nashville TN 37219

WATTS, THOMAS SUMTER, lawyer; b. Statesville, N.C., Mar. 11, 1939; s. Atwell Edwin and Katharine Sumter (Cowan) W.; A.B., Davidson Coll., 1961; LL.B., Wake Forest U., 1964; m. Marguerite E. Peters, Dec. 28, 1963; 1 dau., Mary Katharine. Admitted to N.C. bar, 1964; asso., Small & Small, Elizabeth City, N.C., 1964-66; partner Small, Small & Watts, 1966-70; dist. ct. prosecutor 1st Jud. Dist. N.C., Elizabeth City, 1970, asst. dist. atty., 1970—. Lectr., N.C. Dist. Attys. Assn., 1971—. Trustee N.C. Jr. C. of C. Meml. Found., chmn. bd., 1971-73. Mem. Am., N.C., Pasquotank County (pres. 1969-70), bar assns., N.C. State Bar, U.S. (nat. dir. 1969-71), N.C. (legal counsel 1968-69, spl. asst. to pres. 1971-72), Elizabeth City (Distinguished Service award 1968, Jaycee of Year 1968, pres. 1967-68) jr. chambers commerce, Pi Kappa Phi, Phi Alpha Delta. Democrat. Methodist. Elk. Home: 204 W Church St Elizabeth City NC 27909 Office: 202 E Colonial Av Elizabeth City NC 27909

WAUGH, DORIS HANNER, elementary librarian; b. Greensboro, N.C., June 4, 1928; d. Thomas Benton and Eliabeth (Hanner) Waugh; B.S., Appalachian State Tchrs. Coll., 1950; M.S., U. N.C., 1956. Librarian Black Mountain (N.C.) High Sch., 1950-51, Burlington (N.C.) City Schs., 1951-53, Greensboro Pub. Schs., 1953—. Active Girl Scouts, Brownies; program chmn. ladies aux. Climax Vol. Fire Dept. Mem. Southeastern, N.C. library assns., N.E.A., N.C. Assn. Educators, Assn. Childhood Edn. Methodist. Home: Box 40 Climax NC 27233 Office: 600 W Terrell St Greensboro NC 27406

WAVRO, RICHARD HAROLD, real estate co. exec.; b. Orlando, Fla., Aug. 15, 1939; s. Paul Kenneth and Aileen (Leiden) W.; B.A. with honors, Fla. State U., 1963; m. Susan Varner, Jan. 22, 1963 (div. June 1972); children—William Kendall, Stacey Elizabeth. Pension Cons. Hand & Assos., Houston, 1969-71; treas., chief financial officer Property Investments, Inc., Houston, 1972—; v.p., treas. Gen. Devel. Corp., Houston, 1970—. Financial cons. various small businesses. Mem. Am. Inst. C.P.A.'s, Tex. Soc. C.P.A.'s, Am. Soc. Pension Actuaries, Am. Land Devel. Assn. Mason. Home: 1623 Clarke St Harlingen TX 78550

WAX, GEORGE LOUIS, lawyer; b. New Orleans, Dec. 6, 1928; s. John Edward and Theresa (Schaff) W.; LL.B., Loyola U. of South, 1952, B.C.S., 1960; m. Patricia Ann Delaney, Feb. 20, 1965; children—Louis Jude, Joann Olga. Admitted to La. bar, 1952, practice, New Orleans, 1954—. Served with USNR, 1952-54. Mem. Am., La., New Orleans bar assns., Am. Legion. Roman Catholic. Kiwanian. Clubs: New Orleans Athletic, Suburban Gun and Rod, Pendennis. Home: 5635 Pratt Dr New Orleans LA 70122 Office: First Nat Bank Commerce Bldg New Orleans LA 70112

WAY, JANEY RUTH PHARR (MRS. EUGENE C. WAY), oil co. exec.; b. Nevada, Tex., July 8, 1934; d. Eldon Ray and Lou Evelyn (Deckard) Pharr; B.S., Tex. State Coll. for Women, 1956; m. Eugene C. Way, Oct. 13, 1958; children—Tony Lee, Mark Robert. Tchr. bus. Ferris (Tex.) Sch. System, 1956; sec. to sales mgr. Folding Carrier Corp., Oklahoma City, 1958-62; asst. corporate sec. Quality Products Co., St. Louis, 1965-69, Alco Controls Corp., St. Louis, 1965-69, Columbia Producing Co., N.Y.C., 1965-69; corporate sec. Camm Realty Co., St. Louis, 1967-71, Maguire Oil Co., Dallas, 1969—. Mem. Exec. Secs. (dir. 1974), Bus. and Profl. Women's Club (pres. 1956). Episcopalian (supt. ch. sch. 1971—). Home: 7729 Colebrook St Dallas TX 75217 Office: 4200 1st Nat Bank Bldg Dallas TX 75202

WAYNE, ALAN, educator; b. N.Y.C., June 18, 1909; s. Adolph Otto Johann and Martha (Horvath) Wiesenburg; B.S., Coll. City N.Y., 1931, M.S. in Edn., 1937; postgrad. Columbia, 1945-49, (A.A.A.S. Secondary Sch. fellow) N.Y.U., 1961-68; m. Muriel Rothstein, Aug. 25, 1934; children—Linda (Mrs. Paul Richard Weiss), Susan (Mrs. Lance Kelvin McKee). Tchr. math. and sci. Rhodes Sch., N.Y.C., 1930-45; tchr. math. James Fenimore Cooper Jr. High Sch., N.Y.C., 1940-45, Williamsburgh Vocational High Sch., N.Y.C., 1945-51; asst. prin., supr. math. and sci. Eli Whitney Vocational High Sch., N.Y.C., 1951-72 (on leave). Adj. instr. math. Cooper Union, N.Y.C., 1949-67, adj. asst. prof., 1967-72; instr. math. edn. N.Y.U., 1950-51, Yeshiva U. Grad. Sch., 1959-61; adj. asst. prof. math. Queensborough Community Coll., N.Y.C., 1965-72; editorial cons. vocational-indsl. edn. State U. N.Y., 1949-57; mem. curriculum devel. coms. N.Y.C. Bd. Edn., 1950-70. Vice chmn. finance com. Beacon Sq. Pool Assn.; sec. Richey Symphony Soc. Committeeman, N.Y. County Democratic Com., 1940. Mem. Sch. Sci. and Math. Assn., Council Supervisory Assns., Am. Assn. U. Profs., Am. Math. Soc., Soc. for Indsl. and Applied Math., Math. Assn. Am., Nat. Council Tchrs. Math., Assn. Tchrs. Math. N.Y.C. (pres. 1948-50); exec. bd., historian 1951-71), Assn. Tchrs. Math. N.Y. State (charter, county chmn. 1951-72), Math. Chmns. Assn. N.Y.C. (v.p. 1971-72), Epsilon Pi Tau. Club: N.Y. Riddlers (pres. 1952). Author: Basic Mathematics I, 1951; Basic Mathematics II, 1954; (with Olivo) Basic Applied Science, 1957; (with Bold) Number Systems, 1971. Editor: Metals Technology, 1955. Home: 6614 Springfield Dr Holiday FL 33589

WEABER, GEORGE HAWN, physician; b. Binger, Okla., May 13, 1940; s. Ivan John and Helen (Hawn) W.; B.S., U. Okla., 1962, M.D., 1966. Intern, Baptist Meml. Hosp., Oklahoma City, 1966-67; resident in anesthesiology Parkland Meml. Hosp., Dallas, 1967-69; practice in anesthesiology, Weaber & Lostetter, Arlington, Tex., 1969—; mem. staff Arlington Meml. Hosp., 1969—, Arlington Community Hosp., 1969—. Fellow Am. Coll. Anesthesiologists; mem. Am., Tex. Socs. anesthesiologists, Tarrant County Med. Assn., Okla. U. Alumni Assn., Delta Kappa Epsilon, Phi Beta Pi. Republican. Conglist. Home: 909 Live Oak Lane Arlington TX 76012 Office: 900 W Randol Mill Rd Arlington TX 76010

WEACHTER, EVELYN, librarian; b. Akron, O., Apr. 12, 1908; d. William Clyde and Minnetta (McConnell) Weachter; A.B., Coll. of Wooster, 1932; B.S. in L.S., Columbia, 1940; postgrad. Fitchburg State Coll., 1960-64. With Akron Pub. Library, 1933-45, reference librarian, 1940-43, bus. reference librarian, 1943-45; reference librarian Fitchburg (Mass.) Pub. Library, 1945-55, asst. librarian, 1955-60; head librarian Fitchburg State Coll., 1960-66; now head librarian Cocoa Beach (Fla.) Pub. Library. Instr. reference course Clark U., Worcester, Mass., 1950-51, Mass. U. Extension Service, Cambridge, Mass., 1949-50; author corr. course in reference librarianship for Commonwealth Mass., 1958. Mem. Mass. (chmn. planning com. 1955-56), Fla. library assns., Council State Coll. Librarians (pres. Mass. 1963-64), Brevard County Librarians Assn. Home: Twin Towers 612 N 2020 N Atlantic Av Cocoa Beach FL 32931 Office: 55 S Brevard St Cocoa Beach FL 32931

WEAFER, RICHARD EDWARD, coll. adminstr.; b. Brookline, Mass., June 19, 1924; s. Dominic Edward and Lucy (Slayton) W.; ed. Brescia Coll.; m. Lillian Pauline Payne, Nov. 12, 1946; children—Lucy (Mrs. Gerald Goetz), James, Stephen, Dennis, Janice, Barbara, Richard Edward, Michael, Lillian. Bookkeeper, John L. Denning, Boston, 1946-47, Wathen Coal Co., Owensboro, Ky., 1947-52; accountant Boswell & May, C.P.A.'s, Owensboro, 1952-58; partner firm Boswell & Weafer, C.P.A.'s, Owensboro, 1958-65; mgr. Yeager, Ford & Warren, C.P.A.'s, Owensboro, 1965-69; treas. Brescia Coll., Owensboro, 1969-70, dir. bus. affairs, 1970—, part-time instr., 1958-72. Mem. lay adv. bd. Our Lady of Mercy Hosp., 1962—; mem. Owensboro Catholic High Sch. Bd, 1969—, chmn., 1970-72. Served with AUS, 1942-46. Roman Catholic. Clubs: Civitan (sec.-treas. 1965-67), Serra (treas. 1973-74). Home: 1634 Parrish Av Owensboro KY 42301

WEAGE, J. DAVID, cons. civil engr.; b. Coldwater, Mich., Aug. 26, 1920; s. Emery H. and Mary Ellen (Moffitt) W.; student Tri-State Coll., Angola, Ind., 1944, 45; m. Margarete Anita Loewe, July 22, 1942; children—Tamianne, Deidre (Mrs. Raymond Seitz), Deborah, Stacey. Asst. city engr., Coldwater, 1945-53; sr. engr. Atwell Hicks, Inc., Ann Arbor, 1960-67; v.p. Midwestern Cons., Inc., Ypsilanti, Mich., 1968; partner Smally, Wellford & Nalven, Sarasota, Fla., 1969—. Sec., Planning Commn., Saline, Mich., 1968. Served with AUS, 1940-44. Registered profl. engr., Fla., Mich., Ind. Mem. Sarasota Manatee Engring. Soc., Cons. Engrs. Council. Club: Sarasota Art Assn. Home: 5745 Antietam Dr Sarasota FL 33581 Office: 133 S McIntosh Rd Sarasota FL 33580

WEAR, JENNINGS DARREL, wholesale co. exec.; b. Houston, Ark., June 23, 1909; s. Oscar Allen and Josie Myrtle (Nix) W.; grad. Chillicothe Bus. Coll., 1928; m. Edna Lee Hester, June 6, 1969; children by previous marriage—JoAnn, (Mrs. Kenneth L. Hatter), Marilyn Yvonne (Mrs. Edward M. Eidenschink). With Earl Bros. & Co., Morrilton, Ark., 1928-30; v.p. E.E. Mitchell Co., 1932-40; with Semmes Motor Co., 1940; exec. v.p., treas. F. C. Stearns Hardward Inc., Hot Springs, Ark., 1940—; v.p., treas. F. C. Stearns Real Estate, Inc., 1948—. Sec., Ouachita Area Devel. Council, 1953-54, pres., 1955-56; sec. Hot Springs Municipal Water System, 1954-70; pres. Garland County Indsl. Devel. Corp., 1956-59. Bd. dirs. Ouachita Meml. Hosp., pres. 1954-55. Mem. Hot Springs Jr. C. of C. (life; pres. 1945-46), Hot Springs C. of C. (pres. 1951-52), U. S. C. of C. (membership com. 1968-69). Mason (32 deg., Shriner), Lion (pres. 1948-49), Rotarian (treas. 1957-72). Home: 808 Woodlawn Av Hot Springs AR 71901 Office: PO Box 940 Hot Springs AR 71901

WEAR, JOHN BEENE, mgmt. cons.; b. Olney, Tex., Jan. 21, 1910; s. Joseph B. and Mary (Snodgrass) W.; student U. Tex. at Austin, 1929-30; B.S. in Bus. Adminstrn., So. Meth. U., 1932; m. Elizabeth Ginn, June 27, 1936; 1 dau., Helen Elizabeth (Mrs. William James McCroskey). Pvt. practice accounting, Dallas, 1932-37, mgr. Tex. Employment Commn., 1937-42, chief placement War Manpower Commn., 1942-44, dep. chief examining Civil Service Commn., 1944-65; chief tech. br., 1965-67; ind. mgmt. cons., Dallas, 1968—. Chmn. Golden Cross Founders Found. Mem. Am. Acad. Polit. and Social Sci., Am. Soc. Pub. Adminstrn., Fed. Bus. Assn., Nat. Office Mgmt. Assn., Soc. Personnel Adminstrs., Nat. Rifle Assn. Methodist. Address: 6938 Shook Av Dallas TX 75214

WEARE, BUEL FELLOWS, ret. publishing exec.; b. Morton Park, Ill., Dec. 29, 1902; s. Ely and Mary (Fellows) W.; A.B., Princeton, 1925; M.B.A., Harvard, 1927; m. Nora Borden, Sept. 23, 1938; 1 dau., Mary Owen (Mrs. Paul G. Birdsall). In newspaper work, since 1930; with Des Moines Register and Tribune, 1930-40; mgr., N.Y. Herald Tribune Syndicate, 1946-50; pres. European edit. N.Y. Herald Tribune (Paris), 1950-53; pub. Congressional Quar., also Editorial Research Reports, 1954-73. Served from 1st lt. to col. AUS, 1941-45; in Office of Q.M. Gen., Washington, 1941-42; chief of exec. div., Office of Chief Q.M., Communications Zone hdqrs., Europe, 1942-45. Hon. sec. Howard County Hunt, 1956-66. Mem. Phi Beta Kappa. Republican. Episcopalian. Home: Glenwood MD 21738

WEATHERBY, LOIS MAXINE FLETCHER (MRS. JOSEPH NORMAN WEATHERBY), civic worker; b. Temple, Tex.; d. Omar Lester and Sarah Belle (McDonald) Fletcher; A.A., Ward-Belmont Coll., 1928; B.A. in English, Tex. U., 1930; postgrad. Mary Hardin Baylor Coll., 1931-32, Howard Payne Coll., 1950-51; m. Joseph Norman Weatherby, Feb. 23, 1933; children—Joseph Norman, Sarah Maxine (Mrs. Homer Hilton Stephens). Gray lady Vol. Service, A.R.C., 1942-46; officer, mem. bd. Women's Missionary Union First Bapt. Ch., 1965-69; regent Mary Garland chpt. D.A.R., 1957-60; sec. Hon. Phillip Livingston chpt. Daus. Am. Colonists, 1963-65; charter mem. Feur de Lis chpt. Huegenot Soc. (Austin, Tex.); corr.-sec. Maj. James McGregor chpt. Colonial Dames of XVIII Century (Dallas); mem. San Antonio County chpt. Nat. Soc. Magna Charta Dames, Sovereign Colonial Soc. Am. Royal Descent, Soc. Descs. Knights Most Noble Order of Garter, Plantagenet Soc., Colonial Order of Crown (all Phila.), Sterling C. Robertson chpt. Daus. Rep. of Tex. (Waco), Jr. Service League; charter mem., div. chmn. Women's Aux. Brownwood (Tex.) Community Hosp., 1968—; organizing sr. pres. Tejas Soc. Children Am. Revolution, 1944—; mem. bd. Brownwood Civic Music Assn., 1955-69; officer Women's Assn. Brownwood Country Club, 1950—. Recipient Gen. D. MacArthur Acad. Freedom medal Howard Payne Coll., 1968. Mem. Tex. Ex-Student Assn., Am. Assn. U. Women (past officer), Ashbel Lit. Soc., Brown County Hist Soc., Clan Donald Soc. Tex., Pi Beta Phi (Dallas mother's club). Rotary Ann. (div. chmn. 1967-69). Clubs: Knife and Fork, Investment, Junior 20th Century Study (Brownwood). Home: 2110 Belmeade St Brownwood TX 76801

WEATHERLY, OWEN MILTON, educator; b. nr. Sumter, S.C., Oct. 5, 1915; s. Francis Marion and Eda Bell (Best) W.; A.A., North Greenville Jr. Coll., 1943; B.A. cum laude, Furman U., 1947; M.A., U. Chgo., 1950, Ph.D., 1952; m. Myra Sloan, June 21, 1948; children—Pamela, Marcia, Jan. Ordained to ministry Baptist Ch., 1942; pastor Beech Island (S.C.) Bapt. Ch., 1946-47; dir. youth activities 1st Bapt. Ch., Berwyn, Ill., 1949-50; pastor 2d Bapt. Ch., Richmond, Va., 1952-58, 1st Bapt. Ch., Phila., 1958-64; tchr. lang. arts and social studies Evergreen Park (Ill.) Central Sch., 1951-52; asso. prof. religion and philosophy High Point (N.C.) Coll., 1964-67, prof., 1967—. Served with USAAF, 1943-46. Mem. Am. Philos. Assn., N.C. Philos. Soc., Am. Acad. Religion. Author: The Fulfillment of Life, 1959; The Ten Commandments in Modern Perspective, 1962; Help your Minister to Do His Best, 1965. Home: 1605 Chatham Dr High Point NC 27260

WEATHERLY, TRAVIS EUGENE, ednl. adminstr.; b. Potts Camp, Miss., May 24, 1925; s. Anderson and Mattie Jane (Caviness) W.; student Northwest Miss. Jr. Coll., 1949-50; B.S., Miss. State Coll., 1951, M.S., 1952; postgrad. U. Ga., 1969-70; m. Peggy Joyce Pierce, Aug. 7, 1953; children—Travis Eugene, Edward Anderson. Tchr., Pascagoula (Miss.) High Sch., 1952-57; vocational tchr. Corinth (Miss.) High Sch., 1958-61; draftsman Tyrone Hydraulics, Corinth, 1961-65, sales adminstr., 1965-66; asst. dir. DeKalb Area Tech. Sch., Clarkston, Ga., 1966-69, dir., 1969-72; asst. to pres. DeKalb Community Coll., 1972—. Mem. edn. professions devel. adv. com. U. Ga., 1971. Served with USAAF, 1943-45. Decorated Air medal with 4 oak leaf clusters. Mem. Am., Ga. vocational assns., Nat. Council Local Adminstrs. Mason. Editor: DeKalb Assn. Educators News, 1971-72. Home: 314 Fond du Lac Dr Stone Mountain GA 30083 Office: 555 N Indian Creek Dr Clarkston GA 30021

WEATHERS, BAILEY GRAHAM, physician; b. Shelby, N.C., Dec. 8, 1895; s. John Davidson and Mary Louise (Styers) W.; B.S., Wake Forest Coll., 1927; M.D., Med. Coll. Va., 1929; m. Ora Bumgardner, Dec. 31, 1922; children—Ruth Ann (Mrs. Carl Irvin Grigg), Bailey Graham, John Lewis, Jerry Davidson. Intern, Cook County Gen. Hosp., Chgo., 1935; gen. practice medicine, Stanley, N.C., 1929—; mem. staff Gaston Meml. Hosp., Gastonia, N.C. Served with 30th Arty. Div., U.S. Army, 1917-18. Named Dr. of Yr., Gaston County Med. Soc., 1952, Man of Yr., City of Stanley, 1969. Mem. A.M.A., N.C., Gaston County med. socs., Am. Acad. Gen. Practice (charter mem.). Baptist. Lion (charter mem., 1st pres. Stanley club). Home: 601 Hwy 27 S Stanley NC 28164 Office: 222 S Main St Stanley NC 28164

WEATHERS, BAILEY GRAHAM, JR., physician; b. Stanley, N.C., Apr. 12, 1932; s. Bailey Graham and Ora Edith (Bumbardner) W.; B.S., Wake Forest Coll., 1953; postgrad. So. Bapt. Theol. Sem., 1953-56; M.D., Med. Coll. Va., 1960; m. Wanda Gail Dahmer, Feb. 14, 1970; children by previous marriage—Bailey Graham III, David Gardner, Robert Alfred; 1 foster son, Steven Ray Layell. Intern, Moses H. Cone Hosp., Greensboro, N.C., 1960-61; gen. practice medicine, Farmington, N.C., 1961-67, Stanley, N.C., 1967—; mem. staff Garrison Gen. Hosp., Gastonia, N.C. Profl. artist, 1967—; exhibited paintings and sculpture in shows at Gallery Contemporary Art, Winston-Salem, 1968, 69, 71, Mint Mus. Art, 1968, Festival in the Park, Charlotte, 1969, 70, 71, 72, N.C. Mus. Art, 1970, 73. Fellow Royal Soc. Health; mem. Internat. Assn. Applied Psychology, Am. Acad. Gen. Practice, A.M.A., N.C., Gaston County med. socs., N.C. Asso. Artists, Gaston County Art Assn., Theta Chi. Home: 301 W Chestnut St Stanley NC 28164 Office: 222 S Main St Stanley NC 28164

WEATHERS, ROBERT WAYNE, educator, basketball coach; b. Hattiesburg, Miss., Sept. 16, 1932; s. Roston Alonzo and Virgie Carrie (Rainey) W.; B.S., U. So. Miss., 1954, M.S., 1959; m. Tommie Joan Dixon, Apr. 1, 1956; children—Wendell, Anthony, Robert Wayne II. Freshman basketball coach U. So. Miss., 1955-57, 58-59; basketball coach Picayune High Sch., 1959-60; head basketball coach Miss. Gulf Coast Jr. Coll., Perkinston, 1959—, chmn. dept. health and phys. edn., 1964-73. Mem. Nat. High Sch. Athletic Coaches Assn., Nat. Jr. Coll. Basketball Coaches Assn., Miss. Assn. Coaches. Baptist (finance chmn. 1971-73). Home: Box 101 Perkinston MS 39573

WEATHERS, SAMUEL DEA, JR., govt. ofcl.; b. Louisville, Aug. 5, 1919; s. Samuel Dea and Rebecca Josephine (Crowe) W.; grad. high sch.; m. Josie Lee Rouse, Aug. 5, 1942; children—Henry Lee, Jeffrey Eugene. Letter carrier U.S. Postal Service, Louisville, 1941-56, foreman of mails, 1956-57, asst. supt. Sta. R, 1957-66, supt. Sta. E, 1966-73, mgr. sta. support, 1973—. Mem. Western appeal bd. SSS, 1971—; chmn. bd. mgrs. Chestnut St. br. YMCA; bd. dirs. Met. Bd. Greater Louisville YMCA's. Mem. adv. bd. Mayor's Council-Russell Area Poverty. Served with USNR, 1943-46. Mem. Nat. Assn. Postal Suprs., Nat. Alliance Fed. and Postal Employees, N.A.A.C.P. (life), Urban League. Methodist (trustee). Home: 520 S 21st St Louisville KY 40203 Office: Box 3166 Louisville KY 40201

WEAVER, BARRY ROLAND, resource analyst; b. Tulsa, Okla., Nov. 11, 1933; s. Carmen S. and Ruby (Trent) W.; B.A., U. Ark., 1955; postgrad. U. N.C., 1956-57. Corr. instr. history U. Ark., Fayetteville, 1955-56; research asst. Inst. for Research in Social Sci., Chapel Hill, N.C., 1956-57; exec. dir. Human Engring Lab., Tulsa,

1958-64; sr. test adminstr. Johnson O'Connor Research Found., N.Y.C., 1965; resource analyst Office of Emergency Preparedness, Exec. Office of the Pres., Washington, 1965-70; dir. social services Econ. Opportunity Agy., Fayetteville, Ark., 1973—. Mem. U. Ark. Traffic Bd., 1953-54. Trustee Human Engring Lab., asst. treas., 1959-63; trustee Johnson O'Connor Research Found. Inc., asst. treas., 1959-63; trustee Human Engring. Lab., Ont., asst. treas., 1959-64; trustee Fundacion de Investigaciones Johnson O'Connor, Mexico, 1962-65. Served with AUS, 1957. Named Honorary Citizen of Little Rock, 1963. Mem. Sierra Club (nat. council 1969-70), Wilderness Soc., Met. Washington Coalition for Clean Air (chmn. study strategy com. 1968-70), Nature Conservancy, Friends of Earth, Soc. for Environmental Stablzn. (dir. 1973—), Ozark Soc. (editor Eco-Report), Am. Collegiate Polit. League (pres. 1952-53), Phi Alpha Theta. Democrat. Author tech. reports: Princeton University Aptitude Differences, 1963, Roman Catholic Colleges and Universities, 1963, Research Thesis of the American History Survey, 1964. Editor: Item-by-Item Study of English Vocabulary, 1961. Contbr. to various publs. Address: Eagle's Rest Route 2 Springdale AR 72764

WEAVER, CHARLES EARL, electronic engr., cons.; b. Xenia, O., Aug. 23, 1906; s. Charles Lucian and Sylvia (Turner) W.; diploma Radio Inst. Am., 1926; m. Edith Elizabeth Johnson, July 5, 1928; 1 dau., Janet W. (Mrs. Robert William Tarleton). With Am. Tel. & Tel. Co., Columbus, O., 1928-42, Point Reyes, Cal., 1942-47, tech. asst., N.Y.C., 1947-54; electronic engr. Western Electric Co., Inc., Winston-Salem, N.C., 1954-59; electronic engr. USAF, Andrews AFB, Md., 1954-59, sr. engr., Griffiss AFB, Rome, N.Y., 1959-64; sr. engr. Bell Telephone Labs., Whippany, N.J., 1964-68; communications system cons., 1968—. Def. Communications Agy. rep. U.S. Prep. Group for Internat. Tel. and Tel. Consultative Com., 1963. Mem. I.E.E.E. (asso.), Am. Radio Relay League, Armed Forces Communication and Electronic Assn. Patentee in field. Address: 2161 Sarazen Dr Dunedin FL 33528

WEAVER, DON MELVIN, supt. schs.; b. Temple, Tex., Nov. 8, 1932; s. Leonard Harold and Vivian Edith (Armagost) W.; B.S., Tex. A. and M. Coll., 1957, M. Ed., 1966; m. Janice Ann Taliaferro, Dec. 30, 1957; children—Daryle Don, Ray Lavelle. Tchr. Huckabay, Tex., 1959-63, Priddy, 1963-65; prin. Balmorhea, Tex., 1966-68; supt. schs. Bledsoe (Tex.) Independent Sch. Dist., 1968—; pres. and mgr. Bledsoe Nat. Gas Co., 1968—, Bledsoe Water Supply Corp., 1968—. Served with AUS, 1957-59. Mem. Am. Assn. Sch. Adminstrs., Tex. State Tchrs. Assn., Tex. Assn. Sch. Adminstrs. Baptist. Home: Box 85 Bledsoe TX 79314 Office: Box 85 Bledsoe TX 79314

WEAVER, GEORGE HOMER, mfg. co. exec.; b. Sapulpa, Okla., Jan. 17, 1924; s. John Homer and Lucille Lillian (Bunch) W.; B.A., U. Tulsa, 1948, B. in Mus. Edn., 1950, M. Edn., 1951; m. Jaxine Helen Yeagle, Dec. 23, 1951; children—Lori A., Joni A., Tami A. With Liberty Glass Co., Sapulpa, 1956—, dir. marketing, 1968—, sales mgr., 1969—. Served with AUS, 1941-43: ETO. Decorated Purple Heart. Mem. Phi Mu Alpha, Sigma Phi Epsilon. Clubs: Harvard, Oaks Country (Tulsa). Home: 3707 S Florence Pl Tulsa OK 74105 Office: PO Box 520 Sapulpa OK 74066

WEAVER, HENRY, aircraft parts mfg. co. exec.; b. Dayton, O., Oct. 5, 1916; s. Johnathon Sylvester and Marie Etta (Davis) W.; B.B.A., U. Miami (Fla.), 1945; m. Ruth Esther Heisey, July 26, 1941; children—Pamela, J. Davis. Asst. supt. Pan Am. Airways, Miami, 1941-50; tech. engr. rep. Air Assos., Miami, 1950-53; gen. mgr. So. Engring. Corp., Miami, 1953-56; pres. Wencor Inc., Miami, 1956—, Wencor Mfgs., Griffin, Ga., 1970—, Wencor Ltd., London, Eng., 1970—. Mem. adv. staff U. Miami, U. Fla., 1966—. Flight Safety Found. grantee, 1966. Mem. Value Engring. Soc. Contbr. articles on reliability, inspection and testing of aircraft, hydraulic seals to tech. jours. Home: 1240 Campamento St Coral Gables FL 33156 Office: 1820 NW 42d Av Miami FL 33126

WEAVER, HENRY O'NEIL, oil and gas operator; b. Nashville, Sept. 13, 1907; s. Samuel James and Edith (O'Neil) W.; B.S., U. South, 1928; m. Margaret Warren, Apr. 25, 1941; children—Henry O'Neil, Janet, Nancy. Vice-pres., treas., dir. Western Natural Gas Co., Houston, 1938-63; ind. oil and gas operator, Houston, 1963—; dir. Bank of Tex. Bd. regents U. South, 1963-69; bd. dirs. St. Lukes Hosp., Houston, Retina Research Found., Houston; trustee Kayser Found., Houston. C.P.A., Tex. Mem. Tex. Soc. C.P.A.'s, Petroleum Club, Am. Petroleum Inst. Clubs: Houston Country, Plaza, Coronada. Home: 5207 Bayou Glen Houston TX 77027 Office: 1006 Main St Houston TX 77002

WEAVER, JAMES ELMER, JR., steel co. exec.; b. Dallas, Nov. 27, 1934; s. J. Elmer and Virginia (West) W.; student Tex. Technol. Coll., 1951-54, So. Meth. U., 1954; m. Marilyn Lewis; children—Kitra Kay, Keith Mitchell, Kirsten Ray; stepchildren—Joseph L., Jefferson L., R. Christopher Smith. Salesman, Weaver Iron Works, Inc., Dallas, 1959-63, v.p., 1963-64, pres., 1964—; mgr. S.W.A.K. Co., Irving, Tex., 1967—; partner H & W Devel. Co., 1972—; pres. Hydrotek Distbg. Co., chems., 1973—. Mem. Irving Planning and Zoning Commn., 1964-69, chmn., 1969; pres. Irving Assn. for Retarded Children, 1969-70. Served to capt. USAF, 1954. Mem. Tex. (outstanding local pres. 1962-63, outstanding state chmn. 1963-64), Irving (officer of year 1965-66; v.p. 1965-66) jaycees, Irving C. of C. (dir. 1962-63), Dallas Exec. Assn., Alpha Tau Omega. Republican. Methodist. Mason, Elk, Kiwanian. Office: 3302 Pluto St Dallas TX 75212

WEAVER, JOSEPH DUDLEY, physician; b. nr. Winton, N.C., Sept. 11, 1912; s. Jesse Robert and Claudia C. (Hall) W.; B.S., Howard U., 1934, M.D., 1938; m. Rossie Mae Phenis Clay, Apr. 22, 1958; children—Jesse Robert, Patricia (adopted), Claudia. Intern Freedmen's Hosp., Washington, 1938-39; pvt. practice medicine Hartford, N.C., 1939-46, Ahoskie, 1946—; owner, operator Weaver Clinic, Ahoskie; active staff Roanoke Chowan Hosp., chief staff, 1973; asst. nat. med. dir. Elks; treas. Hobson R. Reynolds Elk's Nat. Shrine, Inc., 1969—. Bd. dirs. N.C. chpt. So. Christian Leadership Conf. Served from 2d lt. (Res.) to 1st lt. M.C., AUS, 1942-44. Named Dr. of Year, Old North State Med. Soc., 1963. Mem. Ahoskie C. of C., Eastern N.C. Med., Dental and Pharm. Soc., Old North State, Hertford County med. socs., Nat. Med. Assn., Med. Soc. State N.C., Acad. Family Physicians, A.M.A., Am. Geriatric Soc., Nat. Rehab. Assn., Kappa Alpha Psi, Beta Kappa Chi. Democrat. Baptist, Mason (32 deg.). Club: Ambassador (pres. 1948—). Home: RFD 2 256-D Ahoskie NC 27910 Office: 111 N Maple St Ahoskie NC 27910

WEAVER, ORDE RICHARD, petroleum co. exec.; b. Orchard, Neb., Apr. 26, 1913; s. George A. and Mae Stella (Knapp) W.; B.S., Neb. State Coll., 1936; M.A., U. Neb., 1946; m. Ann Mae Burkman, Jan. 30, 1970; children—John Charles, Jayne Lonelle. Chief insp. Neb. Def. Corp., Wahoo, 1942-46; mgr. quality control Dept. Army, Ordnance Corps., Neb. Ordnance Plant, Wahoo, 1946-50; mgr. quality control and inspection Nat. Gypsum Co., Wahoo, 1951-54; mgr. quality control Rocket Fuels div. Phillips Petroleum Co., McGregor, Tex., 1954-57, dir. quality control div., Bartlesville, Okla., 1957—. Fellow Am. Soc. Quality Control (v.p. 1970-71, dir. midwest conf. bd. 1959—, Edward J. Oakley award 1971); mem. Phi Delta Kappa. Republican. Presbyn. Mason, Kiwanian. Author: EVOP in Operation, 1966. Home: PO Box 1281 Bartlesville OK 74003 Office: 16 A-1 Phillips Bldg Bartlesville OK 74004

WEAVER, PATSY JEAN, ednl. adminstr.; b. Waterloo, Ark., May 30, 1932; d. Luther P. and Vida (Polk) Weaver; B.S., So. State Coll., Magnolia, Ark., 1954; M.Ed., U. Ark., 1957; postgrad. Auburn U., 1959, 60, U. Ala., 1961-62. Tchr. Harmony Grove High Sch., 1954-55, Camden High Sch., 1955-61; asst. dean of women So. State Coll., Magnolia, Ark., 1962-67, dean of women, 1967—. Mem. Nat., Ark. assns. women deans and counselors, N.E.A., Ark. Edn. Assn., Am., Ark. personnel and guidance assns., Am., Ark. coll. personnel assns., Am. Assn. U. Women, Delta Kappa Gamma. Baptist. Home: 1725 Dogwood Dr Magnolia AR 71753

WEAVER, WILLIAM CHEATHAM, JR., ins. exec.; b. Nashville, Oct. 10, 1912; s. William Cheatham and Irene (Morgan) W.; grad. Peabody Demonstration Sch., 1930; student Vanderbilt U., 1931-32; m. Elizabeth Wade Craig, May 15, 1940; children—William Cheatham III, Elizabeth Craig (Mrs. Raleigh Franklin Lane, Jr.). Mgr. appliance div. McWhorter Weaver & Co., Nashville, later treas., dir., 1932-40, pres., chmn. 1943-51; supr. mortgage loan div. investment dept. Nat. Life & Accident Ins. Co., Nashville, 1940-47, asst. mgr. mortgage loans, 1947-50, asst. v.p., mgr. real estate and mortgage loan dept., 1953-63, financial v.p., 1963-64, sr. v.p. finance, 1964-67, exec. v.p., 1967-69, pres., 1969-72, chmn. bd., chief exec. officer, 1972—; also mem. finance, tax. exec. coms., chmn. finance com.; dir., WSM, Inc., 1963—, v.p., 1964—, chmn. bd., chmn. exec. com., 1972—, chmn. bd., 1972—; chmn. bd. NLT Corp., 1972—; dir. 3d Nat. Bank Nashville, Ralston-Purina Co., 3d Nat. Corp. Trustee, mem. exec. bd., trustee Middle Tenn. council Boy Scouts Am.; trustee Jr. League, Nashville, Ladies Hermitage Assn.; exec. bd. Tenn. Taxpayers Assn.; bd. trust Vanderbilt U.; bd. dirs. Inst. Life Ins.; mem. Monteagle Assembly Endowment Fund Corp.; bd. trust Vanderbilt U. Recipient Silver Beaver, Boy Scouts Am., 1957; named Industrialist of Year, Nashville Bd. Realtors, 1969, Nat. Salesman of Year award Sales and Marketing Execs. Nashville, 1973; Spl. Service award Nashville YMCA, 1973. Mem. Nashville Area C. of C. (bd. govs. 1953-55, chmn. aviation com. 1953), Assn. Tenn. Country Gentlemen, Phi Delta Theta. United Methodist (mem. adminstrv. bd., chmn. 1957-59, chmn. investment com., trustee). Clubs: Belle Meade Country; Cumberland. Home: 416 Jackson Blvd Nashville TN 37250 Office: Nat Life Center Nashville TN 37203

WEAVER, WILLIAM DONALD, clergyman; b. nr. Four Oaks, N.C., May 26, 1934; s. Gertha and Clara Thelma (Denning) W.; student East Carolina U., 1952-53; A.B., Atlantic Christian Coll., 1955; B.D., Lexington Theol. Sem., 1958; m. Joyce Marie Farris, Nov. 2, 1957; children—William Donald, Joyce Dawn. Ordained to ministry Christian Ch., 1957; pastor First Christian Ch., Macclesfield, N.C., 1958-60, First Christian Ch., Jacksonville, N.C., 1960-62, First Christian Ch., Augusta, Ga., 1962-67, dir., 1965-67; pastor First Christian Ch., Robersonville, N.C., 1970—, mem. finance dept., 1971—. Bd. dirs. Martin County Mental Health Assn. Served with USNR, 1967-70. Recipient Navy Chief of Chaplains award, 1967. Mem. Greater Williamston Ministerial Assn. Home: PO Box 867 Robersonville NC 27871 Office: PO Box 755 Robersonville NC 27871

WEAVIL, JAMES COLON, retail store exec.; b. Winston-Salem, N.C., July 21, 1921; s. Ernest Edgar and Vada Belle (Hastings) W.; grad. high sch.; m. Barbara Louise Chambers, Sept. 6, 1947; 1 dau., Michelle. Salesman Vick Paint Co., Winston-Salem, 1938-42, 45-50; field supr. British Am. Tobacco Co., Caracus, Venezuela, 1950; with Ed Kelly Inc., Winston-Salem, 1950—, gen. mgr., 1951—, v.p., 1955-69, exec. v.p., 1969—. Served with USMCR, 1942-45, 50-51. Mem. Winston Salem Retail Mchts. Assn. (bd. dirs., 1969-70). Methodist. Mason. Home: PO Box 96 Clemmons NC 27012 Office: 1122 S Main St Winston-Salem NC 27101

WEBB, DOUGLAS SCHELLING, judge; b. Atmore, Ala., Nov. 25, 1921; s. Alfred Pellar and Ida (Stewart) W.; B.S., U. Ala., 1950, LL.B., 1951; m. Jean Jones, Jan. 31, 1942; children—Letha (Mrs. Emory Lee Head), Douglas Schelling, Jeanie, Alfred Pellar. Admitted to Ala. bar, 1951; pvt. practice law, Atmore, Ala., 1951-66; state senator rep. Baldwin, Monroe, Escambia counties, Ala., 1958-62; judge 21st Jud. Circuit Ct., State Ala., 1965—. Spl. judge Supreme Ct. Ala., 1972, Ala. Ct. Criminal Appeals, 1973. Methodist. Home: Drawer 1059 Atmore AL 36502 Office: PO Box 795 Brewton AL 36426

WEBB, ERNEST PACKARD, publisher; b. Junta, W.Va., Aug. 30, 1907; s. Robert Moses and Josephine (Harvey) W.; student advt. Internat. Corr. Schs., 1946-48, Alexander Hamilton Bus. Sch., 1948-52. Artist, Mountain State Engraving Co., 1929, Huntington Engraving Co. (W. Va.,), 1930, Charleston Engraving Co. (W.Va.), 1931; owner, mgr. Profl. Art Studio, Roanoke, Va., 1931-40; v.p., treas. Roanoke Engraving Co., 1940-48; pres. Va. Engraving Co., Richmond, 1947—; v.p. Dixie Engraving Co., Roanoke, 1961—; pres. W. & H. Corp., Richmond, 1968—. Served with USAAF, 1942-45. Mem. Va., Richmond chambers commerce, Internat. Craftsman's Club. Republican. Baptist. Clubs: Richmond Industrial, Willow Oaks Country, Westwood (Richmond). Home: 2000 Riverside Dr Richmond VA 23225 Office: 2003 Roane St Richmond VA 23222

WEBB, HUBERT JUDSON, scientist, ret. state ofcl.; b. nr. Aiken, S.C., June 8, 1911; s. George R. and Carrie (McCrackan) W.; B.S., Clemson Coll., 1933; Ph.D., Cornell U., 1938; m. Emma Irene McGregor, July 3, 1937; children—Linda (Mrs. Joseph A. Martin), George McGregor, Kennith Edward (dec.). Chief chemist Clemson Coll., 1938-51, dean grad. sci., 1951-55, head agrl. chem. research, 1955-65; dir. environmental health labs. S.C. Bd. Health, Columbia, S.C., 1965-69; asso. dir. S.C. Pollution Control Authority, Columbia, 1969-70, exec. dir., 1970-73; asst. to commr. environmental affairs S.C. Dept. Health and Environmental Control, 1973-74. Fellow A.A.A.S.; mem. Am. Chem. Soc., Am. Soc. Bacteriology, Am. Water Works Assn. (Fuller award 1963), Water Pollution Control Fedn., Sigma Xi, Phi Kappa Phi, Alpha Zeta, Gamma Sigma Delta. Home: 2025 Rolling Hills Rd Columbia SC 29210

WEBB, JAMES KENNETH, dentist; b. Smithville, Tenn., Mar. 7, 1941; s. Thomas Benton and Gladys Gertrude (Gray) W.; B.S., Tenn. Tech., 1962; D.D.S., U. Tenn., 1965; m. Elizabeth Faye Taylor, Sept. 1, 1962; children—Martha Gray, Sarah Elizabeth. Pvt. practice dentistry, Pulaski, Tenn. 1968—. Chmn. Giles County March of Dimes, 1970-71. Bd. dirs. Giles County Mental Health, Giles County Mental Retardation. Served to lt. USPHS, 1965-67. Mem. Am., Tenn., 6th Dist. (pres. 1974-75) dental socs., Am. Legion, Giles County C. of C. (dir.), Xi Psi Phi. Baptist. Rotarian (pres. 1974-75). Home: 109 Tollgate St Pulaski TN 38478 Office: 604 E College St Pulaski TN 38478

WEBB, JAMES SJOBERG, lawyer; b. Macon, Ga., Dec. 2, 1931; s. Jesse Tatum and Dura (Brooks) W.; B.S. (Faculty scholar), U. Tenn., 1956, J.D. summa cum laude, 1956; m. Nina Josephine Holt, June 30, 1956; 1 son, James Sjoberg. Admitted to Tenn. bar, 1956; practiced in N.Y.C., 1956-57, Cleveland, Tenn., 1960-63; asso. Mudge, Stern, Baldwin & Todd, N.Y.C., 1956-57; atty. Bowaters So. Paper Corp., Calhoun, Tenn., 1960-61; partner Bell, Whitson, Painter & Webb, Cleveland, Tenn., 1962-63; v.p. Charleston Hosiery Mills, Cleveland, 1963-73; atty. firm Fillauer, Dietrich, Mobbs, Whitson, Webb & Humberd, 1973—. Trustee Cleveland (Tenn.) Day Sch.; bd. dirs. Bradley-McMinn County Jr. Achievement. Served as capt. USAF, 1957-60. Mem. Tenn. Mfrs. Assn. (mem. indsl. relations com. 1969—), Cleveland Assos. Industries (pres. 1971-73), Cleveland-Bradley County C. of C. (pres. 1969), Cleveland Indsl. Personnel Club (pres. 1968), Order of Coif, Omicron Delta Kappa, Phi Delta Phi, Delta Sigma Pi, Phi Gamma Delta. Republican. Episcopalian (vestryman 1969). Kiwanian, Elk. Club: Cleveland (Tenn.) Golf and Country. Editor-in-chief Tenn. Law Review, 1955-56. Home: Annandale Park Cleveland TN 37311 Office: 90 Ocoee St Cleveland TN 37311

WEBB, JOHN COTHER, mfg. co. exec.; b. Dayton, O., Dec. 29, 1914; s. John Basil and Estelle (Williams) W.; B.A., Oxford U., 1938; B.S. in Elec. Engring., N.Y.U., 1942; m. Gloria Bernal Atristain, Dec. 29, 1951, (dec. 1968); children—John Robert, Gerard Michael. Vice pres. Ferro-Cart Corp. of Am., 1941-44; dir. sales Maguire Industries, 1944-46; chmn. Magnetic Core Corp.; pres. Electro-Metall. Products Inc., 1948-67, Fritzal Corp., Ft. Pierce, Fla., John C. Webb & Assos., Ft. Lauderdale, Fla.; v.p. Fair-Rite Corp., 1951-67; dir. Faradyne Electronics Corp. Mem. Broward Council of 100. Mem. Ossing C. of C. (past pres.), Metals Powder Industry Fedn. (past pres.), I.E.E.E. Clubs: Lions, Ardsley Country, Beach, Rotary (dir.). Author: The New Rubaiyat and Other Verse, 1968. Home: 2782 NE 5th St Pompano Beach FL 33062 Office: PO Box 23039 Fort Lauderdale FL 33307

WEBB, JULIAN, judge; b. Byromville, Ga., Oct. 2, 1911; s. Vester Otis and Flossie (Woodruff) W.; A.B., J.D., Mercer U., 1932; m. Jo Smith, Sept. 25, 1935; children—Joanna (Mrs. Henry Clayton Custer), Julianna (Mrs. Robert Edward Cheshire III). Admitted to Ga. bar, 1932, practiced in Augusta until 1933; in legal dept. Farm Credit Adminstrn., 1933-42; practice law, Donalsonville, Ga., 1943-74; city atty., Donalsonville, 1945-74; atty. Seminole County, 1971-74; mem. Ga. Senate, 1963-74, asst. floor leader, 1963, floor leader, 1964, pres. pro tem, 1967-69; judge Ga. Ct. Appeals, 1974—. Mem. Ga. Constn. Revision Commns., 1963, 69; mem. Ga. Bar Disciplinary Bd., 1964-67, Ga. Gov.'s Jud. Processes Commn., 1971-73, Criminal Law Study Commn., 1972-74. Trustee, chmn. So. Ga. Home for Aging Ams. Mem. Am., Ga. (bd. govs.), Pataula Circuit bar assns., Am. Judicature Soc., State Disciplinary Bd., C. of C. (dir.), Blue Key, Sigma Pi, Phi Alpha Delta. Democrat. Methodist (chmn. Thomasville dist. trustees, del. world conf. 1966). Mason (Shriner), Lion (pres. 1945). Address: 208 E 3d St Donalsonville GA 31745

WEBB, MILTON EVANS, optometrist; b. Sumner-Webb, Miss., Feb. 3, 1912; s. Samuel Evans and Nora Belle (Alford) W.; Dr. Optometry, Ill. Coll. Optometry, 1940; postgrad. Ind. U., 1960-61; m. Ann Sipka, Nov. 30, 1939. Practice optometry, Blytheville, Ark., 1947—. Guest lectr. So. Coll. Optometry, 1962-63. Served with AUS, 1943-46. Fellow Am. Acad. Optometry; mem. Am. (nat. committeeman), Ark. (pres. 1955) optometric assns., N.E. Ark. Optometric Soc. (pres. 1948), Kappa Alpha Phi, Phi Theta Upsilon. Kiwanian. Home: 704 Country Club Rd Blytheville AR 72315 Office: 516 Chickasawba St Blytheville AR 72315

WEBB, RALPH GARNETT, television exec.; b. Whitesboro, Tex., Apr. 25, 1927; s. G. Ralph and Inez (Richards) W.; student Parsons (Kan.) Jr. Coll., 1949, Pathfinder Radio-Television Sch., Kansas City, Mo., 1950; m. Doris Elaine Watson, Dec. 22, 1951; children—James Ralph, Gayle Elaine. Announcer radio sta. KLKC, Parsons, 1948-49, WDAF, Kansas City, Mo., 1949-50, KSET, El Paso, Tex., 1950; program dir. radio sta. KELP, El Paso, 1952-53; producer, dir. sta. KTSM-TV, El Paso, 1953-55; program operations mgr. KWTX Broadcasting Co., Waco, Tex., 1955—. Cons., film producer athletic dept. Baylor U. 1959—; radio and TV adviser Tex. Radio and Film Commn. of Meth. Ch. Mem. Drug Abuse Council, Waco. Bd. dirs. Lions Crippled Camp, Kerrville, Tex.; past bd. dirs. Goodwill Industries McLennan County, March Dimes Waco, Little League Waco; publicity dir. Heart O'Tex. Boy Scouts Scout-o-rama; Past chmn. bd. McLennan County Nat. Found.; mem. council instl. devel. Baylor U.; mem. adv. council Environmental Control, Waco; adv. council VA on Jobs for Returning Vets., Waco. Served with USNR, 1944-46, 50-52. Mem. Alpha Epsilon Rho. Republican. Methodist. Lion. Club: Woodland West Country (dir.). Home: 3900 W Waco Dr Waco TX 76710 Office: 4520 Bosque Blvd Waco TX 76710

WEBB, ROBERT DELWIN, supt. schs.; b. Brownfield, Tex., Mar. 22, 1926; s. Robert E. and Iris (Brannan) W.; B.S., Tex. Technol. Coll., 1949, M.S. in Edn., 1950, Ed.D., 1967; m. Barbara Ann Crowe, Dec. 28, 1954; children—Rhonda Suzanne, Melissa Ann. Tchr. Littlefield (Tex.) Pub. Schs., 1950-51; prin. Brownfield (Tex.) Pub. Schs., 1951-54, curriculum dir., 1955-63; supt. schs., Abernathy, Tex., 1963—. Served with USNR, 1944-46. Mem. West Tex. C. of C. (dir., mem. edn. com. 1963-64), Tex. Tchrs. Assn. (dist. pres. 1971-72), Tex. Assn. Sch. Adminstrs. (chmn. for N.E.A. relations 1971-72). Baptist. Mason (32 deg.), Lion (pres. 1966-67). Home: PO Box 778 Abernathy TX 79311

WEBB, ROBERT ELDRIDGE, journalist; b. Gulfport, Miss., Oct. 9, 1928; s. Otho Barney and Ola (Reagan) W.; B.J., U. Mo., 1949; postgrad. Tulane U., 1951, Yale, 1958, Ariz. State U., 1962; m. Sara Virginia Patton, June 2, 1956; children—John Robert, Mary Virginia. Reporter, Tampa Times, 1949, New Orleans States, 1949-55; with Jackson (Miss.) State Times, 1955-62; statehouse reporter Ariz. Jour., Phoenix, 1962-63; reporter Cin. Enquirer, 1963-64, edn. writer, 1964-66, asst. city editor, 1966-67, polit. writer, columnist, 1967-69, corr., chief Washington Bur., 1969—. Sec., Enquirer Middle Mgmt. Bd., 1969, chmn., 1969; lead writer, lead researcher Enquirer's Govt.-In-Crisis project, 1969. Served with AUS, 1950-51. Mem. White House Corrs. Assn., Ky. Cols., Sigma Delta Chi (a founder Queen City chpt. 1967, pres. 1967-69, Miss. chpt. pres. 1958-59), Tau Kappa Epsilon (nat. pub. relations com. 1965—). Methodist (steward). Club: Nat. Press. Office: Nat Press Bldg Washington DC 20004

WEBB, ROBERT LEE, chem. co. exec.; b. Topeka, Nov. 19, 1926; s. Floyd William and Laura Leona (Arnold) W.; B.S., Washburn U., 1949; m. Mary Elizabeth White, Jan. 25, 1952; children—Robert, Brigitte. Chemist, IH Milling Co., Topeka, 1949-50; research chemist Glidden Co., Jacksonville, Fla., 1950-57, mgr. research and devel. labs., 1957-59, prodn. mgr., 1959-61, asst. tech. dir., 1961, dir. devel., 1961-62; v.p. cons.-research chemistry Terpene Research Inst., Jacksonville, 1962-64; with Union Camp Corp., Jacksonville, 1964, gen. mgr. Terpene and Aromatics div., 1968—. Served with USNR, 1944-46. Mem. Am. Chem. Soc. Luth. Contbr. articles to profl. publs. Patentee in field. Home: 2479 Holly Point Rd E Orange Park FL 32073 Office: 2051 Lane Av N Jacksonville FL 32205

WEBB, ROBERT WATKINS, physician, educator; b. Chickasha, Okla., Jan. 25, 1906; s. Napoleon B. and Mary Elizabeth (White) W.; B.A., So. Meth. U., 1926; M.D., Tulane U., 1933; grad. Washington D.C. Sch. Psychiatry, 1952, Washington D.C. Psychoanalytic Inst., 1952; m. Elisabeth M. Nutting, Sept. 13, 1952. Intern Hotel Dieu Hosp., New Orleans, 1933-34; resident Pa. Hosp. Mental and

Nervous Diseases, Phila., 1934-36, Inst. Pa. Hosp., 1936; asso. physician Silver Hill Found., New Canaan, Conn., 1936-37, resident Payne-Whitney Psychiat. Clinic, N.Y. Hosp., 1937-38; clin. asso. prof. psychiatry Southwestern Med. Sch., Dallas, 1953—; pvt. practice, Dallas, 1939-41, 52—; sr. attending staff physician Parkland Hosp., Dallas, 1953—. Trustee Dallas Art Assn.; bd. dirs. Dallas Theater Center. Served with M.C., AUS, 1941-46. Mem. A.M.A., Internat., Am. psychoanalytic assns., Am. Coll. Psychiatrists, Am. Coll. Psychoanalysts, Tex. Neuropsychiat. Assn., Am., So. psychiat. assns. Home: 5530 Farquhar Lane Dallas TX 75209 Office: 4338 Lemmon Av Dallas TX 75219

WEBB, VAN WYCK HOKE, ins. and railroad exec.; b. Raleigh, N.C., Feb. 18, 1915; s. Alexander and Lydia Maverick (Hoke) W.; B.S., U. N.C., 1936; m. Anna Fawcett Tomlinson, Mar. 22, 1947; children—Van Wyck Hoke, Mary Lovelace, Anna Tomlinson. Teller, N.C. Nat. Bank, Raleigh, 1937-39; spl. agt. N.C. Fire Ins. Rating Bur., Raleigh, 1939-41; state agt. N.Y. Underwriters Ins. Co., Raleigh, 1941-50; asso. mgr. ins. dept. Wachovia Bank & Trust Co., Winston-Salem, N.C., 1950-56; v.p. Dupree & Webb, Inc. Ins., Raleigh, 1956-69, pres., 1969—; v.p. N.C. R.R. Co., Raleigh, 1960—; dir. Troxler Electronic Labs., Raleigh. Bd. dirs. YMCA, 1968—. Served to lt. comdr. USNR, 1942-46; ATO, ETO, PTO. Mem. Ind. Ins. Agts. N.C. (pres. 1965-66, bd. dirs. 1956-67), Chartered Property and Casualty Underwriters, Raleigh C. of C. (exec. com. 1973), Sigma Alpha Epsilon. Democrat. Episcopalian. Kiwanian. Clubs: City, Carolina Country, Sphinx, Raleigh. Home: 2518 Wake Dr Raleigh NC 27608 Office: 336 Fayetteville St Raleigh NC 27601

WEBB, WILLIAM, park adminstr.; b. Glasgow, Ky., Dec. 23, 1933; s. Lawrence Marcus and Mary Elizabeth (Sublett) W.; B.S., Ky. State Coll., 1960; postgrad. Western Ky. State U., 1962; m. Caroleen Bush Woodson, June 22, 1957; children—Ramona Gail, CleAnn Rena. Tchr., coach Jenkins (Ky.) Ind. Sch. System, 1960-66; tchr. sci. Alice Lloyd Coll., Pippa Passe, Ky., 1966; recreation specialist Mammoth Cave (Ky.) Nat. Park, 1966-71; supt. Booker T. Washington Nat. Monument, Hardy, Va., 1971-74, V.I. Nat. Parks, St. Thomas, 1974—. Adviser, Explorer Scouts, Mammoth Cave, Ky., 1968. Served with AUS, 1954-56. Mem. C. of C., Kappa Alpha Psi. Mason. Address: Box 806 St Thomas VI 00801

WEBB, WILLIAM YATES, economist; b. Shelby, N.C., Oct. 12, 1910; s. Edwin Yates and Willie (Simmons) W.; student Wake Forest U., 1928-29; A.B. with honors in Econs., Columbia, 1932, M.A. in Econs., 1933; postgrad. fellow in econs. Duke, 1933-34, N.Y. U., 1934-35, 36-37, Brookings Instn., 1935-36; m. Laura Mae Brown, Oct. 12, 1941; 1 dau., Shirley Webb (Mrs. Moses N. McCall). Economist, tin investigating com. U.S. Ho. Reps., 1934; economist Bituminous Coal Consumers Counsel Dept. Interior, 1937-40; economist, chief oil and gas sect. Census Bur., 1940-42; economist WPB, 1942; economist, indsl. engr. Office Naval Material, 1946-51; indsl. specialist Munitions Bd., Dept. Def., Washington, 1951-53, indsl. specialist Office Asst. Sec. Def., 1954-61; vulnerability analyst Office Civil Def., 1961-65, Office of Sec. Def., 1965-69. Served to comdr. USNR, 1942-46. Mem. Am. Econ. Assn., Am. Inst. Mining, Metall. and Petroleum Engrs., Am. Ordnance Assn., Am. Statis. Assn., Nat. Conf. State Socs. (past pres.), Navy League, Roanoke Island Hist. Soc., N.C. Soc. of Washington (past pres.), Res. Officers Assn., Columbia, Duke, Wake Forest alumni assns., Kappa Alpha, Pi Gamma Mu. Methodist. Clubs: Kenwood Golf and Country (Bethesda, Md.), Nat. Economists. Contbr. articles and book revs. to profl. jours. Home: 3614 Warren St NW Washington DC 20008

WEBER, JOHN ARTHUR, metal co. exec.; b. Ellinwood, Kan., Dec. 9, 1907; s. Frank Joseph and Lena (Berscheidt) W.; B.A., St. Benedicts Coll., 1929; postgrad. Creighton U., 1931, Kan. U., 1933; m. Valerie Ellida Toleik, Feb. 24, 1936 (dec. Jan. 1969); children—John A., Steven G. (dec.), Valerie E. (Mrs. Roy J. Biondi), Babette Marie; m. 2d, Georgia Danner, Dec. 30, 1969. With So. Die Casting & Engring. div. Adams Millis Corp., High Point, N.C., 1960-64, v.p., 1960-65; pres., chmn. bd. dirs. Signal Smelting & Refining Co., Chattanooga, 1965—. Bd. dirs. Hamilton County Republican Club, 1965—. Mem. Soc. Die Casting Engrs. (dir. 1965-68, pres. adv. bd. 1968—), Roman Catholic. Patentee in field. Home: 415 S Palisades Dr Signal Mountain TN 37377 Office: 1207 Fort St Chattanooga TN 37402

WEBER, OTTO JOHN, steamship co. exec.; b. New Haven, Sept. 24, 1915; s. Otto A. and Yvonne (DeMers) W.; B.A., Hobart Coll., 1938; postgrad. U. Cairo, U. Beirut, 1940-41; m. Dorothy Slater Weber, June 15, 1945; children—Karen Slater, Christine DeMers, Melissa Ann. Asst. mgr. Middle East, Socony Vacuum, 1938-41; asst. dir. European Govt. Affairs, Am. Overseas Airline, London, 1946-47; mgr. Am. Export Lines, Inc., Washington, 1948-54; gen. passenger mgr. Am. Export Isbrandtsen Lines, Inc., 1954-65, v.p. passenger traffic, N.Y.C., 1965-68, v.p. Washington, 1968—; pres. U.S. Hydrofoils Co., 1969—; pres. Fla. Hydrofoils, N.Y. Hydrofoils Golden Arrow Hydrafoils Co., Messina, Italy; vice chmn. bd. Hydroplex Corp.; exec. v.p. Norwegian-Caribbean Lines, 1972—. Chmn. Atlantic Passenger Conf. Served to lt. col. USMCR 1941-45. Mem. Nat. Assn. Travel Orgns., Nat. Def. Transp. Assn., Kappa Alpha. Clubs: Propellor of N.Y. (pres.), Downtown Athletic, University; Skal; Fells Brook (pres. 1969). Home: 6900 SW 126th Terrace Miami FL 33156 Office: 100 Biscayne Blvd Miami FL 33132

WEBER, ROGER LEWIS, electronics engr.; b. Keene, N.H., Apr. 29, 1926; s. Gordon Conrad and Marion Rhoda (Morse) W.; B.S. magna cum laude, Am. TV Inst. Tech., 1949; m. Bobbie Jean Walsh, Dec. 31, 1952; children—Michael Lee, Bradley Gordon. Engr., Admiral Corp., 1952-55; sr. engr. Chgo. Aerial Industries, 1955-57; sr. research engr. Warwick Mfg. Corp., 1957-58; sect. supr. Tex. Instruments, Inc., 1958-61; dir. engring. Beta Instruments, Inc., 1961-63; sect. supr. Tex. Instruments, Inc., Dallas, 1963—. Served with USNR, 1944-46. Mem. I.E.E.E., Internat. Soc. for Hybrid Microelectronics, Texins Recreational Assn. (pres. 1970). Mason (Shriner). Club: Texins Rod and Gun (pres. Dallas 1968). Author: Transistor Circuit Design, 1963. Patentee in field. Home: 502 Copper Ridge Dr Richardson TX 75080 Office: PO Box 5012 Dallas TX 75222

WEBSTER, BURNICE HOYLE, physician; b. Leeville, Tenn., Mar. 3, 1910; s. Thomas Jefferson and Martha Anne (Melton) W.; B.A. magna cum laude, Vanderbilt U., 1936, M.D., 1940; D.Sc., Holy Trinity Coll., 1971; m. Georgia Kathryn Foglemann, May 6, 1939; children—Brenda Kathryn, Phillip Hoyle, Adrienne Elise. Intern St. Thomas Hosp., Nashville, 1940-42, resident, 1942-43; practice medicine, specializing in chest disease, Nashville, 1943—; mem. staff St. Thomas, Bapt., Nashville Gen., Westside hosps.; cons. VA Hosp.; asso. in medicine Vanderbilt Med. Sch., 1943—; prof. anatomy Gupton-Jones Sch. Mortuary Sci., 1941-43. Served with USPHS. Fellow Am. Coll. Chest Physicians, Am., Internat. colls. angiology, Royal Soc. Health, Internat. Biog. Assn. (life); mem. Am. Cancer Soc. (dir.), A.M.A., Am. Thoracic Soc., So. Med. Soc., Tenn. Med. Assn., Nashville Acad. Medicine. Research in mycotic and parasitic diseases. Home: 2315 Valley Brook Rd Nashville TN 37215 Office: Mid-State Med Center Nashville TN 37203

WEBSTER, FRANCIS SINCLAIR, III, holding co. exec.; b. Inyokern, Cal., Nov. 13, 1945; s. Francis Sinclair and Virginia Adelaide (Scales) W.; B.A., Rice U., 1967, M.E.E., 1968; m. Pamela Georgeann Brown, Nov. 25, 1967. Elec. engr. space sci. dept. Rice U., 1965-67; with Houston Complex, Inc., 1967—, dir. tech. div., 1969-70, v.p. tech. div., 1970-72, v.p., sec., treas., 1972—. Lectr., U. Houston Sch. Bus. Adminstrn., 1970-71. Mem. S.W. Football Ofcls. Assn. Home: 3122 Groveshire Ct Sugarland TX 77478 Office: 1460 One Allen Center Houston TX 77002

WEBSTER, GEORGE CALVIN, educator; b. South Haven, Mich., July 17, 1924; s. Eugene Homer and Hazel Edna (Empson) W.; B.S., Western Mich. U., 1948, M.S., U. Minn., 1949, Ph.D., 1952; m. Sandra Lee Whitman, Jan. 23, 1960; children—Jeffrey Calvin, Kimberley Ann. Sr. research fellow Cal. Inst. Tech., 1952-55; prof. Ohio State U., 1955-61; vis. prof. U. Wis., 1961-65; chief environmental lab., Cape Kennedy, 1965-71; head dept. biol. scis. Fla. Inst. Tech., Melbourne, 1971—. Cons., NSF, 1959-61; established investigator Am. Heart Assn., 1963-65; USPHS spl. research fellow, 1961-63. Served with USAAF, 1942-45. Decorated Air medal, Purple Heart. Fellow A.A.A.S.; mem. Am. Soc. Biol. Chemists, Biochem. Soc. (Eng.), Am. Soc. Cell Biologists, Am. Chem. Soc. (chmn. Cape Kennedy sect. 1970-71), Fla. Acad. Sci., Sigma Xi. Author: Nitrogen Metabolism in Plants, 1959. Contbr. articles to profl. jours. Home: 389 Chester Dr Cocoa FL 32922 Office: Dept Biol Sci Fla Inst Tech Melbourne FL 32901

WEBSTER, GEORGE DRURY, lawyer; b. Jacksonville, Fla., Feb. 8, 1921; s. George D. and Mary Gaines (Walker) W.; B.A., Maryville Coll., 1941; LL.B., Harvard, 1948; m. Ann Kilpatrick, May 3, 1952; children—Aen Walker, George Drury, Hugh Kilpatrick. Admitted to Ga. bar, 1950, D.C. bar, 1952; atty. tax div. Dept. Justice, 1949-51; practice law, Washington, 1951—; partner Webster & Kilcullen; lectr. tax. insts.; dir. 1st Western Financial Corp. Spl. U.S. ambassador to Liberia, 1972; mem. adv. com. to commr. Internal Revenue Service. Nat. dir. Lawyers for Nixon-Agnew, 1968; nat. co-chmn. Lawyers to Re-elect the Pres., 1972. Bd. dirs. Maryville Coll.; trustee U.S. Naval Acad. Found., Madeira Sch. Served to lt. USNR, 1942-46. Mem. Am. Law Inst., Am. Bar Assn. (council), Nat. Assn. Execs. Club. Clubs: Chevy Chase (Md.); Harvard (N.Y.C. and Washington); Metropolitan (Washington). Author: Associations and the IRS, 1966; Business and Professional Political Action Committees, 1968; The Law of Associations, 1971, 74. Home: 5305 Cardinal Ct Washington DC 20016 also Webster Angus Farm Rogersville TN Office: 1747 Pennsylvania Av NW Washington DC 20006

WEBSTER, JAMES EPPS, motion picture exec.; b. Evansville, Ind., Mar. 6, 1919; s. Robert Byrd and Nancy Elizabeth (Roberts) W.; student Colo. State Coll., 1937-38, U. Tenn., 1939; B.A., U. Chattanooga, 1943; m. Elizabeth Thatcher, May 23, 1944; children—Katherine (Mrs. R.B. Hickey), James L., Lynn. Propr. Running Eagle Trading Post, Bluewater, N.M., 1937-43; with field advt. dept. Proctor & Gamble Co., Cin., 1939-42; asst. mgr. Firestone Stores, Inc., Knoxville, Tenn. 1942; mgr. Rock City Gardens, Lookout Mountain, Tenn., 1945-47; propr. mgr. Lookout Mountain Photo Shop (Tenn.), 1947-50; pres. Camera Mart, Chattanooga, 1950-51; propr. Webster Visual Sales Co., Chattanooga, 1951-65; pres. Continental Film Prodns. Corp., Chattanooga, 1951—, also dir. Served to 1st lt., USAAF, 1943-45. Mem. Soc. Motion Picture and Television Engrs., Aircraft Owners and Pilots Assn., Yucatan Exploring Soc. Clubs: Underwater Archeology and Explorations of Mexico (Mexico City), Fairyland Country (dir. 1960-63), Belle Monte (Lookout Mountain); Explorers of Am. (N.Y.C.); U.S. Polo (Chattanooga). Episcopalian. Home: 1502 Peter Pan Rd Lookout Mountain TN 37350 Office: 2320 Rossville Blvd Chattanooga TN 37408

WEBSTER, LEE RONALD, research firm exec.; b. Detroit, Aug. 21, 1933; s. Alfred Henry and Eva (Lee) W.; B.S. in Mech. Engring., U.S. Mcht. Marine Acad., 1956; postgrad. Adelphi U., 1958-63, N.Y. U., 1963-64; m. Evangeline Josephine Ciraulo, July 14, 1957; children—Leslie Ann, Donna Marie, Danielle, Lee Charles, Angela Patricia. Engring. group leader Sperry Gyroscope Co., Lake Success, L.I., N.Y., 1956-60; supr. reliability, quality control Rep. Aviation Corp., Farmingdale, L.I., 1960-65; mgr. reliability, space information systems div. Fairchild Hiller Corp., Farmingdale and Bladensburg, Md., 1965-66; mgr. systems effectiveness radiation div. Harris Intertupe Corp., Melbourne, Fla., 1966—. Cons. to industry, adj. prof., chmn. dept. systems engring. Fla. Inst. Tech., Melbourne. Mem. I.E.E.E. (sr. mem; chmn. reliability group 1969-70; nat. group performance award 1970), Am. Soc. Quality Control (sr. mem.), Am. Soc. M.E. (exec. com. aerospace div.). Contbr. profl. jours. Home: 7 Shoreview Circle Indialantic FL 32903 Office: PO Box 1823 Melbourne FL 32901

WEBSTER, RONALD ARTHUR, lawyer, county ofcl.; b. nr. Oliver Springs, Tenn., Dec. 21, 1938; s. Paris Guthrie and Myrtle (Hill) W.; B.S., U. Tenn., 1960, J.D., 1962; m. Dianne Sharp Webster, 1967; 1 son, James. Admitted to Tenn. bar, 1963, since practiced in Knoxville; asso. firm Frantz, McConnell, Seymour, 1963-65, Webster & Webster, 1965—; city trial atty. Knoxville, 1965-67; mem. Tenn. Ho. of Reps., 1965-68; now atty. gen. Knox County, Knoxville. Chmn. atty.'s div. East Tenn. Heart Fund, 1964-65. Mem. Knox County Republican Exec. Com., 1960—; mem. Tenn. Rep. Exec. Com.; mem. Knox County Young Republican Club. Mem. Am., Tenn., Knoxville bar assns., Am. Trial Lawyers Assn., Nat. Dist. Attys. Assn., Sigma Chi, Phi Delta Phi, Tau Kappa Alpha. Baptist. Mason (32 deg.). Clubs: Dean Hill, Country. Home: 4120 Maloney Rd Knoxville TN 37920 Office: Criminal Ct Bldg Knoxville TN 37902

WECHSBERG, HENRY, dentist; b. Germany, June 29, 1919 (came to U.S. 1935, naturalized 1941); s. Edward and Sara (Kaufmann) W.; D.D.S., Washington U., 1951; m. Florence Orin, Aug. 18, 1945; children—Orin, Wendy. Pvt. practice dentistry, Miami, Fla., 1951—. Served with CIC, AUS, 1942-45. Recipient award Am. Acad. Dental Medicine. Fellow Royal Soc. Health; mem. Am., Fla., East Coast Dist. dental assns., South Dade Dental Soc., Alpha Omega, Omicron Kappa Upsilon. Jewish religion (temple dir.). Mem. B'nai B'rith. Home: 11031 SW 60th Ct Miami FL 33156 Office: 3542 Coral Way Miami FL 33145

WEDDING, CHARLES RANDOLPH, architect, mayor; b. St. Petersburg, Fla., Nov. 16, 1934; s. Charles Reid and Marion (Whitaker) W.; student McCallie Sch., 1950-52; B.Arch., U. Fla., 1957; m. Audrey Whitsel, Aug. 18, 1956; children—Daryl Leigh, Douglas Randolph, Dorian Blair. Apprentice draftsman, architect Harvard & Jolly, A.I.A., St. Petersburg, Fla., 1957-58, 60; individual practice C. Randolph Wedding, A.I.A., St. Petersburg, 1960—; mayor, St. Petersburg, 1973—. Bd. dirs. Jr. Achievement, St. Petersburg, 1967-68; chmn. bd. Canterbury Sch., 1969-72; chmn. urban renewal Citizen's for Better St. Petersburg, 1965, Bldg. Dept. Survey Team, 1966—; chmn. architects and engrs. United Fund, St. Petersburg, 1965, 66. Trustee Mus. Fine Arts, St. Petersburg, All Children's Hosp., 1970-73. Served to 1st lt. AUS, 1958-60. Recipient Best Multi-Family Housing in Pinellas County award, 1964-68, 65-69; Best Residential Structure award, 1965-69; Outstanding Comml. Structure award, 1964-68, 65-69, Merit Design award Fla. Assn. Architects, 1966. Mem. A.I.A., St. Petersburg Assn. Architects (pres. 1964-66), Com. of 100 (chmn. 1971-72), Suncoasters, C. of C. (treas.), Phi Delta Theta. Episcopalian (vestryman). Rotarian. Home: 990 31st Av NE St Petersburg FL 33703 Office: 2901 58th Av N St Petersburg FL 33714

WEEKS, CHARLES, JR., pub. co. exec.; b. Palo Alto, Cal., Apr. 25, 1919; s. Charles and Mary Alice (Johnson) W.; student U. Fla., 1936-38; m. Patricia Anne Blair, Apr. 7, 1949; children—Patricia Alice, Charles Blair, Clayton Brian, Phyllis Anne. Prin., Fla. Airmotive, Inc., Lantana, Fla., 1946-50; v.p., dir. Perry Publs., Inc., West Palm Beach, Fla., 1950-69; asst. sec., dir. Perry Oceanographics, Inc., Riviera Beach, Fla., 1969—, Perry Ocean Engring., Inc., Riviera Beach, Higgins-McArthur/Longino & Porter, Inc., Atlanta, Palm Beach Cable TV Co., Palm Beach Gardens, Fla., Martin County Cable Co., Inc., Stuart, Fla.; v.p., sec., dir. Perry Bldg. Systems, Inc., Riviera Beach; v.p., dir. Bahama Publishers Ltd., Freeport, Bahamas; asst. treas., dir. Perry Ocean Engring., Inc. Mem. Planning and Zoning Bd., Lantana, 1962-65. Served to 1st lt., pilot, USAF, 1943-46: ETO. Decorated Air medal. Recipient Pilot Safety award Nat. Bus. Aircraft Assn., 1970. Mem. Quiet Birdman. Episcopalian. Democrat. Clubs: Manalapan, LaCoquille (Manalapan, Fla.); Handersonville (N.C.) Country. Home: PO Box 3411 Lantana FL 33462 Office: 100 E 17th St Riviera Beach FL 33404

WEEKS, EDWARD FRANCIS, mus. curator; b. Boston, Apr. 11, 1935; s. Edward Augustus and Frederica (Watriss) W.; student Proctor Acad., 1950-53; B.S., Columbia, 1962; M.A., N.Y. U., 1970; certificate Harvard Inst. for Arts Adminstrn., 1973; m. Janis Hardin, June 21, 1964; 1 son, Edward Augustus. Asst. to dir. Cummer Gallery Art, Jacksonville, Fla., 1962-65; exec. asst. to dir. Albright-Knox Art Gallery, Buffalo, 1967-69; curator High Mus. Art, Atlanta, 1969-70, Birmingham (Ala.) Mus. Art, 1970—. Art adviser Birmingham Civic Center, 1970-73, Downtown Club, Birmingham, 1972—, Eye Found. Hosp., Birmingham, 1972—; mem. Birmingham Festival of Arts Com., 1970-73; co-chmn. for visual arts Birmingham Festival of Art, 1974. Served with AUS, 1965-67. Recipient Best Supporting Actor award Little Theatre of Jacksonville, 1963, Silver Bowl award Festival of Arts, 1973. Mem. Am. Assn. Museums, Southeastern Mus. Conf., Alumni Assn. Inst. Fine Arts N.Y. U. Presbyn. (mem. choir). Club: Birmingham Press. Weekly guest art columnist Birmingham News-Post Herald, 1971—. Home: 201 Mountain Av Birmingham AL 35213 Office: 2000 8th Av N Birmingham AL 35203

WEEKS, ELIE, ret. govt. ofcl., rancher; b. Columbia, Mo., Apr. 12, 1903; s. Raymond and Mary Sophronia (Arnoldia) W.; B.S., U. Va., 1923; postgrad. L'Ecole des Sciences Politique, Paris, France, 1926-27; m. Helen George, Sept. 13, 1930. So. sales mgr. Charles Englehard, Inc., Newark, 1928-30; v.p. Weeks Engring., Richmond, Va., 1931-33; with Fed. Res. Bank, Richmond, 1933-37; sec. Beverley Heating, Richmond, 1937-42; statistician VA, Richmond, 1946-48; asst. sci. dir., tech. adviser U.S. Army Gen. Equipment Test Activity, Ft. Lee, Va., 1948-66; ret., 1966; owner-mgr. plantation and cattle ranch, Manakin-Sabot, Va., 1966—. Mem. Open Spaces Planning Bd. Goochland County, 1972-73; vice chmn. Goochland County Independence Bicentennial Commn., chmn. com. to prepare mil. map Va. Bd. dirs. Family Service Soc., 1969-72. Served with USAAF, 1942-46. Decorated Bronze Star. Mem. Va. Acad. Sci., A.A.A.S., Am. Statis. Soc., Va. Geneal. Soc., Va. Hist. Soc., Alliance Francaise, Va. Mus. Fine Arts, Va. History Fedn., Nat. Trust for Historic Preservation, Am. Boxwood Soc., Goochland County Hist. Soc. (pres. 1968-73, editor-pub. mag. 1968—), S.A.R. (bd. mgrs. Va. soc. 1974—). Club: Soixante Plus, Medmenham, Ruritan (charter mem., past pres. Goochland). Address: Rochambeau Manakin-Sabot VA 23103

WEEKS, GEORGE ELIOT, aerospace engr., educator; b. Montgomery, Ala., July 10, 1939; s. Thomas Powers and Ida Grace (Baker) W.; B.S. in Aerospace Engring., U. Ala., 1960, M.S. in Engring., 1961; Ph.D. in Engring. Mechanics, Va. Poly. Inst., 1967; m. Ann Walton McCraw, Dec. 24, 1962; children—Jeffrey Scott, Robert Powers. Stress analyst Hayes Aircraft, Birmingham, Ala., 1961; prof. aerospace engring. Miss. State U., Starkville, Miss., 1961-63; aerospace technologist NASA, Langley Field, Va., 1963-67; prof. aerospace engring. U. Ala., Tuscaloosa, 1967—. Mem. Am. Inst. Aeros. and Astronautics, Phi Mu Epsilon. Home: Route 2 Moundville AL 35474 Office: PO Box 2908 University of Ala University AL 35486

WEEMS, JOHN EDGAR, coll. pres.; b. Nashville, Feb. 23, 1932; B.S., George Peabody Coll., 1953, M.A., 1956, Ed.D., 1965; m. Frankie Gooch; children—John Mark, David Van, Nancy Carol. Successively mem. exec. tng. program Proctor-Gamble Co., Louisville; asst. prof. bus. adminstrn., dir. admissions, dean students, dir. placement Atlantic Christian Coll., Wilson, N.C.; dean admissions, also registrar Ky. Wesleyan Coll., Owensboro; dean admissions and records Middle Tenn. State U., Murfreesboro, later v.p. finance and adminstrn.; pres. Meredith Coll., Raleigh, N.C., 1972—. Statis. cons. Ohio Valley Conf.; cons. tchr. edn. Nat. Council on Accreditation Tchr. Edn. Commr. Jr.-Pro Football League. Mem. Delta Pi Epsilon, Delta Sigma Phi. Contbr. articles to profl. jours. Address: Meredith Coll Raleigh NC 27602

WEEMS, JOHN EDWARD, writer; b. Grand Prairie, Tex., Nov. 2, 1924; s. J. Eddie and Anna Lee (Scott) W.; B.Journalism, U. Tex., 1948, M.Journalism, 1949; M.A. in L.S., Fla. State U., 1954; m. Jane Ellen Homeyer, Sept. 11, 1946; children—Donald, Carol, Mary, Barbara, Janet. Telegraph editor Temple (Tex.) Daily Telegram, 1950; instr. Cal. State Poly. Coll., San Dimas, 1950-51; night news editor San Angelo (Tex.) Standard-Times, 1951; copy editor Dallas Morning News, 1952-53; asst. prof., head cataloger main library Baylor U., 1954-57; asst. prof. U. Ala., also asst. mgr. Ala. Press Assn., 1957-58; asst. to dir. U. Tex. Press, 1958-68; prof. English Baylor U., 1968-71; reference librarian McLannan Community Coll., Waco, Tex., 1969-70; free-lance writer, 1971—. Served with USNR, 1943-46, 51-52. Am. Philos. Soc. grantee, 1964. Mem. Authors Guild, Tex. Inst. Letters, Am. Assn. U. Profs., Sigma Delta Chi, Beta Phi Mu. Author: A Weekend in September, 1957; The Fate of the Maine, 1958; Race for the Pole, 1960; Peary: The Explorer and the Man, 1967; Men Without Countries, 1969; Dream of Empire (Amon G. Carter award), 1971; To Conquer a Peace: The War Between the United States and Mexico, 1974. Address: 2012 Collins Dr Waco TX 76710 also care Carl Brandt 101 Park Av New York City NY 10017

WEEMS, KYLE RICHARD, lawyer; b. Greeneville, Tenn., May 30, 1937; s. Howard Franklin and Madge Alma (Holland) W.; LL.B., U. Tenn., 1961; m. Catherine Lucille Williams, Dec. 22, 1962; children—Richard Thomas, Catherine Elizabeth. Admitted to Tenn. bar, 1961; practiced in Chattanooga, 1966—; mem. firm Weill, Ellis, Weems & Copeland and predecessor firms, Chattanooga, 1966—, partner, 1969—; chmn. bd., pres. Interdevel. Corp. Co-chmn. Youth for Nixon, U. Tenn., 1960. Served from 1st lt. to capt. AUS, 1962-66. Decorated Army Commendation medal. Mem. Fed. (pres. Chattanooga Chpt. 1973-74), Am. (state membership chmn. Tenn. 1973—), Tenn., Chattanooga bar assns., Am. Judicature Soc., Am. Trial Lawyers Assn., Southeastern Tenn. Bridge Assn. (pres. 1968-70), Pi Kappa Phi, Phi Delta Phi. Presbyn. (chmn. bd. deacons

1971-72). Clubs: Optimist (pres. 1971-72), Expressway (Chattanooga). Home: 125 Ridgeside Rd Chattanooga TN 37411 Office: 11th Floor Vol Bldg Chattanooga TN 37402

WEEMS, WILLIAM CAMPBELL, agrl. machinery co. exec.; b. Houston, Miss., Jan. 12, 1917; s. Ira L. and Lela Ethel (Campbell) W.; B.A., Beloit (Wis.) Coll., 1947; m. Ruth Lois May, Sept. 6, 1941; 1 son, William Campbell. Crane operator Fairbanks Morse Co., Beloit, 1939-47; owner, operator Babcock Trucking Co., Beloit, 1947-49; operations mgr. Rockford (Ill.) terminal Spector Freight System, 1952-67; traffic supr. Warner-Lambert Pharm. Co., Rockford, 1967-70; traffic mgr. Nichols-Homeshield Co., Davenport, Ia., 1970-71; claims and traffic mgr. John Deere Co., Atlanta, 1971—. Active Ken Rock Community Center, Rockford, 1954-58; chmn. B.T. Washington Center Bd., 1956-60; sec. Rockford City Planning Commn., 1961-64. Served with USNR, 1945-46. Home: 55/C Tree View Dr Decatur GA 30034 Office: 5147 Peachtree Indsl Blvd Chamblee GA 30341

WEESNER, MURRELL DAVIS, ednl. adminstr.; b. Morristown, Tenn., Apr. 10, 1927; s. Edwin Davis and Nancy Rebecca (Murrell) W.; A.B., Tusculum Coll., 1950; M.A., Duke, 1956; postgrad. U. Tenn., 1956-61; m. Joan Faulkner, June 21, 1952; children—Rebecca Josephine, Susan, Mary Ellen, Winn Ann. Auditor, U.S. Bur. Census, Washington, 1950; city editor Morristown Sun, 1952-54; reporter Knoxville (Tenn.) Jour., 1954; asst. prin. Morristown-Hamblen High Sch. East. 1954—; auditor The Inn, Buck Hill Falls, Pa., 1955-59; sec. treas. Morristown Employees Credit Union, 1960—. Bd. dirs. Mutual Concert Assn. Mem. Nat., Morristown (treas. 1955-56, pres. 1962, dir. 1973), East Tenn., Tenn. edn. assns., Nat. Assn. Secondary Sch. Prins. (mem. Eastern European study mission 1971), Morristown C. of C. (mem. beautification council 1953—), Morristown Jaycees (distinguished service award 1961), Tusculum Coll. Alumni Assn. (nat. pres. 1972-74, treas. 1956-59). Kiwanian. Home: 433 E 4th North St Morristown TN 37814 Office: 405 S James St Morristown TN 37814

WEHLE, VICTOR OTTO, judge; b. N.Y.C., June 19, 1902; s. Henry J. and Marie (Kuehne) W.; LL.B., Cornell U., 1924; m. Irma E. Anschuetz, Sept. 10, 1932; children—James H., Mary (Mrs. James E. Lewallen), Margaret (Mrs. Leonard Lund), Irma (Mrs. Albert Stephens). Admitted to Fla. bar, 1926; asst. city atty. St. Petersburg, Fla., 1926-28; practice law, St. Petersburg, 1928-45; circuit judge 6th Circuit of Fla., St. Petersburg, 1945-54, 64—; prof. Stetson U. Coll. Law, 1954—. Bd. dirs. Elks Crippled Children's Hosp., Am. Legion Crippled Children's Hosp. Recipient Jr. C. of C. Distinguished Service award, 1945. Mem. Am. Bar Assn., Fla. Bar, Am. Trial Lawyers Assn., Acad. Fla. Trial Lawyers. Lutheran. Mason, Elk, Kiwanian. Home: 920 15th Av North St Petersburg FL 33704 Office: County Bldg St Petersburg FL 33701

WEHRING, CHARLES HENRY, lawyer; b. Corpus Christi, Tex., Apr. 15, 1940; s. Lee Bernard and Willie (Matthews) W.; B.B.A., Tex. A. and M. U., 1962; J.D., U. Tex., 1969; m. Barbara Auguste Hassler, Oct. 20, 1964. Staff accountant U.S. Gen. Accounting Office, 1962-63; tax accountant Peat, Marwick, Mitchell & Co., C.P.A.'s, 1969-72; admitted to Tex. bar, 1969; practiced in Houston, 1972—; asso. atty. firm Foreman, Dyess, Prewett, Rosenberg & Henderson, Houston, 1972—; dir. Wehring Properties, Inc. Served to 1st lt. AUS, 1963-66. Mem. Am., Houston bar assns., State Bar Tex., Houston Estate and Financial Forum, Phi Delta Phi. Home: 3114 Albans St Houston TX 77005 Office: 2900 United Gas Bldg Houston TX 77002

WEIDNER, LARRY WAYNE, physician; b. Shattuck, Okla., Nov. 14, 1938; s. Bill and Sarah (Repp) W.; student Southwestern State Coll., 1956-59; M.D., U. Okla., 1963; m. LuVana Sue Chaney, Oct. 27, 1962; children—Larry Wayne, Bryan. Intern, St. Anthony Hosp., Oklahoma City, 1963-64; resident ophthalmology U. Okla.; gen. practice medicine, Buffalo, Okla., 1964—; partner Hudson-Weidner Clinic, Coldwater, Kan., 1969—; med. flight examiner FAA, 1967—. Pres. Harper County Airport Trust Authority, 1969—; mem. Buffalo Municipal Airport Authority, 1967—. First aid instr. Boy Scouts Am. Mem. Am., Okla. med. assns., N.W. Counties med. assns. (v.p. 1968-69), Am. Acad. Gen. Practice, Buffalo C. of C. (pres. 1969-70), Phi Beta Pi, Beta Beta Beta. Republican. Methodist. Home: 2601 Old Farm Lane Edmond OK 73034

WEIGERS, GORDON ULRICH, paint and coatings co. exec.; b. Hamburg, Germany, Jan. 18, 1929; s. Werner and Ellen (Wasserman) W.; came to U.S., 1939, naturalized, 1943; student Columbia, 1951; B.S. in Mech. Engring., Stevens Inst. Tech., 1952; m. Judith Ann Gordon, Aug. 25, 1956; children—David Gordon, Margaret Ellen. With Am. Cyanamid Co., New Orleans, 1952-54, dept. supt., 1954-63, prodn. mgr. Fortier plant, New Orleans, 1963-68, mgr. distbrn. Indsl. Chem. Div., Wayne, N.J., 1968-69, prodn. mgr. explosives and mining chems. dept., Wayne, 1969-71; mgr. mfg. Napko Corp., Houston, 1971—. Mem. Am. Inst. Chem. Engrs. (chmn. com. safety in air separation and ammonia plants 1958-59), Nat. Paint and Coatings Assn., Houston Soc. Paint Tech. Episcopalian. Club: Galveston Bay Cruising Assn. (Seabrook, Tex.). Home: 18614 Upper Bay Dr Nassau Bay TX 77058 Office: 6300 Sunrise St Houston TX 77021

WEIGESTER, WILLIAM FREDERICK, lawyer; b. Troy, Pa., Jan. 19, 1894; s. William and Susie Jerusha (Smiley) W.; B.S., Pa. State U., 1918; J.D., George Washington U., 1925; m. Margaret Eleanor Ayres, Nov. 24, 1937. Admitted to D.C. bar, 1926; with Standard Oil Devel. Co. (now Esso Research & Engring. Co.), 1927-54, mgr. Washington office, 1936-54; lawyer with Dept. Justice, Washington, 1954-65. Mem. Am., Inter-Am. (chmn. sect. on patents, trademarks and copyrights 1950-54) bar assns., Bar Assn. D.C. (chmn. com. on relations with Inter-Am. Bar Assn. 1950-54, chmn. com. on patents), S.A.R., Newcomen Soc. N.Am., St. Andrews Soc., S.R., Soc. Colonial Wars, Sigma Phi Epsilon. Mason (Shriner). Clubs: Chevy Chase, Metropolitan, Burning Tree, Nat. Press (Washington). Home: 3133 Connecticut Av Washington DC 20008

WEIHE, RUDOLPH GEOFFREY, dentist; b. Oak Park, Ill., Feb. 15, 1944; s. Rudolph George and Violet Ellen (Aikenhead) W.; A.A., St. Petersburg Jr. Coll., 1964; D.D.S., Emory U., 1968; m. Mary Jeannette Chambers, Sept. 28, 1968; Pvt. practice dentistry, Brandon, Fla., 1970—. Served as sr. asst. dental surgeon USPHS, 1968-70. Mem. Am. Soc. Preventive Dentistry, Fla., N.H. dental assns., Hillsborough County Dental Research Group, So. Acad. Clin. Nutrition, Brandon C. of C., Denta Sigma Delta (life). Lutheran. Home: 603 N Sylvan Dr Brandon FL 33511 Office: 110 Knights Av N Brandon FL 33511

WEIHE, RUDOLPH GEORGE, dentist; b. Chgo., June 11, 1913; s. Emil Christian and Elsie Ellen (Gerbing) W.; B.S., U. Ill., 1939, D.D.S., 1941; m. Starr Culver, Oct. 20, 1967; children—Sally (Mrs. Louis L. Wheeler), R. Geoffrey, Bruce. Pvt. practice dentistry, Oak Park, Ill., 1941-60, St. Petersburg, Fla., 1960—. Clin. instr. prosthetics Coll. Dentistry, U. Ill., 1941-47. Mem. budget com. United Fund, Oak Park, Ill., 1955-60. Trustee, Mound Park Hosp. Found., St. Petersburg, sec., 1964—, asso. dir. div. gerontological research, 1970—; bd. dirs. St. Petersburg Meth. Home. Fellow Fla. Acad. Scis.; mem. Fla. Dental Assn. (trustee 1971—, ho. dels. 1971—), Pinellas County Dental Soc. (bd. dirs. 1970—, chmn. ins. council 1967—), West Coast Dental Soc., Emphysema Research Assn. (bd. dirs. 1965—), Gerontological Soc., Fedn. Dentaire Internat., A.A.A.S., U. Ill. Dental Alumni Assn. (pres. 1960-61), Fla. Acad. Dental Practice Adminstrn., Theta Delta Chi. Lutheran. Clubs: St. Petersburg Yacht, Lakewood Country (St. Petersburg). Home: 4726 Sunrise Dr S St Petersburg FL 33705 Office: 415 45th Av S St Petersburg FL 33705

WEIHE, THEODORE EMERALD, optometrist; b. Ocala, Fla., Dec. 8, 1912; s. Frederick Emerald and Effie Lee (Moore) W.; O.D., No. Ill. Coll. Optometry, 1949; m. Edith Mae Whittington, Oct. 24, 1939 (div. June 1969); children—Sandra Lee (Mrs. Walter K. Bruce), Mary Sue (Mrs. Thomas A. Norris), Margie (Mrs. John J. Carroll), Frances (Mrs. David Jessie); m. 2d, Virginia Dare, Sept. 14, 1969. Dance band musician, Fla., Va., 1931-46; seedsman Jackson Grain Co., Tampa, 1941-46; optometrist, Leesburg, Fla., 1949—. Mem. Am., Fla. optometric assns., Mid Fla. Optometric Soc. (pres. 1974-75), Omega Delta. Mason (Shriner, K.T.), Moose, Elk, Lion (treas. 1965—). Home: 1905 Harcourt Dr Leesburg FL 32748 Office: PO Box 479 617 W Dixie Av Leesburg FL 32748

WEIL, CHRISTOPHER MAURICE, lawyer; b. New Orleans, Apr. 5, 1937; s. Maurice K. and Helen (Hyman) W.; LL.B., Washington U., 1961; m. Theanne Kirby, Sept. 5, 1964; children—Jon C., Jennifer P., Timothy M., Andrew J., Ann G. Admitted to Tex. bar, 1961, since practiced in Dallas; asso. firm Akin, Vial, Hamilton, Koch and Tubb, 1961-62; mem. firm Weil and Craig, 1972—. Mem. adv. council Dallas Health and Sci. Mus., 1966-72; bd. dirs. Dallas County Mental Health Assn., 1967-72. Served to lt. USNR, 1965-72. Mem. Dallas (chmn. unauthorized practice com. 1971-73), Mo., Am. bar assns., State Bar Tex., Am. Trial Lawyers Assn., Am. Judicative Soc., Sigma Chi. Clubs: Rush Creek Yacht (mem. bd. govs. 1970-71), City. Home: 3869 Potomac St Dallas TX 75205 Office: 2400 Adolphus Tower Dallas TX 75202

WEILAND, ERIC HUBER, computer process analyst; b. Phila., Nov. 19, 1920; s. Henry and Mary (Huber) W.; student Drexel Inst. Tech., 1939-40, U. Pa., 1951-52; m. Alice JoAnn McReynolds, July 30, 1943; children—Eric Huber, Sunnderland Marie (Mrs. Danny Wilson), Camille (Mrs. Woodrow Anderson). Draftsman, Nicholson File Co., Phila., 1939-40; aero. draftsman Edward C. Budd Mfg. Co., Phila., 1940-41; commd. ensign USN, 1942, advanced through grades to lt. comdr., 1964; ret., 1964; computer process analyst H.K. Porter, Inc. elec. div. Data control sect., Fayetteville, Ark., 1964—. Mem. Am. Radio Relay League. Home: 1016 W California Dr Fayetteville AR 72701 Office: Old Missouri Rd Springdale AR 72756

WEILL, LIGE HARRY, lawyer; b. Chattanooga, Sept. 12, 1916; s. David Robert and Elsie (Wertheimer) W.; B.A., U. Va., 1936; LL.D., J.D., Harvard, 1940; m. Marcelle Baum, Dec. 10, 1947; children—Larry, Flossie, Audrey. Admitted to Tenn. bar, 1939; practiced in Chattanooga, 1940—; mem. firm Weill, Ellis, Weems & Copeland. Dir. Rossville Bank. Past tchr., law div. McKenzie Sch. Bd. dirs. Chattanooga Girls Club. Served to lt. USAAF, World War II. Mem. Am., Tenn. trial lawyers assns., Am. Legion, Am., Tenn., Chattanooga bar assns., Chattanooga Jr. C. of C. (pres.). Jewish religion (past pres. congregation). Home: 1626 Edgewood Circle Chattanooga TN 37405 Office: Volunteer Bldg Chattanooga TN 37402

WEINBERG, ELLSWORTH ARTHUR, lawyer; b. Marlington, W.Va., Oct. 19, 1912; s. Joseph Lionel and Helen (Webb) W.; A.B., U. Balt., 1935; LL.B., So. Meth. U., 1936; m. Mary Caroline Larimore, Aug. 14, 1946; children—Mary Pamela (Mrs. Michael McManus), Ellsworth Arthur. Admitted to Tex. bar, 1936, since practiced in Dallas. Dir. Lumar, Inc., SMC Industries, Inc. Dist. commodore USCG Aux., 1960-62, nat. commodore, 1964-66. Bd. mgmt. Town North br. Dallas YMCA. Served with USNR, 1941-45. Mem. Am., Tex., Dallas bar assns., Am. Judicature Soc. Republican. Episcopalian. Home: 6035 Meadowcrest Dr Dallas TX 75230 Office: Republic Nat Bank Tower Dallas TX 75201

WEINBERG, JERROLD GLADSTONE, lawyer; b. Norfolk, Va., Apr. 5, 1928; s. Charles Paul and Reba (Gladstone) W.; B.S., U. Va., 1947, LL.B., 1950; postgrad. U. Oslo (Norway), 1947; m. Marcia Ellen Moress, Nov. 28, 1954; children—Ellen Jane, Nancy Louise, Andrew Steven. Admitted to Va. bar, 1949; practiced in Norfolk, 1950—; partner firm Stackhouse, Weinberg & Stewart, Norfolk, 1961—. Commr. chancery Circuit Ct. City Norfolk, 1961—. Bd. dirs. Norfolk Forum, Tidewater Vocational Center, Child and Family Service, Norfolk. Served with AUS, 1951-53. Mem. Fed., Am., Norfolk and Portsmouth (pres. 1974) bar assns., Va. State Bar. Jewish religion. Club: Harbor (Norfolk). Home: 1091 Algonquin Rd Norfolk VA 23505 Office: 1400 Virginia Nat Bank Bldg Norfolk VA 23510

WEINBERGER, CASPAR WILLARD, govt. ofcl.; b. San Francisco, Aug. 18, 1917; s. Herman and Cerise Carpenter (Hampson) W.; A.B. magna cum laude, Harvard, 1938, LL.B., 1941; m. Jane Dalton, Aug. 16, 1942; children—Arlin Cerise (Mrs. Richard Paterak), Caspar Willard. Law clk. U.S. Judge William E. Orr, 1945-47; with firm Heller, Ehrman, White & McAuliffe, 1947-69, partner, 1959-69; mem. Cal. Legislature from 21st Dist., 1952-58; vice chmn. Cal. Republican Central Com., 1960-62, chmn., 1962-64; chmn. Com. Cal. govt. Orgn. and Econs., 1967-68; dir. finance Cal., 1968-69; chmn. FTC, 1970; dep. dir. Office Mgmt. and Budget, Washington, 1970-72, dir., 1972-73; counsellor to the Pres., 1973; sec. U.S. Dept. Health, Edn. and Welfare, 1973—. Chmn., Pres.'s Com. on Mental Retardation. Bd. govs. Am. Nat. Red Cross; bd. dirs. Yosemite Inst.; trustee Mech. Inst.; bd. govs. San Francisco Heart Assn.; governing mem. San Francisco YMCA. Served from pvt. to capt., infantry, AUS, 1941-45; PTO. Decorated Bronze Star. Mem. Am. Bar Assn., State Bar Cal. Episcopalian. Clubs: Century (New York); Bohemian (San Francisco); Harvard (San Francisco, Washington); Georgetown (Washington). Writer column on Cal. govt., 1959-68; staff book reviewer San Francisco Chronicle and San Francisco mag. Home: 114 3d St SE Washington DC 20003 Office: care Dept Health Edn Welfare 114 3d St SE Washington DC 20003

WEINER, HAROLD, psychologist; b. Bklyn., Mar. 28, 1932; s. Max and Lillian (Weinstein) W.; B.B.A., Coll. City N.Y., 1953; M.A., U. Md., 1956, Ph.D., 1960; m. Zelda Iris Weiner, June 6, 1959; children—Eric, Kevin, Karen. Dir., Behavioral Research Lab., Am. Inst. for Research, Washington, 1956-61; dir. Operant Conditioning Lab., St. Elizabeth Hosp., Washington, 1961-69 acting asso. for research, 1971—; chief, sect. on operant behavior Nat. Inst. Mental Health, Washington, 1969—; clin. prof. psychiatry George Washington U., 1969—; pvt. practice as behavior therapist, 1972—. Served with AUS, 1954-56. Fellow A.A.A.S., Am. Psychol. Assn. Home: 20 Maplewood Ct Greenbelt MD 20770 Office: St Elizabeth Hosp Washington DC 20032

WEINER, MORTON DAVID, bus. exec.; b. Balt., Aug. 19, 1922; s. Max and Rose (Wolfe) W.; B.S., Towson State Coll., 1942; grad. exec. program, U. Cal. at Los Angeles, 1959; m. Joan M. Maggin; children—Bruce, Susan, Lori, Julie, Jeffrey. Pres., chief operating officer, dir., mem. exec. com. AVNET, Inc., N.Y.C., 1963-69; pres. Morton D. Weiner & Co., investment bankers, N.Y.C., 1969-70; chmn. bd. Nat. Investors Life Ins. Cos., 1970—; pres., chief exec. Norin Corp., North Miami, Fla., 1970—; exec. v.p., dir. Norris Grain Co., 1970—; dir. Maple Leaf Mills, Upper Lakes Shipping Ltd., Toronto, Chgo. Rock Island R.R. Served to capt., Signal Corps, AUS, 1942-46; CBI. Mem. N.A.M. Mason (Shriner). Office: 12100 NE 16th Av North Miami FL 33161

WEINTRAUB, MICHAEL, lawyer, finance co. exec.; b. Miami, Fla., June 5, 1938; s. Joseph and Hortense (Katz) W.; B.A., U. Va., 1960, J.D., 1963; m. Barbara Posthumus, Sept. 5, 1968; 1 stepdau., Lori Ellen Anderson. Admitted to Fla. bar; partner firm Smathers & Thompson, Miami, 1963—; v.p. Atico Financial Corp., Miami, 1967—, also dir.; pres. Pan. Am. Bancshares, Inc., 1969—, also dir.; dir. Pan Am. Bank of Miami. Unit chmn. United Fund. Mem. Citizens Adv. Bd. Variety Childrens Hosp.; bd. dirs. Miami Heart Inst., Mt. Sinai Hosp., A.R.C. Mem. Am., Dade County bar assns., Am. Judicature Soc. Clubs: Westview Country; Ocean Reef Country. Home: 3370 Devon Rd Miami FL 33133 Office: 150 SE Third Av Miami FL 33131

WEINTRAUB, STANLEY, textile co. exec.; b. June 21, 1927; s. Benjamin (N.) and Rebecca (Abramowitz) W.; student Coll. City N.Y., 1946, N.Y. U., 1947; grad. Fashion Inst. Tech., 1949; Mayer Sch. Design, 1953; m. Elayne Star, May 8, 1948; children—Barry, Stacy Jo. With Apollo Knitting Mills, Inc. (became part of Work Wear Corp., Cleve., 1968), Bronx, N.Y., 1946-68, partner, v.p., 1956-64, pres., 1964-68, mng. dir., until 1968; v.p., chief design dir. Work Wear Corp., 1968-73; partner Giamo Knits, Hialeah, Fla., 1973—, also exec. v.p. in charge full prodn., Hallandale, Fla.; chief design dir. for fashion and career apparel Apollo Knitting Mills. Instr., Fashion Inst. Tech., 1950-51; cons. Knitted OTERWEAR Times; fashion and textile cons. textile firms. Home: Hallandale FL 33009 Office: Giamo Knits Inc 1000 E 17th St Hialeah FL 33010

WEIR, CLAYTON J., lawyer; b. McGregor, Ia., July 31, 1901; s. Ithiel and Christina (Tweet) W.; LL.B., Cumberland U., 1931; J.D., Cumberland Sch. Law Samford U., 1969; m. Eva Mae Pate, Dec. 5, 1922; children—Imogene, James. Admitted to Fla. bar, 1931, since practiced in Groveland; also ins. and real estate positions. Mayor, mem. Town Council, Groveland, 1932-40, also former city atty. Democrat. Methodist. Mason, Elk, Kiwanian. Home: Groveland FL 32736

WEIR, DAVIS, finance corp. exec.; b. Mt. Pleasant, Ia., Nov. 4, 1903; s. Adam and Lucy (Davis) W.; grad. high sch.; m. Maurine Sandahl, May 5, 1926. Founder, Am. Finance System, Inc. (formerly State Loan & Finance Corp.), Wilmington, Del., 1930, chmn. bd., 1956—; dir. 1st Nat. Bank of Ft. Lauderdale, (Fla.); mem. adv. bd. Wash. Mut. Investors Fund, 1957—. Trustee Holy Cross Hosp., Ft. Lauderdale. Clubs: Columbia Country, Congressional Country, Fort Lauderdale Yacht, Royal Palm Yacht and Country. Home: 95 Palm Club Pompano Beach FL 33062 Office: 2455 E Sunrise Blvd Fort Lauderdale FL 33304

WEIR, JOHN HOWARD, real estate and banking exec.; b. Binghamton, N.Y., Jan. 18, 1925; s. Milton N. and Mildred L. (Young) W.; student pub., pvt. schs.; m. Jamesena G. Hardee, Aug. 31, 1950; children—Deborah Suzanne, John Howard. Gen. mgr. M. N. Weir & Sons, Inc., Boca Raton, Fla., 1952-58, 61—; v.p., gen. mgr. Arvida Corp., 1958-61; exec. v.p., dir. Boca Raton Nat. Bank, 1961—. v.p., treas., dir. Castleton Industries, Inc., 1968-69; pres. Boca Raton Plaza, Inc., 1962—; sec., dir. Fla. Bancgrowth, Inc., 1963—; partner Milton N. Weir & Sons; pres., dir. Citizens Nat. Bank, Boca Raton; chmn., dir. Fidelity Nat. Bank, Pompano Beach, Fla. Trustee, chmn. Boca Raton Community Hosp. Served with USNR, 1943-46. Mem. Am. Legion, Bankers Club of N.Y. Republican. Presbyn. Mason. Clubs: Miami (Fla.); Wings (N.Y.C.); Royal Palm Yacht and Country (Boca Raton). Home: 272 Coconut Palm Rd Boca Raton FL 33432 Office: 855 S Fed Hwy Boca Raton FL 33432

WEIR, WILLIAM MANNING, real estate firm exec.; b. Binghamton, N.Y., May 17, 1929; s. Milton Nelson and Mildred Lydia (Young) W.; grad high sch.; m. Dorothy Dee Willis, June 18, 1953; children—William Manning, Patricia C. Gen. mgr. Weir Contractors div. M.N. Weir & Sons, Inc., 1954-73; sales mgr. M.N. Weir & Sons, Inc., Boca Raton, Fla., 1973—; v.p. Boca Raton Plaza, Inc., 1962—; dir. Security Exchange Bank, 1965-69; vice chmn., dir. Fidelity Nat. Bank; dir. Boca Raton Nat. Bank, Fidelity Bank West Delray Beach. Served with USCG, 1951-54. Mem. Am. Legion, Nat. Assn. Realtors, Boca Raton C. of C. Republican. Presbyn. Clubs: Royal Palm Yacht and Country (Boca Raton); Ocean Reef (Key Largo). Home: 444 Maya Palm Dr Boca Raton FL 33432 Office: 855 S Federal Hwy Boca Raton FL 33432

WEIR, WILLIAM PATTON, lawyer; b. Hobbs, N.M., Feb. 17, 1940; s. William Neil and Billie Bernice (Patton) W.; B.A., So. Methodist U., 1962, LL.B., 1964; m. Shirley Annette Clark, June 5, 1960; children—Lori Alison, William Nicholas. Sec.-treas. William N. Weir Roofing & Sheet Metal Co., Inc., Arlington, Tex., 1956—; admitted to Tex. bar, 1964, since practiced in Ft. Worth. Mem. Am. (certificate of performance Award of Achievement competition 1969), Ft. Worth-Tarrant County, Ft. Worth-Tarrant County Jr. bar assns., State Bar Tex. Home: 3209 W Biddison St Fort Worth TX 76109 Office: Commerce Bldg Fort Worth TX 76102

WEISLER, JULIAN EARL, II, lawyer; b. Brehnam, Tex., Feb. 8, 1936; s. Julian Earl and Dorothy (Dixon) W.; B.S., U.S. Mil. Acad., 1959; LL.B., U. Tex., 1966; m. Jeraldyne Lehde, Oct. 29, 1968; children—Christina, Caryn. Admitted to Tex. bar, 1966; practiced in Brenham, 1968—; partner, Spinn, Ehlert, Spinn, Weisler & Weisler, Brenham, Tex., 1968—; pres. Stone Abstract Co., 1974—; dir. Ga.-Fla. Oil & Refining Co., Inc. Served to maj. AUS, 1959-68. Decorated Bronze Star medals (2). Mem. State Bar Tex., Washington County Bar Assn. (pres. 1968-71), Brenham C. of C. (pres. 1972). Mason (Shriner), Elk, Lion (pres. 1971). Home: Route 3 Box 458 Brenham TX 77833 Office: PO Drawer 1118 Brenham TX 77833

WEISS, A(DOLPH) KURT, physiologist, educator; b. Graz, Austria, Mar. 22, 1923; s. Alfred and Anna (Giesskann) W.; came to U.S., 1940, naturalized, 1943; B.S., Okla. Baptist U., 1948; M.S., U. Tenn., 1950; Ph.D., U. Rochester, 1953; m. Mary Davis, June 1, 1948; 1 son, Thomas Alfred. Instr. physiology U. Miami (Fla.) Sch. Medicine, 1953-55, asst. prof., 1955-60, asso. prof., 1960-61; prof., head dept. biology Oklahoma City U., 1961-64; asso. prof. physiology and biophysics U. Okla. Health Scis. Center, Oklahoma City, 1961-65, prof., 1966—. Vis. prof. U. W.I., Jamaica, 1959. Served with AUS, 1943-46. Decorated Bronze Star medal with oak leaf cluster. Recipient Research Career Devel. award Nat. Inst. Child Health and Human Devel., 1964-69, citation for service Am. Assn. Ret. Persons and Ret. Tchrs. Assn., 1963. Mem. Soc. Exptl. Biology and Medicine (mem. council 1970-72, chmn. nat. mem. com. 1972-75), Gerontological Soc. (v.p. 1971-72, mem. council 1970-73), Sigma Xi, Phi Kappa Phi. Contbr. articles on endocrinology, gerontology and hypertension to jours. Home: 2224 NW 43rd St Oklahoma City OK 73112

WEISS, ARMAND BERL, economist; b. Richmond, Va., Apr. 2, 1931; s. Maurice Herbert and Henrietta (Shapiro) W.; B.S. in Econs., Wharton Sch. Finance U. Pa., 1953, M.B.A., 1954; D.B.A., George Washington U., 1971; m. Judith Bernstein, May 18, 1957; children—Jo Ann Michele, Rhett Louis. Officer, U.S. Navy, 1954-65; spl. asst. to auditor gen. Navy, 1964-65; sr. economist Center for Naval Analyses, Arlington, Va., 1965-68; project dir. Logistics Mgmt. Inst., Washington, 1968—; sr. v.p. Weiss Pub. Co., Inc., Richmond, Va., 1960—; vis. lectr. George Washington U., 1971. Chmn. U.S. delegation, session chmn. NATO Symposium on Cost-Benefit Analysis, The Hague, Netherlands, 1969, NATO Conf. on Operational Research in Indsl. Systems, St. Louis, France, 1970; pres. Nat. Council Assns. Policy Scis., 1971—; chmn. adv. group Def. Econ. Adv. Council, 1970—; resident asso. Smithsonian Instn., 1973—. Sr. v.p. George Washington U. Sch. Bus. and Govt. Doctoral Assn., 1968-69; del. Pres.'s Mid-Century White House Conf. on Children and Youth, 1950; scoutmaster Japan, U.S., leader World Jamborees, France, Can., U.S., 1945-61; U.S. del. Internat. Conf. on Operations Research, Dublin, Ireland, 1972; organizing com. Internat. Cost-Effectiveness Symposium, Washington, 1970; speaker Internat. Conf. Inst. Mgmt. Scis., Tel Aviv, 1973, del., Mexico City, 1967. Mem. bus. com. Washington Nat. Symphony Orch., 1968-70; exec. com. Mid Atlantic council Union Am. Hebrew Congregations, 1970—; mem. dist. com. Boy Scouts Am., 1972—. Fellow A.A.A.S., Washington Acad. Scis.; mem. Operations Research Soc. Am. (chmn. meetings com. 1969-71; chmn. cost-effectiveness sect. 1969-70), Washington Operations Research Council (editor newsletter 1969—; sec. 1971-72, pres.-elect 1972-73, pres. 1973-74), Internat. Inst. Strategic Studies (London), Inst. for Mgmt. Sci., Am. Econ. Assn., Wharton Grad. Sch. Alumni Assn. (exec. com. 1970-73), Am. Acad. Polit. and Social Sci. Jewish religion (pres. temple 1970-72). Club: Wharton Grad. Sch. Washington (sec. 1967-69, pres. 1969-70). Author: Systems Analysis for Social Problems, 1970; The Relevance of Economic Analysis to Decision Making in the Department of Defense, 1972; Toward More Effective Public Programs: The Role of Analysis and Evaluation, 1973. Editor: Cost-Effectiveness Newsletter, 1966-70, Operations Research/Systems Analysis Today, 1971—; asso. editor Operations Research, 1971—. Home: 6516 Truman Lane Falls Church VA 22043 Office: 4701 Sangamore Rd Washington DC 20016

WEISS, EDWARD HARVEY, psychiatrist; b. N.Y.C., Oct. 2, 1931; s. Maximillian and Sylvia (Herstein) W.; B.A., N.Y. U., 1954; M.D., U. Geneva (Switzerland), 1959; m. Sheila M. O'Reilly, Feb. 21, 1965; children—Matthew, Alexander. Intern Kings County Med. Center Bklyn., 1960-61; resident St. Elizabeth's Hosp., Washington, 1961-63; child psychiatry fellow Childrens Hosp. of D.C., 1963-65; practice medicine specializing in child psychiatry, Washington, 1965—; dir. child psychiatry area C Community Health Center, Washington, 1965-67; dir. regional unit, supervisory cons. therapeutic nursery Alexandria (Va.) Community Mental Health Center, 1967—; asso. prof. psychiatry Georgetown U., Washington, 1965—. Sec.-treas. Washington Council Child Psychiatry, 1971—; Mem. adv. bd. Nat. Child Research Center, Washington, 1972—. Diplomate Am. Bd. Psychiatry with subsplty. in child psychology. Fellow Am. Psychiat. Assn., Am. Acad. Child Psychiatry, Am. Orthopsychiat. Assn.; mem. Washington Psychiat. Soc. (council 1973—), D.C. Med. Soc. (mental health com. 1971—), Va. Assn. Children with Learning Disabilities (adv. bd. 1968-70). Address: 3551 Tilden St NW Washington DC 20008

WEISS, GERALD NAEPHTHALIE, surgeon; b. New Orleans, June 14, 1923; s. Arthur and Amelia (Levy) W.; B.S., Tulane U., 1943, M.D., 1945; m. Elaine Judith Bresler, Feb. 1, 1948; children—Harlan Simon, Gary Neal, Lauren Ruth. Intern, Touro Infirmary, New Orleans, 1945-46, resident in surgery, 1949-51; fellow in surgery Tulane U., New Orleans, 1948-49; vis. surgeon Charity Hosp., New Orleans, 1948-49; physician, surgeon Goldsmith Clinic, Lake Charles, La., 1951-57; practice medicine, specializing in gen. surgery, Lake Charles, 1957—; gen. surgeon Belize Gen. Hosp., British Honduras, Central Am., 1962, Barzilai Govt. Hosp., Afridar, Ashkelon, Israel, 1971; mem. surg. staff Lake Charles Charity Hosp., 1961-69, 72—; clin. instr., dept. surgery Tulane U. Sch. Medicine, 1948-49; instr. dept. zoology McNeese State Coll., 1952-55; clin. instr., dept. surgery La. State U. Sch. Medicine, 1961-64, 66-69, clin. asst. prof., 1973—. Surg. cons. Govt. Brit. Honduras, 1962; teaching faculty Am. Soc. Abdominal Surgeons, 1964—; course instr. Law-Sci. Acad., 1968. Mem. health and safety com. Calcasieu Area Council Boy Scouts Am., 1964-68; pres. S.W. La. chpt. La. Assn. Mental Health, 1961-62; chmn. Calcasieu-Cameron chpt. A.R.C., 1962-63; com. mem. Health Club, YMCA, 1953-60; fleet surgeon Lake Charles chpt. U.S. Power Squadron, 1962-64; mem. pub. health com. Lake Charles Assn. Commerce, 1960-70; pres. Coordinating Council for Community Med. Services, 1970—; chmn. Lake Charles Coordinating Council for Community Emergency Med. Services, 1972—. Dist. del. La. Constnl. Conv., 1973. Bd. dirs., chmn. bd. Research Inst. Quality Health Plans, Inc., 1971—. Served to capt. M.C., USAAF, 1946-49. Recipient Gold medal award Law-Sci. Acad., 1968, Certificate of Merit, Minister of Nat. Defense Guatemala, 1968, Distinguished Service award Salvation Army, 1970. Mem. Am. Soc. Abdominal Surgeons (mem. exec. com. 1967—), A.M.A., So., Pan Am. med. assns., A.C.S. (chmn. Lake Charles Com. on Trauma 1964—), Am. Bd. Surgery, Nat. Bd. Med. Examiners, Law-Sci. Inst., Law-Sci. Acad., Internat. Coll. Surgeons (regent La. 1973—), Am. Physician's Guild, Am. Physicians Fellowship, Southeastern Surg. Congress, La. Physicians Guild (treas. 1968-72), La. State (mem. com. on ins. 1968-72), Orleans Parish, Calcasieu Parish, 7th Dist. med. socs., Alpha Omega Alpha. Kiwanian. Contbr. articles to profl. jours. Inventor stainless steel clip adaptable to biting end several types forceps to prevent gross contamination at exposed cut ends of intestinal viscera. Home: 2001 21st St Lake Charles LA 70601 Office: 1611 Foster St Lake Charles LA 70601

WEISS, JEFFREY J., retail trade co. exec.; b. Bklyn, July 13, 1943; s. Louis M. and Miriam (Solow) W.; student Miami Dade Jr. Coll., 1961-63; m. Glenda Joyce Penner, June 26, 1965; children—Lara J., Gina J. Pres., chmn. bd., founder Atlantic Industries, Inc., Miami, Fla., 1965—; chmn. bd., v.p. Exposition Corp. of Am., Miami, 1968—; v.p., dir. Scarlet O'Hara, 1970—, Glenda Products Inc., 1972—, Gazebo Food Corp., 1973-74; dir. Underwriters Financial of Fla., Inc. Exec. com. Ednl. Community TV, 1973—. Mem. Direct Selling Assn. (dir.), Smithsonian Instn. Home: 8500 SW 85th St Miami FL 33143 Office: 720 NW 27th Av Miami FL 33125

WEISS, WILLIAM LAMOND, research co. exec.; b. Phila., Mar. 3, 1927; s. Andrew F. and Blanche (Trindle) W.; student Pa. Mil. Coll., 1949-52; m. Delores Evelyn Barnes, Mar. 3, 1951; children—Kurt, Eric, Adrian. Specialist in radiation detectors, aircraft nuclear propulsion dept. Gen. Elec. Corp., Evendale, O., 1955-61; chief engr. solid state detectors ORTEC, Inc., Oak Ridge, Tenn., 1961-66, product mgr. mktg. solid state detectors, 1966—. Served with USNR, 1945-46. Mem. I.E.E.E. Contbr. articles to profl. jours. Home: 119 Newell Lane Oak Ridge TN 37830 Office: 100 Midland Rd Oak Ridge TN 37830

WEISSBACH, HERBERT, biochemist; b. N.Y.C., 1932; B.S., Coll. City N.Y.; Ph.D., George Washington U., 1957. With Nat. Heart Inst., 1953—, acting chief Lab. of Clin. Biochemistry, 1968—. Recipient award Am. Soc. Biol. Chemists, Superior Service award U.S. Dept. Health, Edn. and Welfare, 1968, award in enzyme chemistry Am. Chem. Soc., 1970. Mem. A.A.A.S., Am. Soc. for Pharmacology and Exptl. Therapeutics, Am. Soc. Microbiology. Contbr. articles to profl. jours. Editor Jour. Pharmacology and Exptl. Therapeutics, Archives of Biochemistry and Biophysics. Office: Nat Heart Inst 5204 Cedar Lane Bethesda MD 20014*

WEITZ, PAUL JOSEPH, astronaut; b. Erie, Pa., July 25, 1932; s. Paul Joseph and Violet (McClymont) W.; B.S. in Aero. Engring., Pa. State U., 1954; M.S. in Aero. Engring., U.S. Navy Postgrad. Sch., Monterey, Cal., 1964; m. Suzanne Margaret Berry, June 23, 1956; children—Matthew, Cynthia. Commd. ensign U.S. Navy, 1954, advanced through grades to capt., 1973; naval aviator, 1956, with various squadrons, 1956-65; astronaut NASA Manned Spacecraft Center, Houston, 1966—; mem. crew 1st manned mission to Skylab, 1973. Decorated Air medal with 4 gold stars, Navy Commendation medal; Sec. Navy Commendation medal. Mem. Beta Theta Pi. Mason. Home: NASA MSC Code CB Houston TX 77058

WELCH, JAY J., physician; b. Smithfield, Ill., Sept. 19, 1916; s. Alan Richard and Mabel Lee (Hinckle) W.; B.S., U. Ill., 1938; M.B., Northwestern U., 1942, M.D., 1943, M.S., 1949; m. Esther Apperson, Mar. 2, 1946; 1 dau., Sheila (dec.). Intern Wesley Meml. Hosp., Chgo., 1942-43, resident internal medicine, 1946-49; internist Collins-Bellas Clinic, Peoria, Ill., 1953-54, Glenn-Maguire Clinic, Canton, Ill., 1954-58, Greer Clinic, Houston, 1958-59; practice medicine specializing in internal medicine, Houston, 1959—; clin. asso. prof. medicine Baylor U., 1958-66; chief instr. medicine Houston Meml. Hosp. Chmn. bd. dirs. H. Lowrie, Inc.; mng. partner Houston Assos. II. Served with AUS, 1943-46, 49-50, 50-52. Fellow A.C.P.; mem. Am. Soc. Internal Medicine, Am. Inst. Parliamentarians, Fulton County Med. Soc. (pres. 1957), Tex. Soc. Internal Medicine (pres. 1971), Phi Beta Kappa, Alpha Kappa Kappa, Phi Eta Sigma, Phi Lambda Upsilon. Clubs: Houston Toastmasters (area gov. internat. 1957), Houston Yacht, Plaza (Houston). Home: 4711 Ingersoll Av Houston TX 77027 Office: Memorial Professional Bldg Houston TX 77002

WELCH, LOUIE, assn. exec.; b. Lockney, Tex., Dec. 9, 1918; s. Gilford E. and Nora (Shackelford) W.; B.A. magna cum laude, Abilene Christian Coll., 1940; m. Iola Faye Cure, Dec. 17, 1940; children—Guy Lynn, Gary Dale, Louie Gilford, Shannon Austin, Tina Joy. Organized Welch Industries, Inc., Houston 1955, pres., after 1955; pres. Louie Welch & Co., Inc., real estate and investment brokers; pres. Houston C. of C., 1974—. Vice pres. League of Tex. Municipalities, 1957-58, pres., 1958-59. Councilman-at-large City of Houston, 1950-52, 56-62, mayor, 1963-73. Trustee Abilene Christian Coll., South Tex. Jr. Coll.; bd. dirs. Goodwill Industries, Sickle Cell Anemia Found., Houston Symphony, Houston Grand Opera, Energy Research and Edn. Found., Named Key Houstonian, 1973, Distinguished Eagle Scout, 1974; recipient Kennedy Peace medal, 1971, Internat. B'nai B'rith Humanitarian award, 1973. Home: 5013 Happy Hollow Houston TX 77018 Office: Houston C of C Houston TX 77001

WELCH, NATHAN LEE, supt. schs.; b. Abilene, Tex., Jan. 21, 1922; s. Lynton Horace and Beulah (Smith) W.; B.S., W. Tex. State U., 1947, M.Ed., 1953; postgrad. Tex. Tech., 1966—; m. Roberta Walker, Mar. 4, 1944; children—Derrith Lee, Vicki Dawnelle. Prin. elementary sch., Whitharral, Tex., 1946-47, Vega, Tex., 1947-48; asst. coordinator Childress (Tex.) County Vocational Sch., 1948-51; tchr. jr. high sch., Abernathy, Tex., 1951-52; prin. River Rd. Ind. Sch. Dist. Amarillo, Tex., 1952-56; supt. Booker (Tex.) Ind. Sch. Dist., 1956-60, McLean (Tex.), 1960-64; supr. Kress (Tex.) Ind. Sch. Dist., 1964—. Dir. Credit Union Swisher County, 1967—, pres., 1968. Pres., Swisher County Community Action, 1973. Bd. dirs. Hi-Plains Eye Bank, 1970—. Served with USAAF, 1942-46. Mem. Tex., Swisher County tchrs. assns. Mason, Lion (pres. 1967-68). Home: 311 Ripley St Kress TX 79052

WELCH, PORTER PRATHER, banker; b. Lexington, Ky., Dec. 29, 1925; s. Dexter Nathan and Myrtle (Farmer) W.; student Fugazzi Bus. Coll., 1950, Am. Inst. Banking, 1953; m. Betty Jane Price, Jan. 4, 1947; 1 dau., Kathy Ann (Mrs. C. Noel Hall). With Woodford Bank & Trust Co., Versailles, Ky., 1953—, 1st. v.p. 1960-69, pres., 1969—, also dir. Sec. United Fund, Versailles, 1954—; treas. Woodford County Meml. Hosp. Mem. Versailles C. of C. (sec.-treas. 1956—). Kiwanian (pres. 1955). Club: Woodford Hills Country (treas. 1968-71). Home: 241 Morgan St Versailles KY 40383 Office: 101 N Main St Versailles KY 40383

WELD, EDWARD LEE, ednl. adminstr.; b. Kansas City, Mo., Nov. 23, 1912; s. Edward Lee and Nellie Adelia (Nicewarner) W.; B.S., Kansas City Tchrs. Coll., 1935; B.S., U. Kan., 1961; M.S., Kan. State U., 1962; m. Marguerite Davis, June 14, 1941. Asst. prof. mech. engring. Colo. State U., Fort Collins, 1963-65; head engring. techs. Chattanooga State Tech. Inst., 1965-67, dean instrn., 1967-69; dir. Nashville State Tech. Inst., 1969—. Served to 2d lt. USAAF, 1943-45. Registered profl. engr., Tenn., Mo., Colo. Mem. Am. Soc. M.E., Am. Soc. Engring. Edn., Am. Vocational Assn., Nat., Tenn. socs. profl. engrs., Pi Tau Sigma. Kiwanian. Home: 134 Carriage Dr Nashville TN 37221

WELDEN, ARTHUR LUNA, biologist, educator; b. Birmingham, Ala., Jan. 27, 1927; s. Arthur Luna and Mary Woodson (Smith) W.; A.B., Birmingham So. Coll., 1950; M.S., U. Tenn., 1951; Ph.D., U. Ia., 1954; m. Frances Merkl Colvin, Aug. 19, 1950; children—Charles Woodson, Arthur Frederick. Asst. prof. biology Millikin U., Decatur, Ill., 1954-55; instr. botany Tulane U., New Orleans, 1955-59, asst. prof., 1959-64, asso. prof., 1964-68, prof. biology, 1968—. Served with AUS, 1945-47. Am. Philos. Soc. grantee; 1957, NSF grantee, 1960-73. Mem. Sociedad Botanica de Mexico, Mycol. Soc. Am. (councilor 1967-69), Assn. for Tropical Biology, Am. Bot. Soc., Am. Soc. Plant Taxonomy, Internat. Assn. Plant Taxonomy, Assn. Southeastern Biologists. Asso. editor: Tulane Studies in Zoology and Botany. Contbr. articles to profl. jours. Home: 7826 Willow St New Orleans LA 70118

WELDON, HUGH WILSON, utility co. exec.; b. St. Charles, S.C., Dec. 18, 1921; s. Ariel Koga and Daisy (Scott) W.; student Draughons Bus. Coll., 1939-40; m. Jean Elizabeth Mustard, Feb. 12, 1944; children—Hugh, Allan, Richard. Sr. clk. S.C. Electric & Gas Co., Charleston, 1946-47, personnel rep., 1947-49, personnel dir., 1949-59, mgr. employee relations, Columbia, 1959-70, v.p. employee relations, 1970—. Vice pres. Mid-Carolina Council on Alcoholism, 1968—; pres. Univ. Assos., 1968; mem. Central Midlands Regional Planning Council, 1971—. Bd. dirs. Columbia YMCA, 1966—; U.S.O., 1971—. Served with USAAF, 1944-46; PTO; lt. col. USAF Res. (ret.). Mem. Southeastern Electric Exchange and Edison Electric Inst., So. Indsl. Relations Council (dir. 1969—), Sertoma Club (pres. 1969). Presbyn. (elder 1961—, clk. session 1973—). Club: Palmetto. Home: 6319 Whiteoak Rd Columbia SC 29206 Office: 320 Main St Columbia SC 29218

WELDON, JACK GERARD, broadcasting co. exec.; b. N.Y.C., Aug. 2, 1911; s. John B. and Katherine (Osmond) W.; student Columbia, 1929-31; m. Ann Blain, Sept. 11, 1937; children—Ann Stuart (Mrs. Kenneth Michael), John Blain. Announcer various radio stas., N.Y.C., 1927-34; announcer, salesman WDBJ, Roanoke, Va., 1934-39, program dir., 1939-46; exec. v.p., gen. mgr. Old Dominion Broadcasting Corp., WWOD, Lynchburg, 1946-52; exec. rep. A.P., 1952, regional membership exec., 1954-58; gen. mgr. WAIR, Winston-Salem, N.C., 1952-53; sales mgr. WSUN radio, St. Petersburg, Fla., 1958-66; local/regional sales mgr. WLCY-TV, Largo, Fla., 1966—. Tchr. broadcasting, writing, acting, prodn. U. Va. Extension Div., 1942-44. Bd. dirs. Leisure Manor Retirement Facility, 1960-65. Recipient Printer's Ink AFA Silver Medal award, 1965. Mem. Am. Advt. Fedn. (gov. 4th dist. Fla.), Advt. Club (pres. 1965-66). Presbyn. (treas. 1963-65). Home: 5025 39th St S St Petersburg FL 33711 Office: WLCY-TV 11450 Gandy Blvd St Petersburg FL 33702

WELDON, WILSON OSBOURNE, editor, clergyman; b. Camden, S.C., Mar. 15, 1911; s. John Wesley and Leila (Wilson) W.; B.A., U. S.C., 1931; B.D., Duke, 1934; D.D., High Point Coll., 1952; m. Margaret Hammond Lyles, July 19, 1939; children—Nanci Leila (dec.), Wilson Osbourne, Alice Adelaide. Ordained to ministry Meth. Ch., 1938; pastor Meth. chs., China Grove, N.C., 1938-42, High Point, N.C., 1942-48, Meml. Meth. Ch., Thomasville, N.C., 1948-52, 1st Meth. Ch. Gastonia, N.C., 1952-58, Myers Park Meth. Ch., Charlotte, N.C., 1958-63, West Market St. Meth. Ch., Greensboro, N.C., 1963-67; editor Upper Room, Nashville, 1967—. Del., Meth. Ecumenical Conf., Oxford, Eng., 1951, World Meth. Conf., London, Eng., 1966, Denver, 1971, Gen. Conf. Meth. Ch., 1956, 60, 64, 68, 70, 72, Meth. S.E. Jurisdictional Conf., 1952, 56, 60, 64, 68, 72; mem. Gen. Bd. Evangelism, 1960-67; mem. Am. exec. com. World Meth. Council, 1967—. Trustee Greensboro Coll., Scarritt Coll., Nashville, Duke, Junaluska Assembly, Lake Junaluska, N.C. Mem. Lake Junaluska Assos. (pres. 1968—). Mason (32 deg., K.T., Shriner), Rotarian. Author: Thrill of Christian Living, 1966; Discoveries in the Lord's Prayer, 1968; A Plain Man Faces Trouble, 1971; Mark the Road, 1973. Editor: When Fires Burn. Compiler: Breakthru. Home: 1900 Richard Jones Rd Nashville TN 37215 Office: 1908 Grand Av Nashville TN 37203

WELKER, ROBERT LOUIS, educator; b. Clarksville, Tenn., June 26, 1924; s. George Thomas and Emma (Wickham) W.; student Austin Peay State U., 1941-43, U. Conn., 1943-44; B.A., Peabody Coll., 1948; M.A., Vanderbilt U., 1952, Ph.D. (teaching fellow), 1958. Instr. English, Vanderbilt U., Nashville, 1955-56, 57-61, asst. prof., 1961-64; asso. prof. English U. Ala., Huntsville, 1964-66, prof., 1966—, chmn. English dept., 1965—. Served with AUS, 1945-46; ETO. So. Univs. fellow, 1956-57. Mem. Am. Assn. Univ. Profs., Huntsville Lit. Assn. (dir. 1966—, pres. 1971), Modern Lang. Assn., So. Atlantic Modern Lang. Assn. Methodist. Editor: Reality and Myth: Essays in American Literature, 1964; The Sense of Fiction, 1966. Asst. editor Poem, 1967-70, co-editor, 1971-72, editor, 1972—. Home: 600 Franklin St Huntsville AL 35801

WELLBORN, CHARLES TALMADGE, clergyman, educator; b. Alto, Tex., Sept. 24, 1923; s. Charles Floyd and Ethel Berneice (Swanzy) W.; student Kilgore Coll., 1940-42; B.A., Baylor U., 1946, M.A., 1950; M.Div., S.W. Baptist Theol. Sem., 1950; Ph.D. (Cal.-Tex. Found. fellow, Rockefeller Found. fellow), 1964; m. Elizabeth Hood, Mar. 11, 1951; children—Gary Marshall, Jon Richard. Instr., Baylor U., Waco, Tex., 1947-48, asst. prof., 1949-51; sr. minister Univ. Baptist Ch., Waco, Tex., 1951-61; asso. prof. religion Campbell Coll., Buies Creek, N.C., 1964-65; prof. religion Fla. State U., Tallahassee, 1965—. Cons. U.S. Civil Service, 1968—. Trustee, Baylor U., 1958-61. Served with AUS, 1943-45. Decorated Bronze Star medal with oak leaf cluster. Mem. Am. Acad. Religion, Am. Soc. Christian Ethics, Am. Assn. U. Profs., Phi Beta Kappa, Sigma Alpha Epsilon. Baptist. Author: The Challenge of Church Membership, 1956; Twentieth Century Pilgrimage: Walter Lippmann, 1970; Challenge to Morality, 1967. Home: 305 Bradford Rd Tallahassee FL 32303

WELLER, JOHN ALBERT, banker; b. Havana, Cuba, Sept. 29, 1918; s. Albert George and Gladys Eileen (Oates) W.; came to U.S., 1955; naturalized, 1960; B.A. in Bus. Adminstrn., Queen's U., 1943; m. Hedalia Gou, Dec. 12, 1944; children—John Albert, Edward, Gladys. Asst. accountant Bank of Nova Scotia, Havana, Cuba, 1937-46; comml. and polit. adviser Brit. Embassy, Caracas, Venezuela, 1947-55; with First Nat. Bank of Miami (Fla.), 1958—, sr. v.p., 1970—, asst. to chmn. bd. S.E. Bank of Dadeland affiliate, 1972—. Fellow Canadian Bankers Assn.; mem. Latin C. of C. Office: 7200 N Kendall Dr Miami FL 33156

WELLINGTON, JAMES ELLIS, educator; b. Arlington, Mass., July 9, 1921; s. William Edward and Jessie (Dennett) W.; A.B., Dartmouth, 1948; M.A., Boston U., 1950; Ph.D., Fla. State U., 1956; m. Mary Canfield Grier, July 22, 1952; children—Georgia Grier (Mrs. Randall N. Smith), Anne Ross. Instr. dept. English U. Neb., 1950-53; teaching asst., instr. English, Fla. State U., 1953-56; instr., asst. prof. English, U. Miami, Coral Gables, Fla., 1956-63, asso. prof., 1963-70, prof., 1970—. Lang. cons., 1958—. Served with USNR, 1941-46. Mem. Modern Lang. Assn., Renaissance Soc. Am., Malone Soc., Am. Assn. U. Profs., South Atlantic Modern Lang. Assn., Southeastern Renaissance Conf., Augustan Reprint Soc., Delta Upsilon. Democrat. Anglo-Catholic. Author: Alexander Pope's Epistles to Several Persons, 1963; Pope's Eloisa to Abelard, with the Hughes Letters, 1965. Home: 4615 Santa Maria St Coral Gables FL 33146 Office: Dept English U Miami Coral Gables FL 33124

WELLS, ALFRED EUGENE, supt. schs.; b. Springtown, Tex., Oct. 11, 1909; s. Alfred W. and Lillie (Roberts) W.; B.A., Abilene Christian Coll., 1931; M.A., Colo. State Coll. Edn., 1936; m. Zieta Guest, July 11, 1932. Classroom tchr., coach, prin., Albany, Tex., 1931-33; prin. elementary sch., Gladwater, Tex., 1933-40, supt. schs., 1940-42; dir. elementary schs., Gladwater, 1933-40, supt. schs., 1940-42; dir. elementary schs., San Angelo, 1942-45; supt. schs., Sonora, 1945-50; dir. curriculum and instrn., Abilene, 1950-51, supt. schs., 1951—; tchr. summers East Tex. State Tchrs. Coll., 1936-42, Southeastern La. Normal Sch., 1943, Northwestern La. Normal Sch., 1943, San Angelo Jr. Coll., 1944, U. Tex., 1965. Mem. Tex. Elementary Adv. Com., 1936-40; mem. adv. com. Tex. Bd. Edn., 1936-38; chmn. Tex. Textbook Com., 1956; chmn. Tex. Bd. Examiners for Tchr. Edn., 1958-64. Vice pres. Gregg County Tb Assn., chmn. leadership tng. Chisholm Trail council Boy Scouts Am., 1951—. Bd. dirs. West Tex. Rehab. Center, Abilene United Fund. Mem. N.E.A., Tex. Tchrs. Assn. (exec. com. 1963-70, dist. pres.), Am., Tex. (past mem. exec. com., past dist. pres.) assns. sch. adminstrs., Classroom Tchrs. Assn., Tex. Elementary Prins. and Supts. Assn., Nat., Tex. assns. supervision and curriculum devel., Tex. P.T.A. (life), Abilene C. of C. (past dir.). Mem. Ch. of Christ (dir. ch. music). Lion (pres. 1966). Home: 686 Westwood St Abilene TX 79603 Office: Box 981 Abilene TX 79604

WELLS, ALVAN NOBEL, JR., lawyer; b. San Antonio, Oct. 5, 1945; s. A.N. and Fairy (Thompson) W.; J.D., Baylor U., 1970; m. Sylvia Dalton, May 31, 1969. Admitted to Tex. bar, 1970; since practiced in Killeen; partner Lindley, Wells & Michalk, Killeen, 1970—. Legal counsel Fort Hood chpt. Assn. U.S. Army, 1972-74. Chmn. profl. div.

United Fund., 1972. Bell County chmn. for Gov. Briscoe, 1972; pres. Bell County Democratic Club, 1972-73. Mem. Am., Tex. bar assns., Tex. Criminal Def. Lawyers, Tex. Trial Lawyers Assn., Bell, Lampasas, Mills County Bar Assn. (reporter 1972), Baylor U. Law Sch. Alumni (dir.), Phi Alpha Delta, Omicron Delta Kappa, Delta Sigma Pi. Club: Oakridge Country. Home: 3201 Brookbend St Killeen TX 76541 Office: 617 N 8th St Killeen TX 76541

WELLS, BARRY CRAFTON, TV broadcaster; b. McKinney, Tex., June 12, 1939; s. Crafton Oliver and Lois Inez (Latta) W.; B.A., U. Tex., 1962; m. Mary Ruth Dorrill, Jan. 12, 1963; 1 dau., Barri C. Dir. instructional services Sta. KERA-TV, Dallas, 1962—. Tchr. So. Methodist U., Tex. Western U.; cons. Tex. Council Econ. Edn.; TV producer. Judge Ralph Lowell award Reading Advocates of Dallas, 1972—; mem. edn. com. Dallas Mus. Fine Arts, 1971—. Mem. Alpha Phi Omega. Home: 7615 Lavendale St Dallas TX 75230 Office: 3000 Harry Hines Blvd Dallas TX 75230

WELLS, DAMON, JR., investment co. exec.; b. Houston, May 20, 1937; s. Damon and Margaret Corinne (Howze) W.; B.A., magna cum laude, Yale, 1958; B.A., Oxford U., 1964, M.A., 1968; Ph.D., Rice U., 1968. Owner, chief exec. officer Damon Wells Interests, Houston, Tex., 1958—. Bd. dirs. Child Guidance Center of Houston, 1970-73; trustee Christ Ch. Cathedral Endowment Fund, Kinkaid Prep. Sch., Houston, Jefferson Davis Assn. Recipient prize for biography Tex. Writers Roundup, 1971. Mem. Am., So. hist. assns., Am. Assn. State and Local History, English-Speaking Union (nat. dir. 1970-72, v.p. Houston br. 1966-72), Phi Beta Kappa, Pi Sigma Alpha. Episcopalian. Clubs: Coronado, Houston Country, Houston; Garden of the Gods (Colorado Springs, Colo.), Yale (N.Y.C.). Author: Stephen Douglas: The Last Years, 1857-1861, 1971. Home: 2929 Buffalo Speedway Houston TX 77006 Office: River Oaks Bank Bldg 2001 Kirby Dr Houston TX 77019

WELLS, ERNEST HATTON, aerospace technologist, space scis.; b. Crossville, Tenn., Aug. 1, 1921; s. Noah and Chloe (Burges) W.; B.S. in Elec. Engring., Tenn. Tech. U., 1951; m. Signa Faye Stinnett, Dec. 15, 1954; children—David Allen (dec.), William Ernest, Ronald Eston, Robert Lawrence. Instr. radio Tenn. Tech. U., 1947-48; project engr. electronics Airplane & Marine Instruments, Inc., Clearfield, Pa., 1951-53; engr. mine detection ERDL, with research on Greenland Ice Cap, Ft. Belvoir, Va., 1953-55; engr. electronics, radar hdqrs. USMC, Washington, 1955-57; engr. Army Ballistic Missile Agy., Redstone Arsenal, Huntsville, Ala., 1957-62; aerospace technologist NASA, Huntsville, 1962—, former planetary astronomer, exptl. physicist solar research, staff Nuclear and Plasma Physics Lab., now research scientist, environmental sci. Laser Scatter Physics & Astrophysics Lab. Served with USAAF, 1943-46. Decorated Bronze Star with oak leaf cluster. Registered profl. engr., Tenn. Sr. mem. I.E.E.E. Author: Astronomy Finds the Days of Creation; also numerous tech. reports. Home: 712 Kilkenny St U Highland Huntsville AL 35805 Office: NASA MSFC Space Scis Lab S & E-SSL Marshall Space Center AL 35812

WELLS, FRANKLIN BURNHAM, chemist, cons.; b. Chgo., June 9, 1907; s. Albert Jameson and Mary Nancy (Barstow) W.; B.S. in Chem. Engring., U. Ill., 1930; M.Sc. in Organic Chemistry, McGill U. (Can.), 1931, Ph.D. in Organic Chemistry, 1933; m. Mary Lucille Hartley, May 18, 1927; children—Julie (Mrs. John Wehlan), Carolyn (Mrs. Augusto Font III). Analyst, Textile Oils div. Richards Chem. Works, Jersey City, 1934-37, asst. to dir. Lubrication div., 1937-39, dir. Lubrication div., 1940-42; dir. devel. Swan-Finch Oil Corp., Newark, 1939-40; patent devel. research chemist Ellis Foster Co., Montclair, N.J., 1942-46; prof. chemistry and physics, dir. labs. Bloomfield (N.J.) Coll., 1946-51; asst. mgr. Product Devel. div. Trojan Powder Co. (name now Trojan-U.S. Powder Co.), Allentown, Pa., 1951-63; research chemist Picatinny Arsenal, Dover, N.J., 1963-72; ret., 1972; cons. Dept. Army, 1972—. Fellow A.A.A.S., Am. Inst. Chemists, Chem. Soc. (U.K.); mem. Am. Chem. Soc., Am. Ordnance Assn., Bee Research Assn. (U.K.) (hon.), Mich. Beekeepers Assn., Sigma Xi, Alpha Chi Sigma. Republican. Episcopalian. Mason. Abstractor for Chem. Abstracts, Apicultural Abstract (U.K.). Contbr. articles to profl. jours. Patentee on lubricants, rust inhibitors, wetting agts., modified oil varnish bases, apiculture, polyols, silage preservatives, comml. and mil. explosives, also others, in U.S. and fgn. countries. Home: 593 N Avalon St Memphis TN 38112

WELLS, JACK HUBERT, county ofcl., ice mfg. co. exec.; b. Forest Park, Ga., Sept. 15, 1907; s. Emmett Jackson and Mary Frances (Smith) W.; grad. high sch.; m. Mozelle Virginia Moore, Dec. 24, 1927; children—Joel Tommie, Roger Lynn, Carlton Lee, Andrew Michael. With Purity Ice Mfg. Co., Forest Park, 1930—, pres., 1946-68, chmn. bd., 1952—. Chmn., Clayton County Bd. Commrs., 1973—. Mem. So. Ice Exchange (pres. 1962-63), Ga. Ice Mfrs. Assn. (pres. 1962-63), Nat. Ice Assn. (bd. dirs. 1961-66, hon. Life). Baptist (deacon) Kiwanian, Moose. Club: Lakeshore Country. Home: 4775 Courtney Dr Forest Park GA 30050 Office: Clayton County Courthouse Jonesboro GA 30236

WELLS, JOHN HART, ednl. adminstr.; b. Union Level, Va., Dec. 5, 1934; s. Walter James and Vela (Floyd) W.; lit. diploma Ferrum Jr. Coll., 1955; A.B., Atlantic Christian Coll., 1957; M.A., Longwood Coll., 1963; postgrad. U. Va., 1957-70, William and Mary Coll., 1969-71; m. Gladys Rose George, June 27, 1960; children—David Errol, Laura Anne, Janine Elizabeth. Prin., tchr. Boydton (Va.) Elementary Sch., 1957-59; tchr. Buckhorn Elementary Sch., Union Level, 1959-63; prin. LaCrosse (Va.) Elementary Sch., 1963-67; dir. instrn. Lunenburg County Pub. Schs., Victoria, Va., 1967-73, asst. supt. for instrn., 1973—. Served with AUS, 1959-60. Mem. Mecklenburg Edn. Assn. (past treas.), Roanoke River Archeol. Chpt. (past pres.), Archeol. Soc. Va. (dir.). Baptist (deacon). Kiwanian. Home: Box 436 Park Av Victoria VA 23974 Office: Drawer X Victoria VA 23974

WELLS, JOSEPH TYRA, III, accountant; b. Houston, Sept. 3, 1938; s. Joseph Tyra and Leola Arabella (Scharnberg) W.; B.A., Rice U., 1960. With Arthur Anderson & Co., 1960-71, mgr., 1967-71; pvt. practice, Houston, 1971—. C.P.A., Tex. Mem. Am. Inst. C.P.A.'s, Tex. Soc. C.P.A.s. Methodist (treas. eh. 1967—). Club: Bellaire (Tex.) Coin (treas. 1969—). Home: 4316 Stanford St Houston TX 77006 Office: 701 Richmond St Houston TX 77006

WELLS, LEONARD MILTON, city ofcl.; b. Covington, Okla., Nov. 29, 1902; s. Eli Newton and Nancy Jane (Elliott) W.; student Okla. State U., 1922-25; m. Marguerite Hale, Aug. 5, 1928; children—Willia Jane (Mrs. Robert L. Cummins), Robert Milton. Insp., Okla. Hwy. Dept., Okla., 1925-26; partner Wells & Son, Enid, 1926-31; engr. Enid Water Plant, 1931-48; supt. water prodn. City of Enid, 1948-60, dir. pub. works, 1960—. Bd. dirs. Kaw Dam Assn., 1957-72. Mem. Am. Water Works Assn. (pres. Okla. 1967-68, recipient Samuel A. Greeley Local Govt. Service award 1972), Am. Pub. Works Assn., Sigma Nu. Baptist. Rotarian. Home: 409 S Hoover St Enid OK 73701 Office: City Hall Enid OK 73701

WELLS, MARCUS, retail trade co. exec.; b. Charleston, W.Va., Apr. 11, 1908; s. Joseph Wolfe and Anna (Valinsky) W.; B.S.C., U. Cin., 1935; m. Minette Stern, June 3, 1930; children—Richard Allan, Jerry Ames. Div. mdse. mgr. Allied Stores, Cin., 1932-36, Marks-Isaacs, New Orleans, 1936-37; asst. gen. mdse. mgr. Wolff & Mark Co., San Antonio, 1937-40; regional mgr. Sally Frocks, Little Rock, 1940-46; divisional mdse. mgr. E.S. Levy & Co., Inc., Galveston, Tex., 1946—, sr. v.p., 1973—; also dir. Mem. mid-mgmt. com. Galveston Jr. Coll., 1969-72, res. instr., coordinator mid-mgmt., 1971—; chmn. adult edn. Bay Area council Boy Scouts Am., 1949-50; pres. Am. Council for Judaism Galveston, 1951-52. Mem. C. of C. (higher edn. com), Phi Beta Delta. Jewish religion. Mason (32 deg., Shriner). Home: 4527 Av N 1/2 Galveston TX 77550 Office: 2227 Central Plaza Galveston TX 77550

WELLS, RANDY, savings and loan exec.; b. Louisville, Apr. 24, 1940; s. James R. and Marjorie C. (Donoho) W.; student Ind. U., 1964; B.S. in Accounting, Louisville U., 1972. Controller, Norton Hosp., 1964-68, Willett Mfg. Co., 1968-69; v.p. controller S.E. Fed. Savs. and Loan Assn., Louisville, 1969—. Served with USNR, 1958-61. Mem. Nat. Accounting Assn., Louisville Jr. C. of C. Home: 1611 Tunisian Way Louisville KY 40214 Office: 3014 4th St Louisville KY 40208

WELLS, WILLIAM S., mfg. mgmt. cons.; b. Prosser, Wash., May 21, 1921; s. Edgar Ross and Golda Violet (Reist) W.; student Wash. State Coll., 1938-39, Curtiss Wright Tech. Sch., 1940-41, U. Cal. at Berkeley, 1944; m. Ramona D. Conci; children—Moreen (Mrs. Steven C. Foster), Cynthia (Mrs. Terry Robinson), Martin. Engr.-mech. tool planner Douglas Aircraft, Santa Monica and Long Beach, Cal., 1941-47; dir. engring. Frigikar Corp. auto air conditioners, Dallas, 1963-65; pvt. mgmt. cons., Dallas, 1947-63, 65—. Pres., chmn. bd. Effective Research, Inc., Dallas, 1972—, Rankin Mfg. Co., Cedar Falls, Ia., 1958-59. Dir. Dolly Textiles. Active Boy Scouts Am., 1933-54. Named Man of Year State Wash., Nat. C. of C., 1949. Mem. C. of C., Nat. Assn. Watch and Clock Collectors, A.I.M. (fellow pres.'s council, 1973-74), Am. Mgmt. Assn., Soc. Automotive Engrs., Soc. Mfg. Engrs., Am. Soc. Heating, Refrigerating and Air Conditioning Engrs., Alpha Tau Omega. Methodist. Rotarian, Mason. Patentee in field. Home: 10807 Aladdin Dr Dallas TX 75229 Office: PO Box 34313 Dallas TX 75234

WELMAKER, FORREST NOLAN, lawyer; b. McKinney, Tex., Aug. 13, 1925; s. Felix Eustace and Forrest Love (Baker) W.; B.B.A., U. Tex., 1949, J.D., 1953; m. Elizabeth Adele Skillin, Aug. 22, 1959; children—Forrest, Mary Elizabeth, Byron. Admitted to Tex. bar, 1953, since practiced in San Antonio; partner, Clemens, Weiss, Spencer & Welmaker, San Antonio, 1960—. Served with USNR, 1943-46, 50-52. Mem. San Antonio Bar Assn., Res. Officers Assn., Navy League. Kiwanian. Home: 406 Elizabeth Rd San Antonio TX 78209 Office: NBC Bldg San Antonio TX 78205

WELSH, JOHN DICKINSON, theatre dir., educator; b. Richmond, Va., Mar. 22, 1938; s. Virginius Goodwyn and Ann Elizabeth (Dickinson) W.; B.A., U. Richmond, 1960; M.A., Tulane, 1961, Ph.D., 1967; m. Mary Jeanette McWilliams, Sept. 2, 1960; 1 dau., Murray Goodwyn. Instr. theatre and speech Houston Bapt. Coll., 1963-64; guest dir. Barksdale Theatre, Hanover and Hampton, Va., 1965, Swift Creek Mill Playhouse, Colonial Heights, Va., 1974, Barn Playhouse, Richmond, 1974; asso. prof., dir. theatre U. Richmond, 1965—. Nat. Def. Edn. Act fellow, 1960-63. Mem. Am. Theatre Assn., Speech Communication Assn., Am. Assn. U. Profs., So. Speech Communication Assn., So. Theatre Conf. (bus. mgr. So. Theatre 1971-72), Nat. Collegiate Players, Alpha Psi Omega, Omicron Delta Kappa. Home: 802 Hepler Rd Richmond VA 23229 Office: Box 101 U Richmond Richmond VA 23173

WELTIN, WILLIAM LAWRENCE, advt. exec.; b. Chgo., Dec. 2, 1936; s. John Merle and Garnett (Russell) W.; A.B., Dartmouth, 1958; postgrad. Sch. Journalism, U. Mo., 1961-63; div.; children—Laurie Ann, Kimberly Garnet. Copywriter Leo Burnett Co., Chgo., 1963; account exec. Needham, Harper & Steers, Inc., Chgo., 1963-66; v.p., dir. Henderson Advt., Greenville, S.C., 1966-70; pres. Weltin Advt. Agy., Atlanta, 1971—. Vice pres. Greater Atlanta Arts Council, 1969—. Served as capt. USMCR, 1958-61. Mem. Am. Assn. Advt. Agys. (chmn. 1970), Sigma Alpha Epsilon, Kappa Tau Alpha, Alpha Delta Sigma. Republican. Presbyn. Clubs: Cherokee Town and Country, Internat. Golf, Dartmouth Atlanta. Home: 12 Spinning House Pl NW Atlanta GA 30318 Office: 1401 W Paces Ferry Rd NW Atlanta GA 30327

WELTNER, CHARLES LONGSTREET, lawyer; b. Atlanta, Dec. 17, 1927; s. Philip and Sally Cobb (Hull) W.; A.B., Oglethorpe U., 1948; LL.B., Columbia, 1950; m. Juanita McK. Lynn; children by previous marriage—Elizabeth Shirley, Philip II, Susan Martin, Charles Longstreet. Admitted to Ga. bar, 1949; pvt. practice in Atlanta, 1950—; mem. 88th-89th Congresses 5th Dist. Ga. Served to capt. AUS, 1955-57. Democrat. Presbyn. Author: Southener, 1966. Home: 1105 E Rock Springs Rd NE Atlanta GA 30303 Office: 1st Nat Bank Bldg Atlanta GA 30303

WENDE, PHILIP SCOTT, author, illustrator; b. Ogdensburg, N.Y., Jan. 9, 1939; s. Ernest Andrew and Doris (Northrup) W.; student U. Tenn., 1957-58, Ringling Sch. Art, 1958-61; m. Beverly Thera Heacock, Sept. 1, 1962; children—Christopher, Jill, Seth. Recipient citations for merit Soc. Illustrators, 1970-72, Award of Excellence, Communication Arts Mag., 1970, Silver medal Outside N.Y. Communicating Arts Show, 1971. Mem. Soc. Illustrators. Author, illustrator: Hector the Dog Who Loves Fleas, 1967; The Rhinoceros Who Loves Trees, 1967; Hector Has a Flea Circus, 1969; Bird Boy, 1970. Illustrator: The Incredible Thrilling Adventures of the Rock, 1968; Travels of Doctor Dolittle- Doctor Dolittle and the Pirates, 1968; Left and Right with Lion and Ryan, 1969; Gaston's Ghastly Green Thumb, 1969; The Hunter Tick and the Gumberoo, 1971; Why Can't I Be William, 1972. Home and office: 5039 Bedell Rd Roswell GA 30075

WENDLAND, ROBERT ERNEST, farm products mfg. co. exec.; b. Killeen, Tex., June 25, 1900; s. Herman and Mattie Iceley (Wells) W.; student U. Tex., 1918-21; m. NoraLee Mayhew, Aug. 6, 1924; children—Bobbye Lee (Mrs. Charles P. Godbey), Erroll. Grain mcht. Wendland's Farm Products, Inc., Killeen, 1922-28, Temple, Tex., 1928-36, owner, 1957—; owner Wendland Grain Co., Temple, 1936-57; owner Wendland's Farm Products, Inc., Temple, 1957—. Pres., Wendland Trust, Temple, 1949—. Served with U.S. Army, 1918. Mem. Tex. Grain Dealers Assn. (pres. 1934-35), Tex. Feed Mfrs. Assn. (pres. 1944-46), Grain and Feed Dealers Nat. Assn. (dir. 1960-64), Am. Feed Mfg. Assn. (dir. 1953-56, 60-63). Methodist (pres. bd. trustees 1954-74, mem. adminstrv. bd., pres. found. 1936-37). Rotarian. Home: Oakhurst on Midway Dr Temple TX 76501 Office: 405 S 2d St Temple TX 76501

WENTLAND, ROBERT BENEDICT, elec. engr.; b. Milw., May 12, 1924; s. Joseph John and Helen Rose (Warras) W.; B.S., U. Wis., 1949; m. Edith Inez Duncan, Aug. 4, 1962; children—Kathleen (Mrs. William Winstead), Kay; step-children—Lelan, Ralph, Bruce. Operating engr. Halliburton Industries, 1949-50; elec. engr. P.P.G. Industries, Corpus Christi, Tex., 1951-60; utilities engr. Internat. Minerals & Chem. Co., Carlsbad, N.M., 1960-69; sr. prodn. engr. Dow Chem. Co., Freeport, Tex., 1969—. Served to maj. USAAF, World War II. Registered profl. engr., Tex. Mem. I.E.E.E. (chmn. Freeport subsect. 1971-72), Indsl. Mgmt. Club Corpus Christi (past pres.). Home: 204 Carnation St Lake Jackson TX 77566 Office: PO Drawer K Bldg B 101 Freeport TX 77541

WENTWORTH, THEODORE THOMAS, JR., real estate broker, museum ofcl.; b. Mobile, Ala., July 26, 1898; s. Theodore Thomas and Elizabeth (Goodloe) W.; student pub. schs.; m. Rosabel Howington, Sept. 5, 1920; children—Thomas Warren, Aubrey Dean, Jane. Employed in real estate field, 1916—; real estate broker T.T. Wentworth, Jr., Realtor, 1945—; dir., curator T.T. Wentworth, Jr. Museum, Pensacola, 1957—. Mem. Fla. Library and Hist. Commn., 1963-65; charter mem. Pensacola Interstate Fair, 1935—, pres., 1965—. County commr. Escambia County, 1920-24, tax collector, 1928-41. Recipient Award of Merit, D.A.R., 1954, Realtor of Yr. award Pensacola Bd. Realtors, 1960, Liberty Bell award Freedoms Found., 1972, Kiwanian of Yr. award, others. Mem. Nat. Inst. Real Estate Brokers, Nat., Fla. assns. realtors, Pensacola Bd. Realtors (pres. 1960), Am. Assn. State and Local History, Greater Pensacola C. of C., Fla. (v.p.), Pensacola (charter and life mem., pres. 1936-47, pres. emeritus), Jacksonville, Ala., Walton County hist. socs., Hist. Assn. W. Fla., Hist. Assn. S. Fla., Fla. Civil War Centennial Commn., Fla. Sheriffs Assn. (hon.). Methodist (chmn. trustees 1934-58). Mason (32 deg., Shriner), Odd Fellow, Rebekah, Woodman of World, Lion. Home: 8380 Palafox Hwy Pensacola FL 32504 Office: 352-353 Brent Bldg Pensacola FL 32594

WENZE, IRA HARMON, physician; b. Brunswick, Ga., Dec. 10, 1932; s. Frank Smith and Ethel (Jurshial Ponder) W.; B.S., Morehouse Coll., 1954; M.S., U. Mich., 1958; M.D., Meharry Med. Coll., 1967; m. Alberta Brown, Oct. 9, 1961; children—Cornelia, Ira II, Don and Darnell (twins). Instr. biology Fla. A. and M. U., Tallahassee, 1958-63, acting chmn. dept., summer 1963; intern Menorah Med. Center, Kansas City, Mo., 1967-68, resident internal medicine, 1968-69; practice gen. medicine Fort Lauderdale, Fla., 1969—; mem. staff Broward Gen. Med. Center, Fort Lauderdale, Plantation Gen. Hosp., Fort Lauderdale; med. dir. Sweeting Nursing Home, Fort Lauderdale, 1971—, Broward County Sheriff's Dept., Fort Lauderdale, 1971; rheumatologist Broward County Arthritis Found. Served with M.C., AUS, 1954-56. Mem. A.M.A., Alpha Phi Alpha, Beta Kappa Chi. Democrat. Baptist. Home: PO Box 9523 Fort Lauderdale FL 33310 Office: 1433 NW 6th St Fort Lauderdale FL 33311

WERLEIN, PRESLEY EWING, JR., lawyer; b. San Jose, Cal., May 8, 1916; s. Presley Ewing and Sarah Louise (Richard) W.; student, La. State U., 1934-36; J.D., U. Tex., 1940; m. Marjorie Dee Sinclair, Apr. 4, 1943; children—Presley Ewing III, Patricia Louise. Admitted to Tex. bar, 1940, since practiced in Houston. Lectr. Houston Law Sch., 1940-42. Past mem. Tex. Grievance Com. from Dist. 8; past asso. govt. appeal agt. Tex. Draft Bd. 59. Chmn. Harris County Democratic Exec. Com., 1954-58. Trustee, treas. Mus. Med. Sci., 1971—. Served to lt. USNR, 1942-45; PTO. Mem. Houston Bar Assn. (past v.p., dir.), Lawyers Soc. Houston (past pres.), Army-Navy Assn. Houston (past pres. 1973—), Navy League U.S. (v.p. Houston council 1970), Am. Legion (past comdr.), S.A.R. (past chpt. pres.), Delta Kappa Epsilon. Methodist. Clubs: Kiwanis, West Lane Civic (past pres.), Torch of Houston (dir. 1964), Knife and Fork International (past chpt. pres. Houston). Home: 3221 Avalon Houston TX 77019 Office: Esperson Bldg Houston TX 77002

WERMEISTER, JOSEPH ROBERT, wholesale co. exec.; b. Louisville, Aug. 24, 1914; s. Nicholas Alexander and Nora (O'Leary) W.; student U. Louisville, 1936-42; LaSalle Extension U., 1938-46; m. Mary Frances Leatherman, Sept. 9, 1933; children—Joseph Robert, James Richard. Partner, Escott, Grogan & Co. C.P.A.'s, Louisville, 1946-58; mgr. Peat, Marwick, Mitchell & Co., Louisville, 1958-66; sec.-treas. Collins Co., Inc., Louisville, 1966—, also dir. Bd. dirs. Blue Cross Hosp. Plan Ky., St. Mary and Elizabeth Hosp., Louisville. C.P.A., Ky. Mem. Am. Inst. C.P.A.'s, Ky. Soc. C.P.A.'s, Ky. C. of C., Louisville Credit Mgmt. Assn. K.C. (4 deg.), Rotarian (dir.). Home: 1841 Overlook Terrace Louisville KY 40205 Office: PO Box 1977 Louisville KY 40201

WERNER, EDWIN HORNER, safety cons.; b. Staunton, Va., July 24, 1908; s. Phillip Henry and Daisy Rebecca (Horner) W.; B.S. in Elec. Engring., Va. Poly. Inst., 1931; m. Kathleen Rae Barbour, Dec. 26, 1935; 1 dau., Elaine (Mrs. Victor R. Parker). Elec. inspector Edison Gen. Electric Co., Waynesboro, Va., 1931-32; textile supt. E.I. duPont de Nemours & Co., Waynesboro, Va., 1933-40; textile supr. N & W Ry., 1945-61, elec. engr., Roanoke, Va., 1961-62, asst. to supt. motive power, 1963-70, asst. gen. mgr., 1970; safety cons. Sesco Mgmt. Cons., Bristol, Tenn., 1971—. Served to 1st lt. C.E., AUS, 1943-45. Registered profl. engr., Va. Mem. I.E.E.E., Am. Soc. Safety Engrs., Nat. Soc. Profl. Engrs., Va. Soc. Profl. Engrs. Republican. Methodist. Mason. Home: 536 Howard Dr Salem VA 24153 Office: 7th and Cherry Sts Bristol TN 37620

WERNER, HUGO CHARLES, SR., broom mfg. co. exec.; b. San Antonio, Aug. 9, 1910; s. Charles Hugo and Elizabeth (Meyer) W.; grad. high sch.; m. Helen Moore, June 30, 1932; children—Sharron Ann (Mrs. Lyndel L. Rippy), Hugo Charles. Owner Hugo C. Werner Co., Kerrville, Tex., 1945-62; pres., owner All-Tex. Enterprises, San Antonio, 1962-68; owner, gen. mgr. Avalon Industries, Eagle Pass, Tex., 1968—. Mem. Nat. Assn. Ind. Bus., Tex. Mfg. Assn., So. Tex., Eagle Pass (indsl. devel. award 1972) chambers commerce. Mason (32 deg., Shriner), Elk. Clubs: Ft. Duncan, Hill Country Shrine (pres. 1950-51), Maliki Shrine. Home: 2462 Edna St Eagle Pass TX 78852 Office: Box 1183 Eagle Pass TX 78852

WERNER, STANLEY PATRICK, dentist, educator; b. Memphis, Tenn., Sept. 19, 1938; s. Paul Ulrich and Lilla Ruth (Whitehead) W.; student Memphis State U., 1956-57, 59-62; D.D.S. (USPHS fellow), U. Tenn., 1965, M.S. in Orthodontics, 1968; m. Joy Humphries, May 5, 1962; children—Scott Patrick, Kelly Lynn. Instr. U. Tenn. Coll. Dentistry, 1965—; practice of dentistry, specializing in orthodontics, Memphis, 1968—. Served with AUS, 1957-59. Recipient award Internat. Coll. Dentists, 1965. Mem. Am., Memphis dental socs., Tenn. Dental Assn., Memphis Dental Legion, Memphis Soc. Dentistry for Children (sec. treas. 1971—, v.p. 1972) So., Tenn. socs. orthodontists, Am. Assn. Orthodontists, Delta Sigma Delta, Lambda Chi Alpha, Omicron Kappa Upsilon. Republican. Episcopalian. Home: 6227 Lochlevin Cove Memphis TN 38138 Office: 6209 Poplar St Memphis TN 38138

WERNICK, GERALD IRWIN, dentist; b. Watertown, N.Y., Feb. 13, 1934; s. Henry B. and Deborah F. (Fried) W.; grad. Emory U., 1955, D.D.S., 1959; postgrad. endodontics Boston U., 1961-62; m. Violet Konig, Aug. 19, 1956; children—Barbara, Sharon, Jeffrey. Endodontist, Miami Beach, Fla., 1962—; chmn. dept. endodontics Mt. Sinai Hosp., Miami Beach, 1963—. Co-chmn. endodontic sect. Dade County Dental Research Clinic, 1964—; cons. VA Hosp., Miami, 1970—. Chmn. dental div. Greater Miami Combined Jewish Appeal. Served to lt. USNR, 1959-61. Diplomate Am. Bd. Endodontists. Mem. Am. Dental Assn., Am. Assn. Endodontists (editor 1969-71), Fla. Bd. Dentistry (asst. sec.-treas. 1969—), Miami Beach Dental Soc. (pres. 1970-71), Fla. Soc. Endodontists (pres.

1969-74), Fla. Dental Assn., Fla. Acad. Practice Mgmt., N.Y. Acad. Sci., Boston U. Sch. Dentistry Endodontic Alumni Assn. (pres.-elect 1973-74), Alpha Omega (treas. Greater Miami chpt.), Alpha Epsilon Pi. Jewish religion (coordinating v.p. temple 1973). Mason (Shriner). Home: 9375 Balada St Coral Gables FL 33156 Office: 333 Arthur Godfrey Rd Miami Beach FL 33140

WESBROOKS, MARQUIS PERRY, JR., lawyer; b. Burkburnett, Tex., June 14, 1932; s. Marquis Perry and Willie Grace (Barrett) W.; student Midwestern U., 1949-51; B.B.A., U. Tex., 1956, LL.B., 1959, J.D., 1959; m. Shirley Louise Miller, July 10, 1955; children—Lynn Elaine, Mark Doss. Admitted to Tex. bar, 1959, since practiced in Wichita Falls; partner firm Schenk, Wesbrooks, Smith & Douglass, Wichita Falls, 1961—. Chmn. aviation adv. bd. City of Wichita Falls, 1971-73. Served with USN, 1951-55. Mem. State Bar Tex., Wichita County Bar Assn. (dir. 1971-72). Methodist. Home: PO Box 1685 Wichita Falls TX 76308 Office: Oil and Gas Bldg Wichita Falls TX 76301

WESOLOWSKI, ZDZISLAW PAWEL (OGONEZYK), coll. adminstr.; b. Gdynia, Poland, May 7, 1935; s. Stefan P. and Antonia (Kijanczuk) W.; A.A.S., S.I. Community Coll., 1963; B.S. in Bus. State U. N.Y., 1965; M.S., St. Louis U., 1968; m. Lucia Diana Chleva, Nov. 30, 1957; children—Stefan Pawel, Wanda Regina. Staff asst., budget and manpower analyst McDonnell Aircraft Corp., St. Louis, 1964-66; registrar, asst. dean instrn. State U. N.Y., Cobleskill, 1966-69; dir. devel. Alliance Coll., Cambridge Springs, Pa., 1969-71; univ. registrar, dir. admissions Duquesne U., Pitts., 1971-72. Cons. on application of data processing to ednl. adminstrn.; guest lectr. U. Warsaw, summer 1968. Served with USAF, 1954-61. Kosciuszko Found. scholar, 1964. Mem. Kosciuszko Found., Belles Lettres Soc., Polish Nat. Alliance. Contbr. articles to profl. jours. Home: 2211 Av B SW Winter Haven FL 33880

WESSON, HAROLD ROBINSON, cons. engr.; b. Spartanburg, S.C., May 8, 1924; s. William Tillman and Mabel Catherine (Robinson) W.; B.S., U. Tenn., 1950, M.S., 1953; D.Engring., U. Okla., 1970; m. Carolyn Smith, Mar. 25, 1950; children—Harold Robinson, Aubrey Lyle, Cliffie Jane, John Cedomir. Design engr. Union Carbide & Chem. Corp., 1950-52; instr. U. Tenn., 1953; engring. supr. and design specialist Gen. Dynamics, Ft. Worth, 1953-60; pres. Fire Control Engring. Co., Ft. Worth, 1960-68; v.p. Univ. Engrs., Inc., Norman, Okla., 1968-74; pres. Wesson & Assos., Inc., Norman, 1974—. Cons. engr.; instr. mech. engring. U. Tenn., 1952-53. Served with USAAF, 1942-46. Mem. Am. Soc. M.E., A.I.M. (pres.'s council 1964-68), Sigma Xi. Contbr. articles to tech. jours. Patentee in field. Home: 1215 Greenbriar Dr Norman OK 73069 Office: 510 S Webster St Norman OK 73069

WEST, AUBREY IVAN, oil well service co. exec.; b. Pitkin, La., Aug. 20, 1927; s. Lee and Susie (Sweet) W.; student U. Southwestern La., 1947-50; m. Christy Belle Langley, July 29, 1950; children—Christiann, Denise, Llona. Accountant and cost analyst Glaser Constrn. Co., Lafayette, La., 1950-51; with Sladco, Inc., Eunice, La., 1951—, pres., gen. mgr., chief exec. officer, 1970—; with Harris Well Service, Inc., Eunice, 1951—, pres., gen. mgr., chief exec. officer, 1970—. Bd. dirs. Acadiana Health Planning Council. Served with AUS, 1945-47. Mem. Nat. Assn. Oilwell Servicing Contractors (pres. 1973-74), Eunice Jr. C. of C. (pres. 1963-64), Am. Legion (dist. vice comdr. 1955-56). Democrat. Mason, Lion (pres. 1954-55). Home: 340 Great Slave Av Eunice LA 70535 Office: Drawer 949 Eunice LA 70535

WEST, CLAUDE OTIS, retail co. exec.; b. Minden, La., Aug. 26, 1927; s. Herman O. and Gladys (Tatum) W.; B.B.A., La. State U., 1949; postgrad. N.Y. U., 1953-54; m. Leatrice Mae David, Sept. 3, 1946; children—Sandra Lee (Mrs. James M. Jackson), Peggy Ann (Mrs. Charles Waters), Claudia Jane (Mrs. Stephen Lee). Asst. mgr. West Bros., Springhill, La., 1949-51, Bastrop, 1951-52, Stuttgart, Ark., 1952-53, Homer, La., 1953, buyer Gen. Office, DeRidder, La., 1953-56, buyer, v.p. West & Co. of La., Inc., Minden, 1956-65, pres., 1965—; pres. Gibson Products Co. of Camden, Inc., Camden, Ark., 1964—; pres. Gibson Products Co. of Greenwood, Inc., Greenwood, Miss., 1965—; pres. West's Gibson Products Co., Inc., Minden, 1966—; pres. Gibson's Shopping Center of Benton, Inc., Benton, Ark., 1968—; developer West Plaza Shopping Center, Minden, 1966. Dir., Peoples Bank, Minden. Mem. commn. Minden City Airport, 1969—. Sec., treas., West Found., 1957—. Pres. Bossier-Webster Fair and Forrest Festival, 1959; pres. Minden Edn. Found., 1966-67; v.p. Minden Parents League, 1969; mem. exec. bd. Norwela council Boy Scouts Am. Bd. dirs. Glenbrook Sch. Served with USNR, 1945-46. Mem. La. (dir. 1961), Minden (pres. 1960; chmn. long range planning com. 1968-71), U.S. chambers commerce, Am. Legion (post comdr. 1962; club pres. 1964), Lambda Chi Alpha. Baptist (deacon 1957—). Mason, Lion (dir. 1959). Clubs: Minden Tennis and Aquatic (dir. 1968-69), Minden Exchange, One Hundred, Louisi-anne Booster, Pine Hills Country (Minden); Metropolitan Dinner (Greater Shreveport, La.), Holiday In Dixie Ambassadors (Shreveport), Minden Ambassadors. Home: 1110 Madison Av Minden LA 71055 Office: PO Drawer G Minden LA 71055

WEST, DANIEL TONG, automobile dealership owner; b. Ashland, Ky., June 24, 1936; s. William Tong and Doris (Zimmerman) W.; student Centre Coll., Ky., 1953-54; B.S.C., U. Ky., 1960; postgrad. Peabody Coll., 1960, Hofstra Coll., 1967; m. Marilyn Black Striepe, Aug. 24, 1961; children—Laura Anderson, Lindsay Anne. Salesman, Procter & Gamble, Nashville, 1959-60, Northwestern Bell Telephone Co., Mpls., 1960-61; sales mgr. M.H. Graham Corp., Mpls., 1961-63; with Vollrath Co., various locations, 1963-67, Canadian sales mgr., Toronto, Ont., 1965-66, Eastern regional mgr., N.Y.C., 1966-67; v.p. Gen. Equipment & Mfg. Co., Louisville, 1967-71; v.p., dir. Animal Graphics, Inc., Lexington, Ky., 1969, Sta-Tite Mfg. Co., Lexington, Mo., 1969-71; chmn. bd., v.p., dir. Village Den, Inc., Louisville, 1969-73; pres., dir. W.P. Demaree Co., Inc., 1969-73; owner, pres. Shelby County Chrysler-Plymouth-Dodge, Inc., Shelbyville, Ky., 1974—, Dan West's Leasing Inc., Shelbyville, 1974—. Dist. commr. Old Ky. Home council Boy Scouts Am., Seneca dist., 1968-69, chmn. Seneca dist., 1969-71. Served with AUS, 1954-57. Recipient various Boy Scout awards; named Ambassador of Goodwill and Key Holder City Louisville, 1968; Ky. col., 1966. Mem. Petroleum Electric Supply Assn., Phi Delta Theta. Episcopalian. Mason (K.T., Shriner, 32 deg.). Optimist, Rotarian. Home: 1007 Evergreen Rd Anchorage KY 40223 Office: PO Box 284 Hwy 60 West Shelbyville KY 40065

WEST, ELMER GORDON, fed. judge; b. Hyde Park, Mass., Nov. 27, 1914; s. William Albert Howard and Edith Louise (Hall) W.; student Northeastern U., 1934-35, Lamar Jr. Coll., 1935-36; B.S., La. State U., 1941, LL.B., 1942; m. Viola Kay Cayard, Oct. 30, 1942; children—Roger Gordon, Dan Edward. Accountant, Stone & Webster, 1937-42; admitted to La. bar, 1942; mem. firm Long & West, Baton Rouge, 1946-50, Kantrow, Spaht, West & Kleinpeter, and predecessor, Baton Rouge, 1950-61; U.S. dist. judge Eastern Dist. Ct. La., 1961-68, chief judge, 1968-72; U.S. dist. judge Middle Dist. La., 1972—. Atty., La. Revenue Dept., 1946-48, La. inheritance tax collector, 1948-52; asst. prof., spl. lectr. La. State U. Law Sch., 1947-48; mem. Jud. Conf. U.S., 1971-74, mem. com. on operation of jury system, 1972—. Served to lt. USNR, 1942-45. Mem. Am., La., East Baton Rouge bar assns., Am. Judicature Soc., Internat. Assn. Ins. Counsel, Nat. Assn. Compensation Claimants Attys., Alpha Tau Omega, Phi Delta Phi. Episcopalian. Mason. Home: 2629 Lakeshore Dr Baton Rouge LA 70808 Office: Fed Ct Bldg Baton Rouge LA 70801

WEST, EMERY JOSEPH, stockbroker; b. Kingston, Pa., Nov. 24, 1940; s. David Dimon and Elizabeth Irene (Emery) W.; grad. Mercersburg Acad., 1959; student USAF Acad., 1959-62, Northwestern U., 1964; m. Darla Jaton Payne (div.); 1 son, Emery Joseph II. With Tech. Stock Review, Harrisburg, Pa., 1962-63, Grant, Jones & Co., Inc., 1963-64; sr. account exec. W.E. Hutton & Co., Washington, 1964—. Mem. exec. com. D.C. Rep. Com.; mem. D.C. Young Reps. Mem. Assn. Investment Brokers, Bond Club Washington, Financial Analysts Fedn., Nat. Economists Club, Washington Soc. Investment Analysts. Club: Capitol Hill (Washington). Home: 3025 Dumbarton Av NW Washington DC 20007 Office: 1815 H St NW Washington DC 20006

WEST, FRANCIS THORNTON, window and door mfg. co. exec.; b. Salem, Va., Feb. 6, 1920; s. Thomas Fendol and Bentley (Wysor) W.; student Roanoke Coll., 1937-38; m. Nina Penn Moir, Oct. 5, 1940 (div.); children—Suzanne (Mrs. Louis L. Guy, Jr.), Nina (Mrs. James M. Guy), Francis Thornton, Bentley Wysor; m. 2d, Eleanor Eastwick Seeley, May 1, 1970. Sales rep. for several cos., 1938-49; owner West Window Corp., 1949-65; pres. West Window Corp., 1965—; pres. Franklin Finance Co., Inc., Rocky Mount, Va.; dir. 1st Nat. Bank Martinsville & Henry County, Martinsville Cablevision, Inc. Lay del. Diocese Southwestern Va. to Anglican Congress; lay dep. Epis. Gen. Conv.; mem. Diocesan Exec. Bd. Mem. Martinsville City Council, 1966—; vice mayor, Martinsville 1968-72, mayor, 1972—; chmn. adv. com. Patrick-Henry Coll. of U. Va., 1962-71. Mem. C. of C. (pres. 1961-62). Episcopalian. Home: 1012 River Forest Pl Martinsville VA 24112 Office: Drawer 3071 Industrial Park Martinsville VA 24112

WEST, JAMES EDWIN, lawyer; b. Greenwood Junction, Okla., May 9, 1928; s. Dudley G. and Dollye (Quinn) W.; J.S.D., U. Ark., 1952; m. Doris Ann Stevenson, July 24, 1950; children—Carolyn Sue (Mrs. James Richard Wagner), Janice Evonne. Admitted to Ark. bar, 1952; since practiced in Ft. Smith; law clk. U.S. Dist. Judge, 1952-58; asso. Daily & Woods, 1958-61, partner, 1961-70; partner Daily, West, Core & Coffman, 1970—. Chmn. Sebastian County March of Dimes, 1963; chmn. Girls Club Summer Camp Program, 1965. Served with USMCR, 1946-47. Mem. Am., Ark. (pres. 1973-74), Sebastian County (pres. 1961) bar assns., Ark. Bar Found. (pres. 1968), Conf. Local Bar Assns. (pres. 1964-65). Baptist. Club: Fort Smith Toastmasters (pres. 1966). Vice pres. Ark. Law Rev., 1969—. Home: 3201 S Dallas Fort Smith AR 72901 Office: Merchants Bank Bldg Fort Smith AR 72901

WEST, JAMES LEROY, business exec.; b. Gravity, Ia., May 28, 1903; s. Edgar and Anna (Heatherington) W.; student Grinnell Coll., 1919-22, St. Louis U. Sch. Commerce, 1925-26; m. Eunice Pearl East, Jan. 6, 1937. Salesman, Seiberling Rubber Co., Ft. Worth, also Abilene, Tex., 1927-30; mgr. Hinckley-Tandy Leather Co., Houston, 1930-41, partner, 1941-50; dir. Tandy Leather Co., Ft. Worth, 1951-55, v.p., 1955-57, pres., 1957-74; pres., dir. Tandy Corp., Wilmington, Del., 1964-74, vice chmn. bd., 1974—; dir. Continental Nat. Bank. Mem. Ft. Worth Sales Mgrs. Club, Tex. Mfrs. Assn. (State pres. 1968), Newcomen Soc. (honoree 1968). Presbyn. Mason. Home: 6371 Lansdale St Fort Worth TX 76116 Office: 2727 W 7th St Fort Worth TX 76107

WEST, JOHN CARL, gov. S.C.; b. Camden, S.C., Aug. 27, 1922; s. Shelton J. and Mattie (Ratterree) W.; LL.B. magna cum laude, U. S.C., 1948; m. Lois Rhame, Aug. 29, 1942; children—John Carl, Douglas Allen, Shelton Anne. Admitted to S.C. bar, 1948; former atty. firm West Holland, Furman and Cooper, Camden; mem. S.C. Hwy. Commn., 1948-52, vice chmn., 1952; mem. S.C. Senate, 1954-62; lt. gov. S.C., 1967-70, gov., 1970—. Vice-chmn. So. Gov.'s Conf., 1971-72. Chmn., United Cerebral Palsy Dr., S.C., 1964. Trustee Coker Coll. Served with AUS, 1942-46. Mem. Am. Legion, C. of C., Phi Beta Kappa. Presbyn. (deacon, elder). Kiwanian. Office: State House Columbia SC 29201

WEST, JOHN EDWARD, dentist; b. Memphis, Dec. 3, 1921; s. James Leonard and Mary Louise (Ragland) W.; student Ga. Inst. Tech., 1939-40; student Memphis State U., 1939-40; D.D.S., U. Tenn., 1947; m. Josephine Idelia Sullivan, Aug. 26, 1944; 1 dau., Jo Ann (Mrs. Jay Barry Goldman). Pvt. practice dentistry, Memphis, 1947-51; staff dentist VA, Nashville, 1951-56, resident prosthodontics, Memphis, 1956-58, staff prosthodentist, Johnson City, Tenn., 1958-67; chief dental service VA, Beckley, W.Va., 1967-71, VA Center, Johnson City, 1971—. Asst. dist. commr. Boy Scouts Am. Served with AUS, 1942-44. Mem. Am. Dental Assn., Am. Prosthodontics Soc., S.E. Acad. Prosthodontics, Delta Sigma Delta. Presbyn. (deacon). Kiwanian. Address: VA Center Johnson City TN 37684

WEST, OTTIS ANCIL COVINGTON, lawyer; b. Leesville, Tex., Jan. 27, 1911; s. Ancil and Agnes Beatrice (Callaway) W.; LL.B., San Antonio Pub. Sch. Law, 1933; m. Mary Marie Holstein, July 14, 1972. Admitted to Tex. bar, 1934; since practiced in San Antonio; mem. firm West & West, 1934—; magistrate, justice of peace Bexar County (Tex.), 1937-43. Dir. Harlandale State Bank, San Antonio, 1968—. Mem. San Antonio City Council. Served with USNR, 1944-45. Mem. San Antonio Real Estate Bd., Tex. Trial Lawyers Assn., State Bar Tex., Am., San Antonio bar assos., Nat. Home Builders Assn. Mason (Shriner). Home: 805 E Formosa St San Antonio TX 78221 Office: 206 San Pedro Av San Antonio TX 78205

WEST, RHEA HORACE, JR., educator; b. Loudon, Tenn., Oct. 5, 1920; s. Rhea Horace and Verna (Quillen) W.; B.S. in Accounting, U. Tenn., 1947; postgrad. (Sloan fellow, Mass. Inst. Tech. fellow), Mass. Inst. Tech., 1959-60, 63, Case Inst. Tech., summer 1960; Ph.D., U. Ala., 1964. Asso. prof. mgmt. Wake Forest Coll., 1950-51; budget and reports analyst AEC, Oak Ridge, 1951-55; teaching fellow U. Ala., Tuscaloosa, 1956-57; asst. prof. mgmt. U. Ark., Fayetteville, 1957-59; Sloan teaching intern Mass. Inst. Tech., Cambridge, 1959-60; asso. prof. econs. Carson-Newman Coll., Jefferson City, Tenn., 1960-65; prof. mgmt. Ga. State Coll., 1965-70; prof. mgmt., dir. grad. studies Auburn (Ala.) U., 1970—; mgmt. cons.; cons. Cape Kennedy and Huntsville (NASA), Lockheed Aircraft Co., U.S. Civil Service Commn., others. Active Center for Study Democratic Instns., Atlanta High Mus. Art. Served with AUS, 1943-46. Mem. Am. Accounting Assn., Am. Mgmt. Assn., Am. Soc. Personnel Adminstrn. (nat. dir. industry edn. com. 1958-60), Inst. Mgmt. Scis., Soc. Advancement Mgmt., Acad. Mgmt., Soc. Sloan Fellows, Opelika Arts Assn., Acad. Polit. Sci., Am. Acad. Polit. and Social Scis., Am. Assn. U. Profs., Am. Legion, Opelika C. of C., Am. Ordnance Assn., Smithsonian Assos., Am. Acad. Arts and Scis., A.A.A.S., Am. Inst. Aeros. and Astronautics, Am. Inst. Decision Scis., N.Y. Acad. Sics., Internat. Platform Assn., UN Assn. U.S., Newcomen Soc. N.Am., Sigma Iota Epsilon, Alpha Kappa Psi (dist. dir. 1965—), Alpha Phi Omega, Kappa Phi Kappa (pres. 1969-70). Baptist. Kiwanian (pres. 1965). Clubs: Mass. Institute Technology, Harvard Faculty. Book rev. editor Personnel Adminstr., 1960—. Contbr. numerous articles and book revs. to profl. publs. Home: 4819 Skyline Dr Knoxville TN 37914 Office: 212 Thach Hall Auburn U Auburn AL 36830

WEST, ROBERT BURNS, farmer, trucking co. propr.; b. Machipongo, Va., Sept. 27, 1928; s. Harry Clifton and Mary Anne (Downing) W.; student Hampden-Sydney Coll., 1945-46; m. Charlotte Lee Nottingham, Nov. 12, 1945; children—Norwood James, Ronald Nottingham. With H.C. West & Sons, Birds Nest, Va., 1946—, partner, 1948—. Mem. agrl. stblzn. and conservation com. U.S. Dept. Agr., 1970-72. Active Boy Scouts Am., 1956-60. Bd. dirs. A.R.C. Mem. Northampton County Jr. C. of C. (hon.), Eastern Shore C. of C. (dir. 1968-72). Baptist (deacon, 1973—, dir. Sunday sch. 1971—). Club: Red Bank Men's (charter, treas. Marionville, Va.). Address: Birds Nest VA 23307

WEST, STUART JAY, clergyman; b. Grand Island, Neb., Sept. 6, 1938; s. Julian Ralph and Marvel Elaine (Knorr) W.; B.A., Puget Sound Coll. of Bible, Seattle, 1961; B.A., North Park Coll., 1967; M.R.E., No. Baptist Theol. Sem., Chgo., 1969; m. Donna Rae Metzger, Aug. 12, 1969; 1 dau., Rebecca Eilene. Youth minister Normandy Christian Ch., Seattle, 1958-61; minister of youth 1st Christian Ch., Chgo., 1961-69; minister of edn. Nat. City Christian Ch., Washington, 1969—. Mem. Mayor's Prayer Breakfast Com., 1973; mem. 12th St Action Center Com., 1971. Mem. Capital Area Ministerial Assn., Assn. Christian Ch. Educators, Religious Edn. Assn. Home: 5900 N 19th St Arlington VA 22205 Office: National City Christian Church 14th and Thomas Circle NW Washington DC 20005

WEST, THOMAS MOORE, indsl. engr., educator; b. Weston, W.Va., Nov. 10, 1940; s. Stanley Rymer and Dorothy Eloise (Moore) W.; B.S. in Indsl. Engring., U. Tenn., 1963, M.S., 1965; postgrad. (NSF fellow) Ore. State U.; m. Carmen Wessner, Aug. 31, 1967. Operations research analyst Chemstrand Co., Greenville, S.C., 1964-66; instr. engring. Ga. Inst. Tech., Atlanta, 1966-67; asst. prof. engring. U. Tenn., Nashville, 1967—, coordinator indsl. engring., 1969—. Cons. IBM, Burlington, Vt., 1967—, ednl. cons. to U.S. Civil Service Commn. Registered profl. engr., Ore., Tenn. NASA engring. faculty research fellow, 1970. Mem. Am. Inst. Aeros. and Astronautics, Am. Soc. Engring. Edn., Operations Research Soc. Am. Contbr. articles on systems simulation and information systems tech. to tech. jours. Home: 205 E Tennessee Av Oak Ridge TN 37830 Office: 323 McLemore St Nashville TN 37203

WEST, WALTER PRESTON, coll. adminstr.; b. Hopkinsville, Ky., Sept. 16, 1916; s. Robert Cary and Clyde (Carroll) W.; B.A., Maryville Coll., 1938; M.A., George Peabody Coll. for Tchrs., 1948; postgrad. Fla. State U., 1949-50; m. Rowena Sims Grimes, July 2, 1961; stepchildren—Linda Jeanne Grimes, Janet Ellen Grimes. Tchr.-coach Russellville (Ky.) schs., 1938-42; high sch. prin. Russellville, 1946-48, Beattyville, Ky., 1948-49; supr. instrn. schs., Calhoun County, Fla., 1949-50; dir. news service, asst. prof. edn. Florence (Ala.) State Coll., 1950-53; bus. mgr. Highland Park Presbyn. Ch., Dallas, 1953-55; dir. Evening Sch., dir. admissions, asso. prof. edn. Trinity U., San Antonio, 1955—, asst. dean., 1970—; ednl. cons. Caffarelli Ednl. Trust. Served from ensign to lt USNR, 1943-46. Mem. Assn. Coll. Admission Counselors, Pi Gamma Mu, Pi Kappa Delta. Presbyn. (elder). Home: 3602 LaSabre Dr San Antonio TX 78218

WEST, WILLIAM GARRETT, clergyman, educator; b. nr. Princess Anne, Md., Mar. 25, 1913; s. John William and Lenier R. (Garrett) W.; B.A., Lynchburg Coll., 1937; B.D., Yale, 1940, Min. of Div., 1944, S.T.M., 1947, Ph.D., 1949; m. Doris Ewers, June 13, 1938; children—Robert G., Laurie (Mrs. W. Benjamin Johnston). Ordained to ministry Christian Ch., 1937; minister Melrose Av. Christian Ch., Roanoke, Va., 1935-37, Weldermere Beach Community Ch., Melford, Conn., 1937-46, Old Stone Ch., East Haven, Conn., 1940-48, First Christian Ch., Chattanooga, 1948—; faculty Vanderbilt U. Sch. Religion, Pub. Speaking and Homiletics, 1948-53, U. Chattanooga, 1966-68, U. Tenn. at Chattanooga, 1968—. Civilian chaplain 429 Air Base, New Haven, 1942-45; chaplain Chattanooga Scottish Rite Soc. and Alhambra Shrine, 1953; chaplain Chattanooga Police Assn., 1950-58; religious news reporter radio sta. WDEE, 1950—. Gen, chmn. Chattanooga Roundtable Nat. Conf. Christians and Jews, 1954-55; mem. panel of scholars Disciples of Christ or Christian Chs., 1956-62; del. Chs. of Christ in Gt. Britain, 1957, 3d Assembly World Council Chs., New Delhi, 1961. Gen. chmn. Chattanooga Mayor's Com. on UN Day, 1951-52; mem. Council of Community Forges, 1954-60; v.p. Chattanooga Psychiat. Clinic. Bd. dirs. Chattanooga Pub. Library, Disciples Found. at Vanderbilt, Chattanooga Area Found. for Research, Tng., Treatment and Teaching in Mental Health Disciplines, Inc. Mem. Tenn. Assn. Christian Chs. (past pres.), Tenn. Tennis Assn. (past pres.), So. Lawn Tennis Assn. (past mem. exec. com.). Kiwanian. Home: 203 Hillcrest St Chattanooga TN 37411

WESTALL, WILLIAM GLADSTONE, civil engr.; b. Celo, N.C., July 14, 1904; s. Theodore and Hattie Ellen (Autrey) W.; student Wake Forest Coll., 1923-25; C.E., George Washington U., 1934; m. Bethea C. Yeck, Nov. 3, 1932; 1 son, William Grant. Commd. 2d lt. C.E., U.S. Army, 1926, advanced through grades to lt. col. U.S. Air Force, 1951; ret., 1955; asst. mgr. paving bur. Portland Cement Assn., 1955-66; quality control engr. H.B. Zachry, San Antonio, 1967-68; cons. engr., Largo, Fla., 1968—. Decorated Army Commendation medal. Fellow Am. Soc. C.E. Contbr. articles profl. jours.; sect. to McGraw-Hill Handbook of Heavy Construction (Hobbs and Havers), 1971. Home and office: 1700 S Indian Rocks Rd Largo FL 33540

WESTBERRY, ELVIS CLINTON, civil engr.; b. Estelle, S.C., May 29, 1914; s. Clinton and Ethel (Parker) W.; student Internat. Corr. Schs., 1939-43; extension courses U. Fla., 1943, various seminars; m. Margaret Houck, Dec. 12, 1939 (div. Feb. 1945); 1 dau., Melinda (Mrs. Melinda Westberry Warren); m. 2d, Mary Deonacea Safritis, Apr. 12, 1947 (div. Mar. 1966); children—Laurence Elvis, Bianca (Mrs. Douglas Castleberry), Eugenia (Mrs. Robert Ziegler), Candace Marie, Sibyl Ann; m. 3d, Erna Bernice Morris, Apr. 8, 1967 (div. July 1973). Apprentice carpenter Local 627, Jacksonville, Fla., 1933-38; archtl. draftsman Kapalow Engring. Co., Inc., Memphis, 1935-42; apprentice shipfitter, draftsman St. Johns River Shipbuilding Co., 1942-43, liaison coordinator, naval architect's dept., 1943-45; individual practice small home designing, Mandarin, Fla., 1945-50; draftsman, designer Thomas N. Evans, Jr., Jacksonville, 1949-58, George O. Holmes, Jacksonville, 1951-52; sr. draftsman, engring. dept. Nat. Container Corp., Jacksonville, 1952-58; structural designer Evans & Hammond, Inc., Jacksonville, 1958-65; with Dow Chem. Co., Titusville, Fla., 1965-70, engring. technician, 1967, engr., 1967-70; with Pan Am. Airways, Kennedy Space Center, Fla., 1970-74; engr. Planning Research Corp., Kennedy Space Center, 1974—. Registered profl. engr., Fla. Home: 88 Skylark Av Merritt Island FL 32952 Office: Planning Research Corp Kennedy Space Center FL 32899

WESTBROOK, JAMES AUGUSTUS, san. engr.; b. Rocky Mount, N.C., Sept. 19, 1914; s. John Hardy and Ella Blount (Boney) W.; B.S., U. N.C., 1936; M.S., Harvard, 1937; m. Frances Curry Westbrook, Jan. 27, 1944. San. engr. N.C. Bd. Health, Raleigh, 1937-50; with USPHS, various locations, 1950-73, san. engr., Denver, 1964-66, Atlanta, 1966-73; with Robert & Co., Atlanta, 1973—. Instr. Sch. Pub.

Health, U. N.C., Chapel Hill, 1937-50. Diplomate Am. Acad. Environmental Engrs., Fellow Am. Soc. C.E. Methodist. Club: Farmington Country (Charlottesville, Va.). Home: 989 Winding Creek Trail NW Atlanta GA 30328 Office: 96 Poplar St Atlanta GA 30303

WESTBROOK, WILLIAM JERRY, judge; b. Trion, Ga., June 22, 1938; s. Wilmer Carlyle and Dorothy Madalyn (Colbert) W.; student Furman U., 1958; LL.B., J.D., Woodrow Wilson Coll. Law, 1961; m. Judy Gail Woodall, Apr. 29, 1967; children—William J. II, John Parks. Clk., Gulf Oil Corp., 1959-61; admitted to Ga. bar, 1961, U.S. Supreme Ct., 1971; individual practice law, Summerville, Ga., 1964—; judge State Ct., Chattooga County, Ga., 1966-70, 71—, referee Juvenile Ct., 1973—. Sec., Ray's, Inc., Trenton, Ga., 1967—. Served with AUS, 1961-63. Mem. Ga. Bar Assn. (bd. govs. 1968-70, 71-73), Chattooga County Jr. C. of C. Mason. Office: Box 427 Summerville GA 30747

WESTER, JOHN GAY, elec. engr.; b. Mineral Wells, Tex., Aug. 27, 1935; s. S. Gay and Juanita (Johns) W.; B.S., U. Tex., 1960; m. Dianne Williams, May 7, 1971; 1 dau., Regina Gay; children by previous marriage—Linda, Gerald, Julie, Patrick, Glenn James. Engr., Westinghouse Electric Co., Balt., 1960-63; program mgr. airborne infrared mapper and tactical information processing and interpretation system Tex. Instruments, Dallas, also Austin, Tex., 1963-73, program mgr., advanced tech. programs TI Learning Center, 1974—; pres. Tex. Exptl. Engring., 1973—. Served with USCGR, 1953-57. Registered profl. engr., Tex. Mem. Nat., Tex. socs. profl. engrs. Patentee film devel. by laser. Home: 2409 Timbercreek Dr Plano TX 75074 Office: PO Box 5012 Dallas TX 75222

WESTERBURG, LOUIS RICHARD, data processing exec.; b. Foules, La., Oct. 31, 1915; s. William Benjamin and Minnie Mae (Martin) W.; B.S. in Elec. Engring., La. Tech. U., 1956; diploma Air War Coll., 1973; m. Bessie Irene Noble, Nov. 7, 1951; children—Dorothy Rose, Louis Richard. Computer systems design engr. RCA missile test project Air Force Eastern Test Range, Patrick AFB, Fla., 1956-65, project mgr. hdqrs., elec. engr. systems design/implementation, 1965-72, chief data automation div., 1972—. Scout master Boy Scouts Am., Winnsboro, La., 1936-38; cub master Cub Scouts, Melbourne, Fla., 1965-67. County commr., Franklin Parish (La.), 1948-52. Bd. mgrs. YMCA, Brevard County (Fla.), 1964-73; mem. La. Tech. U. Engring. Found., Ruston. Served with USAAF, 1942-45. Decorated D.F.C., Air medal with 4 oak leaf clusters. Registered profl. engr., La. Mem. I.E.E.E., Missile Space and Range Pioneers, Inc., V.F.W. (comdr. post 1931-55). Lion. Home: 106 Av C SW Melbourne FL 32901 Office: Hdqrs Air Force Eastern Test Range Comptroller Office Data Automation Div/ACD Patrick AFB FL 32925

WESTERHOUSE, ROBERT ALLEN, holding co. exec.; b. Eudora, Kan., Feb. 13, 1935; s. Allen H. and Elfrieda Elizabeth (Schlegle) W.; B.S. in E.E., U. Kan., 1962. Tech. rep. Gen. Electric Co., Europe, 1962-65; systems analyst Philco-Ford, 1965-66; regional applications mgr. Sci. Data Systems, 1966-67; v.p. operations Com-Share So., Inc., 1967, v.p. marketing, 1967-68, exec. v.p., 1968-69; pres. Computer Complex, Inc., Houston, 1969-70, chmn. bd., pres., 1970—, also dir. Served with USAF, 1953-57. Mem. I.E.E.E., Assn. Data Processing Service Orgns., Assn. Computing Machinery. Clubs: Houston, The Houston. Home: 819 Edgewick Ct Sugarland TX 77478 Office: 1460 One Allen Center Houston TX 77002

WESTERMAN, HERMAN WILLIAM, chem. co. exec.; b. Bellville, Tex., Jan. 10, 1917; s. Herman and Lula (Viereck) W.; student Draughon's Bus. Coll., 1935-36;; m. Helen Frances Jircik, July 1, 1938; children—Barbara (Mrs. Glenn Shirley Richards), Eric Lane. With Swift & Co., Houston, 1936, Acme Fast Freight, Houston, 1936-41; with Dow Chem. Co., Freeport, Tex., 1941—, So. region traffic mgr., 1965—; exec. v.p., dir. Quintana Enterprises, Inc., Freeport, 1968—; pres., dir. Growman Corp., Lake Jackson, Tex., 1971—; partner Eagle Devel. Co., Lake Jackson, 1971—. Traffic cons. Brazos Harbor Nav. Dist., Freeport, 1952-64. Mem. Am. Soc. Traffic and Transp., S.W. Shippers Adv. Bd. (chmn. chems. and explosives com. 1956—), Tex. Indsl. Traffic League. Club: Houston Traffic. Home: 210 Oak Dr PO Box 576 Lake Jackson TX 77566 Office: Drawer K Freeport TX 77541

WESTFALL, VERNON DALE, aircraft co. exec.; b. Troy, O., Mar. 24, 1920; s. John and Edith Mary (Poorman) W.; Aero. Engr., West Coast U., 1941; m. Barbara Mary Rose, Mar. 3, 1951; 1 son. Michael Todd. Test pilot Hartzell Propeller Co., 1944-47; airline pilot Trans World Airlines, 1947-50; engring. flight test agt. CAA, 1951-53; flight test engr. Northrop Aircraft, 1954-55; chief flight test Cessna Aircraft, 1956-57; v.p. operations Airline Tng., Inc., 1958; dir. sales Lockheed Ga. Co., Marietta, 1959—; pres. Flight Engring. Labs., 1954—; dir. Cargo Masters Inc. Block chmn. Atlanta Republican Com. 1964. Mem. Am. Inst. Aeros. and Astronautics, Instrumentation Soc. Am., Soc. Automotive Engrs. Lutheran (elder 1953-68). Home: 420 N Harbor Dr Atlanta GA 30328 Office: 86 S Cobb Dr Marietta GA 30060

WESTLING, RALPH FORD, purchasing agt.; b. Taylor, Tex., Jan, 6, 1927; s. Frank Albert and Nell Ann Ray (Ford) W.; B.A., U. Tex., 1951, postgrad., 1952; m. Georgia Rose Bailey, Jan. 21, 1956; 1 son, Mark Ford. Office staff Graybar Elec. Co., Inc., San Antonio, 1952-56; purchasing foreman Ed Friedrich, Inc., San Antonio, 1956-61; office mgr. Todd-Ford, Inc., San Antonio, 1962-65; purchasing agt. Steck-Warlick, Austin, Tex., 1966-73, Hart Graphics, Austin, 1974—. Served with AUS, 1944-47. Mem. Purchasing Mgmt. Assn. Austin (pres. 1971), Austin C. of C., Lambda Chi Alpha. Club: Longhorn (Austin). Home: 2710 Pinewood Terrace Austin TX 78757 Office: 8000 Shoalcreek Blvd Austin TX 78767

WESTMORELAND, JAMES CLAUD, bldg. materials and trucking co. exec.; b. Stephens, Ark., July 5, 1926; s. Claudie William and Alta Ruth (Butcher) W.; student La. State U., 1943-44, U. Ark., 1946-47; Accountant, Vets. Vocational Sch., 1949; m. Alys Jo Pagan, Nov. 17, 1946; children—Frances (Mrs. Richard R. Portis), James William. Corporate controller Arkoma Oil Co., Magnolia, Ark., 1950-61; gen. mgr., sec.-treas. Tommy Reynolds Lumber Co., Hamburg, Ark., 1961-67; gen. mgr., asst. sec.-treas. Reynolds Wilson Lumber Co., Corrigan, Tex., 1967-69; gen. mgr. Ga. Pacific Corp., Corrigan, 1969-73; asst. to v.p. La. Pacific Corp., Carthage, Tex., 1973—; gen. mgr. So. div. La. Pacific Trucking Co. Served to lt. col. USAAF, 1944-45. Mem. Tex. Forestry Assn. (dir.), Polk County C. of C., Tex. Mfg. Assn. Republican. Methodist. Mason, Rotarian (v.p. 1966), Lion (pres. 1948-50), Kiwanian (Carthage). Home: 66 Gunston Ct Conroe TX 77301 Office: PO Box 2170 Conroe TX 77301

WESTMORELAND, JOHN SHERRILL, JR., architect; b. Houston, Sept. 4, 1944; s. John Sherrill and Nancy Bernalice (Peake) W.; B.Arch., Tex. A. and M. U., 1967, M.Arch., 1968; m. Janice Leora Johnson, July 23, 1966; 1 dau., Jayna Alice. Programmer The Architects Collaborative, Boston, 1967; archtl. cons. Nat. Insts. Mental Health, Washington, 1968-70; dir. programming Internat. Bldg. Systems, Dallas, 1970-71; dir. archtl. research and planning Presbyn. Hosp., Dallas, 1972; individual practice architecture, Dallas, 1971—; cons. Gerontol. Soc., others. Speaker Tex. Gov.'s Commn. Aging. USPHS fellow, 1967-68. Registered architect, Tex. Mem. A.I.A. (nat. com. architecture for health 1970-71), Nat. Council Archtl. Registration Bds. Mem. Ch. of Nazarene (dir. 1972). Contbr. articles and plans to profl. jours. Home: 2914 Gladiolus Lane Dallas TX 75233 Office: 8210 Walnut Hill Lane Dallas TX 75231

WESTROPE, MARTHA R., psychologist; b. Gaffney, S.C., May 19, 1922; d. Gordon Robert and Hannah (Brown) Westrope; B.S., Winthrop Coll., 1942; M.A., U. N.C., 1944; Ph.D., State U. Ia., 1952; 1 adopted son, Ashley. Psychologist U. Hosps., Iowa City, 1947; clin. psychologist Spartanburg (S.C.) Mental Hygiene Clinic, 1949, 50; chief psychologist S.C. Mental Health Div., Mental Health Commn., 1952-53; chief clin. psychologist Richland County Mental Health Clinic, Columbia, S.C., 1953-55; research psychologist Psychiat. Inst., U. Md., 1955; head psychology sect., psychiatry Med. Sch., U. Miami, 1956-57; chief psychologist Greenville Mental Health Clinic, S.C. Mental Health Commn., 1957-60; individual practice, 1960—; cons. psychologist Clemson (S.C.) Agr. Coll.; vis. lectr. Furman U., 1958-57; instr. Greenville Tech. Edn. Center, 1968; cons. research psychologist, evaluation projects Greenville Community Council, 1957-60, Juvenile Ct., 1957-60; cons. Roger C. Peace Hosp., 1973—. S.C. rep. on So. Regional Edn. Bd. original steering com. on psychol. resources in the South 1953; mem. Greenville Assn. for Retarded Children, 1968; cons. Spartanburg Mental Health Clinic, 1971-73, Greenville Mental Health Clinic, 1973—. Mem. Am., S.C. (rep. to nat. orgn. 1953-54) psychol. assns., Greenville Mental Health Assn., A.A.A.S., Sigma Xi. Home: Route 2 Darien Way Greenville SC 29607 Office: 101 Chapman St Greenville SC 29605

WETHERILL, MELVIN HOWARD, lawyer; b. Lake Charles, La., Oct, 28, 1908; s. John Nathaniel and Katherine (Green) W.; J.D., Tulane U., 1932; m. Claire Winona Chafin, Apr. 12, 1932. Admitted to La. bar, 1933; practiced in Lake Charles, 1933—; municipal atty., Vinton, La., 1933-59; asst. dist. counsel Home Owners Loan Corp., 1935-36; asst. dist. atty. 14th Judicial Dist. La;, 1936, 48-53; atty. for tax collector Calcasieu Parish, La., 1940-41, 42-43, 46-48; spl. asst. to atty. gen. La., 1941; mem. firm Jones, Kimball, Patin, Harper, Tete & Wetherill and predecessor firm, 1953—. Served with AUS, 1943-45; PTO. Mem. Am., La., S.W. La. bar assns., Sigma Alpha Epsilon. Democrat. Methodist. Lion. Home: 613 W McNeese St Lake Charles LA 70601 Office: Gulf Nat Bank Bldg Lake Charles LA 70601

WETHERINGTON, THOMAS IRA, JR., utilities exec.; b. Thonotosassa, Fla., Nov. 6, 1925; s. Thomas Ira and Anne Mae (Milling) W.; student U. Tampa, 1946-49; B.E.E., U. Fla., 1952; m. Adelaide Ann Dingey, Nov. 16, 1946; children—Ellen, Wanda. With Fla. Power Corp., St. Petersburg, 1952—, mgr. sales engring. and research, 1970-71, mgr. application engring. and research, 1971-73, mgr. energy conservation research, 1973—. Mem. adv. com. U. Fla. Air Conditioning Conf. Mem. Mech. Examining Bd., City of St Petersburg. Served with U.S. Mcht. Marines, 1943-46. Mem. Am. Soc. Heating, Refrigeration and Air Conditioning Engrs. (Chmn. tech. com. on service water heating), Nat. Soc. Profl. Engrs., I.E.E.E., Fla. Engring. Soc., St. Petersburg Jr. C. of C. (state dir. 1957-60). Office: 3201 34th St S St Petersburg FL 33733

WETHERINGTON, TOM L., import-export co. exec.; b. Savannah, Ga., Sept. 30, 1926; s. Toy Lee and Edna (Kennedy) W.; B.A., Sussex Coll.; LL.B., LaSalle U., 1974; m. Ruth M. Adams, Feb. 19, 1950; 1 son, Morris Stephen. Mgr. McCrory Corp., Mt. Dora, Fla., 1950-73; pres. Wetherington & Wetherington, Mt. Dora, 1969—; mem. exec. adv. com. Bank of Mt. Dora. Mem. adv. com. distributive edn. Vocational-Tech. Sch., Lake County, Fla., 1972—; active various charity drives. Precinct committeeman Republican party, 1968. Served with AUS, 1940-41, 47-50, USNR, 1941-45. Recipient Red Cross Service award, 1954, Cancer Fund service award, 1974, United Appeal service award, 1968. Mem. Triangle Mchts. Assn. (pres. 1966-67), Mt. Dora C. of C. (pres. 1968). Lutheran (councilman). Mason, Toastmaster (pres. 1955-67), Kiwanian (pres. 1968). Home: 6 McDonald St Mount Dora FL 32757 Office: Golden Triangle Shopping Center Mount Dora FL 32757

WETMORE, JOHN MARSHALL, economist; b. Wichita, Kan., Feb. 16, 1927; s. Z and Mary Lenore (Bass) W.; A.B., U. Kan., 1948, M.A., 1950; postgrad. Harvard, 1951-55; m. Gertrude Emily Natusch, Jan. 12, 1952; children—Karen, Susan, John, Donald. Research fellow U. Minn., St. Paul, 1955-58; economist Fed. Res. Bank, Chgo., 1958-63, Fed. Home Loan Bank Chgo., 1963-67; dir. econ. and research dept. Mortgage Bankers Assn. Am., Washington, 1967—. Mem. Am. Econs. Assn., Nat. Assn. Bus. Economists, Am. Statis. Assn., Am. Finance Assn., Am. Agrl. Econs. Assn., Lambda Alpha. Home: 5305 Bradley Blvd Bethesda MD 20014 Office: 1125 15th St NW Washinton DC 20005

WEXLER, HARVEY JOSEPH, airline exec.; b. N.Y.C., Apr. 25, 1928; s. Samuel and Etta (Saunders) W.; B.S., N.Y.U., 1947; M.B.A., Harvard, 1950. Dir. internat. services Air Transport Assn., Washington, 1958-63; asst. to chmn. bd. Slick Corp., 1963-65; v.p. Continental Airlines, 1965—. Financial and econ. cons., 1950-52; econ. adviser Senate Aviation Sub-Com., 1959-62. Served to capt. USAF, 1952-58. Clubs: Harvard (N.Y.C.); Army-Navy, Harvard Business School (Washington). Home: 2401 Calvert St NW Washington DC 20008 Office: 1025 Connecticut Av NW Washington DC 20006

WEXLER, LEWIS POPE, tire co. exec.; b. Johnson City, Tenn., Nov. 7, 1936; s. Daniel Benjamin and Marie Eloise (Pope) W.; B.A., Washington and Lee U., 1958; student Program Mgmt. Devel., Harvard, 1965; m. Martha Hayes Patton, June 20, 1959; children—Lewis Pope, Lillian, Harrison, Susan. Budget mgr. Goodyear Tire & Rubber Co., Memphis, 1959, budget mgr., asst. store mgr., Nashville, 1959-61; store mgr. Alcoa, Maryville, Tenn., 1961; with Free Service Tire Co., various locations, 1962—, pres., Biltmore and Asheville, N.C., 1970-71, pres. all affiliates, Johnson City, 1971—; dir. 1st Peoples Bank, Johnson City. Bd. dirs. United Fund, 1969, Boys Club, 1969. Methodist. Kiwaian, Elk. Club: Hurtleigh. Home: 106 Belmeade Circle Johnson City TN 37601 Office: 126 Buffalo St Johnson City TN 37601

WEYHRAUCH, ERNEST EMIL, librarian; b. N.Y.C., July 20, 1926; s. Frederick and Martha (Ingber) W.; B.A., N.Y. U., 1945-51; M.S., Columbia, 1959; postgrad Coll. City of N.Y., 1955-57, Ind. U., 1965-66; m. Mary Ekris, July 8, 1955; children—Ernest Christopher, Anne Martha. Tech. asst. N.Y. Pub. Library, 1952-55; tchr. pub. schs., N.Y.C., 1955-57; cataloger, asst.; edn. librarian, chief circulation Bklyn. Coll. Library, 1957-64; edn. librarian Ind. U., 1964-66; dir. libraries Eastern Ky. U., Richmond, 1966—. Mem. Am., Southeastern, Ky. (v.p., pres. elect 1972-73) library assns., Ky. Hist. Soc., Madison County Hist. Soc., Nat., Ky. rifle assns. Contbr. articles to profl. mags. Home: 211 Ridgeway Richmond KY 40475 Office: Eastern Ky University Richmond KY 40475

WEYSHAM, ALCIDE JOHN, lawyer; b. New Orleans, Oct. 17, 1914; s. Arnold J. and Clare (Knight) W.; A.B., Tulane U., 1939, LL.B., 1939; m. Frances Lillian Badalamenti; 1 dau. by previous marriage, Sheryl Clare (Mrs. Robert Fleming, Jr.); stepchildren—Ilene (Mrs. Edmond Catoire III), Alvin Joseph Carriere, Rosalyn Carriere. Admitted to La. bar, 1939, since pvt. practice, New Orleans; counsel criminal div. Legal Aid Bur. New Orleans, 1942-44; asst. counsel New Orleans Levee Bd., 1948-50; atty. fire marshall La., 1950-52. Pres. Central Gentill Civic and Improvement Assn., 1956—; chmn. Citizens' Com. Lake Pontchartrain. Mem. Am., La., New Orleans bar assns., Am. Judicature Soc., Tulane U. Law Alumni Assn., Internat. Platform Assn. Home: 5615 Bancroft Dr New Orleans LA 70122 Office: 4948 Chef Menteur Hwy Suite 316 New Orleans LA 70126

WHALEN, JOSEPH MATTHEW, utility exec.; b. Poplar Bluff, Mo., Aug. 3, 1938; s. John Parsons and Barbara Frances (Bujan) W.; B.A., Vanderbilt U., 1960; postgrad. U. N.C., Chapel Hill, 1963-65; m. Yvonne White, Dec. 27, 1963; 1 son, Michael Scott. Customer service rep. Ark. Power & Light Co., Hot Springs, 1965-66, market research and statistics analyst, Little Rock, 1966-71, asst. mgr. market research, 1971—. Chmn. market research subcom. Middle South Utilities, 1971—; mem. marketing research adv. bd. Electric Energy Assn., 1973-74. Exec. officer Home Builders Assn. Hot Springs, 1966; loaned exec. Pulaski County United Fund, 1969, 70. Served with USNR, 1960-65. Mem. Electric Utility Market Research Council, Am. Marketing Assn., Am. Statis. Assn., Advt. Research Fedn. Home: 4511 Hazelwood Rd North Little Rock AR 72116 Office: Ark Power & Light Co 9th and Louisiana Sts Little Rock AR 72203

WHALEN, MARY O'LEARY (MRS. WILLIAM P. WHALEN), artist; b. Ireland; d. Edward Magawly and Agnes (Manning) Banon; student Manhattanville Coll. Sacred Heart, 1940; m. William P. Whalen, Oct. 28, 1938; 1 dau., Mary Elizabeth. Artist, 1962—; exhibited in group shows Women's Nat. Republican Club, Parrish Art Mus., others. Vice chmn. Internat. Ball, N.Y.C., 1963, 64, 65, 67, 68; co-chmn. Candlelight Ball, N.Y., 1960; com. mem. Gothams, Inc., 1955—; publs. chmn. Manhattanville Coll. Alumnae Rev. 1960-63, editorial staff, 1963—. Bd. dirs. Manhattanville Coll. of Sacred Heart. Mem. art com., membership com. Women's Nat. Republican Club, 1969—. Mem. N.Y. Acad. Scis. (sec. bd. women's aux. 1970-71). Met. Mus. N.Y.C., Parrish Art Mus. Southampton (N.Y.), Hort. Soc. N.Y., Alumnae Assn. Manhattanville Coll., Ladies of Charity, Internat. Platform Assn., Friends of Whitney Mus. Home: Longwood 5IE 11811 Av of the PGA Palm Beach Gardens FL 33403

WHALEY, CHARLES EDWARD, assn. exec.; b. Williamstown, Ky., Feb. 29, 1928; s. Charles Fred and Mary Kathleen (Neal) W.; B.A., U. Ky., 1949; postgrad. U. Louisville, 1961, 65; M.S., Columbia, 1950; M.A., U. Manchester (Eng.), 1957; m. Carol Jean Sutton, Nov. 23, 1957; children—Carrie Elizabeth, Kate Wallace. Reporter, Courier-Jour., Louisville, 1950-60, edn. editor, 1960-64; dir. research and information Ky. Edn. Assn., Louisville, 1964-72, dir. pub. relations and research, 1972—. Chmn. pub. information com. HELP, Louisville, 1964-65; mem. mid-eastern regional com. Selection of Marshall Scholars, 1966-70; chmn. pub. information com. Ky. Sci. and Tech. Council, 1967-71; mem. program and allocations com. Met. United Way, 1972—; mem. edn. com. Louisville and Jefferson County Human Relations Commn., 1973—; mem. Citizens Adv. Council for study of Ky's. found. program for edn., 1971-74. Served with AUS, 1950-52. Mem. Am. Assn. Ednl. Data Systems, Ky. Edn. Assn. (pres. staff orgn. 1970-71), Assn. Marshall Scholars and Alumni (nat. sec. 1965-71), State Edn. Research Staff Assn. (pres. elect 1974—), Pub. Relations Soc. Am. (chmn. edn. com. Bluegrass chpt. 1974—), Edn. Writers Assn., Sigma Delta Chi, Phi Beta Kappa, Sigma Phi Epsilon. Unitarian (pres. bd. trustees 1967-68). Home: 2531 Cherokee Pkwy Louisville KY 40204 Office: 101 W Walnut St Louisville KY 40202

WHALING, ANNE, educator; b. Houston, Mar. 30, 1914; d. Horace Morland and Annie Byrd (Ward) Whaling; B.A., So. Meth. U., 1933, M.A., 1934; Ph.D., Yale, 1946. Cataloger, specialist in music, fgn. langs. So. Meth. U., 1947-55; tchr., English dept. Arlington State Coll., 1955, instr., 1955-57, asst. prof., 1957-60, asso. prof., 1960-68; asso. prof. English, U. Tex. at Arlington, 1968-71, prof., 1971—. Program annotator for chamber music series Dallas Mus. Fine Arts, 1956—; bd. dirs. Dallas Chamber Music Soc., 1954—; chmn. Pro Musica, Dallas, 1960-62. Recipient Decima Lantern award, So. Meth. U., 1933; named Woman of Achievement, So. Meth. U. Assn., 1968. Mem. Am. Studies Assn. Tex. (councilor 1961-62), South Central Modern Lang. Assn., Am. Assn. U. Women (chmn. fellowship com. Dallas br. 1959-64), Music Library Assn., Phi Beta Kappa, Sigma Tau Delta, Delta Kappa Gamma. Methodist. Home: 3320 Daniels Av Dallas TX 75205 Office: Dept English U Tex Arlington TX 76010

WHANG, SANG YOUN, communications co. exec.; b. Korea, Oct. 16, 1931; s. Andrew Chaikyung and Hyun Sook (Kim) W.; came to U.S., 1951; B.S. in E.E. summa cum laude, Poly. Inst. Bklyn., 1956, M.S. in E.E., 1966; m. Mary Alice Pai, Dec. 25, 1955; children—Jeanne, Stephen, Peter. Instr., Poly. Inst. Bklyn., 1956-60; v.p., chief engr. SEG Electronic Co., Inc., Bklyn., 1960-64; tech. specialist Milgo Electronic Co., Miami, 1964-68; v.p., tech. dir. Internat. Communications Corp., 1968—; cons. Compucon Contact Lens Co., Queens, N.Y., 1958—. Bd. dirs. Miami area Korean Student Fund, 1970—. Recipient Presdl. Citation and Medal for Pub. Service, Republic of Korea, 1970. Mem. Korean Assn. of Miami (pres. 1965-70, hon. pres. 1970-73), Tau Beta Pi, Eta Kappa Nu. Democrat. Methodist. Patentee bowling pin setting machine, cornea measuring device, contact lens, electronic filter, data transmission equipment (Modem). Home: 8445 SW 148th Dr Miami FL 33158 Office: 7620 NW 36th Av Miami FL 33147

WHARRAM, KENNETH JONES, physician; b. Painesville, O., Jan. 25, 1915; s. Rutherford Hayes and Theresa Louise (Heider) W.; B.S., Ohio U., 1937; M.D., Ohio State U., 1941; m. Pauline L. Davis, Nov. 12, 1955; children—Kay (Mrs. James A. Johnson), Nancy (Mrs. Stephen G. Johnson), Stephen Paul. Intern, Springfield (O.) City Hosp., 1941-42; practice of medicine, Harlingen, Tex., 1946-55, Lockney, Tex., 1955-57, Nocona, Tex., 1957—; mem. staffs Major Clinic Hosp., Nocona, Bowie (Tex.) Meml. Hosp. Mem. city council, Nocona, 1962—. Served to lt. comdr. M.C., USNR, 1942-46. Mem. A.M.A., Tex. Acad. Gen. Practice, Am. Acad. Family Practice (charter), Tex. Med. Assn., County Med. Soc. Elk, Mason. Home: 303 Carolyn Rd Nocona TX 76255 Office: Box 207 Nocona TX 76255

WHARTON, PORTER, JR., oil co. exec.; b. Elkhart, Ind., Sept. 25, 1922; s. Porter Estle and Clara (Rodewald) W.; A.B., Ind. U., 1949; m. Barbara Dee Dearmin, May 28, 1949; children—Porter III, Sally Dee, Thad Dearmin. Advt. salesman, home bldg. editor Elkhart Truth, 1949-52; pub. relations, advt. exec. Miles Labs., Inc., 1952-59; dir. pub. relations Kerr-McGee Oil Industries, Inc., Oklahoma City, 1960-62, dir. pub. relations, corp. advt., 1962—. Chmn. pub. relations com. United Fund of Elkhart County, 1958-59. Bd. dirs. Elkhart Symphony Soc., 1954-59, treas., 1959. Served with USAAF, 1943-46. Mem. Okla. Petroleum Council, Ind. Petroleum Assn. Am., Mid-Continent Oil and Gas Assn., Okla. Press Assn., Oklahoma City C. of C., Okla. Pub. Relations Assn., Sigma Pi. Clubs: Twin Hills Golf and Country; Oklahoma City Press Club. Died May 10, 1974. Home: 6702 Trenton Rd Oklahoma City OK 73116

WHEAT, LEONARD FREDERICK, economist, govt. ofcl.; b. Sioux City, Ia., Nov. 13, 1931; s. Leonard Benjamin and Gertrude Dorette (Wieland) W.; B.A., U. Minn., 1952, M.Pub. Administrn., 1955; Ph.D. (Littauer fellow, George C. Christian fellow), Harvard, 1958; m. Janis Elizabeth Knudsen, May 9, 1964. Economist Minn. Dept. Taxation, St. Paul, 1954-55; program analyst U.S. Dept. Navy, Washington, 1958-59; budget examiner U.S. Bur. Budget, Washington, 1959-66; economist U.S. Dept. Commerce, Washington, 1966—. Mem. Am. Econ. Assn., Soc. Govt. Economists, Am. Soc. for Pub. Adminstrn., Save Lake Superior Assn., Nat. Parks and Conservation Assn., Nat. Wildlife Fedn., Wilderness Soc., Common Cause. Club: Potomac Appalachian Trail. Author: Paul Tillich's Dialectical Humanism, 1970; Regional Growth and Industrial Location, 1973. Home: 1911 Stirrup Lane Alexandria VA 22308 Office: Econ Devel Adminstrn Commerce Dept Bldg Washington DC

WHEATLEY, DAVID COE, architect; b. St. Louis, Feb. 21, 1929; s. Thomas and Nora (Allen) W.; student Washington U., St. Louis, 1950-53, Frank Lloyd Wright Sch. Architecture, 1953-59; m. Susan Jacobs, Mar. 30, 1957. Staff Architect Frank Lloyd Wright Found., Spring Green, Wis. and Phoenix, 1959-69; architect Wheatley-Merritt Assos., Dallas, 1969-73; v.p. planning and design Centex Homes Corp., Dallas, 1973—. Served with USMC, 1946-49. Mem. A.I.A., Soc. Archtl. Historians. Prin. works include Aitken residence, Woodside, Cal., 1961, Warren residence, St. Joseph, Mich., 1962, Kittleson residence, Scottsdale, Ariz., 1972, Royse residence, LaGrange, Tex., 1973, Menard residence, Hillsboro, Tex., 1973. Home: 3701 Turtle Creek Blvd Dallas TX 75219 Office: 4600 Republic Bank Tower Dallas TX 75201

WHEATLEY, EUGENE AUSTIN, JR., physicist; b. Cin., Aug. 12, 1928; s. Eugene Austin and Grace (Appleton) W.; M.E., U. Cin., 1951, M.S. in Physics, 1954; m. Dolores Gerhardt, June 9, 1956 (div. Dec. 1965); m. 2d, Carol Betty Houck, Nov. 7, 1969. Controls systems engr. Gen. Electric Co., Evendale, O., 1955-58; staff mem. nuclear rocket div. Los Alamos Sci. Lab., 1958-61; asst. sr. engr. NERVA nuclear rocket div. Aerojet Gen. Azusa, Cal., 1961-63; staff mem. AC spark plug div. Gen. Motors, El Segundo, Cal., 1963-64; prin. engr. Saturn V flight evaluation working group Boeing Co., Huntsville, Ala., 1964-69; cons. Code Research Corp., Huntsville, 1970; sr. engr. Skylab, Martin Marietta Corp., Huntsville, 1971—. Mem. Am. Phys. Soc., Am. Nuclear Soc., Am. Soc. M.E., Am. Inst. Aeros. and Astronautics, Internat. Platform Assn., Pi Tau Sigma. Club: Point Aquarius (Ala.) Country. Contbr. articles in field to profl. jours. Home: 1619 Drake Av SE Huntsville AL 35802 Office: Martin Marietta Corp 201 Pinehurst Dr Huntsville AL 35807

WHEATON, ELIZABETH LEE, educator; b. Sherman, Tex.; d. Percival King and Minerva Fay (Ratzel) Fulton; student Rice Inst., 1920-21, San Angelo Coll., 1949-51; certificate S.W. Tex. State Coll., 1922, Kansas City-Horner Conservatory, 1929; B.S., McMurray Coll., 1952; postgrad. A. and I. Coll., 1953-54; m. Grant Wiltsie Wheaton, Dec. 23, 1923. Tchr. pub. schs., Texas City, Tex., 1922-24; tchr. speech, 1922-29, voice and speech, 1929-47; reporter, soc. editor Texas City Sun, 1930-36; corr. Galveston (Tex.) News, 1934; dir. The Texas City Hour, radio sta. KGBC, 1947; elementary tchr. La Feria (Tex.) Pub. Schs., 1952—; tchr. voice, speech, 1956-57; originator, writer, dir., master Story Book Time TV series sta. KRGV-TV, 1957; mem. staff S.W. Writers Conv., Corpus Christi, Tex., 1954—. Mem. Composers, Authors and Artists Am. (chpt. pres.; mem. nat. pub. com. 1960), Tex. Woman's Press Assn., Tex. State Tchrs. Assn., Tex. Poetry Soc., Tex. Inst. Letters, Am. Legion Aux. (pres. LaFeria unit 1960), Tex. State Dept. Music (chmn. 1960), Lower Rio Grande Valley Hist. Soc., Community Concert Assn. (bd. dirs. Harlingen chpt., chmn. La Feria com. 1969—), Poetry Soc. Am. (charter; sec. Lower Rio Grande Valley chpt.), Am. Budgerigar Soc., Tex. Bird Breeders and Fanciers Assn., Tex. Southmost Bird Assn. (sec. 1962), Delta Kappa Gamma (chmn. publicity com.). Author: Mr. George's Joint, 1941; Texas City Remembers, 1948; also poems, articles, revs. in various mags., newspapers. Home: Valley Vista Box 1026 La Feria TX 78559 Office: Sam Houston Sch La Feria TX 78559

WHEATON, GRANT WILTSIE, journalist; b. Kewanee, Ill., Apr. 27, 1895; s. Jeremiah Grant and Myrtle Mable (Hubbard) W.; student Draughan's Bus. Coll., Galveston, Tex., 1920, McMurray Coll., Abilene, Tex., 1951-52; m. Elizabeth Lee Fulton, Dec. 23, 1923. Various positions from sec. to v.p., gen. mgr. to corporate sec., asst. gen. mgr. Texas City (Tex.) Terminal Ry. Co., 1922-48; sec. Terminal Indsl. Land Co., 1943-48; asso. E. Gordon Perry Real Estate, Ins. Agy., San Angelo, Tex., 1948-51; owner Valley Vista Farm, La Feria, Tex., 1953—; originator, mgr., editor Suez Scribblings San Angelo, 1950-51; field editor H. L. Peace Publs., New Orleans, 1953-57; free lance writer, 1957—; staff lectr. Southwestern Writers Conf., Corpus Christi, Tex., 1956-60. Treas. March Dimes, Texas City, 1936-38; dir. La Feria March of Dimes, 1959-66, dir. Cameron County chpt., 1961-67. Served wtih F.A., U.S. Army, 1917-18. Decorated Silver Star medal, Purple Heart. Mem. Lower Rio Grande Valley Hist. Soc., La Feria C. of C., La Feria Live Stock Club, Am. Budgerigar Soc., Tex. Bird Breeders and Fanciers Assn., Tex. Southmost Bird Breeders Assn. (past pres.), Am. Legion, Vets. World War I. Presbyn. (elder). Mason (Shriner), Rotarian. Clubs: La Feria (past pres.), Tip-O-Tex Exhibition Budgie. Contbr. to newspapers, non-fiction mags. Address: Valley Vista Box 1026 La Feria TX 78559

WHEELEN, THOMAS LEO, educator; b. Gardner, Mass., May 30, 1935; s. Thomas Leo and Kathryn Elizabeth (McGrath) W.; student Fordham U., 1953-54; B.B.A. cum laude, Boston Coll., 1957; M.B.A., Babson Coll., 1961; D. Bus. Adminstrn., George Washington U., 1969; m. Margaret A. Doyle, June 25, 1966; children—Kathryn, Thomas Leo II, Richard. Grad. teaching asst. Babson Coll., 1960-61; teaching fellow George Washington U., 1965-68; mfg. tng. program Gen. Electric Co., 1961-64, systems programmer, 1964-65; asst. prof. McIntire Sch. of Commerce, U. Va., 1968-71, asso. prof., 1971-74, prof., 1974—. Cons., liaison faculty FBI Acad. Served to lt. USNR, 1957-60. Mem. Am., So. mgmt. assns., So. Case Research Assn., Acad. Mgmt., Alpha Kappa Psi, Beta Gamma Sigma. Co-editor: Developments in Management Information Systems, 1972. Contbr. articles in field to profl. jours. Home: 1706 Old Forge Rd Charlottesville VA 22901

WHEELER, ARVILLE VANCE, pediatrician, educator; b. Paintsville, Ky., Apr. 3, 1935; s. Arville and Lois Evelyn (Vanc) W.; B.S., Vanderbilt U., 1957, M.D., 1960; m. Elizabeth Mowbray Henderson, Aug. 2, 1956; children—Kathryn Lynn, Vance, Amy. Intern Vanderbilt U. Hosp., Nashville, 1960-61; resident Cin. Children's Hosp., 1961-63; practice medicine, specializing in pediatrics, Nashville, 1966—; mem. staff Cin. Childrens Hosp., 1965-66; clin. asso. prof. pediatrics Vanderbilt Med. Sch., 1966—. Served to capt. USAF, 1963-65. Diplomate Am. Bd. Pediatrics. Fellow Am. Acad. Pediatrics. Home: 4308 Lindawood Dr Nashville TN 37215 Office: 1925 Church St Nashville TN 37215

WHEELER, CHARLES LOVELACE, state ofcl.; b. Upton, Ky., July 30, 1925; s. Joe J. and Ruby (Talley) W.; A.B., Western Ky. State U., 1949; profl. degree So. Regional Tng. Program in Pub. Adminstrn., 1950; m. Patton Galloway, Jan. 12, 1957; children—Barendina Mary, Charles Galloway. Research editor Ky. Legislative Research Commn., 1950-56, dir., 1960-63; research editor Ohio Legislative Service Commn., 1956-58; asst. dir. Ohio Dept. Pub. Welfare, 1959; spl. asst. to Gov. N.C., 1964; dir. N.C. State Commn. Higher Edn. Facilities, Raleigh, 1965—. Sec., N.C. Commn. Interstate Coop., 1964—; vice chmn. Com. State Ofcls. on Suggested State Legislation Council of State Govts., 1962-72; cons. Adv. Commn. on Intergovtl. Relations, 1968—. Trustee Kittrell Coll. Served with AUS, 1943-46. Mem. Assn. Exec. Dirs. Higher Edn. Facilities Commns. (nat. sec. 1967-68, nat. vice chmn. 1968-69, chmn. 1969-70, dir.), Council of State Higher Edn. Agys. (nat. chmn. 1970-71), Nat. Com. Support Pub. Schs. Home: 3211 Burns Pl Raleigh NC 27609 Office: 320 W Jones St Raleigh NC 27602

WHEELER, CLARENCE JOSEPH, JR., physician; b. Dallas, Sept. 25, 1917; s. Clarence Joseph and Sadie Alice (McKinney) W.; B.S. in Math., So. Meth. U., 1941, B.A. in Psychology, 1946; M.D., Johns Hopkins, 1950; m. Alice Mary Freels, Dec. 6, 1942 (dec.); children—Stephen Freels, Clarence Joseph III, Robert McKinney, Thomas Michael, David Ritchey; m. 2d, Jean Grant Faucett, Mar. 2, 1968. Intern Johns Hopkins Hosp., Balt., 1950-51; resident surgery Barnes Hosp., St. Louis, 1951-54; thoracic surgery fellow U. Wis. Hosps., Madison, 1954-55; instr. surgery, 1955-56; practice medicine specializing in gen. and thoracic surgery, Houston, 1956—; clin. instr. surgery Baylor Coll. Medicine, Houston, 1957—; lectr. surgery U. Tex. Postgrad. Med. Sch., Houston, 1957—; mem. active staff Herman Hosp., Houston, 1958—, mem. cardio-vascular research team, 1960—; mem. active staff St. Luke's Hosp., Houston, 1958—, St. Joseph's Hosp., Houston, 1958—, Meml. Hosp., Houston, 1959— Tex. Children's Hosp., Houston, 1960—, Meth. Hosp., 1960—, Ben Taub City-County Hosp., Jefferson Davis Hosp.; now chief of surgery, attending active staff Lewisburg (Tenn.) Community Hosp. Sr. med. office Thua Thien Province, South Vietnam, 1968-70; chief surgery Hue Central Hosp., S. Vietnam, 1968-70; mem. courtesy staff all peripheral outlying hosps.; sr. attending staff Lindley Hosp., Duncan, Okla. Treas. Samuel Clark Ree Sch., P.T.A., Houston, 1959-61; mem. bd. Salvation Army Boys Club, Houston. Served to capt. USMCR, 1942-45; PTO. Decorated D.F.C. (3), Air medal (8), Purple Heart, Navy Commendation medal, Bronze Star, Vietnamese Medal of Health, Vietnamese Medal of Social Welfare. Diplomate Am. Bd. Surgery. Fellow A.C.S., Am. Coll. Chest Physicians, Royal Soc. Medicine; mem. Am., Tex., So., Indsl. med. assns., Harris County, St. Louis, Marshall County (pres.) med. socs., Am., Tex. thoracic socs., Nat. Tb Assn., Am. Assn. History Medicine, Am. Soc. Contemporary Medicine and Surgery, Am., Tex., Houston heart assns., A.A.A.S., Johns Hopkins Med. and Surg. Soc., Southwestern Surg. Congress, Tex. Anti-Tb Assn., Houston Gastroenterological Soc., Houston Surg. Soc., Postgrad Med. Assembly S. Tex., Am. Cancer Soc., Am. Coll. Angiology, Am. Soc. Abdominal Surgeons, Marine Corps, Naval res. officers assns., Nat. Geog. Soc., Kappa Sigma, Phi Chi, Phi Eta Sigma, Kappa Mu Epsilon, Psi Chi. Episcopalian. Rotarian. Club: Internat. Home: Trotwood Apts Apt 63 Columbia TN 38401 Office: Lewisburg Community Hosp Lewisburg TN 37091

WHEELER, JAMES PAUL, lawyer; b. Edgewood, Tex., Nov. 21, 1936; s. Hansel Cleburn and Gladys Inez (Barber) W.; A.A., Paris Jr. Coll., 1957; B.A., in Math., U. Tex., 1959; J.D., So. Meth. U., 1966; m. Patricia Ann Johnson, Mar. 3, 1960; children—Keith Paul, James Patrick, Harlan Clark, Sherri Catherine. Analyst, Western Geophys. Co., Shreveport, La., 1959; engring. mgmt. Tex. Instruments, Inc., Dallas, 1959-68; gen. counsel, sec., dir. Spectronics, Inc., Richardson, Tex., 1968—; admitted to Tex. bar, 1967; pvt. practice law, Mesquite, Tex., 1968—; dir. Wheeler & Lovelace, Optical Services Co. Asso. judge Corporate Ct. City of Mesquite. Mem. State Bar Tex., Am. Bar Assn., Dallas Criminal Bar, Mesquite Bar Assn., Optical Soc. Tex., Mesquite C. of C. (dir. 1972), Mesquite Friends of Library (pres. 1970, bd. dirs.). Democrat. Baptist. Lion. Home: 4721 Shands Dr Mesquite TX 75149 Office: 3318 Hwy 67 E Mesquite TX 75149

WHEELER, MARSHALL RALPH, educator; b. Carlinville, Ill., Apr. 7, 1917; s. Ralph Adelbert and Hester Mae (Ward) W.; student Blackburn Coll., 1935-37; B.A., Baylor U., 1939; postgrad. Tex. A. and M. U., 1939-41; Ph.D. (NRC fellow), U. Tex., 1947; m. Linda Carol Lackner, May 10, 1966; children—Sandra (Mrs. Lee King, Jr.), Karen, Carson. Instr. zoology U. Tex., Austin, 1947-51, asst. prof. 1951-55, asso. prof. 1955-61, prof., 1961—. Gosney fellow Cal. Inst. Tech. Served with USNR, 1941-45. NSF, NIH research grantee. Mem. Entomol. Soc. Am. (editor Annals 1970—), Genetics Soc. Am., Soc. Study Evolution, S. W. Assn. Naturalists (pres. 1961), Am. Soc. Naturalists, Soc. Systematic Zoology, Am. Hemerocallis Soc. Editor: Studies in Genetics, 1960—. Home: 1313 Ardenwood Rd Austin TX 78722

WHEELER, MARY (MRS. RONALD W. WHEELER, JR.), educator; b. Bloomington, Ind., Feb. 27, 1919; d. Claude Elmer and Cordelia (Jones) Cogswell; B.S., Tex. Christian U., 1938, postgrad., 1940-41; M.A., E. Tex. State U., 1963, Ph.D., 1969; m. Ronald W. Wheeler, Jr., Aug. 5, 1938; children—Wendelyn Florence (Mrs. E.D. White) (dec.), Marilyn Anne (Mrs. Jon D. Kindred), Gregg Alan, Carol Kay, Ronald Scott. Employed Frederick Broadcasting Co., radio sta. KTAT, 1948-62, program dir., women's editor, 1948-62, acting mgr., 1950-51, 61-62, bus. mgr., 1956-62; instructional specialist audio-visual edn. E. Tex. State U., Commerce, 1966-68, dir. ednl. TV services, 1968—, asst. prof. audio-visual edn., 1968-73, asso. prof., 1973—. Pres. Teen Town Adult Council; dir. Tillman County Day Nursery. Mem. Am., S.W., Tex. psychol. assns., Tex. Assn. Ednl. Tech. (v.p. 1972-73), Tex. Ednl. TV Assn. (prodn. chmn. 1970-71, curriculum chmn. 1971-72, sec.-treas. 1972-73, v.p. 1973-74), Nat. Assn. Ednl. Broadcasters, Tex. Assn. Coll. Tchrs., Okla. Broadcasters Assn., Philharmonic Music Club (pres. 1957-58), Okla. Fedn. Music Clubs, Past Pres.'s Assembly, C. of C., Univ. Dames (pres.), Tex. State Tchrs. Assn., Tex. Personnel and Guidance Assn., Psychology Club, Mortar Bd., Psi Chi. Mem. Christian Ch. Clubs: Webb Hill Country, Sand Hills Golf and Country; Fort Worth Woman's, Afflatus Culture (rec. sec. 1965-67, pres. 1969-71). Home: 2810 Tanglewood Dr Commerce TX 75428 Office: Audio-Visual Center E Tex State U Commerce TX 75428

WHEELER, MAURICE AULICK, dentist; b. Hazard, Ky., Sept. 17, 1908; s. Peter Taylor and Leora Obra (Aulick) W.; student Georgetown Coll., 1926-29, Transylvania Coll., 1932; D.D.S., U. Louisville, 1934; m. Helen Margaret Brashear, Oct. 6, 1936; children—Jayne (Mrs. John A. Package), James M., Susan (Mrs. James M. Dodson). Pvt. practice dentistry, Hazard, 1934-42, 46-49, Lexington, Ky., 1949—. Served with AUS, 1942-46; lt. col. Res. ret. Mem. Res. Officers Assn. (pres. Hazard chpt. 1946-48), U.S. Mil. Order World Wars (pres. Lexington chpt. 1964). Ret. Officers Assn., Am., Ky. dental assns., Bluegrass, Ky. Mountain (pres. 1937) dental socs., Delta Sigma Delta. Republican. Moose, Lion. Home: 1620 Clayton St Lexington KY 40502 Office: 239 Walton Av Lexington KY 40502

WHEELER, RICHARD HAROLD, radio sta. exec.; b. Albany, N.Y., Nov. 21, 1926; s. Richard Albert and Anne (Gairens) W.; B.A., U. Va., 1950; m. Janet Lee Mitchell, June 7, 1964; children—Stephen, Jeffrey. Newsman, Sta. KOCA, Kilgore, Tex., 1950-51, Sta. WFAA, Dallas, 1951-54, Sta. WFAA-TV, Dallas, 1954-56; news dir. Sta. KOVR-TV, Stockton, Cal., 1956-57, Sta. WFAA-TV, 1957-61, Sta. KOTV-TV, Tulsa, 1961-63, Sta. KRLD-TV-AM, Dallas, 1963-70, Sta. KRLD, Dallas, 1970—. Occasional lectr. area colls., mem. bd. consultants Sta. KSMU, So. Methodist U. Served with AUS, 1945-46. Recipient Best Newscast awards Tex. A.P. Broadcasters Assn., 1972, Dallas Press Club, 1972. Mem. U.P.I. Broadcasters Assn. of Tex. (regional v.p. 1972—, Best Newscast award 1973), U.P.I. Broadcasters Assn. (pres. 1973—). Episcopalian. Clubs: Texas Kennel, North Texas Weimaraner. Home: 13859 Rolling Hills Lane Dallas TX 75240 Office: Station KRLD 7901 Carpenter Freeway Dallas TX 75247

WHEELER, RONALD WENDELL, JR., educator; b. Ft. Worth, June 1, 1914; s. Ronald Whitehead and Kathryn (McMillion) W.; B.A., Tex. Christian U., 1936, M.A., 1940; postgrad. Kilgore Jr. Coll., 1937-38, So. Meth. U., 1938-39, U. Tex., 1940-42, Harvard, 1942-43; Ed.D., U. Okla., 1959; m. Mary Florence Cogswell, Aug. 5, 1938; children—Wendelyn Florence (Mrs. Edwin D. White) (dec.), Marilyn Anne (Mrs. Jon D. Kindred), Gregg Alan, Carol Kay, Ronald Scott. Dir. ofcl. guide band Tex. Central Centennial Expn., Dallas, 1936; music supr., dir. bands Salem Consol. Schs., nr. Troup, Tex., 1936-39; dir. mus. therapy USPHS Hosp., Ft. Worth, 1939-42; partner, gen. mgr. Radio Sta. KTAT, Frederick, Okla., 1948-62, owner, pres., 1956-62; instr. dept. psychology East Tex. State U. at Commerce, 1961-62, asst. prof., 1962-64, asso. prof., 1964-69, prof., 1969—, dir. reading lab., 1963—. Area III adviser S.W. Ednl. Developmental Lab.; tech. asst. Right to Read, Southwestern region U.S. Office Edn. Pres. Tillman County Mental Health Assn., 1958-61. Bd. dirs. Wesley Found., E. Tex. State U. Served to capt. USNR, 1942-48, 50-51. Named commodore Okla. Navy, 1953, adm. of fleet, Okla., 1958. Mem. Am., Southwestern, Tex. psychol. assns., Nat. Reading Conf., Internat. Reading Assn., Coll. Reading Assn., Res. Officers Assn. (liaison officer Greater Dallas chpt.-E. Tex. State U.), N.E.A., Tex. Tchrs. Assn., Tex. Soc. Coll. Profs. Edn., Tex. Assn. Coll. Tchrs. (chpt. pres. 1965-67; mem. state nominating com. state chmn. research com. faculty and classroom, mem. state exec. com. 1968-69), Assn. Higher Edn., Tex. Christian U. Ex-Students Assn., Tex. Christian U. Ex-Letterman's Assn., N.E. Tex. Schs. Men's Club, Lambda Chi Alpha (faculty adviser), Tex. Student Edn. Assn. (faculty adviser), Student Nat. Edn. Assn. (faculty adviser), Am. Legion (post comdr.), V.F.W., Okla. Broadcasters Assn. (dir. 1959-61), C. of C. (pres.), Phi Delta Kappa, Psi Chi. Mem. Christian Ch. (Sunday sch. supt., mem. ch. bd.). Clubs: Webb Hill Country, Sand Hills Golf and Country. Author: Read with Speed; co-author: Reading Laboratory Handbook. Contbr. articles profl. jours. Home: 2810 Tanglewood Dr Commerce TX 75428

WHELAN, RICHARD JAMES, govt. ofcl.; b. Emmett, Kan., June 23, 1931; s. Richard Joseph and Margaret Alma (Cox) W.; A.B. cum laude, Washburn U., 1955; E.Ed., U. Kan., 1966; m. Carol Ann King, Nov. 21, 1959; children—Mark Richard, Cheryl Lynne. Instr. electronics U.S. Army, 1953-54; dir. edn. children's div. Menninger Found., 1959-62; prof., chmn. dept. spl. edn., instr. psychiatry, asst. prof. pediatrics U. Kan. and Kan. U. Med. Center, 1964-72; dir. div. tng. programs, bur. edn. for handicapped U.S. Dept. Health, Edn. and Welfare, Washington, 1972—. Research and evaluation cons. to edn. and mental health agencies; program cons., fed., state and local edn. agencies and univ. tchr. preparation programs. Sec. memtal health com. Kan. Sch. Health Adv. Council, 1962-66. Served with AUS, 1952-54. Mem. Internat. Council Exceptional Children (pres. Kan. Fedn. 1967-69), Phi Kappa Phi, Kappa Sigma. Editor: (with others) Strategies for Teaching Exceptional Children, 1972. Mem. editorial bd. Forum for Residential Therapy, 1963—, Exceptional Children, 1966-72, Focus on Exceptional Children, 1969—. Contbr. articles to profl. jours., chpts. to books. Office: Bur Edn for Handicapped US Office Edn Washington DC 22022

WHELESS, DONALD EDWARD, dentist; b. High Point, N.C., Mar. 16, 1935; s. James Edward and Mary Lee Odell (Webster) W.; B.A., Emory and Henry Coll., 1956; D.D.S., Med. Coll. Va., 1960; m. Jane Lee Davies, Oct. 1, 1960; children—Kellee Susanne, Laurie Elizabeth, Donald Christian. Gen. practice dentistry, Richmond, Va., 1960—. Tchr., Med. Coll. Va., 1960-67; farmer, 1973—; owner Profl. Group. Inc., Richmond, 1973—; pres. Wheelaire, Inc., Richmond, 1973—. Mem. Richmond Dental Soc., So. Crozat Soc., Am. Dental Assn., Fi Phi Alpha, Zi Xi Phi. Mem. Jehovah's Witnesses (minister). Home: Route 2 Powhatan VA 23139 Office: Parham Med Center Richmond VA 23229

WHELESS, THOMAS OMEGA, physician; b. Louisburg, N.C., Sept, 7, 1918; s. Frank Williams and Dona (Purnell) W.; B.S., Wake Forest U., 1939; M.D., Bowman Gray Sch. Medicine, 1943; m. Ruth Lois Brown, Sept. 1, 1945; children—Thomas Omega, Evelyn Kay. Intern, N.C. Bapt. Hosp., Winston-Salem, 1943-44, resident, 1944-45; pvt. practice gen. medicine, Louisburg, N.C., 1947—; instr. obstetrics and gynecology Bowman Gray Sch. Medicine, N.C. Bapt. Hosp., Winston-Salem, 1943-45; mem. staff Franklin Meml. Hosp., Louisburg; med. adviser Local Draft Bd., 1950—; instr. of nurses Franklin Meml. Hosp., Louisburg, 1968—. Bd. trustees Franklin Meml. Hosp., 1951-53. Served with M.C., AUS, 1945-47. Mem. A.M.A., N.C., Franklin County med. socs. Club: Green Hill Country (Louisburg). Home: 106 John St Louisburg NC 27549 Office: 948 N Main St Louisburg NC 27549

WHIDDON, DURELL, lawyer; b. Ashford, Ala., Apr. 11, 1926; s. Freddie Joel and Willie Lee (King) W.; B.A., U. Ala., 1950, LL.B., 1951; m. Martha Kate McGriff, Aug. 3, 1956; children—Bobby P. Hamil, Lisa, Linda. Admitted to Ala. bar, 1951; mem. firm Halstead, Whiddon & Woodham, Abbeville, Ala., Headland, Ala., 1952—. Dir. Wiregrass Bank & Trust Co., Headland. Exec. dir. Headland Housing Authority, 1959—. Dep. dist. atty. Henry County, Ala., 1957—. Served with AUS, 1946-47. Mason, Kiwanian. Home: 101 Whitten St Headland AL 36345 Office: 36 Main St Headland AL 36345 also 19 Kirkland St Abbeville AL 36310

WHIDDON, GENE AUSTIN, lumber co. exec.; b. Lenox, Ga., July 30, 1928; s. Oscar Ray and Mary Alma (Rutherford) W.; student U. Fla., 1946-47; student Broward Bus. Coll., 1947-48, hon. Asso. Bus. Adminstrn., 1962; m. Angelyn Sylvia Gatlin, May 19, 1950; children—Tari Lynn, Gene Austin, Michael Scott. Salesman, Causeway Lumber Co., Inc., Fort Lauderdale, 1950-53, asst. to mgr., 1953-55, sec., treas., gen. mgr., 1955-70, pres., gen. mgr., 1970—; pres. Causeway Lumber Co. of Boca Raton, Inc. (Fla.), 1970—; pres., gen. mgr. Alray Supply, Inc., 1962—; dir. First Nat. Bank, Fort Lauderdale. Chmn. Broward Met. area Nat. Alliance Businessmen, 1972—; mem. Fla. Local Govt. Study Commn., 1972—. Campaign dir. United Fund of Broward County, Fort Lauderdale, 1963, pres., 1964. Bd. dirs. Broward County Citizens Safety Council, 1966-71, A.R.C., Opera Guild of Fort Lauderdale; chmn. bd. dirs. Broward Community Coll. Found.; trustee Stetson U., 1969—; vice chmn. Broward County Adv. Com. to Gov., 1971—. Served with USAF, 1948-50. Named One of Five Outstanding Young Men, Jr. C. of C., Fort Lauderdale, 1960-61; Boss of the Year award PBX Club of Broward County, 1964; Boss of the Year award Fort Lauderdale chpt. Nat. Secretaries Assn., 1965-66; Liberty Bell award Law-Day, Broward County Bar Assn., 1965; Layman of the Year award Kiwanis, 1967; recipient Top Mgmt. award Fort Lauderdale Sales and Marketing Execs. Club, 1965. Mem. Fla. Lumber and Bldg. Material

Dealers Assn. (bd. dirs.; pres. 1968-69), Fla.; State (exec. com. 1970-72), Greater Fort Lauderdale (pres. 1969-72) chambers commerce, Aircraft Owners and Pilots Assn., Christian Businessmen's Com., Execs. Assn. of Fort Lauderdale, Feramo Grotto, Broward Builders Exchange (pres. 1956-57), Gold Key of Nova U. Baptist (deacon, 1955-72, chmn. 1959-60), Kiwanian (pres. 1969-70), Mason (Shriner). Clubs: Metropolitan Dinner (Greater Fort Lauderdale), Lauderdale Yacht, Propeller (Fort Lauderdale), The One Hundred (Broward County, Fla.). Home: 1131 SW 9th Av Fort Lauderdale FL 33315 Office: 2627 S Andrew Av Fort Lauderdale FL 33315

WHINERY, ROBERT, engring. co. exec,; b. N.Y.C., Oct. 24, 1922; s. Samuel Brent and Mabel (Riker) W.; student Newark Coll. Engring., 1940-43; B.M.E., Cornell U., 1944; m. Helen Tarbox McEvoy, Nov. 27, 1948; children—Pamela (Mrs. Keneth H. Knowles), Patricia, Sharon (Mrs. Forest F. Black III), Elizabeth, Andrew. Engr., Standard Oil Devel. Co., Bayway, N.J., 1946-53; sales engr. Mason-Neilan Regulator Co., N.Y.C., 1953-56; br. mgr. Jay Instrument & Splty. Co., Louisville, 1956-59; owner, pres. Whinery Engring. Co., Louisville, 1959—. Served with USNR, 1943-46. Registered profl. engr., Ky. Republican. Episcopalian. Club: Owl Creek Country. Home: PO Box 27 Anchorage KY 40223 Office: PO Box 107 Anchorage KY 40223

WHIPPLE, PAUL WARREN, mgmt. cons.; b. Tonganoxie, Kan., Jan. 21, 1915; s. John Godfrey and Ola (Bull) W.; student Colo. Sch. Mines, 1932-34; B.A. cum laude in English, Willamette U., 1941; M.A. in Pub. Administrn., Am. U., 1950; m. Irma Stark, Nov. 20, 1948; children—Sara Elizabeth, Laura Melanie. Mgmt. analyst U.S. Govt., Washington, 1946-1955, War Dept., 1946-47, Weather Bur., 1947-50, Dept. Agr., 1950-52, Navy Dept., 1952-55; sr. systems analyst Bur. Naval Personnel, Washington, 1955-59; data systems coordinator State of Ore., Salem, 1959-61; computer systems analyst FAA, Washington, 1961-63; data systems cons. HHFA, Washington, 1963-64; asst. mgmt. officer D.C. Govt., Washington, 1964-69, asst. for planning Office Budget and Exec. Mgmt., 1969-72; dir. policy services Nat. Center for Prosecution Mgmt., Washington, 1972—. Served with USAAF, 1942-46; MTO. Mem. Am. Soc. for Pub. Adminstrn., A.A.A.S., Am. Polit. Sci. Assn., Internat. Platform Assn. Unitarian. Club: Torch (pres. 1970-71) (Washington). Contbr. articles profl. jours. Home: 3619 Everett St NW Washington DC 20008 Office: 1900 L St NW Washington DC 20036

WHISENAND, NORMAN ROHRER, accountant; b. Chanute, Kan., Dec. 29, 1916; s. Raymond Duryea and Rita Viola (Rohrer) W.; student LaSalle Extension U., 1954, Odessa Jr. Coll., 1953-54; certificate in pastoral tng. Sems. So. Bapt. Conv., 1968; m. Lucile W. Wood, Mar. 30, 1946 (dec. July 1972); children—Margaret (Mrs. Samuel Wayne Barton), George Raymond; m. 2d, Doris Ann Hanna, Dec. 1, 1972. Self-employed accountant, Odessa, Tex., 1954—. Bd. dirs. Shakespearean Globe Theatre Great S.W., Odessa, Tex. Served with USAAF, World War II. C.P.A., Tex. Mem. Am. Inst. C.P.A.'s, Am. Legion, Air Force Assn., 8th Air Force Assn., Tex. Soc. C.P.A.'s, Odessa C. of C. Presbyn. (deacon 1957-59, elder 1965-66). Home: 1605 W 24th St Odessa TX 79763 Office: 300 N Jackson St Odessa TX 79761

WHISNANT, ISAAC EDWARD, lawyer; b. Clover, S.C., July 22, 1920; s. Isaac Elcana and Emma Grace (Johnson) W.; student St. Mary's U., San Antonio, 1957-59; B.A., U. Md., 1961; J.D., U. Fla., 1965; m. Verna Fae Ray, Aug. 14, 1952; children—William Robert, Sarah Ray. Commd. 2d lt. U.S. Army, 1942, advanced through grades to lt. col., 1951; ret., 1962; admitted to Fla. bar, 1965; v.p., trust officer 1st Nat. Bank of Bradenton (Fla.), 1965-72; practice law, Bradenton, 1972—. Bd. dirs. Fla. West Coast Symphony Orch., 1968-70, Manatee County Soc. Crippled Children and Adults, Happiness House, Manatee County Family YMCA. Decorated Bronze Star. Mem. Am., Fla., Manatee County bar assns., Delta Theta Phi. Presbyn. (elder). Mason, Kiwanian (past dir.). Home: 5611 10th Av Dr W Bradenton FL 33505 Office: 802 12th St W Bradenton FL 33505

WHITACRE, WALTER EMMETT, aero. engr.; b. Detroit, Sept. 28, 1931; s. Arthur James and Reba Adeline (England) W.; B.S. in Aero. Engring., Purdue U., 1959, M.S. in Indsl. Engring., 1968; m. Donna Lee Longstreet, Nov. 26, 1950; children—Donn Arthur, Kirk Alexander, Chris Martin. Project engr. Lockheed Missiles & Space Co., 1959-63; advanced systems engr. Marshall Space Flight Center, NASA, Huntsville, Ala., 1963—. Active Tenn. Valley council Boy Scouts Am. Recipient Valley Scouter award Boy Scouts Am., 1971, Silver Beaver award, 1974. Methodist. Home: 301 Belvidere Dr Huntsville AL 35803 Office: Marshall Space Flight Center Huntsville AL 35812

WHITAKER, HAZEL DEAN HICKS (MRS. WILLIAM M. WHITAKER), educator; b. Germantown, Ky., Jan. 18, 1920; d. Ira and Kemper (Woodward) Hicks; A.B., Morehead State Coll., 1940, M.A., 1950, postgrad. Morehead State U., 1962—; specialist in edn. degree U. Ky., 1962; m. William M. Whitaker, Jan. 4, 1941; 1 son, William M. III. Tchr. pub. schs., Minerva, Ky., 1940-41, Blackey, Ky., 1941-49; prin., Blackey, 1944-47; instr. Morehead (Ky.) State U., 1950-56, asst. prof. edn., 1957-66, asso. prof., 1966—, counselor, 1958-59, acting dir. lab. sch., 1959-61, dir. testing services, 1962—, sch. psychometrist, 1968—. Mem. Ky. Curriculum Com. Mem. Am. Assn. U. Women, Am., Ky. personnel and guidance assns., Nat., Ky. edn. assns., Assn. Student Teaching, Kappa Delta Pi, Delta Kappa Gamma, Delta Zeta. Baptist. Mem. Order Eastern Star. Home: Route 1 Morehead KY 40351

WHITAKER, PHILIP BAILEY, lawyer; b. Chattanooga, June 23, 1933; s. Philip Bailey and Tavenner (Hazlewood) W.; B.A., U. So., 1955; LL.B., U. Va., 1961; m. Ellen Fitzgerald Shutze, Sept. 10, 1960, children—Philip Bailey, Barbara, Charles Newton. Admitted to Tenn. bar. 1961, since practiced in Chattanooga; asso. firm Witt, Gaither, Abernathy and Wilson, 1961-67, partner, 1967—. Head attys. div. Allied Arts Fund, 1972, Heart Fund, 1973. Bd. dirs. Chattanooga Bible Inst.; trustee Baylor Sch. Served as 1st. lt. USAF, 1953-58. Mem. Am., Tenn., Chattanooga bar assns., Phi Beta Kappa. Episcopalian. Clubs: Mountain City, Fairyland, Lookout Mountain Golf. Home: 4 Ft Stephenson Pl Lookout Mountain TN 37350 Office: 1100 Am Nat Bank Bldg Chattanooga TN 37402

WHITAKER, WILLIAM M., JR., radio exec.; b. Blackey, Ky., Aug. 8, 1917; s. William M. and Callie (Caudill) W.; student Alice Lloyd Jr. Coll., Pippa Passes, Ky., 1937-39, Morehead (Ky.) State Coll., 1939-40, 50-52; m. Hazel Dean Hicks, Jan. 4, 1941; 1 son, William M. III. Elementary tchr., Letcher County, Ky., 1939-41; retail mcht., feeds and fertilizer wholesaler, 1941-43; welder insp. Willow Run Bomber Plant, Mich., 1943-44; coal mining co-owner, foreman Caudill & Whitaker Coal Co., Blackey, 1945-49; livestock buying and selling, Morehead, 1950-55; gen. mgr. radio sta. WMOR, 1955—; bldg. constrn., Morehead, 1960—. Mem. Ky. Broadcasters Assn. (past pres.), Morehead C. of C. Democrat. Baptist. Optimist, Lion. Home: Route 1 Forest Hills Subdiv Morehead KY 40351 Office: Radio Sta WMOR Morehead KY 40351

WHITBECK, GARY ALLEN, clergyman, assn. exec.; b. Stillwater, Okla., July 16, 1944; s. Donald Hammond and Mioma T. (Davis) W.; B.A., Phillips U., 1969; M. Div., Brite Div. Sch., Tex. Christian U., 1972; m. Glenda Sue Franks, July 11, 1964; children—Glen Allen, Monica Renee. Ordained to ministry Christian Ch., 1972; minister First Christian Ch., Albany, Tex., 1972—; mgr. Albany C. of C., 1973—. Mem. survey com. Shackelford County Hist. Soc., Albany, 1973—; mem. Albany Ministerial Alliance, 1972—. Home: Box 562 Albany TX 76430 Office: Box 657 Albany TX 76430

WHITCOMB, STANLEY PAGE, JR., land developer; b. Waltham, Mass., July 31, , 1940; s. Stanley Page and Jeannie (Lees) W.; B.S., Babson Coll., 1961; student U. Miami (Fla.), 1965-66; m. Nancy Dee Hellmich, July 2, 1966; children—Frederick C.D., Stanley P. III, Scott Edward. Accountant, Price Waterhouse & Co., Boston, 1961-65; dir. financial services Nat. Airlines, Miami, Fla., 1965-67; controller Coral Ridge Properties subsidiary Westinghouse Corp., Ft. Lauderdale, Fla., 1967-69; exec. v.p. Realtec Inc., Ft. Lauderdale, 1969-71, pres., 1972—, also dir.; pres., treas. Corporate & Profl. Services, Inc., Sarasota, Fla., 1965—; pres., dir. Sapphire Valley Devel. Corp., 1971—, Connestee Falls Devel. Corp., 1971—; pres., dir. Lake Keowee Devel. Corp., 1972—. Mem. Mass., N.Y. socs. C.P.A.'s, Am. Inst. C.P.A.'s, Nat. Assn. Accountants, Greenville, Ft. Lauderdale chambers commerce, Am. Land Devel. Assn., Financial Execs. Inst., Alpha Kappa Psi. Republican. Christian Scientist. Home: 9404 NW 36th Ct Coral Springs FL 33060 also 206 Fairview Av Greenville SC 29601 Office: 3101 N Federal Hwy Ft Lauderdale FL 33306 also 110 Perimeter Rd Greenville SC 29605

WHITE, ALBERT DOUGLAS, wholesale co. exec.; b. Nola, Miss., Jan. 24, 1919; s. Finley Rudolph and Jesse (Lee) W.; student Tex. A. and M. U., 1938-41; m. Dorothy Caven, Sept. 27, 1946; children—Arlis, Barbara, Carla. Gen. mgr. Butane Equipment Co., Inc., Dallas, 1945-49; with Porter Burgess Co., Dallas, 1949—, v.p., 1956-69, exec. v.p. marketing, 1969—; dir. Gt. Nat. Corp., Dallas, Plateau Supply, Inc., Albuquerque, Morton Foods Corp., Dallas. Founder, 1st pres. Okla. Christian Coll. Parents Club, 1969; active Baylor Hosp. Fund drive, 1968, Wadley Research Inst. and Blood Bank Fund, 1968, United Fund, 1971, So. Meth. Univ. Fund, 1970, Okla. Christian Coll. Fund, 1970, Jr. Achievement Fund, 1969, Sustaining Membership Enrollment drive Boy Scouts Am., 1972; v.p. Rosemont Elementary Sch. Dad's Club, 1957. Bd. dirs. Lighthouse for the Blind. Served to capt. AUS, 1941-45. Named Man of the Year, Retailer and Marketing News, 1967; Outstanding Promotion Exec. of Year, Motorola Inc., 1972, 73. Mem. Sales and Marketing Execs. Dallas (pres. 1967-68), Dallas Profl. Salesman Assn. (co-founder 1965), Pi Sigma Epsilon. Mem. Ch. of Christ. Mason (Shriner). Home: 1504 Argonne St Dallas TX 75208 Office: 1233 Levee St Dallas TX 75207

WHITE, ALBERT WYNKOOP, savs. & loan assn. exec.; b. Gentry, Ark., Nov. 15, 1913; s. George Roy and Ione (Wynkoop) W.; student Baker U., 1931-34; B.B.A., U. Kan., 1937; m. Hattie Lorene Stoskopf, Mar. 23, 1940; children—Gretchen (Mrs. Mark L. Perkins), Katrina (Mrs. Bruce L. Graydon). Accountant Cardin Mining & Milling Co., Picher, Okla., 1937-42; mining supt. C G & C Co., Picher, 1942-50; asst. sec., dir. Miami Savs. & Loan Assn. (Okla.), 1950-52, pres., 1952—; dir. Fed. Home Loan Bank of Topeka, Security Mortgage Ins. Co., Baton Rouge, Newman Industries, Miami. Mem. Okla. Savs. and Loan Bd., 1963-73. Chmn. Regional Planning Commn., 1965—. Mem. Okla. Savs. League (pres. 1963-64), Southwestern Savs. Conf. (pres. 1969). Rotarian. Home: 129 D St NW Miami OK 74354 Office: 123 E Central St Miami OK 74354

WHITE, BYRON R., asso. justice U.S. Supreme Ct.; b. Ft. Collins, Colo., June 8, 1917; grad. with honors U. Colo., 1938; Rhodes scholar, Oxford (Eng.) U.; grad. Yale Law Sch.; m. Marion Stearns; children—Charles, Nancy. All-Am. halfback U. Colo., 1937, later played with Pittsburgh Steelers, Detroit Lions of Nat. Profl. League; clk. Chief Justice U.S. Supreme Ct., 1946, 47; dep. atty. gen. U.S., 1961-62; asso. justice U.S. Supreme Ct., 1962—. Chmn. Nat. Citizens for Kennedy, 1960. Served with USNR, World War II; PTO. Mem. Order of Coif, Phi Beta Kappa, Phi Gamma Delta. Home: McLean VA 22101 Office: Supreme Ct US 1 1st St NE Washington DC 20543

WHITE, CARL LUTHER, JR., city ofcl.; b. San Marcos, Tex., July 6, 1931; s. Carl L. and Mildred (Waller) W.; B.B.A., S.W. Tex. State U., 1958; M.B.A., St. Mary's U., 1968; m. Wilma Joyce Gooding, June 1, 1956; children—Tammy, Stacey, Wesley. Controller, Del Rio Loan Co. (Tex.), 1954-57; budget dir. City of San Antonio, 1957-68, asst. finance dir., 1968-71, dir. finance, chief financial officer, 1971—. Prof. accounting San Antonio Coll., 1968—. Mem. Municipal Finance Officers Assn. U.S. and Can., Urban and Regional Information Systems Assn., Nat. Accountants Assn. Home: 11322 Dreamland St San Antonio TX 78230 Office: City Hall San Antonio TX 78218

WHITE, CHARLES ALEXANDER, variety chain stores exec.; b. Greenville, N.C., Sept. 3, 1899; s. Samuel Tilden and Annie (Sheppard) W.; student Mars Hill Coll., 1913, Randolph-Macon Acad., 1914-15, U. N.C., 1916-18; m. Nancy Rogers Lay, June 23, 1925; children—Samuel Tilden II, Barbara Sheppard (Mrs. A. Ward Peacock), Charles Alexander, Elizabeth Atkinson (Mrs. Robert F. Clayton), George Lay, Anna Louise (Mrs. Errol Haun), Nancy Lay (dec.). Ins. adjuster N.J. Fidelity & Plate Glass Ins. Co., N.Y.C., 1919-23; asso. Thomas A. Edison, Inc., East Orange, N.J., 1924-25, Hassell-Dupree Co., Miami, Fla., 1925-26; owner brokerage Charles A. White, Greenville, 1927-29; partner, mgr.-buyer White's Stores, Inc., Greenville, 1930—, pres., 1966—; treas. Carolina Mills Fabrics, Inc. Comdr., Civil Def., Greenville, 1942-55; chmn. Pitt County chpt. N.C. Symphony Soc., 1947-50; mem. adv. bd. East Carolina U. Summer Theatre, 1964-65, 66-68, East Carolina U. Artists Series, 1967-70, chmn., 1971-73; v.p. Pitt County United Fund, 1966-67. Bd. dirs. East Carolina U. Sch. Music Fund, 1971-72; bd. advisers Redevel. Commn. for Central Bus. Dist. Greenville. Mem. Greenville (pres. 1952, dir. 1950-60, 64), N.C. (dir. 1966-72) mchts. assns., C. of C. (pres. 1960; dir. 1957-63, 64), Pitt County Hist. Soc. (pres. 1968-70). Episcopalian. Rotarian. (pres. 1951-52, dir. 1948-56, 65-66). Club: Greenville Music (pres. 1949). Home: 425 W Longmeadow Rd Greenville NC 27834 Office: 601-607 Dickinson Av Greenville NC 27834

WHITE, CHARLES CAVET, JR., dentist; b. Alloy, W.Va., July 31, 1935; s. C.C. and Reva M. (Garrett) W.; A.A., Fla. State U., 1957; D.D.S., Emory U., 1960; m. Fe Thomas, May 2, 1964; children—Charles Cavet, Boyce Thomas, Cassandra Fé. Practice gen. dentistry, Pensacola, Fla., 1962—; staff Bapt., Sacred Heart, Escambia Gen. hosps. Vice pres. Pensacola Symphony, 1962—, chmn. Pensacola div. Nat. Children's Dental Health Week, 1963, '68 Fiesta Art Exhibit, Spanish Village, Pensacola Beach, 1968; mem. Santa Rosa Island Authority Bd., Pensacola Beach, 1969—, chmn., 1972—. Precinct capt. Democratic Party, 1968—. Bd. dirs. Escambia Blood Bank; bd. dirs., past pres. Pensacola Little Theatre; bd. dirs. Pensacola Hist. Soc. and Art Center. Served as lt. USNR, 1960-62. Named Man of Year, Pensacola Jr. C. of C., 1968, Best Dist. Speaker, 1969. Mem. Acad. Gen. Dentistry, Am., Fla. socs. dentistry for children, Pensacola Dental Soc., Fla. State U., Emory U. alumni assns., Navy League, Delta Sigma Delta. Lutheran (pres. 1966-68). Lion, Toastmaster (v.p. bd. 1968—). Club: Pensacola Yacht, Pensacola Racquet Tennis. Home: 3700 Barnwell Circle Pensacola FL 32503 Office: 5228 N Davis Hwy Pensacola FL 32503

WHITE, CHARLES DENNY, clergyman; b. High Point, N.C., Mar. 3, 1914; s. John Charles and Mayme (York) W.; A.B., High Point Coll., 1939, D.D., 1959; B.D., Duke, 1947; m. Julia Lucille Everhart, June 6, 1939 (dec.); children—Charles Denny, Delbert Leon Welch, Judith (Mrs. George W. Ramsey III), LaDean (Mrs. Richard Giles), Zenda R. Welch, David L.; m. 2d, Cornelia Thompson Welch, Mar. 24, 1962. Ordained to ministry Meth. Ch., 1944; pastor All Meth. Ch., Winston Salem, N.C., 1938-41, First-West End Ch., Thomasville, N.C., 1941-43, Duke's Chapel, Durham, N.C., 1943-47, Biltmore Ch., Asheville, N.C., 1947-52, First Meth. Ch., Mt. Holly, 1952-57, Trinity Meth. Ch., Kannapolis, 1957-62, First Meth. Ch., Asheboro, 1962-67; dist. supt. Gastonia Dist., 1967-73, adminstrv. asst. to bishop, 1973—. Sec., Western N.C. Conf. Meth. Ch., 1952-68, Southeastern Jurisdictional Conf., 1960-68; sec. gen. Conf. United Meth. Ch., 1968-71. Trustee Greensboro Coll., Children's Home, Winston-Salem. Mason, Lion, Rotarian. Address: 6800 Abbotswood Dr Charlotte NC 28211

WHITE, CHESTER FURMAN, mfg. co. exec.; b. Greenville, Ala., Sept. 1, 1940; s. Eugene Furman and Lena Mae (Barganier) W.; B.S., U. Ala., 1966, M.B.A. (grad. scholar), 1967; postgrad. N.Y. U., 1971—; m. Maria Nieva Calderon Sanchez, Jan. 26, 1973. Examiner State Ala. Revenue Dept., Montgomery, 1960-65; mgr. internat. taxes Tex. Instruments, Inc., Dallas, 1967-71; supr. internat. tax adminstrn. Pfizer Internat., Inc., N.Y.C., 1972—; chmn. bd. Chester F. White, Inc., Montgomery. Recipient John Burnis Allred award Tex. Soc. C.P.A.'s, 1969, Elijah Watts Sells certificate Am. Inst. C.P.A.'s, 1968, award Ala. Soc. C.P.A.'s, 1966, Austin Gold cup U. Ala., 1966, Mgmt. Com. award Tex. Instruments, 1970, Arthur Young & Co. Accounting award, 1965. Mem. Assn. Internat. Students in Commerce and Econs., Tex. Soc. C.P.A.'s, Am. Inst. C.P.A.'s, Beta Gamma Sigma, Beta Alpha Psi, Omicron Delta Kappa, Alpha Kappa Psi. Home: 3299 Durham Dr Montgomery AL 36109 Office: 235 E 42d St New York City NY 10017

WHITE, CLYDE PARKER, civil engr.; b. Florence, Ala., July 1, 1922; s. John Parker and Mabel Clara (Hipp) W.; student pub. schs., Florence; m. Mary Frances Roberson, July 3, 1950; 1 dau., Mary Lynne (Mrs. Bill Tidwell). Div. engr. Ala. Hwy. Dept., Birmingham, 1941—. Served with C.E., AUS, 1942-45. Mem. Am. Soc. C.E. Club: Birmingham Civitan (dir.). Home: 1412 5th Av W Birmingham AL 35208 Office: PO Box 2745 Birmingham AL 35202

WHITE, DAVID RICHARD, internat. finance co. exec.; b. Springfield, Mo., May 6, 1929; s. Joseph and Helen (Turk) W.; B.A., Va. Mil. Inst., 1952; M.B.A. U. Va., 1960; m. Sophie Ann Ames, Sept. 8, 1957; children—David Richard, Sophie Ann. Asst. sales mgr. Lynchburg Steam Bakery (Va.), 1954-58; trainee White, Weld & Co., N.Y.C., 1960; broker Mason-Hagan, 1961-63; sales mgr., v.p. Craigie, Inc., 1963-70; sr. responsibility corp. finance Craigie, Mason-Hagan, Inc., Richmond, Va., 1971-73; v.p. Starkey Internat. Ltd., Buena Vista, 1973—; dir. Kel-Win Mfg. Co., Trident Corp., Internat. Titanium Ltd., Rush-Hampton Industries, Commonwealth Labs., D-CyclePower Systems. Served to capt. USMCR, 1952-54. Mason (32 deg., Shriner). Clubs: Country of Va. (Va.); Commonwealth (Richmond). Home: 202 Oxford Circle W Richmond VA 23221 Office: Peoples Bank Bldg Buena Vista VA 24416

WHITE, DONALD BURDETT, hotel co. exec.; b. St. Petersburg, Fla., Sept. 22, 1933; s. Amos Burdett and Kathryn (Moran) W.; grad. St. Petersburg Jr. Coll., 1952; B.S., Fla. State U., 1956. With Jack Tar Hotels, Galveston, Tex., 1956-60, mgmt. trainee, 1956-58, traveling accountant, 1958-60; with Internat. Inn, Tampa, Fla., 1960-66, resident mgr., 1961-66; asst. mgr. Hawaiian Village Motel, Tampa, 1966-67, gen. mgr. 1967—. Mem. Tampa C. of C., Fla., Tampa motel and hotel assns., Fla. Motel and Resort Assn. (v.p., 1968-69), Sigma Pi Epsilon. Democrat; Roman Catholic. Home: 1507 W Comanche Av Tampa FL 33603 Office: 2522 N Dale Mabry Tampa FL 33607

WHITE, EDWARD W., JR., oil producer; b. West Palm Beach, Fla., Feb. 21, 1933; s. Edward W. and Jeanne Mary (Kraft) W.; student Loyola U., Chgo., 1951-54; m. M. Carol Anderson, Sept. 8, 1956 (div. May 1972); 1 son, Michael Dennis; m. 2d, Margaret Patricia Rush, Mar. 31, 1973. Owner, E.W. White & Assos., Chgo., 1956-65; founder, pres. Pointer Oil Co., Chgo., 1965—, Pointer Oil Co. Fla., 1971—, Mineral Leasing, Inc., 1970—. Home: 550 Ocean Dr Key Biscayne FL 33149 Office: 104 Crandon Blvd Key Biscayne FL 33149

WHITE, EDWIN DEAN, JR., advt. and public relations agy. exec.; b. Memphis, June 12, 1926; s. Edwin Dean and Martha Zell (Payne) W.; student Tex. A. and M. U., 1944; B.S., B.J., U. Mo., 1949; m. Fannie Kendrick Hill, June 12, 1947; children—Kathryn (Mrs. Thomas Hamm), Dean, Andrew, Leigh. News dir. sta. KCRC, Enid, Okla., 1949-50; mem. news staff sta. WHAS, Louisville, 1950-51; news dir. sta. WMC, Memphis, 1951-55; asst. dir. advt. Nat. Cotton Council, Memphis, 1956-65; advt. dir. Agrico Chem. Co., 1965-69; v.p., Ward Archer & Assos., Memphis, 1969—, also dir.; pres., Delta, Inc., 1953-73. Cons. Community Blood Plan, 1969—. Bd. dirs. Vis. Nurses Assn. Served with USNR, 1944-45. Mem. Radio and Television News Dirs. Assn. (dir. 1953-56), Radio Farm Dirs., Nat. Agrl. Marketing Assn. (dir. 1970), Pub. Relations Soc. Am., Memphis C. of C. (aviation com. 1954-56). Republican. Presbyn. Club: Colonial Country (Memphis). Home: 6110 Macinness Dr Memphis TN 38138 Office: 11 S Orleans St Memphis TN 38101

WHITE, ELBERT ASA, III, pediatrician; b. Corinth, Miss., July 17, 1935; s. Elbert Asa and Mabel (Spencer) W.; A.B., Vanderbilt U., 1957, M.D., 1960; m. Anna Marie Wright, July 22, 1962; children—Laura Spencer, Elbert Asa, John Weston. Intern, Vanderbilt Med. Center, Nashville, 1960-61, resident, 1963-65, chief resident, 1965-66; practice medicine specializing in pediatrics, Corinth, 1966—; staff Magnolia Hosp., Corinth, N.E. Miss. Hosp., Booneville; cons. in pediatrics Project Head Start, N.E. Miss., 1967—. Partner, Radio Corinth, WWTX, 1967—. Founder, Alcorn County Assn. for Handicapped Children, Corinth, 1968; treas. Corinth Theatre-Arts, 1968—, also bd. dirs. Served with M.C., USAF, 1961-63. Named Corinth's Outstanding Young Man, 1969. Diplomate Am. Bd. Pediatrics. Fellow Am. Acad. Pediatrics. Kiwanian (pres. Corinth 1969-70). Home: 1410 Pine Rd Corinth MS 38834 Office: 705 Shiloh Rd Corinth MS 38834

WHITE, ETHYLE HERMAN (MRS. S. ROY WHITE), artist; b. San Antonio, Apr. 10, 1904; d. Ferdinand and Minnie (Simmang) Herman; ed. pvt. schs., instrs.; m. S. Roy White, Mar. 3, 1924; children—De Lois Eileen (Mrs. William Marion Mohrle), Patsyruth (Mrs. Henry Wheeler). Exhibited numerous one-man, group shows, Tex.; represented pub. collections in U.S., pvt. collections in Switzerland, Germany, Sweden. Del. Internat. Com. Centro Studi E. Scambi Internationali. Mem. Anahuac Fine Arts Group, San Antonio, Beaumont, Galveston, Houston art leagues, Daus. Republic Tex., Nat. League Am. Pen Women. Episcopalian. Clubs: Fine Arts (Anahuac); Artist and Craftsmen (Dallas); Conservative Arts (Houston). Author, illustrator: Arabella. Author: Poet's Hour. Home: PO Box 176 Anahuac TX 77514

WHITE, GEORGE PHILLIPS, lawyer; b. Centreville, Ala., Aug. 4, 1915; s. James Bailey and Berta (Jones) W.; LL.B., U. Ala., 1939; m. Betty Ann Poag, Nov. 28, 1952; children—George P. III, Allison, Rachel. Admitted to Ala. bar, 1939; with Employers Liability Assurance Corp., 1940-43; practice law in Centreville, 1946—; dist. atty. Bibb County, 1965—; pres. Abstract Co., Inc.; sec. Centreville Oil Co., Inc., Belcher Motor Co., Inc. Past sec., treas. Bibb County Democratic Exec. Com. Served from ensign to lt. Naval Air Force, USNR, 1943-46; PTO. Decorated Presdl. Unit Citation, 5 battle stars. Mem. 4th Jud. Circuit Bar Assn. (past pres.), Ala. Bar Assn., U. Ala. Alumni Assn. (pres. Bibb County chpt. 1962). Presbyn. Home: 116 Ceder St Centreville AL 35042 Office: 132 Courtsquare E Centreville AL 35042

WHITE, HAROLD TAYLOR, coll. pres.; b. Wiggins, Miss., May 27, 1924; s. Joseph Neal and Atsie (Taylor) W.; B.S., U. So. Miss., 1951, M.A., 1960; m. Annie Jane Carlisle, Sept. 6, 1958; children—Harold Taylor, James Malcolm, Carlisle. Tchr. Perkinston (Miss.) Consol. High Sch., 1948-51; coach Perkinston Jr. Coll., 1951-57, athletic dir., 1958-61, dean men, 1961-64, dir. student personnel, adminstrv. 1964-65; pres. Northeast Miss. Jr. Coll., Bonneville, 1965—. Served with USAAF, 1942-46. Baptist. Home: Cunningham Blvd Bonneville MS 38829

WHITE, HARRY THOMAS, photographer; b. Spartanburg, S.C., Sept. 5, 1930; s. Jimmie A. and Clara (Cothran) W.; student N.Y. Inst. Photography, 1947; student journalism U. N.C., 1950; m. Lillian Ruth Hughes, Mar. 15, 1949; children—Diane Elizabeth, Karen Patryce, Thomas Harry. With editorial staff Spartanburg Herald Jour., 1947-50; organized B. & B. Studios, Inc., Spartanburg, 1950, pres., gen. mgr., 1962—. Pres. Kaminers Art and Frame Co., Spartanburg, 1965—; exec. v.p. Graphico, Inc., 1971—. Recipient awards including Nat. Art League award, 1948, S.C. Press Assn. award, 1949. Mem. Photog. Soc. Am., Nat. Press Photographers Assn., Royal Order of Scotland. Mem. United Methodist Ch. (lay leader). Mason (32 deg. Shriner). Club: Sertoma. Photog. works in traveling photog. exhbns. Home: 230 Cart Dr Spartanburg SC 29302 Office: 268 E Main St Spartanburg SC 29302

WHITE, JACK NOBLE, composer, clergyman, musician; b. Weatherford, Tex., Apr. 25, 1938; s. James F. Cody and Jen (Noble) W., Sr.; B.Mus., Tex. Christian U., 1961; postgrad. Union Theol. Sem., 1962, (fellow) Westminster Choir Coll., 1968; M.A., U. S. Ala., 1972; m. Johanna Parrott, Aug. 2, 1959; children—Stephanie Jeanne, Alicia Kirsten. Organist, choirmaster All Saint's Episcopal Ch., Ft. Worth, 1959-66, St. Paul's Episcopal Ch., Mobile, Ala., 1966—; minister of youth, 1972—; dir. mus. Ft. Worth Country Day Sch., 1963-66; asst. headmaster St. Paul's Day Sch., Mobile, 1966-69, headmaster, 1969-72. Mem. joint commn. on ch. music Episcopal Ch., 1960—, sec., 1963—, cons. radio-tv, films dept., 1964-67, cons. on prayerbook revision, 1966—. Bd. dirs. Mobile Symphony, Mobile '75, Civic Music Assn., Mobile. Mem. Am. Guild Organists, Nat. Assn. Episcopal Schs. Composer: Omnes Gentes, Plaudite, 1968; Destin, 1970; Come Let Us Sing, 1971; Be Joyful, Songs for the Jesus Generation, 1972; (folk opera) Dismas, 1973; Pacific Folk Mass, 1973. Contbr. articles to periodicals. Home: 309 Brawood Dr Mobile AL 36608

WHITE, JAMES WHITCOMB RILEY, publisher; b. Halls, Tenn., Feb. 20, 1919; s. John Lee and Lorene (Mitchell) W.; grad. high sch.; m. Nell Ruth Burnette, Feb. 21, 1943; children—James Timothy, JoMarilyn (Mrs. Stephen Koslow), Gerald Harvey. Pub., Weakley County Press, Martin, Tenn., 1947-63, So. Standard, McMinnville, Tenn., 1955—, Smithville (Tenn.) Rev., 1963—, Warren County Tribune, McMinnville, 1968—; pres. WBMC Radio, McMinnville, 1964—; dir. First Nat. Bank, McMinnville. Pres., Warren County-McMinnville A.R.C., 1958-64. Served with AUS, 1943-45. Mem. Tenn. Press Assn. (pres. 1952-53). Home: 620 W Main St McMinnville TN 37110 Office: Morford St McMinnville TN 37110

WHITE, JERALD RAYMOND, ednl. adminstr.; b. Hominy, Okla., July 4, 1915; s. John William and Opal (Privett) W.; B.Ed., Shenandoah Coll. and Conservatory of Music, 1954; M.Ed., U. Va., 1959, Cert. Advanced Grad. Study in Sch. Adminstrn., 1969; m. Una Vass, Mar. 12, 1938; 1 son, Jerald Raymond Jr. Band dir. Roanoke (Va.) City Schs., 1941-58; asst. prin. Jefferson Sr. High Sch., Roanoke, 1958-61, prin., 1961-66; gen. supr. instrn. Culpeper (Va.) County Schs., 1967-69, dir. instrn., 1969-73, asst. supt., 1973—. Served with AUS, 1945-46. Mem. Phi Delta Kappa. Baptist (deacon, tchr. Sunday sch. 1967—). Mason (Shriner). Rotarian (dir. 1970, chmn. program and music 1971). Home: 2130 Mountain Run Lane Culpeper VA 22701 Office: N Main St Extension Culpeper VA 22701

WHITE, JOHN FRANKLIN, ins. co. exec.; b. Oklahoma City, Mar. 1, 1944; s. John Franklin and Edith Margaret (Carter) W.; student Little Rock U., 1961-63; B.B.A., N. Tex. State U., 1965; m. Rita Mae Hubbard, June 6, 1964; children—Sandy Lynn, Kari Kyle. With Cullum Companies, Inc., 1964-72, chief accountant, 1966-69, treas. subsidiary Page Drugs, Inc., 1969-70, asst. treas. parent co., Dallas, 1970-71, controller subsidiaries A. W. Cullum & Co., Inc., Tom Thumb Stores, Inc., Page Drugs, Inc., 1971-72; dir. accounting Transport Mgmt. Co., Dallas, 1972-74; corporate controller Gulf Ins. Co., Dallas, 1974—. C.P.A., Tex. Mem. Am. Inst. C.P.A.'s, Tex. Soc. C.P.A.'s. Home: 2912 Natalie Rd Plano TX 75074 Office: 305 Cedar Springs Rd Dallas TX 75219

WHITE, JOHN HOXLAND, JR., mus. ofcl.; b. Cin., Nov. 10, 1933; s. John Hoxland and Sarah Christine (Seebaum) W.; B.A., Miami (O.) U., 1958. Mus. aid Smithsonian Instn., Washington, 1958, asst. curator, 1958-67, curator in charge div. transp., 1967-69, chmn. dept. industries, 1969—. Bd. dirs. R.R. Advancement Information Law Found., Nat. Capitol Mus. Transp. Mem. Assn. Pvt. R.R. Car Owners (dir. 1971—), Soc. History Tech. (adv. council 1971—). Author: Cincinnati Locomotive Builders, 1965; American Locomotives 1830-1880: An Engineering History, 1968. Mem. editorial bd. Bus. History Rev., 1969—; editor Bull. Ry. and Locomotive Hist. Soc., 1970—. Contbr. articles to profl. jours. Office: Nat Mus History and Tech Smithsonian Instn 14th St and Constitution Av Washington DC 20560

WHITE, JOSEPH WILLIAM, lawyer; b. Richlands, Va., Jan. 3, 1933; s. Joseph Moss and Josephine Virginia (Brown) W.; B.S., Hampden-Sydney Coll., 1954; M.Litt., U. Pitts., 1960; J.D., U. Va., 1960; m. Joanna Kay Warner, June 13, 1959; children—Ellen Cassell, William Moss, Andrew Warner, Christopher Graham. Admitted to Va. bar, 1960; since practiced in Winchester; partner firm Larrick & White, Winchester, 1964—; dir. Bank Frederick County, W.B.F. White & Sons, Inc. Mem. Winchester Bd. Zoning Appeals, 1966—; mem. Gov's. Hwy. Safety Commn., 1968—. Chmn., City of Winchester, 1968—; mem. Winchester Democratic Com., 1966—. Bd. dirs. Winchester-Frederick County United Givers Fund, Northwestern Workshop, Inc.; bd. dirs., chmn. Winchester-Frederick County chpt. A.R.C. Served to 1st lt. AUS, 1954-57. Mem. Am., Va. State bar assns., Va. State Bar, Va. Trial Lawyers Assn., Winchester-Frederick County Bar Assn. (pres. 1973—), Phi Alpha Delta, Kappa Alpha. Democrat. Methodist. Lion. Club: Golf (Winchester, Va.). Editor Va. Law Weekly, 1959-60. Home: 806 S Stewart St Winchester VA 22601 Office: 35E Boscawen St Winchester VA 22601

WHITE, JOSHUA WARREN, JR., paper co. exec., state legislator; b. Norfolk, Va., Aug. 27, 1916; s. J. Warren and Emily (Johnston) W.; ed. Washington and Lee U., 1939; m. Dorothy Lee Winstead, Aug. 30, 1939; children—Joshua Warren, Dorothy Lee, William Carr, Emily Johnston. With Old Dominion Paper Co., Norfolk, 1946—, treas., 1946—, pres., 1946—; dir. Va. Nat. Bank, Norfolk. Mem. mcht. adv. bd. Union Bay-Camp Paper Corp., N.Y.C., 1959; chmn. mcht. adv. bd. Internat. Paper Co., N.Y.C., 1962. Pres., Young Democratic Clubs Va., 1946; treas., mem. 2d Dist. Dem. Com., 1967—; mem. Ho. of Dels., Va. State Legislature, 1962—; mem. So. Regional Edn. Bd., 1962-69. Bd. dirs. United Communities Fund, Tidewater Cancer Soc.; bd. dirs., mem. exec. com. Norfolk Gen. Hosp.; trustee Tidewater Va. Devel. Council, Jamestown Found.; treas. Edgewater Turney Home for Boys and Girls, 1970—, also bd. dirs. Served as lt. comdr. USNR, 1941-45: PTO. Mem. Nat. (past dir.), Southeastern (past pres.) paper trade assns., Navy League (dir. Hampton Roads council), Norfolk C. of C., Presbyn. (past deacon.). Clubs: Norfolk Yacht and Country, Norfolk German; Virginia (Norfolk); Cedar Point Country (Portsmouth, Va.); Princess Anne Country (Virginia Beach, Va.). Home: 1206 Graydon Av Norfolk VA 23507 Office: 3600 Progress Rd Norfolk VA 23502

WHITE, KENNETH OLIVER, physicist; b. San Diego, May 10, 1940; s. Alford William and Alogene Lila (Evans) W.; B.S., Fresno State Coll., 1962; M.A., N.M. State U., 1965, Ph.D., 1967; m. Dorothy Eloise Wimer, Jan. 1962 (div. Nov. 1970); children—William, Cecelia; m. 2d, Betty Darlene Leeper, Dec. 31, 1970; 1 dau., Jennifer; stepchildren—Annemarie, Margot. Trainee NASA, 1965-67; research physicist Atmospheric Scis. Lab., U.S. Army Electronics Command, White Sands Missile Range, N.M., 1967—. Mem. Am. Phys. Soc., Sigma Pi Sigma. Home: 5205 Fairbanks St Apt 63 El Paso TX 79924 Office: Atmospheric Scis Lab US Army Electronics Command White Sands Missile Range NM 88002

WHITE, LENDELL AARON, microbiologist; b. Sabetha, Kan., Nov. 10, 1926; s. Leonard Aaron and Della C. (Graham) W.; B.A., U. Kan., 1951, M.A., 1955; student Washburn U., 1948-49; m. Helen June Rhodes, Sept. 5, 1948; children—Charles Leonard, Peggy Ann. Bacteriologist, Kan. State pub. Health Labs., Topeka, 1951-53; research asst. U. Kan., Lawrence, 1953-54; supervisory research microbiologist Center for Disease Control, Atlanta, 1955—. Dist. commr. Atlanta area council Boy Scouts Am., 1967-70, asst. council commr., 1970-71. Recipient Silver Beaver award Boy Scouts Am. Served with USNR, 1944-46. Mem. Am. Soc. Microbiologist, Sci. Research Soc. Am. Methodist. Lion. Home: 2534 Wilson Woods Dr Decatur GA 30033 Office: 1600 Clifton Rd Atlanta GA 30333

WHITE, LEONARD ALOYSIOUS, JR., educator; b. Joplin, Mo., June 23, 1933; s. Leonard Aloysious and Louise Clare (Schorgl) W.; B.B.A, Rockhurst Coll., 1954; M.S., St. Louis U., 1961, Ph.D., 1963; m. Katherine C. Kirk, Sept. 28, 1957; children—Linda, Paula, Dale, Thomas, Leslie. Instr., St. Louis U., 1961-63, asst. prof., 1963-65; asso. prof. U. Ark., Fayetteville, 1965-70, prof., 1970—, head dept. econs., 1971—; cons. antitrust cases, 1965—. Served with USNR, 1954-58. NSF grantee, Purchasing Agts. grantee. Mem. Am., Midwest, So. econ. assns., S.W. Social Sci. Assn. Home: 2595 Manor Dr Fayetteville AR 72701

WHITE, LEONARD CECIL, univ. adminstr.; b. Plano, Tex., July 9, 1919; s. Floyd Earl and Bessie Beatrice (Turner) W.; B.S., Tex. Christian U., 1948; m. Clara Ceville Moore, Feb. 12, 1943; children—Stephen Jerome, Susan Erline. Parts dept. Frigidaire Sales Corp., 1939-41, gen. office bookkeeper, 1946; with Tex. Christian U., 1948—, instr. accounting, 1948-49, bus. mgr., treas., 1955—, vice chancellor, 1961—. Dir. Tarrant State Bank. Sec. William C. Connor Found. Served to maj., inf. AUS, 1942-46; PTO. Decorated Purple Heart, Bronze Star; recipient valuable alumni award Tex. Christian U., 1972. C.P.A., Tex. Mem. Nat. Assn. Coll. and Univ. Bus. Officers, Tex. Soc. C.P.A.'s. Mem. Christian Ch. Clubs: South Fort Worth Rotary (pres. 1958-59), Colonial Country (Ft. Worth). Home: 3621 Brighton Rd Fort Worth TX 76109

WHITE, LONNIE JOE, historian, educator; b. Knox City, Tex., Feb. 12, 1931; s. John Alexander and Fannie Melissa (Coates) W.; B.A., West Tex. State Coll., 1951; M.A., Tex. Technol. Coll., 1955; Ph.D., U. Tex., 1961; m. Nancy Louella Evans, June 23, 1951; children—John Evans and Brenda Jo. Teaching asst. history U. Tex., Austin, 1957-61; asst. prof. history Memphis State U., 1961-63, asso. prof. history, 1963-67, prof. history, 1967—. Served with AUS, 1951-53. Am. Philos. Soc. Research grantee, 1963. Mem. Am., So., Western Ark., Tex. State hist. assns., Orgn. Am. Historians, Pi Sigma Alpha, Phi Alpha Theta. Baptist. Author: Politics on the Southwestern Frontier; Arkansas Territory, 1819-1836, 1964; Hostiles and Horse Soldiers; Indian Battles and Campaigns in the West, 1972. Editor: Old Mobeetie, 1877-1885, 1967; The Miles Expedition of 1874-1875, 1971; asso. editor Jour. of West, 1963—. Contbr. numerous articles on history and book revs. to profl. jours. Home: 4272 Rhodes Av Memphis TN 38111

WHITE, LOUISE RUFFIN (MRS. MORRIS EDWARD WHITE), civic worker; b. Como, Miss., Apr. 24, 1898; d. Robert and Kate (Weller) Ruffin; A.B., Miss. State Coll. for Women, 1916; postgrad. Peabody Coll., 1917; m. Morris Edward White, Oct. 8, 1920; children—Louise (Mrs. William Caldwell Cooke), Frances (Mrs. James Klay), Martha (Mrs. Dan Blalock, Jr.). Tchr. math., Aberdeen, Miss., 1917-18, Tarrytown, N.Y., 1918-20. Pres. P.T.A., Tampa, Fla., 1930-32; bd. dirs. YMCA, Tampa, 1932-38, treas., 1933; mem. Tb Bd., Tampa, 1938-41, treas., 1938; treas. Def. Council, Tampa, 1941-46, chmn. county nutrition, 1941-46; mem. Children's Home Bd., Tampa, 1946-56, pres., 1951-52; pres. Chiselers of U. Tampa, 1961-62; mem. Golfview Garden Circle Book Club, Tampa Symphony Club, Tampa Yacht Club, Palma Ceia Golf Club, Rotary Ann, Hillsboro County Bar Aux. (pres. 1963-64), Colonial Dames Am., Inner Wheel Club Lampa U.S.A. Democrat. Episcopalian. Home: 916 Golfview Av Tampa FL 33609

WHITE, MORRIS EDWARD, lawyer; b. Yazoo City, Miss., Aug. 13, 1892; s. Andrew and Fannie (Middleton) W.; B.S., U. Miss., 1913, M.A., 1915, LL.B., 1915; m. Louise Ruffin, Oct. 8, 1920; children—Louise (Mrs. W. C. Cooke), Frances Ruffin (Mrs. James B. Klay), Martha Morris (Mrs. Daniel S. Blalock, Jr.). Admitted to Miss. bar, 1915; practiced in Columbus, 1915-17; mem. firm Bell & White, Greenville, 1919-25; admitted to Fla. bar, 1925, since practiced in Tampa; mem. firm Shackleford, Brown, White & Tillman, 1925-28, Mabry, Reaves, Carlton & White, 1930-44, Fowler, White, Gillen, Yancey & Humkey, 1944-59, Fowler, White, Gillen, Humkey & Trenam, 1959, now mem. firms Fowler, White, Gillen, Kinney, Boggs & Villareal, P.A., Tampa, also Fowler, White, Humkey, Burnett, Hurley & Banick, Miami, Fla. Mem. Hillsborough County Def. Council, 1941-42; bd. dirs. U.S.O., 1941-45; chmn. Hillsborough County Port Authority, 1945-48; pres. Tampa Community Chest, 1938. Served to capt. U.S. Army, 1918. Mem. Am., Fla., Hillsborough County bar assns., Internat. Assn. Ins. Counsel, Maritime Law Assn. U.S., Am. Judicature Soc., Am. Legion (past post comdr.). Episcopalian. Mason (33 deg., Shriner), Rotarian (past pres.; dist. gov. internat. 1948-49). Clubs: University, Palma Ceia Golf and Country, Tampa Yacht and Country. Home: 916 Golfview Av Tampa FL 33609 Office: First Fed Bldg 220 Madison St Tampa FL 33602

WHITE, NATHAN EMMETT, JR., lawyer; b. Dallas, Nov. 28, 1941; s. Nathan Emmett and Martha Eleanor (Scogin) W.; B.B.A., So. Meth. U., 1964; J.D., 1972; postgrad. law studies George Washington U., 1969-71; m. Wanda Joyce Cason, Feb. 28, 1964; children—Steven Kelly, Russell Bradley. Self-employed as C.P.A., Plano, Tex., 1965-66; admitted to Tex. bar, 1972; since practiced in Plano; dir. Precision Mfg. Co., Nathan White Dept. Store, Inc., Ave. K. Devel. Corp. (all Plano). Treas. Plano Heritage Assn., 1973—. Chmn. Collin County (Tex.) Republican Com., 1971—. Bd. dirs. YMCA, Plano, United Fund, Plano. Served to lt. (s.g.) USNR, 1966-71. Mem. Plano C. of C. (dir. 1973—), Sigma Chi. Methodist. Mason, Rotarian. Home: 2700 Arborcove St Plano TX 75074 Office: PO Box 24 Plano TX 75074

WHITE, NELL AMOS (MRS. CHARLES WILLIAM WHITE, SR.), land clearing co. exec.; b. Murphy, N.C., June 14, 1925; d. Charles Nathan and Blanche Elizabeth (Queen) Amos; grad. high sch.; student course Internat. Accountants Soc., 1962; m. Charles William White, Sr., Dec. 31, 1944; children—Charles William II, David, Douglas, Timothy. Sec., bookkeeper Herman H. West & Co., Murphy, 1957-59, sec., treas., 1959—, also dir. Sec., treas. Am. Cancer Soc., Murphy, 1969, 70; mem. Southwestern N.C. Planning and Devel. Commn., 1972. Sec. Cherokee County Republican Party, 1960-65, vice chmn., 1968-71; mem. Cherokee County, N.C., Murphy exec. coms. Republican Party of N.C., 1968-71. Bd. dirs. Cherokee County Housing Corp., Inc., Murphy, Four Sq. Community Action, Inc., Andrews, S.C. Mem. Murphy Bus. and Profl. Women (pres. 1970, 71). Baptist (tchr. Sunday sch. 1961, 62, 67-70; finance com. 1970—). Club: Murphy Band Boosters (sec. 1967, 68). Home: Tanglewood Forest Murphy NC 28906 Office: Herman H West & Co Profl Bldg Murphy NC 28906

WHITE, NOAH WESLEY, ins. co. exec.; b. McKinney, Tex., Oct. 29, 1924; s. Noah and Cecil Vance (Meador) W.; student So. Meth. U., 1946, Tex. Christian U., 1947-48; m. June Wight, July 3, 1943; children—Carolyn (Mrs. Ronald D. Scott), William Wesley. With Agrl. Workers Mut. Auto Ins. Co., Fort Worth, 1948—, asst. sec., 1948-52, treas., dir., 1952-60, v.p., treas., 1960-74, sr. v.p., treas., 1974—; v.p. Nat. Farm Life Ins. Co., 1947—. Served with USAAC, 1943-46. Mem. Tex. Christian U. Alumni Assn. Methodist. Elk. Club: Ridglea Country. Home: 4421 Ridgeton Rd Fort Worth TX 76116 Office: 6001 Bridge St Fort Worth TX 76101

WHITE, ORLANDO HOMER, coll. exec.; b. Charleston, S.C., Mar. 23, 1928; s. Homer S. and Mattie M. (McWhite) W.; B.S., S.C. State Coll., 1953; postgrad. N.Y. U., 1959-61; LL.D., Allen U., 1970; m. Marion Lelia Brown, Nov. 24, 1956; children—Orlando Homer, Lesylee Maurelia Aleson. Acting bus. mgr. Voorhees Coll., Denmark, S.C., 1953, bur. mgr., 1954-73, accountant, purchasing agt., supr. non-acad. personnel, 1954-73; grants coordinator S.C. State Coll. at Orangeburg, 1973—. Mem. Nat., So. assns. coll. and univ. bus. officers, Omega Psi Phi. Episcopalian. Club: Kahine Investment (pres.). Address: 1045 E Calhoun Dr Denmark SC 29042

WHITE, PERRY MERRILL, physician; b. Texarkana, Ark., Oct. 11, 1925; s. Perry Merrill and Mary Gladys (Shelton) W.; B.S., Baylor U., 1948, M.D., 1953; postgrad. Vanderbilt U., 1948-49; m. Lucy Katherine Freeman, Dec. 27, 1947; children—Perry Merrill III, Georgia Lynette, Katherine Landis, John David. Intern, VA Hosp., Houston, 1953-54; practice gen. medicine and surgery, Spearman, Tex., 1955-57; resident orthopedic surgery Talmadge Meml. Hosp., Augusta, Ga., 1957-61; practice medicine, specializing in orthopedic surgery, Atlanta, 1961—; chief Ga. Adult Amputee Clinic; panelist Ga. Dept. Vocational Rehab.; instr. Ga. Baptist Hosp. Orthopedic Surgery Residency Program. Cons. Ga. Crippled Childrens Service. Mem. Circle-R Republican Support Com., North by Northwest Civic Assn. Bd. dirs. Evangelism Internat., Haggai Evangelistic Assn., Atlanta. Served with USNR, 1944-46. Diplomate Am. Bd. Orthopedic Surgery. Fellow Am. Acad. Orthopedic Surgeons; mem. A.M.A., So., Ga., Atlanta med. assns., Eastern Orthopedic Assn., Ga., Atlanta orthopedic socs., Am. Coll. Sports Medicine, Alpha Kappa Kappa. Baptist (deacon). Club: Cherokee Town and Country. Home: 1547 Cave Rd NW Atlanta GA 30327 Office: 340 Boulevard NW Atlanta GA 30312

WHITE, RICHARD CRAWFORD, congressman; b. El Paso, Tex., Apr. 29, 1923; s. James Crawford and Lela (Mueller) W.; B.A., U. Tex., 1946, LL.B., 1949; m. Katherine Huffman, Dec. 18, 1949 (dec. Mar. 1972); children—Rodrick James, Richard Whitman, Raymond Edward; m. 2d, Kathleen Fitzgerald, Sept. 29, 1973. Admitted to Tex. bar, 1949; trial atty., El Paso, 1949-64; mem. 89th-93d congresses from 16th Dist. Tex. Active civic and vets. orgns. Mem. Tex. Ho. of Reps., 1955-58; chmn. El Paso County Democratic Com., 1962-64. Served with USMCR, World War II; PTO. Mem. El Paso County Bar Assn., State Bar Tex., Phi Alpha Delta, Sigma Alpha Epsilon. Episcopalian. Club: 89th Democratic Congress (dir.). Home: 146 US Courthouse El Paso TX 79901 Office: Cannon House Office Bldg Washington DC 20515

WHITE, ROBERT EUGENE, clergyman; b. Lenoir County, N.C., Apr. 12, 1936; s. James Talmadge and Helen Elizabeth (Little) W.; A.B., Atlantic Christian Coll., 1964; M.Div., Lexington Theol. Sem., 1968; m. Emma Ruth Suggs, June 21, 1954; children—Sharon Ruth, Robert Eugene. Ordained to ministry Christian Ch., 1963; minister Hookerton (N.C.)-Airy Grove Unity Ch., 1959-64, Sharpsburg (Ky.) Christian Ch., 1964-68, Broad Street Christian Ch., New Bern, N.C., 1968—. Clin. chaplain Neuse Clinic, New Bern, 1970—; chaplain New Bern Police Dept., 1969—. Mem. gen. bd. Christian Chs. in N.C., 1970—. Mem. New Bern Mental Health Assn., Sigma Pi Alpha. Mason. Contbr. articles to profl. jours. Home: 2108 Steeple Chase Dr New Bern NC 28560 Office: 802 Broad St New Bern NC 28560

WHITE, RUDOLPH ALBERT, coll. adminstr.; b. Townley, Ala., May 3, 1924; s. James and Ada (Castleberry) W.; B.S., U. Ala., 1951, M.S., 1953, Ph.D. (Ford Found. fellow), 1958; m. Virginia Coley, Apr. 29, 1946; children—Larry, Robert. Instr., U. Ala. at Birmingham, 1951-56; asso. prof. Miss. State U., Starkville, 1958-60, prof. econs., dir. grad. studies, 1961-68, cons. Ford Found. project, 1965-68; dir. instrn. U. Ga., Athens, 1969—. Cons., Ford Found. project Savannah State Coll., 1971-73. Served with USNR, 1943-46. Mem. Indsl. Relations Research Assn., So. Econs. Assn., Phi Kappa Phi, Beta Gamma Sigma. Contbr. to profl. jours. Home: 435 Rivermont Rd Athens GA 30601

WHITE, SAMUEL HARVEY, JR., hosp. dir.; b. Ethel, Miss., July 11, 1934; s. Samuel H. and Kathleen (Barnes) W.; B.S., Miss. Coll., 1954; postgrad. Miss. State U., 1954-55; m. Martha Jo Sumrall, June 29, 1961; children—Katherine McLaurin, Isabel Ingram. Sr. accountant Peat, Marwick, Mitchell & Co., Jackson, Miss., 1957-62;

chief accountant Sch., Pictures, Inc., Jackson, 1962-64; asst. treas. Lamar Life Ins. Co., Jackson, 1964-66; asst. dir. Univ. Hosp., Jackson, 1966-74; adminstr. Miss. Meth. Hosp. and Rehab. Center, Jackson, 1974—. Treas., Jackson Men's Y Club, 1966; mem. budget com. Greater Jackson United Givers Fund, 1969. Served with USNR, 1955-57. C.P.A., Miss. Mem. Am. Inst. C.P.A.'s, Miss. Soc. C.P.A.'s (chpt. pres. 1967), Hosp. Financial Mgmt. Assn. (chpt. treas. 1969). Kiwanian (chmn. finance com. 1965). Home: 5901 Medallion Dr Jackson MS 39211 Office: 2500 N State St Jackson MS 39216

WHITE, THOMAS HARRISON, electronics co. exec.; b. Rockville Center, N.Y., Mar. 23, 1942; s. Gifford Elmore and Sarah Ruth (Harrison) W.; student U. Tex., 1959-64; m. Jane Y. Collier, May 12, 1962; children—Judith Susanna, James Taylor. Exec. v.p. White Instruments, Inc., Austin, Tex., 1968—. Mem. I.E.E.E., Audio Engring. Soc. Club: Lake Travis Cruising Assn. (Austin). Home: 2409 Vista Lane Austin TX 78703 Office: PO Box 698 Austin TX 78767

WHITE, THOMAS NICHOLAS, cons.; b. Gorizia, Italy, May 25, 1938; s. Nicholas M. and Olga (Fodor) W.; B.A., George Washington U., 1962, M.A., 1965, postgrad., 1966—; m. Julie Ahlman, Sept. 11, 1971. Research asso. Research & Microfilm Publs., Inc., Washington, 1965-68; research asst. George Washington U., 1966; social sci. analyst U.S. Civil Rights Commn., Washington, 1967; edn. research, planning asso. Washington Pub. Schs., 1968, asst. to asst. supt. for planning and devel., 1969-73; ednl. and mgmt. cons., 1973—; cons. Dept. Edn., Commonwealth of P.R., 1971. Intercollegiate soccer coach George Washington U., Washington, 1964-69. Mem. Am. Polit. Sci. Assn., Am. Acad. Polit. and Social Scis. Home: 2000 N St NW Washington DC 20036

WHITE, THURMAN JAMES, univ. ofcl.; b. Ponca City, Okla., Nov. 7, 1916; s. Charles L. and Winona Faye (Enfield) W.; A.B., Phillips U., 1936; M.S., U. Okla., 1941; Ph.D., U. Chgo., 1950; m. Corrine Laura Hartson, June 13, 1939; children—Sue Ann, Charles Frank. Instr. prison edn. U. Okla., 1937-39, supr. Statewide Mus. Service, 1940-42, dir. audio-visual edn., 1942-46, asst. dir. extension div., 1946-47, acting dir., 1947-48, dir., 1949-50, dean extension div. 1950—, dean Coll. Continuing Edn., 1961—, now v.p. univ., exec. sec. Film Council of Am., 1946-47, bd. trustees, 1950. Mem. Def. Adv. Com. Edn. Armed Forces, 1957-60; exec. vice chmn. 1961 White House Conf. on Aging; mem. UNESCO Com. for Advancement of Adult Edn., mem. nat. adv. council Adult Basic Tchr. Tng. Program, 1966; mem. Pres.'s Nat. Adv. Council on Extension and Continuing Edn.; mem. White House Conf. on Internat. Cooperation, 1965, White House Conf. on Edn., 1965, mem. commn. acad. affairs Am. Council Edn. Bd. dirs. Gt. Books Found., Center Study Liberal Edn. Adults. Mem. N.E.A., Ednl. Screen (mem. editorial bd. 1947-50), Adult Edn. Assn. U.S.A. (pres. 1965-66), C. of C., Okla. Congress Parents and Tchrs. (state bd. mgrs., 1942—), Okla. Edn. Assn., Am. Legion, Okla. Mental Health Assn. (1st v.p.), Nat. U. Extension Assn. (chmn. liberal edn. com., chmn. on Extension Services in Armed Forces, rep. Am. Council on Edn., 1958-60, pres. 1960-61), S.W. Adult Edn. Assn. (exec. com.), Okla. Adult Edn. Assn., Phi Beta Kappa, Phi Delta Kappa, Psi Chi, Pi Kappa Alpha. Clubs: Internat. (Washington); Rotary. Editor: Adult Education. Contbr. articles ednl. jours. Home: 1105 Woodland Dr Norman OK 73069

WHITE, TOM WILLINGHAM, accountant; b. McAllen, Tex., Feb. 16, 1943; s. Louis Thomas and Leota Faye (Grimm) W.; B.B.A., U. Tex., 1965; m. Lauryn G. Longwell, Mar. 8, 1968; 1 son, Brad Edward. Accountant, Haskins & Sells, C.P.A.'s, Houston, 1965-67, Paul Veale, C.P.A., McAllen, Tex., 1967-68; self-employed as C.P.A., Corpus Christi, Tex., 1969—. Bd. dirs., officer Corpus Christi Bus. and Estate Council. C.P.A., Mem. Am. Inst. C.P.A.'s, Tex. Soc. C.P.A.'s (chmn. com. Corpus Christi 1971-73), U. Tex. Ex-Students Assn. (officer Corpus Christi chpt. 1970-71, bd. dirs. 1971-72). Clubs: Mustang, Tex. Pharaoh Valley Country, Conquistadores (Corpus Christi). Home: 55 Townhouse Lane Corpus Christi TX 78412 Office: 2004 Six Hundred Bldg Corpus Christi TX 78401

WHITE, WALTER NYACK, hosp. and nursing home administr.; b. Cagayan, Philippines, Jan. 5, 1933 (came to U.S. 1937); s. Matthew James Walter III and Rita True (Rothgeb) W.; student Otterbein Coll., 1951-53; B.A. in Psychology, U. Va., 1956; postgrad. Med. Coll. Va. Sch. Hosp. Adminstrn., 1958-60; m. Joyce Woodard, Aug. 17, 1962; children—Kenneth Nyack, Kimberly True. Adminstrv. resident U. Va. Hosp., Charlottesville, 1960-61, adminstr. Children's Rehab. Center, 1961-63, adminstrv. asst., 1963-65; adminstr. R.J. Reynolds-Patrick County Meml. Hosp., 1965-69; adminstr. Page Meml. Hosp., Luray, Va., 1969-71; adminstr. Nursing Pavilion, Point Village, Christian and Missionary Alliance Found., Ft. Myers, Fla., 1971; now adminstr. Okeechobee (Fla.) Gen. Hosp. Chmn., Charlottesville-Albermarle Com. on Employment Physically Handicapped, 1963-65; mem. Ednl. TV Authority, Patrick County, Va., 1966-69, chmn., 1967-69; pres. Page County unit Am. Cancer Soc., 1970-71; past pres. Piedmont Tb and Respiratory Disease Assn.; past mem. curriculum devel. com. Lord Fairfax Community Coll. Served with USNR, 1956-58; 1st lt. Res., 1958-64. Mem. Am. Coll. Hosp. Adminstrs., Am. Hosp. Assn., Am. Acad. Med. Adminstrs., U. Va., Otterbein Coll., Med. Coll. Va. alumni Assns., Am., Va. hosp. assns., Am., Fla. nursing home assns. Home: 1307 SE 8th Av Okeechobee Estates Okeechobee FL 33472

WHITE, W(ALTER) PRESTON, JR., lawyer; b. Lynchburg, Va., Apr. 19, 1923; s. Walter Preston and Virginia (Candler) W.; B.S., U. N.C., 1946, J.D., 1949; m. Kathryn Mary Whittle, Oct. 12, 1951; children—Edith Rebecca, Amy Patricia. Admitted to N.C. bar, 1949, Fla. bar, 1961, Ga. bar, 1969; gen. practice, Concord, N.C., 1949-51; spl. atty. Office of Chief Counsel, Internal Revenue Service, Washington, 1951-53, Birmingham, Ala., 1953-56, Jacksonville, Fla., 1956-58, asst. regional counsel, Jacksonville, 1958-62; partner Dowling, White & Mooers, 1962-68; staff asst. to regional counsel Internal Revenue Service, Atlanta, 1968—. Served to 2d lt. USAAC, 1942-46. Mem. Am., N.C., Fed. bar assns., Fla. Bar, Phi Kappa Sigma, Delta Sigma Pi, Delta Theta Phi. Presbyn. Kiwanian. Home: 6851 Roswell Rd NE Atlanta GA 30328 Office: 275 Peachtree St Atlanta GA 32201

WHITE, WILBER SIDNEY, JR., dentist; b. Beaumont, Tex., Mar. 15, 1922; s. Wilber Sample and Florence Viola (Lloyd) W.; A.A., Lamar Jr. Coll., 1941; B.S., Sam Houston State Tchrs. Coll., 1943; Certified in Meteorology, U. Cal. at Los Angeles, 1944; D.D.S., Baylor U., 1950; m. Margaret Culver, June 5, 1949; children—Susan, Mary Katherine, Marilyn, Patricia, David, John, Paul, Sarah. Practice of dentistry, Beaumont, Tex., 1950—; dir. dental clinic City Health Clinic, 1967—; chmn. adv. com. Lamar Sch. Dental Hygiene, 1969—. Bd. dirs. Tex Found. Dental Health and Edn., Tex. Dental Plans, Inc., Citizens Nat. Dental Plan; exec. bd. Southeast Tex. Health Council, 1973—. Served to capt. USAAC, 1943-47; CBI. Fellow Am. Coll. Dentistry; mem. Am. Dental Assn. (mem. council dental health 1971—, alternate ho. dels. 1972—, del. nat. health council), Tex. Dental Assn. (chmn. council dental health 1969-70; v.p. 1971-73), Sabine Dist. Dental Soc. (pres. 1963, gen. chmn. spring clinic meetings 1963—), Am. Acad. Gen. Practice, Internat. Assn. Orthodontists, Tex. Pub. Health Assn., Chgo. Dental Soc. (asso.). Methodist. Mason (K.T., Shriner). Clubs: Sertoma (pres. 1963) Optimist (pres. 1954, lt. gov. 1958) Bus. and Profl. (pres. 1962) (Beaumont). Home: 3495 Kenwood Dr Beaumont TX 77706 Office: PO Box 5453 Beaumont TX 77702

WHITE, WILLIAM BENNY, data processing co. exec.; b. Cullman, Ala., June 23, 1940; s. William Ervin and Myrtle (Scogin) W.; B.S. in E.E., U. Ala., 1963, M.B.A., 1965; m. Janice Deanna Thrower, Sept. 1, 1962; children—William Stephen, Meredith Thrower. Design engr. Rust Engring. Co., Birmingham, Ala., 1963-64, 65-67; marketing rep. IBM Corp., Birmingham 1967—. Named Salesman of Year in Birmingham Area, IBM, 1972. Mem. I.E.E.E. Methodist (mem. ofcl. bd. 1970—, trustee 1971—).

WHITE, WILLIAM D., JR., lawyer; b. Dallas, Dec. 6, 1935; s. William D. and Jean (Tullis) W.; B.B.A., U. Tex., 1958, LL.B., 1960; m. Susan Lay; children—William D. III, David Herrington, Malcolm David, Kathleen Medora, Peggy Herrington, Stephen Andrew, Mimi Herrington. Admitted to Tex. bar, 1960; since practiced in Dallas; asso. firm Turner, White, Atwood, Meer & Francis, Dallas, 1960-63; mng. partner firm White, McElroy, White & Sides, Dallas, 1963—; dir. Transport Life Ins. Co., Ft. Five Resources, Inc., Houston. Active United Way, Heart Assn. Bd. dirs., mem. exec. com. Dallas Services for Visually Impaired Children; bd. dirs., chmn. 1974 sustaining membership campaign Park Cities-North Dallas YMCA. Mem. Am., Dallas bar assns., State Bar Tex., Kappa Sigma. Presbyn. Club: Salesmanship (Dallas). Home: 4224 Versailles St Dallas TX 75205 Office: 2505 Republic Nat Bank Tower Dallas TX 75201

WHITE, WILLIAM SMITH, journalist; b. DeLeon, Tex., May 20, 1907; s. John Van Dyke and Lucia Alberta (Smith) W.; student U. Tex., 1923-26; m. Irene Mason (div. 1945); m. 2d, June McConnell, Apr. 12, 1945; children—Lucia Stanton, Ann Victoria. Successively corr., feature writer, editor, war editor, assault war corr. A.P., 1943-45; Washington staff N.Y. Times, 1945—, senate corr., 1953-56, chief congl. corr., 1956-58, nationally syndicated polit. columnist, 1958; Washington corr. Harper's mag. 1957-58, contbg. editor, 1958-62; regents prof. U. Cal., Berkeley, 1957-58. Served with inf. AUS, 1942. Recipient Pulitzer prize in letters, 1955. Mem. Overseas Writers, Sigma Delta Chi. Clubs: Century (N.Y.C.); Metropolitan, Cosmos (Washington). Author: The Taft Story, 1955; Citadel: The Story of the U.S. Senate, 1957; Majesty and Mischief: A Mixed Tribute to F.D.R., 1961; The Professional: Lyndon B. Johnson, 1964; Home Place, 1963; The Responsibles, 1972. Contbr. mags. Address: 2101 Connecticut Av NW Washington DC 20008

WHITEFIELD, GROCE VESTER, retail co. exec.; b. Forreston, Tex., June 24, 1908; s. John P. and Leah Ellen (Henry) W.; student Abilene Christian Coll., 1925-27, Draughon's Bus. Coll., Dallas, 1927-28; m. Martha Melinda Watkins, May 30, 1936; children—Katherine Anne (Mrs. Curtis Robbins), Dorthy Lee (Mrs. Gary Verett). With M.E. Moses Co., Inc. and Memco Wholesale Co., Dallas, 1935—, controller, treas., 1946—. Bd. dirs. Christian Edn. Found., 1970—; chmn. bd. Christian Coll. of S.W., 1963-68. Served with USNR, 1943-45. Mem. Tex. Retail Assn., Dal-worth Shippers (exec. com., pres. 1967-71). Mem. Ch. of Christ (elder). Club: Spring Valley Country (Dallas). Home: 1625 Glen Valley St Irving TX 75061 Office: 2919 Hansboro Av Dallas TX 75224

WHITEFIELD, NORMAN WAINWRIGHT, educator; b. Sinton, Tex., Feb. 18, 1921; s. Emmit C. and Mable (Howland) W.; B.A., Abilene Christian Coll., 1947; M.A., U. Denver, 1954; postgrad. Case Western Res. U., 1966-68; m. Joyce Fulbright, Dec. 7, 1943. Instr., Abilene (Tex.) Christian Coll., 1948-58, prof., head dept. art, 1958—. Bd. dirs. Abilene Fine Arts Mus. Served with USAAF, 1943-45. Decorated Air medal. Mem. Coll. Art Assn., Soc. for Aesthetics, Soc. Archtl. Historians. Mem. Ch. of Christ. Home: 610 E N 19th St Abilene TX 79601

WHITEHEAD, CLAY THOMAS, govt. ofcl.; b. Neodesha, Kan., Nov. 13, 1938; s. Clay Bell and Helen (Hinton) W.; B.S., Mass. Inst. Tech., 1960, M.S., 1961, Ph.D., 1967; m. Margaret Mahon, May 19, 1973. Tech. aide Bell Telephone Labs., Murray Hill, N.J., 1958-59, sr. tech. aide, 1960; cons. to RAND Corp., Santa Monica, Cal., 1961, 62, 63, organizer policy research program on health services, 1967-69; teaching asst. Mass. Inst. Tech., Cambridge, 1962-63, lectr., 1966-67; mem. Pres.-elect's Task Force on Budget Policies, Washington, 1968-69; spl. asst. to Pres., Washington, 1969-70; dir. Office Telecommunications Policy, Washington, 1970—. Cons. to Bur. Budget, Washington, 1966-68. Served from 1st lt. to capt., AUS, 1963-65. Mem. Yosemite Inst., Sigma Xi, Tau Beta Pi, Eta Kappa Nu. Office: 1800 G St NW Washington DC 20504

WHITEHEAD, H(ARRIS) THORNTON, banker; b. Townsend, Va., Aug. 26, 1918; s. Claude Douvault and Nora (Elliott) W.; B.C.S., Strayer Coll., 1940; m. Karlotta Jacob, May 18, 1962. With Union Trust Co., Washington, 1941—, auditor, 1951-60, comptroller, 1960-64, v.p., comptroller, 1965-70, sr. v.p., 1971—. Mem. Am., D.C. bankers assns., Am. Inst. Banking, Internat. Platform Assn., Washington Bd. Trade, Phi Theta Pi. Republican. Presbyn. Club: Internat. (Washington). Home: 6534 Renwood Lane Annandale VA 22003 Office: 15th and H Sts NW Washington DC 20005

WHITEHEAD, MARVIN DELBERT, educator; b. Paoli, Okla., Dec. 18, 1917; s. Chester Arthur and Lola Elizabeth (Donnell) W.; B.S., Okla. State U., 1939. M.S., 1946; Ph.D., U. Wis., 1949; m. Verna Mae Johnson, Dec. 24, 1942; 1 son, James Mark. Asst. agrl. aide, soil conservation service U.S. Dept. Agr., Okla., 1936-38; asst. in agronomy Okla. State U., 1939-40; sr. seed analyst Fed. State Seed Lab., Ala., 1940-42; asst. plant pathology U. Wis., 1946-48, research fellow, 1948-49; asst. prof. Tex. A. & M. U., 1949-55; asso. prof. U. Mo., 1955-60; prof. botany Edinboro State Coll., 1960-63; prof. plant pathologist Ga. So. Coll., 1963-68; prof. botany Ga. State U., Atlanta, 1968—. Served with USAAF, 1941-46; PTO. Mem. A.A.A.S., Am. Phytopath. Soc., Mycol. Soc. Am., Bot. Soc. Am., Am. Inst. Biol. Sci., Crop Sci. Soc. Am., Am. Soc. Agronomy. Ofcl. Seed Analysis N.Am., Ga. Acad. Sci., Wis. Acad. Scis. Author: College Biology, 1963. Contbr. articles to jours. Home: 817 Clifton Rd NE Atlanta GA 30307

WHITEHEAD, RICHARD HOLMES, univ. ofcl.; b. Largo, Fla., July 9, 1917; s. James George and Janie (Taylor) W.; B.A., U. Fla., 1940, postgrad., 1954-56; grad. certificate in meteorology Cal. Inst. Tech., 1942; m. Martha Dallas Colson, Sept. 29, 1941; children—Carolyn Jo (Mrs. Robert Griffin Harrell), Karen Louise (Mrs. Wayne Lawrence Martin), Barbara Anne (Mrs. Jimmie Melvin Brunson), Shirley Jean. Chief clk. Registrar's Office, U. Fla., Gainesville, 1938-42, asst. registrar, 1946-52, asso. registrar, 1952-65, dean admissions, registrar, 1965—. Served to maj. USAAF, 1942-46. Mem. Am., Fla. (past pres.) assns. collegiate registrars and admissions officers, Assn. Coll. Admission Councillors, Fla. Assn. Ednl. Data Processors, Phi Kappa Phi, Alpha Phi Omega, Phi Gamma Delta. Mem. Ch. of Christ (bishop). Kiwanian. Club: Optimist (past pres.). Home: 923 NW 21st Terrace Gainesville FL 32603

WHITEHOUSE, ULYSSES GRANT, II, chemist, educator; b. Henderson, Ky., July 27, 1917; s. Ulysses Grant and Rosa (Leascher) W.; B.S. magna cum laude, U. Ky., 1940, M.S. magna cum laude (Sullivan Meml. fellow), 1941; M.S. (Chem. Research fellow), U. Ia., 1959; postgrad. (research fellow) Carnegie Inst. Tech., 1948-50; Ph.D. in Chemistry magna cum laude (Dow fellow, Am. Petroleum Inst. fellow), Tex. A. and M. U., 1953, Ph.D. in Oceanography, 1955; m. Doris Yvonne Sheets, Dec. 21, 1954; 1 son, Ulysses Grant III. Research supr. U.S. Rubber Co., Williamsport, Pa., 1942-43; asso. research dir. Carbide & Carbon Chems., Brook, N.J., 1945-47; research scientist div. war research Columbia, N.Y.C., 1943-45; prof., research dir. electron microscopy and colloid sci. Tex. A. and M. U., College Station, 1953—, research project dir., oceanography and colloid chem. cons. Found., 1953—. Dir. research projects NIH, 1959—, Office Naval Research, 1953—, NSF, 1958—, Am. Petroleum Inst., 1951-53; cons. U.S. Corps Engrs., 1954—, Tex. Indsl. Commn., 1960—. Recipient Distinguished Service award Manhattan Project, 1945. Fellow A.A.A.S., Am. Inst. Chemists; mem. Am. Chem. Soc. (tour lectr. 1968-73), Am. Petroleum Inst., Assn. Atomic Scientists, Electron Microscope Soc. Am., Geochem. Soc. Am., Soc. Limnology and Oceanography, Lenshawks Photog. Soc., Profl. Photographers Assn., N.Y, Acad. Sci., Phi Beta Kappa, Sigma Xi, Phi Kappa Phi, Sigma Pi Sigma, Phi Lambda Upsilon, Omicron Delta Kappa, Alpha Chi Sigma. Moose. Club: Brazos Valley Kennel (pres. Bryan 1968-70). Contbr. numerous articles on colloid chemistry, clay mineralogy, phys. chem. to profl. publs. Pioneer colloid chem. interactions in saline waters; biomed. research. Home: 4309 Nagle St Bryan TX 77801 Office: Electron Microscopy Div Tex A and M U College Station TX 77843

WHITEHURST, GEORGE WILLIAM, congressman; b. Norfolk, Va., Mar. 12, 1925; s. Calvert Stanhope and Laura (Tomlinson) W.; B.A., Washington and Lee U., 1950; M.A., U. Va., 1951; student W.Va. U., 1956-57, Ph.D., 1962; m. Jennette Seymour Franks, Aug. 24, 1946; children—Frances Seymour (Mrs. James E. Fitzgerald), Calvert Stanhope. Mem. faculty Old Dominion U., 1950-68, dean students, prof. history, 1963-68; news analyst sta. WTAR-TV, 1962-68; mem. 91st-93d congresses from 2d Dist. Va. Past mem. Mayor Norfolk Commn. Crime and Delinquency, Tidewater Council Health, Recreation and Welfare, Norfolk Council Alcoholism; past pres. Norfolk chpt. Am. Assn. UN, Norfolk Forum; past chmn. Am. Cancer Soc. crusade in Norfolk. Served with USNR, 1943-46. Decorated Air medal with oak leaf cluster. Mem. Am. Hellenic Ednl. and Progressive Assn., V.F.W., Am. Legion, Delta Upsilon. Methodist (past chmn. bd.). Lion, Rotarian. Home: PO Box 685 Sea Pines Sta Virginia Beach VA 23451 also 2300 S 24th St Arlington VA 22206 Office: Cannon House Office Bldg Washington DC 20515

WHITEMAN, HAROLD BARTLETT, JR., coll. pres.; b. Nashville, Apr. 22, 1920; s. Harold Bartlett and Emma Morrow (Anderson) W.; student Montgomery Bell Acad., 1930-34, Taft Sch., 1934-37; A.B., Yale, 1941, Ph.D., 1958; M.A., Vanderbilt U., 1950; m. Edith Uhler Davis, July 13, 1946; children—Bartlett, Maclin, Priscilla. Adminstrv. asst. Pan Am. Airways Africa, Ltd., 1941-42; instr. Taft Sch., 1946-47, trustee, 1950-55; teaching fellow Vanderbilt U., 1947-48; asst. dean freshmen, dean undergrad. affairs, 1948-54; dean of freshmen Yale, 1954-64, lectr. in history, 1956-64, asst. to pres., 1964-67; asst. chancellor N.Y. U., 1967-69, vice chancellor, 1969-71, prof. govt. and internat. relations, 1966-71; pres., prof. history Sweet Briar Coll., 1971—. Bd. dirs. Episcopal Ch. Found.; trustee Chatham Hall, chmn. bd. trustees Berkeley Div. Sch. Served as maj. USAAF, 1942-46. Mem. Phi Beta Kappa, Delta Kappa Epsilon, Scroll and Key. Author: Neutrality 1941, 1941. Editor: Charles Seymour, Letters from the Paris Peace Conf., 1965. Home: Sweet Briar Coll Sweet Briar VA 24595

WHITESCARVER, KENNETH TYREE, mil. acad. pres.; b. Salem, Va., Apr. 3, 1920; s. Kenneth Tyree and Eulalia Elizabeth (Surface) W.; student Roanoke Coll., 1938-40; B.A., Hardin-Simmons U., 1942; J.D., George Washington U., 1954; postgrad. Memphis State U., summers 1969-70; m. Alice Clare King, Mar. 9, 1946; children—Kenneth Tyree, Robert Hunt, William King. Commd. 2d lt. USMC, 1942, advanced through grades to lt. col., 1963; with 3d Marine Div., 1957-58; post legal officer Quantico, Va., 1958-61; with Office Legislative Asst. to comdt. USMC, 1961-63; ret., 1963; admitted to Va. bar, 1954; partner Whitescarver & Scaife, Fredericksburg, 1963-68; pres. Fork Union (Va.) Mil. Acad., 1968—. Substitute county judge, Spotsylvania County, Va., 1963-68; mem. adv. bd. Fork Union br. Nat. Bank & Trust Co. of Charlottesville, 1970—. Chmn., Rappahannock River Basin Area Adv. Com., 1966-68, Rappahannock Area Devel. Commn., 1965-68. Bd. dirs. Frank C. Pratt Mental Health chpt., Piedmont (Va.) Community Coll. (vice chmn), Va. Assn. Ind. Schs.; mem. adv. bd. Salvation Army. Decorated Navy Commendation medal; recipient Judge Adv. Gen. Navy award lit. merit, 1959, Citizenship award City of Fredericksburg, 1968. Mem. Am., Va., 39th Jud. Circuit bar assns., Am., Va. trial lawyers assns., Fredericksburg Area C. of C. (dir., Citizenship award 1966), Am. Legion, Phi Delta Phi. Baptist. Mason (32 degree), K.P. Address: Fork Union VA 23055

WHITESELL, JAMES CLARENCE, food broker; b. St. Joseph, Mo., Apr. 13, 1931; s. David Earl and Emma Gertrude (Derks) W.; student St. Joseph Jr. Coll., 1949-50, U. Mass., 1956-57, Alexander Hamilton Inst., 1960-62; m. Melita Ann Hogan, Sept. 14, 1955; children—Bart, Beth Ann, Susan, Patricia. Salesman, Procter & Gamble, 1950-54, Rath Packing Co., 1954-62, Food Merchandisers, 1962-64; pres., gen. mgr. Splty. Food Sales Co., Inc., Atlanta, 1964—; dir. Belcraft Constrn. Co., Hadacol Corp. Served with USMCR, 1951-53. Mem. Frozen Food Council Ga. (v.p. 1972-73). Elk, K.C. Home: 3470 Crown Point Pl Decatur GA 30032 Office: 1030 White St SW Atlanta GA 30310

WHITESELL, ROBERT WESLEY, social worker; b. Durham, N.C., Dec. 5, 1927; s. Robert Banks and Eula (Walters) W.; A.B., Houghton Coll., 1953; M.S. in Social Work, Richmond Profl. Inst., 1964; m. Agnes Julia Bonesteel, Dec. 20, 1950; children—Carol Elaine, David Robert, Paul Wesley, Elena Marta. Probation officer, supt. juvenile detention home Guilford County Domestic Relations Ct., Greensboro, N.C., 1957-63; coordinator services to children and alcoholics Mecklenburg County Mental Health Clinic, Charlotte, N.C., 1964-67; unit clin. social worker VA Hosp., Salisbury, N.C., 1967—. Field instr. U. N.C., 1966-70. Served with USNR, 1946-48, 53-55. Mem. Nat. Assn. Social Workers, Acad. Certified Social Workers. Home: 5849 Charing Pl Charlotte NC 28211 Office: 1601 Brenner Av Salisbury NC 28144

WHITEWAY, HOWARD EARLE, steel co. exec.; b. Oak Park Ill., May 1, 1927; s. William Earl and Ivy Mae (James) W.; B.A., Westminster Coll., 1950; m. Sue Adelaide Sperry, July 1, 1950; children—Ralph, Paula, Nan. Vice pres. sales Corey Steel Co., Chgo., 1951-66, also dir.; exec. v.p. Jenks Metals Inc., Miami, 1966-69; pres., owner Asso. Steel Co. of Houston, 1969—. Pres. Oak Brook Sch. Bd., 1965. Served with AUS, 1945-46. Mem. Steel Service Center Inst. (pres. Central States chpt. 1965-66, Fla. chpt. 1968-69, Tex. chpt. 1971-72). Rotarian. Home: 11907 Memorial St Houston TX 77024 Office: 7211 Av B Houston TX 77011

WHITFIELD, CARROLL JULIAN, farm implement mfg. co. exec.; b. nr. Cairo, Ga., Feb. 24, 1931; s. Charles and Carolyn Amanda (Bryant) W.; student Middle Ga. Coll., 1948-49; B. M.E., Ga. Inst. Tech., 1955; m. Laura Susan Gandy, Dec. 27, 1955;

children—Amanda Susan, Julia Carol, Miles Gandy. Design engr. Chemstrand Corp., textile machinery mfg., Pensacola, Fla., 1955-56, Timber Fabrications, pre-fabricated truss prodn., Perry, Fla., 1956-57; project engr. Lilliston Corp., farm implements mfg., Albany, Ga., 1957-67; v.p., dir. Kelley Mfg. Co., farm implements, Tifton, Ga., 1967—. Served with AUS, 1956. Mem. Am. Soc. M.E., Am. Soc. Agrl. Engrs., Tau Beta Pi, Pi Tau Sigma. Baptist. Patentee in field. Office: Kelley Mfg Co South Industrial Park PO Box 1145 Tifton GA 31794

WHITFIELD, JACK DUANE, aero. engr.; b. Paoli, Okla., May 16, 1928; s. Lloyd Vernon and Ethel Mae (Wigley) W.; B.S., U. Okla., 1951; M.S., U. Tenn., 1960; D.Sc., Royal Inst. Tech. (Sweden), 1972; m. Marcheta Rae Steward, Sept. 11, 1949; children—Donna Rae, Jeffrey Dwayne, Karen Sue. Engr., Consol. Vultee Aircraft Corp., Daingerfield, Tex., 1951-54; with ARO, Inc., Arnold AFB, Tenn., 1954—, chief von Karman Gas Dynamics Facility, 1968—. Cons. Nat. d'Etudes et de Recherches Aeronautiques, adv. group Aero. Research and Devel., Paris, France, 1960; cons. VITRO/Smith Corp., N.Y.C., 1963. Troop treas. Middle Tenn. council Boy Scouts Am., 1966—; active P.T.A. Served with AUS, 1946-48. Recipient Gen. H. H. Arnold award for contbns. to aerodynamic testing by Tenn. sect. Am. Inst. Aero. and Astronautics, 1968. Mem. Am. Inst. Aero. and Astronautics (sec., treas. 1961-62). Methodist. Lion. Club: Ozarks Wildlife (Little Rock, Ark.). Contbr. articles to profl. jours. Home: 506 Edgewood Dr Tullahoma TN 37388 Office: ARO Inc von Karman Gas Dynamics Facility Arnold AFB TN 37389

WHITFORD, STUART DIAL, cons. engr.; b. Albuquerque, Apr. 30, 1925; s. John Stuart and Ressie Oliver (Dial) W.; B.S. in Chem. Engring., U. Okla., 1949; m. Margaret O'Donnel, Feb. 26, 1960. Supt. water purification City of Oklahoma City, 1949-57; sales engr. Wallace & Tiernan, Inc., San Antonio, 1958-62; sr. devel. engr. United Carbon Co., Aransas Pass, Tex., 1962-70; cons. engr. Seligmann & Pyle, San Antonio, 1970—. Served with USAAF, 1942-45. Decorated Air medal, Purple Heart. Mem. Am. Inst. Chem. Engrs. Republican. Elk. Home: 922 E Ireland St Seguin TX 78155 Office: 419 S Main St San Antonio TX 78204

WHITING, GEORGE WASHINGTON BURKE, internat, shipping co. exec.; b. Phila., Mar. 23, 1921; s. George Burke and Daisy (Gilbert) W.; student Newport Bus. Coll., 1948; B.S., Bryant Coll., 1950; m. Dale Joan Canulla, May 30, 1942; children—Merrily (Mrs. Harvey Karter), Carolyn (Mrs. Charles G. Smith, Jr.), George Washington Burke III, Richard Giles. Pres., Frontier Freight Forwarders, Inc., Miami, Fla., 1955—, Frontier Freight Brokers, Inc., Miami, 1964—, Frontier Travel Agy., Inc., Hialeah, Fla., 1961—. Mem. regional export expansion council U.S. Dept. Commerce, 1971-73. Served with USN, 1939-45. Named Man of Year, Customs Brokers and Forwarders Assn. Miami, 1969-70. Mem. Customs Brokers and Forwarders Assn. Am. (mem. nat. adv. bd. 1962-73), Am. Soc. Travel Agts., Am. Soc. Internat. Execs., D.A.V., Customs Brokers and Forwarders Assn. Miami (pres. 1962-63), Hialeah-Miami Springs C. of C. Democrat. Roman Catholic. Lion. Clubs: Century (Hialeah); Tiger Bay Political (Miami). Home: 15800 SW 97th Av Miami FL 33157 Office: 2150 NW 70th Av Miami FL 33122

WHITINGTON, GENE LUTHER, pediatrician; b. Memphis, May 7, 1929; s. Frank Everett and Mary Lena (Hollingsworth) W.; student Miss. State Coll., 1947-50; M.D., U. Tenn., 1953; m. Martha Gaines, Feb. 4, 1950; children—Peggy (Mrs. Graydon Hartman), Deborah, Gene, Frank. Intern, Brooke Army Hosp., San Antonio, 1953-54; resident John Gaston Hosp., Memphis, 1956-58; practice medicine specializing in pediatrics, Memphis, 1956—; mem. staff LeBonheur, Baptist, Methodist, St. Joseph hosps. (all Memphis); asst. prof. U. Tenn. Med. Sch., 1965—. Owner, Faronic Square Townhouses, 1968—. Rancho Santa Marta, Tampico Mexico, 1969—; partner M & W Farms, Parkin, Ark. Served to capt., M.C., AUS, 1953-56. Fellow Am. Acad. Pediatrics. Home: 981 Palmer St Memphis TN 38116 Office: 1129 Hale St Memphis TN 38116

WHITLEDGE, CLYDE OWEN, computer tape co. exec.; b. Sayre, Okla., Dec. 5, 1921; s. Clarence Othar and Myrta Jay (York) W.; A.A., Sayre Jr. Coll., 1942; B.S. in M.E., U. Okla., 1949; postgrad. So. Meth. U., 1957; m. Kathryn Lucille Kennedy, Apr. 14, 1949; children—Dru Alan, Dana Ann. Air conditioning engr. Lone Star Gas Co., 1949-51; mgr. mfg. missile div. Tex. Instruments, 1951-63; pres. M-H Equipment Co., 1963-65; mgr. mfg. Stanray Corp. div. Traveler Boat Co., 1965-66; chief engr. Magnetic Tape Systems, Geotech. Corp., 1966-67; sr. v.p. Graham Magnetics Mfg., Inc., Graham, Tex., 1967—. Served to lt. (j.g.) USNR, 1942-46. Mem. Okla. U. Alumni Assn., C. of C. (mem. ednl. com. 1969-72; mem. indsl. com. 1969-71), Nat. Soc. Profl. Engrs. Unitarian. Mason. Club: Graham Country. Home: 921 Cherry St Graham TX 76046 Office: Graham TX 76046

WHITLEDGE, ESTHER MAE, constrn. co. exec.; b. Hartshorn, Okla., May 5, 1918; d. Charles N. and Laura Mae (Miller) Whitledge; student LaSalle Extension U. (Chgo.), 1954, U. Tenn., 1958-60. Owner, operator Mae's Service Sta. & Cafe, Portageville, Mo., 1942-44; co-owner Whitledge & Beis Constrn. Co., 1944-46, Twin Oaks Hotel, 1947-51; office mgr., accountant McAlister Constrn. Co., Memphis, 1951—, also corporate officer; corp. sec., treas. Martha-Mac Corp., 1964—; 1st v.p. Central States Dredging Co., Memphis. First v.p. Women's Exec. Council, Memphis, 1965-66. Bd. dirs. Happy Acres Home for Mentally and Physically Retarded Children, pres., 1973; mem. St. Jude Assn. Found. Named Outstanding Woman in civic participation Downtown Assn. Memphis, 1969, Woman of Year Memphis, 1973. Mem. Nat. Assn. Women in Constrn. (pres. 1960-61, nat. conv. chmn. 1964, nat. activities regional chmn. 1965-66, regional dir. 1969), Altrusa Internat. Club: Quota. Home: 4653 Auburn Rd Memphis TN 38116 Office: PO Box 16806 Memphis TN 38116

WHITLEY, ALVIN DONALD, govt. ofcl.; b. Newport News, Va., Sept. 14, 1933; s. Jacob Jordan and Margaret Frances (Mitchell) W.; B.A., U. Richmond, 1956; M.A. (U.S. Navy Pub. Affairs fellow), U. N.C., 1971; m. Betty Lou Evans, Sept. 16, 1956; children—Donald Tabb, Laurie Lynn, Alvin Mitchell. Reporter, Norfolk (Va.) Ledger-Star, 1962-63; pub. information specialist Dept. Army, Ft. Monroe, Va., 1963-65; pub. affairs officer Armed Forces Staff Coll., Norfolk, 1965—. Lectr. journalism Christopher Newport Coll. div. William and Mary Coll., Newport New, 1973. Served with USAF, 1956-62. Recipient citation Va. Pub. Relations Soc., 1968. Mem. Norfolk, Virginia Beach bds. realtors, Sigma Delta Chi, Kappa Sigma, Kappa Tau Alpha. Methodist. Lion. Home: 1045 Patrick Henry Way Virginia Beach VA 23455 Office: Armed Forces Staff Coll Norfolk VA 23511

WHITLEY, ROBERT PATRICK, govt. ofcl.; b. Birmingham, Ala., Apr. 1, 1926; s. Patrick Henry and Mittie (Newton) W.; B.S., Auburn U., 1948; postgrad. U. Okla., 1969—; m. Ruth Marie Schumann, July 21, 1950; children—Jennifer, Amy, Robert Patrick. Aero. research scientist NACA, 1948-51; dir. product assurance Redstone Arsenal, Ala., 1951—. Registered profl. engr., Ala. Mem. Am. Ordnance Assn. (Knowles award and honorarium 1971), Assn. U.S. Army. Home: 4220 Huntington Rd Huntsville AL 35802 Office: Redstone Arsenal AL 35809

WHITLOCK, FRED HENRY, mathematician; b. Winston-Salem, N.C., June 17, 1936; s. Henry Fred and Luvenia (Edwards) W.; B.S., N.C. A. and T. State U., 1959; m. Barbara Hill, Nov. 2, 1962; children—Carlton Fred, Kenneth Henry, Jacquelyn Ewaugh. Mathematician, sci. programmer NASA, Goodard Space Flight Center, Greenbelt, Md., 1962—. Mem. D.C. Young Democrats, 1964-68; mem. S.E. Washington Young Democrats, 1964-68. Served with AUS, 1959-62. Mem. Math. Assn. Am., Assn. for Computing Machinery, Nat. Urban League, Anacostia Civic Assn. Author: Orbit Prediction Accuracy Theory, 1963; Interplanetary Trajectory Encke Method Program, Manual 1, 1967, Manual 2, 1967, Manual for IBM OS/360, 1970; also articles in field. Home: 166 Chesapeake St SW Washington DC 20032 Office: Code 642 Bldg 1 Goodard Space Flight Center Greenbelt MD 20771

WHITLOCK, JAMES EDWARD, state legislator, savs. and loan exec.; b. Lebanon, Ky., Jan. 20, 1934; s. Robert Henry and Carrie (Benningfield) W.; student Bellarmine Coll., 1952-53; B.S., U. Ky., 1960; m. Barbara M. Hazard, Jan. 2, 1956; children—James Edward, Vincent Murrell, Elizebeth, Stephen. Owner real estate, gen. ins. agy., Lebanon, 1961-65; mem. Ky. Ho. of Reps., 1962-68, chief clk., 1968-70; pres., dir. First Fed. Savs. and Loan Assn., Campbellsville, Ky. Mem. Ky. Bldg. and Loan Legislative Com. Served with USMCR, 1954-58. Mem. Am. Legion, Ky. C. of C. K.C. Home: Route 3 Campbellsville KY 42718 Office: 1st and Broadway Campbellsville KY 42718

WHITLOCK, JAMES KENNETH, JR., city ofcl.; b. Hopewell, Va., Oct. 15, 1941; s. James Kenneth and Anne Julia (Baker) W.; B.S., Lamar U., 1963; M.P.A., U. Kan., 1966; m. Susan J. Hutchinson, Jan. 24, 1966; children—James, Steven, Robert Morgan. Asst. city mgr. City of Del City (Okla.), 1967-69, city mgr., 1971—; city mgr. City of Henryetta, 1969-71. Served with AUS, 1967. Mem. City Mgmt. Assn. Okla. (sec.-treas. 1973-74), Internat. City Mgmt. Assn. Baptist. Home: 4305 Angela Dr Del City OK 73115 Office: PO Box 15177 Del City OK 73115

WHITLOCK, JOHN JOSEPH, museum dir.; b. South Bend, Ind., Jan. 7, 1935; s. Joseph Mark and Helen Marcella (Cramer) W.; B.S. in Art, Ball State U., 1957, M.A. in Art, 1963; Ed.D., Ind. U., 1971; m. Sue Ann Kirkman, June 10, 1956; children—Kelly Ann, Michele Lynn, Mark. Tchr. art pub. schs., Union City, Ind., 1957-59; tchr. art, art dir. Madison (Ind.) City Schs., 1959-64; prof. art, dir. gallery Hanover (Ind.) Coll., 1964-69; teaching asso. Ind. U., 1969-70; dir. Burpee Art Mus., Rockford, Ill., 1970-72; prof. arts and humanities Elgin (Ill.) Community Coll., 1970-72; dir. Brooks Meml. Art Gallery, Memphis, 1972—; prof. mus. studies Southwestern Coll., Memphis, 1973-74. Mem. Human Relation Commn. Rockford, 1971-72; mem. pres.'s council Southwestern Coll., 1973—. Mem. Am. Assn. Museums, Assn. Art Mus. Dirs., Tenn. Assn. Museums. Office: Brooks Meml Art Gallery Overton Park Memphis TN 38112

WHITLOCK, (JUDY) MARY ELLEN JENKINS (MRS. DOUGLAS WHITLOCK), social worker; b. Brownville, Neb., Sept. 3, 1906; d. John Crisler and Mabel (Sapp) Jenkins; student Sullins Coll., 1923-24, Ferris Inst., 1924—; A.B., Ind. U., 1927; m. Douglas Whitlock, June 18, 1929; children—Douglas Whitlock II, Marilyn (Mrs. Robert E. Long), Sandra (Mrs. Theodore G. Driscoll, Jr.). Case worker Children's Aid Soc., Detroit, 1927-28, head adoption dept., 1928-29; case supr. Asso. Charities Washington, 1929-32. Mem. Women's Inaugural Com., Washington, 1953, 57. Chmn. women's com. Devereux Found., Devon, Pa., 1959-61. Mem. League Republican Women, Nat. Fedn. Rep. Women. Bd. dirs. Family Service Assn. of Am., Goodwill Industries Assn., Mental Health Assn., Vis. Nurse Assn., Nat. Cathedral Assn. Trustee Family and Child Services, Washington, 1951-65, 1st v.p., 1962-65; v.p. Episcopal Ch. Women of Washington, 1963, pres., 1969-72. Recipient award Alpha Omicron Pi, 1963, award Diocese of Washington, 1973. Mem. Ind. Soc. of Washington (mem. exec. bd. 1932—; recipient award 1962), Indiana U. Alumni Assn., Alpha Omicron Pi. Republican. Episcopalian (vestry-woman 1968-71, 74—). Clubs: Little Garden (pres. 1938-40), Wednesday (pres. 1940-42) (both of Sandy Spring, Md.); International Neighbors (1st pres. 1956-57, sec. 1969—) (Washington); Women of St. Thomas (pres. 1960-62). Home: 2550 Massachusetts Av NW Washington DC 20008

WHITLOW, ETHOLENE RAMSEY (MRS. HOMER P. WHITLOW), educator; b. Franklin County, Va., Aug. 6, 1910; d. Benjamin F. and Lillie (Hodges) Ramsey; student Coll. William and Mary; m. Homer P. Whitlow, Jan. 21, 1933; children—Berger M., Benjamin H., Mary Sue (Mrs. Arthur P. Burgess), D. Ramsey. Tchr., Snow Creek Sch., Martinsville, Va. 1948-58, became prin., 1959; later tchr. Callaway Elementary Sch., Rocky Mounty, Va., Sontag Elementary Sch., Franklin County, Va.; now dir. Audio-Visual Center for Franklin County Schs. Mem. Va., Franklin County (v.p. 1962-64) edn. assns., N.E.A., Internat. Platform Assn., Franklin County Artists Guild. Methodist. Home: RFD 2 Rocky Mount VA 24151

WHITLOW, HUBERT HENRY, JR., librarian; b. Atlanta, Feb. 16, 1930; s. Hubert Henry and Ruby Lee (Simmons) W.; B.A., Emory U., 1951, M.L.S., 1956; M.A., U. Fla., 1967. Asst. catalog humanities librarian U. Ga., Athens, 1956-58; social scis. librarian, 1958-60; res. librarian Emory U., Atlanta, 1961-62, chief serials and binding dept., 1962-64, chief circulation dept., 1964-66, documents librarian, 1966-67, chief circulation dept., 1967-70; librarian Floyd Jr. Coll., Rome, Ga., 1970—. Served with USAF, 1951-55. Home: Route 3 Rome GA 30161 Office: Floyd Junior Coll Library PO Box 1864 Rome GA 30161

WHITMAN, AINSLEY ABBOTT, librarian; b. Pomona, Cal., Sept. 22, 1912; s. William Ainsley and Margaret (Abbott) W.; B.A., San Jose State Coll., 1935; B.S., La. State U., 1936; m. Joyce Bruner Whitman. Librarian, Rayne (La.) High Sch., 1935-37, Poinsett County Library, Harrisburg, Ark., 1937-39; asst. librarian La. Library Commn., Baton Rouge, 1939-40; library asst. San Jose State Coll., 1940-42; librarian Cal. State Poly. Coll., 1946-49, Coll. of Agr., U. Ga., 1949-50, Willamette U., 1950-55, Central State Coll., 1955-57; asst. librarian Jacksonville State Coll., 1957-62; librarian U. N.C. at Asheville, 1962—. Served with M.C., AUS, 1942-46. Mem. N.C., Am., Southeastern library assns., Am. Assn. U. Profs. Democrat. Episcopalian. Home: Apt 2 College Park Apts Asheville NC 28804 Office: D Hiden Ramsey Library Univ of NC Asheville NC 28804

WHITMAN, HOWARD, journalist; b. Cleve., May 6, 1914; s. Lawrence Alvin and Bettie (Goldman) W.; A.B. magna cum laude, Western Res. U., 1935; m. Suzanne Marcia Desberg, Mar. 9, 1938; children—Constance Marcia, Kenneth Jay. Mem. staff N.Y. Herald Tribune, Paris edit., 1936, London Daily Express, 1936-37, N.Y. Daily News, 1937-45; war corr. E.T.O., World War II; specialist on articles on social problems since 1945. Mem. commn. mental health edn. Internat. Congress on Mental Health, 1948; lectr. sex edn., mental health, social problems. Pres. Grand Bahama Mental Health Assn., 1968-69. Comdr. Grand Bahama Boating Squadron, 1968-69. Joint winner Profl. Journalism award for pub. service for series articles in Collier's, Terror In Our Cities, Sigma Delta Chi, 1949-50; winner Parents' mag. book award, 1948-49; winner Freedoms Found. award for article The Truth About Patriotism, 1952, for TV series A Time to Remember, 1956, for TV program The Flag, 1970; Blakeslee award Am. Heart Assn., 1956; TV award Nat. Assn. Mental Health, 1957; First award for program Nervous Tension, Ohio State U. Inst. for Radio and TV, 1961. Clubs: Saugatuck Harbor Yacht (commodore 1965), Palm Beach Nat. Golf. Author: Let's Tell The Truth About Sex, 1948; Terror in the Streets, 1951; A Reporter in Search of God, 1953; Success Is Within You, 1956; A Brighter Later Life, 1961; The Sex Age, 1962; syndicated news series: Vandalism, 1953, The Divorce Dilemma, 1954; Parenthood Without Hokum, 1955; Keeping Our Sanity, 1957; Our Moral Crisis, 1958; Our Drinking Habits, 1958; New Frontiers in Living, 1959; Your Middle Years, 1961; Making Marriage More Rewarding, 1962; Don't Be Nervous, 1963; The American Way of Love, 1964; Our Family Crisis, 1968; appeared NBC-Television series Howard Whitman Talks, 1953; News of Medicine and Health, NBC-TV, 1956; roving editor NBC-TV Home Show, 1957; Dumont television series Probe, 1957-58; Collier's series The Struggle for our Children's Minds, 1954; Better Homes and Gardens series America's Moral Crisis, 1957; commentator WPTV, Palm Beach, 1970. Producer nat. TV series Medical Special Events, 1958-61; News of Your Life, NBC-TV, 1962-64; NBC radio Emphasis, 1964-66, NBC Monitor, 1967-70; News About You, 1970; also nationally syndicated newspaper spls., 1971. Contbr. travel articles to N.Y. Times, nat. mags. Address: 2165 Ibis Isle Rd Palm Beach FL 33480

WHITMER, KENNETH SWEET, ophthalmologist; b. Dayton, O., Jan. 23, 1910; s. Rollo R. and Winifred (Ball) W.; A.B., Miami U. (Oxford, O.), 1931; M.D., Ohio State U., 1936; m. Marcia Ann Butcher, Sept. 14, 1968; children—Cynthia Ann (Mrs. William Thomas), Patricia (Mrs. Darell Hickman), Kenneth Sweet, Carl N. Intern, Jackson Meml. Hosp., 1936-39; resident Detroit Reciving Hosp., 1939-40; pvt. practice medicine specializing in ophthalmology, Miami, Fla., 1940—; mem. staff Childrens, Victoria, Coral Gables hosps., cons. VA Hosp., Miami; clin. prof. ophthalmology U. Miami Sch. Medicine, Served to maj. USAAF, World War II. Mem. Am. Assn. Opthalmology (trustee), Alpha Kappa Kappa, Sigma Chi. Presbyn. Kiwanian (bd. dirs.). Home: 2000 Tigertail St Miami FL 33133 Office: 550 Brickell Av Miami FL 33133

WHITMIRE, BOYCE AUGUSTUS, lawyer; b. Brevard, N.C., Oct. 21, 1905; s. William P. and Annie (Floyd) W.; student U. N.C., 1924-26, Wake Forest U., 1926-28; m. Hazel Patricia Bean, July 1, 1929; children—Boyce Augustus, Jr., William F., Guy P., John F., James T., Patricia L. Admitted to N.C. bar, 1928, since practiced in Hendersonville. Past pres. Hendersonville YMCA. Mem. Henderson County Bd. Edn., 1963-69; mem. N.C. Ho. of Reps., 1959-61; mem. N.C. Senate, 1961-63; mayor, Hendersonville, 1969—. Trustee Western Carolina U., 1963—. Baptist. Mason, Lion (pres. 1946), Elk (exalted ruler 1943-44, pres. N.C. assn. 1946-47). Home: 201 Ewbank Dr Hendersonville NC 28739 Office: 4th Av W Hendersonville NC 28739

WHITMIRE, CHARLES DANIEL, pub. accountant; b. Shepherd, Tenn., July 10, 1921; s. William Madison and Mintie (Lingerfelt) W. ; grad. McKenzie Bus. Coll., 1950; m. Bonnie Bryan, Apr. 7, 1944; children—Alfred, Hayden, Charline (Mrs. Larry T. Elliott). Clk.-typist U.S. Civil Service, 1946; office mgr. Electric Power Coop., Iuka, Miss., 1948-52; office mgr. Hydratane Gas Co., Athens, Tenn., 1953-55; staff accountant W.W. Stribling & Co., C.P.A.'s, 1955-60; sales service mgr. Carpet Mill, Dalton, Ga., 1960-65; treas. World Carpets, Inc., 1965-71; owner C.D. Whitmire and Co., C.P.A.'s, Dalton, 1971—. Served with USAF, 1939-45. C.P.A., Ga. Mem. Am. Inst. C.P.A.'s, Ga. Soc. C.P.A.'s Office: 126 W Gordon St Dalton GA 30720

WHITMORE, ALDEN WILCHER, ednl. adminstr.; b. Broadway, Va., Feb. 16, 1919; s. Allen Wilcher and Kitty (Aldhizer) W.; B.Ed., U. Va., 1943, M.Ed., 1953, Ed.D., 1969; m. Marjorie Evelyn Foltz, Jan. 2, 1942; 1 son, Alden Wilcher. Tchr. social studies, coach, Albemarle and Rockingham Counties, Va., 1946-52; prin. elementary and secondary schs., Amherst County, Va., 1954-56; supervising prin. Lexington (Va.) Pub. Schs., 1956-60; prin. Lexington High Sch., 1960-66; gen. supr. Danville (Va.) City Schs., 1968-72, asst. supt. for personnel, 1972—. Served with AUS, World War II. Decorated Bronze Star medal. Mem. Va., Nat., Danville (pres.) edn. assns., Kappa Delta Pi, Phi Delta Kappa. Baptist (dir. Sunday sch. 1971, deacon 1972—). Club: Lions Internat. (pres. 1964-65, dir. 1962-64, 71—). Home: 110 Briarcliff Pl Danville VA 24541 Office: 313 Municipal Bldg Danville VA 24541

WHITNER, GEORGE CRABTREE, banker; b. Jacksonville, Fla., June 27, 1923; s. John Addison and Eleanor (Crabtree) W.; B.S., U. N.C., 1947; m. Virginia Hilyard, Dec. 3, 1955; children—Banta H., Virginia, Eleanor, John A. Field supt. Whitner & Lawrence, Inc., Fire & Casualty Gen. Agts., 1947-57; agy. supt. N.Y. Underwriters Ins. Co., 1957-58; v.p. Fla. First Nat. Bank Jacksonville, 1958—, dir., 1968—, vice chmn., 1972—; vice chmn., dir. Fla. Bank at Starke, 1970—. Treas., Am. Cancer Soc., 1960-63; pres. Speech & Hearing Center, 1966, Fla. Jr. Coll. at Jacksonville Found., Inc., 1972. Bd. dirs. Travelers Aid. Served to lt. (j.g.) USNR, 1943-46. Mem. Meninak Internat. (treas., dir. Jacksonville 1969—). Clubs: River, Timuquana Country (Jacksonville). Presbyn. Office: 214 Hogan St Jacksonville FL 32202

WHITNEY, A(DELBERT) GRANT, merc., ins. co. exec.; b. Lowell, Mass., July 25, 1917; s. Adelbert Howard and Julie (Sheehan) W.; B.S. in Bus. Adminstrn., Boston U., 1940; m. Lillian Ritch DeArmon, Nov. 17, 1950; children—Julia Woodley, A. Grant, Frank DeArmon. Asst. to v.p. Belk Stores, Charlotte, N.C., 1946-52, asst. to pres., 1952-55, v.p., sec.-treas. Belk Stores Ins. Reciprocal, Belk Underwriters, Inc., Charlotte, 1950-58, exec. v.p., sec.-treas., 1958—; sec.-treas. Archdale Mut. Ins. Co., 1962-65, exec. v.p., sec.-treas., 1965—; gen. mgr. ins. dept. Belk Stores Services, Inc., 1951—, sec., mem. exec. com., 1959-68, v.p., 1964-68; v.p., sec.-treas. Providence Realty Corp., Charlotte, 1950-63, pres., 1959-60, pres., treas., 1964—; v.p. Queen City Investors, Inc., Charlotte, 1959-62; sec. Thrifty Investors, Inc., Charlotte, 1961-62, investment chmn., 1964-65, v.p., 1967-68. Mem. exec. com. Arthritis and Rheumatism Found., Charlotte, 1959-60, dir., 1959-60; mem. exec. bd. Mecklenburg council Boy Scouts Am., 1949—, v.p., 1962-66; chmn. N.C. U.S.O., 1959—; spl. gifts chmn. N.C. div. Am. Cancer Soc., 1967, crusade chmn., 1969, 70, bd. dirs., 1968—; numerous other council offices; program chmn. Charlotte Bi-Centennial Celebration Com., 1968; industry chmn. laymen's nat. com. Nat. Bible Week, 1967-70. Bd. dirs. Mecklenburg Citizens Better Libraries, 1967—; bd. dirs. Charlotte Council on Alcoholism, Goodwill Industries Charlotte, Inc., N.C. Multiple Sclerosis Soc., Festival in the Park; bd. visitors Brevard Music Center; chmn. promotional activities planning com. Downtown Charlotte Assn., 1965-68; parents' council Davidson Coll., 1972—. Served as officer AUS, World War II. Recipient Distinguished Service award Jr. C. of C., 1952; named Charlotte Young Man of Year, 1952; recipient Silver Beaver award Boy Scouts Am., 1956, Soldiers Medal for Heroism U.S. Army; elected to Exec. and Profl. Hall Fame, 1966 mem. selection com., 1967—; recipient Distinguished Service award Charlotte Exchange Club, 1967. Mem. Am. Soc. Ins. Mgmt. (pres. Carolinas chpt. 1963-64, nat. v.p. conf. activities 1965-66, 1st v.p. 1966-67, pres. 1967-68, Man of Yr. award, Pres.'s award 1971), Am. Mgmt. Assn.

(participant confs., seminars), Nat. Assn. Ind. Insurers (v.p. 1953-67), Captive Ins. Cos. Assn. (v.p. 1973—), U.S. (mem. ins. com. 1967-69), Charlotte chambers commerce, Am. Legion, Carolina Carrousel (hon.), Jr. Achievement, Inc., Newcomen Soc. N.Am., Royal Soc. Knights Carrousel (pres. 1955-64, chmn. governing council 1964-68), Soc. 1st Div. Inf., Assn. U.S. Army, Am. Found. Religion and Psychiatry (gov. 1959—), French Fgn. Legion (hon.). Presbyn. (elder). Mason (33 deg., Shriner), Lion. Clubs: Boston University Alumni of the Carolinas, Executives (pres. 1963-64), Myers Park Country, Charlotte City, Goodfellows (Charlotte). Home: 684 Colville Rd Charlotte NC 28207 Office: 308 E 5th St Charlotte NC 28202

WHITNEY, J. WILBUR WAYNE, JR., investment exec.; b. Tulsa, Mar. 22, 1926; B.S., Tulsa U., 1949; m. Blanche Tiffany, Jan. 17, 1947; children—David Michael, Diann Tiffany, J. Wilbur Wayne III. Dist. petroleum engr. Magnolia Petroleum Co., Electra, Tex., 1949-55; gen. prodn. supt. Helmerich & Payne, Inc., Tulsa, 1955-61; pres. Whitney Operating Co., Whitney Engring. Co., Tulsa, 1961-64; pres., dir. White Shield Corp., Tulsa, 1966-70; pvt. investments, 1971— dir. Utica Sq. Nat. Bank, Tulsa. Served with inf. AUS, 1945-46. Mem. Soc. Petroleum Engrs., Am. Petroleum Inst., Ind. Petroleum Assn. Am., Okla. Ind. Producers Assn. (dir.). Home: 3021 S Wheeling St Tulsa OK 74114 Office: 1804 First Nat Bldg Tulsa OK 74103

WHITNEY, JOHN EDWARD, educator; b. Casper, Wyo., July 6, 1926; s. Gary M. and Harriett (Whitney) W.; A.B., U. Cal., Berkeley, 1947, M.A., 1948, Ph.D., 1951; Ph.D., U. Cambridge (Eng.), 1956; m. Barbara Laundrie, June 11, 1949; children—Karen, Kathleen, Eric, Emily, Brian. Research asso. Cedars of Lebanon, Los Angeles, 1951-52, U. Cal., Los Angeles, 1952-54, U. Cambridge (Eng.), 1954-56; mem. faculty U. Ark., Little Rock, 1956—, prof. physiology, head dept., 1962—. Served with USNR, 1944-45. Mem. Am. Physiology Soc., Soc. Exptl. Biology and Medicine, Endocrine Soc., A.A.A.S., Sigma Xi, Alpha Omega Alpha. Home: 7016 Rockwood St Little Rock AR 72207

WHITNEY, PHILIP BLANCHARD, radio sta. exec.; b. Keene, N.H., Sept. 27, 1914; s. Roy V. and Ruth M. (Blanchard) W.; grad. Keene State Coll., 1937; m. Lillian Gatewood, Dec. 31, 1941; children—Cheryl (Mrs. A.L. Humphries), Pamela (Mrs. William Thompson). Engr., Sta. WJEJ, Hagerstown, Md., 1937-39, Sta. WSAL, Salisbury, Md., 1939-40, Sta. WNBX, Springfield, Vt., 1940, Sta. WKNE, Keene, 1940-41; with Sta. WINC, Winchester, Va., 1941—, mgr., 1956—. Chmn. Va. Industry Adv. Com., 1969—. Bd. dirs. Winchester Meml. Hosp. Mem. I.E.E.E., Va. Assn. Broadcasters (pres. 1970), Winchester C. of C. (pres. 1971-72). Rotarian (pres. 1968). Contbr. articles to profl. publs. Home: Route 1 Stephens City VA 22655 Office: PO Box 605 Winchester VA 22601

WHITNEY, RANDALL BROOKS, physician; b. Selma, Ala., July 13, 1933; s. Edwin George and Wanda Livesay (Hess) W.; B.S., Tulane U., 1955, M.D., 1959; m. Martha Carole Bowden, Dec. 21, 1963; children—Aubrey Mark, Lisa Claire, Robin Laurel. Intern, Duval Med. Center, Jacksonville, Fla., 1959-60; resident in gen. practice San Bernardino County (Cal.) Hosp., 1963-65; pvt. practice medicine, Mount Dora, Fla., 1965—. Pres., Parent-Tchr. Orgn., 1969-70. Bd. mgmt. Duval Home for Mentally Retarded, Deland, Fla., 1970—. Recipient Distinguished Service award Mt. Dora Jr. C. of C., 1969. Mem. A.M.A., Fla., So. med. assns., Lake County Med. Soc., Mt. Dora C. of C. (pres. 1969). Democrat. Presbyn. Rotarian. Home: 351 W 10th St Mount Dora FL 32757 Office: 1100 Morningside Dr Mount Dora FL 32757

WHITNEY, WILLIAM BERNARD, educator; b. Kansas City, Kan., Oct. 16, 1905; s. William Baker and Ethel (Reeve) W.; student Garden City Jr. Coll., 1924-26, U. Wis., 1926-27, U. Denver, 1929-30; B.A., U. Tex., 1933, M.S., 1934, Ph.D., 1937; m. Mary Elisabeth Garrett, Feb. 27, 1937; children—Mary Sue (Mrs. Carter Benjamin Kelly), William Bernard, Jesse Garrett. Instr. chemistry U. Tex., 1934-37, prof., 1937-43; supr. chemistry and metall. lab. N.Am. Aviation, Dallas, 1943-45; sr. research chemist Phillips Petroleum Co., Bartlesville, Okla., 1945-69; asso. prof. chemistry Tex. Woman's U., Denton, 1969—. Sec., Limestone Water Co., Bartlesville, 1950-54, pres., 1955-57. Mem. instl. com. Boy Scouts Am., Bartlesville, 1953-56; pres. Washington County (Okla.) Tb Assn., 1956. Fellow Am. Inst. Chemists; mem. A.A.A.S., Am. Chem. Soc., Electro Chem. Soc., Am. Assn. U. Profs., Tex. Assn. Classroom Tchrs., C. of C. (water and sewer com. 1960-69), Republican. Baptist. Rotarian. Contbr. articles to profl. jours. Patentee chems. Home: 208 Pennsylvania St Denton TX 76201

WHITSEL, TRAVIS SEWELL, mgmt. cons.; b. Jackson County, Miss., Aug. 13, 1890; s. Nelson Brown and Myrtle (Sewell) W.; B.S. in Mech. Engring., Purdue U., 1911; m. Irene Tracy, June 11, 1921 (dec. Aug. 1930); children—Travis Sewell, Ruth (Mrs. Norman E. Westphal), Audrey (Mrs. Randolph Wedding), Cynthia (Mrs. William Borden), Joyce (Mrs. Frank W. Bean); m. 2d, Gertrude Ann Louise Van Hermann, Aug. 12, 1933. Rancher nr. Ft. Stockton, Tex., 1904-45; fireman C.I. & L. R.R. Co., 1911-14; tchr. pub. schs., Laketon, Ind., 1914-15; with Union Spl. Machine Co., Chgo., 1919-61, v.p. sales, 1940-61; pvt. practice as mgmt. cons., Chgo. Served to capt. U.S. Army, 1916-19. Mem. Underwear Inst., Internat. Assn. Clothing Designers, Am. Assn. Apparel Mfs. (past chmn. tech. adv. com.), Textile Hall Fame. Clubs: Burning Tree (Washington); Capitol City (Atlanta); Lake Shore (Chgo.); St. Petersburg (Fla.) Yacht; Lakewood Country. Address: 2901 58th Av N St Petersburg FL 33714

WHITT, LONNIE WELDON, cosmetic co. exec.; b. Medina, Tenn., Dec. 17, 1923; s. Thomas Clifford and Emma Jane (Blackwell) W.; student W. Tenn. Bus. Coll., Jackson, 1946-47, Memphis Coll. Accountancy, 1950-54; m. Annie B. Jones, Dec. 14, 1946; children—Lonnie Franklin (dec.), Danny Wayne. Accountant, Firestone Tire & Rubber Co., Memphis, 1948-49; exec. v.p., dir. J. Strickland & Co., Memphis, 1961—; pres. Comml. Towel & Uniform Co., Memphis, 1961-65; exec. v.p., dir. Hoyt Co., Inc., Memphis, 1961—; exec. v.p., dir. Beauty Creations, Inc., Memphis, 1961—; v.p., dir. Elco Co., Inc., Memphis, 1961—, The Loreco Co., Memphis, 1961—. Past dirs. Jr. Achievement, Inc. Served with AUS, 1943-45. Decorated Bronze Star medal. Baptist. Home: 2893 Signal Memphis TN 38127 Office: 1400 Ragan St Memhis TN 38106

WHITTAKER, LEON, educator; b. Benton, La., Oct. 7, 1927; s. Osborne and Mamie (Owens) W.; B.S., Grambling Coll., 1949; M.A., Mich. State U., 1956; Ed.D., Wash. State U., 1966; Certificate, Inst. for Ednl. Mgmt., Harvard, 1973; m. Clarice Jordan, June 8, 1952; children—Lino Gerard, Leona Marie, Sharon Ann, Eric Durand. Tchr., Bossier Parish Sch. Bd., 1949-50, 52-55; counselor, dir. placement Grambling (La.) Coll., 1956-70, dean students, prof. edn., 1970—. Cons. Coll. Placement Services, Inc., 1968—. Served with AUS, 1950-52. Mem. Am. Psychol. Assn., Am. Personnel and Guidance Assn., Grambling C. of C. (pres.), Phi Delta Kappa, Alpha Phi Omega. Mem. Christian M.E. Ch. (steward, lay leader). Mason (Shriner). Home: PO Box 422 Grambling LA 71245

WHITTEMORE, (EDWARD) REED, II, educator, writer; b. New Haven, Sept. 11, 1919; s. Edward Reed and Margaret Eleanor (Carr) W.; A.B., Yale, 1941; student Princeton, 1945-46; m. Helen Lundeen, Oct. 3, 1952; children—Catherine Carr, Edward Reed III, John Lundeen and Margaret Goodhue Whittemore. Mem. faculty Carleton Coll., 1947-67, prof. English, 1962-67, chmn. dept., 1962-64; program asso. Nat. Inst. Pub. Affairs, 1966-68; editor Carleton Miscellany, 1960-64; cons. in poetry Library of Congress, 1964-65; Bain-Swiggett lectr. Princeton U., 1967; prof. U. Md., 1968—; lit. editor New Republic, 1970-74. Served to capt. USAAF, 1941-45. Mem. Assn. Lit. Mags. Am. (dir. 1961-65). Author: Heroes and Heroines, 1947; An American Takes a Walk, 1956; The Self-Made Man, 1959; The Boy From Iowa, 1962; The Fascination of the Abomination, 1963; Poems, New and Selected, 1967; From Zero to the Absolute, 1967; Poems New and Selected, 1968; Fifty Poems Fifty, 1970. Editor: Furioso, 1939-53; Browning, 1960. Home: 3409 Woodley Rd NW Washington DC 20016 Office: Dept English U Md College Park MD 20740

WHITTEMORE, FRANK JACKSON, investment banker; b. Morgan County, Tenn., Jan. 11, 1918; s. Frank and Annie (Penn) W.; B.A., U. N.C., LL.B., 1942; m. Valor M. Snyder (div.); 1 son, Stephan Rand; m. 2d, Ann M. Seaman; children—Derek Letz, Jon Letz, Paula Letz. Various positions family interest in tobacco, comml. banking, savs. & loan assn., mortgage co., farming, ranching, 1939—; exec. v.p., dir. Kassler & Co., mortgage bankers, Denver, 1945-56; pres. dir. Franklin Investment Co., Denver, 1956-62; dir., chmn. bd. Met. Co., other land devel., bldg. cos., 1956—; v.p., asst. to exec. v.p. Douglas L. Elliman & Co., N.Y.C.; asso. Ben G. McGuire & Co., Houston, 1965—; chmn. Intebon Corp., Wilmington, Del.: pres. Met. Mortgage Co., Houston, Franklin Investors, Houston; dir. Continental Corp., Franklin Financial, Atlanta. Cons. various corps., State of Fla., 1963. Served to lt. comdr. USNR, 1942-45. Mem. Am. Savs. and Loan Inst. (pres. 4th dist. 1942), Mortgage Bankers Assn. (pres. Colo. 1955), Internat. Soc. Real Estate Appraisers (pres. Denver 1954), Mil. Order World Wars. Episcopalian (vestryman). Contbr. articles various publs. Office: PO Box 42177 Houston TX 77042

WHITTEMORE, JOE MILES, waste water equipment and supply co. exec.; b. Homer, Ga., Sept. 7, 1936; s. Max Meyerhart and Sarah Gyrr (Bramlett) W.; B.B.A., U. Ga., 1958; m. Patricia Anne Seymour, June 21, 1964; children—Janet Lynn, Joanne Carol. With Ralston Purina Co., various locations, 1958-62, John C. Etheridge, C.P.A., Elberton, Ga., 1962-65; v.p. finance Benson's, Inc., Athens, 1965-71; sec.-treas. Davis Water and Waste Industries, Inc., Thomasville, Ga., 1971-73, v.p. finance and corporate services, 1971-74, sr. v.p., 1974—; dir. Atlas Gravite Co., Elberton, Ga. Bd. dirs., exec. com. Vashti Sch.; bd. dirs. Community Chest, Salvation Army, Athens Boys Club. Mem. Am. Inst. C.P.A.'s, Ga. Soc. C.P.A.'s (pres. Athens chpt.), Financial Execs. Inst. Methodist (ofcl. bd.). Rotarian (dir.). Club: Glen Arver Country. Home: 1202 E Washington St Thomasville GA 31792 Office: Box 1419 Thomasville GA 31792

WHITTEN, JAMIE LLOYD, congressman; b. Cascilla, Miss., Apr. 18, 1910; s. Alymer Guy and Nettie (Early) W.; student lit. and law depts., U. of Miss., 1926-31; m. Rebecca Thompson, June 20, 1940; children—James Lloyd, Beverly Rebecca. Prin. pub. schs., 1931; elected Miss. State Legislature, 1931; dist. atty., 17th Dist. of Miss., 1933, reelected, 1935 and 1939; mem. 77th-93rd congresses from 2d Miss. Dist. Mem. Beta Theta Pi, Phi Alpha Delta, Omicron Delta Kappa. Democrat. Mason. Home: Charleston MS 38921 also 5804 Nebraska Av Washington DC 20015

WHITTINGTON, GLENN ADGER, JR., elec. engr.; b. Darlington, S.C., Aug. 29, 1929; s. Glenn Adger and Leota (Humphries) W.; B.S., Citadel, 1952; m. Marianne Elizabeth May, Oct. 4, 1952; children—Glenn Adger III, Philip, Timothy, Martha Jewell. Elec. engr. C.E., U.S. Army, Jacksonville, Fla., 1955-57; with Sperry Electronic Tube div. Sperry Rand Corp., Gainesville, Fla., 1957—, mgr. microwave tube engring., 1969, dir. engring., 1970—; dir. Steve Spurrier, Inc., Gainesville. Served with AUS, 1953-54; Korea. Mem. I.E.E.E. (sr.), Soc. Am. Mil. Engrs., Assn. Old Crows. Home: 4617 NW 33d Ct Gainesville FL 32601 Office: Microwave Tube Engring Sperry Rand Waldo Rd Gainesville FL 32601

WHITTINGTON, JAMES RICHARD, lawyer; b. San Antonio, May 19, 1945; s. James Connellee and Sara Margaret (Crockett) W.; student U. Tex., 1963-65; B.B.A., Tex. Christian U., 1967; J.D., Tex. Tech U., 1970; m. Mary Bynum Coleman, May 31, 1969. Admitted to Tex. bar, 1970; asso. atty. Johnson, Guthrie & Hunter, Dallas, 1970-71; asso. Hunter, Greenfield & Allen, 1971-72; partner Hunter, Greenfield, Whittington & Vineyard and predecessor firm, 1972—. Adviser to bd. dirs. Garland Foods, Inc., 1970—. Bd. dirs. and mgmt. Camp Grady Spruce br. Dallas YMCA. Mem. Tex., Dallas bar assns., Phi Alpha Delta, Delta Kappa Epsilon. Club: Lancers (Dallas). Home: 6715 Glendora St Dallas TX 75230 Office: Adolphus Tower Dallas TX 75202

WHITTINGTON, PAUL ELVIN, govt. ofcl.; b. Guthrie, W.Va., Oct. 1, 1908; s. James Elvin and Georgianna (Ballard) W.; student W.Va. Inst. Tech., 1928-30, George Washington U., 1941-45; m. Helen Beatrice Tucker, Aug. 27, 1938; children—Judith A. (Mrs. Zar), Dorothy L. Engr., City of Charleston (W.Va.), 1930; engr. W.Va. Dept. Engring., Charleston, 1932-33; mech. engr. Union Carbide and Carbon Co., South Charleston, W.Va., 1934-38, Havens & Emerson, Cleve., 1939; with U.S. Army Materiel Comd., Washington and Natick, Mass., 1939—, mech. engr., Washington, 1966—. Mem. Research Soc. Am. (chpt. pres. 1964, mem. coms.), Psi Delta, Phi Zeta Kappa. Unitarian (bd. sessions ch.). Mason (32 deg.). Patentee life support system for space exploitation including moon walks, other spl. Army equipment. Home: 9208 Forest Haven Dr Alexandria VA 22309 Office: Hdqrs US Army Materiel Command 5001 Eisenhower Av Alexandria VA 22304

WHITTINGTON, TONY BURNICE, ednl. adminstr.; b. Amarillo, Tex., Mar. 21, 1940; s. Claude Burnice and Velda Marjorie (Grounds) W.; B.B.A. in Advt., Tex. Technol. Coll., 1963, M.Ed. in Higher Edn., 1971; m. Judith Lynn Prideaux, Jan. 21, 1967. Asst. dir. pub. relations Children's Hosp., Columbus, O., 1968-69; housing mgr. Tex. Technol. U., Lubbock, 1969—. Served to capt. USAF, 1963-68; Vietnam. Mem. Pub. Relations Soc. Am., Columbus Jr. C. of C., Pub. Relations Soc. Am., Southwest Assn. Coll. and Univ. Housing Officers. Home: 3520 41st St Lubbock TX 79413

WHITTON, PAUL LEWIS, retail co. exec.; b. Appleby, Tex., Aug. 2, 1909; s. Lewis Alexander and Mary Elmira (Ward) W.; B.S., Stephen F. Austin U., 1930; M.Ed., U. Tex., 1935; m. Robbie Katherine Morton, Feb. 20, 1942; children—Paul Lewis, Linda Kay (Mrs. James Martin Hill), James Morton. Tchr., prin., supt. pub. schs., Tex., 1930-66; pres. Miller's Visual Aids, Inc., Fort Worth, 1966—. Served with USAAC, 1942-45. Mem. Tex. Assn. Sch. Adminstrs. (life), Scholarship Soc. of South. Democrat. Methodist. Mason. Club: Optimist (Ft. Worth). Home: 3913 Clayton Rd E Fort Worth TX 76116 Office: 100 N University Dr Fort Worth TX 76107

WHITWORTH, JOE WAYNE, real estate and ins. broker; b. Sulphur Springs, Tex., Aug. 26, 1922; s. Claud Melton and Mary Catherine (Patman) W.; grad. high sch.; m. Ruth Williams, Nov. 16, 1946; children—Joseph Steven, Kim. Salesman, Lemon Ins. Agy., Sulphur Springs, 1945-61; prin. Whitworth Co., Sulphur Springs, 1961—. Served with USAAF, 1942-45. Mem. Hopkin-Franklin-Wood Bd. Realtors (pres. 1965, 71), Hopkin County C. of C. (dir. 1972—). Methodist (lay leader 1973—). Lion (pres. 1968). Home: 612 Plano St Sulphur Springs TX 75482 Office: Box 185-230 Connally St Sulphur Springs TX 75482

WHITWORTH, VIRGIL LEE, photo-geologist; b. Nevada, Mo., Feb. 29, 1896; s. Robert Lee and Cora (Robertson) W.; B.S. in Geology, Mo. Sch. Mines, 1923; refresher course in multiplex machines, 1950. With Roxana (now Shell) Oil Co., 1923-26, Simms Oil Co. (now Tidal Oil), Dallas, 1926-28, Henry L. Doherty & Co., Ft. Worth, 1928-30; chief geologist Tex., Deep Rock Oil Co., Ft. Worth, 1930-31; with Continental Oil Co., Ft. Worth, 1936-42; cons. geologist to Brazilian Govt. and introduced photo-geology to Brazil while with Drilling and Exploration Co. in Brazil, 1946-48, photo-geology for co. in West Tex. area, 1948-49; cons. geologist Washington, 1950-53, Abilene, Tex., 1953-55; with Saxon Exploration Co. and Allison, Prestridge & Anderson Co., 1953-55; engaged in photogeology, Cal., 1955-57; now cons. photogeology, U.S., Can., Alaska; asso. L.B. Oils, Ltd., Can.; cons. Shacron Oil Corp., Photogravity Co., Inc., Houston; with Amuedo & Ivy in cons. capacity; geomorphologist, lectr. in field. Discover oil fields, Tex., oil and gas fields Alta., Can., Tex. Served as capt. Photog. Intelligence, USAAF, 1942-45; CBI. Mem. Am. Assn. Petroleum Geologists, A.A.A.S., Am. Soc. Photogrammetry, Abilene (Tex.) Petroleum Club, Houston Geol. Soc., Internat. Platform Assn., Pi Kappa Alpha. Christian Scientist. Mason (Shriner). Club: Castille (Houston). Houston House 1617 Fannin St Houston TX 77002 Office: Photogravity Co Inc Adair Center 6440 Hillcroft St Houston TX 77017

WHORTON, GARY PAUL, banker; b. New Bern, N.C., Oct. 26, 1943; s. Elmo and Margaurite (Hardy) W.; student South Ga. Coll., 1963; m. Marcia O. Babbitt, Mar. 25, 1967; 1 dau., Jennifer Ann. Teller, 1st Nat. Bank, Brunswick, Ga., 1963-64; bookkeeper 1st Nat. Bank, Merritt Island, Fla., 1965-66; head bookkeeper South Seminole Bank, Fern Park, Fla., 1966; cashier Am. Nat. Bank & Trust, St. Petersburg, Fla., 1967-69, Hendry County Bank, Labelle, Fla., 1969; pres., dir. Beach First Nat. Bank, Ft. Myers Beach, Fla., 1970—; dir. Southwest Fla. Banks, Inc. Bd. dirs. Ft. Myers Beach Library Tax Dist., 1971. Served with AUS, 1963-64. Mem. Ft. Myers Beach C. of C. (dir. 1971). Home: PO Box 4059 Fort Myers Beach FL 33931 Office: 2525 Estero Blvd Ft Myers Beach FL 33931

WHYTE, JAMES LUCAS, publishing co. exec.; b. Highland Park, Mich., Feb. 18, 1927; s. Horace Brittain and Ardelia Mirinda (Lucas) W.; student Albion Coll., 1946-48, Grand Rapids Jr. Coll., 1946-47, Miami Law Sch. 1949-50; B.A., U. Miami, 1951; m. Doris Lucile Newburn, Dec. 17, 1949; children—Michael Brittain, Martha Jean, James Newburn. Reporter, sports editor Hollywood Sun-Tattler, 1951-54, editor, asst. pub., 1954-66; editorial writer Miami (Fla.) News, 1953-54; v.p., gen. mgr. Savannah (Ga.) News-Press, 1966-72; v.p., gen. mgr. Amarillo (Tex.) Globe-News, 1972—. Mem. Amarillo Bd. City Devel. Bd. dirs. United Way of Amarillo, Amarillo YMCA, Llana Estacado council Boy Scouts Am.; trustee St. Anthony's Hosp., West Tex. State U. Found. Served with AUS, 1944-45. Mem. Am. Soc. Newspapers Editors, Amarillo C. of C. (dir. 1973—). Presbyn. (elder 1967-72). Clubs: Amarillo, Amarillo Country. Home: Route 1 Box 338 Tascosa Rd Amarillo TX 79106 Office: 900 Harrison St Amarillo TX 79166

WHYTE, WILLIAM, journalist; b. Jersey City, Oct. 28, 1933; s. William James and Elizabeth (Richmond) W.; B.S., Rutgers U., 1957; m. Bonnie Patricia Smith, Apr. 20, 1963. With U.S. Dept. Agr., Washington, 1957—, editor Agrl. Situation, 1960-64, Employee Newsletter, 1965-67, originator, editor Report on Actions for a Better Environment, Response, 1971—, pesticide information officer, also environmental programs information officer. Cons., contbr. Ency. Americana Yearbook, 1964-68. Mem. Fed. Editors Assn. (pres. 1963-64). Club: Nat. Press (Washington). Home: 1615 Greenbrier Ct Reston VA 22090 Office: US Dept Agr COM Washington DC 20250

WICKER, THOMAS CAREY, JR., judge; b. New Orleans, Aug. 1, 1923; s. Thomas Carey and Mary (Taylor) W.; B.B.A., Tulane U., 1944, LL.B., 1949; m. Lilliemae Hansen, Dec. 20, 1946 (div. June 1965); children—Thomas Carey III, Catherine Anne; m. 2d, Veronica Jean Di-Carlo, Dec. 10, 1965. Admitted to La. bar, 1949; law clk. La. Supreme Ct., New Orleans, 1949-50; asst. U.S. Atty., 1950-53; practiced in New Orleans, 1953-72; mem. firm Simon, Wicker & Wiedemann, 1953-67; partner firm Wicker, Wieldemann & Fransen, 1967-72; dist. judge Jefferson Parish (La.), 1972—. Vice chmn. com. on pattern jury instrns. La. Supreme Ct. Served from ensign to lt. (j.g.), USNR, 1944-46. Mem. Am., La. (chmn. jr. bar sect. 1958-59, gov. 1958, mem. ho. of dels. 1960—, law reform com., chmn. com. on continuing legal edn. 1968, 69), New Orleans (chmn. jr. bar com. 1957-58), Jefferson Parish, Criminal Cts. (exec. com.) bar assns., La., Orleans (mem. bd.) assns. def. counsel, Tulane U. Alumni Assn. (past pres.), Am. Judicature Soc., Order of Coif, Beta Gamma Sigma, Pi Kappa Alpha. Democrat. Episcopalian. Rotarian (pres. 1971-72). Clubs: Metairie (La.) Country; Young Men's Business, Toastmaster's (pres. 1969), Touchdown (past pres.), Green Wave (past pres.) (New Orleans). Home: 3700 Cleveland Pl Metairie LA 70003 Office: New Courthouse Bldg Gretna LA 70053

WICKER, WILLIAM JENNINGS, hosp. adminstr.; b. Newberry, S.C., Dec. 25, 1918; s. Lawrence Pope and Alice (Jennings) W.; B.S., Newberry Coll., 1940; m. Inez Louise McMordie, Mar. 8, 1945; children—Julia Anna, William Jennings. Lab. technician County Meml. Hosp., Newberry, S.C., 1950-55; adminstr. Allendale County Hosp., Fairfax, S.C., 1955—. Served with M.C., AUS, 1941-45; ETO. Mem. Am. Soc. Clin. Pathologists. Methodist. Mason, Lion. Home and office: Box 218 Fairfax SC 29827

WICKMAN, ERNEST NIKOLAJ, transp. co. exec.; b. Ronne, Bornholm, Denmark, Apr. 23, 1909; s. Knud and Karen (Bjornsen) Wichmann; came to U.S., 1927, naturalized, 1934; student Hanover (Ind.) Coll., 1931-33; m. Frances Anne Burke, Sept. 16, 1950. Vice pres. traffic Bowman Transp., Inc., Atlanta, 1952—. Mem. Nat. Classification Com. representing Ala., Washington; treas., bd. govs. So. Motor Carriers Rate Conf. Served with USAAF, 1942-45. Mason (Shriner). Club: Fieldstone Golf and Country (Conyers, Ga.). Home: 6000 Regent Manor Lithonia GA 30058 Office: PO Box 17744 Atlanta GA 30316

WIDDECKE, HENRY AUGUST, JR., banker; b. Bryan, Tex., Jan. 10, 1916; s. Henry August and Josephine (Baker) W.; B.B.A., U. Tex. at Austin, 1938; m. Rogerina Clay, Aug. 20, 1940; children—Patricia (Mrs. Kenneth Edward Linton), Suzanne. Personnel dept. Fed. Reserve Bank, Dallas, 1946-48; v.p. First Nat. Bank, Kansas City, Mo., 1948-53; sr. v.p. The Fort Worth Nat. Bank, 1953—; v.p. Tex. Am. Bancshares, 1973—; dir. Curtis Mathes Corp., Dallas. Bd. dirs. YMCA, pres., 1972-73. Served to lt. comdr. USNR, 1942-45. Mem. Merit System Council, State of Tex. (chmn. 1969—), Am. Inst. Banking, Phi Gamma Delta, Beta Alpha Psi. Methodist. Home: 4108

Warnock Ct Fort Worth TX 76109 Office: 500 Throckmorton St Fort Worth TX 76102

WIDMER, ERNEST CLYDE, cost analyst; b. Daytona Beach, Fla., Mar. 31, 1929; s. Ernest John and Edith (Booth) W.; student Fla. State U., 1951; m. Martha Elizabeth Hunter, Dec. 21, 1951; children—Robert Frederick, Charles Glenn, Jennifer Lynn. Partner, Ernest J. Widmer & Son, Daytona Beach, 1951-67; with FHA Dept. Housing and Urban Devel., 1967—, constrn. cost analyst, 1969—. Mem. Nat. Builders Econ. Council, 1957-59; South Daytona Planning and Zoning Bd., 1958-62; pres. Halifax Children's Mus., 1958, Mus. Arts and Scis., 1959, 60. Mem. Am. Malacological Union, Internat. Oceanographic Found., Daytona Beach Area C. of C. (award 1968, mem. coms. 1961-63). Home: PO Box 814 2360 Holly Leaf Lane Orange Park FL 32073 Office: Peninsula Plaza 661 Riverside Av Jacksonville FL 32204

WIDMER, RICHARD RALPH, advt. exec.; b. Scranton, Pa., Jan. 17, 1947; s. Ralph Wenzel and Helen Virginia (Durning) W.; B.A. in Journalism, Pa. State U., 1968. Account exec. Marsteller Inc., Pitts., 1960-71, Griswold Eshleman Co., Cleve., 1971-72, Royal Caribbean Cruise account Hume-Smith-Mickelberry, Miami, Fla., 1972—. Mem. Am. Advt. Fedn. (Eastern regional v.p. 1970-71, dir. 1971-72, nat. chmn. advt. II div. 1971-72), Pitts. AD II Club (founder, pres. 1969-70), Greater Miami Advt. Fedn. (treas., dir. 1973-74). Home: 301 Manor Pl Coral Gables FL 33133 Office: 1000 Bricknell Av Miami FL 33131

WIDSTROM, NEIL WAYNE, research geneticist; b. Hecla, S.D., Nov. 11, 1933; s. John William and Tena Henrietta (Frohling) W.; B.S., S.D. State U., 1959, Ph.D., 1962; m. Virginia Rose Elder, Sept. 4, 1960; children—Gerald Allen, Jeffrey Lee. Postdoctoral fellow Dept. Genetics, N.C. State U., Raleigh, 1963-64; research geneticist So. Grain Insects Research Lab., U.S. Dept. Agr., Tifton, Ga., 1964—. Pres. P.T.A., 1971-72. Served to cpl. USMCR, 1954-56. Mem. Am. Soc. Agronomy, Genetics Soc. Am., Am. Geneticists Assn., Am. Inst. Biol. Sci., A.A.A.S., Gideons Internat. (chaplain 1971-74), Luth. Laymen's League (bd. govs. Fla-Ga. dist. 1968-72), Am. Contract Bridge League, Sigma Xi, Gamma Sigma Delta. Lutheran (elder 1970-71, pres. ch. 1969, 73). Contbr. articles in field to profl. jours. Home: Route 4 Box 127A Tifton GA 31794 Office: Tifton GA 31794

WIEBUSCH, CHARLES FRED, accoustics specialist; b. Perry, Tex., Mar. 11, 1903; s. Charles Louis and Alvine (Thies) W.; B.A., U. Tex., 1924, M.A., 1925; postgrad. Columbia, 1928-30; m. Agnes Emma Townsend, Sept. 4, 1926. Instr. physics U. Tex., Austin, 1925-27; mem. tech. staff Bell Telephone Labs., Inc., N.Y.C., also Murray Hill, N.J., 1927-45, sta. apparatus engr., 1945-51, dir. underwater systems lab., 1951-62, exec. dir. outside plant and underwater systems div., 1962-67; acoustics cons., Sarasota, Fla., 1967—. Chmn. Com. on Underwater Telecommunications, 1968-70; mem. com. on undersea warfare Nat. Acad. Scis., 1953—. Mem. Zoning Commn., Warren, N.J., 1946-47, chmn. Bd. of Adjustment, 1948-59, mem. Planning Bd., 1949-60. Registered profl. engr., N.Y. Recipient Emile Berliner award Audio Engring. Soc., 1969. Fellow Acoustical Soc. Am.; mem. I.E.E.E., Phi Beta Kappa, Sigma Xi, Tau Beta Pi. Club: Sarasota Yacht. Patentee in audio recording, circuits and underwater ordnance. Address: 819 Mangrove Point Rd Sarasota FL 33581

WIENER, SAMSON, lumber co. exec.; b. Shreveport, La., Dec. 27, 1907; s. Eli and Selma (Loewenstein) W.; B.A., U. Mich., 1928; m. Fan Gardner, Mar. 12, 1939; children—Thomas Eli, Nancy (Mrs. Leon A. Mellow). With Angelina County Lumber Co., Keltys, Tex., 1928-32; co-organizer Wiener Lumber Co., Dallas, 1934, pres., gen. mgr., 1955—, also dir.; v.p., dir. Mellow's Board and Brush, 1966—, Board and Brush of Mesquite, 1969—; dir. Angeline & Neches River R.R. Co., Lufkin, Tex., Lufkin Industries. Trustee Tex. Scottish Rite Hosp. for Crippled Children, pres., 1973—; bd. dirs., mem. exec. com. Dallas Crime Commn.; pres. Dallas Big Bros., 1954-55, bd. dirs.; bd. dirs. Big Bros. Am.; trustee Jewish Welfare Fedn. Found., Dallas; pres. Dallas Big Bros. Found., 1967-69. Recipient Lumberman of Year award Lumbermen's Assn. Tex., 1963; Brotherhood award Nat. Conf. Christians and Jews, 1968. Mem. Lumbermen's Assn. Tex. (pres. 1969-70), Nat. Lumber and Bldg. Material Dealers Assn. (pres. 1969-70), North Dallas C. of C. (bd. dirs. 1968-70), Sigma Alpha Mu. Mason (33 deg., Shriner), Rotarian (pres. Park Cities-Dallas 1950-51); mem. B'nai B'rith. Jewish religion. Clubs: Columbian (sec. 1940). Home: 4408 Lorraine Av Dallas TX 75205 Office: PO Box 35125 Inwood and Maple Avs Dallas TX 75235

WIESE, ELDON CHARLES, marketing adminstr.; b. Moody, Tex., Jan. 7, 1930; s. Charles and Lena Whilemena (Wellman) W.; student South Tex. Coll. Commerce, 1948-50; student U. Houston, 1950-52; m. Mary Frances Stevens, Mar. 3, 1956; children—Carolita Denise, Kim Lisa. Mgr. data processing systems Texaco Inc., Houston, 1947-55, Tulsa, 1955-56; mgr. data processing systems, Am. Petrofina Inc., Dallas, 1956-60; account sales rep. UARCO, Inc., Houston, 1960; sales devel. mgr. Moore Bus. Forms, Inc., Danton, Tex., 1960-71; marketing and sales operations mgr. Ennis Bus. Forms, Inc., Ennis, Tex., 1971—. Mem. Assn. Mgmt. Systems, Am. Mgmt. Assn., Data Processing Mgmt. Assn. (Individual Performance award). Lectr. in field to profl. assns. Home: 230 McMurry St Duncanville TX 75116 Office: 107 N Sherman St Ennis TX 75119

WIESENBURG, KARL, lawyer; b. L.I., N.Y., Aug. 1, 1911; s. Adolph Johann and Martha Mary (Horwath) W.; student pub. schs., N.Y.C.; m. Denise Higginbotham, Dec. 23, 1939; children—Karl, Denis Alan, Martha Ann, Anirah Denise. Admitted to Miss. bar, 1933; practiced in Pascagoula, Miss., 1934—; city atty., Pascagoula and Ocean Springs, 1951-55. Mem. Pascagoula City Council, 1973—; chmn. Pascagoula Democratic Exec. Com., 1950-55; del. Nat. Dem. Conv., Chgo., 1956, Los Angeles, 1960, Miami, 1972. Mem. Miss. Ho. of Reps., 1956-64. Pres., Pascagoula Port Commn., 1939-42, Jackson County chpt. A.R.C., 1947-48. Bd. dirs. Nat. Rivers and Harbors Congress. Served with USCGR, 1929-34, to lt. col. Signal Corps, AUS, 1942-46. Decorated Bronze Star medal. Mem. Fed., Am., Miss., Jackson County (pres.) bar assns., Am. Judicature Soc., Pascagoula C. of C. (dir.), Miss. Rivers and Harbors Assn., V.F.W. (state comdr. 1948-49), Am. Radio Relay League. Roman Catholic (pres. parish council). Kiwanian (past pres.). Home: 525 Spanish Av Pascagoula MS 39567 Office: 3106 Canty St (Box 26) Pascagoula MS 39567

WIESENMAIER, BERNHARD LOUIS, elec. engr.; b. Monroe, Mich., Dec. 8, 1928; s. Louis Carl and Emma Wilhemina (Winkelmann) W.; B.E.E., U. Mich., 1951, postgrad., 1958; m. Ora Lou Slaton, Nov. 22, 1958; children—Thomas David, Julie Lynn. Engr., U.S. Army Ballistic Missile Agy., Redstone Arsenal, Ala., 1953-60; engring. mgr. Marshall Space Flight Center, Huntsville, Ala., 1960—. Served with AUS, 1951-53. Mem. I.E.E.E., Am. Ordnance Assn., Marshall Engr. and Scientist Assn. Lutheran (pres. ch. 1967, 73; sec.-treas. 1968-72). Home: 1203 Appalachee Dr SE Huntsville AL 35801 Office: SS-H-I Marshall Space Flight Center Huntsville AL 35812

WIESER, SIDNEY MALONEY, wholesale feed mfg. and distbg. co. exec.; b. Hamilton, Tex., Oct. 27, 1917; s. Henry M. and Lottie M. (Maloney) W.; student Tex. Christian U., 1936-38; m. Jane Wolfe, June 12, 1940; children—Jean (Mrs. Jack D. Watson), Mary Virginia. Mgr. Hamilton Mill & Elevator Co., 1940-54; pres., gen. mgr. Wieser Mill, Inc., Lampasas, Tex., 1954—; dir. Peoples Nat. Bank, Lampasas, Central Tex. Edn. Corp. Chmn. Salvation Army, 1960—. Mem. Lampasas City Council, 1956-62. Trustee Lampasas Ind. Sch. Dist., 1973—; bd. dirs., vice chmn. Am. Tech. Inst., 1972-74. Mem. Assn. U.S. Army (pres. Central Tex. Ft. Hood chpt. 1968-72), Lampasas C. of C. (pres. 1964-68). Episcopalian (sr. warden). Mason (Shriner). Home: Hwy 281 N Lampasas TX 76550 Office: Box 829 Lampasas TX 76550

WIESNET, DONALD RICHARD, research hydrologist; b. Buffalo, Feb. 7, 1927; s. Charles Anthony and Rose Elizabeth (Hildenbrand) W.; student Syracuse U., 1946-47; B.A., U. Buffalo, 1950, M.A., 1951, postgrad. 1951-52; postgrad. U. Ariz., 1964-65; m. Evelyn Elaine Jordan, Dec. 27, 1952; children—Andrew J., Elizabeth A., Peter C., Ellen E. Geologist U.S. Geol. Survey, Washington, 1952-60; geohydrologist, Washington, also Tucson, Boston, 1960-67; oceanographer, research hydrologist U.S. Naval Oceanographic Office, Washington, 1967-71; sr. research hydrologist NOAA, Environmental Satellite Service, 1971—. Served with USNR, 1944-46. Fellow Geol. Soc. Am.; mem. A.A.A.S., Geol. Soc. Washington, Glaciological Soc., Am. Soc. Photogrammetry, Nat. Water Resources Council (mem. com. hydrology 1968-71). Research and publs. on geology, geohydrology, remote sensing, satellite hydrology, coastal oceanography, geologic cartography. Home: 601 McKinley St NE Vienna VA 22180 Office: 3737 Branch Av SE Washington DC 20031

WIESS, RICHARD THOMAS, dentist; b. Phila., Dec. 31, 1930; s. Louis Charles and Mary Catherine (Dugan) W.; B.A., U. N.C., 1952; D.D.S., 1959; m. Evelyn Adair Beasley, Dec. 22, 1953; children—Sandra Adair, Evelyn Dugan, Mary Julia. Practice dentistry, DeFuniak Springs, Fla., 1959—. Cons. dental hygiene program Pensacola (Fla.) Jr. Coll., 1966-69. Served with USNR, 1952-54. Recipient Best in Show award Walton County Art Show, 1969; 3d place award Bay County Art Show (Fla.), 1970. Mem. Northwest Dist. Dental Soc. (pres. 1969-70), Am. Dental Assn., Fla. Dental Assn., Zi Psi Phi, Kappa Sigma Phi. Presbyn. Lion. 1 Home: S 2d St DeFuniak Springs FL 32433 Office: Circle Dr DeFuniak Springs FL 32433

WIGGINS, ARTHUR WALTER, banker; b. Nashville, Ga., Oct. 6, 1923; s. Oscar Kibbe and Frances (Eldridge) W.; B.S., U. Tampa, 1952; m. Mary Louise Cuddy, Jan. 22, 1956; children—Frances, Arthur Walter, William. Dist. sales mgr. Nat. Airlines, Phila., 1952-57, Northeast Airlines, Tampa, 1957-64; sr. v.p. 1st Nat. Bank Tampa, 1964—. Bd. dirs. Am. Cancer Soc. Hillsborough County, 1968—, Gulf Ridge council Boy Scouts Am., 1969—. Served with AUS, 1941-45. Decorated Bronze Star. Mem. Bank Marketing Assn., Sales and Marketing Execs. Tampa. Lion. Home: 214 Bonnie Brae Temple Terrace FL 33617 Office: 1 First Financial Tower Tampa FL 33602

WIGGINS, BEN T., state ofcl.; b. Augusta, Ga., Nov. 19, 1920; student Spartanburg Jr. Coll., U. Ga., Atlanta Law Sch.; m. Muriel Redfern (dec.); 2 daus. Admitted to Ga. bar, practiced in Toccoa; mem. Ga. Ho. of Reps., 1951-54; exec. sec. to Gov. of Ga., 1955-57; mem. Ga. Pub. Service Commn., 1957—, chmn., 1971—. Chmn. com. on communications Nat. Assn. Regulatory Utility Commrs., 1962—, pres., 1972, also mem. exec. com. Vice pres. Upper Chattahoochee Devel. Assn.; upper region chmn. Chattahoochee River Basin Devel. Commn. Bd. dirs. Greater Atlanta chpt. Leukemia Soc. Am., Inc. Served with USAAF, World War II; ETO. Mem. Ga. Bar Assn., Atlanta Gridiron Soc., Sigma Delta Kappa. Methodist. Mason (Shriner). Address: 244 Washington St SW Atlanta GA 30334

WIGGINS, CHARLES ALFONSA, physician; b. Pennington Gap, Va., Aug. 17, 1943; s. Charlie Lee and Rebecca (McCarroll) W.; A.A., Morristown Coll., 1963; B.A., Fisk U., 1965; M.D., Meharry Med. Coll., 1969. Intern, Hubbard Hosp., Nashville, 1969-70; resident surgery Meharry Med. Coll., Nashville, 1970—; interim med. dir. Delta Health Center, Mound Bayou, Miss., 1973; attending physician Fisk U. Athletic Dept., Nashville, 1969-74, Turney Center for Correction of Youthful Offenders, 1972-74. Mem. R.F. Boyd Med. Soc. Address: Box 465 Meharry Med Coll Nashville TN 37208

WIGGINS, CLIFTON ALLEN, sch. adminstr.; b. Savannah, Ga., June 21, 1912; s. Samuel Sr. and Wilhelmina (Ford) W.; B.S. in Social Studies, Savannah State Coll., 1947; M.A. in Sch. Adminstrn., Atlanta U., 1955; m. George Alma Hayes, Feb. 7, 1938; children—Drusilla Deanna (Mrs. Jimmy Lee Rucker), Ima Wilhemina (Mrs. Sanford Burney, Jr.), Clifftena Allette, Clifton Allen. Asst. prin. Rosenwald Indsl. Sch., Screven, Ga., 1937-41; prin. Clyo High Sch. (Ga.), 1949-56, Central High Sch., Springfield, Ga., 1956-66, Riceboro (Ga.) Elementary Sch., 1966-70; dir. Title I, ESEA, Liberty County Schs., Hinesville, Ga., 1970—. Mem. Selective Service Bd. Recipient Certificate of Merit for Outstanding Bravery, A.R.C., 1939. Mem. N.E.A., Ga. Tchrs. and Edn. Assn. (treas. region 8), Effingham County Tchrs. Assn., Effingham County Prins. Council, Region 8, Ga. prins. councils. Baptist (financial sec.). Mason, Odd Fellow. Home: 1112 W 42d St Savannah GA 31401 Office: Liberty County Bd Edn PO Box 93 Hinesville GA 31313

WIGGINS, MOULTON LEE, bank exec.; b. Peaster, Tex., July 25, 1911; s. John Alexander and Jourdie (Lee) W.; student Weatherford Jr. Coll., 1928-30, U. Tex., 1934-35; m. Clara Elizabeth Wiggins, Jan. 15, 1949. With First Nat. Bank, Munday, Tex., 1935—, pres., chief exec. officer, dir., 1969—. Mem. exec. com. Boy Scouts Am., Munday, 1960-74. Dem. precinct chmn., 1948-62. Recipient Citizen of Year award Chamber of Commerce and Agr., 1967. Mem. C. of C. (dir. 1966-69, pres. 1967-68). Served with inf. AUS, 1941-45. Methodist. Club: Munday Country. Home: 460 S 7th St Munday TX 76371 Office: Box 10 Munday TX 76371

WIGGINS, NORMAN ADRIAN, coll. pres.; b. Burlington, N.C., Feb. 6, 1924; s. Walter James and Margaret (Chason) W.; A.A., Campbell Coll., 1948; B.A., Wake Forest Coll., 1950, LL.B., 1952; LL.M. (Harlan Fiske Stone fellow), Columbia, 1956, J.S.D., 1964; LL.D., Gardner-Webb Coll., 1972; m. Mildred Harmon, Apr. 14, 1948. Admitted to N.C. bar, 1952; asst. trust officer Planters Nat. Bank & Trust Co., Rocky Mount, N.C., 1952-53, asso. trust officer, 1953-55; mem. faculty Wake Forest Coll., Winston-Salem, 1956-67, prof. law, 1962-67, gen. counsel 1964-67; pres. Campbell Coll., Buies Creek, N.C., 1967—. Mem. faculty Cannon Trust Sch., Brevard (N.C.) Coll., 1961—, Nat. Trust Sch., Southwestern U., 1961—; mem. drafting com. N.C. Gen. Statutes Commn., 1958-67; pres. N.C. Assn. Ind. Colls. and Univs., 1971-72; mem. long range planning com. So. Baptist Conv.; mem. faculty Southeastern Trust Sch., 1970—. Chmn. Gov.'s Task Force on Adjudication, Law and Order Com. Chmn. trust faculty Southwestern Grad. Sch. Banking, So. Meth. U., 1965-67, bd. dirs., 1967—; pres. N.C. Found. Ch.-Related Colls., 1969-70. Served with USMCR, 1943-47. Recipient Distinguished Service award Campbell Coll., 1964, Distinguished Alumnus award Phi Alpha Delta, 1966. Mem. N.C. State Bar, N.C. Bar Assn., Nat. Assn. Coll. and Univ. Attys. (exec. bd. 1967—, 2d v.p.), Jay Waugh Evangelistic Assn. (pres. 1965—), Nat. Assn. Coll. and Univ. Attys. (pres. 1972-73), Wake Forest Alumni Assn. (chpt. pres. 1954—), Campbell Coll. Alumni Assn. (v.p. 1958-62). Baptist. Democrat. Author: Wills and Administration of Estates in North Carolina I-II, 1964. Contbr. articles to legal periodicals. Home: Box 127 Buies Creek NC 27506

WIGGS, ASHTON PARKER, educator; b. Pine Level, N.C., Sept. 28, 1928; s. Jasper Joseph and Lucille (Parker) W.; A.B., Atlantic Christian Coll., 1955; postgrad. U. N.C., summer 1956; M.A., E. Carolina U., 1958; m. Jean Vaughan, Aug. 21, 1955; 1 son, Russell Ashton. Forman, Bright Leaf & Burley Tobacco Co., Smithfield, N.C., 1948-50; tchr. Needham Broughton High Sch., Raleigh, N.C., 1956; prin. W. Bertie High Sch., Lewiston, N.C., 1957-59; asst. prof. bus. Atlantic Christian Coll., Wilson, N.C., 1960—. Republican precinct chmn., 1968—; mem. Wilson County Rep. Exec. Com., 1968—. Bd. dirs. United Fund, 1969-70. Served with AUS, 1951-52. Mem. Am. Accounting Assn., Am. Assn. U. Profs., V.F.W., Phi Delta Gamma. Presbyn. (deacon). Mason, Rotarian (chmn. bd. dirs., past pres. Wilson club). Home: 1701 Anderson St Wilson NC 27893 Office: Wilson NC 27893

WIGHTMAN, JOSEPH, educator; b. County of Dorset, Eng., May 18, 1916; s. Joseph and Maud (Pomeroy) W.; B.A., St. Johns Coll., Oxford U., 1938, M.A., 1945; Ph.D., U. S.C., 1961; m. Elaine Taylor, Aug. 5, 1942; children—Robert Mark, Sarah Rosalind. Tchr. Forest Sch., London, Eng., 1938-40, Ilford Grammar Sch. Essex, Eng., 1946-50; head history dept. Weymouth (Dorset, Eng.) Sch., 1950-55, 56-57; guest prof. Erskine Coll., Due West, S.C., 1955-56, prof., dept. history, 1957-63, acad. dean, 1963-66, pres., 1966-73; prof. history, asso. dir. Coastal Carolina Coll., Conway, S.C., 1973—. Served with Brit. Army, 1940-46. Mem. Am. Hist. Assn., S.C. Hist. Assn. Home: Route 6 482 D Conway SC 29526

WIKLER, ABRAHAM, physician; b. N.Y.C., Oct. 12, 1910; s. Isaac and Clara (Wortman) W.; A.B., Columbia Coll., 1930; student Harvard U., 1930-31; M.D., L.I. Coll. Medicine, 1935; m. Ada Fay Fischer, June 15, 1935; children—Marjorie (Mrs. Lester Senechal), Norma, Daniel, Jean. Intern Montefiore Hosp., N.Y.C., 1935-38; with USPHS, 1938-63, asso. dir., chief sect. on exptl. neuropsychiatry Nat. Inst. Mental Health Addiction Research Center, Lexington, Ky., 1943-63; ret., 1963; prof. psychiatry and pharmacology U. Ky. Med. Center, 1963—; mem. staff Univ. Hosp., Lexington. Recipient USPHS Meritorious Service medal, 1963; Ky. Med. Assn. Faculty Sci. Achievement award, 1972. Fellow Am. Psychiat. Assn., Am. Acad. Neurology, Am. Coll. Psychiatrists, Am. Coll. Neuropsychopharmacology; mem. Am. Neurol. Assn., Am. Soc. Pharmacology. Jewish religion. Author: Opiate Addiction, 1953; The Relation of Psychiatry to Pharmacology, 1957; The Addictive States, 1968. Contbr. numerous articles to sci. jours. Home: 1241 Summit Dr Lexington KY 40502 Office: U Ky Med Center Lexington KY 40506

WILBER, GEORGE LEWIN, educator; b. Flint, Mich., July 6, 1918; s. George L. and Etta Matilda (Bacon) W.; B.A., U. Mich., 1944, M.A., 1947; Ph.D., U. Neb., 1952; m. Roberta P. Fisher, Aug. 29, 1941; children—Cynthia, Lane, Brian. Asst. prof. to asso. prof. U. Omaha, 1949-57; prof. Miss. State U., 1957-65, La. State U., 1965-70; prof. demography, dir. Social Welfare Research Inst., U. Ky., Lexington, 1970—. Asso. dir. Nat. Adv. Com. on Rural Poverty, 1966-67. Mem. Population Assn. Am., Am. Sociol. Assn., So. Sociol. Soc., So. Regional Demographic Group. Author: The People Left Behind, 1967. Editor: Rural Poverty in the U.S., 1968. Home: 333 Hightower Rd Lexington KY 40502

WILBOURN, HUGH RANDOLPH, JR., telephone co. exec.; b. Little Rock, Sept. 13, 1915; s. Hugh Randolph and Willye May (Bonner) W.; student Ouachita U., 1932-33; m. Edith K. Morris, June 14, 1936; children—Mary Nell (Mrs. Shaw), Jo Ellen (Mrs. Joe T. Ford), Beverly (Mrs. Phillip T. Pascoe), Hugh Randolph. Plant dept. Southwestern Bell Telephone Co., Little Rock, 1934-44; v.p., gen. mgr. Allied Telephone Co., Little Rock, 1943-62, pres., 1962—, chmn. bd., 1962—; treas. Security Savs. & Loan Assn., Conway, Ark., 1962—. Mem. nat. exec. com. Boy Scouts Am., 1968—. Trustee Ark. Baptist Med. Center. Mem. U.S. Ind. (v.p. 1968—, chmn. legislative com. 1969—), Ark. (pres. 1951-52) telephone assns., Ark. C. of C. (dir.). Baptist (deacon 1954—). Home: 2100 Country Club Lane Little Rock AR 72207 Office: Mart Bldg 3600 Cantrell Rd Little Rock AR 72203

WILBUR, OSCAR MILTON, JR., physician; b. Bangor, Me., Apr. 15, 1921; s. Oscar Milton and Mary (Wentworth) W.; B.A., U. Me., 1944; M.D., Boston U., 1946; m. Louise Wells, Nov. 16, 1946; children—Mary Crosby (Mrs. Charles Carnahan Goetsch), Anne Lawton. Intern Rochester (N.Y.) Gen. Hosp., 1946-47; asst. resident internal medicine Mt. Alto VA Hosp., Washington, 1949-50; asst. resident in pathology, resident in pathology Johns Hopkins Hosp., Balt., 1950-55; asso. pathologist Augustana Hosp., Chgo., 1956; pathologist Hibbing, Minn., 1956-61, Pueblo, Colo., 1962-64, Buffalo, 1965-68, Savannah and Americus, Ga., 1968-70, Cartersville and Canton, Ga., 1973—; instr. pathology Johns Hopkins Sch. Medicine, 1950-55; asst. clin. prof. pathology U. Colo. Sch. Medicine, 1962-64, State U. N.Y. at Buffalo Med. Sch., 1965-68; asst. prof. pathology Emory U. Sch. Medicine, 1971-73. Served to capt. M.C., AUS, 1947-49. Diplomate in path. anatomy, clin. pathology Am. Bd. Pathology. Fellow Am. Soc. Clin. Pathologists, Coll. Am. Pathologists; mem. Internat. Acad. Pathology, Johns Hopkins Med. and Surg. Assn., A.M.A., Am. Assn. Blood Banks, Ga., Bartow County med. socs., Ga. Assn. Pathologists. Republican. Episcopalian. Rotarian. Contbr. papers to Bull. Johns Hopkins Hosp., 1953, 54, 55. Home: 302 W Main St Cartersville GA 30120 Office: Sam Howell Meml Hosp Cartersville GA 30120

WILBURN, JAMES LEWIS, civil and structural engr.; b. Kipling, N.C., Apr. 29, 1916; s. James Carlie and Ruth Ester (Wilder) W.; A.B. in Math., Elon Coll., 1938; postgrad. U. Mich., 1948-49; B.C.E., N.C. State U., 1952; 1 dau., Linda Ellen (Mrs. Don Parker). Civil engr. U.S. Civil Service with AUS, USCG, and USN, 1942-67; structural engr. C.T. Main Cons. Engrs., Charlotte, N.C., 1970—. Instr. math. White Oak (N.C.) Sch., 1938-39. Served with AUS, C.E., 1946-48. Registered profl. engr. N.C., Fla., D.C. Mem. N.C. Soc. Profl. Engrs. Club: Zodiac Social. Home: 1928 Center St Fayetteville NC 28306

WILCOMB, ERNEST FRANCIS, elec. engr.; b. Somerville, Mass., Aug. 11, 1911; s. Francis H. and Rosabel Eleanora (Silver) W.; B.S. in E.E., Tri-State Coll., 1938; postgrad. in radar engring. Bowdoin Coll., 1941; postgrad. in applied math., Adelphi Coll., 1956; m. Lucile Marjory Andrews, Sept. 3, 1949; children—Sarah Conn (Mrs. Francis J. Fabrizio Jr.), Guy Andrews, Keith Jordan. Structural engr. Truscon Steel, Youngstown, O., 1946-47; sr. field test dir. Nat. Bureau Standards, Washington, 1948-51, resident engr., 1951-56; prin. engr., Washington rep. Bendix Corp., 1956-63; gen. mgr., asst. to pres. Airtronics Inc., Bethesda, Md., 1963-64; sr. engr. Raff Analytic Study Assos., Inc., Silver Spring, Md., 1964-68; supr. engr. anti-ship missile def. project Naval Ordnance Systems Command, Washington, 1968—. Vice pres. Phoenix Films, Inc., Chevy Chase, Md., 1965—; owner Center Book Shop, Bethesda, 1970—. Mem. Bethesda P.T.A.

Served to comdr. USN, 1939-46. Recipient NASA Goddard Space Flight Center award, 1968. Registered profl. engr., D.C. Mem. I.E.E.E. (sr.), Assn. Old Crows. Clubs: Lewes (Del.) Yacht; Kenwood Golf and Country (Bethesda). Contbr. articles to profl. jours. Home: 7303 Maple Ave Chevy Chase MD 20015 Office: Code PMO 403-62B Naval Ordnance Systems Command Washington DC 20360

WILCOX, DAVID BERTELL, restaurant and grocery co. exec.; b. Liberty, Mo., May 18, 1930; s. David Bertell and Mary Gertrude (Banks) W.; B.S. in Econs. with high honors, U. Ill., 1956; m. Betsy Ross, Aug. 15, 1955; children—Mary Lou, Julie, Ruth. Mgr. municipal services dept. 1st Nat. Bank, Memphis, 1961-65; asst. sec., treas., controller Graham & Warren, Inc., advt. agy., 1965-67, sec., treas., controller, 1967-70; sec., treas., controller Mitchum Co., 1967-70; asst. sec., treas., controller Mitchum-Thayer, Inc., Paris, Tenn., 1970-71, v.p. adminstrn., 1971-72; pres. Pagliacci, Inc., 1972—; v.p. adminstrn. Jim Adams Inc., 1973—; dir. Puryear Community Devel. Corp., 1967—. Commr., City of Paris, 1970—; mem. Paris Regional Planning Commn.; mem. coms. Henry County Ct. Budget, 1968—, fiscal study com., 1971—, airport com., 1967-69; pres. Paris Little Theater, 1969; dist. chmn. Boy Scouts Am., 1970-71, bd. dirs. West Tenn. council; bd. dirs. Paris-Henry County Youth Center. Served with USNR, 1948-52. Mem. Henry County Plant Mgmt. Assn. (chmn. 1969, 73), Paris C. of C. (treas. 1969-72, dir.), Beta Gamma Sigma, Sigma Iota Epsilon, Chi Gamma Iota. Elk. Home: 307 Jackson St Paris TN 38242 Office: 1301 W Wood St Paris TN 38242

WILCOX, DON CHARLES, economist, educator; b. Mayburg, Pa., May 7, 1934; s. Robert H. and Gladys E. (Miner) W.; B.S., Nicholls State U., 1961; M.A., La. State U., 1962; D.B.A., Miss. State U., 1969; m. Pearl J. Olivier, Feb. 4, 1956; children—Steven, Laurie, Rachel. Asst. prof. econs. La. Tech. U., Ruston, 1962-66, asso. prof., 1967-71, prof., 1971—, dir. div. bus. and econ. research, 1970—. Mem. La. Gov.'s. Council Econ. Advisers, 1972—; asst. dir. La. Coordinating Council for Higher Edn., 1971. Served with USAF, 1952-56. Mem. So. Econs. Assn., Beta Gamma Sigma, Phi Kappa Phi, Omicron Delta Epsilon, Delta Sigma Pi. Home: PO Box 6336 Technical Station Ruston LA 71270

WILCOX, DONALD BROOKS, educator; b. Walden, N.Y., Feb. 23, 1911; s. William W. and Marion Louise (Lawall) W.; B.S. in Indsl. Engring., 1933; B.S. in Mech. Engring., Ga. Inst. Tech., 1939; LL.D., Emory U., 1952; m. Edith Anne Morgan, Nov. 30, 1935; children—Donald B., Ruth Lois (Mrs. Armando P. Romero), Evelyn Louise (Mrs. James Kent Raymond). Instr., Ga. Inst. Tech., Atlanta, 1936-40, prof., 1945-52, indsl. engr., asso. prof. U. Ala., Tuscaloosa, 1941-42, also acting head dept. indsl. engring.; prof. indsl. engring. U. Fla., Gainesville, 1952—. Cons. to Fla. Indsl. Commn., 1954—. Served to capt. USAAF, 1942-45. Registered profl. engr., Fla., Ga. Mem. Am. Inst. Indsl. Engrs., Am. Soc. Engring. Edn., Nat. Soc. Profl. Engrs., Am. Soc. Safety Engrs., Tau Beta Pi. Mason. Home: 1120 NE 5th Terrace Gainesville FL 32601

WILCOX, REX EUGENE, journalist; b. Portland, Ore., May 26, 1915; s. Ralph James and Lida (Riches) W.; student U. Wis., 1939-41, U. Ill., 1942-43, U. Chgo., 1958-59; m. Doris Lucile Haney, July 27, 1937; children—James Hamilton, John Patrick. Pub. relations worker So. Cal. Edison Co., Los Angeles, 1946-52; asst. to editor Ft. Smith (Ark.) Times Record, 1952-59; editor, columnist, lectr. Natchez (Miss.) Times, 1959-61; city editor, editorial writer Palm Beach Post, West Palm Beach, Fla., 1961-70, Palm Beach Times, 1970—. Mem. Internat. Platform Assn., Sigma Delta Chi. Republican. Episcopalian. Mason. Home: 5826 Church Circle W West Palm Beach FL 33405 Office: 2751 S Dixie St West Palm Beach FL 33405

WILD, HARRY EDWARD, JR., civil engr., b. Providence, Sept. 23, 1940; s. Harry Edward and Lula Elizabeth (Johnson) W.; B.C.E., U. Fla., 1966, M. in Bioenvironmental Engring., 1967; m. Ann Elizabeth Johnson, May 22, 1965; children—Elizabeth Ann, Eric Johnson. Engr., Metcalf & Eddy, Inc., Boston, 1967-71; v.p. Briley, Wild & Assos., Daytona Beach, Fla., 1971, pres., 1971—; pres. B & W Properties, Inc., Ormond Beach, Fla., 1972—, also dir. Served with AUS, 1961. Recipient Harrison P. Eddy award Water Pollution Control Fedn., 1972. Registered profl. engr., Fla., Ga., Me. Mem. Am. Pub. Works Assn., Boston Soc. Civil Engrs., Nat. Soc. Profl. Engrs., Air Pollution Control Assn., Fla. Engring. Soc., Am. Water Works Assn., Water Pollution Control Fedn. Clubs: Executive, Halifax. Home: 47 Pine Valley Circle Ormond Beach FL 32074 Office: PO Box 607 Ormond Beach FL 32074

WILDERMAN, EUGENE JOSEPH, electronic engr.; b. Evansville, Ind., Apr. 17, 1941; s. Walter Theodore and Cecelia Frances (Sammet) W.; A.A., Allan Hancock Jr. Coll., 1963; B.S. in E.E. (Samuel E. Orr scholar), U. Evansville, 1969, M.B.A., 1973; m. Barbara Theoann Fenner, May 16, 1964; children—Sharon, Raymond, Janeen. Instrumentation technician Airesearch Mfg. Co., Los Angeles, 1963-68; electronic engr. McDonnell Douglas, St. Louis, 1969; electronic engr. microwave design Gen. Electric Corp., Owensboro, Ky., 1967—. Served with USAF, 1959-63. Mem. Sigma Pi Sigma, Eta Kappa Nu. K.C. Home: 2830 Choctaw Dr Owensboro KY 42301 Office: 316 E 9th St Owensboro KY 42301

WILENSKY, ALVIN, public accountant; b. Scranton, Pa., Nov. 3, 1921; s. Isaac and Sarah (Barnett) W.; A.A., Keystone Jr. Coll., 1941; B.A., Pa. State U., 1943; m. Ruth L. Gross, June 3, 1945; children—Irwin David, Robert Brian Bookkeeper, Charle's Shop, 1941-43; supr. accountant Alberts Kahn & Levess, C.P.A.'s, N.Y.C., 1945-48; pvt. practice pub. accounting, Scranton, 1948-73, merged practice with firm Leidigh & Bisbano, Harrisburg, Pa., 1973; financial adminstr. Cenvill Communities, Inc., West Palm Beach, Fla., 1973, v.p. finance, 1973—; pres. subsidiary Gerald Data Center, Inc., 1973—. Comptroller Cedar Lanes Bowling Stadium, Inc., 1959-68. Instr. accounting Keystone Jr. Coll., 1950-51. Mem. Scranton Mayor's Tax Study Com., 1963-65; mem. dist. dir. profl. adv. com. Internal Revenue Service, Phila., 1961-65. Treas., bd. dirs. United Cerebral Palsy Lackawanna County; bd. dirs. Child Guidance and Psychiat. Clinic, Louis Wolfe Found. Served to 1st lt. USAAF, 1943-45. Decorated Air medal with five oak leaf clusters. C.P.A., Pa. Mem. Am., Pa. (past pres. N.E. chpt., chmn. bd. trustees) insts. C.P.A.'s, Jewish War Vets. (past post comdr.; certificate of outstanding Service 1960), Scranton C. of C., Keystone Jr. Coll. Alumni Assn. (past pres.). Jewish religion (sec., dir. temple). Elk. Club: Glen Oak Country (dir., past treas.). Home: 1723 Consulate Pl West Palm Beach FL 33401 Office: Cenvill Communities Inc West Palm Beach FL 33401 also Connell Bldg Scranton PA 18503

WILEY, FORREST PARKS, biologist, chemist, systems engr.; b. Weldon, N.C., Nov. 1, 1937; s. Joseph Weldon and Georgia (Parks) W.; B.S., Tuskegee Inst., 1966; m. Gloria Jean Chisholm, Dec. 18, 1961; children—Joseph Lamar, John Lamont. Mid-Atlantic regional mgr. Letterflex systems W.R. Grace & Co., Washington Research Center, Columbia, Md., 1967—; dir. research New Ventures, Inc., 1970-73. Bd. dirs. Washington-Tuskegee Housing Found., Tuskegee Alumni Housing Found. Mem. Nat. Geog. Soc., Bot. Soc. Am., Am. Soc. Plant Physiologists, Am. Inst. Biol. Scis., Tuskegee Alumni Assn. (dir.), Washington-Tuskegee Club (dir.), Internat. Platform Assn. Patentee in field. Home: 8408 Barron St Washington DC 20012 Office: Washington Research Center Columbia MD 21044

WILEY, JOSEPH BRANTLEY, judge; b. Birmingham, Ala., Oct. 25, 1922; s. Clarence C. and Lillian (Brantley) W.; A.B., U. Ala., 1947, LL.B., 1949; m. Mary Ann Conrad, Mar. 19, 1949; children—Joseph Brantley, Elizabeth Henderson, James Conrad. Admitted to Ala. bar, 1949; practiced in Troy, Ala., 1949—; city judge, Troy, 1961—; exec. dir. Troy Housing Authority, 1968-71; dir. Troy Broadcasting Corp., Citizens Bank of Troy. Chmn. Choctowhatchee Regional Library, Indsl. Devel. Bd., Troy, 1960-61. Bd. dirs. Pike County Mus. Assn. Served to lt. (j.g.) USNR, 1943-46. Mem. Am., Ala. bar assns., Phi Delta Phi, Sigma Alpha Epsilon. Rotarian (pres. Troy, 1965-66). Home: 312 Flavia Circle Troy AL 36081 Office: 123 Madison St Troy AL 36081

WILHOIT, LOWELL MAINARD, engring. tech. dir.; b. Lutie, Mo., Oct. 6, 1911; s. Joseph S. and Bessie May (Fulton) W.; B.S., Okla. State U., 1936; m. Louise Hillyer, Mar. 27, 1937; children—Jimmy Louise, David Curtis. With Otis Engring. Corp., Dallas, 1936—, v.p. research and engring., 1956-70, sr. v.p., tech. dir., 1970—, also dir. Chmn. spl. awards Dallas Regional Sci. Fair. Registered profl. engr., Tex., Okla., N.M. Fellow Am. Soc. M.E. (Outstanding mech. engr. 1963); mem. Soc. Petroleum Engrs., Am. Petroleum Inst., Dallas Petroleum Engrs. Club. Baptist. Patentee oil field Equipment. Home: 5611 Williamstown Rd Dallas TX 75230 Office: PO Box 34380 Dallas TX 75234

WILHOLD, GILBERT ANTHONY, aero. engr.; b. East St. Louis, Ill., Dec. 9, 1934; s. Gilbert O. and Bernice (Petroski) W.; B.S., St. Louis U., 1957; postgrad. U. Ala., 1960-62; m. Juanita O. Martinez, June 6, 1957; children—Joseph A., Gilbert A., Sherrie G. Engr., McDonnell Aircraft Corp. Mo., 1957-60; engr. Chrysler Corp. Ala., Huntsville, 1960-62; with Marshall Space Flight Center, NASA, 1962—, analytical and theoretical acoustics tech. asst., lab. dir., 1963-66, dep. br. chief unsteady gas dynamics, 1966—. Recipient certificate of recognition Marshall Space Flight Center, 1968; Outstanding Service award NASA, 1969. Registered profl. engr., Ala. Mem. A.A.A.S., Acoustical Soc. Am. Home: 2604 Pitkin Lane Huntsville AL 35810 Office: Marshall Space Flight Center PO Box 3386 Huntsville AL 35810

WILKERSON, JOHN P., lawyer; b. Cuthbert, Ga., Nov. 7, 1918; s. Walter McLendon and Viola (Joyner) W.; student U. Ga., 1946-47; grad. USAAF tech. sch. aircraft engring. Yale, 1945; LL.B., Stetson U., 1949; m. Sarah Terrill Morris, June, 14, 1950; children—Ann Terrill, John Morris, Sarah, Mary. Insp. engring. dept. Brewster Aero. Corp., L.I., N.Y., 1940-43; admitted to Ga. bar, 1948, Fla. bar, 1949; mem. firm Wilkerson & Wilkerson, Atlanta, 1949-51; practiced in Eustis, Fla.; judge municipal ct. Eustis, 1957-59; atty. Town of Tavares (Fla.), 1957-59; citrus grower. Active civic orgns. Served as capt. USAAF, World War II. Mem. Am., Ga., Lake Sumter (pres. 1953-55) bar assns., Fla. Bar, Nat. Hist. Soc. (founder), Republican. Phi Alpha Delta. Episcopalian. Mason (Shriner), Rotarian. Home: Treasure Island FL 32748 Office: Suite 2 Eustis Profl Bldg Eustis FL 32726

WILKERSON, WOODROW WILSON, state ednl. ofcl.; b. Prince Edward County, Va., Apr. 29, 1913; s. John Henry and Betty Maude (Young) W.; B.A. magna cum laude, Hampden-Sydney Coll., 1934, M.A., Coll. William and Mary, 1938; Ed.D., U. Md., 1952; m. Dorothy Price, Sept. 1, 1937; children—Carrington Cabell, Elizabeth Claire (Mrs. Stephen C. Starbuck), Dorothy Swann. Tchr. English, Latin and gen. sci. Lunenburg County, Va., 1934-36; prin. Dillwyn High Sch., Buckingham County, Va., 1936-38, King William (Va.) High Sch., 1938-40, Marion High Sch., Smyth County, Va., 1940-45; asst. supr. secondary edn. Va. Dept. Edn., 1945-47, supr. secondary edn., 1947-57, dir. tech. edn., 1957-58, dir. secondary edn., 1958-60, supt. pub. instrn., 1960—. Commr. from Va. to Edn. Commn. of the States. Hon. life mem. Va. P.T.A., 1962. Mem. So. Assn. Colls. and Secondary Schs. (exec. sec. Va. 1952-57, chmn. central reviewing com. pub. schs., commn. secondary edn. 1956-57), Nat. Assn. Suprs. and Dirs. Secondary Edn. (pres. 1954-55), council Chief State Sch. Officers, State Council Higher Edn., Phi Delta Kappa (Distinguished Service award 1961), Phi Kappa Phi, Omicron Delta Kappa, Sigma Chi. Methodist. Kiwanian. Home: 914 Ridgetop Rd Richmond VA 23229 Office: State Office Bldg Richmond VA 23216

WILKES, CHARLES LATIMER, lawyer; b. Washington, Mar. 7, 1929; s. James Claiborne and Edna (Cross) W.; A.B., Dartmouth, 1950; LL.B., George Washington U., 1954; m. Norma Paige Fitchett, July 17, 1956; children—Charles Latimer, Douglas Hallett, David Claiborne, Karen Elizabeth. Admitted to D.C. bar, 1954, Mich. bar, 1958; practiced in Washington, 1954-57, 60—, Saginaw, Mich., 1958-60; mem. firm Wilkes & Artis, 1954-57, 60—. Dir. Columbia Fed. Savs. & Loan Assn., Washington. Mem. D.C. Hackers License Appeal Bd., 1962—; mem. Nat. Capitol Area council Boy Scouts Am., 1969-73. Mem. Capitol Hill club Republican party. Trustee Fed. City Council, Washington, 1969—, Washington City Orphan Asylum, 1971—; bd. dirs. Met. Washington YMCA and YMCA Found., 1969—. Named Leader of Year, YMCA Met. Washington, 1970. Mem. Bar Assn. D.C. (dir. 1974—), Am. Bar Assn., Barristers, Delta Tau Delta. Republican. Methodist. Mason (32 deg., Jester). Clubs: University, Dartmouth, Lawyers (Washington), Congressional Country. Home: 1004 Woburn Ct McLean VA 22101 Office: 1666 K St NW Washington DC 20006

WILKES, EUGENE PEIRCE, editor emeritus; b. Biloxi, Miss., Aug. 9, 1885; s. George W. and Laurie (Chidsey) W.; ed. Biloxi pub. schs.; m. Loretta V. Voivedich, Oct. 1, 1910; children—Josephine (Mrs. Reicker), Mrs. Robert A. Miller, Walter J. With Biloxi-Gulfport Daily Herald, 1898-70, pres. until 1970; editor Daily Herald, Biloxi and Gulfport. Chmn. Harrison County Pkwy. Commn., pres. Harrison County Devel. Commn., 1963-69; active Boy Scouts Am., 43 years; mem. Gulf Islands Seashore Adv. Commn., 1972-74. Named Outstanding Citizen of Biloxi, Lions, 1935; recipient Laurel Wreath award, 1966, Council cup Boy Scouts Am., 1936. Mem. So. Newspaper Pubs. Assn. (dir.), Miss. Press Assn. (pres.). Rotarian (hon., Paul Harris award), Kiwanian (pres. Gulfport club 1960). Home: 217 Fayard St Biloxi MS 39530

WILKES, GEORGE GARDNER, JR., landscape architect, govt. ofcl.; b. Baton Rouge, Dec. 5, 1927; s. George Gardner and Irene Ola (Sowar) W.; B.S., La. State U., 1952, postgrad., 1953; m. Betty Jay Stokes, June 8, 1949; children—George III, Rebecca Gay. Landscape architect Landscape Service Co., Shreveport, La., 1952-53; pvt. practice landscape architecture, Shreveport, 1953-55, 60-66; chief landscape architect Lamber Landscape Co., Shreveport, 1955-60; chief land planner VA, Atlanta, 1966-72, chief appraiser, 1972—. Served with USNR, 1945-46. Mem. Am. Soc. Landscape Architects. Presbyn. (elder 1971—). Mason (32 deg., Shriner). Home: 1236 Fork Creek Trail Decatur GA 30033 Office: 730 Peachtree St Atlanta GA 30308

WILKEY, MALCOLM RICHARD, judge; b. Murfreesboro, Tenn., Dec. 6, 1918; s. Malcolm Newton and Elizabeth (Gilbert) W.; A.B., Harvard, 1940, LL.B., 1948; m. Emma Secul Depolo, Dec. 21, 1959. Admitted to Tex. bar, 1948, N.Y. bar, 1963, U.S. Supreme Ct. bar, 1952, Ct. of Appeals, D.C. Circuit, 1958; with Butler Binion Rice & Cook, 1948-54, 61-63; U.S. atty. So. Dist. Tex., 1954-58, asst. atty. gen. U.S., 1958-61, sec., asso. gen. counsel, Kennecott Copper Corp. 1963-67, sec., gen. counsel, 1967-70; judge U.S. Ct. Appeals, D.C. Circuit, 1970—. Del. Republican Nat. Conv., 1960. Served from 2d lt. to lt. col. AUS, 1941-45. Fellow Am. Bar Found.; mem. Am. (commn. on nat. inst. justice), Inter-Am. bar assns., Assn. Bar City N.Y., Am. Law Inst., Phi Beta Kappa, Delta Sigma Rho. Clubs: Harvard (N.Y.C.); Metropolitan (Washington). Home: 540 N St SW Washington DC 20024 Office: US Ct Appeals Washington DC 20001

WILKINS, BENJAMIN HARRISON, JR., mfg. co. exec.; b. Nashville, May 28, 1899; s. Benjamin Harrison and Jane Bryan (Weeden) W.; B.S. in Mech. Engring., Ga. Inst. Tech., 1921; m. Mary Boyers McQuiddy, June 29, 1935. With Tenn. Overall Co., Inc., Tullahoma, 1922—, pres., treas., 1941—; with Tenn. Glove Co., Inc., Tullahoma, 1922—, pres., 1941, pres., treas., 1944—; dir. 1st Nat. Bank Tullahoma. Served with U.S. Army, 1918-19; to lt. col. USAF, 1942-46. Mem. Am. Legion (past comdr.), V.F.W. (past comdr.), Tullahoma C. of C. (past pres.), So. Garment mfrs. Assn. (pres. 1956-57). Episcopalian. Mason (Shriner). Club: Tullahoma Golf and Country. Home: 408 N Atlantic St Tullahoma TN 37388 Office: 401 N Atlantic St Tullahoma TN 37388

WILKINS, J. ERNEST, JR., physicist, educator; b. Chgo., Nov. 27, 1923; s. J. Ernest and Lucille Beatrice (Robinson) W.; B.S., U. Chgo., 1940, M.S., 1941, Ph.D. in Math., 1942; B.Mech. Engring., N.Y. U., 1957, M.M.E., 1960; m. Gloria Louise Stewart, June 22, 1947; children—Sharon (Mrs. Thomas Hill), J. Ernest III. Instr. math. Tuskegee (Ala.) Inst., 1943-44; physicist U. Chgo., 1944-46; mathematician Am. Optical Co., N.Y.C., 1946-50; mgr. research and devel. United Nuclear Corp. Am., N.Y.C., 1950-60; asst. lab. dir. Gulf Gen. Atomic, Inc., San Diego, 1960-70; distinguished prof. applied math. physics Howard U., Washington, 1970—. Mem. adv. com. for standard reference materials and methods of measurement AEC, 1964-67, mem. adv. com. nuclear material safeguards, 1967-72; mem. adv. com. for planning and instl. affairs NSF, 1973-74. Fellow A.A.A.S., Am. Nuclear Soc. (pres. 1975). Home: 1403 Romeo Ct McLean VA 22101 Office: Dept Physics Howard University Washington DC 20001

WILKINS, JUDD RICE, microbiologist; b. Chgo., Dec. 12, 1920; s. Lewis Morris and Maude Edith (Wells) W.; B.S., U. Ill., 1946, M.S., 1947, Ph.D., 1950; m. Mary Helen Steinman, Jan. 25, 1950; children—Louise Edith, Ralph Martin. Asst. prof. microbiology U. S.D. Med, Sch., 1950-51; research investigator Upjohn Co., Kalamazoo, 1951-57; project scientist Booz Allen Applied Research, Inc., Bethesda, Md., 1957-64; head dept. microbiology Eye Research Found., Bethesda, 1964-66; microbiologist Langley Research Center, NASA, Hampton, VA, 1966—. Served with AUS, 1943-45. Mem. Am. Soc. for Microbiology, Sigma Xi. Episcopalian. Kiwanian (dir. Bethesda 1966). Research on effect of gravity on growth of microorganisms; devised math. model of incubation period of infectious diseases. Patentee continuous recording nephelometer, antibiotic combinations, lab. instrumentation, microbial detection devices. Home: 313 Beechmount Dr Hampton VA 23369 Office: NASA Langley Research Center Hampton VA 23365

WILKINS, MAURICE LAYNE, aerospace engr.; b. Fayetteville, Ark., Apr. 7, 1941; s. Woodrow and Marion (Phillips) W.; B.S. in Mech. Engring., U. Ark., 1963; m. Estell Gentry, Feb. 1, 1964; children—Scott Allen, Stacy Layne, Aerospace engr. Oklahoma City Air Logistics Center, Tinker AFB, Okla., 1963—. Recipient Silver Zero Defects award Ocama, 1967, Gold Zero Defects award, 1969. Registered profl. engr., Okla. Mem. Soc. Profl. Engrs. and Scientists Tinker AFB, Tinker Mgmt. Club. Baptist. Home: 3701 Greenway Terrace Del City OK 73115 Office: Tinker AFB OK 73145

WILKINS, MICHAEL REAGENE, elec. engr.; b. San Antonio, Apr. 25, 1945; s. Charles Reagene and Helen Maxine (McCann) W.; student San Antonio Coll., 1963-65; B.S., Tex. A & I U., 1969; m. Glynda Cheryl Emery, Aug. 31, 1968. Staff elec. engr. Aluminum Co. Am., Taylor, Tex., 1969-73, sr. staff elec. engr., Rockdale, Tex., 1973-74; elec. engr. Ham-Mer Cons. Engrs., 1974—. Registered profl. engr., Tex. Mem. Tex. Soc. Profl. Engrs., I.E.E.E. Home: Austin TX Office: 5000 E Ben White Blvd Austin TX 78741

WILKINS, RAOUL WHEELER, architect; b. Charlottesville, Va., Aug. 18, 1921; s. John William and Evelyn (Wheeler) W.; B.S., U. Va., 1950; children (by previous marriage)—Susan, Virginia, William; m. 2d, Sandra Leigh Sandlin, Aug. 1, 1970; 1 dau., Elizabeth Mitchell. Draftsman, Ballou & Justice, Richmond, Va., 1950-52, Walford & Wright, Richmond, 1952-57; architect Raoul Wheeler Wilkins, Maidens, Va., 1959—. Served with Combat Engrs., AUS, 1942-45. Registered architect, Va., Tenn., N.C., Md. Mem. A.I.A., Am. Registered Architects, Confederate Hist. Soc. Eng., S.C.V., Order Stars and Bars, S.A.R., Nat. Steeplechase and Hunt Assn., 124th U.S. Cavalry Assn., Am. Legion, U. Va., Greenbrier Mil. (past dir., life) alumni assns., Am. Mus. Natural History, Alpha Rho Chi. Democrat. Methodist. Clubs: Kallikrates, Deep Run Hunt, Farmington Country. Spl. works include shopping centers, apt. projects, townhouses, profl. and comml. bldgs. Home: Pavilion Hill Maidens VA 23102 Office: Route 6 at 522 S Maidens VA 23102

WILKINS, RICHARD COWAN, oil co. exec.; b. Warren, Pa., Aug. 31, 1908; s. Percy Waters and Hariett (Cowan) W.; B.S. in Petroleum Engring., Pa. State U., 1931; m. Sally Lou Darr, Oct. 28, 1938; children—Linda Lou (Mrs. John C. White), Richard Cowan. Engr., geologist Texaco, La., 1931-33, field engr., 1933-35, drilling, prodn. field supt., 1935-46; supt. J.C. Hawkins & Delta Drilling Co., La., Tex., Miss., 1946-50; part owner W. Hawkins Drilling Co., Hawkins-Wilkins Prodn. Co., Houston, 1950-60; cons., ind. oil operator, Houston, 1960-64; eastern regional mgr. Dyna-Drill Co. div. Smith Internat., Houston, 1965—. Mem. Alpha Tau Omega. Mason. Club: Houston. Home: 1225 Wood Hollow Dr Houston TX 77027 Office: Cullen Bank Center 600 Jefferson St Houston TX 77002

WILKINS, RICHARD SANDEFUR, architect, planning cons.; b. Madison, Wis., Sept. 27, 1933; s. Robert Alvin and Alice (Metcalf) W.; B.S., U. Houston, 1957, B.Arch., 1957; m. Beatrice Elaine Bernhausen, Feb. 14, 1964; 1 son, Karl Richard. Architect David D. Red, 1952-55, Suniland Comml. Furnishings, 1955, Robert W. Maurice, 1955-57, 58-60, Raymond Brogniez, 1960-61, Robert W. Maurice, Richard S. Wilkins & Assos., Houston, 1961—. Mem. West University Place City Zoning Bd. Adjustment. Served with AUS, 1957-58. Mem. A.I.A., Tex. Soc. Architects. Kiwanian (pres. Houston 1971-72). Club: Houston Turn Verein. Author: Juveniles of Harris County, 1965. Home: 3305 Amherst St Houston TX 77005 Office: 3222 Mercer St Houston TX 77027

WILKINS, ROBERT PEARCE, lawyer; b. Jesup, Ga., Sept. 10, 1933; s. Ransome Little and Sarah (Pearce) W.; B.S., U. S.C., 1953, LL.B., 1954; LL.M., Georgetown U., 1957; m. Rose Truesdale, Jan. 7, 1956; children—Robert Pearce, Chisolm Wallace, Sarah Ruth, Rose Anne. Admitted to S.C. bar, 1954; atty. Office Gen. Counsel Sec. Army, Washington, 1956; trust officer First Nat. Bank S.C., Columbia,

1957-60; practiced law, 1960-64; partner firm McLain, Sherrill & Wilkins, Columbia, 1964-68, McKay, Sherrill, Walker, Townsend & Wilkins, Columbia, 1969—; pres. Sandlapper Press, Inc., 1967-72, pub. Sandlapper, Mag. of S.C., 1968-72, editor, 1968-69. Lectr. law U. S.C. Law Sch., 1971—. Del., Spl. Liaison Tax Com. Southeastern Region, 1967-70; exec. com. Richland County Republican Com., 1960-64; sec.-treas. Richland County Rep. Club, 1960. Bd. dirs. Central Tb-RD Assn.; trustee Sch. Dist. 1, Lexington County, S.C. Served with AUS, 1954-55. C.L.U., S.C. Mem. Am. (chmn. valuation subcom., estate and gift tax com., taxation sect. 1967-73, vice chmn. service and assistance to law student div. com. gen. practice sect. 1971-72, vice chmn. corporate counsel com. gen. practice sect. 1972—), S.C. (tax coordinating com. 1968-70, chmn. legal econs. com. 1973—), Richland County (chmn. probate sect. 1973—) bar assns., Columbia Jr. C. of C. (sec.-treas. 1958-59), Columbia Estate Planning Council (pres. 1964-65), Am. Y-Flyer Yacht Racing Assn. (area v.p. 1971, internat. dir. 1972-73), Omicron Delta Kappa, Sigma Chi. Clubs: Columbia Sailing (dir. 1968-71), Columbia Tip-Off (dir. 1968-73, pres. 1971-72). Author: Drafting Wills and Trust Agreements in South Carolina. Contbr. articles to publs. Home: Route 7 Lexington SC 29072 Office: 1340 Bull St Columbia SC 29201

WILKINS, RUTH LOIS, mus. curator; b. Boston, Nov. 20, 1926; d. Abraham and Harriett (Olive) Strauss; B.A., Wellesley Coll., 1948 children—Peter Dana, Michael Paul. Adminstrv. asst. Everson Mus. of Art, Syracuse, N.Y., 1959-65, curator of collections, 1966-70; cons. Mus. of Am. China Trade, Milton, Mass., 1971—; curator edn. Kimbell Art Mus., Ft. Worth, Tex., 1971—. Reporter, Council on Museums and Edn. in Visual Arts, N.Y.C., 1973. Recipient Post Standard Woman of Achievement in Arts award, 1968. Co-author: China Trade Silver for the Anglo-American Market, 1971. Editor: American Painting from 1830, 1965; Chinese Art from the Cloud Wampler and other collections, 1968; Everson Dedication, 1968; What is an Art Museum, 1970; American Ship Portraits and Marine Painting, 1970. Contbr. to Kimbell Art Mus. Catalogue of the Collection, 1972. Home: 308 Ridglea Village 6035 Westridge Lane Fort Worth TX 76116 Office: Kimbell Art Mus Will Rogers Rd W Fort Worth TX 76107

WILKINS, WILLIAM THOMAS, JR., investment banker, polit. party ofcl.; b. Cotton Plant, Ark., Jan. 17, 1940; s. William Thomas and Sue Ellen (Brown) W.; student Millsaps Coll., 1958-60; B.Pub. Adminstrn., U. Miss., 1962, M.A., 1966; m. Martha Ann Huddleston, Aug. 18, 1961; children—Martha Ellen, William Thomas IV. Part-time research asst. U. Miss. Bur. Research in Bus. and Govt., 1961-62; field rep., dir. research Miss. Republican Com., Jackson, 1962-64, exec. dir., adminstrv. asst. to state chmn., 1964-73; partner Penantly Plantation, Richwill Devel. Co.; dir. Bank of Olive Branch (Miss.). Exec. dir. So. Assn. Rep. State Chmn., 1969—, So. Rep. Conf., 1969, 71. Mem. Am. Polit. Sci. Assn., Am. Assn. Polit. Consultants, Kappa Sigma, Delta Sigma Phi, Pi Sigma Alpha. Presbyn. Home: 4820 Northampton Dr Jackson MS 39211 Office: PO Box 1178 Jackson MS 39205

WILKINS, WILLIE THOMAS, JR., dentist; b. Durham, N.C., Dec. 10, 1929; s. Willie Thomas and Ida (Boddie) W.; B.S., N.C. Agr. and Tech. State U., 1949; postgrad. Howard U., 1949-50, D.D.S., 1960; postgrad. in oral surgery Georgetown U., 1960-61; m. Burma Louise Whitted, June 23, 1962. Oral surgery intern D.C. Gen. Hosp., Washington, 1960-61; practice dental surgery, Greensboro, N.C., 1961—; chmn. dental affairs L. Richardson Meml. Hosp., Greensboro; active staff Moses Cones Meml. Hosp., Greensboro; staff Evergreen Hosp., Greensboro. Served with AUS, 1952-54; Korea. Recipient Valuable Contbn. award D.C. Dental Soc., 1961. Fellow Am. Sch. Health Assn. (governing council), Royal Soc. Health, Intercontinental Biog. Assn., Acad. Gen. Dentistry; mem. Am., Nat. dental assns., N.C. Dental Soc., Am. Acad. Gen. Dentistry, N.C. Acad. Sci., Am. Soc. Geriatric Dentistry, A.A.A.S., Am. Dental Soc. Anesthesiology, Soc. Advancement Dental Anesthesia, Fedn. Dentaire Internat., Greensboro C. of C. Mem. A.M.E. Ch. (chmn. bd. trustees 1963—). Club: Health. Author: Stabilizing of Replanted or Loose Teeth, 1963. Home: Route 6 Box 198 Greensboro NC 27405 Office: 1607 Asheboro St Greensboro NC 27406

WILKINSON, HAROLD AUSTIN, educator; b. Ft. Worth, Sept. 3, 1919; s. Benjamin Mackenzie and Agnes Beulah (Cox) W.; B.S., Southwestern State Coll., 1949; M.Ed., Tex. Tech. U., 1951, Ed.D., 1961; m. Willie Edwina Evans, June 6, 1943. Tchr., Frederick (Okla.) Pub. Schs., 1942, Hammon (Okla.) Pub. Sch., 1943, Crowell (Tex.) Pub. Sch., 1944-45; store owner, 1946-47; store mgr. Goodyear Tire & Rubber Co., 1947-49; tchr. Lamesa (Tex.) Pub. Sch., 1949-59; mem. faculty Tex. Tech. U., 1959-61; prof. elementary edn. Abilene (Tex.) Christian Coll., 1961—. Cons., lectr. Mem. N.E.A., Tex. Tchrs. Assn., Phi Delta Kappa, Kappa Delta Pi, Phi Alpha Theta. Mem. Ch. of Christ. Rotarian. Home: 926 EN 12th St Abilene TX 79601

WILKINSON, REYMOND WALLACE, oil co. exec.; b. Baton Rouge, June 10, 1927; s. Earl V. and Maydea (Mixon) W.; B.S. in Geology, La. State U., 1949; m. Betty Pecora, Jan. 29, 1949; children—Reymond Neal, Dona Lynn. Seismologist, Keystone Exploration Co., Houston, 1950-52; geophysicist La. Oil Exploration Co., Inc., New Orleans, New Iberia, La., 1952-66, Getty Oil Co., New Orleans, 1966—; also active in real estate investment and devel., So. La. 1966—. Served with USNR, 1945-46: PTO. Mem. New Orleans Geologic Soc., Southeastern Geophys. Soc., Soc. Exploration Geophysicists (gen. chmn. internat. meeting 1970), Permian Basin, Houston geophys. socs. Mason. Home: 2923 Blue Lakes Lane Missouri City TX 77459 Office: One Allen Center PO Box 1404 Houston TX 77001

WILKINSON, ROBERT JOHNSON, assn. exec.; b. Huntington, W.Va., Feb. 23, 1917; s. Robert and Elizabeth (Richmond) W.; LL.B., La Salle U., 1954; B.S. in Law, U. Louisville, 1957; M.Ed., U. Va.; m. Bonny Lyn Todd, Jan. 27, 1961. Corr., United Press, Huntington, 1938-43; with press relations dept. So. Med. Assn., Southeastern Surg. Congress, 1943-53; adminstr. Wilkinson Clinic, 1944-53; exec. sec. Am. Assn. Clinic Physicians and Surgeons, Roanoke, Va., 1950—; exec. sec. Viaud Sch., 1970—, dir. Sch. Law Inst., 1973—; pub. relations dir. Fla. Mil. Acad., Ft. Lauderdale, 1958; mem. faculty Va. Western Community Coll., 1967-70. Mem. Greater Roanoke Citizens Com., 1962-68. Mem. Huntington City Council, 1957-58; del. Democratic Nat. Conv., 1958. Trustee, pres. Wilkinson Found., Inc., 1953—; founder Huntington Clin. Found., Inc., 1948, trustee, sec., 1948-56. Mem. Am. Sch. Law Assn., Am. Personnel and Guidance Assn., Am. Counseling Assn., Am. Assn. U. Profs., Delta Theta Phi, Alpha Theta Nu. Club: University (Huntington). Cons. editor So. Hosps., 1949-69. Contbr. articles to profl. publs. Address: 1812 Carlton Rd SW Roanoke VA 24015

WILKOFF, LEE JOSEPH, microbiologist; b. Youngstown, O., Oct. 17, 1924; s. Irving and Adelaide (Nichol) W.; student North Park Coll., 1942-44; B.S., Roosevelt U., 1948; Ph.D. (Frank G. Logan fellow), U. Chgo., 1953; m. Meryl Louis Traub, Oct. 17, 1953, 1 son, Jay Foster. Biochemist, VA Hosp., Hines, Ill., 1952-54; research asst. dept. medicine U. Chgo., 1954-60; USPHS trainee, 1961-62; dir. microbiol. labs. Woodard Research Corp., Herndon, Va., 1963-64; sr. microbiologist So. Research Inst., Birmingham, Ala., 1964-70, head cell biology div., 1970—. Mem. A.A.A.S., Am. Soc. Microbiology, Soc. for Gen. Microbiology, N.Y. Acad. Scis., Soc. for Exptl. Biology and Medicine, Am. Assn. for Cancer Research, Sigma Xi. Contbr. articles to profl. jours. Home: 1813 Old Creek Trail Vestavia Hills AL 35216 Office: 2000 9th Av S Birmingham AL 35205

WILKS, JAY FREDERICK, lawyer; b. Newport News, Va., May 21, 1938; s. Abe Mark and Rosalie Reiss (Solomon) W.; B.A., Duke, 1960; LL.B. magna cum laude, Washington and Lee U., 1963; m. Marlene Beverly Braver, June 18, 1961; children—David Barney, Reiss Frederick, Jennifer Page. Admitted to Va. bar, 1963; asso. Bangel, Bangel & Bangel, 1963-64; asso. Kaufman, Oberndorfer & Spainhour, Norfolk, Va., 1964-69, partner, 1970—. Mem. Community Relations Com., 1969-73. Bd. dirs. Jewish Family Service, Beth Sholom Home of Va., Tidewater Regional Health Planning Council, United Jewish Fedn. Mem. Am., Va. bar assns., Common Cause, Zeta Beta Tau. Jewish religion (dir. temple). Home: 7366 Chevy Circle Norfolk VA 23505 Office: Va Nat Bank Bldg Norfolk VA 23510

WILKS, STANLEY NEAL, systems analyst; b. London, Eng., Oct. 25, 1932; s. Samuel Stanley and Gena (Orr) W. (parents Am. citizens); B.A., North Tex. State Coll., 1955; postgrad. Cambridge (Eng.) U., 1955-56, Am. U., 1969—; M.A., Columbia, 1961; m. Jocelyn Wilkins, June 28, 1958; children—Elizabeth Anne, Christine Jocelyn, Victoria Lynn, Jeffrey Neal. Mathematician, Nat. Security Agy., Washington, 1956-58; lab. supr. IBM, N.Y.C., 1959-61; program analyst Internat. Electric Corp., Paramus, N.J., 1961-63; sr. analyst Decision Systems, Inc., Paramus, 1963-64; operations research scientist, computer systems specialist System Devel. Corp., Falls Church, Va., 1964-71; computer systems analyst Naval Command Systems Support Activity, Washington, 1971-74; mathematician U.S. Army Concepts Analysis Agy., Bethesda, Md., 1974—. Served with AUS, 1956-58. Mem. Am. Statis. Assn., Assn. Computing Machinery. Home: 3240 N Abingdon St Arlington VA 22207 Office: 8120 Woodmont Av Bethesda MD 20014

WILKS, WILLIAM TAYLOR, univ. adminstr.; b. Berea, Ky., Jan. 11, 1911; s. William Pugh and Mamie (Powell) W.; B.S., Auburn U., 1930, M.S., 1935; Ed.D., Columbia, 1949, postgrad., 1955; m. Gurley Bright, Nov. 26, 1935; 1 dau., Laura Elizabeth. Tchr. sci., Cullman (Ala.) High Sch., 1930-36, Tallassee (Ala.) High Sch., 1936-41, Montgomery (Ala.) High Sch., 1941-42, tchr. sci. Goddard Coll., Plainfield, Vt., 1942-43, 46-47; asst. prof. physics Auburn (Ala.) U., 1943-44; head physics dept. Marion (Ala.) Mil. Inst., 1944-46, asso. prof., 1947-55, prof., head dept., 1955-68; v.p. acad. affairs Troy (Ala.) State U., 1968-72, v.p., 1972—. Chmn., Selective Service Bd. 1953-68, Troy Housing Authority, 1967—. Fellow Ala. Acad. Sci., A.A.A.S.; mem. Troy Tchrs. Assn. (pres. 1952-53), Nat. Sci. Tchrs. Assn. (state dir. 1956-65), Phi Kappa Phi, Omicron Delta Kappa, Kappa Phi Kappa, Kappa Delta Pi, Phi Delta Kappa. Rotarian. Contbr. profl. jours. Home: 202 Highland Av Troy AL 36081

WILLARD, ANNE OLDHAM, phys. therapist; b. Cleve., Aug. 4, 1916; d. John Lorraine and Olga Caroline (Wellington) Oldham; B.A., Rollins Coll., 1940; postgrad. U. Wis., 1942-44, U. Pa., 1959; Ph.D. (hon.), Colo. Christian Coll., 1973; m. Leland Henry Willard, June 8, 1945 (dec. Nov. 1960); children—Dorothy Ann, Byron Keith, David. Phys. therapist Dr. Charles Graybill Meml. Hosp., Lawton, Okla., 1951-53, State of Ala., Gadsden, 1954-57; chief phys. therapist Crippled Children's Soc., Ft. Worth, 1957-60; pvt. practice phys. therapy, Mineral Walls, Tex., 1960-61; head phys. therapist Flow Meml. Hosp., Denton, 1961-71; chief phys. therapist Collin Meml. Hosp., McKinney, Tex., 1971—. Served as 1st lt. AUS, 1940-46. Mem. Internat. Platform Assn., Nat. Wildlife Fedn., Denton Humane Soc., Greater Dallas Great Dane Club, Alpha Phi. Episcopalian. Mem. Order Eastern Star. Club: Soroptimist. Home: Box 850 Denton TX 76201 Office: Phys Therapy Dept Collin Meml Hosp PO Box 703 McKinney TX 75069

WILLARD, HENRY KELLOGG, II, city ofcl.; b. Washington, Aug. 11, 1926; s. Henry Augustus and Abby Fuller (Hooker) W.; grad. Choate Sch., 1944; B.A., Yale, 1950; m. Louise Phelps Brooks, Sept. 1, 1950; children—Henry Augustus III, John Brooks. Intelligence officer CIA, Washington, 1950-52; v.p. Am. Security & Trust Co., Washington, 1952-71, v.p., mgr. internat. dept., 1972—; Presdl. appointee Washington City Council, 1971-72. Trustee Equitable Life Ins. Co., Washington, 1970—. Chmn. finance com. Republican party Washington, 1968-71; mem. Rep. Nat. Finance Com., 1970-71; alternate del. Rep. Conv., 1968. Served with USNR, 1944-46. Clubs: Chevy Chase, Metropolitan (Washington); Nantucket (Mass.) Yacht. Home: 2731 31st Pl NW Washington DC 20008 Office: 15th and Pennsylvania Av NW Washington DC 20005

WILLARD, ISABEL BREWSTER SIMS, oil co. exec.; b. Spartanburg, S.C., Dec. 29, 1910; d. Benjamin Franklin and Helen Gertrude (Knight) Sims; B.A., Converse Coll., 1932; m. William Grant Willard, Mar. 19, 1935 (dec.); children—William Grant III, Benjamin Sims, Dir. Willard Oil Co., Spartanburg, 1958—, mem. exec. com., 1967-70, dir. beautification, recreation and health, 1969—. Head Travellers Aid vols., also Travellers Aid bd. Jr. League, Spartanburg, 1943-50, mem. adv. com., 1968-70; sec., v.p. Ga. Cleveland Home for Old Ladies, Spartanburg, S.C., 1956-58; mem. bd. regents S.C., Gurston Hall, Mus. House and Plantation, Lorton, Va.; mem. 1776 regional task force Appalachian Council Govts. Mem. Nat. Soc. Colonial Dames Am. (mem. S.C. bd. dirs. 1959—, chmn. Spartanburg com. 1958-59), The Assembly (pres. 1958-59), Alumnae Council Converce Coll. Clubs: Country, Piedmont (both Spartanburg). Office: Box 3000 Spartanburg SC 29302

WILLARD, WILLIAM B(RADLEY), banker, estate mgr.; b. Washington, Aug. 17, 1904; s. Henry Kellogg and Helen Wilson (Parker) W.; A.B., Dartmouth, 1926; m. Florence Fatio Keys, Jan. 12, 1929; children—Helen Parker (Mrs. John C. Chapin), Amie Keys (Mrs. Huntington T. Block), William Bradley. Clk., Nat. Met. Bank, Washington, 1926-30; v.p. Nat. Savs. & Trust Co., Washington, 1934-54; trustee Estate of H.K. Willard, Washington, 1926—; mgr., cashier Bank of Guam, 1945-46; chmn. exec. com., dir. Nat. Savs. & Trust Co. Dir. Nat. Capital Area Council Boy Scouts Am., 1937-42, treas., 1941-42; dir. Legal Aid Soc., Washington, 1951-57; pres. Helen Parker Willard Found.; trustee Phi Gamma Delta Ednl. Found. Served with USNR, World War II; now capt. Res. Decorated Bronze Star medal. Mem. Newcomen Soc. N.Am., Oldest Inhabitants D.C., Naval Order U.S., Washington Bd. Trade. Presbyn. (past trustee, treas.). Clubs: Burning Tree, Chevy Chase, Metropolitan. Home: 2615 31st St Washington DC 20008 Office: 509 Walker Bldg 734 15th St NW Washington DC 20005

WILLE, (ROLAND) FRANK, lawyer, govt. ofcl.; b. N.Y.C., Feb. 27, 1931; s. Frank Joseph and Alma (Schutt) W.; grad. Phillips Acad., Andover, Mass., 1947; A.B. cum laude, Harvard, 1951, LL.B. cum laude, 1956; LL.M. in Taxation, N.Y.U., 1960; m. Barbara Bowen McIntosh, July 2, 1969; children—Serena Bowen, Alison Brevard. Admitted to N.Y. bar, 1956; asso. firm Davis Polk Wardwell Sunderland & Kiendl, N.Y.C., 1956-60; asst. counsel to gov. State of N.Y., Albany, 1960-62, 1st asst. counsel, 1962-64; supt. banks State of N.Y., N.Y.C., 1964-70; chmn. Fed. Deposit Ins. Corp., Washington, 1970—, mem. com. on interest and dividends, 1971—. Adv. mem. N.Y. State Joint Legislative Com. on Interstate Co-op; ex officio mem. N.Y. Job Devel. Authority, N.Y. Urban Devel. Corp., 1964-70. Mem. N.Y. County Republican Com., 1959-61. Served to lt. (j.g.) USNR, 1951-54. Mem. N.Y. State Bar Assn., Assn. Bar City N.Y. Home: 4733 Berkeley Terrace NW Washington DC 20007 Office: 550 17th St NW Washington DC 20429

WILLETT, EUGENE PATRICK HENRY, lab. exec.; b. Shawnee, Okla., Dec. 6, 1909; s. Eugene Jerome and Ophelia (Linz) W.; student Belmont Abbey Coll., 1928; m. Carolyn Brockway Chappelle, June 21, 1939, (dec. Jan. 1964); children—Eugene Brockway, Carol Louise, William Charles; m. 3d, Ruby Lee Lester, Mar. 14, 1972. Instrument man, surveyor, chief of party U.S. Engrs. Corps, N.C., S.C., 1929-32, concrete insp., Tuscaloosa (Ala.) Lock and Dam, 1936-38; timber cruiser, chief of party U.S. Forest Service, 1933-36; asst. concrete engr., concrete engr. Harza Engring. Co., 1938-41; concrete engr. U.S. Navy, Charleston, S.C., Bklyn., 1941-43, E.I. DuPont de Nemours, Hanford (Wash.) Engr. Works, 1943-45; engr. Ala. Hwy. Dept., 1946-50; concrete cons. Govt. El Salvador, 1951-53; co-founder, co-owner Dixie Labs, Inc., Mobile, Dothan, Ala., Columbus, Ga., 1953—. Mem. C. of C., Am. Soc. Testing Materials, Am. Concrete Inst., Better Bus. Bur., Baldwin County Hist. Soc., Eastern Shores Art Assn., Am. Welding Soc. Democrat. Roman Catholic. Clubs: Fairhope Yacht, Lake Forest Yacht and Country. Home: 1511 Gloriadale Rd Mobile AL 36609 Office: 604 Loeffler St PO Box 7387 Mobile AL 36607

WILLETT, JAMES MARSHALL, physician, residential instn. ofcl.; b. Walton, Ky., Aug. 2, 1922; s. Dwight Haynes and Sallie Jane (Siler) W.; B.S., Wake Forest Coll., 1948; M.D., U. Tenn., 1948; M.P.H., Johns Hopkins, 1954; m. Lind Prater, Nov. 11, 1948; children—Dwight Haynes, David Prater, Paul Marshall. Intern Methodist Hosp., 1948-49; dir. Carter-Unicoi Johnson Health Dist., 1950-69; supt. Greene Valley Devel. Center, Greenville, Tenn., 1969—. Mem. Elizabethton (Tenn.) Sch. Bd., 1947-49, 67-69. Home: 101 Summit Av Greeneville TN 37743 Office: Box 3087 Greeneville TN 37743

WILLETT, THOMPSON, distilling co. exec.; b. Bardstown, Ky., Jan. 29, 1909; s. A. Lambert and Mary Catherine (Thompson) W.; B.A., Xavier U., Cin., 1931; m. Mary Virginia Sheehan, Jan. 14, 1942; children—Mary Tabitha (Mrs. Francis J. Fisher, Jr.), James L.T., Martha Harriet (Mrs. Even Kulsveen), John David, Susan Virginia (Mrs. Thomas C. Dawson), Richard Francis, Alice Jane. Editor, Loveland (O.) Herald, 1931-32; asst. supt. Bernheim Distilling Co., Louisville, 1933-36; pres. Willett Distilling Co., Bardstown, 1936—, chmn. bd., 1971—. Adviser, Nat. Trust for Historic Preservation, Washington, 1970—. Bd. govs. Xavier U.; bd. advisers Bellarmine Coll., Louisville. Mem. Ky. Distillers Assn. (dir., past pres.), Distilled Spirits Council U.S. (dir.), Ind. Am. Whiskey Assn. N.Y. (v.p.), Newcomen Soc. N.Am. Club: Old Ky. Country. Home: Beechwold E Stephen Foster St Bardstown KY 40004 Office: PO Box 10 Bardstown KY 40004

WILLETTS, FREDERICK, JR., savs. and loan exec.; b. Wilmington, N.C., June 4, 1925; s. Frederick and Eleanor (Harriss) W.; student U. N.C., 1943, U. Ind., 1950-52; m. Helen Messick, June 25, 1948; children—Frederick III, Margaret, Elizabeth. With Coop. Savs. and Loan Assn., Wilmington, 1946—, asst. loan officer, 1946-47, sec., 1947-59, treas., 1947—, exec. v.p., 1959-63, pres., 1964—; pres. N.C. Savs. & Loan League; dir. Am. Mortgage Ins. Co., Raleigh, N.C. Dir. Boys Brigade Clubs Am., Wilmington, 1959-70. Bd. dirs. YMCA, Wilmington. Served with USAAF, 1943-46; PTO. Mem. U.S. Savs. and Loan League (mem. legislative com., sec. Southeast conf. 1973-74), Greater Wilmington C. of C. (pres. 1966), Sigma Alpha Epsilon. Democrat. Episcopalian. Rotarian. Clubs: Carolina Yacht, Surf (Wrightsville Beach, N.C.), Cape Fear Country (Wilmington, N.C.). Home: 1103 Windson Dr Wilmington NC 28401 Office: Coop Savs and Loan Assn 201 Market St Wilmington NC 28401

WILLEY, DOUGLAS JEROME, automobile co. exec.; b. Arlington, Va., Feb. 17, 1924; s. Addison Henry and Lena (Warner) W.; student U. Md., 1941-43, Amherst Coll., 1943-44; A.A. in Fgn. Affairs, George Washington U., 1949; m. June Elizabeth Butscher, Nov. 4, 1944; children—Allen, Ronald, Linda (Mrs. John B. Lowe). With Buick Motor div. Gen. Motors Corp., 1949-57, asst. mgr., Detroit, 1957, cons., 1957-58; pres. Doug Willey Pontiac, Inc., Birmingham, Ala., 1958—, Doug Willey Datsun, Birmingham, 1972—; chmn. bd. Crown Pontiac, St. Petersburg, Fla., 1968—; Crown Datsun, St. Petersburg, 1973—; chmn. bd., pres. Crown Automobile, Birmingham, 1971—, Crown Imported Autos, Inc., St. Petersburg, 1973—; sec., dir. First Standard Life Ins. Co., Phoenix, 1973—; founder, Dealer Mgmt. Analysis Corp., Birmingham, 1967, pres., until 1971; vis. instr. Gen. Motors Inst., 1961-63; cons. in field. Mem. Gen. Motors President's Dealer Adv. Council, 1972-73; mem. retail adv. com. Brand Names Found., 1959—. Bd. govs. St. Bernard (Ala.) Coll. Served to 1st lt. AUS, World War II. Decorated Bronze Star; Medalha de Companha, Medal of Peacemaker (Brazil); knighted by Pope Paul VI, 1969, named knight of St. Gregory. Hon. mem. Soc. 1st Div. Clubs: Vestavia Country (bd. govs.); The Club; Downtown; Relay House; Branchwater Hunt (v.p.); Ocean Reef (Fla.). Home: 3916 Royal Oak Dr Birmingham AL 35243 Office: 3500 6th Av S Birmingham AL 35222

WILLIAMS, ADDISON LE CLERQ, lawyer; b. Denver, Nov. 13, 1900; s. George and Jennie F. (Andre) W.; A.B., U. Colo., 1921, LL.B., 1925; m. Mary T. Hosie, Oct. 7, 1926; 1 dau., Mary Jeanette; m. 2d, Jessie H. Jones, Mar. 26, 1971. Admitted to Fla. bar, 1926; asso. firm Shepard & Wahl, Cocoa, Fla., 1926; mem. firm Pleus, Williams & Pleus, Orlando, Fla., 1927-40; practiced law, 1940-42; mem. firm Johnson & Williams, Orlando, 1942-55, Williams & Chapman, Orlando, 1955—. Pres. McCory Holding Co., 1955—, McCory Properties, Inc., 1955—. Pres. Orlando Jr. Coll., 1944-57, chmn. bd. trustees, 1957-70. Mem. Am., Orange County (pres. 1944) bar assns., Fla. Bar, Orlando C. of C., Phi Kappa Tau, Phi Alpha Delta. Presbyn. Home: 700 Daniels Av Orlando FL 32801 Office: McCory Bldg Orlando FL 32801

WILLIAMS, ALFRED J., storage co. exec.; b. Logan, W.Va., Aug. 22, 1929; s. Alfred Grayson and Opal Lee (Matney) W.; student U. Ky.; m. Joyce Nelson, June 22, 1952; children—Steven A., Michael F. Pres., Barney Williams Co., Inc., Ashland, Ky.; dir. Bank Ashland; chmn. bd. E & I Supply Co., Ashland. Served with USAF, 1948-51. Republican. Baptist. Rotarian. Home: 2722 Auburn Av Ashland KY 41101 Office: 2569 Central Av Ashland KY 41101

WILLIAMS, ALLEN NEWTON, JR., physician; b. Union City, Tenn., Apr. 6, 1920; Allen Newton and Grace (Caldwell) W.; student Memphis State U., 1947-49; M.D., U. Tenn., 1952; m. Frances Marion Baker, Mar. 25, 1950; children—Allen Newton III, Amy Lee, Nancy. Intern, John Gaston Hosp., Memphis, 1952-53; gen. practice medicine, Bemis Clinic, Bemis, Tenn., 1954—; mem. staff Jackson-Madison County Gen. Hosp., Jackson, Tenn. Served to capt. USAAF, 1942-45. Decorated D.F.C. with oak leaf cluster, Air medal with oak leaf cluster. Mem. A.M.A., W. Tenn. Consolidated Med. Soc., Am. Assn. Family Practice, Phi Rho, V.F.W. Methodist. Mason.

Club: Jackson (Tenn.) Golf and Country. Home: 1237 Hollywood St Jackson TN 38301 Office: 219 S Missouri St Bemis TN 38314

WILLIAMS, ANDREW WILLIAM, educator; b. Gastonia, N.C., July 27, 1922; s. Kelley and Elizabeth (Johnson) W.; B.S., N.C. A. and T. State U., 1953; M.S., 1957; postgrad. U. Ill., 1963, U. Mich., 1967-68, U. Tenn., 1966; m. Jacqueline McDonald, Dec. 24, 1943; children—Joseph A., Warren K., Veronica (Mrs. Franklin Biggins). Instr., N.C. A. and T. State U., Greensboro, 1946-56, dept. chmn., 1959—; tchr. trainer in Indonesia, Tuskegee Inst., 1957-59. Cons. mfg. engr. Acme Engring. Co., Greensboro, 1960—. Mem. Bd. Heating Examiners City of Greensboro, 1964—. Served with USNR, 1943-46; PTO. Mem. Soc. Mfg. Engrs. (Joseph A. Siegel Meml. award 1973), Am. Soc. Testing Materials, Am. Def. Preparedness Assn., Nat. Assn. Indsl. Tech., Omega Psi Phi. Presbyn. (deacon). Patentee craniel drill. Home: 2205 New Castle Rd Greensboro NC 27406

WILLIAMS, ASBURY HAMILTON, physician; b. Lake City, S.C., Oct. 24, 1937; s. Eugene Mood and Emera Alyne (Rogers) W.; B.S., Furman U., 1959; M.D., Med. U. S.C., 1963; m. Peggy Rae Kenney, Aug. 9, 1959; children—Asbury Hamilton, Peggy Laura, Suzanne Elizabeth. Intern, Columbia Hosp., Richland County, S.C., 1963-64; practice medicine, Lake City, 1964—; mem. staff Lower Florence County Hosp.; asso. staff McLeod's Infirmary, Saunder's Meml., Williamsburg County hosps. Bd. dirs. Lower Florence County Hosp. Mem. A.M.A., S.C., Florence County, Pee Dee med. assns., Am. Acad. Family Practice, Jr. C. of C. (pres. 1968-69). Republican. Baptist (deacon 1967-70). Home: Lockewood Estates Lake City SC 29560 Office: 101 John St Lake City SC 29560

WILLIAMS, AUDREY ARTHUR, JR., architect; b. Dallas, Mar. 25, 1925; s. Audrey Arthur and Helen Myrtle (Stark) W.; B.S. in Archtl. Constrn., Tex. Agrl. and Mech. U., 1951; m. Martha Louise Thomas, July 2, 1943; 1 dau., Sally Ann (Mrs. James Richard Hewell, Jr.). Architect, Art Williams Jr. & Assos., Architects, Dallas, 1954—. Owner, Art Williams Jr. Interiors; owner Motor Hotel Consultants; pres., dir. Standard Constrn. Co. Waco (Tex.), Am. Motor Inns, Inc., Americana Mortgage & Leasing Corp.; designer numerous bldgs. including motor hotels, restaurants. Served with USAF, 1942-45; ETO. Mem. Nat., Am. insts. architects, Constrn. Specification Inst., Tex. Soc. Architects. Republican. Home: 14140 Rawhide Pkwy Dallas TX 75234 Office: 2880 LBJ Freeway Dallas TX 75234

WILLIAMS, BEN FORREST, JR., curator, art mus.; b. Lumberton, N.C., Dec. 24, 1925; s. Ben Forrest and Mamie (Britt) W.; A.B. in Art and Edn., U. N.C., 1949, grad. tchrs. certificate, 1951; A.A. in Art Criticism and History Art, George Washington U., 1945-47; postgrad. Corcoran Sch. Art, 1942-45, Nat. Sch. Art, 1941-42, Ecole de Louvre (France), 1957, Netherlands Inst. for Art History, 1964; m. Margaret Click, July 2, 1955. Designer U.S. Navy Dept., Washington, 1944-46; color lithographist Nat. Gallery, Washington, 1946; instr. art Corcoran Sch. Art, Washington, 1945-46; instr. art Chapel Hill (N.C.) pub. schs., 1947-48, Ferree Sch. Art, Raleigh, N.C., 1950-52; dir. exhbns. Person Hall Art Gallery, Chapel Hill, 1948-49; exhbn. asso. N.C. State Art Gallery Raleigh, 1950-56; curator art N.C. Mus. Art, Raleigh, 1956—; exhibited paintings and sculpture, Nat. Mus. Art, 1945, Corcoran Gallery, 1945, Phillips Gallery, 1946 (all Washington), Atlanta Art Assn., 1947, Va. Mus., Richmond, 1946, Va. Intermont Gallery, Bristol, 1947, Jacques Seligmann Galleries, N.Y.C., 1948; Weatherspoon Gallery, Greensboro, 1948—, Person Hall Art Gallery, Chapel Hill, 1948-49, Asheville Art Mus., 1949, with Am. Fedn. Arts throughout U.S., 1947. Recipient 1st prize and Painting award, Southeastern Annual Exhibit, Atlanta Art Assn., 1947; 1st Painting award, Washington Art Fair, 1946; 1st prize, Corcoran Sch. Art, 1945, and others. Contbr. articles on art, conservation to profl. jours. Home: 2813 Mayview Rd Raleigh NC 25607 Office: NC Mus of Art Raleigh NC 27601

WILLIAMS, BILL J., dentist; b. Boone, N.C., Mar. 2, 1939; s. Warren Wilson and Elizabeth (Rucker) W.; student U. N.C., 1957-59, Lees McRae Coll., 1959-60, Pfeiffer Coll., 1964; A.B., U. N.C., 1969. Electroceramic researcher Charlotte Chem. Labs. (N.C.), 1964-65; pub. health dentist, Mecklenberg County, Charlotte, 1969; instr. dental hygiene dept. Community Coll. Central Piedmont, Charlotte, 1969-73; mem. vis. staff, dental intern program Charlotte Meml. Hosp.; pvt. practice dentistry, Charlotte, 1970—. Mem. Am. Dental Assn., N.C., 2d Dist., Charlotte dental socs. Baptist. Home: 3912-G Providence Rd Charlotte NC 28211 Office: 2915 Providence Rd Charlotte NC 28211

WILLIAMS, CARLISLE MISTER, JR., county ofcl.; b. Painter, Va., June 27, 1937; s. Carlisle M. and Evelyn (Hickman) W.; student Coll. William and Mary, 1955-56; A.A., Goldey Beacom Jr. Coll., 1958; A.B., E. Carolina U., 1960; m. Dolly Evans Taylor, June 15, 1958; children—Carlisle M. III, Valerie T. Jr. accountant Leatherbury-Broache, Accomac, Va., 1960; accountant Eastern Shore News, Inc., Onancock, Va., 1960-62; bus. mgr. clk. Accomack County Sch. Bd., Accomac, 1962-66, county adminstr. Accomack County, 1966—. Lectr. accounting Eastern Shore Community Coll., 1971—. Sec.-treas. Cedar Island Bridge and Beach Authority, 1968—; coordinator Accomack County Hwy. Safety Commn., 1968—; mem. Com. for Better Schs., 1966-68; dir. Civil Def. for Accomack County, 1971—; chmn. Eastern Shore unit Salvation Army, 1971—. Mem. Va. Assn. County Adminstrs., Onley Recreation Assn., Va., Eastern Shore (pres. 1967-68) jaycees, Eastern Shore C. of C. (dir.), Phi Sigma Pi. Methodist (adminstrv. bd.). Clubs: Eastern Shore Yacht and Country (Onancock). Home: 22 Sturgis St Onancock VA 23417 Office: County Office Bldg Accomac VA 23301

WILLIAMS, CHARLES IVAN, dentist; b. Dallas, Dec. 29, 1943; s. John Groce and Emma Virginia (Fox) W.; student So. Meth. U., 1961-63, Arlington State Coll., summers 1961-63, Dental Sch. U. Tex., 1963-65; D.D.S., Baylor U., 1967; m. Mary Catherine Hollingsworth, Nov. 25, 1965; children—Charles Ivan II, Rachel Dawn. Gen. practice dentistry, Mexia, Tex., 1967—; mem. staff Gen. Mexia Hosp., sec. staff, 1969-74. Mem. Jr. C. of C. (dir.), Am., Tex. dental assns. Mem. Ch. of Nazarene. Rotarian. Home: 214 N Sherman St Mexia TX 76667 Office: 214 N Sherman St Mexia TX 76667

WILLIAMS, CHARLES OLIVER, JR., dentist; b. Greensboro, N.C., Sept. 1, 1939; s. Charles Oliver and Amy (Groves) W.; student U. N.C., 1957-61, Elon Coll., 1961, Wake Forest Coll., 1961, Guilford Coll., 1961; D.M.D., U. Louisville, 1966; m. Nancy Jane McIntosh, July 31, 1965; children—Cristin McIntosh, Charles Oliver III. Practice gen. dentistry, Winnsboro, S.C., 1966—; asso. mem. staff Fairfield Meml. Hosp., Winnsboro. Editor-in-chief S.C. Dental Jour., 1970—, State Publs. Chmn., Nat. Children's Dental Health Week, Fairfield County, 1967; chmn. profl. div. United Fund, Fairfield County, 1967-68; mem. Fairfield County Mental Health Assn., 1970—; spl. lectr., cons. forensic dentistry S.C. Criminal Justice Acad., Columbia. Bd. dirs. Fairfield County Boy Scouts Am. Recipient Dental Editors award Ohio State U., Am. Dental Assn., 1970. Mem. Am., Central Dist., S.C. (Ho. of Dels. 1968—) dental assns., A.A.A.S., Nat. Rehab. Assn., Fairfield Jr. C. of C. (past v.p.), Am. Soc. Dentistry for Children, Southeastern Acad. Prosthodontics, Am. Assn. Dental Editors, Mid-Carolina Dental Study Acad., Federation Dentaire Internat., Royal Soc. Health (Gt. Britain), Order Ky. Cols., Delta Sigma Delta (Nat. Lit. Excellence award 1966). Episcopalian (past sr. warden). Clubs: Winnsboro Cotillion, Fairfield Country (Winnsboro). Home: 203 Carlisle Ct Winnsboro SC 29180 Office: 204 E Washington St Winnsboro SC 29180

WILLIAMS, CHARLOTTE EVELYN FORRESTER (MRS. WALKER ALONZO WILLIAMS), civic worker; b. Kansas City, Mo., Aug. 7, 1905; d. John Dougal and Georgia (Lowerre) Forrester; student U. Kan., 1924-25; m. Walker Alonzo Williams, Sept. 25, 1926; children—Walker Forrester, John Haviland. Trustee, Detroit Grand Opera Assn., 1960—, dir., 1955-60; chmn. Grinnell Opera Scholarship, 1959-65; founder, dir., chmn. adv. bd. Cranbrook Music Guild, Inc., 1952-59, mem., 1952—; bd. dirs. St. Peters Home for Boys, Detroit, 1951-53, Detroit Opera Theater, 1959-61, Severo Ballet, 1959-61; Detroit dist. chmn. Met. Opera Regional Auditions, 1959-65; donor mem. Opera Guild Ft. Lauderdale (Fla.); patron mem. Asol. Festival Theatre Assn., Sarasota, Fla.; trustee Detroit Grand Opera Assn. Mem. Central Opera Service N.Y.C., Debbie-Rand Meml. Service League (life), Fla. Atlantic Music Guild, D.A.R., P.E.O. Mem. Order Eastern Star. Club: Music Study (Boca Raton, Fla.). Home: 1355 Fan Palm Rd Boca Raton FL 33432

WILLIAMS, CLAYTON WHEAT, oil co. exec.; b. Fort Stockton, Tex., Apr. 15, 1895; s. Oscar Waldo and Sallie (Wheat) W.; B.S., Tex. A. and M. U., 1915; m. Chicora Lee Graham, Sept. 10, 1928; children—Clayton Wheat, Janet (Mrs. Robert W. Pollard). With Chino Copper Co., Santa Rita, N.M., 1916-17; elec. engr. Oil Belt Power Co., Eastland, Tex., 1919; county surveyor Pecos County, Tex., 1920; hwy. engring., N.M., Tex., 1921-24; chief engr. Texon Oil & Land Co. and Group No. One Oil Corp., Santa Rita, Tex., 1924-28; ind. oil operator, 1928—; owner, operator 1st ice plant and water works, Crane, Tex., 1927-35; partner ranch, Pecos County, Tex., 1935-54; v.p., dir. Olix Industries (formerly USM Oil Co.), Austin, Tex., 1960—. County commr. Pecos County, 1935-40, 43-50; life mem. Pecos County Sheriff's Posse, 1950—. Tex. Hist. Assn. (life). Served as 2d lt. U.S. Army, 1917-19. Mem. C. of C., Am. Legion, Tex., W. Tex. (exec. com.), Fort Stockton (life) hist. assns. Methodist. Lion, Mason. Author: Never Again, 3 vols., 1969. Home: PO Box 546 Fort Stockton TX 79735 Office: Corner Rooney and 1st St Fort Stockton TX 79735

WILLIAMS, DAVID WILLARD, educator; b. Venedocia, O., Aug. 20; s. David W. and Elizabeth J. (Morgan) W.; B.S.A., Ohio State U., 1915; M.Sc., U. Ill., 1916; postgrad. A. and M. Coll. Tex., 1923, postgrad. U. Chgo., summers, 1927-28; Ingeniero Agronomo, U. Coahuila, Mexico, 1957; LL.D., Austin Coll., 1957; m. Magdalene Rees, Aug. 18, 1921; children—Margaret Ann (Mrs. Walter W. Cardwell, Jr.), Ruth Elizabeth (Mrs. Bruce B. Lawrence), David Willard. Extension animal husbandman U.S. Dept. Agr., Clemson Agrl. Coll., 1917-19; asso. prof. A. and M. Coll. Tex., 1919-20, prof., 1920-22, head dept. animal husbandry, 1922-46, v.p. for agr., 1946-48, vice chancellor for agr., 1948-58, acting pres., 1956-57, vice chancellor emeritus, 1962—. Cattle rancher, 1932-73; cons. U. Ceylon, 1958-62; dir. Bryan Bldg. & Loan. Dept. supt. Southwestern Expn. and Fat Stock Show, 1920-43, chmn. adv. com., 1946-58; pres. Am. Soc. Animal Prodn. rep. Internat. Livestock Breeding Congress, Zurich, Switzerland, 1939; agrl. cons. ECA, Germany, 1949; personnel cons. Fgn. Agr. Service, 1949-58; instnl. rep. Ark., White, Red River Interagy. Com., 1951-58; mem. U.S.-Mexico Joint Tech. Agr. Exchange Com., 1951; cons. to Morocco for AID, 1962; councilor Tex. A. and M. Research Found.; cons. Rockfeller Found., Colombia, 1951; cons. ICA, East Pakistan Agr. and Edn.; cons. agr. Escuela Superior De Agricultura, Mexico, 1954. Hon. v.p. State Fair Tex. Served with CWS, 1918, lt. col. U.S. 1943, 46. Fellow A.A.A.S., Tex. Acad. Sci., Am. Soc. Animal Sci. (past pres.); mem. Tex. Southwestern Cattle Raisers Assn., Tex. Agrl. Workers Assn., Am. Quarter Horse Breeders Assn. (past adv. com.), Bryan C. of C. (past pres.), Ceylon Assn. Advancement Sci. (pres. agr. sect. 1958-59), Nat. Collegiate Athletic Assn. (past v.p. councilman at large), Southwest Athletic Conf. (past pres.), Am. Legion, Sigma Delta Chi, Alpha Gamma Rho (past pres. Ohio), Lambda Gamma Delta. Presbyn. (elder). Mason, Rotarian. Clubs: Nat. Block and Bridle, Saddle and Sirloin (past pres. Ohio). Author: Beef Cattle in the South, 1941; co-author: Livestock and Poultry, 1925; Agriculture in the Southwest, 1940. Home: 500 Fairview St College Station TX 77840

WILLIAMS, DUDLEY RIDAULT, lawyer; b. Martinsville, Va., June 19, 1939; s. Harry Pemberton and Ruth (Thomas) W.; B.A., Howard U., 1961, J.D., 1964; m. Katherine Ann Crowe, Oct. 25, 1969. Admitted to D.C. bar, 1966; partner firm Luck & Williams, Washington, 1966-67; exec. dir. D.C. br. N.A.A.C.P., Washington, 1967-68; dep. dir. D.C. Law Students in Ct., Washington, 1969, dir., 1969—. Legal adviser Pride, Inc., Washington, 1968—; cons. United Planning Orgn., Washington. Mem. S.E. Community Local Devel. Corp., Washington Urban League. Mem. Nat., D.C., Washington bar assns., Jud. Conf. of D.C. Circuit. Democrat. Home: 1209 33d Pl SE Washington DC 20019 Office: 635 F St NW Washington DC 20001

WILLIAMS, E. PAUL, banker; b. Jackson, O., July 24, 1909; s. E. Pratt and Jenny May (Williams) W.; student Washington and Lee U., 1926-28; J.D., U. Ky., 1933; m. Elizabeth Ann DeHart, Mar. 11, 1941; 1 dau., Suzanne. Admitted to Ky. bar, 1934; practiced in Ashland, 1934-42; with 2d Nat. Bank, Ashland, 1946—, exec. v.p., trust officer, 1951-62, pres., 1962-74, chmn. bd., 1974—, also dir.; dir. Mayo Arcade, Collins & Mayo Collieries, Ky. Physicians Mutual. Former mem. Regional Adv. Com. on Banking Policies; dir. Fed. Res. Bank of Cleve., Cin. Bd. dirs. Ky. State Tech. Services; past nat. asso. Boys Club Am.; adv. dir. Kings Daus. Home for Aged; past mem. exec. com. nat. bank div. Am. Bankers Assn.; past chmn. bd. Pikeville Coll., commr. Ky. Indsl. Devel. Found.; commr. Ky. Savs. Bonds. Served with AUS, World War II. Named Boss of Year, 1962. Mem. Am. (govt. relations council), Ky. (past pres.) bankers assns., Ky. C. of C. (treas., dir.), Am. Legion, Sigma Nu. Episcopalian. Mason. Clubs: Kiwanis, Bellefonte Country. Home: 620 Amanda Furnace Dr Ashland KY 41101 Office: 1544 Winchester Av Ashland KY 41101

WILLIAMS, EARL CRANSTON, JR., state ofcl.; b. Corbett, Md., Dec. 26, 1920; s. Earl Cranston and Mildred Cecelia (Nimmo) W.; B.S. in Civil Engring., U. Md., 1950; postgrad. Yale, 1954-55; m. Billie Leona Harris, Mar. 11, 1945; children—Andrea (Mrs. Preston Rotier Perkerson), Linda (Mrs. Stephen Stuart Putney, Janet, Earl Cranston III. With Wichita Falls Pub. Works Dept., 1950-52, city traffic engr., 1952-59; chief traffic engring. div. Montgomery County, Md., 1959-62; state traffic engr. Tenn. Dept. Transp., Nashville, 1962—. Served with USAAF, World War II. Registered profl. engr., Tenn., Tex. Fellow Am. Soc. C.E., Inst. Traffic Engrs. (pres. So. sect. 1969-70); mem. Hwy. Research Bd., Am. Assn. State Hwy. Ofcls. (nat. joint com. on uniform traffic control 1963—), Nat. (pres. North Central Tex. chpt. 1958-59), Tenn. socs. profl. engrs. Home: 3629 Central Av Nashville TN 37205 Office: 212 Doctor's Bldg Nashville TN 37203

WILLIAMS, EARL RAY, educator, economist; b. Granite, Okla., Dec. 7, 1938; s. Bert A. and Minerva (Leonard) W.; B.S., Okla. State U., 1961, M.S., 1963; Ph.D., U. Tenn., 1968; m. Susie Dobson Williams, Sept. 6, 1961; children—Terry, Connie. Teaching, research asst. Okla. State U., Stillwater, 1962; vol. Peace Corps, Colombia, S.Am., 1963-65; asst. agrl. econs. U. Tenn., Knoxville, 1965-68; asst. prof., chmn. dept. econs. Northeastern State Coll., Tahlequah, Okla., 1968-70, asso. prof., 1970-73, prof., 1973—, chmn. bus. div., 1971—. Mem. Air N.G., 1961-63. Mem. Am., So. econ. assns., Southwestern Social Sci. Assn., Adminstrv. Mgmt. Soc., Southwest Bus. Deans Assn., Tahlequah C. of C., Gamma Sigma Delta. Methodist (adminstrv. bd.). Home: 1016 N Cedar Tahlequah OK 74464

WILLIAMS, EBB HARRY, III, lawyer; b. Danville, Va., Dec. 13, 1939; s. Ebb Harry and Lillian Estelle (Shuping) W.; B.A. cum laude, U. Richmond, 1961, J.D. cum laude, 1964; m. Gayle Rae Gowdey, Dec. 31, 1960; children—Kevin Tracy, Christa Gayle. Admitted to Va. bar, 1964; mem. firm Broaddus, Epperly, Broaddus & Williams, Martinsville, Va., 1964-73; individual practice, Martinsville, 1973—. Faculty comml. law Patrick Henry Coll., Martinsville, 1964-73; substitute judge Gen. Dist. Ct. and Juvenile and Domestic Relations cts., Martinsville, Henry County and Patrick County, 1969—. Dist. chmn. Patrick Henry council Boy Scouts Am., 1968-69. Bd. dirs., chmn. Martinsville Henry County Red Cross, 1964-73; bd. assos. Averett Coll., Danville, 1970—. Mem. U. Richmond Alumni Assn. (dir.), Am., Martinsville Henry County (pres. 1973-74), Va. (exec. com. young lawyers sect. 1971-74) bar assns., Va. State Bar (council 1972—, exec. com. 1974—, chmn. 5th dist. com. 1969-70), Am., Va. trial lawyers assns. Baptist (deacon). Home: Chatmoss Plantation Martinsville VA 24112 Office: PO Box 1009 Martinsville VA 24112

WILLIAMS, EDWARD BENNETT, lawyer; b. Hartford, Conn., May 31, 1920; s. Joseph Barnard and Mary (Bennett) W.; A.B. summa cum laude, Coll. Holy Cross, 1941, S.J.D., 1963; LL.B., Georgetown U., 1945; LL.D., Loyola Coll., 1967, Georgetown U., 1968, Fairfield U., 1968, Loyola U., Chgo., 1970, Albertus Magnus Coll., 1971, St. Joseph's Coll., Phila., 1971; Lincoln Coll., 1972; m. Dorothy Adair Guider, May 3, 1946 (dec. May 1959); children—Joseph Barnard, Ellen Adair, Peter Bennett; m. 2d, Agnes Anne Neill, June 11, 1960; children—Edward Neill, Dana Bennett, Anthony Tyler, Kimberly A. Admitted to D.C. bar, 1944, since practiced in Washington; sr. partner firm Williams Connolly & Califano, 1971—; gen. counsel Georgetown U., 1949—; prof. criminal law and evidence Georgetown U. Law Sch., 1946-58; guest prof. U. Frankfurt (Germany), 1954, vis. lectr. Yale Law Sch., 1971. Pres., dir. Washington Redskins, profl. football team, 1965—, Williams Properties, Washington. Chmn. Md. Jud. Selection Commn. for 6th Jud. Dist., 1971; mem. Chief Justice's Com. on Ct. Facilities and Design, 1971—. Served with USAAF, 1941-43. Mem. Am. (chmn. spl. com. on crime prevention and control 1970-71, D.C. (v.p. 1950, 55-56, Lawyer of Year award 1966) bar assns., Am. Coll. Trial Lawyers (regent), Internat. Acad. Trial Lawyers (dir.), U.S. Jud. Conf. (adv. com. on fed. rules of evidence 1965—). Democrat. Roman Catholic. Author: One Man's Freedom, 1962; You in Trial Law, 1963. Home: 8901 Durham Dr Potomac MD 20854 Office: 1000 Hill Bldg Washington DC 20006

WILLIAMS, EDWARD EARL, profl. engr.; b. Rogers, Ark., Mar. 3, 1932; s. Leslie Edward and Jessie (Baldwin) W.; B.S., U. Ark., 1957, M.S., 1960; m. Camilla Ann Harris, Nov. 24, 1971; children—Jennifer Jo, Edward Earl, Nat Allen, Stephanie Darlene. Various positions, Kan., La., 1958-64; sr. design engr. Boeing Co., Huntsville, Ala., 1965-66; sr. staff engr. Sperry Rand Corp., Huntsville, 1965-66; div. head engring. techs. State Tech. Inst., Memphis, 1967-68; tchr. indsl. tech. Ala. A. and M. U., Huntsville, 1968-71; engr. elec. design div. So. div. Naval Facilities Engring. Command, Charleston, S.C., 1971—. Profl. engring. cons. edn., govt., industry. Served with USAF, 1949-53. Registered profl. engr., La., Tex., Okla. Mem. Am. Soc. Engring. Edn., Nat., Ala. socs. profl. engrs., Internat. Platform Assn., V.F.W., Pi Mu Epsilon, Eta Kappa Nu, Tau Beta Pi. Lion. Contbr. articles to profl. jours. Office: Electrical Design Div So Div Naval Facilities Engring Command PO Box 10068 Charleston SC 29411

WILLIAMS, ELLIS KEITH, TV sta. ofcl.; b. Birmingham, Ala., May 26, 1927; s. Christopher Ellis and Carrie Enfield (Watson) W.; B.A., U. Ala., 1949; m. Maxine Roberta Ellenberger, June 27, 1953; children—Mary Enfield, Christopher Keith, Katherine Anne, Kimberly Sue. Film dir. sta. WAFM-TV, Birmingham, 1949-51; program dir. sta. WBRC-TV, Birmingham, 1951-54, sales rep., 1954-68, local sales mgr., asst. gen. sales mgr., 1969—. Vis. lectr. U. Ala., Samford U. Bd. dirs. Ala. Leukemia Soc. Mem. Birmingham Advt. Club (v.p.), Sales and Marketing Execs. (dir.), U. Ala. Alumni Assn. (pres. Jefferson County chpt. 1971), City Salesmen's Club (pres. 1962-63). Presbyn. (elder). Clubs: Exchange (pres. 1957, 64), Touchdown (dir. 1973), Green Valley Country, Downtown (Birmingham). Home: 2736 Cherokee Dr Birmingham AL 35216 Office: Atop Red Mountain Birmingham AL 35209

WILLIAMS, EMIL OTTO NOLTING, utility co. exec.; b. Richmond, Va., July 1, 1909; s. Langbourne Meade and Susanne Catherine (Nolting) W.; B.A., U. Va., 1931; m. Mary Binford Hobson, Apr. 11, 1934; children—E. Otto Nolting, John Langbourne, Julien Hobson. Vice pres., pres. Va. Central Ry., Fredericksburg, Va., 1932-41; pres. Bottled Gas Corp. Va., Richmond, 1941—, also dir.; dir. Commonwealth Natural Gas Corp., Richmond Fredericksburg & Potomac R.R. Treas. Christian Children's Fund. Bd. dirs. Christian Children's Fund, Children's Home Soc. Va.; chmn. bd. govs. St. Christopher's Sch., 1966-68. Served from 1st lt. to capt., Transp. Corps, AUS, 1942-45. Mem. Nat. (dir., pres. 1961), Va. (dir., founder) liquified petroleum gas assns., Phi Kappa Sigma. Episcopalian (trustee, vestryman). Clubs: Country of Va., Commonwealth, Richmond German, Richmond Hundred (Richmond). Home: 6601 River Rd Richmond VA 23229 Office: 1701 Brook Rd Richmond VA 23260

WILLIAMS, ERNEST FRANKLIN, dentist; b. Gallatin, Tenn., Feb. 17, 1917; s. Samuel Watkins and Elizabeth (Franklin) W.; A.B., Ark. Coll., 1938; B.S. in Civil Engring., U. Ark., 1942; postgrad. U. Cal. at Los Angeles, 1943; D.D.S., Washington U., St. Louis, 1950; m. Frances Elizabeth Holloway, June 14, 1948; children—Richard Franklin, Stephen Pryor. Engr., E.I. DuPont Co., Pryor, Okla., 1942; pvt. practice dentistry, Batesville, Ark., 1950—. Mem. Batesville Sch. Dist. Bd., 1969—, pres., 1973-74. Served with USAAF, 1942-46. Mem. Am. Dental Assn., N.E. Ark. Dental Soc. (pres. 1959-60), Sigma Alpha Epsilon, Xi Psi Phi. Methodist. Kiwanian (pres. 1961). Home: 1680 Highland Rd Batesville AR 72501 Office: 359 E Main St Batesville AR 72501

WILLIAMS, ETHEL NAOMI LANGLEY (MRS. LOUIS JOHNSON WILLIAMS), librarian; b. Balt.; d. William Herbert and Carrie Amelia (Sampson) Langley; A.B., Howard U., 1930; B.S. in L.S., Columbia, 1933; m. Louis Johnson Williams, Jan. 13, 1932; 1 dau., Carole Juanita (Mrs. George Jones). Caseworker pub. assistance div. Bd. Pub. Welfare, Washington, 1933-36; searcher Library of Congress, Washington, 1936-40; reference librarian, cataloger Howard U. Library, Washington, 1940-47, librarian Howard U. Sch. of Religion Library, Washington, 1947—. Mem. A.L.A., Am. Theol. Library Assn., D.C. Library Assn., N.A.A.C.P., Washington Urban League. Democrat. Episcopalian. Author: Afro-American Religion: A Bibliography, 1972. Editor: Biographical Directory of Negro Ministers, 1965, 2d edit., 1970. Contbr. weekly book rev. column to Afro-American Newspaper, 1945-46. Home: 1625 Primrose Rd NW Washington DC 20012

WILLIAMS, EVERETT HOLLAND, JR., state ofcl.; b. Jacksonville, Fla., Aug. 7, 1918; s. Everett Holland and Mamie (Whitehead) W.; B.A., U. Fla., 1940; M.S., Johns Hopkins, 1951; m. Bettye Jane Hyatt, July 7, 1942; 1 dau., Patricia A. Statistician, Fla. Bd. Health, Jacksonville, 1940-42, 46-47, dir. vital statistics, 1947—. Served with AUS, 1942-46. Mem. Am., Fla. (sec.) pub. health assns., Am. Assn. Vital Records and Statistics (pres.), Kappa Sigma. Home: 5208 Rollins Av Jacksonville FL 32207 Office: 1217 Pearl St Jacksonville FL 32201

WILLIAMS, FAYETTE CREED, JR., orthodontist; b. Corinth, Miss., June 4, 1933; s. Fayette Creed and Margaret (Schumpert) W.; B.S., U. Tenn., 1955, D.D.S., 1957; m. Mary Elizabeth Phillips, Sept. 3, 1967; 1 dau., Margaret Elizabeth. Resident, U. Ala. Dental Sch., 1957-59; practice dentistry specializing in orthodontics, Tupelo, Miss., 1959—; research asso. U. Ala., 1959-61. Lee County campaign chmn. Tb Christmas Seal drive, 1963-67; Miss. chmn. Project Concern, 1968-69. Named Miss.'s Outstanding Young Man, Miss. Jaycees, 1966. Fellow Am. Coll. Dentists; mem. So. soc. Orthodontists (sec. 1971—), Am. Assn. Orthodontists, Miss. Dental Assn. (editor jour. 1964-69, pres. 1968-69), U. Tenn. Dental Alumni Assn. (pres. 1964-65), Soc. Mayflower Descs. Presbyn. (deacon). Home: 1406 Pinecrest St Tupelo MS 38801 Office: 914 S Gloster St Tupelo MS 38801

WILLIAMS, FREDERICK FRANCIS, mag. editor; b. Liberty, S.C., Oct. 10, 1916; s. Fred Fulton and Bernice (Waldrop) W.; B.A., U. S.C., 1938; m. Margaret Louisa Rollins, June 14, 1940; children—Frederick Francis, Betsy, Louisa. Reporter, Columbia (S.C.) Record, 1938-41; sports editor United Press, Atlanta, 1941-42; owner, pub. The Times, Timmonsville, S.C., 1946-48; sports and city editor, editorial dir. The Statesman, Austin, Tex., 1949-65; editor Chuck Wagon mag., Austin, 1965—. Served with USNR, 1942-45. Recipient award Tex. Soc. Assn. Execs., 1968, editor's award of excellence Internat. Council Indsl. Editors, 1969, award Nat. Restaurant Assn., 1970. Mem. Am. Legion (regional comdr. 1948), Sigma Delta Chi. Episcopalian. Club: Headliners (founder 1955, dir. 1956—) (Austin). Home: 2005 Scenic Dr Austin TX 78703 Office: 2401 S Interstate 35 Austin TX 78741

WILLIAMS, GENE, judge; b. Chgo., June 11, 1916; s. George A. and Marie (Lauletta) W.; J.D., U. Miami, 1939; m. Virginia Handley, Apr. 12, 1946; children—Susan, Judy, Gary. Admitted to Fla. bar, 1939; partner firm Williams & Brion, Miami, Fla., 1939-41, Roth &Williams, Miami, 1946-52; asst. states atty. State of Fla., Miami, 1953-55; judge Criminal Ct. of Record, Miami, 1955-66; judge Circuit Ct., Miami, 1966—. Mem. Dade County Bar Assn. (sec. 1951-53), Ct. of Record Judges Assn. Fla. (pres. 1960-62), U. Miami Alumni Assn. (past dir.), U. Miami Law Alumni Assn. (past dir.), Delta Theta Phi, Lambda Chi Alpha. Episcopalian. Home: 9500 SW 60th Ct Miami FL 33156 Office: Dade County Ct House Miami FL 33136

WILLIAMS, GERALD EDWARD, lawyer; b. Ruleville, Miss., Feb. 14, 1933; s. Edd Noel and Pearl May (Mitchell) W.; B.S. in Bus. Adminstrn., Delta State Coll., 1955; J.D., George Washington U., 1963; m. Peggy Ann Eubank, Sept. 15, 1962; children—Ronald Edward, Richard Mitchell, Kathlyn Noel, Susan Jonell. Auditor U.S. Dept. Agr., Little Rock, also Arlington, Va., 1957-63; admitted to Va. bar, 1963, since practiced in Arlington; with firms E. Eugene Luther, 1963-67, Thomas, Williams, Gwaltney and King, 1968-73, Thomas and Williams, 1973—. Asst. Commonwealth atty., Arlington, 1964-66. Sec. Am. Cancer Soc., 1972, 74; dist. chmn. Boy Scouts Am., 1972-73. Served with USMCR, 1955-57; Korea, Japan. Mem. Va. State Bar, Am., Ark., Arlington County (treas. 1967-71) bar assns., Dist. Atty. Assn., Phi Alpha Delta, Alpha Psi Omega. Mem. Ch. of Christ. Mason. Clubs: Morning Optimist (pres. 1967). Home: 2456 N Lexington St Arlington VA 22207 Office: 2030 16th St Arlington VA 22216

WILLIAMS, GORDON LEE, civil engr.; b. Galbis, Cuba, Dec. 7, 1910 (parents Am. citizens); s. Noah Kellum and Birdie Fay (Pickett) W.; B.S. in Civil Engring., U. Fla., 1932; m. Ethel Cleo Campbell, June 18, 1933; children—Robert, Sarah (Mrs. Allan J. Finnell), Mary Lou (Mrs. Charles J. Thomas). Jr. to asso. engr. U.S. Bur. Reclamation, Nev., Colo., Cal., 1932-41; asso. engr. TVA, Ocoee and Fontana Dams, Tenn., N.C., 1942-45; hydraulic turbine specialist Gen. Electric Co., Rio de Janeiro, Brazil, 1946-49; planning engr. hydroelectric projects Brazilian Light Co., Sao Paulo, 1949-53; engr. Harza Engring. Co., Chgo., 1954-59; project mgr. Devel. & Resources Corp., N.Y.C., 1960-64, Engring. Cons., Inc., Denver, 1965-66; prin. Gordon L. Williams, Miami, Fla., 1968—. Registered profl. engr., Ill. Fellow Am. Soc. C.E. Supr. constrn. Pahlavi Dam, Iran, 1960-64. Address: 13801 SW 100th Av Miami FL 33158

WILLIAMS, HARRY JOHN, accountant; b. West Frankfort, Ill., June 21, 1900; s. George Harry and Lydia (Morgan) W.; student U. Ill., 1920-22; ; m. Helita Eubanks Durham, Oct. 24, 1922; children—Harry John, Patricia (Mrs. Reynold H. Richaud). With Peat, Marwick, Mitchell & Co., C.P.A.'S, 1922-63, partner, 1943-63; accounting adviser Internat. Finance Corp., 1963-67, accounting cons., 1967—. Instr. City Coll. Law and Finance, St. Louis, 1927, Loyola U. of South, New Orleans, 1935. Chmn., Sea Transp. Industry Com., 1952-63; mem. Petroleum Industry Com., 1948-63, chmn. subcom. accounting procedures, 1955-63; mem. Internat. Com. Accounting Cooperation, 1966-72, treas., 1966-67; mem. accountants div. Nat. Fund for Med. Edn., 1955-64; mem. Trade Mission to Orient, 1961. Bd. dirs. Internat. House, New Orleans, 1958-63. C.P.A., Mo., La. Mem. Am. Inst. C.P.A.'s, La. Soc. C.P.A.'s (pres. 1941-42), Nat. Assn. Accountants (pres. New Orleans 1942-43), New Orleans Power Squadron, Grand Isle Tarpon Rodeo (chmn. boat com. 1958-63), Sigma Lambda Epsilon (hon.). Republican. Presbyn. Mason (K.T.). Clubs: Big Ten Universities (pres. 1938), Pickwick, Southern Yacht, Country (New Orleans). Author pamphlets in field. Home: 309 Opal St New Orleans LA 70124

WILLIAMS, HARRY JOHN, JR., accountant; b. Marion, Ill., Mar. 10, 1924; s. Harry John and Helita (Durham) W.; B.B.A., Tulane U., 1948; m. Joanne Elizabeth Schwartz, Nov. 1, 1947; children—Kathleen Anne (Mrs. Frederick Trenchard), Marianne Elizabeth (Mrs. Eugene A. Antoine, Jr.), Barbara Helen (Mrs. Robert Ayuso), Harry John III. With Peat, Marwick, Mitchell & Co., St. Louis, 1948-53; pvt. practice accounting, New Orleans, 1953—; partner Hurdman & Cranston, 1972—). Lectr. Tulane U., 1953-56. Founder, Asso. Regional Accounting Firms, chmn., 1969-71. Served with USNR, 1943-46. Mem. Am. Inst. C.P.A.'s, Soc. La. C.P.A.'s (pres. New Orleans chpt. 1964-65, parliamentarian 1971-72, dir. 1964-65, 71-72, mem. trial bd., 1972—, chmn. 1972-73, chmn. numerous coms.), Accounting Research Assn., New Orleans Estate Planning Council (treas. 1970-71), New Orleans Bd. Trade, Greater New Orleans C. of C., Pi Kappa Alpha. Clubs: Pickwick, Southern Yacht, Internat. House (New Orleans). Methodist. Democrat. Editor: La. C.P.A., 1961-62. Contbr. articles to profl. jours. Home: 6824 Vicksburg St New Orleans LA 70124 Office: Hibernia Bank Bldg New Orleans LA 70112

WILLIAMS, HATCHER CRENSHAW, ednl. adminstr.; b. Oxford, N.C., Nov. 27, 1918; s. John Arrington and Lily Belle (White) W.; A.B., Duke, 1940, M.A., 1949; postgrad. Memphis State U.; m. Jacqueline Ray, Aug. 30, 1944; children—Beverly Royster, John Arrington II, Madge Ray, Margaret Ray. Tchr., Darlington Sch., 1944-53; asst. headmaster, dir. summer session Christchurch Sch., 1953-62; founder, Corolla Acad., Outer Banks, N.C., 1959; asst. headmaster Blue Ridge Sch., Dyke, Va., 1962, headmaster, 1963—. Founder Corolla-in-Eng. Summer Sch., 1964. Bd. govs. Christchurch Sch. Served with USAAF, 1944. Mem. English Speaking Union (dir.). Episcopalian (vestryman 1959-62). Home and office: Blue Ridge School Dyke VA 22935

WILLIAMS, HIRAM DRAPER, painter, educator; b. Indpls., Feb. 11, 1917; s. Earl Boring and Inez Mary (Draper) W.; B.S., Pa. State U., 1950, M.Ed., 1951; m. Avonell Baumunk, July 7, 1941; children—Curtis Earl, Kim Avonell. Tchr. art U. So. Cal., 1953-54, U. Cal. at Los Angeles, summer 1959, U. Tex., 1954-60; mem. faculty U. Fla., 1960—, now prof. of art paintings exhibited Pa. Acad. Fine Arts annuals, Whitney Mus. Am. Art bi-annuals, Corcoran Gallery bi-annuals, U. Ill. bi-annuals, Mus. Modern Art exhibitions, also Nordness Gallery, N.Y.C.; represented in permanent exhbns. Mus. Modern Art, Wilmington Art Center, Whitney Mus. Am. Art, N.Y.C., Sheldon Meml. Art Mus. Milw. Art Center, also pvt. collections. Served to capt. C.E., AUS, World War II; ETO. Tex. Research grantee, 1958; Guggenheim fellow, 1962-63. Author: Notes for a Young Painter, 1963; also articles. Address: 2804 NW 30th Terrace Gainesville FL 32601

WILLIAMS, HOWARD GLENN, accountant; b. Rocky Mount, N.C., June 1, 1938; s. Charles T. and Lucille (Taylor) W.; A.B., E. Carolina Coll., 1963, postgrad. Grad. Sch. Bus., 1963-64; m. Patsy Ann Edwards, June 17, 1967; 1 son, Charles Edwards. Audit mgr. Arthur Andersen & Co., Charlotte, N.C., 1964—. Served with USNR, 1956-60. Mem. N.C. Soc. C.P.A.'s, Am. Inst. C.P.A.'s, Nat. Assn. Accountants, Phi Sigma Pi. Home: 108 Waycross Dr Charlotte NC 28214 Office: 300 S College St Charlotte NC 28282

WILLIAMS, JACK LESLIE, telephone co. exec.; b. Mineola, Tex., Sept. 14, 1944; s. Charles G. and Della Mae (Suggs) W.; student Tyler Jr. Coll., 1964-65; B.B.A., Stephen F. Austin U., 1967; m. Nancy Grace Walters, May 2, 1970. Finance trainee Gulf States United Telephone Co., Tyler, Tex., 1967-69, treasury asst., 1969-70, asst. to treas., 1970, treas., 1970—. Mem. Tyler Jr. C. of C. (dir.). Home: 7 Shady Lane Lake Villages Flint TX 75762 Office: 120 S College St Tyler TX 75701

WILLIAMS, JAMES ALEXANDER, lawyer; b. Pine Bluff, Ark., Oct. 30, 1929; s. Absalom Alexander and Kyle (Baggarly) W.; student U. Ark., 1948; B.A., So. Methodist U., 1951, J.D., 1952, M.L.A., 1971; m. Janet L. Bray, Nov. 27, 1953; children—Laura Kay, Victoria Lynn, Diana Leigh. Admitted to Tex. bar, 1952, since practiced in Dallas; mem. firm Touchstone, Bernays & Johnston, 1955-57; partner firm Bailey, Williams, Westpall & Henderson, 1957—. Bd. dirs. Spl. Care Sch.; bd. mgmt. YMCA. Served to lt. USNR, 1952-55. Mem. Am., Dallas bar assns., State Bar Tex., Dallas, Tex. assns. def. counsel, Internat. Assn. Ins. Counsel, Fedn. Ins. Counsel, Am. Bd. Trial Advocates, Soc. Hosp. Attys., Trial Attys. Am., So. Meth. U. Law Alumni Assn. (pres. 1970-72), Lambda Chi Alpha, Phi Alpha Delta. Democrat. Methodist (chmn. adminstrv. bd. 1973). Club: Exchange (pres. 1967); Dallas; Brookhaven Country. Home: 4630 Northaven Rd Dallas TX 75229 Office: Suite 3900 2001 Bryan Tower Dallas TX 75201

WILLIAMS, JAMES ALLEN, JR., editor; b. Wytheville, Va., Aug. 26, 1907; s. James Allen and Virginia (Tynes) W.; student pub. schs.; m. Dora Emelinee Burgess, June 20, 1928; children—Virginia Elizabeth (Mrs. N.C. Sutherland), Ella Frances (Mrs. Norris Porter) (dec.), James A. III. Printers devil S.W. Va. Enterprise, Wytheville, 1926-31, mech. supt., 1932-38, advt. mgr., 1938-44, mng. editor, 1944-45, editor, gen. mgr., 1945-46, editor-in-chief, mng. editor, gen. mgr., 1946—; editor Bland (Va.) Messenger, 1960—. Bd. dirs. Wythe Community Hosp. Recipient Va. Pub. Relations award, 1968; Freedoms award for editorial, 1969; Resolution for contbn. to state of Va., Va. Legislature, 1969; Congress of Freedom Liberty award, 1972, 73. Mem. 5-State Gt. Lakes to Fla. Hwy. Assn. (pres. 1956—). Wytheville C. of C. (organizer, pres. 1946-53, dir. emeritus 1968), Va. Press Assn. (dir. 1973—, Copeland award 1974). Baptist (trustee). Kiwanian (membership chmn.). Home: 220 10th St Wytheville VA 24382 Office: 275 W Monroe St Wytheville VA 24382

WILLIAMS, JAMES HOWARD, research exec.; b. Wheat, Tenn., Dec. 19, 1920; s. William Wess and Sallie (Shelton) W.; A.B., Carson-Newman Coll., 1942; M.A., George Peabody Coll., 1947; Ph.D., Vanderbilt U., 1956; m. Mary Helen Mewshaw, Aug. 31, 1946; children—James Howard, Edward Robert, Nancy Jean. Instr., dept. sociology U. S.C., 1950-55; asst. dir. Nat. Inst. Mental Health Project, Vanderbilt U. 1956-58; asst. prof. social welfare and sociology Fla. State U., 1958-61; research dir. Fla. Bur. Alcoholic Rehab., Avon Park, 1961—. Social sci. cons. City of Columbia (S.C.) Planning Comm., 1950-55. Served to lt. USNR, 1942-46. Mem. N. Am. Assn. Alcohol Programs, So. Sociol. Soc., Soc. for Study of Social Problems, Am. Sociol. Assn. Nat. Rehab. Assn., Population Assn. Am., Fla. Acad. Sci. Kiwanian (pres. Avon Park club 1970-71). Contbr. articles in field to profl. jours. Home: 91 E Kendall Blvd Avon Park FL 33825 Office: PO Box 1147 Avon Park FL 33825

WILLIAMS, JAMES NEWTON, psychiatrist; b. Richmond, Va., Aug. 29, 1904; s. Samuel Newton and Frances (Kolbe) W.; A.B., Washington and Lee U., 1926; M.D., Med. Coll. Va., 1930; m. Dorothy Henrietta Behle, Aug. 29, 1933; children—James Newton, Dorothy M. Resident psychiatry Med. Coll. Va., Richmond, 1932-35; pvt. practice psychiatry, 1936—; dir. Va. Bd. Mental Hygiene, Richmond, 1935-41; chief neuropsychiat. service U.S. Naval Hosp., Portsmouth, Va. and Newport, R.I., 1950—; dir. Portsmouth Area Counseling and Guidance Clinic, 1950-54, Atlantic Mental Hygiene Center, Virginia Beach, Va., 1960; mem. adv. bd. Atlantic Mental Health Center, Virginia Beach, 1960—, dir.-psychiatrist, 1962—. Mem. adv. bd. Child and Family Service and Travelers Aid, Portsmouth, 1961—, Portsmouth Mental Hygiene Assn., 1960—. Served from lt. to capt., M.C., USNR, 1941-62. Fellow A.C.P., Am. Psychiat. Assn.; mem. A.M.A., Royal Medico Psychol. Assn. (London, Eng.), Med. Soc. Va., C. of C. (exec. bd.). Rotarian (past pres). Contbr. numerous articles to profl. jours. Home: 717 Cardinal Rd Virginia Beach VA 23451 Office: 1876 Wildwood Dr Virginia Beach VA 23454

WILLIAMS, J(AMES) TAYLOR, judge; b. Lynchburg, Va., May 13, 1916; s. William Twyman and Annabel (Lyle) W.; A.B., Hampden-Sydney Coll., 1937; certificate in meteorology Cal. Inst. Tech., 1942; J.D., Washington and Lee U., 1953; m. Eleanor Kathleen Nuckols, June 11, 1942; 1 dau., Kathleen Eleanor. Tchr. Math Whitmell (Va.) Farm-Life Sch., 1937, Cumberland (Va.) High Sch., 1938, Fishburne Mil. Sch., Waynesboro, Va., 1939-41; admitted to Va. bar, 1953; practiced in Cumberland, 1954-55; commonwealth's atty., Cumberland County, 1956-57; judge Cumberland County Cts., Cumberland, 1957-73; chief judge Tenth Dist. Juvenile and Domestic Relations Ct., 1973—. Pres., Cumberland County Indsl. Devel. Corp., 1963—; chmn. Cumberland County Ct. House Restoration Com., 1968-70. Sec., Cumberland County Democratic Com., 1960-73. Bd. dirs. Cumberland Edn. and Recreation Assn. Served to lt. col. AUS, USAAF, 1941-48; ETO. Mem. Assn. County and Municipal Judges, Va. Bar Assn., 5th Jud. Circuit Bar. Assn. (past pres.), Am. Legion (past comdr.), V.F.W., Va. Farm Bur., Chi Phi, Pi Alpha Delta. Democrat. Presbyn. Mason. Clubs: Ruritan (Cumberland); Wedgewood Country (Farmville). Home: US Hwy 60 E Cumberland VA 23040 Office: County Office Bldg Cumberland VA 23040

WILLIAMS, JERRY ALEXANDER, chem. co. exec.; b. Cape Town, South Africa, Oct. 24, 1926; s. William Parkin and Alfa L. (Gunderson) W.; grad. South African Naval Acad., 1943; B.S., U. Ida., 1950; m. Ida-Mae Peterson, Oct. 26, 1946; children—Richard Alexander, Linda Lorene. Came to U.S., 1946, naturalized, 1954. With Shell Chem. Co., 1950-60; with Helena Chem. Co., Memphis, 1961—, chief exec. officer, chmn. bd. dirs., 1964—; chmn. bd. Vicksburg Chem. Co., Transvaal Chem. Co., Eagle River Chem. Co. Served with Royal Navy, 1943-46. Decorated Atlantic Star, African Star. Republican. Christian Scientist. Mason (Shriner). Home: 131 Waring Rd Memphis TN 38117 Office: 100 N Main Bldg Suite 3100 Memphis TN 38113

WILLIAMS, JOHN BARRY, dentist; b. Austin, Tex., May 19, 1928; s. J.B. and Ethyl Lloyd (Clark) W.; B.A., U. Tex., 1948; D.D.S., Baylor U., 1951; m. Marilyn Agnew, June 23, 1951 (div. May 1971); children—John Barry, Marilee. Practice dentistry, Austin, 1954—. Bd. dirs., treas. Child and Family Service, 1959-61. Served with USAF, 1952-54. Fellow Soc. Oral Physiology and Occlusion; mem. Am., Tex. dental assns., Austin Dist. Dental Soc. (v.p. 1963), Acad. Operative Dentistry, Am. Soc. Preventive Dentistry. Home: 7586 Chevy Chase Austin TX 78703 Office: 17 Med Arts Sq Austin TX 78705

WILLIAMS, JOHN RICHARD, electronic scientist; b. Detroit, May 19, 1919; s. Nicolas and Louise (Keydel) W.; B.S., Wayne State U., 1942; m. Mary E. Hornbeck, Aug. 28, 1971. Electronic scientist Naval Research Lab., Washington, 1942—. Mem. Nat. Republican Club. Mem. Am. Ordnance Assn. (life), A.A.A.S. (life), I.E.E.E., Air Force Assn., Assn. Old Crows (charter). Presbyn. (deacon). Clubs: Washington Athletic, Potomac Appalachian Trail. Research and devel. in electronic countermeasures for navy. Home: 2111 Jefferson Davis Hwy Arlington VA 22202 Office: Naval Research Lab Code 5741A Washington DC 20375

WILLIAMS, JOHN WILLIAM, bookstore exec.; b. Red Hill, Va., Nov. 24, 1916; s. John William and Louise Gray (Anderson) W.; grad. Tarleton Bus. Coll., 1936; student U. Va., 2 yrs.; grad. LaSalle U., 1947; m. Laura Elizabeth Kegley, Nov. 6, 1937; children—Elizabeth Byrd (Mrs. Charles Cortez Abbott), Martha Hayes (Mrs. Ward W. Anderson). Clk., Anderson Bros. Bookstores, Inc., Charlottesville, Va., 1936-40, asst. gen. mgr., 1940-41, v.p., 1941-62, pres., gen. mgr., 1962—; asst. sec.-treas. Anderson Realty Corp., Charlottesville, 1938-69, sec.-treas., 1969—, also dir.; dir. Va. Nat. Bank. Asst. varsity, head freshman boxing coach U. Va., 1941-43, head boxing coach, 1953—. Mem. Va. Hosp. Bd., 1963—, vice chmn., 1969; mem. Albemarle County Bd. Pub. Welfare, 1949-61. Mem. Albemarle County Sch. Bd., 1946-49; mem. Albemarle County Bd. Suprs., 1949-64, chmn., 1957-64; a.d.c. to gov. of Va., 1959—; chmn. SSS, Charlottesville, 1970—. Pres. Young Democratic Clubs Va., 1953-55; sec. 8th Congl. Dist. Dem. Com., 1956-66; mem. Va. Dem. Central Com., 1956—, mem. steering com., 1969—; chmn. 7th Congl. Dist. Dem. Com., 1969. Gen. vice chmn. devel. com. U. Va. Grad. Sch. Bus. Served to 1st lt. AUS, 1943-46, col. Va. State Guard. Mem. Va. Coll. Stores Assn. (pres. 1971-72), Nat. Intercollegiate Boxing Coaches Assn. (pres. 1957), Assn. Va. Counties (pres. 1960), U. Va. Alumni Assn., Albemarle Hist. Soc. (pres. 1969), Am. Legion. Rotarian. Clubs: Monticello Guard, Farmington Country. Home: Meadowbrook Heights Charlottesville VA 22901 Office: 1541 W Main St Charlottesville VA 22901

WILLIAMS, JOHNNY KNOTT, supt. schs.; b. Memphis, May 5, 1926; s. Gladstone and Johnny (Knott) W.; B.S., Ark. State Tchrs. Coll., 1950; M.A., George Peabody Coll., 1953; advanced diploma U. Ark., 1967; m. Edna Earle Stephens, Aug. 23, 1953; children—Stephen Gladstone, Jaye Kay, John David, Edward Allen. Tchr., coach, prin. pub. schs., Dumas, Ark., 1950-53, supt. schs., 1954-58; asst. registrar U. Ark., 1958-63; supt. schs. Paragould, Ark., 1963-65, Blytheville, Ark., 1965-70, Pulaski County Spl. Sch. Dist., Little Rock, 1970—. Mem. Ark. State Econ. Edn. Council, 1966-70; bd. dirs. YMCA, Blytheville, Ark., 1966-67. Served with USN, 1943-46. Mem. Ark. Sch. Adminstrs. Assn. (treas. 1966-67, pres. 1970), Ark. Edn. Assn. (mem. legislative com. 1966-67), Miss. County Sch. Adminstrn. (pres. 1966), Nat. Edn. Assn., Am. Assn. Sch. Adminstrs., Phi Delta Kappa. Methodist (bd. dirs., 1966-69). Club: Rotary. Home: 6424 Tulip Rd Little Rock AR 72209 Office: 924 Marshall Little Rock AR 72204

WILLIAMS, JOSEPH R., assn. exec.; b. Yadkinville, N.C., Feb. 1, 1909; s. Samuel Carter and Grace (Redmond) W.; student U. N.C., 1925-28; m. Garnett Kelly, Apr. 19, 1935; children—Phyllis (Mrs. O.J. Hart, Jr.), JoAnn. Asst. sec. N.C. Farm Bur., Greensboro, N.C., 1941-48; exec. sec. Tobacco Bd. Trade, Winston-Salem, N.C., 1948-55; dep., then dir. tobacco div. Agrl. Stblzn. Conservation Service, U.S. Dept. Agr., Washington, 1955-61; agrl. attache, Brussels, Belgium, 1961-63, Salisbury, Rhodesia, 1963-66, Ankara, Turkey, 1966-69; asso. dir. tobacco div. Fgn. Agrl. Service, Washington, 1969-71; mem. exec. com., tobacco growers information com., 1972-73, Nat. Tobacco Tax Council, 1972—. Chmn., Winston-Salem Civic Betterment Com., 1953; chmn. tobacco div. United Givers Fund, 1946-54. Mem. N.C. Senate, 1935-37. Ky. col; recipient Distinguished Service award to agr. N.C. Farm Bur., 1960, Merit certificate U.S. Dept. Agr., 1961. Mem. U.S. C. of C., Mason. Clubs: Foysythe Country (Winston-Salem); Raleigh (N.C.) City. Contbr. articles to profl. jours. Home: 1431 Juliana Pl Alexandria VA 22304 Office: 1107 17th St NW Washington DC 20036

WILLIAMS, LAFAYETTE WESLEY, JR., dentist; b. Valdosta, Ga., Dec. 17, 1937; s. Lafayette Wesley and Ethel Mae (Davis) W.; B.S., Morehouse Coll., 1960; D.D.S., Meharry Med. Coll., 1968; m. Nedra Milicent Huggins, Nov. 28, 1968. Mem. staff Central State Hosp., Milledgeville, Ga., 1968-69; pvt. practice dentistry, Valdosta, 1969—; mem. staff Valdosta Nursing Home, Internat. Nursing Care Center, Valdosta. Mem. Valdosta Black Community Action Group, 1970—. Trustee Lowndes County Progressive Voters League. Mem. Nat., Am. dental assns., Ga., S.W. Dist. dental socs., Valdosta-Lowndes County C. of C., N.A.A.C.P., Beta Kappa Chi, Alpha Phi Alpha. Mason (Shriner, 32 deg.), Elk. Home: 415 Church St Valdosta GA 31601 Office: 415 S Ashley St Valdosta GA 31601

WILLIAMS, LEE ERSKINE, univ. adminstr.; b. Florence, Miss., Apr. 28, 1914; s. Hardy and Miranda (Sanders) W.; B.A., Jackson State U., 1940; M.A., Ohio State U., 1951; Ed.S., George Peabody Coll. Tchrs., 1961; m. Ruth Mae Harris, Mar. 3, 1945; children—Lee Erskine, Kenneth H., Linda Ruth. Mem. faculty Jackson (Miss.) State U., 1940—, coordinator continuing edn. enrichment program and coll. readiness program, 1964-67, asso. dean for adminstrn., 1967-68, dean for adminstrn., 1968-73, v.p. adminstrn. and asst. to pres., 1973—. Cons. evaluation schs. for accreditation by So. Assn. Colls. and Schs.,

1960-64. Chmn. State Accrediting Commn., 1962-66. Gen. Edn. Found. fellow, 1941-42, So. Edn. Found. fellow, 1954-55, Award for Meritorious Service Student N.E.A., 1964. Mem. Miss. Tchrs. Assn., Jackson State Coll. Nat. Alumni Assn. (pres. 1952-64), Phi Delta Kappa (chpt. treas. 1962-64), Phi Beta Sigma (chpt. pres. 1945-55). Baptist (pres. bible class 1954—, trustee). Home: 1101 Wiggins St Jackson MS 39203

WILLIAMS, LELAND HENDRY, ednl. computing co. exec.; b. Columbia, S.C., Feb. 24, 1930; s. Wyman L. and C. Lorraine (Hendry) W.; B.S., U. S.C., 1950; M.S., U. Ga., 1951; Ph.D., Duke, 1961; m. Cornelia Ann Burnett, June 18, 1952; children—Carolyn Leone, Leland Hendry. Mathematician, Redstone Arsenal, Huntsville, Ala., 1951-53; research asso., vis. asst. prof. Duke, Durham, N.C., 1960-62, adj. asso. prof., 1970—; mem. faculty Fla. State U., Tallahassee, 1962-66, asst. dir. computer center, 1964-66, asst. prof. math., 1962-66; asso. prof. math., dir. computer center Auburn (Ala.) U., 1966-70; pres., dir. Triangle Univs. Computation Center, Research Triangle Park, N.C., 1970—. Adj. asso. prof. U. N.C., Chapel Hill, 1970—, N.C. State U., Raleigh, 1970—; cons., lectr. various univs. Mem. Durham Civic Center Commn., 1972-73. Bd. dirs. Auburn United Fund, 1969-70. Served with USNR, 1954-57. Mem. Math. Assn. Am., Am. Sci. Affiliation, Am. Math. Soc., Assn. Computing Machinery (chmn. nat. com. student members 1966-68, nat. council 1968-71, 73-74), A.A.A.S. Home: 2729 Sevier St Durham NC 27705 Office: Box 12076 Research Triangle Park NC 27709

WILLIAMS, LOUIS GRESSETT, educator, biologist; b. Owensboro, Ky., Oct. 28, 1913; s. Walter Wiatt and Ella Mae (Lohrfink) W.; A.B., Marshall U., 1937; M.A., Duke, 1940, Ph.D., 1948; m. Dorothy Belle Huntley, May 31, 1942; children—Louis McGregor, Robert Huntley. Asst. prof. botany U. N.C., Chapell Hill, 1948; asso. prof. biology Furman U., Greenville, S.C., 1948-57; in charge aquatic biology program Nat. Water Quality Network, Taft San. Engring. Center, Cin., 1957-65; in charge plankton biology program Nat. Water Quality Lab., Duluth, Minn., 1965-67; prof. biology U. Ala., University, 1967—. Cons. water pollution, radionuclide contamination. Served to lt. USNR, 1941-45. Carnegie grantee, 1947-48; Ford Found. fellow, 1952. Fellow A.A.A.S., Ecol. Soc. Am., Assn. Southeastern Biologists; mem. Bot. Soc. Am., Phycol. Soc. Am., Internat. Phycol. Soc., Soc. Limnology and Oceanography. Contbr. articles to profl. publs. Home: 1246 Northwood Lake St Northport AL 35476 Office: Dept of Biology PO Box 1927 Universtiy AL 35486

WILLIAMS, MARGARET ANN SCHUMPERT (MRS. FAYETTE CREED WILLIAMS), realty devel. co. exec., club woman; b. Brookhaven, Miss., Aug. 20, 1912; d. Bailey T. and Minnie (Newcomb) Schumpert; student Miss. State Coll. for Women, 1929-31, Randolph-Macon Woman's Coll., 1931-32; m. Fayette Creed Williams, May 24, 1932; children—Fayette Creed, Bailey Robert, John Burton. Sec.-treas., dir. Fontaine Corp., Corinth, Miss., 1963—, Park Devel. Co., Corinth, 1967—, Mid-Town Corp., Corinth, 1962—. Mem. state bd. mgrs. Nat. Soc. Colonial Dames Am., 1941—, state pres., 1962-64; state sec. Soc. Mayflower Descs., 1947-50; mem. N.E. Miss. Hist. Soc., 1966—; mem. Miss. Am. Revolution Bicentennial Commn., now vice chmn. Area chmn. recreation com. Fed. Appalachia Program, Corinth, 1967—; v.p. Jacinto Found., Corinth, 1966-69, pres., 1969-71, bd. dirs., 1964—; bd. dirs. Natchez Trace Pkwy. Assn., Corinth chpt. Boys Club Am., Corinth. Recipient Outstanding Citizen award Corinth Jr. Aux., 1970. Mem. Kappa Alpha Theta. Presbyn. (pres. women of ch. 1966-68). Clubs: Four Seasons Garden, Shakespeare. Home: 1102 Fillmore St Corinth MS 38834

WILLIAMS, MARVIN DALE, JR., clergyman, librarian, archivist; b. Indpls., Oct. 27, 1935; s. Marvin Dale and Betty (Robison) W.; B.A., Butler U., 1958, M.A., 1963; B.D., Christian Theol. Sem., 1962; M.A., George Peabody Coll., 1963; student Am. U., 1966. Ordained to ministry Disciples of Christ Ch., 1962; pastor Olive Christian Ch., Paragon, Ind., 1959-60; periodicals librarian Christian Theol. Sem., Indpls., 1958-62; cataloger Disciples of Christ Hist. Soc., Nashville, Tenn., 1963-65, head tech. services, 1965, dir. library, 1966—, archivist, 1967—. Lilly Endowment scholar, 1962. Mem. Beta Phi Mu, Theta Phi. Editor: Discipliana, 1965—. Home: 422 Acklen Park Dr Nashville TN 37205 Office: 1101 19th Av S Nashville TN 37212

WILLIAMS, MAX, mgr., coach basketball team, real estate exec.; b. 1938; grad. So. Meth. U., 1960; m. Carolyn Cooper; children—Wayne, Laura. Ins. salesman, 1960-62; pres. constrn. co., 1962-65; metal buyer, 1966; gen. mgr. Chaparrals of Am. Basketball Assn., Dallas, 1967—, coach, 1970—; part owner, sr. v.p. Claude R. McClennahan, Inc., 1971—. Address: 2001 McKinney St Dallas TX 75201

WILLIAMS, MAXIE RAYMOND, supt. schs.; b. Johnsonville, Tenn., Aug. 2, 1918; s. Grover Cleveland and Sarah Frances (Moore) W.; B.S., U. Tenn., 1940; M.S., George Washington U., 1965; m. Mary Sue Waldrop, Aug. 8, 1944; children—Maxie Raymond, Gregory Neal. Commd. 2d lt. USMC, 1941, advanced through grades to col., 1967; assigned East Coast, PTO, N. China, 1940's, Washington, Brazil, 6th Fleet, Mediterranean, 1950's, San Juan, P.R., Army War Coll., Vietnam, 1960-67; ret., 1967; prin. Commonwealth High Sch., San Jaun, P.R., 1968-69; supt. Caribbean Consol. Sch., San Juan, 1969—. Vice pres. Rooney Wholesale, San Juan, 1967-68. Vice pres. Travelers Aid; bd. dirs. Salvation Army, Boys Club. Decorated Navy Cross, Joint Services Commendation medal, Navy Commendation medal, Purple Heart with star. Mem. Am. Assn. U. Profs., Am. Assn. Sch. Adminstr., N.E.A., 2d Marine Assn., Inter Am. Edn. Assn., Mil. Order World Wars, Am. Legion, Pvt. Schs. Assn. P.R., Ret. Officers Assn., U. Tenn., George Washington U. alumni assns., Navy League (v.p., dir.). Rotarian (pres. San Jaun 1971-72). Home: Lakeshore Cond 7A 1 Madrid St Santurce PR 00907 Office: 435 Pedro A Espada Hato Rey PR 00918

WILLIAMS, NOLAN EUGENE, educator; b. Whitener, Ark., Aug. 2, 1923; s. Nolan L. and Rubie (Robertson) W.; B.S., Okla. State U., 1947, M.S., 1948; Ph.D., U. Tex., 1957; m. Madelyn Englert, Aug. 28, 1943; children—Janet Kay (Mrs. Richard T. Roessler), Susan E. (Mrs. Richard M. Mayes, Jr.). Asst. prof. accounting U. Tex., Austin, 1950-51; prof., head accounting U. Ark., Fayetteville, 1951—. Part-time accounting and bus.-cons. service, 1947—; partner Fresh-O-Canning Co., Haskell, Okla., 1941-51; vis. prof. Price Waterhouse & Co., Humble Pipe Line Co., U. Ariz. Bd. dirs. Wesley Found. Served with AUS, 1943-45. Decorated Purple Heart. Danforth fellow, 1952-54. Mem. Am. Accounting Assn. (v.p., exec. com. 1965), Am. Inst. C.P.A.'s (com. on auditing procedures 1965-68, nat council 1967-68, 70—), Ark. Soc. C.P.A.'s, Blue Key, Phi Kappa Phi, Beta Gamma Sigma, Beta Alpha Psi (nat. grand council), Delta Sigma Pi. Methodist (mem. bd.). Lion. Club: Fayetteville Country. Home: 512 Adams St Fayetteville AR 72701

WILLIAMS, OLIVER HOYT, psychologist; b. Brashear, Tex., Dec. 18, 1911; s. James Wiley and Maud Dempsy (Williams) W.; A.B., E. Tex. State Tchrs. Coll., 1936; postgrad. U. Colo., summer 1941; M.A., U. Tex., 1949, Ph.D., 1959; m. Corinne Amber Bovenmyer Preston, June 14, 1943. Prin., Waskom (Tex.) High Sch., 1936-38; tchr. sci. Thomas Jefferson High Sch., Port Arthur, Tex., 1938-39; head sci. dept. Commerce (Tex.) High Sch., 1939-42; insp., chief chem. prodn. Dallas Chem. Warfare Procurement Dist., 1942-45; coll. recruiter, coll. relations Phillips Petroleum Co., 1945-46; group adviser Testing and Guidance Bur., dir. Student Employment Bur., asst. registrar grad. admissions, cons.-lectr. Hogg Found., acad. adviser, counselor Alpha Tau Omega, chmn. Faculty Student Cabinet, U. Tex., Austin, 1946-59; asst. prof. edn., dir. guidance edn. Tex. Christian U., 1959-64; prof., chmn. dept. psychology, coll. counselor Geneva Coll., Beaver Falls, Pa., 1964-69; dir. Presbyn. Guidance Center, Synod of Ga., Presbyn. Ch. in U.S., Agnes Scott Coll., Decatur, 1969-70, dir.-counselor, 1970-73, dir.-counselor Career and Personal Counseling Service, Synod of S.E., 1973—. Vis. asst. prof. counseling and guidance Macdonald Coll., Que., summer 1963; vis. asst. prof. Tulane U., summer 1964, vis. asso. prof., summer 1965; projector dir. employment orientation and communication skills Pa. Dept. Labor and Industry Bur. Employment Security, Rochester, summer 1968. Chmn., Christmas Fund com. Tex. Soc. Mental Health, 1954-55, Vol. Services Council, Tex. State Hosps. and Spl. Schs., 1953-56; staff and office chmn., bd. dirs. Tex. Colo. Lakes Area council Girl Scouts U.S.A., 1952-53; program chmn. Austin Personnel Assn., 1954-55; sponsor, adviser Ft. Worth Area Counselors, 1960-64; pres. Mental Health Assn. Austin-Travis County, 1950-51; sec.-treas., v.p. S.W. Placement Assn.; v.p. Boosters Club, Northeastern Sch. Jointure, Darlington, Pa. Bd. dirs. Tex. Soc. Mental Health, William E. Lintz Sheltered Workshop, Rochester, Pa., 1964-67, Beaver County Mental Health Soc. Fellow Coll. Bus. Exchange Program, Sears, Roebuck & Co., Chgo., Dallas, Austin, 1954. Fellow Am. Mgmt. Assn.; mem. Am., Ga. personnel and guidance assns., Nat. (membership coordinator Tex. 1962-63), Ga. (sec.-treas. 1974-75) vocational guidance assns., Internat. Assn. Counseling Services (nominating com. 1972), Hi Pi, Alpha Mu Zeta, Lambda Chi Alpha, Phi Delta Kappa. Contbr. articles to profl. jours. Home: 382 Glenn Circle Decatur GA 30030 Office: 531 Kirk Rd Decatur GA 30030

WILLIAMS, PEELER, JR., educator; b. Lorena, Tex., Nov. 19, 1921; s. Peeler and Gibson Denison (Ross) W.; A.B., Baylor U., 1942, J.D., 1943; LL.M., Harvard, 1947; m. Marguerite Carroll Dunson, Oct. 9, 1943; children—Carol (Mrs. David W. Turner), Peeler III, Brooks, Shapley Ross. Admitted to Tex. bar, 1943, practiced in Waco, 1947-72; mem. firm Sleeper, Williams, Johnston, Helm & Estes, 1947-72; prof. law Baylor U., 1973—. Dir. Amicable Life Ins. Co., 1st Nat. Bank of Waco, Jewell Concrete Products, Inc. Pres. Lighthouse for the Blind, 1950-51, Waco Boys Club, 1949-50, Waco Safety Assn., 1954-55, Goodwill Industries, 1958-59, Waco Symphony Assn., 1971-72; active YMCA, United Fund, Better Bus. Bur. Trustee Waco Sch. Bd., 1952-64, pres., 1964; mem. Brazos River Authority, 1967-69. Trustee Providence Hosp. Found.; mem. adv. bd. Waco Salvation Army, 1949-53. Served to lt. (j.g.), USNR, 1943-46. Named King of Waco, Cotton Palace, 1972. Mem. Am., Tex., Waco-McLennan County bar assns., Waco C. of C., Phi Alpha Delta. Democrat. Episcopalian (sr. warden). Mason (Shriner). Clubs: Waco Tennis Assn., Ridgewood Country. Home: 3804 Castle St Waco TX 76710 Office: Baylor University Waco TX 76703

WILLIAMS, PERCY DON, lawyer; b. Dallas, Sept. 19, 1922; s. Percy Don and Frances (Worrill) W.; B.A., So. Methodist U., 1942, M.A., 1943; LL.B. magna cum laude, Harvard, 1946; m. Helen Lucille Brunsdale, Aug. 4, 1954; children—Anne Lucy, Margaret Frances, Elizabeth Helen. Instr. law So. Meth. U. Sch. Law, 1946-47; asst. prof. law U. Tex. Sch. Law, 1947-48, asso. prof., 1948-49; lectr. law U. Va., 1951; law clk. to Justice Tom C. Clark, Supreme Ct. of U.S., 1949-51; admitted to Tex. bar, 1951; practiced in Houston, 1952—; partner firm Butler, Binion, Rice, Cook & Knapp, 1954-67; pvt. practice, 1967—. Vice pres., bd. dirs. Day Care Assn. of Houston, Child Guidance Clinic, Houston. Mem. Am., Tex., Houston bar assns., Harvard Law Sch. Assn. (pres. Tex. chpt., nat. v.p.), Am. Law Inst., Am. Judicature Soc., Order of Coif, Phi Beta Kappa, Pi Sigma Alpha, Tau Kappa Alpha, Kappa Sigma. Democrat. Clubs: Houston, Forest, Plaza (Houston). Contbr. articles profl. jours. Home: 31 Briar Hollow Lane Houston TX 77027 Office: First City Nat Bank Bldg Houston TX 77002

WILLIAMS, PRYOR ALLEN, JR., dentist; b. Birmingham, Ala., Oct. 12, 1939; s. Pryor Allen and Florence Annette (Ross) W.; B.A., Vanderbilt U., 1959; D.M.D., U. Ala. Sch. Dentistry, 1963; certificate specialization in orthodontics, 1967; m. Sandra Dale Payne, Aug. 23, 1960; children—Pryor Allen, III, Warren Payne, Ashley. Asso. with Dr. Marion F. Dick, specializing in orthodontics, Birmingham, 1967—. Mem. state exec. com. Republican Party Ala., 1970—, mem. finance com., 1970—. Served with Dental Corps, USNR, 1963-65. Mem. Birmingham Dist. Dental Soc., Am., Ala. dental assns., Ala. Orthodontic Soc., So. Soc. Orthodontics, Am. Assn. Orthodontists, Delta Sigma Delta (chpt. pres. 1969-70). Methodist. Kiwanian. Home: 3225 Bonny View Dr Birmingham AL 35226 Office: 2045 Medical Center Dr Birmingham AL 35209 also 1600 Deo Dara Dr Birmingham AL 35226

WILLIAMS, RAY ROBINSON, lawyer; b. Easley, S.C., Mar. 5, 1899; s. G.E.R. and Marinda Jane (Robinson) W.; B.A. magna cum laude, U. S.C., 1923, M.A., LL.B., 1924; m. Genevieve Castleman Groom, Apr. 17, 1929; children—Genevieve Castleman (Mrs. Beecher Allan Bartlett), Mary Ola (Mrs. Horace Lynwood Harper, Jr.), Ray Robinson. Admitted to S.C. bar, 1924, since practiced in Greenville; mem. firm Williams & Henry, 1926—. Past chmn. Greenville County Water Arbitration Bd.; chmn. Greenville County Producers and Consumers Market Commn.; mem. legal coms. serving state. Chmn. Adv. Council for Blind, S.C., 1957—. Mem. S.C. Ho. of Reps., 1937-40, S.C. Senate, 1941-52. Trustee U. S.C., 1937-48. Recipient certificate of commendation for outstanding service to agrl. marketing in S.C., Clemson Coll. and State Agrl. Marketing Commn., 1960. Mem. Am., S.C., Greenville County (pres. 1957) bar assns., Am. Judicature Soc. Baptist. Home: 110 Vannoy St Greenville SC 29601 Office: 513 E Washington St Greenville SC 29601

WILLIAMS, RICHARD ROGER, JR., educator; b. Marshall, Tex., May 5, 1917; s. Richard Roger and Odessa (Herron) W.; B.S., Wiley Coll., 1941; M.S., U. Mich., 1950, postgrad., summers 1951-54, 57-58 (spl. grad. fellow Danforth Found.); postgrad. (Ford Found. grantee) North Tex. State U., summers 1970-71; m. Bernice Lewis, May 17, 1947 (dec. Aug. 1956); 1 son, Richard R. III (dec.); m. 2d, Artie Mosley Price Bennett, Aug. 22, 1957; 1 dau., Kim Aletta Williams; stepchildren—Freddie, Shirley, Teresa. Tchr. math. Galillee High Sch., Hallsville, Tex., 1941-43; instr. math. Wiley Coll., Marshall, 1946-61, asso. prof., 1961-72, chmn. dept. math., 1950-69, chmn. div. natural sci. and math., 1953-58, coordinator div., 1962-69, chmn. Tchr. Edn. Council, 1964-70, bus. mgr., 1969-72, prof. math., 1972—. Ofcl. rep. Am. Assn. Colls. Tchr. Edn. Sustaining mem. East Tex. Area Council Boy Scouts Am. Served with USMCR, 1943-46. Mem. Am. Math. Soc., Am. Assn. U. Profs., Math. Assn. Am., Nat. Inst. Sci., Am. Assn. Sch. Adminstrs., Nat., So. assns. coll. and univ. bus. officers, Beta Kappa Chi, Phi Beta Sigma. Methodist. Co-author: College Algebra, 1956, rev. 1963. Home: 1809 Gatewood St Marshall TX 75670

WILLIAMS, ROBERT EMBERRY, ins. co. exec.; b. Corsicana, Tex., Oct. 9, 1923; s. Robert Henry and Ida Eunice (Honea) W.; B.B.A., So. Meth. U., 1956, M.B.A., 1963; m. Peggy Joyce Bolton, Dec. 23, 1945; children—Richard Dale, Patricia (Mrs. Kenneth Roy Cobler). Enlisted USN, 1946; adminstr., instr. various schs.; ret., 1963; v.p. personnel and tng. Zale Corp., Dallas, 1963-70; dir. human resources Blue Cross-Blue Shield, Dallas, 1970—. Lectr., Dallas County Jr. Coll., 1966-67, Am. Mgmt. Assn. Active United Fund; sponsor Williams award ann. grant to top grad. CPO Acad. USN, Pensacola, Fla., 1968-71; mem. So. Meth. U. Career Hall of Fame. Served with AUS, 1942-45. Mem. Dallas Personnel Assn. (pres. 1973-74), Dallas Retail Personnel Assn. (pres. 1967-68), Am. Soc. Personnel Adminstrn., Sigma Iota Epsilon. Club: North Texas Travel Trailer (pres. 1968). Home: 2018 Cooper Dr Irving TX 75061 Office: 2201 Main St Dallas TX 75201

WILLIAMS, ROBERT MAXWELL, engring. services co. exec.; b. Frostburg, Md., Jan. 10, 1912; s. James Garfield and Myrtle Nina (Davis) W.; student Gen. Motors Inst. Tech., 1930-34; m. Mary Jane Giffin, Aug. 10, 1935; children—Thomas Allan, Linda (Mrs. Frank Leeming). Engr., Gen. Motors Corp., Detroit, 1934-44; chief engr. aviation engine div. Packard Motor Co., Toledo, 1944-48; head engr. Sverdrup & Parcel, Inc., engrs. and architects, St. Louis, 1949-52, asst. to pres., 1952-54; mng. dir. ARO, Inc., Tullahoma, Tenn., 1954-62, pres., 1963—; v.p. Sverdrup & Parcel & Assos., St. Louis, 1962—; dir. 1st Nat. Bank Tullahoma. Dist. chmn. Middle Tenn. council Boy Scouts Am., 1960-71. Asso. fellow Am. Inst. Aeros. and Astronautics; mem. Am. Soc. M.E., Soc. Automotive Engrs., Am. Soc. Metals, Nat. Soc. Profl. Engrs., Tau Beta Pi, Alpha Tau Iota. Mason, Rotarian. Pioneer work in design first Am. turbo-fan engine, 1948. Home: Route 1 Manchester TN 37355 Office: ARO Inc Arnold AFB TN 37389

WILLIAMS, ROGER DAVIS, surgeon; b. Charlotte, N.C., May 26, 1924; s. Edward Eugene and Lucy C. (Davis) W.; B.S., Duke, 1947, M.D., 1947; M.S., Ohio State U., 1951; m. Martha Jeanne Wiedeman, Sept. 7, 1957; children—Diana Lynn, Roger D., George Monroe. Intern, Duke Hosp., 1947-48; resident Ohio State U. Hosps., 1949-54; asst. prof., asso. prof. Ohio State U., 1955-61, prof. surgery, 1961-65; prof. surgery, chmn. dept. surgery U. Tex., Galveston, 1965-67; practice medicine specializing in surgery, Ft. Lauderdale, Fla., 1968—; mem. staff Broward Gen. Med. Center; clin. prof. surgery U. Miami, Fla., 1968—. Mem. adv. group Easter Seal Found., Ft. Lauderdale, 1969—. Bd. dirs. Am. Cancer Soc., Broward County, Fla. Served with USNR, 1952-53. Decorated Bronze Star medal. Mem. Am., Western, Central Surg. assns., Soc. Univ. Surgeons, Am. Assn. Surgery Trauma, Am. Gastroent. Assn., Soc. Surgery Alimentary Tract. Contbr. articles to profl. jours. Home: 2211 SE 20th St Fort Lauderdale FL 33316 Office: 500 SE 17th St Suite 201 Fort Lauderdale FL 33316

WILLIAMS, ROGER JOHN, chemist; b. Ootacumund, India, Aug. 14, 1893 (parents Am. Citizens); s. Robert Runnels and Alice Evelyn (Mills) W.; B.S., U. Redlands, 1914, D.Sc., 1934; postgrad. U. Cal., 1914-15; M.S., U. Chgo., 1918, Ph.D., 1919; D.Sc., Columbia, 1942, Ore. State Coll., 1956; m. Hazel Elizabeth Wood, Aug. 1, 1916 (dec. 1952); children—Roger John, Janet, Arnold; m. 2d, Mabel Phyllis Hobson, May 9, 1953; 1 son (by previous marriage), John W. Hobson. Research chemist Fleischmann Co., Chgo., 1919-20; asst. prof. chemistry U. Ore., 1920-21, asso. prof., 1921-28, prof., 1928-32; prof. chemistry Ore. State Coll., 1932-39, U. Tex., Austin, 1939—; dir. Clayton Found., Biochem. Inst. Tex., 1941-63. Recipient Mead-Johnson award Am. Inst. Nutrition, 1941; Chandler medal Columbia U., 1942. Fellow A.A.A.S.; mem. Am. Chem. Soc. (pres. 1957, S.W. Region award 1950), Am. Soc. Biol. Chemists, Am. Assn. for Cancer Research, Soc. Exptl. Biology and Medicine, Nat., N.Y. acads. scis., Biochem. Soc. London, Phi Beta Kappa, Sigma Xi, Phi Kappa Phi, Phi Sigma, Pi Kappa Delta, Phi Lambda Upsilon. Methodist. Author or co-author books relating to chemistry, latest being: The Biochemistry of B Vitamins (with R. E. Eakin, E. Beerstecher, W. Shive), 1950; Nutrition and Alcoholism, 1951; Free and Unequal, 1953; Biochemical Individuality, 1956; Alcoholism: The Nutritional Approach, 1959; Nutrition in a Nutshell, 1962, You Are Extraordinary, 1967; Nutrition against Disease, 1971. Discoverer pantothenic acid; also made microbiol. study of vitamins, individual metabolic patterns. Office: Clayton Found Biochem Inst U Tex Austin TX 78712

WILLIAMS, SAM HENRY, bank dir.; b. San Augustine, Tex., Jan. 15, 1915; s. Sam Sterling and Jennie Eugene (Henry) W.; student Stephen Austin Coll., 1933; m. Wilda David, Nov. 25, 1943; children—Virginia Ann (Mrs. James Scogin), Bonnie Blue, David S. Salesman, Frito Co., Leesville and Lake Charles, La., 1946-62; pres. Williams Transp. & Storage, Leesville, Lake Charles, 1952—; dir. Mchts. & Farmers Bank, Leesville, 1967—. Mgr. theatre, Leesville, 1946-48; mail contract delivery, 1942-64; pres. Farm Equipment, Inc., 1964—, Am. Moving & Storage, 1968—, Gen. Maintenance & Constrn. Inc., all Leesville, 1968—; owner, operators farms Leesville, La., 1955—, San Augustine, 1954—; owner So. Moving & Storage Co., La. Transfer Co., S.W. Transfer Co., City Transfer Co., Sunshine Transfer Co. Mem. Pub. Affairs Research Council La., C. of C. Democrat. Roman Catholic. K.C., Mason (K.T.). Home: Texas Rd Leesville LA 71446 Office: 301 N 3d Rd Leesville LA 71446 also 202 Stanton Rd New Llano LA

WILLIAMS, SQUIRE NEEDHAM, JR., lawyer; b. Frenchburg, Ky., Nov. 8, 1917; s. Squire Needham and Mary Lee (Spencer) W.; student Berea Coll., 1935-36; A.B., U. Ky., 1939, LL.B., 1942; m. Doris Ellen Macauley, Aug. 24, 1946; children—Janice Lee, Laura Macauley, Kathryn Doris, Squire Needham III. Admitted to Ky. bar, 1942; practiced in Lexington, Ky., 1945-46, Frankfort, Ky., 1955-59, 69—; atty. War Assets Adminstrn., 1947; asst. atty. gen. Commonwealth of Ky., 1948-55; Franklin County judge pro tem and trial commr., 1956-57; spl. circuit judge, 1957-59; judge, chief justice Ct. Appeals Ky., 1959-69. Served as aviator USNR, 1942-45. Mem. Am., Ky. bar assns., V.F.W. Democrat. Presbyn. (elder). Club: Frankfort Country (dir.). Home: 120 W Todd St Frankfort KY 40601 Office: 405 McClure Bldg Frankfort KY 40601

WILLIAMS, STAFFORD HOYT, JR., mech. engr.; b. nr. Grundy, Va., Dec. 27, 1939; s. Stafford Hoyt and Alma Gluck (Pettit) W.; B.S., Va. Poly. Inst., 1962, M.S., 1965; m. Lucretia Dawneda Fowler, Dec. 21, 1961; children—Lucretia Gay, Stafford Hoyt III. Jr. engr. Balt. Gas & Electric Co., summer 1962; project engr. U.S. Air Force Research and Tech. div., Wright-Patterson AFB, O., 1964-67; cons. engr., v.p. charge civil engring. Thompson & Litton, engrs., architects, surveyors and planners, Wise, Va., 1967—; dir. Toliad Properties, Inc. Served from 2d lt. to 1st lt. USAF, 1964-67. Mem. Nat. Soc. Profl. Engrs. (chpt. pres.), Am. Soc. Heating, Refrigeration and Air Conditioning Engrs., Cons. Engrs. Council, Pi Tau Sigma. Mem. Ch. of Christ. Home: PO Box 548 Wise VA 24293 Office: PO Box 1307 Wise VA 24293

WILLIAMS, STEFAN FREEMAN, pub. housing mgr.; b. Alderson, W.Va., May 16, 1939; s. Charles Bliss and Florence Edith (Freeman) W.; grad. Allegheny Coll., 1960; postgrad. Am. U.; m. Beverly Joan Payne, June 19, 1958; children—Stefan Kraig, Alan Bliss, Christopher Martin, Jeffrey Todd. Youth work YMCA, 1952-59; youth counselor

D.C. Dept. Pub. Welfare, 1960-65; mgr. Carl Wilson, Inc., 1965-66; mgmt. aide Nat. Capital Housing Authority, Washington, 1966-68, housing mgr., 1968—. Mem. Council Exceptional Children, U.S., D.C., Capital Hill (nat. dir. 1971-72) jr. chmbers commerce. Episcopalian. Home: 1716 16th St SE Washington DC 20020 Office: 2101 G St NE Washington DC 20002

WILLIAMS, STIRLING BACOT, JR., ednl. adminstr.; b. Memphis, Mar. 28, 1943; s. Stirling Bacot and Mary Virginia (Kendrick) W.; B.A. magna cum laude, U. Miss., 1965, M.Ed., 1966, Ed.D., 1968. Tchr. city schs. Memphis, 1966-67, adminstr., 1968—, asst. prin. Overton High Sch., 1969-74; vice prin. Briarcrest Bapt. High Sch., 1974—; instr. edn. U. Miss., 1967-68; Cons. to various sch. systems; spl. cons. plant mgmt. project Miss. Dept. Edn., 1967-68. Mem. West Tenn. chpt. Arthritis Found. Mem. Am. Assn. Sch. Adminstrs., Nat. Assn. Secondary Sch. Prins., Kappa Delta Pi, Phi Delta Kappa. Baptist (mem. financial planning com. child devel. center 1971-72). Author of various books including Student Activities in the Innovative School, 1969. Contbr. to profl. publs. in field. Home: 3536 Acacia Dr Memphis TN 38116 Office: 842 Sweetbriar Rd Memphis TN 38117

WILLIAMS, T. HARRY, historian, educator, author; b. Vinegar Hill, Ill., May 19, 1909; s. William D. and Emma (Necollins) W.; B.E., Platteville (Wis.) State Tchrs. Coll., 1931; Ph.M., U. Wis., 1932, Ph.D., 1937. Instr. extension div. U. Wis., 1936-38; instr. W.Va. U., summer 1937; instr. and asst. prof. U. Omaha, 1938-41; mem. faculty La. State U., Baton Rouge, 1941—, prof. history, 1948-53, Boyd prof. history, 1953—; Guggenheim fellow, 1957; Harmsworth prof. Am. history Queen's Coll., Oxford (Eng.) U., 1966-67. Mem. hist. adv. com. Dept. of Army, 1955-60. Recipient Lincoln Diploma of Honor, Lincoln Meml. U., 1956, Nat. Book award for history, biography, 1969, Pulitzer Prize, 1969, La. Lit. award, 1969. Mem. Am. Assn. U. Profs., Am. Mil. Inst., Civil War Centennial Assn. (dir.), Soc. Am. Historians, Am., So. (v.p. 1957-58, pres. 1958-59), Mississippi Valley (exec. com. 1955) hist. assns., Orgn. Am. Historians (pres. 1972-73). Author: Lincoln and the Radicals, 1941; Lincoln and His Generals, 1952; P.G.T. Beauregard, 1955; The Union Sundered, 1963; The Union Restored, 1963. Editor: Selected Writings and Speeches of Abraham Lincoln, 1943; With Beauregard in Mexico, 1956; Abraham Lincoln—Selected Speeches, Messages and Letters, 1957; (with others) A History of the United States, 1959; Americans at War, 1960; Romance and Realism in Southern Politics, 1961; Military Memoris of a Confederate by E. Porter Alexander, 1962; McClellan, Sherman and Grant, 1962; Every Man a King, 1964; Hayes: The Diary of a President, 1964; Hayes of the Twenty-third; The Civil War Volunteer Officer, 1965; Huey Long, 1969. Home: 353 Nelson Dr Baton Rouge LA 70808

WILLIAMS, THOMAS EARL, lawyer; b. Corsicana, Tex., Oct. 21, 1924; s. William Archie and Mildred (Gammill) W.; student Tex. A. and M. U., 1942, 43, 46, N. Tex. State U., 1942, Kan. State Coll., 1943; LL.B., Baylor U., 1954, J.D., 1969; m. Johnnie Frances Reynolds, Nov. 10, 1948; children—Stephen Earl, Randolph Walling, Cynthia Ann, Daniel Zachary. Adjuster, Farm Bur. Ins. Co., Waco, Tex., 1954-56, State Farm Ins. Co., McKinney, Tex., 1957; admitted to Tex. bar, 1955; asst. county atty., McKinney, Tex., 1957-60; criminal dist. atty., McKinney, 1960-64; asst. dist. atty., Dallas, 1963-64; practiced in Athens, Tex., 1965—; city atty. Athens, 1967—. Organizer, Amigos Internacionales Corp., 1967—. Served with USAAF, 1943-48; served to 2d lt. AUS, 1948-50. Mem. State Bar of Tex., Am., Henderson County bar assns., Am. Judicature Soc., C. of C. (dir. 1967—). Baptist. Mason (32 deg.). Home: 900 Ward Lane Athens TX 75751 Office: f207 E Corsicana St PO Box 28 Athens TX 75751

WILLIAMS, THOMAS FRASIER, JR., lawyer; b. Washington, Feb. 15, 1939; s. Thomas Frasier and Rachael Victoria (Honeycutt) W.; B.A., Hampden-Sydney Coll., 1962; LL.B., U. Richmond, 1965; m. Elizabeth Archer Cassada, Aug. 11, 1962; children—Elizabeth Carey, Thomas Keller. Admitted to Va. bar, 1965; mem. firm Franklin, Williams and Cowan, and predecessor firm, Fredericksburg, Va., 1965—. Tchr. law course Am. Inst. Banking, 1966-67. Chmn. Fredericksburg Heart Fund, 1966-67. Bd. dirs. New Sch., Salvation Army, Fredericksburg Day Care Center. Mem. Va. State, Fredericksburg bar assns., Va. State Bar, Fredericksburg Area (dir.) Fredericksburg Jr. (pres. 1970-71, Distinguished Service award 1974) chambers commerce. Episcopalian (sr. warden 1973—). Club: Va. Reel Men's (sec. 1973-74) (Fredericksburg). Home: Fredericksburg VA 22401 Office: 321 William St Fredericksburg VA 22401

WILLIAMS, THOMAS STANLEY, packaging mfg. co. exec.; b. Evanston, Ill., Sept. 18, 1919; s. Thomas Samuel and Bertha Ella (Zander) W.; B.S., Tex. A. and M. U., 1941; m. Ethel Naomi Boutwell, June 4, 1941; children—T. Samuel, Gretchen (Mrs. William E. Dunn), Molly (Mrs. David Keebler), Trudi Zander. Pres., gen. mgr. Superior Decals, Inc., Dallas, 1942-48; with Dixico, Inc., Dallas, 1948—, sr. v.p. operations, 1957-64, chmn. exec. com., 1964—; pres. Bancook Maintenance Co., Dallas, 1961-72. Mem. Bd. Edn. Dallas Ind. Sch. Dist., 1971—. Mem. Tex. exec. com. Republican party, 1967-69. Trustee Meth. Hosp. Dallas, C.C. Young Meml. Home, Dallas, Denton Wesley Found., N. Tex. State U. and Tex. Womens U. Served with F.A., AUS, 1941-42. Mem. Flexographic Tech. Assn. Methodist. Mason (Shriner, 32 deg.), Lion. Address: 1024 Knott Pl Dallas TX 75208

WILLIAMS, THOMAS THACKERY, educator; b. Roanoke Rapids, N.C., Mar. 13, 1925; s. George W. and Eliza (Falcon) W.; B.S., N.C. Agrl. and Tech. Coll., 1948; M.S., U. Ill., 1949; Ph.D., Ohio State U., 1955; diploma Case Inst. Tech., 1957; m. Evelyn Moore, Dec. 26, 1952; children—Donna Jean, Thomas Thackery. Asst. dean agr. Tuskegee Inst. (Ala.), 1949-52; mem. faculty So. U., Baton Rouge, 1955—, prof. agrl. econs., 1966—, dir. research and devel., 1967—. Cons. numerous govt. agys.; vis. Fulbright prof. Coll. Agr., Malaysia, 1967; vis. lectr. Interam. Center, Loyola U., New Orleans, 1966—. Found. for Econ. fellow, 1961; Danforth asso., 1963-67. Mem. So. Consumers Coop. (v.p. 1964-66). Home: 2857 77th Av Baton Rouge LA 70807

WILLIAMS, TURNER NELSON, JR., dairy exec.; b. Buena Vista, Ga., May 12, 1920; s. Turner Nelson and Etta (Lowe) W.; B.S., Auburn U., 1940; m. Winifred Greene, Nov. 11, 1944; children—Robert G., Mary, Susan E., Turner Nelson III. Tchr. vocational agr. Marion County High Sch., Buena Vista, Ga., 1946-51; operator Williams Dairy Farm, Ellaville, Ga., 1952—; dir. Wells Dairies Cooperative, Columbus, Ga., 1958—, sec.-treas., 1969—. Owner, mgr. ind. ins. agy., Ellaville, 1957—; dir. Ga. div. Dairymen, Inc., Atlanta, Ga. Milk Producers, Inc. Mem. Schley County Bd. Registrars, 1964-69, chmn., 1972—; chmn. Schley County Bd. Tax Assessors, 1960-70, mem., 1970—; chmn. Schley County Bd. Health, 1969—. Served to 1st lt. 101st Airborne Div., AUS, 1941-46. Mem. Am. Legion. Methodist. Home: Route 2 Ellaville GA 31806 Office: PO Box 404 Ellaville GA 31806

WILLIAMS, TYLER EDWARD, JR., financial mgmt. exec.; b. Chgo., July 10, 1926; s. Tyler Edward and Anne (Salmon) W.; B.S., Ill. Inst. Tech., 1951, M.S., 1956; postgrad. U. Ia.; M.Ed. (Fed. Career Exec. fellow) U. Va., 1972; m. Frances M. Reif, Aug. 27, 1949; children—Tyler Edward III, Michael, Thomas, Margaret, Gerard, Joseph (dec.), John, Mary. Dept. supr. Oscar Mayer & Co., Chgo., 1949-52; indsl. engr. Am. Gage & Machine Co., Chgo., 1952-54; sr. indsl. engr. Bendix Aviation Corp., Davenport, Ia., 1954-55; engr., engring. exec. Ordnance Corps, U.S. Army, Rock Island Arsenal (Ill.), 1955-63, Office Mgmt. and Orgn., Office Sec. Commerce, Washington, 1963-65; with Office Comptroller Army, Washington, 1965-71, dep. dir. budget and manpower Safeguard System Office, Office Chief of Staff, Dept. Army, 1971-73; with Office Sec. Def., 1973—. Served to capt. USNR, 1944—. Registered profl. engr., Ia., Ind. Mem. Am. Soc. Mil. Comptrollers, Am. Soc. Engring. Edn., A.A.A.S., Council Basic Edn., Am. Inst. Indsl. Engrs., Washington Operations Research Soc. Author articles in field. Home: 3312 Prince William Dr Fairfax VA 22030 Office: Office Dep Asst Sec Def Washington DC 20301

WILLIAMS, VICK F(RANKLIN), anatomist; b. Pittsburg, Tex., Apr. 30, 1936; s. Vernon Guinn and Eula (Vick) W.; B.A., Austin Coll., 1958; M.D., U. Tex. Med. Br., 1964, Ph.D., 1964; m. Dorothy Jean Rodina, June 23, 1962; children—Dorothy Jean, Sarah Ellen. Intern in pathology, Charity Hosp. La., New Orleans, 1964-65; instr. in anatomy U. Tex. Southwestern Med. Sch., Dallas, 1965-67, asst. prof. anatomy, 1967-70; asso. prof. anatomy U. Tex. Dental Sch. and U. Tex. Med. Sch., San Antonio, 1970-73; asso. prof. anatomy U. Tex. Health Sci. Center, San Antonio, 1973—. Recipient Borden award for undergrad. research, 1964. Mem. A.A.A.S., Am. Assn. Anatomists, Am. Soc. for Cell Biology, Electron Microscopy Soc. Am., Cajal Club, Nu Sigma Nu, Sigma Xi. Presbyn. Office: 7703 Floyd Curl Dr San Antonio TX 78284

WILLIAMS, VOLIE ADKINS, JR., judge; b. Sanford, Fla., Jan. 10, 1920; s. Volie Adkins and Mary Elizabeth (Miller) W.; Asso. Sci., Marion Inst., 1938-40; LL.B., Stetson U., 1948; m. Constance Lott, Sept. 5, 1946; children—James Lang, Patricia Lee, Penelope, Donald Neal. Admitted to bar, 1948; spl. asst. Atty. Gen. Fla., 1949; mem. Fla. Ho. of Reps., 1950-55; asst. state atty., 1955-57; judge 18th Circuit Ct., Sanford, Fla., 1957—. Served as capt. USAAF, 1944-46; PTO. Decorated Air medal. Mem. Phi Alpha Delta, Sigma Nu. Democrat. Presbyn. Mason (Shriner). Home: 1203 Washington Dr Sanford FL 32771 Office: Brevard County Courthouse Titusville FL 32780 also Seminole County Courthouse Sanford FL 32771

WILLIAMS, WALKER ALONZO, ret. automobile co. exec.; b. Wellington, Mo., June 8, 1901; s. Henry A. and Helen (Walker) W.; student Kan. City Sch. Law, evenings 1921, Kansas City Jr. Coll., evenings, 1921, U. Ill., 1922-23; m. Evelyn Forrester, Sept. 25, 1926; children—Walker Forrester, John Haviland. With traffic dept. Armour Grain Co., Kansas City, Mo., 1920-22; with accounting dept. Am. Can Co., Kansas City, 1924-25; with Kansas City br., Ford Motor Co., 1925-34, asst. br. mgr., Omaha, 1934-39, Kansas City, 1939-41, br. mgr., Salt Lake City, 1941-42, 44-45, Somerville, Mass., 1945-46, Ford sales mgr., Dearborn, Mich., 1946-48, gen. sales mgr. Ford div., 1948-50, v.p. sales and advt. for parent co., 1950-56, v.p., vice chmn. dealer policy bd. for parent co., 1956-58, v.p. parent co., asst. gen. mgr. Lincoln-Mercury div., 1958-61; bus. mgr. Kalunite, Inc., Salt Lake City, 1942-44; ret., 1961. Former mem. Nat. Highway Users Conf. Chmn. Mich. Crusade for Freedom, 1951-52; former mem. Detroit Mayor's Rapid Transit Commn., Detroit Bd. Commerce. Former bd. dirs., gen. chmn. United Found. Detroit; former bd. dirs. Automobile Safety Found. mem. Fla. Atlantic Music Guild, Opera Guild Ft. Lauderdale, Friends of City Center (N.Y.C.), DeMolay Legion of Honor, Phi Gamma Delta. Clubs: Detroit Athletic; Royal Palm Yacht and Country, Boca Raton Hotel and Club (Boca Raton, Fla.); Vermilion Fairways Golf (Cook, Minn.). Home: 1355 Fan Palm Rd Boca Raton FL 33432

WILLIAMS, WALTER ROLLIN, III, educator; b. Norwood, O., Oct. 2, 1933; s. Walter Rollin and Helen Horton (Coons) W.; student Fla. So. Coll., 1953, Fla. State U., 1956; B.S. in Edn., U. Fla., 1955, M.Ed., 1959; Ed.D., U. Md., 1963; m. Janice Louise Southerland, June 16, 1955; children—Walter Rollin IV, David Southerland. Tchr., Leon High Sch., Tallahassee, 1955-56, Rockville (Md.) Jr. High Sch., 1961-62; faculty indsl. edn. Ga. So. Coll., Statesboro, 1962-66; prof., head dept. indsl. edn. Morehead (Ky.) State U., 1966-67; prof., chmn. dept. indsl. edn. E. Tenn. State U., Johnson City, 1967—. Served with USNR, 1956-57. Danforth asso., 1965—. Mem. Tenn. (pres. 1970-71), Am. (Peace Corps rep. 1964-66) indsl. arts assns., Tenn. Edn. Assn. (v.p. 1972-73, pres. dept. higher edn. 1972-73), Am. Council Elementary Sch. Indsl. Arts (sec. 1966), Southeastern Indsl. Arts Conf. (pres. 1967-68), Epsilon Pi Tau (vice chmn. bd. dirs. 1968—), Phi Kappa Phi, Kappa Delta Pi, Phi Delta Kappa, Iota Lambda Sigma. Methodist (chmn. adminstrv. bd. 1972—). Contbr. articles to profl. jours. Home: 1510 Crystal Springs Dr Johnson City TN 37601

WILLIAMS, WALTER WAYLON, lawyer; b. Gause, Tex., Nov. 12, 1933; s. Jesse Nathaniel and Lola Fay (Matthews) W.; B.B.A. with honors, U. Tex. at Austin, 1959, J.D. with honors, 1960; m. Velmalene Von Gonten, Mar. 6, 1953; children—Diana Lee, Virginia Marie. Admitted to Tex. Bar, 1960; since practiced in Houston; mem. firm Fulbright Crooker, Freeman, Bates & Jaworski, 1960-63, Bates & Brock, 1964-66, Brock & Williams, 1966—. Served with AUS, 1953-55. Named Outstanding Soldier of Second Army, 1955. Mem. Am., Houston bar assns., State Bar Tex., Tex. (dir. 1972—), Houston (dir. 1969) trial lawyers assns., Assn. Trial Lawyers Am., Beta Gamma Sigma, Phi Delta Phi, Chancellors. Home: 9607 Meadowglen St Houston TX 77042 Office: 1212 Main St Houston TX 77002

WILLIAMS, WINTON HUGH, civil engr.; b. Tampa, Fla., Feb. 14, 1920; s. Herbert DeMain and Alice (Grant) W.; student U. Tampa, 1948; B.C.E., U. Fla., 1959; grad. U.S. Army Res. Asso. Command and Gen. Staff Coll., Ft. Leavenworth, U.S. Army Logistics Mgmt. Center; m. Elizabeth Walser Seelye, Dec. 18, 1949; children—Jan, Dick, Bill, Ann. Constrn. engr. air fields C.E., U.S. Army, McCoy AFB, Fla., 1959-61, Homestead AFB, Miami, Fla., 1961-62; civil engr. C.E., Jacksonville (Fla.) Dist. Office, 1962-65, chief master planning and layout sect., 1965-70; chief master planning and real estate div. Office of Engr. Hdqrs. USARSO, Ft. Clayton, C.Z., 1970—. Troop com. chmn. Boy Scouts Am., Explorer Scouts, Curundu, C.Z. Served with U.S. Army, World War II, Korean War; ETO, Korea; col. Res. Decorated Breast Order of Yun Hi (Republic China); presdl. citation (Republic Korea). Registered profl. engr., Fla., Panama, C.Z., Republic Panama. Mem. Nat. Soc. Profl. Engrs., Am. Soc. C.E., Fla. Engring. Soc., Prestressed Concrete Inst., Res. Officers Assn. (v.p. chpt.), Soc. Am. Mil. Engrs., U. Tampa Alumni Assn. (nat. council), Theta Chi. Presbyn. (bd. ushers). Lion (dir., scouting instl. rep.). Clubs: Fort Clayton Riding, Gamboa Golf and Country. Home: Box 771 Curundu CZ Office: Office of the Engineer Ft Clayton Canal Zone

WILLIAMS, WOODROW ALLEN, electronics engr.; b. Jackson, Miss., Dec. 12, 1943; s. Austin Woodrow and Dorothy Alice (Brooks) W.; B.E.E., Auburn (Ala.) U., 1969; m. Linda Lee Cates, Oct. 21, 1966; children—Brian Allen, Eric Lee. Student trainee engring. Army Missile Command, Research and Engring. Propulsion Directorate, Redstone Arsenal, Ala., 1963-69, electronics engr., 1969-70, electronics engr.-instrumentation, 1970-73, research electronics engr., 1973—. Named Outstanding I.E.E.E. grad. Auburn U., 1969. Registered profl. engr., Ala. Mem. I.E.E.E., Instrument Soc. Am. (sect. pres., dir. Scholarship Fund for N.Ala. High Sch. Grads., Huntsville sect.), Nat., Ala. socs. profl. engrs., Assn. U.S. Army, Auburn U. Alumni Assn. Baptist. Mason. Home: 509 Harolds Dr Huntsville AL 35806 Office: AMSMI-RKM Bldg 7120 Redstone Arsenal AL 35809

WILLIAMSON, DEFOREST ROY, elec. engr.; b. East Point, Ga., June 16, 1923; s. Roy DeForest and Emma (Parham) W.; B.E.E., Ga. Inst. Tech., 1948; m. Loveniar Almand, Aug. 31, 1946; children—Bruce, Brent. Engr., So. Bell Co., Atlanta, 1949-50; sr. draftsman Ga. Power Co., Atlanta, 1951-55, design engr., 1956-68, project engr. 1969—. Served with C.E., AUS, 1943-46; PTO. Named Ga. Power Co. Engr. of Year, 1970. Mem. I.E.E.E., Ga. Power Co. Engring. Assn. Home: 2442 Plantation Dr East Point GA 30044 Office: Georgia Power Co PO Box 4545 Atlanta GA 30302

WILLIAMSON, HAROLD LAMAR, furniture co. exec.; b. Cordele, Ga,, June 7, 1925; s. Felix Drewry and Ida Florence (Bryan) W.; student Emory U., 1947-48; B.B.A. in Accounting, U. Ga., 1951; m. June Malcom, Apr. 15, 1950; children—Harold Lamar, Malcolm B. Asst. sales mgr. Simmons Co., Atlanta, 1948-57; v.p. Helmly's Furniture Co., Orlando, Fla., 1958-73, Clearwater, Fla., 1960-73, Tampa, Fla., 1962-73, pres., 1973—, also dir. Served with AUS, 1944-46. Mem. Lambda Chi Alpha. Presbyn. Clubs: Winter Park (Fla.) Racquet; University, Citrus (Orlando). Home: 81 Oakleigh Dr Maitland FL 32751 Office: 1028 E Altamonte Dr Altamonte Springs FL 32701

WILLIAMSON, JOHN ALEXANDER, computer co. exec.; b. Birmingham, Ala., Feb. 5, 1918; s. John Kelly and Mary (Lee) W.; A.B., Birmingham-So. Coll., 1939; m. Jean Cochran, Feb. 14, 1948; children—John, Alexander, Linda Sue, Margaret Lee. Mem. parts dept. Gen. Motors Corp., Birmingham, 1935-39, dist. mgr. motor div. Chevrolet, Birmingham, 1945-47; salesman Drennen Motor Co., Birmingham, 1939-40, sales mgr., 1947-56; pres. John Williamson & Assos., mgmt. cons., Birmingham, 1956—; chmn. bd. Computerized Automotive Reporting Service, Inc., Birmingham, 1964—; pres. Key Real Estate & Investment Co., 1960—. Bd. dirs. Birmingham Boys' Club, 1964—; chmn. bd. dirs. New Methodist Hosp., 1967—. Served to capt. USNR, 1940-46, 50-52. Decorated Legion of Merit, Silver Star. Methodist. Clubs: The Club, Birmingham Country. Home: 3012 N Woodridge Rd Birmingham AL 35223 Office: 12 Office Park Circle Birmingham AL 35223

WILLIAMSON, JOHN HENRY, JR., dentist; b. Henrietta, Tex., Sept. 26, 1919; s. John Henry and Zelma (Grimes) W.; B.S., U. Tex., 1942, D.D.S., 1945; m. Marian Irene Broussard, June 20, 1955; 1 son, John Henry III. Asst. mgr. Walgreens, Houston, 1942; instr. U. Tex., 1945-46; pvt. practice dentistry, Galveston, Tex., 1946—. Chmn. adv. com. Galveston Community Coll. Dental Hygiene Sch. Mem. adv. bd. Rainbow Girls. Fellow Am. Coll. Dentists; mem. 9th Dist. Dental Soc. (pres. 1951), Am. Dental Assn., Galveston C. of C., Psi Omega. Baptist. Mason (Shriner). Club: Exchange (Galveston). Home: 27 Colony Park Circle Galveston TX 77550 Office: 1025 25th St Galveston TX 77550

WILLIAMSON, WILLIAM THOMAS, advt. co. exec.; b. Lakeland, Fla., Oct. 24, 1925; s. William Richter and Florence Elizabeth (Bellwood) W.; student Pa. Acad. Fine Arts, 1945-49; m. Edna Pauline Pledger, June 17, 1950; children—Mary Margaret, William Campbell. Artist, Miller & Rhoads, Richmond, Va., 1949-51; layout artist Hecht Co., Washington, 1951-53; designer Kal, Ehrlich & Merrick, Washington, 1953-62, art dir., 1962-68; art dir. Ehrlich, Linkins & Assos., Washington, 1968-69, v.p., 1969-73; v.p., exec. art dir. Ehrlich, Harris, Manes & Assos., Inc., Washington, 1973—. Served with USMCR, 1943-45. Mem. Nat. Symphony Orch. Assn. Home: 2419 N Kenmore St Arlington VA 22207 Office: 4901 Fairmont Av NW Washington DC 20014

WILLIG, BILLY WINSTON, machine shop, foundry exec.; b. Temple, Tex., Mar. 3, 1929; s. Bruno William and Mary (Barth) W.; student San Angelo Jr. Coll., 1946-47; B.S. in Mech. Engring., U. Tex., 1951; m. Lanelle Brooks, Sept. 11, 1951; children—Bruce Wayne, Jana Lynn. With Western Iron Works, San Angelo, Tex., 1951—, gen. mgr., pres., chmn. bd., 1971—. Skipper, Sea Scout Ship 22, Boy Scouts Am., 1965—; chmn. Lake Nasworthy Adv. Bd., 1968-70, Area Environmental Council, 1973, 74—. Trustee San Angelo Ind. Sch. Dist., 1966—, v.p., 1969, 72, sec., treas., 1968, 71, 73; Bd. dirs. San Angelo Govtl. Computer Center, San Angelo Industries. Served with C.E., AUS, 1952-54. Mem. Tex. Mfrs. Assn., Am. Foundry Soc. Presbyn. (deacon, elder, clk. session 1968-71). Mason (Shriner), Rotarian (sec. San Angelo 1973-74). Club: Concho Yacht (past commodore San Angelo). Home: 1618 Shafter St San Angelo TX 76901 Office: 21 E 6th St San Angelo TX 76901

WILLIMON, EDWARD LLOYD, architect, educator; b. Florence, S.C., June 8, 1919; s. Walter Eugene and Lee Oliver (Gregg) W.; B.S., Clemson U., 1942; M.S., Columbia, 1947; M.S., So. Meth. U., 1970; m. Janette Sims, June 20, 1943; children—Laura, Vicki, Mary, Jenny. Archtl. draftsman George Christensen, Architect, 1948-50; self-employed as architect, Dallas, 1950—; asst. prof. geology Bishop Coll., Dallas, 1961—. Served with AUS, 1942-46. Mem. Am. Assn. U. Profs., Paleontol. Soc., Nat. Assn. Geology Tchrs., A.I.A., A.A.A.S., Am. Legion (comdr. 1949-51), Tex. Acad. Sci., Oak Cliff Gem and Mineral Soc. Prin. archtl. works include Brass Craft Western, Lancaster, Tex., Tex. Color Printers, Dallas, Nat. Chemsearch Corp., Irving, Tex. Home: 4137 Fortune Lane Dallas TX 75216 Office: 2450 N Beckley Lancaster TX 75146

WILLIS, BENJAMIN CAWTHON, circuit judge; b. Quincy, Fla., Oct. 7, 1913; s. Lee Lawrence and Etta (Bell) W.; student Emory U., 1930-32; LL.B., U. Fla., 1936; m. Helen Saxon Ausley, Sept. 25, 1940; children—Lee Lawrence II, Benjamin Cawthon. Admitted to Fla. bar, 1936; practiced in Tallahassee, 1936-57; partner firm Messer & Willis, 1942-57; circuit judge 2d Jud. Circuit Fla., Tallahassee, 1957—, presiding judge, 1961-63, 69-71, chief judge, 1971—. Dir. Blue Shield of Fla., Inc. Served as capt. AUS, 1942-46. Mem. Jr. C. of C. (pres. 1938), C. of C. (pres. 1953), Fla. Bar (gov. 1953-54), Tallahassee Bar Assn., Fla. Hist. Soc. Methodist (mem. ofcl. bd.). Clubs: Cotillion, Exchange (pres. 1958-59). Home: 1504 Hickory Av Tallahassee FL 32303 Office: PO Box 24 Tallahassee FL 32302

WILLIS, CECIL, supt. schs.; b. Austin, Tex., Jan. 12, 1918; B.S., Trinity U., 1949, M.S., 1952; postgrad. U. Okla., 1967, Stanford U., 1968; D.Adminstrn., Millard Fillmore Inst.; m. Georgia Robertson. Coach, tchr. Harlandale High Sch., San Antonio, 1939-40, 44-46; football coach, athletic bus. mgr. Trinity U., San Antonio, 1947-50; self-employed businessman, 1950-54; high sch. prin., athletic dir., La Coste, Tex., 1954-55; dir. athletics, coach Huntsville, Tex., 1955-56; supt. schs., Natalia, Tex., 1956-59, New Braunfels, Tex., 1959-61, Brookshire, Tex., 1963-65; supt. schs., Novice (Tex.) Ind. Sch. Dist., 1969-71, Kennedale (Tex.) Ind. Sch. Dist., 1971-72, New Caney (Tex.) Ind. Sch. Dist., 1973-74; dir. edn. Terr. of Guam, 1962-63. Ednl. spl. Exec. Office of Pres. U.S., 1965-69; manpower devel. specialist U.S. Dept. Labor, 1969-70; ednl. cons. Am. Overseas Sch., Rome, Italy, 1965. Served with USAF, 1941-43. Mem. Am., Tex.

assns. sch. adminstrs., N.E.A., Tex. Tchrs. Assn. Home: PO Box 177 New Caney TX 77357 Office: PO Box 53 New Caney TX 77357

WILLIS, DELBERT, newspaper editor; b. Brashear, Tex., Aug. 27, 1914; s. Robert L. and Ella (Ward) Turner; student Harvard, 1949; m. Patricia LeNeve Doss, Jan. 1, 1958; children—Charles Delbert, Danny, Virginia (Mrs. Robert Groom), Priscilla (Mrs. Harold Benefield), Rebecca (Mrs. Jerry Hazelwood). With Ft. Worth Press, 1932—, city editor, 1953-69, mng. editor, 1969-70, editor, 1970—. Adviser Block Partnership; founder Tarrant County Election Bur. Served with inf. AUS, 1942-49; PTO. Decorated Bronze Star medal, Purple Heart; recipient 1st place news writing award Nat. Headliners Club, 1951-53, Tex. Headliner Club, 1965, 66, 73. Nieman fellow, 1948-49. Mem. Sigma Delta Chi. Club: Ft. Worth Press. Contbr. to mags. and jours. Home: 3671 Encanto St Fort Worth TX 76109 Office: Ft Worth Press 5th and Jones Sts Fort Worth TX 76102

WILLIS, JAMES COUSER, JR., state ofcl.; b. Wadesboro, N.C., Sept. 2, 1935; s. James Couser and Myrtle Lee (Pusser) W.; B.S., Clemson U., 1962; postgrad. police adminstrn. Mich. State U., 1964, So. Ill. U. Center for Study Crime, Delinquency and Corrections, 1967, U. Chgo. Center Continuing Edn., Criminal Justice Exec. Inst. program, 1972-73, Mil. Police Civil Disturbance Sch., Ft. Gordon, Ga., 1972, S.C. Midlands Tech. Edn. Center, 1973, Occupational Safety and Health Tng. Inst. U.S. Dept. Labor, 1973; m. Rebecca Ann Hardee, Sept. 16, 1962; 1 son, Kirk James. Forester, U.S. Forest Service, San Juan Nat. Forest, Mancos, Colo., 1962-63; chief police, Loris, S.C., 1964-65; correctional officer S.C. Dept. Corrections, 1965, instn. edn. dir., 1966-67, chief correctional supr., 1967-68, warden Maximum Dentention Retng. Center, 1968-72, correctional tng. coordinator S.C. Criminal Justice Tng. Acad., 1972, safety dir. occupational safety and health div., 1972—. Instr. criminal justice adminstrn. program Sch. Gen. Studies, U. S.C., 1969-71. Served with USAF, 1953-57. Mason. Home: 1924 Pontiac Av Columbia SC 29206 Office: SC Dept Corrections PO Box 766 Columbia SC 29202

WILLIS, LYNWOOD GRAYSON, architect; b. Savannah, Ga., Sept. 17, 1931; s. Charles Wesley and Valeria (Grayson) W.; B.S., Ga. Inst. Tech., 1956; B.Arch., 1957; m. Jane Thompson, July 7, 1954; children—Ellen Kathleen, Linda Jane, Julia Ann, Ashley Grayson. Partner, Willis & Veenstra, Atlanta and Jacksonville, Fla., 1960—, Willis & Veenstra Investment Co., Atlanta, Jacksonville, 1968; gen. partner Heritage Sq. Apts. of Savannah Ltd. (Ga.), 1970—, other apt. complexes, Augusta, Jacksonville, Orlando, Atlanta. Mem. Com. of 100, Jacksonville, 1965-71. Bd. dirs. Vols. Am., Jr. Achievement, Jacksonville. Mem. Nat. Capital Democratic Club, Washington. Founder, Jacksonville Episcopal High Sch., 1966-67. Served with USAF, 1950-51. Recipient Cleve. Found. Structural Design award, 1957, Distinguished Service award Jacksonville Jr. C. of C., 1966. Mem. A.I.A. (Merit award 1971), Alpha Tau Omega. Democrat. Clubs: University, Quarterback, Deerwood, Ponte Vedre (Jacksonville); West Lake Country (Augusta); Chatham (Savannah). Archtl. works include: Fla. Jr. Coll., 1971, U.S. Post Office, 1971, Bapt. Towers, 1971, Jacksonville Gen. Hosp., 1971, Pablo Towers, 1972, 1st Bapt. Ch., 1973, Trinity Bapt. Elementary and High sch., 1972, Intermedic Gen. Hosp., 1973, Piney Is. Devel., 1973 (all Jacksonville); U.S. Post Office and Fed. Office Bldg., Waycross, Ga., 1971. Home: 10411 Deerwood Club Rd Jacksonville FL 32216 Office: 415 E Monroe St Jacksonville FL 32202 also 81 Poplar St Atlanta GA 30303

WILLIS, MAURICE CONNELY, mech. engr.; b. Tulsa, Jan. 10, 1929; s. Maurice Connely and Emma Jean (Orton) W.; B.S., U. Denver, 1953; postgrad. U. Wichita, 1955, U. Colo., 1956, U. Seattle, 1957; M.P.A., U. Okla., 1974; m. Ruth Coners, Oct. 5, 1973; children (by previous marriage)—Diane, Denise, Dana, Michael. With Boeing Airplane Co., Wichita, Kan., 1953-55, Seattle, 1957-58, Vandenburg AFB, Cal., 1962, Sundstrand Denver Corp., 1956-57, IBM, Seattle, 1958-59, Convair div. Gen. Dynamics Astronautics Co., 1959-62; project engr. NASA, 1962-72, launch operations mgr., Huntsville, Ala., 1972—. Pres. Horizon Hills Homeowners Assn.; mem. Conejo Valley Incorporation Com. Served with USNR, 1948-51. Decorated D.F.C., Air medal with three oak leaf clusters. Clubs: Horizon View (pres.), Redstone Yacht (rear commodore, sec.) (Huntsville). Home: 8003 Benaroya Lane Huntsville AL 35802 Office: Marshall Space Flight Center Huntsville AL 35808

WILLIS, MAX CURRY, wreckage co. exec.; b. nr. Fountain Inn, S.C., May 16, 1942; s. William Claude and Cora Nell (Curry) W.; grad. high sch.; m. Phyllis Anne Curry, Nov. 12, 1966; 1 dau., Alecia Curry. Owner Interstate Service Sta., Fountain Inn, 1960-62; with Laurens Glass Works (S.C.), 1962-63; co-owner M & J Auto Wreckage Co., Fountain Inn, 1963—; partner Hayne & Willis Asphalt Co., Laurens, 1972—. Served with U.S. Army, 1964-71. Recipient medal of honor for work done on Shriners Race, 1973. Mem. Fountain Inn Jr. C. of C. Mason (Shriner). Address: Route 2 Fountain Inn SC 29644

WILLIS, ROBERT ALEXANDER, journalist; b. Atlanta, Oct. 8, 1929; s. William Warner and Bonnie (Alexander) W.; A.B. in Journalism, U. Ga., 1950; M.A. in English, State U. Ia., 1951; postgrad. Army Lang. Sch., 1952; m. Mildred Rita Pasquariello, Nov. 5, 1955; children—Michael Bruce, Paula Christine, Daniel Alexander, Jeffrey Thomas. Newsman, A.P., Charlotte, N.C., 1954-62, N.Y.C., 1962-63; tech. writer IBM, Poughkeepsie, N.Y., 1963-64; reporter Ledger-Star, Norfolk, Va., 1964-66, editorial writer 1966-67, spl. writer, 1968-69; asso. editor editorial pages Roanoke (Va.) Times and World News, 1969—. Part-time lectr. English, Old Dominion Coll., Norfolk, 1964-69. Served with AUS, 1951-54. Democrat. Roman Catholic. Home: 3835 Darlington Rd SW Roanoke VA 24018 Office: 201 Campbell Av SW Roanoke VA 24010

WILLIS, W(ILLIAM) EARL, hosp. exec.; b. Chase City, Va., May 9, 1927; s. William Richardson and Edmonia (Jordan) W.; B.S., Va. Commonwealth U., 1951; postgrad. U. Richmond, 1953-54, Med. Coll. Va., 1955-56; m. Mary Jane Bowers, Mar. 21, 1959; children—Elizabeth Ann, Ros Richardson. Hosp. auditor Bur. Hosps. and Nursing Homes, Va. State Health Dept., 1954-55; asst. adminstr. Roanoke Meml. Hosp., 1957-60; adminstr. Southside Community Hosp., Farmville, Va., 1960-63; adminstr. Gen. Hosp., Virginia Beach, Va., 1963—, v.p., 1969—, bd. dirs., 1974—. Bd. dirs. Birchwood Corp., Ocean Sands Corp. Pres., Tidewater Hosps. Council, 1968; mem. exec. com. Virginia Beach Beautification Commn., 1966—; mem. Va. Beach Assn., 1973—. Bd. dirs. Jobs for Vets., Va. Mayor's Task Force, Norfolk Central YMCA; trustee Va. Council Health and Med. Care, Va. Hosp. Research and Ednl. Trust. Served with USNR, 1945-46, 51-52. Fellow Am. Coll. Hosp. Adminstrs.; mem. Va. (sec.-treas. 1971, pres. 1973, mem. exec. com., dir.), Am. hosp. assns., Va. Beach C. of C. (dir., com. of 100). Presbyn. (bd. deacons). Club: Princess Anne Country (Virginia Beach). Home: 1411 Cherry Lane Virginia Beach VA 23454 Office: 1060 1st Colonial Rd Virginia Beach VA 23454

WILLIS, WILLIAM PASCAL, state ofcl.; b. Anadarko, Okla., Oct. 17, 1910; s. Robert Garnet and Lulu (Wyatt) W.; B.A., E. Central State Coll., Ada, Okla., 1935; M.A., Tulsa U., 1948; m. Zelma M. Bynum, Sept. 19, 1935; children—Diane, Joyce (Mrs. Gerald Browder), Billie Jean (Mrs. Alvon Crosslin), Zelma (Mrs. David Bailey), Herbert, William Pascal, Doak. Prin. Spaulding (Okla.) High Sch., 1935-36, Mill Creek High Sch., 1936-37; mayor, Locust Grove, 1937-44; mem. Okla. Ho. of Reps., 1958—, speaker, 1972—. Owner, operator Willis Merc., Tablequah, 1937-56. Served with AUS, 1944. Recipient Tahlequah Outstanding Citizen award Tahlequah Star Citizen, 1965. Mem. Cherokee Hist. Soc. (bd. dirs.), C. of C. Mason (Shriner), Kiwanian. Address: 1 Valley St Tahlequah OK 74464

WILLMOT, WILLIAM CLARENCE, govt. ofcl.; b. Elizabeth, N.J., June 26, 1925; s. Clarence William and Caroline Wienges (Sherman) W.; B. Gen. Studies. Rollins Coll., 1967; M.S., Fla. Inst. Tech., 1970; M.Ed., Stetson U., 1972, M.A., 1974; LL.B., Blackstone Sch. Law, 1958; m. Florence Camilla Veverka, May 22, 1948. Civilian employee Dept. Army, 1947-62; supervisory tech. editor John F. Kennedy Space Center (Fla.), 1964-67, program mgmt. specialist, 1967-72, disaster control officer, 1972—. Mem. Brevard County Mental Health Assn.; mem. planning com. Brevard County Community Shelter Program. Served with AUS, 1943-46. Decorated Bronze Star medal. Mem. Soc. Wireless Pioneers, Soc. Tech. Communication (vice chmn. chpt. 1972-73), Am. Fedn. Govt. Employees, 24th Infantry Div. Assn., Alpha Psi Omega (nat. adv. bd. dirs. 1971-73). Club: Old Timers (Newington, Conn.). Asso. editor No. N.J. Newsletter, 1961-62; mem. editorial com. Space Dimensions, 1963-64. Home: 1630 Venus St Merritt Island FL 32952 Office: John F Kennedy Space Center NASA Kennedy Space Center FL 32952

WILLNER, EUGENE BURTON, fish and seafood co. exec.; b. Chgo., July 27, 1934; s. Fred and Mae (Goodhartz) W.; B.A., Northwestern U., 1956; m. Karen Nell Kaye, Feb. 22, 1962; children—Tracy Fran, Kelly Kaye. Pres., World Wide Fisheries Inc., Chgo., 1956-60; merchandiser Edison Bros. Stores Inc., St. Louis, 1960-66; v.p. Mo. Supreme Life Ins. Co., St. Louis, 1966-67; exec. v.p. Exec. Agys., Inc., St. Louis, 1966-67; pres. Bluff Creek Industries, Inc., Ocean Springs, Miss., 1967-69, Purse String Stores, Inc., Miami, Fla., 1968-69, World Wide Fisheries, Inc., Miami, Fla., 1969-73, Universal Fisheries, Inc., Miami, 1974—; dir. Mo. Supreme Life Ins. Co., Lite Am. Corp. Home: 8400 SW 146th St Miami FL 33158 Office: 1341 NW 22d St Miami FL 33142

WILLOUGHBY, SARAH MARGARET CLAYPOOL, educator; b. Bowling Green, Ky.; d. Austin Burrell and Minerva (Renfrow) Claypool; B.S., Western Ky. U., 1938; Ph.D., Purdue U., 1950; m. John Richard Evans II, Aug. 30, 1938 (dec. Dec. 1942); 1 son, Richard Claypool; m. 2d, O. Glenn Willoughby, June 18, 1948 (div. Aug. 1956); children—Sarah Peyton, Stephen Burrell. Chemist, Devoe-Raynolds, Inc., Louisville, 1941-43; jr. engr. Curtiss-Wright Corp., Louisville, 1943-44; research fellow Purdue U. Sch. Chem. Engring., West Lafayette, Ind., 1946-50; research chemist Monsanto Chem. Co., Boston, 1950-51; asst. prof. chemistry U. Tex., Arlington, 1954-55; asso. prof., 1955—. Profl. engr., Ind., Tex. Fellow Am. Inst. Chemists; mem. Am. Chem. Soc. (sect. sec.-dir. 1967-68), Soc. Women Engrs., Tex. Acad. Sci., Colonial Dames of Am., Magna Charta Dames (chpt. v.p. 1970—, colony regent 1974—), Colonial Order Crown, Descs. of Knights of Garter, Ams. of Royal Descent, Plantagenet Soc., D.A.R. (chpt. regent 1967-69, state bicentennial chmn. 1969-70, nat. v.p. com. 1971-74), Children of Am. Revolution (sr. state pres. 1969-71), Sigma Xi (pres. U. Tex. club, 1966-68), Alpha Chi Omega. Presbyn. Club: Arlington Womens. Co-author: Notes for the Engineer-in-Training Examination, 1st edit., 1966, 2d edit., 1972. Home: 1630 Pecan Park Dr Arlington TX 76012

WILLS, DAVID HILARY, radio commentator; b. Wallasey, Eng., May 15, 1904; s. Thomas A. D. and Isobel (Wardlesworth) W.; B.Engring., Liverpool U., 1924, Ph.D., 1927; postgrad. (Commonwealth Fund fellow in econs.), Harvard, 1931-34; m. Virginia Floyd, 1934; children—Nadia, Jonathan Floyd, Susan; m. 2d, Dorothy Lee Eck, May 8, 1953. Came to U.S., 1940, naturalized, 1944. Jr. engr. Met.-Vickers, Ltd., Eng., 1927-31; asst. chmn. London Daily News, Ltd., 1934-38, finance mgr., 1938-41; mgr. Czechoslovakian Relief Fund News-Chronicle, Prague, 1938-39; editorial writer The Economist, 1934-40; London corr. Christian Sci. Monitor, 1936-40, Washington Post, 1934-37, NBC, 1939-40; dir. information Brit. Supply Council, Washington, 1941-44; commentator radio sta. WMAL, ABC. Washington, 1944-48; chief Washington bur. The Reporter, 1948-50; dir. information IMF, Washington, 1950-52; partner Daveck Assos., Washington, 1952—; commentator fgn. affairs Three Star Extra, NBC, 1953-65. Fellow Royal Econ. Soc. (Eng.), Overseas Writers. Co-author: Total Victory without Atomic War, 1962. Home: 908 Mackall Av McLean VA 22101

WILLS, IRVIN ANDREWS, educator; b. Mendota, Ill., Dec. 21, 1904; s. Edgar Bunker and Margaretta (Moore) W.; B.S., Wheaton Coll., 1927; M.S., State U. Ia., 1932, Ph.D., 1935; m. Ruth Harriet Fisher, July 11, 1934; children—Ruth Elizabeth (Mrs. Paul Perks), Helen Margaret (Mrs. Richard Davis), Paul Irvin. Instr., Valparaiso (Ind.) U., 1927-29; asst. instr. State U. Ia., 1930, asst., 1931, 32-34, research asso., 1934-35; prof. biology John Brown U., Siloam Springs, Ark., 1935-74, dean acad. coll., 1935-54, chmn. nat. sci. div., 1954-72, recipient 30-year Service pin, 1965. Pres. Siloam Springs Camp, Gideons Internat., 1971-73. Recipient 30-year Service pin U.S. Weather Bur., 1973, 25-year award Ark. Dept. Higher Edn., 1960. Fellow Am. Sci. Affiliation, A.A.A.S.; mem. Am. Zoologists, Ark. Edn. Assn., Ark. Acad. Sci. (pres. 1941), Creation Research Soc. Rotarian (pres. Siloam Springs 1950). Home: 225 S Holly St Siloam Springs AR 72761

WILLS, JAMES DONALD, mining engr.; b. Prestonsburg, Ky., Aug. 26, 1940; s. Clayton Edward and Ethel Lorena (Conley) W.; B.S. in Mining Engring. (Princess Coals, Inc. scholar), U. Ky., 1963; m. Alberta Belle Pilcher, Dec. 18, 1965; children—Susan Yvette, Carmen Michelle, Christina Gay. With Princess Coals, Inc., David, Ky., summers 1959-64; engr., asst. to dir. Ky. Div. Reclamation, Frankfort, 1964-66; hwy. design engr. div. design Ky. Dept. Hwys., Frankfort, 1966-68; profl. engr. Ky. Air Pollution Control Commn., Frankfort, 1968-72; environmental engr. Nat. Mines Corp., Wayland, Ky., 1972—. Registered profl. engr., Ky. Mem. Jehovah's Witnesses. Home: PO Box 262 Wayland KY 41666 Office: PO Drawer 295 Wayland KY 41666

WILLS, KEITH CAMERON, clergyman, librarian; b. McCleary, Wash., Aug. 11, 1917; s. Lee Allen and Frances (Mommsen) W.; B.A., U. Wash., 1940; B.D., Southwestern Baptist Sem., 1950, Th.D., 1958; M.A. in L.S. (Lilly Found. fellow), U. Denver, 1966; m. Olin Florine Taylor, Sept. 28, 1944; 1 son, Keith C. Economist, Nat. Housing Agy., Washington, 1941-47; library asst. Southwestern Baptist Sem., Ft. Worth, 1947-51, circulation librarian, 1953-57, reference librarian, 1957-58, dir. libraries, 1966—; librarian Midwestern Baptist Sem., Kansas City, Mo., 1958-66. Mem. Am. Theol. Library Assn. (dir. 1969-71), So. Bapt. Hist. Soc. (dir. 1967—), A.L.A. Club: Civitan. Home: 6133 Wrigley Way Fort Worth TX 76133

WILLS, WILLIAM ERVIN, ins. co. exec.; b. Lynchburg, Va., July 3, 1935; s. Dewitt T. and Mary A. (Tinsley) W.; student Rensselaer Poly. Inst., 1957. U. Richmond, 1958-59; m. Grace Seward, Oct. 23, 1954; children—William Ervin, Robin K., R. Douglas. With Chesapeake Corp., West Point, Va., 1953-63; local agt. State Farm Ins. Cos., West Point, 1963—. Scoutmaster, Robert E. Lee council Boy Scouts Am., 1962-70; chmn. King William County, Va. Heart Assn., 1963-65; mem. West Point Vol. Fire Dept. and Rescue Squad, 1961-73. Mem. West Point Town Council, 1974—. Served with AUS, 1952-53. Mem. West Point Jr. C. of C. (life). Baptist (deacon, mem. finance com. 1972—). Home: Riverview Dr West Point VA 23181 Office: 9th and Main Sts West Point VA 23181

WILLSON, DAVID RICHARD, lumber co. exec.; b. Fort Worth, Jan. 9, 1933; s. James McCrory and Mavis Louise (Terry) W.; B.S., N. Tex. State U., 1954; m. Rochelle Ann Leibovitz, July 20, 1954; children—David Blair, Cynthia Faith. Owner, mgr. Willson & Son-Bldg. Materials, Plainview, Tex., 1956—. Scoutmaster, South Plains council Boy Scouts Am., 1968-71, dist. chmn. camping activities, 1959-60; coach Little League Baseball, 1967-70; bd. commrs. Meth. Home, Waco, Tex., 1971; mem. Plainview Bd. City Devel., 1972-73, Plainview Bicentennial Com., 1973. Trustee McMurry Coll., Abilene, Tex., Mt. Sequoiah Meth. Camp, Fayetteville, Ark., Ceta Canyon Meth. Camp, Canyon, Tex. Served with AUS, 1954-56. Mem. C. of C., Lambda Chi Alpha. Methodist. Mason (Shriner), Rotarian, Toastmaster. Home: Box 1178 1106 Ennis St Plainview TX 79072 Office: 700 E 5th St Plainview TX 79072

WILLSON, MRS. JAMES M., coll. trustee; b. Vashti, Tex., May 11, 1895; d. Richard Everet and Ora Ann (Jetton) Terry; student Seth Ward Coll., 1912, Southwestern U., 1914; A.B., So. Methodist U., 1916; D.Litt., McMurry Coll., 1962; m. James McCorry Willson, June 14, 1919; children—James McCorry, Mavis Louis (Mrs. Robert Neff Arnold), Ora Eugenia (Mrs. Will Addis), David. Tchr. Tex. pub. high schs., 1916-19; trustee Floydada (Tex.) High Sch., 1940. Trustee Tex. Wesleyan Coll., Ft. Worth, 1948-71, Lydia Patterson Inst., El Paso, Tex., 1948—. Recipient Freedoms Found. award, 1960; named Ky. Col. Mem. Am. Legion Aux. (vice chmn. Tex. dept. 1947, chmn. 19th dist. 1945-46, chmn. state child welfare com., 1948, mem. state finance com. 1949-51, dist. pres., state Women's Soc. Christian Service (local pres.). Democrat. Methodist. (dist. sec. young people's supply work). Clubs: Study (pres.), Garden (Floydada). Established (with husband) founds. for youth in various colls. and univs. in S.W. Home: Box 666 Floydada TX 79235

WILLSON, JAMES MCCORRY, lumberman; b. Boonesville, Tex., Dec. 21, 1887; s. David and Sarah Eugenia (Strange) D.; A.B., Southwestern U., 1912; LL.D., Tex. Wesleyan Coll., 1947; L.H.D. (hon.), McMurry Coll., 1956; m. Mavis Louis Terry, June 14, 1919; children—James McCorry, Mavis Louis (Mrs. Robert Arnold), Ora Eugenia (Mrs. Will Addis), David R. Owner lumber yard, 1908—; line yard operator Willson & Son, 1916—; established founds. in numerous colls., instns. Mem. Nat. council Boy Scouts Am. Trustee So. Methodist U., 1930-64; trustee McMurray Coll., 1934—, pres. bd., 1951-54; chmn. jurisdictional bd. hosp. and homes Methodist Ch., 1949-54; chmn. bd. edn. N.W. Tex. Meth. Conf., 1952-54; mem. gen. bd. edn. Meth. Ch., 1960-64; trustee, vice chmn. bd. Meth. Western Assembly, 1934-66, Meth. Hosp., Lubbock, Tex. 1954-71; del. Meth. Gen. Conf., 1934, 38, 40, 44, 48, 52, 56, 60, 64, 66, 68, Uniting Conf., 1939. Served with U.S. Army, World War I. Decorated Purple Heart; recipient Silver Beaver award Boy Scouts Am., Top Leadership award Freedoms Found. Valley Forge, 1960. Mem. West Tex. C. of C. (pres. 1971), V.F.W., Am. Legion (dist. comdr.). Mason (Shriner), Rotarian (dist. gov. 1935-36). Home: 820 Kentucky St Floydada TX 79235 Office: 215 E California St Floydada TX 79235

WILMER, RICHARD HOOKER, lawyer; b. Washington, Oct. 20, 1892; s. William Holland and Re Lewis (Smith) W.; A.B., Yale, 1915; J.D., Columbia, 1917; m. Margaret Van Dyke Grant, June 2, 1917 (dec. Dec. 1973); children—Richard Hooker, John Grant; m. 2d, Frances H. Williams, May 25, 1974. Admitted to D.C. bar, 1917, N.Y. State bar, 1929; asso. firm Minor, Gatley & Rowland, Washington, 1919-24, Cravath, de Gersdorff, Swaine & Wood, N.Y.C., Washington, 1924-29, partner, 1929-42; sr. partner firm Wilmer & Broun, Washington, 1946-62, Wilmer, Cutler & Pickering, Washington, 1962—. Chmn. met. area campaign A.R.C., Washington, 1946. Served as 1st lt., CAC, 1917-19, col. CAC, AUS, 1942-46; chief legal adviser Allied Commn. (Italy), 1944. Decorated Legion of Merit with oak leaf cluster; comdr. Order Saints Mauritius and Lazarus (Italy); chevalier Legion of Honor (France). Mem. Soc. of Cin. (past pres. gen.), Am. Legion, Mil. Order World Wars, Am., D.C. bar assns., Bar Assn. City N.Y., Am. Law Inst., Washington Cathedral. Episcopalian. Clubs: Metropolitan, International (Washington); Chevy Chase. Home: 2600 31st St Washington DC 20008 Office: 1666 K St NW Washington DC 20006

WILSON, BARRY PRESTON, ins. co. exec.; b. Batavia, N.Y., Mar. 16, 1932; s. Wilbur Charles and Gwendolyn Irene (Frey) W.; A.B., Coll. William and Mary, 1953; M.A., Cornell U., 1955; m. Mary Louise Hazelgrove, Jan. 20, 1962; children—Nancy Randolph, Anne Bidgood, Terry Jane, Timothy Bland. News editor Va. Gazette, Williamsburg, 1955-56; staff writer Newport News (Va.) Daily Press, 1958-59; news bur. editor Coll. William and Mary, 1959-60; asst. pub. relations mgr. Group Hospitalization, Inc., Washington, 1960-67, pub. relations mgr., 1967-71, v.p. pub. affairs, 1971—. Mem. communications adv. com. Blue Cross Assn.; adviser health information system Met. Washington Council Govts. Served with AUS, 1956-58. Recipient awards Va. Press Assn., 1956, Advt. Club Washington, 1971, 72, 73, Nat. Outdoor Advt. Assn., 1969. Mem. Pub. Relations Soc. Am. (dir. Nat. Capital chpt.), Am. Soc. Hosp. Pub. Relations Dirs., Sigma Alpha Epsilon, Theta Alpha Phi. Democrat. Episcopalian. Home: 7414 Beverly Manor Dr Annandale VA 22003 Office: 550 12th St SW Washington DC 20024

WILSON, BERNARD EDGAR, ins. co. exec.; b. Chattanooga, Feb. 23, 1912; s. Bernard E. and Lillian (Ledford) W.; B.S., Eastern Ky. State, 1936; M.A., U. Ky., 1938; m. Elizabeth Irene Howard, Apr. 20, 1942; children—Bernard E. III, William Gerald. High sch. athletic coach, Harlan, Ky., 1936-39; athletic dir. Union Coll., 1939-46; head basketball coach Coll. William & Mary, 1946-51; with Commonwealth Life Ins. Co., 1951, successively agt., mgr., dir. agys. of home office, 1951-59, br. mgr., 1959; v.p., dir. agys. Appalachian Nat. Life Ins. Co., 1959-61, dir., 1960-61; v.p., dir. agys. Am. Gen. Life Ins. Co. of Del., 1962-69, sr. v.p., 1969-73, exec. v.p., 1973—; dir., 1962—; exec. v.p., dir. Life & Casualty, 1971—, Am. Gen. of Okla., 1971—; dir. Am. Gen. Life of Tex. Chmn. exec. com. LIAMA, 1970. Trustee Life Underwriters Tng. Council, 1971. Served from 2d lt. to maj. USAF, 1942-46. Mem. Nat., Nashville assns. life underwriters, Newcomen Soc., Nashville Area C. of C., Sales and Marketing Execs. Assn., Gen. Agts. and Mfrs. Assn., Pa. Soc. Methodist. Kiwanian. Clubs: Hillwood Country; Nashville City; Duquesne; Exchange. Home: 1104 Stonewall Jackson Ct Nashville TN 37220 Office: 159 4th Av N Nashville TN 37219

WILSON, CHARLES, congressman; b. Trinity, Tex., June 1, 1933; student Sam Houston State U., Huntsville, Tex., 1951-52; B.S., U.S. Naval Acad., 1956; m. Jerry Carter, 1963. Commd. ensign U.S. Navy, 1956, advanced through grades to lt.; ret., 1960; mem. Tex. Ho. of Reps., 1960-66; mem. Tex. Senate, 1966-72; mem. 93d Congress from 2d Dist. Tex. Mgr. lumber yard. Democrat. Office: 1209 Longsworth House Office Bldg Washington DC 20515•

WILSON, CHARLES, JR., constrn. co. exec.; b. Winston Salem, N.C., Nov. 15, 1920; s. Charles and Lily Lee (Grogan) W.; B.S. in C.E., The Citadel, 1948; m. Frances Ruth Schachte, Nov. 6, 1948; children—Frank G., Charles Lee, Henry S., Cynthia A., Barbara J., Jeffery S. Engr., project mgr. Ruscon Constrn. Co., Charleston, S.C., 1950-57, v.p., project mgr., 1957-67, exec. v.p., gen. mgr., 1967-71, pres., 1971—; partner Carolina Indsl. Developers, Charleston, 1968—; v.p., dir. R.C. Steel Bldg. Co., Inc., Charleston, 1964-73; pres., dir. J.C. Calhoun Homes, Charleston, 1973—. Chmn., St. Andrews Parks and Playground Commn., Charleston, S.C., 1957—. Bd. dirs. Bishop Eng. High Sch., Charleston, 1972—; trustee Carolinas Constrn. Tng. Council, Charlotte, N.C., 1970-73. Served to capt. C.E., AUS, 1943-47, 1951-53. Decorated Bronze Star. Mem. Am. Inst. Constructors, S.C. Soc. Engrs., Soc. Am. Mil. Engrs., Charleston Civil Engrs. Club, Charleston Contractors Assn. (pres. 1967-68). Club: Country (Charleston). Home: 831 St Denis Dr Charleston SC 29407 Office: 149 E Bay St Charleston SC 29401

WILSON, CLAUDE RAYMOND, JR., lawyer; b. Dallas, Feb. 22, 1933; s. Claude Raymond and Lottie (Watts) W.; B.B.A., So. Methodist U., 1954, LL.B., 1956, LL.M., 1958; m. Barbara Jean Cowherd, Apr. 30, 1960; 1 dau., Deidra Nicole. Admitted to Tex. bar, 1956, practiced in Dallas, 1956-60, 65—; lawyer Tex. & Pacific R.R. Co., Dallas, 1958-60; sr. trial atty., chief counsel Internal Revenue Service, Washington, 1960-65; mem. firm Golden, Potts, Boeckman & Wilson, Dallas, 1965—. Bd. dirs., treas. St. Phillips Community Center. Mem. State Bar Tex., Am., Dallas (chmn. sect. taxation 1971-72) bar assns., Tex. Soc. C.P.A.'s (dir. 1973-76, dir. Dallas chpt. 1971-72), Delta Sigma Phi, Delta Theta Phi. Republican. Episcopalian. Mason (K.T., 32 deg., Shriner) Clubs: Chaparral, Royal Oaks Country, Dallas Gun. Home: 4069 Hanover Dallas TX 75225 Office: 2300 Republic Bank Tower Dallas TX 75201

WILSON, CREOLA DANIEL, ret. librarian; b. Galax, Va., Dec. 17, 1901; d. Joseph Emory and Mollie (Ward) Daniel; m. Carl Bain Wilson, Dec. 3, 1924; 1 dau., Betty Jean (Mrs. Louis Franklin Bussler). Tchr., Loudoun County (Va.) Pub. Schs., 1920-24; cataloger Pub. Documents Library, Govt. Printing Office, Washington, 1937-42; librarian U.S. Fish and Wildlife Service, Washington, 1942-44; librarian U.S. Bur. Mines, Washington, 1944-45; subject cataloger, classification specialist Armed Forces Med. Library, Washington, 1945-55; subject cataloger Library of Congress, Washington, 1955-56; asst. librarian St. Elizabeth's Hosp., Washington, 1956-58; subject analyst, chief librarian Def. Documentation Center, Alexandria, Va., 1958-71. Mem. Spl. Libraries Assn. (chmn. Washington chpt. biol. scis. group 1953-54), Med. Library Assn., Loudoun County Hist. Soc., Am. Assn. Ret. Persons, Nat. Assn. Ret. Fed. Employees (pres. Loudoun County chpt. 1973). Democrat. Mem. Soc. of Friends. Home: Route 2 Box 103A Leesburg VA 22075

WILSON, DAVID WINSLOW, advt. agy. exec.; b. Kansas City, Mo., May 22, 1939; s. Edward Graham and Anne Elizabeth (Saunders) W.; B.A. cum laude, U. South, 1961; M.S. in Journalism, Northwestern U., 1963; m. Sandra Slough, Aug. 26, 1961; children—Glen Mackie, Heather Louise. Asst. account exec. Marsteller Inc., Chgo., 1962-66, account exec., 1966-67, dir. collateral, 1967; account exec. Shattuck-Roether Frailey & Wilson, Inc., Orlando, Fla., 1967-70, v.p., 1970—, prin., 1971—. Bd. dirs. Fla. Symphony Orch. Mem. Orlando Area Advt. Club (pres. 1970-71, pres. bd. trustees 1971-72), Orlando Area C. of C., South Seminole C. of C., Antique Airplane Assn., Kappa Sigma. Republican. Episcopalian. Club: Citrus (Orlando). Home: 1121 Glengarry Circle Maitland FL 32751 Office: 601 N Ferncreek St Orlando FL 32803

WILSON, DONALD LEE, lawyer; b. Eufaula, Okla., Dec. 10, 1932; s. Arthur J. and Opal (Bullard) W.; B.A., U. Okla., 1955, LL.B., 1957; LL.M. in Taxation, So. Methodist U., 1964; postgrad. Tex. Christian U., 1968; m. Nancy Caroline Harris, Aug. 15, 1954; children—Wade Harris, Julie Ann, Mary Caroline. Admitted to Okla. bar, 1957, Tex. bar, 1960, U.S. Dist. Ct. No. Dist. Tex., 1960, U.S. Ct. Appeals 5th Circuit, 1960; asso. firm Embry, Crowe, Tolbert, Boxley & Johnson, Oklahoma City, 1959-60; partner firm Brooks, Tarlton, Wilson & Gilbert, Fort Worth, Tex., 1960-69; pres. firm Wilson, McGee, Craig & Owen, Fort Worth, 1969—. Dir. Mgmt. Capital Corp., Fort Worth, Equities Internat. Life, Ins. Co. Chmn. bd. dirs. Tarrant County chpt. Am. Cancer Soc., 1971-72. Served to capt. J.A.G.C., USAF, 1957-59. Mem. State Tex. Bar (chmn. dist. grievance com.), Fort Worth Bus. and Estate Planning Counsel, Fort Worth-Tarrant County, Okla., Am. bar assns., Phi Delta Theta, Phi Beta Kappa, Phi Alpha Delta. Rotarian. Editor-in-chief Okla. Law Rev., 1956. Home: 3817 Mockingbird Lane Fort Worth TX 76109 Office: 711 Fort Worth Nat Bank Bldg Fort Worth TX 76102

WILSON, D(OYCE) JOE, mfg. co. exec.; b. Denton County, Tex., Jan. 2, 1926; s. Walter John and Maggie Lee (Hindsley) W.; grad. Branch Agrl. Coll. Utah, 1944, Alexander Hamilton Inst., 1953; m. Vivian C. Castleberry, Oct. 14, 1944; 1 dau., Linda C. Vice pres., gen. mgr. Plains Dist. Co., Amarillo, Tex., 1948-58, Air-Tex div. Holly Corp., Dallas, 1958-62; pres., founder Remac Corp., Dallas, 1962-69; gen. mgr. Remac div. Sealed Power Corp., Dallas, 1969—; dir., pres., chief exec. officer Penny-Plus Corp., Dallas, 1970—; pres., founder CVS Mfg. Inc., Dallas, 1972—. Served with USAAF, 1943-45. Mem. Jr. C. of C., 1952-58. Lutheran. Elk. Patentee spl. tools for servicing automobile air conditioning. Home: 1702 Glen Valley St Irving TX 75060 Office: 2909 Anode Lane Dallas TX 75220

WILSON, FRANK ELMORE, physician, med. adminstr.; b. Knoxville, Tenn., Jan. 29, 1909; s. Audley Rhea and Edna Lewis (Moore) W.; M.D., U. Tenn., 1933; M.P.H., U. N.C., 1947; m. Esther Hambley, Nov. 28, 1937; 1 son, Lloyd Bonner. Intern Bapt. Meml. Hosp., Memphis, 1934-35; pvt. practice medicine, Mooresville, N.C., 1935-38; pub. health officer several Eastern N.C. counties, 1939-41; dep. nat. med. dir. nat. hdqrs. A.R.C., 1946, nat. med. dir., 1947-49, assisted initial devel. Nat. Blood Program, 1946-47; dep. dir. Washington office A.M.A., 1949-52, dir., 1952-55; exec. v.p., sec. Joint Blood Council, 1955-63; exec. dir. Assn. Mil. Surgeons U.S., Washington, 1963-70; asso. mem. VA Bd. Vets. Appeals, Washington, 1970—; cons. on med. adminstrn. Peruvian Govt., 1959. Dir. Edgecomb County (N.C.) Tb Hosp., 1940; former chmn. Pub. Health Adv. Council, Washington. Served as col. U.S. Army, 1941-46; ETO. Decorated Bronze Star, Diplomate Am. Bd. Preventive Med. and Pub. Health. Fellow Am. Pub. Health Assn.; mem. N.C. Med. Soc. (hon.), So. Med. Assn., A.M.A., Med. Soc. D.C. (chmn. com. pub. health), Am. Med. Writers Assn., Am. Coll. Preventive Medicine (charter), Soc. Med. Cons. Armed Forces, Assn. Mil. Surgeons U.S. (v.p., editorial adv. bd. 1950-70, exec. dir. 1963-70), A.A.A.S., Royal Soc. Health (Eng.), Alpha Omega Alpha, Phi Chi. Presbyn. Kiwanian, Rotarian (pres. Mooresville 1936). Clubs: Army and Navy, Pentagon Officers Athletic (Washington). Contbr. articles to med. jours. on fed. med. legislation. Home: 3283 Arcadia Pl NW Washington DC 20015 Office: VA Central Office Bd Veterans Appeals 811 Vermont Av NW Washington DC 20420

WILSON, FRANK WILEY, judge; b. Knoxville, Tenn., June 21, 1917; s. Frank Caldwell and Mary E. (Wiley) W.; A.B., U. Tenn., 1939, LL.B., 1941; m. Helen E. Warwick, Apr. 6, 1942; children—Frank Carl, William Randall. Admitted to Tenn. bar, 1941, since practiced in Oak Ridge; county atty., Anderson County, Tenn., 1948-50; city atty., Norris, Tenn., 1950-61, U.S. dist. judge Eastern dist. Tenn. So. Div., Chattanooga, 1961—, chief judge, 1970—. Vice pres., dir. Bank of Oak Ridge, 1952-63. Pres. Community Chest; mem. Oak Ridge Bd. Edn. Trustee Siskin Meml. Found. Served with USAAF, 1941-46; MTO. Mem. C. of C. (pres.), Am. Legion (comdr.), Order of Coif, Phi Delta Phi, Phi Kappa Phi. Rotarian (past pres.). Home: Stratford Lane Burnham Woods Signal Mountain TN 37377 Office: US Dist Court Chattanooga TN 37402

WILSON, GEORGE EDWARD, JR., textile co. exec., Republican nat. committeeman; b. Rockwood, Tenn., July 26, 1921; s. George Edward and Madge (Tarwater) W.; grad. Vanderbilt U., 1943; m. Emmie Chalmers Brown, Apr. 26, 1947; children—George Edward III, Emmie N., Madge T. With Roan & Hosiery, Inc., Harriman, Tenn., 1950—, v.p., sec., 1950—. Dir. Hamilton Bank Roane County. Chmn. Tenn. Republican Com., 1963-64; mem. Rep. Nat. Com. for Tenn., 1968—. Bd. dirs. East Tenn. Children's Hosp., Knoxville Symphony Soc., Harriman Gen. Hosp. Served with USCGR, 1943-46. Mem. Tenn. Mfrs. Assn. (pres., dir.), Nat. Assn. Hosiery Mfrs. (dir.), Am. Legion, V.F.W., Vanderbilt U. Alumni Assn. (dir.), Delta Kappa Epsilon. Presbyn. Elk. Clubs: Cherokee Country, City (Knoxville). Home: 702 Cumberland St Harriman TN 37748 Office: PO Box 431 Harriman TN 37748

WILSON, GEORGE HOWARD, state judge; b. Mattoon, Ill., Aug. 21, 1905; s. George Duncan and Helen Maude (Bresee) W.; A.B., Phillips U., 1926; postgrad. U. Mich. Law Sch., 1926-27; LL.B., U. Okla., 1929, J.D., 1970; grad. Nat. Coll. State Trial Judges U. Nev., 1970; m. Myrna Kathryn Reams, June 26, 1929; children—Jane Kathryn, Sandra Kay, Myrna Lee, George Howard II. Admitted to Okla. bar, 1928, U.S. Supreme Ct., in 1934; practiced in Enid, Okla., 1929-52; spl. agt. FBI, U.S. Dept. Justice, 1934-38; city atty., Enid, 1939-42; mem. 81st Congress (1949-51), 8th Dist. Okla.; superior ct. judge, Garfield County, Okla., 1952-68; presiding dist. judge div. 1, 4th Jud. Dist., 1968—. Chief judge Okla. Adminstrv. Zone 1, 1967; pres. Okla. Jud. Conf., 1968; chief judge Ct. of Bank Rev., 1971-73; judge panel 1, div. 2 Okla. Appellate Ct. of Criminal Appeals, 1971-73. Dir. Okla. Crime Commn. 1951-52. Former chmn. Cherokee Strip dist. Boy Scouts Am.; former pres. Enid Community Chest; former pres. bd. dirs. YMCA, Enid, 1968. Served as col. judge adv. gen.'s dept. U.S. Army, 1942-46. Commd. commodore by Okla. gov. 1954; recipient Legionnaire of Honor DeMolay, Distinguished Alumnus award Phillips U., 1972. Mem. Am., Garfield County, Okla. bar assns., Am. Legion, Acacia, Phi Delta Phi, Delta Sigma Rho, Order of Coif. Democrat. Presbyn. (elder). Mason (K.T.). Kiwanian (past lt. gov.). Home: 1724 W Cherokee St Enid OK 73701 Office: Ct House Enid OK 73701

WILSON, HAROLD STALETS, lawyer, state senator; b. Chgo., Sept. 28, 1921 s. Harold B. and Luella (Stalets) W.; B.A., U. Chgo., 1943; LL.B., Harvard, 1953; m. Mary Ellen Rusin, Jan. 19, 1963; children—Jennie Ellen, Janice Mary. Owner, operator Harold's Dept. Store, Amsterdam, N.Y., 1952-59; admitted to Fla. bar, 1960, since practiced in Clearwater; mem. firm Harold S. Wilson, 1967—; mem. Fla. Senate, 1966—; asst. pub. defender, Pinellas County, Fla., 1963-64; asso. municipal judge Indian Rocks Beach, Fla., 1966; city atty., Safety Harbor, Fla., 1962-65. Mem. Pinellas County Mental Health Bd., 1973, Fla. Gov.'s Council on Crime, 1973-74, Fla. Law Revision Council, 1973—. Served with Signal Corps, AUS, 1943-46. Mem. Am., Fla., Largo, Clearwater bar assns., Pinellas County Trial Lawyers Assn., Delta Sigma Pi. Home: 1406 Maple Forest Rd Clearwater FL 33516 Office: 307 S Osceola Av Clearwater FL 33516

WILSON, HENRY PALMER, JR., agrl. scientist; b. Wilmington, Del., Mar. 25, 1942; s. Henry Palmer and Marion (Gilmore) W.; B.S. in Agr., U. Del., 1963, M.S., 1965; Ph.D., Rutgers U., 1967. Plant physiologist Va. Truck and Ornamentals Research Sta., Painter, 1967—. Chmn. coll. scholarship com. Pungoteague chpt. Ruritan Club, 1969-71. Mem. Northeastern (sec. treas.), Am. (mem. newsletter com.) weed sci. socs., Peninsula Hort. Soc., Sigma Xi, Alpha Zeta, Alpha Tau Omega. Moose. Club: Shore Investment (Exmore, Va.). Contbr. articles to profl. jours. Home: Belle Haven VA 23306 Office: PO Box 133 Painter VA 23420

WILSON, HOMER MARVIN, elec. engr.; b. St. Louis, Oct. 3, 1934; s. Homer Marvin and Ogarita (Bailey) W.; student Loughborough Coll., Eng., 1957-58; B.A., Rice U., 1959, B.S. in Elec. Engring., 1960. Tech. mgr. Palmer Nuclear Lab., Princeton, 1961, Bonner Nuclear Lab,, Rice U,, 1961-62; v.p. Tech. Enterprises Corp., Houston, 1962-65; pres. H.M. Wilson Co., Houston, 1965—. Served with AUS, 1955-56. Registered profl. engr., Tex. Mem. I.E.E.E., Soc. Profl. Engrs., Nat. Assn. Corrosion Engrs., Instrument Soc. Am., Aircraft Owners and Pilots Assn. Patentee dual channel well logging system, logging channel disabling circuit, casing collar logging system, well logging system, electrochem. well log, corrosion rate meter, probe assembly for corrosion tests, also others. Home: 206 Marshall St Houston TX 77006 Office: 11501 Chimney Rock Houston TX 77035

WILSON, HOWARD BRUCE, aluminum co. exec.; b. Seattle, Nov. 3, 1924; s. E. Bruce and Olive Grace (Paris) W.; B.A., Colo. State Coll., 1948, M.A., 1950; Ph.D., U. Denver, 1964; children—Howard D., Paris, Jean, Scott. Sr. indsl. engr. Boeing Airplane Co., Wichita, Kan., 1953-56; sr. engr. Martin Co., Denver, 1956-59; mgr. computation Thiokol Chem. Co., Brigham City, Utah, 1959-60; supt. computations Hercules Powder Co., Magna, 1960-64; mgr. computer communications Mobil Oil Co., N.Y.C., 1965-67, Allied Chem. Co., 1967-69; gen. dir. mgmt. information services Reynolds Metals, Richmond, Va., 1969—; dir. Automated Computer Services, Inc., Richmond. Mem. Data Processing Mgmt. Assn. Home: 1834 Ivystone Dr Richmond VA 23233 Office: 6603 W Broad St Richmond VA 23227

WILSON, HOWARD HAZEN, internat. relations writer; b. La Salle, Ill., July 2, 1908; s. George Alexander and Florence Mellen (Hazen) W.; Ph.B. in History, U. Chgo., 1936, Ph.D. in Internat. Relations, 1941; m. Mary Louise Bennett, Dec. 6, 1933; 1 son, Howard Hazen. Asst. economist, internat. econs. U.S. Dept. Commerce, 1942-43; asso. economist U.S. Office Alien Property Custodian, 1943-44; divisional asst. Am. Republics affairs U.S. Dept. State, 1944-46; internat. relations intelligence research Hdqrs. U.S. Air Force, 1951-58, historian, 1958-66 (all Washington). Prof. internat. relations Am. Inst. for Fgn. Trade, 1946-47; lectr. history Am. U., 1950; lectr. internat. law and orgn. Georgetown U., summer 1949; vis. prof. history Shephard Coll., summer 1950. Recipient Honor award Dept. Air Force, 1956. Mem. Am. Soc. Internat. Law, Am. Polit. Sci. Assn., Psi Upsilon. Author 9 books, numerous articles on internat. politics and history (under ofcl. anonymity or security restrictions), 1952-66; bibliography on enemy property control, 1943. Home: 2140 Wyoming Av NW Washington DC 20008

WILSON, J. N. (PETE), supt. schs.; b. Seagraves, Tex., Dec. 17, 1923; s. Edd S. and Ruth W.; m. Jimmie Thomas, Aug. 14, 1947; children—Cynthia (Mrs. Jack Scarborough), Cathy Sue. Prin., coach high sch., Avoca, Tex., 1948-53; bus. mgr., coach Abernathy (Tex.) pub. sch., 1953-62; supt. schs., Petersburg, Tex., 1962—. Pres. Colokan, Inc., Ulysses, Kan., 1966-67. Served with USMCR, 1943-44. Mem. Hale County Tchrs. (pres. 1961-62), N.E.A., Tex., Am. assns. sch. adminstrs., Tex. State Tchrs. Assn., Univ. Interscholastic League (West Tex. rep. legislative council). Mason, Lion. Home: Box 159 Petersburg TX 79250 Office: Box 160 Petersburg TX 79250

WILSON, JACK COOK, physician; b. Little Rock, Nov. 10, 1937; s. Jesse Milton and Ruby Faye (Cook) W.; B.A., Hendrix Coll., 1958; B.S. (HEW-NIH fellow), U. Ark., 1961, M.D., 1963; m. Kay Eloise McSpadden, Aug. 30, 1959; children—Jesse, Matthew, Bruce. Intern, Univ., Hosp., Little Rock, 1963-64; physician Mountain Home (Ark.) Med. Group, 1966—, pres., 1973—; chief staff Baxter Gen. Hosp., Mountain Home, 1967-69, dir. labs., 1969—, bd. dirs., 1967-69. Pres., Pradco, Inc., Mountain Home, 1968—; dir., mem. discount com. 1st Nat. Bank and Trust Co., Mountain Home, 1972—; v.p., dir. Ark.-Mo. Processing Corp., Gassville, Ark., 1973—; dir. Mountain Home Profl. Bldg., Inc., 1970—, sec.-treas., 1973—. Chmn. Baxter County Adv. Health Council, 1968-70, mem., 1971—; coroner Baxter County, 1971—. Served with USAF, 1964-66. Mem. Baxter County Med. Soc. (pres., 1967), Ark. Med. Soc. (del. 1971, 72), A.M.A., Am. Acad. Gen. Practice, Alpha Omega Alpha. Home: 910 Russell St Mountain Home AR 72653 Office: 353 E 8th St Mountain Home AR 72653

WILSON, JAMES WOODFIN, JR., physician; b. Haughton, La., Oct. 28, 1923; s. James Woodfin and Anna Kathleen (Harp) W.; M.D., La. State U., 1948; m. Evoria Anne Dier, June 6, 1954; children—James Woodfin III, Paul Stuart, Roxanne, Barry, Mary Kathleen. Intern Charity Hosp., New Orleans, 1948-49; ships surgeon Alcoa Shipping Co., Miss. Shipping Co., 1949-50; resident internal medicine Confederate Meml. Med. Center, Shreveport, La., 1953-54, chief resident, 1955-56; resident pulmonary disease Essex County Sanitarium, Verona, N.J., 1954-55; practice medicine specializing in internal medicine, Shreveport, 1956—; chief medicine Schumpert Meml. Hosp., 1971-72; instr. medicine Northwestern Sch. Nursing, 1956-60; clin. asst. prof. medicine La. State U. Med. Sch., Shreveport, 1967—. Pres., Caddo Heart Council, 1969-70, 70-71, La. Heart Assn., 1970-71. Served to capt. AUS, 1951-52. Fellow A.C.P., Am. Coll. Chest Physicians; mem. Am. Legion, A.M.A., La., (v.p. 1968-71), So. med. socs. Club: Country (Shreveport). Editor: Shreveport Med. Bull., 1960-62. Contbr. articles to profl. jours. Home: 10501 Ellerbe St Shreveport LA 71106 Office: 925 Olive St Shreveport LA 71104

WILSON, JERRY LEE, research engr.; b. Hope, Ark., June 20, 1939; s. Autrey U. and Cornelia (Lewallen) W.; student So. State Coll., 1957-59; B.S., U. Ark., 1961; postgrad. Mass. Inst. Tech., 1964, U. Ariz., 1968; m. Emily Naron, June 5, 1960; children—David Allen, Mark Andrew. Mech. engr. Little Rock C.E., 1961-63; research engr. U.S. Army Mobility Equipment Research & Devel. Center, Ft. Belvoir, Va., 1963—. Served with AUS, 1957-63. Mem. Am. Soc. Heating, Refrigeration and Air Conditioning Engrs. (asso.), Sci. Research Soc. Home: 5424 Gainsborough Dr Fairfax VA 22030 Office: US Army Mobility Equipment Research and Devel Center Ft Belvoir VA 22060

WILSON, JERRY VERNON, police chief; b. South Hill, Va., Mar. 23, 1928; s. Joseph Eric and Ruth (Plyler) W.; student Am. U. Coll. Continuing Edn., 1956-69; m. Leone Bernice Harris, May 5, 1956; children—Brian Jerry, Kevin Harris. With Met. Police Dept., Washington, 1949—, sgt., 1958-60, lt., 1960, capt., 1961-64, insp., 1964-66, dep. chief, 1966-68, asst. chief, comdr. field operations, 1968, chief of police, 1969—; lectr. So. Police Inst. U. Louisville; lectr. Southwestern police Inst. So. Methodist U. Bd. mgrs. 12th St. br. YMCA. Bd. dirs. Washington Urban Coalition; bd. dirs. D.C. Area br. Nat. Conf. Christians and Jews. Served with USNR, 1943-46, USMCR, 1946-47. Mem. Internat. Assn. Chiefs of Police, Am. Soc. for Pub. Adminstrn., D.C. Govt. Municipal Officers Club (pres. 1968). Methodist. Mason. Home: 4415 Springdale St NW Washington DC 20016 Office: 300 Indiana Av NW Washington DC 20001

WILSON, JOHN HUMAN, II, oil co. exec.; b. Denver, Oct. 4, 1927; s. John Human and Harriette Evarista (Fromhart) W.; Petroleum Refining Engr., Colo. Sch. Mines, 1948; m. Mary Florence Ryan, Nov. 28, 1951; children—Mary Catherine, John Human III, James Ryan, Christopher Michael Thomas. Petroleum engr. Fred M. Manning, Inc., Denver, 1948-50; v.p., chief engr. Wilson Exploration Co., Ft. Worth, 1954—; v.p., dir. Piper Petroleum Co., Ft. Worth, 1956—. Served with AUS, 1950-53. Registered profl. engr, Tex., La., Miss. Mem. Am. Inst. Mining Engrs., Soc. Exploration Geophysicists, Am. Assn. Petroleum Geologists, Sigma Alpha Epsilon, Theta Tau. Clubs: Ft. Worth, River Crest Country. Home: 1515 Thomas Pl Fort Worth TX 76107 Office: 1212 W El Paso St Fort Worth TX 76102

WILSON, JOHN PAGE, mech. engr.; b. Freeport, Ill., July 24, 1922; s. Harold Norman and Nora (Knudstad) W.; B.S., U. Wis., 1943; m. Jane Ann Kiplinger, Aug. 28, 1943; 1 son, Jack K. Student engr., field engr. Babcock & Wilcox Co., N.Y.C., St. Louis, 1946-49; sales engr. A.M. Lockett & Co., Ltd., Dallas, 1949-65; pres. Wilson Co., Addison, Tex., 1965—; chmn. bd. Tex-a-draulics, Inc., Houston; dir. Addison State Bank. Scoutmaster, camping chmn. Dist. 4, Circle 10 council Boy Scouts Am., 1965-68; dir., camping chmn. Camp Fire Girls Met. Dallas. Served to 1st lt. C.E., AUS, 1943-46; PTO. Mem. Am. Soc. M.E. (past chmn. North Tex. sect.), Fluid Power Soc., Tex. Soc. Profl. Engrs., Engrs. Club Dallas. Unitarian. Club: Rush Creek Yacht (Dallas). Home: 6602 Belmead Dr Dallas TX 75230 Office: 16301 Addison Rd Addison TX 75001

WILSON, LEON LANDON, ednl. adminstr.; b. Leslie, Ark., June 15, 1936; s. Zora and Frances Biryal (Matheny) W.; B.S., Memphis State U., 1959, M.A., 1962; Ed.D., U. Ark., 1969; m. Edna M. Jennings, Sept. 3, 1955; children—Ravonda Kay, Kermie Lynn, Ivan Leon, Kenda Beth. Tchr., Marshall (Ark.) Sch. Dist., 1957-59, prin., 1959-62; supt. Leslie (Ark.) Sch. Dist., 1962-65; dir. Ark. Dept. Edn., Little Rock, 1965-69; exec. dir. Central Ark. Ednl. Center, Little Rock, 1969-72; asst. supt. North Little Rock Sch. Dist., 1972—. Vis. prof. State Coll. Ark., Conway, 1970—; cons. Ark. Dept. Edn., 1969—. Mem. N.E.A., Ark. Edn. Assn., Am. Assn. Sch. Adminstrs., Ark. Sch. Adminstrs. Assn., Phi Delta Kappa. Baptist. Lion. Contbr. articles to profl. jours. Home: 805 N Mellon Little Rock AR 72205 Office: 2700 Poplar St North Little Rock AR 72114

WILSON, LEONARD WILLIAM, JR., mobile home mfg. co. exec.; b. Clarendon, Tex., Nov. 28, 1925; s. Leonard W. and Vera Gertrude (March) W.; student So. Meth. U., 1947; m. Barbara Edith Young, July 17, 1946; children—Linda (Mrs. Robert Walker), Leonard Gregory. Mgr., Wilson-Young Lumber, Spur, Tex., 1947-49; regional mgr. Chambers, Inc., lumber, Hobbs, N.M., 1949-51; pres. Mathis-Wilson, Inc., gen. contractors, Lubbock, Tex., 1953-60; sec.-treas. Wilson & Wilson, Inc., Lubbock, 1962—; pres., chmn. bd. Castle Industries, Inc., Lubbock, 1968—, also dir. Rancher, Red River County, Tex., 1965; owner Carriage House Motel, 1970. Served with USNR, 1943-45. Mem. C. of C. Democrat. Baptist. Mason. Clubs: Lubbock Country, Knife & Fork (Lubbock). Home: 4513 9th St Lubbock TX 79416 Office: 5208 34th St Lubbock TX 79407

WILSON, LYLE LAWRENCE, metal bldg. co. exec.; b. Gillette, Wyo., May 6, 1928; s. Robert Walter and Maude (Shannon) W.; B.S. in Civil Engring., U. Wyo., 1950; M.S. in Civil Engring., Ga. Inst.

Tech., 1958; m. Patricia Anne Chittim, Dec. 24, 1948; 1 dau., Shannon Tracey. Design engr. Arctic Contractors, Fairbanks, Point Barrow, Alaska, 1950-52; univ. engr. U. Alaska, College, 1952-54; mem. engring., research, operations and corporate staff Humble Oil & Refining Co., New Orleans, 1957-66; v.p. engring. Am. Bldgs. Co., Eufaula, Ala., 1966—, also dir.; dir. U.S. Golf Co., Eufaula, Viking Hydraulics Inc., Eufaula. Mem. adv. com. Chauncy Parks State Trade Sch. Served to 1st lt. USAF, 1954-56. Recipient M.A. Ferst Sigma Xi Grad. Research award for outstanding research Ga. Inst. Tech., 1958. Registered profl. engr., La., Ark., Miss., Tex., Ala. Mem. Am. Soc. C.E., Tex. Soc. Profl. Engrs., Am. Inst. Steel Constrn. (S.E. regional adv. com., joint research com. on bolted connections with Metal Bldg. Mfrs. Assn., mem. gen. com. steel structures research), Metal Bldg. Mfrs. Assn. (chmn. tech. com.), Sigma Xi, Sigma Phi Epsilon. Republican. Methodist. Lion, Kiwanian. Home: Fox Ridge Rd Eufaula AL 36027 Office: PO Drawer A Eufaula AL 36027

WILSON, MILLARD FILLMORE, educator; b. Sanderson, Fla., Oct. 16, 1911; s. George Washington and Martha Christopher (Houston) W.; B.E., U. Fla., 1939, M.Ed., 1940; postgrad. Duke, 1941; m. Sigrid Claire Devoire, Dec. 2, 1936. Instr. Andrew Jackson Sch., Jacksonville, Fla., 1940-44, dean of men, 1944-48; asso. prof. commerce Catawba Coll., Salisbury, N.C., 1948—, dir. placement office, 1948—, chmn. dept. commerce, 1950. Pres. Rowan County Inter-Civic Council; vice chmn. Rowan County Youth Comm., Rowan County Youth Bd.; mem. nat. speakers bur. Boy Scouts Am., vice chmn. Rowan County council. Named Rowan County Man of Year, 1967. Mem. Am. Acad. Polit. and Social Sci., So. Econ. Assn., Adminstrv. Mgmt. Soc. (pres.), Sales-Marketing Execs. Club (exec. Salisbury), Am. Accounting Assn., Soc. Advt. Mgmt., Acad. Mgmt., Am. Marketing Assn., N.C. Bus. Edn. Council, Internat. Platform Assn., Acad. Certified Adminstrv. Mgrs., Kappa Delta Pi. Christian Scientist. Mason (K.T., Shriner), Lion (pres. Salisbury, zone chmn., dist. gov., internat. counselor). Club: Salisbury Country (dir.). Address: Catawba Coll Salisbury NC 28144

WILSON, OWEN DUNCAN, lawyer; b. Enid, Okla., Feb. 8, 1937; s. Rolland O. and Gladys (Kent) W.; B.A., U. Okla., 1959, LL.B., 1961; m. Mary Elizabeth Donnell, Aug. 23, 1958; children—Philip Owen, Angela Christine. Admitted to Okla. bar, 1961; mem. firm Wilson & Wilson, Enid, 1963—; pres., dir. Wilson Royalty Co., 1963—. Atty. Enid Sch. Bd., 1970—. Served to capt. AUS, 1961-63. Mem. Am., Okla., Garfield County (sec. 1964) bar assns., Sons and Daus. Cherokee Strip Pioneers (pres. 1969), Beta Theta Pi. Methodist. Lion. Home: 1931 Huron St Enid OK 73701 Office: 217 N Independence Enid OK 73701

WILSON, PATRICK JAMES, lawyer; b. Idaho Falls, Ida., Nov. 22, 1923; s. Richard Sheridan and Margaret (Hart) W.; student U. Ida., 1941-43; B.S. cum laude, U. Notre Dame, 1947; LL.B., Georgetown U., 1950; m. Adriana Mercado, June 19, 1949; children—Maria Luisa, Margarita Maria, Richard S. Admitted to P.R. bar, 1950, D.C. bar, 1950; law clk. Supreme Ct. of P.R., San Juan, 1950; practiced in Washington, 1951-54, 59—; asso. firm Ginsberg, Leventhal and Brown, 1951-54; resident partner firm Gadsby & Hannah, P.R., 1959-71; partner Firm O'Neill & Borges, Hato Rey, P.R., 1971—; exec. Mario Mercado e Hijos, Ponce, P.R., 1954-59. Founding dir. Ponce Fed. Savings & Loan Co. (P.R.). Mem. bd. examiners P.R. bar exam. com. Supreme Ct. of P.R., 1964-65. Served with USMCR, 1942-46. Republican. Roman Catholic. Home: Condominium San Geronimo 860 Ashford Av Santurce PR 00907 Office: Chase Manhattan Bank Bldg Hato Rey PR 00918

WILSON, RAY FLOYD, educator; b. Giddings, Tex., Feb. 20, 1926; s. Fred and Beulah (McCloud) W.; B.S. cum laude, Houston-Tillotson Coll., 1950; M.S., Tex. So. U., 1951, J.D. magna cum laude, 1972; Ph.D., U. Tex., 1953; m. Deanovoy Ward, Jan. 3, 1972; children by previous marriage—Ray Floyd II, Freddy O., Roy A., Mercedes L. Asso. prof. chemistry Tex. So. U., Houston, 1953-57, prof., 1957—. Served with USNR, 1944-46. Mem. Am. Chem. Soc., N.Y., Tex. acads. sci., Am. Inst. Chemists, Sigma Xi, Phi Lambda Upsilon, Beta Kappa Chi. Conglist (trustee). Contbr. articles to profl. jours. Home: TSU Box 227 Houston TX 77004 Office: 3201 Wheeler St Houston TX 77004

WILSON, REX WAYNE, elec. engr.; b. Clarksburg, W.Va., July 27, 1941; s. Rex Benton and Pauline (Michael) W.; B.S. in Elec. Engring., W. Va., U., 1963, M.S. in Elec. Engring., 1966; Ph.D., U. Waterloo, Ont., Can., 1973; m. Thelma Irene Eddy, Sept. 6, 1963 (div. Nov. 1969). Radio frequency component engr. Electromagnetic Research Corp., College Park, Md., 1963-64; elec. engr. Control Sci. Corp., Alexandria, Va., 1966; sr. elec. engr. Airtronics Inc., Washington, 1971-74; elec. engr. Vitro Labs., Silver Spring, Md., 1974—. NASA fellow W. Va. U., 1964-66. Mem. I.E.E.E., Measurements and Data Soc., Mensa, Tau Beta Pi, Eta Kappa Nu. Home: 11311 Smithfield Rd Manassas VA 22110 Office: 14000 Georgia Av Silver Spring MD 20906

WILSON, RICHARD CARLTON, educator; b. Greenville, N.C., Oct. 13, 1924; s. Richard Clayton and Myrtle (House) W.; student N.Y.U., 1943-44; B.S., East Carolina Coll., 1948; M.A., U. N.C., 1951, Ph.D., 1958; m. Peggy Ann Tucker, Aug. 24, 1952; children—Richard Carlton, Sherrie Tucker. Tchr. elementary and secondary schs., N.C., 1948-53; elementary sch. prin., Rocky Mount, N.C., 1953-57; asso. prof. Fla. State U., 1958-68; prof., dir. reading U. West Fla., Pensacola, 1968—. Cons. reading and curriculum, 1958—. Served with AUS, 1943-46. Mem. Fla Reading Council (life, pres.), Nat. Council Tchrs. English, Internat. Fla., Leon (pres. 1966-67) reading assns. Clubs: Scenic Hills Country, Current Topics Rocky Mount (pres. 1956). Author: Individualized Reading-A Practical Approach, 1965, rev., 1972; Viewpoints for the Reading Teacher. Editor: Fla. Reading Quar., 1967-71, editorial adviser, 1971—. Contbr. articles to profl. jours. Home: 8901 Scenic Hills Dr Pensacola FL 32504

WILSON, ROBERT E. LEE, III, farmer, mayor; b. Memphis, July 27, 1913; s. Robert E. Lee and Natalie (Armstrong) W.; A.B., Yale, 1936; m. Mildred Martin, Dec. 31, 1962; children—Michael, Stephen, Robert, Frank, Diana, Midlred. Pres., Lee Wilson Co., Wilson, Ark., 1950—, Delta Valley and So. Ry., 1951—; chmn. bd. Bank of Wilson, 1960—; mayor City of Wilson, 1950—; dir. Ark. Power & Light Co., Middle South Utilities, Inc. Justice of peace, Wilson, 1950-72; drainage commr. Mississippi County, Ark., 1952—. Trustee 2 estates for ednl. purposes. Served to capt. AUS, 1941-45. Decorated Bronze Star with two oak leaf clusters. Club: Memphis Country. Home: Wilson AR 72395 Office: Lee Wilson & Co Hwy 61 Wilson AR 72395

WILSON, ROBERT WAYNE, clergyman; b. San Antonio, Oct. 23, 1932; s. Finis Alexander and Willie Faye (Guthrie) W.; ed. Assumption Sem., San Antonio, 1957; M.S. in Psychology, St. John's U., 1964; Ph.D. in Counseling Psychology, N.Y. U., 1974. Joined Diocese Dallas-Ft. Worth, 1950, ordained priest Roman Cath. Ch., 1957; dean students U. Dallas, 1961-64; dir. vocations Cath. Diocese of Dallas-Ft. Worth, 1964-67; pastor St. Rita's Ch., Ranger, Tex., 1967-70, St. John the Apostle Ch., Ft. Worth, 1970—; supt. schs. Catholic Diocese of Ft. Worth, 1970—, pres. senate of priests, 1970—. Pres. senate of priests Diocese of Dallas-Ft. Worth, 1969-70; chmn. Provincial Conf. Priests' Councils, Province of San Antonio, 1971-72. Mem. Am. Psychol. Assn., Nat. Cath. Edn. Assn. (parliamentarian supt.'s dept. 1970-72). K.C. Club: Glen Lakes Country (Dallas). Author: Book of Liturgical Ceremonies, 1956. Contbr. articles to religious publs. Home: 4608 Vance St Fort Worth TX 76118 Office: PO Box 13186 Fort Worth TX 76118

WILSON, SAMUEL, JR., architect; b. New Orleans, Aug. 6, 1911; s. Samuel and Stella (Poupeney) W.; B.Arch., Tulane U., 1931; m. Ellen Elizabeth Latrobe, Oct. 20, 1951. Architect office Moise H. Goldstein, 1930-33, Historic Am. Bldgs. Survey in La., 1934-35; architect office Richard Koch, 1935-42, asso., 1945-55, partner Richard Koch & Samuel Wilson, Jr., New Orleans, 1955-70, Koch & Wilson, Architects, 1971—. Lectr. La. architecture Tulane U. mem. exec. bd. New Orleans area council Boy Scouts Am.; mem. bd. Friends of Cabilde, Maison Hospitaliere; mem. Orleans Parish Landmarks Commn., La. Hist. Preservation and Cultural Commn., 1968-71. Served with USCGR, 1942-45. Edward Langley scholar A.I.A., 1938. Fellow A.I.A.; mem. Soc. Archtl. Historians, La. Landmarks Soc. (pres. 1950-56), Christian Women's Exchange (hon.). Roman Catholic. Club: Boston (New Orleans). Author: A Guide to Architecture of New Orleans, 1699-1959; Plantation Houses on The Battlefield of New Orleans, 1965; The Vieux Carre New Orleans, 1969; Bienvilles New Orleans; co-author Baroness Pontalba's Buildings, 1964; The Basilica on Jackson Square, 1965; The St. Louis Cemeteries of New Orleans, 1963; The Cabildo on Jackson Square, 1970; New Orleans Architecture—Lower Garden District, Vol. I. Editor: Impressions Respecting New Orleans (B. H. B. Latrobe), 1951. Contbr. articles to profl. and hist. publs. Home: 1121 Washington Av New Orleans LA 70130 Office: Masonic Temple Bldg New Orleans LA 70130

WILSON, STEPHEN K., hosp. adminstr.; b. Atlanta, Aug. 3, 1931; s. Henry Louie and Alma (Lewis) W.; student U. Fla., 1948-50, 55-57; B.S., Fla. State U., 1959; M.H.A., Washington U., 1961; m. Patricia Ann Copeland, Aug. 17, 1957; children—Tania Elaine, Stephanie Diane, Krista Ann, Stephen Patrick. Asst. adminstr. Gadsden County Hosp., Quincy, Fla., 1958-59; adminstr. Cape Canaveral Hosp., Cocoa Beach, Fla., 1961-73; adminstr. Ormond Beach (Fla.) Hosp., 1974—. Mem. exec. com. East Central Fla. Hosp. Council, 1969—, pres., 1973. Served with USNR, 1951-55. Mem. Fla., Am. hosp. assns., Am. Coll. Hosp. Adminstrs. Rotarian. (treas. 1965-66, v.p. 1966-67, pres. 1967-68, dir. 1968-69, bull. editor 1969-70). Home: PO Box 1924 1596 John Anderson Dr Ormond Beach FL 32074 Office: Ormond Beach Hosp 264 S Atlantic Av Ormond Beach FL 32074

WILSON, WALTER RALEIGH, JR., optometrist; b. Douglas, Ga., Dec. 7, 1910; s. Walter Raleigh and Bertha Elizabeth (Blackstock) W.; student South Ga. Coll., 1929-30, U. Ga., 1931, George Washington U., 1932-34; D.Optometry, No. Ill. Coll. Optometry, 1939; m. Johnnie Louise Byrd, July 6, 1935; 1 dau., Joanne (Mrs. Edwin Albert Dickey). Practice optometry, Douglas, 1939—. Dir. Farmers Bank, Douglas. Mem. Ga. Bd. Examiners Optometry, 1961-64, 72—. Chmn. Douglas-Coffee County Planning Commn., 1956-72. Mem. Ga. Democratic com., 1971-74. Bd. dirs., v.p. Ga. Lions Lighthouse. Recipient Silver Beaver award Boy Scouts Am., 1954; named Optometrist of Year, 1948, 54, 57. Mem. Ga. Optometric Assn. (pres. 1947-48), Tomb and Key. Baptist (chmn. bd. deacons). Mason (Shriner), Lion (pres. 1946, dist. gov. 1949), Elk. Club: Douglas Golf. Home: 1001 Chester Av Douglas GA 31533 Office: PO Box 511 Douglas GA 31533

WILSON, WESLEY ALLEN, city ofcl.; b. Chipley, Fla., Mar. 16, 1932; s. John William and Leah (Martin) W.; A.A., U. Fla., 1952, postgrad. 1953-54; m. Eleanor Vivian Hasty, July 12, 1952; children—Donna Ellen, Mary Jane. Engring. aide City of Thomasville (Ga.), 1954-55, asst. city engr., 1955-58, city engr., 1958—. Tchr. hwy. tech. Thomas Tech. U., 1968-69. Registered profl. engr., Ga., Fla. Mem. Am. Soc. C.E. (pres. br. 1970), Inst. Municipal Engrs., Am. Pub. Works Assn., Ga. Water Pollution Control Assn. Kiwanian (pres. 1971-72). Methodist. Home: 511 Ernest St Thomasville GA 31792 Office: 144 E Jackson St Thomasville GA 31792

WILSON, WILLIAM EDWARD, rural resource devel. specialist; b. Wedowee, Ala., June 24, 1923; s. James Floyd and Mary Jim (Weathers) W.; B.S., Auburn U., 1949, M.S., 1961; m. Olive Rudine Cooper, May 15, 1946; children—Robert Cooper, Rebecca. Dept. mgr., salesman Guy Hood Feed Seed Fertilizer Co., Gadsden, Ala., 1949-51; farm supt. Ala. Baptist Childrens Home, Troy, 1951-54; asst. county agt. Auburn (Ala.) U. Co-op. Extension Service, 1954-61, specialist in rural resource devel., 1961—. County fund drive chmn. Girl Scouts U.S.A., 1963-64; city chmn. fund drive A.R.C., 1959; organizer, v.p., dir. Clay County Arts and Crafts League, 1970—. Bd. dirs. Tallacoosa Highland Lakes Assn., 1969—, Clay County United Givers Fund, 1967—; bd. dirs., mem. exec. com. Health Planning Assn. Ala. Dist. IV, Ala. Manpower Dist. IV Ancillary Bd., Hugo Black Meml. Library; chmn. Clay County chpt. Nat. Found., 1956—; trustee Clay County High Sch., 1961-65. Served with AUS, 1943-46. Mem. Ashland Jr. C. of C. (dir., sec. 1957-58, pres., 1958-59), Community Devel. Soc. (a founder 1969), Gamma Sigma Delta, Epsilon Sigma Phi. Baptist (Sunday Sch. dir., chmn. bd. deacons 1969-71). Rotarian. Club: Clay County Country (Ashland). Address: PO Box 485 Ashland AL 36251

WILSON, WILLIAM FIGH, mfg. co. exec.; b. Mart, Tex., June 18, 1919; s. Howard Lee and Georgia Louise (Figh) W.; B.B.A., U. Tex., 1940; m. Ella Burndrett, Sept. 12, 1942; children—Fred Lee, Robert Orr. With Shell Oil Co., various locations, 1940-53, mgr. cost accounting, Houston, 1948-51, chief cost analyst, N.Y.C., 1951-53; with Tenneco Inc., various locations, 1953—, dir. systems, Houston, 1968-69, sr. v.p. Newport News Shipbuilding & Dry Dock Co. subsidiary (Va.), 1969—; dir. 1st & Mchts. Nat. Bank, Newport News. Bd. dirs. Riverside Hosp., Newport News, 1970—. Served with AUS, 1942-43. Mem. Sigma Iota Epsilon, Beta Alpha Phi. Methodist. Clubs: James River Country, Huntington. Home: 160 Yeardley Dr Apt 26 Newport News VA 23601 Office: 4101 Washington Av Newport News VA 23607

WILSON, WILLIS TRENT, dentist; b. Stanley, N.C., Aug. 28, 1902; s. William Henry and Sarah (Ashlin) W.; student Va. Poly. Inst., 1922-23; D.D.S., Med. Coll. Va., 1927; m. Emily Louise Lincke, Oct. 27, 1934; children—Christine Lincke (Mrs. Benjamin Bishop Johnson), Willis Trent, Maurice Lincke. Individual practice dentistry, Hopewell, Va., 1927—. Mem. adv. bd. Hopewell br. First Mchts. Nat. Bank. Mem. Am., Southside Va. dental assns., Va., Hopewell (pres. 1960) dental socs. Moose (pres. 1958-61, mem. civic affairs com. 1971-72), Kiwanian (pres. 1930). Home: 2713 Walnut St Hopewell VA 23860 Office: 201 State Planters Bldg Hopewell VA 23860

WILSON, WOODROW HOYT, wholesale co. exec.; b. Seminole, Okla., Nov. 30, 1912; s. Edward Lee and Ethel Mae (Mosier) W.; student Oklahoma City U., 1942-43; m. Lou Baney, Dec. 31, 1953; children—Dolores, Carole Sue; 1 adopted son, Jeffery. With Stevens Products Co., Oklahoma City, 1934-46; with Scrivner Boogaart, Inc., Oklahoma City, 1946—, v.p. J.V. Smith div., 1948—. Served with AUS, 1944-46; ETO. Mem. Okla. Shippers Assn. (v.p. 1954—). Mem. Christian Ch. (deacon). Home: 6468 Sterling Dr Oklahoma City OK 73132 Office: 3421 N Walnut St Oklahoma City OK 73105

WILWERS, EDWARD MATHIAS, educator, artist; b. Chgo., Feb. 4, 1918; s. Michael and Hermina (Meier) W.; B.F.A., Drake U., 1950; M.F.A., Ohio U., 1951; postgrad. U. Wis., 1958; m. Esther M. Mathiesen, May 17, 1943; children—William S., Wendy C. Accounting dept. C.M. St. Paul & P. R.R., Chgo., 1937-42; asst. to sales mgr. Crooks Terminal Warehouses, Inc., Chgo., 1942-43, 46-48; designer, gen. sales mgr. Hutcheson Displays, Inc., Omaha, 1952-59; advt. mgr. D & H Assos., Ogden, Utah, 1959-60; head dept. art Ark. Poly. Coll., Russellville, Ark., 1960—. Exhibited works one-man shows Ohio U., Ark. Poly. Coll., Ark. Found. Arts, Triton Mus. Art, San Jose, Cal.; group shows include Des Moines Art Center, Drake U., Sage Art Gallery, Taos, N.M.; represented in pvt. collections, U.S. and abroad. Served with AUS, 1943-46. Fellow Royal Soc. Arts; mem. Southwestern, Southeastern, Mid-Am. Coll. art confs., Nat. Council Art Adminstrs., Kappa Pi. Home: Route 4 Bayou Lane Russellville AR 72801

WIMBERLY, HARRINGTON, newspaper publisher; b. Hale Center, Tex., June 22, 1901; s. Joe Ed and Margaret (Wilson) W.; A.B., U. Okla., 1924; m. Myrth McCurley, Apr. 22, 1927; children—Janis Myrth, Mary Margaret. Editor, Altus (Okla.) Daily Times-Democrat, 1929-61, Duncan (Okla.) Daily Banner, 1961—. Chmn. Dem. State Com. of Okla., 1944-45; apptd. mem. Fed. Power Commn., 1945. Home: 911 Hillcrest Dr Duncan OK 73533 Office: 1001 Elm St Duncan OK 73533

WIMBERLY, JOHN EVAN, thoracic surgeon; b. Jackson, Miss., May 30, 1938; s. Guilford Evan and Pearl Eugenia (Powers) W.; B.S., Millsaps Coll., 1958; M.D., Baylor U., 1962; m. Clara Irene Smith, July 23, 1960; children—John Evan, Laura Alice, David Lawrence. Surg. intern Vanderbilt U. Hosps., Nashville, 1962-63, resident in gen. and thoracic surgery, 1963-64, 66-69; fellow in thoracic and cardiovascular surgery U. Tex. Hosps., Dallas, 1971-72; practice medicine specializing in thoracic surgery The Med. Center Clinic, Pensacola, Fla., 1969-71, 72—; mem. surg. staff Sacred, Bapt., University hosps. (all in Pensacola, Fla.). Mem. teaching staff, bd. dirs. Pensacola Ednl. Program, 1973—. Served to lt. USNR, 1964-66. Diplomate Am. Bd. Surgery, Am. Bd. Thoracic Surgery. Fellow A.C.S.; mem. Pensacola Surg. Soc. (pres. 1973); A.M.A., Fla. Med. Soc. Contbr. to profl. publs. in field. Home: 3960 Raintree St Pensacola FL 32503 Office: 1750 N Palafox St Pensacola FL 32501

WIMBERLY, JOHN HARRY, gas co. exec.; b. Houston, Dec. 6, 1904; s. Stonewall Jackson and Hallie (Holland) W.; student Rice Inst., 1922; B.B.A., U. Tex., 1927; m. Edith Cooney, Oct. 15, 1931; children—Bryan Holland, Lane Mayfield, Thomas Allan. Auditor Houston Natural Gas Corp., 1931-40, treas., 1940-45, v.p., treas., 1945-47, exec. v.p., 1947-55, pres., 1955—, dir., 1940—, chmn. bd., 1967-73, sr. chmn., 1973—, also sr. chmn. bd. of subsidiaries; pres. Houston Pipe Line Co., 1956-67; dir. Continental Bank of Tex., Houston, Port City State Bank. Pres. Houston Jr. C. of C., 1936. Trustee S.W. Research Inst., Inst. Gas Tech., St. Luke's Episcopal Hosp. Mem. Am. (past dir., past pres.), So. (pres. 1952) gas assns., Tex. Research League (dir.). Episcopalian (pres. churchmen's assns. 1949). Clubs: Houston Country (past pres.), Tejas (Houston). Home: 5421 Sturbridge Dr Houston TX 77027 Office: Houston Natural Gas Bldg PO Box 1188 Houston TX 77002

WIMBERLY, WILLIAM FINCH, agrl. co. exec.; b. Brandon, Tex., Dec. 30, 1928; s. William Finch and Oral Magdalene (Gibson) W.; B.S., Tex. A. and M. U., 1959; children—William Finch III, Brenda Sue. Mgr., High Plains Sesame Growers, Inc. (Tex.), 1959-62; v.p. Tex. Sesame Growers, Inc., 1962-66; exec. v.p. Tex. Sesame div. Paris Milling Co., Muleshoe, Tex., 1966—; sec., dir. Tidwell's, Inc.; dir. Paris Milling Co. Served with USAF, 1952-56. Mem. Nat., Tex. feed and grain assns., Grain Sorghum Producers Assn. (past dir.), Muleshoe C. of C. (dir.), Phi Kappa Phi, Phi Eta Sigma, Alpha Zeta. Methodist. Home: PO Box 789 Muleshoe TX 79347 Office: PO Box 789 Muleshoe TX 79347

WIMPEY, JOHN ANDREW, state ofcl.; b. Blairsville, Ga., Mar. 16, 1927; s. James LaFayette and Thanie Elvira (Cook) W.; A.B., Mercer U., 1950; M.A., George Peabody Coll. Tchrs., 1950, M.Ed., 1954, Ph.D., 1958; postgrad. Harvard, 1958, Columbia, part-time 1961-64; m. Leta Shelby, Nov. 30, 1949; 1 dau., LeAnn (Mrs. Robert James Hulsey). Tchr. pub. schs., Ga., 1949-54; prin., Rhine (Ga.) Schs., 1954-56; prof., head dept. social scis. Belmont Coll., 1958-61; asso. prof. edn. The Citadel, 1961-67; dir. tchr. edn. and certification Ga. Dept. Edn., Atlanta, 1967—. Cons. planning research and evaluation Ga. Dept. Edn., 1971—. Served with AUS, 1945-47. Recipient Gov.'s citation, 1945; named Dodge County Tchr. of Yr., 1956. Mem. N.E.A. (life), Nat. Soc. Study Edn., Assn. Higher Edn., Am. Assn. U. Profs., Nat. Assn. State Dirs. Tchr. Edn. and Certification, Danforth Assos., Phi Delta Kappa. Baptist. Kiwanian. Clubs: Exchange (program chmn. 1968-69), Woodvalley Park (Hapeville, Ga.). Contbr. chpt. to Vital Issues in American Education; articles to profl. jours. Home: 2109 LaVista Circle Hapeville Atlanta GA 30354 Office: State Dept Edn Atlanta GA 30303

WIMPRESS, GORDON DUNCAN, JR., coll. pres.; b. Riverside, Cal., Apr. 10, 1922; s. Gordon Duncan and Maude A. (Waldo) W.; B.A., U. Ore., 1946, M.A., 1951; Ph.D., U. Denver, 1958; LL.D., Monmouth Coll., 1970; L.H.D., Tusculum Coll., 1971; m. Jean Margaret Skerry, Nov. 30, 1946; children—Wendy Jo, Victoria Jean, Gordon Duncan III. Dir. pub. relations, instr. journalism Whittier (Cal.) Coll., 1946-51; asst. to pres. Colo. Sch. Mines, Golden, 1951-59; pres. Monticello Coll., Alton, Ill., 1959-64, Monmouth (Ill.) Coll., 1964-70, Trinity U., San Antonio, 1970—. Mem. adv. council Pres. Assn. Governing Bds. Univs. and Colls.; mem. Nexus com. Presbyn. Coll. Union; mem. adv. com. Character Edn. Project Fund; mem. Burlington No. Scholarship Selection com.; commr. Nat. Commn. Accrediting. Trustee San Antonio Med. Found., Southwest Research Inst., Southwest Tex. Ednl. TV Council, Tex. Bicentennial Citizens' Orgn., Univ. Aviation Found., Inc., World Bus. Council. Served to 1st lt. AUS, 1942-45. Decorated Bronze Star. Mem. Am. Coll. Pub. Relations Assn. (trustee), Am. Alumni Council, Nat. Pilots Assn., Aircraft Owners and Pilots Assn., Assn. Am. Colls., Am. Council on Edn., Sigma Delta Chi, Sigma Upsilon, Pi Gamma Mu, Sigma Phi Epsilon (trustee found.). Presbyn. Rotarian. Clubs: University (Chgo., N.Y. and San Antonio); Argyle; Newcomen; Oak Hills Country; St. Anthony; San Antonio; Texas Internat. Gun. Author: American Journalism Comes of Age, 1950. Office: 715 Stadium Dr San Antonio TX 78212

WINANT, JOHN HALDEMAN, assn. exec.; b. Bklyn., Sept. 3, 1923; s. William Alfred and Hazel Bergen (Hooper) W.; grad. Peddie Sch., 1941; B.A., Williams Coll., 1945; m. Kathryn Pratt Geyer, Sept. 15, 1948; children—Claudia, Peter Bergen. News editor A.P., N.Y.C., 1947-49; mgr. Winant & Co., N.Y.C., 1949-53; v.p. Sprague Electric Co., 1953-71; pres. Nat. Bus. Aircraft Assn., Washington, 1971—. Served with USMCR, 1943-46, 51-52. Decorated Bronze Star medal. Mem. Electronic Industries Assn., Nat. Aviation Club, Delta Kappa Epsilon. Home: 221 Wolfe St Alexandria VA 22314 Office: Pennsylvania Bldg Washington DC 20004

WINCHESTER, ALMA ELIZABETH TATSCH (MRS. CLARENCE FLOYD WINCHESTER), civic worker, radio writer and broadcaster; b. Fredericksburg, Tex.; d. Otto August and Meta (Hohenberger) Tatsch; student Am. Conservatory Music (chgo.), 1937-38; m. Clarence Floyd Winchester, Sept. 25, 1943. Singer Chgo. Civic Opera Jr. Chorus, 1937-38; writer radio script Evans Fur Co., Chgo., 1941-42; writer radio sta. KTSA, San Antonio, 1942-43; womens dir., writer, broadcaster radio sta. KNOE, Monroe, La., 1944-45; writer, music lead in Boyce Smith Show, Sta. WGN, Chgo., 1944; womens dir., writer, broadcaster radio sta. WGGG, Gainesville, Fla., 1948-49; pub. relations Stokeley-Van Camp, Inc., Washington, 1954-55. Mem. Salvation Army Aux., Washington; mem. women's bd. Providence Hosp., Washington; Pan-Am. Liaison Com. Womens Orgns., Washington; mem. Womens Internat. Religious Fellowship in cooperation with UNESCO, UNICEF, Schs., embassies; pres. City of Hope Med. Research chpt. 56, Washington. Mem. Internat. Platform Assn., Los Picaros (hon.), Howard University Faculty Wives. Mem. Christian Ch. Home: 2124 Sudbury Pl NW Washington DC 20012

WINCHESTER, CLARENCE FLOYD, educator; b. Chgo., Oct. 14, 1901; s. Leon Alpheus and Nina Pearl (Thompson) W.; B.S., U. Cal. at Berkeley, 1924, M.S., 1935; Ph.D., U. Mo., 1939; m. Maxine Gertrude Kiefer, Sept. 15, 1924 (div. 1938); 1 dau., Maxine Claire (Mrs. Robert Cloon); m. 2d, Alma Elizabeth Tatsch, Sept. 25, 1943; Tchr. pub. schs., Los Angeles, 1924-28, Palo Verde, Cal., 1928-29, Fresno, Cal., 1929-31; research scientist U. N.H., 1931-32, U. Cal. at Davis, 1932-37, U. Mo., 1937-46; asso. prof. U. Fla., 1946-49; agrl. research scientist, Beltsville, Md., 1949-61; nutritionist U.S. Dept. Interior, 1961-66; lectr. Howard U., Washington, 1966—. Served from 1st lt. to capt. AUS, 1942-46. Fellow Intercontinental Biog. Assn., A.A.A.S., Am. Inst. Chemists; mem. Am. Chem. Soc., Am. Inst. Nutrition, Am. Assn. U. Profs., Assn. Overseas Educators, Am. Soc. Animal Prodn., Sigma Xi, Gamma Sigma Delta, Alpha Chi Sigma, Gamma Alpha. Mason (32 deg.). Home: 2124 Sudbury Pl NW Washington DC 20012 Office: Howard Pl and 4th St NW Washington DC 20001

WINCHESTER, RICHARD LEE, JR., lawyer; b. Memphis, May 21, 1924; s. Cassius Lee and Harriet Haywood (Bond) W.; LL.B., U. Tenn., 1949, J.D., 1965; m. Bette Anne Thompson, July 15, 1944; children—Robin Ann, Richard Lee Jr., John Thompson. Admitted to Tenn. bar, 1949; partner firm Winchester, Walsh & Marshall, Memphis, 1972—; Shelby County atty., 1961-64; city atty., Germantown and Arlington, Tenn., 1966—. Gen. counsel, dir. Quality Concrete Products Co., Ind.; owner Holiday Inn frachise, El Dorado, Ark.; sec. Beachfront Condos, Inc., N.Fla.; dir. First Bank of Germantown; farmer, DeSoto County (Miss.), Carroll County (Tenn.). Chmn., Germantown Planning Commn., 1958-61; mem. Gov.'s Commn. on Human Relations, 1962-68. Vice chmn., treas. Memphis and Shelby County Democratic Exec. Com., 1958-72; state exec. com., pres. Tenn. Young Democrats, 1960-61; del. state and nat. Dem. Convs., 1964-68; nat. elector from Tenn., 1960-72. Pres., bd. dirs. Mid-South Fair Assn.; bd. dirs. Sheltered Occupational Shop, A.R.C.; trustee Episcopal Girls Home; pres. Episcopal Planning Commn. Served to capt. inf. AUS, 1942-46; PTO. Mem. Am. (past del.), Tenn. (past pres. jr. sect.), Memphis and Shelby County (past pres. jr. sect.) bar assns., Am. Judicature Soc., Nat. Assn. Legal Aid and Pub. Defenders, Am. Legion (past post comdr., past state vice comdr.), 40 and 8, V.F.W. (past post vice comdr.) U. Tenn. Alumni Assn. (past bd. govs., 9th Dist. rep.), Sigma Alpha Epsilon, Phi Eta Sigma, Phi Kappa Phi, Omicron Delta Kappa. Episcopalian. Mason (32 degree, Shriner, Jester), Kiwanian. Club: Tennessee. Bd. editors Tenn. Law Rev., 1948-49. Home: 2121 Pete Mitchell Rd Germantown TN 38038 Office: 100 N Main Bldg Memphis TN 38103

WINDECKER, ROLAND THEODORE, elec. engr.; b. Gull Lake, Sask., Can., Jan. 2, 1926; s. Konrad and Freida Emilia (Loos) W.; came to U.S., 1929, naturalized, 1936; B.S. in Elec. Engring. U. Tex., 1946, M.S., 1956; postgrad. Stanford, 1956-58; Ph.D., So. Meth. U., 1970; m. Sara Louise Shepard, Aug. 30, 1952; children—Paula Louise (Mrs. William Bradley Milner), Roland Theodore. Supr. Dow Chem. Co., Freeport, Tex., 1949-56; research asst. Stanford, 1957-58; sr. engr. components div. Tex. Instruments, Inc., Dallas, 1958-72; sr. design engr. Varo, Inc., Garland, Tex., 1972-73; sr. prodn. engr. Mostek Corp., Carrollton, Tex., 1973—. Served with USNR, 1946-48. Registered profl. engr., Tex. Mem. I.E.E.E. (chmn. 1950). Presbyn. (elder 1968—). Contbr. articles on electronic design to profl. publs. Patentee in field. Home: 404 Shadywood Lane Richardson TX 75080 Office: 1215 W Crosby Rd Carrollton TX 75006

WINDHAM, EULA HEARD, librarian; b. Tifton, Ga.; d. William Guy and Eula Beall (Wilson) Windham; A.B., Ga. State Coll. for Women, 1940; postgrad. So. Baptist Theol. Sem., 1945-47; M.R.E., 1950; M.L.S., Emory U., 1956. Tchr. pub. schs. Tifton, 1940-44; bookkeeper State Nat. Bank, Sheffield, Ala., 1944; caseworker Ga. Dept. Pub. Welfare, Tifton, 1945; state jr. leader Ga. Baptist Sunday Sch. Dept., Atlanta, 1947-55; circulation and reference librarian Hardin-Simmons U., Abilene, 1957-60. asst. librarian, 1960-61; librarian Middle Ga. Coll., Cochran, 1961—. Mem. A.L.A., Tex., Southwestern, Abilene, Ga. (exec. bd. 1963—), Southeastern library assns., Ga. Assn. Jr. Colls. (chmn. library div. 1963, 69), Ga. Assn. Educators (local chmn. 1967), Pilot Internat., Beta Sigma Phi. Clubs: XXI (sec. 1960-61), Cochran Women's. Compiler: Library Handbook, 1962, rev., 1973. Contbr. articles to profl. jours. Office: Middle Ga Coll Cochran GA 31014

WINDHAM, ROLAND HERBERT, city ofcl., educator; b. Lamar, S.C., Jan. 21, 1925; s. Theron Earl and Esther Ruth (Yarborough) W.; student Wofford Coll., 1941-43; B.S., U. S.C., 1948, M.Ed., 1949; m. Nancy Kathryn Huntley, Aug. 20, 1950; children—Lucinda Ruth, Roland Herbert, Jane. Tchr. math. Sumter (S.C.) pub. schs., 1948-52; tchr. Clevenger Bus. Coll., Sumter, 1950-52; city clk. City of Sumter, 1952-61, treas., 1952-61, asst. city mgr., 1955-61; city clk., treas., finance officer, asst. city mgr. City of Rock Hill (S.C.), 1961-63; city mgr. City of Aiken (S.C.), 1963—. Lectr. Army Civil Affairs Sch., Ft. Bragg, N.C., 1964-73; staff lectr., bur. pub. affairs U. S.C., Columbia, 1969-73. Served with USNR, 1943-46; Res., ret. Mem. Internat., S.C. (pres. 1967) city mgmt. assns. Rotarian (pres. 1966-67), Kiwanian (pres. 1958). Baptist (chmn. bd. deacons 1971-73, Sunday sch. dept. supt. 1968—, choir mem. 1950—). Home: 908 Whitehall Pl SE Aiken SC 29801 Office: 214 Park Av SW Aiken SC 29801

WINDHAM, WHIT, judge; b. Millport, Ala., Feb. 6, 1897; s. Reuben Vaughn and Martha (Waldrop) W.; A.B., U. Ala., 1918, LL.B., 1925; m. Lavica Margaret Stapp, Apr. 21, 1920; children—Philip, Stephen. Former mem. firms London, Yancy, Smith & Windham and Smith, Windham, Jackson & Rives; judge Circuit Ct., Birmingham, Ala., 1941—. Office: County Courthouse Birmingham AL 35203

WINEGAR, GEORGE LAWRENCE, chem. engr.; b. Rogersville, Tenn., Oct. 4, 1942; s. Harry Cash and Theda Madge (Ringley) W.; B.S. in Chem. Engring., U. Tenn., 1965, M.S. in Chem. Engring., 1967; m. Vivian Jean Taylor, June 19, 1965. Coop. student E.I. duPont de Nemours & Co., Inc., 1961-64; sr. chem. engr. Tenn. Eastman Co., Inc., Kingsport, 1967—. Pres. Tri-Cities Juvenile Residential Treatment Centers, Inc. Chmn. Sullivan County Young Republicans, 1972-73; mem. Sullivan County Rep. Election Commn., 1972—. Named One of Outstanding Young Men of Am., Jaycees, 1970, 71, Kingsport Jaycee of year, 1970, Tenn. Jaycee of Year, 1970. Registered profl. engr., Tenn. Mem. Am. Inst. Chem. Engrs., Kingsport Jaycees (v.p. 1968-69), Sigma Xi, Tau Beta Pi, Alpha Chi Sigma. Baptist. Eagle, Elk. Clubs: Young East Tennesseans (chmn. bd.), Metropolitan Dinner (Kingsport). Home: Route 11 Cliffview Dr Kingsport TN 37663 Office: PO Box 511 Kingsport TN 37662

WINESTONE, ROBERT LOUIS, govt. economist; b. Portland, Ore., Nov. 22, 1915; s. Jacob and Lena (Feldman) W.; B.A., U. Ore., 1939, M.A., 1942; postgrad. U. Minn., 1946-47; Ph.D., Northwestern U., 1954; m. Mildred Rosen, Nov. 27, 1944; children—Jerome Alan, Lee Philip. Tchr. pub. high scho., Portland, 1939-42; instr. U. Minn., Mpls., 1946-47, Northwestern U., Evanston, Ill., 1947-50; asst., prof. Coe Coll., Cedar Rapids, Ia., 1950-51; economist U.S. Dept. Commerce, Washington, 1951-53; asso. prof. U. Wichita, 1953-56; economist Rand Corp., Santa Monica, Cal., 1956-65; economist Research Analysis Corp., McLean, Va., 1966-68; econometrician U.S. Dept. Transp., Washington, 1968—. Lectr. U. Cal. at Los Angeles, 1963-65, Los Angeles State Coll., 1964-65. Pres., Pacific Palisades (Cal.) Democratic Club, 1959-61. Served with AUS, 1942-45. Mem. Am. Assn. U. Profs., Am. Econ. Assn., Artus, Phi Delta Kappa. Democrat. Home: 6504 Callander Dr Bethesda MD 20034 Office: 400 7th St SW Washington DC 20591

WINFIELD, JOHN ANDREW, mech. engr.; b. Petersburg, Va., Feb. 10, 1917; s. Bryant Dewees and Rebecca Beeman (Applewhite) W.; B.S. in Mech. Engring., Clemson U., 1940; postgrad. Emory U., 1968; m. Mary Catherine Lennon, Aug. 17, 1946; children—Catherine (Mrs. Ronald Masden), Marcia (Mrs. Sidney Sparrow). Supr., Bethlehem Steel Co. (Pa.), 1940-42; supr., mgr. Clark Bros. Co., Olean, N.Y., 1946-54; plant mgr. Brunner Co., Gainesville, Ga., 1954-55; mgr. tool design, mgr. standard tool gen. dept., mgr. standard tool control dept. Lockheed Ga. Co., Marietta, 1955—. Mem. adv. bd. North Ga. Tech. Sch., 1957-68; Atlanta/Fulton Co. Vocational and Tech. Sch., 1958-68; mem. Ga. gov.'s staff. 1960-64; dep. chief Civil Def., Olean, 1953. Bd. dirs., founder Ga. Engring. Found., 1972—, v.p., 1972-73, pres., 1973—. Vernon Woods Devel. Corp., 1960. Served to capt. AUS, 1942-46. Decorated Bronze Star medal. Mem. Soc. Mfg. Engrs. (nat. dir. 1967-71), Lockheed Mgmt. Club. Home: 6434 Cherry Tree Lane Atlanta GA 30328 Office: Dept 43-15 Lockheed Ga Co Marietta GA 30060

WINFREY, DORMAN HAYWARD, state librarian; b. Henderson, Tex., Sept. 4, 1924; s. Luke Abel and Linnie (Fears) W.; B.A., U. Tex., 1950, M.A., 1951, Ph.D., 1962; m. Ruth Carolyn Byrd, June 12, 1954; children—Laura, Jennifer. Social sci. research asso. Research in Tex. History, Tex. Hist. Assn. at U. Tex., 1946-58; state archivist, 1958-60; archivist U. Tex., 1960-61; dir., librarian Tex. State Library, 1962—. Chmn. State Bd. Library Examiners, 1962—; chmn. State Records Preservation Adv. Com., 1965—. Served with AUS, 1943-46, ETO. Clara Driscoll scholar for research in Tex. history, 1952-54. Fellow Tex. Hist. Assn. (exec. council, pres. 1971—), Soc. Am. Archivists (council), Am. Assn. for State and Local History (council), mem. Tex. Inst. Letters, Philos. Soc. Tex., Am. Assn. State Libraries (planning com.), A.L.A., Tex. Library Assn., Am., Tex., So. hist. assns., Phi Alpha Theta, Pi Sigma Alpha. Mem. Disciples of Christ Ch. Author, editor: Texas Indian Papers, 1825-1843, 1959; Texas Indian Papers, 1844-1845, 1960; Texas Indian Papers, 1846-1859, 1960; A History of Rusk County, Texas, 1961; Julien Sidney Devereux and His Monte Verdi Plantation, 1964; Indian Papers of Texas and the Southwest, 1825-1916 (5 vols.), 1966; Arturo Toscanini in Texas; The 1950 NBC Symphony Orchestra Tour, 1967; spl. editor Tex. Ency. for Young People, 1964; asso. editor Jr. Historian mag., 1951-58; Seventy-Five Years of Texas History: The Texas State Historical Association, 1897-1972, 1974. Home: 6503 Willamette Dr Austin TX 78723 Office: Tex State Library Box 12927 Capitol Sta Austin TX 78711

WINFREY, ELISHA WILLIAM III, physician; b. Richmond, Va., June 10, 1932; s. Elisha William and Lee (Jones) W.; student Washington and Lee U., 1948-50; A.B., U. Va., 1952, M.D., 1956; Intern, U. Va. Hosp., Charlottesville, 1956-57; resident Vanderbilt U. Hosp., Nashville, 1959-63; resident George Washington U. Hosp., Washington, 1963-65, instr. surgery, 1963-65; practiced medicine specializing in thoracic and cardiovascular surgery in Newport News, Va., 1965—; mem. staff Hampton Va. V.A. Hosp., 1965—. Mem. Adv. Council U. Va., 1966—. Served with USN, 1956-59. Diplomate Am. Bd. Surgery, Am. Bd. Thoracic and Cardiovascular Surgery. Fellow, Am. Coll. Surgeons; mem. So. Thoracic Surgery Assn., Flying Physicians Assn., Aircraft Owners and Pilots Assn., S.E. Va. Radio Control Group, Am. Radio Relay League. Contbr. articles to profl. jours. Home: 16 Conway Rd Newport News VA 23606 Office: 719 J Clyde Morris Blvd Newport News VA 23601

WINGERTER, LORAIN FRANCIS, lawyer, judge; b. New Orleans, Sept. 17, 1917; s. Anthony M. and Vera (Voegtlin) W.; A.B., Loyola at New Orleans, 1938, LL.B., 1940; m. Betty Roden, Nov. 14, 1942; children—Donald S., Martin J. Admitted to La. bar, 1940; practiced in New Orleans, 1945—; judge 2d City Ct., New Orleans, 1948—. Instr. Loyola at New Orleans, 1946-47, asst. prof., 1947-48, asso. prof., 1948; sometimes lectr. Served to lt. USNR, 1942-45. Mem. La., New Orleans bar assns., Am. Judicature Soc. Home: 5815 Sutton Pl New Orleans LA 70114 Office: 526 Verret St New Orleans LA 70114

WINIKATES, CHARLES JOHN, lawyer; b. Chgo., July 21, 1927; s. Henry James and Catherine Therese (O'Reilly) W.; student Loyola U., Chgo.; B.S., U. Ill., 1950; J.D., So. Methodist U., 1950; m. Bonnie Mary Eichorn, Dec. 29, 1956; children—Charles J., Bonnie Mary, Catherine Leslie, Regina Mary, Mary Elizabeth. Admitted to Tex. bar, 1950, since practiced in Dallas; mem. firms Kennemer & Winikates, 1958-62, Cooper & Winikates, 1968—. Dir. Prosper State Bank, Prosper, Tex., 1965—, vice chmn. bd., 1971—; dir. Texmo Corp., Dallas, 1957—, also gen. counsel, 1957—, pres., 1957—. Bd. dirs. Catholic Charities, Diocese of Dallas, 1972—. Served with AUS, 1945-46. Mem. State Bar Tex., Am., Dallas bar assns., Am. Trial Lawyers Assn., Dallas Trial Lawyers Assn., Delta Theta Phi, K.C. Club: Dallas Athletic. Home: 5948 Melshire St Dallas TX 75230 Office: 2535 Republic National Bank Tower Dallas TX 75201

WININGER, DAVID DELEAL, lawyer; b. Birmingham, Ala., Aug. 21, 1941; s. DeLeal Benton and Mary Elizabeth (Smith); B.S., Samford U., 1962; LL.B., Cumberland Sch. Law, 1964; m. Myrna Ann Strong, Aug. 19, 1960; children—David DeLeal, Susan Strong, Kimberly Ann. Admitted to Ala. bar, 1964, U.S. Dist. Ct., 1964, U.S. Supreme Ct., 1970; mem. firm Tarter & Wininger, 1966—. Spl. judge Civil Ct. Jefferson County, Birmingham, 1969—. Pres., Ala. Jr. C. of C. Found. retarded children, 1969-70; v.p. Cystic Fibrosis Found., 1973; legal adviser Ala. Heart Assn., Jefferson County, 1972; bd. advisers Ala. Hist. Commn., 1971-74; chmn. govt. task force Goals for Birmingham, 1969-71. Bd. mgrs. YMCA, 1964-71; trustee Samford U. Scholarship Fund, 1966-67. Mem. Am. Trial Lawyers Assn. (nat. pres. young lawyers sect. 1970-71), Law-Sci. Acad., Lawyers Lit. Soc., Pi Kappa Alpha. Presbyn. (deacon). Mason (Shriner, 32 degree), Eagle. Office: 2101 City Fed Bldg Birmingham AL 35203

WINK, HOWARD LAMAR, JR., mech. engr.; b. Boalsburg, Pa., Dec. 29, 1935; s. Howard Lamar and Anna Beamer (Tawney) W.; B.S. in M.E., Pa. State U., 1957; M.Engr. in Engring. Mgmt., U. Louisville, 1973; m. Joan Bryant Strohecker, Dec. 24, 1959; children—Christine Lynne, Robert Bruce. Mech. engr. facilities planning Ternstedt div. Gen. Motors Corp., Warren, Mich., 1959-63, sr. design engr. product design, 1963-68; project engr. product engring. Refrigerator Products div. Gen. Electric Co., Louisville, 1968-72, mgr. quality improvement design, 1972-73; mgr. design engring. Lithonia Lighting div. Nat. Services Industries, Conyers, Ga., 1973—. Served to 1st lt. Ordnance Corps, AUS, 1957-59. Registered profl. engr., Ky., Ga. Mem. Profl. Engrs. Soc., Soc. Plastics Engrs., Engring. Soc. Detroit. Patentee in field. Home: 4715 Holly Oak Pl Dunwoody GA 30338 Office: Box A Conyers GA 30207

WINKELMAN, DWIGHT WILLIAM, constrn. exec.; b. Lohrville, Ia., Nov. 5, 1901; s. William and Ellen (Cain) W.; B.S., Morningside Coll., 1924, D.Sc. (hon.), 1952; B.A., U. Ia., 1924; D.B.A. (hon.), Syracuse U., 1970; m. Marguerite Powers, Dec. 31, 1930; children—Dwight W. II (dec.), Peter J. Engr., Minder & Cain, 1924; with D.W. Winkelman & Co., Inc., 1927—, chmn. bd., Syracuse, N.Y., 1965—; chmn. bd. D.W. Winkelman Carolina Co., Greensboro, N.C.; dir. Lincoln 1st Bank (Syrac use). Dir. Am. Horse Show and U.S. Equestrian Assn.; trustee, chmn. emeritus Syracuse U. Mem. Am. Soc. C.E. (hon. life). Mason (Shriner, Jester). Clubs: St. Andrews Golf, Delray Beach Yacht, Ocean, Country of Florida (Delray Beach, Fla.); Country of N.C. (Pinehurst); Ocean Reef (Key Largo, Fla.); Onondaga (Syracuse); Skaneateles (N.Y.) Country. Home: 1005 Lewis Cove Delray Beach FL 33444 Office: Box 1366 Syracuse NY 13201

WINKELMAN, HERBERT WILLIAM, accountant; b. Brenham, Tex., Jan. 6, 1902; s. Frederick Henry and Louisa (Jahnke) W.; grad. Blinn Meml. Coll., Brenham, 1918; m. Cordie Louise Dupree, Aug. 4, 1923; 1 dau. Camille (Mrs. F.B. Graham). Accountant, Mattison & Block, Houston, 1920-26; mem. firm J. L. Block & Co., Houston, 1926-29, Winkelman & Tucker, Houston, 1929-33; sr. mem. Winkelman, Davies, Johnson & Watson, and predecessor firm, Houston, 1933—. Mem. Nat., Tex. socs. pub. accountants, Houston Real Estate Bd., Houston Turn Verein. Lutheran. Rotarian. Home: 2102 Bolsover Rd Houston TX 77005 Office: Main Bldg Houston TX 77002

WINKLER, CARL EMIL, elec. engr.; b. Manchester, N.H., Feb. 1, 1928; s. Emil Ernest and Helen L. (Cheney) W.; B.S. in Elec. Engring., U. N.H., 1949; M.S. in Elec. Engring., U. Ala., 1969; m. Margaret Frances Porter, Sept. 15, 1959; 1 dau., Anne Margaret. Engr., Pub. Service Co. N.H., Manchester, 1949-51; elec. engr. U.S. Army, Huntsville, Ala., 1952-60; dep. chief microelectronics br. tech. div. Astrionics Lab., Marshall Space Flight Center, Huntsville, 1960-66, mem. sci. and tech. staff, 1966-70, tech. and sci. staff Space Scis. Lab., 1970—. Served with AUS, 1951-52. Mem. I.E.E.E., Optical Soc. Am., Sigma Xi, Eta Kappa Nu. Mason, Optimist (distinguished pres. Huntsville 1966, distinguished lt. gov. Ala.-Miss. dist. 1967). Patentee static power inverter. Home: 2012 Big Cove Rd SE Huntsville AL 35801 Office: S and E-SSL-X Huntsville AL 35812

WINKLER, THOMAS ROBERT, govt. ofcl.; b. Midland, Mich., Mar. 3, 1930; s. Herman Henry and Cora (Sommerville) W.; B.A., Mich. State U., 1952; m. Virginia Sheila MacDade, Dec. 1, 1957. TV producer, dir. Evening Star Broadcasting Co., 1952; editorial dir. ABC-TV Jimmy Dean Show WMAL-TV, 1961-66; asst. to mgr.-radio code Nat. Assn. Broadcasters, 1966-67, mgr. radio code, 1967-73; broadcast specialist FCC, Washington, 1973—. Bd. dirs. Washington Heart Assn. Mem. Met. Washington Bd. Trade, Nat. TV Acad. Arts and Scis. (dir., pres. Washington chpt. 1971-73, nat. trustee 1971—), Vets. Bedside Network (treas. Washington chpt.). Episcopalian. Home: 3730 N Dittmar Rd Arlington VA 22207 Office: 1919 M St NW Washington DC 20554

WINN, FRED MINOR, JR., mech. engr., engring. co. exec.; b. Tulsa, Dec. 20, 1924; s. Fred Minor and Pearl Alice (Smith) W.; B.S. in Mech. Engring., Rice Inst., 1945; M.M.E., U. Okla., 1949; m. Martha Ann Macdonald, Mar. 19, 1948; children—Scott, Robert, Sherri. Project engr. Rig & Equipment Co., Tulsa, 1947-50; chief engr. Dowell div. Dow Chem. Co., Tulsa, 1953-71; mgr. engring. FWI, Inc., Tulsa, 1971—. Served with USNR, 1943-46, 51-53. Registered profl. engr., Okla. Mem. Am. Soc. M.E., Soc. Automotive Engrs., Hydraulics Inst. Patentee in field. Home: 5822 S 69th East Av Tulsa OK 74145 Office: 3303 Charles Page Blvd Tulsa OK 74127

WINSETT, MARVIN DAVIS, author, poet; b. Van Alstyne, Tex., Feb. 13, 1902; s. Asa and Lily (Gorrell) W.; student So. Methodist U., 1922-24; L.H.D., Universite Libre (Asie), 1968; m. Hettie Lee Bryant, June 20, 1925; children—Betty Lee (Mrs. Wilbur Ausphera Richerson, Jr.), Janis Sue (Mrs. Roger L. Swain). Asst. furniture buyer Sanger Brothers. Dallas, 1925-28; mgr. El Paso and Abilene Sears Roebuck & Co. stores, 1928-30; established advt. agy. under name Marvin Winsett Advt. Agy., 1930, head, 1930-47, owner, 1952-67, partner Winsett, Gidley & Darley Advt. Agy., 1947-52. Pres. Nat. Fedn. State Poetry Socs., 1964-66; Tex. co-chmn. Nat. Poetry Day Com., 1965-67; chmn. Tex. Council Promotion Poetry, 1965—. Apptd. Poet Laureate of Tex., 1962; recipient Deane Settoon Mernagh Sonnet award, 1957; William Lamar Meml. award, 1958; Oread award, 1959; Margaret Royalty Edwards Poetry day award, 1959. Mem. bd. Civilian Def. Vol. Office, 1942-45. Fellow Royal Soc. Arts (Eng.), Internat. Inst. Arts and Letters (life); mem. Acad. Am. Poets (founder), United Poets Laureate Internat. (gold medal and named hon. poet laureate leader 1965), Poetry Soc. Tex. (treas. 1956-61, editor bull. 1962-66, pres. 1962-65), Vachel Lindsay Assn. (adv. bd.), Academie Francaise de la Poesie (fgn. asso.), Chili Appreciation Soc. Internat., Sigma Delta Chi (past sec., treas. Dallas profl. chpt., Key Club mem.), Lambda Chi Alpha. Democrat. Presbyn. Mason (32 deg., Shriner). Club: Dallas Coin. Author: Winding Stairway. A Book of Verse, 1953; Basic Ad Writing, 1954; April Always (verse), 1956; Remembered Earth (verse), 1962; Some Uses of Words, 1969. Contbr. articles and verse to numerous nat. mags. and anthologies Originator Cyclus verse form. Home: 3936 Colgate St Dallas TX 75225

WINSHIP, WADLEIGH CHICHESTER, express co. exec.; b. San Francisco, Oct. 3, 1940; s. Henry Dillon and Anne Eliza (Chichester) W.; student Woodberry Forest (Va.) Sch., 1954-56; grad. Darlington Sch., Rome, Ga., 1959; B.A., U. Ga., 1964; m. Lynne McPherson, Dec. 28, 1970. Exec. trainee G. Hwy. Express, Inc., Atlanta, 1964-68, v.p., 1968—, also dir., mem. exec. com.; pres. SurfAir, Inc., Atlanta, 1970—. Chmn. transp. com. A.R.C., Atlanta, 1968—. Mem. Am. Trucking Assn. (terminal operations council), Atlanta Air Cargo Assn. (charter), Ga. Bus. and Industry Assn. (dir.), Chi Phi. Clubs: Peachtree Golf, Capital City, The Nine O'Clocks, German. Home: 3296 Rilman Rd NW Atlanta GA 30327 Office: 2090 Jonesboro Rd SE Atlanta GA 30315

WINSLOW, LEONARD FRANCIS, JR., land co. exec.; b. Phila., Aug. 13, 1931; s. Leonard Francis and Marjorie Elizabeth (Bloomfield) W.; student Washington and Lee U., 1950-53; B.A., U. Richmond, 1954; m. Mary Hobson Hurt, Oct. 2, 1954;

children—Mary Elizabeth, Leonard Francis III. Vice pres. Leonard F. Winslow Co., Inc., Richmond, Va., 1956-61; sales mgr. Va. Land Co., Charlottesville, 1961—, v.p., 1965-72, pres., 1972—; pres. Tembo Farms, Inc.; dir. First Va. Bank-Monticello Nat. Bank. Pres., Charlottesville-Albemarle Bd. Realtors. Chmn. Chris Greene Lake Fund, 1972—. Served with USNR, 1954-55. Mem. Internat. Real Estate Fedn., Blue Ridge Homebuilders Assn., Izaak Walton League (pres.), Nat. Rifle Assn. (life), Sigma Chi. Episcopalian (vestryman). Elk, Kiwanian (dir. 1956-57). Clubs: Greencroft, Game Coin Internat.; Farmington Country; African Safari (N.Y.C.). Home: Flordon Dr Charlottesville VA 22901 Office: Va Land Co Route 29 N Charlottesville VA 22901

WINSTEAD, BASIL MAYO, food store exec.; b. Dresden, Tenn., Dec. 19, 1913; s. William Almerry and Mary (Cunningham) W.; grad. U.S. Armed Forces Inst., Madison, Wis., 1946; m. Thelma Mae Slaven, Dec. 29, 1945; children—Patricia Ann (Mrs. Dennis Finch), Autumn Frances. Store mgr. Piggly Wiggly Corp., St. Louis, 1928-38, auditor, 1938-41; with Safeway Stores, Inc., Washington, 1949—, v.p., div. mgr., 1965-72, v.p., mgr. Eastern region, 1972—; mng. dir. Safeway Food Stores Ltd., London, Eng., 1962-65; pres., chmn. bd. Holly Enterprises, Wilkesboro, N.C., 1970—. Bd. dirs. Met. Washington Bd. Trade, Downtown Progress, Washington Capital Area council Boy Scouts Am. Served to maj. AUS, 1941-49. Decorated Bronze Star medal, ETO medal with 5 battle stars. Mem. Washington Conv. and Visitors Bur. Home: 4030 N 27th St Arlington VA 22207 Office: Suite 304 Landover Mall Landover MD 20785

WINSTEAD, NASH NICKS, phytopathologist, univ. adminstr.; b. Durham, N.C., June 12, 1925; s. Nash L. and Lizzy (Featherston) W.; B.S., N.C. State U., 1948, M.S., 1951; Ph.D., U. Wis., 1953; m. Geraldine Larkin Kelly, Sept. 17, 1949; 1 dau., Karen Jewell. Asst. prof. plant pathology N.C. State U., Raleigh, 1953-58; asso. prof., 1958-61, prof., 1961—, dir. inst. biol. scis., 1965-67, asst. dir. agrl. exptl. sta., 1965-67, asst. provost, 1967-73, asso. provost, 1973-74, provost, vice chancellor, 1974—. Phillip Found. intern acad. adminstrn. Ind. U., 1965-66. Mem. N.C. Council on Higher Edn. for Adults; inst. rep. So. Assn. for Colls. and Schs., 1967—; mem. Cooperating Raleigh Colls., 1968—, pres., 1971-73. Bd. dirs. N.C. State U. YMCA, 1963-65. Chmn. interaction between protoplasm and toxicants com. So. Regional Edn. Bd., 1964-65. Served with USAAF, 1943-46. Recipient Sigma Xi research award, 1960. Mem. Am. Phytopath. Soc. (chmn. disease, pathogen physiology com. 1965-66), Am. Inst. Biol. Scis., N.C. Acad. Sci., Acad. Deans for So. States, A.A.A.S., Sigma Xi, Phi Kappa Phi. Club: Torch Internat. (sec.). Contbr. to profl. jours. Home: 1109 Glendale Dr Raleigh NC 27612 Office: NC State U Raleigh NC 27607

WINSTEAD, PHILIP CONNOR, JR., univ. adminstr.; b. Mullins, S.C., Dec. 10, 1935; s. Philip Connor and Hilda (Renfrow) W.; A.B., Davidson Coll., 1957; M.A., Appalachian State U., 1964; Ed.D., Duke U., 1966; m. Hazel Jenon Wehunt, May 30, 1961; children—Amoret Beth, Hilda Marie, Mary Connor. Tchr., adminstr. McClenaghan High Sch., Florence, S.C., 1957-64; asst. dir. grad. program edn. Rollins Coll., 1966-68; program asso. higher edn. Regional Edn. Lab. for Carolinas and Va., Durham, N.C., 1968-69, acting dir. Sr. Coll. div., 1969-70; asso. dir. sr. coll. div. Nat. Lab. for Higher Edn., Durham, 1970-71; coordinator institutional planning Furman U., Greenville, S.C., 1972—. Mem. Am. Ednl. Research Assn., Assn. for Instl. Research, Am. Assn. Higher Edn., Am. Assn. Sch. Adminstrs., Am. Assn. U. Profs., Kappa Delta Pi. Research coll. and univ. adminstrn. and organization. Home: 107 Old Mill Rd Taylors SC 29687 Office: Furman U Greenville SC 29613

WINSTON, LOUIS SIMPSON, dentist; b. Alvin, Tex. Feb. 27, 1893; s. LaFayette Fontaine and Jane Elisabeth (Simpson) W.; A.B., Austin Coll., 1915; D.D.S., Tex. Dental Coll., 1923; postgrad. Dewey Sch. Orthodontia, 1923; m. Dorothy Quincy Mills, July 30, 1927; children—Quincy (Mrs. Eldridge Anthony Helwick), Dorothy Ann De Ford. Practice dentistry, specializing in orthodontics, Houston, 1923-48, Sherman, Tex., 1950-54, San Antonio, 1953-63, Schulenburg, Tex., 1968—. Served to ensign USNR, 1917-19. Recipient Meritorious Service award Austin Coll., 1955. Diplomate Am. Bd. Orthodontics; mem. Am. Dental Assn. (life mem.), Houston Dist. Dental Soc. (pres. 1932-33), Am. Assn. Orthodontists (life mem.), Southwestern Soc. Orthodontists (pres. 1933). Presbyn. Kiwanian. Editor, founder monthly publ. of Houston Dist. Dental Soc., 1929. Home: Route 4 Schulenburg TX 78956 Office: 511 Summit St Schulenburg TX 78956

WINSTON, ROBERT TUNSTALL, JR., lawyer; b. Hanover, Va., July 25, 1919; s. Robert Tunstall and Grace Ellen (McKey) W.; B.A., Randolph Macon Coll., 1940; LL.B., Duke U., 1947; m. Elisabeth Joyce Robinson, Feb. 12, 1949; children—Julia R., Frances McKey, Martha L. Admitted to Va. bar, 1947; asso. firm Fred D. Greear, Norton, Va., 1947-48; partner firm Greear, Bowen, Mullins & Winston, 1948-65, 68-70, Kime, Jolly, Winston & Clements, Salem, Va., 1966-67. Chmn. Norton Democratic Com., 1954-56. Mem. scholarship com. Va. Iron Found., 1970—. Served to capt. AUS, 1941-45. Decorated Bronze Star medal. Mem. Am., Wise County (pres. 1963) bar assns., Va. State Bar (mem. council 1968-71), Phi Beta Kappa, Kappa Sigma, Phi Delta Phi. Episcopalian (diocese exec. com. 1965). Kiwanian. Home: 333 Henry St Norton VA 24273 Office: 26 7th St Norton VA 24273

WINTER, TRAVIS ALVIN, banker; b. Wellington, Tex., Feb. 25, 1914; s. Jessie Richard and Minnie Mae (Vaughn) W.; student Draughon's Bus. Coll., 1932-33, Internat. Sch. Commerce, 1934; m. Katie Lena Cary, Oct. 30, 1938. With Dept. Agr., Amherst, Tex, 1934-36, office mgr., Muleshoe, Tex., 1943-53; asst. mgr. Farmers Coop. Gin, Amherst, 1936-43; asst. mgr. White's Concrete Pipe, Littlefield, Tex., 1953-58; with 1st Nat. Bank, Amherst, 1958—, cashier, dir., 1966—; partner Duffy Ins. Agy., Amherst, 1966—. Mason. Home: 519 E 13th St Littlefield TX 79339 Office: 1001 Main St Amherst TX 79312

WINTER, WILLIAM RAYMOND, ret. elec. engr.; b. Worthington, O., Dec. 5, 1913; s. Thomas Raymond and Ada Eltra (Snell) W.; Chem. Engr., Rensselaer Poly. Inst., 1936; postgrad. Columbia, 1937, 40, 46, U. Va., 1955; m. Kathryn Virginia Morgan Winter, Dec. 14, 1940; children—John Staats, Jean Carolyn (Mrs. Gerald K. Bliss). Sales engr. Bklyn. Union Gas Co., 1936-42, dept. head coke oven and light oil plant, 1946-47; sr. engr. research and devel. Cabot Carbon Co., Pampa, Tex., 1947-49; design engr. heating equipment Silent Automatic div. Timken Corp., Jackson, Mich., 1950-55; with Westinghouse Electric Corp., Staunton, Va., 1955-74, mgr. engring. sect. air conditioning equipment, 1957-74. Served to lt. USNR, 1942-45. Mem. Air-Conditioning and Refrigeration Inst. (mem. gen. standards com. 1973—), Am. Soc. Heating, Refrigeration and Air Conditioning Engrs. (mem. various tech. coms.), I.E.E.E. (mem. tech. com. electric space heating and air conditioning 1968-70), Nat. Elec. Mfrs. Assn. (mem. tech. com. electric comfort heating equipment sect. 1961-66). Lion. Club: Stauton Country (pres. 1969-70). Patentee in field. Address: 2708 Cottonwood Lane New Port Richey FL 33552

WINTERHOLLER, JAMES VINCENT, JR., civil engr.; b. Wheeling, W.Va., Sept. 10, 1927; s. James V. and Madelon (Moran) W.; B.S., W.Va. U., 1950; m. Doris J. Gray, Dec. 27, 1954; children—Dana Marie, Deanna Lee. Quality control engr. Wheeling Steel Corp., 1950-53; civil engr. Fla. Rd. Dept., Ft. Lauderdale, 1953-58; co-founder, pres. Fla. Testing & Engring. Co., Ft. Lauderdale, 1958—. Registered profl. engr., Fla. Mem. Fla. Engring. Soc., Nat. Soc. Profl. Engrs. Home: 2611 NE 40th St Fort Lauderdale FL 33308 Office: 6784 NW 17th Av Fort Lauderdale FL 33309

WINTERS, FRANCIS GRAY, utility co. exec.; b. Houston, Mar. 27, 1925; s. William G. and Mary (James) W.; B.S., Rice Inst., 1944; M.S., U. Tex., 1948; m. Nell Mildred Sterquell, June 11, 1949; children—Ann Elizabeth, Susan Kathryn, Janice Carol. Vice pres., gen. mgr., dir. Hull Telephone Co., Houston, 1950-68, Hull Gas Corp., Houston, 1950-57, Hull Water Corp., Houston, 1950-57; v.p., chief engr., dir. Tex. Tel. and Tel. Co., Houston, 1953-64, pres., dir., 1964—. Chmn. telephone technicians tng. com. Tex. A. and M. U., 1965-72, chmn. adv. com. to dean engring. on communications engring. Chmn. nat. fund dr. Rice U., 1973-74. Served as ensign USNR, 1945. Registered profl. engr., Tex. Mem. Am. Soc. M.E., Ind. Telephone Pioneer Assn. (pres. 1972-73), Tex. Soc. Profl. Engrs., Isaak Walton League, Nat. Wildlife Fedn., Wilderness Soc., Tex. Telephone Assn. (dir.), Founders Club of Rice U. (chmn. 1972-73), Pi Tau Sigma, Sigma Phi Epsilon. Presbyn. Rotarian. Clubs: Houston Racquet (pres. 1960), University, Houston. Home: 663 Shartle Circle Houston TX 77024 Office: 5433 Westheimer Houston TX 77027

WINTERS, HAROLD VERNON, banker; b. Morganton, N.C., Dec. 12, 1940; s. Harold Alexander and Frances Livingston (Kincaid) W.; A.B., U. N.C., 1963, M.B.A., 1964; m. Frankie Elizabeth Phillips, June 8, 1963; children—Susan Elizabeth, Harold Alexander II. With Wachovia Bank & Trust Co., Winston-Salem, N.C., 1964—, v.p., 1970—. Mem. budget com. United Fund, Winston-Salem, 1968—, chmn., 1974-75; chmn. budget com. Arts Council, Winston-Salem, 1974. Precinct chmn. Winston-Salem Republican Com., 1969-70. Mem. N.C. Soc. Financial Analysts (pres. 1973-74). Home: 2717 Spring Garden Rd Winston-Salem NC 27106 Office: PO Box 3099 Winston-Salem NC 27102

WINTERS, JAMES COURTLIN, lawyer; b. Houston, Mar. 23, 1923; s. William Gardner and Mary Virginia (James) W.; B.A., Rice U., 1943; LL.B., U. Tex., 1948; m. Bettye Jo Hamm, Sept. 29, 1951; children—Sheryl Leslie, Mallory Leigh. Admitted to Tex. bar, 1948; atty. Blades, Kennerly & Whitworth, Houston, 1948-56; partner Blades, Crain, Slator & Winters, 1956-69, Blades, Crain & Winters, 1969-72, Crain, Winters, Houser & Deaton, 1972-74, Crain, Winters, Deaton, James & Briggs, 1974—. Sec., gen. counsel, dir. Hull Telephone Co., 1948-68; gen. counsel, dir. Boling-Iago Telephone Co., 1955-68, Tex. Tel. & Tel. Co., 1953-68; dir. Spring Branch Bank, Houston, Capital Title Co., Houston, Rollins Terminals Tex., Inc. Democratic precinct chmn. Harris County (Tex.), 1968—; mem. Dem. Exec. Com., 1968—. Served to lt. USNR, 1943-46; ETO. Mem. Am., Houston bar assns., State Bar Tex., Am. Judicature Soc., Sigma Phi Epsilon. Rotarian. Clubs: Houston Racquet (dir.), Houston, Warwick. Home: 6015 Stones Throw Houston TX 77027 Office: 1009 San Jacinto Bldg Houston TX 77002

WINTERS, WILLIAM KYRAN, state ofcl.; b. Albany, N.Y., Dec. 28, 1938; s. William H. and Helen G. (Winters) W.; B.S., Utah State U., 1960; M.S., Kan. State U., 1963; m. Anita E. Eberhard, Aug. 15, 1959; children—Heidi Ann, Gary William. Asst. prof. computer sci. U. Mo., Rolla, 1963-66; operations research analyst U.S. Office Edn., Washington, 1966-67; dir. computer assisted registration U. Tenn., 1967-69; dir. information systems Okla. State Regents for Higher Edn., Oklahoma City, 1970—. Cons., U.S. Office Edn., 1967-70, Okla. State Regents for Higher Edn., 1969. Mem. Am. Statis. Assn., Inst. Math. Statistics, Inst. Mgmt. Sci., A.A.A.S., Assn. for Computing Machinery. Home: 3701 Baird Dr Edmond OK 73034 Office: State Capitol Oklahoma City OK 73105

WINTON, HOWARD PHILLIP, optometrist; b. Springfield, Mo., June 23, 1925; s. George Lecoumpt and Emma Pearl (Schoonover) W.; D. Optometry, No. Ill. Coll. Optometry, 1949; postgrad. Mid West Sch. Optics, 1949-50; L.H.D., Ill. Coll. Optometry, 1965; m. Frances Jeanne Zellweger, June 29, 1946; children—Susan (Mrs. C. A. Rossetter, Jr.), James, Stephen, Gary, Carolyn. Pvt. practice optometry, Jacksonville, Fla., 1950-51, Melbourne, Fla., 1951—. 1st vice chmn. Brevard Econ. Devel. Council. Trustee So. Coll. Optometry, 1966-67; bd. dirs. Minit Saver, Inc., Better Vision Inst. Served with USNR, 1943-46. Fellow Royal Soc. Health, Am. Acad. Optometry, Am. Optometric Assn. (v.p. 1973-74, pres. elect 1974—); mem. Am. Optometric Student Assn. (hon. life), Fla. (Fla. Optometrist of Year 1970, pres. 1965-66), Indian River (pres. 1953) optometric assns., So. Council Optometrists (pres. 1970-71), Melbourne C. of C. (pres. 1963-64). Democrat. Methodist (mem. adminstrv. bd. 1967-72). Rotarian (Outstanding Rotarian 1961-62). Club: Eau Gallie Yacht (Melbourne). Home: 30 E Melbourne St Melbourne FL 32901 Office: PO Box 278 Melbourne FL 32901

WINTTER, ARCHIE HERMAN, mech. engr.; b. Hueytown, Ala., June 25, 1920; s. John Arnold and Ruth (Kinnett) W.; student Birmingham So. Coll., 1946-47; B.S. in Mech. Engring., Auburn U., 1949; m. Helen Eloise West, Aug. 12, 1950; children—Archie Kent, Helen Sue. With Woodward Iron Co. (Ala.), 1949-53, draftsman, 1950-53; with Fairfield (Ala.) works U.S. Steel Corp., 1953-70, head design draftsman, 1963-70; engr. Woodward Co. div. Mead Corp., 1970-71, chief draftsman, 1971—. Served with USAAF, 1941-45. Decorated Air medal. Registered profl. engr., Ala. Mem. Pi Tau Sigma. Baptist. Home: 507 Charleston Dr Bessemer AL 35020 Office: Woodward Co Woodward AL 35189

WIRT, CHARLES ALVIN, mgmt. cons., rep.; b. Cookeville, Tenn., Apr. 16, 1920; s. Alvin Bryan and Conway Lee (Gregg) W.; B.S., U.S. Mil. Acad., 1943; M.S., U.S. Command and Gen. Staff Coll., 1962; m. Jutta E.H. Grunewald, Mar. 22, 1947; children—Pamela Faye, Adrienne Lee. Commd. officer U.S. Army, 1943-63; sr. analyst-tech. research adv. group Tech. Operations, Inc., Hampton, Va., 1963-65; project mgr. TEMPO (Center for Advanced Studies) Gen. Electric Co., Washington, 1965-70; project mgr. Sci. Mgmt. Corp., 1970-72; area rep., mgr. ADCON Corp., Washington, 1972—; cons. in field. Decorated D.S.C., Silver Star, Bronze Star (2), Purple Heart (2). Mem. Operations Research Soc. Am., World War I Aero. Historians, U.S. Army and Army Aviation Assn., Co. Mil. Historians, Pi Kappa Alpha. Home: 929 6th St SW Washington DC 20024

WIRTH, FAY ALLEN, JR., airline exec.; b. Mt. Carmel, Ill., Aug. 22, 1925; s. Fay Allen and Velma Lee (Crawford) W.; student U. Kan., 1943, U. Ill., 1946-49, Xavier U., 1958-60, U. Denver, 1960-61; m. Dorles Marie Lott, Dec. 17, 1950; children—Lisa Lou, William Allen, Melinda Lee. Sr. flight test engr. Gen. Dynamics Co., Ft. Worth, 1952-55; mgr. programming Gen. Electric Co., Cin., 1956-60; mgr. advanced program plans Martin Co., Denver, 1960-63; dir. programs Hoffman Electronics Co., El Monte, Cal., 1963; dir. flight simulator support and sales Am. Airlines Inc., Ft. Worth, 1967—. Served with AUS, 1943-46. Decorated Silver Star medal, Purple Heart. Mem. Am. Inst. Aeros. and Astronautics (adv. council 1969-72), I.E.E.E., Am. Def. Preparedness Assn., Air Force Assn. Republican. Methodist (dist. steward finance com. 1970-73). Rotarian (v.p. 1967). Home: 714 Live Oak Dr Euless TX 76039 Office: American Airlines Inc Greater SW Airport Fort Worth TX 76125

WISE, DONALD ALLEN, librarian; b. Mercedes, Tex., Jan. 25, 1930; s. Lawrence A. and Lucille A. (Crosswhite) W.; B.A., Okla. State U., 1953; M.A., St. Louis U., 1960, postgrad., 1961-63; postgrad. George Washington U., 1965-72; m. June E. Ruth, Sept. 2, 1961; 1 son, Kurt Geoffrey. Employed with U.S. Govt., 1955-60, 63—, head acquisitions sect., geography and map div. Library of Congress, 1970—. Instr. geography St. Louis U., 1960-63; lectr. U.S. Dept. Agr. Grad. Sch., Washington, 1971—. Mem. Arlington County Bicentennial Com., 1972—. Served with AUS, 1953-55. Mem. Assn. Am. Geographers (treas. 1971-74), Spl. Libraries Assn., Am. Congress on Surveying and Mapping, Soc. for History of Discoveries, Am. Assn. State and Local History, Va. History Fedn. (pres. 1973-74), Va., Arlington (pres. 1969-70, archivist 1970—) hist. socs. Presbyn. (elder 1966-69). Home: 5920 4th Rd N Arlington VA 22203 Office: Library of Congress Washington DC 20540

WISE, GORDON TALIAFERRO, banker; b. Amarillo, Tex., Jan. 15, 1934; s. James Marvin and Kathryn Virginia (Charlton) W.; A.B., Princeton, 1956; m. Linda Sue Lewis, Apr. 12, 1957; children—Susan Elizabeth, Margaret Allison, Charles Taliaferro. Account exec. Dittmar & Co., Dallas, 1959-62; mgr. trust investment Tex. Bank and Trust Co., 1962-65; mgr. trust investment dept. First City Nat. Bank of Houston, 1965-73; pres. First Financial Advisors Inc., 1974—. Lectr. Tex. Bankers Assn. trust investment seminar U. Tex. at Austin, 1970. Financial adviser Tex. A. and M. U. Endorment Fund. Mem. investment adv. bd. Tchrs. Retirement System Tex. Served with USAF, 1956-59. Mem. Houston C. of C. (mem. research com. 1970—), Houston Soc. Financial Analysts (pres. 1970-71), Tex. Bankers Assn. (chmn. edn. com. 1972-74). Presbyn. (elder 1962—). Clubs: Houston Racquet; Princeton (N.Y.C.). Home: 5 Sleepy Oaks St Houston TX 77024 Office: Box 2432 First City Nat Bank Bldg Houston TX 77001

WISE, JAMES BERRY, physician; b. Stillwater, Okla., Mar. 15, 1936; s. Paul Conrad and Geneva (Holcomb) W.; B.A., Okla. State U., 1957; M.D., Johns Hopkins, 1961; m. Verena Joss, Sept. 27, 1968; children—Doris Jean, Lee Ann, Ben Paul. Polymer chemist E.I. duPont Co. de Nemours & Co., Inc., Wilmington, Del., 1957; intern, resident Johns Hopkins, 1957-65; postdoctoral research fellow Inst. Ophthalmology, London, Eng., 1965-66; practice medicine, specializing in ophthalmology, Oklahoma City, 1966-67; asst. prof. ophthalmology U. Okla. Med. Sch., Oklahoma City, 1967, asso. prof., 1968—; chief ophthalmology Mercy Hosp., treas. Northwest Eye Physicians Inc. Cons. ophthalmology Oklahoma City VA Hosp. NSF postdoctoral fellow, 1965-66. Diplomate Am. Bd. Ophthalmology. Mem. A.M.A., Okla. State, Oklahoma County med. assns., Am. Acad. Ophthalmol. and Otolarynology, Johns Hopkins Med. and Surg. Soc. Home: 3401 Hickory Stick Rd Oklahoma City OK 73120 Office: 5700 NW Grand Blvd Oklahoma City OK 73112

WISE, JOHN ELWOOD, ednl. adminstr.; b. Carlisle, Pa., June 6, 1920; s. Jacob William and Lynette Olive (Beetem) W.; B.S., U. Md., 1960; M.A. (fellow) U. Ky., 1964; m. Mary Louise Sympson, Nov. 23, 1949; children—John B., Robert K. Enlisted as pvt., U.S. Army, 1941, advanced through grades to col., 1960; with Dept. Army, Washington, 1951-54, NSA, Washington, 1958-61; dir. Research Found. U. Ky., Lexington, 1961-66; v.p. bus. affairs Med. U. S.C., Charleston, 1967—, asst. prof. adminstrv. medicine, 1967-71. Bd. dirs. S.C. League Nursing, 1967-71. Decorated Combat Infantrymen Badge. NIH grantee 1971-72. Mem. Am. Soc. Personnel Adminstrn., Nat. Assn. Coll. and U. Bus. Officers, Charleston C. of C., Phi Delta Kappa. Mason (Shriner). Home: 446 Wampler Dr Charleston SC 29412

WISE, SIDNEY LEE, publisher; b. Swansea, S.C., Jan. 17, 1924; s. Lee R. and Addie (Hyman) W.; student U. Me., 1942-43; B.J., U. S.C., 1946; M. J., Northwestern U., 1947; m. Agnes B. Delaney, Nov. 24, 1951; children—Sidney Lee II, Charlotte D., Marcus B., Winston W., Marian Olivia, Agnes Terry. Pres. Wing Publs., Inc., Columbia, S.C., 1956—, S.C. Mag. Corp., 1956—, Southeastern Press, Inc., 1959—; editor Carolina Law, 1959—; editor S.C. Mag., 1959—. Pres. Columbia Boys Club Am., 1966—. Served with AUS, 1943-46, 1950-51. Decorated Purple Heart with oak leaf cluster, Bronze Star medal, Silver Star medal. Mem. Columbia C. of C., Am. Legion, Blue Key, Kappa Sigma, Kappa Sigma Kappa. Elk, Moose. Club: Exchange. Home: 6915 Sandy Shore Rd Columbia SC 29206 Office: PO Box 3 Columbia SC 29202

WISE, WES, mayor Dallas; b. Shreveport, La., Nov. 25, 1928; s. George Arthur and Myrtle (Hamilton) W.; student N.E. La. U., 1945-46, Kan. State Coll., 1951-52, N.C. State Coll., 1952-53; m. Sally Ann Browning, Sept. 24, 1955; children—Westley, Wynford, Wendy. Broadcaster, KNOE, Monroe, La., 1945-49; baseball broadcaster Liberty Broadcasting System, Dallas, 1949-51; pub. relations dir. Beaumont (Tex.) Baseball Club, 1953-55; sports dir. WFAA-TV, Dallas, 1956-61; news, sports broadcaster KRLD-TV, Dallas, 1961-68; polit. cons. Dallas-Ft. Worth corr. Sports Illustrated Mag., 1960-69; CBS color broadcaster ann. Cotton Bowl Football Classic, 1965-69. Mem. Dallas City Council, 1969-70, mayor, 1971—. Served with AUS, 1951-53. Mem. Press Club Dallas Found. (past pres.), Sigma Delta Xi. Club: Press (past pres.) (Dallas). Home: 10026 Lakedale Dr Dallas TX 75218 Office: World Trade Center Stemmons Freeway Dallas TX 75201

WISEBRAM, JOSHUA HENRY, dept. store exec.; b. Atlanta, Aug.9, 1923; s. Elijah and Nora (Rice) W.; B.S., U. N.C., 1948; m. Jeanne D. Witt, June 16, 1946; children—Diane, Steve. With Wisebram's Dept. Store, Inc., Barnesville, Ga., 1948—, gen. mgr., v.p., 1958—; dir. 1st Nat. Bank Barnesville. Pres., Flint River council Boy Scouts Am., 1969-70. Trustee, Gordon Mil. Coll., chmn., 1964-70. 1955—, Served with AUS, 1942-46. Decorated Bronze Star medal; recipient Silver Beaver award Boy Scouts Am., 1965. Mem. Barnesville C. of C., Am. Legion, Phi Beta Kappa. Rotarian (past pres.), Mason (Shriner). Home: 216 Harrell Circle Barnesville GA 30204 Office: 216 Main St Barnesville GA 30204

WISER, RALPH LLOYD, govt. ofcl.; b. Lyndonville, N.Y., June 30, 1910; s. Floyd J. and Alice (Hook) W.; A.B., George Washington U., 1934, J.D., 1938; m. Mae C. Crosby, Sept. 10, 1938 (dec. 1970); children—Ralph L., Phillip R., Charles S.; m. 2d, Kathleen Harris Andersen, May 27, 1973; 1 stepdau., Greta. With CAB, Washington, 1940—, informal complaint and contract examiner, 1940-42, hearing examiner, 1943—, asso. chief examiner, 1968-71, chief examiner, 1971-72, chief adminstrv. law judge, 1972—. Active Boy Scouts Am. Served to lt. USNR, 1943-46. Mem. Am., Fed. bar assns., Fed. Adminstrv. Law Judges Conf., Delta Theta Phi, Alpha Kappa Psi. Club: Bethesda Country. Home: 3509 Shepherd St Chevy Chase MD 20015 Office: Civil Aeronautics Bd Washington DC 20428

WISHCAMPER, ED NUINEZ, editor; b. Oklahoma City, Dec. 30, 1917; s. Alvin Frank and Annie Serilda (Nuinez) W.; B.A., McMurry Coll., 1938, L.H.D. (hon.), 1971; m. Louise Ernestine Smith, Apr. 19, 1941; children—Jan (Mrs. Hubert G. Wardlaw, Jr.), Joe. Reporter,

Abilene (Tex.) Reporter-News, 1936-46, news editor, 1946-52, asst. mng. editor, 1952, mng. editor, 1953-68, editor, v.p. editorial, 1968—, dir. Reporter Pub. Co., 1953—. Mem. adv. bd. Salvation Army, 1946—; bd. dirs. Taylor County Coliseum, Tex. Election Bur., West Tex. Fair, Abilene Indsl. Found., Tex. Tourist Devel. Agy. Served with USNR, 1941-45. Recipient award for citizen contbg. most to pub. edn. Abilene Pub. Schs., 1958, Liberty Bell award Abilene Bar Assn., 1969, Superior Journalism award Tex. Chiropractic Assn., 1971; Community Service Press award West Tex. C. of C., 1973. Mem. Abilene (pres. 1970), West Tex. (dir.) chambers commerce, Am. Soc. Newspaper Editors, W. Tex. Press Assn. (pres. 1955-56), Tex. A.P. Mng. Editors Assn. (pres. 1959). Baptist (deacon 1958-63). Kiwanian (pres. 1969). Home: 1417 Meadowbrook Dr Abilene TX 79603 Office: Box 30 100 block Cypress St Abilene TX 79604

WISLAR, GEORGE ROWLAND, computer-data processing co. exec.; b. Trenton, N.J., Dec. 12, 1932; s. George Garsed and Marian Beulah (Wakefield) W.; B.A., Yale, 1954; M.B.A., Harvard, 1960; m. Sue Dingman, Dec. 27, 1963; children—Reed W., George G. II, Philip M. Pension adminstr. Bankers Trust Co. N.Y., N.Y.C., 1957-58; registered rep. Kidder, Peabody & Co. N.Y., N.Y.C., 1960-64; with Robinson-Humphrey Co., Inc., Atlanta, 1964-73, sr. v.p., dir., 1969-73; v.p., dir. Nat. Data Corp., Atlanta, 1973—. Served to capt. USMC, 1954-57. Mem. Phi Gamma Delta. Republican. Episcopalian. Clubs: Augusta Nat. Golf; Peachtree Golf, Piedmont Driving, Commerce (Atlanta); University (N.Y.C.). Home: 412 Broadland Rd NW Atlanta GA 30342 Office: Nat Data Corp One Nat Data Plaza Corporate Sq Atlanta GA 30329

WITCHER, JOHN EDGAR, electronics mfg. co. exec.; b. Indpls., May 11, 1938; s. Edgar and Grace Louisa (Shrum) W.; student Rose Poly. Inst., 1956-59; B.S., Ind. U., 1961; LL.B., Blackstone Sch. Law, 1968; m. Marilyn Jean Minor, Jan. 23, 1962; children—John, Mark. With Cummins Engine Co., Inc. and its divisions, Columbus and Seymour, Ind., also Dallas, 1961-70, materials dir., 1968-70; operations mgr. Remcom Mfg. Co., Garland, Tex., 1970-71, v.p. operations, 1971-72; pres. Transtonnics Corp., Garland, Tex., 1973—. Mem. Am. Statistical Assn., Am. Soc. Quality Control. Mason. Home: 3355 Northaven Rd Dallas TX 75229 Office: 2702 Industrial Lane Garland TX 75041

WITHERINGTON, ALBERT SIDNEY, JR., physician; b. Munford, Tenn., Apr. 3, 1914; s. Albert Sidney and Annie Bond (McClanahan) W.; student U. Tenn. at Knoxville, 1933-35, M.D., at Memphis, 1938; m. Eleanor Ruth Snider, June 20, 1945; children—Rosemary (Mrs. Wallace Royce Nelms, Jr.), Albert Sidney III, Annie Laurie. Intern Shreveport (La.) Charity Hosp., 1939; resident Oschner Clinic, New Orleans, 1945-46; practice medicine specializing in gen. practice, Munford, Tenn., 1946—; mem. staff Tipton County Meml. Hosp., Covington, Tenn. Chmn. bd. Tipton Acad., Brighton, Tenn., 1969-71. Served to lt. col. AUS, 1940-45; PTO. Decorated Silver Star. Mem. A.M.A., Tenn. Med. Soc. Presbyn. (edler). Am. party. Home: 253 E Main St Munford TN 38058 Office: 106 W Main St Munford TN 38058

WITHERS, JAMES CLYDE, aircraft co. exec.; b. Buna, Tex., Nov. 5, 1934; s. James William and Vera Idel (Owens) W.; student U.S. Naval Acad., 1952-53; B.S., Am. U., 1956, M.S., 1957, postgrad., 1957-60; m. Helga Tiffany Heppich, Apr. 17, 1969; children—(by previous marriage)—Marc, Chris, Laura. Asst. mgr. materials div. Melpar, Inc., Falls Church, Va., 1954-58; mgr. materials br. Am. Machine and Foundry Co., Alexandria, Va., 1958-61; pres., chief operations officer Gen. Techs. Corp., Reston, Va., 1961—; chmn. bd. Potomac Savs. & Loan Assn. Mem. adv. bd. Va. Poly. Inst., 1969—. Mem. Lakeside Cluster Assn. (pres. 1969-70). Club: Golf and Country (pres. 1970-71) (Reston). Home: 1612 Greenbriar Ct Reston VA 22070 Office: 1821 Michael Faraday Dr Reston VA 22070

WITHERSPOON, ELIZABETH (MRS. JAMES W. WITHERSPOON), ins.-abstract operator; b. Friona, Tex., July 3, 1917; d. James Walter and Cora Mae (Davis) Spradley; student Mary Hardin-Baylor Coll., 1936-37; m. James W. Witherspoon, Feb. 14, 1959; children—Jane (Mrs. D.L. Smith, Jr.), Irene (Mrs. Calvin Couch). Owner-operator Hereford Ins. Agy., 1942-70. Deaf Smith County Abstract Co., 1942-70. Deaf Smith dep. county clk., 1939-41. Mem. Bus. and Profl. Women's Club, C. of C., Wives Club of Legal Profession. Democrat. Clubs: Calliopian, Hereford (Tex.) Country; Amarillo (Tex.). Home: 1712 Plains Hereford TX 79045

WITHERSPOON, JAMES W., lawyer; b. Indianola, Okla., Sept. 20, 1906; s. Ernest and Mary Etta (Stafford) W.; A.B., Montezuma Coll., 1926; LL.B., U. Okla., 1929; m. Margaret Gilliland, July 25, 1930 (dec.); children—Gerald Winfrey (dec.), Eleanor Irene (Mrs. Calvin R. Couch); m. 2d, Elizabeth Womble, Feb. 14, 1959. Admitted to U.S. Supreme Ct. bar, Tex. bar, 1929, since practiced in Hereford; dist. atty., 1933-40, dist. judge, 1940-44; legislative rep. Tex.-N.M. Sugar Beet Growers Assn., now exec. sec. Committeeman state-wide Tex. Hi-Y. Chmn. bd 1st Nat. Bank Hereford; dir. Transport Life Ins. Co., Agri-Basic Corp. Bd. dirs. Tex. A. & M. Coll., 1951-57. Mem. Am. Bar Assn., State Bar Tex., Tex. Assn. Plaintiffs' Attys., Nat. Plaintiffs' Attys. Assn., Am. Judicature Soc., Am. Coll. Probate Counsel, Tex. Bar Found., Am. Trial Lawyers Assn., Nat. Assn. Tax Attys., C. of C., S.A.R., S.C.V., Panhandle Hist. Soc. (dir.), Phi Alpha Delta. Mason (Shriner), Rotarian, Elk. Clubs: Knife and Fork, Amarillo (Hereford). Home: 1712 Plains St Hereford TX 79045 Office: PO Box 1818 Hereford TX 79045

WITHROW, JON RICHARD, geologist; b. Seminole, Okla., Jan. 8, 1933; s. Richard Dean and LoLeta (Carroll) W.; student Seminole Jr. Coll., 1950-51; B.S. in Petroleum Engring., U. Okla., 1954, M. Geol. Engring., 1959; postgrad. U. Tex., 1958; m. Carol Ann Ferguson, Nov. 21, 1960 (div. Nov. 1968); 1 stepdau., Ann Todd. Mem. engr. tng. program Humble Oil & Refining Co., Odessa, Tex., 1954, petroleum engr., asst. to dist. engr., Andrews, Tex., 1954-55, Wink, Tex., 1955-56, petroleum engr., Midland, Tex., 1956-57, Houston, 1957, Midland, 1957-58; petroleum engr., geologist Montgomery Oil Co., El Dorado, Ark., 1959-60; self-employed petroleum engr., geologist, Oklahoma City, 1960-62; mgr. geol. and engring. dept. Sarkeys Enterprises, Oklahoma City, 1962-65; mgr. geol. and engring. dept. Sarkeys, Inc., Oklahoma City, 1965-72, v.p., 1966-72; ind. petroleum geol. engr., 1972—. Registered profl. engr., Okla. Mem. Am. Inst. Mining, Metall, and Petroleum Engrs., Am. Assn. Petroleum Geologists, Nat., Okla. socs. profl. engrs., Oklahoma City Geol. Soc., Oklahoma City Assn. Petroleum Landmen, Oklahoma City Tennis Assn., S.A.R., Sigma Nu, Tau Beta Pi, Pi Epsilon Tau. Republican. Methodist. Club: Oklahoma City Ski. Home: 6307 NW 63d St Oklahoma City OK 73114

WITSIEPE, RALPH ERNEST, elec. products mfg. co. exec.; b. Chgo., Feb. 6, 1928; s. Ralph Ernest and Edna (Hargreaves) W.; student U. Md., 1956-58; m. Lillian Kuleskey, Mar. 10, 1962; children—Kelley L., Robert J. Various worldwide engring. and mgmt. positions Philco Ford Corp., 1953-72; pres. C.T.I. Edn. Products, Inc., Mount Pleasant, S.C., 1972—, dir., 1972—. Served with AUS, 1945-52. Mem. I.E.E.E. (sr.). Home: 688 Molasses Lane Mount Pleasant SC 29464 Office: 695 Coleman Blvd Mount Pleasant SC 29404

WITT, T. FOSTER, JR., banker; b. Richmond, Va., Nov. 4, 1927; s. T. Foster and Isabel (Luke) W.; grad. St. Christopher's Sch., 1946; B.A., Va. Mil. Inst., 1950; LL.B., U. Va., 1955; m. Ann Lane Crittenden, Apr. 13, 1971; children—T. Foster III, Anne Lane. Registered rep. Scott & Stringfellow, 1955-61; trust planner United Va. Bank, Richmond, 1961—; dir. Commonwealth Lab., Inc. Active United Givers Fund; pres. Children's Home Soc. Va. Served to 1st lt., inf. AUS, 1951-53. Chartered financial analyst. Mem. Va. Bar Assn., Richmond Soc. Financial Analysts (past pres.), Va. Mil. Inst. Alumni Assn., English Speaking Union, Assn. Preservation of Va. Antiquities (past dir.), Kappa Alpha, Phi Alpha Delta. Episcopalian. Clubs: Country of Va., Commonwealth, Downtown (past pres.), Bull and Bear (Richmond). Home: 7603 Cornwall Rd Richmond VA 23229 Office: 900 E Main St Richmond VA 23219

WITTKOWER, JAMES ALBERT, mfg. co. exec.; b. Dallas, Jan. 25, 1926; s. Louis David and Orelle Velta (Land) W.; A.A., N.Tex. Agrl. Coll., 1944; B.B.A., So. Methodist U., 1948; M.B.A., Mich. State U., 1968; m. Marilyn Jeannette Bridges, June 28, 1952; children—Lisa Kaye, Melinda Anne, Kathleen Leigh. Various indsl. relations positions Chance Vought Aircraft Corp., Dallas, 1948-63; indsl. relations mgr. Mich. div. Ling-Temco-Vought, Inc., Warren, 1963-69, asst. dir. corp. indsl. relations, Dallas, 1969; dir. adminstrn. LTV Ling Altec, Inc. (name now changed to Altec Corp.), Anaheim, Cal., 1969-73, v.p. adminstrn., Dallas, 1973—. Conf. leader Mich. State U. Seminars, 1966-68, Army Top Mgmt. Sch., Rock Island, Ill., 1965-66; guest lectr. Mich. State U., 1966-68. Mem. personnel adv. com. Dallas Ind. Sch. Dist., 1969; adv. bd. Coro Found., Los Angeles. Served as 1st lt. AUS, 1944-46; PTO. Decorated Purple Heart, Bronze Star. Mem. Am. Soc. Personnel Adminstrn., Advanced Mgmt.-Mich. State U. Club, Inc., Am. Soc. Ins. Mgmt., Personnel and Indsl. Relations Assn. Los Angeles, Delta Sigma Pi. Home: 9722 Highland View Dallas TX 75238 Office: PO Box 30385 Dallas TX 75230

WITTNER, TED PHILIP, ins. exec.; b. Tampa, Sept. 17, 1928; s. Jacob and Helen (Goldman) W.; B.S. in Bus. Adminstrn., U. Fla., 1950; m. Sylvia Heller, Apr. 3, 1954; children—Sharyn (Mrs. Richard Jacobson), Pamela Anne. Mgr., Bell Luggage Co., 1953-54; pvt. life ins. agt., 1955-56; gen. agt. Crown Life Ins. Co., St. Petersburg, Fla., 1956-64; pres. Ted P. Wittner & Assos., 1964-67, pres. Wittner & Co., 1968— (both St. Petersburg.); pres. Crown Life Brokerage Gen. Agts. Assn., 1968-70, Profit Programs Co., St. Petersburg, 1969—; dir. Nat. Bank St. Petersburg, Para-Med. Enterprises, Inc., St. Petersburg. Bd. dirs. Com. of 100; Pinellas County mem. St. Petersburg Civic Adv. Com.; bd. dirs. Pinellas Assn. Retarded Children; bd. dirs., sec.-treas. Menorah Center. Served to 2d lt. USAF, 1950-53. Life and qualifying mem. Million Dollar Round Table. Mem. Gen. Agts. and Mgrs. Conf. (pres. St. Petersburg chpt. 1957), Nat. Assn. Life Underwriters, St. Petersburg Area C. of C. (v.p. 1969-72), Fla. Blue Key. Jewish religion (pres. congregation 1966-68, chmn. bd. 1964-66). Club: Commerce (pres. 1973) St. Petersburg. Home: 6726 10th Av N St Petersburg FL 33710 Office: 3663 Central Av St Petersburg FL 33713

WITTY, ROBERT GEE, ednl. adminstr.; b. Glasgow, Ky., Oct. 6, 1906; s. Robert Lee and Maude Mae (Lawrence) W.; A.B., Willmette U., 1928; postgrad. Princeton Theol. Sem., 1929; B.D., Asbury Theol. Sem., 1932; Ph.D., U. Fla., 1959; m. Katherine Henderson Hoover, Dec. 24, 1943; children—Mary (Mrs. Marty Span), Robert Maxwell, Edith, Daniel, Ann, Robert Earl Hoover. Ordained to ministry Baptist Ch., 1944; pastor Faith Temple, Jacksonville, Fla., 1935-43, Central Bapt. Ch., 1942-70; pres. Luther Rice Sem., 1966—, dean grad. studies, 1964-66; treas. Bapt. Towers, Inc., Jacksonville, 1969—; Bd. dirs. Fredricksburg Bible Inst.; bd. mission Fla. Bapt. Conv., 1970-73. Mem. Pastor's Conf. (pres. 1969-70). Author: Power for Church, 1968; Help Yourself to Happiness, 1969; Church Visitation, 1969; Pastor's Manual for Revival Preparation, 1970; Signs of the Second Coming, 1970; Jesus is Lord, 1971. Home: 357 Tidewater Dr Jacksonville FL 32211 Office: 1050 Hendricks Av Jacksonville FL 32207

WOCHOK, ZACHARY STEPHEN, educator; b. Phila., Dec. 29, 1942; s. Andrew and Mary (Tomaszewsky) W.; B.A., LaSalle Coll., 1964; M.S., Villanova U., 1967; Ph.D. (NIH fellow), U. Conn., 1970; postgrad. (NIH fellow) Yale, 1970-71; m. Barbara Nadya Wylder, Aug. 22, 1970. Asst. prof. biology U. Ala., University, 1971—. Project dir. NSF research grant, 1973-75. Pres., St. Francis Community Council, 1972-73. Mem. Am. Soc. Plant Physiologists, Internat. Assn. Plant Tissue Culture, Bot. Soc. Am., Sigma Xi, Alpha Epsilon Delta. Mem. Ukrainian Catholic Ch. Author: Laboratory Manual for Plant Biology, 1973. Contbr. articles to profl. publs. Home: 11203 Northwood Lake St Northport AL 35476 Office: Biology Dept PO 1927 U Ala University AL 35486

WOERNER, PERRY MONROE, banker; b. Fredericksburg, Tex., Mar. 5, 1924; s. Charles H. and Mary (Ahrens) W.; B.A., Bob Jones U., 1956; postgrad. Nat. Trust Sch. Northwestern U., 1964; m. Bernice Durst, Aug. 14, 1946; children—Rene Sheldon, Hadley Ross, Gaylon Reese. With Schneider Produce Co., 1941-42, Stehling Brothers Mens Clothiers, 1946-47; program clk. U.S. Agr. Dept., 1949-52, adminstrv. asst., 1956-59; with Fredericksburg Nat. Bank, 1959—, asst. cashier, asst. trust officer, 1961-64, trust officer, 1965— (all Fredericksburg). Chmn. service unit Salvation Army, 1959-70; pres. Gillespie County Am. Cancer Soc., 1962-63. Trustee Fredericksburg Ind. Sch. Dist. Served with AUS, 1943-46; PTO. Mem. Am. Inst. Banking, C. of C. (past dir.), S. Central Fedn. Gem and Minerol. Socs. (dir. 1970—), Gillespie County Ministerial Assn. (sec. 1970—). Mem. Emmanuel Gospel Ch. (asso. pastor 1959—). Rotarian. Club: Rockhounds. Home: 407 E College St Fredericksburg TX 78624 Office: 155 E Main St Fredericksburg TX 78624

WOFFORD, CHARLES AUGUSTUS, govt ofcl., judge; b. Atlanta, Nov. 29, 1914; s. James Avery and Ollie Eva (Osborne) W.; LL.B., Atlanta Law Sch., 1943, LL.M., 1945; LL.D., Webster U., 1945; m. Marie Norene Root, July 6, 1936; children—Charles Augustus, Stephanie (Mrs. Roddy Ingraham). Judge municipal Ct., City Atlanta, 1954-58; judge Criminal Ct. Fulton County, 1959-67; judge, Fulton Superior Ct., Atlanta Jud. Circuit, 1967—. Hon. dir. Atlanta Health Council. Charter pres. Ga. Children's Chiropractic Center; bd. dirs. Joseph B. Whitehead Meml. Boys' Club. Mem. Am., Atlanta bar assns., Atlanta Lawyers Club, State Bar Ga., Fulton County Lawyers Assn., Underwater Soc. Am., Peace Officers Assn. Ga., Rack-N-Cue Soc., Atlanta Law Sch. Alumni Assn. (charter pres.), Old War Horse Lawyers Assn., Sigma Delta Kappa (life mem., officer numerous offices). Mason (K.T., 33 deg.), K.P. (chancellor comdr. 1945), Elk, Eagle, Moose; mem. Order Eastern Star. Clubs: Atlanta Athletic, East Lake Country, Lakeside Country (Atlanta). Home: 636 Virginia Av NE Atlanta GA 30306 Office: Fulton County Ct House 136 Pryor St SE Atlanta GA 30303

WOFFORD, CHARLES PARKER, physician; b. Johnson City, Tenn., Dec. 23, 1908; s. George Torrey and Florence Potter (Harris) W.; grad. The Hill Sch., 1928; A.B., Princeton, 1932; M.D., U. Pa., 1936; m. Helen Dyson, June 22, 1935 (dec. 1959); children—Mary (Mrs. Amend), John Charles; m. 2d, Helen Hunter, Apr. 25, 1961. Intern, Phila. Gen. Hosp., 1936-38; fellow internal medicine Cleve. Clinic, 1938-40; pvt. practice internal medicine Johnson City, 1940—; mem. staff Meml. Hosp., Johnson City, chief of medicine. Active Johnson City Symphony Orch., 1971—; mem. exec. council Sequoyah council Boy Scouts Am., 1971—; pres. Johnson City Civil Council, 1955-56. Served to maj. M.C., AUS, 1942-46. Diplomate Am. Bd. Internal medicine. Fellow A.C.P., Am. Acad. Allergy, Am. Assn. Clin. Immunology and Allergy, Am. Coll. Allergy; mem. Southeastern Allergy Assn. (pres. 1956-57), So., Tenn. med. assns., A.M.A., Johnson City C. of C. Clubs: Johnson City Country, Johnson City Apres-ski, Linville Golf, Ponte Vedra, Carolina Caribbean, Unaka Rod and Gun, Hurstleigh. Episcopalian. Home: 3 Llewellyn Wood Johnson City TN 37601 Office: 115 W Fairview Av Johnson City TX 37601

WOHLFORD, JAMES GORDON, ednl. adminstr.; b. Erwin, Tenn., May 24, 1916; s. William Thomas and Ethel (Burkholder) W.; B.E.E., Ga. Inst. Tech., 1941; M.S., Stanford, 1947; m. Mary Waring Green, Mar. 22, 1952; Instr. sch. elec. engring. Ga. Inst. Tech., 1947-48, dir. cooperative div., 1948—. Cons. cooperative edn. Bd. dirs. Villa Internat., Atlanta. Served to capt. AUS, 1941-45. Mem. Am. Soc. Engring. Edn., I.E.E.E., Anak Soc., Koseme Soc., Fulton County Grand Jurors Assn. Presbyn. (deacon 1962-68, elder 1970—). Club: Burns of Atlanta. Home: 2873 W Roxboro Rd NE Atlanta GA 30324 Office: Ga Inst Tech 225 North Av NW Atlanta GA 30332

WOHLSCHLAG, DONALD EUGENE, educator, zoologist, b. Bucyrus, O., Nov. 6, 1918; s. Herman Albert and Agnes Mae (Canode) W.; B.S., Heidelberg Coll., 1940; Ph.D., 1949; m. Elsie Marjorie Baker, June 5, 1943; children—William Eugene, Nancy Sue, Sarah Ann. Research asso. zoology U. Wis., Madison, 1948-49; asst. prof. zoology Stanford, 1949-56, asso. prof., 1956-64, prof., 1964-65; prof. zoology U. Tex., Port Aransas, 1965—, also dir. Marine Sci. Inst., 1965-70. Mem. U.S. Nat. Marine subcom. for internat. biol. program, 1966-71, U.S. Acad. Sci. commn. ecol. research interocean canal, 1969-70, Nat. Sci. Tundra Biome panel, 1971-74, Inst. Ecology Water Ecosystems Commn., 1974—; lab. dir. Nat. Sci. Found. Antarctic biol. lab. support program, also project leader, 1959-65. Served 1st. lt. USAAF, 1942-46. Fellow A.A.A.S., Am. Inst. Fisheries and Research Biologists, Arctic Inst. N.Am.; mem. Am. Inst. Biol. Sci., Am. Fisheries Soc., Am. Soc. Limnology and Oceanography, Am. Soc. Zoology, Ecol. Soc. Am. (pres. western sect. 1965), Am. Soc. Ichthyologyand Herpetology. Lion. Editor: Contributions in Marine Science, 1974—. Contbr. articles to sci. jours. Home: 615 Av C Port Aransas TX 78373

WOLENS, JOSEPH BERNARD, lawyer; b. Corsicana, Tex., Nov. 16, 1932; s. Max and Florence (Franks) W.; B.A. in Philosophy, Rice U., 1953; LL.B., So. Methodist U., 1962, LL.M., 1967; postgrad. Harvard, 1967-68; m. Jacklyn Kless, Dec. 9, 1956; children—Kay, Heidi, Jonathan, Jeoffrey. Admitted to Tex. bar, 1961; jr. exec. and buyer K. Wolens, Inc., Corsicana, 1956-62; mem. law firm Rogers, Eggers, Sherril & Pace, Wichita Falls, Tex., 1962-65; asst. dean and asst. prof. law So. Methodist U., Dallas, 1965-68; mem. law firm Durant, Mankoff, Davis & Wolens, Dallas, 1968—. Legal cons. Harvard Bus. Sch., Cambridge, Mass., 1968-70. Bd. dirs. Akiba Acad. Dallas, 1972—. Served with USNR, 1954-56. Mem. Am., Tex., Dallas Bar assns. Jewish religion (dir. congregation 1966-67, 73—). Mem. Order Woolsack. Contbr. articles to profl. jours. Office: 3434 First National Bank Bldg Dallas TX 75202

WOLF, CLARENCE, JR., stockbroker; b. Phila., May 11, 1908; s. Clarence and Nan (Hogan) W.; student Pa. Mil. Prep. Sch., 1921; grad. Swarthmore (Pa.) Prep. Sch., 1923; m. Alma C. Backhus, Sept. 11, 1942. Founder French-Wolf Paint Products Corp., Phila., 1926, pres. until 1943; admitted to Phila.-Balt. Stock Exchange, 1937; asso. Reynolds Securities Inc., 1944—, rep., Miami Beach, Fla., 1946—, apptd. spl. rep., 1963; dir., vice chmn. bd., mem. exec. com. Amcord, Inc.; dir. George S. MacManus Co., Rand Broadcasting Co., owners radio and TV stas., also hotels, 1946-68. Pres. Normandy Isles Improvement Assn., Miami Beach, 1952-53; mem. Presidents Council Miami Beach, 1952—. Mem. Alumnus Assn. Pa. Mil. Coll. (Fla. dir. 1961—). Clubs: Penn Athletic (Phila.); Variety, Standard (Miami, Fla.). Home: Seacoast Towers 5151 Collins Av Miami Beach FL 33140 Office: care Reynolds Securities 444 Brickell Av Miami FL 33131

WOLF, FREDERICK TAYLOR, botanist, educator; b. Auburn, Ala., July 11, 1915; s. Frederick Adolph and Wynnette (Taylor) W.; student U. N.C., 1931-33; A.B., Harvard, 1935; M.A., U. Wis., 1936, Ph.D., 1938; m. Virginia Hudson Martin, June 10, 1945; children—Ann (Mrs. A.A. Ercelawn), Catherine. NRC fellow Harvard, 1938-39; instr. botany Vanderbilt U., Nashville, 1939-42, asst. prof., 1945-47, asso. prof., 1947-56, prof., 1956—. Served with USAAF, 1942-45. Mem. Tenn. Acad. Sci. (pres. 1955), Soc. Am. Microbiologists (br. chmn. 1952), Bot. Soc. Am. (sect. chmn. 1966), Am. Soc. Plant Physiologists (sect. chmn. 1964), Assn. Southeastern Biologists (v.p. 1956), Sigma Xi. Author: (with F. A. Wolf) The Fungi, 2 vols., 1947. Contbr. articles to profl. publs. Home: 3611 Saratoga Dr Nashville TN 37205

WOLF, HARRY CHARLES, JR., ins. exec.; b. Helena, Ark., Mar. 2, 1908; s. Harry Charles and Lillian Virginia (Cecil) W.; B.S., U. S.C. 1929; m. Rebecca; children—Harry Charles III, Katherine Forsyth. Engr. maintenance of way dept. Pa. R.R., 1929-30; engr., insp. dept. Asso. Factory Mut. Fire Ins. Co., Boston, 1930-31; engr. MFB Mut. Ins. Co. (formerly Firemen's Mut. Ins. Co.), Providence, 1931-36, asst. v.p., 1936-44, v.p., 1944—; asst. v.p. Union Mut. Fire Ins. Co., Providence, 1935-44; pres., treas., dir. Corporate Insurers Service, Inc., Charlotte, N.C., 1947-67; v.p. MFB Mut. Ins. Co., 1968—; pres., dir. Corporate Insurers Service, Inc., 1947—; pres. Corporate Ins. Cons. Internat., Ltd., 1973—. Bd. dirs. Charlotte Council Alcoholism; mem. adv. bd. Mental Health Bd. Charlotte. Mem. Euphradian Lit. Soc., U. S.C., Newcomen Soc., Omicron Delta Kappa. Clubs: Executives, Charlotte Country, Charlotte City. Home: 3821 Arborway Charlotte NC 28211 Office: 139 S Tryon St Charlotte NC 28202

WOLF, HARRY CHARLES, III, architect; b. Charlotte, N.C., June 28, 1935; s. Harry Charles, Jr. and Harriet Aubrey (Howard) W.; B.S., Ga. Inst. Tech., 1958; B. Arch., Mass. Inst. Tech., 1960; m. Janice Grigg, Nov. 13, 1966; children—Harry Charles IV, Harriet Craig. Pres. Wolf Assos., Architects and Planners, Charlotte, 1965—. Mem. Charlotte-Mecklenburg Environmental Council, 1973—, phys. environment subcom. Charlotte-Mecklenburg Citizens Com. Urban Living, 1969; chmn. Joint Coordinating Com. Urban Affairs and Environment, Charlotte, 1969-71. Bd. dirs. Charlotte Nature Museum, 1968-73, pres., 1970-71; bd. dirs. Charlotte Nature Mus. Found., 1969-71, chmn., 1973-75; bd. dirs. Mint Mus. Art. Served with USAF, 1961-62. Recipient Nat. Archtl. Record awards, 1970, 72; Bartlett award Pres.'s Com. Employment Handicapped, 1971, 74; Nat. Plywood Assn. Design citation, 1973. Mem. Am. Inst. Planners (asso.), A.I.A. (nat. honor awards jury 1972; chmn. nat. design com. 1974; chmn. nat. task force Design by Creative Pub. Adminstrn. 1973; pres. Charlotte sect. 1973-74; dir. N.C. chpt. 1973-74; numerous awards 1966, 68, 70, 71, 73, 74), Newcomen Soc. N.Am., Phi Delta Theta. Democrat. Episcopalian. Clubs: Charlotte City, Nocturns (Charlotte); Torch Internat. Important works include N.C. Nat. Bank, Beatties Ford, Latta Arcade, Charlotte, NBT/Williams Cos., Tulsa, Ponte Travers Wolf Devel. plan, Charlotte. Contbr. articles, archtl.

works to profl. jours. Home: 501 Hermitage Ct Charlotte NC 28207 Office: 213 Latta Arcade Charlotte NC 28202

WOLF, LARRY JAMES, newspaper exec.; b. Taylor, Tex., May 4, 1944; s. Harvey Louis and Anita (Conninberg) W.; B.B.A., U. Tex., 1966; m. Charylene Muennink, Aug. 20, 1966; children—Yvonne, Lori. Gen. accounting mgr. Houston Chronicle Pub. Co. Mem. Am. Inst. C.P.A.'s, Tex. Soc. C.P.A.'s. Home: 7602 Redding St Houston TX 77036 Office: 801 Travis St Houston TX 77002

WOLFE, BOBBIE LEE, accountant; b. Beeville, Tex., Oct. 13, 1936; s. Robert E. and Verna Mae (Hudgeons) W.; B.S., Abilene Christian Coll., 1959; m. Lillian Bernice Isaacks, Dec. 3, 1955; children—Shirley, Mary, Charles, Richard, David. Accountant, Smith, Mathis & Wolfe, C.P.A.'s, 1960-69; treas. Gooch Packing Co., Abilene, Tex., 1969-73; now dir.; accountant Wolfe & Roberson, Abilene, 1973—. Treas., Chisholm Trail council Boy Scouts Am., 1971-73; pres. Abilene Bus. and Estate planning council, 1973-74. C.P.A., Tex. Mem. Abilene Jr. C. of C. (treas. 1965). Home: 1538 Richland Dr Abilene TX 79603 Office: 3385 N 3d St Abilene TX 79603

WOLFE, DOUGLAS ARTHUR, ecologist; b. Dayton, O., July 6, 1939; s. Ranald Milton and Julia Marie (Good) W.; B.S. in Zoology, Ohio State U., 1959, M.S. in Physiol. Chemistry, 1961, Ph.D. (NIH fellow), 1964; m. Nancy Suzanne Meeker, July 13, 1959; children—Cynthia Marie, Nicholas Arden, Catherine Anne. Chief biogeochemistry program, radio biol. lab. Bur. Comml. Fisheries, Beaufort, N.C., 1964-71; chief scientist radioecology div. P.R. Nuclear Center, Mayaguez, P.R., 1969-70; dir. div. ecology Atlantic Estuarine Fisheries Center, Nat. Marine Fisheries Service, Beaufort, 1971—. Adj. asso. prof. zoology N.C. State U., Raleigh, 1966—. Mem. Am. Chem. Soc., Am. Soc. Limnology and Oceanography, Ecol. Soc. Am., Atlantic Estuarine Research Soc. (rep. to exec. com. of estuarine research fedn. 1972), Am. Malacological Union, N.C. Shell Club (v.p. 1971-72, pres. 1972-73), Sigma Xi. Contbr. articles to sci. jours. Home: Route 2 Box 184 Beaufort NC 28516 Office: Atlantic Estuarine Fisheries Center Beaufort NC 28516

WOLFE, JOHN ALLEN, cons. firm exec.; b. Riverton, Ia., June 3, 1920; s. Asa Allen and Alice (Thomas) W.; Geol. Engr., Colo. Sch. Mines, 1947, M.S., 1954; children—James Perry, Cynthia (Mrs. J.A. Banghart Jr.), m. 2d, Lenora Irvin, 1969. Dir. exploration Ideal Cement Co., Denver, 1948-65; geol cons., P.I., Latin Am., 1965-68; pres. Mineral Resources Cons., Houston, 1968—; partner Schoenike, Wolfe & Assos., Houston, 1970—; v.p., gen. mgr. Lobo Mines, Inc., Manila, Philippines, 1970—. Lectr., cons. in field; mem. Colo. Mining Industry Devel. Bd., 1963-65. Fellow Geol. Soc. Am.; mem. Am. Mining Congress (gov. 1963-65), Colo. Mining Assn. (pres. 1963), Am. Inst. Mining Engrs., Soc. Econ. Geologists, Am. Inst. Profl. Geologists. Republican. Contbr. articles to profl. jours. Home: care Lobo Mines Inc 504 Manila Banking Bldg Makati Rizal Philippines Office: 5133 Richmond Av Suite 1 Houston TX 77027

WOLFE, PAUL JONES, JR., broadcasting co. exec.; b. Augusta, Ga., Dec. 1, 1940; s. Paul Jones and Pearl (Simon) W.; student Richmond Acad., 1957-59; m. Susan Dale, Sept. 17, 1966; 1 son, David Paul. With sta. WKLE, Washington, Ga., 1959-60; owner, operator sts. WXPQ, Eatonton, Ga., 1966-70; program dir. sta. WJCL-TV, Savannah, Ga., 1970—. Recipient honors for pub. service. Home: 11008 Williamsburg Rd Savannah GA 31406 Office: 10001 Abercorn St Savannah GA 31406

WOLFF, WALTER LEROY, former govt. ofcl.; b. Louisville, Jan. 31, 1910; s. Julius Carl and Alice Louise (Kammerer) W.; B.S. in Mech. Engring., U. Ky., 1932; postgrad. Army Command and Gen. Staff Sch., 1944, U.S. Dept. Agr. Grad. Sch., 1961; m. Mildred Hazel Youngberg, Oct. 9, 1942. Div. engr. Community Pub. Service Co., Winchester, Ky., 1933-35; with Rural Electrification Adminstrn., U.S. Dept. Agr., 1936—, project devel asst., Washington, 1936-37, nat. field rep., Louisville, 1938-41, head acquisition sect., Washington, 1947-49, area dir. telphone program, 1950-60, dep. asst. adminstr. adminstrn. telephone program, 1961-72, ret., 1972. Rep. AID to Hashemite Kingdom, Jordan, 1965. Served to lt. col. AUS, 1942-46. Decorated Army Service medal with oak leaf cluster. Registered profl. valuation engr., Ky., U.S. Mem. Am. Soc. Mil. Engrs., Am. Ordnance Assn., Res. Officers Assn., Rural Electrification Adminstrn. Athletic Assn. (pres. 1952), Am. Legion, Ky. State Soc., Ky. Hist. Soc., Heroes of '76, U. Ky. Alumni Assn. (pres. Washington chpt. 1968-69), Nat. Sojourners (pres. Washington chpt. 3 1970), Lutheran. Mason (Shriner). Club: Agriculture Department, Triangle (pres. 1960). Home: 602 Beverly Dr Alexandria VA 22305

WOLFSON, RICHARD FREDERICK, broadcasting co. exec.; b. Bklyn., Jan. 7, 1923; s. William Leon and Gertrude (Quitman) W.; B.S., Harvard, 1942; LL.B., Yale, 1944; m. Elaine Reinherz, June 6, 1954; children—Lisa Reinherz, Paul Reinherz Quitman. Admitted to N.Y. bar, 1945, Fla. bar. 1956; law clk. to judge U.S. Ct. Appeals, 2d circuit, 1944-45, U.S. Supreme Ct. justice, 1945-47; practiced law, N.Y.C., 1947-52; asst. to pres. Wometco Enterprises, Miami, Fla., 1952-59, v.p., 1959-64, dir., 1959—, sr. v.p., 1964-72, exec. v.p., also gen. counsel, 1972—; dir. City Nat. Bank of Coral Gables (Fla.), Channel 12, Jacksonville, Fla. Chmn. cultural affairs com. Third Century, Inc., 1972—. Bd. dirs. Greater Miami Philharmonic Soc., pres., 1969-72; bd. dirs. Everglades Sch. for Girls, pres., 1971—; bd. dirs. Dade County A.R.C., Pub. Trust Theater, Miami, Friends of Art of Lowe Art Mus., Miami. Guggenheim fellow, 1949-50. Clubs: Miami, Standard of Miami; Coral Gables Country; Westview Country (Miami); Harvard of New York City, Harvard of New York. Author: (with Kurland) Jurisdiction Supreme Court of the United States, 1951. Home: 630 University Dr Coral Gables FL 33134 Office: 306 N Miami Av Miami FL 33128

WOLIN, S. ROGER, airline exec.; b. Rochester, N.Y., Sept. 9, 1909; s. Kief Louis and Ina (Cate) W.; A.B., Union Coll., 1930; m. Dorothy Gibler, Jan. 17, 1946; children—John Anthony, Gregory Chaye, Melissa Conchita. Writer, editor Hearst Newspapers, Rochester, Syracuse, Albany, N.Y., 1929-32; with A.P., Albany, 1932-33. U.P., Washington, 1933-34, Internat. News Service, Washington, 1934-35; pub. relations Pan Am. Airways, Miami, Fla., 1936-41, mgr. pub. relations, Brownsville, Tex., 1941, div. mgr. pub. relations, Mexico City, Mexico, 1942-44, pub. relations mgr. Latin Am. Div., Miami, 1944-64, dir. pub. relations, 1964—. Mem. adv. bd. Biscayne Coll. Mem. Inter-Am. Fla., press assns., Aviation Writers Assn., Internat. Soc. Aviation Writers, Soc. Am. Travel Writers, Pub. Relations Soc. Am., Internat. Pub. Relations Assn., Sigma Delta Chi. Clubs: Nat. Press, Wings; Riviera Country; Coral Gables Country, 200 (dir.). Home: 7677 Ponce de Leon Rd Miami FL 33143 Office: Pan Am Bldg Miami FL 33159

WOLIN, SAMUEL, electronic engr., govt. ofcl.; b. N.Y.C., Feb. 12, 1909; s. Eli and Dina Leah (Levine) W.; B.S. (Tremaine scholar, State scholar of U. State N.Y.), Coll. City N.Y., 1930, M.S., 1931; A.M., Columbia, 1941; m. Dorothy Hirsch, Oct. 25, 1942; children—Eleanor Iris, Karen Barbara, Robert M. Wechsler, Ira L. Blank. Tchr. math., physics and civil service Mondell Engring. Sch., N.Y.C., summers 1930-31; tchr. math. and sci. various high schs., tech. schs., vocational schs., N.Y.C., 1930-42; instr. radio engring. U.S. Army Air Force, Yale, Scott Field, Ill., 1942-44; instr. elec. communications Mass. Inst. Tech., Boston, 1944-45; radio engr. Raytheon Mfg. Co., Waltham, Mass., 1945, RCA Victor div. RCA, Camden, N.J., 1945-46; electronic research engr. Bartol Research Found. of Franklin Inst., Swarthmore, Pa., 1946-47; electronic engr. and scientist U.S. Naval Air Devel. Center, Johnsville, Pa., 1947-57; sr. electronic engr. McDonnell Aircraft Corp., St. Louis, 1957-60, Lockheed Electronics Co., Plainfield, N.J., 1960-61; sr. design staff engr. Vertol div. Boeing Co., Morton, Pa., 1961-63, research engr., Huntsville, Ala., 1966-69; sr. research engr. Brown Engring. Co., Inc., Huntsville, 1963-66; electronic engr. U.S. Army Missile Command, Redstone Arsenal, Ala., 1969—. Mem. I.E.E.E. (sr.), Soc. Indsl. and Applied Math., A.A.A.S., Phi Beta Kappa. Co-author: Techniques for Airborne Radome Design, 1957. Developer procedures for designing radomes. Home: 2107 Wimberley Rd NW Huntsville AL 35805 Office: US Army Missile Command Bldg 5400 Redstone Arsenal AL 35809

WOLKOMIR, NATHAN TULLY, labor union ofcl.; b. Baku, Russia, Oct. 12, 1909; s. Boris and Rose (Silver) W.; came to U.S., 1912, naturalized, 1917; B.S., N.Y.U., 1929, St. Johns U., 1930, St. Francis Coll., N.Y.C., 1930; M.Ed., St. John's Univ., 1940; D.Ed., U. Ill., 1960; m. Louise Orthelia Shimmin, Mar. 10, 1944; 1 dau., Rhya Natalia. Tchr., N.Y.C., 1940-42; ednl. specialist, tng. command USAAF and USAF, 1942-64; mem. Nat. Fedn. Fed. Employees, 1942—, pres. Ill., 1950-52, nat. pres., 1964—. Chmn. Community Concerts, Rantoul, Ill., 1960, Rantoul Recreation Bd., 1961; pres. Chanute AFB Recreation and Welfare Orgn., 1962; mem. President's Com. Hiring Handicapped, 1965. Police commr., Rantoul, 1962. Mem. Soc. Personnel Adminstrn., Soc. Programmed Instrn., Am. Soc. Pub. Adminstrn., Pub. Personnel Assn., Air Force Assn. Mason, Odd Fellow, Moose. Author: (with others) Modern Airmanship, 1957. Home: 1001 Lamberton Dr Silver Spring MD 20902 Office: 1737 H St NW Washington DC 20006

WOLMA, FRED JOHN, physician; b. Albuquerque, Dec. 10, 1916; s. Fred John and Marion (Kitterman) W.; student St. Mary's U., 1933-38; B.A., U. Tex., 1940, M.D., 1943; m. Dorothy Jean Egert, Nov. 19, 1943; children—Fred John, Cynthia Ann. Intern Med. Coll. Va., 1943-44, resident, 1947-48; resident U. Tex. Med. Br., 1948-51; practice medicine, specializing in surgery, Galveston, Tex., 1951—, staff U. Tex. Med. Br. Hosps., Galveston, 1951—, chief div. gen. surgery, 1968—, prof., 1969—. Diplomate Am. Bd. Surgery. Mem. A.C.S., Am. Assn. for Surgery of Trauma, So., Western, Tex. surg. socs.; Sigma Xi, Alpha Omega Alpha. Author: Intravenous Abdominal Aortography and Placentography, 1967; (films) Aortic Reseation for Abdominal Aneurysm, 1956, Bullet Emboli, 1969, Splenic Artery Aneurysms, 1973, Infected Arterial Grafts, 1973. Home: 4404 Sherman St Galveston TX 77550 Office: 800 Mechanic St Galveston TX 77550

WOLSKI, EUGENE JOSEPH, physician; b. Balt., Mar. 29, 1938; s. Milton Joseph and Anna Victoria (Regula) W. ; B.S., Loyola Coll., Balt., 1959; M.D., U. Md., 1963; m. Anne Pauline Cann, Feb. 4, 1961; children—Eugene Joseph, Edward Stephan, Catherine Virginia, Michael Paul. Rotating intern Union Meml. Hosp., Balt., 1963; pvt. med. practice, Lewisville, Tex., 1968—; med. staff Flow Meml. Hosp., Denton, Tex. Mem. adv. council Lewisville Nat. Bank. Served with USNR, 1963-68. Recipient Navy Unit commendation for service in Dominican Republic, 1965. Mem. A.M.A., Tex., So. med. assns., Denton County Med. Soc. Roman Catholic. Home: 124 Red Oak Lane Flower Mound Farms Lewisville TX 75067 Office: Family Med Center 211 Stemmons St Lewisville TX 75067

WOMACK, GEORGE CLEVELAND, bank dir.; b. Natchez, Miss., Sept. 27, 1936; s. Grover Cleveland and Eunice Edna (Richardson) W.; B.S., La. State U., 1959; m. Alma McClure, Sept. 25, 1970; 1 dau., Holly. Mgr., Smithland Plantation, Jonesville, La., 1959-64, owner, 1964—; dir. Catahoula Bank, Jonesville, 1963—. Mem. Catahoula Parish Farm Bur., 1962—. Democrat. Baptist. Home: Star Route B Box 45A Jonesville LA 71343 Office: Catahoula Bank Jonesville LA 71343

WOMACK, NELLEEN RUTH (MRS. AARON M. WOMACK, JR.), librarian; b. Henry Grove, Tex., Jan. 13, 1926; d. George Henry and Nellie (Kirkpatrick) Stroud; student North Tex. State U., 1943-44; B.S. in Edn., East Tex. State U., 1957, M.Ed., 1960, M.L.S., 1967; postgrad., Tex. Women's U., 1965-66; m. Aaron M. Womack, Jr., July 20, 1944; 1 son, Robert Henry. Tchr. pub. elementary schs., Mesquite, Tex., 1957-60, librarian, 1959-60; head librarian Garland (Tex.) High Sch., 1960-63; head librarian Mesquite Pub. Library, 1963—. Chmn. March Dimes, Mesquite, 1967-68. Mem. Tex. Municipal (past pres.), Dallas Met. (past pres.) librarians assns., A.L.A., Dallas County, Tex., Southwest library assns., Bus. and Profl. Women's Club (pres. 1966-67), Mesquite C. of C., Am. Assn. U. Women. Clubs: Mesquite Woman's, Altrusa (pres. 1970-72, recipient Outstanding Performance award 1971) (Mesquite). Home: 520 Kathy Dr Mesquite TX 75149 Office: 300 Grubb Dr Mesquite TX 75149

WOMELDORPH, DONALD EUGENE, JR., statistician; b. Ashland, Ky., June 15, 1940; s. Donald Eugene and Martha Washington (Arnold) W.; B.S., Va. Poly. Inst., 1962; Ph.D., 1966; m. Eileen Fay Payne, Aug. 25, 1962; children—Kristen Anne, Craig Mahlon. Statistician, Phillips Petroleum Co., Bartlesville, Okla., 1966—. Tchr., Okla. State U. Extension, 1969-70. Mem. Am. Statis. Assn., Am. Inst. Chem. Engrs. Democrat. Presbyn. Elk. Home: 1418 Harris Dr Bartlesville OK 74003 Office: 118 RB3 Phillips Research Center Bartlesville OK 74003

WOMER, STANLEY, govt. ofcl.; b. El Paso, Tex., Aug. 3, 1911; s. Melvin and Editha (Dodds) W.; Ph.B., Washburn U., 1934; M.B.A., Northwestern U., 1939; m. Martha M. Ryan, June 4, 1938; children—Marlen (Mrs. Stuart Boyd), Claire (Mrs. George Alkire). Mgmt. cons. Stanley Womer Assos., Phoenix, 1958-67; v.p. Southwestern Research & Investment Co., Phoenix, 1960-64; spl. asst. to Gov. Williams of Ariz., Phoenix, 1967-70; fed. co-chmn. Four Corners Regional Commn., Washington, 1970—. Episcopalian. Home: 2117 E St Washington DC 20037 Office: US Dept Commerce Washington DC 20230

WONG, NATHAN DOON, dentist; b. Kwangtung, China, Mar. 21, 1934 (parents Am. citizens); s. Bing Toy and Yue Hone (Lew) W.; A.A., San Francisco City Coll., 1957; student U. Cal. at Berkeley, 1961-62; D.D.S., Howard U., 1967; postgrad. U. Cal. at Los Angeles, 1971. Intern, St. Elizabeths Hosp., also dental officer Nat. Inst. Mental Health, Dept. Health Edn. and welfare, Washington, 1967-68; staff dentist Group Health Assn., Washington, 1968-71; chief dental services Petersberg (Va.) Tng. Sch. and Hosp., 1971—. Served with AUS, 1958-60. Mem. A.A.A.S., D.C. Dental Soc., Am. Dental Assn., So. Assn. for Instn. Dentists, Mid-Atlantic Chinese-Am. Health Profl. Assn., Omicron Sigma Chi. Home: 311 New Castle Dr Colonial Heights VA 23834 Office: Petersburg Training Sch and Hosp Petersburg VA 23803

WONNACOTT, WILLIAM CURTIS, mus. curator; b. Cleve., May 27, 1946; s. Robert Cliff and Ruth Elaine (Creasman) W.; A.B., Duke, 1968, M.Ed., 1971, M.S., 1973, postgrad., 1973—; m. Barbara Clare Buerger, Oct. 25, 1969. Tchr. sci. Carrington Jr. High Sch., Durham, N.C., 1968-70, asst. prin., 1971; asst. to dir. NSF, Duke, Durham, 1968; curator edn. N.C. Mus. Life and Sci., Durham, 1972—, also collector marine specimens for salt water aquaria. Mem. Kappa Delta Pi, Kappa Sigma. Presbyn. Home: 3109 Sherbon Dr Durham NC 27707 Office: PO Box 8177 Durham NC 27704

WOOD, ALFRED MCCREARY, ret. sales exec.; b. Wildie, Ky., Nov. 1, 1896; s. Henry Hugh and Eliza (Stewart) W.; student U. Ky., 1916-17; B.A., Harvard, 1921; m. Mary Swain, Mar. 11, 1958. With Procter & Gamble Co., 1921-61, salesman, gen. salesman, Kansas City, asst. to gen. sales mgr., Cin., sales supr. Phila., gen. sales supr., N.Y. dist. mgr., Boston, spl. assignment, Dallas, 1921-48, div. mgr., Cin., 1949-61. Served with USN, 1918-19; from maj. to lt. col., USAAF, 1942-45. Decorated Bronze Star, Croix de Guerre with palm. Mem. Am. Acad. Polit. and Social Sci., Newcomen Soc. N.Am., Dallas Council World Affairs (dir.), Sigma Alpha Epsilon. Republican. Presbyn. Mason. Clubs: Harvard (Dallas, Boston), Dallas Country, Dallas. Home: 3525 Turtle Creek Blvd Dallas TX 75219 Office: Tower Petroleum Bldg Dallas TX 75201

WOOD, BEVERLY PRIEST (MRS. FARRIS WILEMAN WOOD), ednl. adminstr.; b. Little Rock, Mar. 24, 1925; d. Glynn and Rubye (Deahl) Priest; student U. Ill., 1944-45; m. Farris Wileman Wood, Jan. 4, 1945. Asst. state editor Ark. Gazette Little Rock, 1945; asso. editor Boone County Headlight, Harrison, Ark., 1946; women's page editor Ark. Farmer, Little Rock, 1949-50; editor Little Rock bur. A.P., 1952-55; with U. Ark. Med. Center, 1962—, pub. information officer, 1965—. Bd. dirs. Vis. Nurse Assn. Pulaski County. Mem. Assn. Am. Med. Colls. (sec. group pub. relations 1973). Presbyn. (v.p. women of ch. 1961). Author: (with K. Johnson) Impact and Promise, 1964, This is a Story About People, 1967. Contbr. articles to profl. publs. Home: 29 Ardmore Dr Little Rock AR 72209 Office: U. Ark Med Center Markham at Hooper Dr Little Rock AR 72201

WOOD, BILLY RAY, supt. schs.; b. Roscoe, Tex., Sept. 19, 1926; s. Henry Elbert and Elize Mae (Webb) W.; B.S., E.Tex. State U., Commerce, 1951, M.Ed., 1956; m. Terry Alene Brookshire, Aug. 20, 1946; children—Terry Darlene (Mrs. Bill Dickey), Rebecca Rae (Mrs. Mike Spikes). Tchr. math. Los Fresnos (Tex.) High Sch., 1946-48, Rockwall Tex., 1949-55; prin. high sch., Rockwall, 1955-58, Ft. Worth, 1958-61; supt. schs., Henrietta, Tex., 1961-72, Memphis, Tex., 1972—. Mem. Gallon Club, A.R.C., 1970—. Served with U.S. Mcht. Marine, 1944-46. Recipient State Distinguished Service award Future Farmers Am., 1969. Mem. Am., Tex. assns. sch. adminstrs., Tex. Tchrs. Assn., Clay County (dir.), Henrietta (past pres.) chambers commerce, Phi Delta Kappa. Kiwanian (past pres., dir.), Rotarian (v.p. 1973). Home: 714 W Main Memphis TX 79245 Office: Box 460 Memphis TX 79245

WOOD, CHARLES HENRY, textile exec.; b. Bklyn., Apr. 12, 1911; s. Matthew Hardenbergh and Mary (Frith) W.; B.A. summa cum laude, Lafayette Coll., 1933; m. Elizabeth Taylor Marsh, Nov. 19, 1933; children—Charles Henry, John Wainwright, Patricia Gretchen (Mrs. James Harrelson). Asst. sec.-treas. Consol. Textile Co., Inc., N.Y.C., 1933-40; asst. controller Esmond Mills (R.I.), 1940-42; sec.-treas. Consol. Textile Co., Inc., 1942-46; controller Blough Mfg. Co., Inc., Harrisburg, Pa., 1946-50; sr. v.p., dir. Oneita Knitting Mills, Andrews, S.C., 1950—. Mem. Nat. Assn. Accountants, Financial Execs. Inst. Mason. Home: Wedgefield Plantation Route 4 Live Oak Rd Georgetown SC 29440 Office: Oneita Knitting Mills Andrews SC 29510

WOOD, CLYDE HARRY, utility co. exec.; b. Fairfield, Ala., Apr. 30, 1931; s. Roy Clyde and Margaret (Falls) W.; E.E., Auburn U., 1960; m. Carolyn McLaughlin, June 3, 1950; children—Larry C., Mark J. Distbn. engr. Ala. Power Co., Birmingham, 1960-63, transmission engr., 1963-65, sr. indsl. engr., 1965-71, asst. mgr. indsl. sales, 1971-73, mgr. indsl. power sales, 1973—. Chmn., Bessemer dist. Boy Scouts Am., 1970-71; sec. Fairfield High Sch. Band Parents, 1971-72, treas., 72—. Served with USNR, 1953-55. Registered profl. engr., Ala. Mem. I.E.E.E. (sr.), Alpha Phi Omega. Club: Glen Oaks Swim (Fairfield, Ala). Home: 613 Glenwood Dr Fairfield AL 35064 Office: 600 N 18th St Birmingham AL 35291

WOOD, DAVID JOSEPH, JR., lawyer; b. Charlottesville, Va., Apr. 18, 1924; s. David Joseph and Margaret Mansfield (Johns) W.; LL.B., U. Va., 1949; m. Helen Maxine Elsea, June 5, 1950; children—Beverley Ann (Mrs. Frank Lane Hereford), Margaret Miller, David Joseph III, Catherine Colston, William Warner. Admitted to Va. Bar, 1949; practiced in Charlottesville, 1949—; mem. firm Wood, Wood & Wood, Charlottesville, 1949—. Dir. Va. Nat. Bank, Peoples Mortgage Corp., Hanckel-Citizens Ins. Corp., Security Storage & Van Lines, Inc., all Charlottesville. Chmn., Charlottesville Redevel. and Housing Authority, 1954-56; asst. sec. Albemarle County (Va.) Electoral Bd., 1969-70; sec. Charlottesville Zoning Bd. Appeals, 1953. Served to lt. (j.g.) USNR, 1942-45. Mem. Charlottesville. Albemarle Bar Assn. (pres. 1971). Club: Farmington Country. Home: 4 Tennis Rd Farmington Charlottesville VA 22903 Office: PO Box 471 Charlottesville VA 22902

WOOD, DICK PENDER, lawyer; b. Abilene, Tex., Sept. 15, 1910; s. Josh and Annie (Pender) W.; B.A., Baylor U., 1931, LL.B., 1933; m. Robena Ashburn, June 10, 1937; children—Dick P., Frank A., Robert F. Admitted to Tex. bar, 1933; pvt. practice law, Dallas, 1933-72; mem. firm. Wood & Wood, 1973—; city atty. University Park, Tex., 1952—. Lectr., Southwestern Grad. Sch. Banking, 1960-71, Nat. Installment Credit Sch., 1965-72, Southwestern Legal Found.; lectr. zoning ordinances, Kan., Tex., Dallas bankers assns. Served with USNR, 1941-44; PTO. Mem. Am., Tex., Dallas bar assns. Baptist. Home: 3518 Caruth Blvd Dallas TX 75225 Office: Dallas Athletic Club Bldg Dallas TX 75201

WOOD, EDMUND REYNOLDS, lawyer; b. Dallas, May 26, 1943; s. Harold Edmund and Ruth Kathryn (Reynolds) W.; B.B.A., So. Methodist U., 1965; J.D., U. Houston, 1970; m. Linda Rebecca Sharrock, Oct. 30, 1965; children—Barry Burke, Mark Sharrock. Admitted to Tex. bar, 1968, since practiced in Dallas; mem. firm Chancellor and Wood, 1968—. Mem. staff state Sentator, 1968; adminstrv. asst., campaign mgr. to Tex. State Senator, 1968-69. Bd. dirs. U. Houston Law Sch. Mem. State Bar Tex., Am., Dallas, Dallas Jr. bar assns., Tex. Trial Lawyers Assn., Delta Sigma Pi, Phi Alpha Delta. Republican. Methodist (adminstrv. bd.). Club: Lakewood Country. Home: 3832 Colgate St Dallas TX 75225 Office: 4925 McKinney Suite 101 Dallas TX 75205

WOOD, ELMER DONOVAN, ret. clergyman; b. Spartanburg, S.C., Aug. 29, 1902; s. David and Sally Selina (Holcombe) W.; B.A., Presbyn. Coll. S.C., 1922; B.D., Columbia Theol. Sem., 1925, M. Div., 1971; postgrad. U. S.C., 1923-24, Princeton Theol. Sem., 1926; m. Sarah Eliza Timmons, Apr. 18, 1925; children—Sally (Mrs. Frank Victor Canfield), Joanna (Mrs. Warner Hale Anthony), Elmer Donovan, Richard H., Kate Sims (Mrs. Romilly Timmins). Ordained to ministry Presbyn. Ch., 1925; pastor in Lockhart, S.C., 1924-25,

Villa Rica, Ga., 1925-26, Gt. Falls, S.C., 1927-28, Mulberry St. Presbyn. Ch., Montgomery, Ala., 1928-30, Broad St. Presbyn. Ch., Mobile, Ala., 1930-31, Monroeville, Ala., 1931-35, El Campo, Tex., 1946-54, Columbia, S.C., 1954-55, West Baton Rouge Presbyn. Ch., Port Allen, La., 1957-69. Chaplain Civilian Conservation Corps, 4th Corp area, 1935-41; tchr., coach Monroeville, 1932-34; chmn. evangelism Brazos (Tex.) Presbytery, 1946-54; chmn. com. ministers annuity La. Presbytery, Synod of La., 1957-62, mem. exam. com., 1957-62, clk. ch. extension com., 1957-62, council mem., 1957—; chaplain, El Campo, Tex. Fireman. Served as chaplain, AUS, 1941-46. Mem. Internat. Platform Assn., Am. Legion (chaplain El Campo), S.A.R. Mason, Elk (chaplain El Campo), Rotarian (pres. El Campo 1947-48. Port Allen 1960-61). Builder chs. in El Campo, Port Allen. Home: PO Box 416 3608 Oak Hill St Zachary LA 70791

WOOD, EVERET HARDENBERGH, ophtalmologist; b. Bklyn., Dec. 3, 1907; s. Matthew Hardenbergh and Mary Stewart (Frith) W.; A.B., Brown U., 1929; M.D., U. Md., 1935; m. Margaret Wilson Fink, Aug. 25, 1934; children—Mary Carolyn (Mrs. L. Norman Herzfeld), Margaret (Mrs. Richard Ricketts), Louise (Mrs. Bernhard Richmann). Intern, Md. Gen. Hosp., Balt., 1935-36; resident L.I. Coll. Hosp., Bklyn., 1936-37, fellow ophthalmology, 1937-39; practice medicine specializing in ophthalmology, Bklyn., 1937-39, Auburn, N.Y., 1939-55, Madison Wis., 1955-57, Brevard, N.C., 1973—; head dept. ophthalmology Lovelace Clinic, Albuquerque, 1957-73; mem. staff Translyvania Community Hosp., Brevard. Instr. ophthalmology Syracuse (N.Y.) Med. Sch., 1953-55, U. Wis., Madison, 1955-57, U. N.M., Albuquerque, 1965-73. Served to maj. M.C. AUS, 1942-46. Diplomate Am. Bd. Ophthalmology. Mem. A.M.A. Am. Acad. Ophthalmology and Otolaryngology (certificate award 1959), Pan Am. Opthal. Soc., Kiwanian. Presbyn. Club: Future Doctors (founder 1959, Albuquerque). Contbr. articles to profl. jours. Address: 205 Park View Brevard NC 28712

WOOD, GEORGE WALLACE III, public relations exec.; b. Kansas City, Kan., Dec. 10, 1929; s. George Wallace and Pauline Bernice (Willett) W.; B.A., So. Meth. U., 1956; m. Holly Sharp, Jan. 26, 1957; 1 son, Robert O'Brien. Disc jockey, KBOX, Dallas, 1953-57, KKYX, San Antonio, 1957-59; program dir. KITE, San Antonio, 1959-60; newscaster WOAI radio, San Antonio, 1960-65; consignee Continental Oil Co., Seguin, 1965-68; dir. community service WOAI TV, 1968-69, sports dir., 1969-74; dir. pub. relations Advt. Center, San Antonio, 1974—. Loaned exec. as mag. job proucurement Nat. Alliance Businessmen; moderator TV 4 Jobs, 1968—. Dir. publicity Tex. Heart Assn., 1973—. Bd. dirs. Seguin Boys Club, 1966-69, Alamo Area council Boy Scouts Am., 1969-71, San Antonio chpt. Am. Heart Assn., 1971—, Muscular Dystrophy Assn., 1971—, Cystic Fibrosis Assn., 1970—, San Antonio Boys Club, 1974—. Served with USAF, 1948-52. Recipient Nat. Service award Nat. Alliance Businessmen, 1970, plaque Tex. Employment Commn., 1973, spl. award V.F.W., 1973 (all for TV 4 Jobs); Named Football Man of Year Pop Warner Jr. League, 1971. Methodist. Free lance writer sports periodicals. Home: 114 Trinity Lane Seguin TX 78155 Office: 246E Century Bldg San Antonio TX 78216

WOOD, GRADY LEE, traffic operations engr.; b. Wausau, Fla., Jan. 26, 1925; s. Julious Lee and Bessie (Curlee) W.; B.S., U. Fla., 1951; m. Juanita Carmilene White, June 6, 1946; children—Charles Larry, Dennis Keith. Design engr. State of Fla., Chipley, Fla., 1946-66, traffic operations engr., 1966—. Bd. dirs. Fla. State Dist. 3 Credit Union; bd. dirs. Washington-Holmes-Jackson County Vocational Tech. Sch. Served with AUS, 1943-46. Decorated Purple Heart medal, Bronze Star medal. Registered profl. engr., Fla. Mem. V.F.W. (comdr. 1951-53), Fla. State Employees Assn. (pres. 1958-61), Fla. Engring. Soc., Nat. Soc. Profl. Engrs. Lion. Club: Quarterback. Home: 501 Coleman Av Chipley FL 32428 Office: PO Box 607 SR 90 Chipley FL 32428

WOOD, JAMES ALLEN, lawyer; b. McMinnville, Tenn., Jan. 14, 1906; s. Ira and Emma (Calhoun) W.; A.B., U. Tenn., 1929; LL.B., U. Tex., 1934; m. Eva Beth Sellers, Dec. 28, 1941; 1 son, Eben Calhoun. Admitted to Tex. bar, 1934; judge 94th Dist. Ct., Nueces County, 1941-43, 45-46; partner law firm Wood, Burney, Nesbitt & Ryan, Corpus Christi, Tex., 1946—. Dir. Merc. Nat. Bank, Gulfway Nat. Bank, Corpus Christi Dir. Nueces River Authority, 1972—. Served to lt. USNR, 1943-45. Fellow Am. Coll. Trial Lawyers; mem. Am., Tex., Nueces County (pres. 1941) bar assns., Tex. Bar Found. Contbr. articles to profl. jours. Home: 458 Dolphin St Corpus Christi TX 78411 Office: Petroleum Tower Corpus Christi TX 78401

WOOD, JAMES POWERS, physician; b. Clinton, Miss., Dec. 29, 1920; s. Arthur Eugene and Anne (Powers) W.; B.A. with distinction, Miss. Coll., 1941; M.D., Tulane U., 1950; m. Carroll Bullock, June 14, 1943; children—James Powers, Anne Carroll, Louise Dampeer, Marshall Bullock. Intern Charity Hosp., New Orleans; gen. practice medicine, Waynesboro, Miss., 1951-53, State Line, Miss., 1953-66, Waynesboro, Miss., 1966—; mem. staffs Wayne Gen. Hosp., Waynesboro, Miss., 1951—, Washington County Hosp., Chatom, Ala., 1953—; trustee Greene County Hosp., Leakesville, Miss., 1958-60. Dir., Consumers Wirebound Box Co., Waynesboro, 1957-58; chmn. bd. AGM Drug Co. Miss., Jackson, Miss.; organizer, chmn. bd. 1st Nat. Bank Way, 1966-68. Chmn. bd. trustees State Line High Sch., 1957-59; mem. Greene County Bd. Edn., 1963-66, Miss. Hosp. Commn., 1964-72, Miss. Oil and Gas Bd., 1970—. Served with USAAF, 1943-46. Decorated Air medal with oak leaf cluster. Hon. col. Miss. Gov.'s staff, 1960-72. Fellow Am. Acad. Family Physicians; mem. Am., Miss. med. assns., So. Miss. Med. Soc., Miss. Acad. Gen. Practice, Alpha Kappa Kappa. Baptist. Home: McIlwain Dr Waynesboro MS 39367 Office: 709 Chickasawhay St Waynesboro MS 39367

WOOD, JUNE POPHAM (MRS. GLEN NORRIS WOOD), educator; b. Houston, Nov. 27, 1920; d. Jesse Lee and Esther Bailey (Brown) Popham; student Sophie Newcomb Coll., 1936, Tex. Christian U., summer 1936; B.A., Baylor U., 1941; M.A., U. Houston, 1958; m. Glen Norris Wood, Aug. 15, 1942; children—Esther Wood (Mrs. Robert Carter Wilson), Glen Norris. Asst. prof. math. U. Houston, 1947-60; prof., chmn. dept. math. South Tex. Jr. Coll., Houston, 1960—. Mem. Com. on Undergrad. Program in Math., 1971—, mem. panel on two-year colls., 1970-73. Sect. chmn. Houston Symphony Soc., 1958; leader Girl Scouts, 1950-51; chmn. March of Dimes, City of Bunker Hill, 1960. Named Outstanding Tchr., Tex. Assn. Jr. Colls., 1970. Mem. Math. Assn. Am. (mem. com. on two yr. colls. 1972-75, mem. Tex. exec. council 1972—, nat. 2d v.p. 1973-75), Tex. Assn. Jr. Coll., South Tex. Jr. Coll. Faculty Assn. (pres. 1967), Alpha Chi. Episcopalian. Author: Introductory Algebra, 1969; (with David Outcalt) A First Course in Algebra, 1971; (with David Outcalt) A Second Course in Algebra, 1974. Book rev. editor Two-Year Coll. Math. Jour. Editorial bd. Two-Year Coll. Math. Jour., 1972—. Home: 10 Carolane Trail Houston TX 77024

WOOD, KATHERINE ALICE, social worker; b. Kingsville, Tex.; d. John J. and Katie (Steves) Wood; student Pan Am. Coll., 1927-29; B.S., S.W. Tex. State Coll., 1936; M.Ed., U. Tex., 1939; postgrad. La. State U., 1941; M.S.W., Tulane U., 1950. Tchr. elementary sch. Palm Garden Sch. Dist., Mercedes, Tex., 1930-34, prin., 1934-37; tchr. social sci. Weslaco (Tex.) Ind. Sch. Dist., 1937-42; field worker Dept. Pub. Welfare, Austin, Tex., 1942-46, supr., 1946-50; supr. casework Houston-Harris County chpt. A.R.C., Houston, 1950-70, dir. service to mil. families, 1970-73, supr. Sheltering Arms, 1973—. Field instr. Worden Sch. Social Service Our Lady of Lake Coll., San Antonio, 1951—, Sch. Social Work, U. Houston, also Prairie View A. and M. Coll. Chmn. interagy. communications com. Community Council, Houston, 1956-58. Mem. Altrusa Club (dir. 1972-73, 1st v.p. 1974-75), Nat. Assn. Social Workers (chmn. nominating com. San Jacinto chpt. 1963-65), Acad. Certified Social Workers, Nat. Conf. on Social Welfare, Council on Social Work Edn., Tex. United Community Services (state bd. 1972—), Houston Bus. and Profl. Women's Club (1st v.p. 1973-74, pres. 1974-75). Home: 1113 Crocker St Houston TX 77019 Office: 5304 Austin St Houston TX 77004

WOOD, MAX PETERSON, elec. products mfg. co. exec.; b. Birmingham, Ala., July 21, 1939; s. Max and Dorothy Marguerite (Peterson) W.; B.E.E., Auburn U., 1962; M.B.A., U. Ala., 1973; m. Susan Carolyn Ray, Mar. 17, 1962; children—Kathleen, Clinton. Asst. sales engr. Westinghouse Power Systems, Chattanooga, 1965-67, sales engr., Atlanta, 1967-68, Birmingham, 1968—. Mem. speaker's bur. United Appeal, 1971-73. Served to capt. AUS, 1963-65. Mem. I.E.E.E. (exec. com. 1970-71, mem. program com. 1972-73), Power Engring. Soc. (vice-chmn. 1973), Lambda Chi Alpha. Methodist. Clubs: Downtown, Club (Birmingham). Home: 542 S Sanders Rd Birmingham AL 35226 Office: PO Box 6098 Birmingham AL 35209

WOOD, ROBERT DONALD, dentist; b. New Augusta, Ind., May 10, 1927; s. Robert Clarence and Lucretia (Wilson) W.; B.S., Ind. U., 1951, D.D.S., 1954, M.S.D., 1962; m. Mary Margaret Newsom, Sept. 12, 1953; children—Eric Kevin, Joseph Duane, Brian Jeffery. Pvt. practice dentistry, Marion, Ind., 1956-60; faculty Meharry Med. Coll. Sch. Dentistry, Nashville, 1962—, asso. prof., chmn. oral medicine and diagnosis, 1969—. Served from 1st lt. to capt. Dental Corps, AUS, 1954-56. Home: 4745 Buena Vista Pike Nashville TN 37218

WOOD, ROBERT GARLAND, physician; b. Lithia, Fla., May 1, 1908; s. Robert Garland and Caddie Blanche (Alderman) W.; student U. Fla., 1925-27; M.D., Tulane, 1932; m. Eunice Luella Holzer, June 27, 1933; children—Florence Jane (Mrs. Gary Omar Dotson), Robert Garland III. Intern, So. Bapt. Hosp., New Orleans, 1931-33; practice gen. medicine, St. Cloud, Fla., 1933—; chief med. dept. Osceola Gen. Hosp., Kissimmee, Fla., 1964-72; vice chief staff St. Cloud Hosp., 1971—. Vice pres., dir. Citizens State Bank, St. Cloud, 1945—. Commr., City of St. Cloud, 1954, utilities commr., 1955-57. Fellow Am. Acad. Family Physicians; mem. Orange County Med. Soc. (v.p. 1946), Osceola County Med. Soc. (pres. 1972), A.M.A., Fla. Med. Assn. (life), So. Med. Assn., Phi Rho Sigma, Chi Phi. Mason. Home: 700 Florida Av St Cloud FL 32769 Office: 1205 Penn Av St Cloud FL 32769

WOOD, RYAN LEE, clergyman; b. Spartanburg, S.C., Feb. 2, 1901; s. David and Sally Selina (Holcombe) W.; B.A., Presbyn. Coll., Clinton, S.C., 1921, D.D., 1950; B.D., Columbia Theol. Sem., Decatur, 1925, M.Div., 1971; m. Mattie Gertrude Timmons, Mar. 15, 1924; children—Ryan Lee, Selina Ellen (Mrs. Ernest Millar Smith), John David, Marion Timmons, Rebecca Holcombe. Prin., athletic coach Williamsburg High Sch., Kingstree, S.C., 1921-22; pastor First Presbyn. Ch., Marion, Ala., 1925-27, Wauchula, Fla., 1927-35, Hyde Park Ch., Tampa, Fla., 1936-42, Meml. Ch., West Palm Beach, 1944-69, Seacrest Blvd. Presbyn. Ch., Delray Beach, Fla., 1971-72, First Presbyn. Ch., North Palm Beach, Fla., 1973—; human relations counselor Rinker Materials Corp., West Palm Beach, 1969; instr. N.T., U. Tampa, 1941, instr. O.T., Palm Beach Jr. Coll., 1948. Moderator Synod Fla. 1958-59. Trustee Columbia Theol. Sem.; mem. St. Lucie County bd. Am. Cancer Soc., Ft. Pierce, Fla. Bd. dirs. Palm Beach County chpt. A.R.C. Served from maj. to lt. col., AUS, 1941-44. Mem. Res. Officers Assn., Assn. U.S. Army, Sons Confederate Vets., Ret. Officers Assn., S.A.R. Mason (32 deg.). Kiwanian, Lion. Home: 4600 Sunrise Blvd Fort Pierce FL 33450 Office: 717 Prosperity Farms Rd North Palm Beach FL 33408

WOOD, WALTER WYVILL, mech. engr.; b. Louisville, Feb. 5, 1928; s. George Twyman and Louise Fairfax (Robertson) W.; B.S. in Mech. Engring., U. Louisville, 1954, M.Engring., 1972; m. Caroline Shelburne Crone, Dec. 29, 1956; children—Victoria Armistead, Walter Wyvill. Product devel. engr. Gamble Bros., Inc., Louisville, 1954-56; sales engr. Air Reduction Sales Co., Louisville, 1956-61; welding engr. Naval Ordnance Sta., Louisville, 1961-62, head prodn. devel. br., 1962-66, head prodn. engring. div., 1966-68, head armament div., 1968-73, dir. engring., 1973—. Bd. dirs. Valley Camp, United Fund Agy. Served with AUS, 1950-52; ETO; lt. col. Res. Registered profl. engr., Ky. Mem. Am. Welding Soc. (past sec., chmn.), Order Ky. Cols., Louisville Engr. and Sci. Councils Soc., Louisville Municipal Harbor Assn., Theta Tau. Democrat. Episcopalian. Home: 209 Kennedy Ct Louisville KY 40206 Office: Southside Dr Louisville KY 40214

WOOD, WILLIAM ANDREW, JR., printing co. exec.; b. Atlanta, Sept. 13, 1919; s. William A. and Naomi (Majors) W.; student U. Ga., 1948; m. Helen C. Kelley, Nov. 19, 1940; children—Elaine (Mrs. Byron Norris), Susan, Shirley, Margaret Kelley. With Foote & Davies div. McCall Printing Co., Doraville, Ga., 1938—, v.p. sales, 1955-69, exec. v.p., 1969-73, v.p. S.E. sales, 1973—. Bd. dirs. DeKalb County chpt. Am. Cancer Soc. Served with USAAF, 1942-45. Mem. Atlanta C. of C., Atlanta Advt. Club, Commerce Club. Kiwanian. Club: Atlanta Athletic. Home: 2050 Amberwood Way NE Atlanta GA 30345 Office: 3101 McCall Dr Doraville GA 30340

WOOD, WILLIAM HUDSON, optometrist; b. Ft. Lauderdale, Fla., May 22, 1926; s. Guy Darracott and Elma (Talley) W.; B.S., Jacksonville U., 1973; O.D., So. Coll. Optometry, 1949; m. Thelma Horton, Mar. 6, 1945; children—Deborah (Mrs. Edward T. Hobin), John Horton, Margaret. Pvt. practice optometry, Jacksonville, Fla., 1950-51; asso. with Wayne W. Wood, Jacksonville, 1971—. Pres. Fla. State Bd. Optometry, 1961. Served with USNR, 1944-46. Mem. N.E. Fla. Optometric Soc. (pres. 1964-65), Am., Fla. optometric assns., Am. Acad. Optometrists. Mason (Shriner). Clubs: Exchange (pres. 1960), Timuquana Country, University, Seminole (Jacksonville). Home: 4429 Sherwood Rd Jacksonville FL 32210 Office: 218 W Adams St Jacksonville FL 32202

WOOD, WILLIAM LEWIS, JR., engring. co. exec.; b. Starkville, Miss., Nov. 15, 1925; s. William Lewis and Helen Rosalie (Young) W.; B.S. in Elec. Engring. U. Tenn., 1949; LL.B., So. Law U., 1958; LL.B. (hon.), Memphis State U., 1968; m. Sara Jane Henderson, Nov. 29, 1946; 1 dau., Jane Ann. Office engr. Ebasco Services, Inc., Forrest City, Ark., 1949-50; elec. engr. gas and water div. Memphis Light, 1952-56; dist. sales mgr. Okonite Co., Memphis, 1956-64; marketing mgr. Allen & Hoshall, cons. engrs., Memphis, 1964—. Mem. So., Tenn. indsl. devel. councils, 1972—. Served with USNR, 1943-46; to 1st. lt., inf. AUS, 1950-52. Decorated Bronze Star medal. Registered profl. engr., Tenn. Mem. I.E.E.E. (pres. Memphis chpt. 1970-71), Memphis C. of C., Kappa Sigma. Episcopalian. Clubs: Engineers (pres. 1973-74), Chickasaw Country. Home: 123 Oak Grove Rd Memphis TN 38117 Office: 2430 Poplar Av Memphis TN 38112

WOODALL, AVIE STELLA JAMES (MRS. HOWARD WOODALL), author; b. Hillsboro, Tex., Jan. 15, 1899; d. Leslie Christopher and Orena Belle (Malone) James; student U. Tex., Famous Writer's Sch.; m. Warren Christopher Proctor, Jan. 20, 1920 (dec.); m. 2d, Howard Woodall, Aug. 5, 1934 (dec.); children—Ruth (Mrs. Raymond P. James), Anna (Mrs. Jean D. Frost), Clara Beth (Mrs. Ben Urban). Free-lance writer and poet published in Christman Ideals, Poet, West Tex. Hist. Year Book, U.D.C. mag., Tex. Methodist, Travis Park News, Air Force Times, others. Mem. Beautify San Antonio Assn. Recipient Council of Pres. award; named alternate poet laureate Tex., 1973. Mem. Poetry Soc. San Antonio (pres.), Stella Woodall Circle (chmn.), Armed Forces Writer's League (past pres.), Am. Poetry League (past nat. v.p.), Internat. Platform Assn., (mem. hospitality com.), Nat. League Am. Pen Women, Nat. Assn. Ret. Fed. Employees, Nat. Soc. Arts and Letters (past 1st v.p.). Methodist. Club: Woman's (chmn. strategy bd. round table). Author: Women of the Bible; Lectures of St. John. Editor, pub. San Antonio Poetry Mag. Home: 3915 SW Military Dr San Antonio TX 78211

WOODALL, NORMAN EUGENE, banker; b. nr. Meridian, Miss., June 10, 1916; s. Albert Edward and Annie (Smith) W.; B.S. in Bus. Adminstrn., Miss. State U., 1939; postgrad. Am. Inst. Banking, 1962, Sch. Banking South La. State U., 1964, Command and Gen. Staff Coll., 1955, Indsl. Coll. Armed Forces, 1970; m. Virginia Dale Willard, Aug. 12, 1967. Adjuster Comml. Credit Co., Jackson, Miss., 1939-41; loan examiner RFC, Birmingham, Ala., 1946-55; with First Nat. Bank Birmingham, 1955—, sr. v.p., 1970—. Served with AUS, 1941-46. Decorated Bronze Star, Legion of Merit, Purple Heart. Mem. Res. Officers Assn., Assn. U.S. Army, Am. Inst. Banking, Miss. State U. Alumni Assn., Birmingham C. of C., Sigma Chi. Clubs: Exchange (bd. govs. 1960-62, 71-72, sec. 1972-73, v.p. 1973-74), The Club, Relay House, Vestavia Country (Birmingham, Ala.). Home: 3422 Loch Ridge Trail Birmingham AL 35216 Office: 1900 5th Av N Birmingham AL 35203

WOODARD, JAMES EDWARD, dentist; b. Ardmore, Tenn., Jan. 14, 1918; s. Bernard Hatcher and Bessie (Carter) W.; A.B., Vanderbilt U., 1940; D.D.S., U. Tenn., 1943; m. Dorothy Louise Carter, Sept. 21, 1946; children—Joseph Anderson, Dorothy Louise, Daniel Carter. Gen. practice dentistry, Columbia, Tenn., 1946—. Mem. Maury County Bd. Health; mem. adv. com. Tenn. Mid-South Regional Med. Program, Tenn. Bd. Dentistry, So. Conf. Dental Deans and Examiners. Mem. Maury County Bd. Edn., 1956—, chmn., 1971—. Bd. dirs. Maury County Bd. Mental Health, Maury County Tb and Health Assn., Tenn. chpt. Am. Cancer Soc. Served with AUS, 1943-46. Mem. Am., Tenn. (trustee 1951-54) dental assns., 6th Dist. Dental Soc. (pres. 1949), U. Tenn. Dental Alumni (chmn. bd. trustees), Am. Coll. Dentists, Pierre Fauchard Acad., Southeastern Acad. Prosthodontics, Omicron Kappa Upsilon, Delta Sigma Delta. Methodist (sec. bd. trustees). Kiwanian (pres. Columbia 1954). Home: 906 Hillcrest Av Columbia TN 38401 Office: 208 W 6th St Columbia TN 38401

WOODARD, MAX WILSON, oil and gas co. exec.; b. Palestine, Tex., Sept. 22, 1938; s. Clyde Burette and Marye Regina (McClung) W.; B.S., Tex. A. and M. U., 1961; m. Emilynn Berry, Aug. 26, 1961; children—Dawn Michele, Melissa Camille. Petroleum engr. Continental Oil Co., Midland, Tex., 1961-66; dist. engr. Tex. Oil & Gas Corp., Amarillo, Tex., 1966-68; pres., Lear Petroleum Corp., Dallas, 1968—; pres., chmn. bd. Producer's Gas Co.; chmn. bd. Lear Petroleum Corp., Dallas. Served as 1st lt. AUS, 1962-64. Mem. Am. Inst. Mining. Metall. and Petroleum Engrs., Ind. Petroleum Assn. Am. Home: 7040 Meadowcreek St Dallas TX 75240 Office: 1907 Elm St Dallas TX 75201

WOODBURY, CHARLES RAY, computer co. exec., elec. engr.; b. Crane, Tex., Oct. 19, 1939; s. William Richard and Verda Doy (Robinson) W.; B.S in Elec. Engring., So. Meth. U., 1963, M.S., 1967; m. Molly Margaret Maule, July 15, 1961; children—Julie Lynn, Richard Edward. Aerosystems engr. Gen. Dynamics Corp., Ft. Worth, 1963-67, sr. aerosystems engr., 1967-68; sec. treas., dir. Octal Systems, Inc., Ft. Worth, 1968—, v.p. engring., 1970—. Registered profl. engr., Tex. Mem. I.E.E.E., Beta Theta Pi. Episcopalian (lay reader 1971— , sr. warden 1972-73). Home: Route 2 Box 229 Alvarado TX 76009 Office: 1801 W Euless Blvd Euless TX 76039

WOODBURY, JAMES HARRY, pub. relations cons.; b. Somerville, Tenn., June 8, 1918; s. James Harry and Mattie Matilda (Anderson) W.; B.S., Memphis State U., 1940; postgrad. U. Miss., 1940-41; m. Ruth Gaskell, Jan. 3, 1941; 1 son, Charles. City hall reporter Memphis Comml. Appeal, 1941-53; partner Archer & Woodbury, Inc., Memphis, 1953-68; dir. pub. service City of Memphis, 1968-71; dir. devel. Memphis State U., 1971-74; pub. relations cons., Gulfport, Miss., 1974—. Pres. Memphis Area Better Bus. Bur., 1965. Chmn. citizen's adv. com. for Shelby County of Tenn. Dept. Pub. Welfare, 1966-68; dir. Memphis Div. Pub. Service. mem. Memphis State Found. Bd.; mem. adv. com. Les Passees Rehab. Center. Bd. dirs. Memphis & Shelby County unit Am. Cancer Soc, Goodwill Industries, Vis. Nurse Assn., Sheltered Occupational Shop. Named outstanding alumnus Memphis State U., 1969. Mem. Memphis State Alumni Assn. (pres. 1968), Pub. Relations Soc. Am. (past pres. Mid South chpt.), Pi Kappa Alpha. Episcopalian. Clubs: Tennessee (v.p. 1969-72), Memphis Press, Kiwanis (Memphis). Home: 145 Bayou Circle Gulfport MS 39501

WOODCOCK, CLARENCE CRANE, JR., internist; b. Nashville, Jan. 7, 1920; s. Clarence Crane and Elizabeth Stokes (Buford) W.; B.A., Vanderbilt U., 1941, M.D., 1944; m. Anita Chandler Green, Sept. 16, 1947; children—Anita F., William C., John R. Intern, Vanderbilt U. Hosp., Nashville, 1944-45; resident VA Hosp., Nashville, 1947-49; pvt. practice medicine specializing in internal medicine, Nashville, 1951—; asso. Miller Clinic, 1958—, chief exec. officer, 1971—; mem. staff Miller, Bapt., Park View hosps., Nashvill. Chmn. trustees Miller Hosp.; trustee Blue Cross Blue Shield Tenn. Served to capt. M.C., AUS, 1945-47, 53. Diplomate Am. Bd. Internal Medicine. Fellow A.C.P., Am. Coll. Chest Physicians; mem. Tenn. Soc. Internal Medicine (pres. elect). Methodist. Home: 247 Ensworth Av Nashville TN 37205 Office: 602 Gallatin Rd Nashville TN 37206

WOODIN, MARTIN DWIGHT, univ. adminstr.; b. Sicily Island, La., July 7, 1915; s. Dwight E. and Gladys Ann (Martin) W.; B.S., La. State U., 1936; M.S., Cornell U., 1939, Ph.D., 1941; m. Virginia Johnson, Sept. 7, 1939 (dec.); children—Rebecca (Mrs. Albin S. Johnson), Pamela (Mrs. James Cangelosi), Linda (Mrs. Vernon Porter Middleton); m. 2d, Elisabeth Wachalik, Oct. 8, 1968. Mem. faculty La. State U., 1941—, prof. agrl. econs., head dept., 1956-59, dir. resident instrn. Coll. Agr., 1959-60, dean at Alexandria, La., 1960-62, exec. v.p. at Baton Rouge, 1962-72, pres. univ. system, 1972—. Dep. dir. La. Civil Def. Agy., 1961—; v.p., exec. com. United Givers Baton Rouge, 1962-67. Sec. La. State U. Found., 1962-72. Served with USNR, 1942-46; PTO. Mem. Am. Agr. Econ. Assn., Am. Marketing Assn., Am. Legion (post comdr.), Sigma Xi, Omicron Delta Kappa, Phi Kappa Phi, Beta Gamma Sigma, Phi Eta Sigma, Gamma Sigma Delta, Alpha Zeta, Pi Gamma Mu. Presbyn. Elk, Rotarian. Author articles in field. Home: 2959 E Lakeshore Dr Baton Rouge LA 70810

WOODLAND, EVERAN CORNELIUS, JR., dentist; b. Norfolk, Va., June 16, 1929; s. Everan Cornelius and Crystal Cecilia (Gilliam) W.; student Georgetown U. Coll. Arts and Scis., 1947-50; D.D.S., Georgetown U., 1954; postgrad. Naval Grad. Dental Sch. and Georgetown U. Grad. Sch., 1964-65; m. Kathleen Ann Donoghue, Nov. 21, 1953; children—Ellen, Neil, Mark, Janet, Laura, Marie. Individual practice dentistry, Kensington, Md., 1957-60; commd. lt. Dental Corps U.S. Navy, 1960, advanced through grades to capt., 1971; with staff submarine base, New London, Conn., 1960-62, U.S.S. Kitty Hawk, 1962-64, Willow Grove, Pa., 1965-68, U.S.S. Grand Canyon, 1968-70; head endodontics Naval Dental Clinic, Naval Base, Newport, R.I., 1970-73; sr. dental officer Naval Sta., Mayport, Fla., 1973—; mem. staff Georgetown U. Sch. Dentistry, 1957-59. Mem. Bucks County council Boy Scouts Am., 1965-68. Bd. dirs. chpt. Navy Relief Soc. Decorated Nat. Def. medal, Viet Nam Service medal, Viet Nam Campaign medal. Mem. Am. Dental Assn., Assn. Mil. Surgeons U.S., U.S. Naval Inst., Delta Sigma Delta. K.C. Home: 1300 Kings Rd Neptune Beach FL 32233 Office: Dental Dept Naval Sta Mayport FL 32228

WOODMAN, DAVID LONGINO, tv exec.; b. Ruston, La., Apr. 14, 1935; s. Longino Alphonse and Farris (Armstrong) W.; student U. Ala., 1952-55, N.E. La. U., 1961-62; m. Lydia Mae Ryan, Apr. 14, 1956; children—Douglas, Leslie, Sharon, Stephanie. Staff announcer WSFA-TV, Montgomery, Ala., 1956-57; with KNOE-TV, Monroe, La., 1957-69, v.p., promotion dir., 1965-69; div. mgr. Success Motivation Inst., Monroe, 1969; with KTVE, El Dorado-Monroe, 1969-70; sports dir. KARK-TV, Little Rock, 1970—. Active United Fund, YMCA, Girl Scouts U.S.A. Bd. dirs. Ventures for Christ. Mem. Nat. Sportscasters and Sportswriters Assn., Fellowship of Christian Athletes. Baptist (deacon 1963—). Club: Sertoma (dist. lt. gov. 1969-70). Home: 6829 Archwood St Little Rock AR 72204 Office: 1001 Spring St Little Rock AR 72203

WOODRESS, FREDERICK ALBERT, found. exec.; b. St. Louis, Jan. 11, 1923; s. James L. and Jessie (Smith) W.; student Antioch Coll., 1941-43; A.B., 1948; student Washington U., 1946; M.S., U. Ky., 1971; m. Anne Loraine Blackmon, Dec. 31, 1953; 1 dau., Cathy Loraine. Stringer, reporter various Ohio and Mo. newspapers, 1939-48; free-lance writer, 1948-49; pub. relations asst. Methodist Div. Fgn. Missions, 1949; reporter, columnist, entertainment editor Birmingham (Ala.) Post-Herald, 1949-55; owner Fred Woodress, pub. relations cons. firm, 1955-69; asst. to chief adminstr. and pub. affairs dir. U. Ala. Med. Center, 1964-69; dir. pub. relations U. Ky., Lexington 1969-71; pub. relations cons. Woodress & Myers, Louisville, 1971-74; supr. Pa. Life Ins. Co., Lexington, 1971-74; dir. marketing Hunter Found. for Health Care, 1974—. Tchr. advt. Birmingham So. Coll., 1958; information specialist U.S. Salvation Army, Haiti, 1963, La., Ark. Salvation Army, New Orleans, 1965. Served with AUS, 1943-46. Mem. Pub. Relations Soc. Am. (v.p. Ala.-Miss. chpt., Presdl. citation 1968, pres. Ala. chpt., nat, membership chmn.). Episcopalian. Author: Impasse pub. in Best One Act Plays, 1949; (with others) 87th Infantry Division History, 1946. Contbr. articles to mags. Home: 3148 Trinity Rd Lexington KY 40503 Office: Hunter Found Security Trust Bldg Lexington Ky 40507

WOODRING, ALVIN JAMES, hosp. adminstr.; b. Detroit, Sept. 27, 1924; s. Alvin and Jean Houston (Mitchell) W.; B.S., Susquehanna U., 1948; m. Evelyn Ellagene Latimer, Oct. 18, 1952; children—James Latimer, Stephen Alvin. Inventory controller Wiedenman & Co., Bloomsburg, Pa., 1948-49, collection mgr. Sears, Roebuck & Co., Greensboro, N.C., 1949-51; asst. adminstr. Anderson (S.C.) Meml. Hosp., 1951-54; adminstr. Fairfield Meml. Hosp., Winnsboro, S.C., 1954-58; asst. dir. U. Fla. Teaching Hosp., Gainesville, 1958-60; adminstr. Tifton (Ga.) County Hosp., 1960-64, Southeastern Ky. Bapt. Hosp., Corbin, 1964—. Served with USAAF, 1942-45. Decorated Air medal with oak leaf cluster, D.F.C. Mem. Am. Coll. Hosp. Adminstrs. Mason. Office: Mitchell St Corbin KY 40701

WOODROW, KENNETH M., psychiatrist; b. Yonkers, N.Y., Mar. 20, 1942; s. Jack H. and Grace (Lewis) W.; grad. Horace Mann Sch., 1960; B.A., Wesleyan U. (Conn.), 1964; M.D., U. Md., 1968; m. Mary Avis Mack, June 9, 1968. Intern, Kaiser Found. Hosp., Oakland, Cal., 1968-69; fellow, resident Stanford (Cal.) Med. Center, 1969-72; research psychiatrist lab. clin. psychopharmacology Nat. Inst. Mental Health, Washington, 1972 clin. asso. St. Elizabeth's Hosp., Washington. Cons. grant rev. dir. NSF, 1970, computer applications clin. medicine Kaiser Permanente Med. Group, 1969. Served with USPHS, 1972—. Recipient Thorndike prize psychology Wesleyan U., 1963. Am. Psychiat. Assn., Com. for Concerned Psychiatrists (exec. com.). Home: 3306 Woodburn Village Dr 32 Annandale VA 22003 Office: Lab Clin Psychopharmacology St Elizabeth Hosp Washington DC 20032

WOODRUFF, EDWIN CUSHING, geophysicist; b. N.Y.C., July 22, 1926; s. George Percy and Margaret (Neville) W.; student Princeton, 1947-50; B.S. in Geology, Marietta Coll., 1953; A.M., U. Mo., 1954; 1 dau., Anne Elizabeth. With Geophys. Service, Inc., Merced, Cal., 1953; grad. asst. U. Mo., 1953-54; with Shell Oil Co., 1954-71, seismologist, 1955-59, geophysicist, party chief, 1959-65, geophysicist, 1965-69, sr. geophysicist, Midland, Tex., 1969-71; sr. geophysicist Basin Geophysical, Inc., Midland, 1971-73; chief geophysicist Am. Quasar Petroleum Co., Midland, 1973—. Instr. Permian Basin Grad. Center, 1972-74. Pres., Lee chpt. Am. Field Service, 1966-68, liaison v.p., 1969-70. Served with USNR, 1944-46. Mem. Permian Basin Aviation Assn. (pres. 1966-67), Am. Assn. Petroleum Geologists, Permian Basin Geophys. Soc. (membership chmn. 1968), West Tex. Geol. Soc. (geothermal survey chmn.), Am. Petroleum Inst., Gamma Alpha, Delta Upsilon. Unitarian. Kiwanian, Toastmaster (pres. 1970). Home: 2900 W Illinois St Midland TX 79701 Office: 606 Vaughn Bldg Midland TX 79701

WOODRUFF, WALLACE JACK, comml laundry sales and leasing co. exec.; b. Louisville, Mar. 3, 1918; s. Wallace G. and Ella (Rebsch) W.; B.S., U. Ky., 1946; m. Mildred Marshall Griffin, Mar. 1, 1943; children—John Steven, Elizabeth Anne. With Kawneer Co., Cynthiana, Ky., 1946-66, successively personnel mgr., plant mgr., sales mgr., plant mgr., works mgr., v.p. and gen. mgr. until 1966; gen. mgr. Archl. div. Gen. Bronze Corp., Miami, Fla., 1966-68; v.p. Miller Distbg. Corp., Miami, 1969—. Mem. Miami Com. of 100. Bd. dirs. Ky. Soc. Crippled Children, Asso. Industries Ky. Served with USNR, 1940-45. Decorated D.F.C., Air medal. Mem. C. of C. (dir., pres.). Baptist. Club: Civitan. Home: 2131 S Bayshore Dr Miami FL 33133 Office: 6300 NW 77th Ct Miami FL 33148

WOODRUM, CLIFTON ALEXANDER III, lawyer, b. Washington, July 23, 1938; s. Clifton Alexander and Margaret Troy (Lanier) W.; A.B., U.N.C., 1961; LL.B., U. Va., 1964; m. Emily Clyde Abbitt, Aug. 10, 1963; children—Robert Hutchins, Meredith Moore, Anne Harris. Admitted to Va. bar, 1964; practiced in Roanoke, Va., 1964—; mem. firm. Dodson, Pence, Coulter, Viar, & Young. Pres., Young Democrat Club Roanoke, 1966; v.p. Young Dem. Clubs Va., 1967, legislative dir., 1966; mem. Roanoke City Dem. Com., 1964—; mem. Va. Dem. Com., 1972—, chmn. 6th dist., 1973—. Bd. dirs. Legal Aid Soc. Roanoke Valley, Nat. Arthritis Found. Mem. Am., Va., Roanoke bar assns., Va. Trial Lawyers Assn., Sigma Alpha Epsilon, Phi Alpha Delta. Episcopal. Home: 2643 Nottingham Rd Roanoke VA 24014 Office: PO Box 1045 Roanoke VA 24005

WOODS, ARTHUR FREDERICK, mfg. co. exec.; b. Syracuse, N.Y., Oct. 7, 1921; s. Charles J. and Ada H. (Frost) W.; B.S., Purdue U., 1943; m. Nancy Woodruff, Aug. 25, 1945; children—Craig A., Bruce F., Wendy Jo. Sales engr. pump dept. Yale & Towne Mfg. Co., Detroit, 1946-49; dist. engr. Marlow Pumps Co., Midland Park, N.J., 1949-53; sales engr. Marlow Pumps div. Bell & Gossett Co., Midland Park, 1953-65; v.p., dir. marketing Marlow div. Internat. Tel. & Tel. Corp., Midland Park, 1965-66, v.p., gen. sales mgr. ITT Fluid Handling div., Morton Grove, Ill., 1966, v.p., dir. marketing, 1966-69, v.p., dir. marketing, pump and compressor group, 1969-71, v.p., gen. mgr. ITT Pneumotive, Monroe, La., 1971-74; v.p., dir. marketing Poly Processing Co., Monroe, 1974—. Served to 1st lt. USAAF, 1942-46. Mem. Asso. Gen. Contractors (chmn. bd. govs. contractors pump bur. 1958-59), Nat. Oil Equipment Jobbers Assn. (chmn. mfrs. com. 1959-60), La. Mfg. Assn. (dist. v.p. 1973-74), Theta Xi. Methodist. Clubs: Bayou De Siard Country (Monroe); Shinnecock Marlin and Tuna (Hampton Bays, N.Y.). Home: 3505 Deborah Dr Monroe LA 71201 Office: 4601 Central Av Monroe LA 71201

WOODS, BARRY ALAN, lawyer; b. N.Y.C., Nov. 21, 1942; s. Harry E. and Lillian (Breath) W.; B.S., N.Y. U., 1965; LL.M. in Taxation, 1969; J.D., Bklyn. Law Sch., 1968; m. Elizabeth Geller, Sept. 8, 1968; 1 dau., Meredith Rose. Admitted to N.Y. State bar, 1968, P.R. bar, 1970; partner firm Baker & Woods, Santurce. Spl. cons. Tax Mgmt., Inc.; mem. tax mgmt. adv. bd. Internat. Taxation. Mem. P.R. Mfg. Assn. (legislative com.), Am. Soc. Internat. Law, Am. Bar Assn., Colegio de Abogados de P.R. Clubs: Guaynabo Riding; Caribe Hilton Swimming and Tennis; Club Nautico de San Juan. Home: 61 Kings Ct Santurce PR 00911 Office: PO Box 10165 Santurce PR 00908

WOODS, BERT EDWARD, optometrist; b. Springtown, Tex., Sept. 2, 1908; s. Albert Franklin and Florence Drucilla (Tate) W.; D.Optometry, Southwestern Optometry Coll., 1929; postgrad. No. Ill. Coll. Optometry, 1931-33, U. Houston, 1964-69, 70; m. Margaret Stroud, Nov. 24, 1943; children—Joe, Paul, Billie (Mrs. Gary M. Dorsey). Pvt. practice optometry, Henderson, Tex., 1936—. Pres., Henderson High Sch. P.T.A., 1961-62; del. Nat. White House Conf. Children and Youth, 1970; del. Tex. Gov.'s Conf. Children and Youth, 1970, 71; mem. Rusk County Child Welfare Bd., 1967-70; bd. dirs. E. Tex. area council Boy Scouts Am., 1946—. Served with AUS, 1944-45. Recipient Silver Beaver award Boy Scouts Am., 1952, Key of Nations award Henderson Lions Club, 1969. Mem. Am. Legion (post comdr. 1949-50), Gideons Internat. (v.p. Henderson 1970-73). Tex. Optometric Assn. (state dir. 1933-38). E. Tex. Optometric Soc. (pres. 1938-43), Am. Optometric Assn. Baptist (Sunday Sch. supt. 1934-36). Lion (pres. Henderson 1957-58, zone chmn. 1955-56, dep. dist. gov. 1956-57). Home: 307 Rogers St Henderson TX 75652 Office: 105 S Marshall St Henderson TX 75652

WOODS, CULLEN CURLEE, dentist; b. Ft. Worth, Mar. 29, 1928; s. Dexter Levert and Margaret Faulds (O'Leary) W.; B.A., Vanderbilt U., 1950; D.D.S., U. Tenn., 1957; m. Jimmie Louise Beckham, Sept. 17, 1950; children—Cullen, Patrick, Susan, Timothy. Dentist, Okla. Health Dept., Shawnee, 1958; individual practice dentistry, Oklahoma City, 1958—. Clin. instr. oral surgery U. Okla. Sch. Medicine, 1969—. Mem. Okla. Dental Polit. Action Com., 1970—, Okla. State Dental Exam. Bd., 1972—; sec.-treas. bd. govs. Registered Dentists Okla., 1973-74. Served with USAF, 1950-54. Mem. Internat., Am., Okla. wildlife fedns., Acad. Gen. Dentistry, Am., Okla. dental assns., Okla. County (dir.; Ho. of Dels.), Deans (hon.) dental socs., Smithsonian Inst., Am. Soc. Implantology, Okla. Peace Officers Assn., YMCA, Omicron Kappa Upsilon. Kiwanian (sec.; pres.), Mason (Shriner). Home: 2321 NW 120th St Oklahoma City OK 73120 Office: 2812 W Hefner Oklahoma City OK 73120

WOODS, EDGAR HALL, mfr.; b. Calyx, Miss., Aug. 13, 1913; s. Edgar Hall and Ida (Lyell) W.; B.S., Marion Inst., 1934; A.B., U. Ky., 1935; m. Irma M. Mihalic, Oct. 12, 1955; children—Charles Scott, Elizabeth Callaway. Cotton planter, 1935-41; adminstr. Munitions Bd. of Standards Agy., 1948-50; v.p. John Deere Plow Co., Balt., 1950-56; gen. sales mgr. Ford Tractor & Implement div., Birmingham, Mich., 1956-58; pres. Midland Ford Tractor Co., St. Louis, 1958-64; pres., dir. Preco, Inc., Los Angeles, 1963—; chmn. bd. D.J. Bricker Lincoln Mercury, Hollywood, Cal., Implement Sales Co., Inc., Memphis; pres., chmn. bd. Midland Mfg. Co., Electric Mills, Miss.; pres. Northcote, Inc., Monterey, Cal. Served with USNR, 1942-46. Decorated Purple Heart. Mem. Am. Soc. Agrl. Engrs., Am. Soc. M.E., Kappa Alpha. Clubs: Northwood (Meridian, Miss.); Jonathan (Los Angeles); Capitol City (Atlanta); Army-Navy (Washington). Home and office: Scooba MS 39358

WOODS, GILBERT WELCH, civil engr.; b. Lamont, Okla., May 3, 1921; s. Elmer Ervin and Hazel (Welch) W.; B.S. in Civil Engring., Okla. U., 1948; m. Wilma Lounsbury, Sept. 25, 1944; 1 dau., Susan. Designer, Okla. Hwy. Dept., 1948-49; hwy. engr. Bur. Pub. Roads, 1949-51; asst. chief engr. Taft & Williamson, cons. engrs., 1951-56; chief civil engr. J.B. Payne & Assos., cons. engrs., 1956-61; chief engr. Serv-Air Inc., Enid, Okla., 1961-72; dir. civil engring. Northrop Worldwide Aircraft Services, 1972—. Served to 1st lt. USAAF, 1942-48. Decorated D.F.C., Air medal with three oak leaf clusters. Registered profl. engr., Okla., Colo. Mem. Am. Soc. Testing and Materials, Nat., Okla. socs. profl. engrs. Mem. Christian Ch. Lion. Home: 1717 E Maple St Enid OK 73701 Office: Northrop Worldwide Aircraft Service Inc Vance AFB Enid OK 73701

WOODS, JERRY DWIGHT, elec. engr.; b. Seminole, Okla., Oct. 10, 1940; s. Lewis Dwight and Helen Elizabeth (Robbins) W.; B.S., Bethany Nazarene Coll., 1972; A.S., Okla. State U., 1971; m. Rose Marie Guzzetti, July 30, 1960; children—Darlene, Jerry Dwight, Timothy, Franklin D. Radar field engr. ITT Gilfillan, Inc., Los Angeles, 1964; traffic control repairman City of Oklahoma City, 1964-65; plant and factory engr. Western Electric Co., Oklahoma City, 1968-71, crossbar switch product engr., 1971—; elec. contractor, El Reno, Okla., Organizing chmn. Southwest Child Guidance Center, 1969, v.p., 1969-70, bd. dirs., 1970-72; pres., organizer John Glenn Elementary Sch. Parent Tchr. Orgn., 1969-70. Served with USAF, 1959-63. Mem. I.E.E.E., Am. Soc. Certified Engring. Technicians, Tau Iota Epsilon. Democrat. Baptist. Clubs: Weokie Archery, Weokie Golf (Oklahoma City). Home: RFD 3 Box 197 El Reno OK 73036 Office: 6655 W Reno Av Oklahoma City OK 73125

WOODS, PAUL RICHARD, pub. relations exec.; b. Pitts., Mar. 4, 1932; s. Edward C. and Sophia Rosalia (Vilary) W.; B.B.A., U. Pitts., 1953; M.B.A., N.Y. U., 1954; postgrad. George Washington U., 1965-66; m. Alice Marie Hughes, July 24, 1954; children—Carol Lyne, Paul Richard, Robert Cameron, Virginia Lee. Credit investigator Dun & Bradstreet, Inc., N.Y.C., 1953-54; regional sales mgr. Cook Electric Co., Rome, N.Y., 1956-59; dir. marketing Lear Siegler Service, Inc., Grand Rapids, Mich., 1959-63, asst. to pres., 1963-64; exec. Paul R. Woods Assos., McLean, Va., 1964—; dir. Shenandoah Airlines, Va. Mgr., Little League, 1969—. Served with USAF, 1954-56. Address: 6227 Nelway Dr McLean VA 22101

WOODS, PENDLETON, ednl. adminstr., author; b. Ft. Smith, Ark., Dec. 18, 1923; s. John Powell and Mabel (Hon) W.; B.A. in Journalism, U. Ark., 1948; m. Lois Robin Freeman, Apr. 3, 1948; children—Margaret, Paul Pendleton, Nancy. Editor, asst. pub. mgr. Okla. Gas & Electric Co., Oklahoma City, 1948-69; dir. Living Legends of Okla., Okla. Christian Coll., Oklahoma City, 1969—. Bd. dirs. Campfire Girls Council, Okla. Jr. Symphony (past pres.), Boy Scout Council; past pres. Oklahoma City Mental Health Clin.; pub. relations chmn. Oklahoma County chpt. A.R.C.; past chmn. Western Heritage award Nat. Cowboy Hall of Fame; past pres. Variety Health Center; dir. Am. Freedom Council. Served with AUS, World War II and Korean; col., state historian Okla. N.G. Named Outstanding Young Man of Year, Oklahoma City Jr. C. of C., 1953; Silver Beaver award Boy Scouts Am., 1963. Mem. Soc. Asso. Indsl. Editors (past v.p.), Advt. Fedn. Am. (past dist. dir.), Central Okla. Indsl. Communicators (past pres., hon. life mem.), Okla. Jr. C. of C. (hon. life; past internat. dir.), Okla. Distributive Edn. Clubs (hon. life), Oklahoma City Advt. Club (past pres.), Okla. Geneal. Soc. (pres.), Okla. Hist. Soc. (publ. editor), Okla. Heritage Assn. (publ. editor), Sigma Delta Chi, Kappa Sigma (nat. commr. publs.). Author: You and Your Company Magazine, 1950; Church of Tomorrow, 1964; Myriad of Sports, 1971. Recorded Sounds of Scouting, 1969; Born Grown, 1974. Home: 541 NW 31st St Oklahoma City OK 73118

WOODS, POWELL, lawyer; b. Ft. Smith, Ark., Jan. 19, 1922; s. John Powell and Mabel Fairfax (Hon) W.; B.A., U. Ark., 1948; LL.B., U. Ark. at Little Rock, 1950; m. Lola Lavoy Keener, June 18, 1954; children—Lola Lavoy, John Powell. Admitted to Ark. bar, 1950; practiced in Ft. Smith, 1950-58; individual practice law, Siloam Springs, 1958—. City atty., Siloam Springs, 1960-62; municipal judge, Siloam Springs, 1963-64. Sec.-treas. Siloam Springs Salvation Army, 1962—. Served with AUS, 1943-45. Mem. Am., Ark., Benton County bar assns., Comml. Law League, Nat. Rifle Assn., C. of C., N.W. Ark. Geol. Soc., Isaac Walton League. Rotarian. Home: 411 S Britt St Siloam Springs AR 72761 Office: 207 S Broadway Siloam Springs AR 72761

WOODS, RILLA MORAN, food services co. exec.; b. Defeated, Tenn., Sept. 14, 1924; d. Ward Romeo and Lydia (Shoemake) Robertson; student George Peabody Coll. for Tchrs., 1957-61; m. Stephen Rogers Woods, Mar. 31, 1972. Various clerical positions, 1941-51; credit mgr., Bookkeeper Ind. Plumbing & Heating Supply Co., Nashville, 1951-58; free lance pub. relations, writing, broadcasting including service as exec. dir. or bus. mgr. Davidson County Easter Seal Soc., Theater Nashville, Nashville Civitan Club, 1958-67; pres., mgr. Moran Assos. Inc., Nashville, 1967-72; pres. Catering Unlimited Inc., Nashville, 1970—. Pres., Nat. Fedn. Democratic Women, 1971—, Tenn. Fedn. Dem. Women, 1970-72, Davidson County Dem. Women, 1969-70; del. Dem. Nat. Conv., 1972; mem. charter commn. Nat. Dem. party, 1972—; Tenn. telethon dir. Dem. Nat. Telethon, 1972. Named Woman of Achievement, Nat. Women Execs., 1969; Outstanding Dem. Woman, Davidson County Dem. Women, 1969. Home: 2004 20th Av S Nashville TN 37212

WOODS, ROBERT JAMES, III, computer co. exec.; b. Memphis, Feb. 23, 1937; s. Robert James, Jr., and Mary Virginia (Allen) W.; B.A., Stanford, 1959; m. Margaret Bostic Schreck, June 18, 1960. Accountant Tenn. Gas Transmission, Houston, 1960-61; systems engr. IBM Corp., Tulsa, 1961-67, mgr. data center, Tulsa, 1967-68; v.p. Mentor Corp., Tulsa, 1968—. Served with USAF, 1959. Mem. Kappa Alpha Order. Republican. Episcopalian. Clubs: Tulsa, Southern Hills Country (Tulsa). Home: 3613 E 49th St Tulsa OK 74135 Office: 10 E 3d St Tulsa OK 74105

WOODSON, HENRY LEE, JR., mgmt. cons.; b. Roanoke, Va., Apr. 12, 1908; s. Henry L. and Estelle (Hancock) W.; B.S. in Elec. Engring., Va. Mil. Inst., 1932; m. Dicie May Cassady, July 1, 1950; children—Douglas Lee, James Neal, Patricia Lea. Asst. city mgr., Roanoke, 1937-45; chief maintenance and operations N.W. Pacific area VA, Seattle, 1945-48; engring. rep. G. F. Muth Co., Washington, 1948-52; chief property mgmt., orgn., methods examiner Office U.S. Housing Adminstr., Washington, 1952-55; adminstr., field mgmt. officer USOM, Pakistan, 1955-56, exec. officer, Turkey, 1956-57; mgr. Washington office Bendix Radio div. Bendix Corp., 1957-67, regional mgr. Bendix Communications div., 1967-73; mgmt. cons., Arlington, Va., 1973—. Mem. Radio Tech. Commn. for Aeros. Served to lt. col. AUS, 1941-46. Mem. I.E.E.E., Am. Helicopter Soc., Am. Congress Mapping and Surveying, A.A.A.S., Nat. Assn. Housing Ofcls., Internat. City Mgrs. Assn., Am. Marketing Assn., Aero Club Washington, Am. Inst. Aeros. and Astronautics, Nat. Space Club, Armed Forces Communications and Electronics Assn., U.S. Naval Inst., Air Force Assn., Assn. Old Crows, Internat. Platform Assn., Fedn. Aeronautique Internationale, Nat. Security Indsl. Assn., Am. Def. Preparedness Assn. (adv. bd.), Armed Forces Mgmt. Assn. (v.p.), Soc. Am. Mil. Engrs., Navy League U.S. (D.C. council), Assn. U.S. Army. Clubs: Army-Navy, MDW Officers, Nat. Aviation, Gaslight. Home: 2401 N Vernon St Arlington VA 22207 Office: PO Box 7140 Arlington VA 22207

WOODSON, SAMUEL PATRICK, JR., bottling co. exec.; b. Roanoke, Va., May 24, 1915; s. Samuel Patrick and Ruby Virginia (Lupton) W.; student U. Tex., 1935; LL.D., Tex. Christian U., 1972; m. Marie Chandler, Feb. 3, 1936; children—Samuel Patrick III, Berry C. With Coca-Cola Bottling Co., 1936—, pres. Ft. Worth Coca-Cola Bottling Co., also 18 other plants in Tex., Okla. and Cal., 1973—; dir. Ft. Worth Nat. Bank. Mem. president's council U. Tex. Med. Sch., Galveston. Bd. dirs. Brown Lupton Found.; trustee Tex. Christian U., Tex. Christian U. Research Found., Arts and Sci. Found. U. Tex. Home: 224 Rivercrest St Fort Worth TX 76106 Office: 123 Hattie St Fort Worth TX 76101

WOODWARD, HARRY EVANS, state ofcl.; b. Clifton Forge, Va., Sept. 9, 1916; s. Harry Evans and Hilda Mitchell (Morris) W.; B.A., U. Va., 1940. With Sales Mgmt. Mag., N.Y.C., 1944-65, spl. features editor, 1950-60, sr. editor, 1960-65; dir. pub. relations and advt. Va. Div. Indsl. Devel., Office Gov., Richmond, 1966—. Founding mem. Alleghany Hist. Soc., 1967—. Mem. exec. bd. Richmond Symphony, 1966-68. Mem. Pub. Relations Soc. Am., Richmond Pub. Relations Assn., Va. Writers Club (bd. dirs. 1970—), English Speaking Union. Episcopalian. Club: 2300. Author: Time of Grace, 1968. Contbr. mags. Home: 3804 Hawthorne Av Richmond VA 23222 Office: Gov's Office Capitol Sq Richmond VA 23219

WOODWARD, RALPH STANLEY, horticulturist; b. Williston, S.C., Oct. 1, 1914; s. Robert Edmond and Clara Mae (Delk) W.; B.S., Clemson Coll., 1936; M.S., La. State U., 1947; m. Eva Francis Rouse, Dec. 18, 1938; children—Ann A., R. Steven. With U. Ark., 1936-39; asst. prof. horticulture La. Poly. Inst. Ruston, 1939-45; prodn. supt. Haitian Govt., 1943-44; horticulturist La. State U., Calhoun, 1945—, supt. expt. sta., 1947—. Mem. Am. Soc. Hort. Sci., Internat. Soc. Hort. Sci., Gamma Sigma Delta. Methodist (lay leader 1960-70). Contbr. articles to profl. publs. Address: N La Exptl Sta Calhoun LA 71225

WOODWARD, WARREN STANTON, assn. exec.; b. Uniontown, Pa., Feb. 4, 1919; s. Alexander and Nellie Alice (Stanton) W.; B.S., Syracuse U., 1939; H.H.D., Lincoln Meml. U., 1971; m. Charlotte

Ingeborg Lund, Dec. 6, 1938 (dec. Apr. 1962); children—Priscilla Celeste (Mrs. David York), Charlotte Stanton (Mrs. Raymond Czwakiel); m. 2d, Gisela Anna Marie Eichler, Nov. 18, 1962. Pub. relations cons., Clinton, N.Y., owner College Inn, Clinton, 1946-54; pres. Woodward Motors, Inc., Utica, N.Y., 1954-63, Woodward Oil Co., Utica, 1959-61, Precision Hardware Corp., Blauvelt, N.Y., 1964-66; nat. exec. sec. S.A.R., Washington, 1966—, also mng. editor mag.; exec. v.p. Cultural Laureate Found. Bd. dirs. Sr. Citizens Program Rockland County, Rockland County (N.Y.) Hist. Area Bd. Rev. Served to lt. USNR, World War II. Decorated comdr. Ordre National (Ivory Coast), comdr. Cross of Merit, Papal Order of Holy Sepulchre. named Hon. Atty. Gen. La., 1964, hon. col. Ky. State Police, 1966; hon. mem. Consul Corps Washington, 1970—. Mem. S.A.R., Am. Soc. French Legion Honor, L'Association Nationale Des Croix De Guerre, Descs. Founders of Hartford (Conn.), Sons and Daus. of Pilgrims, Order Founders and Patriots of Am., S.C.V., Pontifical Tiberina Acad. Rome (fgn. corr.), Academia Mexicana de Genealogia y Heraldia, Washington Family Descs., N.Y. Acad. Scis. Mason (K.T.). Club: Capitol Hill. Editor: Hereditary Register of U.S.A. Address: 2412 Massachusetts Av NW Washington DC 20008

WOODWARD, WILLIAM EDWARD, lawyer; b. Port Arthur, Tex., Jan. 13, 1927; s. Fred Wall and Emma (Wolf) W.; B.A., La. State U., 1956, J.D., 1960; m. Hattie Whittington, Aug. 22, 1964; step-children—Willie L., Robert Lee Sullivan. Admitted to La. bar, 1961; practiced in St. Francisville, La., 1961-62; asso. Richard H. Kilbourne, Clinton, La., 1962-66; practiced in Clinton, 1966—; pub. defender East Feliciana Parish, 1973—. Sec. Silliman Pvt. Sch. Corp., 1965—, bd. dirs., 1966—; chmn. East Feliciana Parish Heart Fund, 1965. Mem., sec. East Feliciana Parish Republican Com., 1967-73. Bd. dirs. Marston Recreational Parks, Inc., Silliman Inst. Served with AUS, 1948-54. Mem. La. Bar. Assn., Am. Judicature Soc., Am. Legion, Pi Gamma Mu, Gamma Eta Gamma. Mem. United Pentecostal Ch. Mem. Woodmen of World. Home: 1548 Horton St Jackson LA 70748 Office: St Helena St Clinton LA 70722

WOODWARD, WILLIAM LEE, banker; b. Lexington, Ky., Jan. 12, 1926; s. Joel Henry and Ophelia Martha (Wallace) W.; A.B., U. Ky., 1950; M.A., 1952; m. Dorothy Dekle, Dec. 31, 1949; children—Pamela, William Lee, Martha. Tchr., Lafayette High Sch., Lexington, 1950-52; prin. Ft. Benning (Ga.) Children's Sch., Columbus, 1952-53; with Lexington Fed. Savs. & Loan, 1953—, exec. v.p., 1964-73, pres., 1973—. Pres., Lexington Deaf Oral Sch., 1968. Trustee Midway (Ky.) Coll., 1969—. Served with USNR, World War II. Clubs: Lexington, Lafayette. Optimist. Office: 2020 Nicholasville Rd Lexington KY 40523

WOODWORTH, LAURENCE NEAL, govt. ofcl.; b. Loudenville, O., Mar. 22, 1918; s. Alfred Ray and Nora (Sheldon) W.; A.B. with high distinction, Ohio No. U., 1940; M.S. (Alfred P. Sloan fellow), U. Denver, 1942; Ph.D., N.Y. U., 1960; m. Margaret Bretz, Sept. 1 1940; children—Laurence, Joseph Ray, Esther Margaret, Melissa Mary. With Civic Research Inst., Kansas City, Mo., 1942-43, Tax Found., Inc., N.Y.C., 1943-44; economist Joint Com. on Internal Revenue Taxation, U.S. Congress, 1944-64, chief staff joint com., 1964—. Mem. Md. Commn. State and County Finance, 1962-64, Md. Gov.'s Fiscal Commn., 1969-70; pres. Md. Municipal League, 1963-64. Mayor, City of Cheverly, Md., 1959-65. Trustee Ohio No. U., Ada. Recipient Outstanding Achievement award Tax Soc. N.Y. U., 1967; Nat. Civil Service Leaguers Career Service award, 1972; Rockefeller Pub. Service award, 1972. Home: 2810 Crest Av Cheverly MD 20785 Office: Longworth House Office Bldg Washington DC 20515

WOODWORTH, TERRANCE CARROLL, govt. ofcl., civil engr.; b. Bar Harbor, Me., May 5, 1941; s. Carroll J. and Hazel (Zande) W.; B.S. in Civil Engring., U. Me., 1963; m. Marylie Dority, Dec. 17, 1966; 1 dau., Susan Carole. Hwy. engr. Fed. Hwy. Adminstrn., Washington, 1963-68, asst. area engr., Atlanta, 1968-69, regional planning engr., 1969—. Bd. dirs. Lockridge Forest Civic Assn., pres., 1972-73, chmn., 1973—. Registered profl. engr. Okla. Mem. Am. Soc. C.E., Toastmasters Internat., Puroga Investment Club (pres. 1969). Home: 3056 Ridge Moore Dr Doraville GA 30340 Office: 1720 Peachtree St Atlanta GA 30309

WOODY, THOMAS BLANTON, safety engr.; b. Abilene, Tex., Dec. 1, 1918; s. John Lunford and Johnnie Ann (Vanlandingham) W.; B.S., North Tex. State U., 1949; M.A. (Edward J. Bond fellow), N.Y. U., 1951; m. Polly Barr Edwards, Sept. 16, 1954; children—Connelly Edwards. Loss prevention engr. Hardward Mut. Ins. Co., Dallas, 1951-52; dir. safety and ins. Continental Carbon Co., Amarillo, Tex., 1952-57; dir. safety and workmen's compensation Murray-Ohio Mfg. Co., Lawrenceburg, Tenn., 1957-60; loss prevention specialist Monsanto, St. Louis, 1960-70; pvt. cons., Pensacola, Fla., 1971; instr. indsl. safety U. West Fla. at Pensacola, spring 1971; div. supr. safety and personnel services Tenneco Chems., Inc., Pensacola, 1972—. Bd. dirs. Morgan County Humane Soc., 1967-68. Served with AUS, 1940-46; PTO. Decorated Purple Heart. Mem. Am. Soc. Safety Engrs. (pres. 1959, 67), Decatur Safety Council (dir. 1965), So. Safety Council (dir. 1968), Ala. Textiles Mfg. Assn. (chmn. safety com. 1963), Nat. Fire Protection Assn., Nat. Rifle Assn., Vets. of Safety, Am. Ex-Prisoners of War, Lost Battalion Assn. Navy League. Lion. Club: Pensacola Country. Home: 2717 Bayou Blvd Pensacola FL 32503 Office: 407 S Pace Blvd Pensacola FL 32502

WOOLDRIDGE, P(OWHATAN) JACK, JR., editor; b. Ft. Smith, Ark., July 22, 1918; s. Powhatan Jack and Dolly (Sorrels) W.; student St. John's Sem., Little Rock, 1937-40; m. Margaret Elizabeth Foalden, Aug. 7, 1965; children—Powhatan Jack III, Michelle Leigh; children by previous marriage-Regina Marie (dec.), Deborah Lorraine; stepchildren—Sharon (Mrs. Aubrey Martin), Wayne D. Bowers. With S.W. Am., Ft. Smith; news editor radio sta. KARK, Little Rock; reporter Houston Press, 1945-46; copy editor Corsicans (Tex.) Daily Sun, 1945-48; editor A.P., Dallas, 1948-50; information specialist OPS, Washington, 1951-52; copy editor Washington bur. Wall Street Jour., 1953-60; asso. editor Nation's Bus., Washington, 1960-62, mng. editor, 1962-64, editor, 1964—. Mem. Am. C. of C. Execs., White House Corrs. Assn., Sigma Delta Chi. Club: Nat. Press. Home: 11231 Sorrel Ridge Lane Oakton VA 22124 Office: 1615 H St Washington DC 20006

WOOLDRIDGE, WILLIAM CHARLES, supt. schs.; b. Petty, Tex., Oct. 2, 1916; s. William Frank and Ada Mary (Baldridge) W.; A.A., Paris Jr Coll., 1936; B.S., East Tex. State U., 1941, M.S., 1949; m. Stella Irene Parsons, May 15, 1942; children—Patricia (Mrs. Robert Carmack), Victoria Elizabeth, William Charles II. Tchr. high sch., prin. Chicota (Tex.) High Sch., 1938-43; tchr. rural sch., Lamar County, Tex., 1936-38, county sch. supt., 1947-54; supt. schs. DeKalb (Tex.) Ind. Sch. Dist., 1954-73; supt. schs., Hallsville, Tex., 1973—. Bd. dirs. Lake Texarkana Water Supply Corp., DeKalb. Indsl. Found., Inc. Served with AUS, 1943-44, USAF, 1944-45, CIC, 1945-46. Named Boss of Year, Am. Bus. Woman's Assn., 1969; recipient Community Service award John H. Moore Am. Legion Post, 1968. Mem. Am., Tex. assns. sch. adminstrs., Tex. Tchrs. Assn. (state exec. com. 1971—), Methodist. Lion. Home: 1012 Creekwood Dr Longview TX 75601 Office: Box 247 Hallsview TX 75650

WOOLFLEY, FRANCIS AUGUSTUS, army officer; b. New Orleans, Apr. 30, 1893; s. Franklin Flanders and Mary Florence (Kessler) W.; grad. Inf. Sch., Ft. Benning, Ga., 1926. Command and Gen. Staff Coll., Ft. Leavenworth, Kan., 1935, Army War Coll., Washington, 1938, Chem. Warfare Sch., Edgewood Arsenal, Md., 1938; m. Rosalie Elizabeth Dufour, June 16, 1920; children—Francis Augustus, Rosalie Elizabeth (Mrs. Allen Henry Johness), Horace Louis. Commd. 2d lt. U.S. Army, 1917, advanced through grades to brig. gen., 1943, inf. advisor to Turkish Army and chief of staff U.S. Army Group, Joint Am. Mil. Mission for Aid to Turkey, Ankara, 1949-52, ret., 1953; dir. La. Civil Def. Agy., 1953-56; asst. adj. gen., dir. La. Civil Def. and dir. Office Emergency Planning for La., 1960-64. Decorated Silver Star with oak leaf cluster, Bronze Star with oak leaf cluster, Legion of Merit, Air medal; Croix de Guerre with palm, chevalier Legion of Honor (France); Croix de Guerre with palm (Belgium); Croix de Guerre (Luxemburg). Mem. S.A.R. (past pres. La. Soc.), Soc. Colonial Wars, Soc. War 1812, Mil. Order World Wars (past comdr.), Am. Legion, Civil War Round Table New Orleans (past pres.). Club: Pendennis (New Orleans). Home: 932 Solomon Pl New Orleans LA 70119

WOOLLEY, CLIFTON WARD, pediatrician; b. Tuscaloosa, Ala., Jan. 15, 1910; s. David Zacchaeus and Mary Benthall (Davis) W.; student Memphis State U., 1930-33; B.S., Union U., 1935; M.D., U. Tenn., 1939; m. Mary Selden Prescott, Sept. 5, 1940; children—Elizabeth (Mrs. Ronald E. Bennett), Martha, John, James Intern, John Gaston Hosp., Memphis, 1939-40, resident, 1941-42, chief resident, 1946; resident Children's Meml. Hosp., Chgo., 1941-42; pub. health officer Maringo County, Linden, Ala., 1940-41; practice medicine specializing in pediatrics, Memphis, 1947—; mem. staffs Baptist Meml., Meth., St. Joseph, John Gaston, LeBonheur hosps. (all Memphis); instr. Tenn. Coll. Medicine, 1947-73; v.p., dir. Die Supplies, Inc., 1963—; physician athletic dept. Memphis State U., 1954—, mem. bd. dirs. 1970—; physician athletic dept. Shelby State Community Coll., 1972—. Bd. advisers Hannibal-LaGrange Coll., 1973—, World Evangelism Found., Dallas, 1970—; trustee Woolley Ednl. Found., Tenn. Baptist Children Homes, Luther Rice Sem., Jacksonville, Fla. Served to maj. AUS, 1942-45. Decorated Silver Star (Luzon). Diplomate Am. Bd. Pediatrics. Fellow Am. Acad. Pediatrics; mem. Am. Tenn., Memphis and Shelby County med. socs., Tenn. Med. Soc., Memphis Pediatrics Soc. (pres. 1952). Baptist (mem. missions com. 1966-70, mem. finance com. 1970—). Contbr. to profl. publs. in field. Home: 3604 Midland Av Memphis TN 38111 Office: 311 Poplar Av Memphis TN 38111

WOOLRICH, WILLIS RAYMOND, instrument co. exec.; b. Mineral Point, Wis., Mar. 1, 1889; s. George and Hannah Martha (Suthers) W.; B.S. in Elec. Engring., U. Wis., 1911, M.E., 1923; m. Neena Rebecca Myhro, Aug. 29, 1914; children—June (Mrs. William S. Morgan), Avis M., Willis Raymond, George Dean, Paul Frederick, Thomas Edwin. Instr. DePaul U., 1911-12; engr. Western Electric Co., 1912-13; asst. methods engr., co-dir. shop schs., Deering br. Internat. Harvester Co., 1913-16; asst. prof. U. Tenn., 1916-24, head dept. mech. engring., 1924-33; dir. small industries div. TVA, 1933-36; dean engring. U. Tex., Austin, 1936-58; interim pres. Middle East Tech. U., Ankara, Turkey, 1959-60; v.p. engring. Indsl. Instrument Corp., Austin, 1960—; prof. mech. engring., U. Tex., 1936-66, dean emeritus, 1959—, also prof. emeritus mech. engring. Tex. chmn. Com. Deferment Scientists and Engrs. Recipient Paul Anderson Gold medal Am. Soc. Heating, Refrigeration and Air Conditioning Engrs., 1968. Mem. A.A.A.S., Am. Soc. Engring. Edn. (nat. pres. 1951-52), Am. Soc. M.E. (past v.p.), Internat. Inst. Refrigeration (internat. v.p. commn. 3). Author profl. articles, handbooks, textbooks. Patentee in food freezing. Home: 4907 Finley Dr Austin TX 78731 Office: PO Box 4647 N Austin PO Austin TX 78751

WOOLRICH, WILLIS RAYMOND, JR., mech. engr.; b. Knoxville, Tenn., July 18, 1919; s. Willis Raymond and Neena (Myhre) W.; B.M.E., U. Tex., 1940, M.M.E., 1946; m. Sarah Louise Weaver, July 4, 1942; children—Willis Raymond III, Sarah Catherine (Mrs. Mathew Monroe Dikeman). Test engr. Gen. Electric Co., Phila., Schenectady, 1940-41; refrigeration engr. Central Power & Light Co., Corpus Christi, Tex., 1946-47; mech. engr. State Bd. Control, Austin, Tex., 1950-53; ty. mgr. Lennox Industries, Houston, 1954-57; mgr. central air conditioners S. Tex. dist. Gen. Elec. Co., Houston, 1958-63; partner Clarke-Woolrich, cons. engrs., 1963-73; chief engr. Mid-South Mfg. Corp., Houston, 1973—; v.p. Smoke-Ban Mfg. Co., Houston, 1968—. Pres. Elec. Engrs. Council Houston. Served with USNR, 1941-45. Mem. Am. Soc. M.E. (sec. 1967-68, vice-chmn. 1968-69, chmn. 1969-70), Tex. Soc. Profl. Engrs., Am. Soc. Oceanography, Pi Tau Sigma. Episcopalian. Mason (32 deg.). Home: 12826 Tosca St Houston TX 77024 Office: 5555 West Loop South Suite 646 Bellaire TX 77401

WOOTAN, LESLEY FRANKLIN, city ofcl.; b. Jayton, Tex., Oct. 12, 1944; s. John Franklin and Emma Alice (Ritchie) W.; B.B.A., N. Tex. State U., 1967; m. Mary Celeste McClellan, Feb. 26, 1965; 1 son, William Franklin. Accountant, Phillips Petroleum Co., Bartlesville, Okla., 1967-68; mem. staff Main, LaFrantz & Co., C.P.A.'s, Dallas, 1970-72; finance dir. City of Sweetwater, Tex., 1972—. Active United Fund, 1972-73, capt., 1973. C.P.A., Tex. Mem. Municipal Finance Officers Assn. Am., Tex. Soc. C.P.A.'s, Am. Inst. C.P.A.'s, Municipal Finance Officers Assn., Tex., Beta Alpha Psi. Kiwanian. Home: 1614 E 14th St Sweetwater TX 79556 Office: PO Box 968 Sweetwater TX 79556

WOOTEN, DON, ry. co. exec.; b. Abilene, Tex., June 2, 1922; s. E.O. and Connie (Harris) W.; B.B.A., U. Tex., 1946; m. Maureen Greer, Jan. 27, 1945; children—Karen Elizabeth (Mrs. William J. Grimes), Bourdon. Pres., H.O. Wooten Grocer Co., Abilene, 1948-60; exec. v.p. Wooten Properties, Inc., Abilene, 1948-63; pres. Roscoe, Snyder & Pacific Ry. Co., Roscoe, Tex., 1948-58, chmn. bd., chief exec. officer, 1958—; v.p. Tex-Hart, Inc., Hart, Tex., 1963—, Reef Oil Corp., Abilene, 1949—; dir. 1st Nat. Bank Abilene, Abilene Savs. & Loan Assn. Pres. Abilene Council Chs., 1964-65; chmn. fund United Fund Abilene, 1965-66; mem. Com. of 75, U. Tex., 1957-58; v.p., dir. Scurry County United Fund, 1968-70, pres., 1970; mem. Merit System Council State Tex., 1958—; mem. adv. council, law study com. Tex. Dept. Mental Health and Mental Retardation, 1965—. Bd. dirs. Tex. Assn. Mental Health, Tex. Good Rds. Assn., Tex. United Community Services, Abilene Council on Alcoholism, A.R.C. Taylor County, Nat., Tex., Abilene assns. mental health, Abilene YMCA. Served with USAAF, 1942-44. Mem. West Tex. C. of C. (mem. exec. com., past pres.). Episcopalian. Home: Bass Ridge Dr Snyder TX 79549 Office: 111 Cypress St Roscoe TX 79545

WOOTEN, JAMES MARTIN, civil engr.; b. Memphis, July 11, 1924; s. William Arthur and Mabel Frances (Martin) W.; B.S. in Civil Engring., Purdue U., 1950; M.S. in Civil Engring., U. Ark., 1967; m. Allie McLane Phelps, Sept. 8, 1949; 1 dau., Ann. Engr., Mosher Steel Co., Dallas, 1950-51; archtl. insp. Gill & Harrell, architects, Dallas, 1951-52; office engr. Ebasco Services Co., Little Rock, 1952-54; chief structural design engr. AFCO Steel Co., Little Rock, 1954—. Served with AUS, 1942-45: ETO. Registered profl. engr., Ark. Mem. Nat., Ark. socs. profl. engrs., Chi Epsilon, Tau Beta Pi, Tau Kappa Epsilon. Home: 1213 Lakeshore Pl North Little Rock AR 72116 Office: PO Box 231 Little Rock AR 72203

WOOTEN, M(ARION) FRANK, JR., city ofcl.; b. Charlotte, N.C., Apr. 8, 1906; s. Marion Frank and Lela (McKamey) W.; B.S. in Civil Engring., U. N.C., 1929; postgrad. Rutgers U. Extension, Europe, 1929, U. N.C., 1932-33; m. Estelle Farmer, June 18, 1934; children—William Scott, Robert Frank. Asso. engr. San. Engring. div., Tenn. Dept. Pub. Health, Nashville, 1929-32; state dir., asst. san. engr. N.C. Dept. Pub. Health and USPHS, Raleigh, N.C., 1933-37; engr. dist. office Frigidaire Corp., Roanoke, Va., 1937-38; sales mgr., engr. Wade Mfg. Co., Charlotte, 1938-39; partner Wooten & Wooten, cons. engrs. and architects, Charlotte, 1939-53; partner Wooten, Wooten & Crosby, 1953-55; v.p., treas. Frank Wooten & Assos., Inc., Charlotte and Orlando, Fla., 1956-61; engr. city Maitland, Fla., 1961-62; dir. pub. works city Winter Park, Fla., 1962-72, city mgr., 1973—. Pres., FEWRO, Inc., Maitland, 1970—. Trustee, Fishburne-Hudgins Ednl. Found., Inc. Registered profl. engr., N.C., S.C., Va., Tenn., Ga., Ala., Miss., Fla. Mem. Inst. Municipal Engring., Nat. (v.p. 1954-55, dir. 1950-53), N.C. (pres. 1950; dir. 1951-52) socs. profl. engrs., Fla. Engring. Soc., Charlotte Engrs. Club (life), Fishburne Alumni Assn. (pres. 1952-56; pres. emeritus 1956—). Methodist (chmn. ofcl. bd., trustee 1960-64). Rotarian. Club: Winter Park University. Home: 930 Pace Av Maitland FL 32751 Office: City Hall Winter Park FL 32789

WOOTEN, SIMEON FRANCIS, JR., banker; b. Tampa, Fla., July 4, 1923; s. Simeon Francis and May (Carter) W.; B.A., U. Fla., 1947, M.B.S., Harvard, 1949; m. Marion McMillin, July 4, 1951; children—Simeon III, Frank, Carter. Landman, Standard Oil Ind., Tulsa, 1951-54; program dir. Apache Corp., Mpls., 1956-58; v.p. Marine Bank & Trust, Tampa, 1958-65, 1st Nat. Bank Fort Lauderdale, Fla., 1967-71; treas. Li'l Gen. Stores, 1965-67; pres. Ocean 1st Nat. Bank, Fort Lauderdale, 1971-73; pres., dir. Southeast Everglades Bank, Fort Lauderdale, 1973—. Bd. govs. United Fund, 1968-71. Served with AUS, 1943-46, 50-52. Mem. Fla. Bankers Assn., Ft. Lauderdale C. of C., Sigma Alpha Epsilon. Republican. Episcopalian. Home: 1735 SE 8th St Fort Lauderdale FL 33316 Office: 1710 S Andrews Av Fort Lauderdale FL 33310

WOOTTON, JANE PENDLETON, physician; b. Cuckoo, Va., Apr. 21, 1939; d. Eugene Barbour and Mildred (McLean) Pendleton, Jr.; B.A., Salem Coll., 1961; M.D. (Nat. Found., Polio Found. scholar, Joseph Collins Found. scholar), Med. Coll. Va., 1965; m. Percy Wootton, June 16, 1962; children—Jane Meredith, Madison Pendleton. Intern Med. Coll. Va., 1965-66, pulmonary fellow, 1966-67; practice medicine, specializing in internal medicine, Richmond, Va., 1972—; physician med. clinic City Health Dept., Richmond, 1972—; mem. courtesy staff Richmond Hosp.; mem. staff Johnston Willis Hosp.; lectr. advanced phys. edn. U. Richmond, 1971. Mem. woman's com. Richmond Symphony, 1967—, Va. Mus. Fine Arts; co-chmn. fund dr. Am. Cancer Soc., Richmond, 1970, bd. dirs., 1967-72. Mem. Med. Soc. Va., Johnston Willis Hosp. Aux. (pres.), Richmond Acad. Medicine, A.M.A., Am. Heart Assn., Women's Aux. Richmond Acad. Medicine, Am. Assn. U. Women. Mem. Christian Ch. (v.p. women's fellowship 1970-71). Clubs: The Country of Virginia, Glenbernie Garden (both Richmond). Home: 509 Tuckahoe Blvd Richmond VA 23226 Office: City Health Dept 1312 Bainbridge St Richmond VA 23113

WOOTTON, PERCY, physician; b. Burkeville, Va., June 14, 1932; s. James Edgar and Annie Winston (Carter) W.; B.S., Lynchburg Coll., 1953; M.D. (Florence Smith Found. Med. scholar), Med. Coll. Va., 1957; m. Barbara Jane Pendleton, June 16, 1962; children—Jane Meredith, Madison Pendleton. Intern, Roanoke Meml. Hosp., 1957-58; jr. asst. resident in medicine Med. Coll. Va., 1958-59, asst. resident in medicine, 1959-60, resident in cardiology, 1962-63; practice medicine, specializing in internal medicine and cardiology, Richmond, Va., 1963—; chief medicine Richmond (Va.) Meml. Hosp., 1971—, mem. exec. com., 1972-74; mem. active staff Johnston Willis, Grace, Stuart Circle, St. Mary's, Retreat for Sick, St. Luke's, Sheltering Arms, Va. Home hosps.; instr. medicine, cardiology Med. Coll. Va., Richmond, 1963—. Physician, Boy Scouts Am., 1963—, Boys Club, Richmond, 1963—. Served to lt. comdr. M.C., USNR, 1960-62. Va. Heart Assn. grantee, 1962-63; Med. Coll. Va. grantee, 1962-63. Fellow Am. Coll. Cardiology; mem. Richmond Soc. Internal Medicine, A.M.A., A.C.P., Am. (mem. clin. council cardiology 1963—), Va. (exec. com. 1972-74, dir. 1969—, del. to Am. assn. 1972-73), Richmond Area (pres. 1972-73, exec. com. 1972-74) heart assns., Med. Soc. Va. (vice councilor 1973-74), Richmond Acad. Medicine (sec. bd. trustees 1972-74), Lynchburg Coll. Alumni Assn. (dir. 1964-74), S.A.R., Mil. Order World Wars, Theta Kappa Psi, Omicron Delta Kappa. Mem. Christian Ch. (deacon 1967—). Mason (Shriner), Rotarian. Clubs: 2300 (dir. 1964-67), Country of Va. (Richmond); Amelia (Va. Country. Home: 509 Tuckahoe Blvd Richmond VA 23226 Office: Profl Bldg Richmond VA 23219

WORDEN, DAVID JOSEPH, clergyman; b. Beatrice, Neb., Jan. 28, 1937; s. Joseph Rogers and Ethel Elenor (Guy) W.; B.Th., N.W. Christian Coll. 1958; postgrad. U. Tex., 1963, 64; M.Div., Tex. Christian U., 1964; m. Jo Ann Debolt, Sept. 8, 1957; children—Lori Ellen, Lisa Ann, Liby Jo. Ordained to ministry Christian Ch., 1958; asso. minister First Christian Ch., The Dalles, Ore., 1959-61; minister First Christian Ch., Allen, Tex., 1961-69, Monica Park Christian Ch., Garland, Tex., 1969—. Pres., Collin County Council on Alcoholism, 1964-66, mem. mayor's Youth Coordinating Com., 1972-73. Bd. dirs. Garland Assistance Program, v.p., 1970—. Recipient Outstanding Achievement award Christian Ch., Tex., 1968. Mem. Assn. Christian Chs. (pres. dist. 17 1966-68). Lion (dist. chaplain 1972-73). Mason. Home: 502 W Celeste Garland TX 75041 Office: 2600 Broadway Garland TX 75041

WORDEN, WILLIAM HENRY, clergyman; b. Ponca City, Okla., July 6, 1921; s. John Luell and Mabel Mary (Kenna) W.; A.B., Phillips U., 1963; m. Edna Darline Harden, Mar. 3, 1942; children—William Henry, Linda, James, Gerald, Kevin. Rollsman, Moore Drydock Co., Oakland, Cal., 1940; prin. W.H. Worden Muskogee, Okla., 1945-47; lab. technician Continental Oil Co., Ponca City, 1947-60; ordained to minstry Christian Ch., 1964; minister Hillside Christian Ch., Ft. Worth, 1964-70, First Christian Ch., Lindsay, Okla., 1970—. Pres., Christian Minister's Fellowship, Ft. Worth, 1969; sec. Ministerial Alliance; moderator Dist. 9 Christian Chs.; dir. Linday Sr. Citizens Center, 1973—. Served with USAAF, 1942-45. Mem. Lindsay C. of C. (exec. com. 1973—); Am. Legion. Mason, Rotarian. Address: 209 SW 4th St Lindsay OK 73052 also 419 Olive Lindsay OK 73052

WORKMAN, DON RAE, banker; b. Plainview, Tex., Feb. 3, 1937; s. C.A. and Elsie Mae (Carpenter) W.; student Lubbock Christian Coll., 1958; B.S., Tex. Tech U., 1960; M.S., Tex. A. and M. U., 1962; m. Almeda Ratliff, Mar. 31, 1961; children—David, Mark. Asst. prof. Tex. A. and M. U., 1962-63; ranch economist State of Tex., 1963-64; v.p., dir. First State Bank, Morton, Tex., 1964-66; v.p. comml. loan dept. First Nat. Bank, Lubbock, Tex., 1966—. Staff mem. Intermediate Banking Sch., Tex. Tech. U., 1974, dean Agrl. Banking Sch., 1973-74; staff mem. Southwestern Grad. Sch. Banking, Banking Sch. of South. Mem. West Tex. Health Planning Council, 1970—; chmn. ABC rodeo, 1971; chmn. state com. Tex. Grain Fed Beef

Promotion, 1971; mem. Gov.'s Traffic Safety Council, 1970; team capt. community div. United Fund, 1970; staff mem. Tex. Youth Council, 1973. Bd. govs. ABC Clubs Am; bd. dirs. West Tex. Water Inst. Mem. Am. Inst. Banking (econs. instr. 1969—), Ranch Hdqrs. Assn. (chmn. annual meeting day 1970), West Tex. C. of C. (regional v.p. 1970—, bd. dirs. 1960-71), Lubbock C. of C. (steering com. agrl. com. 1970). Contbr. articles to profl. pubs. Home: Route 4 Box 176L Lubbock TX 79410 Office: First National Bank PO Box 1241 Lubbock TX 79408

WORLEY, JOHN KYLE, geophysicist; b. Detroit, Aug. 31, 1930; s. John Kyle and Virginia (Fox) W.; student Mass. Inst. Tech., 1948-49; B.S., Wayne State U., 1952; m. Mary Frances O'Flynn, Sept. 7, 1955; 1 dau., Gladys Charmaine (Mrs. Charles Edward Dillon). Seismologist, Geophys. Service, Inc., Dallas, 1953-54; party chief Nancy Exploration Co., Houston, 1955-57; party chief Ray Geophys. Div., Houston, 1957-66, program application geophysicist, 1966-72, mgr. nav./gravity/magnetic dept., 1972—. Mem. Soc. Exploration Geophysicists, Aircraft Owners and Pilots Assn. Home: 15402 W Westwood Circle Houston TX 77071 Office: 6909 SW Freeway Houston TX 77036

WORLEY, WYETH HARDY, dentist; b. Shreveport, La., Sept. 22, 1935; s. Wyeth Bodine and Dessie (Bostick) W.; B.S. in Natural Scis., Centenary Coll., 1957, B.S. in Chemistry, 1959; D.D.S., Loyola U., New Orleans, 1963; m. Jackie Dean Champion, Dec. 26, 1954; children—Susan Elizabeth, Hardy Hayes, Dean Lewis. Practice dentistry, specializing in oral surgery, Shreveport, 1966—; clin. prof. Sch. Medicine, La. State U., Shreveport, 1968—. Cons. Barksdale AFB, 1967—. Diplomate Am. Bd. Oral Surg. Mem. La. (pres.), S.E. Am. socs. oral surgeons, A.M.A., Am., 4th Dist. dental assns., Kappa Sigma. Republican. Baptist. Home: 558 Longleaf St Shreveport LA 71106 Office: 2751 Virginia St Shreveport LA 71103

WORONIAK, ALEXANDER, economist, educator; b. Lviv, Ukraine, Feb. 27, 1918; s. Thomas and Eudoxia (Husar) W.; LL.M., Yohanni Casimiri U. (Lvov, Poland), 1939; M.S., Columbia, 1953, postgrad., 1956-58; m. Maria Zvenyslava Patchovsky, Apr. 27, 1943. Asst. prof. Ivan Franko U., Ukraine, 1940-42; cons., 1942-44; legal counselor, welfare officer UNRRA, IRO, Germany, 1946-50; accountant Advance Solvents & Chem. Corp., N.Y.C., 1950-51, Gregory V. Collins & Co., 1953-54, Radio Clinic, Inc., 1955-57; research asst. Grad. Sch. Bus., Columbia, 1957-58; asst. prof. econs. Cath. U. Am., 1958-67, asso. prof. econs., 1967-71, prof., 1971—; lectr. Howard U., 1963-69; research asso. USAF grant, 1964-69; cons. Rio Bermejo Devel. Project, Argentina, 1967-69, Inst. for Def. Analysis, 1970-71, Stanford Research Inst., 1971—, also bus. firms, 1958—. Bronner scholar, 1951; Ford fellow, 1957. Mem. Am. Econ. Assn., Am. Accounting Assn., Nat. Assn. Accountants, Am. Assn. U. Profs., Assn. Comparative Econs., Assn. Study of Soviet Type Economies, Am. Statis. Assn., Pi Gamma Mu. Author: Labor Mediation and Counseling, 1942; Job Descriptions and Specifications, 1943; Integration of Refugees and Displaced Persons into German Economy, 1949; Business Organization and The Transfer of Technology; Experience of the Soviet Union, 1967; Industrial Concentration in Eastern Europe: The Search for Optimum Size and Efficiency, 1969; Problems and Achievements of Soviet Technology Exports, 1969; Technological Transfer in Eastern Europe: Receiving Countries, 1970; A Microeconomic Approach to the Problem of Regionalism in Soviet Business Management, 1971; Ruble Dollar Conversion Ratio Survey, 1972; Regional Aspects of Soviet Planning and Industrial Organization, 1973. Co-author: The Feasibility of Developing Transfer of Technology Functions, 1967; The Transfer of Technology to Developing Countries, 1967; Valuing Transfer of Military Acquired Skills to Civilian Employment, 1969; Transfer of Technology Functions Extended: The German Case, 1970; Feasibility of Obtaining the 1967 Ruble/Dollar Conversion Ratio, 1973. Home: 1435 Geranium St NW Washington DC 20012 Office: Box 254 Cath U Am Washington DC 20017

WORRELL, ANNE EVERETT ROWELL (MRS. THOMAS EUGENE WORRELL), newspaper exec.; b. Surry, Va., Mar. 7, 1920; d. Charles Gray and Ethel (Roache) Rowell; student Va. Intermont Coll., 1937-39; m. Thomas Eugene Worrell, Sept, 12, 1941; children—Thomas Eugene. Instr., VIRanch Camp, Bristol, Tenn., 1938-39, dir., 1942, 47-51; sec. Gen. Motors Acceptance Corp., Richmond, Va., Washington, 1939-41; feature writer, fashion editor Bristol Herald Courier, Va. Tennessean, Bristol, 1963—; sec.-treas., dir. Worrell Newspapers, Inc., Bristol, 1958—. Pres., Bristol Border Guild, 1959; mem. Va. Mus., 1960—, Carroll Reece Mus., 1968—. Bd. dirs., sec. Bristol chpt. A.R.C., 1966-70; chmn. bd. advisers Va. Intermont Coll., 1973—. Presbyn. Home: 117 Shady Lane Bristol TN 37620 Office: 320 Morrison Blvd Bristol VA 24201

WORRELL, DENNIS LEE, retail exec.; b. Indpls., Nov. 22, 1938; s. Herman A. and Vivian (Anderson) W.; A.B., Columbia, 1960; m. Marie Ann Haspel, June 5, 1958; 1 son, Scott Harrison. Mdse. exec. Lord & Taylor, N.Y.C., 1960-62; personnel mgr., labor relations exec. R.H. Macy & Co., N.Y.C., 1962-67; sr. v.p. Neiman Marcus, Dallas, 1967—. Mem. Nat. Retail Mchts. Assn. (dir.), Dallas Personnel Assn., Am. Soc. Personnel Dirs., Dallas Grand Opera Assn., Dallas Civic Opera Assn. Home: 7419 Carta Valley Dr Dallas TX 75240 Office: Neiman Marcus Main and Ervay Sts Dallas TX 75201

WORRELL, LEE FRANK, educator; b. Orleans, Ind., Feb. 27, 1913; s. Frank S. and Grace (Hollowell) W.; B.S. in Pharmacy, Purdue U., 1935, Ph.D., 1940; m. Mary Dee Pickens, July 15, 1934; 1 dau., Shirley Yvonne (Mrs. Thomas Kauper). Asst., then asso. prof. Drake U. Coll. Pharmacy, 1938-42; from instr. to asso. prof. U. Mich. Coll. Pharmacy, 1942-60; prof. U. Tex. Coll. Pharmacy, Austin, 1960—, dean coll., 1962-66. Bd. dirs. Ann Arbor (Mich.) area United Fund, 1956-60. Mem. Am. Pharm. Assn., Am. Chem. Soc., A.A.A.S., Sigma Xi, Phi Kappa Phi, Rho Chi, Phi Lambda Upsilon. Home: 3411 Foothill Terrace Austin TX 78731

WORRELL, THOMAS EUGENE, newspaper pub.; b. Bristol, Va,, July 30, 1919; s. Howard Hampton and Hester (Denton) W.; B.S., Wake-Forest Coll., 1940; law student George Washington U., 1940-41; m. Anne Rowell, Sept. 12, 1941; 1 son, Thomas Eugene. Admitted to Va. bar, 1941; pvt. practice law, Bristol, 1941, 1946-49; spl. agt. F.B.I., 1942-46; pres. Worrell Newspapers, Inc., pubs. 30 daily and weekly newspapers in 13 states. Bd. advisers U.P.I. Mem. Va. Bar Assn., Va. C. of C. (pres. 1956-58, past dir.). Elk, Kiwanian. Home: 117 Shady Lane Bristol TN 37620 Office: 320 Morrison Blvd Bristol VA 24201

WORSHAM, BERTRAND RAY, psychiatrist; b. Atkins, Ark., Feb. 14, 1926; s. Lewis Henry and Emma Lavada (Burris) W.; B.A., U. Ark., 1951; M.D., 1955; m. Margaret Ann Dickson, June 4, 1948; children—Eric Dickson, Vicki Gayle, William Henry. Intern, Hillcrest Med. Center, Tulsa, 1955-56, resident psychiatry Menninger Sch. Psychiatry, Topeka, 1956-58; resident psychiatry and neurology U. Okla. Sch. Medicine, Oklahoma City, 1958-59; instr., 1959—; practice medicine specializing in psychiatry, Oklahoma City, 1959—; mem. staff Bapt. Med. Center, Coyne-Campbell, Deaconess, Drs. Gen., all Oklahoma City; dir. regional guidance center Okla. Dept. Pub. Health, 1966-70. Cons. Social Security Adminstrn., 1960—, Okla. Health Dept., 1960-73. Elector, Okla. Athletic Hall of Fame, 1969-70; mem. Okla. County Civil Def. Com., 1968-71; Oklahoma City Art Center, Okla. Symphony Soc. Served with USNR, 1944-46; now comdr. Res. Fellow Royal Soc. Health (Eng.); mem. Am., So. med. assns., Am. Psychiatry Alumni Assn., Am. Biog. Assn., Am. Security Council, Oklahoma City C. of C. Home: 9915 N Kelley St Oklahoma City OK 73114 Office: 2600 NW Expressway Oklahoma City OK 73112

WORSHAM, MACKLYNN DUANE, chem. co. exec.; b. Centerville, Ark., Feb. 28, 1923; s. Ray Earnest and Zona Aliene (George) W.; grad. high sch.; m. Floy Elizabeth James, June 1, 1943; children—Judy Ann, Vicky (Mrs. Jack Vawter). Salesman, Steppins & Roberts Inc., Little Rock, 1944-56, sales mgr., 1956-69, v.p., 1969—. Served with USAAF, 1941-45. Decorated Purple Heart medal, three Bronze Star medals. Home: 6040 Wonder Dr Fort Worth TX 76133 Office: 900 N Main St Fort Worth TX 76101

WORTHINGTON, DONALD THOMPSON, govt. ofcl.; b. Lexington, Ky., Nov. 28, 1921; s. John W. and Jennie (Connor) W.; B.S. in Elec. Engring., U. Ky., 1948; postgrad. Coll. Armed Forces, 1963; Va. Poly. Inst., 1972—; m. Nellie D. Palmer, Aug. 6, 1955; children—Donald T., Jr., David Lee. Tech. adviser Rome Air Depot (N.Y.), 1952-54, engr., 1955-62; engr. Def. Communications Agy., Washington, 1962-69, tech. adviser research and devel., 1969-73, chief research and devel. div. Def. Communications Engring. Center, Reston, Va., 1973—. Served with Signal Corps, AUS, 1942-46. Mem. I.E.E.E. (sr. mem.). Mason (Shriner). Contbr. articles to profl. jours. Home: 5516 Flag Run Dr Springfield VA 22151 Office: 1860 Wiehle Av Reston VA 22090

WORTHINGTON, EDDIE LEE, elec. engr.; b. Chickasha, Okla., Jan. 31, 1936; s. Walter Parker and Lois Lou (Erwin) W.; student Cameron State Coll., 1960-61; A.A., Okla. State U., 1957; B.S., 1964; m. Teddy Lou Beneditti, Sept. 20, 1957; children—Brent, Kristi, Kelly. Relay engr. Pub. Service Co. Okla., 1964-67, transmission design engr., 1967-70, scheduling supr., 1970-72, elec. supr. Comanche Power Sta., Lawton, 1972—. Mem. I.E.E.E., Am. Nuclear Soc. Mem. Christian Ch. Home: 4905 Meadowbrook Dr Lawton OK 73501 Office: PO Box 828 Lawton OK 73501

WORTZ, CARL HAGLIN, bus. analyst, cons.; b. Ft. Smith, Ark., May 9, 1921; s. Carl H. Wortz and Ed Dell (Haglin) W.; grad. N.M. Mil. Inst., 1940; Sparton Sch. Aeronautics, 1943; B.S. in Bus., U. Ark., 1947; m. Charlotte Wacker, June 29, 1943; 1 dau., Carolyn Jane. Chmn. bd. Wortz Co., cracker and cookie mfg. co., now ret.; cons., bus. analyst; chmn. bd. Intercontinental Corp., Dallas; dir. Invention Mfg. Co., Arlington, Tex. Served with AUS, 1943-46; CBI. Mem. Sigma Alpha Epsilon. Methodist. Office: PO Box 45565 Dallas TX 75235

WORZEL, JOHN LAMAR, educator; b. West Brighton, S.I., N.Y., Feb. 21, 1919; s. Howard Henry and Marie Alma (Wilson) W.; B.S., Lehigh U., 1940; M.A., Columbia, 1948, Ph.D., 1949; m. Dorothy Crary, Nov. 22, 1941; children—Sandra Lee (Mrs. A.A.J. Browne), Howard H., Richard, William Paddock. Research asso. Woods Hole Oceanographic Inst., 1940-46; mem. faculty Columbia, 1949-72, asst. prof., 1951-52, asso. prof., 1952-57, prof. dept. geology, 1957-72; asst. dir. Lamont-Doherty Geol. Obs., Palisades, N.Y., 1951-64; asso. dir. Lamont-Doherty Geol. Obs., Palisades, N.Y., 1964-72; prof., dep. dir. earth and planetary scis. U. Tex. at Galveston, 1972-74, acting dir. earth and planetary scis. div. Marine Biomed. Inst., 1974, acting dir. Geophysics Lab., Marine Sci. Inst., 1974—. Cons. Office Naval Research, U.S. Navy, 1950-52; chief scientist expdns. at sea. Mem. Rockland County council Boy Scouts Am., 1955-72. Bd. dirs. Palisades Geophys. Inst. Recipient U.S. Navy Meritorious Pub. Service citation, 1964. Fellow Geol. Soc. Am., A.A.A.S., Am. Geophys. Union; mem. Am. Phys. Soc., Seismol. Soc., Am. Soc. Exploration Geophysicists (Distinguished lectr. 1971), Sigma Xi, Pi Mu Epsilon, Tau Beta Pi. Club: Cosmos. Author: Pendulum Gravity Measurements at Sea 1936-59, 1965. Contbr. articles to sci. publs. Home: 3025 Beluche Dr Galveston TX 77550

WOYTYCH, ROBERT LUCIEN, govt. ofcl.; b. Annapolis, Md., Oct. 18, 1915; s. Louis J. and Mary (Brady) W.; student George Washington U., 1935-36; B.A., Benjamin Franklin U., 1942; m. Suzanne Lajoye, June 17, 1939; children—Judith Anne (Mrs. Bruce Henry Danielson), Robert Lucien, Suzanne M. With Immigration and Naturalization Service, 1941—, successively officer in charge, Washington, 1948-54, dist. dir., St. Paul, 1956-59, dist. dir., Washington, 1959-60; supervisory immigrant insp. N.W. Regional Office, St. Paul; 1960-64, dist. dir., Miami, Fla., 1964—. Active Little League, Babe Ruth Baseball, Mpls. Served with AUS, 1945-46. Mem. Am. Legion (past post comdr. Cheverly, Md., chmn. fgn. relations Fla. dept. 1968-69), Dade County Assn. Chiefs of Police (chmn. Greater Miami exec. council 1966-67). Home: 7001 SW 16th Ct West Hollywood FL 33023 Office: Fed Bldg 51 SW 1st Av Miami FL 33130

WRAY, JOSEPH PRESTON, JR., ednl. adminstr.; b. Chesterfield, Va., Mar. 29, 1936; s. Joseph Preston and Mary Nancy (Cannon) W.; A.A., Bluefield Coll., 1956; B.A., U. Richmond, 1958; M.Div., Southeastern Bapt. Theol. Sem., 1963; postgrad. U. Richmond, 1963, Va. Commonwealth U., 1964-66; m. Frances Everlyn Bishop, Aug. 18, 1961; children—Christopher Scott, Monta Elizabeth. Ordained to ministry Bapt. Ch., 1961; pastor Second Bapt. Ch., Dunn, N.C., 1960-62; tchr. English, Hopewell (Va.) High Sch., 1962-65; dir. pub. information Bluefield (Va.) Coll., 1965-73, dir. devel., 1973—. Recipient Man of Year award Bluefield Jr. C. of C., 1968. Mem. Bapt. Gen. Assn. Va. (sesquicentennial com. 1971-73), Am. Alumni Council Nat. Com. Two Year Colls., East River Bapt. Assn. Men's Brotherhood (pres. 1972—, Bluefield Coll. Alumni Assn. (bd. govs. 1966—), Mountain Highlands Archeol. Soc. (bd. govs. 1973-74), Bapt. Pub. Relations Assn., Summit Players, John Rolfe Players, Am. Alumni Council. Baptist (deacon 1968—). Club: Metropolitan (Bluefield). Author: The Bedford Plowboys, 1972. Editor various ednl. publs. Home: 6 Faculty Row Bluefield Coll Campus Bluefield VA 24605

WRAY, ROBERT FREDERICK, city ofcl.; b. Dayton, Ky., Feb. 6, 1935; s. Robert M. and Louise (Rasch) W.; student Va. Poly. Inst., 1953-56; B.S. in Civil Engring., U. Cin., 1959-62; m. Ann Saunders, Nov. 26, 1957; children—Douglas, Louise, Lisa. Asst. engr. W.L. Harper Co., Cin., 1958-60; gen. supt. Eaton Oil Co., Covington, Ky., 1960-64; self-employed as engring. cons., Erlanger, Ky., 1964-68; city mgr. City Covington (Ky)., 1968-71, City of Jacksonville (N.C.), 1971—. Served with USMCR, 1957-59. Mem. Internat. City Mgmt. Assn., Municipal Finance Officers Assn., Ky. Assn. City Mgrs. (v.p. 1968-69). Mem. Christian Ch. Mason. Clubs: Optimist (Covington). Home: 600 River Ct Jacksonville NC 28540 Office: City Hall Jacksonville NC 28540

WREN, WILLIAM MARCEL, feed co. exec.; b. Siler City, N.C., May 22, 1906; s. Lossing Lafayette and Matilda Rose (Folley) W.; A.B., U. Ala., 1929; m. Marion Galloway, Oct. 9, 1948; children—William Galloway, Margaret Matilda. Salesman, Siler City Mills, 1930-37, sec.-treas., 1937-54, pres., chmn. bd., 1954—; pres. Dog Foods Inc., Siler City, 1954—, Champion Milling Co., Dunn, N.C., 1954—, Clinton Grains (N.C.), 1954—, Pine Forest Inc., Siler City, 1960—; dir. 1st Union Nat. Bank of N.C., Charlotte, Cameron Financial Corp., Charlotte. Pres., Wren Found., 1955—, Chatham Hosp., 1958—. Trustee, N.C. Methodist Retirement Home, 1955—, vice chmn., 1972—. Served to lt. comdr., USNR, 1942-45. Mem. Phi Gamma Delta. Republican. Methodist. Clubs: Siler City Country, Dunes Golf and Country, Country of N.C. Home: Pittsboro Rd Siler City NC 27344 Office: PO Box 249 Siler City NC 27344

WRIGHT, ALMA MCINTYRE, publishing co. exec.; b. Knoxville, Tenn., July 31, 1909; d. William Mobry and Theresa (Biagiotti) McIntyre; B.S. in Edn., U. Tenn., 1932; m. Robert Oliver Wright, Feb. 17, 1931; 1 son, Robert Oliver. Writer stories, articles on African violets, house plants, 1947—; editor African Violet mag., 1947-63; exec. dir. African Violet Soc. Am., Inc., 1960-63; pres. Indoor Gardener Pub. Co., Inc., Knoxville, 1963—; editor Gesnerlad-Saintpaulia News, 1963—. Mem. Am. Hort. Soc. (hon. v.p. 1954), African Violet Soc. Am. (hon. life, rec. sec. 1946-48, nat. pres. 1948-49, membership sec. 1953-63), Saintpaulia Internat. (editor publs., rec. sec. 1963—). Editor: Master List of African Violets, 1962; editor for Am., Gesneria Soc. Home: 4752 Calumet Dr Knoxville TN 37919 Office: 1800 Grand Av Knoxville TN 37901

WRIGHT, BENNY WAYNE, mech. engr.; b. Bristol, Tenn., Nov. 30, 1939; s. Robert Kyle and Hazel (Tolliver) W.; B.S. in Mech. Engring., U. Tenn., 1963; m. Patsy Elizabeth Harr, Apr. 16, 1966; children—Kimberly Camille, Brandon Wayne. Mech. engr. Eastman Chem. Products, Inc., Kingsport, Tenn., 1963-68, tech. service engr., 1968—. Registered profl. engrs., Tenn. Mem. Nat., Tenn. socs. profl. engrs., Phi Kappa Phi, Pi Tau Sigma, Tau Beta Pi. Baptist. Home: Route 6 Box 208 Bristol TN 37620 Office: PO Box 431 Kingsport TN 37662

WRIGHT, CARROLL, JR., real estate appraiser and cons.; b. Alexandria, Va., Dec. 10, 1928; s. Carroll and Alice (Barron) W.; B.A., Va. Poly. Inst., 1949; M.A., Am. U., Washington, 1959, postgrad. 1965; m. Laura Beville Hailey, July 23, 1950; children—Carroll Tilden, Laura Alice. Pres., Carroll Wright, Jr. Co., real estate appraisal and counseling, Falls Church, Va., 1967—; real estate appraiser, broker, market analyst, and cons., Washington met. area, also other areas, 1955—; pres., co-founder Am. Real Estate Appraisal Corp., Washington and Falls Church, Va., 1962-67. Mem. faculty Am. U. Pres., Community Projects, Inc. Mem. bd. control George Mason Coll., Fairfax, Va. Served as 1st lt., Inf., AUS, 1950-54; Korea. Mem. Am. Inst. Real Estate Appraisers (pres. Washington met. area chpt. 1971). No. Va. Bd. Realtors, Va. Assn. Assessing Officers (affiliate), Am. Real Estate and Urban Econs. Assn. (affiliate). Rotarian. Club: Washington Golf and Country. Office: Suite 140 1st Va Plaza 6400 Arlington Blvd Falls Church VA 22042

WRIGHT, CHARLES NATHANIEL, health physicist; b. Lynchburg, Va., Feb. 8, 1926; s. Charles Linwood and Lelia Adelaide (Crumpler) W.; B.S. in Chemistry, Lynchburg Coll., 1950; M.S. in Physics (AEC fellow), Vanderbilt U., 1952; m. Nancy Whitsell Dunn, July 15, 1950; children—Linda (Mrs. Russell W. Crider), Mark, Mary, Jonathan. Health physicist E.I. duPont de Nemours & Co., Inc., Savannah River Plant and Lab., Aiden, S.C., 1952—. Cons. radiation, radiol. physics Richmond Labs. Inc., Augusta, Ga., 1961—. Served with USAAF, 1944-46. Mem. Health Physics Soc. (pres. Savannah River chpt. 1968-69, nat. program com. 1962—), Am. Legion. Contbr. articles to profl. jours. Home: 711 Merriwether Dr North Augusta SC 29841 Office: Savannah River Plant Aiken SC 29801

WRIGHT, DAVID WAYNE, JR., carpet mfg. co. exec.; b. Lynchburg, Va., May 29, 1937; s. David Wayne and Nell Chapel (House) W.; B.S., Lynchburg Coll., 1959; M.B.A., U. Va., 1965; m. Bettie Jean Pettyjohn, Aug. 24, 1957; children—Charles Wayne, David Worth, Jeffrey Benedict. Planner, Burlington Industries, Inc., Halifax, Va., 1959-61, systems analyst, Greensboro, N.C., 1965-67, dir. data processing, Monticello, Ark., 1967-71, exec. v.p., 1971—; procedures analyst Sperry Piedmont Co., Charlottesville, Va., 1961-63; dir. Union Bank & Trust Co., Monticello. Pres., bd. dirs. Drew County Mental Retardation Council; co-chmn. Monticello Council on Human Relations. Named Outstanding Young Man of Am., 1972. Mem. Halifax Jr. (sec. pres., dir.), Monticello (dir.) chambers commerce, Asso. Industries Ark. (dir.). Republican. Roman Catholic. Rotarian. Home: PO Box 635 Monticello AR 71655 Office: PO Box 120 Monticello Ark 71655

WRIGHT, DON CONWAY, editorial cartoonist; b. Los Angeles, Jan. 23, 1934; s. Charles and Sally (Olberg) W.; ed. pub. schs.; m. Rita Rose Blondin, Oct. 1, 1960. Mem. staff Miami (Fla.) News, 1952-56, 58—, photo editor, 1960-63, polit. cartoonist, 1963—; rep. permanent exhbn. U. Syracuse. Served with AUS, 1956-58. Recipient Pulitzer prize for editorial cartooning, 1965; Freedoms Found. award for editorial cartoon, 1966; also local citations; named Outstanding Person in Communication Media, Young Democrats Fla., 1966. Mem. Am. Assn. Editorial Cartoonists, Sigma Delta Chi. Home: 11725 SW 88th Av Miami FL 33156 Office: 1 Herald Plaza Miami FL 33101

WRIGHT, ERNEST EDWARD, JR., architect; b. Commerce, Tex., Feb. 17, 1922; s. Ernest Edward and Eva Faye (Browning) W.; B.S., East Tex. State U., 1947; B.Arch., U. Tex., 1951; m. Vera Anderson, Apr. 25, 1942; children—Linda (Mrs. M.A. Russell), Sandra (Mrs. David Ray Oakley). Prin., Wright-Rich & Assos., Dallas, 1953—. Dir. 1st Nat. Bank, Garland, Tex. Mayor, City of Garland, 1958-62. Served with USAAF, 1942-45. Decorated Air medal with two oak leaf clusters. Mem. Garland C. of C. (pres. 1967). Kiwanian. Prin. works include: City Hall, 1972, Meml. Hosp. addition, 1973, 1st Nat. Bank Tower, 1973 (all Garland); Faculty and Office Bldg., U. Tex., Arlington, 1972; Industry and Tech. Bldg., East Tex. State U., Commerce, 1974. Home: 3109 Medina St Garland TX 75041 Office: 2727 Cedar Springs St Dallas TX 75201

WRIGHT, ERNIE EDWARD, lawyer, judge; b. Cisco, Ark., Oct. 31, 1915; s. James Robert and Vindie (Williams) W.; A.B., U. Ark., 1938, LL.B., 1940, J.D., 1969; grad. Nat. Coll. State Trial Judges, 1967; m. Alyce Erline Collins, Aug 22, 1941; children—Warren James, Carolyn Doris. Admitted to Ark. bar, 1940, since practiced in Mountain Home, Ark.; city atty., Mountain Home, 1940-41; pros. atty. 16th Dist. Ark., 1943; chancery judge 11th Dist. Ark., 1955—. Mem. Ark. Tax Commn., 1949; chmn. Baxter County chpt. A.R.C., 1946-47; finance chmn. Boone County unit Am. Cancer Soc., 1955-56; mem. Nat. Com. for Support Pub. Schs., 1964—. Served with USAAF, 1944-45. Mem. Ark. Jud. Council (exec. com. 1963, pres. 1967-68), Nat. Conf. State Trial Judges (Ark. del.), Harrison C. of C. (past dir.), Am. Legion (past dist. comdr.). Methodist. Mason, Rotarian (past pres.), Elk. Home: 522 N Cherry St Harrison AR 72601 Office: Court House Harrison AR 72601

WRIGHT, FLETCHER JOHNSTON, JR., physician; b. Fork Union, Va., Oct. 19, 1910; s. Fletcher J. and Anne (Seay) W.; B.S., U. Richmond, M.D., U. Va., 1934; m. Martha Jeanette Andrews, June 29, 1935; children—Fletcher Johnston, Anne Andrews (Mrs. Edouard B. Steele). Intern, U. Va. Hosp., 1934-35; resident Princeton (W.Va.) Meml. Hosp., 1935-37; pvt. practice, Petersburg, Va., 1937—;

surg. staff Petersburg Hosp., now Petersburg Gen. Hosp., chmn. staff, 1952. Mem. adv. bd. Petersburg Savs. br., also dir. First & Mchts. Nat. Bank. Dir. Va. Blue Shield, 1959-71, pres., 1961-62; mem. bd. Va. Council Health and Med. Care, 1958-64; mem. Va. Study Commn. on Mental Health, 1964, Va. Commn. for Emergency Planning, 1965-66; v.p. Va. Bd. Health, 1967-73, pres., 1973—. Mem. Petersburg City Council, 1968-73, vice mayor, 1970-73. Served from capt. to maj. M.C., AUS, 1942-45; ETO. Mem. Petersburg Med. Faculty (pres. 1946), 4th Dist. Med. Soc. (pres. 1949). Med. Soc. Va. (past exec. com. council, speaker ho. of dels., 1960-62, pres. 1962-63), A.M.A., Am. (state dir. 1955), Va. (pres. 1959-60) acads. gen. practice, Kappa Alpha, Phi Beta Pi. Baptist. Mason. Club: Petersburg Country. Home: 1617 Blair Rd Petersburg VA 23803 Office: 49 S Market St Petersburg 23803

WRIGHT, FRANCIS EVERETT, coll. pres.; b. Dequeen, Ark., Apr. 19, 1915; s. Gerden Gate and Ellen (Beesley) W.; A.B., Baylor U., 1942; M.A., Peabody Coll., 1948, Ed.D. (Algier Sullivan scholar) postgrad. Harvard, 1964; grad. IBM Exec. Computer Course, 1969; m. Mildred Cooper, June 5, 1941; 1 dau., Kay (Mrs. William Stuve). Personnel counselor Northwestern State Coll., Natchitoches, La., 1948-50; dean men Baylor U., Waco, Tex., 1950-52; acad. dean Union U., Jackson, Tenn., 1954-63, pres., 1963-67; pres. Jackson State Community Coll., 1967—. Edn. cons. Child Health Centers Am., 1969—; mem. steering com. Baptist edn. study task force So. Baptist Conv.; mem. Tenn. N.G. Scholarship Com., Programmed Learning for Child Health Centers Am. Com.; chmn. Tenn. Community Coll. President's Council, 1970-71. Mem. policy adv. com. Jackson Civil Def., 1963-68; hon. adv. com. Boys Club of Jackson. Bd. dirs. United Fund, pres., 1971; chmn. bd. dirs. Jackson Rainbow Girls; pres. bd. dirs. Jackson Symphony Orch.; bd. dirs. East Jackson Devel. Council, Jackson Arts Council, Jackson Community Concert, Jackson-Madison County chpt. A.R.C., Jackson-Madison County Diabetic Unit Council; trustee Midwestern Theol. Sem., 1965—, mem. exec. com., 1969—. Served from 1st lt. to maj., USAAF, 1943-46. Recipient Grand Cross Colors, Tenn. Rainbow Girls, 1959—. Mem. Nat. Assn. Higher Edn., Am. Sociol. Soc., Nat. Assn. Student Teaching, N.E.A., Am. Assn. Student Personnel Adminstrs., Jackson Area C. of C. (dir.), So. Assn. Jr. Colls. (exec. com.), Tenn. Jr. Coll. Athletic Assn. (exec. com. 1969-70), Tenn., West Tenn. edn. assns., Phi Delta Kappa, Kappa Sigma. Baptist. Rotarian. Club: West Tenn. Executive (Jackson). Home: PO Box 3254 Jackson TN 38301

WRIGHT, FRANCIS FOLEY, petroleum engring. exec.; b. Port, Okla., Nov. 25, 1911; s. Daniel Proctor and Martha Emma (Foley) W.; A.B., Central State U., 1932; B.S., U. Okla., 1940; grad. Exec. Devel. Program U. Mich., 1958; m. Marion Ernestine Stoker, May 20, 1934; children—Elizabeth (Mrs. David A. Frawley), Martha (Mrs. Benjamin F. Whitney), James. Engring. supr. Sinclair Oil & Gas Co., Oklahoma City, Tulsa, 1938-57, prodn. mgr., Tulsa and Midland, Tex., 1958-61; exec. mgmt. Sinclair Internat., Paris, Brussels, N.Y.C., 1962-69; dist. engr. Atlantic Richfield, Tulsa, 1970—. Named Distinguished Former student Central State U., 1965. Mem. Soc. Petroleum Engrs., Nat. Soc. Profl. Engrs., Am. Petroleum Inst., Tau Beta Pi, Sigma Tau. Mem. Christian Ch. Mason. Club: Tulsa. Home: 8706 E 27th St Tulsa OK 74129 Office: PO Box 521 Tulsa OK 74102

WRIGHT, HELEN MITCHELL PATTON (MRS. J. SKELLY WRIGHT), civic worker; b. Washington, Jan. 15, 1919; d. Raymond Stanton and Virginia (Mitchell) Patton; student Sweet Briar Coll., 1936-38; m. J(ames) Skelly Wright, Feb. 1, 1945; 1 son, James Skelly. Tchr., Washington Sch. for Secretaries, N.Y.C., 1939-40; sec. White House, Washington, 1941-43; sec. to minister econ. warfare Am. embassy, London, Eng., 1943-45; asst. to exec. dir. Senate AEC, U.S. Capitol, Washington, 1946-47. Vice pres. United Fund, New Orleans, 1960-62, Dept. Pub. Welfare, New Orleans, 1954-62, Milne Asylum for Destitute Orphan Boys, 1958-62; mem. Social Welfare Planning Council, New Orleans, 1954-60; v.p. La. Assn. Mental Health, 1960-62. Bd. dirs. Washington Health and Welfare Council, 1962-64, D.C. Assn. Mental Health, 1962-72; Hillcrest Children's Center, 1963-69; dir.-at-large Nat. Assn. Mental Health, 1962-68, 69—, sec., 1968-70, v.p., 1970-71, pres., 1972-73. Home: 5317 Blackistone Washington DC 20016

WRIGHT, JAMES C., JR., congressman; b. Ft. Worth, Dec. 22, 1922; s. James C. and Marie (Lyster) W.; student Weatherford Coll., U. Tex.; m. Betty Hay, Nov. 12, 1972; children by previous marriage—Jimmy, Virginia Sue, Patricia Kay, Alicia Marie. Mem. Tex. Ho. of Reps., 1947-49; mayor City of Weatherford (Tex.), 1950-54; mem. 84th-93d congresses from 12th Tex. Dis., dep. Democratic whip, chmn. pub. works subcom. on investigations and rev. Chmn., Commn. on Hwy. Beautification; mem. Nat. Commn. Water Quality; mem. Ho. of Reps. delegation to U.S. Mexico Interparliamentary Conf., 1963-73. Served with USAAF, World War II. Decorated D.F.C., Legion of Merit; named outstanding young man Tex. Jr. C. of C., 1953. Mem. League Tex. Municipalities (pres. 1953). Presbyn. Author: You and Your Congressman, 1965; The Coming Water Famine, 1966; Of Swords and Plowshares, 1968; co-author Congress and Conscience, 1970. Address: House Office Bldg Washington DC 20515

WRIGHT, JAMES ROBERT, clergyman; b. Iowa Park, Tex., Apr. 6, 1925; s. James Robert and Bonnie (Eddleman) W.; B.A., Tex. Christian U., 1948. B.D., 1950, D.D., 1968; m. Jeanette Myrick, Sept. 12, 1944; children—James Robert III, Jean Elizabeth. Ordained to ministry Christian Ch., 1949; minister Oaks Christian Ch., Houston, 1951-58. First Christian Ch., Fulton, Mo., 1958-61, First Christian Ch., Port Arthur, Tex., 1961—. Mem. adv. com. Port Arthur Community Home, 1971-72; mem. Jefferson County Child Welfare Bd., 1965—. Bd. dirs. S. Jefferson County Mental Health Assn.; trustee Tex. Christian U. Served with USAAF, 1943-45. Recipient award for outstanding leadership Tex. Christian U. Alumni Assn., 1971. Mem. Port Arthur Ministerial Alliance (pres. 1971). Brite Div. Sch. Alumni Assn. (pres. 1971-72). Mason (K.T.), Rotarian (pres. 1974—). Home: 241 4th Av Port Arthur TX 77640 Office: 620 Woodworth Blvd Port Arthur TX 77640

WRIGHT, JAMES SKELLY, judge; b. New Orleans, Jan. 14, 1911; s. James Edward and Margaret (Skelly) W.; Ph.B., Loyola U., 1931, LL.B., 1934; LL.D., Yale, 1961, U. Notre Dame, 1962, Howard U., 1964; m. Helen Mitchell Patton, Feb. 1, 1945; 1 son, James Skelly. Tchr. high sch. 1931-35; lectr. English history Loyola U., 1936-37; admitted to U.S. Supreme Ct. bar; asst. U.S. atty., New Orleans, 1937-46; U.S. atty. East Dist. La., 1948-49, U.S. dist. judge, 1949-62; U.S. circuit judge for D.C., 1962—. Mem. faculty Loyola U. Sch. Law, 1950-62; James Madison lectr. N.Y.U., 1965; Robert L. Jackson lectr. Nat. Coll. State Trial Judges, 1966; lectr. series on law and free soc. U. Tex., 1967; Frank Irvine lectr. Cornell U., 1968; Brainerd Currie lectr. Duke, 1970; mem. com. on ct. adminstrn., chmn. subcom. on fed. jurisdiction Jud. Conf. U.S.; observer U.S. State Dept. Internat. Fisheries Conf., London, 1943. Served as lt. comdr. USCGR, 1942-45. Mem. Am., Fed. (pres. New Orleans), La. (gov.), New Orleans bar assns., Bar Assn. D.C., Am. Law Inst., Am. Judicature Soc., Blue Key, Alpha Delta Gamma (nat. pres.), Phi Delta Phi (hon.). Roman Catholic. Democrat. Home: 5317 Blackistone Rd Washington DC 20016 Office: US Ct House Washington DC 20001

WRIGHT, JANE ELIZABETH, educator; b. Anderson, S.C., Dec. 21, 1918; d. Alvin McLenna and Elisabeth (Robertson) Wright; A.B., Winthrop Coll., 1940; B.S. in L.S., U. N.C., 1950; M.S., Columbia, 1959. Tchr. pub. schs., Anderson, S.C., 1940-44; clk. Shell Oil Co., N.Y.C., 1944-45; transit clk. Carolina Nat. Bank, Anderson, 1945-46; librarian Boys' High Sch., Anderson, 1946-50; asst. librarian Poly. High Sch., Long Beach, Cal., 1950-51; instr. Winthrop Coll., Rock Hill, S.C., 1951-59, asst. prof. Winthrop Coll., 1959-67; grad. asst. Sch. Library Service, Columbia U., 1958-59; asst. prof. Furman U., Greenville, S.C., 1967-70; asso. prof., 1970-73; librarian Brevard (N.C.) Coll., 1973—; vis. asst. prof. Sch. Library Sci., U. N.C. summers, 1961-66, U. Washington, summer 1961, Columbia, 1968; vis. asst. prof. U. N.C. at Greensboro, summer 1969; mem. Cadmus editorial bd. E.M. Hale Pub. Co. Recipient Grolier Americana scholarship, Sch. of Library Service, Columbia U., 1957; HEA grantee Inst. for Tng. in Librarianship, 1970. Mem. Assn. Am. Library Schs., A.L.A. (council 1972-73), Am. Assn. Sch. Librarians, S.C. Edn. Assn., S.C. (treas. 1961-62), N.C., Southeastern library assns., Altrusa (pres. 1972-73), Beta Phi Mu, Delta Kappa Gamma. Home: Box 1183 Brevard NC 28712

WRIGHT, JOHN HERMAN, JR., dentist; b. Hulbert, Okla., Apr. 30, 1934; s. John Herman and Ocie Mae (Disheroon) W.; student U. Okla., 1951-52, Northeastern State Coll., 1952-55; D.D.S., U. Tenn., 1958; m. Patsy Carolyn Hamilton, Oct. 18, 1958; children—Kimberly Kaye, John Herman III, Sylynn Ann. With Okla. State Health Dept., 1958; pvt. practice dentistry, Wagoner, Okla., 1959—; dir. First Wagoner Bank & Trust Co. City councilman, Wagoner, 1960-64; chmn. County Democratic Party 1964-67, dist. coordinator, 1967-70, del. conv., 1964, 68. Bd. dirs. Grand River Dam Authority, vice-chmn., 1971—. Mem. Okla., Am. dental assns., Eastern Dist. Dental Soc., C. of C. Lion. Home: Rural Route 3 Wagoner OK 74467 Office: 1104 W Cherokee St Wagoner OK 74467

WRIGHT, JOHN RICHARD, hotel co. exec.; b. Washington, Jan. 23, 1942; s. John Charles and Gladys Bell (Hartle) W.; student Old Dominion Coll., 1960-66; m. Inabelle Marlene Phillips, Apr. 17, 1965. Owner, operator South Gate Motor Hotel, Inc., Arlington, Va., 1957-61; partner John C. Wright & Son, Leesburg, Va., 1964—; owner, operator Quality Motel Lake Wright, Norfolk, Va., 1964—, Lake Wright Golf Course, 1966—, Country Club Apts., Leesburg, 1970—, Quality Inn, Leesburg, Va., 1972—; sec. Tuscarora, Inc., Leesburg, 1968—. Treas., coach Loudoun County Boy's Midget Football League, Leesburg, 1969—; mem. Loudoun County Parks and Recreation Bd., 1972—, Loudoun County Tourism and Econ. Devel. Com., 1973—. Bd. dirs. John C. Wright Found. Mem. Loudoun County C. of C. (dir.). Presbyn. Optimist, Kiwanian (pres. 1973). Club: Cosmopolitan (Norfolk). Home: 1 Orr Circle Leesburg VA 22075 Office: PO Box 1338 Leesburg VA 22075

WRIGHT, LOUIS CHARLES, judge; b. Gadsden, Ala., May 14, 1922; s. Louis Clifford and Elizabeth (McBrayer) W.; B.S., Auburn U., 1943; LL.B., U. Ala., 1948; m. Maxine McClendon Wright, Mar. 24, 1944; children—Adele (Mrs. Joseph Miller), Louis Charles II, Dennis McClendon. Admitted to Ala. State bar, 1948; pvt. practice law, Gadsden, Ala., 1948-69; dist. atty. Sixteenth Judicial Circuit Ala., 1955-63; mem. Ala. House Reps., 1967-69; presiding judge Ala. Ct. Civil Appeals, Montgomery, 1969—. Served with USNR, 1943-46. Mem. Ala., Am. bar assns., Ala. Defense Lawyers Assn., Etowah County Bar Assn., V.F.W., Am. Legion. Gadsden C. of C., Phi Alpha Delta. Democrat. Baptist. Mason. Club: Internat. Lions. Home: 2347 Wentworth Dr Montgomery AL 36106 Office: Presiding Judge Court of Civil Appeals Judicial Bldg Montgomery AL 36102

WRIGHT, MADISON BROWN, JR., lawyer, ins. co. exec.; b. Orange, Tex., Aug. 29, 1936; s. Madison Brown and Mary Elizabeth (Phillips) W.; student Washington and Lee U., 1954-55, Georgetown U. Sch. Langs. and Linguistics, 1955; B.A., So. Meth. U., 1958, J.D., 1961; m. Lucile Katherine Jones, June 30, 1962; children—Madison Brown III, Katherine Helen. Asst. doorkeeper U.S. Senate, Washington, summers 1955, 56; admitted to Tex. bar; asso. firm Benckenstein and Benckenstein, Beaumont, Tex., 1961-63; asso. Thad Davis, Freeport, Tex., 1963-65; individual practice law, Lake Jackson, Tex., 1965-70; claims counsel Stewart Title Guaranty Co., Co., Houston, 1970—; dir. Brazosport Abstract Co., Freeport, 1967-70; instr. real estate Brazosport Jr. Coll., Freeport, 1968. Instl. rep. explorer scouts Bay Area Council Boy Scouts Am., 1965-68; pres. Brazosport Youth Employment Program, Inc., 1965-70; asst. sec. Brazosport Vocational Student Loan Fund, Inc., 1969-70; chmn. Brazoria County chpt. Nat. Found.-March of Dimes, 1968-70; Lake Jackson chmn. United Fund Brazoria County, 1970; mem. Meml. N.W. Homeowners' Assn., 1971—, parliamentarian, 1973; membership co-chmn. local P.T.A., 1972-73. Precinct chmn. Democratic party, Brazoria County, 1970-71. Bd. dirs. Jr. Achievement Brazoria County, 1968-69, Brazoria County Youth Homes, Inc., 1967-71. Served with USMCR, 1959. Recipient Distinguished Service award U.S. Jaycees, 1969. Mem. State Bar Tex., Am., Brazoria County (sec.-treas. 1964-65, v.p. 1965-66), Houston bar assns., Beta Theta Pi, Alpha Phi Omega, Phi Delta Phi. Episcopalian (vestryman, del. Diocesan council 1972—). Mason (32 deg., K.T.). Clubs: Memorial Northwest. Home: 8002 Beaufort Dr PO Box 214 Spring TX 77373 Office: 2200 West Loop South PO Box 2029 Houston TX 77001

WRIGHT, MARVIN EUGENE, JR., librarian; b. Alexandria, La., Sept. 4, 1936; s. Marvin Eugene and Yvonne (Gravel) W.; B.A., Northwestern State Coll., 1959; M.L.S., La. State U., 1961; J.D., Loyola U. of South, 1974; m. Diana Jane Smith, Aug. 21, 1963; children—Gene Christopher, Amy Carroll. Tchr. Port Sulphur (La.) High Sch., 1959-60; reference librarian Queensboro (N.Y.) Pub. Library, 1961-62; librarian Jackson Parish (La.), Jonesboro, 1962-63; dir. Scottsdale (Ariz.) Pub. Library, 1964-65; asst. librarian New Orleans Pub. Library, 1966-67, librarian, 1967—. Mem. Young Men's Bus. Club, Phi Kappa Phi. Kiwanian. Home: 2124 Gibson St Gretna LA 70053 Office: New Orleans Pub Library 219 Loyola Av New Orleans LA 70140

WRIGHT, MELTON FISHER, supt. schs.; b. Charleston, S.C., Aug. 9, 1922; s. Harold Edward and Marion (Millar) W.; A.B., Bob Jones U., 1945, LL.D., 1961; M.Ed., U. Va., 1951; m. Betty Gearing, Aug. 31, 1945; children—David G., Frank E. Prin., W.H. Keister Sch., Harrisburg, Va., 1951-56, Harrisburg High Sch., 1956-58; dir. instrn. Frederick County, Va., 1958-66, asst. supt., 1966-68, supt. schs., Winchester, 1968—. Mem. Va. Supt. Schs. Adv. Com. Pres., Community Chest, Winchester, 1965. Bd. dirs. Lord Fairfax Community Coll. Kettering Found. fellow, 1970. Mem. No. Va. Div. Supts. Assn. (pres. 1974), Va. Edn. Assn. (pres. 1969), Phi Delta Kappa, Kappa Delta Pi. Club: Stonewall Ruritan (Winchester, Va.). Author: Giant for God, 1951, Into the Light, 1955, Beloved Schoolmaster, 1958, Fortress of Faith, 1960, Thoughts on Education, 1966. Home: PO Box 221 Winchester VA 22601 Office: 36 Whitlock Av Winchester VA 22601

WRIGHT, MURIEL HAZEL, historian; b. Lehigh, Indian Ty.; d. Eliphalet Nott and Ida Belle (Richards) Wright; grad. E. Central State Normal, Ada, Okla., 1912; postgrad. Barnard Coll., Columbia, 1916-17; L.H.D., Oklahoma City U., 1964. Tchr. high sch. and elementary sch. Johnston and Coal counties (Okla.), 1912-24; hist. researcher, writer state histories and articles Okla. Hist. Soc., 1924—, editor The Chronicles of Oklahoma, editor, 1955-73. Mem. hist. adv. panel Gov.'s Council for Cultural Devel., 1964; pres. Nat. Hall of Fame for Famous Am. Indians, Anadarko, Okla., 1965—; mem. Okla. bd. geog. names Okla. Geol. Survey, 1965. Recipient Distinguished Service citation U. Okla., 1948; MacDowell Club award, 1948; named Woman of Year, Oklahoma City Bus. and Profl. Women, 1951; named to Okla. Hall of Fame, 1940; Matrix award Theta Sigma Phi, 1941. Mem. Women in Communications Oklahoma City, Nat. League Am. Pen Women (pres. Oklahoma City br. 1962-64), Am. Historians, Oklahoma City Civil War Round Table (pres. 1963-64), Am. State and Local History, So. Hist. Assn., Soc. Mayflower Descs., U.D.C., D.A.R., Colonial Dames XVII Century, Okla. Hist. Society (hon. life), Alpha Gamma Delta, Delta Kappa Gamma (hon.). Presbyn. Clubs: Red Bud, Women's Dinner, Westerner's Indian Terr. Women's Posse. Author: A Guide to the Indian Tribes of Oklahoma, 1951; The Story of Oklahoma, 1929; Our Oklahoma, 1939; The Oklahoma History, 1955; (with J.B. Thoburn) Oklahoma: A History of the State and Its People, 1929; (with George H. Shirk) Rambler in Oklahoma, 1956; (W. LeRoy H. Fischer) Civil War Sites in Oklahoma, 1967. Address: 7109 NW 14th St Oklahoma City OK 73127

WRIGHT, NATHANIEL LANCASTER, JR., mfg. co. exec.; b. Opelika, Ala., Mar. 29, 1933; s. Nathaniel Lancaster and Marjorie Evelyn (Ramsey) W.; B.Indsl. Mgmt., Auburn U., 1959. Plant engr. Oxford Mfg. Co., Luverne, Ala., 1959-61, plant mgr., Tupelo, Miss., 1962-64; gen. mgr. mfg. Empire Mfg. Co., Winder, Ga., 1964-72; pres. Wright-O-Matic Engring. Corp., Winder, 1968—; cons. gen. mgr. Foster Co., Greenville, Ala., 1973—. Served with USNR, 1953-55 Mem. Am. Apparel Mfrs. Assn. V.F.W., Am. Legion. Republican. Methodist. Elk. Patentee in field. Home: 3567 Carterhill Rd Montgomery AL 36111

WRIGHT, NEEL ALLIE, petrochem. co. exec.; b. Burkburnett, Tex., Mar. 4, 1924; s. Earl Albert and Fannie Lee (Neel) W.; student North Tex. Agrl. Coll., 1942; m. Hazel Jane Libengood, Dec. 19, 1944; children—Lewis Earl, Mark Edward, Jeffery Alan, Carl Neel. With El Paso Natural Gas Co., Oil Center and Jal, N.M., also Midkiff, Tex., 1947-57; with El Paso Products, Odessa, Tex., 1957—, mgr. utility and pollution control, 1970—. Served with USNR, 1943-47, 51-52. Baptist (deacon 1967-74). Mason; mem. Order Eastern Star, Kiwanian (pres. 1970). Home: 1211 E 43d St Odessa TX 79762 Office: Box 3986 Odessa TX 79760

WRIGHT, PETER, labor mgmt. adviser; b. N.Y.C., Jan. 21, 1934; s. Stuyvesant Bayard and Rebecca Addison (Holland) W.; student U. of South, 1952-53, George Washington U., 1953-56, 62-63; m. Carolann Wright, 1956; children—Peter, Andrew S., Edward Stuyvesant. Air Force account Underwood Corp., CIA, Washington, 1953-56; with 1st Fed. Savs. & Loan Assn., Alexandria, Va., 1955; asst. exec. mgr. Truck Body & Equipment Assn., 1956-57; owner, operator Bayard's Bend Farm, 1957-61; pres., dir. Bayard's Bend Farms, Inc., 1960—; dir. supervisory tng. U.S. Dept. Agr., 1961-62, organizational and staffing analyst, 1963-66, personnel staffing specialist, chief tech. services section Far East personnel AID, Washington, 1966-68; supervisory personnel officer Office Personnel and Manpower, Washington, 1968; labor-mgmt. adviser Am. Fedn. Govt. Employees, 1968-69, asst. dir. labor mgmt. dept., chief regulations rev., 1969-71; personnel mgmt., labor relations specialist U.S. Dept. Commerce, Rockville, Md., 1971-73; labor relations specialist Nat. Park Service, Dept. Interior, Washington, 1973—. Vice pres. Belmont Civic Assn., 1965-66; pres. Mason Neck Citizens' Assn., 1972-73. Campaign mgr. City of Alexandria, 1956; city committeeman, 1955-57; v.p. No. Va. Young Republicans, 1956-57; del. state Rep. conv., 1956; Rep. co-committeeman, 1969-71. Mem. Am. Soc. Pub. Adminstrn., Soc. Fed. Labor Relations Profls., Am. Church Union, Am. Guernsey Breeders Assn., Phila. Assemblies, Old Gaffers' Assn. Episcopalian. Toastmaster (ednl. v.p. 1971-72). Home: 10904 Belmont Blvd Lorton VA 22079 Office: Br Labor Relations Nat Park Service 1100 L St NW Washington DC 20240

WRIGHT, PHILLIP DALE, lawyer; b. Gorman, Tex., July 29, 1940; s. W.A. and Mary Vista (Wright) W.; B.S., Central State U., 1963, J.D., Oklahoma City, U., 1967; m. Linda F. Pierce, Sept. 22, 1960; 1 son, Thorold William. Mgr. land dept. Big Chief Drilling Co., Oklahoma City, 1961-68; admitted to Okla. bar, 1967; gen. practice law, Edmond, Okla., 1968—. Part time instr. Central State U., 1971. Mem. Am., Okla., Okla. County bar assns., Am., Okla. trial lawyers assns., Okla., Municipal Judges Assn., Edmond C. of C. (pres. elect 1973-74). Home: 3004 Kelsey Dr Edmond OK 73034 Office: Box 202 Edmond OK 73034

WRIGHT, R(ALEIGH) LEWIS, neurosurgeon; b. Roanoke, Va., Apr. 16, 1931; s. Raleigh Lewis and Mary Lillian (Major) W.; B.A., U. Richmond, 1951; M.D., Med. Coll. Va., 1955; m. Sarah Bird Grant, Sept. 7, 1963; 1 son, Alexander Grant. Intern, Duke U. Hosp., 1955-56, surg. resident, 1956-57; neurosurg. resident Mass. Gen. Hosp., Boston, 1959-63; practice medicine specializing in neurosurgery, Boston, 1964-70, Richmond, Va., 1970—; mem. staff St. Mary's, Retreat, Richmond Meml., Stuart Circle, Grace hosps., Med. Coll. Va.; faculty Harvard Med. Sch., Boston, 1962-70; asst. clin. prof. neurosurgery Med. Coll. Va., 1970—. Served with M.C., USNR, 1957-59. King Trust Fund fellow, 1963-64. Diplomate Am. Bd. Neurol. Surgery, Nat. Bd. Med. Examiners. Fellow A.C.S.; mem. A.M.A., Am. Fedn. Clin. Research, Harvey Cushing Soc., Congress Neurol. Surgeons, Southern Neurosurg. Soc., Microcirculatory Soc., English-Speaking Union, Am. Acad. Neurology, Med. Soc. Va. Assn. for Research in Nervous and Mental Diseases, Richmond Acad. Medicine, Am. Assn. History Medicine. Episcopalian. Club: Salisbury Country. Author: Postoperative Craniotomy Infections, 1966; Septic Complications of Neurosurgical Spinal Procedures, 1970. Contbr. articles to profl. jours. Home: 3505 Old Gun Rd Midlothian VA 23113 Office: 4908 Monument Av Richmond VA 23230

WRIGHT, RICHARD GLENN, financial cons. co. exec.; b. Palestine Tex., Mar. 30, 1929; s. Robinson H. and Mattie L. (Spruill) W.; student Sam Houston State Coll., 1946-48, U. Houston, 1955-59; m. Grace Marie Everts, Dec. 30, 1948; children—Rebecca Lynn, Edie Anne. Accounting supr. Superior Oil Co., 1949-53; ins. auditor Cravens Dargan & Co., 1948-49; with Tenneco, Inc., Houston, 1955-68, banking mgr., 1961-64, asst. treas. subsidiary Tenneco Oil Co., 1964-66, treas., 1966-68; asst. treas. Ashland Oil & Refining Co., (Ky.), 1968-71, also internat. treas.; owner, mgr. R.G. Wright and Co., internat. financial consultants, Houston, 1971-72; v.p. finance, treas. Reed Tool Co., Houston, 1972-73; pres. R.G. Wright Financial Cons. Co., 1973—. Served with AUS, 1953-55. Mem. Am. Petroleum Inst., Am. Mgmt. Assn., U. Houston Coll. Bus Alumni Assn., Nat Assn. Accountants, Internat. Platform Assn. Home: 17906 Canyon Creek St Houston TX 77090 Office: Katy Freeway Houston TX 77002

WRIGHT, ROBERT ERNEST, mfg. co. exec.; b. Oconto, Wis., Nov. 28, 1917; s. Ernest William and Rheua (Nickey) W.; B.S. in Mech. Engring., U. Wis., 1940; m. Janet Christie, Feb. 20, 1943; children—Anne E., William C., Richard C., Robert C. With Monsanto Chem. Co., 1940-51, 64-66, project engr., St. Louis, 1945-47, asst. mgr. design sect., 1947-51, dir. process design, mgmt., internat. engr.,

1964-66; with Chemstrand Corp., 1952-64, dir. engring. and devel., Pensacola, Fla., 1958-62, dir. engring., Decatur, Ala., 1962-64; v.p. engring. Wheeling-Pitts. Steel Corp. (formerly Wheeling Steel Corp.) (W.Va.), 1966-69, v.p. corporate devel., 1969-71; chmn. bd. Black Diamond Enterprises, Inc., Bristol, Va., 1972—, also dir.; dir. Cabana Coach Corp., Portland, Ore. Mem. Am. Soc. M.E., Am. Inst. Chem. Engrs., Nat. Soc. Profl. Engrs., Am. Iron and Steel Inst., Am. Iron and Steel Engrs. Presbyn. (elder). Office: Box 151 Bristol VA 24201

WRIGHT, THOMAS HENRY, bishop; b. Wilmington, N.C., Oct. 16, 1904; s. John Maffitt and Josie Young (Whitaker) W.; A.B., U. of South, 1926, D.D., 1946; B.D., Va. Theol. Sem., Alexandria, 1930, D.D., 1946; D.D., Washington and Lee U., 1940, U. N.C., 1965; ; m. Hannah Hagans Knowlton, Dec. 1, 1937; children—Thomas Henry, Hannah K., James K., John M. Clk., Standard Oil Co. of N.J., Wilmington, 1926-27; ordained to ministry P.E. Ch., 1929; nat. acting sec. of coll. work P.E. Ch., 1933-34; Episcopal chaplain U. N.C., 1931-32, Va. Mil. Inst., 1934-41, Washington and Lee U., 1934-41; rector Robert E, Lee Meml. Ch., Lexington, Va., 1934-41; dean Grace Cathedral, San Francisco, 1941-43; rector St. Mark's Ch., San Antonio, 1943-45; consecrated bishop Diocese of East Carolina, St. James Ch., Wilmington, N.C., 1945—. Rep. of U.S. to World Christian Student Fed. Meeting, Holland, 1932; regional dir. Ch. Soc. for Coll. Work; asso. mem. Forward movement Commn., P.E. Church; chmn. overseas dept. Nat. Council Episcopal Ch.; pres. 4th province Episcopal Ch., 1968—. Trustee U. of South, Va. Sem. Mem. Sigma Nu (former grand chaplain), Sigma Upsilon, Alpha Phi Epsilon, Omicron Delta Kappa (hon.). Democrat. Contbr. articles to profl. jours. Address: Route 1 Box 593 Wilmington NC 28401

WRIGHT, THOMAS WILLIAM DUNSTAN, architect; b. Grand Hotel, Rome, Italy, Jan. 12, 1919; s. Charles Will and Helen Bree (Dunstan) W.; grad. cum laude St. Albans Sch., 1937; A.B. with merit, Harvard, 1941, B.Arch., 1950, M.Arch., 1970; m. Penelope Ladd, Aug. 6, 1942; children—Peter William Dunstan, Felicity, Allegra. Designer, Joseph Saunders, A.I.A., Alexandria, Va., 1950; with Leon Brown, Washington, 1950-53; partner Brown and Wright, architects, Washington, 1953—. Vice chmn. D.C. Commn. on Arts, 1969-72 Met. Washington Planning and Housing Assn., 1955; mem. Commr.'s Planning and Urban Renewal Adv. Council, 1965-68; D.C. Bicentennial Assembly, 1971—. Served to lt. comdr. USAAF, 1941, USNR, 1942-46. Fellow A.I.A. (pres. Washington-Met. chpt. 1969); mem. Soc. Archtl. Historians, Am. Arbitration Assn. (arbitrator 1965—). Club: Cosmos. Contbr. articles to profl. pubs. Home: 4564 Indian Rock Terrace NW Washington DC 20007 Office: 1640 Wisconsin Av NW Washington DC 20007

WRIGHT, WILSON WALKER, lawyer, state ofcl.; b. Washington, Jan. 26, 1930; s. Chester Maynard and June (Walker) W.; student U. Fla., 1948-52; LL.B., U. Miami, 1954; certificate Fla. State U., 1960; m. Patricia Anne Davis, May 14, 1955; children—Randahl June, Lee Anne. Admitted to Fla. bar, 1954; asst. state's atty. gen. State of Fla., Tallahassee, 1957—. Past pres. Leon County Cancer Soc. pres. Leon High Sch. P.T.A., 1973. Past pres. Young Democrats Leon County; state pres. Young Dem. Clubs Fla., 1961-62. Served from 2d lt. to capt., USAF, 1954-57. Named One of Fla.'s 5 Outstanding Young Men, 1961; recipient Good Govt. award Talahassee Jr. C. of C., 1967. Mem. Am., Fla. Govt. bar assns., Fla. Bar, U.S. (past dir.), Fla. (past sec., past editor news), Tallahassee (past pres.) jr. chambers commerce, Sigma Alpha Epsilon, Phi Alpha Delta, Alpha Kappa Psi. Democrat. Kiwanian (past pres. Tallahassee, lt. gov. Fla.). Elk. Contbr. articles to profl. jours. Home: 3375 E Lakeshore Dr Tallahassee FL 32303 Office: 217 S Adams St Tallahassee FL 32304

WU, CHANGSHENG, geophysicist; b. Liaoning, China, Oct. 3, 1923; s. Dee and Jen Shan (Liang) W.; came to U.S., 1945, naturalized, 1954; B.S., U. Tex., 1947; M.A., Rice U., 1963, Ph.D., 1966; m. Judy Tsu, Oct. 25, 1955; children—Johnston L., Constance C. Seismologist, United Geophys. Co., Pasadena, Cal., 1947-52, Precision Exploration Co., Houston, 1953-56; seismic prospecting expert UN, Taiwan, China, 1957-60; teaching asst. Rice U., Houston, 1962-65; research geophysicist Mandrel Industries, Houston, 1965-66; sr. research geophysicist Western Geophys. of Litton Industries, Houston, 1966—. Served with Chinese Army, 1944-46. Mem. I.E.E.E., Soc. Exploration Geophysicists, Canadian, European socs. exploration geophysicists, Sigma Xi. Home: 6522 Redding St Houston TX 77036 Office: 8100 Westpark Dr Houston TX 77042

WUKASCH, MARTIN CHARLES, state ofcl.; b. Austin, Tex., Feb. 20, 1915; s. George Charles and Emma (Hannusch) W.; B. Chem. Engring., U. Tex., 1941; M.S. in pub. health engring. Ga. Inst. Tech., 1950; m. Winifred Ruth Faubion, Sept. 28, 1937; children—Charles, Kenneth, James, Jan. Analyt. chemist Shell Chem. Co., Houston, 1941-42; ordnance research engr. U.S. War Dept., Aberdeen Proving Ground, Md., 1942-45; environmental health engr. Tex. Health Dept., Austin, 1945-48, chief indsl. hygiene sect., 1948-50, chief engr. div. occupational health and radiation control, 1950-60, chief Tex. Radiation Control Agy., 1960-70, dir., 1970—. Mem. faculty U. Tex. Postgrad. Sch. Medicine, 1960—. Bd. dirs. Tex. Luth. Soc. Services. Registered profl. engr., Tex.; certified Bd. Health Physics, Safety Profl. Bd. Fellow Am. Pub. Health Assn. (chmn. radiol. health sect. 1972-73); mem. Am. Acad. Environmental Engrs., Health Physics and Safety Profls. (diplomate indsl. hygiene), Tex. Pub. Health Assn., Travis County, Nat., Tex. socs. profl. engrs., Austin Council on Alcoholism (v.p. 1960-64), Health Physics Soc., Soc. Nuclear Medicine, Southwestern Soc. Nuclear Medicine (2d v.p. 1974-75), Am. Indsl. Hygiene Assn. Home: 6457 Hart Lane Austin TX 78731 Office: 1100 W 49th St Austin TX 78756

WURF, JERRY, labor union ofcl.; b. N.Y.C., May 18, 1919; s. Sigmund and Lena (Tannenbaum) W.; A.B., N.Y.U., 1940; m. Mildred Kiefer, Nov. 26, 1960; children—Susan, Nicholas S., Abigail. Employed in cafeteria, N.Y.C., 1940-43; an organizer local 448 Hotel and Restaurant Employees, 1943, organizer, adminstr. union's Welfare Fund, 1947; organizer in N.Y. for Am. Fedn. State, County and Municipal Employees, 1948-58, exec. dir. dist. council 37, 1959-64, internat. pres., 1964—; lectr. indsl. relations problems Cornell U. Sch. Labor and Indsl. Relations, 1964-70; mem. exec. council AFL-CIO. Trustee Inst. Politics and Planning; mem. exec. com. Com. for Nat. Health Ins., Leadership Conf. on Civil Rights; mem. project adv. com. Washington Center for Met. Studies; co-chmn. urban coalition Panel on Equal Housing Opportunity; co-founder Coalition Am. Employees; mem. exec. bd. Ams. for Democratic Action. Mem. Am. Arbitration Assn. (dir.), Council Fgn. Relations. Home: 3846 Cathedral Av NW Washington DC 20016 Office: 1155 15th St NW Madison Bldg Washington DC 20005

WURZ, JOHN ARNOLD, architect; b. Clarksdale, Miss., Feb. 11, 1936; s. Arnold George and Mildred (Whittle) W.; B.S., Ga. Inst. Tech., 1958, B.Arch., 1959; m. Sally Cooper Fortson, Mar. 20, 1958 (div. July 21, 1973); children—Valli Elizabeth, Susan Priscilla, John Arnold; m. 2d, Janice Beachaump, Dec. 22, 1973. Project mgr. Rich's, Inc., Atlanta, 1962-63; project mgr. Heery & Heery Architects & Engrs., Atlanta, 1963-65, asso. architect, 1965-67, partner, 1967—. Served to capt. USAF, 1959-62. Registered architect, 17 states. Mem. Atlanta Art Assn., Bldg. Research Inst., Ga. Indsl. Devel. Assn., Ga. Tech. Alumni Assn., A.I.A., Sigma Nu Alumni Assn. Club: Cherokee Town and Country. Home: PO Box 7095 Atlanta GA 30309 Office: 880 W Peachtree St NW Atlanta GA 30309

WUST, CARL JOHN, educator, microbiologist; b. Providence, July 2, 1928; s. Louis August and Ida (Jauernig) W.; B.S., Providence Coll., 1950; M.S., Brown U., 1953; Ph.D., Ind. U., 1957; postgrad. (NIH fellow), Yale, 1957-59; m. Barbara Marion Russin, Sept. 5, 1951; children—Carl John, Stephen Louis, Catherine Joanne, Gregory Harold, Elizabeth Diane. Biologist biology div. Oak Ridge Nat. Lab., 1959-70; asso. prof. dept. microbiology U. Tenn., Knoxville, 1970—. Pres., Knoxville Council of the Laity, 1972-73. Mem. Am. Soc. Microbiology, Am. Assn. Immunologists, A.A.A.S., Soc. for Exptl. Biology and Medicine, Am. Acad. for Microbiology, Sigma Xi. K.C. (state dep. 1968-70), Elk. Research studies on antibody biosynthesis. Home: 132 Iroquois Rd Oak Ridge TN 37830 Office: Dept of Microbiology Univ Tenn Knoxville TN 37916

WYATT, PHILIP YATEMAN, JR., dentist; b. Charlottesville, Va., Aug. 6, 1907; s. Philip Yateman and Lula (Kersey) W.; student Va. State Coll., 1922-28; D.D.S., Howard U., 1932; m. Minnie Ella Taylor, Oct. 2, 1934; children—Shirley M. (Mrs. Raymond Mundle), Philip Yateman III, Kenneth Mercer. Gen. practice dentistry, Fredericksburg, Va., 1933—, Alexandria, 1957-59; dir. Hazel Hill Apts. Mem. Va. Human Relations Council, 1940—; co-chmn. Fredericksburg Biracial Commn., 1965. Recipient Man of the Year award Omega Phi Psi, 1969; Dentist of the Year award Old Dominion Dental Soc., 1965-69; citation Richmond Civic Council, 1957; certificate of merit Va. Union U., 1957. Mem. Nat. Dental Assn., Old Dominion Dental Soc. (pres. 1954-57, treas. 1957—), Fredericksburg Dental Soc., N.A.A.C.P. (state pres. 1957-58, city pres. 1957—), Va. Bapt. Tng. Union (pres. 1948-58, chmn. bd. dirs. 1958-62), Bapt. Gen. Conv. Va. (sec. bd. dirs. 1946-60), Alpha Phi Alpha. Democrat. Baptist. (chmn. deacon bd. 1940—). Home: 804 Wolfe St Fredericksburg VA 22401 Office: PO Box 393 also 610 Princess Anne St Fredericksburg VA 22401

WYATT, WILLIAM FRANKLIN, JR., apparel co. exec.; b. Burlington, N.C., Dec. 18, 1927; s. William Franklin and Aetna (Walker) W.; B.S., N.C. State U., 1949; m. Peggy Montgomery Von Canon, Oct. 1, 1949; children—Margaret Elizabeth, William Franklin III, John Walker, Kathryn Rebecca. Owner, Beta Hosiery Co., Sanford, N.C., 1942—; with Wyatt Knitting Co., Sanford, 1949—, pres., 1963—. Mem. Sigma Phi Epsilon. Methodist (steward 1949-57). Rotarian (pres. 1964-65), Elk. Clubs: Central Carolina Beagle, Chicora Riders and Saddle (treas. 1971-72), Associate Investors (treas. 1969-70). Home: Route 3 Sanford NC 27330 Office: 1006 Goldsboro Av Sanford NC 27330

WYATT, WILSON WATKINS, lawyer; b. Louisville, Nov. 21, 1905; s. Richard H. and Mary (Watkins) W.; student U. Louisville, 1922-23, J.D., 1927, LL.D., 1948; LL.D. (hon.), Knox Coll., 1945; m. Anne Kinnaird Duncan, June 14, 1930; children—Mary Anne, Nancy Kinnaird, Wilson Watkins. Admitted to bar, 1927; began practice at Louisville; with Garnett & Van Winkle, 1927-32; individually, 1933-35; trial atty. City Louisville, 1934; partner law firm Peter, Heyburn, Marshall & Wyatt, 1935-41; mayor Louisville, 1941-45; housing expediter, adminstr. Nat. Housing Agy., 1946; sr. partner law firm Wyatt, Grafton & Sloss, 1947—; lt. gov. Ky., 1959-63; spl. emissary from Pres. U.S. to Pres. Indonesia for oil negotiations, Tokyo, 1963. Mem. law faculty Jefferson Sch. Law, 1929-35; dir. Roper Pub. Opinion Research Center, Courier Jour. and Louisville Times Co., WHAS, Inc., Standard Gravure Co., Levy Bros., Inc., Forest Farmers Assn. Spl. rep. Bd. Econ. Warfare, North Africa, 1943; chmn. Louisville Met. Area Def. Council (twice awarded Citation of Merit), 1942-45; pres. Am. Soc. Planning Ofcls., 1943-44, Ky. Municipal League, 1944; pres. Am. Municipal Assn., 1945, Louisville Area Devel. Assn., 1944-45; adv. bd. U.S. Conf. Mayors, 1942-45; v.p. Nat. Municipal League, 1945-72, pres., 1973—; mem. Louisville Sinking Fund Commrs., 1936-38; mem. Louisville Com. on Fgn. Relations (chmn. 1940-41); chmn. Ky. Econ. Devel. Commn., 1960-63. Bd. trustees U. Louisville, 1950-58, chmn. 1951-55; Ky. chmn. Treasury adv. com. U.S. Savs. Bonds Program, 1948-55; bd. dirs. Federalism Seventy-Six. First pres. Young Democrats Club, Louisville-Jefferson County; nat. chmn. Jefferson-Jackson Day Dinners, 1948, 49; del.-at-large nat. convs., 1944—; personal campaign mgr. for Adlai E. Stevenson, 1952, 56; mem. Dem. Nat. Com. Ky., 1960-64. Recipient Distinguished Service award U.S. Treasury, 1955; Citizen of Yr. award Louisville Jaycees, 1972. Mem. English Speaking Union U.S. (nat. dir.), Louisville Area C. of C. (pres. 1972), Am., Fed. Communications, Ky. (sec. 1930-34, commr. 1958), Louisville bar assns., Am. Law Inst. Democrat. Presbyn. Rotarian. Clubs: Pendennis, Louisville Country, Jefferson; Century (N.Y.); Nat. Capitol Democratic, Federal City (Washington). Home: 1001 Alta Vista Rd Louisville KY 40205 Office: Citizens Plaza Louisville KY 40202

WYCHE, CYRIL THOMAS, lawyer; b. Greenville, S.C., Jan. 28, 1926; s. Cyril Granville and Mary (Wheeler) W.; B.S. in Engring., Yale, 1946; LL.B., U. Va., 1949; m. Harriet Smith, June 19, 1948; children—Bradford Wheeler, Sara McCall, Mary Frances. Admitted to S.C. bar, 1949, since practiced in Greenville; partner Wyche, Burgess, Freeman & Parham, 1949—. Dir. Citizens & So. Nat. Bank of S.C., 1957—. Pres., YMCA, Greenville Little Theatre, Arts Festival; v.p. Greenville Symphony. Trustee Greenville Found., Naturaland Trust. Served with USNR, 1944-46. Mem. Am., S.C., Greenville bar assns., Omicron Delta Kappa. Rotarian. Clubs: Greenville Country (dir.), Poinsett. Home: 1140 Parkins Mill Rd Greenville SC 29607 Office: 44 E Camperdown Way Greenville SC 29603

WYLAND, BEN F., clergyman; b. Harlan, Ia., Mar. 16, 1882; s. Frank and Mary (Griffith) W.; Ph.B., U. Ia., 1905; B.D., Yale, 1908; M.Div., 1971; Litt.D., Edward Waters Coll., 1954; m. Ada D. Beach, Jan. 14, 1909; children—Gordon B., Hugh C., Robert B., Molly G.; m. 2d, Mildred E. Oeschger, May 5, 1955. Ordained to ministry Congl. Ch., 1908; pastor, Worcester, Mass., 1918-20, Lincoln, Neb., 1926-36, Bklyn., 1936-39; radio pastor Sta. KFAB, 1926-36; exchange pastor to Eng., 1933; in charge ch. relations for Herbert Hoover's Campaign, Food for Small Democracies, 1940-41; exec. sec. United Chs. Greater St. Petersburg (Fla.), 1948-56, Fla. Council Racial Cooperation, St. Petersburg, 1956—. Chmn. Com. To Preserve Negro Rights; founder Negro Girls Welfare Home, St. Petersburg, St. Petersburg Helping Hand for Sr. Citizens; chmn. United Negro Coll. Fund. Recipient citation from Maj. Gen. Philip Hayes, 3d Service Command; B'nai B'rith Brotherhood award, St. Petersburg, 1954; recipient Oscar, Community Chest dr., 1955; citation Met. Council, Inc., 1958; Bethune Cookman Coll., Edward Waters Coll. Mem. Am. Relief Assn. (dir.), Am. Com. Christian Refugees in Bklyn. (exec. sec.), Bklyn. Fedn. Chs., (dir.), Crime Prevention Soc. (dir.), N.Y.C. Assn. Chs. (pres. bd. dirs.), Congl. Ministers (pres.), Americanization Com. (chmn.), Food Commn. (chmn.), Delta Sigma Phi, Alpha Chi Rho. Mason (32 deg., K.T.), Kiwanian. Home: Apt 107 1898 Shore Dr S St Petersburg FL 33707

WYLIE, JAMES EDWARD, elec. engr.; b. St. Louis, Mo., May 24, 1923; s. Ernest L. and Ruth A. (Calmer) W.; B.S., Mo. Sch. Mines and Metallurgy, 1947; postgrad. Washington U., 1963-64; m. Barbara Lee Zerr, June 4, 1949; children—William, Leslie, Patricia, Paul, David. With Southwestern Bell Telephone Co., 1947—, sr. engr., Little Rock, Ark., 1954-59, plant extension engr., St. Louis, 1959-66, Oklahoma City, 1966—. Served with USNR, 1944-46. Mem. Okla. Soc. Profl. Engrs., Nat. Soc. Profl. Engrs., Engring. Club Oklahoma City, I.E.E.E., Am. Radio Relay League, Nat. Radio Inst., Lambda Chi Alpha, Blue Key. Home: 2712 Meridian Pl Oklahoma City OK 73127 Office: 707 N Robinson St Oklahoma City OK 73102

WYNDLE, GERALD ALLEN, electronics engr.; b. Pueblo, Colo., Oct. 28, 1942; s. Patrick Avery and Margaret Marie (Alitto) W.; A.A., So. Colo. State Coll., 1963; B.S., U. Colo., 1965; m. Patricia Lee Gribben, June 11, 1966; children—Lisa Marie, Tonya Ruth. Electronic engr. Naval Tng. Device Center, Orlando, Fla., 1966-69, project engr., 1969-73, electronics engr., 1973—. Mem. I.E.E.E. Club: Toastmasters. Home: 1946 Bonanza Court Winter Park FL 32789 Office: Naval Tng Equipment Center Orlando FL 32813

WYNN, DOW, city ofcl.; b. Dallas, June 5, 1922; s. Dow and Minnie Gertrude (Barthe) Wynn; student Tex. A. and M. U., 1939-42, Lamar U., 1946-47; m. Audrey L. David, Feb. 14, 1948; children—Ronald S., Virginia (Mrs. Pierce L. Frels), Dow III, Janette E. Indsl. dir. Beaumont (Tex.) C. of C., 1947-49; asst. to dir. Port of Houston, 1949-51; indsl. dir. Houston C. of C., 1951-53; asst. port dir. Port of Freeport, 1954-55; dep. dir. Port of Beaumont, 1955-64; founding port dir. Port of Port Arthur, 1964—. Mem. Gov.'s Adv. Com. Marine Resources, 1970-71; Seagrant Adv. Council Tex., 1971—. Trustee United Community Services. Served to maj. AUS, 1942-46. Mem. Gulf Ports Assn. (dir), Tex. Ports Assn. (pres. 1970-71), Am. Assn. Port Authorities. Roman Catholic (Extraordinary Minister of the Eucharist, 1972-73). Lion, Kiwanian. Club: Propellor of U.S. Home: 2500 Crescent St Groves TX 77619 Office: Box 1428 Port Arthur TX 77640

WYNNE, MICHAEL JAMES, educator; biologist, b. St. Louis, Feb. 4, 1940; s. Edward Joseph and Rose Margaret (Kueter) W.; A.B., Washington U., St. Louis, 1962; Ph.D., U. Cal. at Berkeley, 1967. Asst. prof. biology, phycology U. Tex., Austin, 1969-72, asso. prof. dept. botany, 1972—. Mem. corp. Marine Biol. Lab. Mem. Internat., Brit., Japanese phycological socs., Am. Bot. Soc. (Darbaker prize 1971), Phycological Soc. Am. (sec. 1973—); Phi Beta Kappa, Sigma Xi. Home: 3001 Loyola Lane Austin TX

WYSKIDA, RICHARD MARTIN, educator; elec. engr.; b. Perrysburg, N.Y., Sept. 2, 1935; s. Martin Joseph and Mary (Mirek) W.; B.S. in Elec. Engring., Tri-State Coll., 1960; M.S. in Indsl. Engring., U. Ala., 1964; Ph.D., Okla. State U., 1968; m. Betty Jo Long, Sept. 8, 1962; children—Alan R., Carol A. Elec. engr. Philco Corp., Huntsville, Ala., 1960-62; staff engr. NASA Marshall Space Flight Center, Huntsville, 1962-68; asst. prof. indsl. engring. U. Ala., Huntsville, 1968-72, asso. prof., 1972—, chmn. indsl. and systems engring. dept., 1970-72, chmn. computer sci. program, 1972-73. Cons. U.S. Army Missile Command. Registered profl. engr., Ala. Mem. Am. Soc. Engring. Edn., Am. Inst. Indsl. Engrs., Inst. Mgmt. Sci., Operations Research Soc. Am. Roman Catholic. Home: 225 Spring Valley Court Huntsville AL 35802

WYSOCKI, ROBERT KENNETH, educator; b. Detroit, Nov. 20, 1941; s. Theodore Norbert and Eleanor (Kruk) W.; B.A., U. Dallas, 1964; M.S., So. Meth. U., 1968, Ph.D., 1969; m. Nancy Beatrix Stone, Sept. 5, 1964; children—Michael, Leica, Mark, Jennifer. Quality and reliability engr. Tex. Instruments, Inc., Dallas, 1964-70; asst. prof. quantitative methods, dir. computer center N.E. La. U., Monroe, 1970—. Def. Edn. Act fellow, 1966; USN grantee, 1968. Mem. Am. Statis. Assn., Assn. Instl. Research, Data Mgmt. Processing Assn. Home: 2703 Huntington St Monroe LA 71201

YAMBRUSIC, EDWARD SLAVKO, lawyer; b. Conway, Pa., Mar. 9, 1933; s. Michael Misko and Sylvia Slavica (Yambrusic) Y.; B.A., Duquesne U., 1957; postgrad. Georgetown U., 1959-61; J.D., U. Balt., 1966; postgrad. Cath. U. Am., 1966—; certificate The Hague Acad. Internat. Law, 1967, 69, diploma Center Study and Research. Admitted to U.S. Customs Ct., 1970, Md. bar, 1969; practiced before U.S. Immigration and Naturalization Service, N.Y.C., also Washington, 1966—; copyright atty. Library Congress, U.S. Copyright Office, Washington, 1960—. Served to capt. AUS, 1957-59. Mem. Internat. Law Assn., Am. Bar Assn., Am. Soc. Internat. Law, Internal Fiscal Assn., UN Assn., Center for Study Democratic Instns., Croatian Acad. Am., Croatian Cath. Union, Md. Bar Assn., Assn. Attenders Alumni Hague Acad. Internat. Law, Duquesne U. Tamburitzans Alumni Assn., Pi Gamma Mu. Home: 4720 Massachusetts Av NW Washington DC 20016 Office: US Copyright Office Library Congress Washington DC 20540

YANCEY, ASA GREENWOOD, physician; b. Atlanta, Aug. 19, 1916; s. Arthur H. and Daisy L. (Sherard) Y.; B.S., Morehouse Coll., 1937; postgrad. U. Mich., 1941;; m. Carolyn E. Dunbar, Dec. 28, 1944; children—Arthur H. II, Carolyn L., Caren L., Asa Greenwood. Intern City Hosp., Cleve. 1941-42; resident Freedmen's Hosp., Washington, 1942-45, U.S. Marine Hosp., Boston, 1945; practice medicine specializing in surgery, Atlanta, 1958—; asso. dean Emory U. Sch. Medicine; mem. staff Hughes Spalding, St. Joseph, Ga. Bapt. hosps.; med. dir. Grady Meml. Hosp.; instr. surgery Meharry Med. Coll., 1946-48; chief of surgery VA Hosp., Tuskegee, Ala., 1948-58; asst. prof. surgery Emory U., 1968-73, asso. prof., 1973—. Mem. Atlanta Bd. Edn., 1968—. Trustee Ga. chpt. Am. Cancer Soc. Served to 1st lt. M.C., AUS, 1942. Diplomate Am. Bd. Surgery. Fellow A.C.S.; mem. Nat. Med. Assn. (trustee 1960-66, editorial bd. jour. 1964—), Inst. Medicine, Nat. Acad. Scis. Baptist. Contbr. articles to profl. jours. Home: 2845 Engle Rd NW Atlanta GA 30318 Office: Grady Meml Hosp Atlanta GA 30303

YANCEY, EDWIN LOVELL, agrl. agt.; b. Wedowee, Ala., Nov. 18, 1934; s. James David and Eula Pearl (Huey) Y.; B.S., N.C. State U., 1956, M. Adult Edn. (Kellogg fellow), 1969; m. Betty Anne Williford, Nov. 16, 1956; children—Betty Lael, Elaine Huey, Edwin Lovell. Asst. agrl. extension agt. Johnston County, Smithfield, N.C., 1956-61; service and sales mgr. Benson Feed Mills (N.C.), 1961-63; agrl. extension agt., Smithfield, 1963-69; county extension chmn. Pitt County, Greenville, N.C., 1969—. Ex-officio mem. Pitt County Planning Bd., 1971—; adviser to bd. dirs. Coastal Plain Devel. Assn., 1969—; chmn. Pitt County Rural Devel. Panel, 1970—. Mem. N.C. Assn. County Agrl. Agts. (pres.), Epsilon Sigma Phi. Methodist (chmn. adminstrv. bd.). Kiwanian (v.p. local club). Home: 107 Queen Anne's Rd Greenville NC 27834 Office: PO Box 1427 Greenville NC 27834

YANDA, ALFRED DANIEL, cons. civil engr.; b. Cleve., July 21, 1907; s. George Peter and Therese (Jindrich) Y.; student Ohio State U., 1924-25, John Huntington Poly. Inst., 1937-41, Case Inst. Tech., 1941-42; m. Blanche Theresa Warak, May 11, 1929; 1 son, Alfred Daniel II. Draftsman, party chief Carter & Damerow, Vero Beach, Fla., 1925-27; chief hwy. engr. Cuyahoga County, O., 1927-45; engr. of location, design and planning engr., acting div. engr. State of Ohio, 1945-47; prin. engr. Rapid Transit-Cleve. Transit System, 1947-48; chief hwy. engr. Central Viaduct Inner Belt Freeway, Cleve., 1947-50; cons. civil engr., Vero Beach, Fla., 1950—. Dir. supply State Adj.

Gen's Office, Cleve., 1945-49; lectr. civil engring. Fenn Coll., Cleve., 1953-55. Bd. mgrs. YMCA, Cleve., 1955-63. Registered profl. engr., Ohio, Ky., Ind., Ariz., Fla., Hawaii. Fellow Am. Soc. C.E. (life, pres. Cleve. 1951); mem. Nat. Soc. Profl. Engrs., Fla. Engring. Soc. Unitarian. Rotarian. Home: 576 Cypress Rd Vero Beach FL 32960 Office: 612 Beachland Blvd Vero Beach FL 32960

YANDLE, THOMAS BRUCE, JR., educator; b. Lyons, Ga., Aug. 12, 1933; s. Thomas Bruce and Mollye Lomita (Thompson) Y.; student Young Harris Coll., 1951-52; A.B., Mercer U., 1955; M.B.A., Ga. State U., 1968, Ph.D., 1970; m. Dorothy King Smith, Aug. 28, 1954; children—Kathryn, Thomas Bruce III, Eric. Accountant, sales mgr. Bearings & Drives, Inc., Macon, Ga., 1952-59, exec. v.p., Atlanta, 1960-67; asst. prof. to asso. prof. econs. Clemson (S.C.) U., 1969—, head dept. econs., 1972—. Served to 2d lt. AUS, 1956-57. Mem. Assn. Bearing Specialists (dir. 1966-67), Pub. Choice Soc., Am., So. econ. assns., Omicron Delta Epsilon. Methodist (chmn. ofcl. bd. 1967-69). Home: 323 Tamassee Dr Clemson SC 29631

YANG, TONY TIEN SHENG, educator; b. Tainan, Formosa, May 26, 1928; s. Tsang and Shih Y. (Cheng) Y.; B.S., Nat. Taiwan U., 1953; M.S., U. Okla., 1959, Ph.D., 1968; m. Hsiu-Ying Tsai, Aug. 7, 1959; 1 son, Joseph. Came to U.S., 1957. Project engr., Okla. Dept. Hwys., Oklahoma City, 1958-66, sr. structural engr., 1968-70; prof., chmn. civil and mech. engring. program Fed. City Coll., Washington, 1970-73, prof., chmn. dept. engring. and computer sci., 1973—. Registered profl. engr., D.C., Md., Okla. Mem. Am. Soc. C.E., Am. Concrete Inst. Home: 6108 Beach Tree Dr Alexandria VA 22310 Office: 924 E St NW Washington DC 20004

YARBOROUGH, BETTY HATHAWAY, educator; b. Portsmouth, Va.; d. Joseph Samuel and Isabelle (Rountree) Hathaway; student Coll. William and Mary, 1945-46, M.A. in Guidance, 1955, postgrad., 1956-57; B.A. in English, Edn., Duke, 1948; postgrad. U. Miami (Fla.), 1960, Richmond Profl. Inst., 1963; diploma Edn., U. Va., 1959, Ed.D., 1964; m. Frank Graham Yarborough, July 3, 1949 (div.). Tchr., Cradock High Sch., Portsmouth, 1948-56, head English dept., 1951-56; supr. lang. arts Norfolk County (Va.) Pub. Schs., 1956-57, supr. high schs., dir. developmental reading program, 1957-66; dir. lang. arts Chesapeake (Va.) Pub. Schs., 1966-72. Extension instr. Coll. William and Mary, 1957-67, Hampton Roads Center U. Va., 1965—; vis. instr., asst. reading clinic dir. U. Va., 1959-62; vis. instr. Mich. State U., 1965; vis. instr. Old Dominion Coll., Norfolk, Va., 1967-72, prof. elementary edn., 1972—; diagnostician Psychiat. Assos., Ltd., Portsmouth, 1972—; tchr. adult reading improvement course Norfolk Newspapers, Inc.; project dir. demonstration primary sch. in Chesapeake, 1967-72; dir. diagnostic reading centers, Chesapeake, 1966-72; now prin. investigator Nat. Inst. Edn. research project graded and nongraded instrn. effectiveness. Reading cons. Spong Commn., 1960; dir. workshops, participant tchr. tng. programs Va., N.C., S.C. schs.; chmn. task force reading Regional Edn. Lab. of Carolinas and Va., 1966-67; research English, fgn. lang. instrn. Recipient Ullin W. Leavell award contbn. reading instrn. U. Va., 1967; Outstanding Civic Achievement award Chesapeake C. of C., 1965. Mem. Va. Edn. Assn. (state com. tchr. edn., profl. standards, 1961), Am. Edn. Research Assn., Am. Psychol. Assn., Nat. Council Measurement Edn., Va. Assn. Tchrs. English (sec., treas. 1960-62), Nat. Council Tchrs. English (participant convs. 1960, 62, chmn. composition inst. 1965), Internat. (participant conv. 1966, 70, 71, com. chmn. 1970), Coll. (participant convs. 1969, 70), Va. (pres. 1968-69) reading assns., Nat. Assn. Edn. Young Children, Assn. Childhood Edn. Internat., Va. Ednl. Research Assn. (pres. 1972), Nat. Reading Conf., S. Atlantic Philosophy Edn. Assn., Modern Lang. Assn., Nat. Conf. Research in English (asso.), Council for Exception Children, Kappa Delta Pi, Theta Alpha Phi, Delta Kappa Gamma. Presbyn. Club: Sigma Kappa. Author: Teaching English to Slow Learners, 1962; Guidelines for Improving Spelling Instruction, 1964; Sound and Sense in Spelling textbooks series, 1964, rev. edit., 1968; On Wings on Words, 1970. Contbr. to Ency. Edn., also articles to profl. jours. Home: 3008 Ferguson Dr Portsmouth VA 23703 Office: Hampton Blvd PO Box 6173 Norfolk VA 23508

YARBOROUGH, KEMP PLUMMER, educator; b. Louisburg, N.C., Apr. 29, 1912; s. William Henry and Eloise (Hill) Y.; B.A., U. N.C., 1933; postgrad. law Wake Forest Coll., 1935-36; M.A., U. S.C., 1950; Ph.D., Columbia, 1963; m. Brigitte Margarete Freiin Roeder von Diersburg, Nov. 15, 1947; children—Victoria (Mrs. Kennedy Poyser), William Andrew, Charles Christopher. Admitted to N.C. bar, 1936; practiced law, Louisburg, 1936-41; codification asst. N.C. Dept. Justice, Raleigh, 1941-42; teaching asst. U. S.C., 1948-51; head social studies dept. St. Marys Coll., St. Marys City, Md., 1954-65, dean faculty, 1957-65; asso. prof. Tex. Womans U., Denton, 1965-68, prof. history, 1968—, chmn. dept. history and govt., 1969—. Served with AUS, 1942-48; ETO; also 1951-53; maj. Res. ret. Decorated Bronze Star medal. Mem. Am. Assn. U. Profs., Am. Hist. Assn., Acad. Polit. Sci., Phi Beta Kappa; Phi Alpha Theta. Episcopalian. Home: 2522 Emerson Lane Denton TX 76201

YARBROUGH, DAVID BERTHIER, architect; b. Gainesville, Tex., Nov. 23, 1928; s. Silas McWilliams and Ruby (Gaines) Y.; B.Arch., Tex. A. and M. U., 1952; children—Mark David, Judy Sante (Mrs. Leonard Saphier), Lindsey Dirk, Quinn Payton. With Caudill, Rowlett & Scott, architects, engr., planners, Houston, 1950-61, Harrell & Hamilton, architects, Dallas, 1961-63; pvt. practice as David B. Yarbrough, architect, planner, Dallas, 1963—. Design critic Sch. Architecture, Tex. A. and M. U., College Station, 1954-59, instr. advanced design program, 1963-64; design critic Sch. Architecture Rice U., 1960, Sch. Architecture, Princeton, 1960; cons. environmental awareness Dallas Ind. Sch. Dist., 1972, Gifted Students Found., 1972, Richardson Ind. Sch. Dist., 1972, Baylor U. Environmental Studies Inst., 1972, Channel 13, KERA-TV children's ednl. series, 1972. Mem. City of Richardson Zoning Bd. Adjustment, 1964-65, City Richardson Bldg. Code Bd. Adjustment, 1970-71. Bd. dirs. Hara, Inc., Dallas, 1973-74. Recipient Jaycee of Yr. award Richardson Jr. C. of C., 1963. Mem. A.I.A. (chpt. chmn. com. on registration and profl. practice 1965-66), Tex. Soc. Architects, Amigos Dallas. Home: 911 Waterview Circle Richardson TX 75080 Office: 12800 Hillcrest St Dallas TX 75230

YATES, CHARLES ROBERT, dentist; b. Wedowe, Ala., Mar. 25, 1937; s. Thomas T. and Pauline (Cofield) Y.; B.S., U. Ala., 1961, D.M.D., 1966; m. Delois Marlene Horton, Sept. 21, 1956; children—Stacy Ann, Charles Robert, Dustin Blake. Practice dentistry, Bessemer, Ala., 1966—. Treas. Delta Dental Plans of Ala. Pres. Bessemer Leased Housing Authority, 1971-72. Chmn. adv. com. Park and Recreation Bd., 1971-72. Sec. bd. dirs. YMCA, 1969-72; bd. dirs. Salvation Army; trustee Troy State U., 1969-70. Served with USAF, 1961-62. Mem. Am., Ala. dental assns., Birmingham Dist. Dental Soc., Jr. C of C. (v.p. 1967), Omicron Delta Kappa, Psi Omega (v.p. 1965-66). Baptist (deacon). Lion (pres. 1971-72). Home: 716 Millgray Lane Bessemer AL 35020 Office: 802 Memorial Dr Bessemer AL 35020

YATES, DONALD PITT, supt. schs.; b. Cross Plains, Tenn., Jan. 3, 1929; s. William Herman and Azzie Lee (Pitt) Y.; diploma Martin Coll., 1949; B.S., U. Chattanooga, 1951; M.A., George Peabody Coll., 1952, Ed.S., 1958; Ed.D., U. Tenn., 1968; m. Elsie Arnold, Jan. 1, 1953; 1 dau., Donna Elaine. Tchr., coach schs., Harriman, Tenn., 1954-56; elementary sch. prin., Rockwood, Tenn., 1956-61, supt. schs., 1961-66; cons. sch. planning lab. U. Tenn., 1966-68; supt. schs., Cleveland, Tenn., 1968—. Served with AUS, 1952-54. Mem. Phi Delta Kappa. Methodist. Lion. Home: 3722 Hillside Dr NE Cleveland TN 37311 Office: 190 Church St Cleveland TN 37311

YATES, EDITH OLIVE COE, club woman; b. McPherson, Kan., Dec. 31, 1890; d. James Buchanan and Christine Matilda (Aelmore) Coe; tchrs. certificate U. Tex., 1909; m. Calder Emmet Yates, Apr. 28, 1917; 1 dau., Mildred (Mrs. Herbert Aden Plummer). Auditor 4th dist. Tex. Fedn. Music Clubs, 1946; pres. Dept. Club, Port Arthur, Tex., 1940-41, Symphony Club, 1929-30, 44-45, Griffing Park Garden Club, 1954-55, Country Club Aux., 1941-42, Past Presidents of Symphony Club; del. to 68th Continental Congress of D.A.R., Washington, 1959. Recipient with Dau. of Outstanding Club Family award Tex. Fedn. Women's Clubs, 1958. Mem. Tex. Hist. Assn., Tex. Fedn. Women's Clubs (dist. parliamentarian 1962-64). Travel in U.S., Europe, Can., Mexico, Guatemala. Home: 4200 Griffing Dr Port Arthur TX 77640

YATES, OSCAR WALLACE, JR., cons. engr.; b. Roanoke, Va., Feb. 15, 1931; s. Oscar Wallace and Irene (Frier) Y.; B.S., Va. Poly. Inst., 1953, M.S., 1958; m. Rosa Joan Mitchell, May 31, 1953; children—Deborah Joan, Linda Sue, Jane Lee. Sales engr. Wallace & Tiernan, Inc., Roanoke, 1956-57; civil engr. Wiley & Wilson, Lynchburg, Va., 1957-61; dir. pub. works Prince William County, Manassas, Va., 1961-73; partner O'Donnell, Pietra, Schwenger & Yates, Cons. Engrs., Fairfax, Va., 1973—. Mem. regional san. adv. bd. Washington Met. Council of Govts., 1961-73. Served as commd. officer with AUS, 1954-56. Registered profl. engr., Va., Md., Ky., W. Va., Tenn., D.C. Mem. Va., Am. socs. profl. engrs., Am. Pub. Works Assn., Am. Mgmt. Assn., Am. Soc. C.E., Va. Water Pollution Control Assn., Am. Water Works Assn. Baptist. Home: 9907 Greenview Lane Manassas VA 22110 Office: 3251 Old Lee Hwy Suite 107 Fairfax VA 22030

YATES, SCOTT TUCKER, dept. store exec.; b. Asheboro, N.C., Feb. 5, 1937; s. Frank Ogburn and Sue Ragland (Tucker) Y.; grad. Woodberry Forest Sch., 1955; A.B., U. N.C., 1959; m. Virginia Alexander Shuford, Feb. 3, 1962; children—Virginia Ogburn, Sue Alexander, Scott Tucker, William Shuford, Macon Ferguson. With Belk Yates Co., Asheboro, 1960—, v.p., gen. mgr., 1968—; also dir.; dir. Wachovia Bank & Trust Co., Asheboro, Greyco, Inc., Asheboro. Bd. dirs. Randolph Hosp., Inc., Asheboro, Hope Harbor, Greensboro, N.C. Served with AUS, 19——. Mem. Asheboro C. of C., Full Gospel Businessmen's Fellowship Internat. (pres. Asheboro chpt. 1972—), Alpha Tau Omega. Episcopalian. Mailing Address: Route 2 Lexington Rd Asheboro NC 27203

YEAGER, ARTHUR JOSEPH, coop. assn. exec.; b. Kurten, Tex., May 8, 1908; s. Joe Charlie and Lena (Herzog) Y.; grad. high sch.; m. Johanna Kehlenbrink, Nov. 28, 1935; children—Grace (Mrs. Olley C. Ashley), Elsie (Mrs. Glenn Dressen), Ruth (Mrs. Harry Bostic), Eldon. Cotton gin operator Opersteny Bros. Gin, Kurten, 1930-41, Ward Moring Gin, Brazos County, Tex., 1941-43; gen. mgr. Producer Coop. Assn., Bryan, Tex., 1943—. Mem. adv. bd. Houston Bank for Coops., 1967-70, adv. bd. Farmland Industries, 1966-72, bd. dirs., 1971—. Rural chmn. Brazos County A.R.C., 1952-54. Mem. Brazos County Sch. Bd., 1955—, v.p., 1971. Named Hon. State Farmer Bryan Future Farmers Am., 1961; recipient 4-H award, 1962. Mem. Bryan Young Farmers (life), Bryan C. of C. (chmn. agrl. com. 1957), Tex. Fedn. Coops. (pres. 1971-72), Tex. Feed Control Service (mem. adv. com. 1965-72). Mem. United Ch. of Christ (pres. ch. council 1955-57). Mason (32 deg.). Home: Route 2 Box 143 Bryan TX 77801 Office: PO Box 1108 Bryan TX 77801

YEAGER, KENNETT WILLIAM, govt. ofcl.; b. Pottstown, Pa., Oct. 16, 1917; s. William A. and Edna Mae (Krout) Y.; B.A., U. Pitts., 1938, M.A., 1940, Ph.D., 1949; student U. Pa., 1941-42, U. Wis., summer 1939; m. Margaret L. Oliphant, Sept. 11, 1948; children—Barbara Louise, Margaret Allison. Instr., polit. sci. and econs. Chatham Coll., Pitts., 1942-43; instr. soc. Kent State U., Ohio, 1946-49; asst. prof. sociology George Washington U., Washington, 1949-51; air research specialist Air Force Intelligence Center, Washington, 1951-63; intelligence operations specialist Def. Intelligence Agy., Washington, 1963—. Lectr. sociology U. Md., Am. U. Served with AUS, 1943-46. Mem. Am., Eastern, D.C. sociol. assns., Am. Acad. Polit. and Social Sci. Home: 4771 Kandel Ct Annandale VA 22003 Office: Defense Intelligence Agy Washington DC 20301

YEATES, ZENO LANIER, architect; b. Atlanta, Jan. 9, 1915; s. Zeno Epps and Louise (Ames) Y.; B.S., Miss. State Coll., 1937; B.Arch., U. Pa., 1942; m. Elsie Lankford, June 12, 1947; children—Zeno Ames, Arthur Lankford, Laura. Asso., J. Frazer Smith & Assos., Memphis, 1945-57; pres. Zeno L. Yeates Assos., Memphis, 1958-62; partner Yeates & Gaskill, Memphis, 1963—. Mem. Tenn. Bd. Archtl. and Engring. Examiners, 1957-67. Bd. dirs. Presbyn. Day Sch., Memphis, chmn. bd., 1968—. Mem. A.I.A. (past pres. Memphis chpt., mem. nat. bd. 1975—), Tenn. Soc. Architects (past pres.), Kappa Alpha. Archtl. works include Memphis Meml. Stadium, Shelby County Office Bldg., Meth. Hosp. Sch. Nursing, (all Memphis), Jackson-Madison County Gen. Hosp., Jackson, Tenn. Home: 476 S Goodlett St Memphis TN 38117 Office: 2080 Peabody Memphis TN 38104

YEATMAN, HARRY CLAY, educator; b. Ashwood, Tenn., June 22, 1916; s. T.P. and Mary (Wharton) Y.; A.B., U. N.C., 1939, M.A., 1942, Ph.D., 1956; m. Jean Anderson, 1949; children—Henry Clay III, Jean Hansford. Asst. in zoology U. N.C., Chapel Hill, 1939-42, teaching fellow, 1946-47, instr., 1947-50; asst. prof. biology U. of South, Sewanee, Tenn., 1950-54, asso. prof., 1954-60, prof., 1960—; cons. copepod taxonomy div. Crustacea U.S. Nat. Museum, Woods Hole Oceanographic Instn., U.S. Army, SEATO, others. Chmn. program com. Tech. Aqua Biol. Sta., Tenn. Technol. U., 1970-72. Mem. A.A.A.S., Soc. Systematic Zoology, Soc. Limnology and Oceanography, Soc. Ichthyology and Herpetology, Tenn. Acad. Sci., Am. Ornithologists Union, Phi Beta Kappa, Sigma Xi, Omicron Delta Kappa, Sigma Nu. Contbg. author Fresh Water Biology, 1959, Encyclopedia Science and Technology, 1960—. Contbr. articles to profl. jours. Home: Jumpoff Rd Sewanee TN 37375

YEH, WALTER HUAI-TEH, educator, composer; b. Shanghai, China, Jan. 7, 1911; s. Ziang Tsung and Pei-Yu (Huang) Y.; came to U.S., 1944, naturalized, 1955; A.B., St. John's U. (China), 1933; grad. summa cum laude Nat. Conservatory of Music (China), 1935; M.A. and Mus. M., Eastman Sch. Music, U. Rochester, 1945; A.M., Harvard, 1948, researcher, 1951-54; Ph.D., U. Rochester, 1949; m. Moong Yue, Aug. 8, 1942; children—Peter Wen-chun, Arthur Cho-chun. Prof. flute Nat. Conservatory of Music, China, 1940-44; prof. music, chmn. joint music dept. Allen U., and Benedict Coll., Columbia, S.C., 1954—, chmn. humanities div. Allen U., 1957-60, 63—, chmn. div. fine arts and drama Benedict Coll., 1968-71, 72—, interim pres., 1973. Bd. dirs. Columbia Lyric Theatre, 1972—. Fellow Internat. Inst. Arts and Letters. Rotarian. Composer: Concerto Grosso in F for Oboe, String Quartet and Harp with String Orchestra, 1944; Symphony in D, 1944; Chinese Suite, 1945; Chinese Symphony, 1948; (madrigal) Come Away, Come Away, Death!, 1957; The Cuckoo Chorus, 1958; Hymn for Peace, 1960; And Ruth Said: Intreat Me Not to Leave Thee, 1962; The Solitary Reaper, 1964; She Never Told Her Love, 1965; This Glorious Christmas Night, 1967; Gloria Patri and Kyrie, 1968; The Pattering Rain, 1968; The Lord's Prayer, 1969; We Shall Overcome, 1970; A Tombstone Epitaph, 1971; Alleuia, May Peace Be on Earth, 1972; Farewell for Ever!, 1972; All Glory, Praise and Honor, 1973; Echoes from on the Great Wall, 1974; composer orchestral and choral works, other compositions. Home: 710 Heidt St Columbia SC 29205

YELLOTT, KATHLEEN SIGHTLER, business exec.; b. Birmingham, Ala., Feb. 24, 1905; d. Joseph Edward and Ida Lou (Hutchins) Sightler; student Ala. pub. schs.; m. Wendell W. Smith, Dec. 10, 1922 (dec. Nov. 1928); 1 son, Kenneth H.; m. Charles Lewis, Dec., 12, 1929 (div. Feb. 1938); children—John M., James A.; m. Oscar Yellott, July 1, 1939; 1 adopted son, Phillip Allen. Owner nursing home, Birmingham, 1922, Beaumont, Tex., 1933—. Legislative del. Tex. nursing homes, Washington, 1953-56. Mem. Pvt. Hosps. and Clinics, Tex. Hosp. Assn., Pub. Affairs Forum Lumberton (Tex.), 1972—. Home: Route 3 Box 566 Silsbee TX 77656

YELVERTON, CONLEY WARD, furniture co. exec.; b. St. Augustine, Fla., Aug. 4, 1936; s. Conley Chesler and Frances Elizabeth (Yelverton) Ward; B.S., U. Fla., 1958; m. LaNeeta Maria Pate, Jan. 25, 1957 (div. July 1971); children—Theta Ann, Dione Elizabeth, Debra Alice, Kimma Linn. Self-employed as cons. engr., 1958-60; prodn. mgr., project engr. Multronics, Inc., Sarasota, Fla., and Rockville, Md., 1960-62; prodn. mgr., project engr. Delta Electronics, Inc., Alexandria, Va., 1962-65, chief engr., 1965-68; dir. radio frequency product devel. Aiken Industries, Inc., Alexandria, 1968-69; pres., gen. mgr. Yelverton Furniture Co., Palatka, Fla., 1969—. Engring. cons., 1958—; instr. engring. St. Johns River Coll., 1958-59. Registered profl. engr., Va., Fla. Mem. I.E.E.E., Putnam County C. of C. (dir. 1970-72). Elk (trustee 1970-71, Elk of Year 1970). Home: Harts Point East Palatka FL 32131 Office: 522 St Johns Av Palatka FL 32077

YEO, CEDRIC ARNOLD, edcator; b. Port Hill, P.E.I., Can., Sept. 10, 1905; s. Herbert and Mary Jane Y.; came to U.S., 1940, naturalized, 1948; student Prince of Wales Coll., 1922-25; B.A. with honors, Dalhousie U., 1928; Ph.D., Yale, 1933; postgrad. Oriental Inst., U. Chgo., 1962; m. Ruth Iris Clark, Aug. 8, 1939; children—Helen (Mrs. Michael Chew), Janet (Mrs. Norman Johansen), John Arnold Clark, Tammy Lynn; m. 2d, Jacquelynn Sexton, Nov. 16, 1962. Lectr. classics Kings U., Halifax, N.S., 1936-38, Dalhousie U., Halifax, 1931, 38-40; asst. prof. history The Citadel, Charleston, S.C., 1940-52; asso. prof. classics Memphis State U., 1956-58; prof. history Alice Lloyd Coll., Pippa Passes, Ky., 1961-64, Eastern Ky. U., Richmond, 1965—. Mem. Am. Assn. U. Profs., Am. Hist. Soc., Am. Philol. Assn. Democrat. Mason. Author: A History of the Roman People, 1962. Contbr. articles to profl. jours. Home: 909 Vickers Dr Richmond KY 40475

YEOMAN, WILLIAM F., athletic coach; b. Elnora, Ind., Dec. 26, 1927; s. Cluade Allen and Anna Lillian Y.; B.S., U.S. Mil. Acad., 1950; m. Alma Jean, July 1, 1950; children—William Vance, Gary Layne, Kathy Ann, Carrie Lynn. With U.S. Army in Europe, 1950-53; asst. football coach Mich. State U., 1954-61; head football coach U. Houston, 1962—. Home: 607 Chevy Chase Sugar Land TX 77478 Office: 3855 Holman Houston TX 77004

YERGER, JOHN HENRY, orgn. exec.; b. Reading, Pa., Jan. 4, 1914; s. John Henry and Anna (Long) Y.; A.B., Muhlenberg Coll., 1935; M.S. in Social Service, Boston U., 1942; m. Christine Helen Fegley, June 12, 1937; 1 dau., Pamela Louise. Supr. Pa. Dept. Pub. Assistance, Reading, 1935-40; exec. A.R.C., Boston, Cape Cod, Worcester, Mass., Hudson County, N.J., 1942-50, Niagara Falls (N.Y.) Community Chest, 1950-51; exec. dir. Ottawa (Ont., Can.) Community Chest, 1951-55, United Appeal Met. Toronto (Ont.), 1955-72; v.p. United Way of Am., Alexandria, Va., 1972—. Lectr., Harvard, 1941-42, Clark U., 1946-47, Cornell U., 1950-51, Boston U., 1942, U. Toronto, 1962-72; cons. community orgn. to nat. orgns. and U.S. and Canadian cities, 1945—; chmn. nat. com. bus. leaders Canadian Community Funds, 1964-70, chmn. nat. com. to improve pub. relations, 1964; chmn. Internat. Conf. Community Funds and Councils, Los Angeles, 1972. Mem. Mayor's Civic Com., Toronto, 1958-70; founder Cape Cod Council, 1943. Bd. dirs. Canadian Welfare Council, 1955-72, Met. Toronto Social Planning Council, 1955-72. Served with USCGR, 1943-45. Decorated Most Venerable Order of Hosp. of St. John of Jerusalem in Brit. Realm; Letters of The Kings At Arms, City Ottawa, Can.; recipient citation A.R.C., 1946, Distinguished Service award United Community Fund, 1959, Canadian Red Cross, 1971, Boy Scouts Can., 1971, City Toronto, 1971. Fellow Royal Soc. Health; mem. Internat. Platform Assn., Acad. Certified Social Workers, Canadian Assn. Social Workers, United Community Funds and Councils Am. (adv. com. to corps. 1965-68), Nat. Assn. Social Workers (chmn. Worcester chpt. 1944-45), Nat. Assn. Fund Raisers, Toronto Bd. Trade, Phi Kappa Tau, Tau Kappa Alpha. Lutheran. Clubs: National Club, Canadian (Toronto); Empire of Canada. Contbr. articles to tech. mags. Home: Apt 1104 N Skyline Towers 5601 Seminary Rd Falls Church VA 22041 Office: 801 N Fairfax St Alexandria VA 22314

YERGER, WIRT ADAMS, JR., ins. co. exec.; b. Jackson, Miss., Mar. 18, 1930; s. Wirt Adams and Rivers (Applewhite) Y.; B.B.A., U. Miss., 1952; m. Mary Polk Montague, June 9, 1956; children—Wirt Adams III, Mary Montague, Frank M. With Ross & Yerger Ins. Agy., Jackson, 1954—, v.p., 1957, now pres.; underwriting mem. Lloyd's of London. Founder Miss. Young Republicans, 1956; chmn. Miss. Rep. Com., 1956-66; chmn. So. Assn. Reps., 1961-65; former mem. Rep. Nat. Com. Served to 1st lt., USAAF, 1952-54. Recipient Distinguished Service award Jackson Jr. C. of C., 1956, 60. C.L.U. Mem. Miss. Assn. Ins. Agts. (past pres.). Rotarian. Home: 2457 E Northside Dr Jackson MS 39205 Office: Capital Towers Bldg Jackson MS 39205

YINGLING, DORIS BEAUMONT, nursing sch. adminstr.; b. Balt., Dec. 3, 1918; d. Paul M. and Helen (Beaumont) Yingling; R.N., Union Meml. Hosp., Balt., 1943; B.S., U. Ore., 1944; M.A., U. Md., 1950, Ed.D. 1956; m. Harry Lyons, January 12, 1969. Instr. Sch. Nursing Union Meml. Hosp., 1943-44, instr., supr., 1944-46; cons. Liberty Mut. Ins. Co., Phila., 1946-50; lectr. U. Md., 1950-51; exec. sec. Gov., Md. Commn. Survey of Nursing to Needs and Resources, 1950-53; dean Orvis Sch. Nursing, U. Nev., 1956-57; dean Sch. Nursing, Va. Commonwealth U., Richmond, 1958—. Mem. Gov. Va. Commn. Higher Edn., 1964, Gov. Va. Com. on Nursing, 1966, Adv. Council Practical Nurse Edn., 1965—, Nursing Scholarship Com. Va., 1962—, task force chronic bronchitis Nat. Tb Assn., 1965; cons. div. hosp. and med. facilities Dept. of Health, Edn. and Welfare, 1967. Mem. Va., Richmond (dir. 1962-69) personnel and guidance assns., Instructive Vis. Nurse Assn., Nat., Richmond leagues for nursing, Am., Va. nurses assns., Council Practical Nurse Edn. (chmn. evaluation com. 1966-69), Sigma Theta Tau, Phi Kappa Phi, Alpha Sigma Chi. Contbr. articles to profl. publs. Home: 7618 Idlewyld Rd Richmond VA 23225

YOAKUM, ANNA MARGARET, chemist; b. Loudon, Tenn., Jan. 13, 1933; d. Hugh L. and Emily (Watkins) Yoakum; A.B., Maryville Coll., 1954; M.S., U. Fla., 1956, Ph.D., 1960. Chief chemist, lab. supr. Greenback Industries, Inc., 1956-59; research chemist Chemstrand Research Center, Inc., 1960-64; research staff Oak Ridge Nat. Lab., 1964-69, exec. v.p., lab. dir. Stewart Labs., Inc., Knoxville, 1969—. Fellow Am. Inst. Chemists; mem. Am. Soc. Testing and Materials, Am. Chem. Soc., Soc. Applied Spectroscopy (sect. sec., treas. 1965-68), N.Y. Acad. Scis., Phi Beta Kappa, Sigma Xi, Phi Kappa Phi, Gamma Sigma Epsilon. Methodist. Club: Knoxville Executives. Home: 7844 Ramsgate Dr Knoxville TN 37919 Office: 820 Tulip Av Knoxville TN 37921

YODER, AMOS, govt. ofcl.; b. Falls City, Neb., Mar. 2, 1921; s. Amos H. and Mildred (Johnson) Y.; B.A., Ohio Wesleyan U., 1942; Ph.D., U. Chgo., 1949; m. Janet Lee Tatman, June 15, 1946; children—James Amos, Barbara Ann, Sally Irene. Jr. econ. editor Bd. Econ. Warfare, Washington, 1942-43; economist, fgn. service officer Dept. State, Washington, also Bangkok, Thailand, Tel Aviv, Israel, 1949—, asst. dep. dir., Washington, 1969-71, acting chief, 1971—. Asso. professorial lectr. George Washington U., 1963-64, U. Cal. at Davis, 1964-65. Served with USAAF, 1944-46; ETO, PTO. Recipient Merit Honor award Dept. State, 1967, Meritorious Civilian Service award, 1972. Mem. Nat. Inst. Pub. Affairs, Am. Polit. Sci. Assn., Phi Gamma Delta, Omicron Delta Kappa. Home: 1822 Rupert St McLean VA 22101 Office: Bur Internat Orgn Affairs Dept State Washington DC 20520

YOHN, KENNETH CRAWFORD, physician; b. Dothan, Ala., Nov. 1, 1936; s. Houston Crawford and Julie Lee (Trant) Y.; student Troy State U., 1955-56, Howard Coll., 1956-58; M.D., U. Ala., 1962; postgrad. Naval Aerospace Med. Inst., 1963-64. Intern U.S. Naval Hosp., Portsmouth, Va., 1962-63; student flight surgeon Naval Aerospace Med. Inst., Pensacola, Fla., 1963-64; gen. practice medicine, Eufaula, Ala., 1967—; mem. staff Barbour County Hosp. Served to lt. comdr. M.C., USN, 1962-67. Decorated Air medal. Mem. Am. Acad. Family Physicians (pres. Ala. chpt.), Med. Assn. Ala. (bd. censors), Barbour County Med. Soc. (pres. 1969-71, 72-73), Eufaula C. of C. (dir. 1971—). Baptist (deacon). Office: 108 N Randolph Av Eufaula AL 36027

YOKEL, FELIX YOCHANAN, cons. engr.; b. Vienna, Austria, July 13, 1922; s. Karl and Emma (Hauser) Jokel; came to U.S., 1956, naturalized, 1963; B.S. with highest honors, U. Conn., 1959, M.S., 1961, Ph.D., 1963; m. Susanne Martha Braun, June 26, 1947; children—Uri, Yael, Benjamin. Officer, Israel Def. Force, 1944-50; tech. dir. Hazbani River Diversion Project, Kear-Blum, Israel, 1950-56; chief found. engr. John Clarkson, cons. engr., Albany, N.Y., 1960-64; sr. partner Clarkeson, Clough & Yokel, cons. engrs., Albany, 1964-68; cons. engr. Center for Bldg. Tech., Nat. Bur. Standards, Washington, 1968—. Vice chmn. joint com. on tall bldgs. Am. Soc. C.E.-Internat. Assn. Bridge and Structural Engrs., 1972-74; chmn. Am. Nat. Standards Inst. com., 1973-74. Registered profl. engr., Conn., N.Y., Md., D.C., Vt., Me., R.I., Mass. Mem. Am. Soc. C.E., Am. Concrete Inst., Nat. Soc. Profl. Engrs., Sigma Xi, Phi Kappa Phi, Chi Epsilon, Tau Beta Pi. Home: 8208 Fenway Rd Bethesda MD 20034 Office: Nat Bur Standards Washington DC 20234

YONDORF, WALTER F., electronics co. exec.; b. Nuremberg, Germany, Oct. 2, 1920; s. Emil and Fanny (Rosenzweig) Y.; came to U.S., 1937, naturalized, 1942; student Northwestern U., 1940-42; M.A. (Univ. fellow), U. Chgo., 1957, Ph.D., 1962; m. Anne Louise Lowald, June 30, 1946; children—Barbara Anne, Thomas George, Wendy Alma. Asso. research dir. com. on communications U. Chgo., 1955-57; instr. communications, 1957-59; sr. staff mem. Inst. for Air Weapon Research, 1960-62; with Mitre Corp., electronic systems engrng., McLean, Va., 1962—, tech. dir., 1971—. Chmn. sewer com. Glenview (Ill.) Countryside Civic Assn., 1951-55. Served with AUS, 1942-45. Decorated Bronze Star. Fellow Social Sci. Research Council; mem. Am. Polit. Sci. Assn. Contbr. articles to profl. jours. Home: 5601 Ontario Circle Washington DC 20016 Office: Westgate Research Park McLean VA 22101

YORK, CHARLES IRVING, govt. ofcl.; b. Washington, Sept. 15, 1925; s. Lamar Watson and Helen (Hall) Y.; student Duke, 1943-44; B. Civil Engring., Cath. U., 1951, M. Civil Engring. cum laude, 1956; postgrad. Mass. Inst. Tech., 1960, U. N.M., 1964; grad. Fed. Exec. Inst.; m. Theresa Marie Fritz, Feb. 12, 1952; children—Stephen, Michael, Eileen, Kathleen, Kevin. Engr., George Hyman Constrn. Co., Washington, 1950-52; engr., project mgr. VA, Dept. of Navy, Air Force Ballistic Missile Div., 1952-62; asst. dir. AEC, Washington, 1962—. Cons. civil engr. ballistic missile and space systems divs. USAF, 1958-62; mem. Fed. Constrn. Council, Bldg. Research Adv. Bd. Various adminstrv. positions Boy Scouts Am., 1959-61; athletic coach Pop Warner League, Cath. Youth Orgn., 1960-62; active various ch. activities, bond drs., blood drs. Served to lt. (j.g.) USNR, 1943-47. Recipient Meritorious Civilian Service medal USAF, 1960, Sustained Superior Service award, 1961; Dept. of Commerce Sci. and Tech. fellow, 1966-67. Registered profl. engr., Vt. Mem. Am. Soc. C.E., Am. Assn. Cost Engrs., Am. Inst. Plant Engrs., Nat. Soc. Profl. Engrs., Internat. Conf. Bldg. Ofcls., Sci. Research Soc. Am., Nat. Rifle Assn., Nat. Acad. Sci., Sigma Xi. Club: Senators (Washington). Home: 6012 Kingsford Rd Bethesda MD 20034 Office: AEC Washington DC 20545

YORK, VAUGHN LEROY, banker; b. Bonneyblue, Va., Mar. 19, 1931; s. Harrison and Easter (Cox) Y.; B.S., Lincoln Meml. U., 1958; grad. Sch. Banking of South, La. State U., 1974; m. Joyce Jean Owens, Sept. 2, 1955; children—Nancy Kay, Vaughn Leroy, Jeffrey Thomas. Asst. v.p. Peoples Nat. Bank, LaFollette, Tenn., 1958-63; partner Security Ins. Agy., LaFollette, 1963-64; v.p. Hamilton Nat. Bank, Knoxville, Tenn., 1964-72, v.p., dir. personnel, 1972—. Served with USNR, 1951-54. Mem. Am. Inst. Banking (instr. 1965, gov. 1966-73). Mason, Lion (dir. 1964-65). Home: Route 6 Warrior Trail Concord TN 37720 Office: West Haven Branch Oak Ridge Hwy Knoxville TN 37921

YOUENS, CYNTHIA TANNER, educator; b. Columbus, Tex., Sept. 7, 1905; d. John Osborne and Phyrne (Claiborne) Tanner; B.S., U. Houston, 1951, M.Ed., 1953; m. Willis George Youens, Feb. 13, 1935 (dec.); children—Phyrne (Mrs. Philip Bacon), Leonard Claiborne, John Tanner, Phillip Whitfield. Faculty mem. Alief (Tex.) Sch. (name changed to Cynthia Youens Elementary Sch. in her honor 1974), 1951—. Mem. Internat. Platform Assn., A.A.A.S., Tex. Tchrs. Assn., Tex. Hist. Assn., Women's Aux., Harris County Med. Soc., Kappa Delta Pi. Home: 19 Westlane Houston TX 77019 Office: Cynthia Youens Elementary Sch Alief TX 77411

YOUMANS, CLINTON JAMES, banker; b. Pierce County, Ga., Nov. 17, 1930; s. Clinton and Lucille (Bray) Y.; grad. Sch. of Banking of South, La. State U., 1971; m. Dorothy Ann Stribling, Dec. 16, 1950; children—J. David, L. Alan. With various consumer finance companies, 1952-64; with First Comml. Bank, St. Petersburg, Fla., 1964—, chief exec. officer, 1971—, pres., 1973—, dir., 1973—. Pres. Sulphur Springs Little League, Tampa, 1963-64. Served with USN, 1948-52. Mem. Am. Inst. Banking (chpt. instr. 1964), St. Petersburg C. of C., Com. on 100 Pinellas County. Baptist (deacon 1971-73). Optimist (sec. Tampa 1961-63). Home: 6180 41st Av N St Petersburg FL 33709 Office: 2100 34th St S St Petersburg FL 33733

YOUNG, ANDREW J., JR., clergyman, congressman; b. New Orleans, Mar. 12, 1932; s. Andrew J. and Daisy (Fuller) Y.; student Dillard U., 1947-48; B.S., Howard U., 1951; B.D., Hartford Sem. Found., 1955; m. Jean Childs, June 7, 1954; children—Andrea, Lisa Dow, Paula Jean, Andrew J. III. Ordained to ministry Congl. Ch., 1955; pastor in Thomasville, Ga., 1955-57; asso. dir. dept. youth work Nat. Council Chs., 1957-61; adminstr. Christian edn. program United Ch. Christ, also So. Christian Leadership Conf., 1961-64; mem. staff So. Christian Leadership Conf., 1961-70, exec. dir., 1964-70, exec. v.p., 1967-70; mem. 93d Congress, 5th Dist. Ga., 1973—. Chmn., Atlanta Community Relations Commn., 1970-72. Mem. exec. com. Nat. Urban Coalition, Common Cause; chmn. bd. Delta Ministry of Miss.; bd. dirs. Martin Luther King, Jr. Center for Social Change, Robert F. Kennedy Meml. Found., So. Christian Leadership Conf. Address: 56 Forsyth St NW Atlanta GA 30303

YOUNG, C. W. BILL, congressman; b. Harmarville, Pa., Dec. 16, 1930; m. Marian Ford; children—Pamela Kay, Terry Lee, Kimber. Dist. asst. to Congressman William C. Cramer, 1957-60; mem. Fla. Senate, 1960-70; mem. 92d-93d congresses from 8th Dist. Fla. Mem. Fla. Constn. Revision Commn., 1965-67; chmn. So. Hwy. Policy Com., 1966-68; del. Rep. Nat. Conv., 1968; chmn. Nixon-Agnew campaign 8th Congl. Dist., 1968; mem. Electoral Coll., 1968. Served to sgt. Fla. N.G., 1948-57. Named One of Outstanding Young Men Am., U.S. Jr. C. of C., 1965, Most Valuable Senator, Capitol Press Corps, 1969. Methodist. Home: 4775 Cove Circle St Petersburg FL 33708 also 9001 Captain's Row Alexandria VA 22308

YOUNG, CARLOS LOWERY, furniture co. exec.; b. Shelby, N.C., Sept. 13, 1915; s. H. Fields and Nina (Lowery) Y.; B.S., Davidson Coll., 1936; m. Constance Alice Champion, Apr. 30, 1949; children—Carlos Lowery, Edna Anne, Kathleen Alice, Stephen Lewis. Pres., Young Bros. Inc., Shelby, 1938—; partner Young Bros. Bldg. Fund, Shelby, 1950—, also in real estate interests; dir. First Citizens Bank & Trust Co. Mem. Cleveland County Welfare Bd., 1963-67; mem. Gov.'s Adv. Council on Comprehensive Health Planning N.C., 1967—; mem. N.C. Mental Health Study Commn. Bd. dirs. N.C. Mental Health Assn., Nat. Assn. for Mental Health, N.C. Mental Health Research; trustee Gardner-Webb Coll., Boiling Springs, N.C., Asheville (N.C.) Orthopedic Hosp., Southeastern Bapt. Theol. Sem., Wake Forest, N.C., Bapt. Children's Home; bd. advisers Mars Hill Coll. Served to maj. AUS, 1941-46. Decorated Bronze Star medal; recipient Shelby Outstanding Citizen award, 1970; recipient Distinguished Service medal Jaycees, 1949. Baptist (deacon, mem. gen. bd. N.C. conv.). Mason (Shriner). Home: 922 W Sumter St Shelby NC 28150 Office: 215 S Washington St Shelby NC 28150

YOUNG, CHARLIE ROSS, assn. exec.; b. Vivian, La., Nov. 2, 1923; s. Lawrence Miller and Maude (Crosley) Y.; student U. Mo.; m. Patsy George, Dec. 25, 1946; children—Barbara Ann, John Bruce. Clk. West Tex. Utility Co., McCamey, 1948-50, owner C & R Restaurant, 1950-52; mgr. McCamey C. of C., 1952-56; exec. v.p. Plainview C. of C., 1956-72; exec. dir. Abilene (Tex.) Indsl. Found., Inc., and indsl. dept. C. of C., 1972—. Served with USAAF, 1942-46. Mem. C. of C. Execs. Assn. West Tex. (pres. 1958-59), Tex. C. of C. Mgrs. Assn. (v.p. 1961-62), Am. Legion. Mason. Home: 3900 N 10th St Abilene TX 79603 Office: 341 Hickory St Abilene TX 79604

YOUNG, CLIFFORD AUGUST, JR., air-conditioning co. exec.; b. Cin., June 9, 1942; s. Clifford August and Marie Rosella (Wiegele) Y.; B.S., Ohio State U., 1964; m. Rosemary Segale, June 5, 1965; children—Dana Marie, Todd Clifford. Prodn. supr. Dayton Tire & Rubber Co. (O.), 1964-65; plant mgr. Climate Master Products, Inc., Ft. Lauderdale, Fla., 1969-70; pres. Fla. Heat Pump Corp., mfr. air-conditioners, Pompano Beach, 1970—. Served to 1st lt. AUS, 1966-69. Decorated Army Commendation medal, Bronze Star medal. Mem. Broward Mfrs. Assn., Ohio State Alumni Assn., Sigma Alpha Epsilon. Mason. Home: 6651 NW 20th St Margate FL 33063 Office: 610 SW 12th Av Pompano Beach FL 33060

YOUNG, DORCELL, business exec.; b. Carlton, Tex., Apr. 28, 1925; s. Oscar Eugene and Charlie (Burris) Y.; student Am. Inst. Banking, 1946-51; m. Lou Ann Williamson, June 1, 1947; children—Richard Dee, Debra Lee. With Citizens Nat. Bank, Lubbock, Tex., 1946-61; chief exec. officer First Nat. Bank, Wynnewood, Okla., 1961-63; pres., chmn. bd. First Nat. Bank, Denton, Tex., 1963-71; spl. asst. to pres. Lifetime Security Life Ins. Co., Denton, 1971-72; owner Young Volkswagen Inc., Denton, 1972—; engaged in ranching. Served with USAAF, 1943-45. Decorated Air Medal with 3 oak leaf clusters. Kiwanian. Home: Route 1 Box 35B Aubrey TX 76227 Office: Young Volkswagen Inc 2101 University Dr W Denton TX 76201

YOUNG, EDWARD LUNN, farmer, congressman; b. Ebenezer, S.C., Sept. 7, 1920; s. Fred Hart and Sarah Isabelle (Lunn) Y.; B.S., Clemson Coll., 1941; m. Harriet Gray Yeargin, Aug. 4, 1945; children—Claudia Y. (Mrs. Peter Stone), Harriet, Virginia, Rebbecca. Farmer, Florence, S.C.; mem. 93d Congress from 6th S.C. dist. Pres., Cable Dairy Products Coop., S.C. Jersey Cattle Club, 1946, Florence County Farm Bur., 1954; chmn. Pee Dee Prodn. Credit Assn., Florence Fed. Land Bank Assn., 1964-72, Farm Credit Bd., Columbia, 1968-70. Mem. S.C. Ho. of Reps., 1958-60. Served to maj. USAAF, 1942-46. Decorated Air medal with nine oak leaf clusters, D.F.C.; named Outstanding Young Farmer of Year, S.C. Assn. Young Farmers, 1955, Outstanding Man of Year in Agr. for S.C., Progressive Farmer mag., 1970. Republican. Baptist (chmn. bd. deacons 1950-53). Home: Route 5 Florence SC 29501 Office: 516 Cannon House Office Bldg Washington DC 20515

YOUNG, FREDERICK ANTHONY, optometrist; b. Shelbyville, Ind., July 21, 1903; s. Eden Hampton Davisand Laura (Haehl) Y.; O.D., No. Ill. Coll., 1928; m. Esperance Elizabeth Hilt Fansler, Aug. 6, 1938. Practice optometry, Indpls., 1932-38, Fort Wayne, Ind., 1929-31, Gary, Ind., 1938-42, New Albany, Ind., 1943-59; asso. with Dr. Sol Bizer, Jeffersonville, Ind., 1960—. Active Boy Scouts Am., Cub Scouts. Mem. New Albany C. of C. Am. Optometric Assn., Omega Delta. Christian Scientist. Mason; mem. Order Eastern Star. Clubs: Optomist, Exchange. Home: 4436 Blenheim Rd Louisville KY 40207 Office: 346 Spring St Jeffersonville IN 47130

YOUNG, GALE, physicist; b. Baroda, Mich., Mar. 5, 1912; B.S., Milw. Sch. Engring., 1933; B.S., M.S., U. Chgo., 1936. Asst. in math. biophys. research U. Chgo., 1936-40; head dept. math. and physics Olivet Coll., 1940-42; physicist Manhattan Dist. Project, U. Chgo., 1942-46, Clinton Labs. (Tenn.), 1946-48; tech. dir. Nuclear Devel. Assos., 1948-55; v.p. Nuclear Devel. Corp. Am., 1955-61; v.p. div. United Nuclear Corp., 1961-62; asst. dir. Oak Ridge Nat. Lab., 1962-73; now cons. Mem. sci. adv. bd. USAF, 1954-58. Fellow Am. Phys. Soc.; mem. Am. Nuclear Soc. Address: Oak Ridge National Laboratory Oak Ridge TN 37831*

YOUNG, GEORGE CRESSLER, judge; b. Cin., Aug. 4, 1916; s. George Phillip and Gladys (Cressler) Y.; student Rollins Coll., 1934; A.B., U. Fla., 1938, LL.B., 1940; postgrad. Harvard Coll. Law, 1947; m. Iris June Hart, Oct. 6, 1951; children—George Cressler, Barbara Ann. Admitted to Fla. bar, 1940; asst. city atty., Winter Haven, Fla., 1941-42; asso. in law firm Smathers, Thompson, Maxwell & Dyer, Miami, Fla., 1947; adminstr., also legislative asst. to Senator George Smathers, Fla., 1948-52; asst. U.S. atty., 1952; partner law firm Knight, Kincaid, Young & Harris, 1953-61; U.S. dist. judge Fla., 1961—. Bd. dirs. United Cerebral Palsy Jacksonville, 1953-60. Served from ensign to lt. USNR, 1942-46, ETO, PTO. Mem. Am., Jacksonville (past pres.) bar assns., Fla. Bar (bd. govs. 1961), C. of C. (chmn. nat. affairs com. 1956-57), Phi Beta Kappa, Phi Kappa Phi, Phi Delta Phi, Fla. Blue Key, Sigma Alpha Epsilon. Rotarian. Home: 2424 Shrewsbury Rd Orlando FL 32803 Office: US Ct House Orlando FL 32801

YOUNG, GLEN MURPHY, truck rental co. exec.; b. Tuscaloosa, Ala., Aug. 28, 1924; s. Glenn Jones and Vertrees Elsie (Murphy) Y.; B.S., U. Ala., 1948; m. Patsy Ruth Howard, Feb. 4, 1945; children—Glen Howard, Robert Alan, Patricia Susan. Agt., Internal Revenue Service, U.S. Treasury Dept., Birmingham, Ala., 1948-51; sales mgr. Fairfield Barrell Co., Inc., 1953-55; with Ryder System Inc., 1955—, group v.p. corp. hdqrs., Miami, 1971—, gen. mgr., 1972—; dir. Ryder Truck Rental Ltd., Ryder System N.V.; dir. Ryder System Inc. Republican. Methodist. Home: 9370 Gallardo St Coral Gables FL 33156 Office: 3600 NW 82d Av Miami FL 33152

YOUNG, JACK, dentist, educator; b. Ashland, Ky., Aug. 24, 1920; s. Earnest and Eureka Sarah (Seagraves) Y.; A.A., Ashland Jr. Coll., 1940; postgrad. Moorehead State Tchrs. Coll., 1940-42; D.M.D., U. Louisville, 1951; m. Mildred Evelyn Virgin, Sept. 9, 1944; children—Steven Earnest, Peggy Lynn, James Elwood, John Cameron. Intern, Dr. C.O. Van Antwerp, gen. dentistry, Louisville, 1951-52; individual practice dentistry, 1952-65; prof., div. chmn. spl. edn. Pensacola (Fla.) Jr. Coll., 1965-71, dean Sch. Health Related Edn., 1971—. Mem. task force Northwest Fla. Comprehensive Health Planning Council. Bd. dirs. Escambia Residences, Inc., Am. Cancer Soc. Served with USNR, 1942-45. Fellow Internat. Coll. Dentists; mem. Am., Fla. dental assns., Louisville Dist., Pensacola, Northwest Fla. Dist. dental socs., Am. Vocational Assn. Author: Outline of Oral and Dental Anatomy, 1964; Dissection Guide for Nurses and Dental Hygienists, 1969. Home: 2080 Galt Rd Pensacola FL 32503

YOUNG, JESS WOLLETT, lawyer; b. San Antonio, Sept. 16, 1926; s. James and Zetta (Alonso) Y.; student Southwestern U., 1944, U. Tex., 1946-49; B.A., Trinity U., 1956; LL.B., St. Marys Sch. Law, 1958; m. Mary Alma Keeter, Apr. 17, 1954; children—Zetta, Imogen. Admitted to Tex. bar, 1957; practiced in San Antonio, 1957—; mem. firm Moursund, Ball and Young, 1965—. Dir., Dean L. Leeper Co., Dallas. County judge, Bexar County, Tex., 1964; city atty., Olmos Park, Tex., 1965-70. Precinct committeeman, San Antonio, 1964, 70—; state Democratic committeeman, 1970-72. Served with USNR, 1944-46. Mem. Am., San Antonio bar assns., State Bar Tex., Delta Theta Phi. Clubs: Kiwanis, San Antonio Gun (dir. 1958-63). Democrat. Home: 321 Thelma Dr San Antonio TX 78212 Office: Main Plaza Bldg San Antonio TX 78205

YOUNG, JOE GALBRAITH, retail store ofcl.; b. Whitesburg, Tenn., Aug. 22, 1920; s. Fred Johnson and Chassie O'Dell (Walker) Y.; grad. high sch.; m. Virginia Juanita Greenwell, Oct. 15, 1949. With Dobyns Taylor Hardware Co., Kingsport, Tenn., 1940—, buyer, 1950—. Bd. dirs. Community Chest, 1969-71; pres. Kingsport Mchts. Bur., 1962; mem. Mayor's Adv. Bd., 1971—. Served with USAAF, 1942-46. Mem. V.F.W., Am. Legion. Democrat. Methodist. Elk, Moose. Clubs: Metropolitan Dinner, Kingsport Riding (pres. 1965), Civitan. Home: 704 Fleetwood St Kingsport TN 37660 Office: 120 Broad St Kingsport TN 37660

YOUNG, JOHN, congressman; b. Corpus Christi, Tex., Nov. 10, 1916; s. Philip M. and Catherine J. (Gaffney) Y.; B.A., St. Edward's U., 1937, LL.D., 1961; student law, U. Tex., 1940; m. Jane F. Gallier, Jan. 21, 1950; children—Catherine Gaffney, Nancy Rae, John Andrew, Robert Harold, Mary Patricia. Admitted to Tex. bar, 1940; assf. county atty. Nueces County, Tex., 1946; asst. dist. atty. Fueces County, 1947-50, County atty., 1951-52, county judge, 1953-56; mem. 85th-93d Congresses, 14th Dist. Tex. Served USNR, 1941-45. Decorated Presdl. Unit Citation. Mem. Tex., Nueces County bar assns., U.S. Supreme Ct. Bar, V.F.W., Am. Legion, D.A.V. K.C., Elk, Moose. Home: 941 Delaine St Corpus Christi TX 78411 Office: House Office Bldg Washington DC 20515

YOUNG, JOHN W., astronaut; b. San Francisco, Sept. 24, 1930; s. William H. Young; B.S. in Aero. Engring., Ga. Inst. Tech., 1952; m. Susy Feldman; children—Sandra, John. Joined U.S. Navy, 1952, advanced through the grades to capt.; test pilot, program mgr. F4 weapons systems projects, 1959-62; then maintenance officer Fighter Squadron 143, Naval Air Sta., Miramar, Cal.; astronaut Project Gemini, NASA, made two men 3 orbit flight Mar. 1965, 2d Gemini flight, 1966, Apollo 10 Lunar orbit flight, May 1969; comdr. Apollo 16 Lunar Landing Mission, Apr. 1972. Fellow Am. Astron. Soc.; mem. Am. Inst. Aeros. and Astronautics, Soc. Exptl. Tests Pilots (asso. fellow). Office: Lyndon B Johnson Center NASA Houston TX 77058

YOUNG, JOSEPH LAURIE, educator; b. Huntsville, Tex., Sept. 23, 1924; s. Benjamine Wilkens and Margaret (Cater) Y.; B.Arch., U. Tex., 1950; M.Arch., Ga. Inst. Tech., 1955. Teaching fellow U. Tex., 1947-50; faculty Clemson (S.C.) U. Coll. Architecture, 1950—, prof., 1965—, athletic council, 1963—, faculty adviser Sigma Alpha Epsilon, 1969—. Architect, Greater London Councils, 1956; prof. Middle East Tech. U., Ankara, Turkey, 1963-64. Served with USNR, 1943-46. Hays-Fulbright grantee, 1963-64. Mem. A.I.A. (S.C. pres. 1971), Assn. Collegiate Schs. Architecture, Tau Sigma Delta (grand rec. 1969—), Phi Kappa Sigma. Home: 705 Clemson House Clemson SC 29631

YOUNG, KENNETH EVANS, ednl. adminstr.; b. Toronto, Ont., Can., Mar. 21, 1922; s. John Osborne and Gwendolyn May (Evans) Y.; A.B., San Francisco State Coll., 1943; M.A., Stanford, 1947, Ph.D., 1953; post-doctoral fellow, U. Mich., 1959-60; LL.D., U. Nev., 1972; m. Mae Catherine Wittenmyer, July 1, 1945; 1 son, Bruce Kenneth, Instr. journalism and speech San Francisco State Coll., 1946-48; instr. journalism and English, Cal. State Poly. Coll., 1949-50, asst. prof., then asso. prof. and acting dean arts and scis. Kellogg-Voorhis campus, 1951-57; dean faculty U. Alaska, 1957-59; exec. v.p. U. Nev., 1960-64; pres. State U. N.Y. Coll. at Cortland, 1964-68; v.p., dir. Washington office Am. Coll. Testing Program, 1968—, former mem. bd. dirs. Served with USAAF, 1943-45. Mem. Am. Assn. Higher Edn., Phi Delta Kappa. Home: 4411 Garfield St NW Washington DC 20007 Office: 1 DuPont Circle NW Washington DC 20036

YOUNG, LEO, elec. engr.; b. Vienna, Austria, Aug. 18, 1926; s. Samuel and Marie (Kessler) Y.; came to U.S., 1953, naturalized, 1959; B.A. in Math., Cambridge (Eng.) U., 1945, B.A. in Physics, 1947, M.A., 1950; M.S. in Elec. Engring., Johns Hopkins, 1956, Dr. Eng., 1959; m. Fay Lilian Merskey, Jan. 4, 1953; children—Philip, Sarah, Joseph, Head antenna lab. Decca Radar, Eng., 1951-53; adv. engr. Westinghouse Electric Corp., Balt., 1953-60; program mgr., staff scientist Stanford Research Inst., Menlo Park, Cal., 1960-73; cons.

elec. engr. Naval Research Lab., Washington, 1973—. Fellow I.E.E.E. (dir. 1971—, Microwave prize 1963). Author: (with G.L. Matthaei and E.M.T. Jones) Microwave Filters, Impedance Matching Networks and Coupling Structures, 1964; Systems of Units of Electricity and Magnetism, 1969. Editor: Advances in Microwaves, 8 vols., 1966—; Parallel Coupled Lines and Directional Couplers, 1972; Microwave Filters Using Parallel Coupled Lines, 1972. Contbr. articles on elec. engring. to tech. jours. Home: 6407 Maiden Lane Bethesda MD 20034 Office: Naval Research Lab Washington DC 20375

YOUNG, MARGARET ALETHA MCMULLEN (MRS. HERBERT WILSON YOUNG), social worker; b. Vossburg, Miss., June 13, 1916; d. Grady Garland and Virgie Aletha (Moore) McMullen; B.A. cum laude, Columbia Bible Coll., 1949; grad. Massey Bus. Coll., 1958; M.S.W., Fla. State U., 1965; postgrad. Jacksonville U., 1961-62, Tulane U., 1967; m. Herbert Wilson Young, Aug. 19, 1959. Dir. Christian edn. Eau Claire Presbyn. Ch., Columbia, S.C., 1946-51; tchr. Massey Bus. Coll., Jacksonville, Fla., 1954-57, office mgr., 1957-59; social worker, unit supr. Fla. div. Family Services, St. Petersburg, 1960-66, dist. casework supr., 1966-71; social worker Project Playpen, Inc., 1971—. Mem. Acad. Certified Social Workers, Nat. Assn. Social Workers (pres. Tampa Bay chpt.), Fla. Assn. on Children Under Six. Democrat. Presbyn. Rotary Ann (pres. 1970-71). Home: 330 Roebling Rd N Belleair Clearwater FL 33516 Office: 1250 1/2 Rogers St Clearwater FL 33516

YOUNG, MARJORIE WILLIS, writer, journalist, lectr.; b. Mansfield, O.; d. John Edgar and Mary Adelle (Reiter) Willis; student agr., Cornell U., 1924, Art Students League, 1925-27, Cooper Union, 1925-27, Columbia, 1927, Sorbonne, U. Paris, 1928-30, Japanese Lang. Sch., Tokyo, 1934-35, Columbia, 1943, N.Y.U., 1944; m. James Russell Young, Oct. 2, 1934; 1 son, Willis Patterson. Columnist in Far East, Internat. News Service, 1938-41; feature writer King Features Syndicate, 1939, Saturday Pictorial Rev., 1941-45; asst. tech. dir. motion picture Behind the Rising Sun, 1943; research dept. Believe It or Not, 1946-48; feature editor and columnist The Sunday Star, Wilmington, Del., 1946-48; promotion dir. David McKay Pub. Co., 1945-48; lectr. Nat. Concert and Artists Corp., 1942-43; feature writer Anderson (S.C.) Independent, 1949-73; feature writer Anderson Daily Mail, 1949-73, asso. editor The New South, ann. spl. edit. of Daily Mail, 1966-73; editor The Safety Jour., Anderson, 1953—; program moderator Decorating for a Holiday, sta. WAIM-TV, 1953-54, safety program moderator WAIM-TV, 1953—, program moderator How to Cut and Sew, 1954-55, travel feature program WAIM-WCAC-FM, 1973—; editor Vets. of Safety news page, What's What monthly; dir. Capitol City Communications, Inc. Spl. scroll dir. Chinese War Orphans' Relief, 1941-45; publicity dir. Crusade for Children, State of Del., 1948; publicity chmn. S.C. Indsl. Nurses Assn., 1953; dir. S.C. 4-H Club TV Safety Program, 1953. Bd. dirs. Anderson Heritage, Inc. Recipient various awards for safety activities including Distinguished Service award S.C. Occupational Safety Council, 1973. Mem. U. S.C. Caroliniana Soc., Far East Soc., Writer's Assn. Am., Nat. League Am. Pen Women, Am. Women in Radio and TV, Nat. Recreation Assn., S.C. Recreation Soc. (v.p. and program dir. 1954-56), Anderson County Hist. Soc. (dir.). Am. Soc. Safety Engrs., Am. Soc. Travel Writers, Am. Hort. Council, Vets. Safety Internat., Nat. Press Photographers Assn., D.A.R. Episcopalian. Clubs: Am. Newspaper Women's, Washington Press (Washington); Overseas Press of Am.; Cornell Women's (N.Y.C.). Author: Decorating for Joyful Occasions, 1952; It's Time for Christmas Decorations, 1957; Fodor's Tour Guide of South Carolina, 1966-68, Tour Guide of Georgia, 1966-67. Editor: Textile Leaders, 1963; Japanese American Cook Book, 1972. Home: 2003 Laurel Dr Anderson SC 29621 Office: WAIM-WCAC-FM-WAIM-TV Anderson SC 79621

YOUNG, OLIVER WAYNE, educator; b. McComb, Miss., July 26, 1940; s. William Thomas and Jimmie Elizabeth (Johnson) Y.; A.A., S.W. Miss. Jr. Coll., 1963; B.S., Miss. Coll., 1966; M.S., Miss. State U., 1968; postgrad. U. Miss., 1970-71. Tchr. sci. Bayou View Jr. High Sch., Gulfport, Miss., 1966; instr. biology, basketball coach S.W. Miss. Jr. Coll., Summit, 1966—. Grad. instr. U. Miss. Extension, 1971-72. Bd. dirs. S.W. Miss. Jr. Coll. Found., 1973-74. Served with USNR, 1958-61. Mem. Nat. Assn. Basketball Coaches, Nat. Assn. Biology Tchrs., Nat. Assn. Jr. Coll. Coaches, Miss. Edn. Assn., Miss. Coaches Assn. Lion (2d v.p. 1973-74). Baptist. Address: Southwest Miss Jr Coll Summit MS 39666

YOUNG, PAUL B., lawyer; b. Malvern, Ark., May 12, 1920; ed. Hendrix Coll., Conway, Ark.; J.D., U. Ark., 1947. Admitted to Ark. bar, 1947, since practiced in Pine Bluff. Mem. Am. (mem. corp., banking and bus. law sect.), Jefferson County, Ark. (jr. bar chmn. 1953, pres. 1971-72) bar assns., Phi Alpha Delta. Address: Box 7808 Pine Bluff AR 71601

YOUNG, RALPH ROWLAND, county ofcl.; b. East Orange, N.J., Apr. 4, 1943; s. Rowland Smith and Helen (Hartman) Y.; B.A., U. N.H., 1965; M.A., George Washington U., 1969; m. Judith Corbett, June 19, 1966; children—Kimberly, Jeffrey Corbett. Economist, George Washington U., 1968-69; mgmt. analyst, mgmt. officer, then asst. dir. Office Mgmt. and Budget, computer systems devel. supr. Fairfax County, Va., 1969—. Served to capt. AUS, 1966-68, now Res. Mem. Am. Econ. Assn., Acad. Mgmt., Vienna (Va.) Jaycees, Omicron Delta Epsilon. Home: 1110 Hillcrest Dr Vienna VA 22180 Office: 4100 Chain Bridge Rd Fairfax VA 22030

YOUNG, RAYMOND THEODORE, mfg. co. exec.; b. Waco, Tex., Dec. 29, 1922; s. John Charles and Anna Marie (Huber) Y.; student pub. schs.; m. Frances Marie Markum, Apr. 29, 1958; 1 dau., Mary Catherine. Pres., Young Bros., Inc., contractors, Waco, 1946-62, Slurry Seal, Inc., Waco, 1961—, Ryt, Inc., Waco, 1965—; v.p., dir. Slurry Seal of Mexico, S.A., 1966—. Mem. Pres.'s Regional Export Expansion Council, 1972—. Adv. bd. dirs. Providence Hosp., Waco, 1966-69. Served with USNR, 1942-45. Mem. Internat. Slurry Seal Assn. (organizer 1965, pres. 1965-67). Club: Ridgewood Country (Waco). Patentee in field. Home: 1148 Knotty Oaks Waco TX 76710 Office: PO Box 7677 Waco TX 76710

YOUNG, ROBERT GEORGE, lawyer; b. Atlanta, Mar. 9, 1923; s. Samuel Rollo and Cidney A. (Young) Y.; grad. Ga. Mil. Acad., 1940; A.B., Emory U., 1943; LL.B., U. Ga., 1949; m. Martha Latimer, Dec. 10, 1949; children—John Latimer, R. Carlisle, S. Scott. Admitted to Ga. bar, 1949; asso. Heyman, Howell and Heyman, 1949-51, Heyman and Abram, 1951-53, Marshall, Greene and Neely, 1953-55; partner Heyman, Abram and Young, 1955-63, Edenfield, Heyman and Sizemore, 1963-69, Webb, Parker, Young and Ferguson, 1970—; asst. county atty. Fulton County, Ga., 1966-71, county atty., 1971—. Mem. exec. com. Nat. Assn. of Railroad Trial Counsel, 1965-68. Treas. Fulton County Republican Exec. Com., 1962-64. Served to lt. (j.g.) USNR, 1944-46; PTO. Mem. Am. Bar Assn., Scotch-Irish Soc. U.S., Alpha Tau Omega. Presbyn. Kiwanian. Clubs: Lawyers of Atlanta, Capital City. Home: 3561 Ridgewood Rd NW Atlanta GA 30327 Office: Fulton Fed Bldg Atlanta GA 30303

YOUNG, ROBERT LYLE, engring. educator; b. Neoga, Ill., Apr. 3, 1925; s. Max Dryden and Neva (Higgins) Y.; B.S. in Mech. Engring., Northwestern U., 1946, M.S., 1948, Ph.D., 1953; m. Pyllis Eileen Ralston, Aug. 2, 1946 (dec. Aug. 1968); children—Ronald Lyle, Scott Alan; m. 2d, Martha Moore Robertson, Nov. 15, 1969; 1 stepson, Scotland Randolph Robertson. Instr., then asst. prof. Northwestern U., 1948-57; mem. faculty U. Tenn., 1957—, prof. mech. engring., dep. dir. Space Inst., 1961-71, prof., asso. dean, 1971—; cons. USAF, 1957—. Served with USNR, 1943-46. Mem. Am. Soc. M.E., Am. Inst. Aero. and Astronautics, Am. Soc. Engring. Edn., Sigma Xi. Rotarian. Author: (with E.F. Obert) Elements of Thermodynamics and Heat Transfer, 1961. Contbr. articles to profl. jours. Home: 108 Wilkins Dr Tullahoma TN 37388

YOUNGBLOOD, JOHN L., elec. engr.; b. Elkhart, Tex., Mar. 14, 1941; s. J. Douglas and Hessie B. (Caffy) Y.; B.S., U. Tex., 1963; M.S., Okla. State U., 1965, Ph.D. (Nat. Def. Edn. Act fellow), 1967; m. Larri Sharon Doyle, Aug. 31, 1963; children—John Scott, Jennifer Lynn, Stacy D'Ann, Jay David. Research asst. Okla. State U., Stillwater, 1965-66; project aerosystem engr. Gen. Dynamics, Ft. Worth, 1966-69, group engr., 1969-72, project mgr. Convair aerospace div., 1972—. Mem. faculty elec. engring. U. Tex., Arlington, 1969-70. Mem. I.E.E.E., Eta Kappa Nu, Phi Kappa Phi, Tau Beta Pi, Pi Mu Epsilon. Home: 3008 Santa Fe Trail Fort Worth TX 76116 Office: PO Box 748 Fort Worth TX 76101

YOUNGBLOOD, RAY WILSON, pub. co. exec.; b. Tulia, Tex., Feb. 18, 1931; s. Burk Richard and Jenny Lucile (Wilson) Y.; B.B.A., Tex. Tech U., 1952; postgrad. U. Tex., 1957-58; m. Imogene Price, June 7, 1959; children—Michael Ray, Janet Lynn. Auditor, Peat, Marwick Mitchell & Co., C.P.A.'s, Houston, 1958-65; chief accountant Houston Chronicle Pub. Co., newspaper pub., 1965-66, controller, asst. treas., 1966—; pres. Houston Chronicle Employees Fed. Credit Union, 1970—. Served to 1st lt. USAF, 1952-57. C.P.A., Tex. Mem. Inst. Newspaper Controllers and Finance Officers (dir. 1971—), Am. Inst. C.P.A.'s, Tex. Soc. C.P.A.'s, Nat. Assn. Accountants, Financial Execs. Inst., Delta Sigma Pi. Methodist (mem. meml. drive 1967—). Clubs: Exchange (treas. 1971-72). Home: 13626 Pinerock St Houston TX 77024 Office: 801 Texas Av Houston TX 77002

YOUNGBLOOD, SUE DAVIS (MRS. JACK YOUNGBLOOD), mayor; b. Corsicana, Tex.; d. Plemon B. and Jimmie (McClendon) Davis; student pub. schs.; m. Jack Youngblood, May 25, 1946; children—Gary Jack, David Alan. Partner, office mgr. Youngblood Ins. Agy., Corsicana, Tex., 1954—. City commr., Corsicana, Tex., 1968-71, mayor, 1971—. Bd. dirs. Navarro County Assn. Retarded Children; chmn. bd. Corsicana Pub. Library. Mem. Corsicana C. of C. (ex-officio dir.), Bus. and Profl. Womens Club. Home: 2029 Glennwood Circle Corsicana TX 75110 Office: 615 W 7th Av Corsicana TX 75110

YOUNGBLOOD, THOMAS JEFFERSON, JR., clergyman; b. Covington, Ky., Aug. 1, 1920; s. Thomas Jefferson and Cornelia Ella (Duvall) Y.; student Tex. Wesleyan Coll., 1939-41; A.B., Tex. Christian U., 1948; B.D., Phillips U., 1951; D.D., Atlantic Christian Coll., 1968; m. Katharyn Margaret Lilly, Apr. 6, 1941; children—Thomas Jefferson III, Judy Kaye (Mrs. Frank T. Nickell). Ordained to ministry Christian Ch., 1951; minister Poly. Christian Ch., Ft. Worth, 1946-48, First Christian Ch., Thomas, Okla., 1948-51, First Christian Ch., Arlington, Tex., 1951-60, Hillyer Meml. Christian Ch., Raleigh, N.C., 1960-71, Central Christian Ch., San Antonio, 1971—. Trustee Atlantic Christian Coll., Wilson, N.C., 1963-66, Pension Fund of Christian Ch. (Disciples of Christ), 1965—; bd. mgrs., Unified Promotion Christian Ch. (Disciples of Christ), 1971—. Mem. Pi Gamma Mu. Served with USAAF, 1942-45. Mason, Kiwanian. Home: 2923 Larkwood St San Antonio TX 78209 Office: 720 N Main Av San Antonio TX 78205

YOUNGDAHL, LUTHER W., former gov. Minn., judge; b. Mpls., May 29, 1896; s. John Carl and Elizabeth (Johnson) Y.; U. Minn., 1915-16; A.B., Gustavus Adolphus Coll., 1919; LL.B., Minn. Coll. Law, 1921; numerous hon. degrees; m. Irene Annet Engdahl, June 23, 1923; children—Margaret Louise, Luther William Andrew, Paul David. Asst. city atty. Mpls., 1921-23; practiced law with Judge Tifft, 1923-30; judge, Municipal Ct., Mpls., 1930-36; judge Dist. Ct., Hennepin County, Mpls., 1936-42; asso. justice Minn. Supreme Ct., 1942-46; gov. Minn., 1947-51; judge U.S. Dist. Ct. for D.C., 1951—, sr. judge, 1966—. Chmn. com. on adminstrn. probation system in fed. cts. Nat. Jud. Conf., 1963-66. Mem. Pres.'s Commn. Law Enforcement and Adminstrn. Justice, 1965-67; mem. adv. council judges Nat. Council on Crime and Delinquency, 1953-71; mem. adv. com. on sentencing and rev. Am. Bar Assn. Project on Minimum Standards for Criminal Justice, 1965—. Bd. dirs. Joint Commn. on Correctional Manpower and Tng. Recipient Grand Cross Royal Order North Star, Finnish Order of Lion. Served in World War I. Author: Ramparts We Watch. Home: 4101 Cathedral Av NW Washington DC 20016 Office: US Courthouse Washington DC 20543

YOUNGER, EDWARD FRANKLIN, JR., lawyer; b. Lynchburg, Va., May 1, 1912; s. Edward Franklin and Grace Schenck (Gilliam) Y.; student Hampden-Sydney Coll., 1929-33; A.B., U. Va., 1934, LL.B., 1937, J.D., 1971; m. Nell English, June 29, 1940; children—Katherine Lee, Edward Franklin III, Grace (Mrs. Sheldon M. Rutter), Goerge English. Admitted to Va. bar, 1937, since practiced in Lynchburg; trustee Wage Earner Plans under Chpt. XIII of Bankruptcy Act, 1965—. Sec.-treas. Reams Co., Rock Creek Colliery Co.; dir. Bank of Central Va. Bd. dirs., mem. exec. com. Spring Hill Cemetery Assn.; bd. dirs., sec. Family Service Central Va.; trustee Va. Bapt. Hosp., former pres., now mem. finance com.; bd. dirs. Central Lynchburg, Inc. Served with AUS, 1944-45. Decorated Bronze Star medal, Combat Inf. badge. Mem. Am., Va., Lynchburg bar assns. Baptist (trustee). Rotarian. Clubs: Oakwood Country, Piedmont. Home: 1300 Langhorne Rd Lynchburg VA 24503 Office: 915 1/2 Main St Lynchburg VA 24504

YOUNGER, HAROLD BURRNELL, dentist; b. Morgan, Tex., Sept. 20, 1906; s. Williamson Henry and Stella (McKisick) Y.; D.D.S., Baylor U., 1927; postgrad. So. Methodist U., 1943-44; m. Lois Hortense King, Feb. 21, 1935; 1 dau., Suzanne (Mrs. Aubrey Benjamen/Pinnell, Jr.). Practice dentistry, Dallas, 1927—. Mem. staff Children's Med. Center, Dallas, 1928—, chief dental service, 1935-67, chief emeritus, 1967—; asso. dental research Baylor U., Dallas, 1941-50, lectr., 1957-62, asso. prof., 1962-63, clin. prof., 1963-69; columnist Your Teeth and You, Dallas Morning News, 1960—; mem. Dallas Pub. Health Bd., 1962; chmn. Dallas Health Council, 1956-58; dir. Freeman Meml. Clinic, Dallas, 1953—. Mem. City-County Civil Def. Commn; chief Dallas County (Tex.) Sheriff's Res., 1950-70. Bd. dirs. Dallas Council Social Agys., 1956-60, Dallas Community Chest, 1959-60. maj. gen. Tex. State Guard ret. Fellow Am. Coll. Dentists (pres. Tex. sect. 1957-58); mem. Am. (clinician), Tex., Neb. (hon., clinician), Colo. (clinician), N.M. (clinician) dental assns., Dallas County Dental Soc. (pres. 1959-60), Am. Acad. Oral Medicine, Southwestern Soc. Oral Medicine (pres. 1953-54), Dallas Dentoecon. Soc., Orgn. Tchrs. Dental Practice Adminstrn. (pres. 1966-67), Am. Acad. Dental Practice Adminstrn., Omicron Kappa Upsilon, Delta Sigma Delta. Methodist. Kiwanian (distinguished service award Dallas 1953, pres. Dallas 1969). Contbr. articles and chpts. to profl. publs. Home: 3615 Fairmount St Dallas TX 75219

YOUNKER, SISTER M. MARGUERITE, educator; b. Paducah, Ky.; d. Henry Francis and Rosa (Poat) Younker; Mus.B., Catholic U. of Am., 1927; Mus.M., Am. Conservatory Music (Chgo.), 1939. Tchr., chmn. dept. music Mt. St. Joseph Jr. Coll., Maple Mount, Ky., 1927-49; tchr. Brescia Coll., Owensboro, Ky., 1949—, chmn. dept. music, 1949—. Bd. dirs. Owensboro Symphony Orch. Mem. Nat. Catholic Music Educators Assn., Nat. Music Edn. Assn., Coll. Music Soc., Music Tchrs. Nat. Assn., Ky. Music Tchrs. Assn., Internat. Piano Tchrs. Assn., Am. Musicol. Soc., Ky. Music Educators Assn. Address: Brescia College 120 W 7th St Owensboro KY 42301

YOUNT, JOHN THOMAS, pub. co. exec., author; b. San Angelo, Tex., Apr. 12, 1927; s. Otto and Mary (Lamb) Y.; grad. high sch.; m. Lucille Miller Hopkins, June 8, 1970. Pres., Educator Books, Inc., San Angelo, 1967—; owner Custom Book Bindery of San Angelo, 1971—; editor, pub. Book World mag., 1973—. Served with USNR, 1944-46, 50-54. Author: Bottle Collector's Handbook, 1967; Mail Order Advertising Handbook, 1969; Picture Framing Handbook; Leathercraft Handbook, 1970; Bridge Beginners Handbook, 1971; also children's books. Home: 2206 W Concho St San Angelo TX 76901 Office: 10 N Main St San Angelo TX 76901

YOUNT, LAVINIA ANN CAROTHERS (MRS. JAMES L. YOUNT), civic worker; b. Pitts., Feb. 23, 1927; d. James M. and Lavinia (Jones) Carothers; A.B., Vassar Coll., 1948; postgrad. U. N.C., 1948-50, U. Hawaii, 1950; m. James Locke Yount, Sept. 6, 1949; children—Eric C., Jennifer Ann. Tchr., Punahou Sch., Honolulu, 1951-54. Pres. League Women Voters, Polk County, 1962-65, mem. Fla. bd. dirs., 1965-71, 2d v.p., 1969-71; bd. dirs. United Fund, Winter Haven, Fla., 1969-72; bd. dirs., sec. Ridge Sch., Winter Haven, 1968-70. Presbyn. (elder). Home: Lake Daisy Rd Route 4 Box 130 Winter Haven FL 33880

YOUNTS, CHARLES ALBERT, dentist; b. Temple, Tex., Nov. 17, 1920; s. Charlie and Bessie Mae (Guinn) Y.; student Temple Jr. Coll., 1945-47, U. Houston, 1947-48; D.D.S., U. Tex., 1952; m. Fayola Loretta Schneider, June 25, 1942; children—Timothy, Todd, Tana. Individual practice dentistry, Humble, Tex., 1952—; dir. Am. Nat. Bank, Humble. City councilman, Humble, 1954-61, city judge, 1961-63; mem. Humble Ind. Sch. Dist., 1968—, pres., 1971. Served with USAAF, 1943-46; PTO. Mem. Am., Tex. dental assns., Houston Dist. Dental Soc. K.C., Lion. Home: 513 Lakeland St Humble TX 77338 Office: 110 S Av E Humble TX 77338

YOUNTS, CHARLES ROLPHI, ret. petroleum exec.; b. Pineville, N.C., July 7, 1895; s. William E. and Eunice (Bell) Y.; grad. Bairds U., 1912; L.H.D., Erskine Coll., 1962; m. Willie Antoinette Camp, Mar. 12, 1930. With Standard Oil Co. of N.J. and affiliates, 1912-60; pres. Plantation Pipe Line Co., 1941-59, chmn. bd., 1960. Past moderator Gen. Synod Assn. Ref. Presbyn. Ch., also chmn. trustees, mem. session, Doraville, Ga., treas. retirement plan. Bd. dirs. Blue Ridge Assembly, Inc.; bd. dirs., past pres. Churches Homes for Bus. Girls, Inc., Atlanta; bd. dirs., past chmn. Atlanta chpt. A.R.C.; dir. So. Indsl. Relations Conf.; trustee, treas. Erskine Coll., Due West, S.C.; trustee Met. Atlanta YMCA. Served from pvt. to 1st sgt., U.S. Army, 1917-19. Mem. Newcomen Soc., S.A.R. Mason, Rotarian (Atlanta Armin Maier award for 1949-50). Clubs: Piedmont Driving, Capital City (Atlanta). Home: 3018 Habersham Rd NW Atlanta GA 30305 Office: 140 Peachtree St NW Atlanta GA 30303

YUDKOWKSY, ELIAS B., educator; b. Bklyn., June 3, 1932; student U. Md., 1950-53; D.D.S., Northwestern U., 1957; Ph.D. in Endocrinology (NIH research fellow 1961-68), U. Cal. at San Francisco, 1968. Microbiology lab. technician Northwestern U., 1953-57, instr. oral diagnosis, 1959-61; dental intern Waterbury (Conn.) Gen. Hosp., 1957-58, dir. dental outpatient dept., 1958; practice dentistry, Chgo., 1958-61; research lab. worker, lectr. U. Cal. at San Francisco, 1962-67; asst. sec. Council Dental Research, also asst. dir. Dental Research Information Center Am. Dental Assn., Chgo., 1967-69; asst. dean adminstrn., coordinator Harvard-VA Continuing Edn. Program New Eng., Harvard Sch. Dental Medicine, 1969-70; asso. prof. cell biology Dental Sch., asst. prof. anatomy Med. Sch. Med. U. S.C., Charleston, 1970—. Address: Coll Dental Medicine Med U SC Charleston SC 29401

YURGAITIS, ALEXANDER W., JR., constrn. exec.; b. Front Royal, Va., Sept. 13, 1925; s. Alexander W. and Margaret Elizabeth (Clegg) Y.; student Columbia Tech. Inst., Washington, 1947-48; m. Alice Trigg Swain, Jan. 3, 1951; children—Helen (Mrs. Richard Isley), Diane, Twila, Alexander Thomas. Pres. Yurgaitis Constrn. Co., Inc., Warrenton, Va., 1951—; pres. Yurgaitis Real Estate Co., Bethel Acad. Water Co., Inc.; dir. Peoples Nat. Bank, America, Inc.; pres., dir. Sulphur Springs Investment Co., Inc. Active Boy Scouts Am. Served with USNR, 1944-46; PTO. Mem. Nat. Assn. Realtors, Fauquier Bd. Realtors (pres. 1968-69, dir.), Va. Assn. Realtors (dir. 1968-69), Nat. Inst. Farm and Land Brokers. Democrat. Episcopalian. Clubs: Corinthian Yacht (Washington); Virginia Yacht (Urbanna, Va.); Augusta Country (Staunton, Va.); Fauquier Lions (pres. 1962-63); Fauguier Springs Country (chmn. bd. 1971-72). Home: Bethel Academy Rd Warrenton VA 22186 Office: Rt 1 Warrenton VA 22186

ZABALETA, NICANOR, harpist; b. San Sebastian, Spain, Jan. 7, 1907; s. Pedro and Isabel (Zala) Z.; student Madrid Conservatory Music; studied harp with Marcel Tournier, 1924-28, harmony with Marcel Samuel-Rousseau, counterpoint and fugue with Eugene Cools; m. Graciela Torres, Feb. 22, 1952; children—Pedro, Estela. Came to U.S., 1953. Soloist numerous symphony orchs. including Berlin Philharmonic, Israel Philharmonic, London New Philharmonia, Madrid Nat. Symphony, Paris Orch., Phila. Orch., Tokyo NHK Orch., Budapest Philharmonic, Rome RAI Orch.; performed numerous music festivals at Edinburgh, Venice, Osaka, Berlin, others; also gave 2500 recitals throughout world. Mem. jury Israel 1st Internat. Harp Contest, 1959, Israel 4th Internat. Harp Contest, 1970, Paris 1st Internat. Harp Contest, 1971. Home: 1300 Luchetti Av Santurce PR 00907 Office: PO BOX 886 San Juan PR 00902

ZACHARY, HUGH (PEN NAME ZACH HUGHES), author; b. Holdenville, Okla., Jan. 12, 1928; s. John F. and Ida Louise (Duckworth) Z.; B.A., U. N.C., 1951; m. Elizabeth Wiggs, Jan. 10, 1948; children—Whitney Leigh (Mrs. Allen Walters), Leslie Beth (Mrs. Horace Collier). Engaged in radio-TV broadcasting, 15 years; free lance writer, 1963—. Pres. Ridge Art Assn., Winter Haven, Fla., 1960-61. Served with 82d Airborne Div., U.S. Army, 1946-48. Author: A Feast of Fat Things, 1968; The Beachcombers Handbook of Seafood Cookery, 1970. Address: Pebble Beach Dr Oak Island NC 28461

ZACHERT, VIRGINIA, psychologist, educator; b. Jacksonville, Ala., Mar. 1, 1920; d. Rev. R. E. and Cora H. (Massee) Zachert; student Norman Jr. Coll., 1937; A.B., Ga. State Woman's Coll., 1940; M.A., Emory U., 1947; Ph.D., Purdue U., 1949. Statistician, Davison-Paxon Co., Atlanta, 1941-44; research psychologist Mil. Contracts, Auburn Research Found., Ala. Poly. Inst.; indsl. and research psychologist Sturm & O'Brien, cons. engrs., 1958-59;

research project dir. Western Design, Biloxi, Miss., 1960-61; self-employed cons. psychologist, Norman Park, Ga., 1961-71, Good Hope, Ga., 1971—; research asso. med. edn. Med. Coll. Ga. Augusta, 1963-65, asso. prof., 1965-70, prof., 1970—. Mem. adv. bd. Comdr. Gen. ATC, USAF, 1967-70. Served aerologist USN, 1944-46, aviation psychologist USAF, 1949-54. Diplomate Am. Bd. Profl. Psychologists. Fellow Am. Psychol. Assn.; mem. Am. Statis. Assn., Sigma Xi. Baptist. Author: (with P. L. Wilds) Essentials of Gynecology-Oncology, 1967, Applications of Gynecology-Oncology, 1967. Home: Box 130 Modoc SC 29838 Office: Dept Obstetrics and Gynecology Med Coll Ga Augusta GA 30902

ZACK, PETER GEORGE, physician; b. Pine Bluff, Ark., Nov. 28, 1933; s. George and Eugenia (Paschal) Z.; student Tulane U., 1951-53; B.S., U. Ark., 1955; postgrad. Duke, 1955-56; M.D., U. Ark., 1960; m. Ida Gaile Reynolds, Sept. 3, 1957; children—Peter Gregory, Karen Anne. Intern, Meth. Hosp. Dallas, 1960-61; pediatric resident Children's Med. Center, Dallas, 1963-65; pediatric fellow Mead-Johnson Labs., 1964-65; practice medicine specializing in pediatrics Pediatric Center, Wilmington, N.C., 1971—; mem. staff New Hanover Meml. Hosp.; cons. staff Babies Hosp., Wrightsville, N.C., Cape Fear Hosp., Wilmington. Bd. dirs. local Mental Retardation Assn. Served with USNR, 1961-63. Mem. A.M.A., So. Tenn. med. assns., Hanover County, N.C. med. socs., U. Ark. Alumni Assn. Home: 2001 S Churchill Dr Wilmington NC 28401 Office: 1914 Glen Meade Rd Wilmington NC 28401

ZACKO, GEORGE BERNARD, dentist; b. Pottsville, Pa., Aug. 6, 1932; s. Joseph Charles and Ethel Loretta (Steinheiser) Z.; student Wesleyan U., Middletown, Conn., 1951-54; B.A., Franklin and Marshall Coll., 1956; D.D.S., U. Pa., 1960; m. Donna Cummings, Aug. 7, 1970; children—George Brian, Dorothy Damon (dec.), Patricia Brett, Joseph Christopher. Practice dentistry, Herndon, Va., 1962-66, Reston, Va., 1966—, Sterling, Va., 1971—; pres. Zacko & Shattuck, Inc., corporate group dental practice, 1971—; clin. instr. Georgetown U. Sch. Medicine, 1969-73. Served with USNR, 1960-62. Mem. Am. Dental Assn., Internat. Assn. Orthodontics, Am. Soc. for Study Orthodontia, Acad. Gen. Dentistry, Am. Acad. Dental Group Practice. Republican. Roman Catholic. Rotarian. Home: 2403 Black Cap Lane Reston VA 22070 Office: Reston Med Bldg 1712 Clubhouse Rd Reston VA 22090 also Dulles Internat Med Center Sterling VA 22170

ZAD, MARTIE STEPHEN, journalist; b. Bridgeport, Conn., Aug. 25, 1927; s. Martin Frank and Christina (Mulch) Zadravec; B.S., U. Md., 1953; m. Katharine E. Elson, Dec. 27, 1956; children—Gina, Martin, Lisa, Karen, Sarah, Stefanie. Sports reporter Washington Post, 1950-63, exec. sports editor, 1963-70, asst. mng. editor sports, 1970—. Served with USNR, 1944-46. Home: 3804 Williams Lane Chevy Chase MD 20015 Office: 1515 L St NW Washington DC 20005

ZAGON, IAN STUART, biologist; b. N.Y.C., Mar. 28, 1943; s. Bert and Beatrice (Shaffer) Z.; B.S., U. Wis., 1965; M.S., U. Ill., 1969; Ph.D. (NIH fellow), U. Colo., 1972; m. Eileen Joyce Kostel, Nov. 26, 1964. Teaching asst. U. Ill., Urbana, 1967-68, research asst., 1968-69; asst. prof. biol. structure U. Miami (Fla.), 1972—. Mem. A.A.A.S., Am. Soc. Zoology, Soc. Protozoology, Am. Micros. Soc., Soc. Cell Bilogy, Am. Inst. Biol. Scis., Sigma Xi. Contbr. articles to profl. jours. Home: 7757 SW 86th St Miami FL 33143 Office: Dept Biol Structure U Miami PO Box 875 Biscayne Annex Miami FL 33152

ZAHN, JOSIAH HILLMAN, telephone co. exec.; b. Phila., Aug. 6, 1920; s. George W.A. and Mellie (Crawford) Z.; B.S. in Econs., Wharton Sch., U. Pa., 1942; m. Constance Escott Morgan, Aug. 24, 1944; children—Robert Allen, Elizabeth Carroll. With Bell Telephone Co. Pa., 1945-60, Mich. Bell Telephone Co., 1960-61; with C & P Telephone Cos., 1961—; v.p. pub. relations, 1966—; dir. Equitable Life Ins. Co. Bd. dirs. Washington Bd. Trade, 1962-67, 69-70; trustee Fed. City Council, 1964—; exec. v.p. Nat. Alliance of Businessmen, 1969-70. Bd. dirs. Doctors Hosp. Research Found., 1969—; adv. bd. George Washington U., 1968-70; trustee, treas. Mt. Vernon Coll., 1968-69; bd. dirs. Health Facilities Planning Council, 1962-69, vice chmn., 1969; trustee Washington Tech. Inst., 1967—. Served to lt. USNR, 1942-45. Mem. Md.-D.C. Utilities Assn. (pres. 1968). Lutheran. Club: University (Washington). Home: 5236 Westpath Way Washington DC 20016 Office: 1710 H St NW Washington DC 20006

ZAHRT, MARTHA LEONARD, indsl. editor; b. Dallas; d. Ernest E. and Lily V. (Bell) Leonard; student U. Chgo.; m. Walter S. Zahrt, Sept. 10, 1935 (div. 1946); 1 dau., Kathleen W. With advt. dept. Carson Pirie Scott & Co., Chgo., 1931; asst. to account exec. N.W. Ayer & Son, Inc., Chgo., 1931-36; researcher part-time market survey Tracy Locke Dawson, advt. agy., Dallas, 1936-38; editor employee newspaper Braniff Internat., Dallas, 1945-54, mgr. publs., 1954-70, dir. publs., 1970-73; free lance indsl. editor, pub. relations, 1973—. Nat. chmn. editors com. Savs. Bonds div. U.S. Treasury, 1968-70. Recipient Bronze Medalion S.W. Journalism Forum, 1956; named Editor of Year Dallas Indsl. Editors Assn., 1953. Mem. Greater Dallas Council Chs. (mem. publicity com. 1966—), Internat. Council, Dallas (dir. nat. affairs 1964-65) indsl. editors, Airline Editors Conf., Women in Communications (Matrix award Dallas chpt. 1966, chpt. pres. 1966—, area dir. 1970). Clubs: Braniff International Management (v.p. 1961), Press (Dallas) (charter, treas. 1957, Best Indsl. Newspaper award 1962). Office: Braniff Internat Braniff Bldg Exchange Park Dallas TX 75235

ZAINO, LOUIS FREDERICK, systems analyst; b. Louisville, May 24, 1923; s. Louis and Helen Bertha (Zaugg) Z.; B.S., U. Louisville, 1949; m. Mabel Christine Hickey, July 18, 1947; children—Russell B., Linda D., Jeffrey B. With Louisville & Nashville R.R., Louisville, 1950-69, various accounting positions, 1950-59, programmer, 1959-65, project leader, 1965-67, sect. mgr., 1967-69; mgr. complex systems Cybernetics & Systems, Inc., Louisville, 1969—. Served with AUS, 1943-46: PTO. Mem. Assn. Am. Railroads, Assn. Systems Mgmt., Data Processing Mgmt. Assn. Mem. United Ch. of Christ. Mason. Home: 4504 Walton Ct Louisville KY 40213 Office: 6100 Dutchman's Lane Louisville KY 40205

ZAISER, MARION LLEWELLYN BROWN (MRS. ROBERT ALAN ZAISER), writer, civic worker; b. St. Petersburg, Fla., Jan. 12, 1917; d. Llewellyn Chauncey and Marion Edwina (Ames) Brown; B.A., Sweet Briar Coll., 1938; m. Robert Alan Zaiser, Aug. 26, 1939 (dec. Feb. 1947); children—Alan Robert, Kent Ames. Reporter, features, editorials Evening Ind., St. Petersburg, 1938-39; owner, operator copper tooling studio, 1952-54; dir. pub. information South Pinellas County chpt. A.R.C., 1954-56; sec. Equity Holdings, Inc., St. Petersburg, 1961—, also Brown, Zaiser & Brown; partner Marion B. Zaiser & L.C. Brown, citrus grove. Br. dirs. Nat. League Am. Pen Women, 1962-66, br. pres., 1964-66, state corr. sec., 1966-67; coordinator Ams. Abroad, Am. Field Service, St. Petersburg, 1962-63; active various community drives; pub. relations chmn., bd. dirs. Christmas Toy Shop, Inc., 1958-61, 68-72, rec. sec., 1970-72; chmn. Jr. Red Cross, 1942-44; mem. pub. information com. A.R.C., 1956—, chpt. bd. dirs., 1971-72; sec. Snell Isle Property Owners Assn., 1963-64; den mother Cub Scouts, 1950-55; mem. diocesan Christian edn. com. Episcopal Churchwomen South Fla., 1952-55; mem. St. Petersburg Mus. Fine Arts, All Children's Hosp., Little Theater, 1938-71, YWCA, Sci. Center; mem. Jr. League, 1938-47. Trustee Canterbury Sch. Fla., 1968—. Recipient Pageant award for best biography, 1960, citation Sigma Delta Chi, 1960. Mem. Stuart Soc., Sweet Briar Alumnae Assn. (class sec. 1958-63), Christmas Belles. Republican. Episopalian (mem. altar guild, 1957-62, ch. sch. com. 1966-68, sec. vestry 1971-72). Clubs: Nat. Writers, St. Petersburg Yacht, MacDill AFB Officers. Author: The Beneficient Blaze, 1960. Home: 1248 Monterey Blvd St Petersburg FL 33704

ZALAR, CHARLES, govt. ofcl.; b. Franzdorf, Austria, Sept. 10, 1909; s. Joseph and Marianne (Oblak) Z.; B.S., Belgrade U., 1930; B.A., Ljubljana U., 1931, LL.M., 1935, Ph.D., 1936; postgrad. (scholar) Sorbonne, Paris, 1936-38, Rome U., 1941-43; Ph.D., Georgetown U., 1958; m. Minka Verbic, Aug. 16, 1936; 1 son, Gregory. Came to U.S., 1952, naturalized 1957. Fgn. service officer, Belgrade, Vatican, Paris, 1938-52; research analyst Library of Congress, 1952-62; sci. information adminstr. NSF, Washington, 1962-71, asso. program dir., 1969-72, fgn. sci. adminstr., 1971—, program dir., 1972—. Cons. internat. law, 1946-52. Mem. French Soc. Comparative Legislation, Am. Polit. Sci. Assn., Am. Soc. Internat. Law, Internat. Polit. Sci. Assn., Am. Mil. Inst., A.A.A.S. Author: Yugoslav Communism, 1961. Home: 4545 Connecticut Av NW Washington DC 20008 Office: 1800 G St NW Washington DC 20550

ZANDALL, RICHARD RUDOLPH, program adminstr. in education; b. Gary, Ind., Jan. 22, 1931; s. Rudolph Richard and Anne (Barlock) Z.; grad. Valparaiso Tech. Inst., 1956; m. Kathleen Margaret Sager, Jan. 31, 1959; children—Mary Ann, Laura Louise, Nancy Marie, Margaret Rose. Customer engr. IBM, Chgo., 1956-59, customer engr., computer instr., 1959-62, customer engring. field mgr., 1962-65, fed. region staff systems rep., Washington, 1965-68, edn. industry marketing staff, 1968-74, program adminstr. in edn., 1974—. Served with USAF, 1951-55. Mem. I.E.E.E., Data Processing Mgmt. Assn. Republican. Roman Catholic. K.C. Home: 11221 Hunting Horn Lane Reston VA 22091 Office: 10401 Fernwood Rd Bethesda MD 20034

ZANE, ALAN IRVING, physician; b. Detroit, June 26, 1935; s. Benjamin and Bessie (Popkoff) Z.; M.D., Wayne State U., 1960; m. Audrey Rocklin, Dec. 21, 1958; children—Randall, Cheryl, Robert, Bradley, Susan. Intern Sinai Hosp., Detroit, 1960-61; resident otolaryngology Wayne State U. Affiliated Hosp., Detroit, 1961-65; practice medicine specializing in otolaryngology Hauser Clinic, Detroit, 1967-73, Corpus Christi, Tex., 1973—; mem. staff Meml. Med. Center, Spohn, Doctors, Physicians and Surgeons, Driscoll Children's hosps., all Corpus Christi; asst. prof. Wayne State U. Coll. Medicine, 1967-73, Baylor Coll. Medicine, 1973—. Served with USNR, 1965-67. Diplomate Am. Bd. Otolaryngology. Fellow A.C.S.; mem. A.M.A., Neuces County, Tex. med. socs., Am. Acad. Ophthalmology and Otolaryngology, Phi Delta Epsilon. Jewish religion. Home: 5133 Cape Ann St Corpus Christi TX 78412 Office: Suite 19 3166 Reid St Corpus Christi TX 78404

ZAPOLEON, MARGUERITE WYKOFF, cons., lectr., author; b. Cin., Aug. 18, 1907; d. Fred Clark and Elizabeth (Voth) Wykoff; B.A., engring. degree, U. Cin., 1928; postgrad. Geneva Sch. Internat. Studies, 1927, N.Y. Sch. Social Work, 1928-29, London Sch. Econ. and Polit. Sci., 1932; M.A., Am. U., 1938; m. Louis B. Zapoleon, Oct. 2, 1937 (dec. Dec. 1969). Began career as vocation counselor in the Cin. Pub. Schs., 1929-35; chief of counseling div. D.C. Employment Center, 1935-39; specialist occupational information and guidance service U.S. Office Edn., 1939-43; tng. specialist Hdqrs. ASF, 1943-44; chief employment opportunities br. Women's Bur., Dept. Labor, 1944-51, spl. asst. occupational outlook service Bur. Labor Statistics, 1951-55, spl. asst. to dir. Women's Bur., 1955-60; cons. on labor econs. and vocational guidance, 1960—; lectr., workshop leader, instr. vocational guidance and occupational research colls., univs., Am. Assn. U. Women adult counseling project, 1965; adv. com., panel asso. Assn. Appraisers Earning Capacity, 1964-70; mem. tech. coms., recorder employment sect. White House Conf. on Aging, 1971. Bd. dirs. Am. Soc. Econometric Appraisers, 1967-70, Friends of Everglades; trustee Fla. Council Aging. Mem. Nat. Vocational Guidance Assn. (trustee 1945-51), Council Guidance and Personnel Assn. (v.p. 1947-48), Alliance for Guidance Rural Youth (2d v.p. 1952-60), Am. Personnel and Guidance Assn. (del. to Assembly 1951-60), Am. Econ. Assn., Indsl. Relations Research Assn., Am. Ednl. Research Assns., Nat. Assn. Deans and Counselors of Women. Am. Assn. U. Woman, Nat. League Am. Pen Women, A.A.A.S., Am. Statis. Assn., Internat. Platform Assn., Nature Conservancy (rec. sec. Fla. br. 1972), Fairchild Gardens, Gerontol. Soc., Kappa Kappa Gamma (alumni achievement award 1968). Presbyn. Author: (with Louise Moore) Reference and Related Information: Vocational Guidance for Girls and Women, 1941; Community Occupational Surveys, 1942; The College Girl Looks Ahead to Her Career Opportunities, 1956; Occupational Planning for Women, 1961; Girls and Their Futures, 1963; Wrongful Death of Housewife and Mother, 1965; Economic Aspects of Counseling Adult Women, 1966; also author of numerous govermental pamphlets on occupations and vocational guidance edn. and tng.; articles in profl. jours. Editor: Vocational Guidance Quar., 1953-54. Home: 816 SE Riviera Isle Fort Lauderdale FL 33301

ZAREMBA, SYLVIA ANNE (MRS. ROBERT E. PRESTON), concert pianist, educator; b. Chicopee, Mass.; d. John and Anna (Szot) Zaremba; B.Mus., artist's diploma Curtis Inst. Music, Phila., 1947; m. Robert E. Preston, June 4, 1960. Concert pianist; debut at age 10, Town Hall, N.Y.C.; concertized in U.S., Europe, Central and S.Am.; appearances with symphony orchs., N.Y.C., Chgo., Cleve., Phila., San Antonio, Dallas, Oklahoma City, New Orleans; asst. prof., artist-in-residence U. Okla., 1953-60; asso. prof. music Newcomb Coll., Tulane U., New Orleans, 1964—. Rec. artist, 1958—; soloist Am. Symphony Orch., Carnegie Hall, 1966; artist-in-residence N.H. Music Festival, 1970—. Named Outstanding Faculty Woman U. Okla., 1961. Mem. Pi Kappa Lambda, Mu Phi Epsilon. Home: 5870 Sylvia Dr Lakewood North New Orleans LA 70124

ZARSKY, CLIFFORD LOUIS, constrn. co. exec.; b. Woodsboro, Tex., Sept. 9, 1928; s. Louis J. and Beatrice Marie (St. Onge) Z.; B.A., Mary Knoll Coll., 1951; J.D., U. Tex., 1957; m. Joyce Clarice Ulcak, Feb. 4, 1961; children—Brion Clifford, Louis John, Karen Clarice. Admitted to Tex. bar, 1957; practiced in Austin, 1957-58, Corpus Christi, 1958—; asso. Arthur Mitchel, Austin, 1957, Corpus Christi, 1958; asst. dist. atty., Nueces County, Tex., 1959-61, 1st asst. dist. atty., 1964-68; with Wood Constrn. Co., Seattle, 1962-64; Cliff Zarsky Texan Homes, Inc., Corpus Christi, 1969—; pres., partner Zarsky & Hill, attys., 1968—. Bd. dirs. Corpus Christi (Tex.) Osteopathic Hosp., 1969. Served with USAF, 1952-54. Mem. Am., Tex., Nueces County bar assns., Tex. (v.p. 1972—), Corpus Christi (pres. 1970-71) builders assns. K.C. Clubs: Serra (dist. gov. 1971-72), Sertoma (pres. 1967) (Corpus Christi). Home: 4701 Sea Island Corpus Christi TX 74815 Office: 3840 S Padre Island Dr Corpus Christi TX 74815

ZARZAR, NAKHLEH PACIFICO, state ofcl.; b. Bethlehem, Palestine, Jan. 21, 1932; s. Pacifico Y. and Anita Zarzar; B.A., Am. U. Beirut, 1952, M.D., 1956; m. Doris Azzam, Sept. 23, 1957; children—Michael, Nicholas, David. Intern, Am. U. Hosp., Beirut, Lebanon, 1955-56; resident U. N.C. at Chapel Hill, 1956-59; clin. dir., family sect. John Umstead Hosp., Butner, N.C., 1959-62, entire hosp., 1962-63, supt., 1964-68; interim supt. Dorothea Dix Hosp., Raleigh, N.C., 1966; dep. commr. N.C. Dept. Mental Health, Raleigh, 1966-73, dir. Div. Mental Health Services, 1973—. Clin. asso. prof. U. N.C. Fellow Am. Psychiat. Assn., mem. N.C. Neurophychiat. assn., Am., N.C., Wake County med. assns., Alpha Omega Alpha. Contbr. articles to profl. jours. Home: 4727 Wedgewood St Raleigh NC 27612 Office: PO Box 26327 Raleigh NC 27611

ZAUBER, RAYMOND G., editor; b. Jellico, Tenn., June 25, 1918; s. Milton H. and Mollie Rose (Garber) Z.; student Guilford Coll., 1940-41, U. N.C. at Chapel Hill, 1934-36; m. Eloise Ruth Horstmann, Sept. 30, 1944 (div. Mar. 1968); children—Glenn, Kim, Vonn. With Dallas Times Herald, 1945-46, WBAP News, 1946, Dallas News, 1946-47; pub. Oak Cliff Tribune and subsidiaries, Dallas, 1947—; editor, pub. Grand Prairie Banner, 1948-51, Irving Herald Index, 1948-51; chmn. bd. NewspapeNewspaper Enterprises, Inc., Dallas and Oklahoma City, 1958-65. Founder, commr.'s adv. bd. Dallas Bapt. Coll., 1966-70. Mem. Airport Bd., 1945-74; mem. Interregional Hwy. Council, 1971—, Central Hwy. Com., 1970—. Bd. dirs. Circle council Boy Scouts Am., 1948-50, Oak Cliff YMCA, 1959-62. Served to lt. inf. AUS, World War II; PTO. Recipient cited by Altrusa, Jr. C. of C., and others. Mem. Am. Legion (vice comdr. 1946—), C. of C. (chmn. hwy. com. 1971—), Cedar Crest Golf Assn. (past pres.), Sigma Delta Chi. Kiwanian (Spl. Man of Yr. award). Clubs: Press, Oak Cliff Country, Top o' the Cliff, Exec. 100 (dir.), Cosmopolitan, Singing Hills Country (dir.). Home: 4667 Country Creek Dallas TX 75231 Office: 3333 Tribune Dr Dallas TX 75224

ZEFF, STEPHEN ADDAM, educator; b. Chgo., July 26, 1933; s. Roy David and Hazel (Sex) Z.; B.S., U. Colo., 1955, M.S., 1957; M.B.A., U. Mich., 1960, Ph.D., 1962. Instr. U. Colo., 1955-57; teaching fellow, instr. U. Mich., 1958-61; asst. prof. accounting Tulane U., New Orleans, 1961-63, asso. prof., 1963-67, prof., 1967—; vis. asso. prof. U. Cal., Berkeley, 1964-65, U. Chgo., 1966; vis. prof. Instituto Tecnológico y de Estudios Superiores de Monterrey (Mexico), 1969, spl. lectr., also hon. sr. Fulbright scholar Monash U., Australia, 1972. Mem. Am. Accounting Assn., (dir. edn. 1969-71), Am. Econ. Assn., Nat. Assn. Accountants, Financial Execs. Inst., Am. Inst. Decision Scis. Author: Uses of Accounting for Small Business, 1962, American Accounting Assn. It's First 50 Years, 1966; Forging Accounting Principles in Five Countries: A History and an Analysis of Trends, 1972; Forging Accounting Principles in Australia, 1973. Co-editor: Financial Accounting Theory, Vol. I, 1964, rev., 1973, Vol. II, 1969. Book rev. editor Accounting Rev., 1962-66. Founder, editor Boletin Interamericano de Contabilidad, 1968-71. Contbr. articles to profl. jours. Home: 2231 Marengo St New Orleans LA 70115

ZEGEL, FERDINAND HRANT, physicist; b. N.Y.C., Nov. 26, 1933; s. Ferdinand Jacob and Elinco (Aghamalian) Z.; B.S., Fairfield U., 1955; M.S., Boston Coll., 1958. Supr. Spectrophotometry Lab., Ansco, div. of Gen. Analine and Film Corp., Binghamton N.Y., 1958-59; research physicist Melpar, div. of Westinghouse Air Brake, Fairfax, Va., 1959-61; project engr. U.S. Weather Bur., Washington, 1961-68; mil. signatures specialist U.S. Army Night Vision Lab., Ft. Belvoir, Va., 1968—; chief spectroscopist Beryllium Internat., Washington, 1960-67. Mem. Am. Phys. Soc., Am. Meteorol. Soc., Optical Soc. Am., Soc. for Applied Spectroscopy. Roman Catholic. Contbr. articles in field to profl. jours. Home: 3449 N Randolph St Arlington VA 22207 Office: US Army Night Vision Lab Fort Belvoir VA 22060

ZEIGLER, EUGENE N., lawyer; b. Florence, S.C., July 20, 1921; B.A., U. of South, 1942; LL.B., Harvard, 1949. Admitted to S.C. bar, 1949, since practiced in Florence; spl. judge, 1964, 65. Pres., Florence Museum, 1951-60; founder Pee Dee Area Big Bros. Assn., pres., 1953-55. Mem. S.C. Ho. of Reps., 1961-62, S.C. Senate, 1966-72. Chmn., S.C. Inter-Agy. Council on Arts and Humanities, 1966; mem. S.C. Tri-Centennial and Bi-Centennial commns. Bd. visitors Coker Coll. Recipient Young Man of Year award Jaycees. Mem. Am., Florence County, S.C. bar assns., Am. Judicature Soc., Phi Beta Kappa, Omicron Delta Kappa. Office: 246 W Evans St Florence SC 29501

ZEIGLER, GEORGE MORRIS, real estate co. exec.; b. Pulaski, Tenn., Aug. 10, 1934; s. Denzil H. and Ira Irene (Raines) Z.; B.S., David Lipscomb Coll., 1956; postgrad. U. Md., 1958; m. Sandra Evelyn Lawrence, May 8, 1960; children—George Gavin, Robin Evelyn, Amanda Lawrence. Vice pres. Clark Landstreet Kirkatrick, Inc., 1959-65, First Ala. Securities, Inc., Nashville, 1965-70; pres. Zeigler & Holman, Inc., Nashville, 1970-73; pres. Harpeth Equity Corp., Franklin, Tenn., 1973—. Trustee Harpeth Acad., Franklin, Tenn. Served with AUS, 1956-59. Mem. Nashville Assn. Security Traders (dir. 1969—). Republican. Club: Cumberland (Nashville). Home: Spencer Creek Farm Route 7 Franklin TN 37064 Office: Stahlman Bldg Nashville TN 37201

ZELENY, CHARLES ELLINGSON, psychologist; b. Champaign, Ill., Apr. 24, 1918; s. Charles and Ida (Ellingson) Z.; B.A., U. Ill., 1939, M.A., 1953; m. Marjorie Ann Pfeiffer, Dec. 11, 1950; children—Ann Douglas, Charles Timberlake. Research psychologist Human Resources Research Center, Chanute AFB, Ill., 1949-52; research asst. U. Ill., 1952-54; research psychologist, human factors br. Electronic Warfare Dept., Ft. Huachuca, Ariz., 1954-58, chief of br., 1955-58; program dir. Applied Psychology Corp., Tucson, 1958-63; research psychologist Bendix Corp. Systems Div. Ann Arbor, Mich., 1963-66, project leader, 1965-66; chief of evaluation and selection br., nat. hdqrs. Vols. in Service to Am., Washington, 1966-69, chief vol. placement, 1969-71; policy and program devel. specialist Action Agy., Washington, 1971—. Served with AUS, 1942-46; capt. Res. Mem. A.A.A.S., Am., D.C. psychol. assns., Soc. for Psychol. Study Social Issues, Alpha Kappa Lambda. Conglist. Home: 6825 Wemberly Way McLean VA 22101 Office: 806 Connecticut Av NW Washington DC 20525

ZELENY, MARJORIE PFEIFFER (MRS. CHARLES ELLINGSON ZELENY), psychologist; b. Balt., Mar. 31, 1924; d. Lloyd Armitage and Mable (Willian) Pfeiffer; B.A., U. Md., 1947; M.S., U. Ill., 1949, postgrad., 1951-54; m. Charles Ellingson Zeleny, Dec. 11, 1950; children—Ann Douglas, Charles Timberlake. Vocational counseling psychologist VA, Balt., 1947-48; asst. U. Ill., Urbana, 1948-50, research asso. Bur. Research, 1952-53; chief psychologist dept. neurology and psychiatry Ohio State U. Coll. Medicine, Columbus, 1950-51; research psychologist, cons., Tucson, Washington, 1954—. Mem. Am., D.C. psychol. assns., A.A.A.S., Soc. for Psychol. Study Social Issues, D.A.R., Mortar Bd., Delta Delta Delta, Sigma Delta Epsilon, Psi Chi, Sigma Tau Epsilon. Baptist. Home: 6825 Wemberly Way McLean VA 22101

ZELLER, EMILIO, III, architect; b. Santiago, Dominican Republic, Dec. 13, 1935; s. Emilio, Jr. and Hilda (Cordero Puello) Z.; came to U.S., 1941, naturalized, 1953; B.S., Ga. Inst. Tech., 1957, B.Arch., 1957; m. Frances Faye Andrews, Aug. 12, 1962; children—Melanie, Stephanie, Amy. With Beiswenger-Hoch & J. Brooks Haas, Jacksonville, Fla., 1957-62; pvt. practice architecture, Jacksonville,

1962—; now head Zeller Planners, Jacksonville, 1972—. Active YMCA. Mem. Duval County Republican Exec. Com., 1961-69; v.p. Young Rep. Club, 1968-69, v.p. Duval County Rep. Club, 1970; Goldwater campaign chief Duval County, 1964. Served as capt., C.E., AUS, 1958. Mem. A.I.A., Audubon Soc., Jacksonville Apt. Owners Assn., Theta Chi. Roman Catholic. Clubs: Georgia Tech. Alumni, University, Baymeadows Racquet; South Jacksonville Sertoma. Home: 1237 Northwood Rd Jacksonville FL 32207 Office: 1000 Riverside Av Jacksonville FL 32204

ZENICH, MARGRETT BARTON, information exec.; b. Mead, Okla., Dec. 4, 1915; d. John Dandridge and Inez (Hightower) Barton; B.A., Southeastern State Coll., 1938; postgrad. San Jose State Coll., 1947; B.S. in Library Sci., U. Okla., 1951; spl. student Tex. Western Coll., 1964-65; children—Ruth Ann Linder, Peter Barton Linder, Mary Antoinette Camillo. Tchr., Big Cabin, Okla., 1938-39; Carnegie br. librarian, pub. sch. library, Oklahoma City, 1946-51; spl. services librarian 4th Army White Sands Missle Range, 1951-55, chief tech. library system, 1955-68; chief Sci. and Tech. Information Div., Office of Chief Engrs., Washington. Mem. A.L.A., Spl. Libraries Assn. (sec.-treas. documentation div. 1958-59, pres. Rio Grande chpt. 1967), Am. Assn. Information Sci., Am. Assn. U. Women, PIANC, El Paso County Humane Soc. (dir.), Alpha Phi Sigma. Baptist. Home: 4712 Poplar Dr Alexandria VA 22310 Office: Office Chief Engrs 1000 Independence Av Washington DC 20003

ZENKE, OTTO GEORGE, interior designer; b. Bklyn., May 31, 1904; s. Henry Christian and Susan (Kohler) Z.; student Pratt Inst., N.Y.C., Parsons Sch. Design, N.Y.C. Formerly with Theodore Hofstatter & Co., N.Y.C., B. Altman & Co., N.Y.C., Morrison-Neese, Greensboro, N.C., 1937-50; pres. Otto Zenke, Inc., Greensboro, 1950—. Mem. Am. Inst. Designers, Interior Decorating and Designing Assn. (Brit.). Clubs: Greensboro Country, Greensboro City. Works pub. in House and Garden, House Beautiful, Interior Design and Interiors, Antiques in Interior Decoration (H. Lionel Williams), Archtl. Digest. Address: 220 S Eugene St Greensboro NC 27401

ZENN, FAY MCWHORTER (MRS. PHILIP ZENN, II), club woman; b. Roopville, Ga., Aug. 2, 1916; d. Lorenza B. and Agnes (Ward) McWhorter; R.N., Middle Ga. Hosp., 1937; B.B.A., U. Miami, (Fla.), 1970; m. 2d Philip Zenn II, Feb. 28, 1972; children by previous marriage—William McWhorter, Robert Holder. Supt. hosp., Bremen, Ga., 1938-39. Pres. Fla. Fedn. Garden Clubs, Inc., 1959-61; pres. Fla. chpt. 99's, 1944; editor Fla. Gardener, 1955-57; pres. Fla. Assn. Parliamentarians, 1961-63; past pres. Fla. Atlantic Music, Inc. Mem. Fla. Fedn. Garden Clubs, Nat. Council State Garden Clubs (life), North Broward Soc. of Symphony (life), Women's Aux. Oral Sch. of Ft. Lauderdale (life), Ft. Lauderdale Soc. Symphony Soc. (life), Nature Conservancy (pres. Fla. chpt. 1963-64). Author: Program Patterns, 1958; The New Program Patterns, 1961; Public Relations and Publicity Pointers. Home: 1100 S Ocean Blvd Pompano Beach FL 33062

ZENS, CLARENCE M., editor; b. Racine, Wis., Aug. 17, 1918; s. Henry M. and Elizabeth (Roebling) Z.; student Marquette U., 1936-40; m. Mildred Irene Larson, May 24, 1944; children—Michael Louis, Karen Larson. With Milwaukee Herald-Citizen, 1940-41; news desk Nat. Catholic Welfare Conf. News Service, Washington, 1945-50, asst. to dir. bur. information, 1950-51; mng. editor The Catholic Standard, Washington, 1951-61; fgn. information specialist, U.S. Dept. Commerce, 1961-64; editor, fgn. commerce weekly Internat. Commerce, Washington, 1964—. Cons. internat. trade fairs; free lance writer. Bd. dirs. St. John's Mil. High Sch., Marquette U. Sch. Journalism; mem. nat. adv. bd. Marquette U. Served to 1st lt., USAF, 1941-45. Recipient By-Line award Marquette Sch. Journalism, 1961. Mem. Marquette U. Alumni Assn., Men of St. John's. Author: Saints in Crosswords, 1958. Contbr. articles to Cath. publs. Home: 406 A St SE Washington DC 20003 Office: International Commerce US Dept Commerce Washington DC 20230

ZENS, MILDRED IRENE LARSEN (MRS. CLARENCE MICHAEL ZENS), librarian; b. Racine, Wis., Sept. 14, 1917; d. Lars Anderson and Esther Bolette (Skow) Larsen; student Marquette U., 1936-38; B.A., Lawrence U., 1940; M.A., Catholic U., 1963; postgrad., Wis. U., 1941; m. Clarence Michael Zens, May 24, 1944; children—Michael Louis, Karen Larsen. Tchr., librarian, Calumet, Mich., 1940-41; Frank McKee High Sch., Muskegon, Mich., 1941-43; reporter Jour. Times, Racine, 1944; librarian Am. Alumni Council, Washington, 1963-64; Gonzaga Coll. High Sch., Washington, 1964—. Area dir. Girl Scout ann. cookie drive, 1958-59; dir. County Cub Scouts, 1955-56; organizer Friends of the Library, Fairfax City, Va., 1955-57. Mem. Am., D.C. (publicity dir. 1968-71), Catholic (area dir. 1967-72), library assns., D.C. Assn. Sch. Libraries, Am. Assn. U. Women, Sch. Libraries Assn. Home: 406 A St SE Washington DC 20003 Office: 34th and R St NW Washington DC 20007

ZENTNER, JAMES ROBERT, architect; b. Rowena, Tex., Feb. 27, 1929; s. Anton Joseph and Wilma Crisantha (Huebner) Z.; B.Arch., Tex. A. & M. U., 1951; m. Billie Margaret Wetzel, June 9, 1958; children—James William, Mary Elizabeth, Kyle Robert. Draftsman, Tuckey & Lindberg, Abilene, Tex., 1953-56; asso. Martin & Lemmon architects, Bryan and Andrews, Tex., 1956-58; asso. Leonard R. Mauldin, San Angelo, Tex., 1958-59; partner Chakos, Zentner, Marcum architects, San Angelo, Tex., 1959—. Served with AUS, 1951-53. Mem. A.I.A., Tex. Soc. Architects. Roman Catholic. K.C. Home: 3338 Trinity St San Angelo TX 76901 Office: 3 N A& M St San Angelo TX 76901

ZERFOSS, LESTER FRANK, mgmt. cons., educator; b. Mountaintop, Pa., Nov. 2, 1903; s. Clinton and Mabel (Wilcox) Z.; B.A. cum laude, Pa. State U., 1926, M.Ed., 1934, D.Ed., 1958; m. Harriet Mildred Cary, Dec. 21, 1928; children—Patricia Ann (Mrs. Thomas Sibben), Clinton Cary, Robert Williamson. Coll. tchr., pub. sch. adminstr., Pa., 1928-41; supr. design, devel. Gen. Motors Inst., 1942-46; head supervisory devel. Detroit Edison Co., 1946-52; corporate tng. dir. Am. Enka Corp. (N.C.), 1952-59, dir. indsl. relations, mgmt. services, 1952-66, mgmt. cons. for managerial and tech. devel., 1966—; asso. prof. psychology Asheville-Biltmore Coll., 1966-68; research prof. developmental psychology, dir. mgmt. devel. programs U. N.C. at Asheville, 1968—. Mem. bd., head mgmt. devel. com. N.C. Personnel Bd., 1966-70; cons. to Gov. for mgmt. devel., 1970—; mem. Southeastern Regional Manpower Adv. Com., 1966-70, N.C. Adv. Com. for Community Colls. Trustee Brevard Coll., Asheville-Buncombe Tech. Inst. Mem. Am. Mgmt. Assn., Nat. Soc. Advancement Mgmt. (profl. mgr. citation 1962), Am. Soc. Tng. and Devel., Phi Delta Kappa, Kappa Phi Kappa, Kappa Delta Pi, Delta Sigma Phi. Elk, Rotarian. Author: Developing Professional Personnel in Business, Industry and Government, 1969. Contbg. author: Management Handbook for Plant Engineers, 1973. Contbr. articles to profl. jours. Home: 910 4th Av W Hendersonville NC 28739 Office: Univ of NC Asheville NC 28801

ZIBILICH, BERNICE GOODMAN (MRS. ROBERT J. ZIBILICH), librarian; b. San Antonio, Aug. 26; d. Benjamin and Fannie (Ludwig) Goodman; B.A. cum laude, Our Lady of the Lake Coll., 1941, M.S. in L.S., 1947; m. Robert J. Zibilich, Dec. 20, 1952; children—Franz Ludwig, Gretchen Gwen. Library asst. New Orleans Pub. Library, 1945-46, librarian, 1947-61, head children's services, 1961—; prof. children's lit. Delgado Coll.; lectr. ednl. orgns. on library facilities and services. Coordinator U.S. State Dept. Open Door, 1966-69. Bd. dirs. Council of the Arts for Children, Puppet Playhouse. Mem. Am., Southwestern (publicity chmn. 1971-72), La. (pub. relations com. 1971-73, chmn. publicity 1970-71), Catholic library assns., League of Women Voters, Assn. Childhood Edn. Internat. (award). Clubs: New Orleans Library (sec. 1961-62, v.p., pres. elect 1974), Vista Shores Country (New Orleans). Home: 1350 Filmore Av New Orleans LA 70122 Office: 219 Loyola Av New Orleans LA 70140

ZIBMAN, HENRY MICHAEL, mech. engr.; b. Phila., Dec. 28, 1928; s. David H. and Freda (Halpert) Z.; B.S. in M.E., U. Miami (Fla.), 1951; m. Renie Lee Kleid, May 22, 1954; children—David Neal, Michael Nathan. Combustion control field engr. Leeds & Northrup, Phila., 1951-55; chief engr. Stuart Cooling Corp., Miami, 1955-58; v.p. Miami Air Conditioning, 1958-61; resident dir. IMEC Caribbean Ltd., Port of Spain, Trinidad, 1961-62; chief mech. engr. Oboler and Clarke, Miami Beach, Fla., 1962-66; pres. Zibman, Snyder Stinson cons. engrs., North Miami Beach, Fla., 1966-72; pres. Zibman, Stinson Martinez & Assos., Inc., North Miami Beach, 1972—. Pres., Flight Leasing, Inc., North Miami Beach, 1969-73, Flying Machines, Inc., North Miami Beach, 1974—. Mem. Dade County Mech. Contractors Examining Bd., 1967. Served with AUS, 1946-48. Recipient Appreciation certificate Dade County, 1967. Registered profl. engr., Fla., Ga. Mem. Fla. Inst. Cons. Engrs. (dir. 1973-74), Nat. Soc. Profl. Engrs., Am. Soc. Heating, Refrigerating and Air Conditioning Engrs., Fla. Engring. Soc. K.P., Lion. Office: 1840 NE 153d St North Miami Beach FL 33162

ZIEGLER, GEORGE ELLIOTT, physics cons.; b. Chgo., Apr. 27, 1907; s. George and Sue (Elliott) Z.; B.S., U. Chgo., 1929, M.S., 1930, Ph.D., 1932; postgrad. Mass. Inst. Tech., 1938; m. Ruth Elizabeth Thomas, Mar. 15, 1935; 1 dau., Carol (Mrs. Robert D. Champagne). Chmn. physics research Ill. Inst. Tech., Chgo., 1936-45, asso. prof. physics, 1937-41; exec. scientist Midwest Research Inst., Kansas City, Mo., 1945-48, dir., 1948-51; dir. research, mgr. patents Zonolite div. W.R. Grace & Co., Chgo., 1951-58; individual practice as physics cons., Chgo., 1958-69, Winter Park, Fla., 1969—; pres. Thermal Conduits, Inc., Kirkland, Wash., 1961-70, dir., 1958—; chmn. bd. dirs. Vertecs Corp., Kirkland, 1966-71, dir., 1964—. Recipient award Nat. Def. Research Com., 1945. Registered profl. engr., Mo. Mem. Am. Phys. Soc., I.E.E.E., Am. Chem. Soc., Optical Soc. Am., Am. Soc. Heating, Refrigerating and Air-Conditioning Engrs., Am. Assn. Physics Tchrs., Sigma Xi. Clubs: Physics (pres. 1954) (Chgo.); University (Winter Park). Contbr. articles to profl. jours. Patentee in field. Address: 901 Osceola Av Winter Park FL 32789

ZIEGLER, JAMES CRAIG, computer co. exec.; b. Patterson, N.J., Mar. 11, 1946; s. Walter Herbert and Jean Hilda (Haroldson) Z.; student Ga. Inst. Tech., 1964, Emory U., 1965; m. Cynthia Ann Hubard, June 1972. Programmer, U. Tenn. at Memphis, 1966-68; systems rep. Burroughs Corp., Memphis, 1968-69; dir. advance systems Data Communications Corp., Memphis, 1969-74, v.p., 1974—. Owner, JCZ cons. and design, Memphis, 1972—. Life mem. Am. Civil Liberties Union, 1973—. Comml. pilot. Mem. I.E.E.E., Assn. Computing Machinery (chmn. chpt. 1966-67, 71—), Aircraft Owners and Pilots Assn., Nat. Pilots Assn. Club: Wolf River Soc. Home: 1669 Overton Park Av Memphis TN 38112 Office: 3000 Directors Row Memphis TN 38131

ZIEMANN, ROBERT LEWIS, accountant; b. Southwick, Ida., Jan. 23, 1927; s. Gus H. and Wilda (Keeney) Z.; student Ore. State Coll., 1945-46, U. Ida., 1948-49; B.B.A., U. Houston, 1952. Accountant, Briscoe, House & Stovall, C.P.A.'s, Houston, 1954, Mattison & Riquelmy, C.P.A.'s, Houston, 1954-61, Harris, Kerr, Forster & Co., C.P.A.'s, Houston, 1961-65; self-employed as C.P.A., Houston, 1965—. Served with USAAF, 1946-47. Elk. Address: 1407 Winrock St Houston TX 77027 also PO Box 66681 Houston TX 77006

ZIESENHEIM, JOSEPH C., state ofcl.; b. Houston, Oct. 4, 1918; B.S., U. Pitts., 1940; M.H.A., Baylor U., 1961. Commd. 2d lt. U.S. Army, 1943; advanced through grades to lt. col., 1961; adj. 27th Med. Tng. Bn., Camp Grant, Ill., 1943-44, Ft. Lewis, Wash., 1944, 250th Gen. Hosp., France, 1944-45, 365th Sta. Hosp., 1946; comdr. med. tng. co. Brooke Army Med. Center, Ft. Sam Houston, Tex., 1950; med. adminstrv. asst. 7th Mobile Army Surg. Hosp., Ft. Jackson, S.C., 1951; troop comdr. med. detachment 5th Gen. Hosp., Germany, 1953; comdg. officer 66th Ambulance Train, Germany, 1955; exec. officer U.S. Army Hosp., Sandia Base, Albuquerque, 1956-59; hosp. mgmt. officer U.S. Army Hosp., Ft. Devens, Mass., 1961-62; exec. officer 121st Evacuation Hosp., Korea, 1962-63; comdg. officer 106th Gen. Hosp., William Beaumont Gen. Hosp., El Paso, 1963-64; ret., 1964; adminstr. Fla. Alcoholic Rehab. Program, Avon Park, 1964—. Decorated Croix de Guerre with Silver Star (France). Home: 1016 NW Lakeview Dr Sebring FL Office: Box 1147 Avon Park FL 33825

ZIETZ, ROBERT JOSEPH, librarian; b. Menominee, Mich., Sept. 7, 1922; s. Joseph R. and Mary (Eckert) Z.; B.S., Spring Hill Coll., 1949; M. Library, Emory U., 1950; m. Norma Corners, Nov. 2, 1943; children—Suzanne (Mrs. John N. McAtee), Michael, Stephen, Jan, Jennifer, Kristin. Asst. librarian Spring Hill Coll., Mobile, Ala., 1951-61, librarian, 1961—. Bd. dirs. Mobile Mus. Served with USAAF, 1943-46. Mem. Am., Ala. (pres. 1966-67), Catholic (sect. pres. 1968—), Southeastern, Mobile Bay Area (pres. 1972-73) library assns. Co-author: Writing and Research. Home: 4580 Hawthorne Pl Mobile AL 36608

ZIMMER, JOHN STEPHENS, mech. engr.; b. Argentina, Dec. 10, 1914 (parents Am. citizens); s. Meade Lafayette and Agnes Annie (Stephens) Z.; B.A., Colegio Nacional Cordoba Argentina, 1934; B.S. in Mech. Engring., U. Cin., 1940; m. Antoinette Davis, Nov. 1, 1940; children—Jacqueline (Mrs. Ronald Lane Brown), Ruth (Mrs. Marc Daniel Steck). Test engr. Gen. Electric Co., Schenectady, 1940-42, factory contact engr. industry control, 1942-45, design engr. aircraft control, 1945-55, devel. engr., relay engring., splty. control dept., Waynesboro, Va., 1955—. Mem. I.E.E.E. (sr.). Presbyn. (deacon 1957-58). Lion. Club: Waynesboro Country. Patentee in field. Home: 413 Ellison Lane Waynesboro VA 22980 Office: General Electric Dr Waynesboro VA 22980

ZIMMERER, CARL EDWARD, editor; b. Niles, Mich., Dec. 15, 1912; s. Charles L. and Eva (Gardner) Z.; A.B. magna cum laude, U. Notre Dame, 1934; m. Alice Balcerzak, Aug. 26, 1940; 1 son, Michael G. Reporter South Bend (Ind.) News-Times and South Bend Tribune, 1930-40, book editor, 1935-40; telegraph editor, asst. news editor Courier-Jour., Louisville, 1940-60, chief wire services, stamp and coin columnist, 1960—. Owner, operator Snappy Filler Service, 1950—. Served with U.S. Merchant Marine, 1944-45. Roman Catholic. Club: Big Spring Country. Home: 610 Wataga Dr Louisville KY 40206 Office: 525 W Broadway Louisville KY 40202

ZIMMERMAN, ALVIN LOUIS, lawyer; b. Houston, June 28, 1943; s. Sam Jay and Dorothy (Sakowitz) Z.; B.S., U. Houston, 1964, J.D. (teaching fellow), 1967; m. Ellen Sue Davis, Aug. 22, 1965; children—Brian, Gary. Admitted to Tex. bar, 1967, Fed. bar, 1967, U.S. Supreme Ct. bar, 1968; clk., Judge Ingraham U.S. Dist. Ct., Houston, 1967; asst. atty. gen. Tex., 1967-68; legal counsel, v.p., sec. Sterling Electronics Corp., Houston, 1969—; dir. Mr. Zs Men's & Boy's Clothing, Houston. Adviser, Med. Center Del Oro Hosp., Inc., Houston, 1973-74; mem. opinion com. for Atty. Gen. Tex., 1968. Mem. Maplewood Civic Club, 1969—. Bd. dirs. Anti-Defamation League. Mem. Houston (outstanding chmn. 1973), Am., Tex., Houston bar assns., Am. Judicature Soc., Am. Soc. Corporate Secs. Jewish religion (dir. Men's Club 1970—). Rotarian. Editor Houston Law Rev., 1965-67. Editorial bd. Houston Bar Jour., 1972-74. Home: 7715 Braesview St Houston TX 77071 Office: 4211 Southwest Freeway Houston TX 77025

ZIMMERMAN, GARY EARL, community mental health center exec.; b. Fond du Lac, Wis., Aug. 23, 1939; s. Earl R. and Doris (Brunkhorst) Z.; B.S., U. Wis., 1961, M.S., 1964; M.A., U. Ottawa (Ont., Can.), 1974; m. Marti Zimmerman. Teaching asst. U. Wis., 1963-64; instr., asst. prof. State U. N.Y. at Buffalo, 1964-68; instr. U. Ottawa, 1968-69; asst. prof. Guilford Coll., 1969-70; asst. prof. State U. N.Y., 1970-73; dir. Tri-County Mental Health Center, Bennettsville, S.C., 1973—; psychologist, project adminstr. Community Mental Health Services S.C. Dept. Mental Health, 1973—, mem. staff devel. and in-service tng. adv. com. div. community health services, 1973—. Chmn. Marlboro County (S.C.) Inter-agy. Council, 1973—; chmn. edn. com., cons. Marlboro County Mental Health Assn., 1973—; observer Carnegie Hero Fund Commn., 1972—; linker Nat. Tng. Lab. Applied Behavioral Scis., Washington, 1970—, Nat. Center Voluntary Action, 1973-. Bd. dirs. Chesterfield-Marlboro Econ. Opportunity Council, Inc. Mem. Marlboro County Assn. Retarded Children, Bennettsville C. of C. Episcopalian. Rotarian. Club: Marlboro Country. Contbr. column to Marlboro Herald Adv., 1973—, also commentator radio sta. WBSC. Home: Hidden Valley Apts #6-C Bennettsville SC 29512 Office: Tri-County Mental Health Center 114 S Marlboro St Bennettsville SC 29512

ZIMMERMAN, GUY, JR., psychiatrist; b. Mt. Sterling, Ky., Sept. 15, 1921; s. Couy and Ila (Sec) Z.; B.A., Vanderbilt U., 1943, M.D., 1945; m. Margaret Wells, Dec. 2, 1945; children—Ann (Mrs. Albert Farmer), Guy III, Rex. Intern Jackson Meml. Hosp., 1945-46; resident Warren (Pa.) State Hosp.-U. Pa., 1948-51; clin. dir. Ark. State Hosp., Little Rock, 1952-53; practice medicine specializing in psychiatry, Chattanooga, 1953-70; supt. Moccasin Bend Psychiat. Hosp., Chattanooga, 1971-72; dir. Plateau Mental Health Center, Cookeville, Tenn., 1972—. Served to capt., M.C., AUS, 1943-47. Diplomate Am. Bd. Psychiatry and Neurology. Fellow Am. Psychiat. Assn. Home: 1010 Country Club Rd Cookeville TN 38501 Office: Plateau Mental Health Center Burgess Falls Rd Cookeville TN 38501

ZIMMERMAN, ISAIAH MORRIS, psychotherapist; b. Vladivostok, Russia, Nov. 11, 1928; s. William Isaiah and Pearl (Palkin) Z.; came to U.S., 1947, natrualized, 1953; B.A., U. Cal. at Berkeley, 1951, M.S.W., 1953; Ph.D., Cath. U. Am., 1966; m. Amy Beatrice Kuhn, Aug. 6, 1954; children—Sharon, Carol, Joshua. Commd. 2d lt. Med. Service Corps, U.S. Air Force, 1953, advanced through grades to maj., 1966; assigned USAF Hosp., Lackland AFB, Tex., 1953-56, Office Surgeon Gen. USAF, 1956-63, USAF Hosp., Andrews AFB, Md., 1963-66; ret., 1966; pvt. practice clin. psychology, Washington, 1966—. Dean group psychotherapy tng. program Washington Sch. Psychiatry, 1967-73; cons. group psychotherapy VA, 1965—, behavioral scis. study sect., nat. adv. mental health council NIH, 1956-58, Family Services of Montgomery County (Md.), 1966, alcoholic treatment research NIH, 1973—, Catholic Charities Va., 1973—, others; asso. clin. prof. psychology George Washington U., Washington, 1969—. Fellow Am. Group Psychotherapy Assn., Am. Orthopsychiat. Assn., Am. Psychol. Assn., Am. Anthrop. Assn., Am. Acad. Psychotherapists, Nat. Assn. Social Workers. Club: George Washington Univ. Editorial bd. Pilgrimage, 1973—. Home and office: 5323 Potomac Av NW Washington DC 20016

ZINCK, JAMES HOWARD, dentist; b. Houston, Mar. 29, 1931; s. Howard Abraham and Gertrude Lenard (Lamkin) Z.; student La. State U., 1948-51; D.D.S., Loyola U. South, 1959; m. Jeanne Brulet, Sept. 6, 1952; children—Jean Carol, Julie Ann, Joseph Howard. Individual practice dentistry, Lake Charles, La., 1959-65, Austin, Tex., 1965-68, Luling, Tex., 1968-74; asst. prof. dept. operative dentistry U. Tex. Dental Sch., San Antonio, 1974—. dir. Indsl. Corp., Luling. Trustee Luling Ind. Sch. Dist., 1969-71, v.p., 1970-71. Served with USAF, 1951-54. Research grantee U.S. Govt. Dept. Operative Dentistry, 1958; recipient Cetificate of Merit award Am. Acad. Dentistry, 1959. Mem. Am., Tex. dental assns., Guadalupe Valley Dental Soc., C. Victor Vignes Odontological Soc. (v.p. 1958), 7th Dist. Dental Assn. La. (sec.-treas. 1963, pres. 1964), South Tex. (dir. 1970-71), Luling (dir. 1969-71, pres. 1970) chambers commerce, Luling Thump Assn. (dir. 1969), Alpha Sigma Nu, Omicron Kappa Upsilon, Sigma Alpha Epsilon, Xi Psi Phi. Democrat. Roman Catholic. Lion. Club: Sertoma (Austin, Tex.). Home: 1302 Klondike Dr San Antonio TX 78245 Office: 7703 Floyd Curl Dr San Antonio TX 78229

ZINN, CAROLYN JUNE, educator; b. Takoma Park, Md., June 9, 1933; d. Donald Schaeffer and Erma (Sirbaugh) Zinn; B.A., W.Va. U., 1955, M.A., 1955, Ph.D., 1967; postgrad. (Fulbright scholar) Free U. Brussels (Belgium), 1955-56. Publicity dir., advt. copywriter, asst. book prodn. mgr. Wadsworth Pub. Co., Belmont, Cal., 1959-61; adminstrv. asst. to editorial dir. McGraw-Hill Book Co., Inc., Novato, 1961-63; grad. asst. polit. sci. W.Va. U., 1964-67; asso. prof. polit. sci. Elon (N.C.) Coll., 1967-69; vis. prof. polit. sci. U. N.C. at Chapel Hill, summer 1969; asst. prof. polit. sci. U. Pa., Uniontown, 1969-71; historian, archivist State of W.Va., 1971-73; chmn. div. polit. sci., sociology and geography Ark. State U., 1973—. Pink Lady, Med. Aux. Alamance County-Meml. Hosp. Mem. Am. Polit. Sci. Assn., Phi Beta Kappa, Mortar Bd., Pi Sigma Alpha, Pi Gamma Mu, Phi Alpha Theta, Pi Delta Phi, Kappa Delta Pi, Delta Gamma. Home: 1751 W Nettleton 201D Jonesboro AR 72401 Office: Div Polit Sci Sociology Geography Ark State U State University AR 72467

ZIPFEL, EDWARD WILLIAM, mech. engr.; b. Oak Harbor, O., June 29, 1909; s. William and Freda Wilhelmena (Meinke) Z.; B.Sc., Heidelberg Coll., 1933; m. Vivian A. Kolath, June 29, 1935 (dec.); children—Diane (Mrs. Louis R. Lee), William Edward. Field engr. U.S. Govt., Port Clinton, O., 1934-35; plant engr. Standard Products, Port Clinton, 1936-51, Am. Synthetic Rubber Corp., Louisville, 1951. City engr. Oak Harbor, 1942-51. Mem. Oak Harbor City Council, 1942-51. Mem. Am. Inst. Plant Engrs. (dir., past pres.). Mason. Home: 1134 Audubon Pkwy Louisville KY 40213 Office: 4500 Camp Ground Rd Louisville KY 40201

ZIRKIN, HAROLD, JR., investment counselor; b. Washington, Jan. 6, 1944; s. Harold and Frances Marie (Sarner) Z.; B.S., Syracuse U., 1965; M.B.A., Am. U., 1968; m. Norma Louise Gerstenfield, Aug. 12, 1970; 1 dau., Leslie Frances. Asst. v.p. Nat. Savs. & Trust, Washington, 1965-73; owner H. Zirkin Investments, Washington, 1973—. Chmn. sect. United Givers Fund, 1966-71. Bd. dirs. Children Hearing and Speech Center 1971—. Mem. Washington Soc.

Investment Analysts, Chartered Financial Analysts Inst. Jewish religion (dir. congregation 1971—). Club: Woodmont Country (Rockville, Md.). Home: 7000 Armat Dr Bethesda MD 20034 Office: 733 15th St Suite 624 Washington DC 20005

ZISFEIN, MELVIN BERNARD, govt. ofcl.; b. Phila., May 9, 1926; s. Jacob and Elizabeth (Segal) Z.; B.A., Central High Sch., Phila., 1944; M.S., Mass. Inst. Tech., 1948; m. Elaine J. Feinberg, Dec. 3, 1949; children—James Ira, Carol Ruth. With Naval Aircraft Factory, Phila., 1948-51; chief aerodynamicist Bristol Engring. Co. (Pa.), 1951-52; aerodynamics engr. Lockheed Aircraft Corp., Burbank, Cal., 1952-53; with Bell Aircraft Corp., Buffalo, 1954-60, head aerolasticity and airloads group, 1954-55, chief dynamics sect., 1955-60; gen. mgr. astromechs. research div. Giannini Controls Corp., Malvern, Pa., 1960-66; asso. dir. Franklin Inst. Research Labs., Phila., 1966-71; dep. dir. Nat. Air and Space Mus., Smithsonian Instn., Washington, 1971—. Founding dir. Inst. Devel. Riverine and Estuarine Systems, 1968-69, chmn. tech. bd., 1969-70; chmn. project adv. bd. Reading (Pa.) Municipal Information System, 1970. Fellow Am. Inst. Aeros. and Astronautics (asso.). Clubs: Nat. Aviation, Aerobatics of Am. (hon.) (Washington). Patentee in field. Home: 9204 Bells Mill Rd Potomac MD 20854 Office: Nat Air and Space Museum Smithsonian Instn Washington DC 20560

ZOFFINGER, GEORGE H., telephone co. exec.; b. N.Y.C., Oct. 25, 1927; s. Joseph and Mary (Pearsall) Z.; B.S., Hofstra U., 1955, M.B.A., 1962; m. Patricia Shea, June 18, 1947; children—George, Judy (Mrs. Jim Baker), Billy, James, Thomas, Patricia, Carol. With Bell System, N.Y.C., 1955-67, plant and methods supr., 1965-66, supt. dist. plant, 1966-67; engring. mgr. ITT, Latin Am., 1967-68, dir. telephone operations serving Chile and Peru, N.Y.C., 1968; sr. v.p. operations and engring. P.R. Telephone Co., San Juan, 1968-73, sr. v.p. engring. and planning, 1973—, also dir. Mem. Bd. Caribbean Consol. Sch. System, San Juan, 1965-68. Bd. dirs. Hofstra U., Hempstead, N.Y., 1972-73, Bradley U. Father's Club, 1973-74. Served with USNR, 1945-48. Mem. Sales and Marketing Execs. Assn., Navy League (v.p. 1973-74, dir., 1972-74). Rotarian. Home: 1824 Miosotis St Santa Maria Rio Piedras PR 00926 Office: GPO Box 998 San Juan PR 00936

ZOGG, RICHARD EDWARD, univ. adminstr.; b. Belleville, Ill., Apr. 29, 1924; s. Adolph Gustav and Adalia Susan (Joerg) Z.; A.A., Blackburn Coll., 1943; B.S., U. Ill., 1947; M.B.A., St. Louis U., 1960; m. Marie Annette Flack, July 10, 1948; children—William David, Janice Louise, Paul Alan, Judith Elaine. Head spectrochem. sect. Sinclair Research Labs., Harvey, Ill., 1947-53; asst. to chmn. bd. Midwest Rubber Reclaiming Co., East St. Louis, Ill., 1953-67; lab. adminstr. Brown & Williamson Tobacco Co., Louisville, 1967-70; dir. health scis. labs. U. Louisville, 1970—. Tchr. mgmt. Belleville Jr. Coll., 1963-65, St. Louis U., 1960-67, Bellarmine Coll., 1967-70. Vice-chmn. A.R.C., St. Louis Bi-state chpt., 1966-67; St. Clair County publicity chmn. Am. Heart Assn., 1966-67. Served with USNR, 1944-46. Recipient awards Freedom Found., 1961, 62, St. Louis United Fund, 1963, St. Louis Indsl. Press, 1961. Mem. Am. Assn. Spectrographers (chmn. 1952-53), Am. Chem. Soc., Prodn. Control Soc., Indsl. Press Assn., Assn. Multidisciple Edn. Roman Catholic. Author: Rubberized Playgrounds, 1959; I'll Hire You, 1974. Home: 9211 Trentham Lane Louisville KY 40222

ZON, HENRY, pub. relations co. exec.; b. Vilna, Russia, Oct. 9, 1912 (parents Am. citizens); s. Raphael G. and Anna (Puzyriski) Z.; B.A., U. Minn., 1934; postgrad. London Sch. Econs. and Polit. Sci., 1935; m. Mary Woodbridge Goddard, June 14, 1951; 1 son, Calvin Goddard. Washington corr. labor papers, 1936-42; news editor radio sta. WQQW, 1946-47; pub. relations dir. CIO Polit. Action Com., 1947-55; research and pub. relations dir. AFL-CIO Com. on Polit. Edn., 1955-59; v.p., sec. Maurer, Fleisher, Zon & Assos., Washington, 1959—. Served to 1st lt. USAF, 1942-46. Democrat. Club: Nat. Press. Home: 2220 20th St NW Washington DC 20009 Office: 1120 Connecticut Av NW Washington DC 20037

ZORGER, PAUL HARVEY, elec. engr., research co. exec.; b. Pitts., Jan. 5, 1923; s. Daniel Harvey and Elda Alston (Prentice) Z.; B.S. in Elec. Engring., U. Minn., 1944; B.S. in Edn., Millersville (Pa.) State Coll., 1946; M.S., U. Pa., 1947, Ph.D., 1957; m. Jane Conklin, Nov. 29, 1947; children—Carol Ann, Barbara Ann, David Robert. Tchr. vocation edn. pub. schs., Media, Pa., 1946-47, Hershey Indsl. Sch., 1947-48; tchr., dir. vocational edn. pub. schs., Mechanicsburg, Pa., 1948-49; indsl. engr. Hamilton Watch Co., 1949-52; elec. engr. RCA, 1952-54, Bendix Corp., 1954-58, TRW, 1958-60; tech. dir. Martin Co., 1960-63; staff engr. Vitro Labs., 1963-67; dir. systems support Sanders Assos., 1967-69; dir. systems engring. CEIR, 1963-64; pres. Axiom Systems Corp., Annandale, Va., 1969—, also dir. Mem. faculty grad. schs. Drexel Inst. Tech., 1961-62, Am. U., 1965-67; ednl. cons. to industry, govts., mil. services, 1960—. Mem. electronics adv. council No. Va. Community Coll. Served with AUS, 1942-46. Mem. Am. Soc. Quality Control, I.E.E.E., Am. Inst. Aeros. and Astronautics, N.E.A., Am. Ordnance Assn., Res. Officers Assn. (pres. Robert E. Lee chpt. 1967). Elk. Contbr. articles to profl. publs., also author booklets. Address: 5009 Dodson Dr Annandale VA 22003

ZORN, EUGENE CHRISTIAN, JR., bank economist; b. N.Y.C., Jan. 17, 1916; s. Eugene Christian and Charlotte (Bode) Z.; B.B.A., Coll. City N.Y., 1937; M.S., Columbia, 1942; m. Elizabeth Orban, Aug. 11, 1956; children—Barbara Jean, Robert Eugene. Dept. mgr., dir. research Am. Bankers Assn., N.Y.C., 1940-60; v.p., economist Republic Nat. Bank, Dallas, 1960-66, sr. v.p., economist, 1966—; mem. faculty Southwestern Grad. Sch. Banking. Chmn. U.S. Comptroller Currency Cons. Com. Bank Economists. Served to capt. USAAF, World War II. Mem. Am. Econ. Assn., Am. Finance Assn., Am. Statis. Assn., Am. Mgmt. Assn., Dallas Council World Affairs, Tex. Research League (dir.), Nat. Economists Club, So. Finance Assn., Financial Mgmt. Assn., Am. Bankers Assn. (econ. adv. com.), Nat. Assn. of Bus. Econ., Southwestern Social Sci. Assn., Newcomen Soc., U.S. C. of C. (banking, monetary and fiscal affairs com.), Nat. Planning Assn. (mem. bus. com. on nat. policy), Beta Gamma Sigma. Clubs: Northwood, Economists (Dallas). Home: 4647 Hallmark Dr Dallas TX 75229 Office: Republic Nat Bank Dallas TX 75222

ZORN, WILLIAM EDWARD, city ofcl.; b. Henderson, Tex., Aug. 16, 1911; s. Louis Edward and Margaret (Norvell) Z.; grad. high sch.; m. Hazle Acker, July 4, 1931; children—William Edward, Thomas Lee. Mem. Del Rio Vol. Fire Dept., 1936-51; driver, City Del Rio (Tex.) Fire Dept., 1951-54, chief, 1954—. Instr. Firemen's Tng. Sch., Tex. A. and M. U., mem. adv. bd. Tng. Sch., 1971—. Chmn. Val Verde County chpt. A.R.C., 1958—. Mem. Tex. Firemen's and Fire Marshals' Assn. (pres. 1962-63), Wintergarden Firemen's Assn. (pres. 1940). Mason, Order Hermann Sons. Home: 405 W 5th St Del Rio TX 78840 Office: Central Fire Sta PO Box 543 Del Rio TX 78840

ZUBER, JOHN M., banker; b. Fort Wayne, Ind., 1907; LL.B., Ohio State U., 1929; married. Admitted to Ohio bar, 1929; pvt. practice law, 1929-38; v.p. trust dept. Ohio Citizens Trust, Toledo, 1938-45, Am. Nat. Bank, Indpls., 1945-53, Rep. Nat. Bank Dallas, 1953-69; exec. v.p. First City Nat. Bank, Houston, 1969—. Office: 1001 Main St Houston TX 77002

ZUBER, ORAN HAMILTON, finance and investment exec.; b. Bedias, Tex., Oct. 4, 1910; s. James Andrew and Lillian Gertrude (Owens) Z.; student Sam Houston State U., 1931-32; grad. Sales Analysis Inst., Detroit, 1948, Chrysler Corp. Conf. Bus. Mgmt., Detroit, 1949; m. Minnie Marion Cuthbertson, June 1, 1940; children—Zachary H., Leah Raye (Mrs. Douglas Whitty), Randolph C., Beverly Kaye (Mrs. Lynn Worden). Br. mgr. Universal Credit Co., Houston, 1934-43; sales rep. Gen. Mills Co., Dallas, 1943, Wesson Oil Sales Corp., New Orleans, 1943-44; br. mgr., div. credit mgr., asst. v.p. Comml. Credit Corp., Dallas, 1944-52; v.p. Southwestern Investment Co., Amarillo, Tex., 1952—. Budget com. United Fund, Amarillo, 1965-66; active Operations Drug Alert, Amarillo Area, 1970-72; active Girl Scouts. Bd. dirs. Better Bus. Bur., Amarillo, 1962-63. Mem. Ch. of Christ. Kiwanian; mem. Order of DeMolay (past master counsellor). Office: 205 E 10th St Amarillo TX 79105

ZUBKOFF, MICHAEL, educator; b. N.Y.C., June 2, 1944; s. Harry and Catherine (O'Brien) Z.; B.A., Am. Internat. Coll., 1965; M.A., Columbia, 1966, certificate Internat. Fellows program, 1967, Ph.D., 1969; m. Sandralee Rayner, Feb. 20, 1964; children—Steve, Joel, Lisa. Instr. econs. Harvard-Yale-Columbia Summer Intensive Studies program, 1968-69; research asso. Columbia Conservation Human Resources Project, 1967-69; Woodrow Wilson Found. teaching fellow Fisk U. and Meharry Med. Coll., Nashville, 1969-70; asso. prof. health econs., asso. chmn. dept. family and community health Meharry Med. Coll., 1969—; asso. prof. health econs. Vanderbilt U., 1970—; sr. research asso. Center Policy Research, N.Y.C., 1969. Cons. USPHS, Social Security Joint Commn. on Accreditation Hosps., Nat. Adv. Council on Nursing Home Adminstrn., Milbank Meml. Fund, N.Y.C., Tenn. Group Found. Pres., Med. Com. Human Rights, Nashville, 1971—; co-chmn. Tenn. Cost Containment Commn., 1973; dir. Vanderbilt Summer Program in Israel, 1973. Bd. dirs. Am. Civil Liberties Union, treas., 1972—; bd. dirs. House Between, treas., 1972—. Woodrow Wilson fellow, 1965-67; Fulbright fellow, 1967-68; USPHS fellow, 1968-69. Mem. Am., So. econ. assns., Am. Pub. Health Assn. Contbg. author: Urban Health Services: The Case of New York, 1971; Consumer Incentives for Health Care, 1974; Framework for Government Intervention in the Health Sector, 1974. Contbr. numerous articles to profl. jours. Home: 6952 Highland Park Dr Nashville TN 37205

ZUCKER, ALEXANDER, physicist; b. Zagreb, Yugoslavia, Aug. 1, 1924; s. William and Bertha (Klopfer) Z.; came to U.S., 1939, naturalized, 1943; B.A., U. Vt., 1947; M.S., Yale, 1948, Ph.D., 1950; m. Joan-Ellen Jamieson, Nov. 28, 1953; children—Rebecca Marie, Claire Louise, Susannah Katherine. Research asst. Yale, 1948-50; physicist Oak Ridge Nat. Lab., 1950-53, sr. physicist, 1953-60, asso. div. dir., 1960-70, dir. heavy ion project, 1972-74, asso. dir. phys. scis., 1972—; exec. dir. environmental studies bd. Nat. Acad. Scis.-Nat. Acad. Engring., 1970-72; prof. physics U. Tenn. at Knoxville, 1969-72. Mem. U.S. delegation to USSR on peaceful uses of atomic energy, 1963; del. Pugwash Conf., 1971; mem. com. on nuclear sci. and nuclear physics panel NRC. Served with AUS, 1943-45. Guggenheim fellow, Fulbright research scholar, 1966-67. Fellow Am. Phys. Soc., A.A.A.S.; mem. Phi Beta Kappa, Sigma Xi. Home: 103 Orange Lane Oak Ridge TN 37830 Office: PO Box X Oak Ridge TN 37830

ZUERCHER, WILLIAM ROBERT, hosp. adminstr.; b. Nampa, Ida., Mar. 31, 1937; s. Elliott Howard and Edna Irene (Roth) Z.; B.A., Goshen Coll., 1958; M.H.A., Duke, 1968; m. Mary Joyce Gingerich, June 14, 1958; children—Melanie Alice, Andrea Elizabeth, Edward William. Asst. bus. mgr. Goshen (Ind.) Coll., 1960-62; adminstr. Brook Lane Psychiat. Center, Hagerstown, Md., 1962-66; asst. adminstr. Harlan (Ky.) Appalachian Regional Hosp., 1968-70, adminstr., 1972—; spl. asst. to pres., 1970-72; adminstr. Clover Fork Clinic, Evarts, Ky., 1970-72. Dir., Mennonite Mut. Aid. Assn., Inc., Goshen, Ind., 1967—; pres. Harlan (Ky.) City P.T.A., 1969-71; dir., treas. Mennonite Mental Health Services, Inc., Akron, Pa., 1967—; mem. Cumberland River Mental Health-Mental Retardation Bd., 1971—; nat. chmn. Goshen Coll. Alumni Fund, 1973; mem. ad hoc com. nursing edn. Ky. Council Pub. Higher Edn. Recipient Leadership and Service citation Family Service Agy., Hagerstown, Md., 1969. Mem. Am. Coll. Hosp. Adminstrs., Assn. for Clin. Pastoral Edn., Ky. (chmn. ednl. steering com. 1971, vice chmn. 1974, sec.-treas. Cumberland Hosp. dist. 1973-74, pres. elect 1974-75), Am. (com. community emergency health services 1974) hosp. assns., C. of C. (mem. task force on community improvement 1971). Presbyn. (trustee 1969-71, 73-75). Mennonite (mem., vice chmn. health and welfare com. bd. missions 1968—). Kiwanian. Home: 604 S Main St Harlan KY 40831 Office: Martins Fork Rd Harlan KY 40831

ZUHDI, MOHAMED NAZIH, physician; b. Beirut, Lebanon, May 19, 1925; s. Omar and Lutfiye (Atef) Z.; came to U.S., 1950; B.A., Am. U., Beirut, Lebanon, 1946, M.D., 1950; diploma Instituto Brasileiro de Investigatioes Cardiovascularis, Rio de Janeiro; children by previous marriage—Omar, Nabil, Adam, Leyle; m. 2d, Annette McMichael. Intern St. Vincent's Hosp., N.Y.C., 1950-51, Presbyn.-Columbia Med. Center. N.Y.C., 1951-52; resident Kings County State U. N.Y. Med. Center, N.Y.C., 1952-56, fellow, 1952-53; resident U. Hosp., Mpls., 1956, Oklahoma City, 1957-58; practice medicine specializing in cardiocascular and thoracic surgery, Oklahoma City, 1958—; active thoracic Bapt., Mercy, St. Anthony hosps.; mem. intensive care, inhalation therapy coms. Bapt. Meml. Hosp., Oklahoma City; asst. instr. surgery State U. N.Y., 1955-56. Named Hon. Citizen Brazil. Diplomate Am. Bd. Surgery, Am. Bd. Thoracic Surgery. Fellow A.C.S.; mem. Am., Okla. thoracic socs., Am., So., Okla. med. assns., Internat., Am. colls. angiology, Am. Coll. Chest Physicians, Oklahoma City C. of C., Oklahoma County Med. Soc., Oklahoma City Clin. Soc., Okla. Surg. Assn., Southwestern Sug. Congress, Am. Coll. Cardiology, Am. Soc. Artificial Internal Organs, Soc. Thoracic Surgeons (founder mem.), Internat. Cardiovascular Soc., Okla. Heart Assn., Osler Soc. Research cardiovascular surgery, Am. Assn. Thoracic Surgery, La Sociedad Colombia de Cardiologia (hon.). Contbg. author Cardiac Surgery. Contbr. numerous articles to profl. jours. Home: 7528 NW 150 Route 2 Edmond OK 73034 Office: 1211 N Shartel Oklahoma City OK 73103

ZUNG, MAX MING-KWAI, physician; b. Hankow, China, Oct. 2, 1922; s. Bate and Rose Yu-sun (Fong) Z.; came to U.S., 1937, naturalized, 1952; B.S., Columbia, 1946, M.D., 1950; m. Madeline Elizabeth Roye, May 1, 1965; children—Robert, Richard, Rebecca, Michael. Research asst. dept. biochemistry Coll. Phys. and Surgs., Columbia, 1942-45; intern Orange (N.J.) Meml. Hosp., 1950-51; resident Columbia Presbyn. Med. Center, N.Y.C., 1951-53; sr. attending dept. anesthesia Providence Hosp., Washington, 1954—; dep. rep. subcom. on anesthesia NRC, 1954-55; mem. staff Washington Sanitarium and Hosp., 1953-55, Suburban Hosp., Bethesda, Md., 1953-55. Bd. dirs. Med. Scis. Research Found. Served with USNR, 1953-55. Diplomate Am. Bd. Anesthesiology. Fellow Am. Coll. Anesthesiology; mem. Md.-D.C. Soc. Anesthesiologists (v.p. 1971-73, pres. 1973-75), So. Med. Assn., Am. Soc. Anesthesiologists, Internat. Anesthesia Research Soc. Mem. Chinese Community Ch. (chmn. ch. council 1964-65). Lion. Home: 4117 N Ridgeview Rd Arlington VA 22207 Office: 1150 Varnum St NE Washington DC 20017

ZUNIGA, FRANCISCO, artist; b. San Jose, Costa Rica, Dec. 27, 1912. One-man shows Fine Arts Gallery, San Diego, 1971, Phoenix Art Mus., 1972, De Saissert Art Gallery U. Santa Clara, 1972, Cal. State U. at Fresno, 1972; exhibited in group shows Expn. Central Am. Art, San Jose, 1935, Arts Club, Chgo., 1942, Phila. Mus. Art, 1943, Casa de Arte, Mexico City, 1945, Knoedler Galleries, N.Y.C., 1945, 3d Sculpture Internat., Phila. Mus. Art, 1949; Musee Nacional, San Jose, 1954, Dept. Tourism, San Salvador, El Salvador, Salon Anual Escultura, Mexico City, 1957, 58, Unst der Mexikaner, Cologne, Germany, 1959, Instituto de Bellas Artes, Mexico City, 1960, Galeria Universitaria Aristos, 1963, Latin Am. Artists Art Alliance, Phila., 1964, Phoenix Art Mus., 1964, 72, Gallery Modern Art, Scottsdale, Ariz., 1966, Expn. Art of Mexico, Montreal, Que., Can., 1968, Museo de Arte Moderno, Mexico City, 1968, Musee Middelheim, Antwerp, Belgium, 1971, Fogg Art Mus. Harvard, 1971, 74, Galeria Tasende, Acapulco, Mexico, others; works represented in permanent collections Museo de Arte Moderno, Mexico City, Riverside Musuem, N.Y.C., Phoenix Art Musuem, Museo Nacional de Costa Rica, San Jose, Museo de Arte de Ponce, San Juan, P.R. Address: care Jose Ma Tasende Acapulco Mexico

ZWEIBAN, HERMAN DAVID, stock broker; b. N.Y.C., Oct. 8, 1919; s. Sol and Jennie (Zelekuvitz) Z.; B.S., U. Ill., 1940; m. Ethel Reds Dupler, Dec. 13, 1942; children—Donna (Mrs. Harry R. Price), Glenn. Press., Lee's Furs, Inc., Gary, Ind., 1945-49; v.p. Nancy Lee, Inc., Gary, 1949-58; pres. Greens Furs, Inc., Gary, 1949-63; v.p. Bloom's, Inc., Hammond, Ind., 1950-56, Yousims Furs, Inc., South Bank, Ind., 1950-56; pres. Ben-Her Oil Co., Gary, 1960-63, Norge Village, Gary, 1961-63; v.p. Walston & Co., Dallas, 1964-73, Harris, Upham & Co., Inc., 1973—. Chmn. Lake County (Ind.) Arthritis Fund, 1960-61. Served to capt. USAAF, 1941-45. Mem. U.S. Power Squadron, Gamma Theta Phi, Kappa Tau Alpha. Jewish religion. Mem. B'nai Brith. Club: City (Dallas). Home: 7924 Royal Lane Dallas TX 75230 Office: 2001 Bryan St Dallas TX 75201

PN,789; GV101,204; GV99,3; GV160,0

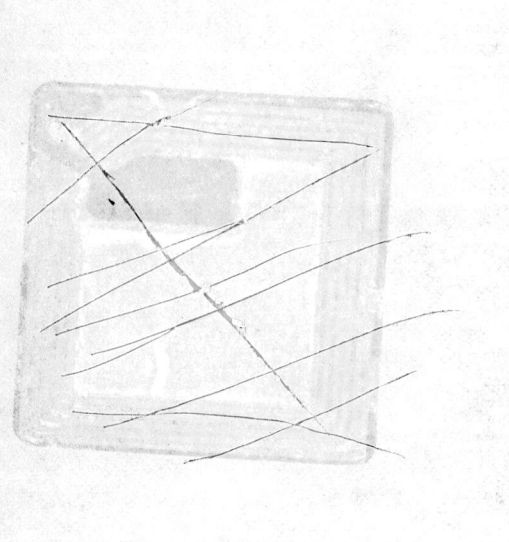